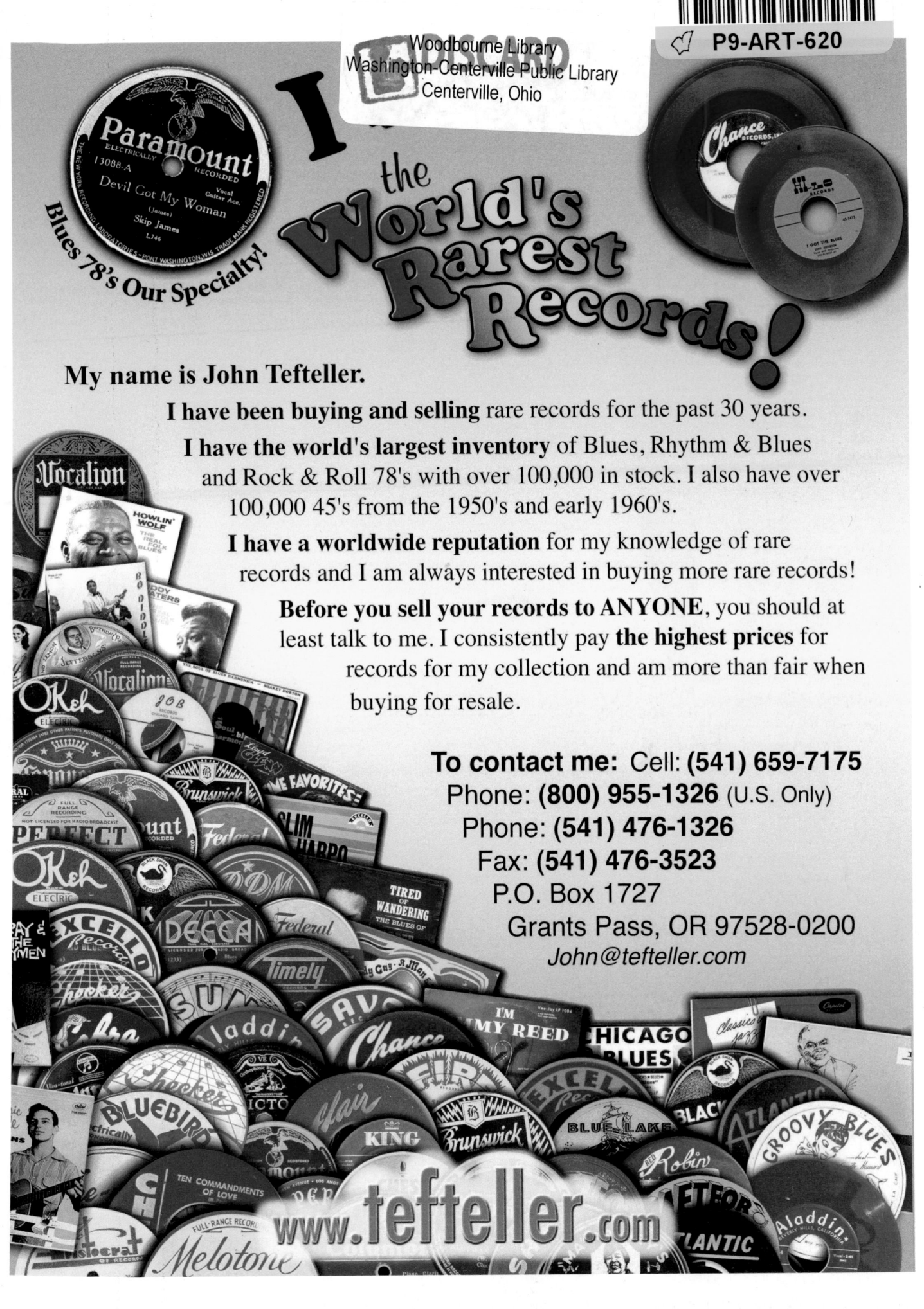

Paramount
13088-A
Devil Got My Woman
(James)
Vocal
Guitar Acc.
Skip James
L746

Blues 78's Our Specialty!

I the World's Rarest Records!

My name is John Tefteller.

I have been buying and selling rare records for the past 30 years.

I have the world's largest inventory of Blues, Rhythm & Blues and Rock & Roll 78's with over 100,000 in stock. I also have over 100,000 45's from the 1950's and early 1960's.

I have a worldwide reputation for my knowledge of rare records and I am always interested in buying more rare records!

Before you sell your records to ANYONE, you should at least talk to me. I consistently pay **the highest prices** for records for my collection and am more than fair when buying for resale.

To contact me: Cell: **(541) 659-7175**
Phone: **(800) 955-1326** (U.S. Only)
Phone: **(541) 476-1326**
Fax: **(541) 476-3523**
P.O. Box 1727
Grants Pass, OR 97528-0200
John@tefteller.com

www.tefteller.com

Goldmine® Record Album

PRICE GUIDE
9th Edition

Dave Thompson

Published by

Krause Publications, a division of F+W Media, Inc.
700 East State Street • Iola, WI 54990-0001
715-445-2214 • 888-457-2873
www.krausebooks.com

To order books or other products call toll-free 1-800-258-0929
or visit us online at www.krausebooks.com

ISBN-13: 978-1-4402-4776-7
ISBN-10: 1-4402-4776-5

Cover Design by Sharon Bartsch
Book Design by Sandi Carpenter
Edited by Paul Kennedy

Printed in the United States of America

10 9 8 7 6 5 4 3 2 1

Special Acknowledgments to:
• Those who worked on this book, including Database Developer Steve Duberstein; Scanning Supervisor Duayne Kett; and Designer Sandi Carpenter.
• Popsike.com, Heritage Auctions, eBay, Etsy.com, Record Collector magazine, VJM, the Recording Industry Association of America, Shutterstock.com, The Audio Preservation Fund and The Library of Congress.
• The fine advertisers who support this book, as well its sister publication, Goldmine magazine.
• You, the dealers, collectors and readers, for your continued interest in records and in this reference.

Connect With Us!

www.goldminemag.com   www.facebook.com/goldminemag   http://twitter.com/Goldmine_mag   http://pinterest.com/goldminemag/

CONTENTS

LISTINGS

INTRODUCTION

Passing of Legends Influence The Record-Collecting Market

Two factors have had a major influence upon record collecting in the years since the last edition of this price guide was published.

The first, and the most pronounced, is the ever-more buoyant market for LPs, both new and old, that accompanies the on-going "vinyl revival"; the other, more specific and less happily, is the spate of high profile deaths that scarred the end of 2015 and early 2016 - most notably those of David Bowie and Prince.

The influence that these two performers had on music in general goes without saying. More pertinently, however, both long ago ascended to the upper echelons of the record collecting world in general, regular fixtures in any Top Ten polls of rock's most collectible artists.

Inevitably, their deaths sent values soaring as fans and collectors alike hastened to pick up the music they were missing; indeed, at least one long-time collector described the activity surrounding the Bowie back catalog as unprecedented since the weeks that followed the deaths of John Lennon (1980) and Elvis Presley (1977).

This frenzy has ebbed somewhat in the months since then, but still we register some remarkable increases in value, not only among the traditional rarities within each artist's catalog, but also among what we might term their "regular" releases - the standard pressings that are the bread-and-butter of the music industry, and of our collections, too. And it is here that the **Album Price Guide** becomes such an invaluable tool for both buyers and sellers, offering an at-a-glance guide not only to the values which each of those releases have attained, but also differentiating between the original release and any reissues that might have followed it.

For example, this edition lists no fewer than a dozen different versions of Bowie's **The Rise and Fall of Ziggy Stardust and the Spiders from Mars** album - less than the 21 different versions of the Beatles' Revolver album that are included, but more than the 10 different editions of **A Date With Elvis Presley**.

Each of these versions has its own unique characteristics, and each has its own value; sometimes negligibly different from another, other times vastly greater or smaller. Being able to tell, as you peruse an auction site or dealer's list, which is which is one of the most powerful tools in any collector's arsenal, but it is one that is all too frequently overlooked.

These statistics have, of course, swollen considerably in recent years, as labels around the world have seized upon the renewed popularity of vinyl with almost the same alacrity as they grasped onto the insurgent compact disc three decades ago.

Back then, as buyers eased themselves into the new format, the question on everybody's lips was "what album would you most like to see reissued on CD?" **Goldmine** magazine even made a regular feature of that question.

Today, that same question is being asked about vinyl, and while it will doubtless take many years more for every request to finally be granted (after all, there are still many pre-CD LPs that have yet to make **the original** transition, let alone flip back again), still we can only look on in astonishment as entire back catalogs are repressed on wax, including many that had never even felt the business end of a stylus before. Major label vinyl production

effectively dried up in the early 1990s, at least in the US, and many of the format's final flourishes are now ranked among the era's most sought-after releases. (Late period mono collectors are excused a sense of **deja vu** here.) These releases, and all of those compact discs that followed are now slowly, but surely, reappearing on vinyl.

Of course there are a great many pros and cons to be weighed. Many of these releases, classic catalog as well as more recent, are being restored to vinyl as fresh (or, at least, recent) digital re-masters, and producer Glyn Johns (the Who, the Beatles, etcetera) is just one of many authoritative voices that have questioned the wisdom of this - "what's the point?" was his succinct summary.

Analogue sound is the natural preserve of vinyl; digital sound belongs to digital media, and the online forums echo with the findings of sundry audiophiles, patiently comparing the sonic range of a modern repressing with its decades-old ancestor, and then arguing over whether it was worth sacrificing the original sound for a **cleaner** sound?

That is not a debate into which the **Album Price Guide** is equipped to wade, and for that reason, we have eschewed the temptation to note whether or not a modern reissue was cut from an analog source or a digital one, just as we have never noted whether a reissue was cut from the original tapes, or from a "needle drop" - that is, recorded directly from an earlier copy of the same record.

The collectors' market, however, made that distinction for itself in the past, and doubtless will do so again in the future. No matter how attractively a reissue might be packaged, if it doesn't sound as good as it should, then its value to all but the most avid will be negligible.

All that said, of course, there have been some remarkable reissues and repackagings offered across the past few years, both within the twice-annual Record Store Day events, and as stand-alone releases, and many of these are included herein. As regards more straightforward reissues, however, and new releases too, we have been forced to exercise considerable discernment.

The vast majority of these, after all, remain readily available at retail prices and outlets and, as such, have had no significant impact on the collectors market beyond, perhaps, reducing the number of casual collectors who might otherwise have been searching for a used copy of a particular old favorite; or, contrarily, increasing the appetite of others to find an original, in the knowledge that it will probably cost less than the reissue. Again, the market will decide what the modern collectibles are, just as it always has, and the Album Price Guide will reflect those decisions in due course.

One final note. As in the past, the pricing in this edition notes only NM values in excess of $10. Albums valued below this threshold are omitted, and this includes variations on a previously noted release - changes in label design that may have followed the original release, for example, revised catalog numbers or artwork, and so forth.

Beyond that, this is - once again - the largest and most up-to-date edition of the **Album Price Guide** that we have ever published, and it remains only to thank all the collectors and enthusiasts out there who have contacted us with their own observations, experiences and, most of all, discoveries. Your contributions, as always, have proven invaluable.

TELL US WHAT YOU THINK

We're always working on the "next" edition of Goldmine's price guides and magazines, which means we're always open for business. What would you like to see in the next book or issue? Do you have proof of a heretofore unknown record? We'd love to hear from you!
- **e-mail:** goldminemag@fwmedia.com.
- **mail:** Goldmine, Attention: Record Price Guides, 700 E. State St., Iola, WI 54990.

We look forward to reading your suggestions. Thank you for the time and thought you put in to sharing your viewpoints!

HOW TO USE THIS BOOK

	Number	Title	Yr	NM
artist name —	QUEEN			
record label —	ELEKTRA			
catalog number —	❏ 5E-513	The Game	1980	10.00
title —	*With dull gray cover; all copies have custom white labels*			
	❏ 5E-513	The Game	1980	15.00
release year —	*– With shiny, mirrorlike cover; all copies have custom white labels*			
	❏ BB-702 [(2)]	Live Killers	1979	12.00
format details —	❏ EQ-5064 [Q]	Queen	1973	40.00
	❏ EKS-75082	Queen II	1974	10.00
value —	*– Butterfly, red or red/black labels*			
	❏ EKS-75082 [DJ]	Queen II	1974	50.00
recording notes —	*– White label promo*			

To the uninitiated, the Goldmine price guide can seem overwhelming. Here are tips to navigate the listings.

The **artist name** (last name first for solo acts) is the first way we break down the listing information. We strive to provide a cross section of artists, genres and formats within our listings. So while you personally may not care about the 1989 album "You Can't Hold Me Back" by Awesome Dre and The Hardcore Committee, or the 1959 album "Torch Time" by Gogi Grant, there are collectors who do – and who may not be as excited about the Lynyrd Skynyrd, Led Zeppelin or Def Leppard listings as you are.

Each artist's listings are subdivided by the **record label** on which the recording was issued. Records sometimes were issued on more than one label; differ-ent labels can mean different values.

Individual listings are preceded by a box (which you can use as a handy check-off for what's in your collec-tion), followed by a **catalog number**. The numerical catalog order is what determines the order of the listings – not titles or release dates.

The second column lists the **title** of the album. Few, if any, records in the import, children's, classical, spoken word or various artist genres appear.

If additional **format details** are available (such as whether a recording was pressed in mono, stereo or quadraphonic sound; if it's a deejay or promo copy; if it includes more than one album, etc.), that information appears in brackets and/or parentheses immediately following the catalog number.

The third column lists the **release year**, which is based on record label information or chart date; this may differ from the date noted on the record itself. Release dates of the albums detailed in this book range from the 1940s to the present, but the majority of our listings are for albums released between 1950 and 1989.

The last column lists the Near Mint **value** for the re-cord. In order for an album to be included in this edition of Goldmine's "Record Album Price Guide," its Near Mint value must be at least $10. This means many common records you own may be excluded from our listings.

Some records have an additional line of italic type under the listing. These **recording notes** offer additional details, such as other featured artists, label variations or the color of the vinyl.

COMMON ABBREVIATIONS AND TERMS

Both (B): An album that is listed in stereo, but has some tracks in monaural sound, too.

Cover or Outer Sleeve: A cardboard cover that protects an LP. Double albums may feature gatefold covers, which fold open, like a book.

Dead Wax: The black, grooveless area surround-ing the label. It may contain engraved mastering numbers and the mastering agent's initials or com-pany name, or even cryptic messages from the band.

Extended Play (EP): A record with four to six tracks; usually less than half the length of a regular album. Rarely used to describe 12-inch records before the 1980s; before that, it refers to 7-inch records.

Inner Sleeve: A paper, plastic or other lightweight sleeve that protects an album inside the cover. May contain liner notes, lyrics or photos.

Monaural or Mono Sound (M): A single-channel audio recording. Virtually all records made before the 1950s were in mono; many records were produced in mono until the late 1960s.

Partial Stereo (P): A record listed as stereo, but only part is "true" two-channel stereo.

Picture Disc (PD): A record featuring graphics as part of the record, not merely on the label area

Promo copy (DJ): A promotional pressing not intended for public sale. Often for radio stations, hence DJ for disc jockey. Not meant for public sale.

Quadraphonic (Q): Records – mostly issued from 1972 to 1976 – that were remixed to play on quadraphonic systems, which feature four speakers.

Rechanneled (RE): A recording listed as stereo, but is all or almost all rechanneled, or "fake," stereo. These recordings were marked as "Duophonic" by Capitol and "Enhanced For Stereo" by Decca, or may be referred to as electronically channeled stereo." Typically, these pressings are less in demand than true mono recordings.

Runout Groove: A loop bordering the label where the needle rides after the last song is played.

Stereophonic Sound (S): A two-channel audio recording. Widespread use of stereo record production began in the mid 1960s. Not all monaural phonographs could play stereo records. If we know an album is all or almost all true stereo, we note it as such. This also appears with certain 45s and EPs from the late 1950s and early 1960s, usually when there is also a mono counterpart.

10-Inch Record (10): A 10-inch record, most of which were from the early years of LPs from 1948 to 1954. These records are difficult to find in top condition.

(2), (3), etc.: The number of records in a set.

THE INDUSTRY STANDARD: GOLDMINE'S GRADING GUIDELINES

BEFORE YOU CAN FIGURE OUT what a record is worth, you need to grade its vinyl, sleeves and labels. Play grading can be a definite advantage for a record that looks much worse than it sounds. When you're visually grading records, use a direct light, such as a 100-watt desk lamp, as less direct lighting can hide defects.

Think like the buyer as you set your grades. If you're on the fence, go with the lower conservative grade under consideration. Records and covers always seem to look better when you're grading them to sell to someone else than when you're on the other side of the table, inspecting a record for purchase. And, if you have a Still Sealed record, subject it to these same grading standards, short of breaking the seal.

MINT (M): Absolutely perfect in every way. Often rumored but rarely seen, Mint should never be used as a grade unless more than one person agrees the item truly is in this condition. There is no hard-and-fast percentage of the Near Mint value these can bring; it is best negotiated between buyer and seller.

- **Overall Appearance:** Looks as if it just came off the manufacturing line.
- **Record:** No scuffs or scratches.
- **Labels:** No writing, stickers or spindle marks. Labels are perfectly placed.
- **Cover/Sleeve:** No blotches, stains, discoloration, stickers, ring wear, dinged corners, sleeve splits or writing.

NEAR MINT (NM) OR MINT MINUS (M-): It's estimated that no more than 2 to 4 percent of all records remaining from the 1950s and 1960s are truly Near Mint. Many dealers won't use a grade higher than this, implying that no record or sleeve is ever truly perfect.

- **Overall Appearance:** Looks as if it were opened for the first time. Includes all original pieces (inner sleeve, lyric sheets, inserts, cover, record, etc.).
- **Record:** Shiny surface, free of visible defects. No surface noise at playback. Records can retain NM condition after many plays provided the record has been played on a properly equipped turntable and has been cared for properly.
- **Labels:** Properly pressed and centered on the record. Free of writing, stickers, spindle marks, blemishes or other markings.
- **Cover/Sleeve:** Free of creases, ring wear and seam splits. Cut-out markings are unacceptable. Picture sleeves look as if no record was ever housed inside. Hint: If you remove a 45 from its picture sleeve and store it separately, you will reduce the potential for damage to the sleeve.

VERY GOOD PLUS (VG+) OR EXCELLENT (E): Except for a few minor condition issues, these records would be Near Mint. Most collectors who want to play their records will be happy with a VG+ record, especially if it is toward the high end of the grade, sometimes called VG++ or E+.

- **Overall Appearance:** Shows slight signs of wear.
- **Record:** May have light scuffs or very light scratches that don't affect the listening experience, or slight warps that don't affect the sound. Expect minor signs of handling, such as telltale marks around the center hole (but the hole is not misshapen). Light ring wear or discoloration may be present, but barely noticeable.
- **Labels:** Free of writing, stickers or major blemishes.
- **Cover/Sleeve:** Outer cover may show some minor seam wear or a split less than one inch long along the bottom, which is the most vulnerable location. A cut-out marking may be present. Picture sleeves may show some slight creasing where it is obvious the record once resided (or still does reside). May show minor seam wear or a split less than 1 inch long along the bottom.

VERY GOOD (VG): VG records have more obvious flaws than records in better condition. That said, VG records – which usually sell for no more than 25 percent of their NM counterparts – are among the biggest bargains in record collecting, because most of the "big money" goes for more perfect copies. For many listeners, a VG record or sleeve will be worth the money. Many collectors who have jukeboxes will use VG records in them and not think twice. They remain a fine listening experience, just not the same as if it were in better shape.

- **Overall Appearance:** Shows signs of wear and handling, including visible groove wear, audible scratches and surface noise, ring wear and seam splits.
- **Record:** Lacks the original glossy finish. Groove wear is evident on sight, and light scratches are deep enough to feel with a fingernail. When played, a VG record has surface noise, and some scratches may be audible, especially during a song's intro and ending, but the noise won't overpower the music otherwise.
- **Labels:** May have minor writing, tape or a sticker.
- **Cover/Sleeve:** Expect obvious signs of human handling and normal wear. Ring wear is expected in the middle or along the edges of the cover where the labels or edges of a record would rest. Seam splits may appear on all three sides, but they won't be obvious. Writing or a price tag may be present. The cover may be dull or discolored, have bent corners, stains or other problems. If the record has more than two of these problems, reduce its grade.

VERY GOOD MINUS (VG–), GOOD PLUS (G+) OR GOOD (G): Good does not necessarily mean bad! A true G to VG- record still plays through without skipping, so it can serve as filler until something better comes along. If the record is common, you may want to pass it up in this condition. If you've sought for a long time, get it cheap and upgrade later. And sellers? Don't expect big profits for records in these grades: They bring 10 to 15 percent of the Near Mint value at most.

- **Overall Appearance:** Shows considerable signs of handling, including groove wear, ring wear, seam splits and damaged labels or covers.
- **Record:** The surface sheen is almost gone, but the record plays through without skipping. Significant surface noise and groove wear..
- **Labels:** Worn, possible stains, heavy writing, or obvious damage caused by someone trying to remove tape or stickers and failing miserably.
- **Cover/Sleeve:** Shows ring wear to the point of distraction, has obvious seam splits and may have even heavier writing, such as huge radio station letters (or the former owner's name) written across the front to deter theft. Expect dinged and dog-eared edges.

FAIR (F) OR POOR (P): These records go for 0 to 5 percent of the Near Mint value – if they go at all. More likely, these records will end up going in the trash, or having their covers, labels or discs turned into kitschy craft items like clocks, journals, purses, jewelry, bowls or coasters.

- **Overall Appearance:** Beat, trashed and dull. Records may lack sleeves or covers (or vice versa). You may want to call a CSI unit to identify "the victim."
- **Record:** Expect the vinyl to be cracked, horrifically scratched and/or impossibly warped. The record will skip and repeat when you attempt to play it.
- **Labels:** Stains, tears, stickers and damage are the least of your problems; the label may be missing some sections altogether.
- **Cover/Sleeve:** So heavily damaged that you almost want to cry. Only the most outrageously rare items ever sell for more than a few cents in this condition– again, if they sell at all.

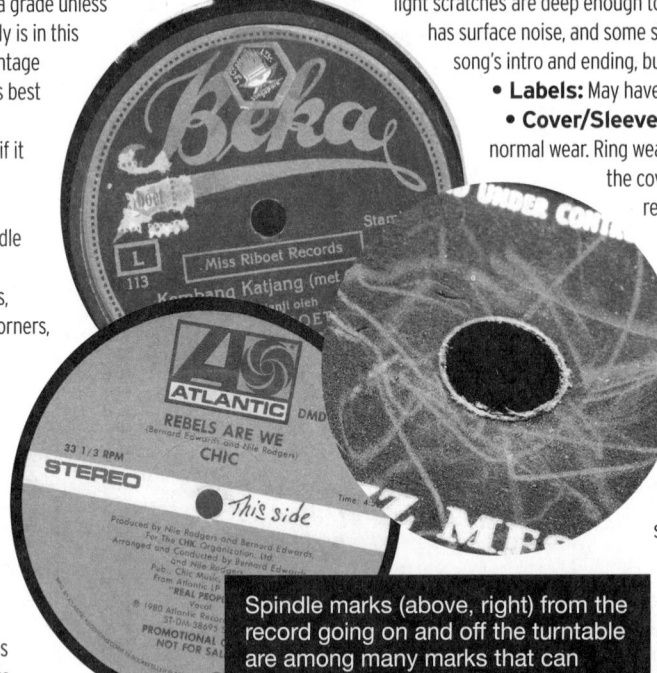

Spindle marks (above, right) from the record going on and off the turntable are among many marks that can help determine a record's grade. The labels also tell a story, and writing (above), stickers and damage (top) all factor into grades.

Number	Title	Yr	NM

A

A.B. SKHY
MGM

❑ SE-4628 [B]	A.B. Skhy	1969	$25
❑ SE-4676 [B]	Ramblin' On	1970	$40

A.F.O. EXECUTIVES WITH TAMI LYNN
A.F.O.

❑ 5002 [M]	A Compendium	1962	$175

A-HA
WARNER BROS.

❑ R114779	Hunting High and Low	1985	$12
—RCA Music Service edition			
❑ 25300	Hunting High and Low	1985	$10
❑ R163775	Scoundrel Days	1986	$12
—RCA Music Service edition			
❑ 25501	Scoundrel Days	1986	$10
❑ R184019	Stay On These Roads	1988	$15
—BMG Direct Marketing edition			
❑ 25733	Stay On These Roads	1988	$12

A-STRINGS, THE
WARNER BROS.

❑ 25759	Home for Christmas	1988	$12

A CAPPELLA CHOIR OF COLUMBIA MUSICAL TREASURIES
COLUMBIA MUSICAL TREASURIES

❑ DS551	The Compleat Alfred Burt Christmas Carols	1969	$18

—Information is as listed on cover; title on record is "Complete" and the group name is "Columbia Musical Treasuries A'Cappella Choir

AALIYAH
BLACKGROUND

❑ 10082	Aaliyah	2001	$18

JIVE

❑ 41533	Age Ain't Nothing But a Number	1994	$15

AALON
ARISTA

❑ AL4127	Cream City	1977	$12

ABBA
ATLANTIC

❑ SD18146	Abba	1975	$15
❑ PR300 [DJ]	Abba	1978	$30
❑ 81675	Abba Live	1986	$15
❑ PR432 [DJ]	A Collection of Hits	1982	$30
❑ SD19115	Arrival	1977	$12
❑ SD18207	Arrival	1977	$15
❑ SD18189	Greatest Hits	1976	$15
❑ SD19114	Greatest Hits	1977	$12
❑ SD16009	Greatest Hits, Vol. 2	1979	$15
❑ 80142	I Love Abba	1984	$12
❑ SD16023	Super Trouper	1980	$12
❑ PR436 [DJ]	The Abba Special	1983	$50
❑ SD19164	The Album	1978	$12
❑ 80036	The Singles -- The First Ten Years	1982	$18
❑ SD19332	The Visitors	1981	$12
❑ SD16000	Voulez-Vous	1979	$12
❑ SD18101 [B]	Waterloo	1974	$18

CBS INTERNATIONAL

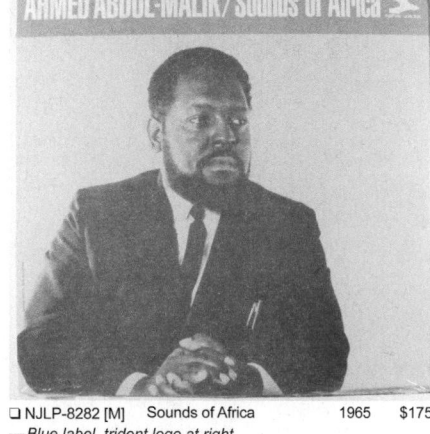

❑ DAL40301 [B]	Gracias Por La Musica	1980	$50

—Spanish-language versions of some of their hits, this LP was pressed in the U.S.

K-TEL

❑ NU9510	The Magic of Abba	1978	$18

NAUTILUS

❑ NR-20	Arrival	1981	$30
—Audiophile vinyl			

POLYDOR

❑ 5499701	The Album	2008	$25

ABBEY TAVERN SINGERS, THE
V.I.P.

❑ 402 [M]	We're Off to Dublin in the Green	1966	$40
❑ S-402 [S]	We're Off to Dublin in the Green	1966	$50

ABBOTT, GREGORY
COLUMBIA

❑ FC44087	I'll Prove It to You	1988	$12
❑ BFC40437	Shake You Down	1986	$12

ABBOTT & COSTELLO
HOLIDAY

❑ HDY-1939	Christmas Stocking	1981	$12

ABC
MERCURY

❑ R143756	Alphabet City	1987	$15
—BMG Direct Marketing edition			
❑ 832391-1	Alphabet City	1987	$12
❑ 814661-1	Beauty Stab	1984	$12
❑ 824904-1	How to Be a Zillionaire	1985	$12
❑ SRM-1-4059	The Lexicon of Love	1982	$12
❑ 822890-1	The Lexicon of Love	1984	$10
—Reissue			
❑ 838646-1	Up	1989	$12

ABDUL, PAULA
VIRGIN

❑ 90943	Forever Your Girl	1988	$12
❑ 91362	Shut Up and Dance	1990	$15
—Red print on cover			
❑ 91362	Shut Up and Dance	1990	$15
—Yellow print on cover			
❑ 91362	Shut Up and Dance	1990	$15
—Purple print on cover			
❑ 91362	Shut Up and Dance	1990	$15
—Blue print on cover			
❑ IP-8128 [B]	Spellbound	1991	$30

—Columbia House edition; the only U.S. vinyl of this LP

ABDUL-MALIK, AHMED
NEW JAZZ

❑ NJLP-8282 [M]	Sounds of Africa	1962	$250
—Purple label			

❑ NJLP-8282 [M]	Sounds of Africa	1965	$175
—Blue label, trident logo at right			
❑ NJLP-8266 [M]	The Music of Ahmed Abdul-Malik	1961	$250
—Purple label			
❑ NJLP-8266 [M]	The Music of Ahmed Abdul-Malik	1965	$175
—Blue label, trident logo at right			

PRESTIGE

❑ PRLP-16003 [M]	Eastern Moods	1963	$300

RCA VICTOR

❑ LPM-2015 [M]	East Meets West	1959	$250
❑ LSP-2015 [S]	East Meets West	1959	$250

RIVERSIDE

❑ RLP 12-287 [M]	Jazz Sahara	1958	$300
❑ RLP-1121 [S]	Jazz Sahara	1959	$300

STATUS

❑ ST-8303 [M]	Spellbound	1965	$100

ABERCROMBIE, JOHN, AND RALPH TOWNER
ECM

❑ 1207	Five Years Later	1981	$25
❑ 1080	Sargasso Sea	1976	$25

ABERCROMBIE, JOHN
ECM

❑ 1133	Arcade	1979	$25
❑ 1117	Characters	1978	$25
❑ 1061	Gateway	1975	$25
❑ 1105	Gateway 2	1977	$25
❑ 1164	John Abercrombie Quartet	1980	$25
❑ 1191	M	1981	$25
❑ 25009	Night	1984	$20
❑ 1047	Timeless	1974	$25

JAM

❑ 5001	Straight Flight	198?	$25

ABOVE THE LAW
RUTHLESS/EPIC

❑ E47934 [EP]	Vocally Pimpin'	1991	$12

RUTHLESS/GIANT

❑ 24477	Black Mafia Life	1992	$15

TOMMY BOY

❑ TB1233	Legends	1998	$18
❑ TB1154	Time Will Reveal	1996	$15

ABRAMS, COLONEL
ACID JAZZ/SCOTTI BROTHERS

❑ 75232	About Romance	1992	$18
—Promo-only vinyl; white label, generic cover			

MCA

❑ 5682	Colonel Abrams	1986	$10
❑ 42029	You and Me Equals Us	1987	$10

ABRAMS, MISS, AND THE STRAWBERRY POINT SCHOOL THIRD GRADE CLASS
REPRISE

❑ MS2098	Abrams, Miss, and the Strawberry Point School Third Grade Class	1972	$15

ABRAMS, MUHAL RICHARD
ARISTA/NOVUS

❑ 3000	Lifea Blinec	1978	$25
❑ 3007	Spiral/Live	1979	$25

BLACK SAINT

❑ BSR 0017	1-OQA + 19	1978	$30
❑ BSR 0061	Blues Forever	1981	$25
❑ BSR 0091	Colors in Thirty-Third	1987	$25
❑ BSR 0051	Duet	1981	$25
—With Amina Claudine Myers			
❑ BSR 0033	Lifelong Ambitions	1980	$25
—With Leroy Jenkins			
❑ BSR 0041	Mama and Daddy	1981	$25
❑ BSR 0071	Rejoicing with the Light	1983	$25
❑ BSR 0003	Sightsong	1975	$30
—Featuring Malachi Favors			
❑ BSR 0032	Spihumonesty	1980	$25
❑ 120103	The Hearinga Suite	1989	$30
❑ BSR 0081	View From Within	1984	$25

DELMARK

❑ DS-413	Levels and Degrees of Light	1968	$25
❑ DS-430	Things to Come From Those Now Gone	1972	$35
❑ DS-423	Young at Heart, Wise in Time	1970	$50

INDIA NAVIGATION

❑ IN-1058	Afrisong	1975	$35

ABSTRAC'
REPRISE

❑ 25997	Abstrac'	1990	$15

ABSTRACTS, THE
POMPEII

❑ 6002 [M]	The Abstracts	1968	$100
—Stereo cover with "DJ Copy Monaural" sticker; white label promo record			
❑ SD6002 [S]	The Abstracts	1968	$40

ACCEPT
EPIC

❑ FE44368	Eat the Heat	1989	$12

PASSPORT

❑ 9849	Accept	1982	$15
❑ PB6010	Breaker	198?	$15

POLYDOR

❑ 815770-1	Accept	1986	$10
❑ 815771-1	I'm a Rebel	1986	$10

Number	Title	Yr	NM
PORTRAIT			
❏ BFR39241	Balls to the Wall	1984	$12
❏ PR39241	Balls to the Wall	1986	$10
❏ 5R40261 [EP]	Kaizoku-Ban	1986	$10
❏ BFR39974	Metal Heart	1985	$12
❏ PR39974	Metal Heart	1986	$10
❏ BFR39215	Restless and Wild	1983	$15
❏ PR39215	Restless and Wild	1986	$10
❏ BFR40354	Russian Roulette	1986	$12
PVC			
❏ 8915	Midnight Highway	198?	$15

AC/DC
Also see GEORDIE.

Number	Title	Yr	NM
ATCO			
❏ SD 36-142	High Voltage	1976	$15
❏ SD 36-151	Let There Be Rock	1977	$15
❏ 91413	The Razors Edge	1990	$18
ATLANTIC			
❏ 80178 [EP]	74 Jailbreak	1984	$12
❏ SD16018	Back in Black	1980	$12
❏ 81828	Blow Up Your Video	1988	$12
❏ SD16033	Dirty Deeds Done Dirt Cheap	1981	$12
❏ 80100	Flick of the Switch	1983	$12
❏ PR562 [DJ]	Flick of the Switch Interview Album	1983	$75
❏ 81263	Fly on the Wall	1985	$12
❏ SD11111	For Those About to Rock We Salute You	1981	$12
❏ SD19244	Highway to Hell	1979	$12
❏ SD19212	If You Want Blood You've Got It	1978	$12
❏ LAAS-001 [DJ]	Live at the Atlantic Studios	1977	$150

— This album has been counterfeited

Number	Title	Yr	NM
❏ SD19180	Powerage	1978	$12
❏ 81650	Who Made Who	1986	$12

EASTWEST

Number	Title	Yr	NM
❏ 61780 [B]	Ballbreaker	1995	$25
EPIC			
❏ E80200 [EP]	74 Jailbreak	2003	$12
❏ 90643 [B]	AC/DC	2003	$250

— Box set with 15 albums on 16 LPs in black slipcase

Number	Title	Yr	NM
❏ E290553 [B]	AC/DC Live	2003	$18
❏ E80207	Back in Black	2003	$15
❏ E80212	Blow Up Your Video	2003	$15
❏ E80202	Dirty Deeds Done Dirt Cheap	2003	$15
❏ E80209	Flick of the Switch	2003	$15
❏ E80210	Fly on the Wall	2003	$15
❏ E80208	For Those About to Rock We Salute You	2003	$15
❏ E80201	High Voltage	2003	$15
❏ E80206	Highway to Hell	2003	$15
❏ E80205	If You Want Blood You've Got It	2003	$15
❏ E80203	Let There Be Rock	2003	$15
❏ E80204	Powerage	2003	$15
❏ E80213	The Razors Edge	2003	$30
❏ E80211	Who Made Who	2003	$15

ACE, JOHNNY

Number	Title	Yr	NM
ABC DUKE			
❏ DLPX-71	Memorial Album	1974	$25
DUKE			
❏ DLP-70 [10]	Memorial Album for Johnny Ace	1955	$1200

— VG value 400; VG+ value 800

Number	Title	Yr	NM
❏ DLP-71 [M]	Memorial Album for Johnny Ace	1956	$500

— With no playing card on front cover

Number	Title	Yr	NM
❏ DLP-71 [M]	Memorial Album for Johnny Ace	1961	$250

— With playing card on front cover

Number	Title	Yr	NM
❏ DLP-71 [M]	Memorial Album for Johnny Ace	1961	$4000

— Playing card cover; red vinyl; VG value 2000; VG+ value 3000

Number	Title	Yr	NM
❏ LP-71 [R]	Memorial Album for Johnny Ace	196?	$50

— Orange label; trail-off number is "LRS-71

Number	Title	Yr	NM
MCA			
❏ 27014	Memorial Album	1983	$10

ACE

Number	Title	Yr	NM
ANCHOR			
❏ ANCL-2001 [B]	Five-a-Side (An Ace Album)	1975	$25
❏ ANCL-2020 [B]	No Strings	1977	$25
❏ ANCL-2013 [B]	Time for Another	1975	$30

ACE JUICE

Number	Title	Yr	NM
CAPITOL			
❏ C1-90925	Ace Juice	1989	$15

ACE SPECTRUM

Number	Title	Yr	NM
ATLANTIC			
❏ SD7299	Inner Spectrum	1974	$25
❏ SD18185	Just Like in the Movies	1976	$25
❏ SD18143	Low Rent Rendezvous	1975	$25

ACKLES, DAVID

Number	Title	Yr	NM
COLUMBIA			
❏ KC32466 [B]	Five & Dime	1973	$25
ELEKTRA			
❏ EKS-75032	American Gothic	1972	$15
❏ EKS-74022	David Ackles	1968	$18
❏ EKS-74060	Subway to the Country	1970	$15

ACKLIN, BARBARA

Number	Title	Yr	NM
BRUNSWICK			
❏ BL754129	Great Soul Hits	1967	$30
❏ BL754187	I Call It Trouble	1972	$25
❏ BL754166	I Did It	1971	$25
❏ BL754137 [B]	Love Makes a Woman	1968	$25
❏ BL754148	Seven Days of Night	1969	$25
❏ BL754156	Someone Else's Arms	1970	$25
CAPITOL			
❏ ST-11377	A Place in the Sun	1975	$15

ACOUSTIC ALCHEMY

Number	Title	Yr	NM
MCA			
❏ 6291	Blue Chip	1989	$25
❏ 42125	Natural Elements	1988	$25
❏ 5816	Red Dust and Spanish Lace	1987	$25

ACUFF, ROY

Number	Title	Yr	NM
CAPITOL			
❏ T617 [M]	Songs of the Smoky Mountains	1955	$75
❏ T1870 [M]	The Best of Roy Acuff	1963	$30
❏ DT1870 [R]	The Best of Roy Acuff	1963	$25
❏ T2103 [M]	The Great Roy Acuff	1964	$30
❏ DT2103 [R]	The Great Roy Acuff	1964	$18
❏ T2276 [M]	The Voice of Country Music	1965	$30
❏ ST2276 [S]	The Voice of Country Music	1965	$40
COLUMBIA			
❏ FC39998	Columbia Historic Edition	1985	$12
❏ CL9010 [10]	Old Time Barn Dance	1949	$175
❏ CL9013 [10]	Songs of the Saddle	1950	$175
❏ CL9004 [10]	Songs of the Smoky Mountains	1949	$250
ELEKTRA			
❏ E-C010/1/1978 [DJ]	An Interview with Roy Acuff	1978	$30
HARMONY			
❏ HL7082 [M]	Great Speckled Bird	1958	$30
❏ HL7294 [M]	That Glory Bound Train	1961	$25
❏ HL7342 [M]	The Great Roy Acuff	196?	$18
❏ HL7376 [M]	Waiting for My Call to Glory	196?	$18
HICKORY			
❏ LPM-119 [M]	Country Music Hall of Fame	1964	$25
❏ LPS-139	Famous Opry Favorites	1967	$25
❏ ST-91297	Famous Opry Favorites	1967	$30

— Capitol Record Club edition

Number	Title	Yr	NM
❏ LPM-125 [M]	Great Train Songs	1965	$25
❏ DT-90698 [R]	Great Train Songs	1965	$30

— Capitol Record Club edition

Number	Title	Yr	NM
❏ LPM-117 [M]	Hand-Clapping Gospel Songs	1963	$30
❏ LPM-109 [M]	King of Country Music -- All-Time Greatest Hits	1962	$30
❏ T-90704 [M]	King of Country Music -- All-Time Greatest Hits	1966	$30

— Capitol Record Club edition

Number	Title	Yr	NM
❏ LPS-145	Living Legend	1968	$25
❏ LPM-H-101 [M]	Once More It's Roy Acuff	1961	$30
❏ LPM-115 [M]	Roy Acuff Sings American Folk Songs	1963	$30
❏ LPM-134 [M]	Roy Acuff Sings Hank Williams	1966	$40
❏ LPS-134 [S]	Roy Acuff Sings Hank Williams	1966	$40
❏ LPM-113 [M]	Roy Acuff -- Star of the Grand Ole Opry	1963	$30
❏ LPS-156	Roy Acuff Time	1970	$25
❏ LPM-114 [M]	The World Is His Stage	1963	$30
❏ LPS-147	Treasury of Country Hits	1969	$25

Number	Title	Yr	NM
METRO			
❏ M508 [M]	Roy Acuff	1965	$18
❏ MS508 [R]	Roy Acuff	1965	$12
MGM			
❏ E-3707 [M]	Favorite Hymns	1958	$50
❏ E-4044 [M]	Hymn Time	1962	$30
❏ SE-4044 [R]	Hymn Time	196?	$25
ROUNDER			
❏ SS-23	1936-1939: Steamboat Whistle Blues	1985	$12
❏ SS-24	1939-1941: Fly Birdie Fly	1985	$12

ADAM AND THE ANTS

Number	Title	Yr	NM
EPIC			
❏ AE1331 [DJ]	Adam and the Ants	1981	$12

— Five-song promo-only sampler

Number	Title	Yr	NM
❏ FE38698	Dirk Wears White Sox	1983	$12

— First U.S. issue of U.K. debut

Number	Title	Yr	NM
❏ PE38698	Dirk Wears White Sox	1984	$10

— Budget-line reissue

Number	Title	Yr	NM
❏ NJE37033	Kings of the Wild Frontier	1981	$15
❏ PE37033	Kings of the Wild Frontier	1985	$10

— Budget-line reissue

Number	Title	Yr	NM
❏ ARE37615	Prince Charming	1981	$12
❏ PE37615	Prince Charming	1984	$10

— Budget-line reissue

ADAMS, BRYAN

Number	Title	Yr	NM
A&M			
❏ SP-4800	Bryan Adams	1980	$15
❏ SP-3100	Bryan Adams	198?	$10

— Budget-line reissue of 4800

Number	Title	Yr	NM
❏ SP-17231 [DJ]	Cuts	1983	$30

— Promo-only four-song sampler from "Cuts Like a Knife" LP

Number	Title	Yr	NM
❏ SP-6-4919	Cuts Like a Knife	1983	$12

— Original with "6" as part of the catalog number

Number	Title	Yr	NM
❏ SP-4919	Cuts Like a Knife	1984	$10

— Reissue without the "6" in the catalog number

Number	Title	Yr	NM
❏ SP-3288	Cuts Like a Knife	198?	$10

— Budget-line reissue of 4919

Number	Title	Yr	NM
❏ SP-3907	Into the Fire	1987	$10
❏ R153919	Into the Fire	1987	$12

— BMG Direct Marketing edition

Number	Title	Yr	NM
❏ SP-5013	Reckless	1984	$10
❏ R151540	Reckless	1984	$12

— RCA Music Service edition

Number	Title	Yr	NM
❏ SP-17321 [DJ]	Retail Sampler	1985	$30

— 10-song collection, a sort of "greatest hits" compilation to that time; promo only

Number	Title	Yr	NM
❏ SP-5327	Waking Up the Neighbours	1991	$25

— Columbia House edition; the only U.S. vinyl of this LP

Number	Title	Yr	NM
❏ SP-4864	You Want It, You Got It	1981	$15
❏ SP-3154	You Want It, You Got It	198?	$10

— Budget-line reissue of 4864

ADAMS, EDIE

Number	Title	Yr	NM
DECCA			
❏ DL4488 [M]	Behind Those Swingin' Doors	1964	$30
❏ DL74488 [S]	Behind Those Swingin' Doors	1964	$30
MGM			
❏ E-3751 [M]	Music to Listen to Records To	1959	$50
❏ SE-3751 [S]	Music to Listen to Records To	1959	$75

ADAMS, FAYE

Number	Title	Yr	NM
COLLECTABLES			
❏ COL-5122	Golden Classics	1988	$12
WARWICK			
❏ W2031 [M]	Shake a Hand	1961	$600

ADAMS, GAYLE

Number	Title	Yr	NM
PRELUDE			
❏ PRL12178	Gayle Adams	1980	$15
❏ PRL14104	Love Fever	1982	$15

ADAMS, GEORGE-DANNIE RICHMOND QUARTET

Number	Title	Yr	NM
SOUL NOTE			
❏ SN-1057	Gentleman's Agreement	1983	$30
❏ SN-1007	Hand to Hand	1980	$30

ADAMS, GEORGE-DON PULLEN QUARTET

Number	Title	Yr	NM
BLUE NOTE			
❏ BLJ-46907	A Song Everlasting	1987	$25
❏ BT-85122	Breakthrough	1986	$25
SOUL NOTE			
❏ SN-1004	Don't Lose Control	198?	$30
❏ SN-1094	Live at the Village Vanguard	1985	$30
❏ 121144-1	Live at the Village Vanguard 2	199?	$25
TIMELESS			
❏ LPSJP-147	Earth Beams	1990	$30

ADAMS, GEORGE

Number	Title	Yr	NM
BLUE NOTE			
B1-91984	Nightingale	1989	$25
— Tenor sax			
ECM			
1141	Sound Suggestions	1979	$30
TIMELESS			
322	Paradise Space Shuttle	1981	$30

ADAMS, JERRI

Number	Title	Yr	NM
COLUMBIA			
CL916 [M]	It's Cool Inside	1956	$40
CL1258 [M]	Play for Keeps	1958	$40

ADAMS, JOHNNY

Number	Title	Yr	NM
ANALOGUE PRODUCTIONS			
APP 028	Johnny Adams Sings Doc Pomus -- The Real Me	199?	$25
ARIOLA AMERICA			
SW50038	After All the Good Is Gone	1978	$18
CHELSEA			
CHL525	Stand By Me	1977	$30
HEP ME			
159	Christmas in New Orleans	197?	$18
ROUNDER			
2049	After Dark	1986	$15
2044	From the Heart	1984	$15
2059	Room with a View of the Blues	1988	$15
2095	Walking on a Tightrope	1989	$15
SSS INTERNATIONAL			
5	Heart and Soul	1969	$25

ADAMS, KAY

Number	Title	Yr	NM
TOWER			
ST5087	Alcohol & Tears	1968	$25
T5069 [M]	Make Mine Country	1967	$30
ST5069	Make Mine Country	1967	$25
T5033 [M]	Wheels & Tears	1966	$30
ST5033 [S]	Wheels & Tears	1966	$30

ADAMS, MIKE, AND THE RED JACKETS

Number	Title	Yr	NM
CROWN			
CLP-5312 [M]	Surfer's Beat	1963	$30
CST-312 [S]	Surfer's Beat	1963	$30
— Black vinyl			
CST-312 [S]	Surfer's Beat	1963	$120
— Red vinyl			
CLP-5255 [M]	Twist Contest	1962	$30
CST-255 [S]	Twist Contest	1962	$30

ADAMS, NANCY

Number	Title	Yr	NM
MEGA			
M31-1018	Nancy Adams and the Deer Creek Fundamentalists	1972	$25

ADAMS, OLETA

Number	Title	Yr	NM
FONTANA			
846346-1	Circle of One	1990	$15

ADAMS, PEPPER, AND FRANK FOSTER

Number	Title	Yr	NM
MUSE			
MR-5313 [B]	Generations	1986	$35

ADAMS, PEPPER, AND JIMMY KNEPPER

Number	Title	Yr	NM
METROJAZZ			
E-1004 [M]	The Pepper-Knepper Quintet	1958	$350
SE-1004 [S]	The Pepper-Knepper Quintet	1959	$350

ADAMS, PEPPER

Number	Title	Yr	NM
BETHLEHEM			
BCP-6056 [M]	Motor City Scene	1961	$250
6056 [B]	Motor City Scene	19–	$500
— red label			
ENJA			
2060	Julian	1976	$35
2074	Twelfth and Pingree	1976	$50
FANTASY			
OJC-031 [M]	10 to 4 at the 5 Spot	198?	$30
— Reissue of Riverside 12-265			
INNER CITY			
IC-3014	Julian	1976	$30
INTERLUDE			
MO-502 [M]	Pepper Adams 5	1959	$150
— Reissue of Mode 112			
ST-1002 [S]	Pepper Adams 5	1959	$75
— Reissue of Mode 112; remixed into stereo; black vinyl			
ST-1002 [S]	Pepper Adams 5	1959	$175
— Orange vinyl			
MODE			
LP-112 [M]	Pepper Adams 5	1957	$300
— With Mel Lewis			
112 [S]	Quintet		$150
MUSE			
MR-5182	Reflectory	1979	$50
MR-5213	The Master	1980	$35
PALO ALTO			
PA-8009	Urban Dreams	1981	$35
PRESTIGE			
PRST-7677 [B]	Encounter	1969	$175
— With Zoot Sims			
REGENT			
MG-6066 [M]	The Cool Sound of Pepper Adams	1958	$180
RIVERSIDE			
RLP 12-265 [M]	10 to 4 at the 5 Spot	1958	$250
RLP-1104 [S]	10 to 4 at the 5 Spot	1959	$150
— black label			
SAVOY			
MG-12211 [M]	The Cool Sound of Pepper Adams	196?	$40
— Reissue of Regent 6066			
SAVOY JAZZ			
SJL-1142	Pure Pepper	198?	$30
— Reissue of Savoy 12211			
WARWICK			
W-2041 [M]	Out of This World	1961	$250
— With Donald Byrd			
WORKSHOP JAZZ			
WSJ-219 [M]	Pepper Adams Plays the Compositions of Charles Mingus	1964	$175
WSJS-219 [S]	Pepper Adams Plays the Compositions of Charles Mingus	1964	$140
219 [S]	Plays Mingus		$150
WORLD PACIFIC			
PJM-407 [M]	Critic's Choice	1957	$400
— With Mel Lewis			
WPM-407 [M]	Critic's Choice	1958	$400
— With Mel Lewis; reissue with new prefix			
ZIM			
ZLS2000 [B]	Ephemera	197?	$150

ADAMS, RYAN

Number	Title	Yr	NM
LOST HIGHWAY			
B0005872-01	29	2005	$25
B0004343-01	Cold Roses	2005	$30
— As "Ryan Adams and the Cardinals			
088170333-1	Demolition	2002	$30
88170235-1	Gold	2002	$175
B0004707-01	Jacksonville City Nights	2005	$30
— As "Ryan Adams and the Cardinals			

Number	Title	Yr	NM
B0001702-1 [10]	Love Is Hell Pts. 1 & 2	2003	$100
— Combination of two EPs on two 10-inch records in gatefold sleeve			
B0001376-01	Rock N Roll	2003	$30

ADC BAND, THE

Number	Title	Yr	NM
COTILLION			
SD16041	Brother Luck	1981	$12
SD5210	Long Stroke	1978	$12
SD5221	Renaissance	1980	$12
SD5232	Roll with the Punches	1982	$12
SD5216	Talk That Stuff	1979	$12

ADDEO, LEO

Number	Title	Yr	NM
RCA CAMDEN			
CAL-807 [M]	Calypso and Other Island Favorites	1963	$15
CAS-807 [S]	Calypso and Other Island Favorites	1963	$18
CAL-901 [M]	Far Away Places	1965	$15
CAS-901 [S]	Far Away Places	1965	$18
CAL-672 [M]	Great Standards with a Hawaiian Touch	1962	$15
CAS-672 [S]	Great Standards with a Hawaiian Touch	1962	$18
CAL-853 [M]	Hawaiian Paradise	1964	$15
CAS-853 [S]	Hawaiian Paradise	1964	$18
CAL-510 [M]	Hawaii in Hi-Fi	1960	$18
CAS-510 [S]	Hawaii in Stereo	1960	$25
CAL-828 [M]	Hello Dolly" and Other Favorites	1964	$15
CAS-828 [S]	Hello Dolly" and Other Favorites	1964	$18
CAL-2134 [M]	Love Is a Hurtin' Thing" and Other Favorites	1966	$15
CAS-2134 [S]	Love Is a Hurtin' Thing" and Other Favorites	1966	$18
CAL-594 [M]	More Hawaii in Hi-Fi	1961	$18
CAS-594 [S]	More Hawaii in Hi-Fi	1961	$25
CAL-977 [M]	Musical Orchids from Hawaii	1966	$15
CAS-977 [S]	Musical Orchids from Hawaii	1966	$18
CAL-726 [M]	Organ and Chimes Play Christmas Carols	1962	$15
CAS-726 [S]	Organ and Chimes Play Christmas Carols	1962	$18
CAL-759 [M]	Songs of Hawaii	1963	$15
CAS-759 [S]	Songs of Hawaii	1963	$18
CAL-2211 [M]	The Magic of Hawaii	1967	$15
CAS-2211 [S]	The Magic of Hawaii	1967	$18
RCA VICTOR			
LPM-2414 [M]	Paradise Regained	1961	$18
LSA-2414 [S]	Paradise Regained	1961	$30

ADDERLEY, CANNONBALL

Number	Title	Yr	NM
AMBASSADOR			
S-98053	The Love Album	197?	$35
BLUE NOTE			
BLP-1595 [M]	Somethin' Else	1958	$1200
— Deep groove" version; W. 63rd St. address on label			
BLP-1595 [M]	Somethin' Else	1958	$250
— Regular version; W. 63rd St. address on label			
BLP-1595 [M]	Somethin' Else	1963	$150
— New York, USA" address on label			
BST-1595 [S]	Somethin' Else	1959	$175
— Deep groove" version; W. 63rd St. address on label			
BST-1595 [S]	Somethin' Else	1959	$200
— Regular version; W. 63rd St. address on label			
BST-81595 [S]	Somethin' Else	1963	$75
— New York, USA" address on label			
BST-81595 [S]	Somethin' Else	1966	$50
— With "A Division of Liberty Records" on label			
BN-LA169-H2	Somethin' Else	1973	$30
— Reissue			
LT-169	Somethin' Else	1981	$25
— Another reissue			
BST-81595	Somethin' Else	1984	$25
— The Finest in Jazz Since 1939" label			
ST-46338	Somethin' Else	1997	$50
— Audiophile reissue			
BST-81595	Somethin' Else	199?	$75
— Classic Records reissue on 180-gram vinyl			
BST-1595 [S]	Somethin' Else	2002	$75
— Classic Records reissue on 200-gram vinyl			
BLP-1595 [M]	Somethin' Else	2002	$150
— Classic Records reissue on 200-gram vinyl			
BLP-1595C	Somethin' Else	2002	$250
— Comparison Pack"; contains both the mono and stereo versions of the LP; Classic Records issue on 200-gram vinyl			
CAPITOL			
T2822 [M]	74 Miles Away -- Walk Tall	1967	$85
ST2822 [S]	74 Miles Away -- Walk Tall	1967	$100
ST2987	Accent on Africa	1968	$100
SWBO-812	Cannonball Adderley and Friends	1971	$100
SVBB-11233	Cannonball Adderley and Friends	1974	$35
— Reissue of 812			
SM-11817	Cannonball Adderley and Friends, Vol. 1	1978	$25
SM-11838	Cannonball Adderley and Friends, Vol. 2	1978	$25
ST-2877	Cannonball Adderley and the Bossa Rio Sextet with Sergio Mendes	1968	$175
— Reissue of 8 of the 10 tracks from Riverside 9455			
T2399 [M]	Cannonball Adderley -- Live!	1965	$100
ST2399 [S]	Cannonball Adderley -- Live!	1965	$150
SM-2399	Cannonball Adderley -- Live!	1976	$25
ST-162	Cannonball in Person	1968	$100
SKAO-404	Country Preacher	1970	$150
SKAO-80404	Country Preacher	1970	$150
— Capitol Record Club edition			
T2203 [M]	Domination	1964	$100
ST2203 [S]	Domination	1964	$150

Number	Title	Yr	NM
❏ ST-484	Experience in E, Tensity, Dialogues	1970	$75
❏ T2216 [M]	Fiddler on the Roof	1965	$100
❏ ST2216 [S]	Fiddler on the Roof	1965	$150
❏ ST-11008	Fiddler on the Roof	1972	$35
—Reissue of 2216			
❏ T2531 [M]	Great Love Themes	1966	$100
❏ ST2531 [S]	Great Love Themes	1966	$150
❏ ST-11121	Happy People	1973	$40
❏ T2284 [M]	Live Session	1965	$100
❏ ST2284 [S]	Live Session	1965	$150
❏ T2663 [M]	Mercy, Mercy, Mercy!	1967	$100
❏ ST2663 [S]	Mercy, Mercy, Mercy!	1967	$85
❏ SM-2663	Mercy, Mercy, Mercy!	1976	$25
❏ SN-16153	Mercy, Mercy, Mercy!	1981	$20
—Budget-line reissue			
❏ ST-8-2663 [S]	Mercy, Mercy, Mercy!	1969	$100
—Capitol Record Club edition			
❏ ST-11484	Music, You All	1975	$85
❏ SN-16002	The Best of Cannonball Adderley	1979	$20
❏ SKAO2939	The Best of Cannonball Adderley	1968	$85
—Black label with colorband			
❏ SKAO-502939	The Best of Cannonball Adderley	1976	$35
—Columbia House edition; orange labels			
❏ SWBO-846	The Black Messiah	1972	$300
❏ SWBB-636	The Price You Got to Pay to Be Free	1971	$300
❏ SABB-11120	The Soul of the Bible	1973	$300
—Reproductions exist			
❏ STBB-697	Walk Tall/Quiet Nights	1971	$100
❏ T2617 [M]	Why Am I Treated So Bad?	1966	$75
❏ ST2617 [S]	Why Am I Treated So Bad?	1966	$100
DOBRE			
❏ 1008	Cannonball, Volume 1	1977	$30
EMARCY			
❏ EMS-2-404	Beginnings	1976	$50
❏ 36043 [B]	Cannonball		$250
—drummer logo			
❏ MG-36135 [M]	Cannonball's Sharpshooters	1958	$250

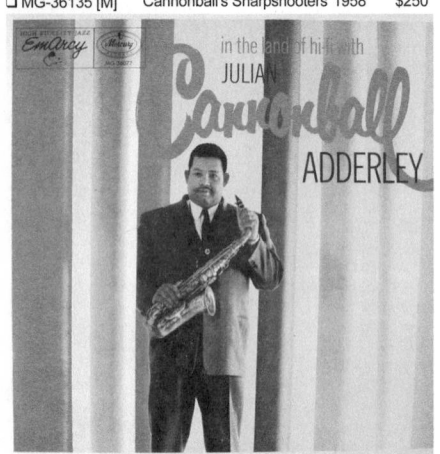

Number	Title	Yr	NM
❏ MG-36077 [M]	In the Land of Hi-Fi	1956	$150
❏ MG-36043 [M]	Julian "Cannonball" Adderley	1955	$175
❏ MG-36063 [M]	Julian "Cannonball" Adderley and Strings	1956	$250
❏ MG-36146 [M]	Jump for Joy	1958	$175
❏ SR-80017 [S]	Jump for Joy	1958	$120
❏ MG-36110 [M]	Sophisticated Swing	1957	$80
EVEREST ARCHIVE OF FOLK & JAZZ			
❏ FS-261	Cannonball Adderley and John Coltrane	1973	$30
—Abridged reissue of Limelight 86009			
❏ FS-291 [B]	Cannonball Adderley with Sergio Mendes	197?	$15
FANTASY			
❏ OJC-258	African Waltz	1987	$25
❏ F-79006	Big Man	1976	$50
❏ OJC-035	Cannonball Adderley Quintet in San Francisco	1982	$25
❏ OJC-142	Cannonball Adderley Sextet In New York	1985	$25
❏ F-9435	Inside Straight	1973	$50
❏ OJC-105	Know What I Mean?	1984	$25
❏ F-9445	Love, Sex and the Zodiac	1974	$200
❏ F-9505	Lovers	1975	$40
❏ FSP2 [DJ]	Musical Highliights from Big Man	1975	$75
❏ OJC-435	Nippon Soul	1990	$35
❏ F-79004	Phenix	1975	$75
❏ OJC-361	Portrait of Cannonball	1989	$25
❏ F-9455	Pyramid	1974	$40
❏ OJC-306	The Cannonball Adderley Quintet Plus	1988	$25
❏ OJC-032	Things Are Getting Better	1982	$25

Number	Title	Yr	NM
LANDMARK			
❏ LLP-1301 [B]	The Cannonball Adderley Collection Vol. 1: Them Dirty Blues	1985	$15
❏ LLP-1302 [B]	The Cannonball Adderley Collection Vol. 2: Cannonball's Bossa Nova	1985	$15
❏ LLP-1303 [B]	The Cannonball Adderley Collection Vol. 3: Jazz Workshop Revisited	1985	$15
❏ LLP-1304 [B]	The Cannonball Adderley Collection Vol. 4: Cannonball and the Poll-Winners	1985	$15
❏ LLP-1305 [B]	The Cannonball Adderley Collection Vol. 5: At the Lighthouse	1985	$15
❏ LLP-1306 [B]	The Cannonball Adderley Collection Vol. 6: Cannonball! Takes Charge	1985	$15
❏ LLP-1307 [B]	The Cannonball Adderley Collection Vol. 7: Cannonball in Europe	1985	$15
LIMELIGHT			
❏ LM82009 [M]	Cannonball and Coltrane	1964	$150
—Reissue of Mercury 20449			
❏ LS86009 [S]	Cannonball and Coltrane	1964	$150
—Reissue of Mercury 60134			
MERCURY			
❏ MG-20449 [M]	Cannonball Adderley Quintet in Chicago	1959	$150
❏ SR-60134 [S]	Cannonball Adderley Quintet in Chicago	1960	$150
❏ MG-20616 [M]	Cannonball En Route	1961	$175
❏ SR-60616 [S]	Cannonball En Route	1961	$150
❏ MG-20531 [M]	Cannonball's Sharpshooters	1960	$175
—Reissue of EmArcy 36135			
❏ SR-60531 [S]	Cannonball's Sharpshooters	1960	$150
❏ SR-60530 [S]	Jump for Joy	1960	$150
❏ MG-20530 [M]	Jump for Joy	1960	$175
—Reissue of EmArcy 36146			
❏ MG-20652 [M]	The Lush Side of Cannonball Adderley	1961	$175
—Reissue of EmArcy 36063			
❏ SR-60652 [R]	The Lush Side of Cannonball Adderley	1961	$150
MILESTONE			
❏ M-47059	Alabama/Africa	1982	$35
❏ M-9030	Cannonball Adderley in New Orleans	197?	$50
❏ M-47039	Coast to Coast	1976	$75
❏ M-47001	Eight Giants	1973	$35
❏ M-47029	The Japanese Concerts	1975	$75
❏ M-9106	The Sextet	198?	$35
❏ M-47053	What I Mean	1979	$35
PABLO LIVE			
❏ 2308238	What Is This Thing Called Soul	1984	$30
PICKWICK			
❏ SPC-3128	I Got It Bad and That Ain't Good	196?	$25
❏ SPC-3255	Quiet Nights of Quiet Stars	196?	$25
—Reissue of eight of the 10 tracks on Riverside 9455; co-credited to Sergio Mendes			
RIVERSIDE			
❏ RLP377 [M]	African Waltz	1961	$250
❏ RS9377 [S]	African Waltz	1961	$250
❏ RLP355 [M]	Cannonball Adderley and the Poll-Winners	1960	$250
❏ RS9355 [S]	Cannonball Adderley and the Poll-Winners	1960	$250
❏ RLP344 [M]	Cannonball Adderley Quintet at the Lighthouse	1960	$250
❏ RS9344 [S]	Cannonball Adderley Quintet at the Lighthouse	1960	$250
❏ RLP 12-311 [M]	Cannonball Adderley Quintet in San Francisco	1959	$300
❏ RLP1157 [S]	Cannonball Adderley Quintet in San Francisco	1959	$300
❏ 6062	Cannonball Adderley Quintet in San Francisco	197?	$35
—Reissue of 1157			
❏ RLP388 [M]	Cannonball Adderley Quintet 1961 Plus	1961	$250
❏ RS9388 [S]	Cannonball Adderley Quintet 1961 Plus	1961	$250
❏ RLP404 [M]	Cannonball Adderley Sextet In New York	1962	$150
—blue label			
❏ RS9404 [S]	Cannonball Adderley Sextet In New York	1962	$250
❏ 6108	Cannonball Adderley Sextet In New York	197?	$35
—Reissue of 9404			
❏ RM499 [M]	Cannonball in Europe	1964	$175
❏ RS9499 [S]	Cannonball in Europe	1964	$175
❏ RLP455 [M]	Cannonball's Bossa Nova	1963	$175
❏ RS9455 [S]	Cannonball's Bossa Nova	1963	$175
❏ RS9416 [S]	Cannonball's Greatest Hits	1962	$250
❏ RLP416 [M]	Cannonball's Greatest Hits	1962	$250
❏ RLP 12-303 [M]	Cannonball Takes Charge	1959	$300
❏ RLP1148 [S]	Cannonball Takes Charge	1959	$300
❏ RLP444 [M]	Jazz Workshop Revisited	1963	$175
❏ RS9444 [S]	Jazz Workshop Revisited	1963	$175
❏ RLP433 [M]	Know What I Mean?	1962	$100
—blue label			
❏ RS9433 [S]	Know What I Mean?	1962	$120

Number	Title	Yr	NM
—black label			
❏ 6051	Know What I Mean?	197?	$35
—Reissue of 9433			
❏ RLP477 [M]	Nippon Soul -- Recorded in Concert in Tokyo	1964	$175
❏ RS9477 [S]	Nippon Soul -- Recorded in Concert in Tokyo	1964	$175
❏ RS3041	Planet Earth	1969	$150
❏ RLP 12-269 [M]	Portrait of Cannonball	1958	$300
❏ RS3038	The Best of Cannonball Adderley	1968	$150
❏ RLP 12-322 [M]	Them Dirty Blues	1960	$250
❏ RLP1170 [M]	Them Dirty Blues	1960	$250
❏ RLP 12-286 [M]	Things Are Getting Better	1959	$175
—blue label			
❏ RLP1128 [S]	Things Are Getting Better	1959	$250
❏ 6122	Things Are Getting Better	197?	$35
—Reissue of 1128			
SAVOY			
❏ MG-12018 [M]	Presenting Cannonball	1955	$175
—Band pictured on cover, red label			
❏ MG-12018 [M]	Presenting Cannonball	196?	$175
—Cannonballs pictured on cover with band members merely listed			
SAVOY JAZZ			
❏ SJL-1195	Discoveries	1987	$35
❏ SJC-401	Presenting Cannonball	1985	$30
—Reissue of Savoy 12018			
❏ SJL-2206	Spontaneous Combustion	1976	$35
SEARS			
❏ SPS-460	Jump for Joy	196?	$35
TRIP			
❏ TLP-5573 [M]	In the Land of Hi-Fi	197?	$35
WING			
❏ SRW-16362 [S]	Cannonball Adderley Quintet	196?	$50
WONDERLAND/RIVERSIDE			
❏ RLP1435 [M]	A Child's Introduction to Jazz	196?	$150
—Adderley narrates an album introducing the works of such artists as Armstrong, Monk, Waller, etc.			
ADDERLEY, CANNONBALL AND NAT			
LIMELIGHT			
❏ LM82032 [M]	Them Adderleys	1966	$150
❏ LS86032 [S]	Them Adderleys	1966	$150
ADDERLEY, NAT			
A&M			
❏ SP-3017	Calling Out Loud	1969	$35
❏ LP-2005 [M]	You, Baby	1968	$75
—Mono is promo only			
❏ SP-3005 [S]	You, Baby	1968	$35
❏ SP9-3005	You, Baby	1983	$35
—Audio Master Plus" reissue			
ATLANTIC			
❏ 1439 [M]	Autobiography	1965	$35
❏ SD1439 [S]	Autobiography	1965	$50
❏ 1475 [M]	Live at Memory Lane	1967	$50
❏ SD1475 [S]	Live at Memory Lane	1967	$35
❏ 1460 [M]	Sayin' Something	1966	$35
❏ SD1460 [S]	Sayin' Something	1966	$50
CAPITOL			
❏ SVBB-11025	Cannonball Adderley Presents Soul Zodiac	1972	$300
EMARCY			
❏ MG-36091 [M]	Introducing Nat Adderley	1955	$300
❏ MG-36100 [M]	To the Ivy League from Nat	1956	$250
FANTASY			
❏ OJC-255	Branching Out	1987	$25
—Reissue of Riverside 12-285			
❏ OJC-648	In the Bag	1991	$30
—Reissue of Jazzland 975			
❏ OJC-363	The Work Song	198?	$25
—Reissue of Riverside 1167			
GALAXY			
❏ 5120	Little New York Midtown Music	197?	$25
JAZZLAND			
❏ JLP-75 [M]	In the Bag	1962	$75
❏ JLP-975 [S]	In the Bag	1962	$40
❏ JLP-47 [M]	Naturally!	1961	$75
❏ JLP-947 [S]	Naturally!	1961	$40
LITTLE DAVID			
❏ LD1012	Hummin'	1975	$30
MILESTONE			
❏ MSP-9009	Natural Soul	1968	$35
❏ MSP-9016	The Scavenger	1968	$35
❏ 47047	Work Songs	197?	$30
PRESTIGE			
❏ 10090	Double Exposure	1974	$30
RIVERSIDE			
❏ RLP 12-285 [M]	Branching Out	1958	$300
❏ RM-474 [M]	Little Big Horn!	1964	$175
❏ RS-9474 [S]	Little Big Horn!	1964	$175

Number	Title	Yr	NM
❏ RLP 12-301 [M]	Much Brass	1959	$300
❏ RLP-1143 [S]	Much Brass	1959	$300
❏ RLP-330 [M]	That's Right!	1960	$250
❏ RS-9330 [S]	That's Right!	1960	$250
❏ RLP 12-318 [M]	The Work Song	1960	$250
❏ RLP-1167 [S]	The Work Song	1960	$250
❏ 6041	The Work Song	197?	$30

— Reissue

SAVOY

| ❏ MG-12021 [M] | That's Nat | 1955 | $175 |

SAVOY JAZZ

| ❏ SJL-1128 | That's Nat | 198? | $25 |

— Reissue of Savoy 12021

STEEPLECHASE

| ❏ SCS-1059 | Don't Look Back | 198? | $25 |

THERESA

| ❏ TR-122 | Blue Autumn | 1987 | $25 |
| ❏ TR-117 | On the Move | 198? | $25 |

WING

| ❏ MGW-60000 [M] | Introducing Nat Adderley | 1956 | $150 |

ADDRISI BROTHERS, THE

BUDDAH

| ❏ BDS-5694 | Addrisi Brothers | 1977 | $12 |

COLUMBIA

| ❏ KC31296 | We've Got to Get It On Again | 1972 | $15 |

ADEVA

CAPITOL

| ❏ C1-93708 | Adeva! | 1990 | $15 |
| ❏ SPRO-79163/4 [DJ] | Love or Lust | 1991 | $18 |

— Full-length LP only issued as a promo on vinyl

ADICTS, THE

CLEOPATRA

| ❏ 3951 [B] | Live and Loud '81 | | $25 |

ADKINS, WENDEL

HITSVILLE

| ❏ H6-406S1 | The Sundowners | 1977 | $18 |

MC

| ❏ MC6-503S1 | The Sundowners | 1977 | $15 |

— Reissue of Hitsville LP

ADRIAN AND THE SUNSETS

SUNSET

| ❏ 63-601 [M] | Breakthrough | 1963 | $100 |

— Black vinyl

| ❏ 63-601 [M] | Breakthrough | 1963 | $175 |

— Multi-color vinyl

| ❏ SD 63-601 [S] | Breakthrough | 1963 | $175 |

— Black vinyl

| ❏ SD 63-601 [S] | Breakthrough | 1963 | $300 |

— Multi-color vinyl

ADVANCEMENT, THE

PHILIPS

| ❏ PHS600328 [B] | The Advancement | 1969 | $150 |

ADVENTURERS, THE (1)

COLUMBIA

| ❏ CL1747 [M] | Can't Stop Twistin' | 1961 | $75 |
| ❏ CS8547 [S] | Can't Stop Twistin' | 1961 | $100 |

ADVENTURES, THE

CHRYSALIS

| ❏ BFV41488 | The Adventures | 1985 | $12 |

ELEKTRA

| ❏ 60772 | Sea of Love | 1988 | $10 |
| ❏ 60772 [DJ] | Sea of Love | 1988 | $15 |

— Ptomo-only audiophile pressing with sticker on cover

ADVENTURES OF STEVIE V

MERCURY

| ❏ 846966-1 | Adventures of Stevie V | 1990 | $15 |

ADVERTS, THE

FIRE

| ❏ FIRELP143 [B] | Crossing The Red Sea With The Adverts | 2016 | $40 |

AEROSMITH

COLUMBIA

| ❏ PC32005 | Aerosmith | 1976 | $12 |

— Without bar code

| ❏ KC32005 | Aerosmith | 1973 | $25 |

— Orange cover with back cover typo "Walking The Dig

| ❏ KC32005 | Aerosmith | 1973 | $18 |

— Orange cover with correct title "Walking The Dog

| ❏ KC32005 [B] | Aerosmith | 1973 | $15 |

— Light blue cover, most (if not all) of which say "Featuring 'Dream On' " on front

| ❏ JC32005 | Aerosmith | 1977 | $10 |
| ❏ PC32005 | Aerosmith | 1984 | $10 |

— With bar code

❏ 88765486131 [B]	Aerosmith	2013	$25
❏ FC36865	Aerosmith's Greatest Hits	1980	$12
❏ PC36865	Aerosmith's Greatest Hits	1984	$10
❏ FC40329	Classics Live	1986	$12
❏ FC40855	Classics Live, Vol. 2	1987	$12
❏ 88883760951 [B]	Draw The Line	2014	$25
❏ JC34856	Draw the Line	1977	$15
❏ PC34856	Draw the Line	198?	$10
❏ FC44487	Gems (1973-1982)	1989	$12
❏ KC32847	Get Your Wings	1974	$15
❏ PC32847	Get Your Wings	1976	$12

— Without bar code

❏ KCQ32847 [Q]	Get Your Wings	1974	$40
❏ JC32847	Get Your Wings	1977	$10
❏ PC32847	Get Your Wings	1984	$10

— With bar code

❏ 88765486151 [B]	Get Your Wings	2013	$25
❏ C87025	Honkin' on Bobo	2004	$18
❏ C62088	Just Push Play	2001	$18
❏ PC235564	Live! Bootleg	1978	$18
❏ FC36050	Night in the Ruts	1979	$12
❏ PC36050	Night in the Ruts	1984	$10
❏ A3S187 [DJ]	Pure Gold from Rock 'n' Roll's Golden Boys	1976	$75

— Pro -only compilation of the first three albums

❏ 88883761441 [B]	Rock In A Hard Place	2014	$25
❏ FC38061	Rock in a Hard Place	1982	$12
❏ PC38061	Rock in a Hard Place	1984	$10
❏ PC34165	Rocks	1976	$15

— Without bar code. Some copies have "Rocks" in quotes on the cover, others don't; no difference in value

| ❏ JC34165 | Rocks | 1976 | $12 |

— Some copies have "Rocks" in quotes on the cover, others don't; no difference in value

| ❏ PC34165 | Rocks | 1984 | $10 |

— With bar code

❏ PCQ34165 [Q]	Rocks	1976	$40
❏ 88883760941 [B]	Rocks	2014	$25
❏ 887654861917 [B]	Toys In The Attic	2013	$25
❏ PC33479	Toys in the Attic	1975	$15

— Without bar code

| ❏ JC33479 | Toys in the Attic | 1977 | $12 |
| ❏ PC33479 | Toys in the Attic | 1984 | $10 |

— With bar code

| ❏ PCQ33479 [Q] | Toys in the Attic | 1975 | $40 |

GEFFEN

❏ GHS24091	Done with Mirrors	1985	$10
❏ GHS24162	Permanent Vacation	1987	$12
❏ GHS24254	Pump	1989	$12
❏ GHS24254	Pump	2008	$25

AESOP'S FABLES

CADET CONCEPT

| ❏ LPS-323 | In Due Time | 1969 | $50 |

AFDEM, JEFF, AND THE SPRINGFIELD FLUTE

BURDETTE

| ❏ 5162 | Something | 1969 | $40 |

AFFECTION COLLECTION, THE

EVOLUTION

| ❏ 2007 | The Affection Collection | 1969 | $25 |

AFFINITY

PARAMOUNT

| ❏ PAS-5027 | Affinity | 1970 | $30 |

AFGHAN WHIGS

COLUMBIA

| ❏ C69450 [B] | 1969 | 1998 | $30 |

SUB POP

| ❏ 353 [B] | Black Love | 1996 | $30 |
| ❏ 130 [B] | Congregation | 1992 | $30 |

— Import only; made in Germany (no U.S. vinyl)

| ❏ 238 [B] | Gentlemen | 1993 | $30 |
| ❏ 60 [B] | Up In It | 1990 | $35 |

— First pressings have orange vinyl and a different sleeve than the black vinyl version

| ❏ 60 [B] | Up In It | 1990 | $18 |

ULTRASUEDE

| ❏ 01 [B] | Big Top Halloween | 1988 | $100 |

— Approximately 2,000 copies were made

AFI

ADELINE

| ❏ ADN30035-1 [B] | Decemberunderground | 2006 | $18 |
| ❏ 026 | Sing the Sorrow | 2003 | $25 |

— All copies on red vinyl

NITRO

| ❏ 15811 | Answer That and Stay Fashionable | 1997 | $15 |

— Reissue; available on black, white, red, tan or gray vinyl

| ❏ 15824 | Black Sails in the Sunset | 1999 | $15 |

— Available on black, lilac or gray vinyl

| ❏ 15815 | Shut Your Mouth and Open Your Eyes | 1997 | $15 |

— Available on black, green, yellow, tan, white or gray vinyl

| ❏ 15835 | The Art of Drowning | 2000 | $15 |

— Available on black, gray, green and purplish vinyl

| ❏ 15805 | Very Proud of Ya | 1996 | $15 |

— Black or blue vinyl

| ❏ 15805 | Very Proud of Ya | 1996 | $12 |

— Any other color vinyl ("Special Colored Vinyl" sticker on cover or shinkwrap)

WINGNUT

| ❏ WLRP-1370 | Answer That and Stay Fashionable | 1995 | $30 |

— First edition: Black vinyl; title on two lines on front cover; no address next to Wingnut logo on back

| ❏ WLRP-1370 | Answer That and Stay Fashionable | 1995 | $30 |

— Second edition: Black vinyl; title on one line on front cover; address next to Wingnut logo on back

| ❏ WLRP-1370 | Answer That and Stay Fashionable | 1995 | $50 |

— Third edition: Same as second edition, except on red vinyl

AFRIKA CORPS

IRON CROSS/DACOIT

| ❏ 0(# unknown) | Music to Kill By | 1977 | $75 |

KLEEN KUT/LIMP

| ❏ 0(# unknown) | Hello World! | 1978 | $25 |

— As "The Korps"; blue vinyl

AFRIQUE

MAINSTREAM

| ❏ S-394 [B] | Soul Makossa | 1973 | $18 |

AFRO-RICAN

LUKE SKYYWALKER

| ❏ 109 | Against All Odds | 1989 | $15 |

AFROS, THE

COLUMBIA

| ❏ C46802 | Kickin' Afrolistics | 1990 | $15 |

Number	Title	Yr	NM

AFTER 7
VIRGIN
❏ 91061	After 7	1989	$12

AFTER THE FIRE
EPIC
❏ FE38282	ATF	1983	$15

AFTERGLOW
BEAT ROCKET
❏ BR127	Afterglow	2001	$15

AFTERNOON DELIGHTS, THE
MCA
❏ 5257	General Hospi-Tale	1981	$12

AFTERSHOCK
VIRGIN
❏ 91341	Aftershock	1990	$12

AGAPE
MARK
❏ MRS-2170 [B]	Gospel Hard Rock	1971	$175
RENRUT
❏ 101 [B]	Victims of Tradition	1972	$175

AGE OF REASON, THE
GEORGETOWNE
❏ (no #)	The Age of Reason	1969	$175

AGENT ORANGE
CLEOPATRA
❏ 5543 [B]	Surf Punks		$25

AGGREGATION, THE
LHI
❏ 12008	Mind Odyssey	1967	$400

AGNOSTIC FRONT
COMBAT
❏ 8204	Liberty and Justice for...	1987	$15
❏ 3022	One Voice	1992	$18
COMBAT CORE
❏ CC8049	Cause for Alarm	1986	$18
❏ CC8046	Victim in Pain	1986	$18
EPITAPH
❏ 86567	Riot Riot Upstart	1999	$15
❏ 86536	Something's Gotta Give	1998	$15
IN EFFECT
❏ 3001	Live at CBGB's	1989	$15

AGUILERA, CHRISTINA
RCA
❏ 82876-82639-1	Back to Basics	2006	$50
—In oversize "album-style" packaging with fold-open cover			
❏ 07863-68037-1	Stripped	2002	$18

AHBEZ, EDEN
DEL-FI
❏ DFLP-1211 [M]	Eden's Island	1960	$175
❏ DFST-1211 [S]	Eden's Island	1960	$250

AIR
ANTILLES
❏ 1007	80 Degrees Below '82	1982	$25
ARISTA/NOVUS
❏ 3014	Air Lore	1980	$15
❏ 3008	Montreux	1979	$15
❏ 3002	Open Air Suit	1978	$15
BLACK SAINT
❏ BSR-0049	Air Mail	198?	$15
❏ BSR-0032	Live Air	198?	$15
❏ BSR-0084	Live at Montreal International Jazz Festival	198?	$12
—As "New Air"			
INDIA NAVIGATION
❏ IN-1064	Air Raid	1976	$18
❏ IN-1057	Air Song	1975	$18
NESSA
❏ 12	Time	1978	$18

AIR SUPPLY
ARISTA
❏ AL-8283	Air Supply	1985	$10
❏ AL-8024	Greatest Hits	1983	$10
❏ AL-8426	Hearts in Motion	1986	$10
❏ AL-4268	Lost in Love	1980	$10
❏ AL-8311	Lost in Love	1985	$10
—Budget-line reissue of 4268			
❏ AL-9587	Now and Forever	1982	$10
❏ AL-8292	Now and Forever	1985	$10

Number	Title	Yr	NM

—Budget-line reissue of 9587			
❏ AL-8528	The Christmas Album	1987	$12
❏ AL-9551	The One That You Love	1981	$10
❏ AL-8312	The One That You Love	1985	$10
—Budget-line reissue of 9551			
COLUMBIA
❏ JC35047	Love and Other Bruises	1977	$18
❏ PC35047	Love and Other Bruises	1981	$10
—Budget-line reissue; much more common than the original "JC" version			
MOBILE FIDELITY
❏ 1-113	The One That You Love	1983	$40
—Audiophile vinyl			
NAUTILUS
❏ NR-31	Lost in Love	1982	$25
—Audiophile vinyl			

AIRBORNE
TIGER LILY
❏ TL14045 [B]	Airborne	1976	$300

AIRTO
ACCORD
❏ SN-7184	Brazilian Heatwave	1982	$25
ARISTA
❏ AL4068	Identity	1975	$25
❏ AL4116	Promises of the Sun	1976	$25
BUDDAH
❏ BDS-21-SK	Natural Feelings	1970	$35
❏ BDS-5085	Seeds on the Ground	1971	$35
❏ BDA-5668	The Essential ... Airto	197?	$35
CTI
❏ 6028	Fingers	1973	$30
❏ CTSQ-6028 [Q]	Fingers	1974	$30
❏ 6020	Free	1972	$30
❏ 8000	Free	197?	$25
—Reissue of 6020			
SALVATION
❏ 701	Virgin Land	1974	$30
WARNER BROS.
❏ BS3084	I'm Fine, How Are You?	1977	$25
❏ BSK3279	Touching You, Touching Me	1979	$25

AIRWAVES
A&M
❏ SP-4689	New Day	1978	$10
❏ SP-4763	Next Stop	1979	$10

AKENS, JEWEL
ERA
❏ EL-110 [M]	The Birds and the Bees	1965	$30
❏ ES-110 [S]	The Birds and the Bees	1965	$150

AKINYELE
VOLCANO
❏ 31153	Aktapuss	1999	$18
❏ 31142	Put It in Your Mouth	1996	$15

AKIYOSHI, TOSHIKO, AND LEON SASH
VERVE
❏ MGV-8236 [M]	Toshiko and Leon Sash at Newport	1958	$175
❏ V-8236 [M]	Toshiko and Leon Sash at Newport	1961	$30

AKIYOSHI, TOSHIKO-LEW TABACKIN BIG BAND
JAM
❏ 03	Farewell to Mingus	1981	$25
❏ 06	Tanuki's Night Out	1982	$25
RCA VICTOR
❏ AFL1-2678	Insights	1978	$30
❏ AFL1-3019	Kogun	1979	$30
—Recorded in 1974			
❏ JPL1-1350	Long Yellow Road	1976	$35
❏ AFL1-1350	Long Yellow Road	1978	$25
—Reissue with new prefix			
❏ CPL2-2242	Road Time	1977	$25
❏ JPL1-0723	Tales of a Courtesan	1976	$35
❏ AFL1-0723	Tales of a Courtesan	1978	$25
—Reissue with new prefix			

AKIYOSHI, TOSHIKO
CANDID
❏ CD-8015 [M]	Toshiko Mariano	1960	$40
❏ CS-9015 [S]	Toshiko Mariano	1960	$50
❏ CD-8012 [M]	Toshiko Mariano Quartet	1960	$40
❏ CS-9012 [S]	Toshiko Mariano Quartet	1960	$50
CONCORD JAZZ
❏ CJ-69	Finesse	1978	$25
❏ CJ-324	Interlude	1987	$25

Number	Title	Yr	NM

DAUNTLESS
❏ DM-4308 [M]	The Country and Western Sounds of Jazz	1963	$40
❏ DS-6308 [S]	The Country and Western Sounds of Jazz	1963	$50
INNER CITY
❏ 6046	Dedications	1977	$30
❏ 6066	Notorious Tourist from the East	1978	$30
METROJAZZ
❏ E-1001 [M]	United Notions	1958	$120
❏ SE-1001 [S]	United Notions	1959	$120
NORGRAN
❏ MGN-22 [10]	Toshiko's Piano	1954	$300
STORYVILLE
❏ STLP-912 [M]	The Toshiko Trio	1956	$250
❏ STLP-918 [M]	Toshiko Akiyoshi, Her Trio, Her Quartet	1957	$75
VEE JAY
❏ LP-2505 [M]	Jazz in Japan	1964	$30
—As "Toshiko Mariano and Her Big Band"			
VERVE
❏ MGV-8273 [M]	The Many Sides of Toshiko	1958	$120
❏ V-8273 [M]	The Many Sides of Toshiko	1961	$30

AKKERMAN, JAN
ATCO
❏ SD7032	Tabernakel	1974	$15
ATLANTIC
❏ SD18210	Eli	1977	$12
❏ SD19159	Jan Akkerman	1978	$12
SIRE
❏ SAS7407	Profile	1973	$18

ALABAMA
ACCORD
❏ SN-7132	Pride of Dixie	1981	$12
ALABAMA
❏ ALA-78-9-01	The Alabama Band	1978	$400
HEARTLAND
❏ HL1186/7	The Very Best of Alabama	1992	$18
LSI
❏ 0177	Deuces Wild	1977	$1200
—As "Wild Country"			
❏ 0275	Wild Country	1975	$1500
—As "Wild Country"; VG value 750; VG+ value 1125			
PLANTATION
❏ 44	Wild Country	1981	$75
RCA
❏ 6825-1-R	Alabama Live	1988	$10
❏ 6495-1-R	Just Us	1987	$10
❏ 9574-1-RDJ [DJ]	Open-Ended Interview	1988	$30
❏ 8587-1-R	Southern Star	1989	$10
❏ 5649-1-R	The Touch	1986	$10
RCA VICTOR
❏ AHL1-5339	40 Hour Week	1985	$10
❏ ASL1-7014	Christmas	1985	$15
—Original copies have gold embossed letters on cover			
❏ ASL1-7014	Christmas	1986	$12
—Later copies have white non-embossed letters on cover			
❏ AHL1-3930	Feels So Right	1981	$10
❏ AHL1-7170	Greatest Hits	1986	$10
❏ AHL1-4229	Mountain Music	1982	$10
❏ AHL1-3644	My Home's in Alabama	1980	$18
❏ AYL1-3644	My Home's in Alabama	1986	$10
—Best Buy Series" reissue			
❏ AHL1-4939	Roll On	1984	$10
❏ AHL1-4663	The Closer You Get	1983	$10
SOUTHWAYS
❏ 101	Pride of Dixie	1981	$12
—Same album as on Accord			

ALAIMO, STEVE
ABC-PARAMOUNT
❏ 501 [M]	Starring Steve Alaimo	1965	$40
❏ S-501 [S]	Starring Steve Alaimo	1965	$50
❏ 551 [M]	Steve Alaimo Sings and Swings	1966	$40
❏ S-551 [S]	Steve Alaimo Sings and Swings	1966	$50
❏ 531 [M]	Where the Action Is	1965	$40
❏ S-531 [S]	Where the Action Is	1965	$50
CHECKER
❏ LP-2986 [M]	Every Day I Have to Cry	1963	$175
❏ LP-2983 [M]	Mashed Potatoes	1962	$175
❏ LP-2981 [M]	Twist with Steve Alaimo	1962	$175
CROWN
❏ CLP-5382 [M]	Steve Alaimo	1963	$30
❏ CST-382 [R]	Steve Alaimo	1963	$18

ALAMO, TONY (2)
ALAMO
❏ SA-253419	Mister D.J.	197?	$15

Number	Title	Yr	NM
❑ TSA-777	Susan, I Love You So Much It Hurts Me	197?	$15
❑ 2233	Tony Alamo Sings Love Songs for Sue ... And You	197?	$15

ALAN, BUDDY, AND DON RICH
CAPITOL
❑ ST-769	We're Real Good Friends	1971	$25

ALAN, BUDDY
CAPITOL
❑ ST-592	Whole Lot of Somethin'	1970	$25

ALARIK, SCOTT
WISCONSIN PUBLIC RADIO
❑ WPRA-2	Simply Christmas	1984	$15

ALARM, THE
I.R.S.
❑ 82018	Change	1989	$12
❑ SP70608	Declaration	1984	$12
❑ 39108	Electric Folklore Live	1988	$12
❑ 42061	Eye of the Hurricane	1987	$12
❑ 5666	Strength	1985	$12
❑ SP70504 [EP]	The Alarm	1984	$14

ALBAM, MANNY
ABC IMPULSE!
❑ AS-19 [S]	Jazz Goes to the Movies	196?	$30

— Reissue of Impulse! AS-19

CORAL
❑ CRL59102 [M]	A Gallery of Gershwin	1958	$40
❑ CRL57231 [M]	Sophisticated Lady -- The Songs of Duke Ellington	1958	$40
❑ CRL59101 [M]	The Blues Is Everybody's Business	195?	$40
❑ CRL57142 [M]	The Jazz Greats of Our Time	1957	$40
❑ CRL57173 [M]	The Jazz Greats of Our Time, Volume 2	1957	$40
❑ CRL57207 [M]	West Side Story	1958	$40

DECCA
❑ DL4517 [M]	Music from West Side Story	1964	$35
❑ DL74517 [S]	Music from West Side Story	1964	$25

DOT
❑ DLP-9004 [M]	Jazz New York	1958	$100
❑ DLP-9008 [M]	Steve's Song	1958	$100

IMPULSE!
❑ A-19 [M]	Jazz Goes to the Movies	1962	$120
❑ AS-19 [S]	Jazz Goes to the Movies	1962	$120

MCA
❑ 1376	The Jazz Greats of Our Time	198?	$30

MERCURY
❑ MG-20325 [M]	With All My Love	1958	$150

RCA VICTOR
❑ LPM-2508 [M]	I Had the Craziest Dream	1962	$25
❑ LSA-2508 [S]	I Had the Craziest Dream	1962	$30
❑ LPM-2432 [M]	More Double Exposure	1961	$25
❑ LSA-2432 [S]	More Double Exposure	1961	$30
❑ LPM-1279 [M]	The Drum Suite	1956	$50
❑ LPM-1211 [M]	The RCA Victor Jazz Workshop	1956	$50

SOLID STATE
❑ SM-17000 [M]	Brass on Fire	1966	$35
❑ SS-18000 [S]	Brass on Fire	1966	$25
❑ SM-17009 [M]	The Soul of the City	1966	$25
❑ SS-18009 [S]	The Soul of the City	1966	$35

TOP RANK
❑ RM-313 [M]	Double Exposure	1960	$40

UNITED ARTISTS
❑ UAL-3079 [M]	Drum Feast	1959	$30
❑ UAS-6079 [S]	Drum Feast	1959	$40

VOCALION
❑ VL3678 [M]	West Side Story	196?	$35

ALBANY, JOE, AND NIELS-HENNING ORSTED PEDERSEN
INNER CITY
❑ IC-2019	Two's Company	1976	$35

STEEPLECHASE
❑ SCS-1019	Two's Company	198?	$35

— Reissue of Inner City 2019

ALBANY, JOE, AND WARNE MARSH
FANTASY
❑ OJC-1749 [M]	The Right Combination	1990	$35

— Reissue of Riverside 12-270

RIVERSIDE
❑ RLP 12-270 [M]	The Right Combination	1958	$300

ALBANY, JOE
ELEKTRA/MUSICIAN
❑ 60161	Portrait of an Artist	1983	$30

INNER CITY
❑ IC-2003	Birdtown Birds	1976	$75

INTERPLAY
❑ IP-7723	Bird Lives!	1979	$50

REVELATION
❑ 25	At Home Alone	197?	$75
❑ 16	Proto-Bopper	197?	$75

RIVERSIDE
❑ RS-3023	The Legendary Jazz Pianist	1968	$150

SEABREEZE
❑ SB-1004	The Albany Touch	1977	$75

STEEPLECHASE
❑ SCS-1003	Birdtown Birds	198?	$35

— Reissue of Inner City 2003

ALBERGHETTI, ANNA MARIA
CAPITOL
❑ T887 [M]	I Can't Resist You	1957	$30
❑ T1379 [M]	Warm and Willing	1960	$25
❑ ST1379 [S]	Warm and Willing	1960	$30

CELEBRITY HOUSE
❑ TW2001	Christmas with Anna Maria Alberghetti	1984	$15

— B-side by Reino Moisio

MERCURY
❑ MG-20056 [M]	Songs by Anna Maria Alberghetti	1955	$30

MGM
❑ E-4001 [M]	Love Makes the World Go 'Round	1962	$25
❑ SE-4001 [S]	Love Makes the World Go 'Round	1962	$30

ALBERT, EDDIE
COLUMBIA
❑ CL2599 [M]	The Eddie Albert Album	1967	$25
❑ CS9399 [S]	The Eddie Albert Album	1967	$25

DOT
❑ DLP-3109 [M]	High Upon a Mountain	1958	$25
❑ DLP-25109 [S]	High Upon a Mountain	1958	$30

HAMILTON
❑ HLP-103 [DJ]	Oh, What a Beautiful Mornin'	1959	$15
❑ HLP-12103 [S]	Oh, What a Beautiful Mornin'	1959	$18

KAPP
❑ KL-1017 [M]	Eddie Albert and Margo	1956	$30
❑ KL-1000 [M]	One God	1954	$30
❑ KL-1083 [M]	September Song	1958	$30

PICCADILLY
❑ PIC-3374	Take Me Home	1980	$18

WONDERLAND
❑ WLP-5000	Eddie Albert Sings and Narrates Americana	1975	$18

ALBERT, MORRIS
RCA VICTOR
❑ APL1-1018	Feelings	1975	$10
❑ APL1-1496	Morris Albert	1976	$10

ALBERT, THE
PERCEPTION
❑ 9 [B]	The Albert	1971	$30

ALBERTI, WILLY
EPIC
❑ LN3662	Marina	1959	$18

ALBERTS, AL
CORAL
❑ CRL57259 [M]	A Man Has Got to Sing	1959	$30
❑ CRL757259 [S]	A Man Has Got to Sing	1959	$30

ALBRIGHT, GERALD
ATLANTIC
❑ 81919	Bermuda Nights	1988	$10
❑ 81813	Just Between Us	1987	$10

ALBRIGHT, LOLA
COLUMBIA
❑ CL1327 [M]	Dreamsville	1959	$40
❑ CS8133 [S]	Dreamsville	1959	$50

ALBRIGHT, MAX
MOTIF
❑ 502 [M]	Mood for Max	1956	$75

ALCATRAZZ
Group featuring YNGWIE J. MALMSTEEM and, later, STEVE VAI, as well as GRAHAM BONNET of Rainbow and MSG fame and members of NEW ENGLAND.

CAPITOL
❑ ST-12477	Dangerous Games	1986	$25
❑ ST-12385	Disturbing the Peace	1985	$25

CLEOPATRA
❑ 8745 [B]	Live '83		$25

ROCSHIRE
❑ 22020	Live Sentence	1984	$25
❑ 22016	No Parole from Rock 'n' Roll	1983	$30

ALCOA SINGERS, THE
ALCOA
❑ 44-4184--J	Old-Fashioned Christmas, An	1979	$15

ALDA, ROBERT
ROULETTE
❑ R-25006 [M]	Robert Alda	1959	$30
❑ SR-25006 [S]	Robert Alda	1959	$30

ALDEN, HOWARD-DAN BARRETT QUINTET
CONCORD JAZZ
❑ CJ-349	Swing Street	1988	$25

ALDEN, HOWARD
CONCORD JAZZ
❑ CJ-378	The Howard Alden Trio	1988	$25

FAMOUS DOOR
❑ HL-154	Swinging Into Prominence	1988	$25

STOMP OFF
❑ SOS-1200	Howard Alden Plays the Music of Harry Reser	1991	$30

ALDRICH, RONNIE
LONDON
❑ LL3383 [M]	Christmas with Ronnie	1964	$12
❑ LL3348 [M]	The Romantic Pianos of Ronnie Aldrich	1964	$15

LONDON PHASE 4
❑ SP-44081 [S]	All-Time Piano Hits	1967	$15
❑ SP44051 [S]	Christmas with Ronnie	1964	$18
❑ SP-44108 [S]	For Young Lovers	196?	$12
❑ 22	Love Story	1971	$18
❑ SP-44062 [S]	Magic Moods	1965	$15
❑ SP-44007 [S]	Melody and Percussion for Two Pianos	1961	$18
❑ SP44018 [S]	Ronnie Aldrich and His Two Pianos	1962	$18
❑ SP-44070 [S]	That Aldrich Feeling	1966	$15
❑ SP-44029 [S]	The Magnificent Pianos of Ronnie Aldrich	1963	$18
❑ SP-44042 [S]	The Romantic Pianos of Ronnie Aldrich	1964	$18
❑ SP-44092 [S]	Two Pianos in Hollywood	196?	$12

ALEEM FEATURING LEROY BURGESS
ATLANTIC
❑ 81622	Casually Formal	1986	$10
❑ 81784	Shock!	1987	$10

ALEONG, ALI, AND THE NOBLES
REPRISE
❑ R-6020 [M]	C'mon Baby, Let's Dance	1962	$30
❑ R9-6020 [S]	C'mon Baby, Let's Dance	1962	$30
❑ R-6011 [M]	Twistin' the Hits	1962	$30
❑ R9-6011 [S]	Twistin' the Hits	1962	$30

VEE JAY
❑ LP-1060 [M]	Come Surf with Me	1963	$30
❑ SR-1060 [S]	Come Surf with Me	1963	$50

ALESS, TONY
ROOST
❑ RST-2202 [M]	Tony Aless and His Long Island Suite	1955	$100

ALESSI
A&M
❑ SP-4608	Alessi	1976	$12
❑ SP-4657	All for a Reason	1977	$12
❑ SP-4713	Driftin'	1978	$12
❑ SP-4776	Words and Music	1979	$12

QWEST
❑ BSK3670	Long Time Friends	1982	$12

ALEXANDER, ARTHUR
DOT
❑ DLP3434 [M]	You Better Move On	1962	$150
❑ DLP25434 [S]	You Better Move On	1962	$160

WARNER BROS.
❑ BS2592	Arthur Alexander	1972	$30

ALEXANDER, BOB
See AL KLINK AND BOB ALEXANDER.

Number	Title	Yr	NM

ALEXANDER, DANIELE
MERCURY
| ❏ 838352-1 | First Move | 1989 | $15 |

ALEXANDER, JOE, AND TIMMONS, BOBBY
JAZZLAND
| ❏ JLP-23 [M] | Blue Jubilee | 1960 | $250 |

—orange label

| ❏ JLP-923 [S] | Blue Jubilee | 1960 | $40 |

ALEXANDER, MONTY, AND ERNEST RANGLIN
PAUSA
| ❏ 7110 | Just Friends | 198? | $25 |

ALEXANDER, MONTY
BASF
❏ 20913	Here Comes the Sun	197?	$30
❏ 25352	Rass!	197?	$30
❏ 25103	We've Only Just Begun	1972	$30
CONCORD JAZZ
❏ CJ-108	Facets	1980	$25
❏ CJ-287	Full Steam Ahead	1985	$25
❏ CJ-231	Reunion in Europe	1984	$25

— With John Clayton and Jeff Hamilton

CONCORD PICANTE
| ❏ CJP-124 | Ivory and Steel | 1981 | $25 |
| ❏ CJP-359 | Jamboree | 1988 | $25 |
MGM
| ❏ SE-4736 | Taste of Freedom | 1971 | $35 |
PABLO
| ❏ 2310826 | Jamento | 1978 | $30 |
| ❏ 2310836 | Monty Alexander in Tokyo | 1979 | $30 |
PACIFIC JAZZ
❏ PJ-86 [M]	Alexander the Great	1966	$25
❏ ST-86 [S]	Alexander the Great	1966	$30
❏ PJ-10094 [M]	Spooky	1966	$25
❏ ST-20094 [S]	Spooky	1966	$30
PAUSA
❏ 7083	Montreux Alexander Live	197?	$30
❏ 7032	Now Is the Time	197?	$30
❏ 7129	With Love	198?	$25
RCA VICTOR
| ❏ LPM-3930 [M] | Zing | 1968 | $75 |
| ❏ LSP-3930 [S] | Zing | 1968 | $35 |
VERVE
| ❏ V6-8790 | This Is Monty Alexander | 1970 | $35 |
VERVE/MPS
| ❏ 821151-1 | The Duke Ellington Songbook | 1984 | $25 |

ALEXANDER, MONTY / NIELS-HENNING ORSTED PEDERSEN / GRADY TATE
SOUL NOTE
| ❏ 121152-1 | Threesome | 198? | $30 |

ALEXANDER, MONTY / RAY BROWN / HERB ELLIS
CONCORD JAZZ
❏ CJ-253	Overseas Special	1983	$25
❏ CJ-136	Trio	1981	$25
❏ CJ-193	Triple Treat	1982	$25
❏ CJ-338	Triple Treat II	1988	$25
❏ CJ-394	Triple Treat III	1989	$25

ALEXANDER, ROLAND
NEW JAZZ
| ❏ NJLP-8267 [M] | Pleasure Bent | 1962 | $175 |

— Purple label

| ❏ NJLP-8267 [M] | Pleasure Bent | 1965 | $175 |

— Blue label, trident at right

ALEXANDER'S TIMELESS BLOOZBAND
SMASK
| ❏ 1001 [M] | Alexander's Timeless Bloozband | 1967 | $250 |
UNI
| ❏ 73021 | For Sale | 1968 | $30 |

ALEXANDRIA, LOREZ
ABC IMPULSE!
| ❏ AS-62 | Alexandria the Great | 1968 | $250 |

— Reissue of Impulse! AS-62

| ❏ AS-76 [B] | More of the Great Lorez Alexandria | 1968 | $250 |

—Reissue of Impulse! AS-76

ARGO
❏ LP-694 [M]	Deep Roots	1962	$140
❏ LPS-694 [S]	Deep Roots	1962	$200
❏ LP-663 [M]	Early in the Morning	1960	$140
❏ LPS-663 [S]	Early in the Morning	1960	$200

— With the Ramsey Lewis Trio

❏ LP-720 [M]	For Swingers Only	1963	$140
❏ LPS-720 [S]	For Swingers Only	1963	$200
❏ LP-682 [M]	Sing No Sad Songs for Me	1961	$140
❏ LPS-682 [S]	Sing No Sad Songs for Me	1961	$200
CADET
| ❏ LPS-682 | Sing No Sad Songs for Me | 1966 | $75 |

— Reissue of Argo 682

DISCOVERY
❏ DS-800	A Woman Knows	1979	$150
❏ DS-905	Harlem Butterfly (Sings the Songs of Johnny Mercer Vol. 2)	1984	$50
❏ DS-782	How Will I Remember You?	1978	$120
❏ DS-826	Lorez Alexandria Sings Johnny Mercer	1981	$75
IMPULSE!
❏ A-62 [M]	Alexandria the Great	1964	$160
❏ AS-62 [S]	Alexandria the Great	1964	$250
❏ A-76 [M]	More of the Great Lorez Alexandria	1965	$160
❏ AS-76 [S]	More of the Great Lorez Alexandria	1965	$250
KING
| ❏ 565 [M] | Lorez Sings Prez | 1956 | $250 |

— Black label, crownless "King

| ❏ 676 [M] | Singing Songs Everyone Knows | 1959 | $250 |

— Black label, crownless "King

| ❏ 657 [M] | The Band Swings, Lorez Sings | 1959 | $250 |

— Black label, crownless "King

| ❏ S-657 [S] | The Band Swings, Lorez Sings | 1959 | $300 |

—Dark blue label, crownless "King

| ❏ 542 [M] | This Is Lorez | 1956 | $250 |

— Black label, crownless "King

MCA
| ❏ 29000 | Alexandria the Great | 198? | $25 |

—Reissue of ABC Impulse! AS-62

PZAZZ
| ❏ LP-320 | Didn't We | 1968 | $150 |
| ❏ LP-324 | In a Different Bag | 1969 | $75 |
TREND
| ❏ TR-547 | Dear to My Heart | 1988 | $35 |
| ❏ TR-538 | Tangerine (Sings the Songs of Johnny Mercer Vol. 3) | 1986 | $35 |

ALFONZO
LARC
| ❏ 8101 | Alfonzo | 1982 | $12 |

ALFRED, CHUZ
SAVOY
| ❏ MG-12030 [M] | Jazz Young Blood | 1955 | $85 |

— With Ola Hanson and Chuck Lee

ALIAS
MERCURY
| ❏ SRM-1-3800 | Contraband | 1979 | $12 |

ALICE IN CHAINS
COLUMBIA
| ❏ C267248 | Alice in Chains | 1995 | $30 |

| ❏ C257804 [B] | Jar of Flies/Sap | 1994 | $35 |

— Two cassette/CD EP releases in one vinyl package

| ❏ CAS2192 [EP] | We Die Young | 1990 | $75 |

—Five-song promo-only issue predating their first LP

ALIEN SEX FIEND
CAROLINE
| ❏ CAROL1370 [B] | Another Planet | 1988 | $30 |
CLEOPATRA
| ❏ CLP2221 [B] | Bat Cave Anthems | 2008 | $30 |
EPITAPH
| ❏ ASFLP2 [B] | Acid Bath | 1985 | $30 |
PVC
| ❏ PVC8960 [B] | Here Cum Germs | 1987 | $40 |
| ❏ PVC6917 [B] | The Impossible Mission | 1987 | $25 |
RELATIVITY
| ❏ EMC8002 [B] | Who's Been Sleeping In My Brain? | 1984 | $40 |

ALIOTTA-HAYNES-JEREMIAH
AMPEX
| ❏ A-10119 | Aliotta-Haynes-Jeremiah | 1970 | $25 |
| ❏ A-10108 | Aliotta-Haynes Music | 1970 | $25 |

— As "Aliota-Haynes

BIG FOOT
| ❏ 714 | Lake Shore Drive | 1978 | $30 |
LITTLE FOOT
| ❏ 711 | Slippin' Away | 1977 | $25 |

ALISHA
MCA
| ❏ 6378 | Bounce Back | 1990 | $12 |
RCA
| ❏ 6248-1-R | Nightwalkin' | 1987 | $12 |
VANGUARD
| ❏ VSD-79456 | Alisha | 1985 | $15 |

ALIVE AND KICKING
ROULETTE
| ❏ SR42052 | Alive and Kicking | 1970 | $25 |

ALL AMERICAN RUMBLERS, THE
GONE
| ❏ LP-5006 [M] | Destination Dixie | 1959 | $50 |

ALL CITY
MCA
| ❏ 8P-4272 | Metropolis Gold | 1998 | $18 |

—Promo version in generic white jacket

| ❏ 11829 | Metropolis Gold | 1998 | $15 |

ALL SPORTS BAND
RADIO
| ❏ SD19321 | All Sports Band | 1981 | $18 |

ALL STARS, THE
GRAMOPHONE
| ❏ 20192 | Boogie Woogie | 196? | $50 |

ALLAN, DAVIE, AND THE ARROWS
TOWER
❏ T5002 [M]	Apache '65	1965	$40
❏ DT5002 [R]	Apache '65	1965	$30
❏ T5078 [M]	Blues Theme	1967	$50
❏ DT5078 [R]	Blues Theme	1967	$40
❏ DT5094 [R]	Cycle-Delic Sounds	1968	$100
❏ T5094 [M]	Cycle-Delic Sounds	1968	$150
❏ T5074 [M]	Devil's Angel	1967	$75
❏ DT5074 [R]	Devil's Angel	1967	$25
❏ T5083 [M]	Mondo Hollywood	1968	$100

Number	Title	Yr	NM
❏ DT5083 [R]	Mondo Hollywood	1968	$25
❏ T5043 [M]	The Wild Angels	1966	$30
❏ DT5043 [R]	The Wild Angels	1966	$25
❏ T5056 [M]	The Wild Angels, Vol. II	1967	$75
❏ DT5056 [R]	The Wild Angels, Vol. II	1967	$25

ALLANSON, SUSIE
ABC
| ❏ ABCD-970 | Susie Allanson | 1976 | $18 |

ELEKTRA
| ❏ 6E-177 | Heart to Heart | 1979 | $12 |

UNITED ARTISTS
| ❏ LT-1059 | Susie | 1980 | $15 |

WARNER BROS.
| ❏ BSK3217 | We Belong Together | 1978 | $12 |

ALLEN, BYRON, TRIO
ESP-DISK'
| ❏ 1005 [M] | The Byron Allen Trio | 1965 | $325 |
| ❏ S-1005 [S] | The Byron Allen Trio | 1965 | $325 |

ALLEN, DAVE
INTERNATIONAL ARTISTS
| ❏ 11 | Color Blind | 1969 | $75 |
— Original pressing
| ❏ 11 | Color Blind | 1979 | $25 |
— Repressing with "RE2" and "Masterfonics" in dead wax

ALLEN, DAVID
EVEREST
| ❏ LP-5224 [M] | David Allen | 1964 | $35 |
| ❏ SD-1224 [S] | David Allen | 1964 | $25 |

PACIFIC JAZZ
| ❏ PJM-408 [M] | A Sure Thing | 1957 | $75 |
| ❏ ST-1006 [S] | A Sure Thing | 1959 | $75 |

WORLD PACIFIC
❏ WP-1295 [M]	David Allen Sings the Jerome Kern Songbook	1960	$150
❏ ST-1295 [S]	David Allen Sings the Jerome Kern Songbook	1960	$150
❏ WP-1250 [M]	Let's Face the Music and Dance	1958	$175

ALLEN, DAYTON
GRAND AWARD
| ❏ GA 33-424 [M] | Why Not? | 1960 | $30 |

ALLEN, DEBBIE
MCA
| ❏ 6317 | Special Look | 1989 | $12 |

ALLEN, DEBORAH
CAPITOL
| ❏ ST-12104 | Trouble in Paradise | 1980 | $15 |

RCA
| ❏ 6239-1-R | Telepathy | 1987 | $12 |

RCA VICTOR
❏ MHL1-8514 [EP]	Cheat the Night	1983	$10
❏ AHL1-5318	Let Me Be the First	1985	$10
❏ AHL1-5806	You Can't Say No	1986	$10

ALLEN, DONNA
21 RECORDS
| ❏ 90548 | Perfect Timing | 1987 | $12 |

OCEANA
| ❏ 91028 | Heaven on Earth | 1988 | $10 |

ALLEN, HENRY "RED", AND KID ORY
VERVE
❏ MGV-1018 [M]	Henry "Red" Allen Meets Kid Ory	1957	$175
❏ V-1018 [M]	Henry "Red" Allen Meets Kid Ory	1961	$25
❏ MGVS-6076 [S]	Henry "Red" Allen Meets Kid Ory	1959	$175
❏ V6-1018 [S]	Henry "Red" Allen Meets Kid Ory	1961	$25
❏ MGV-1020 [M]	We've Got Rhythm	1958	$175
❏ V-1020 [M]	We've Got Rhythm	1961	$25
❏ MGVS-6121 [S]	We've Got Rhythm	1959	$175
❏ V6-1020 [S]	We've Got Rhythm	1961	$25

ALLEN, HENRY "RED", AND RED NORVO
BRUNSWICK
| ❏ BL58044 [10] | Battle of Jazz, Vol. 6 | 1953 | $75 |

ALLEN, HENRY "RED"; JACK TEAGARDEN; KID ORY
VERVE
❏ MGV-8233 [M]	Red Allen, Jack Teagarden & Kid Ory at Newport	1958	$150
❏ V-8233 [M]	Red Allen, Jack Teagarden & Kid Ory at Newport	1961	$25
❏ UMV-2624	Verve at Newport	198?	$25

Number	Title	Yr	NM

ALLEN, HENRY "RED
AMERICAN RECORDING SOCIETY
| ❏ G-436 [M] | Traditional Jazz | 195? | $40 |

COLUMBIA
| ❏ CL2447 [M] | Feelin' Good | 1966 | $35 |
| ❏ CS9247 [S] | Feelin' Good | 1966 | $25 |

PRESTIGE
| ❏ PRST-7755 | Memorial Album | 1968 | $35 |

RCA VICTOR
| ❏ LPV-556 [M] | Henry "Red" Allen | 1965 | $50 |
| ❏ LPM-1509 [M] | Ride, Red, Ride in Hi-Fi | 1957 | $50 |

SWINGVILLE
| ❏ SWLP-2034 [M] | Mr. Allen | 1962 | $40 |
— Purple label
| ❏ SWLP-2034 [M] | Mr. Allen | 1965 | $25 |
— Blue label, trident logo at right
| ❏ SWST-2034 [S] | Mr. Allen | 1962 | $50 |
— Red label
| ❏ SWST-2034 [S] | Mr. Allen | 1965 | $30 |
— Blue label, trident logo at right

TIME-LIFE
| ❏ STL-J-16 | Giants of Jazz | 1981 | $50 |

VERVE
❏ MGV-1025 [M]	Red Allen Plays King Oliver	1959	$150
❏ V-1025 [M]	Red Allen Plays King Oliver	1961	$25
❏ V6-1025 [S]	Red Allen Plays King Oliver	1961	$30

X
| ❏ LVA-3033 [M] | Ridin' with Red | 1955 | $75 |

ALLEN, LEE
EMBER
| ❏ ELP-200 [M] | Walkin' with Mr. Lee | 1958 | $250 |
— Red label
| ❏ ELP-200 [M] | Walkin' with Mr. Lee | 1959 | $50 |
— White "logs" label
| ❏ ELP-200 [M] | Walkin' with Mr. Lee | 1961 | $50 |
— Red and black label

ALLEN, PETER
A&M
❏ SP-4825	Bi-Coastal	1980	$10
❏ SP-4739	I Could Have Been a Sailor	1979	$12
❏ SP-3706	It Is Time for Peter Allen	1977	$15
❏ SP-6508	It Is Time for Peter Allen	198?	$12
— Budget-line reissue of 3706
| ❏ SP-4584 | Taught by Experts | 1976 | $12 |
| ❏ SP-3207 | The Best of Peter Allen | 198? | $10 |

ARISTA
❏ AL1-8275	Captured Live at Carnegie Hall	1985	$15
❏ AL-9613	Not the Boy Next Door	1983	$12
❏ AL-8026	Not the Boy Next Door	198?	$10
— Budget-line reissue of 9613

ALLEN, PHYLICIA
CASABLANCA

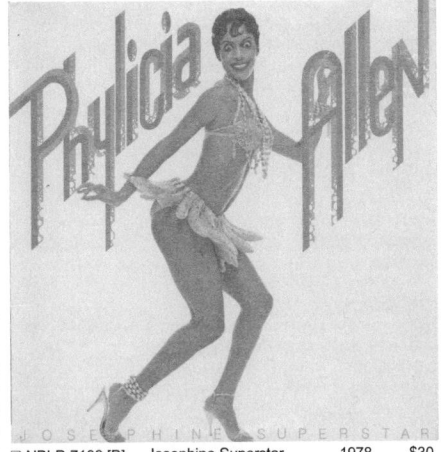

| ❏ NBLP-7108 [B] | Josephine Superstar | 1978 | $30 |

ALLEN, RANCE, GROUP
BELLMARK
| ❏ D1-71806 | Phenomenon | 1991 | $18 |

CAPITOL
| ❏ ST-11613 | Say My Friend | 1977 | $18 |

MYRRH
| ❏ MSB-6736 | Hear My Voice | 1983 | $18 |
| ❏ WR-8243 | I Give Myself to You | 198? | $15 |

STAX
| ❏ MPS-8507 | Ain't No Need of Crying | 198? | $12 |
| ❏ STX-4138 | I Feel Like Going On | 1980 | $15 |

Number	Title	Yr	NM
❏ STX-4127	Smile	1979	$15
❏ STX-4109	Straight from the Heart	1979	$12
❏ MPS-8540	The Best of the Rance Allen Group	1988	$12

TRUTH
| ❏ 4207 | A Soulful Experience | 1975 | $18 |

ALLEN, RAY, AND THE UPBEATS
BLAST
| ❏ BLP-6804 [M] | A Tribute to Six | 1962 | $120 |

ALLEN, RAY
PARAMOUNT
| ❏ PAS-6060 | Ray Allen and the Yonkers Children's Chorus | 1973 | $18 |

ALLEN, REX, JR.
WARNER BROS.
❏ BS2821	Another Goodbye Song	1974	$12
❏ BSK3190	Brand New	1978	$12
❏ BSK3300	Me and My Broken Heart	1979	$12
❏ BSK3403	Oklahoma Rose	1980	$12
❏ BS3054	Rex	1977	$12
❏ BS2958	Ridin' High	1976	$12
❏ BSK3122	The Best of Rex	1977	$12

ALLEN, REX
BUENA VISTA
| ❏ BV-3307 [M] | Rex Allen Sings 16 Golden Hits | 1961 | $40 |

DECCA
❏ DL8776 [M]	Mister Cowboy	1959	$40
❏ DL78776 [S]	Mister Cowboy	1959	$75
❏ DL75011 [S]	The Smooth Country Sound of Rex Allen	1968	$25
❏ DL75205	The Touch of God's Hand	1970	$25
❏ DL8402 [M]	Under Western Skies	1956	$50

HACIENDA
| ❏ WWLP-101 [M] | Rex Allen Sings | 1960 | $250 |

MERCURY
❏ MG-20719 [M]	Faith of a Man	1962	$30
❏ SR-60719 [S]	Faith of a Man	1962	$30
❏ MG-20752 [M]	Rex Allen Sings and Tells Tales	1963	$30
❏ SR-60752 [S]	Rex Allen Sings and Tells Tales	1963	$30

ALLEN, RICHIE
IMPERIAL
❏ LP-9212 [M]	Stranger from Durango	1962	$50
❏ LP-12212 [S]	Stranger from Durango	1962	$75
❏ LP-9243 [M]	Surfer's Slide	1963	$150
❏ LP-12243 [S]	Surfer's Slide	1963	$175
❏ LP-9229 [M]	The Rising Surf	1963	$150
❏ LP-12229 [S]	The Rising Surf	1963	$175

ALLEN, ROSALIE
GRAND AWARD
| ❏ GA-33-330 [M] | Songs of the Golden West | 1957 | $40 |

RCA VICTOR
| ❏ LPM-2313 [M] | Rosalie Allen | 1961 | $25 |
| ❏ LSP-2313 [S] | Rosalie Allen | 1961 | $30 |

WALDORF
| ❏ 150 [10] | Rosalie Allen Sings Country and Western | 1955 | $100 |

ALLEN, STEVE, AND MANNY ALBAM
DOT
| ❏ DLP3194 [M] | ...And All That Jazz | 1959 | $85 |
| ❏ DLP25194 [S] | ...And All That Jazz | 1959 | $85 |

ALLEN, STEVE
CASABLANCA
| ❏ 811366-1 | Funny Fone Calls | 1983 | $10 |
— Reissue of Dot 3472
| ❏ 811367-1 | More Funny Fone Calls | 1983 | $10 |
— Reissue of Dot 3517

CORAL
❏ CRL57048 [M]	Allen Plays Allen	1956	$30
❏ CRL57018 [M]	Jazz for Tonight	1956	$30
❏ CRL57028 [M]	Let's Dance	1956	$30
❏ CRL57004 [M]	Music for Tonight	1955	$30
❏ CRL57138 [M]	Romantic Rendezvous	1957	$25
❏ CRL57442 [M]	Songs Everybody Knows	1964	$18
❏ CRL757442 [R]	Songs Everybody Knows	1964	$15
❏ CRL57019 [M]	Steve Sings	1956	$30
❏ CRL57070 [M]	The Steve Allen Show	1957	$30
❏ CRL57015 [M]	Tonight at Midnight	1956	$30

DECCA
| ❏ DL8151 [M] | Steve Allen's All Star Jazz Concert, Vol. 1 | 1955 | $175 |
| ❏ DL8152 [M] | Steve Allen's All Star Jazz Concert, Vol. 2 | 1955 | $175 |

DOT
❏ DLP3473 [M]	12 Greatest Hits	1963	$25
❏ DLP3480 [M]	Bossa Nova Jazz	1963	$75
❏ DLP25380 [S]	Bossa Nova Jazz	1963	$85

Number	Title	Yr	NM
❏ DLP3538 [M]	Cuano Caliente El Sol and More	1963	$18
❏ DLP25538 [S]	Cuano Caliente El Sol and More	1963	$25
❏ DLP3472 [M]	Funny Fone Calls	1963	$25
❏ DLP3515 [M]	Gravy Waltz and 11 Current Hits!	1963	$75
❏ DLP25515 [S]	Gravy Waltz and 11 Current Hits!	1963	$85
❏ DLP3560 [M]	Great Ragtime Hits	1963	$18
❏ DLP25560 [S]	Great Ragtime Hits	1963	$25
❏ DLP3624 [M]	I Play for You	1965	$15
❏ DLP25624 [S]	I Play for You	1965	$18
❏ DLP3517 [M]	More Funny Fone Calls	1963	$25
❏ DLP3683 [M]	Rhythm and Blues	1966	$15
❏ DLP25683 [S]	Rhythm and Blues	1966	$18
❏ DLP3587 [M]	Songs from the Steve Allen TV Show	1964	$15
❏ DLP25587 [S]	Songs from the Steve Allen TV Show	1964	$18
❏ DLP3597 [M]	Steve Allen, His Piano and Orchestra	1964	$15
❏ DLP25597 [S]	Steve Allen, His Piano and Orchestra	1964	$18
❏ DLP3519 [M]	Steve Allen Plays the Piano Greats	1963	$18
❏ DLP25519 [S]	Steve Allen Plays the Piano Greats	1963	$25
❏ DLP3530 [M]	Steve Allen Sings	1963	$18
❏ DLP25530 [S]	Steve Allen Sings	1963	$25

FORUM

Number	Title	Yr	NM
❏ F-9014 [M]	Steve Allen at the Round Table	196?	$25
❏ FS-9014 [S]	Steve Allen at the Round Table	196?	$18

HAMILTON

Number	Title	Yr	NM
❏ HLP132 [M]	Some of My Favorites	196?	$15
❏ HLP12132 [S]	Some of My Favorites	196?	$18

ROULETTE

Number	Title	Yr	NM
❏ R-25053 [M]	Steve Allen at the Round Table	1959	$30
❏ SR-25053 [S]	Steve Allen at the Round Table	1959	$25

SIGNATURE

Number	Title	Yr	NM
❏ SM1004 [M]	Man in the Street	1959	$30
❏ SM1021 [M]	Monday Nights	1960	$30

ALLEN, TONY
CROWN

Number	Title	Yr	NM
❏ CLP-5231 [M]	Rock and Roll with Tony Allen	1960	$150
—Black label			
❏ CLP-5231 [M]	Rock and Roll with Tony Allen	1961	$75
—Gray label			
❏ CST-240 [S]	Rock and Roll with Tony Allen	1961	$175

ALLEN, WOODY
BELL

Number	Title	Yr	NM
❏ 6008	The Wonderful Wacky World of Woody Allen	1967	$25

CAPITOL

Number	Title	Yr	NM
❏ ST2986	The Third Woody Allen Album	1968	$30

CASABLANCA

Number	Title	Yr	NM
❏ NBLP2-7145	Woody Allen: Stand-Up Comic 1964-1968	1979	$18
—Compilation of material from Colpix and Capitol LPs (different from either UA collection)			

COLPIX

Number	Title	Yr	NM
❏ CP518 [M]	Woody Allen	1964	$30
❏ CP488 [M]	Woody Allen 2	1965	$30
❏ SCP488 [R]	Woody Allen 2	1965	$30

UNITED ARTISTS

Number	Title	Yr	NM
❏ UA-LA849-J2	Woody Allen: Stand-Up Comic 1964-1968	1977	$25
—Compilation of material from Colpix and Capitol LPs (different from UA 9968)			
❏ UAS9968	Woody Allen: The Nightclub Years	1972	$25
—Compilation of material from Colpix and Capitol LPs			

ALLEN AND ROSSI
ABC-PARAMOUNT

Number	Title	Yr	NM
❏ ABC-270 [M]	Hello Dere	1962	$25
❏ ABC-445 [M]	One More Time Hello Dere	1963	$25

MERCURY

Number	Title	Yr	NM
❏ MG-21077 [M]	The Adventures of Batman and Rubin	1966	$40
❏ SR-61077 [S]	The Adventures of Batman and Rubin	1966	$50
—The above LP was written by "Batman" creator Bob Kane as a parody of his own comic book			

REPRISE

Number	Title	Yr	NM
❏ R-6104 [M]	Too Funny for Words	1964	$25

ROULETTE

Number	Title	Yr	NM
❏ R-508 [M]	Dedicated to Our Armed Forces	1967	$25
❏ R-507 [M]	The Truth About the Green Hornet	1966	$25

ALLIN, GG
ALIVE

Number	Title	Yr	NM
❏ 0001 [B]	Brutality and Bloodshed for All	199?	$30
❏ 0012 [B]	Terror in America	199?	$40

BLACK & BLUE

Number	Title	Yr	NM
❏ 006053-X	Always Was, Is and Always Shall Be	1985	$50
—Reissue of Orange original			
❏ 0(# unknown) [B]	Banned in Boston	1989	$30
❏ 0(# unknown) [B]	Eat My Fuc	1988	$25
—Reissue of Blood LP of the same name			

BLOOD

Number	Title	Yr	NM
❏ 0(# unknown) [B]	Eat My Fuc	198?	$80
—Hand-decorated plain cover			

HOMESTEAD

Number	Title	Yr	NM
❏ HMS-069 [B]	You Give Love a Bad Name	1987	$50

ORANGE

Number	Title	Yr	NM
❏ 0(# unknown)	Always Was, Is and Always Shall Be	1980	$150

ALLISON, GENE
VEE JAY

Number	Title	Yr	NM
❏ LP-1009 [M]	Gene Allison	1959	$300
—Maroon label			
❏ LP-1009 [M]	Gene Allison	196?	$150
—Black label, oval or brackets logo			

ALLISON, KEITH
COLUMBIA

Number	Title	Yr	NM
❏ CL2641 [M]	Keith Allison In Action	1967	$30
❏ CS9441 [S]	Keith Allison In Action	1967	$30

ALLISON, LUTHER
DELMARK

Number	Title	Yr	NM
❏ DS-625	Love Me, Mama	1969	$30

GORDY

Number	Title	Yr	NM
❏ G-964	Bad News Is Coming	1973	$12
❏ G-967	Luther's Blues	1974	$12
❏ G-974	Night Life	1976	$12

ALLISON, MOSE
ATLANTIC

Number	Title	Yr	NM
❏ SD1550	Hello There, Universe	1971	$50
❏ 1389 [M]	I Don't Worry About a Thing	1962	$175
❏ SD1389 [S]	I Don't Worry About a Thing	1962	$175
❏ SD1511	I've Been Doin' Some Thinkin'	1969	$75
—1841 Broadway" address on label			
❏ SD1511	I've Been Doin' Some Thinkin'	1976	$30
—75 Rockefeller Plaza" address on label			
❏ 1450 [M]	Mose Alive!	1966	$75
❏ SD1450 [S]	Mose Alive!	1966	$40
—Blue and green label			
❏ SD1450 [S]	Mose Alive!	1969	$50
—Red and green label with "1841 Broadway" address			
❏ SD1627	Mose in Your Ear	1973	$50
—1841 Broadway" address on label			
❏ SD1627	Mose in Your Ear	1976	$30
—75 Rockefeller Plaza" address on label			
❏ 1398 [M]	Swingin' Machine	1963	$50
❏ SD1398 [S]	Swingin' Machine	1963	$30
❏ SD1542	The Best of Mose Allison	1970	$35
❏ 1424 [M]	The Word from Mose	1964	$50
❏ SD1424 [S]	The Word from Mose	1964	$75
❏ SD1584	Western Man	1972	$35
❏ 1456 [M]	Wild Man on the Loose	1966	$75
❏ SD1456 [S]	Wild Man on the Loose	1966	$40
❏ SD1691	Your Mind Is on Vacation	1976	$35

BLUE NOTE

Number	Title	Yr	NM
❏ BLJ-48015	Ever Since the World Ended	1988	$35
❏ B1-93840	My Backyard	1990	$50

COLUMBIA

Number	Title	Yr	NM
❏ CL1565 [M]	I Love the Life I Live	1960	$30
—Red and black label with six "eye" logos			
❏ CS8365 [S]	I Love the Life I Live	1960	$30
—Red and black label with six "eye" logos			
❏ C30564	Retrospective	1971	$35
❏ CL1444 [M]	The Transfiguration of Hiram Brown	1960	$30
❏ CS8240 [S]	The Transfiguration of Hiram Brown	1960	$30

COLUMBIA SPECIAL PRODUCTS

Number	Title	Yr	NM
❏ P13518	V-8 Ford Blues	197?	$35

ELEKTRA/MUSICIAN

Number	Title	Yr	NM
❏ 60237	Lessons in Living	1984	$30
❏ E1-60125	Middle Class White Boy	1983	$30

EPIC

Number	Title	Yr	NM
❏ LA16031 [M]	Take to the Hills	1962	$150
❏ BA17031 [S]	Take to the Hills	1962	$100
❏ LN24183 [M]	V-8 Ford Blues	1966	$150
❏ BN26183 [S]	V-8 Ford Blues	1966	$150

FANTASY

Number	Title	Yr	NM
❏ OJC-075	Back Country Suite	198?	$30
—Reissue of Prestige 7091			
❏ OJC-6004	Greatest Hits	1988	$30
❏ OJC-457	Local Color	1990	$30
—Reissue of Prestige 7121			

ODYSSEY

Number	Title	Yr	NM
❏ 32160294	Mose Goes	1968	$35

PRESTIGE

Number	Title	Yr	NM
❏ PRLP-7189 [M]	Autumn Song	1960	$250
—Yellow label with Bergenfield, NJ address on label			
❏ PRLP-7189 [M]	Autumn Song	196?	$25
—Blue label, trident logo			
❏ PRLP-7091 [M]	Back Country Suite	1957	$300
—With "W. 50th St., NYC" address on label			
❏ PRLP-7152 [M]	Creek Bank	1959	$250
—Yellow label with Bergenfield, NJ address on label			
❏ P-24055	Creek Bank	1975	$75
❏ PRLP-7152 [M]	Creek Bank	196?	$30
—Blue label, trident logo			
❏ PRLP-7423 [M]	Down Home Piano	1966	$25
—Blue label, trident logo at right			
❏ PRST-7423 [S]	Down Home Piano	1966	$30
—Blue label, trident logo at right			
❏ PRLP-7121 [M]	Local Color	1958	$300
—With "W. 50th St., NYC" address on label			
❏ PR-24002	Mose Allison	1972	$75
❏ PRLP-7446 [M]	Mose Allison Plays for Lovers	1967	$30
❏ PRST-7446 [S]	Mose Allison Plays for Lovers	1967	$25
❏ PRLP-7279 [M]	Mose Allison Sings (The Seventh Son)	1963	$40
—Yellow label with Bergenfield, NJ address on label			
❏ PRST-7279 [S]	Mose Allison Sings (The Seventh Son)	1963	$50
—Silver label			
❏ P-10052	Mose Allison Sings (The Seventh Son)	1973	$35
—Reissue of PRST-7279			
❏ PRST-7279 [S]	Mose Allison Sings (The Seventh Son)	196?	$30
—Blue label, trident logo at right			
❏ P-24004	Ol' Devil Mose	1980	$75
❏ PRLP-7215 [M]	Ramblin' with Mose	1961	$250
—Yellow label with Bergenfield, NJ address on label			
❏ PRLP-7215 [M]	Ramblin' with Mose	196?	$30
—Blue label, trident logo			
❏ PRLP-7137 [M]	Young Man Blues	1958	$250
—With "W. 50th St., NYC" address on label			

ALLMAN, DUANE
CAPRICORN

Number	Title	Yr	NM
❏ 2CP 0108	An Anthology	1972	$25
❏ 2CP 0139	An Anthology, Vol. II	1974	$25

POLYDOR

Number	Title	Yr	NM
❏ 827563-1	The Best of Duane Allman	1984	$10
❏ PD-1-6338	The Best of Duane Allman	1981	$15

ALLMAN, DUANE AND GREGG
BOLD

Number	Title	Yr	NM
❏ 33-301 [B]	Duane and Gregg Allman	1972	$30
—Gatefold cover			
❏ 33-301	Duane and Gregg Allman	197?	$25
—Non-gatefold cover			

ALLMAN, GREGG
CAPRICORN

Number	Title	Yr	NM
❏ CP 0116	Laid Back	1973	$15
❏ CP 0181	Playin' Up a Storm	1977	$15
❏ 2CP 0141	The Gregg Allman Tour	1974	$18

EPIC

Number	Title	Yr	NM
❏ FE40531	I'm No Angel	1987	$12
❏ OE44033	Just Before the Bullets Fly	1988	$12

ALLMAN, SHELDON
DEL-FI

Number	Title	Yr	NM
❏ DFLP-1213 [M]	Sing Along with Drac	1961	$40

HIFI

Number	Title	Yr	NM
❏ R-415 [M]	Folk Songs for the 21st Century	1960	$40

ALLMAN AND WOMAN
WARNER BROS.

Number	Title	Yr	NM
❏ BSK3120	Two the Hard Way	1977	$12

ALLMAN BROTHERS BAND, THE
Also see ALLMAN AND WOMAN; THE ALLMAN JOYS; DUANE ALLMAN; DUANE AND GREGG ALLMAN; GREGG ALLMAN; DICKIE BETTS; THE HOUR GLASS.

ARISTA

Number	Title	Yr	NM
❏ AL9564	Brothers of the Road	1981	$12
❏ AL9535	Reach for the Sky	1980	$12

Number	Title	Yr	NM

ATCO
☐ SD 2-805 [B]	Beginnings	1973	$30

☐ SD 33-342 [B]	Idlewild South	1970	$25
☐ SD 33-308 [B]	The Allman Brothers Band	1969	$25

CAPRICORN
☐ 2CX 0132	Beginnings	1974	$18
☐ CPN2 0132	Beginnings	198?	$15
☐ CP 0111 [B]	Brothers and Sisters	1973	$18
☐ CPN 0111	Brothers and Sisters	198?	$10
☐ 2CP 0102 [B]	Eat a Peach	1972	$25
☐ CX4 0102 [Q]	Eat a Peach	1974	$50
☐ CPN2 0102 [B]	Eat a Peach	198?	$18
☐ CPN 0218	Enlightened Rogues	1979	$12
☐ CPN 0197	Idlewild South	1978	$12
☐ CPN 0196	The Allman Brothers Band	1978	$12
☐ SD 2-802 [S]	The Allman Brothers Band at Fillmore East	1971	$25
☐ 2CP 0131 [B]	The Allman Brothers Band at Fillmore East	1974	$30
☐ CX4 0131 [Q]	The Allman Brothers Band at Fillmore East	1974	$100
☐ CPN2 0131 [B]	The Allman Brothers Band at Fillmore East	198?	$25
☐ 2-802 [M]	The Allman Brothers Band at Fillmore East	1971	$300

—Promo only; sticker on front cover says "Promotional DJ Copy Monaural Not for Sale
☐ 2CX 0164	The Road Goes On Forever	1975	$15
☐ CP 0156	Win, Lose or Draw	1975	$12
☐ CPN 0156	Win, Lose or Draw	198?	$10
☐ 2CX 0177	Wipe the Windows, Check the Oil, Dollar Gas	1976	$15

EPIC
☐ E46144	Seven Turns	1990	$18

EPIC LEGACY
☐ 88843043521 [B]	Selections From: Play All Night: Live At The Beacon Theatre 1992	2014	$30

MERCURY
☐ 823-273-1 [B]	Live at the Fillmore East	2015	$40

MOBILE FIDELITY
☐ 1-213	Brothers and Sisters	1994	$75

—Audiophile vinyl
☐ MFSL2-398 [B]	Eat A Peach	2013	$50
☐ 1-157	Eat a Peach	1984	$250

—Audiophile vinyl

NAUTILUS
☐ NR-30	The Allman Brothers Band at Fillmore East	1982	$150

—Audiophile vinyl

POLYDOR
☐ 825092-1	Brothers and Sisters	1985	$10
☐ 839417-1	Dreams	1989	$40
☐ 823654-1	Eat a Peach	1984	$12
☐ 823653-1	The Allman Brothers Band	1984	$10
☐ 823273-1	The Allman Brothers Band at Fillmore East	1984	$12
☐ PD-1-6339	The Best of the Allman Brothers Band	1981	$12
☐ 823708-1	The Best of the Allman Brothers Band	1984	$10

—Reissue of PD-1-6339

ALLMAN JOYS, THE
DIAL
☐ DL6005	Early Allman	1973	$18

ALLSUP, TOMMY
GRT
☐ 20004	Tommy Allsup and the Tennessee Saxes Play the Hits of Tammy Wynette	1970	$25

Number	Title	Yr	NM

METROMEDIA
☐ MM1004	Tommy Allsup and the Nashville Survey Play the Hits of Charley Pride	1969	$30

REPRISE
☐ R6182 [M]	Tommy Allsup Plays the Buddy Holly Songbook	1965	$40
☐ RS6182 [S]	Tommy Allsup Plays the Buddy Holly Songbook	1965	$50

ALMEIDA, LAURINDO, AND CHARLIE BYRD
CONCORD PICANTE
☐ CJP-150	Brazilian Soul	1981	$25
☐ CJP-211	Latin Odyssey	1983	$35
☐ CP-290	Tango	1985	$25

ALMEIDA, LAURINDO
ANGEL
☐ S-36064	Clair de Lune	197?	$30
☐ S-36050	Duets with the Spanish Guitar	197?	$30
☐ S-36051	Duets with the Spanish Guitar, Vol. 2	197?	$30
☐ S-36076	Duets with the Spanish Guitar, Vol. 3	197?	$30
☐ S-37322	Prelude	197?	$35

CAPITOL
☐ T2701 [M]	A Man and a Woman	1967	$85
☐ ST2701 [S]	A Man and a Woman	1967	$85
☐ SM-2701	A Man and a Woman	1976	$25

—Reissue
☐ T2063 [M]	Broadway Solo Guitar	1964	$75
☐ ST2063 [S]	Broadway Solo Guitar	1964	$85
☐ H-193 [10]	Concert Creations for Guitar	1950	$175
☐ P8625 [M]	Concerto de Copacabana	196?	$75
☐ SP8625 [S]	Concerto de Copacabana	196?	$35
☐ SP8636	Concerto for Guitar and Small Orchestra	196?	$35
☐ P8447 [M]	Contemporary Creations for Spanish Guitar	195?	$150
☐ P8532 [M]	Conversations with the Guitar	196?	$100
☐ SP8532 [S]	Conversations with the Guitar	196?	$150
☐ P8467 [M]	Danzas!	196?	$100
☐ PAO8406 [M]	Duets with the Spanish Guitar	1958	$150

—Gatefold cover
☐ P8406 [M]	Duets with the Spanish Guitar	196?	$100

—Regular cover
☐ DP8406 [R]	Duets with the Spanish Guitar	196?	$75
☐ P8461 [M]	For My True Love	1959	$100
☐ SP8461 [S]	For My True Love	1959	$150
☐ T2197 [M]	Guitar from Ipanema	1964	$85
☐ ST2197 [S]	Guitar from Ipanema	1964	$100
☐ P8341 [M]	Guitar Music from the Romantic Era	195?	$150
☐ DP8601 [R]	Guitar Music from the Romantic Era	196?	$75
☐ P8601 [M]	Guitar Music from the Romantic Era	196?	$85

—Reissue of 8341
☐ P8321 [M]	Guitar Music of Latin America	195?	$150
☐ P8295 [M]	Guitar Music of Spain	195?	$150
☐ T1263 [M]	Happy Cha Cha Cha	1959	$100
☐ P8381 [M]	Impressaoes do Brasil	195?	$85
☐ T1946 [M]	It's a Bossa Nova World	1963	$85
☐ ST1946 [S]	It's a Bossa Nova World	1963	$25
☐ SP8497 [S]	Music of the Spanish Guitar	196?	$100
☐ T2419 [M]	New Broadway-Hollywood Hits	1965	$75
☐ ST2419 [S]	New Broadway-Hollywood Hits	1965	$50
☐ T1872 [M]	Ole! Bossa Nova	1963	$50
☐ ST1872 [S]	Ole! Bossa Nova	1963	$25
☐ P8571 [M]	Reverie for Spanish Guitars	196?	$100
☐ SP8571 [S]	Reverie for Spanish Guitars	196?	$150
☐ P8482 [M]	Songs of Enchantment	196?	$50
☐ SP8482 [S]	Songs of Enchantment	196?	$25
☐ T2345 [M]	Suenos (Dreams)	1965	$50
☐ DP8686 [R]	The Best of Laurindo Almeida	1969	$75
☐ STER-291	The Guitar of Laurindo Almeida	1969	$40
☐ P8546 [M]	The Guitar Worlds of Laurindo Almeida	196?	$85
☐ SP8546 [S]	The Guitar Worlds of Laurindo Almeida	196?	$100
☐ P8582 [M]	The Intimate Bach: Duets with the Spanish Guitar Vol. 2	196?	$85
☐ SP8582 [S]	The Intimate Bach: Duets with the Spanish Guitar Vol. 2	196?	$100
☐ ST2866	The Look of Love	1968	$100
☐ P8392 [M]	The New World of the Guitar	195?	$150
☐ P8521 [M]	The Spanish Guitars of Laurindo Almeida	196?	$50
☐ SP8521 [S]	The Spanish Guitars of Laurindo Almeida	196?	$100
☐ P8497 [M]	Villa-Lobos: Music for the Spanish Guitar	196?	$50
☐ P8367 [M]	Vistas d'Espana	195?	$150
☐ T1759 [M]	Viva Bossa Nova!	1962	$50
☐ ST1759 [S]	Viva Bossa Nova!	1962	$25
☐ SM-1759	Viva Bossa Nova!	197?	$25

Number	Title	Yr	NM

CONCORD CONCERTO
☐ CC-2001	First Concerto for Guitar and Orchestra	1980	$25
☐ CC-2003	Laurindo Almeida with Bud Shank	198?	$25

CONCORD JAZZ
☐ CJ-238	Artistry in Rhythm	1984	$25
☐ CJ-84	Chamber Jazz	1979	$35

CORAL
☐ CRL56049 [10]	A Guitar Recital of Famous Serenades	1952	$100
☐ CRL57056 [M]	A Guitar Recital of Famous Serenades	1956	$50

—Maroon label original
☐ CRL57056 [M]	A Guitar Recital of Famous Serenades	196?	$30

—Black label with color bars
☐ CRL56086 [10]	Latin Melodies	1952	$100

CRYSTAL CLEAR
☐ CCS-8007	New Directions	1979	$40

—Direct-to-disc recording
☐ CCS-8001	Virtuoso Guitar	1978	$40

—Direct-to-disc recording; plays at 45 rpm; white vinyl
☐ CCS-8001	Virtuoso Guitar	1978	$30

—Direct-to-disc recording; plays at 45 rpm; black vinyl

DAYBREAK
☐ DR-2013	The Best of Everything	1972	$35

DOBRE
☐ DR1000	Latin Guitar	1977	$50
☐ 1024	Trio	197?	$25

EVEREST
☐ SDBR-3287 [R]	Spanish Guitar Recital	196?	$25

INNER CITY
☐ IC6031	Concierto de Aranjuez	1979	$25

ORION
☐ ORS7259	The Art of Laurindo Almeida	197?	$35

PACIFIC JAZZ
☐ PJLP-7 [10]	Laurindo Almeida Quartet	1953	$250
☐ PJLP-13 [10]	Laurindo Almeida Quartet, Vol. 2	1954	$250
☐ PJ-1204 [M]	Laurindo Almeida Quartet Featuring Bud Shank	1955	$120

—Reissue of 10-inch Pacific Jazz LPs; red vinyl
☐ PJ-1204 [M]	Laurindo Almeida Quartet Featuring Bud Shank	1955	$100

—Reissue of 10-inch Pacific Jazz LPs; black vinyl

PAUSA
☐ PR9009	Brazilliance	1983	$25

—Reissue

PICKWICK
☐ SPC-3172	I Left My Heart in San Francisco	197?	$20

PRO ARTE
☐ PAD-235	3 Guitars 3	1985	$25

—With Sharon Isbin and Larry Coryell

SUTTON
☐ SU247 [M]	Flamenco	196?	$25

TOWER
☐ T5060 [M]	Acapulco '22	1967	$75
☐ DT5060 [R]	Acapulco '22	1967	$50

WARNER BROS.
☐ WS1803	Classical Current: Electronic Excursions	1969	$75

—Original U.S. edition is on a green "W7" label
☐ ST-92083	Classical Current: Electronic Excursions	1969	$150

—Capitol Record Club edition

WORLD PACIFIC
☐ WP-1412 [M]	Brazilliance, Vol. 1	1962	$30

—Reissue of World Pacific 1204
☐ WPS-21412 [S]	Brazilliance, Vol. 1	196?	$150
☐ T90078 [M]	Brazilliance, Vol. 1	196?	$175

—Capitol Record Club edition
☐ WP-1419 [M]	Brazilliance, Vol. 2	1962	$30
☐ ST-1419 [S]	Brazilliance, Vol. 2	1962	$30
☐ WP-1425 [M]	Brazilliance, Vol. 3	1962	$30
☐ ST-1425 [S]	Brazilliance, Vol. 3	1962	$30
☐ PJ-1204 [M]	Laurindo Almeida Quartet Featuring Bud Shank	1958	$175

—Reissue of Pacific Jazz 1204

ALMERICO, TONY
IMPERIAL
☐ LP-9151 [M]	French Quarter Jazz	1961	$175
☐ LP-12072 [S]	French Quarter Jazz	1961	$175

ALMOND, JOHNNY
DERAM
☐ DES18030	Music Machine	1969	$35

ALMOND, MARC
CAPITOL
☐ C1-94404 [B]	Enchanted	1990	$25

Number	Title	Yr	NM
❏ C1-91042 [B]	The Stars We Are	1988	$18

ALMOST BROTHERS, THE
MTM
❏ ST-71056	The Almost Brothers	1986	$10

ALPERT, HERB, AND THE TIJUANA BRASS
A&M
❏ SP-5022	Bullish	1984	$10
❏ SP-4166 [S]	Christmas Album	1968	$15
❏ SP-3113	Christmas Album	198?	$10
— Reissue of SP-4166			
❏ LP166 [M]	Christmas Album	1968	$30
— Mono is white label promo only			
❏ SP-4521	Coney Island	1975	$12
❏ SP-3521	Foursider	1973	$15
❏ SP-6011	Foursider	197?	$12
— Reissue			
❏ LP-112 [M]	Going Places	1965	$12
❏ SP-4112 [S]	Going Places	1965	$15
❏ SP-3264	Going Places	1984	$10
— Reissue			
❏ T-90507 [M]	Going Places	1965	$18
— Capitol Record Club edition			
❏ ST-90507 [S]	Going Places	1965	$25
— Capitol Record Club edition			
❏ SP-4245	Greatest Hits	1970	$12
❏ SP-3267	Greatest Hits	1984	$10
— Reissue			
❏ SP-4627	Greatest Hits, Vol. 2	1976	$12
❏ SP-3269	Greatest Hits, Vol. 2	1984	$10
❏ SP-4134	Herb Alpert's Ninth	1967	$12
❏ LP-103 [M]	Herb Alpert's Tijuana Brass, Volume 2	1963	$18
— Brown label with A&M logo at top			
❏ SP-4103 [S]	Herb Alpert's Tijuana Brass, Volume 2	1963	$18
❏ SP-103 [S]	Herb Alpert's Tijuana Brass, Volume 2	1963	$25
— Original issues had this number			
❏ LP-103 [M]	Herb Alpert's Tijuana Brass, Volume 2	1964	$15
— Brown label with A&M logo at left			
❏ T-90074 [M]	Herb Alpert's Tijuana Brass, Volume 2	1964	$25
— Capitol Record Club edition			
❏ SP-4341	Solid Brass	1972	$12
❏ SP-3268	Solid Brass	1984	$10
❏ LP-124 [M]	Sounds Like	1967	$12
❏ SP-4124 [S]	Sounds Like	1967	$15
❏ LP-108 [M]	South of the Border	1964	$15
❏ SP-4108 [S]	South of the Border	1964	$18
❏ SP-3263	South of the Border	1984	$10
❏ SP-108 [S]	South of the Border	1964	$25
— Original issues had this number			
❏ ST-90073 [S]	South of the Border	1964	$25
— Capitol Record Club edition			
❏ LP-119 [M]	S.R.O.	1966	$12
❏ SP-4119 [S]	S.R.O.	1966	$15
❏ SP-4314	Summertime	1971	$12
❏ SW-93870	Summertime	197?	$15
— Capitol Record Club edition			
❏ SP-4146	The Beat of the Brass	1968	$12
❏ SP-3266 [B]	The Beat of the Brass	1984	$10
— Reissue			
❏ LP-9004 [DJ]	The Best from Herb Alpert & The Tijuana Brass	196?	$18
— Promo-only compilation			
❏ SP-4228	The Brass Are Comin'	1969	$12
❏ SP-4101 [S]	The Lonely Bull	1962	$18
❏ LP-101 [M]	The Lonely Bull	1962	$30
— Originals on yellowish label with brown print			
❏ SP-3101	The Lonely Bull	198?	$10
— Reissue			
❏ SP-101 [S]	The Lonely Bull	1962	$30
— Original editions had this number			
❏ LP-101 [M]	The Lonely Bull	1963	$18
— Second pressings with brown label and A&M logo at top			
❏ LP-101 [M]	The Lonely Bull	1964	$15
— Third pressing with brown label and A&M logo at left			
❏ SP-4190	Warm	1969	$12
❏ LP-114 [M]	What Now My Love	1966	$12
❏ SP-4114 [S]	What Now My Love	1966	$15
❏ SP-3265	What Now My Love	1984	$10
❏ T-90655 [M]	What Now My Love	1966	$15
— Capitol Record Club edition			
❏ LP-110 [M]	Whipped Cream & Other Delights	1965	$12
❏ SP-4110 [S]	Whipped Cream & Other Delights	1965	$15
❏ SP-3157	Whipped Cream & Other Delights	198?	$10
— Reissue			
❏ ST-90387 [S]	Whipped Cream & Other Delights	1965	$18
— Capitol Record Club edition			
❏ SP-3620	You Smile -- The Song Begins	1974	$12

Number	Title	Yr	NM

LONGINES SYMPHONETTE
❏ LWS-500	Treasury of Herb Alpert and the Tijuana Brass	196?	$30
— Also contains music by the Baja Marimba Band; records are individually numbered from 500 through 504			

ALPERT, HERB
A&M
❏ SP-3717	Beyond	1980	$20
❏ SP-4949	Blow Your Own Horn	1983	$20
❏ SP-3731	Fandango	1982	$20
❏ SP-4591	Just You and Me	1976	$25
❏ SP-5125	Keep Your Eye on Me	1987	$20
❏ SP-3728	Magic Man	1981	$20
❏ SP-5273	My Abstract Heart	1989	$20
❏ 7502153451	North on South Street	1991	$30
❏ SP-4790	Rise	1979	$25
❏ SP-3714	Rise	1980	$20
— Reissue of 4790			
❏ SP-5209	Under a Spanish Moon	1988	$20
❏ SP-5082	Wild Romance	1985	$20

MOBILE FIDELITY
❏ Jan-0053	Rise	1981	$75
— Audiophile vinyl			

ALPERT, HERB/HUGH MASEKELA
A&M
❏ SP-3150	Herb Alpert/Hugh Masekela	198?	$20
❏ SP-4727	Main Event	1978	$25

HORIZON
❏ 728	Herb Alpert/Hugh Masekela	1978	$25

ALPERT, TRIGGER
RIVERSIDE
❏ RLP 12-225 [M]	Trigger Happy!	1956	$350
— White label, blue print			
❏ RLP 12-225 [M]	Trigger Happy!	195?	$40
— Blue label with microphone logo			

ALTERED IMAGES
PORTRAIT
❏ BFR38585	Bite	1983	$15
❏ FR37738	Happy Birthday	1982	$15
❏ ARR38110	Pinky Blue	1982	$15

ALVIN, DANNY
JAZZOLOGY
❏ 8 [M]	Danny Alvin and the Kings of Dixieland	1964	$50
❏ S-8 [S]	Danny Alvin and the Kings of Dixieland	1964	$50

STEPHENY
❏ MF-4002 [M]	Club Basin Street	1957	$150

ALVIN, DAVE
EPIC
❏ FE40921	Romeo's Escape	1987	$12

ALWAYS, BILLY
EPIC
❏ FE44332	Watch Out	1988	$10

WAYLO
❏ 12114	Billy Always	1982	$12

AMAZING RHYTHM ACES
ABC
❏ AA-1063	Burning the Ballroom Down	1978	$18

❏ D-913 [B]	Stacked Deck	1975	$25
❏ AA-1123	The Amazing Rhythm Aces	1979	$25
❏ D-940	Too Stuffed to Jump	1976	$18
❏ AB-1005	Toucan Do It Too	1977	$18

Number	Title	Yr	NM

COLUMBIA
❏ JC36083	The Amazing Rhythm Aces	1979	$15
— Reissue of ABC 1123			

WARNER BROS.
❏ BSK3476	How the Hell Do You Spell Rythum?	1980	$15

AMAZULU
MANGO
❏ ILPS9851	Amazula	198?	$12

AMBASSADORS, THE (1)
ARCTIC
❏ ALPS-1005 [B]	Soul Summit	1969	$30

AMBER
TOMMY BOY
❏ 1424	The Hits Remixed	2000	$25

AMBOY DUKES, THE
Also see CACTUS; TED NUGENT.
DISCREET
❏ DS2181	Call of the Wild	1974	$18
— As "Ted Nugent and the Amboy Dukes"			
❏ DS2203	Tooth, Fang and Claw	1974	$18
— As "Ted Nugent and the Amboy Dukes"			

MAINSTREAM
❏ S-414	Dr. Slingshot	1975	$18
❏ S-2-801	Journeys and Migrations	1974	$30
— Reissue of 6112 and 6118			
❏ S-6112 [B]	Journey to the Center of the Mind	1968	$50

❏ S-6118 [B]	Migration	1968	$50
❏ S-421	Ted Nugent and the Amboy Dukes	1976	$30
— Reissue of early material			
❏ 56104 [M]	The Amboy Dukes	1967	$175
❏ S-6104 [S]	The Amboy Dukes	1967	$50
❏ S-6125	The Best of the Original Amboy Dukes	1969	$30

POLYDOR
❏ 24-4012	Marriage on the Rocks/Rock Bottom	1970	$30
❏ 24-4035	Survival of the Fittest/Live	1971	$30
— As "Ted Nugent and the Amboy Dukes"			

AMBROSE, AMANDA
DUNWICH
❏ 668 [M]	Amanda	1966	$18
❏ S-668 [S]	Amanda	1966	$25

AMBROSE SLADE
See SLADE.

AMBROSIA
20TH CENTURY
❏ T-434	Ambrosia	1975	$15
— Original cover with black border			
❏ T-434	Ambrosia	1975	$12
— New cover without black border			
❏ T-510	Somewhere I've Never Traveled	1976	$15
— Fold-open cover in the shape of a pyramid			
❏ T-510	Somewhere I've Never Traveled	1976	$12
— Standard cover			

NAUTILUS
❏ NR-23	Life Beyond L.A.	1981	$30
— Audiophile vinyl			

Number	Title	Yr	NM

WARNER BROS.

❏ BSK3181	Ambrosia	1978	$10

— *Reissue of 20th Century 434*

❏ BSK3135	Life Beyond L.A.	1978	$12
❏ BSK3368	One Eighty	1980	$12
❏ BSK3638	Road Island	1982	$12

AMECHE, DON, AND FRANCES LANGFORD

COLUMBIA

❏ CL1692	The Bickersons	1962	$25

— *Live-in-the-studio recordings from 1961*

❏ CL1883	The Bickersons Fight Back	1962	$25

— *More live-in-the-studio recordings from 1961*

❏ G30523 [B]	The Bickersons Rematch	1970	$18

— *Compilation of the earlier Columbia LPs*

RADIOLA

❏ MR1115	The Bickersons	198?	$15

— *Compilation of radio shows*

RADIOLA/MURRAY HILL

❏ 3MH36721	Return of the Bickersons	1987	$25

— *Compilation of radio shows*

AMELING, ELLY

CBS MASTERWORKS

❏ M36677	Christmas with Elly Ameling	1980	$15

AMERICA

CAPITOL

❏ SOO-12098	Alibi	1980	$12
❏ SN-16275	Alibi	1982	$10
❏ ST-12422	In Concert	1985	$12
❏ ST-12370	Perspective	1984	$12
❏ SO-11950	Silent Letter	1979	$12
❏ ST-12209	View from the Ground	1982	$12
❏ SN-16350	View from the Ground	1985	$10
❏ ST-12277	Your Move	1983	$12
❏ SN-16361	Your Move	1985	$10

WARNER BROS.

❏ BS2576	America	1971	$30

— *First pressings omit "A Horse with No Name"*

❏ BS2576	America	1972	$15

— *With "A Horse with No Name" mentioned on front cover; green label*

❏ BS2576	America	1972	$18

— *Transitional edition includes "A Horse with No Name" but doesn't mention it on the front cover*

❏ BSK3136	America/Live	1977	$15
❏ BSK3017	Harbor	1977	$15
❏ BS2728	Hat Trick	1973	$15
❏ BS2852	Hearts	1975	$15
❏ BS42852 [Q]	Hearts	1975	$40
❏ BS2932	Hideaway	1976	$15
❏ BS2894	History/America's Greatest Hits	1975	$15
❏ BSK3110	History/America's Greatest Hits	1977	$12

— *Reissue of BS 2894 with "Burbank" palm trees label (later white labels are $8 NM)*

❏ BS2808	Holiday	1974	$15
❏ BS42808 [Q]	Holiday	1974	$40
❏ BS2655	Homecoming	1972	$15

AMERICAN BLUES, THE
Early incarnation of ZZ TOP.

KARMA

❏ 1001 [B]	The American Blues Is Here	1967	$500

UNI

❏ 73044 [B]	The American Blues Do Their Thing	1968	$150

Number	Title	Yr	NM

AMERICAN BLUES EXCHANGE, THE

TAYL

❏ TLS-1	Blueprints	1969	$400

AMERICAN BREED, THE

ACTA

❏ 8003 [M]	Bend Me, Shape Me	1968	$25
❏ 38003 [S]	Bend Me, Shape Me	1968	$30
❏ 8008 [M]	Lonely Side of the City	1969	$50

— *In stereo cover with "Monaural" sticker; record is regular yellow label*

❏ 38008 [S]	Lonely Side of the City	1969	$25
❏ 38006 [S]	Pumpkin, Powder, Scarlet & Green	1968	$25
❏ 8006 [M]	Pumpkin, Powder, Scarlet & Green	1968	$50

— *Stock label; the cover is the same as stereo but with a "Monaural" sticker attached*

❏ 8002 [M]	The American Breed	1967	$25
❏ 38002 [S]	The American Breed	1967	$30

AMERICAN DREAM, THE

AMPEX

❏ A-10101 [B]	The American Dream	1970	$30

— *Produced by Todd Rundgren*

AMERICAN EAGLE

DECCA

❏ DL75258	American Eagle	1971	$25

AMERICAN FLYER

UNITED ARTISTS

❏ UA-LA650-G	American Flyer	1976	$15
❏ UA-LA720-G	Spirit of a Woman	1977	$15

AMERICAN JAZZ ENSEMBLE, THE

EPIC

❏ LA16040 [M]	New Dimensions	1962	$50
❏ BA17040 [S]	New Dimensions	1962	$75

RCA VICTOR

❏ LPM-2557 [M]	The American Jazz Ensemble in Rome	1962	$25
❏ LSP-2557 [S]	The American Jazz Ensemble in Rome	1962	$30

AMERICAN MUSIC CLUB

ALIAS

❏ A015 [B]	Everclear	1991	$18

FRONTIER

❏ 4619-1-L	California	1988	$15
❏ 4612-1-L	Engine	1987	$15

REPRISE

❏ 45721	San Francisco	1994	$15

AMERICAN REVOLUTION, THE

FLICK DISC

❏ FL-45,002 [M]	The American Revolution	1968	$50

— *White label promo in stereo cover with "Not for Sale DJ Monaural" sticker on front*

❏ FLS-45,002 [S]	The American Revolution	1968	$30

AMERICA'S MOST WANTED

TRIAD

❏ 2222	Criminals	1991	$18

AMES, ED

RCA CAMDEN

❏ ACL1-0244	Do You Hear What I Hear?	1973	$15
❏ CAS-2536	Ed Ames	1972	$15
❏ CAS-2598	Somewhere, My Love	1972	$15

RCA VICTOR

❏ LPM-4028 [M]	Apologize	1968	$25
❏ LSP-4028 [S]	Apologize	1968	$12
❏ LSP-4128	A Time for Living, A Time for Hope	1969	$12
❏ LSP-4385	Christmas Is the Warmest Time of the Year	1970	$25
❏ LPM-3838 [M]	Christmas with Ed Ames	1967	$18
❏ LSP-3838 [S]	Christmas with Ed Ames	1967	$15
❏ LSP-4634	Ed Ames	1972	$18
❏ LSP-4683	Ed Ames Remembers Jim Reeves	1972	$18
❏ LPM-3460 [M]	It's a Man's World	1965	$15
❏ LSP-3460 [S]	It's a Man's World	1965	$18
❏ LSP-4249	Love of the Common People	1969	$12
❏ LPM-3636 [M]	More I Cannot Wish You	1966	$12
❏ LSP-3636 [S]	More I Cannot Wish You	1966	$15
❏ LPM-3774 [M]	My Cup Runneth Over	1967	$12
❏ LSP-3774 [S]	My Cup Runneth Over	1967	$15
❏ LPM-3390 [M]	My Kind of Songs	1965	$15
❏ LSP-3390 [S]	My Kind of Songs	1965	$18
❏ LPM-2781 [M]	Opening Night	1963	$15
❏ LSP-2781 [S]	Opening Night	1963	$18
❏ ANL1-1780	Pure Gold	1976	$12
❏ LSP-4381	Sing Away the World	1970	$12
❏ LSP-4808	Songs from "Lost Horizon	1973	$18
❏ LSP-4184	The Best of Ed Ames	1969	$12

Number	Title	Yr	NM

❏ LPM-2944 [M]	The Ed Ames Album	1964	$15
❏ LSP-2944 [S]	The Ed Ames Album	1964	$18
❏ LSP-4079	The Hits of Broadway and Hollywood	1968	$12
❏ ANL1-2891	The Impossible Dream	1978	$12
❏ LSP-4453	The Songs of Bacharach and David	1971	$12
❏ LSP-4172	The Windmills of Your Mind	1969	$12
❏ VPS-6023	This Is Ed Ames	1970	$25
❏ LPM-3834 [M]	Time, Time	1967	$15
❏ LSP-3834 [S]	Time, Time	1967	$12
❏ LPM-3913 [M]	When the Snow Is On the Roses	1967	$15
❏ LSP-3913 [S]	When the Snow Is On the Roses	1967	$12
❏ LPM-3961 [M]	Who Will Answer? And Other Songs of Our Time	1968	$18
❏ LSP-3961 [S]	Who Will Answer? And Other Songs of Our Time	1968	$12

AMES, NANCY

EPIC

❏ LN24197 [M]	As Time Goes By	1967	$15
❏ BN26197 [S]	As Time Goes By	1967	$18
❏ LN24189 [M]	Latin Pulse	1966	$15
❏ BN26189 [S]	Latin Pulse	1966	$18
❏ BN26378	Nancy Ames at the Americana	1968	$15
❏ LN24238 [M]	Spiced with Brazil	1967	$15
❏ BN26238 [S]	Spiced with Brazil	1967	$18

LIBERTY

❏ LRP-3329 [M]	I Never Will Marry	1964	$18
❏ LST-7329 [S]	I Never Will Marry	1964	$25
❏ LRP-3400 [M]	Let It Be Me	1965	$18
❏ LST-7400 [S]	Let It Be Me	1965	$25
❏ LRP-3299 [M]	Portrait of Nancy	1963	$18
❏ LST-7299 [S]	Portrait of Nancy	1963	$25
❏ LRP-3276 [M]	The Incredible Nancy Ames	1963	$18
❏ LST-7276 [S]	The Incredible Nancy Ames	1963	$25
❏ LRP-3369 [M]	This Is the Girl That Is	1964	$18
❏ LST-7369 [S]	This Is the Girl That Is	1964	$25

SUNSET

❏ SUM-1109 [M]	The Versatile Nancy Ames	196?	$15
❏ SUS-5109 [S]	The Versatile Nancy Ames	196?	$18

AMES BROTHERS, THE

CORAL

❏ CRL57031 [M]	Ames Brothers Concert	1956	$30
❏ CRL56097 [10]	Favorite Songs	1954	$50
❏ CRL56050 [10]	Favorite Spirituals	1952	$50
❏ CRL56079 [10]	Home on the Range	1952	$50
❏ CRL56025 [10]	Hoop-De-Hoo	1951	$50
❏ CRL56017 [10]	In the Evening by the Moonlight	1951	$50
❏ CRL57176 [M]	Love Serenade	1958	$30
❏ CRL57054 [M]	Love's Old Sweet Song	1956	$30
❏ CRL56080 [10]	Merry Christmas	1952	$50
❏ CRL57338 [M]	Our Golden Favorites	1960	$30
❏ CRL56024 [10]	Sentimental Me	1951	$50
❏ CRL56014 [10]	Sing a Song of Christmas	1950	$50
❏ CRL57166	Sounds of Christmas Harmony	1957	$30
❏ CRL56042 [10]	Sweet Leilani	1951	$50

EPIC

❏ LN24036 [M]	Hello Italy	1962	$18
❏ BN26036 [S]	Hello Italy	1962	$25
❏ LN24069 [M]	Knees Up Mother Brown	1963	$18
❏ BN26069 [S]	Knees Up Mother Brown	1963	$25

MCA

❏ 1510 [R]	The Ames Brothers	197?	$12

RCA CAMDEN

❏ CAL-571 [M]	The Ames Brothers -- Sweet and Swing	1958	$18

RCA SPECIAL PRODUCTS

❏ DVL2-0207	All Their Greatest Hits	1976	$18

RCA VICTOR

❏ LPM-1680 [M]	Destination Moon	1958	$30
❏ LSP-1680 [S]	Destination Moon	1958	$30
❏ LPM-2981 [M]	Down Memory Lane with the Ames Brothers	1964	$15
❏ LSP-2981 [S]	Down Memory Lane with the Ames Brothers	1964	$18
❏ LPM-1142 [M]	Exactly Like You	1955	$30
❏ LPM-1954 [M]	Famous Hits of Famous Quartets	1959	$25
❏ LSP-1954 [S]	Famous Hits of Famous Quartets	1959	$30
❏ LPM-2876 [M]	For Sentimental Reasons	1964	$15
❏ LSP-2876 [S]	For Sentimental Reasons	1964	$18
❏ LPM-1157 [M]	Four Brothers	1955	$30
❏ LPM-2100 [M]	Hello, Amigos	1960	$25
❏ LSP-2100 [S]	Hello, Amigos	1960	$30
❏ LPM-3186 [10]	It Must Be True	1954	$50
❏ LPM-1855 [M]	Smoochin' Time	1958	$30
❏ LSP-1855 [S]	Smoochin' Time	1958	$30
❏ LPM-1487 [M]	Sweet Seventeen	1957	$30
❏ LPM-1998 [M]	The Ames Brothers Sing the Best in the Country	1959	$25
❏ LSP-1998 [S]	The Ames Brothers Sing the Best in the Country	1959	$30
❏ LPM-1228 [M]	The Ames Brothers with Hugo Winterhalter	1956	$30
❏ LPM-1859 [M]	The Best of the Ames Brothers	1958	$30

Number	Title	Yr	NM
❏ LSP-1859(e) [R]	The Best of the Ames Brothers	196?	$25
❏ ANL1-1095e	The Best of the Ames Brothers	1975	$12
❏ LPM-2273 [M]	The Best of the Bands	1960	$25
❏ LSP-2273 [S]	The Best of the Bands	1960	$30
❏ LPM-2182 [M]	The Blend and the Beat	1960	$25
❏ LSP-2182 [S]	The Blend and the Beat	1960	$30
❏ LPM-1541 [M]	There'll Always Be a Christmas	1957	$30
❏ VPS-6068	This Is the Ames Brothers	1972	$18

Number	Title	Yr	NM
❏ LPM-2009 [M]	Words and Music	1959	$25
❏ LSP-2009 [S]	Words and Music	1959	$30

READER'S DIGEST
| ❏ RDA-160 | Sentimentally Yours | 1981 | $30 |

VOCALION
| ❏ VL73788 [R] | Christmas Harmony | 196? | $15 |
— Reissue of some Coral tracks
| ❏ VL3617 [M] | The Ames Brothers | 196? | $18 |
| ❏ VL73818 | The Ames Brothers Featuring Ed Ames | 196? | $12 |

AMESBURY, BILL
CAPITOL
| ❏ ST-11528 | Can You Feel It | 1976 | $15 |

CASABLANCA
| ❏ NB9005 | Jus' a Taste of the Kid | 1974 | $15 |

AMG
304 ENTERTAINMENT
| ❏ 54433 | Bitch Betta Have My Money | 2000 2001 | $18 |

AMISH, THE
SUSSEX
| ❏ SUX-7016 [B] | The Amish | 1972 | $30 |

AMMONS, ALBERT, AND PETE JOHNSON
RCA VICTOR
| ❏ LPT-9 [10] | 8 to the Bar | 1952 | $200 |

AMMONS, ALBERT
BLUE NOTE
| ❏ BLP-7017 [10] | Boogie Woogie Classics | 1951 | $300 |

COMMODORE
| ❏ XFL-15357 [M] | The Boogie Woogie and the Blues | 198? | $30 |

MERCURY
| ❏ MG-25012 [10] | Boogie Woogie Piano | 1950 | $300 |

AMMONS, ALBERT / MEADE LUX LEWIS
MOSAIC
| ❏ MR3-103 | The Complete Blue Note Recordings of Albert Ammons and Meade Lux Lewis | 198? | $50 |
— Limited edition of 5,000

AMMONS, GENE, AND JAMES MOODY
PRESTIGE
| ❏ P-10065 | Chicago Concert | 1973 | $75 |

AMMONS, GENE, AND RICHARD "GROOVE" HOLMES
PACIFIC JAZZ
| ❏ PJ-32 [M] | Groovin' with Jug | 1961 | $175 |
| ❏ ST-32 [S] | Groovin' with Jug | 1961 | $120 |

AMMONS, GENE, AND SONNY STITT
CADET
| ❏ LP-785 [M] | Jug and Sonny | 1967 | $40 |
| ❏ LPS-785 [S] | Jug and Sonny | 1967 | $75 |
— Fading blue label
| ❏ LPS-785 [S] | Jug and Sonny | 197? | $35 |
— Yellow and pink label (reissue)

CHESS
| ❏ LP1445 [M] | Jug and Sonny | 1960 | $175 |
| ❏ CH-91549 | Jug and Sonny | 198? | $25 |

PRESTIGE
❏ PRST-7823	Blues Up and Down Vol. 1	1969	$50
❏ PRLP-107 [10]	Gene Ammons vs. Sonny Stitt: Battle of the Saxes	1951	$300
❏ PRLP-7234 [M]	Soul Summit	1962	$175
❏ PRST-7234 [S]	Soul Summit	1962	$175
❏ PRLP-7454 [M]	Soul Summit	1967	$50
❏ PRST-7454 [S]	Soul Summit	1967	$35
❏ P-10100	Together Again for the Last Time	197?	$50
❏ PRST-7606	We'll Be Together Again	1969	$40
❏ PRST-10019	You Talk That Talk!	1970	$40

VERVE
❏ V-8426 [M]	Boss Tenors	1962	$75
❏ V6-8426 [S]	Boss Tenors	1962	$75
❏ V-8468 [M]	Boss Tenors in Orbit	1962	$75
❏ V6-8468 [S]	Boss Tenors in Orbit	1962	$75
❏ 2V6S-8812 [S]	Prime Cuts	1972	$50

AMMONS, GENE
ANALOGUE PRODUCTIONS
| ❏ AP 038 [M] | The Soulful Moods of Gene Ammons | 199? | $75 |
— 180-gram reissue of Moodsville 28

ARGO
❏ 697 [M]	Dig Him	1962	$120
❏ S-697 [S]	Dig Him	1962	$150
❏ 698 [M]	Just Jug	1962	$100
❏ S-698 [S]	Just Jug	1962	$40

CADET
❏ 2CA-60038	Early Visions	1975	$35
❏ LP-783 [M]	Makes It Happen	1967	$40
❏ LPS-783 [S]	Makes It Happen	1967	$50
— Fading blue label (original)
| ❏ CA-783 [S] | Makes It Happen | 197? | $35 |
— Yellow and pink label (reissue)

CHESS
| ❏ CH2-92514 | Early Visions | 198? | $30 |
— Reissue of Cadet 60038
| ❏ LP1442 [M] | Soulful Saxophone | 1959 | $140 |
— Black vinyl
| ❏ LP1442 [DJ] | Soulful Saxophone | 1959 | $175 |
— White label promo; multicolor swirl vinyl

EMARCY
| ❏ EMS-2-400 | The "Jug" Sessions | 1976 | $50 |
| ❏ MG-26031 [10] | With or Without | 1954 | $300 |

ENJA
| ❏ 3093 | Gene Ammons in Sweden | 1981 | $35 |

FANTASY
❏ OJC-014	All-Star Sessions	1982	$25
❏ OJC-351	Bad! Bossa Nova	198?	$25
❏ OJC-192	Blue Gene	1985	$25
❏ OJC-297	Boss Tenor	1988	$25
❏ OJC-244	Funky	1987	$25
❏ OJC-6005	Gene Ammons' Greatest Hits, Vol. 1: The Sixties	1988	$30
❏ OJC-129	Jammin' in Hi-Fi	198?	$25
❏ OJC-211	Jammin' with Gene	1986	$25
❏ OJC-395	Live in Chicago	198?	$25
❏ OJC-651	The Big Sound	1991	$30
❏ OJC-013	The Happy Blues	198?	$25

MOODSVILLE
| ❏ MVLP-18 [M] | Nice and Cool | 1961 | $175 |
— Originals have green label
| ❏ MVLP-18 [M] | Nice and Cool | 1965 | $40 |
— Second editions have blue label with trident at right
| ❏ MVLP-28 [M] | The Soulful Moods of Gene Ammons | 1963 | $175 |
— Originals have green label
| ❏ MVLP-28 [M] | The Soulful Moods of Gene Ammons | 1965 | $40 |
— Second editions have blue label with trident at right
| ❏ MVST-28 [S] | The Soulful Moods of Gene Ammons | 1963 | $175 |

PRESTIGE
| ❏ PRLP-7369 [M] | Angel Eyes | 1965 | $150 |
— Originals have blue label with trident at right
| ❏ PRST-7369 [S] | Angel Eyes | 1965 | $120 |
— Originals have blue label with trident at right
| ❏ PRLP-7257 [M] | Bad! Bossa Nova | 1962 | $175 |
— Originals have yellow label, Bergenfield, N.J. address; some copies have a cover calling this "Jungle Soul! (ca' purange)

Number	Title	Yr	NM
❏ PRST-7257 [S]	Bad! Bossa Nova	1962	$50
— Originals have silver label
| ❏ P-10070 | Big Bad Jug | 1973 | $40 |
| ❏ PRST-10006 | Black Cat | 1970 | $75 |
— Original on purple label
| ❏ PRST-10006 | Black Cat | 1973 | $75 |
— Second edition on green label
| ❏ PRLP-7146 [M] | Blue Gene | 1958 | $350 |
— Originals have yellow label, Bergenfield, N.J. address
| ❏ MPP-2514 | Blue Groove | 1982 | $30 |
| ❏ PRLP-7445 [M] | Boss Soul! | 1967 | $150 |
— Originals have blue label with trident at right
| ❏ PRST-7445 [S] | Boss Soul! | 1967 | $150 |
— Originals have blue label with trident at right
| ❏ PRLP-7180 [M] | Boss Tenor | 1960 | $250 |
— Originals have yellow label, Bergenfield, N.J. address
| ❏ PRST-7180 [S] | Boss Tenor | 1960 | $250 |
— Originals have silver label
| ❏ PRLP-7534 [M] | Boss Tenor | 1967 | $150 |
— Reissue of 7180; originals have blue label with trident at right
| ❏ PRST-7534 [S] | Boss Tenor | 1967 | $75 |
— Reissue of 7180; originals have blue label with trident at right
❏ P-10080	Brasswind	1974	$75
❏ P-10021	Brother Jug	1970	$40
❏ PRST-10010	Chase!	1970	$75
❏ P-10040	Free Again	1972	$75
❏ PRLP-7083 [M]	Funky	1957	$300
— Originals have yellow label, "W. 50th St., NYC" address
| ❏ PRLP-107 [10] | Gene Ammons | 1951 | $300 |
| ❏ PRLP-7050 [M] | Gene Ammons All Star Session | 1951 | $300 |
— Compilation of Prestige 107 and 127, yellow label
❏ P-10078	Gene Ammons and Friends at Montreux	1973	$35
❏ PRLP-127 [10]	Gene Ammons Favorites, Volume 2	1952	$300
❏ PRLP-149 [10]	Gene Ammons Favorites, Volume 3	1953	$300
❏ PRLP-211 [10]	Gene Ammons Jazz Session	1955	$300
❏ PRLP-7495 [M]	Gene Ammons Live in Chicago	1967	$150
— Originals have blue label with trident at right
| ❏ PRST-7495 [S] | Gene Ammons Live in Chicago | 1967 | $40 |
— Originals have blue label with trident at right
❏ P-10093	Goodbye	1975	$50
❏ PRST-10058	Got My Own	1973	$75
❏ P-10084	Greatest Hits	1974	$75
❏ PRLP-7201 [M]	Groove Blues	1961	$150
— Originals have yellow label, Bergenfield, N.J. address
| ❏ PRLP-7039 [M] | Hi Fidelity Jam Session | 1956 | $300 |
| ❏ PRLP-7110 [M] | Jammin' in Hi-Fi with Gene Ammons | 1957 | $300 |
— Originals have yellow label, "W. 50th St., NYC" address
| ❏ PRLP-7060 [M] | Jammin' with Gene | 1956 | $650 |
| ❏ PRST-7192 [S] | Jug | 1960 | $250 |
— Originals have silver label
| ❏ PRLP-7192 [M] | Jug | 1960 | $250 |
— Originals have yellow label, Bergenfield, N.J. address
| ❏ PRST-7192 [S] | Jug | 1972 | $75 |
— Reissue; trident logo at top
❏ P-24021	Jug and Dodo	1972	$50
❏ P-24036	Juganthology	197?	$50
❏ PRST-7552	Jungle Soul	1968	$40
— Reissue of 7257
| ❏ PRLP-7287 [M] | Late Hour Special | 1964 | $40 |
— Originals have yellow label, Bergenfield, N.J. address
| ❏ PRST-7287 [S] | Late Hour Special | 1964 | $150 |
— Originals have silver label
❏ P-10022	My Way	197?	$50
❏ P-7862	Night Lights	1985	$30
❏ PRLP-7060 [M]	Not Really the Blues	1960	$250
— Retitled version of "Jammin' with Gene"

Number	Title	Yr	NM
❑ PRLP-7270 [M]	Preachin'	1963	$120
—Originals have yellow label, Bergenfield, N.J. address			
❑ PRST-7270 [S]	Preachin'	1963	$140
—Originals have silver label			
❑ PRLP-7400 [M]	Sock!	1966	$150
—Originals have blue label with trident at right			
❑ PRST-7400 [S]	Sock!	1966	$120
—Originals have blue label with trident at right			
❑ PRLP-7275 [M]	Soul Summit, Volume 2	1963	$120
—Originals have yellow label, Bergenfield, N.J. address			
❑ PRST-7275 [S]	Soul Summit, Volume 2	1963	$140
—Originals have silver label			
❑ PRLP-112 [10]	Tenor Sax Favorites, Volume 1	1951	$300
❑ PRST-7774	The Best of Gene Ammons	1970	$50
❑ PRST-7708	The Best of Gene Ammons for Beautiful People	1969	$50
❑ PRLP-7132 [M]	The Big Sound	1958	$300
—Originals have yellow label, "W. 50th St., NYC" address			
❑ P-24098	The Big Sound of Gene Ammons	1981	$50
❑ P-10023	The Boss Is Back	197?	$50
—Reissue of 7739			
❑ PRST-7739	The Boss Is Back!	1970	$75
❑ P-24079	The Gene Ammons Story: Gentle Jug	197?	$50
❑ P-24071	The Gene Ammons Story: Organ Combos	197?	$75
❑ P-24058	The Gene Ammons Story: The 78 Era	197?	$50
❑ PRLP-7039 [M]	The Happy Blues	1960	$250
—Retitled version of "Hi Fidelity Jam Session			
❑ PRST-7654	The Happy Blues -- Jam Session, Vol. 1	1969	$75
—Second reissue of 7039			
❑ PRLP-7176 [M]	The Twister	1960	$250
—Originals have yellow label, Bergenfield, N.J. address; reissue of 7110			
❑ PRLP-7238 [M]	Twistin' the Jug	1962	$250
—Originals have yellow label, Bergenfield, N.J. address			
❑ PRST-7238 [S]	Twistin' the Jug	1962	$120
—Originals have silver label			
❑ PRLP-7208 [M]	Up Tight!	1961	$175
—Originals have yellow label, Bergenfield, N.J. address			
❑ PRST-7208 [S]	Up Tight!	1961	$175
—Originals have silver label			
❑ PRLP-7320 [M]	Velvet Soul	1964	$120
—Originals have yellow label, Bergenfield, N.J. address			
❑ PRST-7320 [S]	Velvet Soul	1964	$175
—Originals have silver label			
❑ PRLP-7320 [M]	Velvet Soul	1965	$40
—Blue label with tridenr at right			
❑ PRST-7320 [S]	Velvet Soul	1965	$150
—Blue label with trident at right			
❑ PRLP-7050 [M]	Woofin' and Tweetin'	1960	$250
—Retitled version of "Gene Ammons All Star Session			
ROOTS			
❑ 1002	Swinging the Jugg	1976	$50
SAVOY			
❑ MG-14033 [M]	Golden Saxophone	1961	$150
❑ SJL-1103	Red Top	1976	$30
STATUS			
❑ 18	Nice & Cool	197?	$35
TRIP			
❑ TLP-5578 [M]	Light, Bluesy and Moody	197?	$30
UPFRONT			
❑ UPF-116	Nothing But Soul	1968	$35
—Reissue of Vee-Jay material			
VEE JAY			
❑ LP-3024 [M]	Juggin' Around	1961	$175
❑ LPS-3024 [S]	Juggin' Around	1961	$175
WING			
❑ MGW-12156 [M]	Light, Bluesy and Moody	1963	$175
—Reissue of EmArcy 10-inch LP			
❑ SRW-16156 [R]	Light, Bluesy and Moody	1963	$35
AMON DUUL			
PROPHESY			
❑ PHS-1003 [B]	Amon Duul	1969	$150
AMON DUUL II			
ATCO			
❑ SD 36-108	Hijack	1975	$18
❑ SD 36-119	Made in Germany	1976	$18
CLEOPATRA			
❑ CLP1712 [B]	Dance of the Lemmings	2014	$40
❑ CLP1804 [B]	Duulirium	2014	$30
❑ CLP1715 [B]	Phallus Dei	2014	$40
❑ CLP1720 [B]	Viva La Trance	2014	$40
❑ CLP1587LP [B]	Wolf City	2014	$40
UNITED ARTISTS			
❑ UAS-5586 [B]	Carnival in Babylon	1972	$35
❑ UAS-9954 [B]	Dance of the Lemmings	1971	$40
❑ UA-LA198-F [B]	Viva La Trance	1974	$35
❑ UA-LA017-F [B]	Wolf City	1973	$35

Number	Title	Yr	NM
AMOS, TORI			
Also see Y KANT TORI READ. Also, any picture disc of any of her albums is a bootleg, no matter what they purport to be.			
ATLANTIC			
❑ 82862	Boys for Pele	1996	$25
—Clear vinyl			
❑ 83095	From the Choirgirl Hotel	1998	$30
❑ 82567	Under the Pink	1995	$30
—Limited edition on pink vinyl			
UNIVERSAL REPUBLIC			
❑ 1290601	Abnormally Attracted to Sin	2009	$30
AMRAM, DAVID			
ELEKTRA/MUSICIAN			
❑ 60195	Latin Jazz Celebration	1983	$25
FLYING FISH			
❑ FC-27753	Autobiography	198?	$25
❑ FF-094	Friends, At Home/Around the World	1979	$25
❑ FF-057	Havana/New York	1978	$30
❑ FC-27752	No More Walls	198?	$25
AMRAM-BARROW QUARTET, THE			
DECCA			
❑ DL8558 [M]	Jazz Studio No. 6	1957	$120
AMUZEMENT PARK			
ATLANTIC			
❑ 80126	All Points Bulletin	1984	$12
OUR GANG			
❑ 30001	Amuzement Park	1983	$18
AMY, CURTIS, AND DUPREE BOLTON			
PACIFIC JAZZ			
❑ PJ-70 [M]	Katanga!	1963	$30
❑ ST-70 [S]	Katanga!	1963	$75
—Red vinyl			
❑ ST-70 [S]	Katanga!	1963	$30
—Black vinyl			
AMY, CURTIS, AND FRANK BUTLER			
PACIFIC JAZZ			
❑ PJ-19 [M]	Groovin' Blue	1961	$30
❑ ST-19 [S]	Groovin' Blue	1961	$40
AMY, CURTIS, AND PAUL BRYANT			
KIMBERLY			
❑ 2020 [M]	This Is the Blues	1963	$25
❑ 11020 [S]	This Is the Blues	1963	$30
PACIFIC JAZZ			
❑ PJ-26 [M]	Meetin' Here	1961	$30
❑ ST-26 [S]	Meetin' Here	1961	$40
❑ PJ-9 [M]	The Blues Message	1960	$30
❑ ST-9 [S]	The Blues Message	1960	$40
AMY, CURTIS, AND VICTOR FELDMAN			
PACIFIC JAZZ			
❑ PJ-46 [M]	Way Down	1962	$30
❑ ST-46 [S]	Way Down	1962	$30
AMY, CURTIS			
PACIFIC JAZZ			
❑ PJ-62 [M]	Tippin' On Through -- Recorded "Live" at the Lighthouse	1962	$30
❑ ST-62 [S]	Tippin' On Through -- Recorded "Live" at the Lighthouse	1962	$30
PALOMAR			
❑ G-24003 [M]	Sounds of Hollywood and Broadway	1965	$35
❑ GS-34003 [S]	Sounds of Hollywood and Broadway	1965	$25
VERVE			
❑ V-8684 [M]	Mustang	1966	$35
❑ V6-8684 [S]	Mustang	1966	$25
ANA			
PARC			
❑ FZ40668	Ana	1987	$12
ANACOSTIA			
MCA			
❑ 2269	Anacostia	1977	$15
TABU			
❑ JZ35570	Anacostia	1978	$12
ANCIENT GREASE			
MERCURY			
❑ SR-61305	Women and Children First	1970	$30

Number	Title	Yr	NM
ANDERS & PONCIA			
WARNER BROS.			
❑ WS1778	The Anders & Poncia Album	1969	$30
ANDERSEN, ARLID			
ECM			
❑ 1236	A Molde Concert	1981	$30
❑ 1127	Green Shading Into Blue	1978	$30
❑ 1082	Shimri	1976	$30
ANDERSEN, ERIC			
ARISTA			
❑ AL4033	Be True to You	1975	$12
❑ AL4075	Sweet Surprise	1976	$12
❑ AL4128	The Best Songs	1977	$12
COLUMBIA			
❑ KC31062	Blue River	1972	$12
❑ PC31062	Blue River	197?	$10
—Reissue			
VANGUARD			
❑ VSD6540	A Country Dream	1969	$20
❑ VRS9206 [M]	'Bout Changes and Things	1966	$25
❑ VSD79206 [S]	'Bout Changes and Things	1966	$30
❑ VSD79236	'Bout Changes and Things, Take 2	1968	$25
❑ VSD79271	More Hits from Tin Can Alley	1969	$18
❑ VSD7/8	The Best of Eric Andersen	1971	$18
❑ VRS9157 [M]	Today Is the Highway	1965	$25
❑ VSD79157 [S]	Today Is the Highway	1965	$25
WARNER BROS.			
❑ WS1748	Avalanche	1968	$18
❑ WS1806	Eric Andersen	1969	$18
ANDERSON, AL			
Also see NRBQ; THE WILDWEEDS.			
TWIN/TONE			
❑ TTR88110	Party Favors	1989	$15
VANGUARD			
❑ VSD-79324	Al Anderson	1973	$25
ANDERSON, BILL, AND JAN HOWARD			
DECCA			
❑ DL75293	Bill & Jan (Or Jan & Bill)	1972	$25
❑ DL4959 [M]	For Loving You	1967	$30
❑ DL74959 [S]	For Loving You	1967	$25
❑ DL75184	If It's All the Same to You	1970	$25
ANDERSON, BILL, AND MARY LOU TURNER			
MCA			
❑ 2298	Billy Boy & Mary Lou	1977	$15
❑ 2182	Sometimes	1976	$15
ANDERSON, BILL			
DECCA			
❑ DL75275	Always Remember	1971	$15
❑ DL75161	Bill Anderson's Christmas	1969	$18
❑ DL4859 [M]	Bill Anderson's Greatest Hits	1967	$25
❑ DL74859 [S]	Bill Anderson's Greatest Hits	1967	$25
❑ DL75315	Bill Anderson's Greatest Hits, Vol. 2	1971	$15
❑ DL4600 [M]	Bill Anderson Showcase	1964	$18
❑ DL74600 [S]	Bill Anderson Showcase	1964	$25
❑ DL4499 [M]	Bill Anderson Sings	1964	$18
❑ DL74499 [S]	Bill Anderson Sings	1964	$25
❑ DL4192 [M]	Bill Anderson Sings Country Songs	1962	$25
❑ DL74192 [S]	Bill Anderson Sings Country Songs	1962	$30
❑ DL75344	Bill Anderson Sings For "All the Lonely Women in the World	1972	$15
❑ DL4686 [M]	Bright Lights and Country Music	1965	$18
❑ DL74686 [S]	Bright Lights and Country Music	1965	$25
❑ DL75383	Don't She Look Good	1972	$15
❑ DL4646 [M]	From This Pen	1965	$18
❑ DL74646 [S]	From This Pen	1965	$25
❑ DL4855 [M]	Get While the Gettin's Good	1967	$18
❑ DL74855 [S]	Get While the Gettin's Good	1967	$25
❑ DL75056	Happy State of Mind	1968	$18
❑ DL4886 [M]	I Can Do Nothing Alone	1967	$30
❑ DL74886 [S]	I Can Do Nothing Alone	1967	$25
❑ DL4771 [M]	I Love You Drops	1966	$18
❑ DL74771 [S]	I Love You Drops	1966	$25
❑ DL75206	Love Is a Sometimes Thing	1970	$15
❑ DL75142	My Life/But You Know I Love You	1969	$18
❑ DL75339	Singing His Praise	1972	$15
❑ DL4427 [M]	Still	1963	$25
❑ DL74427 [S]	Still	1963	$30
❑ DXSA7198	The Bill Anderson Story	1969	$18
❑ DL75254	Where Have All Our Heroes Gone?	1971	$15
❑ DL74998	Wild Weekend	1968	$18
MCA			
❑ 320	Bill	1973	$15
❑ 13	Bill Anderson's Greatest Hits	1973	$12
—Reissue of Decca 74859			
❑ 454	Every Time I Turn the Radio On/Talk to Me Ohio	1974	$12

Number	Title	Yr	NM
❑ 3075	Ladies' Choice	1979	$12
❑ 694	Ladies' Choice	198?	$10
—Reissue			
❑ 2371	Love and Other Sad Stories	1977	$12
❑ 693	Love and Other Sad Stories	198?	$10
—Reissue			
❑ 3214	Nashville Mirrors	1980	$12
❑ 766	Nashville Mirrors	198?	$10
—Reissue			
❑ 2222	Peanuts & Diamonds & Other Jewels	1975	$12
❑ 2264	Scorpio	1976	$12
❑ 4001	The Bill Anderson Story	1973	$15
—Reissue of Decca 7198			
❑ 416	Whispering" Bill Anderson	1974	$15
❑ 35032	Whispering	197?	$12
MCA CORAL			
❑ 20002	I Can Do Nothing	1973	$12
VOCALION			
❑ VL3835 [M]	Bill Anderson's Country Style	196?	$15
❑ VL73835 [S]	Bill Anderson's Country Style	196?	$18
❑ VL73927	Just Plain Bill	197?	$12

ANDERSON, CARL
EPIC

Number	Title	Yr	NM
❑ BFE40410	Carl Anderson	1986	$10
❑ BFE39217	On & On	1984	$12
❑ BFE39889	Protocol	1985	$12
GRP			
❑ 9612	Pieces of a Heart	1990	$18
POLYDOR			
❑ 835693-1	An Act of Love	1988	$10

ANDERSON, CASEY
ATCO

Number	Title	Yr	NM
❑ 33-176 [M]	Blues Is a Woman Gone	1965	$25
❑ SD 33-176 [S]	Blues Is a Woman Gone	1965	$30
❑ 33-172 [M]	Live at the Ice House	1965	$25
❑ SD 33-172 [S]	Live at the Ice House	1965	$30
❑ 33-166 [M]	More Pretty Girls Than One	1964	$25
❑ SD 33-166 [S]	More Pretty Girls Than One	1964	$30

Number	Title	Yr	NM
❑ 33-149 [M]	The Bag I'm In	1962	$25
❑ SD 33-149 [S]	The Bag I'm In	1962	$30
CHELSEA			
❑ CHL551	Passing Time	1976	$25
EDGE			
❑ ER-742	Good Old Boys	1974	$25
ELEKTRA			
❑ EKL-192 [M]	Goin' Places	1960	$25
❑ EKS-7192 [S]	Goin' Places	1960	$30
FORUM CIRCLE			
❑ FCS-9108 [S]	Casey Anderson Sings Folk Songs	196?	$15
❑ FC-9108 [M]	Casey Anderson Sings Folk Songs	196?	$18
—Reissue of Urania album with one track deleted			
SUPERSTAR			
❑ SSR-73-1	The Kind of Man I Am	196?	$30
URANIA			
❑ UR9024 [M]	Casey Sings Out	196?	$40

ANDERSON, CAT
CLASSIC JAZZ

Number	Title	Yr	NM
❑ CJ-142	Cat Speaks	1979	$30
EMARCY			
❑ MG-36142 [M]	Cat on a Hot Tin Roof	1958	$250
INNER CITY			
❑ 1143	Cat Anderson	198?	$25
MERCURY			
❑ MG-20522 [M]	Cat on a Hot Tin Roof	1959	$150

Number	Title	Yr	NM
❑ SR-60199 [S]	Cat on a Hot Tin Roof	1959	$150

ANDERSON, CHRIS
JAZZLAND

Number	Title	Yr	NM
❑ JLP-57 [M]	Inverted Images	1961	$30
❑ JLP-957 [S]	Inverted Images	1961	$40

ANDERSON, DAVE & BARB
FELLOWSHIP

Number	Title	Yr	NM
❑ F-234	Road in Winter	1980	$12

ANDERSON, ERNESTINE
CONCORD JAZZ

Number	Title	Yr	NM
❑ CJ-319	Be Mine Tonight	1987	$50
❑ CJ-214	Big City	1983	$50
❑ CJ-31	Hello Like Before	1977	$50
❑ CJ-54	Live from Concord to London	1978	$75
❑ CJ-147	Never Make Your Move Too Soon	1982	$50
❑ CJ-109	Sunshine	1980	$50
❑ CJ-263	When the Sun Goes Down	1985	$50
MERCURY			
❑ MG-20400 [M]	Ernestine Anderson	1959	$150
❑ SR-60074 [S]	Ernestine Anderson	1959	$300
❑ MG-20492 [M]	Fascinating Ernestine	1959	$175
❑ SR-60171 [S]	Fascinating Ernestine	1959	$300
❑ MG-20354 [M]	Hot Cargo	1958	$250
❑ MG-20582 [M]	Moanin'	1960	$150
❑ SR-60242 [S]	Moanin'	1960	$175
❑ MG-20496 [M]	My Kinda Swing	1959	$250
❑ SR-60175 [S]	My Kinda Swing	1959	$300
SUE			
❑ LP1015 [M]	The New Sound of Ernestine Anderson	1963	$50
WING			
❑ MGW-12281 [M]	My Kinda Swing	1964	$35
❑ SRW-16281 [S]	My Kinda Swing	1964	$50

ANDERSON, HERB OSCAR
VERVE

Number	Title	Yr	NM
❑ V-5021 [M]	What Would I Be	1967	$25
❑ V6-5021 [S]	What Would I Be	1967	$30

ANDERSON, IVIE, AND LENA HORNE
JAZZTONE

Number	Title	Yr	NM
❑ J-1262 [M]	Lena and Ivie	1956	$40

ANDERSON, JOHN
MCA

Number	Title	Yr	NM
❑ 42218	10	1988	$10
❑ 42037	Blue Skies Again	1988	$10
WARNER BROS.			
❑ 23912	All the People Are Talkin'	1983	$10
❑ 25373	Countrified	1986	$10
❑ 25099	Eye of a Hurricane	1984	$10
❑ 25169	Greatest Hits	1984	$10
❑ BSK3599	I Just Came Home to Count the Memories	1981	$12
❑ BSK3459	John Anderson	1980	$15
❑ BSK3547	John Anderson 2	1981	$12
❑ 25211	Tokyo, Oklahoma	1985	$10
❑ 23721	Wild & Blue	1982	$10

ANDERSON, JON

Also see ANDERSON BRUFORD WAKEMAN HOWE; JON AND VANGELIS; YES.

ATLANTIC

Number	Title	Yr	NM
❑ SD19355	Animation	1982	$12
❑ SD18180 [B]	Olias of Sunhillow	1976	$18

Number	Title	Yr	NM
❑ SD16021 [B]	Song of Seven	1980	$15

Number	Title	Yr	NM
COLUMBIA			
❑ BFC40910	In the City of Angels	1988	$12
ELEKTRA			
❑ 60469	3 Ships	1985	$15

ANDERSON, JUDY
GUINNESS

Number	Title	Yr	NM
❑ GNS36018 [B]	Right Time Of The Night	1977	$50

ANDERSON, LAURIE
WARNER BROS.

Number	Title	Yr	NM
❑ BSK3674	Big Science	1982	$12
❑ WBMS-134-2 [DJ]	Home of the Brave Interview	1986	$30
—Part of the Warner Bros. Music Show series			
❑ 25400	Home of the Brave (Soundtrack)	1986	$12
❑ 25077 [DJ]	Mister Heartbreak	1984	$18
—Quiex II" audiophile pressing			
❑ 25077	Mister Heartbreak	1984	$12
❑ PRO-A-2123 [EP]	Selections from Mister Heartbreak	1984	$10
—Promo-only sampler with three songs (Excellent Birds/ Sharkey's Day/Sharkey's Night)			
❑ PRO-A-2229 [DJ]	Selections from United States Live	1984	$15
—Promo-only sampler with eight tracks			
❑ 25900	Strange Angels	1989	$15
❑ 25192	United States Live	1984	$40
—Boxed set			

ANDERSON, LEROY
DECCA

Number	Title	Yr	NM
❑ DL8121 [M]	Blue Tango and Other Favorites	1955	$25
❑ DL8193 [M]	Christmas Carols	1955	$25
❑ DL8925 [M]	Christmas Festival	1959	$15
❑ DL78925 [S]	Christmas Festival	1959	$18
❑ DL9749 [M]	Leroy Anderson "Pops" Concert	195?	$25
❑ DL8954 [M]	Leroy Anderson Conducts His Music	1959	$25
❑ DL78954 [S]	Leroy Anderson Conducts His Music	1959	$30
❑ DL7509 [10]	Leroy Anderson Conducts His Own Compositions, Volume 1	195?	$30
❑ DL7519 [10]	Leroy Anderson Conducts His Own Compositions, Volume 2	195?	$30
❑ DL8865 [M]	Leroy Anderson Conducts Leroy Anderson	1958	$18
❑ DL78865 [S]	Leroy Anderson Conducts Leroy Anderson	1958	$25
❑ DL4335 [M]	New Music of Leroy Anderson	1962	$18
❑ DL74335 [S]	New Music of Leroy Anderson	1962	$25
MCA			
❑ 531	Leroy Anderson Conducts His Music	197?	$15
—Reissue of Decca 78954; black label with rainbow			
❑ 555	Leroy Anderson Conducts Leroy Anderson	197?	$15
—Reissue of Decca 78665; black label with rainbow			
PICKWICK			
❑ SPC-1036	Christmas Festival	197?	$18

ANDERSON, LIZ
RCA VICTOR

Number	Title	Yr	NM
❑ LPM-3852 [M]	Cookin' Up Hits	1967	$30
❑ LSP-3852 [S]	Cookin' Up Hits	1967	$25
❑ LSP-4346	Husband Hunting	1970	$25
❑ LSP-4222	If the Creek Don't Rise	1969	$25
❑ LSP-4014	Like a Merry-Go-Round	1968	$25
❑ LPM-3769 [M]	Liz Anderson Sings	1967	$30
❑ LSP-3769 [S]	Liz Anderson Sings	1967	$25
❑ LPM-3908 [M]	Liz Anderson Sings Her Favorites	1968	$40
❑ LSP-3908 [S]	Liz Anderson Sings Her Favorites	1968	$25

ANDERSON, LYNN
CHART

Number	Title	Yr	NM
❑ CHS-1017	At Home with Lynn	1969	$18
❑ CHS-1008	Big Girls Don't Cry	1969	$18
❑ CHS-1037	I'm Alright	1970	$15
❑ CHS-1050	Lynn Anderson	1972	$18
❑ CHS-1040	Lynn Anderson's Greatest Hits	1971	$15
❑ CHS-1043	Lynn Anderson with Strings	1971	$15
❑ CHM-1004 [M]	Promises, Promises	1968	$25
❑ CHS-1004 [S]	Promises, Promises	1968	$18
❑ CHM-1001 [M]	Ride, Ride, Ride	1967	$25
❑ CHS-1001 [S]	Ride, Ride, Ride	1967	$18
❑ CHS-1032	Songs My Mother Wrote	1970	$15
❑ CHS-1022	Songs That Made Country Girls Famous	1970	$15
❑ CHS-1009	The Best of Lynn Anderson	1969	$18
❑ CHS-1028	Uptown Country Girl	1970	$15
❑ CHS-1013	With Love, From Lynn	1969	$18

Number	Title	Yr	NM
COLUMBIA			
❏ PC34089	All the King's Horses	1976	$12
❏ KC30957	Christmas Album	1971	$15
❏ 3C30957	Christmas Album	198?	$10
— Reissue of KC 30957			
❏ KC31316	Cry	1972	$12
❏ FC37354	Encore	1981	$12
❏ PC37354	Encore	1983	$10
— Budget-line reissue			
❏ JC36568	Even Cowgirls Get the Blues	1980	$12
❏ KC35445	From the Inside	1978	$12
❏ C30925	How Can I Unlove You	1971	$12
❏ JC34871	I Love What Love Is Doing to Me/He/He Ain't You	1977	$12
❏ KC33691	I've Never Loved Anyone More	1975	$12
❏ KC32078	Keep Me in Mind	1973	$12
❏ KC31647	Listen to a Country Song	1972	$12
❏ KC31641	Lynn Anderson's Greatest Hits	1972	$12
❏ PC31641	Lynn Anderson's Greatest Hits	197?	$10
— Reissue			
❏ PC34308	Lynn Anderson's Greatest Hits Volume II	1976	$12
❏ C30099	No Love at All	1970	$15
❏ JC35776	Outlaw Is Just a State of Mind	1979	$12
❏ KC32719	Queens of Country	1974	$12
❏ C30411	Rose Garden	1970	$12
❏ PC30411	Rose Garden	197?	$10
— Reissue			
❏ KC32941	Smile for Me	1974	$12
❏ CS1025	Stay There 'Til I Get There	1970	$15
❏ CG30902	The World of Lynn Anderson	1971	$15
❏ KC32429	Top of the World	1973	$12
❏ KC33293	What a Man, My Man Is	1974	$12
❏ PC34439	Wrap Your Love All Around Your Man	1977	$12
❏ C30793	You're My Man	1971	$12
COLUMBIA LIMITED EDITION			
❏ LE10053	Stay Here 'Til I Get There	197?	$12
HARMONY			
❏ KH32433	Singing My Song	1973	$10
MERCURY			
❏ 834625-1	What She Does Best	1988	$10
MOUNTAIN DEW			
❏ 7047	Lynn Anderson	197?	$12
PERMIAN			
❏ 8205	Back	1983	$12
PICKWICK			
❏ SPC-3267	Flower of Love	197?	$10
❏ SPC-3296	It Makes You Happy	197?	$10
❏ PTP-2049	Lynn Anderson	1973	$15
TIME-LIFE			
❏ STW-112	Country Music	1981	$12

ANDERSON, MARIAN

Number	Title	Yr	NM
RCA VICTOR RED SEAL			
❏ LRM-7006 [10]	Eleven Great Spirituals	1951	$50
❏ LSC-2592 [S]	He's Got the Whole World in His Hands	1962	$25
— Originals with "shaded dog" label			
❏ LM7008 [10]	Marian Anderson Sings Christmas Carols	1954	$50
❏ LSC-2613 [S]	Marian Anderson Sings Christmas Carols	1961	$25
— Originals with "shaded dog" label			
❏ LSC-2613 [S]	Marian Anderson Sings Christmas Carols	1965	$30
— Second pressings with "white dog" label			
❏ LM-110 [10]	Spirituals	1956	$50
❏ LM-2032 [M]	Spirituals	1956	$40

ANDERSON, MICHAEL

Number	Title	Yr	NM
A&M			
❏ SP-5203	Sound Alarm	1988	$10

ANDERSON, MILDRED

Number	Title	Yr	NM
BLUESVILLE			
❏ BVLP-1017 [M]	No More in Life	1961	$50
— Blue and silver label			
❏ BVLP-1017 [M]	No More in Life	1964	$30
— Blue label with trident logo			
❏ BVLP-1004 [M]	Person to Person	1960	$50
— Blue and silver label			
❏ BVLP-1004 [M]	Person to Person	1964	$30
— Blue label with trident logo			

ANDERSON, PINK, AND REV. GARY DAVIS

Number	Title	Yr	NM
RIVERSIDE			
❏ RLP 12-611 [M]	Carolina Street Ballads/Harlem Street Spirituals	196?	$75

ANDERSON, PINK

Number	Title	Yr	NM
BLUESVILLE			
❏ BVLP-1071 [M]	Ballad and Folk Singer	1963	$150
— Blue label, silver print			

Number	Title	Yr	NM
❏ BVLP-1071 [M]	Ballad and Folk Singer	1964	$30
— Blue label with trident logo			
❏ BVLP-1038 [M]	Carolina Blues Man	1961	$120
— Blue label, silver print			
❏ BVLP-1038 [M]	Carolina Blues Man	1964	$30
— Blue label with trident logo			
❏ BVLP-1051 [M]	Medicine Show Man	1962	$150
— Blue label, silver print			
❏ BVLP-1051 [M]	Medicine Show Man	1964	$30
— Blue label with trident logo			

ANDERSON, RAY

Number	Title	Yr	NM
GRAMAVISION			
❏ R1-79453	What Because	1990	$30
MINOR MUSIC			
❏ MM-007	You Be	1986	$30
SOUL NOTE			
❏ SN-1087	Right Down Your Alley	1985	$30

ANDERSON, SUNSHINE

Number	Title	Yr	NM
SOULIFE/ATLANTIC			
❏ 93011	Your Woman	2001	$18

ANDERSON BRUFORD WAKEMAN HOWE

Number	Title	Yr	NM
ARISTA			
❏ 90126	Anderson Bruford Wakeman Howe	1989	$10

ANDERZA, EARL

Number	Title	Yr	NM
PACIFIC JAZZ			
❏ PJ-65 [M]	Outa Sight	1963	$30
❏ ST-65 [S]	Outa Sight	1963	$30

ANDRE'S CUBAN ALL-STARS

Number	Title	Yr	NM
CLEF			
❏ MGC-515 [10]	Cubano	1954	$300
— This was reissued on 12-inch as part of a JACK COSTANZO album.			

ANDREWS, ERNIE

Number	Title	Yr	NM
DISCOVERY			
❏ 825	From the Heart	198?	$30
GENE NORMAN PRESENTS			
❏ GNP-42 [M]	Ernie Andrews	1959	$40
❏ GNP-28 [M]	In the Dark	1957	$40
❏ GNP-43 [M]	Travelin' Light	1959	$40
❏ GNPS-10008 [S]	Travelin' Light	1959	$40
GNP CRESCENDO			
❏ GNPS-10008 [S]	Travelin' Light	196?	$35

ANDREWS, GAYLE

Number	Title	Yr	NM
HI-LIFE			
❏ HL-54 [M]	Love's a Snap	195?	$30

ANDREWS, JULIE

Number	Title	Yr	NM
COLUMBIA			
❏ CL1712 [M]	Broadway's Fair Julie	1962	$25
— Red and black label with six "eye" logos			
❏ CS8512 [S]	Broadway's Fair Julie	1962	$30
— Red and black label with six "eye" logos			
❏ CL1886 [M]	Don't Go In the Lion's Cage Tonight	1963	$25

Number	Title	Yr	NM
❏ CS8686 [S]	Don't Go In the Lion's Cage Tonight	1963	$30
RCA VICTOR			
❏ LPM-3829 [M]	A Christmas Treasure	1967	$18
❏ LSP-3829 [S]	A Christmas Treasure	1967	$18
❏ LPM-1681 [M]	Julie Andrews Sings	1958	$30
❏ LSP-1681 [S]	Julie Andrews Sings	1958	$50

Number	Title	Yr	NM
❏ LPM-1403 [M]	The Lass with the Delicate Air	1957	$40
— With pale blue jacket and the words "Julie Andrews" in a picture frame			
❏ LPM-1403 [M]	The Lass with the Delicate Air	1958	$30
— With altered cover; "RE" on jacket			
❏ LSP-1403 [S]	The Lass with the Delicate Air	1958	$75

ANDREWS, LEE, AND THE HEARTS

Number	Title	Yr	NM
COLLECTABLES			
❏ COL-5028	Biggest Hits	198?	$15
❏ COL-5003	Gotham Recording Sessions	1982	$15
LOST-NITE			
❏ LP-101 [M]	Biggest Hits	1964	$150
— Yellow vinyl			
❏ LP-101 [M]	Biggest Hits	1964	$50
— Black vinyl			
❏ LP-113 [M]	Lee Andrews and the Hearts Live	1965	$50
❏ LLP-1 [10]	The Best of Lee Andrews and the Hearts, Volume 1	1981	$15
— Red vinyl; in die-cut cover with sticker			
❏ LLP-2 [10]	The Best of Lee Andrews and the Hearts, Volume 2	1981	$15
— Red vinyl; in die-cut cover with sticker			

ANDREWS, RUBY

Number	Title	Yr	NM
ABC			
❏ AB-1002	Genuine Ruby	1977	$18
ICHIBAN			
❏ 1104	Kiss This	1991	$18
ZODIAC			
❏ ZS1001	Everybody Saw You	1970	$100

ANDREWS SISTERS, THE

Also see PATTY ANDREWS; BING CROSBY.

Number	Title	Yr	NM
ABC			
❏ 4003	Sixteen Great Performances	1975	$15
CAPITOL			
❏ T860 [M]	Fresh and Fancy Free	1957	$30
❏ T790 [M]	The Andrews Sisters in Hi-Fi	1957	$30
❏ T973 [M]	The Dancing Twenties	1957	$30
❏ T1924 [M]	The Hits of the Andrews Sisters	1963	$25
❏ DT1924 [R]	The Hits of the Andrews Sisters	1963	$15
DECCA			
❏ DL5264 [10]	Berlin Songs	1951	$40
❏ DL5282 [10]	Christmas Cheer	1950	$40
— Also see "Crosby, Bing			
❏ DL5155 [10]	Club 15	1951	$40
❏ DL4019 [M]	Curtain Call	1956	$30
❏ DL5306 [10]	I Love to Tell the Story	1952	$40
❏ DL8354 [M]	Jingle Bells	1956	$30
❏ DL5423 [10]	My Isle of Golden Dreams	1953	$40
❏ DL5438 [10]	Sing, Sing, Sing	1953	$40
❏ DL5120 [10]	The Andrews Sisters	1951	$40
❏ DL8360 [M]	The Andrews Sisters -- By Popular Demand	1957	$30
❏ DL5065 [10]	Tropical Songs	1950	$40
DOT			
❏ DLP3567 [M]	Great Country Hits	1963	$15
❏ DLP25567 [S]	Great Country Hits	1963	$18
❏ DLP3452 [M]	Great Golden Hits	1962	$18
❏ DLP25452 [S]	Great Golden Hits	1962	$25
❏ DLP3529 [M]	Present	1963	$15
❏ DLP25529 [S]	Present	1963	$18
❏ DLP3632 [M]	The Andrews Sisters Go Hawaiian	1964	$15
❏ DLP25632 [S]	The Andrews Sisters Go Hawaiian	1964	$18
❏ DLP3406 [M]	The Andrews Sisters' Greatest Hits	1962	$18
❏ DLP25406 [S]	The Andrews Sisters' Greatest Hits	1962	$25
HAMILTON			
❏ HLP124 [M]	Pennsylvania Polka	196?	$15
❏ HLP12124 [S]	Pennsylvania Polka	196?	$18
MCA			
❏ 27082	Boogie Woogie Bugle Girls	1980	$10
— Reissue of Paramount 6075			
❏ 24015	Christmas	1987	$10
— Reissue			
❏ 739	Near You	198?	$10
— Reissue of Vocalion album			
❏ 908	Rarities	198?	$10
❏ 27081	Sixteen Great Performances	1980	$10
— Reissue of ABC 4003			
❏ 2-4024	The Best of the Andrews Sisters	1973	$18
❏ 2-4093	The Best of the Andrews Sisters, Vol. 2	197?	$18
PARAMOUNT			
❏ PAS-6075	Boogie Woogie Bugle Girls	1973	$15
❏ PAS-1023	In the Mood	1974	$18

Number	Title	Yr	NM

PICKWICK

❑ PC-3094 [M]	Don't Sit Under the Apple Tree	196?	$18
❑ SPC-3094 [S]	Don't Sit Under the Apple Tree	196?	$15
❑ SPC-3382	Sing! Sing! Sing!	197?	$12

VOCALION

| ❑ VL3611 [M] | Near You | 196? | $15 |

ANDY AND THE BEY SISTERS

PRESTIGE

❑ PRLP-7346 [M]	Now! Hear!	1964	$40
❑ PRST-7346 [S]	Now! Hear!	1964	$50
❑ PRLP-7411 [M]	'Round About Midnight	1965	$40
❑ PRST-7411 [S]	'Round About Midnight	1965	$50

ANGEL

CASABLANCA

❑ NBLP7021 [B]	Angel	1975	$18
❑ NBLP7028 [B]	Helluva Band	1976	$18
❑ NBLP7203	Live Without a Net	1980	$18
❑ NBLP7043	On Earth As It Is in Heaven	1977	$15
❑ NBLP7127	Sinful	1979	$15
❑ NBLP7085	White Hot	1977	$15

ANGELI, PIER

ROULETTE

| ❑ R-25051 [M] | Italia Con Pier Angeli | 1959 | $30 |
| ❑ SR-25051 [S] | Italia Con Pier Angeli | 1959 | $30 |

ANGELOU, MAYA

LIBERTY

| ❑ LRP-3028 [M] | Miss Calypso | 1958 | $150 |

ANGELS, THE (1)

ASCOT

| ❑ AM13009 [M] | The Angels Sing -- Twelve of Their Greatest Hits | 1964 | $35 |
| ❑ ALS16009 [S] | The Angels Sing -- Twelve of Their Greatest Hits | 1964 | $50 |

CAPRICE

| ❑ LP1001 [M] | …And the Angels Sing | 1962 | $120 |
| ❑ SLP1001 [S] | …And the Angels Sing | 1962 | $250 |

COLLECTABLES

| ❑ COL-5085 | My Boyfriend's Back: Golden Classics | 198? | $12 |

SMASH

| ❑ MGS-27048 [M] | A Halo to You | 1964 | $40 |
| ❑ SRS-67048 [S] | A Halo to You | 1964 | $75 |

— *Some copies distributed with Netherlands Philips 842 948 edition vinyl instead of US.*

| ❑ MGS-27039 [M] | My Boyfriend's Back | 1963 | $40 |
| ❑ SRS-67039 [S] | My Boyfriend's Back | 1963 | $75 |

ANGRY SAMOANS

BAD TRIP

❑ (# unknown) [B]	Back from Samoa	1982	$50
❑ 01 [EP]	Different World/Unhinged + 4	1986	$75
❑ 201 [EP]	Inside My Brain	1981	$30
❑ 201 [EP]	Inside My Brain	1981	$75

— *Original with heavy gray cardboard cover*

| ❑ 02 [B] | The Mistaken | 1987 | $75 |

— *As "The Mistaken"; 1,000 copies made*

PVC

| ❑ 8955 [B] | Inside My Brain | 1987 | $30 |

— *Reissue*

| ❑ 8965 [B] | STP Not LSD | 1988 | $25 |
| ❑ 6915 [B] | Yesterday Started Tomorrow | 1987 | $30 |

ANIMALS, THE

Includes "Eric Burdon and the Animals." Also see ERIC BURDON; ERIC BURDON AND WAR; ALAN PRICE.

ABKCO

| ❑ AB-4226 | The Best of the Animals | 1973 | $15 |
| ❑ AB-4324 [M] | The Best of the Animals | 1987 | $12 |

— *With alternate version of "We Gotta Get Out of This Place"*

ACCORD

| ❑ SN-7193 | Looking Back | 1981 | $10 |
| ❑ SN-7235 | The Animals with Eric Burdon | 1982 | $10 |

I.R.S.

| ❑ SP70043 | Rip It to Shreds: Their Greatest Hits Live | 1984 | $12 |
| ❑ SP70037 | The Ark | 1983 | $12 |

JET/UA

| ❑ JT-LA790-H | Before We Were So Rudely Interrupted | 1977 | $12 |

— *As "The Original Animals"*

| ❑ JT-LA790-H | Before We Were So Rudely Interrupted | 1977 | $150 |

— *White label test pressing with promo letter signed by Danny Goldberg*

MGM

| ❑ E-4414 [M] | Animalism | 1966 | $150 |

— *Yellow label promo*

❑ E-4414 [M]	Animalism	1966	$30
❑ SE-4414 [S]	Animalism	1966	$30
❑ E-4384 [M]	Animalization	1966	$30
❑ E-4384 [M]	Animalization	1966	$150

— *Yellow label promo*

| ❑ SE-4384 [P] | Animalization | 1966 | $30 |

— *All stereo except "Inside Looking Out," which is rechanneled.*

| ❑ T90923 [M] | Animalization | 1966 | $50 |

— *Capitol Record Club edition*

| ❑ ST90923 [P] | Animalization | 1966 | $50 |

— *Capitol Record Club edition*

| ❑ E-4305 [M] | Animal Tracks | 1965 | $175 |

— *Yellow label promo*

❑ E-4305 [M]	Animal Tracks	1965	$40
❑ SE-4305 [R]	Animal Tracks	1965	$30
❑ T90571 [M]	Animal Tracks	1965	$50

— *Capitol Record Club edition*

❑ E-4433 [M]	Eric Is Here	1967	$50
❑ SE-4433 [S]	Eric Is Here	1967	$25
❑ E-4553 [M]	Every One of Us	1968	$100

— *Mono is promo only (yellow label)*

| ❑ SE-4553 [S] | Every One of Us | 1968 | $30 |
| ❑ ST-91550 [S] | Every One of Us | 1968 | $40 |

— *Capitol Record Club edition; black label*

❑ SE-4602	Greatest Hits of Eric Burdon and the Animals	1969	$18
❑ SE-4591 [B]	Love Is	1968	$75
❑ E-4264 [M]	The Animals	1964	$250

— *Yellow label promo*

| ❑ E-4264 [M] | The Animals | 1964 | $30 |

— *The House of the Rising Sun" is the edited 45 version*

| ❑ SE-4264 [R] | The Animals | 1964 | $30 |

— *The House of the Rising Sun" is the edited 45 version (rechanneled, like the rest of the LP)*

| ❑ T90687 [M] | The Animals | 1966 | $50 |

— *Capitol Record Club edition*

| ❑ E-4281 [M] | The Animals On Tour | 1965 | $150 |

— *Yellow label promo*

❑ E-4281 [M]	The Animals On Tour	1965	$30
❑ SE-4281 [R]	The Animals On Tour	1965	$30
❑ T90414 [M]	The Animals On Tour	1965	$50

— *Capitol Record Club edition*

| ❑ ST90414 [R] | The Animals On Tour | 1965 | $40 |

— *Capitol Record Club edition*

❑ E-4454 [M]	The Best of Eric Burdon and the Animals, Vol. 2	1967	$25
❑ SE-4454 [P]	The Best of Eric Burdon and the Animals, Vol. 2	1967	$25
❑ T-91156 [M]	The Best of Eric Burdon and the Animals, Vol. 2	1967	$30

— *Capitol Record Club edition*

| ❑ E-4324 [M] | The Best of the Animals | 1966 | $100 |

— *Yellow label promo*

| ❑ SE-4324 [R] | The Best of the Animals | 1966 | $30 |
| ❑ E-4324 [M] | The Best of the Animals | 1966 | $25 |

— *This album was the first to contain the full-length version of "House of the Rising Sun."*

| ❑ KAO90622 [M] | The Best of the Animals | 1966 | $40 |

— *Capitol Record Club edition*

| ❑ SKAO90622 [R] | The Best of the Animals | 1966 | $40 |

— *Capitol Record Club edition; black label*

| ❑ SKAO90622 [R] | The Best of the Animals | 1969 | $30 |

— *Capitol Record Club edition; blue and gold label*

❑ SE-4537 [S]	The Twain Shall Meet	1968	$30
❑ E-4537 [M]	The Twain Shall Meet	1968	$100
❑ E-4484 [M]	Winds of Change	1967	$30
❑ SE-4484 [S]	Winds of Change	1967	$30

PICKWICK

| ❑ SPC-3330 | The Early Animals with Eric Burdon | 1971 | $10 |

POLYDOR

| ❑ 829091-1 | Animalization | 1986 | $10 |

RHYTHM AND BLUES RECORDS

| ❑ 33XXR&B2 [M] | We're Gonna Howl Tonight | 2015 | $40 |

— *Record Store Day exclusive*

SCEPTER CITATION

| ❑ CTN-18026 | The Best of the Animals | 1972 | $10 |

SPRINGBOARD

| ❑ SPB-4025 | The Best of the Animals | 1972 | $10 |
| ❑ SPB-4065 | The Night Time Is the Right Time | 1973 | $10 |

WAND

| ❑ WDS-690 [B] | In the Beginning | 1970 | $12 |

ANIMATED EGG, THE

ALSHIRE

| ❑ SF-32700 [B] | The Animated Egg | 1967 | $175 |

ANIMOTION

CASABLANCA

| ❑ 826691-1 | Strange Behavior | 1986 | $10 |

MERCURY

| ❑ 822580-1 | Animotion | 1984 | $10 |

POLYDOR

| ❑ 837314-1 | Animotion | 1989 | $15 |

— *Featuring "Room to Move*

ANKA, PAUL

ABC-PARAMOUNT

❑ 353 [M]	Anka at the Copa	1960	$30
❑ S-353 [S]	Anka at the Copa	1960	$40
❑ 420 [M]	Diana	1962	$30
❑ S-420 [S]	Diana	1962	$30
❑ ABC360 [M]	It's Christmas Everywhere	1960	$30
❑ ABCS360 [S]	It's Christmas Everywhere	1960	$40

❑ 296 [M]	My Heart Sings	1959	$30
❑ S-296 [S]	My Heart Sings	1959	$50
❑ 240 [M]	Paul Anka	1958	$50
❑ 409 [M]	Paul Anka Sings His Big, Big 15, Volume III	1962	$30
❑ S-409 [S]	Paul Anka Sings His Big, Big 15, Volume III	1962	$30
❑ 323 [M]	Paul Anka Sings His Big 15	1960	$50
❑ S-323 [R]	Paul Anka Sings His Big 15	196?	$30
❑ S-390 [S]	Paul Anka Sings His Big 15, Vol. 2	1961	$40
❑ 390 [M]	Paul Anka Sings His Big 15, Vol. 2	1961	$30
❑ 347 [M]	Paul Anka Swings for Young Lovers	1960	$30
❑ S-347 [S]	Paul Anka Swings for Young Lovers	1960	$40
❑ 371 [M]	Strictly Instrumental	1961	$30
❑ S-371 [S]	Strictly Instrumental	1961	$40

ACCORD

| ❑ SN-7117 | She's a Lady | 1981 | $10 |

BUDDAH

❑ BDS5114	Jubilation	1972	$15
❑ BDS5093	Paul Anka	1971	$15
❑ BDS5667	The Essential Paul Anka	1974	$18
❑ BDS5622	This Is Anka	1974	$18

COLUMBIA

| ❑ FC39323 | Paul Anka Live | 1984 | $10 |
| ❑ FC38442 | Walk a Fine Line | 1983 | $10 |

LIBERTY

| ❑ LN-10149 | Feelings | 1982 | $10 |

— *Budget-line reissue*

| ❑ LN-10000 | Paul Anka: His Best | 1980 | $10 |

— *Budget-line reissue*

| ❑ LN-10220 | The Painter | 1983 | $10 |

— *Budget-line reissue*

| ❑ LN-10001 | The Times of Your Life | 1980 | $10 |

— *Budget-line reissue*

PAIR

| ❑ PDL2-1129 | Songs I Write and Sing | 1986 | $15 |

PICKWICK

❑ PTP-2087	Paul Anka Way	197?	$12
❑ SPC-3508	Puppy Love	1975	$10
❑ SPC-3523	She's a Lady	1975	$10

RANWOOD

| ❑ 8203 | The Very Best of Paul Anka | 1981 | $10 |

RCA CAMDEN

| ❑ ACL1-0616 | My Way | 1974 | $10 |

RCA VICTOR

❑ AFL1-3926	Both Sides of Love	1981	$12
❑ LPM-2996 [M]	Excitement on Park Avenue	1964	$18
❑ LSP-2996 [S]	Excitement on Park Avenue	1964	$25
❑ LSP-4142	Goodnight My Love	1969	$18
❑ AFL1-3382	Headlines	1979	$12
❑ LPM-2575 [M]	Let's Sit This One Out	1962	$25
❑ LSP-2575 [S]	Let's Sit This One Out	1962	$30
❑ LSP-4250	Life Goes On	1969	$18
❑ AFL1-2892	Listen to Your Heart	1978	$12
❑ LPM-2614 [M]	Our Man Around the World	1963	$25
❑ LSP-2614 [S]	Our Man Around the World	1963	$30
❑ LSP-4300	Paul Anka 70s	1970	$18
❑ LPM-3875 [M]	Paul Anka Live	1967	$18
❑ LSP-3875 [S]	Paul Anka Live	1967	$25

Number	Title	Yr	NM
❑ LPM-2691 [M]	Paul Anka's 21 Golden Hits	1963	$25
❑ LSP-2691 [S]	Paul Anka's 21 Golden Hits	1963	$30

—*LPM/LSP-2691 has re-recorded versions of ABC-Paramount hits*

❑ AYL1-3808	Paul Anka's 21 Golden Hits	1980	$10

—*Best Buy Series" reissue*

❑ ANL1-1584	Paul Anka Sings His Favorites	1976	$12
❑ ANL1-0896	Remember Diana	1975	$12
❑ ANL1-1054	She's a Lady	1975	$12
❑ LSP-4203	Sincerely	1969	$18
❑ LPM-2744 [M]	Songs I Wish I'd Written	1963	$18
❑ LSP-2744 [S]	Songs I Wish I'd Written	1963	$25
❑ ANL1-2482	Songs I Wish I'd Written	1977	$12
❑ LPM-3580 [M]	Strictly Nashville	1966	$18
❑ LSP-3580 [S]	Strictly Nashville	1966	$25
❑ LPM-2502 [M]	Young, Alive and In Love!	1962	$30

—*With portrait of Paul Anka on front cover*

❑ LPM-2502 [M]	Young, Alive and In Love!	1962	$18

—*With portrait of Paul Anka on back cover*

❑ LSP-2502 [S]	Young, Alive and In Love!	1962	$30

—*With portrait of Paul Anka on front cover*

❑ LSP-2502 [S]	Young, Alive and In Love!	1962	$25

—*With portrait of Paul Anka on back cover*

RHINO

❑ RNLP-70220	The Best of Paul Anka (14 Original Hits, 1957-1961)	1986	$12

RIVIERA

❑ 047 [M]	Paul Anka and Others	1959	$175

—*With Paul Anka's RPM recordings plus tracks by other artists*

SIRE

❑ SASH-3704	Paul Anka Gold	1974	$18
❑ SBK6043	The Vintage Years 1957-1961	1978	$15

UNITED ARTISTS

❑ UA-LA314-G	Anka	1974	$12
❑ UA-LA367-G	Feelings	1975	$12
❑ UA-LA922-H	Paul Anka: His Best	1978	$12
❑ UA-LA746-H	The Music Man	1977	$12
❑ UA-LA653-H [Q]	The Painter	1976	$18

—*All copies are quadraphonic*

❑ UA-LA569-G	Times of Your Life	1975	$12

ANN-MARGRET

LHI

❑ S-12007	The Cowboy and the Lady	1969	$40

—*With Lee Hazlewood*

MCA

❑ 3226	Ann-Margret	1980	$15

RCA VICTOR

❑ LPM-2399 [M]	And Here She Is…	1961	$30
❑ LSP-2399 [S]	And Here She Is…	1961	$40
❑ LPM-2659 [M]	Bachelor's Paradise	1963	$30

❑ LSP-2659 [S]	Bachelor's Paradise	1963	$40
❑ LPM-2453 [M]	On the Way Up	1961	$30
❑ LSP-2453 [S]	On the Way Up	1961	$40
❑ LPM-3710 [M]	Songs from The Swinger and Others	1966	$75
❑ LSP-3710 [S]	Songs from The Swinger and Others	1966	$100
❑ LPM-2551 [M]	The Vivacious One	1962	$30
❑ LSP-2551 [S]	The Vivacious One	1962	$40

ANNA MARIE

Female singer, possibly Anna Marie Wooldridge, who later recorded as ABBEY LINCOLN.

VESTA

❑ LP-101 [10]	Anna Marie	1955	$100

Number	Title	Yr	NM

ANNE G.

ATLANTIC

❑ 81946	On a Mission	1989	$12

ANNETTE

BUENA VISTA

❑ BV-3301 [M]	Annette	1959	$120
❑ BV-3324 [M]	Annette at Bikini Beach	1964	$50
❑ STER-3324 [S]	Annette at Bikini Beach	1964	$150
❑ BV-4037	Annette Funicello	1972	$50
❑ BV-3320 [M]	Annette on Campus	1964	$50
❑ STER-3320 [S]	Annette on Campus	1964	$150
❑ BV-3302 [M]	Annette Sings Anka	1960	$150
❑ BV-3327 [M]	Annette Sings Golden Surfin' Hits	1964	$150
❑ STER-3327 [S]	Annette Sings Golden Surfin' Hits	1964	$175
❑ BV-3325 [M]	Annette's Pajama Party	1964	$40
❑ STER-3325 [S]	Annette's Pajama Party	1964	$150
❑ BV-3316 [M]	Beach Party	1963	$75
❑ STER-3316 [S]	Beach Party	1963	$150
❑ BV-3305 [M]	Dance Annette	1961	$85
❑ BV-3303 [M]	Hawaiiannette	1960	$85
❑ BV-3304 [M]	Italiannette	1960	$85
❑ BV-3314 [M]	Muscle Beach Party	1963	$85
❑ STER-3314 [S]	Muscle Beach Party	1963	$175
❑ BV-3328 [M]	Something Borrowed, Something Blue	1964	$75
❑ STER-3328 [P]	Something Borrowed, Something Blue	1964	$150
❑ BV-3313 [M]	Teen Street	1962	$85
❑ BV-3312 [M]	The Story of My Teens	1962	$85

RHINO

❑ RNDF-206	The Best of Annette	1984	$15
❑ RNLP-702 [PD]	The Best of Annette	1984	$30

ANNETTE / HAYLEY MILLS

Also see each artist's individual listings.

DISNEYLAND

❑ DL-3508 [M]	Annette and Hayley Mills (Singing 10 of Their Greatest All-Time Hits)	1964	$1000

—*TV offer; issued with paper jacket. Though the cover says "Buena Vista Records Presents," the label is the yellow Disneyland label*

ANONYMOUS

A-MAJOR

❑ AMLS-1002	Inside the Shadow	1976	$300

ANOTHER BAD CREATION

MOTOWN

❑ MOT-6318	Coolin' at the Playground Ya' Know!	1991	$18

—*Columbia House edition; only U.S. vinyl version of this record*

❑ 374636363-1 [DJ]	It Ain't What U Wear, It's How U Play It	1993	$18

—*Vinyl is promo only; in black company sleeve*

ANQUETTE

LUKE SKYYWALKER

❑ 103	Respect	1988	$12

ANSWERED QUESTIONS

EMI

❑ E1-93198	Happiness Is...	1990	$15

ANT, ADAM

EPIC

❑ ARE38370	Friend or Foe	1982	$12

❑ FE39108 [B]	Strip	1984	$12
❑ BFE40159	Vive Le Rock	1985	$10

MCA

❑ 6315	Manners & Physique	1989	$12

Number	Title	Yr	NM

ANT TRIP CEREMONY

C.R.C.

❑ 2129	24 Hours	1970	$750

—*Originals have thick cover and black vinyl*

ANTHEM

BUDDAH

❑ BDS-5071	Anthem	1971	$25

ANTHONY, C.J.

KMA

❑ 004	Luv's Invitation	1989	$15

ANTHONY, MARC

COLUMBIA

❑ C69726	Marc Anthony	1999	$15

ANTHONY, MARK

TABU

❑ FZ44311	Jumpin' Off	1988	$10

ANTHONY, RAY

AERO SPACE

❑ RA1007	Around the World	197?	$25
❑ RA1028	Let's Go Dancing	197?	$30

—*Green vinyl; Arthur Murray promotional item; add 25 percent if certificate for a free dance lesson is included*

CAPITOL

❑ T1371 [M]	Arthur Murray Favorites – Fox Trots	1960	$75
❑ H362 [10]	Campus Rumpus	195?	$100
❑ T2043 [M]	Charade and Other Top Themes	1964	$75
❑ ST2043 [S]	Charade and Other Top Themes	1964	$85
❑ T1420 [M]	Dancing Alone Together	1960	$75

—*Black colorband label, Capitol logo at left*

❑ ST1420 [S]	Dancing Alone Together	1960	$85

—*Black colorband label, Capitol logo at left*

❑ T1420 [M]	Dancing Alone Together	1962	$40

—*Black colorband label, Capitol logo at top*

❑ ST1420 [S]	Dancing Alone Together	1962	$75

—*Black colorband label, Capitol logo at top*

❑ T1028 [M]	Dancing Over the Waves	1958	$85
❑ T723 [M]	Dream Dancing	1956	$85
❑ T1608 [M]	Dream Dancing Medley	1961	$75
❑ ST1608 [S]	Dream Dancing Medley	1961	$85
❑ T2457 [M]	Dream Dancing Today	1966	$75
❑ ST2457 [S]	Dream Dancing Today	1966	$85
❑ M-11978	Fox Trots	1979	$25
❑ H258 [10]	Fox Trots	195?	$75
❑ T563 [M]	Golden Horn	1955	$85
❑ T2530 [M]	Hit Songs to Remember	1966	$75
❑ ST2530 [S]	Hit Songs to Remember	1966	$85
❑ H292 [10]	Houseparty Hop	195?	$85

—*Reissue of L 292; purple label; "This Album Contains 8 Selections" on upper right back cover*

❑ L292 [10]	Houseparty Hop	195?	$100

—*Original issue; maroon label; "In addition to the selections listed, this long playing record contains: PERDIDO - WAGON WHEELS" under the title on back cover*

❑ T1783 [M]	I Almost Lost My Mind	1962	$75
❑ ST1783 [S]	I Almost Lost My Mind	1962	$85
❑ H476 [10]	I Remember Glenn Miller	1954	$85
❑ T749 [M]	Jam Session at the Tower	1956	$85
❑ T1304 [M]	Like Wild!	1959	$75
❑ ST1304 [S]	Like Wild!	1959	$85
❑ T917 [M]	Moments Together	1958	$85
❑ T1252 [M]	More Dream Dancing	1959	$75
❑ ST1252 [S]	More Dream Dancing	1959	$85
❑ T2150 [M]	My Love, Forgive Me	1964	$75
❑ ST2150 [S]	My Love, Forgive Me	1964	$50
❑ T1066 [M]	Ray Anthony Plays Steve Allen	1958	$50
❑ T1917 [M]	Smash Hits of '63	1963	$75
❑ ST1917 [S]	Smash Hits of '63	1963	$50
❑ T1200 [M]	Sound Spectacular	1959	$50
❑ T831 [M]	Star Dancing	1957	$50
❑ T2188 [M]	Swim, Swim, C'mon, Let's Swim	1964	$75
❑ ST2188 [S]	Swim, Swim, C'mon, Let's Swim	1964	$50
❑ T969 [M]	The Dream Girl	1958	$85
❑ T1477 [M]	The Hits of Ray Anthony	1960	$75
❑ T1421 [M]	The New Ray Anthony Show	1960	$75
❑ ST1421 [S]	The New Ray Anthony Show	1960	$50
❑ T1668 [M]	Twist with Ray Anthony	1961	$75
❑ ST1668 [S]	Twist with Ray Anthony	1961	$50
❑ T1752 [M]	Worried Mind	1962	$75
❑ ST1752 [S]	Worried Mind	1962	$75
❑ T866 [M]	Young Ideas	1957	$75

Number	Title	Yr	NM
CIRCLE			
❑ CLP-96	Sweet and Swingin' 1949-1953	1987	$25
HINDSIGHT			
❑ HSR-240	Young Man with a Horn	1988	$25
RANWOOD			
❑ 8153	Golden Hits	197?	$25
❑ 8083	I Get the Blues When It Rains	197?	$25
❑ 8059	Love Is for the Two of Us	197?	$25
❑ R.8033	Now	197?	$25
—Cover uses "R." prefix, label uses "RLP" prefix			
ANTHONY AND THE CAMP			
WARNER BROS.			
❑ 25648	Suspense	1988	$10
ANTHRAX			
ISLAND			
❑ 90584	Among the Living	1987	$10
❑ 848804-1 [B]	Attack of the Killer B's	1991	$25
❑ 90685 [EP]	I'm the Man	1987	$10

Number	Title	Yr	NM
❑ 846480-1 [B]	Persistence of Time	1990	$18
❑ 90480	Spreading the Disease	1985	$10
❑ PR2563 [DJ]	Statements of Euphoria	1988	$18
—Promo-only interview album			
❑ 91004 [B]	State of Euphoria	1988	$10
MEGAFORCE			
❑ MRS-05 [EP]	Armed & Dangerous	1985	$25
❑ CAROL-1382 [EP]	Armed & Dangerous	198?	$10
—Reissue of 5			
❑ MRI-469 [B]	Fistful of Metal	1983	$25
❑ CAROL-1383	Fistful of Metal	198?	$10
—Reissue of 469			
ANTI-FLAG			
CLEOPATRA			
❑ 9555 [B]	Die For The Government		$25
ANTI NOWHERE LEAGUE			
CLEOPATRA			
❑ CLP2066 [B]	We Are... The League... Un-cut	2015	$25
—restores originally scheduled 1980 running order			
GWR			
❑ 1238	The Perfect Crime	1987	$18
WXYZ			
❑ FEP1301 [EP]	I Hate...People	1982	$14
❑ COPE4	We Are ... The League	1982	$18
ANTISEEN			
BONA FIDE/CHOPPER			
❑ (# unknown)	Honor Among Thieves	1987	$15
REPO			
❑ (# unknown)	The Raw Shit	1986	$15
—Pink vinyl			
ANTOINETTE			
NEXT PLATEAU			
❑ 1015	Who's the Boss?	1989	$12

Number	Title	Yr	NM
ANVIL			
ENIGMA/METAL BLADE			

Number	Title	Yr	NM
❑ 7-73336 [B]	Pound for Pound	1988	$25
❑ ST-73267 [B]	Strength of Steel	1987	$25
AORTA			
COLUMBIA			
❑ CS9785	Aorta	1969	$30
HAPPY TIGER			
❑ HT-1010	Aorta 2	1970	$40
APACHE			
TOMMY BOY			
❑ 1068	Apache	1993	$18
APHRODITE'S CHILD			
VERTIGO			
❑ VEL-2-500	666 (The Apocalypse of John)	1972	$150
APOLLO 100			
MEGA			
❑ 31-1010	Joy	1972	$12
APOLLONIA			
WARNER BROS.			
❑ 25594	Apollonia	1988	$10
❑ 25108	Apollonia 6	1984	$10
APPALOOSA			
COLUMBIA			
❑ CS9819	Appaloosa	1969	$18
—Produced by Al Kooper			
APPLE PIE MOTHERHOOD BAND, THE			
ATLANTIC			
❑ SD8233	Apple Pie	1969	$30
❑ SD8189	The Apple Pie Motherhood Band	1968	$30
APPLEJACKS, THE (1)			
CAMEO			
❑ C-1004 [M]	Alone Together	1958	$50
—As "Dave Appell"			
APPLES IN STEREO, THE			
SPINART			
❑ spart42	Fun Trick Noisemaker	1995	$12
❑ spart72	Her Wallpaper Reverie	1999	$12
❑ spart48	Science Faire	1996	$12
❑ spart83	The Discovery of a World Inside the Moone	2000	$12
❑ spart57	Tone Soul Evolution	1997	$12
APPLETREE THEATRE CO.			
VERVE FORECAST			
❑ FTS-3042	Playback	1968	$50
—RICK NELSON appears on this album			
APPLEYARD, PETER			
AUDIO FIDELITY			
❑ AFLP-1901 [M]	The Vibe Sound of Peter Appleyard	1958	$40
❑ AFSD-5901 [S]	The Vibe Sound of Peter Appleyard	1958	$40
APRIL WINE			
AQUARIUS			
❑ AQR504	Electric Jewels	1973	$18
❑ AQR505	Live	1974	$18

Number	Title	Yr	NM
ATLANTIC			
❑ SD19303	Stand Back	1981	$12
—Reissue of Big Tree 89506			
BIG TREE			
❑ BTS2012	April Wine	1972	$25
❑ 89506	Stand Back	1975	$18
CAPITOL			
❑ ST-12311	Animal Grace	1984	$12
❑ ST-11852	First Glance	1979	$15
❑ SN-16245	First Glance	1982	$10
—Budget-line reissue			
❑ ST-12013	Harder...Faster	1979	$12
❑ SN-16322	Harder...Faster	1984	$10
—Budget-line reissue			
❑ ST-12218	Power Play	1982	$12
❑ SN-16344	Power Play	1984	$10
—Budget-line reissue			
❑ SPRO-9632/3 [DJ]	Summer Tour 1981	1981	$25
—Promo-only sampler			
❑ SOO-12125	The Nature of the Beast	1981	$12
❑ SN-16379	The Nature of the Beast	1986	$10
—Budget-line reissue			
❑ C1-48418	Walking Through Fire	1988	$15
LONDON			
❑ PS699	Live at the El Mocambo	1977	$18
❑ PS675	The Whole World's Goin' Crazy	1976	$18
AQUARIAN DREAM			
BUDDAH			
❑ BDS-5672	Norman Connors Presents Aquarian Dream	1976	$15
ELEKTRA			
❑ 6E-205	Chance to Dance	1979	$12
❑ 6E-152	Fantasy	1978	$12
AQUARIANS			
UNI			
❑ 73053	Jungle Grass	1969	$18
AQUATONES, THE			
FARGO			
❑ 3001 [M]	The Aquatones Sing	1964	$500
RELIC/FARGO			
❑ 5033 [M]	The Aquatones Sing	198?	$10
ARABIAN PRINCE			
ORPHEUS			
❑ D1-75614	Brother Arab	1989	$12
ARBORS, THE			
DATE			
❑ TEM3003 [M]	A Symphony for Susan	1967	$25
❑ TES4003 [S]	A Symphony for Susan	1967	$25
❑ TES4017 [B]	The Arbors Featuring I Can't Quit Her and The Letter	1969	$25
❑ TEM3011 [M]	Valley of the Dolls	1967	$30
❑ TES4011 [S]	Valley of the Dolls	1967	$30
ARCADIA			
CAPITOL			
❑ R134433	So Red the Rose	1985	$15
—RCA Music Service edition			
❑ SV-12428	So Red the Rose	1985	$12
ARCHER, FRANCES, AND BEVERLY GILE			
DISNEYLAND			
❑ EB-1347/8 [10]	A Child's Garden of Verses	1955	$175
—The very first LP released on Disneyland Records			
❑ WDL-3004 [M]	A Child's Garden of Verses	1956	$30
—Reissue of 1347/8			
❑ WDL-1008 [M]	A Child's Garden of Verses	1959	$25
—Reissue of 3004			
❑ DQ-1241 [M]	A Child's Garden of Verses	1964	$25
—Reissue of 1008			
❑ ST-3802 [M]	A Child's Garden of Verses	1971	$30
—Reissue of 1241			
❑ WDL-3023 [M]	Community Concert	1958	$30
❑ WDL-3006 [M]	Folk Songs from the Far Corners	1957	$30
❑ DQ-1226 [M]	Songs from All Around the World	1962	$25
—Black and white back cover (original)			
ARCHIES, THE			
51 WEST			
❑ 16002	The Archies	1979	$12
ACCORD			
❑ SN-7149	Straight A's	1981	$12
CALENDAR			
❑ KES-103 [B]	Everything's Archie	1969	$30
❑ KES-101 [B]	The Archies	1968	$30

Number	Title	Yr	NM
KIRSHNER			
❏ KES-103 [DJ]	Everything's Archie Box	1969	$150
— Box with LP, photos, press kit and buttons			
❏ KES-105 [B]	Jingle Jangle	1969	$30
❏ KES-107 [B]	Sunshine	1970	$30
❏ KES-109 [B]	The Archies Greatest Hits	1970	$30
❏ KES-110	This Is Love	1971	$30
ARDEN, TONI			
DECCA			
❏ DL8875 [M]	Besame	1959	$25
— Black label, silver print			
❏ DL78875 [S]	Besame	1959	$30
— Maroon label, silver print			
❏ DL4375 [M]	Italian Gold	196?	$15
❏ DL74375 [S]	Italian Gold	196?	$18
❏ DL8651 [M]	Miss Toni Arden	1957	$30
— Black label, silver print			
❏ DL8765 [M]	Sing a Song of Italy	1958	$30
— Black label, silver print			
❏ DL78765 [S]	Sing a Song of Italy	1959	$30
— Maroon label, silver print			
HARMONY			
❏ HL7212 [M]	Exciting Toni Arden	196?	$25
AREA CODE 615			
POLYDOR			
❏ 24-4002 [B]	Area Code 615	1969	$30
❏ 24-4025 [B]	A Trip in the Country	1970	$30
ARENA BRASS, THE			
EPIC			
❏ LN24039 [M]	The Lonely Bull	1962	$15
❏ BN26039 [S]	The Lonely Bull	1962	$18
ARGENT			
Rod Argent's group after THE ZOMBIES broke up.			
EPIC			
❏ KE31556	All Together Now	1972	$25
— Yellow label			
❏ KE31556	All Together Now	1973	$15
— Orange label			
❏ PE33955	Anthology	1976	$18
— Orange label			
❏ PE33955	Anthology	1979	$12
— Dark blue label			
❏ BN26525	Argent	1970	$25
— Yellow label			
❏ BN26525	Argent	1973	$15
— Orange label			

Number	Title	Yr	NM
❏ E30128 [B]	A Ring of Hands	1971	$25
— Yellow label			
❏ KE30128	A Ring of Hands	1973	$15
— Orange label			
❏ PE33422	Circus	1975	$25
— Orange label			
❏ PEG33079 [B]	Encore -- Live in Concert	1975	$30
— Orange labels			
❏ KE32195	In Deep	1973	$25
— Orange label			
❏ PEQ32195 [Q]	In Deep	1974	$75
❏ KE32195	In Deep	1973	$30
— Yellow label			
❏ PE32573	Nexus	1974	$25
— Orange label			
UNITED ARTISTS			
❏ UA-LA560-G	Counterpoint	1975	$15
ARGO, TONY			
SAVOY			
❏ MG-12157 [M]	Jazz Argosy	1960	$40

Number	Title	Yr	NM
ARISTOCATS, THE			
HIFI			
❏ J-610 [M]	Boogie and Blues	1959	$30
❏ JS-610 [S]	Boogie and Blues	1959	$40
ARISTOCRATS OF DIXIELAND, THE			
AUDIOPHILE			
❏ AP-129	Florida Blues	1979	$25
ARLEN, HAROLD, AND "FRIEND"			
The "Friend" is BARBRA STREISAND.			
COLUMBIA MASTERWORKS			
❏ OL6520 [M]	Harold Sings Arlen	1966	$30
❏ OS2920 [S]	Harold Sings Arlen	1966	$40
— Gray label with "360 Sound" in white			
ARMAGEDDON (1)			
AMOS			
❏ 73075	Armageddon	1970	$30
ARMAGEDDON (2)			
With KEITH RELF, ex-member of THE YARDBIRDS; his last material before his death. Also see CAPTAIN BEYOND.			
A&M			
❏ SP-4513 [B]	Armageddon	1975	$35
ARMATRADING, JOAN			
A&M			
❏ SP-4525	Back to the Night	1975	$15
❏ SP-3141	Back to the Night	1980	$10
— Reissue			
❏ 7502152981	Hearts and Flowers	1990	$18
❏ SP-3302 [EP]	How Cruel	1979	$10
❏ SP-12400 [EP]	How Cruel	1984	$10
— Reissue			
❏ SP-4588	Joan Armatrading	1976	$12
❏ SP-3228	Joan Armatrading	1984	$10
— Reissue			
❏ SP-8414 [DJ]	Joan Armatrading Live at the Bijou Café	1977	$25
— Promo-only "Superstars Radio Network" issue			
❏ SP-4809	Me Myself I	1980	$12
❏ SP-5040	Secret Secrets	1985	$12
❏ SP-4663	Show Some Emotion	1977	$12
❏ SP-3273	Show Some Emotion	1984	$10
— Reissue			
❏ SP-5130	Sleight of Hand	1986	$12
❏ SP-4912	The Key	1983	$12
❏ SP-5211	The Shouting Stage	1988	$12
❏ SP-4732	To the Limit	1978	$12
❏ SP-4987	Track Record	1984	$12
❏ SP-4876	Walk Under Ladders	1981	$12
❏ SP-4382	Whatever's For Us	1974	$15
❏ SP-3227	Whatever's For Us	1984	$10
— Reissue			
ARMEN, KAY			
DECCA			
❏ DL8835 [M]	Golden Songs of Tin Pan Alley	1959	$25
❏ DL78835 [S]	Golden Songs of Tin Pan Alley	1959	$30
MGM			
❏ E-3276 [M]	If You Believe	1955	$30
❏ E-277 [10]	Kay Armen Sings "For No One But You"	1955	$40
ARMORED SAINT			
CHRYSALIS			
❏ BFV41516	Delirious Nomad	1985	$12
❏ FV41476	March of the Saint	1984	$12
❏ BFV41601	Raising Fear	1987	$12
ENIGMA/METAL BLADE			
❏ 72301 [EP]	Live: Saints Will Conquer	1988	$12
METAL BLADE			
❏ MBR1009 [EP]	Armored Saint	1983	$50
ARMS, RUSSELL			
ERA			
❏ EL-20013 [M]	Where Can a Wanderer Go	1957	$30
ARMSTRONG, LIL HARDIN			
RIVERSIDE			
❏ RLP-401 [M]	Lil Armstrong and Her Orchestra	1962	$175
❏ RLP-9401 [R]	Lil Armstrong and Her Orchestra	1962	$175
❏ RLP 12-120 [M]	Satchmo and Me	1956	$300
— White label, blue print			
❏ RLP 12-120 [M]	Satchmo and Me	195?	$40
— Blue label with microphone logo at top			

Number	Title	Yr	NM
ARMSTRONG, LOUIS, AND DUKE ELLINGTON			
MOBILE FIDELITY			
❏ 2-155	The Great Reunion	1984	$175
— Audiophile vinyl			
PICKWICK			
❏ PC-3033	Louis Armstrong and Duke Ellington	196?	$25
ROULETTE			
❏ RE-108	The Duke Ellington-Louis Armstrong Era	1973	$35
❏ R52103 [M]	The Great Reunion	1963	$50
❏ SR52103 [S]	The Great Reunion	1963	$75
❏ R52074 [M]	Together for the First Time	1961	$75
❏ SR52074 [S]	Together for the First Time	1961	$50
ARMSTRONG, LOUIS, AND OSCAR PETERSON			
VERVE			
❏ MGV-8322 [M]	Louis Armstrong Meets Oscar Peterson	1959	$150
❏ MGVS-6062 [S]	Louis Armstrong Meets Oscar Peterson	1960	$150
❏ V-8322 [M]	Louis Armstrong Meets Oscar Peterson	1961	$50
❏ V6-8322 [S]	Louis Armstrong Meets Oscar Peterson	1961	$35
ARMSTRONG, LOUIS, AND SIDNEY BECHET			
JOLLY ROGER			
❏ 5029 [M]	Louis Armstrong and Sidney Bechet	195?	$40
ARMSTRONG, LOUIS, AND THE MILLS BROTHERS			
DECCA			
❏ DL5509 [10]	Louis Armstrong and the Mills Brothers	1954	$175

Number	Title	Yr	NM
ARMSTRONG, LOUIS			
ABC			
❏ S-650	What a Wonderful World	1968	$75
ACCORD			
❏ SN-7161	Mr. Music	1982	$25
AMSTERDAM			
❏ AMS12009	Louis Armstrong and His Friends	1970	$35
AUDIO FIDELITY			
❏ AFLP-2128 [M]	Ain't Gonna Give Nobody None of My Jelly Roll	1964	$35
❏ AFSD-6128 [S]	Ain't Gonna Give Nobody None of My Jelly Roll	1964	$50
❏ AFLP-1924 [M]	Louie and the Dukes of Dixieland	1960	$75
❏ AFSD-5924 [S]	Louie and the Dukes of Dixieland	1960	$40
❏ AFSD-6241	Louis Armstrong	196?	$35
❏ AFLP-1930 [M]	Louis Armstrong Plays King Oliver	1960	$75
❏ AFSD-5930 [S]	Louis Armstrong Plays King Oliver	1960	$40
❏ AFLP-2132 [M]	The Best of Louis Armstrong	1964	$35
❏ AFSD-6132 [S]	The Best of Louis Armstrong	1964	$50
BIOGRAPH			
❏ C-5	Great Soloists	1973	$30
❏ C-6	Louis Armstrong Plays the Blues	1973	$30
BLUEBIRD			
❏ 9759-1-RB	Louis Armstrong & His Orchestra 1932-33: Laughin' Louie	1989	$30
❏ 5920-1-RB	Pops: The 1940s Small Band Sides	1987	$35
❏ 8310-1-RB	What a Wonderful World	1988	$25
❏ AXM2-5519	Young Louis (1932-1933)	1984	$30
BRUNSWICK			
❏ BL58004 [10]	Armstrong Classics	1950	$200
❏ BL754136	I Will Wait for You	1968	$35

Number	Title	Yr	NM
BUENA VISTA			
❑ BV-4044	Disney Swings the Satchmo Way	1968	$40
CHIAROSCURO			
❑ 2003	Great Alternatives	1977	$30
❑ 2002	Snake Rag	1977	$30
❑ 2006	Sweetheart	1977	$30
CLEOPATRA			
❑ 4806 [B]	Live In Paris '65		$25
COLUMBIA			
❑ CL840 [M]	Ambassador Satch	1956	$40
❑ CL591 [M]	Louis Armstrong Plays W.C. Handy	1954	$120
—Maroon label, gold print (original)			
❑ CL591 [M]	Louis Armstrong Plays W.C. Handy	1955	$50
—Red and black label with six "eye" logos			
❑ CL6335 [10]	Louis Armstrong Plays W.C. Handy, Volume 2	1955	$50
❑ CL2638 [M]	Louis Armstrong's Greatest Hits	1967	$50
❑ CS9438 [R]	Louis Armstrong's Greatest Hits	1967	$30
❑ PC9438 [R]	Louis Armstrong's Greatest Hits	198?	$20
—Budget-line reissue			
❑ CL1077 [M]	Satchmo the Great	1957	$75
❑ CL708 [M]	Satch Plays Fats	1955	$50
—Red and black label with six "eye" logos			
G30416	The Genius of Louis Armstrong, Vol. 1	1971	$35
❑ ML4383 [M]	The Louis Armstrong Story, Volume 1: Louis Armstrong and His Hot Five	1951	$150
—Green label, gold or silver print			
❑ CL851 [M]	The Louis Armstrong Story, Volume 1: Louis Armstrong and His Hot Five	1956	$75
—Red and black label with six "eye" logos; reissue of 4383			
❑ CL851 [M]	The Louis Armstrong Story, Volume 1: Louis Armstrong and His Hot Five	197?	$30
—Orange label			
❑ ML4384 [M]	The Louis Armstrong Story, Volume 2: Louis Armstrong and His Hot Seven	1951	$150
—Green label, gold or silver print			
❑ CL852 [M]	The Louis Armstrong Story, Volume 2: Louis Armstrong and His Hot Seven	1956	$75
—Red and black label with six "eye" logos; reissue of 5484			
❑ ML4385 [M]	The Louis Armstrong Story, Volume 3: Louis Armstrong and Earl Hines	1951	$150
—Green label, gold or silver print			
❑ CL853 [M]	The Louis Armstrong Story, Volume 3: Louis Armstrong and Earl Hines	1956	$75
—Red and black label with six "eye" logos; reissue of 4385			
❑ CL853 [M]	The Louis Armstrong Story, Volume 3: Louis Armstrong and Earl Hines	197?	$30
—Orange label reissue			
❑ ML4386 [M]	The Louis Armstrong Story, Volume 4: Louis Armstrong Favorites	1951	$150
—Green label, gold or silver print			
❑ CL854 [M]	The Louis Armstrong Story, Volume 4: Louis Armstrong Favorites	1956	$75
—Red and black label with six "eye" logos; reissue of 4386			
COLUMBIA JAZZ MASTERPIECES			
❑ CJ40242	Louis Armstrong Plays W.C. Handy	1986	$25
❑ CJ40378	Satch Plays Fats	1986	$25
COLUMBIA MUSICAL TREASURIES			
❑ P4M5676	40 Greatest Hits	197?	$50
COLUMBIA SPECIAL PRODUCTS			
❑ JCL708 [M]	Satch Plays Fats	196?	$30
—Special Collector's Series" reissue			
DECCA			
❑ DL74330 [R]	A Musical Autobiography, 1928-1930	1962	$30
❑ DL4227 [M]	I Love Jazz	1962	$50
❑ DL74227 [R]	I Love Jazz	1962	$30
❑ DL8284 [M]	Jazz Classics	1956	$175
—Black label, silver print			
❑ DL8284 [M]	Jazz Classics	1960	$35
—Black label with color bars			
❑ DL5280 [10]	Jazz Concert	1950	$175
❑ DL4245 [M]	King Louis	1962	$50
❑ DL74245 [R]	King Louis	1962	$30
❑ DL5532 [10]	Latter-Day Louis	1954	$175
❑ DL8488 [M]	Louis and the Angels	1957	$120
—Black label, silver print			
❑ DL8488 [M]	Louis and the Angels	1960	$35
—Black label with color bars			
❑ DL8781 [M]	Louis and the Good Book	1958	$150
—Black label, silver print			
❑ DL8741 [M]	Louis and the Good Book	1960	$35
—Black label with color bars			

Number	Title	Yr	NM
❑ DL8168 [M]	Louis Armstrong at the Crescendo, Volume 1	1955	$175
—Black label, silver print			
❑ DL8169 [M]	Louis Armstrong at the Crescendo, Volume 2	1955	$150
—Black label, silver print			
❑ DL5536 [10]	Louis Armstrong-Gordon Jenkins	1954	$175
❑ DL5279 [10]	New Orleans Days	1950	$250
❑ DL8283 [M]	New Orleans Jazz	1956	$120
—Black label, silver print			
❑ DL8283 [M]	New Orleans Jazz	1960	$35
—Black label with color bars			
❑ DL8329 [M]	New Orleans Nights	1957	$120
—Black label, silver print			
❑ DL8329 [M]	New Orleans Nights	1960	$35
—Black label with color bars			
❑ DL8329 [M]	New Orleans Nights	1960	$35
—Black label with color bars			
❑ DL5225 [10]	New Orleans to New York	1950	$250
❑ DL9225 [M]	Rare Items (1935-1944)	196?	$50
❑ DL79225 [R]	Rare Items (1935-1944)	196?	$30
❑ DX155 [M]	Satchmo, A Musical Autobiography	1956	$200
—Black labels, silver print			
❑ DXM155 [M]	Satchmo, A Musical Autobiography	1960	$40
—Black labels with color bars			
❑ DL8963 [M]	Satchmo, A Musical Autobiography, 1923-1925	1960	$75
❑ DL78963 [R]	Satchmo, A Musical Autobiography, 1923-1925	196?	$30
❑ DL4230 [M]	Satchmo, A Musical Autobiography, 1926-1927	1962	$75
❑ DL4330 [M]	Satchmo, A Musical Autobiography, 1928-1930	1962	$75
❑ DL4331 [M]	Satchmo, A Musical Autobiography, 1930-1934	1962	$75
❑ DL8041 [M]	Satchmo at Pasadena	1954	$175
—Black label, silver print			
❑ DL8041 [M]	Satchmo at Pasadena	1960	$35
—Black label with color bars			
❑ DX108 [M]	Satchmo at Symphony Hall	1954	$175
—Black labels, silver print			
❑ DL8037 [M]	Satchmo at Symphony Hall, Volume 1	1954	$175
—Black label, silver print			
❑ DL8037 [M]	Satchmo at Symphony Hall, Volume 1	1960	$35
—Black label with color bars			
❑ DL8038 [M]	Satchmo at Symphony Hall, Volume 2	1954	$175
—Black label, silver print			
❑ DL8038 [M]	Satchmo at Symphony Hall, Volume 2	1960	$35
—Black label with color bars			
❑ DL8840 [M]	Satchmo in Style	1958	$150
—Black label, silver print			
❑ DL8840 [M]	Satchmo in Style	1960	$35
—Black label with color bars			
❑ DL8330 [M]	Satchmo on Stage	1957	$120
—Black label, silver print			
❑ DL8330 [M]	Satchmo on Stage	1960	$35
—Black label with color bars			
❑ DL8327 [M]	Satchmo's Collector's Items	1957	$120
—Black label, silver print			
❑ DL8327 [M]	Satchmo's Collector's Items	1960	$35
—Black label with color bars			
❑ DL5401 [10]	Satchmo Serenades	1952	$175
❑ DL8211 [M]	Satchmo Serenades	1956	$175
—Black label, silver print			
❑ DL8211 [M]	Satchmo Serenades	1960	$35
—Black label with color bars			
❑ DL4137 [M]	Satchmo's Golden Favorites	1961	$50
❑ DL74137 [R]	Satchmo's Golden Favorites	1961	$30
❑ DL8126 [M]	Satchmo Sings	1955	$175
—Black label, silver print			
❑ DL8126 [M]	Satchmo Sings	1960	$35
—Black label with color bars			
❑ DXB183 [M]	The Best of Louis Armstrong	196?	$75
❑ DXSB7183 [R]	The Best of Louis Armstrong	196?	$35
❑ DL9233 [M]	Young Louis the Sideman (1924-1927)	196?	$50
❑ DL79233 [R]	Young Louis the Sideman (1924-1927)	196?	$30
DISNEYLAND			
❑ STER-1341	The Wonderful World of Walt Disney	1971	$50
—Reissue of Buena Vista 4044			
EVEREST			
❑ 3312 [R]	In Memoriam	1971	$25
EVEREST ARCHIVE OF FOLK & JAZZ			
❑ 258	Louis "Satchmo" Armstrong	197?	$30
❑ 312	Louis Armstrong, Vol. 2	197?	$25
GNP CRESCENDO			
❑ 11001	An Evening with Louis Armstrong	1977	$35
❑ 9050	Pasadena Concert, Vol. II	1987	$25

Number	Title	Yr	NM
HARMONY			
❑ HS11316	Louis Armstrong	197?	$30
❑ KH31236	The Louis Armstrong Saga	1971	$30
IAJRC			
❑ LP-29	Oregon State Fair, 1960	198?	$25
JOLLY ROGER			
❑ 5009 [10]	Louis Armstrong	1954	$150
KAPP			
❑ KL-1364 [M]	Hello, Dolly!	1964	$30
❑ KS-3364 [S]	Hello, Dolly!	1964	$18
MCA			
❑ 1304	Back in New York	197?	$25
❑ 538	Hello, Dolly!	197?	$25
—Reissue of Kapp LP			
❑ 1300	Louis and the Good Book	197?	$25
—Reissue of Decca 8741			
❑ 2-4013	Louis Armstrong at the Crescendo	197?	$30
—Reissue of Decca 8168/8169 in one sleeve			
❑ 42328	Louis Armstrong of New Orleans	1990	$30
❑ 1306	Louis with Guest Stars	197?	$25
❑ 1335	Old Favorites	197?	$25
❑ 10006	Satchmo, A Musical Autobiography	197?	$75
—Reissue of Decca 155			
❑ 2-4057	Satchmo at Symphony Hall	197?	$30
—Reissue of Decca 108			
❑ 1334	Satchmo For Ever!	197?	$25
❑ 1322	Satchmo's Collector's Items	197?	$25
—Reissue of Decca 8327			
❑ 1316	Satchmo Serenades	197?	$25
—Reissue of Decca 8211			
❑ 1312	Swing That Music!	197?	$25
❑ 2-4035	The Best of Louis Armstrong	197?	$30
—Reissue of Decca 7183			
❑ 25204	What a Wonderful World	1988	$25
—Reissue of ABC 650			
❑ 1301	Young Louis the Sideman	197?	$25
—Reissue of Decca 9233			
MERCURY			
❑ MG-21081 [M]	Louis Armstrong Sings Louis Armstrong	1965	$150
❑ SR-61081 [S]	Louis Armstrong Sings Louis Armstrong	1965	$150
METRO			
❑ M-510 [M]	Hello, Louis	1965	$175
❑ MS-510 [S]	Hello, Louis	1965	$300
MILESTONE			
❑ 2010	Early Portrait	1969	$25
❑ 47017	Louis Armstrong and King Oliver	197?	$30
MOSAIC			
❑ MQ8-146	The Complete Decca Studio Recordings of Louis Armstrong and the All-Stars	199?	$175
PABLO			
❑ 2310941	Mack the Knife	1990	$30
PAIR			
❑ PDL2-1042	The Jazz Legend	1986	$30
PAUSA			
❑ 9018	The Greatest of Louis Armstrong	1983	$25
RCA VICTOR			
❑ LPM-2322 [M]	A Rare Batch of Satch	1961	$75
❑ VPM-6044	July 4, 1900/July 6, 1971	1971	$50
❑ LPM-2971 [M]	Louis Armstrong in the '30s/ in the '40s	1964	$50
❑ LSP-2971(e) [R]	Louis Armstrong in the '30s/ in the '40s	1964	$30
❑ LJM-1005 [M]	Louis Armstrong Sings the Blues	1954	$150
❑ LPT7 [10]	Louis Armstrong Town Hall Concert	1951	$175
❑ LPM-1443 [M]	Town Hall Concert Plus	1957	$150
RIVERSIDE			
❑ RLP 12-122 [M]	Louis Armstrong 1923	1956	$300
—White label, blue print			
❑ RLP 12-122 [M]	Louis Armstrong 1923	195?	$40
—Blue label			
❑ RLP-1001 [10]	Louis Armstrong Plays the Blues	1953	$300
❑ RLP-1029 [10]	Louis Armstrong with King Oliver's Creole Jazz Band 1923	1953	$300
❑ RLP 12-101 [M]	The Young Louis Armstrong	1956	$300
—White label, blue print			
❑ RLP 12-101 [M]	The Young Louis Armstrong	195?	$40
—Blue label			
SEAGULL			
❑ LG-8206	Greatest Hits: Live in Concert	198?	$30
STORYVILLE			
❑ 4012	Louis Armstrong and His All-Stars	1980	$25

Number	Title	Yr	NM
SWING			
❑ SW-8450	Louis and the Big Bands	1984	$25
TIME-LIFE			
❑ STBB-22	Big Bands: Louis Armstrong	1985	$35
❑ STL-J-01	Giants of Jazz	1978	$50
VANGUARD			
❑ VSD91/92	Essential Louis Armstrong	1977	$35
❑ VMS73129	Essential Louis Armstrong, Vol. 1	1986	$20
VERVE			
❑ MGV-4035 [M]	I've Got the World on a String	1959	$150
❑ MGVS-6101 [S]	I've Got the World on a String	1960	$150
❑ V-4035 [M]	I've Got the World on a String	1961	$50
❑ V6-4035 [S]	I've Got the World on a String	1961	$35
❑ MGVS-4035	I've Got the World on a String	199?	$75
—Classic Records reissue			
❑ MGV-4012 [M]	Louis Under the Stars	1957	$175
❑ MGVS-6044 [S]	Louis Under the Stars	1960	$150
❑ V-4012 [M]	Louis Under the Stars	1961	$50
❑ V6-4012 [S]	Louis Under the Stars	1961	$35
❑ MGV-4012 [S]	Louis Under the Stars	199?	$75
—180-gram reissue; distributed by Classic Records			
❑ V-8595 [M]	The Best of Louis Armstrong	1964	$35
❑ V6-8595 [S]	The Best of Louis Armstrong	1964	$35
❑ SW-90658 [S]	The Best of Louis Armstrong	1964	$100
—Capitol Record Club edition			
❑ V-8569 [M]	The Essential Louis A.	1963	$30
❑ V6-8569 [S]	The Essential Louis A.	1963	$35
VOCALION			
❑ VL73851 [R]	Here's Louis Armstrong	196?	$25
❑ VL3851 [M]	Here's Louis Armstrong	196?	$35
❑ VL73871 [R]	The One and Only Louis Armstrong	1968	$25
WING			
❑ SR-16381	Great Louis	196?	$25
ARMSTRONG, LOUIS/AL HIRT			
MURRAY HILL			
❑ 930633	Louis Armstrong and Al Hirt Play Dixieland Trumpet	197?	$50
ARMSTRONG, VANESSA BELL			
JIVE			
❑ 1251-1-J [EP]	Gospel Sampler	1989	$15
—Promo-only four-song sampler			
❑ 1074-1-J	Vanessa Bell Armstrong	1987	$12
ARNAZ, DESI			
RCA VICTOR			
❑ LPM-3096 [10]	Babalu!	1954	$120
ARNELL, GINNY			
MGM			
❑ E-4228 [M]	Meet Ginny Arnell	1964	$30
❑ SE-4228 [S]	Meet Ginny Arnell	1964	$40
ARNOLD, BILLY BOY			
See BILLY BOY			
ARNOLD, BUDDY			
ABC-PARAMOUNT			
❑ ABC-114 [M]	Wailing	1956	$75
ARNOLD, EDDY			
K-TEL			
❑ WC307	The Living Legend of Eddy Arnold	1974	$12
MGM			
❑ SE-4916	I Wish I Had Loved You Better	1974	$15
❑ SE-4912	She's Got Everything I Need	1974	$15
❑ SE-4878	So Many Ways/If the Whole World Stopped Lovin'	1973	$15
❑ MG-1-4992	The Wonderful World of Eddy Arnold	1975	$15
❑ MJB-5107	World of Hits	1976	$15
PAIR			
❑ PDL2-1000	The Mellow Side of Eddy Arnold	1986	$15
RCA			
❑ 9963-1-R	Hand-Holdin' Songs	1990	$18
RCA CAMDEN			
❑ CAL-741 [M]	Country Songs I Love to Sing	1963	$18
❑ CAS-741(e) [R]	Country Songs I Love to Sing	1966	$12
❑ CAL-471 [M]	Eddy Arnold (That's How Much I Love You)	1959	$25
❑ CAS-471(e) [R]	Eddy Arnold (That's How Much I Love You)	1966	$12
❑ CAL-799 [M]	Eddy's Songs	1964	$18
❑ CAS-799(e) [R]	Eddy's Songs	1966	$12
❑ CAL-897 [M]	I'm Throwing Rice (At the Girl That I Love) And Other Favorites	1966	$18
❑ CAS-897(e) [R]	I'm Throwing Rice (At the Girl That I Love) And Other Favorites	1966	$12
❑ CAL-563 [M]	More Eddy Arnold	1960	$25
❑ CAS-563(e) [R]	More Eddy Arnold	1966	$12
❑ CAS-2501	Then You Can Tell Me Goodbye	197?	$12
RCA VICTOR			
❑ LPM-1293 [M]	A Dozen Hits	1956	$50
❑ AHL1-3606	A Legend and His Lady	1980	$12
❑ LPM-1377 [M]	A Little on the Lonely Side	1956	$50
❑ LPM-3117 [10]	All-Time Favorites	1953	$150
❑ LPM-1223 [M]	All-Time Favorites	1955	$50
—New version of LPM 3117			
❑ LSP-1223(e) [R]	All-Time Favorites	1975	$12
—Tan label; thin vinyl			
❑ LSP-1223(e) [R]	All-Time Favorites	1967	$15
—Black label; dog on top			
❑ LPM-3031 [10]	All-Time Hits from the Hills	1952	$150
❑ AHL1-3914	A Man for All Seasons	1980	$12
❑ LPM-3230 [10]	An American Institution	1954	$150
❑ LPM-3230	An American Institution Booklet	1954	$50
❑ LPM-3027 [10]	Anytime	1952	$120
—Label calls this "Country Classics"			
❑ LPM-1224 [M]	Anytime	1955	$50
—New version of LPM 3027			
❑ LPM-2578 [M]	Cattle Call	1962	$30
❑ LSP-2578 [S]	Cattle Call	1962	$30
❑ LSP-2578 [S]	Cattle Call	1967	$18
—Reissue with "Country Music Hall of Fame" on front cover and "RE" on back cover; black label			
❑ LSP-2578 [S]	Cattle Call	1969	$15
—Reissue with "Country Music Hall of Fame" on front cover and "RE" on back cover; orange label			
❑ LPM-2554 [M]	Christmas with Eddy Arnold	1962	$25
❑ LSP-2554 [S]	Christmas with Eddy Arnold	1962	$30
—Original cover; "Living Stereo" on label			
❑ PRS-346	Christmas with Eddy Arnold	1971	$18
—Special-products issue			
❑ LSP-2554 [S]	Christmas with Eddy Arnold	1967	$18
—Second cover with Eddy standing in front of a Christmas tree; "Country Music Hall of Fame" on front cover and "RE" on back cover			
❑ ANL1-1926	Christmas with Eddy Arnold	1976	$12
—Reissue of LSP-2554 with similar cover to the second edition			
❑ AHL1-4661	Close Enough to Love	1983	$12
❑ AHL1-5467	Collector's Series	1985	$12
❑ AHL1-4263	Don't Give Up on Me	1981	$12
❑ APL1-1817	Eddy	1976	$15
❑ LSP-4738	Eddy Arnold Sings for Housewives and Other Ladies	1972	$15
❑ LPM-2185 [M]	Eddy Arnold Sings Them Again	1960	$30
❑ LSP-2185 [S]	Eddy Arnold Sings Them Again	1960	$30
❑ LPM-2629 [M]	Faithfully Yours	1963	$30
❑ LSP-2629 [S]	Faithfully Yours	1963	$30
❑ LPM-2811 [M]	Folk Song Book	1964	$25
❑ LSP-2811 [S]	Folk Song Book	1964	$30
—Black label, dog on top			
❑ LSP-2811 [S]	Folk Song Book	1971	$12
—Orange label, thin vinyl			
❑ LPM-1928 [M]	Have Guitar, Will Travel	1959	$30
❑ LSP-1928 [S]	Have Guitar, Will Travel	1959	$30
❑ APL1-2277	I Need You All the Time	1977	$15
❑ LPM-3507 [M]	I Want to Go with You	1966	$15
❑ LSP-3507 [S]	I Want to Go with You	1966	$18
—Black label, dog on top			
❑ LSP-3507 [S]	I Want to Go with You	1971	$12
—Orange label, thin vinyl			
❑ LPM-2337 [M]	Let's Make Memories Tonight	1961	$25
❑ LSP-2337 [S]	Let's Make Memories Tonight	1961	$30
❑ LPM-3753 [M]	Lonely Again	1967	$25
❑ LSP-3753 [S]	Lonely Again	1967	$18
—Black label, dog on top			
❑ LSP-3753 [S]	Lonely Again	1971	$12
—Orange label, thin vinyl			
❑ LSP-4304	Love & Guitars	1970	$15
—Orange label, rigid vinyl			
❑ LSP-4304	Love & Guitars	1971	$12
—Orange label, thin vinyl			
❑ LSP-4625	Loving Her Was Easier	1971	$15
❑ LPM-1575 [M]	My Darling, My Darling	1957	$40
❑ LPM-3466 [M]	My World	1965	$15
❑ LSP-3466 [S]	My World	1965	$18
❑ LPM-2471 [M]	One More Time	1961	$25
❑ LSP-2471 [S]	One More Time	1961	$30
❑ LSP-2471 [S]	One More Time	1967	$18
—Reissue with "Country Music Hall of Fame" on front cover and "RE" on back cover			
❑ LPM-2596 [M]	Our Man Down South	1962	$30
❑ LSP-2596 [S]	Our Man Down South	1962	$30
❑ LPM-2951 [M]	Pop Hits from the Country Side	1964	$25
❑ LSP-2951 [S]	Pop Hits from the Country Side	1964	$30
❑ LSP-2951 [S]	Pop Hits from the Country Side	1967	$18
—Reissue with "Country Music Hall of Fame" on front cover and "RE" on back cover			
❑ LSP-4471	Portrait of My Woman	1971	$15
❑ LPM-1733 [M]	Praise Him, Praise Him	1958	$40
❑ ANL1-1078	Pure Gold	1975	$12
❑ AHL1-3358	Somebody	1979	$12
❑ LPM-3715 [M]	Somebody Like Me	1966	$15
❑ LSP-3715 [S]	Somebody Like Me	1966	$18
❑ LSP-3715 [S]	Somebody Like Me	1967	$15
—Reissue with "Country Music Hall of Fame" on front cover and "RE" on back cover			
❑ LPM-2909 [M]	Sometimes I'm Happy, Sometimes I'm Blue	1964	$25
❑ LSP-2909 [S]	Sometimes I'm Happy, Sometimes I'm Blue	1964	$30
❑ LSP-4110	Songs of the Young World	1969	$18
❑ LSP-4390	Standing Alone	1970	$15
❑ LPM-3565 [M]	The Best of Eddy Arnold	1967	$25
❑ LSP-3565 [S]	The Best of Eddy Arnold	1967	$18
❑ AYL1-3675	The Best of Eddy Arnold	1980	$10
—Best Buy Series" reissue			
❑ LSP-4320	The Best of Eddy Arnold, Volume II	1970	$15
❑ AYL1-3937	The Best of Eddy Arnold, Volume II	1981	$10
—Best Buy Series" reissue			
❑ LPM-1225 [M]	The Chapel on the Hill	1955	$50
—New version of LPM 3031			
❑ LPM-3361 [M]	The Easy Way	1965	$18
❑ LSP-3361 [S]	The Easy Way	1965	$25
❑ LPM-3931 [M]	The Everlovin' World of Eddy Arnold	1968	$40
❑ LSP-3931 [S]	The Everlovin' World of Eddy Arnold	1968	$18
❑ LSP-4179	The Glory of Love	1969	$18
❑ DPL2-0051	The Greatest of Eddy Arnold	1973	$18
—Special products issue; "Tele House Inc. Presents" on labels			
❑ LPM-3622 [M]	The Last Word in Lonesome	1966	$15
❑ LSP-3622 [S]	The Last Word in Lonesome	1966	$18
❑ CPL2-4885	The Legendary Performances (1945-1971)	1983	$15
❑ LSP-4009 [S]	The Romantic World of Eddy Arnold	1968	$18
❑ LPM-4009 [M]	The Romantic World of Eddy Arnold	1968	$175
❑ LSP-4231	The Warmth of Eddy	1969	$18
❑ APL1-0239	The World of Eddy Arnold	1973	$15
❑ VPS-6032	This Is Eddy Arnold	1972	$18
❑ LPM-2036 [M]	Thereby Hangs a Tale	1959	$30
❑ LSP-2036 [S]	Thereby Hangs a Tale	1959	$30
❑ LPM-3869 [M]	Turn the World Around	1967	$25
❑ LSP-3869 [S]	Turn the World Around	1967	$18
❑ LSP-4089	Walkin' in Love Land	1968	$18
❑ LPM-1111 [M]	Wanderin' with Eddy Arnold	1955	$50
❑ LPM-3219 [10]	When It's Roundup Time in Heaven	1954	$150
❑ LPM-1484 [M]	When They Were Young	1956	$50
❑ LPM-2268 [M]	You Gotta Have Love	1960	$30
❑ LSP-2268 [S]	You Gotta Have Love	1960	$30
READER'S DIGEST			
❑ RDA168-A	Welcome to My World	1975	$50
—Box set with booklet; prefix on labels is "RD 4			
TIME-LIFE			
❑ STW-120	Country Music	1981	$12
ARNOLD, HARRY			
ATCO			
❑ 33-120 [M]	I Love Harry Arnold (And All That Jazz)	1960	$40
EMARCY			
❑ MG-36139 [M]	Harry Arnold and His Orchestra	1958	$175
❑ SR-80006 [S]	Harry Arnold and His Orchestra	1958	$175
JAZZLAND			
❑ JLP-65 [M]	Harry Arnold's Great Big Band and Friends	1962	$30
❑ JLP-965 [S]	Harry Arnold's Great Big Band and Friends	1962	$30
JAZZTONE			
❑ J-1270 [M]	The Jazztone Mystery Band	1957	$40
RIVERSIDE			
❑ RM-7536 [M]	Dancing on Broadway to the Music of Cole Porter	196?	$25
❑ RS-97536 [S]	Dancing on Broadway to the Music of Cole Porter	196?	$30
❑ RM-7526 [M]	Let's Dance on Broadway	196?	$25
❑ RS-97526 [S]	Let's Dance on Broadway	196?	$30
ARNOLD, P.P.			
IMMEDIATE			
❑ Z1252016 [B]	Kafunta	1968	$30
ARPEGGIO			
POLYDOR			
❑ PD-1-6230	Breakout	1980	$12
❑ PD-1-6180	Let the Music Play	1979	$12

Number	Title	Yr	NM

ARRESTED DEVELOPMENT
CHRYSALIS
❏ F1-21929	3 Years, 5 Months, & 2 Days in the Life of...	1992	$30
❏ F1-29274	Zingalamaduni	1994	$25

ARRINGTON, STEVE
ATLANTIC
❏ 81245	Dancin' in the Key of Life	1985	$10
❏ 80727	Positive Power	1984	$10
❏ 80049	Steve Arrington's Hall of Fame: I	1983	$10
❏ 81643	The Jammin' National Anthem	1986	$10

MANHATTAN
❏ MLT-46903	Jam Packed	1987	$10

ARS NOVA
ATLANTIC
❏ SD8221	Sunshine and Shadows	1969	$25

ELEKTRA
❏ EKS-74020	Ars Nova	1968	$25

ART BEARS
RALPH
❏ RR7905 [B]	Winter Songs	1979	$30

ART ENSEMBLE OF CHICAGO
AECO
❏ 04	Kabalaba	1978	$35

ARISTA/FREEDOM
❏ AL1903	The Paris Session	197?	$35

ATLANTIC
❏ SD1639	Bap-Tizum	1973	$35
❏ SD1651	Fanfare for the Warriors	1974	$35
❏ 90046	Fanfare for the Warriors	1983	$25
— Reissue of 1651			

DELMARK
❏ DS-432/433	Live at Mandel Hall	1974	$35

DIW
❏ 8014	Ancient to the Future	1987	$25
❏ 8038	Art Ensemble of Soweto	1990	$30
❏ 8005	Live in Japan	1986	$25
❏ 8011	Naked	1987	$25
❏ 8033	The Alternate Express	1989	$30
❏ 8021/22	The Complete Live in Japan	198?	$35

ECM
❏ 1167	Full Force	1980	$30
❏ 1126	Nice Guys	1979	$30
❏ 25014	The Third Decade	1985	$25
❏ 1211	Urban Bushmen	1982	$35

INNER CITY
❏ 1004	Certain Blacks	197?	$30

NESSA
❏ N-4	Les Stances a Sophie	1970	$30
— With Fontella Bass			
❏ N-5	Old/Quartet	1975	$25
❏ N-3	People in Sorrow	1969	$30

PAULA
❏ LPS-4001	Chi-Congo	197?	$35

PRESTIGE
❏ 10049	Art Ensemble of Chicago with Fontella Bass	1972	$35
❏ 10064	Phase One	197?	$35

ART IN AMERICA
PAVILLION
❏ BFZ38517	Art in America	1983	$12

ART OF LOVIN'
MAINSTREAM
❏ S-6113	Art of Lovin'	1968	$300

ART OF NOISE
CHINA
❏ 839404-1	Below the Waste	1989	$18
❏ R143956	In No Sense? Nonsense!	1987	$15
— BMG Direct Marketing edition			
❏ OV41570	In No Sense? Nonsense!	1987	$12
❏ BFV41528	In Visible Silence	1986	$12
❏ FV41567	Re-Works of The Art of Noise	1986	$15
❏ R100848	The Best of The Art of Noise	1988	$15
— BMG Direct Marketing edition			
❏ 837367-1	The Best of The Art of Noise	1988	$12

ISLAND
❏ 90137	Art of Noise	1984	$15
❏ 90179	(Who's Afraid of?) The Art of Noise!	1984	$12
❏ 842473-1	(Who's Afraid of?) The Art of Noise!	1990	$12
— Reissue of Island 90179			

ARTER, CARL
EARWIG
❏ LPS-4905	Song from Far Away	1986	$25

ARTHUR, BROOKS
VERVE
❏ V-8650 [M]	Sole Forms	1966	$35
❏ V6-8650 [S]	Sole Forms	1966	$35
❏ V6-8779	Traces	1969	$35

ARTHUR
LHI
❏ 12000	Dreams and Images	1968	$85

ARTISTICS, THE
BRUNSWICK
❏ BL54123 [M]	I'm Gonna Miss You	1967	$30
❏ BL754123 [S]	I'm Gonna Miss You	1967	$30
❏ BL754168	I Want You to Make My Life Over	1970	$30

❏ BL754195 [B]	Look Out	1973	$25
❏ BL754139	The Articulate Artistics	1968	$30
❏ BL754153	What Happened	1969	$30

OKEH
❏ OKM-12119 [M]	Get My Hands on Some Lovin'	1967	$100
❏ OKS-14119 [S]	Get My Hands on Some Lovin'	1967	$100

ARTISTS UNITED AGAINST APARTHEID
MANHATTAN
❏ ST-53019	Sun City	1985	$15
❏ SPRO-9538 [DJ]	Voices of Sun City	1985	$30
— Promo album of interviews with participants in the benefit LP			

ARVON, BOBBY
FIRST ARTISTS
❏ 4001	Until Now	1978	$15

ARZACHEL
ROULETTE
❏ SR42036 [B]	Arzachel	1969	$250

A'S, THE
ARISTA
❏ AL9554	A Woman's Got the Power	1981	$12
❏ AB4238	The A's	1979	$12
❏ CP705 [10]	The A's E.P.	1979	$15
— Red vinyl with three songs from their first album			

ASGAERD
THRESHOLD
❏ THS6 [B]	In the Realm of Asgaerd	1972	$30

ASH, DANIEL
BEGGARS BANQUET
❏ 3014-1-R [B]	Coming Home	1991	$25

ASH, MARVIN
CAPITOL
❏ H188 [10]	Honky Tonk Piano	1950	$150

DECCA
❏ DL8346 [M]	New Orleans at Midnight	1957	$40

JAZZ MAN
❏ LPJM-335 [10]	Marvin Ash	1954	$50

JUMP
❏ JL-4 [10]	Marvin Ash	1954	$50

ASHANTI
MURDER, INC.
❏ 314586830-1	Ashanti	2002	$25
❏ B0000143-01 [B]	Chapter II	2003	$18
❏ B0003409-01	Concrete Rose	2004	$18

ASHBY, DOROTHY
ARGO
❏ LP-690 [M]	Dorothy Ashby	1962	$30
❏ LPS-690 [S]	Dorothy Ashby	1962	$30

ATLANTIC
❏ 1447 [M]	The Fantastic Jazz Harp of Dorothy Ashby	1966	$35
❏ SD1447 [S]	The Fantastic Jazz Harp of Dorothy Ashby	1966	$25

CADET
❏ LPS-809	Afro-Harping	1968	$35
❏ LP-690 [M]	Dorothy Ashby	1966	$30
— Reissue of Argo LP-690			
❏ LPS-690 [S]	Dorothy Ashby	1966	$35
— Reissue of Argo LPS-690			
❏ LPS-825	Dorothy's Harp	1969	$35
❏ LPS-841	Rubaiyat	1970	$35

CHESS
❏ CH-91555	Afro-Harping	198?	$25
— Reissue of Cadet 809			

JAZZLAND
❏ JLP-61 [M]	Soft Winds	1961	$30
❏ JLP-961 [S]	Soft Winds	1961	$30

NEW JAZZ
❏ NJLP-8209 [M]	In a Minor Groove	1958	$175
— Purple label			
❏ NJLP-8209 [M]	In a Minor Groove	1965	$175
— Blue label, trident logo at right			

PRESTIGE
❏ PRLP-7639	Dorothy Plays for Beautiful People	1969	$35
— Reissue of New Jazz 8209			
❏ PRLP-7140 [M]	Hip Harp	1958	$250
❏ PRLP-7638	The Best of Dorothy Ashby	1969	$35
— Reissue of 7140			

REGENT
❏ MG-6039 [M]	Dorothy Ashby -- Jazz Harpist	1957	$75

SAVOY
❏ MG-12212 [M]	Dorothy Ashby -- Jazz Harpist	196?	$35
— Reissue of Regent 6039			

ASHBY, HAROLD
GEMINI
❏ GMLP-60-1	The Viking	1988	$25

PROGRESSIVE
❏ PRO-7040	Presenting Harold Ashby	1979	$25

ASHBY, IRVING
AUDIOPHILE
❏ AP-133	Memoirs	1980	$25

ASHES
VAULT
❏ 125	Ashes	1971	$150
— Recorded in 1968 but released in 1971			

ASHFORD AND SIMPSON
CAPITOL
❏ ST-12282	High Rise	1983	$10
❏ C1-46946	Love Or Physical	1989	$12
❏ ST-12469	Real Love	1986	$10
❏ ST-12366	Solid	1984	$10
❏ ST-12207	Street Opera	1982	$10

WARNER BROS.
❏ HS3458	A Musical Affair	1980	$12
❏ BS2858	Come As You Are	1976	$12
❏ BS2739	Gimme Something Real	1973	$12
❏ BSK3219	Is It Still Good to Ya	1978	$12
❏ BS2789	I Wanna Be Selfish	1974	$12
❏ 2BS3524	Performance	1981	$15
❏ BS3088	Send It	1977	$12
❏ BS2992	So So Satisfied	1977	$12
❏ BSK3357	Stay Free	1979	$12

ASHKAN
SIRE
❏ SES-97107	In from the Cold	1970	$40

ASHLEY, LEON, AND MARGIE SINGLETON
ASHLEY
❏ A-3695	New Brand of Country	197?	$18

ASHLEY, LEON
ASHLEY
❏ 54001	The Best of Leon Ashley	197?	$18

Number	Title	Yr	NM
HILLTOP			
❏ JS-6069	Flower of Love	1968	$18
RCA VICTOR			
❏ LPM-3900 [M]	Laura (What's He Got That I Ain't Got)	1967	$35
❏ LSP-3900 [S]	Laura (What's He Got That I Ain't Got)	1967	$25

ASHLEY, STEVE

Number	Title	Yr	NM
GULL			
❏ GU6406S1 [B]	Speedy Return	1976	$35
❏ GU401V1 [B]	Stroll On	1975	$40

ASHTON, GARDNER AND DYKE

Number	Title	Yr	NM
CAPITOL			
❏ ST-563	Resurrection Shuffle	1971	$15
❏ SW-827	The Last Rebel	1971	$15
❏ SMAS-862 [B]	What a Bloody Long Day It's Been	1972	$18

ASHWORTH, ERNEST

Number	Title	Yr	NM
HICKORY			
❏ LPM-118 [M]	Hits of Today and Tomorrow	1964	$30

ASIA
Includes members of KING CRIMSON, EMERSON, LAKE AND PALMER and YES.

Number	Title	Yr	NM
GEFFEN			
❏ GHS4008	Alpha	1983	$10
— White label with pinstripes			
❏ GHS4008 [DJ]	Alpha	1983	$30
— Promo on "Quiex II" vinyl			

Number	Title	Yr	NM
❏ GHS2008 [B]	Asia	1982	$10
— White label with pinstripes			
❏ GHS2008 [DJ]	Asia	1982	$30
— Promo on "Quiex II" vinyl			
❏ GHS24072	Astra	1985	$10
❏ GHS24298	Then and Now	1990	$15

ASLEEP AT THE WHEEL

Number	Title	Yr	NM
ARISTA			
❏ AL-8550	Keepin' Me Up Nights	1990	$15
CAPITOL			

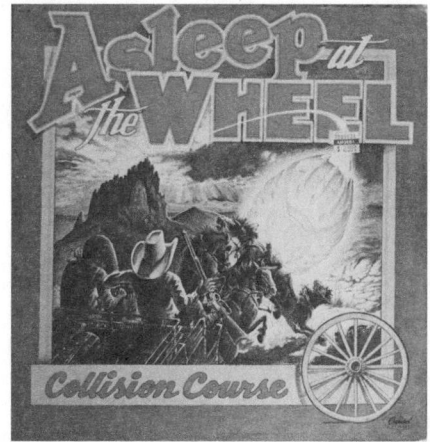

Number	Title	Yr	NM
❏ SW-11726 [B]	Collision Course	1978	$15
❏ ST-11945	Served Live	1979	$15
❏ SN-16306	Served Live	1984	$10
— Budget-line reissue			
❏ ST-11441	Texas Gold	1975	$15
❏ ST-11620	The Wheel	1977	$15
❏ ST-11548	Wheelin' and Dealin'	1976	$15

Number	Title	Yr	NM
CAPITOL SPECIAL MARKETS			
❏ SL-8138	Drivin'	1980	$15
DOT/MCA			
❏ 39036	Asleep at the Wheel	1985	$12
EPIC			
❏ BFE40681	10	1987	$10
❏ KE33097	Asleep at the Wheel	1974	$18
❏ PE33097	Asleep at the Wheel	197?	$10
— Reissue			
❏ BG33782	Fathers and Sons	1974	$30
— With Bob Wills			
❏ EG33782	Fathers and Sons	197?	$15
— Reissue			
❏ FE44213	Western Standard Time	1988	$10
LIBERTY			
❏ LN-10296	Comin' Right At Ya!	1986	$10
— Budget-line reissue			
MCA			
❏ 5131	Framed	1980	$12
❏ 742	Framed	1982	$10
— Reissue of 5131			
UNITED ARTISTS			
❏ UA-LA038-F	Comin' Right At Ya!	1973	$25

ASMUSSEN, SVEND

Number	Title	Yr	NM
ANGEL			
❏ ANG.60010 [10]	Rhythm Is Our Business	1955	$85
❏ ANG.60000 [10]	Svend Asmussen and His Unmelancholy Danes	1955	$85
BRUNSWICK			
❏ BL58051 [10]	Hot Fiddle	1953	$100
DOCTOR JAZZ			
❏ FW39150	June Night	1983	$30
EPIC			
❏ LN3210 [M]	Skol!	1955	$150

ASMUSSEN, SVEND / STEPHANE GRAPPELLI

Number	Title	Yr	NM
STORYVILLE			
❏ SLP-4088	Two of a Kind	198?	$30

ASSAULT AND BATTERY

Number	Title	Yr	NM
ATTITUDE			
❏ 14001	Assault and Battery	1992	$18

ASSEMBLED MULTITUDE, THE

Number	Title	Yr	NM
ATLANTIC			
❏ SD8262 [B]	The Assembled Multitude	1970	$18

ASSOCIATION, THE
COLUMBIA

Number	Title	Yr	NM
❏ KC31348 [B]	Waterbeds in Trinidad	1972	$12
HITBOUND/REALISTIC			
❏ 51-3022	New Memories	1983	$15
PAIR			
❏ PDL2-1061	Songs That Made Them Famous	1986	$15
VALIANT			
❏ VLM-5002 [M]	And Then…Along Comes The Association	1966	$25
❏ VLS-25002 [S]	And Then…Along Comes The Association	1966	$30
❏ VLM-5004 [M]	Renaissance	1966	$25
— With no blurb for "No Fair at All" on cover			
❏ VLM-5004 [M]	Renaissance	1967	$18
— With blurb for "No Fair at All" on cover			
❏ VLS-25004 [S]	Renaissance	1966	$30
— With no blurb for "No Fair at All" on cover			
❏ VLS-25004 [S]	Renaissance	1967	$25
— With blurb for "No Fair at All" on cover			

Number	Title	Yr	NM
WARNER BROS.			
❏ WS1702 [S]	And Then…Along Comes The Association	1967	$15
— With "W7" logo on green label			
❏ WS1702 [S]	And Then…Along Comes The Association	1967	$25
— Gold label			
❏ W1702 [M]	And Then…Along Comes The Association	1967	$25
❏ WS1733	Birthday	1968	$15
— With "W7" logo on green label			
❏ WS1786	Goodbye Columbus	1969	$15
— With "W7" logo on green label			
❏ WS1767	Greatest Hits	1968	$15
— With "W7" logo on green label			
❏ WS1767 [B]	Greatest Hits	197?	$10
— Any later pressing (LP in print until the late 1980s)			
❏ ST-91586	Greatest Hits	1968	$25
— Capitol Record Club edition			
❏ W1696 [M]	Insight Out	1967	$18
❏ WS1696 [S]	Insight Out	1967	$25
— Gold label			
❏ WS1696 [S]	Insight Out	1968	$15
— With "W7" logo on green label			
❏ ST-91317 [S]	Insight Out	1967	$30
— Capitol Record Club edition			
❏ WS1704	Renaissance	1967	$15
❏ WS1927	Stop Your Motor	1971	$15
❏ 2WS1868	The Association "Live	1970	$18
❏ STBO-93249	The Association "Live	1970	$25
— Capitol Record Club edition			
❏ WS1800	The Association	1969	$15
— With "W7" logo on green label			

ASTAIRE, FRED

Number	Title	Yr	NM
CHOREO			
❏ A-1 [M]	Three Evenings with Fred Astaire	1961	$40
CLEF			
❏ MGC-662 [M]	The Fred Astaire Story, Volume 1	1955	$300
— Reissue of Mercury 1001			
❏ MGC-663 [M]	The Fred Astaire Story, Volume 2	1955	$300
— Reissue of Mercury 1002			
❏ MGC-664 [M]	The Fred Astaire Story, Volume 3	1955	$300
— Reissue of Mercury 1003			
❏ MGC-665 [M]	The Fred Astaire Story, Volume 4	1955	$300
— Reissue of Mercury 1004			
DRG			
❏ DARC-3-1102	The Astaire Story	197?	$75
EPIC			
❏ LN3103 [M]	Nothing Thrilled Us Half As Much	1955	$250
❏ FLM13103 [M]	Nothing Thrilled Us Half As Much	196?	$150
— Reissue of 3103			
❏ FLS15103 [R]	Nothing Thrilled Us Half As Much	196?	$85
❏ LN3137 [M]	The Best of Fred Astaire	1955	$250
KAPP			
❏ KL-1165 [M]	Fred Astaire Now	1959	$75
❏ KS-3165 [S]	Fred Astaire Now	1959	$75
MCA			
❏ 1552	Fred Astaire Sings	198?	$30
MERCURY			
❏ MGC-1001/4 [M]	The Fred Astaire Story	1953	$1000
— Spiral-bound four-record set, pressed on blue vinyl, autographed by Fred Astaire			
❏ MGC-1001 [M]	The Fred Astaire Story, Volume 1	1954	$600
❏ MGC-1002 [M]	The Fred Astaire Story, Volume 2	1954	$300
❏ MGC-1003 [M]	The Fred Astaire Story, Volume 3	1954	$300
❏ MGC-1004 [M]	The Fred Astaire Story, Volume 4	1954	$300
VERVE			
❏ MGV-2114 [M]	Easy to Dance With	1958	$175
❏ MGV-2010 [M]	Mr. Top Hat	1956	$250
VOCALION			
❏ VL3716 [M]	Fred Astaire	1964	$35

ASTLEY, JON

Number	Title	Yr	NM
ATLANTIC			
❏ 81740	Everyone Loves the Pilot (Except the Crew)	1987	$10
❏ 81882	The Compleat Angler	1988	$10

ASTLEY, RICK

Number	Title	Yr	NM
RCA			
❏ 8589-1-R	Hold Me in Your Arms	1989	$10
❏ 6822-1-R	Whenever You Need Somebody	1988	$10

Number	Title	Yr	NM

ASTRONAUTS, THE (1)
RCA VICTOR

Number	Title	Yr	NM
❑ LPM-2858 [M]	Competition Coupe	1964	$75
❑ LSP-2858 [S]	Competition Coupe	1964	$100
❑ LPM-3454 [M]	Down the Line	1966	$30
❑ LSP-3454 [S]	Down the Line	1966	$40
❑ LPM-2782 [M]	Everything Is A-OK!	1964	$50
❑ LSP-2782 [S]	Everything Is A-OK!	1964	$75
❑ LPM-3359 [M]	Favorites for You from Us	1965	$30
❑ LSP-3359 [S]	Favorites for You from Us	1965	$40
❑ PRM-183 [M]	Rockin' with the Astronauts	1965	$30
—Promo only			
❑ LPM-2760 [M]	Surfin' with the Astronauts	1963	$75
❑ LSP-2760 [S]	Surfin' with the Astronauts	1963	$100
❑ LPM-3307 [M]	The Astronauts Go, Go, Go	1965	$30
❑ LSP-3307 [S]	The Astronauts Go, Go, Go	1965	$40
❑ LPM-2903 [M]	The Astronauts Orbit Kampus	1964	$40
❑ LSP-2903 [S]	The Astronauts Orbit Kampus	1964	$50
❑ LPM-3733 [M]	Travelin' Men	1967	$50
❑ LSP-3733 [S]	Travelin' Men	1967	$30

ASTRONAUTS, THE (1) / THE LIVERPOOL FIVE
RCA VICTOR

Number	Title	Yr	NM
❑ PRS-251 [S]	Stereo Festival	1967	$175
—Special-prodcuts edition			

ASWAD
MANGO

Number	Title	Yr	NM
❑ MLPS9399	Aswad	1976	$12
❑ MLPS9833	Crucial Tracks (The Best of Aswad)	1989	$12
❑ MLPS9810	Distant Thunder	1988	$12
❑ MLPS9723	Live & Direct	1983	$12
❑ MLPS9711	New Chapter of Dub	1982	$12
❑ MLPS9780	Rebel Souls	1984	$12
❑ 539867-1	Showcase	1990	$12
—Originally issued in 1981			
❑ 539883-1	Too Wicked	1990	$12
❑ 539866-1	To the Top	1990	$12
—Originally issued in 1986			

ASYLUM CHOIR
LEON RUSSELL and MARC BENNO.
MCA

Number	Title	Yr	NM
❑ 684	Asylum Choir II	1979	$10
—Reissue of Shelter 52010			

SHELTER

Number	Title	Yr	NM
❑ SW-8910	Asylum Choir II	1971	$18
❑ 52010	Asylum Choir II	1977	$12
—Reissue of 2120			
❑ SR2120	Asylum Choir II	1974	$15
—Reissue of 8910			

SMASH

Number	Title	Yr	NM
❑ SRS-67107 [B]	Look Inside the Asylum Choir	1968	$50
—Front cover has a roll of toilet paper			
❑ SRS-67107	Look Inside the Asylum Choir	197?	$18
—Front cover has a photo of Leon and Marc			

AT THE DRIVE-IN
FEARLESS

Number	Title	Yr	NM
❑ F 034	In/Casino/Out	1998	$10
❑ F 040 [10]	Vaya	1999	$12
—Seven-song EP			

VIRGIN/GRAND ROYAL

Number	Title	Yr	NM
❑ 49999	Relationship of Command	2000	$12

ATCHER, BOB
COLUMBIA

Number	Title	Yr	NM
❑ HL9006 [10]	Early American Folk Songs	1949	$100
❑ HL9013 [10]	Songs of the Saddle	1949	$100
❑ CL2232 [M]	The Dean of Cowboy Singers	1964	$30
❑ CS9032 [R]	The Dean of Cowboy Singers	1964	$18

HARMONY

Number	Title	Yr	NM
❑ HL7313 [M]	Bob Atcher's Best	1964	$25

ATENSION
ISLAND

Number	Title	Yr	NM
❑ 91053	D.O.A. (Def On Arrival)	1989	$12

ATKINS, CHET, AND DOC WATSON
RCA VICTOR

Number	Title	Yr	NM
❑ AHL1-3701	Reflections	1980	$12

ATKINS, CHET, AND LES PAUL
RCA VICTOR

Number	Title	Yr	NM
❑ APL1-1167	Chester and Lester	1976	$15
❑ AYL1-3682	Chester and Lester	1980	$10
—Best Buy Series" reissue			
❑ APL1-2786	Guitar Monsters	1978	$15

ATKINS, CHET
COLUMBIA

Number	Title	Yr	NM
❑ FC44323	Chet Atkins, C.G.P.	1989	$10
❑ PC39003	East Tennessee Christmas	1983	$12
❑ FC40593	Sails	1987	$10
❑ FC39591	Stay Tuned	1985	$12
❑ FC40256	Street Dreams	1986	$10
❑ FC38536	Work It Out with Chet Atkins C.G.P.	1983	$12
❑ PC38536	Work It Out with Chet Atkins C.G.P.	1985	$10
—Budget-line reissue			

DOLTON

Number	Title	Yr	NM
❑ BLP-16506 [M]	Play Guitar with Chet Atkins	1967	$75
❑ BST-17506 [S]	Play Guitar with Chet Atkins	1967	$30

PAIR

Number	Title	Yr	NM
❑ PDL2-1115	Guitar for All Seasons	1986	$15
❑ PDL2-1047	Tennessee Guitar Man	1985	$15

RCA CAMDEN

Number	Title	Yr	NM
❑ CAL-2182 [M]	Chet	1967	$15
❑ CAS-2182 [S]	Chet	1967	$18
❑ CAL-659 [M]	Chet Atkins and His Guitar	196?	$18
❑ CAS-659(e) [R]	Chet Atkins and His Guitar	1964	$15
❑ CAS-2523	Chet 'n Boots	1972	$15
❑ CAS-2600	Finger Pickin' Good	1973	$12
❑ CAL-753 [M]	Guitar Genius	196?	$18
❑ CAS-753(e) [R]	Guitar Genius	196?	$15
❑ ACL1-7042	Love Letters	197?	$12
❑ CAL-981 [M]	Music from Nashville, My Home Town	1966	$15
❑ CAS-981 [S]	Music from Nashville, My Home Town	1966	$18
❑ CAS-2555	Nashville Gold	1972	$15
❑ CAS-2296	Relaxin' with Chet	1969	$15

RCA RED SEAL

Number	Title	Yr	NM
❑ LSC-3104	Chet Picks On the Pops	1969	$18
—With the Boston Pops Orchestra, Arthur Fiedler, conductor			
❑ LM-2870 [M]	The "Pops" Goes Country	1966	$18
❑ LSC-2870 [S]	The "Pops" Goes Country	1966	$25
—Above two with the Boston Pops Orchestra, Arthur Fiedler, conductor			

RCA VICTOR

Number	Title	Yr	NM
❑ CPL1-2503	A Legendary Performer	1977	$15
❑ APL1-0159	Alone	1973	$15
❑ LPM-1090 [M]	A Session with Chet Atkins	1954	$75
—Red cover			
❑ LPM-1090 [M]	A Session with Chet Atkins	1961	$25
—Woman and guitars cover			
❑ LSP-1090(e) [R]	A Session with Chet Atkins	1967	$12
❑ LPM-2601 [M]	Back Home Hymns	1962	$25
❑ LSP-2601 [S]	Back Home Hymns	1962	$30
❑ LPM-2549 [M]	Caribbean Guitar	1962	$25
❑ LSP-2549 [S]	Caribbean Guitar	1962	$30
❑ APL1-0645	Chat Atkins Goes to the Movies	1973	$15
❑ LPM-1544 [M]	Chet Atkins at Home	1957	$50
—Title in block letters on cover			
❑ LPM-1544 [M]	Chet Atkins at Home	1961	$25
—Title in script on cover			
❑ LSP-1544(e) [R]	Chet Atkins at Home	1967	$12
❑ LPM-3079 [10]	Chet Atkins' Gallopin' Guitar	1952	$175
❑ LPM-1993 [M]	Chet Atkins in Hollywood	1959	$30
—Night-time cover			
❑ LPM-1993 [M]	Chet Atkins in Hollywood	1961	$25
—Daylight "blonde" cover			
❑ LSP-1993 [S]	Chet Atkins in Hollywood	1959	$50
—Night-time cover			
❑ LSP-1993 [S]	Chet Atkins in Hollywood	1961	$30
—Daylight "blonde" cover			
❑ LPM-1197 [M]	Chet Atkins in Three Dimensions	1956	$50
—Black-and-white guitar cover			
❑ LPM-1197 [M]	Chet Atkins in Three Dimensions	1961	$25
—Red guitar cover			
❑ LSP-1197(e) [R]	Chet Atkins in Three Dimensions	1967	$12
❑ APL1-0545	Chet Atkins Picks On Jerry Reed	1974	$15
❑ LPM-3531 [M]	Chet Atkins Picks On the Beatles	1966	$30
❑ LSP-3531 [S]	Chet Atkins Picks On the Beatles	1966	$30
❑ LPM-3818 [M]	Chet Atkins Picks the Best	1967	$30
❑ LSP-3818 [S]	Chet Atkins Picks the Best	1967	$15
❑ ANL1-0981	Chet Atkins Picks the Best	1975	$12
❑ LSP-4754	Chet Atkins Picks the Hits	1973	$18
❑ LPM-2232 [M]	Chet Atkins' Workshop	1961	$25
❑ LSP-2232 [S]	Chet Atkins' Workshop	1961	$30
❑ LPM-2423 [M]	Christmas with Chet Atkins	1961	$25
❑ LSP-2423 [S]	Christmas with Chet Atkins	1961	$30
❑ ANL1-1935	Christmas with Chet Atkins	1976	$10
—Reissue of LSP-2423			
❑ LPM-3885 [M]	Class Guitar	1967	$30
❑ LSP-3885 [S]	Class Guitar	1967	$15
❑ AHL1-5495	Collector's Series	1985	$12
❑ LPM-2450 [M]	Down Home	1962	$25
❑ LSP-2450 [S]	Down Home	1962	$30
❑ LPM-1383 [M]	Finger Style Guitar	1956	$50
—Chet's face not visible on cover			
❑ LPM-1383 [M]	Finger Style Guitar	1961	$25
—Chet's face visible on cover			

Number	Title	Yr	NM
❑ LSP-1383(e) [R]	Finger Style Guitar	1962	$15
❑ LSP-4464	For the Good Times	1971	$18
❑ LPM-3647 [M]	From Nashville with Love	1966	$15
❑ LSP-3647 [S]	From Nashville with Love	1966	$18
❑ AHL1-4724	Great Hits of the Past	1983	$12
❑ LPM-2783 [M]	Guitar Country	1964	$18
❑ LSP-2783 [S]	Guitar Country	1964	$25
❑ LPM-1577 [M]	Hi-Fi in Focus	1957	$50
—No guitars on cover			

Number	Title	Yr	NM
❑ LPM-1577 [M]	Hi-Fi in Focus	1957	$25
—Guitar on cover			
❑ LSP-1577(e) [R]	Hi-Fi in Focus	196?	$12
❑ LPM-4017 [M]	Hometown Guitar	1968	$100
❑ LSP-4017 [S]	Hometown Guitar	1968	$18
❑ LPM-2025 [M]	Hum & Strum Along	1959	$30
—Add $10 NM if instruction book is included			
❑ LSP-2025 [S]	Hum & Strum Along	1959	$40
—Add $10 NM if instruction book is included			
❑ LPM-3728 [M]	It's a Guitar World	1967	$30
❑ LSP-3728 [S]	It's a Guitar World	1967	$15
❑ LSP-4135	Lover's Guitar	1968	$18
❑ LSP-4396	Me & Jerry	1971	$18
—With Jerry Reed			
❑ LPM-2103 [M]	Mister Guitar	1959	$30
—Lone guitar on cover			
❑ LPM-2103 [M]	Mister Guitar	1961	$25
—Guitar and woman on cover			
❑ LSP-2103 [S]	Mister Guitar	1959	$50
—Lone guitar on cover			
❑ LSP-2103 [S]	Mister Guitar	1961	$30
—Guitar and woman on cover			
❑ LPM-3429 [M]	More of That "Guitar Country	1965	$18
❑ LSP-3429 [S]	More of That "Guitar Country	1965	$25
❑ LPM-3316 [M]	My Favorite Guitars	1965	$18
❑ LSP-3316 [S]	My Favorite Guitars	1965	$25
❑ AHL1-2405	My Guitar	1977	$15
❑ VPXS-6079	Now & Then	1972	$18
❑ LPM-2616 [M]	Our Man in Nashville	1963	$25
❑ LSP-2616 [S]	Our Man in Nashville	1963	$30
❑ LPM-2908 [M]	Progressive Pickin'	1964	$18
❑ LSP-2908 [S]	Progressive Pickin'	1964	$25
❑ LSP-4061	Solid Gold '68	1968	$18
❑ LSP-4244	Solid Gold '69	1969	$15
❑ LPM-3992 [M]	Solo Flights	1968	$50
❑ LSP-3992 [S]	Solo Flights	1968	$15
❑ AHL1-4044	Still Country — After All These Years	1981	$12
❑ LPM-3169 [10]	Stringin' Along with Chet Atkins	1953	$150
❑ LPM-1236 [M]	Stringin' Along with Chet Atkins	1956	$50
—Orange cover			
❑ LPM-1236 [M]	Stringin' Along with Chet Atkins	1961	$25
—Full-color cover			
❑ LSP-1236(e) [R]	Stringin' Along with Chet Atkins	1967	$12
❑ APL1-0329	Superpickers	1974	$15
❑ APD1-0329 [Q]	Superpickers	1974	$30
❑ LPM-2719 [M]	Teen Scene	1963	$25
❑ LSP-2719 [S]	Teen Scene	1963	$30
❑ LPM-2161 [M]	Teensville	1960	$30
—Title overlaps cover photo			
❑ LPM-2161 [M]	Teensville	1961	$25
—Title in black strip at top of cover photo			
❑ LSP-2161 [S]	Teensville	1960	$50
—Title overlaps cover photo			
❑ LSP-2161 [S]	Teensville	1961	$30
—Title in black strip at top of cover photo			
❑ LPM-2887 [M]	The Best of Chet Atkins	1964	$18
❑ LSP-2887 [S]	The Best of Chet Atkins	1964	$25
❑ APL1-1985	The Best of Chet Atkins	1975	$15
❑ LPM-3558 [M]	The Best of Chet Atkins, Volume 2	1966	$15
❑ LSP-3558 [S]	The Best of Chet Atkins, Volume 2	1966	$18
❑ AHL1-3505	The Best of Chet On The Road…Live	1980	$15

Number	Title	Yr	NM
❏ AHL1-3302	The First Nashville Guitar Quartet	1979	$15
❏ AYL1-3741	The First Nashville Guitar Quartet	1981	$10
—Best Buy Series" reissue			
❏ LPM-2346 [M]	The Most Popular Guitar	1961	$25
❏ LSP-2346 [S]	The Most Popular Guitar	1961	$30
❏ APL1-1233	The Night Atlanta Burned	1975	$15
❏ LPM-2175 [M]	The Other Chet Atkins	1960	$25
❏ LSP-2175 [S]	The Other Chet Atkins	1960	$30
❏ VPS-6030	This Is Chet Atkins	1972	$18
❏ LPM-2678 [M]	Travelin'	1963	$25
❏ LSP-2678 [S]	Travelin'	1963	$30
❏ LSP-4331	Yestergroovin'	1970	$15
TIME-LIFE			
❏ STW-117	Country Music	1981	$15

ATKINS
WARNER BROS.
| ❏ BSK3659 | Atkins | 1982 | $12 |

ATLANTA
MCA
| ❏ 5576 | Atlanta | 1985 | $10 |
| ❏ 5463 | Pictures | 1984 | $10 |

ATLANTA DISCO BAND, THE
ARIOLA AMERICA
| ❏ SW-50004 | Bad Luck | 1975 | $12 |

ATLANTA RHYTHM SECTION
COLUMBIA
❏ FC37550 [B]	Quinella	1981	$12
❏ PC37550	Quinella	1982	$10
—Budget-line reissue			
DECCA
| ❏ DL75265 | Atlanta Rhythm Section | 1972 | $30 |
| ❏ DL75390 | Back Up Against the Wall | 1973 | $30 |
MCA
| ❏ 2-4114 | Atlanta Rhythm Section | 1977 | $15 |
| —Combines the two Decca LPs into one package | | | |
MOBILE FIDELITY
| ❏ Jan-0038 | Champagne Jam | 1981 | $40 |
| —Audiophile vinyl | | | |
POLYDOR
| ❏ PD-2-6236 | Are You Ready! | 1979 | $15 |
| ❏ PD-1-6080 | A Rock and Roll Alternative | 1977 | $12 |

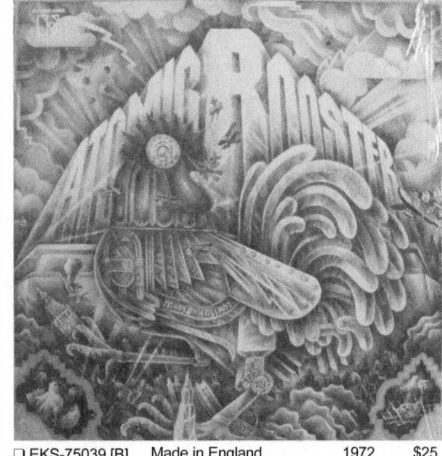

CHAMPAGNE JAM • ATLANTA RHYTHM SECTION Polydor

❏ PD-1-6134 [B]	Champagne Jam	1978	$12
❏ PD6041	Dog Days	1975	$12
❏ PD-1-6060	Red Tape	1976	$12
❏ PD-1-6285	The Boys from Doraville	1980	$12
❏ PD6027	Third Annual Pipe Dream	1974	$12
❏ PD-1-6200	Underdog	1979	$12

ATLANTIC STARR
A&M
❏ SP-5019	As the Band Turns	1985	$10
❏ SP-4711	Atlantic Starr	1978	$12
❏ SP-3166	Atlantic Starr	198?	$10
—Budget-line reissue of 4711			
❏ SP-4883	Brilliance	1982	$10
❏ SP-4833	Radiant	1981	$10
❏ SP-5141	Secret Lovers: The Best of Atlantic Starr	1986	$10
❏ SP-4764	Straight to the Point	1979	$12
❏ SP-3167	Straight to the Point	198?	$10
—Budget-line reissue of 4764			
❏ SP-4948	Yours Forever	1983	$10
WARNER BROS.
| ❏ 25660 | All in the Name of Love | 1987 | $10 |
| ❏ 25849 | We're Movin' Up | 1989 | $12 |

Number	Title	Yr	NM

ATOMIC ROOSTER
CLEOPATRA
| ❏ CLP1772 [B] | Death Walks Behind You | 2014 | $30 |
ELEKTRA
❏ EKS-75074	Atomic Rooster IV	1973	$18
❏ EKS-74094	Death Walks Behind You	1971	$25
❏ EKS-74109	In Hearing Of Atomic Rooster	1971	$25

| ❏ EKS-75039 [B] | Made in England | 1972 | $25 |

ATTILA
BACK-TRAC
| ❏ P18808 | Attila | 1985 | $12 |
EPIC
| ❏ E30030 [B] | Attila | 1970 | $40 |

ATTITUDE
ATLANTIC
| ❏ 80096 | Pump the Nation | 1983 | $15 |

ATTITUDES
DARK HORSE
| ❏ SP-22008 | Attitudes | 1976 | $15 |
| ❏ DH3021 | Good News | 1977 | $12 |

AU GO-GO SINGERS, THE
With Stephen Stills and Richie Furay, later of BUFFALO SPRINGFIELD.
ROULETTE
| ❏ R25280 [M] | They Call Us the Au Go-Go Singers | 1964 | $50 |

| ❏ SR25280 [S] | They Call Us the Au Go-Go Singers | 1964 | $80 |

AUDIENCE
ELEKTRA
| ❏ EKS-74100 [B] | House on the Hill | 1971 | $35 |
| ❏ EKS-75026 [B] | Lunch | 1972 | $35 |

AUDIO TWO
FIRST PRIORITY
| ❏ 91358 | I Don't Care -- The Album | 1990 | $100 |
| ❏ 90907 | What More Can I Say? | 1988 | $100 |

AUGER, BRIAN, TRINITY
ATCO
| ❏ SD 33-273 | Definitely What! | 1969 | $15 |

Number	Title	Yr	NM

HEADFIRST			
❏ 9702	Search Party	1981	$18
POLYDOR			
❏ PD-1-6505	Genesis	1975	$15
RCA VICTOR			
❏ LSP-4540	A Better Land	1971	$12
❏ LSP-4372	Befour	1970	$12
❏ LSP-4462	Brian Auger's Oblivion Express	1971	$12
—Starting here, group is "Oblivion Express"			
❏ AFL1-4462	Brian Auger's Oblivion Express	197?	$10
—Reissue			
❏ APL1-0140	Closer To It	1973	$12
❏ AFL1-0140	Closer To It	197?	$10
—Reissue			
❏ CPL1-0645	Live Oblivion	1974	$12
❏ ANL1-2481	Live Oblivion	1977	$10
—Reissue			
❏ CPL2-1230	Live Oblivion, Vol. 2	1976	$18
❏ APL1-1210	Reinforcements	1975	$12
❏ LSP-4703	Second Wind	1972	$12
❏ AFL1-4703	Second Wind	197?	$10
—Reissue			
❏ CPL1-0454	Straight Ahead	1974	$12
❏ AFL1-0454	Straight Ahead	197?	$10
—Reissue			
❏ AFL1-2249	The Best of Brian Auger	1977	$12
SPRINGBOARD			
❏ SPB-4044	Brian Auger	1973	$10
—Reissue of early material			
WARNER BROS.			
❏ BS2981	Happiness Heartaches	1977	$12

AUGER, BRIAN AND JULIE TIPPETTS
WARNER BROS.
| ❏ BSK3153 [B] | Encore | 1978 | $15 |

AUGUST, JAN
MERCURY
❏ SR60618 [S]	Accent!	1961	$25
❏ MG20618 [M]	Accent!	1961	$18
❏ SR60082 [S]	Cha Cha Charm	1959	$25
❏ MG20408 [M]	Cha Cha Charm	1959	$18
❏ MG20160 [M]	Christmas Favorites	1955	$30
❏ MG20272 [M]	Cocktails and Conversation	195?	$25
❏ MG20744 [M]	Jan August Plays a Collection of 27 Popular Classical Melodies	196?	$18
❏ SR60744 [S]	Jan August Plays a Collection of 27 Popular Classical Melodies	196?	$25
❏ MG20513 [M]	Jan August Plays Great Piano Hits	195?	$18
❏ SR60189 [S]	Jan August Plays Great Piano Hits	195?	$25
❏ MG20072 [M]	Jan August Plays Songs to Remember	1955	$30
❏ MG20667 [M]	Jan August Styles the Great International Hits	196?	$18
❏ SR60667 [S]	Jan August Styles the Great International Hits	196?	$25
❏ MG20659 [M]	Jan August Styles the Great Pop Piano Classics	196?	$18
❏ SR60659 [S]	Jan August Styles the Great Pop Piano Classics	196?	$25
❏ MG20273 [M]	Keyboard Waltzes	195?	$25
❏ MG20274 [M]	Latin Rhythms	195?	$25
❏ MG20078 [M]	Music for the Quiet Hour	1955	$30
❏ MG25087 [10]	Piano Favorites	195?	$30
❏ MG25136 [10]	Piano Poetry	195?	$30
❏ MG20147 [M]	Piano Roll Blues	1955	$30
WING			
❏ MGW12175 [M]	Christmas Favorites	196?	$15
❏ MGW12129 [M]	Music for the Quiet Hour	196?	$15
❏ SRW16129 [R]	Music for the Quiet Hour	196?	$12
❏ MGW12254 [M]	The Piano Wizardry of Jan August	196?	$15
❏ SRW16254 [R]	The Piano Wizardry of Jan August	196?	$12

AUGUST SONS
EYES IN THE WOODS
| ❏ (# unknown) [EP] | I Am Not a Vampire | 1989 | $40 |

AULD, GEORGIE
ABC-PARAMOUNT
| ❏ ABC-287 [M] | Georgie Auld Plays for Melancholy Babies | 1958 | $40 |
| ❏ ABCS-287 [S] | Georgie Auld Plays for Melancholy Babies | 1959 | $30 |
ALLEGRO
| ❏ 3102 [M] | Jazz Concert | 1953 | $40 |
APOLLO
| ❏ LAP-102 [10] | Concert in Jazz | 1951 | $100 |
CORAL
❏ CRL57029 [M]	Lullaby of Broadway	1956	$40
❏ CRL56085 [10]	Manhattan	1953	$100
❏ CRL57032 [M]	Misty	1956	$40
❏ CRL56060 [10]	Tenderly	1952	$100

Number	Title	Yr	NM

DISCOVERY
❏ DL3007 [10]	That's Auld	1950	$300

EMARCY
| ❏ MG-36090 [M] | Dancing in the Land of Hi-Fi | 1956 | $250 |
| ❏ MG-36060 [M] | In the Land of Hi-Fi | 1955 | $40 |

JARO
| ❏ JAM-5003 [M] | Hawaii on the Rocks | 1959 | $30 |

MUSICRAFT
| ❏ 501 | Georgie Auld and His Orchestra, Vol. 1 | 197? | $25 |
| ❏ 509 | Georgie Auld and His Orchestra, Vol. 2 | 197? | $25 |

PHILIPS
❏ PHM200096 [M]	Georgie Auld Plays to the Winners	1963	$35
❏ PHS600096 [S]	Georgie Auld Plays to the Winners	1963	$25
❏ PHM200116 [M]	Here's to the Losers	1963	$35
❏ PHS600116 [S]	Here's to the Losers	1963	$25

ROOST
| ❏ RST-403 [10] | Georgie Auld Quintet | 1951 | $100 |

TOP RANK
| ❏ RM-333 [M] | Good Enough to Keep | 1960 | $40 |
| ❏ RM-306 [M] | The Melody Lingers On | 1959 | $40 |

UNITED ARTISTS
| ❏ UAL-3068 [M] | Manhattan with Strings | 1959 | $40 |
| ❏ UAS-6068 [S] | Manhattan with Strings | 1959 | $30 |

XANADU
| ❏ 190 | Homage | 197? | $25 |

AUM
FILLMORE
| ❏ Z30002 [B] | Resurrection | 1970 | $40 |

SIRE

| ❏ SES-97007 [B] | Bluesvibes | 1969 | $50 |

AURRA
DREAM
| ❏ DA-3503 | Aurra | 1980 | $18 |

SALSOUL
❏ SA-8551	A Little Love	1982	$15
❏ SA-8559	Live and Let Live	1983	$15
❏ SA-8538	Send Your Love	1981	$15

AUSTIN, BOBBY
CAPITOL
❏ T2773 [M]	Apartment No. 9	1967	$30
❏ ST2773 [S]	Apartment No. 9	1967	$25
❏ ST2915	Old Love Never Dies	1968	$25

AUSTIN, CLAIRE
CONTEMPORARY
| ❏ C-5002 [M] | When Your Lover Has Gone | 1956 | $250 |

FANTASY
| ❏ OJC-1711 | When Your Lover Has Gone | 198? | $30 |
| —Reissue of Contemporary 5002 | | | |

GHB
| ❏ S-22 | Claire Austin and the Great Excelsior Band | 197? | $35 |

GOOD TIME JAZZ
| ❏ L-24 [10] | Claire Austin Sings the Blues | 1954 | $120 |

JAZZOLOGY
| ❏ 52 | Goin' Crazy | 197? | $35 |

AUSTIN, DONALD
EASTBOUND
| ❏ EB-9005 | Crazy Legs | 1973 | $30 |

AUSTIN, GENE
DECCA
| ❏ DL8433 [M] | My Blue Heaven | 1957 | $40 |

DOT
| ❏ DLP3300 [M] | Great Hits | 1960 | $25 |
| ❏ DLP25300 [S] | Great Hits | 1960 | $30 |

FRATERNITY
| ❏ F-1006 [M] | Gene Austin and His Lonesome Road | 1957 | $25 |

RCA VICTOR
❏ LPM-3200 [10]	My Blue Heaven	1953	$75
❏ LPM-2490 [M]	My Blue Heaven	1961	$30
❏ LPM-1549 [M]	Restless Heart	1957	$40
❏ VPM-6065	This Is Gene Austin	1972	$25

X
| ❏ LVA-1007 [M] | Gene Austin Sings All-Time Favorites | 1954 | $40 |

AUSTIN, PATTI
CTI
❏ JZ36503	Body Language	1980	$12
❏ PZ36503	Body Language	198?	$10
—Budget-line reissue			
❏ 5001	End of a Rainbow	1976	$12
❏ 5006	Havana Candy	1977	$12
❏ 7086	Live at the Bottom Line	1979	$12

GRP
| ❏ GR-9603 | Love Is Gonna Getcha | 1990 | $12 |

QWEST
❏ QWS3591	Every Home Should Have One	1981	$10
❏ 25276	Gettin' Away with Murder	1985	$10
❏ 23974	Patti Austin	1984	$10
❏ 25698	The Real Me	1988	$10

AUSTIN, SIL
MERCURY
❏ MG-20320 [M]	Everything's Shakin'	1958	$80
❏ SR-60755 [S]	Folk Songs	1963	$25
❏ MG-20755 [M]	Folk Songs	1963	$18
❏ MG-20663 [M]	Golden Saxophone Hits	1961	$30
❏ SR-60663 [S]	Golden Saxophone Hits	1961	$30
❏ MG-20424 [M]	Sil Austin Plays Pretty for the People	1959	$40
❏ SR-60096 [S]	Sil Austin Plays Pretty for the People	1959	$75
—Black label			
❏ SR-60096 [S]	Sil Austin Plays Pretty for the People	1965	$30
—Red label, white "MERCURY" at top			
❏ SR-60096 [S]	Sil Austin Plays Pretty for the People	1974	$12
—Chicago styline" label			
❏ MG-21126 [M]	Sil Austin Plays Pretty for the People Again	1967	$25
❏ SR-61126 [S]	Sil Austin Plays Pretty for the People Again	1967	$30
❏ MG-20925 [M]	Sil Austin Plays Pretty Melodies of the World	1964	$25
❏ SR-60925 [S]	Sil Austin Plays Pretty Melodies of the World	1964	$30
❏ MG-20237 [M]	Slow Walk Rock	1957	$80
❏ MG-20576 [M]	Soft, Plaintive and Moody	1960	$40
❏ SR-60236 [S]	Soft, Plaintive and Moody	1960	$75

SSS INTERNATIONAL
❏ 4 [B]	Honey Sax	1969	$25
❏ 14	Sil and Silver Screen	1971	$18
❏ 8	Soft Soul with Strings	1970	$18
❏ 23	Songs of Gold	1971	$18

WING
| ❏ SRW-16227 [S] | Everything's Shakin' | 196? | $18 |
| ❏ SRW-16369 [S] | Sil Austin Again Plays Pretty for the People | 196? | $18 |

AUSTRALIAN ALL STARS, THE
BETHLEHEM
| ❏ BCP-6070 [M] | Jazz for Beach-Niks | 1963 | $250 |
| ❏ BCP-6073 [M] | Jazz for Surf-Niks | 1963 | $250 |

AUSTRALIAN JAZZ QUARTET, THE
BETHLEHEM
❏ BCP-1031 [10]	The Australian Jazz Quartet	195?	$75
❏ BCP-6003 [M]	The Australian Jazz Quartet	1955	$300
❏ BCP-6002	The Australian Jazz Quartet	197?	$35
—Reissue distributed by RCA Victor			
❏ BCP-6012 [M]	The Australian Jazz Quartet at the Varsity Drag	1956	$250
❏ BCP-6029 [M]	The Australian Jazz Quartet In Free Style	1959	$250
❏ BCP-6022 [M]	The Australian Jazz Quartet Plays the Best of Broadway Musical Hits	1957	$300
❏ BCP-6015 [M]	The Australian Jazz Quartet Plus One	1957	$300
❏ BCP-6002 [M]	The Australian Jazz Quartet/ Quintet	1955	$300
❏ BCP-6030 [M]	Three Penny Opera	1959	$250

AUTOGRAPH
RCA
| ❏ 5796-1-R | Loud and Clear | 1987 | $10 |

RCA VICTOR

AUTOGRAPH

| ❏ AFL1-5423 [B] | Sign In Please | 1984 | $10 |
| ❏ AFL1-7009 | That's the Stuff | 1985 | $10 |

AUTOMATIC MAN
ISLAND
| ❏ ILPS9397 | Automatic Man | 1976 | $12 |
| ❏ ILPS9429 | Visitors | 1977 | $12 |

AUTOSALVAGE
RCA VICTOR
| ❏ LPM-3940 [M] | Autosalvage | 1968 | $300 |
| ❏ LSP-3940 [S] | Autosalvage | 1968 | $150 |

AUTRY, GENE
CBS SPECIAL PRODUCTS
❏ P18964	Famous Favorites	1985	$12
❏ P18737	Golden Hits	1985	$12
❏ P18963	His Golden Hits	1985	$12

CHALLENGE
| ❏ CHL-600 [M] | Christmas with Gene Autry | 1958 | $50 |

COLUMBIA
❏ JL8012 [10]	Champion	1950	$175
❏ CL(# unk) [10]	Easter Favorites	1949	$175
❏ CL2568 [10]	Easter Favorites	1955	$120
—House Party Series" issue			
❏ CL677 [M]	Gene Autry and Champion -- Western Adventures	1955	$120
❏ JL8001 [10]	Gene Autry at the Rodeo	1949	$175
❏ CS1035	Gene Autry's Country Music Hall of Fame Album	1970	$18
❏ CL1575 [M]	Gene Autry's Greatest Hits	1961	$30
—Red and black label with six "eye" logos			
❏ CL6020 [10]	Gene Autry's Western Classics	1949	$175
❏ HL9001 [10]	Gene Autry's Western Classics, Volume 1	1949	$175
❏ HL9002 [10]	Gene Autry's Western Classics, Volume 2	1949	$175
❏ CL6137 [10]	Merry Christmas	1950	$175
❏ CL2547 [10]	Merry Christmas with Gene Autry	1954	$120
—House Party Series" release			
❏ JL8009 [10]	Stampede	1949	$175

COLUMBIA SPECIAL PRODUCTS
| ❏ P15766 | Christmas Favorites | 1981 | $15 |
| ❏ P15767 | Everyone's a Child at Christmas | 1981 | $15 |

GRAND PRIX
| ❏ KX-11 [M] | The Original Gene Autry Sings Rudolph the Red-Nosed Reindeer and Other Christmas Favorites | 1961 | $18 |
| ❏ KS-X11 [S] | The Original Gene Autry Sings Rudolph the Red-Nosed Reindeer and Other Christmas Favorites | 1961 | $25 |

GUSTO
| ❏ 1038 | Christmas Classics | 1978 | $12 |

HARMONY
❏ HL7376 [M]	Back in the Saddle Again	1966	$25
❏ HS11276 [R]	Back in the Saddle Again	1966	$18
❏ HL9505 [M]	Gene Autry and Champion -- Western Adventures	1959	$30
❏ HL7332 [M]	Gene Autry's Great Western Hits	1965	$30
❏ HL7399 [M]	Gene Autry Sings	1966	$25
❏ HS11199 [R]	Gene Autry Sings	1966	$18
❏ HL9550 [M]	The Original Rudolph the Red-Nosed Reindeer and Other Children's Christmas Favorites	1964	$30

Number	Title	Yr	NM
❑ HS14450 [R]	The Original Rudolph the Red-Nosed Reindeer and Other Children's Christmas Favorites	1964	$15
MELODY RANCH			
❑ 101 [M]	Melody Ranch	1965	$40
MURRAY HILL			
❑ 897296	Melody Ranch Radio Show	197?	$75
— Compilation of some of Gene's radio shows in a box set			
RCA VICTOR			
❑ LPM-2623 [M]	Gene Autry's Golden Hits	1962	$30
❑ LSP-2623 [S]	Gene Autry's Golden Hits	1962	$40
REPUBLIC			
❑ RLP6018 [M]	Christmas with Gene Autry	1976	$15
❑ 6012	Cowboy Hall of Fame	1976	$25
❑ 6011	South of the Border, All American Cowboy	1976	$25

AVALANCHE (1)
ABC

Number	Title	Yr	NM
❑ AB-1000	Avalanche	1976	$18

AVALANCHES, THE
WARNER BROS.

Number	Title	Yr	NM
❑ W1525 [M]	Ski Surfin'	1963	$40
❑ WS1525 [S]	Ski Surfin'	1963	$75

AVALON, FRANKIE
ABC

Number	Title	Yr	NM
❑ ABCX-805 [R]	16 Greatest Hits	1974	$15
CHANCELLOR			
❑ CHL5022 [M]	And Now About Mr. Avalon	1961	$30
❑ CHLS5022 [S]	And Now About Mr. Avalon	1961	$40
❑ CHL5018 [M]	A Whole Lotta Frankie	1961	$30
❑ CHL5032 [M]	Cleopatra Plus 13 Other Great Hits	1963	$30
❑ CHLS5032 [S]	Cleopatra Plus 13 Other Great Hits	1963	$40
❑ CHL5001 [M]	Frankie Avalon	1958	$50
— Pink label			
❑ CHL5001 [M]	Frankie Avalon	1959	$40
— Black label			
❑ CHL5031 [M]	Frankie Avalon's Christmas Album	1962	$30
❑ CHLS5031 [S]	Frankie Avalon's Christmas Album	1962	$40
❑ CHL5025 [M]	Italiano	1962	$30
❑ CHLS5025 [S]	Italiano	1962	$40
❑ CHL5011 [M]	Summer Scene	1960	$30
❑ CHLS5011 [S]	Summer Scene	1960	$40
❑ CHLX5004 [M]	Swingin' on a Rainbow	1959	$40
❑ CHLXS5004 [S]	Swingin' on a Rainbow	1959	$50
❑ CHL5002 [M]	The Young Frankie Avalon	1959	$50
— Pink label			

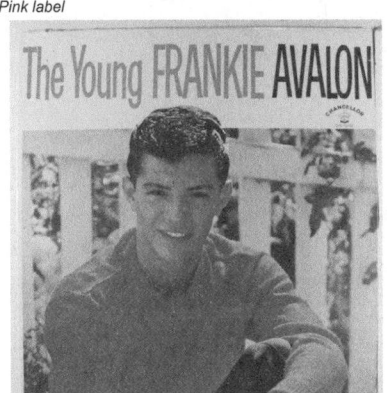

Number	Title	Yr	NM
❑ CHL5002 [M]	The Young Frankie Avalon	1959	$40
— Black label			
❑ CHLS5002 [S]	The Young Frankie Avalon	1959	$75
— Pink label			
❑ CHLS5002 [S]	The Young Frankie Avalon	1959	$50
— Black label			
❑ 69801 [M]	Young and In Love	1960	$100
— LP in felt cover and 3-D portrait, all in box			
❑ 69801 [M]	Young and In Love	1960	$40
— LP without the box			
❑ CHL5027 [M]	You're Mine	1962	$30
❑ CHLS5027 [S]	You're Mine	1962	$40
DE-LITE			
❑ 2020	Venus	1976	$18
❑ 9504	You're My Life	1977	$18
EVEREST			
❑ 4187	Greatest Hits	1982	$12
LIBERTY			
❑ LN-10193	Songs from Muscle Beach Party	1981	$10
— Budget-line reissue			

Number	Title	Yr	NM
MCA			
❑ 27096	The Best of Frankie Avalon	1985	$10
METROMEDIA			
❑ MD-1034	I Want You Near Me	1970	$18
SUNSET			
❑ SUS-5244	Frankie Avalon	1969	$18
TRIP			
❑ 1621	16 Greatest Hits of Frankie Avalon	1977	$12
UNITED ARTISTS			
❑ UAL-3382 [M]	Frankie Avalon's 15 Greatest Hits	1964	$25
❑ UAS-6382 [S]	Frankie Avalon's 15 Greatest Hits	1964	$30
❑ UAL-3371 [M]	Songs from Muscle Beach Party	1964	$30
❑ UAS-6371 [S]	Songs from Muscle Beach Party	1964	$30
❑ UA-LA450-F	The Very Best of Frankie Avalon	1975	$15

AVALON, FRANKIE AND FABIAN
MCA

Number	Title	Yr	NM
❑ 27097	The Greatest of Frankie Avalon and Fabian	1985	$12

AVENGERS
4 MEN WITH BEARDS

Number	Title	Yr	NM
❑ 4M519LP [B]	The Avengers		$25
CD PRESENTS			
❑ 007	Avengers	1983	$30
— Red vinyl			
❑ 007	Avengers	1983	$25
— Black vinyl			
GO			
❑ 005	Avengers	1983	$120
LOOKOUT!			
❑ 217 [B]	The Avengers Died for Your Sins	1999	$12
WHITE NOISE			
❑ 02 [EP]	Avengers	1978	$150

AVENGERS VI, THE
MARK 56

Number	Title	Yr	NM
❑ 536	Good Humor Presents Real Cool Hits	1966	$300
— Custom pressing for the Good Humor ice cream company			

AVERAGE, JOHNNY, BAND
BEARSVILLE

Number	Title	Yr	NM
❑ BRK3514	Some People	1981	$18

AVERAGE WHITE BAND
ARISTA

Number	Title	Yr	NM
❑ AB9594	Cupid's in Fashion	1981	$12
❑ AB9523	Shine	1980	$12
ATLANTIC			
❑ SD7308	Average White Band	1974	$12
❑ QD7308 [Q]	Average White Band	1975	$40
❑ SD19116	Average White Band	1977	$10
— Reissue			
❑ SD19105	Benny and Us	1977	$12
— With Ben E. King			

Number	Title	Yr	NM
❑ SD18140 [B]	Cut the Cake	1975	$12
❑ SD19207	Feel No Fret	1979	$12
❑ SD 2-1002	Person to Person	1977	$15
❑ SD18179	Soul Searching	1976	$12
❑ SD19266	Volume VIII	1980	$12
❑ SD19162	Warmer Communications	1978	$12
MCA			
❑ 475	Put It Where You Want It	1975	$12

Number	Title	Yr	NM
— Reissue of MCA 345			
❑ 345	Show Your Hands	1973	$30
MOBILE FIDELITY			
❑ 1-245	Average White Band	1996	$35
— Audiophile vinyl			
TRACK			
❑ 58830	Aftershock	1988	$12

AVILA, BOBBY ROSS
RCA

Number	Title	Yr	NM
❑ 9913-1-R	Bobby Ross Avila	1989	$18

AVONS, THE (1)
HULL

Number	Title	Yr	NM
❑ HLP-1000 [M]	The Avons	1960	$700

AWESOME DRE AND THE HARDCORE COMMITTEE
BENTLEY

Number	Title	Yr	NM
❑ 12001	You Can't Hold Me Back	1989	$25

AXE
ATCO

Number	Title	Yr	NM
❑ 90099	Nemesis	1983	$10
❑ SD 38-148	Offering	1982	$10
MCA			
❑ 3171	Axe	1979	$12
❑ 3224 [B]	Living on the Edge	1980	$12

AXTON, HOYT
A&M

Number	Title	Yr	NM
❑ SP-4571	Fearless	1976	$12
❑ SP-4376	Less Than a Song	1973	$12
❑ SP-4402	Life Machine	1974	$12
❑ SP-3155	Life Machine	198?	$10
— Budget-line reissue			
❑ SP-4669	Road Songs	1977	$12
❑ SP-3182	Road Songs	198?	$10
— Budget-line reissue			
❑ SP-4510	Southbound	1975	$12
ACCORD			
❑ SN-7197	Heartbreak Hotel	1982	$12
ALLEGIANCE			
❑ AV-5023	Down and Out	1984	$12
BRYLEN			
❑ BN4400	Double Dare	1982	$15
CAPITOL			
❑ SMAS-850	Country Anthem	1971	$15
❑ ST-788	Joy to the World	1971	$15
COLUMBIA			
❑ CS9766	My Griffin Is Gone	1969	$18
❑ KC33103	My Griffin Is Gone	1975	$12
❑ PC33103	My Griffin Is Gone	1979	$10
— Budget-line reissue			
EXODUS			
❑ EX-301 [M]	Hoyt Axton Sings Bessie Smith	1966	$25
❑ EXS-321 [M]	Saturday's Child	1966	$25
— Cover says stereo, record plays mono			
HORIZON			
❑ WP-1601 [M]	Greenback Dollar	1963	$25
— Black label; two fewer songs than "The Balladeer			
❑ WP-1601 [S]	Greenback Dollar	1963	$30
— Blue label; two fewer songs than "The Balladeer			
❑ WP-1621 [M]	Saturday's Child	1963	$30
❑ SWP-1621 [S]	Saturday's Child	1963	$30
❑ WP-1601 [M]	The Balladeer	1962	$30
— Black label			
❑ WP-1601 [S]	The Balladeer	1962	$30
— Same number as mono, but with blue label			
❑ WP-1613 [M]	Thunder 'N Lightnin'	1963	$30
❑ SWP-1613 [S]	Thunder 'N Lightnin'	1963	$30
JEREMIAH			
❑ JH-5000	A Rusty Old Halo	1979	$15
❑ JH-5001	Where Did the Money Go?	1980	$15
MCA			
❑ 2319	Free Sailin'	1978	$12
❑ 648	Free Sailin'	198?	$10
— Budget-line reissue			
❑ 2263	Snow Blind Friend	1977	$12
❑ 647	Snow Blind Friend	198?	$10
— Budget-line reissue			
SURREY			
❑ S-1005 [M]	Mr. Greenback Dollar Man	1965	$25
❑ SS-1005 [S]	Mr. Greenback Dollar Man	1965	$30
VEE JAY			
❑ LP-1126 [M]	Greenback Dollar	1965	$25
❑ LPS-1126 [S]	Greenback Dollar	1965	$30
❑ LP-1098 [M]	Hoyt Axton Explodes!	1964	$30
❑ LPS-1098 [R]	Hoyt Axton Explodes!	1964	$25
❑ LP-1127 [M]	Saturday's Child	1965	$25
❑ LPS-1127 [S]	Saturday's Child	1965	$30

Number	Title	Yr	NM

— Reissue of Horizon 1621

❏ LP-1118 [M]	The Best of Hoyt Axton	1965	$25
❏ LPS-1118 [S]	The Best of Hoyt Axton	1965	$30
❏ LP-1128 [M]	Thunder 'N Lightnin'	1965	$25
❏ LPS-1128 [S]	Thunder 'N Lightnin'	1965	$30

— Reissue of Horizon 1613

VEE JAY/DYNASTY

| ❏ VJS-7306 | Bessie Smith… My Way | 1974 | $18 |

VEE JAY INTERNATIONAL

| ❏ VJS-2-1005 | Gold | 1974 | $25 |

— Compilation of older Vee Jay material

| ❏ LP-6001 | Long Old Road | 1977 | $18 |

AYCOCK, EARL

MERCURY

| ❏ MG-20282 [M] | Earl Aycock | 1958 | $30 |

AYERS, ROY, AND WAYNE HENDERSON

POLYDOR

| ❏ PD-1-6276 | Prine Time | 1980 | $25 |
| ❏ PD-1-6179 | Step Into Our Life | 1978 | $25 |

AYERS, ROY

ATLANTIC

❏ SD1692	Daddy Bug & Friends	1976	$30
❏ SD1538	Daddy Bug	1969	$50
❏ SD1514	Stoned Soul Picnic	1968	$50
❏ 1488 [M]	Virgo Vibes	1967	$50
❏ SD1488 [S]	Virgo Vibes	1967	$18

COLUMBIA

| ❏ FC39422 | In the Dark | 1984 | $25 |

ICHIBAN

| ❏ ICH-1028 | Drive | 198? | $25 |
| ❏ ICH-1040 | Wake Up | 198? | $25 |

POLYDOR

❏ PD-1-6327	Africa, Center of the World	1981	$25
❏ PD6046	A Tear to a Smile	1975	$25
❏ PD6032	Change Up the Groove	1974	$25
❏ PD-1-6070	Everybody Loves the Sunshine	1976	$25
❏ PD-1-6348	Feeling Good	1982	$25
❏ PD-1-6204	Fever	1979	$25
❏ PD5022	He's Coming	1972	$30
❏ PD-1-6126	Let's Do It	1978	$25
❏ PD-1-6108	Lifeline	1977	$25
❏ PD-1-6301	Love Fantasy	1980	$25
❏ PD6057	Mystic Voyage	1976	$25
❏ PD-1-6246	No Stranger to Love	1979	$25
❏ PD5045	Red, Black and Green	1973	$30
❏ PD-1-6078	Red, Black and Green	1976	$25

— Reissue of 5045

❏ PD-1-6091	Vibrations	1977	$25
❏ PD6016	Virgo Red	1973	$30
❏ PD-1-6159	You Send Me	1978	$25

UNITED ARTISTS

| ❏ UAL-3325 [M] | West Coast Vibes | 1964 | $50 |
| ❏ UAS-6325 [S] | West Coast Vibes | 1964 | $75 |

AYLER, ALBERT

ABC IMPULSE!

❏ AS-9155 [S]	Live at the Village Vanguard	1968	$160
❏ IA-9336	Live at the Village Vanguard	1978	$35
❏ AS-9165	Love Cry	1968	$250
❏ AS-9191	Music Is the Healing Force of the Universe	1969	$250

❏ AS-9175 [B]	New Grass	1969	$250
❏ AS-9257	Re-evaluations: The Impulse Years	1974	$35
❏ AS-9208	The Last Album	1971	$250

ARISTA/FREEDOM

| ❏ AL1000 | Vibrations | 1976 | $35 |
| ❏ AL1018 | Witches and Devils | 1977 | $35 |

Number	Title	Yr	NM

ESP-DISK'

| ❏ 1010 [M] | Bells | 1965 | $300 |

— Black vinyl

| ❏ 1010 [M] | Bells | 1965 | $600 |

— A multitude of color vinyl pressings were produced between release and 1974, including: black without any lettering; blue with white silk screened lettering; blue/black splash with white silk screened lettering; clear with/without red silk screened lettering; gold with red silk screened lettering; grey marbled with red/white silk screened lettering; maroon with white silk screened lettering; orange without lettering; red without lettering violet with white silk screened lettering; yellow without lettering.

❏ S-1010 [S]	Bells	1965	$300
❏ 1016 [M]	New York Eye and Ear Control	1966	$75
❏ S-1016 [S]	New York Eye and Ear Control	1966	$150
❏ ESP-3030	Prophecy	1975	$40
❏ 1020 [M]	Spirits Rejoice	1966	$700
❏ S-1020 [S]	Spirits Rejoice	1966	$350
❏ 1002 [M]	Spiritual Unity	1965	$1000

FANTASY

| ❏ 6016 [M] | My Name Is Albert Ayler | 196? | $25 |
| ❏ 86016 [S] | My Name Is Albert Ayler | 196? | $30 |

GNP CRESCENDO

| ❏ GNPS-9022 | The First Recordings | 1973 | $30 |

IMPULSE!

| ❏ A-9155 [M] | Live at the Village Vanguard | 1967 | $160 |
| ❏ AS-9155 [S] | Live at the Village Vanguard | 1967 | $160 |

MCA

| ❏ 4129 | Live at the Village Vanguard | 198? | $30 |

— Reissue of ABC Impulse 9336

AZ

NOO TRYBE

| ❏ 56715 | Pieces of a Man | 1998 | $18 |

AZAMA, ETHEL

LIBERTY

❏ LRP-3142 [M]	Cool Heat	1960	$40
❏ LST-7142 [S]	Cool Heat	1960	$50
❏ LRP-3104 [M]	Exotic Dreams	1959	$25
❏ LST-7104 [S]	Exotic Dreams	1959	$30

AZIMUTH

ECM

❏ 1099	Azimuth	1977	$12
❏ 1289	Azimuth '85	1985	$12
❏ 1163	Depart	1979	$12
❏ 1130	The Touchstone	1978	$12

AZITIS

ELCO

| ❏ SC-EC-5555 | Help! | 197? | $500 |

AZTEC CAMERA

SIRE

| ❏ 25285 [10] | Backwards and Forwards | 1985 | $18 |

— Ten-inch record in a 12-inch cover

❏ 23899	High Land, Hard Rain	1983	$15
❏ 25183	Knife	1984	$15
❏ 25646	Love	1987	$12
❏ 26211	Stray	1990	$12

AZTEC TWO-STEP

ELEKTRA

| ❏ EKS-75031 [B] | Aztec Two-Step | 1972 | $18 |

FLYING FISH

| ❏ 505 | See It Was Like This… An Acoustic Retrospective | 1991 | $12 |

RCA VICTOR

❏ AFL1-2453	Adjoining Suites	1978	$15
❏ APL1-1161	Second Step	1975	$15
❏ APL1-1497	Two's Company	1976	$15

REFLEX

| ❏ 8601 | Living in America | 1986 | $12 |

WATERHOUSE

| ❏ 9 | The Times of Our Lives | 1980 | $18 |

AZTECA

COLUMBIA

❏ KC31776	Azteca	1972	$15
❏ CQ31776 [Q]	Azteca	1974	$40
❏ KC32451	Pyramid of the Sun	1973	$15

AZTECS, THE

WORLD ARTISTS

| ❏ WAM-2001 [M] | Live at the Ad Lib Club of London | 1964 | $75 |

— Features Beatles on the cover endorsing the band

Number	Title	Yr	NM

AZYMUTH

INTIMA

| ❏ D1-73517 | Tudo Bern | 1989 | $15 |

MILESTONE

❏ M-9169	Carioca	1989	$15
❏ M-9109	Cascades	1982	$12
❏ M-9156	Crazy Rhythm	1988	$12
❏ M-9128	Flame	1984	$12
❏ M-9089	Light as a Feather	1979	$15
❏ M-9097	Outubro	1980	$15
❏ M-9134	Spectrum	1985	$12
❏ M-9101	Telecommunication	1982	$12
❏ M-9143	Tightrope Walker	1987	$12

B

B-52'S, THE

MOBILE FIDELITY

| ❏ MOFI1-023 [B] | Cosmic Thing | 197? | $40 |

REPRISE

| ❏ 25854 [B] | Cosmic Thing | 1989 | $15 |
| ❏ 44519 | Time Capsule -- The Mixes | 1998 | $18 |

— Numbered as if it were a 12-inch single, this contains remixes of seven songs from the "best of" CD compilation, so we've listed it under LPs; issued in orange vinyl cover

WARNER BROS.

| ❏ 25504 | Bouncing Off the Satellites | 1986 | $12 |
| ❏ R154582 | Bouncing Off the Satellites | 1986 | $15 |

— RCA Music Service edition

❏ MINI3641 [EP]	Mesopotamia	1982	$10
❏ MINI3596 [EP]	Party Mix	1981	$15
❏ BSK3355	The B-52's	1979	$12
❏ 23819	Whammy!	1983	$12
❏ BSK3471	Wild Planet	1980	$15

— Originals have red custom labels (deduct 33% for later pressings)

B.G. KNOCC OUT & DRESTA

OUTBURST

| ❏ 527899-1 | Real Brothas | 1995 | $18 |

B.G. THE PRINCE OF RAP

EPIC

| ❏ E48667 | The Power of Rhythm | 1991 | $15 |

B-H-Y

SALSOUL

| ❏ SA-8524 | B-H-Y | 1979 | $15 |

B.T. EXPRESS

COAST TO COAST

| ❏ FZ38001 | Keep It Up | 1982 | $12 |

COLLECTABLES

| ❏ COL-5190 | Golden Classics: Express | 198? | $12 |

COLUMBIA

❏ JC36333	B.T. Express 1980	1980	$12
❏ PC34178	Energy to Burn	1976	$12
❏ PCQ34178 [Q]	Energy to Burn	1976	$20
❏ PC34702	Function at the Junction	1977	$12
❏ JC36923	Greatest Hits	1980	$12
❏ JC35078	Shout!	1978	$12

ROADSHOW

| ❏ 41001 | Non-Stop | 1975 | $15 |

ROADSHOW/SCEPTER

| ❏ 5117 | Do It ('Til You're Satisfied) | 1974 | $15 |

Number	Title	Yr	NM
B ANGIE B			
CAPITOL			
❑ C1-95236	B Angie B	1990	$15
BABASIN, HARRY			
MODE			
❑ LP-119 [M]	Jazz Pickers	1957	$150
NOCTURNE			
❑ NLP-3 [10]	Harry Babasin Quartet	1954	$175
BABASIN, HARRY/TERRY GIBBS			
PREMIER			
❑ PM-2010 [M]	Pick 'n' Pat	1963	$35
❑ PS-2010 [R]	Pick 'n' Pat	1963	$25
BABE RUTH			
CAPITOL			
❑ ST-11515	Kids Stuff	1976	$25
HARVEST			
❑ ST-11275	Amar Caballero	1974	$30
❑ ST-11367	Babe Ruth	1975	$18
❑ SW-11151	First Base	1973	$40
❑ ST-11451	Stealin' Home	1975	$18
BABES IN TOYLAND			
REPRISE			
❑ 45868 [B]	Nemesisters	1995	$25
TWIN/TONE			
❑ TTR89183 [B]	Spanking Machine	1990	$35
BABY			
CHELSEA			
❑ CHL-517	Where Did All the Money Go	1976	$16
LONE STARR			
❑ 9782	Baby	1974	$30
BABY GRAND			
ARISTA			
❑ AL4148	Baby Grand	1977	$25
BABY HUEY			
CURTOM			
❑ CRS-8007	The Living Legend	1970	$40
BABY RAY			
IMPERIAL			
❑ LP-9335 [M]	Where Soul Lives	1967	$30
❑ LP-12335 [S]	Where Soul Lives	1967	$30
BABYFACE			
ARISTA			
❑ 12667	Face2Face	2001	$18
EPIC			
❑ E53558	For the Cool in You	1993	$15
❑ E67293	The Day	1996	$12
SOLAR			
❑ ST-72552	Lovers by Babyface	1987	$15
❑ FZ45288	Tender Lover	1989	$12
BABYLON A.D.			
ARISTA			
❑ AL8580	Babylon A.D.	1989	$12
BABYS, THE			
Also see JOHN WAITE; BAD ENGLISH.			
CHRYSALIS			
❑ CHR1351	Anthology	1981	$12
❑ PV41351	Anthology	198?	$10
—Reissue of 1351			
❑ CHR1150	Broken Heart	1977	$12

Number	Title	Yr	NM
❑ PV41150 [B]	Broken Heart	1983	$10
—Reissue of 1150			
❑ CHR1195	Head First	1979	$12
❑ FV41195	Head First	1983	$10
—Reissue of 1195			
❑ CHR1305	On the Edge	1980	$12
❑ PV41305	On the Edge	1983	$10
—Reissue of 1305			
❑ CHR1129	The Babys	1976	$15
❑ PV41129	The Babys	1983	$10
—Reissue of 1129			
❑ CHR1267	Union Jacks	1980	$12
❑ PV41267	Union Jacks	1983	$10
—Reissue of 1267			
BACH, STEVE			
CAFÉ			
❑ 59-00733	Holiday	1986	$30
❑ 59-00736	Zero Gravity	1987	$30
EAGLE			
❑ SM-4220	Child's Play	1986	$30
SOUNDWINGS			
❑ SW-2112	More Than a Dream	1989	$30
BACH CHOIR, THE			
PETERS INTERNATIONAL			
❑ PLE 091	Carols for Choirs	1976	$15
BACHARACH, BURT			
A&M			
❑ SP-3501	Burt Bacharach	1971	$12
❑ SP-3661	Burt Bacharach's Greatest Hits	1973	$12
❑ SP-4622	Futures	1977	$12
❑ SP-3527	Living Together	1973	$12
❑ SP-4188	Make It Easy on Yourself	1969	$12
❑ SP-131 [M]	Reach Out	1967	$15
❑ SP-4131 [S]	Reach Out	1967	$15
❑ SP-3709	Woman	1979	$12
COLUMBIA			
❑ C97734	At This Time	2005	$12
KAPP			
❑ KS-3577	Burt Bacharach Plays His Hits	1969	$15
MCA			
❑ 65	Burt Bacharach Plays His Hits	1973	$10
—Reissue of Kapp LP			
BACHAUER, GINA, AND SIR JOHN GIELGUD			
MERCURY LIVING PRESENCE			
❑ SR90391 [S]	Collaboration in Poetry and Music	196?	$30
—Maroon label, no "Vendor: Mercury Record Corporation			
BACHAUER, GINA			
MERCURY LIVING PRESENCE			
❑ SR90381 [S]	Beethoven: Piano Concerto No. 4; Piano Sonata in E	196?	$40
—With Antal Dorati/London Symphony Orchestra; maroon label, no "Vendor: Mercury Record Corporation			
❑ SR90321 [S]	Beethoven: Piano Concerto No. 5 "Emperor	196?	$75
—With Stanislaw Skrowaczewski/London Symphony Orchestra; maroon label, no "Vendor: Mercury Record Corporation			
❑ SR90301 [S]	Brahms: Piano Concerto No. 2	196?	$30
—With Stanislaw Skrowaczewski/London Symphony Orchestra; maroon label, no "Vendor: Mercury Record Corporation			
❑ SR90368 [S]	Chopin: Piano Concerto No. 1; Nocturne; Three Etudes	196?	$40
—Maroon label, no "Vendor: Mercury Record Corporation			
❑ SR90368 [S]	Chopin: Piano Concerto No. 1; Nocturne; Three Etudes	196?	$30
—Maroon label, with "Vendor: Mercury Record Corporation			
❑ SR90432 [S]	Chopin: Piano Concerto No. 2 in F; Fantasy in F	1965	$40
—Maroon label, no "Vendor: Mercury Record Corporation			
BACHELORS, THE (1)			
LONDON			
❑ PS528 [S]	Bachelors '68	1968	$15
❑ LL3528 [M]	Bachelors '68	1968	$25
❑ LL3393 [M]	Back Again	1964	$18
❑ PS393 [P]	Back Again	1964	$25
—I Wouldn't Trade You for the World" is rechanneled.			
❑ LL3518 [M]	Golden All Time Hits	1967	$18
❑ PS518 [P]	Golden All Time Hits	1967	$18
❑ LL3460 [M]	Hits of the 60's	1966	$18
❑ PS460 [S]	Hits of the 60's	1966	$25
❑ LL3435 [M]	Marie	1965	$18
❑ PS435 [P]	Marie	1965	$25
—Marie" is rechanneled			
❑ LL3418 [M]	No Arms Can Ever Hold You	1965	$18

Number	Title	Yr	NM
❑ PS418 [S]	No Arms Can Ever Hold You	1965	$25
❑ LL3353 [M]	Presenting the Bachelors	1964	$18
❑ PS353 [S]	Presenting the Bachelors	1964	$30
❑ LL3491 [M]	The Bachelors' Girls	1966	$15
❑ PS491 [P]	The Bachelors' Girls	1966	$25
—Marie" is rechanneled			
❑ PS611	Under and Over	1972	$12
BACHMAN, RANDY			
Also see GUESS WHO; BACHMAN-TURNER OVERDRIVE; IRONHORSE.			
POLYDOR			
❑ PD-1-6141	Survivor	1978	$15
BACHMAN-TURNER OVERDRIVE			
Also see RANDY BACHMAN; GUESS WHO.			
COMPLEAT			
❑ CPL1-1010	Bachman-Turner Overdrive	1984	$10
MCA/CURB			
❑ 5760	Live! Live! Live!	1986	$10
MERCURY			
❑ SRM-1-673	Bachman-Turner Overdrive	1973	$15
—Red label			
❑ SRM-1-673	Bachman-Turner Overdrive	1974	$12
—Chicago skyline label			
❑ SRM-1-696	Bachman-Turner Overdrive II	1973	$15
—Red label			
❑ SRM-1-696	Bachman-Turner Overdrive II	1974	$12
—Chicago skyline label			
❑ SRM-1-1101	Best of B.T.O. (So Far)	1976	$12
❑ 822786-1	Best of B.T.O. (So Far)	1984	$10
—Reissue of 1101			
❑ SRM-1-1027	Four Wheel Drive	1975	$12
❑ SRM-1-3700	Freeways	1977	$12
❑ SRM-1-1067	Head On	1975	$12
❑ SRM-1-1004 [B]	Not Fragile	1974	$15
❑ SRM-1-3748	Rock N' Roll Nights	1979	$12
❑ SRM-1-3713	Street Action	1978	$12
BACHS, THE			
ROTO			
❑ PR-1044	Out of the Bachs	1968	$4000
—VG value 2000, VG+ value 3000			
BACK PORCH MAJORITY, THE			
EPIC			
❑ LN24134 [M]	Live from Ledbetter's	1965	$18
❑ BN26134 [S]	Live from Ledbetter's	1965	$25
❑ LN24149 [M]	Riverboat Days	1965	$18
❑ BN26149 [S]	Riverboat Days	1965	$25
❑ LN24184 [M]	That's the Way It's Gonna Be	1966	$18
❑ BN26184 [S]	That's the Way It's Gonna Be	1966	$25
❑ LN24319 [M]	Willy Nilly Wonder of Illusion	1967	$25
❑ BN26319 [S]	Willy Nilly Wonder of Illusion	1967	$18
BACK STREET CRAWLER			
ATCO			
❑ SD 36-138 [B]	2nd Street	1976	$15
❑ SD 36-125	The Band Plays On	1975	$15
EPIC			
❑ PE34900	Crawler	1977	$12
—Epic titles as "Crawler			
❑ JE35482	Snake, Rattle and Roll	1978	$12
BACK TO THE BIBLE MUSICIANS			
BACK TO THE BIBLE			
❑ 876B-1547	Music of Christmas	1971	$12
BACKBEAT BAND			
VIRGIN			
❑ SPRO-14124 [DJ]	Backbeat (Original Soundtrack)	1994	$18
—Green vinyl in plastic sleeve			
BACKUS, JIM			
RCA VICTOR			
❑ LPM-1362 [M]	Mr. Magoo in Hi-Fi	1957	$50
BACON FAT			
BLUE HORIZON			
❑ BH-4807	Grease One for Me	1970	$30
BAD AZZ			
PRIORITY			
❑ 50741	Word on Tha Streets	1998	$15
BAD BOY			
UNITED ARTISTS			
❑ UA-LA869-H	Back to Back	1978	$15

Number	Title	Yr	NM
❏ UA-LA781-G	The Band That Milwaukee Made Famous	1977	$15

BAD BRAINS
BAD BRAINS
❏ 003 [EP]	I and I Survive/Destroy Babylon	1983	$40

CAROLINE
❏ CAROL-1375 [B]	Quickness	1989	$30
❏ CAROL-1613	Rock for Light	1990	$16

—Reissue of PVC 8917 with three bonus tracks
❏ CAROL-1617 [B]	The Youth Are Getting Restless	1990	$25

IMPORTANT
❏ 003 [EP]	I and I Survive/Destroy Babylon	1983	$30

MAVERICK
❏ 45882	God of Love	1995	$25

PVC

❏ 8917 [B]	Rock for Light	1983	$50

ROIR
❏ 8223 [B]	Bad Brains	1997	$18

—First issued in the early 1980s on cassette only, this is a limited vinyl reissue

SST
❏ 065	I Against I	199?	$12

— With back cover bar code
❏ 065 [B]	I Against I	1986	$40

— No back cover bar code
❏ 160 [B]	Live	1988	$30
❏ 228 [10]	Spirit Electricity	1991	$12

VICTORY
❏ VR64 [10]	The Omega Sessions	1997	$18

BAD COMPANY
Also see FREE, PAUL RODGERS; THE FIRM.

ATCO
❏ 91371	Holy Water	1990	$18

ATLANTIC
❏ 81625	10 from 6 (The Best of Bad Company)	1986	$12
❏ 81884	Dangerous Age	1988	$12
❏ 81684	Fame and Fortune	1987	$12

RHINO
❏ R1554483 [B]	Live 1977	2016	$30
❏ R18413 [B]	Straight Shooter	2014	$25

SWAN SONG
❏ SS8410	Bad Company	1974	$12
❏ SS8501	Bad Company	1977	$10
❏ SS8500	Burnin' Sky	1977	$12
❏ SS8506	Desolation Angels	1979	$12
❏ R1551262 [B]	Rock 'n' Roll Fantasy The Very Best Of Bad Company	2016	$30
❏ 90001	Rough Diamonds	1982	$12
❏ SS8415	Run with the Pack	1976	$12
❏ SS8503	Run with the Pack	1977	$10

Number	Title	Yr	NM

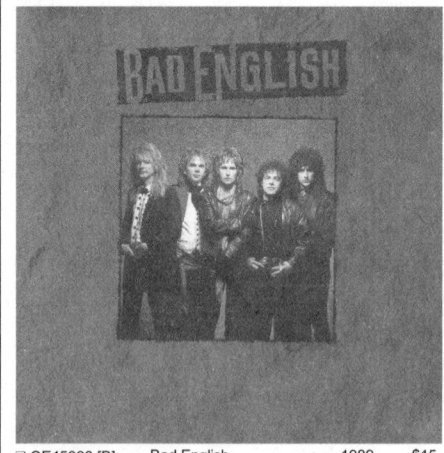

❏ SS8413 [B]	Straight Shooter	1975	$12
❏ SS8502	Straight Shooter	1977	$10
❏ R1547492 [B]	Straight Shooter	2015	$40

—180g

BAD ENGLISH
Also see JOHN WAITE; THE BABYS.

EPIC

❏ OE45083 [B]	Bad English	1989	$15

BAD MANNERS
MCA
❏ 5218	Bad Manners	1981	$18
❏ 5415	Klass	1983	$18

PORTRAIT
❏ BFR39413	Forging Ahead	1984	$15
❏ BFR40070	Mental Notes	1985	$15

BAD RELIGION
ATLANTIC
❏ 83094	No Substance	1998	$25

❏ 82658 [B]	Stranger Than Fiction	1994	$30

—Issued on red vinyl
❏ 82870	The Gray Race	1996	$25

Number	Title	Yr	NM

—Issued on gray vinyl
❏ 83303	The New America	2000	$18

EPITAPH
❏ 86409 [B]	Against the Grain	1990	$30
❏ 86443	All Ages	1995	$15
❏ 86416 [B]	Generator	1992	$25
❏ E-86416-1 [B]	Generator	2014	$30
❏ EPI-BRLP-1	How Could Hell Be Any Worse?	1982	$150

—Original edition with lyric sheet. Some copies have personal notes or autographs scribbled on the inner sleeves by the band members; these can bring significantly more than this.
❏ 86407	How Could Hell Be Any Worse?	1989	$30

—Reissue of Epitaph BRLP-1
❏ EPI-BRLP-2	Into the Unknown	1983	$250
❏ 86406	No Control	1989	$18
❏ 86420 [B]	Recipe for Hate	1993	$25
❏ 86404	Suffer	1988	$18
❏ 86694	The Empire Strikes First	2004	$15
❏ 86635	The Process of Belief	2002	$18

BADAROU, WALLY
ISLAND
❏ 90495	Echoes	1986	$12

BADFINGER
APPLE
❏ SW3411	Ass	1973	$25
❏ ST3364	Magic Christian Music	1970	$30

—With Capitol logo on Side 2 bottom
❏ ST3364	Magic Christian Music	1970	$25
❏ ST-3355	Maybe Tomorrow	1969	$2000

—As "The Iveys"; album not released in US; price is for an LP slick, which does exist

❏ SKAO3367 [B]	No Dice	1970	$30
❏ SW3387	Straight Up	1971	$75

ELEKTRA
❏ 6E-175	Airwaves	1979	$15

RADIO
❏ RR16030	Say No More	1981	$12

RYKO ANALOGUE
❏ RALP10189 [B]	Day After Day	1990	$40

—Limited edition on clear vinyl with obi

WARNER BROS.
❏ BS2762	Badfinger	1974	$18
❏ BS2827	Wish You Were Here	1974	$18

BADGER
ATCO
❏ SD7022 [B]	One Live Badger	1973	$16

EPIC
❏ KE32831	White Lady	1974	$18

BADLANDS
Also see BLACK SABBATH; OZZY OSBOURNE; KISS.
ATLANTIC
❏ 81966	Badlands	1989	$12

CMH
❏ 6254	Badlands	198?	$12

BADU, ERYKAH
MOTOWN
❏ 012-153287-1	Mama's Gun	2000	$18

—Comes in generic sleeve with large center hole; red vinyl

UNIVERSAL/KEDAR
❏ 53027	Baduizm	1997	$12

—Comes in generic sleeve with large center hole
❏ 53109	Live	1997	$18

—Comes in generic sleeve with large center hole

Number	Title	Yr	NM

BAERWALD, DAVID
A&M
| ❏ 7502152891 | Bedtime Stories | 1990 | $18 |

BAEZ, JOAN
A&M
❏ SP-4339	Come From the Shadows	1972	$12
❏ QU-54339 [Q]	Come From the Shadows	1974	$40
❏ SP-3103	Come From the Shadows	198?	$10
—Budget-line reissue			
❏ SP-4527	Diamonds and Rust	1975	$12
❏ QU-54527 [Q]	Diamonds and Rust	1975	$40
❏ SP-3233	Diamonds and Rust	198?	$10
—Budget-line reissue			
❏ SP-3704	From Every Stage	1976	$15
❏ SP-6506	From Every Stage	198?	$12
—Reissue			
❏ SP-3614	Gracias A La Vida	1974	$15
❏ SP-4603	Gulf Winds	1976	$12
❏ SP-4668	The Best of Joan C. Baez	1977	$12
❏ SP-3234	The Best of Joan C. Baez	198?	$10
—Budget-line reissue			
❏ SP-4390	Where Are You Now, My Son?	1973	$12

BOOK-OF-THE-MONTH
| ❏ 40-5711 | Satisfied Mind | 1979 | $30 |
| *—With booklet* | | | |

GOLD CASTLE
❏ D1-71321	Diamonds and Rust in the Bullring	1989	$15
❏ D1-71309	Recently	1989	$15
—Reissue of 171 009			
❏ 171009	Recently	1988	$12
❏ D1-71324	Speaking of Dreams	1989	$15

MOBILE FIDELITY
| ❏ 1-238 | Diamonds and Rust | 1996 | $75 |
| *—Audiophile vinyl* | | | |

NAUTILUS
| ❏ NR-12 | Diamonds and Rust | 1980 | $40 |
| *—Audiophile vinyl* | | | |

PORTRAIT
| ❏ PR34697 | Blowin' Away | 1977 | $12 |
| ❏ JR35766 | Honest Lullaby | 1979 | $12 |

SQUIRE
| ❏ SQ-33001 [M] | The Best of Joan Baez | 1963 | $25 |

VANGUARD
| ❏ VSD-79306/7 | Any Day Now | 1969 | $30 |

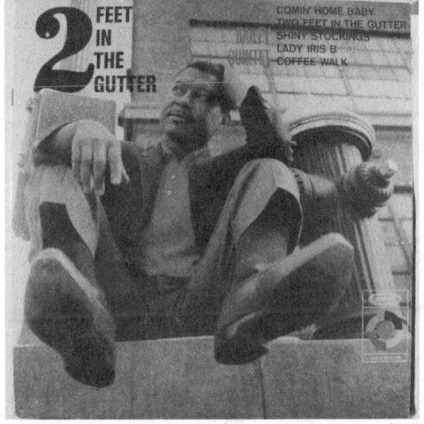

❏ VSD-79275 [B]	Baptism	1968	$25
❏ VSD-6570/1	Blessed Are...	1971	$18
—Add 50 percent if bonus 7-inch single, "Maria Dolores"/"Plane Wreck at Los Gatos (Deportee)," and its special sleeve are still in the package			
❏ VSD6570/1 [B]	Blessed Are...	2014	$40
❏ VSQ-40001/2 [Q]	Blessed Are	1973	$40
❏ VSD-79313	Carry It On	1971	$30
—Soundtrack album			
❏ VSD-79308	David's Album	1969	$15
❏ VRS-9200 [M]	Farewell, Angelina	1965	$20
❏ VSD-79200 [S]	Farewell, Angelina	1965	$25
❏ VSD-79332	Hits/Greatest & Others	1973	$12
❏ VSQ-40032 [Q]	Hits/Greatest & Others	1973	$40
❏ VRS-9240 [M]	Joan	1967	$18
❏ VSD-79240 [S]	Joan	1967	$25
❏ VRS-9078 [M]	Joan Baez	1960	$40
❏ VSD-2077 [S]	Joan Baez	1960	$50
❏ VRS-9094 [M]	Joan Baez, Vol. 2	1961	$40
❏ VSD-2097 [S]	Joan Baez, Vol. 2	1961	$40
❏ VRS-9160 [M]	Joan Baez/5	1964	$25
❏ VSD-79160 [S]	Joan Baez/5	1964	$35
❏ VRS-9112 [M]	Joan Baez In Concert	1962	$30
❏ VSD-2122 [S]	Joan Baez In Concert	1962	$40
❏ VRS-9113 [M]	Joan Baez In Concert, Part 2	1963	$25
❏ VSD-2123 [S]	Joan Baez In Concert, Part 2	1963	$30
❏ VRS-9230 [M]	Noel	1966	$20
❏ VSD-79230 [S]	Noel	1966	$25
❏ VSD-79310	One Day at a Time	1970	$15
❏ VSD-49/50	The Contemporary Ballad Book	1974	$15
❏ VSD-105/6	The Country Music Album	1979	$15
❏ VSD-6560/1	The First 10 Years	1970	$18
❏ VSD-41/42	The Joan Baez Ballad Book	1972	$15
❏ VMS-73107	The Joan Baez Ballad Book, Vol. 1	1985	$12
❏ VMS-73115	The Joan Baez Ballad Book, Vol. 2	1985	$12
❏ VSD-79/80	The Love Song Album	197?	$15
❏ VMS-73119	The Night They Drove Old Dixie Down	198?	$12
❏ VSD-79446/7	Very Early Joan	1981	$15

BAG, THE
DECCA
| ❏ DL75057 | Real | 1968 | $18 |

BAGDASARIAN, ROSS
LIBERTY
| ❏ LRP-3451 [M] | The Crazy, Mixed-Up World of Ross Bagdasarian | 1966 | $40 |
| ❏ LST-7451 [S] | The Crazy, Mixed-Up World of Ross Bagdasarian | 1966 | $50 |

BAGLEY, DON
DOT
❏ DLP-3070 [M]	Basically Bagley	1957	$50
❏ DLP-25070 [S]	Basically Bagley	1959	$100
❏ DLP-9007 [M]	The Soft Sell	1959	$150
❏ DLP-29007 [S]	The Soft Sell	1959	$100
REGENT
| ❏ MG-6061 [M] | Jazz on the Rocks | 1957 | $75 |
SAVOY
| ❏ MG-12210 [M] | Jazz on the Rocks | 196? | $25 |

BAGWELL, WENDY
CANAAN
❏ 8331	And That's a Fact With My Hand Up	196?	$18
❏ 9765	Bust Out Laffin'	197?	$15
❏ 9869	The Known Comic	197?	$15
❏ 9679	This, That and the Other	1971	$18
❏ 9699	You Won't Believe This	197?	$18

BAHAMADIA
CHRYSALIS
| ❏ SPRO-10478 | Kollage | 1996 | $25 |
| *—Promo-only full-length vinyl issue* | | | |
GOOD VIBE
| ❏ 2021 | B.B. Queen | 2000 | $18 |

BAILES BROTHERS, THE
AUDIO LAB
| ❏ AL-1511 [M] | Avenues of Prayer | 1959 | $250 |

BAILEY, BENNY
ARGO
| ❏ LP-668 [M] | The Music of Quincy Jones | 1961 | $30 |
| ❏ LPS-668 [S] | The Music of Quincy Jones | 1961 | $30 |
CANDID
| ❏ CD-8011 [M] | Big Brass | 1960 | $30 |
| ❏ CS-9011 [S] | Big Brass | 1960 | $40 |
GEMINI
| ❏ GMLP-69-1 | While My Lady Sleeps | 1990 | $30 |
SABA
| ❏ 15158 [S] | Soul Eyes | 1968 | $300 |

BAILEY, BUSTER
FELSTED
| ❏ FAJ-7003 [M] | All About Memphis | 1959 | $40 |
| ❏ SJA-2003 [S] | All About Memphis | 1959 | $40 |

BAILEY, DAVE
EPIC
❏ LA16011 [M]	Gettin' Into Something	1960	$175
❏ BA17011 [S]	Gettin' Into Something	1960	$250
—yellow label			
❏ LA16008 [M]	One Foot in the Gutter	1960	$175
❏ BA17008 [S]	One Foot in the Gutter	1960	$250
❏ BA17008 [S]	One Foot in the Gutter	199?	$75
—Classic Records reissue			
❏ LA16021 [M]	Two Feet in the Gutter	1961	$175
❏ BA17021 [S]	Two Feet in the Gutter	1961	$175
JAZZ LINE
| ❏ 33-01 [M] | Bash! | 1961 | $350 |
JAZZTIME
❏ JT-003 [M]	Reaching Out	1961	$350
❏ JS-003 [S]	Reaching Out	1961	$175
—Reissued under GRANT GREEN's name			

BAILEY, J.R.
MAM
| ❏ 9 | Just Me 'N' You | 1974 | $15 |

BAILEY, MILDRED
ALLEGRO
❏ 3119 [M]	Mildred Bailey Sings	1955	$75
❏ 4009 [10]	Mildred Bailey Songs	1952	$100
❏ 4040 [10]	Mildred Bailey Songs	1954	$100
COLUMBIA
❏ C3L22	Her Greatest Performances	1962	$50
—With booklet; originals have red labels with "Guaranteed High Fidelity" at bottom			
❏ CL6094 [10]	Serenade	1950	$75
DECCA
| ❏ DL5133 [10] | Mildred Bailey Memorial Album | 1950 | $120 |
| ❏ DL5387 [10] | The Rockin' Chair Lady | 195? | $75 |
EVEREST ARCHIVE OF FOLK & JAZZ
| ❏ 269 | Mildred Bailey | 197? | $30 |
HINDSIGHT
| ❏ HSR-133 | Mildred Bailey 1944 | 198? | $25 |
MONMOUTH-EVERGREEN
| ❏ 6814 | All of Me | 196? | $35 |
REGENT
| ❏ MG-6032 [M] | Me and the Blues | 1957 | $50 |
ROYALE
| ❏ VLP6078 [10] | Mildred Bailey Sings | 195? | $100 |
SAVOY
| ❏ MG-12219 [M] | Me and the Blues | 196? | $25 |
SAVOY JAZZ
| ❏ SJL-1151 | The Majestic Mildred Bailey | 198? | $30 |
SUNBEAM
| ❏ 209 | Radio Show 1944-45 | 197? | $30 |

BAILEY, PEARL, AND LOUIS BELLSON
EVEREST ARCHIVE OF FOLK & JAZZ
| ❏ FS284 [R] | Pearl Bailey and Louis Bellson | 197? | $25 |

BAILEY, PEARL
COLUMBIA
| ❏ CL6099 [10] | Pearl Bailey Entertains | 1950 | $150 |
| ❏ CL985 [M] | The Definitive Pearl Bailey | 1957 | $75 |
CORAL
| ❏ CRL57162 [M] | Cultured Pearl | 1958 | $40 |

Number	Title	Yr	NM
❏ CRL56078 [10]	I'm with You	1954	$150
❏ CRL57037 [M]	Pearl Bailey	1957	$40
❏ CRL56068 [10]	Say Si Si	1953	$150
MERCURY			
❏ MG-20277 [M]	The Intoxicating Pearl Bailey	1957	$150

❏ MG-20187 [M]	The One and Only Pearl Bailey Sings	1956	$40
PROJECT 3			
❏ PR5022SD	The Real Pearl	1968	$35
RCA VICTOR			
❏ LSP-4529	Pearl's Pearls	1971	$35
ROULETTE			
❏ R-25195 [M]	All About Good Little Girls and Bad Little Boys	1963	$50
—Originals have a pink and orange label			
❏ SR-25195 [S]	All About Good Little Girls and Bad Little Boys	1963	$75
—Originals have a pink and orange label			
❏ R-25222 [M]	C'est La Vie	1963	$50
—Originals have a pink and orange label			
❏ SR-25222 [S]	C'est La Vie	1963	$75
—Originals have a pink and orange label			
❏ R-25181 [M]	Come On, Let's Play with Pearlie Mae	1962	$50
—Originals have a white label with colored spokes			
❏ SR-25181 [S]	Come On, Let's Play with Pearlie Mae	1962	$75
—Originals have a white label with colored spokes			
❏ R-25300 [M]	For Women Only	1965	$35
❏ SR-25300 [S]	For Women Only	1965	$50
❏ R-25167 [M]	Happy Sounds	1962	$50
—Originals have a white label with colored spokes			
❏ SR-25167 [S]	Happy Sounds	1962	$75
—Originals have a white label with colored spokes			
❏ R-25101 [M]	More Songs for Adults Only	1960	$50
—Originals have a white label with colored spokes			
❏ SR-25101 [S]	More Songs for Adults Only	1960	$75
—Originals have a white label with colored spokes			
❏ R-25125 [M]	Naughty But Nice	1960	$50
—Originals have a white label with colored spokes			
❏ SR-25125 [S]	Naughty But Nice	1960	$75
—Originals have a white label with colored spokes			
❏ R-25012 [M]	Pearl Bailey A Broad	1957	$75
—Black label original			
❏ SR-25012 [R]	Pearl Bailey A Broad	196?	$30
❏ R-25016 [M]	Pearl Bailey Sings for Adults Only	1959	$50
—Originals have a white label with colored spokes			
❏ SR-25016 [S]	Pearl Bailey Sings for Adults Only	1959	$75
—Originals have a white label with colored spokes			
❏ R-25063 [M]	Pearl Bailey Sings Porgy and Bess and Other Gershwin Melodies	1959	$50
—Originals have a white label with colored spokes			
❏ SR-25063 [S]	Pearl Bailey Sings Porgy and Bess and Other Gershwin Melodies	1959	$75
—Originals have a white label with colored spokes			
❏ R-25155 [M]	Pearl Bailey Sings Songs of Harold Arlen	1961	$50
—Originals have a white label with colored spokes			
❏ SR-25155 [S]	Pearl Bailey Sings Songs of Harold Arlen	1961	$75
—Originals have a white label with colored spokes			
❏ R-25271 [M]	Songs by James Van Heusen	1964	$35
❏ SR-25271 [S]	Songs by James Van Heusen	1964	$50
❏ R-25116 [M]	Songs of the Bad Old Days	1960	$50
—Originals have a white label with colored spokes			
❏ SR-25116 [S]	Songs of the Bad Old Days	1960	$75
—Originals have a white label with colored spokes			
❏ SR5004	Songs of the Bad Old Days	1976	$30
❏ R-25037 [M]	St. Louis Blues	1958	$75

Number	Title	Yr	NM
—Black label original			
❏ SR-25037 [S]	St. Louis Blues	1959	$75
—Originals have a white label with colored spokes			
❏ R-25144 [M]	The Best of Pearl Bailey	1961	$50
—Originals have a white label with colored spokes			
❏ SR-25144 [S]	The Best of Pearl Bailey	1961	$75
—Originals have a white label with colored spokes			
❏ SR-25144 [S]	The Best of Pearl Bailey	1964	$35
—Orange and yellow "roulette wheel" label			
❏ R-25259 [M]	The Risque World of Pearl Bailey	1964	$35
❏ SR-25259 [S]	The Risque World of Pearl Bailey	1964	$50
VOCALION			
❏ VL3621 [M]	Gems by Pearl Bailey	1958	$75

BAILEY, PHILIP
COLUMBIA

❏ FC39542	Chinese Wall	1984	$12
❏ FC38725	Continuation	1983	$12
❏ PC38725	Continuation	198?	$10
—Budget-line reissue with new prefix			
❏ FC40209	Inside Out	1986	$12
HORIZON			
❏ SP-754	Triumph	1986	$12
MYRRH			
❏ 7-01-683406	Triumph	1986	$18
—Released simultaneously with the Horizon issue, this version was found in Christian bookstores			
❏ 7-01-679606-X	Wonders of His Love	1984	$15
MYRRH/A&M			
❏ WR-8448	Family Affair	1989	$15

BAILEY, RAZZY
MCA

❏ 5615	Arrival	1986	$10
❏ 5544	Cut from a Different Stone	1985	$10
RCA VICTOR			
❏ AHL1-4423	A Little More Razz	1982	$10
❏ AHL1-4228	Feelin' Right	1982	$10
❏ AHL1-4679	Greatest Hits	1983	$10
❏ AHL1-3391	If Love Had a Face	1979	$12
❏ AHL1-4026	Makin' Friends	1981	$10
❏ AHL1-3688	Razzy	1980	$10
❏ AHL1-4936	The Midnight Hour	1984	$10

BAILEY, VICTOR
ATLANTIC

❏ 81978	Bottoms Up	1989	$30

BAILLARGEON, HELENE
FOLKWAYS

❏ FW829 [10]	Christmas Songs of French Canada	195?	$75
❏ FC7229	Christmas Songs of French Canada	195?	$75

BAILLIE AND THE BOYS
RCA

❏ 6272-1-R	Baillie and the Boys	1987	$10
❏ 8454-1-R	Turn the Tide	1989	$12

BAIN, BOB
CAPITOL

❏ T1500 [M]	Guitar De Amor	1961	$30
❏ ST1500 [S]	Guitar De Amor	1961	$40
❏ T1201 [M]	Latin Love	1959	$30
❏ ST1201 [S]	Latin Love	1959	$40
❏ T965 [M]	Rockin', Rollin' and Strollin'	1958	$100

BAIO, SCOTT
RCA VICTOR

❏ NFL1-8025	Scott Baio	1982	$15
❏ AYL1-4763	Scott Baio	1983	$10
—Reissue of 8025			
❏ AFL1-4696	The Boys Are Out Tonight	1983	$15
❏ AYL1-5111	The Boys Are Out Tonight	1985	$10
—Reissue of 4696			

BAJA MARIMBA BAND, THE
A&M

❏ SP-4298	As Time Goes By	1971	$12
❏ LP-104 [M]	Baja Marimba Band	1964	$15
—Original pressing with A&M logo at top			
❏ SP-104 [S]	Baja Marimba Band	1964	$18
—Original number; has A&M logo at top			
❏ LP-104 [M]	Baja Marimba Band	1964	$12
—Reissue with A&M logo at left			
❏ SP-4104 [S]	Baja Marimba Band	1964	$15
—Reissue; has A&M logo at left			
❏ LP-109 [M]	Baja Marimba Band Rides Again	1965	$12
❏ SP-4109 [S]	Baja Marimba Band Rides Again	1965	$15
❏ SP-109 [S]	Baja Marimba Band Rides Again	1965	$18

Number	Title	Yr	NM
—Original issues had this number			
❏ SP-4150	Do You Know the Way to San Jose?	1968	$12
❏ SP-113 [M]	For Animals Only	1965	$12
❏ SP-4113 [S]	For Animals Only	1965	$15
❏ SP-3523	Foursider	1972	$15
❏ SP-4136	Fowl Play	1968	$12
❏ SP-4200	Fresh Air	1969	$12
❏ SP-4248	Greatest Hits	1970	$12
❏ SP-123 [M]	Heads Up	1967	$15
❏ SP-4123 [S]	Heads Up	1967	$15
❏ SP-4167	Those Were the Days	1969	$12
❏ SP-118 [M]	Watch Out!	1966	$12
❏ SP-4118 [S]	Watch Out!	1966	$15

BAKER, ANITA
BEVERLY GLEN

❏ 10002	The Songstress	1983	$15
ELEKTRA			
❏ 60922	Compositions	1990	$12
❏ 60827	Giving You the Best That I Got	1988	$10
❏ 60444	Rapture	1986	$10

BAKER, ARTHUR
A&M

❏ SP-5262	Merge	1989	$15

BAKER, BUDDY
VERVE

❏ MGV-2006 [M]	Two in Love	1956	$250
❏ V-2006 [M]	Two in Love	1961	$25

BAKER, BUTCH
MERCURY

❏ 834777-1	We Will	1989	$12

BAKER, CHET, AND ART PEPPER
PACIFIC JAZZ

❏ PJ-18 [M]	Picture of Health	1961	$50
❏ PJ-1234 [M]	Playboys	1957	$350
—Pacific Jazz records come in World Pacific covers			
WORLD PACIFIC			
❏ WP-1234 [M]	Playboys	1958	$175
❏ PJ-1234 [M]	Playboys	1958	$300

BAKER, CHET, AND LEE KONITZ
INDIA NAVIGATION

❏ IN-1052	In Concert	198?	$30

BAKER, CHET, AND PAUL BLEY
STEEPLECHASE

❏ SCS-1207	Diane	198?	$25

BAKER, CHET, JIM HALL; HUBERT LAWS
CTI

❏ 9007	Studio Trieste	1983	$25

BAKER, CHET
ANALOGUE PRODUCTIONS

❏ AAPJ-016	Chet	199?	$30
—Audiophile reissue			
ARTISTS HOUSE			
❏ 9411	Once Upon a Summertime	1978	$30
BAINBRIDGE			
❏ 1040	Albert's House	198?	$25
BLUEBIRD			
❏ 2001-1-RB	The Italian Sessions	1990	$30
BLUE NOTE			
❏ B1-92932	Let's Get Lost/The Best of Chet Baker	1989	$30
BOPLICITY			
❏ BOP-13	Cool Out	198?	$25
CADENCE JAZZ			
❏ CJ-1019	Improviser	198?	$25
COLPIX			
❏ CP-476 [M]	Chet Baker Sings and Plays	1964	$40
❏ SCP-476 [S]	Chet Baker Sings and Plays	1964	$50
COLUMBIA			
❏ CL549 [M]	Chet Baker and Strings	1954	$100
—Maroon label, gold print			
❏ CL549 [M]	Chet Baker and Strings	1955	$75
—Red and black label with six "eye" logos			
CROWN			
❏ CLP-5317 [M]	Chet Baker Quintette	196?	$25
❏ CST-317 [R]	Chet Baker Quintette	196?	$35
CTI			
❏ 6050	She Was Too Good to Me	1974	$30
ENJA			
❏ 4016	Peace	1982	$25
❏ R1-79600	The Last Great Concert: My Favorite Songs Vol. 1	1989	$30

Number	Title	Yr	NM
❑ R1-79624	The Last Great Concert: My Favorite Songs Vol. 2	1989	$30
FANTASY			
❑ OJC-087	Chet	198?	$30
— Reissue of Riverside 1135			
❑ OJC-370	Chet Baker in Milan	198?	$30
— Reissue of Jazzland 18			
❑ OJC-207	Chet Baker in New York	1985	$50
— Reissue of Riverside 1119			
❑ OJC-137	Chet Baker Plays the Best of Lerner and Loewe	198?	$30
— Reissue of Riverside 1152			
❑ OJC-492	Chet Baker with Fifty Italian Strings	1991	$30
— Reissue of Jazzland 921			
❑ OJC-303	It Could Happen to You -- Chet Baker Sings	1988	$25
— Reissue of Riverside 1120			
❑ OJC-405	Once Upon a Summertime	1989	$25
— Reissue of Galaxy 5150			
GALAXY			
❑ 5150	Once Upon a Summertime	1977	$35
HARMONY			
❑ HL7320 [M]	Love Walked In	1962	$25
HORIZON			
❑ 726	You Can't Go Home Again	1977	$30
INNER CITY			
❑ 1120	Broken Wing	198?	$25
JAZZLAND			
❑ JLP-11 [M]	Chet Baker and Orchestra	1960	$40
❑ JLP-911 [S]	Chet Baker and Orchestra	1960	$40
❑ JLP-18 [M]	Chet Baker in Milan	1960	$40
❑ JLP-918 [S]	Chet Baker in Milan	1960	$40
❑ JLP-21 [M]	Chet Baker with Fifty Italian Strings	1960	$40
❑ JLP-921 [S]	Chet Baker with Fifty Italian Strings	1960	$40
LIMELIGHT			
❑ LM-82003 [M]	Baby Breeze	1964	$30
❑ LS-86003 [S]	Baby Breeze	1964	$30
❑ LM-82019 [M]	Baker's Holiday	1965	$30
❑ LS-86019 [S]	Baker's Holiday	1965	$30
MOSAIC			
❑ MR4-113	The Complete Pacific Jazz Live Recordings of the Chet Baker Quartet with Russ Freeman	199?	$100
❑ MR4-122	The Complete Pacific Jazz Studio Recordings of the Chet Baker Quartet with Russ Freeman	199?	$120
PACIFIC JAZZ			
❑ PJ-1224 [M]	Chet Baker and Crew	1956	$120
❑ PJ-1229 [M]	Chet Baker Big Band	1957	$120
❑ PJLP-9 [10]	Chet Baker Ensemble	1954	$250
❑ PJ-1218 [M]	Chet Baker in Europe	1956	$400
❑ PJLP-3 [10]	Chet Baker Quartet	1953	$250
❑ PJLP-6 [10]	Chet Baker Quartet Featuring Russ Freeman	1953	$250
❑ PJLP-15 [10]	Chet Baker Sextet	1954	$250
❑ PJLP-11 [10]	Chet Baker Sings	1954	$250
❑ PJ-1222 [M]	Chet Baker Sings	1956	$400
❑ PJ-1202 [M]	Chet Baker Sings and Plays with Bud Shank, Russ Freeman and Strings	1955	$120
❑ PJ-1203 [M]	Jazz at Ann Arbor	1955	$175
❑ PJ-1206 [M]	The Trumpet Artistry of Chet Baker	1955	$120
PAUSA			
❑ 9011	The Trumpet Artistry of Chet Baker	198?	$25
PRESTIGE			
❑ PRLP-7512 [M]	Boppin' with the Chet Baker Quintet	1967	$30
❑ PRST-7512 [M]	Boppin' with the Chet Baker Quintet	1967	$25
❑ PRLP-7478 [M]	Comin' On with the Chet Baker Quintet	1967	$30
❑ PRST-7478 [M]	Comin' On with the Chet Baker Quintet	1967	$25
❑ PRLP-7496 [M]	Cool Burnin' with the Chet Baker Quintet	1967	$30
❑ PRST-7496 [M]	Cool Burnin' with the Chet Baker Quintet	1967	$25
❑ PRLP-7460 [M]	Groovin' with the Chet Baker Quintet	1966	$25
❑ PRST-7460 [S]	Groovin' with the Chet Baker Quintet	1966	$30
❑ PRLP-7449 [M]	Smokin' with the Chet Baker Quintet	1966	$25
❑ PRST-7449 [S]	Smokin' with the Chet Baker Quintet	1966	$30
RIVERSIDE			
❑ RLP 12-299 [M]	Chet	1959	$250
— blue label			
❑ RLP-1135 [S]	Chet	1959	$300
❑ RLP 12-281 [M]	Chet Baker in New York	1958	$300
— blue label			
❑ RLP-1119 [S]	Chet Baker in New York	1959	$300
❑ 6095	Chet Baker in New York	197?	$30
— Reissue			

Number	Title	Yr	NM
❑ RLP1119 [B]	Chet Baker in New York	2015	$25
❑ RLP 12-307 [M]	Chet Baker Plays Lerner and Loewe	1959	$250
— blue label			
❑ RLP-1152 [S]	Chet Baker Plays Lerner and Loewe	1959	$300
❑ RLP 12-278 [M]	It Could Happen to You -- Chet Baker Sings	1958	$250

It could happen to you CHET BAKER sings (RIVERSIDE RLP-1120)

Number	Title	Yr	NM
❑ RLP-1120 [S]	It Could Happen to You -- Chet Baker Sings	1959	$40
SCEPTER			
❑ 540 [M]	Angel Eyes	1966	$25
❑ S-540 [S]	Angel Eyes	1966	$30
STEEPLECHASE			
❑ SCS-1142	Daybreak	1981	$30
❑ SCS-1131	No Problem	198?	$30
❑ SCS-1180	Someday My Prince Will Come	198?	$25
❑ SCS-1122	The Touch of Your Lips	1980	$30
❑ SCS-1168	This Is Always	198?	$25
TIMELESS			
❑ LPSJP-251	As Time Goes By	1990	$30
❑ LPSJP-252	Cool Cat: Chet Baker Plays, Chet Baker Sings	1990	$30
❑ LPSJP-192	Mr. B.	1990	$30
TRIP			
❑ 5569	Chet Baker Sings and Plays Billie Holiday	197?	$25
VERVE			
❑ V6-8798	Blood, Chet and Tears	1969	$35
WORLD PACIFIC			
❑ WP-1224 [M]	Chet Baker and Crew	1958	$175
— Reissue of Pacific Jazz 1224			
❑ ST-1004 [S]	Chet Baker and Crew	1959	$175
❑ WP-1229 [M]	Chet Baker Big Band	1958	$175
— Reissue of Pacific Jazz 1229			
❑ WP-1218 [M]	Chet Baker in Europe	1958	$175
— Reissue of Pacific Jazz 1218			
❑ WP-1222 [M]	Chet Baker Sings	1958	$120
— Reissue of Pacific Jazz 1222			
❑ WP-1826 [M]	Chet Baker Sings	1964	$150
— Reissue of World Pacific 1222			
❑ ST-1826 [R]	Chet Baker Sings	1964	$150
❑ WP-1202 [M]	Chet Baker Sings and Plays with Bud Shank, Russ Freeman and Strings	1958	$175
— Reissue of Pacific Jazz 1202			
❑ WP-1852 [M]	Double Shot	1967	$150
❑ WPS-21852 [S]	Double Shot	1967	$150
❑ WP-1842 [M]	Hat's Off	1966	$150
❑ WPS-21842 [S]	Hat's Off	1966	$150
❑ WPS-21859 [S]	In the Mood	1968	$150
❑ WP-1858 [M]	Into My Life	1967	$150
❑ WPS-21858 [S]	Into My Life	1967	$150
❑ WP-1203 [M]	Jazz at Ann Arbor	1958	$175
— Reissue of Pacific Jazz 1203			
❑ WP-1249 [M]	Pretty/Groovy	1958	$250
❑ WP-1847 [M]	Quietly, There	1966	$150
❑ WPS-21847 [S]	Quietly, There	1966	$150
❑ WP-1206 [M]	The Trumpet Artistry of Chet Baker	1958	$175
— Reissue of Pacific Jazz 1206			
WORLD PACIFIC JAZZ			
❑ ST-20138 [R]	Chet Baker Plays and Sings	1968	$150
— Compilation of 1950s Pacific Jazz material			

BAKER, DAVID, AND HIS 21ST CENTURY BEBOP BAND

Number	Title	Yr	NM
LAUREL			
❑ LR-503	David Baker and His 21st Century Bebop Band	1984	$30
❑ LR-504	RSVP	1985	$30
❑ LR-505	Struttin'	1986	$30

Number	Title	Yr	NM
BAKER, GEORGE, SELECTION			
COLOSSUS			
❑ CS-1002	Little Green Bag	1970	$25
WARNER BROS.			
❑ BS2905	Paloma Blanca	1975	$18

BAKER, GINGER, 'S AIR FORCE
Includes records credited only to Ginger Baker. Also see BLIND FAITH; CREAM.

Number	Title	Yr	NM
ATCO			
❑ SD 2-703	Ginger Baker's Air Force	1970	$25
❑ SD 33-343	Ginger Baker's Air Force 2	1971	$15
❑ SD7012	Stratavarious	1972	$15
AXIOM			
❑ 539864-1	Middle Passage	1990	$18
CELLULOID			
❑ CEL-6126	Horses and Trees	1986	$12
POLYDOR			
❑ 3504	Ginger Baker At His Best	1973	$18
SIRE			
❑ SASD-7532	Eleven Sides of Baker	1977	$12

Number	Title	Yr	NM
BAKER, JOSEPHINE			
COLUMBIA			
❑ FL9533 [10]	Chansons Americaines	1951	$150
❑ FL9532 [10]	Josephine Baker	1951	$150
COLUMBIA MASTERWORKS			
❑ ML2609 [10]	Chansons Americaines	1952	$100
❑ ML2613 [10]	Encores Americaines	1952	$100
❑ ML2608 [10]	Josephine Baker Sings	1952	$100
JOLLY ROGER			
❑ 5015 [10]	Josephine Baker	1951	$50
MERCURY			
❑ MG-25151 [10]	Avec Josephine Baker	1952	$175
❑ MG-25105 [10]	The Inimitable Josephine Baker	1952	$175
RCA VICTOR RED SEAL			
❑ LSC-2427 [S]	The Fabulous Josephine Baker	1960	$50
— Original with "shaded dog" label			
❑ LM-2427 [M]	The Fabulous Josephine Baker	1960	$25
— Original with "shaded dog" label			

Number	Title	Yr	NM
BAKER, LAVERN			
ATCO			
❑ SD 33-372	Her Greatest Recordings	1971	$15
ATLANTIC			
❑ 8030 [M]	Blues Ballads	1959	$250
— Black label			
❑ 8030 [M]	Blues Ballads	1960	$175
— White "bullseye" label			
❑ 8030 [M]	Blues Ballads	1960	$30
— Red and purple label, "fan" logo in white			
❑ 8030 [M]	Blues Ballads	1963	$25
— Red and purple label, "fan" logo in black			
❑ 8002 [M]	LaVern	1956	$300
— Black label			
❑ 8002 [M]	LaVern	1960	$30
— Red and purple label, "fan" logo in white			
❑ 8002 [M]	LaVern	1963	$25
— Red and purple label, "fan" logo in black			
❑ 8007 [M]	LaVern Baker	1957	$300
— Black label			
❑ 8007 [M]	LaVern Baker	1960	$30
— Red and purple label, "fan" logo in white			
❑ 8007 [M]	LaVern Baker	1963	$25
— Red and purple label, "fan" logo in black			
❑ 1281 [M]	LaVern Baker Sings Bessie Smith	1958	$300
— Black label			
❑ 1281 [M]	LaVern Baker Sings Bessie Smith	1960	$300
— Red and purple label, "fan" logo in white			
❑ 1281 [M]	LaVern Baker Sings Bessie Smith	1963	$50
— Red and purple label, "fan" logo in black			
❑ SD1281 [S]	LaVern Baker Sings Bessie Smith	1959	$300
— Green label			
❑ SD1281 [S]	LaVern Baker Sings Bessie Smith	1960	$300
— Green and blue label, "fan" logo in white			
❑ SD1281 [S]	LaVern Baker Sings Bessie Smith	1963	$75
— Green and blue label, "fan" logo in black			
❑ 90980	LaVern Baker Sings Bessie Smith	1989	$30
— Reissue of SD 1281			
❑ 8036 [M]	Precious Memories	1959	$250
— Black label			
❑ 8036 [M]	Precious Memories	1960	$175
— White "bullseye" label			
❑ 8036 [M]	Precious Memories	1960	$30

Number	Title	Yr	NM
—Red and purple label, "fan" logo in white			
❏ 8036 [M]	Precious Memories	1963	$25
—Red and purple label, "fan" logo in black			
❏ SD8036 [S]	Precious Memories	1959	$300
—Green label			
❏ SD8036 [S]	Precious Memories	1960	$250
—White "bullseye" label			
❏ SD8036 [S]	Precious Memories	1960	$40
—Green and blue label, "fan" logo in white			
❏ SD8036 [S]	Precious Memories	1963	$30
—Green and blue label, "fan" logo in black			
❏ 8050 [M]	Saved	1961	$150
—Red and purple label, "fan" logo in white			
❏ 8050 [M]	Saved	1963	$25
—Red and purple label, "fan" logo in black			
❏ SD8050 [S]	Saved	1961	$175
—Green and blue label, "fan" logo in white			
❏ SD8050 [S]	Saved	1963	$30
—Green and blue label, "fan" logo in black			
❏ 8071 [M]	See See Rider	1962	$150
—Red and purple label, "fan" logo in white			
❏ 8071 [M]	See See Rider	1963	$25
—Red and purple label, "fan" logo in black			
❏ SD8071 [S]	See See Rider	1962	$175
—Green and blue label, "fan" logo in white			
❏ SD8071 [S]	See See Rider	1963	$30
—Green and blue label, "fan" logo in black			
❏ 8078 [M]	The Best of LaVern Baker	1963	$175
—Red and purple label, "fan" logo in black			
BRUNSWICK			
❏ BL754160	Let Me Belong to You	1970	$25

BAKER, MICKEY "GUITAR"
Also see MICKEY AND SYLVIA.

ATLANTIC

Number	Title	Yr	NM
❏ 8035 [M]	The Wildest Guitar	1959	$175
—Black label			
❏ 8035 [M]	The Wildest Guitar	1960	$50
—Red and purple label, "fan" logo in white			
❏ SD8035 [S]	The Wildest Guitar	1959	$300
—Green label			
❏ SD8035 [S]	The Wildest Guitar	1960	$100
—Green and blue label, "fan" logo in white			

KICKING MULE

❏ 142	The Blues and Jazz Guitar of Mickey Baker	1978	$15
❏ 140	The Jazz Rock Guitar of Mickey Baker	1978	$15

KING

❏ 839 [M]	But Wild	1963	$400
—Black label, no crown			
❏ 839 [M]	But Wild	196?	$100
—Blue label with crown			
❏ S-839 [R]	But Wild	196?	$40

BAKER, RONNIE

WARNER BROS.

❏ W1212 [M]	Oh, Johnny!	1958	$30
❏ WS1212 [S]	Oh, Johnny!	1959	$50

BAKER, SHORTY, AND DOC CHEATHAM

SWINGVILLE

❏ SVLP-2021 [M]	Shorty & Doc	1961	$50
—Purple label			
❏ SVLP-2021 [M]	Shorty & Doc	1965	$30
—Blue label with trident logo at right			

BAKER, SHORTY

KING

❏ 608 [M]	Broadway Beat	1958	$100

BAKER GURVITZ ARMY, THE

ATCO

❏ SD 36-123	Elysian Encounters	1975	$12
❏ SD 36-137 [B]	Hearts On Fire	1976	$12

JANUS

❏ JXS-7015	The Baker Gurvitz Army	1975	$15

BALAAM AND THE ANGEL

VIRGIN

❏ 90869	Live Free or Die	1988	$12
❏ 90574	The Greatest Story Ever Told	1986	$12

BALANCE

PORTRAIT

❏ NFR37357	Balance	1981	$10
❏ ARR38019	In for the Count	1982	$10

BALDRY, LONG JOHN

ASCOT

❏ AM-13022 [M]	Long John's Blues	1965	$50
❏ AS-16022 [R]	Long John's Blues	1965	$40

CASABLANCA

Number	Title	Yr	NM
❏ NBLP7012	Good to Be Alive	1975	$15
❏ NBLP7035	Welcome to the Club	1976	$15

EMI AMERICA

❏ SW-17015	Baldry's Out	1979	$12
❏ SW-17038	Long John Baldry	1980	$12

UNITED ARTISTS

❏ UAS-5543 [M]	Long John's Blues	1971	$15
—Reissue of Ascot 13022			

WARNER BROS.

❏ BS2614 [B]	Everything Stops for Tea	1973	$18
❏ WS1921 [B]	It Ain't Easy	1971	$18

BALDWIN, BOB

ATLANTIC

❏ 82098	Rejoice	1990	$30

MALACO

❏ MJ-1501	I've Got a Long Way to Go	1988	$25

BALES, BURT

ABC-PARAMOUNT

❏ ABC-181 [M]	Jazz from the San Francisco Waterfront	1957	$40

CAVALIER

❏ 5007 [10]	On the Waterfront	195?	$75

EUPHONIC

❏ ESR-1210 [M]	New Orleans Ragtime	196?	$30

GOOD TIME JAZZ

❏ L-19 [10]	New Orleans Joys	1954	$50

BALES & LINGLE

GOOD TIME JAZZ

❏ L-12025 [M]	They Tore My Playhouse Down	1955	$50

BALIN, MARTY

EMI AMERICA

❏ SPRO-9673 [DJ]	Balin	1981	$25
—Red vinyl			
❏ ST-17054	Balin	1981	$12
❏ ST-17088 [B]	Lucky	1983	$12

BALL, KENNY

JAZZOLOGY

❏ 65	In Concert in the USA, Volume 1	1979	$25
❏ 66	In Concert in the USA, Volume 2	1979	$25

KAPP

❏ KL-1340 [M]	Big Ones	1963	$35
❏ KS-3340 [S]	Big Ones	1963	$50
❏ KL-1392 [M]	For the Jet Set	1964	$35
❏ KS-3392 [S]	For the Jet Set	1964	$50
❏ KL-1285 [M]	It's Trad	1962	$50
❏ KS-3285 [S]	It's Trad	1962	$50
❏ KL-1276 [M]	Midnight in Moscow	1962	$50
❏ KS-3276 [S]	Midnight in Moscow	1962	$50
❏ KL-1314 [M]	More	1963	$35
❏ KS-3314 [S]	More	1963	$50
❏ KL-1294 [M]	Recorded Live	1962	$50
❏ KS-3294 [S]	Recorded Live	1962	$50
❏ KL-1348 [M]	Washington Square and the Best of Kenny Ball	1964	$35
❏ KS-3348 [S]	Washington Square and the Best of Kenny Ball	1964	$50

BALL, MARCIA

CAPITOL

❏ ST-11752	Circuit Queen	1978	$15

BALL, ROCKY, AND THE RAZ'MATAZ JAZZ BAND

BONFIRE

❏ 502	For Your Listening Pleasure	198?	$25
❏ 501	Hot Dixieland Jazz	198?	$25
❏ 503	Salute to Li'l Wally	198?	$25

BALL, RONNIE

SAVOY

❏ MG-12075 [M]	All About Ronnie	1956	$40

BALLADEERS, THE

DEL-FI

❏ DFLP-1204 [M]	Alive-O!	1959	$40
❏ DFST-1204 [S]	Alive-O!	1959	$75

BALLARD, FRANK

PHILLIPS INTERNATIONAL

❏ 1985 [M]	Rhythm-Blues Party	1962	$5000
—VG value 2500; VG+ value 3750			

BALLARD, HANK, AND THE MIDNIGHTERS

KING

❏ 981 [M]	24 Great Songs	1968	$40
❏ 950 [M]	24 Hit Tunes	1966	$75

Number	Title	Yr	NM
❏ 896 [M]	A Star in Your Eyes	1964	$150
❏ 867 [M]	Biggest Hits	1963	$150

❏ 759 [M]	Dance Along	1961	$120
❏ 927 [M]	Glad Songs, Sad Songs	1965	$80
❏ 793 [M]	Jumpin' Hank Ballard	1962	$150
❏ 748 [M]	Let's Go Again	1961	$120
❏ 700 [M]	Mr. Rhythm and Blues	1960	$175
❏ 618 [M]	Singin' and Swingin'	1959	$300
❏ 740 [M]	Spotlight on Hank Ballard	1961	$175
❏ KS-740 [S]	Spotlight on Hank Ballard	1961	$300
❏ 815 [M]	The 1963 Sound of Hank Ballard	1963	$150
❏ 674 [M]	The One and Only Hank Ballard	1959	$300
—Brown cover			
❏ 674 [M]	The One and Only Hank Ballard	1960	$175
—Green cover			
❏ 781 [M]	The Twistin' Fools	1962	$150
❏ 913 [M]	Those Lazy, Lazy Days	1965	$80
❏ KSD-1052	You Can't Keep a Good Man Down	1969	$50

BALLARD, KAYE

UNITED ARTISTS

❏ UAL-3165 [M]	Ha-Ha Boo-Hoo	1960	$25
❏ UAS-6165 [S]	Ha-Ha Boo-Hoo	1960	$30
❏ UAL-3155 [M]	Kaye Ballard Live?	1960	$25
❏ UAS-6155 [S]	Kaye Ballard Live?	1960	$30
❏ UAL-3043 [M]	Kaye Ballard Swings	1959	$25
❏ UAS-6043 [S]	Kaye Ballard Swings	1959	$30

BALLARD, RUSS
Member of ARGENT.

EMI AMERICA

❏ ST-17108	Russ Ballard	1984	$10
❏ ST-17162	The Fire Still Burns	1985	$10

EPIC

❏ JE35035	At the Third Stroke	1978	$12
❏ JE36993	Into the Fire	1981	$12
❏ JE36186	Russ Ballard & the Barnet Dogs	1980	$12
❏ KE33252 [B]	Russ Ballard	1974	$15
❏ PE34093	Winning	1976	$12

BALLIN' JACK

COLUMBIA

❏ C30344	Ballin' Jack	1971	$12
❏ KC31468	Buzzard Luck	1972	$12

MERCURY

❏ SRM-1-672	Special Pride	1973	$12

BALLOU, MONTE, AND HIS NEW CASTLE JAZZ BAND

GHB

❏ GHB-155	They're Moving Willie's Grave to Dig a Sewer	1986	$25

BALMER, DAN

CMG

❏ CML-8013	Becoming Became	1989	$30

BALTIMORA

MANHATTAN

❏ ST-53026	Living in the Background	1986	$12

BAMBAATAA, AFRIKA, AND THE SOUL SONIC FORCE

CAPITOL

❏ C1-90157	The Light	1988	$15

TOMMY BOY

❏ TBLP-1008	Beware (The Funk Is Everywhere)	1986	$18
❏ TBEP-1052 [EP]	Don't Stop...Planet Rock (The Remix EP)	1992	$12

Number	Title	Yr	NM
❑ TBLP-1457	Looking for the Perfect Beat 1980-1985	2001	$18
❑ TBLP-1007	Planet Rock -- The Album	1986	$18

BANANA AND THE BUNCH
WARNER BROS.

Number	Title	Yr	NM
❑ BS2626	Mid Mountain Ranch	1972	$15

BANANA SPLITS, THE
DECCA

Number	Title	Yr	NM
❑ DL75075 [B]	We're the Banana Splits	1969	$250

BANANARAMA
LONDON

Number	Title	Yr	NM
❑ 820036-1	Bananarama	1984	$15
— Original edition without "The Wild Life"			
❑ 820165-1	Bananarama	1984	$12
— Revised edition with "The Wild Life" added			
❑ 810102-1	Deep Sea Skiving	1983	$15
❑ R100616	The Greatest Hits Collection	1988	$15
— BMG Direct Marketing edition			
❑ 828158-1	The Greatest Hits Collection	1988	$12
❑ 828013-1	True Confessions	1986	$12
❑ R150257	Wow!	1987	$15
— BMG Direct Marketing edition			
❑ 828061-1	Wow!	1987	$12

BANCHEE
ATLANTIC

Number	Title	Yr	NM
❑ SD8240	Banchee	1969	$50
— With insert			

POLYDOR

Number	Title	Yr	NM
❑ 24-4066	Thinkin'	1971	$50

BAND, THE
Also see RICK DANKO; BOB DYLAN; RONNIE HAWKINS AND THE HAWKS; LEVON AND THE HAWKS; LEVON HELM; ROBBIE ROBERTSON.

CAPITOL

Number	Title	Yr	NM
❑ SKBO-11856	Anthology	1978	$18
❑ SN-16010	Anthology, Volume 1	1980	$10
— Budget-line reissue			
❑ SN-16011	Anthology, Volume 2	1980	$10
— Budget-line reissue			
❑ SMAS-651	Cahoots	1971	$18
❑ SN-16003 [B]	Cahoots	1980	$10
— Budget-line reissue			
❑ SO-11208	Islands	1977	$15
❑ SN-16007	Islands	1980	$10
— Budget-line reissue			
❑ SW-11214	Moondog Matinee	1973	$18
— Includes tear-off wraparound cover			
❑ SW-11214	Moondog Matinee	1973	$12
— Without tear-off wraparound cover			
❑ SN-16004	Moondog Matinee	1980	$10
— Budget-line reissue			
❑ SKAO2955	Music from Big Pink	1968	$30
— Black label with colorband			
❑ SKAO2955	Music from Big Pink	1969	$18
— Lime green label			
❑ SKAO2955	Music from Big Pink	1971	$18
— Red label, purple "C" logo at top			
❑ ST-11440	Northern Lights-Southern Cross	1975	$15
❑ SN-16005	Northern Lights-Southern Cross	1980	$10
— Budget-line reissue			
❑ SABB-11045	Rock of Ages	1972	$25
❑ SN-16008	Rock of Ages, Volume 1	1980	$10
— Budget-line reissue			
❑ SN-16009	Rock of Ages, Volume 2	1980	$10
— Budget-line reissue			

Number	Title	Yr	NM
❑ SW-425	Stage Fright	1970	$18
— Includes tear-off wraparound cover			
❑ SW-425	Stage Fright	1970	$12
— Without tear-off wraparound cover			
❑ SN-16006	Stage Fright	1980	$10
— Budget-line reissue			
❑ STAO-132	The Band	1969	$18
— Lime green label			
❑ SN-16296	The Band	198?	$10
— Budget-line reissue			
❑ STAO-8-0132	The Band	1969	$150
— Capitol Record Club edition with black rainbow label; we don't know if any standard versions of this album exist with this label			
❑ ST-11553	The Best of the Band	1976	$15
❑ SN-16331	The Best of the Band	198?	$10
— Budget-line reissue			

MOBILE FIDELITY

Number	Title	Yr	NM
❑ Jan-0039	Music from Big Pink	1981	$50
— Audiophile vinyl			
❑ MFSL1-346 [B]	Music from the Big Pink	2012	$50
❑ MFSL2-348 [B]	Rock Of Ages: The Band In Concert	2012	$75
❑ MFSL1-419 [B]	The Band	2013	$50

RHINO

Number	Title	Yr	NM
❑ R13146 [B]	The Last Waltz	2013	$40

RHINO HANDMADE

Number	Title	Yr	NM
❑ RHM1-7801	The Last Waltz	2003	$75
— Box set with remixed version of the album, booklet, facsimiles of tickets, posters and other ephemera, many bonus photos, and a reproduction of the cover signed by Robbie Robertson			

WARNER BROS.

Number	Title	Yr	NM
❑ 3WS3146	The Last Waltz	1978	$25
❑ PRO-A-737 [DJ]	The Last Waltz Sampler	1978	$25

BAND OF GOLD
RCA VICTOR

Number	Title	Yr	NM
❑ AFL1-5360	Love Songs Are Back Again	1984	$12

BANDANA
WARNER BROS.

Number	Title	Yr	NM
❑ 25115	Bandana	1985	$10

BANDIT
ABC

Number	Title	Yr	NM
❑ ABCD-918	Bandit	1975	$15

ARIOLA AMERICA

Number	Title	Yr	NM
❑ SW-50042	Partners in Crime	1978	$12

ARISTA

Number	Title	Yr	NM
❑ AL4113	Bandit	1976	$12

BANDITS, THE
WORLD PACIFIC

Number	Title	Yr	NM
❑ T-1833 [M]	The Electric 12 String	1964	$25
❑ ST-1833 [S]	The Electric 12 String	1964	$30

BANDWAGON, THE
EPIC

Number	Title	Yr	NM
❑ BN26426	Johnny Johnson and the Bandwagon	1969	$25

BANDY, MOE, AND JOE STAMPLEY
COLUMBIA

Number	Title	Yr	NM
❑ FC38316	Greatest Hits	1983	$10
❑ FC37003	Hey Joe!/Hey Moe!	1981	$10
❑ PC37003	Hey Joe!/Hey Moe!	198?	$10
— Budget-line reissue			
❑ JC36202	Just Good Ol' Boys	1979	$12
❑ PC36202	Just Good Ol' Boys	198?	$10
— Budget-line reissue			
❑ FC39955	Live from Bad Bob's, Memphis	1985	$10
❑ FC39426	The Good Ol' Boys -- Alive and Well	1984	$10
❑ PC39426	The Good Ol' Boys -- Alive and Well	1986	$10
— Budget-line reissue			

BANDY, MOE
COLUMBIA

Number	Title	Yr	NM
❑ FC39906	Barroom Roses	1985	$10
❑ PC34874	Cowboys Ain't Supposed to Cry	1977	$15
— No bar code on back cover			
❑ FC38726	Devoted to Your Memory	1983	$10
❑ PC37350	Encore	1981	$10
❑ JC36789	Following the Feeling	1980	$12
❑ FC38315	Greatest Hits	1983	$10
❑ KC34091	Hank Williams, You Wrote My Life	1976	$15
— No bar code on back cover			
❑ PC34091	Hank Williams, You Wrote My Life	198?	$10
— With bar code on back cover			

Number	Title	Yr	NM
❑ KC34285	Here I Am Drunk Again	1976	$15
— No bar code on back cover			
❑ PC34443	I'm Sorry for You, My Friend	1977	$15
— No bar code on back cover			
❑ FC38199	I Still Love You in the Same Ol' Way	1982	$10
❑ KC35779	It's a Cheating Situation	1979	$12
❑ PC35779	It's a Cheating Situation	198?	$10
— Budget-line reissue			
❑ FC40140	Keepin' It Country	1986	$10
❑ KC35534	Love Is What Life's All About	1978	$15
❑ PC38652	Moe Bandy Sings the Songs of Hank Williams	1983	$10
❑ FC39275	Motel Matches	1984	$10
❑ JC36228	One of a Kind	1980	$12
❑ FC37568	Rodeo Romeo	1981	$10
❑ PC37568	Rodeo Romeo	198?	$10
— Budget-line reissue			
❑ FC38009	She's Not Really Cheatin' (She's Just Gettin' Even)	1982	$10
❑ PC38009	She's Not Really Cheatin' (She's Just Gettin' Even)	198?	$10
— Budget-line reissue			
❑ KC35288	Soft Lights and Hard Country Music	1978	$15
❑ PC34715	The Best of Moe Bandy Volume One	1977	$15
— No bar code on back cover			
❑ PC34715	The Best of Moe Bandy Volume One	198?	$10
— With bar code on back cover			
❑ JC36487	The Champ	1980	$12

CURB

Number	Title	Yr	NM
❑ 10609	Many Mansions	1989	$12
❑ 10600	No Regrets	1988	$12

GRC

Number	Title	Yr	NM
❑ 10016	Bandy the Rodeo Clown	1975	$18
❑ 10005	I Just Started Hatin' Cheatin' Songs Today	1974	$18
❑ 10007	It Was Always So Easy (To Find an Unhappy Woman)	1975	$18

MCA

Number	Title	Yr	NM
❑ 5914	You Haven't Heard the Last of Me	1987	$10

BANG, BILLY
CELLULOID

Number	Title	Yr	NM
❑ CELL-5004	Outline #12	198?	$30

SOUL NOTE

Number	Title	Yr	NM
❑ SN-1036	Invitation	1982	$30
❑ 121136	Live at Carlos 1	1987	$30
❑ SN-1016	Rainbow Gladiator	1981	$30
❑ SN-1086	The Fire from Within	1985	$30

BANG
CAPITOL

Number	Title	Yr	NM
❑ ST-11015	Bang	1972	$30
❑ SMAS-11110	Mother/Bow to the Music	1972	$30
❑ ST-11190	Music	1973	$30

BANG TANGO
MCA

Number	Title	Yr	NM
❑ 6300 [B]	Psycho Cafe	1989	$12

WORLD OF HURT

Number	Title	Yr	NM
❑ WEP1000 [EP]	Live Injection	1989	$18

BANGLES
COLUMBIA

Number	Title	Yr	NM
❑ BFC39220	All Over the Place	1984	$15
❑ PC39220	All Over the Place	1986	$10
— Reissue with new prefix and longer bar code			
❑ BFC40039	Different Light	1986	$15
❑ FC40039	Different Light	1986	$10
— Reissue with new prefix; "02" added to bar code on back cover			

Number	Title	Yr	NM
❑ OC44056 [B]	Everything	1988	$12

Number	Title	Yr	NM
❑ CAS2270 [DJ]	Interchords	1986	$30
—Promo-only interview album			

FAULTY PRODUCTS
❑ FEP1302 [EP]	Bangles	1982	$25

I.R.S.
❑ SP-70506 [EP]	Bangles	1983	$15
—Reissue of Faulty Products EP			

BANGOR FLYING CIRCUS
ABC DUNHILL
❑ DS-50069	Bangor Flying Circus	1969	$18

BANJO KINGS, THE
GOOD TIME JAZZ
❑ L-12029 [M]	Nostalgia Revisited	1956	$40
❑ L-15 [10]	The Banjo Kings	1953	$50
❑ L-12015 [M]	The Banjo Kings	1955	$50
❑ L-12015 [M]	The Banjo Kings, Vol. 1	198?	$25
—Reissue with revised title and thinner vinyl			
❑ L-25 [10]	The Banjo Kings, Vol. 2	1954	$50
❑ L-12047 [M]	The Banjo Kings Enjoy the Good Old Days	1958	$40
❑ S-12047 [S]	The Banjo Kings Enjoy the Good Old Days	1959	$30
❑ L-12036 [M]	The Banjo Kings Go West	1957	$40

BANKS, ANT
JIVE
❑ 41496	Sittin' on Something Phat	1993	$18
—Vinyl may be promo only			
❑ 41534	The Big Badass	1994	$18
—Vinyl may be promo only			

PRIORITY
❑ 50698	Big Thangs	1997	$18

BANKS, DARRELL
ATCO
❑ 33-216 [M]	Darrell Banks Is Here	1967	$30
❑ SD 33-216 [S]	Darrell Banks Is Here	1967	$30

VOLT
❑ VOS-6002	Here to Stay	1969	$30

BANKS, PATRYCE "CHOC'LET"
T-ELECTRIC
❑ 3243	She's Back and Ready...	1980	$18

BANKS, PETER
CAPITOL/SOVEREIGN
❑ SMAS-11217	Two Sides of Peter Banks	1973	$18

BANKS, RON
CBS ASSOCIATED
❑ FZ39148	Truly Bad	1983	$12

BANKS, ROSE
MOTOWN
❑ M6-845S1	Rose	1976	$15

BANKS, TONY
ATLANTIC
❑ 82007	Bankstatement	1989	$12
—As "Bankstatement			
❑ 81680	Soundtracks	1986	$10
❑ 80071	The Fugitive	1983	$10

CHARISMA
❑ CA-1-2207 [B]	A Curious Feeling	1979	$15

BANKS AND HAMPTON
WARNER BROS.
❑ BS2993	Passport to Ecstasy	1977	$12

BANNON, R.C.
COLUMBIA
❑ KC35346	R.C. Bannon Arrives	1978	$15

BANTAMS, THE
WARNER BROS.
❑ W1625 [M]	Beware the Bantams	1966	$25
❑ WS1625 [S]	Beware the Bantams	1966	$30

BAR-KAYS, THE
ATCO

Number	Title	Yr	NM
❑ SD 33-289	Soul Finger	1968	$30

MERCURY
❑ 836774-1	Animal	1989	$12
❑ SRM-1-3844	As One	1980	$12
❑ 824727-1	Banging the Wall	1985	$12
❑ 830305-1	Contagious	1987	$12
❑ 818478-1	Dangerous	1984	$12
❑ SRM-1-1181	Flying High on Your Love	1977	$12
❑ SRM-1-3781	Injoy	1979	$12
❑ SRM-1-3732	Light of Life	1978	$12
❑ SRM-1-4028	Nightcruising	1981	$12
❑ SRM-1-4065	Propositions	1982	$12
❑ SRM-1-1099	Too Hot to Stop	1976	$12

STAX
❑ MPS-8510	Cold Blooded	1981	$12
❑ 4130	Gotta Groove	1979	$12
❑ 4106	Money Talks	1978	$12
❑ MPS-8542	The Best of the Bar-Kays	1988	$12

VOLT
❑ 6011	Black Rock	1971	$30
❑ 9504	Cold Blooded	1974	$30
❑ VOS-8001	Do You See What I See	1972	$30
❑ 6004	Gotta Groove	1969	$30
❑ 417 [M]	Soul Finger	1967	$40
❑ S-417 [S]	Soul Finger	1967	$40

BARBARIANS, THE
LAURIE
❑ LLP-2033 [M]	Are You a Boy or Are You a Girl?	1966	$150
❑ SLP-2033 [S]	Are You a Boy or Are You a Girl?	1966	$120

RHINO
❑ RNLP 008	The Barbarians	1979	$15

BARBARIN, PAUL, AND PUNCH MILLER
ATLANTIC
❑ 1410 [M]	Paul Barbarin and Punch Miller	1963	$25
❑ SD1410 [S]	Paul Barbarin and Punch Miller	1963	$30

BARBARIN, PAUL
ATLANTIC
❑ 1215 [M]	New Orleans Jazz	1955	$300
—Black label			
❑ 1215 [M]	New Orleans Jazz	1961	$175
—Multi-color label, white "fan" logo at right			
❑ 1215 [M]	New Orleans Jazz	1963	$35
—Multi-color label, black "fan" logo at right			
❑ SD1215 [S]	New Orleans Jazz	1959	$300
—Green label			
❑ SD1215 [S]	New Orleans Jazz	1961	$175
—Multi-color label, white "fan" logo at right			
❑ SD1215 [S]	New Orleans Jazz	1963	$35
—Multi-color label, black "fan" logo at right			

CIRCLE
❑ 408 [10]	Paul Barbarin's New Orleans Band	1951	$175

CONCERT HALL JAZZ
❑ 1006 [10]	New Orleans Jamboree	1954	$50

GHB
❑ GHB-140 [M]	Bourbon St. Beat	197?	$30
—Reissue of Southland LP			
❑ GHB-2 [M]	Paul Barbarin and His New Orleans Jazz Band	1962	$25

JAZZTONE
❑ J-1205 [M]	New Orleans Jamboree	1955	$50

NOBILITY
❑ 708	Last Journey of a Jazzman	196?	$25

SOUTHLAND
❑ SLP-237 [M]	Bourbon St. Beat	195?	$40

STORYVILLE
❑ 4049 [M]	Jazz from New Orleans	198?	$25

BARBARIN, PAUL / JOHNNY ST. CYR
SOUTHLAND
❑ SLP-212 [M]	Paul Barbarin and His Jazz Band/Johnny St. Cyr and His Hot Five	1955	$50

BARBARIN, PAUL / SHARKEY BONANO
RIVERSIDE
❑ RLP 12-217 [M]	New Orleans Contrasts	1955	$300
—White label, blue print			
❑ RLP 12-217 [M]	New Orleans Contrasts	195?	$40
—Blue label with microphone logo			

BARBARY, RICHARD
A&M
❑ SP-3010	Soul Machine	1969	$50

BARBER, AVA
RANWOOD
❑ 8170	Grits	1977	$15
❑ 8180	You're Gonna Love Love	1978	$15

BARBER, CHRIS
ATLANTIC
❑ 1292 [M]	Here Is Chris Barber	1959	$300

COLPIX
❑ CP-404 [M]	Chris Barber Plays "Trad	1959	$75

GHB
❑ GHB-40 [M]	Collaboration	1967	$35

LAURIE
❑ LLP-1009 [M]	Chris Barber's "American" Jazz Band	1962	$75
❑ 1001 [M]	Petite Fleur	1959	$40
❑ LLP-1003 [M]	Trad Jazz Volume 1	1960	$75

BARBER, GLENN
HICKORY
❑ LPS-152	New Star	1970	$18
❑ LPS-167	The Best of Glenn Barber	1973	$18

HICKORY/MGM
❑ H3F-4510	Glenn Barber	1974	$18

BARBER, PATRICIA
PREMONITION
❑ PREM737-1	Café Blue	199?	$30
—Audiophile vinyl			
❑ 90747	Companion	1999	$30
—Audiophile vinyl			
❑ PREM747-1	Modern Cool	1998	$30
—Audiophile vinyl			
❑ 27290	Nightclub	2000	$30
—Audiophile vinyl			

BARBIERI, GATO & DOLLAR BRAND
ARISTA FREEDOM
❑ AL1003	Confluence	1975	$35

BARBIERI, GATO
A&M
❑ SP-4597	Caliente!	1976	$25
❑ SP-3247	Caliente!	198?	$20
—Reissue of 4597			
❑ SP-4774	Euphoria	1979	$25
❑ SP-3188	Euphoria	198?	$20
—Reissue of 4774			
❑ SP-3029	Fire and Passion	1970	$75
❑ SP-9-3029	Fire and Passion	1984	$35
—Audio Master Plus" reissue			
❑ SP-4655	Ruby, Ruby	1977	$25
❑ SP-4710	Tropico	1978	$25

ABC IMPULSE!
❑ ASD-9303	Chapter Four -- Alive in New York	1975	$250
❑ AS-9248	Chapter One -- Latin America	1973	$250
❑ ASD-9279	Chapter Three -- Viva Emiliano Zapata	1974	$250
❑ AS-9263	Chapter Two -- Hasta Siempre	1974	$250

BLUEBIRD
❑ 6995-1-RB	Third World Revisited	1988	$30

DOCTOR JAZZ
❑ FW40183	Apasionado	1986	$25
❑ W2X39204	Gato...Para Los Amigos	1985	$30

Number	Title	Yr	NM

ESP-DISK'
❏ 1049	In Search of the Mystery	1968	$150

FANIA
❏ JM608	Gato = Bahia	1982	$30

FLYING DUTCHMAN
❏ FD10117	3rd World	1970	$50
❏ BXL1-2826	3rd World	1978	$25
—Reissue of 10117			
❏ AYL1-3815	3rd World	1980	$20
—Budget-line reissue			
❏ FD10158	Bolivia	1973	$75
❏ BXL1-2830	Bolivia	1978	$25
—Reissue of 10158			
❏ BDL1-1147	El Gato	1976	$30
❏ AYL1-3817	El Gato	1980	$20
—Budget-line reissue			
❏ FD10151	El Pampero	1973	$50
❏ BXL1-2828	El Pampero	1978	$25
—Reissue of 10151			
❏ FD10144	Fenix	1972	$50
❏ BXL1-2827	Fenix	1978	$25
—Reissue of 10144			
❏ FD10165	The Legend of Gato Barbieri	1974	$50
❏ FD10156	Under Fire	1973	$50
❏ BXL1-2829	Under Fire	1978	$25
—Reissue of 10156			
❏ BDL1-0550	Yesterdays	1974	$30
❏ AYL1-3816	Yesterdays	1980	$20
—Budget-line reissue			

MCA
❏ 29003	Chapter Four -- Alive in New York	1981	$25
—Reissue of Impulse 9303			
❏ 29002	Chapter Two -- Hasta Siempre	1981	$20
—Reissue of Impulse 9263			

QUINTESSENCE
❏ QJ-25281	Gato Barbieri	1979	$25
—Reissue of 1974 recordings			

UNITED ARTISTS
❏ UA-LA045-H	Last Tango in Paris	1973	$35

BARBOSA-LIMA, CARLOS, AND SHARON ISBIN

CONCORD CONCERTO
❏ CC-2012	Rhapsody in Blue/West Side Story	1988	$25

CONCORD PICANTE
❏ CJP-320	Brazil, With Love	1987	$25

BARBOSA-LIMA, CARLOS

CONCORD CONCERTO
❏ CC-2008	Carlos Barbosa-Lima Plays The Entertainer and Other Works by Scott Joplin	1985	$25
❏ CC-2005	Carlos Barbosa-Lima Plays the Music of Jobim and Gershwin	1983	$25
❏ CC-2006	Carlos Barbosa-Lima Plays the Music of Luiz Bonfa and Cole Porter	1984	$25
❏ CC-2009	Impressions	1991	$30

BARBOUR, KEITH

EPIC
❏ BN26485	Echo Park	1969	$25

BARCLAY JAMES HARVEST

HARVEST
❏ SW-11145 [B]	Baby James Harvest	1973	$25

MCA
❏ 2302	Gone to Earth	1977	$12
❏ 2234 [B]	Octoberon	1976	$12

POLYDOR
❏ PD-6508	Everyone Is Everybody Else	1974	$15
❏ PD-1-6267	Eyes of the Universe	1980	$12
❏ PD-6517	Time Honoured Ghosts	1975	$15
❏ PD-1-6173	XII	1978	$12

SIRE
❏ SI-4904	Back Again	1971	$18
❏ SES-97026	Barclay James Harvest	1970	$25
❏ SI-5904	Other Short Stories	1972	$18

BARDENS, PETE

CAPITOL
❏ ST-12555	Seen One Earth	1987	$12
❏ C1-48967	Speed of Light	1988	$12

BARDEUX

ENIGMA
❏ D1-73312	Bold As Love	1988	$12
❏ 7735221	Shangri-La	1989	$12

BARDOT, BRIGITTE & GAINSBOURG SERGE

4 MEN WITH BEARDS
❏ 4M178LP [B]	Bonnie and Clyde		$25

BARDOT, BRIGITTE

DOT
❏ DLP-3120 [M]	La Belle Bardot	1958	$150

PHILIPS
❏ PCC204 [M]	Brigitte Bardot Sings	1963	$30
❏ PCC604 [S]	Brigitte Bardot Sings	1963	$40

BARE, BOBBY, AND SKEETER DAVIS

RCA VICTOR
❏ LPM-3336 [M]	Tunes for Two	1965	$25
❏ LSP-3336 [S]	Tunes for Two	1965	$30
❏ LSP-4335	Your Husband, My Wife	1970	$18

BARE, BOBBY, NORMA JEAN, & LIZ ANDERSON

RCA VICTOR
❏ LPM-3764 [M]	The Game of Triangles	1967	$30
❏ LSP-3764 [S]	The Game of Triangles	1967	$25

BARE, BOBBY

COLUMBIA
❏ FC37719	Ain't Got Nothin' to Lose	1982	$12
❏ FC37157	As Is	1981	$12
❏ KC35314	Bare	1977	$12
❏ FC38311	Biggest Hits	1982	$12
❏ JC36323	Down & Dirty	1978	$12
❏ PC36323	Down & Dirty	198?	$10
—Budget-line reissue			
❏ FC38670	Drinkin' from the Bottle, Singin' from the Heart	1983	$12
❏ JC36785	Drunk & Crazy	1980	$12
❏ FC37351	Encore	1981	$12
❏ PC37351	Encore	198?	$10
—Budget-line reissue			

HILLTOP
❏ 6026	Tender Years	196?	$15

MERCURY
❏ SR-61290	This Is Bare Country	1970	$25
❏ SR-61363	What Am I Gonna Do?	1972	$25
❏ SR-61316	Where Have All the Seasons Gone	1971	$25

PICKWICK
❏ ACL-7003	500 Miles Away from Home	1975	$12

RCA CAMDEN
❏ CAS-2290	Folsom Prison Blues	1969	$15
❏ CAS-2465	I'm a Long Way from Home	1971	$15
❏ ACL1-0150	Memphis, Tennessee	1973	$15

RCA VICTOR
❏ LPM-2835 [M]	500 Miles Away from Home	1964	$25
❏ LSP-2835 [S]	500 Miles Away from Home	1964	$30
❏ LPM-3831 [M]	A Bird Named Yesterday	1967	$30
❏ LSP-3831 [S]	A Bird Named Yesterday	1967	$25
❏ CPL2-0290	Bobby Bare Sings Lullabys, Legends and Lies	1973	$25
❏ AHL1-5469	Collector's Series	1985	$12
❏ LPM-3395 [M]	Constant Sorrow	1965	$25
❏ LSP-3395 [S]	Constant Sorrow	1965	$30
❏ APL1-1222	Cowboys and Daddys	1975	$15
❏ LPM-2776 [M]	Detroit City" and Other Hits	1963	$25
❏ LSP-2776 [S]	Detroit City" and Other Hits	1963	$30
❏ AYL1-4118	Greatest Hits	1982	$10
❏ APL1-0906 [B]	Hard Time Hungrys	1975	$15
❏ APL1-0040	I Hate Goodbyes/Ride Me Down Easy	1973	$18
❏ LSP-4177	(Margie's At) The Lincoln Park Inn (And Other Controversial Country Songs)	1969	$25
❏ APL1-2179	Me and McDill	1977	$15
❏ LSP-4422	Real Thing	1970	$18
❏ APL1-0700	Singin' in the Kitchen	1974	$18
❏ ANL1-0560	Sunday Morning	1974	$12
❏ LPM-3515 [M]	Talk Me Some Sense	1966	$25
❏ LSP-3515 [S]	Talk Me Some Sense	1966	$30
❏ LPM-3479 [M]	The Best of Bobby Bare	1965	$25
❏ LSP-3479 [S]	The Best of Bobby Bare	1965	$30
❏ LPM-3994 [M]	The Best of Bobby Bare -- Volume 2	1968	$40
❏ LSP-3994 [S]	The Best of Bobby Bare -- Volume 2	1968	$25
❏ LPM-3896 [M]	The English Country Side	1967	$40
❏ LSP-3896 [S]	The English Country Side	1967	$25
❏ LPM-3618 [M]	The Streets of Baltimore	1966	$25
❏ LSP-3618 [S]	The Streets of Baltimore	1966	$30
❏ LPM-2955 [M]	The Travelin' Bare	1964	$25
❏ LSP-2955 [S]	The Travelin' Bare	1964	$30
❏ APL1-1786	The Winner and Other Losers	1976	$15
❏ LPM-3688 [M]	This I Believe	1966	$25
❏ LSP-3688 [S]	This I Believe	1966	$30
❏ VPS-6090	This Is Bobby Bare	1972	$25

UNITED ARTISTS
❏ UA-LA621-G	Bare Country	1977	$15

BARGE, GENE

CHECKER
❏ LP-2994 [M]	Dance with Daddy G	1965	$50

BARKER, WARREN

WARNER BROS.
❏ W1205 [M]	The King and I" for Orchestra	1958	$30
❏ WS1205 [S]	The King and I" for Orchestra	1958	$30
❏ W1290 [M]	TV Guide -- Top TV Themes	1959	$30
❏ WS1290 [S]	TV Guide -- Top TV Themes	1959	$40
❏ B1308 [M]	William Holden Presents a Musical Touch of Far Away Places	1959	$75
❏ BS1308 [S]	William Holden Presents a Musical Touch of Far Away Places	1959	$40

BARLOW, RANDY

GAZELLE
❏ 6021	Arrival	1976	$18

PAID
❏ 2002	Dimensions	1981	$15

REPUBLIC
❏ RLP6023	Fall in Love with Me	1978	$15
❏ RLP6024	Randy Barlow Featuring Sweet Melinda	1979	$15

BARNABY BYE

ATLANTIC
❏ SD7273	Room to Grow	1973	$15
❏ SD18104	Touch	1974	$15

BARNES, CHERYL

OPTIMISM
❏ OP-3105	Cheryl	198?	$30

BARNES, EMIL

AMERICAN MUSIC
❏ LP-641 [10]	New Orleans Trad Jazz	1952	$50

JAZZOLOGY
❏ JCE-34 [M]	Emil Barnes and His New Orleans Music	197?	$30
❏ JCE-23 [M]	Too Well Thou Lov'st	1967	$30

BARNES, GEORGE, AND KARL KRESS

STASH
❏ ST-222	Two Guitars	198?	$25
❏ ST-228	Two Guitars and a Horn	198?	$25

UNITED ARTISTS
❏ UAL3335 [M]	Town Hall Concert	1963	$75
❏ UAS6335 [S]	Town Hall Concert	1963	$75

BARNES, GEORGE

DECCA
❏ DL8658 [M]	Guitars -- By George	1957	$120
—Black label, silver print			

GRAND AWARD
❏ GA 33-358 [M]	Guitar in Velvet	195?	$30

MERCURY
❏ MG-20956 [M]	Guitar Galaxies	1962	$150
❏ SR-60956 [S]	Guitar Galaxies	1962	$150
❏ PPS-2011 [M]	Guitar Galaxies	196?	$150
❏ PPS-6011 [S]	Guitar Galaxies	196?	$150

BARNES, J.J.

VOLT
❏ VOS-6001	Rare Stamps	1969	$30
—With Steve Mancha			

BARNES, JIMMY

GEFFEN
❏ GHS24146	Freight Train Heart	1988	$10
❏ GHS24089	Jimmy Barnes	1986	$10

BARNES, MAE

ATLANTIC
❏ ALS-404 [10]	Fun with Mae Barnes	1953	$400

VANGUARD
❏ VRS-9036 [M]	Meet Mae Barnes	1958	$150

BARNES, SIDNEY

PARACHUTE
❏ 9009	Footstomp'n Music	1978	$15

BARNET, CHARLIE

AIRCHECK
❏ 5	Charlie Barnet and His Orchestra 1945	197?	$25
❏ 30	Charlie Barnet On the Air Vol. 2	198?	$25

Number	Title	Yr	NM

ALAMAC
| ❏ QSR2446 | Charlie Barnet & His Orchestra 1949 | 198? | $25 |

AVA
| ❏ A-10 [M] | Charlie Barnet !?!?!?!?!?!?! | 1962 | $30 |
| ❏ AS-10 [S] | Charlie Barnet !?!?!?!?!?!?! | 1962 | $30 |

BLUEBIRD
❏ AXM2-5526	The Complete Charlie Barnet Vol. 1, 1935-37	197?	$35
❏ AXM2-5577	The Complete Charlie Barnet Vol. 2, 1939	197?	$35
❏ AXM2-5581	The Complete Charlie Barnet Vol. 3, 1939-40	197?	$35
❏ AXM2-5585	The Complete Charlie Barnet Vol. 4, 1940	197?	$35
❏ AXM2-5587	The Complete Charlie Barnet Vol. 5, 1940-41	197?	$35
❏ AXM2-5590	The Complete Charlie Barnet Vol. 6, 1940-41	197?	$35

BRIGHT ORANGE
| ❏ XBO-706 [S] | The Stereophonic Sound of the Charlie Barnet Orchestra | 196? | $35 |

CAPITOL
❏ H235 [10]	Big Bands	195?	$150
❏ T624 [M]	Classics in Jazz	1955	$100
❏ T1403 [M]	Jazz Oasis	1960	$50
❏ ST1403 [S]	Jazz Oasis	1960	$75
❏ H325 [10]	The Modern Idiom	1952	$300

CHOREO
| ❏ A-10 [M] | Charlie Barnet !?!?!?!?!?!?! | 196? | $25 |
| ❏ AS-10 [S] | Charlie Barnet !?!?!?!?!?!?! | 196? | $30 |

— Some copies have Choreo logo on front cover, but Ava labels and back cover

CIRCLE
| ❏ CLP-65 | Charlie Barnet and His Orchestra 1941 | 198? | $25 |

CLEF
❏ MGC-164 [10]	Charlie Barnet Dance Session, Vol. 1	1954	$300
❏ MGC-165 [10]	Charlie Barnet Dance Session, Vol. 2	1954	$300
❏ MGC-114 [10]	Charlie Barnet Plays Charlie Barnet	1953	$300
❏ MGC-139 [10]	Dance with Charlie Barnet	1953	$300
❏ MGC-638 [M]	One Night Stand	1955	$250

COLUMBIA
| ❏ CL639 [M] | Town Hall Jazz Concert | 1955 | $75 |

— Maroon label, gold print
| ❏ CL639 [M] | Town Hall Jazz Concert | 195? | $40 |

— Black and red label with six "eye" logos

CREATIVE WORLD
| ❏ ST1056 | Charlie Barnet Big Band 1967 | 197? | $30 |

— Reissue of Vault LPS-9004

CROWN
❏ CLP-5114 [M]	A Tribute to Harry James	195?	$25
❏ CLP-5127 [M]	Charlie Barnet Presents a Salute to Harry James	195?	$25
❏ CLP-5134 [M]	On Stage with Charlie Barnet	1959	$25

DECCA
| ❏ DL8098 [M] | Hop on the Skyliner | 195? | $50 |

EVEREST
❏ LPBR-5008 [M]	Cherokee	1958	$30
❏ SDBR-1008 [S]	Cherokee	1959	$25
❏ LPBR-5059 [M]	More Charlie Barnet	196?	$25
❏ SDBR-5059 [S]	More Charlie Barnet	196?	$30

HEP
| ❏ 2005 | Live at Basin Street East | 198? | $25 |

MCA
| ❏ 2-4069 | The Best of Charlie Barnet | 1975 | $30 |

— Black rainbow labels
| ❏ 2-4069 | The Best of Charlie Barnet | 1980 | $25 |

— Blue rainbow labels

MERCURY
| ❏ MGC-114 [10] | Charlie Barnet Plays Charlie Barnet | 1952 | $300 |

RCA VICTOR
❏ LPV-551 [M]	Charlie Barnet (Volume 1)	1968	$25
❏ LPV-567 [M]	Charlie Barnet (Volume 2)	1969	$25
❏ LPM-1091 [M]	Redskin Romp	1955	$75
❏ LPT-3062 [10]	Rockin' in Rhythm	195?	$100
❏ LPM-2081 [M]	The Great Dance Bands	1960	$25

SUNSET
| ❏ SUS-5150 | Cherokee | 1967 | $30 |

SWING
| ❏ 103 [M] | Charlie Barnet and His Orchestra | 195? | $40 |

TIME-LIFE
| ❏ STBB-07 | Big Bands: Charlie Barnet | 1983 | $35 |

VAULT
| ❏ LP-9004 [M] | Charlie Barnet Big Band 1967 | 1967 | $25 |
| ❏ LPS-9004 [S] | Charlie Barnet Big Band 1967 | 1967 | $35 |

VERVE
❏ MGV-2007 [M]	Dance Bash	1956	$175
❏ V-2007 [M]	Dance Bash	1961	$25
❏ MGV-2027 [M]	Dancing Party	1956	$175
❏ V-2027 [M]	Dancing Party	1961	$25
❏ MGV-2031 [M]	For Dancing Lovers	1956	$175
❏ V-2031 [M]	For Dancing Lovers	1961	$25
❏ MGV-2040 [M]	Lonely Street	1957	$175
❏ V-2040 [M]	Lonely Street	1961	$25

BARNETT, BOBBY

SIMS
| ❏ LP-198 [M] | Bobby Barnett at the World Famous Crystal Palace, Tombstone, Arizona | 1964 | $30 |

BARNUM, H.B.

CAPITOL
❏ T2289 [M]	Big Hits of Detroit	1965	$18
❏ ST2289 [S]	Big Hits of Detroit	1965	$25
❏ T2278 [M]	Golden Boy	1965	$18
❏ ST2278 [S]	Golden Boy	1965	$25
❏ T2583 [M]	Pop and Ice Cream Sodas	1966	$18
❏ ST2583 [S]	Pop and Ice Cream Sodas	1966	$25

BAROQUE ENSEMBLE OF THE MERSEYSIDE KAMMERMUSIKGESELLSCHAFT, THE

ELEKTRA
| ❏ EKL-306 [M] | The Baroque Beatles Book | 1966 | $30 |
| ❏ EKS-7306 [S] | The Baroque Beatles Book | 1966 | $30 |

BAROQUES, THE

CHESS
| ❏ LP-1516 [M] | The Baroques | 1967 | $100 |
| ❏ LPS-1516 [S] | The Baroques | 1967 | $150 |

BARR, WALT

MUSE
❏ 5238	Artful Dancer	1980	$35
❏ 5210	East Winds	1979	$35
❏ 5172	First Visit	1978	$35

BARRABAS

ATCO
❏ SD 36-110	Barrabas	1974	$12
❏ SD 36-118	Heart of the City	1975	$12
❏ SD 36-136	Watch Out	1976	$12

RCA VICTOR
| ❏ LSP-4861 | Wild Safari | 1973 | $15 |

BARRACUDAS, THE

JUSTICE
| ❏ JLP-143 | A Plane View | 1968 | $300 |

BARRETT, DAN

CONCORD JAZZ
| ❏ CJ-331 | Strictly Instrumental | 1988 | $25 |

BARRETT, EMMA

GHB
| ❏ 142 [M] | Emma Barrett at Disneyland | 1969 | $30 |

— Reissue of Southland 242
| ❏ 141 [M] | Sweet Emma Barrett and Her New Orleans Music | 1969 | $30 |

— Reissue of Southland 241

NOBILITY
| ❏ 711 [M] | The Bell Gal and Her New Orleans Jazz | 196? | $25 |

RIVERSIDE
| ❏ RLP-364 [M] | Sweet Emma | 1960 | $250 |
| ❏ RS-9364 [R] | Sweet Emma | 196? | $25 |

SOUTHLAND
| ❏ 242 [M] | Emma Barrett at Disneyland | 1967 | $25 |
| ❏ 241 [M] | Sweet Emma Barrett and Her New Orleans Music | 1964 | $25 |

BARRETT, RONA

MISS RONA
| ❏ MRR1001 | Miss Rona Sings Hollywood's Greatest Hits | 1974 | $40 |

BARRETT, SUSAN

CAPITOL
| ❏ T1266 [M] | Mixed Emotions | 1959 | $50 |

RCA VICTOR
| ❏ LPM-3738 [M] | Susan Barrett | 1967 | $40 |
| ❏ LSP-3738 [S] | Susan Barrett | 1967 | $30 |

BARRETT, SYD
Member of the earliest incarnation of PINK FLOYD.

CAPITOL

| ❏ C1-91206 [B] | Opel | 1989 | $25 |

HARVEST
❏ RP1543314 [B]	Barrett	2014	$30
❏ RP1543315 [B]	The Madcap Laughs	2014	$30
❏ SABB-11314	The Madcap Laughs/Barrett	1974	$30

BARRETTO, RAY

ATLANTIC
❏ SD19198	Can You	1978	$30
❏ SD19140	Eye of the Beholder	1977	$30
❏ SD 2-509	Tomorrow: Ray Barretto Live	197?	$35

CTI
| ❏ 9002 | La Cuna | 198? | $25 |

FANIA
❏ SLP-346 [B]	Acid	196?	$25
❏ SLP-388	Barretto Head Sounds	197?	$25
❏ SLP-410	From the Beginning	197?	$25
❏ SLP-362	Hard Hands	1970	$25
❏ SLP-391	Power	197?	$25
❏ SLP-403	The Message	197?	$25
❏ SLP-378	Together	197?	$25

FANTASY
| ❏ 24713 | Carnaval | 197? | $35 |

TICO
❏ LP-1087 [M]	Charanga Moderna	1962	$25
❏ SLP-1087 [S]	Charanga Moderna	1962	$30
❏ LP-1114 [M]	Guajira y Guaguanco	1964	$25
❏ SLP-1114 [S]	Guajira y Guaguanco	1964	$30
❏ LP-1102 [M]	La Moderna De Siempre	1963	$25
❏ SLP-1102 [S]	La Moderna De Siempre	1963	$30
❏ CLP-1314	Lo Mejor De Ray Barretto	1973	$35
❏ SLP-1205	Something to Remember	1969	$35
❏ LP-1099 [M]	The Hit Latin Style of Ray Barretto	1963	$25
❏ SLP-1099 [S]	The Hit Latin Style of Ray Barretto	1963	$30

BARRON, BILL

AUDIO FIDELITY
| ❏ AFLP-2123 [M] | Now Hear This! | 1964 | $25 |
| ❏ AFSD-6123 [S] | Now Hear This! | 1964 | $30 |

DAUNTLESS
| ❏ DM-4312 [M] | West Side Story Bossa Nova | 1963 | $30 |
| ❏ DS-6312 [S] | West Side Story Bossa Nova | 1963 | $30 |

MUSE
| ❏ 5235 | Jazz Caper | 1978 | $30 |
| ❏ 5306 | Variations in Blue | 1983 | $30 |

SAVOY
❏ MG-12183 [M]	Hot Line	1965	$175
❏ MG-12163 [M]	Modern Windows	1962	$175
❏ MG-12303	Motivation	197?	$35
❏ MG-12160 [M]	The Tenor Stylings of Bill Barron	1961	$40

SAVOY JAZZ
| ❏ SJL-1184 | Nebulae | 1987 | $25 |
| ❏ SJL-1160 | The Hot Line | 1986 | $25 |

BARRON, KENNY, AND TED DUNBAR

MUSE
| ❏ MR-5140 | In Tandem | 1975 | $30 |

BARRON, KENNY

BLACK HAWK
| ❏ 50601 | 1 + 1 + 1 | 1986 | $30 |

CRISS CROSS
| ❏ 3008 | Green Chimneys | 1984 | $30 |

EASTWIND
| ❏ 709 | Spiral | 1982 | $30 |

Number	Title	Yr	NM
LIMETREE			
❏ 20	Landscape	1984	$30
MUSE			
❏ MR-5220	Golden Lotus	1980	$30
❏ MR-5080	Lucifer	1975	$30
❏ MR-5044	Peruvian Blue	1974	$30
❏ MR-5014	Sunset to Dawn	1973	$30
WHY NOT			
❏ 25032	Imo Live	1982	$30
WOLF			
❏ 1203	Innocence	1978	$35
XANADU			
❏ 188	Kenny Barron at the Piano	1981	$30
BARROW, KEITH			
CAPITOL			
❏ ST-12112	Just As I Am	1980	$15
COLUMBIA			
❏ PC34465	Keith Barrow	1976	$15
❏ JC35597	Physical Attraction	1978	$15
BARRY, CLAUDJA			
CHRYSALIS			
❏ CHR1232	Boogie Woogie Dancin' Shoes	1979	$15
❏ CHR1251	Feel the Fire	1980	$15
EPIC			
❏ FE40622	I, Claudja	1987	$12
PERSONAL			
❏ 59801 [EP]	No La De Da Part 2	1983	$15
SALSOUL			
❏ SA5525	Claudja	1977	$15
❏ SA5512	Sweet Dynamite	1977	$15
BARRY, GENE			
RCA VICTOR			
❏ LPM-2975 [M]	The Star of "Burke's Law" Sings of Love and Things	1964	$30
❏ LSP-2975 [S]	The Star of "Burke's Law" Sings of Love and Things	1964	$30
BARRY, JEFF			
A&M			
❏ SP-4393 [B]	Walkin' in the Sun	1973	$30
BARRY, JOHN			
BULLDOG			
❏ BDL-1036 [B]	Bond by Barry	198?	$12
COLUMBIA			
❏ CL2493 [M]	Great Movie Sounds of John Barry	1966	$18
❏ CS9293 [S]	Great Movie Sounds of John Barry	1966	$25
❏ C1003	Ready When You Are, Mr. J.B.	1970	$12
❏ CL2708 [M]	You Only Live Twice	1967	$18
❏ CS9508 [S]	You Only Live Twice	1967	$25
UNITED ARTISTS			
❏ UAL3424 [M]	Goldfinger and Other Favorites	1965	$15
❏ UAS6424 [S]	Goldfinger and Other Favorites	1965	$18
BARRY, LEN			
BUDDAH			
❏ BDS-5105	Ups & Downs	1972	$18
DECCA			
❏ DL4720 [M]	1-2-3	1965	$30
❏ DL74720 [P]	1-2-3	1965	$40
—Lip Sync" is rechanneled			
RCA VICTOR			
❏ LPM-3823 [M]	My Kind of Soul	1967	$30
❏ LSP-3823 [S]	My Kind of Soul	1967	$25
BARRY AND THE TAMERLANES			
VALIANT			
❏ LP-406 [M]	I Wonder What She's Doing Tonight	1963	$175
❏ LPS-406 [S]	I Wonder What She's Doing Tonight	1963	$300
BARRY SISTERS, THE			
ABC			
❏ ABCS-597 [S]	A Time to Remember	1967	$15
❏ ABC-597 [M]	A Time to Remember	1967	$18
❏ ABCS-578 [S]	Something Spanish	1966	$18
❏ ABC-578 [M]	Something Spanish	1966	$15
ABC-PARAMOUNT			
❏ ABCS-516 [S]	The Barry Sisters Sing Fiddler on the Roof	1965	$18
❏ ABC-516 [M]	The Barry Sisters Sing Fiddler on the Roof	1965	$15

Number	Title	Yr	NM
CADENCE			
❏ CLP-4001 [M]	The Barry Sisters Sing All Time Yiddish Favorites	1958	$18
—Reissue of 1017			
❏ CLP-1017 [M]	The Barry Sisters Sing All Time Yiddish Favorites	1957	$25
ROULETTE			
❏ SR-25060 [S]	At Home with the Barry Sisters	1959	$25
❏ R-25060 [M]	At Home with the Barry Sisters	1959	$18
❏ R-25157 [M]	Shalom	1962	$18
❏ SR-25157 [S]	Shalom	1962	$25
❏ SR-25136 [S]	Side by Side	1960	$25
❏ R-25136 [M]	Side by Side	1960	$18
❏ SR-25198 [S]	The Barry Sisters in Israel	1963	$25
❏ R-25198 [M]	The Barry Sisters in Israel	1963	$18
❏ R-25258 [M]	The World of the Barry Sisters	1964	$15
❏ SR-25258 [S]	The World of the Barry Sisters	1964	$18
❏ SR-25156 [S]	We Belong Together	1961	$25
❏ R-25156 [M]	We Belong Together	1961	$18
BARRYMORE, LIONEL, AS EBENEZER SCROOGE			
MGM			
❏ CH112 [10]	A Christmas Carol	1952	$40
BARTEL, JON, THING			
CAPITOL			
❏ ST-274	The Jon Bartel Thing	1969	$30
BARTHOLOMEW, DAVE			
BROADMOOR			
❏ BR-1201	Dave Bartholomew's New Orleans Jazz Band	1981	$18
IMPERIAL			
❏ LP-9162 [M]	Fats Domino Presents Dave Bartholomew	1961	$175
❏ LP-12076 [S]	Fats Domino Presents Dave Bartholomew	1961	$250
❏ LP-9217 [M]	New Orleans House Party	1963	$175
❏ LP-12217 [S]	New Orleans House Party	1963	$250
BARTLEY, CHARLENE			
RCA VICTOR			
❏ LPM-1478 [M]	Weekend of a Private Secretary	1957	$50
BARTLEY, CHRIS			
VANDO			
❏ VAS-60000 [S]	The Sweetest Thing This Side of Heaven	1967	$40
❏ VA-60000 [M]	The Sweetest Thing This Side of Heaven	1967	$50
BARTON, LOU ANN			
ANTONE'S			
❏ ANT 0009	Read My Lips	1989	$12
ASYLUM			
❏ 60032	Old Enough	1982	$18
SPINDLETOP			
❏ 107	Forbidden Tones	1986	$15
BARTZ, GARY			
ARISTA			
❏ AL4263	Bartz	1979	$15
CAPITOL			
❏ SW-11789	Love Affair	1978	$15
❏ ST-11647	My Sanctuary	1977	$15
CATALYST			
❏ 7610	Ju Ju Man	1976	$15
MILESTONE			
❏ 9018	Another Earth	1969	$25
❏ 9031	Harlem Bush Music -- Taifa	1971	$25
❏ 9032	Harlem Bush Music -- Uhuru	1972	$25
❏ 9027	Home!	1970	$25
❏ 9006	Libra	1968	$25
PRESTIGE			
❏ 10068	Follow the Medicine Man	197?	$35
❏ 66001	I've Known Rivers	197?	$25
❏ 10057	Juju St. Songs	197?	$35
❏ 10083	Singerella -- A Ghetto Fairy Tale	197?	$35
❏ 10092	The Shadow 'Do	1975	$35
VEE JAY			
❏ VJS-3068	Love Song	1977	$30
BAS NOIR			
ATLANTIC			
❏ 4503 [DJ]	Bas Noir	1992	$18
—Vinyl is promo only			
BASE, ROB, AND D.J. E-Z ROCK			
PROFILE			
❏ PRO-1267	It Takes Two	1988	$15
❏ PRO-1285	The Incredible Base	1989	$15

Number	Title	Yr	NM
BASEMENT JAXX			
ASTRALWERKS			
❏ 6270	Remedy	1999	$18
BASIA			
EPIC			
❏ EAS2821 [EP]	Basia	1988	$18
—Promo-only four-song sampler			
❏ E45472	London Warsaw New York	1990	$12
❏ FE40767	Time and Tide	1988	$10
BASIE, COUNT, AND BILLY ECKSTINE			
ROULETTE			
❏ R52029 [M]	Basie/Eckstine, Incorporated	1959	$75
❏ SR52029 [S]	Basie/Eckstine, Incorporated	1959	$40
❏ SR42017	Count Basie and Billy Eckstine	1968	$35
—Reissue			
BASIE, COUNT, AND DIZZY GILLESPIE			
PABLO			
❏ 2310833	The Gifted Ones	1979	$25
VERVE			
❏ V-8560 [M]	The Count Basie Band and the Dizzy Gillespie Band at Newport	1963	$50
❏ V6-8560 [S]	The Count Basie Band and the Dizzy Gillespie Band at Newport	1963	$75
BASIE, COUNT, AND DUKE ELLINGTON			
ACCORD			
❏ SN-7200	Heads of State	1982	$25
BASIE, COUNT, AND JOE WILLIAMS			
CLEF			
❏ MGC-678 [M]	Count Basie Swings/Joe Williams Sings	1955	$300
ROULETTE			
❏ R52093 [M]	Back to Basie and Blues	1963	$75
❏ SR52093 [S]	Back to Basie and Blues	1963	$75
❏ R52033 [M]	Everyday I Have the Blues	1959	$75
❏ SR52033 [S]	Everyday I Have the Blues	1959	$40
❏ R52054 [M]	Just the Blues	1960	$75
❏ SR52054 [S]	Just the Blues	1960	$40
❏ R52021 [M]	Memories Ad Lib	1959	$75
❏ SR52021 [S]	Memories Ad Lib	1959	$40
VANGUARD			
❏ VRS-8508 [M]	A Night at Count Basie's	1955	$200
VERVE			
❏ MGV-8063 [M]	Count Basie Swings/Joe Williams Sings	1957	$300
—Reissue of Clef 678			
❏ V-8488 [M]	Count Basie Swings/Joe Williams Sings	1962	$75
—Reissue of 8063			
❏ V6-8488 [R]	Count Basie Swings/Joe Williams Sings	1962	$30
❏ UMV-2650	The Greatest	1981	$25
❏ MGV-2016 [M]	The Greatest! Count Basie Swings/Joe Williams Sings Standards	1956	$150
❏ MGVS-6006 [S]	The Greatest! Count Basie Swings/Joe Williams Sings Standards	1960	$150
BASIE, COUNT, AND MAYNARD FERGUSON			
ROULETTE			
❏ R52117 [M]	Big Band Scene '65	1965	$50
❏ SR52117 [S]	Big Band Scene '65	1965	$75
BASIE, COUNT, AND OSCAR PETERSON			
PABLO			
❏ 2310843	Night Rider	1979	$25
❏ 2310722	Satch" and "Josh	1975	$30
❏ 2310802	Satch and Josh Again	1978	$25
❏ 2310896	The Timekeepers	198?	$30
❏ 2310923	Yessir, That's My Baby	1987	$25
BASIE, COUNT, AND SAMMY DAVIS, JR.			
VERVE			
❏ V-8605 [M]	Our Shining Hour	1965	$35
❏ V6-8605 [S]	Our Shining Hour	1965	$50
BASIE, COUNT, AND THE MILLS BROTHERS			
Also see each artist's individual listings.			
DOT			
❏ DLP-25838	The Board of Directors	1968	$85
BASIE, COUNT; JOE WILLIAMS; LAMBERT, HENDRICKS AND ROSS			
ROULETTE			
❏ R52018 [M]	Sing Along with Basie	1959	$50
❏ SR52018 [S]	Sing Along with Basie	1959	$75

BASIE, COUNT

Number	Title	Yr	NM
ABC			
❑ 4001	16 Great Performances	1974	$30
❑ AC-30004	The ABC Collection	1976	$30
ABC IMPULSE!			
❑ AS-15 [S]	Count Basie and the Kansas City Seven	1968	$30
❑ IA-9351	Retrospective Sessions	1978	$30
ABC-PARAMOUNT			
❑ ABC-570 [M]	Basie's Swingin' -- Voices Singin'	1966	$50
❑ ABCS-570 [S]	Basie's Swingin' -- Voices Singin'	1966	$75
ACCORD			
❑ SN-7183	Command Performance	1981	$25
ALAMAC			
❑ QSR-2412	Count Basie and His Orchestra 1937	198?	$25
AMERICAN RECORDING SOCIETY			
❑ G-422 [M]	Basie's Best	1957	$40
❑ G-401 [M]	Count Basie	1956	$40
❑ G-435 [M]	Mainstream Jazz Swing	1957	$40
❑ G-402 [M]	The Band That Swings the Blues	1956	$40
BASF			
❑ 25111	Basic Basie	1973	$35
BOOK-OF-THE-MONTH CLUB			
❑ 91-6545	The Early Years	1982	$75
—Alternate number: P3-16389			
BRIGHT ORANGE			
❑ XBO-702	Count Basie Featuring B.B. King	196?	$50
BRUNSWICK			
❑ BL58019 [10]	Basie's Best	195?	$150
❑ BL754127	Basie's in the Bag	196?	$35
❑ BL54012 [M]	Count Basie	1957	$40
BULLDOG			
❑ BDL-2020	20 Golden Pieces of Count Basie	1980	$30
CLEF			
❑ MGC-666 [M]	Basie	1955	$350
❑ MGC-749 [M]	Basie in Europe	1956	$0
—Canceled; released as Verve 8199			
❑ MGC-633 [M]	Basie Jazz	1954	$350
❑ MGC-729 [M]	Basie Rides Again!	1956	$300
❑ MGC-723 [M]	Basie Roars Again	1956	$300
❑ MCG-120 [10]	Count Basie and His Orchestra Collates	1953	$350
❑ MGC-148 [10]	Count Basie Big Band	1954	$350
❑ MGC-626 [M]	Count Basie Dance Session #1	1954	$350
❑ MGC-647 [M]	Count Basie Jazz Session #2	1955	$350
❑ MCG-146 [10]	Count Basie Sextet	1954	$350
❑ MGC-722 [M]	The Band of Distinction	1956	$300
❑ MGC-685 [M]	The Count	1956	$300

Number	Title	Yr	NM
❑ MGC-724 [M]	The King of Swing	1956	$75
❑ MGC-706 [M]	The Swinging Count	1956	$300
COLISEUM			
❑ 51003 [S]	The Happiest Millionaire	1968	$35
❑ 41003 [M]	The Happiest Millionaire	1968	$40
COLUMBIA			
❑ CL2560 [10]	Basie Bash	1956	$175
❑ CL901 [M]	Blues By Basie	1956	$40
❑ CL754 [M]	Classics	1955	$120
❑ CL6079 [10]	Dance Parade	1949	$200
❑ CL997 [M]	One O'Clock Jump	1956	$40
❑ G31224	Super Chief	1972	$35
COLUMBIA JAZZ MASTERPIECES			
❑ CJ40608	The Essential Count Basie, Volume 1	1987	$25
❑ CJ40835	The Essential Count Basie, Volume 2	1987	$25

Number	Title	Yr	NM
❑ CJ44150	The Essential Count Basie, Volume 3	1988	$25
COLUMBIA JAZZ ODYSSEY			
❑ PC36824	Blues By Basie	1981	$20
COLUMBIA SPECIAL PRODUCTS			
❑ P14355	The Count	198?	$20
COMMAND			
❑ 33-905 [M]	Broadway Basie's...Way	1966	$30
❑ RS905SD [S]	Broadway Basie's...Way	1966	$35
❑ CQ-40004 [Q]	Broadway Basie's...Way	1972	$75
❑ 33-912 [M]	Hollywood... Basie's Way	1967	$35
❑ RS912SD [S]	Hollywood... Basie's Way	1967	$30
DAYBREAK			
❑ 2005	Have a Nice Day	1971	$30
DECCA			
❑ DL8049 [M]	Count Basie and His Orchestra	1954	$175
❑ DL78049 [R]	Count Basie and His Orchestra	196?	$30
❑ DL5111 [10]	Count Basie at the Piano	1950	$300
❑ DXB170 [M]	The Best of Count Basie	196?	$75
❑ DXSB7170 [R]	The Best of Count Basie	196?	$35
DOCTOR JAZZ			
❑ FW39520	Afrique	1985	$25
—Reissue of Flying Dutchman 10138			
DOT			
❑ DLP-25938	Standing Ovation	1969	$85
❑ DLP-25902	Straight Ahead	1969	$85
EMARCY			
❑ MG-26023 [10]	Jazz Royalty	1954	$250
EMUS			
❑ ES12011	Basie at Birdland	197?	$25
EPIC			
❑ LN3169 [M]	Basie's Back in Town	1955	$250
❑ LN3107 [M]	Lester Leaps In	1955	$250
—With Lester Young			
❑ LN3168 [M]	Let's Go to Prez	1955	$250
—With Lester Young			
❑ LN1117 [10]	Rock the Blues	1955	$300
❑ LG1021 [10]	The Old Count and the New Count -- Basie	1954	$300
EVEREST ARCHIVE OF FOLK & JAZZ			
❑ FS-318	Savoy Ballroom 1937	197?	$25
FANTASY			
❑ OJC-416	88 Basie Street	198?	$30
❑ OJC-379	Basie Big Band Montreux '77	1989	$25
—Reissue of Pablo Live 2308 209			
❑ OJC-600	Kansas City 3/For the Second Time	1991	$30
—Reissue of Pablo 2310 878			
❑ OJC-449	Kansas City 6	1990	$30
—Reissue of Pablo 2310 871			
FLYING DUTCHMAN			
❑ FD10138	Afrique	1972	$75
FORUM			
❑ F-9032 [M]	Kansas City Suite	196?	$30
❑ SF-9032 [S]	Kansas City Suite	196?	$35
—Reissue of Roulette 52056			
❑ F-9063 [M]	Not Now -- I'll Tell You When	196?	$30
❑ SF-9063 [S]	Not Now -- I'll Tell You When	196?	$35
—Reissue of Roulette 52044			
❑ F-9060 [M]	One More Time	196?	$30
❑ SF-9060 [S]	One More Time	196?	$35
—Reissue of Roulette 52024			
GROOVE MERCHANT			
❑ 2001	Evergreens	1972	$30
HAPPY TIGER			
❑ 1007	Basie on the Beatles	196?	$75
HARMONY			
❑ HL7229 [M]	Basie's Best	1960	$35
❑ HS11371	Just in Time	1970	$30
IMPULSE!			
❑ A-15 [M]	Count Basie and the Kansas City Seven	1962	$250
❑ AS-15 [S]	Count Basie and the Kansas City Seven	1962	$160
INTERMEDIA			
❑ QS-5039	The Classic Count	198?	$25
❑ QS-5028	The Deacon	198?	$25
JAZZ ARCHIVES			
❑ JA-41	At the Famous Door, 1938-1939	198?	$25
❑ JA-16	The Count at the Chatterbox, 1937	198?	$25
JAZZ MAN			
❑ 5006	Ain't It the Truth	198?	$25
JAZZ PANORAMA			
❑ 1803 [10]	Count Basie and Lester Young	1951	$200
MCA			
❑ 718	16 Greatest Performances	198?	$20

Number	Title	Yr	NM
❑ 29003	Count Basie and the Kansas City Seven	198?	$20
❑ 4108	Good Morning Blues	197?	$30
❑ 42324	One O'Clock Jump	1990	$30
❑ 4130	Retrospective Sessions	198?	$25
❑ 4163	Showtime	198?	$25
❑ 29005	Standing Ovation	198?	$20
❑ 29004	Straight Ahead	198?	$20
❑ 4050	The Best of Count Basie	197?	$30
MCA/IMPULSE!			
❑ 5656	Count Basie and the Kansas City Seven	1986	$20
MERCURY			
❑ MG-25105 [10]	Count Basie and His Kansas City Seven	1952	$300
❑ MGC-120 [10]	Count Basie and His Orchestra Collates	1952	$300
METRO			
❑ M-516 [M]	Count Basie	1965	$300
❑ MS-516 [S]	Count Basie	1965	$175
MGM			
❑ GAS-126	Count Basie (Golden Archive Series)	1970	$35
MOBILE FIDELITY			
❑ 1-237	April in Paris	1995	$120
—Audiophile vinyl			
❑ 1-129	Basie Plays Hefti	1985	$175
—Audiophile vinyl			
MOSAIC			
❑ MR12-135	The Complete Roulette Live Recordings of Count Basie and His Orchestra	199?	$250
❑ MQ15-149	The Complete Roulette Studio Recordings of Count Basie and His Orchestra	199?	$300
PABLO			
❑ 2310901	88 Basie Street	1984	$50
❑ 2310925	Basie and His Friends	1988	$30
❑ 2310745	Basie and Zoot	1976	$50
❑ 2310756	Basie Big Band	1975	$50
❑ 2310786	Basie Jam #2	1977	$35
❑ 2310840	Basie Jam #3	1979	$30
❑ 2310718	Basie Jam	1975	$35
❑ 2310750	Basie Jam/Montreux '75	1976	$30
❑ 2310924	Count Basie Get Together	1987	$25
❑ 2310920	Fancy Pants	1987	$25
❑ 2310874	Farmers Market Barbecue	1982	$25
❑ 2310712	For the First Time	1974	$30
❑ 2310767	I Told You So	1976	$30
❑ 2310871	Kansas City 6	198?	$25
❑ 2310859	Kansas City Shout	1980	$30
—With Joe Turner and Eddie "Cleanhead" Vinson			
❑ 2310891	Me & You	1983	$25
❑ 2310919	Mostly Blues...And Some Others	1987	$25
❑ 2310797	Prime Time	1977	$30
❑ 2310852	The Best of Basie	1980	$25
❑ 2405408	The Best of the Count Basie Band	198?	$25
❑ 2310709	The Bosses	1974	$30
PABLO LIVE			
❑ 2308207	Basie Big Band Montreux '77	1977	$30
❑ 2308209	Basie Jam/Montreux '77	1977	$30
❑ 2308246	Live in Japan, 1978	198?	$25
PABLO TODAY			
❑ 2312126	Kansas City 5	198?	$25
❑ 2312112	On the Road	1980	$25
❑ 2312131	Warm Breeze	198?	$25
PAIR			
❑ PDL2-1045	Basic Basie	1986	$30
PAUSA			
❑ 7105	High Voltage	198?	$25
PICKWICK			
❑ SPC-3500	Everything's Coming Up Roses	197?	$25
❑ SPC-3028 [S]	His Hits of the 60's	196?	$30
❑ PC-3028 [M]	His Hits of the 60's	196?	$35
PRESTIGE			
❑ 24109	Reunions	197?	$30
QUINTESSENCE			
❑ 25151	Everything's Coming Up Roses	197?	$25
RCA CAMDEN			
❑ CAL-497 [M]	Basie's Basement	1959	$75
❑ CAL-514 [M]	Count Basie in Kansas City	1959	$75
❑ CAL-395 [M]	The Count	1958	$75
RCA VICTOR			
❑ LPM-1112 [M]	Count Basie	1955	$600
—Andy Warhol cover			
❑ LPV-514 [M]	Count Basie in Kansas City	1965	$75
❑ AFM1-5180	Kansas City Style	1985	$25
REPRISE			
❑ R-6153 [M]	Pop Goes the Basie	1965	$35
❑ RS-6153 [S]	Pop Goes the Basie	1965	$50
❑ R-6070 [M]	This Time by Basie! Hits of the 50's and 60's	1963	$50
❑ R9-6070 [S]	This Time by Basie! Hits of the 50's and 60's	1963	$75

Number	Title	Yr	NM

ROULETTE

Number	Title	Yr	NM
❏ R52113 [M]	Back with Basie	1964	$50
❏ SR52113 [S]	Back with Basie	1964	$75
❏ R52003 [M]	Basie	1958	$150
— White label with colored "spokes			
❏ SR52003 [S]	Basie	1958	$120
— Black vinyl; white label with colored "spokes			
❏ SR52003 [S]	Basie	1958	$300
— Red vinyl; white label with colored "spokes			
❏ R52003 [M]	Basie	1964	$75
— Orange and yellow "roulette wheel" label			
❏ R52003 [M]	Basie	2003	$75
— 200-gram vinyl reissue; distributed by Classic Records			
❏ SR52003 [S]	Basie	1964	$40
— Orange and yellow "roulette wheel" label			
❏ R52065 [M]	Basie at Birdland	1961	$75
❏ SR52065 [S]	Basie at Birdland	1961	$75
❏ R52011 [M]	Basie Plays Hefti	1958	$75
❏ SR52011 [S]	Basie Plays Hefti	1958	$75
❏ R52056 [M]	Benny Carter's Kansas City Suite	1960	$75
❏ SR52056 [S]	Benny Carter's Kansas City Suite	1960	$75
❏ R52028 [M]	Breakfast, Dance & Barbeque	1959	$75
❏ SR52028 [S]	Breakfast, Dance & Barbeque	1959	$75
❏ R52032 [M]	Chairman of the Board	1959	$75
❏ SR52032 [S]	Chairman of the Board	1959	$75
❏ R52099 [M]	Count Basie in Sweden	1963	$50
❏ SR52099 [S]	Count Basie in Sweden	1963	$75
❏ R52036 [M]	Dance Along with Basie	1959	$50
❏ SR52036 [S]	Dance Along with Basie	1959	$75
❏ R52106 [M]	Easin' It	1963	$50
❏ SR52106 [S]	Easin' It	1963	$75
❏ RE-102	Echoes of an Era (The Count Basie Years)	1971	$35
❏ RE-107	Echoes of an Era (The Vocal Years)	1971	$35
❏ SR42009	Fantail	1968	$35
❏ RE-124	Kansas City Suite/Easin' It	1973	$35
❏ R52044 [M]	Not Now -- I'll Tell You When	1960	$75
❏ SR52044 [S]	Not Now -- I'll Tell You When	1960	$75
❏ R52024 [M]	One More Time	1959	$75
❏ SR52024 [S]	One More Time	1959	$75
❏ R52051 [M]	String Along with Basie	1960	$75
❏ SR52051 [S]	String Along with Basie	1960	$75
❏ R52081 [M]	The Best of Basie	1962	$35
❏ SR52081 [S]	The Best of Basie	1962	$50
❏ R52089 [M]	The Best of Basie, Volume 2	1962	$35
❏ SR52089 [S]	The Best of Basie, Volume 2	1962	$50
❏ RE-118	The Best of Count Basie	1971	$35
❏ RB-1 [M]	The Count Basie Story	1960	$40
❏ SRB-1 [S]	The Count Basie Story	1960	$150
❏ SR42015	The Kid from Red Bank	1968	$35
❏ R52086 [M]	The Legend	1962	$50
❏ SR52086 [S]	The Legend	1962	$75
❏ R52111/3 [M]	The World of Count Basie	1964	$40
❏ SR52111/3 [S]	The World of Count Basie	1964	$150

SOLID STATE

Number	Title	Yr	NM
❏ SS-18032	Basie Meets Bond	1968	$35
— Reissue of United Artists LP			

TIME-LIFE

Number	Title	Yr	NM
❏ STBB-08	Big Bands: Count Basie	1983	$35
❏ STL-J-22	Giants of Jazz	1982	$50

UNITED ARTISTS

Number	Title	Yr	NM
❏ UAL-3480 [M]	Basie Meets Bond	1966	$75
❏ UAS-6480 [S]	Basie Meets Bond	1966	$75

UPFRONT

Number	Title	Yr	NM
❏ UPF-142	Count Basie and His Orchestra	1969	$30

VEE JAY

Number	Title	Yr	NM
❏ VJS-3054	I Got Rhythm	198?	$30

VERVE

Number	Title	Yr	NM
❏ VE-2-2517	16 Men Swinging	197?	$30
❏ MGV-8012 [M]	April in Paris	1957	$175
❏ V-8012 [M]	April in Paris	1961	$75
❏ UMV-1-2641	April in Paris	198?	$25
❏ 821291-1	Basic Basie	198?	$30
❏ V6-8783	Basie	1969	$35
❏ MGV-8199 [M]	Basie in London	1957	$150
❏ V-8199 [M]	Basie in London	1961	$50
❏ V-8597 [M]	Basie Land	1964	$35
❏ V6-8597 [S]	Basie Land	1964	$50
❏ V-8616 [M]	Basie Picks the Winners	1965	$35
❏ V6-8616 [S]	Basie Picks the Winners	1965	$50
❏ MGV-8108 [M]	Basie Rides Again!	1957	$300
— Reissue of Clef 729			
❏ V-8108 [M]	Basie Rides Again!	1961	$50
❏ MGV-8018 [M]	Basie Roars Again	1957	$300
— Reissue of Clef 723			
❏ V-8018 [M]	Basie Roars Again	1961	$50
❏ V-8687 [M]	Basie's Beat	1967	$50
❏ V6-8687 [S]	Basie's Beat	1967	$35
❏ V-8659 [M]	Basie's Beatle Bag	1966	$75
❏ V6-8659 [S]	Basie's Beatle Bag	1966	$40
❏ MGV-8243 [M]	Count Basie at Newport	1958	$175
❏ MGVS-6024 [S]	Count Basie at Newport	1960	$150
❏ V-8243 [M]	Count Basie at Newport	1961	$50
❏ V6-8243 [S]	Count Basie at Newport	1961	$50
❏ UMV-1-2619	Count Basie at Newport	198?	$25
❏ MGV-8291 [M]	Hall of Fame	1958	$150
❏ V-8291 [M]	Hall of Fame	1961	$50

Number	Title	Yr	NM
❏ 825194-1	High Voltage (Basic Basie Vol. 2)	198?	$25
❏ VSP-12 [M]	Inside Basie, Outside	1966	$35
❏ VSPS-12 [S]	Inside Basie, Outside	1966	$50
❏ V-8549 [M]	Li'l Ol' Groovemaker…Basie!	1963	$50
❏ V6-8549 [S]	Li'l Ol' Groovemaker…Basie!	1963	$75
❏ V-8563 [M]	More Hits of the 50's and 60's	1963	$50
❏ V6-8563 [S]	More Hits of the 50's and 60's	1963	$75
❏ V-8511 [M]	On My Way and Shoutin' Again!	1963	$35
❏ V6-8511 [S]	On My Way and Shoutin' Again!	1963	$50
❏ VE-2-2542	Paradise Squat	197?	$30
❏ MGV-8103 [M]	The Band of Distinction	1957	$300
— Reissue of Clef 722			
❏ V-8103 [M]	The Band of Distinction	1961	$50
❏ MGV-8070 [M]	The Count	1957	$300
— Reissue of Clef 120			
❏ V-8070 [M]	The Count	1961	$50
❏ V-8407 [M]	The Essential Count Basie	1961	$35
❏ V6-8407 [S]	The Essential Count Basie	1961	$50
❏ MGV-8104 [M]	The King of Swing	1957	$300
— Reissue of Clef 724			
❏ V-8104 [M]	The King of Swing	1961	$50
❏ V6-8831	The Newport Years	1973	$30
❏ MGV-8090 [M]	The Swinging Count!	1957	$300
— Reissue of Clef 706			
❏ V-8090 [M]	The Swinging Count!	1961	$50
❏ V-8596 [M]	Verve's Choice -- Best of Count Basie	1964	$35
❏ V6-8596 [S]	Verve's Choice -- Best of Count Basie	1964	$50

BASIL, TONI

CHRYSALIS

Number	Title	Yr	NM
❏ FV41449	Toni Basil	1983	$12
❏ PV41449	Toni Basil	1986	$10
— Reissue with new prefix			
❏ CHR1410	Word of Mouth	1982	$15
❏ FV41410	Word of Mouth	1983	$12
— Reissue of 1410			
❏ PV41410	Word of Mouth	1986	$10
— Reissue with new prefix			

BASIN STREET SIX, THE

CIRCLE

Number	Title	Yr	NM
❏ L-403 [10]	Dixieland from New Orleans	1951	$50

EMARCY

Number	Title	Yr	NM
❏ MG-26012 [10]	The Basin Street Six	1954	$300

MERCURY

Number	Title	Yr	NM
❏ MG-20151 [M]	Strictly Dixie	195?	$150
❏ MG-25111 [10]	The Basin Street Six	1951	$150

BASKERVILLE HOUNDS, THE

DOT

Number	Title	Yr	NM
❏ DLP-3823 [M]	The Baskerville Hounds (Featuring Space Rock, Part 2)	1967	$120
❏ DLP-25823 [S]	The Baskerville Hounds (Featuring Space Rock, Part 2)	1967	$150

BASS, FONTELLA

CHECKER

Number	Title	Yr	NM
❏ LP-2997 [M]	The "New" Look	1966	$150
— Blue label with red and black checkers			
❏ LP-2997 [M]	The "New" Look	1967	$40
— Blue and white label			
❏ LPS-2997 [S]	The "New" Look	1966	$100
— Blue label with red and black checkers			
❏ LPS-2997 [S]	The "New" Look	1967	$40
— Blue and white label			

PAULA

Number	Title	Yr	NM
❏ LPS-2203	Free	1971	$15

BASS, MARTHA AND FONTELLA

SOUL NOTE

Number	Title	Yr	NM
❏ SN-1006	From the Root to the Source	197?	$30

BASSEY, SHIRLEY

APPLAUSE

Number	Title	Yr	NM
❏ APLP1005	Shirley Bassey	1982	$12

EPIC

Number	Title	Yr	NM
❏ LN3834 [M]	The Bewitching Shirley Bassey	1962	$25

LIBERTY

Number	Title	Yr	NM
❏ LWB-715	Greatest Hits	198?	$12
❏ LN-10252	Greatest Hits	198?	$10
❏ LN-10180	I, Capricorn	198?	$10
❏ LWB-111	Live at Carnegie Hall	198?	$12
❏ LN-10262	Shirley Means Bassey	198?	$10
❏ LM-1013	Something Else	198?	$10
❏ LN-10104	The Best of Shirley Bassey	1980	$10
❏ LN-10012	The Magic Is You	1980	$10
❏ LW-847	Yesterdays	198?	$10

MERCURY

Number	Title	Yr	NM
❏ 838033-1	La Mujer	1989	$15

MGM

Number	Title	Yr	NM
❏ E-4301 [M]	Golden Sound	1965	$15
❏ SE-4301 [S]	Golden Sound	1965	$18
❏ E-3862 [M]	The Fabulous Shirley Bassey	1960	$25
❏ SE-3862 [S]	The Fabulous Shirley Bassey	1960	$30

PAIR

Number	Title	Yr	NM
❏ PDL2-1057	Sassy Bassey	1986	$15

PHILIPS

Number	Title	Yr	NM
❏ PHM200168 [M]	Spectacular Shirley Bassey	1965	$15
❏ PHS600168 [S]	Spectacular Shirley Bassey	1965	$18

PICKWICK

Number	Title	Yr	NM
❏ SPC-3303	How About You	197?	$12

SPRINGBOARD

Number	Title	Yr	NM
❏ SPB-4045	This Is My Life	197?	$10

UNITED ARTISTS

Number	Title	Yr	NM
❏ UAS5643	And I Love You So	1972	$12
❏ UAL3565 [M]	And We Were Lovers	1967	$15
❏ UAS6565 [S]	And We Were Lovers	1967	$18
❏ UAS6713	Does Anybody Miss Me?	1969	$15
❏ UA-LA542-G	Good, Bad But Beautiful	1975	$12
❏ UA-LA715-H2	Greatest Hits	1976	$18
❏ UAS5565	I, Capricorn	1971	$12
❏ UAL3463 [M]	In Person	1965	$15
❏ UAS6463 [S]	In Person	1965	$18
❏ UA-LA111-H2	Live at Carnegie Hall	1973	$18
❏ UA-LA605-G	Love, Life and Feelings	1976	$12
❏ UA-LA055-F	Never, Never, Never	1973	$12
❏ UA-LA214-G	Nobody Does It Like Me	1974	$12
❏ UAL3169 [M]	Shirley Bassey	1962	$18
❏ UAS6169 [S]	Shirley Bassey	1962	$25
❏ UAL3419 [M]	Shirley Bassey Belts the Best	1965	$15
❏ UAS6419 [S]	Shirley Bassey Belts the Best	1965	$18
❏ UAS6765	Shirley Bassey Is Really "Something	1970	$12
❏ UAL3237 [M]	Shirley Bassey Sings the Hits from "Oliver	1962	$18
❏ UAS6237 [S]	Shirley Bassey Sings the Hits from "Oliver	1962	$25
❏ UAL3545 [M]	Shirley Means Bassey	1966	$15
❏ UAS6545 [S]	Shirley Means Bassey	1966	$18
❏ LM-1013	Something Else	1979	$12
❏ UAS6797	Something Else	1971	$12
❏ UA-LA926-H	The Magic Is You	1978	$12
❏ UAS6675	This Is My Life	1969	$15
❏ UA-LA847-H	Yesterdays	1977	$12
❏ UA-LA751-H	You Take My Heart Away	1977	$12

BASSO-VALDAMBRINI OCTET, THE

VERVE

Number	Title	Yr	NM
❏ MGV-20009 [M]	Jazz Festival, Milan	1960	$150
❏ V-20009 [M]	Jazz Festival, Milan	1961	$25
❏ MGV-20011 [M]	The New Sound from Italy	1960	$150
❏ MGVS-6152 [S]	The New Sound from Italy	1960	$150
❏ V-20011 [M]	The New Sound from Italy	1961	$25
❏ V6-20011 [S]	The New Sound from Italy	1961	$25

BASTARDS, THE

TREEHOUSE

Number	Title	Yr	NM
❏ 016	Monticallo	1989	$15

BAT BOYS, THE

DESIGN

Number	Title	Yr	NM
❏ DLP249 [B]	Batman - Batman Theme: as on the ABC T.V. television series Batman!		$30

BATDORF & RODNEY

ARISTA

Number	Title	Yr	NM
❏ AL4041	Life Is You	1975	$12

ASYLUM

Number	Title	Yr	NM
❏ SD5056	Batdorf & Rodney	1972	$12

ATLANTIC

Number	Title	Yr	NM
❏ SD8298	Off the Shelf	1971	$15

BATORS, STIV

BOMP!

Number	Title	Yr	NM
❏ 4015 [B]	Disconnected	1980	$30
❏ 4043 [10]	Disconnected	1993	$18
— Reissue of 4015 on 10-inch vinyl			
❏ 4046 [10]	L.A. L.A.	1993	$18

BATTERED ORNAMENTS

HARVEST

Number	Title	Yr	NM
❏ SKAO-422 [B]	Mantle-Piece	1970	$175

BATTIN, SKIP

SIGNPOST

Number	Title	Yr	NM
❏ SP8408	Skip Battin	1972	$15

Number	Title	Yr	NM

BATTLE, KATHLEEN
ANGEL
❑ DS-37363	A Christmas Celebration	1986	$12

BAUDUC, RAY, AND NAPPY LAMARE
CAPITOL
| ❑ T877 [M] | Riverboat Dandies | 1957 | $85 |
MERCURY
| ❑ SR-60186 [S] | On a Swinging Date | 1960 | $150 |
| ❑ MG-0(# unknown) [M] | On a Swinging Date | 1960 | $150 |

BAUER, BILLY
AD LIB
| ❑ AAL-5501 [10] | Let's Have a Session | 1955 | $250 |
INTERPLAY
| ❑ IP-8603 | Anthology | 198? | $30 |
NORGRAN
| ❑ MGN-1082 [M] | Billy Bauer Plectrist | 1956 | $100 |
VERVE
❑ MGV-8172 [M]	Billy Bauer Plectrist	1957	$100
— yellow label			
❑ V-8172 [M]	Billy Bauer Plectrist	1961	$25

BAUGH, PHIL
ERA
| ❑ ES-801 | California Guitar | 1969 | $30 |
LONGHORN
| ❑ LP-02 [M] | Country Guitar | 1965 | $50 |
TORO
| ❑ T-502 [M] | Country Guitar II | 1965 | $40 |

BAUHAUS
4 MEN WITH BEARDS
| ❑ 4M512LP [B] | Burning From The Inside | | $25 |
| ❑ 4M511LP [B] | The Sky's Gone Out | | $25 |
A&M
| ❑ SP-4953 | Burning from the Inside | 1983 | $25 |
| ❑ SP4918 [B] | The Sky's Gone Out | 1982 | $25 |
BEGGARS BANQUET
| ❑ 9804-1-H | Swing the Heartache/The BBC Sessions | 1989 | $25 |

BAXTER, DUKE
VMC
| ❑ VS-138 | Everybody Knows Matilda | 1969 | $25 |

BAXTER, LES
CAPITOL
❑ T1117 [M]	African Jazz	1958	$75
❑ T1388 [M]	Baxter's Best	1960	$30
❑ DT1388 [R]	Baxter's Best	1960	$18
❑ SM-1388	Baxter's Best	197?	$10
❑ T733 [M]	Caribbean Moonlight	1956	$40
❑ T1537 [M]	Jewels of the Sea	1961	$30
❑ ST1537 [S]	Jewels of the Sea	1961	$40
❑ T594 [M]	Kaleidoscope	1955	$40
❑ T10015 [M]	La Femme	1956	$40
❑ H288 [10]	Le Sacre Du Sauvage	1952	$100
❑ T288 [M]	Le Sacre Du Sauvage	1954	$40
❑ T1088 [M]	Love Is a Fabulous Thing	1958	$40
❑ T843 [M]	Midnight on the Cliffs	1957	$40
❑ H0(# unknown) [10]	Music for Peace of Mind	1953	$100
❑ H2000 [10]	Music Out of the Moon	1953	$100
❑ T390 [M]	Music Out of the Moon/ Music for Peace of Mind	1954	$40
❑ T868 [M]	Ports of Pleasure	1957	$40
❑ M-11702	Ritual of the Savage	1977	$12
❑ DT288 [R]	Ritual of the Savage (Le Sacre Du Sauvage)	196?	$15
❑ T780 [M]	'Round the World	1957	$40
❑ T1012 [M]	Selections from "South Pacific	1958	$40
❑ T774 [M]	Skins!	1957	$40
❑ T968 [M]	Space Escapade	1958	$40
❑ T655 [M]	Tamboo!	1955	$40
❑ T1846 [M]	The Original Quiet Village	1963	$25
❑ ST1846 [S]	The Original Quiet Village	1963	$30
❑ LAL486 [M]	The Passions	1954	$40
❑ T1661 [M]	The Sensational Les Baxter	1962	$30
❑ ST1661 [S]	The Sensational Les Baxter	1962	$30
❑ SQBO-90984	The Sounds of Adventure	1967	$30
— Capitol Record Club exclusive			
❑ T474 [M]	Thinking of You	1954	$40
❑ H474 [10]	Thinking of You	1954	$50
GNP CRESCENDO
❑ GNPS-2047	Aftrican Blue	1969	$15
❑ GNP-2036 [M]	Brazil Now	1967	$18
❑ GNPS-2036 [S]	Brazil Now	1967	$15
❑ GNPS-2042	Love Is Blue	1968	$15
❑ GNPS-2053	Moon Rock	1969	$15
PICKWICK
| ❑ PC-3048 [M] | I Could Have Danced All Night | 196? | $18 |
| ❑ SPC-3048 [S] | I Could Have Danced All Night | 196? | $15 |

| ❑ PC-3011 [M] | The Fabulous Sounds of Les Baxter | 196? | $18 |
| ❑ SPC-3011 [S] | The Fabulous Sounds of Les Baxter | 196? | $18 |
REPRISE
❑ R-6079 [M]	Academy Award Winners '63	1963	$18
❑ R9-6079 [S]	Academy Award Winners '63	1963	$25
❑ R-6048 [M]	The Primitive and the Passionate	1962	$18
❑ R9-6049 [S]	The Primitive and the Passionate	1962	$25
❑ R-6100 [M]	The Soul of the Drums	1963	$18
❑ R9-6100 [S]	The Soul of the Drums	1963	$25
❑ R-6036 [M]	Voices in Rhythm	1961	$18
❑ R9-6036 [S]	Voices in Rhythm	1961	$25

BAXTER
PARAMOUNT
| ❑ PAS-6050 | Baxter | 1973 | $25 |

BAY CITY JAZZ BAND, THE
GOOD TIME JAZZ
| ❑ S-10053 [S] | Golden Days | 1969 | $35 |
| ❑ L-12017 [M] | The Bay City Jazz Band | 1955 | $40 |

BAY CITY ROLLERS
ARISTA
| ❑ AL4049 [B] | Bay City Rollers | 1975 | $15 |

❑ AL4093 [B]	Dedication	1976	$15
❑ AB4241 [B]	Elevator	1979	$15
— As "The Rollers			
❑ AB4158	Greatest Hits	1977	$12
❑ AB7004 [B]	It's a Game	1977	$15
❑ AL4071 [B]	Rock N' Roll Love Letter	1976	$15
❑ AB4194 [B]	Strangers in the Wind	1978	$15

BAYETE
PRESTIGE
| ❑ 10062 | Seeking Other Beauty | 1973 | $30 |
| ❑ 10045 | Worlds Around the Sun | 1972 | $75 |

BAYSIDERS, THE
EVEREST
| ❑ LPBR-5124 [M] | Over the Rainbow | 1961 | $250 |
| ❑ BRST-1124 [S] | Over the Rainbow | 1961 | $300 |

BBC SYMPHONY ORCHESTRA (ANTAL DORATI, CONDUCTOR)
MERCURY LIVING PRESENCE
❑ SR90416 [S]	Bartok: The Miraculous Mandarin	196?	$50
— Maroon label, no "Vendor: Mercury Record Corporation			
❑ SR90416 [S]	Bartok: The Miraculous Mandarin	196?	$30
— Maroon label, with "Vendor: Mercury Record Corporation			
❑ SR90416 [S]	Bartok: The Miraculous Mandarin	196?	$18
— Third edition: Dark red (not maroon) label			

BE-BOP DELUXE
CAPITOL
❑ SN-16025	Axe Victim	1980	$10
— Reissue of Harvest 11689			
❑ SN-16023	Drastic Plastic	1980	$10
— Reissue of Harvest 11750			
❑ SN-16024	Futurama	1980	$10
— Reissue of Harvest 11432			
❑ SN-16026	Modern Music	1980	$10
— Reissue of Harvest 11575			
❑ SN-16022 [M]	Sunburst Finish	1980	$10
— Reissue of Harvest 11478			
❑ SPRO-8486 [DJ]	Sunburst Finish	1975	$30
— Specially banded version for radio			

HARVEST
❑ SM-11689	Axe Victim	1977	$12
— Their first UK album; first US issue has "SM" prefix			
❑ SPRO-8531 [DJ]	Be-Bop's Biggest	1978	$30
— Promo-only compilation			
❑ SW-11750	Drastic Plastic	1978	$12
❑ ST-11432	Futurama	1975	$12
❑ SKBB-11666	Live! In the Air Age	1977	$15
❑ ST-11575	Modern Music	1976	$12
❑ ST-11478	Sunburst Finish	1975	$12
❑ SKBO-11870	The Best Of & The Rest Of Be-Bop Deluxe	1979	$15

BEACH BOYS, THE
ANALOGUE PRODUCTIONS
❑ APP061S [B]	Little Deuce Coup	2015	$20
— 200g			
❑ AAPP060S [B]	Surfer Girl	2015	$20
— 200g			
ASYLUM
| ❑ R113793 | Surf's Up | 1972 | $175 |
| — RCA Record Club edition, pressed with wrong labels | | | |
BROTHER
❑ T9001 [M]	Smiley Smile	1967	$40
— No mention of Barry Turnbull on cover			
❑ T9001 [M]	Smiley Smile	1967	$30
— Title for this album by Barry Turnbull" on back cover			
❑ ST9001 [R]	Smiley Smile	1967	$25
— No mention of Barry Turnbull on cover			
❑ ST9001 [R]	Smiley Smile	1967	$18
— Title for this album by Barry Turnbull" on back cover			
BROTHER/REPRISE
❑ MS2251	15 Big Ones	1976	$15
❑ R130223	15 Big Ones	1976	$18
— RCA Record Club edition			
❑ 2MS2083	Carl and the Passions "So Tough"/Pet Sounds	1972	$30
❑ 2MS2083 [DJ]	Carl and the Passions "So Tough"/Pet Sounds	1972	$50
— White label promo			
❑ 2MS2167	Friends & Smiley Smile	1974	$18
❑ MS2223	Good Vibrations -- Best of the Beach Boys	1975	$15
❑ MSK2280	Good Vibrations -- Best of the Beach Boys	1978	$12
❑ MS2118 [DJ]	Holland	1973	$40
— White label promo; includes bonus white-label promo EP, "Mount Vernon and Fairway," in picture sleeve, taped to back cover			
❑ MS2118	Holland	1973	$18
— Includes bonus stock-copy EP, "Mount Vernon and Fairway," in picture sleeve, taped to back cover			
❑ MS2118 [DJ]	Holland	1973	$500
— Test pressing with "We Got Love," deleted from promos and stock copies			
❑ MSK2258	Love You	1977	$15
❑ MSK2268	M.I.U. Album	1978	$15
❑ MS2197 [M]	Pet Sounds	1974	$25
❑ RS-6382 [DJ]	Sunflower	1970	$50
— White label promo			

❑ RS-6382 [B]	Sunflower	1970	$30
❑ SKAO-93352	Sunflower	1970	$250
— Capitol Record Club edition			
❑ RS6453 [DJ]	Surf's Up	1971	$40
— White label promo			
❑ RS6453	Surf's Up	1971	$25
❑ R113793	Surf's Up	1972	$30
— RCA Record Club edition			
❑ 2RS6484 [DJ]	The Beach Boys In Concert	1973	$40
— White label promo			
❑ 2RS6484	The Beach Boys In Concert	1973	$25
❑ R223569	The Beach Boys In Concert	1973	$30
— RCA Record Club edition			
❑ 2MS2166	Wild Honey & 20/20	1974	$18

Number	Title	Yr	NM

CAPITOL

Number	Title	Yr	NM
☐ SKAO-133	20/20	1969	$25

—Black label with colorband

| ☐ SKAO-133 | 20/20 | 1969 | $18 |

—Starline" label

| ☐ SKAO-8-0133 | 20/20 | 1969 | $30 |

—Capitol Record Club edition; black label

| ☐ SKAO-8-0133 | 20/20 | 1970 | $40 |

—Capitol Record Club edition; lime label

| ☐ C1-29638 | 20/20 | 1994 | $18 |
| ☐ T2110 [M] | All Summer Long | 1964 | $50 |

— With "Don't Break Down" erroneously listed on front cover

| ☐ T2110 [M] | All Summer Long | 1964 | $30 |

— With "Don't Back Down" correctly listed on front cover

| ☐ ST2110 [S] | All Summer Long | 1964 | $50 |

— With "Don't Break Down" erroneously listed on front cover

| ☐ ST2110 [S] | All Summer Long | 1964 | $30 |

— With "Don't Back Down" correctly listed on front cover

☐ SN-16016 [S]	All Summer Long	1980	$10
☐ C1-29631 [S]	All Summer Long	1994	$18
☐ SF-501	All Summer Long	1970	$12

— Individual record from above set

| ☐ SF-8-0501 | All Summer Long | 1971 | $12 |

— Capitol Record Club edition

| ☐ SF-500501 | All Summer Long | 1971 | $12 |

— Columbia Record Club edition

| ☐ STBB-500 | All Summer Long/California Girls | 1970 | $25 |

—Lime labels; "Special Double Play" pack; two separate LPs (abridged versions of "All Summer Long" and "Summer Days [And Summer Nights!!]") bound together

| ☐ STBB-500 | All Summer Long/California Girls | 1971 | $30 |

— Red labels; "Special Double Play" pack; two separate LPs (abridged versions of "All Summer Long" and "Summer Days [And Summer Nights!!]") bound together

| ☐ R233593 | American Summer | 1975 | $30 |

— RCA Music Service exclusive

☐ ST-11584	Beach Boys '69 (The Beach Boys Live in London)	1976	$15
☐ SN-12011	Beach Boys '69 (The Beach Boys Live in London)	1979	$12
☐ SN-16134	Beach Boys '69 (The Beach Boys Live in London)	1981	$10
☐ C1-29634	Beach Boys '69 (The Beach Boys Live in London)	1994	$18
☐ TAO2198 [M]	Beach Boys Concert	1964	$30

— With bound-in booklet

| ☐ STAO2198 [S] | Beach Boys Concert | 1964 | $30 |

— With bound-in booklet

| ☐ STAO-8-2198 [S] | Beach Boys Concert | 196? | $100 |

— Capitol Record Club edition

☐ SM-2198	Beach Boys Concert	197?	$12
☐ C1-90427	Beach Boys Concert	1994	$18
☐ MAS2398 [M]	Beach Boys Party!	1965	$40

— With sheet of photos

| ☐ MAS2398 [M] | Beach Boys Party! | 1965 | $30 |

— Without sheet of photos

| ☐ DMAS2398 [R] | Beach Boys Party! | 1965 | $30 |

— With sheet of photos

| ☐ DMAS2398 [R] | Beach Boys Party! | 1965 | $30 |

— Without sheet of photos

☐ DN-16272 [R]	Beach Boys Party!	1982	$10
☐ C1-29640 [M]	Beach Boys Party!	1994	$18
☐ T2545 [M]	Best of the Beach Boys	1966	$25

— Black label with colorband

| ☐ T2545 [M] | Best of the Beach Boys | 1966 | $18 |

— Black "The Star Line" label

| ☐ T2545 [M] | Best of the Beach Boys | 1967 | $30 |

— Red and white "Starline" label

| ☐ DT2545 [P] | Best of the Beach Boys | 1966 | $18 |

— Black label with colorband

| ☐ DT2545 [P] | Best of the Beach Boys | 1966 | $15 |

— Black "The Star Line" label

| ☐ DT2545 [P] | Best of the Beach Boys | 1967 | $18 |

— Red and white "Starline" label

| ☐ DT2545 [P] | Best of the Beach Boys | 1970 | $15 |

— Green "Starline" label

| ☐ DT2545 [P] | Best of the Beach Boys | 1973 | $12 |

— Orange label, "Capitol" on bottom

| ☐ DT2545 [P] | Best of the Beach Boys | 1978 | $12 |

— Purple label, large Capitol logo

| ☐ DT2545 [P] | Best of the Beach Boys | 1983 | $12 |

— Black label, print in colorband

| ☐ C1-91318 [R] | Best of the Beach Boys | 1988 | $15 |

— Purple label, small Capitol logo

| ☐ R123946 | Best of the Beach Boys | 197? | $18 |

— RCA Music Service edition

| ☐ DT-502545 [P] | Best of the Beach Boys | 197? | $18 |

— Columbia Record Club edition

| ☐ DT2706 [P] | Best of the Beach Boys, Vol. 2 | 1973 | $12 |

— Orange label, "Capitol" on bottom

| ☐ T2706 [M] | Best of the Beach Boys, Vol. 2 | 1967 | $30 |
| ☐ DT2706 [P] | Best of the Beach Boys, Vol. 2 | 1967 | $18 |

— Red and while "Starline" label

| ☐ DT2706 [P] | Best of the Beach Boys, Vol. 2 | 1970 | $15 |

— Green "Starline" label

| ☐ DT2706 [P] | Best of the Beach Boys, Vol. 2 | 1978 | $12 |

— Purple label, large Capitol logo

| ☐ DN-16318 [R] | Best of the Beach Boys, Vol. 2 | 1984 | $10 |
| ☐ DT-502706 [P] | Best of the Beach Boys, Vol. 2 | 197? | $18 |

— Columbia Record Club edition

☐ N-16273	Be True to Your School	1983	$10
☐ DN-16017 [R]	California Girls	1980	$10
☐ SF-502	California Girls	1970	$12

— Individual record from above set

| ☐ SF-8-0502 | California Girls | 1971 | $12 |

— Capitol Record Club edition

| ☐ SF-500502 | California Girls | 1971 | $12 |

— Columbia Record Club edition

| ☐ SWBB-253 | Close-Up | 1969 | $30 |

— Reissue of "Surfin' U.S.A." and "All Summer Long" in one package; black labels with colorband

| ☐ SWBB-253 | Close-Up | 1970 | $40 |

— Lime labels

| ☐ DN-16019 [R] | Dance, Dance, Dance | 1981 | $10 |
| ☐ SF-703 | Dance, Dance, Dance | 1971 | $12 |

— Individual record from above set

| ☐ SF-8-0703 | Dance, Dance, Dance | 1971 | $12 |

— Capitol Record Club edition

| ☐ SVBB-11307 | Endless Summer | 1974 | $25 |

— Orange labels, "Capitol" on bottom; with poster

| ☐ SVBB-511307 | Endless Summer | 197? | $30 |

— Columbia Record Club edition

| ☐ R223559 | Endless Summer | 197? | $30 |

— RCA Music Service edition

| ☐ SVBB-11307 | Endless Summer | 1978 | $18 |

— Purple labels, large Capitol logo

| ☐ SVBB-11307 | Endless Summer | 1983 | $15 |

— Black labels, print in colorband

| ☐ SVBB-11307 | Endless Summer | 1988 | $15 |

— Purple labels, small Capitol logo

☐ ST2895	Friends	1968	$30
☐ SN-16157	Friends	1981	$10
☐ C1-29637	Friends	1994	$18
☐ SN-16018 [P]	Fun, Fun, Fun	1980	$10

— Reissue of "Shut Down, Vol. 2"

| ☐ SF-702 | Fun, Fun, Fun | 1971 | $12 |

— Individual record from above set

| ☐ SF-8-0702 | Fun, Fun, Fun | 1971 | $12 |

— Capitol Record Club edition

| ☐ STBB-701 | Fun, Fun, Fun/Dance, Dance, Dance | 1970 | $25 |

— Lime labels; "Special Double Play" pack; two separate LPs (abridged versions of "Shut Down, Volume 2" and "The Beach Boys Today!") bound together

| ☐ STBB-701 | Fun, Fun, Fun/Dance, Dance, Dance | 1971 | $30 |

— Red labels; "Special Double Play" pack; two separate LPs (abridged versions of "Shut Down, Volume 2" and "The Beach Boys Today!") bound together

| ☐ ST-442 | Good Vibrations | 1970 | $25 |

— Lime label (original)

| ☐ ST-8-0442 | Good Vibrations | 1970 | $30 |

— Capitol Record Club edition

| ☐ ST-442 | Good Vibrations | 1972 | $30 |

— Red or orange label

☐ T1998 [M]	Little Deuce Coupe	1963	$40
☐ ST1998 [S]	Little Deuce Coupe	1963	$40
☐ SM-1998 [S]	Little Deuce Coupe	197?	$12
☐ SN-16013 [S]	Little Deuce Coupe	1980	$10
☐ C1-29630 [S]	Little Deuce Coupe	1994	$18
☐ STBK-12396	Made in U.S.A.	1986	$15
☐ T2458 [M]	Pet Sounds	1966	$40
☐ DT2458 [R]	Pet Sounds	1966	$30
☐ SN-16156 [M]	Pet Sounds	1981	$10
☐ C1-48421 [M]	Pet Sounds	1994	$18
☐ C1-21241 [S]	Pet Sounds	1999	$18

— True stereo version on heavyweight vinyl

| ☐ 09463-51370-1-9 | Pet Sounds | 2006 | $30 |

— Limited two-record edition; one record is on yellow vinyl and contains the original mono mix; the other is on green vinyl and contains the 2003 stereo mix

☐ ST-12293	Rarities	1983	$18
☐ T2027 [M]	Shut Down, Volume 2	1964	$40
☐ ST2027 [P]	Shut Down, Volume 2	1964	$40
☐ C1-29629 [M]	Shut Down, Volume 2	1994	$18
☐ PRO3133 [DJ]	Silver Platter Service from Hollywood: The Beach Boys Christmas Special	1964	$250
☐ T/DT2580	Smile	1966	$1000

— Unreleased; price is for cover slick, which has been counterfeited

| ☐ T/DT2580 [B] | Smile Booklet | 1966 | $400 |

— Printed for insertion into unreleased "Smile" LP; counterfeits exist

☐ SN-16158 [M]	Smiley Smile	1981	$10
☐ C1-29635 [M]	Smiley Smile	1994	$18
☐ ST-8-2891 [R]	Smiley Smile	1968	$300

— Capitol Record Club edition

| ☐ SVBB-11384 | Spirit of America | 1975 | $18 |

— Orange labels, "Capitol" on bottom

| ☐ SVBB-511384 | Spirit of America | 1975 | $25 |

— Columbia Record Club edition

| ☐ SVBB-11384 | Spirit of America | 1978 | $15 |

— Purple labels, large Capitol logo

| ☐ SVBB-11384 | Spirit of America | 1983 | $12 |

— Black labels, print in colorband

| ☐ SVBB-11384 | Spirit of America | 1988 | $12 |

— Purple labels, small Capitol logo

| ☐ DKAO2893 [B] | Stack-o-Tracks | 1968 | $150 |

— With sheet music booklet

| ☐ DKAO2893 | Stack-o-Tracks | 1968 | $50 |

— Without sheet music booklet

| ☐ DKAO-8-2893 | Stack-o-Tracks | 1968 | $250 |

— Capitol Record Club edition

☐ C1-29641	Stack-o-Tracks	1994	$18
☐ C1-92639	Still Cruisin'	1989	$15
☐ T2354 [M]	Summer Days (And Summer Nights!!)	1965	$30
☐ DT2354 [R]	Summer Days (And Summer Nights!!)	1965	$50

— With "New Improved Full Dimensional Stereo" banner

| ☐ DT2354 [R] | Summer Days (And Summer Nights!!) | 1965 | $30 |

— With "Duophonic" banner

☐ C1-29633 [M]	Summer Days (And Summer Nights!!)	1994	$18
☐ SVBB-12220	Sunshine Dream	1982	$15
☐ T1981 [M]	Surfer Girl	1963	$40

— With reference to The Four Freshmen in liner notes

| ☐ T1981 [M] | Surfer Girl | 1963 | $40 |

— With reference to "their other new single record, 'Little Deuce Coupe'" in liner notes

| ☐ ST1981 [S] | Surfer Girl | 1963 | $50 |

— With reference to The Four Freshmen in liner notes

| ☐ ST1981 [S] | Surfer Girl | 1963 | $50 |

— With reference to "their other new single record, 'Little Deuce Coupe'" in liner notes

☐ SM-1981 [S]	Surfer Girl	197?	$12
☐ SN-16014 [S]	Surfer Girl	1980	$10
☐ C1-29628 [S]	Surfer Girl	1994	$18
☐ ST1995 [B]	Surfing's Greatest Hits	1963	$10

— split LP with Dick Dale & his Del-Tones, plus one track by Frank N. Stein & The Abominable Surf Men

| ☐ T1808 [M] | Surfin' Safari | 1962 | $40 |
| ☐ DT1808 [R] | Surfin' Safari | 1962 | $100 |

— With "Capitol Full Dimensional Stereo" banner under the "Duophonic" banner

| ☐ DT1808 [R] | Surfin' Safari | 1962 | $30 |

— With only the "Duophonic" banner at top

☐ SM-1808 [R]	Surfin' Safari	197?	$12
☐ N-16012 [M]	Surfin' Safari	1980	$10
☐ C1-29661 [M]	Surfin' Safari	1994	$18
☐ SY-4572 [R]	Surfin' Safari	197?	$15

— Orange label, Capitol logo at bottom; reissue of DT-1808 with completely different back cover and the words "... A Collector's Item ... Special Collections of Classic Hit Recordings by the Brightest Stars ..."

☐ T1890 [M]	Surfin' U.S.A.	1963	$40
☐ ST1890 [S]	Surfin' U.S.A.	1963	$50
☐ SM-1890 [S]	Surfin' U.S.A.	197?	$12
☐ SN-16015 [S]	Surfin' U.S.A.	1980	$10
☐ C1-48422 [S]	Surfin' U.S.A.	1994	$18
☐ 509994 63199 1 3 [B]	That's Why God Made The Radio	2012	$35
☐ T2164 [M]	The Beach Boys' Christmas Album	1964	$50
☐ ST2164 [S]	The Beach Boys' Christmas Album	1964	$50
☐ SM-2164	The Beach Boys' Christmas Album	197?	$12
☐ R133854	The Beach Boys' Christmas Album	197?	$18

— RCA Music Service edition

| ☐ TCL2813 [M] | The Beach Boys Deluxe Set | 1967 | $300 |

— Black border on box; albums have "T" prefixes

| ☐ DTCL2813 [R] | The Beach Boys Deluxe Set | 1967 | $50 |

— Maroon border on box; custom pressings of LPs with "DTCL" prefixes

| ☐ DTCL-8-2813 [R] | The Beach Boys Deluxe Set | 1967 | $175 |

— Capitol Record Club edition; blue border on box; custom pressings of LPs with "DTCL" prefixes

☐ T2269 [M]	The Beach Boys Today!	1965	$30
☐ DT2269 [R]	The Beach Boys Today!	1965	$30
☐ DT-8-2269 [R]	The Beach Boys Today!	1965	$100

— Capitol Record Club edition

| ☐ C1-29632 [M] | The Beach Boys Today! | 1994 | $18 |
| ☐ DKAO2945 [P] | The Best of the Beach Boys, Vol. 3 | 1968 | $18 |

— Black label with colorband

| ☐ DKAO2945 [P] | The Best of the Beach Boys, Vol. 3 | 1969 | $25 |

— Starline" label

☐ T2859 [M]	Wild Honey	1967	$40
☐ ST2859 [S]	Wild Honey	1967	$25
☐ SN-16159 [S]	Wild Honey	1981	$10
☐ C1-29636 [S]	Wild Honey	1994	$18

CAPITOL SPECIAL MARKETS

| ☐ SL-8114 | Beach Boys Super Hits | 1978 | $12 |

Number	Title	Yr	NM
❑ SLB-6994	Golden Years of the Beach Boys	1975	$25
❑ SL-9431	Good Vibrations from the Beach Boys	1986	$18

— Special issue for Sunkist

Number	Title	Yr	NM
❑ SLB-8134	The Beach Boys	1980	$25

CARIBOU

❑ FZ36283 [DJ]	Keepin' the Summer Alive	1980	$18

— White label promo

❑ FZ36283	Keepin' the Summer Alive	1980	$12
❑ JZ35752	L.A. (Light Album)	1979	$12
❑ JZ35752 [DJ]	L.A. (Light Album)	1979	$18

— White label promo

❑ PZ35752	L.A. (Light Album)	1980	$10

— Budget-line reissue

❑ Z2X37445	Ten Years of Harmony (1970-1980)	1981	$15
❑ BFZ39946	The Beach Boys	1985	$12
❑ PZ39946	The Beach Boys	1988	$10

— Budget-line reissue

DCC COMPACT CLASSICS

❑ LPZ-2006 [M]	Pet Sounds	1995	$120

— Audiophile vinyl

ERA

❑ HTE-805 [M]	The Beach Boys' Biggest Beach Hits	1969	$18

— Also contains non-Beach Boys filler

EVEREST

❑ 4108 [M]	Rare Early Recordings	1981	$10

GATEWAY

❑ GSLP-10104 [M]	Surfing with the Beach Boys, the Marketts and the Frogmen	1979	$10

MOBILE FIDELITY

❑ 1-116	Surfer Girl	1984	$40

— Audiophile vinyl

ORBIT

❑ OR688 [M]	The Beach Boys' Greatest Hits 1961-1963	1972	$15

— Also contains non-Beach Boys filler

PAIR

❑ PDL2-1068	For All Seasons	1986	$18
❑ PDL2-1084	Golden Harmonies	1986	$18

PICKWICK

❑ SPC-3269	Good Vibrations	1971	$12
❑ PTP-2059 [B]	High Water	1973	$15
❑ SPC-3562	Little Deuce Coupe	1975	$12
❑ SPC-3221	Summertime Blues	1970	$12
❑ SPC-3351	Surfer Girl	1973	$12
❑ SPC-3309	Wow! Great Concert!	1972	$12

READER'S DIGEST

❑ RBA-178	Their Greatest Hits and Finest Performances	1989	$50

— Box set

SCEPTER CITATION

❑ CTN-18004 [M]	The Best of the Beach Boys (1961-1963)	1972	$15

— Also contains non-Beach Boys filler

SEARS

❑ SPS-609	Summertime Blues	1970	$50

SPRINGBOARD

❑ SPB-4021 [M]	The Beach Boys 1961	1977	$10

— Also contains non-Beach Boys filler

SUNDAZED

❑ LP5005 [B]	Lost & Found!	1991	$15

— Colored vinyl (red, yellow and light blue are known); first LP issue of the 1961 sessions from the master tapes; three tracks are stereo

TIME-LIFE

❑ SRNR-03	The Beach Boys: 1963-1967	1986	$18

— 2 LPs in box with fold-open liner notes; second cover has a portrait of the Beach Boys

❑ SRNR-03	The Beach Boys: 1963-1967	1986	$30

— 2 LPs in box with fold-open liner notes; original cover portrays the Beach Boys surfing

WAND

❑ WDS-688 [M]	The Beach Boys' Greatest Hits 1961-1963	1972	$15

— Also contains non-Beach Boys filler

BEACHWOOD SPARKS

SUB POP

❑ SP503 [B]	Beachwood Sparks	2000	$18

BEACON STREET UNION, THE
Also see EAGLE.

MGM

❑ SE-4568 [S]	The Clown Died in Marvin Gardens	1968	$30
❑ E-4568 [M]	The Clown Died in Marvin Gardens	1968	$50

— May be promo only (yellow label)

❑ E-4517 [M]	The Eyes of the Beacon Street Union	1967	$30
❑ SE-4517 [S]	The Eyes of the Beacon Street Union	1967	$30

BEAL, JEFF

ANTILLES

❑ 90625	Liberation	1987	$25
❑ 91237	Perpetual Motion	1989	$25

BEAN, BILLY

RIVERSIDE

❑ RLP-380 [M]	The Trio	1961	$250
❑ RS-9380 [S]	The Trio	1961	$250

BEANS

AVALANCHE

❑ 9200	Beans	1971	$25

BEARFOOT

EPIC

❑ KE32146	Bearfoot	1973	$15

BEARS, THE
Also see ADRIAN BELEW; KING CRIMSON.

I.R.S.

❑ 42139	Rise and Shine	1988	$12
❑ 42011	The Bears	1987	$15

BEASLEY, JIMMY

CROWN

❑ CLP-5014 [M]	The Fabulous Jimmy Beasley	1957	$175

— Black label

❑ CLP-5247 [M]	Twist with Jimmy Beasley	1962	$40

— Gray label

MODERN

❑ MLP-1214 [M]	The Fabulous Jimmy Beasley	1956	$400

BEASLEY, WALTER

MERCURY

❑ 838912-1	Just Kickin' It	1989	$15

POLYDOR

❑ 833866-1	Walter Beasley	1987	$10

BEASLEY, WATSON

WARNER BROS.

❑ BSK3445	Watson Beasley	1980	$12

BEAST

COTILLION

❑ SD9012	Beast	1969	$18

EVOLUTION

❑ 2017	Beast	1970	$18

BEASTIE BOYS
Also see COUNTRY MIKE.

CAPITOL

❑ C1-98938 [B]	Check Your Head	1992	$75
❑ C137716 [B]	Hello Nasty	1998	$30
❑ SPRO79461 [DJ]	Hip Hop Sampler	1994	$100

— Promo-only compilation of remixes and rarities; 1,250 copies were pressed; only the Side 1 number is listed above (the other three sides are numbered SPRO-79463, SPRO-79472 and SPRO-79473); this album has been counterfeited; there are several differences; most notably that authentic copies have gatefold sleeves, and the counterfeits have single-pocket sleeves

❑ SPRO79461 [DJ]	Hip Hop Sampler	1994	$100

— This album has been counterfeited; there are several differences, most notably that authentic copies have gatefold sleeves, and the counterfeits have single-pocket sleeves

❑ C1-28599	III Communications	1994	$25
❑ C1-92844	Paul's Boutique	1989	$30

— Multi-gatefold edition (number on record is 91743, the same as single gatefold edition)

❑ C1-91743 [B]	Paul's Boutique	1989	$18

— Single gatefold edition

❑ C1-22940	The Sounds of Science	2000	$175

— Boxed set with hardbound booklet; released a year after a similar CD compilation

❑ C1-84571	To the 5 Boroughs	2004	$30

DEF JAM

❑ BFC40238	Licensed to III	1986	$25
❑ FC40238	Licensed to III	1986	$18

— Second pressing, with "02" added to bar code on back cover

GRAND ROYAL

❑ GR 026 [EP]	Aglio E Olio	1995	$18
❑ GR 066	Check Your Head	1998	$30

— Vinyl reissue of Capitol 98938

❑ GR 061 [B]	Hello Nasty	1998	$50

— Limited edition on yellow vinyl

❑ GR 006	III Communication	1994	$30
❑ GR 065	Paul's Boutique	1999	$25

— Reissue of original multi-gatefold edition

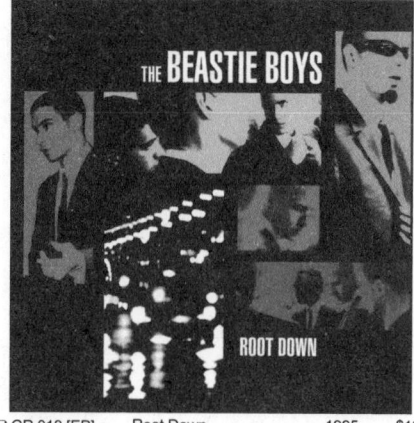

❑ GR 018 [EP]	Root Down	1995	$18

— Black vinyl

❑ GR 018 [EP]	Root Down	1995	$30

— Blue vinyl

❑ GR 071 [EP]	Scientists of Sound	2000	$15

— Remix album

❑ GR 003 [B]	Some Old Bullshit	1994	$30
❑ GR 013	The In Sound from Way Out!	1996	$100

— Original editions were limited to 5,000 and have a sticker indicating this on the back cover

❑ GR 013	The In Sound from Way Out!	1999	$30

— Second editions were not limited and have no sticker on the back cover

RAT CAGE

❑ 026 [EP]	Cookypuss	1983	$40

BEAT, THE

COLUMBIA

❑ JC36195	The Beat	1979	$15
❑ ARC36794	The Kids Are the Same	1982	$12

PASSPORT

❑ 5002 [EP]	To Beat or Not to Beat	1983	$10

BEAT FARMERS

MCA CURB

❑ L33-17381 [EP]	Home of Country Dick	1987	$30

— Promo-only compilation with four non-LP songs

❑ 6296	Poor and Famous	1989	$15

❑ 5993 [B]	The Pursuit of Happiness	1987	$15
❑ 5759 [B]	Van Go	1986	$15

RHINO

❑ RNOR-021 [EP]	Bigger Stones	1985	$18

— Promo-only four-song sampler from RNLP-853

❑ RNLP-853	Tales of the New West	1985	$15

BEAT HAPPENING

K

❑ 1 [B]	Beat Happening		$30
❑ KLP-06	Black Candy	1989	$15
❑ KLP-03	Dreamy	199?	$12

— Reissue

❑ KLP-02	Jamboree	199?	$12

— Reissue

❑ KLP-07	You Turn Me On	199?	$12

— Reissue

Number	Title	Yr	NM

K/ROUGH TRADE

| ❏ ROUGH US30 | Jamboree | 198? | $18 |

SUB POP

❏ SP98 [B]	Dreamy	1991	$30
❏ SP167 [B]	You Turn Me On	1992	$30
—*Most copies are on red vinyl*			

BEAT OF THE EARTH, THE

ARDISH

| ❏ AS-001 | The Beat of the Earth | 1968 | $300 |
| ❏ AS-0001 | The Beat of the Earth | 1968 | $400 |

BEAT RODEO

COYOTE

| ❏ 002 [EP] | Steve Almaas/Beat Rodeo | 1982 | $15 |

I.R.S.

| ❏ 5774 | Home in the Heart of the Beat | 1986 | $12 |
| ❏ 39020 | Staying Out Late with Beat Rodeo | 1989 | $15 |

BEATLE BUDDIES, THE

DIPLOMAT

| ❏ D-2313 [M] | The Beatle Buddies | 1964 | $18 |
| ❏ DS-2313 [S] | The Beatle Buddies | 1964 | $25 |

BEATLES, THE

Also see PETE BEST; GEORGE HARRISON; JOHN LENNON; PAUL McCARTNEY; RINGO STARR.

| ❏ 94638241317 [B] | A Hard Day's Night | 2012 | $30 |

APPLE

❏ SO-383	Abbey Road	1969	$85
—*With Capitol logo on Side 2 bottom; "Her Majesty" is NOT listed on either the jacket or the label*			
❏ SO-383	Abbey Road	1969	$40
—*With Capitol logo on Side 2 bottom; "Her Majesty" IS listed on both the jacket and the label*			
❏ SO-383	Abbey Road	1969	$25
—*With "Mfd. by Apple" on label; "Her Majesty" is NOT listed on the label*			
❏ SO-383 [B]	Abbey Road	1969	$30
—*With "Mfd. by Apple" on label; "Her Majesty" IS listed on the label*			
❏ SO-383	Abbey Road	1975	$30
—*With "All Rights Reserved" on label, either in black print or in light print along label edge (both versions exist)*			
❏ PCS7088 [B]	Abbey Road	2012	$30
❏ C1-8-34445 [B]	Anthology 1	1995	$75
—*All copies distributed in the U.S. were manufactured in the U.K. with no distinguishing marks (some LPs imported directly from the U.K. have "Made in England" stickers, which can be removed easily)*			
❏ C1-8-34448	Anthology 2	1996	$40
❏ SPRO11206/7 [EP]	Anthology 2 Sampler	1996	$175
—*Promo-only collection sent to college radio stations*			
❏ C1-8-34451	Anthology 3	1996	$30
❏ SW-385 [B]	Hey Jude	1970	$75
—*Label calls the LP "The Beatles Again"; record is "SO-385" (this could be found in retail stores as late as 1973)*			
❏ SW-385	Hey Jude	1970	$30
—*Label calls the LP "The Beatles Again"; record is "SW-385"*			
❏ SW-385	Hey Jude	1970	$30
—*With Capitol logo on Side 2 bottom; label calls the LP "Hey Jude"*			
❏ SW-385	Hey Jude	1970	$25
—*With "Mfd. by Apple" on label; label calls the LP "Hey Jude"*			
❏ SW-385	Hey Jude	1975	$30
—*With "All Rights Reserved" on label; label calls the LP "Hey Jude"*			
❏ AR-34001	Let It Be	1970	$30
—*Red Apple label; originals have "Bell Sound" stamped in trail-off area, counterfeits do not*			
❏ PCS7096 [B]	Let It Be	2012	$30
❏ C1-8-31796 [B]	Live at the BBC	1994	$100
❏ 5099963380613 [B]	Magical Mystery Tour	2014	$30
❏ 94638246510 [B]	Magical Mystery Tour	2012	$30
❏ 5.09991E+12 [M]	Mono Masters	2014	$85
❏ 5099969943515 [B]	Past Masters	2012	$40
❏ 5099963380415 [M]	Revolver	2014	$30
❏ 5099963380514 [M]	Sgt. Pepper's Lonely Hearts Club Band	2014	$30
❏ SWBO-101 [B]	The Beatles	1968	$1000
—*Numbered copy; includes four individual photos and large poster (included in value); because the white cover shows ring wear so readily, this is an EXTREMELY difficult album to find in near-mint condition; second pressing labels have Side 1, Song 5 correctly listed as "The Continuing Story of Bungalow Bill"; VG value 37.50; VG+ value 75*			
❏ SWBO-101	The Beatles	197?	$75
—*Un-numbered copy; includes four individual photos and large poster (included in value)*			
❏ SWBO-101	The Beatles	1975	$80
—*With "All Rights Reserved" on labels; title in black on cover; photos and poster of thinner stock than originals*			
❏ SWBO-101 [B]	The Beatles	1968	$1500
—*Numbered copy; includes four individual photos and large poster (included in value); because the white cover shows*			

---

ring wear so readily, this is an EXTREMELY difficult album to find in near-mint condition; first pressing label has Side 1, Song 5 incorrectly listed as "Bungalow Bill"; VG value 60; VG+ value 120

❏ PMC7067/8 [M]	The Beatles		$40
❏ PCS7067-8 [B]	The Beatles	2012	$50
❏ SKBO-3403 [P]	The Beatles 1962-1966	1975	$50
—*Custom red Apple labels with "All Rights Reserved" on labels*			
❏ SKBO-3403 [P]	The Beatles 1962-1966	1973	$30
—*Custom red Apple labels. "Love Me Do" and "I Want to Hold Your Hand" are rechanneled. "She Loves You," "A Hard Day's Night," "I Feel Fine" and "Ticket to Ride" are mono; "From Me to You," "Can't Buy Me Love" and everything else is stereo.*			
❏ C1-97036 [B]	The Beatles 1962-1966	1993	$30
—*Custom red Apple labels; red vinyl; all copies pressed in U.K; U.S. versions have a bar-code sticker over the international bar code on back cover. "Love Me Do," "Please Please Me," "From Me to You" and "She Loves You" are mono; all others are stereo.*			
❏ SKBO-3404 [B]	The Beatles 1967-1970	1973	$30
—*Custom blue Apple labels. "Hello Goodbye" and "Penny Lane" are mono, all others stereo.*			
❏ SKBO-3404 [B]	The Beatles 1967-1970	1975	$50
—*Custom blue Apple labels with "All Rights Reserved" on labels*			
❏ C1-97039	The Beatles 1967-1970	1993	$30
—*Custom blue Apple labels; blue vinyl; all copies pressed in U.K.; U.S. versions have a bar-code sticker over the international bar code on back cover*			
❏ -0 [DJ]	The Beatles Again	1970	$8000
—*Prototypes with "The Beatles Again" on cover; not released to the general public*			
❏ SO-385 [DJ]	The Beatles Again	1970	$10000
—*Prototype covers with "The Beatles Again" on cover; not released to the general public. This is NOT a standard issue! VG value 4000; VG+ value 6000*			

❏ SBC-100 [M]	The Beatles' Christmas Album	1970	$1200
—*Fan club issue of the seven Christmas messages; very good counterfeits exist*			
❏ 5099963379716 [M]	The Beatles In Mono	2014	$350
❏ SW-153 [P]	Yellow Submarine	1969	$50
—*With Capitol logo on Side 2 bottom. "Only a Northern Song" is rechanneled.*			
❏ SW-153 [P]	Yellow Submarine	1971	$25
—*With "Mfd. by Apple" on label*			
❏ SW-153 [P]	Yellow Submarine	1975	$30
—*With "All Rights Reserved" on label*			

APPLE/CAPITOL

❏ ST2228 [P]	Beatles '65	1968	$40
—*With Capitol logo on Side 2 bottom*			
❏ ST2228 [P]	Beatles '65	1971	$25
—*With "Mfd. by Apple" on label*			
❏ ST2228 [P]	Beatles '65	1975	$30
—*With "All Rights Reserved" on label*			
❏ ST2358 [P]	Beatles VI	1969	$40
—*With Capitol logo on Side 2 bottom*			
❏ ST2358 [P]	Beatles VI	1971	$25
—*With "Mfd. by Apple" on label*			
❏ ST2358 [P]	Beatles VI	1975	$30
—*With "All Rights Reserved" on label*			
❏ SMAS2386 [P]	Help!	1969	$40
—*With Capitol logo on Side 2 bottom*			
❏ SMAS2386 [P]	Help!	1971	$25
—*With "Mfd. by Apple" on label*			
❏ SMAS2386 [P]	Help!	1975	$30
—*With "All Rights Reserved" on label*			
❏ SMAL2835 [P]	Magical Mystery Tour	1969	$50
—*With Capitol logo on Side 2 bottom; with 24-page booklet*			
❏ SMAL2835 [P]	Magical Mystery Tour	1971	$25
—*With "Mfd. by Apple" on label; with 24-page booklet*			
❏ SMAL2835 [P]	Magical Mystery Tour	1975	$30
—*With "All Rights Reserved" on label; with 24-page booklet*			

❏ ST2047 [P]	Meet the Beatles!	1968	$40
—*With Capitol logo on Side 2 bottom*			
❏ ST2047 [P]	Meet the Beatles!	1971	$25
—*With "Mfd. by Apple" on label*			
❏ ST2047 [P]	Meet the Beatles!	1975	$30
—*With "All Rights Reserved" on label*			
❏ ST2576 [S]	Revolver	1971	$25
—*With "Mfd. by Apple" on label*			
❏ ST2576 [S]	Revolver	1969	$40
—*With Capitol logo on Side 2 bottom*			
❏ ST2576 [S]	Revolver	1975	$30
—*With "All Rights Reserved" on label*			
❏ ST2442 [S]	Rubber Soul	1969	$40
—*With Capitol logo on Side 2 bottom*			
❏ ST2442 [S]	Rubber Soul	1971	$25
—*With "Mfd. by Apple" on label*			
❏ ST2442 [S]	Rubber Soul	1975	$30
—*With "All Rights Reserved" on label*			
❏ SMAS2653 [S]	Sgt. Pepper's Lonely Hearts Club Band	1969	$40
—*With Capitol logo on Side 2 bottom*			
❏ SMAS2653 [S]	Sgt. Pepper's Lonely Hearts Club Band	1971	$30
—*With "Mfd. by Apple" on label*			
❏ SMAS2653 [S]	Sgt. Pepper's Lonely Hearts Club Band	1975	$30
—*With "All Rights Reserved" on label*			
❏ ST2108 [S]	Something New	1968	$40
—*With Capitol logo on Side 2 bottom*			
❏ ST2108 [S]	Something New	1971	$25
—*With "Mfd. by Apple" on label*			
❏ ST2108 [S]	Something New	1975	$30
—*With "All Rights Reserved" on label*			
❏ 0(no cat #)	The Beatles 10th Anniversary Box Set	1974	$2000
—*VG value 1000; VG+ value 1500*			
❏ ST2080 [P]	The Beatles' Second Album	1968	$40
—*With Capitol logo on Side 2 bottom*			
❏ ST2080 [P]	The Beatles' Second Album	1971	$25
—*With "Mfd. by Apple" on label*			
❏ ST2080 [P]	The Beatles' Second Album	1975	$30
—*With "All Rights Reserved" on label*			
❏ 0(no cat #)	The Beatles Special Limited Edition	1974	$1200
❏ STBO2222 [P]	The Beatles' Story	1968	$75
—*With Capitol logo on bottom of B-side of both records*			
❏ STBO2222 [P]	The Beatles' Story	1971	$30
—*With "Mfd. by Apple" on labels*			
❏ STBO2222 [P]	The Beatles' Story	1975	$40
—*With "All Rights Reserved" on labels*			
❏ ST2309 [P]	The Early Beatles	1969	$40
—*With Capitol logo on Side 2 bottom*			
❏ ST2309 [P]	The Early Beatles	1971	$25
—*With "Mfd. by Apple" on label*			
❏ ST2309 [P]	The Early Beatles	1975	$30
—*With "All Rights Reserved" on label*			
❏ ST2553 [P]	Yesterday and Today	1969	$40
—*With Capitol logo on Side 2 bottom*			
❏ ST2553 [P]	Yesterday and Today	1971	$25
—*With "Mfd. by Apple" on label*			
❏ ST2553 [S]	Yesterday and Today	1971	$30
—*With "Mfd. by Apple" on label; all 11 tracks are in true stereo. Check for a triangle in the record's trail-off area.*			
❏ ST2553 [P]	Yesterday and Today	1975	$30
—*With "All Rights Reserved" on label*			

APPLE FILMS

❏ KAL4 [DJ]	The Yellow Submarine (A United Artists Release)	1969	$2000
—*One-sided LP with radio spots for movie*			
❏ KAL 004 [DJ]	The Yellow Submarine (A United Artists Release)	1969	$3000
—*One-sided LP with radio spots for movie; VG value 1000; VG+ value 1500*			

ATCO

❏ -0 [M-DJ]	Ain't She Sweet	1964	$1000
—*White label promo*			
❏ 33-169 [M]	Ain't She Sweet	1964	$300
❏ 33-169 [M]	Ain't She Sweet	1964	$1500
—*White label promo*			
❏ SD 33-169 [P]	Ain't She Sweet	1964	$500
—*Tan and purple label; all four Beatles tracks are rechanneled*			

Number	Title	Yr	NM
❏ SD 33-169 [P]	Ain't She Sweet	1969	$500

— *Yellow label*

AUDIOFIDELITY

Number	Title	Yr	NM
❏ PHX-339 [M]	First Movement	1982	$15

— *Contains eight Decca audition tracks*

❏ PD-339 [M]	First Movement	1982	$40

— *Contains eight Decca audition tracks; picture disc*

AUDIO RARITIES

❏ AR-2452 [M]	The Complete Silver Beatles	1982	$18

— *Contains 12 Decca audition tracks*

BACKSTAGE

❏ -0 [DJ]	Like Dreamers Do	1982	$50

— *White vinyl promo in white sleeve*

❏ -0 [DJ]	Like Dreamers Do	1982	$50

— *Gray vinyl promo in white sleeve*

❏ BSR-1111 [M]	Like Dreamers Do	1982	$75

— *Two picture discs (10 of 15 Decca audition tracks on one, interviews on the other) and one white-vinyl record (same contests as musical picture disc)*

❏ BSR-1111 [M]	Like Dreamers Do	1982	$150

— *Same as above, except colored-vinyl LP is gray*

❏ BSR-1111 [DJ]	Like Dreamers Do	1982	$50

— *White vinyl promo in white sleeve*

❏ BSR-1111 [DJ]	Like Dreamers Do	1982	$50

— *Gray vinyl promo in white sleeve*

❏ 2-201 [M]	Like Dreamers Do	1982	$75

— *Non-gatefold package*

❏ 2-201 [M]	Like Dreamers Do	1982	$40

— *Gatefold package, individually numbered (numbers under 100 increase value significantly)*

❏ BSR-1165 [PD]	The Beatles Talk with Jerry G.	1982	$30

— *Picture disc*

❏ BSR-1175 [PD]	The Beatles Talk with Jerry G., Vol. 2	1983	$30

— *Picture disc*

CAPITOL

❏ SV-12245 [P]	20 Greatest Hits	1982	$25

— *Purple label, large Capitol logo. "Love Me Do" and "She Loves You" are rechanneled, the other 18 tracks are stereo*

❏ SV-12245 [P]	20 Greatest Hits	1983	$25

— *Black label, print in colorband*

❏ SV-12245 [P]	20 Greatest Hits	1988	$30

— *Purple label, small Capitol logo*

❏ SO-383	Abbey Road	1976	$15

— *Orange label*

❏ SO-383 [B]	Abbey Road	1978	$12

— *Purple label, large Capitol logo*

❏ SO-383	Abbey Road	1983	$18

— *Black label, print in colorband*

❏ C1-46446	Abbey Road	1988	$30

— *New number; purple label, small Capitol logo*

❏ C1-46446	Abbey Road	1995	$15

— *Apple logo restored to back cover on reissue*

❏ SEAX-11900 [PD]	Abbey Road	1978	$40

— *Picture disc; deduct 25% for cut-outs*

❏ SJ-383	Abbey Road	1984	$30

— *New prefix; black label, print in colorband*

❏ SW-11921 [P]	A Hard Day's Night	1979	$15

— *Purple label, large Capitol logo*

❏ SW-11921 [P]	A Hard Day's Night	1983	$18

— *Black label, print in colorband*

❏ SW-11921 [P]	A Hard Day's Night	1988	$30

— *Purple label, small Capitol logo*

❏ CLJ-46437 [M]	A Hard Day's Night	1987	$25

— *Black label, print in colorband; first Capitol version of original British LP*

❏ CLJ-46437 [M]	A Hard Day's Night	1988	$30

— *Purple label, small Capitol logo*

❏ C1-46437 [M]	A Hard Day's Night	1995	$15

— *New prefix; Apple logo on back cover*

❏ T2228 [M]	Beatles '65	1964	$175
❏ ST2228 [P]	Beatles '65	1964	$150

— *Black label with colorband. "She's a Woman" and "I Feel Fine" are rechanneled.*

❏ ST2228 [P]	Beatles '65	1969	$40

— *Lime green label*

❏ ST2228 [P]	Beatles '65	1976	$15

— *Orange label*

❏ ST2228 [P]	Beatles '65	1978	$12

— *Purple label, large Capitol logo*

❏ ST2228 [P]	Beatles '65	1983	$18

— *Black label, print in colorband*

❏ C1-90446 [P]	Beatles '65	1988	$30

— *New number; purple label, small Capitol logo*

❏ ST2228 [P]	Beatles '65	1968	$50

— *Black colorband label; border print adds "A Subsidiary of Capitol Industries Inc.*

❏ CLJ-46438 [M]	Beatles for Sale	1987	$25

— *Black label, print in colorband; first Capitol version of original British LP*

❏ CLJ-46438 [M]	Beatles for Sale	1988	$30

— *Purple label, small Capitol logo*

❏ C1-46438 [M]	Beatles for Sale	1995	$15

— *New prefix; Apple logo on back cover*

❏ T2358 [M]	Beatles VI	1965	$175

— *With "See label for correct playing order" on back cover*

❏ T2358 [M]	Beatles VI	1965	$120

— *With song titles listed in correct order on back cover*

❏ ST2358 [P]	Beatles VI	1965	$100

— *Black label with colorband; with "See label for correct playing order" on back cover*

❏ ST2358 [P]	Beatles VI	1965	$150

— *Black label with colorband; with song titles listed in correct order on back cover. "Yes It Is" is rechanneled.*

❏ ST-8-2358 [P]	Beatles VI	1965	$600

— *Capitol Record Club edition; black label with colorband*

❏ ST-8-2358 [P]	Beatles VI	1969	$500

— *Capitol Record Club edition; lime green label*

❏ ST2358 [P]	Beatles VI	1969	$40

— *Lime green label*

❏ ST2358 [P]	Beatles VI	1976	$15

— *Orange label*

❏ ST2358 [P]	Beatles VI	1978	$12

— *Purple label, large Capitol logo*

❏ ST2358 [M]	Beatles VI	1983	$18

— *Black label, print in colorband; plays in mono despite label designation*

❏ ST2358 [M]	Beatles VI	1988	$100

— *Purple label, small Capitol logo; plays in mono despite label designation*

❏ C1-90445 [M]	Beatles VI	1988	$30

— *New number; purple label, small Capitol logo; plays in mono despite label designation*

❏ ST2358 [P]	Beatles VI	1968	$75

— *Black colorband label; border print adds "A Subsidiary of Capitol Industries Inc.*

❏ MAS2386 [M]	Help!	1965	$250
❏ SMAS2386 [P]	Help!	1965	$150

— *Black label with colorband. Has incidental music by George Martin. "Ticket to Ride" is rechanneled.*

❏ SMAS-8-2386 [P]	Help!	1965	$500

— *Capitol Record Club edition; black label with colorband; no "8" on cover*

❏ SMAS-8-2386 [P]	Help!	1965	$800

— *Capitol Record Club edition; black label with colorband; with "8" on cover*

❏ SMAS-8-2386 [P]	Help!	197?	$700

— *Longines Symphonette edition; with "Mfd. by Longines" and "8" on cover*

❏ SMAS-8-2386 [P]	Help!	1969	$300

— *Capitol Record Club edition; lime green label; no "8" on cover*

❏ SMAS-8-2386 [P]	Help!	1969	$500

— *Capitol Record Club edition; lime green label; with "8" on cover*

❏ SMAS2386 [P]	Help!	1969	$40

— *Lime green label*

❏ SMAS2386 [P]	Help!	1976	$15

— *Orange label*

❏ SMAS2386 [P]	Help!	1978	$12

— *Purple label, large Capitol logo*

❏ SMAS2386 [P]	Help!	1983	$18

— *Black label, print in colorband*

❏ C1-90454 [P]	Help!	1988	$30

— *New number; purple label, small Capitol logo*

❏ CLJ-46439 [S]	Help!	1987	$25

— *Black label, print in colorband; first Capitol version of original British LP*

❏ CLJ-46439 [S]	Help!	1988	$30

— *Purple label, small Capitol logo*

❏ C1-46439 [S]	Help!	1995	$15

— *New prefix; Apple logo on back cover*

❏ SMAS2386 [P]	Help!	1968	$50

— *Black colorband label; border print adds "A Subsidiary of Capitol Industries Inc.*

❏ SW-385	Hey Jude	1976	$15

— *Orange label (all Capitol label versions call the LP "Hey Jude")*

❏ SW-385	Hey Jude	1978	$12

— *Purple label, large Capitol logo*

❏ SW-385	Hey Jude	1983	$50

— *Black label, print in colorband*

❏ SJ-385	Hey Jude	1984	$30

— *New prefix; black label, print in colorband*

❏ C1-90442	Hey Jude	1988	$30

— *New number; purple label, small Capitol logo*

❏ SW-11922	Let It Be	1979	$18

— *Purple label, large Capitol logo; with poster and custom innersleeve*

❏ SW-11922	Let It Be	1983	$18

— *Black label, print in colorband; add 33% if poster is included*

❏ SW-11922	Let It Be	1988	$30

— *Purple label, small Capitol logo; add 20% if poster and custom innersleeve are included*

❏ C1-46447	Let It Be	1995	$15

— *New number (the only 1995 reissue with a completely new number)*

❏ SKBL-11711 [P]	Love Songs	1977	$35

— *With booklet and embossed, leather-like cover. "P.S. I Love You" and "Yes It Is" are rechanneled.*

❏ SKBL-11711 [P]	Love Songs	1988	$30

— *With booklet, but without embossed cover*

❏ MAL2835 [M]	Magical Mystery Tour	1967	$700

— *With 24-page book bound into center of gatefold*

❏ SMAL2835 [P]	Magical Mystery Tour	1967	$250

— *Black label with colorband; with 24-page booklet. "Penny Lane," "Baby You're a Rich Man" and "All You Need Is Love" is rechanneled, as is the second half of "I Am the Walrus" (every "stereo" version of "Walrus" is this way)*

❏ SMAL2835 [P]	Magical Mystery Tour	1969	$75

— *Lime green label; with 24-page booklet*

❏ SMAL2835 [P]	Magical Mystery Tour	1976	$15

— *Orange label; with 24-page booklet*

❏ SMAL2835 [P]	Magical Mystery Tour	1978	$12

— *Purple label, large Capitol logo; this edition did not come with booklet*

❏ SMAL2835 [P]	Magical Mystery Tour	1983	$18

— *Black label, print in colorband; no booklet*

❏ C1-48062 [P]	Magical Mystery Tour	1988	$30

— *New number; purple label, small Capitol logo; no booklet*

❏ C1-48062 [P]	Magical Mystery Tour	1992	$15

— *With Apple logo on back cover; reissue restores booklet to package*

❏ SMAL2835 [P]	Magical Mystery Tour	1968	$150

— *Black colorband label; border print adds "A Subsidiary of Capitol Industries Inc."; with 24-page booklet*

❏ T2047 [M]	Meet the Beatles!	1964	$300

— *Black label with colorband; "Beatles!" on cover in tan to brown print; label has "ASCAP" after every title except "I Want to Hold Your Hand" (BMI); no producer credit on back cover (this is the second edition of this LP)*

❏ T2047 [M]	Meet the Beatles!	1965	$175

— *Black label with colorband; "Beatles!" on cover in green print; most of these have "Produced by George Martin" on lower left of back cover; many of these have a label giving "BMI" credit to every song except "Don't Bother Me" and "Till There Was You"*

❏ ST2047 [P]	Meet the Beatles!	1964	$250

— *Black label with colorband; "Beatles!" on cover in tan to brown print; label has "ASCAP" after every title except "I Want to Hold Your Hand" (BMI); no producer credit on back cover (this is the second edition of this LP)*

❏ ST2047 [P]	Meet the Beatles!	1965	$150

— *Black label with colorband; "Beatles!" on cover in green print; most of these have "Produced by George Martin" on lower left of back cover; many of these have a label giving "BMI" credit to every song except "Don't Bother Me" and "Till There Was You"*

❏ ST-8-2047 [P]	Meet the Beatles!	1969	$500

— *Capitol Record Club edition; black label with colorband*

❏ ST-8-2047 [P]	Meet the Beatles!	1969	$250

— *Capitol Record Club edition; lime green label*

❏ ST2047 [P]	Meet the Beatles!	1969	$40

— *Lime green label*

❏ ST2047 [P]	Meet the Beatles!	1976	$15

— *Orange label*

❏ ST2047 [P]	Meet the Beatles!	1978	$12

— *Purple label, large Capitol logo*

❏ ST2047 [P]	Meet the Beatles!	1983	$18

— *Black label, print in colorband*

❏ C1-90441 [P]	Meet the Beatles!	1988	$30

— *New number; purple label, small Capitol logo*

❏ T2047 [M]	Meet the Beatles!	1964	$450

— *Black label with colorband; "Beatles!" on cover in tan to brown print; no producer credit on back cover; "ASCAP" and "BMI" credits are missing on the label (this is the first edition of the LP)*

❏ ST2047 [P]	Meet the Beatles!	1964	$500

— *Black label with colorband; "Beatles!" on cover in tan to brown print; "ASCAP" and "BMI" credits are missing on the label; no producer credit on back cover (this is the first edition of the LP)*

❏ ST2047 [P]	Meet the Beatles!	1968	$75

— *Black colorband label; border print adds "A Subsidiary of Capitol Industries Inc.*

❏ T2047 [M]	Meet the Beatles!	1964	$175

— *Black label with colorband; "Beatles!" on cover in tan to brown print; some labels have "ASCAP" after every title except "I Want to Hold Your Hand"; other labels have "ASCAP" after every title except "I Want to Hold Your Hand," "I Saw Her Standing There" and "I Wanna Be Your Man"; still other labels have "ASCAP" after every title except "I Want to Hold Your Hand" and "I Wanna Be Your Man"; most of the back covers add "Produced by George Martin" to lower left*

❏ ST2047 [P]	Meet the Beatles!	1964	$250

— *Black label with colorband; "Beatles!" on cover in tan to brown print; some labels have "ASCAP" after every title except "I Want to Hold Your Hand"; other labels have "ASCAP" after every title except "I Want to Hold Your Hand," "I Saw Her Standing There" and "I Wanna Be Your Man"; still other labels have "ASCAP" after every title except "I Want to Hold Your Hand" and "I Wanna Be Your Man"; back cover adds "Produced by George Martin" to lower left*

Number	Title	Yr	NM
❏ C1-91135 [B]	Past Masters Volume 1 and 2	1988	$30

—*Some early tracks are in mono, but "This Boy," "She's a Woman," "Yes It Is," and "The Inner Light" are in stereo.*

❏ CLJ-46435 [M]	Please Please Me	1987	$25

—*Black label, print in colorband; first Capitol version of original British LP*

❏ CLJ-46435 [M]	Please Please Me	1988	$30

—*Purple label, small Capitol logo*

❏ C1-46435 [M]	Please Please Me	1995	$15

—*New prefix; Apple logo on back cover*

❏ -0 [DJ]	Rarities	1979	$300

—*Green label; withdrawn before official release; all known copies have a plain white sleeve*

❏ SPRO-8969	Rarities	1978	$50

—*Purple label, large Capitol logo; part of the U.S. box set The Beatles Collection (BC-13)*

❏ SN-12009 [DJ]	Rarities	1979	$500

—*Green label; withdrawn before official release; all known copies have a plain white sleeve*

❏ SHAL-12060 [B]	Rarities	1980	$25

—*Black label with colorband. First pressing says that "There's a Place" debuts in stereo (false) and that the screaming at the end of "Helter Skelter" was a "classic Lennon statement" (it's actually Ringo).*

❏ SHAL-12060 [B]	Rarities	1980	$18

—*Same as above, with errors deleted and "Produced by George Martin" added to back cover*

❏ -0 [DJ]	Reel Music	1982	$40

—*Yellow vinyl promo; numbered back cover with 12-page booklet*

❏ -0 [DJ]	Reel Music	1982	$25

—*Yellow vinyl promo; plain white cover with 12-page booklet*

❏ SV-12199 [DJ]	Reel Music	1982	$40

—*Yellow vinyl promo; numbered back cover with 12-page booklet*

❏ SV-12199 [DJ]	Reel Music	1982	$25

—*Yellow vinyl promo; plain white cover with 12-page booklet*

❏ SV-12199	Reel Music	1982	$12

—*Standard issue with 12-page booklet*

❏ T2576 [M]	Revolver	1966	$300
❏ ST2576 [S]	Revolver	1966	$150

—*Black label with colorband*

❏ ST-8-2576 [S]	Revolver	1966	$400

—*Capitol Record Club edition; black label with colorband*

❏ ST-8-2576 [S]	Revolver	1969	$120

—*Capitol Record Club edition; lime green label*

❏ ST-8-2576 [S]	Revolver	1973?	$250

—*Longines Symphonette edition; orange label (a very late issue, as the club closed in 1974)*

❏ ST2576 [S]	Revolver	1969	$40

—*Lime green label*

❏ ST2576 [S]	Revolver	1970	$300

—*Red label with "target" Capitol at top (same design as lime green label)*

❏ ST2576 [S]	Revolver	1976	$15

—*Orange label*

❏ SW2576 [S]	Revolver	1978	$12

—*Purple label, large Capitol logo*

❏ SW2576 [S]	Revolver	1983	$18

—*Black label, print in colorband*

❏ C1-90452 [S]	Revolver	1988	$30

—*New number; purple label, small Capitol logo*

❏ CLJ-46441 [S]	Revolver	1987	$25

—*Black label, print in colorband; first Capitol version of original British LP*

❏ CLJ-46441 [S]	Revolver	1988	$30

—*Purple label, small Capitol logo*

❏ C1-46441 [S]	Revolver	1995	$15

—*New prefix; Apple logo on back cover*

❏ ST2576 [S]	Revolver	1968	$50

—*Black colorband label; border print adds "A Subsidiary of Capitol Industries Inc.*

❏ SKBO-11537	Rock 'n' Roll Music	1976	$30
❏ SN-16020 [B]	Rock 'n' Roll Music, Volume 1	1980	$15
❏ SN-16021 [B]	Rock 'n' Roll Music, Volume 2	1980	$15
❏ T2442 [M]	Rubber Soul	1965	$175
❏ ST2442 [S]	Rubber Soul	1965	$75

—*Black label with colorband*

❏ ST-8-2442 [S]	Rubber Soul	1965	$400

—*Capitol Record Club edition; black label with colorband*

❏ ST-8-2442 [S]	Rubber Soul	1969	$300

—*Capitol Record Club edition; lime green label*

❏ ST-8-2442 [S]	Rubber Soul	1969	$300

—*Longines Symphonette edition (will be stated on label); lime green label*

❏ ST2442 [S]	Rubber Soul	1969	$40

—*Lime green label*

❏ ST2442 [S]	Rubber Soul	1976	$15

—*Orange label*

❏ SW2442 [S]	Rubber Soul	1978	$12

—*Purple label, large Capitol logo*

❏ SW2442 [S]	Rubber Soul	1983	$18

—*Black label, print in colorband*

Number	Title	Yr	NM
❏ C1-90453 [S]	Rubber Soul	1988	$30

—*New number; purple label, small Capitol logo*

❏ CLJ-46440 [S]	Rubber Soul	1987	$25

—*Black label, print in colorband; first Capitol version of original British LP*

❏ CLJ-46440 [S]	Rubber Soul	1988	$30

—*Purple label, small Capitol logo*

❏ C1-46440 [S]	Rubber Soul	1995	$15

—*New prefix; Apple logo on back cover*

❏ ST2442 [S]	Rubber Soul	1968	$50

—*Black colorband label; border print adds "A Subsidiary of Capitol Industries Inc.*

❏ MAS2653 [M]	Sgt. Pepper's Lonely Hearts Club Band	1967	$500
❏ SMAS2653 [S]	Sgt. Pepper's Lonely Hearts Club Band	1967	$250

—*Black label with colorband*

❏ SMAS2653 [S]	Sgt. Pepper's Lonely Hearts Club Band	1969	$75

—*Lime green label*

❏ SMAS2653 [S]	Sgt. Pepper's Lonely Hearts Club Band	1976	$15

—*Orange label*

❏ SMAS2653 [S]	Sgt. Pepper's Lonely Hearts Club Band	1978	$12

—*Purple label, large Capitol logo. Many copies from 1978 had a "The Original Classic" sticker on shrink wrap; it was added at the time of the release of the bomb movie version of Sgt. Pepper. Double the value if the sticker is still there.*

❏ SMAS2653 [S]	Sgt. Pepper's Lonely Hearts Club Band	1983	$18

—*Black label, print in colorband; some of these had "The Original Classic" stickers, too. Add $10 to value if it is there.*

❏ C1-46442 [S]	Sgt. Pepper's Lonely Hearts Club Band	1988	$30

—*New number; purple label, small Capitol logo*

❏ C1-46442 [S]	Sgt. Pepper's Lonely Hearts Club Band	1995	$15

—*With Apple logo on back cover*

❏ SEAX-11840 [PD]	Sgt. Pepper's Lonely Hearts Club Band	1978	$25

—*Picture disc; deduct 25% for cut-outs*

❏ SMAS2653 [S]	Sgt. Pepper's Lonely Hearts Club Band	1968	$150

—*Black colorband label; border print adds "A Subsidiary of Capitol Industries Inc.*

❏ 2653	Sgt. Pepper's Lonely Hearts Club Band Cut-Out Inserts	1967	$3
❏ 2653	Sgt. Pepper's Lonely Hearts Club Band Special Inner Sleeve	1967	$18

—*Red-pink psychedelic sleeve only issued with 1967 (mono and stereo) editions*

❏ T2108 [M]	Something New	1964	$250
❏ ST2108 [S]	Something New	1964	$150

—*Black label with colorband*

❏ ST-8-2108 [S]	Something New	1964	$300

—*Capitol Record Club edition; black label with colorband*

❏ ST-8-2108 [S]	Something New	1969	$175

—*Capitol Record Club edition; lime green label*

❏ ST-8-2108 [S]	Something New	1969	$300

—*Longines Symphonette edition (will be stated on label); lime green label*

❏ ST2108 [S]	Something New	1969	$40

—*Lime green label*

❏ ST2108 [S]	Something New	1976	$15

—*Orange label*

❏ ST2108 [S]	Something New	1978	$12

—*Purple label, large Capitol logo*

❏ ST2108 [S]	Something New	1983	$18

—*Black label, print in colorband*

❏ C1-90443 [S]	Something New	1988	$30

—*New number; purple label, small Capitol logo*

❏ ST2108 [S]	Something New	1968	$50

—*Black colorband label; border print adds "A Subsidiary of*

Capitol Industries Inc.

Number	Title	Yr	NM
❏ SWBO-101	The Beatles	1976	$30

—*Orange label; with photos and poster*

❏ C1-46443	The Beatles	1995	$25

—*With Apple logo on back cover*

❏ SWBO-101	The Beatles	1978	$30

—*Purple label, large Capitol logo; with photos and poster (some copies have four photos as one perforated sheet)*

❏ SWBO-101	The Beatles	1983	$40

—*Black label, print in colorband; with photos and poster (some copies have four photos as one perforated sheet)*

❏ C1-46443	The Beatles	1988	$50

—*New number; purple label, small Capitol logo; with photos and poster (some copies have four photos as one perforated sheet)*

❏ SEBX-11841	The Beatles	1978	$50

—*White vinyl; with photos and poster (with number "SEBX-11841" on each)*

❏ SKBO-3403 [P]	The Beatles 1962-1966	1976	$30

—*Red labels*

❏ SKBO-3403 [P]	The Beatles 1962-1966	1976	$30

—*Blue labels (error pressing)*

❏ SEBX-11842 [P]	The Beatles 1962-1966	1978	$40

—*Red vinyl*

❏ C1-90435 [P]	The Beatles 1962-1966	1988	$30

—*New number; purple labels, small Capitol logo*

❏ SKBO-3404 [B]	The Beatles 1967-1970	1976	$25

—*Blue labels*

❏ SEBX-11843 [B]	The Beatles 1967-1970	1978	$40

—*Blue vinyl*

❏ C1-90438 [B]	The Beatles 1967-1970	1988	$30

—*New number; purple labels, small Capitol logo*

❏ -0 [DJ]	The Beatles at the Hollywood Bowl	1977	$500

—*Advance tan label promo in plain white jacket*

❏ SMAS-11638	The Beatles at the Hollywood Bowl	1977	$30

—*Originals with embossed title and ticket on front cover*

❏ SMAS-11638 [DJ]	The Beatles at the Hollywood Bowl	1977	$500

—*Advance tan label promo in plain white jacket*

❏ SMAS-11638	The Beatles at the Hollywood Bowl	1980	$18

—*Second pressing without embossed title and ticket*

❏ SMAS-11638	The Beatles at the Hollywood Bowl	1989	$40

—*With UPC code on back cover*

❏ BC-13 [B]	The Beatles Collection	1978	$300

—*American versions have "EMI" and "BC-13" on box spine; imports go for less*

❏ 0(no cat #)	The Beatles Collection Platinum Series	1984	$800
❏ BBX1-91302	The Beatles Deluxe Box Set	1988	$300

❏ T2080 [M]	The Beatles' Second Album	1964	$300
❏ ST2080 [P]	The Beatles' Second Album	1964	$150

—*Black label with colorband. "She Loves You," "I'll Get You" and "You Can't Do That" are rechanneled*

❏ ST-8-2080 [P]	The Beatles' Second Album	1964	$600

—*Capitol Record Club edition; black label with colorband*

❏ ST-8-2080 [P]	The Beatles' Second Album	1969	$400

—*Capitol Record Club edition; lime green label*

❏ ST2080 [P]	The Beatles' Second Album	1969	$40

—*Lime green label*

❏ ST2080 [P]	The Beatles' Second Album	1976	$15

—*Orange label*

❏ ST2080 [P]	The Beatles' Second Album	1978	$12

—*Purple label, large Capitol logo*

❏ ST2080 [P]	The Beatles' Second Album	1983	$18

—*Black label, print in colorband*

❏ C1-90444 [P]	The Beatles' Second Album	1988	$30

—*New number; purple label, small Capitol logo*

❏ ST2080 [P]	The Beatles' Second Album	1968	$50

—*Black colorband label; border print adds "A Subsidiary of*

Number	Title	Yr	NM

Capitol Industries Inc.

❑ TBO2222 [M] The Beatles' Story 1964 $300
❑ STBO2222 [P] The Beatles' Story 1964 $300
—*Black label with colorband. Some of the musical snippets are rechanneled.*
❑ STBO2222 [P] The Beatles' Story 1969 $50
—*Lime green label*
❑ STBO2222 [P] The Beatles' Story 1976 $25
—*Orange label*
❑ STBO2222 [P] The Beatles' Story 1978 $25
—*Purple label, large Capitol logo*
❑ STBO2222 [P] The Beatles' Story 1983 $40
—*Black label, print in colorband*
❑ STBO2222 [P] The Beatles' Story 1968 $150
—*Black colorband label; border print adds "A Subsidiary of Capitol Industries Inc.*
❑ T2309 [M] The Early Beatles 1965 $300
❑ ST2309 [P] The Early Beatles 1965 $150
—*Black label with colorband. "Love Me Do" and "P.S. I Love You" are rechanneled.*
❑ ST2309 [P] The Early Beatles 1969 $40
—*Lime green label*
❑ ST2309 [P] The Early Beatles 1976 $15
—*Orange label*
❑ ST2309 [P] The Early Beatles 1978 $12
—*Purple label, large Capitol logo*
❑ ST2309 [P] The Early Beatles 1983 $30
—*Black label, print in colorband*
❑ ST2309 [P] The Early Beatles 1968 $50
—*Black colorband label; border print adds "A Subsidiary of Capitol Industries Inc.*
❑ CLJ-46436 [M] With the Beatles 1987 $25
—*Black label, print in colorband; first Capitol version of original British LP*
❑ CLJ-46436 [M] With the Beatles 1988 $30
—*Purple label, small Capitol logo*
❑ C1-46436 [M] With the Beatles 1995 $15
—*New prefix; Apple logo on back cover*
❑ SW-153 [P] Yellow Submarine 1976 $15
—*Orange label*
❑ SW-153 [P] Yellow Submarine 1978 $12
—*Purple label, large Capitol logo*
❑ SW-153 [P] Yellow Submarine 1983 $18
—*Black label, print in colorband*
❑ C1-46445 [P] Yellow Submarine 1988 $30
—*New number; purple label, small Capitol logo*
❑ C1-46445 [P] Yellow Submarine 1995 $15
—*Reissue has the British liner notes, which include a review of the White Album.*
❑ T2553 [M] Yesterday and Today 1966 $4000
—*First state" butcher cover (never had other cover on top); cover will be the same size as other Capitol Beatles LPs; VG value 2000; VG+ value 3000*
❑ T2553 [M] Yesterday and Today 1966 $1500
—*Second state" butcher cover (trunk cover pasted over original cover)*
❑ T2553 [M] Yesterday and Today 1966 $1200
—*Third state" butcher cover (trunk cover removed, leaving butcher cover intact); cover will be about 3/16-inch narrower than other Capitol Beatles LPs; value is highly negotiable depending upon the success of removing the paste-over; VG value 400; VG+ value 800*

❑ T2553 [M] Yesterday and Today 1966 $250
—*Trunk cover*
❑ T2553 [P] Yesterday and Today 1966 $12000
—*First state" butcher cover (never had other cover on top); cover will be the same size as other Capitol Beatles LPs; VG value 4000; VG+ value 6000*
❑ ST2553 [P] Yesterday and Today 1966 $1000
—*Second state" butcher cover (trunk cover pasted over original cover)*
❑ ST-8-2553 [P] Yesterday and Today 1966 $350
—*Capitol Record Club edition; black label with colorband*
❑ ST2553 [P] Yesterday and Today 1966 $1500
—*Third state" butcher cover (trunk cover removed, leaving butcher cover intact); cover will be about 3/16-inch narrower than other Capitol Beatles LPs; value is highly negotiable depending upon the success of removing the paste-over*
❑ ST2553 [P] Yesterday and Today 1966 $100
—*Trunk cover; black label with colorband (all later variations have the trunk cover). "I'm Only Sleeping," "Dr. Robert" and*

"And Your Bird Can Sing" are rechanneled.
❑ ST-8-2553 [S] Yesterday and Today 1969 $175
—*Capitol Record Club edition; lime green label; all 11 tracks are in true stereo! (We don't know if the same is true of the black label version.)*
❑ ST2553 [P] Yesterday and Today 1969 $40
—*Lime green label*
❑ ST2553 [P] Yesterday and Today 1976 $15
—*Orange label; it's possible that this and all future pressings have all 11 tracks in true stereo, but we don't know.*
❑ ST2553 [P] Yesterday and Today 1978 $12
—*Purple label, large Capitol logo*
❑ ST2553 [P] Yesterday and Today 1983 $18
—*Black label, print in colorband*
❑ C1-90447 [P] Yesterday and Today 1988 $30
—*New number; purple label, small Capitol logo; stereo content uncertain*
❑ ST2553 [P] Yesterday and Today 1968 $50
—*Black colorband label; border print adds "A Subsidiary of Capitol Industries Inc.*

CICADELIC
❑ 1963 All Our Loving 1986 $15
❑ 1964 East Coast Invasion 1985 $15
❑ 1967 From Britain with Beat! 1987 $15
❑ 1968 Here, There and Everywhere 1988 $15
❑ 1960 Moviemania 1987 $15
❑ 1961 Not a Second Time 1987 $15
❑ 1965 Round the World 1986 $15
❑ 1962 Things We Said Today 1986 $15
❑ 1966 West Coast Invasion 1985 $15

CLARION
❑ 601 [M] The Amazing Beatles and Other Great English Group Sounds 1966 $150
❑ SD601 [P] The Amazing Beatles and Other Great English Group Sounds 1966 $250
—*All four Beatles tracks are rechanneled*

GREAT NORTHWEST
❑ GNW4007 Beatle Talk 1978 $12
❑ GNW4007 Beatle Talk 1978 $50
—*Columbia Record Club edition; "CRC" on spine*

HALL OF MUSIC
❑ HM-1-2200 [M] Live 1962, Hamburg, Germany 1981 $50
—*Only American LP with the original Eurpoean contents -- "I Saw Her Standing There," "Twist and Shout," "Ask Me Why" and "Reminiscing" replace the four songs listed with the Lingasong issue*

I-N-S RADIO NEWS
❑ -0 [DJ] Beatlemania Tour Coverage 1964 $1500
—*Promo-only open-end interview with script in plain white jacket*
❑ DOC-1 [DJ] Beatlemania Tour Coverage 1964 $1500
—*Promo-only open-end interview with script in plain white jacket; VG value 750; VG+ value 1125*

LINGASONG
❑ -07001 [DJ] Live at the Star Club in Hamburg, Germany, 1962 1977 $300
—*Promo only on blue vinyl*
❑ -07001 [DJ] Live at the Star Club in Hamburg, Germany, 1962 1977 $250
—*Promo only on red vinyl*
❑ -07001 [DJ] Live at the Star Club in Hamburg, Germany, 1962 1977 $40
—*Promo on black vinyl; "D.J. Copy Not for Sale" on labels*
❑ LS-2-7001 [R] Live at the Star Club in Hamburg, Germany, 1962 1977 $25
—*American version contains "I'm Gonna Sit Right Down and Cry," "Where Have You Been All My Life," "Till There Was You," and "Sheila," not on imports*
❑ LS-2-7001 [DJ] Live at the Star Club in Hamburg, Germany, 1962 1977 $300
—*Promo only on blue vinyl*
❑ LS-2-7001 [DJ] Live at the Star Club in Hamburg, Germany, 1962 1977 $250
—*Promo only on red vinyl*
❑ LS-2-7001 [DJ] Live at the Star Club in Hamburg, Germany, 1962 1977 $40
—*Promo on black vinyl; "D.J. Copy Not for Sale" on labels*

LLOYDS
❑ ER-MC-LTD The Great American Tour -- 1965 Live Beatlemania Concert 1965 $600
—*Another interview album from the Ed Rudy people, with a live Beatles show in the background and the songs poorly overdubbed by the Liverpool Lads*

METRO
❑ M-563 [M] This Is Where It Started 1966 $150
—*Reissue of MGM album with two of the "others" tracks deleted*
❑ MS-563 [R] This Is Where It Started 1966 $175
—*In stereo cover*
❑ MS-563 [R] This Is Where It Started 1966 $250
—*In mono cover with "Stereo" sticker*

MGM
❑ E-4215 [M] The Beatles with Tony Sheridan and Their Guests 1964 $250
—*Without "And Guests" on cover*
❑ E-4215 [M] The Beatles with Tony Sheridan and Their Guests 1964 $300
—*With "And Guests" on cover*
❑ SE-4215 [R] The Beatles with Tony Sheridan and Their Guests 1964 $600
—*With "And Guests" on cover*
❑ SE-4215 [R] The Beatles with Tony Sheridan and Their Guests 1964 $800
—*Without "And Guests" on cover*

MOBILE FIDELITY
❑ Jan-0023 Abbey Road 1979 $50
—*Audiophile vinyl*
❑ 1-103 [S] A Hard Day's Night 1987 $50
—*Audiophile vinyl; British version of album*
❑ 1-104 [S] Beatles for Sale 1986 $100
—*Audiophile vinyl; British version of album*
❑ 1-105 [S] Help! 1985 $40
—*Audiophile vinyl; British version of album*
❑ 1-109 Let It Be 1987 $50
—*Audiophile vinyl; gatefold cover*
❑ 1-109 Let It Be 1987 $300
—*Audiophile vinyl; regular cover*
❑ Jan-0047 [P] Magical Mystery Tour 1980 $150
—*Audiophile vinyl; yes, this contains the rechanneled stereo versions of "Penny Lane," "Baby You're a Rich Man" and "All You Need Is Love"*
❑ 1-101 [S] Please Please Me 1986 $50
—*Audiophile vinyl; British version of album. "Love Me Do" and "P.S. I Love You" are rechanneled.*
❑ 1-107 [S] Revolver 1986 $40
—*Audiophile vinyl; British version of album*
❑ 1-106 [S] Rubber Soul 1985 $150
—*Audiophile vinyl; British version of album*
❑ 1-100 [S] Sgt. Pepper's Lonely Hearts Club Band 1985 $175
—*Audiophile vinyl*
❑ UHQR 1-100 [S] Sgt. Pepper's Lonely Hearts Club Band 1982 $400
—*Ultra High Quality release with special cover; numbered edition of 5,000; numbers under 100 fetch even more*
❑ Feb-0072 The Beatles 1982 $50
—*Audiophile vinyl; not issued with photos or poster*
❑ BC-1 The Beatles Collection 1982 $800
❑ 1-102 [S] With the Beatles 1986 $300
—*Audiophile vinyl; British version of album. Limited run because of a damaged stamper that was not replaced.*
❑ 1-108 [S] Yellow Submarine 1987 $150
—*Audiophile vinyl*

ORANGE
❑ -0 [DJ] The Silver Beatles 1985 $300
—*Test pressing; white cover with title sticker*
❑ -0 [DJ] The Silver Beatles 1985 $400
—*Test pressing; full cover cover slick folded around a white cover. Both contain all 15 Decca audition tracks*
❑ ORC-12880 [DJ] The Silver Beatles 1985 $300
—*Test pressing; white cover with title sticker*
❑ ORC-12880 [DJ] The Silver Beatles 1985 $400
—*Test pressing; full cover cover slick folded around a white cover. Both contain all 15 Decca audition tracks*

PARLOPHONE
❑ 5099963380019 [M] A Hard Day's Night 2014 $30
❑ 5099963380118 [M] Beatles For Sale 2014 $30
❑ 94638241416 [B] Beatles for Sale 2012 $30
❑ 5099963380217 [M] Help! 2014 $30
❑ 94638241515 [B] Help! 2012 $30
❑ 5099963379815 [M] Please Please Me 2014 $30
❑ 94638241614 [B] Please Please Me 2012 $30
❑ 94638241713 [B] Revolver 2012 $30
❑ 5099963380316 [M] Rubber Soul 2014 $30
❑ 94638241812 [B] Rubber Soul 2012 $30
❑ 5099963379914 [M] With The Beatles 2014 $30
❑ 94638242017 [B] With The Beatles 2012 $30

PBR INTERNATIONAL
❑ 7005/6 The David Wigg Interviews (The Beatles Tapes) 1978 $100
—*Blue vinyl*
❑ 7005/6 The David Wigg Interviews (The Beatles Tapes) 1980 $75
—*Black vinyl*

PHOENIX
❑ P20-623 20 Hits, Beatles 1983 $25
—*With 12 Decca audition tracks, four Beatles/Tony Sheridan tracks, and four Tony Sheridan solo tracks*
❑ P20-629 20 Hits, Beatles 1983 $25
—*With 20 live Hamburg tracks*
❑ PHX-352 [M] Silver Beatles, Volume 1 1982 $15
—*Contains seven Decca audition tracks*
❑ PHX-353 [M] Silver Beatles, Volume 2 1982 $15
—*Contains seven Decca audition tracks (different seven than Phoenix 352)*

Number	Title	Yr	NM
PICKWICK			
❏ BAN-90051 [M]	Recorded Live in Hamburg, Vol. 1	1978	$30
❏ BAN-90061 [M]	Recorded Live in Hamburg, Vol. 2	1978	$30
❏ BAN-90071 [M]	Recorded Live in Hamburg, Vol. 3	1978	$40
❏ SPC-3661 [M]	The Beatles' First Live Recordings, Volume 1	1979	$15
❏ SPC-3662 [M]	The Beatles' First Live Recordings, Volume 2	1979	$15
❏ PTP-2098 [M]	The Historic First Live Recordings	1980	$25

— Same contents as Lingasong LP, plus "Hully Gully"

POLYDOR			
❏ 24-4504 [P]	The Beatles -- Circa 1960 – In the Beginning Featuring Tony Sheridan	1970	$30

— Originals have gatefold cover

❏ SKAO-93199 [P]	The Beatles -- Circa 1960 – In the Beginning Featuring Tony Sheridan	1970	$40

— Capitol Record Club edition

❏ 24-4504 [P]	The Beatles -- Circa 1960 – In the Beginning Featuring Tony Sheridan	197?	$40

— Some copies of the record contain only the title "The Beatles -- In the Beginning"

❏ PD-4504 [P]	The Beatles -- Circa 1960 – In the Beginning Featuring Tony Sheridan	1981	$15

— Reissue without gatefold cover

❏ 825073-1 [P]	The Beatles -- Circa 1960 – In the Beginning Featuring Tony Sheridan	1988	$25

— Reissue with new number

RADIO PULSEBEAT NEWS			
❏ 3	1965 Talk Album – Ed Rudy with New U.S. Tour	1965	$175

— The Beatles" in black print under front cover photo (other versions appear to be bootlegs)

❏ 2	The American Tour with Ed Rudy	1964	$150

— Yellow label; some copies came with a special edition of Teen Talk magazine (add 50%)

❏ 2	The American Tour with Ed Rudy	1980	$30

— Blue label; authorized reissue with Beatles' photo on cover

RAVEN/PVC			
❏ 8911 [DJ]	Talk Downunder	1981	$100

— Promo only in white cover with title sticker. Label reads "For Radio Play Only

❏ 8911	Talk Downunder	1981	$12
❏ 8911 [DJ]	Talk Downunder	1981	$100

— Promo only in white cover with title sticker. Label reads "For Radio Play Only

SAVAGE			
❏ BM-69 [M]	The Savage Young Beatles	1964	$175

— Orange label; no legitimate copy says "Stereo" on cover

❏ BM-69 [M]	The Savage Young Beatles	1964	$1500

— Yellow label, glossy orange cover

SILHOUETTE			
❏ SM-10015	Golden Beatles	1985	$18
❏ SM-10015	Golden Beatles	1985	$100

— Gold vinyl

❏ -0 [DJ]	The British Are Coming	1984	$40

— White label promo; no numbered sticker

❏ SM-10013	The British Are Coming	1984	$18

— Interview album with numbered sticker (very low numbers increase the value)

❏ SM-10013	The British Are Coming	1984	$100

— Same as above, but on red vinyl

❏ SM-10013 [DJ]	The British Are Coming	1984	$40

— White label promo; no numbered sticker

❏ PD-83010 [PD]	The British Are Coming	1985	$30

— Picture disc

❏ SM-10004 [PD]	Timeless	1981	$25

— Picture disc

❏ SM-10004 [PD]	Timeless	1981	$30

— Picture disc with all interviews

— Picture disc with interviews plus remakes of "Imagine" and "Let It Be" (by non-Beatles)

❏ SM-10010 [PD]	Timeless II	1982	$25

— Picture disc with mostly interviews

STERLING			
❏ 8895-6481	I Apologize	1966	$300

— Same as above, but without photo

❏ 8895-6481	I Apologize	1966	$400

— One-sided LP with John Lennon's "apology" for supposed anti-Christian remarks; includes photo

UNITED ARTISTS			
❏ UAL3366 [M-DJ]	A Hard Day's Night	1964	$3500

— White label promo

❏ UAL3366 [M]	A Hard Day's Night	1964	$3000

— White label promo

❏ UAL3366 [M]	A Hard Day's Night	1964	$300

— With "I Cry Instead" listing

❏ UAL3366 [M]	A Hard Day's Night	1964	$300

— With "I'll Cry Instead" listing

Number	Title	Yr	NM
❏ UAS6366 [P]	A Hard Day's Night	1964	$300

— With "I Cry Instead" listing

❏ UAS6366 [P]	A Hard Day's Night	1964	$300

— With "I'll Cry Instead" listing. Has incidental music by George Martin. All eight Beatles tracks are rechanneled; Martin's are in true stereo.

❏ UAS6366 [P]	A Hard Day's Night	1964	$15000

— Pink vinyl; only one copy known, probably privately (and secretly) done by a pressing-plant employee; VG value 6000; VG+ value 9000

❏ UAS6366 [P]	A Hard Day's Night	1968	$50

— Pink and orange label

❏ UAS6366 [P]	A Hard Day's Night	1970	$50

— Black and orange label

❏ UAS6366 [P]	A Hard Day's Night	1971	$25

— Tan label

❏ UAS6366 [P]	A Hard Day's Night	1975	$25

— Tan label with "All Rights Reserved" in perimeter print

❏ UAS6366 [P]	A Hard Day's Night	1977	$25

— Sunrise label. Note: Any of the variations from 1968 on can have titles of songs incorrectly listed as "I Cry Instead" and "Tell Me Who," or only one can be wrong, or neither can be wrong. No difference in value at this time.

❏ T-90828 [M]	A Hard Day's Night	1964	$1500

— Capitol Record Club edition; VG value 750; VG+ value 1125

❏ ST-90828 [P]	A Hard Day's Night	1964	$750

— Capitol Record Club edition

❏ -0 [DJ]	United Artists Presents A Hard Day's Night	1964	$1500

— Radio spots for movie

❏ -0 [DJ]	United Artists Presents A Hard Day's Night	1964	$2500

— Open-end interview with script

❏ SP-2362/3 [DJ]	United Artists Presents A Hard Day's Night	1964	$2000

— Radio spots for movie

❏ SP-2359/60 [DJ]	United Artists Presents A Hard Day's Night	1964	$2000

— Open-end interview with script; VG value 1000; VG+ value 1500

❏ -0A/B [DJ]	United Artists Presents Help!	1965	$2000

— Radio spots for movie

❏ -0INT [DJ]	United Artists Presents Help!	1965	$2500

— Open-end interview with script (red label)

❏ -0Show [DJ]	United Artists Presents Help!	1965	$3500

— One-sided interview with script (blue label)

❏ UA-Help-0A/B [DJ]	United Artists Presents Help!	1965	$2000

— Radio spots for movie; VG value 500; VG+ value 1000

❏ UA-Help-0INT [DJ]	United Artists Presents Help!	1965	$2000

— Open-end interview with script (red label); VG value 1000; VG+ value 1500

❏ UA-Help-0Show [DJ]	United Artists Presents Help!	1965	$3000

— One-sided interview with script (blue label); VG value 1500; VG+ value 2250

UNITED DISTRIBUTORS			
❏ UDL-2333 [M]	Dawn of the Silver Beatles	1981	$50

— With numbered registration card (deduct 20% if missing)

❏ UDL-2333 [M]	Dawn of the Silver Beatles	1981	$75

— Hand-stamped numbers on back cover and label; contains 10 Decca audition tracks

❏ UDL-2382 [M]	Lightning Strikes Twice	1981	$75

— Side 1 has five Beatles' Decca audition tracks; Side 2 has live Elvis Presley performances from 1955

VEE JAY			
❏ PRO202 [DJ]	Hear the Beatles Tell All	1964	$10000

— White label promo with blue print

❏ PRO202 [M]	Hear the Beatles Tell All	1964	$250

— With "PRO" prefix on label

❏ 202 [M]	Hear the Beatles Tell All	1964	$350

— Without "PRO" prefix on label

❏ PRO202 [DJ]	Hear the Beatles Tell All	1964	$18000

— White label promo with blue print; VG value 6000; VG+ value 12000

❏ PRO202 [M]	Hear the Beatles Tell All	1979	$12

— Authorized reissue; every copy with the word "Stereo" on the front cover is this edition, though the record still plays in mono (no 1964 copies have "Stereo" on the cover)

❏ PRO202 [PD]	Hear the Beatles Tell All	1987	$25

— Shaped picture disc with same recordings as the black vinyl versions

❏ LP1062 [M]	Introducing the Beatles	1964	$5000

— Ad back" cover; with "Love Me Do" and "P.S. I Love You"; oval Vee Jay logo with colorband only!; VG value 1500; VG+ value 2750

❏ SR1062 [B]	Introducing the Beatles	1964	$12000

— Ad back" cover; with "Love Me Do" and "P.S. I Love You" (both mono); oval Vee Jay logo with colorband only!; VG value 4000; VG+ value 8000

❏ LP1062 [M]	Introducing the Beatles	1964	$1500

— Blank back cover; with "Love Me Do" and "P.S. I Love You"; oval Vee Jay logo with colorband only!; VG value 400; VG+ value 800

Number	Title	Yr	NM
❏ SR1062 [B]	Introducing the Beatles	1964	$2500

— Blank back cover; with "Love Me Do" and "P.S. I Love You"; oval Vee Jay logo with colorband only!

❏ LP1062 [B]	Introducing the Beatles	1964	$1000

— Blank back cover; with "Please Please Me" and "Ask Me Why"; oval Vee Jay logo with colorband only!

❏ LP1062 [M]	Introducing the Beatles	1964	$1000

— Song titles cover; with "Love Me Do" and "P.S. I Love You"; oval Vee Jay logo with colorband only!

❏ SR1062 [B]	Introducing the Beatles	1964	$10000

— Song titles cover; with "Love Me Do" and "P.S. I Love You"; oval Vee Jay logo with colorband only!; VG value 3000; VG+ value 5500; This album has been heavily counterfeited; please check the label of your copy before contacting the author. If the words "Introducing the Beatles" are above the center hole of the record, and the words "The Beatles" are below, it is automatically a counterfeit and almost worthless.

❏ LP1062 [M]	Introducing the Beatles	1964	$400

— Song titles cover; with "Please Please Me" and "Ask Me Why"; oval Vee Jay logo with colorband

❏ LP1062 [M]	Introducing the Beatles	1964	$300

— Song titles cover; with "Please Please Me" and "Ask Me Why"; brackets Vee Jay logo with colorband (most common authentic version)

❏ LP1062 [M]	Introducing the Beatles	1964	$300

— Song titles cover; with "Please Please Me" and "Ask Me Why"; plain Vee Jay logo on solid black label

❏ LP1062 [M]	Introducing the Beatles	1964	$300

— Song titles cover; with "Please Please Me" and "Ask Me Why"; oval Vee Jay logo on solid black label

❏ LP1062 [M]	Introducing the Beatles	1964	$1000

— Song titles cover; with "Please Please Me" and "Ask Me Why"; brackets Vee Jay logo on solid black label

❏ SR1062 [S]	Introducing the Beatles	1964	$1600

— Song titles cover; with "Please Please Me" and "Ask Me Why"; oval Vee Jay logo with colorband

❏ SR1062 [S]	Introducing the Beatles	1964	$1500

— Song titles cover; with "Please Please Me" and "Ask Me Why"; brackets Vee Jay logo with colorband

❏ SR1062 [S]	Introducing the Beatles	1964	$1600

— Song titles cover; with "Please Please Me" and "Ask Me Why"; plain Vee Jay logo on solid black label

❏ LP1085 [M]	Jolly What! The Beatles and Frank Ifield on Stage	1964	$350

— Man in Beatle wig cover; originals have printing on spine and a dark blue/purple background (counterfeits have a black background and no spine print)

❏ SR1085 [B]	Jolly What! The Beatles and Frank Ifield on Stage	1964	$600

— Man in Beatle wig cover; "Stereo" on both cover and label. "From Me to You" is mono.

❏ LP1092 [M]	Songs, Pictures and Stories of the Fabulous Beatles	1964	$500

— See above; brackets Vee Jay logo with colorband

❏ LP1092 [M]	Songs, Pictures and Stories of the Fabulous Beatles	1964	$500

— See above; plain Vee Jay logo on solid black label

❏ LP1092 [M]	Songs, Pictures and Stories of the Fabulous Beatles	1964	$500

— See above; oval Vee Jay logo on solid black label

❏ VJS1092 [S]	Songs, Pictures and Stories of the Fabulous Beatles	1964	$2500

— See above; brackets Vee Jay logo with colorband; VG value 800; VG+ value 1600

❏ LP1092 [M]	Songs, Pictures and Stories of the Fabulous Beatles	1964	$500

— All copies have gatefold cover with 2/3 width on front; also, all copies have "Introducing the Beatles" records. Oval Vee Jay logo with colorband.

❏ VJS1092 [S]	Songs, Pictures and Stories of the Fabulous Beatles	1964	$2500

— All copies have gatefold cover with 2/3 width on front; also, all copies have "Introducing the Beatles" records. Oval Vee Jay logo with colorband; VG value 800; VG+ value 1600

Number	Title	Yr	NM

☐ VJS1092 [S] — Songs, Pictures and Stories of the Fabulous Beatles — 1964 — $2500

—*See above; plain Vee Jay logo on solid black label. NOTE: Any non-gatefold copy or any copy called "Songs and Pictures of the Fabulous Beatles" is a counterfeit; VG value 800; VG+ value 1600*

☐ LP1085 [M] — The Beatles and Frank Ifield on Stage — 1964 — $6000

—*Portrait of Beatles cover; counterfeits are poorly reproduced and have no spine print; VG value 2000; VG+ value 3500*

☐ SR1085 [B] — The Beatles and Frank Ifield on Stage — 1964 — $12000

—*Portrait of Beatles cover; "Stereo" on both cover and label; VG value 4000; VG+ value 8000*

☐ DX-30 [M] — The Beatles vs. The Four Seasons — 1964 — $1000

—*Combines "Introducing the Beatles" with "Golden Hits of the Four Seasons" (Vee Jay 1065)*

☐ DXS-30 [S] — The Beatles vs. The Four Seasons — 1964 — $5000

—*Combines "Introducing the Beatles" with "Golden Hits of the Four Seasons" (Vee Jay 1065); VG value 1500; VG+ value 2250*

☐ DX(S)-30 [B] — The Beatles vs. The Four Seasons Poster — 1964 — $350

BEATNUTS, THE
LOUD/RELATIVITY
Number	Title	Yr	NM
☐ 1722	A Musical Massacre	1999	$15
☐ 1906	Take It or Squeeze It	2001	$15

RELATIVITY
☐ 1114 [EP]	Intoxicated Demons	1994	$12
☐ 1508	Stone Crazy	1997	$15
☐ 1621 [EP]	The Beatnuts Remix EP: The Spot	1998	$12
☐ 1179	The Beatnuts (Street Level)	1994	$15

BEATS INTERNATIONAL
ELEKTRA
| ☐ 60921 | Let Them Eat Bingo | 1990 | $18 |

BEAU BRUMMELS, THE
ACCORD
| ☐ SN-7175 | Just a Little | 1982 | $12 |

AUTUMN
☐ LP103 [M]	Introducing the Beau Brummels	1965	$75
☐ SLP103 [S]	Introducing the Beau Brummels	1965	$100
☐ LP104 [M]	The Beau Brummels, Volume 2	1965	$75
☐ SLP104 [S]	The Beau Brummels, Volume 2	1965	$100

JAS
| ☐ 5000 | Original Hits of the Beau Brummels | 1976 | $18 |

POST
| ☐ 6000 [B] | The Beau Brummels Sing | 196? | $25 |

RHINO
☐ RNLP-104	From the Vaults	1981	$15
☐ RNLP-102	Introducing the Beau Brummels	1981	$12
☐ RNLP-101	The Best of the Beau Brummels	1981	$12
☐ RNLP-70171	The Best of the Beau Brummels (Golden Archive Series)	1986	$12

SUNDAZED
| ☐ LP5089 | Gentle Wanderin' Ways | 2001 | $15 |
| ☐ LP5088 | North Beach Legends | 2001 | $15 |

VAULT
☐ SLP-121	Beau Brummels, Vol. 44	1968	$30
☐ LP-114 [M]	Best of the Beau Brummels	1967	$30
☐ SLP-114 [S]	Best of the Beau Brummels	1967	$30

WARNER BROS.
☐ W1644 [M]	Beau Brummels '66	1966	$25
☐ WS1644 [S]	Beau Brummels '66	1966	$30
☐ WS1760	Bradley's Barn	1968	$30
☐ BS2842	The Beau Brummels	1975	$25
☐ W1692 [M]	Triangle	1967	$25
☐ WS1692 [S]	Triangle	1967	$30

BEAU COUP
AMHERST
| ☐ AMH3316 | Born and Raised on Rock-n-Roll | 1987 | $18 |

BEAUREGARDE
EMPIRE
| ☐ 0(no cat #) | Beauregarde | 1969 | $150 |

SOUND
| ☐ 7104 [B] | Beauregarde | 1969 | $150 |

BEAUTIFUL SOUTH, THE
ELEKTRA
| ☐ 60917 | Welcome to the Beautiful South | 1989 | $18 |

BEAUVOIR, JEAN
COLUMBIA
Number	Title	Yr	NM
☐ BFC40403	Drums Along the Mohawk	1986	$10
☐ BFC40621	Jacknifed	1988	$10

BEAVER, PAUL
RAPTURE
| ☐ 11111 | Perchance to Dream | 196? | $50 |

BEAVER AND KRAUSE
LIMELIGHT
| ☐ 86069 | Ragnarok -- Electronic Funk | 1969 | $30 |

WARNER BROS.
☐ BS2624	All Good Men	1972	$18
☐ WS1909 [B]	Gandharva	1970	$18
☐ WS1850	In a Wild Sanctuary	1969	$18

BEBOP AND BEYOND
CONCORD JAZZ
| ☐ CJ-244 | Bebop and Beyond | 1984 | $35 |

BECHET, SIDNEY, AND BOB WILBER
COMMODORE
| ☐ 15774 | New Orleans Style Old and New | 198? | $25 |

BECHET, SIDNEY, AND BUNK JOHNSON
JAZZ ARCHIVES
| ☐ JA-48 | Bechet, Bunk and Boston 1945 | 198? | $25 |

BECHET, SIDNEY, AND EDDIE CONDON
SAVOY
| ☐ MG-12208 [M] | We Dig Dixieland | 196? | $25 |

BECHET, SIDNEY, AND MARTIAL SOLAL
WORLD PACIFIC
| ☐ PJ-1236 [M] | Young Ideas | 1957 | $300 |
| ☐ WP-1236 [M] | Young Ideas | 1957 | $300 |
—*Reissue with new prefix*

BECHET, SIDNEY, AND MARTY MARSALA
JAZZ ARCHIVES
| ☐ JA-44 | Jazz from California | 198? | $25 |

BECHET, SIDNEY, AND MEZZ MEZZROW
CLASSIC JAZZ
| ☐ 28 | Sidney Bechet and Mezz Mezzrow | 198? | $30 |

JAZZ ARCHIVES
| ☐ JA-39 | Really the Blues Concert | 198? | $25 |

BECHET, SIDNEY, AND MUGGSY SPANIER
ALLEGRO ELITE
| ☐ 4123 [10] | Bechet-Spanier Quartet | 1956 | $40 |

BECHET, SIDNEY, AND WINGY MANONE
JAZZ ARCHIVES
| ☐ JA-29 | Together at Town Hall, 1947 | 198? | $25 |

BECHET, SIDNEY
ATLANTIC
| ☐ 1206 [M] | Sidney Bechet Duets | 1956 | $300 |
—*With Muggsy Spanier*
| ☐ ALS-118 [10] | Sidney Bechet Solos | 1952 | $350 |

BLUEBIRD
| ☐ AXM2-5516 | Master Musician | 1976 | $50 |
| ☐ 6590-1-RB | The Legendary Sidney Bechet | 198? | $25 |

BLUE NOTE
☐ BLP-7008 [10]	Days Beyond Recall	1951	$500
☐ BLP-7026 [10]	Dixie by the Fabulous Sidney Bechet	1953	$500
☐ BLP-1203 [M]	Giant of Jazz, Volume 1	1955	$1200
—*Deep groove" version; Lexington Ave. address on label*
| ☐ BLP-1203 [M] | Giant of Jazz, Volume 1 | 1955 | $500 |
—*Deep groove" edition, W. 63rd St. address on label*
| ☐ BST-81203 [R] | Giant of Jazz, Volume 1 | 1968 | $50 |
—*With "A Division of Liberty Records" on label*
| ☐ BLP-1203 [M] | Giant of Jazz, Volume 1 | 1963 | $250 |
—*New York, USA" on label*
| ☐ BLP-1204 [M] | Giant of Jazz, Volume 2 | 1955 | $1500 |
—*Deep groove" version (deep indentation under label on both sides)*
| ☐ BLP-1204 [M] | Giant of Jazz, Volume 2 | 1955 | $1000 |
—*Regular edition, Lexington Ave. address on label*
| ☐ BST-81204 [R] | Giant of Jazz, Volume 2 | 1968 | $50 |
—*With "A Division of Liberty Records" on label*
| ☐ BST-81204 [R] | Giant of Jazz, Volume 2 | 1971 | $35 |
—*With "A Division of United Artists Records" on label*
| ☐ BLP-7002 [10] | Jazz Classics, Volume 1 | 1950 | $500 |
| ☐ BLP-1201 [M] | Jazz Classics, Volume 1 | 1955 | $800 |
—*Deep groove" version; Lexington Ave. address on label*
| ☐ BLP-1201 [M] | Jazz Classics, Volume 1 | 1958 | $250 |
—*Deep groove" edition, W. 63rd St. address on label*
| ☐ BST-81201 [R] | Jazz Classics, Volume 1 | 1968 | $50 |
—*With "A Division of Liberty Records" on label*
| ☐ BLP-1201 [M] | Jazz Classics, Volume 1 | 1963 | $175 |
—*New York, USA" on label*
| ☐ BLP-7003 [10] | Jazz Classics, Volume 2 | 1950 | $500 |
| ☐ BLP-1202 [M] | Jazz Classics, Volume 2 | 1955 | $1000 |
—*Deep groove" version; Lexington Ave. address on label*
| ☐ BLP-1202 [M] | Jazz Classics, Volume 2 | 1958 | $800 |
—*Deep groove" edition, W. 63rd St. address on label*
| ☐ BST-81202 [R] | Jazz Classics, Volume 2 | 1968 | $50 |
—*With "A Division of Liberty Records" on label*
| ☐ BLP-1202 [M] | Jazz Classics, Volume 2 | 1963 | $250 |
—*New York, USA" on label*
☐ BLP-7024 [10]	Jazz Festival Concert, Paris 1952 -- Volume 1	1953	$500
☐ BLP-7025 [10]	Jazz Festival Concert, Paris 1952 -- Volume 2	1953	$500
☐ BLP-7029 [10]	Olympia Concert, Paris 1954 -- Volume 1	1954	$500
☐ BLP-7030 [10]	Olympia Concert, Paris 1954 -- Volume 2	1954	$500
☐ BLP-7001 [10]	Sidney Bechet's Blue Note Jazz Men	1950	$1000
☐ BLP-7014 [10]	Sidney Bechet's Blue Note Jazz Men, Volume 2	1951	$500
☐ BLP-7009 [10]	Sidney Bechet with the Blue Note Jazz Men	1951	$500
☐ BLP-1207 [M]	The Fabulous Sidney Bechet	1956	$1500
—*Deep groove" version; Lexington Ave. address on label*
| ☐ BLP-1207 [M] | The Fabulous Sidney Bechet | 1956 | $800 |
—*Deep groove" edition, W. 63rd St. address on label*
| ☐ BST-81207 [R] | The Fabulous Sidney Bechet | 1968 | $30 |
—*With "A Division of Liberty Records" on label*
| ☐ BLP-7020 [10] | The Fabulous Sidney Bechet and His Hot Six | 1952 | $500 |
| ☐ BLP-7022 [10] | The Port of Harlem Six | 1952 | $500 |

BRUNSWICK
| ☐ BL54037 [M] | Sidney Bechet in Paris | 1958 | $100 |
| ☐ BL54048 [M] | The Sidney Bechet Story | 1959 | $75 |

COLUMBIA
| ☐ CL836 [M] | Grand Master of the Soprano Sax and Clarinet | 1956 | $75 |
—*Red and black label with six "eye" logos*
| ☐ CL1410 [M] | Sidney Bechet In Concert at the Brussels Fair | 1960 | $40 |
—*Red and black label with six "eye" logos*

COMMODORE
| ☐ FL-20020 [10] | New Orleans Style, Old and New | 1952 | $300 |

DIAL
| ☐ LP-301 [10] | Black Stick | 195? | $600 |
| ☐ LP-302 [10] | Sidney Bechet with Wally Bishop's Orchestra | 195? | $600 |

EVEREST ARCHIVE OF FOLK & JAZZ
| ☐ FS-323 | Sidney Bechet Volume 2 | 197? | $30 |
| ☐ FS-228 | Sidney Bechet with Guest Artist Lionel Hampton | 1969 | $30 |

GNP CRESCENDO
| ☐ GNP-9012 | Sidney Bechet | 197? | $30 |
| ☐ GNP-9037 | The Legendary Sidney Bechet | 1976 | $30 |

GOOD TIME JAZZ
| ☐ L-12013 [M] | King of the Soprano Saxophone | 1955 | $75 |

JAZZOLOGY
| ☐ J-35 | The Genius of Sidney Bechet | 197? | $30 |

JAZZ PANORAMA
| ☐ 1801 [10] | Sidney Bechet, Vol. 1 | 1951 | $250 |
| ☐ 1809 [10] | Sidney Bechet, Vol. 2 | 1951 | $250 |

JOLLY ROGER
| ☐ 5028 [10] | Sidney Bechet | 1954 | $100 |

LONDON
| ☐ WV91050 [10] | La Nuit Est Une Sorciere | 1955 | $100 |

MCA
| ☐ 1330 | Blackstick | 198? | $25 |

MOSAIC
| ☐ MR6-110 | The Complete Blue Note Recordings of Sidney Bechet | 198? | $300 |
—*Limited edition of 7,500*

RCA VICTOR
| ☐ LPV-510 [M] | Bechet of New Orleans | 1965 | $30 |
—*Purple label original*
| ☐ LPV-510 [M] | Bechet of New Orleans | 1969 | $25 |
—*Orange label reissue*
☐ LPV-535 [M]	Blue Bechet	1966	$30
☐ LPT-22 [10]	Sidney Bechet	1951	$300
☐ LPT-31 [10]	Treasury of Immortal Performances	1951	$300

Number	Title	Yr	NM
REPRISE			
❏ R-6076 [M]	The Immortal Sidney Bechet	1963	$30
❏ R9-6076 [R]	The Immortal Sidney Bechet	1963	$25
RIVERSIDE			
❏ RLP-2516 [10]	Sidney Bechet and His Soprano Sax	1955	$300
RONDO-LETTE			
❏ A24 [M]	Jam Session Vintage 1946	1953	$40
SAVOY			
❏ MG-15013 [10]	Sidney Bechet	1952	$300
STINSON			
❏ 46 [R]	Haitian Moods	196?	$30
STORYVILLE			
❏ 4028	Sessions	198?	$25
❏ STLP-902 [M]	Sidney Bechet at Storyville	1955	$75
❏ STLP-301 [10]	Sidney Bechet at Storyville, Vol. 1	1954	$250
❏ STLP-306 [10]	Sidney Bechet at Storyville, Vol. 2	1954	$250
TIME-LIFE			
❏ STL-J-09	Giants of Jazz	1980	$50
X			
❏ LVA-3024 [10]	Sidney Bechet and His New Orleans Feetwarmers	1954	$120

BECHET, SIDNEY / OMER SIMEON

Number	Title	Yr	NM
JAZZTONE			
❏ J-1213 [M]	Jazz A La Creole	1955	$50

BECK, BOGERT & APPICE
Also see JEFF BECK; VANILLA FUDGE; CACTUS.

Number	Title	Yr	NM
EPIC			
❏ KE32140	Beck, Bogert & Appice	1973	$18
— Yellow label			
❏ KE32140	Beck, Bogert & Appice	1973	$12
— Orange label			
❏ CQ32140 [Q]	Beck, Bogert & Appice	1973	$40
❏ PE32140	Beck, Bogert & Appice	198?	$10
— Budget-line reissue			

BECK, JEFF
Includes the Jeff Beck Group, of whom ROD STEWART was lead singer. Also see BECK, BOGERT AND APPICE; THE YARDBIRDS. (HONEYDRIPPERS; THE YARDBIRDS.)

Number	Title	Yr	NM
ACCORD			
❏ SN-7141	Early Anthology	1981	$12
ANALOGUE PRODUCTIONS			
❏ AAPP078-45 [B]	Blow By Blow	2015	$50
— 45rpm			
EPIC			
❏ BN26478	Beck-Ola	1969	$18
— Yellow label			
❏ BN26478	Beck-Ola	1973	$12
— Orange label			
❏ PE26478	Beck-Ola	197?	$10
— Reissue with new prefix			
❏ PE33409	Blow by Blow	1975	$12
— Orange label, no bar code on cover			
❏ PEQ33409 [Q]	Blow by Blow	1975	$40
❏ HE43409	Blow by Blow	1980	$30
— Half-speed mastered edition			
❏ PE33409	Blow by Blow	198?	$10
— Reissue with dark blue label and bar code on cover			
❏ AS151 [DJ]	Everything You Always Wanted to Hear by Jeff Beck But Were Afraid to Ask For	1977	$25
— Promo-only sampler			
❏ AS151 [DJ]	Everything You Always Wanted to Hear by Jeff Beck But Were Afraid to Ask For	1977	$25
— Promo-only sampler			
❏ FE39483	Flash	1985	$12
❏ KE31331	Jeff Beck Group	1972	$18
— Yellow label			
❏ KE31331	Jeff Beck Group	1973	$12
— Orange label			
❏ EQ31331 [Q]	Jeff Beck Group	1972	$40
❏ PE31331	Jeff Beck Group	198?	$10
— Budget-line reissue			
❏ FE44313	Jeff Beck's Guitar Shop	1989	$18
❏ PE34433	Jeff Beck with the Jan Hammer Group Live	1977	$12
— Orange label, no bar code on cover			
❏ PE34433	Jeff Beck with the Jan Hammer Group Live	198?	$10
— Reissue with dark blue label and bar code on cover			
❏ KE30993	Rough and Ready	1971	$18
— Yellow label			
❏ KE30993	Rough and Ready	1973	$12
— Orange label			
❏ EQ30993 [Q]	Rough and Ready	1972	$40
❏ PE30973	Rough and Ready	198?	$10
— Budget-line reissue			
❏ A2S850 [DJ]	Then and Now	1981	$30
— Promo-only sampler			

Number	Title	Yr	NM
❏ A2S850 [DJ]	Then and Now	1981	$30
— Promo-only sampler			
❏ FE35684	There and Back	1980	$12
❏ PE35684	There and Back	1985	$10
— Budget-line reissue			
❏ BN26413 [S]	Truth	1968	$25
— Yellow label			
❏ BN26413 [B]	Truth	1973	$12
— Orange label			
❏ PE26413	Truth	198?	$10
— Reissue with new prefix			
❏ BN26413 [M]	Truth	1968	$300
— Mono is promo only with stereo number; cover has "Mono" sticker covering the word "Stereo"			
❏ BG33779 [B]	Truth/Beck-Ola	1975	$18
❏ PE33849	Wired	1976	$12
— Orange label, no bar code on cover			
❏ PEQ33849 [Q]	Wired	1976	$40
❏ PE33849	Wired	1979	$10
— Reissue with dark blue label; with or without bar code on cover			
❏ HE43849	Wired	198?	$30
— Half-speed mastered edition			
FRIDAY MUSIC			
❏ FRM26478 [B]	Beck-Ola	2015	$25

BECK, JOE

Number	Title	Yr	NM
CTI			
❏ 8002	Beck & Sanborn	1979	$25
— Reissue of Kudu 21 with new title			
CTI/CBS ASSOCIATED			
❏ FZ40805	Beck & Sanborn	1987	$25
KUDU			
❏ 21	Beck	1975	$30
POLYDOR			
❏ PD-1-6092	Watch the Time	1976	$25

BECK, PIA

Number	Title	Yr	NM
EPIC			
❏ LN3269 [M]	Dutch Treat	1956	$100

BECK

Number	Title	Yr	NM
BONG LOAD			
❏ BL12 [B]	Mellow Gold	1993	$75

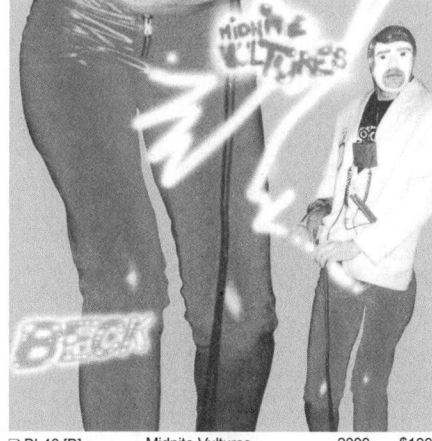

Number	Title	Yr	NM
❏ BL46 [B]	Midnite Vultures	2000	$100
❏ BL39	Mutations	1999	$50
— Includes bonus 7-inch single with sleeve			
❏ BL30 [B]	Odelay	1996	$50
DGC			
❏ B0004372-01	Sea Change	2006	$18
— CD version issued in 2002			
FINGERPAINT			
❏ 02 [10]	A Western Harvest Field by Moonlight	1992	$85
— First 3,000 contain a unique insert fingerpainted by Beck and friends at the record release party			
❏ 02 [10]	A Western Harvest Field by Moonlight	1995	$50
— Later pressings do not contain a fingerpainted insert			
FLIPSIDE			
❏ 660 [B]	Stereopathetic Soulmanure	2000	$30
— Vinyl issue of 1994 CD compilation			
ILIAD/K			
❏ 1282901	One Foot in the Grave	2009	$30
— Expanded two LP edition			
INTERSCOPE			
❏ B0003546-1	Guero	2005	$30
❏ B0005650-01	Guerolito	2006	$18

Number	Title	Yr	NM
❏ 1163001 [B]	Modern Guilt	2008	$25
K			
❏ KLP28	One Foot in the Grave	1994	$50

BECK FAMILY, THE

Number	Title	Yr	NM
LEJOINT			
❏ LEJ-17001	Dancin' on the Ceiling	1979	$12

BECKMEIER BROTHERS

Number	Title	Yr	NM
CASABLANCA			
❏ NBLP-7147	Beckmeier Brothers	1979	$15

BEDIENT, JACK

Number	Title	Yr	NM
EXECUTIVE PRODUCTIONS			
❏ 0(no cat #) [M]	Jack Bedient	196?	$100
FANTASY			
❏ 3365 [M]	Live at Harvey's	1965	$75
SATORI			
❏ LP1001 [M]	Where Did She Go?	1967	$250
TROPHY			
❏ 101 [M]	Two Sides of Jack Bedient	1964	$75

BEDLAM
Includes RAINBOW and BLACK SABBATH drummer Cozy Powell.

Number	Title	Yr	NM
CHRYSALIS			
❏ CHR-1048	Bedlam	1973	$30

BEE, CELI

Number	Title	Yr	NM
APA			
❏ 77002	Alternating Currents	1978	$18
❏ 77005	Blow My Mind	1979	$18
❏ 77001	Celi Bee and the Buzzy Bunch	1977	$18
❏ 77003	Fly Me on the Wings of Love	1979	$18

BEE, DAVID

Number	Title	Yr	NM
BALLY			
❏ BAL-12005 [M]	Belgian Jazz	1956	$30
JUBILEE			
❏ JLP-1076 [M]	Dixieland at the World's Fair	1958	$30

BEE, MOLLY

Number	Title	Yr	NM
ACCORD			
❏ 7901	Sounds Fine to Me	1982	$12
CAPITOL			
❏ T1097 [M]	Young Romance	1958	$40
GRANITE			
❏ 1002	Good Golly Ms. Molly	1974	$15
MGM			
❏ E-4303 [M]	It's Great, It's Molly Bee	1965	$25
❏ SE-4303 [S]	It's Great, It's Molly Bee	1965	$30
❏ E-4423 [M]	Swingin' Country	1967	$25
❏ SE-4423 [S]	Swingin' Country	1967	$30

BEE GEES
Also see BARRY GIBB; MAURICE GIBB; ROBIN GIBB.

Number	Title	Yr	NM
ATCO			
❏ 33-353 [M]	2 Years On	1971	$150
— White label promo only; "DJ Copy Monaural" sticker on cover			
❏ SD 33-353 [S]	2 Years On	1971	$15
❏ 33-223 [M]	Bee Gees' 1st	1967	$50
❏ SD 33-223 [S]	Bee Gees' 1st	1967	$25
— Brown and purple label original			
❏ SD 33-223	Bee Gees' 1st	1969	$12
— Yellow label reissue			
❏ 33-292 [M]	Best of Bee Gees	1969	$150
— White label promo only			
❏ SD 33-292 [S]	Best of Bee Gees	1969	$15
❏ SD 33-327	Cucumber Castle	1970	$15
❏ 33-233 [M]	Horizontal	1968	$150
❏ SD 33-233 [S]	Horizontal	1968	$25
— Brown and purple label original			
❏ SD 33-233	Horizontal	1969	$12
— Yellow label reissue			
❏ 33-253 [M]	Idea	1968	$150
— White label promo only			
❏ SD 33-253 [S]	Idea	1968	$25
— Brown and purple label original			
❏ SD 33-253	Idea	1969	$12
— Yellow label reissue			
❏ SD 2-702 [B]	Odessa	1969	$100
— Red felt cover			
❏ SD 2-702	Odessa	1969	$100
— Record club editions with plain red cover			
❏ 33-264 [M]	Rare, Precious & Beautiful	1968	$50
— White label promo only			
❏ SD 33-264 [R]	Rare, Precious & Beautiful	1968	$18
— Brown and purple label original			
❏ SD 33-264	Rare, Precious & Beautiful	1969	$12
— Yellow label reissue			

Number	Title	Yr	NM
❑ 33-321 [M]	Rare, Precious & Beautiful, Volume 2	1970	$50

— *White label promo only*

Number	Title	Yr	NM
❑ SD 33-321 [R]	Rare, Precious & Beautiful, Volume 2	1970	$15
❑ SD7012	To Whom It May Concern	1972	$15
❑ SD7003	Trafalgar	1971	$15

MOBILE FIDELITY

❑ 1-263 [B]	Trafalgar	1996	$100

— *Audiophile vinyl*

NAUTILUS

❑ NR-42 [B]	Living Eyes	1982	$250

— *Record was never released; value is for test pressings*

❑ NR-17	Spirits Having Flown	1981	$30

PICKWICK

❑ BAN-90021 [R]	Monday's Rain	1978	$10

— *Reissue of Australian recordings*

❑ BAN-90041 [R]	Peace of Mind	1978	$10

— *Reissue of Australian recordings; tracks on this LP were making their first appearance in the U.S.*

❑ BAN-90031 [R]	Take Hold of That Star	1978	$10

— *Reissue of Australian recordings*

❑ BAN-90011 [R]	Turn Around, Look at Me	1978	$10

— *Reissue of Australian recordings*

RSO

❑ RS-1-3006	Bee Gees Gold, Volume One	1976	$12
❑ 823659-1	Bee Gees Gold, Volume One	1984	$10
❑ RS-2-4200	Bee Gees' Greatest	1979	$15
❑ 825390-1	Bee Gees' Greatest	1984	$12

— *Gatefold replaced by single-pocket cover*

❑ SO874	Best of Bee Gees	1973	$12

— *Reissue of Atco SD 33-292*

❑ SO875	Best of Bee Gees, Vol. 2	1973	$12
❑ RS-1-3003	Children of the World	1976	$12
❑ 823658-1	Children of the World	1984	$10
❑ RS-2-3901	Here At Last...Bee Gees... Live	1977	$15
❑ 823274-1	Here At Last...Bee Gees... Live	1984	$12
❑ SO870 [S]	Life in a Tin Can	1973	$12

— *Side 1 master number is "ST-SO-722677"; Side 2 master number is "ST-SO-722678*

❑ SO870 [M]	Life in a Tin Can	1973	$175

— *Mono is white label promo only; cover has red "d/j copy monaural" sticker on front; Side 1 master number is "SO-14153"; Side 2 master number is "SO-14154*

❑ RS-1-3098	Living Eyes	1981	$12

❑ SO4807 [B]	Main Course	1975	$12
❑ RS-1-3024	Main Course	1977	$10
❑ SO4800	Mr. Natural	1974	$12
❑ RS-1-3007	Odessa	1976	$12

— *Condensed version of Atco original*

❑ PRO33 [DJ]	Saturday Night Fever Special Disco Versions	1978	$50

— *Promo-only sampler; contains an otherwise unavailable extended version of "Stayin' Alive"*

❑ PRO 033 [DJ]	Saturday Night Fever Special Disco Versions	1978	$50

— *Promo-only sampler; contains an otherwise unavailable extended version of "Stayin' Alive"*

❑ PRO0 [DJ]	Select Disco Cuts from "Spirits Having Flown"	1979	$30
❑ RPO1008 [DJ]	Select Disco Cuts from "Spirits Having Flown"	1979	$30
❑ RS-1-3041	Spirits Having Flown	1979	$12

— *Some pressings have a cardboard innersleeve, others a paper innersleeve. No difference in value.*

❑ RS-1-3042 [PD]	Spirits Having Flown	1979	$18
❑ -0 [DJ]	The Words and Music of Maurice, Barry and Robin Gibb	1979	$50

— *Promo-only publisher's sampler*

Number	Title	Yr	NM
❑ SMP-1 [DJ]	The Words and Music of Maurice, Barry and Robin Gibb	1979	$50

— *Promo-only publisher's sampler*

❑ -0 [DJ]	Unichappell Publisher's Sampler	1980	$50
❑ PUB-1000 [DJ]	Unichappell Publisher's Sampler	1980	$50

WARNER BROS.

❑ 25541	E.S.P.	1987	$12
❑ 25887	One	1989	$15

BEEBE, JIM, 'S CHICAGO JAZZ
DELMARK

❑ DS-219	Cornet Chop Suey	1980	$25

— *With Tommy Bridges*

❑ DS-218	Saturday Night Function	1979	$25

BEENIE MAN
ARTISTS ONLY

❑ 31	Y2K	1999	$15

VIRGIN

❑ 49093	Art & Life	2000	$18

VP

❑ 1413	Beenie Man Meets Mad Cobra	1995	$15
❑ 1605	Best of Beenie Man	2000	$18
❑ 1547	Doctor	1999	$15
❑ 1486	Maestro	199?	$15
❑ 1513	Many Moods of Moses	1998	$15

BEERS FAMILY, THE
BIOGRAPH

❑ BLP-12033	The Seasons of Peace -- A Great Family Sings	1971	$15

— *Evelyne and Bob Beers; Martha and Eric Nagler; Bill, Janet, Susan, Joe, Becky and John Boyer (all related). In all, 15 songs are on this LP, the following of which are Christmas-related:*

COLUMBIA MASTERWORKS

❑ ML6335 [M]	Christmas with the Beers Family	1966	$15

— *Evelyne, Bob and Martha Beers*

❑ MS6935 [S]	Christmas with the Beers Family	1966	$18

— *Same as above, but in stereo*

BEETHOVEN SOUL
DOT

❑ DLP-3821 [M]	Beethoven Soul	1967	$30
❑ DLP-25821 [S]	Beethoven Soul	1967	$30

BEGINNING OF THE END, THE
ALSTON

❑ SD 33-379 [B]	Funky Nassau	1971	$25

BEIDERBECKE, BIX
BLUEBIRD

❑ 6845-1-R	Bix Lives!	1989	$30

COLUMBIA

❑ GL507 [M]	The Bix Beiderbecke Story, Volume 1: Bix and His Gang	1952	$50

— *Black label, silver print*

❑ CL507 [M]	The Bix Beiderbecke Story, Volume 1: Bix and His Gang	1953	$40

— *Maroon label, gold print*

❑ CL844 [M]	The Bix Beiderbecke Story, Volume 1: Bix and His Gang	1956	$30

— *Red and black label with six "eye" logos*

❑ CL844 [M]	The Bix Beiderbecke Story, Volume 1: Bix and His Gang	1963	$25

— *Guaranteed High Fidelity" label*

❑ CL844 [M]	The Bix Beiderbecke Story, Volume 1: Bix and His Gang	1966	$35

— *360 Sound" label*

❑ CL844 [M]	The Bix Beiderbecke Story, Volume 1: Bix and His Gang	1970	$30

— *Orange label*

❑ GL508 [M]	The Bix Beiderbecke Story, Volume 2: Bix and Tram	1952	$50

— *Black label, silver print*

❑ CL508 [M]	The Bix Beiderbecke Story, Volume 2: Bix and Tram	1953	$40

— *Maroon label, gold print*

❑ CL845 [M]	The Bix Beiderbecke Story, Volume 2: Bix and Tram	1956	$30

— *Red and black label with six "eye" logos*

❑ CL845 [M]	The Bix Beiderbecke Story, Volume 2: Bix and Tram	1963	$25

— *Guaranteed High Fidelity" label*

❑ CL845 [M]	The Bix Beiderbecke Story, Volume 2: Bix and Tram	1966	$35

— *360 Sound" label*

❑ CL845 [M]	The Bix Beiderbecke Story, Volume 2: Bix and Tram	1970	$30

— *Orange label*

Number	Title	Yr	NM
❑ GL509 [M]	The Bix Beiderbecke Story, Volume 3: The Whiteman Years	1952	$50

— *Black label, silver print*

❑ CL509 [M]	The Bix Beiderbecke Story, Volume 3: The Whiteman Years	1953	$40

— *Maroon label, gold print*

❑ CL846 [M]	The Bix Beiderbecke Story, Volume 3: The Whiteman Years	1956	$30

— *Red and black label with six "eye" logos*

❑ CL846 [M]	The Bix Beiderbecke Story, Volume 3: The Whiteman Years	1963	$25

— *Guaranteed High Fidelity" label*

❑ CL846 [M]	The Bix Beiderbecke Story, Volume 3: The Whiteman Years	1966	$35

— *360 Sound" label*

❑ CL846 [M]	The Bix Beiderbecke Story, Volume 3: The Whiteman Years	1970	$30

— *Orange label*

COLUMBIA MASTERWORKS

❑ ML4811 [M]	The Bix Beiderbecke Story, Volume 1	1950	$150
❑ ML4812 [M]	The Bix Beiderbecke Story, Volume 2	1950	$150
❑ ML4813 [M]	The Bix Beiderbecke Story, Volume 3	1950	$150

EVEREST ARCHIVE OF FOLK & JAZZ

❑ 317	Bix Beiderbecke	197?	$25

JAZZ TREASURY

❑ S-1003	Bix Beiderbecke with the Wolverines	197?	$30

JOLLY ROGER

❑ 5010 [10]	Bix Beiderbecke	1954	$50

MILESTONE

❑ 47019	Bix Beiderbecke and the Chicago Cornets	197?	$35

OLYMPIC

❑ 7130	Bix Beiderbecke and the Wolverines 1924	198?	$25

RCA VICTOR

❑ LPM-2323 [M]	The Bix Beiderbecke Legend	1961	$30

— *Long Play" on label*

❑ LPM-2323 [M]	The Bix Beiderbecke Legend	1963	$35

— *Mono" or "Monaural" on label*

RIVERSIDE

❑ RLP-1050 [10]	Bix Beiderbecke and the Wolverines	1954	$300
❑ RLP 12-123 [M]	Bix Beiderbecke and the Wolverines	1956	$300

— *White label, blue print*

❑ RLP 12-123 [M]	Bix Beiderbecke and the Wolverines	195?	$30

— *Blue label with microphone logo*

❑ RLP-1023 [10]	Early Bix	1954	$300

TIME-LIFE

❑ STL-J-04	Giants of Jazz	1979	$50

BEIRACH, RICHIE, AND JOHN ABERCROMBIE
PATHFINDER

❑ PTF-8701	Emerald City	1988	$25

BEIRACH, RICHIE
ECM

❑ 1142	Elm	1979	$30
❑ 1054	Eon	197?	$35
❑ 1104	Hubris	1977	$30

MAGENTA

❑ MA-0202	Breathing of Statues	1985	$25

PATHFINDER

❑ PTF-8617	Antarctica	1987	$25

BEL-AIRE GIRLS, THE
EVEREST

❑ LPBR-5081 [M]	The Bel-Aire Girls Sing Along with the Teen-Agers	1960	$75
❑ STBR-1081 [S]	The Bel-Aire Girls Sing Along with the Teen-Agers	1960	$100

BEL-AIRE POPS ORCHESTRA, THE
LIBERTY

❑ LRP-3414 [M]	Jan and Dean's Pop Symphony No. 1	1965	$120
❑ LST-7414 [S]	Jan and Dean's Pop Symphony No. 1	1965	$250

BELAFONTE, HARRY
COLUMBIA

❑ FC37489	Loving You Is Where I Belong	1981	$12

Number	Title	Yr	NM
DCC COMPACT CLASSICS			
❑ LPZ-2039	Jump Up Calypso	1997	$75
—Audiophile vinyl			
EMI			
❑ E1-92247	Belafonte '89	1989	$15
EMI MANHATAN			
❑ E1-46971	Paradise in Gazankulu	1988	$15
PAIR			
❑ PDL2-1060	The Belafonte Song Book	1986	$15
RCA CAMDEN			
❑ ACL1-0502	Abraham, Martin and John	1974	$12
❑ CAS-2599		1972	$12
RCA CUSTOM EDITION			
❑ DRL1-0068	I Wish You a Merry Christmas	1973	$18
—Reissue of LSP-2424 with two tracks deleted			
RCA VICTOR			
❑ CPL1-2469	A Legendary Performer	1977	$12
❑ LPM-1402 [M]	An Evening with Belafonte	1957	$30
❑ LSP-1402(e) [R]	An Evening with Belafonte	1960	$15
—Dog on top			
❑ LSP-1402(e) [R]	An Evening with Belafonte	1969	$12
—Orange label			
❑ ANL1-1434	An Evening with Belafonte	1976	$12
—Reissue of LSP-1402			
❑ LPM-3420 [M]	An Evening with Belafonte/Makeba	1965	$18
❑ LSP-3420 [S]	An Evening with Belafonte/Makeba	1965	$25
—With Miriam Makeba			
❑ LPM-3415 [M]	An Evening with Belafonte/Mouskouri	1966	$18
❑ LSP-3415 [S]	An Evening with Belafonte/Mouskouri	1966	$25
—With Nana Mouskouri			
❑ LPM-2309 [M]	At Home and Abroad	1961	$25
❑ LSP-2309 [S]	At Home and Abroad	1961	$30
❑ LPM-2953 [M]	Ballads, Blues and Boasters	1964	$18
❑ LSP-2953 [S]	Ballads, Blues and Boasters	1964	$25
❑ LPM-1150 [M]	Belafonte	1955	$50
❑ LSP-1150(e) [R]	Belafonte	196?	$15
❑ LOC-6006 [M]	Belafonte at Carnegie Hall	1959	$30
❑ LSO-6006 [S]	Belafonte at Carnegie Hall	1959	$150
❑ LSO-6006 [S]	Belafonte at Carnegie Hall	1996	$40
—Classic Records reissue on audiophile vinyl			
❑ LOC-6009 [M]	Belafonte at the Greek Theatre	1964	$25
❑ LSO-6009 [S]	Belafonte at the Greek Theatre	1964	$50
❑ VPSX-6077	Belafonte Live	1972	$18
❑ LPM-3779 [M]	Belafonte on Campus	1967	$15
❑ LSP-3779 [S]	Belafonte on Campus	1967	$18
❑ LOC-6007 [M]	Belafonte Returns to Carnegie Hall	1960	$25
❑ LSO-6007 [S]	Belafonte Returns to Carnegie Hall	1960	$50
—The above LP also has tracks by Odetta, Miriam Makeba and The Chad Mitchell Trio (the latter for the first time on record)			
❑ LSO-6007	Belafonte Returns to Carnegie Hall	1996	$40
—Classic Records reissue on audiophile vinyl			
❑ LPM-3938 [M]	Belafonte Sings of Love	1968	$18
❑ LSP-3938 [S]	Belafonte Sings of Love	1968	$18
❑ LPM-1505 [M]	Belafonte Sings of the Caribbean	1957	$30
❑ LSP-1505(e) [R]	Belafonte Sings of the Caribbean	196?	$15
❑ LOP-1006	Belafonte Sings the Blues	1958	$30
—Original issue			
❑ LPM-1972 [M]	Belafonte Sings the Blues	1959	$25
—Reissue of LOP-1006			
❑ LSP-1972 [S]	Belafonte Sings the Blues	1959	$30
❑ LSP-1972	Belafonte Sings the Blues	199?	$30
—Classic Records reissue on audiophile vinyl			
❑ LSP-4301	By Request	1970	$15

| ❑ LPM-1248 [M] | Calypso | 1956 | $30 |

Number	Title	Yr	NM
❑ LSP-1248(e) [R]	Calypso	196?	$15
❑ AYL1-3801(e) [R]	Calypso	1980	$10
❑ AFL1-1248	Calypso	1977	$12
—Reissue with new prefix			
❑ LSP-4521	Calypso Carnival	1971	$15
❑ LPM-3658 [M]	Calypso in Brass	1967	$15
❑ LSP-3658 [S]	Calypso in Brass	1967	$18
❑ LSP-4255	Homeward Bound	1969	$18
❑ LPM-3571 [M]	In My Quiet Room	1966	$15
❑ LSP-3571 [S]	In My Quiet Room	1966	$18
❑ LPM-2388 [M]	Jump Up Calypso	1961	$25
❑ LSP-2388 [S]	Jump Up Calypso	1961	$30
❑ LPM-1927 [M]	Love Is a Gentle Thing	1959	$25
❑ LSP-1927 [S]	Love Is a Gentle Thing	1959	$30
❑ LPM-1022 [M]	Mark Twain" and Other Folk Favorites	1954	$50
❑ LSP-1022(e) [R]	Mark Twain" and Other Folk Favorites	196?	$15
❑ LPM-2022 [M]	My Lord What a Mornin'	1960	$25
❑ LSP-2022 [S]	My Lord What a Mornin'	1960	$30
❑ APL1-0094	Play Me	1973	$15
❑ LOC-1507 [M]	Porgy and Bess	1959	$25
❑ LSO-1507 [S]	Porgy and Bess	1959	$30
❑ AYL1-3860(e) [R]	Pure Gold	1980	$10
❑ ANL1-0979	Pure Gold	1975	$12
❑ LPM-2695 [M]	Streets I Have Walked	1963	$25
❑ LSP-2695 [S]	Streets I Have Walked	1963	$30
❑ LPM-2194 [M]	Swing Dat Hammer	1961	$25
❑ LSP-2194 [S]	Swing Dat Hammer	1961	$30
❑ LPM-2574 [M]	The Many Moods of Belafonte	1962	$25
❑ LSP-2574 [S]	The Many Moods of Belafonte	1962	$30
—Living Stereo" on label, "RCA Victor" in silver			
❑ LSP-2574 [S]	The Many Moods of Belafonte	196?	$25
—Stereo" on black label, "RCA Victor" in white			
❑ LSP-2574 [S]	The Many Moods of Belafonte	1969	$15
—Orange label			
❑ LPM-2449 [M]	The Midnight Special	1962	$30
❑ LSP-2449 [S]	The Midnight Special	1962	$40
—The above LP features Bob Dylan on harmonica on the title track, his first appearance on record			
❑ ANL1-2324	The Midnight Special	1976	$12
—Reissue of LSP-2449			
❑ VPS-6024	This Is Harry Belafonte	1970	$18
❑ LPM-2626 [M]	To Wish You a Merry Christmas	1962	$25
—Reissue of LPM-1887 with new cover and one additional track			
❑ LSP-2626 [S]	To Wish You a Merry Christmas	1962	$30
❑ LPM-1887 [M]	To Wish You a Merry Christmas	1958	$30
❑ LSP-1887 [S]	To Wish You a Merry Christmas	1958	$40
❑ LSP-4481	Warm Touch	1971	$15
TIME-LIFE			
❑ SLGD-17	Legendary Singers: Harry Belafonte	1986	$18

BELEW, ADRIAN
Member of THE BEARS; KING CRIMSON; also briefly guitarist for FRANK ZAPPA and DAVID BOWIE.

Number	Title	Yr	NM
ATLANTIC			
❑ 81959	Mr. Music Head	1989	$12
❑ 82099	Young Lions	1990	$15
ISLAND			
❑ 90551	Desire Caught by the Tail	1986	$12
❑ IL9751	Lone Rhino	1982	$15

| ❑ 90108 [B] | Twang Bar King | 1983 | $12 |

BELEW, CARL, AND BETTY JEAN ROBINSON

DECCA			
❑ DL75337	When My Baby Sings His Song	1972	$18

Number	Title	Yr	NM
BELEW, CARL			
BUCKBOARD			
❑ BBS1014	Singing My Song	197?	$12
DECCA			
❑ DL4074 [M]	Carl Belew	1960	$30
❑ DL74074 [S]	Carl Belew	1960	$30
HILLTOP			
❑ JM-6013 [M]	Another Lonely Night	1965	$25
❑ JS-6013 [S]	Another Lonely Night	1965	$25
PICCADILLY			
❑ 3356	Big Time Gambling Man	198?	$12
RCA VICTOR			
❑ LPM-3381 [M]	Am I That Easy to Forget?	1965	$25
❑ LSP-3381 [S]	Am I That Easy to Forget?	1965	$30
❑ LPM-2848 [M]	Hello Out There	1964	$25
❑ LSP-2848 [S]	Hello Out There	1964	$30
❑ LPM-3919 [M]	Twelve Shades of Belew	1968	$50
❑ LSP-3919 [S]	Twelve Shades of Belew	1968	$25
VOCALION			
❑ VL73774 [S]	Country Songs	196?	$15
❑ VL3774 [M]	Country Songs	196?	$15
❑ VL3791 [M]	Lonely Street	1967	$18
❑ VL73791 [S]	Lonely Street	1967	$15
WRANGLER			
❑ WR1007 [M]	Carl Belew	1962	$30
❑ WRS31007 [S]	Carl Belew	1962	$40
BELGRAVE, MARCUS			
TRIBE			
❑ 2228	Gemini II	1975	$35
BELL, AARON			
HERALD			
❑ HLP-0100 [M]	Three Swinging Bells	1955	$85
LION			
❑ L-70111 [M]	Music from "77 Sunset Strip	1959	$30
❑ L-70112 [M]	Music from "Peter Gunn	1959	$30
❑ L-70113 [M]	Music from "Victory at Sea	1959	$30
RCA VICTOR			
❑ LPM-1876 [M]	After the Party's Over	1958	$50
BELL, ARCHIE, AND THE DRELLS			
ATLANTIC			
❑ SD8204	I Can't Stop Dancing	1968	$30
❑ SD8226	There's Gonna Be a Showdown	1969	$30
❑ 8181 [M]	Tighten Up	1968	$50
❑ SD8181 [S]	Tighten Up	1968	$30
PHILADELPHIA INT'L.			
❑ PZ34855	Hard Not to Like It	1977	$12
❑ JZ36096 [B]	Strategy	1979	$12
❑ PZ34323	Where Will You Go When the Party's Over	1976	$12
TSOP			
❑ PZ33844	Dance Your Troubles Away	1975	$12
BELL, CHARLES			
ATLANTIC			
❑ 1400 [M]	Another Dimension	1963	$175
❑ SD1400 [S]	Another Dimension	1963	$175
COLUMBIA			
❑ CL1582 [M]	The Charles Bell Contemporary Jazz Quartet	1961	$250
❑ CS8382 [S]	The Charles Bell Contemporary Jazz Quartet	1961	$250
GATEWAY			
❑ 7012 [M]	Charles Bell in Concert	1964	$35
❑ S-7012 [S]	Charles Bell in Concert	1964	$25

Number	Title	Yr	NM

BELL, DEE
CONCORD JAZZ
Number	Title	Yr	NM
❑ CJ-206	Let There Be Love	1982	$25

BELL, DELIA
WARNER BROS.
| ❑ 23838 | Delia Bell | 1983 | $12 |

BELL, FREDDIE, AND THE BELL BOYS
20TH FOX
| ❑ TF-4146 [M] | Bells Are Swinging | 1964 | $30 |
| ❑ TFS-4146 [S] | Bells Are Swinging | 1964 | $30 |
MERCURY
| ❑ MG-20289 [M] | Rock and Roll... All Flavors | 1957 | $250 |

BELL, GRAEME
ANGEL
| ❑ ANG.60002 [10] | Inside Jazz Down Under | 1954 | $75 |
JAZZOLOGY
| ❑ J-75 | Graeme Bell Jazz | 197? | $30 |

BELL, JERRY
MCA
| ❑ 5180 | Winter Love Affair | 1981 | $18 |

BELL, MADELINE
PHILIPS
| ❑ PHS600271 | I'm Gonna Make You Love Me | 1968 | $15 |

BELL, MAGGIE
ATLANTIC
| ❑ SD7293 | Queen of the Night | 1974 | $15 |
SWAN SONG
| ❑ SS8412 [B] | Suicide Sal | 1975 | $18 |

BELL, MARTY
RIVERSIDE
❑ RLP 12-206 [M]	The Voice of Marty Bell	1956	$300
— White label, blue print			
❑ RLP 12-206 [M]	The Voice of Marty Bell	1957	$300
— Blue label, microphone logo			

BELL, VINCENT
DECCA
❑ DL75212	Airport Love Theme	1970	$18
❑ DL4938 [M]	Pop Goes the Electric Sitar	1967	$25
❑ DL74938 [S]	Pop Goes the Electric Sitar	1967	$18
MUSICOR
❑ MM-3009 [M]	51 Motion Picture Favorites	1963	$18
❑ MS-3009 [S]	51 Motion Picture Favorites	1963	$25
❑ MM-3047 [M]	Big 16 Guitar Favorites	1965	$18
❑ MS-3047 [S]	Big 16 Guitar Favorites	1965	$25
VERVE
| ❑ V-8574 [M] | Whistle Stop | 1964 | $18 |
| ❑ V6-8574 [S] | Whistle Stop | 1964 | $25 |

BELL, WILLIAM
KAT FAMILY
| ❑ FZ38643 | Survivor | 1983 | $12 |
MERCURY
| ❑ SRM-1-1146 [B] | Coming Back for More | 1977 | $12 |
| ❑ SRM-1-1193 | It's Time You Took Another Listen | 1978 | $12 |
STAX
❑ ST-2014 [M]	Bound to Happen	1969	$50
— Mono is promo only			
❑ STS-2014 [S]	Bound to Happen	1969	$30
❑ STS-3005	Phases of Reality	1973	$25
❑ STS-5502	Relating	1974	$25
❑ 719 [M]	Soul of a Bell	1967	$40
❑ S-719 [S]	Soul of a Bell	1967	$50
❑ MPS-8541	The Best of William Bell	1988	$12
❑ STS-2037	Wow...	1971	$30
WRC
| ❑ WL-3007 | On a Roll | 1986 | $15 |

BELL & JAMES
A&M
❑ SP-4728	Bell & James	1978	$12
❑ SP-4834	In Black & White	1981	$12
❑ SP-4784	Only Make Believe	1979	$12

BELL BIV DEVOE
MCA
❑ 10682	Hootie Mack	1993	$15
❑ 6387	Poison	1990	$15
❑ 10345	WBBD -- Bootcity! The Remix Album	1991	$15

BELLAMY BROTHERS, THE
ELEKTRA
| ❑ 60210 | Strong Weakness | 1982 | $12 |
| ❑ E1-60099 | When We Were Boys | 1982 | $12 |

MCA CURB
Number	Title	Yr	NM
❑ 5721	Country Rap	1987	$12
❑ 42039	Crazy from the Heart	1987	$12
❑ 1462	Greatest Hits	1985	$10
— Reissue of Warner Bros. 23697			
❑ 42298	Greatest Hits Volume III	1989	$12
❑ 5812	Greatest Hits Volume Two	1986	$12
❑ 5586	Howard & David	1985	$12
❑ 42224	Rebels Without a Clue	1988	$12
❑ 5489	Restless	1984	$12
❑ 1441	Restless	1985	$10
— Reissue of MCA 5489			
WARNER BROS.
❑ BSK3176	Friends	1978	$12
❑ 23697	Greatest Hits	1982	$12
❑ BS2941	Let Your Love Flow	1976	$12
❑ BS3034	Plain & Fancy	1977	$12
❑ BSK3491	Sons of the Sun	1980	$12
❑ 60210	Strong Weakness	1983	$10
— Reissue of Elektra 60210			
❑ BSK3347	The Two and Only	1979	$12
❑ BSK3408	You Can Get Crazy	1980	$12

BELLE, REGINA
COLUMBIA
| ❑ BFC40537 | All By Myself | 1987 | $10 |
| ❑ FC44367 | Stay with Me | 1989 | $12 |

BELLE AND SEBASTIAN
MATADOR
❑ OLE429 [B]	Fold Your Hands Child, You Walk Like a Peasant	2000	$25
❑ OLE296 [B]	If You're Feeling Sinister	1996	$40
❑ OLE311 [B]	The Boy with the Arab Strap	1998	$30
❑ OLE361 [B]	Tigermilk	1999	$40
— First U.S. release of their rare U.K. debut; issued in loose bag			

BELLE EPOQUE
BIG TREE
| ❑ BT76008 | Miss Broadway | 1978 | $12 |
SHADY BROOK
| ❑ SB 33-009 | Miss Broadway | 1977 | $15 |

BELLE STARS, THE
WARNER BROS.
| ❑ 23866 | The Belle Stars | 1983 | $12 |

BELLETTO, AL
CAPITOL
❑ T751 [M]	Half and Half	1956	$100
❑ T6514 [M]	Sounds and Songs	1955	$150
❑ T6506 [M]	The Al Belletto Sextette	1955	$150
❑ T901 [M]	Whisper Not	1957	$175
KING
| ❑ 716 [M] | The Big Sound | 1961 | $50 |

BELLS, THE (1)
POLYDOR
| ❑ 24-4510 | Fly, Little White Dove, Fly | 1971 | $18 |
| ❑ 24-5503 | Love, Luck & Lollypops | 1972 | $18 |

BELLSON, LOUIS, AND GENE KRUPA
ROULETTE
| ❑ R-52098 [M] | The Mighty Two | 1962 | $25 |
| ❑ SR-52098 [S] | The Mighty Two | 1962 | $30 |

BELLSON, LOUIS, AND LALO SCHIFRIN
ROULETTE
| ❑ R-52120 [M] | Explorations | 1964 | $35 |
| ❑ SR-52120 [S] | Explorations | 1964 | $25 |

BELLSON, LOUIS, AND WALFREDO DE LOS REYES
FANTASY
| ❑ OJC-632 | Edue Ritmos Cubanos | 1991 | $30 |
| — Reissue of Pablo 2310 807 | | | |
PABLO
| ❑ 2310807 | Edue Ritmos Cubanos | 1978 | $30 |

BELLSON, LOUIS
ABC IMPULSE!
| ❑ AS-9107 [S] | Thunderbird | 1968 | $30 |
| — Reissue of Impulse AS-9107 | | | |
CAPITOL
| ❑ H348 [10] | Just Jazz All-Stars | 1952 | $300 |
CONCORD JAZZ
❑ CJ-36	150 M P H	1977	$30
❑ CJ-105	Dynamite!	1979	$30
❑ CJ-350	Live at the Jazz Showcase	1988	$30
❑ CJ-157	London Scene	198?	$30
❑ CJ-64	Prime Time	1978	$30
❑ CJ-73	Raincheck	1978	$30
❑ CJ-141	Side Track	198?	$30

Number	Title	Yr	NM
❑ CJ-20	The Louis Bellson 7 Live at the Concord Festival	1977	$30
DISCWASHER
| ❑ 002 | Note Smoking | 1979 | $30 |
| — Direct-to-disc recording | | | |
IMPULSE!
| ❑ A-9107 [M] | Thunderbird | 1966 | $120 |
| ❑ AS-9107 [S] | Thunderbird | 1966 | $120 |
NORGRAN
❑ MGN-1085 [M]	Concerto for Drums	1956	$0
— Canceled			
❑ MGN-1007 [M]	Journey Into Love	1954	$300
❑ MGN-1011 [M]	Louis Bellson and His Drums	1954	$300

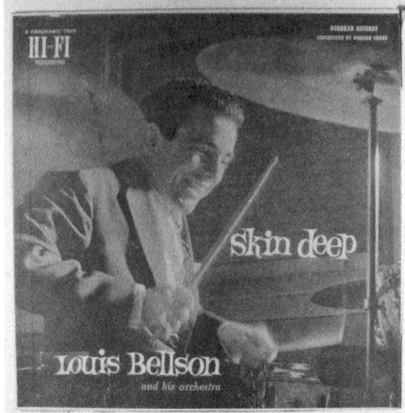

❑ MGN-1046 [M]	Skin Deep	1955	$150
❑ MGN-7 [10]	The Amazing Artistry of Louis Bellson	1954	$250
❑ MGN-1020 [M]	The Driving Louis Bellson	1955	$250
❑ MGN-14 [10]	The Exciting Mr. Bellson (And His Big Band)	1954	$250
❑ MGN-1099 [M]	The Hawk Talks	1956	$100
— Reissue of 1020			
PABLO
❑ 2310899	Cool, Cool Blue	198?	$30
❑ 2310755	Explosion	1975	$35
❑ 2310838	Jam	1979	$30
❑ 2310880	London Gig	198?	$30
❑ 2310834	Matterhorn	1979	$30
❑ 2310813	Sunshine Rock	1978	$30
❑ 2405407	The Best of Louis Bellson	198?	$30
PROJECT 3
| ❑ PR5029SD | Breakthrough! | 1968 | $35 |
ROULETTE
❑ R-65002 [M]	Around the World in Percussion	1962	$25
❑ SR-65002 [S]	Around the World in Percussion	1962	$30
❑ R-52087 [M]	Big Band Jazz from the Summit	1962	$25
❑ SR-52087 [S]	Big Band Jazz from the Summit	1962	$30
SEAGULL
| ❑ LG-8208 | Louis Bellson and Orchestra | 198? | $25 |
VERVE
❑ MGV-8016 [M]	Concerto for Drums	1957	$50
— Reissue of Norgran 1011			
❑ V-8016 [M]	Concerto for Drums	1961	$25
❑ MGV-8354 [M]	Drummer's Holiday	1959	$150
❑ V-8354 [M]	Drummer's Holiday	1959	$150
❑ MGV-8193 [M]	Drumorama!	1957	$150
❑ V-8193 [M]	Drumorama!	1957	$150
❑ MGV-8258 [M]	Let's Call It Swing	1958	$175
❑ V-8258 [M]	Let's Call It Swing	1958	$175
❑ MGV-8256 [M]	Louis Bellson at the Flamingo	1958	$120
❑ V-8256 [M]	Louis Bellson at the Flamingo	1958	$120
❑ MGV-2131 [M]	Louis Bellson Swings Jules Styne	1960	$150
❑ MGVS-6138 [S]	Louis Bellson Swings Jules Styne	1960	$150
❑ V-2131 [M]	Louis Bellson Swings Jules Styne	1960	$150
❑ V6-2131 [S]	Louis Bellson Swings Jules Styne	1960	$150
❑ MGV-8280 [M]	Music, Romance and Especially Love	1958	$120
❑ V-8280 [M]	Music, Romance and Especially Love	1958	$120
❑ MGV-8137 [M]	Skin Deep	1957	$50
— Reissue of Norgran 1046			
❑ V-8137 [M]	Skin Deep	1957	$150
❑ MGV-2123 [M]	The Brilliant Bellson Sound	1960	$120
❑ MGVS-6093 [S]	The Brilliant Bellson Sound	1960	$120
❑ V-2123 [M]	The Brilliant Bellson Sound	1960	$120
❑ V6-2123 [S]	The Brilliant Bellson Sound	1960	$120
❑ MGV-8186 [M]	The Hawk Talks	1957	$300
— Reissue of Norgran 1099			
❑ V-8186 [M]	The Hawk Talks	1957	$175

Number	Title	Yr	NM

VOSS
| ❑ VLP1-42936 | Note Smoking | 1988 | $25 |

— Reissue of Discwasher 002

BELLSON, LOUIS/ RAY BROWN/PAUL SMITH
PAUSA
| ❑ 7167 | Intensive Care | 1978 | $30 |

VOSS
| ❑ VLP1-42933 | Intensive Care | 1988 | $25 |

— Reissue

BELLUS, TONY
NRC
| ❑ LPA-8 [M] | Robbin' the Cradle | 1960 | $250 |

— Blue label
| ❑ LPA-8 [M] | Robbin' the Cradle | 1960 | $150 |

— Black label

SHI-FI
| ❑ LP-11 [M] | Gems of Tony Bellus | 196? | $75 |

BELLY
SIRE
| ❑ 45833 | King | 1995 | $15 |

BELMONTS, THE
BUDDAH

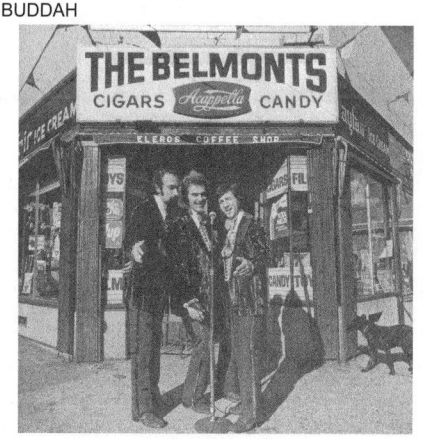

| ❑ BDS-5123 [B] | Cigars, Acapella, Candy | 1972 | $50 |

DOT
| ❑ DLP-25949 [B] | Summer Love | 1969 | $30 |

SABINA
| ❑ SALP-5001 [M] | The Belmonts' Carnival of Hits | 1962 | $175 |

STRAWBERRY
| ❑ 6001 | Cheek to Cheek | 1978 | $18 |

BELOVED, THE
ATLANTIC
| ❑ 82047 | Happiness | 1990 | $15 |

BELVIN, JESSE
CROWN
| ❑ CLP-5145 [M] | The Casual Jesse Belvin | 1959 | $80 |

— Black label
| ❑ CLP-5145 [M] | The Casual Jesse Belvin | 196? | $18 |

— Gray label
| ❑ CLP-5187 [M] | The Unforgettable Jesse Belvin | 1959 | $80 |

— Black label
| ❑ CLP-5187 [M] | The Unforgettable Jesse Belvin | 196? | $18 |

— Gray label

RCA CAMDEN
| ❑ CAL-960 [M] | Jesse Belvin's Best | 1966 | $15 |
| ❑ CAS-960 [S] | Jesse Belvin's Best | 1966 | $18 |

RCA VICTOR
❑ LPM-2089 [M]	Just Jesse Belvin	1959	$40
❑ LSP-2089 [S]	Just Jesse Belvin	1959	$75
❑ LPM-2105 [M]	Mr. Easy	1960	$30
❑ LSP-2105 [S]	Mr. Easy	1960	$40

SPECIALTY
| ❑ SP-7003 | The Blues Balladeer | 1990 | $18 |

BENATAR, PAT
CHRYSALIS
❑ F1-21715	Best Shots	1989	$15
❑ CHE1275	Crimes of Passion	1980	$10
❑ CHE1275	Crimes of Passion	1980	$30

— Error pressing: White label (not a promo) with photo of Pat leaning on a barre, as on regular copies, but with no blue at all, and with no butterfly or "Chrysalis" on label

Number	Title	Yr	NM

| ❑ FV41275 | Crimes of Passion | 1983 | $10 |

— Reissue of 1275
| ❑ CHR1396 | Get Nervous | 1982 | $10 |
| ❑ FV41396 | Get Nervous | 1983 | $10 |

— Reissue of 1396

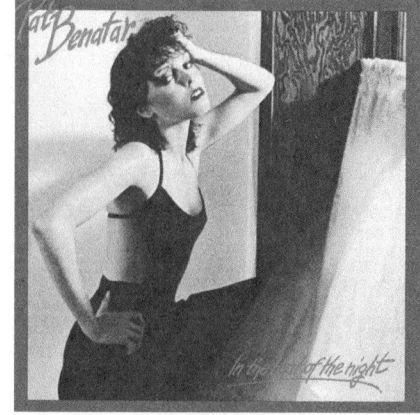

| ❑ CHR1236 [B] | In the Heat of the Night | 1979 | $10 |
| ❑ FV41236 | In the Heat of the Night | 1983 | $10 |

— Reissue of 1236
❑ FV41444	Live from Earth	1983	$10
❑ CHR1346	Precious Time	1981	$10
❑ FV41346	Precious Time	1983	$10

— Reissue of 1346
❑ FV41507	Seven the Hard Way	1985	$10
❑ FV41471	Tropico	1984	$10
❑ FV41628	Wide Awake in Dreamland	1988	$10

MOBILE FIDELITY
| ❑ Jan-0057 | In the Heat of the Night | 1981 | $40 |

— Audiophile vinyl

BENAY, BEN
CAPITOL
| ❑ T2484 [M] | The Big Blues Harmonica of Ben Benay | 1966 | $25 |
| ❑ ST2484 [S] | The Big Blues Harmonica of Ben Benay | 1966 | $30 |

BENDIX, WILLIAM
CRICKET
| ❑ CR-30 [M] | William Bendix Sings and Tells Famous Pirate Stories | 1959 | $40 |

BENEDICTINE MONKS OF SANTO DOMINGO DE SILOS, THE
MUSICAL HERITAGE SOCIETY
| ❑ 923698X | Chant | 1994 | $18 |

— The only U.S. vinyl version of this surprising hit compilation album

BENEDICTINE MONKS OF ST. PROCOPIUS ABBEY
(NO LABEL)
| ❑ U-51773/4 | Christmas at St. Procopius Abbey | 197? | $15 |

BENEKE, TEX/RAY EBERLE/THE MODERNAIRES
COLUMBIA
| ❑ CL2392 [M] | Christmas Serenade in the Glenn Miller Style | 1965 | $15 |
| ❑ CS9192 [S] | Christmas Serenade in the Glenn Miller Style | 1965 | $18 |

BENET, VICKI
DECCA
❑ DL8381 [M]	The French Touch	1957	$40
❑ DL8987 [M]	Vicki Benet a Paris	1959	$30
❑ DL78987 [S]	Vicki Benet a Paris	1959	$40
❑ DL8233 [M]	Woman of Paris	1956	$40

LIBERTY
| ❑ LRP-3103 [M] | Sing to Me of Love | 1960 | $30 |
| ❑ LST-7103 [S] | Sing to Me of Love | 1960 | $30 |

BENNETT, BETTY
ATLANTIC
| ❑ 1226 [M] | Nobody Else But Me | 1956 | $300 |

— Black label
| ❑ 1226 [M] | Nobody Else But Me | 1961 | $175 |

— Multicolor label, white "fan" logo

KAPP
| ❑ KL-1052 [M] | Blue Sunday | 1957 | $40 |

TREND
| ❑ TL-1006 [10] | Betty Bennett Sings Previn Arrangements | 1954 | $120 |

Number	Title	Yr	NM

UNITED ARTISTS
| ❑ UAL-3070 [M] | I Love to Sing | 1959 | $40 |
| ❑ UAS-6070 [S] | I Love to Sing | 1959 | $50 |

BENNETT, BOYD
KING
| ❑ 395-594 [M] | Boyd Bennett | 1955 | $4000 |

— VG value 1500; VG+ value 2750

BENNETT, CONNIE, WITH BILL SMITH AND THE HARLEM-AIRES
HOLLYWOOD
| ❑ LPH-30 [M] | Rhythm 'N Blues in the Night | 1957 | $500 |

— Photo of Julie "Catwoman" Newmar on front cover

BENNETT, JOE, AND THE SPARKLETONES
MCA
| ❑ 1553 | Black Slacks | 1983 | $18 |

BENNETT, MAX
BETHLEHEM
❑ BCP-48 [M]	Johnny Jaguar	1957	$300
❑ BCP-50 [M]	Max Bennett Plays	1957	$120
❑ BCP-1028 [10]	Max Bennett Quintet	1955	$300

PALO ALTO
| ❑ TBA-216 | The Drifter | 1986 | $25 |

BENNETT, RICHARD RODNEY
AUDIOPHILE
| ❑ AP-168 | Harold Arlen's Songs | 1982 | $25 |
| ❑ AP-206 | Take Love Easy | 1985 | $25 |

DRG
| ❑ SL-5182 | A Different Side of Sondheim | 1978 | $25 |
| ❑ DRG-6102 | Special Occasions | 1979 | $25 |

BENNETT, TONY, AND BILL EVANS
DRG
| ❑ MRS-901 | Together Again | 1985 | $20 |

FANTASY
| ❑ F-9489 | The Tony Bennett/Bill Evans Album | 1975 | $30 |

IMPROV
| ❑ 7117 | Together Again | 1978 | $30 |

MOBILE FIDELITY
| ❑ 1-117 | The Tony Bennett/Bill Evans Album | 1981 | $40 |

— Audiophile vinyl

BENNETT, TONY, AND COUNT BASIE
COLUMBIA
| ❑ CL1294 [M] | Tony Bennett In Person | 1959 | $75 |
| ❑ CS8104 [S] | Tony Bennett In Person | 1959 | $40 |

COLUMBIA LIMITED EDITION
| ❑ LE10125 | Tony Bennett In Person | 197? | $30 |

ROULETTE
❑ R25231 [M]	Bennett and Basie Strike Up the Band	1963	$50
❑ SR25231 [S]	Bennett and Basie Strike Up the Band	1963	$75
❑ R25072 [M]	Count Basie Swings/Tony Bennett Sings	1961	$75
❑ SR25072 [S]	Count Basie Swings/Tony Bennett Sings	1961	$75

BENNETT, TONY
COLUMBIA
| ❑ C30240 | All Time Hall of Fame Hits | 1971 | $15 |
| ❑ PC30240 | All Time Hall of Fame Hits | 197? | $12 |

— Reissue with new prefix

Number	Title	Yr	NM
☐ CL2507 [10]	Alone at Last with Tony Bennett	1955	$75
☐ CL1471 [M]	Alone Together	1960	$30
☐ CS8262 [S]	Alone Together	1960	$40
☐ CL1559 [M]	A String of Harold Arlen	1961	$25
☐ CS8359 [S]	A String of Harold Arlen	1961	$30
☐ CL2560 [M]	A Time for Love	1966	$15
☐ CS9360 [S]	A Time for Love	1966	$18
☐ CL6221 [10]	Because of You	1952	$100
☐ CL2550 [10]	Because of You	1956	$75
☐ FC44029	Bennett/Berlin	1987	$25
☐ C63668	Bennett Sings Ellington -- Hot and Cool	1999	$30
☐ CL1292 [M]	Blue Velvet	1958	$30
☐ CL621 [M]	Cloud Seven	1955	$40
☐ CL2773 [M]	For Once in My Life	1967	$30
☐ CS9573 [S]	For Once in My Life	1967	$18
☐ CL1301 [M]	Hometown, My Hometown	1959	$30
☐ CS8107 [S]	Hometown, My Hometown	1959	$40
☐ CL2343 [M]	If I Ruled the World -- Songs for the Jet Set	1965	$15
☐ CS9143 [S]	If I Ruled the World -- Songs for the Jet Set	1965	$18
☐ CL1869 [M]	I Left My Heart in San Francisco	1962	$18
☐ CS8669 [S]	I Left My Heart in San Francisco	1962	$25
☐ PC8669	I Left My Heart in San Francisco	198?	$10

— Reissue with new prefix

☐ CG33612	I Left My Heart in San Francisco/Tony Sings the Great Hits of Today!	1975	$18
☐ CS9882	I've Gotta Be Me	1969	$18
☐ CL2000 [M]	I Wanna Be Around	1963	$18
☐ CS8800 [S]	I Wanna Be Around	1963	$30
☐ CL1186 [M]	Long Ago and Far Away	1958	$30
☐ GP14	Love Songs	1969	$18
☐ C30558	Love Story	1971	$15
☐ CL1535 [M]	More Tony's Greatest Hits	1961	$25
☐ CS8335 [S]	More Tony's Greatest Hits	1961	$30
☐ CL1763 [M]	Mr. Broadway	1962	$18
☐ CS8563 [S]	Mr. Broadway	1962	$25
☐ CL1658 [M]	My Heart Sings	1961	$25
☐ CS8458 [S]	My Heart Sings	1961	$30
☐ CS9739	Snowfall: The Tony Bennett Christmas Album	1968	$15
☐ C31219	Summer of '42	1972	$15
☐ FC40344	The Art of Excellence	1986	$25
☐ CL1079 [M]	The Beat of My Heart	1957	$30
☐ CL2141 [M]	The Many Moods of Tony	1964	$18
☐ CS8941 [S]	The Many Moods of Tony	1964	$25
☐ CL2472 [M]	The Movie Song Album	1966	$15
☐ CS9272 [S]	The Movie Song Album	1966	$18
☐ CL2056 [M]	This Is All I Ask	1963	$18
☐ CS8856 [S]	This Is All I Ask	1963	$25
☐ CL1429 [M]	To My Wonderful One	1960	$30
☐ CS8226 [S]	To My Wonderful One	1960	$40
☐ CL938 [M]	Tony	1956	$30
☐ C2L23 [M]	Tony Bennett at Carnegie Hall	1962	$25
☐ C2S823 [S]	Tony Bennett at Carnegie Hall	1962	$30
☐ CL1905 [M]	Tony Bennett at Carnegie Hall Vol. 1	1963	$18
☐ CS8705 [S]	Tony Bennett at Carnegie Hall Vol. 1	1963	$25
☐ CG40424	Tony Bennett Jazz	1987	$30
☐ C30280	Tony Bennett's "Something	1971	$15
☐ KG31494	Tony Bennett's All-Time Greatest Hits	1972	$18
☐ CS9814	Tony Bennett's Greatest Hits, Volume IV	1969	$18
☐ CL2653 [M]	Tony Makes It Happen!	1967	$18
☐ CS9453 [S]	Tony Makes It Happen!	1967	$18
☐ CL1229 [M]	Tony's Greatest Hits	1958	$30
☐ CS8652 [R]	Tony's Greatest Hits	1962	$18
☐ CL2373 [M]	Tony's Greatest Hits, Volume III	1965	$15
☐ CS9173 [S]	Tony's Greatest Hits, Volume III	1965	$18
☐ CL1446 [M]	Tony Sings for Two	1960	$30
☐ CS8242 [S]	Tony Sings for Two	1960	$40
☐ CS9980	Tony Sings the Great Hits of Today!	1970	$15
☐ CL2175 [M]	When Lights Are Low	1964	$18
☐ CS8975 [S]	When Lights Are Low	1964	$25
☐ CL2285 [M]	Who Can I Turn To	1964	$18
☐ CS9085 [S]	Who Can I Turn To	1964	$25
☐ KC31460	With Love	1972	$15
☐ CS9678	Yesterday I Heard the Rain	1968	$18

COLUMBIA LIMITED EDITION

☐ LE10057	For Once in My Life	197?	$12

COLUMBIA SPECIAL PRODUCTS

☐ CSR8107 [S]	Hometown, My Town	196?	$15
☐ CSM552 [M]	Singer Presents Tony Bennett	1966	$18
☐ CSS552 [S]	Singer Presents Tony Bennett	1966	$25
☐ C11264	This Is All I Ask	1972	$15

— Distributed by Arc-Jay-Kay Distributing Co." on upper back cover

DRG

☐ MRS-910	Make Magnificent Music	1985	$25
☐ DARC-2-2102	The Rodgers and Hart Songbook	1986	$35

HARMONY

☐ HS11340	Just One of Those Things	1969	$12

Number	Title	Yr	NM
☐ KH30758	The Very Thought of You	1971	$12
☐ KH32171	Tony	1973	$12

IMPROV

☐ 7123	Beautiful Music	1979	$30
☐ 7112	Life Is Beautiful	1975	$30
☐ 7120	Tony Bennett Sings More Rodgers and Hart	1978	$30
☐ 7113	Tony Bennett Sings Rodgers and Hart	197?	$30

MGM

☐ SE-4929	Greatest Hits, Vol. 7	1973	$15

PAIR

☐ PDL2-1102	All-Time Favorites	1986	$15

TIME-LIFE

☐ SLGD-10	Legendary Singers: Tony Bennett	1986	$18

VERVE

☐ MV-5094	Listen Easy	1973	$15
☐ MV-5088	The Good Things in Life	1972	$15

BENNO, MARC

A&M

☐ SP-4364	Ambush	1972	$15
☐ SP-4767	Lost in Austin	1979	$12
☐ SP-4273	Marc Benno	1970	$15
☐ SP-4303	Minnows	1971	$15

BENOIT, DAVID

AVI

☐ AV-6074	Can You Imagine	1980	$15
☐ AV-8620	Christmastime	1985	$15
☐ AV-6138	Digits	1984	$15
☐ AV-6025	Heavier Than Yesterday	1977	$20
☐ AV-6214	Stages	1983	$15
☐ AV-8712	Waves of Raves	1986	$15

GRP

☐ 1047	Every Step of the Way	1987	$15
☐ 1035	Freedom at Midnight	1986	$15
☐ 9621	Inner Motion	1990	$15
☐ 9587	Urban Daydreams	1989	$15
☐ 9595	Waiting for Spring	1989	$15

SPINDLETOP

☐ STP-104	This Side Up	1986	$15

BENSON, GEORGE, AND EARL KLUGH

WARNER BROS.

☐ 25580 [B]	Collaboration	1987	$12

BENSON, GEORGE

A&M

☐ SP-3014	Shape of Things to Come	1969	$50

— Brown label

☐ SP-3014	Shape of Things to Come	1976	$30

— Silvery label with fading "A&M" logo

☐ SP9-3014	Shape of Things to Come	1983	$35

— Audio Master Plus" reissue

☐ SP-3020	Tell It Like It Is	1969	$50

— Brown label

☐ SP-3020	Tell It Like It Is	1976	$30

— Silvery label with fading "A&M" logo

☐ SP9-3020	Tell It Like It Is	1984	$35

— Audio Master Plus" reissue

☐ SP-3203	The Best of George Benson	1983	$25
☐ SP-3028	The Other Side of Abbey Road	1970	$75

— Brown label

☐ SP-3028	The Other Side of Abbey Road	1976	$30

— Silvery label with fading "A&M" logo

☐ SP9-3028	The Other Side of Abbey Road	1984	$35

— Audio Master Plus" reissue

COLUMBIA

☐ CG33569	Benson Burner	1976	$30
☐ CL2613 [M]	The George Benson Cook Book	1967	$50
☐ CS9413 [S]	The George Benson Cook Book	1967	$50

— Red "360 Sound" label

☐ CS9413	The George Benson Cook Book	1976	$25

— Orange label

☐ PC9413	The George Benson Cook Book	198?	$20

— Reissue with new prefix

☐ CL2525 [M]	The Most Exciting New Guitarist on the Jazz Scene Today -- It's Uptown	1966	$50
☐ CS9325 [S]	The Most Exciting New Guitarist on the Jazz Scene Today -- It's Uptown	1966	$50

— Red "360 Sound" label

☐ CS9325	The Most Exciting New Guitarist on the Jazz Scene Today -- It's Uptown	1976	$25

— Orange label

Number	Title	Yr	NM
☐ PC9325	The Most Exciting New Guitarist on the Jazz Scene Today -- It's Uptown	198?	$20

— Reissue with new prefix

CTI

☐ 6045	Bad Benson	1974	$30
☐ 6069	Benson & Farrell	1976	$30
☐ 6009	Beyond the Blue Horizon	1971	$30
☐ 6033	Body Talk	1973	$30
☐ CTSQ-6033 [Q]	Body Talk	1973	$75
☐ 8030	Cast Your Fate to the Wind	1982	$25
☐ 6072	George Benson In Concert -- Carnegie Hall	1976	$30
☐ 6062	Good King Bad	1976	$30
☐ 8031	Summertime: In Concert	198?	$25
☐ 8014	Take Five	198?	$25
☐ 6015	White Rabbit	1972	$30
☐ 8009	White Rabbit	198?	$25

FANTASY

☐ OJC-461	The New Boss Guitar of George Benson	1990	$30

— Reissue of Prestige 7310

MOBILE FIDELITY

☐ Jan-0011	Breezin'	1979	$120

— Audiophile vinyl

POLYDOR

☐ PD-1-6084	Blue Benson	1976	$25

PRESTIGE

☐ 24072	George Benson & Jack McDuff	1976	$35
☐ PRLP-7310 [M]	The New Boss Guitar of George Benson	1964	$75
☐ PRST-7310 [S]	The New Boss Guitar of George Benson	1964	$40

VERVE

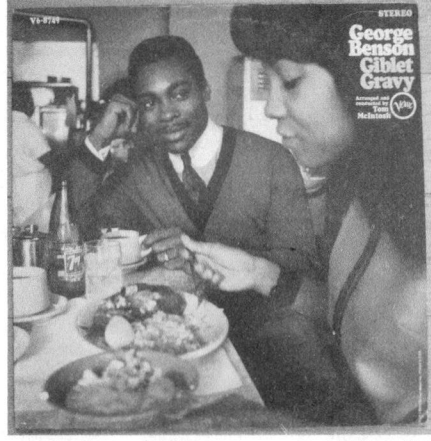

☐ V6-8749 [B]	Giblet Gravy	1968	$25
☐ V6-8771	Goodies	1969	$50

WARNER BROS.

☐ 25178	20/20	1985	$25
☐ 26295	Big Boss Band	1990	$35
☐ BS2919	Breezin'	1976	$35

— With no mention of "This Masquerade" on front cover

☐ BS2919	Breezin'	1976	$25

— With "Contains This Masquerade" on front cover

☐ BSK3111	Breezin'	1977	$20

— Reissue of 2919

☐ HS3453	Give Me the Night	1980	$25
☐ BSK2983	In Flight	1977	$25
☐ 23744	In Your Eyes	1983	$25
☐ 2BSK3277	Livin' Inside Your Love	1979	$30
☐ 25907	Tenderly	1989	$25
☐ 2HS3577	The George Benson Collection	1981	$30
☐ 25705	Twice the Love	1988	$25
☐ 2WS3139	Weekend in L.A.	1978	$30
☐ 25475	While the City Sleeps…	1986	$25

BENTON, BARBI

PLAYBOY

☐ PB406	Barbi Benton	1975	$18
☐ PB404	Barbi Doll	1974	$18
☐ PB411	Something New	1976	$18

BENTON, BROOK

ALLEGIANCE

☐ AV-5033	Memories Are Made of This	1986	$12

ALL PLATINUM

☐ 3015	This Is Brook Benton	1976	$15

COTILLION

☐ SD9018	Brook Benton Today	1970	$15
☐ SD9002	Do Your Own Thing	1969	$15
☐ SD9028	Home Style	1970	$15
☐ SD9050	Story Teller	1971	$15
☐ SD9058	The Gospel Truth	1972	$15

Number	Title	Yr	NM
EPIC			
❑ LN3573 [M]	Brook Benton At His Best	1959	$50
HARMONY			
❑ HL7346 [M]	The Soul of Brook Benton	196?	$15
❑ HS11146 [R]	The Soul of Brook Benton	196?	$15
HMC			
❑ 830724	Beautiful Memories of Christmas	1983	$15
MERCURY			
❑ MG-20830 [M]	Best Ballads of Broadway	1963	$25
❑ SR-60830 [S]	Best Ballads of Broadway	1963	$30
❑ MG-20886 [M]	Born to Sing the Blues	1964	$25
❑ SR-60886 [S]	Born to Sing the Blues	1964	$30
❑ MG-20464 [M]	Endlessly	1959	$30
❑ SR-60146 [S]	Endlessly	1959	$40
❑ MG-20607 [M]	Golden Hits	1961	$25
❑ SR-60607 [S]	Golden Hits	1961	$30
❑ MG-20774 [M]	Golden Hits, Volume 2	1963	$25
❑ SR-60774 [S]	Golden Hits, Volume 2	1963	$30
❑ MG-20619 [M]	If You Believe	1961	$25
❑ SR-60619 [S]	If You Believe	1961	$30
❑ MG-20421 [M]	It's Just a Matter of Time	1959	$40
❑ SR-60077 [S]	It's Just a Matter of Time	1959	$50
❑ 822321-1	It's Just a Matter of Time: His Greatest Hits	1984	$12
❑ MG-20918 [M]	On the Country Side	1964	$18
❑ SR-60918 [S]	On the Country Side	1964	$25
❑ MG-20740 [M]	Singing the Blues -- Lie to Me	1962	$25
❑ SR-60740 [S]	Singing the Blues -- Lie to Me	1962	$30
❑ MG-20565 [M]	So Many Ways I Love You	1960	$30
❑ SR-60225 [S]	So Many Ways I Love You	1960	$40
❑ MG-20602 [M]	Songs I Love to Sing	1960	$30
❑ SR-60602 [S]	Songs I Love to Sing	1960	$40
❑ MG-20641 [M]	The Boll Weevil Song and 11 Other Great Hits	1961	$25
❑ SR-60641 [S]	The Boll Weevil Song and 11 Other Great Hits	1961	$30
❑ MG-20673 [M]	There Goes That Song Again	1962	$25
❑ SR-60673 [S]	There Goes That Song Again	1962	$30
❑ MG-20934 [M]	This Bitter Earth	1964	$18
❑ SR-60934 [S]	This Bitter Earth	1964	$25
MGM			
❑ SE-4874	Something for Everyone	1973	$15
MUSICOR			
❑ 4603	The Best of Brook Benton	1977	$15
OLDE WORLD			
❑ OWR7707	Hot and Sensitive	1978	$0
—Unreleased?			
PAIR			
❑ PDL2-1100	Brook Benton's Best	1986	$15
RCA CAMDEN			
❑ CAL-564 [M]	Brook Benton	1960	$18
❑ CAS-2431	I Wanna Be with You	1970	$15
RCA VICTOR			
❑ APL1-1044	Book Benton Sings a Love Story	1975	$12
❑ LPM-3526 [M]	Mother Nature, Father Time	1965	$18
❑ LSP-3526 [S]	Mother Nature, Father Time	1965	$25
❑ LPM-3590 [M]	My Country	1966	$18
❑ LSP-3590 [S]	My Country	1966	$25
❑ LPM-3514 [M]	That Old Feeling	1966	$18
❑ LSP-3514 [S]	That Old Feeling	1966	$25
REPRISE			
❑ R-6268 [M]	Laura (What's He Got That I Ain't Got)	1967	$35
❑ RS-6268 [S]	Laura (What's He Got That I Ain't Got)	1967	$18
RHINO			
❑ RNFP71497	The Brook Benton Anthology (1959-1970)	1986	$15
WING			
❑ MGW-12314 [M]	Brook Benton	1966	$15
❑ SRW-16314 [S]	Brook Benton	1966	$15
BENTON, WALTER			
JAZZLAND			
❑ JLP-28 [M]	Out of This World	1960	$500
—orange label			
❑ JLP-928 [S]	Out of This World	1960	$150
—black label			
BERBERIAN, JOHN, WITH THE ROCK EAST ENSEMBLE			
MAINSTREAM			
❑ S-6123	Impressions East	1969	$120
VERVE FORECAST			
❑ FTS-3073 [B]	Middle Eastern Rock	1969	$75
BERG, BOB			
RED			
❑ VPA-178	Steppin' -- Live in Europe	1985	$30
XANADU			
❑ 159	New Birth	1978	$35

Number	Title	Yr	NM
BERG, GERTRUDE			
AMY			
❑ 8007 [M]	How to Be a Jewish Mother	1965	$30
BERGAMO, JOHN			
CMP			
❑ CMP-27-ST	On the Edge	1987	$25
BERGEN, FRANCES			
COLUMBIA			
❑ CL873 [M]	The Beguiling Miss Bergen	1956	$30
BERGEN, POLLY			
COLUMBIA			
❑ CL1300 [M]	All Alone by the Telephone	1959	$25
❑ CS8100 [S]	All Alone by the Telephone	1959	$30
❑ CL994 [M]	Bergen Sings Morgan	1957	$30
❑ CL1632 [M]	Do Re Mi" and "Annie Get Your Gun	1961	$25
❑ CS8432 [S]	Do Re Mi" and "Annie Get Your Gun	1961	$30
❑ CL1451 [M]	Four Seasons of Love	1960	$25
❑ CS8246 [S]	Four Seasons of Love	1960	$30
❑ CL1218 [M]	My Heart Sings	1959	$25
❑ CS8018 [S]	My Heart Sings	1959	$30
❑ CL1138 [M]	Polly and Her Pop	1958	$30
❑ CL1031 [M]	The Party's Over	1957	$30
JUBILEE			
❑ JGL-14 [10]	Polly Bergen	1955	$50
PHILIPS			
❑ PHM200084 [M]	Act One -- Sing, Too	1963	$18
❑ PHS600084 [S]	Act One -- Sing, Too	1963	$25
BERGER, BENGT			
ECM			
❑ 1179	Bitter Funeral Beer	1981	$30
BERGER, KARL			
CMC			
❑ 00101	Peace Church	197?	$25
ENJA			
❑ 2022	With Silence	1974	$35
ESP-DISK'			
❑ 1041 [M]	Karl Berger	1967	$300
❑ S-1041 [S]	Karl Berger	1967	$300
MILESTONE			
❑ MSP-9026	Tune In	1969	$35
BERGMAN, BORAH			
CHIAROSCURO			
❑ 158	Bursts of Joy	1979	$30
❑ 125	Discovery	1973	$35
❑ 118	Solo	1972	$35
SOUL NOTE			
❑ SN-1030	New Frontier	1984	$30
❑ SN-1080	Upside Down Visions	1985	$30
BERIGAN, BUNNY, AND WINGY MANONE			
X			
❑ LVA-3034 [10]	Swing Session 1934	1954	$100
BERIGAN, BUNNY			
BIOGRAPH			
❑ C-10	Bunny Berigan 1932-37	197?	$30
BLUEBIRD			
❑ AXM2-5584	The Complete Bunny Berigan, Volume 1	197?	$35
❑ 5657-1-RB	The Complete Bunny Berigan, Volume 2	1987	$35
❑ 9953-1-RB	The Complete Bunny Berigan, Volume 3	1990	$35
EPIC			
❑ LA16004 [M]	Bunny Berigan and His Boys	196?	$25
❑ LN3109 [M]	Take It, Bunny!	1955	$150
HINDSIGHT			
❑ HSR-239	Bunny Berigan 1937-38	1988	$25
JAZZ ARCHIVES			
❑ JA-11	Down by the Old Mill Stream	198?	$25
MCA			
❑ 1362	Decca/Champion Sessions	198?	$30
RCA CAMDEN			
❑ CAL-550 [M]	Bunny	195?	$25
RCA VICTOR			
❑ LPV-550 [M]	Bunny	1966	$25
❑ LPT-10 [10]	Bunny Berigan 1937-38	1951	$100
❑ LPT-1003 [M]	Bunny Berigan Plays Again	1952	$50
❑ LPM-2078 [M]	Great Dance Bands of the 30s and 40s	1959	$40
TIME-LIFE			
❑ STL-J-25	Giants of Jazz	1982	$50

Number	Title	Yr	NM
BERIGAN, BUNNY/JACK TEAGARDEN			
FOLKWAYS			
❑ FJ-2819	The Big Band Sound of Bunny Berigan and Jack Teagarden	1982	$30
BERK, DICK, AND THE JAZZ ADOPTION AGENCY			
DISCOVERY			
❑ DS-890	Big Jake	1986	$25
❑ DS-922	More Birds Less Feathers	1987	$25
❑ DS-877	The Rare One	1985	$25
TREND			
❑ 550	Lover	198?	$25
BERLE, MILTON			
FORUM			
❑ F-9005 [M]	Songs My Mother Loved	1963	$25
ROULETTE			

Number	Title	Yr	NM
❑ R-25018 [M]	Songs My Mother Loved	1957	$40
BERLIN			
CLEOPATRA			
❑ 3741 [B]	Greatest Hits		$25
ENIGMA			
❑ 3 [EP]	Pleasure Victim	1982	$30
—Original issue			
GEFFEN			
❑ R100731	Best of Berlin 1979-1988	1988	$25
—BMG Direct Marketing edition			
❑ GHS24187	Best of Berlin 1979-1988	1988	$18
❑ R153624	Count Three and Pray	1986	$12
—RCA Music Service edition			
❑ GHS24121	Count Three and Pray	1986	$10
❑ GHS4025	Love Life	1984	$12
❑ GHS2036 [EP]	Pleasure Victim	1982	$10
❑ PRO-A-2121 [EP]	Selections from Love Life	1984	$15
—Four-song promo sampler (Touch/Now It's My Turn/In My Dreams/No More Words)			
BERLINER, JAY			
MAINSTREAM			
❑ 384	Bananas Not Equal	1973	$35
BERLINER, PAUL, AND KUDU			
FLYING FISH			
❑ FF-092	The Sun Rises Later Here	1979	$35
BERMAN, SHELLEY			
METRO			
❑ M-546 [M]	Let Me Tell You a Funny Story	1965	$18
❑ MS-546 [R]	Let Me Tell You a Funny Story	1965	$15
VERVE			
❑ MGV-15027 [M]	A Personal Appearance	1961	$25
❑ V-15027 [M]	A Personal Appearance	1962	$18
❑ V6-15027 [R]	A Personal Appearance	196?	$15
❑ V-15048 [M]	Great Moments in Comedy	1965	$25
❑ V6-15048 [R]	Great Moments in Comedy	1965	$18
❑ MGV-15008-2 [M]	Inside and Outside Shelley Berman	1959	$30
❑ V-15008-2 [M]	Inside and Outside Shelley Berman	1962	$25
❑ MGV-15003 [M]	Inside Shelley Berman	1959	$30
❑ V-15003 [M]	Inside Shelley Berman	1962	$18
❑ V6-15003 [R]	Inside Shelley Berman	196?	$15
❑ V-15036 [M]	New Sides	1962	$18
❑ V6-15036 [R]	New Sides	196?	$15
❑ MGV-15007 [M]	Outside Shelley Berman	1959	$30
❑ V-15007 [M]	Outside Shelley Berman	1962	$18
❑ V6-15007 [R]	Outside Shelley Berman	196?	$15
❑ MGV-15013 [M]	The Edge of Shelley Berman	1960	$30
❑ V-15013 [M]	The Edge of Shelley Berman	1962	$18

Number	Title	Yr	NM
❏ V6-15013 [R]	The Edge of Shelley Berman	196?	$15
❏ V-15043 [M]	The Sex Life of the Primate (And Other Bits of Gossip)	1964	$25
❏ V6-15043 [R]	The Sex Life of the Primate (And Other Bits of Gossip)	1964	$18

BERMAN, SONNY
ESOTERIC

Number	Title	Yr	NM
❏ ES-532 [M]	Sonny Berman 1946	1954	$120

BERNARD, ROD
JIN

❏ LP-4007 [M]	Rod Bernard	196?	$75

BERNARDI, HERSCHEL
COLUMBIA

❏ C30004	Show Stopper	1970	$25

COLUMBIA MASTERWORKS

❏ OL6610 [M]	Fiddler on the Roof	1966	$25
❏ OS3010 [S]	Fiddler on the Roof	1966	$30

BERNE, TIM, AND BILL FRISELL
EMPIRE

❏ EPC72K	...Theoretically	1984	$50

MINOR MUSIC

❏ 08	…Theoretically	1986	$35

BERNE, TIM
COLUMBIA

❏ FC40530	Fulton Street Maul	1987	$30
❏ FC44073	Sanctified Dreams	1987	$30

EMPIRE

❏ EPC36K	7X	1980	$50
❏ EPC60K-2	Songs and Rituals in Real Time	1982	$75
❏ EPC48K	Spectres	1981	$50
❏ EPC24K	The Five Year Plan	1979	$50

JMT

❏ 834431-1	Fractured Fairy Tales	1989	$35

SOUL NOTE

❏ SN-1091	Mutant Variations	1984	$30
❏ SN-1061	The Ancestors	1983	$30

BERNHARDT, WARREN
ARISTA/NOVUS

❏ AN3011	Floating	1979	$30
❏ AN3020	Manhattan Update	1980	$30
❏ AN3001	Solo Piano	1978	$30

BERNHART, MILT
DECCA

❏ DL9214 [M]	The Sounds of Bernhart	1959	$100
❏ DL79214 [S]	The Sounds of Bernhart	1959	$100

RCA VICTOR

❏ LPM-1123 [M]	Modern Brass	1955	$300

BERNSTEIN, LEONARD
COLUMBIA

❏ CL919 [M]	What Is Jazz?	1956	$150
—Red and black label with six "eye" logos			

BERRY, BILL
CONCORD JAZZ

❏ CJ-27	Hello Rev	1977	$30
❏ CJ-75	Shortcake	1978	$30

DIRECTIONAL SOUND

❏ 5002 [M]	Jazz and Swinging Percussion	1963	$25
❏ S-5002 [S]	Jazz and Swinging Percussion	1963	$30

PARADE

❏ SP-353 [M]	Broadway Escapades	196?	$25

REAL TIME

❏ 101 [B]	For Duke	1980	$200
—Direct-to-disc recording			

BERRY, BROOKS, AND SCRAPPER BLACKWELL
BLUESVILLE

❏ BVLP-1074 [M]	My Heart Struck Sorrow	1963	$100
—Blue label, silver print			
❏ BVLP-1074 [M]	My Heart Struck Sorrow	1964	$30
—Blue label with trident logo			

BERRY, CHU
COMMODORE

❏ XFL15353	A Giant of the Tenor Sax	198?	$25
❏ DL-30017 [M]	Chu Berry	1959	$100
❏ FL-20024 [10]	Chu Berry Memorial	1952	$300

ENCORE

❏ EE22007	Chu (1936-1940)	1968	$35

EPIC

❏ LG3124 [M]	Chu	1955	$175

MAINSTREAM

❏ 56038 [M]	Sittin' In	1965	$30
❏ S-6038 [R]	Sittin' In	1965	$35

BERRY, CHUCK
ACCORD

❏ SN-7171	Toronto Rock 'N' Roll Revival, Vol. 2	1982	$12
❏ SN-7172	Toronto Rock 'N' Roll Revival, Vol. 3	1982	$12

ATCO

❏ SD 38-118	Rockit	1979	$15

CHESS

❏ LP-1426 [M]	After School Session	1958	$250
❏ LPS-1426 [R]	After School Session	196?	$15
❏ CH-9284	After School Session	1989	$12
—Reissue of 1426			
❏ LPS-1550	Back Home	1970	$25
❏ CH-50043	Chuck Berry/Bio	1973	$25
❏ LP-1495 [M]	Chuck Berry in London	1965	$30
❏ LPS-1495 [S]	Chuck Berry in London	1965	$40
❏ LP-1435 [M]	Chuck Berry Is On Top	1959	$180
❏ LPS-1435 [R]	Chuck Berry Is On Top	196?	$15
❏ CH-9256	Chuck Berry Is On Top	1987	$12
—Reissue of 1435			
❏ LP-1480 [M]	Chuck Berry On Stage	1963	$120
❏ LPS-1480 [R]	Chuck Berry On Stage	196?	$15
❏ LP-1514 [M]	Chuck Berry's Golden Decade	1967	$40
❏ LPS-1514 [R]	Chuck Berry's Golden Decade	1967	$25
—Old cover does not have a pink radio			
❏ 2CH-1514 [R]	Chuck Berry's Golden Decade	1972	$18
—New cover has a pink radio			
❏ 2CH-60023	Chuck Berry's Golden Decade, Vol. 2	1973	$30
❏ 2CH-60028	Chuck Berry's Golden Decade, Vol. 3	1974	$30
❏ LP-1485 [M]	Chuck Berry's Greatest Hits	1964	$120
❏ LPS-1485 [R]	Chuck Berry's Greatest Hits	196?	$15
❏ LP-1465 [M]	Chuck Berry Twist	1962	$150
❏ LP-1498 [M]	Fresh Berry's	1965	$30
❏ LPS-1498 [S]	Fresh Berry's	1965	$40
❏ CH-9318	Missing Berries: Rarities, Volume 3	1990	$12
❏ LP-1465 [M]	More Chuck Berry	1963	$120
—Retitled version of above			
❏ LPS-1465 [R]	More Chuck Berry	196?	$15
❏ CH-9190	More Rock 'n' Roll Rarities	1986	$12
❏ LP-1456 [M]	New Juke Box Hits	1961	$180
❏ CH-9171	New Juke Box Hits	1986	$12
—Reissue of 1456			
❏ LP-1432 [M]	One Dozen Berrys	1958	$250
❏ LPS-1432 [R]	One Dozen Berrys	196?	$15
❏ CH-9259	Rockin' at the Hop	1987	$12
—Reissue of 1448			

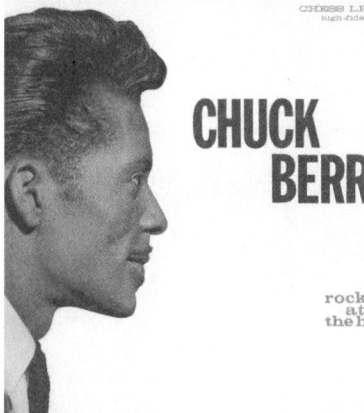

CHESS LP 1448
high-fidelity

CHUCK BERRY

rockin' at the hops

❏ LP-1448 [M]	Rockin' at the Hops	1960	$180
❏ CH2-92521	Rock 'n' Roll Rarities	1986	$18
❏ CH-50008	San Fransisco Dues	1971	$25
❏ LP-1488 [M]	St. Louis to Liverpool	1964	$75
❏ LPS-1488 [S]	St. Louis to Liverpool	1964	$100
❏ CH-9186	St. Louis to Liverpool	1988	$12
—Reissue of 1488			
❏ CH6-80001	The Chess Box	1989	$50
❏ CH2-92500	The Great Twenty-Eight	1983	$15
❏ CH-60020	The London Chuck Berry Sessions	1972	$25
❏ CH-9295	The London Chuck Berry Sessions	1989	$12
—Reissue of 60020			

EVEREST ARCHIVE OF FOLK & JAZZ

❏ FS-321	Chuck Berry's Greatest Hits	1976	$12

GUSTO

❏ 0004	The Best of the Best of Chuck Berry	198?	$12

MERCURY

❏ MG-21123 [M]	Chuck Berry in Memphis	1967	$25
❏ SR-61123 [S]	Chuck Berry in Memphis	1967	$18
❏ MG-21103 [M]	Chuck Berry's Golden Hits	1967	$25
❏ SR-61103 [S]	Chuck Berry's Golden Hits	1967	$18
❏ 826256-1	Chuck Berry's Golden Hits	1985	$10
—Reissue			
❏ SR-61223	Concerto in B Goode	1969	$25
❏ SR-61176	From St. Louie to Frisco	1968	$25
❏ MG-21138 [M]	Love at the Fillmore Auditorium	1967	$25
❏ SR-61138 [S]	Love at the Fillmore Auditorium	1967	$25
❏ SRM-2-6501	St. Louis to Frisco to Memphis	1972	$25

PICKWICK

❏ PTP-2061	Flashback	1975	$15
❏ SPC-3327	Johnny B. Goode	1973	$12
❏ SPC-3345	Sweet Little Rock and Roller	1974	$12
❏ SPC-3392	Wild Berrys	1974	$12

QUICKSILVER

❏ QS-1017	Live Hits	198?	$12

SSS INTERNATIONAL

❏ 36	Chuck Berry Live	1981	$12

BERRY, KEN
BARNABY

❏ Z30094	Ken Berry, R.F.D.	1970	$30
❏ Z30014	R.F.D.	1970	$30

BERRY, MIKE
EPIC

❏ JE36071	I'm a Rocker	1979	$12

SIRE

❏ SASD7524	Rocks in My Head	1976	$18

BERRY, RICHARD
CROWN

❏ CLP-5371 [M]	Richard Berry and the Dreamers	1963	$75
❏ CST-371 [R]	Richard Berry and the Dreamers	1963	$40

PAM

❏ 1001	Live at the Century Restaurant	1968	$40
❏ 1002	Wild Berry	196?	$40

BERRY, SCOTT WITH TOUCH
TIGER LILY

❏ TL14005 [B]	Morning Glory	1976	$150

BERT, EDDIE
DISCOVERY

❏ DL-3020 [M]	Eddie Bert Quintet	1953	$300

JAZZTONE

❏ J-1223 [M]	Modern Moods	1956	$250

SAVOY

❏ MG-12019 [M]	Encore	1955	$120
❏ MG-12015 [M]	Musician of the Year	1955	$85

SAVOY JAZZ

❏ SJL-1186	Kaleidoscope	198?	$25

SOMERSET

❏ SF-5200 [M]	Like Cool	1958	$40
—Reissue of Trans World LP			

TRANS WORLD

❏ TWLP-208 [M]	Let's Dig Bert	1955	$150

BERTONCINI, GENE, AND MICHAEL MOORE
OMNISOUND

❏ GJB-3333	Bridges	198?	$30
❏ GJB-3334	Close Ties	198?	$30

STASH

❏ ST-258	O Grande Amor: A Bossa Nova Collection	1986	$25
❏ ST-272	Strollin'	1987	$25

BERTONCINI, GENE
EVOLUTION

❏ 3001	Evolution	1969	$35

BEST, JOHNNY/DICK CATHCART
MERCURY

❏ PPM-2009 [M]	Dixieland	1961	$150
❏ PPS-6009 [S]	Dixieland (Left and Right)	1961	$150
—Odd record with Best's band in the left channel and Cathcart's in the right!			

BEST, PETER (1)
PHOENIX

❏ PHX-340	The Beatle That Time Forgot	1982	$15

Number	Title	Yr	NM

SAVAGE
❏ BM-71 — Best of the Beatles — 1966 — $250
—Authentic copies have white circle around the word "Savage" and white circle around Pete Best's head on the album cover.

BETH, KAREN
DECCA
❏ DL75247 — Harvest — 1970 — $18
❏ DL75148 — The Joys of Life — 1969 — $18

BETHLEHEM CHOIR, THE
COMPOSE
❏ S98022 — The Bethlehem Choir with Organ and Chimes — 1967 — $15

BETTER THAN EZRA
ELEKTRA
❏ 61944 — Friction, Baby — 1996 — $15

BETTERS, HAROLD
GATEWAY
❏ GLP-7014 [M] — Do Anything You Wanna — 1966 — $25
❏ GS-7014 [S] — Do Anything You Wanna — 1966 — $35
❏ GLP-7008 [M] — Even Better — 1966 — $25
❏ GS-7008 [S] — Even Better — 1966 — $35
❏ GLP-7001 [M] — Harold Betters at the Encore — 1964 — $25
❏ GS-7001 [S] — Harold Betters at the Encore — 1964 — $35
❏ GLP-7009 [M] — Harold Betters Meets Slide Hampton — 1966 — $25
❏ GS-7009 [S] — Harold Betters Meets Slide Hampton — 1966 — $35
❏ 7021 — Jazz Showcase — 197? — $30
❏ GLP-7015 [M] — Swingin' on the Railroad — 1966 — $25
❏ GS-7015 [S] — Swingin' on the Railroad — 1966 — $35
❏ GLP-7004 [M] — Take Off — 1964 — $25
❏ GS-7004 [S] — Take Off — 1964 — $35
❏ 7017 — The Best of Betters — 197? — $30
REPRISE
❏ R-6241 [M] — Funk City Express — 1966 — $35
❏ RS-6241 [S] — Funk City Express — 1966 — $25
❏ R-6208 [M] — Out of Sight and Sound — 1966 — $35
❏ RS-6208 [S] — Out of Sight and Sound — 1966 — $25
❏ R-6195 [M] — Ram-Bunk-Shush — 1965 — $35
❏ RS-6195 [S] — Ram-Bunk-Shush — 1965 — $25

BETTS, DICKEY
ARISTA
❏ AL4168 — Atlanta's Burning Down — 1978 — $12
❏ AL4123 — Dickey Betts & Great Southern — 1977 — $12
CAPRICORN
❏ CP 0123 — Highway Call — 1974 — $15
—As "Richard Betts
EPIC
❏ FE44289 — Pattern Disruptive — 1988 — $12

BETTY BOO
SIRE
❏ 26360 — Boomania — 1990 — $15

BEVEL, CHARLES
A&M
❏ SP-4412 — Meet "Mississippi Charles — 1973 — $15

BEVERLY HILL BILLIES, THE
RAR-ARTS
❏ 1000 [M] — Those Fabulous Beverly Hill Billies — 1961 — $150
—Gold vinyl

BIANCO
RCA/READER'S DIGEST
❏ CPM-104 [M] — Joy to the World — 1962 — $18
❏ CSP-104 [S] — Joy to the World — 1962 — $25

BICKERT, ED, AND DON THOMPSON
SACKVILLE
❏ 4010 — Dance to the Lady — 198? — $25
❏ 4005 — Ed Bickert & Don Thompson — 198? — $25

BICKERT, ED
CONCORD JAZZ
❏ CJ-232 — Bye Bye Baby — 1983 — $25
❏ CJ-216 — Ed Bickert at Toronto's Bourbon Street — 1982 — $25
❏ CJ-284 — I Wished on the Moon — 1985 — $25
❏ CJ-380 — Third Floor Richard — 1989 — $25
PM
❏ PMR-010 — Ed Bickert — 1976 — $30

BIDDU ORCHESTRA
EPIC
❏ PE33903 — Biddu Orchestra — 1975 — $12
❏ PE34723 — Eastern Man — 1977 — $12

❏ PE34230 — Rain Forest — 1976 — $12

BIELEFELDER KINDERCHOR, THE
CAPITOL
❏ T10308 [M] — A German Christmas — 196? — $18

BIG AUDIO DYNAMITE
Includes records as "Big Audio Dynamite II" and "Big Audio." Features Mick Jones, formerly of THE CLASH.
COLUMBIA
❏ FC45212 — Megatop Phoenix — 1989 — $12
❏ BFC40445 — No. 10 Upping Street — 1986 — $15
❏ BFC40705 — No. 10 Upping Street — 1986 — $12
—Reissue with extra track, "Badrock City
❏ C46147 [B] — The Globe — 1991 — $25
❏ BFC40220 — This Is Big Audio Dynamite — 1985 — $12
❏ FC44074 — Tighten Up Vol. 88 — 1988 — $12
RADIOACTIVE
❏ 11280 — F-Punk — 1995 — $18

BIG BEATS, THE
LIBERTY
❏ LRP-3407 [M] — The Big Beats Live — 1965 — $30
❏ LST-7407 [S] — The Big Beats Live — 1965 — $40

BIG BLACK
HOMESTEAD
❏ HMS 043 [B] — Atomizer — 1986 — $50
❏ HMS 007 [EP] — Racer X — 1983 — $150
❏ HMS 044 [B] — The Hammer Party — 1986 — $75
RUTHLESS
❏ 0(# unknown) [EP] — Bulldozer — 1983 — $100
❏ 0(# unknown) [EP] — Lungs — 1982 — $175
TOUCH & GO
❏ TG93 [B] — Atomizer — 1992 — $30
—Reissue of Homestead 043
❏ TG111 — Boxes — 1992 — $150
—Box set containing the Pigpile LP, video, T-shirt and poster
❏ TG90 [EP] — Bulldozer — 1992 — $30
—Reissue
❏ TG20 [EP] — Headache — 1987 — $30
❏ TG20 [EP] — Headache — 1987 — $150
—With "gross" cover (different from regular issue), red vinyl record, bonus 7-inch single, book and poster
❏ TG89 [EP] — Lungs — 1992 — $30
—Reissue
❏ TG81 [B] — Pigpile — 1992 — $30
❏ TG91 [EP] — Racer X — 1992 — $30
—Reissue of Homestead 007
❏ TG24 [B] — Songs About Fucking — 1987 — $75
❏ 0(no cat #) [DJ] — The Incredibly Corporate Whorish Big Black Interview Album — 1987 — $85
UNI
❏ 73134 — Big Black and the Blues — 1972 — $18
❏ 73018 — Elements of Now — 1968 — $18
❏ 73033 — Lion Walk — 1969 — $18

BIG BOPPER
MERCURY
❏ MG-20402 [M] — Chantilly Lace — 1959 — $500
—Black label
❏ MG-20402 [M] — Chantilly Lace — 1964 — $250
—Red label with black or black & white Mercury logo at top
❏ MG-20402 [M] — Chantilly Lace — 196? — $30
—Red label with twelve Mercury logos on label edge
❏ MG-20402 [M] — Chantilly Lace — 1975 — $18
—Chicago skyline label
❏ 832902-1 [M] — Chantilly Lace — 1988 — $18
—New number, black label
PICKWICK
❏ SPC-3365 — Chantilly Lace — 1973 — $18
RHINO
❏ R1-70164 — Helloooo Baby! The Best of the Big Bopper 1954-1959 — 1989 — $15

BIG BOYS
ENIGMA
❏ E-1128 — Lullabies Help the Brain Grow — 1984 — $18
—Reissue of Moment 002
❏ 72028 — No Matter How Long the Line Is at the Cafeteria, There's Always a Seat — 1984 — $30
MOMENT
❏ 01 — Fun, Fun, Fun — 1982 — $100
❏ 002 — Lullabies Help the Brain Grow — 1983 — $50
RAT RACE
❏ RRR80351 — Recorded Live at Raul's — 1980 — $100
—One side features the Big Boys; the other side, the Dicks

UNSEEN HAND
❏ UHT727-3 — Wreck Collection — 1988 — $18

❏ JWP3405 — Where's My Towel/Industry Standard — 1981 — $75

BIG BROTHER
ALL-AMERICAN
❏ 5770 — Big Brother — 1970 — $300

BIG BROTHER AND THE HOLDING COMPANY
Also see JANIS JOPLIN.
COLUMBIA
❏ C30222 — Be a Brother — 1970 — $25
❏ C30631 — Big Brother and the Holding Company — 1971 — $25
—Reissue of Mainstream LP with two extra tracks
❏ KCS9700 [M] — Cheap Thrills — 1968 — $300
—White label "Special Mono Radio Station Copy" with stereo number
❏ KCS9700 [S] — Cheap Thrills — 1968 — $30
—Red "360 Sound" label
❏ KCS9700 — Cheap Thrills — 1970 — $15
—Orange label
❏ PC9700 — Cheap Thrills — 198? — $10
—Reissue with new prefix
❏ KCL2900 [M] — Cheap Thrills — 1968 — $500
—Red label stock copy has been confirmed
❏ C30738 — How Hard It Is — 1971 — $25
COLUMBIA SPECIAL PRODUCTS
❏ P13313 — Big Brother and the Holding Company — 197? — $18
LEGACY
❏ KC2900 [B] — Cheap Thrills — 2012 — $30
MAINSTREAM
❏ 56099 [M] — Big Brother and the Holding Company — 1967 — $175
❏ S-6099 [S] — Big Brother and the Holding Company — 1967 — $50
RHINO
❏ RNLP121 — Live — 1984 — $25
—Recorded 1966

BIG BUB
KEDAR/UNIVERSAL
❏ 53074 — Timeless — 1997 — $12

BIG CHIEF
GET HIP
❏ GH-1004 [B] — Drive It Off — 1991 — $18
SUB POP
❏ SP147 [B] — Face — 1992 — $25

BIG COUNTRY
MERCURY
❏ 822831-1 — Steeltown — 1984 — $12
❏ 812870-1 — The Crossing — 1983 — $12
—Embossed print on front cover
❏ 812870-1 — The Crossing — 198? — $10
—No embossed print on front cover
❏ 826844-1 — The Seer — 1986 — $12
❏ 818835-1 [EP] — Wonderland — 1984 — $10
REPRISE
❏ 25787 — Peace in Our Time — 1988 — $12

BIG DADDY
REGENT
❏ MG-6106 [M] — Twist Party — 1962 — $80
RHINO
❏ RNLP-852 — Big Daddy — 198? — $12
❏ RNLP-854 — Meanwhile... Back in the States — 1985 — $12

BIG ED
NO LIMIT/PRIORITY
❏ P1-50729 — The Assassin — 1998 — $15

BIG FOOT
WINRO
❏ 1004 — Big Foot — 1969 — $30

BIG HEAD TODD AND THE MONSTERS
BIG
❏ BR-0001 — Another Mayberry — 1989 — $18
GIANT
❏ 24580 — Strategem — 1994 — $18

BIG L
COLUMBIA
❏ C53795 — Lifestylez Ov Da Poor and Dangerous — 1995 — $18
RAWKUS
❏ RWK1178 — The Big Picture 1974-1999 — 2000 — $18

Number	Title	Yr	NM
BIG LADY K			
PRIORITY			
❏ SL57109	Bigger Than Life	1990	$15
BIG MAYBELLE			
BRUNSWICK			
❏ BL754142	The Gospel Soul of Big Maybelle	1968	$40
❏ BL54107 [M]	What More Can a Woman Do	1962	$50
❏ BL754107 [S]	What More Can a Woman Do	1962	$80
EPIC			
❏ EE22011 [M]	Gabbin' Blues	196?	$30
—Reissue of Okeh recordings			
PARAMOUNT			
❏ PAS-1011	The Last of Big Maybelle	1973	$30
ROJAC			
❏ R522 [M]	Got a Brand New Bag	1967	$40
❏ RS522 [S]	Got a Brand New Bag	1967	$40
❏ RS123	Saga of the Good Life and Hard Times	196?	$40
SAVOY			
❏ MG-14005 [M]	Big Maybelle Sings	1957	$300
❏ MG-14011 [M]	Blues, Candy and Big Maybelle	1958	$300
SAVOY JAZZ			
❏ SJL-1168	Blues, Candy and Big Maybelle	1986	$12
—Reissue of 14011			
❏ SJL-1143	Roots of Rock 'n' Roll Vol. 13: Blues & Early Soul	1985	$12
SCEPTER			
❏ S-522 [M]	The Soul of Big Maybelle	1964	$40
❏ SS-522 [S]	The Soul of Big Maybelle	1964	$50
BIG NOISE			
ATCO			
❏ 91296	Bang!	1989	$12
BIG NOYD			
TOMMY BOY			
❏ 1156	Episodes of a Hustla	1996	$15
BIG PIG			
A&M			
❏ SP-6-5185	Bonk	1988	$12
BIG PUNISHER			
LOUD			
❏ 67512	Capital Punishment	1998	$18
❏ 1963	Endangered Species	2001	$15
❏ C263843	Yeeeah Baby	2000	$18
BIG RIC			
SCOTTI BROTHERS			
❏ BFZ38864	Big Ric	1983	$12
BIG STAR			
4 MEN WITH BEARDS			
❏ 4M240 [B]	#1 Record	2014	$25
❏ 4M-142	3rd	2006	$18
—Reissue on 180-gram vinyl			
❏ 4M241 [B]	Radio City	2014	$25
ARDENT			

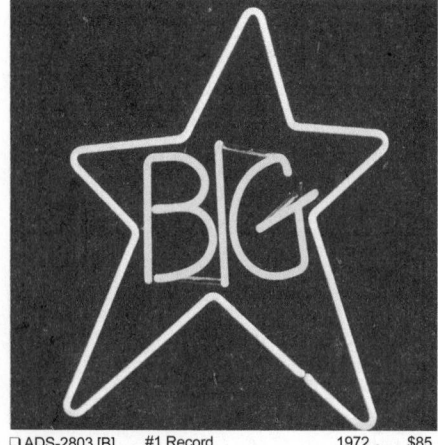

❏ ADS-2803 [B]	#1 Record	1972	$85
❏ ADS-1501	Radio City	1974	$50
DBK WORKS			
❏ DBK115	In Space	2005	$18

Number	Title	Yr	NM
PVC			
❏ 7903	Big Star's Third	1978	$40
❏ 8933	Sister Lovers	1985	$18
—Reissue of PVC 7903 with new title			
BIG THREE, THE			
FM			
❏ 311 [M]	Live at the Recording Studio	1964	$30
❏ S-311 [S]	Live at the Recording Studio	1964	$40
❏ 307 [M]	The Big Three	1963	$30
❏ S-307 [S]	The Big Three	1963	$40
ROULETTE			
❏ R-42000 [M]	The Big Three Featuring Cass Elliot	1967	$25
❏ SR-42000 [S]	The Big Three Featuring Cass Elliot	1967	$30
BIG TROUBLE			
EPIC			
❏ BFC40850	Big Trouble	1987	$10
BIG WHEELIE AND THE HUB CAPS			
SCEPTER			
❏ SPS-5109	Solid Grease!	1973	$15
BIGARD, BARNEY, AND ART HODES			
DELMARK			
❏ DS-211	Bucket's Got a Hole In It	1969	$35
BIGARD, BARNEY			
LIBERTY			
❏ LRP-3072 [M]	Jazz Hall of Fame	1957	$40
BIGARD, BARNEY/ALBERT NICHOLAS			
RCA VICTOR			
❏ LPV-566 [M]	Barney Bigard/Albert Nicholas	1966	$25
BIGELOW, ARTHUR LYNDS			
COLUMBIA			
❏ CL750 [M]	Christmas Carillon	1955	$30
BIGGS, E. POWER			
COLUMBIA MASTERWORKS			
❏ ML5567 [M]	Joyeaux Noel: Twelve Noels by Louis Clark Daquin	1960	$18
❏ MS6167 [S]	Joyeaux Noel: Twelve Noels by Louis Clark Daquin	1960	$25
COLUMBIA SPECIAL PRODUCTS			
❏ P14076	Music for a Merry Christmas	1977	$12
BIGGS, RICHARD KEYS			
CAPITOL			
❏ T9013 [M]	Christmas Bells	1954	$25
COLUMBIA			
❏ CL6076 [10]	An Organ Concert of Carols	1950	$40
BIKINI KILL			
KILL ROCK STARS			
❏ 204 [EP]	Bikini Kill	1991	$60
❏ 218 [B]	Pussy Whipped	1993	$30
❏ 260	Reject All-American	1996	$12
BILK, ACKER, AND BENT FABRIC			
ATCO			
❏ 33-175 [M]	Together	1965	$30
❏ SD 33-175 [S]	Together	1965	$35
BILK, ACKER, AND KEN COLYER			
STOMP OFF			
❏ SOS-1119	It Looks Like a Big Time Tonight	198?	$25
BILK, ACKER			
ATCO			
❏ 33-144 [M]	Above the Stars	1962	$35
❏ SD 33-144 [S]	Above the Stars	1962	$50
❏ 33-181 [M]	Acker Bilk in Paris	1966	$30
❏ SD 33-181 [S]	Acker Bilk in Paris	1966	$35
❏ 33-168 [M]	A Touch of Latin	1964	$30
❏ SD 33-168 [S]	A Touch of Latin	1964	$35
❏ 33-158 [M]	Call Me Mister	1963	$35
❏ SD 33-158 [S]	Call Me Mister	1963	$50
❏ 33-170 [M]	Great Themes from Great Foreign Films	1965	$30
❏ SD 33-170 [S]	Great Themes from Great Foreign Films	1965	$35
❏ 33-197 [M]	Mood for Love	1966	$30
❏ SD 33-197 [S]	Mood for Love	1966	$35
❏ 33-150 [M]	Only You	1963	$35
❏ SD 33-150 [S]	Only You	1963	$50
❏ 33-129 [M]	Stranger on the Shore	1961	$35
❏ SD 33-129 [S]	Stranger on the Shore	1961	$50
GNP CRESCENDO			
❏ GNPS-2191	Acker Bilk Plays Lennon and McCartney	1988	$30

Number	Title	Yr	NM
❏ GNPS-2116	The Best of Acker Bilk: His Clarinet and Strings	198?	$25
❏ GNPS-2171	The Best of Acker Bilk: His Clarinet and Strings, Volume 2	198?	$25
REPRISE			
❏ R-6031 [M]	A Stranger No More	1962	$50
❏ RS-6031 [R]	A Stranger No More	1962	$35
BILLION DOLLAR BABIES			
Members of ALICE COOPER's band.			
POLYDOR			
❏ PRO 022 [DJ]	Battle Axe	1977	$30
—Promo-only sampler			
❏ PD-1-6100 [B]	Battle Axe	1977	$30
BILLY BOY			
PRESTIGE			
❏ PRLP-7389 [M]	Blues on the South Side	1965	$40
—As "Billy Boy Arnold			
❏ PRST-7389 [S]	Blues on the South Side	1965	$50
—As "Billy Boy Arnold			
BILLY HILL			
REPRISE			
❏ 25915	I Am Just a Rebel	1989	$12
BILLY SATELLITE			
CAPITOL			
❏ ST-12340	Billy Satellite	1984	$12
BIOHAZARD			
WARNER BROS.			
❏ 45595	State of the World Address	1994	$12
—Orange vinyl; comes in stickered clear vinyl cover			
BIRCHWOOD CHORALE			
PICKWICK			
❏ SPC-1031	Holiday Greetings	1980	$10
BIRCHWOOD POPS ORCHESTRA			
PICKWICK			
❏ SPC-1030	A Christmas Card	1980	$10
❏ SPC-1029	Silent Night	1980	$10
BIRDSONG, EDWIN			
ABC DUNHILL			
❏ DSX-51036	Can't Stop the Madness	1974	$18
PHILADELPHIA INT'L.			
❏ JZ35758 [B]	Edwin Birdsong	1978	$15
POLYDOR			
❏ PD-5057	Super Natural	1973	$15
❏ 24-4071	What It Is	1971	$15
SALSOUL			
❏ SA-8550 [B]	Funktaztic	1981	$15
BIRKIN, JANE, AND SERGE GAINSBOURG			
FONTANA			
❏ SRF-67610	Je T'aime	1970	$25
LIGHT IN THE ATTIC			
❏ LITA048 [B]	Jane Birkin - Serge Gainsbourg	2010	$30
—includes 7" single			
BIRTH CONTROL			
PROPHESY			
❏ PRS-1002	Birth Control: A New German Rock Group	1970	$40
BIS			
CAPITOL			
❏ 96439	Social Dancing	1999	$12
GRAND ROYAL			
❏ GR 060	Intendo	1998	$12
❏ GR 045	The New Transistor Heroes	1997	$12
❏ GR 040 [10]	This Is Teen-C Power	1997	$10
BISHOP, BOB			
ABC			
❏ ABCS-667	Somewhere in the Country	1969	$18
BISHOP, ELVIN			
ALLIGATOR			
❏ AL-4767	Big Fun	1987	$12
CAPRICORN			
❏ CPN-0215	Hog Heaven	1978	$15
❏ CP 0176	Hometown Boy Makes Good!	1976	$15
❏ CP 0151	Juke Joint Jump	1975	$15
❏ CP 0134 [B]	Let It Flow	1974	$15
❏ 2CP 0185	Live! Raisin' Hell	1977	$18
❏ CP 0165	Struttin' My Stuff	1975	$15
❏ CPN-0165	Struttin' My Stuff	1980	$12
—Reissue with revised prefix and Polygram distribution			

Number	Title	Yr	NM

EPIC
❑ KE31563	Rock My Soul	1972	$18
❑ PE33693	The Best of Elvin Bishop	1975	$15

FILLMORE
❑ F30001	Elvin Bishop Group	1969	$25
❑ Z30239	Feel It	1970	$25

BISHOP, JOEY
ABC
❑ ABCS-656	Joey Bishop Sings Country and Western	1968	$30

BISHOP, JOHN
TANGERINE
❑ TRCS-1508	Bishop's Whirl	1969	$35
❑ TRCS-1513	John Bishop Plays His Guitar	1970	$35

BISHOP, STEPHEN
ABC
❑ AA-1082	Bish	1977	$10
❑ ABCD-954	Careless	1976	$10

ATLANTIC
❑ PRO(# unknown) [DJ]	Bish Is Back!	1989	$25
—Promo-only interview and music album			
❑ 81970	Bowling in Paris	1989	$12

MCA
❑ 37022	Bish	1980	$10
—Reissue of ABC 1082 (includes copies with gold stamped number on cover)			
❑ 37021	Careless	1980	$10
—Reissue of ABC 954 (includes copies with gold stamped number on cover)			

RHINO
❑ R1-70833	The Best of Bish	1988	$12

WARNER BROS.
❑ BSK3473	Red Cab to Manhattan	1980	$10
❑ PRO-A-907 [EP]	Red Cab to Manhattan Sampler	1980	$15
—Promo-only sampler (Big House; Let Her Go; The Story of a Boy in Love; Sex Kittens Go to College)			

BISHOP, WALTER, JR.
BLACK JAZZ
❑ 2	Coral Keys	1972	$35
❑ QD-14 [Q]	Keeper of My Soul	1974	$40

COTILLION
❑ SD236 [B]	Walter Bishop [aka Summertime]	1969	$300

INTERPLAY
❑ IP-8605	Just in Time	1988	$25

JAZZTIME
❑ JT-002 [M]	Speak Low	1961	$2000
❑ JS-002 [S]	Speak Low	1961	$300

MUSE
❑ 5151	Cubicle	1978	$30
❑ 5183	Hot House	1979	$30
❑ 5142	Soul Village	1977	$30
❑ 5066	Speak Low	1976	$30
—Reissue of Jazztime JS-002			
❑ 5060	Valley Land	1976	$30

PRESTIGE
❑ PRST-7730	The Walter Bishop Trio 1965	1969	$25

SEABREEZE
❑ 1002	Soliloquy	1975	$30

XANADU
❑ 114	Bish Bash	1977	$30

BIT 'A SWEET
ABC
❑ S-640	Hypnotic 1	1968	$40

BIVONA, GUS
MERCURY
❑ MG-20157 [M]	Hey, Dig That Crazy Band	195?	$30

BIZARROS, THE
MERCURY
❑ SRM-1-3776	The Bizarros	1979	$18

BJOERLING, JUSSI
RCA VICTOR RED SEAL
❑ LSC-2570 [S]	The Incomparable Jussi Bjoerling	1962	$25
—Original with "shaded dog" label			

BJORK
ELEKTRA
❑ ED6059 [DJ]	Homogenic	1997	$30
—WEA Manufacturing test pressing; regular promos are not			

Number	Title	Yr	NM
known to exist; the LP was not issued in the U.S. on vinyl			
❑ 61897	Telegram	1997	$15

BLAC MONKS
RAP-A-LOT
❑ 13153 [EP]	Hot Club Wax	1998	$18
—Promo-only sampler			
❑ 7082	Secrets of the Hidden Temple	1994	$18

BLACK, BILL, 'S COMBO
COLUMBIA
❑ CS1055	Basic Black	1970	$15
❑ CS9848	Black with Sugar	1969	$15
❑ CS9957	Raindrops Keep Fallin' on My Head	1970	$15

HI
❑ HL-12032 [M]	All Timers	1966	$15
❑ SHL-32032 [S]	All Timers	1966	$18
❑ 6005	Award Winners	1978	$12
❑ HL-12015 [M]	Bill Black Plays the Blues	1964	$18
❑ SHL-32015 [S]	Bill Black Plays the Blues	1964	$25
❑ HL-12017 [M]	Bill Black Plays Tunes by Chuck Berry	1964	$18
❑ SHL-32017 [S]	Bill Black Plays Tunes by Chuck Berry	1964	$25
❑ HL-12020 [M]	Bill Black's Combo Goes Big Band	1964	$18
❑ SHL-32020 [S]	Bill Black's Combo Goes Big Band	1964	$25
❑ HL-12013 [M]	Bill Black's Combo Goes West	1963	$18
❑ SHL-32013 [S]	Bill Black's Combo Goes West	1963	$25
❑ HL-12012 [M]	Bill Black's Greatest Hits	1963	$18
❑ SHL-32012 [S]	Bill Black's Greatest Hits	1963	$25
❑ XSHL-32078	Bill Black's Greatest Hits, Vol. 2	1973	$15
❑ HL-12006 [M]	Bill Black's Record Hop	1961	$30
❑ SHL-32006 [S]	Bill Black's Record Hop	1961	$30
❑ HL-12033 [M]	Black Lace	1966	$15
❑ SHL-32033 [S]	Black Lace	1966	$18
❑ SHL-32104	It's Honky Tonk Time	1976	$15
❑ HL-12036 [M]	King of the Road	1966	$15
❑ SHL-32036 [S]	King of the Road	1966	$18
❑ HL-12006 [M]	Let's Twist Her	1961	$18
—Retitled version of above			
❑ SHL-32006 [S]	Let's Twist Her	1961	$25
—Retitled version of above			
❑ 8004	Memphis Tennessee	1977	$12
❑ SHL-32061	More Magic	1971	$15
❑ HL-12023 [M]	More Solid and Raunchy	1965	$18
❑ SHL-32023 [S]	More Solid and Raunchy	1965	$25
❑ HL-12005 [M]	Movin'	1961	$25
❑ SHL-32005 [S]	Movin'	1961	$30
❑ HL-12027 [M]	Mr. Beat	1965	$18
❑ SHL-32027 [S]	Mr. Beat	1965	$25
❑ HL-12002 [M]	Saxy Jazz	1960	$40
❑ SHL-32002 [R]	Saxy Jazz	1964	$25
❑ HL-12001 [M]	Smokie	1960	$75
—Black label with red and silver logo			
❑ HL-12001 [M]	Smokie	1960	$40
—Orange and white label			
❑ SHL-32001 [R]	Smokie	1964	$25
❑ XSHL-32088	Solid and Country	1974	$15
❑ HL-12003 [M]	Solid and Raunchy	1960	$40
❑ SHL-32003 [R]	Solid and Raunchy	1964	$25
❑ SHL-32052	Solid and Raunchy The 3rd	1969	$18
❑ HL-12047 [M]	Soulin' the Blues	1968	$18
❑ SHL-32047 [S]	Soulin' the Blues	1968	$18
❑ HL-12004 [M]	That Wonderful Feeling	1961	$25
❑ SHL-32004 [S]	That Wonderful Feeling	1961	$30
❑ HL-12041 [M]	The Beat Goes On	1967	$18
❑ SHL-32041 [S]	The Beat Goes On	1967	$18
❑ HL-12009 [M]	The Untouchable Sound of Bill Black	1962	$18
❑ SHL-32009 [S]	The Untouchable Sound of Bill Black	1962	$25
❑ SHL-32093	The World's Greatest Honky Tonk Band	1975	$15
❑ HL-12044 [M]	Turn Your Lovelight On	1967	$18
❑ SHL-32044 [S]	Turn Your Lovelight On	1967	$18

MEGA
❑ MLPS-600	Bill Black Is Back	1973	$15
❑ 31-1014	Juke Box Favorites	1972	$15
❑ 51-5008	Rock 'n' Roll Forever	1973	$15
❑ 31-1008	The Memphis Scene	1971	$15

BLACK, CILLA
CAPITOL
❑ T2308 [M]	Is It Love?	1965	$30
❑ ST2308 [S]	Is It Love?	1965	$40

BLACK, CLINT
RCA
❑ 9668-1-R	Killin' Time	1989	$18
❑ R124690	Put Yourself in My Shoes	1990	$50
—Released on vinyl only through BMG Direct Marketing			

BLACK, FRANK
SPINART
❑ spart67	Frank Black and the Catholics	1998	$15

Number	Title	Yr	NM
❑ spart70	Pistolero	1999	$15

BLACK, JEANNE
CAPITOL
❑ T1513 [M]	A Little Bit Lonely	1961	$25
❑ ST1513 [S]	A Little Bit Lonely	1961	$30

BLACK BOTTOM STOMPERS (ENGLAND)
STOMP OFF
❑ SOS-1045	Stomp Off, Let's Go	1982	$25

BLACK BOTTOM STOMPERS (SWITZERLAND)
STOMP OFF
❑ SOS-1130	Four O'Clock Blues	1987	$25

BLACK BOX
RCA
❑ 2221-1-R	Dreamland	1990	$15

BLACK CROWES, THE
AMERICAN
❑ 43000 [B]	Amorica	1994	$30
—All copies of the vinyl LP retained the cover that was censored on most cassette and CD copies			

DEF AMERICAN
❑ 24278	Shake Your Money Maker	1990	$15

BLACK EYED PEAS
INTERSCOPE
❑ 90152	Behind the Front	1998	$15
❑ 490661	Bridging the Gap	2000	$15

BLACK FLAG
Note: Most, if not all, the below records on SST remain in print on vinyl. Not all editions are identical, but until we know the differences, we can't differentiate values. (One of the most obvious indicators of a reissue is the presence of a bar code on the back cover.)

SST
❑ 081 [EP]	Annihilate This Week	1986	$30
❑ 007	Damaged	198?	$12
—Reissue of Unicorn 9502			
❑ 015 [B]	Everything Went Black	1982	$40
❑ 026 [B]	Family Man	1984	$40
❑ 226 [EP]	I Can See You	1989	$30
❑ 045 [B]	In My Head	1985	$30
❑ 003 [EP]	Jealous Again	1980	$40
❑ 907 [10]	Jealous Again	199?	$10
—10-inch reissue of 003			
❑ 035 [B]	Loose Nut	1985	$35
❑ 023 [B]	My War	1984	$35
❑ 916 [10]	Nervous Breakdown	199?	$10
—10-inch reissue of 001 (7-inch EP)			

❑ 029 [B]	Slip It In	1984	$35
❑ 021 [B]	The First Four Years	1983	$30
❑ 037 [EP]	The Process of Weeding Out	1985	$30
❑ 924 [10]	The Process of Weeding Out	199?	$10
—10-inch reissue of 037			
❑ 166 [B]	Wasted Again	1987	$30
❑ 060	Who's Got the 10 1/2?	1986	$15

UNICORN/SST
❑ 9502	Damaged	1981	$30
—First pressings had stickers on the front and back covers -- the one on the back begins "As a parent...			
❑ 9502 [B]	Damaged	198?	$18
—With no stickers on cover			

BLACK HEART
GUINNESS
❑ GNS36025 [B]	Jigsaw	1977	$175

Number	Title	Yr	NM

BLACK HEAT
ATLANTIC
❏ SD7237	Black Heat	1972	$15
❏ SD18128	Keep On Burnin'	1975	$15
❏ SD7294	No Time to Burn	1974	$15

BLACK ICE
HDM
❏ 2001	Black Ice	1977	$18
❏ 2003	I Judge the Funk	1978	$18
MONTAGE
❏ ST-72003	Black Ice	1981	$18

BLACK IVORY
BUDDAH
❏ BDS-5658	Black Ivory	1976	$12
❏ BDS-5644	Feel It	1975	$12
❏ BDS-5722	Hangin' Heavy	1979	$12
TODAY
❏ 1008	Baby, Won't You Change Your Mind	1972	$15
❏ 1005	Don't Turn Around	1972	$15

BLACK KEYS, THE
FAT POSSUM
❏ 0371-1 [B]	Thickfreakness	2003	$18

BLACK LIGHTNING
TOWER
❏ ST5129	Shades of Black Lightning	1968	$25

BLACK MERDA
CHESS
❏ LP-1551	Black Merda	1970	$50

BLACK MOON
PRIORITY
❏ 50039	War Zone	1999	$15
WRECK
❏ 02002	Enta Da Stage	1993	$18

BLACK 'N BLUE
Includes Tommy Thayer, now in KISS.
GEFFEN
❏ GHS24041	Black 'N Blue	1984	$10
❏ GHS24180	In Heat	1988	$10
❏ GHS24111	Nasty Nasty	1986	$10
❏ GHS24075	Without You	1985	$10

BLACK OAK ARKANSAS
Includes drummer Tommy Aldridge of PAT TRAVERS and WHITESNAKE fame.
ATCO
❏ SD 36-111	Ain't Life Grand	1975	$15
❏ SD 33-354	Black Oak Arkansas	1971	$18
❏ SD7035	High on the Hog	1973	$18
❏ SD7008	If An Angel Came to See You, Would You Make Her Feel at Home?	1972	$18
❏ SD 33-381 [S]	Keep the Faith	1972	$18
❏ 33-381 [M]	Keep the Faith	1972	$100

—White label promo, "DJ Copy Monaural" sticker on cover; no stock copies were issued in mono

❏ SD 36-128	Live! Mutha	1976	$15
❏ SD7019	Raunch 'n' Roll/Live	1973	$18
❏ QD7019 [Q]	Raunch 'n' Roll/Live	1974	$40
❏ SD 36-101	Street Party	1974	$15
❏ SD 36-150	The Best of Black Oak Arkansas	1976	$15
CAPRICORN
❏ CP 0207	I'd Rather Be Sailing	1978	$15
❏ CP 0191	Race with the Devil	1977	$15
MCA
❏ 2224	10 Year Overnight Success	1977	$15
❏ 2199	Balls of Fire	1976	$15
❏ 2155	X-Rated	1975	$15
❏ 704	X-Rated	198?	$10

—Budget-line reissue

STAX
❏ STS-5504	Early Times	1974	$18

BLACK PEARL
ATLANTIC
❏ SD8220	Black Pearl	1969	$30
PROPHESY
❏ PRS-1001	Black Pearl -- Live!	1970	$30

BLACK RANDY AND THE METROSQUAD
DANGERHOUSE
❏ PCP725	Pass the Dust, I Think I'm Bowie	1980	$50

BLACK ROB
BAD BOY
❏ 73026	Life Story	2000	$18

Number	Title	Yr	NM

BLACK ROSE
With CHER on lead vocals.
CASABLANCA
❏ NBLP7234	Black Rose	1980	$30

—Promo copies, with "DJ" and "Promotional Copy Not for Sale" on label, go for less

BLACK SABBATH
Also see OZZY OSBOURNE; DIO; DEEP PURPLE; TRAPEZE.
I.R.S.
❏ 82002	Headless Cross	1989	$12
NEMS
❏ NEL6003 [B]	Paranoid	2011	$25
RHINO
❏ R1552926 [B]	Master of Reality	2016	$25

—180g

❏ R13186 [B]	Never Say Die!	2013	$30
❏ R1552927 [B]	Paranoid	2016	$40

—180g

❏ R12969 [B]	Technical Ecstasy	2013	$30
❏ R12923 [B]	We Sold Our Souls for Rock'n'Roll	2013	$40
WARNER BROS.
❏ R1552928 [B]	Black Sabbath	2016	$40

—180 gram

WARNER BROS.
❏ WS1871 [B]	Black Sabbath	1970	$30

—Green label

❏ WS1871	Black Sabbath	1973	$12

—Burbank" palm trees label

❏ WS1871	Black Sabbath	1979	$10

—White or tan label

❏ BS2602 [B]	Black Sabbath, Vol. 4	1972	$30

—Green label

❏ BS2602	Black Sabbath, Vol. 4	1973	$12

—Burbank" palm trees label

❏ BS2602	Black Sabbath, Vol. 4	1979	$10

—White or tan label

❏ 23978	Born Again	1983	$12
❏ BSK3372	Heaven and Hell	1980	$15
❏ 23742	Live Evil	1983	$18
❏ BS2562 [B]	Master of Reality	1971	$30

—Green label

❏ BS2562	Master of Reality	1973	$12

—Burbank" palm trees label

❏ BS2562	Master of Reality	1979	$10

—White or tan label

❏ BS2562	Master of Reality Poster	1971	$30
❏ BSK3605	Mob Rules	1981	$15
❏ BSK3186	Never Say Die!	1978	$15
❏ WS1887	Paranoid	1971	$18

—Green label

❏ WS1887	Paranoid	1973	$12

—Burbank" palm trees label

❏ WS41887 [Q]	Paranoid	1974	$175

—All quad copies have "Burbank" palm trees label

❏ BSK3104	Paranoid	1978	$12

—Reissue; "Burbank" palm trees label

❏ BSK3104	Paranoid	1979	$10

—Reissue; white or tan label

❏ BS2695	Sabbath Bloody Sabbath	1974	$18

—Burbank" palm trees label

❏ BS2695	Sabbath Bloody Sabbath	1979	$10

—White or tan label

❏ BS2822	Sabotage	1975	$18

—Burbank" palm trees label

❏ BS2822	Sabotage	1979	$10

—White or tan label

❏ 25337	Seventh Star	1986	$12
❏ BS2969	Technical Ecstasy	1976	$18

—Burbank" palm trees label

❏ BS2969	Technical Ecstasy	1979	$10

—White or tan label

❏ 25548	The Eternal Idol	1987	$12
❏ 2BS2923	We Sold Our Souls for Rock 'N' Roll	1975	$25

—Burbank" palm trees label

❏ 2BS2923	We Sold Our Souls for Rock 'N' Roll	1979	$12

—White or tan label

BLACK SHEEP
With Lou Gramm, pre-FOREIGNER.
CAPITOL
❏ ST-11369	Black Sheep	1974	$25
❏ ST-11447	Encouraging Words	1975	$25

BLACK SHEEP (1)
MERCURY
❏ 848368-1	A Wolf in Sheep's Clothing	1991	$18
❏ 522685-1	Non-Fiction	1994	$18

—May be promo only

Number	Title	Yr	NM

BLACK SHEEP (2)
ENIGMA
❏ 72071	Trouble in the Streets	1985	$10

BLACK UHURU
HEARTBEAT
❏ HB-18	Guess Who's Coming to Dinner	198?	$18
ISLAND
❏ 90180	Anthem	1983	$12
❏ IL-9752	Chill Out	1982	$12
MANGO
❏ MLPS-9823	Anthem	198?	$10

—Reissue of Island 90180

❏ MLPS-9625	Red	1980	$12

—Black vinyl

❏ MLPS-9625	Red	1980	$18

—Red vinyl

❏ MLPS-9791	Reggae Greats	1984	$15
❏ MLPS-9593	Sinsimella	1980	$12
❏ MLPS-9696	Tear It Up	1982	$12
❏ MLPS-9756	The Dub Factor	1982	$15
MESA
❏ R1-79021	Now	1990	$18
❏ R1-79022	Now Dub	1990	$18
RAS
❏ 3015	Brutal	1986	$12
❏ 3020	Brutal Dub	1986	$15
❏ 3025	Positive	1987	$15

BLACK VELVET
OKEH
❏ OKS14130	Love City	1969	$30

BLACKBYRDS, THE
FANTASY
❏ F-9535	Action	1977	$30
❏ F-9602	Better Days	1980	$30
❏ F-9490	City Life	1975	$35
❏ F-9472	Flying Start	1974	$35
❏ FPM-4004 [Q]	Flying Start	1975	$40
❏ F-9570	Night Grooves	1978	$30
❏ F-9444	The Blackbyrds	1974	$35
❏ F-9518	Unfinished Business	1976	$35

BLACKFOOT, J.
EDGE
❏ 001	U-Turn	1987	$15
SOUND TOWN
❏ ST8002	City Slicker	1983	$15
❏ ST8013	Physical Attraction	1984	$15

BLACKFOOT, J.D.
FANTASY
❏ F-9468	Song of Crazy Horse	1974	$25
❏ F-9487	Southbound and Gone	1975	$25
MERCURY
❏ SR-61288	The Ultimate Prophecy	1970	$175

BLACKFOOT
Rick Medlocke, both formerly and later of LYNYRD SKYNYRD, was in this group.
ANTILLES
❏ AN7076	No Reservations	1975	$18
ATCO
❏ SD 32-107	Marauder	1981	$12
❏ 90080	Siogo	1983	$12
❏ SD 38-112	Strikes	1979	$12
❏ SD 32-101	Tomcattin'	1980	$12
❏ 90218	Vertical Smiles	1984	$12
ATLANTIC
❏ 81743	Rick Medlocke and Blackfoot	1987	$15
EPIC
❏ PE34378	Flyin' High	1976	$18

—Orange label

BLACKHORSE
DSDA
❏ 01	Blackhorse	1979	$85

—With insert

BLACKJACK
With Bruce Kulick (later of KISS) and Michael Bolotin (better known as MICHAEL BOLTON). The group on 20th Century is a different band.
POLYDOR
❏ PD-1-6215	Blackjack	1979	$15
❏ PD-1-6279	Worlds Apart	1980	$18

BLACKMAN, CINDY
MUSE
❏ MR-5341	Arcane	1988	$30

Number	Title	Yr	NM

BLACKMAN, HONOR
LONDON
| ❏ LL3408 [M] | Everything I've Got | 1964 | $40 |
| ❏ PS408 [S] | Everything I've Got | 1964 | $75 |

BLACKSMOKE
CHOCOLATE CITY
| ❏ 2001 | Blacksmoke | 1976 | $25 |

BLACKSTREET
INTERSCOPE
| ❏ INT-90071 | Another Level | 1996 | $25 |
| ❏ INT2-90274 | Finally | 1999 | $18 |

BLACKWELL, OTIS
DAVIS
| ❏ 109 [M] | Singin' the Blues | 1956 | $500 |
INNER CITY
| ❏ 1032 | These Are My Songs | 1977 | $25 |

BLACKWELL, SCRAPPER
BLUESVILLE
❏ BVLP-1047	Mr. Scrapper's Blues	1962	$180
—Blue label, silver print			
❏ BVLP-1047	Mr. Scrapper's Blues	1964	$40
—Blue label with trident logo			

BLACKWOOD, R.W.
CAPITOL
| ❏ ST-11563 | We Can Feel Love | 1976 | $12 |

BLACKWOOD BROTHERS, THE
VOICE BOX
| ❏ VB 0779 | Merry Christmas from the Blackwood Brothers | 1979 | $15 |

BLADES, JIMMY, AND CHARLES SMART
LONDON
❏ LB82 [10]	Christmas Chimes	195?	$40
—Back cover with liner notes and no reference to other LPs			
❏ LB82 [10]	Christmas Chimes	195?	$30
—Back cover with liner notes and other Christmas LPs mentioned			
RICHMOND
| ❏ B20063 [M] | Christmas Chimes | 196? | $15 |
| —Reissue of London 82; artist credited only as "Organ and Chimes | | | |

BLADES, RUBEN
ELEKTRA
❏ ED5299 [DJ]	A Conversation with Ruben Blades/Songs and Interview	1988	$18
❏ 60721	Agua de Luna	1987	$12
❏ 60795	Antecedente	1988	$12
❏ 60352	Buscando America	1984	$12
❏ 60432	Escenas	1985	$12
❏ 60754	Nothing But the Truth	1988	$12
❏ 60754 [DJ]	Nothing But the Truth	1988	$18
—Promo-only white label audiophile edition			
FANIA
| ❏ JM-576 | Maestra Vida | 1980 | $18 |
| ❏ JM-577 | Maestra Vida, Second Part | 1980 | $18 |

BLADES OF GRASS, THE
JUBILEE
| ❏ JGS-8007 | The Blades of Grass Are Not for Smoking | 1968 | $18 |

BLAINE, HAL
ABC DUNHILL
❏ DS-50035	Have Fun!!! Play Drums!!!	1968	$50
—With instruction booklet			
❏ DS-50035	Have Fun!!! Play Drums!!!	1968	$40
—Without instruction booklet			
DUNHILL
❏ D-50002 [M]	Drums! Drums! A-Go-Go	1966	$30
❏ DS-50002 [S]	Drums! Drums! A-Go-Go	1966	$40
❏ D-50019 [M]	Psychedelic Percussion	1967	$40
❏ DS-50019 [S]	Psychedelic Percussion	1967	$75
RCA VICTOR
| ❏ LPM-2834 [M] | Deuces, "T's," Roadsters & Drums | 1963 | $150 |
| ❏ LSP-2834 [S] | Deuces, "T's," Roadsters & Drums | 1963 | $175 |

BLAIR, SALLIE
BETHLEHEM
| ❏ BCP-6009 [M] | Squeeze Me | 1957 | $300 |
MGM
| ❏ E-3723 [M] | Hello, Tiger! | 1959 | $40 |
| ❏ SE-3723 [S] | Hello, Tiger! | 1959 | $50 |

BLAKE, BETTY
BETHLEHEM
❏ BCP-6058 [M]	Betty Blake Sings in a Tender Mood	1962	$400
—red label			
❏ BCPS-6058 [S]	Betty Blake Sings in a Tender Mood	1962	$300

BLAKE, EUBIE
BIOGRAPH
| ❏ 1011 | Blues & Ragtime | 1972 | $30 |
| ❏ 1012 | Blues & Spirituals | 1972 | $30 |
COLUMBIA
❏ C2S847	The Eighty-Six Years of Eubie Blake	1969	$25
—Red "360 Sound" labels			
❏ C2S847	The Eighty-Six Years of Eubie Blake	1970	$35
—Orange labels			
EUBIE BLAKE MUSIC
❏ EBM-4	Early Rare Recordings	197?	$30
❏ EBM-7	Early Rare Recordings, Vol. 2	197?	$30
❏ EBM-8	Eubie Blake and His Proteges	197?	$30
❏ EBM-1	Eubie Blake Featuring Ivan Harold Browning	197?	$30
❏ EBM-3	Eubie Blake with Edith Wilson and Ivan Harold Browning	197?	$30
❏ EBM-6	Introducing Jim Hession	197?	$30
❏ EBM-5	Live Concert	197?	$30
❏ EBM-2	Rags to Classics: Charlestown Rag	197?	$30
❏ EBM-9	Song Hits	197?	$30
QUICKSILVER
| ❏ QS-9003 | Tricky Fingers | 198? | $25 |

BLAKE, HARRIETTE
HARRIETTE BLAKE
| ❏ HBLP-002 | My Way | 1978 | $18 |
| ❏ HBLP-001 | This Is My Life | 1976 | $18 |

BLAKE, RAN
ARISTA/NOVUS
| ❏ AN3019 | Film Noir | 1980 | $30 |
| ❏ AN3006 | Rapport | 1978 | $30 |
ESP-DISK'
| ❏ 1011 [M] | Ran Blake Plays Solo Piano | 1965 | $300 |
| ❏ S-1011 [S] | Ran Blake Plays Solo Piano | 1965 | $300 |
GC
| ❏ 4176 | Take One | 197? | $30 |
| ❏ 4177 | Take Two | 197? | $30 |
GM RECORDINGS
| ❏ GM-3007 | Painted Rhythms: The Compleat Ran Blake, Vol. 1 | 1987 | $30 |
| ❏ GM-3008 | Painted Rhythms: The Compleat Ran Blake, Vol. 2 | 1989 | $30 |
IAI
| ❏ 373842 | Breakthru | 1976 | $30 |
MILESTONE
| ❏ MSP-9021 | The Blue Potato | 1969 | $35 |
OWL
❏ 029	Portrait of Doktor Mabuse	1978	$35
❏ 012	The Realization of a Dream	1978	$35
❏ 017	Third Stream Recompositions	1977	$35
❏ 041	Vertigo	1986	$35
SOUL NOTE
| ❏ SN-1027 | Duke Dreams | 198? | $30 |
| ❏ SN-1077 | Suffield Gothic | 1983 | $30 |

BLAKE AND HINES
MOTOWN
| ❏ 6224ML | Blake and Hines | 1987 | $12 |

BLAKE BABIES
CHEWBUD
| ❏ CBTW-001 [EP] | Nicely, Nicely | 1987 | $40 |
| —1,000 copies pressed | | | |
MAMMOTH
❏ MR0016 [B]	Earwig	1989	$18
❏ MR0025 [EP]	Rosy Jack World	1991	$18
—Red vinyl			
❏ MR0022 [B]	Sunburn	1990	$18

BLAKEY, ART, AND THE JAZZ MESSENGERS
ABC IMPULSE!
❏ AS-45 [S]	A Jazz Message	1968	$30
—Reissue of Impulse AS-45			
❏ AS-7 [S]	Art Blakey!!!! Jazz Messengers!!!!	1968	$30
—Reissue of Impulse AS-7			
BETHLEHEM
| ❏ BCP-6027 [M] | Art Blakey's Big Band | 1958 | $300 |
| ❏ BCPS-6027 [S] | Art Blakey's Big Band | 1959 | $250 |

❏ BCP-6023 [M]	Hard Drive	1957	$100
❏ BCP-6037	Hard Drive	197?	$30
—Reissue of 6023, distributed by RCA Victor			
❏ BCP-6015	The Finest of Art Blakey	197?	$30
—Reissue of 6027, distributed by RCA Victor			
BLUEBIRD
| ❏ 6286-1-RB | Theory of Art | 1987 | $25 |
BLUE NOTE
❏ BLP-5037 [10]	A Night at Birdland, Volume 1	1954	$400
—original cover. Deduct 50% for W 63rd address			
❏ BLP-1521 [M]	A Night at Birdland, Volume 1	1956	$300
—Deep groove" version (deep indentation under label on both sides)			
❏ BLP-1521 [M]	A Night at Birdland, Volume 1	1956	$800
—Regular version, Lexington Ave. address on label			
❏ BLP-1521 [M]	A Night at Birdland, Volume 1	1957	$350
—With W. 63rd St. address on label			
❏ BLP-1521 [M]	A Night at Birdland, Volume 1	1963	$250
—With "New York, USA" address on label			
❏ BST-81521 [R]	A Night at Birdland, Volume 1	1968	$75
—With "A Division of Liberty Records" on label			
❏ BLP-1521 [M]	A Night at Birdland, Volume 1	1967	$150
—A Division of Liberty Records" on label			
❏ BLP-5038 [10]	A Night at Birdland, Volume 2	1954	$800
❏ BLP-1522 [M]	A Night at Birdland, Volume 2	1956	$300
—Deep groove" version (deep indentation under label on both sides)			
❏ BLP-1522 [M]	A Night at Birdland, Volume 2	1956	$1000
—Regular version, Lexington Ave. address on label			
❏ BLP-1522 [M]	A Night at Birdland, Volume 2	1957	$750
—With W. 63rd St. address on label			
❏ BLP-1522 [M]	A Night at Birdland, Volume 2	1963	$500
—With "New York, USA" address on label			
❏ BST-81522 [R]	A Night at Birdland, Volume 2	1968	$25
—With "A Division of Liberty Records" on label			
❏ BLP-5039 [10]	A Night at Birdland, Volume 3	1954	$300
❏ BLP-4049 [M]	A Night in Tunisia	1960	$300
—Deep groove" version (deep indentation under label on both sides)			
❏ BLP-4049 [M]	A Night in Tunisia	1960	$175
—Regular version, with W. 63rd St. address on label			
❏ BLP-4049 [M]	A Night in Tunisia	1963	$75
—With "New York, USA" address on label			
❏ BST-84049 [S]	A Night in Tunisia	1960	$75
—With W. 63rd St. address on label			
❏ BST-84049 [S]	A Night in Tunisia	1963	$25
—With "New York, USA" address on label			
❏ BST-84049 [S]	A Night in Tunisia	196?	$30
—With "A Division of Liberty Records" on label			
❏ B1-84049	A Night in Tunisia	1989	$25
—The Finest in Jazz Since 1939" reissue			
❏ BLP-4003 [M]	Art Blakey and the Jazz Messengers	1958	$300
—Deep groove" version (deep indentation under label on both sides)			
❏ BLP-4003 [M]	Art Blakey and the Jazz Messengers	1958	$250
—Regular version, with W. 63rd St. address on label			
❏ BLP-4003 [M]	Art Blakey and the Jazz Messengers	1963	$75
—With "New York, USA" address on label			

Number	Title	Yr	NM
❏ BST-4003 [S]	Art Blakey and the Jazz Messengers	1959	$250

—*Deep groove" version (deep indentation under label on both sides)*

Number	Title	Yr	NM
❏ BST-4003 [S]	Art Blakey and the Jazz Messengers	1959	$100

—*Regular version, with W. 63rd St. address on label*

❏ BST-4003 [S]	Art Blakey and the Jazz Messengers	1963	$25

—*With "New York, USA" address on label*

❏ BST-84003 [S]	Art Blakey and the Jazz Messengers	196?	$30

—*With "A Division of Liberty Records" on label*

❏ BLP-1507 [M]	At the Café Bohemia, Volume 1	1956	$300

—*Deep groove" version (deep indentation under label on both sides)*

❏ BLP-1507 [M]	At the Café Bohemia, Volume 1	1956	$250

—*Regular version, Lexington Ave. address on label*

❏ BLP-1507 [M]	At the Café Bohemia, Volume 1	1957	$150

—*With W. 63rd St. address on label*

❏ BLP-1507 [M]	At the Café Bohemia, Volume 1	1963	$75

—*With "New York, USA" address on label*

❏ BST-81507 [R]	At the Café Bohemia, Volume 1	1968	$25

—*With "A Division of Liberty Records" on label*

❏ BST-81507 [M]	At the Café Bohemia, Volume 1	1985	$25

—*The Finest in Jazz Since 1939" reissue*

❏ BLP-1508 [M]	At the Café Bohemia, Volume 2	1956	$250

—*Regular version, Lexington Ave. address on label*

❏ BLP-1508 [M]	At the Café Bohemia, Volume 2	1956	$350

—*Deep groove" version (deep indentation under label on both sides)*

❏ BLP-1508 [M]	At the Café Bohemia, Volume 2	1957	$150

—*With W. 63rd St. address on label*

❏ BLP-1508 [M]	At the Café Bohemia, Volume 2	1963	$75

—*With "New York, USA" address on label*

❏ BST-81508 [R]	At the Café Bohemia, Volume 2	1968	$25

—*With "A Division of Liberty Records" on label*

❏ B1-81508	At the Café Bohemia, Volume 2	1987	$25

—*The Finest in Jazz Since 1939" reissue*

❏ BLP-4015 [M]	At the Jazz Corner of the World, Volume 1	1958	$150

—*Deep groove" version (deep indentation under label on both sides)*

❏ BLP-4015 [M]	At the Jazz Corner of the World, Volume 1	1958	$175

—*Regular version, with W. 63rd St. address on label*

❏ BLP-4015 [M]	At the Jazz Corner of the World, Volume 1	1963	$75

—*With "New York, USA" address on label*

❏ BST-84015 [S]	At the Jazz Corner of the World, Volume 1	1959	$350

—*Deep groove" version (deep indentation under label on both sides)*

❏ BST-84015 [S]	At the Jazz Corner of the World, Volume 1	1959	$75

—*Regular version, with W. 63rd St. address on label*

❏ BST-84015 [S]	At the Jazz Corner of the World, Volume 1	1963	$25

—*With "New York, USA" address on label*

❏ BST-84015 [S]	At the Jazz Corner of the World, Volume 1	196?	$30

—*With "A Division of Liberty Records" on label*

❏ BLP-4016 [M]	At the Jazz Corner of the World, Volume 2	1958	$250

—*Deep groove" version (deep indentation under label on both sides)*

❏ BLP-4016 [M]	At the Jazz Corner of the World, Volume 2	1958	$175

—*Regular version, with W. 63rd St. address on label*

❏ BLP-4016 [M]	At the Jazz Corner of the World, Volume 2	1963	$75

—*With "New York, USA" address on label*

❏ BST-84016 [S]	At the Jazz Corner of the World, Volume 2	1959	$350

—*Deep groove" version (deep indentation under label on both sides)*

❏ BST-84016 [S]	At the Jazz Corner of the World, Volume 2	1959	$75

—*Regular version, with W. 63rd St. address on label*

❏ BST-84016 [S]	At the Jazz Corner of the World, Volume 2	1963	$25

—*With "New York, USA" address on label*

❏ BST-84016 [S]	At the Jazz Corner of the World, Volume 2	196?	$30

—*With "A Division of Liberty Records" on label*

❏ BST-84016 [S]	At the Jazz Corner of the World, Volume 2	197?	$25

—*New darker label; with "United Artists Music and Records Group" on label*

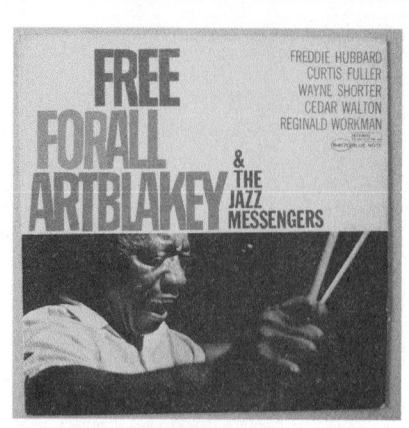

FREDDIE HUBBARD
CURTIS FULLER
WAYNE SHORTER
CEDAR WALTON
REGINALD WORKMAN

FREE FOR ALL ART BLAKEY & THE JAZZ MESSENGERS

Number	Title	Yr	NM
❏ BLP-4104 [M]	Buhaina's Delight	1962	$75

—*With "New York, USA" on label*

❏ BST-84104 [S]	Buhaina's Delight	1962	$40

—*With "New York, USA" address on label*

❏ BST-84104 [S]	Buhaina's Delight	196?	$30

—*With "A Division of Liberty Records" on label*

❏ BLP-4170 [M]	Free for All	1965	$75
❏ BST-84170 [S]	Free for All	1965	$40

—*With "New York, USA" address on label*

❏ BST-84170 [S]	Free for All	196?	$30

—*With "A Division of Liberty Records" on label*

❏ BLP-4004 [M]	Holiday for Skins, Volume 1	1958	$250

—*Deep groove" version (deep indentation under label on both sides)*

❏ BLP-4004 [M]	Holiday for Skins, Volume 1	1958	$175

—*Regular version, with W. 63rd St. address on label*

❏ BLP-4004 [M]	Holiday for Skins, Volume 1	1963	$75

—*With "New York, USA" address on label*

❏ BST-4004 [S]	Holiday for Skins, Volume 1	1959	$175

—*Deep groove" version (deep indentation under label on both sides)*

❏ BST-4004 [S]	Holiday for Skins, Volume 1	1959	$120

—*Regular version, with W. 63rd St. address on label*

❏ BST-4004 [S]	Holiday for Skins, Volume 1	1963	$25

—*With "New York, USA" address on label*

❏ BST-84004 [S]	Holiday for Skins, Volume 1	196?	$30

—*With "A Division of Liberty Records" on label*

❏ BLP-4005 [M]	Holiday for Skins, Volume 2	1958	$250

—*Deep groove" version (deep indentation under label on both sides)*

❏ BLP-4005 [M]	Holiday for Skins, Volume 2	1958	$175

—*Regular version, with W. 63rd St. address on label*

❏ BLP-4005 [M]	Holiday for Skins, Volume 2	1963	$75

—*With "New York, USA" address on label*

❏ BST-4005 [S]	Holiday for Skins, Volume 2	1959	$175

—*Deep groove" version (deep indentation under label on both sides)*

❏ BST-4005 [S]	Holiday for Skins, Volume 2	1959	$120

—*Regular version, with W. 63rd St. address on label*

❏ BST-4005 [S]	Holiday for Skins, Volume 2	1963	$25

—*With "New York, USA" address on label*

❏ BST-84005 [S]	Holiday for Skins, Volume 2	196?	$30

—*With "A Division of Liberty Records" on label*

❏ BLP-4193 [M]	Indestructible	1966	$75
❏ BST-84193 [S]	Indestructible	1966	$40

—*With "New York, USA" address on label*

❏ BST-84193 [S]	Indestructible	196?	$30

—*With "A Division of Liberty Records" on label*

❏ BST-84193 [S]	Indestructible	1986	$25

—*The Finest in Jazz Since 1939" reissue*

❏ BLP-4245 [M]	Like Someone in Love	1967	$100
❏ BST-84245 [S]	Like Someone in Love	1967	$40

—*With "New York, USA" address on label*

❏ BST-84245 [S]	Like Someone in Love	196?	$30

—*With "A Division of Liberty Records" on label*

❏ B1-84245	Like Someone in Love	1989	$25

—*The Finest in Jazz Since 1939" reissue*

❏ BN-LA473-4047	Live Messengers	1975	$35
❏ BLP-4054 [M]	Meet You at the Jazz Corner of the World, Volume 1	1960	$150

—*With W. 63rd St. address on label*

❏ BLP-4054 [M]	Meet You at the Jazz Corner of the World, Volume 1	1963	$75

—*With "New York, USA" address on label*

❏ BST-84054 [S]	Meet You at the Jazz Corner of the World, Volume 1	1960	$75

—*With W. 63rd St. address on label*

❏ BST-84054 [S]	Meet You at the Jazz Corner of the World, Volume 1	1963	$25

—*With "New York, USA" address on label*

❏ BST-84054 [S]	Meet You at the Jazz Corner of the World, Volume 1	196?	$30

—*With "A Division of Liberty Records" on label*

❏ BLP-4055 [M]	Meet You at the Jazz Corner of the World, Volume 2	1960	$150

—*With W. 63rd St. address on label*

Number	Title	Yr	NM
❏ BLP-4055 [M]	Meet You at the Jazz Corner of the World, Volume 2	1963	$75

—*With "New York, USA" address on label*

❏ BST-84055 [S]	Meet You at the Jazz Corner of the World, Volume 2	1960	$75

—*With W. 63rd St. address on label*

❏ BST-84055 [S]	Meet You at the Jazz Corner of the World, Volume 2	1963	$25

—*With "New York, USA" address on label*

❏ BST-84055 [S]	Meet You at the Jazz Corner of the World, Volume 2	196?	$30

—*With "A Division of Liberty Records" on label*

❏ B1-46516	Moanin'	199?	$35

—*Audiophile reissue of 84003*

❏ BLP-4090 [M]	Mosaic	1961	$175

—*With 61st St. address on label*

❏ BLP-4090 [M]	Mosaic	1963	$75

—*With "New York, USA" address on label*

❏ BST-84090 [S]	Mosaic	1961	$120

—*With 61st St. address on label*

❏ BST-84090 [S]	Mosaic	1963	$25

—*With "New York, USA" address on label*

❏ BST-84090 [S]	Mosaic	196?	$30

—*With "A Division of Liberty Records" on label*

❏ B1-46523	Mosaic	199?	$35

—*Audiophile reissue*

❏ LT-1065	Once Upon a Groove	1980	$25
❏ BLP-1554 [M]	Orgy in Rhythm, Volume 1	1957	$750

—*Deep groove" version (deep indentation under label on both sides)*

❏ BLP-1554 [M]	Orgy in Rhythm, Volume 1	1957	$250

—*Regular version, with W. 63rd St. address on label*

❏ BLP-1554 [M]	Orgy in Rhythm, Volume 1	1963	$175

—*With "New York, USA" address on label*

❏ BST-81554 [R]	Orgy in Rhythm, Volume 1	1968	$25

—*With "A Division of Liberty Records" on label*

❏ BLP-1555 [M]	Orgy in Rhythm, Volume 2	1957	$300

—*Regular version, with W. 63rd St. address on label*

❏ BLP-1555 [M]	Orgy in Rhythm, Volume 2	1957	$850

—*Deep groove" version (deep indentation under label on both sides)*

❏ BLP-1555 [M]	Orgy in Rhythm, Volume 2	1963	$175

—*With "New York, USA" address on label*

❏ BST-81555 [R]	Orgy in Rhythm, Volume 2	1968	$25

—*With "A Division of Liberty Records" on label*

❏ BST-84347	Roots and Herbs	1970	$30

—*With "Liberty/UA" on label*

❏ BLP-4097 [M]	The African Beat	1961	$175

—*With 61st St. address on label*

❏ BLP-4097 [M]	The African Beat	1963	$75

—*With "New York, USA" address on label*

❏ BST-84097 [S]	The African Beat	1961	$75

—*With 61st St. address on label*

❏ BST-84097 [S]	The African Beat	1963	$30

—*With "New York, USA" address on label*

❏ BST-84097 [S]	The African Beat	196?	$30

—*With "A Division of Liberty Records" on label*

❏ B1-93205	The Best of Art Blakey and the Jazz Messengers	1989	$30
❏ BLP-4029 [M]	The Big Beat	1960	$300

—*Deep groove" version (deep indentation under label on both sides)*

❏ BLP-4029 [M]	The Big Beat	1960	$175

—*Regular version, with W. 63rd St. address on label*

❏ BLP-4029 [M]	The Big Beat	1963	$75

—*With "New York, USA" address on label*

❏ BST-84029 [S]	The Big Beat	1960	$75

—*With W. 63rd St. address on label*

❏ BST-84029 [S]	The Big Beat	1963	$25

—*With "New York, USA" address on label*

❏ BST-84029 [S]	The Big Beat	196?	$30

—*With "A Division of Liberty Records" on label*

❏ BST-84029 [S]	The Big Beat	1985	$25

—*The Finest in Jazz Since 1939" reissue*

❏ BLP-4156 [M]	The Freedom Rider	1964	$75
❏ BST-84156 [S]	The Freedom Rider	1964	$40

—*With "New York, USA" address on label*

❏ BST-84156 [S]	The Freedom Rider	196?	$30

—*With "A Division of Liberty Records" on label*

❏ BST-84258 [S]	The Witch Doctor	1969	$25

—*With "A Division of Liberty Records" on label*

CADET

❏ LP-4049 [M]	Tough!	1966	$30
❏ LPS-4049 [S]	Tough!	1966	$30

CATALYST

❏ 7902	Jazz Messengers '70	197?	$30

COLUMBIA

❏ CL1002 [M]	Drum Suite	1957	$75

—*Red and black label with six "eye" logos*

❏ CL1002 [M]	Drum Suite	200?	$30

—*180-gram reissue*

❏ CL1040 [M]	Hard Bop	1957	$75

—*Red and black label with six "eye" logos*

❏ CL897 [M]	The Jazz Messengers	1956	$100

Number	Title	Yr	NM
—Red and black label with six "eye" logos			
❏ FC38036	The Original Jazz Messengers -- A Quarter Century Ago	1982	$25

CONCORD JAZZ
❏ CJ-68	In This Korner	1978	$35
❏ CJ-196	Keystone 3	1982	$25
❏ CJ-307	Live at Kimball's	1986	$25
❏ CJ-256	New York Scene	1984	$25
❏ CJ-168	Straight Ahead	1981	$25

ELEKTRA
❏ EKL-120 [M]	A Midnight Session with the Jazz Messengers	1957	$100

EMARCY
❏ MG-26030 [10]	Blakey	1954	$500

EPIC
❏ LA16017 [M]	Art Blakey in Paris	1961	$75
❏ BA17017 [S]	Art Blakey in Paris	1961	$100
❏ LA16009 [M]	Paris Concert	1960	$75
❏ BA17009 [S]	Paris Concert	1960	$100

EVEREST ARCHIVE OF FOLK & JAZZ
❏ 332	Jazz Messengers	197?	$25

FANTASY
❏ OJC-038	Caravan	198?	$25
❏ OJC-145	Kyoto	198?	$25
❏ OJC-090	Ugetsu	198?	$25

GNP CRESCENDO
❏ GNPS-2182	Live at Sweet Basil	1986	$25

IMPULSE!
❏ A-45 [M]	A Jazz Message	1963	$250
❏ AS-45 [S]	A Jazz Message	1963	$160
❏ A-7 [M]	Art Blakey!!!! Jazz Messengers!!!!	1961	$120
❏ AS-7 [S]	Art Blakey!!!! Jazz Messengers!!!!	1961	$160

JOSIE
❏ JOZ-3501 [M]	Cu-Bop	1962	$40
—Reissue of Jubilee LP			
❏ JS-3501 [S]	Cu-Bop	1962	$30

JUBILEE
❏ JLP-1049 [M]	Cu-Bop	1958	$100

LIMELIGHT
❏ LM-82034 [M]	Buttercorn Lady	1966	$25
❏ LS-86034 [S]	Buttercorn Lady	1966	$30
❏ LM-82038 [M]	Hold On, I'm Coming	1966	$25
❏ LS-86038 [S]	Hold On, I'm Coming	1966	$30
❏ LM-82001 [M]	'S Make It	1965	$25
❏ LS-86001 [S]	'S Make It	1965	$30
❏ LM-82019 [M]	Soul Finger	1965	$25
❏ LS-86019 [S]	Soul Finger	1965	$30

MCA IMPULSE!
❏ MCA-5648	A Jazz Message	1986	$20
—Reissue			

MILESTONE
❏ 47008	Thermo	197?	$35

MOSAIC
❏ MR10-141	The Complete Blue Note Recordings of Art Blakey's 1960 Jazz Messengers	199?	$175

ODYSSEY
❏ PC36809	Hard Bop	1981	$25
❏ PC37021	The Jazz Messengers	1981	$25

PACIFIC JAZZ
❏ PJM-402 [M]	Ritual	1957	$100
❏ PJ-15 [M]	Ritual	1961	$40
—Reissue of 402			

PRESTIGE
❏ 10076	Anthenagin	197?	$30
❏ 10067	Buhaina	197?	$30
❏ 10047	Child's Dance	197?	$15

RCA VICTOR
❏ LPM-2654 [M]	A Night in Tunisia	1963	$40
—Reissue of Vik 1115			
❏ LSP-2654 [R]	A Night in Tunisia	1963	$25

RIVERSIDE
❏ RS-438 [M]	Caravan	1962	$250
❏ RS-9438 [S]	Caravan	1962	$250
❏ 6074	Caravan	197?	$30
❏ RS-493 [M]	Kyoto	1966	$150
❏ RS-9493 [S]	Kyoto	1966	$150
❏ RS-464 [M]	Ugetsu	1963	$175
❏ RS-9464 [S]	Ugetsu	1963	$175
❏ RS-3022	Ugetsu	1968	$150

ROULETTE
❏ SR-5003	Backgammon	1976	$30
❏ SR-5008	Gypsy Folk Tales	1977	$30

SAVOY
❏ MG-12171 [M]	Art Blakey and the Jazz Messengers	1960	$30

SAVOY JAZZ
❏ SJL-1112	Mirage	1977	$35

SOLID STATE
❏ SS-18033	Three Blind Mice	1969	$30

Number	Title	Yr	NM

SOUL NOTE
❏ 121155-1	I Get a Kick Out of You	1990	$30
❏ 121105-1	Not Yet	1989	$30

TIMELESS
❏ SJP-307	Feel the Wind	1990	$30
❏ 301	In My Prime, Vol. 1	1979	$30
❏ 317	Reflections in Blue	1980	$30

TRIP
❏ 5019	Art Blakey and the Jazz Messengers	197?	$25
❏ 5034	Art Blakey and the Jazz Messengers Live	197?	$25
❏ 5505	Buttercorn Lady	197?	$25

UNITED ARTISTS
❏ UAJ-14002 [M]	Three Blind Mice	1962	$40
❏ UAJS-15002 [S]	Three Blind Mice	1962	$50
❏ UAS-5633	Three Blind Mice	197?	$25

VEE JAY
❏ VJS-3066	Bag of Blues Featuring Buddy DeFranco	1977	$30

VIK
❏ LX-1115 [M]	A Night in Tunisia	1958	$150
❏ LX-1103 [M]	Art Blakey and the Jazz Messengers Play Selections from Lerner and Loewe	1957	$150

BLAKEY, ART, AND THE JAZZ MESSENGERS/ELMO HOPE

PACIFIC JAZZ
❏ PJ-33 [M]	The Jazz Messengers and Elmo Hope	1962	$40

BLAKEY, ART, AND THE JAZZ MESSENGERS/MAX ROACH

CHESS
❏ CH2-92511	Percussion Discussion	198?	$35

BLAKEY, ART, AND THE JAZZ MESSENGERS WITH THELONIOUS MONK

ATLANTIC
❏ 1278 [M]	Art Blakey's Jazz Messengers with Thelonious Monk	1958	$300
—Black label			
❏ 1278 [M]	Art Blakey's Jazz Messengers with Thelonious Monk	1960	$300
—Multicolor label, white "fan" logo			
❏ 1278 [M]	Art Blakey's Jazz Messengers with Thelonious Monk	1963	$175
—Multicolor label, black "fan" logo			
❏ SD1278 [S]	Art Blakey's Jazz Messengers with Thelonious Monk	1959	$300
—Green label			
❏ SD1278 [S]	Art Blakey's Jazz Messengers with Thelonious Monk	1960	$300
—Multicolor label, white "fan" logo			
❏ SD1278 [S]	Art Blakey's Jazz Messengers with Thelonious Monk	1963	$175
—Multicolor label, black "fan" logo			

ODYSSEY
❏ 32160246	Art Blakey with the Original Jazz Messengers	1968	$35

BLANC, MEL

CAPITOL
❏ H-436 [10]	Party Panic	1953	$150

BLANCHARD, JACK, AND MISTY MORGAN

MEGA
❏ 31-1009	Two Sides	1972	$15

WAYSIDE
❏ WWS 33-001	Birds of a Feather	1970	$18

BLANCHARD, PIERRE

SUNNYSIDE
❏ SSC-1023	Music for String Quartet, Jazz Trio, Violin and Lee Konitz	1988	$25

BLANCHARD, TERENCE, AND DONALD HARRISON

COLUMBIA
❏ FC44216	Black Pearl	1988	$25
❏ FC40830	Crystal Star	1987	$25
❏ BFC40335	Nascence	1986	$25

GEORGE WEIN COLLECTION
❏ GW-3008	Discernment	1986	$30
❏ GW-3002	New York Second Line	1984	$30

BLAND, BOBBY, AND B.B. KING

ABC DUNHILL
❏ DSY-50190	Together for the First Time... Live	1974	$18

ABC IMPULSE!
❏ 9317	Together Again...Live	1976	$15

Number	Title	Yr	NM

COMMAND
❏ CQDY-40012 [Q]	Together for the First Time... Live	1974	$40

MCA
❏ 27012	Together Again...Live	198?	$10
—Reissue of ABC Impulse! 9317			
❏ 4160	Together for the First Time... Live	198?	$12
—Reissue of ABC Dunhill 50190			

BLAND, BOBBY

ABC
❏ AA-1075	Come Fly with Me	1978	$12
❏ D-895	Get On Down with Bobby Bland	1975	$15
❏ AB-1018	Reflections in Blue	1977	$12

ABC DUKE
❏ DLP-78	Ain't Nothing You Can Do	1974	$15
❏ DLP-88	A Touch of the Blues	1974	$15
❏ DLP-77	Call On Me/That's the Way Love Is	1974	$15
❏ DLP-75	Here's the Man!!!	1974	$15
❏ DLP92-2	Introspective of the Early Years	1974	$25
❏ DLP-89	Spotlighting the Man	1974	$15
❏ DLP-84	The Best of Bobby Bland	1974	$15
❏ DLP-86	The Best of Bobby Bland, Volume 2	1974	$15
❏ DLP-79	The Soul of the Man	1974	$15
❏ DLPS-74	Two Steps from the Blues	197?	$15

ABC DUNHILL
❏ DSX-50169	Dreamer	1974	$18
❏ DSX-50163	His California Album	1973	$18

BLUESWAY
❏ BLS-6065	Call On Me	197?	$18

DUKE
❏ DLP-78 [M]	Ain't Nothing You Can Do	1964	$100
❏ DLPS-78 [S]	Ain't Nothing You Can Do	1964	$120
❏ DLP-88 [M]	A Touch of the Blues	1968	$30
❏ DLPS-88 [S]	A Touch of the Blues	1968	$25
❏ DLP-77 [M]	Call On Me/That's the Way Love Is	1963	$150
❏ DLPS-77 [S]	Call On Me/That's the Way Love Is	1963	$175
❏ DLP-75 [M]	Here's the Man!!!	1962	$250
—Purple and yellow label			
❏ DLP-75 [M]	Here's the Man!!!	1962	$150
—Orange label			
❏ DLPS-75 [S]	Here's the Man!!!	1962	$250
—With spoken intro to "36-22-36			
❏ DLPS-75 [S]	Here's the Man!!!	196?	$150
—Without spoken intro to "36-22-36			
❏ DLPS-90	If Loving You Is Wrong	1970	$25
❏ DLPS-89	Spotlighting the Man	1969	$25
❏ DLP-84 [M]	The Best of Bobby Bland	1967	$25
❏ DLPS-84 [P]	The Best of Bobby Bland	1967	$30
❏ DLP-86 [M]	The Best of Bobby Bland, Volume 2	1968	$30
❏ DLPS-86 [P]	The Best of Bobby Bland, Volume 2	1968	$25
❏ DLP-79 [M]	The Soul of the Man	1966	$100
❏ DLPS-79 [S]	The Soul of the Man	1966	$120
❏ DLP-74 [M]	Two Steps from the Blues	1961	$300
—Purple and yellow label			
❏ DLP-74 [M]	Two Steps from the Blues	1962	$300
—Orange label, red vinyl			
❏ DLP-74 [M]	Two Steps from the Blues	1962	$150
—Orange label, black vinyl			
❏ DLPS-74 [R]	Two Steps from the Blues	196?	$75

MCA
❏ 27040	Ain't Nothing You Can Do	198?	$10
—Reissue of Duke 78			
❏ 27047	A Touch of the Blues	1984	$10
—Reissue of Duke 88			
❏ 27042	Call On Me/That's the Way Love Is	1984	$10
—Reissue of Duke 77			
❏ 27044	Come Fly with Me	1984	$10
—Reissue of ABC 1075			
❏ 27038	Here's the Man!!!	198?	$10
—Reissue of Duke 75			
❏ 5297	Here We Go Again	1982	$12
❏ 3157	I Feel Good, I Feel Fine	1979	$12
❏ 27073	I Feel Good, I Feel Fine	1985	$10
—Reissue of MCA 3157			
❏ 4172	Introspective of the Early Years	198?	$12
—Reissue of Duke 92			
❏ 27043	Reflections in Blue	1984	$10
—Reissue of ABC 1018			
❏ 27048	Spotlighting the Man	1984	$10
—Reissue of Duke 89			
❏ 5145	Sweet Vibrations	1980	$12
❏ 27076	Sweet Vibrations	198?	$10
—Reissue of 5145			
❏ 5425	Tell Mr. Bland	1983	$12
❏ 27013	The Best of Bobby Bland	198?	$10
—Reissue of Duke 84			

Number	Title	Yr	NM
❑ 27045	The Best of Bobby Bland, Volume 2	1984	$10
—Reissue of Duke 86			
❑ 27041	The Soul of the Man	1984	$10
—Reissue of Duke 79			
❑ 5233	Try Me, I'm Real	1981	$12
❑ 27036	Two Steps from the Blues	198?	$10
—Reissue of Duke 74			
❑ 5503	You've Got Me Loving You	1984	$12

BLASSIE, FRED
RHINO
❑ RNLP-813 [PD]	I Bite the Songs	1985	$25

BLAST, C.L.
COTILLION
❑ SD5222	I Wanna Get Down	1980	$15

BLASTERS, THE
Also see DAVE ALVIN. The group on Crown is not the same as the others.

CROWN
❑ CLP-5392 [M]	Sounds of the Drags	1963	$25
❑ CST-392 [S]	Sounds of the Drags	1963	$30
ROLLIN' ROCK
❑ 021	American Music	1980	$85
SLASH
❑ 25093	Hard Line	1985	$12
❑ 23818	Non Fiction	1983	$12
❑ 23735 [EP]	Over There: Live at the Venue, London	1982	$12
❑ BKS3680	The Blasters	1982	$12
—With blue labels; reissue of 109			
❑ SR109	The Blasters	1981	$18
WARNER BROS.
❑ WBMS-130 [DJ]	Music and Interviews	1985	$40
—Part of "The Warner Bros. Music Show" series; one side is The Blasters; the other side is The Smiths, which accounts for this piece's value			

BLAYLOCK, BILL & WILLIS, CLAY
GUINNESS
❑ GNS36071 [B]	Bill Blaylock & Clay Willis	1977	$25

BLAZING REDHEADS
REFERENCE RECORDINGS
❑ RR-26	Blazing Redheads	1988	$25
❑ RR-41	Crazed Women	1991	$25

BLEND, THE
MCA
❑ 3175	Anytime Delight	1979	$12
❑ 3058	The Blend	1978	$12

BLESSED END
TNS
❑ 248	Movin' On	1971	$300

BLEU, MIKKI
EMI
❑ E1-91171	I Promise	1989	$18

BLEY, CARLA
ECM
❑ 25003	Heavy Heart	1984	$25
ECM/WATT
❑ ECM W-14	Heavy Heart	1983	$30
❑ ECM W-122-Jan	I Hate to Sing	1982	$30
❑ ECM W-12	Live!	1982	$30
❑ ECM W-11	Social Studies	1980	$30
JCOA
❑ 3-LP-EOTH	Escalator Over the Hill	1971	$30
WATT
❑ 6	Dinner Music	1976	$35
❑ 8	European Tour 1977	1978	$35
❑ 9	Musique Mecanique	1979	$35
❑ 1	Tropic Appetites	1974	$35

BLEY, PAUL, AND GARY PEACOCK
ECM
❑ 1003ST	Paul Bley with Gary Peacock	1973	$35
—Original issue, made in Germany?			

BLEY, PAUL, AND NIELS-HENNING ORSTED PEDERSEN
INNER CITY
❑ IC-2005	Paul Bley and Niels-Henning Orsted Pedersen	1973	$35
STEEPLECHASE
❑ SCS-1005	Paul Bley and Niels-Henning Orsted Pedersen	198?	$30

Number	Title	Yr	NM

BLEY, PAUL; GARY PEACOCK; BARRY ALTSCHUL
IAI
❑ 373849	Japan Suite	1977	$35
❑ 373844	Virtuosi	1976	$35

BLEY, PAUL
ARISTA/FREEDOM
❑ AL1901	Copenhagen and Haarlem	197?	$50
DEBUT
❑ DLP-7 [10]	Introducing Paul Bley	1954	$600
ECM
❑ 1010ST	Ballads	1973	$50
—Original issue, made in Germany?			
❑ 1320	Fragments	198?	$35
—Made in Germany			
❑ 1023ST	Open to Love	1974	$35
—Original issue, made in Germany?			
❑ ECM-1-1023	Open to Love	197?	$30
—Distributed by Polydor			
EMARCY
❑ MG-36092 [M]	Paul Bley	1955	$250
ESP-DISK'
❑ 1008 [M]	Barrage	1965	$300
❑ S-1008 [S]	Barrage	1965	$300
❑ 1021 [M]	Closer	1966	$300
❑ S-1021 [S]	Closer	1966	$300
FANTASY
❑ OJC-201	Introducing Paul Bley	198?	$175
—Reissue of Debut 7			
GENE NORMAN
❑ GNP-31 [M]	Solemn Meditation	1957	$100
GNP CRESCENDO
❑ GNPS-31 [R]	Solemn Meditation	197?	$35
❑ GT-3002	Solemn Meditation	198?	$35
IAI
❑ 373840	Alone Again	1975	$35
❑ 373853	Axis	1978	$50
❑ 373839	Quiet Song	1975	$35
—With Jimmy Giuffre and Bill Connors			
❑ 373841	Turning Point	1975	$30
—With John Gilmore			
INNER CITY
❑ IC-1007	Live at the Hillcrest 1958	197?	$35
LIMELIGHT
❑ LS-86060	Mr. Joy	1968	$200
MILESTONE
❑ MSP-9046	Paul Bley and Scorpio	1973	$120
—Reproductions exist			
❑ MSP-9033	Synthesizer Show	1970	$175
OWL
❑ 034	Tears	1984	$40
SAVOY
❑ MG-12182 [M]	Footloose!	1964	$100
SAVOY JAZZ
❑ SJL-1148	Floater	1984	$35
❑ SJL-1175	Syndrome	1987	$35
❑ SJL-1192	Turns	1988	$35
SOUL NOTE
❑ SN-1140	Paul Bley Group	1986	$35
❑ SN-1085	Sonor	1984	$35
❑ SN-1090	Tango Palace	1985	$35
STEEPLECHASE
❑ SCS-1214	My Standard	198?	$35
❑ SCS-1205	Questions	198?	$50
❑ SCS-1236	Solo Piano	198?	$50
❑ SCS-1246	The Nearness of You	198?	$35
TRIP
❑ TLP-5587	Mr. Joy	197?	$35
WING
❑ MGW-60001 [M]	Paul Bley	1956	$120

BLEYER, ARCHIE
CADENCE
❑ CLP-3044 [M]	Moonlight Serenade	1962	$25
❑ CLP-25044 [S]	Moonlight Serenade	1962	$30

BLIGE, MARY J.
GEFFEN
❑ 1033301	Growing Pains	2008	$25
MCA
❑ 111929	Mary	1999	$18
❑ 112616	No More Drama	2001	$18
—Original edition			
❑ 112808	No More Drama (2002)	2002	$15
—Revised edition			
❑ 11606	Share My World	1997	$18
UPTOWN
❑ 11156	My Life	1994	$18
❑ 10681	What's the 411?	1992	$18

Number	Title	Yr	NM

BLIND FAITH
Also see GINGER BAKER'S AIR FORCE; ERIC CLAPTON; STEVE WINWOOD.
ATCO
❑ 33-304A [M]	Blind Faith	1969	$500
—White label promo only			
❑ SD 33-304A [S]	Blind Faith	1969	$30
—Cover with naked girl on Side 1 and same scene without girl on Side 2			
❑ SD 33-304B [S]	Blind Faith	1969	$18
—Cover with band photo on Side 1 and song lyrics on Side 2			
MOBILE FIDELITY
❑ 1-186	Blind Faith	1985	$40
—Audiophile vinyl			
RSO
❑ RS-1-3016	Blind Faith	1977	$12
—Reissue with naked girl on one side and band photo on the other			
❑ 825094-1	Blind Faith	1986	$10

BLIND MELON
CAPITOL
❑ 28732	Soup	1995	$18

BLINK 182
KUNG FU
❑ 78765 [B]	Buddha	1998	$18
—Reissue of 1995 album			

BLITZ
CLEOPATRA
❑ 8096 [B]	Warriors		$25

BLOCKER, DAN, AND JOHN MITCHUM
Also see LORNE GREENE, MICHAEL LANDON AND DAN BLOCKER.
RCA VICTOR
❑ LPM-2896 [M]	Our Land -- Our Heritage	1964	$30
❑ LSP-2896 [S]	Our Land -- Our Heritage	1964	$40

BLOCKER, DAN
TREY
❑ TLP-903 [M]	Tales for Young 'Uns	1961	$50

BLODWYN PIG
JETHRO TULL related.
A&M
❑ SP-4210	Ahead Rings Out	1969	$18
❑ SP-3180	Ahead Rings Out	1982	$12
—Budget-line reissue			
❑ SP-4243	Getting to This	1970	$18

BLOND
FONTANA
❑ SRF-67067	Blond	1969	$25

BLONDE ON BLONDE
JANUS
❑ JLP-3003	Contrasts	1969	$30

BLONDIE
CHRYSALIS
❑ CHS24PDJ [DJ]	At Home with Debbie Harry and Chris Stein	1981	$75
—Open-end interview with script			
❑ CHE1290	Autoamerican	1980	$12
❑ PV41290	Autoamerican	1983	$10
—Reissue			
❑ CHR1165	Blondie	1977	$15
—Reissue of Private Stock album			
❑ PV41165	Blondie	1983	$10
—Reissue			
❑ CHE1225	Eat to the Beat	1979	$12
❑ PV41225	Eat to the Beat	1983	$10
—Reissue			
❑ R200816	Once More into the Bleach	1988	$25
—BMG Music Service edition			
❑ V2X41658	Once More into the Bleach	1988	$18
—Remixes of Blondie and Debbie Harry tracks			
❑ CHR1192	Parallel Lines	1978	$18
—First pressing, with 3:54 version of "Heart of Glass"			
❑ CHR1192	Parallel Lines	1979	$12
—Second pressing, with 5:50 version of "Heart of Glass" (Disco Version)			
❑ CHP5001 [PD]	Parallel Lines	1979	$30
—Picture disc			
❑ FV41192	Parallel Lines	1983	$10
—Reissue			
❑ PV41192	Parallel Lines	1986	$10
—Reissue			
❑ CHR1166	Plastic Letters	1977	$25
—Green label			

Number	Title	Yr	NM

❏ PV41166 [B]	Plastic Letters	1983	$10
— Reissue			
❏ CHR1166	Plastic Letters	1977	$15
— Blue and white label			
❏ CHS1337	The Best of Blondie	1981	$12
❏ FV41337	The Best of Blondie	1983	$10
— Reissue			
❏ PV41337	The Best of Blondie	1986	$10
— Reissue			
❏ CHR1384	The Hunter	1982	$10
❏ PV41384	The Hunter	1983	$10
— Reissue			
❏ F132748	The Remix Project: Remixed, Remade, Remodeled	1995	$18

MOBILE FIDELITY

❏ Jan-0050 [B]	Parallel Lines	1980	$50
— Audiophile vinyl			

PRIVATE STOCK

❏ PS-2023 [B]	Blondie	1976	$35

BLOOD, SWEAT AND TEARS

ABC

❏ 1015	Brand New Day	1977	$25

CBS SPECIAL PRODUCTS

❏ P16660	Musically Speaking	1982	$25

COLUMBIA

❏ CS9720	Blood, Sweat and Tears	1969	$35
— Red "360 Sound" label			
❏ CS9720	Blood, Sweat and Tears	1970	$25
— Orange label			
❏ PC9720	Blood, Sweat and Tears	1980	$20
❏ CQ30994 [Q]	Blood, Sweat and Tears	1972	$40
❏ KC30090	Blood, Sweat and Tears 3	1970	$25
❏ PC30090	Blood, Sweat and Tears 3	1986	$20
❏ KC31170	Blood, Sweat and Tears' Greatest Hits	1972	$25
— With the single versions of "You've Made Me So Very Happy," "Spinning Wheel," and "And When I Die" (all in mono)			
❏ CQ31170 [Q]	Blood, Sweat and Tears' Greatest Hits	1972	$40
❏ PC31170	Blood, Sweat and Tears' Greatest Hits	1980	$20
❏ PCQ31170 [Q]	Blood, Sweat and Tears' Greatest Hits	1976	$75
— Reissue with new prefix			
❏ KC30590	BS&T: 4	1971	$25
❏ CS9616 [S]	Child Is Father to the Man	1968	$35
— Red "360 Sound" label			
❏ CS9616	Child Is Father to the Man	1970	$25
— Orange label			
❏ PC9619	Child Is Father to the Man	1980	$20
❏ HC49619	Child Is Father to the Man	1981	$150
— Half-speed mastered edition			
❏ CS9616 [M]	Child Is Father to the Man	1968	$350
— White label promo only, "Special Mono Radio Station Copy" sticker on cover, with same number as stereo edition			
❏ PC32929	Mirror Image	1974	$25
❏ CQ32929 [Q]	Mirror Image	1974	$40
❏ PC34233	More Than Ever	1976	$25
❏ KC31780	New Blood	1972	$25
❏ PC33484	New City	1975	$25
❏ PCQ33484 [Q]	New City	1975	$40
❏ KC32180	No Sweat	1973	$25

DIRECT DISK

❏ SD-16605	Blood, Sweat and Tears	1981	$120

MCA

❏ 3227	Blood, Sweat and Tears	1981	$0
— Canceled?			
❏ L33-1865 [DJ]	Nuclear Blues	1980	$35
— Promo only on gold vinyl			
❏ 3061	Nuclear Blues	1980	$25

MOBILE FIDELITY

❏ 1-251	Blood, Sweat and Tears	1996	$150
— Audiophile vinyl; fewer than 2,000 pressed			

Number	Title	Yr	NM

BLOODROCK
GRAND FUNK and TERRY KNIGHT related.

CAPITOL

❏ ST-435	Bloodrock	1970	$18
❏ ST-491	Bloodrock 2	1970	$18
❏ ST-765	Bloodrock 3	1971	$18
❏ SM-765	Bloodrock 3	197?	$12
— Reissue with new prefix			
❏ SVBB-11038	Bloodrock Live	1972	$25
— Original edition has a lime green label			
❏ SM-11417	Bloodrock 'N' Roll	1975	$15
❏ SW-11109	Bloodrock Passage	1972	$18
❏ SMAS-645	Bloodrock U.S.A.	1971	$18
❏ SM-645	Bloodrock U.S.A.	197?	$12
— Reissue with new prefix			
❏ SMAS-11259	Whirlwind Tongues	1973	$18

BLOODSTONE

LONDON

❏ PS671	Do a Thing?	1976	$18
❏ APS647	I Need Time	1974	$25
❏ XPS620	Natural High	1973	$25
❏ PS654	Riddle of the Sphinx	1975	$18
❏ XPS634	Unreal	1973	$25

MOTOWN

❏ M7-909	Don't Stop!	1978	$15

T-NECK

❏ FZ39146	Bloodstone's Party	1984	$12
❏ PZ40016	Greatest Hits	1985	$10
❏ PZ40042	Lullaby of Broadway	1985	$10
❏ FZ38115	We Go a Long Way Back	1982	$12

BLOODSUCKERS

GUINNESS

❏ GNS36077 [B]	Bloodsuckers	1977	$50

BLOODY MARY

FAMILY PRODUCTIONS

❏ FPS-2707	Bloody Mary	1972	$30

BLOOM, BOBBY

BUDDAH

❏ BDS-5072	Where Are We Going	1971	$15

L&R

❏ LR-1035	The Bobby Bloom Album	1970	$18

BLOOMFIELD, MIKE, AND AL KOOPER

COLUMBIA

❏ KGP6	The Live Adventures of Mike Bloomfield & Al Kooper	1969	$30
— Red "360 Sound" labels			
❏ PG6	The Live Adventures of Mike Bloomfield & Al Kooper	197?	$15
— Reissue with new prefix			

BLOOMFIELD, MIKE, AND NICK GRAVENITES

COLUMBIA

❏ CS9899 [B]	My Labors	1969	$18
— Red "360 Sound" label			
❏ CS9899 [B]	My Labors	1970	$15
— Orange label			

BLOOMFIELD, MIKE

COLUMBIA

❏ C237578	Bloomfield	1982	$15
❏ CS9883	It's Not Killing Me	1969	$18
— Red "360 Sound" label			

HARMONY

❏ KH30395	It's Not Killing Me	1971	$12

SUNDAZED

❏ LP5105	I'm Cutting Out	2001	$15

TAKOMA

❏ C-1059	Analine	1977	$20
❏ TAK-7059	Analine	198?	$15
❏ C-1070	Between a Hard Place and the Ground	1979	$15
❏ TAK-7070	Between a Hard Place and the Ground	198?	$12
❏ TAK-7091	Cruisin' for a Bruisin'	198?	$15
❏ C-1063	Michael Bloomfield	1978	$15
❏ TAK-7063	Michael Bloomfield	198?	$15

WATERHOUSE

❏ 11	Living in the Fast Lane	1981	$12

BLOOMFIELD, MIKE/AL KOOPER/STEVE STILLS

COLUMBIA

❏ CS9701	Super Session	1968	$25
— Red "360 Sound" label			
❏ CS9701	Super Session	1970	$12
— Orange label			
❏ CQ30991 [Q]	Super Session	1971	$40
❏ PC9701	Super Session	198?	$10
— Reissue with new prefix			

Number	Title	Yr	NM

MOBILE FIDELITY

❏ 1-178 [B]	Super Session	198?	$75
— Audiophile vinyl			

BLOOMFIELD, MIKE/JOHN PAUL HAMMOND/DR. JOHN

COLUMBIA

❏ KC32172	Triumvirate	1973	$15

BLOSSOMS, THE

LION

❏ 1007	Shockwave	1972	$18

BLOW, KURTIS

MERCURY

❏ 826141-1	America	1985	$12
❏ 834692-1	Back by Popular Demand	1988	$12
❏ SRM-1-4020	Deuce	1981	$12
❏ 822420-1	Ego Trip	1984	$12
❏ 830215-1	Kingdom Blow	1986	$12
❏ SRM-1-3854	Kurtis Blow	1980	$15
❏ 812757-1	Party Time?	1983	$12
❏ MX-1-505 [EP]	Tough	1982	$12

BLOW MONKEYS

RCA

❏ NFL1-8065	Animal Magic	1986	$12
❏ MFL1-8527 [EP]	Forbidden Fruit	1985	$12
❏ 6246-1-R	She Was Only a Grocer's Daughter	1987	$12

BLU, PEGGI

CAPITOL

❏ ST-12550	Blu Blowin'	1987	$12

BLUE, DAVID

ASYLUM

❏ 7E-1043	Com'n Back for More	1975	$12
❏ 7E-1077	Cupid's Arrow	1976	$12
❏ SD5052	Stories	1972	$15
❏ SD5066	The Nice Baby and the Angel	1973	$15

ELEKTRA

❏ EKM-4003 [M]	David Blue	1966	$30
❏ EKS-74003 [S]	David Blue	1966	$30

REPRISE

❏ RS6296	These 23 Days in September	1968	$18

BLUE

ROCKET

❏ PIG-2290	Another Night Time Flight	1977	$18

RSO

❏ SO873	Blue	1973	$15

BLUE ANGEL
Features CYNDI LAUPER.

POLYDOR

❏ PD-1-6300	Blue Angel	1980	$25

BLUE BARONS, THE

PHILIPS

❏ PHM200017 [M]	Twist to the Great Blues Hits	1962	$25
❏ PHS600017 [S]	Twist to the Great Blues Hits	1962	$30

BLUE BEATS, THE

A.A.

❏ 133 [M]	The Beatle Beat	1964	$40

BLUE BIRD SOCIETY ORCHESTRA, THE

STASH

❏ ST-268	The Blue Bird Society Orchestra	1987	$25

BLUE BOYS, THE

RCA VICTOR

❏ LPM-3794 [M]	Hit After Hit	1967	$30
❏ LSP-3794 [S]	Hit After Hit	1967	$25
❏ LPM-3529 [M]	Sounds of Jim Reeves	1966	$25
❏ LSP-3529 [S]	Sounds of Jim Reeves	1966	$30
❏ LPM-3696 [M]	The Blue Boys in Person	1967	$25
❏ LSP-3696 [S]	The Blue Boys in Person	1967	$30
❏ LPM-3331 [M]	We Remember Jim	1965	$30
❏ LSP-3331 [S]	We Remember Jim	1965	$30

BLUE CHEER

CAROLINE

❏ CAROL1395	The Beast Is Back	1989	$15
— Reissue			

MEGAFORCE

❏ MRI1069	The Beast Is Back	1984	$18

PHILIPS

❏ PHS600333	Blue Cheer	1970	$40
❏ PHS600305	New! Improved! Blue Cheer	1969	$40

Number	Title	Yr	NM
❑ PHS600350	Oh! Pleasant Hope	1971	$40
❑ PHS600278	Outsideinside	1968	$40
❑ PHS600347	The Original Human Being	1970	$40
❑ PHM200264 [M]	Vincebus Eruptum	1968	$175
❑ PHS600264 [S]	Vincebus Eruptum	1968	$40

RHINO

❑ RNLP70130	Louder Than God (The Best of Blue Cheer, 1968-1969)	1986	$15

BLUE DIAMONDS, THE
LONDON

❑ LL3235 [M]	Ramona1	1963	$30

BLUE JAYS, THE (1)
MILESTONE

❑ 1001 [M]	The Blue Jays Meet Little Caesar and the Romans	1962	$150

BLUE MAGIC
ATCO

❑ SD7038	Blue Magic	1974	$15
❑ SD 36-140	Mystic Dragons	1976	$15
❑ SD 36-103	The Magic of the Blue	1974	$15
❑ SD 38-104	The Message	1977	$15
❑ SD 36-120	Thirteen Blue Magic Lane	1975	$15

CAPITOL

❑ ST-12143	Welcome Back	1981	$12

COLLECTABLES

❑ COL-5031	The Magic of the Blue: Greatest Hits	198?	$12

COLUMBIA

❑ C45092	From Out of the Blue	1989	$15

MIRAGE

❑ 90074	Magic #	1983	$12

OMNI

❑ 90527	Greatest Hits	1986	$12

BLUE MERCEDES
MCA

❑ 42143	Rich and Famous	1988	$10

BLUE MINK
MCA

❑ 332	Blue Mink	1973	$15

PHILIPS

❑ PHS600323	Melting Pot	1970	$18
❑ PHS600339	Real Mink	1970	$18

BLUE MURDER
GEFFEN

❑ GHS24212	Blue Murder	1989	$12

BLUE NILE, THE
A&M

❑ SP-6-5087	A Walk Across the Rooftops	1983	$12
❑ SP-5284	Hats	1990	$18

BLUE NOTES, THE (1)
COLLECTABLES

❑ COL-5006	The Early Years	1982	$15

BLUE OYSTER CULT
COLUMBIA

❑ PC34164	Agents of Fortune	1976	$12

—*Original gatefold with no bar code on cover*

❑ PC34164 [B]	Agents of Fortune	198?	$10

—*Budget-line reissue with bar code*

❑ KC31063	Blue Oyster Cult	1972	$15
❑ PC31063	Blue Oyster Cult	197?	$10

—*Reissue with new prefix*

Number	Title	Yr	NM
❑ FC39979	Club Ninja	1986	$12
❑ JC36550	Cultosaurus Erectus	1980	$12
❑ PC36550	Cultosaurus Erectus	198?	$10

—*Budget-line reissue*

❑ KG37946	Extraterrestrial Live	1982	$15
❑ FC37389	Fire of Unknown Origin	1981	$12
❑ PC37389	Fire of Unknown Origin	1984	$10

—*Budget-line reissue*

❑ FC40618	Imaginos	1988	$12
❑ JC36009	Mirrors	1979	$12
❑ PC36009	Mirrors	198?	$10

—*Budget-line reissue*

❑ KG33371	On Your Feet or On Your Knees	1975	$18
❑ KC32858	Secret Treaties	1974	$15
❑ CQ32858 [Q]	Secret Treaties	1974	$50
❑ PC32858	Secret Treaties	197?	$10

—*Reissue with new prefix*

❑ JC35563	Some Enchanted Evening	1978	$12
❑ PC35563	Some Enchanted Evening	198?	$10

—*Budget-line reissue*

❑ JC35019	Spectres	1977	$12
❑ PC35019	Spectres	198?	$10

—*Budget-line reissue*

❑ FC38947	The Revolution by Night	1983	$12
❑ PC38947	The Revolution by Night	1985	$10

—*Budget-line reissue*

❑ KC32017	Tyranny and Mutation	1973	$15
❑ CQ32017 [Q]	Tyranny and Mutation	1973	$50
❑ PC32017	Tyranny and Mutation	197?	$10

—*Reissue with new prefix*

BLUE RIDGE MOUNTAIN BOYS, THE
TIME

❑ T-2103 [M]	Bluegrass Down Home	1963	$18
❑ ST-2103 [S]	Bluegrass Down Home	1963	$25
❑ T-2083 [M]	Hootenanny and Bluegrass	1963	$18
❑ ST-2083 [S]	Hootenanny and Bluegrass	1963	$25

BLUE RIDGE QUARTET, THE
MARK IV

❑ 1118	Another Christmas with the Blue Ridge Quartet	197?	$12
❑ 21027	Christmas with the Blue Ridge Quartet	197?	$12

BLUE SKY BOYS, THE
CAPITOL

❑ T2483 [M]	Presenting the Blue Sky Boys	1966	$25
❑ ST2483 [S]	Presenting the Blue Sky Boys	1966	$30

PINE MOUNTAIN

❑ PMR257	Together Again	198?	$15

RCA CAMDEN

❑ CAL-797 [M]	The Blue Sky Boys	1963	$25
❑ CAS-797(e) [R]	The Blue Sky Boys	1963	$18

ROUNDER

❑ 0236	1964	198?	$18

STARDAY

❑ SLP-205 [M]	Rare Treasury of Old Song Gems	1962	$40
❑ SLP-269 [M]	The Blue Sky Boys	1964	$40
❑ SLP-257 [M]	Together Again	1963	$40

BLUE STARS
EMARCY

❑ MG-36067 [M]	Lullaby of Birdland	1956	$250

BLUE STEEL
ASYLUM

❑ 6E-308	Nothing But Time	1981	$12

INFINITY

❑ INF-9018	No More Lonely Nights	1979	$12

BLUE SWEDE
EMI

❑ ST-11266	Hooked on a Feeling	1974	$12
❑ ST-11346	Out of the Blue	1975	$12

BLUE THINGS, THE
RCA VICTOR

❑ LPM-3603 [M]	The Blue Things	1966	$300
❑ LSP-3603 [S]	The Blue Things	1966	$300

BLUE VELVET BAND, THE
WARNER BROS.

❑ WS1802	Sweet Moments	1969	$30

BLUE ZONE U.K.
ARISTA

❑ AL8552	Big Thing	1988	$15

Number	Title	Yr	NM

BLUEGRASS HOPPERS, THE
CUCA

❑ 1160	The Country's Come to Town	196?	$30

BLUES BOY WILLIE
ICHIBAN

❑ 1064	Be-Who?	1990	$12
❑ 1038	Strange Things Happening	1989	$12

BLUES BROTHERS
ATLANTIC

❑ SD19331	Best of the Blues Brothers	1981	$12
❑ SD19217	Briefcase Full of Blues	1978	$12
❑ SD16025	Made in America	1980	$12
❑ SD16017	The Blues Brothers	1980	$12

—*Movie soundtrack; also includes tracks by Aretha Franklin, Ray Charles and James Brown*

BLUES CLIMAX
HORNE

❑ JC-333	Blues Climax	1969	$75

BLUES IMAGE
ATCO

❑ SD 33-300	Blues Image	1969	$30
❑ SD 33-317	Open	1970	$25
❑ SD 33-346	Red, White and Blues Image	1971	$25

BLUES MAGOOS
ABC

❑ S-710	Gulf Coast Bound	1970	$25
❑ S-697	Never Goin' Back to Georgia	1969	$25

MERCURY

❑ SR-61167	Basic Blues Magoos	1968	$30
❑ MG-21104 [M]	Electric Comic Book	1967	$30
❑ SR-61104 [S]	Electric Comic Book	1967	$40
❑ 21104/61104	Electric Comic Book Comic Book	1967	$18
❑ MG-21096 [M]	Psychedelic Lollipop	1966	$40

—*With "21096" in trail-off; this record is mono*

❑ SR-61096 [S]	Psychedelic Lollipop	1966	$50
❑ SR-61096	Psychedelic Lollipop	197?	$15

—*Reissue on Chicago skyline label*

❑ MG-21096 [S]	Psychedelic Lollipop	1966	$40

—*With "2/61096" in trail-off; this record plays stereo, though labeled mono*

BLUES PROJECT, THE
CAPITOL

❑ ST-782	Lazarus	1971	$15
❑ SMAS-11017	The Blues Project	1972	$15

MCA

❑ 8003	Reunion in Central Park	1975	$18

—*Reissue of Sounds of the South LP; black rainbow labels*

❑ 25984	Reunion in Central Park	1987	$15

—*Reissue of MCA 8003; blue rainbow labels*

MGM

❑ M3G-4953	Archetypes	1974	$15
❑ GAS-118	The Blues Project	1970	$15

RHINO

❑ R1-70165	No Time Like the Right Time: The Best of the Blues Project	1989	$15

SOUNDS OF THE SOUTH

❑ MCA2-8003	Reunion in Central Park	1973	$25

—*Yellow labels*

VERVE

❑ 827918-1	Projections	1986	$10

—*Reissue*

VERVE FOLKWAYS

❑ FT-3000 [M]	Live at the Café a Go Go	1966	$35
❑ FTS-3000 [S]	Live at the Café a Go Go	1966	$35
❑ FT-3008 [M]	Projections	1966	$40
❑ FTS-3008 [S]	Projections	1966	$40

VERVE FORECAST

❑ FTS-3077	Best of the Blues Project	1969	$18
❑ FTS-3069	Flanders/Kalb/Katz, Etc.	1969	$18
❑ FT-3000 [M]	Live at the Café a Go Go	1967	$20

—*Reissue of Verve Folkways 3000*

❑ FTS-3000 [S]	Live at the Café a Go Go	1967	$25

—*Reissue of Verve Folkways 3000*

❑ FTS-3046	Planned Obsolescence	1968	$18
❑ FT-3008 [M]	Projections	1967	$20

—*Reissue of Verve Folkways 3008*

❑ FTS-3008 [S]	Projections	1967	$25

—*Reissue of Verve Folkways 3008*

❑ FT-3025 [M]	The Blues Project Live at Town Hall	1967	$25
❑ FTS-3025 [S]	The Blues Project Live at Town Hall	1967	$18

Number	Title	Yr	NM

BLUES TRAVELER
A&M
| ☐ 7502153081 | Blues Traveler | 1990 | $18 |

BLUIETT, HAMIET
BLACK SAINT
| ☐ BSR-0014 | Resolution | 198? | $30 |
CHIAROSCURO
| ☐ CH-182 | Orchestra, Duo and Sextet | 1978 | $30 |
INDIA NAVIGATION
☐ IN-1030	Birthright	1977	$30
☐ IN-1025	Endangered Species	1976	$30
☐ IN-1039	S.O.S.	1979	$30
SOUL NOTE
| ☐ SN-1018 | Dangerously Suite | 198? | $30 |
| ☐ SN-1088 | Ebu | 1985 | $30 |

BLUNSTONE, COLIN
4 MEN WITH BEARDS
| ☐ 4M237 [B] | One Year | 2013 | $30 |
EPIC
☐ KE31994 [B]	Ennismore	1972	$18
☐ KE32962 [B]	Journey	1974	$18
☐ E30974 [B]	One Year	1972	$18
ROCKET
| ☐ BXL1-2093 | Never Even Thought | 1978 | $12 |

BLUNT, JAMES
CUSTARD/ATLANTIC
| ☐ R1-73396 | Back to Bedlam | 2006 | $25 |

BLYTH, ANN
EVEREST
| ☐ LPBR-5113 [M] | Hail Mary | 1960 | $30 |
| ☐ SDBR-1113 [S] | Hail Mary | 1960 | $40 |

BLYTHE, ARTHUR
ADELPHI
| ☐ 5008 | Bush Baby | 1978 | $30 |
COLUMBIA
☐ FC37427	Blythe Spirit	1981	$25
☐ FC40237	Da-Da	1986	$25
☐ FC38163	Elaborations	1982	$25
☐ JC36583	Illusions	1980	$25
☐ PC36583	Illusions	198?	$20
—Budget-line reissue			
☐ JC36300	In the Tradition	1979	$25
☐ JC35638	Lenox Avenue Breakdown	1979	$25
☐ FC38661	Light Blue	1983	$25
☐ FC39411	Put Sunshine In It	1984	$25
INDIA NAVIGATION
| ☐ IN-1038 | Metamorphosis | 1979 | $30 |
| ☐ IN-1029 | The Grip | 1977 | $30 |

BLYTHE, JIMMY
EUPHORIA
| ☐ EES-101 | Messin' Around | 198? | $30 |
| ☐ EES-102 | Messin' Around, Vol. 2 | 198? | $30 |
RIVERSIDE
| ☐ RLP-1031 [10] | Chicago Stomps and the Dixie Four | 1954 | $300 |
| ☐ RLP-1036 [10] | Jimmy Blythe's State Street Ramblers | 1954 | $300 |

BLYTHE, STERLING
CROWN
| ☐ CLP-5179 [M] | Sterling Blythe Sings | 1963 | $25 |
SAGE & SAND
☐ C-14 [M]	A Night at the Showboat	1962	$40
—Red vinyl; label print is red and black			
☐ C-14 [M]	A Night at the Showboat	196?	$30
—Red vinyl; label print is multi-colored			

BO GRUMPUS
ATCO
| ☐ 33-246 [M] | Bo Grumpus | 1968 | $30 |
| ☐ SD 33-246 [S] | Bo Grumpus | 1968 | $25 |

BOA
SNAKEFIELD
| ☐ SN-001 | Wrong Road | 1971 | $500 |

BOB AND EARL
CRESTVIEW
| ☐ CRS-3055 | Bob & Earl | 1969 | $30 |
TIP
| ☐ TLP-1011 [M] | Harlem Shuffle | 1964 | $30 |
| ☐ TLS-9011 [S] | Harlem Shuffle | 1964 | $50 |

BOB AND RAY
RCA VICTOR
☐ LPM-2131 [M]	Bob and Ray on a Platter	1960	$30
☐ LSP-2131 [S]	Bob and Ray on a Platter	1960	$50
☐ LPM-1773 [M]	Bob and Ray Throw a Stereo Spectacular	1958	$30
☐ LSP-1773 [S]	Bob and Ray Throw a Stereo Spectacular	1958	$100
☐ LSP-1773 [S]	Bob and Ray Throw a Stereo Spectacular	199?	$30
—Classic Records reissue			
UNICORN
| ☐ UN1001 [10] | Write If You Get Work | 1954 | $75 |

BOB B. SOXX AND THE BLUE JEANS
PHILLIES
| ☐ PHLP-4002 [M] | Zip-a-Dee Doo-Dah | 1963 | $500 |

BOBBY AND THE MIDNITES
ARISTA
| ☐ AL9568 | Bobby and the Midnites | 1981 | $12 |
COLUMBIA
| ☐ BFC39276 | Where the Beat Meets the Street | 1984 | $12 |

BOBBY JIMMY AND THE CRITTERS
MACOLA
| ☐ MRC 0989 | Back and Proud | 1987 | $12 |
| ☐ MRC 0933 | Roaches: The Beginning | 1986 | $12 |
RAPSUR
| ☐ RP10009 | Ugly Knuckle Butt | 1985 | $30 |

BOBBY M
GORDY
| ☐ 6023GL | Blow | 1982 | $15 |

BOBO, WILLIE
BLUE NOTE
| ☐ BN-LA711-H2 | Tomorrow Is Here | 1977 | $40 |
COLUMBIA
☐ JC36108	Bobo	1979	$75
—Reproductions exist			
☐ JC35734	Hell of an Act to Follow	1978	$40
—Reproductions exist			
MGM
☐ LAT-10012	Spanish Blues Band	197?	$40
☐ LAT-10007	Spanish Grease	197?	$40
☐ LAT-10011	Uno, Dos, Tres	197?	$40
ROULETTE
| ☐ R-52097 [M] | Bobo's Beat | 1962 | $120 |
| ☐ SR-52097 [S] | Bobo's Beat | 1962 | $175 |
SUSSEX
| ☐ SXBS-7003 | Do What You Want to Do | 1971 | $40 |
| —Reproductions exist | | | |
TICO
☐ T-1108 [M]	Do That Thing	1963	$120
☐ ST-1108 [S]	Do That Thing	1963	$175
—Reproductions exist			
TRIP
| ☐ 5013 | Latin Beat | 1974 | $25 |
VERVE
☐ V6-8772	A New Dimension	1969	$150
☐ V-8699 [M]	Bobo Motion	1967	$40
☐ V6-8699 [S]	Bobo Motion	1967	$40
☐ V-8781	Evil Ways	1969	$40
☐ V-8669 [M]	Feelin' So Good	1966	$40
☐ V6-8669 [S]	Feelin' So Good	1966	$150
☐ V-8685 [M]	Juicy	1967	$40
☐ V6-8685 [S]	Juicy	1967	$40
☐ V6-8736 [S]	Spanish Blues Band	1968	$40
☐ V-8736 [M]	Spanish Blues Band	1968	$120
—May be promo only			
☐ V-8631 [M]	Spanish Grease	1965	$75
☐ V6-8631 [S]	Spanish Grease	1965	$40
☐ V-8648 [M]	Uno, Dos, Tres	1966	$75
☐ V6-8648 [S]	Uno, Dos, Tres	1966	$40

BOCAGE, PETER
JAZZOLOGY
| ☐ JCE-32 | Peter Bocage with His Creole Serenaders | 1979 | $25 |
| ☐ JCE-29 | San Jacinto Hall | 1978 | $25 |
RIVERSIDE
| ☐ RLP-379 [M] | Peter Bocage with His Creole Serenaders | 1961 | $250 |
| ☐ RLP-9379 [S] | Peter Bocage with His Creole Serenaders | 1961 | $250 |

BOCIAN, MICHAEL
GM RECORDINGS
| ☐ GM-3002 | For This Gift | 1982 | $25 |

BOCK, FRED
IMPACT
| ☐ R3479 | Upon a Midnight Clear | 1977 | $15 |

BODACIOUS D.F.
RCA VICTOR
☐ APL1-0206	Bodacious D.F.	1973	$18
☐ AFL1-0206	Bodacious D.F.	1977	$12
☐ AYL1-4243	Bodacious D.F.	1982	$10
—Best Buy Series" reissue			

BODEANS
SLASH
☐ 25876	Home	1989	$15
☐ 25403	Love & Hope & Sex & Dreams	1986	$12
☐ R153192	Outside Looking In	1987	$15
—BMG Direct Marketing edition			
☐ 25629	Outside Looking In	1987	$12

BODY
MCA
| ☐ 42058 | Body | 1987 | $12 |

BODY COUNT
VIRGIN
| ☐ 39802 | Born Dead | 1994 | $18 |

BOETCHER, CURT
ELEKTRA
| ☐ EKS-75037 | There's an Innocent Face | 1972 | $25 |

BOFFALONGO
UNITED ARTISTS
| ☐ UAS-6770 | Beyond Your Head | 1970 | $25 |
| ☐ UAS-6726 | Boffalongo | 1969 | $25 |

BOFILL, ANGELA
ARISTA
☐ AL8-8258	Let Me Be the One	1984	$12
☐ AL9576	Something About You	1981	$12
☐ AL8-8125	Something About You	198?	$10
—Reissue of 9576			
☐ AL8-8198	Teaser	1983	$12
☐ AL8-8396	Tell Me Tomorrow	1985	$12
☐ AL8-8425	The Best of Angela Bofill	1986	$12
☐ AL9616	Too Tough	1983	$12
☐ AL8-8000	Too Tough	198?	$10
—Reissue of 9616			
ARISTA/GRP
☐ GL5501	Angel of the Night	1979	$15
☐ GL8-8060	Angel of the Night	198?	$10
—Reissue of 5501			
☐ GL5000	Angie	1978	$15
☐ GLB-8302	Angie	198?	$10
—Reissue of 5000			
CAPITOL
| ☐ C1-48335 | Intuition | 1988 | $12 |

BOGARDE, DIRK
LONDON
| ☐ LL3187 [M] | Lyrics for Lovers | 1960 | $30 |
| ☐ PS210 [S] | Lyrics for Lovers | 1960 | $30 |

BOGGUSS, SUZY
CAPITOL
☐ C1-90237	Somewhere Between	1989	$18
☐ C1-590237	Somewhere Between	1989	$18
—Columbia House edition			

BOHANNON, GEORGE
WORKSHOP JAZZ
| ☐ WSJ-207 [M] | Boss Bossa Nova | 1963 | $100 |

BOHANNON
COMPLEAT
| ☐ CPL-1-1003 | Make Your Body Move | 1983 | $12 |
| ☐ CPL-1-1005 | The Bohannon Drive | 1984 | $15 |
DAKAR
☐ DK76917	Bohannon	1975	$18
☐ DK76919	Dance Your Ass Off	1976	$18
☐ DK76921	Gittin' Off	1976	$25
☐ 76916	Insides Out	1974	$15
☐ 6910	Keep On Dancing	1973	$15
MCA
| ☐ 42310 | Here Comes Bohannon | 1989 | $15 |
MERCURY
☐ SRM-1-3762	Cut Loose	1979	$12
☐ SRM-1-3813	Music in the Air	1980	$12
☐ SRM-1-3710	On My Way	1978	$12
☐ SRM-1-1159	Phase II	1977	$12
☐ SRM-1-3728	Summertime Groove	1978	$12
☐ SRM-1-3778	Too Hot to Hold	1979	$12
PHASE II
☐ FZ37695	Alive	1981	$12
☐ FZ38113	Bohannon Fever	1982	$12
☐ JW36867	One Step Ahead	1980	$12

Number	Title	Yr	NM

BOHEMIAN VENDETTA
MAINSTREAM
❏ 56106 [M]	Bohemian Vendetta	1968	$500
❏ S-6106 [S]	Bohemian Vendetta	1968	$500

BOLCOM, WILLIAM
JAZZOLOGY
| ❏ JCE-72 | William Bolcom Plays His Own Rags | 198? | $25 |

NONESUCH
| ❏ N-71257 | Heliotrope Bouquet (Piano Rags, 1900-70) | 1971 | $30 |
| ❏ N-71299 | Pastimes and Piano Rags | 1972 | $30 |

BOLD
ABC
| ❏ ABCS-705 | Bold | 1969 | $85 |

BOLDER DAMN
HIT
| ❏ HRI-5061 | Mourning | 1971 | $1000 |

BOLGER, RAY
DISNEYLAND
| ❏ ST-3930 [M] | The Story of the Scarecrow of Oz | 1965 | $30 |

BOLIN, TOMMY
Also see THE JAMES GANG; ZEPHYR; DEEP PURPLE.
CLEOPATRA
| ❏ 2076 [B] | Savannah Woman - Demos And Jam Sessions | | $25 |

COLUMBIA
❏ PC34329	Private Eyes	1976	$15
— Original with no bar code on cover			
❏ PC34329	Private Eyes	198?	$10
— With bar code on cover			

GEFFEN
| ❏ 3GHS24248 | The Ultimate Tommy Bolin | 1989 | $30 |

NEMPEROR
| ❏ NE436 [B] | Teaser | 1975 | $18 |
| ❏ PZ37534 | Teaser | 1982 | $10 |

BOLL WEEVIL JAZZ BAND
GHB
❏ 89	Red Hot in Memphis	197?	$25
❏ 31 [M]	Volume 1	1966	$30
❏ 32 [M]	Volume 2: Just a Little While	1966	$30
❏ 33 [M]	Volume 3: One More Time	1966	$30
❏ 34 [M]	Volume 4: One More Time Again	1966	$30
❏ 48	Volume 5: A Hot Band Is Hard to Find	1968	$25

BOLLING, CLAUDE
BALLY
| ❏ BAL-12003 [M] | French Jazz | 1956 | $40 |

CBS
❏ FM42474	Bolling Plays Ellington, Vol. 1	1988	$25
❏ FM42476	Bolling Plays Ellington, Vol. 2	1988	$25
❏ FM42318	Suite No. 2 for Flute and Jazz Piano Trio	1987	$25

CBS MASTERWORKS
❏ FM39245	Big Band	1985	$25
❏ M336845	Bolling	1981	$30
— Combines 33233, 35128, and 35864 in one box			
❏ FM36691	California Suite	1980	$25
— With Hubert Laws and Shelly Manne; not the same as the original soundtrack recording			
❏ FM37264	Concerto for Classic Guitar and Jazz Piano	1981	$25
— With Alexandre Lagoya; reissue of RCA Red Seal 0149			
❏ FM39244	Jazz A La Francaise	1985	$25
❏ FM39059	Suite for Cello and Jazz Piano Trio	1984	$25
— With Yo-Yo Ma, others			
❏ FM37798	Suite for Chamber Orchestra and Jazz Piano Trio	1982	$25
❏ FM36731	Toot Suite for Trumpet and Jazz Piano	1980	$25
— With Maurice Andre			

COLUMBIA
❏ PC33277	Original Ragtime	1975	$25
❏ FM39009	Original Ragtime	1984	$20
— Reissue of 33277			

COLUMBIA MASTERWORKS
❏ M35864	Picnic Suite for Flute, Guitar and Jazz Piano	1979	$25
— With Jean-Pierre Rampal and Alexandre Lagoya			
❏ M33233	Suite for Flute and Jazz Piano	1975	$25
— With Jean-Pierre Rampal			
❏ M35128	Suite for Violin and Jazz Piano	1978	$25

Number	Title	Yr	NM

| — With Pinchas Zuckerman | | | |

DRG
| ❏ SL-5201 | Nuances | 1986 | $25 |

JAZZ MAN
| ❏ 5018 | Rolling with Bolling | 198? | $25 |
| — Reissue of Omega OSL-6 | | | |

MERCURY
| ❏ 812569-1 | Bolling Blues | 1983 | $25 |

OMEGA
| ❏ OKL-6 [M] | Rolling with Bolling | 1960 | $30 |
| ❏ OSL-6 [S] | Rolling with Bolling | 1960 | $30 |

PHILIPS
| ❏ PHM200204 [M] | Two-Beat Mozart | 1966 | $35 |
| ❏ PHS600204 [S] | Two-Beat Mozart | 1966 | $25 |

RCA RED SEAL
| ❏ FRL1-0149 | Concerto for Classic Guitar and Jazz Piano | 1973 | $30 |
| — With Alexandre Lagoya | | | |

BOLTON, MICHAEL
COLUMBIA
❏ BFC39328	Everybody's Crazy	1985	$12
❏ BFC38357	Michael Bolton	1983	$12
❏ PC38357	Michael Bolton	1985	$10
— Reissue with new prefix			
❏ OC45012	Soul Provider	1989	$12
❏ FC40473	The Hunger	1987	$12
❏ C46771	Time, Love and Tenderness	1991	$18

RCA VICTOR
| ❏ APL1-1551 [B] | Every Day of My Life | 1976 | $30 |
| — As "Michael Bolotin" | | | |

| ❏ APL1-0992 [B] | Michael Bolotin | 1975 | $30 |
| — As "Michael Bolotin" | | | |

BOMBERS
WEST END
| ❏ WE-104 | Bombers | 1978 | $18 |
| ❏ WE-106 | Bombers 2 | 1979 | $18 |

BON JOVI, JON
MERCURY
| ❏ 846473-1 | Blaze of Glory (Young Guns II) | 1990 | $18 |

BON JOVI
MERCURY
❏ 824509-1	7800 Fahrenheit	1985	$10
❏ 814982-1	Bon Jovi	1984	$10
❏ 836345-1	New Jersey	1988	$10
❏ 836499-1 [B]	New Jersey	1988	$30
— Picture disc in plastic sleeve			
❏ 830264-1	Slippery When Wet	1986	$10
❏ 830822-1 [B]	Slippery When Wet	1986	$30
— Picture disc in plastic cover			

BONADUCE, DANNY
LION
| ❏ LN-1015 | Danny Bonaduce | 1973 | $75 |

BONANO, SHARKEY, AND LIZZIE MILES
CAPITOL
❏ T792 [M]	A Night in Old New Orleans	1956	$85
❏ H367 [10]	Midnight on Bourbon Street	1952	$100
❏ T367 [M]	Midnight on Bourbon Street	1954	$85

BONANO, SHARKEY
CAPITOL
| ❏ T266 [M] | Kings of Dixieland | 1954 | $85 |
| ❏ H266 [10] | Sharkey's Southern Comfort | 1951 | $100 |

Number	Title	Yr	NM

CIRCLE
| ❏ LP-422 [10] | Sharkey Bonano | 1951 | $50 |

GMB
| ❏ 122 | Sharkey Bonano and His Kings of Dixieland | 198? | $25 |

ROULETTE
| ❏ R-25112 [M] | Dixieland at the Roundtable | 1960 | $30 |

SOUTHLAND
❏ 222 [M]	Kings of Dixieland	1959	$30
❏ SLP-205 [10]	New Orleans Dixieland Session	1954	$50
❏ 205 [M]	New Orleans Jam Session	1961	$30

BOND, ANGELO
ABC
| ❏ D-889 | Bondage | 1975 | $12 |

BOND, BOBBY
SOMERSET
| ❏ SF24400 [S] | Bobby Bond Sings the Roger Miller Songbook | 1966 | $18 |
| ❏ P24400 [M] | Bobby Bond Sings the Roger Miller Songbook | 1966 | $15 |

TIME
| ❏ 52122 [M] | On the Country Side | 1964 | $15 |
| ❏ S-2122 [S] | On the Country Side | 1964 | $18 |

BOND, EDDIE
PHILLIPS INT'L.
| ❏ PLP-1980 [M] | The Greatest Country Gospel Hits | 1961 | $400 |

BOND, GRAHAM
MERCURY
| ❏ SR-61327 [B] | Holy Magick | 1970 | $50 |
| ❏ SRM-1-612 [B] | We Put Our Magick on You | 1971 | $40 |

PULSAR
| ❏ 10604 [B] | Love Is the Law | 1969 | $75 |
| ❏ 10606 [B] | Mighty Graham Bond | 1969 | $50 |

WARNER BROS.
| ❏ 2LS2555 [B] | Solid Bond | 1971 | $30 |

BOND, JAMES, SEXTETTE
MIRWOOD
| ❏ M-7001 [M] | The James Bond Songbook | 1966 | $30 |
| ❏ S-7001 [S] | The James Bond Songbook | 1966 | $30 |

BOND, JOHNNY
CMH
| ❏ 6213 | The Return of the Singing Cowboy | 1981 | $12 |
| ❏ 6212 | The Singing Cowboy Again | 1981 | $12 |

HARMONY
| ❏ HL7353 [M] | Bottled in Bond | 1965 | $25 |
| ❏ HL7308 [M] | Johnny Bond's Best | 1964 | $25 |

NASHVILLE
| ❏ 2054 | Three Sheets to the Wind | 196? | $18 |

SHASTA
| ❏ LP-516 | Johnny Bond Rides Again | 197? | $18 |

STARDAY
❏ SLP-378 [M]	Bottles Up	1966	$30
❏ SLP-416	Drink Up and Go Home	1968	$18
❏ SLP-354 [M]	Famous Hot Rodders I Have Known	1965	$40
❏ SLP-472	Here Come the Elephants	1971	$18
❏ SLP-298 [M]	Hot Rod Lincoln	1964	$50
❏ SLP-456	Old, New, Patriotic and Blue	1970	$18
❏ SLP-227 [M]	Songs That Made Him Famous	1963	$40
❏ SLP-333 [M]	Ten Little Bottles	1965	$30
❏ SLP-402 [M]	Ten Nights in a Barroom	1967	$25
❏ SLP-147 [M]	That Wild, Wicked But Wonderful Wesy	1961	$50
❏ SLP-444	The Best of Johnny Bond	1969	$18
❏ 954	The Best of Johnny Bond	1976	$12
❏ SLP-388 [M]	The Branded Stock of Johnny Bond	1966	$25
❏ SLP-368 [M]	The Man Who Comes Around	1966	$30

BONDS, GARY U.S.
EMI AMERICA
❏ SO-17051	Dedication	1981	$12
❏ SPRO-9666 [EP]	Dedication Sampler	1981	$18
— Promo-only sampler with limited-edition number on pink sticker			
❏ SO-17068	On the Line	1982	$12

LEGRAND
❏ LLP-3001 [M]	Dance 'Til Quarter to Three	1961	$150
❏ LLP-3003 [M]	Greatest Hits of Gary U.S. Bonds	1962	$80
❏ LLP-3002 [M]	Twist Up Calypso	1962	$80

MCA
| ❏ 905 | The Best of Gary U.S. Bonds | 1984 | $12 |

PHOENIX
| ❏ PRT 0072 | Standing in the Line of Fire | 1984 | $12 |

Number	Title	Yr	NM
RHINO			
❏ RNLP-805	Certified Soul	1981	$12
BONE THUGS-N-HARMONY			
RUTHLESS			
❏ C263581	BTNH Resurrection	2000	$18
❏ 5539	E. 1999 Eternal	1995	$18
❏ 6340	The Art of War	1997	$18
❏ C69715	The Collection: Volume One	1998	$15
❏ C285172	The Collection: Volume Two	2000	$18
BONEY M			
ATCO			
❏ SD 36-143	Take the Heat Off Me	1976	$18
ATLANTIC			
❏ SD19145	Love for Sale	1977	$18
SIRE			
❏ SRK6062	Nightflight to Venus	1978	$12
BONFA, LUIZ			
ATLANTIC			
❏ 8028 [M]	The Fabulous Guitar of Luiz Bonfa/Amor!	1959	$300
— Black label			
❏ 8028 [M]	The Fabulous Guitar of Luiz Bonfa/Amor!	1960	$300
— White "bullseye" label			
❏ 8028 [M]	The Fabulous Guitar of Luiz Bonfa/Amor!	1961	$175
— Multicolor label, white "fan" logo at right			
❏ 8028 [M]	The Fabulous Guitar of Luiz Bonfa/Amor!	1963	$50
— Multicolor label, black "fan" logo at right			
❏ SD8028 [S]	The Fabulous Guitar of Luiz Bonfa/Amor!	1959	$300
— Green label			
❏ SD8028 [S]	The Fabulous Guitar of Luiz Bonfa/Amor!	1960	$300
— White "bullseye" label			
❏ SD8028 [S]	The Fabulous Guitar of Luiz Bonfa/Amor!	1961	$175
— Multicolor label, white "fan" logo at right			
❏ SD8028 [S]	The Fabulous Guitar of Luiz Bonfa/Amor!	1963	$50
— Multicolor label, black "fan" logo at right			
CAPITOL			
❏ T10134 [M]	Brazilian Guitar	1958	$75
— Turquoise label			
DOT			
❏ DLP-25848	Black Orpheus Impressions	1969	$85
❏ DLP-25881	Bonfa	1969	$85
❏ DLP-3804	Luiz Bonfa	1967	$85
❏ DLP-25804 [S]	Luiz Bonfa	1967	$85
❏ DLP-25825	Luiz Bonfa Plays Great Songs	1968	$85
EPIC			
❏ LN24124 [M]	Softly	1964	$85
❏ BN26124 [S]	Softly	1964	$50
PHILIPS			
❏ PHM200199 [M]	Braziliana	1965	$30
❏ PHS600199 [S]	Braziliana	1965	$35
❏ PHM200087 [M]	Brazil's King of the Bossa Nova and Guitar	1963	$35
❏ PHS600087 [S]	Brazil's King of the Bossa Nova and Guitar	1963	$25
❏ PHM200208 [M]	The Brazilian Scene	1966	$30
❏ PHS600208 [S]	The Brazilian Scene	1966	$35
RCA VICTOR			
❏ LSP-4376	The New Face of Bonfa	1970	$35
VERVE			
❏ V-8522 [M]	Luiz Bonfa Plays and Sings Bossa Nova	1963	$35
❏ V6-8522 [S]	Luiz Bonfa Plays and Sings Bossa Nova	1963	$25
BONFIRE, MARS			
COLUMBIA			
❏ CS9834	Faster Than the Speed of Life	1969	$30
— Reissue of Uni 73027 with slight alterations			
UNI			
❏ 73027	Mars Bonfire	1968	$40
BONHAM, TRACY			
ISLAND			
❏ 524187-1	The Burdens of Being Upright	1996	$18
— With Jason Bonham, son of John Bonham (Led Zeppelin) on drums.			
BONHAM			
As in Jason Bonham, John Bonham's son. Jason also drummed with UFO and is currently with FOREIGNER.			
WTG			
❏ P45009	The Disregard of Timekeeping	1989	$18

Number	Title	Yr	NM
BONNEMERE, EDDIE			
PRESTIGE			
❏ PRLP-7354 [M]	Jazz Oriented	1965	$25
❏ PRST-7354 [S]	Jazz Oriented	1965	$30
ROOST			
❏ RST-2236 [M]	Piano Bon Bons	1959	$30
❏ SLP-2236 [S]	Piano Bon Bons	1959	$40
❏ RST-419 [10]	Piano Mambo with Bonnemere	1954	$50
❏ RST-2241 [M]	The Sound of Memory	1960	$30
❏ SLP-2241 [S]	The Sound of Memory	1960	$40
BONNEVILLES, THE			
More than one group.			
DRUM BOY			
❏ DLM-1001 [M]	Meet the Bonnevilles	1963	$150
❏ DLS-1001 [S]	Meet the Bonnevilles	1963	$175
JUSTICE			
❏ JLP-146	Bringing It Home	196?	$500
BONNIE LOU			
KING			
❏ 595 [M]	Bonnie Lou Sings	1958	$175
BONNIWELL, T.S.			
CAPITOL			
❏ ST-377	Close	1969	$85
BONOFF, KARLA			
COLUMBIA			
❏ JC34672	Karla Bonoff	1977	$12
❏ PC34672	Karla Bonoff	198?	$10
— Budget-line reissue			
❏ JC35799	Restless Nights	1979	$12
❏ PC35799	Restless Nights	198?	$10
— Budget-line reissue			
❏ FC37444	Wild Heart of the Young	1982	$10
GOLD CASTLE			
❏ 171014-1	New World	1987	$15
BONZO DOG BAND, THE			
IMPERIAL			
❏ LP12370 [S]	Gorilla	1968	$30
— With booklet			
❏ LP12370 [S]	Gorilla	1968	$25
— Without booklet			
❏ LP9370 [M]	Gorilla	1968	$100
— With booklet			
❏ LP9370 [M]	Gorilla	1968	$50
— Without booklet			
❏ LP12457	Keynsham	1969	$25
❏ LP12445	Tadpoles	1969	$25
❏ LP12432	Urban Spaceman	1968	$30
— With booklet			
❏ LP12432	Urban Spaceman	1968	$25
— Without booklet			
LIBERTY			
❏ LN-10206	Some of the Best of the Bonzo Dog Band	1983	$10
UNITED ARTISTS			
❏ UAS5584	Let's Make Up and Be Friendly	1972	$18
❏ UAS5517	The Beast of the Bonzos	1971	$18
❏ UA-LA321-H2	The History of the Bonzos	1974	$18
BOO-YAA T.R.I.B.E.			
4TH & B'WAY			
❏ 4017	New Funky Nation	1990	$18
BOOGIE BOYS, THE			
CAPITOL			
❏ ST-12409	City Life	1985	$15
❏ C1-46917	Romeo Knight	1988	$12
❏ ST-12488	Survival of the Freshest	1986	$15
BOOGIE DOWN PRODUCTIONS			
B BOY			
❏ BB2000	A Man and His Music	1997	$18
❏ BB4787	Criminal Minded	1987	$15
— Reissued in 1997 with the same number			
❏ BB5787	Criminal Minded Instrumental	1987	$15
— Reissued in 1997 with the same number			
JIVE			
❏ 1097-1-J	By All Means Necessary	1988	$12
❏ 1358-1-J	Edutainment	1990	$18
❏ 1187-1-J	Ghetto Music: The Blueprint of Hip-Hop	1989	$12
LANDSPEED			
❏ LSR8806	Best of B-Boy Records	2000	$25
BOOGIE KINGS, THE			
MONTEL			
❏ LP-109 [M]	Blue Eyed Soul	1967	$30

Number	Title	Yr	NM
❏ LP-104 [M]	The Boogie Kings	1966	$40
BOOGIEMONSTERS			
PENDULUM			
❏ 56045	God Sound	1997	$15
❏ E1-29607	Riders of the Storm: The Underwater Album	1994	$18
BOOK OF LOVE			
SIRE			
❏ 25355	Book of Love	1986	$12
❏ 25700	Lullaby	1988	$12
BOOKER T. AND PRISCILLA			
A&M			
❏ SP-3504	Booker T. and Priscilla	1971	$18
❏ SP-4413	Chronicles	1973	$12
❏ SP-4351	Home Grown	1972	$12
BOOKER T. AND THE MG'S			
A&M			
❏ SP-4874	I Want You	1981	$12
— As "Booker T. Jones			
❏ SP-4798	The Best of You	1979	$12
— As "Booker T. Jones			
❏ SP-4720	Try and Love Again	1978	$12
— As "Booker T. Jones			
ASYLUM			
❏ 7E-1093	Universal Language	1977	$12
ATLANTIC			
❏ 8202 [M]	The Best of Booker T. and the MG's	1968	$50
— Mono is white label promo only			
❏ 81285	The Best of Booker T. and the MG's	1985	$10
❏ SD8202 [S]	The Best of Booker T. and the MG's	1968	$25
EPIC			
❏ KE33143	Evergreen	1974	$15
MCA			
❏ 6282	The Runaway	1989	$15
— As "Booker T. Jones			
STAX			
❏ ST-711 [M]	And Now…Booker T. and the MG's	1966	$50
❏ STS-711 [S]	And Now…Booker T. and the MG's	1966	$100
❏ STS-2033	Booker T. and the MG's Greatest Hits	1970	$18
❏ MPS-8505	Booker T. and the MG's Greatest Hits	1981	$12
❏ STS-724 [S]	Doin' Our Thing	1968	$50
❏ ST-724 [M]	Doin' Our Thing	1968	$100
❏ STX-4104	Free Ride	1978	$12
❏ ST-701 [M]	Green Onions	1962	$80
❏ STS-701 [R]	Green Onions	1966	$50

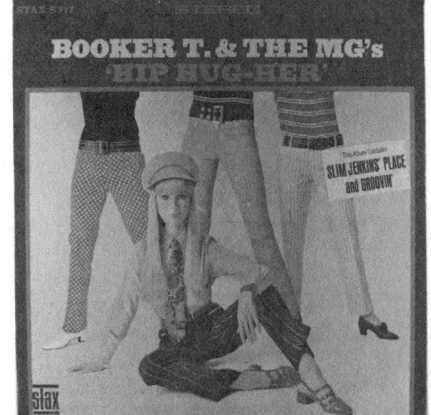

Number	Title	Yr	NM
❏ ST-717 [M]	Hip Hug-Her	1967	$40
❏ STS-717 [S]	Hip Hug-Her	1967	$50
❏ ST-713 [M]	In the Christmas Spirit	1966	$400
— Fingers and piano keys cover			
❏ ST-713 [M]	In the Christmas Spirit	1967	$300
— Same as above; Santa Claus cover			
❏ STS-713 [S]	In the Christmas Spirit	1966	$400
— Fingers and piano keys cover			
❏ STS-713 [S]	In the Christmas Spirit	1967	$250
— Santa Claus cover			
❏ STS-2027 [B]	McLemore Avenue	1970	$35
❏ MPS-8552	McLemore Avenue	1990	$15
— Reissue of 2027			
❏ STS-2035 [S]	Melting Pot	1971	$18
❏ MPS-8521 [B]	Melting Pot	198?	$12
— Reissue of 2035			
❏ STM-2035 [M]	Melting Pot	1971	$40
— Mono is white label promo only			

Number	Title	Yr	NM
❏ ST-705 [M]	Soul Dressing	1965	$80
❏ STS-705 [R]	Soul Dressing	1966	$50
❏ STS-2001	Soul Limbo	1968	$30
❏ STX-4113	Soul Limbo	198?	$12
—Reissue of 2001			
❏ STS-2009	The Booker T. Set	1969	$30
❏ MPS-8531	The Booker T. Set	1987	$12
—Reissue of 2009			
❏ STS-2006	Uptight	1969	$30
SUNDAZED			
❏ LP5043	And Now! Booker T. and the MG's	2000	$18
—Reissue on 180-gram vinyl			
❏ LP5079	Green Onions	2002	$15
—Reissue on 180-gram vinyl			
❏ LP5080	Hip Hug-Her	2002	$15
—Reissue on 180-gram vinyl			
❏ LP5053	In the Christmas Spirit	2000	$18
—Reissue on 180-gram vinyl			
❏ LP5042	Soul Dressing	2000	$18
—Reissue on 180-gram vinyl			

BOOMERANG

RCA VICTOR

Number	Title	Yr	NM
❏ LSP-4577	Boomerang	1971	$25

BOOMTOWN RATS, THE
Includes (Sir!) BOB GELDOF.

COLUMBIA

Number	Title	Yr	NM
❏ JC35750	A Tonic for the Troops	1979	$12
❏ PC35750	A Tonic for the Troops	198?	$10
—Budget-line reissue			
❏ FC39335	In the Long Grass	1985	$12
❏ PC39335	In the Long Grass	198?	$10
—Budget-line reissue			
❏ JC37062	Mondo Bongo	1981	$15
—With poster			
❏ PC37062	Mondo Bongo	198?	$10
—Budget-line reissue			
❏ 5C38591 [EP]	Ratrospective	1983	$12
❏ 5C38097 [EP]	The Boomtown Rats	1982	$10
❏ JC36248	The Fine Art of Surfacing	1979	$12
❏ PC36248	The Fine Art of Surfacing	198?	$10
—Budget-line reissue			
❏ FC38195	V Deep	1982	$12
❏ PC38195	V Deep	198?	$10
—Budget-line reissue			

MERCURY

Number	Title	Yr	NM
❏ SRM-1-1188	The Boomtown Rats	1977	$18

BOONE, DANIEL

MERCURY

Number	Title	Yr	NM
❏ SRM-1-649	Beautiful Sunday	1972	$12

BOONE, DEBBY

CAPITOL

Number	Title	Yr	NM
❏ ST-41005	Choose Life	198?	$12
❏ ST-41029	Surrender	198?	$12

LAMB & LION

Number	Title	Yr	NM
❏ LLR3008	Choose Life	1985	$15
❏ 83011	Friends for Life	198?	$15
❏ 1046	With My Song	1980	$15

MCA

Number	Title	Yr	NM
❏ 1457	Best of Debby Boone	198?	$10
❏ 962	You Light Up My Life	198?	$10
—Reissue of Warner Bros. 3118			

WARNER BROS.

Number	Title	Yr	NM
❏ BSK3301	Debby Boone	1979	$12
❏ BSK3419	Love Has No Reason	1980	$12
❏ BSK3130	Midstream	1978	$12
❏ BSK3501	Savin' It Up	1981	$12
❏ BS3118	You Light Up My Life	1977	$12

BOONE, LARRY

MERCURY

Number	Title	Yr	NM
❏ 834377-1	Larry Boone	1988	$10
❏ 836710-1	Swingin' Doors, Sawdust Floors	1989	$12

BOONE, PAT, FAMILY

THISTLE

Number	Title	Yr	NM
❏ TR-1001	The Boone Family Christmas	1975	$15

BOONE, PAT

ABC

Number	Title	Yr	NM
❏ 4006	16 Great Performances	1975	$10

BIBLE VOICE

Number	Title	Yr	NM
❏ 7076	The Solution to Crisis-America	1970	$12

DOT

Number	Title	Yr	NM
❏ DLP-3814 [M]	15 Hits of Pat Boone	1967	$15
❏ DLP-25814 [S]	15 Hits of Pat Boone	1967	$12
❏ DLP-3601 [M]	Blest Be the Tie That Binds	1965	$12

Number	Title	Yr	NM
❏ DLP-25601 [S]	Blest Be the Tie That Binds	1965	$15
❏ DLP-3594 [M]	Boss Beat	1964	$12
❏ DLP-25594 [S]	Boss Beat	1964	$15
❏ DLP-3770 [M]	Christmas Is a-Comin'	1966	$12
❏ DLP-25770 [S]	Christmas Is a-Comin'	1966	$15
❏ DLP-3346 [M]	Great! Great! Great!	1961	$15
❏ DLP-25346 [S]	Great! Great! Great!	1961	$20
❏ DLP-3685 [M]	Great Hits of 1965	1965	$12
❏ DLP-25685 [S]	Great Hits of 1965	1965	$15
❏ DLP-3234 [M]	He Leadeth Me	1960	$15
❏ DLP-25234 [S]	He Leadeth Me	1960	$20
❏ DLP-3030 [M]	Howdy!	1956	$50
—Maroon label			
❏ DLP-3030 [M]	Howdy!	1957	$30
—Black label			
❏ DLP-3798 [M]	How Great Thou Art	1967	$15
❏ DLP-25798 [S]	How Great Thou Art	1967	$12
❏ DLP-3068 [M]	Hymns We Love	1957	$25
❏ DLP-25068 [S]	Hymns We Love	1959	$30
❏ DLP-3399 [M]	I'll See You in My Dreams	1961	$12
❏ DLP-25399 [S]	I'll See You in My Dreams	1961	$15
❏ DLP-3475 [M]	I Love You Truly	1962	$12
❏ DLP-25475 [S]	I Love You Truly	1962	$15
❏ DLP-3805 [M]	I Was Kaiser Bill's Batman	1967	$15
❏ DLP-25805 [S]	I Was Kaiser Bill's Batman	1967	$12
❏ DLP-3876 [M]	Look Ahead	1968	$15
❏ DLP-25876 [S]	Look Ahead	1968	$12
❏ DLP-3748 [M]	Memories	1966	$12
❏ DLP-25748 [S]	Memories	1966	$15
❏ DLP-3384 [M]	Moody River	1961	$12
❏ DLP-25384 [S]	Moody River	1961	$15
❏ DLP-3270 [M]	Moonglow	1960	$15
❏ DLP-25270 [S]	Moonglow	1960	$20
—Black vinyl			
❏ DLP-25270 [S]	Moonglow	1960	$50
—Blue vinyl			
❏ DLP-3650 [M]	My 10th Anniversary with Dot Records	1965	$12
❏ DLP-25650 [S]	My 10th Anniversary with Dot Records	1965	$15
❏ DLP-3386 [M]	My God and I	1961	$12
❏ DLP-25386 [S]	My God and I	1961	$15
❏ DLP-3606 [M]	Near You	1965	$12
❏ DLP-25606 [S]	Near You	1965	$15
❏ DLP-3050 [M]	Pat	1957	$25
❏ DLP-3012 [M]	Pat Boone	1956	$50
—Maroon label			
❏ DLP-3012 [M]	Pat Boone	1957	$30
—Black label			
❏ DLP-25573 [R]	Pat Boone	1964	$12
❏ DLP-3402 [M]	Pat Boone Reads from the Holy Bible	1962	$15
❏ DLP-3455 [M]	Pat Boone's Golden Hits	1962	$12
❏ DLP-25455 [S]	Pat Boone's Golden Hits	1962	$15
❏ DLP-3504 [M]	Pat Boone Sings "Days of Wine and Roses" and Other Great Movie Themes	1963	$12
❏ DLP-25504 [S]	Pat Boone Sings "Days of Wine and Roses" and Other Great Movie Themes	1963	$15
❏ DLP-3158 [M]	Pat Boone Sings	1959	$20
❏ DLP-25158 [S]	Pat Boone Sings	1959	$25
❏ DLP-3501 [M]	Pat Boone Sings Guess Who?	1963	$50
❏ DLP-25501 [S]	Pat Boone Sings Guess Who?	1963	$80
❏ DLP-3077 [M]	Pat Boone Sings Irving Berlin	1958	$20
❏ DLP-25077 [S]	Pat Boone Sings Irving Berlin	1959	$25
❏ DLP-3071 [M]	Pat's Great Hits	1957	$25
❏ DLP-25071 [P]	Pat's Great Hits	1959	$30
❏ DLP-3261 [M]	Pat's Great Hits Volume 2	1960	$15
❏ DLP-25261 [S]	Pat's Great Hits Volume 2	1960	$20
❏ DLP-3199 [M]	Side by Side	1959	$20
❏ DLP-25199 [S]	Side by Side	1959	$25
❏ DLP-3513 [M]	Sing Along Without Pat Boone	1963	$12
❏ DLP-25513 [S]	Sing Along Without Pat Boone	1963	$15
❏ DLP-3118 [M]	Star Dust	1958	$20
❏ DLP-25118 [S]	Star Dust	1959	$25
❏ DLP-3180 [M]	Tenderly	1959	$20
❏ DLP-25180 [S]	Tenderly	1959	$25
❏ DLP-3626 [M]	The Golden Era of Country Hits	1965	$12
❏ DLP-25626 [S]	The Golden Era of Country Hits	1965	$15
❏ DLP-3582 [M]	The Lord's Prayer And Other Great Hymns	1964	$12
❏ DLP-25582 [S]	The Lord's Prayer And Other Great Hymns	1964	$15
❏ DLP-3520 [M]	The Star Spangled Banner	1963	$12
❏ DLP-25520 [S]	The Star Spangled Banner	1963	$15
❏ DLP-3546 [M]	The Touch of Your Lips	1963	$12
❏ DLP-25546 [S]	The Touch of Your Lips	1963	$15
❏ DLP-3285 [M]	This and That	1960	$15
❏ DLP-25285 [S]	This and That	1960	$20
❏ DLP-3534 [M]	Tie Me Kangaroo Down, Sport	1963	$12
❏ DLP-25534 [S]	Tie Me Kangaroo Down, Sport	1963	$15
❏ DLP-3222 [M]	White Christmas	1959	$25
❏ DLP-25222 [S]	White Christmas	1959	$30
❏ DLP-3667 [M]	Winner of the Reader's Digest Poll	1965	$12
❏ DLP-25667 [S]	Winner of the Reader's Digest Poll	1965	$15
❏ DLP-3764 [M]	Wish You Were Here, Buddy	1966	$12
❏ DLP-25764 [S]	Wish You Were Here, Buddy	1966	$15

Number	Title	Yr	NM
❏ DLP-3121 [M]	Yes Indeed!	1958	$20
❏ DLP-25121 [S]	Yes Indeed!	1959	$25
HAMILTON			
❏ HLP-118 [M]	12 Great Hits	196?	$12
❏ HLP-12118 [S]	12 Great Hits	196?	$12
HITSVILLE			
❏ H6-405	Texas Woman	1976	$15
LAMB & LION			
❏ 1008	All in the Boone Family	1972	$10
❏ 1007	Born Again	197?	$10
❏ 1005	Christian People, Vol. 1	197?	$10
❏ 1002	New Songs of the Jesus People	197?	$12
❏ 1004	Pat Boone and the First Nashville Jesus Band	197?	$10
❏ 1013	S-A-V-E-D	197?	$10
❏ 1016	Songs from the Inner Court	197?	$10
❏ 1006	The Family Who Prays	197?	$10
❏ 5000	The Pat Boone Family in the Holy Land	197?	$10
MCA			
❏ 658	16 Great Performances	1980	$10
❏ 6020	The Best of Pat Boone	1980	$15
❏ 15028 [S]	White Christmas	198?	$10
—Reissue of Dot LP			
MELODYLAND			
❏ 6-501	The Country Side of Pat Boone	1975	$15
MGM			
❏ SE-4899	I Love You More and More Every Day	1973	$10
PARAMOUNT			
❏ 1043	Pat Boone's Greatest Hits	1974	$15
❏ 1024	Pat Boone's Greatest Hymns	1974	$15
PICKWICK			
❏ SPC-3123	Canadian Sunset	196?	$10
❏ SPC-3145	Favorite Hymns	197?	$10
❏ SPC-3597	Great Hits	1978	$10
❏ SPC-3107	Love Me Tender	196?	$10
❏ SPC-3568	The Old Rugged Cross	1978	$10
❏ SPC-3079	True Love	196?	$10
❏ SPC-1024	White Christmas	1979	$10
❏ SPC-3219	You've Lost That Lovin' Feeling	197?	$10
SUPREME			
❏ SS-2060	Rapture	1970	$12
TETRAGRAMMATON			
❏ T-118	Departure	1969	$12
WORD			
❏ WST-8711	He Leadeth Me	197?	$12
❏ WST-8664	Hymns We Love	197?	$12
❏ WST-8738	I Believe	198?	$10
❏ WST-8536	The Pat Boone Family	1970	$10
❏ WST-8725	The Star-Spangled Banner	197?	$12

BOONE, RANDY

DECCA

Number	Title	Yr	NM
❏ DL4663 [M]	Ramblin' Randy	1965	$25
❏ DL74663 [S]	Ramblin' Randy	1965	$30
❏ DL4619 [M]	Singing Star of The Virginian	1965	$30
❏ DL74619 [S]	Singing Star of The Virginian	1965	$35

BOOT

AGAPE

Number	Title	Yr	NM
❏ 2601	Boot	1972	$30

GUINNESS

Number	Title	Yr	NM
❏ GNS36002 [B]	Turn the Other Cheek	1977	$50

BOOT CAMP CLIK

PRIORITY

Number	Title	Yr	NM
❏ 50646	For the People	1997	$15
❏ 23052	Greatest Hits: Basic Training	2000	$15

BOOTH, TONY

CAPITOL

Number	Title	Yr	NM
❏ ST-11270	Happy Hour	1974	$18
❏ ST-11126	Lonesone 7-7203	1972	$18
❏ ST-11076	The Key's in the Mailbox	1972	$18
❏ ST-11210	This Is Tony Booth	1973	$18
❏ ST-11160	When a Man Loves a Woman (The Way That I Love You)	1973	$18
❏ ST-11352	Workin' at the Car Wash Blues	1974	$18

MGM

Number	Title	Yr	NM
❏ SE-4704	On the Right Track	1970	$25

BOOTSY'S RUBBER BAND

WARNER BROS.

Number	Title	Yr	NM
❏ BS2972	Ahh... The Name Is Bootsy, Baby!	1977	$18
❏ BSK3093	Bootsy? Player of the Year	1978	$18
—With perforated punch-out glasses intact			
❏ BSK3093	Bootsy? Player of the Year	1978	$12
—Without punch-out glasses			

Number	Title	Yr	NM
❑ BS2920	Stretchin' Out in Bootsy's Rubber Band	1976	$18
❑ BSK3295	This Boot Is Make for Fonk-n	1979	$18
— With 8-page coloring book			
❑ BSK3295	This Boot Is Make for Fonk-n	1979	$12
— Without coloring book			
❑ BSK3433	Ultra Wave	1980	$18
— As "Bootsy"			

BOOTY PEOPLE
ABC
❑ AB-998	Booty People	1977	$18

BORCHERS, BOBBY
PLAYBOY
❑ KZ34829	Bobby Borchers	1977	$15
❑ KZ35027	Denim and Rhinestones	1977	$15

BORDERSONG
REAL GOOD
❑ 1001	Morning	1975	$80

BORESON, STAN, AND DOUG SETTERBERG
GOLDEN CREST
❑ CR31021	Stan and Doug Yust Go Nuts at Christmas	1970	$15

BORNAND COLLECTION, THE
BORNAND MUSIC BOX
❑ AB-3/90-5611	The Original Music Box Medley of Christmas Songs	1977	$15
— Book-of-the-Month Club pressing			

BORODIN STRING QUARTET
MERCURY LIVING PRESENCE
❑ SR90309 [S]	Shostakovich: String Quartets No. 4 and 8	196?	$80
— Maroon label, no "Vendor: Mercury Record Corporation"			

BOSTIC, EARL
GRAND PRIX
❑ K-404 [M]	The Earl of Bostic	196?	$35
❑ KS-404 [R]	The Earl of Bostic	196?	$30
❑ K-416 [M]	Wild Man	196?	$35
❑ KS-416 [R]	Wild Man	196?	$30

KING
❑ K-5010X	14 Original Greatest Hits	1977	$30
❑ 947 [M]	24 Songs That Earl Loved the Most	1966	$40
❑ 597 [M]	Alto Magic in Hi-Fi	1958	$175
❑ KS-597 [S]	Alto Magic in Hi-Fi	1959	$300
❑ 395-515 [M]	Alto-Tude	1956	$200
❑ 395-503 [M]	Bostic for You	1956	$200
❑ 613 [M]	Bostic Workshop	1959	$150
❑ KS-613 [S]	Bostic Workshop	1959	$200
❑ 786 [M]	By Popular Demand	1961	$150
❑ 558 [M]	C'mon and Dance with Earl Bostic	1956	$175
❑ KS-558 [S]	C'mon and Dance with Earl Bostic	1959	$300
❑ 395-525 [M]	Dance Time	1956	$175
❑ 395-500 [M]	Dance to the Best of Bostic	195?	$100
— Second cover with girl in a swimsuit pictured			
❑ 395-500 [M]	Dance to the Best of Bostic	1956	$200
— Original cover with Earl Bostic pictured			
❑ 295-64 [10]	Earl Bostic and His Alto Sax	1951	$250
— Black vinyl			
❑ 295-64 [10]	Earl Bostic and His Alto Sax	1951	$400
— Red vinyl			
❑ 295-65 [10]	Earl Bostic and His Alto Sax	1951	$250
— Black vinyl			
❑ 295-65 [10]	Earl Bostic and His Alto Sax	1951	$400
— Red vinyl			
❑ 295-66 [10]	Earl Bostic and His Alto Sax	1951	$250
— Black vinyl			
❑ 295-66 [10]	Earl Bostic and His Alto Sax	1951	$400
— Red vinyl			
❑ 295-72 [10]	Earl Bostic and His Alto Sax	1952	$250
❑ 295-76 [10]	Earl Bostic and His Alto Sax	1952	$250
❑ 295-77 [10]	Earl Bostic and His Alto Sax	1952	$250
❑ 295-78 [10]	Earl Bostic and His Alto Sax	1952	$250
❑ 295-79 [10]	Earl Bostic and His Alto Sax	1952	$250
❑ 295-103 [10]	Earl Bostic and His Alto Sax	1954	$250
❑ 827 [M]	Earl Bostic Plays Bossa Nova	1963	$150
❑ 295-95 [10]	Earl Bostic Plays the Old Standards	1954	$250
❑ KS-1048 [S]	Harlem Nocturne	1969	$75
❑ 571 [M]	Hits of the Swing Age	1957	$175
❑ 705 [M]	Hit Tunes of Big Broadway Shows	1960	$150
❑ KS-705 [S]	Hit Tunes of Big Broadway Shows	1960	$175
❑ 395-547 [M]	Invitation to Dance	1956	$175
❑ 846 [M]	Jazz As I Feel It	1963	$150
❑ 395-529 [M]	Let's Dance with Earl Bostic	1956	$175
❑ 662 [M]	Musical Pearls	1960	$150
❑ KS-662 [S]	Musical Pearls	1960	$175

Number	Title	Yr	NM
❑ 583 [M]	Showcase of Swinging Dance Hits	1958	$175
❑ 838 [M]	Songs of the Fantastic Fifties, Volume 2	1963	$150
❑ 620 [M]	Sweet Tunes from the Roaring Twenties	1959	$150
❑ KS-620 [S]	Sweet Tunes from the Roaring Twenties	1959	$200
❑ 602 [M]	Sweet Tunes of the Fantastic Fifties	1959	$150

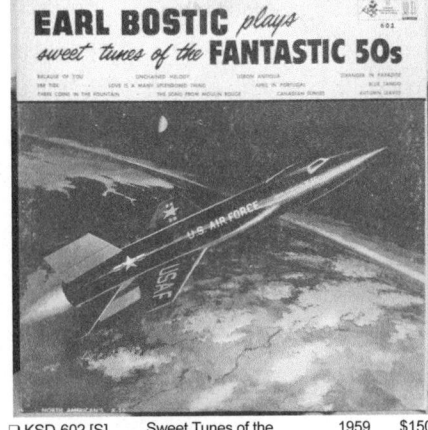

❑ KSD-602 [S]	Sweet Tunes of the Fantastic Fifties	1959	$150
❑ 640 [M]	Sweet Tunes of the Sentimental Forties	1960	$150
❑ KS-640 [S]	Sweet Tunes of the Sentimental Forties	1960	$175
❑ 632 [M]	Sweet Tunes of the Swinging Thirties	1959	$150
❑ KS-632 [S]	Sweet Tunes of the Swinging Thirties	1959	$200
❑ 881 [M]	The Best of Earl Bostic, Volume 2	1964	$150
❑ 921 [M]	The Great Hits of 1964	1964	$150
❑ 900 [M]	The New Sound	1964	$150

PHILIPS
❑ PHM200262 [M]	The Song Is Not Ended	1967	$75
❑ PHS600262 [S]	The Song Is Not Ended	1967	$75

BOSTIC, EARL/JIMMY LUNCEFORD
ALLEGRO ELITE
❑ 4053 [10]	Earl Bostic/Jimmy Lunceford Orchestras	195?	$40

BOSTIC, SAM
ATLANTIC
❑ 81232	Circuitry Starring Sam Bostic	1985	$10

BOSTON
Also see ORION THE HUNTER.
EPIC
❑ HE34188	Boston	1981	$50
— First edition of the half-speed mastered edition			
❑ HE44188	Boston	1982	$40
— Second edition of the half-speed mastered edition			
❑ PE34188	Boston	1976	$12
— Original edition; orange label			
❑ JE34188	Boston	1977	$10
— Second edition; orange label, different prefix			
❑ JE34188	Boston	1979	$10
— Third edition; dark blue label			
❑ E9934188	Boston	1978	$25
— Picture disc			
❑ HE45050	Don't Look Back	1982	$50
— Half-speed mastered edition			
❑ FE35050	Don't Look Back	1978	$12
— Original edition; orange label			
❑ FE35050	Don't Look Back	1979	$10
— Second edition; dark blue label			

FRIDAY MUSIC
❑ 88875015111 [B]	Don't Look Back	2015	$25
— clear vinyl			

MCA
❑ 6188	Third Stage	1986	$10
❑ 10973	Walk On	1994	$30

MOBILE FIDELITY
❑ 1-249 [B]	Boston	1996	$100
— Audiophile vinyl			

BOSTON CAMERATA, THE
NONESUCH
❑ H-71315	A Medieval Christmas	1975	$15
❑ H-71354	Sing We Noel: Christmas Music from England and Early America	1978	$15

Number	Title	Yr	NM

BOSTON POPS ORCHESTRA (ARTHUR FIEDLER, CONDUCTOR)
Perhaps the most popular orchestra and conductor in American history, Fiedler and the Pops released literally hundreds of albums, of which the below are merely a sample. Most of these are from the "golden age of stereo" and also exist in monaural, but the mono versions are in much less demand than the stereo editions.

DEUTCHE GRAMMOPHON
❑ 2584024	White Christmas	198?	$12
— Reissue of Polydor LP			

FLEETWOOD
❑ FMS1016	An Evening with Arthur Fiedler and the Boston Pops	1976	$15
— Side 1: Great Songs for All Seasons; Side 2: Great Songs of Christmas (reissue of Polydor recordings)			

POLYDOR
❑ 24-5004	A Christmas Festival	1970	$12

RCA GOLD SEAL
❑ AGL1-3436	Pops Christmas Party	1979	$12
— Reissue of LSC-2329			

RCA VICTOR RED SEAL
❑ LSC-2439 [S]	All-Time Favorites	1960	$25
— Original with "shaded dog" label			
❑ LSC-2213 [S]	Boston Tea Party	1959	$25
— Original with "shaded dog" label			
❑ LSC-2621 [S]	Chopin: Les Sylphides; Prokofiev: Love for Three Oranges	1962	$30
— Original with "shaded dog" label			
❑ LSC-6082 [S]	Everything But the Beer	1959	$150
— Original with "shaded dog" label			
❑ LSC-2549 [S]	Family Fun	1961	$40
— Original with "shaded dog" label			
❑ LSC-2586 [S]	Gershwin: Piano Concerto	1962	$25
— Earl Wild, piano; originals with "shaded dog" label			
❑ LSC-2586 [S]	Gershwin: Piano Concerto	199?	$30
— Earl Wild, piano; Classic Records reissue			
❑ LSC-2367 [S]	Gershwin: Rhapsody in Blue; An American in Paris	1960	$25
— Earl Wild, piano; originals with "shaded dog" label			
❑ LSC-2235 [S]	Good Music to Have Fun With	1959	$30
— Original with "shaded dog" label			
❑ LSC-2125 [S]	Grieg: Music from Peer Gynt	1958	$25
— Original with "shaded dog" label			
❑ LSC-2100 [S]	Hi-Fi Fiedler	1958	$30
— Original with "shaded dog" label			
❑ LSC-2240 [S]	Kay, Hershey: Stars and Stripes	1959	$40
— Original with "shaded dog" label			
❑ LSC-2229 [S]	Marches in Hi-Fi	1959	$25
— Original with "shaded dog" label			
❑ LSC-2702 [S]	Milhaud: A Frenchman in New York; Gershwin: An American in Paris	1963	$30
— Original with "shaded dog" label			
❑ LSC-2470 [S]	More Classical Music for People Who Hate Classical Music	1961	$40
— Original with "shaded dog" label			
❑ LSC-2380 [S]	Music from Million Dollar Movies	1960	$25
— Original with "shaded dog" label			
❑ LSC-2486 [S]	Music of Frank Loesser	1961	$40
— Original with "shaded dog" label			
❑ LSC-1817 [S]	Offenbach: Gaite Parisienne	1958	$400
— Original with "shaded dog" label			
❑ LSC-1817 [S]	Offenbach: Gaite Parisienne	199?	$30
— Classic Records reissue			
❑ LSC-2267 [S]	Offenbach: Gaite Parisienne; Khachatourian: Gayne Suite	1959	$25
— Original with "shaded dog" label			
❑ LSC-1990 [S]	Offenbach: In America	1958	$40
— Original with "shaded dog" label			
❑ LSC-1990 [S]	Offenbach: In America	1964	$50
— Second pressing with "white dog" label; a rare case where the second edition is more desirable than the first			
❑ LSC-2202 [S]	Pops Caviar	1959	$25
— Original with "shaded dog" label			
❑ LSC-2329 [S]	Pops Christmas Party	1959	$40
— Original copies have "shaded dog" with small "RCA Victor" logo; large "Living Stereo" on front cover			
❑ LSC-2329 [S]	Pops Christmas Party	1964	$25
— Second editions have "white dog" with large "RCA Victor" logo; small "Living Stereo" on front cover			
❑ LSC-3324	Pops Goes Christmas	1972	$12
— Compilation of older Christmas recordings			
❑ LSC-2270 [S]	Pops Stoppers	1959	$25
— Original with "shaded dog" label			
❑ LSC-2637 [S]	Rodgers: No Strings; State Fair	1962	$25
— Original with "shaded dog" label			
❑ LSC-2294 [S]	Rodgers: Slaughter on Tenth Avenue	1959	$25
— Original with "shaded dog" label			

Number	Title	Yr	NM
❑ LSC-2084 [S]	Rossini-Respighi: La Boutique Fantasque	1958	$120
—Original with "shaded dog" label			
❑ LSC-2596 [S]	Saint-Saens: Carnival of the Animals; Britten: Young Person's Guide to the Orchestra	1962	$75
—Original with "shaded dog" label			
❑ LSC-2320 [S]	Song of India	1959	$25
—Original with "shaded dog" label			
❑ LSC-2130 [S]	Strauss, Johann: Orchestral Music from Gypsy Baron and Die Fledermaus	1958	$25
—Original with "shaded dog" label			
❑ LSC-2052 [S]	Tchaikovsky: The Nutcracker (selections)	1958	$25
—Original with "shaded dog" label			
❑ LSC-2442 [S]	The Music of Franz Liszt	1960	$25
—Original with "shaded dog" label			
❑ LSC-2028 [S]	Waltzes by the Strauss Family	1958	$25
—Original with "shaded dog" label			
READER'S DIGEST			
❑ RBA-060-D	A Christmas Festival	1988	$12

BOSTON SYMPHONY ORCHESTRA (AARON COPLAND, CONDUCTOR)
RCA VICTOR RED SEAL

Number	Title	Yr	NM
❑ LSC-2401 [S]	Copland: Appalachian Spring; The Tender Land Suite	1960	$25
—Original with "shaded dog" label			

BOSTON SYMPHONY ORCHESTRA (CHARLES MUNCH, CONDUCTOR)
RCA VICTOR RED SEAL

Number	Title	Yr	NM
❑ LSC-6140 [S]	Bach: Brandenburg Concertos No. 1-6	196?	$175
—Original with "shaded dog" label			
❑ LSC-2233 [S]	Beethoven: Symphony No. 3	1959	$50
—Original with "shaded dog" label			
❑ LSC-2228 [S]	Berlioz: Harold in Italy	1959	$25
—Original with "shaded dog" label			
❑ LSC-2438 [S]	Berlioz: Overtures	1960	$80
—Original with "shaded dog" label			
❑ LSC-1900 [S]	Berlioz: Symphonie Fantastique	199?	$30
—Classic Records issue. This album is not known to have been issued in stereo before this.			
❑ LSC-1900 [S]	Berlioz: Symphonie Fantastique	1958	$0
—No mention of Classic Records on cover. Unknown; "if a copy did exist it could fetch up to $25,000 or more," according to at least one audiophile source			
❑ LSC-2608 [S]	Berlioz: Symphonie Fantastique	1962	$30
—Original with "shaded dog" label			
❑ LSC-2352 [S]	Blackwood: Symphony No. 1; Haieff: Symphony No. 2	1960	$75
—Original with "shaded dog" label			
❑ LM-2352 [M]	Blackwood: Symphony No. 1; Haieff: Symphony No. 2	1960	$25
❑ LSC-2097 [S]	Brahms: Symphony No. 1	1958	$175
—Original with "shaded dog" label			
❑ LSC-2297 [S]	Brahms: Symphony No. 4	1959	$30
—Original with "shaded dog" label			
❑ LSC-2647 [S]	Chausson: Symphony in B-flat; Franck: Le Chasseur Maudit	1962	$40
—Original with "shaded dog" label			
❑ LSC-2282 [S]	Debussy: Images	1959	$100
—Original with "shaded dog" label			
❑ LM-2282 [M]	Debussy: Images	1959	$25
❑ LSC-2111 [S]	Debussy: La Mer	1958	$50
—Original with "shaded dog" label			
❑ LSC-2629 [S]	Dvorak: Symphony No. 4 (8) in G	1962	$50
—Original with "shaded dog" label			
❑ LSC-2131 [S]	Franck: Symphony in D	1958	$25
—Original with "shaded dog" label			
❑ LSC-2371 [S]	Mahler: Songs of a Wayfarer	1960	$30
—Original with "shaded dog" label			
❑ LSC-2520 [S]	Mendelssohn: Symphony No. 3 "Scotch"; Scherzo from Octet in E-flat	1961	$25
—Original with "shaded dog" label			
❑ LSC-2221 [S]	Mendelssohn: Symphony No. 4 and No. 5	1959	$25
—Original with "shaded dog" label			
❑ LDS-2625 [S]	Milhaud: La Creation du Monde; Suite Provencale	1962	$250
—Original with "shaded dog" label			
❑ LSC-2625 [S]	Milhaude: La Creation Du Monde	1962	$250
—With "shaded dog" or "white dog" label			
❑ LSC-2625 [S]	Milhaude: La Creation Du Monde	199?	$30
—Classic Records reissue			
❑ LSC-2567 [S]	Poulenc: Organ Concerto; Stravinsky: Jeu de Cartes	1961	$40

Number	Title	Yr	NM
—Original with "shaded dog" label			
❑ LSC-1984 [S]	Ravel: Bolero; La Valse; Rapsodie Espagnole; Debussy: Prelude	1958	$100
—Original with "shaded dog" label			
❑ LSC-2271 [S]	Ravel: Concerto in G; d'Indy: Symphony on a French Mountain Air	1959	$150
—Original with "shaded dog" label			
❑ LSC-2271 [S]	Ravel: Concerto in G; d'Indy: Symphony on a French Mountain Air	199?	$30
—Classic Records reissue			
❑ LSC-1893 [S]	Ravel: Daphnis and Chloe	1958	$400
—Original with "shaded dog" label			
❑ LSC-1893 [S]	Ravel: Daphnis and Chloe	199?	$30
—Classic Records reissue			
❑ LSC-2568 [S]	Ravel: Daphnis et Chloe	1961	$25
—Original with "shaded dog" label			
❑ LSC-2341 [S]	Saint-Saens: Symphony No. 3	1960	$25
—Original with "shaded dog" label			
❑ LSC-2522 [S]	Schubert: Symphony No. 2; Beethoven: Prometheus Ballet Excerpts	1961	$25
—Original with "shaded dog" label			
❑ LSC-2344 [S]	Schubert: Symphony No. 9	1960	$40
—Original with "shaded dog" label			
❑ LSC-2344 [S]	Schubert: Symphony No. 9	1964	$30
—Second edition with "white dog" label			
❑ LSC-2474 [S]	Schumann: Symphony No. 1	1961	$25
—Original with "shaded dog" label			
❑ LSC-2565 [S]	Tchaikovsky: Romeo and Juliet; Strauss, Richard: Till Eulenspiegel	1961	$40
—Original with "shaded dog" label			
❑ LSC-2105 [S]	Tchaikovsky: Serenade for Strings	1958	$40
—Original with "shaded dog" label			
❑ LSC-2683 [S]	Tchaikovsky: Symphony No. 6	1962	$25
—Original with "shaded dog" label			
❑ LSC-2292 [S]	The French Touch	1959	$250
—Original with "shaded dog" label			

BOSTON SYMPHONY ORCHESTRA (ERICH LEINSDORF, CONDUCTOR)
RCA VICTOR RED SEAL

Number	Title	Yr	NM
❑ LSC-2707 [S]	Prokofiev: Symphony No. 5	1963	$25
—Original with "shaded dog" label			

BOSTON SYMPHONY ORCHESTRA (PIERRE MONTEUX, CONDUCTOR)
RCA VICTOR RED SEAL

Number	Title	Yr	NM
❑ LSC-2376 [S]	Stravinsky: Petrouchka	1960	$150
—Original with "shaded dog" label			
❑ LSC-2376 [S]	Stravinsky: Petrouchka	1964	$50
—Second edition with "white dog" label			
❑ LSC-2369 [S]	Tchaikovsky: Symphony No. 4	1959	$50
—Original with "shaded dog" label			
❑ LSC-2369 [S]	Tchaikovsky: Symphony No. 4	199?	$30
—Classic Records reissue			
❑ LSC-2239 [S]	Tchaikovsky: Symphony No. 5	1959	$30
—Original with "shaded dog" label			
❑ LSC-2239 [S]	Tchaikovsky: Symphony No. 5	1964	$25
—Second edition with "white dog" label			
❑ LSC-1901 [S]	Tchaikovsky: Symphony No. 6 "Pathetique"	1958	$50
—Original with "shaded dog" label			
❑ LSC-1901 [S]	Tchaikovsky: Symphony No. 6 "Pathetique"	199?	$30
—Classic Records reissue			

BOSTON TEA PARTY, THE
FLICK DISC

Number	Title	Yr	NM
❑ 45000	The Boston Tea Party	1968	$75

BOSWELL, CONNEE
DECCA

Number	Title	Yr	NM
❑ DL8356 [M]	Connee	1956	$175
❑ DL5390 [10]	Connee Boswell	1951	$250
❑ DL5445 [10]	Singing the Blues	1952	$175
DESIGN			
❑ DLP-68 [M]	Connee Boswell Sings Irving Berlin	196?	$30
❑ DLPS-68 [R]	Connee Boswell Sings Irving Berlin	196?	$20
❑ DLP-101 [M]	The New Sound of Connee Boswell	196?	$30
❑ DLPS-101 [R]	The New Sound of Connee Boswell	196?	$20
RCA VICTOR			
❑ LPM-1426 [M]	Connee Boswell and the Original Memphis Five	1957	$40

BOTHWELL, JOHNNY
BRUNSWICK

Number	Title	Yr	NM
❑ BL58033 [10]	Presenting Johnny Bothwell	1953	$150

BOTICELLI, ANTHONY
CAROLEER

Number	Title	Yr	NM
❑ X1702 [M]	Christmas Favorites	196?	$15
❑ SX1702 [M]	Christmas Favorites	196?	$18
—Same as above, but in stereo			

BOTTARI, SONNY
GUINNESS

Number	Title	Yr	NM
❑ GNS36049 [B]	Never Look Back	1977	$20
❑ GNS36050 [B]	Pickin' Up The Pieces	1977	$20

BOULEZ, PIERRE
COLUMBIA MASTERWORKS

Number	Title	Yr	NM
❑ MQ32160 [Q]	Boulez Conducts Boulez: Le Marteau Sans Maitre / Livre Pour Cordes	1973	$30
❑ M32160 [B]	Boulez Conducts Boulez (Le Marteau Sans Maître / Livre Pour Cordes	1973	$20
❑ M233303 [B]	Conducts Schoenberg – Gurre-Lieder	1975	$20
❑ MS7356 [B]	Et Exspecto Resurrectionem Mortuorum / Couleurs De La Cité Céleste	1966	$12
❑ M37850 [B]	Rituel / Eclat-Multiples	1983	$20
MACE			
❑ MXX9043 [B]	Structures For Two Pianos: First And Second Books	1965	$20
TURNABOUT			
❑ TV34081 [B]	Le Marteau Sans Maître	1964	$15

BOUNTY KILLER
TVT

Number	Title	Yr	NM
❑ 6420	5th Element	1999	$15
❑ 6370	Next Millennium	1998	$15

BOURBON STREET STOMPERS, THE
TIME

Number	Title	Yr	NM
❑ 52118 [M]	We Like Dixieland	196?	$35
❑ S-2118 [S]	We Like Dixieland	196?	$25

BOW STREET RUNNERS, THE
B.T. PUPPY

Number	Title	Yr	NM
❑ BTPS-1026	The Bow Street Runners	1969	$1000
SUNDAZED			
❑ LP5029	The Bow Street Runners	199?	$12
—Reissue of B.T. Puppy LP			

BOW WOW WOW
HARVEST

Number	Title	Yr	NM
❑ SK-12234	12 Original Recordings	1982	$18
RCA VICTOR			
❑ AFL1-4375	I Want Candy	1982	$15
❑ DJL1-4193 [DJ]	RCA Special Radio Series	1981	$30
❑ AFL1-4147	See Jungle, See Jungle! Go Join Your Gang, Yeah! City All Over, Go Ape Crazy	1981	$15
❑ CPL1-4314 [EP]	The Last of the Mohicans	1982	$12
❑ AFL1-4570	When the Going Gets Tough, the Tough Get Going	1983	$12

BOWEN, JIMMY
DECCA

Number	Title	Yr	NM
❑ DL4816 [M]	Margie Bowes Sings	1967	$25
REPRISE			
❑ R-6210 [M]	Sunday Morning with the Comics	1966	$30
❑ RS-6210 [S]	Sunday Morning with the Comics	1966	$40
ROULETTE			
❑ R25004 [M]	Jimmy Bowen	1957	$300
—Black and silver label			
❑ R25004 [M]	Jimmy Bowen	1958	$175
—Red label			
❑ R25004 [M]	Jimmy Bowen	198?	$15
—Reissue for Publishers Central Bureau (it says so on the jacket)			

BOWES, MARGIE
DECCA

Number	Title	Yr	NM
❑ DL4816 [M]	Margie Bowes Sings	1967	$25
❑ DL74816 [S]	Margie Bowes Sings	1967	$18
❑ DL75023	Today's Country Sound	1968	$18

BOWIE, DAVID
COLUMBIA

Number	Title	Yr	NM
❑ 88875065901 [B]	A Reality Tour	2016	$100
—blue vinyl, Friday Music ltd edition			
❑ 88875173871 [B]	Blackstar	2016	$250
—clear vinyl			
❑ 88875173871 [B]	Blackstar	2016	$100
—Gatefold sleeve, vinyl in clear plastic wallet, and 16 page			

Number	Title	Yr	NM
booklet			
❏ C86630	Heathen	2002	$75
❏ 88765 461861 [B]	The Next Day	2013	$60
DERAM			
❏ DE16003 [M]	David Bowie	1967	$600
❏ DES18003 [S]	David Bowie	1967	$375
EMI			
❏ DBZSX40 [B]	The Rise And Fall Of Ziggy Stardust And The Spiders From Mars	2012	$60
EMI AMERICA			
❏ R153730	Let's Dance	1983	$15
—RCA Music Service edition			
❏ SO-17093 [B]	Let's Dance	1983	$12
❏ SPRO0 [DJ]	Let's Talk	1983	$50
—Promo-only interview album			
❏ SPRO9960/1 [DJ]	Let's Talk	1983	$50
—Promo-only interview album			
❏ R174212	Never Let Me Down	1987	$25
—BMG Direct Marketing edition			
❏ PJ-17267	Never Let Me Down	1987	$25
❏ -0 [DJ]	Never Let Me Down: The Interview	1987	$100
❏ SPRO-79112/3 [DJ]	Never Let Me Down: The Interview	1987	$100
❏ SJ-17138	Tonight	1984	$20
FRIDAY MUSIC			
❏ FRM40711 [B]	1.Outside	2015	$100
—white vinyl			
❏ FRM42627 [B]	Earthling	2015	$35
❏ FRM86630 [B]	Heathen	2015	$35
❏ FRM48155 [B]	Hours...	2015	$50
—blue vinyl			
❏ FRM90576 [B]	Reality	2015	$35
—clear vinyl			
LONDON			
❏ PS628/9	Images 1966-1967	1973	$60
—Original pressings have dark blue and silver labels. Later pressings, if any, are worth at least 50% less.			
❏ LC50007	Starting Point	1977	$15
MERCURY			
❏ SR61246 [B]	Man of Words, Man of Music	1969	$700
❏ SR61325	The Man Who Sold the World	1970	$100
—An often-counterfeited album; originals have matrix numbers stamped in the trail-off area			
MOBILE FIDELITY			
❏ Jan-0083	Let's Dance	1984	$125
—Audiophile vinyl			
❏ Jan-0064	The Rise and Fall of Ziggy Stardust and the Spiders from Mars	1983	$150
—Audiophile vinyl			
PARLOPHONE			
❏ DBXL1 [B]	Five Years 1969-1973	2015	$300
—box set includes 2003 mix of Ziggy Stardust and double compilation LP Recall 1, plus regular studio and live LPs 1969-1973			
❏ 8.25646E+11 [B]	Hunky Dory	2016	$25
❏ 8.25647E+11 [B]	The Man Who Sold The World	2016	$50
—picture disc			
❏ 8.25646E+11 [B]	The Man Who Sold The World	2016	$25
❏ 8.25646E+11 [B]	The Rise And Fall Of Ziggy Stardust And The Spiders From Mars	2016	$25
❏ PAR9835 [B]	Who Can I Be Now? (1974 to 1976)	2016	$250
RCA RED SEAL			
❏ ARL1-2743	Peter and the Wolf	1978	$50
—With the Philadelphia Orchestra conducted by Eugene Ormandy; green vinyl			
❏ ARL1-2743	Peter and the Wolf	1978	$50
—With the Philadelphia Orchestra conducted by Eugene Ormandy; black vinyl			
RCA VICTOR			
❏ - [DJ]	1980 All Clear	1980	$130
❏ DJL1-3545 [DJ]	1980 All Clear	1980	$150
—Promo-only compilation			
❏ LSP-4852	Aladdin Sane	1973	$25
—Orange label is original (deduct 50% for tan labels)			
❏ AFL1-4852	Aladdin Sane	1977	$25
—Reissue			
❏ AYL1-3890	Aladdin Sane	1980	$20
—Reissue			
❏ - [DJ]	An Evening with David Bowie	1978	$150
—Live concert for "Superstars Radio Network			
❏ DJL1-3016 [DJ]	An Evening with David Bowie	1978	$150
—Music and interview for "Superstars Radio Network			
❏ - [DJ]	Bowie Now	1978	$185
❏ DJL1-2697 [DJ]	Bowie Now	1978	$175
❏ APL1-1732 [B]	Changesonebowie	1976	$40
❏ AFL1-1732	Changesonebowie	1978	$30

Number	Title	Yr	NM
—Reissue			
❏ AQL1-1732	Changesonebowie	1984	$25
—Reissue			
❏ AFL1-4202	Changestwobowie	1981	$40
❏ DJL1-3829 [DJ]	College Radio Series	1980	$80
❏ CPL1-4346 [EP]	David Bowie in Berthold Brecht's Baal	1982	$50
❏ [DJ]	David Bowie Special	1976	$0
—This album has been listed elsewhere, but we can't confirm its existence. The numbering doesn't even make sense.			
❏ CPL2-0771	David Live	1974	$60
—At time of release, available with either orange or tan labels			
❏ CPL2-0771	David Live	1976	$35
—Reissue with black label, dog near top			
❏ CPL1-0576 [B]	Diamond Dogs	1974	$5000
—Original copies have cover with dog's genitals clearly visible. Almost all were destroyed prior to release.			
❏ CPL1-0576	Diamond Dogs	1974	$40
—Standard issue, with dog's genitals airbrushed			
❏ AYL1-3889	Diamond Dogs	1980	$25
—Reissue			
❏ AFL1-4919	Fame and Fashion	1984	$20
❏ AFL1-4792	Golden Years	1983	$20
❏ AFL1-2522	Heroes	1977	$50
❏ AYL1-3857	Heroes	1980	$30
—Reissue			
❏ LSP-4623	Hunky Dory	1972	$65
❏ AYL1-3844	Hunky Dory	1980	$30
—Reissue			
❏ AQL1-3254	Lodger	1979	$40
❏ AYL1-4234	Lodger	1981	$25
—Reissue			
❏ APL1-2030	Low	1977	$50
❏ AYL1-3856	Low	1980	$30
—Reissue			

Number	Title	Yr	NM
❏ APL1-0291 [B]	Pin Ups	1973	$60
❏ AFL1-0291	Pin Ups	1978	$30
—Reissue			
❏ AYL1-4653	Pin Ups	1982	$25
—Reissue			
❏ AQL1-3647	Scary Monsters	1980	$50
❏ - [DJ]	Scary Monsters Interview	1980	$125
❏ DJL1-3840 [DJ]	Scary Monsters Interview	1980	$125
❏ LSP-4813	Space Oddity	1973	$50
—Reissue of Mercury SR-61246; add 1/3 if bonus poster is enclosed			
❏ DJL1-3829 [DJ]	Special Radio Series	1980	$150
—Same material as DJL1-3829			
❏ - [DJ]	Special Radio Series, Volume 1	1980	$150
❏ CPL2-2913	Stage	1978	$40
❏ APL1-1327	Station to Station	1976	$50
—Originals have a brown label			
❏ APL1-1327	Station to Station	1976	$35
—Black label			
❏ AQK1-1327	Station to Station	1984	$25
—Reissue			
❏ LSP-4816	The Man Who Sold the World	1973	$50
—Reissue of Mercury SR-61325; add 1/3 if bonus poster is enclosed			
❏ LSP-4702	The Rise and Fall of Ziggy Stardust and the Spiders from Mars	1972	$75
—Orange label			
❏ AFL1-4702	The Rise and Fall of Ziggy Stardust and the Spiders from Mars	1977	$25
—Reissue			
❏ AYL1-3843	The Rise and Fall of Ziggy Stardust and the Spiders from Mars	1980	$25
—Reissue			
❏ LSP-4702	The Rise and Fall of Ziggy Stardust and the Spiders from Mars	1975	$35
—Tan label			

Number	Title	Yr	NM
❏ APL1-0998	Young Americans	1975	$50
—At time of release, available with either orange or tan label			
❏ APL1-0998	Young Americans	1976	$35
—Black label			
❏ AQK1-0998	Young Americans	1984	$25
—Reissue			
❏ - [DJ]	Ziggy Stardust, The Motion Picture	1983	$80
—Promo version on clear vinyl			
❏ CPL2-4862 [DJ]	Ziggy Stardust, The Motion Picture	1983	$80
—Promo version on clear vinyl			
❏ CPL2-4862	Ziggy Stardust, The Motion Picture	1983	$50
RYKO ANALOGUE			
❏ RALP 0135 [B]	Aladdin Sane	1990	$50
—Clear vinyl with "Limited Edition" obi			
❏ RALP 0171 [B]	Changesbowie	1990	$80
—Clear vinyl with "Limited Edition" obi			
❏ RALP 0138/9 [B]	David Live	1990	$175
—Clear vinyl with "Limited Edition" obi			
❏ RALP 0137 [B]	Diamond Dogs	1990	$100
—Clear vinyl with "Limited Edition" obi; genitals on dog are restored			
❏ RALP 0133 [B]	Hunky Dory	1990	$150
—Clear vinyl with "Limited Edition" obi			
❏ RALP 0136 [B]	Pin Ups	1990	$150
—Clear vinyl with "Limited Edition" obi			
❏ RALP 0120/1/2 [B]	Sound + Vision	1989	$600
—Six-LP box set on clear vinyl with three gatefold cardboard inner sleeves			
❏ RALP 0131	Space Oddity	1990	$125
—Clear vinyl with "Limited Edition" obi			
❏ RALP 0132 [B]	The Man Who Sold the World	1990	$150
—Clear vinyl with "Limited Edition" obi			
❏ -0 [DJ]	The Rise and Fall of Ziggy Stardust and the Spiders from Mars	1990	$150
—Special promo-only package with both the LP and CD versions			
❏ RALP 0134 [B]	The Rise and Fall of Ziggy Stardust and the Spiders from Mars	1990	$175
—Clear vinyl with "Limited Edition" obi			
❏ LSD-4702 [DJ]	The Rise and Fall of Ziggy Stardust and the Spiders from Mars	1990	$200
—Special promo-only package with both the LP and CD versions			
SANCTUARY			
❏ BMG16004v [B] 1966		2016	$20

BOWIE, LESTER, AND PHILIP WILSON

IAI

❏ 373854	Duet	1978	$30

BOWIE, LESTER

Trumpeter and fluegel horn player. Also see ART ENSEMBLE OF CHICAGO.

BLACK SAINT

❏ BSR-0020	Fifth Power	197?	$30

ECM

❏ 23789	All the Magic	1984	$25
❏ 25034	I Only Have Eyes for You	1985	$25
❏ 1209	The Great Pretender	1981	$30

MUSE

❏ MR-5055	Fast Last!	1975	$30
❏ MR-5337	Hello Dolly	1987	$25
❏ MR-5081	Rope-a-Dope	1975	$30

NESSA

❏ N-1	Numbers 1 and 2	1968	$30

VENTURE

❏ 90650	Twilight Dreams	1988	$25

BOWIE, PAT

PRESTIGE

❏ PRLP-7437 [M]	Feelin' Good	1967	$30
❏ PRST-7437 [S]	Feelin' Good	1967	$30
❏ PRLP-7385 [M]	Out of Sight	1965	$30
❏ PRST-7385 [S]	Out of Sight	1965	$30

BOWLES, RICK

POLYDOR

❏ PD-1-6352	Free for the Evening	1982	$12

BOWMAN, DON

LONE STAR

❏ 4605	Still Fighting Mental Health	1979	$18

RCA VICTOR

❏ LPM-3646 [M]	Don Bowman Recorded Almost Live	1966	$25

Number	Title	Yr	NM
❏ LSP-3646 [S]	Don Bowman Recorded Almost Live	1966	$30
❏ LPM-3345 [M]	Fresh from the Funny Farm	1965	$25
❏ LSP-3345 [S]	Fresh from the Funny Farm	1965	$30
❏ LPM-3795 [M]	From Mexico with Laughs Featuring the Tijuana Drum and Bugle Corps	1967	$30
❏ LSP-3795 [S]	From Mexico with Laughs Featuring the Tijuana Drum and Bugle Corps	1967	$25
❏ LPM-3920 [M]	Funny Folk Flops	1968	$50
❏ LSP-3920 [S]	Funny Folk Flops	1968	$25
❏ LPM-3495 [M]	Funny Way to Make an Album	1966	$25
❏ LSP-3495 [S]	Funny Way to Make an Album	1966	$30
❏ LPM-2831 [M]	Our Man in Trouble	1964	$25
❏ LSP-2831 [S]	Our Man in Trouble	1964	$30

BOWN, PATTI
COLUMBIA
| ❏ CL1379 [M] | Patti Bown Plays Big Piano | 1959 | $30 |

BOX OF FROGS
Featuring ex-members of THE YARDBIRDS.
EPIC
| ❏ BFE39327 [B] | Box of Frogs | 1984 | $15 |
| ❏ EAS1904 [DJ] | Interchords | 1984 | $25 |
—Promo-only interview album
| ❏ BFE39923 [B] | Strange Land | 1986 | $15 |

BOX TOPS, THE
BELL
❏ 6017	Cry Like a Baby	1968	$25
❏ 6032	Dimensions	1969	$25
❏ 6023	Non-Stop	1968	$25
❏ 6025	The Box Tops Super Hits	1968	$25
❏ 6011 [M]	The Letter/Neon Rainbow	1967	$30
❏ S-6011 [S]	The Letter/Neon Rainbow	1967	$25
RHINO
❏ RNLP-161	The Greatest Hits	1982	$15

BOXCAR WILLIE
AHMC
| ❏ AA118 | Marty Martin Sings Country Music | 1976 | $50 |
—As "Marty Martin"; he changed his name to "Boxcar Willie" after one of his early songs
MAIN STREET
❏ 73002	Best of Boxcar, Vol. 1	1982	$15
❏ 73000	King of the Road	1981	$15
❏ 73001	Last Train to Heaven	1982	$15
❏ 9309	... Not the Man I Used to Be	1984	$12

BOY GEORGE
Also see CULTURE CLUB. (SC2)
Also see CULTURE CLUB.
VIRGIN
| ❏ R100843 | High Hat | 1989 | $15 |
—BMG Direct Marketing edition
| ❏ 91022 | High Hat | 1989 | $12 |
| ❏ R153255 | Sold | 1987 | $15 |
—BMG Direct Marketing edition
| ❏ 90617 | Sold | 1987 | $12 |

BOY MEETS GIRL
A&M
| ❏ SP-6-5046 | Boy Meets Girl | 1985 | $12 |
RCA
| ❏ 8414-1-R | Reel Life | 1988 | $10 |

BOYCE, TOMMY, AND BOBBY HART
A&M
❏ SP-4162	It's All Happening on the Inside	1968	$25
❏ LP-143 [M]	I Wonder What She's Doing Tonite?	1968	$35
❏ SP-4143 [S]	I Wonder What She's Doing Tonite?	1968	$25
❏ LP-126 [M]	Test Patterns	1967	$30
❏ SP-4126 [S]	Test Patterns	1967	$25

BOYCE, TOMMY
RCA CAMDEN
| ❏ CAL-2202 [M] | Tommy Boyce | 1967 | $25 |
| ❏ CAS-2202 [S] | Tommy Boyce | 1967 | $30 |

BOYD, BILL, AND HIS COWBOY RAMBLERS
BLUEBIRD
| ❏ AXM2-5503 | Bill Boyd and His Cowboy Ramblers | 197? | $25 |

BOYD, BILLY
CROWN
| ❏ CLP-5170 [M] | Twangy Guitars | 1960 | $75 |
—Black label, silver print
| ❏ CLP-5170 [M] | Twangy Guitars | 1961 | $25 |
—Gray label

Number	Title	Yr	NM
❏ CST-196 [R]	Twangy Guitars	196?	$50
—Red vinyl			
❏ CST-196 [R]	Twangy Guitars	196?	$15
—Black vinyl			

BOYD, BOBBY
TIGER LILY
| ❏ TL14066 [B] | Bobby Boyd | 1976 | $2,000 |

BOYD, EDDIE
EPIC
| ❏ BN26409 | 7936 South Rhodes | 1968 | $30 |
LONDON
| ❏ PS554 | I'll Dust My Broom | 1969 | $30 |

BOYD, JIMMY
COLUMBIA
| ❏ CL6270 [10] | Christmas with Jimmy Boyd | 1953 | $150 |
| ❏ CL2543 [10] | I Saw Mommy Kissing Santa Claus | 1955 | $40 |
—House Party Series" reissue

BOYD, LIONA
CBS
| ❏ FM37248 | A Guitar for Christmas | 1981 | $15 |

BOYD, ROCKY
JAZZTIME
| ❏ JT-001 [M] | Ease It | 1961 | $1000 |
—"deep groove"
| ❏ JS-001 [S] | Ease It | 1961 | $300 |

BOYER, CHARLES
VALIANT
| ❏ VLM-5001 [M] | Where Does Love Go? | 1966 | $30 |
| ❏ VLS-25001 [S] | Where Does Love Go? | 1966 | $30 |

BOYER, DAVE
WORD
| ❏ 8612 | Christmas with Dave Boyer | 198? | $12 |

BOYLAN, TERENCE
ASYLUM
| ❏ 6E-201 | Suzy | 1980 | $12 |
| ❏ 7E-1091 | Terence Boylan | 1977 | $12 |

BOYS, THE
MOTOWN
| ❏ 6260 | Messages from the Boys | 1988 | $12 |
| ❏ 6302 | The Boys | 1990 | $18 |

BOYS BAND, THE
ELEKTRA
| ❏ E1-60047 | The Boys Band | 1982 | $15 |

BOYS CLUB
MCA
| ❏ 42242 | Boys Club | 1988 | $10 |

BOYS DON'T CRY
ATLANTIC
| ❏ 81795 | Boys Don't Cry | 1987 | $10 |
PROFILE
| ❏ PRO1219 | Boys Don't Cry | 1986 | $12 |

BOYS ON THE BLOCK
FANTASY
| ❏ F-9656 | Blockbuster | 1987 | $12 |

BOYS TOWN CHOIR, THE
MASTERTONE
| ❏ MS-102 | Christmas at Boys Town | 1964 | $25 |
—Some copies contain a concert program

BOYZ II MEN
MOTOWN
| ❏ 31453 0819-1 | Evolution | 1997 | $15 |
| ❏ -0 [DJ] | II | 1994 | $30 |
—Vinyl is promo only; in Motown company cover
| ❏ 31453 0323-1 [DJ] | II | 1994 | $30 |
—Vinyl is promo only; in Motown company cover

BR5-49
ARISTA NASHVILLE
| ❏ 18862 | Big Backyard Beat Show | 1999 | $15 |
—Originally issued on CD and cassette in 1998
| ❏ 18818 | BR5-49 | 1999 | $15 |
—Originally issued on CD and cassette in 1996
| ❏ 10800 [EP] | Live from Robert's | 1999 | $12 |
—Originally issued on CD and cassette in 1996

Number	Title	Yr	NM
BRACE, JANET			
ABC-PARAMOUNT			
❏ ABC-116 [M]	Special Delivery	1956	$50

BRACKEEN, CHARLES
SILKHEART
❏ SH-110	Attainment	198?	$30
❏ SH-105	Bannar	198?	$30
❏ SH-111	Worshippers Come Nigh	198?	$30
STRATA-EAST
❏ 19736	Rhythm X	1974	$30

BRACKEEN, JOANNE
ANTILLES
| ❏ 1001 | Special Identity | 198? | $25 |
CHOICE
❏ CRS1024	Prism	1978	$30
❏ CRS1009	Snooze	1976	$30
❏ CRS1016	Tring-a-Ling	1977	$30
COLUMBIA
❏ JC36593	Ancient Dynasty	1980	$25
❏ JC36075	Keyed In	1979	$25
CONCORD JAZZ
❏ CJ-316	Fi-Fi Goes to Heaven	1987	$25
❏ CJ-280	Havin' Fun	1985	$25
PAUSA
❏ 7045	Mythical Magic	1979	$30
TIMELESS
❏ TI-302	Aft	1980	$30

BRADDOCK, BOBBY
ELEKTRA
| ❏ 6E-187 | Between the Lines | 1979 | $15 |
| ❏ 6E-224 | Love Bomb | 1980 | $15 |
RCA VICTOR
| ❏ MHL1-8524 [EP] | Hardpore Cornography | 1984 | $10 |

BRADEN, JOHN
A&M
| ❏ SP-4172 | John Braden | 1969 | $18 |

BRADFORD, ALEX
CHECKER
| ❏ LP-10041 [M] | Alex Bradford | 196? | $30 |
SPECIALTY
| ❏ SP-2108 [M] | Too Close to Heaven | 1959 | $150 |
VEE JAY
| ❏ LP-5023 [M] | One Step | 1962 | $40 |
| ❏ LP-5056 [M] | The Soul of Alex Bradford | 1964 | $40 |

BRADFORD, BOBBY
Also see JOHN CARTER AND BOBBY BRADFORD.
Trumpeter.
EMANEM
| ❏ 3302 | Love's Dream | 1976 | $25 |
NESSA
| ❏ N-17 | Bobby Bradford with John Stevens and the Spontaneous Music Ensemble, Vol. 1 | 198? | $25 |
| ❏ N-18 | Bobby Bradford with John Stevens and the Spontaneous Music Ensemble, Vol. 2 | 198? | $25 |
SOUL NOTE
| ❏ 121168-1 | One Night Stand | 1990 | $30 |

BRADFORD, CLEA
CADET
| ❏ LPS-810 | Her Point of View | 1969 | $35 |
MAINSTREAM
| ❏ 56042 [M] | Clea Bradford Now | 1965 | $30 |
| ❏ S-6042 [S] | Clea Bradford Now | 1965 | $30 |
NEW JAZZ
| ❏ NJLP-8320 [M] | Clea Bradford with Clark Terry | 1963 | $0 |
—Canceled
STATUS
| ❏ ST-8320 [M] | Clea Bradford with Clark Terry | 1965 | $40 |
TRU-SOUND
| ❏ TRU-15005 [M] | These Dues | 1962 | $50 |

BRADFORD, PERRY
CRISPUS ATTUCKS
| ❏ 101 [M] | The Perry Bradford Story | 1957 | $75 |

BRADFORD, SCOTT
PROBE
| ❏ 4509 | Rock Slides | 1969 | $25 |

Number	Title	Yr	NM

BRADLEY, HAROLD
COLUMBIA
❏ CS8814 [S]	Bossa Nova Goes to Nashville	1963	$18
❏ CL2014 [M]	Bossa Nova Goes to Nashville	1963	$15
❏ CL2456 [M]	Guitar for Lovers Only	1966	$15
❏ CS9256 [S]	Guitar for Lovers Only	1966	$18
❏ CL2073 [M]	Misty Guitar	1963	$15
❏ CS8873 [S]	Misty Guitar	1963	$18

HARMONY
❏ H31324	Guitar for Sentimental Lovers	1971	$15

BRADLEY, JAMES
MALACO
❏ 6358	James Bradley	1979	$18

BRADLEY, OWEN
CORAL
❏ CRL56065 [10]	Cherished Hymns	195?	$75
❏ CRL56012 [10]	Christmas Time	1950	$100
❏ CRL56035 [10]	Lazy River	195?	$75
❏ CRL57071 [M]	Organ and Chimes Played by Owen Bradley	1956	$30
❏ CRL56047 [10]	Singin' in the Rain	195?	$75
❏ CRL56022 [10]	Strauss Waltzes	195?	$75

DECCA
❏ DL8724 [M]	Bandstand Hop	1958	$30
❏ DL8868 [M]	Big Guitar	1958	$30
❏ DL78868 [S]	Big Guitar	1958	$40
❏ DL8652 [M]	Joyous Bells of Christmas	1957	$30
❏ DL4078 [M]	Paradise Island	1960	$25
❏ DL74078 [S]	Paradise Island	1960	$30

BRADLEY, WILL
EPIC
❏ LG1005 [10]	Boogie Woogie	1954	$300
❏ LN3115 [M]	Boogie Woogie	1955	$150
❏ LN3199 [M]	The House of Bradley	1955	$150
❏ LN1127 [10]	The House of Bradley	1954	$300

RCA VICTOR
❏ LPM-2098 [M]	Big Band Boogie	1960	$40
❏ LSP-2098 [S]	Big Band Boogie	1960	$50

WALDORF MUSIC HALL
❏ MH 33-132 [10]	Jazz -- Dixieland and Chicago Style	195?	$40
❏ MH 33-122 [10]	Jazz Encounter	195?	$40

BRADSHAW, EVANS
RIVERSIDE
❏ RLP 12-263 [M]	Look Out for Evans Bradshaw	1958	$75
❏ RLP 12-296 [M]	Pieces of Eighty-Eight	1959	$300
❏ RLP-1136 [S]	Pieces of Eighty-Eight	1959	$300

BRADSHAW, TINY
KING
❏ 953 [M]	24 Great Songs	1966	$40
❏ 653 [M]	Great Composer	1960	$300
❏ 295-74 [10]	Off and On	1955	$1000
❏ 395-501 [M]	Selections	1956	$700

BRADSHAW, TERRY
BENSON
❏ R-3702	Until You	1980	$18

HEART WARMING
❏ 3735	Here in My Heart	1983	$18

MERCURY
❏ SRM-1-1073	I'm So Lonesome I Could Cry	1976	$25

BRADY BUNCH, THE
PARAMOUNT
❏ PAS-6032	Meet the Brady Bunch	1972	$50
❏ PAS-5026	Merry Christmas from the Brady Bunch	1971	$100
❏ PAS-6058	The Brady Bunch Phonograph Record	1973	$100
❏ PAS-6037	The Kids from the Brady Bunch	1972	$40

BRAFF, RUBY, AND DICK HYMAN
CONCORD JAZZ
❏ CJ-393	Music from My Fair Lady	1989	$30

GEORGE WEIN COLLECTION
❏ GW-3003	America the Beautiful	198?	$25

BRAFF, RUBY, AND ELLIS LARKINS
CHIAROSCURO
❏ 117	The Grand Reunion	1972	$35

VANGUARD
❏ VRS-8019 [10]	Inventions in Jazz -- Volume 1	1955	$160
❏ VRS-8020 [10]	Inventions in Jazz -- Volume 2	1955	$160
❏ VRS-8516 [M]	Pocketful of Dreams	1957	$100

❏ VRS-8507 [M]	Two By Two	1956	$100

BRAFF, RUBY, AND GEORGE BARNES
CHIAROSCURO
❏ 126	Live at the New School	1975	$35
❏ 121	The Ruby Braff-George Barnes Quartet	1973	$35

CONCORD JAZZ
❏ CJ-5	The Ruby Braff-George Barnes Quartet Plays Gershwin	1975	$30
❏ CJ-7	The Ruby Braff-George Barnes Quartet Salutes Rodgers and Hart	1976	$30

BRAFF, RUBY, AND SCOTT HAMILTON
CONCORD JAZZ
❏ CJ-274	A First	1985	$25
❏ CJ-296	A Sailboat in the Moonlight	1986	$25

BRAFF, RUBY; PEE WEE RUSSELL; BOBBY HENDERSON
VERVE
❏ MGV-8241 [M]	The Ruby Braff Octet with Pee Wee Russell and Bobby Henderson at Newport	1958	$150
❏ V-8241 [M]	The Ruby Braff Octet with Pee Wee Russell and Bobby Henderson at Newport	1961	$30

BRAFF, RUBY
ABC-PARAMOUNT
❏ ABC-141 [M]	Ruby Braff Featuring Dave McKenna	1956	$40

AMERICAN RECORDING SOCIETY
❏ G-445 [M]	Hey, Ruby	1957	$40

BETHLEHEM
❏ BCP-6043	Adoration of the Melody	197?	$35
—Reissue material, distributed by RCA Victor			
❏ BCP-1034 [10]	Ball at Bethlehem	1955	$300
❏ BCP-82 [M]	Handful of Cool Jazz	1958	$250
❏ BCP-1032 [10]	Holiday in Braff	1955	$300
❏ BCP-5 [M]	Omnibus	1955	$300
❏ BCP-1005 [10]	Ruby Braff Quartet	1954	$300
❏ BCP-6043 [M]	The Best of Braff	1960	$250

BLACK LION
❏ 127	Hear Me Talkin'	197?	$30

CHIAROSCURO
❏ 115	International Quartet Plus Three	1972	$35

CONCERT HALL JAZZ
❏ 1210 [M]	Little Big Horn	1955	$75

CONCORD JAZZ
❏ CJ-381	Me, Myself and I	1989	$30

EPIC
❏ LN3377 [M]	Braff!	1957	$150

FINESSE
❏ FW37988	Very Sinatra	1983	$30

JAZZTONE
❏ J-1210 [M]	Little Big Horn	1955	$50

RCA VICTOR
❏ LPM-1966 [M]	Easy Now	1959	$30
❏ LSP-1966 [S]	Easy Now	1959	$40
❏ LPM-1510 [M]	Hi-Fi Salute to Bunny	1957	$40
❏ LPM-1332 [M]	The Magic Horn of Ruby Braff	1956	$40
❏ LPM-1008 [M]	To Fred Astaire with Love	1955	$75

SACKVILLE
❏ 3022	Ruby Braff with the Ed Bickert Trio	198?	$25

STEREO-CRAFT
❏ RTN-507 [M]	You're Getting to Be a Habit with Me	1959	$75
❏ RTS-507 [S]	You're Getting to Be a Habit with Me	1959	$40

STORYVILLE
❏ STLP-320 [10]	Hustlin' and Bustlin'	1955	$100
❏ STLP-908 [M]	Hustlin' and Bustlin'	1956	$50

UNITED ARTISTS
❏ UAL-3045 [M]	Blowing Around the Around	1959	$30
❏ UAS-6045 [S]	Blowing Around the Around	1959	$40
❏ UAL-4093 [M]	Ruby Braff-Marshall Brown Sextet	1960	$30
❏ UAS-5093 [S]	Ruby Braff-Marshall Brown Sextet	1960	$40

VANGUARD
❏ VRS-8504 [M]	The Ruby Braff Special	1955	$150

WARNER BROS.
❏ W1273 [M]	Ruby Braff Goes Girl Crazy	1959	$30
❏ WS1273 [S]	Ruby Braff Goes Girl Crazy	1959	$40

BRAGG, BILLY, AND WILCO
ELEKTRA
❏ 62204 [B]	Mermaid Avenue	1998	$18

BRAGG, BILLY
CD PRESENTS
❏ CD 027	Brewing Up with Billy Bragg	1984	$18
❏ CD 035 [B]	Life's a Riot Etc. (With the Between the Wars EP)	1985	$25

ELEKTRA
❏ 60726	Back to Basics	1987	$15
❏ 60787 [EP]	Help Save the Youth of America	1988	$10
❏ 60502	Talking to the Taxman About Poetry	1986	$15
❏ 61935 [B]	William Bloke	1996	$25
❏ 60824	Workers Playtime	1988	$12

BRAINBOX
CAPITOL
❏ ST-596	Brainbox	1970	$18

BRAINS, THE
LANDSLIDE
❏ LM1201 [EP]	Dancing Under Streetlights	1982	$18

MERCURY
❏ SRM-1-4012	Electronic Eden	1981	$12
❏ SRM-1-3835	The Brains	1980	$15

BRAINSTORM
TABU
❏ JZ35749	Funky Entertainment	1979	$18
❏ JZ35327	Journey to the Night	1978	$18
❏ BQL1-2048	Stormin'	1977	$25

BRAINTICKET
CLEOPATRA
❏ 7058 [B]	Cottonwoodhill		$25
❏ 6611 [B]	Live In Rome 1973		$25
❏ 9024 [B]	Psychonaut		$25

BRAITH, GEORGE
BLUE NOTE
❏ BLP-4171 [M]	Extension	1964	$150
—With "New York, USA" on label			
❏ BST-84171 [S]	Extension	1964	$100
—With "New York, USA" on label			
❏ BST-84171 [S]	Extension	1966	$25
—With "A Division of Liberty Records" on label			
❏ BLP-4161 [M]	Soul Stream	1964	$150
—With "New York, USA" on label			
❏ BST-84161 [S]	Soul Stream	1964	$150
—With "New York, USA" on label			
❏ BST-84161 [S]	Soul Stream	1966	$40
—With "A Division of Liberty Records" on label			
❏ BLP-4148 [M]	Two Souls in One	1963	$100
—With "New York, USA" on label			
❏ BST-84148 [S]	Two Souls in One	1963	$50
—With "New York, USA" on label			
❏ BST-84148 [S]	Two Souls in One	1966	$25
—With "A Division of Liberty Records" on label			

PRESTIGE
❏ PRLP-7474 [M]	Laughing Soul	1967	$30
❏ PRST-7474 [S]	Laughing Soul	1967	$25
❏ PRLP-7515 [M]	Musart	1967	$30
❏ PRST-7515 [S]	Musart	1967	$25

BRAITHWAITE, DARYL
CBS ASSOCIATED
❏ FZ45206	Edge	1989	$12

BRAM TCHAIKOVSKY
Also see DUCKS DELUXE; THE MOTORS.

ARISTA
❏ AB4292	Funland	1981	$12

POLYDOR
❏ PD-1-6273	Pressure	1980	$12
❏ PD-1-6211	Strange Man, Changed Man	1979	$15

BRAMLETT, BONNIE
CAPRICORN
❏ CP 0148	It's Time	1975	$15
❏ CP 0169	Lady's Choice	1976	$15
❏ CP 0190	Memories	1978	$15

COLUMBIA
❏ KC31786	Sweet Bonnie Bramlett	1973	$18

BRAMLETT, DELANEY
COLUMBIA
❏ KC32420	Moblus Strip	1973	$15
❏ KC31631	Some Things Coming	1972	$15

MGM
❏ M3G-5011	Giving Birth to a Song	1975	$12

PRODIGAL
❏ P6-10017S1	Class Reunion	1977	$12

Number	Title	Yr	NM

BRANCH, CLIFF
SUTRA
| ❑ SUT1020 | All About Love | 1988 | $15 |

BRAND, OSCAR
ABC-PARAMOUNT
| ❑ ABC-388 [M] | Oscar Brand Sings for Adults | 1961 | $30 |
| ❑ ABCS-388 [S] | Oscar Brand Sings for Adults | 1961 | $30 |
AUDIO FIDELITY
❑ AFLP-2121 [M]	Bawdy Hootenanny	1964	$25
❑ AFSD-6121 [S]	Bawdy Hootenanny	1964	$30
❑ AFLP-1884 [M]	Bawdy Sea Shanties (Vol. 5)	1959	$30
❑ AFSD-5884 [S]	Bawdy Sea Shanties (Vol. 5)	1959	$30
❑ AFLP-1906 [M]	Bawdy Songs and Backroom Ballads, Vol. I	195?	$30
❑ AFLP-1806 [M]	Bawdy Songs and Backroom Ballads, Vol. II	195?	$30
❑ AFLP-1824 [M]	Bawdy Songs and Backroom Ballads, Vol. III	195?	$30
❑ AFSD-5824 [S]	Bawdy Songs and Backroom Ballads, Vol. III	196?	$30
❑ AFLP-1847 [M]	Bawdy Songs and Backroom Ballads, Vol. IV	195?	$30
❑ AFSD-5847 [S]	Bawdy Songs and Backroom Ballads, Vol. IV	195?	$30
❑ AFLP-1952 [M]	Bawdy Songs Goes to College	1961	$30
❑ AFSD-5952 [S]	Bawdy Songs Goes to College	1961	$30
❑ AFLP-1920 [M]	Bawdy Western Songs (Vol. VI)	1960	$30
❑ AFSD-5920 [S]	Bawdy Western Songs (Vol. VI)	1960	$30
❑ AFLP-1966 [M]	Rollicking Sea Shanties	1962	$30
❑ AFSD-5966 [S]	Rollicking Sea Shanties	1962	$30
❑ AFLP-1971 [M]	Sing Along Bawdy Songs and Backroom Ballads	1962	$30
❑ AFSD-5971 [S]	Sing Along Bawdy Songs and Backroom Ballads	1962	$30
CAEDMON
| ❑ TC1658 | Singing Is Believing: Songs of the Advent Season | 1980 | $15 |
CHESTERFIELD
| ❑ CMS-101 [10] | Backroom Ballads | 195? | $50 |
DECCA
| ❑ DL4275 [M] | Folk Songs for Fun | 1962 | $25 |
| ❑ DL74275 [S] | Folk Songs for Fun | 1962 | $30 |
ELEKTRA
❑ EKL-228 [M]	A Snow Job for Skiers	1963	$25
❑ EKS-7228 [S]	A Snow Job for Skiers	1963	$30
❑ EKL-183 [M]	Boating Songs and All That Bilge	1960	$25
❑ EKS-7183 [S]	Boating Songs and All That Bilge	1960	$30
❑ EKL-242 [M]	Cough: Army Songs Out of the Barracks Bag	1963	$25
❑ EKS-7242 [S]	Cough: Army Songs Out of the Barracks Bag	1963	$30
❑ EKL-169 [M]	Every Inch a Sailor	1960	$25
❑ EKS-7169 [S]	Every Inch a Sailor	1960	$30
❑ EKL-204 [M]	For Doctors Only	1961	$25
❑ EKS-7204 [S]	For Doctors Only	1961	$30
❑ EKL-178 [M]	Out of the Blue: Songs of a Fighting Airforce	1960	$25
❑ EKS-7178 [S]	Out of the Blue: Songs of a Fighting Airforce	1960	$30
❑ EKL-237 [M]	Songs Fore Golfers	1963	$25
❑ EKS-7237 [S]	Songs Fore Golfers	1963	$30
❑ EKL-188 [M]	Sports Car Songs for Big Wheels	1960	$30
❑ EKS-7188 [S]	Sports Car Songs for Big Wheels	1960	$30
❑ EKL-174 [M]	Tell It to the Marines	1960	$25
❑ EKS-7174 [S]	Tell It to the Marines	1960	$30
❑ EKL-168 [M]	The Wild Blue Yonder	1959	$25
❑ EKS-7168 [S]	The Wild Blue Yonder	1959	$30
❑ EKL-198 [M]	Up in the Air: Songs for the Madcap Airman	1961	$25
❑ EKS-7198 [S]	Up in the Air: Songs for the Madcap Airman	1961	$30
FOLKWAYS
| ❑ FA5280 [M] | Election Songs of the United States | 1960 | $40 |
KAPP
| ❑ KS-3629 | Oscar Brand "Live" On Campus | 1970 | $18 |
RIVERSIDE
❑ RLP 12-825 [M]	Absolute Nonsense	195?	$30
❑ RLP 12-630 [M]	American Drinking Songs	1956	$30
❑ RLP1419	Everybody Sing, Vol. 2	196?	$18
❑ RLP 12-639 [M]	G.I. -- American Army Songs	195?	$30
❑ RLP1438	Oscar Brand's Children's Concert	196?	$18
❑ RLP 12-835 [M]	Songs Inane Only	1959	$30
❑ RLP 12-844 [M]	Songs of the U.S. Army	1960	$30
ROULETTE
| ❑ SR-42060 | Brand X | 1971 | $18 |
TRADITION
❑ RLP1014 [M]	Laughing America	195?	$30
❑ TLP1022 [M]	Pie in the Sky	195?	$30
❑ TLP2053	The Best of Oscar Brand	1967	$25

Number	Title	Yr	NM

BRAND NEW HEAVIES, THE
DELICIOUS VINYL
| ❑ 14243 | Brother Sister | 1994 | $18 |
| ❑ 71807 [B] | Heavy Rhyme Experience -- Vol. 1 | 1998 | $25 |
— Originally issued in 1992
| ❑ 71806 [B] | The Brand New Heavies | 1998 | $18 |
— Originally issued in 1991
| ❑ 846874-1 | The Brand New Heavies | 1991 | $18 |

BRAND NUBIAN
ARISTA
| ❑ 19024 | Foundation | 1998 | $18 |
ELEKTRA
❑ 61682	Everything Is Everything	1994	$18
❑ 61381	In God We Trust	1993	$18
❑ 60946	One for All	1990	$18

BRAND X
PASSPORT
❑ PB9845	Do They Hurt?	1980	$12
❑ PB6016	Is There Anything About?	1982	$12
❑ PB9824	Livestock	1977	$12
❑ PB9829	Masques	1978	$12
❑ PB9822	Moroccan Roll	1977	$12
— Reissue of 98022
❑ PP-98022	Moroccan Roll	1977	$15
❑ PB9840	Product	1979	$12
❑ PB9819	Unorthodox Behaviour	1977	$12
— Reissue of 98019
| ❑ PPSD-98019 [B] | Unorthodox Behaviour | 1976 | $18 |

BRANDMEIER, JONATHON
BRANDMEIER
| ❑ BPI2004 | Almost Live | 1984 | $25 |

BRANDOS, THE
RELATIVITY
| ❑ 88561-8192-1 | Honor Among Thieves | 1987 | $10 |

BRANDY
ATLANTIC
| ❑ PR5970 [DJ] | Brandy | 1994 | $18 |
— Vinyl is promo only
| ❑ 83493 | Full Moon | 2002 | $18 |
| ❑ 83039 | Never S-a-y Never | 1998 | $18 |

BRANIGAN, LAURA
ATLANTIC
❑ SD19289	Branigan	1982	$10
❑ 80052	Branigan 2	1983	$10
❑ 81265	Hold Me	1985	$10
❑ 82086	Laura Branigan	1990	$15
❑ 80147	Self Control	1984	$10
❑ 81747	Touch	1987	$10

BRANNEN, JOHN
APACHE
| ❑ D1-71650 | Mystery Street | 1988 | $12 |

BRASS COMPANY, THE
SACKVILLE
| ❑ 3006 | Sangoma | 198? | $25 |
STRATA-EAST
| ❑ 19752 | Colors | 1974 | $25 |

BRASS CONSTRUCTION
CAPITOL
❑ ST-12423	Conquest	1985	$10
❑ ST-12268	Conversations	1983	$10
❑ ST-12324	Renegades	1984	$10
LIBERTY
| ❑ LT-51121 | Attitudes | 1982 | $12 |
| ❑ LT-1060 | Brass Construction 6 | 1981 | $10 |
— Reissue of United Artists 1060
UNITED ARTISTS
❑ UA-LA545-G	Brass Construction	1976	$12
❑ LT-977	Brass Construction 5	1979	$12
❑ LT-1060	Brass Construction 6	1980	$15
❑ UA-LA677-G	Brass Construction II	1976	$12
❑ UA-LA775-H	Brass Construction III	1977	$12
❑ UA-LA916-H	Brass Construction IV	1978	$12

BRASS ENSEMBLE OF THE JAZZ AND CLASSICAL MUSIC SOCIETY, THE
COLUMBIA
| ❑ CL941 [M] | Music for Brass | 1956 | $120 |

BRASS RING, THE
ABC DUNHILL
❑ DS-50034	Gazpacho	1968	$15
❑ DS-50044	Only Love	1969	$15
❑ DS-50051	The Best of the Brass Ring	1970	$12

Number	Title	Yr	NM

DUNHILL
❑ D50012 [M]	Lara's Theme	1966	$15
❑ DS50012 [S]	Lara's Theme	1966	$18
❑ ST-91039 [S]	Lara's Theme	1966	$25
— Capitol Record Club edition
❑ D50008 [M]	Love Theme from The Flight of the Phoenix	1966	$15
❑ DS50008 [S]	Love Theme from The Flight of the Phoenix	1966	$18
❑ D50015 [M]	Sunday Night at the Movies	1967	$15
❑ DS50015 [S]	Sunday Night at the Movies	1967	$18
❑ D50017 [M]	The Dis-Advantages of You	1967	$15
❑ DS50017 [S]	The Dis-Advantages of You	1967	$18
❑ D50023 [M]	The Now Sound	1967	$15
❑ DS50023 [S]	The Now Sound	1967	$18
PROJECT 3
| ❑ 5067 | The Brass Ring | 1972 | $12 |

BRASSELLE, KEEFE
CORAL
| ❑ CRL57295 [M] | Minstrel Man | 1959 | $25 |
| ❑ CRL757295 [S] | Minstrel Man | 1959 | $30 |

BRAUFMAN, ALAN
INDIA NAVIGATION
| ❑ IN-1024 | Valley of Search | 197? | $30 |

BRAUN, BOB
DECCA
| ❑ DL4339 [M] | Till Death Do Us Part | 1962 | $25 |
| ❑ DL74339 [S] | Till Death Do Us Part | 1962 | $30 |
UNITED ARTISTS
| ❑ UAS6664 | Christmas in Your Heart | 1968 | $15 |

BRAUTIGAN, RICHARD
HARVEST
| ❑ ST-424 | Listening to Richard Brautigan | 1970 | $30 |

BRAVE BELT
Also see RANDY BACHMAN; BACHMAN-TURNER OVERDRIVE.
REPRISE
❑ MS2210	Bachman-Turner-Bachman As Brave Belt	1974	$12
❑ RS6447	Brave Belt	1971	$15
❑ MS2057	Brave Belt II	1972	$15

BRAXTON, ANTHONY, AND DEREK BAILEY
EMANEM
| ❑ 3313 | Duo 1 | 197? | $35 |
| ❑ 3314 | Duo 2 | 197? | $35 |
INNER CITY
| ❑ 1041 | Live at Wigmor | 198? | $30 |

BRAXTON, ANTHONY, AND MUHAL RICHARD ABRAMS
ARISTA
| ❑ AL4101 | Duets | 1976 | $35 |

BRAXTON, ANTHONY
ANTILLES
| ❑ 1005 | Six Compositions: Quartet | 1981 | $30 |
ARISTA
❑ AL4064	5 Pieces 1975	1975	$35
❑ A2L8602	Alto Sax Improvisations '79	1979	$35
❑ AL4080	Creative Orchestra Music 1976	1976	$35
❑ AL4181	For Trio	1978	$35
❑ AL4032	New York, Fall 1974	1975	$35
❑ AL5002	The Montreux/Berlin Concerts	1977	$25
ARISTA FREEDOM
| ❑ AL1902 | The Complete Braxton 1971 | 1978 | $25 |
BLACK SAINT
❑ BSR-0066	Four Compositions: Quartet 1983	1983	$30
❑ BSR-0086	Four Compositions: Quartet 1984	1985	$30
❑ 120116-1	Six Monk Compositions	1987	$30
BLUEBIRD
| ❑ 6626-1-RB | Anthony Braxton Live | 1988 | $25 |
CONCORD JAZZ
| ❑ CJ-213 | A Ray Brown 3 | 1982 | $30 |
DELMARK
❑ DS-420/1	For Alto	1971	$30
❑ DS-415	Three Compositions of New Jazz	1969	$25
❑ DS-428	Together Alone	1973	$25
— With Joseph Jarman
HAT HUT
❑ 1984	Composition 98	1981	$35
❑ 1995/96	Open Aspects '82	1982	$35
❑ 2019	Performance	1983	$35

Number	Title	Yr	NM
INNER CITY			
❑ 2015	In the Tradition	197?	$35
❑ IC2045	In the Tradition, Vol. 2	1976	$35
❑ 1008	Saxophone Improvisations -- Series F	197?	$35
MAGENTA			
❑ MA-0203	Seven Standards 1985	1986	$30
❑ MA-0205	Seven Standards 1985, Volume 2	1986	$30
SACKVILLE			
❑ 3007	Trio and Duet	198?	$25
SOUND ASPECTS			
❑ SAS-009	Anthony Braxton with the Robert Schumann Quartet	1986	$30
STEEPLECHASE			
❑ SCS-1015	In the Tradition	198?	$25
❑ SCS-1045	In the Tradition, Volume 2	198?	$25
BRAXTON, TONI			
LAFACE			
❑ 26069	The Heat	2000	$25
BRAZOS VALLEY BOYS, THE			
WARNER BROS.			
❑ W1679 [M]	The Countrypolitan Sound	1967	$25
❑ WS1679 [S]	The Countrypolitan Sound	1967	$30
❑ W1686 [M]	The Gold Standard Collection	1967	$25
❑ WS1686 [S]	The Gold Standard Collection	1967	$30
❑ W1664 [M]	Where Is the Circus	1966	$25
❑ WS1664 [S]	Where Is the Circus	1966	$30
BREAD, LOVE AND DREAMS			
LONDON			
❑ PS566	Bread, Love and Dreams	1969	$30
BREAD			
ELEKTRA			
❑ 60414	Anthology of Bread	1985	$12
❑ EKS-75015	Baby I'm-a Want You	1971	$18
— Gatefold with raised photo on front			
❑ EKS-75015	Baby I'm-a Want You	197?	$12
— Front photo is not raised			
❑ EQ-5015 [Q]	Baby I'm-a Want You	1974	$40
❑ EKS-74044	Bread	1969	$18
— Red label with large stylized "E"			
❑ EKS-74044	Bread	1971	$12
— Butterfly label			
❑ BRD-1 [DJ]	Bread	1971	$25
— In-store sampler; very similar to the future LP "The Best of Bread			
❑ EKS-75047	Guitar Man	1972	$15
❑ 7E-1094	Lost Without Your Love	1976	$12
❑ EKS-74086	Manna	1971	$15
❑ EKS-74076	On the Waters	1970	$18
— Red label with large stylized "E"			
❑ EKS-74076	On the Waters	1971	$12
— Butterfly label			
❑ EKS-75056	The Best of Bread	1973	$15
❑ 6E-108 [B]	The Best of Bread	1977	$10
— Reissue of 75056			
❑ EQ-5056 [Q]	The Best of Bread	1973	$40
❑ 7E-1005	The Best of Bread, Volume 2	1974	$15
❑ 6E-110	The Best of Bread, Volume 2	1977	$10
— Reissue of 7E-1005			
BREAKFAST CLUB			
MCA			
❑ 5821	Breakfast Club	1987	$10
BREAKSTONE, JOSHUA			
CONTEMPORARY			
❑ C-14025	Echoes	1987	$25
❑ C-14040	Evening Star	1988	$25
❑ C-14050	Self-Portrait in Swing	1989	$25
BREAKWATER			
ARISTA			
❑ AB4208	Breakwater	1978	$40
— Value is for originals; this album has been reissued to look like the original, but has a reissue sticker on the back of sealed copies			
❑ AB4264	Splashdown	1980	$40
BREAM, JULIAN			
RCA VICTOR RED SEAL			
❑ LDS-2656 [S]	An Evening of Elizabethan Music	1962	$40
— Original with "shaded dog" label			
❑ LSC-2487 [S]	Giuliani: Guitar Concerto; Arnold: Guitar Concerto	1961	$30
— Original with "shaded dog" label			
❑ LSC-2606 [S]	Popular Classics for Spanish Guitar	1962	$30
— Original with "shaded dog" label			

Number	Title	Yr	NM
❑ LSC-2448 [S]	The Art of Julian Bream	1960	$30
— Original with "shaded dog" label			
❑ LDS-2560 [S]	The Golden Age of English Lute Music	1961	$30
— Original with "shaded dog" label			
BREATHE			
A&M			
❑ SP-5163	All That Jazz	1988	$10
❑ 7502153201	Peace of Mind	1990	$15
BREATHLESS			
EMI AMERICA			
❑ SW-17013	Breathless	1979	$18
❑ SW-17041	Nobody Leaves This Song Alive	1980	$18
BRECKER, MICHAEL			
GRP			
❑ GR-9622	Now You See It (Now You Don't)	1990	$20
MCA IMPULSE!			
❑ 42229	Don't Try This at Home	1989	$20
❑ 5980	Michael Brecker	1987	$15
BRECKER, RANDY, AND ELIANE ELIAS			
PASSPORT			
❑ PJ-88013	Amanda	1987	$12
BRECKER, RANDY			
MCA			
❑ 6334	Toe to Toe	1990	$20
PASSPORT			
❑ PJ-88039	In the Idiom	1988	$20
SOLID STATE			
❑ SS-18051	Score	1969	$30
BRECKER BROTHERS, THE			
ARISTA			
❑ AL4061	Back to Back	1976	$25
❑ AQ4061 [Q]	Back to Back	1976	$75
❑ AB4272	Détente	1979	$25
❑ AL4122	Don't Stop the Music	1977	$25
❑ AB4185	Heavy Metal Be-Bop	1978	$25
❑ AL9550	Straphangin'	1981	$30
❑ AL4037	The Brecker Brothers	1975	$30
BREEDLOVE, JIMMY			
RCA CAMDEN			
❑ CAL-430 [M]	Rock 'N' Roll Hits	1958	$40
BREEN, BOBBY			
LONDON			
❑ LB270 [10]	Songs at Yuletide	1953	$50
BREGMAN, BUDDY			
VERVE			
❑ MGV-2094 [M]	Dig Buddy Bregman in Hi-Fi	1959	$150
❑ V-2094 [M]	Dig Buddy Bregman in Hi-Fi	1961	$25
❑ MGV-2064 [M]	Funny Face	1958	$175
❑ V-2064 [M]	Funny Face	1961	$25
❑ MGV-2042 [M]	Swingin' Kicks	1957	$175
❑ MGVS-6013 [S]	Swingin' Kicks	1960	$100
❑ V-2042 [M]	Swingin' Kicks	1961	$25
❑ V6-2042 [S]	Swingin' Kicks	1961	$35
❑ MGV-2093 [M]	The Gershwin Anniversary Album	1959	$150
❑ V-2093 [M]	The Gershwin Anniversary Album	1961	$25
WORLD PACIFIC			
❑ WP-1263 [M]	Swingin' Standards	1959	$150
❑ ST-1024 [S]	Swingin' Standards	1959	$150
BREL, JACQUES			
COLUMBIA			
❑ AWS324 [B]	American Debut	1960	$25
— original release; deduct 25% for 1973 reissue			
PHILIPS			
❑ PCC634 [B]	If You Go Away: Jacques Brel Is Alive And Singing In Paris	1967	$30
— original release; deduct 25% for 1975 reissue			
❑ PCC620 [B]	The Poetic World of Jacques Brel		$30
REPRISE			
❑ RS6246 [B]	Encore!	1967	$15
❑ RS6187 [B]	Jacques Brel	1966	$15
VANGUARD			
❑ VSD79265 [B]	Le Formidable	1967	$50
BREMERS, BEVERLY			
SCEPTER			
❑ SPS-5102	I'll Make You Music	1972	$12

Number	Title	Yr	NM
BRENDA AND HERB (THE EXCITERS)			
DRIVE			
❑ 109	In Heat Again	1978	$15
BRENDA AND THE BIG DUDES			
CAPITOL			
❑ ST-12482	Weekend Special	1986	$12
BRENDA AND THE TABULATIONS			
CHOCOLATE CITY			
❑ 2002	I Keep Coming Back for More	1977	$12
DIONN			
❑ LPM-2000 [M]	Dry Your Eyes	1967	$40
❑ LPS-2000 [S]	Dry Your Eyes	1967	$50
TOP & BOTTOM			
❑ 100	Brenda and the Tabulations	1970	$25
BRENNAN, WALTER			
DOT			
❑ DLP-3309 [M]	Dutchman's Gold	1960	$30
❑ DLP-25309 [S]	Dutchman's Gold	1960	$30
EVEREST			
❑ LPBR-5123 [M]	The President: A Musical Biography of Our Chief Executive	1960	$30
❑ SDBR-1123 [S]	The President: A Musical Biography of Our Chief Executive	1960	$30
❑ LPBR-5103 [M]	World of Miracles	1960	$30
❑ SDBR-1103 [S]	World of Miracles	1960	$30
HAMILTON			
❑ HLP-159 [M]	Dutchman's Gold	1965	$15
❑ HLP-12159 [S]	Dutchman's Gold	1965	$15
LIBERTY			
❑ LRP-3372 [M]	Gunfight at the O.K. Corral	1964	$25
❑ LST-7372 [S]	Gunfight at the O.K. Corral	1964	$30
❑ LRP-3266 [M]	Mama Sang a Song	1963	$25
❑ LST-7266 [S]	Mama Sang a Song	1963	$30
❑ LRP-3233 [M]	Old Rivers	1962	$25
❑ LST-7233 [S]	Old Rivers	1962	$30
❑ LRP-3317 [M]	Talkin' from the Heart	1964	$25
❑ LST-7317 [S]	Talkin' from the Heart	1964	$30
❑ LRP-3241 [M]	The President: A Musical Biography of Our Chief Executive	1962	$18
— Reissue of Everest 5123			
❑ LST-7241 [S]	The President: A Musical Biography of Our Chief Executive	1962	$25
— Reissue of Everest 1123			
❑ LRP-3257 [M]	'Twas the Night Before Christmas Back Home	1962	$25
❑ LST-7257 [S]	'Twas the Night Before Christmas Back Home	1962	$30
❑ LRP-3244 [M]	World of Miracles	1962	$18
— Reissue of Everest 5103			
❑ LST-7244 [S]	World of Miracles	1962	$25
— Reissue of Everest 1103			
LONDON			
❑ PS577	Yesterday, When I Was Young	1970	$18
R.P.C.			
❑ 108 [M]	By the Fireside	1961	$30
❑ 108S [S]	By the Fireside	1961	$40
SUNSET			
❑ SUM-1100 [M]	Country Heart	1966	$15
❑ SUS-5100 [S]	Country Heart	1966	$15
❑ SUS-5269	God and Country	1970	$12
UNITED ARTISTS			
❑ UA-LA438-E	The Very Best of Walter Brennan	1975	$15
BRESH, TOM			
ABC			
❑ AB-1055	Portrait	1978	$15
ABC DOT			
❑ DO-2084	Kicked Back	1977	$15
FARR			
❑ FL1000	Homemade Love	1976	$18
BREWER, TERESA, AND COUNT BASIE			
DOCTOR JAZZ			
❑ FW38836	Songs of Bessie Smith	1984	$20
FLYING DUTCHMAN			
❑ FD10161	Songs of Bessie Smith	1973	$30
BREWER, TERESA, AND MERCER ELLINGTON			
DOCTOR JAZZ			
❑ FW40031	The Cotton Connection	1985	$25
BREWER, TERESA, AND STEPHANE GRAPPELLI			
DOCTOR JAZZ			
❑ FW38448	On the Road Again	198?	$25

Number	Title	Yr	NM

BREWER, TERESA, AND SVEND ASMUSSEN

DOCTOR JAZZ

Number	Title	Yr	NM
❏ FW40233	On the Good Ship Lollipop	1987	$25

BREWER, TERESA

AMSTERDAM

Number	Title	Yr	NM
❏ 12013	Music, Music, Music	1973	$12
❏ 12015	Teresa Brewer In London	1974	$12
❏ 12012	The Doo Dah Song	1973	$12

COLUMBIA

Number	Title	Yr	NM
❏ PC37363	A Sophisticated Lady	198?	$10

—*Budget-line reissue*

| ❏ FC37363 | A Sophisticated Lady | 1981 | $12 |

CORAL

Number	Title	Yr	NM
❏ CRL56072 [10]	A Bouquet of Hits	1952	$40
❏ CRL57374 [M]	Aloha from Teresa	1961	$25
❏ CRL757374 [S]	Aloha from Teresa	1961	$30
❏ CRL57414 [M]	Don't Mess with Tess	1962	$25
❏ CRL757414 [S]	Don't Mess with Tess	1962	$30
❏ CRL57135 [M]	For Teenagers in Love	1957	$30
❏ 57297 [M]	Heavenly Lover	1959	$25
❏ CRL57179 [M]	Miss Music	1958	$30
❏ CRL57027 [M]	Music, Music, Music	1955	$30
❏ CRL57351	My Golden Favorites	1960	$25
❏ CRL757351 [R]	My Golden Favorites	1960	$25
❏ CRL57329 [M]	Naughty, Naughty, Naughty	1960	$25
❏ CRL757329 [S]	Naughty, Naughty, Naughty	1960	$30
❏ CRL57315 [M]	Ridin' High	1960	$25
❏ CRL757315 [S]	Ridin' High	1960	$30
❏ CRL57361 [M]	Songs Everybody Knows	1961	$25
❏ CRL757361 [S]	Songs Everybody Knows	1961	$30
❏ CRL57053 [M]	Teresa	1956	$30
❏ CRL57245 [M]	Teresa Brewer and the Dixieland Band	1958	$25
❏ CRL757245 [S]	Teresa Brewer and the Dixieland Band	1958	$30
❏ CRL57144 [M]	Teresa Brewer At Christmas Time	1957	$30
❏ CXB7 [M]	The Best of Teresa Brewer	1965	$25
❏ CXSB7 [P]	The Best of Teresa Brewer	1965	$25
❏ CRL56093 [10]	Till I Waltz Again with You	1953	$40
❏ CRL57232 [M]	Time for Teresa	1958	$30
❏ CRL57297 [M]	When Your Lover Has Gone	1958	$25
❏ CRL757297 [S]	When Your Lover Has Gone	1959	$30

DOCTOR JAZZ

Number	Title	Yr	NM
❏ ASLP804	Good News	198?	$12
❏ FW40951	Good News	198?	$10
❏ FW38534	I Dig Big Band Singers	1983	$12
❏ W2X39521	Live at Carnegie Hall and Montreux, Switzerland	1984	$15
❏ FW40232	Midnight Café	1986	$12

FLYING DUTCHMAN

Number	Title	Yr	NM
❏ BSL1-0577	Good News	1974	$15

LONDON

Number	Title	Yr	NM
❏ APB-1006 [10]	Teresa Brewer	1951	$50

PHILIPS

Number	Title	Yr	NM
❏ PHM200163 [M]	Dear Heart/Goldfinger	1965	$15
❏ PHS600163 [S]	Dear Heart/Goldfinger	1965	$18
❏ PHM200216 [M]	Gold Country	1966	$15
❏ PHS600216 [S]	Gold Country	1966	$18
❏ PHM200147 [M]	Golden Hits of 1964	1964	$15
❏ PHS600147 [S]	Golden Hits of 1964	1964	$18
❏ PHM200119 [M]	Moments to Remember	1964	$15
❏ PHS600119 [S]	Moments to Remember	1964	$18
❏ PHM200200 [M]	Songs for Our Fighting Men	1966	$15
❏ PHS600200 [S]	Songs for Our Fighting Men	1966	$18
❏ PHM200062 [M]	Teresa Brewer's Greatest Hits	1962	$18
❏ PHS600062 [S]	Teresa Brewer's Greatest Hits	1962	$25
❏ PHM200099 [M]	Terrific Teresa	1963	$18
❏ PHS600099 [S]	Terrific Teresa	1963	$25
❏ PHM200230 [M]	Texas Leather and Mexican Lace	1967	$18
❏ PHS600230 [S]	Texas Leather and Mexican Lace	1967	$15

PROJECT 3

Number	Title	Yr	NM
❏ 5108	Come Follow the Band	1982	$12

RCA VICTOR

Number	Title	Yr	NM
❏ ANL1-1131	The Best of Teresa Brewer	1975	$12

SIGNATURE

Number	Title	Yr	NM
❏ PW40113	Teresa Brewer At Christmas Time	1985	$12

—*Reissue of Coral 57144*

| ❏ FW39421 | Teresa Brewer In London | 1984 | $10 |

—*Reissue of Amsterdam 12015*

VOCALION

Number	Title	Yr	NM
❏ VL73847 [R]	Here's Teresa Brewer	1969	$12
❏ VL3693 [M]	Teresa Brewer	1966	$15

BREWER AND SHIPLEY

A&M

Number	Title	Yr	NM
❏ SP-4154	Down in L.A.	1968	$18

CAPITOL

Number	Title	Yr	NM
❏ ST-11261	ST-11261	1974	$12
❏ ST-11402	Welcome to Riddle Bridge	1975	$12

KAMA SUTRA

Number	Title	Yr	NM
❏ KSBS-2058	Rural Space	1972	$15
❏ KSBS-2039	Shake Off the Demon	1971	$15
❏ KSBS-2024	Tarkio	1970	$15

—*LP label calls this "Tarkio Road*

| ❏ KSBS2613-2 | The Best... Brewer & Shipley | 1976 | $18 |
| ❏ KSBS-2016 | Weeds | 1969 | $15 |

BRIAN AND BRENDA

ROCKET

Number	Title	Yr	NM
❏ PIG-2291	Supersonic Lover	1977	$18

BRIARWOOD SINGERS, THE

UNITED ARTISTS

Number	Title	Yr	NM
❏ UAL3318 [M]	Well, Well, Well!	1963	$15
❏ UAS6318 [S]	Well, Well, Well!	1963	$18

BRICK

BANG

Number	Title	Yr	NM
❏ FZ38170	After 5	1982	$12
❏ BLP-409	Brick	1977	$15
❏ BLP-408	Good High	1976	$15

—*Beware of sealed copies -- this album has been "reissued" to look exactly like the original*

❏ JZ35969	Stoneheart	1979	$12
❏ FZ37471	Summer Heat	1981	$12
❏ JZ36262	Waiting on You	1980	$12

MAGIC CITY

Number	Title	Yr	NM
❏ MCR1001	Too Tuff	1988	$12

BRICKELL, EDIE, & NEW BOHEMIANS

GEFFEN

Number	Title	Yr	NM
❏ GHS24304	Ghost of a Dog	1990	$18
❏ R100789	Shooting Rubberbands at the Stars	1988	$15

—*BMG Direct Marketing edition*

| ❏ GHS24192 | Shooting Rubberbands at the Stars | 1988 | $12 |

BRICKLIN

A&M

Number	Title	Yr	NM
❏ SP-5124	Bricklin	1986	$10

BRIDES OF FUNKENSTEIN, THE

ATLANTIC

Number	Title	Yr	NM
❏ SD19201 [B]	Funk or Walk	1978	$25
❏ SD19261 [B]	Never Buy Texas from a Cowboy	1980	$25

BRIDGES, ALICIA

POLYDOR

Number	Title	Yr	NM
❏ PD-1-6158	Alicia Bridges	1978	$12
❏ PD-1-6219	Play It As It Lays	1979	$12

SECOND WAVE

Number	Title	Yr	NM
❏ 22007	Hocus Pocus	1984	$15

BRIDGEWATER, DEE DEE

ATLANTIC

Number	Title	Yr	NM
❏ SD18188	Dee Dee Bridgewater	1976	$15

ELEKTRA

Number	Title	Yr	NM
❏ 6E-188	Bad for Me	1979	$12
❏ 6E-306	Dee Dee Bridgewater	1980	$12
❏ 6E-119	Just Family	1978	$12

MCA/IMPULSE

Number	Title	Yr	NM
❏ MCA-6331	Live in Paris	1989	$15

BRIGADE, THE

BAND'N VOCAL

Number	Title	Yr	NM
❏ 1066	Last Laugh	1970	$2000

—*VG value 1000; VG+ value 1500*

BRIGATI

ASYLUM

Number	Title	Yr	NM
❏ 7E-1074	Lost in the Wilderness	1976	$18

BRIGG

SUSQUEHANNA

Number	Title	Yr	NM
❏ LP-301	Brigg	1973	$250

BRIGGS, ANNE

4 MEN WITH BEARDS

Number	Title	Yr	NM
❏ 4M164LP [B]	Anne Briggs		$25
❏ 4M165LP [B]	The Time Has Come		$25

BRIGGS, KAREN

VITAL

Number	Title	Yr	NM
❏ VTL-009	Karen	1996	$25

BRIGHT, RONNELL

REGENT

Number	Title	Yr	NM
❏ MG-6041 [M]	Bright's Spot	1957	$150

SAVOY

Number	Title	Yr	NM
❏ MG-12206 [M]	Bright's Spot	196?	$75

—*Reissue of Regent LP*

VANGUARD

Number	Title	Yr	NM
❏ VRS-8512 [M]	Bright's Flight	1957	$175

BRIGHTER SIDE OF DARKNESS

20TH CENTURY

Number	Title	Yr	NM
❏ T-405	Love Jones	1973	$30

BRIGMAN, GEORGE

SOLID

Number	Title	Yr	NM
❏ SR-001	Jungle Rot	1975	$120

BRIGNOLA, NICK

BEE HIVE

Number	Title	Yr	NM
❏ BH-7000	Baritone Madness	1977	$30
❏ BH-7010	Burn Brigade	1979	$30

DISCOVERY

Number	Title	Yr	NM
❏ DS-917	Northern Lights	1986	$25

INTERPLAY

Number	Title	Yr	NM
❏ IP-7719	New York Bound	198?	$30

SEA BREEZE

Number	Title	Yr	NM
❏ SB-2003	L.A. Bound	198?	$30

BRILEY, MARTIN

MERCURY

Number	Title	Yr	NM
❏ 822423-1	Dangerous Moments	1984	$12
❏ SRM-1-4026	Fear of the Unknown	1981	$15
❏ 810332-1	One Night with a Stranger	1983	$12

BRILL, MARTY

MERCURY

Number	Title	Yr	NM
❏ MG-20178 [M]	The Roving Balladeer	1957	$30

BRIMSTONE

PEPPERMINT

Number	Title	Yr	NM
❏ 1022	Paper Winged Dreams	1973	$500

BRINSLEY SCHWARZ

CAPITOL

Number	Title	Yr	NM
❏ ST-589 [B]	Brinsley Schwarz	1970	$30
❏ SWBC-11869 [B]	Brinsley Schwarz	1978	$25
❏ ST-744 [B]	Despite It All	1971	$30

LIBERTY

Number	Title	Yr	NM
❏ LN10146	Nervous on the Road	1981	$12

—*10-track reissue*

| ❏ LN10145 | Silver Pistol | 1980 | $12 |

—*10-track reissue*

UNITED ARTISTS

Number	Title	Yr	NM
❏ UAS-5647 [B]	Nervous on the Road	1972	$30
❏ UAS-5566 [B]	Silver Pistol	1972	$30

BRISKER, GORDON

DISCOVERY

Number	Title	Yr	NM
❏ DS-923	About Charlie	1987	$25
❏ DS-938	New Beginning	1987	$25

SEA BREEZE

Number	Title	Yr	NM
❏ SB-2016	Cornerstone	1985	$25

BRISTOL, JOHNNY

ATLANTIC

Number	Title	Yr	NM
❏ SD18197	Bristol's Creme	1976	$12
❏ SD19184	Strangers	1978	$12

HANDSHAKE

Number	Title	Yr	NM
❏ FW37666	Free to Be Me	1981	$12

MGM

Number	Title	Yr	NM
❏ M3G-4983	Feeling the Magic	1975	$15
❏ M3G-4959	Hang On In There Baby	1974	$15

BRITISH LIONS

RSO

Number	Title	Yr	NM
❏ RS-1-3032 [B]	British Lions	1978	$15

BRITNY FOX

COLUMBIA

Number	Title	Yr	NM
❏ FC45300	Boys in Heat	1989	$15
❏ BFC44140	Britny Fox	1988	$12

BRITT, ELTON

ABC-PARAMOUNT

Number	Title	Yr	NM
❏ ABC-322 [M]	Beyond the Sunset	1960	$30
❏ ABCS-322 [S]	Beyond the Sunset	1960	$40
❏ ABC-331 [M]	I Heard a Forest Praying	1960	$30
❏ ABCS-331 [S]	I Heard a Forest Praying	1960	$40
❏ ABC-566 [M]	Somethin' for Everybody	1966	$30
❏ ABCS-566 [S]	Somethin' for Everybody	1966	$40
❏ ABC-521 [M]	The Singing Hills	1965	$30
❏ ABCS-521 [S]	The Singing Hills	1965	$40
❏ ABC-293 [M]	The Wandering Cowboy	1959	$30
❏ ABCS-293 [S]	The Wandering Cowboy	1959	$40

RCA VICTOR

Number	Title	Yr	NM
❏ LPM-2669 [M]	The Best of Elton Britt	1963	$30
❏ LPM-3222 [10]	Yodel Songs	1954	$120
❏ LPM-1288 [M]	Yodel Songs	1956	$75

Number	Title	Yr	NM

BRITT, PAT
CATALYST
❏ 7612 — Starsong — 1976 — $30
CRESTVIEW
❏ CR-3075 [M] — Jazz from San Francisco — 1967 — $25
❏ CRS-3075 [S] — Jazz from San Francisco — 1967 — $35
VEE JAY
❏ VJS-3064 — Jazz from San Francisco — 1975 — $30
❏ VJS-3070 — Jazzman — 1975 — $30

BRITT, TINA
MINIT
❏ LP-24023 — Blue All the Way — 1968 — $25

BROADBENT, ALAN
DISCOVERY
❏ DS-929 — Everything I Love — 1987 — $25
GRANITE
❏ 7901 — Palette — 1979 — $30
TREND
❏ TR-546 — Another Time — 1988 — $25

BROCAS HELM
GARGOYLE
❏ 138801 — Black Death — 1988 — $50

BROCK, B., AND THE SULTANS
CROWN
❏ CLP-5399 [M] — Do the Beetle — 1964 — $40
❏ CST-399 [S] — Do the Beetle — 1964 — $50

BROCK, HERBIE
SAVOY
❏ MG-12069 [M] — Brock's Tops — 1956 — $40
❏ MG-12066 [M] — Herbie Brock Solo — 1956 — $40

BROCK, JIM
REFERENCE RECORDINGS
❏ RR-31 — Tropic Affair — 198? — $35

BRODIE, HUGH, AND IMPULSE
CADENCE JAZZ
❏ CJ-1004 — Live and Cooking at the Wild Oat — 1981 — $20

BROKENSHA, JACK
SAVOY
❏ MG-12180 — And Then I Said — 1962 — $30

BROLIN, JAMES
ARTCO
❏ LPC-1099 — James Brolin Sings — 1974 — $30

BROMBERG, DAVID
COLUMBIA
❏ C31104 — David Bromberg — 1972 — $15
❏ PC31104 — David Bromberg — 198? — $10
— Budget-line reissue
❏ KC31753 — Demon in Disguise — 1973 — $15
❏ PC31753 — Demon in Disguise — 198? — $10
— Budget-line reissue
❏ PC33397 — Midnight on the Water — 1975 — $15
— Original with no bar code
❏ PC33397 — Midnight on the Water — 198? — $10
— Budget-line reissue with bar code
❏ PC34467 — The Best of David Bromberg: Out of the Blues — 1976 — $15
— Original with no bar code
❏ PC34467 — The Best of David Bromberg: Out of the Blues — 198? — $10
— Budget-line reissue with bar code
❏ KC32717 — Wanted Dead or Alive — 1974 — $15
FANTASY
❏ 9555 — Bandit in a Bathing Suit — 1978 — $12
❏ 79007 — How Late'll Ya Play 'Til? — 1976 — $18
❏ 9572 — My Own House — 1979 — $12
❏ 9540 — Reckless Abandon — 1977 — $15
❏ 9590 — You Should See the Rest of the Band — 1980 — $12
ROUNDER
❏ 3110 — Sideman Serenade — 1989 — $15

BRONSKI BEAT
MCA
❏ 39038 [EP] — Hundreds & Thousands — 1985 — $12
❏ 5538 — The Age of Consent — 1984 — $10
❏ 25052 — The Age of Consent — 198? — $10
— Reissue of 5538
❏ 5751 — Truthdare Doubledare — 1986 — $10

BROOD, HERMAN
ARIOLA AMERICA
❏ OL-1500 [B] — Go Nutz — 1980 — $15
❏ SW-50059 [B] — Herman Brood & His Wild Romance — 1979 — $15

BROOKINS, ROBERT
MCA
❏ 5824 — In the Night — 1986 — $15
❏ 42250 — Let It Be Me — 1988 — $12

BROOKLYN BRIDGE, THE
BUDDAH
❏ BDS-5107 — Bridge in Blue — 1972 — $25
❏ BDS-5034 — Brooklyn Bridge — 1969 — $25
❏ BDS-5065 — The Brooklyn Bridge — 1970 — $25
❏ BDS-5042 — The Second Brooklyn Bridge — 1969 — $25
COLLECTABLES
❏ COL-5015 — The Greatest Hits — 198? — $15
— As "Johnny Maestro and the Brooklyn Bridge"

BROOKLYN DREAMS
CASABLANCA
❏ NBLP-7165 — Joy Ride — 1979 — $15
❏ NBLP-7135 — Sleepless Nights — 1979 — $15
❏ NBLP-7226 — Won't Let Go — 1980 — $12
MILLENNIUM
❏ MNLP-8002 — Brooklyn Dreams — 1977 — $15

BROOKMEYER, BOB, AND BILL EVANS
UNITED ARTISTS
❏ UAL-3044 [M] — The Ivory Hunters -- Double Barreled Piano — 1959 — $50
❏ UAS-6044 [S] — The Ivory Hunters -- Double Barreled Piano — 1959 — $40

BROOKMEYER, BOB, AND MEL LEWIS
GRYPHON
❏ 912 — Live at the Village Vanguard — 1980 — $30

BROOKMEYER, BOB, AND ZOOT SIMS
JAZZTONE
❏ J-1239 [M] — Bob Brookmeyer and Zoot Sims — 1956 — $40
STORYVILLE
❏ STLP-907 [M] — Tonight's Jazz Today — 1956 — $100
❏ STLP-914 [M] — Whoo-eeee! — 1956 — $175

BROOKMEYER, BOB; JIM HALL; JIMMY RANEY
KIMBERLY
❏ 2021 [M] — Brookmeyer and Guitars — 1963 — $30
❏ 11021 [S] — Brookmeyer and Guitars — 1963 — $25
WORLD PACIFIC
❏ PJ-1239 [M] — The Street Swingers — 1957 — $350
❏ WP-1239 [M] — The Street Swingers — 1958 — $300
— Reissue with new prefix

BROOKMEYER, BOB
ATLANTIC
❏ 1320 [M] — Portrait of the Artist — 1960 — $300
— Black label
❏ 1320 [M] — Portrait of the Artist — 1961 — $175
— Multicolor label, white "fan" logo at right
❏ SD1320 [S] — Portrait of the Artist — 1960 — $300
— Green label
❏ SD1320 [S] — Portrait of the Artist — 1961 — $175
— Multicolor label, white "fan" logo at right
CLEF
❏ MGC-644 [M] — Bob Brookmeyer Plays Bob Brookmeyer and Some Others — 1955 — $300
❏ MGC-732 [M] — The Modernity of Bob Brookmeyer — 1956 — $300
COLUMBIA
❏ CL2237 [M] — Bob Brookmeyer and Friends — 1965 — $35
❏ CS9037 [S] — Bob Brookmeyer and Friends — 1965 — $25
CROWN
❏ CLP-5318 [M] — Bob Brookmeyer — 196? — $35
FANTASY
❏ OJC-1729 — The Dual Role of Bob Brookmeyer — 1990 — $30
— Reissue of Prestige 7066
FINESSE
❏ FW37488 — Through a Looking Glass — 198? — $25
GRYPHON
❏ 785 — Bob Brookmeyer's Small Band — 1978 — $35
MERCURY
❏ MG-20600 [M] — Jazz Is a Kick — 1960 — $150
❏ SR-60600 [S] — Jazz Is a Kick — 1960 — $150
NEW JAZZ
❏ NJLP-8294 [M] — Revelation — 1963 — $175
— Purple label
❏ NJLP-8294 [M] — Revelation — 1965 — $175
— Blue label, trident logo at right
ODYSSEY
❏ PC36804 — Bob Brookmeyer and Friends — 1980 — $25
— Reissue of Columbia 9037
PACIFIC JAZZ
❏ PJLP-16 [10] — Bob Brookmeyer Quartet — 1954 — $175
PRESTIGE
❏ PRLP-214 [10] — Bob Brookmeyer with Jimmy Raney — 1955 — $300
❏ PRLP-7066 [M] — The Dual Role of Bob Brookmeyer — 1956 — $300
SONET
❏ 778 — Back Again — 1979 — $30
STORYVILLE
❏ STLP-305 [10] — Bob Brookmeyer Featuring Al Cohn — 1954 — $300
TODAY'S JAZZ
❏ J-1239 [M] — Bob Brookmeyer and Zoot Sims — 196? — $30
TRIP
❏ 5568 — Jazz Is a Kick — 197? — $25
UNITED ARTISTS
❏ UAL-4008 [M] — Kansas City Revisited — 1959 — $50
❏ UAS-5008 [S] — Kansas City Revisited — 1959 — $40
VERVE
❏ V-8413 [M] — 7 X Wilder — 1961 — $150
❏ V6-8413 [S] — 7 X Wilder — 1961 — $150
❏ V-8455 [M] — Gloomy Sunday and Other Bright Moments — 1962 — $30
❏ V6-8455 [S] — Gloomy Sunday and Other Bright Moments — 1962 — $30
❏ MGV-8385 [M] — The Blues, Hot and Cold — 1960 — $100
❏ V-8385 [M] — The Blues, Hot and Cold — 1961 — $30
❏ V6-8385 [S] — The Blues, Hot and Cold — 1961 — $30
❏ MGV-8111 [M] — The Modernity of Bob Brookmeyer — 1957 — $300
❏ V-8111 [M] — The Modernity of Bob Brookmeyer — 1961 — $175
❏ V-8498 [M] — Trombone Jazz Samba — 1962 — $30
❏ V6-8498 [S] — Trombone Jazz Samba — 1962 — $30
VIK
❏ LX-1071 [M] — Brookmeyer — 1957 — $50
WORLD PACIFIC
❏ PJ-1233 [M] — Traditionalism Revisited — 1958 — $175

BROOKS, CECIL, III
MUSE
❏ MR-5377 — The Collective — 1989 — $30

BROOKS, DONNA
DAWN
❏ DLP-1105 [M] — I'll Take Romance — 1956 — $120

BROOKS, DONNIE
ERA
❏ EL-105 [M] — The Happiest — 1961 — $175

BROOKS, ELKIE
A&M
❏ SP-4554 — Rich Man's Woman — 1975 — $12
❏ SP-4695 — Shooting Star — 1977 — $12
❏ SP-4631 — Two Days Away — 1977 — $12

BROOKS, GARTH
CAPITOL
❏ C1-90897 — Garth Brooks — 1989 — $30
— Non-record club edition
❏ C1-590897 — Garth Brooks — 1989 — $25
— Columbia House edition
❏ 1P-8042 — No Fences — 1990 — $40
— Columbia House version; cover photo is the size of CD cover
CAPITOL NASHVILLE
❏ R173266 — No Fences — 1990 — $75
— BMG Direct Marketing version has a large cover photo
❏ C1-596330 — Ropin' the Wind — 1991 — $50
— Only released on U.S. vinyl by Columbia House

BROOKS, HADDA
CROWN
❏ CLP-5010 [M] — Femme Fatale — 1957 — $75
— Black label; reissue of Modern LP
❏ CLP-5374 [M] — Hadda Brooks Sings and Swings — 1963 — $30
— Gray label
MODERN
❏ MLP-1210 [M] — Femme Fatale — 1956 — $250

Number	Title	Yr	NM

BROOKS, HADDA / PETE JOHNSON
CROWN
| CLP-5058 [M] | Boogie | 1958 | $50 |

BROOKS, JOHN BENSON
DECCA
| DL5018 [M] | Avant Slant | 1968 | $40 |

— White label promo only; in stereo cover with "Monaural" sticker on front

| DL75018 [S] | Avant Slant | 1968 | $25 |

RIVERSIDE
| RLP 12-276 [M] | The Alabama Concerto | 1958 | $300 |
| RLP-1123 [S] | The Alabama Concerto | 1959 | $300 |

VIK
| LX-1083 [M] | Folk Jazz U.S.A. | 1957 | $40 |

BROOKS, KAREN
WARNER BROS.
25051	Hearts of Fire	1984	$10
25277	I Will Dance with You	1985	$10
23676	Walk On	1983	$10

BROOKS, RANDY
CIRCLE
| CLP-035 | Randy Brooks and His Orchestra 1945-47 | 198? | $25 |

DECCA
| DL8201 [M] | Trumpet Moods | 195? | $30 |

BROOKS, ROY
IM-HOTEP
| CS-030 | Ethnic Expressions | 197? | $35 |

MUSE
| MR-5003 | Free Slave | 197? | $35 |

WORKSHOP JAZZ
| WSJ-220 [M] | Roy Brooks Beat | 1964 | $50 |
| WSJS-220 [S] | Roy Brooks Beat | 1964 | $75 |

BROOKS, TINA
BLUE NOTE
| BLP-4052 [M] | Back to the Tracks | 1960 | $3500 |

— Released canceled, test pressings exist

| BST-84052 [S] | Back to the Tracks | 1960 | $0 |

— Canceled

| BST-84052 [S] | Back to the Tracks | 199? | $40 |

— Classic Records reissue; first U.S. vinyl issue

| BLP-4041 [M] | True Blue | 1960 | $3000 |

— Deep Groove, W 63rd address

| BST-84041 [S] | True Blue | 1960 | $0 |

— Canceled

| B1-28975 | True Blue | 1994 | $25 |

MOSAIC
| MR4-106 | The Complete Blue Note Recordings of the Tina Brooks Quintets | 1984 | $175 |

BROOM, BOBBY
ARISTA
| AL8-8253 | Bobby Broom | 1984 | $12 |

ARISTA/GRP
| GL5504 | Clean Sweep | 1981 | $12 |

BROONZY, BIG BILL
BIOGRAPH
| C-15 | Big Bill Broonzy 1932-1942 | 197? | $12 |

CHESS
| LP-1468 [M] | Big Bill Broonzy and Washboard Sam | 1962 | $160 |

COLUMBIA
| WL111 [M] | Big Bill's Blues | 1958 | $150 |

DIAL
| LP-306 [10] | Blues Concert | 1952 | $175 |

EMARCY
| MG-36137 [M] | Blues by Broonzy | 1958 | $150 |
| MG-26034 [10] | Folk Blues | 1954 | $120 |

EPIC
| EE22017 [M] | Big Bill's Blues | 196? | $25 |

EVEREST ARCHIVE OF FOLK & JAZZ
| 213 | Big Bill Broonzy | 1967 | $15 |

FOLKWAYS
FA-2315 [M]	Big Bill Broonzy	1957	$100
31005 [R]	Big Bill Sings Country Blues	196?	$20
FA-2326 [M]	Country Blues	1957	$75
FG-3586 [M]	His Songs and Story	195?	$50

GNP CRESCENDO
| 10004 | Feeling Low Down | 1974 | $12 |
| 10009 | Lonesome Road Blues | 1975 | $12 |

MERCURY
MG-20822 [M]	Big Bill Broonzy -- Memorial	1963	$30
SR-60822 [R]	Big Bill Broonzy -- Memorial	1963	$25
MG-20905 [M]	Remembering Big Bill Broonzy	1964	$30
SR-60905 [R]	Remembering Big Bill Broonzy	1964	$25

PERIOD
| SLP-1209 [M] | Big Bill Broonzy Sings and Josh White Comes a-Visiting | 1958 | $80 |
| SLP-1114 [M] | Big Bill Broonzy Sings (Blues) | 1956 | $175 |

PORTRAIT MASTERS
| RJ44089 | Big Bill's Blues | 1988 | $18 |

— Reissue of Columbia 111

SMITHSONIAN FOLKWAYS
| SF-40023 | Big Bill Broonzy Sings Folk Songs | 1989 | $15 |

VERVE
MGV-3001 [M]	Last Session, Vol. 1	1959	$50
MGV-3002 [M]	Last Session, Vol. 2	1959	$50
MGV-3003 [M]	Last Session, Vol. 3	1959	$50
MGV-3000-5 [M]	The Big Bill Broonzy Story	1959	$250

YAZOO
| L-1035 | Do That Guitar Rag | 197? | $18 |
| L-1011 [B] | The Young Big Bill Broonzy | 1969 | $18 |

BROS
EPIC
| BFE44285 | Push | 1988 | $12 |

BROTH
MERCURY
| SR-61298 | Broth | 1970 | $25 |

BROTHER BEYOND
CAPITOL
| C1-92940 | Get Even | 1989 | $15 |

BROTHER BONES
TEMPO
| 7004 [M] | Bones on the Beat | 1958 | $175 |

BROTHER FOX AND TAR BABY
CAPITOL
| ST-544 | Brother Fox and Tar Baby | 1970 | $30 |

ORACLE
| 1001 | Brother Fox and Tar Baby | 1969 | $30 |

BROTHER MATTHEW
ABC-PARAMOUNT
| ABC-121 | Brother Matthew | 1956 | $50 |

BROTHER TO BROTHER
SUGAR HILL
| SH259 | Brother to Brother 2 | 1981 | $15 |

TURBO
7013	In the Bottle	1974	$18
7015	Let Your Mind Be Free	1976	$18
7018	Shades in Creation	1977	$18

BROTHERHOOD
MCA
| 828 | Brotherhood | 198? | $10 |

— Budget-line reissue of 2373

| 2373 | Brotherhood | 1978 | $12 |

BROTHERHOOD OF MAN, THE
DERAM
| DES18046 | United We Stand | 1970 | $18 |

PYE
| 12134 | Save Your Kisses for Me | 1976 | $15 |

BROTHERS FOUR, THE
COLUMBIA
CL2502 [M]	A Beatles' Songbook (The Brothers Four Sing Lennon/McCartney)	1966	$18
CS9302 [S]	A Beatles' Songbook (The Brothers Four Sing Lennon/McCartney)	1966	$25
CL2702 [M]	A New World's Record	1967	$30

— Original cover has a flopped image on the front cover, which makes it appear as if the guitarist is left-handed

| CS9502 [S] | A New World's Record | 1967 | $25 |

— Original cover has a flopped image on the front cover, which makes it appear as if the guitarist is left-handed

| CS9502 [S] | A New World's Record | 1967 | $15 |

— Corrected cover, with the guitarist using his right hand, as he does in real life

| CL2702 [M] | A New World's Record | 1967 | $18 |

— Corrected cover, with the guitarist using his right hand, as he does in real life

CL1578 [M]	B.M.O.C. (Best Music On/Off Campus)	1961	$15
CS8378 [S]	B.M.O.C. (Best Music On/Off Campus)	1961	$18
CL1946 [M]	Cross Country Concert	1963	$15
CS8746 [S]	Cross Country Concert	1963	$18
CS9818	Let's Get Together	1969	$15
CL2213 [M]	More Big Folk Hits	1964	$15
CS9013 [S]	More Big Folk Hits	1964	$18
CL1479 [M]	Rally 'Round the Brothers Four	1960	$15
CS8270 [S]	Rally 'Round the Brothers Four	1960	$18
CL1625 [M]	Roamin'	1961	$15
CS8425 [S]	Roamin'	1961	$18
CL2033 [M]	The Big Folk Hits	1963	$15
CS8833 [S]	The Big Folk Hits	1963	$18
CL1402 [M]	The Brothers Four	1960	$15
CS8197 [S]	The Brothers Four	1960	$18
CL1828 [M]	The Brothers Four: In Person	1962	$15
CS8628 [S]	The Brothers Four: In Person	1962	$18
CL1803 [M]	The Brothers Four's Greatest Hits	1962	$15
CS8603 [S]	The Brothers Four's Greatest Hits	1962	$18

— Red "360 Sound" label

| CS8603 | The Brothers Four's Greatest Hits | 1970 | $12 |

— Orange label

| PC8603 | The Brothers Four's Greatest Hits | 198? | $10 |

— Reissue with new prefix

CL2128 [M]	The Brothers Four Sing of Our Times	1964	$15
CS8928 [S]	The Brothers Four Sing of Our Times	1964	$18
CL1697 [M]	The Brothers Four Song Book	1961	$15
CS8497 [S]	The Brothers Four Song Book	1961	$18
CL2305 [M]	The Honey Wind Blows	1965	$15
CS9105 [S]	The Honey Wind Blows	1965	$18
CL2379 [M]	Try to Remember	1965	$15
CS9179 [S]	Try to Remember	1965	$18

FANTASY
| 8400 | The Brothers Four 1970 | 1970 | $12 |

FIRST AMERICAN
7722	Greenfields and Other Gold	1980	$15
7728	New Gold	1981	$12
7705	The Brothers Four Now	1978	$12

HARMONY
| HS11341 | Four Strong Winds | 1969 | $12 |
| H31505 | Great Songs of Our Times | 1972 | $12 |

BROTHERS JOHNSON, THE
A&M
| PR-4714 [DJ] | Blam!! | 1978 | $25 |

— Promo-only picture disc

| SP-4714 | Blam!! | 1978 | $12 |
| SP-17049 [DJ] | Blam!! Radio Special | 1978 | $25 |

— Promo-only music and interview record

SP-4927	Blast! (The Latest and the Greatest)	1982	$12
SP-5162	Kickin'	1988	$12
SP-3716	Light Up the Night	1980	$12
SP-4567	Look Out for #1	1976	$12
SP-4965	Out of Control	1984	$12
SP-4644	Right on Time	1977	$12
SP-3724	Winners	1981	$12

BROUSSARD, JULES
HEADFIRST
| 796 | Jules Broussard | 198? | $30 |

BROWER, JOHNNY
GUINNESS
| GNS36028 [B] | Swamp Witches And Other Creatures | 1977 | $50 |

BROWN, AL
AMY
| A-1 [M] | Madison Dance Party | 1960 | $40 |
| AS-1 [S] | Madison Dance Party | 1960 | $75 |

BROWN, ARTHUR, THE CRAZY WORLD OF
GULL
| GU6-405 | Dance | 1975 | $15 |

PASSPORT
| 98003 | Journey | 1974 | $15 |

— As Arthur Brown's Kingdom Come

TRACK
| SD8198 | The Crazy World of Arthur Brown | 1968 | $30 |

BROWN, BOBBY
DESTINY
| 4001 | Bobby Brown Live | 1972 | $150 |
| 4002 | The Enlightening Beam of Axonda | 1972 | $120 |

MCA
10417	Bobby	1992	$18
6342	Dance! ... Ya Know It!	1989	$15
42185	Don't Be Cruel	1988	$10

Number	Title	Yr	NM
❑ 11691	Forever	1997	$18
❑ 5827	King of Stage	1986	$10
❑ 10974	Remixes N the Key of B	1993	$18

— *Issued in generic black cardboard sleeve*

BROWN, BOOTS / DAN DREW
GROOVE
❑ LG-1000 [M]	Rock That Boat	1955	$300

BROWN, BUSTER
COLLECTABLES
❑ COL-5110	Golden Classics: The New King of the Blues	198?	$12

FIRE
❑ FLP-102 [M]	The New King of the Blues	1961	$700

— *White and red label*
❑ FLP-102 [M]	The New King of the Blues	1961	$400

— *Red and black label, purple cover*
❑ FLP-102 [M]	The New King of the Blues	1961	$300

— *Red and black label, white cover*

SOUFFLE
❑ 2014	Get Down	1973	$15

BROWN, CHARLES
ALADDIN
❑ LP-702 [10]	Mood Music	1952	$7500

— *Red vinyl; VG value 3000; VG+ value 5250*
❑ LP-702 [10]	Mood Music	1952	$4000

— *Black vinyl; VG value 1500; VG+ value 2750*
❑ LP-809 [M]	Mood Music	1956	$0

— *Unreleased?*

ALLIGATOR
❑ AL-4771	One More for the Road	1989	$30

BIG TOWN
❑ 1003	Merry Christmas Baby	1977	$30
❑ 1005	Music Maestro Please	1978	$25

BLUESWAY
❑ BLS-6039	Charles Brown -- Legend	1970	$75

BULLSEYE BLUES
❑ BB-9501	All My Life	1990	$50

IMPERIAL
❑ LP-9178 [M]	Charles Brown Sings Million Sellers	1961	$400

JEWEL
❑ 5006	Blues 'N' Brown	1972	$30

KING
❑ 775 [M]	Charles Brown Sings Christmas Songs	1961	$300
❑ KS-775 [S]	Charles Brown Sings Christmas Songs	1963	$300

— *Stereo copies (whether true stereo or rechanneled, we don't know) exist on blue labels with "King" in block letters (no crown)*
❑ 878 [M]	The Great Charles Brown	1963	$250

MAINSTREAM
❑ 56035 [M]	Ballads My Way	1965	$50
❑ S-6035 [S]	Ballads My Way	1965	$75
❑ 56007 [M]	Boss of the Blues	1965	$50
❑ S-6007 [S]	Boss of the Blues	1965	$75

MOSAIC
❑ MQ7-153	The Complete Aladdin Recordings of Charles Brown	1994	$175

SCORE
❑ SLP-4011 [M]	Driftin' Blues	1958	$400
❑ SLP-4036 [M]	More Blues with Charles Brown	1959	$0

— *Unreleased*

BROWN, CHUCK AND THE SOUL SEARCHERS
Records on the Polydor and Sussex labels were credited simply to "Soul Searchers."
SOURCE
❑ SOR-3076	Bustin' Loose	1979	$15
❑ SOR-3234	Funk Express	1980	$18

SUSSEX
❑ SRA-8030 [B]	Salt of the Earth	1974	$120

— *Reproductions exist*
❑ SXBS-7020 [B]	We the People	1972	$120

— *Reproductions exist*

BROWN, CLIFFORD, AND ART FARMER
PRESTIGE
❑ PRLP-167 [10]	Clifford Brown and Art Farmer with the Swedish All Stars	1953	$300

BROWN, CLIFFORD, AND MAX ROACH
ELEKTRA/MUSICIAN
❑ 60026	Pure Genius	1982	$30

EMARCY
❑ MG-36037 [M]	A Study in Brown	1955	$700

Number	Title	Yr	NM
❑ MG-36008 [M]	Brown and Roach Incorporated	1955	$300
❑ MG-26043 [10]	Clifford Brown and Max Roach	1954	$600
❑ MG-36036 [M]	Clifford Brown and Max Roach	1955	$650
❑ MG-36070 [M]	Clifford Brown and Max Roach at Basin Street	1956	$250

GENE NORMAN
❑ GNP-5 [10]	Clifford Brown and Max Roach, Vol. 1	1954	$300
❑ GNP-7 [10]	Clifford Brown and Max Roach, Vol. 2	1954	$300
❑ GNP-125 [10]	Gene Norman Presents Max Roach and Clifford Brown	1954	$400
❑ GNP-18 [M]	The Best of Max Roach and Clifford Brown In Concert	1955	$300

MAINSTREAM
❑ MRL-386 [M]	Daahoud	197?	$30

TRIP
❑ 5550	All Stars	197?	$25
❑ 5530	A Study in Brown	197?	$25
❑ 5537	Best Coast Jazz	197?	$25
❑ 5520	Brown and Roach Incorporated	197?	$25
❑ 5511 [B]	Clifford Brown and Max Roach at Basin Street	197?	$25
❑ 5540	Jordu	197?	$25

BROWN, CLIFFORD
BLUE NOTE
❑ BST-84428	Alternate Takes	198?	$30
❑ BN-LA267-H2	Brownie Eyes	1974	$30
❑ BLP-1526 [M]	Clifford Brown Memorial Album	1956	$800

— *Deep groove" version (deep indentation under label on both sides)*
❑ BLP-1526 [M]	Clifford Brown Memorial Album	1956	$175

— *Regular edition, Lexington Ave. address on label*
❑ BLP-1526 [M]	Clifford Brown Memorial Album	196?	$175

— *With W. 63rd St. address on label*
❑ BLP-1526 [M]	Clifford Brown Memorial Album	196?	$75

— *With "New York, USA" address on label*
❑ BST-81526 [R]	Clifford Brown Memorial Album	1967	$30

— *With "A Division of Liberty Records" on label*
❑ BST-81526	Clifford Brown Memorial Album	1985	$25

— *The Finest in Jazz Since 1939" reissue*
❑ BLP-5047 [10]	Clifford Brown Quartet	1954	$500
❑ BLP-5032 [10]	New Star on the Horizon	1953	$500

COLUMBIA
❑ KC32284	The Beginning and the End	1973	$35
❑ C32284	The Beginning and the End	197?	$30

— *Reissue with new prefix*

EMARCY
❑ 36039 [M]	Best Coast Jazz		$120

— *Blue label, Silver lettering, Deep Groove, small drummer logo.*
❑ MG-36102 [M]	Clifford Brown All Stars	1956	$250
❑ MG-36005 [M]	Clifford Brown with Strings	1955	$250

— *drummer logo*

FANTASY
❑ OJC-359	Clifford Brown Big Band in Paris	198?	$25
❑ OJC-017	Clifford Brown Memorial	198?	$25
❑ OJC-357	Clifford Brown Quartet in Paris	198?	$25
❑ OJC-358	Clifford Brown Sextet in Paris	198?	$25

JAZZTONE
❑ J-1281 [M]	Jazz Messages	195?	$40

LIMELIGHT
❑ 2-8201 [M]	The Immortal Clifford Brown	1965	$40
❑ 2-8601 [R]	The Immortal Clifford Brown	1965	$30

MERCURY
❑ MG-20827 [M]	Remember Clifford	1963	$150
❑ SR-60827 [R]	Remember Clifford	1963	$150

MOSAIC
❑ MR5-104	The Complete Blue Note and Pacific Jazz Recordings of Clifford Brown	198?	$100

NEW JAZZ
❑ NJLP-8301 [M]	Clifford Brown	1963	$0

— *Canceled*

PACIFIC JAZZ
❑ PJ-3 [M]	Jazz Immortal	1956	$150
❑ LN-10126	Jazz Immortal	198?	$25
❑ PJLP-19 [10]	The Clifford Brown Ensemble	1955	$300

PRESTIGE
❑ PRLP-16008 [M]	Clifford Brown	1964	$40
❑ PRST-7840	Clifford Brown Big Band in Paris	1970	$30
❑ 24020	Clifford Brown in Paris	1971	$35
❑ PRLP-7055 [M]	Clifford Brown Memorial	1956	$300

Number	Title	Yr	NM
❑ PRST-7662 [R]	Clifford Brown Memorial Album	1969	$30
❑ PRST-7761	Clifford Brown Quartet in Paris	1969	$30
❑ PRST-7794	Clifford Brown Sextet in Paris	1970	$30

TRIP
❑ 5502	Clifford Brown with Strings	197?	$25

BROWN, DENNIS
A&M
❑ SP-4850	Foul Play	1981	$15
❑ SP-4886	Love Has Found Its Way	1982	$15
❑ SP-4964	The Prophet Rides Again	1983	$15

RAS
❑ 3207	Brown Sugar	1986	$18

VP
❑ 1478	Could It Be	1996	$12

BROWN, DON
1ST AMERICAN
❑ 7711	Come On	1978	$12
❑ 7701	I Can't Say No	1977	$12

BROWN, DONALD
MUSE
❑ MR-5385	Sources of Inspiration	198?	$25

SUNNYSIDE
❑ SSC-1025	Early Bird	1988	$25

BROWN, FOXY (1)
DEF JAM
❑ 558933-1	Chyna Doll	1999	$18

VIOLATOR
❑ 533684-1	Ill Na Na	1996	$18

BROWN, FOXY (2)
RAS
❑ 3059	Foxy	198?	$15
❑ 3070	My Kind of Girl	198?	$12

BROWN, HYLO
CAPITOL
❑ T1168 [M]	Hylo Brown	1959	$100

STARDAY
❑ SLP-185 [M]	Bluegrass Balladeer	1962	$40
❑ SLP-204 [M]	Bluegrass Goes to College	1962	$40
❑ SLP-220 [M]	Hylo Brown Meets the Lonesome Pine Fiddlers	1963	$40
❑ SLP-249 [M]	Sing Me a Bluegrass Song	1963	$40

BROWN, JAMES
CLEOPATRA
❑ 2061 [B]	Cold Sweat Live		$25
❑ 3038 [B]	Live In New York 1980		$25
❑ 7500 [B]	New York City Soul Break Out!		$25

HRB
❑ 1004	The Fabulous James Brown	1974	$30

KING
❑ KSD-1092	Ain't It Funky	1970	$40
❑ KS-1040	A Soulful Christmas	1968	$100
❑ 1010 [M]	Christmas Songs	1966	$150

— *Wreath on gray wall, no song titles on back*
❑ 1010 [M]	Christmas Songs	1967	$150

— *Wreath on white wall, song titles are on back*
❑ KS-1010 [S]	Christmas Songs	1966	$175

— *Wreath on gray wall, no song titles on back*
❑ KS-1010 [S]	Christmas Songs	1967	$150

— *Wreath on white wall, song titles are on back*
❑ 1020 [M]	Cold Sweat	1967	$85
❑ KS-1020 [S]	Cold Sweat	1967	$80
❑ 780 [M]	Excitement	1963	$175

— *Third title; "crownless" King label*
❑ 780 [M]	Excitement	1966	$50

— *Third title; "crown" King label*
❑ KS-1051	Gettin' Down To It	1969	$50
❑ 780 [M]	Good Good Twistin'	1962	$250

— *Good Good Twistin'" on either label or cover, or both*
❑ KSD-1124	Hey America!	1970	$40
❑ LPS-1030	I Can't Stand Myself (When You Touch Me)	1968	$50
❑ LPS-1031	I Got the Feelin'	1968	$50
❑ 946 [M]	I Got You (I Feel Good)	1966	$150

— *Crownless" King label*
❑ 946 [M]	I Got You (I Feel Good)	1966	$40

— *Crown" King label*
❑ LPS-946 [S]	I Got You (I Feel Good)	1966	$175

— *Crownless" King label*
❑ LPS-946 [S]	I Got You (I Feel Good)	1966	$50

— *Crown" King label*
❑ 985 [M]	It's a Man's Man's Man's World	1966	$50
❑ KS-985 [S]	It's a Man's Man's Man's World	1966	$80

Number	Title	Yr	NM
❑ KSD-1063	It's a Mother	1969	$40
❑ KSD-1095	It's a New Day So Let a Man Come In	1970	$40
❑ 804 [M]	James Brown & His Famous Flames Tour the U.S.A.	1962	$300

— Crownless" King label

❑ 804 [M]	James Brown & His Famous Flames Tour the U.S.A.	1966	$50

— Crown" King label

❑ KSD-1055	James Brown Plays & Directs The Popcorn	1969	$40
❑ LPS-1034	James Brown Plays Nothing But Soul	1968	$50
❑ LPS-1024	James Brown Presents His Show of Tomorrow	1968	$50

— Various-artists album

❑ 771 [M]	Jump Around	1963	$250

— Third title

❑ KS-771 [S]	Jump Around	1963	$300

— Stereo copies of King 771 only exist with this title

❑ 826 [M]	Live at the Apollo	1963	$250

— Custom back cover; "crownless" King label

❑ 826 [M]	Live at the Apollo	1963	$175

— Other King albums on back cover; "crownless" King label

❑ 826 [M]	Live at the Apollo	1966	$50

— Crown" King label

❑ KS-826 [S]	Live at the Apollo	1963	$300

— Custom back cover; "crownless" King label

❑ KS-826 [S]	Live at the Apollo	1963	$250

— Other King albums on back cover; "crownless" King label

❑ KS-826 [S]	Live at the Apollo	1966	$80

— Crown" King label

❑ 826 [M]	Live at the Apollo	1963	$800

— White label promo, banded for airplay

❑ LPS-1022	Live at the Apollo, Volume II	1968	$80
❑ 1018 [M]	Live at the Garden	1967	$500

— Black label promo; banded for airplay

❑ 1018 [M]	Live at the Garden	1967	$150
❑ KS-1018 [S]	Live at the Garden	1967	$150
❑ 961 [M]	Mighty Instrumentals	1966	$150
❑ LPS-961	Mighty Instrumentals	1966	$175
❑ 771 [M]	Night Train	1961	$300

— Original title

❑ 938 [M]	Papa's Got a Brand New Bag	1965	$100

— Red cover; "crownless" King label

❑ 938 [M]	Papa's Got a Brand New Bag	1966	$50

— Green cover; "crownless" King label

❑ 938 [M]	Papa's Got a Brand New Bag	1966	$40

— Crown" King label

❑ LPS-938 [P]	Papa's Got a Brand New Bag	1965	$150

— Red cover; "crownless" King label

❑ LPS-938 [P]	Papa's Got a Brand New Bag	1966	$75

— Green cover; "crownless" King label

❑ LPS-938 [P]	Papa's Got a Brand New Bag	1966	$50

— Crown" King label

❑ 610 [M]	Please Please Please	1958	$1200

— Woman's and man's legs" cover; "King" on label is two inches wide

❑ 610 [M]	Please Please Please	1961	$1000

— Woman's and man's legs" cover; "King" on label is three inches wide

❑ 909 [M]	Please Please Please	1964	$150

— Reissue of 610; "crownless" King label

❑ 909 [M]	Please Please Please	1966	$50

— Crown" King label

❑ 851 [M]	Prisoner of Love	1963	$250

— Custom back cover; "crownless" King label

❑ 851 [M]	Prisoner of Love	1963	$150

— Other King albums on back cover; "crownless" King label

❑ 851 [M]	Prisoner of Love	1966	$50

— Crown" King label

❑ 883 [M]	Pure Dynamite! Live at the Royal	1964	$800

— White label promo; banded for airplay

❑ 883 [M]	Pure Dynamite! Live at the Royal	1964	$250

— Crownless" King label

❑ 883 [M]	Pure Dynamite! Live at the Royal	1966	$50

— Crown" King label

❑ 1016 [M]	Raw Soul	1967	$50
❑ KS-1016 [P]	Raw Soul	1967	$80
❑ KS-1047	Say It Loud -- I'm Black and I'm Proud	1969	$50
❑ KSD-1115	Sex Machine	1970	$50
❑ KSD-1110	Sho Is Funky Down Here	1971	$40
❑ 780 [M]	Shout and Shimmy	1962	$300

— Shout and Shimmy" on both cover and label

❑ KSD-1100	Soul on Top	1970	$40
❑ KSD-1127	Super Bad	1971	$40
❑ 743 [M]	The Amazing James Brown	1961	$500

— James Brown in suit" cover

❑ 743 [M]	The Amazing James Brown	1963	$175

— White title cover; "crownless" King label

❑ 743 [M]	The Amazing James Brown	1966	$500

— White title cover with "James Brown" in huge letters; "crown" King label

❑ 919 [M]	The Unbeatable James Brown -- 16 Hits	1964	$150

— Reissue of 635; "crownless" King label

❑ 919 [M]	The Unbeatable James Brown -- 16 Hits	1966	$50

— Crown" King label

❑ 683 [M]	Think!	1960	$900

— Baby" cover; "King" on label is two inches wide

❑ 683 [M]	Think!	1961	$600

— Baby" cover; "King" on label is three inches wide

❑ 683 [M]	Think!	1963	$150

— James Brown photo cover; "crownless" King label

❑ 683 [M]	Think!	1966	$50

— James Brown photo cover; "crown" King label

❑ LPS-1038 [B]	Thinking About Little Willie John and a Few Nice Things	1968	$50
❑ 635 [M]	Try Me!	1959	$900

— Woman with cigarette and gun" cover; "King" on label is two inches wide

❑ 635 [M]	Try Me!	1961	$600

— Woman with cigarette and gun" cover; "King" on label is three inches wide

❑ 771 [M]	Twist Around	1962	$300

— Second title

POLYDOR

❑ 821231-1	Ain't That a Groove: The James Brown Story 1966-1969	1984	$18
❑ PD-6014	Black Caesar	1973	$50
❑ PD-1-6093	Bodyheat	1976	$40
❑ 827439-1	Dead on the Heavy Funk: The James Brown Story 1974-1978	1985	$18
❑ 821232-1	Doing It to Death: The James Brown Story 1970-1973	1984	$18
❑ PD-1-6054	Everybody's Doin' the Hustle & Dead On the Double Bump	1975	$40
❑ PD2-3004	Get On the Good Foot	1972	$75
❑ PD-1-6071	Get Up Offa That Thing	1976	$40
❑ PD-2-9001	Hell	1974	$100
❑ PD-1-6059	Hot	1976	$40
❑ 24-4054	Hot Pants	1971	$40
❑ 829624-1	In the Jungle Groove	1986	$18
❑ PD-1-6140	Jam/1980s	1978	$40
❑ PD-2-6290	James Brown…Live/Hot on the One	1980	$50
❑ 829417-1	James Brown's Funky People	1986	$18

— Various-artists LP

❑ 835857-1	James Brown's Funky People 2	1988	$18

— Various-artists compilation

❑ SC-5401	James Brown Soul Classics	1972	$30
❑ 8434791 [S]	Live at the Apollo	2008	$25
❑ 837126-1	Motherlode	1988	$18
❑ PD-1-6111	Mutha's Nature	1977	$40
❑ PD-1-6318	Nonstop!	1981	$30
❑ PD-1-6258	People	1980	$30
❑ PD-1-6039	Reality	1975	$40
❑ 25-3003	Revolution of the Mind -- Live at the Apollo, Volume III	1971	$75
❑ PD-2-9004	Sex Machine Live	1976	$50

❑ PD-1-6042 [B]	Sex Machine Today	1975	$40
❑ PD-6015	Slaughter's Big Rip-Off	1973	$50
❑ 829254-1	Solid Gold: 30 Golden Hits	1985	$25
❑ SC-5402	Soul Classics, Volume 2	1973	$30
❑ PD-1-6181	Take a Look at Those Cakes	1978	$30
❑ PD-1-6340	The Best of James Brown	1981	$25
❑ 823275-1	The Best of James Brown	1984	$15

— Reissue of 6340

❑ PD-1-6212	The Original Disco Man	1979	$30
❑ PD2-3007	The Payback	1973	$50
❑ PD-5028	There It Is	1972	$40

RHINO

❑ RNLP-219	Greatest Hits (1964-1968)	1986	$18
❑ R1-70219	Greatest Hits (1964-1968)	1988	$15

— Reissue of 219

❑ RNLP-217	Live at the Apollo, Volume 2, Part 1	1985	$18
❑ R1-70217	Live at the Apollo, Volume 2, Part 1	1988	$15

— Reissue of 217

❑ RNLP-218	Live at the Apollo, Volume 2, Part 2	1985	$18
❑ R1-70218	Live at the Apollo, Volume 2, Part 2	1988	$15

— Reissue of 218

❑ R170194	Santa's Got a Brand New Bag	1986	$12

— Reissue of King material

SCOTTI BROTHERS

❑ FZ40380	Gravity	1986	$15
❑ FZ44241	I'm Real	1988	$15
❑ 75225-1	Love Overdue	1991	$25
❑ FZ45164	Soul Session Live	1989	$18

SMASH

❑ MGS-27057 [M]	Grits & Soul	1965	$30
❑ SRS-67057 [S]	Grits & Soul	1965	$40
❑ MGS-27084 [M]	Handful of Soul	1966	$30
❑ SRS-67084 [S]	Handful of Soul	1966	$40
❑ MGS-27072 [M]	James Brown Plays James Brown -- Today & Yesterday	1965	$30
❑ SRS-67072 [S]	James Brown Plays James Brown -- Today & Yesterday	1965	$40
❑ MGS-27080 [M]	James Brown Plays New Breed	1966	$30
❑ SRS-67080 [S]	James Brown Plays New Breed	1966	$40
❑ MGS-27093 [M]	James Brown Plays the Real Thing	1967	$30
❑ SRS-67093 [S]	James Brown Plays the Real Thing	1967	$40
❑ SRS-67109	James Brown Sings Out of Sight	1968	$30

— Abridged reissue of 67058

❑ MGS-27058 [M]	Out of Sight	1965	$150
❑ SRS-67058 [S]	Out of Sight	1965	$175
❑ MGS-27054 [M]	Showtime	1964	$30
❑ SRS-67054 [S]	Showtime	1964	$40
❑ MGS-27087 [M]	The James Brown Show	1967	$30

— Various-artists LP

❑ SRS-67087 [S]	The James Brown Show	1967	$40

— Various-artists LP

SOLID SMOKE

❑ SS-8013	Can Your Heart Stand It	1981	$15
❑ SS-8006	Live and Lowdown at the Apollo, Vol. 1	1980	$15
❑ SS-8023	The Federal Years, Part 1	198?	$15
❑ SS-8024	The Federal Years, Part 2	198?	$15

SUNDAZED

❑ LP5470 [B]	Love Power Peace	2014	$75

T.K.

❑ 615	Soul Syndrome	1980	$30

BROWN, JIM ED, AND HELEN CORNELIUS

RCA VICTOR

❑ APL1-2399	Born Believer	1977	$15
❑ AHL1-3999	Greatest Hits	1981	$12
❑ AYL1-4392	Greatest Hits	1982	$10

— Reissue of 3999

❑ APL1-2024	I Don't Want to Have to Marry You	1976	$15
❑ AHL1-2781	I'll Never Be Free	1978	$15
❑ AHL1-3562	One Man, One Woman	1980	$12
❑ AHL1-3258	You Don't Bring Me Flowers	1979	$12

BROWN, JIM ED

RCA CAMDEN

❑ CAS-2549	Country Cream	1972	$12
❑ CAS-2496	Gentle on My Mind	1971	$12
❑ ACL1-0197	Hey Good Lookin'	1973	$12
❑ ACL1-0618	The Three Bells	1974	$12

RCA VICTOR

❑ LPM-3569 [M]	Alone with You	1966	$25
❑ LSP-3569 [S]	Alone with You	1966	$30
❑ LSP-4525	Angel's Sunday	1971	$18
❑ APL1-0172	Bar-Rooms & Pop-A-Tops	1973	$18
❑ APL1-0324	Best of Jim Ed Brown	1973	$18
❑ LPM-3942 [M]	Bottle, Bottle	1968	$40
❑ LSP-3942 [S]	Bottle, Bottle	1968	$25
❑ LSP-4755	Brown Is Blue	1972	$18
❑ LSP-4011	Country's Best on Record	1968	$25
❑ LSP-4713	Evening	1972	$18
❑ LPM-3853 [M]	Gems by Jim	1967	$30
❑ LSP-3853 [S]	Gems by Jim	1967	$25
❑ LSP-4262	Going Up the Country	1970	$18
❑ APL1-0572	It's That Time of Night	1974	$18
❑ ANL1-1215	It's That Time of Night	1975	$12

— Reissue of 0572

❑ LSP-4175	Jim Ed Sings the Browns	1969	$25
❑ LSP-4366	Just for You	1970	$18
❑ LPM-3744 [M]	Just Jim	1967	$30
❑ LSP-3744 [S]	Just Jim	1967	$25
❑ LSP-4461	Morning	1971	$18
❑ LSP-4614	She's Leavin'	1971	$18
❑ LSP-4130	This Is My Best!	1968	$25

BROWN, JULIE

RHINO

❑ RNEP610 [EP]	Goddess in Progress	1984	$18

SIRE

❑ 25634	Trapped in the Body of a White Girl	1987	$15

Number	Title	Yr	NM

BROWN, LAWRENCE
ABC IMPULSE!
| ❑ AS-89 | Inspired Abandon | 1968 | $30 |

CLEF
| ❑ MGC-682 [M] | Slide Trombone | 1955 | $300 |

IMPULSE!
| ❑ A-89 [M] | Inspired Abandon | 1965 | $120 |
| ❑ AS-89 [S] | Inspired Abandon | 1965 | $120 |

VERVE
| ❑ MGV-8067 [M] | Slide Trombone | 1957 | $150 |
| ❑ V-8067 [M] | Slide Trombone | 1961 | $25 |

BROWN, LES, AND VIC SCHOEN
KAPP
❑ KRL-4504 [M]	Impact! Band Meets Band	196?	$50
— Reissue of KDL-7003			
❑ KRS-4504 [S]	Impact! Band Meets Band	196?	$75
— Reissue of KDS-7003			
❑ KDL-7003 [M]	Stereophonic Suite for Two Bands	195?	$75
❑ KDS-7003 [S]	Stereophonic Suite for Two Bands	195?	$40

MCA
| ❑ 1548 | Stereophonic Suite for Two Bands | 198? | $30 |

BROWN, LES
CAPITOL
❑ T657 [M]	College Classics	1955	$85
— Turquoise or gray label			
❑ T886 [M]	Composer's Holiday	1957	$75
— Turquoise or gray label			
❑ T959 [M]	Concert Modern	1958	$75
— Turquoise or gray label			
❑ T746 [M]	Les Brown's in Town	1956	$75
— Turquoise or gray label			
❑ T659 [M]	The Les Brown All Stars	1955	$85
— Turquoise or gray label			
❑ T1174 [M]	The Les Brown Story	1959	$75
— Black colorband label, logo at left			
❑ ST1174 [S]	The Les Brown Story	1959	$75
— Black colorband label, logo at left			
❑ SM-1174	The Les Brown Story	1976	$20
— Reissue with new prefix			

CIRCLE
| ❑ CLP-90 | Les Brown and His Orchestra 1946 | 1986 | $25 |

COLUMBIA
❑ CL1497 [M]	Bandland	1960	$35
— Red and black label with six "eye" logos			
❑ CS8288 [S]	Bandland	1960	$25
— Red and black label with six "eye" logos			
❑ CL6159 [10]	Classics in Rhythm	195?	$40
❑ CL6060 [10]	Dance Parade	1949	$40
❑ CL539 [M]	Dance with Les Brown	1954	$40
— Maroon label, gold print			
❑ CL2030 [M]	Explosive Sound	1964	$35
— "Guaranteed High Fidelity" on label			
❑ CS8830 [S]	Explosive Sound	1964	$25
— 360 Sound Stereo" in black on label			
❑ CL2512 [10]	I've Got My Love to Keep Me Warm	1955	$50
❑ CL1818 [M]	Revolution in Sound	1962	$35
— Red and black label with six "eye" logos			
❑ CS8618 [S]	Revolution in Sound	1962	$25
— Red and black label with six "eye" logos			
❑ CL649 [M]	Sentimental Journey	1955	$40
— Maroon label, gold print			
❑ CL649 [M]	Sentimental Journey	1955	$40
— Red and black label with six "eye" logos			
❑ CL2561 [10]	The Cool Classics	1955	$50
❑ CS8394 [S]	The Lerner and Loewe Bandbook	1960	$25
— Red and black label with six "eye" logos			
❑ CL(# unk) [M]	The Lerner and Loewe Bandbook	1960	$35
— Red and black label with six "eye" logos			
❑ CL2119 [M]	The Young Beat	1964	$35
— Guaranteed High Fidelity" on label			
❑ CS8919 [S]	The Young Beat	1964	$25
— 360 Sound Stereo" in black on label			
❑ CL6123 [10]	Your Dance Date with Les Brown	1950	$40

COLUMBIA SPECIAL PRODUCTS
| ❑ P14361 | Sentimental Journey | 198? | $25 |

CORAL
❑ CRL56108 [10]	Invitation	1954	$50
❑ CRL57311 [M]	Jazz Song Book	1959	$30
❑ CRL757311 [S]	Jazz Song Book	1959	$30
❑ CX-1 [M]	Les Brown Concert at the Palladium	1953	$75
❑ CRL57000 [M]	Les Brown Concert at the Palladium, Part 1	1954	$40
❑ CRL57001 [M]	Les Brown Concert at the Palladium, Part 1	1954	$40

Number	Title	Yr	NM
❑ CRL56094 [10]	Les Dance	1953	$50
❑ CRL56116 [10]	Les Dream	1954	$50
❑ CRL57165 [M]	Love Letters in the Sand	1957	$30
❑ CRL57058 [M]	More from Les	1956	$30
❑ CRL56077 [10]	Musical Weather Vane	1953	$50
❑ CRL57051 [M]	Open House	1956	$30
❑ CRL56026 [10]	Over the Rainbow	1951	$50
❑ CRL57300 [M]	Swing Song Book	1959	$30
❑ CRL757300 [S]	Swing Song Book	1959	$30
❑ CRL56030 [10]	The Sound of Renown	1951	$50
❑ CRL57030 [M]	The Sound of Renown	1955	$40
❑ CRL56109 [10]	Time to Dance	1954	$50
❑ CRL56046 [10]	You're My Everything	1952	$150

DAYBREAK
| ❑ 2007 | New Horizons | 1972 | $30 |

DECCA
❑ DL4768 [M]	A Sign of the Times	1966	$30
❑ DL74768 [S]	A Sign of the Times	1966	$35
❑ DL4607 [M]	In Town	1965	$30
❑ DL74607 [S]	In Town	1965	$35
❑ DL4965 [M]	The World of the Young	1968	$25
❑ DL74965 [S]	The World of the Young	1968	$30

FANTASY
| ❑ F-9650 | Digital Swing | 1987 | $30 |

GREAT AMERICAN
| ❑ 1010 | Les Brown Goes Direct to Disc | 1981 | $25 |

HARMONY
❑ HL7335 [M]	Hits from The Sound of Music, My Fair Lady, Camelot and Others	1965	$30
❑ HS11135 [S]	Hits from The Sound of Music, My Fair Lady, Camelot and Others	1965	$30
❑ HL7100 [M]	Les Brown's Greatest	196?	$30
❑ HL7211 [M]	Sentimental Journey	196?	$30
❑ KH32015	The Beat of the Bands	1972	$25

HINDSIGHT
❑ HSR-103	Les Brown and His Orchestra 1944-45	198?	$25
❑ HSR-131	Les Brown and His Orchestra 1949	198?	$25
❑ HSR-199	Les Brown and His Orchestra 1956-57	198?	$25
❑ HSR-132	Les Brown and His Orchestra Vol. 3	198?	$25

INSIGHT
| ❑ 213 | Les Brown and His Orchestra, 1949 | 198? | $25 |

MCA
| ❑ 4070 | The Best of Les Brown | 1974 | $30 |

TIME-LIFE
| ❑ STBB-11 | Big Bands: Les Brown | 1984 | $35 |

VOCALION
| ❑ VL3618 [M] | Les Dance | 196? | $30 |

BROWN, MARION, AND ELLIOTT SCHWARTZ
CENTURY
| ❑ 41746 | Soundways | 1973 | $35 |

BROWN, MARION, AND GUNTER HAMPEL
IAI
| ❑ 373855 | Reeds 'n Vibes | 1978 | $30 |

BROWN, MARION
ABC IMPULSE!
❑ AS-9252	Geechee Recollections	1973	$30
❑ AS-9275	Sweet Earth Flying	1974	$30
❑ AS-9139	Three for Shepp	1968	$30
❑ ASD-9304	Vista	1975	$30

ARISTA FREEDOM
| ❑ AL1904 | Duets | 1975 | $35 |
| ❑ AL1001 | Porto Novo | 1975 | $30 |

ECM
| ❑ 1004 | Afternoon of a Georgia Faun | 197? | $35 |

ESP-DISK'
❑ 1022 [M]	Marion Brown Quartet	1966	$25
❑ S-1022 [S]	Marion Brown Quartet	1966	$35
❑ 1040 [M]	Why Not?	1967	$150
❑ S-1040 [S]	Why Not?	1967	$150

IMPULSE!
| ❑ A-9139 [M] | Three for Shepp | 1967 | $120 |
| ❑ AS-9139 [S] | Three for Shepp | 1967 | $250 |

SWEET EARTH
| ❑ SER-1001 | Solo Saxophone | 1978 | $30 |

TIMELESS
| ❑ TI-314 | La Placita – Live in Willisau | 197? | $30 |

BROWN, MARTI
ATLANTIC
| ❑ SD7278 | Ms. Marti Brown | 1973 | $18 |

BROWN, MAXINE (1)
COLLECTABLES
| ❑ COL-5116 | Golden Classics | 198? | $15 |

Number	Title	Yr	NM

COMMONWEALTH UNITED
| ❑ CU-6001 | We'll Cry Together | 1969 | $25 |

GUEST STAR
| ❑ GS-1911 [M] | Maxine Brown | 1964 | $15 |

WAND
❑ WD-684 [M]	Maxine Brown's Greatest Hits	1967	$25
❑ WDS-684 [S]	Maxine Brown's Greatest Hits	1967	$30
❑ WD-663 [M]	Spotlight on Maxine Brown	1965	$30
❑ WDS-663 [S]	Spotlight on Maxine Brown	1965	$40
❑ LP-656 [M]	The Fabulous Sound of Maxine Brown	1963	$50
❑ WDS-656 [S]	The Fabulous Sound of Maxine Brown	1963	$75
❑ DT-91012 [R]	The Fabulous Sound of Maxine Brown	196?	$50
— Capitol Record Club edition			

BROWN, MAXINE (2)
Also see THE BROWNS. Not to be confused with the R&B singer of the same name, whose biggest hit was "All in My Mind."
CHART
| ❑ 1012 | Sugar Cane Country | 1969 | $25 |

BROWN, MEL
ABC
| ❑ AA-1103 | Actor of Music | 1978 | $30 |

ABC IMPULSE!
❑ AS-9249 [Q]	Big Foot Country Girl	1974	$40
❑ A-9180 [M]	Blues for We	1969	$250
❑ AS-9180 [S]	Blues for We	1969	$250
❑ A-9152 [M]	Chicken Fat	1967	$120
❑ AS-9152 [S]	Chicken Fat	1967	$250
❑ AS-9209	Fifth	1971	$250
❑ AS-9186	I'd Rather Suck My Thumb	1970	$250
❑ A-9169 [M]	The Wizard	1968	$160
❑ AS-9169 [S]	The Wizard	1968	$250

BLUESWAY
| ❑ 6064 | 18 Pounds of Uncleaned Chittlins | 1973 | $35 |

BROWN, MILTON
MCA
| ❑ 1509 | Milton Brown and His Brownies: Pioneer Western Swing Band | 198? | $30 |

BROWN, NAPPY
BLACK TOP
| ❑ BT-1039 | Something Gonna Jump Out the Bushes | 1987 | $18 |

ICHIBAN
| ❑ ICH-1056 | Apples and Lemons | 1990 | $15 |

KING SNAKE/ICHIBAN
| ❑ ICH-9006 | Aw! Shucks | 1991 | $18 |

LANDSLIDE
| ❑ LD1008 | Tore Up | 1984 | $18 |

MELTONE
| ❑ 1502 | Deep Sea Diver | 1989 | $18 |

SAVOY
❑ 14427	Nappy Brown	1977	$15
❑ MG-14002 [M]	Nappy Brown Sings	1958	$400
❑ MG-14025 [M]	The Right Time	1960	$300

SAVOY JAZZ
| ❑ SJL-1149 | Don't Be Angry | 1984 | $12 |

BROWN, O'CHI
MERCURY
| ❑ 826962-1 | O'Chi | 1986 | $15 |

BROWN, ODELL
CADET
❑ LP-800 [M]	Ducky	1967	$50
❑ LPS-800 [S]	Ducky	1967	$35
❑ LPS-838	Free Delivery	1970	$35
❑ LP-788 [M]	Mellow Yellow	1967	$50
❑ LPS-788 [S]	Mellow Yellow	1967	$35
❑ LPS-823	Odell Brown Plays Otis Redding	1969	$35
❑ LP-775 [M]	Raising the Roof	1966	$35
❑ LPS-775 [S]	Raising the Roof	1966	$50

PAULA
| ❑ 4005 | Odell Brown | 1974 | $30 |

BROWN, OSCAR, JR.
ATLANTIC
❑ SD1649	Brother Where Are You	1973	$35
❑ SD18106	Fresh	1974	$30
❑ SD1629	Movin' On	1972	$35

COLUMBIA
❑ CL1774 [M]	Between Heaven and Hell	1962	$30
— Red and black label with six "eye" logos			
❑ CS8574 [S]	Between Heaven and Hell	1962	$30
— Red and black label with six "eye" logos			

Number	Title	Yr	NM
❑ CL1873 [M]	In a New Mood	1963	$25
—Red label, "Guaranteed High Fidelity" in black			
❑ CS8673 [S]	In a New Mood	1963	$30
—Red label, "360 Sound Stereo" in black			
❑ CL2025 [M]	Oscar Brown Jr. Tells It Like It Is	1964	$25
—Red label, "Guaranteed High Fidelity" in black			
❑ CS8825 [S]	Oscar Brown Jr. Tells It Like It Is	1964	$30
—Red label, "360 Sound Stereo" in black			
❑ CL1577 [M]	Sin and Soul	1960	$30
—Red and black label with six "eye" logos			
❑ CS8377 [S]	Sin and Soul	1960	$30
—Red and black label with six "eye" logos			
FONTANA			
❑ MGF-27549 [M]	Finding a New Friend	1966	$35
❑ SRF-67549 [S]	Finding a New Friend	1966	$25
❑ MGF-27540 [M]	Mr. Oscar Brown Goes to Washington	1965	$35
❑ SRF-67540 [S]	Mr. Oscar Brown Goes to Washington	1965	$25

BROWN, PETE
BETHLEHEM

❑ BCP-1011 [10]	Peter the Great	1954	$300
VERVE			
❑ MGV-8365 [M]	From the Heart	1958	$175
❑ MGVS-6133 [S]	From the Heart	1960	$120
❑ V-8365 [M]	From the Heart	1962	$25
❑ V6-8365 [S]	From the Heart	1962	$35

BROWN, PETE/JONAH JONES
BETHLEHEM

❑ BCP-4 [M]	Jazz Kaleidoscope	1957	$300

BROWN, PETER
DRIVE

❑ 104	Do Ya Wanna Get Funky with Me? (A Fantasy Love Affair)	1977	$12

— The actual title is "A Fantasy Love Affair," but the placement of the words "Do Ya Wanna Get Funky with Me?" along the upper edge of the front cover makes it seem as if that is the title

❑ 108	Stargazer	1979	$12
RCA VICTOR			
❑ AFL1-4604	Back to the Front	1983	$12

BROWN, PUD, AND EDDIE MILLER
NEW ORLEANS JAZZ

❑ NORJC-001	Jazz for Two	198?	$25

BROWN, PUD
JAZZOLOGY

❑ J-166	Pud Brown Plays Clarinet	198?	$25

BROWN, RANDY
CHOCOLATE CITY

❑ CCLP-2010	Midnight Desire	1980	$18
PARACHUTE			
❑ RRLP-9012	Intimately	1979	$12
❑ RRLP-9005	Welcome to My Room	1978	$18
STAX			
❑ MPS-8512	Check It Out	1981	$18

BROWN, RAY, AND JIMMIE ROWLES
CONCORD JAZZ

❑ CJ-66	As Good As Gold	1977	$30
❑ CJ-122	Tasty	1979	$30

BROWN, RAY
BLUESWAY

❑ BLS-6056	Hard Times	1971	$35
CONCORD JAZZ			
❑ CJ-375	Bam Bam Bam	1989	$30
❑ CJ-19	Brown's Bag	1976	$30
❑ CJ-293	Don't Forget the Blues	1986	$25
❑ CJ-213	Ray Brown 3	1982	$25
❑ CJ-268	Soular Energy	1985	$25
❑ CJ-102	The Ray Brown Trio Live at the Concord Jazz Festival	1979	$30
❑ CJ-315	The Red Hot Ray Brown Trio	1987	$25
CONTEMPORARY			
❑ C-7641	Something for Lester	1978	$25
FANTASY			
❑ OJC-412	Something for Lester	1990	$30
NORGRAN			
❑ MGN-1105 [M]	Bass Hit!	1956	$0
—Canceled; released on Verve 8022			
VERVE			
❑ MGV-8022 [M]	Bass Hit!	1957	$120
—yellow label			
❑ V-8022 [M]	Bass Hit!	1961	$25

Number	Title	Yr	NM
❑ MGV-8390 [M]	Jazz Cello	1960	$150
❑ V-8390 [M]	Jazz Cello	1961	$25
❑ V-8580 [M]	Much in Common	1964	$30
❑ V6-8580 [S]	Much in Common	1964	$30
—With Milt Jackson			
❑ V-8615 [M]	Ray Brown/Milt Jackson	1965	$30
❑ V6-8615 [S]	Ray Brown/Milt Jackson	1965	$30
❑ V-8444 [M]	Ray Brown with the All Star Big Band Featuring Cannonball Adderley	1962	$30
❑ V6-8444 [S]	Ray Brown with the All Star Big Band Featuring Cannonball Adderley	1962	$30
❑ MGV-8290 [M]	This Is Ray Brown	1958	$250
❑ V-8290 [M]	This Is Ray Brown	1961	$150
❑ UMV-2117	This Is Ray Brown	198?	$25
❑ VSP-10 [M]	Two for the Blues	1966	$30
❑ VSPS-10 [S]	Two for the Blues	1966	$35

BROWN, REUBEN, AND RICHIE COLE
ADELPHIA

❑ AD-5001	Starburst	1976	$30

BROWN, RONNIE
PHILIPS

❑ PHM200130 [M]	Jazz for Everyone	1964	$35
❑ PHS600130 [S]	Jazz for Everyone	1964	$25

BROWN, ROY
BLUESWAY

❑ BLS-6056	Hard Times	1973	$30
❑ BLS-6019	The Blues Are Brown	1968	$30
EPIC			
❑ E30473	Live at Monterey	1971	$30
INTERMEDIA			
❑ QS-5027	Good Rockin' Tonight	198?	$12
KING			
❑ KS-1130	Hard Luck Blues	1971	$30
❑ 956 [M]	Roy Brown Sings 24 Hits	1966	$50
❑ KS-956 [R]	Roy Brown Sings 24 Hits	1966	$50

BROWN, ROY / WYNONIE HARRIS
KING

❑ 607 [M]	Battle of the Blues	1958	$600
❑ 627 [M]	Battle of the Blues, Volume 2	1959	$800

BROWN, ROY / WYNONIE HARRIS / EDDIE VINSON
KING

❑ 668 [M]	Battle of the Blues, Volume 4	1960	$2500

BROWN, RUTH
ATLANTIC

❑ 1308 [M]	Last Date with Ruth Brown	1959	$300
—Black label			
❑ 1308 [M]	Last Date with Ruth Brown	1961	$50
—Red and purple label, "fan" logo in white			
❑ SD1308 [S]	Last Date with Ruth Brown	1959	$300
—Green label			
❑ SD1308 [S]	Last Date with Ruth Brown	1961	$175
—Blue and green label, "fan" logo in white			
❑ 8026 [M]	Miss Rhythm	1959	$250
—Black label			
❑ 8026 [M]	Miss Rhythm	1960	$175
—White "bullseye" label			
❑ 8026 [M]	Miss Rhythm	1961	$50
—Red and purple label, "fan" logo in white			
❑ 8004 [M]	Ruth Brown	1957	$250
—Black label			
❑ 8004 [M]	Ruth Brown	1960	$175
—White "bullseye" label			
❑ 8004 [M]	Ruth Brown	1961	$50
—Red and purple label, "fan" logo in white			
❑ 8080 [M]	The Best of Ruth Brown	1963	$40
DOBRE			
❑ 1041	You Don't Know Me	1978	$30
FANTASY			
❑ F-9662	Blues on Broadway	1989	$30
❑ F-9661	Have a Good Time	1988	$30
ICHIBAN			
❑ SPEG-4023	Brown, Black and Beautiful	198?	$30
MAINSTREAM			
❑ 56034 [M]	Ruth Brown '65	1965	$75
❑ S-6034 [S]	Ruth Brown '65	1965	$75
❑ 369	Softly	1972	$30
PHILIPS			
❑ PHM200028 [M]	Along Comes Ruth	1962	$40
❑ PHS600028 [S]	Along Comes Ruth	1962	$50
❑ PHM200055 [M]	Gospel Time	1962	$30
❑ PHS600055 [S]	Gospel Time	1962	$40
SKYE			
❑ SK-13	Black Is Brown and Brown Is Beautiful	1970	$35

Number	Title	Yr	NM
BROWN, SHEREE			
CAPITOL			
❑ ST-12153	Straight Ahead	1981	$18
❑ ST-12229	The Music	1982	$18

BROWN, SHIRLEY
ARISTA

❑ AL4129	Shirley Brown	1977	$25
MALACO			
❑ 7451	Fire & Ice	1989	$15
❑ 7467	Joy & Pain	1993	$18
❑ 7459	Timeless	1991	$15
SOUND TOWN			
❑ ST8008	Intimate Storm	1984	$18
STAX			
❑ STX-4126	For the Real Feeling	1979	$15
TRUTH			
❑ 4206	Woman to Woman	1975	$18

BROWN, T. GRAHAM
CAPITOL

❑ ST-12552	Brilliant Conversationalist	1987	$10
❑ C1-48621	Come As You Were	1988	$10
❑ ST-12487	I Tell It Like It Used to Be	1986	$10

BROWN, TED
CRISS CROSS

❑ 1031	Free Spirit	1988	$30
VANGUARD			
❑ VRS-8515 [M]	Free Wheeling	1956	$1000

BROWN, WINI
SAVOY JAZZ

❑ SJL-1163 [M]	Miss Brown for You	1986	$25

BROWN SUGAR
CHELSEA

❑ BCL1-0368	Brown Sugar Featuring Clydie King	1973	$25

BROWNE, BRIAN
JAZZIMAGE

❑ JZ-105	Beatles	198?	$35

BROWNE, JACKSON
ASYLUM

❑ SD5067	For Everyman	1973	$15
❑ 5E-511	Hold Out	1979	$12
❑ SD5051	Jackson Browne (Saturate Before Using)	1972	$25
—Burlap cover, opens at top; white label with "Asylum Records" logo in a circle at top			
❑ SD5051	Jackson Browne (Saturate Before Using)	1972	$15
—Burlap cover; "clouds" label			
❑ SD5051	Jackson Browne (Saturate Before Using)	1972	$16
—Burlap cover, opens at right side; white label with "Asylum Records" logo in a circle at top			
❑ SD5051	Jackson Browne (Saturate Before Using)	1972	$10
—Standard cover			
❑ 7E-1017	Late for the Sky	1974	$15
❑ EQ-1017 [Q]	Late for the Sky	1974	$75
❑ 60268	Lawyers in Love	1983	$12
❑ 60457	Lives in the Balance	1986	$12
❑ 6E-113	Running on Empty	1977	$12
❑ 7E-1079	The Pretender	1976	$15
❑ 6E-107	The Pretender	1977	$12
—Reissue of 7E-1079			
ELEKTRA			
❑ 60830	World in Motion	1989	$12
MOBILE FIDELITY			
❑ Jan-0055	The Pretender	1981	$50
—Audiophile vinyl			
NINA MUSIC PUBLISHING			
❑ 0(no cat #) [B]	Songs by Jackson Browne	1967	$2500
—Publisher's demo in plain cardboard jacket; three sides performed by Jackson Browne, one side by Steve Noonan; VG value 1000; VG+ value 1500			

BROWNE, TOM
ARISTA

❑ AL8107	Rockin' Radio	1983	$10
❑ AL8-8249	Tommy Gun	1984	$10
ARISTA/GRP			
❑ GL5003	Browne Sugar	1979	$12
❑ GL5008	Love Approach	1980	$12
❑ GL5502	Love Approach	1981	$10
—Reissue of 5008			
❑ GL5503	Magic	1981	$12
❑ GL5507	Yours Truly	1981	$25
MALACO			
❑ MJ-1500	No Longer I	1989	$15

Number	Title	Yr	NM
BROWNMARK			
MOTOWN			
❏ MOT-6277	Good Feeling	1989	$15
❏ MOT-6251	Just Like That	1988	$12
BROWNS, THE			
RCA CAMDEN			
❏ CAL-2142 [M]	Big Ones from the Country	1967	$15
❏ CAS-2142 [S]	Big Ones from the Country	1967	$12
❏ CAL-885 [M]	I Heard the Bluebirds Sing	1965	$15
❏ CAS-885 [S]	I Heard the Bluebirds Sing	1965	$15
❏ CAS-2262	The Browns Sing a Harvest of Country Songs	1968	$12
RCA VICTOR			
❏ LPM-2784 [M]	Grand Ole Opry Favorites	1963	$18
❏ LSP-2784 [S]	Grand Ole Opry Favorites	1963	$25
❏ LPM-1438 [M]	Jim Edward, Maxine and Bonnie Brown	1957	$50
❏ LPM-2333 [M]	Our Favorite Folk Songs	1961	$25
❏ LSP-2333 [S]	Our Favorite Folk Songs	1961	$30
❏ LPM-3668 [M]	Our Kind of Country	1966	$18
❏ LSP-3668 [S]	Our Kind of Country	1966	$25
❏ LPM-2144 [M]	Sweet Sounds by the Browns	1959	$30
❏ LSP-2144 [S]	Sweet Sounds by the Browns	1959	$40
❏ LPM-3561 [M]	The Best of the Browns	1966	$18
❏ LSP-3561 [S]	The Best of the Browns	1966	$25
❏ ANL1-1083	The Best of the Browns	1975	$12
❏ LPM-2260 [M]	The Browns Sing Their Hits	1960	$25
❏ LSP-2260 [S]	The Browns Sing Their Hits	1960	$30
❏ LPM-2345 [M]	The Little Brown Church Hymnal	1961	$25
❏ LSP-2345 [S]	The Little Brown Church Hymnal	1961	$30
❏ LPM-3798 [M]	The Old Country Church	1967	$25
❏ LSP-3798 [S]	The Old Country Church	1967	$18
❏ LPM-2860 [M]	This Young Land	1964	$18
❏ LSP-2860 [S]	This Young Land	1964	$25
❏ LPM-2987 [M]	Three Shades of Brown	1964	$18
❏ LSP-2987 [S]	Three Shades of Brown	1964	$25
❏ LPM-2174 [M]	Town and Country	1960	$25
❏ LSP-2174 [S]	Town and Country	1960	$30
❏ LPM-3423 [M]	When Love Is Gone	1965	$18
❏ LSP-3423 [S]	When Love Is Gone	1965	$25
BROWN'S FERRY FOUR, THE			
KING			
❏ 551 [M]	Sacred Songs	1957	$100
❏ 590 [M]	Sacred Songs	1958	$100
❏ 943	Wonderful Sacred Songs	1964	$30
BROWNSVILLE STATION			
BIG TREE			
❏ BTS-2010	A Night on the Town	1972	$15
❏ BT89510	Motor City Connection	1975	$15
❏ BT89500	School Punks	1974	$15
❏ BTS-2102	Yeah!	1973	$15
EPIC			
❏ JE35606	Air Special	1978	$16
❏ JE35606 [DJ]	Air Special	1978	$25
—Orange vinyl promo			
PALLADIUM			
❏ P-1004	Brownsville Station	1970	$30
PRIVATE STOCK			
❏ PS-2026	Brownsville Station	1977	$12
WARNER BROS.			
❏ WS1888	No B.S.	1970	$18
BRUBECK, DAVE			
ATLANTIC			
❏ SD1684	All the Things We Are	1976	$30
❏ SD1660	Brother, The Great Spirit Made Us All	1974	$30
❏ SD 2-317	The Art of Dave Brubeck: The Fantasy Years	1975	$35
❏ SD1607	The Last Set at Newport	1972	$30
❏ SD1606	Truth Is Fallen	1972	$30
❏ SD1645	Two Generations of Brubeck	1974	$30
❏ SD1641	We're All Together Again for the First Time	1973	$30
BOOK-OF-THE-MONTH			
❏ 80-5547	Early Fantasies	1980	$50
COLUMBIA			
❏ G30625	Adventures in Time	1971	$35
❏ KG32761	All-Time Greatest Hits	1974	$35
❏ CL932 [M]	American Jazz Festival at Newport '56	1956	$150
—Red/black label with six "eye" logos			
❏ CL932 [M]	American Jazz Festival at Newport '56	1962	$50
—Red "Guaranteed High Fidelity" label			
❏ CL2348 [M]	Angel Eyes	1965	$50
—Red "Guaranteed High Fidelity" label			
❏ CL2348 [M]	Angel Eyes	1966	$30
—Red "360 Sound" label			
❏ CS9148 [S]	Angel Eyes	1965	$75
—Red label, "360 Sound" in black			
❏ CS9148 [S]	Angel Eyes	1966	$35
—Red label, "360 Sound" in white			

Number	Title	Yr	NM
❏ CL2602 [M]	Anything Goes! Dave Brubeck Quartet Plays Cole Porter	1966	$35
❏ CS9402 [S]	Anything Goes! Dave Brubeck Quartet Plays Cole Porter	1966	$50
—Red "360 Sound" label			
❏ CS9402	Anything Goes! Dave Brubeck Quartet Plays Cole Porter	1971	$30
—Orange label			
❏ PC9402	Anything Goes! Dave Brubeck Quartet Plays Cole Porter	1981	$20
—Reissue with new prefix			
❏ PC37022	A Place in Time	1981	$25
—Reissue of Odyssey LP			
❏ CL1466 [M]	Bernstein Plays Brubeck Plays Bernstein	1960	$75
—Red/black label with six "eye" logos			
❏ CL1466 [M]	Bernstein Plays Brubeck Plays Bernstein	1962	$35
—Red "Guaranteed High Fidelity" label			
❏ CL1466 [M]	Bernstein Plays Brubeck Plays Bernstein	1966	$30
—Red "360 Sound" label			
❏ CS9749	Blues Roots	1969	$35
—Red "360 Sound" label			
❏ CS9749	Blues Roots	1971	$30
—Orange label			
❏ CL1998 [M]	Bossa Nova U.S.A.	1963	$50
—Red "Guaranteed High Fidelity" label			
❏ CL1998 [M]	Bossa Nova U.S.A.	1966	$30
—Red "360 Sound" label			
❏ CS8798 [S]	Bossa Nova U.S.A.	1963	$75
—Red label, "360 Sound" in black			
❏ CS8798 [S]	Bossa Nova U.S.A.	1966	$35
—Red label, "360 Sound" in white			
❏ CL1963 [M]	Brandenburg Gate Revisited	1963	$50
—Red "Guaranteed High Fidelity" label			
❏ CL1963 [M]	Brandenburg Gate Revisited	1966	$30
—Red "360 Sound" label			
❏ CS8763 [S]	Brandenburg Gate Revisited	1963	$75
—Red label, "360 Sound" in black			
❏ CS8763 [S]	Brandenburg Gate Revisited	1966	$35
—Red label, "360 Sound" in white			
❏ CL2695 [M]	Bravo Brubeck!	1967	$50
❏ CS9495 [S]	Bravo Brubeck!	1967	$35
—Red "360 Sound" label			
❏ CS9495	Bravo Brubeck!	1971	$30
—Orange label			
❏ CL1553 [M]	Brubeck and Rushing	1961	$75
—Red/black label with six "eye" logos			
❏ CL1553 [M]	Brubeck and Rushing	1962	$50
—Red "Guaranteed High Fidelity" label			
❏ CL1553 [M]	Brubeck and Rushing	1966	$30
—Red "360 Sound" label			
❏ CS8353 [S]	Brubeck and Rushing	1961	$75
—Red/black label with six "eye" logos			
❏ CS8353 [S]	Brubeck and Rushing	1962	$50
—Red label, "360 Sound" in black			
❏ CS8353 [S]	Brubeck and Rushing	1966	$35
—Red label, "360 Sound" in white			
❏ KC32143	Brubeck at the Berlin Philharmonic	1973	$30
❏ CS9897	Brubeck in Amsterdam	1969	$35
—Red "360 Sound" label			
❏ CS9897	Brubeck in Amsterdam	1971	$30
—Orange label			
❏ KG31298	Brubeck On Campus	1972	$35
❏ CS8257 [S]	Brubeck Plays Bernstein Plays Brubeck	1960	$75
—Red/black label with six "eye" logos			
❏ CS8257 [S]	Brubeck Plays Bernstein Plays Brubeck	1962	$50
—Red label, "360 Sound" in black			
❏ CS8257 [S]	Brubeck Plays Bernstein Plays Brubeck	1966	$35
—Red label, "360 Sound" in white			
❏ CS8257	Brubeck Plays Bernstein Plays Brubeck	1971	$30
—Orange label			
❏ CL878 [M]	Brubeck Plays Brubeck	1956	$120
—Red/black label with six "eye" logos			
❏ CL878 [M]	Brubeck Plays Brubeck	1962	$50
—Red "Guaranteed High Fidelity" label			
❏ CL878 [M]	Brubeck Plays Brubeck	1966	$30
—Red "360 Sound" label			
❏ CL622 [M]	Brubeck Time	1955	$120
—Red/black label with six "eye" logos			
❏ CL622 [M]	Brubeck Time	1962	$50
—Red "Guaranteed High Fidelity" label			
❏ CL622 [M]	Brubeck Time	1966	$30
—Red "360 Sound" label			
❏ CS9704	Compadres	1968	$35
—Red "360 Sound" label			
❏ CS9704	Compadres	1971	$30
—Orange label			

Number	Title	Yr	NM
❏ CL1775 [M]	Countdown -- Time in Outer Space	1962	$75
—Red/black label with six "eye" logos			
❏ CL1775 [M]	Countdown -- Time in Outer Space	1962	$35
—Red "Guaranteed High Fidelity" label			
❏ CL1775 [M]	Countdown -- Time in Outer Space	1966	$30
—Red "360 Sound" label			
❏ CS8575 [S]	Countdown -- Time in Outer Space	1962	$40
—Red/black label with six "eye" logos			
❏ CS8575 [S]	Countdown -- Time in Outer Space	1962	$50
—Red label, "360 Sound" in black			
❏ CS8575 [S]	Countdown -- Time in Outer Space	1966	$35
—Red label, "360 Sound" in white			
❏ CL590 [M]	Dave Brubeck at Storyville: 1954	1954	$175
—Dark red label, gold print; released at the same time as 6330 and 6331			
❏ CL590 [M]	Dave Brubeck at Storyville: 1954	1955	$150
—Red/black label with six "eye" logos			
❏ CL590 [M]	Dave Brubeck at Storyville: 1954	1962	$50
—Red "Guaranteed High Fidelity" label			
❏ CL590 [M]	Dave Brubeck at Storyville: 1954	1966	$30
—Red "360 Sound" label			
❏ CL6330 [10]	Dave Brubeck at Storyville: 1954, Volume 1	1954	$175
❏ CL6331 [10]	Dave Brubeck at Storyville: 1954, Volume 2	1954	$175
❏ CL2484 [M]	Dave Brubeck's Greatest Hits	1966	$35
❏ CS9284 [S]	Dave Brubeck's Greatest Hits	1966	$50
—Red "360 Sound" label			
❏ CS9284	Dave Brubeck's Greatest Hits	1971	$30
—Orange label			
❏ PC9284	Dave Brubeck's Greatest Hits	1981	$20
—Reissue with new prefix			
❏ CL1059 [M]	Dave Digs Disney	1957	$40
—Red/black label with six "eye" logos			
❏ CL1059 [M]	Dave Digs Disney	1962	$50
—Red "Guaranteed High Fidelity" label			
❏ CL1059 [M]	Dave Digs Disney	1966	$30
—Red "360 Sound" label			
❏ CS8090 [S]	Dave Digs Disney	1959	$150
—Red/black label with six "eye" logos			
❏ CS8090 [S]	Dave Digs Disney	1962	$75
—Red label, "360 Sound" in black			
❏ CS8090 [S]	Dave Digs Disney	1966	$35
—Red label, "360 Sound" in white			
❏ CL1347 [M]	Gone with the Wind	1959	$40
—Red/black label with six "eye" logos			
❏ CL1347 [M]	Gone with the Wind	1962	$50
—Red "Guaranteed High Fidelity" label			
❏ CL1347 [M]	Gone with the Wind	1966	$30
—Red "360 Sound" label			
❏ CS8156 [S]	Gone with the Wind	1959	$150
—Red/black label with six "eye" logos			
❏ CS8156 [S]	Gone with the Wind	1962	$75
—Red label, "360 Sound" in black			
❏ CS8156 [S]	Gone with the Wind	1966	$35
—Red label, "360 Sound" in white			
❏ CS8156	Gone with the Wind	1971	$30
—Orange label			
❏ CG33666	Gone with the Wind/Time Out	1975	$35
❏ CL2712 [M]	Jackpot	1967	$50
❏ CS9512 [S]	Jackpot	1967	$35
—Red "360 Sound" label			
❏ CL699 [M]	Jazz: Red Hot and Cool	1955	$120
—Red/black label with six "eye" logos			
❏ CL699 [M]	Jazz: Red Hot and Cool	1962	$50
—Red "Guaranteed High Fidelity" label			
❏ CL699 [M]	Jazz: Red Hot and Cool	1966	$30
—Red "360 Sound" label			
❏ CS8645 [R]	Jazz: Red Hot and Cool	1963	$35
—Red label, "360 Sound" in black			
❏ CS8645 [R]	Jazz: Red Hot and Cool	1966	$30
—Red label, "360 Sound" in white			
❏ CL566 [M]	Jazz Goes to College	1954	$175
—Dark red label, gold print; released at the same time as 6321 and 6322			
❏ CL566 [M]	Jazz Goes to College	1955	$150
—Red/black label with six "eye" logos			
❏ CL566 [M]	Jazz Goes to College	1962	$50
—Red "Guaranteed High Fidelity" label			
❏ CL566 [M]	Jazz Goes to College	1966	$30
—Red "360 Sound" label			
❏ CL6321 [10]	Jazz Goes to College, Volume 1	1954	$200

Number	Title	Yr	NM
❑ CL6322 [10]	Jazz Goes to College, Volume 2	1954	$200
❑ CL1034 [M]	Jazz Goes to Junior College	1957	$40
—Red/black label with six "eye" logos			
❑ CL1034 [M]	Jazz Goes to Junior College	1962	$50
—Red "Guaranteed High Fidelity" label			
❑ CL1034 [M]	Jazz Goes to Junior College	1966	$30
—Red "360 Sound" label			
❑ CL1251 [M]	Jazz Impressions of Eurasia	1958	$40
—Red/black label with six "eye" logos			
❑ CL1251 [M]	Jazz Impressions of Eurasia	1962	$50
—Red "Guaranteed High Fidelity" label			
❑ CL1251 [M]	Jazz Impressions of Eurasia	1966	$30
—Red "360 Sound" label			
❑ CS8058 [S]	Jazz Impressions of Eurasia	1959	$150
—Red/black label with six "eye" logos			
❑ CS8058 [S]	Jazz Impressions of Eurasia	1962	$75
—Red label, "360 Sound" in black			
❑ CS8058 [S]	Jazz Impressions of Eurasia	1966	$35
—Red label, "360 Sound" in white			
❑ CL2212 [M]	Jazz Impressions of Japan	1964	$50
—Red "Guaranteed High Fidelity" label			
❑ CL2212 [M]	Jazz Impressions of Japan	1966	$30
—Red "360 Sound" label			
❑ CS9012 [S]	Jazz Impressions of Japan	1964	$75
—Red label, "360 Sound" in black			
❑ CS9012 [S]	Jazz Impressions of Japan	1966	$35
—Red label, "360 Sound" in white			
❑ CS9012	Jazz Impressions of Japan	1971	$30
—Orange label			
❑ PC9012	Jazz Impressions of Japan	1981	$20
—Reissue with new prefix			
❑ CL2275 [M]	Jazz Impressions of New York	1965	$50
—Red "Guaranteed High Fidelity" label			
❑ CL2275 [M]	Jazz Impressions of New York	1966	$30
—Red "360 Sound" label			
❑ CS9075 [S]	Jazz Impressions of New York	1965	$75
—Red label, "360 Sound" in black			
❑ CS9075 [S]	Jazz Impressions of New York	1966	$35
—Red label, "360 Sound" in white			
❑ CS9075	Jazz Impressions of New York	1971	$30
—Orange label			
❑ PC9075	Jazz Impressions of New York	1981	$20
—Reissue with new prefix			
❑ CL984 [M]	Jazz Impressions of the U.S.A.	1957	$150
—Red/black label with six "eye" logos			
❑ CL984 [M]	Jazz Impressions of the U.S.A.	1962	$50
—Red "Guaranteed High Fidelity" label			
❑ CL984 [M]	Jazz Impressions of the U.S.A.	1966	$30
—Red "360 Sound" label			
❑ CL2437 [M]	My Favorite Things	1966	$35
❑ CS9237 [S]	My Favorite Things	1966	$50
—Red "360 Sound" label			
❑ CL1249 [M]	Newport 1958	1958	$40
—Red/black label with six "eye" logos			
❑ CL1249 [M]	Newport 1958	1962	$50
—Red "Guaranteed High Fidelity" label			
❑ CL1249 [M]	Newport 1958	1966	$30
—Red "360 Sound" label			
❑ CS8082 [S]	Newport 1958	1959	$150
—Red/black label with six "eye" logos			
❑ CS8082 [S]	Newport 1958	1962	$75
—Red label, "360 Sound" in black			
❑ CS8082 [S]	Newport 1958	1966	$35
—Red label, "360 Sound" in white			
❑ CL1439 [M]	Southern Scene	1960	$75
—Red/black label with six "eye" logos			
❑ CL1439 [M]	Southern Scene	1962	$35
—Red "Guaranteed High Fidelity" label			
❑ CL1439 [M]	Southern Scene	1966	$30
—Red "360 Sound" label			
❑ CS8235 [S]	Southern Scene	1960	$75
—Red/black label with six "eye" logos			
❑ CS8235 [S]	Southern Scene	1962	$50
—Red label, "360 Sound" in black			
❑ CS8235 [S]	Southern Scene	1966	$35
—Red label, "360 Sound" in white			
❑ CL2316 [M]	Take Five	1965	$50
—Red "Guaranteed High Fidelity" label			
❑ CL2316 [M]	Take Five	1966	$30
—Red "360 Sound" label			
❑ CS9116 [S]	Take Five	1965	$75
—Red label, "360 Sound" in black			
❑ CS9116 [S]	Take Five	1966	$35
—Red label, "360 Sound" in white			
❑ C2L26 [M]	The Dave Brubeck Quartet at Carnegie Hall	1963	$75
—Red "Guaranteed High Fidelity" label			

Number	Title	Yr	NM
❑ C2L26 [M]	The Dave Brubeck Quartet at Carnegie Hall	1966	$35
—Red "360 Sound" label			
❑ C2S826 [S]	The Dave Brubeck Quartet at Carnegie Hall	1963	$75
—Red label, "360 Sound" in black			
❑ C2S826 [S]	The Dave Brubeck Quartet at Carnegie Hall	1966	$50
—Red label, "360 Sound" in white			
❑ C2S826	The Dave Brubeck Quartet at Carnegie Hall	1971	$35
—Orange label			
❑ CL1168 [M]	The Dave Brubeck Quartet in Europe	1958	$40
—Red/black label with six "eye" logos			
❑ CL1168 [M]	The Dave Brubeck Quartet in Europe	1962	$50
—Red "Guaranteed High Fidelity" label			
❑ CL1168 [M]	The Dave Brubeck Quartet in Europe	1966	$30
—Red "360 Sound" label			
❑ CS9672	The Last Time We Saw Paris	1968	$35
—Red "360 Sound" label			
❑ CS9572	The Last Time We Saw Paris	1971	$30
—Orange label			
❑ CL1454 [M]	The Riddle	1960	$75
—Red/black label with six "eye" logos			
❑ CL1454 [M]	The Riddle	1962	$35
—Red "Guaranteed High Fidelity" label			
❑ CL1454 [M]	The Riddle	1966	$30
—Red "360 Sound" label			
❑ CS8248 [S]	The Riddle	1960	$75
—Red/black label with six "eye" logos			
❑ CS8248 [S]	The Riddle	1962	$50
—Red label, "360 Sound" in black			
❑ CS8248 [S]	The Riddle	1966	$35
—Red label, "360 Sound" in white			
❑ C30522	The Summit Sessions	1971	$30
❑ CL2127 [M]	Time Changes	1964	$50
—Red "Guaranteed High Fidelity" label			
❑ CL2127 [M]	Time Changes	1966	$30
—Red "360 Sound" label			
❑ CS8927 [S]	Time Changes	1964	$75
—Red label, "360 Sound" in black			
❑ CS8927 [S]	Time Changes	1966	$35
—Red label, "360 Sound" in white			
❑ CL1690 [M]	Time Further Out	1961	$75
—Red/black label with six "eye" logos			
❑ CL1690 [M]	Time Further Out	1962	$35
—Red "Guaranteed High Fidelity" label			
❑ CL1690 [M]	Time Further Out	1966	$30
—Red "360 Sound" label			
❑ CS8490 [S]	Time Further Out	1961	$75
—Red/black label with six "eye" logos			
❑ CS8490 [S]	Time Further Out	1962	$50
—Red label, "360 Sound" in black			
❑ CS8490 [S]	Time Further Out	1966	$35
—Red label, "360 Sound" in white			
❑ CS8490	Time Further Out	1971	$30
—Orange label			
❑ PC8490	Time Further Out	1981	$20
—Reissue with new prefix			
❑ CL2512 [M]	Time In	1966	$35
❑ CS9312 [S]	Time In	1966	$50
—Red "360 Sound" label			
❑ CS9312	Time In	1971	$30
—Orange label			
❑ PC9312	Time In	1981	$20
—Reissue with new prefix			
❑ CL1397 [M]	Time Out	1960	$75
—Red/black label with six "eye" logos			

Number	Title	Yr	NM
❑ CS8192 [S]	Time Out	1960	$30
—Red/black label with six "eye" logos			
❑ PC8192	Time Out	1981	$20
—Reissue with new prefix			
❑ CS8192	Time Out	1995	$75
—Audiophile vinyl, distributed by Classic Records			
❑ CL1397 [M]	Time Out Featuring "Take Five	1962	$35
—Red "Guaranteed High Fidelity" label; beginning with this issue, the cover was altered to emphasize the hit			
❑ CL1397 [M]	Time Out Featuring "Take Five	1966	$30
—Red "360 Sound" label			
❑ CS8192 [S]	Time Out Featuring "Take Five	1962	$50
—Red label, "360 Sound" in black; beginning with this issue, the cover was altered to emphasize the hit			
❑ CS8192 [S]	Time Out Featuring "Take Five	1966	$35
—Red label, "360 Sound" in white			
❑ CS8192	Time Out Featuring "Take Five	1971	$30
—Orange label			
❑ CL1609 [M]	Tonight Only!	1961	$75
—Red/black label with six "eye" logos			
❑ CL1609 [M]	Tonight Only!	1962	$35
—Red "Guaranteed High Fidelity" label			
❑ CL1609 [M]	Tonight Only!	1966	$30
—Red "360 Sound" label			
❑ CS8409 [S]	Tonight Only!	1961	$75
—Red/black label with six "eye" logos			
❑ CS8409 [S]	Tonight Only!	1962	$50
—Red label, "360 Sound" in black			
❑ CS8409 [S]	Tonight Only!	1966	$35
—Red label, "360 Sound" in white			
COLUMBIA JAZZ MASTERPIECES			
❑ CJ40627	Gone with the Wind	1987	$25
❑ CJ45149	Jazz Goes to College	1989	$25
❑ CJ40455	The Dave Brubeck Quartet Plays Music from West Side Story and Other Shows and Films	1987	$25
❑ CJ40585	Time Out	1987	$25
COLUMBIA LIMITED EDITION			
❑ LE10013	Gone with the Wind	197?	$25
CONCORD JAZZ			
❑ CJ-103	Back Home	1979	$25
❑ CJ-317	Blue Rondo	1987	$25
❑ CJ-198	Concord on a Summer Night	1982	$25
❑ CJ-259	For Iola	1985	$25
❑ CJ-353	Moscow Night	1988	$25
❑ CJ-178	Paper Moon	1982	$25
❑ CJ-299	Reflections	1986	$25
❑ CJ-129	Tritonis	1980	$25
CROWN			
❑ CLP5470 [M]	Dave Brubeck and the George Nielson Quartet	196?	$35
❑ CLP-5406 [M]	The Greats	196?	$35
DECCA			
❑ DL710181	Brubeck/Mulligan/Cincinnati	1971	$30
❑ DL710175	The Gates of Justice	1969	$30
❑ DXSA7202	The Light in the Wilderness	1968	$35
—Records are individually numbered "DL 710,155" and "DL 710,156			
DIRECT DISK			
❑ 106	A Cut Above	1979	$75
FANTASY			
❑ 3249 [M]	Brubeck & Desmond at Wilshire-Ebell	1957	$200
—Dark red vinyl			
❑ 3249 [M]	Brubeck & Desmond at Wilshire-Ebell	195?	$75
—Black vinyl, red label, non-flexible vinyl			
❑ 3249 [M]	Brubeck & Desmond at Wilshire-Ebell	196?	$40
—Black vinyl, red label, flexible vinyl			
❑ 3301 [M]	Brubeck A La Mode	1960	$120
—Red vinyl			
❑ 3301 [M]	Brubeck A La Mode	1960	$40
—Black vinyl, red label, non-flexible vinyl			
❑ 3301 [M]	Brubeck A La Mode	196?	$75
—Black vinyl, red label, flexible vinyl			
❑ 8047 [S]	Brubeck A La Mode	1962	$150
—Blue vinyl			
❑ 8047 [S]	Brubeck A La Mode	196?	$75
—Black vinyl, blue label, non-flexible vinyl			
❑ 8047 [S]	Brubeck A La Mode	196?	$50
—Black vinyl, blue label, flexible vinyl			
❑ OJC-200	Brubeck A La Mode	1985	$25
❑ 8095 [S]	Brubeck and Desmond at Wilshire-Ebell	1962	$150
—Blue vinyl			
❑ 8095 [S]	Brubeck and Desmond at Wilshire-Ebell	1962	$75
—Black vinyl, blue label, non-flexible vinyl			
❑ 8095 [S]	Brubeck and Desmond at Wilshire-Ebell	196?	$50

Number	Title	Yr	NM
—Black vinyl, blue label, flexible vinyl			
❏ 3229 [M]	Brubeck-Desmond	1956	$200
—Dark red vinyl; reissue of 3-5			
❏ 3229 [M]	Brubeck-Desmond	195?	$75
—Black vinyl, red label, non-flexible vinyl			
❏ 3229 [M]	Brubeck-Desmond	196?	$40
—Black vinyl, red label, flexible vinyl			
❏ 8092 [R]	Brubeck-Desmond	1962	$40
—Blue vinyl			
❏ 8092 [R]	Brubeck-Desmond	1962	$50
—Black vinyl, blue label, non-flexible vinyl			
❏ 8092 [R]	Brubeck-Desmond	196?	$35
—Black vinyl, blue label, flexible vinyl			
❏ 24727	Brubeck-Desmond	1982	$35
❏ 3240 [M]	Brubeck Desmond: Jazz at Storyville	1957	$200
—Dark red vinyl; reissue of 3-8			
❏ 3240 [M]	Brubeck Desmond: Jazz at Storyville	195?	$75
—Black vinyl, red label, non-flexible vinyl			
❏ 3240 [M]	Brubeck Desmond: Jazz at Storyville	196?	$40
—Black vinyl, red label, flexible vinyl			
❏ 3332 [M]	Brubeck Tjader	1962	$120
—Red vinyl			
❏ 3332 [M]	Brubeck Tjader	1962	$40
—Black vinyl, red label, non-flexible vinyl			
❏ 3332 [M]	Brubeck Tjader	196?	$75
—Black vinyl, red label, flexible vinyl			
❏ 8074 [R]	Brubeck Tjader	1962	$40
—Blue vinyl			
❏ 8074 [R]	Brubeck Tjader	1962	$50
—Black vinyl, blue label, non-flexible vinyl			
❏ 8074 [R]	Brubeck Tjader	196?	$35
—Black vinyl, blue label, flexible vinyl			
❏ 3-3 [10]	Dave Brubeck Octet	1951	$175
❏ 3239 [M]	Dave Brubeck Octet	1956	$200
—Dark red vinyl; reissue of 3-3			
❏ 3239 [M]	Dave Brubeck Octet	195?	$75
—Black vinyl, red label, non-flexible vinyl			
❏ 3239 [M]	Dave Brubeck Octet	196?	$40
—Black vinyl, red label, flexible vinyl			
❏ 8094 [R]	Dave Brubeck Octet	1962	$40
—Blue vinyl			
❏ 8094 [R]	Dave Brubeck Octet	1962	$50
—Black vinyl, blue label, non-flexible vinyl			
❏ 8094 [R]	Dave Brubeck Octet	196?	$35
—Black vinyl, blue label, flexible vinyl			
❏ 3259 [M]	Dave Brubeck Plays and Plays and Plays and…	1958	$120
—Red vinyl			
❏ 3259 [M]	Dave Brubeck Plays and Plays and Plays and Plays and…	195?	$40
—Black vinyl, red label, non-flexible vinyl			
❏ 3259 [M]	Dave Brubeck Plays and Plays and Plays and…	196?	$75
—Black vinyl, red label, flexible vinyl			
❏ 3230 [M]	Dave Brubeck Quartet	1956	$200
—Dark red vinyl; reissue of 3-7			
❏ 3230 [M]	Dave Brubeck Quartet	195?	$75
—Black vinyl, red label, non-flexible vinyl			
❏ 3230 [M]	Dave Brubeck Quartet	196?	$40
—Black vinyl, red label, flexible vinyl			
❏ 8093 [R]	Dave Brubeck Quartet	1962	$40
—Blue vinyl			
❏ 8093 [R]	Dave Brubeck Quartet	1962	$50
—Black vinyl, blue label, non-flexible vinyl			
❏ 8093 [R]	Dave Brubeck Quartet	196?	$35
—Black vinyl, blue label, flexible vinyl			
❏ 3-5 [10]	Dave Brubeck Quartet with Paul Desmond	1952	$175
❏ 3-7 [10]	Dave Brubeck Quartet with Paul Desmond	1952	$175
❏ 3-1 [10]	Dave Brubeck Trio	1951	$175
❏ 3-2 [10]	Dave Brubeck Trio	1951	$175
❏ 3-4 [10]	Dave Brubeck Trio	1952	$175
❏ 3204 [M]	Dave Brubeck Trio	1956	$200
—Dark red vinyl; reissue of 3-1			
❏ 3204 [M]	Dave Brubeck Trio	195?	$75
—Black vinyl, red label, non-flexible vinyl			
❏ 3204 [M]	Dave Brubeck Trio	196?	$40
—Black vinyl, red label, flexible vinyl			
❏ 3205 [M]	Dave Brubeck Trio: Distinctive Rhythm Instrumentals	1956	$200
—Dark red vinyl; reissue of 3-2			
❏ 3205 [M]	Dave Brubeck Trio: Distinctive Rhythm Instrumentals	195?	$75
—Black vinyl, red label, non-flexible vinyl			
❏ 3205 [M]	Dave Brubeck Trio: Distinctive Rhythm Instrumentals	196?	$40
—Black vinyl, red label, flexible vinyl			
❏ 3331 [M]	Dave Brubeck Trio Featuring Cal Tjader	1962	$120

Number	Title	Yr	NM
—Red vinyl			
❏ 3331 [M]	Dave Brubeck Trio Featuring Cal Tjader	1962	$40
—Black vinyl, red label, non-flexible vinyl			
❏ 3331 [M]	Dave Brubeck Trio Featuring Cal Tjader	196?	$75
—Black vinyl, red label, flexible vinyl			
❏ 8073 [R]	Dave Brubeck Trio Featuring Cal Tjader	1962	$40
—Blue vinyl			
❏ 8073 [R]	Dave Brubeck Trio Featuring Cal Tjader	1962	$50
—Black vinyl, blue label, non-flexible vinyl			
❏ 8073 [R]	Dave Brubeck Trio Featuring Cal Tjader	196?	$35
—Black vinyl, blue label, flexible vinyl			
❏ MPF-4528	Greatest Hits from the Fantasy Years	1987	$25
❏ 3-11 [10]	Jazz at Oberlin	1953	$250
—Red vinyl			
❏ 3245 [M]	Jazz at Oberlin	1957	$200
—Dark red vinyl; reissue of 3-11			
❏ 3245 [M]	Jazz at Oberlin	195?	$75
—Black vinyl, red label, non-flexible vinyl			
❏ 3245 [M]	Jazz at Oberlin	196?	$40
—Black vinyl, red label, flexible vinyl			
❏ 8069 [R]	Jazz at Oberlin	1962	$40
—Blue vinyl			
❏ 8069 [R]	Jazz at Oberlin	196?	$50
—Black vinyl, blue label, non-flexible vinyl			
❏ 8069 [R]	Jazz at Oberlin	196?	$35
—Black vinyl, blue label, flexible vinyl			
❏ OJC-046	Jazz at Oberlin	198?	$25
—Reissue of 3245			
❏ 3-11 [10]	Jazz at Oberlin	1953	$200
—Black vinyl			
❏ 3-8 [10]	Jazz at Storyville	1953	$175
❏ 8080 [R]	Jazz at Storyville	1962	$40
—Blue vinyl			
❏ 8080 [R]	Jazz at Storyville	1962	$50
—Black vinyl, blue label, non-flexible vinyl			
❏ 8080 [R]	Jazz at Storyville	196?	$35
—Black vinyl, blue label, flexible vinyl			
❏ 3-10 [10]	Jazz at the Blackhawk	1953	$175
❏ 3210 [M]	Jazz at the Blackhawk	1956	$200
—Dark red vinyl; reissue of 3-10			
❏ 3210 [M]	Jazz at the Blackhawk	195?	$75
—Black vinyl, red label, non-flexible vinyl			
❏ 3210 [M]	Jazz at the Blackhawk	196?	$40
—Black vinyl, red label, flexible vinyl			
❏ 3-13 [10]	Jazz at the College of the Pacific	1954	$175
❏ 3223 [M]	Jazz at the College of the Pacific	1956	$200
—Dark red vinyl; reissue of 3-13			
❏ 3223 [M]	Jazz at the College of the Pacific	195?	$75
—Black vinyl, red label, non-flexible vinyl			
❏ 3223 [M]	Jazz at the College of the Pacific	196?	$40
—Black vinyl, red label, flexible vinyl			
❏ 8078 [R]	Jazz at the College of the Pacific	1962	$40
—Blue vinyl			
❏ 8078 [R]	Jazz at the College of the Pacific	196?	$50
—Black vinyl, blue label, non-flexible vinyl			
❏ 8078 [R]	Jazz at the College of the Pacific	196?	$35
—Black vinyl, blue label, flexible vinyl			
❏ OJC-047	Jazz at the College of the Pacific	198?	$25
—Reissue of 3223			
❏ OJC-236	Near Myth	1986	$25
—Reissue of Fantasy 3319			
❏ 3319 [M]	Near-Myth	1961	$120
—Red vinyl			
❏ 3319 [M]	Near-Myth	1961	$40
—Black vinyl, red label, non-flexible vinyl			
❏ 3319 [M]	Near-Myth	196?	$75
—Black vinyl, red label, flexible vinyl			
❏ 8063 [S]	Near-Myth	1962	$150
—Blue vinyl			
❏ 8063 [S]	Near-Myth	196?	$75
—Black vinyl, blue label, non-flexible vinyl			
❏ 8063 [S]	Near-Myth	196?	$50
—Black vinyl, blue label, flexible vinyl			
❏ 3-16 [10]	Old Sounds from San Francisco	1954	$300
—Red or purple vinyl			
❏ 3-20 [10]	Paul and Dave's Jazz Interwoven	1955	$175
❏ 3268 [M]	Re-Union	1958	$120
—Red vinyl			
❏ 3268 [M]	Re-Union	195?	$40
—Black vinyl, red label, non-flexible vinyl			
❏ 3268 [M]	Re-Union	196?	$75
—Black vinyl, red label, flexible vinyl			
❏ 8007 [S]	Re-Union	1962	$150

Number	Title	Yr	NM
—Blue vinyl			
❏ 8007 [S]	Re-Union	196?	$75
—Black vinyl, blue label, non-flexible vinyl			
❏ 8007 [S]	Re-Union	196?	$50
—Black vinyl, blue label, flexible vinyl			
❏ OJC-150	Re-Union	198?	$25
❏ 24728	Stardust	198?	$35
❏ OJC-101	The Dave Brubeck Octet	198?	$25
—Reissue of Fantasy 3239			
❏ 24726	The Dave Brubeck Trio	198?	$35
❏ 3298 [M]	Two Knights at the Black Hawk	1959	$120
—Red vinyl			
❏ 3298 [M]	Two Knights at the Black Hawk	1959	$40
—Black vinyl, red label, non-flexible vinyl			
❏ 3298 [M]	Two Knights at the Black Hawk	196?	$75
—Black vinyl, red label, flexible vinyl			
❏ 8081 [R]	Two Knights at the Blackhawk	1962	$40
—Blue vinyl			
❏ 8081 [R]	Two Knights at the Blackhawk	1962	$50
—Black vinyl, blue label, non-flexible vinyl			
❏ 8081 [R]	Two Knights at the Blackhawk	196?	$35
—Black vinyl, blue label, flexible vinyl			

HARMONY
Number	Title	Yr	NM
❏ HS11336	Gone with the Wind	1969	$30
❏ HS11253	Instant Brubeck	1968	$30

HORIZON
Number	Title	Yr	NM
❏ SP-703	1975: The Duets	1975	$30
❏ SP-714	The Dave Brubeck Quartet 25th Anniversary	1976	$30

JAZZTONE
Number	Title	Yr	NM
❏ J-1272 [M]	Best of Brubeck	195?	$40

MOBILE FIDELITY
Number	Title	Yr	NM
❏ 1-216	We're All Together Again for the First Time	1994	$120
—Audiophile vinyl			

MOON
Number	Title	Yr	NM
❏ 028	St. Louis Blues	1992	$50

ODYSSEY
Number	Title	Yr	NM
❏ 32160248	A Place in Time	1968	$30

TOMATO
Number	Title	Yr	NM
❏ 7018	The New Brubeck Quartet at Montreux	1978	$30

BRUCE, ED
EPIC
Number	Title	Yr	NM
❏ KE35541	Cowboys and Dreamers	1978	$12
❏ KE35043	Tennesseean	1977	$12

MCA
Number	Title	Yr	NM
❏ 3242	Ed Bruce	1980	$12
❏ 27068	Ed Bruce	198?	$10
—Reissue of 3242			
❏ 5577	Greatest Hits	1985	$12
❏ 5323	I Write It Down	1982	$12
❏ 5188	One to One	1981	$12
❏ 5511	Tell 'Em I've Gone Crazy	1984	$12
❏ 5416	You're Not Leaving Here Tonight	1983	$12

MONUMENT
Number	Title	Yr	NM
❏ SLP-18118	Shades	1969	$25

RCA VICTOR
Number	Title	Yr	NM
❏ AHL1-5324	Homecoming	1985	$12
❏ LPM-3948 [M]	If I Could Just Go Home	1968	$50
❏ LSP-3948 [S]	If I Could Just Go Home	1968	$30
❏ AHL1-5808	Night Things	1986	$12

UNITED ARTISTS
Number	Title	Yr	NM
❏ UA-LA613-G	Ed Bruce	1976	$15

BRUCE, JACK
Ex-member of CREAM.
ATCO
Number	Title	Yr	NM
❏ SD 33-365	Harmony Row	1971	$18
❏ SD 33-306	Songs for a Tailor	1969	$18
❏ SD 33-349	Things We Like	1971	$18

EPIC
Number	Title	Yr	NM
❏ FE45279	A Question of Time	1989	$18
❏ JE36827	I've Always Wanted to Do This	1980	$12

POLYDOR
Number	Title	Yr	NM
❏ PD2-3505	Jack Bruce At His Best	1972	$18

RSO
Number	Title	Yr	NM
❏ RS-1-3021	How's Tricks	1977	$12
❏ SO4805	Out of the Storm	1974	$12

BRUCE, JACK/ROBIN TROWER
CHRYSALIS
Number	Title	Yr	NM
❏ CHR1352	Truce	1982	$12
❏ PV41352	Truce	1983	$10
—Reissue			

Number	Title	Yr	NM

BRUCE, LENNY
BIZARRE
❏ 2XS6329	The Berkeley Concert	1969	$75

DOUGLAS

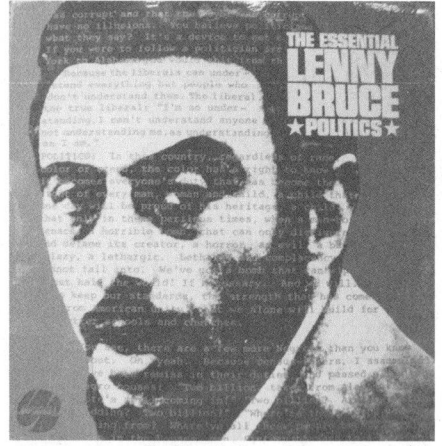

❏ 788 [B]	The Essential Lenny Bruce Politics	1968	$30
❏ 2 [B]	To Is a Preposition, Come Is a Verb	196?	$30
❏ Z30872	What I Was Arrested For	1971	$35

—Reissue of 2

FANTASY
❏ 7007 [M]	I Am Not a Nut, Elect Me	1960	$200

—Opaque, non-flexible red vinyl

❏ 7007 [M]	I Am Not a Nut, Elect Me	1960	$40

—Non-flexible black vinyl

❏ 7007 [M]	I Am Not a Nut, Elect Me	1962	$40

—Translucent, flexible red vinyl

❏ 7007 [M]	I Am Not a Nut, Elect Me	1962	$50

—Flexible black vinyl

❏ 7001 [M]	Interviews of Our Times	1959	$200

—Opaque, non-flexible red vinyl; tan cover with Lenny Bruce's name blacked out throughout the back

❏ 7001 [M]	Interviews of Our Times	1959	$40

—Non-flexible black vinyl; cover changed to blue tint

❏ 7001 [M]	Interviews of Our Times	1962	$40

—Translucent, flexible red vinyl

❏ 7001 [M]	Interviews of Our Times	1962	$50

—Flexible black vinyl

❏ 7011 [M]	Lenny Bruce, American	1961	$200

—Opaque, non-flexible red vinyl

❏ 7011 [M]	Lenny Bruce, American	1961	$40

—Non-flexible black vinyl

❏ 7011 [M]	Lenny Bruce, American	1962	$40

—Translucent, flexible red vinyl

❏ 7011 [M]	Lenny Bruce, American	1962	$50

—Flexible black vinyl

❏ 34201	Lenny Bruce at the Curran Theater	1971	$40
❏ 7017	Thank You Masked Man	1971	$35
❏ 7012 [M]	The Best of Lenny Bruce	1962	$150

—Red vinyl

❏ 7012 [M]	The Best of Lenny Bruce	1962	$25

—Black vinyl

❏ FP-1 [DJ]	The Promo Album	196?	$250

—Promo-only compilation of material from albums 7001, 7003, 7007 and 7011

❏ 79003	The Real Lenny Bruce	1975	$50
❏ 7003 [M]	The Sick Humor of Lenny Bruce	1959	$200

—Opaque, non-flexible red vinyl

❏ 7003 [M]	The Sick Humor of Lenny Bruce	1959	$40

—Non-flexible black vinyl

❏ 7003 [M]	The Sick Humor of Lenny Bruce	1962	$40

—Translucent, flexible red vinyl

❏ 7003 [M]	The Sick Humor of Lenny Bruce	1962	$25

—Flexible black vinyl

LENNY BRUCE
❏ LB-3001/2 [M]	Lenny Bruce Is Out Again	196?	$300

—Privately pressed version with white labels and Lenny's address on cover

❏ LB-9001/2 [10]	Warning: Sale of This Album...	1962	$500

—Privately pressed LP with routines used as evidence in Lenny's obscenity trial

PHILLIES
❏ PHLP-4010 [M]	Lenny Bruce Is Out Again	1966	$200

—Reissue of Lenny Bruce 3001/2

UNITED ARTISTS
❏ UAS9800	Lenny Bruce/Carnegie Hall	1972	$75

❏ UAL3580 [M]	The Midnight Concert	1967	$75
❏ UAS6794	The Midnight Concert	1972	$35

—Reissue of 6580

❏ UAS6580	The Midnight Concert	1967	$50

WARNER/SPECTOR
❏ SP9101	The Law, the Language and Lenny Bruce	1975	$35

BRUEL, MAX
EMARCY
❏ MG-36062 [M]	Cool Bruel	1955	$250

BRUFORD, BILL
EDITIONS EG
❏ EGS48	Earthworks	1987	$12
❏ EGS67	Master Strokes 1978-1985	198?	$12
❏ EGS106	The Bruford Tapes	1979	$12

POLYDOR
❏ PD-1-6149	Feels Good to Me	1977	$12
❏ PD-1-6261	Gradually Going Tornado	1980	$12
❏ PD-1-6205	One of a Kind	1979	$12

BRUNEL, BUNNY
INNER CITY
❏ 1162	Ivanhoe	198?	$25
❏ 1102	Touch	198?	$25

BRUNIOUS, WENDELL
GHB
❏ GHB-194	Wendell Brunious and His New Orleans Jazz Band in the Tradition	198?	$25

BRUNIS, GEORG
COMMODORE
❏ FL-20008 [10]	King of the Tailgate Trombone	1950	$100
❏ DL30015 [M]	King of the Tailgate Trombone	1959	$40

JAZZOLOGY
❏ J-012	Georg Brunis and His Rhythm Kings	1965	$35

JOLLY ROGER
❏ 5024 [10]	Georg Brunis and the New Orleans Rhythm Kings	1954	$50

RIVERSIDE
❏ RLP-1024 [10]	Georg Brunis and the Original New Orleans Rhythm Kings	1954	$300

BRUNSON, FRANKIE
GEE
❏ GLP-704 [M]	Big Daddy's Blues	1959	$100
❏ SGLP-704 [S]	Big Daddy's Blues	1959	$120

BRUNSON, TYRONE
BELIEVE IN A DREAM
❏ FZ39197	Fresh	1984	$12

MCA
❏ 5968	Love Triangle	1987	$12
❏ 5810	The Method	1986	$12

BRUSH ARBOR
CAPITOL
❏ ST-11158	Brush Arbor	1973	$18
❏ ST-11209	Brush Arbor 2	1973	$18

LIGHT
❏ LS-5873	Live	1985	$15

MONUMENT
❏ KZ34251	Page One	1977	$18
❏ 6637	Page One	1977	$15

—Reissue of 34251

❏ 7613	Straight	1978	$15

MYRRH
❏ MSB-6664	Hero	198?	$15
❏ MSB-6624	Hide Away	1979	$15

BRUTE FORCE
B.T. PUPPY
❏ BTPS-1015	Extemporaneous	1971	$300

COLUMBIA
❏ CL2615 [M]	I, Brute Force -- Confections of Love	1967	$30
❏ CS9415 [S]	I, Brute Force -- Confections of Love	1967	$25

EMBRYO
❏ 522	Brute Force	1970	$25

—Different band

BRYAN, JOY
CONTEMPORARY
❏ M-3604 [M]	Make the Man Love Me	1961	$250
❏ S-7604 [S]	Make the Man Love Me	1961	$250

MODE
❏ LP-108 [M]	Joy Bryan Sings	1957	$100

BRYANT, ANITA
CARLTON
❏ LP-118 [M]	Anita Bryant	1959	$25
❏ STLP-118 [S]	Anita Bryant	1959	$30
❏ LP-127 [M]	Hear Anita Bryant in Your Home Tonight	1960	$25
❏ STLP-127 [S]	Hear Anita Bryant in Your Home Tonight	1960	$30
❏ LP-132 [M]	In My Little Corner of the World	1961	$25
❏ STLP-132 [S]	In My Little Corner of the World	1961	$30

COLUMBIA
❏ CL1767 [M]	Abiding Love	1962	$18
❏ CS8567 [S]	Abiding Love	1962	$25
❏ CL1956 [M]	Anita Bryant's Greatest Hits	1963	$15
❏ CS8756 [S]	Anita Bryant's Greatest Hits	1963	$18
❏ CL2035 [M]	As Long As He Needs Me	1963	$15
❏ CS8835 [S]	As Long As He Needs Me	1963	$18
❏ CL2069 [M]	Country's Best	1964	$15
❏ CS8869 [S]	Country's Best	1964	$18
❏ CL2720 [M]	Do You Hear What I Hear?	1967	$18
❏ CS9520 [S]	Do You Hear What I Hear?	1967	$12
❏ CS9642	How Great Thou Art	1968	$15
❏ CL2706 [M]	I Believe	1967	$18
❏ CS9506 [S]	I Believe	1967	$15
❏ CL1885 [M]	In a Velvet Mood	1962	$18
❏ CS8685 [S]	In a Velvet Mood	1962	$18
❏ CS9607	In Remembrance of You (The Story of a Love Affair)	1968	$15
❏ CL1719 [M]	Kisses Sweeter Than Wine	1961	$18
❏ CS8519 [S]	Kisses Sweeter Than Wine	1961	$25
❏ CL2573 [M]	Mine Eyes Have Seen the Glory	1966	$15
❏ CS9373 [S]	Mine Eyes Have Seen the Glory	1966	$18
❏ CL2222 [M]	World of Lonely People	1964	$15
❏ CS9022 [S]	World of Lonely People	1964	$18

COLUMBIA SPECIAL PRODUCTS
❏ CSS900	The Sunshine Tree	1970	$15

HARMONY
❏ HL9557 [M]	ABC Stories of Jesus	196?	$15
❏ HS11280	Anita Bryant	1968	$12
❏ HS11395	A World Without Love	1970	$12
❏ HS11330	Little Things Mean a Lot	1969	$12
❏ H31181	You'll Never Walk Alone	1972	$12

MYRRH
❏ MSB-6513	Naturally	197?	$15

WORD
❏ WST-8532	Abide with Me	1970	$15
❏ WST-8571	Battle Hymn of the Republic	1972	$15
❏ WST-8652	Hymns	1976	$15
❏ WST-8540	Love Lifted Me	1971	$15
❏ WST-8670	Old Fashioned Prayin'	1977	$15
❏ 8785	Singing a New Song	198?	$12
❏ WST-8558	The Miracle of Christmas	197?	$12
❏ WST-8631	This Is My Story	1975	$15

BRYANT, BOBBY
CADET
❏ LP-795 [M]	Ain't Doing Too B-A-D, Bad	1967	$25
❏ LPS-795 [S]	Ain't Doing Too B-A-D, Bad	1967	$35
❏ CA-50011	Swahili Strut	1972	$30

VEE JAY
❏ VJS-3059	Big Band Blues	1974	$25

WORLD PACIFIC
❏ ST-20159	The Jazz Excursion Into "Hair	1969	$150

BRYANT, BOUDLEAUX
MONUMENT
❏ MLP-8007 [M]	Boudleaux Bryant's Best Sellers	1963	$25
❏ SLP-18007 [S]	Boudleaux Bryant's Best Sellers	1963	$30

BRYANT, CLORA
MODE
❏ LP-106 [M]	Gal with a Horn	1957	$175

BRYANT, JIMMY
CAPITOL
❏ T1314 [M]	Country Cabin Jazz	1960	$100
❏ ST1314 [S]	Country Cabin Jazz	1960	$150

DOLTON
❏ BLP-16505 [M]	Play Country Guitar with Jimmy Bryant	196?	$75
❏ BST-17505 [S]	Play Country Guitar with Jimmy Bryant	196?	$30

IMPERIAL
❏ LP-9310 [M]	Bryant's Back in Town	1966	$25
❏ LP-12310 [S]	Bryant's Back in Town	1966	$30
❏ LP-9315 [M]	Laughing Guitar, Crying Guitar	1966	$25
❏ LP-12315 [S]	Laughing Guitar, Crying Guitar	1966	$30
❏ LP-9360 [M]	That Fastest Guitar in the Country	1967	$30

Number	Title	Yr	NM
❏ LP-12360 [S]	That Fastest Guitar in the Country	1967	$25
❏ LP-9338 [M]	We Are Young	1967	$25
❏ LP-12338 [S]	We Are Young	1967	$30

BRYANT, LEON

DE-LITE
| ❏ DSR8501 | Leon Bryant | 1981 | $15 |

BRYANT, PAUL

FANTASY
❏ 3363 [M]	Groove Time	1964	$25
❏ 8363 [S]	Groove Time	1964	$30
❏ 3357 [M]	Something's Happening	1963	$25
❏ 8357 [S]	Something's Happening	1963	$30

PACIFIC JAZZ
| ❏ PJ-12 [M] | Burnin' | 1961 | $40 |

BRYANT, RAY

ATLANTIC
| ❏ SD1626 | Alone at Montreux | 1972 | $30 |
| ❏ SD1564 | MCMLXX | 1970 | $35 |

CADET
❏ LP-767 [M]	Gotta Travel On	1966	$35
❏ LPS-767 [S]	Gotta Travel On	1966	$50
❏ 50052	In the Cut	1974	$30
❏ 50038	It Was a Very Good Year	1973	$35
❏ LP-778 [M]	Lonesome Traveler	1966	$35
❏ LPS-778 [S]	Lonesome Traveler	1966	$50
❏ LP-781 [M]	Slow Freight	1967	$35
❏ LPS-781 [S]	Slow Freight	1967	$50
❏ LPS-830	Sound Ray	1969	$35
❏ LP-801 [M]	Take a Bryant Step	1967	$50
❏ LPS-801 [S]	Take a Bryant Step	1967	$35
❏ LP-793 [M]	The Ray Bryant Touch	1967	$50
❏ LPS-793 [S]	The Ray Bryant Touch	1967	$35
❏ LPS-818	Up Above the Rock	1968	$35

CLASSIC JAZZ
| ❏ 130 | Hot Turkey | 198? | $25 |

COLUMBIA
❏ CL1633 [M]	Con Alma	1961	$50
❏ CS8433 [S]	Con Alma	1961	$75
❏ CL1746 [M]	Dancing the Big Twist	1962	$50
❏ CS8546 [S]	Dancing the Big Twist	1962	$75
❏ CL1867 [M]	Hollywood Jazz Beat	1962	$50
❏ CS8667 [S]	Hollywood Jazz Beat	1962	$75
❏ CL1449 [M]	Little Susie	1960	$50
❏ CS8244 [S]	Little Susie	1960	$75
❏ CL1476 [M]	The Madison Time	1960	$75
❏ CS8276 [S]	The Madison Time	1960	$75

COLUMBIA JAZZ MASTERPIECES
| ❏ CJ44058 | Con Alma | 1988 | $25 |

EMARCY
❏ 836368-1	Golden Earrings	1989	$30
❏ 832235-1	Ray Bryant Plays Basie and Ellington	1987	$30
❏ 832589-1	The Ray Bryant Trio Today	1988	$30

EPIC
| ❏ LN3279 [M] | Ray Bryant Trio | 1956 | $300 |

FANTASY
❏ OJC-213	Alone with the Blues	1987	$25
—Reissue			
❏ OJC-371	Montreux '77	1989	$25
—Reissue of Pablo Live 2308 201			

NEW JAZZ
❏ NJLP-8213 [M]	Alone with the Blues	1959	$250
—Purple label			
❏ NJLP-8213 [M]	Alone with the Blues	1965	$175
—Blue label with trident logo			
❏ NJLP-8227 [M]	Ray Bryant Trio	1959	$175
—Purple label; reissue of Prestige 7098			
❏ NJLP-8227 [M]	Ray Bryant Trio	1965	$175
—Blue label with trident logo			

PABLO
❏ 2310820	All Blues	1978	$25
❏ 2310764	Here's Ray Bryant	1976	$25
❏ 2310860	Potpourri	1981	$25
❏ 2310798	Solo Flight	1977	$25
❏ 2405402	The Best of Ray Bryant	198?	$25

PABLO LIVE
| ❏ 2308201 | Montreux '77 | 1977 | $25 |

PRESTIGE
❏ PRLP-7837	Alone with the Blues	1971	$35
—Reissue of New Jazz 8213			
❏ PRT-7837	Alone with the Blues	1973	$30
—Reissue; "Distributed by Fantasy Records, Berkeley, California" on label			
❏ 24038	Me and the Blues	1973	$35
❏ PRLP-7098 [M]	Ray Bryant Trio	1957	$1000

SIGNATURE
| ❏ SM-6008 [M] | Ray Bryant Plays | 1960 | $500 |
| ❏ SS-6008 [S] | Ray Bryant Plays | 1960 | $300 |

SUE
❏ LP-1032 [M]	Cold Turkey	1964	$40
❏ LPS-1032 [S]	Cold Turkey	1964	$150
❏ LP-1016 [M]	Groove House	1963	$40

Number	Title	Yr	NM
❏ LPS-1016 [S]	Groove House	1963	$150
❏ LP-1019 [M]	Live at Basin Street	1964	$40
❏ LPS-1019 [S]	Live at Basin Street	1964	$150
❏ STLP-1036 [M]	Ray Bryant Soul	1965	$40
❏ STLPS-1036 [S]	Ray Bryant Soul	1965	$150

BRYANT, RUSTY

DOT
❏ DLP-3006 [M]	All Night Long	1956	$100
—Maroon label			
❏ DLP-3353 [M]	America's Greatest Jazz	1961	$85
❏ DLP-25353 [S]	America's Greatest Jazz	1961	$85
❏ DLP-3079 [M]	Rusty Bryant Plays Jazz	1957	$100

FANTASY
| ❏ OJC-331 | Rusty Bryant Returns | 1988 | $25 |
| —Reissue of Prestige 7626 | | | |

PRESTIGE
❏ 10013	Fire Eater	1972	$30
❏ 10073	For the Good Times	1974	$30
❏ 10053	Friday Night Funk	1973	$30
❏ PRST-7735	Night Train Now!	1970	$30
❏ PRST-7626	Rusty Bryant Returns	1969	$30
❏ PRST-7798	Soul Liberation	1971	$30
❏ 10085	Until It's Time for You to Go	1974	$30
❏ 10037	Wild Fire	1972	$30

BRYANT, SHARON

WING
| ❏ 837313-1 | Here I Am | 1989 | $12 |

BRYCE, SHERRY

MGM
| ❏ M3G-5000 | This Song's for You | 1975 | $18 |
| ❏ M3G-4967 | Treat Me Like a Lady | 1974 | $18 |

BRYNNER, YUL

VANGUARD
| ❏ VRS-9256 [M] | The Gypsy and I | 1967 | $30 |
| ❏ VSD-79256 [S] | The Gypsy and I | 1967 | $40 |

BRYSON, PEABO, AND ROBERTA FLACK

ATLANTIC
| ❏ SD7000 | Live and More | 1980 | $15 |
| —As "Roberta Flack and Peabo Bryson" | | | |

CAPITOL
| ❏ ST-12284 | Born to Love | 1983 | $10 |

BRYSON, PEABO

BULLET
| ❏ 7000 | Peabo | 1976 | $25 |

CAPITOL
❏ C1-90461	All My Love	1989	$12
❏ ST-11875	Crosswinds	1978	$12
❏ ST-12241	Don't Play with Fire	1982	$10
❏ ST-12179	I Am Love	1981	$12
❏ SOO-12063	Paradise	1980	$12
❏ ST-11729	Reaching for the Sky	1978	$12
❏ SJ-12348	The Peabo Bryson Collection	1984	$12
❏ ST-12138	Turn the Hands of Time	1981	$12

COLUMBIA
| ❏ C46823 | Can You Stop the Rain | 1991 | $18 |

ELEKTRA
❏ 60753	Positive	1988	$10
❏ 60484	Quiet Storm	1986	$10
❏ 60362	Straight from the Heart	1983	$10
❏ 60427	Take No Prisoners	1985	$10

BUA, GENE

HERITAGE
| ❏ 35004 | Love of Life | 1973 | $25 |

BUBBLE GUM MACHINE, THE

SENATE
| ❏ 21002 [M] | The Bubble Gum Machine | 1968 | $30 |
| ❏ S-21002 [S] | The Bubble Gum Machine | 1968 | $30 |

BUBBLE PUPPY, THE
Also see DEMIAN.

INTERNATIONAL ARTISTS
❏ 10	A Gathering of Promises	1969	$150
—Original does not have "Masterfonics" in the dead wax			
❏ 10	A Gathering of Promises	1979	$30
—Reissue has "Masterfonics" in the dead wax			

BUBBLES, JOHN W.

VEE JAY
| ❏ VJ-1109 [M] | Bubbles, John W., That Is | 1964 | $25 |

BUCCI, JOE

CAPITOL
| ❏ T1840 [M] | Wild About Basie | 1963 | $75 |
| ❏ ST1840 [S] | Wild About Basie | 1963 | $100 |

Number	Title	Yr	NM

BUCHANAN, ROY

ALLIGATOR
❏ AL-4747	Dancing on the Edge	1986	$12
❏ AL-4756	Hot Wires	1988	$12
❏ AL-4741	When a Guitar Plays the Blues	1985	$12

ATLANTIC
❏ SD18170	A Street Called Straight	1976	$15
❏ SD18219	Loading Zone	1977	$15
❏ SD19138	Loading Zone	1978	$10
—Reissue of 18219			
❏ SD19170	You're Not Alone	1978	$15

BIOYA
| ❏ MM-519 | Buch and the Snake Stretchers | 1971 | $300 |

POLYDOR
❏ PD-6035	In the Beginning	1974	$18
❏ PD-6048	Live Stock	1975	$18
❏ PD-5033	Roy Buchanan	1972	$18
❏ PD-5046	Second Album	1973	$18
❏ PD-6020	That's What I Am Here For	1974	$18

WATERHOUSE
| ❏ 12 | My Babe | 1981 | $12 |

BUCHANAN BROTHERS

EVENT
| ❏ ES-101 | Medicine Man | 1969 | $30 |

BUCK, GARY

TOWER
| ❏ T5054 [M] | Country Scene | 1967 | $25 |
| ❏ DT5054 [R] | Country Scene | 1967 | $18 |

BUCKACRE

MCA
| ❏ 2365 | Buckacre | 1978 | $12 |
| ❏ 2218 | Morning Comes | 1976 | $12 |

BUCKAROOS, THE

CAPITOL
❏ T2722 [M]	America's Most Wanted Band	1967	$25
❏ ST2722 [S]	America's Most Wanted Band	1967	$30
❏ ST2902	A Night on the Town with Buck Owens' Buckaroos	1968	$30
❏ ST-194	Anywhere U.S.A.	1969	$30
❏ ST2973	Meanwhile Back at the Ranch	1968	$30
❏ ST-322	Roll Your Own with Buck Owens' Buckaroos	1969	$30
❏ ST-440	Rompin' and Stompin'	1970	$25
❏ ST-767	The Buckaroos Play the Hits	1971	$25
❏ ST-860	The Buckaroos Play the Songs of Merle Haggard	1971	$30
❏ T2828 [M]	The Buck Owens' Buckaroos Strike Again!	1968	$40
❏ ST2828 [S]	The Buck Owens' Buckaroos Strike Again!	1968	$30
❏ T2436 [M]	The Buck Owens Song Book	1966	$25
❏ ST2436 [S]	The Buck Owens Song Book	1966	$30

BUCKINGHAM, LINDSEY
Also see FLEETWOOD MAC.

ASYLUM
| ❏ 512970 | Gift of Screws | 2008 | $25 |
| ❏ 5E-561 | Law and Order | 1981 | $12 |

ELEKTRA
| ❏ 60363 | Go Insane | 1984 | $12 |

BUCKINGHAM NICKS
Lindsey Buckingham and Stephanie (later known as Stevie) Nicks. Also see FLEETWOOD MAC.

POLYDOR
❏ PD-5058 [B]	Buckingham Nicks	1973	$75
—Gatefold cover			
❏ PD-5058	Buckingham Nicks	1975	$15
—Regular cover			

BUCKINGHAMS, THE (1)

COLUMBIA
❏ CS9703	In One Ear and Gone Tomorrow	1968	$25
❏ KG33333	Made in Chicago	1975	$25
❏ CS9598 [S]	Portraits	1968	$25
❏ CL2798 [M]	Portraits	1968	$30
❏ CS9812	The Buckinghams Greatest Hits	1969	$25
—Red "360 Sound" label			
❏ CS9812	The Buckinghams Greatest Hits	1970	$15
—Orange label			
❏ PC9812	The Buckinghams Greatest Hits	198?	$10
—Reissue with new prefix			
❏ CL2669 [M]	Time & Charges	1967	$30
❏ CS9469 [S]	Time & Charges	1967	$25

Number	Title	Yr	NM
U.S.A.			
❑ 107 [M]	Kind of a Drag	1967	$700
— With "I'm a Man"			
❑ 107 [M]	Kind of a Drag	1967	$50
— Without "I'm a Man"			
❑ 107 [S]	Kind of a Drag	1967	$40
— No known stereo copy has "I'm a Man"			

BUCKLEY, LORD

Number	Title	Yr	NM
CRESTVIEW			
❑ CRV-801 [M]	The Best of Lord Buckley	1963	$150
❑ CRV7-801 [S]	The Best of Lord Buckley	1963	$120
ELEKTRA			
❑ EKS-74047	The Best of Lord Buckley	1969	$75
— Reissue of Crestview 7-801			
RCA VICTOR			
❑ LPM-3246 [10]	Hipsters, Flipsters and Finger Poppin' Daddies, Knock Me Your Lobes	1955	$600
REPRISE			
❑ RS6389	A Most Immaculately Hip Aristocrat	1970	$150
— Reissue of Straight 1054			
STRAIGHT			
❑ STS-1054	A Most Immaculately Hip Aristocrat	1970	$175
VAYA			
❑ 1715 [10]	Euphoria	195?	$600
— Red vinyl			
❑ 101/2 [M]	Euphoria, Volume 1	1955	$300
❑ 107/8 [M]	Euphoria, Volume 2	1955	$400
WORLD PACIFIC			
❑ WPS-21889	Bad Rapping of the Marquis de Sade	1969	$300
❑ WP-1849 [M]	Blowing His Mind (and Yours, Too)	1966	$300
❑ WPS-21879	Buckley's Best	1968	$175
❑ WP-1815 [M]	Lord Buckley in Concert	1964	$250
— Reissue of 1279			
❑ WP-1279 [M]	The Way Out Humor of Lord Buckley	1959	$350
— With "Far Out Humor" on the back cover			
❑ WP-1279 [M]	The Way Out Humor of Lord Buckley	1959	$350
— With correct "Way Out Humor" on the back cover			

BUCKLEY, TIM

Number	Title	Yr	NM
4 MEN WITH BEARDS			
❑ 4M133LP [B]	Blue Afternoon		$25
❑ 4M132LP [B]	Goodbye and Hello		$25
❑ 4M145LP [B]	Happy Sad		$25
❑ 4M146LP [B]	Lorca		$25
❑ 4M134LP [B]	Starsailor		$25
DISCREET			
❑ DS2201 [B]	Look at the Fool	1974	$25
❑ MS2157 [B]	Sefronia	1973	$25
ELEKTRA			
❑ EKL-4028 [M]	Goodbye and Hello	1968	$50
— Reissue of 318; may not exist with this number			
❑ EKS-74028 [S]	Goodbye and Hello	1968	$25
— Brown labels; reissue of 7318			
❑ EKS-74028 [S]	Goodbye and Hello	1975	$12
— Butterfly label with Warner Communications logo			
❑ EKL-318 [M]	Goodbye and Hello	1967	$30
— Original issue			
❑ EKS-7318 [S]	Goodbye and Hello	1967	$30
— Original issue; tan/brown/silvery label			
❑ EKS-74045	Happy Sad	1969	$25
❑ EKS-74074	Lorca	1970	$25
❑ EKL-4004 [M]	Tim Buckley	1966	$30
❑ EKS-74004 [S]	Tim Buckley	1966	$25
RHINO			
❑ RNLP-112	The Best of Tim Buckley	1985	$12
STRAIGHT			
❑ STS-1060	Blue Afternoon	1969	$30
TPM/RHINO EXCLUSIVE			
❑ 2631	Greetings from L.A.	2008	$12
❑ 74004	Tim Buckley	2008	$12
WARNER BROS.			
❑ WS1842	Blue Afternoon	1970	$18
❑ BS2631	Greetings from L.A.	1972	$18
❑ WS1881	Starsailor	1970	$18

BUCKNER, MILT

Number	Title	Yr	NM
ARGO			
❑ LP-702 [M]	Midnight Mood	1962	$35
❑ LPS-702 [S]	Midnight Mood	1962	$25
❑ LP-660 [M]	Mighty High	1960	$35
❑ LPS-660 [S]	Mighty High	1960	$25
❑ LP-670 [M]	Please Mr. Organ Player	1960	$35
❑ LPS-670 [S]	Please Mr. Organ Player	1960	$25
BASF			
❑ 20631	Chords	1972	$35

Number	Title	Yr	NM
BETHLEHEM			
❑ BCP-6072 [M]	The New World of Milt Buckner	1963	$250
CAPITOL			
❑ T722 [M]	Rockin' Hammond	1956	$100
— Turquoise or gray label			
❑ T642 [M]	Rockin' with Milt	1955	$100
— Turquoise or gray label			
❑ T938 [M]	Send Me Softly	1958	$100
— Turquoise or gray label			
CLASSIC JAZZ			
❑ 141	Green Onions	198?	$25
JAZZ MAN			
❑ 5012	Rockin' Again	198?	$30
PRESTIGE			
❑ PRST-7668	Milt Buckner in Europe '66	1969	$35
REGENT			
❑ MG-6004 [M]	Organ -- Sweet 'n' Swing	195?	$30
SAVOY			
❑ MG-15023 [10]	Milt Buckner Piano	1953	$120

BUCKNER, TEDDY

Number	Title	Yr	NM
AIRCHECK			
❑ 10	Teddy Buckner and His Orchestra 1955	198?	$25
DIXIELAND JUBILEE			
❑ DJ-505 [M]	A Salute to Louis Armstrong	1959	$25
❑ DJS-505 [S]	A Salute to Louis Armstrong	1959	$35
❑ DJ-503 [M]	In Concert at the Dixieland Jubilee	195?	$25
❑ DJS-503 [R]	In Concert at the Dixieland Jubilee	196?	$30
❑ DJ-504 [M]	Teddy Buckner and His Dixieland Band	195?	$25
❑ DJS-504 [R]	Teddy Buckner and His Dixieland Band	195?	$30
❑ DJ-507 [M]	Teddy Buckner and the All Stars	1959	$25
❑ DJS-507 [S]	Teddy Buckner and the All Stars	1959	$35
❑ DJS-516	Teddy Buckner at the Crescendo	196?	$35
❑ DJ-510 [M]	Teddy Buckner on the Sunset Strip	1960	$25
❑ DJS-510 [S]	Teddy Buckner on the Sunset Strip	1960	$35
GENE NORMAN			
❑ GNP-(# unk) [10]	Dixieland Jubilee	195?	$50
— Red vinyl			
❑ GNP-11 [M]	Teddy Buckner	1955	$50
GNP CRESCENDO			
❑ GNP-68 [M]	Midnight in Moscow	1962	$30
❑ GNPS-68 [S]	Midnight in Moscow	1962	$35

BUCKNER & GARCIA

Number	Title	Yr	NM
COLUMBIA			
❑ RC37041	Pac-Man Fever	1982	$12
— With video games inner sleeve			

BUCKSHOT LEFONQUE

Number	Title	Yr	NM
COLUMBIA			
❑ C257322	Buckshot LeFonque	1994	$20
❑ C67584	Music Evolution	1997	$15
❑ CAS8780 [EP]	Music Evolution (Sampler)	1997	$12
— Promo only; five songs			
❑ CAS6566 [EP]	Selections from Buckshot LeFonque	1995	$12
— Promo only; five songs			

BUCKWHEAT

Number	Title	Yr	NM
LONDON			
❑ PS595	Buckwheat	1971	$18
❑ XPS621	Charade	1972	$15
❑ XPS635	Hot Tracks	1973	$15
❑ PS609	Movin' On	1972	$15

BUCKWHEAT ZYDECO

Number	Title	Yr	NM
BLACK TOP			
❑ 1024 [B]	100% Fortified Zydeco	1983	$18
BLUES UNLIMITED			
❑ 5006	Ils Sont Partis	1981	$25
❑ 5017	People's Choice	1982	$25
ISLAND			
❑ 90622	On a Night Like This	1987	$12
❑ 90968 [B]	Taking It Home	1988	$12
ROUNDER			
❑ 2045	Turning Point	1984	$18
❑ 2051	Waitin' for My Ya Ya	1985	$18

BUD AND TRAVIS

Number	Title	Yr	NM
LIBERTY			
❑ LRP-3125 [M]	Bud and Travis	1959	$30
❑ LST-7125 [S]	Bud and Travis	1959	$40
❑ LDM-11001 [M]	Bud and Travis...In Concert	1960	$30
❑ LDS-12001 [S]	Bud and Travis...In Concert	1960	$30

Number	Title	Yr	NM
❑ LRP-3222 [M]	Bud and Travis In Concert at the Santa Monica Civic Auditorium, Vol. 2	1961	$25
❑ LST-7222 [S]	Bud and Travis In Concert at the Santa Monica Civic Auditorium, Vol. 2	1961	$30
❑ LRP-3386 [M]	Bud and Travis In Person (At the Cellar Door)	1964	$25
❑ LST-7386 [S]	Bud and Travis In Person (At the Cellar Door)	1964	$30
❑ LRP-3295 [M]	Naturally	1963	$25
❑ LST-7295 [S]	Naturally	1963	$30
❑ LRP-3341 [M]	Perspective on Bud and Travis	1964	$25
❑ LST-7341 [S]	Perspective on Bud and Travis	1964	$30
❑ LRP-3138 [M]	Spotlight On Bud and Travis	1960	$25
❑ LST-7138 [S]	Spotlight On Bud and Travis	1960	$30
❑ LRP-3398 [M]	The Latin Album	1965	$25
❑ LST-7398 [S]	The Latin Album	1965	$30
SUNSET			
❑ SUM-1154 [M]	Bud and Travis	1967	$15
❑ SUS-5154 [S]	Bud and Travis	1967	$15

BUDD, HAROLD

Number	Title	Yr	NM
ADVANCE RECORDINGS			
❑ FGR16 [B]	The Oak Of The Golden Dreams	1971	$800
CANTIL			
❑ 384 [B]	Abandoned Cities	1984	$75
❑ 181 [B]	The Serpent (In Quicksilver)	1981	$50
EDITIONS EG			
❑ EGED46 [B]	Lovely Thunder	1986	$100
❑ EGS301 [B]	The Pavilion of Dreams	1981	$60
— US release for 1978 LP on the UK Obscure label			
OPAL			
❑ 9 25766-1 [B]	The White Arcades	1988	$50

BUDDIES, THE

Number	Title	Yr	NM
WING			
❑ MGW-12306 [M]	Go Go with the Buddies	1965	$50
❑ SRW-16306 [S]	Go Go with the Buddies	1965	$100
❑ MGW-12293 [M]	The Buddies and the Compacts	1965	$50
❑ SRW-16293 [S]	The Buddies and the Compacts	1965	$100

BUDGIE

Number	Title	Yr	NM
A&M			
❑ SP-4618 [B]	Bandolier	1975	$50
❑ SP-4593 [B]	If I Were Brittania I'd Waive the Rules	1976	$30
❑ SP-4675 [B]	Impeckable	1978	$35
KAPP			
❑ KS-3656 [B]	Budgie	1971	$150
❑ KS-3669 [B]	Squawk	1972	$100
MCA			
❑ 429 [B]	In for the Kill	1973	$75

BUDIMIR, DENNIS

Number	Title	Yr	NM
MAINSTREAM			
❑ 56059 [M]	Creeper	1966	$25
❑ S-6059 [S]	Creeper	1966	$30
REVELATION			
❑ REV-M-1 [M]	Alone Together	1967	$30
❑ REV-1 [S]	Alone Together	1967	$25
❑ REV-4	A Second Coming	1968	$25
❑ REV-14	Session with Albert	1971	$25
❑ REV-8	Sprung Free!	1969	$25

BUDWIG, MONTY

Number	Title	Yr	NM
CONCORD JAZZ			
❑ CJ-79	Dig	198?	$25

BUFFALO NICKEL JUGBAND, THE

Number	Title	Yr	NM
HAPPY TIGER			
❑ 1018	The Buffalo Nickel Jugband	1971	$30

BUFFALO SOLDIERS

Number	Title	Yr	NM
CREW LA-POO			
❑ E3002	Penny	1990	$15

BUFFALO SPRINGFIELD

Number	Title	Yr	NM
ATCO			
❑ 33-200 [M]	Buffalo Springfield	1967	$300
— With "Baby Don't Scold Me"			
❑ SD 33-200 [S]	Buffalo Springfield	1967	$250
— With "Baby Don't Scold Me"			
❑ 33-200A [M]	Buffalo Springfield	1967	$100
— With "For What It's Worth" replacing "Baby Don't Scold Me"			
❑ SD 33-200A [S]	Buffalo Springfield	1967	$30
— With "For What It's Worth" replacing "Baby Don't Scold Me"; purple and brown label			
❑ SD 33-200A [S]	Buffalo Springfield	1969	$18
— Reissue on yellow label			
❑ SD 2-806	Buffalo Springfield	1973	$25
— Yellow label			

Number	Title	Yr	NM
❑ SD 33-200A [S]	Buffalo Springfield	197?	$10
—Later white or gray label			
❑ SD 2-806	Buffalo Springfield	197?	$15
—Later white or gray label			
❑ 33-226 [M]	Buffalo Springfield Again	1967	$175
❑ SD 33-226 [S]	Buffalo Springfield Again	1967	$30
—Purple and brown label			
❑ SD 33-226 [S]	Buffalo Springfield Again	1969	$18
—Reissue on yellow label			
❑ SD 33-226 [S]	Buffalo Springfield Again	197?	$10
—Later white or gray label			
❑ SD 33-256 [S]	Last Time Around	1968	$30
—Purple and brown label			
❑ 33-256 [M]	Last Time Around	1968	$175
—White label promo only			
❑ SD 33-256 [S]	Last Time Around	1969	$18
—Reissue on yellow label			
❑ SD 33-256 [S]	Last Time Around	197?	$10
—Later white or gray label			
❑ 33-283 [M]	Retrospective/The Best of Buffalo Springfield	1969	$150
—White label promo only			
❑ SD 33-283 [S]	Retrospective/The Best of Buffalo Springfield	1969	$25
—Yellow label			
❑ SD 38-105 [S]	Retrospective/The Best of Buffalo Springfield	197?	$10
—Reissue of 33-283			

BUFFALO TOM
SST
❑ 250	Buffalo Tom	1989	$18

BUFFETT, JIMMY
ABC
❑ AB-990	Changes in Latitudes, Changes in Attitudes	1977	$15
❑ D-914	Havana Daydreamin'	1976	$15
❑ AA-1046	Son of a Son of a Sailor	1978	$15
❑ -0 [DJ]	Special Jimmy Buffett Sampler	1978	$25
❑ SPDJ-43 [DJ]	Special Jimmy Buffett Sampler	1978	$25
❑ AK-1008	You Had to Be There	1978	$18

ABC DUNHILL
❑ DSD-50183	A1A	1975	$18
❑ DSX-50150	A White Sport Coat and a Pink Crustaceon	1974	$18
❑ DSD-50132	Living and Dying in 3/4 Time	1973	$18

BARNABY
❑ Z30093	Down to Earth	1970	$150
❑ BR-6014	High Cumberland Jubilee	1975	$40

MCA
❑ 37027	A1A	1981	$10
❑ 37026	A White Sport Coat and a Pink Crustaceon	1981	$10
❑ 37150	Changes in Latitudes, Changes in Attitudes	1982	$10
❑ 5169	Coconut Telegraph	1981	$12
❑ 5730	Floridays	1986	$12
❑ 37023	Havana Daydreamin'	1981	$10
❑ 42093	Hot Water	1988	$12
❑ 5600	Last Mango in Paris	1985	$12
❑ 37025	Living and Dying in 3/4 Time	1981	$10
❑ 6314	Off to See the Lizard	1989	$12
❑ 5447	One Particular Harbour	1983	$12
❑ 5512	Riddles in the Sand	1984	$12
❑ 5285	Somewhere Over China	1982	$12
❑ 37246	Somewhere Over China	1984	$10
❑ 5633	Songs You Know By Heart – Jimmy Buffett's Greatest Hit(s)	1985	$12
❑ 37024	Son of a Son of a Sailor	1981	$10
❑ 5102	Volcano	1979	$12
❑ 37156	Volcano	1982	$10
❑ 2-6005	You Had to Be There	1981	$12

BUG ALLEY
P.M.
❑ PMR-019	Bug Alley	1980	$35

BUGALOOS, THE
CAPITOL
❑ SW-621	The Bugaloos	1970	$30

BUGGLES, THE
CARRERE
❑ ARZ37926	Adventures in Modern Recording	1982	$18

ISLAND
❑ ILPS9585	The Age of Plastic	1980	$18
❑ 90090	The Age of Plastic	1983	$12
—Reissue			

BUGGS, THE
CORONET
❑ CX-212 [M]	The Beatle Beat	1964	$25
❑ CXS-212 [R]	The Beatle Beat	1964	$15

Number	Title	Yr	NM

BUGNON, ALEX
ORPHEUS
❑ D1-75615	Head Over Heels	1990	$18
❑ D1-75602	Love Season	1989	$12

BUILT TO SPILL
UP
❑ 018 [10]	Built to Spill Caustic Resin	1995	$10
—Four-track 10-inch EP with Caustic Resin			
❑ 069	Keep It Like a Secret	1999	$12
❑ 083	Live	2000	$15
❑ 033	Perfect from Now On	1997	$15
❑ 006	There's Nothing Wrong with Love	1995	$12

BULLDOG
BUDDAH
❑ BDS-5600	Smasher	1974	$18

DECCA
❑ DL75370	Bulldog	1972	$25

BULLETBOYS
WARNER BROS.
❑ 25782	Bulletboys	1988	$10
❑ R134757	Freakshow	1991	$25
—BMG Direct Marketing version; not issued on vinyl to stores			

BUMBLE BEE UNLIMITED
RCA VICTOR
❑ AFL1-3407	Sting Like a Bee	1979	$30

BUNCH, JOHN
AUDIOPHILE
❑ AP-184	Jubilee	1982	$25

CHIAROSCURO
❑ 144	John Bunch Plays Music of Kurt Weill	1975	$30

CONCORD JAZZ
❑ CJ-328	The Best Thing for You	1987	$25

FAMOUS DOOR
❑ 107	John's Bunch	1976	$30
❑ 114	John's Other Bunch	1977	$30
❑ 118	Slick Funk	1978	$30

BUNCH, THE
A&M
❑ SP-4354	The Bunch	1973	$30

BUNKER, LARRY
VAULT
❑ LP-9005 [M]	Live at Shelly's Manne-Hole	1966	$25
❑ LPS-9005 [S]	Live at Shelly's Manne-Hole	1966	$35

BUNKERS, THE
RCA VICTOR
❑ APL1-0102	Archie and Edith Side by Side	1973	$25

BUONO, VICTOR
DORE
❑ 325	Heavy!	1971	$18

BUOYS, THE
SCEPTER
❑ SPS-593	Timothy	1971	$30

BURCH, VERNON
CHOCOLATE CITY
❑ CCLP-2009	Get Up	1979	$18
❑ CCLP-2005	Love-a-Thon	1978	$18
❑ CCLP-2014	Steppin' Out	1980	$18

COLUMBIA
❑ PC34701	When I Get Back Home	1977	$18

SRI
❑ SW-70005	Playing Hard to Get	1982	$15

UNITED ARTISTS
❑ UA-LA342-G	I'll Be Your Sunshine	1975	$18

BURDON, ERIC, AND THE ANIMALS
SUNDAZED
❑ LP5488 [B]	The Twain Shall Meet	2015	$25

BURDON, ERIC, AND WAR
ABC
❑ D-988	Love Is All Around	1976	$15
—As "War Featuring Eric Burdon"			

LAX
❑ PW37109	Spill the Wine	1981	$12
—Reissue of MGM 4663 with new title			

MGM
❑ SE-4663	Eric Burdon Declares "War	1970	$18
❑ SE-4710-2	The Black Man's Burdon	1970	$25
—Add 50% if the package includes an "Official War Bond," entitling the bearer to $1 off any Eric Burdon and War concert before December 31, 1973			

BURDON, ERIC
CAPITOL
❑ S?A?11426	Stop	1975	$25
—Cover shaped like a hexagon			
❑ ST-11426	Stop	1975	$15
—Regular square cover			
❑ ST-11359	Sun Secrets	1974	$15

GNP CRESCENDO
❑ GNPS-2194	Wicked Man	1988	$12

LAX
❑ PW37110	Sun Secrets	1981	$12
—Reissue of Capitol 11359			

STRIPED HORSE
❑ SHL2006	I Used to Be an Animal	1988	$12

BURGER, JACK
HIFI
❑ R-803 [M]	Let's Play Bongos!	1957	$40
❑ R-809 [M]	Let's Play Congas	1958	$30
❑ RS-809 [S]	Let's Play Congas	1959	$40
❑ R-804 [M]	The End on Bongos!	1957	$40

BURGESS, WILMA
DECCA
❑ DL4788 [M]	Don't Touch Me	1966	$18
❑ DL74788 [S]	Don't Touch Me	1966	$25
❑ DL75090	Parting Is Such Sweet Sorrow	1968	$25
❑ DL4935 [M]	Tear Time	1967	$30
❑ DL74935 [S]	Tear Time	1967	$25
❑ DL75024	The Tender Lovin' Country Sound	1968	$25
❑ DL4852 [M]	Wilma Burgess Sings Misty Blue	1967	$18
❑ DL74852 [S]	Wilma Burgess Sings Misty Blue	1967	$25

BURGHOFF, GARY
SHALOM
❑ 651	Gary Burghoff and His Mardi Gras Celebration Band	1983	$40

BURKE, CHRIS, AND HIS NEW ORLEANS MUSIC
GHB
❑ 175	True to New Orleans	1985	$25

BURKE, RAY
NEW ORLEANS
❑ 7202	Speakeasy Boys (1937-49)	198?	$25

SOUTHLAND
❑ SLP-209 [10]	Contemporary New Orleans Jazz	1955	$250

BURKE, SOLOMON
ABC DUNHILL
❑ DSX-50161	I Have a Dream	1974	$15

AMHERST
❑ AMH-1018	Please Don't You Say Goodbye to Me	1978	$15

APOLLO
❑ ALP-498 [M]	Solomon Burke	1962	$500

ATLANTIC
❑ 8085 [M]	If You Need Me	1963	$50
❑ SD8085 [S]	If You Need Me	1963	$100
❑ SD8185	I Wish I Knew	1968	$30
❑ SD8158	King Solomon	1968	$30
❑ 8096 [M]	Rock N' Soul	1964	$50
❑ SD8096 [S]	Rock N' Soul	1964	$100
❑ 8067 [M]	Solomon Burke's Greatest Hits	1962	$50
❑ SD8067 [S]	Solomon Burke's Greatest Hits	1962	$100
❑ 8109 [M]	The Best of Solomon Burke	1965	$30
❑ SD8109 [S]	The Best of Solomon Burke	1965	$40

BELL
❑ 6033	Proud Mary	1969	$25

CHESS
❑ CH-19002	Back to My Roots	1976	$15
❑ CH-60042	Music to Make Love By	1975	$15

CLARION
❑ 607 [M]	I Almost Lost My Mind	1966	$25
❑ SD607 [S]	I Almost Lost My Mind	1966	$30

DBK WORKS
❑ 104	Don't Give Up on Me	2003	$25

INFINITY
❑ INF-9024	Sidewalks, Fences and Walls	1979	$15

Number	Title	Yr	NM
KENWOOD			
❏ LP-498 [M]	Solomon Burke	1964	$250
— Reissue of Apollo 498			
MGM			
❏ SE-4767	Electronic Magnetism	1971	$18
❏ SE-4830	King Heavy	1972	$18
PRIDE			
❏ 0011	The History of Solomon Burke	1972	$18
ROUNDER			
❏ 2053	A Change Is Gonna Come	1986	$12
❏ 2042/3	Soul Alive!	1984	$15
SAVOY			
❏ 14679	Into My Life	1982	$12
❏ 14660	Solomon Burke	1981	$12
❏ 14717	Take Me, Shake Me	1983	$12

BURKE, VINNIE
Number	Title	Yr	NM
ABC-PARAMOUNT			
❏ ABC-139 [M]	The Vinnie Burke All Stars	1956	$50
❏ ABC-170 [M]	The Vinnie Burke String Jazz Quartet	1957	$50
BETHLEHEM			
❏ BCP-1010 [10]	East Coast Jazz 2	1954	$300

BURNETT, CARL
Number	Title	Yr	NM
DISCOVERY			
❏ 819	Carl Burnett Plays the Music of Richard Rodgers	198?	$25

BURNETT, CAROL
Number	Title	Yr	NM
DECCA			
❏ DL4049 [M]	Carol Burnett Remembers How They Stopped the Show	1960	$30
❏ DL74049 [S]	Carol Burnett Remembers How They Stopped the Show	1960	$40
❏ DL4437 [M]	Let Me Entertain You	1964	$25
❏ DL74437 [S]	Let Me Entertain You	1964	$30
RCA VICTOR			
❏ LPM-3839 [M]	Carol Burnett Sings	1967	$25
❏ LSP-3839 [S]	Carol Burnett Sings	1967	$25

BURNETT, T-BONE
Number	Title	Yr	NM
COLUMBIA			
❏ BFC40792	Talking Animals	1988	$12
MCA			
❏ 5809	T-Bone Burnett	1986	$10
TAKOMA			
❏ 7080	Truth Decay	1980	$15
UNI			
❏ 73125	The B-52 Band and the Fabulous Skyhawks	1972	$30
— As "J. Henry Burnett"			
WARNER BROS.			

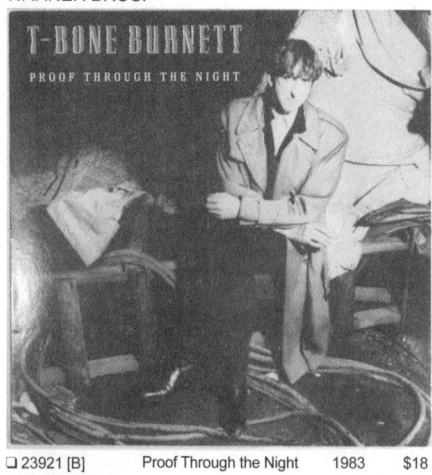

Number	Title	Yr	NM
❏ 23921 [B]	Proof Through the Night	1983	$18
— Quiex II vinyl promo			
❏ 23691	Trap Door	1982	$12

BURNETTE, BILLY
Number	Title	Yr	NM
COLUMBIA			
❏ JC36792	Billy Burnette	1980	$12
❏ FC37460	Gimme You	1981	$12
ENTRANCE			
❏ Z31228	Billy Burnette	1972	$25
MCA CURB			
❏ 5604	Try Me	1985	$12

Number	Title	Yr	NM
POLYDOR			
❏ PD-1-6187	Billy Burnette	1979	$12

BURNETTE, BILLY JOE
Number	Title	Yr	NM
GUSTO			
❏ 994	Welcome Home, Elvis	1977	$18

BURNETTE, DORSEY
Number	Title	Yr	NM
CALLIOPE			
❏ CAL7006	Things I Treasure	1977	$15
CAPITOL			
❏ ST-11219	Dorsey Burnette	1973	$18
❏ ST-11094	Here and Now	1972	$18
DOT			
❏ DLP-3456 [M]	Dorsey Burnette Sings	1963	$40
❏ DLP-25456 [S]	Dorsey Burnette Sings	1963	$50
ERA			
❏ ES-800 [M]	Dorsey Burnette's Greatest Hits	1969	$30
❏ EL-102 [M]	Tall Oak Tree	1960	$175
❏ ES-102 [S]	Tall Oak Tree	1960	$300
GUSTO			
❏ 0050	The Golden Hits of Dorsey Burnette	197?	$15

BURNETTE, DORSEY AND JOHNNY
Number	Title	Yr	NM
SOLID SMOKE			
❏ SS-8005	Together Again	1978	$18

BURNETTE, JOHNNY
Number	Title	Yr	NM
CORAL			
❏ CRL57080 [M]	Johnny Burnette & the Rock 'N' Roll Trio	1956	$6000
— Originals have maroon labels, machine-stamped (not engraved) numbers in the dead wax, printing on jacket's spine and "Printed in U.S.A." in lower right of back cover; VG value 2000; VG+ value 4000			
LIBERTY			
❏ LRP-3179 [M]	Dreamin'	1960	$40
❏ LST-7179 [S]	Dreamin'	1960	$75
❏ LRP-3183 [M]	Johnny Burnette	1961	$40
❏ LST-7183 [S]	Johnny Burnette	1961	$75
❏ LRP-3206 [M]	Johnny Burnette's Hits and Other Favorites	1962	$40
❏ LST-7206 [S]	Johnny Burnette's Hits and Other Favorites	1962	$50
❏ LRP-3190 [M]	Johnny Burnette Sings	1961	$40
❏ LST-7190 [S]	Johnny Burnette Sings	1961	$75
❏ LRP-3255 [M]	Roses Are Red	1962	$40
❏ LST-7255 [S]	Roses Are Red	1962	$50
❏ LRP-3389 [M]	The Johnny Burnette Story	1964	$40
❏ LST-7389 [S]	The Johnny Burnette Story	1964	$50
MCA			
❏ 1513	Listen to Johnny Burnette and the Rock 'N' Roll Trio	1982	$12
SOLID SMOKE			
❏ SS-8001	Tear It Up	1978	$30
— Blue vinyl			
❏ SS-8001	Tear It Up	1978	$18
— Black viinyl			
SUNSET			
❏ SUM-1179 [M]	Dreamin'	1967	$18
❏ SUS-5179 [S]	Dreamin'	1967	$25
UNITED ARTISTS			
❏ UA-LA432-G	The Very Best of Johnny Burnette	1975	$12

BURNETTE, ROCKY
Number	Title	Yr	NM
EMI AMERICA			
❏ SW-17033	The Son of Rock and Roll	1980	$12
THE GOODS			
❏ 0(# unknown)	Heart Stopper	1982	$18

BURNETTE, SMILEY
Number	Title	Yr	NM
CRICKET			
❏ CR-11 [M]	Rodeo Songaree	1959	$30
STARDAY			
❏ SLP-191 [M]	Ole Frog	1962	$40

BURNING SENSATIONS
Number	Title	Yr	NM
CAPITOL			
❏ DLP-15009 [EP]	Burning Sensations	1983	$12
❏ ST-12300	Burning Sensations	1983	$15

BURNS, DAVE
Number	Title	Yr	NM
VANGUARD			
❏ 9111 [B]	Dave Burns	1962	$300
❏ VR9143 [M]	Warming Up	1964	$300

BURNS, GEORGE
Number	Title	Yr	NM
BUDDAH			
❏ BDS-5127	A Musical Trip with George Burns	1972	$15
— Reissue of 5027			

Number	Title	Yr	NM
❏ BDS-5025	George Burns Sings	1969	$18
MERCURY			
❏ SRM-1-6001	George Burns in Nashville	1981	$12
❏ SRM-1-5025	I Wish I Was Eighteen Again	1980	$12
❏ SRM-1-4061	Young at Heart	1982	$12
PRIDE			
❏ PRD-0011	An Evening with George Burns	1974	$25

BURNS, RALPH
Number	Title	Yr	NM
BETHLEHEM			
❏ BCP-68 [M]	Bijou	1957	$300
CLEF			
❏ MGC-115 [10]	Free Forms	1953	$300
DECCA			
❏ DL8235 [M]	Jazz Studio 5	1956	$175
❏ DL9068 [M]	New York's a Song	1959	$100
❏ DL79068 [S]	New York's a Song	1959	$100
❏ DL9215 [M]	Porgy and Bess	1959	$100
❏ DL79215 [S]	Porgy and Bess	1959	$100
❏ DL8555 [M]	The Masters Revisited	1957	$120
❏ DL9207 [M]	Very Warm for Jazz	1959	$100
❏ DL79207 [S]	Very Warm for Jazz	1959	$150
EPIC			
❏ LN24015 [M]	Swingin' Down the Lane	1962	$75
❏ BN26015 [S]	Swingin' Down the Lane	1962	$100
JAZZTONE			
❏ J-1228 [M]	Spring Sequence	1956	$50
MERCURY			
❏ MGC-115 [10]	Free Forms	1952	$300
MGM			
❏ E-3616 [M]	The Swinging Seasons	1958	$50
❏ SE-3616 [S]	The Swinging Seasons	1959	$40
NORGRAN			
❏ MGN-1028 [M]	Ralph Burns Among the JATP's	1955	$120
PERIOD			
❏ SPL-1109 [10]	Bijou	1955	$120
❏ SPL-1105 [10]	Spring Sequence	1955	$120
VERVE			
❏ MGV-8121 [M]	Ralph Burns Among the JATP's	1957	$150
❏ V-8121 [M]	Ralph Burns Among the JATP's	1961	$25
WARWICK			
❏ W-5001 [M]	Where There's Burns There's Fire	1961	$150
❏ W-5001ST [S]	Where There's Burns There's Fire	1961	$140

BURNS, RALPH/BILLIE HOLIDAY
Number	Title	Yr	NM
CLEF			
❏ MGC-718 [M]	The Free Forms of Ralph Burns/The Songs of Billie Holiday	1956	$300
VERVE			
❏ MGV-8098 [M]	Jazz Recital	1957	$175
❏ V-8098 [M]	Jazz Recital	1961	$25

BURNS, RANDY
Number	Title	Yr	NM
ESP-DISK'			
❏ 1089	Evening of the Magician	1968	$175
❏ 2007	Song for an Uncertain Lady	1971	$50
❏ 1039	Songs of Love and War	1966	$150
MERCURY			
❏ SR-61329	Randy Burns and the Skydog Band	1971	$30
POLYDOR			
❏ PD-5030	I'm a Lover, Not a Fool	1972	$15
❏ PD-5049	Still On Our Feet	1973	$15

BURNS, RON
Number	Title	Yr	NM
ROULETTE			
❏ R-52095 [M]	Skin Burns	1963	$25
❏ SR-52095 [S]	Skin Burns	1963	$30

BURNSIDE, R.L.
Number	Title	Yr	NM
FAT POSSUM			
❏ 80301-1 [B]	Mr Wizard	1997	$18
❏ 80307-1 [B]	Too Bad Jim	1994	$18

BURNT SUITE
Number	Title	Yr	NM
B.J.W.			
❏ 9	Burnt Suite	1972	$250

BURRELL, DAVE
Number	Title	Yr	NM
ARISTA FREEDOM			
❏ AL1906	High Won/High Two	1975	$35
DOUGLAS			
❏ SD798	High	1969	$25
HAT ART			
❏ 2025	Windward Passages	1987	$35
— Reissue of Hat Hut 05			

Number	Title	Yr	NM
HAT HUT			
❏ 05	Windward Passages	1979	$50
BURRELL, KENNY, AND GROVER WASHINGTON. JR.			
BLUE NOTE			
❏ BT-85106	Togethering	1985	$25
BURRELL, KENNY, AND JIMMY RANEY			
PRESTIGE			
❏ PRLP-7119 [M]	Two Guitars	1957	$300
BURRELL, KENNY, AND JOHN COLTRANE			
FANTASY			
❏ OJC-300	Kenny Burrell and John Coltrane	1987	$25
❏ OJC-079	The Cats	198?	$25
— Reissue of New Jazz 8217			
NEW JAZZ			
❏ NJLP-8276 [M]	Kenny Burrell with John Coltrane	1962	$250
— Purple label			
❏ NJLP-8276 [M]	Kenny Burrell with John Coltrane	1965	$175
— Blue label with trident logo			
❏ NJLP-8217 [M]	The Cats	1959	$1500
— Purple label			
❏ NJLP-8217 [M]	The Cats	1965	$175
— Blue label with trident logo			
PRESTIGE			
❏ 24059	Kenny Burrell & John Coltrane	197?	$35
— Reissue of New Jazz and Prestige LPs in one package			
❏ PRLP-7532 [M]	Kenny Burrell Quintet with John Coltrane	1967	$75
❏ PRST-7532 [S]	Kenny Burrell Quintet with John Coltrane	1967	$50
BURRELL, KENNY; TINY GRIMES; BILL JENNINGS			
STATUS			
❏ ST-8318 [M]	Guitar Soul	1965	$40
BURRELL, KENNY			
ARGO			
❏ LP-655 [M]	A Night at the Vanguard	1959	$150
❏ LPS-655 [S]	A Night at the Vanguard	1959	$120
BLUE NOTE			
❏ BLP-1596 [M]	Blue Lights, Volume 1	1958	$800
— Deep groove" version (deep indentation under label on both sides). Andy Warhol cover.			
❏ BST-1596 [S]	Blue Lights, Volume 1	1959	$400
— Deep groove" version (deep indentation under label on both sides).			
❏ BLP-1596 [M]	Blue Lights, Volume 1	1958	$300
— Regular version, W. 63rd St., NYC address on label			
❏ BST-1596 [S]	Blue Lights, Volume 1	1959	$140
— Regular version, W. 63rd St., NYC address on label			
❏ BLP-1596 [M]	Blue Lights, Volume 1	1963	$150
— New York, USA address on label			
❏ BST-1596 [S]	Blue Lights, Volume 1	1963	$75
— New York, USA address on label			
❏ BST-81596 [S]	Blue Lights, Volume 1	1967	$35
— A Division of Liberty Records" on label			
❏ BLP-1597 [M]	Blue Lights, Volume 2	1958	$750
— Deep groove" version (deep indentation under label on both sides). Andy Warhol cover.			
❏ BST-1597 [S]	Blue Lights, Volume 2	1959	$400
— Deep groove" version (deep indentation under label on both sides).			
❏ BLP-1597 [M]	Blue Lights, Volume 2	1958	$140
— Regular version, W. 63rd St., NYC address on label			
❏ BST-1597 [S]	Blue Lights, Volume 2	1959	$140
— Regular version, W. 63rd St., NYC address on label			
❏ BLP-1597 [M]	Blue Lights, Volume 2	1963	$150
— New York, USA address on label			
❏ BST-1597 [S]	Blue Lights, Volume 2	1963	$75
— New York, USA address on label			
❏ BST-81597 [S]	Blue Lights, Volume 2	1967	$35
— A Division of Liberty Records" on label			
❏ B1-85137	Generation	1987	$25
❏ BLP-1523 [M]	Introducing Kenny Burrell	1956	$500
— Deep groove" version (deep indentation under label on both sides).			
❏ BLP-1523 [M]	Introducing Kenny Burrell	1956	$1500
— Regular version, Lexington Ave. address on label			
❏ BLP-1523 [M]	Introducing Kenny Burrell	1957	$800
— W. 63rd St., NYC address on label			
❏ BLP-1523 [M]	Introducing Kenny Burrell	1963	$250
— New York, USA address on label			
❏ BST-81523 [R]	Introducing Kenny Burrell	1967	$30
— A Division of Liberty Records" on label			
❏ BLP-1543 [M]	Kenny Burrell, Volume 2	1957	$1500
— Deep groove" version (deep indentation under label on both			

Number	Title	Yr	NM
sides). Andy Warhol cover.			
❏ BLP-1543 [M]	Kenny Burrell, Volume 2	1957	$1000
— Regular version, Lexington Ave. address on label. Andy Warhol cover.			
❏ BLP-1543 [M]	Kenny Burrell, Volume 2	1957	$800
— W. 63rd St., NYC address on label. Andy Warhol cover.			
❏ BLP-1543 [M]	Kenny Burrell, Volume 2	1963	$400
— New York, USA address on label. Andy Warhol cover.			
❏ BST-81543 [R]	Kenny Burrell, Volume 2	1967	$30
— A Division of Liberty Records" on label			
❏ BLP-4123 [M]	Midnight Blue	1963	$150
— New York, USA address on label			
❏ BST-84123 [S]	Midnight Blue	1963	$40
— New York, USA address on label			
❏ BST-84123 [S]	Midnight Blue	1967	$35
— A Division of Liberty Records" on label			
❏ BST-84123	Midnight Blue	1985	$25
— The Finest in Jazz Since 1939" reissue			
❏ BLP-4021 [M]	On View at the Five Spot Café	1960	$250
— Deep groove" version (deep indentation under label on both sides)			
❏ BLP-4021 [M]	On View at the Five Spot Café	1960	$140
— Regular version, W. 63rd St., NYC address on label			
❏ BST-84021 [S]	On View at the Five Spot Café	1960	$120
— W. 63rd St., NYC address on label			
❏ BLP-4021 [M]	On View at the Five Spot Café	1963	$150
— New York, USA address on label			
❏ BST-84021 [S]	On View at the Five Spot Café	1963	$75
— New York, USA address on label			
❏ BST-84021 [S]	On View at the Five Spot Café	1967	$35
— A Division of Liberty Records" on label			
❏ B1-90260	Pieces of Blue and the Blues	1988	$25
CADET			
❏ LP-779 [M]	Have Yourself a Soulful Little Christmas	1966	$35
❏ LPS-779 [S]	Have Yourself a Soulful Little Christmas	1966	$50
❏ LP-769 [M]	Men at Work	1965	$35
— Reissue of Argo 655			
❏ LPS-769 [S]	Men at Work	1965	$50
— Reissue of Argo 655			
❏ LP-798 [M]	Ode to 52nd Street	1967	$50
❏ LPS-798 [S]	Ode to 52nd Street	1967	$35
❏ LP-772 [M]	The Tender Gender	1966	$35
❏ LPS-772 [S]	The Tender Gender	1966	$50
CHESS			
❏ CH-9316	A Night at the Vanguard	1990	$30
— Reissue of Argo 655			
❏ CH-60019	Cool Cookin'	1973	$35
❏ CH2-92509	Recapitulation	198?	$30
COLUMBIA			
❏ CL1703 [M]	Weaver of Dreams	1961	$50
❏ CS8503 [S]	Weaver of Dreams	1961	$75
CONCORD JAZZ			
❏ CJ-121	Moon and Sand	1980	$25
❏ CJ-45	Tin Tin Deo	1978	$25
❏ CJ-83	When Lights Are Low	1978	$25
CONTEMPORARY			
❏ C-14058	Guiding Spirit	1990	$30
CTI			
❏ 6011	God Bless the Child	1970	$30
DENON			
❏ 7533	Lush Life	1979	$35
❏ 7541	'Round Midnight	1979	$35
FANTASY			
❏ OJC-456	All Day Long	1990	$30
❏ OJC-427	All Night Long	1990	$30
❏ F-9427	Both Feet on the Ground	1973	$30
❏ 79005	Ellington Is Forever	1975	$35
❏ 79008	Ellington Is Forever, Vol. 2	197?	$35
❏ MPF-4506	For Duke	1981	$25
❏ OJC-019	Kenny Burrell	198?	$25
— Reissue of Prestige 7088			
❏ F-9417	'Round Midnight	1972	$30
❏ F-9514	Sky Street	1975	$30
❏ F-9558	Stormy Monday	1978	$30
❏ OJC-216	Two Guitars	198?	$25
❏ F-9458	Up the Street	1974	$30
KAPP			
❏ KL-1326 [M]	Lotta Bossa Nova	1962	$50
❏ KS-3326 [S]	Lotta Bossa Nova	1962	$75
MOODSVILLE			
❏ MVLP-29 [M]	Bluesy Burrell	1963	$40
— Green label			
❏ MVST-29 [S]	Bluesy Burrell	1963	$40
— Green label			
❏ MVLP-29 [M]	Bluesy Burrell	1965	$50
— Blue label with trident logo			
❏ MVST-29 [S]	Bluesy Burrell	1965	$75
— Blue label with trident logo			

Number	Title	Yr	NM
MUSE			
❏ 5317	A La Carte	1984	$25
❏ 5281	Groovin' High	1983	$25
❏ 5144	Handcrafted	1979	$25
❏ 5241	Kenny Burrell in New York	1982	$25
❏ 5264	Listen to the Dawn	1982	$25
❏ 5216	Live at the Village Vanguard	1979	$25
PAUSA			
❏ 9000	Midnight	198?	$25
PRESTIGE			
❏ 24025	All Day Long & All Night Long	197?	$35
— Reissue of both albums in one package			
❏ PRLP-7081 [M]	All Day Long	1957	$400
— Actually an all-star session; reissued as a Kenny Burrell album, thus it is listed here			
❏ PRLP-7277 [M]	All Day Long	1963	$150
— Reissue of 7081			
❏ PRST-7277 [R]	All Day Long	1963	$50
❏ PRLP-7073 [M]	All Night Long	1957	$300
— Actually an all-star session; reissued as a Kenny Burrell album, thus it is listed here			
❏ PRLP-7289 [M]	All Night Long	1964	$150
— Reissue of 7073			
❏ PRST-7289 [R]	All Night Long	1964	$50
❏ PRLP-7308 [M]	Blue Moods	1964	$75
— Reissue of 7088			
❏ PRST-7308 [R]	Blue Moods	1964	$50
❏ PRLP-7347 [M]	Crash	1964	$75
❏ PRST-7347 [S]	Crash	1964	$50
❏ PRLP-7088 [M]	Kenny Burrell	1957	$300
❏ PRST-7578	Out of This World	1968	$35
— Reissue of Moodsville 29			
❏ PRLP-7315 [M]	Soul Call	1964	$75
❏ PRST-7315 [S]	Soul Call	1964	$75
❏ PRLP-7448 [M]	The Best of Kenny Burrell	1967	$75
❏ PRST-7448 [S]	The Best of Kenny Burrell	1967	$50
SAVOY JAZZ			
❏ SJL-1120	Monday Stroll	1978	$25
— Reissue			
VERVE			
❏ V-8656 [M]	A Generation Ago Today	1966	$35
❏ V6-8656 [S]	A Generation Ago Today	1966	$50
❏ V6-8773	Asphalt Canyon Suite	1969	$35
❏ V-8553 [M]	Blue Bash!	1963	$50
❏ V6-8553 [S]	Blue Bash!	1963	$75
❏ V-8746 [M]	Blues-- The Common Ground	1968	$50
❏ V6-8746 [S]	Blues-- The Common Ground	1968	$35
❏ V-8612 [M]	Guitar Forms	1965	$35
❏ V6-8612 [S]	Guitar Forms	1965	$50
❏ UMV-2070	Guitar Forms	198?	$25
— Reissue of 8612			
❏ V6-8751	Night Song	1968	$35
VOSS			
❏ VLP1-42930	Heritage	1988	$25
BURRELL			
VIRGIN			
❏ 90890	Burrell	1988	$12
BURRITO BROTHERS, THE			
See THE FLYING BURRITO BROTHERS.			
BURROUGH, ROSLYN			
SUNNYSIDE			
❏ SSC-1009	Love Is Here	1985	$25
BURROUGHS, WILLIAM			
ESP-DISK'			
❏ 1050 [M]	Call Me Burroughs	1967	$250
SUPERIOR VIADUCT			
❏ SV094 [B]	Call Me Burroughs	2016	$30
BURROWS, ABE			
COLUMBIA			
❏ CL6128 [10]	Abe Burrows Sings?	1950	$40
DECCA			
❏ DL5288 [10]	The Girl with the 3 Blue Eyes	1951	$40
BURTNICK, GLEN			
A&M			
❏ SP-5166	Heroes and Zeros	1987	$10
❏ SP-5114	Talking in Code	1986	$10
BURTON, ANN			
INNER CITY			
❏ 6026	By Myself Alone	1974	$30
BURTON, GARY, AND CHICK COREA			
ECM			
❏ 1024ST	Crystal Silence	1973	$30
— Original edition; made in Germany?			

Number	Title	Yr	NM
❏ 1140	Duet	1978	$30
❏ ECM2-1182	Gary Burton and Chick Corea In Concert	1979	$35
—Distributed by Warner Bros.			
❏ 23797	Lyric Suite for Sextet	1983	$25
—Distributed by Warner Bros.			
❏ 1260	Lyric Suite for Sextet	1983	$30
—Made in Germany			

BURTON, GARY; SONNY ROLLINS; CLARK TERRY
RCA VICTOR
Number	Title	Yr	NM
❏ LPM-2725 [M]	Three in Jazz	1963	$35
❏ LSP-2725 [S]	Three in Jazz	1963	$25

BURTON, GARY
ATLANTIC
Number	Title	Yr	NM
❏ SD1598	Alone at Last	1971	$30
❏ SD1577	Gary Burton with Keith Jarrett	1971	$30
❏ SD1560	Good Vibes	1970	$30
❏ SD1597	Paris Encounter	1972	$30
❏ SD1531	Throb	1969	$30
❏ SD 2-321	Turn of the Century	1976	$35
BLUEBIRD
| ❏ 6280-1-RB | Artist's Choice | 1987 | $25 |
ECM
❏ 1072	Dreams So Real	1976	$30
❏ 1184	Easy As Pie	1979	$30
❏ 1055	Hotel Hello	1974	$30
❏ 1092	Passengers	1977	$30
❏ 1226	Picture This	1980	$30
❏ 25024	Real Life Hits	1985	$25
❏ 1051	Ring	1975	$30
❏ 1040	Seven Songs for Quartet and Chamber Orchestra	1974	$30
❏ 1030	The New Quartet	1973	$30
❏ 1111	Times Square	1978	$30
GRP
| ❏ GR-9598 | Reunion | 1990 | $30 |
| ❏ GR-9569 | Times Like These | 1988 | $25 |
RCA CAMDEN
| ❏ ACL1-0200 | Norwegian Wood | 1973 | $25 |
RCA VICTOR
❏ LSP-3988	A Genuine Tong Funeral	1968	$35
❏ LSP-4098	Country Roads and Other Places	1969	$35
❏ LPM-3835 [M]	Duster	1967	$25
❏ LSP-3835 [S]	Duster	1967	$35
❏ LPM-3985 [M]	Gary Burton Quartet In Concert	1968	$30
❏ LSP-3985 [S]	Gary Burton Quartet In Concert	1968	$35
❏ LPM-3901 [M]	Lofty Fake Anagram	1967	$25
❏ LSP-3901 [S]	Lofty Fake Anagram	1967	$35
❏ LPM-2420 [M]	New Vibe Man in Town	1961	$25
❏ LSP-2420 [S]	New Vibe Man in Town	1961	$30
❏ LPM-2880 [M]	Something's Coming	1964	$25
❏ LSP-2880 [S]	Something's Coming	1964	$30
❏ LPM-3719 [M]	Tennessee Firebird	1966	$35
❏ LSP-3719 [S]	Tennessee Firebird	1966	$25
❏ LPM-3360 [M]	The Groovy Sound of Music	1965	$35
❏ LSP-3360 [S]	The Groovy Sound of Music	1965	$25
❏ LPM-3642 [M]	The Time Machine	1966	$35
❏ LSP-3642 [S]	The Time Machine	1966	$25
❏ LPM-2665 [M]	Who Is Gary Burton?	1963	$50
❏ LSP-2665 [S]	Who Is Gary Burton?	1963	$75

BURTON, JAMES
A&M
Number	Title	Yr	NM
❏ SP-4293	James Burton	1971	$30

BURTON, JENNY
ATLANTIC
Number	Title	Yr	NM
❏ 80122	In Black and White	1984	$10
❏ 81238	Jenny Burton	1985	$10
❏ 81690	Souvenirs	1986	$10

BURTON, JOE
ACE
Number	Title	Yr	NM
❏ LP-1002 [M]	Joe Burton Plays	1959	$0
—Canceled?			
CORAL
❏ CRL57175 [M]	Here I Am in Love Again	1958	$40
❏ CRL757175 [S]	Here I Am in Love Again	1959	$30
❏ CRL57098 [M]	Joe Burton Session	1957	$40
JODAY
| ❏ J-1000 [M] | The Subtle Sound of Joe Burton | 1963 | $35 |
| ❏ JS-1000 [S] | The Subtle Sound of Joe Burton | 1963 | $25 |
REGENT
| ❏ MG-6036 [M] | Jazz Pretty | 1957 | $50 |

BUS BOYS
ARISTA
Number	Title	Yr	NM
❏ AL9569	American Worker	1982	$15
❏ AL8-8030	American Worker	198?	$10

Number	Title	Yr	NM
—Reissue			
❏ AB4280	Minimum Wage Rock 'n' Roll	1980	$15
❏ AL5-8324	Minimum Wage Rock 'n' Roll	198?	$10
—Second reissue of 4280			
❏ AL8-8054	Minimum Wage Rock 'n' Roll	198?	$10
—First reissue of 4280			
VOSS/CHRYSALIS
| ❏ 72915 | Money Don't Make No Man | 1988 | $15 |

BUSH, CHARLIE
REVELATION
Number	Title	Yr	NM
❏ REV-33	Local Living Legend	1979	$30

BUSH, JOHNNY
HILLTOP
Number	Title	Yr	NM
❏ JS-6081	You Ought to Hear Me Cry	197?	$18
MILLION
| ❏ 1001 | The Best of Johnny Bush | 1972 | $30 |
POWER PAK
| ❏ PO-217 | Bush Country | 197? | $15 |
RCA VICTOR
❏ APL1-0216	Here Comes the World Again	1973	$18
❏ APL1-0369	Texas Dance Hall Girl	1974	$18
❏ LSP-10002	Whiskey River/There Stands the Glass	1973	$18
STOP
❏ 10014	Johnny Bush	1970	$25
❏ 10002	Sound of a Heartache	1968	$30
❏ 1028	The Greatest Hits of Johnny Bush	1972	$25
❏ 10005	Undo the Right	1968	$25
❏ 10008	You Gave Me a Mountain	1969	$25
WHISKEY RIVER
| ❏ 8024 | Live at Dance Town USA | 1979 | $18 |

BUSH, KATE
COLUMBIA
Number	Title	Yr	NM
❏ OC44164	The Sensual World	1989	$15
EMI AMERICA
❏ ST-17171 [B]	Hounds of Love	1985	$40
—Marbled vinyl			
❏ ST-17171	Hounds of Love	1985	$12
—Black vinyl			
❏ MLP-19004 [EP]	Kate Bush	1983	$18
❏ SMAS-17008	Lionheart	1978	$18
❏ ST-17115	Never for Ever	1983	$12
❏ ST-17084	The Dreaming	1982	$12
❏ SW-17003	The Kick Inside	1978	$12
—Reissue of Harvest release			
❏ PWAS-17242	The Whole Story	1986	$18
HARVEST
| ❏ SW-11761 | The Kick Inside | 1978 | $30 |
STEVE STROUT & ASSOC.
| ❏ SSA3021 | Kate Bush Radio Special: Self-Portrait | 1978 | $450 |
| —Uses The Kick Inside cover with special wrapper band | | | |

BUSH
TRAUMA
Number	Title	Yr	NM
❏ INT2-90161	Deconstructed	1997	$18
❏ INT-90091	Razorblade Suitcase	1996	$18
❏ IS-92531	Sixteen Stone	1996	$18
—Distributed by Revelation			

BUSHKIN, JOE
ATLANTIC
Number	Title	Yr	NM
❏ ALR-108 [10]	I Love a Piano	1950	$300
❏ 81621	Play It Again, Joe	1985	$25
CAPITOL
❏ T832 [M]	A Fellow Needs a Girl	1957	$75
—Turquoise or gray label			
❏ T1094 [M]	Blue Angels	1959	$40
—Black colorband label, logo at left			
❏ ST1094 [S]	Blue Angels	1959	$75
—Black colorband label, logo at left			
❏ T911 [M]	Bushkin Spotlights Berlin	1958	$75
—Turquoise or gray label			
❏ T711 [M]	Midnight Rhapsody	1956	$75
—Turquoise or gray label			
❏ T759 [M]	Skylight Rhapsody	1956	$75
—Turquoise or gray label			
COLUMBIA
❏ CL6201 [10]	After Hours	195?	$50
❏ CS9615	Doctor Dolittle	1968	$30
❏ CL6152 [10]	Piano Moods	195?	$50
DECCA
| ❏ DL4731 [M] | Night Sounds of San Francisco | 1965 | $30 |
| ❏ DL74731 [S] | Night Sounds of San Francisco | 1965 | $35 |
EPIC
| ❏ LN3345 [M] | Piano After Midnight | 1956 | $75 |

Number	Title	Yr	NM
REPRISE
| ❏ R-6119 [M] | In Concert, Town Hall | 1964 | $35 |
| ❏ RS-6119 [S] | In Concert, Town Hall | 1964 | $25 |
ROYALE
| ❏ 18118 [10] | Joe Bushkin | 195? | $50 |

BUSSE, HENRY
HINDSIGHT
Number	Title	Yr	NM
❏ HSR-122	The Uncollected Henry Busse and His Orchestra, 1935	1978	$25

BUSTA RHYMES
ELEKTRA
Number	Title	Yr	NM
❏ 62517 [B]	Anarchy	2000	$18
❏ 62211	E.L.E. (Extinction Level Event)	1998	$18
❏ 61742	The Coming	1996	$18
❏ ED6052 [DJ]	When Disaster Strikes	1997	$25
—Promo-only version			
❏ 62064	When Disaster Strikes	1997	$18
J
| ❏ 20009 [B] | Genesis | 2001 | $25 |

BUSY BEE
UNI
Number	Title	Yr	NM
❏ 2	Running Thangs	1988	$12

BUTCHER, JON, AXIS
CAPITOL
Number	Title	Yr	NM
❏ ST-12425	Along the Axis	1985	$10
❏ C1-90238	Pictures from the Front	1989	$15
❏ ST-12542	Wishes	1987	$10
POLYDOR
| ❏ 810059-1 | Jon Butcher Axis | 1983 | $12 |
| ❏ 817493-1 | Stare at the Sun | 1984 | $12 |

BUTERA, SAM, AND THE WITNESSES
CAPITOL
Number	Title	Yr	NM
❏ T1098 [M]	The Big Horn	1958	$30
❏ ST1098 [S]	The Big Horn	1959	$40
❏ T1521 [M]	The Big Sax and the Big Voice	1960	$30
❏ ST1521 [S]	The Big Sax and the Big Voice	1960	$30
DOT
❏ DLP-3381 [M]	Apache	1961	$25
❏ DLP-25381 [S]	Apache	1961	$30
❏ DLP-3272 [M]	The Wildest Clan	1960	$25
❏ DLP-25272 [S]	The Wildest Clan	1960	$30

BUTLER, ARTIE
A&M
Number	Title	Yr	NM
❏ SP-2007 [M]	Have You Met Miss Jones?	1968	$50
—Mono appears to be promo only, in stereo cover with "Monaural" sticker			
❏ SP-3007 [S]	Have You Met Miss Jones?	1968	$30

BUTLER, BILLY
FANTASY
Number	Title	Yr	NM
❏ OJC-334	Guitar Soul	1988	$30
—Reissue of Prestige 7734			
OKEH
| ❏ OKM12115 [M] | Right Track | 1966 | $50 |
| ❏ OKS14115 [S] | Right Track | 1966 | $75 |
PRESTIGE
❏ PRST-7734	Guitar Soul	1969	$30
❏ PRST-7854	Night Life	1971	$30
❏ PRST-7622	This Is Billy Butler	1968	$30
❏ PRST-7797	Yesterday, Today and Tomorrow	1970	$75

Number	Title	Yr	NM

BUTLER, CARL, AND PEARL

CHART
❏ 1051	Temptation Keeps Twistin' Her Arm	1972	$18

COLUMBIA
❏ CL2640 [M]	Avenue of Prayer	1967	$25
❏ CS9440 [S]	Avenue of Prayer	1967	$18
❏ CS1039	Carl and Pearl Butler's Greatest Hits	1970	$18
❏ CS9769	Honky Tonkin'	1969	$18
❏ CL2125 [M]	Loving Arms	1964	$25
❏ CS8925 [S]	Loving Arms	1964	$30
❏ CS9651	Our Country World	1968	$18
❏ CL2308 [M]	The Old and the New	1965	$18
❏ CS9108 [S]	The Old and the New	1965	$25

HARMONY
❏ H31182	Watch and Pray	1972	$15

BUTLER, CARL

COLUMBIA
❏ CL2002 [M]	Don't Let Me Cross Over	1963	$25
❏ CS8802 [S]	Don't Let Me Cross Over	1963	$30

HARMONY
❏ H30674	For the First Time	1971	$15
❏ HL7385 [M]	The Great Carl Butler Sings	1966	$15
❏ HS11185 [S]	The Great Carl Butler Sings	1966	$18

BUTLER, FRANK

XANADU
❏ 152	The Stepper	1977	$25
❏ 169	Wheelin' and Dealin'	1978	$25

BUTLER, FREDDIE

KAPP
❏ KS-3519	With a Dab of Soul	1968	$30

BUTLER, JERRY, AND BRENDA LEE EAGER

MERCURY
❏ SRM-1-660	The Love We Have	1973	$18

BUTLER, JERRY

ABNER
❏ R-2001 [M]	Jerry Butler, Esq.	1959	$400

BUDDAH
❏ BDS-4001	The Very Best of Jerry Butler	1969	$18

FOUNTAIN
❏ FR 2-82-1	Ice 'n Hot	1982	$12

MERCURY
❏ SR-61234	Ice On Ice	1969	$18
❏ SR-61151	Jerry Butler's Golden Hits Live	1968	$18
❏ SR-61320	Jerry Butler Sings Assorted Sounds	1971	$18
❏ MG-21146 [M]	Mr. Dream Merchant	1967	$25
❏ SR-61146 [S]	Mr. Dream Merchant	1967	$18
❏ 822212-1	Only the Strong Survive: The Great Philadelphia Hits	1984	$12
❏ SRM-1-1006	Sweet Sixteen	1974	$18
❏ SR-61281	The Best of Jerry Butler	1970	$18
❏ 810369-1	The Best of Jerry Butler	1983	$12
❏ SR-61198	The Ice Man Cometh	1968	$18
❏ SRM-1-689	The Power of Love	1973	$18
❏ SR-61347	The Sagittarius Movement	1971	$18
❏ MG-21005 [M]	The Soul Artistry of Jerry Butler	1967	$25
❏ SR-61005 [S]	The Soul Artistry of Jerry Butler	1967	$18
❏ SR-61171 [B]	The Soul Goes On	1968	$18
❏ SRM-2-7502	The Spice of Life	1972	$25
❏ SR-61269	You & Me	1970	$18

MOTOWN
❏ M6-892	It All Comes Out in My Songs	1977	$12
❏ M6-850	Love's on the Menu	1976	$15
❏ M6-878	Suite for the Single Girl	1977	$12

PHILADELPHIA INT'L.
❏ JZ35510	Nothing Says I Love You Like I Love You	1978	$12
❏ JZ36413	The Best Love I Ever Had	1979	$12

RHINO
❏ RNLP-216	The Best of Jerry Butler (1958-1969)	1984	$12

TRADITION
❏ TLP-2068	Starring Jerry Butler	1969	$18

TRIP
❏ 8011	All Time Hits	1972	$18

UNITED ARTISTS
❏ UA-LA498-E	The Very Best of Jerry Butler	1975	$12

VEE JAY
❏ LP-1038 [M]	Aware of Love	1961	$40
❏ SR-1038 [S]	Aware of Love	1961	$50
❏ LP-1057 [M]	Folk Songs	1963	$30
❏ SR-1057 [S]	Folk Songs	1963	$30
❏ LP-1075 [M]	For Your Precious Love	1963	$30
❏ SR-1075 [S]	For Your Precious Love	1963	$30
❏ LP-1076 [M]	Giving Up On Love/Need to Belong	1963	$30
❏ VJS-1076 [S]	Giving Up On Love/Need to Belong	1963	$30
❏ LP-1029 [M]	He Will Break Your Heart	1960	$100
❏ D1-74807	He Will Break Your Heart	1989	$15
❏ LP-1027 [M]	Jerry Butler, Esquire	1960	$175

—Reissue of Abner 2001
❏ VJLP2-1003	Jerry Butler Gold	198?	$18
❏ LP-1034 [M]	Love Me	1961	$50

—Reissue of 1027
❏ LP-1046 [M]	Moon River	1962	$40
❏ SR-1046 [S]	Moon River	1962	$50
❏ VJLP-1046	Moon River	1985	$12

—Reissue of original 1046; has softer vinyl
❏ LP-1119 [M]	More of the Best of Jerry Butler	1965	$30
❏ VJS-1119 [S]	More of the Best of Jerry Butler	1965	$30
❏ LP-1048 [M]	The Best of Jerry Butler	1962	$30
❏ SR-1048 [P]	The Best of Jerry Butler	1962	$30
❏ VJLP-1048	The Best of Jerry Butler	1985	$12

—Reissue of original 1048; has softer vinyl

BUTLER, JONATHAN

JIVE
❏ 1361-1-J	Heal Our Land	1990	$15
❏ 1032-1-J	Jonathan Butler	1987	$15
❏ 1136-1-J	More Than Friends	1988	$12

JIVE/ARISTA
❏ JL8-8408	Introducing Jonathan Butler	1986	$12

BUTLER, LARRY

IMPERIAL
❏ LP-12410	A Thing Called Love	1968	$18
❏ LP-9354 [M]	Take Me	1967	$25
❏ LP-12354 [S]	Take Me	1967	$18

UNITED ARTISTS
❏ UA-LA739-G	Larry Butler and Friends	1977	$15

BUTLIN CHORAL SOCIETY, THE

RICHMOND
❏ B20028 [M]	Carol Singing at Kingsway Hall	195?	$0

BUTTERFIELD, BILLY

CAPITOL
❏ H424 [10]	Classics in Jazz	195?	$100
❏ H201 [10]	Stardusting	1950	$100

CIRCLE
❏ CLP-037	Billy Butterfield with Ted Easton's Jazz Band	1977	$35

COLUMBIA
❏ CL1514 [M]	Billy Blows His Horn	1960	$25
❏ CS8314 [S]	Billy Blows His Horn	1960	$30
❏ CL1673 [M]	The Golden Horn	1961	$25

—Red and black label with six "eye" logos
❏ CS8473 [S]	The Golden Horn	1961	$30

—Red and black label with six "eye" logos
❏ CS8473 [S]	The Golden Horn	196?	$25

—360 Sound Stereo" on label

EPIC
❏ LA16026 [M]	Billy Plays Bix	1962	$75
❏ BA17026 [S]	Billy Plays Bix	1962	$100

ESSEX
❏ 403 [M]	Billy Butterfield at Amherst	1955	$50
❏ 401 [M]	Billy Butterfield at Princeton	1955	$50
❏ 404 [M]	Billy Butterfield at Rutgers	1955	$50
❏ 402 [M]	Billy Butterfield Goes to NYU	1955	$50
❏ ESLP-111 [10]	Far Away Places	195?	$50

HINDSIGHT
❏ HSR-173	Billy Butterfield 1946	198?	$25

JAZZOLOGY
❏ J-117	Just Friends	1984	$30
❏ J-93	Watch What Happens	198?	$25

JOY
❏ JL-1003 [M]	The New Dance Sound of Billy Butterfield	196?	$40

RCA VICTOR
❏ LPM-1699 [M]	A Lovely Way to Spend an Evening	1958	$30
❏ LSP-1699 [S]	A Lovely Way to Spend an Evening	1958	$40
❏ LPM-1566 [M]	A Touch of the Blues	1958	$40
❏ LPM-1212 [M]	New York Land Dixie	1956	$40
❏ LPM-1590 [M]	Thank You for a Lovely Evening	1958	$30
❏ LPM-1441 [M]	They're Playing Our Song	1957	$40

SOMERSET
❏ P-2200 [M]	I'm In the Mood for the Magic Trumpet of Billy Butterfield and His Orchestra	196?	$35

WESTMINSTER
❏ WL-3020 [10]	Billy Butterfield	1954	$50
❏ WL-6006 [M]	Dancing for Two in Love	1955	$50

BUTTERFIELD, ERSKINE

CIRCLE
❏ CLP-062	Tuesday and Ten	198?	$25

DAVIS
❏ JD-104 [M]	Piano Cocktail	1951	$40

BUTTERFIELD, PAUL

AMHERST
❏ AMH-3305	The Legendary Paul Butterfield Rides Again	1986	$15

BEARSVILLE
❏ BR2170	It All Comes Back	1973	$15
❏ BRK6995	North-South	1978	$15
❏ BR2119	Paul Butterfield's Better Days	1973	$15
❏ BR6960	Put It In Your Ear	1976	$15

ELEKTRA
❏ EKL-315 [M]	East-West	1966	$25

—Gold label with guitar player
❏ EKL-315 [M]	East-West	1967	$18

—Brown label
❏ EKS-7315 [S]	East-West	1966	$30

—Gold label with guitar player
❏ EKS-7315 [S]	East-West	1967	$25

—Brown label
❏ EKS-7315 [S]	East-West	1969	$18

—Red label with large stylized "E
❏ EKS-7315 [S]	East-West	1971	$15

—Butterfly label
❏ 7E-2005	Golden Butter/The Best of the Paul Butterfield Blues Band	1972	$30
❏ EKS-74025	In My Own Dream	1968	$25

—Brown label
❏ EKS-74025	In My Own Dream	1969	$18

—Red label with large stylized "E
❏ EKS-74025	In My Own Dream	1971	$15

—Butterfly label
❏ EKS-74053	Keep On Moving	1969	$25

—Red label with large stylized "E
❏ EKS-74053	Keep On Moving	1971	$15

—Butterfly label
❏ EKS-75013	Sometimes I Just Feel Like Smilin'	1971	$25
❏ 7E-2001	The Butterfield Blues Band/ Live	1970	$30
❏ EKL-294 [M]	The Paul Butterfield Blues Band	1965	$25

—Gold label with guitar player
❏ EKS-7294 [S]	The Paul Butterfield Blues Band	1965	$30

—Gold label with guitar player
❏ EKL-294 [M]	The Paul Butterfield Blues Band	1966	$18

—Brown label
❏ EKS-7294 [S]	The Paul Butterfield Blues Band	1966	$25

—Brown label
❏ EKS-7294 [S]	The Paul Butterfield Blues Band	1969	$18

—Red label with large stylized "E
❏ EKS-7294 [S]	The Paul Butterfield Blues Band	1971	$15

—Butterfly label
❏ EKL-4015 [M]	The Resurrection of Pigboy Crabshaw	1967	$30
❏ EKS-74015 [S]	The Resurrection of Pigboy Crabshaw	1967	$25

—Brown label
❏ EKS-74015 [S]	The Resurrection of Pigboy Crabshaw	1969	$18

—Red label with large stylized "E
❏ EKS-74015 [S]	The Resurrection of Pigboy Crabshaw	1971	$15

—Butterfly label

RHINO
❏ RNLP-70878	It All Comes Back	1987	$10

—Reissue of Bearsville 2170
❏ RNLP-70880	North-South	1987	$10

—Reissue of Bearsville 6995
❏ RNLP-70877	Paul Butterfield's Better Days	1987	$10

—Reissue of Bearsville 2119
❏ RNLP-70879	Put It In Your Ear	1987	$10

—Reissue of Bearsville 6960

SUNDAZED
❏ LP5096	East-West	2001	$15

—Reissue on 180-gram vinyl
❏ LP5095 [S]	The Paul Butterfield Blues Band	2001	$15

—Reissue on 180-gram vinyl

BUTTHOLE SURFERS

ALTERNATIVE TENTACLES
❏ VIRUS32 [EP]	Brown Reason to Live	198?	$10

—Black vinyl
❏ VIRUS32 [EP]	Brown Reason to Live	1983	$25

Number	Title	Yr	NM
— Retitled version of debut EP with brown swirl vinyl			
❏ VIRUS32 [EP]	Butthole Surfers	1983	$30
— Original pressing of debut EP with no title			
❏ VIRUS39 [EP]	Live PCPPEP	1984	$10
CAPITOL			
❏ C1-29842 [B]	Electriclarryland	1996	$30
❏ C1-98798	Independent Worm Saloon	1993	$18
HOLLYWOOD			
❏ 41447-1	Weird Revolution	2001	$18
— Pressed in Germany for U.S. release			
LATINO BUGGERVEIL			
❏ LBV 07	Humpty Dumpty LSD	2002	$25
ROUGH TRADE			
❏ R260	Pioughd	1990	$25
TOUCH & GO			
❏ 14 [EP]	Cream Corn from the Socket of Davis	1985	$30
— Yellow vinyl in green generic sleeve with sticker			
❏ 14 [EP]	Cream Corn from the Socket of Davis	1985	$25
—Red vinyl			
❏ 14 [EP]	Cream Corn from the Socket of Davis	1985	$12
— Black vinyl			
❏ 29	Hairway to Steven	1988	$12
❏ 19	Locust Abortion Technician	1987	$12
❏ 5	Psychic...Powerless...Another Man's Sac	1985	$12
— Reissue on black vinyl			
❏ 5	Psychic...Powerless...Another Man's Sac	1985	$25
— Original on clear vinyl			
❏ 8	Rembrandt Pussyhorse	1986	$12
— Black vinyl			
❏ 8	Rembrandt Pussyhorse	1986	$40
— Red vinyl; supposedly only 100 were pressed			
❏ 50	Widowermaker!	1989	$12

BUTTS BAND

BLUE THUMB

| ❏ BTS-53 | Butts Band | 1973 | $15 |
| ❏ BTS-6018 | Hear and Now | 1975 | $15 |

BUZZCOCKS, THE

4 MEN WITH BEARDS

| ❏ 4M505LP [B] | Singles Going Steady | | $25 |

GO-KART

| ❏ GK 058 | Modern | 1999 | $12 |

I.R.S.

❏ SP-009	A Different Kind of Tension	1980	$18
— Original issue			
❏ SP-75009	A Different Kind of Tension	1981	$12
— Reissue of SP-009			
❏ -0 [DJ]	Are Everything/Strange Thing + 4	1980	$18
— Red vinyl; no cover; some come with numbered sticker			
❏ SP-70507 [EP]	Parts 1-3	1984	$12
❏ SP-70955 [DJ]	Parts 1-3	1981	$30
— Original issue; six-song promo on red vinyl in plastic cover with numbered sticker			
❏ SP-001	Singles Going Steady	1979	$18
— Original issue			
❏ SP-75001	Singles Going Steady	1981	$12
— Reissue of SP-001			

BWP

NO FACE

| ❏ C47068 | The Bytches | 1991 | $18 |

BY ALL MEANS

ISLAND

| ❏ 91319 | Beyond a Dream | 1989 | $18 |
| ❏ 90898 | By All Means | 1988 | $10 |

BYARD, JAKI, AND RAN BLAKE

SOUL NOTE

| ❏ SN-1022 | Improvisations | 198? | $30 |

BYARD, JAKI

MUSE

| ❏ 5173 | Family Man | 1978 | $35 |
| ❏ 5007 | There'll Be Some Changes Made | 1974 | $25 |

NEW JAZZ

❏ NJLP-8256 [M]	Here's Jaki	1961	$150
— Purple label			
❏ NJLP-8256 [M]	Here's Jaki	1965	$175
— Blue label with trident logo at right			
❏ NJLP-8273 [M]	Hi-Fly	1962	$175
— Purple label			
❏ NJLP-8273 [M]	Hi-Fly	1965	$175
— Blue label with trident logo at right			

Number	Title	Yr	NM
PRESTIGE			
❏ PRLP-7463 [M]	Freedom Together	1967	$40
—Blue label with trident logo at right			
❏ PRST-7463 [S]	Freedom Together	1967	$40
— Blue label with trident logo at right			
❏ PRST-7463 [S]	Freedom Together	1968	$30
— Blue label with trident logo in circle at top			
❏ 24086	Giant Steps	197?	$25
❏ PRST-7573	Jaki Byard with Strings!	1968	$30
❏ PRLP-7419 [M]	Live!	1966	$30
— Blue label with trident logo at right			
❏ PRST-7419 [S]	Live!	1966	$40
— Blue label with trident logo at right			
❏ PRST-7419 [S]	Live!	1968	$30
— Blue label with trident logo in circle at top			
❏ PRLP-7477 [M]	Live! Volume 2	1967	$40
— Blue label with trident logo at right			
❏ PRST-7477 [S]	Live! Volume 2	1967	$40
— Blue label with trident logo at right			
❏ PRST-7477 [S]	Live! Volume 2	1968	$30
— Blue label with trident logo in circle at top			
❏ PRLP-7524 [M]	On the Spot	1967	$50
— Blue label with trident logo at right			
❏ PRST-7524 [S]	On the Spot	1967	$40
— Blue label with trident logo at right			
❏ PRST-7524 [S]	On the Spot	1968	$30
— Blue label with trident logo in circle at top			
❏ PRLP-7397 [M]	Out Front	1965	$30
— Blue label with trident logo at right			
❏ PRST-7397 [S]	Out Front	1965	$40
— Blue label with trident logo at right			
❏ PRST-7397 [S]	Out Front	1968	$30
— Blue label with trident logo in circle at top			
❏ PRST-7686	Solo Piano	1969	$30
❏ PRST-7615	The Jaki Byard Experience	1969	$30
❏ PRST-7550	The Sunshine of My Soul	1968	$30
SOUL NOTE			
❏ 121125	Foolin' Myself	199?	$30
❏ SN-1075	Phantasies	1985	$30
❏ 121175	Phantasies II	199?	$30
❏ SN-1031	To Them -- To Us	198?	$30

BYAS, DON, AND BUD POWELL

COLUMBIA

| ❏ JC35755 | A Tribute to Cannonball | 1979 | $30 |

BYAS, DON

ATLANTIC

| ❏ ALR-117 [10] | Don Byas Solos | 1952 | $350 |

BATTLE

| ❏ B-6121 [M] | April in Paris | 1963 | $30 |
| ❏ BS-6121 [S] | April in Paris | 1963 | $40 |

BLACK LION

| ❏ 160 | Anthropology | 1973 | $35 |

DIAL

| ❏ LP-216 [10] | Tenor Saxophone Concerto | 1951 | $400 |

DISCOVERY

| ❏ 3022 [10] | Don Byas with Beryl Booker | 1954 | $300 |

EMARCY

| ❏ MG-26026 [10] | Don Byas Sax | 1954 | $250 |

GNP CRESCENDO

| ❏ GNP-9027 | Don Byas | 197? | $30 |

NORGRAN

| ❏ MGN-12 [10] | In France "Don Byas Et Ses Rhythmes | 1954 | $300 |

ONYX

| ❏ 208 | Midnight at Minton's | 197? | $35 |

PRESTIGE

❏ PRST-7598	Don Byas In Paris	1969	$25
❏ PRST-7692 [B]	Don Byas Meets Ben Webster	1969	$150
—aka Ben Webster Meets Don Byas			

REGENT

| ❏ MG-6044 [M] | Jazz Free and Easy | 1957 | $100 |

SAVOY

❏ MG-9007 [10]	Don Byas Sax	1952	$175
❏ MG-12203	Jazz Free and Easy	196?	$50
❏ SJL-2213	Savoy Jam Party	197?	$35
❏ MG-15043 [10]	Tenor Sax Solos	1955	$120

SEECO

| ❏ SLP-35 [10] | Don Byas Favorites | 1955 | $175 |

BYAS, DON/ BERNARD PEIFFER

CLEF

| ❏ MGC-748 [M] | Jazz from Saint-Germain Des Pres | 1956 | $0 |
| *—Canceled* | | | |

VERVE

| ❏ MGV-8119 [M] | Jazz from Saint-Germain Des Pres | 1957 | $175 |
| ❏ V-8119 [M] | Jazz from Saint-Germain Des Pres | 1961 | $25 |

Number	Title	Yr	NM
BYAS, DON/BUDDY TATE			
ALLEGRO			
❏ 1741 [M]	All Star Jazz	1956	$40
BYERS, BILLY; JOE NEWMAN; EDDIE BERT			
JAZZTONE			
❏ J-1276 [M]	East Coast Sounds	1959	$75
BYERS, BILLY			
CONCERT HALL JAZZ			
❏ 1217 [M]	Byers' Guide	1955	$100
MERCURY			
❏ PPM-2028 [M]	Impressions of Duke Ellington	196?	$25
❏ PPS-6028 [S]	Impressions of Duke Ellington	196?	$150
RCA VICTOR			
❏ LPM-1269 [M]	The Jazz Workshop	1956	$100
WING			
❏ SRW-16398 [S]	Impressions of Duke Ellington	196?	$20
BYERS, BRENDA			
MTA			
❏ 5016	Thank You for Loving Me	1969	$25
❏ 5013	The Auctioneer	1968	$25
BYRD, BILLY			
REPRISE			
❏ R-6040 [M]	Lonesome Country Songs	1962	$25
❏ R9-6040 [S]	Lonesome Country Songs	1962	$30
WARNER BROS.			
❏ W1327 [M]	I Love a Guitar	1960	$25
❏ WS1327 [S]	I Love a Guitar	1960	$30
❏ W1576 [M]	The Golden Guitar of Billy Byrd	1964	$25
❏ WS1576 [S]	The Golden Guitar of Billy Byrd	1964	$30
BYRD, BOBBY			
KING			
❏ KS-1118	I Need Help	1970	$250
BYRD, CHARLIE, AND FATHER MALCOLM BOYD			
COLUMBIA			
❏ CL2548 [M]	Are You Running With Me, Jesus?	1966	$35
❏ CS9348 [S]	Are You Running With Me, Jesus?	1966	$50
❏ CL2657 [M]	Happening Prayers for Now	1967	$35
❏ CS9457 [S]	Happening Prayers for Now	1967	$35
BYRD, CHARLIE, HERB ELLIS & BARNEY KESSEL			
CONCORD JAZZ			
❏ CJD-1002	Straight Tracks	1986	$50
—Direct-to-disc recording			
❏ C-4	The Great Guitars	197?	$30
❏ C-23	The Great Guitars	197?	$30
❏ CJ-209	The Great Guitars at Charlie's Georgetown	1982	$25
❏ CJ-131	The Great Guitars at the Winery	1981	$25
BYRD, CHARLIE			
COLUMBIA			
❏ CS9841	Aquarius	1969	$35
❏ C30380	A Stroke of Genius	1971	$30
❏ CL2504 [M]	A Touch of Gold	1966	$30
❏ CS9304 [S]	A Touch of Gold	1966	$35
❏ CL2337 [M]	Brazilian Byrd	1965	$35
— Guaranteed High Fidelity" on label			
❏ CL2337 [M]	Brazilian Byrd	1965	$30
—360 Sound Mono" on label			
❏ CS9137 [S]	Brazilian Byrd	1965	$50
— Red label, "360 Sound" in black			
❏ CS9137 [S]	Brazilian Byrd	1965	$35
— Red label, "360 Sound" in white			
❏ PC9137	Brazilian Byrd	198?	$20
— Reissue with new prefix			
❏ CS9137	Brazilian Byrd	1971	$25
— Orange label			
❏ CL2592 [M]	Byrdland	1967	$50
❏ CS9392 [S]	Byrdland	1967	$35
❏ CL2555 [M]	Christmas Carols for Solo Guitar	1966	$35
❏ CS9355 [S]	Christmas Carols for Solo Guitar	1966	$50
❏ CS9667	Delicately	1968	$35
❏ G30622	For All We Know	1971	$35
❏ CS9627 [M]	Hit Trip	1968	$75
— Special Mono Radio Station Copy" with white label			
❏ CS9627 [S]	Hit Trip	1968	$35
❏ CL2652 [M]	Hollywood Byrd	1967	$50
❏ CS9452 [S]	Hollywood Byrd	1967	$35
❏ CS9869	Let Go	1969	$35
❏ CS1053	Let It Be	1970	$30
❏ CL2692 [M]	More Brazilian Byrd	1967	$50

Number	Title	Yr	NM
❑ CS9492 [S]	More Brazilian Byrd	1967	$35
❑ C31025	Onda Nuevo	1972	$30
❑ CS9582	Sketches of Brazil (Music of Villa Lobos)	1968	$35
❑ CS9747	The Great Byrd	1968	$35
❑ CS9970	The Greatest Hits of the 60's	1970	$30
❑ CG31967	The World of Charlie Byrd	1972	$35
❑ CL2435 [M]	Travellin' Man Recorded Live	1966	$30
❑ CS9235 [S]	Travellin' Man Recorded Live	1966	$35

CONCORD JAZZ

❑ CJ-82	Blue Byrd	1979	$25
❑ CJ-304	Byrd & Brass	1986	$25
❑ CJ-252	Isn't It Romantic	1984	$25
❑ CJ-374	It's a Wonderful World	1989	$30

CONCORD PICANTE

❑ P-173	Brazilville	1981	$25
❑ P-114	Sugarloaf Suite	1980	$25

CRYSTAL CLEAR

❑ 8002	Charlie Byrd	1979	$75

—Direct-to-disc recording; plays at 45 rpm

FANTASY

❑ OJC-107	Bossa Nova Pelos Passaros	198?	$25

—Reissue of Riverside 436

❑ OJC-262	Byrd at the Gate	1987	$25

—Reissue of Riverside 9467

❑ F-9466	Byrd by the Sea	1974	$30
❑ F-9429	Crystal Silence	1973	$30
❑ F-9496	Top Hat	1975	$30

IMPROV

❑ 7116	Charlie Byrd Swings Downtown	1977	$30

MILESTONE

❑ 47049	Charlie Byrd in Greenwich Village	1978	$35
❑ 47005	Latin Byrd	1973	$35

MOBILE FIDELITY

❑ 1-515	Byrd at the Gate	1982	$150

—Audiophile vinyl

OFFBEAT

❑ OLP-3009 [M]	Blues Sonata	1960	$75
❑ OS-93009 [S]	Blues Sonata	1960	$75
❑ OJ-3007 [M]	Charlie's Choice	1960	$75
❑ OS-93007 [S]	Charlie's Choice	1960	$75
❑ OJ-3001 [M]	Jazz at the Show Boat, Volume 1	1959	$75
❑ OS-93001 [S]	Jazz at the Show Boat, Volume 1	1959	$75
❑ OJ-3005 [M]	Jazz at the Show Boat, Volume 2	1959	$75
❑ OS-93005 [S]	Jazz at the Show Boat, Volume 2	1959	$75
❑ OJ-3006 [M]	Jazz at the Show Boat, Volume 3	1959	$75
❑ OS-93006 [S]	Jazz at the Show Boat, Volume 3	1959	$75

PICKWICK

❑ SPC-3042	Byrd and the Herd	196?	$30

RIVERSIDE

❑ RM-453 [M]	Blues Sonata	1963	$175
❑ RS-9453 [S]	Blues Sonata	1963	$175
❑ 6054	Blues Sonata	197?	$25
❑ RM-436 [M]	Bossa Nova Pelos Passaros	1962	$250
❑ RS-9436 [S]	Bossa Nova Pelos Passaros	1962	$250
❑ RM-467 [M]	Byrd at the Gate	1964	$175
❑ RS-9467 [S]	Byrd at the Gate	1964	$175
❑ RM-449 [M]	Byrd in the Wind	1963	$175
❑ RS-9449 [S]	Byrd in the Wind	1963	$175
❑ RS-3044	Byrd Man with Strings	1969	$150
❑ RM-481 [M]	Byrd Song	1966	$150
❑ RS-9481 [S]	Byrd Song	1966	$25
❑ RM-448 [M]	Byrd's Word	1963	$175
❑ RS-9448 [S]	Byrd's Word	1963	$175
❑ RM-452 [M]	Charlie Byrd at the Village Vanguard	1963	$175
❑ RS-9452 [S]	Charlie Byrd at the Village Vanguard	1963	$175
❑ RM-427 [M]	Latin Impressions	1962	$175
❑ RS-9427 [S]	Latin Impressions	1962	$175
❑ RM-450 [M]	Mr. Guitar	1963	$175
❑ RS-9450 [S]	Mr. Guitar	1963	$175
❑ RM-454 [M]	Once More! Bossa Nova	1963	$175
❑ RS-9454 [S]	Once More! Bossa Nova	1963	$175
❑ RM-498 [M]	Solo Flight	1967	$150
❑ RS-9498 [S]	Solo Flight	1967	$150
❑ RM-451 [M]	The Guitar Artistry of Charlie Byrd	1963	$175
❑ RS-9451 [S]	The Guitar Artistry of Charlie Byrd	1963	$175
❑ RS-3005	The Guitar Artistry of Charlie Byrd	1968	$150

SAVOY

❑ MG-12116 [M]	Blues for Night People	1957	$40
❑ MG-12099 [M]	Jazz Recital	1957	$40

SAVOY JAZZ

❑ SJL-1131	First Flight	1980	$25
❑ SJL-1121	Midnight Guitar	1980	$25

BYRD, DONALD; HANY MOBLEY; KENNY BURRELL

STATUS

Number	Title	Yr	NM
❑ ST-8317 [M]	Donald Byrd, Hank Mobley & Kenny Burrell	1965	$40

BYRD, DONALD

AMERICAN RECORDING SOCIETY

❑ G-437 [M]	Modern Jazz	1957	$300

BLUE NOTE

❑ BLP-4124 [M]	A New Perspective	1964	$250
❑ BST-84124 [S]	A New Perspective	1964	$175

—New York, USA" address on label

❑ BST-84124 [S]	A New Perspective	1967	$75

—A Division of Liberty Records" on label

❑ BST-84124	A New Perspective	198?	$30

—The Finest in Jazz Since 1939" reissue

❑ BST-84124 [S]	A New Perspective	1973	$12

—A Division of United Artists Records Inc." on label

❑ BN-LA047-F	Black Byrd	1973	$35
❑ LO-047	Black Byrd	1981	$20

—Reissue of LA047

❑ BLP-4259 [M]	Blackjack	1967	$150
❑ BST-84259 [S]	Blackjack	1967	$50
❑ BLP-4048 [M]	Byrd in Flight	1960	$350

—Deep groove" version (deep indentation under label on both sides)

❑ BLP-4048 [M]	Byrd in Flight	1960	$175

—W. 63rd St., NYC address on label

❑ BLP-4048 [M]	Byrd in Flight	1963	$150

—New York, USA" address on label

❑ BST-84048 [S]	Byrd in Flight	1960	$120

—W. 63rd St., NYC address on label

❑ BST-84048 [S]	Byrd in Flight	1963	$75

—New York, USA" address on label

❑ BST-84048 [S]	Byrd in Flight	1967	$30

—A Division of Liberty Records" on label

❑ BLP-4019 [M]	Byrd in Hand	1959	$350

—Deep groove" version (deep indentation under label on both sides)

❑ BLP-4019 [M]	Byrd in Hand	1959	$175

—W. 63rd St., NYC address on label

❑ BLP-4019 [M]	Byrd in Hand	1963	$150

—New York, USA" address on label

❑ BST-84019 [S]	Byrd in Hand	1959	$120

—W. 63rd St., NYC address on label

❑ BST-84019 [S]	Byrd in Hand	1963	$75

—New York, USA" address on label

❑ BST-84019 [S]	Byrd in Hand	1967	$30

—A Division of Liberty Records" on label

❑ BST-84007 [S]	Byrd in Hand	1967	$30

—A Division of Liberty Records" on label

❑ BST-84019	Byrd in Hand	198?	$25

—The Finest in Jazz Since 1939" reissue

❑ BN-LA633-G	Caricatures	1976	$35
❑ LT-991	Chant	1980	$30
❑ LT-1096	Creeper	1981	$30
❑ BLP-4060 [M]	Donald Byrd at the Half Note Café, Volume 1	1961	$175

—W. 63rd St., NYC address on label

❑ BLP-4060 [M]	Donald Byrd at the Half Note Café, Volume 1	1963	$150

—New York, USA" address on label

❑ BST-84060 [S]	Donald Byrd at the Half Note Café, Volume 1	1961	$120

—W. 63rd St., NYC address on label

❑ BST-84060 [S]	Donald Byrd at the Half Note Café, Volume 1	1963	$75

—New York, USA" address on label

❑ BST-84060 [S]	Donald Byrd at the Half Note Café, Volume 1	1967	$30

—A Division of Liberty Records" on label

❑ BLP-4061 [M]	Donald Byrd at the Half Note Café, Volume 2	1961	$175

—W. 63rd St., NYC address on label

❑ BLP-4061 [M]	Donald Byrd at the Half Note Café, Volume 2	1963	$150

—New York, USA" address on label

❑ BST-84061 [S]	Donald Byrd at the Half Note Café, Volume 2	1961	$120

—W. 63rd St., NYC address on label

❑ BST-84061 [S]	Donald Byrd at the Half Note Café, Volume 2	1963	$75

—New York, USA" address on label

❑ BST-84061 [S]	Donald Byrd at the Half Note Café, Volume 2	1967	$30

—A Division of Liberty Records" on label

❑ BN-LA700-G	Donald Byrd's Best	1976	$35
❑ BST-84349	Electric	1970	$50
❑ B1-36195	Electric Byrd	1996	$35
❑ BST-84380	Ethiopian Nights	1972	$50
❑ BST-84319	Fancy Free	1969	$50
❑ B1-89796	Fancy Free	1993	$35
❑ BLP-4118 [M]	Free Form	1963	$150
❑ BST-84118 [S]	Free Form	1963	$75

—New York, USA" address on label

❑ BST-84118 [S]	Free Form	1967	$30

—A Division of Liberty Records" on label

❑ BST-84118	Free Form	1986	$25

—The Finest in Jazz Since 1939" reissue

❑ BLP-4026 [M]	Fuego	1960	$300

—Deep groove" version (deep indentation under label on both sides)

❑ BLP-4026 [M]	Fuego	1960	$175

—W. 63rd St., NYC address on label

❑ BLP-4026 [M]	Fuego	1963	$150

—New York, USA" address on label

❑ BST-84026 [S]	Fuego	1959	$120

—W. 63rd St., NYC address on label

❑ BST-84026 [S]	Fuego	1963	$75

—New York, USA" address on label

❑ BST-84026 [S]	Fuego	1967	$30

—A Division of Liberty Records" on label

❑ BLP-4188 [M]	I'm Tryin' to Get Home	1965	$150
❑ BST-84188 [S]	I'm Tryin' to Get Home	1965	$75

—New York, USA" address on label

❑ BST-84188 [S]	I'm Tryin' to Get Home	1967	$30

—A Division of Liberty Records" on label

❑ BST-84188	I'm Tryin' to Get Home	1986	$25

—The Finest in Jazz Since 1939" reissue

❑ B1-31875	Kofi	1995	$35
❑ BLP-4238 [M]	Mustang!	1966	$150
❑ BST-84238 [S]	Mustang!	1966	$75

—New York, USA" address on label

❑ BST-84238 [S]	Mustang!	1967	$30

—A Division of Liberty Records" on label

❑ BLP-4007 [M]	Off to the Races	1959	$250

—Deep groove" version (deep indentation under label on both sides)

❑ BLP-4007 [M]	Off to the Races	1959	$175

—W. 63rd St., NYC address on label

❑ BLP-4007 [M]	Off to the Races	1963	$150

—New York, USA" address on label

❑ BST-4007 [S]	Off to the Races	1959	$175

—Deep groove" version (deep indentation under label on both sides)

❑ BST-4007 [S]	Off to the Races	1959	$120

—W. 63rd St., NYC address on label

❑ BST-4007 [S]	Off to the Races	1963	$75

—New York, USA" address on label

❑ BN-LA549-G	Places and Spaces	1975	$35
❑ LW-549	Places and Spaces	1981	$20

—Reissue of LA549

❑ BLP-4101 [M]	Royal Flush	1962	$150
❑ BST-84101	Royal Flush	1962	$75

—New York, USA" address on label

❑ BST-84101 [S]	Royal Flush	1967	$30

—A Division of Liberty Records" on label

❑ BN-LA368-G	Sleeping Into Tomorrow	1975	$35

❑ BST-84292 [B]	Slow Drag	1968	$25
❑ BN-LA140-G	Street Lady	1974	$35
❑ LN-10054	Street Lady	1981	$20

—Budget-line reissue

❑ BLP-4075 [M]	The Cat Walk	1961	$175

—61st St, New York address on label

❑ BLP-4075 [M]	The Cat Walk	1963	$150

—New York, USA" address on label

❑ BST-84075 [S]	The Cat Walk	1961	$120

—61st St, New York address on label

❑ BST-84075 [S]	The Cat Walk	1963	$75

—New York, USA" address on label

❑ BST-84075 [S]	The Cat Walk	1967	$30

—A Division of Liberty Records" on label

DELMARK

❑ DS-407	First Flight	1990	$30

DISCOVERY

❑ 869	September Afternoon	198?	$25

Number	Title	Yr	NM

ELEKTRA

Number	Title	Yr	NM
❏ 6E-247	Donald Byrd and 125th St., N.Y.C.	1980	$25
❏ 5E-531	Love Byrd	1981	$25
❏ 6E-144	Thank You for F.U.M.L. (Funking Up My Life)	1978	$25
❏ 60188	Words, Sounds, Colors and Shapes	1982	$25

LANDMARK

| ❏ LLP-1523 | Getting Down to Business | 1990 | $30 |
| ❏ LLP-1516 | Harlem Blues | 1988 | $25 |

SAVOY

| ❏ MG-12032 [M] | Byrd's Word | 1956 | $200 |
| ❏ MG-12064 [M] | The Jazz Message of Donald Byrd | 1956 | $250 |

SAVOY JAZZ

| ❏ SJL-1101 | Long Green | 198? | $25 |
| ❏ SJL-1114 | Star Eyes | 198? | $25 |

TRANSITION

❏ TRLP-17 [M]	Byrd Blows on Beacon Hill	1956	$2500
❏ TRLP-5 [M]	Byrd Jazz	1956	$1400
❏ TRLP-4 [M]	Byrd's Eye View	1956	$1400

TRIP

| ❏ 5000 | Two Sides of Donald Byrd | 1974 | $35 |

VERVE

| ❏ V-8609 [M] | Up with Donald Byrd | 1965 | $50 |
| ❏ V6-8609 [S] | Up with Donald Byrd | 1965 | $75 |

BYRD, GARY

RCA VICTOR

| ❏ LSP-4657 | The Gary Byrd Experience | 1972 | $30 |

BYRD, JERRY

DECCA

❏ DL8643 [M]	Hi-Fi Guitar	1958	$40
❏ DL4078 [M]	Paradise Island	1961	$25
❏ DL74078 [S]	Paradise Island	1961	$30

MERCURY

❏ MG-20856 [M]	Blue Hawaiian Steel Guitar	1963	$30
❏ SR-60856 [S]	Blue Hawaiian Steel Guitar	1963	$40
❏ MG-25169 [10]	Byrd's Expedition	1954	$100
❏ MG-25134 [10]	Guitar Magic	1954	$100
❏ MG-20693 [M]	Hawaiian Golden Hits	1962	$30
❏ SR-60693 [S]	Hawaiian Golden Hits	1962	$40
❏ MG-25077 [10]	Nani Hawaii	1953	$100
❏ MG-20230 [M]	On the Shores of Waikiki	1960	$30
❏ SR-60230 [S]	On the Shores of Waikiki	1960	$40
❏ MG-20345 [M]	Steel Guitar Favorites	1961	$30
❏ SR-60345 [S]	Steel Guitar Favorites	1961	$40
❏ MG-20932 [M]	The Man of Steel	1964	$25
❏ SR-60932 [S]	The Man of Steel	1964	$30

MONUMENT

❏ MLP-8014 [M]	Admirable Byrd	1963	$25
❏ SLP-18014 [S]	Admirable Byrd	1963	$30
❏ MLP-8009 [M]	Byrd of Paradise	1962	$25
❏ SLP-18009 [S]	Byrd of Paradise	1962	$30
❏ MLP-4008 [M]	Memories of Maria	1962	$25
❏ SLP-14008 [S]	Memories of Maria	1962	$30

BYRD, JOE, AND THE FIELD HIPPIES

COLUMBIA MASTERWORKS

| ❏ MS7317 | The American Metaphysical Circus | 1969 | $40 |

BYRD, SENATOR ROBERT

COUNTY

| ❏ 769 | Mountain Fiddler | 1978 | $30 |

BYRDS, THE

SUNDAZED

| ❏ S189 | Lazy Days/Reputation | 2007 | $3 |

— *Outtake versions from the "Sweetheart of the Rodeo" sessions*

| ❏ S189 [PS] | Lazy Days/Reputation | 2007 | $3 |

ASYLUM

| ❏ 5058 [M] | Byrds | 1973 | $100 |

— *Mono is white label promo only; "dj copy monaural" sticker on stereo cover*

| ❏ SD5058 [S] | Byrds | 1973 | $15 |

COLUMBIA

| ❏ CS9942 [S] | Ballad of Easy Rider | 1969 | $25 |

— *Red "360 Sound" label*

| ❏ CS9942 [S] | Ballad of Easy Rider | 1971 | $12 |

— *Orange label*

| ❏ PC9942 | Ballad of Easy Rider | 1984 | $10 |

— *Reissue with new prefix*

| ❏ KC30640 | Byrdmaniax | 1971 | $15 |
| ❏ CS9755 [S] | Dr. Byrds and Mr. Hyde | 1969 | $25 |

— *Red "360 Sound" label*

| ❏ CS9755 [S] | Dr. Byrds and Mr. Hyde | 1971 | $12 |

— *Orange label*

| ❏ PC9755 [S] | Dr. Byrds and Mr. Hyde | 198? | $10 |

— *Reissue with new prefix*

❏ C31050	Farther Along	1971	$15
❏ CL2549 [M]	Fifth Dimension (5D)	1966	$30
❏ CS9349 [S]	Fifth Dimension (5D)	1966	$30

— *Red "360 Sound" label*

| ❏ CS9349 [S] | Fifth Dimension (5D) | 1971 | $12 |

— *Orange label*

| ❏ PC9349 [S] | Fifth Dimension (5D) | 198? | $10 |

— *Reissue with new prefix*

| ❏ CL2372 [M] | Mr. Tambourine Man | 1965 | $40 |

— *"Guaranteed High Fidelity" on label*

| ❏ CL2372 [M] | Mr. Tambourine Man | 1966 | $30 |

— *360 Sound Mono" on label*

| ❏ CS9172 [S] | Mr. Tambourine Man | 1965 | $40 |

— *Red label, "360 Sound" in black*

| ❏ CS9172 [S] | Mr. Tambourine Man | 1966 | $30 |

— *Red label, "360 Sound" in white*

| ❏ CS9172 [S] | Mr. Tambourine Man | 1971 | $12 |

— *Orange label*

| ❏ PC9172 [S] | Mr. Tambourine Man | 198? | $10 |

— *Reissue with new prefix*

| ❏ CG33645 | Mr. Tambourine Man/Turn! Turn! Turn! | 1976 | $18 |
| ❏ KC32183 | Preflyte | 1973 | $15 |

— *Reissue of Together LP*

| ❏ C32183 | Preflyte | 197? | $12 |

— *Reissue with new prefix*

| ❏ CS9670 [M] | Sweetheart of the Rodeo | 1968 | $250 |

— *Special Mono Radio Station Copy" with white label*

| ❏ CS9670 [M] | Sweetheart of the Rodeo | 1968 | $25 |

— *Red "360 Sound" label*

| ❏ CS9670 [S] | Sweetheart of the Rodeo | 1971 | $12 |

— *Orange label*

| ❏ PC9670 [S] | Sweetheart of the Rodeo | 198? | $10 |

— *Reissue with new prefix*

| ❏ KC31795 | The Best of the Byrds (Greatest Hits, Volume II) | 1972 | $15 |
| ❏ C31795 | The Best of the Byrds (Greatest Hits, Volume II) | 197? | $12 |

— *Reissue with new prefix*

| ❏ PC31795 | The Best of the Byrds (Greatest Hits, Volume II) | 198? | $10 |

— *Reissue with another new prefix*

| ❏ CL2716 [M] | The Byrds' Greatest Hits | 1967 | $30 |
| ❏ CS9516 [S] | The Byrds' Greatest Hits | 1967 | $25 |

— *Red "360 Sound" label*

| ❏ KCS9516 [S] | The Byrds' Greatest Hits | 1971 | $12 |

— *Orange label*

| ❏ PC9516 [S] | The Byrds' Greatest Hits | 197? | $10 |

— *Reissue with another new prefix*

| ❏ PC36293 | The Byrds Play Dylan | 1980 | $12 |
| ❏ G30127 | The Byrds (Untitled) | 1970 | $25 |

— *With "Kathleen" listed on back cover (it is not on the set)*

| ❏ G30127 | The Byrds (Untitled) | 1970 | $18 |

— *Without "Kathleen" listed on back cover*

| ❏ CL2775 [M] | The Notorious Byrd Brothers | 1968 | $175 |
| ❏ CS9575 [S] | The Notorious Byrd Brothers | 1968 | $25 |

— *Red "360 Sound" label*

| ❏ CS9575 [S] | The Notorious Byrd Brothers | 1971 | $12 |

— *Orange label*

| ❏ PC9575 [S] | The Notorious Byrd Brothers | 198? | $10 |

— *Reissue with new prefix*

| ❏ FC37335 | The Original Singles Volume 1 (1965-1967) | 1981 | $12 |
| ❏ PC37335 | The Original Singles Volume 1 (1965-1967) | 1985 | $10 |

— *Budget-line reissue*

| ❏ CL2454 [M] | Turn! Turn! Turn! | 1965 | $30 |
| ❏ CS9254 [S] | Turn! Turn! Turn! | 1965 | $30 |

— *Red "360 Sound" label*

| ❏ CS9254 [S] | Turn! Turn! Turn! | 1971 | $12 |

— *Orange label*

| ❏ PC9254 [S] | Turn! Turn! Turn! | 198? | $10 |

— *Reissue with new prefix*

| ❏ CL2642 [M] | Younger Than Yesterday | 1967 | $30 |
| ❏ CS9442 [S] | Younger Than Yesterday | 1967 | $30 |

— *Red "360 Sound" label*

| ❏ CS9442 [S] | Younger Than Yesterday | 1971 | $12 |

— *Orange label*

| ❏ PC9442 [S] | Younger Than Yesterday | 198? | $10 |

— *Reissue with new prefix*

COLUMBIA LIMITED EDITION

| ❏ LE10215 | Farther Along | 197? | $18 |

— *Reissue of 31050*

PAIR

| ❏ PDL2-1040 | The Very Best of the Byrds | 1986 | $15 |

RE-FLYTE

| ❏ MH-70318 | Never Before | 1987 | $15 |

— *Released by Muuray Hill Records via mail order*

RHINO

| ❏ R1-70244 | In the Beginning | 1988 | $12 |

SUNDAZED

| ❏ LP5059 | Fifth Dimension | 1999 | $18 |

— *Reissue on 180-gram vinyl*

| ❏ LP5199 [M] | Fifth Dimension | 2006 | $18 |

— *Reissue on 180-gram vinyl*

| ❏ LP5057 | Mr. Tambourine Man | 1999 | $18 |

— *Reissue on 180-gram vinyl*

| ❏ LP5197 [M] | Mr. Tambourine Man | 2006 | $18 |

— *Reissue on 180-gram vinyl*

❏ LP5061	Sanctuary	2000	$15
❏ LP5065	Sanctuary II	2000	$15
❏ LP5066	Sanctuary III	2001	$15
❏ LP5090	Sanctuary IV	2002	$15
❏ LP5130	The Columbia Singles '65-'67	2001	$18
❏ LP5201 [M]	The Notorious Byrd Brothers	2006	$18

— *Reissue on 180-gram vinyl*

| ❏ LP5114 | The Preflyte Sessions | 2001 | $18 |
| ❏ LP5058 | Turn! Turn! Turn! | 1999 | $18 |

— *Reissue on 180-gram vinyl*

| ❏ LP5198 [M] | Turn! Turn! Turn! | 2006 | $18 |

— *Reissue on 180-gram vinyl*

| ❏ LP5060 | Younger Than Yesterday | 1999 | $18 |

— *Reissue on 180-gram vinyl*

| ❏ LP5200 [M] | Younger Than Yesterday | 2006 | $18 |

— *Reissue on 180-gram vinyl*

TOGETHER

| ❏ ST-T-1001 | Preflyte | 1969 | $30 |

BYRNE, BOBBY; WILL BRADLEY; BUD FREEMAN

GRAND AWARD

| ❏ GA 33-313 [M] | Jazz, Dixieland-Chicago | 1955 | $50 |

BYRNE, BOBBY

COMMAND

❏ RS 33-894 [M]	1966 -- Magnificent Movie Themes	1966	$30
❏ RS894SD [S]	1966 -- Magnificent Movie Themes	1966	$35
❏ RS928SD	Sound in the 8th Dimension	1968	$100

GRAND AWARD

❏ GA 33-381 [M]	Great Song Hits of the Glenn Miller Orchestra	1958	$30
❏ GA207SD [S]	Great Song Hits of the Glenn Miller Orchestra	1958	$40
❏ GA 33-382 [M]	Great Song Hits of the Tommy and Jimmy Dorsey Orchestras	1958	$30
❏ GA206SD [S]	Great Song Hits of the Tommy and Jimmy Dorsey Orchestras	1958	$40
❏ GA 33-392 [M]	Great Themes of America's Greatest Bands	1958	$30
❏ GA225SD [S]	Great Themes of America's Greatest Bands	1959	$40
❏ GA 33-416 [M]	The Jazzbone's Connected to the Trombone	1959	$40
❏ GA248SD [S]	The Jazzbone's Connected to the Trombone	1959	$50

WALDORF MUSIC HALL

| ❏ MH 33-121 [10] | Dixieland Jazz | 195? | $50 |

BYRNE, DAVID, AND RYUICHI SAKAMOTO

VIRGIN

| ❏ 2204 [DJ] | The Making of The Last Emperor: An Interview with... | 1988 | $30 |

BYRNE, DAVID

Also see TALKING HEADS.

ECM

| ❏ 25022 | Music for The Knee Plays | 1985 | $18 |

LUAKA BOP

| ❏ 25990 | Rei Momo | 1989 | $15 |
| ❏ 26799 | Uh-Oh | 1992 | $15 |

SIRE

| ❏ SRK6093 | My Life in the Bush of Ghosts | 1981 | $30 |

— *With Brian Eno*

| ❏ SRK3645 | The Catherine Wheel | 1981 | $12 |

— *Songs and music from the Broadway play of the same name*

Number	Title	Yr	NM
VIRGIN			
PR2204 [DJ]	The Making of The Last Emperor: An Interview with David Byrne and Ryuichi Sakamoto	1988	$30

BYRNES, EDD
WARNER BROS.

Number	Title	Yr	NM
W1309 [M]	Kookie	1959	$150
WS1309 [S]	Kookie	1959	$120
W/WS1309	Kookie Bonus Photo	1959	$50

BYRON, GEORGE
ATLANTIC

Number	Title	Yr	NM
1293 [M]	Premiere Performance	1958	$300

—*Black label*

Number	Title	Yr	NM
SD1293 [S]	Premiere Performance	1958	$50

—*Green label*

C

C.A. QUINTET, THE
CANDY FLOSS

Number	Title	Yr	NM
7764	A Trip Through Hell	1969	$1500

—*VG value 500; VG+ value 1000*

SUNDAZED

Number	Title	Yr	NM
LP-5037 [B]	Trip Thru Hell	1997	$18

C.C.S.
RAK

Number	Title	Yr	NM
KZ31569	C.C.S.	1972	$25
Z30559	Whole Lotta Love	1971	$25

C.K. STRONG
EPIC

Number	Title	Yr	NM
BN26473	C.K. Strong	1969	$25

CABARET VOLTAIRE
CAROLINE

Number	Title	Yr	NM
CAROL2451 [EP]	Drinking Gasoline	1985	$18
CAROL1331	The Covenant, the Sword, and the Arm of the Lord	1985	$12
CAROL2452 [EP]	The Drain Train	1986	$25

GIANT

Number	Title	Yr	NM
GR-16009	Eight Crepuscule Tracks	1988	$18

MANHATTAN

Number	Title	Yr	NM
MLT-46999	Code	1987	$18

RESTLESS

Number	Title	Yr	NM
71475	Listen Up with Cabaret Voltaire	1990	$12
71476	The Living Legends	1990	$12

ROUGH TRADE

Number	Title	Yr	NM
ROUGH US-24	Hai! Live in Japan	1982	$25
ROUGH US-15 [B]	Red Mecca	1981	$25
ROUGH US-9 [B]	The Voice of America	1980	$30
TRADE US-12 [EP]	Three Crepuscule Tracks	1981	$25

CABLES, GEORGE
CONTEMPORARY

Number	Title	Yr	NM
C-14030	By George: The Music of George Gershwin	1987	$25
C-14001	Cables' Vision	1979	$35

—*Pianist.*

Number	Title	Yr	NM
C-14015	Circle	198?	$30
C-14014	Phantom of the City	198?	$30

CABO FRIO
ZEBRA

Number	Title	Yr	NM
ZEB-5990	Cabo Frio	198?	$25
ZR-5002	Just Having Fun	198?	$30
ZEB-5685	Right On the Money	1986	$25

CABOT, SEBASTIAN
MGM

Number	Title	Yr	NM
E-4431 [M]	Sebastian Cabot, Actor; Bob Dylan, Poet: A Dramatic Reading with Music	1967	$30
SE-4431 [S]	Sebastian Cabot, Actor; Bob Dylan, Poet: A Dramatic Reading with Music	1967	$40

CACIA, PAUL
HAPPY HOUR

Number	Title	Yr	NM
HH6001	Paul Cacia Presents The Alumni Tribute to Stan Kenton	198?	$25
HH5004	Quantum Leap	198?	$25

—*Trumpeter and bandleader.*

Number	Title	Yr	NM
OUTSTANDING			
OUTS-056	Quantum Leap	1986	$30

CACTUS
With Tim Bogert and Carmen Appice, ex-VANILLA FUDGE.
ATCO

Number	Title	Yr	NM
SD 33-340	Cactus	1970	$25
SD 33-356	One Way...Or Another	1971	$25
SD7011 [B]	'Ot 'N' Sweaty	1972	$25
SD 33-377	Restrictions	1971	$25

CLEOPATRA

Number	Title	Yr	NM
6804 [B]	Ultra Sonic Boogie 1971		$40

CADETS, THE
CROWN

Number	Title	Yr	NM
CLP-5015 [M]	Rockin' 'n' Reelin'	1957	$300

—*Black label*

Number	Title	Yr	NM
CLP-5370 [M]	The Cadets	1963	$175
CST-370 [R]	The Cadets	1963	$150

MODERN

Number	Title	Yr	NM
LPM-1215 [M]	Rockin' 'n' Reelin'	1956	$0

—*Canceled*

RELIC

Number	Title	Yr	NM
5025	The Cadets' Greatest Hits	197?	$15

CADILLACS, THE
HARLEM HIT PARADE

Number	Title	Yr	NM
5009	Cruisin' with the Cadillacs	197?	$12

JUBILEE

Number	Title	Yr	NM
JGM-1089 [M]	The Crazy Cadillacs	1959	$300

—*Flat black label*

Number	Title	Yr	NM
JGM-1089 [M]	The Crazy Cadillacs	1960	$150

—*Glossy black label*

Number	Title	Yr	NM
JGM-1045 [M]	The Fabulous Cadillacs	1957	$400

—*Blue label*

Number	Title	Yr	NM
JGM-1045 [M]	The Fabulous Cadillacs	1959	$300

—*Flat black label*

THE FABULOUS CADILLACS

Number	Title	Yr	NM
JGM-1045 [M]	The Fabulous Cadillacs	1960	$150

—*Glossy black label*

Number	Title	Yr	NM
JGM-5009 [M]	Twisting with the Cadillacs	1962	$250

MURRAY HILL

Number	Title	Yr	NM
1285	The Cadillacs	198?	$40

—*Box set*

Number	Title	Yr	NM
1195	The Very Best of the Cadillacs	198?	$18

CADILLACS, THE/ THE ORIOLES
JUBILEE

Number	Title	Yr	NM
JGM-1117 [M]	The Cadillacs Meet the Orioles	1961	$250

CAESAR, SHIRLEY
REJOICE

Number	Title	Yr	NM
WR8347	Christmasing	1986	$12

CAFÉ NOIR
GAJO

Number	Title	Yr	NM
GR-1001	Café Noir	1988	$25

CAFFERTY, JOHN, AND THE BEAVER BROWN BAND
SCOTTI BROTHERS

Number	Title	Yr	NM
BFZ38929	Eddie and the Cruisers (Soundtrack)	1983	$15

—*With original prefix*

Number	Title	Yr	NM
FZ38929	Eddie and the Cruisers (Soundtrack)	1984	$10

—*With altered prefix*

Number	Title	Yr	NM
FZ40980	Roadhouse	1988	$12
FZ39405	Tough All Over	1985	$10

CAGE, JOHN
ANGEL

Number	Title	Yr	NM
S36059 [B]	Three Dances & Four Organs	1973	$40

—*one side only. Side two features Steve Reich*

COLUMBIA MASTERWORKS

Number	Title	Yr	NM
M2S819 [B]	Music For Keyboard 1935 - 1948	1970	$50
MS7051 [B]	New Electronic Music From Leaders Of The Avant-Garde	1967	$50

—*also credits Henri Pousseur, Milton Babbitt*

COMPOSERS RECORDINGS INC

Number	Title	Yr	NM
CRISD199 [B]	Sonatas And Interludes For Prepared Piano (1946-48)	1965	$100

DIAL

Number	Title	Yr	NM
19-20 [B]	Sonatas And Interludes For Prepared Piano		$150
19 [B]	Sonatas And Interludes For Prepared Piano Volume One	1951	$100
20 [B]	Sonatas And Interludes For Prepared Piano Volume Two	1951	$100

FINNADAR

Number	Title	Yr	NM
QD9006 [Q]	Wound / Winter Music	1974	$50

—*one side only. Side one by George Flynn*

MAINSTREAM

Number	Title	Yr	NM
MS5005 [B]	Circles / Frammento / Aria With Fontana Mix	1970	$30

—*Luciano Berio - E. E. Cummings / Sylvano Bussotti*

MODERN HARMONIC

Number	Title	Yr	NM
MH8020 [B]	John Cage Meets Sun Ra The Complete Concert June 8, 1986 Coney Island, NY	2016	$40

NEW WORLD

Number	Title	Yr	NM
NW214 [B]	The Music Of John Cage And Harry Partch	1978	$50

—*one side only. Side one by Harry Partch*

Number	Title	Yr	NM
no labelno cat [B]	The 25-Year Retrospective Concert Of The Music Of John Cage	1959	$300

—*box set*

TIME

Number	Title	Yr	NM
58003 [B]	Circles / Frammento / Aria With Fontana Mix	1962	$30

—*also credited: Luciano Berio - E. E. Cummings / Sylvano Bussotti*

TOMATO

Number	Title	Yr	NM
TOM21101 [B]	Etudes Australes For Piano	1979	$50
TOM7016 [B]	John Cage	1978	$50
TOM-21001 [B]	Sonatas And Interludes / A Book Of Music	1977	$80

TURNABOUT

Number	Title	Yr	NM
TVS34610 [B]	Black Angels (Images 1) / String Quartet In Four Parts	1976	$30

—*one side only; side one by George Crumb*

Number	Title	Yr	NM
TV4046 [B]	Electronic Music	1967	$50

—*also credited to Luciano Berio, Ilhan Mimaroglu*

CAGE, JOHN / PISTON, WALTER
COLUMBIA

Number	Title	Yr	NM
ML4495 [B]	Modern American Music Series	1953	$50

CAGE, JOHN AND FOXX, LUKAS
NONESUCH

Number	Title	Yr	NM
H71202 [B]	Concerto For Prepared Piano & Orchestra / Baroque Variations	1968	$50

CAGE, JOHN AND HILLER, LEJAREN
NONESUCH

Number	Title	Yr	NM
H71224 [B]	HPSCHD / String Quartet No. 2	1969	$40

—*also credited to Ben Johnston*

CAGE, JOHN AND TUDOR, DAVID
COMMUNICATING THE GOSPEL TODAY

Number	Title	Yr	NM
no cat [B]	Sounds	1968	$1500

—*side one only; side two features Country Joe and the Fish*

EVEREST

Number	Title	Yr	NM
3132 [B]	Variations IV Volume I	1965	$40
3230 [B]	Variations IV Volume II	1965	$40

FOLKWAYS

Number	Title	Yr	NM
FT3704 [B]	Indeterminacy: New Aspect Of Form In Instrumental And Electronic Music	1959	$150

—*box set*

CAGE, JOHN AND WOLFF, CHRISTIAN
MAINSTREAM

Number	Title	Yr	NM
MS5015 [B]	John Cage - Christian Wolff	1970	$50

TIME

Number	Title	Yr	NM
58009 [M]	John Cage - Christian Wolff	1963	$75
S8009 [B]	John Cage - Christian Wolff	1963	$50

Number	Title	Yr	NM

CAGLE, BUDDY
IMPERIAL
Number	Title	Yr	NM
❑ LP-9361 [M]	Longtime Traveling	1967	$30
❑ LP-12361 [S]	Longtime Traveling	1967	$30
❑ LP-9348 [M]	Mi Casa, Tu Casa	1967	$25
❑ LP-12348 [S]	Mi Casa, Tu Casa	1967	$30
❑ LP-9318 [M]	The Way You Like It	1966	$25
❑ LP-12318 [S]	The Way You Like It	1966	$30
❑ LP-12374	Through a Crack in a Boxcar Door	1968	$30

CAHEN, FRANCOIS
INNER CITY
Number	Title	Yr	NM
❑ 1118	Great Winds	1979	$35

—*Pianist, former member of French progressive rock band Magma.*

CAIN, JACKIE, AND ROY KRAL
ABC-PARAMOUNT
Number	Title	Yr	NM
❑ ABC-163 [M]	Bits and Pieces	1957	$50
❑ ABC-207 [M]	Free and Easy	1958	$50
❑ ABC-267 [M]	In the Spotlight	1959	$40
❑ ABCS-267 [S]	In the Spotlight	1959	$50
❑ ABC-120 [M]	The Glory of Love	1956	$50
AUDIOPHILE
| ❑ AP-230 | One More Rose (A Tribute to the Lyrics of Alan Jay Lerner) | 1988 | $25 |
BRUNSWICK
| ❑ BL54026 [M] | Jackie Cain and Roy Kral | 1957 | $50 |
CAPITOL
| ❑ ST2936 | Grass | 1968 | $85 |
COLUMBIA
❑ CL1704 [M]	Double Take	1961	$30
❑ CS8504 [S]	Double Take	1961	$30
❑ CL1934 [S]	Jackie and Roy Kral Like And Sing Songs by Dory And André Previn	1963	$25

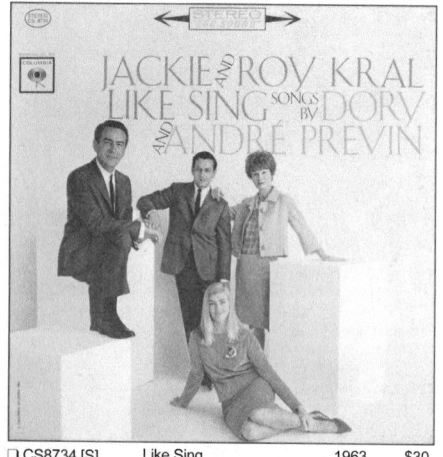

Number	Title	Yr	NM
❑ CS8734 [S]	Like Sing	1963	$30
❑ CL1469 [M]	Sweet and Low Down	1960	$30
❑ CS8260 [S]	Sweet and Low Down	1960	$30
CONCORD JAZZ
❑ CJ-149	East of Suez	1981	$30
❑ CJ-186	High Standards	198?	$30
❑ CJ-115	Star Sounds	1979	$30
CONTEMPORARY
| ❑ C-14046 | Full Circle | 1989 | $30 |
CTI
| ❑ 6040 | A Wilder Alias | 1974 | $35 |
| ❑ 6019 | Time and Love | 1972 | $35 |
DISCOVERY
| ❑ 907 | We've Got It: The Music of Cy Coleman | 1986 | $25 |
FANTASY
| ❑ F-9643 | Bogie | 1986 | $25 |
FINESSE
| ❑ FW38324 | A Stephen Sondheim Collection | 1983 | $25 |
MCA
| ❑ 4169 | Jackie & Roy | 198? | $30 |
REGENT
| ❑ MG-6057 [M] | Jackie & Roy | 1957 | $50 |
ROULETTE
| ❑ R-25278 [M] | By Jupiter & Girl Crazy | 1964 | $25 |
| ❑ SR-25278 [S] | By Jupiter & Girl Crazy | 1964 | $30 |
SAVOY
| ❑ MG-12198 [M] | Jackie and Roy | 196? | $25 |
STORYVILLE
| ❑ STLP-322 [10] | Jackie & Roy | 1955 | $120 |

Number	Title	Yr	NM
❑ STLP-915 [M]	Sing Baby, Sing!	1956	$75
❑ STLP-904 [M]	Storyville Presents Jackie & Roy	1955	$85
STUDIO 7
| ❑ 402 | By the Sea | 1978 | $30 |
VERVE
❑ V-8668 [M]	Changes	1966	$25
❑ V6-8668 [S]	Changes	1966	$30
❑ V-8688 [M]	Lovesick	1967	$30
❑ V6-8688 [S]	Lovesick	1967	$25

CAIN
A.S.I.
Number	Title	Yr	NM
❑ 204	A Pound of Flesh	1974	$85
❑ 214 [B]	Stinger	1975	$40

CAIOLA, AL
ATCO
| ❑ 33-117 [M] | Music for Space Squirrels | 1960 | $30 |
| ❑ SD 33-117 [S] | Music for Space Squirrels | 1960 | $30 |
AVALANCHE
| ❑ 9201 | The Magnificent Seven | 1972 | $15 |
| ❑ AV-LA058-F | The Magnificent Seven Ride '73 | 1973 | $12 |
AVCO EMBASSY
| ❑ 33019 | Bonanza Guitars/50 Years of the Greatest Country Music | 1971 | $12 |
BAINBRIDGE
❑ 1030	Guitar of Plenty	1980	$10
❑ 1023	Italian Guitars	198?	$10
❑ 1010	Soft Guitars	198?	$10
CHANCELLOR
| ❑ CHL-5008 [M] | Great Pickin' | 1960 | $75 |
| ❑ CHS-5008 [S] | Great Pickin' | 1960 | $75 |
PICKWICK
| ❑ SPC-3034 | Italian Style | 196? | $15 |
RCA CAMDEN
❑ CAS-2569	Music from "The Godfather"	1972	$12
❑ CAL-710 [M]	The Guitar Style of Al Caiola	1962	$15
❑ CAS-710 [S]	The Guitar Style of Al Caiola	1962	$18
RCA VICTOR
| ❑ LPM-2031 [M] | High Strung | 1959 | $30 |
| ❑ LSP-2031 [S] | High Strung | 1959 | $30 |
ROULETTE
❑ SR-42008	Roman Guitar	1968	$12
❑ R25108 [M]	Salute Italia	1960	$25
❑ SR25108 [S]	Salute Italia	1960	$30
SAVOY
| ❑ MG-12033 [M] | Deep in a Dream | 1955 | $50 |
| ❑ MG-12057 [M] | Serenade in Blue | 1956 | $40 |
SUNSET
| ❑ SUS-5292 | Guitar in Love | 1970 | $12 |
TIME
❑ 52101 [M]	Gershwin and Guitars	1961	$25
❑ S-2101 [S]	Gershwin and Guitars	1961	$30
❑ 52000 [M]	Percussion and Guitars	1960	$25
❑ S-2000 [S]	Percussion and Guitars	1960	$30
❑ 52006 [M]	Percussion Espanol	1960	$25
❑ S-2006 [S]	Percussion Espanol	1960	$30
❑ 52026 [M]	Percussion Espanol, Vol. 2	1960	$25
❑ S-2026 [S]	Percussion Espanol, Vol. 2	1960	$30
❑ 52039 [M]	Spanish Guitars	1960	$25
❑ S-2039 [S]	Spanish Guitars	1960	$30
UNITED ARTISTS
❑ UAL-3330 [M]	50 Fabulous Guitar Favorites	1964	$15
❑ UAS-6330 [S]	50 Fabulous Guitar Favorites	1964	$18
❑ UAL-3354 [M]	50 Fabulous Italian Favorites	1964	$15
❑ UAS-6354 [S]	50 Fabulous Italian Favorites	1964	$18
❑ UAL-3256 [M]	Acapulco 1922 and The Lonely Bull	1963	$15
❑ UAS-6256 [S]	Acapulco 1922 and The Lonely Bull	1963	$18
❑ UAL-3276 [M]	Ciao	1963	$15
❑ UAS-6276 [S]	Ciao	1963	$18
❑ UAL-3255 [M]	City Guy Goes Country	1963	$15
❑ UAS-6255 [S]	City Guy Goes Country	1963	$18
❑ UAL-3299 [M]	Cleopatra and All That Jazz	1963	$75
❑ UAS-6299 [S]	Cleopatra and All That Jazz	1963	$75
❑ UAL-3280 [M]	Give Me the Simple Life	1963	$15
❑ UAS-6280 [S]	Give Me the Simple Life	1963	$18
❑ UAL-3240 [M]	Golden Guitar	1962	$15
❑ UAS-6240 [S]	Golden Guitar	1962	$18
❑ UAL-3142 [M]	Golden Instrumental Hits	1961	$15
❑ UAS-6142 [S]	Golden Instrumental Hits	1961	$18
❑ UAL-3403 [M]	Guitar for Lovers	1965	$15
❑ UAS-6403 [S]	Guitar for Lovers	1965	$18
❑ UAL-3405 [M]	Have Guitar Will Travel	1965	$15
❑ UAS-6405 [S]	Have Guitar Will Travel	1965	$18
❑ UAL-3161 [M]	Hit Instrumentals from TV Westerns	1961	$18
❑ UAS-6161 [S]	Hit Instrumentals from TV Westerns	1961	$25
❑ UAS-6712	Let the Sunshine In	1969	$12
❑ UAL-3228 [M]	Midnight Dance Party	1962	$15
❑ UAS-6228 [S]	Midnight Dance Party	1962	$18
❑ UAL-3362 [M]	On the Trail	1964	$15

Number	Title	Yr	NM
❑ UAS-6362 [S]	On the Trail	1964	$18
❑ UAL-3263 [M]	Paradise Village	1963	$15
❑ UAS-6263 [S]	Paradise Village	1963	$18
❑ UAL-3180 [M]	Solid Gold Guitar	1962	$15
❑ UAS-6180 [S]	Solid Gold Guitar	1962	$18
❑ UAL-3418 [M]	Solid Gold Guitar Goes Hawaiian	1965	$15
❑ UAS-6418 [S]	Solid Gold Guitar Goes Hawaiian	1965	$18
❑ UAL-3435 [M]	Sounds for Spies and Private Eyes	1965	$18
❑ UAS-6435 [S]	Sounds for Spies and Private Eyes	1965	$25
❑ UAL-3310 [M]	The Best of Al Caiola	1964	$15
❑ UAS-6310 [S]	The Best of Al Caiola	1964	$18
❑ UAL-3133 [M]	The Magnificent Seven	1960	$25
❑ UAS-6133 [S]	The Magnificent Seven	1960	$30
❑ UAL-3389 [M]	Tuff Guitar	1965	$15
❑ UAS-6389 [S]	Tuff Guitar	1965	$18
❑ UAL-3454 [M]	Tuff Guitar English Style	1966	$15
❑ UAS-6454 [S]	Tuff Guitar English Style	1966	$18

CAJUN PETE
MERCURY
Number	Title	Yr	NM
❑ MG-20633 [M]	Tales of the Bayou	1961	$25
❑ SR-60633 [S]	Tales of the Bayou	1961	$30

CAKE, THE
DECCA
| ❑ DL75039 [S] | A Slice of the Cake | 1968 | $30 |
| ❑ DL5039 [M] | A Slice of the Cake | 1968 | $50 |

—*Mono is white label promo only*

| ❑ DL4927 [M] | The Cake | 1967 | $25 |
| ❑ DL74927 [S] | The Cake | 1967 | $30 |

CALAMITY JANE
COLUMBIA
| ❑ FC37626 | Calamity Jane | 1981 | $12 |

CALDWELL, BOBBY
Also see CAPTAIN BEYOND.
CLOUDS
| ❑ 8804 | Bobby Caldwell | 1978 | $25 |

—*Gold vinyl*

| ❑ 8804 | Bobby Caldwell | 1978 | $15 |

—*Black vinyl*

| ❑ 8810 [B] | Cat in the Hat | 1980 | $18 |
POLYDOR
| ❑ PD-1-6347 | Carry On | 1982 | $12 |

CALDWELL, LOUISE HARRISON
RECAR
| ❑ 2012 [M] | All About the Beatles | 1965 | $250 |

—*With insert*

| ❑ 2012 [M] | All About the Beatles | 1965 | $175 |

—*Without insert*

CALE, J.J.
MCA
| ❑ 37102 | 5 | 1981 | $10 |

—*Reissue of Shelter 3163*

| ❑ 37104 | Naturally | 1981 | $10 |

—*Reissue of Shelter 52009*

| ❑ 37106 | Okie | 1981 | $10 |

—*Reissue of Shelter 52019*

| ❑ 37105 | Really | 1981 | $10 |

—*Reissue of Shelter 52012*

| ❑ 5158 | Shades | 1981 | $12 |
| ❑ 37103 | Troubadour | 1981 | $10 |

—*Reissue of Shelter 52002*

MERCURY
| ❑ 811152-1 | #8 | 1983 | $12 |
| ❑ 810313-1 | 5 | 1983 | $10 |

—*Reissue of MCA 37102*

| ❑ SRM-1-4038 | Grasshopper | 1982 | $12 |
| ❑ 822888-1 | Grasshopper | 1985 | $10 |

—*Reissue of 4038*

| ❑ 810314-1 | Really | 1983 | $10 |

—*Reissue of MCA 37105*

| ❑ 818633-1 | Special Edition | 1984 | $12 |
SHELTER
| ❑ 3163 [B] | 5 | 1979 | $15 |
| ❑ 2122 | Naturally | 1974 | $15 |

—*Reissue of SW-8908*

| ❑ SW-8908 | Naturally | 1971 | $18 |
| ❑ 52009 | Naturally | 1977 | $12 |

—*Reissue of 2122*

| ❑ 2107 | Okie | 1974 | $18 |
| ❑ 52015 | Okie | 1977 | $12 |

—*Reissue of 2107*

| ❑ SW-8912 | Really | 1972 | $18 |
| ❑ 2123 | Really | 1974 | $15 |

—*Reissue of 8912*

| ❑ 52012 | Really | 1977 | $12 |

—*Reissue of 2123*

| ❑ 52002 | Troubadour | 1976 | $18 |

Number	Title	Yr	NM
SILVERTONE			
❏ 1306-1-J	Travel-Log	1990	$15
CALE, JOHN			
Also see THE VELVET UNDERGROUND.			
4 MEN WITH BEARDS			
❏ 4M125LP [B]	Paris 1919		$25
A&M			
❏ SP-4849 [B]	Honi Soit	1981	$25
ANTILLES			
❏ AN-7063 [B]	Guts	198?	$20
—Reissue of Island 9459			
COLUMBIA			
❏ CS1037	Vintage Violence	1970	$100
—Red "360 Sound" label			
❏ CS1037	Vintage Violence	1971	$50
—Orange label			
ISLAND			
❏ IT-8401 [B]	Caribbean Sunset	1984	$20
❏ ILPS9301	Fear	1975	$100
❏ ILPS9459	Guts	1977	$50
❏ IXP-2 [DJ]	Hear Fear	1975	$120
—Promo-only interview album			
❏ ILPS9350 [B]	Helen of Troy	1975	$100
❏ IT-8402 [B]	John Cale Comes Alive	1984	$30
❏ ILPS9317 [B]	Slow Dazzle	1975	$100
OPAL/WARNER BROS.			
❏ 26024 [B]	Words for the Dying	1989	$30
PASSPORT			
❏ PB6019 [B]	Music for a New Society	1982	$30
PVC			
❏ 8947	Artificial Intelligence	1985	$18
REPRISE			
❏ MS2131	Paris, 1919	1973	$150
❏ MS2079	The Academy in Peril	1972	$150
SPY/I.R.S.			
❏ SP-004 [B]	Sabotage/Live	1980	$40
WAX CATHEDRAL			
❏ MELT012 [B]	Fear	2015	$25
❏ MELT014 [B]	Helen of Troy	2015	$30
❏ MELT013 [B]	Slow Dazzle	2015	$25
CALE, JOHN AND RILEY, TERRY			
COLUMBIA			
❏ C30131 [B]	Church of Anthrax	1971	$50
CALICO			
UNITED ARTISTS			
❏ UA-LA454-G	Calico	1975	$18
❏ UA-LA659-G	Calico, Vol. 2	1976	$18
CALIFORNIA, RANDY			
EPIC			
❏ KE31755	Kapt. Kopter & the Fabulous Twirly Birds	1972	$30
—Yellow label			
❏ KE31755	Kapt. Kopter & the Fabulous Twirly Birds	1973	$15
—Orange label			
CALIFORNIA POPPY PICKERS, THE			
ALSHIRE			
❏ S-5153	Blue-Eyed Soul	1969	$30
❏ S-5167	Honky Tonk Women	1970	$40
❏ S-5163	Today's Chart Busters	1969	$25
CALIFORNIA RAMBLERS, THE			
BIOGRAPH			
❏ 12021	Hallelujah, Vol. 2 1925-29	197?	$25
❏ 12020	Miss Annabelle Lee 1925-27	197?	$25
CALIMAN, HADLEY			
CATALYST			
❏ 0(# unknown)	Celebration	1977	$30
❏ 7604	Projecting	1976	$30
MAINSTREAM			
❏ MRL-318	Hadley Caliman	1971	$25
❏ MRL-342	Iapetus	1972	$25
CALL, THE			
ELEKTRA			
❏ 60739	Into the Woods	1987	$12
❏ R141152	Reconciled	1986	$15
—RCA Music Service edition			
❏ 60440	Reconciled	1986	$12
MCA			
❏ 6303	Let the Day Begin	1989	$12
❏ 10033	Red Moon	1990	$15
MERCURY			
❏ 810307-1	Modern Romans	1983	$12
❏ SRM-1-4037	The Call	1982	$15

Number	Title	Yr	NM
❏ 822868-1	The Call	1984	$10
—Reissue of 4037			
❏ 818793-1	The Scene Beyond Dreams	1984	$15
CALLENDER, BOBBY			
MGM			
❏ SE-4557	Rainbow	1968	$175
CALLENDER, RED			
CROWN			
❏ CLP-5012 [M]	Callender Speaks Low	1957	$50
❏ CLP-5025 [M]	Swingin' Suite	1957	$40
LEGEND			
❏ 1005	Basin Street Bass	197?	$30
METROJAZZ			
❏ E-1007 [M]	The Lowest	1958	$120
❏ SE-1007 [S]	The Lowest	1959	$120
MODERN			
❏ MLP-1201 [M]	Swingin' Suite	1956	$100
RED			
❏ KM2248	Red Callender Speaks Low	1978	$35
CALLIOPE			
BUDDAH			
❏ BDS-5023	Steamed	1968	$25
CALLOWAY, CAB			
BRUNSWICK			
❏ BL58101 [10]	Cab Calloway	1954	$150
COLUMBIA			
❏ CG32593	The Hi De Ho Man	1973	$25
CORAL			
❏ CRL57408 [M]	Blues Make Me Happy	1962	$30
❏ CRL757408 [S]	Blues Make Me Happy	1962	$30
EPIC			
❏ LN3265 [M]	Swing Showman	1957	$150
GLENDALE			
❏ GLS9007	Cab Calloway	1984	$25
GONE			
❏ LP-101 [M]	Cotton Club Revue '58	1958	$100
MCA			
❏ 1344	Mr. Hi-De-Ho	198?	$25
P.I.P.			
❏ 6801	Cab Calloway '68	1968	$50
RCA VICTOR			
❏ LPM-2021 [M]	Hi De Hi De Ho	1958	$30

Number	Title	Yr	NM
❏ LSP-2021 [S]	Hi De Hi De Ho	1958	$40
VOCALION			
❏ VL73820	The Blues	196?	$30
CALLOWAY			
SOLAR			
❏ FZ75310	All the Way	1989	$18
CAMARATA			
BUENA VISTA			
❏ BV-3319 [M]	33 Great Walt Disney Motion Picture Melodies	1963	$30
❏ STER-3319 [S]	33 Great Walt Disney Motion Picture Melodies	1963	$30
❏ BV-4023 [M]	Camarata Conducts a Modern Interpretation of Snow White and the Seven Dwarfs	1963	$30
—Gatefold cover			
❏ BV-4023 [M]	Camarata Conducts a Modern Interpretation of Snow White and the Seven Dwarfs	1967	$25

Number	Title	Yr	NM
—Regular cover			
❏ STER-4023 [S]	Camarata Conducts a Modern Interpretation of Snow White and the Seven Dwarfs	1963	$40
—Gatefold cover			
❏ STER-4023 [S]	Camarata Conducts a Modern Interpretation of Snow White and the Seven Dwarfs	1967	$30
—Regular cover			
❏ BV-4048	Camarata Featuring Tutti's Trombones	1970	$25
❏ BV-4047	Camarata Featuring Tutti's Trumpets	1970	$25
—Reissue of 3011			
❏ BV-3322 [M]	In the Still of the Night	1959	$25
❏ STER-3322 [S]	In the Still of the Night	1960	$30
❏ BV-3321 [M]	The Changing Seasons	1964	$25
❏ STER-3321 [S]	The Changing Seasons	1964	$30
❏ BV-3330 [M]	Tinpanorama	1965	$25
DISNEYLAND			
❏ DQ-1232 [M]	A Child's Introduction to Melody and Instruments of the Orchestra	1963	$25
❏ WDL-3021 [M]	Autumn	1958	$25
❏ STER-3021 [S]	Autumn	1959	$30
❏ WDL-4009 [M]	Camarata Interprets Music from Cinderella and Bambi	1957	$75
❏ 0(# unknown) [M]	Music of the Seasons	1959	$40
—Box set with mono versions of 3021, 3026, 3027 and 3032			
❏ 0(# unknown) [S]	Music of the Seasons	1959	$100
—Box set with stereo versions of 3021, 3026, 3027 and 3032			
❏ WDL-3032 [M]	Spring	1958	$25
❏ STER-3032 [S]	Spring	1959	$30
❏ WDL-3027 [M]	Summer	1958	$25
❏ STER-3027 [S]	Summer	1959	$30
❏ WDL-3011 [M]	Tutti's Trumpets	1957	$25
❏ STER-3011 [S]	Tutti's Trumpets	1959	$30
❏ WDL-3026 [M]	Winter	1958	$25
❏ STER-3026 [S]	Winter	1959	$30
CAMBRIDGE, GODFREY			
EPIC			
❏ FLM13108 [M]	Godfrey Cambridge Toys with the World	1966	$25
❏ FLS15108 [S]	Godfrey Cambridge Toys with the World	1966	$25
❏ FLM13101 [M]	Ready or Not...Here's Godfrey Cambridge	1964	$25
❏ FLS15101 [S]	Ready or Not...Here's Godfrey Cambridge	1964	$25
❏ FLM13115 [M]	The Godfrey Cambridge Show Live at the Aladdin	1968	$25
❏ FLS15115 [S]	The Godfrey Cambridge Show Live at the Aladdin	1968	$25
❏ FLM13102 [M]	Them Cotton Pickin' Days Is Over	1965	$25
❏ FLS15102 [S]	Them Cotton Pickin' Days Is Over	1965	$25
CAMEL			
ARISTA			
❏ AB4206	Breathless	1979	$12
❏ AB4254	I Can See Your House from Here	1980	$12
JANUS			
❏ 7009	Mirage	1974	$15
❏ 7024	Moonmadness	1976	$15
❏ 7035	Rain Dances	1977	$15
❏ 7016	The Snow Goose	1975	$15
LONDON			
❏ 820166-1	Pressure Points	1987	$12
PASSPORT			
❏ PB-9855	Mirage	198?	$10
—Reissue of Janus 7009			
❏ PB-9857	Moonmadness	198?	$10
—Reissue of Janus 7024			
❏ PB-6008	Nude	198?	$12
❏ PB-9858	Rain Dances	198?	$10
—Reissue of Janus 7035			
❏ PB-6013	The Single Factor	198?	$12
❏ PB-9856	The Snow Goose	198?	$10
—Reissue of Janus 7016			
CAMEO			
ATLANTA ARTISTS			
❏ 836002-1	Machismo	1988	$12
❏ 846297-1	Real Men..Wear Black	1990	$15
❏ 814984-1	She's Strange	1984	$12
❏ 824546-1	Single Life	1985	$12
❏ 811072-1	Style	1983	$12
❏ 830265-1	Word Up!	1986	$12
CHOCOLATE CITY			
❏ CCLP2021	Alligator Woman	1982	$15
❏ CCLP2011	Cameosis	1980	$15
❏ CCLP2003	Cardiac Arrest	1977	$15
❏ CCLP2016	Feel Me	1980	$15
❏ CCLP2019	Knights of the Sound Table	1981	$15
❏ CCLP2008	Secret Omen	1979	$15
❏ CCLP2006	Ugly Ego	1978	$15
❏ CCLP2004	We All Know Who We Are	1978	$15

Number	Title	Yr	NM

CAMERON, BRUCE
DISCOVERY
| ❏ 793 | With All My Love | 198? | $25 |
SEA BREEZE
| ❏ 9801 | Jet Away | 198? | $25 |

CAMERON, DOUG
SPINDLETOP
| ❏ STP-103 | Freeway Mentality | 1986 | $30 |

CAMERON, JOHN
DERAM
| ❏ DES18033 | Off Centre | 1969 | $25 |

CAMILO, MICHEL
EPIC
| ❏ OE45295 | On Fire | 1989 | $75 |
PORTRAIT
| ❏ OR44482 | Michael Camilo | 1988 | $25 |

CAMP, HAMILTON
ELEKTRA
| ❏ EKL-278 [M] | Paths of Victory | 1965 | $40 |
| ❏ EKS-7278 [S] | Paths of Victory | 1965 | $50 |
WARNER BROS.
| ❏ WS1737 | Here's to You | 1967 | $30 |
| ❏ WS1753 | Welcome to Hamilton Camp | 1969 | $25 |

CAMP, RED
COOK
❏ LP-5005 [M]	Camp Has a Ball	1957	$50
❏ LP-1087 [10]	Camp Inventions: Bold New Design for Jazz Piano	1955	$75
❏ LP-1089 [10]	Red Camp	1955	$75

CAMPBELL, ALEX
STARDAY
| ❏ SLP-214 [M] | 16 Radio Favorites | 1963 | $30 |
| ❏ SLP-342 [M] | Travel On | 1965 | $30 |

CAMPBELL, ARCHIE, AND LORENE MANN
RCA VICTOR
| ❏ LSP-4086 | Archie and Lorene Tell It Like It Is | 1968 | $25 |

CAMPBELL, ARCHIE
RCA VICTOR
❏ LPM-3504 [M]	Have a Laugh on Me	1966	$25
❏ LSP-3504 [S]	Have a Laugh on Me	1966	$30
❏ LPM-3780 [M]	Kids I Love 'Em	1967	$30
❏ LSP-3780 [S]	Kids I Love 'Em	1967	$25
❏ LPM-3699 [M]	The Cockfight and Other Tall Tales	1967	$25
❏ LSP-3699 [S]	The Cockfight and Other Tall Tales	1967	$30
❏ LPM-3892 [M]	The Golden Years	1967	$30
❏ LSP-3892 [S]	The Golden Years	1967	$25
STARDAY
❏ SLP-167 [M]	Bedtime Stories for Adults	1962	$30
❏ SLP-162 [M]	Make Friends with Archie Campbell	1962	$30
❏ SLP-377 [M]	The Grand Ole Opry's Good Humor Man	1966	$30
❏ SLP-223 [M]	The Joker Is Wild	1963	$30

CAMPBELL, CECIL
STARDAY
| ❏ SLP-254 [M] | Steel Guitar Jamboree | 1963 | $40 |

CAMPBELL, CHOKER
MOTOWN
| ❏ M-620 [M] | Hits of the Sixties | 1964 | $150 |
| ❏ MS-620 [S] | Hits of the Sixties | 1964 | $175 |

CAMPBELL, DICK
MERCURY
| ❏ MG-21060 [M] | Dick Campbell Sings Where It's At | 1966 | $30 |
| ❏ SR-61060 [S] | Dick Campbell Sings Where It's At | 1966 | $40 |

CAMPBELL, EDDIE C.
ROOSTER BLUES
| ❏ 7602 | King of the Jungle | 1986 | $18 |

CAMPBELL, GLEN, AND BOBBIE GENTRY
CAPITOL
❏ ST2928	Bobbie Gentry & Glen Campbell	1968	$18
❏ ST 8-2928	Bobbie Gentry & Glen Campbell	1968	$25
— *Capitol Record Club edition*			

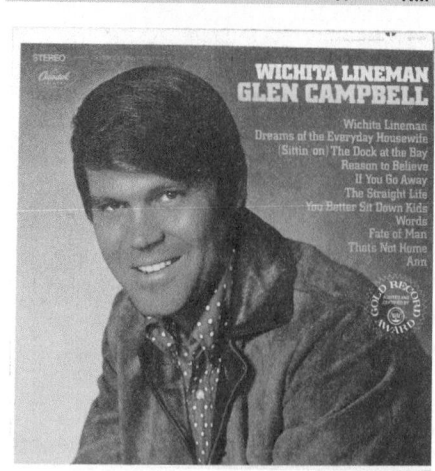

CAMPBELL, GLEN
ATLANTIC AMERICA
❏ 90483	It's Just a Matter of Time	1985	$10
❏ 90164	Letter to Home	1984	$10
❏ 90016	Old Home Town	1983	$10
CAPITOL
❏ ST2907	A New Place in the Sun	1968	$18
❏ SW-11407	Arkansas	1975	$12
❏ SM-11407	Arkansas	1977	$10
— *Reissue with new prefix*			
❏ SW-11722	Basic	1978	$12
❏ T1810 [M]	Big Bluegrass Special	1962	$100
— *As "The Green River Boys Featuring Glen Campbell*			
❏ ST1810 [S]	Big Bluegrass Special	1962	$150
— *As "The Green River Boys Featuring Glen Campbell*			
❏ SW-11516	Bloodline	1976	$12
❏ T2679 [M]	Burning Bridges	1967	$18
❏ ST2679 [S]	Burning Bridges	1967	$18
❏ T2851 [M]	By the Time I Get to Phoenix	1967	$18
❏ ST2851 [S]	By the Time I Get to Phoenix	1967	$18
❏ SM-12040	By the Time I Get to Phoenix	1979	$10
— *Reissue of 2851*			
❏ ST-210	Galveston	1969	$18
❏ SN-16259	Galveston	1982	$10
— *Budget-line reissue*			
❏ T2809 [M]	Gentle on My Mind	1967	$18
❏ ST2809 [S]	Gentle on My Mind	1967	$18
❏ SM-11960	Gentle on My Mind	1979	$10
— *Reissue of 2809*			
❏ STBO-268	Glen Campbell -- "Live"	1969	$25
❏ SW-752	Glen Campbell's Greatest Hits	1971	$15
❏ SN-16297	Glen Campbell's Greatest Hits	1984	$10
— *Budget-line reissue*			
❏ SW-11117	Glen Travis Campbell	1972	$12
❏ SN-16031	Glen Travis Campbell	1980	$10
— *Budget-line reissue*			
❏ ST2878 [S]	Hey, Little One	1968	$18
❏ T2878 [M]	Hey, Little One	1968	$30
❏ SN-16258	Hey Little Girl	1982	$10
— *Budget-line reissue*			
❏ SOO-12008	Highwayman	1979	$12
❏ SW-11293	Hosuton (I'm Comin' to See You)	1974	$12
❏ SW-11185	I Knew Jesus (Before He Was a Star)	1973	$12
❏ SW-11253	I Remember Hank Williams	1973	$12
❏ SOO-12124	It's the World Gone Crazy	1981	$12
❏ SWAK-93157	Limited Collector's Edition	1970	$25
— *Capitol Record Club exclusive; includes tour program*			
❏ SWBC-11707	Live at the Royal Festival Hall	1977	$15
❏ SW-443	Oh Happy Day	1970	$15
❏ SW-11336	Reunion (The Songs of Jimmy Webb)	1974	$12
❏ SW-11430	Rhinestone Cowboy	1975	$12
❏ SN-16029	Rhinestone Cowboy	1980	$10
— *Budget-line reissue*			
❏ SOO-12075	Somethin' 'Bout You Baby I Like	1980	$12
❏ SO-11601	Southern Nights	1977	$12
❏ SN-16030	Southern Nights	1980	$10
— *Budget-line reissue*			
❏ ST2978	That Christmas Feeling	1968	$18
❏ T2023 [M]	The Astounding 12-String Guitar of Glen Campbell	1964	$18
❏ ST2023 [S]	The Astounding 12-String Guitar of Glen Campbell	1964	$25
❏ ST-11577	The Best of Glen Campbell	1976	$12
❏ SN-16335	The Best of Glen Campbell	1984	$10
— *Budget-line reissue*			
❏ T2392 [M]	The Big Bad Rock Guitar of Glen Campbell	1965	$18
❏ ST2392 [S]	The Big Bad Rock Guitar of Glen Campbell	1965	$25

Number	Title	Yr	NM
❏ SW-493	The Glen Campbell Goodtime Album	1970	$15
❏ SW-733	The Last Time I Saw Her	1971	$15
❏ SM-733	The Last Time I Saw Her	1977	$10
— *Reissue with new prefix*			
❏ T1881 [M]	Too Late to Worry, Too Blue to Cry	1963	$25
❏ ST1881 [S]	Too Late to Worry, Too Blue to Cry	1963	$30
❏ SW-389	Try a Little Kindness	1970	$15
❏ SM-389	Try a Little Kindness	1977	$10
— *Reissue with new prefix*			
❏ ST-103 [B]	Wichita Lineman	1968	$18
❏ SM-103	Wichita Lineman	1977	$10
— *Reissue with new prefix*			
❏ SN-16160	Wichita Lineman	1981	$10
— *Budget-line reissue*			
❏ ST-8-0103	Wichita Lineman	1968	$25
— *Capitol Record Club edition*			

LONGINES SYMPHONETTE
| ❏ LS-218 | Glen Campbell's Golden Favorites | 1972 | $30 |
MCA
| ❏ 42210 | Light Years | 1988 | $10 |
| ❏ 42009 | Still Within the Sound of My Voice | 1987 | $10 |
PAIR
| ❏ PDL2-1089 | All-Time Favorites | 1986 | $15 |
PICKWICK
❏ SPC-3134	A Satisfied Mind	197?	$10
❏ SPC-3346	I'll Paint You a Song	197?	$10
❏ PTP-2048	Only the Lonely	197?	$12
❏ PC-3052 [M]	The 12 String Guitar of Glen Campbell	196?	$15
❏ SPC-3052 [S]	The 12 String Guitar of Glen Campbell	196?	$12
❏ SPC-3274	The Glen Campbell Album	197?	$10
STARDAY
| ❏ SLP-437 | Country Music Star #1 | 1969 | $18 |
| ❏ SLP-424 | Country Soul | 1968 | $18 |
SURREY
| ❏ S1007 [M] | Country Shindig | 196? | $15 |

CAMPBELL, JO ANN
ABC-PARAMOUNT
| ❏ 393 [M] | Twistin' and Listenin' | 1962 | $100 |
| ❏ S-393 [S] | Twistin' and Listenin' | 1962 | $150 |
CAMEO
| ❏ C-1026 [M] | All the Hits of Jo Ann Campbell | 1962 | $50 |
| ❏ SC-1026 [S] | All the Hits of Jo Ann Campbell | 1962 | $150 |
CORONET
| ❏ CX-199 [M] | Starring Jo Ann Campbell | 196? | $25 |
| ❏ CXS-199 [R] | Starring Jo Ann Campbell | 196? | $15 |
END
| ❏ LP-306 [M] | I'm Nobody's Baby | 1959 | $175 |

CAMPBELL, JOHN
CONTEMPORARY
| ❏ C-14053 | After Hours | 1989 | $30 |
| ❏ C-14061 | Turning Point | 1991 | $35 |

CAMPER VAN BEETHOVEN
INDEPENDENT PROJECT
❏ 016	Telephone Free Landslide Victory	1985	$100
— *Letterpress cover, "First Edition: June 1985" on back (numbered edition from 1-1,250); the basic color scheme is white, black and flourescent orange on brown chipboard*			
❏ 016	Telephone Free Landslide Victory	1985	$75
— *Letterpress cover, "Second Edition: 1175 cp./September 1985" on back (numbered edition from 1251-2425)*			
❏ 016	Telephone Free Landslide Victory	1985	$80
— *Letterpress cover, "First Edition: June 1985" on back (un-numbered promo); the basic color scheme is red, black and flourescent orange on brown chipboard*			
❏ 016	Telephone Free Landslide Victory	1985	$50
— *Letterpress cover, "Second Edition: 1175 cp./September 1985" on back (un-numbered promo)*			
❏ 016	Telephone Free Landslide Victory	1985	$30
— *Manufactured and Distributed within the United States of America by Rough Trade" on back cover; non-letterpress edition; several color schemes exist, all of equal value*			
PITCH A TENT
❏ 02	Camper Van Beethoven	1986	$18
❏ 01	II & III	1985	$18
❏ 05 [EP]	Vampire Can Mating Oven	1987	$18
VIRGIN
| ❏ 91289 | Key Lime Pie | 1989 | $12 |
| ❏ 90918 | Our Beloved Revolutionary Sweetheart | 1988 | $12 |

Number	Title	Yr	NM

CAMPI, RAY
ROLLIN' ROCK
| ☐ 023 | Rockabilly Music | 1979 | $15 |

ROUNDER
| ☐ 3047 | Gone, Gone, Gone | 198? | $12 |
| ☐ 3046 | Rockin' at the Ritz | 198? | $12 |

CAMPUS SINGERS, THE
ARGO
☐ LP-4033 [M]	Road of Blue	1964	$25
☐ LPS-4033 [S]	Road of Blue	1964	$30
☐ LP-4023 [M]	The Campus Singers at the Fickle Pickle	1963	$25
☐ LPS-4023 [S]	The Campus Singers at the Fickle Pickle	1963	$30

CAN
CLEOPATRA
| ☐ 3016 [B] | Inner Space | | $25 |
| ☐ 3043 [B] | Out Of Reach | | $25 |

MUTE
| ☐ 9033-1 | Sacrilege | 1997 | $30 |
— Album of remixes

CANADIAN ALL STARS, THE
DISCOVERY
| ☐ DL-3025 [10] | The Canadian All Stars | 1954 | $300 |

CANADIAN BEADLES, THE
TIDE
| ☐ 2005 [M] | Three Faces North | 1964 | $50 |

CANADIAN BRASS, THE
FM/CBS
| ☐ FM39740 | A Canadian Brass Christmas | 1985 | $12 |

RCA RED SEAL
| ☐ ARL1-4132 | Christmas with the Canadian Brass | 1981 | $12 |

CANADIAN SWEETHEARTS, THE
A&M
| ☐ LP-106 [M] | Introducing the Canadian Sweethearts | 1964 | $40 |
| ☐ SP-4106 [S] | Introducing the Canadian Sweethearts | 1964 | $50 |

CANAL STREET RAGTIMERS
GHB
| ☐ 4 [M] | Canal Street Ragtimers | 196? | $30 |
— Members: Roy Bower, Tony Smith, Martin Rodger, Chris Brown, John Featherhouse, Derek Gracie, Colin Knight, Derek Hamer

CANARIES, THE
B.T. PUPPY
| ☐ BTS-1007 | Flying High with the Canaries | 1970 | $150 |

CANDIDO
ABC-PARAMOUNT
☐ ABC-125 [M]	Candido Featuring Al Cohn	1956	$50
☐ ABC-453 [M]	Candido's Comparsa	1963	$25
☐ ABCS-453 [S]	Candido's Comparsa	1963	$30
☐ ABC-236 [M]	In Indigo	1958	$50
☐ ABCS-236 [S]	In Indigo	1959	$40
☐ ABC-286 [M]	Latin Fire	1959	$40
☐ ABCS-286 [S]	Latin Fire	1959	$50
☐ ABC-180 [M]	The Volcanic Candido	1957	$50

BLUE NOTE
| ☐ BST-84357 | Beautiful | 1970 | $35 |

POLYDOR
| ☐ PD-5063 | Drum Fever | 1973 | $30 |

RCA VICTOR
| ☐ LPM-2027 [M] | Beautiful | 1959 | $30 |
| ☐ LSP-2027 [S] | Beautiful | 1959 | $40 |

ROULETTE
| ☐ R-52078 [M] | Conga Soul | 1962 | $25 |
| ☐ SR-52078 [S] | Conga Soul | 1962 | $30 |

SOLID STATE
| ☐ SS-18066 | The Thousand Finger Man | 1969 | $35 |

CANDLEBOX
MAVERICK
| ☐ 46076 | Lucy/Candlebox | 1995 | $30 |
— First two albums packaged together in gatefold sleeve (neither available separately in U.S.)

CANDOLI, CONTE, AND FRANK ROSOLINO
RCA VICTOR
| ☐ TPL1-1509 | Conversation | 197? | $30 |

CANDOLI, CONTE, AND PHIL WOODS
PAUSA
| ☐ PR-7189 | Old Acquaintance | 1986 | $25 |

CANDOLI, CONTE, AND STAN LEVEY
BETHLEHEM
| ☐ BCP-9 [M] | West Coasting | 1956 | $300 |

CANDOLI, CONTE
ANDEX
| ☐ A-3002 [M] | Mucho Calor | 1958 | $50 |
| ☐ AS-3002 [S] | Mucho Calor | 1959 | $40 |

BETHLEHEM
| ☐ BCP-1016 [10] | Sincerely, Conte Candoli | 1954 | $300 |
| ☐ BCP-30 [M] | Toots Sweet | 1956 | $300 |

CROWN
| ☐ CLP-5162 [M] | Little Band, Big Jazz | 1960 | $25 |
| ☐ CST-190 [R] | Little Band, Big Jazz | 196? | $30 |
— Black vinyl
| ☐ CST-190 [R] | Little Band, Big Jazz | 196? | $30 |
— Red vinyl

GROOVE
| ☐ 1003 [M] | Cool Gabriels | 1956 | $500 |
— Warhol cover

CANDOLI, PETE
DECCA
| ☐ DL4761 [M] | Moscow Mule (And Many More Kicks) | 1966 | $35 |
| ☐ DL74761 [S] | Moscow Mule (And Many More Kicks) | 1966 | $25 |

KAPP
| ☐ KL-1230 [M] | For Pete's Sake | 1960 | $25 |
| ☐ KS-3230 [S] | For Pete's Sake | 1960 | $30 |

SOMERSET
| ☐ SF-17200 [M] | Blues, When Your Lover Has Gone | 1963 | $25 |
| ☐ SFS-17200 [S] | Blues, When Your Lover Has Gone | 1963 | $30 |

CANDOLI BROTHERS, THE
DOT
☐ DLP-3168 [M]	Bell, Book and Candoli	1959	$85
☐ DLP-25168 [S]	Bell, Book and Candoli	1959	$85
☐ DLP-3062 [M]	The Brothers Candoli	1957	$150

IMPULSE!
| ☐ 29064 | The Brothers Candoli | 198? | $25 |

MERCURY
| ☐ MG-20515 [M] | Two for the Money | 1959 | $150 |
| ☐ SR-60191 [S] | Two for the Money | 1959 | $150 |

WARNER BROS.
| ☐ W1462 [M] | The Brothers Candoli | 1962 | $25 |
| ☐ WS1462 [S] | The Brothers Candoli | 1962 | $30 |

CANDY STORE, THE
DECCA
| ☐ DL75147 | Turned-On Christmas | 1969 | $30 |

CANDYMEN, THE
ABC
☐ 616 [M]	The Candymen	1967	$30
☐ S-616 [S]	The Candymen	1967	$25
☐ S-633	The Candymen Bring You Candypower	1968	$25

DIPLOMAT
| ☐ FM100 | The Twist | 196? | $25 |

CANNED HEAT
ACCORD
| ☐ SN-7144 | Captured Live | 1981 | $12 |

ATLANTIC
| ☐ SD7289 | One More River to Cross | 1973 | $18 |

CLEOPATRA
| ☐ CLP1790 [B] | Live at Topanga Corral | 2014 | $25 |

DALI
| ☐ DCLP-89022 | Reheated | 1990 | $18 |

JANUS
| ☐ JLS-3009 | Vintage -- Canned Heat | 1969 | $18 |

LIBERTY
| ☐ LST-7541 [S] | Boogie with Canned Heat | 1968 | $25 |
| ☐ LN-10105 | Boogie with Canned Heat | 1981 | $10 |
— Budget-line reissue
| ☐ LRP-3541 [M] | Boogie with Canned Heat | 1968 | $50 |
— Stock copy in stereo cover with "Audition Mono LP Not for Sale" sticker
☐ LRP-3526 [M]	Canned Heat	1967	$50
☐ LST-7526 [S]	Canned Heat	1967	$25
☐ LST-11000	Canned Heat Cook Book (The Best of Canned Heat)	1969	$25
☐ LN-10106	Canned Heat Cook Book (The Best of Canned Heat)	1981	$10
— Budget-line reissue

☐ LST-11002	Future Blues	1970	$18
☐ LST-7618	Hallelujah	1969	$25
☐ LST-27200	Living the Blues	1968	$30

PICKWICK
| ☐ SPC-3614 | Boogie | 1978 | $12 |
| ☐ SPC-3364 | Live at Topanga Canyon | 197? | $12 |

SCEPTER CITATION
| ☐ CTN-18017 | The Best of Canned Heat | 1972 | $12 |

SUNSET
| ☐ SUS-5298 | Collage | 1971 | $12 |

TAKOMA
| ☐ 7066 | The Human Condition | 1980 | $15 |

UNITED ARTISTS
| ☐ LM-1015 | Boogie with Canned Heat | 1980 | $15 |
— Reissue of Liberty 7541
☐ UAS-5509	Canned Heat Concert (Recorded Live in Europe)	1971	$18
☐ UAS-5557	Historical Figures and Ancient Heads	1972	$18
☐ UAS-9955	Living the Blues	1971	$25
— Reissue of Liberty 27200
| ☐ UA-LA049-F | The New Age | 1973 | $18 |

WAND
| ☐ WDS-693 | Live at Topanga Canyon | 1970 | $30 |

CANNED HEAT AND JOHN LEE HOOKER
See JOHN LEE HOOKER AND CANNED HEAT

CANNIBAL AND THE HEADHUNTERS
DATE
| ☐ TEM3001 [M] | Land of 1000 Dances | 1966 | $30 |
| ☐ TES4001 [S] | Land of 1000 Dances | 1966 | $40 |

RAMPART
| ☐ RM-3302 [M] | Land of 1000 Dances | 1965 | $50 |
| ☐ RS-3302 [S] | Land of 1000 Dances | 1965 | $80 |

CANNON, ACE
ALLEGIANCE
| ☐ AV-5024 | Ace in the Whole | 1986 | $10 |

HI
☐ HL-12025 [M]	Ace Cannon Live	1965	$18
☐ SHL-32025 [S]	Ace Cannon Live	1965	$25
☐ SHL-32072/3	Aces Back to Back	1972	$18
☐ HL-12016 [M]	Aces Hi	1964	$25
☐ SHL-32016 [S]	Aces Hi	1964	$30
☐ 6006	After Hours	1978	$12
☐ SHL-32076	Baby Don't Get Hooked on Me	1973	$12
☐ SHL-32067	Blowing Wild	1971	$15
☐ SHL-32071	Cannon Country	1972	$15
☐ 8008	Cannon Country	1979	$12
☐ HL-12022 [M]	Christmas Cheer	1964	$25
☐ SHL-32022 [S]	Christmas Cheer	1964	$30
☐ SHL-32060	Cool 'n Saxy	1971	$15
☐ SHL-32080	Country Comfort	1974	$12
☐ SHL-32046	In the Spotlight	1968	$18
☐ HL-12008 [M]	Looking Back	1962	$30
☐ SHL-32008 [S]	Looking Back	1962	$30
☐ HL-12040 [M]	Memphis Golden Hits	1967	$25
☐ SHL-32040 [S]	Memphis Golden Hits	1967	$18
☐ HL-12028 [M]	Nashville Hits	1965	$18
☐ SHL-32028 [S]	Nashville Hits	1965	$25
☐ SHL-32101	Peace in the Valley	1976	$12
☐ 8003	Sax Man	1977	$12
☐ SHL-32090	Super Sax Country Style	1975	$12
☐ HL-12030 [M]	Sweet and Tuff	1966	$18
☐ SHL-32030 [S]	Sweet and Tuff	1966	$25
☐ SHL-32086	That Music City Feeling	1974	$12
☐ SHL-32051	The Ace of Sax	1969	$18
☐ HL-12019 [M]	The Great Show Tunes	1964	$25
☐ SHL-32019 [S]	The Great Show Tunes	1964	$30
☐ SHL-32057	The Happy and Mellow Sax of Ace Cannon	1970	$15
☐ SHL-32043	The Incomparable Sax of Ace Cannon	1968	$18
☐ HL-12035 [M]	The Misty Sax of Ace Cannon	1967	$25
☐ SHL-32035 [S]	The Misty Sax of Ace Cannon	1967	$18
☐ HL-12014 [M]	The Moanin' Sax of Ace Cannon	1963	$30
☐ SHL-32014 [S]	The Moanin' Sax of Ace Cannon	1963	$30
☐ HL-12007 [M]	Tuff Sax	1962	$30
☐ SHL-32007 [S]	Tuff Sax	1962	$30

CANNON, FREDDY
RHINO
| ☐ RNLP-210 | 14 Booming Hits | 1982 | $12 |

SWAN
☐ LP-507 [M]	Freddy Cannon at Palisades Park	1962	$175
☐ LP-511 [M]	Freddy Cannon Steps Out	1963	$175
☐ LP-504 [M]	Happy Shades of Blue	1960	$175
☐ LP-505 [M]	Solid Gold Hits	1961	$175
☐ LP-502 [M]	The Explosive! Freddy Cannon	1960	$120
☐ LPS-502 [S]	The Explosive! Freddy Cannon	1960	$300

WARNER BROS.
| ☐ W1612 [M] | Action! | 1965 | $30 |

Number	Title	Yr	NM
❏ WS1612 [S]	Action!	1965	$40
❏ W1544 [M]	Freddie Cannon	1964	$30
❏ WS1544 [S]	Freddie Cannon	1964	$40
❏ W1628 [M]	Freddy Cannon's Greatest Hits	1966	$30
❏ WS1628 [S]	Freddy Cannon's Greatest Hits	1966	$40

CANNON, GUS
STAX
Number	Title	Yr	NM
❏ ST-702 [M]	Walk Right In	1962	$600

CANO, EDDIE
ATCO
Number	Title	Yr	NM
❏ 33-184 [M]	On Broadway	1966	$12
❏ SD 33-184 [S]	On Broadway	1966	$15
DUNHILL			
❏ D-50018 [M]	Brought Back Live from P.J.'s	1967	$15
❏ DS-50018 [S]	Brought Back Live from P.J.'s	1967	$12
GNP CRESCENDO			
❏ GNP-77 [M]	A Taste of Cano	1963	$15
❏ GNPS-77 [S]	A Taste of Cano	1963	$18
PICKWICK			
❏ SPC-3017	25 Latin Dance Favorites	196?	$12
RCA VICTOR			
❏ LPM-1672 [M]	Time for Cha Cha Cha	1958	$18
REPRISE			
❏ R-6124 [M]	Broadway -- Right Now!	1964	$15
❏ R9-6124 [S]	Broadway -- Right Now!	1964	$18
❏ R-6068 [M]	Cano Plays Mancini	1963	$15
❏ R9-6068 [S]	Cano Plays Mancini	1963	$18
❏ R-6105 [M]	Danke Schoen	1963	$15
❏ R9-6105 [S]	Danke Schoen	1963	$18
❏ R-6030 [M]	Eddie Cano at P.J.'s	1962	$15
❏ R9-6030 [S]	Eddie Cano at P.J.'s	1962	$18
❏ R-6055 [M]	Here Is the Fabulous Eddie Cano	1963	$15
❏ R9-6055 [S]	Here Is the Fabulous Eddie Cano	1963	$18
❏ R-6145 [M]	The Sound of Music	1965	$15
❏ RS-6145 [S]	The Sound of Music	1965	$18

CANTELON, WILLARD
SUPREME
Number	Title	Yr	NM
❏ M-113 [M]	L.S.D. Battle for the Mind	1966	$30
❏ S-113 [S]	L.S.D. Battle for the Mind	1966	$40

CANTOR, EDDIE
VIK
Number	Title	Yr	NM
❏ LXA-1119 [M]	The Best of Eddie Cantor	1957	$50

CANTRELL, LANA
RCA VICTOR
Number	Title	Yr	NM
❏ LPM-3947 [M]	Act III	1968	$18
❏ LSP-3947 [S]	Act III	1968	$15
❏ LPM-3755 [M]	And Then There Was Lana	1967	$18
❏ LSP-3755 [S]	And Then There Was Lana	1967	$15
❏ LPM-3862 [M]	Another Shade of Lana	1967	$18
❏ LSP-3862 [S]	Another Shade of Lana	1967	$15
❏ LSP-4026	Lana!	1968	$15
❏ LSP-4121	Now or Then	1969	$15
❏ LSP-4263	The 6th Lana	1970	$15

CANTRELL, LAURA
SUNDAZED
Number	Title	Yr	NM
❏ LP-5163	When the Roses Bloom Again	2003	$18

CANYON
16TH AVENUE
Number	Title	Yr	NM
❏ D1-70552	I Guess I Just Missed You	1988	$12
❏ D1-70556	Radio Romance	1989	$12

CAPALDI, JIM
ANTILLIES
Number	Title	Yr	NM
❏ 7050	Short Cut Draw Blood	198?	$10
— Reissue of Island 9336			
ATLANTIC			
❏ 80059	Fierce Heart	1983	$12
❏ 80182	One Man Mission	1984	$12
ISLAND			
❏ SW-9314	Oh How We Danced	1972	$15
❏ ILPS9336	Short Cut Draw Blood	1976	$12
❏ 91024	Some Came Running	1988	$12
❏ ILPS9254	Whale Meat Again	1974	$12
RSO			
❏ RS-1-3037	Daughter of the Night	1978	$12
❏ RS-1-3050	Electric Nights	1979	$12
❏ RPO1015 [EP]	Special A.O.R. Sampler	1979	$18
— Promo-only collection			

CAPERS, VALERIE
ATLANTIC
Number	Title	Yr	NM
❏ SD3003	Portrait in Soul	1970	$35

CAPITAL CITY ROCKETS
Featuring Eric Moore of THE GODZ.
ELEKTRA
Number	Title	Yr	NM
❏ EKS-75079	Capital City Rockets	1973	$25

CAPITOLS, THE (1)
ATCO
Number	Title	Yr	NM
❏ 33-190 [M]	Dance the Cool Jerk	1966	$40
❏ SD 33-190 [S]	Dance the Cool Jerk	1966	$50
❏ 33-201 [M]	We Got a Thing That's in the Groove	1966	$40
❏ SD 33-201 [S]	We Got a Thing That's in the Groove	1966	$50
COLLECTABLES			
❏ COL-5105	Golden Classics	1988	$12
SOLID SMOKE			
❏ 8019	The Capitols: Their Greatest Hits	1983	$15

CAPP-PIERCE JUGGERNAUT, THE
CONCORD JAZZ
Number	Title	Yr	NM
❏ CJ-40	Juggernaut	1979	$30
— Frank Capp and Nat Pierce, leaders			
❏ CJ-336	Live at the Alley Cat	1988	$25
❏ CJ-72	Live at the Century Plaza	1980	$30
❏ CJ-183	The Juggernaut Orchestra Strikes Again	1981	$30

CAPRARO, JOE
SOUTHLAND
Number	Title	Yr	NM
❏ 220 [M]	Dixieland	1959	$25

CAPRIS, THE (1)
AMBIENT SOUND
Number	Title	Yr	NM
❏ FW37714	There's a Moon Out Again	1982	$18
COLLECTABLES			
❏ COL-5016	There's a Moon Out Tonight	198?	$15

CAPRIS, THE (2)
COLLECTABLES
Number	Title	Yr	NM
❏ COL-5000	Gotham Recording Stars	198?	$15

CAPTAIN AND TENNILLE
A&M
Number	Title	Yr	NM
❏ SP-4667	Captain & Tennille's Greatest Hits	1977	$12
❏ SP-3105	Captain & Tennille's Greatest Hits	198?	$10
— Reissue of 4667			
❏ SP-4700	Come In From the Rain	1977	$12
❏ SP-4707	Dream	1978	$12
❏ SP-3405	Love Will Keep Us Together	1975	$15
❏ SP-4552	Love Will Keep Us Together	1975	$12
— Reissue of 3405			
❏ QU-54552 [Q]	Love Will Keep Us Together	1975	$20
❏ SP-4561	Por Amor Vivremos	1975	$15
❏ SP-4570	Song of Joy	1976	$12
CASABLANCA			
❏ NBLP7250	Keeping Our Love Warm	1980	$12
❏ NBLP7188	Make Your Move	1979	$12

CAPTAIN BEEFHEART
Also see FRANK ZAPPA.
4 MEN WITH BEARDS
Number	Title	Yr	NM
❏ 4M211LP [B]	Doc At The Radar Station		$25
❏ 4M212LP [B]	Ice Cream For Crow		$25
A&M			
❏ SP-12510 [EP]	The Legendary A&M Sessions	1984	$18
BLUE THUMB			
❏ BTS-1	Strictly Personal	1968	$50
— Black label, unbanded sides			
❏ BTS-1	Strictly Personal	1969	$30
— White label, unbanded sides			
❏ BTS-1	Strictly Personal	197?	$25
— White label, banded sides			
BUDDAH			
❏ BDS-5077	Mirror Man	1971	$50
— Die-cut gatefold cover			
❏ BDS-5077 [B]	Mirror Man	197?	$30
— Regular cover			
❏ BDM-1001 [M]	Safe As Milk	1967	$150
❏ BDS-5001 [S]	Safe As Milk	1967	$75
❏ BDS-5063 [B]	Safe As Milk	1969	$30
❏ 1001/5001 [B]	Safe As Milk "Baby Jesus" Bumper Sticker	1967	$30
MERCURY			
❏ SRM-1-1018	Bluejeans and Moonbeams	1975	$25
❏ SRM-1-709	Unconditionally Guaranteed	1974	$25
REPRISE			
❏ MS2115	Clear Spot	1972	$30
❏ RS6420	Lick My Decals Off, Baby	1970	$30
❏ MS2050	The Spotlight Kid	1971	$30
❏ 2MS2027 [B]	Trout Mask Replica	1970	$40
— Stock copy with 2027 labels and 2027 jacket			

RHINO
Number	Title	Yr	NM
❏ R16420 [B]	Lick My Decals Off, Baby	2016	$25
STRAIGHT			
❏ RS-1053	Lick My Decals Off, Baby	1970	$50
❏ 2 STS-1053	Trout Mask Replica	1969	$300
— Stock copy with 1053 labels (this has been confirmed to exist)			
❏ 2MS2027 [DJ]	Trout Mask Replica	1969	$175
— White label promo with 2027 labels inside 1053 jacket			
❏ 2MS2027	Trout Mask Replica	1969	$75
— Stock copy with 2027 labels inside 1053 jacket			
❏ 2 STS-1053 [DJ]	Trout Mask Replica	1969	$250
— White label promo with 1053 labels			
SUNDAZED			
❏ LP5460 [B]	Safe As Milk	2013	$30
VERVE FORECAST			
❏ FTS-3054	Captain Beefheart and the Magic Band	1968	$0
— Canceled			
VIRGIN			
❏ VA13148	Doc at the Radar Station	1980	$15
VIRGIN/EPIC			
❏ ARE38274	Ice Cream for Crow	1982	$15
WARNER BROS.			
❏ 0(no cat #)	Bat Chain Puller	1978	$400
— Test pressing with different selections than stock version			
❏ BSK3256	Shiny Beast (Bat Chain Puller)	1978	$18

CAPTAIN BEYOND
Also see DEEP PURPLE; ARMAGEDDON; IRON BUTTERFLY.
CAPRICORN
Number	Title	Yr	NM
❏ CP 0105	Captain Beyond	1972	$30
— Original covers are 3-D			
❏ CP 0105	Captain Beyond	1972	$18
— Later covers are normal			
❏ CP 0115	Sufficiently Breathless	1973	$18
CLEOPATRA			
❏ CLP1716 [B]	Captain Beyond	2014	$25
❏ CLP0150 [B]	Captain Beyond	2013	$30
❏ CLP0296 [B]	Live In Texas October 6, 1973	2013	$30
❏ CLP0149 [B]	Sufficiently Breathless	2013	$30
WARNER BROS.			
❏ BS3047	Dawn Explosion	1977	$15

CAPTAIN SKY
AVI
Number	Title	Yr	NM
❏ 6077	Pop Goes the Captain	1979	$18
❏ 6042	The Adventures of Captain Sky	1978	$40
❏ 6100	The Return of Captain Sky	1981	$30
TEC			
❏ 1202	Concerned Party No. 1	1980	$25

CARA, IRENE
ELEKTRA
Number	Title	Yr	NM
❏ 60724	Carasmatic	1987	$12
GEFFEN			
❏ GHS4021	What a Feelin'	1983	$10
NETWORK			
❏ E1-60003	Anyone Can See	1982	$12

CARAM, ANA
CHESKY
Number	Title	Yr	NM
❏ JR-28	Rio After Dark	199?	$30
— Audiophile vinyl			

CARAMIA, TONY
STOMP OFF
Number	Title	Yr	NM
❏ SOS-1209	Hot Ivories	1991	$35

CARAVAN, JIMMY
TOWER
Number	Title	Yr	NM
❏ T5103 [M]	Look Into the Flower	1968	$50
❏ ST5103 [S]	Look Into the Flower	1968	$25
VAULT			
❏ 9007	Hey Jude	1969	$25

CARAVAN
4 MEN WITH BEARDS
Number	Title	Yr	NM
❏ 4M237 [B]	If I Could Do It All Over Again, I'd Do It All Over You	2013	$25
ARISTA			
❏ AL4088	Blind Dog at St. Dunstans	1976	$12
BTM			
❏ 5000	Cunning Stunts	1975	$12

Number	Title	Yr	NM

LONDON

Number	Title	Yr	NM
❏ XPS650	Caravan and the New Symphonia	1974	$18
❏ XPS637	For Girls Who Grow Plump in the Night	1973	$18
❏ PS582	If I Could Do It All Over Again…	1971	$18
❏ PS593	In the Land of the Grey & Pink	1971	$18
❏ LC50011 [B]	The Best of Caravan	1978	$25
❏ XPS615	Waterloo Lily	1972	$18

VERVE FORECAST

❏ FTS-3066 [B]	Caravan	1969	$75

CARAVELLES, THE (1)

SMASH

❏ MGS-27044 [M]	You Don't Have to Be a Baby to Cry	1963	$75
❏ SRS-67044 [R]	You Don't Have to Be a Baby to Cry	1963	$75

CARBO, GLADYS

SOUL NOTE

❏ 121197	Street Cries	1990	$30

CARE PACKAGE

LIBERTY

❏ LST-7647	Keep On Keepin' On	1970	$30

CAREFREES, THE

LONDON

❏ LL3379 [M]	From England! The Carefrees	1964	$100
❏ PS379 [S]	From England! The Carefrees	1964	$150

CAREY, DAVE

LAURIE

❏ LLP-1004 [M]	Bandwagon Plus 2	1959	$30

CAREY, MARIAH

COLUMBIA

❏ C269670	#1's	1998	$25
❏ C47980	Emotions	1991	$18
❏ C45202	Mariah Carey	1990	$25
❏ C53205	Music Box	1993	$18
❏ C263800	Rainbow	1999	$18

ISLAND

❏ 440 063467-1	Charmbracelet	2002	$18
❏ B0003943-01	The Emancipation of Mimi	2005	$18
❏ B0003943-01	The Emancipation of Mimi	2005	$18

VIRGIN

❏ SPRO-16452 [DJ]	Glitter	2001	$25

— *Promo-only version*

❏ 10797	Glitter	2001	$18

CAREY, MUTT, AND PUNCH MILLER

SAVOY

❏ MG-12038 [M]	Jazz -- New Orleans	1955	$150
❏ MG-12050 [M]	Jazz -- New Orleans, Vol. 2	1955	$150

SAVOY JAZZ

❏ SJC-415	New Orleans Jazz	1985	$25

CAREY, MUTT

RIVERSIDE

❏ RLP-1042 [10]	Mutt Carey Plays the Blues	1954	$300

CARGILL, FIDELIA B. (THE CHRISTMAS LADY)

(NO LABEL)

❏ 5-5945	Bringing In Christmas	196?	$18

— *Title on jacket; title on label is "Bring In Christmas"*

CARGILL, HENSON

ATLANTIC

❏ SD7279	This Is Henson Cargill Country	1973	$15

HARMONY

❏ KH31397	Welcome to My World	1972	$12

MEGA

❏ 31-1016	On the Road	1972	$18

MONUMENT

❏ SLP-18103	Coming On Strong	1968	$25
❏ SLP-18117	None of My Business	1969	$25
❏ SLP-18094	Skip a Rope	1968	$25
❏ SLP-18137	Uncomplicated	1970	$25

CARISI, JOHN

COLUMBIA

❏ CL1419 [M]	The New Jazz Sound of "Show Boat"	1960	$30
❏ CS(# unk) [S]	The New Jazz Sound of "Show Boat"	1960	$30

Number	Title	Yr	NM

CARLILE, TOM

DOOR KNOB

❏ 1006	The Tom Carlile Feel	198?	$18

CARLIN, GEORGE

ATLANTIC

❏ SD19326	A Place for My Stuff	1981	$12

EARDRUM

❏ 1001	Carlin On Campus	1984	$12
❏ 90523	Playin' with Your Head	1986	$12
❏ 90972	What Am I Doing in New Jersey	1988	$12

ERA

❏ EL103 [M]	George Carlin and Jack Burns At the Playboy Club Tonight	1960	$30
❏ E600	The Original George Carlin	1972	$15

LAFF

❏ A219	Killer Carlin	1981	$12

— *Reissue of Era material*

LITTLE DAVID

❏ LD1008	An Evening with Wally Londo	1975	$12
❏ LD1004	Class Clown	1972	$12

❏ LD7214 [B]	FM & AM	1972	$12
❏ LD1076	Indecent Exposure (Some of the Best of George Carlin)	1978	$12
❏ LD1005	Occupation: Foole	1973	$12
❏ LD1075	On the Road	1977	$12
❏ 90241	The George Carlin Collection	1984	$10
❏ LD3003	Toledo Window Box	1974	$12
❏ 90129	Toledo Window Box	1983	$10

— *Reissue of 3003*

RCA CAMDEN

❏ CAS-2566	Take-Offs and Put-Ons	1972	$12

RCA VICTOR

❏ LPM-3772 [M]	Take-Offs and Put-Ons	1967	$25
❏ LSP-3772 [S]	Take-Offs and Put-Ons	1967	$18

CARLISLE, BELINDA

I.R.S.

❏ R114824	Belinda	1986	$15

— *RCA Music Service edition*

❏ 5741	Belinda	1986	$12

MCA

❏ R143541	Heaven on Earth	1987	$15

— *BMG Direct Marketing edition*

❏ 42080	Heaven on Earth	1987	$12
❏ R173667	Runaway Horses	1989	$15

— *BMG Direct Marketing edition*

❏ 6339	Runaway Horses	1989	$12

CARLISLE, BILL

HICKORY

❏ LPS-129 [S]	The Best of Bill Carlisle	1967	$30
❏ LPM-129 [M]	The Best of Bill Carlisle	1967	$30

CARLISLE, CLIFF

OLD TIMEY

❏ 103	Cliff Carlisle, Volume 1	198?	$15
❏ 104	Cliff Carlisle, Volume 2	198?	$15

CARLISLE BROTHERS, THE

KING

❏ 643 [M]	Fresh from the Country	1959	$50

MERCURY

❏ MG-20359 [M]	On Stage with the Carlisles	1958	$50

Number	Title	Yr	NM

CARLOS, WALTER

CBS MASTERWORKS

❏ M39340	Digital Moonscapes	1984	$12

— *As "Wendy Carlos*

COLUMBIA

❏ KG31236	Sonic Seasonings	1972	$18
❏ KC31480	Walter Carlos' Clockwork Orange	1972	$15

COLUMBIA MASTERWORKS

❏ KM32659	More Switched-On Bach	1974	$15
❏ MS7194	Switched-On Bach	1968	$18

— *Standing Bach" cover; gray label with "360 Sound Stereo*

❏ MS7194	Switched-On Bach	1970	$15

— *Gray label with orange Columbia logos and no "360 Sound Stereo*

❏ HM47194	Switched-On Bach	198?	$30

— *Half-speed mastered edition*

❏ MS7194	Switched-On Bach	1968	$50

— *Sitting Bach" (sometimes called "Constipated Bach") cover that was quickly replaced; gray label with "360 Sound Stereo*

❏ MS7194	Switched-On Bach	198?	$18

— *Later reissue under the name "Wendy Carlos"; bar code on back cover*

❏ M2X35895	Switched-On Brandenburgs	1979	$18
❏ HM45950	Switched-On Brandenburgs Vol. 1	1980	$150

— *Half-speed mastered edition*

❏ MS7286	The Well-Tempered Synthesizer	1969	$18

— *Gray label with "360 Sound Stereo*

❏ MS7286	The Well-Tempered Synthesizer	1970	$15

— *Gray label with orange Columbia logos and no "360 Sound Stereo*

❏ M32088	Walter Carlos By Request	1973	$15

CARLTON, CARL

20TH CENTURY

❏ T-628	Carl Carlton	1981	$12

ABC

❏ D-857	Everlasting Love	1974	$15
❏ D-910	I Wanna Be with You	1975	$15

BACK BEAT

❏ BBLX-71	Can't Stop a Man in Love	1973	$18

CASABLANCA

❏ 822705-1	Private Property	1985	$12

RCA VICTOR

❏ AFL1-4425	The Bad C.C.	1982	$12

CARLTON, LARRY

BLUE THUMB

❏ BTS-46	Singing/Playing	1972	$35

GRP

❏ 9611	Collection	1990	$30

MCA

❏ 5689	Alone/But Never Alone	1986	$20
❏ 6322	Christmas at Our House	1989	$25
❏ 42003	Discovery	1987	$20
❏ 6237	On Solid Ground	1989	$20

UNI

❏ 73036	With a Little Help from My Friends	1968	$50

WARNER BROS.

❏ 23834	Friends	1983	$20
❏ BSK3221	Larry Carlton	1978	$25
❏ BSK3635	Sleepwalk	1981	$25
❏ BSK3380	Strikes Twice	1980	$25

CARMEN, ERIC

Also see CYRUS ERIE; THE QUICK; RASPBERRIES.

ARISTA

❏ AB4124	Boats Against the Current	1977	$10
❏ AB4184	Change of Heart	1978	$10
❏ AL4057	Eric Carmen	1975	$15

— *Shiny, simulated gold foil cover*

❏ AL4057	Eric Carmen	1975	$10

— *Regular non-shiny gold cover*

❏ AQ4057 [Q]	Eric Carmen	1975	$30
❏ AL8547	The Best of Eric Carmen	1988	$18

— *Original copies do not contain "Make Me Lose Control*

❏ AL8547	The Best of Eric Carmen	1988	$10

— *Reissues add "Make Me Lose Control*

❏ AL9513	Tonight You're Mine	1980	$10

GEFFEN

❏ GHS24042	Eric Carmen	1985	$10

CARMEN

EPIC

❏ BN26479	Carmen	1969	$25

CARMICHAEL, HOAGY

BIOGRAPH

❏ 37	Stardust (1927-30)	198?	$25

Number	Title	Yr	NM
BLUEBIRD			
❏ 8333-1-RB	Stardust, And Much More	1989	$30
BOOK-OF-THE-MONTH			
❏ 61-5450	Hoagy Carmichael	1984	$30
DECCA			
❏ DL5068 [10]	Stardust Road	1950	$175
❏ DL8588 [M]	Stardust Road	1958	$150
GOLDEN			
❏ LP-198-18 [M]	Havin' a Party	1958	$30
JAZZTONE			
❏ J-1266 [M]	Hoagy Sings Carmichael	1957	$30
KIMBERLY			
❏ 2023 [M]	The Legend of Hoagy Carmichael	1962	$30
❏ 11023 [R]	The Legend of Hoagy Carmichael	196?	$25
MCA			
❏ 20196	Hong Kong Blues	198?	$25
❏ 1507	Stardust Road	198?	$25
PACIFIC JAZZ			
❏ PJ-1223 [M]	Hoagy Sings Carmichael	1956	$75
PAUSA			
❏ 9006	Hoagy Sings Carmichael	1982	$25
RCA VICTOR			
❏ CPL1-3370(e)	A Legendary Performer and Composer	1979	$35
❏ LPT-3072 [10]	Old Rockin' Chair	1953	$100
TOTEM			
❏ 1039	The 1944-45 V-Disc Sessions	198?	$25

CARMICHAEL, JUDY

Number	Title	Yr	NM
STATIRAS			
❏ SLP-8074	Jazz Piano	1985	$30
❏ SLP-8078	Pearls	1986	$30
❏ SLP-8072	Two-Handed Stride	1985	$30

CARMICHAEL, RALPH

Number	Title	Yr	NM
CAPITOL			
❏ T1819 [M]	I Can Dream, Can't I?	1963	$15
❏ ST1819 [S]	I Can Dream, Can't I?	1963	$18

CARN, DOUG, AND JEAN CARN

Number	Title	Yr	NM
BLACK JAZZ			
❏ 3	Infant Eyes	1971	$35
❏ QT-16 [Q]	Revelation	1973	$40
❏ QD-8 [Q]	Spirit of the New Land	1972	$40
OVATION			
❏ 1702	Higher Ground	197?	$30

CARN, DOUG

Number	Title	Yr	NM
SAVOY			
❏ MG-12195	The Doug Carn Trio	1969	$25
TABLIGHI			
❏ 100	Ah Rahman!	1978	$30

CARNES, KIM

Number	Title	Yr	NM
A&M			
❏ SP-4548	Kim Carnes	1975	$15
❏ SP-4606	Sailin'	1976	$15
❏ SP-3114	Sailin'	198?	$10
—Budget-line reissue			
❏ SP-3204	The Best of Kim Carnes	1982	$12
AMOS			
❏ AAS7016 [B]	Rest on Me	1971	$30
EMI AMERICA			
❏ SO-17159	Barking at Airplanes	1985	$12
❏ SO-17107	Café Racers	1983	$12
❏ ST-17198	Light House	1986	$10
❏ SO-17052	Mistaken Identity	1981	$12
❏ SW-17030	Romance Dance	1980	$12
❏ SW-17004	St. Vincent's Court	1978	$12
❏ SO-17078	Voyeur	1982	$12
MCA			
❏ 914	The Early Years	1984	$10
❏ 42200	View from the House	1988	$10
MOBILE FIDELITY			
❏ Jan-0073	Mistaken Identity	1982	$50
—Audiophile vinyl			

CARNEY, ART

Number	Title	Yr	NM
COLUMBIA			
❏ CL2595 [10]	Doodle-Li-Boops and Rhinocelopes	1955	$100

CARNEY, HARRY

Number	Title	Yr	NM
CLEF			
❏ MGC-640 [M]	Harry Carney with Strings	1955	$175
VERVE			
❏ MGV-2028 [M]	Moods for Girl and Boy	1957	$300
—Reissue of Clef 640			
❏ V-2028 [M]	Moods for Girl and Boy	1957	$175

CARNIVAL

Number	Title	Yr	NM
WORLD PACIFIC			
❏ ST-21894	The Carnival	1969	$15

CAROLEERS, THE

Number	Title	Yr	NM
ALLEGRO ROYALE			
❏ 1295 [M]	An Hour of Christmas Music	195?	$25
—B-side by anonymous "Organ and Chimes			
PARADE			
❏ XSP417 [M]	Christmas with the Caroleers	195?	$18

CAROLERS, THE

Number	Title	Yr	NM
VANGUARD CARDINAL			
❏ VCS10015	A Music Box of Christmas Carols	1967	$20
—With Music Boxes from the Borland Collection…also see "Welch Chorale, The			

CAROLINA SLIM

Number	Title	Yr	NM
SHARP			
❏ 2002 [M]	Blues from the Cotton Fields	195?	$300

CARP
Actor Gary Busey was in this group.

Number	Title	Yr	NM
EPIC			
❏ E30212	Carp	1970	$30

CARPENTER, IKE

Number	Title	Yr	NM
ALADDIN			
❏ LP-811 [M]	Lights Out	1957	$0
—Unreleased			
DISCOVERY			
❏ DL3003 [10]	Dancers in Love	1949	$300
INTRO			
❏ 950 [10]	Lights Out	1952	$300
SCORE			
❏ SLP-4010 [M]	Lights Out	1957	$175

CARPENTER, MARY CHAPIN

Number	Title	Yr	NM
COLUMBIA			
❏ FC40758	Hometown Girl	1987	$12
❏ FC44228	State of the Heart	1989	$12
❏ LLR001 [B]	The Things That We Are Made Of	2016	$25

CARPENTERS

Number	Title	Yr	NM
A&M			
❏ SP-4581	A Kind of Hush	1976	$15
❏ SP-3197	A Kind of Hush	1982	$10
—Reissue of 4581			
❏ SP-5172	An Old Fashioned Christmas	1987	$10
—Reissue of 3270 (record still says 3270 but cover is 5172)			
❏ SP-3270	An Old-Fashioned Christmas	1984	$12
❏ SP-3511	A Song for You	1972	$15
❏ QU-53511 [Q]	A Song for You	1974	$0
—Not released			
❏ SMAS-94398	A Song for You	1972	$25
—Capitol Record Club edition; unlike the standard edition, the cover is smooth and not textured			
❏ SP-3502 [B]	Carpenters	1971	$15
❏ QU-53502 [Q]	Carpenters	1974	$0
—Not released			
❏ SP-4726	Christmas Portrait	1978	$18
❏ SP-3210	Christmas Portrait	198?	$10
—Reissue of SP-4726			
❏ SP-4271	Close to You	1970	$15
❏ QU-54271 [Q]	Close to You	1974	$0
—Not released			
❏ SP-3184	Close to You	1982	$10
—Reissue of 4271			
❏ SP-4530	Horizon	1975	$15
❏ QU-54530 [Q]	Horizon	1975	$40
❏ SP-3723	Made in America	1981	$15
❏ SP-3519	Now & Then	1973	$15
❏ QU-53519 [Q]	Now & Then	1974	$40
❏ SP-4205	Offering	1969	$100
❏ SP-4703	Passage	1977	$15
❏ SP-3199	Passage	1982	$10
—Reissue of 4703			
❏ SP-3601	The Singles 1969-1973	1973	$15
❏ QU-53601 [Q]	The Singles 1969-1973	1974	$40
❏ SP-4205	Ticket to Ride	1970	$15
—Reissue of "Offering" with new title and cover			
❏ SP-4954	Voice of the Heart	1983	$15
❏ SP-6601	Yesterday Once More	1985	$18

CARR, CATHY

Number	Title	Yr	NM
DOT			
❏ DLP-3674 [M]	Ivory Tower	1966	$30
❏ DLP-25674 [S]	Ivory Tower	1966	$30
FRATERNITY			
❏ 1005 [M]	Ivory Tower	1957	$120

ROULETTE

Number	Title	Yr	NM
❏ R25077 [M]	Shy	1959	$40
❏ SR25077 [S]	Shy	1959	$50

CARR, GEORGIA

Number	Title	Yr	NM
TOPS			
❏ L-1617 [M]	Songs by a Moody Miss	195?	$30
VEE JAY			
❏ LP-1105 [M]	Rocks in My Bed	1964	$25
❏ VJS-1105 [S]	Rocks in My Bed	1964	$30

CARR, HELEN

Number	Title	Yr	NM
BETHLEHEM			
❏ BCP-1027 [10]	Down in the Depths on the 90th Floor	1955	$300
❏ BCP-45 [M]	Why Do I Love You	1956	$300

CARR, IAN, AND NUCLEUS

Number	Title	Yr	NM
CAPITOL			
❏ ST-11771	In Flagrante Delicto	1978	$30
❏ ST-11916	Out of the Long Dark	1979	$30

CARR, JAMES

Number	Title	Yr	NM
GOLDWAX			
❏ 3002S	A Man Needs a Woman	1968	$175
❏ 3001S	You Got My Mind Messed Up	1968	$175

CARR, JOE "FINGERS

Number	Title	Yr	NM
CAPITOL			
❏ T280 [M]	Bar Room Piano	1952	$30
❏ T1151 [M]	Fingers" and the Flapper	1959	$25
❏ ST1151 [S]	Fingers" and the Flapper	1959	$30
❏ T527 [M]	Fireman's Ball	1954	$30
❏ T443 [M]	Joe "Fingers" Carr and His Ragtime Band	1954	$30
❏ T1217 [M]	Joe "Fingers" Carr and His Swingin' String Band	1959	$25
❏ ST1217 [S]	Joe "Fingers" Carr and His Swingin' String Band	1959	$30
❏ T345 [M]	Roughhouse Piano	1953	$30
WARNER BROS.			
❏ W1386 [M]	The World's Greatest Ragtime Piano Player	1960	$18
❏ WS1386 [S]	The World's Greatest Ragtime Piano Player	1960	$25

CARR, JOYCE

Number	Title	Yr	NM
AUDIOPHILE			
❏ AP-148	Joyce Carr	198?	$30
SEECO			
❏ 440 [M]	Make The Man Love Me	1960	$325

CARR, LARRY

Number	Title	Yr	NM
AUDIOPHILE			
❏ AP-223	Fit as a Fiddle	198?	$30

CARR, LEROY

Number	Title	Yr	NM
COLUMBIA			
❏ CL1911 [M]	Blues Before Sunrise	1962	$30
❏ CS8511 [R]	Blues Before Sunrise	1962	$25

CARR, LODI

Number	Title	Yr	NM
LAURIE			
❏ LLP-1007 [M]	Lady Bird	1960	$30

CARR, RICHARD

Number	Title	Yr	NM
AUDIOPHILE			
❏ AP-194	Afternoon in New York	1984	$30
PROGRESSIVE			
❏ P-7047	String Vibrations	1986	$30

CARR, VIKKI

Number	Title	Yr	NM
COLUMBIA			
❏ KC31470	Canta En Espanol	1972	$12
❏ PC33340	Hoy (Today)	1975	$12
❏ KG32656	Live at the Greek Theatre	1973	$15
❏ CG33609	Love Story/The First Time Ever	1976	$15
❏ KC32251	Ms. America	1973	$12
❏ KC32860	One Hell of a Woman	1974	$12
❏ C31040	Superstar	1971	$12
❏ KC31453	The First Time Ever (I Saw Your Face)	1972	$12
❏ C30662	Vikki Carr's Love Story	1971	$12
LIBERTY			
❏ LRP-3314 [M]	Color Her Great	1963	$18
❏ LST-7314 [S]	Color Her Great	1963	$25
❏ LRP-3354 [M]	Discovery!	1964	$18
❏ LST-7354 [S]	Discovery!	1964	$25
❏ LRP-3383 [M]	Discovery! Volume Two	1964	$18
❏ LST-7383 [S]	Discovery! Volume Two	1964	$25
❏ LST-7565	Don't Break My Pretty Balloon	1969	$18
❏ LST-7604	For Once in My Life	1969	$18
❏ LRP-3506 [M]	Intimate Excitement	1967	$25
❏ LST-7506 [S]	Intimate Excitement	1967	$18

Number	Title	Yr	NM
❏ LRP-3533 [M]	It Must Be Him	1967	$25
❏ LST-7533 [S]	It Must Be Him	1967	$18
❏ LST-11001	Nashville by Carr	1970	$18
❏ LRP-3420 [M]	The Anatomy of Love	1965	$18

❏ LST-7420 [S]	The Anatomy of Love	1965	$25
❏ LN-10108	The Best of Vikki Carr	1981	$10
❏ LRP-3456 [M]	The Way of Today	1966	$18
❏ LST-7456 [S]	The Way of Today	1966	$25
❏ LST-7548 [S]	Vikki	1968	$18
❏ LRP-3548 [M]	Vikki	1968	$30

—Mono stock copy inside stereo cover with "Audition Mono LP Not for Sale" sticker

PAIR

❏ PDL2-1082	From the Heart	1986	$15

PICKWICK

❏ SPC-3587	Intimate	1978	$10
❏ SPC-3613	Unforgettable	1978	$10

SUNSET

❏ SUS-5228	That's All	1969	$12
❏ SUS-5293	Unforgettable	1971	$12

UNITED ARTISTS

❏ LM-1006	It Must Be Him	1980	$12

—Abridged reissue of Liberty 7533

❏ UAS-5581	The Best of Vikki Carr	1972	$15
❏ UA-LA244-G	The Very Best of Vikki Carr	1974	$12
❏ UAS-6813	The Ways to Love a Man	1972	$12
❏ UA-LA089-G	Vikki Carr's Golden Songbook/Superpak	1973	$15

CARRACK, PAUL

CHRYSALIS

❏ F1-21709	Groove Approved	1989	$15
❏ BFV41578	One Good Reason	1987	$10
❏ 6V41663	The Carrack Collection	1988	$12

EPIC

❏ ARE38161	Suburban Voodoo	1982	$10

CARRASCO, JOE "KING", AND THE CROWNS

HANNIBAL

❏ HNBL-1308	Joe "King" Carrasco and the Crowns	1980	$18
❏ HNEP-3301 [EP]	Party Safari	1981	$18

MCA

❏ 5404	Party Weekend	1983	$15
❏ 5308	Synapse Gap	1982	$18

ROUNDER

❏ 9012	Bandido Rock	1987	$12

CARRINGTON, TERRI LYNN

VERVE

❏ 837697-1	Real Life Story	1989	$35

CARROLL, ANDREA /BEVERLY WARREN

B.T. PUPPY

❏ BTS-1017	Andrea Carroll and Beverly Warren Side By Side	1971	$175

CARROLL, BAIKIDA

HAT HUT

❏ 0M/N	The Spoken Word	197?	$25

SOUL NOTE

❏ SN-1023	Shadows & Reflections	198?	$30

CARROLL, BARBARA

ATLANTIC

❏ ALR-132 [10]	Piano Panorama	195?	$100

BLUE NOTE

❏ BN-LA645-H2	Barbara Carroll	1976	$35

DISCOVERY

❏ DS-847	Barbara Carrol at the Piano	1980	$35

KAPP

❏ KL-1113 [M]	Flower Drum Song	1958	$30
❏ KS-(# unk) [S]	Flower Drum Song	1958	$30
❏ KL-1193 [M]	Satin Doll	1959	$30

LIVINGSTON

❏ 1081 [10]	Barbara Carroll Trio	1953	$150

RCA VICTOR

❏ LJM-1001 [M]	Barbara Carroll Trio	1954	$50
❏ LPM-1137 [M]	Have You Met Miss Carroll?	1956	$50
❏ LPM-1396 [M]	It's a Wonderful World	1957	$50
❏ LJM-1023 [M]	Lullabies in Rhythm	1955	$75
❏ LPM-1296 [M]	We Just Couldn't Say Goodbye	1956	$50

SESAC

❏ N-3201 [M]	Why Not?	1959	$75
❏ SN-3201 [S]	Why Not?	1959	$40

UNITED ARTISTS

❏ UA-LA778-H	From the Beginning	1978	$20

VERVE

❏ MGV-2095 [M]	Barbara	1958	$175
❏ V-2095 [M]	Barbara	1961	$25
❏ MGV-2063 [M]	Funny Face	1957	$175

—Orange label

❏ MGV-2063 [M]	Funny Face	1957	$175

—Black label

❏ MGV-2092 [M]	The Best of George and Ira Gershwin	1958	$120
❏ V-2092 [M]	The Best of George and Ira Gershwin	1961	$25

WARNER BROS.

❏ W1710 [M]	Barbara Carroll Live! Her Piano and Trio	1967	$50
❏ WS1710 [S]	Barbara Carroll Live! Her Piano and Trio	1967	$50
❏ W1543 [M]	Hello Dolly" and "What Makes Sammy Run	1964	$35
❏ WS1543 [S]	Hello Dolly" and "What Makes Sammy Run	1964	$50

CARROLL, BARBARA/MARY LOU WILLIAMS

ATLANTIC

❏ 1271 [M]	Ladies in Jazz	1958	$300

—Black label

❏ 1271 [M]	Ladies in Jazz	1961	$175

—Multi-color label, white "fan" logo

CARROLL, CORKY

CASUAL TUNA

❏ 0(# unknown)	A Surfer for President	1979	$40

RURAL

❏ RR-001	Laid Back	1971	$85

CARROLL, DAVID

AMBASSADOR

❏ S-98051	All Time Great Hits	196?	$12

MERCURY

❏ PPS-2022 [M]	All the World Dances	196?	$18
❏ PPS-6022 [S]	All the World Dances	196?	$25
❏ SR-60873 [S]	All the World Dances	196?	$25
❏ MG-20873 [M]	All the World Dances	196?	$18
❏ MG-20351 [M]	Dance and Stay Young	195?	$18
❏ SR-60027 [S]	Dance and Stay Young	1959	$25
❏ MG-20109 [M]	Dancer's Delight	195?	$25
❏ SR-60690 [S]	David Carroll Galaxy	196?	$25
❏ MG-20690 [M]	David Carroll Galaxy	196?	$18
❏ MG-20301 [M]	Dreams	195?	$25
❏ MG-20286 [M]	Feathery Feeling	195?	$18
❏ SR-60026 [S]	Feathery Feeling	1959	$25
❏ MG-20935 [M]	Golden Oldies for Today's Teens	196?	$15
❏ SR-60935 [S]	Golden Oldies for Today's Teens	196?	$18
❏ MG-20846 [M]	Happy Feet	196?	$18
❏ SR-60846 [S]	Happy Feet	196?	$25
❏ MG-20962 [M]	House Party Discotheque	196?	$15
❏ SR-60962 [S]	House Party Discotheque	196?	$18
❏ PPS-2000 [M]	Latin Percussion	196?	$18
❏ PPS-6000 [S]	Latin Percussion	196?	$25
❏ MG-20281 [M]	Let's Dance	195?	$18
❏ SR-60001 [S]	Let's Dance	1959	$25
❏ MG-20470 [M]	Let's Dance Again	195?	$18
❏ SR-60152 [S]	Let's Dance Again	1959	$25
❏ MG-20649 [M]	Let's Dance Dance Dance	196?	$18
❏ SR-60649 [S]	Let's Dance Dance Dance	196?	$25
❏ MG-20739 [M]	Let's Dance to America's Waltz Favorites	196?	$18
❏ SR-60739 [S]	Let's Dance to America's Waltz Favorites	196?	$25
❏ MG-20688 [M]	Let's Dance to the Movie Themes	196?	$18
❏ MG-60688 [S]	Let's Dance to the Movie Themes	196?	$25
❏ MG-20660 [M]	Mexico and 11 Other Great Hits	196?	$18
❏ SR-60660 [S]	Mexico and 11 Other Great Hits	196?	$25
❏ MG-20926 [M]	Music Makes Me Want to Dance!	196?	$15
❏ SR-60926 [S]	Music Makes Me Want to Dance!	196?	$18
❏ MG-20166 [M]	Percussion in Hi-Fi	195?	$18
❏ SR-60003 [S]	Percussion in Hi-Fi	1959	$25

❏ MG-20867 [M]	Percussion Orientale	196?	$18
❏ SR-60867 [S]	Percussion Orientale	196?	$25
❏ PPS-2008 [M]	Percussion Parisienne	196?	$18
❏ PPS-6008 [S]	Percussion Parisienne	196?	$25
❏ MG-20955 [M]	Percussion Parisienne	196?	$15
❏ SR-60955 [S]	Percussion Parisienne	196?	$18
❏ MG-20389 [M]	RePercussion	195?	$18
❏ SR-60029 [S]	RePercussion	1959	$25
❏ MG-20156 [M]	Serenade to a Princess	195?	$25
❏ MG-20154 [M]	Shimmering Strings	195?	$25
❏ MG-20411 [M]	Show Stoppers from the Fabulous Fifties	195?	$18
❏ SR-60060 [S]	Show Stoppers from the Fabulous Fifties	1959	$25
❏ MG-20503 [M]	Solo Encores	195?	$18
❏ SR-60180 [S]	Solo Encores	195?	$25
❏ SR-60786 [S]	Today's Top Hits	196?	$25
❏ MG-20786 [M]	Today's Top Hits	196?	$18
❏ MG-20064 [M]	Toe-Tappers	195?	$25
❏ MG-20086 [M]	Waltzes, Wine and Candlelight	195?	$25

WING

❏ MGW-12146 [M]	Contrasts	195?	$18
❏ SRW-12508 [S]	Contrasts	195?	$18
❏ MGW-12106 [M]	Dance Date	195?	$18
❏ SRW-16106 [S]	Dance Date	195?	$18
❏ SRW-16367	Let's Dance	196?	$15
❏ MGW-12256 [M]	Waltzes	196?	$15
❏ SRW-16256 [S]	Waltzes	196?	$15

CARROLL, DIAHANN, AND ANDRE PREVIN

UNITED ARTISTS

❏ UAL3069 [M]	Diahann Carroll and Andre Previn	1960	$25
❏ UAS6069 [S]	Diahann Carroll and Andre Previn	1960	$30
❏ UAL4021 [M]	Porgy and Bess	1959	$25
❏ UAS5021 [S]	Porgy and Bess	1959	$30

CARROLL, DIAHANN

ATLANTIC

❏ 8048 [M]	Fun Life	1961	$25
❏ SD8048 [S]	Fun Life	1961	$30

RCA CAMDEN

❏ CAL-695 [M]	Show-Stoppers (She's Diahann Carroll)	1961	$15

RCA VICTOR

❏ LPM-1467 [M]	Diahann Carroll Sings Harold Arlen	1957	$40

UNITED ARTISTS

❏ UAL3080 [M]	Diahann Carroll at the Persian Room	1960	$25
❏ UAS6080 [S]	Diahann Carroll at the Persian Room	1960	$30

VIK

❏ LXA-1131 [M]	Best Beat Forward	1958	$30

CARROLL, JIM, BAND

ATCO

❏ SD 38-132	Catholic Boy	1980	$25
❏ SD 38-145	Dry Dreams	1982	$16

ATLANTIC

❏ 80123	I Write Your Name	1984	$18

CARROLL, JIM

A&M

❏ SP-4323	Jim Carroll	1971	$15

CARROLL, JOE

CHARLIE PARKER

❏ PLP-802 [M]	The Man with the Happy Sound	1962	$30
❏ PLP-802S [S]	The Man with the Happy Sound	1962	$30

EPIC

❏ LN3272 [M]	Joe Carroll	1956	$150

CARROLL, JOHNNY

HMG/HIGHTONE

❏ HT6602	Texabilly	1997	$12

CARROLL BROTHERS, THE

CAMEO

❏ C-1015 [M]	College Twist Party	1962	$30
❏ SC-1015 [S]	College Twist Party	1962	$40

CARS, THE

DCC COMPACT CLASSICS

❏ LPZ-2056	The Cars Greatest Hits	1998	$30

—Audiophile vinyl

ELEKTRA

❏ 5E-507	Candy-O	1979	$12

—No title and artist listed on front cover (information was on a sticker on the shrink wrap)

❏ R123334	Candy-O	1979	$15

—RCA Music Service edition has "The Cars Candy-O" printed on upper left front cover

Number	Title	Yr	NM
❑ R161593	Door to Door	1987	$12
—BMG Direct Marketing edition			
❑ 60747	Door to Door	1987	$10
❑ R153702	Greatest Hits	1985	$15
—RCA Music Service edition			
❑ 60464	Greatest Hits	1985	$12
❑ R143650	Heartbeat City	1984	$12
—RCA Music Service edition			
❑ 60296	Heartbeat City	1984	$10
❑ 60296 [DJ]	Heartbeat City	1984	$18
—Promo-only audiophile pressing on Quiex II vinyl			
❑ 5E-514	Panorama	1980	$12
❑ 5E-567	Shake It Up	1981	$12
❑ 5E-567 [PD]	Shake It Up	1981	$40
—Promo-only picture disc with blank back			
❑ 5E-567 [PD]	Shake It Up	1981	$50
—Promo-only picture disc with "KMET-FM" imprinted on back			
❑ R144033	The Cars	1978	$15
—RCA Music Service edition			
❑ 6E-135	The Cars	1978	$12

NAUTILUS

❑ NR-49	Candy-O	1982	$30
—Audiophile "Super Disc"			
❑ NR-14	The Cars	1981	$30
—Audiophile "Super Disc"			

CARSON, ERNIE, AND BOB GREEN

GHB

❑ 56	Strutters, Volume 1	197?	$25
❑ 57	Strutters, Volume 2	197?	$25

CARSON, ERNIE

GHB

❑ 95	Brother Lowdown	197?	$25
❑ 125	Ernie Carson and the Original Cottonmouth Jazz Band at the Hookers' Ball	1980	$25
❑ 162	Southern Comfort	198?	$25

JAZZOLOGY

❑ JCE-5	Eleanor Buck, A Celebration Service, Sept. 18, 1983	1984	$25
❑ J-89	Ernie Carson and Rhythm	1983	$25
❑ 54	Ernie Carson and the Capitol City Jazz Band	198?	$25
❑ J-45	The Carson-Bornemann All Stars	198?	$25

CARSON, MARTHA

CAPITOL

❑ T1607 [M]	A Talk with the Lord	1961	$30
❑ ST1607 [S]	A Talk with the Lord	1961	$30
❑ T1507 [M]	Satisfied	1960	$30
❑ ST1507 [S]	Satisfied	1960	$30

RCA VICTOR

❑ LPM-1145 [M]	Journey to the Sky	1955	$40
❑ LPM-1490 [M]	Rock-a My Soul	1957	$50

SIMS

❑ LP-100 [M]	Martha Carson	196?	$30

CARSON, WAYNE

MONUMENT

❑ Z30906	Life Lines	1972	$18

CARTER, ANITA

CAPITOL

❑ ST-11085	So Much Love	1972	$18

MERCURY

❑ MG-20847 [M]	Anita of the Carter Family	1964	$30
❑ SR-60847 [S]	Anita of the Carter Family	1964	$30
❑ MG-20770 [M]	Folk Songs Old and New	1963	$30
❑ SR-60770 [S]	Folk Songs Old and New	1963	$30

CARTER, BENNY; BEN WEBSTER; BARNEY BIGARD

SWINGVILLE

❑ SVLP-2032 [M]	B.B.B. & Co.	1962	$40
—Purple label			
❑ SVST-2032 [S]	B.B.B. & Co.	1962	$50
—Red label			
❑ SVLP-2032 [M]	B.B.B. & Co.	1965	$25
—Blue label, trident logo at right			
❑ SVST-2032 [S]	B.B.B. & Co.	1965	$30
—Blue label, trident logo at right			

CARTER, BENNY; COLEMAN HAWKINS; BEN WEBSTER

BLUEBIRD

❑ 9683-1-RB	Three Great Swing Saxophonists	1989	$30

CARTER, BENNY

20TH CENTURY-FOX

❑ TFM-3134 [M]	Benny Carter in Paris	1963	$25
❑ TFS-4134 [S]	Benny Carter in Paris	1963	$30

ABC IMPULSE!

Number	Title	Yr	NM
❑ AS-9116 [S]	Additions to Further Definitions	1968	$30
❑ AS-12 [S]	Further Definitions	1968	$30

ANALOGUE PRODUCTIONS

❑ AP-13	Jazz Giant	199?	$30
—Audiophile reissue			

AUDIO LAB

❑ AL-1505 [M]	The Fabulous Benny Carter	1959	$175

CLEF

❑ MGC-141 [10]	Cosmopolite	1953	$350

CONCORD JAZZ

❑ CJ-285	A Gentleman and His Music	1985	$25

CONTEMPORARY

❑ C-3555 [M]	Jazz Giant	1958	$300
❑ S-7028 [S]	Jazz Giant	1960	$300
—Reissue of Stereo Records 7028			
❑ S-7555 [S]	Jazz Giant	197?	$30
—Reissue of 7028			
❑ M-3561 [M]	Swingin' the Twenties	1959	$300
❑ S-7561 [S]	Swingin' the Twenties	1959	$300

FANTASY

❑ OJC-167	Jazz Giant	198?	$25
—Reissue of Contemporary 7555			
❑ OJC-374	Montreux '77	1988	$25
—Reissue of Pablo Live 2308 204			
❑ OJC-339	Swingin' the Twenties	198?	$25
—Reissue of Contemporary 7561			

HINDSIGHT

❑ HSR-218	Benny Carter and His Orchestra 1944	1985	$25

IMPULSE!

❑ A-9116 [M]	Additions to Further Definitions	1966	$120
❑ AS-9116 [S]	Additions to Further Definitions	1966	$160
❑ A-12 [M]	Further Definitions	1962	$120
❑ AS-12 [S]	Further Definitions	1962	$120

MCA

❑ 29066	Additions to Further Definitions	198?	$20
❑ 29006	Further Definitions	198?	$20

MCA IMPULSE!

❑ MCA-5651	Further Definitions	1986	$25

MOVIETONE

❑ 1020 [M]	Autumn Leaves	1967	$25
❑ 72020 [S]	Autumn Leaves	1967	$35

MUSICAL HERITAGE SOCIETY

❑ MHS912375Z	In the Mood for Swing	1989	$30

NORGRAN

❑ MGN-1058 [M]	Alone Together	1956	$300
—With Oscar Peterson			
❑ MGN-1025 [M]	Benny Carter	1955	$0
—Canceled			
❑ MGN-1015 [M]	Benny Carter Plays Pretty	1955	$250
❑ MGN-1070 [M]	Cosmopolite	1956	$300
❑ MGN-1044 [M]	New Jazz Sounds	1955	$300
—With Dizzy Gillespie, Bill Harris			
❑ MGN-21 [10]	The Formidable Benny Carter	1954	$300
❑ MGN-10 [10]	The Urbane Mr. Carter	1954	$300

PABLO

❑ 2310926	Benny Carter Meets Oscar Peterson	1987	$25
❑ 2310781	Cater, Gillespie, Inc.	1976	$30
—With Dizzy Gillespie			
❑ 2310935	My Kind of Trouble	1989	$30
❑ 2405409	The Best of Benny Carter	198?	$25
❑ 2310768	The King	1975	$30
❑ 2310922	Wonderland	1987	$25

PABLO LIVE

❑ 2308216	Live and Well in Japan	1979	$30
❑ 2308204	Montreux '77	1978	$30

PRESTIGE

❑ PR-7643	Benny Carter 1933	1969	$35
❑ 2513	Opening Blues	198?	$25

STEREO RECORDS

❑ S-7028 [S]	Jazz Giant	1959	$40

STORYVILLE

❑ 4047	Summer Serenade	1981	$25

SWING

❑ SW-8403	Benny Carter and His Orchestra 1938 and 1946	1985	$25

TIME-LIFE

❑ STL-J-10	Giants of Jazz	1980	$50

UNITED ARTISTS

❑ UAL-4017 [M]	Aspects	1960	$30
❑ UAS-5017 [S]	Aspects	1960	$40
❑ UAL-3055 [M]	Can Can" and "Anything Goes	1959	$30
❑ UAS-6055 [S]	Can Can" and "Anything Goes	1959	$40
❑ UAL-4073 [M]	Can Can" and "Anything Goes	1960	$25

Number	Title	Yr	NM
❑ UAS-5073 [S]	Can Can" and "Anything Goes	1960	$30
❑ UAL-4080 [M]	Jazz Calendar	1960	$25
❑ UAS-5080 [S]	Jazz Calendar	1960	$30
❑ UAL-4094 [M]	Sax A La Carter	1961	$25
❑ UAS-5094 [S]	Sax A La Carter	1961	$30

VERVE

❑ MGV-8148 [M]	Alone Together	1957	$300
—Reissue of Norgran 1058			
❑ V-8148 [M]	Alone Together	1961	$75
❑ MGV-8160 [M]	Cosmopolite	1957	$250
—Reissue of Norgran 1070			
❑ V-8160 [M]	Cosmopolite	1961	$25
❑ MGV-2025 [M]	Moonglow -- Love Songs by Benny Carter	1957	$250
—Reissue of Norgran 1015			
❑ V-2025 [M]	Moonglow -- Love Songs by Benny Carter	1961	$25
❑ MGV-8135 [M]	New Jazz Sounds	1957	$300
—Reissue of Norgran 1044			
❑ V-8135 [M]	New Jazz Sounds	1961	$25

CARTER, BETTY

ABC IMPULSE!

❑ AS-9321	What a Little Moonlight	197?	$250

ABC-PARAMOUNT

❑ ABC-363 [M]	The Modern Sound of Betty Carter	1960	$250
❑ ABCS-363 [S]	The Modern Sound of Betty Carter	1960	$250

ATCO

❑ 33-152 [M]	'Round Midnight	1963	$50
❑ SD 33-152 [S]	'Round Midnight	1963	$75

BET-CAR

❑ 1001	Betty Carter	1970	$30
❑ MK1003	The Audience with Betty Carter	1980	$25
❑ 1002	The Betty Carter Album	197?	$30

PEACOCK

❑ PLP-90 [M]	Out There with Betty Carter	1958	$120

ROULETTE

❑ SR-5000	Finally	1969	$30
❑ SR-5005	Now It's My Turn	1976	$25
❑ SR-5001 [B]	'Round Midnight	1975	$25

UNITED ARTISTS

❑ UAL3379 [M]	Inside Betty Carter	1964	$50
❑ UAS6379 [S]	Inside Betty Carter	1964	$75
❑ UAS-5639	Inside Betty Carter	1971	$25
—Reissue of 6379			

VERVE

❑ 843991-1	Droppin' Things	1990	$35
❑ 835661-1	Look What I Got	1988	$30
❑ 835684-1	The Audience with Betty Carter	1988	$35
—Reissue of Bet-Car 1003			
❑ 835682-1	The Betty Carter Album	1988	$30
—Reissue of Bet-Car 1002			

CARTER, CALVIN

VEE JAY

❑ LP-1041 [M]	Twist with Calvin Carter	1962	$150
❑ SR-1041 [S]	Twist with Calvin Carter	1962	$175

CARTER, CARLENE

EPIC

❑ BFE38663	C'est C Bon	1983	$12

WARNER BROS.

❑ BSK3616	Blue Nun	1981	$12
❑ BSK3204	Carlene Carter	1979	$12

CARTER, CLARENCE

ABC

❑ X-943	A Heart Full of Song	1976	$18
❑ X-896	Loneliness & Temptation	1975	$18
❑ X-833	Real	1974	$18

ATLANTIC

❑ 8267 [M]	Patches	1970	$75
—Mono is white label promo only; "d/j copy monaural" sticker on stereo cover			
❑ SD8267 [S]	Patches	1970	$30
❑ SD8238	Testifyin'	1969	$30
❑ SD8282	The Best of Clarence Carter	1971	$25
❑ SD8199	The Dynamic Clarence Carter	1969	$30
❑ SD8192	This Is Clarence Carter	1968	$30

FAME

❑ FM-LA186-F	Sixty Minutes	1973	$18

ICHIBAN

❑ ICH-1068	Between a Rock and a Hard Place	1989	$15
❑ ICH-1003	Dr. C.C.	1986	$15
❑ ICH-1016	Hooked on Love	1987	$15
❑ ICH-1001	Messin' with My Mind	1986	$15
❑ ICH-1116	The Best of Clarence Carter: The Dr.'s Greatest Presciptions	1991	$15

Number	Title	Yr	NM
❑ ICH-1032	Touch of Blues	1988	$15

VENTURE

❑ VL1005	Let's Burn	1980	$12
❑ VL1009	Mr. Clarence Carter In Person	1981	$12

CARTER, JACK

AAMCO

❑ ALP-316 [M]	Broadway A La Carter	1958	$30

CARTER, JOHN, AND BOBBY BRADFORD

FLYING DUTCHMAN

❑ FDS-108	Flight for Four	1969	$25
❑ FD-10108	Flight for Four	1971	$35
—Reissue of 108			
❑ FDS-128	Self Determination Music	1970	$25
❑ FD-10128	Self Determination Music	1971	$35
—Reissue of 128			

REVELATION

❑ 18	Secrets	1978	$35
❑ 9	The New Art Ensemble	1977	$35

CARTER, JOHN

BLACK SAINT

❑ BSR-0057	Dauwhe	1983	$30
❑ BSR-0047	Night Fire	1982	$30

FLYING DUTCHMAN

❑ FDS-109	John Carter	1969	$25

GRAMAVISION

❑ 18-8603	Castles of Ghana	1986	$30
❑ 18-8704	Dance of the Love Ghosts	1987	$30
❑ 18-8809	Ghosts	1988	$30
❑ 79422	Shadows on the Wall	1989	$30

CARTER, JUNE

COLUMBIA

❑ KC33686	Appalachian Pride	1975	$18
—As "June Carter Cash"			

CARTER, LYNDA

EPIC

❑ JE35308	Portrait	1978	$18
❑ 35308 [PD]	Portrait	1978	$75
—Picture disc version			

CARTER, MEL

AMOS

❑ 7010	This Is My Life	1971	$15

DERBY

❑ LPM-702 [M]	When a Boy Falls in Love	1963	$300

IMPERIAL

❑ LP-9300 [M]	All of a Sudden My Heart Sings	1966	$18
❑ LP-12300 [S]	All of a Sudden My Heart Sings	1966	$25
❑ LP-9319 [M]	Easy Listening	1966	$18
❑ LP-12319 [S]	Easy Listening	1966	$25
❑ LP-9289 [M]	Hold Me, Thrill Me, Kiss Me	1965	$18
❑ LP-12289 [S]	Hold Me, Thrill Me, Kiss Me	1965	$25

SUNSET

❑ SUS-5295	Easy Goin'	1970	$12
❑ SUS-5227	Mel Carter	1968	$12

CARTER, MOTHER MAYBELLE

AMBASSADOR

❑ 98069 [M]	Mother Maybelle Carter	195?	$175

COLUMBIA

❑ CL2475 [M]	A Living Legend	1965	$25
❑ CS9275 [S]	A Living Legend	1965	$30
❑ KG32436	Mother Maybelle Carter	1973	$30

KAPP

❑ KL-1413 [M]	Queen of the Autoharp	1964	$25
❑ KS-3413 [S]	Queen of the Autoharp	1964	$30

SMASH

❑ MGS-27025 [M]	Mother Maybelle Carter and Her Autoharp	1963	$25
❑ SRS-67025 [S]	Mother Maybelle Carter and Her Autoharp	1963	$30
❑ MGS-27041 [M]	Pickin' and Singin'	1963	$25
❑ SRS-67041 [S]	Pickin' and Singin'	1963	$30

CARTER, RON, AND JIM HALL

CONCORD JAZZ

❑ CJ-245	Live at Village West	1983	$35
❑ CJ-270	Telephone	1985	$35

CARTER, RON; HERBIE HANCOCK; TONY WILLIAMS

MILESTONE

❑ M-9105	Third Plane	1981	$30

Number	Title	Yr	NM

CARTER, RON

CTI

❑ 6037	All Blues	1974	$50
❑ 6027	Blues Farm	1973	$50
❑ 8001	Blues Farm	1979	$35
—Reissue of 6027			
❑ 6051	Spanish Blue	1975	$50
❑ 6064	Yellow and Green	1976	$50

ELEKTRA/MUSICIAN

❑ 60214	Etudes	1984	$30

EMARCY

❑ 836366-1	All Alone	1988	$30

EMBRYO

❑ SD521	Uptown Conversation	1970	$25

FANTASY

❑ OJC-432	Where?	1990	$30

KUDU

❑ 25	Anything Goes	1976	$35

MILESTONE

❑ M-9086	A Song for You	1978	$30
❑ M-9096	New York Slick	1979	$35
❑ M-9088	Parade	1978	$30
❑ M-9107	Parfait	1981	$30
❑ M-9073	Pastels	1976	$30
❑ M-9099	Patrao	1980	$35
❑ M-9082	Peg Leg	1977	$30
❑ M-55004	Piccolo	1977	$50
❑ M-9092	Pick 'Em	1979	$30
❑ M-9100	Super Strings	1981	$30

NEW JAZZ

❑ NJLP-8265 [M]	Where?	1961	$250
—With Eric Dolphy and Mal Waldron; purple label			
❑ NJLP-8265 [M]	Where?	1965	$175
—With Eric Dolphy and Mal Waldron;; blue label, trident logo at right			

RSO

❑ RS-1-3085	Empire Jazz	1980	$50

CARTER FAMILY, THE

ACME

❑ LP-1 [M]	All Time Favorites	1960	$250
❑ LP-2 [M]	In Memory of A.P. Carter	1960	$250

COLUMBIA

❑ CL2617 [M]	Country Album	1967	$30
❑ CS9417 [S]	Country Album	1967	$25
❑ KC34266	Country's First Family	1976	$25
❑ CL2319 [M]	The Best of the Carter Family	1965	$18
❑ CS9119 [S]	The Best of the Carter Family	1965	$25
❑ KC33084	Three Generations	1974	$25
❑ KC31454	Travelin' Minstrel Band	1972	$25

DECCA

❑ DL4404 [M]	A Collection of Favorites by the Carter Family	1963	$30
❑ DL4557 [M]	More Favorites by the Carter Family	1964	$30

LIBERTY

❑ LRP-3230 [M]	The Carter Family Album	1962	$30
❑ LST-7230 [S]	The Carter Family Album	1962	$40

RCA CAMDEN

❑ CAL-2473 [M]	Lonesome Pine Special	1971	$15
❑ CAS-2554(e) [R]	More Golden Gems from the Original Carter Family	1972	$12
❑ ACL1-0047 [R]	My Old Cottage Home	1973	$12
❑ CAL-586 [M]	The Original and Great Carter Family	1960	$18
—Two-tone blue label with "RCA Camden" at top			
❑ CAL-586 [M]	The Original and Great Carter Family	1969	$12
—All-blue label with "RCA" on its side at left and "Camden" straight at right (reissue)			

Number	Title	Yr	NM

RCA VICTOR

❑ LPM-2772 [M]	'Mid the Green Fields of Virginia	1963	$40
❑ LSP-2772 [R]	'Mid the Green Fields of Virginia	1963	$25

STARDAY

❑ SLP-248 [M]	Echoes of the Carter Family	1963	$40

CARTOONE

ATLANTIC

❑ SD8219	Cartoone	1969	$25

CARTWRIGHT, ANGELA

STAR-BRIGHT

❑ HLP-102 [M]	Angela Cartwright Sings	1959	$50

CARTWRIGHT, JOHN

ALLEGRO

❑ 1684 [M]	Christmas Grand Organ and Chimes	1956	$18

CARTWRIGHT, LIONEL

MCA

❑ 42276	Lionel Cartwright	1989	$15

CARVER, JOHNNY

ABC

❑ ABCX-812	Double Exposure	1974	$15
❑ ABCD-843	Please Don't Tell (That Sweet Ole Lady of Mine)	1974	$15
❑ ABCD-864	Strings	1975	$15
❑ ABCX-792	Tie a Yellow Ribbon Around the Ole Oak Tree	1973	$15

ABC DOT

❑ DO-2042	Afternoon Delight	1976	$15
❑ DO-2083	The Best of Johnny Carver	1977	$15

HARMONY

❑ KH32476	I Start Thinking About You	1973	$15

IMPERIAL

❑ LP-12412	Leaving Again	1968	$25
❑ LP-12347 [S]	Really Country	1967	$25
❑ LP-9347 [M]	Really Country	1967	$30
❑ LP-12380	You're in Good Hands with Johnny Carver	1968	$25

CARVIN, MICHAEL

INNER CITY

❑ 2038	The Camel	1975	$35

MUSE

❑ MR-5370	Between You and Me	1989	$30
❑ MR-5352	First Time	1988	$25

STEEPLECHASE

❑ SCS-1038	The Camel	198?	$25

CARY, DICK

BELL

❑ BLP-44 [M]	Hot and Cool	1961	$75

CIRCLE

❑ CLP-018	The Amazing Dick Cary	198?	$25

FAMOUS DOOR

❑ HL-140	California Doings	1980	$30

GOLDEN CREST

❑ GC-3024 [M]	Dixieland Goes Progressive	1958	$50

STEREOCRAFT

❑ RTN-106 [S]	Hot and Cool	196?	$30

CASADESUS, JEAN

RCA VICTOR RED SEAL

❑ LSC-2415 [S]	Debussy: Preludes, Book 1	1960	$40
—Original with "shaded dog" label			

CASCADES, THE

UNI

❑ 73069	Maybe the Rain Will Fall	1969	$30

VALIANT

❑ W405 [M]	Rhythm of the Rain	1963	$175
❑ WS405 [S]	Rhythm of the Rain	1963	$300

CASE, ALLEN

COLUMBIA

❑ CS8202 [S]	The Deputy" Sings	1960	$30
❑ CL1406 [M]	The Deputy" Sings	1960	$25

CASEY, AL
STACY

Number	Title	Yr	NM
STM-100 [M]	Surfin' Hootenanny	1963	$300
STS-100 [S]	Surfin' Hootenanny	1963	$400

SUNDAZED
Number	Title	Yr	NM
LP-5026 [B]	Surfin' Hootenanny	1996	$12

—green and red vinyl pressings

5531 [B]	Surfin' Hootenanny	2016	$25

—green vinyl

CASEY, AL (2)
MOODSVILLE
Number	Title	Yr	NM
MVLP-12 [M]	The Al Casey Quartet	1960	$150

—Green label

MVLP-12 [M]	The Al Casey Quartet	1965	$75

—Blue label, trident logo at right

SWINGVILLE
SVLP-2007 [M]	Buck Jumpin'	1960	$150

—Purple label

SVLP-2007 [M]	Buck Jumpin'	1965	$75

—Blue label, trident logo at right

CASH, ALVIN
MAR-V-LUS
Number	Title	Yr	NM
1827 [M]	Twine Time	1965	$30

CASH, JOHNNY, AND JUNE CARTER
COLUMBIA
Number	Title	Yr	NM
CL2728 [M]	Carryin' On with Johnny Cash and June Carter	1967	$35
CS9528 [S]	Carryin' On with Johnny Cash and June Carter	1967	$25
KC32443	Johnny Cash and His Woman	1973	$18

CASH, JOHNNY
ACCORD
Number	Title	Yr	NM
SN-7134	I Walk the Line	1983	$12
SN-7208	Years Gone By	1983	$12

ALLEGIANCE
AV-5017	The First Years	1986	$12

AMERICAN
C69691 [B]	American III: Solitary Man	2000	$85
440-063336-1	American IV: The Man Comes Around	2002	$25
B0019507-01 [B]	American IV: The Man Comes Around	2014	$35
45520 [B]	American Recordings	1994	$150
B0002769-01	American V: A Hundred Highways	2006	$15
43097	Unchained	1996	$120

ARCHIVE OF FOLK MUSIC
278	Johnny Cash	198?	$15

CACHET
9001	A Believer Sings the Truth	1979	$18

CLEOPATRA
1996 [B]	Hayride Anthology		$30

—picture disc

COLUMBIA
PC38074	A Believer Sings the Truth	1985	$10

—Reissue of Priority 38074

KC32091	Any Old Wind That Blows	1973	$15
KC31332	A Thing Called Love	1972	$15
C2L38 [M]	Ballads of the True West	1965	$30
C2S838 [S]	Ballads of the True West	1965	$30
CL2248 [M]	Bitter Tears (Ballads of the American Indian)	1964	$18
CS9048 [S]	Bitter Tears (Ballads of the American Indian)	1964	$25
CL1930 [M]	Blood, Sweat & Tears	1963	$25
CS8730 [S]	Blood, Sweat & Tears	1963	$30
KC32898	Children's Album	1974	$15
JC36866	Classic Christmas	1980	$15
FC37355	Encore	1981	$12
CL2492 [M]	Everybody Loves a Nut	1966	$18
CS9292 [S]	Everybody Loves a Nut	1966	$25
C32951	Five Feet High and Rising	1974	$15
CL2647 [M]	From Sea to Shining Sea	1967	$50
CS9447 [S]	From Sea to Shining Sea	1967	$25
KC31256	Give My Love to Rose	1972	$15
KC35646	Gone Girl	1978	$15
KCS9943	Hello, I'm Johnny Cash	1970	$15
FC40056	Highwayman	1985	$12

—Waylon Jennings/Willie Nelson/Johnny Cash/Kris Kristofferson

C45240	Highwayman 2	1990	$18

—Waylon Jennings/Willie Nelson/Johnny Cash/Kris Kristofferson

CL1284 [M]	Hymns by Johnny Cash	1959	$30
CS8125 [S]	Hymns by Johnny Cash	1959	$40
CL1722 [M]	Hymns from the Heart	1962	$25
CS8522 [S]	Hymns from the Heart	1962	$30
CL2190 [M]	I Walk the Line	1964	$18
CS8990 [S]	I Walk the Line	1964	$25
S30397	I Walk the Line	1970	$15

—Soundtrack from movie

KC35313	I Would Like to See You Again	1978	$12
FC38696	Johnny 99	1983	$12
PC38696	Johnny 99	1986	$10

—Budget-line reissue

KC31645	Johnny Cash: America (A 200-Year Salute in Story and Song)	1972	$15
CS9639 [M]	Johnny Cash at Folsom Prison	1968	$50

—White label promo with stereo number; "Special Mono Radio Station Copy" sticker on cover

CS9639 [M]	Johnny Cash at Folsom Prison	1968	$25

—Red label with "360 Sound Stereo" at bottom

CL2839 [M]	Johnny Cash at Folsom Prison	1968	$175

—Red label with "Mono" at bottom; this is a stock copy

CG33639	Johnny Cash at Folsom Prison/Johnny Cash at San Quentin	1974	$18
CS9827	Johnny Cash at San Quentin	1969	$15
CQ30961 [Q]	Johnny Cash at San Quentin	1971	$30
FC38317	Johnny Cash's Biggest Hits	1982	$12
CL2678 [M]	Johnny Cash's Greatest Hits, Volume 1	1967	$25
CS9478 [S]	Johnny Cash's Greatest Hits, Volume 1	1967	$25
JC35637	Johnny Cash's Greatest Hits, Volume 3	1978	$15
C33087	Johnny Cash Sings Precious Memories	1974	$15
KC33370	John R. Cash	1975	$15
KC33814	Look at Them Beans	1975	$15
KC30550	Man in Black	1971	$15
CL2446 [M]	Mean as Hell	1965	$18
CS9246 [S]	Mean as Hell	1965	$25
CL1463 [M]	Now, There Was a Song!	1960	$30
CS8254 [S]	Now, There Was a Song!	1960	$40
KC34193	One Piece at a Time	1976	$15
CL2309 [M]	Orange Blossom Special	1965	$18
CS9109 [S]	Orange Blossom Special	1965	$25
FC39951	Rainbow	1985	$12
CL1464 [M]	Ride This Train	1960	$30
CS8255 [S]	Ride This Train	1960	$40
CS8255 [S]	Ride This Train	197?	$12

—Reissue on orange label

CL2052 [M]	Ring of Fire (The Best of Johnny Cash)	1963	$25

CS8853 [S]	Ring of Fire (The Best of Johnny Cash)	1963	$30
JC36779	Rockabilly Blues	1980	$12
JC36086	Silver	1979	$15
CL1339 [M]	Songs of Our Soil	1959	$30
CS8148 [S]	Songs of Our Soil	1959	$40
KC34088	Strawberry Cake	1976	$15
C32240	Sunday Morning Coming Down	1973	$15
CL2537 [M]	That's What You Get for Lovin' Me	1966	$18
CS9337 [S]	That's What You Get for Lovin' Me	1966	$25
FC38094	The Adventures of Johnny Cash	1982	$12
FC37179	The Baron	1981	$12
CL2117 [M]	The Christmas Spirit	1963	$30
CS8917 [S]	The Christmas Spirit	1963	$30
CL1253 [M]	The Fabulous Johnny Cash	1958	$25
CS8122 [S]	The Fabulous Johnny Cash	1959	$40
C32253	The Gospel Road	1973	$15
CG32253	The Gospel Road	1973	$30
STS2004	The Heart of Johnny Cash	196?	$25

—"Columbia Star Series" release; has "360 Sound" labels

KCS9726	The Holy Land	1969	$18
KC30887	The Johnny Cash Collection (His Greatest Hits, Volume II)	1971	$15
C30100	The Johnny Cash Show	1970	$15
KC33086	The Junkie and the Juicehead	1974	$15
JC34314	The Last Gunfighter Ballad	1977	$15
CL1622 [M]	The Lure of the Grand Canyon	1961	$40

—Cash narrates; with Andre Kostelanetz and His Orchestra

CS8422 [S]	The Lure of the Grand Canyon	1961	$50

—Cash narrates; with Andre Kostelanetz and His Orchestra

C32917	The Ragged Old Flag	1974	$15
JC34833	The Rambler	1977	$15
CL1802 [M]	The Sound of Johnny Cash	1962	$25
CS8602 [S]	The Sound of Johnny Cash	1962	$30
GP29	The World of Johnny Cash	1970	$18

COLUMBIA LIMITED EDITION
LE10063 [S]	The Fabulous Johnny Cash	197?	$18

—Reissue of 8122

COLUMBIA SPECIAL PRODUCTS
P13043	Destination Victoria Station	1977	$40

—Alternate number is "VS 150

P13832	Hello, I'm Johnny Cash	1977	$15
363	Legends and Love Songs	196?	$25

DORAL/CSP
0(# unknown)	Doral Presents Johnny Cash	1972	$40

—Mail-order offer from Doral cigarettes

EVEREST
276	Johnny Cash	19??	$15

FRIDAY MUSIC
FRM30550 [B]	Man in Black	2016	$30

—blue vinyl

HARMONY
KH32388	Ballads of the American Indian	1973	$15
HS11249	Golden Sounds of Country Music	1968	$15
HS11342	Johnny Cash	1969	$15
KH31602	The Johnny Cash Songbook	1972	$15
KH30138	The Walls of a Prison	1970	$15
KH30916	Understand Your Man	1971	$15

MERCURY
832031-1	Johnny Cash Is Coming to Town	1987	$12
834778-1	Water from the Wells of Home	1988	$12

MUSIC WORLD ENTERTAINMENT
CR9295121	Johnny Cash Remixed	2008	$30

PAIR
PDL2-1107	Classic Cash	1986	$18

POWER PAK
246	Country Gold	198?	$12

PRIORITY
PU38074	A Believer Sings the Truth	1982	$15

—Reissue of Cachet album

PU33087	Johnny Cash Sings Precious Memories	1982	$15

—Reissue of Columbia album of the same name

UG32253	The Gospel Road	1981	$18

—Reissue of Columbia album of the same name

RHINO
RNLP70229	The Vintage Years	1987	$15

SHARE
5001	Folsom Prison Blues	197?	$15
5000	I Walk the Line	197?	$15
5003	Johnny Cash Sings the Greatest Hits	197?	$15
5002	The Blue Train	197?	$15

SUN
SLP-1270 [M]	All Aboard the Blue Train	1963	$50
DT-91458 [R]	All Aboard the Blue Train	196?	$30

—Capitol Record Club edition

LP-140	Folsom Prison Blues	1979	$12
LP-105	Get Rhythm	1969	$15
LP-139	I Walk the Line	1979	$12
LP-126	Johnny Cash: The Man, The World, His Music	1971	$25
SLP-1240 [M]	Johnny Cash's Greatest!	1959	$50
SLP-1245 [M]	Johnny Cash Sings Hank Williams	1960	$50
SLP-1245 [R]	Johnny Cash Sings Hank Williams	196?	$25

—Reissue in rechanneled stereo; front cover says "STEREO

DT-91284 [R]	Johnny Cash Sings Hank Williams	196?	$30

—Capitol Record Club edition

Number	Title	Yr	NM
❏ T-91284 [M]	Johnny Cash Sings Hank Williams	196?	$40
—Capitol Record Club edition			
❏ LP-142	Johnny Cash Sings the Greatest Hits	1979	$12
❏ LP-118	Johnny Cash -- The Legend	1970	$25
❏ SLP-1220 [M]	Johnny Cash with His Hot and Blue Guitar	1956	$150
❏ SLP-1220 [R]	Johnny Cash with His Hot and Blue Guitar	196?	$25
—Reissue in rechanneled stereo; front cover says "STEREO			
❏ SLP-1255 [M]	Now Here's Johnny Cash	1961	$50
❏ SLP-1255 [R]	Now Here's Johnny Cash	196?	$25
—Reissue in rechanneled stereo; front cover says "STEREO			
❏ DT-90678 [R]	Now Here's Johnny Cash	1966	$25
—Capitol Record Club edition			
❏ LP-100	Original Golden Hits, Volume I	1969	$15
❏ ST-92085	Original Golden Hits, Volume I	1969	$25
—Capitol Record Club edition; uses older Sun label			
❏ LP-101	Original Golden Hits, Volume II	1969	$15
❏ ST-92086	Original Golden Hits, Volume II	1969	$25
—Capitol Record Club edition; uses older Sun label			
❏ LP-127	Original Golden Hits, Volume III	1972	$15
❏ LP-106	Showtime	1969	$15
❏ LP-104	Story Songs of the Trains and Rivers	1969	$15
❏ 1002	Superbilly (1955-58)	198?	$12
❏ LP-141	The Blue Train	1979	$12
❏ SQBO-93213	The Greatness of Johnny Cash	197?	$25
—Capitol Record Club exclusive			
❏ 1006	The Original Johnny Cash	1980	$12
❏ SLP-1275 [M]	The Original Sun Sound of Johnny Cash	1965	$50
❏ LP-122	The Rough Cut King of Country Music	1971	$15
❏ LP-115	The Singing Story Teller	1970	$15
❏ SLP-1235 [M]	The Songs That Made Him Famous	1958	$150
❏ SLP-1235 [R]	The Songs That Made Him Famous	196?	$25
—Reissue in rechanneled stereo; front cover says "STEREO			
❏ DT-90668 [R]	The Songs That Made Him Famous	1966	$30
—Capitol Record Club edition			
❏ T-90668 [M]	The Songs That Made Him Famous	1966	$40
—Capitol Record Club edition			
❏ LP1220 [B]	With His Hot And Blue Guitar	2014	$30
SUNDAZED			
❏ LP-5176	Blood, Sweat & Tears	2003	$18
—Reissue on 180-gram vinyl			
❏ LP-5170	Town Hall Party Live! 1958	2003	$18
—Reissue on 180-gram vinyl			
❏ LP-5171	Town Hall Party Live! 1959	2003	$18
—Reissue on 180-gram vinyl			
❏ LP5238 [B]	With His Hot and Blue Guitar	2016	$25
TIME-LIFE			
❏ TLCS-3	Country & Western Classics	1982	$25
❏ STW-108	Country Music	1981	$15
WORD			
❏ WR-8333	Believe in Him	1986	$15

CASH, JOHNNY/TAMMY WYNETTE
COLUMBIA MUSICAL TREASURIES

❏ P4S5376	The King/The Queen	1969	$30

—Box set; two records by Johnny Cash, two records by Tammy Wynette; records are individually numbered from DS 562 through DS 565

❏ DS608	The King/The Queen	1969	$18

—One record by Johnny Cash, the other by Tammy Wynette

CASH, ROSEANNE
COLUMBIA

❏ OC45054	Hits 1979-1989	1989	$15
❏ AS1527 [DJ]	Interview with Martha Hume	1982	$30
—Generic cover with sticker			
❏ FC40777	King's Record Shop	1987	$12
❏ FC39463	Rhythm and Romance	1985	$12
❏ JC36155	Right or Wrong	1980	$12
❏ PC36155	Right or Wrong	1984	$10
—Budget-line reissue with new prefix and "02" added to bar code			
❏ JC36965	Seven Year Ache	1981	$12
❏ HC46965	Seven Year Ache	1981	$50
—Half-speed mastered edition			
❏ PC36965	Seven Year Ache	1984	$10
—Budget-line reissue with new prefix and "02" added to bar code			
❏ FC37570	Somewhere in the Stars	1982	$12
❏ PC37570	Somewhere in the Stars	1984	$10
—Budget-line reissue with new prefix and "02" added to bar code			

CASH, TOMMY
ELEKTRA

❏ CM-5	Only a Stone	1975	$18

EPIC

❏ E30860	American Way of Life	1971	$18
❏ E30556	Cash Country	1971	$18
❏ E30107	Rise and Shine	1970	$18
❏ BN26535	Six White Horses	1970	$18
❏ KE31747	That Certain One	1972	$18
❏ KE31995	The Best of Tommy Cash, Volume I	1972	$18
❏ BN26484	Your Lovin' Takes the Leavin' Out of Me	1969	$25

MONUMENT

❏ 7619	The New Spirit	1978	$15

UNITED ARTISTS

❏ UAS-6628	Here Comes Tommy Cash	1968	$25

CASHMAN, PISTILLI AND WEST
ABC

❏ ABCS-629	Bound to Happen	1968	$25

CAPITOL

❏ ST-211	Cashman, Pistilli, and West	1969	$18

CASHMAN, TERRY
LIFESONG

❏ LS8137	Talkin' Baseball	1981	$18
❏ LS6006	Terry Cashman	1976	$15
❏ PZ34999	Terry Cashman	1977	$12
—Reissue of 6006			

CASHMAN AND WEST
ABC DUNHILL

❏ DSX-50126	A Song or Two	1972	$15
❏ DSX-50179	Lifesong	1974	$15
❏ DSX-50141	Moondog Serenade	1973	$15

CASIMIR, JOHN
JAZZOLOGY

❏ JCE-5	Casimir's Paragon Jazz Band	1967	$35
❏ JCE-21	Tomorrow Tomorrow	1967	$35

CASINOS, THE (1)
FRATERNITY

❏ LP-1019 [M]	Then You Can Tell Me Goodbye	1967	$40
❏ LPS-1019 [S]	Then You Can Tell Me Goodbye	1967	$75

CASIOPEA
ALFA

❏ AAA10002	Eyes of the Mind	1981	$35

MILESTONE

❏ M-9133	Zoom	1985	$30

CASSELL, PETE
HILLTOP

❏ 6023	The Legend of Pete Cassell	1965	$30

CASSIDY, DAVID
BELL

❏ 1312	Cassidy Live	1974	$40
❏ 6070	Cherish	1972	$30
❏ 1321	David Cassidy's Greatest Hits	1974	$20
❏ 1132 [B]	Dreams Are Nothing More Than Wishes	1973	$25
❏ 1109	Rock Me Baby	1972	$30

RCA VICTOR

❏ APL1-1852	Gettin' It in the Street	1976	$40
❏ APL1-1309	Home Is Where the Heart Is	1976	$25
❏ APL1-1066	The Higher They Climb…	1975	$30
—Black vinyl			
❏ APL1-1066	The Higher They Climb…	1975	$150
—Blue vinyl			

CASSIDY, EVA
S&P

❏ 501	Songbird	2004	$30
—180-gram edition			

CASSIDY, SHAUN
WARNER BROS.

❏ BSK3126	Born Late	1977	$10
❏ HS3265	Live/That's Rock and Roll	1979	$12
❏ BSK3351	Room Service	1979	$12
❏ BS3067	Shaun Cassidy	1977	$10
❏ BSK3222	Under Wraps	1978	$10
❏ BSK3451	Wasp	1980	$18

CASTELLES, THE
COLLECTABLES

❏ COL-5002	The Sweet Sounds of the Castelles	198?	$15

CASTELLS, THE
ERA

❏ EL-109 [M]	So This Is Love	1962	$120
❏ ES-109 [S]	So This Is Love	1962	$400

CASTLE, LEE
CELEBRITY

❏ CEL-203 [M]	World Famous Dixieland Favorites	1952	$40

DAVIS

❏ JD-105 [M]	Dixieland Heaven	1951	$75

CASTLE, PAULA
BETHLEHEM

❏ BCP-1036 [10]	Paula Castle	1955	$500

CASTOR, JIMMY, BUNCH
ATLANTIC

❏ SD18124	Butt Of Course	1975	$12
❏ SD18186	E-Man Groovin'	1976	$12
❏ SD19111	Maximum Stimulation	1977	$12
❏ SD18150	Supersound	1975	$12
❏ SD7305	The Everything Man	1974	$12

COTILLION

❏ SD5215	The Jimmy Castor Bunch	1979	$15

DRIVE

❏ 407	Let It Out	1978	$15

LONG DISTANCE

❏ 1201	C	1980	$15

RCA VICTOR

❏ APD1-0103 [Q]	Dimension III	1973	$30
—All copies are quadraphonic			
❏ LSP-4640	It's Just Begun	1972	$18
❏ LSP-4783	Phase Two	1972	$18
❏ APL1-0313	The Everything Man	1974	$18

SMASH

❏ MGS-27091 [M]	Hey Leroy!	1967	$40
❏ SRS-67091 [S]	Hey Leroy!	1967	$40

CASTRO, JOE
ATLANTIC

❏ 1324 [M]	Groove Funk Soul	1960	$300
—Black label			
❏ SD1324 [S]	Groove Funk Soul	1960	$300
—Green label			
❏ 1264 [M]	Mood Jazz	1957	$300
—Black label			
❏ 1264 [M]	Mood Jazz	1961	$175
—Multicolor label with white "fan" logo			
❏ SD1264 [S]	Mood Jazz	1959	$300
—Green label			
❏ SD1264 [S]	Mood Jazz	1961	$175
—Multicolor label with white "fan" logo			

CAT MOTHER AND THE ALL NIGHT NEWS BOYS
POLYDOR

❏ 24-4023	Albion Doo-Wah	1970	$18
❏ PD-5017	Cat Mother	1972	$18
❏ PD-5042	Last Chance Dance	1972	$18
❏ 24-4001 [B]	The Street Giveth…And the Street Taketh Away	1969	$35
—Produced by Jimi Hendrix			

CATALINAS, THE (1)
Studio band of Los Angeles session pros.
RIC

❏ M-1006 [M]	Fun, Fun, Fun	1964	$150
❏ S-1006 [S]	Fun, Fun, Fun	1964	$175

CATALYST
COBBLESTONE

❏ 9018	Catalyst	1972	$25

MUSE

❏ MR-5069	A Tear and a Smile	1975	$35
❏ MR-5170	Catalyst	198?	$30
❏ MR-5025	Perception	1973	$35
❏ MR-5042	Unity	1974	$35

CATANOOGA CATS, THE
FORWARD

❏ ST-F-1018	The Catanooga Cats	1969	$40

CATAPILLA
VERTIGO

❏ 1006 [B]	Catapilla	1971	$300

CATES, GEORGE
CORAL

❏ CRL57220 [M]	Exciting	1958	$30
❏ CRL57126 [M]	Under European Skies	1957	$40

DOT

❏ DLP-3564 [M]	Hit Songs -- Hit Sounds	1964	$15

Number	Title	Yr	NM
❑ DLP-25564 [S]	Hit Songs -- Hit Sounds	1964	$18
❑ DLP-3355 [M]	Polynesian Percussion	1961	$15
❑ DLP-25355 [S]	Polynesian Percussion	1961	$25
❑ DLP-3400 [M]	Take Five	1961	$15
❑ DLP-25400 [S]	Take Five	1961	$25
❑ DLP-25464 [S]	Third Man Theme	1962	$18
❑ DLP-3464 [M]	Third Man Theme	1962	$15
❑ DLP-25422 [S]	Twistin' 12 Great Hits	1962	$25
❑ DLP-3422 [M]	Twistin' 12 Great Hits	1962	$18

HAMILTON

❑ HLP-161 [M]	1965's Great Hits	1966	$18
❑ HLP-12161 [S]	1965's Great Hits	1966	$25
❑ HLP-127 [M]	The Great Hit Sounds of George Cates	1964	$12
❑ HLP-12127 [S]	The Great Hit Sounds of George Cates	1964	$15

RANWOOD

❑ 8039	Hawaii	1969	$15

CATES SISTERS, THE

OVATION

❑ 1740	Steppin' Out	1979	$15

—As "The Cates

CATHCART, DICK

WARNER BROS.

❑ W1275 [M]	Bix/MCMLIX	1959	$30
❑ WS1275 [S]	Bix/MCMLIX	1959	$30

CATHERINE, PHILIP

WARNER BROS.

❑ BS2950	Nairam	1977	$35

CATHERINE WHEEL, THE

MERCURY

❑ 526850-1 [B]	Happy Days	1995	$30

—Clear vinyl

CATHY JEAN AND THE ROOMATES

VALMOR

❑ 789 [M]	At the Hop!	1961	$900
❑ 78 [M]	Great Oldies	1962	$800

—Reissue of 789 with titles on cover and no group shot

CATINGUB, MATT

REFERENCE RECORDINGS

❑ RR-14	Your Friendly Neighborhood Big Band	1985	$50

—Plays at 45 rpm

SEA BREEZE

❑ SB-2025	Hi-Tech Big Band	1985	$25
❑ SB-3006	In the Land of the Long White Cloud	1990	$30
❑ SB-2013	My Mommy and Me	1983	$25

CATO, CONNIE

CAPITOL

❑ ST-11387	Good Hearted Woman	1975	$15
❑ ST-11312	Super Connie Cato	1974	$15
❑ ST-11606	Whoever Finds This, I Love You	1977	$15

CAUTHEN, STEVE

BAREBACK

❑ BB3334	...And Steve Cauthen Sings Too!	1977	$25

CAVALIERE, FELIX

BEARSVILLE

❑ BR6958	Destiny	1975	$15
❑ BR6955	Felix Cavaliere	1974	$15

EPIC

❑ JE35990	Castles in the Air	1979	$12

CAVANAUGH, PAGE

CAPITOL

❑ T879 [M]	Fats Sent Me	1957	$75
❑ T1001 [M]	Swingin' Down the Road from Paris to Rome	1958	$85

X

❑ LX-3027 [10]	Page Cavanaugh Trio	1954	$50

CAVE, NICK, AND THE BAD SEEDS

ANTI

❑ 86668	Nocturama	2003	$18

—Actually contains two records, but the second record is a single-sided disc with one song

ENIGMA

❑ 775401-1	Tender Prey	1988	$30

HOMESTEAD

❑ HMS 065 [B]	Kicking Against the Pricks	1986	$40
❑ HMS 026 [B]	The Firstborn is Dead	1985	$40
❑ HMS 073	Your Funeral, My Trial	1986	$40

CELEBRATION FEATURING MIKE LOVE

PACIFIC ARTS

❑ 122	Celebration	1978	$18

CELESTIN, OSCAR

FOLKLYRIC

❑ 9030	Oscar "Papa" Celestin and His New Orleans Jazz Band	198?	$25

IMPERIAL

❑ LP-9149 [M]	Birth of the Blues	1961	$175
❑ LP-9125 [M]	Dixieland King	1961	$175
❑ LP-12062 [S]	Dixieland King	1961	$175
❑ LP-9199 [M]	Oscar "Papa" Celestin's New Orleans Jazz Band	1962	$175
❑ LP-12199 [S]	Oscar "Papa" Celestin's New Orleans Jazz Band	1962	$175

JAZZOLOGY

❑ JCE-28	Ragtime Band	1968	$25

SOUTHLAND

❑ SLP-206 [10]	Papa's Golden Wedding	1955	$150

CELL BLOCK SEVEN

DIXIELAND JUBILEE

❑ DJ-506 [M]	A Dixieland Riot	195?	$50
❑ DJS-506 [R]	A Dixieland Riot	196?	$30

CENTAURUS

AZRA

❑ 61549	Centaurus	1978	$50

—Issued on clear vinyl

CENTIPEDE

RCA VICTOR

❑ CPL2-5042	Septober Energy	1974	$40

CENTRAL NERVOUS SYSTEM

MUSIC FACTORY

❑ MFS-12003 [S]	I Could Have Danced All Night	1968	$25
❑ MF-12003 [M]	I Could Have Danced All Night	1968	$35

—White label promo only (no stock copies were issued in mono)

CENTURIONS, THE

DEL-FI

❑ DFLP-1228 [M]	Surfer's Pajama Party	1963	$150
❑ DFST-1228 [S]	Surfer's Pajama Party	1963	$250

—Above has the same title and number, and almost the same cover, as the album of the same name by Bruce Johnston, but the contents are different

CENTURY 22 FEATURING GEORGE SHAW

TBA

❑ TB-209	Flight 2201	198?	$25

CERRONE

ATLANTIC

❑ SD19250	Cerrone V -- Angelina	1979	$12

COTILLION

❑ SD5202	Cerrone 3 -- Supernature	1977	$15
❑ SD5208	Cerrone IV -- The Golden Touch	1978	$15
❑ SD9917	Cerrone's Paradise	1977	$15
❑ SD9913	Love in C Minor	1977	$15

PAVILLION

❑ FZ38159	Back Track	1982	$15

PURE

❑ PE2250-1	Best of Cerrone Remixes	1995	$18

CESANA

MODERN

❑ M-100 [M]	Tender Emotions	1964	$25

CETERA, PETER

FULL MOON

❑ FMH3624	Peter Cetera	1981	$12

WARNER BROS.

❑ 25704	One More Story	1988	$10
❑ 25474	Solitude/Solitaire	1986	$10

CEYLEIB PEOPLE, THE

VAULT

❑ LP-117 [M]	Tanyet	1968	$250

—With Ry Cooder

❑ LP-117 [S]	Tanyet	1968	$175

—with Ry Cooder

CHACKSFIELD, FRANK

COMPLEAT

❑ 671020-1	TV's Golden Hits	198?	$15

EXCELSIOR

❑ XRP-7005	After the Lovin'	1980	$15
❑ XRP-7008	Dust in the Wind	1980	$15
❑ XRP-7001	Great Film Music	1980	$12
❑ XRP-7004	In the Country	1980	$15
❑ XRP-7009	Love Is in the Air	1980	$15
❑ XRP-7006	Sunflower	1980	$15
❑ XRP-7007	Weekend in New England	1980	$15

LONDON

❑ CHA-S-1	Academy Award Hit Songs 1934-1967	1969	$15
❑ LL3347 [M]	Best of the New Film Themes	196?	$12
❑ PS347 [S]	Best of the New Film Themes	196?	$15
❑ LL1509 [M]	Broadway Melodies	195?	$15
❑ LL3322 [M]	Ebb Tide	196?	$12
❑ PS322 [S]	Ebb Tide	196?	$15
❑ LL3038 [M]	Evening in London	195?	$15
❑ PS135 [S]	Evening in London	195?	$18
❑ LL997 [M]	Evening in Paris	195?	$18
❑ LL1205 [M]	Evening in Rome	195?	$18
❑ PS126 [S]	Evening in Rome, Evening in Paris	195?	$18
❑ LL1041 [M]	Frank Chacksfield and His Orchestra, Vol. 1	195?	$18
❑ PS436 [S]	Great Country and Western Hits	1965	$15
❑ LL3436 [M]	Great Country and Western Hits	1965	$12
❑ LL3330 [M]	Here's Love	196?	$12
❑ PS330 [S]	Here's Love	196?	$15
❑ LL3102/3 [M]	Hollywood Almanac -- Award Winners 1934-1957	195?	$18
❑ PS320/1 [S]	Hollywood Almanac -- Award Winners 1934-1957	195?	$25
❑ PS122 [S]	Immortal Serenades	195?	$18
❑ LL3061 [M]	Immortal Serenades	195?	$15
❑ LL3257 [M]	King of Kings and Other Film Spectaculars	196?	$12
❑ PS246 [S]	King of Kings and Other Film Spectaculars	196?	$15
❑ LL3298 [M]	Lawrence of Arabia and Other Themes	196?	$12
❑ PS298 [S]	Lawrence of Arabia and Other Themes	196?	$15
❑ PS145 [S]	Love Letters in the Sand	195?	$18
❑ LL3027 [M]	Love Letters in the Sand	195?	$15
❑ LL1614 [M]	Lovely Lady -- The Music of Jimmy McHugh	195?	$15
❑ PS304 [S]	Magic Strings	196?	$15
❑ LL3304 [M]	Magic Strings	196?	$12
❑ LL1440 [M]	Mean to Me	195?	$18
❑ LL1588 [M]	Mediterranean Moonlight	195?	$15
❑ PS316 [S]	Music from "She Loves Me	196?	$15
❑ LL3316 [M]	Music from "She Loves Me	196?	$12
❑ LL1203 [M]	Music of George Gershwin	195?	$18
❑ PS120 [S]	Music of George Gershwin	195?	$18
❑ LL1062 [M]	Music of Noel Coward	195?	$18
❑ LL3158 [M]	On the Beach	1960	$15
❑ PS203 [S]	On the Beach	1960	$18
❑ SPC21092	Opera's Golden Moments	197?	$12
❑ LL1538 [M]	South Sea Island Magic	195?	$15
❑ PS416 [S]	The First Hits of 1965	1965	$15
❑ LL3416 [M]	The First Hits of 1965	1965	$12
❑ LL3431 [M]	The New Limelight	1965	$12
❑ LL1440 [M]	Velvet	195?	$18
❑ LL1603 [M]	Waltzes to Remember	195?	$15
❑ LL1355 [M]	You	195?	$18

LONDON PHASE 4

❑ SP-44158	Chacksfield Plays Bacharach	197?	$18
❑ SP-44151	Chacksfield Plays Simon and Garfunkel and Jim Webb	1970	$18
❑ SP-44142	Chacksfield Plays the Beatles' Songbook	1970	$18
❑ SP-44112	Foreign Film Festival	196?	$18
❑ SP-44090	France	196?	$18
❑ SP-44275	Frank Chacksfield Plays Hoagy Carmichael	197?	$18
❑ SP-44254	Frank Chacksfield Plays Irving Berlin	197?	$18
❑ SP-44249	Frank Chacksfield Plays Lerner and Loewe	197?	$18
❑ SP-44223	Frank Chacksfield Plays Rodgers and Hart	1975	$18
❑ SP-44059	Globetrotting	196?	$18
❑ SP-44087	Hawaii	196?	$18
❑ SP-44102	Music from Doctor Dolittle	196?	$18
❑ SP-44141	New York	196?	$18
❑ SP-44194	The Glory That Was ... Gershwin	1973	$15
❑ SW-95146	The Glory That Was ... Gershwin	1973	$18

—Longines Symphonette Record Club edition

❑ SP-44077	The Great TV Themes	196?	$18
❑ SP-44213	The Incomparable Jerome Kern	1974	$18
❑ SP-44185	The Music of Cole Porter	1972	$18
❑ SP-44053	The New Ebb Tide	1964	$18
❑ SP-44066 [S]	The New Limelight	1965	$18
❑ SP-44289	Vintage '52	1977	$18

MCA

❑ 5239	Love Songs	1981	$15

PHOENIX 20

❑ P20-604	How Deep Is Your Love	1980	$10

PICKWICK

❑ SPC-3231	Ebb Tide	197?	$10

Number	Title	Yr	NM
RICHMOND			
☐ S30078 [S]	Ebb Tide	1960	$15
☐ B20078 [M]	Ebb Tide	1960	$12
☐ B20073 [M]	Great Strauss Waltzes	1960	$12
☐ S30073 [S]	Great Strauss Waltzes	1960	$15
☐ S30087 [S]	Love Themes from Great Operas	196?	$15
☐ B20087 [M]	Love Themes from Great Operas	196?	$12
☐ S30045 [S]	Million Sellers	195?	$15
☐ B20045 [M]	Million Sellers	195?	$12
☐ S30095 [S]	Movie Themes	196?	$15
☐ B20095 [M]	Movie Themes	196?	$12
☐ B20056 [M]	Music for a Merry Christmas	1959	$12
☐ S30056 [S]	Music for a Merry Christmas	1959	$15
☐ S30093 [S]	My Gypsy Love	196?	$15
☐ B20093 [M]	My Gypsy Love	196?	$12
☐ B20059 [M]	Porgy and Bess/Show Boat	1960	$12
☐ S30059 [S]	Porgy and Bess/Show Boat	1960	$15
☐ B20080 [M]	Songs of Sunny Italy	196?	$12
☐ S30080 [S]	Songs of Sunny Italy	196?	$15
☐ B20046 [M]	South Pacific	195?	$12
☐ S30046 [S]	South Pacific	195?	$15
☐ B20086 [M]	The Best of Herbert and Romberg	196?	$12
☐ S30086 [S]	The Best of Herbert and Romberg	196?	$15
STARBORNE			
☐ SB-9002	Mirrors	1980	$30
☐ SB-9003	People in Love	1980	$30

CHAD AND JEREMY
CAPITOL

Number	Title	Yr	NM
☐ TT2546 [M]	More Chad and Jeremy	1966	$12
☐ STT2546 [P]	More Chad and Jeremy	1966	$15
☐ T2470 [M]	The Best of Chad and Jeremy	1966	$12
—Black label with colorband			
☐ ST2470 [P]	The Best of Chad and Jeremy	1966	$15
—Black label with colorband			
☐ T2470 [M]	The Best of Chad and Jeremy	1967	$10
—Starline" label			
☐ ST2470 [P]	The Best of Chad and Jeremy	1967	$12
—Starline" label			
☐ SN-16135 [P]	The Best of Chad and Jeremy	1980	$10
—Budget-line reissue			

COLUMBIA

Number	Title	Yr	NM
☐ CL2374 [M]	Before and After	1965	$25
☐ CS9174 [S]	Before and After	1965	$30
☐ CL2564 [M]	Distant Shores	1966	$25
☐ CS9364 [P]	Distant Shores	1966	$30
—Distant Shores" is rechanneled			
☐ CL2398 [M]	I Don't Want to Lose You Baby	1966	$30
☐ CS9198 [S]	I Don't Want to Lose You Baby	1966	$40
☐ CL2671 [M]	Of Cabbages and Kings	1967	$40
☐ CS9471 [S]	Of Cabbages and Kings	1967	$30
☐ CS9699 [S]	The Arc	1968	$30
—Some copies spell the LP title this way on the cover			
☐ CL2899 [M]	The Ark	1968	$75
☐ CS9699 [S]	The Ark	1968	$30
—Correct spelling of LP title on cover			

FIDU

| ☐ FM-101 [M] | 5 + 10 = 15 Fabulous Hits | 1966 | $12 |
| ☐ FS-101 [M] | 5 + 10 = 15 Fabulous Hits | 1966 | $15 |

HARMONY

| ☐ HS11357 [S] | Chad and Jeremy | 1973 | $10 |

ROCSHIRE

| ☐ XR-22018 [B] | Chad Stuart and Jeremy Clyde | 1983 | $12 |

Number	Title	Yr	NM
WORLD ARTISTS			
☐ WAM-2005 [M]	Chad and Jeremy Sing for You	1965	$15
☐ WAS-3005 [S]	Chad and Jeremy Sing for You	1965	$18
☐ WAM-2002 [M]	Yesterday's Gone	1964	$15
☐ WAS-3002 [P]	Yesterday's Gone	1964	$18
—"Yesterday's Gone" is rechanneled.			

CHAIRMEN OF THE BOARD
INVICTUS

☐ ST-9801	Bittersweet	1972	$40
☐ ST-7300 [B]	Chairmen of the Board (Featuring "Give Me Just a Little More Time")	1970	$50
☐ SKAO-7304	In Session	1970	$40
☐ KZ32526 [B]	Skin I'm In	1974	$20
☐ ST7300 [B]	The Chairmen of the Board	1970	$10
☐ KZ32526 [B]	The Skin I'm In	1974	$50

CHAKACHAS, THE
POLYDOR

| ☐ PD-5504 | Jungle Fever | 1972 | $18 |

CHAKIRIS, GEORGE
CAPITOL

☐ T1750 [M]	George Chakiris	1962	$18
☐ ST1750 [S]	George Chakiris	1962	$25
☐ T2391 [M]	It's Been a Swingin' Summer	1965	$15
☐ ST2391 [S]	It's Been a Swingin' Summer	1965	$18
☐ T1813 [M]	Memories Are Made of These	1963	$18
☐ ST1813 [S]	Memories Are Made of These	1963	$25

HORIZON

| ☐ WP-1610 [M] | The Gershwin Songbook | 1962 | $18 |
| ☐ ST-1610 [S] | The Gershwin Songbook | 1962 | $25 |

CHALKER, CURLY
COLUMBIA

| ☐ CL2596 [M] | Big Hits on Big Steel | 1965 | $25 |
| ☐ CS9396 [S] | Big Hits on Big Steel | 1965 | $30 |

CHALLENGERS, THE (1)
FANTASY

| ☐ F-9443 | Where Were You in the Summer of '62 | 1973 | $15 |

GNP CRESCENDO

☐ GNP-609 [M]	25 Great Instrumental Hits	1967	$30
☐ GNPS-609 [S]	25 Great Instrumental Hits	1967	$25
☐ GNP-2030 [M]	Billy Strange and the Challengers	1966	$25
☐ GNPS-2030 [S]	Billy Strange and the Challengers	1966	$30
☐ GNP-2025 [M]	California Kicks	1966	$25
☐ GNPS-2025 [S]	California Kicks	1966	$30
☐ GNPS-2045	Light My Fire with Classical Gas	1968	$25
☐ GNPS-2093	Sidewalk Surfing	1975	$15
☐ GNP-2010 [M]	The Challengers at the Teenage Fair	1965	$25
☐ GNPS-2010 [S]	The Challengers at the Teenage Fair	1965	$30
☐ GNP-2018 [M]	The Man from U.N.C.L.E.	1965	$30
☐ GNPS-2018 [S]	The Man from U.N.C.L.E.	1965	$30
☐ GNPS-2056 [B]	Vanilla Funk	1970	$25
☐ GNP-2031 [M]	Wipe Out	1966	$25
☐ GNPS-2031 [S]	Wipe Out	1966	$30

RHINO

| ☐ RNLP-053 | Best of the Challengers | 1982 | $12 |

TRIUMPH

| ☐ TR-100 [M] | The Challengers Go Sidewalk Surfing | 1965 | $25 |
| ☐ TRS-100 [S] | The Challengers Go Sidewalk Surfing | 1965 | $30 |

VAULT

☐ LP-107 [M]	K-39	1964	$100
☐ VS-101 [S]	(Lloyd Thaxton Goes) Surfin' with the Challengers	1963	$300
—Either title; orange vinyl			
☐ LP-101 [M]	Lloyd Thaxton Goes Surfin' with the Challengers	1963	$75
—Original title			
☐ VS-101 [S]	(Lloyd Thaxton Goes) Surfin' with the Challengers	1963	$300
—Either title; red vinyl			
☐ VS-101 [S]	Lloyd Thaxton Goes Surfin' with the Challengers	1963	$150
—Original title; black vinyl			
☐ VS-101 [S]	(Lloyd Thaxton Goes) Surfin' with the Challengers	1963	$300
—Either title; yellow vinyl			
☐ VS-101 [S]	(Lloyd Thaxton Goes) Surfin' with the Challengers	1963	$300
—Either title; blue vinyl			
☐ LP-100 [M]	Surfbeat	1963	$50
☐ VS-100 [S]	Surfbeat	1963	$100
—Black vinyl			

Number	Title	Yr	NM
☐ VS-100 [S]	Surfbeat	1963	$300
—Orange vinyl			
☐ VS-100 [S]	Surfbeat	1963	$300
—Red vinyl			
☐ VS-100 [S]	Surfbeat	1963	$300
—Yellow vinyl			
☐ LP-101 [M]	Surfin' with the Challengers	1963	$50
—Altered title			
☐ VS-101 [S]	Surfin' with the Challengers	1963	$100
—Altered title; black vinyl			
☐ LP-110 [M]	The Challengers A-Go-Go	1966	$30
☐ VS-110 [S]	The Challengers A-Go-Go	1966	$40
☐ LP-111 [M]	The Challengers' Greatest Hits	1967	$30
☐ VS-111 [S]	The Challengers' Greatest Hits	1967	$30
☐ LP-102 [M]	The Challengers On The Move	1963	$40
☐ VS-102 [S]	The Challengers On The Move	1963	$75
☐ LP-109 [M]	The Surf's Up	1965	$40
☐ VS-109 [S]	The Surf's Up	1965	$75

CHALLIS, BILL
CIRCLE

| ☐ CLP-71 | Bill Challis and His Orchestra: 1936 | 198? | $25 |
| ☐ CLP-72 | Bill Challis and His Orchestra: More 1936 | 198? | $25 |

CHALOFF, SERGE
CAPITOL

☐ M-11032	Blue Serge	1972	$35
—Capitol Jazz Classics, Vol. 7			
☐ T742 [M]	Blue Serge	1956	$350
—Turquoise label			
☐ T742 [M]	Blue Serge	1959	$150
—Black colorband label, logo at left			
☐ T6510 [M]	Boston Blow-Up	1955	$300

MOSAIC

| ☐ MQ5-147 | The Complete Serge Chaloff Sessions | 1993 | $120 |

STORYVILLE

| ☐ STLP-350 [10] | Serge & Boots | 1955 | $300 |
| ☐ STLP-317 [10] | The Fable of Mable | 1954 | $300 |

CHALOFF, SERGE/OSCAR PETTIFORD
MERCER

| ☐ LP-1003 [10] | New Stars, New Sounds, Volume 2 | 1951 | $300 |

CHAMAELEON CHURCH
Chevy Chase was in this group.

MGM

| ☐ SE-4574 [B] | Chamaeleon Church | 1968 | $25 |

CHAMBERLAIN, RICHARD
METRO

| ☐ M-564 [M] | Richard Chamberlain Sings | 1966 | $15 |
| ☐ MS-564 [S] | Richard Chamberlain Sings | 1966 | $15 |

MGM

☐ E-4287 [M]	Joy in the Morning	1965	$18
☐ SE-4287 [S]	Joy in the Morning	1965	$25
☐ T90512 [M]	Richard Chamberlain Sings	1965	$30
—Capitol Record Club edition			
☐ ST90512 [S]	Richard Chamberlain Sings	1965	$30
—Capitol Record Club edition			
☐ E-4088 [M]	Richard Chamberlain Sings	1962	$18
☐ SE-4088 [S]	Richard Chamberlain Sings	1962	$25
☐ E-4185 [M]	Twilight of Honor	1963	$18
☐ SE-4185 [S]	Twilight of Honor	1963	$25

Number	Title	Yr	NM

CHAMBERLAND, LINC
MUSE
❏ MR-5064	A Place Within	1976	$30
❏ MR-5263	Yet to Come	1981	$25

CHAMBERS, JOE, AND LARRY YOUNG
MUSE
❏ MR-5165	Double Exposure	1977	$15

CHAMBERS, JOE
MUSE
❏ MR-5035	The Almoravid	197?	$30

CHAMBERS, PAUL, AND JOHN COLTRANE
BLUE NOTE
❏ BN-LA451-H2	High Step	1975	$75

— *Reissue of Blue Note 1534 plus other material*

CHAMBERS, PAUL
BLUE NOTE
❏ BLP-1569 [M]	Bass on Top	1957	$500

— *Deep groove" version; W. 63rd St. address on label*
❏ BLP-1569 [M]	Bass on Top	1957	$400

— *Regular version, W. 63rd St. address on label*
❏ BLP-1569 [M]	Bass on Top	1963	$250

— *New York, USA" address on label*
❏ BST-1569 [S]	Bass on Top	1959	$700

— *Deep groove" version, W. 63rd St. address on label*
❏ BST-1569 [S]	Bass on Top	1959	$400

— *Regular version, W. 63rd St. address on label*
❏ BST-1569 [S]	Bass on Top	1963	$130

— *New York, USA" address on label*
❏ BST-81569 [S]	Bass on Top	196?	$50

— *A Division of Liberty Records" on label*
❏ BLP-1564 [M]	Paul Chambers Quintet	1957	$400

— *Deep groove" version, W. 63rd St. address on label*
❏ BLP-1564 [M]	Paul Chambers Quintet	1957	$250

— *Regular version, W. 63rd St. address on label*
❏ BLP-1564 [M]	Paul Chambers Quintet	1963	$100

— *New York, USA" address on label*
❏ BST-1564 [S]	Paul Chambers Quintet	1959	$300

— *Deep groove" version, W. 63rd St. address on label*
❏ BST-1564 [S]	Paul Chambers Quintet	1959	$175

— *Regular version, W. 63rd St. address on label*
❏ BST-1564 [S]	Paul Chambers Quintet	1963	$30

— *New York, USA" address on label*
❏ BST-81564 [S]	Paul Chambers Quintet	196?	$50

— *A Division of Liberty Records" on label*
❏ BLP-1534 [M]	Whims of Chambers	1956	$1200

— *Deep groove" version, Lexington Ave. address on label*
❏ BLP-1534 [M]	Whims of Chambers	1958	$750

— *Deep groove" version, W. 63rd St. address on label*
❏ BLP-1534 [M]	Whims of Chambers	1963	$175

— *New York, USA" address on label*
❏ BST-81534 [R]	Whims of Chambers	196?	$50

— *A Division of Liberty Records" on label*
EPITAPH
❏ E-4001	Paul Chambers 1935-1969	1975	$50

IMPERIAL
❏ LP-9182 [M]	A Jazz Delegation from the East: Chambers' Music	1961	$175
❏ LP-12182 [S]	A Jazz Delegation from the East: Chambers' Music	1961	$175

JAZZ: WEST
❏ JWLP7 [M]	A Jazz Delegation from the East	1956	$1500

JAZZ WEST
❏ JWLP-7 [M]	A Jazz Delegation from the East	1956	$600

SCORE
❏ SLP-4033 [M]	A Jazz Delegation from the East: Chambers' Music	1958	$100

TRIP
❏ 5026	Just Friends	197?	$35

VEE JAY
❏ LP-3012 [M]	First Bassman	1960	$50
❏ SR-3012 [S]	First Bassman	1960	$100
❏ VJS-3012 [S]	First Bassman	198?	$35

— *Reissue on thinner vinyl*
❏ LP-1014 [M]	Go	1959	$300
❏ SR-1014 [S]	Go	1959	$150
❏ VJS-1014 [S]	Go	198?	$35

— *Reissue on thinner vinyl*

CHAMBERS BROTHERS, THE
AVCO
❏ 69003	Night Move	1975	$25
❏ 11013	Unbonded	1974	$15

COLUMBIA
❏ CS9671	A New Time -- A New Day	1968	$25
❏ KGP20	Love, Peace and Happiness	1969	$30
❏ C30032	New Generation	1970	$18
❏ KC31158	Oh My God	1972	$0

Number	Title	Yr	NM
—*Canceled*			
❏ C30871	The Chambers Brothers' Greatest Hits	1971	$18
❏ PC30871	The Chambers Brothers' Greatest Hits	198?	$10

— *Reissue with new prefix*
❏ CL2722 [M]	The Time Has Come	1967	$30
❏ CS9522 [S]	The Time Has Come	1967	$25

— *Red "360 Sound" label*
❏ CS9522	The Time Has Come	1971	$15

— *Orange label*
❏ PC9522	The Time Has Come	198?	$10

— *Reissue with new prefix*
❏ CG33642	The Time Has Come/A New Time -- A New Day	1975	$18

FANTASY
❏ 24718	The Best of the Chambers Brothers	1973	$18

FOLKWAYS
❏ 31008	Groovin' Time	1968	$20

ROXBURY
❏ RLX-106	Live In Concert on Mars	1976	$30

VAULT
❏ VS-128	Feelin' the Blues	1969	$18
❏ LP-9003 [M]	People Get Ready	1966	$25
❏ LPS-9003 [S]	People Get Ready	1966	$30
❏ VS-135 [B]	The Chambers Brothers Greatest Hits	1970	$25
❏ LP-115 [M]	The Chambers Brothers Now	1967	$18
❏ VS-115 [S]	The Chambers Brothers Now	1967	$18
❏ VS-120	The Chambers Brothers Shout	1968	$18

CHAMBLEE, EDDIE
EMARCY
❏ MG-36124 [M]	Chamblee Music	1958	$250
❏ MG-36131 [M]	Doodlin'	1958	$250
❏ SR-80007 [S]	Doodlin'	1959	$250

MERCURY
❏ SR-60127 [S]	Chamblee Music	1960	$150

PRESTIGE
❏ PRLP-7321 [M]	The Rocking Tenor Sax of Eddie Chamblee	1964	$30

— *Yellow label*
❏ PRST-7321 [S]	The Rocking Tenor Sax of Eddie Chamblee	1964	$30

— *Silver label*

CHAMPLIN, BILL
ELEKTRA
❏ 5E-563	Runaway	1981	$12

FULL MOON/EPIC
❏ JE35367	Single	1978	$18

CHAMPS, THE
CHALLENGE
❏ CHL-614 [M]	All American Music from the Champs	1962	$120
❏ CHS-2514 [S]	All American Music from the Champs	1962	$250
❏ CHL-605 [M]	Everybody's Rockin' with the Champs	1959	$250
❏ CHS-2500 [S]	Everybody's Rockin' with the Champs	1959	$300
❏ CHL-601 [M]	Go Champs Go	1958	$2400

— *Blue vinyl; VG value 800; VG+ value 1600*
❏ CHL-601 [M]	Go Champs Go	1958	$300
❏ CHL-613 [M]	Great Dance Hits	1962	$120
❏ CHS-2513 [S]	Great Dance Hits	1962	$250

CHANCE
MERCURY
❏ 826029-1	Chance	1986	$10

CHANCLER, NDUGU
MCA
❏ 6302	Old Friends, New Friends	1989	$30

CHANDLER, GENE, AND JERRY BUTLER
MERCURY
❏ SR-61330	Gene & Jerry -- One & One	1971	$18

CHANDLER, GENE
20TH CENTURY
❏ T-625	Ear Candy	1980	$12
❏ T-605	Gene Chandler '80	1980	$12
❏ T-629	Here's to Love	1981	$12
❏ T-598	When You're #1	1979	$12

BRUNSWICK
❏ BL54124 [M]	The Girl Don't Care	1967	$30
❏ BL754124 [S]	The Girl Don't Care	1967	$25
❏ BL754131	There Was a Time	1968	$25
❏ BL754149	The Two Sides of Gene Chandler	1969	$25

Number	Title	Yr	NM

CHECKER
❏ LP-3003 [M]	The Duke of Soul	1967	$50
❏ LPS-3003 [R]	The Duke of Soul	1967	$30

CHI-SOUND
❏ T-578	Get Down	1978	$12

CONSTELLATION
❏ LP1425 [M]	Gene Chandler -- Live On Stage in '65	1965	$50
❏ LP1421 [M]	Greatest Hits by Gene Chandler	1964	$50
❏ LP1423 [M]	Just Be True	1964	$50

MERCURY
❏ SR-61304	The Gene Chandler Situation	1970	$18

SOLID SMOKE
❏ SS-8027	Stroll On with the Duke	198?	$12

UPFRONT
❏ UPF105	Duke of Earl	197?	$12

VEE JAY
❏ LP-1040 [M]	The Duke of Earl	1962	$120
❏ SR-1040 [S]	The Duke of Earl	1962	$800

— *Stereophonic" on front cover; top back cover contains note that begins: "Important Notice...This is a Stereophonic Record"; "Stereo" on record labels*
❏ SR-1040 [S]	The Duke of Earl	1962	$300

— *Stereo" sticker on mono cover; "Stereo" on record labels*
❏ SR-1040 [M]	The Duke of Earl	1962	$50

— *Stereophonic" on front; no "Important Notice..." on back; record plays mono. Most labels are all-black with "VJ" in brackets. This was a semi-authorized reissue after ex-Vee Jay executives bought the company's remnants in bankruptcy court in 1966.*
❏ VJLP-1040	The Duke of Earl	198?	$12

— *Mid-1980s authorized reissue*

CHANDLER, JEFF
LIBERTY
❏ LRP-3067 [M]	Jeff Chandler Sings to You	1957	$40
❏ LRP-3074 [M]	Warm and Easy	1958	$40

SUNSET
❏ SUS-5127	Sincerely Yours	1969	$15

CHANNEL, BRUCE
SMASH
❏ MGS-27008 [M]	Hey! Baby (And 11 Other Songs About Your Baby)	1962	$150
❏ SRS-67008 [R]	Hey! Baby (And 11 Other Songs About Your Baby)	1962	$75

CHANNELS, THE (1)
COLLECTABLES
❏ COL-5012	New York's Finest: The Best of Earl Lewis and the Channels	198?	$15

LOST-NITE
❏ LLP-15 [10]	The Channels	1981	$15

— *Red vinyl*
❏ LLP-16 [10]	The Channels	1981	$15

— *Red vinyl*

CHANNING, CAROL
CAEDMON
❏ TC1303	The Year Without a Santa Claus and Other Stories for Christmas	1969	$15

— *Spoken-word recordings*
COMMAND
❏ 33-880 [M]	Carol Channing Entertains	1966	$18
❏ 880SD [S]	Carol Channing Entertains	1966	$25

PLANTATION
❏ PLP-527	Carol Channing With the Original Country Cast	1978	$25

VANGUARD
❏ VRS-9056 [M]	Carol Channing	1959	$50
❏ VSD-2041 [S]	Carol Channing	1959	$75

CHANTAYS
DOT
❏ DLP3516 [M]	Pipeline	1963	$50
❏ DLP25516 [S]	Pipeline	1963	$100
❏ DLP3771 [M]	Two Sides of the Chantays	1966	$50
❏ DLP25771 [S]	Two Sides of the Chantays	1966	$100

DOWNEY
❏ DLP-1002 [M]	Pipeline	1963	$220
❏ DLPS-1002 [S]	Pipeline	1963	$350

CHANTELS, THE
CARLTON
❏ LP-144 [M]	The Chantels On Tour/Look in My Eyes	1962	$250
❏ STLP-144 [P]	The Chantels On Tour/Look in My Eyes	1962	$400

— *Eight tracks are true stereo, two are mono, two are rechanneled*

Number	Title	Yr	NM

END
| ❏ LP-312 [M] | There's Our Song Again | 1962 | $120 |
| ❏ LP-301 [M] | We Are the Chantels | 1958 | $1500 |

—Group photo on front cover; gray label with "11-17-58" in trail-off wax; VG value 500; VG+ value 1000

| ❏ LP-301 [M] | We Are the Chantels | 1959 | $400 |

—Jukebox on front cover; gray label, "11-17-58" in trail-off wax

| ❏ LP-301 [M] | We Are the Chantels | 1962 | $250 |

—Jukebox on front cover; gray label, "1962" in trail-off wax

| ❏ LP-301 [M] | We Are the Chantels | 1965 | $150 |

—Jukebox on front cover; gray label, "8-65" in trail-off wax

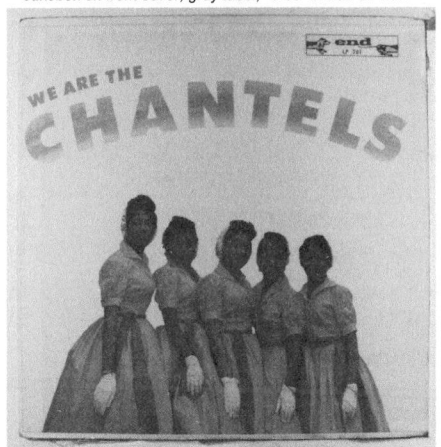

| ❏ LP-301 [M] | We Are the Chantels | 1965 | $100 |

—Jukebox on front cover; multicolor label, "8-65" in trail-off wax

| ❏ END-301 [R] | We Are the Chantels | 197? | $30 |

—Reissue in rechanneled stereo; orange bar through center hole and "END" on both sides of center hole

FORUM
| ❏ F-9104 [M] | The Chantels Sing Their Favorites | 1964 | $50 |
| ❏ FS-9104 [R] | The Chantels Sing Their Favorites | 1964 | $30 |

CHAPARRAL BROTHERS, THE
CAPITOL
| ❏ ST2922 | Introducing the Chaparral Brothers | 1968 | $25 |
| ❏ ST-551 | Just for the Record | 1970 | $18 |

CHAPEL SINGERS OF THE MORNING CHAPEL HOUR
MORNING CHAPEL HOUR
| ❏ KM5539 | O Come, O Come Immanuel | 197? | $12 |

CHAPIN, HARRY
BOARDWALK
| ❏ FW36872 | Sequel | 1980 | $12 |
ELEKTRA
❏ 60413	Anthology of Harry Chapin	1985	$12
❏ 9E-301	Dance Band on the Titanic	1977	$15
❏ 7E-2009	Greatest Stories Live	1976	$15
❏ 8E-6003	Greatest Stories Live	1978	$12

—Reissue of 7E-2009

❏ EKS-75023	Heads and Tales	1972	$12
❏ BB-703	Legends of the Lost and Found -- New Greatest Stories Live	1979	$15
❏ 6E-142	Living Room Suite	1978	$12
❏ 7E-1082	On the Road to Kingdom Come	1976	$12
❏ 7E-1041	Portrait Gallery	1975	$12
❏ EKS-75065	Short Stories	1973	$12
❏ EKS-75042	Sniper and Other Love Songs	1972	$12
❏ 7E-1012	Verities & Balderdash	1974	$12

CHAPIN, JIM
CLASSIC JAZZ
| ❏ 6 [M] | Jim Chapin Sextet | 197? | $25 |
| ❏ 7 [M] | Skin Tight | 197? | $25 |
PRESTIGE
| ❏ PRLP-213 [10] | Jim Chapin Sextet | 1955 | $300 |

CHAPINS, THE
ROCK-LAND
| ❏ RR-66 [M] | Chapin Music | 1966 | $85 |

—As "The Chapin Brothers"; both mono and stereo, same price

CHAPMAN, BETH NIELSEN
CAPITOL
| ❏ ST-12050 | Hearing It First | 1980 | $50 |

CHAPMAN, GARY
RCA
| ❏ 6375-1-R | Everyday Man | 1988 | $12 |

CHAPMAN, MARSHALL
EPIC
❏ JE35341	Jaded Virgin	1978	$12
❏ JE36192	Marshall	1979	$12
❏ PE34422	Me, I'm Feelin' Free	1977	$12
ROUNDER
| ❏ 3069 | Take It On Home | 1982 | $15 |

CHAPMAN, TRACY
ELEKTRA
| ❏ 60888 | Crossroads | 1989 | $15 |
| ❏ R142496 | Crossroads | 1989 | $15 |

—BMG Direct Marketing edition

| ❏ R153582 | Tracy Chapman | 1988 | $15 |

—BMG Direct Marketing edition

| ❏ 60774 | Tracy Chapman | 1988 | $12 |

CHARIOT
NATIONAL GENERAL
| ❏ NG-2003 [B] | Chariot | 1971 | $125 |

CHARIOTEERS, THE
COLUMBIA
| ❏ CL6014 [10] | Sweet and Low | 1949 | $300 |
HARMONY
| ❏ HL7089 [M] | The Charioteers with Billy Williams | 1957 | $150 |

CHARISMA
ROULETTE
| ❏ SR-42037 [B] | Charisma | 1970 | $30 |

CHARITY
UNI
| ❏ 73061 | Charity Now | 1969 | $30 |

CHARLATANS, THE
PHILIPS
| ❏ PHS600309 | The Charlatans | 1969 | $150 |

CHARLEE
AMERAMA
| ❏ 1005 | Standing in Your Shoes | 1977 | $18 |

CHARLENE
MOTOWN
❏ 6007ML	Charlene	1981	$12
❏ 6090ML	Hit and Run Lover	1985	$12
❏ 6027ML	Used to Be	1982	$12
PRODIGAL
| ❏ P6-10015 | Charlene | 1976 | $25 |
| ❏ P6-10018 | Songs of Love | 1977 | $25 |

CHARLES, BOBBY
CHESS
| ❏ CH9175 | Chess Masters | 1984 | $18 |

CHARLES, RAY, AND BETTY CARTER
ABC
| ❏ S-385 [S] | Ray Charles and Betty Carter | 1967 | $50 |

—Reissue of ABC-Paramount ABCS-385

ABC-PARAMOUNT
| ❏ ABC-385 [M] | Ray Charles and Betty Carter | 1961 | $120 |
| ❏ ABCS-385 [S] | Ray Charles and Betty Carter | 1961 | $175 |
DCC COMPACT CLASSICS
| ❏ LPZ-2005 | Ray Charles and Betty Carter | 1995 | $175 |

—Audiophile vinyl

DUNHILL COMPACT CLASSICS
| ❏ DZL-039 | Ray Charles and Betty Carter | 1988 | $35 |

—Clear vinyl reissue

CHARLES, RAY, AND CLEO LAINE
RCA VICTOR
| ❏ CPL2-1831 | Porgy & Bess | 1976 | $35 |
| ❏ DJL1-2163 | Porgy & Bess | 1976 | $50 |

—Promo-only excerpts from 2-record set

CHARLES, RAY, AND MILT JACKSON
ATLANTIC
| ❏ 1279 [M] | Soul Brothers | 1958 | $300 |

—Black label

| ❏ 1279 [M] | Soul Brothers | 1960 | $300 |

—Red and white label, white fan logo on right

| ❏ 1279 [M] | Soul Brothers | 1962 | $175 |

—Red and white label, black fan logo on right

| ❏ SD1279 [S] | Soul Brothers | 1959 | $300 |

—Green label

| ❏ SD1279 [S] | Soul Brothers | 1960 | $300 |

—Blue and green label, white fan logo on right

| ❏ SD1279 [S] | Soul Brothers | 1962 | $175 |

—Blue and green label, black fan logo on right

| ❏ 1360 [M] | Soul Meeting | 1961 | $175 |

—Red and white label, white fan logo on right

| ❏ 1360 [M] | Soul Meeting | 1962 | $175 |

—Red and white label, black fan logo on right

| ❏ SD1360 [S] | Soul Meeting | 1961 | $175 |

—Blue and green label, white fan logo on right

| ❏ SD1360 [S] | Soul Meeting | 1962 | $175 |

—Blue and green label, black fan logo on right

CHARLES, RAY, SINGERS
ABC
| ❏ X-772 | Moods of Love | 1973 | $12 |
ATCO
| ❏ SD 33-263 | Memories of a Middle-Aged Movie Fan | 1970 | $12 |
COMMAND
❏ 33-870 [M]	Al-Di-La and Other Extra Special Songs for Young Lovers	1964	$12
❏ SD870 [S]	Al-Di-La and Other Extra Special Songs for Young Lovers	1964	$15
❏ SD923	At the Movies	1968	$12
❏ 33-876 [M]	Command Performances	1965	$12
❏ SD876 [S]	Command Performances	1965	$15
❏ 33-896 [M]	Command Performances Vol. 2	1966	$12
❏ SD896 [S]	Command Performances Vol. 2	1966	$15
❏ CQ-40005 [Q]	Love Me with All of Your Heart	1972	$20
❏ SD936	MacArthur Park	1969	$12
❏ SD949	Move Me, O Wondrous Music	1969	$12
❏ 33-898 [M]	One of Those Songs	1966	$12
❏ SD898 [S]	One of Those Songs	1966	$15
❏ 33-845 [M]	Paradise Islands	1962	$12
❏ SD845 [S]	Paradise Islands	1962	$15
❏ 33-839 [M]	Rome Revisited	1962	$12
❏ SD839 [S]	Rome Revisited	1962	$15
❏ 33-866 [M]	Something Special for Young Lovers	1964	$12
❏ SD866 [S]	Something Special for Young Lovers	1964	$15
❏ 33-827 [M]	Something Wonderful	1961	$12
❏ SD827 [S]	Something Wonderful	1961	$15
❏ 33-886 [M]	Songs for Latin Lovers	1965	$12
❏ SD886 [S]	Songs for Latin Lovers	1965	$15
❏ 33-874 [M]	Songs for Lonesome Lovers	1964	$12
❏ SD874 [S]	Songs for Lonesome Lovers	1964	$15
❏ 33-914 [M]	Special Something	1967	$15
❏ SD914 [S]	Special Something	1967	$12
❏ SD926	Take Me Along	1968	$12
❏ 33-903 [M]	What the World Needs Now Is Love	1966	$12
❏ SD903 [S]	What the World Needs Now Is Love	1966	$15
❏ 33-890 [M]	Young Lovers on Broadway	1965	$12
❏ SD890 [S]	Young Lovers on Broadway	1965	$15
DECCA
❏ DL8988 [M]	Deep Night	1960	$15
❏ DL78988 [S]	Deep Night	1960	$18
❏ DL8787 [M]	Highest Fidelity -- Love and Marriage	1958	$15
❏ DL78787 [S]	Highest Fidelity -- Love and Marriage	1958	$18
❏ DL8874 [M]	In the Evening by the Moonlight	1959	$15
❏ DL78874 [S]	In the Evening by the Moonlight	1959	$18
❏ DL8838 [M]	Sunrise Serenade	1958	$15
❏ DL78838 [S]	Sunrise Serenade	1958	$18
❏ DL8940 [M]	We Gather Together -- Beloved Hymns	1959	$15
❏ DL78940 [S]	We Gather Together -- Beloved Hymns	1959	$18
MCA
| ❏ 4162 | The Best of the Ray Charles Singers | 1980 | $12 |
METRO
| ❏ M-507 [M] | Spring, Spring, Spring | 1965 | $12 |
| ❏ MS-507 [S] | Spring, Spring, Spring | 1965 | $12 |
MGM
❏ E-4163 [M]	Autumn Moods	1963	$15
❏ SE-4163 [S]	Autumn Moods	1963	$15
❏ E-4166 [M]	Christmas at Home	1963	$15
❏ SE-4166 [S]	Christmas at Home	1963	$15
❏ E-3568 [M]	Here's to My Lady	1957	$18

—Yellow label

| ❏ E-3568 [M] | Here's to My Lady | 1960 | $15 |

—Black label

| ❏ E-4164 [M] | Songs for a Lazy Summer Afternoon | 1963 | $15 |
| ❏ SE-4164 [S] | Songs for a Lazy Summer Afternoon | 1963 | $15 |

Number	Title	Yr	NM
E-4257 [M]	The Very Best of the Ray Charles Singers	1964	$15
SE-4257 [S]	The Very Best of the Ray Charles Singers	1964	$15
E-4165 [M]	We Love Paris	1963	$15
SE-4165 [S]	We Love Paris	1963	$15
E-3387 [M]	Winter Wonderland	1956	$18

— *Yellow label*

E-3387 [M]	Winter Wonderland	1960	$15

— *Black label*

SOMERSET

Number	Title	Yr	NM
P-21400 [M]	Quiet Moments for Young Lovers	196?	$12
SF-21400 [S]	Quiet Moments for Young Lovers	196?	$12
P-21500 [M]	Young Lovers in Far Away Places	196?	$12
SF-21500 [S]	Young Lovers in Far Away Places	196?	$12

VOCALION

Number	Title	Yr	NM
VL3784 [M]	Love Is a Many-Splendored Thing	196?	$12
VL73784 [S]	Love Is a Many-Splendored Thing	196?	$12

CHARLES, RAY

ABC

Number	Title	Yr	NM
H-731	A 25th Anniversary in Show Business Salute to Ray Charles	1971	$18
X-781/2	All-Time Great Country & Western Hits	1973	$18
590X [M]	A Man and His Soul	1967	$18
S-590X [S]	A Man and His Soul	1967	$25
X-755	A Message from the People	1972	$15
S-625	A Portrait of Ray	1968	$15
S-544 [S]	Crying Time	1967	$15
S-355 [S]	Dedicated to You	1967	$15
S-695	Doing His Thing	1969	$15
S-495 [S]	Have a Smile with Me	1967	$15
S-675	I'm All Yours -- Baby!	1969	$15
S-465 [S]	Ingredients in a Recipe for Soul	1967	$15
S-707	Love Country Style	1971	$15
S-410 [S]	Modern Sounds in Country and Western Music	1967	$15
S-435 [S]	Modern Sounds in Country and Western Music (Volume Two)	1967	$15
S-415 [S]	Ray Charles' Greatest Hits	1967	$15
595 [M]	Ray Charles Invites You to Listen	1967	$25
S-595 [S]	Ray Charles Invites You to Listen	1967	$18
ST-91233 [S]	Ray Charles Invites You to Listen	1967	$18

— *Capitol Record Club edition*

S-500 [S]	Ray Charles Live in Concert	1967	$15
S-550 [S]	Ray's Moods	1967	$15
S-480 [S]	Sweet & Sour Tears	1967	$15
S-335 [S]	The Genius Hits the Road	1967	$15
QBO-91036 [M]	The Ray Charles Story	1967	$30

— *Capitol Record Club exclusive*

SQBO-91036 [S]	The Ray Charles Story	1967	$30

— *Capitol Record Club exclusive*

X-765	Through the Eyes of Love	1972	$15
S-520 [S]	Together Again	1967	$15
S-726	Volcanic Action of My Soul	1971	$15

ABC IMPULSE!

Number	Title	Yr	NM
AS-2 [S]	Genius + Soul = Jazz	1968	$30

ABC-PARAMOUNT

Number	Title	Yr	NM
520 [M]	Country & Western Meets Rhythm & Blues	1965	$18
S-520 [S]	Country & Western Meets Rhythm & Blues	1965	$25
544 [M]	Crying Time	1966	$18
S-544 [S]	Crying Time	1966	$25
T-90625 [M]	Crying Time	1966	$25

— *Capitol Record Club edition*

ST-90625 [S]	Crying Time	1966	$25

— *Capitol Record Club edition*

355 [M]	Dedicated to You	1961	$25
S-355 [S]	Dedicated to You	1961	$30
495 [M]	Have a Smile with Me	1964	$25
S-495 [S]	Have a Smile with Me	1964	$30
465 [M]	Ingredients in a Recipe for Soul	1963	$25
S-465 [S]	Ingredients in a Recipe for Soul	1963	$30
410 [M]	Modern Sounds in Country and Western Music	1962	$30
S-410 [S]	Modern Sounds in Country and Western Music	1962	$30
435 [M]	Modern Sounds in Country and Western Music (Volume Two)	1962	$25
S-435 [S]	Modern Sounds in Country and Western Music (Volume Two)	1962	$30
415 [M]	Ray Charles' Greatest Hits	1962	$25
S-415 [S]	Ray Charles' Greatest Hits	1962	$30
500 [M]	Ray Charles Live in Concert	1965	$18
S-500 [S]	Ray Charles Live in Concert	1965	$25
T-90144 [M]	Ray Charles Live in Concert	1965	$25

— *Capitol Record Club edition*

ST-90144 [S]	Ray Charles Live in Concert	1965	$25

— *Capitol Record Club edition*

Number	Title	Yr	NM
550 [M]	Ray's Moods	1966	$18
S-550 [S]	Ray's Moods	1966	$25
ST-90929 [S]	Ray's Moods	1966	$30

— *Capitol Record Club edition*

480 [M]	Sweet & Sour Tears	1964	$25
S-480 [S]	Sweet & Sour Tears	1964	$30
335 [M]	The Genius Hits the Road	1960	$25
S-335 [S]	The Genius Hits the Road	1960	$30
520 [M]	Together Again	196?	$18

— *Retitled version of "Country and Western Meets Rhythm and Blues"*

S-520 [S]	Together Again	196?	$25

— *Retitled version of "Country and Western Meets Rhythm and Blues"*

ST-90847 [S]	Together Again	1966	$30

— *Capitol Record Club edition*

ATLANTIC

Number	Title	Yr	NM
SD19251	Ain't It So	1979	$15
SD19281	Brother Ray Is At It Again	1980	$15
8054 [M]	Do the Twist!	1961	$30

— *Red and white label, white fan logo on right*

8054 [M]	Do the Twist!	1962	$25

— *Red and white label, black fan logo on right*

8006 [M]	Hallelujah! I Love Her So	1962	$25

— *Red and white label, white fan logo on right; retitled version*

SD19199	Love and Peace	1978	$15
3700	Ray Charles: A Life in Music	198?	$50
1289 [M]	Ray Charles at Newport	1958	$300

— *Black label*

1289 [M]	Ray Charles at Newport	1960	$300

— *Red and white label, white fan logo on right*

1289 [M]	Ray Charles at Newport	1962	$175

— *Red and white label, black fan logo on right*

SD1289 [S]	Ray Charles at Newport	1959	$300

— *Green label*

SD1289 [S]	Ray Charles at Newport	1960	$300

— *Blue and green label, white fan logo on right*

SD1289 [S]	Ray Charles at Newport	1962	$175

— *Blue and green label, black fan logo on right*

8039 [M]	Ray Charles In Person	1960	$40

— *Black label*

8039 [M]	Ray Charles In Person	1960	$30

— *Red and white label, white fan logo on right*

8039 [M]	Ray Charles In Person	1962	$25

— *Red and white label, black fan logo on right*

SD 2-503	Ray Charles Live	1973	$18
8006 [M]	Ray Charles (Rock and Roll)	1957	$125

— *Black label*

8006 [M]	Ray Charles (Rock and Roll)	1960	$30

— *Red and white label, white fan logo on right*

SD1543	The Best of Ray Charles	1970	$30
1369 [M]	The Genius After Hours	1961	$175

— *Red and white label, white fan logo on right*

1369 [M]	The Genius After Hours	1962	$175

— *Red and white label, black fan logo on right*

SD1369 [S]	The Genius After Hours	1961	$175

— *Blue and green label, white fan logo on right*

SD1369 [S]	The Genius After Hours	1962	$175

— *Blue and green label, black fan logo on right*

90464	The Genius After Hours	1986	$25

— *Reissue*

1312 [M]	The Genius of Ray Charles	1960	$300

— *Black label*

1312 [M]	The Genius of Ray Charles	1960	$300

— *White "bullseye" label*

1312 [M]	The Genius of Ray Charles	1960	$300

— *Red and white label, white fan logo on right*

1312 [M]	The Genius of Ray Charles	1962	$25

— *Red and white label, black fan logo on right*

SD1312 [S]	The Genius of Ray Charles	1960	$300

— *Green label*

SD1312 [S]	The Genius of Ray Charles	1960	$300

— *White "bullseye" label*

SD1312 [S]	The Genius of Ray Charles	1960	$300

— *Blue and green label, white fan logo on right*

SD1312 [S]	The Genius of Ray Charles	1962	$175

— *Blue and green label, black fan logo on right*

SD1312 [S]	The Genius of Ray Charles	1968	$50

— *Brown and purple label*

8052 [M]	The Genius Sings the Blues	1961	$30

— *Red and white label, white fan logo on right*

8052 [M]	The Genius Sings the Blues	1962	$25

— *Red and white label, black fan logo on right*

SD7101	The Great Hits of Ray Charles Recorded on 8-Track Stereo	1966	$30
1259 [M]	The Great Ray Charles	1957	$300

— *Black label*

1259 [M]	The Great Ray Charles	1960	$300

— *Red and white label, white fan logo on right*

1259 [M]	The Great Ray Charles	1962	$175

— *Red and white label, black fan logo on right*

SD1259 [S]	The Great Ray Charles	1959	$300

— *Green label*

SD1259 [S]	The Great Ray Charles	1960	$300

— *Blue and green label, white fan logo on right*

SD1259 [S]	The Great Ray Charles	1962	$175

— *Blue and green label, black fan logo on right*

2-900 [M]	The Ray Charles Story	1962	$40
8063 [M]	The Ray Charles Story, Volume 1	1962	$25
8064 [M]	The Ray Charles Story, Volume 2	1962	$25
8083 [M]	The Ray Charles Story, Volume 3	1963	$25
8094 [M]	The Ray Charles Story, Volume 4	1964	$25
SD8094 [S]	The Ray Charles Story, Volume 4	1964	$30
SD19142	True to Life	1977	$15
8029 [M]	What'd I Say	1959	$50

— *Black label*

8029 [M]	What'd I Say	1960	$40

— *White "bullseye" label*

8029 [M]	What'd I Say	1960	$30

— *Red and white label, white fan logo on right*

8029 [M]	What'd I Say	1962	$25

— *Red and white label, black fan logo on right*

8025 [M]	Yes, Indeed!	1958	$50

— *Black label; cover has screaming girls*

8025 [M]	Yes, Indeed!	1960	$30

— *Red and white label, white fan logo on right; cover has screaming girls*

8025 [M]	Yes, Indeed!	1962	$25

— *Red and white label, black fan logo on right; cover has Ray on it*

BARONET

Number	Title	Yr	NM
B-111 [M]	The Artistry of Ray Charles	196?	$30
BS-111 [R]	The Artistry of Ray Charles	196?	$25
B-117 [M]	The Great Ray Charles	196?	$30
BS-117 [R]	The Great Ray Charles	196?	$25

BLUESWAY

Number	Title	Yr	NM
6053	The Genius Live	1973	$15

COLUMBIA

Number	Title	Yr	NM
FC38990	Do I Ever Cross Your Mind	1984	$12
FC39415	Friendship	1985	$12
AS1920 [DJ]	Friendship Radio Show	1984	$25
FC40338	From the Pages of My Mind	1986	$12
FC45062	Seven Spanish Angels and Other Hits (1982-1986)	1989	$15
FC40125	The Spirit of Christmas	1985	$12
FC38293	Wish You Were Here Tonight	1983	$12
PC38293	Wish You Were Here Tonight	1985	$10

— *Budget-line reissue*

CORONET

Number	Title	Yr	NM
CX-173 [M]	Ray Charles	196?	$30
CXS-173 [R]	Ray Charles	196?	$25

CROSSOVER

Number	Title	Yr	NM
9000	Come Live with Me	1974	$15
9007	My Kind of Jazz, Part 3	1976	$30
9005	Renaissance	1975	$15

DCC COMPACT CLASSICS

Number	Title	Yr	NM
LPZ-2012	Greatest Country and Western Hits	1995	$150

— *Audiophile vinyl*

DUNHILL COMPACT CLASSICS

Number	Title	Yr	NM
DZL-038	Genius + Soul = Jazz	1988	$35

— *Clear vinyl reissue*

EVEREST ARCHIVE OF FOLK & JAZZ

Number	Title	Yr	NM
244	Ray Charles	1970	$15
292	Ray Charles, Vol. 2	197?	$12
358	Rockin' with Ray	1979	$12

HOLLYWOOD

Number	Title	Yr	NM
505 [M]	The Fabulous Ray Charles	1959	$175
504 [M]	The Original Ray Charles	1959	$175

IMPULSE!

Number	Title	Yr	NM
A-2 [M]	Genius + Soul = Jazz	1961	$250
AS-2 [S]	Genius + Soul = Jazz	1961	$120

Number	Title	Yr	NM
INTERMEDIA			
❏ QS-5013	Goin' Down Slow	198?	$12
LONGINES SYMPHONETTE			
❏ 95647	The Greatest Hits of Ray Charles	1974	$40
PAIR			
❏ PDL2-1139	The Real Ray Charles	1986	$15
PREMIER			
❏ PS-6001 [R]	Fantastic Ray Charles	196?	$25
❏ PM2004 [M]	The Great Ray Charles	196?	$30
❏ PS2004 [R]	The Great Ray Charles	196?	$25
RHINO			
❏ R1-70097	Greatest Hits, Volume 1	1988	$12
❏ R1-70098	Greatest Hits, Volume 2	1988	$12
❏ R1-70099	Modern Sounds in Country and Western Music	1988	$12
TANGERINE			
❏ 1512	My Kind of Jazz	1970	$30
❏ 1516	My Kind of Jazz No. II	1973	$30
WARNER BROS.			
❏ 26343	Would You Believe?	1990	$18

CHARLES, RAY / HARRY BELAFONTE

Number	Title	Yr	NM
CORONET			
❏ CX-203 [M]	The Greatest Ever	196?	$15
❏ CXS-203 [R]	The Greatest Ever	196?	$12

CHARLES, RAY/IVORY JOE HUNTER/JIMMY RUSHING

Number	Title	Yr	NM
DESIGN			
❏ DLP-909 [M]	Three of a Kind	196?	$15
❏ DLS-909 [R]	Three of a Kind	196?	$12

CHARLES, SONNY

Number	Title	Yr	NM
HIGHRISE			
❏ HR-102	The Sun Still Shines	1982	$15

CHARLES, TEDDY

Number	Title	Yr	NM
ATLANTIC			
❏ 1229 [M]	The Teddy Charles Tentet	1956	$300
—Black label			
❏ 1229 [M]	The Teddy Charles Tentet	1961	$175
—Multicolor label with white "fan" logo			
❏ 1274 [M]	Word from Bird	1956	$300
—Black label			
❏ 1274 [M]	Word from Bird	1961	$175
—Multicolor label with white "fan" logo			
BETHLEHEM			
❏ BCP-6044 [M]	On Campus -- Ivy League Jazz Concert	1960	$50
❏ BCP-6032 [M]	Salute to Hamp	1959	$250
ELEKTRA			
❏ EKL-136 [M]	Vibe-Rant	1957	$300
FANTASY			
❏ OJC-122	Collaboration: West	198?	$25
—Reissue of Prestige 7028			
JOSIE			
❏ JOZ-3505 [M]	Teddy Charles Trio Plays Duke Ellington	1963	$30
❏ JJS-3505 [S]	Teddy Charles Trio Plays Duke Ellington	1963	$30
JUBILEE			
❏ JLP-1047 [M]	Three for Duke	1957	$50
❏ JGS-1047 [S]	Three for Duke	1959	$40
NEW JAZZ			
❏ NJLP-1106 [10]	Teddy Charles New Directions Quartet	1955	$600
PRESTIGE			
❏ PRLP-7028 [M]	Collaboration: West	1956	$300
—Yellow label with 446 W. 50th St. address			
❏ PRLP-7028 [M]	Collaboration: West	196?	$30
—Blue label, trident logo on right			
❏ PRLP-7078 [M]	Evolution	1957	$300
—Yellow label			
❏ PRLP-7078 [M]	Evolution	196?	$30
—Blue label, trident logo on right			
❏ PRLP-143 [10]	New Directions Vol. 1	1953	$300
❏ PRLP-150 [10]	New Directions Vol. 2	1953	$300
❏ PRLP-164 [10]	New Directions Vol. 3	1953	$300
❏ PRLP-169 [10]	New Directions Vol. 4	1954	$300
❏ PRLP-178 [10]	New Directions Vol. 5	1954	$300
—With Bob Brookmeyer			
❏ PRLP-132 [10]	Teddy Charles and His Trio	1952	$400
❏ PRLP-206 [10]	Teddy Charles New Directions Quartet	1955	$300
—Reissue of New Jazz 1106			
SAVOY			
❏ MG-12174 [M]	The Vibe-Rant Quintet	1961	$30
—Reissue of Elektra LP			
SOUL NOTE			
❏ 121183	Live at the Verona Jazz Festival, 1988	1990	$30

Number	Title	Yr	NM
UNITED ARTISTS			
❏ UAL-3365 [M]	Russia Goes Jazz	1964	$30
❏ UAS-6365 [S]	Russia Goes Jazz	1964	$30
WARWICK			
❏ W-2033 [M]	Jazz in the Garden of the Museum of Modern Art	1960	$50

CHARLES RIVER VALLEY BOYS, THE

Number	Title	Yr	NM
ELEKTRA			
❏ EKL-4006 [M]	Beatle Country	1967	$25
❏ EKS-74006 [S]	Beatle Country	1967	$30

CHARLESTON CITY ALL-STARS

Number	Title	Yr	NM
ABC WESTMINSTER GOLD			
❏ WGAS-68004	The Roaring 20's, Volume 2	197?	$30
GRAND AWARD			
❏ GA 33-411 [M]	Dixieland	1959	$30
❏ GA243SD [S]	Dixieland	1959	$35
❏ GA 33-327 [M]	The Roaring 20's	1957	$35
❏ GA201SD [S]	The Roaring 20's	1958	$30
❏ GA 33-340 [M]	The Roaring 20's, Volume 2	1957	$35
❏ GA211SD [S]	The Roaring 20's, Volume 2	1958	$30
❏ GA 33-353 [M]	The Roaring 20's, Volume 3	1957	$35
❏ GA229SD [S]	The Roaring 20's, Volume 3	1958	$30
❏ GA 33-370 [M]	The Roaring 20's, Volume 4	1958	$35
WALDORF MUSIC HALL			
❏ MH 33-142 [M]	The Roaring Twenties	195?	$50

CHARQUET & CO.

Number	Title	Yr	NM
STOMP OFF			
❏ SOS-1008	Crazy Quilt	197?	$30
❏ SOS-1053	Everybody Stomp	198?	$25
❏ SOS-1076	Jungle Jamboree	198?	$25
❏ SOS-1039	Live at Joseph Lam Club	198?	$25
❏ SOS-1195	You'll Long for Me	198?	$25

CHARTERS, ANN

Number	Title	Yr	NM
GNP CRESCENDO			
❏ GNPS-9021	A Joplin Bouquet	197?	$25
❏ GNPS-9032	The Genius of Scott Joplin	197?	$25
KICKING MULE			
❏ 101	Scott Joplin and His Friends	198?	$25

CHARTS, THE

Number	Title	Yr	NM
COLLECTABLES			
❏ COL-5029	Greatest Hits	1986	$15
LOST-NITE			
❏ LLP-10 [10]	The Charts	1981	$15
—Red vinyl			

CHASE, CAROL

Number	Title	Yr	NM
CASABLANCA			
❏ NBLP-7237	Chase Is On	1980	$15
❏ CAC-6001	Sexy Songs	1980	$15

CHASE, LINCOLN

Number	Title	Yr	NM
LIBERTY			
❏ LRP-3076 [M]	The Explosive Lincoln Chase	1958	$50

CHASE

Number	Title	Yr	NM
EPIC			
❏ E30472	Chase	1971	$25
❏ EQ30472 [Q]	Chase	1973	$75
❏ EG33737	Chase/Ennea	1976	$25
❏ KE31097	Ennea	1972	$25
❏ KE32572	Pure Music	1974	$25
❏ EQ32572 [Q]	Pure Music	1974	$75

CHEAP TRICK
Also see FUSE.

Number	Title	Yr	NM
EPIC			
❏ FE36498	All Shook Up	1980	$12
❏ PE36498	All Shook Up	1984	$10
❏ E46013	Busted	1990	$15
❏ PE34400 [B]	Cheap Trick	1976	$18
—Originals have orange labels			
❏ PE34400	Cheap Trick	1979	$10
—Later editions have dark blue labels; may or may not have bar code on back			
❏ FE35795 [B]	Cheap Trick at Budokan	1979	$15
—Orange label; came with gold-colored obi (add 5/6 if there) and booklet (deduct 1/6 if missing)			
❏ FE35795 [B]	Cheap Trick at Budokan	1979	$18
—Dark blue label; some copies came with gold-colored obi (add 100% if there) and all came with booklet (deduct 20% if missing)			
❏ FE35795 [DJ]	Cheap Trick at Budokan	1979	$25
—White label promo			
❏ PE35795	Cheap Trick at Budokan	1984	$10
❏ FE35773	Dream Police	1979	$12
—Despite lower number, this came out after Epic 35795			
❏ PE35773	Dream Police	1984	$10
❏ PE38541 [EP]	Found All the Parts	1983	$10
—Six-song reissue of Epic/Nu-Disk release on 12-inch LP			
❏ AS518 [DJ]	From Tokyo to You	1979	$50
—Promo-only sampler from Cheap Trick at Budokan			
❏ JE35312	Heaven Tonight	1978	$15
—Originals have orange labels			
❏ PE35312	Heaven Tonight	1979	$10
—Later editions have dark blue labels; may or may not have bar code			
❏ JE34884	In Color	1977	$15
—Originals have orange labels			
❏ PE34884	In Color	1979	$10
—Later editions have dark blue labels; may or may not have bar code on back			
❏ OE40922	Lap of Luxury	1988	$12
❏ FE38794	Next Position Please	1983	$12
❏ PE38794	Next Position Please	1985	$10
❏ FE38021	One on One	1982	$12
❏ PE38021	One on One	1984	$10
❏ FE39592	Standing on the Edge	1985	$12
❏ PE39592	Standing on the Edge	1987	$10
❏ FE40405	The Doctor	1986	$12
❏ PE40405	The Doctor	1987	$10
—Reissue with new prefix on cover			
EPIC/NU-DISK			
❏ 4E36453 [10]	Found All the Parts	1980	$30
—10-inch, four-track EP with bonus 45, "Everything Works If You Let It" (AE7 1206)			

CHEATHAM, DOC, AND SAMMY PRICE

Number	Title	Yr	NM
SACKVILLE			
❏ 3029	Black Beauty	198?	$30
❏ 3013	Doc & Sammy	198?	$30
❏ 3024	Sweet Substitute	198?	$30

CHEATHAM, DOC

Number	Title	Yr	NM
CLASSIC JAZZ			
❏ 113	Good for What Ails Ya	1977	$30

CHEATHAM, JEANNIE AND JIMMY

Number	Title	Yr	NM
CONCORD JAZZ			
❏ CJ-373	Back to the Neighborhood	1989	$30
❏ CJ-321	Homeward Bound	1987	$25
❏ CJ-297	Midnight Mama	1986	$25
❏ CJ-258	Sweet Baby Blues	1985	$25

CHECKER, CHUBBY

Number	Title	Yr	NM
ABKCO			
❏ 4219	Chubby Checker's Greatest Hits	1972	$25
EVEREST			
❏ 4111	Chubby Checker's Greatest Hits	1981	$15
MCA			
❏ 5291	The Change Has Come	1982	$12
PARKWAY			
❏ P7014 [M]	All the Hits (For Your Dancin' Party)	1962	$30
❏ P7030 [M]	Beach Party	1963	$30
❏ SP7030 [S]	Beach Party	1963	$40
❏ P7026 [M]	Chubby Checker In Person	1963	$30
❏ SP7026 [S]	Chubby Checker In Person	1963	$40
—The above record is labeled "Twist It Up"			
❏ P7022 [M]	Chubby Checker's Biggest Hits	1962	$30
❏ SP7022 [R]	Chubby Checker's Biggest Hits	1962	$30
❏ P7048 [M]	Chubby Checker's Eighteen Golden Hits	1966	$30
❏ SP7048 [P]	Chubby Checker's Eighteen Golden Hits	1966	$40
❏ P7036 [M]	Chubby Checker With Sy Oliver and His Orchestra	1964	$30
❏ SP7036 [S]	Chubby Checker With Sy Oliver and His Orchestra	1964	$40
❏ P7045 [M]	Discotheque	1965	$30

Number	Title	Yr	NM
❏ SP7045 [S]	Discotheque	1965	$40
❏ P7040 [M]	Folk Album	1964	$30
❏ SP7040 [S]	Folk Album	1964	$40
❏ P7009 [M]	For Teen Twisters Only	1962	$30
❏ SP7009 [S]	For Teen Twisters Only	1962	$40
❏ P7002 [M]	For Twisters Only	1960	$40
— All-orange label			
❏ P7002 [M]	For Twisters Only	1962	$30
— Orange and yellow label			
❏ P7003 [M]	It's Pony Time	1961	$40
— All-orange label			
❏ P7003 [M]	It's Pony Time	1962	$30
— Orange and yellow label			
❏ P7027 [M]	Let's Limbo Some More	1963	$30
❏ SP7027 [S]	Let's Limbo Some More	1963	$40
❏ P7004 [M]	Let's Twist Again	1961	$40
— All-orange label			
❏ P7004 [M]	Let's Twist Again	1962	$30
— Orange and yellow label			
❏ P7020 [M]	Limbo Party	1962	$30
❏ SP7020 [S]	Limbo Party	1962	$40
❏ P7008 [M]	Twistin' Round the World	1962	$30
❏ SP7008 [B]	Twistin' Round the World	1962	$40
❏ P7001 [M]	Twist with Chubby Checker	1962	$30
— Orange and yellow label			
❏ P7001 [M]	Twist with Chubby Checker	1960	$40
— All-orange label			
❏ P7007 [M]	Your Twist Party	1961	$40
— All-orange label			
❏ P7007 [M]	Your Twist Party	1962	$30
— Orange and yellow label			

CHECKMATES, THE
JUSTICE

❏ JLP-149	The Checkmates	1966	$400

CHECKMATES LTD., THE
A&M

❏ SP-4183	Love Is All I Have to Give	1969	$30

CAPITOL

❏ T2840 [M]	Live at Caesar's Palace	1968	$30
❏ ST2840 [S]	Live at Caesar's Palace	1968	$25

FANTASY

❏ 9541	We Got the Moves	1978	$18

CHEECH AND CHONG
MCA

❏ 5640	Get Out of My Room	1985	$10

ODE

❏ SP-77014 [B]	Big Bambu	1972	$18
— Add 50% if rolling paper is still enclosed			
❏ SP-77010	Cheech and Chong	1971	$15
❏ PE34947	Cheech and Chong	1977	$12
— Reissue of 77010			
❏ SP-77025 [B]	Cheech and Chong's Wedding Album	1974	$18
❏ PE34954	Cheech and Chong's Wedding Album	1977	$12
— Reissue of 77025			
❏ SP-77019 [B]	Los Cochinos	1973	$18
❏ PE34951	Los Cochinos	1977	$12
— Reissue of 77019			
❏ SP-77040 [B]	Sleeping Beauty	1976	$18
❏ PE34960	Sleeping Beauty	1977	$12
— Reissue of 77040			

WARNER BROS.

❏ BSK3251	Big Bambu	1978	$10
❏ BSK3250	Cheech and Chong	1978	$10
❏ BSK3614	Cheech and Chong's Greatest Hit	1982	$10
❏ BSK3253	Cheech and Chong's Wedding Album	1978	$10
❏ HS3391	Let's Make a New Dope Deal	1980	$12
❏ BSK3252	Los Cochinos	1978	$10
❏ BSK3254	Sleeping Beauty	1978	$10
❏ BSK3249	Up in Smoke	1978	$12

CHELSEA

Future Kiss member Peter Criss (as "Peter Cris") played drums on this LP.

DECCA

❏ DL75262	The Chelsea Album	1972	$150

CHEMICAL BROTHERS, THE
ASTRALWERKS

❏ ASW6180	Dig Your Own Hole	1997	$18
❏ ASW6157 [B]	Exit Planet Dust	1995	$30
❏ ASW47610	Surrender	1999	$18

CHER
ATCO

❏ SD 33-298 [S]	3614 Jackson Highway	1969	$25
❏ 33-298 [M]	3614 Jackson Highway	1969	$30
— White label promo only (no stock copies issued in mono)			

CASABLANCA

❏ NBLP-7184	Prisoner	1980	$12
❏ NBLP-7133	Take Me Home	1979	$12
❏ NBPIX-7133 [PD]	Take Me Home	1979	$50

COLUMBIA

❏ FC38096	I Paralyze	1982	$12

GEFFEN

❏ GHS24164	Cher	1987	$12
❏ GHS24239	Heart of Stone	1989	$18
— Original cover with Cher in heart-shaped pose next to "skeleton rock"			
❏ GHS24239	Heart of Stone	1989	$12
— Later cover with larger picture of Cher and no rock			

IMPERIAL

❏ LP-9292 [M]	All I Really Want to Do	1965	$25
❏ LP-12292 [S]	All I Really Want to Do	1965	$30
❏ LP-12373 [M]	Backstage	1968	$50
— Stereo cover with designate mono sticker attached; label is stock			
❏ LP-12373 [S]	Backstage	1968	$25

❏ LP-9320 [M]	Cher	1966	$18
❏ LP-12320 [S]	Cher	1966	$25
❏ LP-12406	Cher's Golden Greats	1968	$25
❏ LP-9301 [M]	The Sonny Side of Cher	1966	$25
❏ LP-12301 [S]	The Sonny Side of Cher	1966	$30
❏ LP-9358 [M]	With Love -- Cher	1967	$18
❏ LP-12358 [S]	With Love -- Cher	1967	$25

KAPP

❏ KS-3649	Cher	1971	$25
— Original title of LP (without "Gypsys, Tramps & Thieves" title on front cover)			
❏ KRS-5514	Foxy Lady	1972	$18
❏ SW-94485	Foxy Lady	1972	$25
— Capitol Record Club edition			
❏ KS-3649	Gypsys, Tramps & Thieves	1971	$18
— Retitled version of above LP; red and orange swirl label			
❏ KRS-5549	Gypsys, Tramps & Thieves	1972	$18
— Reissue of 3649; black label			

LIBERTY

❏ LN-10110	The Very Best of Cher, Vol. 1	1981	$10
❏ LN-10111	The Very Best of Cher, Vol. 2	1981	$10

MCA

❏ 2101	Bittersweet White Light	1973	$15
❏ 624	Cher	197?	$12
❏ 2113	Dark Lady	1974	$15
❏ 2127	Greatest Hits	1974	$15
❏ 37028	Greatest Hits	1981	$10
— Reissue of MCA 2127			
❏ 2104	Half-Breed	1973	$15

PICKWICK

❏ SPC-3619	This Is Cher	1978	$12

SPRINGBOARD

❏ SPB-4028	Cher's Greatest Hits	197?	$12
❏ SPB-4029	Cher Sings the Hits	197?	$12

SUNSET

❏ SUS-5276	This Is Cher	1970	$18

UNITED ARTISTS

❏ UXS-88	Cher Superpak	1971	$25
❏ UXS-89	Cher Superpak, Vol. II	1972	$25
— The above are reissues of Imperial recordings			
❏ UA-LA237-G	The Very Best of Cher	1974	$15
❏ UA-LA377-E	The Very Best of Cher	1975	$12
❏ UA-LA435-E	The Very Best of Cher, Vol. 2	1975	$15

WARNER BROS.

❏ BS3046	Cherished	1977	$15
❏ BS2898	I'd Rather Believe in You	1976	$15
❏ BS2850	Stars	1975	$15

CHEROKEE
ABC

❏ ABCS-719	Cherokee	1970	$25

CHERRY, DON
BLUE NOTE

❏ BST84226 [B]	Complete Communion	2015	$20

COLUMBIA

❏ CL893 [M]	Swingin' for Two	1956	$30

MONUMENT

❏ SLP-18124	Don Cherry	1970	$15
❏ MLP-8049 [M]	Don Cherry Smashes	1966	$15
❏ SLP-18049 [S]	Don Cherry Smashes	1966	$18
❏ SLP-18088	Let It Be Me	1968	$15
❏ SLP-18109	Take a Message to Mary	1969	$15
❏ MLP-8075 [M]	There Goes My Everything	1967	$18
❏ SLP-18075 [S]	There Goes My Everything	1967	$15
❏ KZG32334 [B]	The World of Don Cherry	1972	$18
❏ 8601	The World of Don Cherry	197?	$15
— Reissue of 32334			

CHERRY, DON (2)

Jazz trumpeter, also father of 1980s hitmaker Neneh Cherry and 1990s hitmaker Eagle-Eye Cherry.

A&M

❏ SP-5258	Art Deco	1989	$50

ANTILLES

❏ AN7034	The Eternal Now	197?	$150

ATLANTIC

❏ SD18217	Hear and Now	1977	$150

BASF

❏ 20680	Eternal Rhythm	1972	$75

BLUE NOTE

❏ BLP-4226 [M]	Complete Communion	1966	$250
— New York, USA" address on label			
❏ BST-84226 [S]	Complete Communion	1966	$120
— New York, USA" address on label			
❏ BST-84226 [S]	Complete Communion	1968	$40
— A Division of Liberty Records" on label			
❏ BLP-4247 [M]	Symphony for Improvisers	1966	$250
— New York, USA" address on label			
❏ BST-84247 [S]	Symphony for Improvisers	1966	$120
— New York, USA" address on label			
❏ BST-84247 [S]	Symphony for Improvisers	1968	$40
— A Division of Liberty Records" on label			
❏ BST-84311	Where Is Brooklyn?	1969	$120
— A Division of Liberty Records" on label			

ECM

❏ ECM1-1230	El Corazon	1982	$35
— With Ed Blackwell; distributed by Warner Bros.			

HORIZON

❏ SP-717	Don Cherry	1976	$75

INNER CITY

❏ IC1009	Togetherness	197?	$50

JCOA

❏ 1006	Relativity Suite	1974	$150

MOSAIC

❏ MQ3-145	The Complete Blue Note Recordings of Don Cherry	199?	$120

PICCADILLY

❏ PIC-3515	Tibet	1981	$75

CHERRY, NENEH
VIRGIN

❏ R174031	Raw Like Sushi	1989	$15
— BMG Direct Marketing edition			
❏ 91252	Raw Like Sushi	1989	$12

CHERRY PEOPLE, THE

ANGEL related.

HERITAGE

❏ HT35000 [M]	The Cherry People	1968	$50
— Stereo cover with "Mono" and "DJ" stickers attached; all records appear to be white label promos			
❏ HTS35000 [S]	The Cherry People	1968	$25

CHESKY, DAVID, BAND
COLUMBIA

❏ JC36799	Rush Hour	1980	$25

CHESNUT, JIM
ABC HICKORY

❏ AH-44004	Let Me Love You Now	1977	$15
❏ AH-44012	Show Me a Sign	1978	$15

CHESS, TUBBY, AND HIS CANDY STRIPE TWISTERS
GRAND PRIX

❏ K-187 [M]	Do the Twist	1962	$25
❏ KS-187 [S]	Do the Twist	1962	$30

CHESTER, BOB
CIRCLE

❏ 44	Bob Chester and His Orchestra: 1940-41	198?	$25

Number	Title	Yr	NM
74	Bob Chester and His Orchestra: More 1940-41	198?	$25

CHESTER, GARY
DCP

Number	Title	Yr	NM
DCL3803 [M]	Yeah, Yeah, Yeah	1964	$25
DCS6803 [S]	Yeah, Yeah, Yeah	1964	$30

CHEVALIER, MAURICE
CAPITOL

Number	Title	Yr	NM
T10360 [M]	The Young Chevalier	196?	$25

EPIC

FXS15117	Maurice Chevalier at 80	1968	$25

LONDON

GH46001/4 [M]	60 Years of Song	1966	$40
GHS56001/4 [S]	60 Years of Song	1966	$50

MGM

E-3773 [M]	A Tribute to Al Jolson	1959	$30

— Yellow label original

SE-3773 [S]	A Tribute to Al Jolson	1959	$30

— Yellow label original

E-3801 [M]	Life Is Just a Bowl of Cherries	1960	$25
SE-3801 [S]	Life Is Just a Bowl of Cherries	1960	$30
E-3738 [M]	Maurice Chevalier Sings Broadway	1959	$30

— Yellow label original

SE-3738 [S]	Maurice Chevalier Sings Broadway	1959	$30

— Yellow label original

E-4015 [M]	Maurice Chevalier Sings Lerner, Loewe & Chevalier	1962	$25
SE-4015 [S]	Maurice Chevalier Sings Lerner, Loewe & Chevalier	1962	$30
E-4120 [M]	Paris to Broadway	1963	$25
SE-4120 [S]	Paris to Broadway	1963	$30
E-3835 [M]	Thank Heaven for Little Girls	1960	$25
SE-3835 [S]	Thank Heaven for Little Girls	1960	$30
E-4205 [M]	The Very Best of Maurice Chevalier	1964	$18
SE-4205 [S]	The Very Best of Maurice Chevalier	1964	$25
E-3703 [M]	Today	1958	$30

— Yellow label original

SE-3703 [S]	Today	1958	$30

— Yellow label original

E-3702 [M]	Yesterday	1958	$30

— Yellow label original

SE-3702 [S]	Yesterday	1958	$30

— Yellow label original

2E-5 [M]	Yesterday…Today	1958	$40

— Yellow label original; also released separately as 3702 and 3703

2SE-5 [S]	Yesterday…Today	1958	$75

— Yellow label original; also released separately as 3702 and 3703

RCA VICTOR

LPM-2076 [M]	Thank Heaven for Maurice Chevalier	1960	$30
LSP-2076 [S]	Thank Heaven for Maurice Chevalier	1960	$30

TIME

52072 [M]	Maurice Chevalier	1963	$25
S-2072 [S]	Maurice Chevalier	1963	$30

CHEVRONS, THE
TIME

T-10008 [M]	Sing-a-Long Rock & Roll	1961	$100

CHI-LITES, THE
BRUNSWICK

BL754188	A Letter to Myself	1973	$30

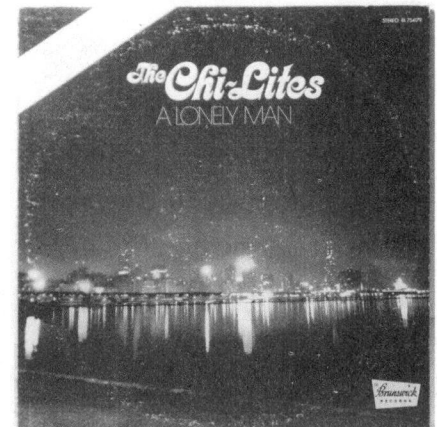

BL754179 [B]	A Lonely Man	1972	$30

Number	Title	Yr	NM
BL754197	Chi-Lites	1973	$30
BL754170	(For God's Sake) Give More Power to the People	1971	$30
BL754152	Give It Away	1969	$30
BL754204	Half a Love	1975	$30
BL754165	I Like Your Lovin', Do You Like Mine?	1970	$30
BL754184	The Chi-Lites Greatest Hits	1972	$30
BL754208	The Chi-Lites Greatest Hits, Volume 2	1976	$30
BL754200	Toby	1974	$30

CHI-SOUND

T-619	Heavenly Body	1980	$18
T-635	Me and You	1982	$18

EPIC

PE38627	Greatest Hits	1983	$12

ICHIBAN

ICH-1057	Just Say You Love Me	198?	$12

LARC

8103	Bottom's Up	1983	$15

MERCURY

SRM-1-1147	Fantastic	1977	$18
SRM-1-1118	Happy Being Lonely	1976	$18

PRIVATE I

FZ39316	Steppin' Out	1984	$12
PZ39316	Steppin' Out	1985	$10

— Budget-line reissue

CHIC
ATLANTIC

80107	Believer	1983	$10
SD19209	C'est Chic	1978	$10
SD19153	Chic	1977	$10
SD16011	Les Plus Grands Succes de Chic -- Chic's Greatest Hits	1979	$10
SD16016	Real People	1980	$10
SD16003	Risque	1979	$10
SD19323	Take It Off	1981	$10
80031	Tongue in Chic	1982	$10

CHICAGO
ACCORD

SN-7140	Toronto Rock 'n Roll Revival, 1982 Part I		$30

— Reissue of Magnum LP

COLUMBIA

KGP24	Chicago	1970	$40

— Red labels with "360 Sound" at bottom; label and spine call the album "Chicago"

(no #)	Chicago	1976	$300

— Promo-only set: The first 10 Chicago LPs with gold stamps on covers, box, side panel and wraparound

FC36105	Chicago 13	1979	$15
C4X30865	Chicago at Carnegie Hall	1971	$75

— With box, 4 posters and program; deduct for missing items

C4Q30865 [Q]	Chicago at Carnegie Hall	1971	$0

— Scheduled but never released

KG30863	Chicago at Carnegie Hall, Vol. 1 & 2	1971	$35

— First half of the 4-LP box, possibly for Columbia Record Club only

KG30864	Chicago at Carnegie Hall, Vol. 3 & 4	1971	$35

— Second half of the 4-LP box, possibly for Columbia Record Club only

FC37682	Chicago -- Greatest Hits, Volume II	1981	$15
KGP24	Chicago II	1970	$35

— Orange labels

GQ33258 [Q]	Chicago II	1975	$40
KGP24	Chicago II	1970	$75

— Red labels with "360 Sound" at bottom; label and spine call the album "Chicago II"

C230110	Chicago III	1971	$35
C2Q30110 [Q]	Chicago III	1974	$40
PC33900	Chicago IX -- Chicago's Greatest Hits	1975	$12
PCQ33900 [Q]	Chicago IX -- Chicago's Greatest Hits	1975	$40
HC43900	Chicago IX -- Chicago's Greatest Hits	1982	$30

— Half-speed mastered edition

GP8	Chicago Transit Authority	1969	$75

— Red labels with "360 Sound" at bottom

GP8	Chicago Transit Authority	1970	$35

— Orange labels; most copies add a Roman numeral "I" to the title on spine

GQ33255 [Q]	Chicago Transit Authority	1975	$40
KC31102	Chicago V	1972	$18

Number	Title	Yr	NM
CQ31102 [Q]	Chicago V	1974	$40
KC32400	Chicago VI	1973	$15
CQ32400 [Q]	Chicago VI	1974	$40
C232810	Chicago VII	1974	$18
C2Q32810 [Q]	Chicago VII	1974	$40
PC33100	Chicago VIII	1975	$15
PCQ33100 [Q]	Chicago VIII	1975	$40
PC34200	Chicago X	1976	$12
PCQ34200 [Q]	Chicago X	1976	$40
HC44200	Chicago X	1982	$40

— Half-speed mastered edition

JC34860	Chicago XI	1977	$12
FC36517	Chicago XIV	1980	$15
FC35512	Hot Streets	1978	$12
PC38590	If You Leave Me Now	1982	$15
PC39579	Take Me Back to Chicago	1983	$15

FULL MOON

23689	Chicago 16	1982	$10

MAGNUM

MR604	Chicago Transit Authority Live in Concert	1978	$50

— Taken from their 1969 Toronto Rock 'n Roll Revival performance

MOBILE FIDELITY

2-128	Chicago Transit Authority	1983	$175

— Audiophile vinyl

REPRISE

25714	Chicago 19	1988	$10
26080	Greatest Hits 1982-1989	1989	$12
R110533	Twenty 1	1991	$25

— BMG Direct Marketing version

WARNER BROS.

25060	Chicago 17	1984	$10
25060 [DJ]	Chicago 17	1984	$25

— Promo pressing on Quiex II vinyl

25509	Chicago 18	1986	$10

CHICAGO HOT SIX
GHB

176	Stompin' at the Good Time	1982	$25

CHICAGO RHYTHM
JAZZOLOGY

J-157	Caution Blues	198?	$25
J-127	'Round Evening	198?	$25

STOMP OFF

SOS-1026	Chicago Rhythm	198?	$25
SOS-1164	Made in Chicago	1989	$30
SOS-1059	One in a Million	1982	$25

CHICAGO SYMPHONY ORCHESTRA (FRITZ REINER, CONDUCTOR)
RCA VICTOR RED SEAL

LM-1934 [M]	Bartok: Concerto for Orchestra	1958	$15
LSC-1934 [S]	Bartok: Concerto for Orchestra	1958	$40

— Original with "shaded dog" label

LSC-1934 [S]	Bartok: Concerto for Orchestra	199?	$30

— Classic Records reissue

LSC-2374 [S]	Bartok: Music for Strings, Percussion and Celesta	1959	$40

— Original with "shaded dog" label

LSC-2374 [S]	Bartok: Music for Strings, Percussion and Celesta	199?	$30

— Classic Records reissue

LSC-2343 [S]	Beethoven: Symphony No. 5	1960	$25

— Original with "shaded dog" label

LMD-2614 [M]	Beethoven: Symphony No. 6 "Pastorale"	1962	$40

— Gatefold with bound-in booklet

LSCD-2614 [S]	Beethoven: Symphony No. 6 "Pastorale"	1962	$150

— Gatefold with bound-in booklet

LSC-2614 [S]	Beethoven: Symphony No. 6 "Pastorale"	1962	$25

— Original with "shaded dog" label; non-gatefold edition

LSC-1991 [S]	Beethoven: Symphony No. 7	1958	$40

Number	Title	Yr	NM
— *Original with "shaded dog" label*			
❏ LSC-2209 [S]	Brahms: Symphony No. 3	1959	$40
❏ LSC-2209 [S]	Brahms: Symphony No. 3	1964	$25
— *Second edition with "white dog" label*			
❏ LSC-2222 [S]	Debussy: Iberia	1958	$250
— *Original with "shaded dog" label*			
❏ LSC-2222 [S]	Debussy: Iberia	199?	$30
— *Classic Records reissue*			
❏ LSC-2462 [S]	Debussy: La Mer; Strauss, Richard: Don Juan	1961	$50
— *Original with "shaded dog" label*			
❏ LSC-2462 [S]	Debussy: La Mer; Strauss, Richard: Don Juan	1964	$40
— *Second edition with "white dog" label*			
❏ LSC-2214 [S]	Dvorak: Symphony No. 9 "From the New World"	1959	$25
— *Original with "shaded dog" label*			
❏ LSC-2423 [S]	Festival	1960	$175
— *Original with "shaded dog" label*			
❏ LSC-2423 [S]	Festival	199?	$30
— *Classic Records reissue*			
❏ LSC-2251 [S]	Hovhaness: Mysterious Mountain; Stravinsky: Divertimento	1959	$50
— *Original with "shaded dog" label*			
❏ LSC-2251 [S]	Hovhaness: Mysterious Mountain; Stravinsky: Divertimento	1964	$25
— *Second edition with "white dog" label*			
❏ LSC-2364 [S]	Mahler: Symphony No. 4	1960	$30
— *Original with "shaded dog" label*			
❏ LSC-2364 [S]	Mahler: Symphony No. 4	199?	$30
— *Classic Records reissue*			
❏ LSC-2201 [S]	Mussorgsky-Ravel: Pictures at an Exhibition	1959	$50
— *Original with "shaded dog" label*			
❏ LSC-2201 [S]	Mussorgsky-Ravel: Pictures at an Exhibition	1964	$40
— *Second edition with "white dog" label*			
❏ LSC-2395 [S]	Prokofiev: Alexander Nevsky	1960	$75
— *Original with "shaded dog" label*			
❏ LSC-2395 [S]	Prokofiev: Alexander Nevsky	1964	$75
— *Second edition with "white dog" label*			
❏ LSC-2150 [S]	Prokofiev: Lieutenant Kije; Stravinsky: Song of the Nightingale	1958	$40
— *Original with "shaded dog" label*			
❏ LSC-2150 [S]	Prokofiev: Lieutenant Kije; Stravinsky: Song of the Nightingale	1964	$40
— *Second edition with "white dog" label*			
❏ LSC-2441 [S]	Reiner Conducts Wagner	1960	$40
— *Original with "shaded dog" label*			
❏ LSC-2441 [S]	Reiner Conducts Wagner	1964	$40
— *Second edition with "white dog" label*			
❏ LSC-2436 [S]	Respighi: Pines of Rome; Fountains of Rome	1960	$30
— *Original with "shaded dog" label*			
❏ LSC-2436 [S]	Respighi: Pines of Rome; Fountains of Rome	199?	$30
— *Classic Records reissue*			
❏ LSC-2446 [S]	Rimsky-Korsakov: Scheherazade	1960	$150
— *Original with "shaded dog" label*			
❏ LSC-2446 [S]	Rimsky-Korsakov: Scheherazade	199?	$30
— *Classic Records reissue*			
❏ LSC-2446 [S]	Rimsky-Korsakov: Scheherazade	1964	$300
— *Second edition with "white dog" label; a rare instance where a later edition is more desirable than the original*			
❏ LSC-2318 [S]	Rossini: Overtures	1959	$30
— *Original with "shaded dog" label*			
❏ LSC-2516 [S]	Schubert: Symphonies No. 5 and 8	1961	$25
— *Original with "shaded dog" label*			
❏ LSC-2230 [S]	Spain	1958	$150
— *Original with "shaded dog" label*			
❏ LSC-2230 [S]	Spain	1964	$80
— *Second issue with "white dog" label*			
❏ LSC-2230 [S]	Spain	199?	$30
— *Classic Records reissue*			
❏ LSC-2609 [S]	Strauss, Richard: Also Sprach Zarathustra	1962	$40
— *Original with "shaded dog" label*			
❏ LSC-2609 [S]	Strauss, Richard: Also Sprach Zarathustra	1964	$25
— *Second edition with "white dog" label*			
❏ LDS-2384 [S]	Strauss, Richard: Don Quixote	1960	$80
— *Original with "shaded dog" label*			
❏ LSS-2384 [S]	Strauss, Richard: Don Quixote	1960	$120
— *Original with "shaded dog" label; limited edition of 200 in box with booklet*			
❏ LM-1806 [M]	Strauss: Also Sprach Zarathustra	1955	$18
❏ LSC-1806 [S]	Strauss: Also Sprach Zarathustra	1958	$300

Number	Title	Yr	NM
— *Original with "shaded dog" label*			
❏ LSC-1806 [S]	Strauss: Also Sprach Zarathustra	199?	$30
— *Classic Records reissue*			
❏ LSC-2500 [S]	Strauss: Waltzes	1960	$40
— *Original with "shaded dog" label*			
❏ LSC-2500 [S]	Strauss: Waltzes	199?	$30
— *Classic Records reissue*			
❏ LSC-2500 [S]	Strauss: Waltzes	1964	$40
— *Second edition with "white dog" label*			
❏ LSC-2241 [S]	Tchaikovsky: 1812 Overture	1958	$500
— *Original with "shaded dog" label*			
❏ LSC-2241 [S]	Tchaikovsky: 1812 Overture	199?	$30
— *Classic Records reissue*			
❏ LSC-2216 [S]	Tchaikovsky: Symphony No. 6 "Pathetique"	1959	$25
— *Original with "shaded dog" label*			
❏ LSC-2328 [S]	Tchaikovsky: The Nutcracker	1959	$50
— *Original with "shaded dog" label*			
❏ LSC-2496 [S]	The Heart of the Symphony	1961	$40
— *Original with "shaded dog" label*			
❏ LSC-2183 [S]	The Reiner Sound	1958	$150
— *Original with "shaded dog" label*			
❏ LSC-2183 [S]	The Reiner Sound	199?	$30
— *Classic Records reissue*			
❏ LSC-2112 [S]	Vienna	1958	$40
— *Original with "shaded dog" label*			

CHICAGO SYMPHONY ORCHESTRA (PIERRE MONTEUX, CONDUCTOR)
RCA VICTOR RED SEAL

Number	Title	Yr	NM
❏ LSC-2514 [S]	Franck: Symphony in D	1961	$25
— *Original with "shaded dog" label*			

CHICKEN SHACK
Also see CHRISTINE McVIE; features Stan Webb.

BLUE HORIZON

Number	Title	Yr	NM
❏ BH7706	100-Ton Chicken	1969	$30
❏ BH4809	Accept Chicken Shack	1970	$30
❏ BH7705	O.K. Ken?	1969	$30

DERAM

| ❏ DES18063 | Imagination Lady | 1972 | $25 |

EPIC

| ❏ LN24414 [M] | Forty Blue Fingers, Freshly Packed and Ready to Serve | 1968 | $300 |
| ❏ BN26414 [S] | Forty Blue Fingers, Freshly Packed and Ready to Serve | 1968 | $30 |

LONDON

| ❏ XPS632 | Unlucky Boy | 1973 | $25 |

CHICKENFOOT
Supergroup featuring Sammy Hagar, Joe Satriani, Michael Anthony and Chad Smith; also see VAN HALEN; RED HOT CHILI PEPPERS; MONTROSE.

REDLINE ENTERTAINMENT

| ❏ 20092 | Chickenfoot | 2009 | $30 |

CHIEFTAINS, THE
COLUMBIA

Number	Title	Yr	NM
❏ JC36401	Boil the Breakfast Early	1981	$15
❏ PC36401	Boil the Breakfast Early	198?	$10
— *Budget-line reissue*			
❏ JC35612	The Chieftains 7	1979	$15
❏ PC35612	The Chieftains 7	198?	$10
— *Budget-line reissue*			
❏ JC35726	The Chieftains 8	1980	$15

ISLAND

❏ ILPS9432	Bonaparte's Retreat	1977	$15
❏ ILPS9364	The Chieftains 1	1976	$15
— *Black label original; first US issue*			
❏ ILPS9365	The Chieftains 2	1976	$15
— *Black label original; first US issue*			
❏ ILPS9379	The Chieftains 3	1976	$15
— *Black label original; first US issue*			
❏ ILPS9380	The Chieftains 4	1976	$15
— *Black label original; first US issue*			
❏ ILPS9334	The Chieftains 5	1975	$15
— *Black label original*			
❏ ILPS9501	The Chieftains Live	1978	$15

RCA

| ❏ 7858-1-R | A Chieftains Celebration | 1989 | $15 |
| ❏ 6358-1-R | Celtic Wedding | 1987 | $12 |

SHANACHIE

❏ 79026	Bonaparte's Retreat	198?	$12
— *Reissue of Island 9432*			
❏ 79019	Cotton-Eyed Joe	198?	$12
❏ 79051	The Ballad of Iron Horse	198?	$12
❏ 79021	The Chieftains 1	1982	$12
— *Reissue of Island 9364*			
❏ 79022	The Chieftains 2	198?	$12
— *Reissue of Island 9365*			
❏ 79023	The Chieftains 3	198?	$12
— *Reissue of Island 9379*			

Number	Title	Yr	NM
❏ 79024	The Chieftains 4	198?	$12
— *Reissue of Island 9380*			
❏ 79025	The Chieftains 5	198?	$12
— *Reissue of Island 9334*			
❏ 79050	The Chieftains in China	198?	$12
❏ 79036	Year of the French	1983	$12

CHIFFONS, THE
B.T. PUPPY

| ❏ S-1011 | My Secret Love | 1970 | $400 |

COLLECTABLES

| ❏ COL-5042 | Golden Classics | 198? | $15 |

LAURIE

❏ 4001	Everything You Always Wanted to Hear by the Chiffons	1975	$25
❏ LLP-2018 [M]	He's So Fine	1963	$120
❏ DT-90075 [R]	He's So Fine	1965	$250
— *Capitol Record Club edition*			
❏ LLP-2020 [M]	One Fine Day	1963	$250
❏ LLP-2036 [M]	Sweet Talkin' Guy	1966	$150
❏ SLP-2036 [S]	Sweet Talkin' Guy	1966	$175
❏ ST-90779 [S]	Sweet Talkin' Guy	1966	$250
— *Capitol Record Club edition*			

CHILD, DESMOND, AND ROUGE
CAPITOL

❏ SPRO8993 [DJ]	AOR Sampler	1978	$18
— *Five-song promo-only sampler*			
❏ ST-11908	Desmond Child and Rouge	1978	$18
❏ ST-11999	Runners in the Night	1979	$15
❏ SPRO8995 [DJ]	Soul Sampler	1978	$18
— *Five-song promo-only sampler*			

CHILD, JANE
WARNER BROS.

| ❏ 25858 | Jane Child | 1989 | $15 |

CHILDERS, BUDDY
LIBERTY

| ❏ LJH-6013 [M] | Buddy Childers Quartet | 1957 | $150 |
| ❏ LJH-6009 [M] | Sam Songs | 1956 | $150 |

TREND

| ❏ TR-539 | Just Buddy's | 1986 | $50 |

CHILDRE, LEW
STARDAY

| ❏ SLP-153 [M] | Old Time Get Together | 1961 | $30 |

CHILDREN, THE
ATCO

| ❏ SD 33-271 | Rebirth | 1968 | $30 |

CINEMA

| ❏ CLP-1 | Rebirth | 1968 | $250 |

CHILDREN'S CHOIR OF ALL NATIONS, THE
WARNER BROS.

| ❏ W1231 [M] | Some Children See Him | 1958 | $25 |

CHILDS, BILLY
WINDHAM HILL

| ❏ WH-0113 | Take For Example This | 1988 | $30 |
| ❏ WH-0118 | Twilight Is Upon Us | 1989 | $30 |

CHILDS, SUE
STUDIO 4

| ❏ 200 [M] | Sue Childs | 195? | $300 |

CHILES AND PETTIFORD
ATLANTIC

| ❏ 8111 [M] | Live at Jilly's | 1965 | $40 |
| ❏ SD8111 [S] | Live at Jilly's | 1965 | $50 |

CHILLIWACK
A&M

| ❏ SP-4375 [B] | All Over You | 1972 | $30 |
| ❏ SP-3509 | Chilliwack | 1971 | $30 |

MILLENNIUM

| ❏ BXL1-7766 | Opus X | 1982 | $12 |
| ❏ BXL1-7759 | Wanna Be a Star | 1981 | $12 |

MUSHROOM

❏ MRS-5015	Breakdown in Paradise	1980	$15
❏ MRS-5006	Dreams, Dreams, Dreams	1977	$15
❏ MRS-5011	Lights from the Valley	1978	$15

PARROT

| ❏ PAS71040 | Chilliwack | 1970 | $30 |

SIRE

| ❏ SASD-7506 | Chilliwack | 1975 | $18 |
| ❏ SASD-7511 | Rockerbox | 1976 | $18 |

Number	Title	Yr	NM

CHINA CRISIS

A&M
❏ SP-5225	Diary of a Hollow Horse	1989	$15
❏ SP-5148	What Price Paradise	1986	$12

VIRGIN
❏ 90632	Difficult Shapes and Passive Rhythms Some People Think It's Fun to Entertain	1987	$12

— First U.S. issue of 1981 U.K. debut

WARNER BROS.
❏ 25296	Flaunt the Imperfection	1985	$12
❏ 25062	Working with Fire and Steel	1983	$12

CHIPMUNKS, THE, DAVID SEVILLE AND

LIBERTY
❏ LRP-3170 [M]	Around the World with the Chipmunks	1960	$40

— Original cover features "realistic" chipmunks on and near a plane

❏ LRP-3170 [M]	Around the World with the Chipmunks	1961	$25

— Second cover features the "cartoon" Chipmunks on and near a camel

❏ LST-7170 [S]	Around the World with the Chipmunks	1960	$50

— Original covers have "realistic" chipmunks on and near a plane.

❏ LST-7170 [S]	Around the World with the Chipmunks	1960	$30

— Second cover features the "cartoon" Chipmunks on and near a camel

❏ LRP-3256 [M]	Christmas with the Chipmunks	1962	$30
❏ LST-7256 [S]	Christmas with the Chipmunks	1962	$30
❏ LM-1070	Christmas with the Chipmunks	1980	$10

— Reissue with two tracks omitted

❏ LRP-3334 [M]	Christmas with the Chipmunks, Vol. 2	1963	$30
❏ LST-7334 [S]	Christmas with the Chipmunks, Vol. 2	1963	$30
❏ LRP-3132 [M]	Let's All Sing with the Chipmunks	1959	$75

— Red vinyl

❏ LRP-3132 [M]	Let's All Sing with the Chipmunks	1959	$30

— Black vinyl; original cover features "realistic" chipmunks and no reference to "The Alvin Show

❏ LRP-3132 [M]	Let's All Sing with the Chipmunks	1961	$25

— Second cover features the "cartoon" Chipmunks and a reference to "The Alvin Show

❏ LST-7132 [S]	Let's All Sing with the Chipmunks	1959	$100

— Red vinyl

❏ LST-7132 [S]	Let's All Sing with the Chipmunks	1959	$40

— Black vinyl; original cover features "realistic" chipmunks and no reference to "The Alvin Show

❏ LST-7132 [S]	Let's All Sing with the Chipmunks	1961	$30

— Second cover features the "cartoon" Chipmunks and a reference to "The Alvin Show

❏ LRP-3159 [M]	Sing Again with the Chipmunks	1960	$40

— Original cover features "realistic" chipmunks

❏ LRP-3159 [M]	Sing Again with the Chipmunks	1961	$25

— Second cover features the "cartoon" Chipmunks

❏ LST-7159 [S]	Sing Again with the Chipmunks	1960	$50

— Original cover features "realistic" chipmunks

❏ LST-7159 [S]	Sing Again with the Chipmunks	1961	$30

— Second cover features the "cartoon" Chipmunks

❏ LRP-3209 [M]	The Alvin Show	1961	$30
❏ LST-7209 [S]	The Alvin Show	1961	$30
❏ LRP-3424 [M]	The Chipmunks A-Go-Go	1965	$25
❏ LST-7424 [S]	The Chipmunks A-Go-Go	1965	$30
❏ LRP-3388 [M]	The Chipmunks Sing the Beatles Hits	1964	$30
❏ LST-7388 [S]	The Chipmunks Sing the Beatles Hits	1964	$40
❏ LRP-3405 [M]	The Chipmunks Sing with Children	1965	$25
❏ LST-7405 [S]	The Chipmunks Sing with Children	1965	$30
❏ LRP-3229 [M]	The Chipmunks Songbook	1962	$30
❏ LST-7229 [S]	The Chipmunks Songbook	1962	$30

MISTLETOE
❏ MLP-1216	Christmas with the Chipmunks	197?	$10

— Reissue of Liberty LST-7256

❏ MLP-1217	Christmas with the Chipmunks, Vol. 2	197?	$10

— Reissue of Liberty LST-7334

PICKWICK
❏ SPC-1034	Christmas with the Chipmunks	1980	$12
❏ SPC-1035	The Twelve Days of Christmas with The Chipmunks	1980	$12

— Reissue of "Christmas with the Chipmunks, Vol. 2

SUNSET
❏ LST-7334 [S]	Christmas with the Chipmunks, Vol. 2	1968	$25

— Budget-line reissue of Liberty LST-7334

❏ LST-7424 [S]	The Chipmunks A-Go-Go	196?	$18

— Same cover as Liberty 7424, but with "SUNSET" sticker at upper right

UNITED ARTISTS
❏ UA-LA352-E2	Christmas with the Chipmunks	1974	$25

— Entire contents of both original Liberty LPs

CHIPMUNKS, THE

EXCELSIOR
❏ X-6008	Chipmunk Punk	1980	$18

RCA VICTOR
❏ AQL1-4041	A Chipmunk Christmas	1981	$18

— With booklet

❏ AFL1-4304	Chipmunk Rock	1982	$12
❏ AFL1-4376	The Chipmunks Go Hollywood	1983	$12
❏ AFL1-4027	Urban Chipmunk	1981	$12

CHITTISON, HERMAN

AUDIOPHILE
❏ AP-39 [M]	The Melody Lingers On	1986	$25

COLUMBIA
❏ CL6134 [10]	Herman Chittison	1950	$50
❏ CL6182 [10]	Herman Chittison Trio	1951	$50

ROYALE
❏ 1824 [10]	Cocktail Time	195?	$40

CHOATES, HARRY

D
❏ 7000 [M]	Jole Blon	196?	$40

CHOCO AND HIS MALIMBA DRUM RHYTHMS

AUDIO FIDELITY
❏ AFLP-2102 [M]	African Latin Voodoo Drums	1962	$30
❏ AFSD-6102 [S]	African Latin Voodoo Drums	1962	$35

CHOCOLATE WATCH BAND, THE

RHINO
❏ RNLP-108	The Best of the Chocolate Watch Band	1983	$15

TOWER
❏ T5096 [M]	No Way Out	1967	$500
❏ ST5096 [S]	No Way Out	1967	$500
❏ ST5153	One Step Beyond	1969	$300
❏ T5106 [M]	The Inner Mystique	1968	$500
❏ ST5106 [S]	The Inner Mystique	1968	$500

CHOIR, THE

SUNDAZED
❏ LP5009	Choir Practice	1992	$12

CHOIR OF LONDON, THE

ACORN
❏ 693	Favorite Christmas Songs	196?	$18

CHOIR OF THE BELLA VISTA CHILDREN'S HOME, THE

FOLKWAYS
❏ FC7714 [M]	Villancicos: Spanish Christmas Songs for Children	1967	$20

CHORDETTES, THE

BARNABY
❏ BR-4003	All the Very Best of the Chordettes	1976	$15

CADENCE
❏ CLP-3020 [M]	Barbershop Harmony	1958	$40
❏ CLP-1002 [10]	Close Harmony	1955	$50
❏ CLP-3056 [M]	Never on Sunday	1962	$25
❏ CLP-25056 [S]	Never on Sunday	1962	$30
❏ CLP-3001 [M]	The Chordettes	1957	$40

COLUMBIA
❏ CL6218 [10]	Harmony Encores	1952	$50
❏ CL6111 [10]	Harmony Time	1950	$50
❏ CL6170 [10]	Harmony Time, Vol. 2	1951	$50
❏ CL956 [M]	Listen	1955	$50
❏ CL2519 [10]	The Chordettes	1955	$40
❏ CL6285 [10]	Your Requests	1953	$50

HARMONY
❏ HL7164 [M]	The Chordettes	196?	$18

RHINO
❏ R1-70849	The Best of the Chordettes	1989	$15

CHOSEN FEW, THE

MAPLE
❏ 6000	Takin' All the Love I Can	196?	$25

RCA VICTOR
❏ LSP-4242	The Chosen Few	1969	$25

CHRIST GABRIEL JAZZ MISSIONARY GROUP

MUSICMASTER RECORDS
❏ no number [B]	Christ Gabriel Jazz Missionary Group	1974	$1500

CHRISTIAN, CHARLIE

COLUMBIA
❏ G30779	Solo Flight -- The Genius of Charlie Christian	1972	$25

COLUMBIA JAZZ MASTERPIECES
❏ CJ40846	Charlie Christian -- The Genius of the Electric Guitar	1986	$35

COUNTERPOINT
❏ 548 [M]	The Harlem Jazz Scene 1941	195?	$75

ESOTERIC
❏ ESJ-1 [10]	Jazz Immortal	1951	$250

— Red vinyl

❏ ES-548 [M]	The Harlem Jazz Scene 1941	1956	$100

EVEREST ARCHIVE OF FOLK & JAZZ
❏ 219	Charlie Christian	197?	$25

CHRISTIAN DEATH

CLEOPATRA
❏ 3296 [B]	Sleepless Nights - Live 1990		$25

EPITAPH
❏ 80103-1LP [B]	Only Theatre of Pain	1997	$25

FRONTIER
❏ FLP1007 [B]	Only Theatre of Pain	1982	$150

— with double sided insert

FUTURE
❏ FL2LP [B]	Only Theatre of Pain	1983	$100

— with double sided black insert

IMPORTANT
❏ IRD014 [B]	Ashes	1985	$50

— includes 16 page booklet

LSR
❏ NOS1055-1LP [B]	Ashes	1989	$30
❏ NOS1054-1LP [B]	Catastrophe Ballet	1989	$30

— includes eight page booklet

NORMAL
❏ 15 [B]	Ashes	1986	$40

— includes 12 page booklet

❏ 15 [B]	Ashes	1988	$40

— gatefold sleeve

❏ 84 [B]	Deathwish	1990	$30
❏ 56 [B]	Only Theatre of Pain	1987	$30

CHRISTIE, LOU

51 WEST
❏ P18260	Lou Christie Does Detroit	1983	$18

BUDDAH
❏ BDS-5052	I'm Gonna Make You Mine	1969	$18
❏ BDS-5073	Paint America Love	1971	$18

CO & CE
❏ LP-1231 [M]	Lou Christie Strikes Back	1966	$40

— The front cover and spine use this title, but the back cover and label use "Lou Christie Strikes Again

COLPIX
❏ CP-4001 [M]	Lou Christie Strikes Again	1966	$30
❏ SCP-4001 [S]	Lou Christie Strikes Again	1966	$50

MGM
❏ E-4360 [M]	Lightnin' Strikes	1966	$18
❏ SE-4360 [S]	Lightnin' Strikes	1966	$25
❏ E-4394 [M]	Painter of Hits	1966	$18
❏ SE-4394 [S]	Painter of Hits	1966	$25

RHINO
❏ R1-70246	EnLightnin'Ment: The Best of Lou Christie	1988	$15

ROULETTE
❏ R25208 [M]	Lou Christie	1963	$50

— Blue background on front cover

❏ R25208 [M]	Lou Christie	1963	$40

— White wall in background on front cover

❏ SR25208 [S]	Lou Christie	1963	$100

— Blue background on front cover

❏ SR25208 [S]	Lou Christie	1963	$75

— White wall in background on front cover

❏ R25332 [M]	Lou Christie Strikes Again	1966	$30
❏ SR25332 [S]	Lou Christie Strikes Again	1966	$30

SPIN-O-RAMA
❏ M-173 [M]	Starring Lou Christie and the Classics	1966	$25

Number	Title	Yr	NM
❏ S-173 [R]	Starring Lou Christie and the Classics	1966	$15

— *The above LP also includes other artists*

THREE BROTHERS

| ❏ THB-2000 | Lou Christie | 1973 | $25 |

CHRISTIE

EPIC

| ❏ E30403 | Yellow River | 1970 | $18 |

CHRISTMAS REVELS, THE

REVELS

| ❏ RC1087 | Christmas Day in the Morning: A Revels Celebration of the Winter Solstice | 1987 | $15 |
| ❏ RC1078 | The Christmas Revels | 1978 | $15 |

— *Various spoken and musical bits by a collection of artists under one umbrella*

| ❏ RC1082 | Wassail! Wassail! | 1982 | $15 |

CHRISTOPHER, JORDAN

UNITED ARTISTS

| ❏ UAL3479 [M] | Jordan Christopher Has the Knack | 1966 | $25 |
| ❏ UAS6479 [S] | Jordan Christopher Has the Knack | 1966 | $30 |

CHRISTOPHER (1)

BELL

| ❏ 1203 | R.P.M. | 1970 | $25 |

CHRISTOPHER (2)

Band from North Carolina.

CHRIS-TEE

| ❏ 12411 | What'cha Gonna Do | 1969 | $3000 |

— *100 copies were pressed; VG value 1500; VG+ value 2250*

CHRISTOPHER (3)
)
Band from Texas.

METROMEDIA

| ❏ 1024 | Christopher | 1970 | $400 |

CHRISTY, JUNE

CAPITOL

| ❏ T1308 [M] | Ballads for Night People | 1959 | $150 |

— *Black label with colorband, Capitol logo at left*

| ❏ ST1308 [S] | Ballads for Night People | 1959 | $75 |

— *Black label with colorband, Capitol logo at left*

❏ T1845 [M]	Big Band Specials	1962	$100
❏ ST1845 [S]	Big Band Specials	1962	$150
❏ T1586 [M]	Do-Re-Mi	1961	$75

— *Black label with colorband, Capitol logo at left*

| ❏ ST1586 [S] | Do-Re-Mi | 1961 | $175 |

— *Black label with colorband, Capitol logo at left*

| ❏ T656 [M] | Duets | 1955 | $85 |

— *Turquoise label*

| ❏ T902 [M] | Gone for the Day | 1957 | $75 |

— *Turquoise label*

| ❏ T1202 [M] | June Christy Recalls Those Kenton Days | 1959 | $150 |

— *Black label with colorband, Capitol logo at left*

| ❏ ST1202 [S] | June Christy Recalls Those Kenton Days | 1959 | $85 |

— *Black label with colorband, Capitol logo at left*

| ❏ T833 [M] | June -- Fair and Warmer! | 1957 | $85 |

— *Turquoise label*

| ❏ T1076 [M] | June's Got Rhythm | 1958 | $150 |

— *Black label with colorband, Capitol logo at left*

| ❏ ST1076 [S] | June's Got Rhythm | 1958 | $85 |

— *Black label with colorband, Capitol logo at left*

| ❏ T1498 [M] | Off Beat | 1961 | $85 |

— *Black label with colorband, Capitol logo at left*

| ❏ ST1498 [S] | Off Beat | 1961 | $175 |

— *Black label with colorband, Capitol logo at left*

| ❏ TBO1327 [M] | Road Show | 1960 | $150 |

— *Black label with colorband, Capitol logo at left*

| ❏ STBO1327 [S] | Road Show | 1960 | $85 |

— *Black label with colorband, Capitol logo at left*

❏ T2410 [M]	Something Broadway, Something Latin	1965	$150
❏ ST2410 [S]	Something Broadway, Something Latin	1965	$150
❏ H516 [10]	Something Cool	1954	$300
❏ T516 [M]	Something Cool	1955	$175

— *Turquoise label; blue-green cover with June's eyes closed*

| ❏ T516 [M] | Something Cool | 1959 | $150 |

— *Black label with colorband, logo at left; with original blue-green cover with June's eyes closed*

| ❏ SM-516 [S] | Something Cool | 197? | $25 |
| ❏ ST516 [S] | Something Cool | 1960 | $50 |

— *Re-recording of the original mono LP; issued with different cover than original mono LP, in color with June's eyes open; black label, Capitol logo at left*

Number	Title	Yr	NM
❏ T516 [M]	Something Cool	1962	$50

— *Black label with colorband, logo at top; issued with different cover than original mono LP, in color with June's eyes open*

| ❏ T1605 [M] | That Time of Year | 1961 | $85 |
| ❏ ST1605 [S] | That Time of Year | 1961 | $175 |

— *Black label with colorband, Capitol logo at left*

| ❏ T1693 [M] | The Best of June Christy | 1962 | $150 |

— *Black label with colorband*

| ❏ ST1693 [S] | The Best of June Christy | 1962 | $150 |

— *Black logo with colorband*

| ❏ SM-11961 | The Best of June Christy | 1979 | $25 |
| ❏ T1398 [M] | The Cool School | 1960 | $150 |

— *Black label with colorband, Capitol logo at left*

| ❏ ST1398 [S] | The Cool School | 1960 | $75 |

— *Black label with colorband, Capitol logo at left*

❏ T1953 [M]	The Intimate June Christy	1963	$100
❏ ST1953 [S]	The Intimate June Christy	1963	$150
❏ T725 [M]	The Misty Miss Christy	1956	$85

— *Turquoise label*

| ❏ T1114 [M] | The Song Is June! | 1959 | $150 |

— *Black label with colorband, Capitol logo at left*

| ❏ ST1114 [S] | The Song Is June! | 1959 | $85 |

— *Black label with colorband, Capitol logo at left*

| ❏ T1006 [M] | This Is June Christy! | 1958 | $85 |

— *Turquoise label*

DISCOVERY

❏ DS-836	Impromptu	1982	$30
❏ DS-911	Interlude	1986	$25
❏ DS-919	The Misty Miss Christy	1986	$25

HINDSIGHT

| ❏ HSR-219 | June Christy, Vol. 1 | 1986 | $25 |
| ❏ HSR-235 | June Christy, Vol. 2 | 1988 | $25 |

PAUSA

| ❏ 9039 | Big Band Specials | 198? | $25 |

CHROME

CLEOPATRA

❏ 7287 [B]	3rd From The Sun		$25
❏ 2075 [B]	Alien Soundtracks		$25
❏ CLP3239 [B]	Blood on the Moon	2008	$40

— *US release of 1981 UK LP*

❏ 7286 [B]	Half Machine Lip Moves		$25
❏ CLP1310 [B]	Read Only Memory	2014	$25
❏ CLP3026 [B]	Red Exposure	2008	$40

— *US reissue of 1980 UK release on Beggars Banquet*

| ❏ CLP1000 [B] | The Visitation | 2013 | $30 |

SIREN RECORDS

❏ DE777 [B]	3rd from the Sun	1982	$100
❏ DE21-22SEC-L [B]	Alien Soundtracks	1977	$150
❏ DE333SEC [B]	Half Machine Lip Moves	1979	$150
❏ DE444 [B]	Read Only Memory	1979	$150
❏ DE1000 [B]	The Visitation	1976	$150

TOUCH & GO

| ❏ T&G057 [B] | Alien Soundtracks | 1990 | $30 |
| ❏ TG058 [B] | Half Machine Lip Moves | 1991 | $25 |

CHRYSALIS

MGM

| ❏ SE-4547 | Definition | 1968 | $30 |
| ❏ SE-4547 [M] | Definition | 1968 | $85 |

CHRYSANTHEMUM RAGTIME BAND

STOMP OFF

❏ SOS-1047	Bringin' 'Em Back Alive!	1983	$25
❏ SOS-1079	Come On and Hear	1984	$25
❏ SOS-1168	Dancing on the Edge of the World	1988	$25
❏ SOS-1196	Joy Rag	1989	$25
❏ SOS-1123	Preserves	1987	$25

CHUCK WAGON GANG, THE

HARMONY

| ❏ HL7355 | Christmas with the Chuck Wagon Gang | 196? | $15 |
| ❏ HS11155 [R] | Christmas with the Chuck Wagon Gang | 196? | $15 |

CHURCH, THE
Features Steven Kilbey and Marty Willson-Piper.

ARISTA

| ❏ AL8579 | Gold Afternoon Fix | 1990 | $12 |
| ❏ R171667 | Gold Afternoon Fix | 1990 | $15 |

— *BMG Direct Marketing edition*

| ❏ AL8567 | Heyday | 1988 | $12 |

— *Reissue of Warner Bros. 25370*

| ❏ AL8563 | Of Skins and Heart | 1988 | $12 |

— *First U.S. issue of first Australian album*

| ❏ AL8566 | Remote Luxury | 1988 | $12 |

— *Reissue of Warner Bros. 25152*

| ❏ AL8565 | Seance | 1988 | $12 |

— *First U.S. issue of third Australian album*

| ❏ 18727-1 | Sometime Anywhere | 1994 | $18 |
| ❏ R173703 | Starfish | 1988 | $15 |

— *BMG Direct Marketing edition*

| ❏ AL8521 | Starfish | 1988 | $12 |

Number	Title	Yr	NM
❏ ADP9713 [DJ]	Sum of the Parts	1988	$40

— *Interviews and live acoustic tracks*

| ❏ ADP9713 [DJ] | Sum of the Parts | 1988 | $40 |

— *Interviews and live acoustic tracks*

| ❏ AL8564 | The Blurred Crusade | 1988 | $12 |

— *First U.S. issue of second Australian album*

CAPITOL

| ❏ ST-12193 | The Church | 1982 | $18 |

WARNER BROS.

| ❏ 25370 | Heyday | 1985 | $18 |
| ❏ 25152 | Remote Luxury | 1984 | $18 |

CINDERELLA

MERCURY

❏ 848018-1	Heartbreak Station	1990	$15
❏ 834612-1	Long Cold Winter	1988	$10
❏ 830076-1	Night Songs	1986	$10
❏ 832255-1 [PD]	Night Songs	1987	$25

— *Picture disc in plastic sleeve with sticker*

| ❏ 522947-1 | Still Climbing | 1995 | $15 |

— *Numbered limited edition on clear vinyl; CD version issued in late 1994*

CIRCLE

ECM

| ❏ 1018/19 ST | Paris Concert | 197? | $25 |

— *Original issue, made in Germany?*

| ❏ ECM2-1018 | Paris Concert | 1972 | $20 |

— *Distributed by Polydor*

CIRCUS

METROMEDIA

| ❏ 7401 | Circus | 1973 | $85 |

CIRCUS MAXIMUS
Group features JERRY JEFF WALKER.

VANGUARD

| ❏ VRS-9260 [M] | Circus Maximus | 1967 | $50 |

| ❏ VSD-79260 [S] | Circus Maximus | 1967 | $75 |
| ❏ VSD-79274 | Neverland Revisited | 1968 | $50 |

CIRILLO, WALLY/BOBBY SCOTT

SAVOY

| ❏ MG-15055 [10] | Cirillo and Scott | 1955 | $100 |

CISSEL, CHUCK

ARISTA

| ❏ AL9581 | If I Had the Chance | 1982 | $30 |
| ❏ AB4257 | Just for You | 1979 | $18 |

CITIZEN KING

WARNER BROS.

| ❏ PRO-A-9653 [DJ] | Mobile Estates | 1999 | $15 |

— *Promo version in generic white sleeve with sticker*

| ❏ 47023 | Mobile Estates | 1999 | $15 |

— *Stock version in full-color jacket*

CITY, THE
CAROLE KING was a member.

ODE

| ❏ Z1244012 | Now That Everything's Been Said | 1968 | $100 |

— *Color front cover*

| ❏ Z1244012 | Now That Everything's Been Said | 1971 | $15 |

— *Black & white front cover*

CITY BOY

ATLANTIC

| ❏ SD19285 | Heads Are Rolling | 1980 | $12 |

Number	Title	Yr	NM
❏ SD19249	The Day the Earth Caught Fire	1979	$12

MERCURY

Number	Title	Yr	NM
❏ SRM-1-3737	Book Early	1978	$12
❏ SRM-1-1098	City Boy	1976	$15
❏ SRM-1-1121	Dinner at the Ritz	1977	$15
❏ SRM-1-1182 [B]	Young Men Gone West	1977	$15

CIVIL WARS, THE

COLUMBIA

Number	Title	Yr	NM
❏ C-375352 [B]	Barton Hollow	2013	$40
❏ 88843 04141 [B]	Live at Eddie's Attic	2014	$30
❏ 88883 738501 [B]	The Civil Wars	2013	$40

SENSIBILITY

Number	Title	Yr	NM
❏ 796745099323 [B]	A Place at the Table (with T-Bone Burnett)	20123	$40
❏ [B]	Barton Hollow	2011	$75
❏ 001 [B]	Unplugged on VH1	2013	$40

CLANCY BROTHERS, THE

COLUMBIA

Number	Title	Yr	NM
❏ CS9876	Christmas	1969	$15

CLANTON, DARRELL

AUDIOGRAPH

Number	Title	Yr	NM
❏ 6012	Alive	1983	$15

CLANTON, JIMMY

ACE

Number	Title	Yr	NM
❏ 1008 [M]	Jimmy's Blue	1960	$40
❏ 1007 [M]	Jimmy's Happy	1960	$40
❏ DLP-100 [M]	Jimmy's Happy/Jimmy's Blue	1960	$400

— The "Happy" album is red vinyl, the "Blue" album is blue

Number	Title	Yr	NM
❏ DLP-100 [M]	Jimmy's Happy/Jimmy's Blue	1960	$175

— Black vinyl; also released as two separate albums, 1007 and 1008

Number	Title	Yr	NM
❏ DLP-100	Jimmy's Happy/Jimmy's Blue Poster	1960	$100
❏ 1001 [M]	Just a Dream	1959	$120
❏ 1011 [M]	My Best to You	1960	$150
❏ 1014 [M]	Teenage Millionaire	1961	$150

Number	Title	Yr	NM
❏ 1026 [M]	Venus in Blue Jeans	1962	$150

PHILIPS

Number	Title	Yr	NM
❏ PHM200154 [M]	The Best of Jimmy Clanton	1964	$30
❏ PHS600154 [S]	The Best of Jimmy Clanton	1964	$30

CLANTON, JIMMY/BRISTOW HOOPER

DESIGN

Number	Title	Yr	NM
❏ DLP-176 [M]	Jimmy Clanton and Bristow Hooper	196?	$18
❏ DLS-176 [R]	Jimmy Clanton and Bristow Hooper	196?	$12

CLAP

NOVA SOL

Number	Title	Yr	NM
❏ 1001	Have You Reached Yet?	1972	$1000

CLAPTON, ERIC

Also see BLIND FAITH; CREAM; DEREK AND THE DOMINOS; GEORGE HARRISON AND FRIENDS; B.B. KING; JOHN MAYALL; THE YARDBIRDS.

ATCO

Number	Title	Yr	NM
❏ -0 [DJ]	Eric Clapton	1970	$150

— Mono pressing is promo only

Number	Title	Yr	NM
❏ 33-329 [DJ]	Eric Clapton	1970	$150

— Mono pressing is promo only

Number	Title	Yr	NM
❏ SD 33-329	Eric Clapton	1970	$25
❏ SD 33-329	Eric Clapton	1970	$250

— Odd pressing with alternate takes of "After Midnight" and "Blues Power" plus remixes of other tracks. Look for "CTH" in trail-off area.

Number	Title	Yr	NM
❏ SD 2-803	History of Eric Clapton	1972	$25

— Contains tracks from the Yardbirds, John Mayall's Bluesbreakers, Cream, Blind Faith, and solo records

DUCK

Number	Title	Yr	NM
❏ 25476	August	1986	$12
❏ 25166	Behind the Sun	1985	$12
❏ 23773	Money and Cigarettes	1983	$12

MOBILE FIDELITY

Number	Title	Yr	NM
❏ 1-220	Eric Clapton	1995	$50

— Audiophile vinyl

NAUTILUS

Number	Title	Yr	NM
❏ NR-32	Just One Night	1981	$175

— Audiophile vinyl

POLYDOR

Number	Title	Yr	NM
❏ 1775318	461 Ocean Boulevard	2008	$25
❏ 24-5526	Clapton	1973	$18

— Compiles tracks from his first solo album plus Derek and the Dominos

Number	Title	Yr	NM
❏ 835261-1	Crossroads	1988	$50

— Box set; contains material from all phases of his career

Number	Title	Yr	NM
❏ PD3503	Eric Clapton at His Best	1972	$25

— Compiles tracks from his first solo album plus Derek and the Dominos

Number	Title	Yr	NM
❏ SKBO-94837	Eric Clapton at His Best	1972	$30

— Capitol Record Club edition

Number	Title	Yr	NM
❏ 8171881	Slowhand	2008	$25

— Audiophile vinyl

REPRISE

Number	Title	Yr	NM
❏ W1-26420	24 Nights	1991	$30

— Vinyl copies released only through Columbia House

Number	Title	Yr	NM
❏ 45735-1 [B]	From the Cradle		$30
❏ 26074	Journeyman	1989	$15
❏ 48423-1	Me and Mr. Johnson	2004	$25

— Regular edition on 140-gram vinyl; distributed by Classic Records

Number	Title	Yr	NM
❏ 48423-1 SV	Me and Mr. Johnson	2004	$30

— 200-gram vinyl edition, distributed by Classic Records

RHINO

Number	Title	Yr	NM
❏ R1537929 [B]	Crossroads Guitar Festival 2013	2014	$30

RSO

Number	Title	Yr	NM
❏ SO4801	461 Ocean Boulevard	1974	$18

— With "Give Me Strength"

Number	Title	Yr	NM
❏ SO4801 [B]	461 Ocean Boulevard	1974	$30

— With "Better Make It Through the Day

Number	Title	Yr	NM
❏ QD4801 [Q]	461 Ocean Boulevard	1974	$50
❏ RS-1-3023	461 Ocean Boulevard	1977	$15

— Reissue of RSO 4801

Number	Title	Yr	NM
❏ 811697-1	461 Ocean Boulevard	198?	$10

— Reissue of RSO 3023

Number	Title	Yr	NM
❏ RX-1-3095	Another Ticket	1981	$12
❏ 827579-1	Another Ticket	1985	$10

— Reissue of RSO 3095

Number	Title	Yr	NM
❏ RS-1-3039	Backless	1978	$15
❏ SO4809	E.C. Was Here	1975	$15
❏ RS-1-3008	Eric Clapton	1977	$15

— Reissue of Atco LP of the same name

Number	Title	Yr	NM
❏ 825093-1	Eric Clapton	1984	$10

— Reissue of RSO 3008

Number	Title	Yr	NM
❏ SO877	Eric Clapton's Rainbow Concert	1973	$18
❏ RS-2-4202	Just One Night	1980	$18
❏ 825391-1	Just One Night	1984	$12

— Reissue of RSO 4202

Number	Title	Yr	NM
❏ 1009 [DJ]	Limited Backless	1978	$40

— White vinyl promo

Number	Title	Yr	NM
❏ RPO-1009 [DJ]	Limited Backless	1978	$50

— White vinyl promo

Number	Title	Yr	NM
❏ RS-1-3004	No Reason to Cry	1976	$15
❏ 35 [DJ]	Slowhand	1977	$30

— White vinyl promo

Number	Title	Yr	NM
❏ RS-1-3030 [B]	Slowhand	1977	$15
❏ PRO 035 [DJ]	Slowhand	1977	$40

— White vinyl promo sampler

Number	Title	Yr	NM
❏ 823276-1	Slowhand	1983	$10

— Reissue of RSO 3030

Number	Title	Yr	NM
❏ SO4806	There's One in Every Crowd	1975	$15
❏ QD4806 [Q]	There's One in Every Crowd	1975	$40
❏ RS-1-3099	Time Pieces/The Best of Eric Clapton	1982	$12
❏ 825382-1	Time Pieces/The Best of Eric Clapton	1984	$10

— Reissue of RSO 3099

CLARINET SUMMIT

INDIA NAVIGATION

Number	Title	Yr	NM
❏ IN-1062	In Concert at the Public Theater, Vol. 1	1985	$30
❏ IN-1067	In Concert at the Public Theater, Vol. 2	1985	$30

CLARK, ALICE

MAINSTREAM

Number	Title	Yr	NM
❏ MRL-362	Alice Clark	1972	$25

CLARK, CHRIS

MOTOWN

Number	Title	Yr	NM
❏ M-664 [M]	Soul Sounds	1967	$50
❏ MS-664 [S]	Soul Sounds	1967	$75

WEED

Number	Title	Yr	NM
❏ 801	C.C. Rides Again	1969	$100

CLARK, CLAUDINE

CHANCELLOR

Number	Title	Yr	NM
❏ CHL-5029 [M]	Party Lights	1962	$300

CLARK, DAVE, FIVE

CORTLEIGH

Number	Title	Yr	NM
❏ C-1073 [M]	The Dave Clark Five with Ricky Astor	1964	$30

— With two early DC5 tracks and assorted other stuff by other artists

Number	Title	Yr	NM
❏ CS-1073 [R]	The Dave Clark Five with Ricky Astor	1964	$18

— With two early DC5 tracks and assorted other stuff by other artists

CROWN

Number	Title	Yr	NM
❏ CLP-5473 [M]	Chaquita/In Your Heart	1964	$30

— With two early DC5 tracks and assorted other stuff by other artists

Number	Title	Yr	NM
❏ CST-473 [R]	Chaquita/In Your Heart	1964	$18

— With two early DC5 tracks and assorted other stuff by other artists

Number	Title	Yr	NM
❏ CLP-5400 [M]	The Dave Clark Five with the Playbacks	1964	$30

— With two early DC5 tracks and assorted other stuff by other artists

Number	Title	Yr	NM
❏ CST-400 [R]	The Dave Clark Five with the Playbacks	1964	$18

— With two early DC5 tracks and assorted other stuff by other artists

Number	Title	Yr	NM
❏ CST-644 [R]	The Dave Clark Five with the Playbacks	196?	$15

— Reissue

CUSTOM

Number	Title	Yr	NM
❏ CS1098 [R]	The Dave Clark Five with the Playbacks	196?	$15

— Reissue

EPIC

Number	Title	Yr	NM
❏ LN24236 [M]	5 by 5	1967	$35
❏ BN26236 [S]	5 by 5	1967	$40
❏ LN24117 [M]	American Tour	1964	$40
❏ BN26117 [R]	American Tour	1964	$30

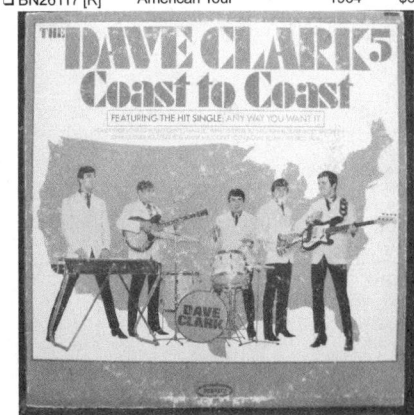

Number	Title	Yr	NM
❏ LN24128 [M]	Coast to Coast	1965	$40
❏ BN26128 [R]	Coast to Coast	1965	$30
❏ LN24354 [M]	Everybody Knows	1968	$50
❏ BN26354 [S]	Everybody Knows	1968	$40
❏ LN24093 [M]	Glad All Over	1964	$100

— Group photo, no instruments

Number	Title	Yr	NM
❏ BN26093 [R]	Glad All Over	1964	$50

— Group photo, no instruments

Number	Title	Yr	NM
❏ LN24093 [M]	Glad All Over	1964	$40

— Group photo with instruments

Number	Title	Yr	NM
❏ BN26093 [R]	Glad All Over	1964	$30

— Group photo with instruments

Number	Title	Yr	NM
❏ KEG33459 [M]	Glad All Over Again	1975	$50
❏ LN24162 [M]	Having a Wild Weekend	1965	$40
❏ BN26162 [R]	Having a Wild Weekend	1965	$30
❏ LN24178 [M]	I Like It Like That	1965	$40
❏ BN26178 [R]	I Like It Like That	1965	$30
❏ LN24221 [M]	More Greatest Hits	1966	$30
❏ BN26221 [R]	More Greatest Hits	1966	$25
❏ LN24212 [M]	Satisfied with You	1966	$30
❏ BN26212 [R]	Satisfied with You	1966	$30
❏ EG30434 [M]	The Dave Clark Five	1971	$150

— Twenty hits and near-hits, all in true stereo! Yellow label.

Number	Title	Yr	NM
❏ EG30434 [S]	The Dave Clark Five	1973	$100

— Twenty hits and near-hits, all in true stereo! Orange label.

Number	Title	Yr	NM
❏ XEM0 [DJ]	The Dave Clark Five Interview	1964	$600

Number	Title	Yr	NM
❏ XEM77238/9 [DJ]	The Dave Clark Five Interview	1964	$600
❏ LN24104 [M]	The Dave Clark Five Return	1964	$40
❏ BN26104 [R]	The Dave Clark Five Return	1964	$30
❏ LN24185 [M]	The Dave Clark Five's Greatest Hits	1966	$30
❏ BN26185 [R]	The Dave Clark Five's Greatest Hits	1966	$25
— Yellow label			
❏ BN26185 [R]	The Dave Clark Five's Greatest Hits	1973	$40
— Orange label			
❏ LN24198 [M]	Try Too Hard	1966	$30
❏ BN26198 [R]	Try Too Hard	1966	$30
❏ LN24139 [M]	Weekend in London	1965	$40
❏ BN26139 [R]	Weekend in London	1965	$30
❏ LN24312 [M]	You Got What It Takes	1967	$30
❏ BN26312 [S]	You Got What It Takes	1967	$40

CLARK, DEE
ABNER

Number	Title	Yr	NM
❏ LP-2000 [M]	Dee Clark	1959	$120
❏ SR-2000 [S]	Dee Clark	1959	$350

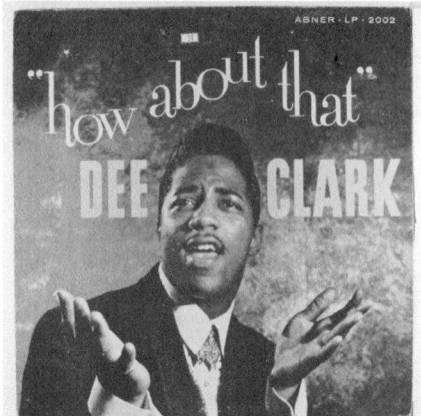

Number	Title	Yr	NM
❏ LP-2002 [M]	How About That	1960	$100
❏ SR-2002 [S]	How About That	1960	$120

SOLID SMOKE
❏ 8026	His Best Recordings	1983	$12

SUNSET
❏ SUS-5217	Wondering	1968	$15

VEE JAY
❏ LP-1037 [M]	Hold On, It's Dee Clark	1961	$50
❏ SR-1037 [S]	Hold On, It's Dee Clark	1961	$150
❏ LP-1047 [M]	The Best of Dee Clark	1964	$50
❏ SR-1047 [S]	The Best of Dee Clark	1964	$150
❏ VJLP-1047	The Best of Dee Clark	1986	$15
— Authorized reissue			
❏ LP-1019 [M]	You're Looking Good	1960	$50

CLARK, DICK
See VARIOUS ARTISTS COLLECTIONS.

CLARK, DOTTIE
MAINSTREAM
❏ 56006 [M]	I'm Lost	1966	$25
❏ S-6006 [S]	I'm Lost	1966	$30

CLARK, DOUG, AND THE HOT NUTS
GROSS
❏ 108	Freak Out	196?	$30
❏ 107	Hell Night	196?	$30
❏ 103	Homecoming	196?	$30
❏ 101	Nuts to You	196?	$30
❏ 102	On Campus	196?	$30
❏ 105	Panty Raid	196?	$30
❏ 104	Rush Week	1967	$30
❏ 106	Summer Session	196?	$30
❏ 109	With a Hat On	196?	$30

CLARK, GENE
4 MEN WITH BEARDS
❏ 4M116LP [B]	Gene Clark (White Light)		$25
❏ 4M200LP [B]	No Other		$25

A&M
❏ SP-4292	White Light	1971	$18

ASYLUM
❏ 7E-1016	No Other	1974	$40

COLUMBIA
❏ KC31123	Early L.A. Sessions	1972	$18
❏ CL2618 [M]	Gene Clark with the Gosdin Brothers	1967	$30
❏ CS9418 [S]	Gene Clark with the Gosdin Brothers	1967	$50

RSO
❏ RS-1-3011	Two Sides to Every Story	1976	$25

SUNDAZED
Number	Title	Yr	NM
❏ LP5062	Gene Clark with the Gosdin Brothers	2000	$18
— Reissue of Columbia LP			

TAKOMA
❏ TAK-7112	Firebyrd	1984	$15

CLARK, GUY
4 MEN WITH BEARDS
❏ 4M236 [B]	Old No. 1	2014	$30

RCA VICTOR
❏ APL1-1303	Old No. 1	1976	$25
❏ AHL1-1303	Old No. 1	198?	$12
— Reissue with new prefix			
❏ APL1-1944	Texas Cookin'	1976	$25

SUGAR HILL
❏ SH-1025	Old Friends	198?	$15

WARNER BROS.
❏ 23880	Better Days	1983	$15
❏ BSK3241	Guy Clark	1978	$18
❏ WBMS-105 [DJ]	On the Road, Live!	198?	$75
— Part of "The Warner Bros. Music Show" series; promo only			
❏ BSK3381	South Coast of Texas	1981	$18

CLARK, JOHN
ECM
❏ 1176	Faces	1981	$30

CLARK, KEN, AND DON ANTHONY
STARDAY
❏ SLP-114 [M]	Fiddlin' Country Style	1959	$40

CLARK, PETULA
COCA-COLA
❏ 103 [DJ]	Petula Clark Swings the Jingle	1966	$175
❏ 103 [DJ]	Petula Clark Swings the Jingle	1966	$175

GNP CRESCENDO
❏ 2069	Live at the Royal Albert Hall	1972	$12
❏ 2170	The Greatest Hits of Petula Clark	1984	$10

IMPERIAL
❏ LP-9079 [M]	Pet Clark	1959	$50
❏ LP-12027 [S]	Pet Clark	1959	$100
❏ LP-9281 [M]	Uptown with Petula Clark	1965	$25
— Reissue of Imperial 9079			
❏ LP-12281 [S]	Uptown with Petula Clark	1965	$30
— Reissue of Imperial 12079			

JANGO
❏ 779	Give It a Try	1986	$12

LAURIE
❏ LLP-2032 [M]	In Love!	1965	$18
❏ ST-90497 [S]	In Love!	1965	$25
— Capitol Record Club edition			
❏ SLP-2032 [S]	In Love!	1965	$18
❏ T-90497 [M]	In Love!	1965	$25
— Capitol Record Club edition			

MGM
❏ SE-4859	Pet Clark Now	1972	$12

PREMIER
❏ PM-9016 [M]	The English Sound Starring Petula Clark	1965	$15
❏ PS-9016 [S]	The English Sound Starring Petula Clark	1965	$18

ROULETTE
❏ 1	Petula	1975	$25

SUNSET
❏ SUM-1101 [M]	This Is Petula Clark	1965	$15
❏ SUS-5101 [S]	This Is Petula Clark	1965	$18

WARNER BROS.
❏ W1673 [M]	Color My World/Who Am I	1967	$12
❏ WS1673 [S]	Color My World/Who Am I	1967	$15
❏ W1590 [M]	Downtown	1965	$18
— Originals have gray labels			
❏ W1590 [M]	Downtown	1966	$15
— Reissues have gold labels			
❏ WS1590 [S]	Downtown	1965	$25
— Originals have gold labels			
❏ WS1765	Greatest Hits, Volume I	1968	$12
❏ ST-91598	Greatest Hits, Volume I	1968	$18
— Capitol Record Club edition			
❏ SQBO-93215 [P]	Hits...My Way	1969	$30
— Capitol Record Club exclusive; "The Other Man's Grass Is Always Greener" is rechanneled.			
❏ W1645 [M]	I Couldn't Live Without Your Love	1966	$12
❏ WS1645 [S]	I Couldn't Live Without Your Love	1966	$15
❏ W1598 [M]	I Know a Place	1965	$18
— Originals have gray labels			
❏ W1598 [M]	I Know a Place	1966	$15
— Reissues have gold labels			

Number	Title	Yr	NM
❏ WS1598 [S]	I Know a Place	1965	$25
— Originals have gold labels			
❏ WS1598 [S]	I Know a Place	1968	$15
— Green label with "W7" logo in box at top			
❏ WS1823	Just Pet	1969	$12
❏ WS1862	Memphis	1970	$12
❏ W1630 [M]	My Love	1966	$12

Number	Title	Yr	NM
❏ WS1630 [S]	My Love	1966	$15
❏ W1743 [M]	Petula	1968	$15
❏ WS1743 [S]	Petula	1968	$15
❏ WS1789	Portrait of Petula	1969	$12
❏ W1719 [M]	The Other Man's Grass Is Always Greener	1968	$15
❏ WS1719 [P]	The Other Man's Grass Is Always Greener	1968	$15
— The Other Man's Grass Is Always Greener" is rechanneled.			
❏ W1698 [M]	These Are My Songs	1967	$12
❏ WS1698 [S]	These Are My Songs	1967	$15
❏ ST-91348 [S]	These Are My Songs	1967	$18
— Capitol Record Club edition			
❏ W1608 [M]	The World's Greatest International Hits	1965	$18
— Originals have gray labels			
❏ W1608 [M]	The World's Greatest International Hits	1965	$15
— Reissues have gold labels			
❏ WS1608 [S]	The World's Greatest International Hits	1965	$25
— Originals have gold labels			
❏ WS1865	Warm and Tender (The Song of My Life)	1971	$12

CLARK, ROY, AND BUCK TRENT
ABC
❏ AY-1084	Banjo Bandits	1978	$12

ABC DOT
❏ 2015	A Pair of Fives (Banjos, That Is)	1975	$12

CLARK, ROY
ABC
❏ AB-1053	Labor of Love	1978	$12

ABC DOT
❏ DOSD-2010	Classic Clark	1974	$12
❏ DOSD-2041	Heart to Heart	1975	$12
❏ DO-2099	Hookin' It	1977	$12
— Reissue of Record 2 of 2072			
❏ DO-2072	My Music and Me/Vocal & Instrumental	1977	$15
❏ DOSD-2005	Roy Clark, Family & Friends	1974	$12
❏ DOSD-2054	Roy Clark In Concert	1976	$12
❏ DOSD-2030	Roy Clark's Greatest Hits -- Volume 1	1975	$12
❏ DOSD-2001	Roy Clark/The Entertainer	1974	$12

CAPITOL
❏ T2031 [M]	Happy to Be Unhappy	1964	$25
❏ ST2031 [S]	Happy to Be Unhappy	1964	$30
❏ T2452 [M]	Roy Clark Sings Lonesome Love Ballads	1966	$25
❏ ST2452 [S]	Roy Clark Sings Lonesome Love Ballads	1966	$30
❏ SM-11412	So Much to Remember	1975	$12
❏ T2535 [M]	Stringing Along with the Blues	1966	$25
❏ ST2535 [S]	Stringing Along with the Blues	1966	$30
❏ SABB-11264	The Entertainer of the Year	1974	$18
❏ SKAO-369	The Greatest!	1969	$15
❏ SM-369	The Greatest!	197?	$12
— Reissue with new prefix			
❏ SN-16161	The Greatest!	198?	$10
❏ T1780 [M]	The Lightning Fingers of Roy Clark	1962	$25
❏ ST1780 [S]	The Lightning Fingers of Roy Clark	1962	$30
❏ SN-16227	The Lightning Fingers of Roy Clark	198?	$10
❏ T2425 [M]	The Roy Clark Guitar Spectacular	1965	$25

Number	Title	Yr	NM
❏ ST2425 [S]	The Roy Clark Guitar Spectacular	1965	$30
❏ SM-2425	The Roy Clark Guitar Spectacular	197?	$12
—Reissue with new prefix			
❏ T1972 [M]	The Tip of My Fingers	1963	$25
❏ ST1972 [S]	The Tip of My Fingers	1963	$30
❏ SM-12032	The Tip of My Fingers	1980	$10
CHURCHILL			
❏ 9421	The Roy Clark Show Live from Austin City Limits	1982	$12
❏ 9425	Turned Loose	1982	$12
DOT			
❏ DOS-26010	Come Live with Me	1973	$15
❏ DLP-25895	Do You Believe This Roy Clark	1968	$15
❏ DLP-25980	I Never Picked Cotton	1970	$15
❏ DOS-25997	Roy Clark Country!	1972	$15
❏ ST-94463	Roy Clark Country!	1972	$18
—Capitol Record Club edition			
❏ DOS-26005	Roy Clark Live!	1972	$15
❏ DOS-26018	Roy Clark's Family Album	1973	$15
❏ DOS-26008	Roy Clark/Superpicker	1973	$15
❏ DOS-25986	The Best of Roy Clark	1971	$15
❏ DLP-25972	The Everlovin' Soul of Roy Clark	1969	$15
❏ ST-93117	The Everlovin' Soul of Roy Clark	1969	$18
—Capitol Record Club edition with old-style black Dot label with multi-color logo			
❏ DOS-25990	The Incredible Roy Clark	1971	$15
❏ DOS-25993	The Magnificent Sanctuary Band	1971	$15
❏ DLP-25977	The Other Side of Roy Clark	1970	$15
❏ DOS-000112	The Special Talents of Roy Clark	1973	$15
❏ DLP-25863	Urban, Suburban	1968	$15
❏ DLP-25953	Yesterday, When I Was Young	1969	$15
HILLTOP			
❏ 6094	He'll Have to Go	1970	$12
❏ 6154	Honky Tonk	197?	$12
❏ 6046	Roy Clartk	196?	$18
❏ 6080	Silver Threads and Golden Needles	1970	$12
❏ 6135	Take Me As I Am	197?	$12
MCA			
❏ 37131	A Pair of Fives (Banjos, That Is)	198?	$10
❏ 811	Back to the Country	198?	$10
❏ 37130	Banjo Bandits	198?	$10
—With Buck Trent			
❏ 676	Heart to Heart	1980	$10
❏ 677	Hookin' It	1980	$10
❏ 675	Labor of Love	1980	$10
❏ 3161	Makin' Music	1980	$12
—With Gatemouth Brown			
❏ 37142	My Music	198?	$10
❏ 3189	My Music	1980	$12
❏ 37132	Roy Clark In Concert	198?	$10
❏ 37134	Roy Clark Live!	198?	$10
❏ 27050	Roy Clark's Greatest Hits -- Volume 1	198?	$10
❏ 679	Roy Clark/Superpicker	198?	$10
❏ 27015	The Best of Roy Clark	198?	$10
❏ 678	Yesterday, When I Was Young	198?	$10
PAIR			
❏ PDL2-1088	Country Standard Time	1986	$15
PICKWICK			
❏ PTP-2043	Roy Clark	1973	$15
❏ PTP-2093	The Entertainer of the Year	1978	$15
SONGBIRD			
❏ 5260	The Last Word in Jesus Is Us	1981	$12
TOWER			
❏ DT5118 [R]	In the Mood	1968	$18
❏ T5055 [M]	Roy Clark Live	1967	$18
❏ ST5055 [S]	Roy Clark Live	1967	$25
WORD			
❏ 8654	Roy Clark Sings Gospel	1975	$15

CLARK, SANFORD

Number	Title	Yr	NM
LHI			
❏ 12003	Return of the Fool	1968	$75

CLARK, SONNY

Number	Title	Yr	NM
BLUE NOTE			
❏ BLP-1588 [M]	Cool Struttin'	1958	$5000
—Deep groove" version (deep indentation under label on both sides)			
❏ BLP-1588 [M]	Cool Struttin'	1958	$800
—Regular version, W. 63rd St. address on label			
❏ BLP-1588 [M]	Cool Struttin'	1963	$300
—New York, USA" address on label			
❏ BST-1588 [S]	Cool Struttin'	1959	$4000
—Deep groove" version (deep indentation under label on both sides)			
❏ BST-1588 [S]	Cool Struttin'	1959	$250
—Regular version, W. 63rd St. address on label			

Number	Title	Yr	NM
❏ BST-1588 [S]	Cool Struttin'	1963	$150
—New York, USA" address on label			
❏ BST-81588 [S]	Cool Struttin'	1967	$75
—A Division of Liberty Records" on label			
❏ BST-81588 [S]	Cool Struttin'	1970	$50
—Mostly black label, "Liberty/UA" at bottom			
❏ BLJ-81588	Cool Struttin'	1987	$30
—The Finest in Jazz Since 1939" reissue			
❏ BST-1588-45 [S]	Cool Struttin'	200?	$250
—Classic Records box set of four 45 rpm 12-inch records			
❏ BST-1588 [S]	Cool Struttin'	1997	$175
—180-gram reissue; distributed by Classic Records			
❏ BLP-1592 [M]	Cool Struttin' -- Volume 2	1959	$0
—Canceled			
❏ BST-1592 [S]	Cool Struttin' -- Volume 2	1959	$0
—Canceled			
❏ BLP-1570 [M]	Dial "S" for Sonny	1957	$3500
—Deep groove" version; W. 63rd St. address on label			
❏ BLP-1570 [M]	Dial "S" for Sonny	1957	$250
—Regular version, W. 63rd St. address on label			
❏ BLP-1570 [M]	Dial "S" for Sonny	1963	$175
—New York, USA" address on label			
❏ BST-1570 [S]	Dial "S" for Sonny	1959	$350
—Deep groove" version; W. 63rd St. address on label			
❏ BST-1570 [S]	Dial "S" for Sonny	1959	$250
—Regular version, W. 63rd St. address on label			
❏ BST-1570 [S]	Dial "S" for Sonny	1963	$150
—New York, USA" address on label			
❏ BST-81570 [S]	Dial "S" for Sonny	1967	$75
—A Division of Liberty Records" on label			
❏ BLP-4091 [M]	Leapin' and Lopin'	1961	$250
—W. 63rd St. address on label			
❏ BLP-4091 [M]	Leapin' and Lopin'	1963	$250
—New York, USA" address on label			
❏ BST-84091 [S]	Leapin' and Lopin'	1961	$175
—W. 63rd St. address on label			
❏ BST-84091 [S]	Leapin' and Lopin'	1963	$50
—New York, USA" address on label			
❏ BST-84091 [S]	Leapin' and Lopin'	1967	$75
—A Division of Liberty Records" on label			
❏ BLP-1579 [M]	Sonny Clark Trio	1958	$800
—Deep groove" version; W. 63rd St. address on label			
❏ BLP-1579 [M]	Sonny Clark Trio	1958	$300
—Regular version, W. 63rd St. address on label			

sonny clark

with paul chambers 'philly' joe jones | blue note 1579

Number	Title	Yr	NM
❏ BLP-1579 [M]	Sonny Clark Trio	1963	$100
—New York, USA" address on label			
❏ BST-1579 [S]	Sonny Clark Trio	1959	$500
—Deep groove" version; W. 63rd St. address on label			
❏ BST-1579 [S]	Sonny Clark Trio	1959	$300
—Regular version, W. 63rd St. address on label			
❏ BST-1579 [S]	Sonny Clark Trio	1963	$100
—New York, USA" address on label			
❏ BST-81579 [S]	Sonny Clark Trio	1967	$75
—A Division of Liberty Records" on label			
❏ BLP-1576 [M]	Sonny's Crib	1957	$3000
—Deep groove" version; W. 63rd St. address on label			
❏ BLP-1576 [M]	Sonny's Crib	1957	$300
—Regular version, W. 63rd St. address on label			
❏ BLP-1576 [M]	Sonny's Crib	1963	$300
—New York, USA" address on label			
❏ BST-1576 [S]	Sonny's Crib	1959	$1250
—Deep groove" version; W. 63rd St. address on label			
❏ BST-1576 [S]	Sonny's Crib	1959	$300
—Regular version, W. 63rd St. address on label			
❏ BST-1576 [S]	Sonny's Crib	1963	$250
—New York, USA" address on label			
❏ BST-81576 [S]	Sonny's Crib	1967	$75
—A Division of Liberty Records" on label			
TIME			
❏ T-70010 [M]	Sonny Clark Trio	1960	$1200
❏ ST-70010 [S]	Sonny Clark Trio	1960	$500

Number	Title	Yr	NM
❏ 52101 [M]	Sonny Clark Trio	1962	$30
❏ S-2101 [S]	Sonny Clark Trio	1962	$30
XANADU			
❏ 121	Memorial Album	1975	$35

CLARK, SPENCER

Number	Title	Yr	NM
AUDIOPHILE			
❏ 131	Spencer Clark and His Bass Sax Play Sweet & Hot	1978	$30

CLARK, YODELING SLIM

Number	Title	Yr	NM
CONTINENTAL			
❏ C-1505 [M]	Cowboy and Yodel Songs	1962	$40
MASTERSEAL			
❏ MS-57 [M]	Cowboy Songs	1963	$30
❏ MS-135 [M]	Cowboy Songs Vol. 2	1964	$30
❏ MS-112 [M]	Songs by Yodeling Slim Clark	1964	$30
PALOMINO			
❏ 306 [M]	I Feel a Trip Coming On	1966	$40
❏ 307 [M]	Old Chestnuts	1967	$40
❏ 311 [M]	The Ballad of Billy Venero	1968	$40
❏ 310 [M]	Yodeling Slim Clark Happens Again	1967	$40
❏ 314 [M]	Yodeling Slim Clark's 50th Anniversary Album	1968	$50
—Gold vinyl			
❏ 301 [M]	Yodeling Slim Clark Sings and Yodels Favorite Montana Slim Songs of the Mountains and Plains, Vol. 1	1966	$75
❏ 303 [M]	Yodeling Slim Clark Sings and Yodels Favorite Montana Slim Songs of the Mountains and Plains, Vol. 2	1966	$40
❏ 300 [M]	Yodeling Slim Clark Sings the Legendary Jimmie Rodgers Songs	1966	$75
PLAYHOUSE			
❏ 2017 [10]	Western Songs and Dances	1954	$50

CLARK SISTERS, THE

Number	Title	Yr	NM
CORAL			
❏ CRL57290 [M]	Beauty Shop Beat	1960	$25
❏ CRL757290 [S]	Beauty Shop Beat	1960	$30
DOT			
❏ DLP-3104 [M]	Sing, Sing, Sing	1957	$30
❏ DLP-3137 [M]	The Clark Sisters Swing Again	1958	$30
❏ DLP-25137 [S]	The Clark Sisters Swing Again	1958	$30

CLARKE, ALLAN

Number	Title	Yr	NM
ASYLUM			
❏ 7E-1056	I've Got Time	1976	$12
ATLANTIC			
❏ SD19175	I Wasn't Born Yesterday	1978	$12
ELEKTRA			
❏ 6E-267	Legendary Heroes	1980	$12
EPIC			
❏ KE31757	My Real Name Is 'Arold	1972	$18

CLARKE, BUCK

Number	Title	Yr	NM
ARGO			
❏ LP-4007 [M]	Drum Sum	1961	$30
❏ LPS-4007 [S]	Drum Sum	1961	$30
❏ LP-4021 [M]	The Buck Clarke Sound	1963	$30
❏ LPS-4021 [S]	The Buck Clarke Sound	1963	$30
OFFBEAT			
❏ OLP-3003 [M]	Cool Hands	1960	$30
❏ OS-93003 [S]	Cool Hands	1960	$40

CLARKE, KEN

Number	Title	Yr	NM
MGM			
❏ E-205 [10]	Jazz Piano	1953	$50

CLARKE, KENNY, AND ERNIE WILKINS

Number	Title	Yr	NM
SAVOY			
❏ MG-12007 [M]	Plenty for Kenny	1955	$100

CLARKE, KENNY

Number	Title	Yr	NM
BLUE NOTE			
❏ BLP4092 [B]	The Golden Eight	1961	$150
EPIC			
❏ LN3376 [M]	Kenny Clarke Plays Andre Hodeir	1957	$100
PRESTIGE			
❏ PRST-7605	Paris Bebop Sessions	1969	$35
SAVOY			
❏ MG-12017 [M]	Bohemia After Dark	1955	$100
❏ MG-15051 [10]	Kenny Clarke	195?	$250
❏ MG-15053 [10]	Kenny Clarke, Vol. 2	195?	$250
❏ MG-12065 [M]	Klook's Clique	1956	$150
❏ MG-12006 [M]	Telefunken Blues	1955	$100

Number	Title	Yr	NM

SAVOY JAZZ
| ❏ SJL-1111 | Kenny Clarke Meets the Detroit Jazzmen | 198? | $25 |

SOUL NOTE
| ❏ SN-1078 | Pieces of Time | 1983 | $30 |

SWING
| ❏ SW-8411 | Kenny Clarke in Paris Vol. 1 | 1986 | $25 |

CLARKE, STANLEY, AND GEORGE DUKE

EPIC
❏ FE36918	The Clarke/Duke Project	1981	$75
❏ PE36918	The Clarke/Duke Project	198?	$20
— Budget-line reissue			
❏ FE38934	The Clarke/Duke Project II	1983	$25

CLARKE, STANLEY
Also see RETURN TO FOREVER.

EPIC
❏ FE40040	Find Out!	1985	$25
❏ FE40275	Hideaway	1986	$25
❏ PE36974	Journey to Love	1981	$20
— Reissue of Nemperor 433			
❏ FE38086	Let Me Know You	1982	$75
❏ JE36506	Rocks, Pebbles and Sand	1980	$25
❏ PE36975	School Days	1981	$20
— Reissue of Nemperor 900			
❏ PE36973	Stanley Clarke	1981	$20
— Reissue of Nemperor 431			
❏ FE38688	Time Exposure	1984	$25

NEMPEROR
❏ KZ235680	I Wanna Play for You	1979	$35
❏ NE433	Journey to Love	1975	$30
❏ JZ35303	Modern Man	1978	$25
— Original issue			
❏ PZ35303	Modern Man	1985	$20
— Reissue with new prefix and bar code			
❏ NE439	School Days	1976	$30
❏ SD900	School Days	1978	$25
— Reissue of 439			
❏ NE431	Stanley Clarke	1974	$30

POLYDOR
❏ PD-5531	Children of Forever	1973	$35
❏ 827559-1	Children of Forever	1985	$20
— Reissue			

PORTRAIT
| ❏ FR40923 | If This Bass Could Only Talk | 1988 | $25 |

CLARKE-BOLAND BIG BAND, THE
KENNY CLARKE and Francy Boland.

ATLANTIC
❏ 1401 [M]	Jazz Is Universal	1963	$50
❏ SD1401 [S]	Jazz Is Universal	1963	$50
❏ 1404 [M]	The Clarke-Boland Big Band	1963	$50
❏ SD1404 [S]	The Clarke-Boland Big Band	1963	$50

BASF
| ❏ 29686 | All Smiles | 1972 | $35 |
| ❏ 25102 | The Big Band Sound | 1971 | $25 |

BLACK LION
| ❏ 131 | At Her Majesty's Pleasure | 1974 | $35 |

BLUE NOTE
❏ BLP-4092 [M]	The Golden Eight	1961	$250
— As "Kenny Clarke-Francy Boland & Co."; W. 63rd St. address on label			
❏ BLP-4092 [M]	The Golden Eight	1963	$250
— As "Kenny Clarke-Francy Boland & Co."; "New York, USA" address on label			
❏ BST-84092 [S]	The Golden Eight	1961	$175
— As "Kenny Clarke-Francy Boland & Co."; W. 63rd St. address on label			
❏ BST-84092 [S]	The Golden Eight	1963	$100
— As "Kenny Clarke-Francy Boland & Co."; "New York, USA" address on label			
❏ BST-84092 [S]	The Golden Eight	1967	$75
— As "Kenny Clarke-Francy Boland & Co."; "A Division of Liberty Records" on label			

COLUMBIA
| ❏ CL2314 [M] | Now Hear Our Meanin' | 1965 | $35 |
| ❏ CS9114 [S] | Now Hear Our Meanin' | 1965 | $25 |

MUSE
| ❏ MR-5056 | Open Door | 197? | $30 |

PAUSA
| ❏ 7097 | Sax No End | 198? | $25 |

POLYDOR
| ❏ 24-4501 | Volcano | 1970 | $35 |

PRESTIGE
❏ PRST-7634	Fire, Heat, Soul and Guts	1969	$35
❏ PRST-7760	Latin Kaleidoscope	1970	$35
❏ PRST-7699	Let's Face the Music	1969	$35

CLARY, ROBERT

ATLANTIC
| ❏ 8053 [M] | Livin' It Up at the Playboy Club | 1961 | $30 |
| ❏ SD8053 [S] | Livin' It Up at the Playboy Club | 1961 | $40 |

EPIC
| ❏ LN3281 [M] | Hooray for Love | 1956 | $30 |
| ❏ LN3171 [M] | Meet Robert Clary | 1955 | $30 |

MERCURY
| ❏ MG-20367 [M] | Gigi Sung by Robert Clary | 1958 | $25 |
| ❏ SR-60042 [S] | Gigi Sung by Robert Clary | 1958 | $30 |

CLASH, THE
Also see JOE STRUMMER; BIG AUDIO DYNAMITE.

EPIC
❏ PE38540	Black Market Clash	1982	$12
— 12-inch version of 10-inch record			
❏ -0 [DJ]	Combat Rock	1982	$40
— Camouflage green vinyl promo			
❏ FE37689	Combat Rock	1982	$18
— First pressings (with custom labels) contain a commercial in the middle of the song "Inoculated City			
❏ AS 99-1592 [PD]	Combat Rock	1982	$40
— Promo-only picture disc			
❏ AS 99-1595 [DJ]	Combat Rock	1982	$30
— Camouflage green vinyl promo			
❏ FE37689	Combat Rock	1982	$12
— Second and later pressings (with standard dark blue labels) delete commercial during "Inoculated City			

❏ FE40017 [B]	Cut the Crap	1985	$12
❏ JE35543 [DJ]	Give 'Em Enough Rope	1978	$30
— White label promo; timing strip; back cover has one incorrect song title			
❏ JE35543	Give 'Em Enough Rope	1978	$18
— Script cover; orange label			
❏ JE35543 [DJ]	Give 'Em Enough Rope	1978	$30
— White label promo; timing strip; back cover has one incorrect song title			
❏ JE35543	Give 'Em Enough Rope	1978	$18
— Block letters on cover; orange label			
❏ AS952 [DJ]	If Music Could Talk (Interchords)	1981	$30
— Promo-only interview record			
❏ AS952 [DJ]	If Music Could Talk (Interchords)	1981	$40
— Promo-only interview record			
❏ E236238 [DJ]	London Calling	1980	$30
— White label promo			
❏ E236329 [B]	London Calling	1979	$30
❏ E236238 [DJ]	London Calling	1980	$30
— White label promo			
❏ E3X37037	Sandinista!	1981	$30
❏ AS913 [DJ]	Sandinista Now!	1981	$25
— Promo-only sampler			
❏ AS913 [DJ]	Sandinista Now!	1981	$50
— Promo-only sampler			
❏ JE36060	The Clash	1979	$18
❏ PE36060	The Clash	1979	$10
— Budget-line reissue; no bonus single			
❏ E244025	The Story of the Clash, Vol. 1	1988	$18
❏ AS1594 [DJ]	The World According to the Clash	1982	$40
— Promo-only sampler			
❏ AS1594 [DJ]	The World According to the Clash	1982	$40
— Promo-only sampler			

EPIC LEGACY
| ❏ E353191 [10] | Super Black Market Clash | 1993 | $30 |

EPIC NU-DISK
| ❏ 4E36846 [10] | Black Market Clash | 1980 | $30 |

CLASS-AIRES, THE

HONEY BEE
| ❏ 0(# unknown) | Tears Start to Fall | 195? | $300 |

CLASSIC JAZZ ENSEMBLE

DELMARK
| ❏ DE-221 | Classic Blues | 1989 | $25 |

CLASSIC JAZZ QUARTET, THE

JAZZOLOGY
| ❏ J-139 | The Classic Jazz Quartet | 1985 | $25 |

STOMP OFF
| ❏ SOS-1125 | MCMLXXXVI | 1986 | $25 |

CLASSICS IV
ATLANTA RHYTHM SECTION related.

ACCORD
| ❏ SN-7107 | Stormy | 1981 | $12 |

IMPERIAL
❏ LP-16000	Dennis Yost & the Classics IV/Golden Greats - Volume I	1969	$25
❏ LP-12407	Mamas and Papas/Soul Train	1969	$25
❏ LP-12371 [S]	Spooky	1968	$25
❏ LP-9371 [M]	Spooky	1968	$40
— Mono has stock copy label inside stereo cover with white "Monaural" sticker			
❏ LP-12429	Traces	1969	$25

LIBERTY
| ❏ LST-11003 | Song | 1970 | $18 |
| ❏ LN-10109 | The Very Best of the Classics IV | 198? | $10 |

MGM SOUTH
| ❏ 702 | Dennis Yost and the Classics IV | 1973 | $18 |

UNITED ARTISTS
| ❏ UA-LA446-E | The Very Best of the Classics IV | 1975 | $15 |

CLAUSON, WILLIAM

CAPITOL
| ❏ T10158 [M] | Concert | 195? | $30 |
| ❏ T10176 [M] | Scandinavia | 195? | $30 |

RCA VICTOR
| ❏ LPM-1286 [M] | Folk Songs | 1956 | $30 |

CLAY, CASSIUS

COLUMBIA
| ❏ CL2093 [M] | I Am the Greatest! | 1963 | $75 |
| ❏ CS8893 [S] | I Am the Greatest! | 1963 | $100 |

CLAY, JAMES, AND DAVID "FATHEAD" NEWMAN

FANTASY
| ❏ OJC-257 | The Sound of the Wide Open Spaces!!! | 1987 | $30 |

RIVERSIDE
❏ RLP 12-327 [M]	The Sound of the Wide Open Spaces!!!	1960	$250
— Blue label			
❏ RLP-1178 [S]	The Sound of the Wide Open Spaces!!!	1960	$250
— Black label			

CLAY, JAMES

RIVERSIDE
❏ RLP-349 [M]	A Double Dose of Soul	1961	$120
— Blue label			
❏ RS-9349 [S]	A Double Dose of Soul	1961	$250
— Black label			

CLAY, OTIS

HI
| ❏ HLP6003 [B] | I Can't Take It | 1977 | $18 |
| ❏ SHL32075 | Trying to Live My Life Without You | 1972 | $25 |

ROOSTER BLUES
| ❏ R-7609 | Soul Man: Live in Japan | 1985 | $18 |

CLAY, TOM

MOWEST
| ❏ 103 | What the World Needs Now Is Love | 1971 | $18 |

CLAYDERMAN, RICHARD

COLUMBIA
| ❏ PC40190 | A Romantic Christmas | 1985 | $12 |

CLAYTON, BUCK, AND BUDDY TATE

PRESTIGE
| ❏ 24040 | Kansas City Nights | 1974 | $35 |

SWINGVILLE
| ❏ SVLP-2017 [M] | Buck and Buddy | 1961 | $50 |

Number	Title	Yr	NM
—Purple label			
❏ SVLP-2017 [M]	Buck and Buddy	1965	$30
—Blue label, trident logo at right			
❏ SVLP-2030 [M]	Buck and Buddy Blow the Blues	1962	$40
—Purple label			
❏ SVLP-2030 [M]	Buck and Buddy Blow the Blues	1965	$25
—Blue label, trident logo at right			
❏ SVST-2030 [S]	Buck and Buddy Blow the Blues	1962	$50
—Red label			
❏ SVST-2030 [S]	Buck and Buddy Blow the Blues	1965	$30
—Blue label, trident logo at right			

CLAYTON, BUCK; RUBY BRAFF; MEL POWELL
VANGUARD
❏ VRS-8514 [M]	Buckin' the Blues	1957	$100
❏ VRS-8008 [10]	Buck Meets Ruby	1954	$150
❏ VRS-8517 [M]	Buck Meets Ruby and Mel	1957	$100

CLAYTON, BUCK
ALLEGRO ELITE
| ❏ 4121 [10] | Buck Clayton All Stars | 195? | $40 |

CHIAROSCURO
❏ 132	A Buck Clayton Jam Session	1974	$30
❏ 143	A Buck Clayton Jam Session, Vol. II	1975	$30
❏ 152	A Buck Clayton Jam Session, Vol. III: Jazz Party Time	1976	$30
❏ 163	A Buck Clayton Jam Session, Vol. IV: Jay Hawk	1977	$30

COLUMBIA
❏ CL882 [M]	All the Cats Join In	1956	$40
—Red and black label with six "eye" logos			
❏ CL614 [M]	Buck Clayton Jams Benny Goodman	1955	$75
—Maroon label, gold print			
❏ CL614 [M]	Buck Clayton Jams Benny Goodman	1955	$40
—Red and black label with six "eye" logos			
❏ CL567 [M]	How Hi the Fi: A Jam Session	1954	$50
—Maroon label, gold print			
❏ CL6326 [10]	How Hi the Fi: A Jam Session	1954	$75
❏ CL567 [M]	How Hi the Fi: A Jam Session	1955	$40
—Red and black label with six "eye" logos			
❏ CL808 [M]	Jazz Spectacular	1956	$40
—Red and black label with six "eye" logos			
❏ CL701 [M]	Jumpin' at the Woodside	1955	$50
—Red and black label with six "eye" logos			
❏ CL6325 [10]	Moten Swing -- Sentimental Journey	1954	$75
❏ CL1320 [M]	Songs for Swingers	1959	$30
—Red and black label with six "eye" logos			
❏ CS8123 [S]	Songs for Swingers	1959	$30
—Red and black label with six "eye" logos			
❏ CL548 [M]	The Huckle-Buck and Robbins' Nest: A Jam Session	1954	$50
—Maroon label, gold print			
❏ CL548 [M]	The Huckle-Buck and Robbins' Nest: A Jam Session	1955	$40
—Red and black label with six "eye" logos			

COLUMBIA JAZZ MASTERPIECES
| ❏ CJ44291 | Jam Sessions from the Vaults | 1988 | $30 |

FANTASY
| ❏ OJC-1709 | The Classic Swing of Buck Clayton | 1985 | $30 |

INNER CITY
| ❏ 7009 | Passport to Paradise | 1980 | $25 |

JAZZTONE
| ❏ J-1225 [M] | Meet Buck Clayton | 1956 | $40 |

STASH
| ❏ ST-281 | A Swingin' Dream | 1989 | $30 |

STEEPLECHASE
| ❏ SCC-6006/7 | Copenhagen Concert | 198? | $35 |

VANGUARD
| ❏ 103/104 | Essential Buck Clayton | 197? | $35 |

CLAYTON, BUCK/WILD BILL DAVISON
JAZZTONE
| ❏ J-1267 [M] | Singing Trumpets | 1957 | $40 |

CLAYTON, KID
FOLKWAYS
| ❏ FJ-2859 | The First Kid Clayton Session (1952) | 1983 | $30 |

JAZZOLOGY
| ❏ JCE-22 | Exit Stares | 1967 | $30 |

Number	Title	Yr	NM
CLAYTON, MERRY			
MCA			
❏ 3200	Emotion	1980	$12
ODE			
❏ SP-77001	Gimme Shelter	1970	$18
❏ SP-77030	Keep Your Eye on the Sparrow	1975	$15
❏ PE34957	Keep Your Eye on the Sparrow	1977	$10
❏ SP-77012	Merry Clayton	1971	$15
❏ PE34948	Merry Clayton	1977	$10

CLAYTON, PAUL
ELEKTRA
| ❏ EKL-155 [M] | Bobby Burns' Merry Muses | 1958 | $30 |
| ❏ EKL-147 [M] | Unholy Matrimony | 1958 | $30 |

FOLKWAYS
❏ FA-2106 [M]	Bay State Ballads	1956	$100
❏ FW-8708 [M]	British Broadside Ballads in Popular Tradition	1957	$40
❏ FA-2007 [M]	Cumberland Mountain Folksongs	1957	$80
❏ FA-2429 [M]	Foc'sle Songs and Shanties	1959	$40
❏ FA-2310 [M]	Folk Ballads of the English-Speaking World	1956	$80
❏ FA-2110 [M]	Folksongs and Ballads of Virginia	1956	$75

MONUMENT
| ❏ MLP-8017 [M] | Folk Singer | 1965 | $25 |
| ❏ SLP-18017 [S] | Folk Singer | 1965 | $30 |

RIVERSIDE
❏ RLP 12-615 [M]	Bloody Ballads	1957	$30
❏ RLP 12-648 [M]	Timber-r-r! -- Folk Songs and Ballads of the Lumberjack	1958	$30
❏ RLP 12-640 [M]	Wanted for Murder -- American Folksongs of Outlaws and Desperadoes	1958	$30

STINSON
| ❏ SLP-70 [10] | Waters of Tyme -- English North Country Songs | 1958 | $40 |
| ❏ SLP-69 [10] | Whaling Songs and Ballads | 1958 | $40 |

TRADITION
| ❏ TLP-1005 [M] | Whaling and Sailing Songs from the Days of Moby Dick | 1956 | $30 |

CLAYTON, STEVE
SOVEREIGN
| ❏ SOV-501 | All Aglow Again | 1986 | $25 |
| ❏ SOV-500 | Inner Spark | 1985 | $25 |

CLAYTON-THOMAS, DAVID
ABC
| ❏ AA-1104 | Clayton | 1978 | $12 |
COLUMBIA
| ❏ KC31000 | David Clayton-Thomas | 1972 | $18 |
| ❏ KC31700 | Tequila Sunrise | 1972 | $18 |
DECCA
| ❏ DL75146 | David Clayton-Thomas! | 1969 | $25 |
RCA VICTOR
| ❏ APL1-0173 | David Clayton-Thomas | 1973 | $15 |
| ❏ APD1-0173 [Q] | David Clayton-Thomas | 1973 | $30 |

CLAYTON BROTHERS, THE
CONCORD JAZZ
| ❏ CJ-138 | It's All in the Family | 1980 | $25 |
| ❏ CJ-89 | The Clayton Brothers | 1978 | $25 |

CLEAN LIVING
VANGUARD
| ❏ VSD-79318 [B] | Clean Living | 1972 | $15 |
| ❏ VSD-79334 [B] | Meadow Muffin | 1973 | $15 |

CLEANLINESS AND GODLINESS SKIFFLE BAND,
VANGUARD
| ❏ VSD-79285 | Greatest Hits | 1968 | $30 |

CLEAR LIGHT
ELEKTRA
| ❏ EKL-4011 [M] | Clear Light | 1967 | $50 |
| ❏ EKS-74011 [S] | Clear Light | 1967 | $35 |
SUNDAZED
| ❏ LP5125 | Clear Light | 2002 | $15 |
| *—Reissue on 180-gram vinyl* | | | |

CLEARY, DON
PALOMINO
| ❏ 302 [M] | Don Cleary Sings Traditional Cowboy Songs | 1966 | $50 |

CLEAVER, ELDRIDGE
MORE
| ❏ 4000 [M] | Soul On Wax | 1968 | $30 |

Number	Title	Yr	NM
CLEFTONES, THE			
GEE			
❏ GLP-707 [M]	For Sentimental Reasons	1961	$300
❏ SGLP-707 [S]	For Sentimental Reasons	1961	$1200
❏ GLP-705 [M]	Heart and Soul	1961	$250
❏ SGLP-705 [S]	Heart and Soul	1961	$500

CLEMENT, JACK
ELEKTRA
| ❏ 6E-122 | All I Want to Do in Life | 1978 | $15 |

CLEMENTS, BOOTS
WEST
| ❏ WLP1005 | Walkin' Proud | 1986 | $12 |

CLEMENTS, VASSAR
FLYING FISH
❏ 038	Bluegrass Session	197?	$12
❏ 101	Hillbilly Jazz	197?	$18
❏ 385	Hillbilly Jazz Rides Again	1986	$12
❏ 073	Nashville Jam	197?	$15
❏ 232	Vassar	1980	$12
MCA
❏ 2270	Vassar Clements Band	1977	$18
❏ 695	Vassar Clements Band	198?	$10
—Budget-line reissue of 2270			
MERCURY
| ❏ SRM-1-1058 | Superbow | 1975 | $15 |
| ❏ SRM-1-1022 | Vassar Clements | 1975 | $15 |
MIND DUST
| ❏ MDM1002 | Westport Drive | 1984 | $15 |
ROUNDER
| ❏ 0016 | Crossing the Catskills | 198? | $15 |

CLEMONS, CLARENCE
COLUMBIA
❏ FC40917	A Night with Mr. C.	1989	$15
❏ FC40010	Hero	1985	$12
❏ BFC38933	Rescue	1983	$12

CLEVELAND, JAMES (REV.)
APOLLO
| ❏ LP-509 | In the Beginning | 197? | $18 |
HOB
❏ 239	Give Glory to God	197?	$18
❏ 233	Love of God	197?	$18
—With the Voices of Tabernacle			
❏ 253	The Best of James Cleveland	197?	$18
KENWOOD
| ❏ LP-509 | In the Beginning | 197? | $18 |
SAVOY
❏ MG-14260	Amazing Grace	197?	$25
—With the Southern California Community Choir			
❏ MG-14311	Down Memory Lane	197?	$18
❏ SL14412	Give It To Me	197?	$15
❏ MG-14352	God Has Smiled on Me	1975	$15
❏ MG-14131	He Leadeth Me	196?	$30
❏ MG-14282	I'll Do His Will	197?	$18
—With the Southern California Community Choir			
❏ SGL-7035	It's a New Day	1979	$18
—With the Southern California Community Choir			
❏ SGL-7071	I Want to Be Ready When You Come	1981	$25
—With the Los Angeles Chapter of the GMWA			
❏ MG-14159	Jame Cleveland in Hollywood	196?	$30
❏ MG-14211	James Cleveland and the Cleveland Singers	196?	$25
❏ MG-14265	James Cleveland and the Cleveland Singers	197?	$25
❏ SGL-7046	James Cleveland and the Voices of Cornerstone	1979	$18
❏ MG-14226	James Cleveland and the Voices of Tabernacle	196?	$25
❏ SGL-7059	James Cleveland Sings with the World's Greatest Choirs	1980	$18
❏ DBL-7014	Live at Carnegie Hall	1977	$18
❏ SGL-7038	Lord Let Me Be an Instrument	1979	$18
—With the Charles Fold Singers			
❏ MG-14195	Merry Christmas from James Cleveland and the Angelic Choir	196?	$30
❏ MG-14076	Peace Be Still	1964	$30
—With the Angelic Choir			
❏ MG-14269	Somehow I Can Sing	197?	$18
❏ MG-14176	Songs My Mother Taught Me	196?	$30
❏ SGL-7103	The Last Live Recording of the King of Gospel Music	1991	$18
—With the L.A. Gospel Messengers			
❏ SL14425	The Lord Is My Life	197?	$15
❏ MG-14252	The One and Only	197?	$25
❏ MG-14068	The Soul of James Cleveland	196?	$30
❏ MG-14085	The Sun Will Shine After Awhile	196?	$30
❏ SL14438	Think of His Goodness to You	197?	$15

Number	Title	Yr	NM
❏ SGL-7072	This, Too, Will Pass	1981	$25
— *With the Charles Fold Singers*			
❏ MG-14360	To the Glory of God	1975	$15
— *With the Southern California Community Choir*			
❏ SL14541	Victory Shall Be Mine	197?	$15
— *With the Salem Inspirational Choir*			
❏ DBL-7020	Volume 3/Recorded Live in Cincinnati, Ohio/(Is There Any Hope for) Tomorrow	1978	$18
— *With the Charles Fold Singers*			
❏ MG-14096	Volume 4	196?	$30
❏ MG-14205	Volume 8 -- Part 1	196?	$30
— *With the Angelic Choir*			
❏ SGL-7066	Where Is Your Faith	1981	$18
— *With the Southern California Community Choir*			

UPFRONT
Number	Title	Yr	NM
❏ UPF-163	I Walk with God	197?	$15
❏ UPF-190	Rev. James Cleveland	197?	$15

CLEVELAND, JIMMY
EMARCY
Number	Title	Yr	NM
❏ MG-36126 [M]	Cleveland Style	1958	$250
❏ MG-36066 [M]	Introducing Jimmy Cleveland and His All Stars	1956	$85
❏ MG-26003 [M]	Rhythm Crazy	1964	$150

MERCURY
Number	Title	Yr	NM
❏ MG-20442 [M]	A Map of Jimmy Cleveland	1959	$150
❏ SR-60117 [S]	A Map of Jimmy Cleveland	1959	$150
❏ MG-20553 [M]	Cleveland Style	1960	$150
❏ SR-60121 [S]	Cleveland Style	1959	$175

CLIBURN, VAN
RCA VICTOR RED SEAL
Number	Title	Yr	NM
❏ LM-2680 [M]	Beethoven: Piano Concerto No. 4	1963	$15
❏ LSC-2680 [S]	Beethoven: Piano Concerto No. 4	1963	$18
— *Shaded dog" pressing ("Living Stereo" on label)*			
❏ LSC-2680 [S]	Beethoven: Piano Concerto No. 4	1965	$15
— *White dog" pressing ("Stereo" on label)*			
❏ LSC-2680 [S]	Beethoven: Piano Concerto No. 4	1969	$12
— *No dog" pressing ("RCA" sideways at left)*			
❏ LM-2562 [M]	Beethoven: Piano Concerto No. 5 (Emperor Concerto)	1961	$18
❏ LSC-2562 [S]	Beethoven: Piano Concerto No. 5 (Emperor Concerto)	1961	$25
— *Shaded dog" pressing ("Living Stereo" on label)*			
❏ LSC-2562 [S]	Beethoven: Piano Concerto No. 5 (Emperor Concerto)	1964	$25
— *White dog" pressing ("Stereo" on label)*			
❏ LSC-2562 [S]	Beethoven: Piano Concerto No. 5 (Emperor Concerto)	1969	$15
— *No dog" pressing ("RCA" sideways at left)*			
❏ LM-2581 [M]	Brahms: Piano Concerto No. 2	1962	$18
❏ LSC-2581 [S]	Brahms: Piano Concerto No. 2	1962	$25
— *Shaded dog" pressing ("Living Stereo" on label)*			
❏ LSC-2581 [S]	Brahms: Piano Concerto No. 2	1965	$18
— *White dog" pressing ("Stereo" on label)*			
❏ LSC-2581 [S]	Brahms: Piano Concerto No. 2	1969	$15
— *No dog" pressing ("RCA" sideways at left)*			
❏ LSC-2581 [S]	Brahms: Piano Concerto No. 2	1976	$10
— *Late dog" pressing (dog near top)*			
❏ LM-2576 [M]	My Favorite Chopin	1962	$18
❏ LSC-2576 [S]	My Favorite Chopin	1962	$25
— *Shaded dog" pressing ("Living Stereo" on label)*			
❏ LSC-2576 [S]	My Favorite Chopin	1965	$18
— *White dog" pressing ("Stereo" on label)*			
❏ LSC-2576 [S]	My Favorite Chopin	1969	$15
— *No dog" pressing ("RCA" sideways at left)*			
❏ LSC-2576 [S]	My Favorite Chopin	1976	$10
— *Late dog" pressing (dog near top)*			
❏ LM-2507 [M]	Prokofiev: Piano Concerto No. 3; MacDowell: Piano Concerto No. 2	1961	$18
❏ LSC-2507 [S]	Prokofiev: Piano Concerto No. 3; MacDowell: Piano Concerto No. 2	1961	$30
— *Shaded dog" pressing ("Living Stereo" on label)*			
❏ LSC-2507 [S]	Prokofiev: Piano Concerto No. 3; MacDowell: Piano Concerto No. 2	1965	$30
— *White dog" pressing ("Stereo" on label)*			
❏ LSC-2507 [S]	Prokofiev: Piano Concerto No. 3; MacDowell: Piano Concerto No. 2	1969	$15
— *No dog" pressing ("RCA" sideways at left)*			
❏ LM-2601 [M]	Rachmaninoff: Piano Concerto No. 2	1962	$18
❏ LSC-2601 [S]	Rachmaninoff: Piano Concerto No. 2	1962	$25
— *Shaded dog" pressing ("Living Stereo" on label)*			
❏ LSC-2601 [S]	Rachmaninoff: Piano Concerto No. 2	1962	$18
— *White dog" pressing ("Stereo" on label)*			

Number	Title	Yr	NM
❏ LSC-2601 [S]	Rachmaninoff: Piano Concerto No. 2	1969	$15
— *No dog" pressing ("RCA" sideways at left)*			
❏ LM-2355 [M]	Rachmaninoff: Piano Concerto No. 3	1959	$25
❏ LSC-2355 [S]	Rachmaninoff: Piano Concerto No. 3	1959	$30
— *Shaded dog" pressing ("Living Stereo" on label)*			
❏ LSC-2355 [S]	Rachmaninoff: Piano Concerto No. 3	1965	$18
— *White dog" pressing ("Stereo" on label)*			
❏ LSC-2355 [S]	Rachmaninoff: Piano Concerto No. 3	1969	$15
— *No dog" pressing ("RCA" sideways at left)*			
❏ ARP1-4688	Rachmaninoff: Piano Concerto No. 3	198?	$12
— *Half-speed mastered reissue*			
❏ LM-2455 [M]	Schumann: Piano Concerto in A Minor	1960	$18
❏ LSC-2455 [S]	Schumann: Piano Concerto in A Minor	1960	$25
— *Shaded dog" pressing ("Living Stereo" on label)*			
❏ LSC-2455 [S]	Schumann: Piano Concerto in A Minor	1965	$18
— *White dog" pressing ("Stereo" on label)*			
❏ LSC-2455 [S]	Schumann: Piano Concerto in A Minor	1969	$15
— *No dog" pressing ("RCA" sideways at left)*			
❏ LM-2252 [M]	Tchaikovsky: Piano Concerto No. 1	1958	$25
❏ LSC-2252 [S]	Tchaikovsky: Piano Concerto No. 1	1958	$30
— *Shaded dog" pressing ("Living Stereo" on label)*			
❏ LSC-2252 [S]	Tchaikovsky: Piano Concerto No. 1	1965	$18
— *White dog" pressing ("Stereo" on label)*			
❏ LSC-2252 [S]	Tchaikovsky: Piano Concerto No. 1	1969	$15
— *No dog" pressing ("RCA" sideways at left)*			
❏ LSC-2252 [S]	Tchaikovsky: Piano Concerto No. 1	1976	$10
— *Late dog" pressing (dog near top)*			
❏ ARP1-4441	Tchaikovsky: Piano Concerto No. 1	198?	$12
— *Half-speed mastered reissue*			
❏ LSC-3323	The World's Favorite Piano Music	196?	$15

CLIFF, JIMMY
A&M
Number	Title	Yr	NM
❏ SP-4251	Wonderful World, Beautiful People	1970	$30
❏ SP-3189	Wonderful World, Beautiful People	198?	$10
— *Reissue of 4251*			

COLUMBIA
Number	Title	Yr	NM
❏ FC40002	Cliff Hanger	1985	$12
❏ FC40845	Hanging Fire	1988	$12
❏ FC38099	Special	1982	$12
❏ PC38099	Special	198?	$10
— *Budget-line reissue*			
❏ FC38986	The Power and the Glory	1983	$12
❏ PC38996	The Power and the Glory	1985	$10
— *Budget-line reissue*			

ISLAND
Number	Title	Yr	NM
❏ SW-9343	Struggling Man	1973	$25

MANGO
Number	Title	Yr	NM
❏ ILPS9235	Struggling Man	197?	$15
— *Reissue of Island SW-9343*			

MCA
Number	Title	Yr	NM
❏ 5217	Give the People What They Want	1981	$15
❏ 820	Give the People What They Want	198?	$10
— *Reissue of 5217*			
❏ 5153	I Am the Living	1980	$15
❏ 813	I Am the Living	198?	$10
— *Reissue of 5153*			

REPRISE
Number	Title	Yr	NM
❏ MS2218 [B]	Follow My Mind	1975	$18
❏ MS2256	In Concert: The Best of Jimmy Cliff	1976	$18
❏ MS2188	Music Maker	1974	$18
❏ MS2147	Unlimited	1973	$18

VEEP
Number	Title	Yr	NM
❏ VPS-16536	Can't Get Enough of It	1969	$40

WARNER BROS.
Number	Title	Yr	NM
❏ BSK3240	Give Thankx	1978	$15

CLIFFORD, BUZZ
COLUMBIA
Number	Title	Yr	NM
❏ CL1616 [M]	Baby Sittin' with Buzz	1961	$150
❏ CS8416 [S]	Baby Sittin' with Buzz	1961	$175

DOT
Number	Title	Yr	NM
❏ DLP-25965	See Your Way Clear	1969	$30

CLIFFORD, DOUG
FANTASY
Number	Title	Yr	NM
❏ 9411	Cosmo	1972	$18

CLIFFORD, MIKE
UNITED ARTISTS
Number	Title	Yr	NM
❏ UAL-3409 [M]	For the Love of Mike	1965	$25
❏ UAS-6409 [S]	For the Love of Mike	1965	$30

CLIFTON, BILL, AND THE DIXIE MOUNTAIN BOYS
STARDAY
Number	Title	Yr	NM
❏ SLP-271 [M]	Code of the Mountains	1965	$30
❏ SLP-111 [M]	Mountain Folk Songs	1959	$40
❏ SLP-213 [M]	Soldier, Sing Me a Song	1963	$30
❏ SLP-159 [M]	The Bluegrass Sound of Bill Clifton	1961	$30
❏ SLP-146 [M]	The Carter Family Memorial Album	1961	$30

CLIFTON, BILL
COLUMBIA
Number	Title	Yr	NM
❏ CL6166 [10]	Piano Moods	1951	$50

CLIMAX
ROCKY ROAD
Number	Title	Yr	NM
❏ 3506	Climax	1972	$18

CLIMAX BLUES BAND
SIRE
Number	Title	Yr	NM
❏ SES-4901	#3	1971	$18
❏ SAS-2-7411	FM/Live	1973	$18
❏ 2XS6013	FM/Live	1977	$15
❏ SASD-7523	Gold Plated	1976	$15
❏ SR6004	Lot of Bottle	1977	$12
❏ SRK3334	Real to Reel	1979	$12
❏ SES-7402	Rich Man	1972	$18
❏ SAS-7501	Sense of Direction	1974	$15
❏ SRK6056	Shine On	1978	$12
❏ SASD-7507	Stamp Album	1975	$15
❏ SR6016	Stamp Album	1977	$12
❏ SES-97013	The Climax Chicago Blues Band	1969	$18
❏ SR6003	The Climax Chicago Blues Band	1978	$12
❏ SES-97023	The Climax Chicago Blues Band Plays On	1970	$18
❏ SR6033	The Climax Chicago Blues Band Plays On	1978	$12
❏ SES-5903	Tightly Knit	1972	$18
❏ SR6008	Tightly Knit	1977	$12

VIRGIN/EPIC
Number	Title	Yr	NM
❏ FE38631	Sample and Hold	1983	$12

WARNER BROS.
Number	Title	Yr	NM
❏ BSK3493	Flying the Flag	1981	$15
❏ BSK3623	Lucky for Some	1982	$12

CLINE, PATSY
ACCORD
Number	Title	Yr	NM
❏ SN-7153	Let the Teardrops Fall	1981	$12

ALLEGIANCE
Number	Title	Yr	NM
❏ AV-5021	Stop, Look and Listen	198?	$12

CLEOPATRA
Number	Title	Yr	NM
❏ 8726 [B]	Walkin' After Midnight		$30
— *picture disc*			

DECCA
Number	Title	Yr	NM
❏ DL4508 [M]	A Portrait of Patsy Cline	1964	$30
❏ DL74508 [S]	A Portrait of Patsy Cline	1964	$40
❏ DL8611 [M]	Patsy Cline	1957	$150
— *Black label with silver print*			
❏ DL8611 [M]	Patsy Cline	1960	$50
— *Black label with color bars*			
❏ DL4854 [M]	Patsy Cline's Greatest Hits	1967	$25
❏ DL74854 [S]	Patsy Cline's Greatest Hits	1967	$30
❏ DL4202 [M]	Patsy Cline Showcase	1961	$40

Number	Title	Yr	NM
❏ DL74202 [S]	Patsy Cline Showcase	1961	$50
❏ DL4282 [M]	Sentimentally Yours	1962	$30
❏ DL74282 [S]	Sentimentally Yours	1962	$40
❏ DL4586 [M]	That's How a Heartache Begins	1964	$30
❏ DL74586 [S]	That's How a Heartache Begins	1964	$40

Number	Title	Yr	NM
❏ DXB176 [M]	The Patsy Cline Story	1963	$40
❏ DXSB7176 [S]	The Patsy Cline Story	1963	$50
EVEREST			
❏ 5204 [M]	Encores	1962	$25
❏ 1204 [R]	Encores	1962	$15
❏ 5200 [M]	Golden Hits	1962	$25
❏ 1200 [R]	Golden Hits	1962	$15
❏ ST-90070 [R]	Golden Hits	1962	$18
—*Capitol Record Club edition*			
❏ 5217 [M]	In Memoriam	1963	$25
❏ 1217 [R]	In Memoriam	1963	$15
❏ 5223 [M]	Legend	1963	$25
❏ 5229 [M]	Reflections	1964	$25
❏ 1229 [R]	Reflections	1964	$15
HILLTOP			
❏ 6148	Country Music Hall of Fame	197?	$12
❏ 6016 [M]	I Can't Forget You	1966	$15
❏ S-6016 [R]	I Can't Forget You	1966	$12
❏ JS-6072	In Care of the Blues	1969	$12
❏ S-6039	Stop the World	1968	$12
❏ 6001 [M]	Today, Tomorrow, Forever	1965	$15
❏ S-6001 [R]	Today, Tomorrow, Forever	1965	$12
MCA			
❏ 3263	Always	1980	$18
❏ 27069	Always	198?	$10
❏ 224	A Portrait of Patsy Cline	1973	$15
—*Reissue of Decca 74508; black label with rainbow*			
❏ 738	Here's Patsy Cline	198?	$12
—*Reissue of Vocalion 73753*			
❏ 42142	Live at the Opry	1988	$12
❏ 42284	Live Volume 2	1989	$15
❏ 12	Patsy Cline's Greatest Hits	1973	$15
—*Reissue of Decca 74854; black label with rainbow*			
❏ 12	Patsy Cline's Greatest Hits	1977	$12
—*Tan label*			
❏ 12	Patsy Cline's Greatest Hits	1980	$10
—*Blue label with rainbow*			
❏ 87	Patsy Cline Showcase	1973	$15
—*Reissue of Decca 74202; black label with rainbow*			
❏ 90	Sentimentally Yours	1973	$15
—*Reissue of Decca 74282; black label with rainbow*			
❏ 1440	Stop, Look and Listen	198?	$10
❏ 6149	Sweet Dreams -- The Life and Times of Patsy Cline	1985	$12
❏ 736	The Great Patsy Cline	198?	$12
—*Reissue of Vocalion 73872*			
❏ 4038	The Patsy Cline Story	1974	$18
—*Reissue of Decca 7176; black labels with rainbow*			
❏ 1463	Today, Tomorrow and Forever	198?	$10
METRO			
❏ M-540 [M]	Gotta Lot of Rhythm in My Soul	1965	$15
❏ MS-540 [R]	Gotta Lot of Rhythm in My Soul	1965	$12
RHINO			
❏ R1-70048	Her First Recordings, Vol. 1: Walkin' Dreams	1989	$15
❏ R1-70049	Her First Recordings, Vol. 2: Hungry for Love	1989	$15
❏ R1-70050	Her First Recordings, Vol. 3: The Rockin' Side	1989	$15
SEARS			
❏ SPS-112	I Can't Forget You	1968	$30
❏ SPS-127	In Care of the Blues	1968	$30
❏ SP-102 [M]	Walkin' After Midnight	196?	$30
❏ SPS-102 [R]	Walkin' After Midnight	196?	$25
VOCALION			
❏ VL73872	Country Great!	1969	$12
❏ VL3753 [M]	Here's Patsy Cline	1965	$15
❏ VL73753 [R]	Here's Patsy Cline	1965	$12

CLINTON, GEORGE

Number	Title	Yr	NM
550 MUSIC			
❏ B267144	T.A.P.O.A.F.O.M. -- The Awesome Power of a Fully Operational Mothership	1996	$18
—*Red vinyl*			
ABC			
❏ D-831	The George Clinton Band Arrives	1974	$18
CAPITOL			
❏ ST-12246	Computer Games	1982	$12
❏ C1-33911	Greatest Funkin' Hits	1996	$15
—*Red vinyl*			
❏ ST-12481	R&B Skeletons in the Closet	1986	$12
❏ ST-12417	Some of My Best Jokes Are Friends	1985	$12
❏ CJ-48424	The Best of George Clinton	1987	$12
❏ MLP-15021 [EP]	The Mothership Connection Live from Houston, Texas	1986	$18
❏ ST-12308	You Shouldn't-Nuf Bit Fish	1984	$12
INVICTUS			
❏ ST-9815	Black Vampire	1973	$25
PAISLEY PARK			
❏ PRO-A-6537 [DJ]	Hey Man... Smell My Finger	1993	$30
—*Promo-only vinyl issue*			
❏ 25994	The Cinderella Theory	1989	$15

Number	Title	Yr	NM
WARNER BROS.			
❏ 25887	George Clinton Presents Our Gang Funky	1988	$12
❏ 25991	Under a Nouveau Groove	1989	$12

CLINTON, LARRY

Number	Title	Yr	NM
CIRCLE			
❏ 58	Larry Clinton and His Orchestra 1941 and 1949	198?	$25
EVEREST			
❏ LPBR-5096 [M]	My Million Sellers	196?	$25
❏ SDBR-1096 [S]	My Million Sellers	196?	$30
HINDSIGHT			
❏ HSR-109	Larry Clinton and His Orchestra 1937-38	198?	$25
RCA CAMDEN			
❏ CAL-434 [M]	Dance Date	1958	$50
SUNBEAM			
❏ 208	Larry Clinton and His Orchestra 1937-41	198?	$25

CLIQUE, THE (1)

Number	Title	Yr	NM
WHITE WHALE			
❏ WWS-7126	The Clique	1969	$25

CLOONEY, ROSEMARY, AND BING CROSBY

Number	Title	Yr	NM
CAPITOL			
❏ T2300 [M]	That Travelin' Two-Beat	1965	$25
❏ ST2300 [S]	That Travelin' Two-Beat	1965	$75
RCA CAMDEN			
❏ CAS-2330	Rendezvous	1968	$18
RCA VICTOR			
❏ LPM-1854 [M]	Fancy Meeting You Here	1958	$25
❏ LSP-1854 [S]	Fancy Meeting You Here	1958	$30

CLOONEY, ROSEMARY

Number	Title	Yr	NM
COLUMBIA			
❏ CL2572 [10]	A Date with the King	1956	$50
❏ CL872 [M]	Blue Rose	1956	$40
❏ CL2569 [10]	Children's Favorites	1955	$75
❏ CL969 [M]	Clooney Tunes	1957	$100
❏ CL6224 [10]	Hollywood's Best	1952	$75
❏ CL585 [M]	Hollywood's Best	1955	$75
❏ CL2597 [10]	My Fair Lady	1956	$50
❏ CL2581 [10]	On Stage	1956	$50
❏ CL1006 [M]	Ring Around the Rosie	1957	$40
—*With the Hi-Lo's*			
❏ CL6297 [10]	Rosemary Clooney (While We're Young)	1954	$75
❏ CL1230 [M]	Rosie's Greatest Hits	1958	$40
—*Six "eye" logos on label*			
❏ CL1230 [M]	Rosie's Greatest Hits	1962	$30
—*Guaranteed High Fidelity" on label*			
❏ CL1230 [M]	Rosie's Greatest Hits	1965	$25
—*360 Sound Mono" on label*			
❏ CL2525 [10]	Tenderly	1955	$75
❏ CL6338 [10]	White Christmas	1954	$120
COLUMBIA SPECIAL PRODUCTS			
❏ P13085	Blue Rose	197?	$15
❏ P14382	Come On-a My House	197?	$15
❏ P13083	Hollywood's Best	197?	$15
CONCORD JAZZ			
❏ CJ-47	Everything's Coming Up Rosie	1978	$15
❏ CJ-81	Here's to My Lady	1979	$15
❏ CJ-226	My Buddy	1984	$15
—*With Woody Herman*			
❏ CJ-282	Rosemary Clooney Sings Ballads	1985	$15
❏ CJ-185	Rosemary Clooney Sings Cole Porter	1982	$15
❏ CJ-210	Rosemary Clooney Sings Harold Arlen	1983	$15
❏ CJ-112	Rosemary Clooney Sings Ira Gershwin	1980	$15
❏ CJ-333	Rosemary Clooney Sings the Lyrics of Johnny Mercer	1988	$15
❏ CJ-255	Rosemary Clooney Sings the Music of Irving Berlin	1985	$15
❏ CJ-308	Rosemary Clooney Sings the Music of Jimmy Van Heusen	1987	$15
❏ CJ-60	Rosie Sings Bing	1979	$15
❏ CJ-364	Show Tunes	1989	$15
❏ CJ-144	With Love	1981	$30
CORAL			
❏ CRL57266 [M]	Swing Around Rosie	1959	$30
❏ CRL757266 [S]	Swing Around Rosie	1959	$40
HARMONY			
❏ HL7213 [M]	Hollywood Hits	195?	$30
❏ HL7454 [M]	Mixed Emotions	1968	$25
❏ HS11254 [M]	Mixed Emotions	1968	$15
❏ HL7123 [M]	Rosemary Clooney in High Fidelity	195?	$30
❏ HL9501 [M]	Rosemary Clooney Sings for Children	196?	$25
HINDSIGHT			
❏ HSR-234	Rosemary Clooney 1951-1952	1988	$12

Number	Title	Yr	NM
HOLIDAY			
❏ 1946	Christmas with Rosemary Clooney	1981	$12
MGM			
❏ E-3782 [M]	Hymns from the Heart	1959	$30
❏ SE-3782 [S]	Hymns from the Heart	1959	$40
❏ E-3687 [M]	Oh, Captain!	1958	$40
❏ E-3834 [M]	Rosie Clooney Swings Softly	1960	$30
❏ SE-3834 [S]	Rosie Clooney Swings Softly	1960	$40
MISTLETOE			
❏ MLP-1234	Christmas with Rosemary Clooney	1978	$15
RCA VICTOR			
❏ LPM-2133 [M]	A Touch of Tabasco	1960	$25
❏ LSP-2133 [S]	A Touch of Tabasco	1960	$30
❏ LPM-2212 [M]	Clap Hands, Here Comes Rosie	1960	$25
❏ LSP-2212 [S]	Clap Hands, Here Comes Rosie	1960	$30
❏ LPM-2565 [M]	Country Hits from the Heart	1963	$25
❏ LSP-2565 [S]	Country Hits from the Heart	1963	$30
❏ LPM-2265 [M]	Rosie Solves the Swingin' Riddle	1961	$25
❏ LSP-2265 [S]	Rosie Solves the Swingin' Riddle	1961	$30
REPRISE			
❏ R-6088 [M]	Love	1963	$30
❏ R9-6088 [S]	Love	1963	$40
❏ R-6108 [M]	Thanks for Nothing	1964	$30
❏ RS-6108 [S]	Thanks for Nothing	1964	$40
TIME-LIFE			
❏ SLGD-16	Legendary Singers: Rosemary Clooney	1986	$20

CLOONEY SISTERS, THE
Also see ROSEMARY CLOONEY.

Number	Title	Yr	NM
EPIC			
❏ LN3160 [M]	The Clooney Sisters with Tony Pastor	1956	$75

CLOUD, BRUCE

Number	Title	Yr	NM
CAPITOL			
❏ ST-343	California Soul	1969	$25

CLOVER, TIMOTHY

Number	Title	Yr	NM
TOWER			
❏ ST5114	A Harvard Square Affair	1968	$25

CLOVER

Number	Title	Yr	NM
FANTASY			
❏ 8395	Clover	1969	$30
❏ 8405	Forty-Niner	1970	$30

CLOVERS, THE

Number	Title	Yr	NM
ATCO			
❏ SD 33-374	Their Greatest Recordings/ The Early Years	1971	$15
ATLANTIC			
❏ 8034 [M]	Dance Party	1959	$400
—*Black label*			
❏ 8034 [M]	Dance Party	1960	$300
—*White "bullseye" label*			
❏ 8034 [M]	Dance Party	1961	$250
—*Red and white label*			

Number	Title	Yr	NM
❏ 1248 [M]	The Clovers	1956	$600
❏ 8009 [M]	The Clovers	1957	$400
—*Reissue of 1248 on the "pop" series; black label*			
❏ 8009 [M]	The Clovers	1960	$300
—*White "bullseye" label*			
❏ 8009 [M]	The Clovers	1961	$250
—*Red and white label*			
GRAND PRIX			
❏ K-428 [M]	The Original Love Potion Number Nine	1964	$30
❏ KS-428 [R]	The Original Love Potion Number Nine	1964	$15
POPLAR			
❏ 1001 [M]	The Clovers In Clover	1958	$400
UNITED ARTISTS			
❏ UAL-3099 [M]	Love Potion Number Nine	1959	$300

Number	Title	Yr	NM
❏ UAS-6099 [S]	Love Potion Number Nine	1959	$500
❏ UAL-3033 [M]	The Clovers In Clover	1959	$300
❏ UAS-6033 [R]	The Clovers In Clover	196?	$250

CLOWER, JERRY

DECCA

Number	Title	Yr	NM
❏ DL75286	From Yazoo City, Mississippi Talkin'	1971	$15
❏ DL75342	Mouth of Mississippi	1972	$15

MCA

Number	Title	Yr	NM
❏ 5602	An Officer and a Ledbetter	1985	$12
❏ 42178	Classic Clower	1988	$12
❏ 317	Clower Power	1973	$12
❏ 417	Country Ham	1974	$12
❏ 5321	Dogs I Have Known	1982	$12
❏ 33	From Yazoo City, Mississippi Talkin'	1973	$12

— *Reissue of Decca 75286*

Number	Title	Yr	NM
❏ 3152	Greatest Hits	1979	$12
❏ 5422	Live at Cleburne, Texas	1983	$12
❏ 3062	Live from the Stage of the Grand Ole Opry!	1979	$12
❏ 486	Live in Picayune	1975	$12
❏ 5215	More Good 'Uns	1981	$12
❏ 47	Mouth of Mississippi	1973	$12

— *Reissue of Decca 75342*

Number	Title	Yr	NM
❏ 2281	On the Road	1978	$12
❏ 5773	Runaway Truck	1986	$12
❏ 5491	Starke Raving	1984	$12
❏ 2205	The Ambassador of Goodwill	1976	$12
❏ 3247	The Ledbetter Olympics	1980	$12
❏ 42034	Top Gum	1987	$12

WORD

Number	Title	Yr	NM
❏ WSB-8737	Ain't God Good!	197?	$15

CLUB NOUVEAU

RIP-IT

Number	Title	Yr	NM
❏ 9004	Everything Is Black	1995	$18

WARNER BROS.

Number	Title	Yr	NM
❏ 25531	Life, Love & Pain	1986	$10
❏ 25687	Listen to the Message	1988	$10
❏ 25991	Under a Nouveau Groove	1989	$12

CLUSTER & ENO

4 MEN WITH BEARDS

Number	Title	Yr	NM
❏ 4M141LP [B]	Cluster & Eno		$25

CLUSTER

4 MEN WITH BEARDS

Number	Title	Yr	NM
❏ 4M140LP [B]	Cluster '71		$25
❏ 4M162LP [B]	Sowiesoso		$25

COASTERS, THE

ATCO

Number	Title	Yr	NM
❏ 33-135 [M]	Coast Along with the Coasters	1962	$150

— *Gold and gray label*

Number	Title	Yr	NM
❏ SD 33-135 [P]	Coast Along with the Coasters	1962	$175

— *Purple and brown label; "Wait a Minute" is rechanneled*

Number	Title	Yr	NM
❏ 33-123 [M]	One By One	1960	$175

— *Yellow "harp" label*

Number	Title	Yr	NM
❏ SD 33-123 [S]	One By One	1960	$400

— *Yellow "harp" label*

Number	Title	Yr	NM
❏ 33-123 [M]	One By One	196?	$75

— *Gold and gray label*

Number	Title	Yr	NM
❏ SD 33-123 [S]	One By One	196?	$175

— *Purple and brown label*

Number	Title	Yr	NM
❏ 33-101 [M]	The Coasters	1958	$300

— *Yellow "harp" label*

Number	Title	Yr	NM
❏ 33-101 [M]	The Coasters	196?	$75

— *Gold and dark blue label*

Number	Title	Yr	NM
❏ 33-111 [M]	The Coasters' Greatest Hits	1959	$175

— *Yellow "harp" label*

Number	Title	Yr	NM
❏ 33-111 [M]	The Coasters' Greatest Hits	196?	$75

— *Gold and gray label*

Number	Title	Yr	NM
❏ SD 33-371	Their Greatest Recordings/ The Early Years	1971	$25

CLARION

Number	Title	Yr	NM
❏ 605 [M]	That Is Rock and Roll	1965	$40
❏ SD605 [S]	That Is Rock and Roll	1965	$50

KING

Number	Title	Yr	NM
❏ KS-1146	The Coasters On Broadway	1971	$30

POWER PAK

Number	Title	Yr	NM
❏ 310	Greatest Hits	198?	$12

TRIP

Number	Title	Yr	NM
❏ 8028	It Ain't Sanitary	197?	$15

COATES, JOHN, JR.

OMNISOUND

Number	Title	Yr	NM
❏ 1021	After the Before	1978	$30
❏ 1015	Alone and Live at the Deer Head	1977	$30
❏ 1022	In the Open Space	1979	$35
❏ 1038	Pocono Friends	1981	$35
❏ 1045	Pocono Friends Encore	1982	$30

Number	Title	Yr	NM
❏ 1024	Rainbow Road	1979	$30
❏ 1004	The Jazz Piano of John Coates, Jr.	197?	$30
❏ 1032	Tokyo Concert	1980	$30

SAVOY

Number	Title	Yr	NM
❏ MG-12082 [M]	Portrait	1956	$40

COBB, ARNETT; DIZZY GILLESPIE; JEWEL BROWN

FANTASY

Number	Title	Yr	NM
❏ F-9659	Show Time	1987	$30

COBB, ARNETT

APOLLO

Number	Title	Yr	NM
❏ LAP-105 [10]	Swingin' with Arnett Cobb	1952	$300

BEE HIVE

Number	Title	Yr	NM
❏ BH-7017	Keep On Pushin'	1985	$30

CLASSIC JAZZ

Number	Title	Yr	NM
❏ 102	The Wild Man from Texas	1976	$35

FANTASY

Number	Title	Yr	NM
❏ OJC-219	Party Time	198?	$25
❏ OJC-323	Smooth Sailing	1988	$25

HOME COOKING

Number	Title	Yr	NM
❏ HCS-114	The Wild Man from Texas	1990	$30

— *Reissue of Classic Jazz 102*

MOODSVILLE

Number	Title	Yr	NM
❏ MVLP-14 [M]	Ballads by Cobb	1961	$50

— *Green label*

Number	Title	Yr	NM
❏ MVLP-14 [M]	Ballads by Cobb	1965	$30

— *Blue label, trident logo at right*

MUSE

Number	Title	Yr	NM
❏ MR-5191	Live at Sandy's	1977	$30
❏ MR-5236	More Live at Sandy's	1979	$30

PRESTIGE

Number	Title	Yr	NM
❏ PRLP-7151 [M]	Blow, Arnett, Blow	1959	$250

— *Yellow label*

Number	Title	Yr	NM
❏ PRLP-7151 [M]	Blow, Arnett, Blow	1963	$30

— *Blue label, trident logo at right*

Number	Title	Yr	NM
❏ PRST-7151 [R]	Blow, Arnett, Blow	196?	$30
❏ PRST-7835	Go Power!	1970	$35
❏ PRLP-7175 [M]	More Party Time	1960	$250

— *Yellow label*

Number	Title	Yr	NM
❏ PRLP-7175 [M]	More Party Time	1963	$30

— *Blue label, trident logo at right*

Number	Title	Yr	NM
❏ PRLP-7216 [M]	Movin' Right Along	1961	$150

— *Yellow label*

Number	Title	Yr	NM
❏ PRLP-7216 [M]	Movin' Right Along	1963	$30

— *Blue label, trident logo at right*

Number	Title	Yr	NM
❏ PRLP-7165 [M]	Party Time	1959	$250

— *Yellow label*

Number	Title	Yr	NM
❏ PRLP-7165 [M]	Party Time	1963	$30

— *Blue label, trident logo at right*

Number	Title	Yr	NM
❏ PRLP-7227 [M]	Sizzlin'	1962	$175

— *Yellow label*

Number	Title	Yr	NM
❏ PRLP-7227 [M]	Sizzlin'	1963	$25

— *Blue label, trident logo at right*

Number	Title	Yr	NM
❏ PRST-7227 [S]	Sizzlin'	1962	$175

— *Silver label*

Number	Title	Yr	NM
❏ PRST-7227 [S]	Sizzlin'	1963	$30

— *Blue label, trident logo at right*

Number	Title	Yr	NM
❏ PRLP-7184 [M]	Smooth Sailing	1960	$250

— *Yellow label*

Number	Title	Yr	NM
❏ PRLP-7184 [M]	Smooth Sailing	1963	$30

— *Blue label, trident logo at right*

Number	Title	Yr	NM
❏ PRST-7711	The Best of Arnett Cobb	1969	$35

PROGRESSIVE

Number	Title	Yr	NM
❏ 7037	Arnett Cobb Is Back!	1978	$30
❏ 7054	Funky Butt	1981	$30

COBB, JUNIE C.

RIVERSIDE

Number	Title	Yr	NM
❏ RLP-415 [M]	Junie C. Cobb and His New Hometown Band	1962	$175
❏ RS-9415 [S]	Junie C. Cobb and His New Hometown Band	1962	$175

COBHAM, BILLY, AND GEORGE DUKE

ATLANTIC

Number	Title	Yr	NM
❏ SD18194	Live On Tour in Europe	1976	$25

COBHAM, BILLY

ATLANTIC

Number	Title	Yr	NM
❏ SD18149	A Funky Thide of Sings	1975	$30
❏ SD7300	Crosswinds	1974	$35

— *Original pressings have "1841 Broadway" address on label*

Number	Title	Yr	NM
❏ SD19174	Inner Conflicts	1978	$30
❏ SD18166	Life & Times	1976	$30
❏ SD18139	Shabazz (Recorded Live in Europe)	1975	$35
❏ SD7268	Spectrum	1973	$35

— *Original pressings have "1841 Broadway" address on label*

Number	Title	Yr	NM
❏ SD19238	The Best of Billy Cobham	1979	$30
❏ SD18121	Total Eclipse	1974	$35

COLUMBIA

Number	Title	Yr	NM
❏ JC35993	B.C.	1979	$30
❏ JC34939	Magic	1977	$30
❏ JC35457	Simplicity of Expression – Depth of Thought	1978	$30
❏ JC36400	The Best of Billy Cobham	1980	$30

ELEKTRA/MUSICIAN

Number	Title	Yr	NM
❏ 60123	Observations &	1982	$35
❏ 60233	Smokin'	1983	$35

GRP

Number	Title	Yr	NM
❏ GR-9575	Billy's Best Hits	1988	$25
❏ GR-1040	Picture This	1987	$25
❏ GR-1027	Power Play	1986	$25
❏ GR-1020	Warning	1986	$30

COCHRAN, CHARLES

AUDIOPHILE

Number	Title	Yr	NM
❏ AP-177	Haunted Heart	1982	$30

COCHRAN, EDDIE

EMI AMERICA

Number	Title	Yr	NM
❏ SQ17245	On the Air	1987	$18

LIBERTY

Number	Title	Yr	NM
❏ LRP-3172 [M]	Eddie Cochran (12 of His Biggest Hits)	1960	$120
❏ LN-10204	Great Hits	198?	$10
❏ LRP-3220 [M]	Never to Be Forgotten	1962	$150
❏ LRP-3061 [M]	Singin' to My Baby	1957	$800

— *Green label*

Number	Title	Yr	NM
❏ LRP-3061 [M]	Singin' to My Baby	1960	$300

— *Black label*

Number	Title	Yr	NM
❏ LN-10137	Singin' to My Baby	198?	$15

— *Budget-line reissue*

SUNSET

Number	Title	Yr	NM
❏ SUM-1123 [M]	Summertime Blues	1966	$40
❏ SUS-5123 [R]	Summertime Blues	1966	$30

UNITED ARTISTS

Number	Title	Yr	NM
❏ UAS-9959 [B]	Legendary Masters Series #4	1972	$30
❏ UA-LA428-E	The Very Best of Eddie Cochran	1975	$15

COCHRAN, HANK

CAPITOL

Number	Title	Yr	NM
❏ ST-11807	With a Little Help from His Friends	1978	$15

ELEKTRA

Number	Title	Yr	NM
❏ 6E-277	Make the World Go Away	1980	$12

MONUMENT

Number	Title	Yr	NM
❏ SLP-18089	The Heart of Hank	1968	$25

RCA VICTOR

Number	Title	Yr	NM
❏ LPM-3431 [M]	Going in Training	1965	$25
❏ LSP-3431 [S]	Going in Training	1965	$30
❏ LPM-3303 [M]	Hits from the Heart	1965	$25
❏ LSP-3303 [S]	Hits from the Heart	1965	$30

COCHRAN, TODD

VITAL

Number	Title	Yr	NM
❏ VTL-001	Todd	1991	$25

COCHRAN, WAYNE

BETHLEHEM

Number	Title	Yr	NM
❏ 10002	High and Ridin'	1970	$18

CHESS

Number	Title	Yr	NM
❏ LPS-1519	Wayne Cochran!	1968	$40

EPIC

Number	Title	Yr	NM
❏ KE30889	Cochran	1972	$18

KING

Number	Title	Yr	NM
❏ KS-1116	Alive and Well	1970	$25

COCHRANE, MICHAEL

SOUL NOTE

Number	Title	Yr	NM
❏ SN-1151	Elements	198?	$30

Number	Title	Yr	NM

COCKBURN, BRUCE

EPIC

| ❏ KE31768 | Sunwheel Dance | 1972 | $25 |
| ❏ E30812 | True North | 1971 | $25 |

GOLD CASTLE

| ❏ D1-71320 | Big Circumstance | 1988 | $10 |
| ❏ 171009-1 | Dancing in the Dragon's Jaws | 1987 | $10 |

— Reissue of Gold Mountain GM-3276

| ❏ 171010-1 | Stealing Fire | 1987 | $10 |

— Reissue of Gold Mountain GM-80012

| ❏ 171008-1 | The Trouble with Normal | 1987 | $10 |

— Reissue of Gold Mountain GM-3283

| ❏ 171005-1 | Waiting for a Miracle | 1987 | $15 |

GOLD MOUNTAIN

| ❏ GM-3276 | Dancing in the Dragon's Jaws | 1985 | $10 |

— Reissue of Millennium BXL1-7747

| ❏ GM-80012 | Stealing Fire | 1984 | $10 |
| ❏ GM-3283 | The Trouble with Normal | 1985 | $10 |

ISLAND

❏ ILTA9475	Circles in the Stream	1977	$18
❏ ILSP9528	Furhter Adventures of	1978	$15
❏ ILTN9463	In the Falling Dark	1976	$15

MCA

| ❏ 5772 | World of Wonders | 1986 | $10 |

MILLENNIUM

❏ BXL1-7747 [B]	Dancing in the Dragon's Jaws	1979	$12
❏ BXL1-7752	Humans	1980	$12
❏ BXL1-7761	Inner City Front	1981	$12
❏ DJL1-3830 [DJ]	RCA College Radio Series, Vol. II	1980	$25

— Promo-only music and interview

| ❏ DJL1-3583 [DJ] | RCA Special Radio Series | 1980 | $25 |

— Promo-only music and interview

| ❏ BXL1-7757 | Resume | 1981 | $12 |
| ❏ DJL1-0(# unknown) [DJ] | Selected Cuts from 1980 U.S. Tour | 1980 | $50 |

— Promo-only four-song live EP

COCKER, JOE

A&M

❏ SP-3633	I Can Stand a Little Rain	1974	$12
❏ SP-3175	I Can Stand a Little Rain	1980	$10
❏ SP-4529	Jamaica Say You Will	1975	$12
❏ SP-4368	Joe Cocker	1972	$15

— Brown label

| ❏ SP-4368 | Joe Cocker | 1974 | $12 |

— Silver label

| ❏ SP-4224 | Joe Cocker! | 1969 | $15 |

— Brown label

| ❏ SP-4224 | Joe Cocker! | 1974 | $12 |

— Silver label

| ❏ QU-54224 [Q] | Joe Cocker! | 1974 | $0 |

— Not released

❏ SP-4670	Joe Cocker's Greatest Hits	1977	$12
❏ SP-3257	Joe Cocker's Greatest Hits	1982	$10
❏ SP-6002	Mad Dogs and Englishmen	1970	$18

— Brown labels

| ❏ SP-6002 | Mad Dogs and Englishmen | 1974 | $15 |

— Silver labels

| ❏ SP-4574 | Stingray | 1976 | $12 |
| ❏ SP-4182 | With a Little Help from My Friends | 1969 | $15 |

— Brown label

| ❏ SP-4182 | With a Little Help from My Friends | 1974 | $12 |

— Silver label

| ❏ SP-3106 | With a Little Help from My Friends | 1980 | $10 |
| ❏ QU-54182 [Q] | With a Little Help from My Friends | 1974 | $0 |

— Not released

ASYLUM

| ❏ DP-400 [PD] | Luxury You Can Afford | 1978 | $18 |
| ❏ 6E-145 | Luxury You Can Afford | 1978 | $12 |

CAPITOL

❏ ST-12335	Civilized Man	1984	$12
❏ ST-12394	Cocker	1986	$12
❏ C1-92861	One Night of Sin	1989	$15
❏ CLT-48285	Unchain My Heart	1988	$12

ISLAND

| ❏ 90096 | One More Time | 1983 | $12 |
| ❏ IL9750 | Sheffield Steel | 1982 | $12 |

MOBILE FIDELITY

| ❏ 1-223 | Sheffield Steel | 1995 | $40 |

— Audiophile vinyl

COCTEAU TWINS

CAPITOL

| ❏ C1-90892 | Blue Bell Knoll | 1988 | $15 |
| ❏ SPRO79066/7 [DJ] | Cocteau Twins | 1991 | $75 |

— Promo-only 10-song collection

| ❏ C1-93669 | Heaven Or Las Vegas | 1990 | $18 |

RELATIVITY/4AD

| ❏ 88561-8141-1 [EP] | Love's Easy Tears | 1986 | $15 |
| ❏ 88561-8143-1 | The Moon and the Melodies | 1987 | $50 |

— With Harold Budd

| ❏ EMC8040 | The Pink Opaque | 1986 | $15 |

CODONA

ECM

❏ 1132	Codona	1979	$30
❏ 1177	Codona 2	1980	$30
❏ 23785	Codona 3	1983	$30

COE, DAVID ALLAN

COLUMBIA

❏ FC40571	A Matter of Life... And Death	1987	$12
❏ FC38318	Biggest Hits	1982	$12
❏ FC38535	Castles in the Sand	1983	$12
❏ PC38535	Castles in the Sand	1985	$10

— Budget-line reissue with new prefix

| ❏ JC36277 | Compass Point | 1980 | $12 |
| ❏ PC36277 | Compass Point | 198? | $10 |

— Budget-line reissue with new prefix

❏ FC45057	Crazy Daddy	1989	$12
❏ FC38093	D.A.C.	1982	$12
❏ FC39617	Darlin', Darlin'	1985	$12
❏ PC34310	David Allan Coe Rides Again	1977	$12
❏ FC37352	Encore	1981	$12
❏ PC37352	Encore	198?	$10

— Budget-line reissue with new prefix

❏ KC35306	Family Album	1978	$12
❏ KC239585	For the Record -- The First 10 Years	1984	$15
❏ KC35627	Greatest Hits	1978	$12
❏ PC35627	Greatest Hits	198?	$10

— Budget-line reissue

❏ FC38926	Hello In There	1983	$12
❏ KC35535	Human Emotions -- Happy Side/Su-I-Side	1978	$12
❏ JC36970	Invictus (Means) Unconquered	1981	$12
❏ PC36970	Invictus (Means) Unconquered	198?	$10

— Budget-line reissue with new prefix

| ❏ JC36489 | I've Got Something to Say | 1980 | $12 |
| ❏ PC36489 | I've Got Something to Say | 198? | $10 |

— Budget-line reissue with new prefix

| ❏ FC39269 | Just Divorced | 1984 | $12 |
| ❏ PC39269 | Just Divorced | 1986 | $10 |

— Budget-line reissue with new prefix

❏ PC33916	Longhaired Redneck	1976	$12
❏ KC32942	Mysterious Rhinestone Cowboy	1974	$15
❏ PC32942	Mysterious Rhinestone Cowboy	197?	$12

— Early reissue with new prefix and no bar code

| ❏ KC33085 | Once Upon a Rhyme | 1975 | $15 |
| ❏ PC33085 | Once Upon a Rhyme | 197? | $12 |

— Early reissue with new prefix and no bar code

| ❏ FC37736 | Rough Rider | 1982 | $12 |
| ❏ PC37736 | Rough Rider | 198? | $10 |

— Budget-line reissue with new prefix

❏ FC40346	Son of the South	1986	$12
❏ KC35789	Spectrum, VII	1979	$12
❏ PC34780	Tattoo	1977	$12
❏ FC37454	Tennessee Whiskey	1981	$12
❏ PC37454	Tennessee Whiskey	198?	$10

— Budget-line reissue with new prefix

| ❏ FC40195 | Unchained | 1985 | $12 |

PAIR

| ❏ PDL2-1075 | Best of David Allan Coe | 1986 | $15 |

PLANTATION

| ❏ 507 | Texas Moon | 197? | $18 |

SSS INTERNATIONAL

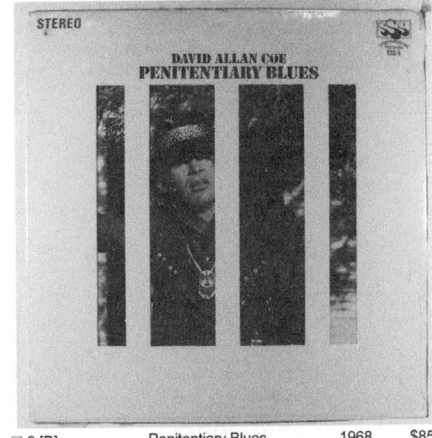

| ❏ 9 [B] | Penitentiary Blues | 1968 | $85 |
| ❏ SSS31 | Requiem for a Harlequin | 1973 | $320 |

COE, JIMMY

DELMARK

| ❏ DL-443 | After Hours Joint | 1989 | $25 |

COFFEY, DENNIS

ORPHEUS

| ❏ D1-75617 | Under the Moonlight | 1989 | $15 |

SUSSEX

❏ SUX-7021	Electric Coffey	1972	$15
❏ SUX-7004	Evolution	1971	$15
❏ SUX-7010	Goin' for Myself	1972	$15
❏ SUX-8031	Instant Coffey	1974	$15

WESTBOUND

❏ W-212	Finger Lickin' Good	1975	$12
❏ WD300	Home	1977	$12
❏ 6105	The Sweet Taste of Sin	1978	$12

COHEN, LEONARD

COLUMBIA

❏ FC44191	I'm Your Man	1988	$12
❏ CL2733 [M]	Leonard Cohen	1967	$250
❏ CS9533 [S]	Leonard Cohen	1967	$15

— Red "360 Sound" label

| ❏ CS9533 [S] | Leonard Cohen | 1970 | $12 |

— Orange label

| ❏ PC9533 | Leonard Cohen | 198? | $10 |

— Reissue with new prefix

❏ KC31724	Leonard Cohen: Live Songs	1973	$15
❏ KC33167	New Skin for the Old Ceremony	1974	$15
❏ JC36264	Recent Songs	1979	$12
❏ PC36264	Recent Songs	198?	$10

— Budget-line reissue

| ❏ CS9767 | Songs From a Room | 1969 | $15 |

— Red "360 Sound" label

| ❏ CS9767 | Songs From a Room | 1970 | $12 |

— Orange label

| ❏ PC9767 | Songs From a Room | 198? | $10 |

— Reissue with new prefix

| ❏ C30103 | Songs of Love and Hate | 1971 | $15 |
| ❏ PC30103 | Songs of Love and Hate | 198? | $10 |

— Budget-line reissue

| ❏ C85953 | Ten New Songs | 2001 | $25 |
| ❏ PC34077 | The Best of Leonard Cohen | 1975 | $12 |

— No bar code

| ❏ PC34077 | The Best of Leonard Cohen | 198? | $10 |

— Reissue with bar code

PASSPORT

| ❏ PB-6045 | Various Positions | 1985 | $12 |

WARNER BROS.

| ❏ BSK3125 | Death of a Ladies' Man | 1977 | $12 |

COHEN, MYRON

AUDIO FIDELITY

| ❏ 701 [M] | Myron Cohen | 196? | $25 |

RCA VICTOR

❏ LPM-3534 [M]	Everybody Gotta Be Someplace	1966	$15
❏ LSP-3534 [S]	Everybody Gotta Be Someplace	1966	$18
❏ LPM-3791 [M]	It's Not a Question	1967	$15
❏ LSP-3791 [S]	It's Not a Question	1967	$18
❏ VPS-6052	This Is Myron Cohen	1972	$18

COHN, AL, AND BILLY MITCHELL

XANADU

| ❏ 185 | Night Flight to Dakar | 1980 | $25 |
| ❏ 180 | Xanadu in Africa | 1979 | $25 |

COHN, AL, AND JIMMY ROWLES

XANADU

| ❏ 145 | Heavy Love | 1978 | $25 |

COHN, AL, AND ZOOT SIMS

ABUNDANT SOUNDS

| ❏ 1 [M] | Either Way | 1960 | $200 |

CORAL

| ❏ CRL57171 [M] | Al and Zoot | 1958 | $200 |

MCA

| ❏ 1377 | Al Cohn Quintet Featuring Zoot Sims | 198? | $30 |

MERCURY

| ❏ MG-20606 [M] | You 'n Me | 1960 | $150 |
| ❏ SR-60606 [S] | You 'n Me | 1960 | $175 |

MUSE

| ❏ MR-5016 | Body and Soul | 1974 | $35 |
| ❏ MR-5356 | Body and Soul | 1988 | $25 |

— Reissue of 5016

RCA VICTOR

| ❏ LPM-1282 [M] | From A to Z | 1956 | $175 |

SONET

| ❏ 684 | Motoring Along | 197? | $30 |

Number	Title	Yr	NM
TRIP			
❑ 5548	You 'n Me	197?	$25
ZIM			
❑ 2002	Either Way	197?	$30

COHN, AL; RICH KAMUCA; BILL PERKINS

Number	Title	Yr	NM
RCA VICTOR			
❑ LPM-1162 [M]	The Brothers	1955	$175

COHN, AL; SCOTT HAMILTON; BUDDY TATE

Number	Title	Yr	NM
CONCORD JAZZ			
❑ CJ-172	Tour de Force	198?	$25

COHN, AL

Number	Title	Yr	NM
BIOGRAPH			
❑ 12063	Be Loose	197?	$25
CONCORD JAZZ			
❑ CJ-155	Nonpareil	1981	$25
❑ CJ-194	Overtures	1982	$25
❑ CJ-241	Standards of Excellence	1983	$25
CORAL			
❑ CRL57118 [M]	Al Cohn Quintet	1957	$50
DAWN			
❑ DLP-1110 [M]	Cohn on the Saxophone	1956	$120
PRESTIGE			
❑ PRST-7819	Broadway 1954	1970	$30
PROGRESSIVE			
❑ PLP-3002 [10]	Al Cohn Quartet	1953	$300
❑ PLP-3004 [10]	Al Cohn Quintet	1953	$300
RCA VICTOR			
❑ LPM-1161 [M]	Four Brass, One Tenor	1956	$100
❑ LJM-1024 [M]	Mr. Music	1955	$100
❑ LPM-2312 [M]	Son of Drum Suite	1960	$40
❑ LSP-2312 [S]	Son of Drum Suite	1960	$50
❑ LPM-1207 [M]	That Old Feeling	1956	$100
❑ LPM-1116 [M]	The Natural Seven	1955	$100
SAVOY			
❑ MG-12048 [M]	Cohn's Tones	1956	$100
SAVOY JAZZ			
❑ SJL-1126	The Progressive	197?	$25
TIMELESS			
❑ LPSJP-259	Rifftide	1990	$30
XANADU			
❑ 138	America	1976	$25
❑ 179	No Problem	1979	$25
❑ 110	Play It Now	1975	$25

COHN, AL/SHORTY ROGERS

Number	Title	Yr	NM
RCA VICTOR			
❑ LJM-1020 [M]	East Coast -- West Coast Scene	1954	$250

COHN, STEVE

Number	Title	Yr	NM
CADENCE JAZZ			
❑ CJ-1020	Shapes Sounds Theories	198?	$20

COIL, PAT

Number	Title	Yr	NM
SHEFFIELD LABS			
❑ TLP-34	Just Ahead	1993	$75
—Audiophile vinyl			
❑ TLP-31	Steps	1991	$40
—Audiophile vinyl			

COKER, DOLO

Number	Title	Yr	NM
XANADU			
❑ 178	All Alone	1979	$25
❑ 142	California Hard	1976	$25
❑ 139	Dolo!	1976	$25
❑ 153	Third Down	1977	$25

COKER, JERRY

Number	Title	Yr	NM
FANTASY			
❑ 3214 [M]	Modern Music from Indiana University	1956	$250
—Red vinyl			
❑ 3214 [M]	Modern Music from Indiana University	1957	$300
—Black vinyl			
REVELATION			
❑ 45	A Re-Emergence	1983	$30
❑ 47	Rebirth	1984	$30

COLA, GEORGE "KID SHEIK"

Number	Title	Yr	NM
GHB			
❑ GHB-187	Kid Sheik in England	1986	$25
❑ GHB-47	Kid Sheik Plays Blues and Standards	197?	$25
❑ GHB-76	Stompers	197?	$25
JAZZOLOGY			
❑ JCE-31	Kid Sheik and Sheik's Swingers	1967	$30

COLBY, MARK

Number	Title	Yr	NM
COLUMBIA			
❑ JC35725	One Good Turn	1979	$25
❑ JC35298	Serpentine Fire	1978	$25

COLD BLOOD

Number	Title	Yr	NM
ABC			
❑ D-917	Lydia Pense and Cold Blood	1976	$12
REPRISE			
❑ MS2074	First Taste of Sin	1972	$15
❑ MS2130	Thriller!	1973	$15
SAN FRANCISCO			
❑ SD200	Cold Blood	1969	$25
❑ SD205	Sisyphus	1970	$25
WARNER BROS.			
❑ BS2806	Lydia	1974	$12

COLD SWEAT

Number	Title	Yr	NM
JMT			
❑ 834426-1	Cold Sweat Plays J.B.	1989	$35

COLDCUT

Number	Title	Yr	NM
TOMMY BOY			
❑ 25974	What's That Noise?	1989	$15

COLDER, BEN

See SHEB WOOLEY.

COLE, BUDDY

Number	Title	Yr	NM
COLUMBIA			
❑ CL1224 [M]	Pipes & Chimes of Christmas	1958	$25
—Red label with six "eye" logos			
❑ CS8032 [S]	Pipes & Chimes of Christmas	1958	$30
—Red and black label with six "eye" logos			
PICKWICK			
❑ SPCX-1001	Christmas Organ and Chimes	196?	$15

COLE, COZY

Number	Title	Yr	NM
AUDITION			
❑ 33-5943 [M]	Cozy Cole	1955	$150
BETHLEHEM			
❑ BCP-21 [M]	Jazz at the Metropole Café	1955	$300
CHARLIE PARKER			
❑ PLP-403 [M]	A Cozy Conaption of Carmen	1962	$50
❑ PLP-403S [S]	A Cozy Conaption of Carmen	1962	$75
COLUMBIA			
❑ CL2553 [M]	It's a Rockin' Thing	1965	$35
❑ CS9353 [S]	It's a Rockin' Thing	1965	$50
CORAL			
❑ CRL57423 [M]	Drum Beat Dancing Feet	1962	$35
❑ CRL757423 [S]	Drum Beat Dancing Feet	1962	$25
❑ CRL57457 [M]	It's a Cozy World	1964	$35
❑ CRL757457 [S]	It's a Cozy World	1964	$50
FELSTED			
❑ 7002 [M]	Cozy's Caravan/Earl's Backroom	1958	$150
❑ 2002 [S]	Cozy's Caravan/Earl's Backroom	1958	$40
GRAND AWARD			
❑ GA 33-334 [M]	After Hours	1956	$40
KING			
❑ 673 [M]	Cozy Cole	1959	$120
❑ KS-673 [S]	Cozy Cole	1959	$300
LOVE			
❑ 500M [M]	Topsy	1959	$200
❑ 500S [S]	Topsy	1959	$250
PARIS			
❑ 122 [M]	Cozy Cole and His All-Stars	1958	$150
PLYMOUTH			
❑ P 12-155 [M]	Cozy Cole and His All Stars	195?	$30
SAVOY			
❑ MG-12197 [M]	Concerto for Cozy	196?	$50
WHO'S WHO IN JAZZ			
❑ 21003	Lionel Hampton Presents Cozy Cole & Marty Napoleon	1977	$25

COLE, COZY/JIMMY MCPARTLAND

Number	Title	Yr	NM
WALDORF MUSIC HALL			
❑ MH 33-162 [10]	After Hours	195?	$50

COLE, HOLLY

Number	Title	Yr	NM
BLUE NOTE JAZZ			
❑ JP-5003	Temptation	2001	$40
—Audiophile edition issued by Classic Records (CD was issued in 1995)			

COLE, IKE

Number	Title	Yr	NM
DEE GEE			
❑ LPM-4001 [M]	Ike Cole's Tribute to His Brother Nat	1966	$40
❑ ST-4001 [S]	Ike Cole's Tribute to His Brother Nat	1966	$50
DOT			
❑ DLP-25943	Picture This!	1969	$30
GUEST STAR			
❑ G-1502 [M]	Ike Cole -- The Brother of Nat King Cole	196?	$18
❑ GS-1502 [S]	Ike Cole -- The Brother of Nat King Cole	196?	$18
PROMENADE			
❑ 2099 [M]	Ike Cole Sings	196?	$18
UNITED ARTISTS			
❑ UAL-3569 [M]	Same Old You	1967	$30
❑ UAS-6569 [S]	Same Old You	1967	$30

COLE, JERRY

Number	Title	Yr	NM
BEAT ROCKET			
❑ BR117	Guitars A-Go-Go!	2000	$15
❑ BR118	Wild Strings!	2001	$15
CAPITOL			
❑ T2061 [M]	Hot Rod Dance Party	1964	$100
❑ ST2061 [S]	Hot Rod Dance Party	1964	$150
❑ (S)T2061	Hot Rod Dance Party Bonus Photo	1964	$30
❑ T2044 [M]	Outer Limits	1963	$50
❑ ST2044 [S]	Outer Limits	1963	$100
❑ T2112 [M]	Surf Age	1964	$150
—With bonus single by Dick Dale, "Thunder Wave"/"Spanish Kiss"			
❑ ST2112 [S]	Surf Age	1964	$120
—With bonus single by Dick Dale, "Thunder Wave"/"Spanish Kiss"			
❑ T2112 [M]	Surf Age	1964	$100
—With bonus single missing			
❑ ST2112 [S]	Surf Age	1964	$150
—With bonus single missing			
LIBERTY			
❑ LRP-3362 [M]	Sounds of the Big Irons	1964	$50
❑ LST-7362 [S]	Sounds of the Big Irons	1964	$75

COLE, JOHNNY

Number	Title	Yr	NM
CROWN			
❑ CMX100	Famous Christmas Carols	196?	$15
❑ CLP5081 [M]	Famous Christmas Carols	196?	$15
—Same as Crown CMX 100			
❑ CLP5132 [M]	Wishing You a Merry Christmas	196?	$15
—Same as Crown 165, but in mono			
❑ 165 [S]	Wishing You a Merry Christmas	196?	$18
CUSTOM			
❑ CS6 [S]	12 Days of Christmas	196?	$15
—Reissue of Crown 165 with new title			
YULETIDE SERIES			
❑ YS-216	12 Days of Christmas	197?	$12
—Reissue of Custom album of the same name			
❑ YS-211	Famous Christmas Carols	197?	$12
—Reissue of Crown LP of the same name			
❑ YS-213	Rudolph the Red-Nosed Reindeer	197?	$12

COLE, MARIA

Number	Title	Yr	NM
KAPP			
❑ 102 [10]	Maria Cole	1954	$50

COLE, NAT KING

First renowned as a piano player in The King Cole Trio, then as a male singer. The other members of the Trio were Oscar Moore (guitar) and Wesley Prince (bass).

Number	Title	Yr	NM
CAMAY			
❑ CA-3004	Nat King Cole	196?	$15
CAPITOL			
❑ ST-12219	16 Grandes Exitos	1982	$12
❑ DN-16165	A Blossom Fell	1981	$10
❑ W782 [M]	After Midnight	1956	$75
—Turquoise label			
❑ W782 [M]	After Midnight	1958	$150
—Black label with colorband, "Capitol" at left			
❑ W782 [M]	After Midnight	1962	$100
—Black label with colorband, "Capitol" at top			
❑ SM-11796	After Midnight	1978	$12
❑ W1220 [M]	A Mis Amigos	1959	$30
—Black label with colorband, "Capitol" at left			
❑ W1220 [M]	A Mis Amigos	1962	$25
—Black label with colorband, "Capitol" at top			
❑ SW1220 [S]	A Mis Amigos	1959	$40
—Black label with colorband, "Capitol" at left			
❑ SW1220 [S]	A Mis Amigos	1962	$30
—Black label with colorband, "Capitol" at top			
❑ SN-16136	A Mis Amigos	1980	$10

Number	Title	Yr	NM
❏ T680 [M]	Ballads of the Day	1956	$40

— *Turquoise label*

Number	Title	Yr	NM
❏ T680 [M]	Ballads of the Day	1958	$30

— *Black label with colorband, "Capitol" at left*

❏ T680 [M]	Ballads of the Day	1962	$25

— *Black label with colorband, "Capitol" at top*

❏ DT680 [R]	Ballads of the Day	1963	$18

— *Black label with colorband*

❏ T2820 [M]	Beautiful Ballads	1967	$18
❏ ST2820 [S]	Beautiful Ballads	1967	$15
❏ DWBB-252	Close-Up	1969	$18

— *Reissue of 680 and 1891*

❏ W1031 [M]	Cole Espanol	1958	$30

— *Black label with colorband, "Capitol" at left*

❏ W1031 [M]	Cole Espanol	1962	$25

— *Black label with colorband, "Capitol" at top*

❏ DW1031 [R]	Cole Espanol	196?	$18

— *Black label with colorband*

❏ SM-1031	Cole Espanol	197?	$10

— *Reissue with new prefix*

❏ N-16166	Cole Espanol	1981	$10
❏ T1838 [M]	Dear Lonely Hearts	1962	$18
❏ ST1838 [S]	Dear Lonely Hearts	1962	$25
❏ H9110 [10]	Eight Top Pops	1954	$50
❏ W1249 [M]	Every Time I Feel the Spirit	1960	$30

— *Black label with colorband, "Capitol" at left*

❏ SW1249 [S]	Every Time I Feel the Spirit	1960	$30

— *Black label with colorband, "Capitol" at left*

❏ H213 [10]	Harvest of Hits	1950	$300

— *Original; purple label*

❏ L213 [10]	Harvest of Hits	195?	$75

— *Reissue; maroon label, "H" mechanically crossed out on back cover with "L" stamped next to it*

❏ T2454 [M]	Hymns and Spirituals	1966	$15
❏ ST2454 [S]	Hymns and Spirituals	1966	$18
❏ T2118 [M]	I Don't Want to Be Hurt Anymore	1964	$18
❏ ST2118 [S]	I Don't Want to Be Hurt Anymore	1964	$25
❏ T592 [M]	Instrumental Classics	1955	$85
❏ W903 [M]	Just One of Those Things	1957	$40

— *Turquoise or gray label*

❏ W903 [M]	Just One of Those Things	1958	$30

— *Black label with colorband, "Capitol" at left*

❏ W903 [M]	Just One of Those Things	1962	$25

— *Black label with colorband, "Capitol" at top*

❏ SW903 [S]	Just One of Those Things	1959	$30

— *Black label with colorband, "Capitol" at left*

❏ SW903 [S]	Just One of Those Things	1962	$25

— *Black label with colorband, "Capitol" at top*

❏ W2008 [M]	Let's Face the Music	1963	$18
❏ SW2008 [S]	Let's Face the Music	1963	$25
❏ T2361 [M]	Looking Back	1965	$15
❏ ST2361 [S]	Looking Back	1965	$18
❏ SM-11882	Looking Back	1979	$12
❏ T2195 [M]	L-O-V-E	1965	$18
❏ ST2195 [S]	L-O-V-E	1965	$25
❏ SWAK-11355	Love Is Here to Stay	1974	$15
❏ W824 [M]	Love Is the Thing	1957	$40

— *Turquoise or gray label*

❏ W824 [M]	Love Is the Thing	1958	$30

— *Black label with colorband, "Capitol" at left*

❏ W824 [M]	Love Is the Thing	1962	$25

— *Black label with colorband, "Capitol" at top*

❏ SW824 [S]	Love Is the Thing	1959	$30

— *Black label with colorband, "Capitol" at left*

❏ SW824 [S]	Love Is the Thing	1962	$25

— *Black label with colorband, "Capitol" at top*

❏ SW824 [S]	Love Is the Thing	1969	$15

— *Lime green label*

❏ SM-824	Love Is the Thing	197?	$10

— *Reissue with new prefix*

❏ SN-16163	Love Is the Thing	1981	$10
❏ W1749 [M]	More Cole Espanol	1962	$30

— *Black label with colorband, "Capitol" at left*

Number	Title	Yr	NM
❏ W1749 [M]	More Cole Espanol	1963	$18

— *Black label with colorband, "Capitol" at top*

❏ SW1749 [S]	More Cole Espanol	1962	$30

— *Black label with colorband, "Capitol" at left*

❏ SW1749 [S]	More Cole Espanol	1963	$25

— *Black label with colorband, "Capitol" at top*

❏ SM-1749	More Cole Espanol	197?	$10

— *Reissue with new prefix*

❏ SN-16167	More Cole Espanol	1981	$10
❏ W2117 [M]	My Fair Lady	1964	$18
❏ SW2117 [S]	My Fair Lady	1964	$25

— *Black label with colorband*

❏ SW2117 [S]	My Fair Lady	1969	$15

— *Lime green label*

❏ SM-2117	My Fair Lady	197?	$10

— *Reissue with new prefix*

❏ H156 [10]	Nat King Cole at the Piano	1950	$300
❏ MAS2434 [M]	Nat King Cole at the Sands	1966	$15
❏ SMAS2434 [S]	Nat King Cole at the Sands	1966	$18
❏ SM-2434	Nat King Cole at the Sands	197?	$10

— *Reissue with new prefix*

❏ SKAO-373	Nat King Cole's Greatest	1969	$15
❏ H420 [10]	Nat King Cole Sings for Two in Love	1953	$175

— *Original; purple label*

❏ T420 [M]	Nat King Cole Sings for Two in Love	1955	$85

— *Turquoise label*

❏ T420 [M]	Nat King Cole Sings for Two in Love	1958	$150

— *Black label with colorband, "Capitol" at left*

❏ T420 [M]	Nat King Cole Sings for Two in Love	1962	$100

— *Black label with colorband, "Capitol" at top*

❏ DT420 [R]	Nat King Cole Sings for Two in Love	1963	$50

❏ L420 [10]	Nat King Cole Sings for Two in Love	195?	$50

— *Reissue; maroon label, back cover probably has "H" mechanically crossed out with "L" stamped next to it*

❏ W1675 [M]	Nat King Cole Sings/George Shearing Plays	1962	$150

— *Black label with colorband, "Capitol" at left*

❏ W1675 [M]	Nat King Cole Sings/George Shearing Plays	1963	$50

— *Black label with colorband, "Capitol" at top*

❏ SW1675 [S]	Nat King Cole Sings/George Shearing Plays	1962	$150

— *Black label with colorband, "Capitol" at left*

❏ SW1675 [S]	Nat King Cole Sings/George Shearing Plays	1963	$100

— *Black label with colorband, "Capitol" at top*

❏ SM-1675	Nat King Cole Sings/George Shearing Plays	197?	$20

— *Reissue with new prefix*

❏ W1713 [M]	Nat King Cole Sings the Blues	1962	$100

— *Black label with colorband, "Capitol" at left*

❏ SW1713 [S]	Nat King Cole Sings the Blues	1962	$150

— *Black label with colorband, "Capitol" at left*

❏ W1929 [M]	Nat King Cole Sings the Blues, Volume 2	1963	$50
❏ SW1929 [S]	Nat King Cole Sings the Blues, Volume 2	1963	$100
❏ T1891 [M]	Nat King Cole's Top Pops	1963	$18
❏ DT1891 [R]	Nat King Cole's Top Pops	1963	$15
❏ T2348 [M]	Nature Boy	1965	$18
❏ DT2348 [R]	Nature Boy	1965	$15
❏ H332 [10]	Penthouse Serenade	1951	$250

— *Original; purple label*

❏ T332 [M]	Penthouse Serenade	1955	$40
❏ L332 [10]	Penthouse Serenade	195?	$50

— *Reissue; maroon label, "H" mechanically crossed out on back cover with "L" stamped next to it*

❏ T1793 [M]	Ramblin' Rose	1962	$18
❏ ST1793 [S]	Ramblin' Rose	1962	$25
❏ SN-16032	Ramblin' Rose	1980	$10
❏ T2680 [M]	Sincerely, Nat King Cole	1967	$18
❏ ST2680 [S]	Sincerely, Nat King Cole	1967	$15
❏ T2340 [M]	Songs from "Cat Ballou" and Other Motion Pictures	1965	$15
❏ ST2340 [S]	Songs from "Cat Ballou" and Other Motion Pictures	1965	$18
❏ SM-11804	Songs from "Cat Ballou" and Other Motion Pictures	1978	$12
❏ W993 [M]	St. Louis Blues	1958	$50

— *Turquoise or gray label*

❏ W993 [M]	St. Louis Blues	1962	$40

— *Black label with colorband, "Capitol" at left*

❏ SW993 [S]	St. Louis Blues	1959	$50

— *Black label with colorband, "Capitol" at left*

❏ SN-16137	St. Louis Blues	1980	$10
❏ W1331 [M]	Tell Me About Yourself	1960	$30

— *Black label with colorband, "Capitol" at left*

❏ SW1331 [S]	Tell Me About Yourself	1960	$30

— *Black label with colorband, "Capitol" at left*

❏ W514 [M]	Tenth Anniversary Album	1955	$85

— *Gray label; released simultaneously with H1-514 and H2-514*

❏ H1-514 [10]	Tenth Anniversary Album, Part 1	1954	$175

Number	Title	Yr	NM

— *Contains Side 1 of W 514*

❏ H2-514 [10]	Tenth Anniversary Album, Part 2	1954	$175

— *Contains Side 2 of W 514*

❏ T2759 [M]	Thank You Pretty Baby	1967	$18
❏ ST2759 [S]	Thank You Pretty Baby	1967	$15
❏ SKAO2944	The Best of Nat King Cole	1968	$15
❏ SN-16036	The Best of Nat King Cole	1980	$10
❏ N-16260	The Best of the King Cole Trio -- Volume 1	1982	$20
❏ N-16281	The Best of the King Cole Trio -- Volume 2	1982	$20
❏ W1967 [M]	The Christmas Song	1962	$18

— *Reissue of W 1444 with title song added and another deleted*

❏ SW1967 [S]	The Christmas Song	1962	$18

— *Black label with colorband*

❏ SW1967 [S]	The Christmas Song	1969	$15

— *Lime-green label*

❏ SW1967 [S]	The Christmas Song	1971	$15

— *Red label*

❏ SW1967 [S]	The Christmas Song	1973	$12

— *Orange label, "Capitol" at bottom*

❏ SM-1967 [S]	The Christmas Song	197?	$10

— *Budget-line reissue*

❏ T2558 [M]	The Great Songs!	1966	$15
❏ ST2558 [S]	The Great Songs!	1966	$18
❏ H8 [10]	The King Cole Trio	1950	$300
❏ H29 [10]	The King Cole Trio, Volume 2	1950	$300
❏ H59 [10]	The King Cole Trio, Volume 3	1950	$300
❏ H177 [10]	The King Cole Trio, Volume 4	1950	$300
❏ W1444 [M]	The Magic of Christmas	1960	$25
❏ SW1444 [S]	The Magic of Christmas	1960	$25
❏ SQBO-93741	The Man and His Music	197?	$25

— *Capitol Record Club exclusive; with booklet*

❏ TCL2873 [M]	The Nat King Cole Deluxe Set	1968	$30
❏ STCL2873 [P]	The Nat King Cole Deluxe Set	1968	$30
❏ WCL1613 [M]	The Nat King Cole Story	1961	$30
❏ SWCL1613 [S]	The Nat King Cole Story	1961	$30
❏ W1926 [M]	The Nat King Cole Story, Volume 1	1962	$15
❏ SW1926 [S]	The Nat King Cole Story, Volume 1	1962	$18
❏ SN-16033	The Nat King Cole Story, Volume 1	1980	$10
❏ W1927 [M]	The Nat King Cole Story, Volume 2	1963	$15
❏ SW1927 [S]	The Nat King Cole Story, Volume 2	1963	$18
❏ SN-16034	The Nat King Cole Story, Volume 2	1980	$10
❏ W1928 [M]	The Nat King Cole Story, Volume 3	1963	$15
❏ SW1928 [S]	The Nat King Cole Story, Volume 3	1963	$18
❏ SN-16035	The Nat King Cole Story, Volume 3	1980	$10
❏ H220 [10]	The Nat King Cole Trio	1950	$250
❏ T2311 [M]	The Nat King Cole Trio	1965	$75
❏ W689 [M]	The Piano Style of Nat King Cole	1956	$85

— *Turquoise label*

❏ W689 [M]	The Piano Style of Nat King Cole	1958	$150

— *Black label with colorband, "Capitol" at left*

❏ W689 [M]	The Piano Style of Nat King Cole	1962	$100

— *Black label with colorband, "Capitol" at top*

❏ ST-310	There! I've Said It Again	1969	$15
❏ SQBO91278	The Swingin' Moods of Nat King Cole	1967	$150

— *Capitol Record Club exclusive*

❏ W1574 [M]	The Touch of Your Lips	1961	$25

— *Black label with colorband, "Capitol" at left*

❏ W1574 [M]	The Touch of Your Lips	1962	$18

— *Black label with colorband, "Capitol" at top*

❏ SW1574 [S]	The Touch of Your Lips	1961	$30

— *Black label with colorband, "Capitol" at left*

❏ SW1574 [S]	The Touch of Your Lips	1962	$25

— *Black label with colorband, "Capitol" at top*

❏ SQBO90938	The Velvet Moods of Nat King Cole	1967	$30

— *Capitol Record Club exclusive*

❏ W1084 [M]	The Very Thought of You	1958	$30

— *Black label with colorband, "Capitol" at left*

❏ W1084 [M]	The Very Thought of You	1962	$25

— *Black label with colorband, "Capitol" at top*

❏ SW1084 [S]	The Very Thought of You	1959	$30

— *Black label with colorband, "Capitol" at left*

❏ SW1084 [S]	The Very Thought of You	1962	$25

— *Black label with colorband, "Capitol" at top*

❏ T2529 [M]	The Vintage Years	1966	$15
❏ T870 [M]	This Is Nat "King" Cole	1957	$40

— *Turquoise or gray label*

❏ T870 [M]	This Is Nat "King" Cole	1958	$30

— *Black label with colorband, "Capitol" at left*

❏ T870 [M]	This Is Nat "King" Cole	1962	$25

— *Black label with colorband, "Capitol" at top*

❏ DT870 [R]	This Is Nat "King" Cole	1963	$18

Bottom-left partial entries:

❏ W824 [M]	Love Is the Thing	1962	$25

— *Black label with colorband, "Capitol" at top*

❏ SW824 [S]	Love Is the Thing	1959	$30

— *Black label with colorband, "Capitol" at left*

❏ SW824 [S]	Love Is the Thing	1962	$25

— *Black label with colorband, "Capitol" at top*

❏ SW824 [S]	Love Is the Thing	1969	$15

— *Lime green label*

❏ SM-824	Love Is the Thing	197?	$10

— *Reissue with new prefix*

❏ SN-16163	Love Is the Thing	1981	$10
❏ W1749 [M]	More Cole Espanol	1962	$30

— *Black label with colorband, "Capitol" at left*

Number	Title	Yr	NM
—Black label with colorband			
❏ T1932 [M]	Those Lazy-Hazy-Crazy Days of Summer	1963	$18
❏ ST1932 [S]	Those Lazy-Hazy-Crazy Days of Summer	1963	$25
❏ W1190 [M]	To Whom It May Concern	1959	$30
—Black label with colorband, "Capitol" at left			
❏ SW1190 [S]	To Whom It May Concern	1959	$40
—Black label with colorband, "Capitol" at left			
❏ M-11033 [M]	Trio Days	1972	$50
❏ H357 [10]	Unforgettable	1952	$75
❏ T357 [M]	Unforgettable	1955	$40
—Turquoise label			
❏ T357 [M]	Unforgettable	1958	$30
—Black label with colorband, "Capitol" at left			
❏ T357 [M]	Unforgettable	1962	$25
—Black label with colorband, "Capitol" at top			
❏ DT357 [R]	Unforgettable	1965	$15
❏ SM-357	Unforgettable	197?	$10
—Reissue with new prefix			
❏ SN-16162	Unforgettable	1981	$10
❏ T591 [M]	Vocal Classics	1955	$40
❏ DN-16164	Walkin' My Baby Back Home	1981	$10
❏ STBB-503	Walkin' My Baby Back Home/A Blossom Fell	1970	$18
❏ W1120 [M]	Welcome to the Club	1959	$30
—Black label with colorband, "Capitol" at left			
❏ SW1120 [S]	Welcome to the Club	1959	$40
—Black label with colorband, "Capitol" at left			
❏ W1859 [M]	Where Did Everyone Go?	1963	$18
❏ SW1859 [S]	Where Did Everyone Go?	1963	$25
❏ WAK1392 [M]	Wild Is Love	1960	$30
—Black label with colorband, "Capitol" at left			
❏ SWAK1392 [S]	Wild Is Love	1960	$30
—Black label with colorband, "Capitol" at left			
❏ SN-16037	Wild Is Love	1980	$10
DCC COMPACT CLASSICS			
❏ LPZ-2029	Love Is the Thing	1997	$120
—Audiophile vinyl			
❏ LPZ-2061	The Greatest Hits	1998	$120
—Audiophile vinyl			
❏ LPZ-2047	The Very Thought of You	1998	$150
—Audiophile vinyl			
DECCA			
❏ DL8260 [M]	In the Beginning	1956	$175
—Black label, silver print			
❏ DL8260 [M]	In the Beginning	1960	$75
—Black label with color bars			
EVEREST ARCHIVE OF FOLK & JAZZ			
❏ 290	Nature Boy	197?	$25
MARK 56			
❏ 739	Early 1940s	197?	$35
MCA			
❏ 4020	From the Very Beginning	1973	$30
MOBILE FIDELITY			
❏ Jan-0081	Nat King Cole Sings/George Shearing Plays	1981	$150
—Audiophile vinyl			
MOSAIC			
❏ MR27-138	The Complete Capitol Recordings of the Nat King Cole Trio	1991	$800
PAIR			
❏ PDL2-1026	Love Moods	1986	$15
❏ PDL2-1128	Tenderly	1986	$15
❏ PDL2-1025	Weaver of Dreams	1986	$15
PICKWICK			
❏ SPC-3046 [B]	Love Is a Many Splendored Thing	196?	$12
❏ SPC-3249	Nature Boy	197?	$12
❏ PTP-2058	Nature Boy	1973	$15
❏ SPC-3105	Stay As Sweet As You Are	196?	$12
❏ SPC-3071	When You're Smiling	196?	$12
❏ SPC-3154	You're My Everything	197?	$12
SAVOY JAZZ			
❏ SJL-1205	Nat King Cole & The King Cole Trio	1989	$30
SCORE			
❏ SLP-4019 [M]	The King Cole Trio and Lester Young	1957	$175
TIME-LIFE			
❏ SLGD-01	Legendary Singers: Nat King Cole	1985	$35
❏ SLGD-15	Legendary Singers: Nat King Cole: Take Two	1986	$35
TRIP			
❏ 7	The Nat "King" Cole Trio	197?	$30
VERVE			
❏ VSP-14 [M]	Nat Cole at JATP	1966	$35
❏ VSPS-14 [R]	Nat Cole at JATP	1966	$30
❏ VSP-25 [M]	Nat Cole at JATP 2	1966	$35
❏ VSPS-25 [R]	Nat Cole at JATP 2	1966	$30

COLE, NATALIE, AND PEABO BRYSON

CAPITOL

Number	Title	Yr	NM
❏ SOO-12025	We're the Best of Friends	1979	$12

COLE, NATALIE

CAPITOL

Number	Title	Yr	NM
❏ ST-12242	A Collection	1982	$12
❏ SN-16310	A Collection	1985	$10
—Budget-line reissue			
❏ ST-12079	Don't Look Back	1980	$12
❏ ST-12165	Happy Love	1981	$12
❏ SO-11928	I Love You So	1979	$12
❏ ST-11429	Inseparable	1975	$12
❏ SN-16038	Inseparable	198?	$10
—Budget-line reissue			
❏ ST-11517	Natalie	1976	$12
❏ SKBL-11709	Natalie..Live!	1978	$15
❏ SW-11708	Thankful	1978	$12
❏ SO-11600	Unpredictable	1977	$12
ELEKTRA			
❏ 61049	Unforgettable	1991	$25
EMI			
❏ E1-48902	Good to Be Back	1989	$12
EPIC			
❏ FE38280	I'm Ready	1983	$12
MANHATTAN			
❏ 53051	Everlasting	1987	$12
MOBILE FIDELITY			
❏ Jan-0032 [B]	Thankful	1980	$25
—Audiophile vinyl			
MODERN			
❏ 90270	Dangerous	1985	$12

COLE, RICHIE, AND BOOTS RANDOLPH

PALO ALTO

Number	Title	Yr	NM
❏ PA-8041	Yakety Madness	1983	$25

COLE, RICHIE, AND ERIC KLOSS

MUSE

Number	Title	Yr	NM
❏ MR-5082	Battle of the Saxes	1976	$25

COLE, RICHIE, AND HANK CRAWFORD

MILESTONE

Number	Title	Yr	NM
❏ M-9180	Bossa International	1990	$30

COLE, RICHIE, AND PHIL WOODS

MUSE

Number	Title	Yr	NM
❏ MR-5237	Side by Side	1980	$25

COLE, RICHIE

ADELPHI

Number	Title	Yr	NM
❏ AD5001	Starburst	1976	$25
CONCORD JAZZ			
❏ CJ-314	Pure Imagination	1987	$25
MILESTONE			
❏ M-9152	Popbop	1987	$25
❏ M-9162	Signature	1988	$25
MUSE			
❏ MR-5270	Alive at the Village Vanguard	1981	$25
❏ MR-5155	Alto Madness	1977	$25
❏ MR-5245	Cool "C"	1981	$25
❏ MR-5207	Hollywood Madness	1979	$25
❏ MR-5192	Keeper of the Flame	1978	$25
❏ MR-5119	New York Afternoon	1976	$25
❏ MR-5295	Some Things Speak for Themselves	1982	$25
PALO ALTO			
❏ PA-8036	Alto Annie's Theme	1983	$25
❏ PA-8070	Bossa Nova Eyes	1985	$25
❏ PA-8023	Return to Alto Acres	1982	$25

COLE, TONY

20TH CENTURY

Number	Title	Yr	NM
❏ T-403	If the Music Stops	1972	$15
❏ T-416	Magnificently Mad	1973	$15

COLEMAN, ALBERT, 'S ATLANTA POPS

EPIC

Number	Title	Yr	NM
❏ FE38630	Classic Country	1983	$10
❏ FE38154	Just Hooked on Country	1982	$10

COLEMAN, BILL

BLACK LION

Number	Title	Yr	NM
❏ 128	London!	197?	$30
❏ 212	Mainstream at Montreux	1974	$30
DRG			
❏ SL-5200	Blowing for the Cats: The Final Big Band Sessions	198?	$25
SWING			
❏ SW-8410	Bill Coleman with George Duvivier & Co.	198?	$25
❏ SW-8402	Paris 1936-38	198?	$25

COLEMAN, CY

BENIDA

Number	Title	Yr	NM
❏ LP-1023A [10]	Cy Coleman	1955	$75
CAPITOL			
❏ T1952 [M]	Piano Witchcraft	1963	$50
❏ ST1952 [S]	Piano Witchcraft	1963	$75
❏ T2355 [M]	The Art of Love	1965	$85
❏ ST2355 [S]	The Art of Love	1965	$50
COLUMBIA			
❏ C32804	Broadway Tunesmith	1973	$25
❏ CL2578 [M]	If My Friends Could See Me Now	1966	$30
❏ CS9378 [S]	If My Friends Could See Me Now	1966	$35
DRG			
❏ SL-5205	Comin' Home	1988	$25
EVEREST			
❏ LPBR-5092 [M]	Playboy's Penthouse	196?	$30
❏ SDBR-1092 [S]	Playboy's Penthouse	196?	$30
MGM			
❏ SE-4501	Ages of Rock	1968	$30
WESTMINSTER			
❏ WLP-15001 [M]	Cool Coleman	195?	$40

COLEMAN, EARL

ATLANTIC

Number	Title	Yr	NM
❏ SD8172	Love Songs	1968	$35
FANTASY			
❏ OJC-187	Earl Coleman Returns	1986	$25
PRESTIGE			
❏ PRLP-7045 [M]	Earl Coleman Returns	1956	$300
—Yellow label			
❏ PRLP-7045 [M]	Earl Coleman Returns	196?	$30
—Blue label, trident logo at right			
STASH			
❏ 243	Stardust	1984	$25
XANADU			
❏ 147	A Song for You	1978	$30
❏ 175	There's Something About an Old Love	1979	$30

COLEMAN, ERNIE

WARNER BROS.

Number	Title	Yr	NM
❏ W1261 [M]	Be Gentle, Please	1959	$75
❏ WS1261 [S]	Be Gentle, Please	1959	$75

COLEMAN, GEORGE

THERESA

Number	Title	Yr	NM
❏ TR-126	George Coleman at Yoshi's	1989	$30
❏ TR-120	Manhattan Panorama	1986	$25
TIMELESS			
❏ 312	Meditation	197?	$30

COLEMAN, GLORIA

ABC IMPULSE!

Number	Title	Yr	NM
❏ AS-47	Soul Sisters	1968	$30
IMPULSE!			
❏ A-47 [M]	Soul Sisters	1963	$120
❏ AS-47 [S]	Soul Sisters	1963	$120
MAINSTREAM			
❏ MRL-322	Gloria Coleman Sings and Swings -- Organ	1972	$30

COLEMAN, ORNETTE

ABC IMPULSE!

Number	Title	Yr	NM
❏ AS-9187	Crisis	1969	$120
❏ AS-9178	Ornette at 12	1968	$120
ANTILLES			
❏ AN-2001	Of Human Feelings	198?	$35
ARISTA FREEDOM			
❏ AL1900	The Great London Concert	1978	$25
ARTISTS HOUSE			
❏ 1	Body Meta	1977	$25
❏ 6	Soapsuds	1978	$25
ATLANTIC			
❏ 1327 [M]	Change of the Century	1960	$300
—Multicolor label, white "fan" logo			
❏ 1327 [M]	Change of the Century	1963	$50
—Multicolor label, black "fan" logo			
❏ SD1327 [S]	Change of the Century	1960	$300
—Multicolor label, white "fan" logo			
❏ SD1327 [S]	Change of the Century	1963	$50
—Multicolor label, black "fan" logo			
❏ SD1327 [S]	Change of the Century	1969	$30
—Red and green label, "1841 Broadway" on label			
❏ 1327 [M]	Change of the Century	1960	$300
—Black label			
❏ SD1327 [S]	Change of the Century	1960	$300
—Green label			
❏ SD1327 [S]	Change of the Century	1976	$25
❏ 1364 [M]	Free Jazz	1961	$175

Number	Title	Yr	NM
—Multicolor label, white "fan" logo			
❑ 1364 [M]	Free Jazz	1963	$25
—Multicolor label, black "fan" logo			
❑ SD1364 [S]	Free Jazz	1961	$175
—Multicolor label, white "fan" logo			
❑ SD1364 [S]	Free Jazz	1963	$50
—Multicolor label, black "fan" logo			
❑ SD1364 [S]	Free Jazz	1969	$30
—Red and green label			
❑ 1378 [M]	Ornette	1961	$175
—Multicolor label, white "fan" logo			
❑ 1378 [M]	Ornette	1963	$35
—Multicolor label, black "fan" logo			
❑ SD1378 [S]	Ornette	1961	$175
—Multicolor label, white "fan" logo			
❑ SD1378 [S]	Ornette	1963	$25
—Multicolor label, black "fan" logo			
❑ SD1378 [S]	Ornette	1969	$30
—Red and green label			
❑ 90530	Ornette	198?	$25
—Reissue of 1378			
❑ 1394 [M]	Ornette on Tenor	1962	$175
—Multicolor label, black "fan" logo			
❑ SD1394 [S]	Ornette on Tenor	1962	$175
—Multicolor label, black "fan" logo			
❑ SD1394 [S]	Ornette on Tenor	1969	$30
—Red and green label			
❑ SD1572	The Art of Improvisors	1971	$35
❑ SD1558	The Best of Ornette Coleman	1970	$35
❑ 1317 [M]	The Shape of Jazz to Come	1959	$100
—Bullseye" label			
❑ 1317 [M]	The Shape of Jazz to Come	1960	$300
—Multicolor label, white "fan" logo			
❑ 1317 [M]	The Shape of Jazz to Come	1963	$35
—Multicolor label, black "fan" logo			
❑ SD1317 [S]	The Shape of Jazz to Come	1959	$300
—Bullseye" label			
❑ SD1317 [S]	The Shape of Jazz to Come	1960	$300
—Multicolor label, white "fan" logo			
❑ SD1317 [S]	The Shape of Jazz to Come	1963	$25
—Multicolor label, black "fan" logo			
❑ SD1317 [S]	The Shape of Jazz to Come	1969	$30
—Red and green label			
❑ 1353 [M]	This Is Our Music	1960	$300
—Multicolor label, white "fan" logo			
❑ 1353 [M]	This Is Our Music	1963	$35
—Multicolor label, black "fan" logo			
❑ SD1353 [S]	This Is Our Music	1960	$300
—Multicolor label, white "fan" logo			
❑ SD1353 [S]	This Is Our Music	1963	$25
—Multicolor label, black "fan" logo			
❑ SD1353 [S]	This Is Our Music	1969	$30
—Red and green label			
❑ SD1588	Twins	1972	$35
❑ SD8810	Twins	198?	$30
BLUE NOTE			
❑ BST-84356	Love Call	1970	$25
❑ BST-84287	New York Is Now!	1968	$30
❑ BLP-4224 [M]	Ornette Coleman at the Golden Circle, Stockholm, Volume 1	1965	$75
❑ BST-84224 [S]	Ornette Coleman at the Golden Circle, Stockholm, Volume 1	1965	$40
—New York, USA" on label			
❑ BST-84224 [S]	Ornette Coleman at the Golden Circle, Stockholm, Volume 1	1967	$35
—A Division of Liberty Records" on label			
❑ BLP-4225 [M]	Ornette Coleman at the Golden Circle, Stockholm, Volume 2	1965	$75
❑ BST-84225 [S]	Ornette Coleman at the Golden Circle, Stockholm, Volume 2	1965	$40
—New York, USA" on label			
❑ BST-84225 [S]	Ornette Coleman at the Golden Circle, Stockholm, Volume 2	1967	$35
—A Division of Liberty Records" on label			
❑ BLP-4246 [M]	The Empty Foxhole	1966	$75
❑ BST-84246 [S]	The Empty Foxhole	1966	$40
—New York, USA" on label			
❑ BST-84246 [S]	The Empty Foxhole	1967	$30
—A Division of Liberty Records" on label			
❑ B1-28982	The Empty Foxhole	1994	$35
❑ BLP-4210 [M]	Town Hall Concert, Volume 1	1965	$0
—Canceled			
❑ BST-84210 [S]	Town Hall Concert, Volume 1	1965	$0
—Canceled			
❑ BLP-4211 [M]	Town Hall Concert, Volume 2	1965	$0
—Canceled			
❑ BST-84211 [S]	Town Hall Concert, Volume 2	1965	$0
—Canceled			
COLUMBIA			
❑ FC38029	Broken Shadows	198?	$30

Number	Title	Yr	NM
❑ KC31061	Science Fiction	1972	$25
❑ CG33669	Science Fiction/Skies of America	1976	$25
❑ KC31562	Skies of America	1972	$25
CONTEMPORARY			
❑ C-3551 [M]	The Music of Ornette Coleman -- Something Else!	1958	$300
❑ S-7551 [S]	The Music of Ornette Coleman -- Something Else!	1959	$300
❑ M-3569 [M]	Tomorrow Is the Question	1959	$300
❑ S-7569 [S]	Tomorrow Is the Question	1959	$300
ESP-DISK'			
❑ 1006 [M]	Town Hall Concert, December 1962	1965	$250
❑ S-1006 [S]	Town Hall Concert, December 1962	1965	$175
❑ S1006 [B]	Town Hall Concert, December 1962	1965	$1200

—Promo with blank white labels. Includes ESP press release and original inner sleeve with essay "The New Music" by Robert Ostermann and ESP catalogue. Cover is silkscreened. Back cover is blank.

Number	Title	Yr	NM
FANTASY			
❑ OJC-163	The Music of Ornette Coleman -- Something Else!	198?	$30
—Reissue of Contemporary 7551			
❑ OJC-342	Tomorrow Is the Question	198?	$30
—Reissue of Contemporary 7569			
FLYING DUTCHMAN			
❑ 123	Friends and Neighbors	1970	$25
❑ FD-10123	Friends and Neighbors	1972	$35
—Reissue of 123			
HORIZON			
❑ 722	Dancing in Your Head	1977	$35
IAI			
❑ 373852	Classics, Volume 1	197?	$25
INNER CITY			
❑ 1001	Live at the Hillcrest Club 1958	197?	$25
MOON			
❑ MLP-022	Broken Shadows	1992	$35
PORTRAIT			
❑ OR44301	Virgin Beauty	1988	$35
RCA VICTOR			
❑ LPM-2982 [M]	The Music of Ornette Coleman	1964	$30
❑ LSP-2982 [S]	The Music of Ornette Coleman	1964	$30

Number	Title	Yr	NM
COLEMAN, STEVE			
JMT			
❑ 850001	Motherland Pulse	1985	$35
❑ 860005	On the Edge of Tomorrow	1986	$35
❑ 834425-1	Strata Institute Cipher Syntax	1988	$30
❑ 870010	World Expansion	1987	$35
NOVUS			
❑ 63180-1 [EP]	A Tale of 3 Cities The EP	1995	$30

Number	Title	Yr	NM
COLES, JOHNNY			
BLUE NOTE			
❑ BLP-4144 [M]	Little Johnny C	1963	$175
—New York, USA" on label			
❑ BST-84144 [S]	Little Johnny C	1963	$50
—New York, USA" on label			
❑ BST-84144 [S]	Little Johnny C	1967	$35
—A Division of Liberty Records" on label			
EPIC			
❑ LA16015 [M]	The Warm Sound	1961	$1000
—deep groove			
❑ BA17015 [M]	The Warm Sound	1961	$300
MAINSTREAM			
❑ MRL-346	Katumbo (Dance)	1972	$25

Number	Title	Yr	NM
COLIANNI, JOHN			
CONCORD JAZZ			
❑ CJ-367	Blues-O-Matic	1989	$30
❑ CJ-309	John Colianni	1987	$25

Number	Title	Yr	NM
COLINA, MICHAEL			
PRIVATE MUSIC			
❑ 2041-1-P	The Shadow of Urbano	1988	$25

Number	Title	Yr	NM
COLLAGE, THE			
SMASH			
❑ SRS-67101	The Collage	1968	$25

Number	Title	Yr	NM
COLLECTIVE SOUL			
ATLANTIC			
❑ 82984-1	Disciplined Breakdown	1997	$15

COLLECTORS, THE
Early incarnation of CHILLIWACK.

Number	Title	Yr	NM
WARNER BROS.			
❑ WS1774	Grass and Wild Strawberries	1969	$30
❑ W1746 [M]	The Collectors	1968	$50
—May be white label promo only			
❑ WS1746 [S]	The Collectors	1968	$30

Number	Title	Yr	NM
COLLEGIANS, THE (1)			
LOST-NITE			
❑ LLP-5 [10]	The Best of the Collegians	1981	$12
—Red vinyl			
WINLEY			
❑ LP-6004 [M]	Sing Along with the Collegians	195?	$400

Number	Title	Yr	NM
COLLETTE, BUDDY			
ABC-PARAMOUNT			
❑ ABC-179 [M]	Calm, Cool and Collette	1957	$75
CHALLENGE			
❑ CHL-603 [M]	Everybody's Buddy	1958	$50
CONTEMPORARY			
❑ C-3522 [M]	Man of Many Parts	1956	$250
❑ S-7522 [S]	Man of Many Parts	1959	$300
❑ C-3531 [M]	Nice Day with Buddy Collette	1957	$300
❑ S-7531 [S]	Nice Day with Buddy Collette	1959	$300
CROWN			
❑ CLP-5019 [M]	Bongo Madness	195?	$30
DIG			
❑ LP-101 [M]	Tanganyika	1956	$150
DOOTO			
❑ DTL-245 [M]	Buddy's Best	1957	$150
—Red vinyl			
❑ DTL-245 [M]	Buddy's Best	1957	$75
—Black vinyl			
EMARCY			
❑ MG-36133 [M]	Swingin' Shepherds	1958	$250
❑ SR-80005 [S]	Swingin' Shepherds	1959	$250
FANTASY			
❑ OJC-239	Man of Many Parts	198?	$25
INTERLUDE			
❑ MO-505 [M]	Modern Interpretations of Porgy & Bess	196?	$30
❑ ST-1005 [S]	Modern Interpretations of Porgy & Bess	196?	$40
LEGEND			
❑ 1004	Now and Then	1974	$30
MERCURY			
❑ MG-20447 [M]	At the Cinema	1959	$150
❑ SR-60132 [S]	At the Cinema	1959	$150
MUSIC & SOUND			
❑ 1001	Polynesia	196?	$30
❑ S-1001 [S]	Polynesia	196?	$40
RGB			
❑ 2001	Block Buster	1975	$30
SOUL NOTE			
❑ 121165	Flute Talk	1990	$35
SPECIALTY			
❑ SP-5002 [M]	Jazz Loves Paris	1960	$50
SURREY			
❑ S-1009 [M]	Buddy Collette on Broadway	1965	$35
❑ SS-1009 [S]	Buddy Collette on Broadway	1965	$25
TAMPA			
❑ TP-34 [M]	Star Studded Cast	1959	$175
WORLD PACIFIC			
❑ WP-1823 [M]	Warm Winds	1964	$150
❑ ST-1823 [S]	Warm Winds	1964	$150

Number	Title	Yr	NM
COLLIE, MAX, AND HIS RHYTHM ACES			
GHB			
❑ GHB-63	On Tour in the U.S.A.	198?	$25

Number	Title	Yr	NM
COLLIER, MITTY			
CHESS			
❑ LP-1492 [M]	Shades of a Genius	1965	$100
❑ LPS-1492 [S]	Shades of a Genius	1965	$120

Number	Title	Yr	NM
COLLINS, AARON			
CROWN			
❑ CLP-5028 [M]	Calypso U.S.A.	1958	$600

Number	Title	Yr	NM
COLLINS, AL "JAZZBO			
ABC IMPULSE!			
❑ AS-9150 [S]	A Lovely Bunch of Al "Jazzbo" Collins	1968	$35
CORAL			
❑ CRL57035 [M]	East Coast Jazz Scene	1956	$100
EVEREST			
❑ LPBR-5097 [M]	Swingin' at the Opera	1960	$30
❑ SDBR-1097 [S]	Swingin' at the Opera	1960	$40

Number	Title	Yr	NM

IMPULSE!
| ❏ A-9150 [M] | A Lovely Bunch of Al "Jazzbo" Collins | 1967 | $160 |
| ❏ AS-9150 [S] | A Lovely Bunch of Al "Jazzbo" Collins | 1967 | $120 |

OLD TOWN
| ❏ LP-2001 [M] | In the Purple Grotto | 1961 | $30 |

COLLINS, ALBERT

ALLIGATOR
❏ AL-4752	Cold Snap	1986	$12
❏ AL-4730	Don't Lose Your Cool	1983	$12
❏ AL-4719	Frostbite	1980	$12
❏ AL-4725	Frozen Alive!	1981	$12
❏ AL-4713	Ice Pickin'	1978	$12
❏ AL-4733	Live in Japan	1984	$12
❏ AL-4743	Showdown!	1985	$12

— *With Robert Cray and Johnny Copeland*

BLUE THUMB
| ❏ BTS8 | Truckin' with Albert Collins | 1969 | $30 |

— *Reissue of TCF Hall LP*

IMPERIAL
❏ LP-12428	Love Can Be Found Anywhere	1968	$30
❏ LP-12449	The Compleat Albert Collins	1970	$30
❏ LP-12438	Trash Talkin'	1969	$30

MOBILE FIDELITY
| ❏ 1-226 | Cold Snap | 1995 | $40 |

— *Audiophile vinyl*
| ❏ 1-217 | Showdown! | 1995 | $40 |

— *With Robert Cray and Johnny Copeland; audiophile vinyl*

TCF HALL
| ❏ 8002 [M] | The Cool Sound of Albert Collins | 1965 | $300 |

TUMBLEWEED
| ❏ TWS-103 | There's Gotta Be a Change | 1971 | $18 |

COLLINS, BOOTSY

COLUMBIA
| ❏ FC44107 | What's Bootsy Doin'? | 1988 | $12 |

WARNER BROS.
| ❏ BSK3667 | The One Giveth, The Count Taketh Away | 1982 | $12 |

COLLINS, BRIAN

ABC
| ❏ AC-1029 | The ABC Collection | 1977 | $18 |

ABC DOT
| ❏ DOSD-2008 | That's the Way Love Should Be | 1974 | $18 |

DOT
| ❏ DLP-26017 | This Is Brian Collins | 1973 | $18 |

COLLINS, CAL

CONCORD JAZZ
❏ CJ-95	Blues on My Mind	1979	$25
❏ CJ-119	By Myself	1980	$25
❏ CJ-71	Cal Collins In San Francisco	1978	$25
❏ CJ-59	Cincinnati to L.A.	1977	$25
❏ CJ-166	Cross Country	1981	$25
❏ CJ-137	Interplay	1981	$25

FAMOUS DOOR
| ❏ HL-123 | Ohio Boss Guitar | 198? | $25 |

PAUSA
| ❏ 7159 | Milestones | 198? | $25 |

COLLINS, DAVE AND ANSIL

BIG TREE
| ❏ 2005 [B] | Double Barrel | 1971 | $75 |

COLLINS, DICK

RCA VICTOR
| ❏ LJM-1019 [M] | Horn of Plenty | 1955 | $150 |
| ❏ LJM-1027 [M] | King Richard the Swing Hearted | 1955 | $150 |

COLLINS, DOROTHY

CORAL
❏ CRL57105 [M]	Dorothy Collins at Home	1957	$30
❏ CRL57150 [M]	Picnic	1958	$30
❏ CRL57106 [M]	Songs by Dorothy Collins	1957	$30

EVEREST
| ❏ LPBR-5026 [M] | Singing and Swinging | 196? | $25 |
| ❏ SDBR-1026 [S] | Singing and Swinging | 196? | $30 |

TOP RANK
| ❏ TM-340 [M] | A New Way to Travel | 1959 | $30 |

COLLINS, JOYCE

DISCOVERY
| ❏ 828 | Moment to Moment | 198? | $25 |

JAZZLAND
| ❏ JLP-24 [M] | The Girl Here Plays Mean Piano | 1960 | $30 |

Number	Title	Yr	NM
❏ JLP-924 [S]	The Girl Here Plays Mean Piano	1960	$30

COLLINS, JUDY

DCC COMPACT CLASSICS
| ❏ LPZ-2067 | Colors of the Day/The Best of Judy Collins | 1998 | $30 |

— *Audiophile vinyl*

DIRECT DISK
| ❏ SD-16607 | Judith | 1980 | $40 |

— *Audiophile vinyl*

ELEKTRA
| ❏ 7E-1076 | Bread and Roses | 1976 | $12 |
| ❏ EKS-75030 | Colors of the Day/The Best of Judy Collins | 1972 | $15 |

— *Butterfly label, no Warner Communications logo*
| ❏ EKS-75030 | Colors of the Day/The Best of Judy Collins | 1975 | $10 |

— *Any label with Warner Communications logo*

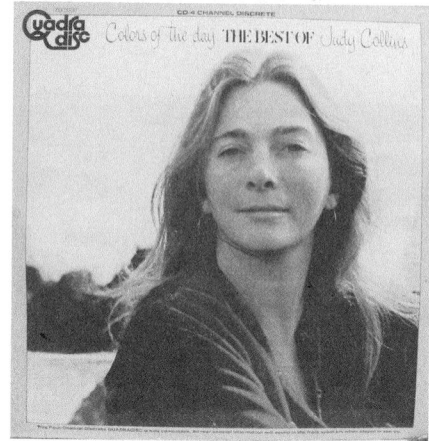

| ❏ EQ-5030 [Q] | Colors of the Day/The Best of Judy Collins | 1973 | $40 |
| ❏ EKL-222 [M] | Golden Apples of the Sun | 1962 | $30 |

— *Guitar player" label*
| ❏ EKL-222 [M] | Golden Apples of the Sun | 1966 | $25 |

— *Gold/tan label*
| ❏ EKS-7222 [R] | Golden Apples of the Sun | 196? | $15 |

— *Gold/tan label or red label with large stylized "E*
| ❏ EKS-7222 [R] | Golden Apples of the Sun | 1971 | $12 |

— *Butterfly label, no Warner Communications logo*
| ❏ EKS-7222 [R] | Golden Apples of the Sun | 1975 | $10 |

— *Any label with Warner Communications logo*
❏ 6E-171	Hard Times for Lovers	1979	$12
❏ 60304	Home Again	1985	$12
❏ EKL-320 [M]	In My Life	1966	$25
❏ EKS-7320 [S]	In My Life	1966	$30
❏ EKS-74027	In My Life	1968	$25

— *Reissue of 7320; gold/tan label*
| ❏ EKS-74027 | In My Life | 1969 | $18 |

— *Red label with large stylized "E*
| ❏ EKS-74027 | In My Life | 1971 | $15 |

— *Butterfly label, no Warner Communications logo*
| ❏ EKS-74027 | In My Life | 1975 | $10 |

— *Any label with Warner Communications logo*
❏ 7E-1032	Judith	1975	$15
❏ EQ-1032 [Q]	Judith	1975	$40
❏ 6E-111	Judith	1977	$10

— *Reissue of 7E-1032*
| ❏ DS500 | Judy | 1969 | $18 |

— *Columbia Record Club exclusive; red label with large stylized "E*
| ❏ EKL-243 [M] | Judy Collins #3 | 1963 | $30 |

— *Guitar player" label*
| ❏ EKL-243 [M] | Judy Collins #3 | 1966 | $25 |

— *Gold/tan label*
| ❏ EKS-7243 [S] | Judy Collins #3 | 1963 | $40 |

— *Guitar player" label*
| ❏ EKS-7243 [S] | Judy Collins #3 | 1966 | $30 |

— *Gold/tan label*
| ❏ EKS-7243 [S] | Judy Collins #3 | 1969 | $18 |

— *Red label with large stylized "E*
| ❏ EKS-7243 [S] | Judy Collins #3 | 1971 | $12 |

— *Butterfly label, no Warner Communications logo*
| ❏ EKS-7243 [S] | Judy Collins #3 | 1975 | $10 |

— *Any label with Warner Communications logo*
| ❏ JC-1 [DJ] | Judy Collins | 1967 | $18 |

— *Promo-only compilation of six songs, each in mono on one side, stereo on the other*
| ❏ EKL-280 [M] | Judy Collins' Concert | 1964 | $30 |

— *Guitar player" label*
| ❏ EKL-280 [M] | Judy Collins' Concert | 1966 | $25 |

— *Gold/tan label*
| ❏ EKS-7280 [S] | Judy Collins' Concert | 1964 | $40 |

— *Guitar player" label*

Number	Title	Yr	NM
❏ EKS-7280 [S]	Judy Collins' Concert	1966	$30

— *Gold/tan label*
| ❏ EKS-7280 [S] | Judy Collins' Concert | 1969 | $18 |

— *Red label with large stylized "E*
| ❏ EKS-7280 [S] | Judy Collins' Concert | 1971 | $15 |

— *Butterfly label, no Warner Communications logo*
| ❏ EKS-7280 [S] | Judy Collins' Concert | 1975 | $10 |

— *Any label with Warner Communications logo*
| ❏ EKL-300 [M] | Judy Collins' Fifth Album | 1965 | $30 |

— *Guitar player" label*
| ❏ EKL-300 [M] | Judy Collins' Fifth Album | 1966 | $25 |

— *Gold/tan label*
| ❏ EKS-7300 [S] | Judy Collins' Fifth Album | 1965 | $40 |

— *Guitar player" label*
| ❏ EKS-7300 [S] | Judy Collins' Fifth Album | 1966 | $30 |

— *Gold/tan label*
| ❏ EKS-7300 [S] | Judy Collins' Fifth Album | 1969 | $18 |

— *Red label with large stylized "E*
| ❏ EKS-7300 [S] | Judy Collins' Fifth Album | 1971 | $15 |

— *Butterfly label, no Warner Communications logo*
| ❏ EKS-7300 [S] | Judy Collins' Fifth Album | 1975 | $10 |

— *Any label with Warner Communications logo*
| ❏ EKS-75014 | Living | 1971 | $15 |

— *Butterfly label, no Warner Communications logo*
| ❏ EKS-75014 | Living | 1975 | $10 |

— *Any label with Warner Communications logo*
| ❏ EKL-209 [M] | Maid of Constant Sorrow | 1961 | $40 |

— *Guitar player" label*
| ❏ EKL-209 [M] | Maid of Constant Sorrow | 1966 | $25 |

— *Gold/tan label*
| ❏ EKS-7209 [R] | Maid of Constant Sorrow | 1966 | $15 |

— *Gold/tan label or red label with large stylized "E*
| ❏ EKS-7209 [R] | Maid of Constant Sorrow | 1971 | $12 |

— *Butterfly label, no Warner Communications logo*
| ❏ EKS-7209 [R] | Maid of Constant Sorrow | 1975 | $10 |

— *Any label with Warner Communications logo*
| ❏ EKS-7209 [R] | Maid of Constant Sorrow | 1964 | $25 |

— *Guitar player" label (first edition)*
| ❏ EKS-74055 | Recollections | 1969 | $18 |

— *Red label with large stylized "E*
| ❏ EKS-74055 | Recollections | 1971 | $15 |

— *Butterfly label, no Warner Communications logo*
| ❏ EKS-74055 | Recollections | 1975 | $10 |

— *Any label with Warner Communications logo*
❏ 6E-253	Running for My Life	1980	$12
❏ 8E-6002	So Early in the Spring: The First 15 Years	1977	$15
❏ 60001	Times of Our Lives	1982	$12
❏ EKS-75053	True Stories and Other Dreams	1973	$15

— *Butterfly label*
| ❏ EKS-75053 | True Stories and Other Dreams | 1980 | $10 |

— *Red or red/black label*
| ❏ EKS-75010 | Whales & Nightingales | 1970 | $15 |

— *Butterfly label, no Warner Communications logo*
| ❏ EKS-75010 | Whales & Nightingales | 1975 | $10 |

— *Any label with Warner Communications logo*
| ❏ EKS-74033 | Who Knows Where the Time Goes | 1968 | $25 |

— *Gold/tan label*
| ❏ EKS-74033 | Who Knows Where the Time Goes | 1969 | $18 |

— *Red label with large stylized "E*
| ❏ EKS-74033 | Who Knows Where the Time Goes | 1971 | $15 |

— *Butterfly label, no Warner Communications logo*
| ❏ EKS-74033 | Who Knows Where the Time Goes | 1975 | $10 |

— *Any label with Warner Communications logo*
| ❏ EKL-4012 [M] | Wildflowers | 1967 | $30 |
| ❏ EKS-74012 [S] | Wildflowers | 1967 | $25 |

— *Gold/tan label*
| ❏ EKS-74012 [S] | Wildflowers | 1969 | $18 |

— *Red label with large stylized "E*
| ❏ EKS-74012 [S] | Wildflowers | 1971 | $15 |

— *Butterfly label, no Warner Communications logo*
| ❏ EKS-74012 [S] | Wildflowers | 1975 | $10 |

— *Any label with Warner Communications logo*

GOLD CASTLE
❏ D1-71318	Sanity and Grace	1989	$15
❏ 171002	Trust Your Heart	1988	$15
❏ D1-71302	Trust Your Heart	1989	$15

— *Reissue of 171002*

PAIR
| ❏ PDL2-1141 | Her Finest Hour | 1986 | $15 |

WARNER SPECIAL PRODUCTS
| ❏ 61-6462 | Judy Collins | 1981 | $100 |

— *Book-of-the-Month Club exclusive*

COLLINS, LEE

NEW ORLEANS
| ❏ 7203 [M] | Night at Victory Club | 198? | $25 |

Number	Title	Yr	NM

COLLINS, LYN
PEOPLE
| ❏ PE-6605 | Check Me Out | 1975 | $150 |

— This album has been "reissued"; be careful of sealed copies

| ❏ PE-5602 | Think (About It) | 1972 | $175 |

— This album has been "reissued"; be careful of sealed copies

COLLINS, PHIL
Also see GENESIS; BRAND X; BRIAN ENO. Phil also drummed in ROBERT PLANT's solo band.
ATLANTIC
| ❏ 82050 | ... But Seriously | 1989 | $15 |
| ❏ PR759 [DJ] | Collins on Collins: Exclusive Candid Interview | 1985 | $30 |

— Promo-only interview album with cue sheets

❏ SD16029	Face Value	1981	$10
❏ 80035	Hello, I Must Be Going!	1982	$10
❏ 81240	No Jacket Required	1985	$10
❏ 82157	Serious Hits... Live!	1990	$25

COLLINS, SHIRLEY & GRAHAM, DAVY
4 MEN WITH BEARDS
| ❏ 4M802LP [B] | Folk Roots, New Routes | 20.00 | $ |

COLLINS, SHIRLEY AND DOROTHY
HARVEST
| ❏ SKAO-370 | Anthems in Eden | 1969 | $50 |

COLLINS, TOMMY
CAPITOL
❏ T1125 [M]	Light of the Lord	1959	$150
❏ T1436 [M]	Songs I Love to Sing	1961	$50
❏ ST1436 [S]	Songs I Love to Sing	1961	$75
❏ T1196 [M]	This Is Tommy Collins	1959	$75
❏ T776 [M]	Words and Music Country Style	1957	$150
COLUMBIA
❏ CL2510 [M]	The Dynamic Tommy Collins	1966	$30
❏ CS9310 [S]	The Dynamic Tommy Collins	1966	$40
❏ CL2778 [M]	Tommy Collins On Tour -- His Most Requested Songs	1968	$75
❏ CS9578 [S]	Tommy Collins On Tour -- His Most Requested Songs	1968	$30
STARDAY
| ❏ SLP-474 | Tommy Collins Callin' | 1972 | $25 |
TOWER
❏ T5021 [M]	Let's Live a Little	1966	$30
❏ DT5021 [R]	Let's Live a Little	1966	$25
❏ T5107 [M]	Shindig	1967	$40
❏ DT5107 [R]	Shindig	1967	$25

COLMAN, RONALD
DECCA
| ❏ DLP8010 [M] | A Christmas Carol/Mr. Pickwick's Christmas | 1949 | $25 |

— Side 2 read by Charles Laughton

MCA
| ❏ 15010 | A Christmas Carol/Mr. Pickwick's Christmas | 1973 | $12 |

— Side 2 read by Charles Laughton; reissue of Decca LP

COLONNA, JERRY
DECCA
| ❏ DL5540 [10] | Music? For Screaming!!! | 1955 | $175 |
LIBERTY
| ❏ SL-9004 [M] | Along the Dixieland Hi-Fi Way | 1957 | $40 |
| ❏ LRP-3046 [M] | Let's All Sing with Jerry Colonna | 1957 | $40 |

COLOSSEUM
Gary Moore and Don Airey are Colosseum alumni.
ABC DUNHILL
❏ DSX-50101 [B]	Daughter of Time	1971	$30
❏ DS-50079 [B]	The Grass Is Green	1970	$30
❏ DS-50062 [B]	Those Who Are About to Die Salute You	1969	$30
WARNER BROS.
| ❏ 2WS1942 [B] | Colosseum Live | 1972 | $30 |
| ❏ PRO500 [DJ] | Colosseum Live | 1972 | $30 |

— Highlights for radio

COLOURS
DOT
| ❏ DLP-25935 | Atmosphere | 1969 | $30 |
| ❏ DLP-3854 [M] | Colours | 1968 | $50 |

— Record has a black label, resembling a stock copy, but it is in a stereo cover with "Monaural" and "Promotional Copy Not for Sale" stickers on front

| ❏ DLP-25854 [S] | Colours | 1968 | $30 |

COLTER, JESSI
CAPITOL
❏ ST-11543	Diamond in the Rough	1976	$12
❏ ST-11363	I'm Jessi Colter	1975	$12
❏ ST-11477	Jessi	1976	$12

❏ ST-11583	Mirriam	1977	$12
❏ ST-12185	Ridin' Shotgun	1981	$12
❏ ST-11863	That's the Way a Cowboy Rocks and Rolls	1978	$12
❏ ST-511863	That's the Way a Cowboy Rocks and Rolls	1978	$15

— Columbia House edition

RCA VICTOR
| ❏ LSP-4333 | Country Star | 1970 | $25 |

COLTRANE, ALICE, AND CARLOS SANTANA
Also see ALICE COLTRANE; SANTANA.
COLUMBIA
| ❏ PC32900 | Illuminations | 1974 | $50 |

— No bar code on cover

COLTRANE, ALICE
ABC IMPULSE!
❏ AS-9156	A Monastic Trio	1968	$160
❏ AS-9185	Huntington Ashram Monastery	1969	$250
❏ AS-9203	Journey in Satchidananda	1970	$250
❏ AS-9224	Lord of Lords	1972	$160
❏ AS-9196	Ptah the El Daoud	1969	$250
❏ AS-9232	Reflection On Creation and Space	1973	$250
❏ AS-9210	Universal Consciousness	1971	$250
❏ AS-9218	World Galaxy	1972	$160
GRP/IMPULSE!
| ❏ IMP-228 | Journey in Satchidanada | 1997 | $35 |

— 180-gram reissue

WARNER BROS.
❏ BS2916	Eternity	1975	$50
❏ BS2986	Radha-Krsna Nama Sankirtana	1976	$75
❏ BS3077	Transcendence	1977	$50
❏ 2WB3218	Transfiguration	1978	$40

COLTRANE, CHI
COLUMBIA
| ❏ KC31275 | Chi Coltrane | 1972 | $15 |
| ❏ KC32463 | Let It Ride | 1973 | $15 |

COLTRANE, JOHN
ABC IMPULSE!
❏ AS-6 [S]	Africa/Brass	1968	$250
❏ AS-9273	Africa/Brass, Volume 2	1974	$160
❏ AS-77 [S]	A Love Supreme	1968	$250

— Black label with red border

| ❏ AS-77 [S] | A Love Supreme | 1978 | $30 |

— abc" musical note at top of yellow, red, purple "target" label

| ❏ AS-77 [S] | A Love Supreme | 1974 | $35 |

— Green, blue, purple "target" label

| ❏ AS-95 [S] | Ascension | 1968 | $250 |

— With "Edition II" in dead wax; black label with red ring

| ❏ AS-95 [S] | Ascension | 1978 | $30 |

— abc" musical note at top of yellow, red, purple "target" label

| ❏ AS-32 [S] | Ballads | 1968 | $250 |

— Black label with red ring

| ❏ AS-32 [S] | Ballads | 1973 | $150 |

— All-black label

| ❏ AS-21 [S] | Coltrane | 1968 | $250 |

— Black label with red ring

| ❏ AS-50 [S] | Coltrane Live at Birdland | 1968 | $250 |

— Black label with red ring

| ❏ AS-50 [S] | Coltrane Live at Birdland | 1975 | $35 |

— Green blue, purple "target" label

| ❏ IA-9246 | Concert Japan | 1973 | $35 |

| ❏ AS-9148 [B] | Cosmic Music | 1969 | $250 |

— Credited to "Alice and John Coltrane"; reissue of Coltrane LP

| ❏ AS-66 [S] | Crescent | 1968 | $250 |

— Black label with red ring

| ❏ AS-30 [S] | Duke Ellington and John Coltrane | 1968 | $250 |

— Black label with red ring

| ❏ AS-30 [S] | Duke Ellington and John Coltrane | 1973 | $120 |

— All-black label

| ❏ AS-9120 [S] | Expression | 1968 | $250 |

— Black label with red ring

❏ IA-9332	First Meditations	1978	$30
❏ AS-9200	Greatest Years	1971	$250
❏ AS-9223	Greatest Years, Volume 2	1973	$35
❏ IA-9278	Greatest Years, Volume 3	1974	$35
❏ AS-42 [S]	Impressions	1968	$250

— Black label with red ring

❏ AS-9225	Infinity	1973	$30
❏ IA-9277	Interstellar Space	1974	$30
❏ AS-40 [S]	John Coltrane + Johnny Hartman	1968	$250

— Black label with red ring

| ❏ AS-40 [S] | John Coltrane + Johnny Hartman | 1975 | $35 |

— Green blue, purple "target" label

| ❏ AS-9106 [S] | Kulu Se Mama | 1968 | $250 |

— Black label with red ring

| ❏ AS-10 [S] | Live at the Village Vanguard | 1968 | $250 |
| ❏ AS-9124 [S] | Live at the Village Vanguard Again! | 1968 | $250 |

— Black label with red ring

| ❏ AS-9124 [S] | Live at the Village Vanguard Again! | 1975 | $35 |

— Green, blue and purple "target" label

| ❏ AS-9202 | Live in Seattle | 1971 | $250 |
| ❏ AS-9110 [S] | Meditations | 1968 | $250 |

— Black label with red ring

| ❏ AS-9110 [S] | Meditations | 1975 | $35 |

— Green, blue and purple "target" label

| ❏ AS-9110 [S] | Meditations | 1978 | $30 |

— abc" musical note at top of yellow, red, purple "target" label

| ❏ AS-94 [S] | New Thing at Newport | 1968 | $250 |

— Black label with red ring

| ❏ AS-9140 [S] | Om | 1968 | $250 |

— Black label with red ring

❏ AS-9161	Selflessness	1969	$250
❏ AS-9161	Sun Ship	1971	$250
❏ IA-9306	The Gentle Side of John Coltrane	1976	$35
❏ AS-85 [S]	The John Coltrane Quartet Plays	1968	$250

— Black label with red ring

❏ IZ-9345	The Mastery of John Coltrane Vol. 1: Feelin' Good	1978	$30
❏ IZ-9346	The Mastery of John Coltrane Vol. 2: Different Drum	1978	$30
❏ IA-9360	The Mastery of John Coltrane Vol. 3: Jupiter Variation	1978	$30
❏ IZ-9361	The Mastery of John Coltrane Vol. 4: Trane's Moods	1978	$30
❏ IA-9325	The Other Village Vanguard Tapes	1977	$35
❏ AS-9195	Transition	1969	$250
ATLANTIC
| ❏ 1354 [M] | Coltrane Jazz | 1960 | $300 |

— Orange and purple label, white fan logo

| ❏ 1354 [M] | Coltrane Jazz | 1962 | $150 |

— Orange and purple label, black fan logo

| ❏ SD1354 [S] | Coltrane Jazz | 1960 | $400 |

— Green and blue label, white fan logo

| ❏ SD1354 [S] | Coltrane Jazz | 1962 | $100 |

— Green and blue label, black fan logo

| ❏ SD1354 [S] | Coltrane Jazz | 1969 | $40 |

— Red and green label

| ❏ 1382 [M] | Coltrane Plays the Blues | 1962 | $250 |
| ❏ SD1382 [S] | Coltrane Plays the Blues | 1962 | $300 |

— Green and blue label, black fan logo

| ❏ SD1382 [S] | Coltrane Plays the Blues | 1969 | $75 |

— Red and green label

| ❏ 1419 [M] | Coltrane's Sound | 1964 | $100 |
| ❏ SD1419 [S] | Coltrane's Sound | 1964 | $150 |

— Green and blue label, black fan logo

| ❏ SD1419 [S] | Coltrane's Sound | 1969 | $30 |

— Red and green label

| ❏ 90462 | Countdown | 1986 | $25 |
| ❏ 1311 [M] | Giant Steps | 1959 | $1400 |

— Black label

| ❏ 1311 [M] | Giant Steps | 1960 | $300 |

— Orange and purple label, white fan logo

| ❏ 1311 [M] | Giant Steps | 1962 | $100 |

— Orange and purple label, black fan logo

| ❏ SD1311 [S] | Giant Steps | 1959 | $300 |

— Green label

| ❏ SD1311 [S] | Giant Steps | 1960 | $300 |

— Green and blue label, white fan logo

| ❏ SD1311 [S] | Giant Steps | 1962 | $150 |

— Green and blue label, black fan logo

| ❏ SD1311 [S] | Giant Steps | 1969 | $30 |

— Red and green label

| ❏ SD1311 [S] | Giant Steps | 1959 | $300 |

— Bullseye" label

| ❏ 1361 [M] | My Favorite Things | 1961 | $300 |

— Orange and purple label, white fan logo

Number	Title	Yr	NM
❑ 1361 [M]	My Favorite Things	1962	$175
—Orange and purple label, black fan logo			
❑ SD1361 [S]	My Favorite Things	1961	$175
—Green and blue label, white fan logo			
❑ SD1361 [S]	My Favorite Things	1962	$175
—Green and blue label, black fan logo			
❑ SD1361 [S]	My Favorite Things	1969	$30
—Red and green label			
❑ 1373 [M]	Ole' Coltrane	1961	$300
—Orange and purple label, white fan logo			
❑ 1373 [M]	Ole' Coltrane	1962	$175
—Orange and purple label, black fan logo			
❑ SD1373 [S]	Ole' Coltrane	1961	$300
—Green and blue label, white fan logo			
❑ SD1373 [S]	Ole' Coltrane	1962	$175
—Green and blue label, black fan logo			
❑ SD1373 [S]	Ole' Coltrane	1969	$30
—Red and green label			
❑ SD 2-313	The Art of John Coltrane	1973	$35
❑ 1451 [M]	The Avant Garde	1966	$175
❑ SD1451 [S]	The Avant Garde	1966	$175
—Green and blue label, black fan logo			
❑ SD1451 [S]	The Avant Garde	1969	$25
—Red and green label			
❑ 90041	The Avant-Garde	1983	$25
❑ SD1541	The Best of John Coltrane	1970	$30
❑ SD1553	The Coltrane Legacy	1971	$30

ATLANTIC/RHINO
| ❑ R1-71984 | The Heavyweight Champion: The Complete Atlantic Recordings | 1995 | $300 |
| —Box set with liner notes; albums pressed on 150-gram vinyl | | | |

ATLANTIC/RHINO HANDMADE
❑ RHM1-7784	The Heavyweight Champion: The Complete Atlantic Recordings (Year 2000 Second Edition)	2000	$250
— Year 2000 Second Edition" at lower right back cover; limited, numbered edition of 1,500 copies on 180-gram vinyl			
❑ RHM1-7784	The Heavyweight Champion: The Complete Atlantic Recordings (Year 2000 Second Edition)	2000	$250
— Year 2000 Second Edition" on lower left back cover; limited edition of 1,500, un-numbered, on 180-gram vinyl; pressed in the U.S. for export			

BLUE NOTE
❑ BLP-1577 [M]	Blue Train	1957	$1500
—Deep groove" version; W. 63rd St., NYC address on label			
❑ BLP-1577 [M]	Blue Train	1957	$300
—Regular version, W. 63rd St., NYC address on label			
❑ BST-1577 [S]	Blue Train	1957	$4000
—Deep groove" version; W. 63rd St., NYC address on label			
❑ BST-1577 [S]	Blue Train	1959	$250
—Regular version, W. 63rd St., NYC address on label			
❑ BLP-1577 [M]	Blue Train	1965	$400
—New York, USA" address on label			
❑ BST-1577 [S]	Blue Train	1965	$300
—New York, USA" address on label			
❑ BST-81577	Blue Train	1967	$75
—A Division of Liberty Records" on label			
❑ BST-81577	Blue Train	198?	$30
—The Finest in Jazz Since 1939" reissue			
❑ B1-81577	Blue Train	1988	$30
—Reissue with new prefix			
❑ B1-46095	Blue Train	1997	$35
—180-gram reissue			

COLTRANE
| ❑ AU-4950 | Cosmic Music | 1966 | $300 |
| ❑ AU-5000 | Cosmic Music | 1966 | $250 |

DCC COMPACT CLASSICS
| ❑ LPZ-2032 | Lush Life | 1997 | $120 |
| —Audiophile vinyl | | | |

FANTASY
❑ OJC-415	Bahia	1990	$30
❑ OJC-352	Black Pearls	1989	$25
❑ OJC-460	Cattin' with Coltrane and Quinichette	1990	$30
❑ OJC-020	Coltrane	198?	$25
❑ OJC-393	Dakar	1989	$25
❑ OJC-394	Last Trane	1989	$25
❑ OJC-131	Lush Life	198?	$25
❑ OJC-078	Settin' the Pace	198?	$25
❑ OJC-021	Soultrane	198?	$25
❑ OJC-246	Standard Coltrane	1987	$25
❑ OJC-127	Tenor Conclave	1991	$30
❑ OJC-189	Traneing In	1986	$25

GRP/IMPULSE!
❑ GR-155	A Love Supreme	1995	$35
❑ GR-156	Ballads	1995	$35
❑ IMP-215	Coltrane	1997	$35
❑ IMP-198	Coltrane Live at Birdland	1997	$35
❑ IMP-200	Crescent	1997	$35
❑ IMP-166	Duke Ellington and John Coltrane	1997	$35
❑ GR-157	John Coltrane + Johnny Hartman	1995	$35

Number	Title	Yr	NM
❑ IMP-213	Live at the Village Vanguard Again!	1997	$35
❑ IMP-169	Stellar Regions	1995	$35
❑ IMP-167	Sun Ship	1997	$35
❑ IMP-214	The John Coltrane Quartet Plays	1997	$35

IMPULSE!
❑ A-6 [M]	Africa/Brass	1961	$500
❑ AS-6 [S]	Africa/Brass	1961	$250
❑ A-77 [M]	A Love Supreme	1965	$250
❑ AS-77 [S]	A Love Supreme	1965	$300
❑ B002391101 [B]	A Love Supreme: The Complete Masters	2016	$50
❑ A-95 [M]	Ascension	1965	$300
—Without "Edition II" in dead wax			
❑ A-95 [M]	Ascension	1966	$250
—With "Edition II" in dead wax			
❑ AS-95 [S]	Ascension	1965	$180
—Without "Edition II" in dead wax			
❑ AS-95 [S]	Ascension	1966	$250
—With "Edition II" in dead wax			
❑ A-32 [M]	Ballads	1963	$160
❑ AS-32 [S]	Ballads	1963	$250
❑ A-21 [M]	Coltrane	1962	$160
❑ AS-21 [S]	Coltrane	1962	$250
❑ A-50 [M]	Coltrane Live at Birdland	1963	$160
❑ AS-50 [S]	Coltrane Live at Birdland	1963	$250
❑ SMAS-90232 [S]	Coltrane Live at Birdland	1964	$300
—Capitol Record Club edition			
❑ A-66 [M]	Crescent	1964	$160
❑ AS-66 [S]	Crescent	1964	$250
❑ A-30 [M]	Duke Ellington and John Coltrane	1963	$250
❑ AS-30 [S]	Duke Ellington and John Coltrane	1963	$450
❑ A-9120 [M]	Expression	1967	$250
❑ AS-9120 [S]	Expression	1967	$160
❑ SMAS-91288 [S]	Expression	1967	$300
—Capitol Record Club edition			
❑ A-42 [M]	Impressions	1963	$250
❑ AS-42 [S]	Impressions	1963	$160
❑ A-40 [M]	John Coltrane + Johnny Hartman	1963	$250
❑ AS-40 [S]	John Coltrane + Johnny Hartman	1963	$250
❑ A-9106 [M]	Kulu Se Mama	1966	$250
❑ AS-9106 [S]	Kulu Se Mama	1966	$250
❑ A-10 [M]	Live at the Village Vanguard	1962	$250
❑ AS-10 [S]	Live at the Village Vanguard	1962	$1200
❑ A-9124 [M]	Live at the Village Vanguard Again!	1967	$300
❑ AS-9124 [S]	Live at the Village Vanguard Again!	1967	$250
❑ A-9110 [M]	Meditations	1966	$160
❑ AS-9110 [S]	Meditations	1966	$250
❑ A-94 [M]	New Thing at Newport	1965	$250
❑ AS-94 [S]	New Thing at Newport	1965	$160
❑ A-9140 [M]	Om	1967	$300

❑ AS-9140 [S]	Om	1967	$160
❑ A-85 [M]	The John Coltrane Quartet Plays	1965	$250
❑ AS-85 [S]	The John Coltrane Quartet Plays	1965	$160

MCA
❑ 29007	Africa/Brass	1981	$20
❑ 29008	Africa/Brass, Volume 2	1981	$20
❑ 29017	A Love Supreme	1981	$20
❑ 29020	Ascension	1981	$20
❑ 29012	Ballads	1981	$20
❑ 29011	Coltrane	1981	$20
❑ 29015	Coltrane Live at Birdland	1981	$20
❑ 4135	Concert Japan	1981	$25
❑ 29025	Cosmic Music	1981	$20
❑ 29016	Crescent	1981	$20
❑ 29032	Duke Ellington and John Coltrane	1981	$20
❑ 29023	Expression	1981	$20
❑ 29030	First Meditations	1981	$20
❑ 4131	Greatest Years	1981	$25
❑ 4132	Greatest Years, Volume 2	1981	$25
❑ 4133	Greatest Years, Volume 3	1981	$25

Number	Title	Yr	NM
❑ 29014	Impressions	1981	$20
❑ 29029	Interstellar Space	1981	$20
❑ 29013	John Coltrane + Johnny Hartman	1981	$20
❑ 29021	Kulu Se Mama	1981	$20
❑ 29009	Live at the Village Vanguard	1981	$20
❑ 29010	Live at the Village Vanguard Again!	1981	$20
❑ 4134	Live in Seattle	1981	$25
❑ 29022	Meditations	1981	$20
❑ 29019	New Thing at Newport	1981	$20
❑ 29024	Om	1981	$20
❑ 29026	Selflessness	1981	$20
❑ 29028	Sun Ship	1981	$20
❑ 4136	The Gentle Side of John Coltrane	1981	$25
❑ 29018	The John Coltrane Quartet Plays	1981	$20
❑ 4138	The Mastery of John Coltrane Vol. 1: Feelin' Good	1981	$25
❑ 4139	The Mastery of John Coltrane Vol. 2: Different Drum	1981	$25
❑ 29031	The Mastery of John Coltrane Vol. 3: Jupiter Variation	1981	$20
❑ 4140	The Mastery of John Coltrane Vol. 4: Trane's Moods	1981	$25
❑ 4137	The Other Village Vanguard Tapes	1981	$25
❑ 29027	Transition	1981	$20

MCA/IMPULSE!
❑ 42231	Africa/Brass	1988	$25
❑ 42232	Africa/Brass, Volume 2	1988	$12
❑ 5660	A Love Supreme	1986	$25
❑ 5885	Ballads	1987	$25
❑ 5883	Coltrane	1987	$25
❑ 33109	Coltrane Live at Birdland	198?	$25
❑ 5889	Crescent	1987	$25
❑ 39103	Duke Ellington and John Coltrane	1988	$25
❑ 5887	Impressions	1987	$25
❑ 5661	John Coltrane + Johnny Hartman	1986	$25
❑ 39136	Live at the Village Vanguard	1988	$25
❑ 39118	Om	1988	$25
❑ 33110	The John Coltrane Quartet Plays	198?	$25

ORIGINAL JAZZ CLASSICS
| ❑ OJC131 [B] | Lush Life | 2015 | $30 |

PABLO
| ❑ 2405417 | The Best of John Coltrane | 198? | $25 |

PABLO LIVE
❑ 2620101	Afro Blue Impressions	198?	$30
❑ 2308227	Bye Bye Blackbird	1981	$30
❑ 2308222	European Tour	1981	$30
❑ 2308217	The Paris Concert	1980	$30

PRESTIGE
❑ PRLP-7353 [M]	Bahia	1965	$75
❑ PRST-7353 [S]	Bahia	1965	$75
❑ 24110	Bahia	198?	$30
❑ PRLP-7316 [M]	Black Pearls	1964	$40
—Yellow label			
❑ PRST-7316 [S]	Black Pearls	1964	$40
—Silver label			
❑ PRLP-7316 [M]	Black Pearls	1964	$75
—Blue label with trident logo			
❑ PRST-7316 [S]	Black Pearls	1964	$75
—Blue label with trident logo			
❑ 24037	Black Pearls	1974	$35
❑ PRLP-7158 [M]	Cattin' with Coltrane and Quinichette	1959	$450
—Yellow label			
❑ PRLP-7158 [M]	Cattin' with Coltrane and Quinichette	1964	$30
—Blue label with trident logo			
❑ PRLP-7105 [M]	Coltrane	1957	$1200
—Yellow label			
❑ PRLP-7105 [M]	Coltrane	1964	$75
—Blue label with trident logo			
❑ PRLP-7280 [M]	Dakar	1963	$40
—Yellow label			
❑ PRST-7280 [S]	Dakar	1963	$40
—Silver label			
❑ PRLP-7280 [M]	Dakar	1964	$75
—Blue label with trident logo			
❑ PRST-7280 [S]	Dakar	1964	$75
—Blue label with trident logo			
❑ 24104	Dakar	198?	$30
❑ 24003	John Coltrane	1972	$35
❑ PRLP-7123 [M]	John Coltrane and the Red Garland Trio	1957	$650
—Yellow label			
❑ PRLP-7426 [M]	John Coltrane Plays for Lovers	1966	$75
❑ PRST-7426 [S]	John Coltrane Plays for Lovers	1966	$75
❑ PRLP-7188 [M]	Lush Life	1960	$250
—Yellow label			
❑ PRLP-7188 [M]	Lush Life	1964	$75
—Blue label with trident logo			
❑ PRST-7581 [R]	Lush Life	1968	$30

Number	Title	Yr	NM
❑ PRLP-7247 [M]	Mating Call	1962	$175

— Yellow label

❑ PRST-7247 [R]	Mating Call	196?	$75

— Silver label

❑ PRLP-7247 [M]	Mating Call	1964	$75

— Blue label with trident logo

❑ PRST-7247 [R]	Mating Call	1964	$50

— Blue label with trident logo

❑ PRST-7725	Mating Call	1970	$30
❑ 24014	More Lasting Than Bronze	1973	$35
❑ 24084	On a Misty Night	198?	$30
❑ 24094	Rain or Shine	198?	$30
❑ PRLP-7213 [M]	Settin' the Pace	1961	$250

— Yellow label

❑ PRLP-7213 [M]	Settin' the Pace	1964	$75

— Blue label with trident logo

❑ PRLP-7142 [M]	Soultrane	1958	$500

— Yellow label

❑ PRLP-7531 [M]	Soultrane	1967	$75
❑ PRLP-7142 [M]	Soultrane	1964	$75

— Blue label with trident logo

❑ PRST-7531 [R]	Soultrane	1967	$30
❑ PRLP-7243 [M]	Standard Coltrane	1962	$175

— Yellow label

❑ PRST-7243 [S]	Standard Coltrane	1962	$175

— Silver label

❑ PRLP-7243 [M]	Standard Coltrane	1964	$75

— Blue label with trident logo

❑ PRST-7243 [S]	Standard Coltrane	1964	$75

— Blue label with trident logo

❑ PRLP-7268 [M]	Stardust	1963	$40

— Yellow label

❑ PRST-7268 [S]	Stardust	1963	$40

— Silver label

❑ PRLP-7268 [M]	Stardust	1964	$75

— Blue label with trident logo

❑ PRST-7268 [S]	Stardust	1964	$75

— Blue label with trident logo

❑ PRLP-7249 [M]	Tenor Conclave	1962	$175

— Yellow label

❑ PRST-7249 [R]	Tenor Conclave	196?	$75

— Silver label

❑ PRLP-7249 [M]	Tenor Conclave	1964	$75

— Blue label with trident logo

❑ PRST-7249 [R]	Tenor Conclave	1964	$50

— Blue label with trident logo

❑ PRLP-7292 [M]	The Believer	1964	$40

— Yellow label

❑ PRST-7292 [S]	The Believer	1964	$40

— Silver label

❑ PRLP-7292 [M]	The Believer	1964	$75

— Blue label with trident logo

❑ PRST-7292 [S]	The Believer	1964	$75

— Blue label with trident logo

❑ PRST-7609 [R]	The First Trane	1969	$30
❑ PRLP-7378 [M]	The Last Trane	1965	$75
❑ PRST-7378 [S]	The Last Trane	1965	$75
❑ PRST-7825	The Master	1971	$30
❑ 24056	The Stardust Session	197?	$35
❑ PRLP-7123 [M]	Traneing In	1964	$75

— Blue label with trident logo; reissue with new title

❑ PRST-7651 [R]	Traneing In	1969	$30
❑ PRST-7746	Trane's Reign	1970	$30
❑ PRST-7670 [R]	Two Tenors	1969	$30
❑ 24069	Wheelin'	197?	$30

RHINO

❑ R1-75203	Giant Steps	2003	$35

— Reissue on 180-gram vinyl

SOLID STATE

❑ SM-17025 [M]	Coltrane Time	1968	$75
❑ SS-18025 [S]	Coltrane Time	1968	$35

TRIP

❑ 5001	Trane Tracks	1974	$35

UNITED ARTISTS

❑ UAJ-14001 [M]	Coltrane Time	1962	$40
❑ UAJS-15001 [S]	Coltrane Time	1962	$150
❑ UAS-5638	Coltrane Time	1972	$30

— Reissue of 15001

COLUMBIA CHOIR, THE

COLUMBIA

❑ CL1051 [M]	The Christmas Mood	1957	$30

— Expanded version of 10-inch LP with B-side instrumentals

❑ CL(# unk) [10]	The Christmas Mood	1954	$50

— First appearance of the "Albert Burt Carols" on record

❑ CL2546 [10]	The Christmas Mood	1955	$40

— House Party Series" reissue

COLUMBO, CHRIS

STRAND

❑ SL-1044 [M]	Jazz Rediscovered	1962	$30
❑ SLS-1044 [S]	Jazz Rediscovered	1962	$40
❑ SL-1095 [M]	Summertime	1963	$30
❑ SLS-1095 [S]	Summertime	1963	$40

COLUMBUS BOYCHOIR

DECCA

Number	Title	Yr	NM
❑ DL8920 [M]	Joy to the World	1959	$18
❑ DL78920 [S]	Joy to the World	1959	$25

COLVIN, SHAWN

COLUMBIA

❑ FC45209	Steady On	1989	$15

COLWELL-WINFIELD BLUES BAND, THE

VERVE FORECAST

❑ FTS-3056	Cold Wind Blues	1968	$25

ZA-ZOO

❑ 1	Live Bust	1971	$250

COLYER, KEN

GHB

❑ 161	Live at the 100 Club	198?	$25

LONDON

❑ LL1340 [M]	Back to the Delta	1956	$40
❑ LL1618 [M]	Club Session with Colyer	1957	$40
❑ PB904 [10]	New Orleans to London	1954	$150

STORYVILLE

❑ SLP-144	Ken's Early Days	197?	$30

COMBUSTIBLE EDISON

SUB POP

❑ SP244	I, Swinger	1994	$12
❑ SP313	Schizophonic	1996	$12
❑ SP431	The Impossible World	1998	$15

COME

MATADOR

❑ OLE 045 [B]	11:11	1992	$18
❑ OLE108	Don't Ask, Don't Tell	1994	$12
❑ OLE254	Gently Down the Stream	1998	$15
❑ OLE192	Near Life Experience	1996	$12
❑ OLE126 [10]	String	1995	$18

— Four-song 10-inch EP

COMFORTABLE CHAIR, THE

ODE

❑ Z1244005	The Comfortable Chair	1968	$25

COMMANDER CODY AND HIS LOST PLANET AIRMEN

ARISTA

❑ AB4183	Flying Dreams	1978	$18
❑ AL4125	Rock 'N' Roll Again	1977	$12

BLIND PIG

❑ BP-2086	Let's Rock	1986	$12

MCA

❑ 660	Country Casanova	1980	$10

— Reissue of Paramount 6054

❑ 661	Hot Licks, Cold Steel & Truckers Favorites	1980	$10

— Reissue of Paramount 6031

❑ 659	Live from Deep in the Heart of Texas	1980	$10

— Reissue of Paramount 1017

❑ 37101	Lost in the Ozone	1980	$10

— Reissue of Paramount 6017

PARAMOUNT

❑ PAS-6054	Country Casanova	1973	$15
❑ PAS-6031	Hot Licks, Cold Steel & Truckers Favorites	1972	$15
❑ PAS-1017	Live from Deep in the Heart of Texas	1974	$15
❑ PAS-6017	Lost in the Ozone	1971	$18

WARNER BROS.

❑ BS2847	Commander Cody and His Lost Planet Airmen	1975	$12
❑ BS2883	Tales from the Ozone	1975	$12
❑ 2LS2939	We've Got a Live One Here!	1976	$15

COMMANDERS, THE

DECCA

❑ DL8117 [M]	Dance Party	1955	$175

— Led by Eddie Grady

COMMODORES

MOTOWN

❑ PR39 [DJ]	1978 Platinum Tour	1978	$25

— Promo-only compilation

❑ 6028ML	All the Great Hits	1982	$12
❑ 6044ML2	Anthology	1983	$15
❑ M6-820	Caught in the Act	1975	$12
❑ M5-240V1	Caught in the Act	1982	$10
❑ M7-884	Commodores	1977	$12
❑ M5-222V1	Commodores	1982	$10
❑ 6054ML	Commodores 13	1983	$12
❑ M7-912	Commodores' Greatest Hits	1978	$12
❑ M9-894	Commodores Live!	1977	$15
❑ M8-939	Heroes	1980	$12
❑ M6-867	Hot on the Tracks	1976	$12

Number	Title	Yr	NM
❑ 5257ML	Hot on the Tracks	1983	$10
❑ M8-955	In the Pocket	1981	$12
❑ M5-121V1	Machine Gun	1981	$12

— Reissue

❑ M6-798	Machine Gun	1974	$18
❑ M8-926	Midnight Magic	1979	$12
❑ M6-848	Movin' On	1975	$12
❑ M5-179V1	Movin' On	1981	$10
❑ M7-902	Natural High	1978	$12
❑ 5293ML [B]	Natural High	1983	$10
❑ 6124ML	Nightshift	1985	$12

POLYDOR

❑ 835369-1	Rock Solid	1988	$12
❑ 831194-1	United	1986	$12

COMMON PEOPLE, THE

CAPITOL

❑ ST-266	Of the People/By the People/For the People/From the Common People	1969	$250

COMMUNARDS

MCA

❑ 5794	Communards	1986	$12
❑ 42106	Red	1987	$12

COMO, PERRY

PAIR

❑ PDL2-1112	Blue Skies	1986	$15
❑ PDL2-1001	Easy Listening	1986	$15
❑ PDL2-1038	Love Moods	1986	$15

PICKWICK

❑ CAS-660 [R]	Perry Como Sings Merry Christmas Music	1977	$10

— Reissue of RCA Camden CAS-660 with another new cover

RCA

❑ 6368-1-R	Perry Como Today	1988	$12

RCA CAMDEN

❑ CAL-742 [M]	An Evening with Perry Como	196?	$18
❑ CAL-511 [M]	Como's Wednesday Night Music Hall	1959	$25
❑ CAS-2482	Door of Dreams	1971	$12
❑ CAL-403 [M]	Dream Along with Me	1957	$25
❑ CAS-403(e) [R]	Dream Along with Me	1962	$12
❑ CAL-582 [M]	Dreamer's Holiday	1960	$18
❑ CAS-2609	Dream On Little Dreamer	1972	$12
❑ CXS-9002	Easy Listening	1972	$15
❑ CAL-2122 [M]	Hello Young Lovers	1967	$18
❑ CAS-2122 [R]	Hello Young Lovers	1967	$12
❑ CAL-805 [M]	Love Makes the World Go 'Round	1964	$15
❑ CAS-805 [S]	Love Makes the World Go 'Round	1964	$12
❑ CAL-694 [M]	Make Someone Happy	1962	$15
❑ CAL-941 [M]	No Other Love	1966	$15
❑ CAS-941 [S]	No Other Love	1966	$12
❑ CAL-440 [M]	Perry Como Sings Just for You	1958	$18
❑ CAS-440(e) [R]	Perry Como Sings Just for You	1962	$12
❑ CAL-660 [M]	Perry Como Sings Merry Christmas Music	1961	$15

— Reissue of RCA Victor LPM-1243 with new cover

❑ CAS-660(e) [R]	Perry Como Sings Merry Christmas Music	1961	$12
❑ CAL-858 [M]	Somebody Loves Me	1965	$15
❑ CAS-858 [S]	Somebody Loves Me	1965	$12
❑ CAS-2299	The Lord's Prayer	1968	$12
❑ CAS-2547	The Shadow of Your Smile	1972	$12
❑ CAL-2201 [M]	You Are Never Far Away	1968	$18
❑ CAS-2201 [S]	You Are Never Far Away	1968	$12

RCA CUSTOM EDITION

❑ DRL1-0010	Seattle	1973	$15

RCA SPECIAL PRODUCTS

❑ DPL1-0193	By Special Request	1974	$15

— Sold only at Sylvania dealers

RCA VICTOR

❑ CPL1-1752	A Legendary Performer	1976	$12
❑ APL1-0100	And I Love You So	1973	$12
❑ APD1-0100 [Q]	And I Love You So	1974	$20
❑ AYL1-3672	And I Love You So	1980	$10

— Reissue

❑ LPM-3133 [10]	Around the Christmas Tree	1953	$40
❑ LPM-3035 [10]	A Sentimental Date with Perry Como	1952	$40
❑ LPM-1177 [M]	A Sentimental Date with Perry Como	1956	$30
❑ LPM-2567 [M]	By Request	1962	$18
❑ LSP-2567 [S]	By Request	1962	$25
❑ LPM-3224 [10]	Como's Golden Records	1954	$40
❑ LOP-1007	Como's Golden Records	1958	$30
❑ LPM-1981 [M]	Como's Golden Records	1959	$25

— Reissue of LOP-1007

❑ LSP-1981(e) [R]	Como's Golden Records	1962	$15
❑ AFL1-1981	Como's Golden Records	1977	$12

— Reissue with new prefix

❑ AYL1-3802	Como's Golden Records	1981	$10

— Reissue

❑ LPM-2010 [M]	Como Swings	1959	$25
❑ LSP-2010 [S]	Como Swings	1959	$30
❑ ANL1-2485	Especially for You	1977	$12

Number	Title	Yr	NM
❑ LPM-2343 [M]	For the Young at Heart	1960	$18
❑ LSP-2343 [S]	For the Young at Heart	1960	$25
❑ LPM-3124 [10]	Hits from Broadway Shows	1953	$40
❑ LPM-1191 [M]	Hits from Broadway Shows	1956	$30
❑ LPM-3188 [10]	I Believe	1954	$40
❑ LPM-1172 [M]	I Believe	1956	$30
❑ LSP-1172(e) [R]	I Believe	1962	$15
❑ LSP-4539	I Think of You	1971	$18
❑ AFL1-4539	I Think of You	1977	$12
—Reissue with new prefix			
❑ LSP-4473	It's Impossible	1970	$18
❑ AFL1-4473	It's Impossible	1977	$12
—Reissue with new prefix			
❑ AYL1-3804	It's Impossible	1981	$10
—Reissue			
❑ AYL1-4526	I Wish It Could Be Christmas Forever	1982	$12
❑ APL1-0863	Just Out of Reach	1975	$12
❑ APD1-0863 [Q]	Just Out of Reach	1975	$20
❑ LPM-3552 [M]	Lightly Latin	1966	$15
❑ LSP-3552 [S]	Lightly Latin	1966	$18
❑ LSP-4052	Look to Your Heart	1968	$18
❑ LPM-51 [10]	Merry Christmas	1951	$40
❑ ANL1-2969(e)	Over the Rainbow	1976	$12
❑ CPL1-0585	Perry	1974	$12
❑ APD1-0585 [Q]	Perry	1974	$20
❑ AFL1-3629	Perry Como	1980	$12
❑ LSPX-1001	Perry Como at the International Hotel, Las Vegas	1970	$18
❑ LPM-3608 [M]	Perry Como in Italy	1966	$15
❑ LSP-3608 [S]	Perry Como in Italy	1966	$18
❑ LPM-1243 [M]	Perry Como Sings Merry Christmas Music	1956	$30
❑ ANL1-0972	Pure Gold	1975	$12
❑ LPM-1176	Relaxing with Perry Como	1956	$30
❑ LOP-1004	Saturday Night with Mr. C.	1958	$30
❑ LPM-1971 [M]	Saturday Night with Mr. C.	1959	$25
—Reissue of LOP-1004			
❑ LSP-1971 [S]	Saturday Night with Mr. C.	1958	$30
❑ LPM-2066 [M]	Season's Greetings from Perry Como	1959	$25
—Later front covers have "LPM-2066" in upper right, inside RCA Victor box			
❑ LSP-2066 [S]	Season's Greetings from Perry Como	1959	$30
❑ LPM-2066 [M]	Season's Greetings from Perry Como	1959	$30
—Original front covers have "LPM-2066" in lower left corner			
❑ LSP-4183	Seattle	1969	$18
❑ LPM-2390 [M]	Sing to Me, Mr. C.	1961	$18
❑ LSP-2390 [S]	Sing to Me, Mr. C.	1961	$25
❑ AFL1-4272	So It Goes	1983	$12
❑ LPM-1085 [M]	So Smooth	1955	$30
❑ LPM-3044 [10]	Supper Club Favorites	1952	$40
❑ LPM-2630 [M]	The Best of Irving Berlin's Songs from "Mr. President	1962	$18
❑ LSP-2630 [S]	The Best of Irving Berlin's Songs from "Mr. President	1962	$25
❑ LSP-4016	The Perry Como Christmas Album	1968	$15
❑ ANL1-1929	The Perry Como Christmas Album	1976	$10
—Budget-line reissue of LSP-4016			
❑ LPM-3396 [M]	The Scene Changes	1965	$15
❑ LSP-3396 [S]	The Scene Changes	1965	$18
❑ LPM-2708 [M]	The Songs I Love	1963	$18
❑ LSP-2708 [S]	The Songs I Love	1963	$25
❑ ACL1-0444	The Sweetest Sounds	1974	$12
❑ VPS-6026	This Is Perry Como	1970	$18
❑ VPS-6067	This Is Perry Como, Volume 2	1972	$18
❑ LPM-3013 [10]	TV Favorites	1952	$40
❑ LPM-1463 [M]	We Get Letters	1957	$30
❑ LPM-1885 [M]	When You Come to the End of the Day	1958	$25
❑ LSP-1885 [S]	When You Come to the End of the Day	1958	$30
❑ AFL1-2641	Where You're Concerned	1978	$12
❑ AYL1-3803	Where You're Concerned	1981	$10
—Reissue			

READER'S DIGEST
| ❑ RDA-144/D | Christmas with Perry Como | 1983 | $12 |

TIME-LIFE
| ❑ SLGD-04 | Legendary Singers: Perry Como | 1985 | $18 |

COMPETITORS, THE
DOT
| ❑ DLP-3542 [M] | Hits of the Street and Strip | 1963 | $175 |
| ❑ DLP-25542 [S] | Hits of the Street and Strip | 1963 | $250 |

COMPOSER'S WORKSHOP ENSEMBLE, THE
STRATA-EAST
| ❑ 1972-3 | The Composer's Workshop Ensemble | 197? | $30 |
| ❑ 7422 | (We've Been) Around | 1974 | $30 |

COMPTON BROTHERS, THE
DOT
❑ DLP-25974	Haunted House/Charlie Brown	1970	$25
❑ DLP-25867	Off the Top of...	1968	$25
❑ DLP-25998	Yellow River	1972	$25

COMSTOCK, BOBBY
ASCOT
| ❑ AM-13026 [M] | Out of Sight | 1966 | $30 |
| ❑ AS-16026 [S] | Out of Sight | 1966 | $30 |

CON BRIO
PLUG
| ❑ PLUG-4 | Con Brio | 1986 | $30 |

CONCORD ALL STARS, THE
CONCORD JAZZ
| ❑ CJ-348 | Ow! | 1988 | $25 |
| ❑ CJ-347 | Take 8 | 1988 | $25 |

CONCORD FESTIVAL ALL STARS, THE
CONCORD JAZZ
| ❑ CJ-366 | 20th Anniversary | 1989 | $30 |

CONCORD JAZZ ALL STARS, THE
CONCORD JAZZ
| ❑ CJ-182 | The Concord Jazz All Stars at Northsea Jazz Festival | 1982 | $30 |
| ❑ CJ-205 | The Concord Jazz All Stars at Northsea Jazz Festival, Vol. 2 | 1982 | $30 |

CONCORD SUPER BAND, THE
CONCORD JAZZ
| ❑ CJ-120 | CSB II | 1980 | $35 |
| ❑ CJ-80 | The Concord Super Band in Tokyo | 1979 | $35 |

CONCRETE BLONDE
I.R.S.
❑ X1-13037	Bloodletting	1990	$40
—Stock copy; red vinyl			
❑ 82037 [DJ]	Bloodletting	1990	$30
—Promo only, sticker on generic cover, black vinyl			
❑ 5835	Concrete Blonde	1987	$15
❑ 82001	Free	1989	$15

CONCRETE COWBOY BAND
EXCELSIOR
| ❑ 88007 | Concrete Cowboys | 1981 | $15 |

CONDELLO
SCEPTER
| ❑ SPS-542 | Phase 1 | 1968 | $85 |
| —Avaliable in mono and stereo; both same price | | | |

CONDON, EDDIE
ATLANTIC
| ❑ 90461 | That Toddlin' Town: Chicago Jazz Revisited | 1986 | $25 |

CHIAROSCURO
❑ 154	Eddie Condon in Japan	1978	$30
❑ 108	Town Hall Concerts, Volume 1	197?	$30
❑ 113	Town Hall Concerts, Volume 2	197?	$30

COLUMBIA
❑ CL719 [M]	Bixieland	1955	$50
—Red and black label with six "eye" logos			
❑ CL632 [M]	Chicago Style Jazz	1955	$50
—Red and black label with six "eye" logos			
❑ CL881 [M]	Eddie Condon's Treasury of Jazz	1956	$40
—Red and black label with six "eye" logos			
❑ CL616 [M]	Jammin' at Condon's	1955	$75
—Maroon label, gold print			
❑ CL616 [M]	Jammin' at Condon's	1955	$50
—Red and black label with six "eye" logos			
❑ CL1089 [M]	The Roaring Twenties	1958	$40
—Red and black label with six "eye" logos			
❑ KG31564	The World of Eddie Condon	1972	$50
❑ PG31564	The World of Eddie Condon	197?	$35
—Reissue with new prefix			

COMMODORE
❑ XFL-16568	A Good Band Is Hard to Find	198?	$25
❑ FL20022 [M]	Ballin' the Jack	195?	$50
❑ FL30010 [M]	Condon A La Carte	195?	$75
❑ XFL-15355	The Liederkranz Sessions	198?	$25
❑ XFL-14427	Windy City Seven/Jam Sessions at Commodore	198?	$25

DECCA
❑ DL8281 [M]	A Night at Eddie Condon's	1956	$120
❑ DL5137 [10]	George Gershwin Jazz Concert	1950	$175
❑ DL9234 [M]	Gershwin Program (1941-1945)	1968	$30
❑ DL79234 [R]	Gershwin Program (1941-1945)	1968	$30
❑ DL8282 [M]	Ivy League Jazz	195?	$40
❑ DL5195 [10]	Jazz Band Ball (Volume 1)	1951	$250
❑ DL5203 [10]	Jazz Concert at Eddie Condon's	1951	$250
❑ DL5218 [10]	Jazz Concert at Eddie Condon's	1950	$175
❑ DL5246 [10]	We Call It Music	1951	$250

DESIGN
| ❑ DLP-47 [M] | Confidentially...It's Condon | 196? | $30 |
| ❑ DLP-148 [M] | Eddie Condon & Dixieland All Stars | 196? | $30 |

DOT
| ❑ DLP-3141 [M] | Dixieland Dance Party | 1958 | $100 |

EPIC
| ❑ LA16024 [M] | Midnight in Moscow | 1962 | $85 |
| ❑ BA17024 [S] | Midnight in Moscow | 1962 | $50 |

JAZZOLOGY
❑ J-101/2	1944 Jam Sessions	198?	$35
❑ JCE-10	Eddie Condon Concert	196?	$35
❑ J-50	Eddie Condon Jazz	197?	$35
❑ J-73	The Spirit of Condon	1979	$30
❑ JCE-1001/2	Town Hall Concerts, Volume 1	1988	$35
❑ JCE-1003/4	Town Hall Concerts, Volume 2	1988	$35
❑ JCE-1005/6	Town Hall Concerts, Volume 3	1988	$35
❑ JCE-1007/8	Town Hall Concerts, Volume 4	1990	$35
❑ JCE-1009/10	Town Hall Concerts, Volume 5	1990	$35
❑ JCE-1011/12	Town Hall Concerts, Volume 6	1990	$35
❑ JCE-1013/14	Town Hall Concerts, Volume 7	1992	$35

JAZZ PANORAMA
| ❑ 1805 [10] | Eddie Condon | 1951 | $40 |

JOLLY ROGER
| ❑ 5025 [10] | Eddie Condon | 1954 | $75 |
| ❑ 5018 [10] | Eddie Condon and His Orchestra Featuring Pee Wee Russell | 1954 | $75 |

MAINSTREAM
| ❑ 56024 [M] | Eddie Condon: A Legend | 1965 | $30 |
| ❑ S-6024 [R] | Eddie Condon: A Legend | 1965 | $35 |

MCA
| ❑ 4071 | The Best of Eddie Condon | 197? | $35 |
| —Black rainbow labels | | | |

MCA CORAL
| ❑ 20013 | Sunny Day | 198? | $25 |

MGM
| ❑ E-3651 [M] | Eddie Condon Is Uptown Now | 1960 | $30 |
| ❑ SE-3651 [S] | Eddie Condon Is Uptown Now | 1960 | $30 |

MOSAIC
| ❑ MQ7-152 | The Complete CBS Recordings of Eddie Condon and His All-Stars | 199? | $120 |

SAVOY
| ❑ MG-12055 [M] | Ringside at Condon's | 1956 | $40 |

TRIP
| ❑ 5800 | Eddie Condon and His Jazz Concert Orchestra | 197? | $35 |

WARNER BROS.
| ❑ W1315 [M] | That Toddlin' Town | 1959 | $75 |
| ❑ WS1315 [S] | That Toddlin' Town | 1959 | $40 |

X
| ❑ LX-3005 [M] | Eddie Condon's Hot Shots | 1954 | $50 |

CONLEE, JOHN
16TH AVENUE
| ❑ D1-70555 | Fellow Travelers | 1989 | $12 |

ABC
| ❑ AY-1105 | Rose Colored Glasses | 1978 | $15 |

COLUMBIA
| ❑ FC40442 | American Travelers | 1987 | $10 |
| ❑ FC40257 | Harmony | 1986 | $10 |

MCA
❑ 5521	Blue Highway	1984	$10
❑ 5310	Busted	1982	$12
❑ 5818	Conlee Country	1986	$10
❑ 3174	Forever	1979	$12
❑ 3246	Friday Night Blues	1980	$12
❑ 27029	Friday Night Blues	198?	$10
—Budget-line reissue			
❑ 5642	Greatest Hits Volume 2	1985	$10
❑ 5434	In My Eyes	1983	$10
❑ 948	In My Eyes	1986	$10
—Budget-line reissue			
❑ 5405	John Conlee's Greatest Hits	1983	$12
❑ AY-1105	Rose Colored Glasses	1979	$12
—Reissue of ABC 1105			
❑ 3281	Rose Colored Glasses	1980	$10
—Reissue of 1105			
❑ 5699	Songs for the Working Man	1986	$10
❑ 5213	With Love...	1981	$12

Number	Title	Yr	NM

CONLEY, ARTHUR

ATCO
☐ SD 33-276 [S]	More Sweet Soul	1969	$30
☐ 33-276 [M]	More Sweet Soul	1969	$80

— Mono is white label promo only; "d/j copy monaural" sticker on stereo cover
| ☐ 33-220 [M] | Shake, Rattle & Roll | 1967 | $40 |
| ☐ SD 33-220 [S] | Shake, Rattle & Roll | 1967 | $30 |

| ☐ SD 33-243 [S] | Soul Directions | 1968 | $30 |
| ☐ 33-243 [M] | Soul Directions | 1968 | $75 |

— Mono is white label promo only; "Mono" sticker over the word "Stereo" on front cover
| ☐ 33-215 [M] | Sweet Soul Music | 1967 | $40 |
| ☐ SD 33-215 [S] | Sweet Soul Music | 1967 | $30 |

CONLEY, EARL THOMAS

RCA
| ☐ 6824-1-R | The Heart of It All | 1988 | $10 |
| ☐ 5619-1-R | Too Many Times | 1986 | $10 |

RCA VICTOR
☐ AHL1-4713	Don't Make It Easy for Me	1983	$10
☐ AHL1-4135	Fire & Smoke	1981	$10
☐ AYL1-5118	Fire & Smoke	1984	$10

— "Best Buy Series" reissue
☐ AHL1-7032	Greatest Hits	1985	$10
☐ AHL1-4348	Somewhere Between Right and Wrong	1982	$10
☐ AYL1-5156	Somewhere Between Right and Wrong	1984	$10

— "Best Buy Series" reissue
| ☐ AHL1-5175 | Treadin' Water | 1984 | $10 |

SUNBIRD
| ☐ 50105 | Blue Pearl | 1980 | $18 |

CONNELLY, PEGGY

BETHLEHEM
| ☐ BCP-53 [M] | That Old Black Magic | 1957 | $300 |

CONNICK, HARRY, JR.

COLUMBIA
☐ FC44369	20	1988	$30
☐ C269794	30	2001	$35
☐ BFC40702	Harry Connick, Jr.	1987	$15
☐ C46223	Lofty's Roach Souffle	1990	$20
☐ C86077	Songs I Heard	2001	$20
☐ C46146	We Are in Love	1990	$20
☐ SC45319	When Harry Met Sally... (soundtrack)	1989	$30
☐ 474551-1	When My Heart Finds Christmas	1993	$18

— Vinyl version is European import only

CONNIFF, RAY

COLUMBIA
☐ PC34477	After the Lovin'	1977	$12
☐ KC31629	Alone Again (Naturally)	1972	$12
☐ CQ31629 [Q]	Alone Again (Naturally)	1972	$20
☐ FC44152	Always in My Heart	1988	$12
☐ KC33564	Another Somebody Done Somebody Wrong Song	1975	$12
☐ CQ33564 [Q]	Another Somebody Done Somebody Wrong Song	1975	$20
☐ CS1022	Bridge Over Troubled Water	1970	$12
☐ CL1252 [M]	Broadway in Rhythm	1959	$18
☐ CS8064 [S]	Broadway in Rhythm	1959	$25

— Red and black label with six "eye" logos
☐ C32413	Charlotte's Web	1973	$12
☐ PC38300	Christmas Album	1982	$12
☐ PC39470	Christmas Caroling	1984	$12
☐ CL1390 [M]	Christmas with Conniff	1959	$18
☐ CS8185 [S]	Christmas with Conniff	1959	$15
☐ CL1163 [M]	Concert in Rhythm	1958	$18
☐ CS8022 [S]	Concert in Rhythm	1958	$25

— Red and black label with six "eye" logos

| ☐ PC8022 | Concert in Rhythm | 1988 | $10 |

— Reissue with new prefix
☐ CL1415 [M]	Concert in Rhythm – Volume II	1960	$15
☐ CS8212 [S]	Concert in Rhythm – Volume II	1960	$18
☐ G30122	Concert in Stereo/Live at the Sahara/Tahoe	1970	$18
☐ CS8155 [S]	Conniff Meets Butterfield	1959	$30

— Red and black label with six "eye" logos
| ☐ CL1004 [M] | Dance the Bop | 1957 | $30 |

— Red and black label with six "eye" logos; includes instruction booklet
☐ CL2608 [M]	En Espanol	1967	$15
☐ CS9408 [S]	En Espanol	1967	$12
☐ CL2210 [M]	Friendly Persuasion	1964	$12
☐ CS9110 [S]	Friendly Persuasion	1964	$15
☐ C30755	Great Contemporary Instrumental Hits	1971	$12
☐ CL2461 [M]	Happiness Is	1966	$12
☐ CS9261 [S]	Happiness Is	1966	$15
☐ KC32553	Harmony	1973	$12
☐ CQ32553 [Q]	Harmony	1973	$20
☐ CL2747 [M]	Hawaiian Album	1967	$15
☐ CS9547 [S]	Hawaiian Album	1967	$12
☐ PC9547	Hawaiian Album	198?	$10

— Reissue with new prefix
☐ CL2406 [M]	Here We Come a-Caroling	1965	$15
☐ CS9206 [S]	Here We Come a-Caroling	1965	$12
☐ GP3	Here We Come a-Caroling/ Ray Conniff's World of Hits	1968	$18
☐ CL1310 [M]	Hollywood in Rhythm	1959	$18
☐ CS8117 [S]	Hollywood in Rhythm	1959	$25

— Red and black label with six "eye" logos
☐ CS9661	Honey	1968	$12
☐ KC32090	I Can See Clearly Now	1973	$12
☐ KC31220	I'd Like to Teach the World to Sing	1972	$12
☐ CS9777	I Love How You Love Me	1969	$12
☐ CL2264 [M]	Invisible Tears	1964	$12
☐ CS9064 [S]	Invisible Tears	1964	$15
☐ CL2795 [M]	It Must Be Him	1968	$18
☐ CS9595 [S]	It Must Be Him	1968	$12
☐ CL1334 [M]	It's the Talk of the Town	1959	$15
☐ CS8143 [S]	It's the Talk of the Town	1959	$18
☐ PC36255	I Will Survive	1979	$12
☐ KC34040	I Write the Songs	1976	$12
☐ CQ34040 [Q]	I Write the Songs	1976	$20
☐ CS9920	Jean	1969	$12
☐ CL2022 [M]	Just Kiddin' Around	1963	$15
☐ CS8822 [S]	Just Kiddin' Around	1963	$18
☐ CQ33332 [Q]	Laughter in the Rain	1975	$20
☐ CL2352 [M]	Love Affair	1965	$12
☐ CS9152 [S]	Love Affair	1965	$15
☐ C30498	Love Story	1971	$12
☐ CQ30498 [Q]	Love Story	1972	$20
☐ KC31473	Love Theme from "The Godfather"	1972	$12
☐ CQ31473 [Q]	Love Theme from "The Godfather"	1972	$20
☐ KC33884	Love Will Keep Us Together	1975	$12
☐ CQ33884 [Q]	Love Will Keep Us Together	1975	$20
☐ CL1574 [M]	Memories Are Made of This	1961	$15
☐ CS8374 [S]	Memories Are Made of This	1961	$18
☐ CL2366 [M]	Music from Mary Poppins, The Sound of Music, My Fair Lady & Other Great Movie Themes	1965	$12
☐ CS9166 [S]	Music from Mary Poppins, The Sound of Music, My Fair Lady & Other Great Movie Themes	1965	$15
☐ JC36749	Perfect "10" Classics	1980	$12
☐ JC35659	Ray Conniff Plays the Bee Gees and Other Hits	1978	$12
☐ CS9839	Ray Conniff's Greatest Hits	1969	$12
☐ PC9839	Ray Conniff's Greatest Hits	198?	$10

— Reissue with new prefix
☐ CL2500 [M]	Ray Conniff's World of Hits	1966	$15
☐ CS9300 [S]	Ray Conniff's World of Hits	1966	$12
☐ CL1878 [M]	Rhapsody in Rhythm	1962	$15
☐ CS8678 [S]	Rhapsody in Rhythm	1962	$18
☐ CL1137 [M]	'S Awful Nice	1958	$18
☐ CS8001 [S]	'S Awful Nice	1958	$25

— Red and black label with six "eye" logos
☐ CL1490 [M]	Say It With Music (A Touch of Latin)	1960	$15
☐ CS8282 [S]	Say It With Music (A Touch of Latin)	1960	$18
☐ FC40384	Say You, Say Me	1986	$12
☐ CL1776 [M]	'S Continental	1962	$15
☐ CS8576 [S]	'S Continental	1962	$18
☐ KC34170	Send In the Clowns	1976	$12
☐ CQ34170 [Q]	Send In the Clowns	1976	$20
☐ CL1074 [M]	'S Marvelous	1957	$18
☐ CS8037 [S]	'S Marvelous	1958	$25

— Red and black label with six "eye" logos
☐ CL1642 [M]	Somebody Loves Me	1961	$15
☐ CS8442 [S]	Somebody Loves Me	1961	$18
☐ CL2519 [M]	Somewhere My Love	1966	$15
☐ CS9319 [S]	Somewhere My Love	1966	$12
☐ PC9319	Somewhere My Love	198?	$10

— Reissue with new prefix
☐ CG33603	Somewhere My Love/Bridge Over Troubled Water	1975	$15
☐ CL1720 [M]	So Much in Love	1962	$15
☐ CS8520 [S]	So Much in Love	1962	$18
☐ CL2150 [M]	Speak to Me of Love	1964	$12

☐ CS8950 [S]	Speak to Me of Love	1964	$15
☐ KC34312	S.W.A.T.	1976	$12
☐ CQ34312 [Q]	S.W.A.T.	1976	$20
☐ CL925 [M]	'S Wonderful!	1956	$25

— Red and black label with six "eye" logos
☐ CL1949 [M]	The Happy Beat	1963	$15
☐ CS8749 [S]	The Happy Beat	1963	$18
☐ KC33139	The Happy Sound	1974	$12
☐ CQ33139 [Q]	The Happy Sound	1974	$20
☐ FC38072	The Nashville Connection	1981	$12
☐ KC32802	The Way We Were	1974	$12
☐ CQ32802 [Q]	The Way We Were	1974	$20
☐ CL2676 [M]	This Is My Song	1967	$15
☐ CS9476 [S]	This Is My Song	1967	$12
☐ CS9712	Turn Around Look at Me	1968	$12
☐ C30410	We've Only Just Begun	1970	$12
☐ CL1892 [M]	We Wish You a Merry Christmas	1962	$18
☐ CS8692 [S]	We Wish You a Merry Christmas	1962	$15
☐ KC32376	You Are the Sunshine of My Life	1973	$12
☐ CL2118 [M]	You Make Me Feel So Young	1964	$15
☐ CS8918 [S]	You Make Me Feel So Young	1964	$18
☐ CL1489 [M]	Young at Heart	1960	$15
☐ CS8281 [S]	Young at Heart	1960	$18

COLUMBIA RECORD CLUB
| ☐ D267 [M] | Ray Conniff's World of Favorites | 196? | $15 |
| ☐ DS267 [S] | Ray Conniff's World of Favorites | 196? | $18 |

HARMONY
| ☐ HS11346 [B] | Love Is a Many-Splendored Thing | 1969 | $12 |
| ☐ KH30134 | The Impossible Dream | 1970 | $12 |

CONNOR, CHRIS, AND MAYNARD FERGUSON

ATLANTIC
| ☐ 8049 [M] | Double Exposure | 1961 | $175 |

— Multi-color label, white "fan" logo
| ☐ 8049 [M] | Double Exposure | 196? | $30 |

— Multi-color label, black "fan" logo
| ☐ SD8049 [S] | Double Exposure | 1961 | $175 |

— Multi-color label, white "fan" logo
| ☐ SD8049 [S] | Double Exposure | 196? | $35 |

— Multi-color label, black "fan" logo
| ☐ 90143 | Double Exposure | 198? | $25 |

— Reissue

ROULETTE
| ☐ R52068 [M] | Two's Company | 1961 | $30 |

— White label with colored spokes
| ☐ SR52068 [S] | Two's Company | 1961 | $40 |

— White label with colored spokes

CONNOR, CHRIS

ABC
| ☐ ABC-585 [M] | Chris Connor Now | 1966 | $25 |
| ☐ ABCS-585 [S] | Chris Connor Now | 1966 | $30 |

ABC-PARAMOUNT
| ☐ ABC-529 [M] | Gentle Bossa Nova | 1965 | $25 |
| ☐ ABCS-529 [S] | Gentle Bossa Nova | 1965 | $30 |

APPLAUSE
| ☐ APLP-1020 | Chris Connor Live | 1982 | $20 |

ATLANTIC
| ☐ 1286 [M] | A Jazz Date with Chris Connor | 1958 | $300 |

— Black label
| ☐ 1286 [M] | A Jazz Date with Chris Connor | 196? | $25 |

— Multi-color label, white "fan" logo
| ☐ 1286 [M] | A Jazz Date with Chris Connor | 196? | $30 |

— Multi-color label, black "fan" logo
| ☐ 8046 [M] | A Portrait of Chris | 1960 | $300 |

— Multi-color label, white "fan" logo
| ☐ 8046 [M] | A Portrait of Chris | 196? | $30 |

— Multi-color label, black "fan" logo
| ☐ SD8046 [S] | A Portrait of Chris | 1960 | $300 |

— Multi-color label, white "fan" logo
| ☐ SD8046 [S] | A Portrait of Chris | 196? | $35 |

— Multi-color label, black "fan" logo
| ☐ 1307 [M] | Ballads of the Sad Café | 1959 | $300 |

— Black label
| ☐ 1307 [M] | Ballads of the Sad Café | 196? | $25 |

— Multi-color label, white "fan" logo
| ☐ 1307 [M] | Ballads of the Sad Café | 196? | $30 |

— Multi-color label, black "fan" logo
| ☐ SD1307 [S] | Ballads of the Sad Café | 1959 | $300 |

— Green label
| ☐ SD1307 [S] | Ballads of the Sad Café | 196? | $30 |

— Multi-color label, white "fan" logo
| ☐ SD1307 [S] | Ballads of the Sad Café | 196? | $35 |

— Multi-color label, black "fan" logo
| ☐ 1228 [M] | Chris Connor | 1956 | $300 |

— Black label
| ☐ 1228 [M] | Chris Connor | 196? | $25 |

Number	Title	Yr	NM
—*Multi-color label, white "fan" logo*			
❏ 1228 [M]	Chris Connor	196?	$30
—*Multi-color label, black "fan" logo*			
❏ SD1228 [S]	Chris Connor	1958	$300
—*Green label*			
❏ SD1228 [S]	Chris Connor	196?	$30
—*Multi-color label, white "fan" logo*			
❏ SD1228 [S]	Chris Connor	196?	$35
—*Multi-color label, black "fan" logo*			
❏ 2-601 [M]	Chris Connor Sings the George Gershwin Almanac of Song	1957	$300
—*Black label*			
❏ 2-601 [M]	Chris Connor Sings the George Gershwin Almanac of Song	196?	$40
—*Multi-color label, white "fan" logo*			
❏ 2-601 [M]	Chris Connor Sings the George Gershwin Almanac of Song	196?	$25
—*Multi-color label, black "fan" logo*			
❏ 1309 [M]	Chris Connor Sings the George Gershwin Almanac of Song, Vol. 1	1959	$300
—*Black label*			
❏ 1309 [M]	Chris Connor Sings the George Gershwin Almanac of Song, Vol. 1	196?	$25
—*Multi-color label, white "fan" logo*			
❏ 1309 [M]	Chris Connor Sings the George Gershwin Almanac of Song, Vol. 1	196?	$30
—*Multi-color label, black "fan" logo*			
❏ 1310 [M]	Chris Connor Sings the George Gershwin Almanac of Song, Vol. 2	1959	$300
—*Black label*			
❏ 1310 [M]	Chris Connor Sings the George Gershwin Almanac of Song, Vol. 2	196?	$25
—*Multi-color label, white "fan" logo*			
❏ 1310 [M]	Chris Connor Sings the George Gershwin Almanac of Song, Vol. 2	196?	$30
—*Multi-color label, black "fan" logo*			
❏ 1290 [M]	Chris Craft	1958	$300
—*Black label*			
❏ 1290 [M]	Chris Craft	196?	$25
—*Multi-color label, white "fan" logo*			
❏ 1290 [M]	Chris Craft	196?	$30
—*Multi-color label, black "fan" logo*			
❏ 8040 [M]	Chris In Person	1959	$300
—*Black label*			
❏ 8040 [M]	Chris In Person	196?	$25
—*Multi-color label, white "fan" logo*			
❏ 8040 [M]	Chris In Person	196?	$30
—*Multi-color label, black "fan" logo*			
❏ SD8040 [S]	Chris In Person	1959	$300
—*Green label*			
❏ SD8040 [S]	Chris In Person	196?	$30
—*Multi-color label, white "fan" logo*			
❏ SD8040 [S]	Chris In Person	196?	$35
—*Multi-color label, black "fan" logo*			
❏ 8061 [M]	Free Spirits	1962	$175
—*Multi-color label, black "fan" logo*			
❏ SD8061 [S]	Free Spirits	1962	$175
—*Multi-color label, black "fan" logo*			
❏ 1240 [M]	He Loves Me, He Loves Me Not	1956	$300
—*Black label*			
❏ 1240 [M]	He Loves Me, He Loves Me Not	196?	$25
—*Multi-color label, white "fan" logo*			
❏ 1240 [M]	He Loves Me, He Loves Me Not	196?	$30
—*Multi-color label, black "fan" logo*			
❏ SD1240 [S]	He Loves Me, He Loves Me Not	1958	$300
—*Green label*			
❏ SD1240 [S]	He Loves Me, He Loves Me Not	196?	$30
—*Multi-color label, white "fan" logo*			
❏ SD1240 [S]	He Loves Me, He Loves Me Not	196?	$35
—*Multi-color label, black "fan" logo*			
❏ 1240 [M]	He Loves Me, He Loves Me Not	1960	$300
—*White "bullseye" label*			
❏ SD1240 [S]	He Loves Me, He Loves Me Not	1960	$300
—*White "bullseye" label*			
❏ 8014 [M]	I Miss You So	1957	$300
—*Black label*			
❏ 8014 [M]	I Miss You So	196?	$25
—*Multi-color label, white "fan" logo*			
❏ 8014 [M]	I Miss You So	196?	$30
—*Multi-color label, black "fan" logo*			
❏ 8014 [M]	I Miss You So	1960	$300
—*White "bullseye" label*			
❏ 8032 [M]	Witchcraft	1959	$300

Number	Title	Yr	NM
—*Black label*			
❏ 8032 [M]	Witchcraft	196?	$50
—*Multi-color label, white "fan" logo*			
❏ 8032 [M]	Witchcraft	196?	$30
❏ SD8032 [S]	Witchcraft	1959	$300
—*Green label*			
❏ SD8032 [S]	Witchcraft	196?	$75
—*Multi-color label, white "fan" logo*			
❏ SD8032 [S]	Witchcraft	196?	$35
—*Multi-color label, black "fan" logo*			
❏ 8032 [M]	Witchcraft	1960	$300
—*White "bullseye" label*			

AUDIOPHILE
❏ AP-208	Sweet and Swinging	199?	$35

BAINBRIDGE
❏ 6230	Sketches	198?	$25
—*Reissue of Stanyan 10029*			

BETHLEHEM
❏ BCP-56 [M]	Chris	1957	$300
❏ BCP-1002 [10]	Chris Connor Sings Lullabys for Lovers	1954	$300
❏ BCP-1001 [10]	Chris Connor Sings Lullabys of Birdland	1954	$300
❏ BCP-6004 [M]	Chris Connor Sings Lullabys of Birdland	1955	$300
❏ BCP-6004 [M]	Chris Connor Sings Lullabys of Birdland	1984	$15
—*Reissue*			
❏ BCP-6010	Cocktails and Dusk	197?	$30
❏ 2BP-1001	The Finest	197?	$35
❏ BCP-20 [M]	This Is Chris	1955	$300

CLARION
❏ 611 [M]	Chris Connor Sings George Gershwin	1966	$20
—*Abbreviated version of Atlantic 2-601*			
❏ SD611 [R]	Chris Connor Sings George Gershwin	1966	$12

CONTEMPORARY
❏ C-14023	Classic	1987	$30
❏ C-14038	New Again	1988	$30

FM
❏ 312 [M]	A Weekend in Paris	1964	$50
❏ S-312 [S]	A Weekend in Paris	1964	$75
❏ 300 [M]	Chris Connor at the Village Gate	1963	$50
❏ S-300 [S]	Chris Connor at the Village Gate	1963	$75

PROGRESSIVE
❏ 7028	Sweet and Singing	1979	$30

STANYAN
❏ 10029	Sketches	1972	$35

STASH
❏ 232	Love Being Here with You	1984	$30

CONNORS, BILL

ECM
❏ 1120	Of Mist and Melting	1977	$35
❏ 1158	Swimming with a Hole in My Body	1979	$30
❏ 1057	Theme to the Gaurdian	197?	$35

PATHFINDER
❏ PTF-8707	Assembler	1987	$25
❏ PTF-8620	Double Up	1986	$25
❏ PTF-8503	Step It	1985	$25

CONNORS, NORMAN

ACCORD
❏ SN-7210	Just Imagine	1982	$20

ARISTA
❏ AB4216	Invitation	1979	$25
❏ AL9575	Mr. C.	1981	$25
❏ AL9534	Take It to the Limit	1980	$25
❏ AB4177	This Is Your Life	1978	$25

BUDDAH
❏ BDS-5674	Dance of Magic	1977	$50
—*Reissue of Cobblestone 9024*			
❏ BDS-5675	Dark of Light	1977	$50
—*Reissue of Cobblestone 9035*			
❏ BDS-5142	Love from the Sun	1973	$30
❏ BDS-5682	Romantic Journey	1977	$25
❏ BDS-5643	Saturday Night Special	1975	$25
❏ BDS-5611	Slewfoot	1974	$30
❏ BDS-5716	The Best of Norman Connors & Friends	1978	$25
❏ BDS-5655	You Are My Starship	1976	$25

CAPITOL
❏ C1-48515	Passion	1988	$25

COBBLESTONE
❏ 9024	Dance of Magic	1972	$75
❏ 9035	Dark of Light	1973	$75

CONNY

CAPITOL
❏ T10253 [M]	Germany's Greatest Record Star	1960	$30

CONSTANTINE, EDDIE

KAPP
❏ KL-1018 [M]	La Grande Sensation de la Paris	1957	$30

MERCURY
❏ MG-20339 [M]	The Rage of Paris	1958	$30

CONTEMPORARY JAZZ ENSEMBLE, THE

PRESTIGE
❏ PRLP-163 [10]	New Sounds from Rochester	1953	$350

CONTI, ROBERT

DISCOVERY
❏ 834	Robert Conti Jazz Quintet	1981	$30

TREND
❏ TR-540	Laura	1986	$30
❏ TR-519	Solo Guitar	198?	$25
—*Direct-to-disc recording*			

CONTI, TOM

CAEDMON
❏ TC1657	Charles Dickens' "A Christmas Carol	1980	$15
—*Spoken-word recording*			

CONTINENTAL OCTETTE, THE

CROWN
❏ CLP-5220 [M]	Modern Jazz Greats	196?	$25

CONTOURS, THE

GORDY
❏ G901 [M]	Do You Love Me?	1962	$500

MOTOWN
❏ M5-188V1	Do You Love Me?	1981	$12

CONWAY, JULIE

HARMONY
❏ HL7143 [M]	Good Housekeeping's Plan for Reducing Off-the-Record	1960	$25

CONWELL, JAMES

GUINNESS
❏ GNS36007 [B]	Let It All Out	1977	$150

COODER, RY

MOBILE FIDELITY
❏ Jan-0085	Jazz	198?	$400
—*Audiophile vinyl*			

REPRISE
❏ MS2117	Boomer's Story	1973	$15
❏ MS2254	Chicken Skin Music	1976	$15
❏ MS2052	Into the Purple Valley	1972	$15
❏ MS2179 [B]	Paradise and Lunch	1974	$15
❏ RS-6402	Ry Cooder	1969	$18
—*Two-tone orange label with "r:" and "W7" logos*			
❏ RS-6402 [B]	Ry Cooder	1970	$15
—*No "W7" on label; one-tone orange (almost tan) label*			
❏ PRO588 [DJ]	The Ry Cooder Radio Show	1976	$150

WARNER BROS.
❏ BSK3358	Bop Till You Drop	1979	$12
❏ BSK3489	Borderline	1980	$12
❏ 25399	Crossroads	1986	$12
❏ 25639	Get Rhythm	1987	$12
❏ BSK3197	Jazz	1978	$12
❏ 25996	Johnny Handsome	1989	$12
❏ 25270	Paris, Texas	1984	$12
❏ BS3059	Show Time	1977	$12
❏ HS3448	The Long Riders	1980	$12
❏ BSK3651	The Slide Area	1982	$12

COOK, JUNIOR

JAZZLAND
❏ JLP-58 [M]	Junior's Cookin'	1961	$300
❏ JLP-958 [S]	Junior's Cookin'	1961	$175

MUSE
❏ MR-5159	Good Cookin'	1979	$30
❏ MR-5218	Something's Cookin'	1981	$30

COOKE, ALISTAIR

COLUMBIA MASTERWORKS
❏ ML4970 [M]	An Evening with Alistair Cooke	1955	$40

COOKE, SAM

51 WEST
❏ Q16032	My Foolish Heart	198?	$15

ABKCO
❏ 9899-1 [B]	Ain't That Good News	2014	$40
❏ 2970-1	Sam Cooke at the Copa	1988	$15
—*Reissue*			
❏ 1124-1	Sam Cooke's Night Beat	1995	$15
—*Reissue*			

FAMOUS

Number	Title	Yr	NM
512	Cha-Cha-Cha	1969	$40
505	Only Sixteen	1969	$40
502	Sam's Songs	1969	$40
508	So Wonderful	1969	$40
509	You Send Me	1969	$40

KEEN

Number	Title	Yr	NM
A-2003 [M]	Encore	1958	$250
86101 [M]	Hit Kit	1959	$300
86103 [M]	I Thank God	1960	$400
A-2001 [M]	Sam Cooke	1958	$250
86106 [M]	The Wonderful World of Sam Cooke	1960	$350
A-2004 [M]	Tribute to the Lady	1959	$175
AS-2004 [S]	Tribute to the Lady	1959	$250

PAIR

Number	Title	Yr	NM
PDL2-1006	You Send Me	1986	$18

RCA CAMDEN

Number	Title	Yr	NM
CAS-2433	Sam Cooke	1970	$15
CAL-2264 [M]	The One and Only Sam Cooke	1967	$25
CAS-2264 [R]	The One and Only Sam Cooke	1967	$15
CAS-2610	The Unforgettable Sam Cooke	1972	$15
ACS1-0445	You Send Me	1974	$15

RCA VICTOR

Number	Title	Yr	NM
LPM-2899 [M]	Ain't That Good News	1964	$30
LSP-2899 [S]	Ain't That Good News	1964	$40
LPM-2221 [M]	Cooke's Tour	1960	$40
LSP-2221 [S]	Cooke's Tour	1960	$50
LPM-2236 [M]	Hits of the 50's	1960	$40
LSP-2236 [S]	Hits of the 50's	1960	$50
AFL1-5181	Live at the Harlem Square Club, 1963	1985	$15
LPM-2673 [M]	Mr. Soul	1963	$30
LSP-2673 [S]	Mr. Soul	1963	$40
LPM-2392 [M]	My Kind of Blues	1961	$40
LSP-2392 [S]	My Kind of Blues	1961	$50

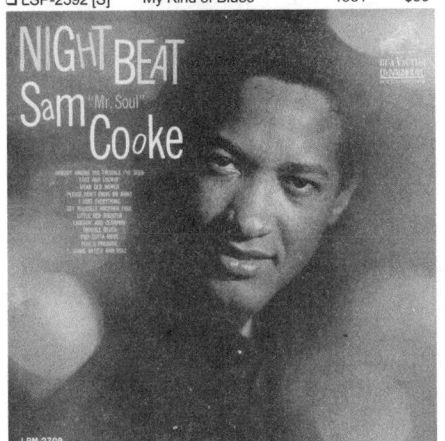

Number	Title	Yr	NM
LPM-2709 [M]	Night Beat	1963	$30
LSP-2709 [S]	Night Beat	1963	$40
LPM-2970 [M]	Sam Cooke at the Copa	1964	$30
LSP-2970 [S]	Sam Cooke at the Copa	1964	$40
ANL1-2658	Sam Cooke at the Copa	1977	$15

—Reissue of LSP-2970

Number	Title	Yr	NM
LPM-3367 [M]	Shake	1965	$30
LSP-3367 [S]	Shake	1965	$30
LPM-2293 [M]	Swing Low	1960	$40
LSP-2293 [S]	Swing Low	1960	$50
LPM-2625 [M]	The Best of Sam Cooke	1962	$30
LSP-2625 [R]	The Best of Sam Cooke	1962	$25
AFL1-2625	The Best of Sam Cooke	1977	$15

—Reissue with new prefix

Number	Title	Yr	NM
AYL1-3863	The Best of Sam Cooke	1981	$10

—Budget-line reissue

Number	Title	Yr	NM
LPM-3373 [M]	The Best of Sam Cooke, Volume 2	1965	$30
LSP-3373 [S]	The Best of Sam Cooke, Volume 2	1965	$30
CPL2-7127	The Man and His Music	1986	$18
LPM-3991 [M]	The Man Who Invented Soul	1968	$50
LSP-3991 [S]	The Man Who Invented Soul	1968	$30
LPM-3517 [M]	The Unforgettable Sam Cooke	1966	$25
LSP-3517 [S]	The Unforgettable Sam Cooke	1966	$30
VPS-6027	This Is Sam Cooke	1970	$25
LPM-3435 [M]	Try a Little Love	1965	$30
LSP-3435 [S]	Try a Little Love	1965	$30
LPM-2555 [M]	Twistin' the Night Away	1962	$40
LSP-2555 [S]	Twistin' the Night Away	1962	$50

SPECIALTY

Number	Title	Yr	NM
SPS-2106	Sam Cooke and the Soul Stirrers	1970	$18
SPS-2146	That's Heaven to Me	197?	$18
SPS-2116	The Gospel Soul of Sam Cooke, Vol. 1	1970	$18
SPS-2128	The Gospel Soul of Sam Cooke, Vol. 2	197?	$18
SPS-2119	Two Sides of Sam Cooke	1970	$18

TRIP

Number	Title	Yr	NM
8030	The Golden Sound of Sam Cooke	1972	$18

UPFRONT

Number	Title	Yr	NM
160	The Billie Holiday Story	1973	$18

COOKIES, THE/LITTLE EVA/CAROLE KING

DIMENSION

Number	Title	Yr	NM
DLP-6001 [M]	The Dimension Dolls, Vol. 1	1964	$350

COOL, CALVIN, AND THE SURF KNOBS

CHARTER

Number	Title	Yr	NM
CLP-103 [M]	The Surfer's Beat	1963	$40
CLS-103 [S]	The Surfer's Beat	1963	$50

COOL BRITONS, THE

BLUE NOTE

Number	Title	Yr	NM
BLP-5052 [10]	New Sounds from Olde England	1954	$300

COOLEY, SPADE

COLUMBIA

Number	Title	Yr	NM
CL9007 [10]	Sagebrush Swing	1949	$250

DECCA

Number	Title	Yr	NM
DL5563 [10]	Dance-O-Rama	1955	$300

RAYNOTE

Number	Title	Yr	NM
R-5007 [M]	Fidoolin'	1959	$40
RS-5007 [S]	Fidoolin'	1959	$50

ROULETTE

Number	Title	Yr	NM
R25145 [M]	Fidoolin'	1961	$30
SR25145 [S]	Fidoolin'	1961	$40

COOLIDGE, RITA

A&M

Number	Title	Yr	NM
SP-4616 [B]	Anytime...Anywhere	1977	$12
SP-3163	Anytime…Anywhere	198?	$10

—Budget-line reissue

Number	Title	Yr	NM
SP-3627	Fall Into Spring	1974	$12
SP-3238	Greatest Hits	198?	$10

—Budget-line reissue

Number	Title	Yr	NM
SP-4836	Greatest Hits	1981	$12
SP-3727	Heartbreak Radio	1981	$12
SP-5003	Inside the Fire	1984	$12
SP-4531	It's Only Love	1975	$12
SP-4669	Love Me Again	1978	$12
SP-4914	Never Let You Go	1983	$12
SP-4325	Nice Feelin'	1971	$12
SP-3130	Nice Feelin'	198?	$10

—Budget-line reissue

Number	Title	Yr	NM
SP-4291	Rita Coolidge	1971	$12
SP-3107	Rita Coolidge	198?	$10

—Budget-line reissue

Number	Title	Yr	NM
SP-4781	Satisfied	1979	$12
SP-4370	The Lady's Not for Sale	1972	$12

NAUTILUS

Number	Title	Yr	NM
NR-16	Anytime…Anywhere	1981	$30

—Audiophile vinyl

COON, JACKIE

SEA BREEZE

Number	Title	Yr	NM
SB-1009	Jazzin' Around	1987	$25

COOPER, ALICE

ACCORD

Number	Title	Yr	NM
SN-7162	Toronto Rock 'n' Roll Revival 1969	1981	$15

ATLANTIC

Number	Title	Yr	NM
SD18130	Welcome to My Nightmare	1975	$12
SD19157	Welcome to My Nightmare	1978	$10

—Reissue of 18130

EPIC

Number	Title	Yr	NM
E46786 [B]	Hey Stoopid	1991	$30
OE45137	Trash	1989	$15

FRIDAY MUSIC

Number	Title	Yr	NM
FRM2803 [B]	Greatest Hits	2013	$30
FRM2567 [B]	Killer	2012	$25

MCA

Number	Title	Yr	NM
5761	Constrictor	1986	$10
42091	Raise Your Fist and Yell	1987	$10

MOBILE FIDELITY

Number	Title	Yr	NM
Jan-0063	Welcome to My Nightmare	1980	$75

—Audiophile vinyl

PAIR

Number	Title	Yr	NM
PDL2-1163	A Man Called Alice	1987	$18

STRAIGHT

Number	Title	Yr	NM
WS1845 [DJ]	Easy Action	1970	$150

—White label promo

Number	Title	Yr	NM
WS1845	Easy Action	1970	$50

—Pink label stock copy; "Alice Cooper" in black on cover

Number	Title	Yr	NM
WS1845	Easy Action	1970	$30

—Pink label stock copy; "Alice Cooper" in white on cover

Number	Title	Yr	NM
WS1883 [DJ]	Love It to Death	1971	$150

—White label promo

Number	Title	Yr	NM
WS1883	Love It to Death	1971	$50

—Pink label stock copy

Number	Title	Yr	NM
STS-1051 [DJ]	Pretties for You	1969	$250

—White label promo

Number	Title	Yr	NM
STS-1051	Pretties for You	1969	$175

—Yellow label stock copy

Number	Title	Yr	NM
WS1840 [B]	Pretties for You	1970	$85

—Pink label stock copy

TPM/RHINO EXCLUSIVE

Number	Title	Yr	NM
1845	Easy Action	2008	$12
1883	Love It to Death	2008	$12
1840	Pretties for You	2008	$12

WARNER BROS.

Number	Title	Yr	NM
BS2896	Alice Cooper Goes to Hell	1976	$12
W2803	Alice Cooper's Greatest Hits	1974	$12
BS42803 [Q]	Alice Cooper's Greatest Hits	1974	$0

—Not released

Number	Title	Yr	NM
BSK3107	Alice Cooper's Greatest Hits	1977	$10

—Reissue of BS 2803

Number	Title	Yr	NM
BS2685	Billion Dollar Babies	1973	$15

—Green "WB" label

Number	Title	Yr	NM
BS42685 [Q]	Billion Dollar Babies	1974	$75
23969	Da Da	1983	$12
BSK3436	Flush the Fashion	1980	$12
BSK3263	From the Inside	1978	$12
BS2567	Killer	1971	$30

—Early copies have an attached 1972 calendar/poster

Number	Title	Yr	NM
BS2567	Killer	1972	$15

—Later copies no longer have the calendar/poster

Number	Title	Yr	NM
BSK3027	Lace and Whiskey	1977	$12
WS1883 [B]	Love It To Death	2010	$30
WS1883 [B]	Love It to Death	1971	$50

—Version 1: Green "WB" label; cover has Alice's thumb sticking out in such a way that it appears to be another part of the body

Number	Title	Yr	NM
WS1883	Love It to Death	1971	$25

—Version 2: Green "WB" label; same as above, but has a white box reading "Contains the Hit 'I'm Eighteen'"

Number	Title	Yr	NM
WS1883	Love It to Death	1971	$25

—Version 3: Green "WB" label; cover has large white areas at top and bottom with lower half of the photo cropped out

Number	Title	Yr	NM
WS1883	Love It to Death	1971	$15

—Version 4: Green "WB" label; with "I'm Eighteen" box and Alice's protruding thumb airbrushed off the cover

Number	Title	Yr	NM
BS2748	Muscle of Love	1973	$12
BS42748 [Q]	Muscle of Love	1974	$100
WS1840	Pretties for You	1973	$25

—Burbank" palm trees label; comes in Straight cover

Number	Title	Yr	NM
WS1840	Pretties for You	1971	$30

—Green label; comes in "Straight" cover

Number	Title	Yr	NM
BS2623	School's Out	1972	$40

—With paper panties intact; back cover does not list song titles

Number	Title	Yr	NM
BS2623	School's Out	1972	$25

—Back cover does not list song titles, but panties are missing

Number	Title	Yr	NM
BS2623	School's Out	1972	$30

—With paper panties intact; back cover lists song titles

Number	Title	Yr	NM
BS2623	School's Out	1972	$15

—No panties, with song titles listed

Number	Title	Yr	NM
BSK3581	Special Forces	1981	$12
PRO789 [DJ]	The Alice Cooper Radio Show	1978	$30
BSK3138	The Alice Cooper Show	1977	$12
23719 [B]	Zipper Catches Skin	1982	$12

COOPER, BOB

CAPITOL

Number	Title	Yr	NM
H6501 [10]	Bob Cooper	1954	$175
T6501 [M]	Bob Cooper	1955	$100
T1586 [M]	Do Re Mi	1961	$75
ST1586 [S]	Do Re Mi	1961	$75
H6513 [10]	Shifting Winds	1955	$150
T6513 [M]	Shifting Winds	1955	$100

CONTEMPORARY

Number	Title	Yr	NM
C-3544 [M]	Coop!	1958	$300
S-7012 [S]	Coop!	1959	$300

—Reissue of Stereo Records 7012

Number	Title	Yr	NM
C-14017	In a Mellotone	1986	$25

DISCOVERY

Number	Title	Yr	NM
822	Bob Cooper Plays the Music of Michel Legrand	1981	$30

FANTASY

Number	Title	Yr	NM
OJC-161	Coop!	198?	$25

STEREO RECORDS

Number	Title	Yr	NM
S-7012 [S]	Coop!	1958	$50

TREND

Number	Title	Yr	NM
TR-518	Tenor Sax Impressions	198?	$25

—Direct-to-disc recording

WORLD PACIFIC

Number	Title	Yr	NM
WPM-411 [M]	Bob Cooper Swings TV	1958	$175

Number	Title	Yr	NM

COOPER, JACKIE
DOT
| ❏ DLP-3146 [M] | The Movies Swing! | 1958 | $30 |

COOPER, JEROME
ABOUT TIME
| ❏ 1008 | Outer and Interactions | 1988 | $25 |
| ❏ 1002 | The Unpredictability of Predictability | 1979 | $25 |

HAT HUT
| ❏ 07 | For the People | 1980 | $30 |

COOPER, LES, AND THE SOUL ROCKERS
EVERLAST
| ❏ ELP-202 [M] | Wiggle Wobble | 1963 | $50 |

COOPER, PAT
UNITED ARTISTS
❏ UAS6690	More Saucy Stories from... Pat Cooper	1969	$15
❏ UAL3446 [M]	Our Hero...Pat Cooper	1966	$15
❏ UAS6446 [S]	Our Hero...Pat Cooper	1966	$18
❏ UAL3548 [M]	Spaghetti Sauce & Other Delights	1966	$15
❏ UAS6548 [S]	Spaghetti Sauce & Other Delights	1966	$18
❏ UAS6600	You Don't Have to Be Italian To Like Pat Cooper	1968	$15

COOPER, WILMA LEE AND STONEY
DECCA
| ❏ DL4784 [M] | Wilma Lee and Stoney Cooper Sing | 1966 | $25 |
| ❏ DL74784 [S] | Wilma Lee and Stoney Cooper Sing | 1966 | $30 |

HARMONY
| ❏ HL7233 [M] | Sacred Songs | 1960 | $30 |

HICKORY
❏ LP-106 [M]	Family Favorites	1962	$40
❏ LP-112 [M]	New Songs of Inspiration	1962	$40
❏ LP-100 [M]	There's a Big Wheel	1960	$50

COPAS, COWBOY, AND HAWKSHAW HAWKINS
KING
❏ 984 [M]	24 Great Hits	1968	$30
❏ 835 [M]	In Memory	1963	$40
❏ 850 [M]	The Legend of Cowboy Copas and Hawkshaw Hawkins	1964	$40

COPAS, COWBOY
KING
❏ 824 [M]	As You Remember Cowboy Copas	1963	$40
❏ 720 [M]	Broken Hearted Melodies	1960	$100
❏ 817 [M]	Country Gentleman of Song	1963	$40
❏ 894 [M]	Cowboy Copas Hymns	1964	$40
❏ 553 [M]	Cowboy Copas Sings His All-Time Hits	1957	$150
❏ 556 [M]	Favorite Sacred Songs	1957	$100
❏ 619 [M]	Sacred Songs by Cowboy Copas	1959	$100
❏ 714 [M]	Tragic Tales of Love and Life	1960	$100

STARDAY
❏ SLP-118 [M]	All Time Country Music Great	1960	$40
❏ SLP-212 [M]	Beyond the Sunset	1963	$40
❏ SLP-208 [M]	Country Music Entertainer #1	1963	$40
❏ SLP-144 [M]	Cowboy Copas	1961	$40
❏ SLP-268 [M]	Cowboy Copas and His Friends	1964	$40
❏ SLP-133 [M]	Inspirational Songs	1961	$40
❏ SLP-175 [M]	Mister Country Music	1962	$40
❏ SLP-157 [M]	Opry Star Spotlight on Cowboy Copas	1962	$40
❏ SLP-184 [M]	Songs That Made Him Famous	1962	$40
❏ SLP-247 [M]	Star of the Grand Ole Opry	1963	$40
❏ SLP-458	The Best of Cowboy Copas	1970	$18
❏ SLP-347 [M]	The Cowboy Copas Story	1965	$30
❏ SLP (9)-347 [R]	The Cowboy Copas Story	1965	$30
❏ SLP-317 [M]	The Legend Lives On	1965	$30
❏ SLP-234 [M]	The Unforgettable Cowboy Copas	1963	$40

COPAS, COWBOY/HAWKSHAW HAWKINS/PATSY CLINE
STARDAY
| ❏ SLP-346 [M] | Gone But Not Forgotten | 1965 | $30 |

COPE, JULIAN
Also see THE TEARDROP EXPLODES.

ISLAND
❏ 91025	My Nation Underground	1988	$12
❏ PR126667 [EP]	Peggy Suicide (Sampler)	1991	$18
—Promo only; 6 tracks			
❏ 90571	Saint Julian	1987	$12
❏ 90560 [EP]	World Shut Your Mouth (Julian Cope)	1987	$10

COPELAND, RUTH
INVICTUS
| ❏ SMAS9802 [B] | I Am What I Am | 1971 | $50 |
| ❏ ST7303 [B] | Self Portrait | 1970 | $30 |

RCA
| ❏ APL11236 [B] | Take Me to Baltimore | | $10 |

COPELAND, STEWART
Also see KLART KENT; THE POLICE.

A&M
| ❏ SP-6-4983 | Rumble Fish | 1983 | $15 |
| ❏ SP-5084 | The Rhythmatist | 1985 | $12 |

I.R.S.
| ❏ 42099 | The Equalizer and Other Cliffhangers | 1988 | $12 |

COPPER PLATED INTEGRATED CIRCUIT, THE
COMMAND
| ❏ RS-945SD | Plugged In Pop | 1969 | $30 |

COPPERPENNY
RCA VICTOR
| ❏ LSP-4291 [B] | Copperpenny | 1970 | $25 |

CORBIN, HAROLD
ROULETTE
| ❏ R-52079 [M] | Soul Brother | 1961 | $30 |
| ❏ SR-52079 [S] | Soul Brother | 1961 | $30 |

CORBIN/HANNER
ALFA
❏ AAA-10003	For the Sake of the Song	1981	$15
—As "Corbin-Hanner Band			
❏ AAA-11008	Son of America	1982	$15
—As "Corbin-Hanner Band			

CORBITT, JERRY & DANIELS, CHARLIE
TIGER LILY
| ❏ TL14001 [B] | Corbitt & Daniels Live I | 1976 | $50 |

CORCORAN, CORKY
C.C. PRODUCTION
| ❏ 4012 [M] | Corky Corcoran Plays Everywhere | 1974 | $15 |

CELESTIAL
❏ Vol.1 [M]	Sounds of Jazz	1958	$300
—Red vinyl			
❏ Vol.1 [M]	Sounds of Jazz	1958	$250
—Black vinyl			

EPIC
| ❏ LN3319 [M] | The Sound of Love | 1956 | $175 |

RCS
| ❏ 2555 [M] | Corky Corcoran Plays Something | 197? | $30 |

CORDIALS, THE
CATAMOUNT
| ❏ 902 | Blue Eyed Soul | 1967 | $30 |

COREA, CHICK, AND LIONEL HAMPTON
WHO'S WHO IN JAZZ
| ❏ WWLP21016 | Live at Midem | 1980 | $35 |

COREA, CHICK; HERBIE HANCOCK; KEITH JARRETT; MCCOY TYNER
ATLANTIC
| ❏ SD1696 | Corea/Hancock/Jarrett/Tyner | 1976 | $30 |

COREA, CHICK
51 WEST
| ❏ Q16078 | Jazzman | 1979 | $35 |

ATLANTIC
| ❏ SD 2-305 | Inner Space | 1973 | $35 |

BLUE NOTE
❏ BN-LA395-H2	Chick Corea	1975	$35
—"The Blue Note Reissue Series" labels			
❏ LWB-395	Chick Corea	1981	$25
—Reissue with new prefix			
❏ BN-LA472-H2	Circling In	1976	$50
—"The Blue Note Reissue Series" labels			
❏ BN-LA882-4047	Circulus	1978	$50
❏ B1-90055	Now He Sings, Now He Sobs	1988	$30
—Reissue; "The Finest in Jazz Since 1939" on label			
❏ BST-84353	Song of Singing	1970	$40
—A Division of Liberty Records" on label			
❏ BST-84353	Song of Singing	1984	$50
—Reissue, "The Finest in Jazz Since 1939" on label			

ECM
❏ 1009ST	A.R.C.	197?	$35
—Original issue, made in Germany?			
❏ ECM1-1009	A.R.C.	1977	$30
—Distributed by Polydor			
❏ 25005	Children's Songs	1984	$25
—Distributed by Warner Bros.			
❏ 1267	Children's Songs	1984	$30
—Made in Germany			
❏ 1014ST	Piano Improvisations, Vol. 1	1974	$35
—Original edition; made in Germany?			
❏ ECM-1-1014	Piano Improvisations, Vol. 1	1977	$30
—Distributed by Polydor			
❏ 1020ST	Piano Improvisations, Vol. 2	197?	$35
—Original edition; made in Germany?			
❏ ECM1-1020	Piano Improvisations, Vol. 2	1977	$30
—Distributed by Polydor			
❏ 25035	Septet	1985	$25
—Distributed by Warner Bros.			
❏ 1297	Septet	1985	$30
—Made in Germany			
❏ 1232	Trio Music	198?	$30
❏ 25013	Voyage	1985	$25
—Distributed by Warner Bros.			
❏ 1282	Voyage	1985	$30
—Made in Germany			

ELEKTRA/MUSICIAN
| ❏ 60167 | Again & Again | 1984 | $25 |

GROOVE MERCHANT
❏ 4406	Piano Giants	197?	$50
❏ 2202	Sundance	1972	$75
❏ GM530	Sundance	1974	$35
—Reissue of 2202			

GRP
❏ GR-1053	Eye of the Beholder	1988	$25
❏ GR-9601	Inside Out	1991	$35
❏ GR-1036	Light Years	1987	$25
❏ GR-9582	The Chick Corea Akoustic Band	1989	$30
❏ GRP-A-1026	The Chick Corea Elektric Band	1987	$25

MUSE
| ❏ MR5011 | Bliss! | 1973 | $50 |

PACIFIC JAZZ
| ❏ LN-10057 | Now He Sings, Now He Sobs | 1981 | $25 |
| —Reissue of Solid State 18039 | | | |

POLYDOR
❏ PD-1-6208	Delphi I	1979	$25
❏ PD-2-6334	Delphi II & III	1982	$35
❏ PD-1-6160	Friends	1978	$25
❏ PD-2-9003	My Spanish Heart	1976	$35
❏ PD-1-6176	Secret Agent	1979	$25
❏ PD-6062	The Leprechaun	1976	$25
❏ PD-1-6130	The Mad Hatter	1978	$25

QUINTESSENCE
| ❏ QJ-25011 | Before Forever | 1978 | $30 |

SOLID STATE
| ❏ SS-18055 | Chick Corea "Is | 1969 | $50 |
| ❏ SS-18039 | Now He Sings, Now He Sobs | 1969 | $50 |

VORTEX
| ❏ 2004 | Tones for Joan's Bones | 1971 | $75 |

WARNER BROS.
❏ BSK3425	Tap Step	1980	$25
❏ BSK3552	Three Quartets	1981	$25
❏ 23699	Touchstone	1983	$25

COREY, JILL
COLUMBIA
| ❏ CL1095 [M] | Sometimes I'm Happy, Sometimes I'm Blue | 1957 | $75 |

CORNELIUS BROTHERS AND SISTER ROSE
UNITED ARTISTS
| ❏ UAS-5568 | Cornelius Brothers and Sister Rose | 1972 | $18 |
| ❏ UA-LA593-G | Greatest Hits | 1976 | $15 |

CORNELL, DON
ABC-PARAMOUNT
| ❏ ABC-537 [M] | Incomparable | 1966 | $15 |
| ❏ ABCS-537 [S] | Incomparable | 1966 | $18 |

CORAL
| ❏ CRL57055 [M] | Don | 1955 | $30 |
| ❏ CRL57133 [M] | For Teenagers Only | 1957 | $30 |

DOT
| ❏ DLP-3160 [M] | Don Cornell's Great Hits | 1959 | $30 |
| ❏ DLP-25160 [S] | Don Cornell's Great Hits | 1959 | $30 |

MOVIETONE
| ❏ 71013 [M] | I Wish You Love | 1966 | $15 |
| ❏ S-72013 [S] | I Wish You Love | 1966 | $18 |

SIGNATURE
| ❏ SM-1001 [M] | Don Cornell Sings Love Songs | 1960 | $25 |
| ❏ SS-1001 [S] | Don Cornell Sings Love Songs | 1960 | $30 |

Number	Title	Yr	NM

VOCALION
| VL3657 [M] | Don Cornell | 196? | $15 |

CORNELLS, THE
GAREX
| LPGA-100 [M] | Beach Bound | 1963 | $500 |

SUNDAZED
| LP-5013 | Surf Fever! | 199? | $12 |

CORPORATION, THE
AGE OF AQUARIUS
| 4150 | Get On Our Swing | 1968 | $30 |
| 4250 | Hassles in My Mind | 1969 | $30 |

CAPITOL
| ST-175 | The Corporation | 1969 | $50 |

CORPUS
ACORN
1001 [B]	Creation: A Child	1971	$600
— Banded tracks			
1001 [B]	Creation: A Child	1971	$300
— Second pressing, green/pink label, unbanded			

CORTEZ, DAVE "BABY"
CHESS
| LP-1473 [M] | Rinky Dink | 1962 | $50 |

CLOCK
C-331 [M]	Dave "Baby" Cortez	1960	$40
CS-331 [S]	Dave "Baby" Cortez	1960	$50
MGC-20647 [M]	Dave "Baby" Cortez	1961	$30
SRC-60647 [S]	Dave "Baby" Cortez	1961	$40

CORONET
| CX-201 [M] | The Whistling Organ | 196? | $18 |

DESIGN
| DLP-163 [R] | The Happy Organ | 1962 | $15 |

METRO
| M-550 [M] | The Fabulous Organ of Dave "Baby" Cortez | 1965 | $18 |
| MS-550 [R] | The Fabulous Organ of Dave "Baby" Cortez | 1965 | $15 |

RCA VICTOR
| LPM-2099 [M] | The Happy Organ | 1959 | $100 |
| LSP-2099 [S] | The Happy Organ | 1959 | $150 |

ROULETTE
R-25328 [M]	In Orbit with Dave "Baby" Cortez	1966	$25
SR-25328 [S]	In Orbit with Dave "Baby" Cortez	1966	$30
R-25298 [M]	Organ Shindig	1965	$25
SR-25298 [S]	Organ Shindig	1965	$30
R-25315 [M]	Tweety Pie	1966	$25
SR-25315 [S]	Tweety Pie	1966	$30

T-NECK
| TNS-3005 | The Isley Brothers Way | 1970 | $25 |

CORWIN, BOB
RIVERSIDE
RLP 12-220 [M]	Bob Corwin Quartet with Don Elliott	1956	$300
— White label, blue print			
RLP 12-220 [M]	Bob Corwin Quartet with Don Elliott	1957	$300
— Blue label with microphone logo			

CORYELL, LARRY, AND ALPHONSE MOUZON
ATLANTIC
| SD18220 | Back Together Again | 1977 | $30 |

CORYELL, LARRY, AND BRIAN KEANE
FLYING FISH
| FF-337 | Just Like Being Born | 1985 | $30 |

CORYELL, LARRY, AND PHILIP CATHERINE
ELEKTRA
| 6E-153 | Splendid | 1978 | $30 |
| 6E-123 | Twin House | 1977 | $30 |

CORYELL, LARRY, AND STEVE KAHN
ARISTA
| AB4156 | Two for the Road | 1978 | $30 |

CORYELL, LARRY
ARISTA
AL4077	Aspects	1976	$35
AL4052	Level One	1975	$35
AL4108	The Lion and the Ram	1977	$35

ARISTA/NOVUS
| AN3005 | European Imperssions | 1978 | $30 |
| AN3017 | Tributaries | 1979 | $30 |

CONCORD JAZZ
| CJ-289 | Together | 1986 | $25 |

Number	Title	Yr	NM

FLYING DUTCHMAN
| FD-10139 | Barefoot Boy | 1971 | $35 |
| 51-1000 | Fairyland | 1971 | $25 |

MEGA
| 607 | Fairyland | 197? | $35 |
| — Reissue of Flying Dutchman 51-1000 | | | |

MUSE
MR-5303	Comin' Home	1985	$25
MR-5319	Equipoise	1986	$25
MR-5350	Toku Do	1988	$30

RCA VICTOR
| AYL1-3961 | Barefoot Boy | 198? | $20 |
| — Reissue of Flying Dutchman 10139 | | | |

SHANACHIE
| 97005 | The Dragon Gate | 1990 | $35 |

STEEPLECHASE
| SCS-1187 | A Quiet Day in Spring | 1983 | $25 |

VANGUARD
VSD-79360	Another Side of Larry Coryell	1975	$35
VSD-79375	Basics	1976	$30
VSD-6547	Coryell	1969	$75
VSD-79342	Introducing the Eleventh House	1974	$35
VSQ-40036 [Q]	Introducing the Eleventh House	1974	$30
VSD-6509	Lady Coryell	1969	$40
VSD-79410	Larry Coryell and the Eleventh House at Montreux	1978	$30
VSD-6573	Larry Coryell at the Village Gate	1971	$35
VSQ-40006 [Q]	Larry Coryell at the Village Gate	197?	$30
VSD-79319	Offering	1972	$35
VSQ-40013 [Q]	Offering	197?	$30
VSD-79367	Planet End	1975	$30
VSD-79426	Return	1979	$30
VSD-6558	Spaces	1970	$35
VSD-79345	Spaces	1974	$30
— Reissue of 6558 with new cover			
VSD-75/76	The Essential Larry Coryell	1975	$35
VSD-79329	The Real Great Escape	1973	$35
VSQ-40023 [Q]	The Real Great Escape	197?	$30
VSD-79353	The Restful Mind	1975	$30

COSBY, BILL
CAPITOL
ST-11530	Bill Cosby Is Not Himself These Days, Rat Own, Rat Own, Rat Own	1976	$12
ST-11731	Bill's Best Friend	1978	$12
ST-11683	Let's Boogie (Disco Bill)	1977	$12
ST-11590	My Father Confused Me… What Must I Do? What Must I Do?	1977	$12

GEFFEN
| GHS24104 | Those of You With or Without Children, You'll Understand | 1986 | $12 |

MCA
8005	Bill	197?	$15
333	Fat Albert	1973	$12
553	For Adults Only	197?	$10
— Reissue of Uni 73112			
554	Inside the Mind of Bill Cosby	197?	$10
— Reissue of Uni 73139			
169	When I Was a Kid	197?	$10
— Reissue of Uni 73100			

MOTOWN
6026ML	Bill Cosby "Himself	1982	$12
5364ML	Bill Cosby "Himself	198?	$12
— Reissue of 6026 with new cover			

TETRAGRAMMATON
| TD-5100 | 8:15 12:15 | 1969 | $25 |

UNI
73066	Bill Cosby	1969	$12
73101	Bill Cosby Talks to Kids About Drugs	1971	$18
73112	For Adults Only	1971	$12
73139	Inside the Mind of Bill Cosby	1972	$12
73082	Live" Madison Square Garden Center	1970	$12
73100	When I Was a Kid	1971	$12

WARNER BROS.
WS1757	200 M.P.H.	1968	$15
W1518 [M]	Bill Cosby Is a Very Funny Fellow Right!	1964	$18
W1728 [M]	Bill Cosby Sings/Hooray for the Salvation Army Band	1968	$18
WS1728 [S]	Bill Cosby Sings/Hooray for the Salvation Army Band	1968	$15
W1709 [M]	Bill Cosby Sings/Silver Throat	1967	$18
WS1709 [S]	Bill Cosby Sings/Silver Throat	1967	$15
W1567 [M]	I Started Out as a Child	1964	$18
WS1567 [S]	I Started Out as a Child	1964	$25
— Gold label			
WS1770 [B]	It's True! It's True!	1969	$15
WS1836	More of the Best of Bill Cosby	1970	$15

Number	Title	Yr	NM

PRO249 [DJ]	Radio Sampler Album -- The Best of Bill Cosby	1969	$25
— Promo LP with edits of 12 tracks for radio use			
PRO249 [DJ]	Radio Sampler Album -- The Best of Bill Cosby	1969	$25
— Promo LP with edits of 12 tracks for radio use			
W1691 [M]	Revenge	1967	$18
WS1798 [B]	The Best of Bill Cosby	1969	$15
W1734 [M]	To Russell, My Brother, Whom I Slept With	1968	$18
WS1734 [S]	To Russell, My Brother, Whom I Slept With	1968	$15
W1606 [M]	Why Is There Air?	1965	$18
WS1606 [S]	Why Is There Air?	1965	$25
— Gold label			
W1634 [M]	Wonderfulness	1966	$18
WS1634 [S]	Wonderfulness	1966	$18
— Gold label			

COSMIC, MICHAEL
COSMIC RECORDS
| 85 [B] | Peace In The World | | $2000 |
| — handmade cover | | | |

COSMIC TWINS, THE
STRATA-EAST
| SES-7410 | The Waterbearers | 1974 | $30 |

COSTA, DON
ABC-PARAMOUNT
ABC-362 [M]	Don Costa Conducts His 15 Hits	1961	$30
ABC-107 [M]	Music to Break a Lease	1956	$30
ABC-212 [M]	Music to Break a Sub-Lease	1958	$30

COLUMBIA
CL2041 [M]	Hits! Hits! Hits!	1963	$18
CS8841 [S]	Hits! Hits! Hits!	1963	$30
CS8680 [S]	Hollywood Premiere	1962	$30
CL1880 [M]	Hollywood Premiere	1962	$18

DCP INTERNATIONAL
DCL3806 [M]	Don Costa Plays Music from Umbrellas of Cherbourg and Other Film Music	1965	$15
DCS6806 [S]	Don Costa Plays Music from Umbrellas of Cherbourg and Other Film Music	1965	$18
DCL3802 [M]	The Golden Touch	1964	$15
DCS6802 [S]	The Golden Touch	1964	$18

HARMONY
| HL7347 [M] | Days of Wine and Roses and Other Great Hits | 1965 | $15 |
| HS11147 [S] | Days of Wine and Roses and Other Great Hits | 1965 | $18 |

MERCURY
| SR61177 | Instrumental Versions of Simon and Garfunkel | 1968 | $25 |
| SR61216 | The Don Costa Concept | 1969 | $25 |

UNITED ARTISTS
WW7501 [M]	Echoing Voices and Trombones	1960	$25
WWS8501 [S]	Echoing Voices and Trombones	1960	$30
UAL3134 [M]	Magnificent Motion Picture Music	1960	$18
UAS6134 [S]	Magnificent Motion Picture Music	1960	$25
WW3513 [M]	The Sound of the Million Sellers	1960	$18
WWS8513 [S]	The Sound of the Million Sellers	1960	$30
UAL3119 [M]	The Unforgiven	1960	$25

VERVE
| V-8702 [M] | Modern Delights | 1967 | $25 |
| V6-8702 [S] | Modern Delights | 1967 | $18 |

COSTA, EDDIE, AND ART FARMER
PREMIER
| PM-2002 [M] | In Their Own Sweet Way | 1962 | $50 |
| PMS-2002 [R] | In Their Own Sweet Way | 196? | $30 |

COSTA, EDDIE
CORAL
| CRL57230 [M] | Guys and Dolls Like Vibes | 1958 | $250 |

DOT
| DLP-3206 [M] | The House of Blue Lights | 1959 | $600 |
| DLP-25206 [S] | The House of Blue Lights | 1959 | $500 |

INTERLUDE
MO-508 [M]	Eddie Costa Quintet	1959	$150
— Reissue of Mode 118			
ST-1008 [S]	Eddie Costa Quintet	1959	$75

JOSIE
| JOZ-3509 [M] | Eddie Costa with the Burke Trio | 1963 | $25 |
| JSS-2509 [S] | Eddie Costa with the Burke Trio | 1963 | $30 |

JUBILEE
| JLP-1025 [M] | Eddie Costa Quintet with the Vinnie Burke Trio | 1956 | $75 |

Number	Title	Yr	NM

MODE
| ❏ LP-118 [M] | Eddie Costa Quintet | 1957 | $300 |

COSTA, EDDIE/MAT MATTHEWS AND DON ELLIOTT
VERVE
| ❏ MGV-8237 [M] | Eddie Costa with Rolf Kuhn and Dick Johnson/Mat Matthews and Don Elliott at Newport | 1958 | $175 |
| ❏ V-8237 [M] | Eddie Costa with Rolf Kuhn and Dick Johnson/Mat Matthews and Don Elliott at Newport | 1961 | $30 |

COSTA, JOHNNY
CORAL
| ❏ CRL57117 [M] | The Most Beautiful Girl in the World | 1957 | $30 |

SAVOY
| ❏ MG-15056 [10] | Johnny Costa | 1955 | $100 |
| ❏ MG-12052 [M] | The Amazing Johnny Costa | 1956 | $50 |

SAVOY JAZZ
| ❏ SJL-1190 | Neighborhood | 198? | $25 |

COSTANZO, JACK
GENE NORMAN
| ❏ GNP-19 [M] | Mr. Bongo | 1955 | $75 |

LIBERTY
❏ LRP-3137 [M]	Afro Can-Can	1960	$30
❏ LST-7137 [S]	Afro Can-Can	1960	$30
❏ LRP-3109 [M]	Bongo Fever	1959	$30
❏ LST-7109 [S]	Bongo Fever	1959	$30
❏ LRP-3093 [M]	Latin Fever	1958	$30
❏ LST-7020 [S]	Latin Fever	1958	$30
❏ LRP-3177 [M]	Learn-Play Bongos	1960	$30
❏ LRP-3195 [M]	Naked City	1961	$30
❏ LST-7195 [S]	Naked City	1961	$30

NORGRAN
| ❏ MGN-32 [10] | Afro-Cubano | 1954 | $300 |

SUNSET
| ❏ SUM-1134 [M] | Bongo Fever | 196? | $30 |
| ❏ SUS-5134 [S] | Bongo Fever | 196? | $30 |

COSTANZO, JACK/ANDRE'S CUBAN ALL STARS
NORGRAN
| ❏ MGN-1067 [M] | Afro-Cubano | 1956 | $350 |

—Combined reissue of Norgran 32 (by the former) and Clef 515 (by the latter)

VERVE
| ❏ MGV-8157 [M] | Afro-Cubano | 1957 | $250 |
| ❏ V-8157 [M] | Afro-Cubano | 1961 | $75 |

COSTELLO, ELVIS
COLUMBIA
| ❏ AS1318 [DJ] | Almost Blue | 1981 | $75 |

—Radio sampler with introductions by Elvis before each track
| ❏ FC37562 | Almost Blue | 1981 | $12 |
| ❏ PC37562 | Almost Blue | 1984 | $10 |

—Budget-line reissue with new prefix
| ❏ AS1318 [DJ] | Almost Blue: Elvis Introduces His Favorite Country Songs | 1981 | $85 |

—Radio sampler with introductions by Elvis before each track
| ❏ JC35709 [DJ] | Armed Forces | 1979 | $18 |

—White label promo, includes bonus 7" single
| ❏ JC35709 [DJ] | Armed Forces | 1979 | $18 |

—White label promo; add 20 percent if bonus 7-inch single is there; add another 33 percent if the 7-inch's picture sleeve is there
| ❏ JC35709 | Armed Forces | 1979 | $12 |

—Stock copy; add 30 percent if bonus 7-inch single is there; add another 50 percent if the 7-inch's picture sleeve is there
| ❏ PC35709 | Armed Forces | 1984 | $10 |

—Budget-line reissue with new prefix; not issued with bonus single
❏ FC40518	Blood & Chocolate	1986	$12
❏ JC36347	Get Happy!!	1980	$12
❏ PC36347	Get Happy!!	1984	$10

—Budget-line reissue with new prefix
| ❏ FC39429 | Goodbye Cruel World | 1984 | $12 |
| ❏ PC39429 | Goodbye Cruel World | 198? | $10 |

—Budget-line reissue with new prefix
| ❏ FC38157 | Imperial Bedroom | 1982 | $12 |
| ❏ HC48157 | Imperial Bedroom | 1982 | $50 |

—Half-speed mastered edition
| ❏ PC38157 | Imperial Bedroom | 1984 | $10 |

—Budget-line reissue with new prefix
| ❏ FC40173 | King of America | 1986 | $12 |

—By "The Costello Show Featuring Elvis Costello"
| ❏ PC40173 | King of America | 198? | $12 |

—By "The Costello Show Featuring Elvis Costello"; budget-line reissue with new prefix
| ❏ AS529 [EP] | Live at Hollywood High | 1978 | $25 |

—Promo-only 12-inch version of 7-inch single
| ❏ JC35037 | My Aim Is True | 1977 | $18 |

—First pressings have yellow back covers
| ❏ JC35037 [B] | My Aim Is True | 1978 | $12 |

—Second pressings have a white back cover and no bar code
| ❏ PC35037 | My Aim Is True | 1984 | $10 |

—Budget-line reissue with new prefix
| ❏ 0(no cat #) [PD] | My Aim Is True/This Year's Model | 1978 | $150 |

—Promo-only picture disc; contains six songs from one album and six from the other
| ❏ FC38897 | Punch the Clock | 1983 | $12 |
| ❏ JC36839 | Taking Liberties | 1980 | $12 |

—With custom old-style Columbia label
| ❏ JC36839 | Taking Liberties | 1980 | $10 |
| ❏ PC36839 | Taking Liberties | 1984 | $10 |

—Budget-line reissue with new prefix
❏ FC40101	The Best of Elvis Costello	1985	$15
❏ AS958 [DJ]	The Elvis Costello Interview with Tom Snyder	1981	$50
❏ JC35331	This Year's Model	1978	$15

—With "Costello" replacing "Columbia" on labels
| ❏ JC35331 | This Year's Model | 1978 | $12 |

—With standard Columbia label
| ❏ PC35331 | This Year's Model | 1984 | $10 |

—Budget-line reissue with new prefix
❏ AS958 [DJ]	Tom Snyder Interview	1981	$25
❏ JC37051	Trust	1981	$12
❏ PC37051	Trust	1984	$10

—Budget-line reissue with new prefix

COSTELLO
| ❏ AS847 [EP] | Taking Liberties | 1980 | $18 |

—Promo-only four-song sampler' "Costello" is where "Columbia" would normally be on the 78-rpm-style label

DEUTSCHE GRAMMAPHON
| ❏ 00289 479 6062 [B] | Live With The Metropole Orkest - My Flame Burns Blue | 2016 | $40 |

—blue vinyl

LOST HIGHWAY
| ❏ B0003905-1 [10] | Delta-Verite: The Clarksdale Sessions | 2005 | $75 |
| ❏ B0003905-1 [10] | Delta-Verite: The Clarksdale Sessions | 2005 | $75 |

—Black vinyl; this album has been counterfeited; originals have a white border around all four sides of the front cover and the words "The Round-Up Factor" at the bottom of the back cover, and counterfeits do not; also, counterfeits use the catalog number "CN-005" and have white labels
| ❏ B0002593-01 | The Delivery Man | 2004 | $25 |

MOBILE FIDELITY
❏ MFSL1-355 [B]	Almost Blue	2012	$40
❏ MFSL1-433 [B]	Blood and Chocolate	2015	$40
❏ 1-432 [B]	Goodbye Cruel World	2015	$30
❏ MFSL1-353 [B]	Imperial Bedroom	2012	$50
❏ MFSL1-389 [B]	Punch The Clock	2013	$40
❏ MFSL1-340 [B]	Trust	2015	$30

RHINO
| ❏ R1-74285 | My Aim Is True | 2003 | $18 |

—180-gram vinyl; first U.S. issue of British track lineup

WARNER BROS.
| ❏ 46198 | All This Useless Beauty | 1996 | $150 |
| ❏ R100841 | Spike | 1989 | $15 |

—BMG Direct Marketing edition
| ❏ 25848 | Spike | 1989 | $12 |
| ❏ -03488 [DJ] | Spike -- The Elvis Costello Hour | 1989 | $30 |

—Music and conversation; generic gatefold sleeve with sticker on cover
| ❏ PRO-A-3488 [DJ] | The Elvis Costello Hour | 1989 | $40 |

—Music and interview; generic gatefold sleeve with sticker on cover

COTTON, GENE
ABC
| ❏ D-933 | For All the Young Writers | 1975 | $12 |
| ❏ D-983 | Rain On | 1977 | $12 |

ARIOLA AMERICA
| ❏ SW-50070 | No Strings Attached | 1979 | $12 |
| ❏ SW-50031 | Save the Dancer | 1978 | $12 |

KNOLL
| ❏ 1001 | Eclipse of the Blue Moon | 1981 | $12 |

MYRRH
| ❏ MSB-6517 | In the Gray of the Morning | 1973 | $15 |
| ❏ MSB-6524 | Liberty | 1974 | $15 |

COTTON, JAMES
ALLIGATOR
| ❏ AL-4737 | High Compression | 1984 | $12 |
| ❏ AL-4746 | Live from Chicago | 1986 | $12 |

ANTONE'S
| ❏ ANT-0007 | James Cotton Live | 1988 | $15 |

BLIND PIG
| ❏ BP-2587 | Take Me Back | 1987 | $12 |

BUDDAH
| ❏ BDS-5620 | 100% Cotton | 1974 | $15 |

| ❏ BDS-5650 | High Energy | 1975 | $15 |
| ❏ BDS-5661 | Live & On the Move! | 1976 | $18 |

CAPITOL
| ❏ ST-814 | Taking Care of Business | 1971 | $18 |
| ❏ SM-814 | Taking Care of Business | 197? | $12 |

—Reissue with new prefix

INTERMEDIA
| ❏ QS-5006 | Dealing with the Devil | 198? | $12 |
| ❏ QS-5011 | Two Sides of the Blues | 198? | $12 |

VANGUARD
| ❏ VSD-79283 | Cut You Loose! | 1969 | $18 |

VERVE FORECAST
| ❏ FTS-3038 [B] | Pure Cotton | 1968 | $25 |

| ❏ FT-3023 [M] | The James Cotton Blues Band | 1967 | $30 |
| ❏ FTS-3023 [S] | The James Cotton Blues Band | 1967 | $25 |

COTTON, JOSIE
ELEKTRA
| ❏ 60140 | Convertible Music | 1982 | $15 |
| ❏ 60309 | From the Hip | 1984 | $15 |

COTTON PICKERS, THE
PHILIPS
| ❏ PHM200025 [M] | Country Guitar | 1962 | $25 |
| ❏ PHS600025 [S] | Country Guitar | 1962 | $30 |

COTTRELL, LOUIS
NOBILITY
| ❏ LP-703 | Dixieland Hall Presents Louis Cottrell and His New Orleans Jazz | 197? | $35 |

RIVERSIDE
| ❏ RLP-385 [M] | Bourbon Street | 1961 | $250 |
| ❏ RS-9385 [S] | Bourbon Street | 1961 | $250 |

COTTRELL, LOUIS/'HERB HALL
GHB
| ❏ 156 | Clarinet Legends | 198? | $25 |

COUCH, ORVILLE
VEE JAY
| ❏ VJLP-1087 [M] | Hello Trouble | 1964 | $25 |
| ❏ VJS-1087 [S] | Hello Trouble | 1964 | $40 |

COUGAR, JOHN(NY)
RIVA
| ❏ RVL7051 [B] | American Fool | 2016 | $25 |

COULSON, DEAN, McGUINNESS, FLINT
SIRE
| ❏ SAS-7405 [B] | Lo and Behold | 1972 | $30 |

COULTER, CLIFF
ABC IMPULSE!
| ❏ AS-9216 | Do It Now! | 1972 | $250 |
| ❏ AS-9197 | Eastside San Jose | 1971 | $250 |

COULTER, PHIL
SHANACHIE
| ❏ 53005 | Phil Coulter's Christmas | 1983 | $12 |

COUNCE, CURTIS
ANALOGUE PRODUCTIONS
| ❏ AP-3006 | You Get More Bounce with Curtis Counce | 199? | $35 |

BOPLICITY
| ❏ BOP-7 | Exploring the Future | 198? | $30 |

—Reissue of Dooto LP

Number	Title	Yr	NM
CONTEMPORARY			
❏ M-3574 [M]	Carl's Blues	1960	$150
❏ S-7574 [S]	Carl's Blues	1960	$120
❏ C-7539	Counceltation	197?	$25
—Retitled version of "You Get More Bounce with Curtis Counce"			
❏ C-3526 [M]	Curtis Counce Group	1957	$150
❏ S-7526 [S]	Curtis Counce Group	1959	$300
❏ S-7526 [S]	Landslide	196?	$30
—Retitled version of "Curtis Counce Group"			
❏ C-7655	Sonority	198?	$25
❏ M-3539 [M]	You Get More Bounce with Curtis Counce	1957	$300
❏ S-7539 [S]	You Get More Bounce with Curtis Counce	1959	$300
DOOTO			
❏ DTL-247 [M]	Exploring the Future	1958	$50
FANTASY			
❏ OJC-423	Carl's Blues	1990	$30
—Reissue of Contemporary 7574			
❏ OJC-159	You Get More Bounce with Curtis Counce	198?	$25
—Reissue of Contemporary 7539			

COUNT FIVE, THE

Number	Title	Yr	NM
DOUBLE SHOT			
❏ DSM-1001 [M]	Psychotic Reaction	1966	$75
❏ DSS-5001 [R]	Psychotic Reaction	1966	$30

COUNTING CROWS

Number	Title	Yr	NM
DGC			
❏ 24975	Recovering the Satellites	1996	$18
❏ DGC2-24975	Recovering the Satellites	1996	$50
❏ 069490415-1	This Desert Life	1999	$50
— Side 2 of the second record is blank			

COUNTRY ALL-STARS, THE

Number	Title	Yr	NM
RCA VICTOR			
❏ LPM-3167 [10]	String Dustin'	1953	$175

COUNTRY CUT-UPS, THE

Number	Title	Yr	NM
TOWN HOUSE			
❏ 1000 [M]	The Country Cut-Ups Go to College	195?	$100

COUNTRY GENTLEMEN, THE

Number	Title	Yr	NM
CIMARRON			
❏ 2001 [M]	Songs of the Pioneers	1962	$40
MERCURY			
❏ MG-20858 [M]	Folk Session Inside	1963	$25
❏ SR-60858 [S]	Folk Session Inside	1963	$30
STARDAY			
❏ SLP-174 [M]	Bluegrass at Carnegie Hall	1962	$40
❏ SLP-311 [M]	Songs of the Pioneers	1965	$30
❏ SLP-109 [M]	Traveling Dobro Blues	1959	$50

COUNTRY GOSPELAIRES, THE

Number	Title	Yr	NM
STARDAY			
❏ SLP-105 [M]	The Church Back Home	1959	$30

COUNTRY JOE AND THE FISH

Number	Title	Yr	NM
COMMUNICATING THE GOSPEL TODAY			
❏ no cat [B]	Sounds	1968	$1500
—side two only; side one features John Cage and David Tudor			
CUSTOM FIDELITY			
❏ CFS-2348	Joe McDonald	1968	$1000
—Recorded in 1964, 200 copies were pressed for Joe McDonald; VG value 500; VG+ value 750			
FANTASY			
❏ 9525	Goodbye Blues	1977	$12
❏ 9586	Leisure Suite	1980	$12
❏ 9511	Love Is a Fire	1976	$12
❏ 9495	Paradise with an Ocean View	1975	$12
❏ 9530	Reunion	1977	$15
❏ 9544	Rock and Roll Music From the Planet Earth	1978	$12
FIRST AMERICAN			
❏ PIC-3309	The Early Years	1979	$12
MOBLIE FIDELITY			
❏ 1-056	Paradise with an Ocean View	1981	$30
—Audiophile vinyl			
VANGUARD			
❏ VSD-6555	C.J. Fish	1970	$25
❏ VSD-6545	Country Joe & The Fish/ Greatest Hits	1969	$25
❏ VSD-79348	Country Joe	1974	$15
❏ VRS-9244 [M]	Electric Music for the Mind and Body	1967	$175
— Black label (unverified)			
❏ VRS-9244 [M]	Electric Music for the Mind and Body	1967	$150
— Gold label			

Number	Title	Yr	NM
❏ VSD-79244 [S]	Electric Music for the Mind and Body	1967	$75
— Black label (unverified)			
❏ VSD-79244 [S]	Electric Music for the Mind and Body	1967	$50
— Gold label			
❏ VSD-79299	Here We Are Again	1969	$25
❏ VSD-79304	Hold On It's Coming	1971	$18
❏ VSD79266 [B]	I-Feel-Like-I'm-Fixin'-To-Die	2013	$30
❏ VRS-9266 [M]	I-Feel-Like-I'm-Fixin'-to-Die	1967	$75
❏ VSD-79266 [S]	I-Feel-Like-I'm-Fixin'-to-Die	1967	$40
❏ 9266/79266 [B]	I-Feel-Like-I'm-Fixin'-to-Die "Fish Game" Poster	1967	$40
❏ VSD-79316	Incredible! Live!	1972	$15
❏ VSD-79328	Paris Sessions	1973	$15
❏ VSD-85/86	The Essential Country Joe	1977	$15
❏ VSD-27/28	The Life and Times of Country Joe & the Fish From Haight-Ashbury to Woodstock	1971	$25
❏ VSQ-40004/5 [Q]	The Life and Times of Country Joe & the Fish From Haight-Ashbury to Woodstock	197?	$50
❏ VSD-6546	Thinking of Woody	1969	$18
❏ VSD-79277	Together	1968	$30
❏ VSD79277 [B]	Together	2015	$25
— Record Store Day			
❏ VSD-6557	Tonight I'm Singing Just for You	1970	$18
❏ VSD-79315	War, War, War	1971	$18

COUNTRY MIKE
Actually Mike D of BEASTIE BOYS.

Number	Title	Yr	NM
GRAND ROYAL			
❏ CM-1	Country Mike's Greatest Hits	2000	$250
— Black vinyl; this album has been counterfeited; originals have a white border around all four sides of the front cover and the words "The Round-Up Factor" at the bottom of the back cover, and counterfeits do not; also, counterfeits use the catalog number "CN-005" and have white labels			
❏ CM-1	Country Mike's Greatest Hits	2000	$300
— Red vinyl			

COUNTS, THE (2)
Detroit-based funk group.

Number	Title	Yr	NM
AWARE			
❏ 2006	Funk Pump	1975	$25
❏ 2002	Love Sign	1973	$30
WESTBOUND			
❏ 2011	What's Up Front That Counts	1972	$30

COURTLAND, JEROME

Number	Title	Yr	NM
JUBILEE			
❏ LP22 [10]	Through a Long and Sleepless Night	1955	$40

COURTNEY, LOU

Number	Title	Yr	NM
EPIC			
❏ KE33011	I'm in Need of Love	1974	$15
RCA VICTOR			
❏ APL1-1969	Buffalo Smoke	1976	$15
RIVERSIDE			
❏ 92000	Skate Now (Shing-a-Ling)	1967	$30

COUSIN WILBUR

Number	Title	Yr	NM
C.W.			
❏ 100 [M]	The Cousin Wilbur Show	195?	$50

COUSINS, THE (2)

Number	Title	Yr	NM
PARKWAY			
❏ P-7005 [M]	Music of the Strip	1961	$25
❏ SP-7005 [S]	Music of the Strip	1961	$30

COVAY, DON

Number	Title	Yr	NM
ATLANTIC			
❏ 8104 [M]	Mercy	1965	$40
❏ SD8104 [S]	Mercy	1965	$50
❏ 8120 [M]	See Saw	1966	$40
❏ SD8120 [S]	See Saw	1966	$50
❏ SD8237	The House of Blue Lights	1969	$30
JANUS			
❏ 3038	Different Strokes for Different Folks	1972	$18
MERCURY			
❏ 835030-1	Checkin' In with Don Covay	1988	$12
❏ SRM-1-1020	Hot Blood	1974	$15
❏ SRM-1-653	Super Dude I	1973	$15
PHILADELPHIA INT'L.			
❏ PZ33958	Travelin' In Heavy Traffic	1977	$12

COVEN
Features Jinx Dawson.

Number	Title	Yr	NM
BUDDAH			
❏ BDS-5614	Blood on the Snow	1974	$30

Number	Title	Yr	NM
MERCURY			
❏ SR61239 [B]	Witchcraft Destroys Minds and Reaps Souls	1969	$175
MGM			
❏ SE-4801 [B]	Coven	1971	$75

COWARD, NOEL, AND GERTRUDE LAWRENCE

Number	Title	Yr	NM
RCA VICTOR			
❏ LPM-1156 [M]	Noel and Gertie	1955	$30

COWARD, NOEL

Number	Title	Yr	NM
COLUMBIA MASTERWORKS			
❏ ML5063 [M]	Noel Coward at Las Vegas	1955	$30

COWBOY JUNKIES

Number	Title	Yr	NM
LATENT RECORDINGS			
❏ LATEX4	Whites Off Earth Now!!	1986	$30
—Canada-only release			
RCA			
❏ 8568-1-R	The Trinity Session	1988	$18
❏ 8568-1-R	The Trinity Session	1997	$40
—Classic Records reissue on audiophile vinyl			

COWELL, STANLEY

Number	Title	Yr	NM
ARISTA FREEDOM			
❏ AL1009	Beautiful Circles	197?	$30
❏ AL1032	Blues for the Viet Cong	197?	$30
ECM			
❏ 1026	Illusion Suite	1973	$30
GALAXY			
❏ 5125	Equipoise	1979	$30
❏ 5131	New World	1979	$30
❏ 5111	Talkin' Bout Love	1978	$30
❏ 5104	Waiting for ...	1977	$30
STRATA-EAST			
❏ SES-19743	Musa-Ancestral Streams	1974	$25
❏ SES-19765	Regeneration	1976	$25

COWSILL, BILL

Number	Title	Yr	NM
MGM			
❏ SE-4706	Nervous Breakthrough	1970	$18

COWSILLS, THE

LONDON

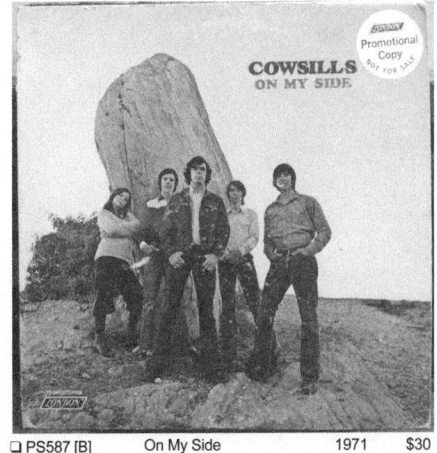

Number	Title	Yr	NM
❏ PS587 [B]	On My Side	1971	$30
MGM			
❏ E-4554 [M]	Captain Sad and His Ship of Fools	1968	$40
—Mono appears to be yellow label promo only			
❏ SE-4554 [S]	Captain Sad and His Ship of Fools	1968	$18
❏ SE-4639	II X II	1969	$25
❏ SE-4597	The Best of the Cowsills	1968	$18
❏ E-4498 [M]	The Cowsills	1967	$25
❏ SE-4498 [S]	The Cowsills	1967	$18
❏ GAS-103	The Cowsills (Golden Archive Series)	1970	$18
❏ SE-4619	The Cowsills in Concert	1969	$18
❏ E-4534 [M]	We Can Fly	1968	$30
—Appears to exist only as a yellow label promo			
❏ SE-4534 [S]	We Can Fly	1968	$18
WING			
❏ SRW-16354	The Cowsills Plus the Lincoln Park Zoo	1968	$15

COX, DANNY

Number	Title	Yr	NM
PIONEER			
❏ 2125	Sunny	1968	$30
TOGETHER			
❏ 1011	Birth Announcement	1969	$30

Number	Title	Yr	NM

COX, IDA
FANTASY
| ❏ OJC-1758 | Blues for Rampart Street | 198? | $35 |

— *Reissue of Riverside 9374*

RIVERSIDE
| ❏ RLP-374 [M] | Blues for Rampart Street | 1961 | $250 |
| ❏ RS-9374 [S] | Blues for Rampart Street | 1961 | $250 |

COX, KENNY, CONTEMPORARY JAZZ QUINTET
BLUE NOTE
| ❏ BST-84302 | Introducing Kenny Cox | 1969 | $85 |
| ❏ BST-84339 | Multidirection | 1970 | $85 |

COX, SONNY
CADET
| ❏ LP-765 [M] | The Wailer | 1966 | $35 |
| ❏ LPS-765 [S] | The Wailer | 1966 | $25 |

COXON'S ARMY
Pat Benatar was in this group. Also see PAT BENATAR.
SAM MILLER EXCHANGE
| ❏ 0(no cat #) | Live from Sam Miller's Exchange Cafe | 1974 | $300 |

— *Original is on Sam Miller Exchange purple label*

TRACE
| ❏ 0(no cat #) | Live from Sam Miller's Exchange Cafe | 1975 | $300 |

— *Reprint is on black Trace label*

COYNE, KEVIN
4 MEN WITH BEARDS
| ❏ 4M191LP [B] | Case History | | $25 |

VIRGIN
| ❏ PZ34757 [B] | In Living Black and White | 1976 | $18 |

— *single LP version of UK 2LP*
| ❏ VR13-106 [B] | Marjory Razorblade | 1973 | $30 |

— *single disc version of UK 2LP*
| ❏ VR13-117 [B] | Matching Head and Feet | 1975 | $30 |

CRABBY APPLETON
ELEKTRA
| ❏ EKS-74067 [B] | Crabby Appleton | 1970 | $18 |
| ❏ EKS-74106 | Rotten to the Core! | 1971 | $18 |

CRACK THE SKY
GRUDGE
| ❏ 4500-1-F | From the Greenhouse | 1989 | $12 |

LIFESONG
| ❏ LS6005 | Animal Notes | 1976 | $18 |
| ❏ PZ34998 | Animal Notes | 1977 | $12 |

— *Reissue of 6004*
| ❏ LS6000 | Crack the Sky | 1975 | $18 |
| ❏ PZ34994 | Crack the Sky | 1977 | $12 |

— *Reissue of 6000*
❏ PZ35620	Live Sky	1978	$15
❏ LS8133	Photoflamingo	1981	$12
❏ LS6015	Safety in Numbers	1978	$18
❏ PZ35041	Safety in Numbers	1978	$12

— *Reissue of 6015*

CRACKER
VIRGIN
| ❏ 39012 | Kerosene Hat | 1993 | $18 |
| ❏ 41498 | The Golden Age | 1996 | $25 |

— *Classic Records/Rock the House edition on audiophile vinyl*

CRACKERBASH
EMPTY
| ❏ MT-179 | Crackerbash | 1992 | $15 |
| ❏ MT-239 [10] | Tin Toy | 1993 | $15 |

CRADDOCK, BILLY "CRASH"
ABC
❏ X-777	Afraid I'll Want to Love Her One More Time	1973	$30
❏ AB-1078	Billy "Crash" Craddock Sings His Greatest Hits	1978	$12
❏ X-850	Greatest Hits -- Volume One	1975	$15
❏ X-788	Mr. Country Rock	1973	$18
❏ X-817	Rub It In	1974	$18

— *Black label*
| ❏ X-817 | Rub It In | 1974 | $15 |

— *Multicolor label*
| ❏ ABCD-875 | Still Thinkin' Bout You | 1975 | $15 |
| ❏ X-777 | Two Sides of "Crash" | 1973 | $18 |

— *Retitled version of above*

ABC DOT
❏ 2063	Crash	1976	$15
❏ DOSD-2040	Easy As Pie	1976	$15
❏ 2082	Live!	1977	$15

ATLANTIC
| ❏ 82012 | Back on Track | 1989 | $15 |

CAPITOL
❏ ST-11758	Billy "Crash" Craddock	1978	$12
❏ ST-12054	Changes	1980	$12
❏ ST-12304	Greatest Hits	1983	$12
❏ ST-11946	Laughing and Crying, Living and Dying	1979	$12
❏ ST-12249	The New Will Never Wear Off	1981	$12
❏ SW-11853	Turning Up and Turning On	1978	$12

CARTWHEEL
| ❏ 193 | Knock Three Times | 1971 | $25 |
| ❏ 05001 | You Better Move On | 1972 | $25 |

CHART
| ❏ 1053 | The Best of Billy Crash Craddock | 1973 | $18 |

HARMONY
| ❏ KH32186 | Billy "Crash" Craddock | 1973 | $15 |

KING
| ❏ 912 [M] | I'm Tore Up | 1964 | $150 |

MCA
| ❏ 663 | Billy "Crash" Craddock Sings His Greatest Hits | 1981 | $10 |

— *Reissue of ABC 1078*
| ❏ 664 | Easy As Pie | 1981 | $10 |

— *Reissue of ABC Dot 2040*
| ❏ 662 | Greatest Hits -- Volume One | 1981 | $10 |

— *Reissue of ABC 850*
| ❏ 665 | Live! | 1981 | $10 |

— *Reissue of ABC Dot 2082*
| ❏ 4165 | The Best of Billy "Crash" Craddock | 198? | $15 |
| ❏ 666 | The First Time | 1981 | $10 |

MCA DOT
| ❏ 39054 | Crash Craddock | 1986 | $12 |

STARDAY
| ❏ 3005 | 16 Favorite Hits | 1978 | $12 |

CRAM, PAUL
ONARI/A&M
| ❏ 06 | Blue Tales in Time | 1982 | $30 |

CRAMER, FLOYD
MGM
❏ E-4223 [M]	Floyd Cramer Goes Honky Tonkin'	1964	$18
❏ SE-4223 [R]	Floyd Cramer Goes Honky Tonkin'	1964	$15
❏ SE-4666	Floyd Cramer Goes Honky Tonkin'	1970	$15

— *Reissue of 4223*
| ❏ E-3502 [M] | That Honky-Tonk Piano | 1957 | $40 |

PAIR
| ❏ PDL2-1049 | Country Classics | 1986 | $15 |

RCA
| ❏ 5621-1-R | Our Class Reunion | 1987 | $12 |

RCA CAMDEN
❏ CXS-9016	A Date with Floyd Cramer	1972	$18
❏ CAS-2508	Almost Persuaded	1971	$15
❏ CAL-2104 [M]	Distinctive Piano Styling	196?	$15
❏ CAS-2104 [S]	Distinctive Piano Styling	196?	$15
❏ ACL2-0128	Floyd Cramer Plays the Big Hits	1973	$15
❏ CAL-2152 [M]	Night Train	1967	$15
❏ CAS-2152 [S]	Night Train	1967	$15
❏ ACL1-0563	Spotlight On Floyd Cramer	1974	$12
❏ CAL-874 [M]	The Magic Touch	1965	$15
❏ CAS-874(e) [P]	The Magic Touch	1965	$15

— *Even though this album is labeled "Stereo Electronically Reprocessed," nine of the 10 tracks are in true stereo*

RCA VICTOR
❏ LPM-2466 [M]	America's Biggest Selling Pianist	1962	$18
❏ LSP-2466 [S]	America's Biggest Selling Pianist	1962	$25
❏ LSP-4821	Best of the Class of…	1973	$18
❏ AHL1-4119	Best of the West	1982	$12
❏ LPM-3405 [M]	Class of '65	1965	$15
❏ LSP-3405 [S]	Class of '65	1965	$18
❏ LPM-3650 [M]	Class of '66	1966	$15
❏ LSP-3650 [S]	Class of '66	1966	$18
❏ LPM-3827 [M]	Class of '67	1967	$18
❏ LSP-3827 [S]	Class of '67	1967	$18
❏ LPM-4025 [M]	Class of '68	1968	$50
❏ LSP-4025 [S]	Class of '68	1968	$18
❏ LSP-4162	Class of '69	1969	$18
❏ LSP-4437	Class of '70	1970	$18
❏ LSP-4590	Class of '71	1971	$18
❏ LSP-4772	Class of '72	1972	$18
❏ APL1-0299	Class of '73	1973	$15
❏ APD1-0299 [Q]	Class of '73	1973	$20
❏ APL1-1191	Class of '74 and '75	1975	$12
❏ APD1-1191 [Q]	Class of '74 and '75	1975	$20
❏ AHL1-5452	Collector's Series	1985	$12
❏ LPM-2701 [M]	Comin' On	1963	$18
❏ LSP-2701 [S]	Comin' On	1963	$25
❏ LPM-2800 [M]	Country Piano -- City Strings	1964	$18
❏ LSP-2800 [S]	Country Piano -- City Strings	1964	$25
❏ LPM-2883 [M]	Cramer at the Console	1964	$18
❏ LSP-2883 [S]	Cramer at the Console	1964	$25
❏ AHL1-3613	Dallas	1980	$12
❏ LSP-4676	Detours	1972	$18
❏ APL1-2278	Floyd Cramer & the Keyboard Kick Band	1977	$12
❏ APL1-1541	Floyd Cramer Country	1976	$12
❏ APD1-1541 [Q]	Floyd Cramer Country	1976	$20
❏ LPM-2428 [M]	Floyd Cramer Gets Organized	1962	$18
❏ LSP-2428 [S]	Floyd Cramer Gets Organized	1962	$25
❏ APL1-0661	Floyd Cramer In Concert	1974	$15
❏ ANL1-3469	Floyd Cramer In Concert	1979	$10
❏ LPM-3925 [M]	Floyd Cramer Plays Country Classics	1968	$25
❏ LSP-3925 [S]	Floyd Cramer Plays Country Classics	1968	$18
❏ LSP-4220	Floyd Cramer Plays More Country Classics	1969	$18
❏ LPM-3811 [M]	Floyd Cramer Plays the Monkees	1967	$30
❏ LSP-3811 [S]	Floyd Cramer Plays the Monkees	1967	$18
❏ LSP-4367	Floyd Cramer with the Music City Pops	1970	$18
❏ AYL1-4008	Great Country Hits	1981	$10
❏ LPM-2151 [M]	Hello Blues	1960	$18
❏ LSP-2151 [S]	Hello Blues	1960	$25
❏ LPM-3746 [M]	Here's What's Happening!	1967	$18
❏ LSP-3746 [S]	Here's What's Happening!	1967	$18
❏ ANL1-2344	Hits from Country Hall	1977	$12
❏ LPM-3318 [M]	Hits from the Country Hall of Fame	1965	$18
❏ LSP-3318 [S]	Hits from the Country Hall of Fame	1965	$25
❏ LPM-2544 [M]	I Remember Hank Williams	1962	$18
❏ LSP-2544 [S]	I Remember Hank Williams	1962	$25
❏ LPM-2350 [M]	Last Date	1961	$25
❏ LSP-2350 [S]	Last Date	1961	$30
❏ AHL1-3487	Last Date	1979	$12
❏ AHL1-2644	Looking for Mr. Goodbar	1978	$12
❏ LSP-4070	MacArthur Park	1968	$18
❏ LPM-2359 [M]	On the Rebound	1961	$18
❏ LSP-2359 [S]	On the Rebound	1961	$25
❏ APL1-0893	Piano Masterpieces (1900-75)	1975	$12
❏ APD1-0893 [Q]	Piano Masterpieces (1900-75)	1975	$20
❏ AYL1-3745	Piano Masterpieces (1900-75)	1980	$10
❏ LSP-4500	Sounds of Sunday	1971	$18
❏ APD1-0155 [Q]	Super Country Hits	1973	$20

— *All copies are in quadraphonic*
❏ AHL1-3209	Super Hits	1979	$12
❏ LPM-2642 [M]	Swing Along	1963	$18
❏ LSP-2642 [S]	Swing Along	1963	$25
❏ LPM-2888 [M]	The Best of Floyd Cramer	1964	$15
❏ LSP-2888 [S]	The Best of Floyd Cramer	1964	$18
❏ AYL1-3900	The Best of Floyd Cramer	1981	$10
❏ LSP-4091	The Best of Floyd Cramer, Volume 2	1969	$18
❏ LPM-3533 [M]	The Big Ones	1966	$15
❏ LSP-3533 [S]	The Big Ones	1966	$18
❏ LSP-4312	The Big Ones, Volume II	1970	$18
❏ APL1-0469	The Young and the Restless	1974	$15
❏ APD1-0469 [Q]	The Young and the Restless	1974	$20
❏ VPS-6031	This Is Floyd Cramer	1970	$25
❏ LPM-3828 [M]	We Wish You a Merry Christmas	1967	$30
❏ LSP-3828 [S]	We Wish You a Merry Christmas	1967	$15

CRAMPS, THE
ENIGMA
| ❏ 21 | Smell of Female | 1983 | $18 |
| ❏ 268 [DJ] | Stay Sick! | 1990 | $25 |

— *Promo-only version*
| ❏ 73543 | Stay Sick! | 1990 | $18 |
| ❏ EPRO268 [DJ] | Stay Sick! | 1990 | $30 |

— *Promo-only version*

EPITAPH
| ❏ 86516 | Big Beat from Badsville | 1997 | $15 |
| ❏ 86449 | Flamejob | 199? | $15 |

— *Reissue of Medicine Label 24592*

I.R.S.
| ❏ SP-70042 | Bad Music for Bad People | 1984 | $18 |
| ❏ SP-70501 [EP] | Gravest Hits | 198? | $12 |

— *Reissue of 501*
❏ SP-501 [EP]	Gravest Hits	1979	$35
❏ SP-70016	Psychedelic Jungle	1981	$25
❏ SP-007 [B]	Songs the Lord Taught Us	1980	$35
❏ SP-70007	Songs the Lord Taught Us	198?	$15

— *Reissue of 007*

MEDICINE LABEL
| ❏ 24592 [B] | Flamejob | 1994 | $30 |

CRANBERRIES, THE
ISLAND
| ❏ 524234-1 | To the Faithful Departed | 1996 | $15 |

— *Yellow vinyl, fold-open poster-bag cover; British import for distribution in U.S. (no "Made in England" stickers)*

Number	Title	Yr	NM

CRANE, BOB
EPIC

❑ LN24224 [M]	The Funny Side of TV	1966	$30
❑ BN26224 [S]	The Funny Side of TV	1966	$30

CRANE, LES
WARNER BROS.

❑ BS2570	Desiderata	1971	$12
❑ SW-94266	Desiderata	1972	$15
— Capitol Record Club edition			

CRAWFORD, HANK, AND JIMMY MCGRIFF
MILESTONE

❑ M-9177	On the Blue Side	1990	$30
❑ M-9142	Soul Survivors	1986	$25
❑ M-9153	Steppin' Up	1988	$25

CRAWFORD, HANK
ATLANTIC

❑ 1455 [M]	After Hours	1966	$35
❑ SD1455 [S]	After Hours	1966	$50
❑ 1436 [M]	Dig These Blues	1965	$35
❑ SD1436 [S]	Dig These Blues	1965	$50
❑ SD1503	Double Cross	1968	$75
❑ 1387 [M]	From the Heart	1962	$175
❑ SD1387 [S]	From the Heart	1962	$175
❑ 1356 [M]	More Soul	1960	$300
— Purple and red label, white fan logo			
❑ SD1356 [S]	More Soul	1960	$300
— Green and blue label, white fan logo			
❑ 1356 [M]	More Soul	1962	$175
— Purple and red label, black fan logo			
❑ SD1356 [S]	More Soul	1962	$175
— Green and blue label, black fan logo			
❑ 1470 [M]	Mr. Blues	1967	$50
❑ SD1470 [S]	Mr. Blues	1967	$35
❑ SD1523	Mr. Blues Plays Lady Soul	1969	$35
❑ 1405 [M]	Soul of the Ballad	1963	$35
❑ SD1405 [S]	Soul of the Ballad	1963	$50
❑ SD 2-315	The Art of Hank Crawford	1973	$35
❑ SD1557	The Best of Hank Crawford	1970	$35
❑ 1372 [M]	The Soul Clinic	1961	$175
— Purple and red label, white fan logo			
❑ SD1372 [S]	The Soul Clinic	1961	$175
— Green and blue label, white fan logo			
❑ 1372 [M]	The Soul Clinic	1962	$175
— Purple and red label, black fan logo			
❑ SD1372 [S]	The Soul Clinic	1962	$175
— Green and blue label, black fan logo			
❑ 1423 [M]	True Blue	1964	$35
❑ SD1423 [S]	True Blue	1964	$50

COTILLION

❑ SD18003	It's a Funky Thing to Do	1971	$50

KUDU

❑ KU-39	Cajun Sunrise	1979	$35
❑ KU-19	Don't You Worry 'Bout a Thing	1975	$50
❑ KU-33	Hank Crawford's Back	1977	$35
❑ KU-06	Help Me Make It Through the Night	1972	$50
❑ KU-26	I Hear a Symphony	1976	$50
❑ KU-35	Tico Rico	1977	$35
❑ KU-08	We've Got a Good Thing	1973	$50
❑ KU-15	Wildflower	1974	$50

MILESTONE

❑ M-9129	Down on the Deuce	1985	$25
❑ M-9182	Groove Master	1990	$30
❑ M-9119	Indigo Blue	1984	$25
❑ M-9112	Midnight Ramble	1983	$25
❑ M-9149	Mr. Chips	1987	$25
❑ M-9168	Night Beat	1988	$25
❑ M-9140	Roadhouse Symphony	1986	$25

MOBILE FIDELITY

❑ 1-224	Soul of the Ballad	1995	$75
— Audiophile vinyl			

CRAWFORD, JESSE
DECCA

❑ DL8794 [M]	Christmas	1958	$15
❑ DL78794 [S]	Christmas	1958	$18

DESIGN

❑ DLPX-7 [M]	Organ and Chimes for Christmas	196?	$15
— Same recordings as Promenade LP, but in slightly different order			
❑ SDLPX-7 [S]	Organ and Chimes for Christmas	196?	$18
— Same as above, but in stereo			

DIPLOMAT

❑ SX1010 [S]	Organ and Chimes	196?	$18
— Textured cover; same order and contents as Promenade LP			

PROMENADE

❑ CH-1000 [M]	Organ and Chimes for Christmas	196?	$15

CRAWFORD, JOHNNY
DEL-FI

❑ DFLP-1223 [M]	A Young Man's Fancy	1962	$30
❑ DFST-1223 [S]	A Young Man's Fancy	1962	$40
❑ DFLP-1248 [M]	Greatest Hits, Volume 2	1964	$25
❑ DFST-1248 [S]	Greatest Hits, Volume 2	1964	$30
❑ DFLP-1229 [M]	His Greatest Hits	1963	$30
❑ DFST-1229 [S]	His Greatest Hits	1963	$40
❑ DFLP-1224 [M]	Rumors	1963	$30
❑ DFST-1224 [S]	Rumors	1963	$40
❑ DFLP-1220 [M]	The Captivating Johnny Crawford	1962	$40

GUEST STAR

❑ GS-1470 [M]	Johnny Crawford	196?	$25
❑ GSS-1470 [S]	Johnny Crawford	196?	$30

RHINO

❑ RNDF-202	The Best of Johnny Crawford	1982	$15

SUPREME

❑ M-110 [M]	Songs from "The Restless Ones	1965	$25
❑ MS-210 [S]	Songs from "The Restless Ones	1965	$30

CRAWFORD, RAY
CANDID

❑ CJM-8028 [M]	Smooth Groove	1963	$30
❑ CJS-9028 [S]	Smooth Groove	1963	$30

DOBRE

❑ 1021	One Step at a Time	1978	$30

CRAYTON, PEE WEE
CROWN

❑ CLP-5175 [M]	Pee Wee Crayton	1959	$150
— Black label			

❑ CLP-5175 [M]	Pee Wee Crayton	196?	$25
— Gray label			

VANGUARD

❑ VSD-6566 [B]	The Things I Used to Do	1971	$18

CRAZY ELEPHANT
BELL

❑ 6034	Crazy Elephant	1969	$25

CRAZY HORSE
Also see NEIL YOUNG.

EPIC

❑ KE31710	Crazy Horse at Crooked Lake	1972	$18
— Yellow label			
❑ KE31710	Crazy Horse at Crooked Lake	1973	$15
— Orange label			

RCA VICTOR

❑ AFL1-3054	Crazy Moon	1978	$15

REPRISE

❑ RS6438	Crazy Horse	1971	$18
❑ MS2059	Loose	1972	$18

CRAZY JOE AND THE VARIABLE SPEED BAND
CASABLANCA

❑ NBLP7254	Crazy Joe and the Variable Speed Band	1980	$18

CRAZY OTTO
DECCA

❑ DL8113 [M]	Crazy Otto	1955	$25
— Black label, silver print			
❑ DL8113 [M]	Crazy Otto	1960	$15
— Black label with color bars			
❑ DL8163 [M]	Crazy Otto Rides Again	1956	$25
❑ DL8627 [M]	Crazy Otto's Back in Town	1957	$18
❑ DL8919 [M]	Golden Award Songs	1960	$18
❑ DL78919 [S]	Golden Award Songs	1960	$25
❑ DL4157 [M]	Have Piano, Will Travel	1961	$18
❑ DL74157 [S]	Have Piano, Will Travel	1961	$25
❑ DL8737 [M]	Honky Tonk Piano	1958	$18
❑ DL8367 [M]	Not So Crazy	1956	$25

MGM

❑ E-4150 [M]	Crazy Otto Plays Crazy Tunes	1963	$15
❑ SE-4150 [S]	Crazy Otto Plays Crazy Tunes	1963	$18

VOCALION

❑ VL3663 [M]	Crazy Otto Goes Sentimental	196?	$15

CREACH, PAPA JOHN
BUDDAH

❑ BDS-5649	I'm the Fiddle Man	1975	$15
❑ BDS-5660	Rock Father	1977	$15

DJM

❑ 11	Cat & Fiddle	1977	$15
❑ 18	Inphasion	1978	$15

GRUNT

❑ FTR-1009	Filthy!	1972	$18
❑ BXL1-1009	Filthy!	197?	$15
— Reissue with new prefix			
❑ FTR-1003	Papa John Creach	1971	$18
❑ BXL1-1003	Papa John Creach	197?	$15
— Reissue with new prefix			
❑ BFL1-0418	Playing My Fiddle for You	1974	$18

CREAM
Also see GINGER BAKER'S AIR FORCE; JACK BRUCE; ERIC CLAPTON.

ATCO

❑ SD 33-291	Best of Cream	1969	$30
❑ 33-232 [M]	Disraeli Gears	1967	$175
❑ SD 33-232 [S]	Disraeli Gears	1967	$30
— Purple and brown labels			
❑ SD 33-232 [S]	Disraeli Gears	1969	$18
— Yellow labels			
❑ 33-206 [M]	Fresh Cream	1967	$50
❑ SD 33-206 [S]	Fresh Cream	1967	$30
— Purple and brown labels			
❑ SD 33-206 [S]	Fresh Cream	1969	$18
— Yellow labels			
❑ SD7001	Goodbye	1969	$30
— Purple and brown labels; deduct 33% if poster is missing			
❑ SD7001	Goodbye	1969	$18
— Yellow labels			

❑ SD 33-328 [B]	Live Cream	1970	$30
❑ SD7005	Live Cream -- Volume II	1972	$30
❑ 2-700 [M]	Wheels of Fire	1968	$500
— White label promo; no stock copies are mono			
❑ SD 2-700 [S]	Wheels of Fire	1968	$50
— Purple and brown labels; foil-like cover			
❑ SD 2-700 [S]	Wheels of Fire	1969	$25
— Yellow labels; dull gray cover			

DCC COMPACT CLASSICS

❑ LPZ-2015	Fresh Cream	1996	$150
— Audiophile vinyl			

MOBILE FIDELITY

❑ 1-264 [B]	Goodbye	1996	$0
— Audiophile vinyl; canceled			
❑ Feb-0066	Wheels of Fire	1980	$175
— Audiophile vinyl			

POLYDOR

❑ 1775315 [S]	Disraeli Gears	2008	$25
❑ 24-3502	Heavy Cream	1972	$18
❑ 24-5529	Off the Top	1973	$18

Number	Title	Yr	NM
❑ 8275781 [S]	Wheels of Fire	2009	$30
REPRISE			
❑ 494616-1 [B]	Royal Albert Hall - London - May 2-3-5-6 05	2013	$100
❑ 49416-1	Royal Albert Hall London May 2-3-5-6 2005	2005	$50
—Box set; contains three 180-gram LPs, each in its own cardboard cover, plus a 12x12 cardboard poster and bubble padding			
RSO			
❑ RS-1-3012	Best of Cream	1977	$15
❑ 15 [DJ]	Classic Cuts	1978	$40
—Promo-only compilation			
❑ 015 [DJ]	Classic Cuts	1978	$40
—Promo-only compilation			
❑ RS-1-3010	Disraeli Gears	1977	$15
❑ RS-1-3009	Fresh Cream	1977	$15
❑ RS-1-3013	Goodbye	1977	$15
❑ RS-1-3014	Live Cream	1977	$15
❑ RS-1-3015	Live Cream -- Volume 2	1977	$15
❑ RS-2-3802	Wheels of Fire	1977	$18
SPRINGBOARD			
❑ SPB4037	Early Cream	1972	$18

CREATION OF SUNLIGHT
WINDI

Number	Title	Yr	NM
❑ 1001 [B]	Creation of Sunlight	1968	$2000

CREATIVE CONSTRUCTION COMPANY
MUSE

Number	Title	Yr	NM
❑ MR-5071	Volume 1	1975	$35
❑ MR-5097	Volume 2	1976	$35

CREATIVE SOURCE
POLYDOR

Number	Title	Yr	NM
❑ PD-1-6065	Consider the Source	1976	$15
❑ PD-1-6052	Pass the Feelin' On	1975	$15
SUSSEX			
❑ SUS-8027	Creative Source	1973	$18
❑ SUS-8035	Migration	1974	$18

CREEDENCE CLEARWATER REVIVAL
Also see DOUG CLIFFORD; JOHN FOGERTY; TOM FOGERTY; TOMMY FOGERTY AND THE BLUE VELVETS; THE GOLLIWOGS.

4 MEN WITH BEARDS

Number	Title	Yr	NM
❑ 4M224LP [B]	Live In Europe		$30
❑ 4M224 [B]	Live in Europe	2014	$30
❑ 4M225LP [B]	The Concert		$25
ANALOGUE PRODUCTIONS			
❑ AAPP-8387	Bayou Country	2002	$30
—Audiophile edition on heavy vinyl			
❑ AAPP-8402	Cosmo's Factory	2002	$30
—Audiophile edition on heavy vinyl			
❑ AAPP-8382	Creedence Clearwater Revival	2002	$30
—Audiophile edition on heavy vinyl			
❑ AAPP-8393	Green River	2002	$30
—Audiophile edition on heavy vinyl			
❑ AAPP-9404	Mardi Gras	2002	$30
—Audiophile edition on heavy vinyl			
❑ AAPP-8397	Willie and the Poor Boys	2002	$30
—Audiophile edition on heavy vinyl			
DCC COMPACT CLASSICS			
❑ LPZ-2019	Willie and the Poor Boys	1996	$50
—Audiophile vinyl			
FANTASY			
❑ -0 [DJ]	Bayou Country	1969	$100
—White label promo			
❑ F-8387 [DJ]	Bayou Country	1969	$100
—White label promo			
❑ F-8387	Bayou Country	1969	$18
—Dark blue label			
❑ F-8387	Bayou Country	1973	$12
—Brown label			
❑ ORC-4513	Bayou Country	1981	$10
—Reissue of 8387			
❑ 8387 [B]	Bayou Country	2015	$30
—ltd edition, clear vinyl			
❑ F-9621	Chooglin'	1982	$10
❑ CCR-3	Chronicle, Volume 2	1987	$18
❑ CCR-2	Chronicle (The 20 Greatest Hits)	1976	$18
—Brown labels			
❑ CCR-2	Chronicle (The 20 Greatest Hits)	1979	$15
—Whitish or light blue labels			
❑ -0 [DJ]	Cosmo's Factory	1970	$100
—White label promo			
❑ F-8402 [DJ]	Cosmo's Factory	1970	$100
—White label promo			
❑ F-8402	Cosmo's Factory	1970	$18
—Dark blue label			
❑ F-8402	Cosmo's Factory	1973	$12

Number	Title	Yr	NM
—Brown label			
❑ ORC-4516	Cosmo's Factory	1981	$10
—Reissue of 8402			
❑ 8402 [B]	Cosmo's Factory	2015	$50
—Ltd edition of 1000, 80 gram translucent red vinyl			
❑ -0 [DJ]	Creedence Clearwater Revival	1968	$100
—White label promo			
❑ F-8382 [DJ]	Creedence Clearwater Revival	1968	$100
—White label promo			
❑ F-8382	Creedence Clearwater Revival	1968	$30
—With no reference to "Susie Q" on the front cover			
❑ F-8382	Creedence Clearwater Revival	1968	$18
—With "Susie Q" mentioned on the front cover; dark blue label			
❑ F-8382	Creedence Clearwater Revival	1973	$12
—Brown label			
❑ ORC-4512	Creedence Clearwater Revival	1981	$10
—Reissue of 8382			
❑ CCR-68	Creedence Clearwater Revival 1968/69	1981	$15
—Compilation of 8382 and 8387			
❑ CCR-69	Creedence Clearwater Revival 1969	1981	$15
—Compilation of 8393 and 8397			
❑ CCR-70	Creedence Clearwater Revival 1970	1981	$15
—Compilation of 8402 and 8410			
❑ MPF-4509	Creedence Country	1981	$12
❑ F-9418	Creedence Gold	1972	$12
❑ FPM-4001 [Q]	Creedence Gold	1975	$75
❑ -0 [DJ]	Green River	1969	$100
—White label promo			
❑ F-8393 [DJ]	Green River	1969	$100
—White label promo			
❑ F-8393	Green River	1969	$18
—Dark blue label			
❑ F-8393	Green River	1973	$12
—Brown label			
❑ ORC-4514	Green River	1981	$10
—Reissue of 8393			
❑ CCR-1	Live in Europe	1973	$15
❑ ORC-4526	Live in Europe	1986	$12
❑ F-9404	Mardi Gras	1972	$18
—Dark blue label			
❑ F-9404	Mardi Gras	1973	$12
—Brown label			
❑ ORC-4518	Mardi Gras	1981	$10
—Reissue of 9404			
❑ F-9430	More Creedence Gold	1973	$12
❑ F-8410	Pendulum	1970	$18
—Dark blue label			
❑ F-8410	Pendulum	1973	$12
—Brown label			
❑ ORC-4517	Pendulum	1981	$10
—Reissue of 8410			
❑ MPF-4501	The Concert	1981	$12
—Retitled version			
❑ MPF-4522	The Movie Album	1985	$10
❑ MPF-4501	The Royal Albert Hall Concert	1980	$18
—Album withdrawn and changed when it was discovered this didn't come from the Royal Albert Hall			
❑ -0 [DJ]	Willy and the Poor Boys	1969	$100
—White label promo			
❑ F-8397 [DJ]	Willy and the Poor Boys	1969	$100
—White label promo			
❑ F-8397	Willy and the Poor Boys	1969	$18
—Dark blue label			
❑ F-8397	Willy and the Poor Boys	1973	$12
—Brown label			
❑ ORC-4515	Willy and the Poor Boys	1981	$10
—Reissue of 8397			
❑ 8397 [B]	Willy and the Poor Boys	2015	$25
—blue vinyl			
HEARTLAND			
❑ HR2039	Creedence Clearwater Revival	1990	$18
K-TEL			
❑ NU9360	The Best of Creedence Clearwater Revival -- 20 Super Hits	1978	$18
MOBILE FIDELITY			
❑ Jan-0037	Cosmo's Factory	1979	$80
—Audiophile vinyl			
TIME-LIFE			
❑ SCLR-18	Classic Rock: Creedence Clearwater Revival	1989	$18

CREEKMORE, TOM
DISCOVERY

Number	Title	Yr	NM
❑ DS-791	She Is It	198?	$25

CREME SODA
TRINITY

Number	Title	Yr	NM
❑ CST-11	Tricky Zingers	1977	$250
—With white cover			
❑ CST-11	Tricky Zingers	1975	$400
—With photo of group on cover			

CRENSHAW, MARSHALL
WARNER BROS.

Number	Title	Yr	NM
❑ 25319	Downtown	1985	$12
❑ 23873	Field Day	1983	$12
❑ 25908	Good Evening	1989	$12
❑ BSK3673	Marshall Crenshaw	1982	$12
❑ 25583	Mary Jean and 9 Others	1987	$12

CREQUE, NEAL
COBBLESTONE

Number	Title	Yr	NM
❑ 9023	Contrast!	1972	$30
❑ 9005	Creque	1971	$35
MUSE			
❑ MR-5226	Black Velvet Rose	1980	$25
❑ MR-5029	Neal Creque and the Hands of Time	1973	$30

CRESCENDOS, THE (1)
GUEST STAR

Number	Title	Yr	NM
❑ G-1453 [M]	Oh Julie	1962	$50
❑ GS-1453 [R]	Oh Julie	1962	$25

CRESTS, THE
COED

Number	Title	Yr	NM
❑ LPC-904 [M]	The Best of the Crests/16 Fabulous Hits	1961	$400
—Label simply calls this "16 Fabulous Hits			
❑ LPC-901 [M]	The Crests Sing All Biggies	1960	$400
—Yellow label, black print			
❑ LPC-901 [M]	The Crests Sing All Biggies	1960	$250
—Red label			
COLLECTABLES			
❑ COL-5009	Greatest Hits	1982	$15
POST			
❑ 3000	The Crests Sing	196?	$40
RHINO			
❑ R1-70948	The Best of the Crests	1989	$15

CRETONES, THE
PLANET

Number	Title	Yr	NM
❑ P-15	Snap! Snap!	1981	$15
❑ P-5	Thin Red Line	1980	$12

CREVELING, CAROLE
EUTERPE

Number	Title	Yr	NM
❑ ETP-101 [M]	Carole Creveling	1955	$75

CREW CUTS, THE
CAMAY

Number	Title	Yr	NM
❑ CA-1002 [M]	The Great New Sound of the Crew Cuts	196?	$25
❑ CA-3002 [S]	The Great New Sound of the Crew Cuts	196?	$30
MERCURY			
❑ MG-20143 [M]	Crew Cut Capers	1956	$50
❑ MG-20199 [M]	Music A La Carte	1957	$50
❑ MG-20144 [M]	Rock and Roll Bash	1956	$100
❑ MG-20067 [M]	The Crew Cuts Go Longhair	1955	$50
❑ MG-25200 [10]	The Crew Cuts On Campus	1956	$100
❑ MG-20140 [M]	The Crew Cuts On Campus	1956	$50
PICADILLY			
❑ PIC-3560	The Wonderful Happy Crazy Innocent World	1980	$12
RCA VICTOR			
❑ LPM-1933 [M]	Surprise Package	1958	$30
❑ LSP-1933 [S]	Surprise Package	1959	$40
❑ PR-129 [M]	The Crew Cuts Have a Ball	1960	$30
—Produced for Ebonite bowling balls; Side 2 has "Bowling Tips by Top Stars			
❑ LPM-2037 [M]	The Crew Cuts Sing	1959	$30
❑ LSP-2037 [S]	The Crew Cuts Sing	1959	$40
❑ PR-102 [M]	The Crew Cuts Sing Out!	1960	$30
❑ LPM-2067 [M]	You Must Have Been a Beautiful Baby	1960	$30
❑ LSP-2067 [S]	You Must Have Been a Beautiful Baby	1960	$40
WING			
❑ MGW-12180 [M]	High School Favorites	196?	$25
❑ MGW-12125 [M]	Rock and Roll Bash	196?	$30
❑ MGW-12177 [M]	The Crew Cuts	196?	$25
❑ MGW-12145 [M]	The Crew Cuts On Campus	196?	$25
❑ MGW-12195 [M]	The Crew Cuts Sing the Masters	196?	$25

Number	Title	Yr	NM

CREWE, BOB
CGC
| ❏ 1000 | Let Me Touch You | 1970 | $15 |

DYNO VOICE
❏ DV-1902 [M]	Music to Watch Birds By	1967	$18
❏ DV-31902 [S]	Music to Watch Birds By	1967	$15
❏ DV-9003 [M]	Music to Watch Girls By	1967	$18
❏ DVS-9003 [S]	Music to Watch Girls By	1967	$15
❏ DV-1906 [M]	The Bob Crewe Generation In Classic Form	1968	$18
❏ DV-31906 [S]	The Bob Crewe Generation In Classic Form	1968	$15

ELEKTRA
| ❏ 7E-1103 | Motivation | 1977 | $15 |
| ❏ 7E-1083 | Street Talk | 1976 | $15 |

PHILIPS
❏ PHM200150 [M]	All the Song Hits of the Four Seasons	1964	$30
❏ PHS600150 [S]	All the Song Hits of the Four Seasons	1964	$30
❏ PHM200238 [M]	Bob Crewe Plays the Four Seasons' Hits	1967	$25
❏ PHS600238 [S]	Bob Crewe Plays the Four Seasons' Hits	1967	$18

WARWICK
❏ W-2034 [M]	Crazy in the Heart	1961	$30
❏ WST-2034 [S]	Crazy in the Heart	1961	$50
❏ W-2009 [M]	Kicks	1960	$30
❏ WST-2009 [S]	Kicks	1960	$50

CRICKETS, THE (1)
BARNABY
| ❏ Z30268 | Rockin' 50's Rock 'N' Roll | 1970 | $30 |

BRUNSWICK

❏ BL54038 [M]	The "Chirping" Crickets	1958	$600
—Regular cover			
❏ BL54038 [M]	The "Chirping" Crickets	1957	$800
—Textured cover			
❏ BL54038 [M]	The "Chirping" Crickets	1958	$1500
—promo, yellow label			

CORAL
| ❏ CRL57320 [M] | In Style with the Crickets | 1960 | $250 |
| ❏ CRL757320 [S] | In Style with the Crickets | 1960 | $400 |

EPIC
| ❏ FE44446 | T-Shirt | 1988 | $18 |

LIBERTY
❏ LRP-3351 [M]	California Sun/She Loves You	1964	$150
❏ LST-7351 [S]	California Sun/She Loves You	1964	$175
❏ LRP-3272 [M]	Something Old, Something New, Something Blue, Somethin' Else	1962	$175
❏ LST-7272 [S]	Something Old, Something New, Something Blue, Somethin' Else	1962	$250

VERTIGO
| ❏ VEL-1020 | Remnants | 1973 | $25 |

CRICKETS, THE (2)
RELIC
| ❏ LP-5040 | The Crickets Featuring Dean Barlow | 1987 | $12 |

CRIME
PLANET PIMP
| ❏ OTD 005 | Love Us or Hate Us, We Don't Give a Fuck | 1992 | $15 |

CRINER, CLYDE
NOVUS
| ❏ 3029-1-N | Behind the Sun | 1988 | $25 |
| ❏ 3066-1-N | The Color of Dark | 1989 | $30 |

TERRA
| ❏ T-4 | New England | 1985 | $30 |

CRISPELL, MARILYN
BLACK SAINT
❏ BSR-0069	Live in Berlin	1984	$30
❏ 120069	Live in Berlin	198?	$25
—Reissue of 0069			

CADENCE JAZZ
| ❏ CJR-1015 | Spirit Music | 1983 | $25 |

CRISS, GARY
SALSOUL
| ❏ SA8504 | Rio de Janeiro | 1978 | $25 |

CRISS, PETER
Also see CHELSEA; KISS.

CASABLANCA
❏ NBLP-7240	Out of Control	1980	$30
❏ NBLP-7122	Peter Criss	1978	$25
❏ NBPIX-7122 [PD]	Peter Criss	1978	$50

CRISS, SONNY, AND KENNY DORHAM
ABC IMPULSE!
| ❏ IA-9337 | Bopmasters | 197? | $250 |
MCA
| ❏ 4141 | Bopmasters | 198? | $30 |
| —Reissue of ABC Impulse! 9337 | | | |

CRISS, SONNY
ABC IMPULSE!
| ❏ AS-9326 | The Joy of Sax | 197? | $35 |
| ❏ AS-9312 | Warm and Sonny | 197? | $35 |
CLEF
| ❏ MGC-122 [10] | Sonny Criss Collates | 1953 | $350 |
FANTASY
❏ OJC-655	Portrait of Sonny Criss	1991	$30
—Reissue of Prestige 7526			
❏ OJC-430	This Is Sonny Criss!	1990	$30
—Reissue of Prestige 7511			
IMPERIAL
❏ LP-9205 [M]	Criss Cross	1963	$150
❏ LP-12205 [R]	Criss Cross	1963	$175
❏ LP-9020 [M]	Go Man: It's Sonny Criss & Modern Jazz	1956	$1300
❏ LP-9006 [M]	Jazz U.S.A.	1956	$300
❏ LP-9024 [M]	Sonny Criss Plays Cole Porter	1956	$500
MERCURY
| ❏ MGC-122 [10] | Sonny Criss Collates | 1953 | $0 |
| —Cover exists, but all known copies contain Clef labels | | | |
MUSE
| ❏ MR-5068 | Crisscraft | 1975 | $35 |
| ❏ MR-5089 | Out of Nowhere | 1976 | $35 |
PABLO
| ❏ 2310929 | Intermission Riff | 1988 | $25 |
PEACOCK
| ❏ PLP-91 [M] | At the Crossroads | 1959 | $350 |
PRESTIGE
❏ PRST-7742	Hits of the 60s	1970	$35
❏ PRST-7628	I'll Catch the Sun	1969	$25
❏ PRLP-7526 [M]	Portrait of Sonny Criss	1967	$30
❏ PRST-7526	Portrait of Sonny Criss	1967	$30
❏ PRST-7610	Rockin' in Rhythm	1969	$25
❏ PRST-7576	Sonny's Dream	1968	$25
❏ PRST-7558	The Beat Goes On	1968	$25
❏ PRLP-7511 [M]	This Is Sonny Criss!	1966	$30
❏ PRST-7511 [S]	This Is Sonny Criss!	1966	$30
❏ PRLP-7530 [M]	Up, Up and Away	1967	$40
❏ PRST-7530 [S]	Up, Up and Away	1967	$30
XANADU
| ❏ 200 | Memorial Album | 198? | $25 |
| ❏ 105 | Saturday Morning | 197? | $35 |

CRITTERS, THE
KAPP
| ❏ KL-1485 [M] | Younger Girl | 1966 | $30 |
| ❏ KS-3485 [S] | Younger Girl | 1966 | $40 |
PROJECT 3
| ❏ PR4002SD | The Critters | 1969 | $30 |
| ❏ PR4001SD | Touch 'n Go with the Critters | 1968 | $30 |

CRITTERS, THE /THE YOUNG RASCALS/LOU CHRISTIE
BOUTIQUE
| ❏ CA-1079 [M] | A Taste of the Critters & The Young Rascals & Lou Christie | 1966 | $40 |

CROCE, JIM
21 RECORDS
❏ 90469	Down the Highway	1985	$12
❏ 90467	Photographs & Memories/ His Greatest Hits	1985	$10
❏ 90468	Time in a Bottle -- Jim Croce's Greatest Love Songs	1985	$10
ABC
❏ ABCX-797	I Got a Name	1973	$18
❏ ABCX-769	Life and Times	1973	$18
❏ ABCD-835	Photographs & Memories/ His Greatest Hits	1974	$18
❏ ABCX-756	You Don't Mess Around with Jim	1972	$25
—Original covers have no green box advertising "Time in a Bottle"			
❏ ABCX-756	You Don't Mess Around with Jim	1973	$18
—Posthumous covers have a green box advertising "Time in a Bottle"			
CAPITOL
| ❏ SMAS-315 | Jim and Ingrid Croce | 1970 | $30 |
COMMAND
❏ QD-40008 [Q]	I Got a Name	1974	$40
❏ QD-40007 [Q]	Life and Times	1974	$40
❏ QD-40020 [Q]	Photographs & Memories/ His Greatest Hits	1974	$40
❏ QD-40006 [Q]	You Don't Mess Around with Jim	1974	$40
—Without border around outside of front cover			
❏ QD-40006 [Q]	You Don't Mess Around with Jim	1974	$40
—With wide border around the outside of front cover			
CROCE
| ❏ 101 | Facets | 1966 | $300 |
DCC COMPACT CLASSICS
| ❏ LPZ-2054 | His Greatest Recordings | 1998 | $40 |
| —Audiophile vinyl | | | |
LIFESONG
❏ JZ35571	Bad, Bad Leroy Brown: Jim Croce's Greatest Character Songs	1978	$12
❏ JZ35009	I Got a Name	1978	$12
❏ JZ35008	Life and Times	1978	$12
❏ JZ35010	Photographs & Memories/ His Greatest Hits	1978	$12
❏ LS900	The Faces I've Been	1975	$18
❏ LS6007	Time in a Bottle -- Jim Croce's Greatest Love Songs	1976	$15
❏ JZ35000	Time in a Bottle -- Jim Croce's Greatest Love Songs	1978	$12
❏ JZ34993	You Don't Mess Around with Jim	1978	$12
MOBILE FIDELITY
| ❏ Jan-0079 | You Don't Mess Around with Jim | 1981 | $40 |
| —Audiophile vinyl | | | |
PICKWICK
| ❏ SPC-3332 | Another Day, Another Town | 1973 | $12 |
| —Reissue of Capitol LP | | | |

CROME SYRCUS, THE
COMMAND
| ❏ RS925SD | The Love Cycle | 1968 | $85 |

CRONHAM, CHARLES R.
WING
| ❏ MGW12173 [M] | Christmas Carols with Organ and Chimes | 195? | $18 |

CROOK, HAL
OMNISOUND
| ❏ 1039 | Hello Heaven | 198? | $25 |

CROOKS, RICHARD
CATHEDRAL
| ❏ ARC012/20/1943 | The Voice of Firestone -- Christmas 1943 Radio Broadcast | 1978 | $18 |

CROPPER, STEVE
MCA
| ❏ 5340 | Night After Night | 1982 | $12 |
| ❏ 5171 | Playin' My Thang | 1980 | $12 |
VOLT
| ❏ VOS-6006 [B] | With a Little Help from My Friends | 1970 | $30 |

CROSBY, BING, AND FRED ASTAIRE
UNITED ARTISTS
| ❏ UA-LA588-H | A Couple of Song and Dance Men | 1976 | $30 |

CROSBY, BING, AND LOUIS ARMSTRONG
CAPITOL
| ❏ SM-11735 | Bing Crosby and Louis Armstrong | 1977 | $25 |

Number	Title	Yr	NM
MGM			
❏ E-3882 [M]	Bing and Satchmo	1960	$35
❏ SE-3882 [S]	Bing and Satchmo	1960	$50
CROSBY, BING			
20TH CENTURY			
❏ T-551	A Holiday Toast	1977	$15
AMOS			
❏ AAS-7001	Hey Jude/Hey Bing!	1969	$15
BIOGRAPH			
❏ C-13	Bing Crosby 1929-33	1973	$30
❏ M-1	When the Blue of the Night Meets the Gold of the Day	197?	$25
BRUNSWICK			
❏ BL58000 [10]	Bing Crosby, Volume 1	1950	$150
❏ BL58001 [10]	Bing Crosby, Volume 2	1950	$150
❏ BL54005 [M]	The Voice of Bing in the 1930s	1957	$75
CAPITOL			
❏ SM-11738	Bing Crosby Classics, Vol. 1	1977	$12
❏ SM-11739	Bing Crosby Classics, Vol. 2	1977	$12
❏ SM-11740	Bing Crosby Classics, Vol. 3	1977	$12
❏ SM-11732	Bing Crosby's Christmas Classics	1977	$12

— A Capitol Re-Issue"; same recordings as on Warner Bros. 1484

❏ T2346 [M]	Great Country Hits	1965	$18
❏ ST2346 [S]	Great Country Hits	1965	$25
❏ SM-11737	Great Country Hits	1977	$12
❏ T2300 [M]	That Travelin' Two-Beat	1965	$18
❏ ST2300 [S]	That Travelin' Two-Beat	1965	$25
❏ SM-11736	That Travelin' Two-Beat	1977	$12
COLUMBIA			
❏ C35093	Bing Crosby Collection, Vol. 1	1977	$25
❏ C35094	Bing Crosby Collection, Vol. 2	1977	$25
❏ C2L43	Bing in Hollywood 1930-1934	196?	$35

— Red "360 Sound" labels

❏ C2L43	Bing in Hollywood 1930-1934	1971	$30

— Orange labels

❏ CL6027 [10]	Crosby Classics	1949	$150
❏ CL6105 [10]	Crosby Classics, Volume 2	1950	$150
❏ CL2502 [10]	Der Bingle	1955	$50
❏ C4X44229	The Crooner: The Columbia Years	1988	$40
COLUMBIA SPECIAL PRODUCTS			
❏ P14369	Bing	197?	$25
❏ CE2E-201	The Bing Crosby Story, Volume 1	1974	$15

— Reissue of Encore E2E-201

DAYBREAK			
❏ 2006	A Time to Be Jolly	1971	$15
❏ 2014	Bing and Basie	1972	$30
DECCA			
❏ DL8419 [M]	A Christmas Sing with Bing Around the World	1957	$40
❏ DL78419 [R]	A Christmas Sing with Bing Around the World	196?	$12
❏ DL8318 [M]	Anything Goes	1956	$50
❏ DL8687 [M]	Around the World	1958	$40
❏ DL5028 [10]	Auld Lang Syne	1950	$50
❏ DL5351 [10]	Beloved Hymns	1951	$50
❏ DX151 [M]	Bing: A Musical Autobiography	195?	$175
❏ DL9054 [M]	Bing: A Musical Autobiography 1927-1934	1961	$40
❏ DL9064 [M]	Bing: A Musical Autobiography 1934-1941	1961	$40
❏ DL9067 [M]	Bing: A Musical Autobiography 1941-44	1961	$40
❏ DL9077 [M]	Bing: A Musical Autobiography 1944-47	1961	$40
❏ DL9078 [M]	Bing: A Musical Autobiography 1947-1953	1961	$40
❏ DL5390 [10]	Bing and Connee	1953	$175

— With Connee Boswell

❏ DL5323 [10]	Bing and the Dixieland Bands	1951	$250
❏ DL8493 [M]	Bing and the Dixieland Bands	1957	$40
❏ DL8780 [M]	Bing in Paris	1958	$40
❏ DL4258 [M]	Bing's Hollywood: Accentuate the Positive	1962	$30
❏ DL4264 [M]	Bing's Hollywood: Anything Goes	1962	$30
❏ DL4259 [M]	Bing's Hollywood: Blue Skies	1962	$30
❏ DL4260 [M]	Bing's Hollywood: But Beautiful	1962	$30
❏ DL4262 [M]	Bing's Hollywood: Cool of the Evening	1962	$30
❏ DL4253 [M]	Bing's Hollywood: East Side of Heaven	1962	$30
❏ DL4250 [M]	Bing's Hollywood: Easy to Remember	1962	$30
❏ DL4256 [M]	Bing's Hollywood: Holiday Inn	1962	$30
❏ DL4255 [M]	Bing's Hollywood: Only Forever	1962	$30
❏ DL4251 [M]	Bing's Hollywood: Pennies from Heaven	1962	$30

❏ DL4252 [M]	Bing's Hollywood: Pocket Full of Dreams	1962	$30
❏ DL4261 [M]	Bing's Hollywood: Sunshine Cake	1962	$30
❏ DL4257 [M]	Bing's Hollywood: Swinging on a Star	1962	$30
❏ DL4254 [M]	Bing's Hollywood: The Road Begins	1962	$30
❏ DL4263 [M]	Bing's Hollywood: Zing a Little Zong	1962	$30
❏ DL5220 [10]	Bing Sings Hits	1950	$50
❏ DL5520 [10]	Bing Sings the Hits	1954	$50
❏ DL5355 [10]	Bing Sings Victor Herbert	1951	$50
❏ DL8269 [M]	Blue Hawaii	1956	$40
❏ DL5102 [10]	Blue of the Night	1950	$50
❏ DL5042 [10]	Blue Skies	1950	$50
❏ DLP5020 [10]	Christmas Greetings	1949	$75
❏ DL5064 [10]	Cole Porter Songs	1950	$175
❏ DL6009 [10]	Collector's Classics: Anything Goes/Two for Tonight	1951	$75
❏ DL6014 [10]	Collector's Classics: Big Broadcast of 1936	1951	$75
❏ DL6008 [10]	Collector's Classics: Mississippi/Here Is My Heart	1951	$75
❏ DL6012 [10]	Collector's Classics: Paris Honeymoon	1951	$75
❏ DL6010 [10]	Collector's Classics: Rhythm on the Range/Pennies from Heaven	1951	$75
❏ DL6015 [10]	Collector's Classics: The Road to Singapore/If I Had My Way	1951	$75
❏ DL6013 [10]	Collector's Classics: The Star Maker/Doctor Rhythm	1951	$75
❏ DL6011 [10]	Collector's Classics: Waikiki Wedding	1951	$75
❏ DL5556 [10]	Country Girl/Little Boy Lost/ Anything Goes	1954	$50
❏ DL5331 [10]	Country Style	1951	$50
❏ DL5107 [10]	Cowboy Songs	1950	$50
❏ DL5129 [10]	Cowboy Songs, Volume 2	1950	$50
❏ DL5063 [10]	Don't Fence Me In	1950	$50
❏ DL5340 [10]	Down Memory Lane	1951	$50
❏ DL5343 [10]	Down Memory Lane, Volume 2	1951	$50
❏ DL5119 [10]	Drifting and Dreaming	1950	$50
❏ DL8268 [M]	Drifting and Dreaming	1956	$40
❏ DLP5011 [10]	El Bingo	1949	$50
❏ DL5299 [10]	Favorite Hawaiian Songs	1951	$50
❏ DL34522	Favorite Songs of Christmas	1968	$18

— Decca Records Custom Division pressing

❏ DL5052 [10]	Going My Way/The Bells of St. Mary's	1950	$75
❏ DL5302 [10]	Go West, Young Man	1951	$50
❏ DL5122 [10]	Hawaiian Songs	1950	$50
❏ DL8272 [M]	High Tor	1956	$400
❏ DL5298 [10]	Hits from Broadway Shows	1951	$50
❏ DLP5000 [10]	Hits from Musical Comedies	1949	$50
❏ DL4281 [M]	Holiday in Europe	1962	$30
❏ DL74281 [R]	Holiday in Europe	1962	$18
❏ DL8210 [M]	Home on the Range	1956	$40
❏ DL6001 [10]	Ichabod/Rip Van Winkle	1950	$50
❏ DL9106 [M]	Ichabod/Rip Van Winkle	1962	$30
❏ DL79106 [R]	Ichabod/Rip Van Winkle	1962	$12
❏ DL8846 [M]	In a Little Spanish Town	1959	$30
❏ DLP5001 [10]	Jerome Kern Songs	1949	$50
❏ DL5417 [10]	Just for You	1952	$50
❏ DL8110 [M]	Lullaby Time	1955	$40
❏ DLP5019 [10]	Merry Christmas	1949	$75

— Original editions have a light blue-green cover and "DLP" prefix

❏ DL8128 [M]	Merry Christmas	1955	$40

— Expanded version of 10-inch LP; all-black label

❏ DL78128 [R]	Merry Christmas	196?	$12
❏ DL8128 [M]	Merry Christmas	1960	$30

— Reissue on black label with color bars

❏ DL8178 [M]	Merry Christmas	196?	$75

— Black label with color bars; at least one copy is known to exist on red vinyl

❏ DL5019 [10]	Merry Christmas	1950	$50

— Second editions have a blue-green cover, but a "DL" prefix on the record, though not necessarily on the cover

❏ DL5019 [10]	Merry Christmas	1951	$40

— Third editions have a brand-new red and green cover

❏ DL5284 [10]	Mr. Music	1950	$50
❏ DL4086 [M]	My Golden Favorites	1961	$30
❏ DL8575 [M]	New Tricks	1957	$40
❏ DX152 [M]	Old Masters	195?	$175
❏ DL8207 [M]	Shillelaghs and Shamrocks	1956	$40
❏ DL78207 [R]	Shillelaghs and Shamrocks	196?	$12
❏ DL5508 [10]	Some Fine Old Chestnuts	1953	$50
❏ DL8374 [M]	Some Fine Old Chestnuts	1957	$40
❏ DL5499 [10]	Song Hits of Paris/Le Bing	1953	$50
❏ DL8352 [M]	Song I Wish I Had Sung... The First Time Around	1956	$40
❏ DL5081 [10]	Songs by Gershwin	1950	$50
❏ DL4415 [M]	Songs Everybody Knows	1964	$30
❏ DL74415 [R]	Songs Everybody Knows	1964	$18
❏ DL78352 [R]	Songs I Wish I Had Sung... The First Time Around	196?	$12
❏ DL5126 [10]	Stardust	1950	$250
❏ DLP5010 [10]	Stephen Foster Songs	1949	$50
❏ DL5037 [10]	St. Patrick's Day	1950	$50
❏ DL5039 [10]	St. Valentine's Day	1950	$50
❏ DL8781 [M]	That Christmas Feeling	1958	$30

— Expanded version of DL 5020; all-black label, textured cover

❏ DL78781 [R]	That Christmas Feeling	196?	$12
❏ DL8781 [M]	That Christmas Feeling	1960	$25

— Reissue on black label with color bars, smooth cover

❏ DXB184 [M]	The Best of Bing	1965	$30
❏ DXSB7184 [R]	The Best of Bing	1965	$18
❏ DL8020 [M]	The Man Without a Country/ What So Proudly We Hail	1950	$40
❏ DL5444 [10]	The Road to Bali	1952	$75
❏ DL74283 [R]	The Small One	1962	$12
❏ DL5272 [10]	Top o' the Morning/The Emperor Waltz	1950	$50
❏ DL8365 [M]	Twilight on the Trail	1957	$40
❏ DL4283	Two Favorite Stories by Bing Crosby	1962	$30
❏ DL6000 [10]	Two Favorite Stories by Bing Crosby	1950	$75
❏ DL5310 [10]	Way Back Home	1951	$50
❏ DL5403 [10]	When Irish Eyes Are Smiling	1952	$50
❏ DL8262 [M]	When Irish Eyes Are Smiling	1956	$40
❏ DL78262 [R]	When Irish Eyes Are Smiling	196?	$12
❏ DL5326 [10]	Yours Is My Heart Alone	1951	$50
ENCORE			
❏ E2E-201	The Bing Crosby Story, Volume 1	1968	$18
❏ E2E-202	The Bing Crosby Story, Volume 2	1968	$18
FOX AMERICAN			
❏ SMF210	Bing Crosby Sings Christmas	1978	$12

— Side 1 from radio show Dec. 19, 1951; Side 2 from radio show Dec. 14, 1949

GNP CRESCENDO			
❏ GNP-9044	The Radio Years, Vol. 1	1985	$10
❏ GNP-9046	The Radio Years, Vol. 2	1986	$10
❏ GNP-9047	The Radio Years, Vol. 3	1986	$10
❏ GNP-9048	The Radio Years, Vol. 4	1986	$10
GOLDEN			

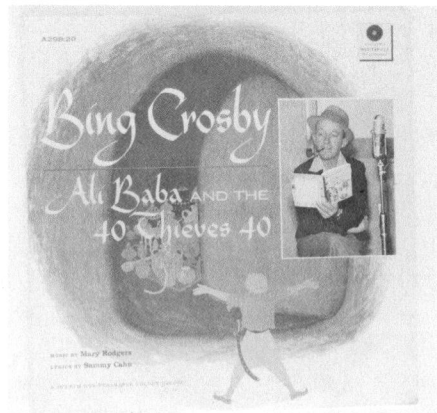

❏ A298:20 [M]	Ali Baba and the 40 Thieves	1957	$30
❏ A298:21 [M]	How Lovely Is Christmas/A Christmas Story	195?	$30
HARMONY			
❏ HL7094 [M]	Crosby Classics	1958	$35
❏ HS11313 [R]	Crosby Classics	196?	$25
LONDON			
❏ PS679	Feels Good	1977	$15
MARK 56			
❏ 762	Original Radio Broadcasts	197?	$12
MCA			
❏ 15018 [R]	A Christmas Sing with Bing Around the World	197?	$10

— Reissue of Decca DL7-8419

❏ 3031	Bing Crosby's Greatest Hits	1977	$12
❏ 37076	Bing Crosby's Greatest Hits	198?	$10
❏ 915	Hey Bing!	198?	$12
❏ 15024 [R]	Merry Christmas	197?	$10

— Reissue of Decca DL7-8128

❏ 1502	Rare 1930-31 Brunswick Recordings	198?	$25
❏ 177	Shillelaghs and Shamrocks	1973	$12
❏ 15019 [R]	That Christmas Feeling	1973	$10

— Reissue of Decca DL7-8781

❏ 2-4045	The Best of Bing	197?	$15

— Black labels with rainbow; gatefold cover

❏ 2-4045	The Best of Bing	197?	$12

— Blue labels with rainbow; regular cover

❏ 15017	Two Favorite Stories by Bing Crosby	197?	$12

— Reissue of Decca DL 4283

❏ 519	When Irish Eyes Are Smiling	197?	$12
METRO			
❏ M-523 [M]	Bing Crosby	1965	$15
❏ MS-523 [S]	Bing Crosby	1965	$18
MGM			
❏ E-3890 [M]	Senor Bing	1961	$18
❏ SE-3890 [S]	Senor Bing	1961	$25
❏ E-4129 [M]	The Great Standards	1963	$18

Number	Title	Yr	NM
❏ SE-4129 [S]	The Great Standards	1963	$25
❏ E-4203 [M]	The Very Best of Bing Crosby	1964	$18
❏ SE-4203 [S]	The Very Best of Bing Crosby	1964	$25

MOBILE FIDELITY

❏ 1-260	Bing Sings Whilst Bregman Swings	1996	$40

— Audiophile vinyl

MURRAY HILL

❏ 894637	Bing Crosby and His Friends	197?	$30

PHILCO

❏ LP436 [10]	Crosby Classics	195?	$40

— Custom item for Philco (front cover has "Philco: Famous for Quality the World Over")

PICKWICK

❏ SPC-3583	Thoroughly Modern Bing	1978	$10

P.I.P.

❏ 6802	Thoroughly Modern Bing	1971	$15

POLYDOR

❏ PD-1-6128	Seasons: The Closing Chapter	1978	$15

RCA VICTOR

❏ CPL1-2086(e)	A Legendary Performer	1976	$12
❏ LPM-1473 [M]	Bing with a Beat	1957	$75
❏ LPM-1854 [M]	Fancy Meeting You Here	1958	$25
❏ LSP-1854 [S]	Fancy Meeting You Here	1958	$30
❏ AFL1-1854	Fancy Meeting You Here	1977	$12
❏ LPM-2071 [M]	Young Bing Crosby	1959	$25

READER'S DIGEST

❏ RDA-175	Christmas with Bing	1980	$12

— Repackage of Warner Bros. and Capitol recordings

REPRISE

❏ R-6106 [M]	Return to Paradise Islands	1964	$18
❏ R9-6106 [S]	Return to Paradise Islands	1964	$25

SPOKANE

❏ 21	Bing Crosby & the Music Maids	197?	$12
❏ 1	Bing Crosby On the Air, 1934 and 1938	197?	$12
❏ 12	Bing in the 30's	197?	$12
❏ 14	Bing in the 30s, Vol. 2	197?	$12
❏ 24	Bing in the 30s, Vol. 3	1986	$10
❏ 25	Bing in the 30s, Vol. 4	1986	$10
❏ 26	Bing in the 30s, Vol. 5	1986	$10
❏ 27	Bing in the 30s, Vol. 6	1986	$10
❏ 5	Der Bingle, Vol. 1	197?	$12
❏ 10	Der Bingle, Vol. 2	197?	$12
❏ 20	Der Bingle, Vol. 3	197?	$12
❏ 15	Holiday Inn/The Bells of St. Mary's	197?	$12
❏ 16	Kraft Music Hall Highlights	197?	$12
❏ 19	Kraft Music Hall Highlights, Vol. 2	197?	$12

SUNBEAM

❏ 502	Distinctively Bing, Vol. 1	197?	$12
❏ 504	Distinctively Bing, Vol. 2	197?	$12

TIME-LIFE

❏ SLGD-06	Legendary Singers: Bing Crosby	1985	$18

UNITED ARTISTS

❏ UA-LA554-G	That's What Life Is All About	1976	$15

VERVE

❏ MGV2020 [M]	Bing Sings Whilst Bregman Swings	1956	$250
❏ V-2020 [M]	Bing Sings Whilst Bregman Swings	1961	$75

VOCALION

❏ VL3603 [M]	Bing Crosby Sings	195?	$18
❏ VL73603 [R]	Bing Crosby Sings	196?	$12

WARNER BROS.

❏ 2W1401 [M]	101 Gang Songs	1961	$25
❏ 2WS1401 [S]	101 Gang Songs	1961	$30
❏ W1484 [M]	I Wish You a Merry Christmas	1962	$18
❏ WS1484 [S]	I Wish You a Merry Christmas	1962	$25
❏ W1435 [M]	Join Bing and Sing Along	1962	$18
❏ WS1435 [S]	Join Bing and Sing Along	1962	$25
❏ W1422 [M]	Join Bing in a Gang Song Sing-Along	1961	$18
❏ WS1422 [S]	Join Bing in a Gang Song Sing-Along	1961	$25
❏ W1363 [M]	Join with Bing and Sing Along	1960	$18
❏ WS1363 [S]	Join with Bing and Sing Along	1960	$25
❏ W1482 [M]	On the Happy Side	1962	$18
❏ WS1482 [S]	On the Happy Side	1962	$25

X

❏ XLVA-4250 [M]	Young Bing Crosby	1955	$150

CROSBY, BOB

AIRCHECK

❏ 17	Bob Crosby and His Orchestra 1940	197?	$25

CAPITOL

❏ H293 [10]	Bob Crosby and His Bobcats	1952	$100
❏ T293 [M]	Bob Crosby and His Bobcats	1955	$85
❏ T1556 [M]	The Hits of Bob Crosby's Bobcats	1961	$50

CIRCLE

❏ 1	Bob Crosby and His Orchestra 1938	198?	$25
❏ 34	Bob Crosby and His Orchestra 1938-39	198?	$25

COLUMBIA

❏ CL766 [M]	The Bob Crosby Show	1956	$30

CORAL

❏ CRL57060 [M]	Bobcats' Blues	1956	$40
❏ CRL57061 [M]	Bobcats On Parade	1956	$40
❏ CRL57089 [M]	Bob Crosby 1936-1956	1957	$40
❏ CRL57062 [M]	Bob Crosby in Hi-Fi	1956	$40
❏ CRL56003 [10]	Dixieland Jazz 1	1950	$50
❏ CRL56018 [10]	Marches in Dixieland Style	1950	$50
❏ CRL56039 [10]	St. Louis Blues	1950	$50
❏ CRL56006 [10]	Swinging at the Sugar Bowl	1950	$50
❏ CRL57005 [M]	The Bobcats' Ball	1955	$50
❏ CRL57170 [M]	The Bobcats in Hi-Fi	1958	$40

DECCA

❏ DL8061 [M]	Bob Crosby's Bobcats	1954	$175
❏ DL4856 [M]	Bob Crosby's Bobcats -- Their Greatest Hits	1967	$30
❏ DL74856 [R]	Bob Crosby's Bobcats -- Their Greatest Hits	1967	$30
❏ DL8042 [M]	Five Feet of Swing	1954	$175

DOT

❏ DLP-3278 [M]	Bob Crosby's Great Hits	196?	$85
❏ DLP-25278 [S]	Bob Crosby's Great Hits	196?	$85
❏ DLP-3382 [M]	C'est Si Bon	196?	$85
❏ DLP-25382 [S]	C'est Si Bon	196?	$85
❏ DLP-3170 [M]	Petite Fleur	1959	$85
❏ DLP-25170 [S]	Petite Fleur	1959	$30
❏ DLP-3136 [M]	South Pacific Blows Warm	1958	$85
❏ DLP-25136 [S]	South Pacific Blows Warm	1959	$85

HINDSIGHT

❏ HSR-192	Bob Crosby and His Orchestra 1941-42	198?	$20
❏ HSR-209	Bob Crosby and His Orchestra 1952-53	1985	$20

MCA

❏ 253	Bob Crosby's Bobcats -- Their Greatest Hits	1974	$25
❏ 4083	The Best of Bob Crosby	1974	$30

MONMOUTH-EVERGREEN

❏ 7026	Mardi Gras Parade	1970	$35
❏ 6815	The Bob Crosby Orchestra Live	1968	$35

PAUSA

❏ 9034	This Hits of Bob Crosby's Bobcats	198?	$25

— Reissue of Capitol 1556

SUNBEAM

❏ 216	The Bob Crosby Orchestra 1938-39	197?	$25

TIME-LIFE

❏ STBB-14	Big Bands: Bob Crosby	1984	$35

CROSBY, DAVID

A&M

❏ SP-5232	Oh Yes I Can	1989	$12

ATLANTIC

❏ SD7203	If I Could Only Remember My Name...	2000	$30

— Classic Records reissue on audiophile vinyl

❏ SD7203	If I Could Only Remember My Name…	1971	$18

CROSBY, GARY

VERVE

❏ MGV-2112 [M]	Gary Crosby Belts the Blues	1959	$150

CROSBY, STILLS, NASH & YOUNG

ATLANTIC

❏ -0 [DJ]	4 Way Street	1971	$50

— White label stereo promo

❏ PR18102 [DJ]	A Rap with C, S, N & Y	1974	$50

— Promo-only interview album

❏ PR165 [M]	Celebration/CSNY Month	1974	$300

— Promo-only LP in mono

❏ PR165 [S-DJ]	Celebration/CSNY Month	1974	$50

— Promo-only LP in stereo

❏ SD7200 [DJ]	Deja Vu	1970	$75

— White label stereo promo

CROSBY, STILLS, NASH & YOUNG

Also see DAVID CROSBY; GRAHAM NASH; STEPHEN STILLS; NEIL YOUNG.

ATLANTIC

❏ SD 2-902	4 Way Street	1971	$25
❏ 2-902 [M]	4 Way Street	1971	$250

— White label promo; no stock copies are mono

❏ SD 2-902 [DJ]	4 Way Street	1971	$50

— White label stereo promo			
❏ 81888	American Dream	1988	$12
❏ PR18102 [DJ]	A Rap with C, S, N & Y	1974	$50

— Promo-only interview album

❏ PR165 [M]	Celebration/CSNY Month	1974	$300

— Promo-only LP in mono

❏ PR165 [S]	Celebration/CSNY Month	1974	$50

— Promo-only LP in stereo

❏ 7200 [M]	Deja Vu	1970	$350

— White label promo; no stock copies are mono

❏ SD7200 [DJ]	Deja Vu	1970	$75

— White label stereo promo

❏ SD7200	Deja Vu	1970	$18

— Pasted-on front cover photo must still be intact

❏ SD19118	Deja Vu	1977	$12

— Reissue of 7200, this time with photo as part of the cover rather than as a paste-on

❏ SD18100	So Far	1974	$15
❏ SD19119	So Far	1977	$12

— Reissue of 18100

MOBILE FIDELITY

❏ Jan-0088	Deja Vu	198?	$250

— Audiophile vinyl

CROSBY, STILLS AND NASH

Also see DAVID CROSBY; GRAHAM NASH; STEPHEN STILLS.

ATLANTIC

❏ 80075	Allies	1983	$15
❏ SD8229	Crosby, Stills & Nash	1969	$25
❏ SD19117	Crosby, Stills & Nash	1977	$12

— Reissue of 8229

❏ SD8229	Crosby, Stills & Nash	2000	$30

— Classic Records reissue on 180-gram vinyl

❏ SD19104	CSN	1977	$15
❏ SD19360	Daylight Again	1982	$15
❏ 82107	Live It Up	1990	$18
❏ SD16026	Replay	1980	$15

— Also has solo cuts by Stephen Stills

NAUTILUS

❏ NR-48	Crosby, Stills and Nash	1982	$175

— Audiophile vinyl

CROSS, CHRISTOPHER

REPRISE

❏ 25685	Back of My Mind	1988	$12

WARNER BROS.

❏ 23757	Another Page	1983	$10
❏ BSK3383	Christopher Cross	1979	$10
❏ 25341	Every Turn of the World	1985	$10

CROSS COUNTRY

ATCO

❏ SD7024 [S]	Cross Country	1973	$18
❏ 7024 [M]	Cross Country	1973	$40

— Mono is white label promo only; "d/j copy monaural" sticker on cover

CROSSE, JON

JAZZ CAT

❏ JCR-101	Lullabies Go Jazz	1986	$25

CROSSFIRE

HEADFIRST

❏ HF9704	East of Where	198?	$25

CROSSFIRES, THE (1)

RHINO

❏ RNLP-019	Out of Control	1981	$12

CROSSFIRES, THE (3)

STRAND

❏ SL-1083 [M]	Limbo Rock	1963	$25
❏ SLS-1083 [S]	Limbo Rock	1963	$30

CROSSING POINT

CLAY PIGEON

❏ CP-1027	Listener Friendly	1986	$35

OPTIMISM

❏ OP-5001	Listener Friendly	1988	$25
❏ OP-5002	Point of No Return	1988	$25

CROSSINGS

IRIS

❏ IL-1001	Child's Play	198?	$25
❏ IL-1000	Crossings of the Spirit	198?	$25

CROSTON, JILL

See LACY J. DALTON.

CROTHERS, CONNIE, AND RICHARD TABNICK

NEW ARTISTS

❏ NA-1003	Duo Dimension	1987	$25

Number	Title	Yr	NM

CROTHERS, CONNIE
INNER CITY
| ❏ IC-2022 | Perception | 1974 | $35 |

JAZZ
| ❏ JR-4 | Solo | 1980 | $35 |

NEW ARTISTS
| ❏ NA-1002 | Concert at Cooper Union | 198? | $25 |

STEEPLECHASE
| ❏ SCS-1022 | Perception | 1986 | $30 |

CROTHERS, CONNIE/LENNY POPKIN QUARTET
NEW ARTISTS
| ❏ NA-1005 | Love Energy | 1989 | $30 |

CROTHERS, SCATMAN
CRAFTSMAN
| ❏ 8036 [M] | Gone with the Scat Man | 1960 | $30 |

DOOTO
| ❏ DTL814 [M] | Comedy Sweepstakes | 1961 | $30 |

MOTOWN
| ❏ M777L | Big Ben Sings | 1973 | $25 |

TOPS
| ❏ 1511 [M] | Rock and Roll with Scat Man | 1956 | $100 |

CROW, ALVIN
POLYDOR
| ❏ PD-1-6102 | High Riding | 1977 | $18 |

CROW
BLACK SABBATH's first single was a cover of this band's "Evil Woman."
AMARET
❏ AST-5012	Best of Crow	1972	$18
❏ ST-5006	Crow By Crow	1970	$25
❏ ST-5002 [B]	Crow Music	1969	$30
❏ ST-5013	David Crow d/b/a Crow	1973	$18
❏ ST-5009	Mosaic	1971	$25

CROWDED HOUSE
CAPITOL
❏ R133277	Crowded House	1987	$15
—BMG Direct Marketing edition			
❏ ST-12485	Crowded House	1987	$12
❏ R114827	Temple of Low Men	1988	$15
—BMG Direct Marketing edition			
❏ C1-48763	Temple of Low Men	1988	$15
❏ C1-93559	Woodface	1991	$18

CROWELL, RODNEY
COLUMBIA
❏ CAS2001 [DJ]	Dialog with T-Bone Burnett	1989	$30
—Promo-only interview record			
❏ FC44076	Diamonds and Dirt	1988	$12
❏ FC45242	Keys to the Highway	1989	$15
❏ FC40116	Street Language	1986	$10
❏ CAS2456 [DJ]	Street Language Interchords	1986	$30
—Promo-only interview record			

WARNER BROS.
❏ BSK3228	Ain't Living Long Like This	1978	$18
❏ BSK3407	But What Will the Neighbors Think	1980	$12
❏ BSK3587	Rodney Crowell	1981	$12

CROWLEY, ALEISTER
CLEOPATRA
| ❏ 5570 [B] | The Evil Beast | | $30 |

CROWLEY, J.C.
RCA
| ❏ 8370-1-R | Beneath the Texas Moon | 1988 | $12 |

CROWN HEIGHTS AFFAIR
DE-LITE
❏ 9512	Dance Lady Dance	1979	$12
❏ 2022	Do It	1977	$12
❏ 2017	Dreaming a Dream	1975	$12
❏ 9506	Dream World	1978	$12
❏ 2021	Foxy Lady	1976	$12
❏ 9517	Sure Shot	1980	$12
❏ 8504	Think Positive	1982	$12

RCA VICTOR
❏ APL1-0492	Crown Heights Affair	1974	$15
❏ ANL1-2660	Crown Heights Affair	1977	$10
—Reissue of above LP			

CROWS, THE / THE HARPTONES
ROULETTE
| ❏ RE-114 | Echoes of a Rock Era: The Groups | 1973 | $25 |

CRUCIFIX
UNIVERSAL
| ❏ RON2 [EP] | Crucifix | 1982 | $40 |

CRUDUP, ARTHUR
COLLECTABLES
| ❏ COL-5130 | Mean Ol' Frisco | 1988 | $12 |

DELMARK
| ❏ DS-621 | Crudup's Mood | 1969 | $40 |
| ❏ DS-614 | Look on Yonder's Wall | 1969 | $40 |

FIRE
| ❏ 103 [M] | Mean Ol' Frisco | 1960 | $900 |

RCA VICTOR
| ❏ LVP-573 | Father of Rock and Roll | 1971 | $25 |

TRIP
| ❏ 7501 | Mean Ol' Frisco | 1975 | $18 |

CRUM, SIMON
See FERLIN HUSKY.

CRUSADERS, THE (1)
ABC BLUE THUMB
❏ 6022	Chain Reaction	1975	$25
❏ BT-6001	Crusaders 1	1975	$30
❏ SPMK-42 [DJ]	Crusaders In-Store Sampler Album	1978	$50
—Promo-only issue			
❏ 6029	Free As the Wind	1977	$25
❏ BA-6030	Images	1978	$25
❏ BT-6010	Scratch	1975	$25
—Reissue			
❏ BTSY-9002	Southern Comfort	1974	$30
❏ 6027	The Best of the Crusaders	1976	$30
❏ 6024	Those Southern Knights	1976	$25

APPLAUSE
| ❏ APBL-2313 | Powerhouse | 197? | $30 |
| —Reissue of Pacific Jazz 20136 | | | |

BLUE NOTE
❏ LT-1046	Live Sides	1980	$25
❏ BN-LA170-H2	Tough Talk	1974	$30
❏ BN-LA530-H2	Young Rabbits	1977	$30
❏ LWB-530	Young Rabbits	1981	$25
—Reissue of BN-LA530-H2			

BLUE THUMB
❏ BT-6001	Crusaders 1	1972	$35
❏ BT-6010	Scratch	1974	$30
❏ BT-7000	The 2nd Crusade	1973	$35
❏ BTSA1 [DJ]	The Crusaders Promotional Album	1973	$50
—Promo-only album contains one side of material from "Crusaders 1" and one side from "The 2nd Crusade"			
❏ BT-6007	Unsung Heroes	1973	$30

CHISA
❏ 804	Old Socks, New Shoes… New Socks, Old Shoes	1970	$30
—As "Jazz Crusaders			
❏ 807	Pass the Plate	1971	$30

CRUSADERS
❏ 16002	Ongaku-Kai: Live in Japan	1982	$75
—Audiophile vinyl			
❏ 16000	Street Life	1982	$75
—Audiophile vinyl			

LIBERTY
| ❏ LST-11005 | Give Peace a Chance | 1970 | $35 |
| —As "Jazz Crusaders | | | |

MCA
❏ 6015	2nd Crusade	198?	$25
—Reissue of Blue Thumb 7000			
❏ 37146	Chain Reaction	198?	$20
—Reissue of Blue Thumb 6022			
❏ 6014	Crusaders 1	198?	$25
—Reissue of Blue Thumb 6001			
❏ 37073	Free As the Wind	198?	$20
—Reissue of Blue Thumb 6029			
❏ 5429	Ghetto Blaster	1984	$25
❏ 37074	Images	198?	$20
—Reissue of Blue Thumb 6030			
❏ 42168	Life in the Modern World	1988	$25
❏ 5124	Rhapsody and Blues	1980	$25
❏ 37174	Rhapsody and Blues	198?	$20
—Reissue of 5124			
❏ 8017	Royal Jam	1982	$30
❏ 37072	Scratch	198?	$20
—Reissue of Blue Thumb 6010			
❏ 6016	Southern Comfort	198?	$25
—Reissue of Blue Thumb 9002			
❏ 5254	Standing Tall	1981	$25
❏ 37240	Standing Tall	1985	$20
—Reissue of 5254			
❏ 3094	Street Life	1979	$25
❏ 6006	The Best of the Crusaders	1980	$25
—Reissue of Blue Thumb 6027			
❏ 5781	The Good and Bad Times	1987	$25

❏ 42087	The Vocal Album	1988	$25
❏ 37147	Those Southern Knights	198?	$20
—Reissue of Blue Thumb 6024			

MOBILE FIDELITY
| ❏ Jan-0010 | Chain Reaction | 1979 | $40 |
| —Audiophile vinyl | | | |

MOTOWN
| ❏ M796 | The Crusaders At Their Best | 1973 | $30 |
| ❏ M5-195V1 | The Crusaders At Their Best | 1981 | $25 |

MOWEST
| ❏ 118 | Hollywood | 1972 | $30 |

PACIFIC JAZZ
❏ PJ-10092 [M]	Chili Con Soul	1965	$50
❏ ST-20092 [S]	Chili Con Soul	1965	$75
❏ T-90598 [M]	Chili Con Soul	1965	$150
—Capitol Record Club edition			
❏ PJ-27 [M]	Freedom Sound	1961	$75
❏ ST-27 [S]	Freedom Sound	1961	$75
❏ PJ-76 [M]	Heat Wave	1963	$75
❏ ST-76 [S]	Heat Wave	1963	$75
❏ ST-20131	Lighthouse '68	1968	$50
❏ PJ-10098 [M]	Live at the Lighthouse '66	1966	$50
❏ ST-20098 [S]	Live at the Lighthouse '66	1966	$75
❏ PJ-43 [M]	Lookin' Ahead	1962	$75
❏ ST-43 [S]	Lookin' Ahead	1962	$75
—Black vinyl			
❏ ST-43 [S]	Lookin' Ahead	1962	$120
—Yellow vinyl			
❏ ST-20136	Powerhouse	1968	$50
❏ PJ-83 [M]	Stretchin' Out	1964	$75
❏ ST-83 [S]	Stretchin' Out	1964	$75
❏ PJ-10106 [M]	Talk That Talk	1966	$50
❏ ST-20106 [S]	Talk That Talk	1966	$75
❏ ST-20175	The Best of the Jazz Crusaders	1969	$50
❏ PJ-10115 [M]	The Festival Album	1967	$75
❏ ST-20115 [S]	The Festival Album	1967	$50
❏ PJ-57 [M]	The Jazz Crusaders at the Lighthouse	1962	$75
❏ ST-57 [S]	The Jazz Crusaders at the Lighthouse	1962	$75
❏ ST-90481 [S]	The Jazz Crusaders at the Lighthouse	1965	$150
—Capitol Record Club edition			
❏ ST-20165	The Jazz Crusaders at the Lighthouse '69	1969	$50
❏ PJ-87 [M]	The Thing	1964	$75
❏ ST-87 [S]	The Thing	1964	$75
❏ PJ-68 [M]	Tough Talk	1963	$75
❏ ST-68 [S]	Tough Talk	1963	$75
❏ PJ-10124	Uh Huh	1967	$75
❏ ST-20124	Uh Huh	1967	$50

PAUSA
| ❏ 9005 | The Best of the Jazz Crusaders | 1979 | $25 |
| —As "Jazz Crusaders | | | |

WORLD PACIFIC JAZZ
| ❏ ST-20098 [S] | Live at the Lighthouse '66 | 1970 | $150 |
| —Reissue with "Liberty/UA" on label | | | |

CRYAN' SHAMES, THE
COLUMBIA
❏ CL2786 [M]	A Scratch in the Sky	1967	$30
❏ CS9586 [S]	A Scratch in the Sky	1967	$25
❏ CL2589 [M]	Sugar & Spice	1967	$35
❏ CS9389 [S]	Sugar & Spice	1967	$25
❏ CS9719	Synthesis	1969	$25

CRYSTAL, BILLY
A&M
| ❏ SP-5096 | Mahvelous! | 1985 | $12 |

CRYSTAL
BLACKHAWK
| ❏ BKH-51501 | Clear | 1986 | $25 |

CRYSTAL MANSION, THE
CAPITOL
| ❏ ST-227 | The Crystal Mansion | 1969 | $25 |

CRYSTALS, THE (1)
PHILLES
❏ PHLP-4001 [M]	He's a Rebel	1963	$600
❏ PHLP-4003 [M]	The Crystals Sing the Greatest Hits, Vol. 1	1963	$600
❏ PHLP-4000 [M]	Twist Uptown	1962	$600
❏ T-90722 [M]	Twist Uptown	1965	$600
—Capitol Record Club edition			
❏ DT-90722 [R]	Twist Uptown	1965	$1200
—Capitol Record Club edition			

CUBER, RONNIE
XANADU
| ❏ 135 | Cuber Libre | 1976 | $35 |
| ❏ 156 | The Eleventh Day of Aquarius | 1978 | $35 |

Number	Title	Yr	NM

CUBY AND THE BLIZZARDS
PHILIPS
☐ PHS600307	Cuby and the Blizzards Live	1969	$25
☐ PHS600331	King of the World	1970	$25

CUFF LINKS, THE (1)
DECCA
☐ DL75235	The Cuff Links	1970	$25
☐ DL75160	Tracy	1969	$25

CUGAT, XAVIER
COLUMBIA
☐ CL1016 [M]	Bread, Love and Cha Cha Cha	1957	$15
☐ CL718 [M]	Cha Cha Cha	1956	$30

— Red and black label with six "eye" logos

☐ CL6077 [10]	Conga with Cugat	1949	$50

☐ CL1094 [M]	Cugat Cavalcade	1958	$30

— Red and black label with six "eye" logos

☐ CS8055 [S]	Cugat Cavalcade	1959	$30

— Red and black label with six "eye" logos

☐ CL6021 [10]	Cugat's Favorite Rhumbas	1949	$50
☐ CL6005 [10]	Cugat's Rhumba	1948	$50
☐ CL6121 [10]	Dance Date	1950	$50
☐ CL537 [M]	Dance with Cugat	1953	$40

— Maroon label, gold print

☐ CL537 [M]	Dance with Cugat	1955	$30

— Red and black label with six "eye" logos

☐ CL579 [M]	Favorite Rhumbas	1954	$40

— Maroon label, gold print

☐ CL579 [M]	Favorite Rhumbas	1955	$30

— Red and black label with six "eye" logos

☐ CL579 [M]	Favorite Rhumbas	1962	$18

— Red "Guaranteed High Fidelity" label

☐ CL579 [M]	Favorite Rhumbas	1965	$15

— Red "Mono 360 Sound" label

☐ CL2506 [10]	Mambo!	1955	$50
☐ CL6213 [10]	Mambo at the Waldorf	1951	$50
☐ CL732 [M]	Mambo at the Waldorf	1956	$30

— Red and black label with six "eye" logos

☐ CL733 [M]	Merengue by Cugat	1956	$30

— Red and black label with six "eye" logos

☐ CL733 [M]	Merengue by Cugat	1962	$18

— Red "Guaranteed High Fidelity" label

☐ CL733 [M]	Merengue by Cugat	1965	$15

— Red "Mono 360 Sound" label

☐ CS8646 [R]	Merengue by Cugat	1963	$15
☐ CL626 [M]	Mucho Mucho Mambo	1955	$40

— Maroon label, gold print

☐ CL626 [M]	Mucho Mucho Mambo	1955	$30

— Red and black label with six "eye" logos

☐ CL610 [M]	Ole	1955	$40

— Maroon label, gold print

☐ CL610 [M]	Ole	1955	$30

— Red and black label with six "eye" logos

☐ GL515 [M]	Relaxing with Cugat (Quiet Music, Volume VI)	1952	$50

— Original copies have black label, silver print and a "GL" prefix

☐ CL515 [M]	Relaxing with Cugat (Quiet Music, Volume VI)	1953	$40

— Second editions have maroon label, gold print and a "CL" prefix

☐ CL6036 [10]	Rhumba with Cugat	1949	$50
☐ CL6236 [10]	Samba with Cugat	1951	$50
☐ CL6234 [10]	Tango with Cugat	1951	$50
☐ CL6086 [10]	Tropical Bouquet	1950	$50
☐ CL1143 [M]	Waltzes! But By Cugat	1959	$30

— Red and black label with six "eye" logos

☐ CS8059 [S]	Waltzes! But By Cugat	1959	$30

— Red and black label with six "eye" logos

DECCA
☐ DL4799 [M]	Bang Bang	1966	$18
☐ DL74799 [S]	Bang Bang	1966	$25

☐ DL4740 [M]	Dance Party	1966	$18
☐ DL74740 [S]	Dance Party	1966	$25
☐ DL4672 [M]	Feeling Good	1965	$18
☐ DL74672 [S]	Feeling Good	1965	$25
☐ DL4851 [M]	Xavier Cugat Today	1967	$18
☐ DL74851 [S]	Xavier Cugat Today	1967	$25

MERCURY
☐ MG-20888 [M]	Cugat Caricatures	1964	$18
☐ SR-60888 [S]	Cugat Caricatures	1964	$25
☐ PPS-2021 [M]	Cugat Plays Continental Favorites	1961	$25
☐ PPS-6021 [S]	Cugat Plays Continental Favorites	1961	$30
☐ MG20065 [M]	Cugat's Favorites	1955	$30
☐ MG-20798 [M]	Cugat's Golden Goodies	1963	$25
☐ SR-60798 [S]	Cugat's Golden Goodies	1963	$30
☐ MG-20832 [M]	Cugi's Cocktails	1963	$25
☐ SR-60832 [S]	Cugi's Cocktails	1963	$30
☐ MG25149 [10]	Dance with Cugat/The Great Latin-American Rhythms of Xavier Cugat	195?	$40
☐ MG25120 [10]	Here's Cugat	195?	$40
☐ MG20108 [M]	Mambo!/Music for Latin Lovers	1957	$30
☐ MG25168 [10]	Mambos by Cugat	195?	$40
☐ PPS-2015 [M]	The Best of Cugat	1961	$25
☐ PPS-6015 [S]	The Best of Cugat	1961	$30
☐ MG-20870 [M]	The Best of Cugat	1964	$18

— Reissue of 2015

☐ SR-60870 [S]	The Best of Cugat	1964	$25

— Reissue of 6015

☐ MG-20745 [M]	The Most Popular Movie Themes As Styled by Cugat	1961	$25
☐ SR-60745 [S]	The Most Popular Movie Themes As Styled by Cugat	1961	$30
☐ MG-20705 [M]	Twist with Cugat	1962	$25
☐ SR-60705 [S]	Twist with Cugat	1962	$30
☐ PPS-2003 [M]	Viva Cugat!	1961	$25
☐ PPS-6003 [S]	Viva Cugat!	1961	$30
☐ MG-20868 [M]	Viva Cugat!	1964	$18

— Reissue of 2003

☐ SR-60868 [S]	Viva Cugat!	1964	$25

— Reissue of 6003

RCA VICTOR
☐ LPM-1987 [M]	Chili Con Cugie	1959	$25
☐ LSP-1987 [S]	Chili Con Cugie	1959	$30
☐ LPM-2173 [M]	Cugat in France, Spain and Italy	1960	$25
☐ LSP-2173 [S]	Cugat in France, Spain and Italy	1960	$30
☐ LPM-1894 [M]	Cugat in Spain	1959	$25
☐ LSP-1894 [S]	Cugat in Spain	1959	$30
☐ ANL1-1310	Pure Gold	1976	$10
☐ LPT-11 [10]	Tangos	195?	$40
☐ LPM-1882 [M]	The King Plays Some Aces	1958	$25
☐ LSP-1882 [S]	The King Plays Some Aces	1958	$30

CULLEY, FRANK "FLOORSHOW
BATON
☐ BL1201 [M]	Rock 'n Roll: Instrumentals for Dancing the Lindy Hop	1955	$600

— B-side tracks by Buddy Tate Orchestra

CULLUM, JIM (JR.)
JAZZOLOGY
☐ 132	Life in Memphis	198?	$25

STOMP OFF
☐ SOS-1148	Super Satch	1987	$25

CULLUM, JIM (SR.)
AUDIOPHILE
☐ 107 [B]	Eloquent Clarinet	1972	$35
☐ 117	Jazz -- The Music of Jim Cullum, Sr.	1972	$30

CULT, THE
Features Billy Duffy and Ian Astbury.
SIRE
☐ R184083	Electric	1987	$15

— RCA Music Service edition

☐ 25555	Electric	1987	$12
☐ R134608	Love	1985	$15

— RCA Music Service edition

☐ 25259	Love	1985	$12
☐ R101015	Sonic Temple	1989	$15

— BMG Direct Marketing edition

☐ 25871 [B]	Sonic Temple	1989	$12

WARNER BROS.
☐ -0 [DJ]	Electric Interview	1987	$40
☐ WBMS-147 [DJ]	Electric Interview	1987	$50

— Part of "The Warner Bros. Music Show" series

CULTURE CLUB
VIRGIN/EPIC
☐ QE39107	Colour by Numbers	1983	$12
☐ 9E9-39237 [PD]	Colour by Numbers	1983	$30

— Picture disc in plastic sleeve

☐ OE40345	From Luxury to Heartache	1986	$12
☐ ARE38398	Kissing to Be Clever	1982	$15

— First pressings have nine tracks and do not contain "Time (Clock of the Heart)"

☐ FE38398	Kissing to Be Clever	1983	$12

— This version has 10 tracks with the addition of "Time (Clock of the Heart)" as the first song on side 2

☐ FE40913	This Time: The First Four Years	1987	$15
☐ OE39881	Waking Up with the House on Fire	1984	$12
☐ 9E9-40005 [PD]	Waking Up with the House on Fire	1984	$30

CUMBERLAND THREE, THE
ROULETTE
☐ R25132 [M]	Civil War Almanac, Volume 1: The Yankees	1960	$25
☐ SR25132 [S]	Civil War Almanac, Volume 1: The Yankees	1960	$30
☐ R25133 [M]	Civil War Almanac, Volume 2: The Rebels	1960	$25
☐ SR25133 [S]	Civil War Almanac, Volume 2: The Rebels	1960	$30
☐ R25121 [M]	Folk Scene U.S.A.	1960	$25
☐ SR25121 [S]	Folk Scene U.S.A.	1960	$30

CUMMINGS, BURTON
ALFA
☐ AAB-11007	Sweet Sweet	1981	$12

PORTRAIT
☐ PR34261	Burton Cummings	1976	$12
☐ PRQ34261 [Q]	Burton Cummings	1976	$50
☐ JR35481	Dream of a Child	1978	$12
☐ PR34698	My Own Way to Rock	1977	$12

CUNHA, RICK
GRC
☐ GA-5004	Cunha Songs	1974	$15

SIERRA
☐ 8707	Moving Pictures	1980	$15

CUNIMONDO, FRANK
MONDO
☐ M-101	Communication	197?	$25
☐ M-104	Echoes	197?	$25
☐ M-103	Introducing Lynn Marino	197?	$25
☐ M-105	Sagittarius	197?	$25
☐ M-102	The Lamp Is Low	197?	$25
☐ S1-90175	The Top Shelf Collection	197?	$25

CUNNINGHAM, J.C.
VIVA
☐ 25173	J.C. Cunningham	1984	$10

CUNTS
PRAVDA
☐ 633	Decade of Fun: 1978-1988	1988	$15

CUOZZO, MIKE
JUBILEE
☐ JLP-1027 [M]	Mike Cuozzo	1957	$150

Number	Title	Yr	NM

SAVOY
| ❏ MG-12051 [M] | Mighty Mike | 1956 | $150 |

CURB, MIKE
COBURT
| ❏ CO1002 | Come Together | 1970 | $12 |
| ❏ CO1003 | Sweet Gingerbread Man | 1970 | $12 |

MGM
❏ SE-4761	Burning Bridges and Other Great Motion Picture Themes	1971	$12
❏ SE-4785	Put Your Hand in the Hand	1971	$12
❏ SE-4821	Softly Whispering I Love You	1972	$12
❏ SE-4844	Song for a Young Love	1972	$12
❏ SE-4804	The Mike Curb Congregation Sing Their Hits from the Glen Campbell Show	1971	$12

WARNER BROS.
| ❏ BS3129 | The Mike Curb Congregation | 1977 | $12 |

CURE, THE
A&M
| ❏ SP-6020 [B] | Happily Ever After | 1981 | $75 |
| ❏ SP-4902 [B] | Pornography | 1982 | $75 |

ELEKTRA
❏ 62236 [B]	Bloodflowers	2000	$100
❏ 60786	Boys Don't Cry	1988	$20
— Reissue of PVC 7916			
❏ R101109	Disintegration	1989	$20
— BMG Direct Marketing edition			
❏ 60855	Disintegration	1989	$20
❏ 60783 [B]	Faith	1988	$40
— Reissue of third U.K. album			
❏ 62117	Galore: The Singles 1987-1997	1997	$100
❏ 60737 [DJ]	Kiss Me, Kiss Me, Kiss Me	1987	$40
— Promo-only audiophile pressing			
❏ R242404	Kiss Me, Kiss Me, Kiss Me	1987	$50
— BMG Direct Marketing edition			
❏ 60737	Kiss Me, Kiss Me, Kiss Me	1987	$20
❏ 60737 [DJ]	Kiss Me, Kiss Me, Kiss Me	1987	$75
— Promo-only audiophile pressing			
❏ 60978	Mixed Up	1990	$40
— LP version has one extra track not on CD or cassette			
❏ R274190	Mixed Up	1990	$30
— BMG Direct Marketing edition			
❏ 60785	Pornography	1988	$20
— Reissue of A&M SP-4902			
❏ 60784 [B]	Seventeen Seconds	1988	$30
— Reissue of second U.K. album			
❏ R150024	Standing on a Beach -- The Singles	1986	$20
— BMG Direct Marketing edition			
❏ 60477	Standing on a Beach -- The Singles	1986	$40
❏ 60435 [B]	The Head on the Door	1985	$40
❏ 61744	Wild Mood Swings	1996	$40

GEFFEN
| ❏ B0002870-1 | The Cure | 2004 | $40 |

PVC
| ❏ 7916 [B] | Boys Don't Cry | 1980 | $75 |
| — revised version of first U.K. album | | | |

RHINO
| ❏ R160737 [B] | Kiss Me Kiss Me Miss Me | 2013 | $40 |

SIRE
❏ 25076	Japanese Whispers	1983	$25
❏ 25086 [B]	The Top	1984	$40
❏ 23928 [EP]	The Walk	1983	$30

CURIOSITY KILLED THE CAT
MERCURY
| ❏ 842010-1 | Get Ahead | 1989 | $15 |
| ❏ 832025-1 | Keep Your Distance | 1987 | $12 |

CURLESS, DICK, AND KAY ADAMS
TOWER
| ❏ T5025 [M] | A Devil Like Me Needs an Angel Like You | 1966 | $30 |
| ❏ DT5025 [R] | A Devil Like Me Needs an Angel Like You | 1966 | $25 |

CURLESS, DICK
CAPITOL
❏ ST-792	Comin' On Country	1971	$25
❏ ST-689	Doggin' It	1971	$25
❏ ST-552	Hard, Hard Travelin' Man	1970	$25
❏ ST-11119	Live at the Wheeling Truck Driver's Jamboree	1973	$25
❏ ST-11087	Stonin' Around	1972	$25
❏ ST-11211	The Last Blues Song	1973	$30
— First cover shows Dick Curless with an eye patch			
❏ ST-11211	The Last Blues Song		$25
— Second cover shows Dick Curless with no eye patch			
❏ ST-11011	Tombstone Every Mile	1972	$18
— Reissue of Tower DT 5005			

TIFFANY
❏ 1016 [M]	Dick Curless Sings Songs of the Open Country	1958	$150
❏ 1033 [M]	I Love to Tell a Story	1960	$150
❏ 1028 [M]	Singing Just for Fun	1959	$150

TOWER
❏ T5066 [M]	All of Me Belongs to You	1967	$30
❏ ST5066 [S]	All of Me Belongs to You	1967	$30
❏ T5016 [M]	At Home with Dick Curless	1966	$30
❏ DT5016 [R]	At Home with Dick Curless	1966	$25
❏ T5012 [M]	Hymns	1965	$30
❏ DT5012 [R]	Hymns	1965	$25
❏ ST5089 [S]	Ramblin' Country	1967	$30
❏ T5089 [M]	Ramblin' Country	1967	$30
❏ ST5108	The Long Lonesome Road	1968	$30
❏ T5013 [M]	The Soul of Dick Curless	1966	$30
❏ DT5013 [R]	The Soul of Dick Curless	1966	$25
❏ ST5139	The Wild Side of Town	1969	$30
❏ T5005 [M]	Tombstone Every Mile	1965	$30
❏ DT5005 [R]	Tombstone Every Mile	1965	$25
❏ T5015 [M]	Travelin' Man	1966	$30
❏ DT5015 [R]	Travelin' Man	1966	$25

CURRAN, ED
SAVOY
| ❏ MG-12191 [M] | Elysa | 1967 | $25 |

CURRENT EVENTS
VERVE FORECAST
| ❏ 839388-1 | Current Events | 1989 | $35 |

CURRIE, CHERIE AND MARIE
Lead singer of the RUNAWAYS plus her sister.
CAPITOL

| ❏ ST-12022 [B] | Messin' with the Boys | 1979 | $25 |

CURSON, TED
ARISTA FREEDOM
| ❏ AL1030 | Flip Top | 197? | $35 |
| ❏ AL1021 | Tears | 197? | $35 |

ATLANTIC
| ❏ 1441 [M] | The New Thing and the Blue Thing | 1965 | $25 |
| ❏ SD1441 [S] | The New Thing and the Blue Thing | 1965 | $30 |

AUDIO FIDELITY
| ❏ AFLP-2123 [M] | Now Hear This | 1964 | $25 |
| ❏ AFSD-6123 [S] | Now Hear This | 1964 | $30 |

FANTASY
| ❏ OJC-1744 | Fire Down Below | 1990 | $30 |

INDIA NAVIGATION
| ❏ IN-1054 | Blue Piccolo | 1976 | $35 |

INNER CITY
| ❏ IC1017 | Jubilant Power | 1976 | $30 |

INTERPLAY
❏ 7716	Blowin' Away	1978	$30
❏ 7726	I Heard Mingus	1980	$30
❏ 7722	The Trio	1979	$30

OLD TOWN
| ❏ LP-2003 [M] | Plenty of Horn | 1961 | $700 |

PRESTIGE
❏ PRLP-7263 [M]	Fire Down Below	1963	$30
— Yellow label, Bergenfield, N.J. address			
❏ PRLP-7263 [M]	Fire Down Below	1965	$25
— Blue label with trident logo at right			
❏ PRST-7263 [S]	Fire Down Below	1963	$40
— Silver label, Bergenfield, N.J. address			
❏ PRST-7263 [S]	Fire Down Below	1965	$30
— Blue label with trident logo at right			

CURTIS, KEN
CAPITOL
| ❏ T2418 [M] | Gunsmoke's Festus | 1965 | $30 |
| ❏ ST2418 [S] | Gunsmoke's Festus | 1965 | $40 |

DOT
| ❏ DLP-25859 | Gunsmoke's Festus Calls Out Ken Curtis | 1968 | $30 |

CURTIS, MAC
EPIC
| ❏ BN26419 | The Sunshine Man | 1969 | $25 |

HMG/HIGHTONE
| ❏ HT6601 | Rockabilly Uprising: The Best of Mac Curtis | 1997 | $12 |

ROLLIN' ROCK
❏ LP-007	Good Rockin' Tomorrow	1975	$40
❏ LP-002	Ruffabilly	1975	$40
❏ LP-002	Ruffabilly	1977	$25
— Reissue			

CURTIS, SONNY
ELEKTRA
❏ 6E-283	Love Is All Around	1980	$12
❏ 6E-349	Rollin'	1981	$12
❏ 6E-227	Sonny Curtis	1979	$12

IMPERIAL
| ❏ LP-9276 [M] | Beatle Hits Flamenco Style | 1964 | $40 |
| ❏ LP-12276 [S] | Beatle Hits Flamenco Style | 1964 | $50 |

VIVA
| ❏ V-36012 | The First of Sonny Curtis | 1968 | $30 |
| ❏ V-36021 | The Sonny Curtis Style | 1969 | $30 |

CUTTING CREW
VIRGIN
❏ R163456	Broadcast	1987	$12
— BMG Direct Marketing edition			
❏ 90573	Broadcast	1987	$10
❏ R101103	The Scattering	1989	$15
— BMG Direct Marketing edition			
❏ 91239	The Scattering	1989	$12

CYKLE, THE
LABEL
| ❏ 9-261 | The Cykle | 1969 | $500 |

CYMANDE
JANUS
| ❏ 3044 | Cymande | 1972 | $12 |
| ❏ 3054 | Second Time Round | 1973 | $12 |

CYMARRON
ENTRANCE
| ❏ Z30962 | Rings | 1971 | $15 |

CYMBAL, JOHNNY
KAPP
| ❏ KL-1324 [M] | Mr. Bass Man | 1963 | $50 |
| ❏ KS-3324 [S] | Mr. Bass Man | 1963 | $80 |

CYMBAL & CLINGER
CHELSEA
| ❏ 1002 | Cymbal & Clinger | 1972 | $15 |

CYMONE, ANDRE
COLUMBIA
❏ FC40037	A.C.	1985	$12
❏ FC38123	Livin' in the New Wave	1982	$12
❏ FC38902	Survivin' in the 80's	1983	$12

CYRILLE, ANDREW, AND MILFORD GRAVES
IPS
| ❏ 001 | Dialogue of the Drums | 1974 | $25 |

CYRILLE, ANDREW; JEANNE LEE; JIMMY LYONS
BLACK SAINT
| ❏ BSR-0030 | Nuba | 198? | $30 |

CYRILLE, ANDREW
BLACK SAINT
| ❏ BSR-0025 | Metamusician's Stomp | 1979 | $15 |

ICTUS
| ❏ 09 | The Loop | 197? | $35 |

IPS
| ❏ 02 | Celebration | 1977 | $35 |
| ❏ 03 | Junction | 1978 | $35 |

SOUL NOTE
❏ SN-1078	Pieces of Time	198?	$30
❏ SN-1012	Special People	1981	$30
❏ SN-1062	The Navigator	1982	$30

Number	Title	Yr	NM

CYRKLE, THE
COLUMBIA

Number	Title	Yr	NM
❏ CL2632 [M]	Neon	1967	$18
❏ CS9432 [S]	Neon	1967	$25
❏ CL2544 [M]	Red Rubber Ball	1966	$25
❏ CS9344 [S]	Red Rubber Ball	1966	$30

CYRUS, BILLY RAY
MERCURY

❏ 1P-8218	Some Gave All	1992	$30

— Only released on vinyl through Columbia House

D

DA COSTA, PAULINHO
FANTASY

❏ OJC-630	Agora	1991	$30

PABLO

❏ 2310785	Agora	1976	$35

PABLO TODAY

❏ 2312102	Happy People	1979	$30

D'ABO, MIKE
A&M

❏ SP-3634 [B]	Broken Rainbows	1974	$18
❏ SP-4346 [B]	Down at Rachel's Place	1972	$18

DADDY COOL
REPRISE

❏ RS6471	Daddy Who? Daddy Cool!	1971	$18
❏ MS2088	Teenage Heaven	1972	$25

DADDY DEWDROP
SUNFLOWER

❏ SNF-5006	Daddy Dewdrop	1971	$25

DADDY WARBUCKS
TIGER LILY

❏ TL14007 [B]	Daddy Warbucks 1	1976	$500

DAFT PUNK
VIRGIN

❏ 49606 [B]	Discovery	2001	$25
❏ 42609	Homework	1997	$18

DAGRADI, TONY
GRAMAVISION

❏ 8103	Lunar Eclipse	1982	$30
❏ 8001	Oasis	1981	$30

ROUNDER

❏ 2071	Dreams of Love	1988	$25

DAHL, STEVE
HILARIA

❏ SD1983 [EP]	Pet Fishsticks	1983	$15

DAHLANDER, NILS-BERTIL "BERT"
EVERYDAY

❏ EDLP528	Talkin' Jazz: Untitled #1	1990	$35

— As "Bert Dahlander"

VERVE

❏ MGV-8253 [M]	Skol	1958	$150
❏ V-8253 [M]	Skol	1961	$25

DAILEY, ALBERT
COLUMBIA

❏ KC31278	Day After the Dawn	1973	$35

MUSE

❏ MR-5256	Textures	198?	$25

STEEPLECHASE

❏ SCS-1107	That Old Feeling	198?	$25

DAILEY, DON
CROWN

❏ CLP-5314 [M]	Surf Stompin'	1963	$30
❏ CST-314 [R]	Surf Stompin'	1963	$18

DAILY, PETE
CAPITOL

❏ H385 [10]	Dixie by Daily	1953	$100
❏ T385 [M]	Dixie by Daily	1954	$75
❏ H183 [10]	Dixieland Band	1950	$100
❏ T183 [M]	Dixieland Band	1954	$75

DAILY, PETE/PHIL NAPOLEON
DECCA

❏ DL5261 [10]	Pete Daily/Phil Napoleon	195?	$50

DAKUS, WES
KAPP

Number	Title	Yr	NM
❏ KL-1536 [M]	Wes Dakus' Rebels	1967	$30
❏ KS-3536 [S]	Wes Dakus' Rebels	1967	$30

DALE, DICK, AND THE DEL-TONES
CAPITOL

❏ T2002 [M]	Checkered Flag	1963	$75
❏ ST2002 [S]	Checkered Flag	1963	$100
❏ T1930 [M]	King of the Surf Guitar	1963	$100
❏ ST1930 [S]	King of the Surf Guitar	1963	$120
❏ T2053 [M]	Mr. Eliminator	1964	$75
❏ ST2053 [S]	Mr. Eliminator	1964	$150
❏ T2293 [M]	Rock Out -- Live at Ciro's	1965	$150
❏ ST2293 [S]	Rock Out -- Live at Ciro's	1965	$175
❏ T2111 [M]	Summer Surf	1964	$150

— With bonus single by Jerry Cole, "Racing Waves"/"Movin' Surf," in front cover pocket

❏ T2111 [M]	Summer Surf	1964	$50

— Without bonus single

❏ ST2111 [S]	Summer Surf	1964	$120

— With bonus single by Jerry Cole, "Racing Waves"/"Movin' Surf," in front cover pocket

❏ ST2111 [S]	Summer Surf	1964	$80

— Without bonus single

CLOISTER

❏ CLP-6301 [M]	Silver Sounds of the Surf	1963	$250

— With tracks by the Stompers

DELTONE

❏ LPM-1001 [M]	Surfer's Choice	1962	$175
❏ T1886 [M]	Surfer's Choice	1962	$75
❏ DT1886 [R]	Surfer's Choice	1962	$40

DUB TONE

❏ LP-1246 [M]	The Surf Family	1964	$30

— With tracks by the Hollywood Surfers

GNP CRESCENDO

❏ GNPS-2095	Greatest Hits	1975	$15

RHINO

❏ RNLP-70074 [B]	King of the Surf Guitar: The Best of Dick Dale and the Del-Tones, 1961-1964	1986	$18

DALE, KENNY
CAPITOL

❏ ST-11673	Bluest Heartache	1977	$15
❏ ST-11762	Red Hot Memory	1978	$15
❏ ST-12126	When It's Just You and Me	1980	$15

DALE
PAISLEY PARK

❏ 25577	Riot in English	1988	$12

DALE AND GRACE
MICHELLE

❏ 100 [M]	I'm Leaving It Up to You	1964	$175

MONTEL

❏ 100 [M]	I'm Leaving It Up to You	1964	$175

DALEY, JOE
RCA VICTOR

❏ LPM-2763 [M]	Joe Daley at Newport '63	1963	$25
❏ LSP-2763 [S]	Joe Daley at Newport '63	1963	$30

DALLAS, DEAN, AND THE DOUGHBOYS
CUMBERLAND

❏ MGC-29516 [M]	Golden Country Hits	1965	$25
❏ SRC-69516 [S]	Golden Country Hits	1965	$30

DALLAS, MARIA
RCA VICTOR

❏ LPM-3950 [M]	Tumblin' Down	1968	$40

Number	Title	Yr	NM
❏ LSP-3950 [S]	Tumblin' Down	1968	$25

DALLWITZ, DAVE
STOMP OFF

❏ SOS-1112	Elephant Stomp	1987	$25
❏ SOS-1098	Nostalgia	1985	$25

DALTO, JORGE
CONCORD PICANTE

❏ CJP-275	Urban Oasis	1985	$25

DALTON, KAREN
CAPITOL

❏ ST271	It's So Hard to Tell	1969	$150

JUST SUNSHINE/PARAMOUNT

❏ PAS6008	In My Own Time	1972	$50

DALTON, KATHY
DISCREET

❏ MS2168	Amazing	1973	$25
❏ DS2208	Boogie Bands and One Night Stands	1974	$15

DALTON, LACY J.
COLUMBIA

❏ FC37975	16th Avenue	1982	$10
❏ FC40780	Blue Eyed Blues	1987	$10
❏ FC40028	Can't Run Away from Your Heart	1985	$10
❏ FC38604	Dream Baby	1983	$10
❏ FC38883	Greatest Hits	1984	$10
❏ JC36763	Hard Times	1980	$12
❏ PC36763	Hard Times	1985	$10

— Budget-line reissue with new prefix

❏ FC40393	Highway Diner	1986	$10
❏ JC36322	Lacy J. Dalton	1980	$12
❏ PC36322	Lacy J. Dalton	198?	$10

— Budget-line reissue with new prefix

❏ FC37327	Takin' It Easy	1981	$10
❏ PC37327	Takin' It Easy	1985	$10

— Budget-line reissue with new prefix

HARBOR

❏ 001	Jill Croston	1978	$30

— As "Jill Croston

UNIVERSAL

❏ 42294	Survivor	1989	$12

DALTREY, ROGER
Also see THE WHO.
ATLANTIC

❏ 81759	Can't Wait to See the Movie	1987	$12
❏ 80128	Parting Should Be Painless	1984	$12
❏ 81269	Under a Raging Moon	1985	$12

MCA

❏ 5301	Best Bits	1982	$12
❏ 2349	Daltrey	1977	$12

— Reissue of Track 328

❏ 37032	Daltrey	1980	$10

— Budget-line reissue

❏ 2271 [B]	One of the Boys	1977	$18
❏ 37031	One of the Boys	1980	$10

— Budget-line reissue

❏ 2147 [B]	Ride a Rock Horse	1975	$18
❏ 37030	Ride a Rock Horse	1980	$10

— Budget-line reissue

POLYDOR

❏ PD-1-6284	McVicar	1980	$12

TRACK

❏ 328	Daltrey	1973	$15

D'AMBROSIO, MEREDITH
PALO ALTO

❏ 8019	Little Jazz Bird	1982	$30

SHIAH

❏ SR-109	Another Time	198?	$35

SPRING INC.

❏ 0SPR	Lost in His Arms	1978	$35

SUNNYSIDE

❏ SSC-1017	Another Time	1987	$25
❏ SSC-1011	It's Your Dance	1985	$25
❏ SSC-1018	Lost in His Arms	1987	$25
❏ SSC-1039	South to a Warmer Place	1989	$30
❏ SSC-1028	The Cove	1988	$25

DAMERON, TADD
FANTASY

❏ OJC-055	Fontainebleu	198?	$30

— Reissue of Prestige 7037

❏ OJC-212	Mating Call	198?	$30

— Reissue of Prestige 7070

❏ OJC-143	The Magic Touch of Tadd Dameron	198?	$30

— Reissue of Riverside 9419

Number	Title	Yr	NM
JAZZLAND			
❏ JLP-50 [M]	Fats Navarro Featured with the Tadd Dameron Quintet	1962	$175
❏ JLP-68 [M]	The Tadd Dameron Band	1962	$175
MILESTONE			
❏ M-47041	Fats Navarro Featured with the Tadd Dameron Band	1977	$50
NEW JAZZ			
❏ NJLP-8300 [M]	Dameronia	1963	$0

—Canceled; reassigned to Prestige 16007

Number	Title	Yr	NM
PRESTIGE			
❏ PRLP-159 [10]	A Study in Dameronia	1953	$600
❏ PRLP-16007 [M]	Dameronia	1964	$150
❏ PRLP-7037 [M]	Fontainebleu	1956	$300
❏ PRLP-7070 [M]	Mating Call	1956	$300

—Reissued as 7247 and 7725 as a John Coltrane LP; see his listings

Number	Title	Yr	NM
❏ PRST-7842	Memorial Album	1970	$35
RIVERSIDE			
❏ RS-3019	Good Bait	1968	$150
❏ RLP-419 [M]	The Magic Touch of Tadd Dameron	1962	$175
❏ RS-9419 [S]	The Magic Touch of Tadd Dameron	1962	$175

DAMIAN, MICHAEL

Number	Title	Yr	NM
CYPRESS			
❏ YL9-0130	Where Do We Go from Here	1989	$15

D'AMICO, HANK

Number	Title	Yr	NM
BETHLEHEM			
❏ BCP-1006 [10]	Hank's Holiday	1954	$300

DAMIN EIH, A.L.K. AND BROTHER CLARK

Number	Title	Yr	NM
DEMELOT			
❏ 7310	Never Mind	1973	$175

DAMITA JO

Number	Title	Yr	NM
ABC-PARAMOUNT			
❏ 378 [M]	The Big Fifteen	1961	$100
❏ S-378 [S]	The Big Fifteen	1961	$150
EPIC			
❏ LN24244 [M]	If You Go Away	1967	$25
❏ BN26244 [S]	If You Go Away	1967	$18
❏ LN24202 [M]	Midnight Session	1966	$18
❏ BN26202 [S]	Midnight Session	1966	$25
❏ LN24164 [M]	One More Time with Feeling	1965	$18
❏ BN26164 [S]	One More Time with Feeling	1965	$25
❏ LN24131 [M]	This Is Damita Jo	1965	$18
❏ BN26131 [S]	This Is Damita Jo	1965	$25
MERCURY			
❏ MG-20703 [M]	Damita Jo Live at the Diplomat	1962	$30
❏ SR-60703 [S]	Damita Jo Live at the Diplomat	1962	$30
❏ MG-20642 [M]	I'll Save the Last Dance for You	1961	$30
❏ SR-60642 [S]	I'll Save the Last Dance for You	1961	$40
❏ MG-20734 [M]	Sing a Country Song	1962	$30
❏ SR-60734 [S]	Sing a Country Song	1962	$30
❏ MG-20818 [M]	This One's for Me	1963	$25
❏ SR-60818 [S]	This One's for Me	1963	$30
RANWOOD			
❏ RLP.8037	Miss Damita Jo	1968	$18
RCA CAMDEN			
❏ CAL-900 [M]	Go Go with Damita Jo	196?	$18
❏ CAS-900(e) [R]	Go Go with Damita Jo	196?	$15
SUNSET			
❏ SUS-5198	The Irresistible Damita Jo	1968	$15
VEE JAY			
❏ LP-1137 [M]	Damita Jo Sings	1965	$30
❏ LPS-1137 [S]	Damita Jo Sings	1965	$50
WING			
❏ WC-16333	This One's for Me	196?	$15

DAMNATION OF ADAM BLESSING, THE

Number	Title	Yr	NM
UNITED ARTISTS			
❏ UAS-6738 [B]	The Damnation of Adam Blessing	1970	$35
❏ UAS-6773 [B]	The Second Damnation	1970	$35
❏ UAS-5533 [B]	Which Is the Justice, Which Is the Thief	1971	$35

DAMNED, THE

Number	Title	Yr	NM
CLEOPATRA			
❏ 8110 [B]	Punk & Nasty		$25
❏ CLP8360 [B]	Punk Oddities & Rare Tracks 1977-1982	2014	$25
❏ 8360 [B]	Pure Punk 1977-1982		$30

—picture disc

Number	Title	Yr	NM
❏ 2021 [B]	Recorded Live At Woolwich Coronet - Thursday 11 July 1985		$25
❏ 8119 [B]	The Chaos Years - Live & Studio Demos 1977-1982		$25

Number	Title	Yr	NM
FRONTIER			
❏ 1003	Damned Damned Damned	1987	$18

—Reissue of 1976-77 material

Number	Title	Yr	NM
I.R.S.			
❏ SP-70012	The Black Album	1980	$15
MCA			
❏ 5966 [B]	Anything	1987	$18
❏ 2-8024	Light at the End of the Tunnel	1988	$18
❏ 39039 [B]	Phantasmagoria	1986	$25

DAMON, LIZ, 'S ORIENT EXPRESS

Number	Title	Yr	NM
MAKAHA			
❏ MS-5003	Liz Damon's Orient Express	1970	$25
WHITE WHALE			
❏ WWS5003	Liz Damon's Orient Express	1971	$15

DAMON

Number	Title	Yr	NM
ANKH			
❏ 968	Song of a Gypsy	1969	$1500

—Gatefold cover

Number	Title	Yr	NM
❏ 968	Song of a Gypsy	1969	$1500

—Regular cover

DAMONE, VIC

Number	Title	Yr	NM
APPLAUSE			
❏ 1018	Over the Rainbow	197?	$12
CAPITOL			
❏ T1646 [M]	Linger Awhile with Vic Damone	1962	$15
❏ ST1646 [S]	Linger Awhile with Vic Damone	1962	$18
❏ T1811 [M]	My Baby Loves to Swing	1963	$15
❏ ST1811 [S]	My Baby Loves to Swing	1963	$18
❏ T2123 [M]	On the Street Where You Live	1964	$15
❏ ST2123 [S]	On the Street Where You Live	1964	$18
❏ T1691 [M]	Strange Enchantment	1962	$15
❏ ST1691 [S]	Strange Enchantment	1962	$18
❏ T1944 [M]	The Liveliest	1963	$15
❏ ST1944 [S]	The Liveliest	1963	$18
❏ T1748 [M]	The Lively Ones	1962	$15
❏ ST1748 [S]	The Lively Ones	1962	$18
COLUMBIA			
❏ CL1088 [M]	Angela Mia	1957	$25
❏ CS8046 [S]	Angela Mia	1959	$30
❏ CL1174 [M]	Closer Than a Kiss	195?	$25
❏ CS8019 [S]	Closer Than a Kiss	1959	$30
❏ CL1573 [M]	On the Swingin' Side	1961	$18
❏ CS8373 [S]	On the Swingin' Side	1961	$25

Number	Title	Yr	NM
❏ CL900 [M]	That Towering Feeling!	1956	$30
❏ CL1368 [M]	This Game of Love	1960	$18
❏ CS8169 [S]	This Game of Love	1960	$25
HARMONY			
❏ HL7328 [M]	The Best of Vic Damone	196?	$15
❏ HS11128 [S]	The Best of Vic Damone	196?	$15
❏ HL7431 [M]	Vic Damone Sings	196?	$15
❏ HS11231 [S]	Vic Damone Sings	196?	$15
HOLIDAY			
❏ HDY1936	Christmas with Vic Damone	1981	$12
MERCURY			
❏ MG-25133 [10]	April in Paris	1952	$40
❏ MG-25092 [10]	Christmas Favorites	1951	$40
❏ MG-20193 [M]	My Favorites	1957	$30
❏ MG-25054 [10]	Song Hits	1950	$40
❏ MG-25131 [10]	The Night Has a Thousand Eyes	1952	$40
❏ MG-25028 [10]	Vic Damone	1950	$40
❏ MG-25029 [10]	Vic Damone	1950	$40
❏ MG-25045 [10]	Vic Damone	1950	$40
❏ MG-25156 [10]	Vic Damone	1952	$40
❏ MG-25100 [10]	Vic Damone and Others	1952	$40
❏ MG-25132 [10]	Vocals by Vic	1952	$40

Number	Title	Yr	NM
❏ MG-20163 [M]	Yours for a Song	1957	$30
RANWOOD			
❏ 8204	The Best of Vic Damone – Live	198?	$12
RCA VICTOR			
❏ LPM-3916 [M]	A Damone Type of Thing	1968	$18
❏ LSP-3916 [S]	A Damone Type of Thing	1968	$18
❏ LPM-3765 [M]	On the South Side of Chicago	1967	$15
❏ LSP-3765 [S]	On the South Side of Chicago	1967	$18
❏ LPM-3671 [M]	Stay with Me	1966	$15
❏ LSP-3671 [S]	Stay with Me	1966	$18
❏ ANL1-2462	The Best of Vic Damone	1977	$12
❏ LSP-3984	Why Can't I Walk Away	1968	$18
REBECCA			
❏ 1212	Feelings	1976	$12
❏ 1213	Inspiration	19??	$12
❏ 100	Let's Fall in Love Again	1981	$15
UNITED TALENT			
❏ 4501	Don't Let Me Go	1969	$15
WARNER BROS.			
❏ W1607 [M]	Country Love Songs	1965	$15
❏ WS1607 [S]	Country Love Songs	1965	$18
❏ W1602 [M]	You Were Only Fooling	1965	$15
❏ WS1602 [S]	You Were Only Fooling	1965	$18
WING			
❏ MGW12113 [M]	I'll Sing for You	196?	$15
❏ SRW16113 [R]	I'll Sing for You	196?	$15
❏ MGW12157 [M]	Tenderly	196?	$15
❏ SRW16157 [R]	Tenderly	196?	$15
❏ MGW12182 [M]	Yours for a Song	196?	$15
❏ SRW16182 [R]	Yours for a Song	196?	$15

DAN AND DALE

Number	Title	Yr	NM
DIPLOMAT			
❏ D-2364 [M]	Country & Western Hits	196?	$12
❏ DS-2364 [S]	Country & Western Hits	196?	$15
❏ D-2361 [M]	Country and Western Waltzes	196?	$12
❏ DS-2361 [S]	Country and Western Waltzes	196?	$15
❏ D-2340 [M]	Dear Heart, Willow Weep for Me and Other Love Songs	196?	$12
❏ DS-2340 [S]	Dear Heart, Willow Weep for Me and Other Love Songs	196?	$15
❏ DS-2343 [S]	Themes from Goldfinger and Zorba the Greek	196?	$15
❏ D-2343 [M]	Themes from Goldfinger and Zorba the Greek	196?	$12
❏ D-2390 [M]	The Nearness of You	196?	$12
❏ DS-2390 [S]	The Nearness of You	196?	$15
TIFTON			
❏ M-8002 [M]	Batman and Robin	1966	$30
❏ S-78002 [S]	Batman and Robin	1966	$40

DANA, BILL
See JOSE JIMENEZ.

DANA, VIC

Number	Title	Yr	NM
DOLTON			
❏ BLP-2041 [M]	Crystal Chandelier	1966	$18
❏ BST-8041 [S]	Crystal Chandelier	1966	$25
❏ BLP-2048 [M]	Golden Greats	1966	$18
❏ BST-8048 [S]	Golden Greats	1966	$25
❏ BLP-2049 [M]	Little Altar Boy and Other Christmas Songs	1966	$18
❏ BST-8049 [S]	Little Altar Boy and Other Christmas Songs	1966	$25
❏ BLP-2036 [M]	Moonlight and Roses	1965	$18
❏ BST-8036 [S]	Moonlight and Roses	1965	$25
❏ BLP-2026 [M]	More	1963	$18
❏ BST-8026 [S]	More	1963	$25
❏ BLP-2032 [M]	Now	1964	$18
❏ BST-8032 [S]	Now	1964	$25
❏ BLP-2034 [M]	Red Roses for a Blue Lady	1965	$18
❏ BST-8034 [S]	Red Roses for a Blue Lady	1965	$25
❏ BLP-2028 [M]	Shangri-La	1964	$18
❏ BST-8028 [S]	Shangri-La	1964	$25
❏ BLP-2013 [M]	This Is Vic Dana	1961	$75
❏ BST-8013 [S]	This Is Vic Dana	1961	$30
❏ BLP-2046 [M]	Town and Country	1966	$18
❏ BST-8046 [S]	Town and Country	1966	$25
❏ BLP-2015 [M]	Warm and Wild	1962	$18
❏ BST-8015 [S]	Warm and Wild	1962	$25
LIBERTY			
❏ LST-8063	If I Never Knew Your Name	1969	$15
❏ BST-8049 [S]	Little Altar Boy and Other Christmas Songs	1967	$15

—Liberty record in Dolton cover

Number	Title	Yr	NM
SUNSET			
❏ SUM-1182 [M]	On the Country Side	1967	$12
❏ SUS-5182 [S]	On the Country Side	1967	$15
❏ SUM-1130 [M]	Warm and Wonderful	196?	$12
❏ SUS-5130 [S]	Warm and Wonderful	196?	$15

DANCY, MEL

Number	Title	Yr	NM
MAINSTREAM			
❏ MRL-378	A Little Lovin'	1972	$30

Number	Title	Yr	NM
D'ANDREA, FRANCO			
RED			
❑ NS-201	My One and Only Love	198?	$30
❑ NS-202	No Idea of Time	1985	$30
DANE, BARBARA			
BARBARY COAST			
❑ 33014 [M]	Trouble in Mind	1959	$40
— Reissue of San Francisco LP			
CAPITOL			
❑ T1758 [M]	On My Way	1962	$150
❑ ST1758 [S]	On My Way	1962	$85
DOT			
❑ DLP-3177 [M]	Living with the Blues	1959	$175
❑ DLP-25177 [S]	Living with the Blues	1959	$100
FOLKWAYS			
❑ FA-2468	Barbara Dane and the Chambers Brothers	1966	$175
❑ FA-2471	Folk Songs	1966	$75
HORIZON			
❑ WP-1602 [M]	When I Was a Young Girl	1962	$75
❑ WPS-1602 [S]	When I Was a Young Girl	1962	$40
— Black vinyl			
❑ WPS-1602 [S]	When I Was a Young Girl	1962	$120
— Gold vinyl			
PAREDON			
❑ 1003	FTA! Songs of the GI Resistance	1970	$35
❑ 1014	I Hate the Capitalist System	1973	$35
❑ 1046	When We Make It Through	1982	$35
SAN FRANCISCO			
❑ 33014 [M]	Trouble in Mind	1957	$120
D'ANGELO			
VIRGIN			
❑ 48499	Voodoo	2000	$18
❑ SPRO14969 [DJ]	Voodoo DJ Soul Essentials	2000	$25
— Six-song promo-only sampler			
DANIEL, TED			
UJAMAA			
❑ 1001	Ted Daniel	197?	$30
DANIELS, CHARLIE, BAND			
KAMA SUTRA			
❑ KSBS EP-10 [PS] Volunteer Jam		1974	$3
— Picture sleeve with above bonus disc			
❑ KSBS EP-10	Volunteer Jam Part (1)/ Volunteer Jam Part (2)/ Volunteer Jam Part (3)	1974	$3
— Small hole, plays at 33 1/3 rpm; not issued separately; only released as bonus with Fire on the Mountain LP			
CAPITOL			
❑ ST-790	Charlie Daniels	1971	$30
❑ SN-16039	Charlie Daniels	1979	$10
— Budget-line reissue			
❑ ST-11414	Charlie Daniels	1975	$15
— Reissue of ST-790			
EPIC			
❑ FE38795	A Decade of Hits	1983	$12
❑ JE34365	Fire on the Mountain	1976	$12
— Reissue of Kama Sutra 2603 without bonus EP; orange label, no bar code on cover			
❑ PE34365	Fire on the Mountain	198?	$10
— Budget-line reissue			
❑ HE44365	Fire on the Mountain	1982	$40
— Half-speed mastered edition			
❑ FE36571 [B]	Full Moon	1980	$12
❑ PE36571	Full Moon	198?	$10
— Budget-line reissue			
❑ JE34377	High Lonesome	1976	$12
— Orange label, no bar code on cover			
❑ PE34377	High Lonesome	198?	$10
— Budget-line reissue			
❑ FE44324	Homesick Man	1988	$10
❑ AS586 [DJ]	Interchords	1979	$18
— Music and interviews; promo only			
❑ FE39878	Me and the Boys	1985	$12
❑ PE39878	Me and the Boys	198?	$10
— Budget-line reissue			
❑ JE34970	Midnight Wind	1977	$12
— Orange label, no bar code on cover			
❑ PE34970	Midnight Wind	198?	$10
— Budget-line reissue			
❑ JE35751	Million Mile Reflections	1979	$12
❑ PE35751	Million Mile Reflections	198?	$10
— Budget-line reissue			
❑ HE45751	Million Mile Reflections	1982	$40
— Half-speed mastered edition			
❑ JE34402	Nightrider	1977	$12
— Reissue of Kama Sutra 2607; orange label, no bar code on cover			
❑ PE34402	Nightrider	198?	$10

Number	Title	Yr	NM
— Budget-line reissue			
❑ FE40760	Powder Keg	1987	$10
❑ PE34150	Saddle Tramp	1976	$12
— Orange label, no bar code on cover			
❑ PE34150	Saddle Tramp	198?	$10
— With bar code on cover			
❑ FE45316	Simple Man	1989	$15
❑ JE34665	Te John, Grease and Wolfman	1977	$12
— Reissue of Kama Sutra 2060; orange label, no bar code on cover			
❑ PE34665	Te John, Grease and Wolfman	198?	$10
— Budget-line reissue			
❑ EAS1780 [DJ]	The Charlie Daniels Story	1990	$18
— Promo-only interview/radio show			
❑ JE34369	Uneasy Rider	1976	$12
— Reissue of Kama Sutra 2071 with new name; orange label, no bar code on cover			
❑ PE34369	Uneasy Rider	198?	$10
— Budget-line reissue			
❑ JE34664	Whiskey	1977	$12
— Reissue of Kama Sutra 2076 with new name; orange label, no bar code on cover			
❑ PE34664	Whiskey	198?	$10
— Budget-line reissue			
❑ FE37694	Windows	1982	$12
❑ PE37694	Windows	198?	$10
— Budget-line reissue			
KAMA SUTRA			
❑ KSBS2603	Fire on the Mountain	1974	$18
— Includes bonus EP, "Volunteer Jam" (deduct 20% if missing)			
❑ KSBS2071	Honey in the Rock	1973	$18
❑ KSBS2607	Nightrider	1975	$18
❑ KSBS2060	Te John, Grease and Wolfman	1972	$18
❑ KSBS2076	Way Down Yonder	1974	$18
MOBILE FIDELITY			
❑ 1-176	Million Mile Reflections	1984	$50
— Audiophile vinyl			
DANIELS, EDDIE			
CHOICE			
❑ 1002	A Flower for All Seasons	1974	$30
COLUMBIA			
❑ JC36290	Morning Thunder	1980	$25
GRP			
❑ GR-9584	Blackwood	1989	$30
❑ GR-1024	Breakthrough	198?	$25
❑ GR-1050	Memos from Paradise: The Music of Roger Kellaway	1988	$25
❑ GR-1034	To Bird with Love	1987	$25
MUSE			
❑ MR-5154	Brief Encounter	1978	$30
PRESTIGE			
❑ PRLP-7506 [M]	First Prize	1967	$40
❑ PRST-7506 [S]	First Prize	1967	$30
DANIELS, HALL			
JUMP			
❑ JL-9 [10]	Hall Daniels Septet	1955	$100
— Issued on blue vinyl			
DANIELS, MIKE, AND HIS DELTA JAZZMEN			
STOMP OFF			
❑ SOS-1203	Together Again -- Thirty Years On!	1991	$30
DANIELS, SLOPPY			
DOOTO			
❑ DTL-266 [M]	Sloppy's House Party	1959	$30
DANKO, HAROLD, AND KIRK LIGHTSEY			
SUNNYSIDE			
❑ SSC-1004	Shorter by Two	1985	$25
DANKO, HAROLD, AND RUFUS REID			
SUNNYSIDE			
❑ SSC-1001	Mirth Song	1985	$25
DANKO, HAROLD			
DREAMSTREET			
❑ 104	Coincidence	1980	$30
INNER CITY			
❑ IC-1069	Chasin' Bad Guys	1979	$30
❑ IC-1029	Harold Danko Quartet Featuring Gregory Herbert	1978	$30
SUNNYSIDE			
❑ SSC-1033	Alone But Not Forgotten	1989	$30
❑ SSC-1008	Ink and Water	1985	$25
DANKO, RICK			
Also see THE BAND.			

Number	Title	Yr	NM
ARISTA			
❑ AB4141	Rick Danko	1977	$15
DANKWORTH, JOHN			
DRG			
❑ MRS-507	Movies 'N' Me	198?	$25
FONTANA			
❑ SRF-67603	The Sophisticated Johnnie Dankworth	1969	$25
❑ MGF-27543 [M]	Zodiac Variations	1966	$35
❑ SRF-67543 [S]	Zodiac Variations	1966	$50
IAJRC			
❑ LP39	Johnny Dankworth's Big Band In the Fifties	198?	$25
MCA CLASSICS			
❑ 25932	Crossing Over the Bridge	1987	$25
ROULETTE			
❑ R-52059 [M]	Collaboration	1961	$25
❑ SR-52059 [S]	Collaboration	1961	$30
❑ R-52040 [M]	England's Ambassador of Jazz	1960	$25
❑ SR-52040 [S]	England's Ambassador of Jazz	1960	$30
❑ R-52096 [M]	Jazz from Abroad	1963	$25
❑ SR-52096 [S]	Jazz from Abroad	1963	$30
VERVE			
❑ MG V-20006 [M]	5 Steps to Dankworth	1957	$175
— Also contains several tracks by others who are performing songs Dankworth wrote			
DANKWORTH, JOHN/BILLY STRAYHORN			
ROULETTE			
❑ RE-121	Echoes of an Era	1973	$35
DANNY AND THE JUNIORS			
MCA			
❑ 1555	Rockin' with Danny and the Juniors	1987	$12
DANTE, RON			
HANDSHAKE			
❑ JW37341	Street Angel	1981	$15
KIRSHNER			
❑ KES-106	Ron Dante Brings You Up	1970	$25
DANTE			
MADISON			
❑ MA-LP1002 [M]	Dante and the Evergreens	1961	$550
DANZIG, GLENN			
Also see DANZIG; THE MISFITS. This is Glenn's classical album.			
PLAN 9			
❑ PL9-11 [B]	Black Aria	1992	$35
DANZIG			
Glenn Danzig was also in MISFITS and SAMHAIN.			
AMERICAN			
❑ 45647 [B]	4	1994	$30
DEF AMERICAN			
❑ DEF24208 [B]	Danzig	1988	$40
❑ DEF24281 [B]	Lucifuge	1990	$40
DAPOGNY, JIM, AND BUTCH THOMPSON			
STOMP OFF			
❑ SOS-1183	How Could We Be So Blue?	1988	$25
DAPOGNY, JIM			
JAZZOLOGY			
❑ J-140	Back Home in Illinois	1984	$25
❑ J-120	Jim Dapogny's Chicago Jazz Band	1983	$25
D'ARBY, TERENCE TRENT			
COLUMBIA			
❑ BFC40964	Introducing the Hardline According to Terence Trent D'Arby	1987	$15
❑ C45351	Neither Fish Nor Flesh	1989	$12
DARCEL, DENISE			
CAMEO			
❑ C-1002 [M]	Banned in Boston	1958	$40
DARCH, BOB			
UNITED ARTISTS			
❑ UAL-3120 [M]	Ragtime Piano	1960	$25
❑ UAS-6120 [S]	Ragtime Piano	1960	$30
DARDANELLE			
AUDIOPHILE			
❑ AP-191	A Woman's Intuition	198?	$25
❑ AP-214	Down Home	1985	$25
❑ AP-145	Echoes Singing Ladies	1982	$25

Number	Title	Yr	NM
❏ AP-32	Gold Braid	1983	$25
STASH			
❏ ST-202	Songs for New Lovers	1978	$25
❏ ST-217	The Colors of My Life	198?	$25

DARDANELLE AND VIVIAN LORD
STASH

Number	Title	Yr	NM
❏ ST-231	The Two of Us	1983	$25

DARENSBOURG, JOE
GHB

Number	Title	Yr	NM
❏ 90	Barrelhousin' with Joe	197?	$25
GNP CRESCENDO			
❏ GNP-515	Petite Fleur	197?	$25
❏ GNP-514	Yellow Dog Blues	197?	$25

DARGO, PHIL
GUINNESS

Number	Title	Yr	NM
❏ GNS36039 [B]	California Road	1977	$25

DARIN, BOBBY
ATCO

Number	Title	Yr	NM
❏ 33-102 [M]	Bobby Darin	1958	$150
— Yellow "harp" label			
❏ 33-102 [M]	Bobby Darin	1962	$30
— Gold and dark blue label			
❏ 33-140 [M]	Bobby Darin Sings Ray Charles	1962	$30
❏ SD 33-140 [S]	Bobby Darin Sings Ray Charles	1962	$30
❏ 33-122 [M]	Darin at the Copa	1960	$40
— Yellow "harp" label			
❏ 33-122 [M]	Darin at the Copa	1962	$25
— Gold and dark blue label			
❏ SD 33-122 [S]	Darin at the Copa	1960	$100
— Yellow "harp" label			
❏ SD 33-122 [S]	Darin at the Copa	1962	$30
— Purple and brown label			
❏ SP1001 [M]	For Teenagers Only	1960	$175
— Gatefold with fold-open poster and paper insert			
❏ SP1001 [M]	For Teenagers Only	1960	$85
— With extras missing			
❏ 33-124 [M]	It's You or No One	1960	$40
— Yellow "harp" label			
❏ 33-124 [M]	It's You or No One	1962	$25
— Gold and dark blue label			
❏ SD 33-124 [S]	It's You or No One	1960	$100
— Yellow "harp" label			
❏ SD 33-124 [S]	It's You or No One	1962	$30
— Purple and brown label			
❏ 33-134 [M]	Love Swings	1961	$40
— Yellow "harp" label			
❏ 33-134 [M]	Love Swings	1962	$25
— Gold and dark blue label			
❏ SD 33-134 [S]	Love Swings	1961	$50
— Yellow "harp" label			
❏ SD 33-134 [S]	Love Swings	1962	$30
— Purple and brown label			
❏ 33-104 [M]	That's All	1959	$40
— Yellow "harp" label			
❏ 33-104 [M]	That's All	1962	$25
— Gold and dark blue label			
❏ SD 33-104 [S]	That's All	1959	$150
— Yellow "harp" label			
❏ SD 33-104 [S]	That's All	1962	$30
— Purple and brown label			
❏ 33-125 [M]	The 25th Day of December	1960	$50
— Yellow "harp" label			
❏ SD 33-125 [S]	The 25th Day of December	1960	$75
— Yellow "harp" label			
❏ 33-125 [M]	The 25th Day of December	1962	$25
— Gold and dark blue label			
❏ SD 33-125 [S]	The 25th Day of December	1962	$30
— Gold and dark blue label			
❏ 33-131 [M]	The Bobby Darin Story	1961	$40
— Yellow "harp" label; white cover			
❏ 33-131 [M]	The Bobby Darin Story	1962	$25
— Gold and dark blue label; black cover			
❏ SD 33-131 [S]	The Bobby Darin Story	1961	$50
— Yellow "harp" label; white cover			
❏ SD 33-131 [S]	The Bobby Darin Story	1962	$30
— Purple and brown label; black cover			
❏ SD 33-131	The Bobby Darin Story	1969	$15
— Yellow label, "Atco" on left			
❏ SD 33-131	The Bobby Darin Story	1978	$10
— Any later Atco label			
❏ 33-146 [M]	Things & Other Things	1962	$30
❏ SD 33-146 [S]	Things & Other Things	1962	$30
❏ 33-115 [M]	This Is Darin	1960	$40
— Yellow "harp" label			
❏ 33-115 [M]	This Is Darin	1962	$25
— Gold and dark blue label			
❏ SD 33-115 [S]	This Is Darin	1960	$100
— Yellow "harp" label			

Number	Title	Yr	NM
❏ SD 33-115 [S]	This Is Darin	1960	$30
— Purple and brown label			
❏ 33-138 [M]	Twist with Bobby Darin	1961	$40
— Yellow "harp" label			
❏ 33-138 [M]	Twist with Bobby Darin	1962	$25
— Gold and dark blue label			
❏ SD 33-138 [S]	Twist with Bobby Darin	1961	$50
— Yellow "harp" label			
❏ SD 33-138 [S]	Twist with Bobby Darin	1962	$30
— Purple and brown label			
❏ 33-126 [M]	Two of a Kind	1961	$40
— Yellow "harp" label			
❏ 33-126 [M]	Two of a Kind	1962	$25
— Gold and dark blue label			
❏ SD 33-126 [S]	Two of a Kind	1961	$50
— Yellow "harp" label			
❏ SD 33-126 [S]	Two of a Kind	1962	$30
— Purple and brown label			
❏ 90484	Two of a Kind	1986	$12
❏ 33-167 [M]	Winners	1964	$30
❏ SD 33-167 [S]	Winners	1964	$30
ATLANTIC			
❏ 8154 [M]	Bobby Darin Sings Doctor Dolittle	1967	$18
❏ SD8154 [S]	Bobby Darin Sings Doctor Dolittle	1967	$18
❏ 8135 [M]	If I Were a Carpenter	1967	$18
❏ SD8135 [S]	If I Were a Carpenter	1967	$50
— Inexplicably rare in stereo			
❏ 8126 [M]	In a Broadway Bag	1966	$18
❏ SD8126 [S]	In a Broadway Bag	1966	$25
❏ 8142 [M]	Inside Out	1967	$18
❏ SD8142 [S]	Inside Out	1967	$30
❏ 8121 [M]	The Shadow of Your Smile	1966	$18
❏ SD8121 [S]	The Shadow of Your Smile	1966	$25
BAINBRIDGE			
❏ 6220	Bobby Darin at the Copa	1981	$12
CAPITOL			
❏ T1942 [M]	18 Yellow Roses	1963	$18
❏ ST1942 [S]	18 Yellow Roses	1963	$25
❏ T2084 [M]	As Long As I'm Singing	1964	$0
— Canceled			
❏ ST2084 [S]	As Long As I'm Singing	1964	$250
— Canceled; price is for an acetate, which is known to exist			
❏ T1826 [M]	Earthy	1963	$18
❏ ST1826 [S]	Earthy	1963	$25
❏ T2194 [M]	From Hello Dolly to Goodbye Charlie	1964	$18
❏ ST2194 [S]	From Hello Dolly to Goodbye Charlie	1964	$25
❏ T2007 [M]	Golden Folk Hits	1963	$18
❏ ST2007 [S]	Golden Folk Hits	1963	$25
❏ W1791 [M]	Oh! Look at Me Now	1962	$25
❏ SW1791 [S]	Oh! Look at Me Now	1962	$30
❏ T1791 [M]	Oh! Look at Me Now	1962	$18
❏ ST1791 [S]	Oh! Look at Me Now	1962	$25
❏ T2571 [M]	The Best of Bobby Darin	1966	$18
❏ ST2571 [S]	The Best of Bobby Darin	1966	$18
❏ T2322 [M]	Venice Blue	1965	$18
❏ ST2322 [S]	Venice Blue	1965	$25
❏ T1866 [M]	You're the Reason I'm Living	1963	$18
❏ ST1866 [S]	You're the Reason I'm Living	1963	$25
CLARION			
❏ 603 [M]	Clementine	1966	$25
❏ SD603 [S]	Clementine	1966	$30
DIRECTION			
❏ 1936	Born Walden Robert Cassotto	1968	$30
❏ 1937	Commitment	1969	$30
MOTOWN			
❏ M753L	Bobby Darin	1972	$25
❏ M6-813L	Darin 1936-1973	1974	$18
❏ M5-185V1	Darin 1936-1973	1981	$15
— Reissue			
❏ MS-739	Finally	1972	$500
— Unreleased; value is for RCA test pressing			

DARIUS
CHARTMAKER

Number	Title	Yr	NM
❏ 1102	Darius	1968	$500

DARK
CMP

Number	Title	Yr	NM
❏ 28	Dark	1987	$30

DARLING, DAVID
ECM

Number	Title	Yr	NM
❏ 1219	Cycles	198?	$25
❏ 1161	Journal October	1980	$30

DARLING, DENVER
AUDIO LAB

Number	Title	Yr	NM
❏ AL-1507 [M]	Songs of the Trail	1958	$150

DARNEL, BILL
X

Number	Title	Yr	NM
❏ LVA-(# unk) [10]	Bill Darnel Sings	1955	$40

Number	Title	Yr	NM
DARR, ALICE			
CHARLIE PARKER			
❏ PLP-611 [M]	I Only Know How to Cry	1962	$30
❏ PLP-611S [S]	I Only Know How to Cry	1962	$40

DARRELL, JOHNNY
CAPRICORN

Number	Title	Yr	NM
❏ CP 0154	Water Glass Full of Whiskey	1975	$12
SUNSET			
❏ SUS-5232	The Johnny Darrell Sound	1969	$12
UNITED ARTISTS			
❏ UAS6752	California Stop-Over	1970	$25
❏ UAS6594 [S]	Ruby, Don't Take Your Love to Town	1967	$25
❏ UAL3594 [M]	Ruby, Don't Take Your Love to Town	1967	$30
❏ UAS6759	The Best of Johnny Darrell, Volume 1	1970	$18
❏ UAS6634	The Son of Hickory Holler's Tramp	1968	$25
❏ UAS6707	Why You Been Gone So Long	1969	$25
❏ UAS6660	With Pen in Hand	1968	$25

DARREN, JAMES
COLPIX

Number	Title	Yr	NM
❏ CP-418 [M]	Gidget Goes Hawaiian (James Darren Sings the Movies)	1961	$30
❏ SCP-418 [S]	Gidget Goes Hawaiian (James Darren Sings the Movies)	1961	$40
❏ CP-406 [M]	James Darren (Album No. 1)	1960	$50
— Black vinyl			
❏ CP-406 [M]	James Darren (Album No. 1)	1960	$175
— Green vinyl			
❏ CP-424 [M]	James Darren Sings for All Sizes	1962	$30
❏ SCP-424 [S]	James Darren Sings for All Sizes	1962	$40
❏ CP-428 [M]	Love Among the Young	1962	$30
❏ SCP-428 [S]	Love Among the Young	1962	$40
KIRSHNER			
❏ KES-116	Love Songs from the Movies	1972	$18
❏ KES-115	Mammy Blue	1971	$18
WARNER BROS.			
❏ W1668 [M]	James Darren/All	1967	$18
❏ WS1668 [S]	James Darren/All	1967	$25

DARREN, JAMES/ SHELLEY FABARES/PAUL PETERSEN
COLPIX

Number	Title	Yr	NM
❏ CP-468 [M]	More Teenage Triangle	1964	$40
❏ SCP-468 [P]	More Teenage Triangle	1964	$75
❏ CP-444 [M]	Teenage Triangle	1963	$40
❏ SCP-444 [R]	Teenage Triangle	1963	$40

DARRIEU, DANIELLE
LONDON

Number	Title	Yr	NM
❏ LB-616 [10]	Le Voix de France	1954	$50

DARRIEUX, DANIELLE
CAPITOL

Number	Title	Yr	NM
❏ T10319 [M]	Incomparable Danielle Darrieux	1963	$25
❏ ST10319 [S]	Incomparable Danielle Darrieux	1963	$30

DARTELLS, THE
DOT

Number	Title	Yr	NM
❏ DLP-3522 [M]	Hot Pastrami	1963	$30
❏ DLP-25522 [S]	Hot Pastrami	1963	$40

DARTMOUTH INDIAN CHIEFS
TRANSITION

Number	Title	Yr	NM
❏ TRLP-23 [M]	Chiefly Jazz	1956	$120

DARTS, THE
DEL-FI

Number	Title	Yr	NM
❏ DFLP-1244 [M]	Hollywood Drag	1963	$75
❏ DFST-1244 [S]	Hollywood Drag	1963	$100

DASH, JULIAN
MASTER JAZZ

Number	Title	Yr	NM
❏ 8106	Portrait	1970	$25

DASHIEL, BUD, AND THE KINSMEN
WARNER BROS.

Number	Title	Yr	NM
❏ W1429 [M]	Folk Music in a Contemporary Manner	1961	$30
❏ WS1429 [S]	Folk Music in a Contemporary Manner	1961	$30
❏ W1432 [M]	Live Concert Extraordinaire -- Bud Dashiel and the Kinsmen Sing Everybody's Hits	1961	$30

Number	Title	Yr	NM
❏ WS1432 [S]	Live Concert Extraordinaire -- Bud Dashiel and the Kinsmen Sing Everybody's Hits	1961	$30

DAUGHERTY, JACK

A&M
| ❏ SP-3038 | Jack Daugherty and the Class of '71 | 1971 | $25 |

MONTEREY
| ❏ 100 | Carmel by the Sea | 1976 | $35 |

DAUGHTERS OF ALBION, THE

FONTANA
| ❏ SRF-67586 | The Daughters of Albion | 1968 | $40 |

DAVE & SUGAR

RCA VICTOR
❏ APL1-1818	Dave & Sugar	1976	$12
❏ AHL1-3915	Dave & Sugar/Greatest Hits	1981	$12
❏ AHL1-3823	New York Wine Tennessee Shine	1980	$12
❏ AHL1-3360	Stay with Me/Golden Tears	1979	$12
❏ APL1-2861	Tear Time	1978	$12
❏ APL1-2477	That's the Way Love Should Be	1976	$12

DAVE DEE, DOZY, BEAKY, MICK & TICH

FONTANA
| ❏ MGF-27567 [M] | Greatest Hits | 1967 | $40 |
| ❏ SRF-67567 [P] | Greatest Hits | 1967 | $40 |
—Bend It" and "Hold Tight" are rechanneled.

IMPERIAL
| ❏ LP-12402 [P] | Time to Take Off | 1968 | $75 |
—Zabadak" is rechanneled.

DAVENPORT, WALLACE

GHB
| ❏ 146 | Darkness on the Delta | 198? | $25 |

DAVEY AND THE BADMEN

GOTHIC
| ❏ KRW-054 | Wanted | 1963 | $250 |

DAVID, THE

V.M.C.
| ❏ 124 | Another Day, Another Lifetime | 1968 | $250 |
—Mono and stereo versions same price

DAVID AND DAVID

A&M
| ❏ R183799 | Boomtown | 1987 | $15 |
—RCA Music Service edition
| ❏ SP5134 | Boomtown | 1986 | $12 |

DAVID AND JONATHAN

CAPITOL
| ❏ T2473 [M] | Michelle | 1966 | $18 |
| ❏ ST2473 [S] | Michelle | 1966 | $25 |

DAVIDSON, JOHN

20TH CENTURY
| ❏ T-512 | Every Time I Sing | 1976 | $12 |
| ❏ T-429 | Touch Me | 1974 | $12 |

ACCORD
| ❏ SN-7202 | Closeup | 1981 | $10 |

COLPIX
| ❏ CP-485 [M] | The Young Warm Sound of John Davidson | 1964 | $18 |
| ❏ SCP-485 [S] | The Young Warm Sound of John Davidson | 1964 | $25 |

COLUMBIA
❏ CL2734 [M]	A Kind of Hush	1967	$12
❏ CS9534 [S]	A Kind of Hush	1967	$15
❏ C30098	Everything Is Beautiful	1970	$12
❏ CS9654	Goin' Places	1968	$12
❏ PC36956	Incredible	1981	$10
❏ CS9795	John Davidson	1969	$12
❏ CL2648 [M]	My Best to You	1967	$12
❏ CS9448 [S]	My Best to You	1967	$15
❏ CS9859	My Cherie Amour	1969	$12
❏ CS9864	My Christmas Favorites	1969	$15
❏ CL2580 [M]	The Time of My Life	1966	$12
❏ CS9380 [S]	The Time of My Life	1966	$15

MERCURY
| ❏ SRM-1-658 | Well, Here I Am | 1973 | $12 |

DAVIDSON, LOWELL

ESP-DISK'
| ❏ 1012 [M] | Lowell Davidson Trio | 1965 | $150 |
| ❏ S-1012 [S] | Lowell Davidson Trio | 1965 | $150 |

DAVIE, HUTCH

ATCO
| ❏ 33-105 [M] | Much Hutch | 1958 | $75 |

DAVIES, DAVE
Also see THE KINKS.

RCA VICTOR
| ❏ AFL1-3603 | AFL1-3603 | 1980 | $12 |
| ❏ AFL1-4036 | Glamour | 1981 | $12 |

WARNER BROS.
| ❏ 23917 | Chosen People | 1983 | $12 |

DAVIES, GAIL

LIFESONG
| ❏ KZ35504 | Gail Davies | 1978 | $18 |

MCA
| ❏ 42274 | Pretty Words | 1989 | $12 |

RCA VICTOR
| ❏ AHL1-5187 | Where Is a Woman to Go | 1984 | $10 |

WARNER BROS.
❏ BSK3636	Givin' Herself Away	1982	$12
❏ BSK3509	I'll Be There	1981	$12
❏ BSK3395	The Game	1980	$12
❏ 23972	What Can I Say	1983	$12

DAVIS, ANTHONY

GRAMAVISION
❏ 8101	Episteme	1981	$30
❏ 8303	Hemispheres	1983	$30
❏ 8201	I've Known Rivers	1982	$30
❏ 8401	Middle Passage	1984	$30
❏ R1-79441	Trio Squared	1989	$30
❏ 8612	Undine	1986	$30

INDIA NAVIGATION
❏ IN-1041	Hidden Voices	1979	$35
❏ IN-1047	Lady in the Mirror	1980	$35
❏ IN-1036	Songs for the Old World	1978	$35
❏ IN-1056	Variations in Dream-Time	1981	$35

PAUSA
| ❏ 7120 | Under the Double Moon | 198? | $25 |

SACKVILLE
| ❏ 3020 | Of Blues and Dreams | 198? | $25 |

DAVIS, ART

INTERPLAY
| ❏ 7728 | Reemergence | 197? | $30 |

SOUL NOTE
| ❏ 121143 | Life | 198? | $30 |

DAVIS, BOB

STEPHENY
| ❏ MF-4000 [M] | Jazz in Orbit | 1958 | $75 |
| ❏ MFS-8003 [S] | Jazz in Orbit | 1960 | $50 |

ZEPHYR
| ❏ 12001 [M] | Jazz from the North Coast | 1959 | $50 |

DAVIS, CHARLES

STRATA-EAST
| ❏ 7425 | Ingia! | 1974 | $35 |

WEST 54
| ❏ 8006 | Dedicated to Tadd | 1979 | $30 |

DAVIS, DANNY, AND THE NASHVILLE BRASS

PICKWICK
| ❏ ACL-7034 | Down Yonder | 197? | $10 |
| ❏ ACL-7048 | Super Country | 1977 | $10 |

RCA SPECIAL PRODUCTS
| ❏ DPL1-0176 | America 200 Years Young | 1976 | $18 |
—Available only at Amana dealers

RCA VICTOR
❏ APL1-0565	Bluegrass Country	1974	$12
❏ APD1-0565 [Q]	Bluegrass Country	1974	$20
❏ APL1-0232	Cairbbean Cruise	1973	$12
❏ APD1-0232 [Q]	Cairbbean Cruise	1973	$20
❏ LSP-4377	Christmas with Danny Davis and the Nashville Brass	1970	$12
❏ ANL1-1930	Christmas with Danny Davis and the Nashville Brass	1976	$10
—Reissue of LSP-4377
❏ APL1-2980	Cookin' Country	1978	$12
❏ AHL1-4022	Cotton Eyed Joe	1981	$12
❏ LSP-4424	Down Homers	1970	$12
❏ APL1-1043	Dream Country	1975	$12
❏ APD1-1043 [Q]	Dream Country	1975	$18
❏ APL1-1240	Gold	1975	$12
❏ APD1-1240 [Q]	Gold	1975	$18
❏ AHL1-3415	Great Songs of the Big Band Era	1979	$12
❏ APL1-2721	How I Love Them Ol' Songs	1977	$12
❏ LSP-4720	Live -- In Person	1972	$12
❏ APL1-2310	Live Vegas	1977	$12
❏ LSP-4176	More Nashville Sounds	1969	$12
❏ LSP-4232	Movin' On	1969	$12
❏ ANL1-0902	Orange Blossom Special	1974	$12

Number	Title	Yr	NM
❏ LSP-4475	Somethin' Else	1971	$12
❏ APL1-1986	Super	1976	$12
❏ LSP-4571	Super Country	1971	$12
❏ APL1-1578	Texas	1976	$12
❏ APD1-1578 [Q]	Texas	1976	$18
❏ APL1-0425	The Best of Danny Davis and the Nashville Brass	1973	$12
❏ APL1-0774	The Latest and Greatest	1974	$12
❏ APD1-0774 [Q]	The Latest and Greatest	1974	$20
❏ LSP-4059	The Nashville Sound	1969	$12
❏ APD1-0034 [Q]	Travelin'	1973	$18
❏ LSP-4803	Turn On Some Happy!	1972	$12
❏ LSP-4627	Turns to Gold	1972	$12
❏ LSP-4334	You Ain't Heard Nothin' Yet	1970	$12

DAVIS, EDDIE "LOCKJAW", AND HARRY "SWEETS" EDISON

PABLO
| ❏ 2310882 | Jazz at the Philharmonic 1983 | 1983 | $30 |

STORYVILLE
| ❏ 4004 | Eddie "Lockjaw" Davis and Harry "Sweets" Edison | 197? | $30 |

DAVIS, EDDIE "LOCKJAW", AND JOHNNY GRIFFIN

FANTASY
| ❏ OJC-264 | Griff & Lock | 1987 | $25 |

JAZZLAND
❏ JLP-60 [M]	Blues Up and Down	1961	$40
❏ JLP-960 [S]	Blues Up and Down	1961	$50
❏ JLP-42 [M]	Griff & Lock	1961	$40
❏ JLP-942 [S]	Griff & Lock	1961	$50
❏ JLP-39 [M]	Lookin' at Monk	1961	$40
❏ JLP-939 [S]	Lookin' at Monk	1961	$50
❏ JLP-76 [M]	Tough Tenor Favorites	1962	$40
❏ JLP-976 [S]	Tough Tenor Favorites	1962	$50
❏ JLP-31 [M]	Tough Tenors	1960	$40
❏ JLP-931 [S]	Tough Tenors	1960	$50

MILESTONE
| ❏ 47035 | The Toughest Tenors | 198? | $35 |

PAUSA
| ❏ 7062 | The Tough Tenors Again 'n' Again | 197? | $25 |

PRESTIGE
❏ PRLP-7282 [M]	Battle Stations	1963	$30
❏ PRST-7282 [S]	Battle Stations	1963	$40
❏ 24099	Live at Minton's	197?	$35
❏ PRLP-7407 [M]	The Breakfast Show	1965	$30
—Reissue of 7191
❏ PRST-7407 [S]	The Breakfast Show	1965	$30
❏ PRLP-7309 [M]	The First Set -- Recorded Live at Minton's	1964	$30
❏ PRST-7309 [S]	The First Set -- Recorded Live at Minton's	1964	$40
❏ PRLP-7357 [M]	The Late Show -- Recorded Live!	1965	$30
❏ PRST-7357 [S]	The Late Show -- Recorded Live!	1965	$30
❏ PRLP-7330 [M]	The Midnight Show at Minton's Playhouse	1964	$30
❏ PRST-7330 [S]	The Midnight Show at Minton's Playhouse	1964	$30
❏ PRLP-7191 [M]	The Tenor Scene	1961	$175

DAVIS, EDDIE "LOCKJAW", AND SHIRLEY SCOTT

FANTASY
| ❏ OJC-216 | Jaws | 198? | $25 |
| ❏ OJC-322 | Jaws in Orbit | 1988 | $25 |

MOODSVILLE
| ❏ MVLP-4 [M] | Eddie "Lockjaw" Davis with Shirley Scott | 1960 | $50 |
—Green label
| ❏ MVLP-4 [M] | Eddie "Lockjaw" Davis with Shirley Scott | 1965 | $30 |
—Blue label, trident logo on right
| ❏ MVLP-30 [M] | Misty | 1963 | $50 |
—Green label
| ❏ MVLP-30 [M] | Misty | 1965 | $30 |
—Blue label, trident logo on right
| ❏ MVST-30 [S] | Misty | 1963 | $50 |
—Green label
| ❏ MVST-30 [S] | Misty | 1965 | $30 |
—Blue label, trident logo on right

PRESTIGE
❏ PRLP-7178 [M]	Bacalao	1960	$100
❏ PRLP-7154 [M]	Jaws	1959	$250
❏ PRLP-7171 [M]	Jaws in Orbit	1959	$250
❏ PRLP-7301 [M]	Smokin'	1964	$40
❏ PRST-7301 [S]	Smokin'	1964	$30
❏ PRST-7710	The Best of Eddie "Lockjaw" Davis with Shirley Scott	1970	$35

DAVIS, EDDIE "LOCKJAW"

BETHLEHEM
| ❏ BCP-6035 [M] | Eddie's Function | 197? | $35 |
—Reissue material, distributed by RCA Victor
| ❏ BCP-6069 [M] | The Best of Eddie "Lockjaw" Davis | 1963 | $250 |

Number	Title	Yr	NM
BCPS-6069 [R]	The Best of Eddie "Lockjaw" Davis	196?	$25
CLASSIC JAZZ			
116	Sweet and Lovely	197?	$30
ENJA			
3097	Jaws' Blues	1981	$30
FANTASY			
OJC-403	Afro-Jaws	1989	$30
OJC-384	Montreux '77	1989	$30
OJC-629	Straight Ahead	1991	$30
OJC-652	The Eddie "Lockjaw" Davis Cookbook, Vol. 1	1991	$30
OJC-653	The Eddie "Lockjaw" Davis Cookbook, Vol. 2	1991	$30
OJC-429	Trane Whistle	1990	$30
INNER CITY			
IC-2058	Swingin' Till the Girls Come Home	1976	$35
JAZZLAND			
JLP-97 [M]	Alma Alegre	1962	$30
JLP-997 [S]	Alma Alegre	1962	$30
KING			
599 [M]	Big Beat Jazz	1958	$150
566 [M]	Jazz with a Beat	1957	$150
395-526 [M]	Jazz with a Horn	1957	$150
395-506 [M]	Modern Jazz Expression	1956	$300
637 [M]	This and That	1959	$150
606 [M]	Uptown	1958	$150
MUSE			
MR-5202	Heavy Hitter	1979	$30
PABLO			
2310778	Straight Ahead	197?	$35
2405414	The Best of Eddie "Lockjaw" Davis	198?	$25
PABLO LIVE			
2308214	Montreux '77	1978	$30
PRESTIGE			
PRLP-7242 [M]	Goin' to the Meeting	1962	$175
PRST-7242 [S]	Goin' to the Meeting	1962	$175
PRST-7660	In the Kitchen	1969	$35

— *Reissue of 7141 in (rechanneled?) stereo*

Number	Title	Yr	NM
PRLP-7261 [M]	I Only Have Eyes for You	1963	$40
PRST-7261 [S]	I Only Have Eyes for You	1963	$50
PRST-7834	Stolen Moments	197?	$35

— *Reissue of 7206 in (rechanneled?) stereo*

Number	Title	Yr	NM
PRLP-7141 [M]	The Eddie "Lockjaw" Davis Cookbook	1958	$250

— *Cover photo features Davis with no hat*

Number	Title	Yr	NM
PRLP-7141 [M]	The Eddie "Lockjaw" Davis Cookbook	1959	$50

— *Cover photo features Davis with hat*

Number	Title	Yr	NM
24039	The Eddie "Lockjaw" Davis Cookbook	197?	$50
PRLP-7161 [M]	The Eddie "Lockjaw" Davis Cookbook, Vol. 2	1959	$150
PRLP-7219 [M]	The Eddie "Lockjaw" Davis Cookbook, Vol. 3	1961	$175
PRST-7219 [S]	The Eddie "Lockjaw" Davis Cookbook, Vol. 3	1961	$175
PRST-7782	The Rev.	197?	$35

— *Reissue of 7161 in (rechanneled?) stereo*

Number	Title	Yr	NM
PRLP-7271 [M]	Trackin'	1963	$40
PRST-7271 [S]	Trackin'	1963	$50
PRLP-7206 [M]	Trane Whistle	1961	$175
RCA VICTOR			
LPM-3652 [M]	Lock the Fox	1966	$25
LSP-3652 [S]	Lock the Fox	1966	$30
LPM-3882 [M]	Love Calls	1967	$30
LSP-3882 [S]	Love Calls	1967	$25
LPM-3741 [M]	The Fox and the Hounds	1967	$30
LSP-3741 [S]	The Fox and the Hounds	1967	$25
RIVERSIDE			
RLP-373 [M]	Afro-Jaws	1961	$250
RS-9373 [S]	Afro-Jaws	1961	$250
RLP-430 [M]	Jawbreakers	1962	$175
RS-9430 [S]	Jawbreakers	1962	$175
ROOST			
RST-2227 [M]	Eddie Davis Trio	1957	$150
LP-422 [10]	Goodies	1954	$175
ROULETTE			
R-52007 [M]	Count Basie Presents Eddie Davis	1958	$75

— *White label with color spokes*

Number	Title	Yr	NM
R-52007 [M]	Count Basie Presents Eddie Davis	1963	$30

— *Orange and yellow "roulette wheel" label*

Number	Title	Yr	NM
SR-52007 [S]	Count Basie Presents Eddie Davis	1959	$50

— *White label with color spokes*

Number	Title	Yr	NM
SR-52007 [S]	Count Basie Presents Eddie Davis	1963	$25

— *Orange and yellow "roulette wheel" label*

Number	Title	Yr	NM
R-52019 [M]	Eddie Davis Trio	1959	$75

— *White label with color spokes*

Number	Title	Yr	NM
R-52019 [M]	Eddie Davis Trio	1963	$30

— *Orange and yellow "roulette wheel" label*

Number	Title	Yr	NM
SR-52019 [S]	Eddie Davis Trio	1959	$50

— *White label with color spokes*

Number	Title	Yr	NM
SR-52019 [S]	Eddie Davis Trio	1963	$25

— *Orange and yellow "roulette wheel" label*

Number	Title	Yr	NM
STEEPLECHASE			
SCS-1181	All of Me	198?	$25
SCS-1058	Swingin' Till the Girls Come Home	198?	$25

DAVIS, EDDY

Number	Title	Yr	NM
JAZZOLOGY			
J-67	Eddy Davis and His Hot Jazz Orchestra	1979	$25
J-88	Eddy Davis and His Hot Jazz Orchestra	1982	$25

DAVIS, JACKIE

Number	Title	Yr	NM
CAPITOL			
T815 [M]	Chasing Shadows	1957	$75

— *Turquoise or gray label*

Number	Title	Yr	NM
T1180 [M]	Jackie Davis Meets the Trombones	1959	$75

— *Black colorband label, logo at left*

DAVIS, JESSE ED

Number	Title	Yr	NM
ATCO			
SD 33-346	Jesse Ed Davis	1970	$18
SD 33-382	Ululu	1972	$18
EPIC			
KE32133	Keep On Comin'	1973	$15

DAVIS, JIMMIE

Number	Title	Yr	NM
DECCA			
DL4868 [M]	Going Home for Christmas	1967	$18
DL74868 [S]	Going Home for Christmas	1967	$15
DL8786 [M]	Hail Him with a Song	1958	$30
DL8572 [M]	Hymn Time	1957	$30
DL4587 [M]	It's Christmas Time Again	1964	$15
DL74587 [S]	It's Christmas Time Again	1964	$18
DL8174 [M]	Near the Cross	1955	$30
DL8953 [M]	Suppertime	1960	$25
DL78953 [S]	Suppertime	1960	$30
DL8729 [M]	The Door Is Always Open	1958	$30
DL8896 [M]	You Are My Sunshine	1959	$25
DL78896 [S]	You Are My Sunshine	1959	$30

DAVIS, JOHNNY "SCAT

Number	Title	Yr	NM
KING			
626 [M]	Here's Lookin' Atcha	1959	$100

DAVIS, LINK

Number	Title	Yr	NM
MERCURY			
SR-61243	Cajun Crawdaddy	1969	$25

DAVIS, MAC

Number	Title	Yr	NM
ACCORD			
SN-7165	Little Touch of Love	1981	$10
SN-7189	With Love	1981	$10
ALLEGIANCE			
AV-5031	Losers	198?	$10
AV-5019	Volume XC	198?	$10
CASABLANCA			
NBLP7207	It's Hard to Be Humble	1980	$10
NBLP7257	Midnight Crazy	1981	$10
NBLP7239	Texas in My Rear View Mirror	1980	$10
822638-1	The Very Best and More	1984	$10
COLUMBIA			
PC32927	All the Love in the World	1975	$12
PCQ32927 [Q]	All the Love in the World	1975	$20
KC31770	Baby Don't Get Hooked on Me	1972	$12
CQ31770 [Q]	Baby Don't Get Hooked on Me	1972	$20
PC33551	Burnin' Thing	1975	$12
JC35284	Fantasy	1978	$12
PC34105	Forever Lovers	1976	$12
PCQ34105 [Q]	Forever Lovers	1976	$0

— *Not released*

Number	Title	Yr	NM
JC36317	Greatest Hits	1979	$12
PC36317	Greatest Hits	198?	$10

— *Budget-line reissue*

Number	Title	Yr	NM
C30926	I Believe in Music	1971	$12
KC32206	Mac Davis	1973	$12
CS9969	Song Painter	1970	$18

— *Red "360 Sound" label*

Number	Title	Yr	NM
CS9969	Song Painter	1974	$12

— *Orange label*

Number	Title	Yr	NM
KC32582	Stop and Smell the Roses	1974	$12
PC32582	Stop and Smell the Roses	1986	$10

— *Budget-line reissue*

Number	Title	Yr	NM
CQ32582 [Q]	Stop and Smell the Roses	1974	$20
PC34313	Thunder in the Afternoon	1976	$12
PCQ34313 [Q]	Thunder in the Afternoon	1976	$20
FC38950	Who's Lovin' You	1983	$10
PC38950	Who's Lovin' You	198?	$10

— *Budget-line reissue*

Number	Title	Yr	NM
MCA			
5718	Somewhere in America	1986	$10
5590	Till I Made It with You	1985	$10
SPRINGBOARD			
SPB-4024	Mac Davis	197?	$10
TRIP			
9502	Mac Davis	1973	$10

DAVIS, MARTHA
Also see THE MOTELS.

Number	Title	Yr	NM
CAPITOL			
CLT-48054	Policy	1988	$15
CLT-79197/8 [DJ]	Policy (Radio Cue Card)	1987	$30

DAVIS, MAXWELL

Number	Title	Yr	NM
ALADDIN			
LP-709 [10]	Maxwell Davis	1955	$400
LP-804 [M]	Maxwell Davis	1956	$250
SCORE			
SLP-4106 [M]	Blue Tango	1957	$250

DAVIS, MEL

Number	Title	Yr	NM
EPIC			
LN3268 [M]	Trumpet with a Soul	1956	$100
RCA CAMDEN			
CAL-2127 [M]	The Big Ones of '66	1966	$30
CAS-2127 [S]	The Big Ones of '66	1966	$35
TIME			
52087 [M]	Shoot the Trumpet Player	1962	$25
S-2087 [S]	Shoot the Trumpet Player	1962	$30
52117 [M]	We Like Broadway	1963	$25
S-2117 [S]	We Like Broadway	1963	$30

DAVIS, MILES, AND JOHN COLTRANE

Number	Title	Yr	NM
MOODSVILLE			
MVLP-32 [M]	Miles Davis and John Coltrane Play Richard Rodgers	1963	$150

— *Green label*

Number	Title	Yr	NM
MVLP-32 [M]	Miles Davis and John Coltrane Play Richard Rodgers	1965	$75

— *Blue label, trident logo at right*

Number	Title	Yr	NM
PRESTIGE			
PRLP-7322 [M]	Miles Davis and John Coltrane Play Rodgers and Hart	1964	$40
PRST-7322 [R]	Miles Davis and John Coltrane Play Rodgers and Hart	1964	$50

DAVIS, MILES, AND MARCUS MILLER

Number	Title	Yr	NM
WARNER BROS.			
25655	Music from Siesta	1987	$35

DAVIS, MILES, AND TADD DAMERON

Number	Title	Yr	NM
COLUMBIA			
JC34804	Paris Festival International, May 1949	1978	$50

DAVIS, MILES, AND THELONIOUS MONK

Number	Title	Yr	NM
COLUMBIA			
CL2178 [M]	Miles and Monk at Newport	1964	$40

— *Guaranteed High Fidelity" on label*

Number	Title	Yr	NM
CL2178 [M]	Miles and Monk at Newport	1965	$75

— *360 Sound Mono" on label*

Number	Title	Yr	NM
CS8978 [S]	Miles and Monk at Newport	1964	$120

— *360 Sound Stereo" in black on label*

Number	Title	Yr	NM
CS8978 [S]	Miles and Monk at Newport	1965	$75

— *360 Sound Stereo" in white on label*

Number	Title	Yr	NM
KCS8978	Miles and Monk at Newport	1974	$25

— *Orange label, new prefix*

Number	Title	Yr	NM
PC8978	Miles and Monk at Newport	1977	$20

— *Orange label, new prefix; some have bar codes*

Number	Title	Yr	NM
PC8978	Miles and Monk at Newport	199?	$30

— *180-gram reissue*

DAVIS, MILES

Number	Title	Yr	NM
ALA			
AJ-503	Archives of Jazz, Vol. 3	198?	$30
BLUE NOTE			
BLP-5022 [10]	Miles Davis, Vol. 2	1953	$1000
BLP-5040 [10]	Miles Davis, Vol. 3	1954	$1000
BLP-1501 [M]	Miles Davis, Volume 1	1955	$800

— *Deep groove" version; Lexington Ave. address on label*

Number	Title	Yr	NM
BLP-1501 [M]	Miles Davis, Volume 1	1958	$800

— *Deep groove" version, W. 63rd St. address on label*

Number	Title	Yr	NM
BLP-1501 [M]	Miles Davis, Volume 1	1958	$200

— *Regular version, W. 63rd St. address on label*

Number	Title	Yr	NM
BLP-1501 [M]	Miles Davis, Volume 1	1963	$100

— *New York, USA" address on label*

Number	Title	Yr	NM
BLP-1501 [M]	Miles Davis, Volume 1	1966	$150

— *With "A Division of Liberty Records" on label*

Number	Title	Yr	NM
BLP-81501 [B]	Miles Davis, Volume 1	1968	$75

— *Rechanneled stereo version of 1501*

Number	Title	Yr	NM
❏ BST-81501	Miles Davis, Volume 1	1985	$30

— The Finest in Jazz Since 1939" reissue label

❏ BLP-1502 [M]	Miles Davis, Volume 2	1955	$500

— Deep groove" version; Lexington Ave. address on label

❏ BLP-1502 [M]	Miles Davis, Volume 2	1955	$550

— Deep groove" version; W. 63rd St. address on label

❏ BLP-1502 [M]	Miles Davis, Volume 2	1958	$200

— Regular version, W. 63rd St. address on label

❏ BLP-1502 [M]	Miles Davis, Volume 2	1963	$100

— With New York, USA address on label

❏ BLP-1502 [M]	Miles Davis, Volume 2	1966	$150

— With "A Division of Liberty Records" on label

❏ BLP-81502 [B]	Miles Davis, Volume 2	1968	$75

— Rechanneled stereo version of 1502

❏ BST-81502	Miles Davis, Volume 2	1985	$30

— The Finest in Jazz Since 1939" reissue label

❏ BLP-5013 [10]	Miles Davis (Young Man with a Horn)	1952	$1000

BOOK-OF-THE-MONTH CLUB

❏ 91-7725	Master of Styles	198?	$40

CAPITOL

❏ T762 [M]	Birth of the Cool	1956	$300

— Turquoise label

❏ T1974 [M]	Birth of the Cool	1963	$75

— Reissue of 762; black label with rainbow ring, Capitol logo at top

❏ DT1974 [R]	Birth of the Cool	1963	$85
❏ T762 [M]	Birth of the Cool	1958	$300

— Black label wirh rainbow ring, Capitol logo at left

❏ T762 [M]	Birth of the Cool	2003	$40

— Classic Records reissue on 200-gram vinyl

❏ H459 [10]	Classics in Jazz	1954	$300

— First 33 1/3 rpm issue of some of the "Birth of the Cool" sessions

❏ M-11026 [M]	The Complete Birth of the Cool	1972	$100
❏ N-16168 [M]	The Complete Birth of the Cool	198?	$25

— Budget-line reissue

CHARLIE PARKER

❏ PLP-824	Many Miles of Davis	196?	$150

COLUMBIA

❏ PG33967	Agharta	1976	$40
❏ KC30455	A Tribute to Jack Johnson	1971	$50

— Original issue

❏ PC30455	A Tribute to Jack Johnson	1977	$20

— Orange label, new prefix; some with bar codes

❏ PC30455	A Tribute to Jack Johnson	199?	$30

— 180-gram reissue

❏ C2X45332	Aura	1989	$75
❏ C32025	Basic Miles -- The Classic Performances of Miles Davis	1973	$50

— Original prefix

❏ PC32025	Basic Miles -- The Classic Performances of Miles Davis	198?	$20

— Budget-line reissue; bar code on cover

❏ PC32025	Basic Miles -- The Classic Performances of Miles Davis	199?	$30

— 180-gram reissue

❏ CG32866	Big Fun	1974	$75

— Original prefix

❏ PG32866	Big Fun	1977	$35

— Orange labels, new prefix

❏ GP26	Bitches Brew	1970	$120

— 360 Sound Stereo" on red labels

❏ GP26	Bitches Brew	1970	$75

— Orange labels; no bar code on cover

❏ GQ30997 [Q]	Bitches Brew	1972	$175
❏ PG26	Bitches Brew	1977	$50

— Orange labels, new prefix; some have bar code on cover

❏ KC236278	Circle in the Round	1980	$50
❏ FC38991	Decoy	1984	$30

— Original issue

❏ FC38991	Decoy	199?	$30

— 180-gram reissue

❏ KC236472	Directions	1981	$50
❏ CL2350 [M]	E.S.P.	1965	$75

— Guaranteed High Fidelity" on label

❏ CL2350 [M]	E.S.P.	1965	$50

— 360 Sound Mono" on label

❏ CS9150 [S]	E.S.P.	1965	$120

— 360 Sound Stereo" in black on label

❏ CS9150 [S]	E.S.P.	1965	$150

— 360 Sound Stereo" in white on label

❏ CS9150	E.S.P.	1971	$50

— Orange label

❏ KCS9150	E.S.P.	1974	$35

— Orange label, new prefix

❏ PC9150	E.S.P.	1977	$20

— Orange label, new prefix; some have bar code on back

❏ PC9150	E.S.P.	199?	$30

— 180-gram reissue

❏ J1	Facets	1973	$30
❏ CS9750	Filles de Kilimanjaro	1969	$50

— 360 Sound Stereo" on red label

❏ CS9750	Filles de Kilimanjaro	1971	$30

— Orange label

❏ KCS9750	Filles de Kilimanjaro	1974	$25

— Orange label, new prefix

❏ PC9750	Filles de Kilimanjaro	1977	$20

— Orange label, new prefix; some have bar codes

❏ PC9750	Filles de Kilimanjaro	199?	$30

— 180-gram reissue

❏ CL2453 [M]	Four" & More -- Recorded Live in Concert	1966	$75
❏ CS9253 [S]	Four" & More -- Recorded Live in Concert	1966	$75

— 360 Sound Stereo" on red label

❏ CS9253	Four" & More -- Recorded Live in Concert	1971	$35

— Orange label

❏ KCS9253	Four" & More -- Recorded Live in Concert	1974	$30

— Orange label, new prefix

❏ PC9253	Four" & More -- Recorded Live in Concert	1977	$20

— Orange label, new prefix; some have bar codes

❏ PC9253	Four" & More -- Recorded Live in Concert	199?	$30

— 180-gram reissue

❏ KG33236	Get Up With It	1974	$75

— Original prefix

❏ PG33236	Get Up With It	1977	$50

— Orange labels, new prefix

❏ C238506	Heard 'Round the World	1983	$50
❏ CS9875	In a Silent Way	1969	$40

— 360 Sound Stereo" on red label

❏ CS9875	In a Silent Way	1971	$50

— Orange label

❏ KCS9875	In a Silent Way	1974	$30

— Orange label, new prefix

❏ PC9875	In a Silent Way	1977	$20

— Orange label, new prefix; some have bar codes

❏ KG32092	In Concert	1973	$75
❏ PG32092	In Concert	1977	$35

— Orange labels, new prefix

❏ S30455	Jack Johnson	1971	$150

— Original issue on gray "Masterworks" label

❏ C32470	Jazz at the Plaza, Vol. 1	1973	$50

— Original prefix

❏ PC32470	Jazz at the Plaza, Vol. 1	1977	$20

— Reissue with new prefix; some have bar codes

❏ PC32470	Jazz at the Plaza, Vol. 1	199?	$30

— 180-gram reissue

❏ CL1268 [M]	Jazz Track	1958	$200

— Red and black label with six "eye" logos; with abstract drawing on cover

❏ CL1268 [M]	Jazz Track	1958	$140

— Red and black label with six "eye" logos; with Miles and a woman on cover

❏ CL1355 [M]	Kind of Blue	1959	$600

— Red and black label with six "eye" logos

❏ CL1355 [M]	Kind of Blue	1963	$150

— Guaranteed High Fidelity" on label

❏ CL1355 [M]	Kind of Blue	1965	$75

— 360 Sound Mono" on label

❏ CS8163 [S]	Kind of Blue	1959	$300

— Black and red label with "Stereo Fidelity" at top and "Columbia" in white at bottom; six white "eye" logos on label

❏ CS8163 [S]	Kind of Blue	1963	$120

— 360 Sound Stereo" in black on label

❏ CS8163 [S]	Kind of Blue	1965	$40

— 360 Sound Stereo" in white on label

❏ CS8163	Kind of Blue	1971	$50

— Orange label

❏ KCS8163	Kind of Blue	1974	$30

— Orange label, new prefix

❏ PC8163	Kind of Blue	1977	$20

— Orange label, new prefix; some have bar codes

❏ CS8163	Kind of Blue	1997	$175

— Contains both the original Side 1, which was mastered slightly fast, and the "correct" Side 1 (as Side 3), with an alternate take of "Flamenco Sketches" on Side 4 (at 45 rpm); distributed by Classic Records

❏ CS8163	Kind of Blue	2002	$300

— Blue vinyl; 200-gram edition; distributed by Classic Records; approximately 100 copies were pressed

❏ CS8163	Kind of Blue	2002	$250

— Blue vinyl; 180-gram edition; distributed by Classic Records; 500 copies were pressed

❏ CS8163-45	Kind of Blue	1999	$200

— Distributed by Classic Records; pressed on four single-sided 12-inch 45 rpm records

❏ CS8163	Kind of Blue	2001	$75

— 200-gram pressing; distributed by Classic Records; contains Side 1 at its "correct" speed

❏ 88697680571 [B]	Kind of Blue	2015	$25

— blue vinyl

❏ C238266	Live at the Plugged Nickel	1982	$50
❏ G30954	Live-Evil	1971	$75

— Original edition

❏ GQ30954 [Q]	Live-Evil	1973	$175
❏ CL1041 [M]	Miles Ahead	1957	$250

— Red and black label with six "eye" logos; cover has a while woman and her child on a sailboat

❏ CL1041 [M]	Miles Ahead	1957	$200

— Red and black label with six "eye" logos; cover has Miles Davis blowing his trumpet

❏ CL1041 [M]	Miles Ahead	1963	$40

— Guaranteed High Fidelity" on label

❏ CL1041 [M]	Miles Ahead	1965	$75

— 360 Sound Mono" on label

❏ CS8633 [R]	Miles Ahead	1963	$50

— Rechanneled stereo version of 1041; "360 Sound Stereo" in black on label

❏ CS8633	Miles Ahead	1971	$30

— Orange label

❏ KCS8633	Miles Ahead	1974	$25

— Orange label, new prefix

❏ PC8633	Miles Ahead	1977	$20

— Orange label, new prefix; some have bar codes

❏ CS8633 [R]	Miles Ahead	1963	$35

— 360 Sound Stereo" in white on label

❏ CL1812 [M]	Miles Davis at Carnegie Hall	1962	$150

— Red and black label with six "eye" logos

❏ CL1812 [M]	Miles Davis at Carnegie Hall	1963	$75

— Guaranteed High Fidelity" on label

❏ CL1812 [M]	Miles Davis at Carnegie Hall	1965	$50

— Mono" on label

❏ CS8612 [S]	Miles Davis at Carnegie Hall	1962	$120

— Red and black label with six "eye" logos

❏ CS8612 [S]	Miles Davis at Carnegie Hall	1962	$75

— 360 Sound Stereo" in black on label

❏ CS8612 [S]	Miles Davis at Carnegie Hall	1965	$75

— 360 Sound Stereo" in white on label

❏ CS8612	Miles Davis at Carnegie Hall	1971	$35

— Orange label

❏ KCS8612	Miles Davis at Carnegie Hall	1974	$30

— Orange label, new prefix

❏ PC8612	Miles Davis at Carnegie Hall	1977	$20

— Orange label, new prefix; may have bar code on back cover

❏ PC8612	Miles Davis at Carnegie Hall	199?	$30

— 180-gram vinyl reissue

❏ G30038	Miles Davis at Fillmore	1970	$75

— Original prefix

❏ CG30038	Miles Davis at Fillmore	197?	$35

— Later prefix

❏ J17	Miles Davis at Newport	1973	$30
❏ CS9808	Miles Davis' Greatest Hits	1969	$50

— 360 Sound Stereo" on red label

❏ CS9808	Miles Davis' Greatest Hits	1971	$30

— Orange label

❏ KCS9808	Miles Davis' Greatest Hits	1974	$25

— Orange label, new prefix

❏ PC9808	Miles Davis' Greatest Hits	1977	$20

— Orange label, new prefix; some have bar codes

❏ PC9808	Miles Davis' Greatest Hits	199?	$30

— 180-gram reissue

❏ CL2183 [M]	Miles Davis in Europe	1964	$40

— Guaranteed High Fidelity" on label

❏ CL2183 [M]	Miles Davis in Europe	1965	$75

— 360 Sound Mono" on label

❏ CS8983 [S]	Miles Davis in Europe	1964	$40

— 360 Sound Stereo" in black on label

❏ CS8983 [S]	Miles Davis in Europe	1965	$75

— 360 Sound Stereo" in white on label

❏ CS8983	Miles Davis in Europe	1971	$35

— Orange label

❏ KCS8983	Miles Davis in Europe	1974	$30

— Orange label, new prefix

❏ PC8983	Miles Davis in Europe	1977	$20

— Orange label, new prefix; some have bar codes

❏ PC8983	Miles Davis in Europe	199?	$30

— 180-gram reissue

❏ CL1669 [M]	Miles Davis in Person, Vol. 1 (Friday Nights at the Blackhawk, San Francisco)	1961	$75

— Red and black label with six "eye" logos; later pressings may exist

❏ CS8469 [S]	Miles Davis in Person, Vol. 1 (Friday Nights at the Blackhawk, San Francisco)	1961	$75

— Red and black label with six "eye" logos; later pressings may exist

❏ CL1670 [M]	Miles Davis in Person, Vol. 2 (Saturday Nights at the Blackhawk, San Francisco)	1961	$75

— Six "eye" logos on label; later pressings may exist

❏ CS8470 [S]	Miles Davis in Person, Vol. 2 (Saturday Nights at the Blackhawk, San Francisco)	1961	$75

— Six "eye" logos on label; later pressings may exist

❏ C2L20 [M]	Miles Davis in Person (Friday & Saturday Nights at the Blackhawk, San Francisco)	1961	$150

— Six "eye" logos on label

Number	Title	Yr	NM
❑ C2L20 [M]	Miles Davis in Person (Friday & Saturday Nights at the Blackhawk, San Francisco)	1963	$75
—Guaranteed High Fidelity" on label			
❑ C2L20 [M]	Miles Davis in Person (Friday & Saturday Nights at the Blackhawk, San Francisco)	1965	$75
—Mono" on label			
❑ C2S820 [S]	Miles Davis in Person (Friday & Saturday Nights at the Blackhawk, San Francisco)	1961	$120
—Red and black label with six "eye" logos			
❑ C2S820 [S]	Miles Davis in Person (Friday & Saturday Nights at the Blackhawk, San Francisco)	1963	$75
—360 Sound Stereo" in black on label			
❑ C2S820 [S]	Miles Davis in Person (Friday & Saturday Nights at the Blackhawk, San Francisco)	1965	$75
—360 Sound Stereo" in white on label			
❑ C2S820	Miles Davis in Person (Friday & Saturday Nights at the Blackhawk, San Francisco)	1971	$35
—Orange labels			
❑ CL2828 [M]	Miles in the Sky	1968	$175
❑ CS9628 [S]	Miles in the Sky	1968	$75
—360 Sound Stereo" on red label			
❑ CS9628	Miles in the Sky	1971	$35
—Orange label			
❑ KCS9628	Miles in the Sky	1974	$30
—Orange label, new prefix			
❑ PC9628	Miles in the Sky	1977	$20
—Orange label, new prefix; some have bar codes			
❑ PC9628	Miles in the Sky	199?	$30
—180-gram reissue			
❑ CL2601 [M]	Miles Smiles	1966	$40
❑ CS9401 [S]	Miles Smiles	1966	$75
—360 Sound Stereo" on red label			
❑ CS9401	Miles Smiles	1971	$35
—Orange label			
❑ KCS9401	Miles Smiles	1974	$30
—Orange label, new prefix			
❑ PC9401	Miles Smiles	1977	$20
—Orange label, new prefix; some have bar codes			
❑ PC9401	Miles Smiles	199?	$30
—180-gram reissue			
❑ A2S1374 [DJ]	Miles to Go	1982	$40
—Promo-only compilation			
❑ CL1193 [M]	Milestones	1958	$175
—Red and black label with six "eye" logos			
❑ CL1193 [M]	Milestones	1963	$40
—Guaranteed High Fidelity" on label			
❑ CL1193 [M]	Milestones	1965	$75
—360 Sound Mono" on label			
❑ CL2628 [M]	Milestones	1967	$75
—Reissue of 1193?			
❑ CS8021 [S]	Milestones	1959	$250
—Red and black label with six "eye" logos			
❑ CS8021 [S]	Milestones	1963	$200
—360 Sound Stereo" in black on label			
❑ CS8021 [S]	Milestones	1965	$120
—360 Sound Stereo" in white on label			
❑ CS9428 [R]	Milestones	1967	$75
—360 Sound Stereo" on red label; reissue of 8021			
❑ KCS9428	Milestones	1974	$30
—Orange label, new prefix			
❑ PC9428	Milestones	1977	$20
—Orange label, new prefix; some have bar codes			
❑ CS9428	Milestones	1971	$35
—Orange label			
❑ CL2306 [M]	My Funny Valentine	1965	$75
—Guaranteed High Fidelity" on label			
❑ CL2306 [M]	My Funny Valentine	1965	$50
—Mono" on label			
❑ CS9106 [S]	My Funny Valentine	1965	$75
—360 Sound Stereo" in black on label			
❑ CS9106 [S]	My Funny Valentine	1965	$50
—360 Sound Stereo" in white on label			
❑ CS9106	My Funny Valentine	1971	$30
—Orange label			
❑ KCS9106	My Funny Valentine	1974	$25
—Orange label, new prefix			
❑ PC9106	My Funny Valentine	1977	$20
—Orange label, new prefix			
❑ CL2794 [M]	Nefertiti	1968	$150
❑ CS9594 [S]	Nefertiti	1968	$50
—360 Sound Stereo" on red label			
❑ CS9594	Nefertiti	1971	$30
—Orange label			
❑ KCS9594	Nefertiti	1974	$25
—Orange label, new prefix			
❑ PC9594	Nefertiti	1977	$20
—Orange label, new prefix			
❑ KC31906	On the Corner	1972	$30
❑ PC31906	On the Corner	1977	$20
—Orange label, new prefix			
❑ CL1274 [M]	Porgy and Bess	1958	$150
—Six "eye" logos on label			
❑ CL1274 [M]	Porgy and Bess	1963	$75
—Guaranteed High Fidelity" on label			
❑ CL1274 [M]	Porgy and Bess	1965	$50
—Mono" on label			
❑ CS8085 [S]	Porgy and Bess	1959	$150
—Six "eye" logos on label			
❑ CS8085 [S]	Porgy and Bess	1963	$75
—360 Sound Stereo" in black on label			
❑ CS8085 [S]	Porgy and Bess	1965	$50
—360 Sound Stereo" in white on label			
❑ CS8085	Porgy and Bess	1971	$30
—Orange label			
❑ KCS8085	Porgy and Bess	1974	$25
—Orange label, new prefix			
❑ PC8085	Porgy and Bess	1977	$20
—Orange label, new prefix			
❑ CL2106 [M]	Quiet Nights	1964	$75
—Guaranteed High Fidelity" on label			
❑ CL2106 [M]	Quiet Nights	1965	$50
—Mono" on label			
❑ CS8906 [S]	Quiet Nights	1964	$75
—360 Sound Stereo" in black on label			
❑ CS8906 [S]	Quiet Nights	1965	$50
—360 Sound Stereo" in white on label			
❑ CS8906	Quiet Nights	1971	$30
—Orange label			
❑ KCS8906	Quiet Nights	1974	$25
—Orange label, new prefix			
❑ PC8906	Quiet Nights	1977	$20
—Orange label, new prefix			
❑ CL949 [M]	'Round About Midnight	1957	$150
—Six "eye" logos on label			
❑ CL949 [M]	'Round About Midnight	1963	$75
—Guaranteed High Fidelity" on label			
❑ CL949 [M]	'Round About Midnight	1965	$50
—Mono" on label			
❑ CS8649 [R]	'Round About Midnight	1963	$30
—Rechanneled stereo version of 949			
❑ CS8649	'Round About Midnight	1971	$30
—Orange label			
❑ KCS8649	'Round About Midnight	1974	$25
—Orange label, new prefix			
❑ PC8649	'Round About Midnight	1977	$20
—Orange label, new prefix			
❑ CL2051 [M]	Seven Steps to Heaven	1963	$75
—Guaranteed High Fidelity" on label			
❑ CL2051 [M]	Seven Steps to Heaven	1965	$50
—Mono" on label			
❑ CS8851 [S]	Seven Steps to Heaven	1963	$75
—360 Sound Stereo" in black on label			
❑ CS8851 [S]	Seven Steps to Heaven	1965	$50
—360 Sound Stereo" in white on label			
❑ CS8851	Seven Steps to Heaven	1971	$30
—Orange label			
❑ KCS8851	Seven Steps to Heaven	1974	$25
—Orange label, new prefix			
❑ PC8851	Seven Steps to Heaven	1977	$20
—Orange label, new prefix			
❑ CL1480 [M]	Sketches of Spain	1960	$150
—Six "eye" logos on label			
❑ CL1480 [M]	Sketches of Spain	1963	$75
—Guaranteed High Fidelity" on label			

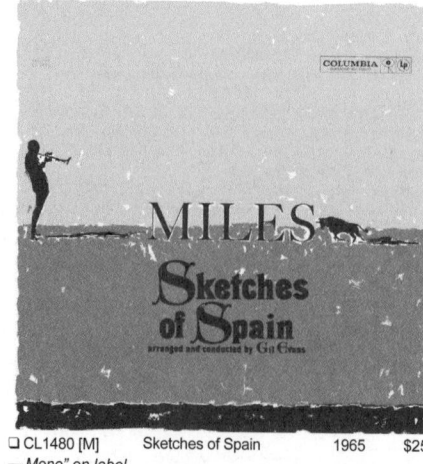

Number	Title	Yr	NM
❑ CL1480 [M]	Sketches of Spain	1965	$25
—Mono" on label			
❑ CS8271 [S]	Sketches of Spain	1960	$175
—Red and black label with six "eye" logos			
❑ CS8271 [S]	Sketches of Spain	1963	$75
—360 Sound Stereo" in black on label			
❑ CS8271 [S]	Sketches of Spain	1965	$50
—360 Sound Stereo" in white on label			
❑ CS8271	Sketches of Spain	1971	$30
—Orange label			
❑ KCS8271	Sketches of Spain	1974	$25
—Orange label, new prefix			
❑ PC8271	Sketches of Spain	1977	$20
—Orange label, new prefix			
❑ CS8271 [S]	Sketckes of Spain	1999	$75
—Audiophile reissue; distributed by Classic Records			
❑ CL1656 [M]	Someday My Prince Will Come	1961	$40
—Six "eye" logos on label			
❑ CL1656 [M]	Someday My Prince Will Come	1963	$75
—Guaranteed High Fidelity" on label			
❑ CL1656 [M]	Someday My Prince Will Come	1965	$50
—Mono" on label			
❑ CS8456 [S]	Someday My Prince Will Come	1961	$40
—Six "eye" logos on label			
❑ CS8456 [S]	Someday My Prince Will Come	1963	$75
—360 Sound Stereo" in black on label			
❑ CS8456 [S]	Someday My Prince Will Come	1965	$50
—360 Sound Stereo" in white on label			
❑ CS8456 [B]	Someday My Prince Will Come	1971	$15
—Orange label			
❑ KCS8456	Someday My Prince Will Come	1974	$25
—Orange label, new prefix			
❑ PC8456	Someday My Prince Will Come	1977	$20
—Orange label, new prefix			
❑ CL2732 [M]	Sorcerer	1967	$75
❑ CS9532 [S]	Sorcerer	1967	$50
—360 Sound Stereo" on red label			
❑ CS9532	Sorcerer	1971	$30
—Orange label			
❑ KCS9532	Sorcerer	1974	$25
—Orange label, new prefix			
❑ PC9532	Sorcerer	1977	$20
—Orange label, new prefix			
❑ FC38657	Star People	1983	$25
❑ C5X45000	The Columbia Years 1955-1985	1988	$120
❑ FC36790	The Man with the Horn	1981	$30
—Original edition			
❑ HC46790	The Man with the Horn	1982	$150
—Half-Speed Mastered" on cover			
❑ PC36790	The Man with the Horn	198?	$20
—Budget-line reissue with new prefix			
❑ PC36790	The Man with the Horn	199?	$30
—180-gram reissue			
❑ C6X36976	The Miles Davis Collection Vol. 1: 12 Sides of Miles	1980	$200
❑ PC34396	Water Babies	1977	$30
—Original has no bar code			
❑ PC34396	Water Babies	198?	$20
—Reissue with bar code			
❑ C238005	We Want Miles	1982	$30
❑ FC40023	You're Under Arrest	1985	$25

COLUMBIA JAZZ MASTERPIECES

Number	Title	Yr	NM
❑ CJ44151	Ballads	1988	$25
❑ CJ44151	Ballads	199?	$30
—180-gram reissue			
❑ C2J40577	Bitches Brew	1987	$35
❑ CJ40645	Cookin' at the Plugged Nickel	1987	$35
❑ CJ40580	In a Silent Way	1987	$25

Number	Title	Yr	NM
❏ CJ40580	In a Silent Way	199?	$30

— 180-gram reissue

| ❏ CJ40579 | Kind of Blue | 1987 | $35 |

— Reissue; when this version of the album was prepared, Columbia discovered that all of Side 1 on the original LP was mastered at the wrong speed; this album was the first time it was mastered "correctly

| ❏ CJ40609 | Live Miles: More Music from the Legendary Carnegie Hall Concert | 1987 | $25 |
| ❏ CJ40609 | Live Miles: More Music from the Legendary Carnegie Hall Concert | 199? | $30 |

— 180-gram reissue

| ❏ CJ40784 | Miles Ahead | 1987 | $25 |
| ❏ CJ40784 | Miles Ahead | 199? | $30 |

— 180-gram reissue

| ❏ CJ44052 | Miles and Coltrane | 1988 | $25 |
| ❏ CJ44052 | Miles and Coltrane | 199? | $30 |

— 180-gram reissue

| ❏ CJ44257 | Miles Davis in Person, Vol. 1 (Friday Nights at the Blackhawk, San Francisco) | 1988 | $25 |
| ❏ CJ44257 | Miles Davis in Person, Vol. 1 (Friday Nights at the Blackhawk, San Francisco) | 199? | $30 |

— 180-gram reissue

❏ CJ44425	Miles Davis in Person, Vol. 2 (Saturday Nights at the Blackhawk, San Francisco)	1989	$25
❏ CJ40837	Milestones	1987	$25
❏ CJ40837	Milestones	199?	$30

— 180-gram reissue

❏ CJ40647	Porgy and Bess	1987	$25
❏ CJ40610	'Round About Midnight	1987	$25
❏ CJ40578	Sketches of Spain	1987	$25
❏ CJ40947	Someday My Prince Will Come	1987	$25

COLUMBIA LIMITED EDITION

| ❏ LE10018 | Miles Davis in Person, Vol. 1 (Friday Nights at the Blackhawk, San Francisco) | 197? | $35 |
| ❏ LE10076 | Miles Davis in Person, Vol. 2 (Saturday Nights at the Blackhawk, San Francisco) | 197? | $35 |

COLUMBIA SPECIAL PRODUCTS

| ❏ P13811 | Facets | 1977 | $30 |

CONTEMPORARY

| ❏ C-7645 | Miles Davis and the Lighthouse All-Stars At Last! | 1985 | $35 |

DEBUT

| ❏ DEB120 [M] | Blue Moods | 1955 | $400 |

EVEREST ARCHIVE OF FOLK & JAZZ

| ❏ FS-283 | Miles Davis | 197? | $25 |

FANTASY

| ❏ OJC-245 | Bags Groove | 1987 | $30 |

— Reissue of Prestige 7109

| ❏ OJC-093 | Blue Haze | 198? | $30 |

— Reissue of Prestige 7054

| ❏ 6001 [M] | Blue Moods | 1962 | $350 |

— Reissue of Debut album; red vinyl

| ❏ 6001 [M] | Blue Moods | 1963 | $140 |

— Black vinyl, red label

| ❏ 86001 [R] | Blue Moods | 1962 | $120 |

— Blue vinyl

| ❏ 86001 [R] | Blue Moods | 1963 | $75 |

— Black vinyl, blue label

| ❏ OJC-043 | Blue Moods | 198? | $30 |

— Reissue of Fantasy 6001

| ❏ OJC-071 | Collectors' Item | 198? | $30 |

— Reissue of Prestige 7044

| ❏ OJC-128 | Cookin' with the Miles Davis Quintet | 198? | $30 |

— Reissue of Prestige 7094

| ❏ OJC-005 | Dig Miles Davis/Sonny Rollins | 198? | $30 |

— Reissue of Prestige 7012

| ❏ OJC-053 | Miles Davis and Horns | 198? | $30 |

— Reissue of Prestige 7025

| ❏ OJC-480 | Miles Davis and the Lighthouse All-Stars At Last! | 1991 | $30 |

— Reissue of Contemporary 7645

| ❏ OJC-012 | Miles Davis and the Milt Jackson Quintet/Sextet | 198? | $25 |

— Reissue of Prestige 7034

| ❏ OJC-347 | Miles Davis and the Modern Jazz Giants | 198? | $30 |

— Reissue of Prestige 7150

| ❏ OJC-006 | Miles -- The New Miles Davis Quintet | 198? | $30 |

— Reissue of Prestige 7014

| ❏ OJC-190 | Relaxin' with the Miles Davis Quintet | 1985 | $25 |

— Reissue of Prestige 7129

| ❏ OJC-391 | Steamin' with the Miles Davis Quintet | 1989 | $25 |

— Reissue of Prestige 7200

| ❏ OJC-004 | The Musings of Miles | 198? | $30 |

— Reissue of Prestige 7007

Number	Title	Yr	NM
❏ OJC-213	Walkin'	1987	$25

— Reissue of Prestige 7076

| ❏ OJC-296 | Workin' with the Miles Davis Quintet | 1987 | $25 |

— Reissue of Prestige 7166

FONTANA

| ❏ MGF-27532 [M] | Jazz on the Screen | 1965 | $40 |

— With Art Blakey and the Jazz Messengers

| ❏ SRF-67532 [S] | Jazz on the Screen | 1965 | $40 |

JAZZ HERITAGE

| ❏ 913427F [M] | Dig Miles Davis/Sonny Rollins | 198? | $35 |

— Mail-order reissue

MOBILE FIDELITY

❏ MFSL1-376 [B]	Four & More - Recorded Live In Concert	2013	$50
❏ MFSL1-377 [B]	In A Silent Way	2013	$50
❏ MFSL-245011 [B]	Kind of Blue	2015	$75

— remastered, 45rpm

❏ MFSL1-374 [B]	Milestones	2013	$50
❏ MFSL1-373 [B]	Round About Midnight	2013	$75
❏ MFSL1-375 [B]	Sketches of Spain	2013	$50
❏ 1-177	Someday My Prince Will Come	1985	$175

— Audiophile vinyl

MOSAIC

❏ MQ11-164	Miles Davis & Gil Evans: The Complete Columbia Studio Recordings	1996	$400
❏ MQ6-183	The Complete Bitches Brew Sessions	1999	$200
❏ MQ6-220	The Complete Blackhawk Sessions	2003	$200
❏ MQ9-191	The Complete Columbia Recordings of Miles Davis with John Coltrane	2000	$170
❏ MQ5-209	The Complete In a Silent Way Sessions (September 1968-February 1969)	2002	$175
❏ MQ10-158	The Complete Plugged Nickel Sessions	1995	$300
❏ MQ10-177	The Complete Studio Recordings of the Miles Davis Quintet 1965-June 1968	1998	$175

ORIGINAL JAZZ CLASSICS

| ❏ OJC190 [B] | Relaxing with the Miles Davis Quintet | 2015 | $20 |

— clear vinyl

PAIR

| ❏ PDL2-1095 | Best of Miles Davis | 1986 | $30 |

PHILIPS

| ❏ 836305-1 | Elevator to the Scaffold (L'Ancenseur Pour L'Echafaud) | 198? | $30 |

— Reissue of Columbia 1268

PRESTIGE

| ❏ PRLP-7076 [M] | All Stars | 1957 | $500 |

— With W. 50th St. address on yellow label

| ❏ PRLP-7076 [M] | All Stars | 196? | $40 |

— With trident on blue label

| ❏ PRLP-7076 [M] | All Stars | 1958 | $300 |

— With Bergenfield, N.J. address on yellow label

| ❏ PRLP-7109 [M] | Bags Groove | 1957 | $300 |

— With W. 50th St. address on yellow label

| ❏ PRLP-7109 [M] | Bags Groove | 196? | $40 |

— With trident on blue label

| ❏ PRLP-7109 [M] | Bags Groove | 1958 | $300 |

— With Bergenfield, N.J. address on yellow label

| ❏ PRLP-7054 [M] | Blue Haze | 1956 | $300 |

— With W. 50th St. address on yellow label

| ❏ PRLP-7054 [M] | Blue Haze | 196? | $40 |

— With trident on blue label

❏ PRLP-140 [10]	Blue Period	1953	$300
❏ P-12	Chronicle: The Complete Prestige Recordings	1980	$300
❏ PRLP-7044 [M]	Collectors' Item	1956	$300

— With W. 50th St. address on yellow label

| ❏ PRLP-7044 [M] | Collectors' Item | 196? | $40 |

— With trident on blue label

❏ P-24022	Collector's Items	1973	$50
❏ PRST-7744 [R]	Conception	1970	$50
❏ PRLP-7094 [M]	Cookin' with the Miles Davis Quintet	1957	$500

— With W. 50th St. address on yellow label

| ❏ PRLP-7094 [M] | Cookin' with the Miles Davis Quintet | 196? | $40 |

— With trident on blue label

| ❏ PRLP-7094 [M] | Cookin' with the Miles Davis Quintet | 1958 | $300 |

— With Bergenfield, N.J. address on yellow label

| ❏ P-24054 | Dig | 197? | $35 |
| ❏ PRLP-7281 [M] | Diggin' | 1963 | $200 |

— Reissue of 7012; with Bergenfield, NJ address on yellow label

| ❏ PRLP-7281 [M] | Diggin' | 196? | $40 |

— With trident on blue label

| ❏ PRST-7281 [R] | Diggin' | 1963 | $75 |
| ❏ PRLP-7012 [M] | Dig Miles Davis/Sonny Rollins | 1956 | $1250 |

Number	Title	Yr	NM

— Gray cover

| ❏ PRLP-7012 [M] | Dig Miles Davis/Sonny Rollins | 1957 | $300 |

— Color cover; yellow label with W. 50th St. address

| ❏ PRLP-7168 [M] | Early Miles | 1959 | $250 |

— Reissue of 7025; with Bergenfield, NJ address on yellow label

| ❏ PRLP-7168 [M] | Early Miles | 196? | $40 |

— With trident on blue label

| ❏ PRST-7674 [R] | Early Miles | 1969 | $35 |

— Reissue of 7168

❏ P-24064	Green Haze	1976	$50
❏ PRLP-7373 [M]	Jazz Classics	1965	$75
❏ PRST-7373 [R]	Jazz Classics	1965	$50
❏ PRST-7822 [R]	Miles Ahead!	1971	$35
❏ PR-24001	Miles Davis	1972	$50
❏ PRLP-196 [10]	Miles Davis All Stars, Volume 1	1955	$350
❏ PRLP-200 [10]	Miles Davis All Stars, Volume 2	1955	$350
❏ PRLP-7025 [M]	Miles Davis and Horns	1956	$400

— Yellow label with W. 50th St. address

| ❏ PRLP-7025 [M] | Miles Davis and Horns | 1958 | $300 |

— Yellow label, Bergenfield, N.J. address

| ❏ PRLP-7034 [M] | Miles Davis and the Milt Jackson Quintet/Sextet | 1956 | $400 |

— With W. 50th St. address on yellow label

| ❏ PRLP-7034 [M] | Miles Davis and the Milt Jackson Quintet/Sextet | 196? | $40 |

— With trident on blue label

| ❏ PRLP-7034 [M] | Miles Davis and the Milt Jackson Quintet/Sextet | 1958 | $300 |

— Yellow label with Bergenfield, N.J. address

| ❏ PRLP-7150 [M] | Miles Davis and the Modern Jazz Giants | 1958 | $300 |

— With Bergenfield, NJ address on yellow label

| ❏ PRLP-7150 [M] | Miles Davis and the Modern Jazz Giants | 196? | $40 |

— With trident on blue label

| ❏ PRST-7650 [R] | Miles Davis and the Modern Jazz Giants | 1969 | $50 |

— Reissue of 7150

| ❏ 16-3 [M] | Miles Davis and the Modern Jazz Giants | 1957 | $1000 |

— This album plays at 16 2/3 rpm and is marked as such; white label

❏ PRLP-161 [10]	Miles Davis Featuring Sonny Rollins	1953	$350
❏ PRLP-7457 [M]	Miles Davis' Greatest Hits	1967	$75
❏ PRST-7457 [R]	Miles Davis' Greatest Hits	1967	$35
❏ PRLP-154 [10]	Miles Davis Plays Al Cohn Compositions	1953	$350
❏ PRLP-7352 [M]	Miles Davis Plays for Lovers	1965	$75
❏ PRST-7352 [R]	Miles Davis Plays for Lovers	1965	$50
❏ PRLP-7322 [M]	Miles Davis Plays Richard Rodgers	1964	$75
❏ PRST-7322 [R]	Miles Davis Plays Richard Rodgers	1964	$50
❏ PRLP-185 [10]	Miles Davis Quintet	1954	$300
❏ PRLP-187 [10]	Miles Davis Quintet Featuring Sonny Rollins	1954	$300
❏ PRLP-182 [10]	Miles Davis Sextet	1954	$300
❏ PRLP-7014 [M]	Miles -- The New Miles Davis Quintet	1956	$300

— Yellow label with W. 50th St. address

| ❏ PRST-7540 [R] | Odyssey | 1968 | $30 |

— Reissue of 7034

| ❏ PRST-7847 | Oleo | 1972 | $30 |
| ❏ PRLP-7129 [M] | Relaxin' with the Miles Davis Quintet | 1957 | $600 |

— With W. 50th St. address on yellow label

| ❏ PRLP-7129 [M] | Relaxin' with the Miles Davis Quintet | 196? | $40 |

— With trident on blue label

| ❏ PRLP-7129 [M] | Relaxin' with the Miles Davis Quintet | 1957 | $300 |

— With Bergenfield, NJ address on yellow label

| ❏ PRST-7580 [R] | Steamin' | 1968 | $30 |

— Reissue of 7200

| ❏ PRLP-7200 [M] | Steamin' with the Miles Davis Quintet | 1961 | $750 |

— With Bergenfield, NJ address on yellow label

| ❏ PRLP-7200 [M] | Steamin' with the Miles Davis Quintet | 196? | $75 |

— With trident on blue label

| ❏ PRLP-7221 [M] | The Beginning | 1962 | $175 |

— Reissue of 7007; with Bergenfield, NJ address on yellow label

| ❏ PRLP-7221 [M] | The Beginning | 196? | $75 |

— With trident on blue label

| ❏ PRLP-7007 [M] | The Musings of Miles | 1955 | $400 |

— Yellow label with W. 50th St. address

| ❏ PRLP-124 [10] | The New Sounds of Miles Davis | 1952 | $350 |
| ❏ PRLP-7254 [M] | The Original Quintet | 1963 | $150 |

— Reissue of 7014; with Bergenfield, NJ address on yellow label

| ❏ PRLP-7254 [M] | The Original Quintet | 196? | $75 |

— With trident on blue label

❏ PRST-7254 [R]	The Original Quintet	1963	$50
❏ 24012	The Tallest Trees	1972	$35
❏ 24077	Tune Up	197?	$30
❏ PRST-7608 [R]	Walkin'	1969	$30

Number	Title	Yr	NM
— Reissue of 7076			
❑ 24034	Workin' and Steamin'	1973	$35
❑ PRLP-7166 [M]	Workin' with the Miles Davis Quintet	1959	$250
— With Bergenfield, NJ address on yellow label			
❑ PRLP-7166 [M]	Workin' with the Miles Davis Quintet	196?	$75
— With trident on blue label			
SAVOY JAZZ			
❑ SJL-1196	First Miles	1989	$30
TRIP			
❑ 5015	Miles of Jazz	1974	$25
UNITED ARTISTS			
❑ UAS-9952	Miles Davis	1972	$50
— Reissue of Blue Note material			
WARNER BROS.			
❑ 25873	Amandla	1989	$50
❑ 26938	Doo-Bop	1992	$35
❑ 25490	Tutu	1986	$25

DAVIS, PAUL

Number	Title	Yr	NM
ARISTA			
❑ AL9578	Cool Night	1981	$12
❑ AL8376	Cool Night	198?	$10
— Reissue of 9578			
BANG			
❑ BLPS-223	A Little Bit of Paul Davis	1970	$100
❑ JZ36094	Paul Davis	1980	$12
❑ 401	Ride 'Em Cowboy	1974	$15
❑ 410	Singer of Songs -- Teller of Tales	1977	$15
❑ 405	Southern Tracks and Fantasies	1976	$15
❑ PZ37973	The Best of Paul Davis	1982	$12

DAVIS, REVEREND GARY

Number	Title	Yr	NM
BLUESVILLE			
❑ BVLP-1032 [M]	A Little More Faith	1961	$150
— Blue label, silver print			
❑ BVLP-1032 [M]	A Little More Faith	1964	$30
— Blue label with trident logo			
❑ BVLP-1015 [M]	Harlem Street Singer	1961	$150
— Blue label, silver print			
❑ BVLP-1015 [M]	Harlem Street Singer	1964	$30
— Blue label with trident logo			
❑ BVLP-1049 [M]	Say No to the Devil	1962	$150
— Blue label, silver print			
❑ BVLP-1049 [M]	Say No to the Devil	1964	$30
— Blue label with trident logo			
FOLKLORE			
❑ F-14033 [M]	Guitar and Banjo	196?	$40
❑ F-14028 [M]	Pure Religion	196?	$40
STINSON			
❑ SLP-56 [10]	The Singing Reverend	195?	$150

DAVIS, RICHARD

Number	Title	Yr	NM
BASF			
❑ 20725	Muses for Richard Davis	1973	$35
COBBLESTONE			
❑ 9003	Philosophy of the Spiritual	1972	$35
GALAXY			
❑ 5102	Fancy Free	1978	$25
MUSE			
❑ MR-5093	As One	1977	$30
❑ MR-5027	Dealin'	1974	$30
❑ MR-5002	Epistrophy & Now's the Time	1973	$30
❑ MR-5115	Harvest	1978	$30
❑ MR-5180	Way Out West	198?	$25
❑ MR-5083	With Understanding	1976	$30
PAUSA			
❑ 7022	Jazz Wave	197?	$25

DAVIS, SAMMY, JR., AND CARMEN MCRAE

Number	Title	Yr	NM
DECCA			
❑ DL8490 [M]	Boy Meets Girl	1957	$175

DAVIS, SAMMY, JR., AND COUNT BASIE

Number	Title	Yr	NM
MGM			
❑ SE-4825	Sammy Davis Jr. and Count Basie	1972	$25
— Reissue of Verve LP?			
VERVE			
❑ V-8605 [M]	Our Shining Hour	1965	$30
❑ V6-8605 [S]	Our Shining Hour	1965	$35

DAVIS, SAMMY, JR.

Number	Title	Yr	NM
DECCA			
❑ DL8779 [M]	All the Way And Then Some	1958	$30
❑ DL4381 [M]	Forget-Me-Nots for First Nighters	1963	$18
❑ DL74381 [S]	Forget-Me-Nots for First Nighters	1963	$25
❑ DL8351 [M]	Here's Looking at You	1956	$30
❑ DL8981 [M]	I Got a Right to Swing	1960	$50
❑ DL78981 [S]	I Got a Right to Swing	1960	$75
❑ DL8641 [M]	It's All Over But the Swingin'	1957	$30
❑ DL8170 [M]	Just for Lovers	1955	$30
❑ DL8676 [M]	Mood to Be Wooed	1958	$150
❑ DL4153 [M]	Mr. Entertainment	1961	$18
❑ DL74153 [S]	Mr. Entertainment	1961	$25
❑ DL8854 [M]	Porgy and Bess	1959	$25
❑ DL78854 [S]	Porgy and Bess	1959	$30
❑ DL8841 [M]	Sammy Davis, Jr., at Town Hall	1959	$25
❑ DL78841 [S]	Sammy Davis, Jr., at Town Hall	1959	$30
❑ DL8486 [M]	Sammy Swings	1957	$30
❑ DL8118 [M]	Starring Sammy Davis, Jr.	1955	$30
❑ DXB192 [M]	The Best of Sammy Davis, Jr.	1966	$18
❑ DXSB7192 [S]	The Best of Sammy Davis, Jr.	1966	$25
❑ DL8921 [M]	The Sammy Awards	1960	$25
❑ DL78921 [S]	The Sammy Awards	1960	$30
❑ DL4582 [M]	Try a Little Tenderness	1965	$15
❑ DL74582 [S]	Try a Little Tenderness	1965	$18
HARMONY			
❑ HS11365	Let There Be Love	1970	$12
❑ HS11299	The Great Sammy Davis, Jr.	196?	$15
❑ H30568	What Kind of Fool Am I	1971	$12
MCA			
❑ 4109	Sammy Davis Jr. At His Greatest	1975	$15
MGM			
❑ SE-4852	Portrait of Sammy Davis, Jr.	1972	$12
❑ SE-4832	Sammy Davis Jr. Now	1972	$12
❑ M3G-4965	That's Entertainment	1974	$12
MOTOWN			
❑ 4519ML	Hello Detroit!	1984	$12
❑ MS710	Something for Everyone	1970	$15
PICKWICK			
❑ SPC-3002	The Many Faces of Sammy Davis, Jr.	196?	$12
REPRISE			
❑ R-6033 [M]	All Star Spectacular	1962	$18
❑ R9-6033 [S]	All Star Spectacular	1962	$25
❑ R-6082 [M]	As Long As She Needs Me	1963	$18
❑ R9-6082 [S]	As Long As She Needs Me	1963	$25
❑ R-6126 [M]	California Suite	1964	$18
❑ RS-6126 [S]	California Suite	1964	$25
❑ R-6159 [M]	If I Ruled the World	1965	$15
❑ RS-6159 [S]	If I Ruled the World	1965	$18
❑ RS-6324	I've Gotta Be Me	1969	$15
❑ RS-6308	Lonely Is the Name	1968	$15
❑ R-2010 [M]	Sammy Davis, Jr., Belts the Best of Broadway	1962	$18
❑ R9-2010 [S]	Sammy Davis, Jr., Belts the Best of Broadway	1962	$25
❑ RS-6410	Sammy Davis, Jr., Steps Out	1970	$15
❑ RS-6291	Sammy Davis, Jr.'s Greatest Hits	1968	$15
❑ R-6236 [M]	Sammy Davis. Jr., Sings/ Laurindo Almeida Plays	1966	$30
❑ RS-6236 [S]	Sammy Davis, Jr., Sings/ Laurindo Almeida Plays	1966	$35
❑ R-6063 [M]	Sammy Davis Jr. at the Cocoanut Grove	1963	$25
❑ R9-6063 [S]	Sammy Davis Jr. at the Cocoanut Grove	1963	$30
❑ R-6095 [M]	Sammy Davis Jr. Salutes the Stars of the London Palladium	1964	$18
❑ RS-6095 [S]	Sammy Davis Jr. Salutes the Stars of the London Palladium	1964	$25
❑ R-6131 [M]	Sammy Davis Jr. Sings the Big Ones for Young Lovers	1964	$15
❑ RS-6131 [S]	Sammy Davis Jr. Sings the Big Ones for Young Lovers	1964	$18
❑ R-6264 [M]	Sammy Davis Jr. Sings the Complete Dr. Dolittle	1967	$25
❑ RS-6264 [S]	Sammy Davis Jr. Sings the Complete Dr. Dolittle	1967	$15
❑ R-6169 [M]	Sammy's Back on Broadway	1965	$15
❑ RS-6169 [S]	Sammy's Back on Broadway	1965	$18
❑ R-6237 [M]	That's All	1967	$18
❑ RS-6237 [S]	That's All	1967	$25
❑ RS-6339	The Goin's Great	1969	$15
❑ R-6164 [M]	The Nat Cole Song Book	1965	$15
❑ RS-6164 [S]	The Nat Cole Song Book	1965	$18
❑ R-6188 [M]	The Sammy Davis, Jr., Show	1965	$15
❑ RS-6188 [S]	The Sammy Davis, Jr., Show	1965	$18
❑ R-6114 [M]	The Shelter of Your Arms	1964	$18
❑ RS-6114 [S]	The Shelter of Your Arms	1964	$25
❑ R-6214 [M]	The Sounds of '66	1966	$15
❑ RS-6214 [S]	The Sounds of '66	1966	$18

THE WHAM OF SAM

SAMMY DAVIS JR.

Number	Title	Yr	NM
❑ R-2003 [M]	The Wham of Sam	1961	$18
❑ R9-2003 [S]	The Wham of Sam	1961	$25
❑ R-6096 [M]	Treasury of Golden Hits	1964	$18
❑ RS-6096 [S]	Treasury of Golden Hits	1964	$25
❑ R-6051 [M]	What Kind of Fool Am I and Other Show-Stoppers	1962	$18
❑ R9-6051 [S]	What Kind of Fool Am I and Other Show-Stoppers	1962	$25
❑ R-6144 [M]	When the Feeling Hits You	1965	$15
❑ RS-6144 [S]	When the Feeling Hits You	1965	$18
WARNER BROS.			
❑ BSK3128	Live Performance	1977	$12
WARNER SPECIAL PRODUCTS			
❑ OP-1501	The Sound of Sammy	1978	$12
— Special item for Alka-Seltzer			

DAVIS, SKEETER, AND NRBQ

Number	Title	Yr	NM
ROUNDER			
❑ 3092	She Sings, They Play	1986	$15

DAVIS, SKEETER

Number	Title	Yr	NM
GUSTO			
❑ 0014	Best of the Best	1978	$12
RCA CAMDEN			
❑ CAL-899 [M]	Blueberry Hill and Other Favorites	1965	$15
❑ CAS-899 [S]	Blueberry Hill and Other Favorites	1965	$18
❑ CAS-2367	Easy to Love	1970	$15
❑ CAS-2517	Foggy Mountain Top	1971	$15
❑ ACL1-0622	He Wakes Me with a Kiss	1974	$12
❑ CAL-818 [M]	I Forgot More Than You'll Ever Know	196?	$15
❑ CAS-818(e) [R]	I Forgot More Than You'll Ever Know	196?	$18
❑ CAS-2607	The End of the World	1972	$12
RCA VICTOR			
❑ LSP-4310	A Place in the Country	1970	$18
❑ LSP-4642	Bring It on Home	1972	$18
❑ LPM-2736 [M]	Cloudy, With Occasional Tears	1963	$30
❑ LSP-2736 [S]	Cloudy, With Occasional Tears	1963	$30
❑ LPM-3763 [M]	Hand in Hand with Jesus	1967	$30
❑ LSP-3763 [S]	Hand in Hand with Jesus	1967	$25
❑ LPM-2327 [M]	Here's the Answer	1961	$30
❑ LSP-2327 [S]	Here's the Answer	1961	$30
❑ LSP-4818	Hillbilly Singer	1972	$18
❑ APL1-0322	I Can't Believe That It's All Over	1974	$15
❑ LPM-2197 [M]	I'll Sing You a Song and Harmonize, Too	1960	$30
❑ LSP-2197 [S]	I'll Sing You a Song and Harmonize, Too	1960	$30
❑ LPM-3667 [M]	I Love Flatt & Scruggs	1968	$25
❑ LSP-4382	It's Hard to Be a Woman	1970	$18
❑ LPM-2980 [M]	Let Me Get Close to You	1964	$25
❑ LSP-2980 [S]	Let Me Get Close to You	1964	$30
❑ LSP-4557	Love Takes a Lot	1971	$18
❑ LSP-4200	Maryfrances	1969	$25
❑ LPM-3667 [M]	My Heart's in the Country	1966	$25
❑ LSP-3667 [S]	My Heart's in the Country	1966	$30
❑ LPM-3567 [M]	Singin' in the Summer Sun	1966	$25
❑ LSP-3567 [S]	Singin' in the Summer Sun	1966	$30
❑ LSP-4486	Skeeter	1971	$18
❑ LPM-3790 [M]	Skeeter Davis Sings Buddy Holly	1967	$50
❑ LSP-3790 [S]	Skeeter Davis Sings Buddy Holly	1967	$40
❑ LSP-4732	Skeeter Sings Dolly	1972	$18
❑ LPM-3463 [M]	Skeeter Sings Standards	1965	$25
❑ LSP-3463 [S]	Skeeter Sings Standards	1965	$30
❑ LPM-3374 [M]	The Best of Skeeter Davis	1965	$25
❑ LSP-3374 [S]	The Best of Skeeter Davis	1965	$30
❑ APL1-0190	The Best of Skeeter Davis, Volume 2	1973	$15
❑ LSP-4124	The Closest Thing to Love	1969	$25
❑ LPM-2699 [M]	The End of the World	1963	$30
❑ LSP-2699 [S]	The End of the World	1963	$30

Number	Title	Yr	NM
❏ LPM-3876 [M]	What Does It Take (To Keep a Man Like You Satisfied)	1967	$30
❏ LSP-3876 [S]	What Does It Take (To Keep a Man Like You Satisfied)	1967	$25
❏ LPM-3960 [M]	Why So Lonely?	1968	$50
❏ LSP-3960 [S]	Why So Lonely?	1968	$25
❏ LPM-3382 [M]	Written by the Stars	1965	$25
❏ LSP-3382 [S]	Written by the Stars	1965	$30

DAVIS, SPENCER, GROUP
ALLEGIANCE
❏ AV-442	Crossfire	1983	$12

DATE
❏ TES-4021 [B]	Funky	1971	$300

—*Deleted almost immediately upon release*

MEDIARTS
❏ 41-11	It's Been So Long	1971	$15

RHINO
❏ RNLP117	The Best of the Spencer Davis Group	1983	$10
❏ RNLP70172	The Best of the Spencer Davis Group (Golden Archive Series)	1987	$15

UNITED ARTISTS
❏ UAL3578 [M]	Gimme Some Lovin'	1967	$100
❏ UAS6578 [S]	Gimme Some Lovin'	1967	$40
❏ ST-91127 [R]	Gimme Some Lovin'	1967	$50

—*Capitol Record Club edition*

❏ UAS6691	Heavies	1969	$25
❏ UAL3589 [M]	I'm a Man	1967	$75
❏ UAS6589 [P]	I'm a Man	1967	$50
❏ UAS6641 [P]	The Spencer Davis Group's Greatest Hits	1968	$30
❏ UA-LA433-E	The Very Best of the Spencer Davis Group	1975	$12
❏ UAS6652	With Their New Face On	1968	$25

VERTIGO
❏ VEL-1015 [B]	Gluggo	1973	$50
❏ VEL-1021 [B]	Living in a Back Street	1974	$35

DAVIS, STANTON
OUTRAGEOUS
❏ 2	Better Days	1977	$35

DAVIS, TYRONE
COLUMBIA
❏ JC36230	Can't You Tell It's Me	1979	$15
❏ FC37366	Everything in Place	1981	$15
❏ JC35305	I Can't Go On This Way	1978	$15
❏ JC36598	I Just Can't Keep On Going	1980	$15
❏ JC35723	In the Mood with Tyrone Davis	1979	$15
❏ PC34654	Let's Be Closer Together	1977	$15
❏ PC34268	Love and Touch	1976	$15
❏ PC37979	The Best of Tyrone Davis	1982	$12

DAKAR
❏ DK-9005	Can I Change My Mind	1969	$30
❏ DK-76915	Homewrecker	1975	$25
❏ DK-76901	I Had It All the Time	1972	$30
❏ DK-76909	It's All in the Game	1974	$25
❏ DK-9027	Turn Back the Hands of Time	1970	$30
❏ DK-76918	Turning Point	1976	$25
❏ DK-76902	Tyrone Davis' Greatest Hits	1972	$30
❏ DK-76904	Without You in My Life	1973	$30

EPIC
❏ PE38626	Tyrone Davis' Greatest Hits	1983	$10

HIGHRISE
❏ 103	Tyrone Davis	1982	$12

ICHIBAN
❏ ICH1103	I'll Always Love You	1991	$15

DAVIS, WALTER, JR.
BLUE NOTE
❏ BLP-4018 [M]	Davis Cup	1959	$1000

—*Deep groove" version (deep indentation under label on both sides)*

❏ BLP-4018 [M]	Davis Cup	1959	$175

—*Regular version with W. 63rd St. address on label*

❏ BLP-4018 [M]	Davis Cup	1964	$75

—*With New York, USA address on label*

❏ BST-84018 [S]	Davis Cup	1959	$75

—*Regular version with W. 63rd St. address on label*

❏ BST-84018 [S]	Davis Cup	1964	$25

—*With New York, USA address on label*

❏ BST-84018 [S]	Davis Cup	1967	$35

—*With "A Division of Liberty Records" on label*

❏ B1-32098	Davis Cup	1995	$35

RED
❏ VPA-150	A Being Such As You	198?	$30
❏ VPA-153	Blues Walk	198?	$30

DAVIS, WILD BILL
CORAL
❏ CRL57427 [M]	Lover	1962	$25
❏ CRL757427 [S]	Lover	1962	$30

❏ CRL57417 [M]	One More Time	1962	$25
❏ CRL757417 [S]	One More Time	1962	$30

EPIC
❏ LN3308 [M]	Evening Concerto	1956	$150
❏ LN1004 [10]	Here's Wild Bill Davis	1954	$250
❏ LN1121 [M]	On the Loose	1955	$150
❏ LN3118 [M]	Wild Bill Davis at Birdland	1955	$300

EVEREST
❏ LPBR-5094 [M]	Dance the Madison	1960	$30
❏ SDBR-1094 [S]	Dance the Madison	1960	$30
❏ LPBR-5125 [M]	Dis Heah	1961	$30
❏ SDBR-1125 [S]	Dis Heah	1961	$30
❏ LPBR-5052 [M]	Flying High	1959	$30
❏ SDBR-1052 [S]	Flying High	1959	$30
❏ LPBR-5014 [M]	My Fair Lady	1958	$30
❏ SDBR-1014 [S]	My Fair Lady	1959	$30
❏ LPBR-5116 [M]	Organ Grinder's Swing	1960	$30
❏ SDBR-1116 [S]	Organ Grinder's Swing	1960	$30
❏ LPBR-5133 [M]	The Music from "Milk and Honey"	1961	$30
❏ SDBR-1133 [S]	The Music from "Milk and Honey"	1961	$30

IMPERIAL
❏ LP-9015 [M]	Wild Bill Davis in Hollywood	1956	$250
❏ LP-9010 [M]	Wild Bill Davis on Broadway	1956	$250
❏ LP-9201 [M]	Wild Wild Wild Wild Wild	1963	$175
❏ LP-12201 [R]	Wild Wild Wild Wild Wild	1963	$200

RCA VICTOR
❏ LSP-4139	Doin' His Thing	1969	$35
❏ LPM-3314 [M]	Free, Frantic and Funky	1965	$35
❏ LSP-3314 [S]	Free, Frantic and Funky	1965	$25
❏ LPM-3578 [M]	Live at Count Basie's	1966	$35
❏ LSP-3578 [S]	Live at Count Basie's	1966	$25
❏ LPM-3799 [M]	Midnight to Dawn	1967	$25
❏ LSP-3799 [S]	Midnight to Dawn	1967	$35

SUNSET
❏ SUS-5191	Flying Home	196?	$35

TANGERINE
❏ 1509	Wonderful World	197?	$35

DAVISON, WILD BILL, AND EDDIE MILLER
REALTIME
❏ 306	Wild Bill Davison and Eddie Miller Play Hoagy Carmichael	198?	$25

DAVISON, WILD BILL, AND RALPH SUTTON
STORYVILLE
❏ 4027	Together Again	197?	$25

DAVISON, WILD BILL
AIRCHECK
❏ 31	Wild Bill Davison	198?	$25

AUDIOPHILE
❏ AP-149	Beautifully Wild	197?	$30

CHIAROSCURO
❏ 124	Live at the Rainbow Room	197?	$35

CIRCLE
❏ LP-405 [10]	Showcase	1951	$100

COLUMBIA
❏ CL871 [M]	Pretty Wild: Wild Bill Davison with Strings	1956	$40
❏ CL983 [M]	Wild Bill Davison with Strings Attached	1957	$40

COMMODORE
❏ FL-20000 [10]	Dixieland Jazz Jamboree	1950	$150
❏ FL-30009 [M]	Mild and Wild	1959	$75
❏ XFL-14939	That's a-Plenty	198?	$25

DIXIELAND JUBILEE
❏ DJ-508 [M]	Greatest of the Greats	1958	$30
❏ DJS-508 [S]	Greatest of the Greats	1958	$30

JAZZOLOGY
❏ J-22	After Hours	196?	$35
❏ J-18	Blowin' Wild	1966	$35
❏ J-37	Jazz on a Saturday Afternoon, Vol. 1	197?	$30
❏ J-38	Jazz on a Saturday Afternoon, Vol. 2	197?	$30
❏ J-39	Jazz on a Saturday Afternoon, Vol. 3	197?	$30
❏ J-128	Lady of the Evening	1986	$25
❏ J-133	Live in Memphis	1986	$25
❏ J-14 [M]	Rompin' and Stompin'	196?	$25
❏ JCE-14 [S]	Rompin' and Stompin'	196?	$30
❏ J-25	Surfside Jazz	196?	$35
❏ J-151	Wild Bill Davison and His 75th Anniversary Jazz Band	1986	$25
❏ J-103	Wild Bill Davison and His Jazz Band	198?	$25
❏ J-70	Wild Bill Davison and the Classic Jazz Collegium	197?	$30
❏ J-30	Wild Bill Davison at Bull Run	1968	$35
❏ J-121	Wild Bill Davison In London	1987	$25
❏ J-2 [M]	Wild Bill Davison's Jazzologists	1962	$50
❏ JCE-2 [S]	Wild Bill Davison's Jazzologists	1962	$30

❏ J-160	Wild Bill Davison with Freddy Randall and His Band	198?	$25

REGENT
❏ MG-6026 [M]	When the Saints Go Marching In	196?	$50

RIVERSIDE
❏ RLP 12-211 [M]	Sweet and Hot	1956	$300

—*White label, blue print*

❏ RLP 12-211 [M]	Sweet and Hot	195?	$30

—*Blue label, microphone logo at top*

SACKVILLE
❏ 3002	The Jazz Giants	198?	$25

SAVOY
❏ MG-12214 [M]	Dixieland	1969	$35
❏ MG-12035 [M]	Jazz at Storyville	1955	$85
❏ MG-12055 [M]	Ringside at Condon's	1955	$85

—*Reissue of two 10-inch LPs (15029 and 15030) that are listed in the Various Artists Collection area*

SAVOY JAZZ
❏ SJL-2229	Individualism	198?	$35
❏ SJC-403	Ringside at Condon's	198?	$25

STORYVILLE
❏ 4048	But Beautiful	197?	$25
❏ 4029	Papa Bue's Viking Jazz Band	197?	$25
❏ 4005	Wild Bill Davison with Eddie Condon's All Stars	197?	$25

DAWE, TIM
STRAIGHT
❏ STS-1058 [B]	Penrod	1969	$150

WARNER BROS.
❏ WS1841	Penrod	1970	$18

DAWN (1)
ARISTA
❏ AL4045	Greatest Hits	1975	$12
❏ AQ4045 [Q]	Greatest Hits	1975	$20
❏ AL4059	Skybird	1975	$12
❏ A2L9006	The World of Tony Orlando and Dawn	1977	$15

BELL
❏ 1320	Candida & Knock Three Times	1974	$12

—*Reissue of 6052*

❏ 6052	Candida	1970	$15
❏ 6069	Dawn Featuring Tony Orlando	1971	$15
❏ 1130	Dawn's New Ragtime Follies	1973	$12
❏ 1317	Prime Time	1974	$12
❏ 1322	Tony Orlando & Dawn II	1974	$12

—*Reissue of 6069*

❏ 1112	Tuneweaving	1973	$12

ELEKTRA
❏ 7E-1034	He Don't Love You (Like I Love You)	1975	$12
❏ EQ-1034 [Q]	He Don't Love You (Like I Love You)	1975	$20
❏ 7E-1049	To Be with You	1976	$12
❏ EQ-1049 [Q]	To Be with You	1976	$20

DAWSON, SID
DELMAR
❏ DL-109 [10]	Sid Dawson's Riverboat Gamblers	195?	$75

DAY, BOBBY
CLASS
❏ LP-5002 [M]	Rockin' with Robin	1959	$400

COLLECTABLES
❏ COL-5074	Golden Classics	198?	$12

RENDEZVOUS
❏ M-1312 [M]	Rockin' with Robin	196?	$150

RHINO
❏ RNDF-208	The Best of Bobby Day	1984	$15

DAY, CORA LEE
ROULETTE
❏ R-52048 [M]	My Crying Hour	1960	$30
❏ SR-52048 [S]	My Crying Hour	1960	$40

DAY, DENNIS
DESIGN
❏ DLPX-1 [M]	Dennis Day Sings "Christmas Is for the Family"	195?	$25

—*Cover features Jack Benny as Santa; he also appears briefly on the LP*

❏ DLP-X-17 [M]	White Christmas	1965	$15
❏ SDLP-X-17 [S]	White Christmas	1965	$18

GLENDALE
❏ 6029	Christmas Winterland	19??	$12

Number	Title	Yr	NM

STEREO-SPECTRUM

| ❏ SDLPX-1 [S] | Dennis Day Sings "Christmas Is for the Family | 195? | $30 |

— *Same as Design 1*

DAY, DORIS

COLUMBIA

❏ CL1614 [M]	Bright and Shiny	1960	$25
❏ CS8414 [S]	Bright and Shiny	1960	$30
❏ CL6248 [10]	By the Light of the Silvery Moon	1953	$75
❏ CL6273 [10]	Calamity Jane	1953	$75
❏ CL1232 [M]	Cuttin' Capers	1959	$25
❏ CS8078 [S]	Cuttin' Capers	1959	$30

❏ CL942 [M]	Day By Day	1957	$30
❏ CL1053 [M]	Day By Night	1958	$30
❏ CS8089 [S]	Day By Night	1959	$30
❏ CL624 [M]	Day Dreams	1955	$50

— *Red label, gold print*

| ❏ CL624 [M] | Day Dreams | 1956 | $30 |

— *Six "eye" logos on label*

| ❏ CL749 [M] | Day in Hollywood | 1956 | $30 |
| ❏ CL1210 [M] | Doris Day's Greatest Hits | 1958 | $30 |

— *Six "eye" logos on label*

| ❏ CS8635 [P] | Doris Day's Greatest Hits | 1962 | $25 |

— *360 Sound Stereo" in black at bottom*

| ❏ CL1210 [M] | Doris Day's Greatest Hits | 1962 | $15 |

— *Guaranteed High Fidelity" or "Mono" on label*

| ❏ PC8635 | Doris Day's Greatest Hits | 198? | $10 |

— *Budget-line reissue*

| ❏ CL1752 [M] | Duet | 1962 | $25 |

— *With Andre Previn*

| ❏ CS8552 [S] | Duet | 1962 | $30 |

— *With Andre Previn*

❏ C2L5 [M]	Hooray for Hollywood	1959	$40
❏ C2S805 [S]	Hooray for Hollywood	1959	$50
❏ CL1366 [M]	Hooray for Hollywood, Volume 1	1959	$25
❏ CS8066 [S]	Hooray for Hollywood, Volume 1	1959	$30
❏ CL1367 [M]	Hooray for Hollywood, Volume 2	1959	$25
❏ CS8067 [S]	Hooray for Hollywood, Volume 2	1959	$30
❏ CL1660 [M]	I Have Dreamed	1961	$25
❏ CS8460 [S]	I Have Dreamed	1961	$30
❏ CL6198 [10]	I'll See You in My Dreams	1951	$75
❏ CL2310 [M]	Latin for Lovers	1965	$15
❏ CS9110 [S]	Latin for Lovers	1965	$25
❏ CL2518 [10]	Lights, Camera, Action	1955	$75
❏ DD1 [M]	Listen to Day	1960	$25
❏ DDS1 [S]	Listen to Day	1960	$30
❏ CL2131 [M]	Love Him!	1964	$25
❏ CS8931 [S]	Love Him!	1964	$25
❏ CL710 [M]	Love Me or Leave Me	1955	$75

— *Red label, gold print*

| ❏ CL710 [M] | Love Me or Leave Me | 1956 | $30 |

— *Six "eye" logos on label*

| ❏ CL710 [M] | Love Me or Leave Me | 1962 | $25 |

— *Guaranteed High Fidelity" or "Mono" on label*

❏ CS8773 [S]	Love Me or Leave Me	1963	$15
❏ CL6168 [10]	Lullaby of Broadway	1951	$75
❏ CL6186 [10]	On Moonlight Bay	1951	$75
❏ CL2360 [M]	Sentimental Journey	1965	$15
❏ CS9160 [S]	Sentimental Journey	1965	$20
❏ CL1470 [M]	Show Time	1960	$25
❏ CS8261 [S]	Show Time	1960	$25
❏ CL6149 [10]	Tea for Two	1950	$75
❏ CL2226 [M]	The Doris Day Christmas Album	1964	$15
❏ CS9026 [S]	The Doris Day Christmas Album	1964	$25
❏ CL1438 [M]	What Every Girl Should Know	1960	$25
❏ CS8234 [S]	What Every Girl Should Know	1960	$30
❏ CL2266 [M]	With a Smile and a Song	1965	$30
❏ CS9066 [S]	With a Smile and a Song	1965	$35
❏ CL1904 [M]	You'll Never Walk Alone	1962	$35

| ❏ CS8704 [S] | You'll Never Walk Alone | 1962 | $50 |
| ❏ CL6339 [10] | Young at Heart | 1954 | $120 |

— *Six songs by Doris Day, two by Frank Sinatra*

| ❏ CL6106 [10] | Young Man with a Horn | 1950 | $200 |
| ❏ CL582 [M] | Young Man with a Horn | 1954 | $40 |

— *Reissue of 6106; red label, gold print*

| ❏ CL6071 [10] | You're My Thrill | 1949 | $120 |

COLUMBIA LIMITED EDITION

| ❏ LE10197 | The Doris Day Christmas Album | 197? | $12 |

COLUMBIA SPECIAL PRODUCTS

| ❏ P13346 | The Doris Day Christmas Album | 197? | $12 |

— *Reissue of CS 9026*

| ❏ C10988 | The Doris Day Christmas Album | 197? | $12 |

— *Reissue of CS 9026*

| ❏ P213231 | The Magic of Doris Day | 1976 | $20 |
| ❏ XTV82021/2 [M] | Wonderful Day | 1961 | $40 |

HARMONY

❏ HL9559 [M]	Do Re Mi (And Other Children's Favorites)	196?	$15
❏ HS14559 [S]	Do Re Mi (And Other Children's Favorites)	196?	$15
❏ HL7392 [M]	Great Movie Hits	1966	$15
❏ HS11192 [R]	Great Movie Hits	1966	$15
❏ KH31498	Softly, As I Leave You	1972	$12
❏ HS11382	The Magic of Doris Day	1970	$15
❏ HS11282	Whatever Will Be, Will Be (Que Sera, Sera)	1968	$15

HEARTLAND

| ❏ HL1102/3 | The Best of Doris Day | 1990 | $20 |

— *Mail-order offer; alternate number is CBS Special Products P2 22031*

HINDSIGHT

| ❏ HSR-200 | Doris Day with Van Alexander's Orchestra | 198? | $12 |

DAY, JIMMY

PHILIPS

❏ PHM200016 [M]	Golden Steel Guitar Hits	1962	$30
❏ PHS600016 [S]	Golden Steel Guitar Hits	1962	$30
❏ PHM200075 [M]	Steel and Strings	1963	$30
❏ PHS600075 [S]	Steel and Strings	1963	$30

DAY BLINDNESS

STUDIO 10

| ❏ DBX-101 | Day Blindness | 1969 | $75 |

DAYNE, TAYLOR

ARISTA

| ❏ AL-8581 | Can't Fight Fate | 1989 | $12 |
| ❏ AL-8529 | Tell It to My Heart | 1987 | $12 |

DAZZ BAND

20TH CENTURY

| ❏ T-594 | Dazz | 1979 | $18 |

— *As "Kinsman Dazz*

| ❏ T-594 | Kinsman Dazz | 1978 | $18 |

— *As "Kinsman Dazz*

GEFFEN

| ❏ GHS24110 | Wild and Free | 1986 | $10 |

MOTOWN

❏ 5387ML	Greatest Hits	1986	$10
❏ 6149ML	Hot Spot	1985	$12
❏ M8-946M1	Invitation to Love	1980	$15
❏ 6084ML	Joystick	1983	$12
❏ 6117ML	Jukebox	1984	$12
❏ 5350ML	Keep It Live	1984	$10

— *Reissue of 6004*

❏ 6004ML	Keep It Live	1982	$12
❏ M8-957M1	Let the Music Play	1981	$12
❏ 6031ML	On the One	1983	$12

RCA

| ❏ 6928-1-R | Rock the Room | 1988 | $10 |

DB'S, THE

BEARSVILLE

| ❏ 25146 | Like This | 1984 | $18 |

I.R.S.

| ❏ 42055 | The Sound of Music | 1987 | $15 |

RHINO

| ❏ R1-70891 | Like This | 1988 | $12 |

— *Reissue of Bearsville LP*

DE-FENDERS, THE

DEL-FI

| ❏ DFLP-1242 [M] | Drag Beat | 1963 | $50 |
| ❏ DFST-1242 [S] | Drag Beat | 1963 | $75 |

WORLD PACIFIC

| ❏ WP-1810 [M] | The De-Fenders Play the Big Ones | 1963 | $50 |
| ❏ ST-1810 [S] | The De-Fenders Play the Big Ones | 1963 | $175 |

— *Red vinyl*

| ❏ ST-1810 [S] | The De-Fenders Play the Big Ones | 1963 | $175 |

— *Green vinyl*

| ❏ ST-1810 [S] | The De-Fenders Play the Big Ones | 1963 | $80 |

— *Black vinyl*

DE LA SOUL

TOMMY BOY

| ❏ TB1019 | 3 Feet High and Rising | 1989 | $25 |

— *Original edition*

| ❏ TB1019 | 3 Feet High and Rising | 2001 | $18 |

— *Reissue, expanded to a two-disc set*

| ❏ TB1362 | AOI: Bionix | 2001 | $18 |
| ❏ TB1443 [DJ] | AOI: Bionix//Edited | 2001 | $18 |

— *Promo-only "clean" version*

❏ TB1546	AOI: Bionix Instrumentals	2002	$18
❏ TB1361	Art Official Intelligence: Mosaic Thump	2000	$18
❏ TB1437	Art Official Intelligence: Mosaic Thump Instrumentals	2000	$18
❏ TB1063 [DJ]	Buhloone Mindstate	1993	$30

— *Vinyl appears to be promo only*

| ❏ TB1093 [DJ] | Clear Lake Auditorium | 1994 | $30 |

— *Promo-only on clear vinyl (black vinyl editions are counterfeits)*

| ❏ TB1029 [B] | De La Soul Is Dead | 1991 | $30 |
| ❏ TB1041 [DJ] | De La Soul Is Dead | 1991 | $35 |

— *Promo-only two-record set*

| ❏ TB1149 | Stakes Is High | 1996 | $18 |
| ❏ TB1175 [DJ] | Stakes Is High Sampler | 1996 | $30 |

— *Promo only; contains eight songs from the full-length edition*

DEAD BOYS

BOMP!

| ❏ 4017 | Night of the Living Dead Boys | 1981 | $18 |

SIRE

| ❏ SRK-6054 | We Have Come for Your Children | 1978 | $30 |
| ❏ SRK-6054 | We Have Come for Your Children | 1978 | $50 |

— *With original title Down To Kill on label*

| ❏ SR-6038 [B] | Young, Loud & Snotty | 1977 | $35 |

DEAD KENNEDYS

Featuring Jello Biafra.

ALTERNATIVE TENTACLES

| ❏ VIRUS50 [B] | Bedtime for Democracy | 1986 | $35 |

— *Originals have a newspaper insert*

| ❏ VIRUS45 [B] | Frankenchrist | 1985 | $75 |

— *Originals have a poster of H.R. Giger's painting Landscape #20, which was involved in an obscenity trial. The poster is still available, but only by mailing in a coupon inside the LP.*

| ❏ VIRUS1 | Fresh Fruit for Rotting Vegetables | 1988 | $25 |

— *Reissue of I.R.S. album*

❏ VIRUS57	Give Me Convenience or Give Me Death	1987	$18
❏ VIRUS5 [EP]	In God We Trust, Inc.	1981	$50
❏ VIRUS27 [B]	Plastic Surgery Disasters	1982	$40

FAULTY

| ❏ 70014 | Fresh Fruit for Rotting Vegetables | 1982 | $40 |

— *With nursing home photo on back cover, no reference to I.R.S. on label or cover*

I.R.S./FAULTY PRODUCTS

| ❏ SP-70014 [B] | Fresh Fruit for Rotting Vegetables | 1980 | $75 |

— *Originals have an orange cover "to distinguish it from imports*

| ❏ SP-70014 | Fresh Fruit for Rotting Vegetables | 1980 | $25 |

— *Reissues have a black front cover, same as imports; it was changed at the insistence of band member Jello Biafra*

DEAD MILKMEN, THE

ENIGMA

| ❏ 73351 | Beelzebubba | 1988 | $18 |
| ❏ D1-73260 | Bucky Fellini | 1988 | $18 |

FEVER/ENIGMA

| ❏ 72054 | Big Lizard in My Backyard | 1985 | $25 |

RESTLESS

| ❏ 72131 | Eat Your Paisley | 1988 | $18 |

DEAD OR ALIVE

EPIC

❏ FE40572	Mad, Bad and Dangerous to Know	1986	$15
❏ OE45224	Nude	1989	$15
❏ EAS2668 [DJ]	Radio Special with Pete Burns	1986	$80

— *Promo-only music and interviews*

❏ OE44255	Rip It Up	1988	$15
❏ BFE39274	Sophisticated Boom Boom	1984	$15
❏ FE39274	Sophisticated Boom Boom	1985	$10

Number	Title	Yr	NM
—Reissue with new prefix			
❑ BFE40119	Youthquake	1985	$12
❑ FE40119	Youthquake	1985	$10
—Reissue with new prefix			

DEADLY ONES, THE
VEE JAY
❑ LP-1090 [M]	It's Monster Surfing Time	1964	$300
❑ LPS-1090 [S]	It's Monster Surfing Time	1964	$350

DEAL, BILL, AND THE RHONDELS
HERITAGE
❑ HTS35006	The Best of Bill Deal and the Rhondels	1970	$30
❑ HTS35003	Vintage Rock	1969	$30
RHINO
❑ RNLP-70129	The Best of Bill Deal and the Rhondels (1969-1970)	1986	$12

DEAN, ALAN
DESIGN
❑ DLP-102 [M]	Songs of Faith	1959	$15
❑ SDLP-300 [S]	The Lord's Prayer	1969	$12
GRAND PRIX
❑ K-184 [M]	Songs of Faith	196?	$12
❑ KS-184 [S]	Songs of Faith	196?	$15
INTERNATIONAL AWARD SERIES
❑ AKS-184 [S]	Songs of Faith	196?	$15
❑ AK-184 [M]	Songs of Faith	196?	$12
MGM
❑ E-3461 [M]	Heart and Soul	1956	$30
STEREO-SPECTRUM
❑ SS-45 [S]	Songs of Faith	1959	$18

DEAN, EDDIE
SAGE AND SAND
❑ C-1 [M]	Greatest Westerns	1956	$50
❑ C-5 [M]	Hi-Country	1957	$50
❑ C-16 [M]	Hillbilly Heaven	1961	$30
SOUND
❑ LP-603 [M]	Greatest Westerns	1957	$30

DEAN, JIMMY
COLUMBIA
❑ CL1735 [M]	Big Bad John and Other Fabulous Songs and Tales	1961	$25
—With the version of "Big Bad John" containing the lyric "At the bottom of this mine lies a big, big man"; confirmed copies have trail-off numbers of "XLP-54925-1F" and "XLP-54925-1J"			
❑ CS8535 [S]	Big Bad John and Other Fabulous Songs and Tales	1961	$30
—It's possible that two different editions exist, one with the "hell of a man" lyrics of "Big Bad John" and the other with the "big, big man" lyrics, but this has not been confirmed.			
❑ CL1735 [M]	Big Bad John and Other Fabulous Songs and Tales	1961	$30
—With the version of "Big Bad John" containing the lyric "At the bottom of this mine lies one hell of a man"; confirmed copies have a trail-off number of "XLP-54925-2A" and "XLP-54925-2B			
❑ CS9677 [M]	Dean's List	1968	$30
—White label promo; "Special Mono Radio Station Copy" sticker on cover			
❑ CS9677 [S]	Dean's List	1968	$18
❑ CL2027 [M]	Everybody's Favorite	1963	$18
❑ CS8827 [S]	Everybody's Favorite	1963	$25
❑ CL2404 [M]	Jimmy Dean's Christmas Card	1965	$18
❑ CS9204 [S]	Jimmy Dean's Christmas Card	1965	$18
❑ CL2485 [M]	Jimmy Dean's Greatest Hits	1966	$18
❑ CS9285 [S]	Jimmy Dean's Greatest Hits	1966	$18
❑ PC9285	Jimmy Dean's Greatest Hits	198?	$10
—Budget-line reissue			
❑ CL1025 [M]	Jimmy Dean's Hour of Prayer	1957	$40
❑ CS9424 [R]	Jimmy Dean's Hour of Prayer	1966	$15
❑ CL1894 [M]	Portrait of Jimmy Dean	1962	$25
❑ CS8694 [S]	Portrait of Jimmy Dean	1962	$30
❑ CL2188 [M]	Songs We All Love Best	1964	$18
❑ CS8988 [S]	Songs We All Love Best	1964	$25
❑ CL2538 [M]	The Big Ones	1966	$18
❑ CS9338 [S]	The Big Ones	1966	$18
❑ CL2401 [M]	The First Thing Every Morning	1965	$18
❑ CS9201 [S]	The First Thing Every Morning	1965	$25
CROWN
❑ 291	Jimmy Dean and the Western Gentlemen	196?	$15
GRT
❑ 8014	I.O.U.	1977	$12
HARMONY
❑ HL7268 [M]	Hymns	1960	$18
❑ HS11042 [R]	Hymns	1960	$15
❑ HL7408 [M]	Mr. Country Music	1967	$15
❑ HS11208 [S]	Mr. Country Music	1967	$15

Number	Title	Yr	NM
❑ HS11270	The Country's Favorite Son	1968	$15
HILLTOP
❑ 6004	Golden Favorites	196?	$15
KING
❑ 686 [M]	Favorites of Jimmy Dean	1961	$75
MERCURY
❑ MG-20319 [M]	Jimmy Dean Sings His Television Favorites	1957	$40
RCA VICTOR
❑ LPM-3999 [M]	A Thing Called Love	1968	$30
❑ LSP-3999 [S]	A Thing Called Love	1968	$18
❑ LSP-4434	Country Boy and Country Girl	1970	$18
❑ LSP-4323	Dean of Country	1970	$18
❑ LSP-4511	Everybody Knows	1971	$18
❑ LPM-3727 [M]	Jimmy Dean Is Here	1967	$18
❑ LSP-3727 [S]	Jimmy Dean Is Here	1967	$18
❑ LPM-3824 [M]	Most Richly Blesed	1967	$25
❑ LSP-3824 [S]	Most Richly Blesed	1967	$18
❑ LSP-4035	Speaker of the House	1968	$18
❑ LPM-3890 [M]	The Jimmy Dean Show	1967	$25
❑ LSP-3890 [S]	The Jimmy Dean Show	1967	$18
❑ LSP-4618	These Hands	1972	$18
SEARS
❑ 105	Jimmy Dean's Golden Favorites	196?	$18
SPIN-O-RAMA
❑ 137	Country Round-Up Featuring Jimmy Dean	196?	$15
❑ 108	Featuring the Coutnry Singing of Jimmy Dean	196?	$15
WING
❑ MGW-12292 [M]	Jimmy Dean Sings His Television Favorites	196?	$18
❑ SRW-16292 [R]	Jimmy Dean Sings His Television Favorites	196?	$15
WYNCOTE
❑ 9032	Country Favorites	196?	$15

DEAN, JIMMY / JOHNNY HORTON
LA BREA
❑ L8014 [M]	Bummin' Around with Jimmy Dean and Johnny Horton	1961	$100
STARDAY
❑ SLP-325 [M]	Bummin' Around with Jimmy Dean and Johnny Horton	1965	$30

DEAN, JIMMY / MARVIN RAINWATER
PREMIER
❑ 9054	Nashville Showtime	196?	$15

DEAN, PETER
AUDIO FIDELITY
❑ AFSD-6280	Peter Dean in Fun City	197?	$35
BUDDAH
❑ BDS-5613	Four or Five Times	1974	$35
INNER CITY
❑ IC-4002	Only Time Will Tell	1979	$30
MONMOUTH-EVERGREEN
❑ 7092	Where Did the Magic Go	198?	$30
PROJECT 3
❑ PR5075SD	Ding Dong Daddy!	196?	$35

DEAN, SUZANNE
NOVA
❑ 8808-1	Dreams Come True	198?	$25
❑ 9028-1	I Wonder	1988	$25

DEANGELIS, JIM, AND TONY SIGNA
STATIRAS
❑ SLP-8075	Gridlock	1985	$25

DEARANGO, BILL
EMARCY
❑ MG-26020 [10]	Bill DeArango	1954	$300

DEARIE, BLOSSOM
CAPITOL
❑ T2086 [M]	May I Come In	1964	$85
❑ ST2086 [S]	May I Come In	1964	$40
❑ SM-2086	May I Come In	1976	$25
—Reissue with new prefix			
DAFFODIL
❑ BMD-102	1975	1975	$35
❑ BMD-101	Blossom Dearie Sings	197?	$35
❑ BMD-109	Chez Wahlberg, Part I	198?	$30
❑ BMD-108	Et Tu Bruce (Volume VIII)	198?	$25
❑ BMD-103	My New Celebrity Is You	197?	$25
❑ BMD-105	Needlepoint Magic	198?	$30
❑ BMD-107	Positively Volume VII	198?	$25
❑ BMD-106	Simply Volume VI	1983	$25
❑ BMD-110	Songs of Chelsea	1987	$25
❑ BMD-104	Winchester in Apple Blossom Time	197?	$50

Number	Title	Yr	NM
DRG
❑ DARC-1105	Blossom Dearie On Broadway	1980	$35
FONTANA
❑ MGF-27562 [M]	Blossom Time	1966	$35
❑ SRF-67562 [S]	Blossom Time	1966	$25
VERVE
❑ MGV-2037 [M]	Blossom Dearie	1957	$175
❑ V-2037 [M]	Blossom Dearie	1961	$25
❑ UMV-2639	Blossom Dearie	198?	$25
❑ MGV-2109 [M]	Blossom Dearie Sings Comden & Green	1959	$175
❑ MGVS-6050 [S]	Blossom Dearie Sings Comden & Green	1960	$175
❑ V-2109 [M]	Blossom Dearie Sings Comden & Green	1961	$25
❑ V6-2109 [S]	Blossom Dearie Sings Comden & Green	1961	$30
❑ MGV-2133 [M]	Broadway Song Hits	1960	$120
❑ MGVS-6139 [S]	Broadway Song Hits	1960	$120
❑ V-2133 [M]	Broadway Song Hits	1961	$25
❑ V6-2133 [S]	Broadway Song Hits	1961	$30
❑ MGV-2081 [M]	Give Him the Ooh-La-La	1958	$150
❑ V-2081 [M]	Give Him the Ooh-La-La	1961	$25
❑ MGV-2125 [M]	My Gentleman Friend	1959	$150
❑ MGVS-6112 [S]	My Gentleman Friend	1960	$150
❑ V-2125 [M]	My Gentleman Friend	1961	$25
❑ V6-2125 [S]	My Gentleman Friend	1961	$30
❑ MGV-2111 [M]	Once Upon a Summertime	1958	$120
❑ MGVS-6020 [S]	Once Upon a Summertime	1960	$150
❑ V-2111 [M]	Once Upon a Summertime	1961	$25
❑ V6-2111 [S]	Once Upon a Summertime	1961	$30
❑ 827757-1	Once Upon a Summertime	1986	$25

DEATH CAB FOR CUTIE
BARSUK
❑ BARK47	Plans	2005	$30
❑ BARK21	The Photo Album	2001	$50

❑ BARK11 [B]	We Have the Facts and We're Voting Yes	2000	$50
SONIC BOOM
❑ SBR 002	Something About Airplanes	1998	$50
—Blue marbled vinyl			
❑ SBR 012	Transatlanticism	2004	$25

DEAUVILLE, RONNIE
ERA
❑ 20002 [M]	Smoke Dreams	1957	$40
IMPERIAL
❑ LP-9060 [M]	Romance	1959	$30
❑ LP-12009 [S]	Romance	1959	$30

DEBARGE, CHICO
KEDAR
❑ 53088	Long Time No See	1997	$15
MOTOWN
❑ 6214ML	Chico DeBarge	1986	$10
❑ 6249ML	Kiss Serious	1987	$10

DEBARGE, EL
GORDY
❑ 6181GL	El DeBarge	1986	$10
MOTOWN
❑ PR-189 [DJ]	El Elaborates!	1986	$30
—Promo-only interview and music album			
❑ MOT-6264	Gemini	1989	$12

DEBARGE
GORDY
❑ 6012GL	All This Love	1982	$10
❑ 6061GL	In a Special Way	1983	$10
❑ 6123GL	Rhythm of the Night	1985	$10
❑ G8-1003M1	The DeBarges	1981	$15

Number	Title	Yr	NM

MOTOWN
| ❏ 5335ML | The DeBarges | 1985 | $10 |

—Reissue of Gordy 1003

STRIPED HORSE
| ❏ SHL2004 | Bad Boys | 1987 | $12 |

DEBRIS
STATIC DISPOSAL
| ❏ 00 [B] | Debris | 1976 | $120 |

DECARLO, YVONNE
MASTERSEAL
| ❏ MS33-1869/70 [M] | Yvonne DeCarlo Sings | 1957 | $100 |

DECARO, NICK
A&M
| ❏ SP-4176 | Happy Heart | 1969 | $12 |

DECASTRO SISTERS, THE
ABBOTT
| ❏ 5002 [M] | The DeCastro Sisters | 1956 | $75 |

CAPITOL
❏ T1402 [M]	The DeCastros Sing	1960	$30
❏ ST1402 [S]	The DeCastros Sing	1960	$30
❏ T1501 [M]	The Rockin' Beat	1961	$30
❏ ST1501 [S]	The Rockin' Beat	1961	$30

DECAUTER, KOEN, AND ORANGE KELLIN
GHB
| ❏ GHB-242 | New Orleans Swing with Koen DeCauter and Orange Kellin: A Little Piece of Paradise | 1990 | $30 |

DECEMBER BAND, THE
GHB
| ❏ GHB-197 | The December Band, Volume 1 | 1986 | $25 |
| ❏ GHB-198 | The December Band, Volume 2 | 1986 | $25 |

DECEMBER'S CHILDREN
MAINSTREAM
| ❏ S-6128 | December's Children | 1970 | $175 |

DEDRICK, RUSTY
4 CORNERS OF THE WORLD
| ❏ FC-4207 [M] | The Big Band Sound | 1964 | $35 |
| ❏ FCS-4207 [S] | The Big Band Sound | 1964 | $25 |

COUNTERPOINT
| ❏ 552 [M] | Salute to Bunny | 1957 | $50 |

ESOTERIC
| ❏ ESJ-9 [10] | Rhythm and Winds | 1955 | $150 |

KEYNOTE
| ❏ 1103 [M] | Rusty Dedrick | 1955 | $85 |

MONMOUTH-EVERGREEN
| ❏ 6918 | Harold Arlen in Hollywood | 1969 | $35 |
| ❏ 7035 | Many Facets, Many Friends | 1970 | $35 |

MONUMENT
| ❏ MLP-6502 [M] | A Jazz Journey | 1965 | $35 |
| ❏ SLP-16502 [S] | A Jazz Journey | 1965 | $25 |

DEE, DUANE
CAPITOL
| ❏ ST2931 | My Shining Hour | 1968 | $18 |

DEE, JOEY, AND THE STARLITERS
FORUM
| ❏ FC9099 [M] | Joey Dee and the Starliters | 1963 | $15 |
| ❏ FCS9099 [S] | Joey Dee and the Starliters | 1963 | $15 |

JUBILEE
| ❏ JGM-8000 [M] | Hitsville | 1966 | $30 |
| ❏ JGS-8000 [S] | Hitsville | 1966 | $30 |

ROULETTE
❏ R-25171 [M]	All the World Is Twistin'	1962	$30
❏ SR-25171 [S]	All the World Is Twistin'	1962	$40
❏ R-25173 [M]	Back at the Peppermint Lounge -- Twistin'	1962	$30
❏ SR-25173 [S]	Back at the Peppermint Lounge -- Twistin'	1962	$40
❏ R-25221 [M]	Dance, Dance, Dance	1963	$30
❏ SR-25221 [S]	Dance, Dance, Dance	1963	$40
❏ R-25166 [M]	Doin' the Twist at the Peppermint Lounge	1961	$40
❏ SR-25166 [S]	Doin' the Twist at the Peppermint Lounge	1961	$50
❏ R-25197 [M]	Joey Dee	1963	$30
❏ SR-25197 [S]	Joey Dee	1963	$30

SCEPTER
| ❏ S503 [M] | The Peppermint Twisters | 1962 | $30 |
| ❏ SS503 [S] | The Peppermint Twisters | 1962 | $35 |

DEE, KIKI
LIBERTY
| ❏ LST-7613 | Patterns | 1969 | $18 |
| ❏ LN-10148 | Patterns | 1981 | $10 |

—Budget-line reissue

RCA VICTOR
| ❏ AFL1-4180 | Perfect Timing | 1981 | $12 |

ROCKET
❏ PIG-458	I've Got the Music In Me	1974	$15
❏ BXL1-2257	Kiki Dee	1977	$12
❏ PIG-395	Loving and Free	1973	$12
❏ BXL1-3011	Stay with Me	1979	$12

TAMLA
| ❏ TS303 [B] | Great Expectations | 1970 | $30 |

DEE, LENNY
DECCA
❏ DL4429 [M]	By Popular Dee-Mand	1963	$12
❏ DL74429 [S]	By Popular Dee-Mand	1963	$15
❏ DL8628 [M]	Dee-Day	1957	$15
❏ DL8718 [M]	Dee-Latin Hi-Fi Organ	1958	$15
❏ DL8275 [M]	Dee-Licious	1956	$15
❏ DL8114 [M]	Dee-Lightful	1955	$18
❏ DL8165 [M]	Dee-Lirious	1956	$15
❏ DL8308 [M]	Dee-Most	1956	$15
❏ DL75196	Easy Come, Easy Go	1970	$12
❏ DL75320	Easy Lovin'	1972	$12
❏ DL4994 [M]	Gentle on My Mind	1968	$15
❏ DL74994 [S]	Gentle on My Mind	1968	$12
❏ DL4112 [M]	Golden Organ Favorites	1961	$12
❏ DL74112 [S]	Golden Organ Favorites	1961	$15
❏ DL4146 [M]	Happy Holi-Dee	1961	$12
❏ DL74146 [S]	Happy Holi-Dee	1961	$15
❏ DL8406 [M]	Hi-Dee-Fi	1957	$15
❏ DL4818 [M]	In the Mood	1967	$12
❏ DL74818 [S]	In the Mood	1967	$15
❏ DL4365 [M]	Lenny Dee Down South	1963	$12
❏ DL74365 [S]	Lenny Dee Down South	1963	$15
❏ DL4315 [M]	Lenny Dee In Hollywood	1962	$12
❏ DL74315 [S]	Lenny Dee In Hollywood	1962	$15
❏ DL8857 [M]	Lenny Dee Plays the Hits	1959	$15
❏ DL78857 [S]	Lenny Dee Plays the Hits	1959	$18
❏ DL75112	Little Green Apples	1969	$12
❏ DL8796 [M]	Mellow-Dee	1959	$15
❏ DL78796 [S]	Mellow-Dee	1959	$18
❏ DL4572 [M]	Most Requested	1964	$12
❏ DL74572 [S]	Most Requested	1964	$15
❏ DL4880 [M]	Moving On	1967	$12
❏ DL78880 [S]	Moving On	1967	$15
❏ DL8497 [M]	Mr. Dee Goes to Town	1957	$15
❏ DL4706 [M]	My Favorite Things	1966	$12
❏ DL74706 [S]	My Favorite Things	1966	$15
❏ DL4946 [M]	Relaxin'	1968	$15
❏ DL74946 [S]	Relaxin'	1968	$12
❏ DL75255	Remember Me	1971	$12
❏ DL4498 [M]	Something Special	1964	$12
❏ DL74498 [S]	Something Special	1964	$15
❏ DL8978 [M]	Songs Everybody Knows	1960	$12
❏ DL78978 [S]	Songs Everybody Knows	1960	$15
❏ DL75152	Spinning Wheel	1969	$12
❏ DL4632 [M]	Sweethearts on Parade	1965	$12
❏ DL74632 [S]	Sweethearts on Parade	1965	$15
❏ DXS7199	The Best of Lenny Dee	1968	$15
❏ DL8913 [M]	The Lenny Dee Show	1960	$12
❏ DL78913 [S]	The Lenny Dee Show	1960	$15
❏ DL4654 [M]	The Lenny Dee Tour	1965	$12
❏ DL74654 [S]	The Lenny Dee Tour	1965	$15
❏ DL75073	Turn Around, Look at Me	1969	$12
❏ DL75366	Where Is the Love	1972	$12

MCA
| ❏ 476 | City Lights | 1974 | $10 |
| ❏ 290 | Easy Come, Easy Go | 1973 | $10 |

—Reissue of Decca 75196
| ❏ 297 | Easy Lovin' | 1973 | $10 |

—Reissue of Decca 75320
| ❏ 271 | Gentle on My Mind | 1973 | $10 |

—Reissue of Decca 74994
| ❏ 182 | Golden Organ Favorites | 1973 | $10 |

—Reissue of Decca 74112
| ❏ 2162 | I'll Play for You | 1975 | $10 |
| ❏ 172 | In the Mood | 1973 | $10 |

—Reissue of Decca 74818
❏ 379	Lenny	1973	$10
❏ 334	Lenny Dee	1973	$10
❏ 279	Little Green Apples	1973	$10

—Reissue of Decca 75112
| ❏ 2236 | Misty Blue | 1976 | $10 |
| ❏ 231 | Most Requested | 1973 | $10 |

—Reissue of Decca 74572
| ❏ 241 | My Favorite Things | 1973 | $10 |

—Reissue of Decca 74706
❏ 2370	Organ Celebration	1978	$10
❏ 2301	Organ Magic	1977	$10
❏ 26	Remember Me	1971	$10

—Reissue of Decca 75255
| ❏ 334 | Sing" and Others | 1973 | $10 |
| ❏ 221 | Something Special | 1973 | $10 |

—Reissue of Decca 74498
| ❏ 533 | Songs Everybody Knows | 1975 | $10 |

—Reissue of Decca 78978
| ❏ 455 | Steppin' Out with Lenny Dee | 1974 | $10 |

Number	Title	Yr	NM

| ❏ 2200 | Take It to the Limit | 1976 | $10 |
| ❏ 4042 | The Best of Lenny Dee | 197? | $12 |

—Reissue of Decca 7179
| ❏ 4084 | The Best of Lenny Dee, Volume II | 1977 | $12 |
| ❏ 504 | Where Is the Love | 1974 | $10 |

—Reissue of Decca 75366

VOCALION
❏ VL3782 [M]	Here's Lenny Dee at the Organ	1967	$12
❏ VL73782 [S]	Here's Lenny Dee at the Organ	1967	$12
❏ VL73817	Organ Special	1968	$12
❏ VL73819	Varieties	1969	$12

DEEE-LITE
ELEKTRA
❏ 61526	Dewdrops in the Garden	1994	$15
❏ 61313	Infinity Within	1992	$15
❏ 60957	World Clique	1990	$12

DEEP, THE
PARKWAY
| ❏ P7051 [M] | Psychedelic Moods | 1966 | $300 |
| ❏ SP7051 [S] | Psychedelic Moods | 1966 | $500 |

DEEP PURPLE
Also see BLACK SABBATH; TOMMY BOLIN; CAPTAIN BEYOND; GILLAN; IAN GILLAN BAND; RAINBOW; TRAPEZE; WHITESNAKE.

DCC COMPACT CLASSICS
| ❏ LPZ-2052 | Made in Japan | 1998 | $40 |

—Audiophile vinyl

EAGLE ROCK
| ❏ ER20083-1 | Rapture of the Deep | 2005 | $25 |

FRIDAY MUSIC
| ❏ FRM10370 [B] | Last Concert in Japan | 2012 | $30 |

HARVEST
| ❏ SHVL793 [B] | Fireball | 2016 | $25 |

—180 gram
| ❏ SHVL777 [B] | In Rock | 2016 | $25 |

—180g

MERCURY
❏ 835897-1	Nobody's Perfect	1988	$12
❏ 824003-1	Perfect Strangers	1984	$12
❏ 831318-1	The House of Blue Light	1987	$10

PARLOPHONE
| ❏ 2564633757 [B] | Shades of Deep Purple | 2014 | $35 |

RCA
| ❏ 2421-1-R | Slaves and Masters | 1990 | $18 |

RHINO
| ❏ R1-75622 | Machine Head | 2003 | $18 |

—180-gram reissue

SCEPTER CITATION
| ❏ CTN-18010 | The Best of Deep Purple | 1972 | $25 |

TETRAGRAMMATON
❏ T-131 [B]	Concerto for Group and Orchestra	1970	$300
❏ T-119	Deep Purple	1969	$30
❏ T-102	Shades of Deep Purple	1968	$30
❏ T-107	The Book of Taliesyn	1968	$30

WARNER BROS.
❏ W2766	Burn	1974	$12
❏ WS1860 [B]	Concerto for Group and Orchestra	1970	$18
❏ WS1877 [B]	Deep Purple in Rock	1970	$18
❏ BS2564 [B]	Fireball	1971	$18
❏ BS2607 [B]	Machine Head	1972	$18

—Original copies have green "WB" labels
| ❏ BS2607 | Machine Head | 1973 | $12 |

—"Burbank" labels
❏ BS2607 [Q]	Machine Head	1974	$175
❏ BSK3100	Machine Head	1976	$10
❏ 2WS2701 [B]	Made in Japan	1973	$30
❏ 2WS2701 [B]	Made in Japan	1979	$18

—White labels
| ❏ 2LS2644 | (Purple Passages) | 1972 | $18 |
| ❏ BS2678 | Who Do We Think We Are! | 1973 | $15 |

—Original copies have green "WB" labels
| ❏ BS2678 | Who Do We Think We Are! | 1973 | $12 |

—"Burbank" labels

WARNER BROS./PURPLE
❏ PR2895	Come Taste the Band	1975	$12
❏ PRK3486	Deepest Purple: The Best of Deep Purple	1980	$12
❏ PR2995	Made in Europe	1976	$12
❏ PR2832	Stormbringer	1974	$12
❏ PR42832 [Q]	Stormbringer	1974	$100
❏ PRK3223	When We Rock, We Rock, and When We Roll	1978	$12

DEEP RIVER BOYS, THE
QUE
| ❏ FLS-104 [M] | Midnight Magic | 1957 | $175 |

Number	Title	Yr	NM
RCA CAMDEN			
CAL-303 [M]	Presenting the Deep River Boys	1957	$75

—Reissue of "X" album

Number	Title	Yr	NM
WALDORF MUSIC HALL			
MH 33-108 [10]	The Deep River Boys Sing Songs of Jubilee	1954	$300

—Photo of group on cover

Number	Title	Yr	NM
MH 33-108 [10]	The Deep River Boys Sing Songs of Jubilee	195?	$175

—Cartoon on cover

Number	Title	Yr	NM
X			
LXA-1019 [M]	Presenting the Deep River Boys	1956	$120

DEERFIELD

Number	Title	Yr	NM
FLAT ROCK			
FRS-1	Nil Desperandum	1971	$250

DEES, RICK

Number	Title	Yr	NM
ATLANTIC			
81288	I'm Not Crazy	1985	$15
81231	Put It Where the Moon Don't Shine	1984	$15
NO BUDGET			
NBR102	Hurt Me Baby -- Make Me Write Bad Checks!	1983	$18
RSO			

Number	Title	Yr	NM
RS-1-3017 [B]	The Original Disco Duck	1976	$30

DEES, SAM

Number	Title	Yr	NM
ATLANTIC			
SD18134	The Show Must Go On	1975	$175

DEF LEPPARD
Also see DIO.

Number	Title	Yr	NM
MERCURY			
SRM-1-4021	High 'n' Dry	1981	$15

—Chicago skyline label

Number	Title	Yr	NM
818836-1	High 'n' Dry	1984	$10

—Altered version of 4021; "Bringin' on the Heartbreak" is remixed, and "Me & My Wine" is added

Number	Title	Yr	NM
830675-1	Hysteria	1987	$10
832962-1 [PD]	Hysteria	1987	$40

—Limited-edition picture disc in plastic sleeve

Number	Title	Yr	NM
1775319	Hysteria	2008	$25
SRM-1-3828	On Through the Night	1980	$15

—Chicago skyline label

Number	Title	Yr	NM
822533-1	On Through the Night	198?	$10

—Reissue of 3828

Number	Title	Yr	NM
810308-1	Pyromania	1983	$10
810308-1	Pyromania	2008	$25

DEFRANCESCO, JOEY

Number	Title	Yr	NM
COLUMBIA			
FC44463	All of Me	1989	$35

DEFRANCO, BUDDY, AND TOMMY GUMINA

Number	Title	Yr	NM
MERCURY			
MG-20743 [M]	Kaleidoscope	1962	$150
SR-60743 [S]	Kaleidoscope	1962	$150
MG-20833 [M]	Polytones	1963	$150
SR-60833 [S]	Polytones	1963	$150
MG-20685 [M]	Presenting the Buddy DeFranco-Tommy Gumina Quintet	1962	$150
SR-60685 [S]	Presenting the Buddy DeFranco-Tommy Gumina Quintet	1962	$150
MG-20900 [M]	The Girl from Ipanema	1964	$150
SR-60900 [S]	The Girl from Ipanema	1964	$150

DEFRANCO, BUDDY

Number	Title	Yr	NM
CHOICE			
1008	Free Sail	1974	$35
1017	Waterbed	1977	$30
CLASSIC JAZZ			
33	Buddy DeFranco and Jim Gillis	1978	$30
CLEF			
MGC-149 [10]	The Buddy DeFranco Quartet	1954	$0

—Canceled; reassigned to Norgran 3

Number	Title	Yr	NM
DECCA			
DL4031 [M]	Pacific Standard Swingin' Time	1961	$25
DL74031 [S]	Pacific Standard Swingin' Time	1961	$30
DOT			
DLP-9006 [M]	Cross-Country Suite	1958	$100
GENE NORMAN			
GNP-2 [10]	Buddy DeFranco Takes You to the Stars	1954	$120
HAMILTON			
HL-133 [M]	Cross-Country Suite	1964	$25
HS-12133 [R]	Cross-Country Suite	1964	$30
MGM			
E-3396 [M]	Buddy DeFranco	1956	$100
E-253 [10]	Buddy DeFranco with Strings	1954	$150
E-177 [10]	King of the Clarinet	1952	$120
MOSAIC			
MR5-117	The Complete Recordings of the Buddy DeFranco Quartet/Quintet with Sonny Clark	199?	$150
NORGRAN			
MGN-1096 [M]	Autumn Leaves	1956	$250
MGN-1105 [M]	Broadway Showcase	1956	$0

—Canceled; reassigned to Verve 2033

Number	Title	Yr	NM
MGN-1012 [M]	Buddy DeFranco and His Clarinet	1954	$250
MGN-1016 [M]	Buddy DeFranco and Oscar Peterson Play George Gershwin	1955	$250
MGN-1026 [M]	Buddy DeFranco Quartet	1955	$250
MGN-1079 [M]	In a Mellow Mood	1956	$175
MGN-1068 [M]	Jazz Tones	1956	$175
MGN-1069 [M]	Mr. Clarinet	1956	$175
MGN-1094 [M]	Odalisque	1956	$175
MGN-16 [10]	Pretty Moods by Buddy DeFranco	1954	$175
MGN-3 [10]	The Buddy DeFranco Quartet	1954	$300
MGN-1085 [M]	The Buddy DeFranco Wailers	1956	$175
MGN-1006 [M]	The Progressive Mr. DeFranco	1954	$120
PABLO			
2310906	Mr. Lucky	198?	$30
PROGRESSIVE			
7014	Like Someone in Love	1979	$30
SONET			
724	Boronquin	197?	$30
VERVE			
MGV-8183 [M]	Autumn Leaves	1957	$250

—Reissue of Norgran 1096

Number	Title	Yr	NM
V-8183 [M]	Autumn Leaves	1961	$75
MGV-8315 [M]	Bravura	1959	$175
MGVS-6051 [S]	Bravura	1960	$120
V-8315 [M]	Bravura	1961	$25
V6-8315 [S]	Bravura	1961	$25
MGV-2033 [M]	Broadway Showcase	1957	$175
V-2033 [M]	Broadway Showcase	1961	$25
MGV-8384 [M]	Buddy DeFranco	1960	$0

—Canceled

Number	Title	Yr	NM
MGVS-6167 [S]	Buddy DeFranco	1960	$0

—Canceled

Number	Title	Yr	NM
MGV-8210 [M]	Buddy DeFranco and the Oscar Peterson Quartet	1958	$175
V-8210 [M]	Buddy DeFranco and the Oscar Peterson Quartet	1961	$25
MGV-2090 [M]	Buddy DeFranco Plays Artie Shaw	1958	$175
V-2090 [M]	Buddy DeFranco Plays Artie Shaw	1961	$25
MGV-2089 [M]	Buddy DeFranco Plays Benny Goodman	1958	$175
V-2089 [M]	Buddy DeFranco Plays Benny Goodman	1961	$25
MGV-8382 [M]	Closed Session	1960	$150
MGVS-6165 [S]	Closed Session	1960	$150
V-8382 [M]	Closed Session	1961	$25
V6-8382 [S]	Closed Session	1961	$25
UMV-2632	Closed Session	198?	$25
MGV-8221 [M]	Cooking the Blues	1958	$175
V-8221 [M]	Cooking the Blues	1961	$25
MGV-8363 [M]	Generalissimo	1960	$175
MGVS-6132 [S]	Generalissimo	1960	$175
V-8363 [M]	Generalissimo	1961	$25
V6-8363 [S]	Generalissimo	1961	$25
MGV-2108 [M]	I Hear Benny Goodman and Artie Shaw	1958	$175

Number	Title	Yr	NM
MGVS-6032 [S]	I Hear Benny Goodman and Artie Shaw	1960	$150
MGV-8279 [M]	I Hear Benny Goodman and Artie Shaw	1958	$0

—Canceled; issued as 2108

Number	Title	Yr	NM
V-2108 [M]	I Hear Benny Goodman and Artie Shaw	1961	$25
V6-2108 [S]	I Hear Benny Goodman and Artie Shaw	1961	$25
MGV-8169 [M]	In a Mellow Mood	1957	$300

—Reissue of Norgran 1079

Number	Title	Yr	NM
V-8169 [M]	In a Mellow Mood	1961	$25
MGV-8158 [M]	Jazz Tones	1957	$300

—Reissue of Norgran 1068

Number	Title	Yr	NM
V-8158 [M]	Jazz Tones	1961	$25
MGV-8383 [M]	Live Date!	1960	$150
MGVS-6166 [S]	Live Date!	1960	$150
V-8383 [M]	Live Date!	1961	$25
V6-8383 [S]	Live Date!	1961	$25
MGV-8159 [M]	Mr. Clarinet	1957	$175

—Reissue of Norgran 1069

Number	Title	Yr	NM
V-8159 [M]	Mr. Clarinet	1961	$25
MGV-8182 [M]	Odalisque	1957	$175

—Reissue of Norgran 1094

Number	Title	Yr	NM
V-8182 [M]	Odalisque	1961	$25
MGV-8224 [M]	Sweet and Lovely	1958	$175
V-8224 [M]	Sweet and Lovely	1961	$25
MGV-8175 [M]	The Buddy DeFranco Wailers	1957	$250

—Reissue of Norgran 1085

Number	Title	Yr	NM
V-8175 [M]	The Buddy DeFranco Wailers	1961	$25
MGV-2022 [M]	The George Gershwin Songbook	1956	$250

—Reissue of Norgran 1016

Number	Title	Yr	NM
MGV-8375 [M]	Wholly Cats	1960	$75
MGVS-6150 [S]	Wholly Cats	1960	$75
V-8375 [M]	Wholly Cats	1961	$50
V6-8375 [S]	Wholly Cats	1961	$50

DEFRANCO FAMILY, THE

Number	Title	Yr	NM
20TH CENTURY			
T-422	Heartbeat, It's a Lovebeat	1973	$12
T-441	Save the Last Dance for Me	1974	$12

DEGEN, BOB

Number	Title	Yr	NM
ENJA			
3015	Chartreuse	198?	$25
INNER CITY			
IC-3027	Children of the Night	1978	$30

DEHAVEN, DOC

Number	Title	Yr	NM
CUCA			
K-3000 [M]	Dixieland Treasure	1962	$25
K-3100 [M]	Doc DeHaven On Location	1963	$25
K-3200 [M]	Doc Swings a Little	1964	$25
K-3400 [M]	Erle of Madison	1967	$25
K-3300 [M]	Just Off State Street	1966	$25
KS-3300 [S]	Just Off State Street	1966	$30

DEHAVEN, PENNY

Number	Title	Yr	NM
MAIN STREET			
9310	Penny DeHaven	1984	$12
UNITED ARTISTS			
UAS-6821	Penny DeHaven	1972	$18

DEJOHN SISTERS, THE

Number	Title	Yr	NM
EPIC			
LN1116 [M]	The DeJohn Sisters	195?	$30
UNITED ARTISTS			
UAL-3103 [M]	Yes Indeed	1960	$25
UAS-6103 [S]	Yes Indeed	1960	$30

DEJOHNETTE, JACK

Number	Title	Yr	NM
COLUMBIA			
C31176	Compost (Take Off Your Body)	1971	$25
ECM			
25010	Album Album	1984	$25
23790	Inflation Blues	1983	$25
1128	New Directions	1978	$30
1157	New Directions in Europe	1980	$30
1103	New Rags	1977	$30
1079	Pictures	1976	$30
1152	Special Edition	1980	$30
1189	Tin Can Alley	1981	$30
1074	Untitled	1976	$30
IMPULSE!/MCA			
5992	Irresistible Force	1987	$25
LANDMARK			
LLP-1504	The Piano Album	1985	$25
MCA			
42313	Parallel Realities	1990	$35
42160	Zebra	1986	$25
MILESTONE			
MSP-9029	Have You Heard?	1970	$35
MSP-9022	The DeJohnette Complex	1969	$25

Number	Title	Yr	NM

PRESTIGE
❏ 10094	Cosmic Chicken	1975	$35
❏ 10081	Sorcery	1974	$35

DEKKER, DESMOND, AND THE ACES
BULLDOG
| ❏ 1037 | The Israelites | 198? | $12 |
UNI
| ❏ 73059 | Israelites | 1969 | $30 |

DEL AMITRI
A&M
| ❏ SP-5287 | Waking Hours | 1990 | $15 |
CHRYSALIS
| ❏ BFV41499 | Del Amitri | 1985 | $15 |

DEL FUEGOS, THE
RCA
| ❏ 9860 | Smoking in the Fields | 1989 | $12 |
SLASH
❏ 25339	Boston, Mass.	1985	$12
❏ 25540	Stand Up	1987	$12
❏ 25174	The Longest Day	1984	$12

DEL LORDS, THE
Also see THE DICTATORS.
EMI AMERICA
| ❏ ST-17183 | Johnny Comes Marching Home | 1986 | $15 |
ENIGMA
| ❏ D1-73326 | Based on a True Story | 1988 | $12 |

DEL SATINS
B.T. PUPPY
| ❏ BTS-1019 | Out to Lunch | 1972 | $300 |

DEL VIKINGS, THE
COLLECTABLES
| ❏ COL-5010 | The Best of the Dell-Vikings | 198? | $15 |
DOT
| ❏ DLP-3685 [M] | Come Go with Me | 1966 | $250 |
| ❏ DLP-25685 [R] | Come Go with Me | 1966 | $175 |
LUNIVERSE
| ❏ LP-1000 [M] | Come Go with the Del Vikings | 1957 | $500 |
—*Eight tracks, cover is composed of slicks. Counterfeits have more tracks and a preprinted cover (not slicks)*
MERCURY
| ❏ MG-20353 [M] | A Swinging, Singing Record Session | 1958 | $250 |
| ❏ MG-20314 [M] | They Sing -- They Swing | 1957 | $300 |

DEL VIKINGS, THE / THE SONNETS
CROWN
| ❏ CLP-5368 [M] | The Del Vikings and the Sonnets | 1963 | $40 |

DELANEY, JACK
SOUTHLAND
❏ LP-201 [10]	Jack Delaney and George Girard in New Orleans	1954	$50
❏ LP-214 [M]	Jack Delaney and the New Orleans Jazz Babies	195?	$40
❏ LP-214 [10]	Jack Delaney with Lee Collins	1954	$50

DELANEY AND BONNIE
ATCO
| ❏ SD 33-383 | Country Life | 1972 | $25 |
| ❏ SD 33-326 | Delaney & Bonnie & Friends On Tour with Eric Clapton | 1970 | $30 |
— *Yellow label original*
| ❏ SD 33-326 | Delaney & Bonnie & Friends On Tour with Eric Clapton | 197? | $12 |
— *Later pressings on other labels*
❏ SD 33-358	Motel Shot	1971	$30
❏ SD7014 [B]	The Best of Delaney and Bonnie	1972	$25
❏ SD 33-341 [S]	To Bonnie from Delaney	1970	$30
❏ 33-341 [M]	To Bonnie from Delaney	1970	$100
— *White label promo; no stock copies were issued in mono*
COLUMBIA
| ❏ KC31377 | D&B Together | 1972 | $25 |
ELEKTRA
| ❏ EKS-74039 | Accept No Substitute -- The Original Delaney & Bonnie & Friends | 1969 | $30 |
GNP CRESCENDO
| ❏ GNPS-2054 | Genesis | 1970 | $25 |
STAX
| ❏ STS-2026 | Home | 1969 | $30 |

DELEGATES, THE (1)
MAINSTREAM
| ❏ 100 | The Delegates | 1973 | $25 |

DELEGATES, THE (2)
See BILLY LARKIN.

DELFONICS, THE
ARISTA
| ❏ AL8333 | The Best of the Delfonics | 198? | $12 |
COLLECTABLES
| ❏ COL-5109 | Golden Classics | 198? | $12 |
KORY
| ❏ 1002 | The Best of the Delfonics | 1977 | $15 |
PHILLY GROOVE
❏ 1501	Alive & Kicking	1974	$50
❏ 1150	La La Means I Love You	1968	$100
❏ 1154	Tell Me This Is a Dream	1972	$50
❏ 1153	The Delfonics	1970	$50
❏ 1152	The Delfonics Super Hits	1969	$50
❏ 1151	The Sexy Sound of Soul	1969	$100
POOGIE
| ❏ 121680 | The Delfonics Return | 1981 | $15 |

DELICATO, PAUL
ARTISTS OF AMERICA
| ❏ AOA5002 | Cara Mia | 1976 | $15 |
| ❏ AOA5001 | Ice Cream Sodas and Lollipops | 1975 | $15 |
AVI
| ❏ 6029 | Off on an Island | 1978 | $15 |

DELIRIUM TREMOLO
STOMP OFF
| ❏ SOS-1177 | Banjophobia | 1987 | $25 |

DELL, FRANK
GUINNESS
| ❏ GNS36001 [B] | Yesterday's People | 1977 | $175 |

DELLER, ALFRED
VANGUARD
| ❏ VRS-499 [M] | The Holly and the Ivy -- Christmas Songs of Old England | 1956 | $100 |
| ❏ VRS-479 [M] | The Three Ravens | 195? | $40 |

DELLS, THE, AND THE DRAMATICS
CADET
| ❏ 60027 | The Dells Vs. the Dramatics | 1974 | $30 |

DELLS, THE
20TH CENTURY
| ❏ T-618 | I Touched a Dream | 1980 | $15 |
| ❏ T-633 | Whatever Turns You On | 1981 | $15 |
ABC
| ❏ AA-1113 | Face to Face | 1978 | $15 |
| ❏ AA-1100 | New Beginnings | 1978 | $15 |
BUDDAH
| ❏ BDS-5053 | The Dells | 1969 | $18 |
CADET
❏ 50004	Freedom Means	1971	$30
❏ 50037	Give Your Baby a Standing Ovation	1973	$30
❏ LPS-837	Like It Is, Like It Was	1970	$50
❏ LPS-829	Love Is Blue	1969	$50
❏ 50021	Sweet As Funk Can Be	1972	$30
❏ 50046	The Dells	1973	$30
❏ LPS-824	The Dells Greatest Hits	1969	$50
❏ 60036	The Dells' Greatest Hits, Vol. 2	1975	$25
❏ LPS-822	The Dells Musical Menu/ Always Together	1969	$50
❏ 50017	The Dells Sing Dionne Warwicke's Greatest Hits	1972	$30
❏ 60030	The Mighty Mighty Dells	1974	$30
❏ LPS-804	There Is	1968	$50
CHESS
| ❏ CH-9103 | The Dells | 198? | $12 |
— *Reissue*
| ❏ CH-9288 | There Is | 1989 | $12 |
— *Reissue of Cadet 804*
LOST-NITE
| ❏ LLP-21 [10] | The Dells | 1981 | $18 |
— *Red vinyl, generic red cover*
MERCURY
❏ SRM-1-3711	Love Connection	1977	$18
❏ SRM-1-1084	No Way Back	1976	$18
❏ SRM-1-1145	They Said It Couldn't Be Done	1977	$18
❏ SRM-1-1059	We Got to Get Our Thing Together	1975	$18
PRIVATE I
| ❏ BFZ39309 | One Step Closer | 1984 | $12 |

SOLID SMOKE
| ❏ 8029 | Breezy Ballads and Tender Tunes: The Best of the Early Years (1955-65) | 1984 | $12 |
UPFRONT
| ❏ UPF-105 | Stay In My Corner | 1968 | $18 |
URGENT
| ❏ URG-4108 | The Second Time | 1991 | $15 |
VEE JAY
❏ LP1141 [M]	It's Not Unusual	1965	$150
❏ LPS1141 [S]	It's Not Unusual	1965	$175
❏ LP1010 [M]	Oh What a Nite	1959	$800
— *Maroon label*

| ❏ LP1010 [M] | Oh What a Nite | 1961 | $300 |
— *Black label with colorband*
| ❏ VJLP-1010 | Oh What a Nite | 198? | $12 |
— *Late-80s reissue on reactivated Vee Jay label. "Trade Mark Reg." on label.*
VJ INTERNATIONAL
| ❏ 7305 | The Dells In Concert | 197? | $15 |
ZOO
| ❏ 11023 | I Salute You | 1992 | $18 |

DELMORE BROTHERS, THE
KING
❏ 983 [M]	24 Great Country Songs	1966	$30
❏ KS-983 [R]	24 Great Country Songs	1966	$25
❏ 785 [M]	30th Anniversary Album	1962	$100
❏ 910 [M]	In Memory	1964	$40
❏ 920 [M]	In Memory, Volume 2	1964	$40
❏ 589 [M]	Songs by the Delmore Brothers	1958	$175

DEMANO, HANK
FREEWAY
| ❏ FLJP-1 [M] | Hank DeMano Quartet | 1955 | $75 |

DEMENSIONS, THE
CORAL
| ❏ CRL57430 [M] | My Foolish Heart | 1963 | $175 |
| ❏ CRL757430 [S] | My Foolish Heart | 1963 | $300 |

DEMERLE, LES
DOBRE
| ❏ 1020 | Transfusion | 1978 | $30 |
PALO ALTO
| ❏ 8008 | On Fire | 1981 | $30 |

DEMIAN
Includes members of BUBBLE PUPPY.
ABC
| ❏ ABCS-718 | Demian | 1970 | $150 |

DENNIS, JOHN
DEBUT
| ❏ DEB-121 [M] | New Piano Expressions | 1955 | $175 |

DENNIS, MATT
JUBILEE
| ❏ JLP-1105 [M] | Welcome Matt Dennis | 1959 | $50 |
| ❏ JGS-1105 [S] | Welcome Matt Dennis | 1959 | $75 |
KAPP
| ❏ KL-1024 [M] | Matt Dennis Plays and Sings Matt Dennis | 1956 | $75 |
MCA
| ❏ 1547 | Matt Dennis Plays and Sings Matt Dennis | 198? | $30 |
RCA VICTOR
| ❏ LPM-1134 [M] | Dennis, Anyone? | 1955 | $50 |
| ❏ LPM-1322 [M] | Play Melancholy Baby | 1956 | $75 |

Number	Title	Yr	NM
❏ LPM-1065 [M]	She Dances Overhead	1954	$40

DENNY, DOTTY
A440
❏ AJ-506 [M]	Dotty Digs Duke	1954	$150
❏ AJ-505 [M]	Tribute to Edgar Sampson	1954	$150

DENNY, MARTIN
FIRST AMERICAN
❏ 7743	From Hawaii With Love	1981	$12

LIBERTY
❏ LRP-3415 [M]	20 Golden Hawaiian Hits	1965	$15
❏ LST-7415 [S]	20 Golden Hawaiian Hits	1965	$18
❏ LRP-3111 [M]	Afro-Desia	1959	$30
— Turquoise label			
❏ LRP-3111 [M]	Afro-Desia	1960	$25
— Black rainbow label			
❏ LST-7111 [S]	Afro-Desia	1959	$40
— All-black label			
❏ LST-7111 [S]	Afro-Desia	1960	$30
— Black rainbow label			
❏ LRP-3277 [M]	Another Taste of Honey	1963	$18
❏ LST-7277 [S]	Another Taste of Honey	1963	$25
❏ LRP-3328 [M]	A Taste of Hits	1964	$15
❏ LST-7328 [S]	A Taste of Hits	1964	$18
❏ LRP-3237 [M]	A Taste of Honey	1962	$18
❏ LST-7237 [S]	A Taste of Honey	1962	$25
❏ LRP-3034 [M]	Exotica	1957	$40
— Turquoise label			
❏ LRP-3034 [M]	Exotica	1960	$30
— Black rainbow label			
❏ LST-7034 [R]	Exotica	1958	$30
— All-black label			
❏ LST-7034 [R]	Exotica	1960	$25
— Black rainbow label			
❏ LRP-3116 [M]	Exotica, Vol. III	1959	$30
— Turquoise label			
❏ LRP-3116 [M]	Exotica, Vol. III	1960	$25
— Black rainbow label			
❏ LST-7116 [S]	Exotica, Vol. III	1959	$40
— All-black label			
❏ LST-7116 [S]	Exotica, Vol. III	1960	$30
— Black rainbow label			
❏ LRP-3077 [M]	Exotica, Volume II	1957	$30
— Turquoise label			
❏ LRP-3077 [M]	Exotica, Volume II	1960	$25
— Black rainbow label			
❏ LST-7006 [S]	Exotica, Volume II	1958	$40
— All-black label			
❏ LST-7006 [S]	Exotica, Volume II	1960	$30
— Black rainbow label			
❏ LRP-3513 [M]	Exotica Classica	1967	$15
❏ LST-7513 [S]	Exotica Classica	1967	$18
❏ LM-1009	Exotica Vol. 1	1982	$10
— Reissue of United Artists 1009			
❏ LST-7621 [S]	Exotic Moog	1969	$40
❏ LRP-3168 [M]	Exotic Percussion	1961	$25
❏ LST-7168 [S]	Exotic Percussion	1961	$30
❏ LRP-3158 [M]	Exotic Sounds from the Silver Screen	1960	$25
❏ LST-7158 [S]	Exotic Sounds from the Silver Screen	1960	$30
❏ LRP-3163 [M]	Exotic Sounds Visit Broadway	1960	$25
❏ LST-7163 [S]	Exotic Sounds Visit Broadway	1960	$30
❏ LRP-3081 [M]	Forbidden Island	1958	$30
— Turquoise label; woman in jungle on cover			
❏ LRP-3081 [M]	Forbidden Island	1960	$25
— Black rainbow label; white foil on cover			
❏ LST-7001 [S]	Forbidden Island	1958	$40
— All-black label; woman in jungle on cover			
❏ LST-7001 [S]	Forbidden Island	1960	$30
— Black rainbow label; white foil on cover			
❏ LRP-3467 [M]	Golden Greats	1966	$15
❏ LST-7467 [S]	Golden Greats	1966	$18
❏ LRP-3488 [M]	Hawaii	1967	$15
❏ LST-7488 [S]	Hawaii	1967	$18
❏ LRP-3445 [M]	Hawaiian A-Go-Go	1966	$15
❏ LST-7445 [S]	Hawaiian A-Go-Go	1966	$18
❏ LRP-3394 [M]	Hawaii Tattoo	1964	$15
❏ LST-7394 [S]	Hawaii Tattoo	1964	$18
❏ LRP-3102 [M]	Hypnotique	1958	$30
— Turquoise label			
❏ LRP-3102 [M]	Hypnotique	1960	$25
— Black rainbow label			
❏ LST-7102 [S]	Hypnotique	1958	$40
— All-black label			
❏ LST-7102 [S]	Hypnotique	1960	$30
— Black rainbow label			
❏ LRP-3378 [M]	Latin Village	1964	$15
❏ LST-7378 [S]	Latin Village	1964	$18
❏ LRP-3438 [M]	Martin Denny	1965	$15
❏ LST-7438 [S]	Martin Denny	1965	$18
❏ LRP-3087 [M]	Primitiva	1958	$30
— Turquoise label			
❏ LRP-3087 [M]	Primitiva	1960	$25
— Black rainbow label			

Number	Title	Yr	NM
❏ LST-7023 [S]	Primitiva	1958	$40
— All-black label			
❏ LST-7023 [S]	Primitiva	1960	$30
— Black rainbow label			
❏ LRP-3122 [M]	Quiet Village	1959	$30
— Turquoise label			
❏ LRP-3122 [M]	Quiet Village	1960	$25
— Black rainbow label			
❏ LST-7122 [S]	Quiet Village	1959	$40
— All-black label			
❏ LST-7122 [S]	Quiet Village	1960	$30
— Black rainbow label			
❏ L-5502 [M]	The Best of Martin Denny	1962	$18
❏ S-6602 [S]	The Best of Martin Denny	1962	$25
❏ LRP-3141 [M]	The Enchanted Sea	1959	$30
— Turquoise label			
❏ LRP-3141 [M]	The Enchanted Sea	1960	$25
— Black rainbow label			
❏ LST-7141 [S]	The Enchanted Sea	1959	$40
— All-black label			
❏ LST-7141 [S]	The Enchanted Sea	1960	$30
— Black rainbow label			
❏ LRP-3224 [M]	The Exotic Sounds of Martin Denny In Person	1962	$18
❏ LST-7224 [S]	The Exotic Sounds of Martin Denny In Person	1962	$25
❏ LRP-3307 [M]	The Versatile Martin Denny	1963	$18
❏ LST-7307 [S]	The Versatile Martin Denny	1963	$25

SUNSET
❏ SUS-5199	Exotic Night	1969	$15
❏ SUM-1102 [M]	Paradise Moods	196?	$15
❏ SUS-5102 [S]	Paradise Moods	196?	$15
❏ SUM-1169 [M]	Sayonara	1967	$15
❏ SUS-5169 [S]	Sayonara	1967	$15

UNITED ARTISTS
❏ LM-1009	Exotica Vol. 1	1980	$12
— Reissue of Liberty 7034			
❏ UA-LA234-G	The Very Best of Martin Denny	1974	$12
❏ UA-LA383-E	The Very Best of Martin Denny	1975	$12

DENNY, SANDY
A&M
❏ SP-4371	Sandy	1972	$18
❏ SP-4317	The Northstar Grassman and the Ravens	1971	$18

CARTHAGE
❏ CGLP-4425	Like an Old Fashioned Waltz	1985	$12
— Reissue of Island 9340			
❏ CGLP-4423	Rendezvous	1985	$12
— Reissue of Island 9433			
❏ CGLP-4429	The Northstar Grassman and the Ravens	1985	$12
— Reissue of A&M 4317			

HANNIBAL
❏ HNBX-5301	Who Knows Where the Time Goes	198?	$25

ISLAND
❏ SW-9340	Like an Old Fashioned Waltz	1974	$18
❏ ILPS9433	Rendezvous	1977	$18

DENVER, JOHN, AND THE MUPPETS
RCA VICTOR
❏ AFL1-3451	A Christmas Together	1979	$15

DENVER, JOHN
HJD
❏ 66 [B]	John Denver Sings	1966	$1000
— Private issue of 300 or so, made by JD as Christmas gifts to friends.			

MERCURY
❏ SRM-1-704	Beginnings	1972	$25
— With illustration on cover			
❏ SRM-1-704	Beginnings	1974	$15
— With mountain scene on cover			

RCA
❏ 7624-1-R	Back Home Again	1988	$12
— Last vinyl reissue			
❏ 7631-1-R	Poems, Prayers and Promises	1988	$12
— Last vinyl reissue			
❏ 7632-1-R	Rocky Mountain High	1988	$12
— Last vinyl reissue			

RCA VICTOR
❏ LSP-4607	Aerie	1971	$15
— Orange label			
❏ LSP-4607	Aerie	1975	$12
— Tan label or black label, dog near top			
❏ AFL1-4607	Aerie	197?	$10
— Reissue			
❏ CPL2-0764	An Evening with John Denver	1975	$15
— Orange or tan labels			

Number	Title	Yr	NM
❏ CPL2-0764	An Evening with John Denver	1976	$12
— Black label, dog near top			
❏ AQL1-3449	Autograph	1980	$10
❏ AYL1-5193	Back Home Again	198?	$10
— Best Buy Series" reissue			
❏ CPL1-0548	Back Home Again	1974	$12
— Orange or tan label			
❏ CPL1-0548	Back Home Again	1976	$10
— Black label, dog near top			
❏ AFL1-0548	Back Home Again	197?	$10
— Reissue			
❏ AQL1-0548	Back Home Again	197?	$10
— Later reissue			
❏ AFL1-5458	Dreamland Express	1985	$10
❏ APL1-0101	Farewell Andromeda	1973	$15
— Orange label			
❏ APL1-0101	Farewell Andromeda	1975	$12
— Tan label or black label, dog near top			
❏ AYL1-5195	Farewell Andromeda	198?	$10
— Best Buy Series" reissue			
❏ AFL1-4683	It's About Time	1983	$10
❏ AYL1-5192	I Want to Live	198?	$10
— Best Buy Series" reissue			
❏ AFL1-2521	I Want to Live	1977	$10
❏ AQL1-3075	John Denver	1979	$10
❏ CPL1-0374	John Denver's Greatest Hits	1974	$12
— Orange label			
❏ CPL1-0374	John Denver's Greatest Hits	1975	$10
— Tan label or black label, dog near top			
❏ APL1-0374	John Denver's Greatest Hits	197?	$10
— Reissue			
❏ AQL1-0374	John Denver's Greatest Hits	197?	$10
— Later reissue			
❏ CPL1-2195	John Denver's Greatest Hits, Volume 2	1977	$12
❏ AQL1-2195	John Denver's Greatest Hits, Volume 2	197?	$10
— Reissue			
❏ AJL1-5313	John Denver's Greatest Hits, Volume 3	1984	$10
❏ AFL1-5811	One World	1986	$10
❏ LSP-4499	Poems, Prayers and Promises	1971	$15
— Orange label			
❏ LSP-4499	Poems, Prayers and Promises	1975	$12
— Tan label or black label, dog near top			
❏ AFL1-4499	Poems, Prayers and Promises	197?	$10
— Reissue			
❏ AYL1-5189	Poems, Prayers and Promises	198?	$10
— Best Buy Series" reissue			
❏ LSP-4207	Rhymes & Reasons	1969	$18
— Orange label, non-flexible vinyl			
❏ APL1-1201	Rocky Mountain Christmas	1975	$12
— Tan label			
❏ AFL1-1201	Rocky Mountain Christmas	197?	$10
— Reissue			
❏ APL1-1201	Rocky Mountain Christmas	1976	$10
— Black label, dog near top			
❏ LSP-4731	Rocky Mountain High	1972	$15
— Orange label			
❏ LSP-4731	Rocky Mountain High	1975	$12
— Tan label or black label, dog near top			
❏ AFL1-4731	Rocky Mountain High	197?	$10
— Reissue			
❏ AQL1-4731	Rocky Mountain High	197?	$10
— Later reissue			
❏ AYL1-5190	Rocky Mountain High	198?	$10
— Best Buy Series" reissue			
❏ AFL1-4256	Seasons of the Heart	1982	$10
❏ AFL1-4055	Some Days Are Diamonds	1981	$10
❏ AYL1-5194	Spirit	198?	$10
— Best Buy Series" reissue			
❏ APL1-1694	Spirit	1976	$12
— Originals are black label, dog near top			
❏ AFL1-1694	Spirit	197?	$10
— Reissue			
❏ LSP-4278	Take Me to Tomorrow	1970	$18
— Orange label, non-flexible vinyl			
❏ APL2-1263	The John Denver Gift Pak	1974	$30
— Contains "Rocky Mountain Christmas" and "Windsong" in a special Christmas sleeve.			
❏ DJL-5398 [DJ]	The John Denver Holiday Radio Show	1984	$25
❏ DJL-0075 [DJ]	The John Denver Radio Show	1973	$30
❏ DJL-0683 [DJ]	The Second John Denver Radio Show	1974	$30
❏ LSP-4414	Whose Garden Was This?	1970	$18
— Orange label, non-flexible vinyl			
❏ AYL1-5191	Windsong	198?	$10
— Best Buy Series" reissue			
❏ APL1-1183	Windsong	1975	$12
— Tan label			
❏ APL1-1183	Windsong	1976	$10

Number	Title	Yr	NM
—Black label, dog near top			
❏ AFL1-1183	Windsong	197?	$10
—Reissue			
❏ AQL1-1183	Windsong	197?	$10
—Later reissue			

DEODATO
ATLANTIC
❏ 82048	Somewhere Out There	1989	$30

CTI
❏ 7081	2001	1977	$25
❏ CTS-6029	Deodato 2	1973	$30
❏ CTSQ-6029 [Q]	Deodato 2	1973	$75
❏ CTS-6021	Prelude	1972	$30
❏ CTSQ-6021 [Q]	Prelude	1973	$75
❏ 8021	Prelude	198?	$20
—Reissue of 6021			

MCA
❏ 457	Artistry	1974	$25
❏ 491	First Cuckoo	1975	$25
❏ 2219	Very Together	1976	$25
❏ 697	Very Together	198?	$20
—Reissue of 2219			
❏ 410	Whirlwinds	1974	$25

WARNER BROS.
❏ BSK3649	Happy Hour	1981	$25
❏ BSK3321	Knights of Fantasy	1979	$25
❏ BSK3132	Love Island	1978	$25
❏ 25175	Motion	1984	$25
❏ BSK3467	Night Cruiser	1980	$30

DEODATO/AIRTO
CTI
❏ CTS-6041	In Concert	1974	$30
❏ CTSQ-6041 [Q]	In Concert	1974	$75

DEPARIS, SIDNEY
BLUE NOTE
❏ B-6501	DeParis Dixie	1969	$25
❏ BLP-7016 [10]	Sidney DeParis' Blue Note Stompers	1951	$300

DEPARIS, SIDNEY/JAMES P. JOHNSON
BLUE NOTE
❏ B-6506	Original Blue Note Jazz, Volume 3	1969	$25

DEPARIS, WILBUR, AND JIMMY WITHERSPOON
ATLANTIC
❏ 1266 [M]	New Orleans Blues	1957	$300
—Black label			
❏ 1266 [M]	New Orleans Blues	1961	$175
—Multicolor label, white "fan" logo			
❏ 1266 [M]	New Orleans Blues	1964	$30
—Multicolor label, black "fan" logo			

DEPARIS, WILBUR
A440
❏ AJ-503 [10]	New New Orleans Jazz	1954	$75

ATLANTIC
❏ 1233 [M]	Marchin' and Swingin'	1956	$300
—Black label			
❏ 1233 [M]	Marchin' and Swingin'	1961	$175
—Multicolor label, white "fan" logo			
❏ 1233 [M]	Marchin' and Swingin'	1964	$35
—Multicolor label, black "fan" logo			
❏ SD1233 [S]	Marchin' and Swingin'	1958	$300
—Green label			
❏ SD1233 [S]	Marchin' and Swingin'	1961	$175
—Multicolor label, white "fan" logo			
❏ SD1233 [S]	Marchin' and Swingin'	1964	$35
—Multicolor label, black "fan" logo			
❏ 1219 [M]	New New Orleans Jazz	1956	$300
—Black label			
❏ 1219 [M]	New New Orleans Jazz	1961	$175
—Multicolor label, white "fan" logo			
❏ 1219 [M]	New New Orleans Jazz	1964	$35
—Multicolor label, black "fan" logo			
❏ SD1219 [S]	New New Orleans Jazz	1958	$300
—Green label			
❏ SD1219 [S]	New New Orleans Jazz	1961	$175
—Multicolor label, white "fan" logo			
❏ SD1219 [S]	New New Orleans Jazz	1964	$35
—Multicolor label, black "fan" logo			
❏ SD1552	Over and Over Again	1970	$35
❏ 1300 [M]	Something Old, New, Gay, Blue	1958	$300
—Black label			
❏ 1300 [M]	Something Old, New, Gay, Blue	1961	$175
—Multicolor label, white "fan" logo			
❏ 1300 [M]	Something Old, New, Gay, Blue	1964	$35
—Multicolor label, black "fan" logo			
❏ SD1300 [S]	Something Old, New, Gay, Blue	1958	$300
—Green label			
❏ SD1300 [S]	Something Old, New, Gay, Blue	1961	$175
—Multicolor label, white "fan" logo			
❏ SD1300 [S]	Something Old, New, Gay, Blue	1964	$35
—Multicolor label, black "fan" logo			
❏ 1318 [M]	That's a-Plenty	1959	$300
—Black label			
❏ 1318 [M]	That's a-Plenty	1961	$175
—Multicolor label, white "fan" logo			
❏ 1318 [M]	That's a-Plenty	1964	$35
—Multicolor label, black "fan" logo			
❏ SD1318 [S]	That's a-Plenty	1959	$300
—Green label			
❏ SD1318 [S]	That's a-Plenty	1961	$175
—Multicolor label, white "fan" logo			
❏ SD1318 [S]	That's a-Plenty	1964	$35
—Multicolor label, black "fan" logo			
❏ 1336 [M]	The Wild Jazz Age	1960	$300
—Multicolor label, white "fan" logo			
❏ 1336 [M]	The Wild Jazz Age	1964	$35
—Multicolor label, black "fan" logo			
❏ SD1336 [S]	The Wild Jazz Age	1960	$300
—Multicolor label, white "fan" logo			
❏ SD1336 [S]	The Wild Jazz Age	1964	$25
—Multicolor label, black "fan" logo			
❏ ALS-143 [10]	Wilbur DeParis, Volume 2	1953	$300
❏ ALS-141 [10]	Wilbur DeParis and His Rampart Street Ramblers	1952	$350
❏ 1253 [M]	Wilbur DeParis at Symphony Hall	1957	$300
—Black label			
❏ 1253 [M]	Wilbur DeParis at Symphony Hall	1961	$175
—Multicolor label, white "fan" logo			
❏ 1253 [M]	Wilbur DeParis at Symphony Hall	1964	$35
—Multicolor label, black "fan" logo			
❏ SD1253 [S]	Wilbur DeParis at Symphony Hall	1958	$300
—Green label			
❏ SD1253 [S]	Wilbur DeParis at Symphony Hall	1961	$175
—Multicolor label, white "fan" logo			
❏ SD1253 [S]	Wilbur DeParis at Symphony Hall	1964	$35
—Multicolor label, black "fan" logo			
❏ 1363 [M]	Wilbur DeParis on the Riviera	1961	$175
—Multicolor label, white "fan" logo			
❏ 1363 [M]	Wilbur DeParis on the Riviera	1964	$35
—Multicolor label, black "fan" logo			
❏ SD1363 [S]	Wilbur DeParis on the Riviera	1961	$175
—Multicolor label, white "fan" logo			
❏ SD1363 [S]	Wilbur DeParis on the Riviera	1964	$50
—Multicolor label, black "fan" logo			
❏ 1288 [M]	Wilbur DeParis Plays Cole Porter	1958	$300
—Black label			
❏ 1288 [M]	Wilbur DeParis Plays Cole Porter	1961	$175
—Multicolor label, white "fan" logo			
❏ 1288 [M]	Wilbur DeParis Plays Cole Porter	1964	$35
—Multicolor label, black "fan" logo			

HERITAGE
❏ SS-1207 [M]	Wilbur DeParis	1956	$150

DEPAUR CHORUS, THE
COLUMBIA
❏ CL923 [M]	Calypso Christmas	1956	$40
❏ CL725 [M]	The Spirit of Christmas/God Is With Us	1955	$30

COLUMBIA MASTERWORKS
❏ AL45 [10]	Swing Low	1953	$75
❏ ML2119 [10]	Work Songs and Spirituals	195?	$75

MERCURY LIVING PRESENCE
❏ SR90418 [S]	Danse Calinda! Creole Songs, Work Songs and Spirituals	196?	$50
—Maroon label, no "Vendor: Mercury Record Corporation			
❏ SR90418 [S]	Danse Calinda! Creole Songs, Work Songs and Spirituals	196?	$30
—Maroon label, with "Vendor: Mercury Record Corporation			
❏ SR90382 [S]	Songs of New Nations	196?	$75
—Maroon label, no "Vendor: Mercury Record Corporation			
❏ SR90382 [S]	Songs of New Nations	196?	$40
—Maroon label, with "Vendor: Mercury Record Corporation			

DEPECHE MODE
MUTE
❏ WBA1234300 [B]	Exciter	2014	$30
❏ MUTEL5	The Singles 86-98	1998	$30
—Numbered, limited box set pressed in England with U.S. bar code sticker			

SIRE
❏ 25853	101	1989	$18
❏ 23751	A Broken Frame	1982	$15
❏ 25429	Black Celebration	1986	$12
❏ R143674 [B]	Catching Up with Depeche Mode	1985	$25
—RCA Music Service edition			
❏ 25346	Catching Up with Depeche Mode	1985	$12
❏ R100560 [B]	Catching Up with Depeche Mode	1990	$25
—BMG Direct Marketing edition; reissue			
❏ 23900	Construction Time Again	1983	$15
❏ R100598	Music for the Masses	1988	$15
—BMG Direct Marketing edition			
❏ 25614	Music for the Masses	1987	$12
❏ 25124	People Are People	1984	$12
❏ PRO-A-5192 [DJ]	Selections from the Commercially Available Limited Edition Box Sets One and Two	1991	$40
—Promo-only sampler			
❏ PRO-A-5242 [DJ]	Selections from the Commercially Available Limited Edition Box Set Three	1991	$40
❏ 25194	Some Great Reward	1984	$15
❏ SRK3642	Speak & Spell	1981	$18
❏ WBA1234364 [B]	Ultra	2014	$35
❏ 26081	Violator	1990	$18
❏ R173408	Violator	1990	$18
—BMG Direct Marketing edition			
❏ WBA1233980 [B]	Violator	2014	$35

DEPENDABLES, THE
UNITED ARTISTS
❏ UAS-6799	Klaatu Berrada Niktu	1971	$25

DEPUTIES, THE
FARON YOUNG
❏ 002 [M]	Sounds of the Deputies	1965	$30

DEREK AND THE DOMINOS
Also see ERIC CLAPTON.
ATCO
❏ 2-704 [M]	Layla and Other Assorted Love Songs	1970	$800
—White label promo only			
❏ SD 2-704 [DJ]	Layla and Other Assorted Love Songs	1970	$250
—White label promo			
❏ SD 2-704 [S]	Layla and Other Assorted Love Songs	1970	$30

DIRECT DISK
❏ SD-16629	Layla and Other Assorted Love Songs	1981	$175
—Audiophile vinyl			

MOBILE FIDELITY
❏ 2-239	Derek and the Dominos in Concert	1996	$150
—Audiophile vinyl			

MOTOWN
❏ 5310373	Layla and Other Assorted Love Songs	2008	$30

POLYDOR
❏ PD2-3501	Layla and Other Assorted Love Songs	1972	$25

RSO
❏ SO 2-8800	Derek and the Dominos in Concert	1973	$25
❏ RS-2-3801	Layla and Other Assorted Love Songs	1977	$18

DERISE, JOE
AUDIOPHILE
❏ AP-153	House of Flowers	1981	$30
❏ AP-231	Joe DeRise Sings and Plays the Jimmy Van Heusen Anthology, Vol. 1	1989	$25
❏ AP-232	Joe DeRise Sings and Plays the Jimmy Van Heusen Anthology, Vol. 2	1989	$25
❏ AP-233	Joe DeRise Sings and Plays the Jimmy Van Heusen Anthology, Vol. 3	1989	$25
❏ AP-174	The Blues Are Out of Town	1982	$30
❏ AP-215	The Joe DeRise Tentette Is Mad About You	1986	$25

BETHLEHEM
❏ BCP-1039 [10]	Joe DeRise Sings	1955	$300
❏ BCP-51 [M]	Joe DeRise with the Australian Jazz Quintet	1956	$300

Number	Title	Yr	NM
INNER CITY			
❑ IC-4003	I'll Remember Suzanne	1979	$30
DERRINGER, RICK			

Also see THE McCOYS; DIO, BLACK SABBATH; DUST; ALCATRAZZ; PAT BENATAR; includes records as DERRINGER

Number	Title	Yr	NM
BLUE SKY			
❑ KZ32481	All American Boy	1973	$18
❑ ZQ32481 [Q]	All American Boy	1974	$40
❑ PZ32481	All American Boy	197?	$10
— Reissue with new prefix			
❑ PZ34181	Derringer	1976	$15
❑ PZ34848	Derringer Live	1977	$15
— Without bar code			
❑ PZ34848	Derringer Live	198?	$10
— Reissue with bar code			
❑ JZ36551	Face to Face	1980	$12
❑ JZ36092	Guitars and Women	1979	$12
❑ JZ35075	If I Weren't So Romantic I'd Shoot You	1978	$12
❑ PRO265	Live in Cleveland	1977	$25
— Promo			
❑ PZ33423	Spring Fever	1975	$15
❑ PZQ33423 [Q]	Spring Fever	1975	$40
❑ PZ34470	Sweet Evil	1977	$18
PASSPORT			
❑ PB-6025	Good Dirty Fun	1983	$12
DES PLANTES, TED			
JAZZOLOGY			
❑ J-125	Ted Des Plantes and His Buddies	1983	$25
STOMP OFF			
❑ SOS-1136	Swedish-American Hot Jazz Collaboration	1987	$25
DESANTO, SUGAR PIE			
CHECKER			
❑ LP-2979 [M]	Sugar Pie DeSanto	1961	$250
DESARIO, TERI			
CASABLANCA			
❑ NBLP-7231	Caught	1980	$15
❑ NBLP-7178	Moonlight Madness	1979	$12
❑ NBLP-7115	Pleasure Train	1978	$15
DAYSPRING			
❑ 701-411301-1	Call to Us All	1983	$15
❑ 701-413101-X	Voices in the Wind	1985	$15
DESCENDANTS OF MIKE & PHOEBE, THE			
STRATA-EAST			
❑ SES-19744	A Spirit Speaks	1973	$75
DESCENDENTS			
EPITAPH			
❑ 86481 [B]	Everything Sucks	1996	$18
FAT WRECK CHORDS			
❑ FAT673	Cool to Be You	2004	$15
NEW ALLIANCE			
❑ NAR-025	Bonus Fat	1985	$18
❑ NAR-029	Enjoy!	1986	$18
❑ NAR-026	I Don't Want to Grow Up	1985	$18
❑ NAR-012	Milo Goes to College	1982	$18
SST			
❑ 112	All	1987	$15
❑ 144	Bonus Fat	198?	$15
❑ 242	Enjoy!	1989	$15
❑ 205	Hallraker Live!	1988	$15
❑ 143	I Don't Want to Grow Up	198?	$15
❑ 163	Liveage!	1988	$15
❑ 142	Milo Goes to College	198?	$15
❑ 259	Somery	1991	$18
DESERT ROSE BAND, THE			
MCA			
❑ 42169	Running	1988	$10
❑ 5991	The Desert Rose Band	1987	$10
DESHANNON, JACKIE			
AMHERST			
❑ AMH1016	Quick Touches	1978	$15
❑ AMX1010	You're the Only Dancer	1977	$15
ATLANTIC			
❑ SD7231	Jackie	1972	$15
❑ SD7303	Your Baby Is a Lady	1974	$15
CAPITOL			
❑ ST-772	Songs	1971	$15
COLUMBIA			
❑ PC33500	New Arrangement	1975	$15
IMPERIAL			
❑ LP-9328 [M]	Are You Ready for This?	1966	$18
❑ LP-12328 [S]	Are You Ready for This?	1966	$25
❑ LP-9352 [M]	For You	1967	$18
❑ LP-12352 [S]	For You	1967	$25
❑ LP-9296 [M]	In the Wind	1965	$25

Number	Title	Yr	NM
— Black and pink label			
❑ LP-9296 [M]	In the Wind	1966	$18
— Black and green label			
❑ LP-12296 [S]	In the Wind	1965	$30
— Black and pink label			
❑ LP-12296 [S]	In the Wind	1966	$25
— Black and green label			
❑ LP-12415	Laurel Canyon	1969	$18
❑ LP-12386	Me About You	1968	$18
❑ LP-9344 [M]	New Image	1967	$18
❑ LP-12344 [S]	New Image	1967	$25
❑ LP-12442	Put a Little Love in Your Heart	1969	$18
❑ LP-9286 [M]	This Is Jackie DeShannon	1965	$25
— Black and pink label			
❑ LP-9286 [M]	This Is Jackie DeShannon	1966	$18
— Black and green label			
❑ LP-12286 [S]	This Is Jackie DeShannon	1965	$30
— Black and pink label			
❑ LP-12286 [S]	This Is Jackie DeShannon	1966	$25
— Black and green label			
❑ LP-12453	To Be Free	1970	$18
❑ LP-12404	What the World Needs Now Is Love	1968	$18
❑ LP-9294 [M]	You Won't Forget Me	1965	$25
— Black and pink label			
❑ LP-9294 [M]	You Won't Forget Me	1966	$18
— Black and green label			
❑ LP-12294 [S]	You Won't Forget Me	1965	$30
— Black and pink label			
❑ LP-12294 [S]	You Won't Forget Me	1966	$25
— Black and green label			
LIBERTY			
❑ LRP-3390 [M]	Breakin' It Up on the Beatles Tour!	1964	$40
❑ LST-7390 [S]	Breakin' It Up on the Beatles Tour!	1964	$50
❑ LRP-3320 [M]	Jackie DeShannon	1963	$40
❑ LST-7320 [S]	Jackie DeShannon	1963	$50
❑ LN-10265	Jackie DeShannon	1985	$10
❑ LN-10179	The Very Best of Jackie DeShannon	1983	$10
— Reissue of United Artists 434			
SUNSET			
❑ SUS-5322	Jackie DeShannon	1970	$15
❑ SUS-5225	Lonely Girl	1968	$15
UNITED ARTISTS			
❑ UA-LA434-E	The Very Best of Jackie DeShannon	1975	$15
DESMARAIS, LORRAINE			
JAZZIMAGE			
❑ JZ-106	Andiamo	1985	$30
❑ JZ-100	Lorraine Desmarais Trio	1984	$30
DESMOND, JOHNNY			
COLUMBIA			
❑ CL1477 [M]	Blue Smoke	1960	$18
❑ CS8268 [S]	Blue Smoke	1960	$25
❑ CL1399 [M]	Once Upon a Time	1959	$25
❑ CS8194 [S]	Once Upon a Time	1959	$30
CORAL			
❑ CRL57073 [M]	Desmo Sings Desmond	195?	$50
❑ CRL57130 [M]	Easy Come Easy Go	195?	$40
❑ CRL56124 [10]	Hearts and Flowers	1955	$75
❑ CRL57079 [M]	Souvenir d'Italie	195?	$40
CORONET			
❑ CXS-236 [S]	Johnny Desmond In Las Vegas!	196?	$12
CRAFTSMEN			
❑ C-8019 [M]	Hymns	196?	$12
❑ C-8030 [M]	Johnny Desmond Sings for Dancing	196?	$12
EVON			
❑ 343 [M]	Johnny Desmond Sings Hymns for You	196?	$12
GOLDEN TONE			
❑ C-4045 [M]	Dance Party Featuring Johnny Desmond	196?	$12
❑ 14045 [M]	Dance Party Featuring Johnny Desmond	196?	$15
❑ 9628S [S]	Hymns	196?	$15
❑ C-4031 [M]	Hymns	196?	$12
LION			
❑ L-70061 [M]	Dreams of Paris	1958	$18
MAYFAIR			
❑ 9628S [S]	Hymns	1958	$18
— Yellow vinyl			
❑ 9635S [S]	Johnny Desmond Swings	1958	$18
— Yellow vinyl			
MGM			
❑ E-186 [10]	Hands Across the Table	1952	$40
❑ E-3561 [M]	Hands Across the Table	1957	$30
MOVIETONE			
❑ 71011 [M]	Johnny Desmond On Location	1966	$15

Number	Title	Yr	NM
❑ S-72011 [S]	Johnny Desmond On Location	1966	$18
PICKWICK			
❑ SPC-3558	Hymns for the Family	197?	$12
RONDO			
❑ 9762 [S]	Dance Party Featuring Johnny Desmond	196?	$15
❑ 1762 [M]	Dance Party Featuring Johnny Desmond	196?	$12
TOPS			
❑ 1762 [M]	Dance Party Featuring Johnny Desmond	196?	$12
❑ 9762 [S]	Dance Party Featuring Johnny Desmond	196?	$15
❑ L1628 [M]	Hymns	1958	$12
❑ L1635 [M]	Johnny Desmond Swings	1958	$15
VENISE			
❑ 7013 [M]	So Nice!	196?	$12
❑ 10013 [S]	So Nice!	196?	$18
— Yellow vinyl			
VOCALION			
❑ VL3773 [M]	Johnny Desmond	1966	$15
❑ VL73773 [R]	Johnny Desmond	1966	$12
DESMOND, PAUL			
A&M			
❑ SP-3032	Bridge Over Troubled Water	1970	$50
❑ SP-3024	From the Hot Afternoon	1969	$35
❑ SP9-3024	From the Hot Afternoon	198?	$50
— Audio Master Plus" reissue			
❑ SP-3015	Summertime	1969	$35
ARTISTS HOUSE			
❑ AH2	Paul Desmond	1978	$25
CTI			
❑ CTS-6059	Pure Desmond	1975	$25
❑ CTS-6039	Skylark	1974	$25
CTI/CBS ASSOCIATED			
❑ FZ40806	Pure Desmond	1987	$25
— Reissue of CTI 6059			
❑ FZ44170	Skylark	1988	$25
— Reissue of CTI 6039			
DISCOVERY			
❑ 840	East of the Sun	198?	$25
FANTASY			
❑ 3-21 [10]	Paul Desmond	1955	$200
❑ 3235 [M]	Paul Desmond Quartet Featuring Don Elliott	1956	$175
— Red vinyl			
❑ 3235 [M]	Paul Desmond Quartet Featuring Don Elliott	1957	$40
— Black vinyl, red label, non-flexible vinyl			
❑ 3235 [M]	Paul Desmond Quartet Featuring Don Elliott	1962	$50
— Black vinyl, red label, flexible vinyl			
❑ OJC-119	Paul Desmond Quartet Featuring Don Elliott	198?	$25
— Reissue of Fantasy 3235			
FINESSE			
❑ FW37487	Paul Desmond and the Modern Jazz Quartet	1981	$25
HORIZON			
❑ 850	Paul Desmond Live	1976	$35
MOSAIC			
❑ MR6-120	The Complete Recordings of the Paul Desmond Quartet with Jim Hall	199?	$300
RCA CAMDEN			
❑ ACL1-0201	Samba de Orfeo	1973	$25
RCA VICTOR			
❑ LPM-3320 [M]	Boss Antigua	1965	$50
❑ LSP-3320 [S]	Boss Antigua	1965	$75
❑ LPM-2438 [M]	Desmond Blue	1961	$75
❑ LSP-2438 [S]	Desmond Blue	1961	$75
❑ LPM-3480 [M]	Easy Living	1965	$50
❑ LSP-3480 [S]	Easy Living	1965	$75
❑ LPM-3407 [M]	Glad to Be Unhappy	1965	$50
❑ LSP-3407 [S]	Glad to Be Unhappy	1965	$75
❑ ANL1-2807	Pure Gold	1978	$25
❑ LPM-2569 [M]	Take Ten	1962	$75
❑ LSP-2569 [S]	Take Ten	1962	$75
❑ LPM-2654 [M]	Two of a Mind	1963	$75
❑ LSP-2654 [S]	Two of a Mind	1963	$75
WARNER BROS.			
❑ W1356 [M]	First Place Again	1960	$75
❑ WS1356 [S]	First Place Again	1960	$75
DESOUZA, RAUL			
CAPITOL			
❑ SW-11774	Don't Ask My Neighbors	1978	$30
❑ ST-11648	Sweet Lucy	1977	$75
❑ ST-11918	'Til Tomorrow Comes	1979	$30
MILESTONE			
❑ 9061	Colors	1975	$35

Number	Title	Yr	NM

DESPAIR [AKA THE VIBRATORS]
CLEOPATRA
| ❏ 6613 [B] | The Birth Of The Vibrators 1973-1975 | | $25 |

DESTINY'S CHILD
COLUMBIA
| ❏ CAS56652 [DJ] | Holiday Sampler | 2001 | $18 |

— *Contains 8 tracks -- 3 versions of "Emotion," 3 versions of "8 Days of Christmas" and 2 versions of "Sexy Daddy"*

❏ C261063	Survivor	2001	$18
❏ C269870	The Writing's on the Wall	1999	$18
❏ C286431	This Is the Remix	2002	$18
❏ DES-01 [DJ]	This Is the Remix Sampler	2002	$18

— *Five-song sampler*

DETERGENTS, THE
ROULETTE
| ❏ R25308 [M] | The Many Faces of the Detergents | 1965 | $120 |
| ❏ SR25308 [R] | The Many Faces of the Detergents | 1965 | $150 |

DETROIT
PARAMOUNT
| ❏ PAS-6010 | Detroit | 1971 | $18 |

DETROIT CITY LIMITS, THE
OKEH
| ❏ OKS14127 | 98c + Tax | 1968 | $30 |

DETROIT EMERALDS
WESTBOUND
❏ 2006	Do Me Right	1971	$40
❏ 302	Feel the Need	1977	$18
❏ 2018	I'm in Love with You	1973	$40
❏ 6101	Let's Get Together	1978	$18
❏ 2013	You Want It, You Got It	1972	$40

DETROIT SYMPHONY ORCHESTRA (PAUL PARAY, CONDUCTOR)
MERCURY LIVING PRESENCE
| ❏ SR90318 [S] | Ballet Highlights from French Opera | 196? | $175 |

— *Maroon label, no "Vendor: Mercury Record Corporation*

| ❏ SR90318 [S] | Ballet Highlights from French Opera | 196? | $150 |

— *Maroon label, with "Vendor: Mercury Record Corporation*

| ❏ SR90205 [S] | Beethoven: Symphonies No. 1 and 2 | 196? | $120 |

— *Maroon label, no "Vendor: Mercury Record Corporation*

| ❏ SR90254 [S] | Berlioz: Symphonie Fantastique | 196? | $120 |

— *Maroon label, no "Vendor: Mercury Record Corporation*

| ❏ SR90254 [S] | Berlioz: Symphonie Fantastique | 196? | $25 |

— *Maroon label, with "Vendor: Mercury Record Corporation*

| ❏ SR90375 [S] | Berlioz: Symphonie Fantastique; Le Corsair Overture; Royal Hunt and Storm | 196? | $50 |

— *Maroon label, no "Vendor: Mercury Record Corporation*

| ❏ SR90001 [S] | Bizet: Carmen Suite | 1959 | $50 |

— *Maroon label, no "Vendor: Mercury Record Corporation*

| ❏ SR90374 [S] | Bizet: Carmen Suite; L'Arlesienne Suites No. 1 and 2; Chabrier: Espana; Bourree; Marche | 196? | $25 |

— *Maroon label, no "Vendor: Mercury Record Corporation*

| ❏ SR90203 [S] | Bouquet de Paray | 196? | $75 |

— *Maroon label, no "Vendor: Mercury Record Corporation*

| ❏ SR90203 [S] | Bouquet de Paray | 196? | $30 |

— *Maroon label, with "Vendor: Mercury Record Corporation*

| ❏ SR90212 [S] | Chabrier: Espana; Suite Pastorale; Fete Polonaise; Overture to "Gwendoline"; Danse Slave | 196? | $120 |

— *Maroon label, no "Vendor: Mercury Record Corporation*

| ❏ SR90212 [S] | Chabrier: Espana; Suite Pastorale; Fete Polonaise; Overture to "Gwendoline"; Danse Slave | 199? | $30 |

— *Classic Records reissue*

| ❏ SR90017 [S] | Chausson: Symphony in B-flat | 1959 | $40 |

— *Maroon label, no "Vendor: Mercury Record Corporation*

| ❏ SR90359 [S] | Curtain Up! Heroic Overtures | 196? | $30 |

— *Maroon label, no "Vendor: Mercury Record Corporation*

| ❏ SR90010 [S] | Debussy: La Mer; Iberia | 1959 | $100 |

— *Maroon label, no "Vendor: Mercury Record Corporation*

| ❏ SR90372 [S] | Debussy: La Mer; Petite Suite; Iberia; Prelude | 196? | $40 |

— *Maroon label, no "Vendor: Mercury Record Corporation*

| ❏ SR90281 [S] | Debussy: Nocturnes; Ravel: Daphnis et Chloe Suite 2 | 196? | $300 |

— *Maroon label, no "Vendor: Mercury Record Corporation*

| ❏ SR90262 [S] | Dvorak: Symphony No. 9 "From the New World | 196? | $175 |

— *Maroon label, no "Vendor: Mercury Record Corporation*

| ❏ SR90285 [S] | Franck: Symphony in D | 196? | $50 |

— *Maroon label, no "Vendor: Mercury Record Corporation*

| ❏ SR90285 [S] | Franck: Symphony in D | 196? | $25 |

— *Maroon label, with "Vendor: Mercury Record Corporation*

| ❏ SR90247 [S] | French Overtures | 196? | $100 |

— *Maroon label, no "Vendor: Mercury Record Corporation*

| ❏ SR90129 [S] | Haydn: Symphony No. 96; Mozart: Symphony No. 35 | 1960 | $40 |

— *Maroon label, no "Vendor: Mercury Record Corporation*

| ❏ SR90174 [S] | Mendelssohn: A Midsummer Night's Dream; Symphony No. 5 | 196? | $40 |

— *Maroon label, no "Vendor: Mercury Record Corporation*

| ❏ SR90174 [S] | Mendelssohn: A Midsummer Night's Dream; Symphony No. 5 | 196? | $30 |

— *Maroon label, with "Vendor: Mercury Record Corporation*

| ❏ SR90191 [S] | Ouvertures Francaises | 196? | $175 |

— *Maroon label, no "Vendor: Mercury Record Corporation*

| ❏ SR90215 [S] | Overtures | 196? | $75 |

— *Maroon label, no "Vendor: Mercury Record Corporation*

| ❏ SR90377 [S] | Overtures and Excerpts from French Opera | 196? | $40 |

— *Maroon label, no "Vendor: Mercury Record Corporation*

| ❏ SR90128 [S] | Paray: Mass for Joan of Arc | 1960 | $25 |

— *Maroon label, no "Vendor: Mercury Record Corporation*

| ❏ SR90019 [S] | Rachmaninoff: Symphony No. 2 | 1959 | $40 |

— *Maroon label, no "Vendor: Mercury Record Corporation*

| ❏ SR90005 [S] | Ravel: Bolero; Ma Mere L'Oye; Chabrier: Bourree Fantasque | 1959 | $30 |

— *Maroon label, no "Vendor: Mercury Record Corporation*

| ❏ SR90213 [S] | Ravel: La Tombeau de Couperin; Valses Nobles et Sentimentales; Debussy: Petite Suite; Prelude | 196? | $250 |

— *Maroon label, no "Vendor: Mercury Record Corporation*

| ❏ SR90373 [S] | Ravel: Ma Mere L'Oye; Pavane; Tombeau de Couperin; Valses Nobles et Sentimentales | 196? | $30 |

— *Maroon label, no "Vendor: Mercury Record Corporation*

| ❏ SR90313 [S] | Ravel: Rapsodie Espagnole; La Valse; Pavane; Alborada; Ibert: Escales | 196? | $500 |

— *Maroon label, no "Vendor: Mercury Record Corporation*

| ❏ SR90012 [S] | Saint-Saens: Symphony No. 3 | 1959 | $85 |

— *Maroon label, no "Vendor: Mercury Record Corporation*

| ❏ SR90331 [S] | Saint-Saens: Symphony No. 3; Chausson: Symphony in B-flat | 196? | $30 |

— *Maroon label, no "Vendor: Mercury Record Corporation*

| ❏ SR90177 [S] | Schmitt: Tragedie de Salome; Strauss, Richard: Salome-Dance; Lalo: Namouna, Suite 1 | 196? | $100 |

— *Maroon label, no "Vendor: Mercury Record Corporation*

| ❏ SR90330 [S] | Schumann: Symphonies No. 1 and 3 | 196? | $30 |

— *Maroon label, no "Vendor: Mercury Record Corporation*

| ❏ SR90330 [S] | Schumann: Symphonies No. 1 and 3 | 196? | $30 |

— *Maroon label, with "Vendor: Mercury Record Corporation*

| ❏ SR90198 [S] | Schumann: Symphony No. 1; Manfred Overture | 196? | $30 |

— *Maroon label, no "Vendor: Mercury Record Corporation*

| ❏ SR90102 [S] | Schumann: Symphony No. 2 | 1960 | $40 |

| ❏ SR90102 [S] | Schumann: Symphony No. 2 | 196? | $30 |

— *Maroon label, with "Vendor: Mercury Record Corporation*

| ❏ SR90133 [S] | Schumann: Symphony No. 3 "Rhenish | 1960 | $25 |

— *Maroon label, no "Vendor: Mercury Record Corporation*

| ❏ SR90204 [S] | Sibelius: Symphony No. 2 | 196? | $150 |

— *Maroon label, no "Vendor: Mercury Record Corporation*

| ❏ SR90204 [S] | Sibelius: Symphony No. 2 | 196? | $50 |

— *Maroon label, with "Vendor: Mercury Record Corporation*

| ❏ SR90204 [S] | Sibelius: Symphony No. 2 | 196? | $25 |

— *Third edition: Dark red (not maroon) label*

| ❏ SR90269 [S] | Suppe: Overtures | 196? | $30 |

| ❏ SR90269 [S] | Suppe: Overtures | 196? | $25 |

— *Maroon label, no "Vendor: Mercury Record Corporation*

| ❏ SR90211 [S] | Vive La Marche! | 196? | $30 |

— *Maroon label, no "Vendor: Mercury Record Corporation*

| ❏ SR90107 [S] | Wagner: Dawn & Sigfried's Rhine Journey, etc. | 196? | $25 |

— *Maroon label, no "Vendor: Mercury Record Corporation*

| ❏ SR90232 [S] | Wagner: Rienzi Overture; Magic Fire Music; Flying Dutchman Overture; Meistersinger Excerpts | 196? | $30 |

— *Maroon label, no "Vendor: Mercury Record Corporation*

DEUCE
REDWOOD
| ❏ R-8602 | Deuce | 1986 | $30 |

— *Jean Fineberg and Ellen Seeling*

DEUCE COUPES, THE
May be two different groups.
CROWN
| ❏ CLP-5393 [M] | The Shut Downs | 1963 | $25 |
| ❏ CST-393 [S] | The Shut Downs | 1963 | $30 |
DEL-FI
| ❏ DFLP-1243 [M] | Hotrodder's Choice | 1963 | $50 |
| ❏ DFST-1243 [S] | Hotrodder's Choice | 1963 | $75 |

DEUCHAR, JIMMY
CONTEMPORARY
| ❏ C-3529 [M] | Pub Crawling | 1957 | $300 |
DISCOVERY
| ❏ DL-2004 [10] | New Sounds from England | 1953 | $100 |

DEVAUGHN, WILLIAM
ROXBURY
| ❏ RLX-100 | Be Thankful For What You Got | 1974 | $15 |

DEVIANTS, THE
CLEOPATRA
| ❏ CLP1803 [B] | Ptooff! | 2014 | $25 |
SIRE
❏ SES-97005 [B]	Disposable	1969	$250
❏ SES-97016 [B]	No. 3	1969	$250
❏ SES-97001 [B]	Ptoof!	1968	$300

DEVILED HAM
SUPER K
| ❏ SKS-6003 | I Had Too Much to Dream Last Night | 1968 | $30 |

DEVIL'S ANVIL, THE
COLUMBIA
| ❏ CL2664 [M] | Hard Rock from the Middle East | 1967 | $150 |
| ❏ CS9464 [S] | Hard Rock from the Middle East | 1967 | $150 |

DEVO
DUTCH EAST INDIA
| ❏ DE-112008-1 | Smooth Noodle Maps | 1991 | $30 |

— *Red vinyl, 1,000 copies pressed*

ENIGMA
| ❏ 73514 | Now It Can Be Told! | 1989 | $15 |
| ❏ EPRO326 [DJ] | Smooth Noodle Maps | 1990 | $25 |

— *Promo only, no picture cover*

| ❏ 73303 | Total Devo | 1988 | $15 |

JACKPOT
| ❏ JPR028 [B] | Live At Max's Kansas City - November 15, 1977 | 2014 | $30 |

WARNER BROS.
| ❏ MINI3548 [EP] | Dev-O Live | 1981 | $12 |

— *All copies came in plastic sleeve*

❏ BSK3337	Duty Now for the Future	1979	$15
❏ BSK3435	Freedom of Choice	1980	$12
❏ PRO-A-928 [EP]	Freedom of Choice/Whip It/ Be Still/Gates of Steel	1980	$16

— *Promo version of "Dev-O Live*

| ❏ BSK3595 | New Traditionalists | 1981 | $25 |

— *First pressings include bonus 45 (EP 3595) and poster; deduct 1/3 if missing*

| ❏ 23741 [B] | Oh No! It's Devo | 1982 | $12 |
| ❏ W1-23741 | Oh No! It's Devo | 1982 | $15 |

— *Columbia House version, no easel cutout on back cover*

| ❏ BSK3239 | Q: Are We Not Men? A: We Are Devo! | 1978 | $18 |
| ❏ 25097 | Shout | 1984 | $15 |

Number	Title	Yr	NM

DEVOL, FRANK
ABC-PARAMOUNT

Number	Title	Yr	NM
❏ 534 [M]	Italian Romance American Style	1966	$15
❏ S-534 [S]	Italian Romance American Style	1966	$18
❏ 513 [M]	Theme from "Peyton Place" and 11 Other Great Themes	1965	$15
❏ S-513 [S]	Theme from "Peyton Place" and 11 Other Great Themes	1965	$18

COLUMBIA

❏ CL1371 [M]	Fabulous Hollywood	1959	$18
❏ CS8172 [S]	Fabulous Hollywood	1959	$25
❏ CL1451 [M]	Four Seasons of Love	1960	$18
❏ CS0(# unknown) [S]	Four Seasons of Love	1960	$25
❏ CL1482 [M]	More Old Sweet Songs	1960	$18
❏ CS8273 [S]	More Old Sweet Songs	1960	$25
❏ CL1108 [M]	Portraits	1957	$18
❏ C2L12 [M]	The Columbia Album of Irving Berlin	1958	$30
❏ C2S812 [S]	The Columbia Album of Irving Berlin	1958	$40
❏ CL1260 [M]	The Columbia Album of Irving Berlin, Volume 1	1958	$18
❏ CS8044 [S]	The Columbia Album of Irving Berlin, Volume 1	1958	$25
❏ CL1261 [M]	The Columbia Album of Irving Berlin, Volume 2	1958	$18
❏ CS8045 [S]	The Columbia Album of Irving Berlin, Volume 2	1958	$25
❏ CL1413 [M]	The Old Sweet Songs	1960	$18
❏ CS8209 [S]	The Old Sweet Songs	1960	$25
❏ CL1543 [M]	The Old Sweet Songs of Christmas	1960	$18
❏ CS8343 [S]	The Old Sweet Songs of Christmas	1960	$18

COLUMBIA SPECIAL PRODUCTS

❏ EN216437	The Columbia Album of Irving Berlin	1983	$15

HARMONY

❏ HL7356 [M]	The Old Sweet Songs of Christmas	196?	$15
❏ HS11156 [S]	The Old Sweet Songs of Christmas	196?	$18

DEVORZON, BARRY
ARISTA

❏ AL4104	Nadia's Theme	1976	$12

DEVROE, BILLY, AND THE DEVILAIRES
TAMPA

❏ TP-31 [M]	Billy Devroe and the Devilaires, Vol. 1	1957	$40
❏ TP-39 [M]	Billy Devroe and the Devilaires, Vol. 2	1958	$40

DEWITT, GEORGE
EPIC

❏ LN3562 [M]	George DeWitt Sings That Tune	1959	$25
❏ BN531 [S]	George DeWitt Sings That Tune	1959	$30

DEWITT, LEW
COMPLEAT

❏ 671018-1	On My Own	1986	$15

DEXTER, AL
CAPITOL

❏ T1701 [M]	Al Dexter Sings and Plays His Greatest Hits	1962	$30
❏ ST1701 [S]	Al Dexter Sings and Plays His Greatest Hits	1962	$40

COLUMBIA

❏ CL9005 [10]	Songs of the Southwest	195?	$50

HARMONY

❏ HL7293 [M]	Pistol Packin' Mama	1961	$25

DEXY'S MIDNIGHT RUNNERS
CAPITOL

❏ SN-16288	Searching for the Young Soul Rebels	1983	$12

—Budget-line reissue

EMI AMERICA

❏ SW-17042	Searching for the Young Soul Rebels	1980	$18

MERCURY

❏ 822989-1	Don't Stand Me Down	1985	$12
❏ SRM-1-4069	Too-Rye-Ay	1982	$12

PARLOPHONE

❏ 2564629701 [B]	Searching For The Young Soul Rebels	2014	$25

DEYOUNG, CLIFF
MCA

❏ 432	Cliff DeYoung	1974	$12
❏ 387	Sunshine	1973	$18

DEYOUNG, DENNIS
A&M

❏ SP-5109	Back to the World	1986	$10
❏ SP-5006	Desert Moon	1984	$10

DIALOGUE
COLD

❏ 0(no cat #)	Dialogue	1974	$175

— White cover with insert

❏ 0(no cat #)	Dialogue	1972	$175

— Orange cover with insert

DIALS, THE
TIME

❏ 52100 [M]	It's Monkey Time	1964	$30
❏ S-2100 [S]	It's Monkey Time	1964	$30

DIAMOND, GREGG
MARLIN

❏ 2217	Star Cruiser	1978	$18

MERCURY

❏ SRM-1-3757	Hardware	1979	$15

POLYDOR

❏ PD-1-6123	Bionic Boogie	1978	$15

— As "Bionic Boogie"

❏ PD-1-6162	Hot Butterfly	1978	$15

— As "Gregg Diamond Bionic Boogie"

❏ PD-1-6237	Tiger Tiger	1979	$15

DIAMOND, LEO
ABC-PARAMOUNT

❏ ABC-303 [M]	Subliminal Sounds	1960	$30
❏ ABCS-303 [S]	Subliminal Sounds	1960	$40

RCA VICTOR

❏ LPM-1165 [M]	Skin Diver Suite and Other Selections	1955	$75

REPRISE

❏ R-6002 [M]	Exciting Sounds of the South Seas	1961	$30
❏ R9-6002 [S]	Exciting Sounds of the South Seas	1961	$30
❏ R-6024 [M]	Off Shore	1962	$30
❏ R9-6024 [S]	Off Shore	1962	$30
❏ R-6009 [M]	Themes from Great Foreign Films	1961	$30
❏ R9-6009 [S]	Themes from Great Foreign Films	1961	$30

DIAMOND, NEIL
BANG

❏ BLPS224 [P]	Do It!	1971	$75
❏ BLPS224	Do It!	1974	$15

— Later pressing on blue "clouds" label

❏ BLPS-227 [S]	Double Gold	1973	$100
❏ BLPS227	Double Gold	1974	$18

— Later pressing on blue "clouds" label

❏ BLP217 [M]	Just for You	1967	$100

— With blurb for "Thank the Lord for the Night Time" on cover

❏ BLPS217 [P]	Just for You	1967	$150

— With blurb for "Thank the Lord for the Night Time" on cover

❏ BLPS217 [P]	Just for You	1968	$100

— With blurb for "Shilo" pasted over "Thank the Lord for the Night Time" blurb

❏ BLPS217 [P]	Just for You	1970	$25

— With blurb for "Shilo" imprinted on cover

❏ BLPS217	Just for You	1974	$15

— Later pressing on blue "clouds" label

❏ BLPS219 [P]	Neil Diamond's Greatest Hits	1968	$100

— First editions have the single version of "Solitary Man" in rechanneled stereo

❏ BLPS219 [P]	Neil Diamond's Greatest Hits	196?	$25

— Later editions have an alternate take of "Solitary Man" in true stereo

❏ BLPS219	Neil Diamond's Greatest Hits	1974	$15

— Later pressing on blue "clouds" label

❏ BLPS221 [S]	Shilo	1970	$100
❏ BLPS221	Shilo	1974	$15

— Later pressing on blue "clouds" label

❏ BLP214 [M]	The Feel of Neil Diamond	1966	$150

— All tracks play mono

❏ BLP214 [P]	The Feel of Neil Diamond	1966	$175

— Album is labeled mono, but plays in stereo

❏ BLPS214 [P]	The Feel of Neil Diamond	1966	$150

— Album is labeled stereo and plays in stereo (except "Solitary Man," "Do It," "I'll Come Running" are rechanneled)

❏ BLPS214	The Feel of Neil Diamond	1974	$15

— Later pressing on blue "clouds" label

CAPITOL

❏ SWAV-12120	The Jazz Singer	1980	$12

COLUMBIA

❏ TC38068	12 Greatest Hits, Vol. II	1982	$12
❏ HC48068	12 Greatest Hits, Vol. II	1982	$150

— Half-speed mastered edition

❏ 8-2876-77507-1	12 Songs	2006	$25

❏ PC33965	Beautiful Noise	1976	$15

— Originals have no bar code

❏ PC38792	Classics -- The Early Years	1983	$12

— Possibly a reissue of Frog King 1

❏ OC40368	Headed for the Future	1986	$10
❏ TC38359	Heartlight	1982	$12
❏ HC48359	Heartlight	1982	$40

— Half-speed mastered edition

❏ AS 99-1586 [DJ]	Heartlight	1982	$30

— Promo-only picture disc

❏ CG240990	Hot August Night II	1987	$15
❏ JC34990	I'm Glad You're Here with Me Tonight	1977	$15
❏ KS32550	Jonathan Livingston Seagull	1973	$15

— With booklet

❏ HC42550	Jonathan Livingston Seagull	1982	$50

— Half-speed mastered edition

❏ KC34181	Love at the Greek	1977	$18
❏ C48610	Lovescape	1991	$30
❏ TC37628	On the Way to the Sky	1981	$12
❏ HC47628	On the Way to the Sky	1982	$30

— Half-speed mastered edition

❏ QC39199	Primitive	1984	$12
❏ 9C939915 [PD]	Primitive	1984	$25
❏ FC36121	September Morn	1979	$15
❏ PC32919	Serenade	1974	$15
❏ PCQ32919 [Q]	Serenade	1974	$40
❏ OC45025	The Best Years of Our Lives	1988	$10
❏ FC35625	You Don't Bring Me Flowers	1978	$15
❏ HC45625	You Don't Bring Me Flowers	1982	$40

— Half-speed mastered edition

DIRECT DISK

❏ SD16612	His 12 Greatest Hits	1982	$50

— Audiophile vinyl

FROG KING

❏ AAR-1	Early Classics	1972	$40

— Compilation of Bang material for Columbia Record Club; includes songbook (deduct 25% if missing)

MCA

❏ 2227	And the Singer Sings His Song	1976	$18
❏ 37060	And the Singer Sings His Song	1980	$10
❏ 37209	Gold	1981	$10
❏ 8000	Hot August Night	1972	$25
❏ 6896	Hot August Night	1980	$15

— Reissue of MCA 2-8000

❏ 5239	Love Songs	1981	$12
❏ 2005	Moods	1973	$12
❏ 37194	Moods	1981	$10
❏ 2007	Neil Diamond/Gold	1973	$12
❏ 2106	Neil Diamond/His 12 Greatest Hits	1974	$18
❏ 5219	Neil Diamond/His 12 Greatest Hits	1981	$12

— Reissue of MCA 2106

❏ 1489	Neil Diamond/His 12 Greatest Hits	1987	$10

— Reissue of MCA 5219

❏ 37252	Neil Diamond/His 12 Greatest Hits	198?	$10

— Reissue of MCA 5219

❏ 2103	Rainbow	1973	$18

— Compilation of Uni tracks

❏ 37059	Rainbow	1980	$10
❏ 2008	Stones	1973	$12
❏ 37195	Stones	1981	$10
❏ 2011	Sweet Caroline (Brother Love's Travelling Salvation Show)	1973	$12
❏ 37057	Sweet Caroline/Brother Love's Travelling Salvation Show	1980	$10
❏ 2013	Tap Root Manuscript	1973	$12
❏ 37196	Tap Root Manuscript	1981	$10
❏ 2006	Touching You Touching Me	1973	$12
❏ 37058	Touching You Touching Me	1980	$10
❏ 37056	Velvet Gloves and Spit	1980	$10

MOBILE FIDELITY

❏ Feb-0024 [B]	Hot August Night	1979	$75

— Audiophile vinyl

❏ Jan-0071	The Jazz Singer	1981	$30

— Audiophile vinyl

SILVER EAGLE

❏ MSM-35151	The Neil Diamond Collection	1988	$30

— Mail-order offer; contains material from his Uni period

UNI

❏ 73047	Brother Love's Travelling Salvation Show	1969	$30

— First editions do not include "Sweet Caroline"

❏ 73047	Brother Love's Travelling Salvation Show	1969	$25

— Later editions add "Sweet Caroline"

❏ 93047	Brother Love's Travelling Salvation Show	1971	$18

— Reissue of the version with "Sweet Caroline," with new number

❏ 93136	Moods	1972	$25
❏ ND-11 [DJ]	Neil Diamond DJ Sampler	1970	$300
❏ 73084	Neil Diamond/Gold	1970	$25

Number	Title	Yr	NM
❑ 1913 [DJ]	Open-End Interview with Neil Diamond	1971	$300
❑ 93106	Stones	1971	$25
❑ 73092	Tap Root Manuscript	1970	$25
❑ ST-93501	Tap Root Manuscript	1970	$30
— Capitol Record Club issue			
❑ 73071	Touching You Touching Me	1969	$25
❑ 93071	Touching You Touching Me	1971	$18
— Reissue of 73071			
❑ 73030	Velvet Gloves and Spit	1968	$30
— First editions do not include "Shilo			
❑ 73030-N	Velvet Gloves and Spit	1970	$25
— Later editions add a new recording of "Shilo			
❑ 93030-N	Velvet Gloves and Spit	1971	$18
— Reissue of the version with "Shilo" added, with new number			

DIAMONDS, THE (1)
MERCURY
Number	Title	Yr	NM
❑ MG-20213 [M]	Collection of Golden Hits	1956	$120
❑ MG-20480 [M]	Songs from the Old West	1959	$100
❑ SR-60159 [S]	Songs from the Old West	1959	$120
❑ MG-20309 [M]	The Diamonds	1957	$120
❑ MG-20368 [M]	The Diamonds Meet Pete Rugolo	1958	$100
❑ SR-60076 [S]	The Diamonds Meet Pete Rugolo	1959	$120

RHINO
| ❑ RNDF-209 | The Best of the Diamonds | 1984 | $15 |

WING
| ❑ MGW-12178 [M] | Pop Hits by the Diamonds | 1962 | $30 |
| ❑ MGW-12114 [M] | The Diamonds: America's Famous Song Stylists | 1959 | $30 |

DIAZ MENA, ANTONIO
AUDIO FIDELITY
| ❑ AFLP-2117 [M] | Eso Es En Latin Jazz Man | 1963 | $35 |
| ❑ AFSD-6117 [S] | Eso Es En Latin Jazz Man | 1963 | $25 |

DIBANGO, MANU
ATLANTIC
| ❑ SD7276 | Makossa Man | 1974 | $12 |
| ❑ SD7267 | Soul Makossa | 1973 | $12 |
ISLAND
| ❑ ILPS9526 | Afrovision | 1976 | $15 |

DICK AND DEEDEE
LIBERTY
| ❑ LRP-3236 [M] | Tell Me/The Mountain's High | 1962 | $50 |
| ❑ LST-7236 [R] | Tell Me/The Mountain's High | 1962 | $40 |
WARNER BROS.
❑ W1623 [M]	Song We've Sung on "Shindig	1966	$30
❑ WS1623 [S]	Song We've Sung on "Shindig	1966	$30
❑ W1586 [M]	Thou Shalt Not Steal	1965	$30
❑ WS1586 [S]	Thou Shalt Not Steal	1965	$30
❑ W1538 [M]	Turn Around	1964	$30
❑ WS1538 [S]	Turn Around	1964	$30
❑ W1500 [M]	Young and In Love	1963	$30
❑ WS1500 [S]	Young and In Love	1963	$30

DICKENS, JIMMY
COLUMBIA
❑ CS9648 [S]	Big Man in Country Music	1968	$30
❑ CS9648 [M]	Big Man in Country Music	1968	$100
— White label promo with stereo number and "Mono" on label; "Special Mono Radio Station Copy" sticker and timing strip on front cover			
❑ CL1545 [M]	Big Songs by Little Jimmy Dickens	1960	$30
❑ CS8345 [S]	Big Songs by Little Jimmy Dickens	1960	$40
❑ CL2288 [M]	Handle with Care	1964	$30
❑ CS9088 [S]	Handle with Care	1964	$30
❑ CL2551 [M]	Little Jimmy Dickens' Greatest Hits	1966	$30
❑ CS9351 [S]	Little Jimmy Dickens' Greatest Hits	1966	$30
❑ CL1887 [M]	Little Jimmy Dickens Sings Out Behind the Barn	1962	$30
❑ CS8687 [S]	Little Jimmy Dickens Sings Out Behind the Barn	1962	$40
❑ CL2442 [M]	May the Bird of Paradise Fly Up Your Nose	1965	$30
❑ CS9242 [S]	May the Bird of Paradise Fly Up Your Nose	1965	$30
❑ CL1047 [M]	Raisin' the Dickens	1957	$100
❑ CL9053 [10]	The Old Country Church	1954	$120
DECCA
❑ DL75091	Jimmy Dickens Comes Callin'	1968	$25
❑ DL75133	Jimmy Dickens' Greatest Hits	1969	$25
❑ DL4967 [M]	Jimmy Dickens Sings	1967	$30
❑ DL74967 [S]	Jimmy Dickens Sings	1967	$25

DICKENSON, VIC, AND JOE THOMAS
ATLANTIC
| ❑ 1303 [M] | Mainstream | 1958 | $300 |
| — Black label | | | |

Number	Title	Yr	NM
❑ 1303 [M]	Mainstream	1961	$175
— Multicolor label, white "fan" logo			
❑ SD1303 [S]	Mainstream	1958	$300
— Green label			
❑ SD1303 [S]	Mainstream	1961	$175
— Multicolor label, white "fan" logo			

DICKENSON, VIC
JAZZTONE
| ❑ J-1259 [M] | Slidin' Swing | 1956 | $40 |
SACKVILLE
| ❑ 2015 | Just Friends | 198? | $30 |
SONET
| ❑ 720 | Trombone Cholly | 197? | $25 |
STORYVILLE
| ❑ STLP-920 [M] | Vic's Boston Story | 1957 | $40 |
VANGUARD
❑ VRS-99/100	The Essential Vic Dickenson	197?	$35
❑ VRS-8001 [10]	Vic Dickenson Septet, Volume 1	1953	$50
❑ VRS-8002 [10]	Vic Dickenson Septet, Volume 2	1953	$50
❑ VRS-8012 [10]	Vic Dickenson Septet, Volume 3	1954	$50
❑ VRS-8013 [10]	Vic Dickenson Septet, Volume 4	1954	$50
❑ VRS-8520 [M]	Vic Dickenson Showcase, Volume 1	1958	$100
❑ VRS-8521 [M]	Vic Dickenson Showcase, Volume 2	1958	$100

DICKERSON, DWIGHT
DISCOVERY
| ❑ DS-792 | Sooner or Later | 1978 | $30 |

DICKERSON, WALT
AUDIO FIDELITY
❑ AFLP-2131 [M]	Unity	1963	$25
❑ AFSD-6131 [S]	Unity	1963	$30
❑ AFLP-2217 [M]	Vibes in Motion	1968	$30
— Reissue of Dauntless 4313			
❑ AFSD-6217 [S]	Vibes in Motion	1968	$35
— Reissue of Dauntless 6313			
DAUNTLESS
| ❑ DM-4313 [M] | Jazz Impressions of "Lawrence of Arabia | 1963 | $30 |
| ❑ DS-6313 [S] | Jazz Impressions of "Lawrence of Arabia | 1963 | $30 |
INNER CITY
| ❑ IC-2042 | Peace | 1976 | $35 |
MGM
| ❑ E-4358 [M] | Impressions of "A Patch of Blue | 1965 | $25 |
| ❑ SE-4358 [S] | Impressions of "A Patch of Blue | 1965 | $30 |
NEW JAZZ
❑ NJLP-8268 [M]	A Sense of Direction	1962	$175
— Purple label			
❑ NJLP-8268 [M]	A Sense of Direction	1965	$175
— Blue label, trident logo at right			
❑ NJLP-8275 [M]	Relativity	1962	$175
— Purple label			
❑ NJLP-8275 [M]	Relativity	1965	$175
— Blue label, trident logo at right			
❑ NJLP-8254 [M]	This Is Walt Dickerson	1961	$300
— Purple label			
❑ NJLP-8254 [M]	This Is Walt Dickerson	1965	$175
— Blue label, trident logo at right			
❑ NJLP-8283 [M]	To My Queen	1962	$175
— Purple label			
❑ NJLP-8283 [M]	To My Queen	1965	$175
— Blue label, trident logo at right			
SOUL NOTE
| ❑ SN-1028 | Life Rays | 1982 | $30 |
STEEPLECHASE
❑ SCS-1089	Divine Gemini	197?	$30
❑ SCS-1146	I Hear You John	198?	$30
❑ SCS-1115	Landscape with Open Door	1978	$30
❑ SCS-1042	Peace	197?	$25
— Reissue of Inner City 2042			
❑ SCS-1070	Serendipity	197?	$30
❑ SCD-17002	Shades of Love	198?	$30
— Direct-to-disc recording			
❑ SCS-1213	Tenderness	198?	$30
❑ SCS-1112	To My Queen Revisited	1978	$30
❑ SCS-1130	To My Son	1979	$30
❑ SCS-1126	Visions	1979	$30

DICKIE, NEVILLE
STOMP OFF
❑ SOS-1052	Eye Openers	1982	$25
❑ SOS-1176 [B]	Neville Dickie Meets Fats, the Lion and the Lamb	1988	$25
❑ SOS-1096	Taken in Stride	1986	$25

DICKIES, THE
Famously covered BLACK SABBATH'S "Paranoid."

A&M
Number	Title	Yr	NM
❑ SP-4796	Dawn of the Dickies	1979	$18
❑ SP-4742	The Incredible Shrinking Dickies	1979	$25
— First pressing on yellow vinyl			
❑ SP-4742	The Incredible Shrinking Dickies	1979	$18
ENIGMA
| ❑ D1-73322 [EP] | Killer Klowns (From Outer Space) | 1988 | $10 |
| ❑ D1-73289 | Second Coming | 1989 | $10 |
PVC
| ❑ 6903 | Stukas Over Disneyland | 1983 | $15 |
TAANG!
| ❑ 56 [B] | Locked and Loaded | 1991 | $25 |
TRIPLE X
| ❑ 51168 | Idjit Savant | 1994 | $18 |

DICKS, THE
ALTERNATIVE TENTACLES
| ❑ VIRUS43 | These People | 1985 | $18 |
RADICAL
| ❑ RRR80351 | Recorded Live at Raul's | 1980 | $75 |
| — One side features the Big Boys; the other side, the Dicks | | | |
SST
| ❑ 017 | Kill from the Heart | 1983 | $30 |

DICKY DOO AND THE DON'TS
UNITED ARTISTS
❑ UAL-3097 [M]	Teen Scene	1959	$40
❑ UAS-6097 [S]	Teen Scene	1959	$50
❑ UAL-3094 [M]	The Madison and Other Dances	1959	$40
❑ UAS-6094 [S]	The Madison and Other Dances	1959	$50

DICTATORS, THE
ASYLUM
| ❑ 6E-147 | Bloodbrothers | 1978 | $18 |
| ❑ 7E-1109 | Manifest Destiny | 1977 | $16 |
EPIC
| ❑ KE33348 | The Dictators Go Girl Crazy | 1975 | $25 |

DIDDLEY, BO
ACCORD
| ❑ SN-7182 | Toronto Rock and Roll Revival, Vol. 5 | 1982 | $25 |
CHECKER
❑ LP2989 [M]	16 All Time Greatest Hits	1964	$100
❑ LPS2989 [R]	16 All Time Greatest Hits	1964	$40
❑ LP2996 [M]	500% More Man	1965	$75
❑ LPS2996 [R]	500% More Man	1965	$30
❑ LP2984 [M]	Bo Diddley	1962	$150

CHESS LP 1431 — Hi-Fidelity — BO DIDDLEY

❑ LP1431 [M]	Bo Diddley	1958	$300
❑ LP2985 [M]	Bo Diddley and Company	1963	$120
❑ LP2977 [M]	Bo Diddley Is a Gunslinger	1961	$300
❑ LP2980 [M]	Bo Diddley Is a Lover	1961	$250
❑ LP2982 [M]	Bo Diddley's a Twister	1962	$175
❑ LP2988 [M]	Bo Diddley's Beach Party	1963	$150
❑ LP2987 [M]	Boss Man	1967	$100
— Reissue of Chess 1431			
❑ LPS3007 [R]	Boss Man	1967	$50
❑ LP1436 [M]	Go Bo Diddley	1959	$400
❑ LP3006 [M]	Go Bo Diddley	1967	$50
— Reissue of 1436			
❑ LPS3006 [R]	Go Bo Diddley	1967	$40
❑ LP2974 [M]	Have Guitar, Will Travel	1960	$250
❑ LP2992 [M]	Hey! Good Lookin'	1965	$100
❑ LPS2992 [R]	Hey! Good Lookin'	1965	$30
❑ LP2982 [M]	Road Runner	1967	$150

Number	Title	Yr	NM
—Reissue of "Bo Diddley's a Twister			
❏ LPS-2982 [R]	Road Runner	1967	$50
❏ LP2976 [M]	Spotlight on Bo Diddley	1960	$250
❏ LP2987 [M]	Surfin' with Bo Diddley	1964	$120
❏ LPS2987 [R]	Surfin' with Bo Diddley	1964	$30
❏ LPS3013	The Black Gladiator	1968	$30
❏ LP3001 [M]	The Originator	1966	$30
❏ LPS3001 [S]	The Originator	1966	$40
CHESS			
❏ CH50001	Another Dimension	1971	$40
❏ CH50047	Big Bad Bo	1974	$30
❏ LP1431 [M]	Bo Diddley	1958	$500
❏ CH-9194	Bo Diddley	1986	$12
—Reissue of 1431			
❏ CH-9285	Bo Diddley Is a Gunslinger	1989	$12
—Reissue of Checker 2977			
❏ CH-9196	Go Bo Diddley	1986	$12
—Reissue of Checker 1436			
❏ 2CH60005	Got My Own Bag of Tricks	1972	$30
❏ CH-9187	Have Guitar, Will Travel	1985	$12
—Reissue of Checker 2974			
❏ CH-9106	His Greatest Sides, Vol. 1	1984	$12
❏ CH-9264	Spotlight on Bo Diddley	1987	$12
—Reissue of Checker 2976			
❏ CH3-19502	The Chess Box	1990	$40
❏ CH50029	The London Bo Diddley Sessions	1973	$30
❏ CH-9296	The London Bo Diddley Sessions	1989	$12
—Reissue of 50029			
❏ CH50016	Where It All Began	1972	$40
CLEOPATRA			
❏ 8837 [B]	I'm A Man - Live '84		$25
—picture disc			
RCA VICTOR			
❏ APL1-1229	The 20th Anniversary of Rock and Roll	1976	$25
SUNDAZED			
❏ LP5443 [B]	Bo Diddley	2014	$30
❏ LP [B]	Bo Diddley's Beach Party	2014	$30

DIDDLEY, BO/CHUCK BERRY
Also see each artist's individual listings.

Number	Title	Yr	NM
CHECKER			
❏ LP2991 [M]	Two Great Guitars	1964	$75
❏ LPS2991 [R]	Two Great Guitars	1964	$40
❏ 2991 [B]	Two Great Guitars	1964	$175
CHESS			
❏ CH-9170 [B]	Two Great Guitars	1985	$12
—Reissue of Checker 2991			

DIDDLEY, BO/MUDDY WATERS/HOWLIN' WOLF
Also see each artist's individual listings.

Number	Title	Yr	NM
CHECKER			
❏ LP3010 [M]	Super, Super Blues Band	1968	$50
❏ LPS3010 [S]	Super, Super Blues Band	1968	$40
CHESS			
❏ CH-9169	Super, Super Blues Band	1985	$12
—Reissue of Checker 3010			

DIDDLEY, BO/MUDDY WATERS/LITTLE WALTER
Also see each artist's individual listings.

Number	Title	Yr	NM
CHECKER			
❏ LP3008 [M]	Super Blues Band	1968	$50
❏ LPS3008 [S]	Super Blues Band	1968	$40
CHESS			
❏ CH-9168	Super Blues Band	1985	$12
—Reissue of Checker 3008			

DIDO

Number	Title	Yr	NM
ARISTA			
❏ RTH-2015	Life for Rent	2004	$30
—Audiophile edition on 200-gram vinyl			
❏ RTH-2003	No Angel	2001	$30
—Audiophile edition on 200-gram vinyl			

DIESEL

Number	Title	Yr	NM
REGENCY			
❏ SD19315	Watts in a Tank	1981	$12
—Reissue, distributed by Atlantic			
❏ 9603	Watts in a Tank	1981	$15
—Original release, distributed by JEM			

DIETRICH, MARLENE

Number	Title	Yr	NM
CAPITOL			
❏ T10443 [M]	Marlene Dietrich's Berlin	1966	$25
❏ ST10443 [S]	Marlene Dietrich's Berlin	1966	$30
❏ T10397 [M]	Marlene (Songs in German by the Inimitable Dietrich)	1965	$25
❏ ST10397 [S]	Marlene (Songs in German by the Inimitable Dietrich)	1965	$30
❏ STCR-300	The Magic of Marlene	1969	$40
—All three of her Capitol LPs in one box			
❏ T10282 [M]	Wiedersehn Mit Marlene	1961	$25
❏ ST10282 [S]	Wiedersehn Mit Marlene	1961	$30

Number	Title	Yr	NM
CLEOPATRA			
❏ 3671 [B]	Lili Marlene		$25
❏ 8142 [B]	Lili Marlene		$30
—picture disc			
COLUMBIA			
❏ CL1275 [M]	Lili Marlene	1959	$50
❏ CL105 [10]	Overseas -- Songs for the O.S.S.	1953	$150
❏ C32245	The Best of Marlene Dietrich	1973	$15
COLUMBIA MASTERWORKS			
❏ ML4975 [M]	At the Café de Paris	1955	$50
❏ OL6430 [M]	Dietrich in London	1966	$30
❏ OS2830 [S]	Dietrich in London	1966	$30
❏ WL164 [M]	Dietrich in Rio	195?	$40
❏ WS316 [S]	Dietrich in Rio	195?	$50
DECCA			
❏ DL8465 [M]	Marlene Dietrich	1957	$40
—Black label, silver print			
❏ DL8465 [M]	Marlene Dietrich	196?	$30
—Black label with color bars			
❏ DL78465 [R]	Marlene Dietrich	196?	$25
❏ DL5100 [10]	Souvenir Album	1950	$100
MURRAY HILL/CSP			
❏ P314689	The Legendary Marlene Dietrich	1978	$30
VOX			
❏ VS-3040 [10]	Marlene Dietrich Sings	1950	$100

DIFFORD AND TILBROOK

Number	Title	Yr	NM
A&M			
❏ SP-4985	Difford and Tilbrook	1984	$12

DIGA RHYTHM BAND, THE
Also see THE GRATEFUL DEAD.

Number	Title	Yr	NM
ROUND			
❏ RX-110	The Diga Rhythm Band	1976	$30

DIGABLE PLANETS

Number	Title	Yr	NM
PENDULUM			
❏ E1-30654	Blowout Comb	1994	$15
❏ 61414	Reachin' (A New Refutation of Time and Space)	1993	$15

DIGGS, DAVID

Number	Title	Yr	NM
INSTANT JOY			
❏ 1002	Supercook!	198?	$25
PALO ALTO			
❏ 8037	Realworld	198?	$25
PBR			
❏ 12	Elusion	1979	$30
❏ 9	Out on a Limb	197?	$30
TBA			
❏ TB-213	Right Before Your Eyes	1986	$25
❏ TB-207	Streetshadows	1985	$25

DIGITAL UNDERGROUND

Number	Title	Yr	NM
CRITIQUE			
❏ 15452	Future Rhythm	1996	$15
JAKE			
❏ INT2-92061	Who Got the Gravy?	1998	$18
TOMMY BOY			
❏ TB1470	No Nose Job: The Legend of Digital Underground	2001	$18
❏ TB1026 [B]	Sex Packets	1990	$18
❏ TB1045	Sons of the P.	1991	$15
❏ TB964 [EP]	This Is an E.P. Release	1991	$18

DILCHER, CHERYL

Number	Title	Yr	NM
A&M			
❏ SP-4394	Butterfly	1973	$30
❏ SP-3640	Magic	1974	$25
AMPEX			
❏ A-10109	Special Songs	1970	$50
BUTTERFLY			
❏ FLY 003	Blue Sailor	1977	$25
—Clear vinyl			
❏ FLY 003	Blue Sailor	1977	$15
—Black vinyl			

DILL, DANNY

Number	Title	Yr	NM
LIBERTY			
❏ LRP-3301 [M]	Folk Songs from the Country	1963	$25
❏ LST-7301 [S]	Folk Songs from the Country	1963	$30
MGM			
❏ E-3819 [M]	Folk Songs from the Wild West	1960	$25
❏ SE-3819 [S]	Folk Songs from the Wild West	1960	$30

DILLARD, DOUG

Number	Title	Yr	NM
TOGETHER			
❏ STT-1003	The Banjo Album	1970	$100

Number	Title	Yr	NM
DILLARD, VARETTA			
SAVOY JAZZ			
❏ SJL-1203	Mercy, Mr. Percy, Volume 1	1989	$15

DILLARD AND CLARK

Number	Title	Yr	NM
A&M			
❏ SP-4158	The Fantastic Expedition of Dillard and Clark	1968	$25
—Brown label			

DILLARDS, THE

Number	Title	Yr	NM
ANTHEM			
❏ ANS-5901	Roots and Branches	1972	$18
CRYSTAL CLEAR			
❏ CCS-5007	Mountain Rock	1979	$30
—Direct-to-disc recording			
ELEKTRA			
❏ EKL-232 [M]	Back Porch Bluegrass	1963	$30
❏ EKS-7232 [S]	Back Porch Bluegrass	1963	$30
—Mandolin-player label			
❏ EKS-74054	Copperfields	1969	$25
—Red label with large stylized "E" on top			
❏ EKL-285 [M]	Pickin' and Fiddlin'	1965	$25
❏ EKS-7285 [S]	Pickin' and Fiddlin'	1965	$30
—Mandolin-player label			
❏ EKL-265 [M]	The Dillards, Live!!! Almost!!!	1964	$25
❏ EKS-7265 [S]	The Dillards, Live!!! Almost!!!	1964	$30
—Mandolin-player label			
❏ EKS-74035	Wheatstraw Suite	1968	$25
—Tan label with large stylized "E" on top			
❏ EKS-74035	Wheatstraw Suite	1969	$18
—Red label with large stylized "E" on top			
FLYING FISH			
❏ FF 082	Decade Waltz	1979	$15
❏ FF215	Homecoming and Family Reunion	1979	$15
❏ FF 040	The Dillards Vs. the Incredible L.A. Time Machine	1977	$15
POPPY			
❏ PP-LA175-F	Tribute to the American Duck	1973	$18

DILLER, PHYLLIS

Number	Title	Yr	NM
COLUMBIA			
❏ CS9623	Born to Sing	1969	$25

DILLON, DEAN

Number	Title	Yr	NM
CAPITOL			
❏ C1-48920	Slick Nickel	1988	$10

DILS, THE

Number	Title	Yr	NM
LOST			
❏ 001	The Dils	1990	$15
TRIPLE X			
❏ 51003	The Dils Live	1987	$18
—White vinyl			

DIMENSIONS, THE

Number	Title	Yr	NM
(NO LABEL)			
❏ 0(# unknown)	From All Dimensions	1966	$800

DIMEOLA, AL

Number	Title	Yr	NM
COLUMBIA			
❏ JC35277	Casino	1978	$25
❏ PC35277	Casino	1980	$20
—Budget-line reissue			
❏ HC46454	Electric Rendezvous	198?	$50
—Half-speed mastered edition			
❏ FC37654	Electric Rendezvous	1982	$25
❏ PC37654	Electric Rendezvous	198?	$20
—Budget-line reissue			
❏ HC44461	Elegant Gypsy	198?	$40
—Half-speed mastered edition			
❏ PC34461	Elegant Gypsy	1976	$25
—Original issue with no bar code			
❏ JC35561	Elegant Gypsy	197?	$20
—Reissue with new prefix			
❏ PC35561	Elegant Gypsy	198?	$20
—Budget-line reissue with bar code			
❏ HC47152	Friday Night in San Francisco	198?	$50
—Half-speed mastered edition			
❏ PC34074	Land of the Midnight Sun	1976	$25
—Original issue with no bar code			
❏ PC34074	Land of the Midnight Sun	1980	$20
—Budget-line reissue with bar code			
❏ FC38944	Scenario	1983	$25
❏ C2X36270	Splendido Hotel	1980	$30
❏ FC38373	Tour de Force -- "Live"	1982	$25
EMI-MANHATTAN			
❏ MLT-46995	Tirami Su	1987	$25

Number	Title	Yr	NM

MANHATTAN
| ❏ ST-53002 | Cielo E Terra | 1985 | $25 |
| ❏ ST-53011 | Soaring Through a Dream | 1987 | $25 |

DINNING, MARK

MGM
❏ E-3828 [M]	Teen Angel	1960	$100
❏ SE-3828 [S]	Teen Angel	1960	$175
❏ E-3855 [M]	Wanderin'	1960	$100
❏ SE-3855 [S]	Wanderin'	1960	$120

DINNING SISTERS, THE

CAPITOL
| ❏ H318 [10] | The Dinning Sisters | 195? | $50 |

DINO, DESI AND BILLY

REPRISE
❏ R6176 [M]	I'm a Fool	1965	$25
❏ RS6176 [S]	I'm a Fool	1965	$30
❏ R6198 [M]	Memories Are Made of This	1966	$25
❏ RS6198 [S]	Memories Are Made of This	1966	$30
❏ R6194 [M]	Our Time's Coming	1966	$25
❏ RS6194 [S]	Our Time's Coming	1966	$30
❏ R6224 [M]	Souvenir	1966	$25
❏ RS6224 [S]	Souvenir	1966	$30
❏ R/RS6224	Souvenir Bonus Photo Sheet	1966	$10

DINOSAUR JR

HOMESTEAD
| ❏ 015-2 | Dinosaur | 1985 | $50 |
| —Released under the name "Dinosaur" | | | |

RHINO VINYL
❏ 77630	Green Mind	2006	$18
—Reissue on 180-gram vinyl			
❏ 77631	Where You Been	2006	$18
—Reissue of Sire 45108 on 180-gram vinyl			

SIRE
❏ 26479 [B]	Green Mind	1991	$50
❏ 45108 [B]	Where You Been	1993	$25
❏ 45719 [B]	Without a Sound	1994	$25

SST
❏ 216	Bug	1988	$12
❏ 152 [EP]	Dinosaur Jr	1987	$15
—Originals on purple swirl vinyl			
❏ 910 [10]	Dinosaur Jr	1987	$10
❏ 275 [EP]	Fossils	1991	$18
❏ 925 [10]	Fossils	1991	$18
❏ 244 [EP]	Just Like Heaven	1989	$10
❏ 914 [10]	Just Like Heaven	1989	$10
❏ 130	You're Living All Over Me	1987	$25
—First released under the name "Dinosaur"			
❏ 130	You're Living All Over Me	1987	$18
—As "Dinosaur Jr"; purple swirl vinyl			
❏ 130	You're Living All Over Me	1987	$12
—As "Dinosaur Jr"; black vinyl			

DIO, RONNIE

JOVE
| ❏ J-108 | Dio at Domino's | 1963 | $250 |

DIO
Also see RONNIE DIO; ELF; RAINBOW; BLACK SABBATH.

WARNER BROS.
❏ WB25612	Dream Evil	1987	$10
❏ WB23836	Holy Diver	1983	$12
❏ WB25443	Intermission	1986	$10
❏ W1262121	Lock Up The Wolves	1990	$14
❏ WB25292	Sacred Heart	1985	$10
❏ WB25100	The Last in Line	1984	$12

DION

ARISTA
| ❏ AL8549 | Yo Frankie | 1989 | $12 |

COLLECTABLES
| ❏ 5027 | Runaround Sue | 198? | $12 |

COLUMBIA
❏ KC31942	Dion's Greatest Hits	1973	$25
❏ PC31942	Dion's Greatest Hits	198?	$10
—Budget-line reissue			
❏ CL2107 [M]	Donna the Prima Donna	1963	$30
❏ CS8907 [S]	Donna the Prima Donna	1963	$40
❏ CL2010 [M]	Ruby Baby	1963	$30
❏ CS8810 [S]	Ruby Baby	1963	$40
❏ CS9773	Wonder Where I'm Bound	1969	$25

DAYSPRING
❏ DST-4022	Inside Job	1980	$15
❏ WR-8111	I Put Away My Idols	198?	$15
❏ DST-4027	Only Jesus	198?	$15
❏ 7-01-412901-5	Seasons	1984	$15
❏ WR-8112	Seasons (The Best of Dion)	198?	$15

LAURIE
❏ LES-4004	Abraham, Martin and John	197?	$15
—Reissue of SLP-2047			
❏ LLP2004 [M]	Alone with Dion	1960	$250
—With three wallet-size photos on inside strip (deduct 50% if missing)			
❏ SLP2047 [B]	Dion	1968	$25
❏ ST-91577	Dion	1968	$30
—Capitol Record Club edition			
❏ LLP2013 [M]	Dion Sings His Greatest Hits	1962	$80
❏ SLP2013 [R]	Dion Sings His Greatest Hits	196?	$50
❏ T-90366 [M]	Dion Sings His Greatest Hits	1965	$120
—Capitol Record Club edition			
❏ DT-90366 [R]	Dion Sings His Greatest Hits	1965	$120
—Capitol Record Club edition			
❏ LLP2019 [M]	Dion Sings the 15 Million Sellers	1963	$50
❏ SLP2019 [R]	Dion Sings the 15 Million Sellers	196?	$30
❏ LES-4013	Dion Sings the Hits of the 50's and 60's	1978	$15
❏ LLP2017 [M]	Dion Sings to Sandy (And All His Other Girls)	1963	$50
❏ LLP2015 [M]	Love Came to Me	1963	$80
❏ LLP2012 [M]	Lovers Who Wander	1962	$80
❏ LLP2022 [M]	More of Dion's Greatest Hits	196?	$50
❏ SLP2022 [R]	More of Dion's Greatest Hits	196?	$30
❏ T-91128 [M]	More of Dion's Greatest Hits	196?	$120
—Capitol Record Club edition			
❏ DT-91128 [R]	More of Dion's Greatest Hits	196?	$120
—Capitol Record Club edition			
❏ LLP2009 [M]	Runaround Sue	1961	$800
—Colored vinyl (gold, green or blue)			
❏ LLP2009 [M]	Runaround Sue	1961	$150
—Black vinyl			
❏ T-91027 [M]	Runaround Sue	196?	$120
—Capitol Record Club edition			
❏ DT-91027 [R]	Runaround Sue	196?	$120
—Capitol Record Club edition			
❏ LLP2009 [M]	Runaround Sue	1962	$100
—Black vinyl; with sticker on front cover: "Includes the Hit Singles 'The Majestic'/'The Wanderer'"			

LIFESONG
| ❏ JZ35356 | Return of the Wanderer | 1978 | $15 |

WARNER BROS.
❏ WS1945	Sanctuary	1971	$18
❏ WS1826	Sit Down, Old Friend	1969	$25
❏ BS2954	Streetheart	1976	$18
❏ BS2642	Suite for Late Summer	1972	$18
❏ WS1872	You're Not Alone	1971	$18

WORD
| ❏ WR-8285 | Kingdom in the Streets | 1985 | $15 |

DION AND THE BELMONTS

ABC
| ❏ 599 [M] | Together Again | 1967 | $30 |
| ❏ S-599 [S] | Together Again | 1967 | $40 |

ARISTA
| ❏ A2L8206 | 24 Original Classics | 1984 | $15 |

COLLECTABLES
❏ 5041	20 Golden Classics	198?	$12
❏ 5025	Presenting Dion & The Belmonts	198?	$12
❏ 5026	Wish Upon a Star	198?	$12

LAURIE
❏ SLP6000	60 Greatest Hits	197?	$30
—In box			
❏ SLP6000	60 Greatest Hits	197?	$25
—In regular cover			
❏ LES4002	Everything You Always Wanted to Hear by Dion and the Belmonts	197?	$18
❏ LLP1002 [M]	Presenting Dion & The Belmonts	1959	$300
❏ LLP2002 [M]	Presenting Dion & The Belmonts	1960	$175
❏ SLP2002 [R]	Presenting Dion & The Belmonts	196?	$900
—Despite its rechanneled stereo sound, this record is collectible because of its utter rarity			

| ❏ LLP2016 [M] | Together" On Records -- By Special Request | 1963 | $50 |
| ❏ LLP2006 [M] | Wish Upon a Star | 1960 | $175 |

PAIR
| ❏ PDL2-1142 | The Best of Dion and the Belmonts | 1986 | $15 |

PICKWICK
| ❏ SPC-3521 | Doo Wop | 1975 | $12 |
| —Reissue of ABC tracks | | | |

RHINO
| ❏ RNLP70228 | Reunion -- Live at Madison Square Garden -- 1972 | 1987 | $12 |
| —Reissue of ABC tracks | | | |

WARNER BROS.
| ❏ BS2664 | Reunion -- Live at Madison Square Garden -- 1972 | 1973 | $18 |

DIRE STRAITS
Also see MARK KNOPFLER.

WARNER BROS.
❏ 25264 [DJ]	Brothers in Arms	1985	$100
—Promo on Quiex II vinyl			
❏ 25264	Brothers in Arms	1985	$12
❏ 49377-1	Brothers in Arms	2006	$30
—Remastered reissue; contains the full-length version of the album as it appears on the CD version, with longer versions of five songs			
❏ HS3330	Communique	1979	$12
❏ BSK3266	Dire Straits	1979	$12
❏ WBMS-109 [DJ]	Dire Straits Live	1980	$150
—The Warner Bros. Music Show" promo			
❏ 25085 [DJ]	Dire Straits Live -- Alchemy	1984	$75
—Promo on Quiex II vinyl			
❏ 25085	Dire Straits Live -- Alchemy	1984	$15
❏ 23728 [DJ]	Love Over Gold	1982	$75
—Promo on Quiex II vinyl; the times of the songs are listed differently than on stock copies, for they are not rounded to the nearest 0 or 5			
❏ 23728	Love Over Gold	1982	$12
—On U.S. stock copies, the times of the songs as listed on the labels are rounded to the nearest 0 or 5			
❏ BSK3480	Making Movies	1980	$12
❏ 25794 [B]	Money for Nothing	1989	$18
❏ 26680	On Every Street	1991	$30
❏ PRO-A-2149 [EP]	Selectins from Dire Straits Live -- Alchemy	1984	$18
—Three-song promo-only sampler			
❏ 29800 [EP]	Twisting by the Pool	1983	$10
—Also known as "ExtendeDancEPlay"			

DIRECT FLIGHT

DIRECT DISC
| ❏ DD-104 | Spectrum | 1980 | $75 |
| —Direct-to-disc recording | | | |

DIRKSEN, SENATOR EVERETT MCKINLEY

CAPITOL
❏ T2792 [M]	Everett McKinley Dirksen at Christmas Time	1967	$30
❏ ST2792 [S]	Everett McKinley Dirksen at Christmas Time	1967	$25
❏ T2643 [M]	Gallant Men	1966	$18
❏ ST2643 [S]	Gallant Men	1966	$18
❏ T2754 [M]	Man Is Not Alone	1967	$25
❏ ST2754 [S]	Man Is Not Alone	1967	$18

DIRT BAND, THE
See NITTY GRITTY DIRT BAND.

DIRTY BLUES BAND, THE

BLUESWAY
| ❏ BLS-6020 | Stone Dirt | 1968 | $25 |
| ❏ BLS-6010 | The Dirty Blues Band | 1968 | $25 |

DIRTY DOZEN JAZZ BAND, THE

COLUMBIA
| ❏ FC45042 | Voodoo | 1989 | $35 |

GEORGE WEIN COLLECTION
| ❏ GW-3005 | My Feet Can't Fail Me Now | 1984 | $30 |

ROUNDER
| ❏ 2052 | Live: Mardi Gras in Montreux | 1986 | $30 |

DISCO-TEX AND THE SEX-O-LETTES

CHELSEA
❏ CHL555	A Piece of the Rock	1977	$12
❏ CHL505	Disco-Tex and His Sex-O-Lettes	1975	$12
❏ CHL516	Manhattan Millionaire	1976	$12

DITMARS, IVAN

CROWN
❏ 5049 [M]	Joy to the World	196?	$15
—Same as Crown CST 8, but in mono			
❏ CST8 [S]	Joy to the World	196?	$18
❏ CMX800 [M]	Joy to the World	196?	$15

Number	Title	Yr	NM
YULETIDE SERIES			
❏ YS-218 [S]	Joy to the World	197?	$12
—Same as Crown CST 8			
DITMAS, BRUCE			
CHIAROSCURO			
❏ 195	Aeray Dust	1977	$35
DIVINYLS			
CHRYSALIS			
❏ BFV41404	Desperate	1983	$12
❏ BFV41627	Temperamental	1989	$15
❏ BFV41511	What a Life!	1985	$15
DIXIE CHICKS			
COLUMBIA			
❏ C286840	Home	2002	$18
DIXIE CUPS, THE			
ABC-PARAMOUNT			
❏ 525 [M]	Riding High	1965	$75
❏ S-525 [S]	Riding High	1965	$100
RED BIRD			
❏ RB 20-100 [M]	Chapel of Love	1964	$75
❏ RBS 20-100 [S]	Chapel of Love	1964	$100
❏ RB 20-103 [M]	Iko Iko	1965	$175
DIXIE DREGS, THE			
Also see KANSAS; DEEP PURPLE.			
DIRECT DISK			
❏ SD-16620	Dregs of the Earth	1980	$40
—Audiophile vinyl			
(NO LABEL)			
❏ 0	The Great Spectacular Dixie Dregs	1975	$250
DIXIE SMALL FRY, THE			
LIBERTY			
❏ LRP-3057 [M]	The Dixie Small Fry in Hi-Fi	1957	$40
❏ LST-7010 [S]	The Dixie Small Fry in Hi-Fi	1958	$40
DIXIE STOMPERS, THE			
DELMAR			
❏ DL-204 [M]	Jazz at Westminster College	195?	$75
—Blue vinyl; label says "DL-201" though cover says "204			
❏ DL-112 [10]	The Dixie Stompers Play New Orleans Jazz	195?	$100
❏ DL-113 [10]	Wake the Levee	195?	$100
RCA VICTOR			
❏ LPM-1212 [M]	New York Land Dixie	1956	$100
DIXIEBELLES, THE			
SOUND STAGE 7			
❏ SSM-5000 [M]	Down at Papa Joe's	1963	$40
❏ SSS-15000 [R]	Down at Papa Joe's	1963	$30
DIXIELAND RHYTHM KINGS, THE			
BLACKBIRD			
❏ 12006	A Trip to Waukesha	197?	$35
EMPIRICAL			
❏ LP-102 [10]	The Dixieland Rhythm Kings	1954	$100
GHB			
❏ GHB-7	The Dixieland Rhythm Kings	1963	$35
RIVERSIDE			
❏ RLP 12-210 [M]	Dixieland in Hi-Fi	1956	$300
—White label, blue print			
❏ RLP 12-210 [M]	Dixieland in Hi-Fi	1957	$300
—Blue label, microphone logo			
❏ RLP 12-289 [M]	Jazz in Retrospect	1959	$300
❏ RLP-2505 [10]	New Orleans Jazz Party	1954	$300
❏ RLP 12-259 [M]	The Dixieland Rhythm Kings at the Hi-Fi Jazz Band Ball	1958	$300
DIXON, BILL			
CADENCE JAZZ			
❏ CJ-1024/25	Collection	1985	$25
RCA VICTOR			
❏ LPM-3844 [M]	Intents and Purposes	1967	$30
❏ LSP-3844 [S]	Intents and Purposes	1967	$25
SAVOY			
❏ MG-12184	The Bill Dixon 7-Tette	1964	$25
SOUL NOTE			
❏ SN-1008	Bill Dixon in Italy, Volume 1	1980	$30
❏ SN-1011	Bill Dixon in Italy, Volume 2	1981	$30
❏ SN-1037/38	Nov-81	1982	$35
❏ 121138	Son of Sisyphus	1990	$35
❏ 121111	Thoughts	1987	$30
DIXON, ERIC			
MASTER JAZZ			
❏ 8124	Eric's Edge	197?	$35

Number	Title	Yr	NM
DIXON, WILLIE, AND MEMPHIS SLIM			
BATTLE			
❏ BV-6122 [M]	In Paris	1963	$30
❏ BVS-6122 [S]	In Paris	1963	$40
VERVE			
❏ MGV-3007 [M]	Blues Every Which Way	1961	$120
DIXON, WILLIE			
BLUESVILLE			
❏ BVLP-1003 [M]	Willie's Blues	1960	$175
—Blue and silver label			
❏ BVLP-1003 [M]	Willie's Blues	1964	$40
—Blue label, trident logo at right			
CHESS			
❏ CH3-16500	The Chess Box: Willie Dixon	1988	$30
COLUMBIA			

❏ CS9987 [B]	I Am the Blues	1970	$30
—Red label, "360 Sound"			
DIZRHYTHMIA			
ANTILLES			
❏ 91026	Disrhythmia	1988	$25
DJAVAN			
COLUMBIA			
❏ FC44276	Bird of Paradise	1988	$25
DMZ			
Features Jeff "Mono Man" Conolly, later of THE LYRES.			
4 MEN WITH BEARDS			
❏ 4M528LP [B]	DMZ		$25
BOMP			
❏ VXS200004	Relics	1981	$30
SIRE			
❏ SRK6051	DMZ	1978	$35
DO-RE-MI CHILDREN'S CHORUS, THE			
KAPP			
❏ KS-3368 [S]	More of the Christmas Songs Children Love to Sing	1964	$18
—Same as KL-1368, but in stereo			
❏ KL-1368 [M]	More of the Christmas Songs Children Love to Sing	1964	$15
MCA			
❏ 15008	Do You Hear What I Hear?	1973	$12
—Reissue of Kapp KS-3368			
DOBBINS, BILL			
ADVENT			
❏ 5003	Textures	1974	$35
OMNISOUND			
❏ 1036	Dedications	1980	$25
❏ 1041	Where One Relaxes	1981	$25
TELARC			
❏ 5003	Textures	198?	$25
—Reissue of Advent LP			
DOBKINS, CARL, JR.			
DECCA			
❏ DL8938 [M]	Carl Dobkins, Jr.	1959	$150
❏ DL78938 [S]	Carl Dobkins, Jr.	1959	$175
DOC HOLLIDAY			
METROMEDIA			
❏ 1017	Doc Holliday	1973	$25

Number	Title	Yr	NM
DOCTOR AND THE MEDICS			
I.R.S.			
❏ 53228	More/Stare Crazy	1987	$10
❏ 42026	I Keep Thinking It's Tuesday	1987	$15
❏ 5797	Laughing at the Pieces	1986	$12
DOCTOR ROSS			
FORTUNE			
❏ F-3011 [M]	Doctor Ross, The Harmonica Boss	1962	$50
❏ FS-3011 [S]	Doctor Ross, The Harmonica Boss	1962	$150
TESTAMENT			
❏ 2206 [M]	Doctor Ross	196?	$25
DOCTORS OF MADNESS, THE			
UNITED ARTISTS			
❏ UA-LA871J2 [B]	Doctors of Madness	1978	$40
—2LP compilation of first 2 UK LPs			
DODD, BILLY			
JAZZOLOGY			
❏ J-161	Billy Dodd's Swing All-Stars, Volume One	198?	$25
❏ J-162	Billy Dodd's Swing All-Stars, Volume Two	198?	$25
❏ J-130	Doctor Billy Dodd and Friends	1985	$25
DODD, DICK			
TOWER			
❏ ST5142	The First Evolution of Dick Dodd	1968	$50
DODD, JIMMIE			
DISNEYLAND			
❏ DQ-1302 [M]	Favorite Hymns for Family Singing	1967	$25
—Reissue of 1014			
❏ WDL-1014 [M]	Jimmie Dodd Sings His Favorite Hymns	1959	$30
—Reissue of 3014 with new number			
❏ WDL-3014 [M]	Jimmie Dodd Sings His Favorite Hymns	1958	$30
❏ DQ-1235 [M]	Sing Along with Jimmie Dodd	1963	$30
IMPERIAL			
❏ LP-9089 [M]	Lonely Guitar	1959	$40
❏ LP-9121 [M]	Swing-A-Spell	1960	$40
❏ LP-12058 [S]	Swing-A-Spell	1960	$50
DODD, KEN			
LIBERTY			
❏ LRP-3442 [M]	Tears and The River	1966	$18
❏ LST-7442 [S]	Tears and The River	1966	$25
DODDS, BABY			
AMERICAN MUSIC			
❏ 1 [M]	Baby Dodds No. 1	1951	$50
❏ 2 [M]	Baby Dodds No. 2	1951	$50
❏ 3 [M]	Baby Dodds No. 3	1951	$50
FOLKWAYS			
❏ FP-30 [10]	Footnotes to Jazz, Vol. 1 -- Baby Dodds' Drum Solos	1951	$100
GHB			
❏ GHB-50	Jazz A La Creole	1969	$35
DODDS, JOHNNY, AND KID ORY			
EPIC			
❏ LN3207 [M]	Johnny Dodds and Kid Ory	1956	$250
❏ LA16004 [M]	Johnny Dodds and Kid Ory	1960	$150
DODDS, JOHNNY			
BIOGRAPH			
❏ 12024	Johnny Dodds and Tommy Ladner, 1923-28	198?	$25
BRUNSWICK			
❏ BL58016 [10]	The King of New Orleans Clarinets	1951	$150
HERWIN			
❏ 115	Paramount Recordings Vol. 1: 1926-1929	198?	$30
JOLLY ROGER			
❏ 5012 [10]	Johnny Dodds	1954	$50
MCA			
❏ 42326	South Side Chicago Jazz	1990	$35
❏ 1328	Spirit of New Orleans	198?	$25
MILESTONE			
❏ M-2011	Chicago Mess Around	1968	$25
❏ M-2002 [M]	The Immortal Johnny Dodds	1967	$25
RCA VICTOR			
❏ LPV-558 [M]	Sixteen Rare Recordings	1965	$30
RIVERSIDE			
❏ RLP 12-135 [M]	In the Alley: Johnny Dodds, Volume 2	1961	$250

Number	Title	Yr	NM
❑ RLP-1002 [10]	Johnny Dodds, Volume 1	1953	$300
❑ RLP-1015 [10]	Johnny Dodds, Volume 2	1953	$300
❑ RLP 12-104 [M]	Johnny Dodds' New Orleans Clarinet	1956	$300
—White label, blue print			
❑ RLP 12-104 [M]	Johnny Dodds' New Orleans Clarinet	195?	$40
—Blue label with microphone logo			
TIME-LIFE			
❑ STL-J-26	Giants of Jazz	1982	$25
X			
❑ LX-3006 [10]	Johnny Dodds' Washboard Band	1954	$75

DODDS, JOHNNY/JIMMY NOONE
BRUNSWICK

Number	Title	Yr	NM
❑ BL58046 [10]	Battle of Jazz, Volume 8	1953	$175

DODDS, MALCOLM
RCA CAMDEN

Number	Title	Yr	NM
❑ CAL-873 [M]	Happiness Is a Thing Called Love	196?	$18
❑ CAS-873 [S]	Happiness Is a Thing Called Love	196?	$15

DODSON, MARGE
COLUMBIA

Number	Title	Yr	NM
❑ CL1309 [M]	In the Still of the Night	1959	$30
❑ CL1458 [M]	New Voice in Town	1960	$30
❑ CS8258 [S]	New Voice in Town	1960	$40

DOGGETT, BILL
ABC-PARAMOUNT

Number	Title	Yr	NM
❑ 507 [M]	Wow!	1965	$50
❑ S-507 [S]	Wow!	1965	$75
AFTER HOURS			
❑ AFT-4112	The Right Choice	1991	$35
COLUMBIA			
❑ CL2082 [M]	Fingertips	1963	$50
❑ CS8882 [S]	Fingertips	1963	$75
❑ CL1814 [M]	Oops!	1962	$50
❑ CS8614 [S]	Oops!	1962	$75
❑ CL1942 [M]	Prelude to the Blues	1963	$50
❑ CS8742 [S]	Prelude to the Blues	1963	$75
KING			
❑ K-5009	14 Original Greatest Hits	1977	$25
❑ 395-600 [M]	A Bill Doggett Christmas	1959	$40
❑ 295-89 [10]	All-Time Christmas Favorites	1955	$250
❑ 830 [M]	American Songs in the Bossa Nova Style	1963	$40
❑ 395-533 [M]	A Salute to Ellington	1958	$120
❑ 395-523 [M]	As You Desire	1957	$120
❑ KLP-523 [M]	As You Desire	1987	$25
—Reissue with "Highland Records" on label			
❑ 723 [M]	Back Again with More	1960	$150
❑ 641 [M]	Big City Dance Party	1959	$150
❑ 295-82 [10]	Bill Doggett -- His Organ and Combo	1955	$300
❑ 295-83 [10]	Bill Doggett -- His Organ and Combo, Volume 2	1955	$300
❑ 667 [M]	Bill Doggett On Tour	1959	$150
❑ 959 [M]	Bonanza of 24 Hit Songs	1966	$75
❑ 759 [M]	Bonanza of 24 Songs	1960	$150
❑ 395-563 [M]	Candle Glow	1958	$120
❑ 395-532 [M]	Dame Dreaming	1958	$120
❑ KLP-532 [M]	Dame Dreaming	1987	$25
—Reissue with "Highland Records" on label			
❑ 395-585 [M]	Dance Awhile	1959	$120
❑ KLP-585 [M]	Dance Awhile	1987	$25
—Reissue with "Highland Records" on label			
❑ 395-531 [M]	Everybody Dance to the Honky Tonk	1958	$120
❑ 706 [M]	For Reminiscent Lovers, Romantic Songs	1960	$150
❑ 633 [M]	High and Wide	1959	$150
❑ 395-609 [M]	Hold It	1959	$120
❑ KS-1078	Honky Tonk Popcorn	1969	$150
❑ 395-514 [M]	Hot Doggett	1957	$120
❑ 868 [M]	Impressions	1964	$40
❑ 395-502 [M]	Moondust	1957	$120
❑ KS-1101	Ram-Bunk-Shush	1970	$75
❑ KS-1104	Sentimental Journey	1970	$75
❑ 295-102 [10]	Sentimentally Yours	1956	$175
❑ KS-1108	Soft	1970	$75
❑ 395-582 [M]	Swingin' Easy	1959	$120
❑ 908 [M]	The Best of Bill Doggett	1964	$40
❑ 395-557 [M]	The Doggett Beat for Dancing Feet	1958	$120
❑ KLP-557 [M]	The Doggett Beat for Dancing Feet	1987	$25
—Reissue with "Highland Records" on label			
❑ 778 [M]	The Many Moods of Bill Doggett	1960	$150
❑ KLP-778 [M]	The Many Moods of Bill Doggett	1987	$25
—Reissue with "Highland Records" on label			
❑ KS-1097	The Nearness of You	1970	$75
POWER PAK			
❑ 269	Hold It!	197?	$25

Number	Title	Yr	NM
ROULETTE			
❑ R25330 [M]	Honky Tonk A La Mod	1966	$50
❑ SR25330 [S]	Honky Tonk A La Mod	1966	$75
STARDAY			
❑ 3023	16 Bandstand Favorites	197?	$25
WARNER BROS.			
❑ W1404 [M]	3,046 People Danced 'Til 4 AM	1960	$50
❑ WS1404 [S]	3,046 People Danced 'Til 4 AM	1960	$75
❑ W1452 [M]	Bill Doggett Swings	1962	$50
❑ WS1452 [S]	Bill Doggett Swings	1962	$75
❑ W1421 [M]	The Band with the Beat	1961	$50
❑ WS1421 [S]	The Band with the Beat	1961	$75
WHO'S WHO IN JAZZ			
❑ 21002	Lionel Hampton Presents Bill Doggett	1977	$30

DOGGY STYLE
CLEOPATRA

Number	Title	Yr	NM
❑ 6537 [B]	Punkers Anthem		$25

DOHENY, NED
ASYLUM

Number	Title	Yr	NM
❑ SD5059	Ned Doheny	1973	$25
COLUMBIA			
❑ PC34259	Hard Candy	1976	$18

DOHERTY, DENNY
ABC DUNHILL

Number	Title	Yr	NM
❑ DS-50096	Watcha' Gonna Do?	1970	$18
EMBER			
❑ EMS-1036	Waiting for a Song	1975	$15

DOJO
ECLIPSE

Number	Title	Yr	NM
❑ ES-7309	Down for the Last Time	1971	$30

DOKY, NIELS LAN
MILESTONE

Number	Title	Yr	NM
❑ M-9178	Dreams	1990	$35
STORYVILLE			
❑ SLP-4160	Daybreak	1989	$30
❑ SLP-4117	Here or There	1986	$25
❑ SLP-4140	The Target	1987	$25
❑ SLP-4144	The Truth	1988	$25

DOLBY, THOMAS
CAPITOL

Number	Title	Yr	NM
❑ ST-12309	The Flat Earth	1984	$12

Number	Title	Yr	NM
❑ ST12271 [B]	The Golden Age of Wireless	1983	$12
EMI MANHATTAN			
❑ E1-48075	Aliens Ate My Buick	1988	$12
HARVEST			
❑ MLP15007 [EP]	Blinded by Science	1983	$15
❑ ST12271	The Golden Age of Wireless	1982	$15

DOLCE, JOE
MONTAGE

Number	Title	Yr	NM
❑ ST-72002	Christmas Album	1981	$15

DOLDINGER, KLAUS
PHILIPS

Number	Title	Yr	NM
❑ PHM200125 [M]	Dig Doldinger	1966	$25
❑ PHS600125 [S]	Dig Doldinger	1966	$30
WORLD PACIFIC			
❑ WPS-20176	Blues Happening	1969	$150

DOLENZ, JONES, BOYCE & HART
CAPITOL

Number	Title	Yr	NM
❑ ST-11513	Dolenz, Jones, Boyce & Hart	1976	$18

DOLLAR, JOHNNY
DATE

Number	Title	Yr	NM
❑ TEM3009 [M]	Johnny Dollar	1967	$30
❑ TES4009 [S]	Johnny Dollar	1967	$25

DOLPHY, ERIC
BLUE NOTE

Number	Title	Yr	NM
❑ BT-85131	Other Aspects	1987	$25
❑ BLP-4163 [M]	Out to Lunch!	1964	$175
❑ BST-84163 [S]	Out to Lunch!	1964	$100
—"New York, USA" on label			
❑ BST-84163 [S]	Out to Lunch!	1966	$75
—"A Division of Liberty Records" on label			
❑ BST-84163 [S]	Out to Lunch!	1970	$50
—Mostly black label with "Liberty/UA" at bottom			
❑ BST-84163 [S]	Out to Lunch!	1971	$35
—"A Division of United Artists" on label			
❑ BST-84163 [S]	Out to Lunch!	1985	$30
—"The Finest in Jazz Since 1939" reissue			
❑ B1-46524	Out to Lunch!	199?	$35
—Reissue of 84163			
❑ BST-84163 [S]	Out to Lunch!	1973	$30
—Dark blue label with black stylized "b" at upper right			
CELLULOID			
❑ CELL-5014	Conversations	198?	$25
❑ CELL-5015	Iron Man	198?	$25
DOUGLAS			
❑ SD785	Iron Man	1969	$30
❑ KZ30873	Iron Man	1971	$25
❑ 6002	Jitterbug Waltz	197?	$35
EPITAPH			
❑ E-4010	Eric Dolphy 1928-1964	1975	$35
EVEREST ARCHIVE OF FOLK & JAZZ			
❑ FS-227	Eric Dolphy and Cannonball Adderley	1968	$30
EXODUS			
❑ EX-6005 [M]	The Memorial Album	1966	$25
—Reissue of Vee Jay LP-2503			
❑ EXS-6005 [S]	The Memorial Album	1966	$25
—Reissue of Vee Jay LPS-2503			
FANTASY			
❑ OJC-133	Eric Dolphy at the Five Spot	198?	$25
—Reissue of New Jazz 8260			
❑ OJC-247	Eric Dolphy at the Five Spot, Volume 2	198?	$25
—Reissue of Prestige 7294			
❑ OJC-413	Eric Dolphy in Europe, Volume 1	1990	$30
—Reissue of Prestige 7304			
❑ OJC-414	Eric Dolphy in Europe, Volume 2	1990	$30
—Reissue of Prestige 7350			
❑ OJC-415	Eric Dolphy in Europe, Volume 3	1990	$30
—Reissue of Prestige 7366			
❑ OJC-353	Eric Dolphy Memorial Album	198?	$25
—Reissue of Prestige 7334			
❑ OJC-400	Far Cry	1989	$30
—Reissue of New Jazz 8270			
❑ OJC-023	Out There	198?	$25
—Reissue of New Jazz 8252			
❑ OJC-022	Outward Bound	198?	$25
—Reissue of New Jazz 8236			
FM			
❑ 308 [M]	Conversations	1963	$40
❑ S-308 [S]	Conversations	1963	$50
FONTANA			
❑ 822226-1	Last Date	1986	$25
GM			
❑ GM-3005	Vintage Dolphy	1986	$35
INNER CITY			
❑ IC-3017	The Berlin Concerts	1978	$35
LIMELIGHT			
❑ LM-82013 [M]	Last Date	1964	$30
❑ LS-86013 [S]	Last Date	1964	$40
NEW JAZZ			
❑ NJLP-8260 [M]	Eric Dolphy at the Five Spot	1961	$650
—Purple label			
❑ NJLP-8260 [M]	Eric Dolphy at the Five Spot	1965	$175
—Blue label, trident logo at right			
❑ NJLP-8270 [M]	Far Cry	1962	$400
—Purple label			
❑ NJLP-8270 [M]	Far Cry	1965	$175
—Blue label, trident logo at right			
❑ NJLP-8252 [M]	Out There	1960	$300
—Purple label			
❑ NJLP-8252 [M]	Out There	1965	$175
—Blue label, trident logo at right			

Number	Title	Yr	NM
❑ NJLP-8236 [M]	Outward Bound	1960	$450

PRESTIGE

Number	Title	Yr	NM
❑ 24027	Copenhagen Concert	197?	$25
❑ MPP-2517	Dash One	198?	$25
❑ 24008	Eric Dolphy	197?	$25
❑ PRLP-7294 [M]	Eric Dolphy at the Five Spot, Volume 2	1964	$400
— Yellow label			
❑ PRLP-7294 [M]	Eric Dolphy at the Five Spot, Volume 2	1965	$25
— Blue label, trident logo at right			
❑ PRST-7294 [S]	Eric Dolphy at the Five Spot, Volume 2	1964	$50
— Silver label			
❑ PRST-7294 [S]	Eric Dolphy at the Five Spot, Volume 2	1965	$30
— Blue label, trident logo at right			
❑ PRLP-7304 [M]	Eric Dolphy in Europe, Volume 1	1964	$40
— Yellow label			
❑ PRLP-7304 [M]	Eric Dolphy in Europe, Volume 1	1965	$25
— Blue label, trident logo at right			
❑ PRST-7304 [S]	Eric Dolphy in Europe, Volume 1	1964	$50
— Silver label			
❑ PRST-7304 [S]	Eric Dolphy in Europe, Volume 1	1965	$30
— Blue label, trident logo at right			
❑ PRLP-7350 [M]	Eric Dolphy in Europe, Volume 2	1965	$25
❑ PRST-7350 [S]	Eric Dolphy in Europe, Volume 2	1965	$30
❑ PRLP-7366 [M]	Eric Dolphy in Europe, Volume 3	1965	$25
❑ PRST-7366 [S]	Eric Dolphy in Europe, Volume 3	1965	$30
❑ PRLP-7334 [M]	Eric Dolphy Memorial Album	1964	$25
❑ PRST-7334 [S]	Eric Dolphy Memorial Album	1964	$30
❑ PRST-7747	Far Cry	1970	$35
❑ 34002	Great Concert	1974	$30
❑ PRLP-7382 [M]	Here and There	1965	$25
❑ PRST-7382 [S]	Here and There	1965	$30
❑ PRST-7611	Live at the Five Spot, Volume 1	1969	$35
❑ PRST-7826	Live at the Five Spot, Volume 2	1971	$35
❑ 24053	Magic	197?	$35
❑ PRST-7652	Out There	1969	$35
❑ PRLP-7311 [M]	Outward Bound	1964	$50
— Yellow label			
❑ PRLP-7311 [M]	Outward Bound	1965	$30
— Blue label, trident logo at right			
❑ PRST-7311 [S]	Outward Bound	1964	$40
— Silver label			
❑ PRST-7311 [S]	Outward Bound	1965	$25
— Blue label, trident logo at right			
❑ P-24070	Status	1977	$35
❑ PRST-7843	Where?	1971	$35

TRIP

Number	Title	Yr	NM
❑ 5506	Last Date	197?	$30
❑ 5012	The Greatness of Eric Dolphy	197?	$30

VEE JAY

Number	Title	Yr	NM
❑ LP-2503 [M]	The Memorial Album	1964	$30
❑ LPS-2503 [S]	The Memorial Album	1964	$40

DOMINGO, PLACIDO, AND THE VIENNA CHOIR BOYS

RCA RED SEAL

Number	Title	Yr	NM
❑ ARL1-3835	Placido Domingo and the Vienna Choir Boys	1980	$12

DOMINGO, PLACIDO

CBS

Number	Title	Yr	NM
❑ FM37245	Christmas with Placido Domingo	1981	$15
— dark front cover			
❑ FM37245	Christmas with Placido Domingo	1982	$12
— white front cover			

CBS MASTERWORKS

Number	Title	Yr	NM
❑ HM47243	Perhaps Love	1982	$25
— Half-speed mastered edition			

DOMINO, FATS

ABC

Number	Title	Yr	NM
❑ S-479 [S]	Fats on Fire	1967	$18
❑ S-510 [S]	Get Away with Fats Domino	1967	$18
❑ ST-90167 [S]	Get Away with Fats Domino	1969	$30
— Capitol Record Club edition; reissue			
❑ S-455 [S]	Here Comes... Fats Domino	1967	$18

ABC-PARAMOUNT

Number	Title	Yr	NM
❑ 479 [M]	Fats on Fire	1964	$25
❑ S-479 [S]	Fats on Fire	1964	$30
❑ 510 [M]	Get Away with Fats Domino	1965	$25
❑ S-510 [S]	Get Away with Fats Domino	1965	$30
❑ T-90167 [M]	Get Away with Fats Domino	1965	$30
— Capitol Record Club edition			
❑ ST-90167 [S]	Get Away with Fats Domino	1965	$30
— Capitol Record Club edition			
❑ 455 [M]	Here Comes... Fats Domino	1963	$25
❑ S-455 [S]	Here Comes... Fats Domino	1963	$30

ATLANTIC

Number	Title	Yr	NM
❑ 81751	Live in Montreux	1987	$15

COLUMBIA

Number	Title	Yr	NM
❑ C35996	When I'm Walking	1979	$12
— Reissue of Harmony LP			
❑ PC35996	When I'm Walking	1986	$10
— Budget-line reissue			

COLUMBIA SPECIAL PRODUCTS

Number	Title	Yr	NM
❑ P213197	The Legendary Music Man	1976	$18
— Candelite Music TV offer			

EVEREST ARCHIVE OF FOLK & JAZZ

Number	Title	Yr	NM
❑ 280	Fats Domino	1974	$12
❑ 330	Fats Domino, Vol. II	1975	$12

GRAND AWARD

Number	Title	Yr	NM
❑ 267 [M]	Fats Domino	196?	$25
❑ S-267 [R]	Fats Domino	196?	$12

HARLEM HIT PARADE

Number	Title	Yr	NM
❑ 5005	Fats' Hits	197?	$12

HARMONY

Number	Title	Yr	NM
❑ HS11343	When I'm Walking	1969	$15

IMPERIAL

Number	Title	Yr	NM
❑ LP-9127 [M]	A Lot of Dominos	1960	$150
— Black label with stars on top			
❑ LP-9127 [M]	A Lot of Dominos	1964	$30
— Black and pink label			
❑ LP-9127 [M]	A Lot of Dominos	1967	$25
— Black and green label			
❑ LP-12066 [S]	A Lot of Dominos	1961	$175
— Black label with silver top			
❑ LP-12066 [S]	A Lot of Dominos	1964	$40
— Black and pink label			
❑ LP-12066 [S]	A Lot of Dominos	1967	$30
— Black and green label			
❑ LP-9009 [M]	Fats Domino Rock and Rollin'	1956	$175
— Maroon label			
❑ LP-9009 [M]	Fats Domino Rock and Rollin'	1958	$100
— Black label with stars on top			
❑ LP-9009 [M]	Fats Domino Rock and Rollin'	1964	$30
— Black and pink label			
❑ LP-9009 [M]	Fats Domino Rock and Rollin'	1967	$25
— Black and green label			
❑ LP-12388 [R]	Fats Domino Rock and Rollin'	1968	$15
— Rechanneled reissue of 9009			
❑ LP-9062 [M]	Fats Domino Swings	1959	$150
— Black label with stars on top			
❑ LP-9062 [M]	Fats Domino Swings	1964	$30
— Black and pink label			
❑ LP-9062 [M]	Fats Domino Swings	1967	$25
— Black and green label			
❑ LP-12091 [R]	Fats Domino Swings	1964	$25
— Black and pink label			
❑ LP-12091 [R]	Fats Domino Swings	1967	$18
— Black and green label			
❑ LP-9248 [M]	Here He Comes Again	1963	$50
— Black label with stars on top			
❑ LP-9248 [M]	Here He Comes Again	1964	$30
— Black and pink label			
❑ LP-9248 [M]	Here He Comes Again	1967	$25
— Black and green label			
❑ LP-12248 [R]	Here He Comes Again	1964	$25
— Black and pink label			
❑ LP-12248 [R]	Here He Comes Again	1967	$18
— Black and green label			
❑ LP-9038 [M]	Here Stands Fats Domino	1957	$175
— Maroon label			
❑ LP-9038 [M]	Here Stands Fats Domino	1958	$100
— Black label with stars on top			
❑ LP-9038 [M]	Here Stands Fats Domino	1964	$30
— Black and pink label			
❑ LP-9038 [M]	Here Stands Fats Domino	1967	$25
— Black and green label			
❑ LP-12390 [R]	Here Stands Fats Domino	1968	$15
— Rechanneled reissue of 9038			
❑ LP-9138 [M]	I Miss You So	1961	$150
— Black label with stars on top			
❑ LP-9138 [M]	I Miss You So	1964	$30
— Black and pink label			
❑ LP-9138 [M]	I Miss You So	1967	$25
— Black and green label			
❑ LP-12398 [R]	I Miss You So	1968	$15
— Rechanneled reissue of 9138			
❑ LP-9208 [M]	Just Domino	1962	$50
— Black label with stars on top			
❑ LP-9208 [M]	Just Domino	1964	$30
— Black and pink label			
❑ LP-9208 [M]	Just Domino	1967	$25
— Black and green label			
❑ LP-9239 [M]	Let's Dance with Domino	1963	$50
— Black label with stars on top			
❑ LP-9239 [M]	Let's Dance with Domino	1964	$30
— Black and pink label			
❑ LP-9239 [M]	Let's Dance with Domino	1967	$25
— Black and green label			
❑ LP-9065 [M]	Let's Play Fats Domino	1959	$150
— Black label with stars on top			
❑ LP-9065 [M]	Let's Play Fats Domino	1964	$30
— Black and pink label			
❑ LP-9065 [M]	Let's Play Fats Domino	1967	$25
— Black and green label			
❑ LP-12395 [R]	Let's Play Fats Domino	1968	$15
— Rechanneled reissue of 9065			
❑ LP-9153 [M]	Let the Four Winds Blow	1961	$150
— Black label with stars on top			
❑ LP-9153 [M]	Let the Four Winds Blow	1964	$30
— Black and pink label			
❑ LP-9153 [M]	Let the Four Winds Blow	1967	$25
— Black and green label			
❑ LP-12073 [S]	Let the Four Winds Blow	1961	$175
— Black label with silver top			
❑ LP-12073 [S]	Let the Four Winds Blow	1964	$40
— Black and pink label			
❑ LP-12073 [S]	Let the Four Winds Blow	1967	$30
— Black and green label			
❑ LP-9103 [M]	Million Record Hits	1960	$150
— Black label with stars on top			
❑ LP-9103 [M]	Million Record Hits	1964	$30
— Black and pink label			
❑ LP-9103 [M]	Million Record Hits	1967	$25
— Black and green label			
❑ LP-12103 [R]	Million Record Hits	1964	$25
— Black and pink label			
❑ LP-12103 [R]	Million Record Hits	1967	$18
— Black and green label			
❑ LP-9195 [M]	Million Sellers by Fats	1962	$50
— Black label with stars on top			
❑ LP-9195 [M]	Million Sellers by Fats	1964	$30
— Black and pink label			
❑ LP-9195 [M]	Million Sellers by Fats	1967	$25
— Black and green label			
❑ LP-12195 [R]	Million Sellers by Fats	1964	$25
— Black and pink label			
❑ LP-12195 [R]	Million Sellers by Fats	1967	$18
— Black and green label			
❑ LP-9004 [M]	Rock and Rollin' with Fats Domino	1956	$175
— Maroon label			
❑ LP-9004 [M]	Rock and Rollin' with Fats Domino	1958	$100
— Black label with stars on top			
❑ LP-9004 [M]	Rock and Rollin' with Fats Domino	1964	$30
— Black and pink label			
❑ LP-9004 [M]	Rock and Rollin' with Fats Domino	1967	$25
— Black and green label			
❑ LP-12387 [R]	Rock and Rollin' with Fats Domino	1968	$15
— Rechanneled reissue of 9004			
❑ LP-9055 [M]	The Fabulous Mr. D.	1958	$150
— Black label with stars on top			
❑ LP-9055 [M]	The Fabulous Mr. D.	1964	$30
— Black and pink label			
❑ LP-9055 [M]	The Fabulous Mr. D.	1967	$25
— Black and green label			
❑ LP-12394 [R]	The Fabulous Mr. D.	1968	$15
— Rechanneled reissue of 9055			
❑ LP-9040 [M]	This Is Fats	1957	$175
— Maroon label			
❑ LP-9040 [M]	This Is Fats	1958	$100
— Black label with stars on top			
❑ LP-9040 [M]	This Is Fats	1964	$30
— Black and pink label			
❑ LP-9040 [M]	This Is Fats	1967	$25
— Black and green label			
❑ LP-12391 [R]	This Is Fats	1968	$15
— Rechanneled reissue of 9040			
❑ LP-9028 [M]	This Is Fats Domino!	1957	$175
— Maroon label			
❑ LP-9028 [M]	This Is Fats Domino!	1958	$100
— Black label with stars on top			
❑ LP-9028 [M]	This Is Fats Domino!	1964	$30
— Black and pink label			
❑ LP-9028 [M]	This Is Fats Domino!	1967	$25
— Black and green label			
❑ LP-12389 [R]	This Is Fats Domino!	1968	$15
— Rechanneled reissue of 9028			
❑ LP-9170 [M]	Twistin' the Stomp	1962	$75
— Black label with stars on top			
❑ LP-9170 [M]	Twistin' the Stomp	1964	$30
— Black and pink label			

Number	Title	Yr	NM
❏ LP-9170 [M]	Twistin' the Stomp	1967	$25
—Black and green label			
❏ LP-9227 [M]	Walking to New Orleans	1963	$50
—Black label with stars on top			
❏ LP-9227 [M]	Walking to New Orleans	1964	$30
—Black and pink label			
❏ LP-9227 [M]	Walking to New Orleans	1967	$25
—Black and green label			
❏ LP-12227 [R]	Walking to New Orleans	1964	$25
—Black and pink label			
❏ LP-12227 [R]	Walking to New Orleans	1967	$18
—Black and green label			
❏ LP-9164 [M]	What a Party	1962	$75
—Black label with stars on top			
❏ LP-9164 [M]	What a Party	1964	$30
—Black and pink label			
❏ LP-9164 [M]	What a Party	1967	$25
—Black and green label			

LIBERTY

❏ LWB-122	Cookin' with Fats (Superpak)	1981	$15
—Budget-line reissue of UA 122			
❏ LWB-9958	Legendary Masters	1981	$12
—Budget-line reissue of UA 9958			
❏ LN-10135	Let's Play Fats Domino	1981	$10
—Budget-line reissue			
❏ LM-1027	Million Sellers by Fats	1981	$10
—Budget-line reissue of UA 1027			
❏ LN-10136	The Fabulous Mr. D.	1981	$10
—Budget-line reissue			

MCA/SILVER EAGLE

❏ 6170	Greatest Hits	198?	$12

MERCURY

❏ MG-21039 [M]	Fats Domino '65	1965	$30
❏ SR-61039 [S]	Fats Domino '65	1965	$40
❏ 21065/61065	Southland U.S.A.	1966	$0
—Canceled			

PICKWICK

❏ SPC-3111	Blueberry Hill	197?	$12

❏ SPC-3295 [B]	My Blue Heaven	1971	$12
❏ SPC-3165	When My Dreamboat Comes Home	197?	$12

QUICKSILVER

❏ QS-1016	Live Hits	198?	$12

REPRISE

❏ RS6439	Fats	1970	$500
—Officially unreleased, test pressings and coverless stock copies are known to exist			
❏ RS6304	Fats Is Back	1968	$30

SEARS

❏ SPS-473	Blueberry Hill!	1970	$30

SUNSET

❏ SUS-5299 [R]	Ain't That a Shame	1970	$15
❏ SUM-1103 [M]	Fats Domino	1966	$15
❏ SUS-5103 [R]	Fats Domino	1966	$15
❏ SUM-1158 [M]	Stompin' Fats Domino	1967	$15
❏ SUS-5158 [R]	Stompin' Fats Domino	1967	$15
❏ SUS-5200 [P]	Trouble in Mind	1968	$25

UNITED ARTISTS

❏ UA-LA122-F2	Cookin' with Fats (Superpak)	1974	$30
❏ UA-LA122-F2 [DJ]	Cookin' with Fats (Superpak)	1974	$300
—Promo with one black vinyl record and one colored vinyl record			
❏ UAS-9958	Legendary Masters	1972	$18
❏ LM-1027	Million Sellers by Fats	1980	$12
❏ UAMG-104 [DJ]	The Fats Domino Sound	1973	$40
—Promo compilation of 30 excerpts of Fats hits			
❏ UA-LA233-G	The Very Best of Fats Domino	1974	$15

DOMINOES, THE
See BILLY WARD AND THE DOMINOES.

DOMNERUS, ARNE

PRESTIGE

❏ PRLP-134 [10]	New Sounds from Sweden, Volume 4	1952	$350

RCA CAMDEN

❏ CAL-417 [M]	Swedish Modern Jazz	1958	$75

RCA VICTOR

❏ LPT-3032 [10]	Around the World in Jazz	1953	$300

DOMNERUS, ARNE/LARS GULLIN

PRESTIGE

❏ PRLP-133 [10]	New Sounds from Sweden, Volume 3	1952	$350

DON, DICK & JIMMY

CROWN

❏ CLP-5005 [M]	Spring Fever	1958	$40

DOT

❏ DLP-3152 [M]	Don, Dick & Jimmy	1959	$30

MODERN

❏ MLP-1205 [M]	Spring Fever	1957	$120

VERVE

❏ MGV-2084 [M]	Medium Rare	1958	$40
❏ MGV-2107 [M]	Songs for the Hearth	1959	$40

DON AND DEWEY

SPECIALTY

❏ SPS-2131	They're Rockin' Til Midnight, Rollin' Til Dawn	1970	$30
—Original labels are black and gold			

DON AND EDDIE

MODERN

❏ M7014 [M]	Rock and Roll Party	1963	$40

DON AND THE GOODTIMES

BEAT ROCKET

❏ BR-130	The Original Northwest Sound of Don and the Goodtimes	2000	$15

BURDETTE

❏ 300 [M]	Don and the Goodtimes' Greatest Hits	1966	$175
❏ 300S [S]	Don and the Goodtimes' Greatest Hits	1966	$300
—LP plays true stereo			
❏ 300S [R]	Don and the Goodtimes' Greatest Hits	1966	$150
—LP plays rechanneled stereo			

EPIC

❏ LN24311 [M]	So Good	1967	$30
❏ BN26311 [S]	So Good	1967	$40

PICCADILLY

❏ 3394	Goodtime Rock 'n' Roll	1980	$30

WAND

❏ WDS-679	Where the Action Is	1969	$30

DON ARMANDO'S SECOND AVENUE RHUMBA BAND

ZE

❏ 33-005	Don Armando's Second Avenue Rhumba Band	1979	$25

DONAHUE, SAM

CAPITOL

❏ H626 [10]	Classics in Jazz	1955	$100
❏ H613 [10]	For Young Moderns in Love	1955	$150
❏ T613 [M]	For Young Moderns in Love	1956	$75

DONALD, BARBARA

CADENCE JAZZ

❏ CJ-1011	Olympia Live	198?	$25
❏ CJ-1017	Past & Tomorrows	198?	$25

DONALDSON, BO, AND THE HEYWOODS

ABC

❏ D-824	Bo Donaldson and the Heywoods	1974	$12

CAPITOL

❏ ST-11501	Farther On	1976	$18

FAMILY PRODUCTIONS

❏ FPS-2711	Special Someone	1972	$18

DONALDSON, BOBBY

GOLDEN CREST

❏ GC-1003	Unlimited	196?	$25

SAVOY

❏ MG-12128 [M]	Dixieland Jazz Party	1958	$40
❏ SST-13003 [S]	Dixieland Jazz Party	1959	$30

WORLD WIDE

❏ 20005	Bobby Donaldson and the 7th Avenue Stompers	196?	$25

DONALDSON, LOU

ARGO

❏ LP-747 [M]	Cole Slaw	1965	$75
❏ LPS-747 [S]	Cole Slaw	1965	$75
❏ LP-734 [M]	Possum Head	1964	$75
❏ LPS-734 [S]	Possum Head	1964	$75
❏ LP-724 [M]	Signifyin'	1963	$75
❏ LPS-724 [S]	Signifyin'	1963	$75

BLUE NOTE

❏ BLP-4263 [M]	Alligator Boogaloo	1967	$175
❏ BST-84263 [S]	Alligator Boogaloo	1967	$150
—With "A Division of Liberty Records" on label			
❏ BLP-1593 [M]	Blues Walk	1958	$350
—"Deep groove" version; W. 63rd St. address on label			
❏ BLP-1593 [M]	Blues Walk	1958	$300
—Regular version with W. 63rd St. address on label			
❏ BLP-1593 [M]	Blues Walk	1963	$100
—With New York, USA address on label			
❏ BST-1593 [S]	Blues Walk	1959	$500
—"Deep groove" version (deep indentation under label on both sides)			
❏ BST-1593 [S]	Blues Walk	1959	$150
—Regular version with W. 63rd St. address on label			
❏ BST-1593 [S]	Blues Walk	1963	$50
—With New York, USA address on label			
❏ BST-81593 [S]	Blues Walk	1967	$30
—With "A Division of Liberty Records" on label			
❏ BST-81593	Blues Walk	1985	$30
—The Finest in Jazz Since 1939" reissue			
❏ BST-84370	Cosmos	1971	$35
❏ BST-84337	Everything I Play Is Funky	1970	$150
—With "A Division of Liberty Records" on label			
❏ B1-31248	Everything I Play Is Funky	1995	$35
—Reissue of 84337			
❏ BLP-4125 [M]	Good Gracious	1963	$175
❏ BST-84125 [S]	Good Gracious	1963	$150
—With "New York, USA" on label			
❏ BST-84125 [S]	Good Gracious	1967	$50
—With "A Division of Liberty Records" on label			
❏ BLP-4079 [M]	Gravy Train	1962	$250
—With W. 63rd St. address on label			
❏ BLP-4079 [M]	Gravy Train	1963	$200
—With New York, USA address on label			
❏ BST-84079 [S]	Gravy Train	1962	$200
—With W. 63rd St. address on label			
❏ BST-84079 [S]	Gravy Train	1963	$150
—With New York, USA address on label			
❏ BST-84079 [S]	Gravy Train	1967	$75
—With "A Division of Liberty Records" on label			
❏ BLP-4066 [M]	Here 'Tis	1961	$250
—With W. 63rd St. address on label			
❏ BLP-4066 [M]	Here 'Tis	1963	$175
—With New York, USA address on label			
❏ BST-84066 [S]	Here 'Tis	1961	$200
—With W. 63rd St. address on label			
❏ BST-84066 [S]	Here 'Tis	1963	$150
—With New York, USA address on label			
❏ BST-84066 [S]	Here 'Tis	1967	$25
—With "A Division of Liberty Records" on label			
❏ BST-84318	Hot Dog	1969	$150
—With "A Division of Liberty Records" on label			
❏ B1-28267	Hot Dog	1994	$35
—Reissue of 84318			
❏ BLP-4012 [M]	LD + 3	1959	$400
—"Deep groove" version; W. 63rd St. address on label			
❏ BLP-4012 [M]	LD + 3	1959	$250
—Regular version with W. 63rd St. address on label			
❏ BLP-4012 [M]	LD + 3	1963	$100
—With New York, USA address on label			
❏ BST-4012 [S]	LD + 3	1960	$300
—"Deep groove" version; W. 63rd St. address on label			
❏ BST-4012 [S]	LD + 3	1960	$175
—Regular version with W. 63rd St. address on label			
❏ BST-4012 [S]	LD + 3	1963	$75
—With New York, USA address on label			
❏ BLP-4053 [M]	Light Foot	1960	$120
—With W. 63rd St. address on label			
❏ BLP-4053 [M]	Light Foot	1963	$250
—With New York, USA address on label			
❏ BST-84053 [S]	Light Foot	1960	$200
—With W. 63rd St. address on label			
❏ BST-84053 [S]	Light Foot	1963	$150
—With New York, USA address on label			
❏ BLP-5030 [10]	Lou Donaldson-Clifford Brown	1954	$500
❏ BLP-1537 [M]	Lou Donaldson Quartet/Quintet/Sextet	1957	$1200
—"Deep groove" version; Lexington Ave. address on label			
❏ BLP-1537 [M]	Lou Donaldson Quartet/Quintet/Sextet	1958	$800
—"Deep groove" version; W. 63rd St. address on label			

Number	Title	Yr	NM
❏ BLP-1537 [M]	Lou Donaldson Quartet/ Quintet/Sextet	1958	$200
— Regular version with W. 63rd St. address on label			
❏ BLP-1537 [M]	Lou Donaldson Quartet/ Quintet/Sextet	1963	$100
— With New York, USA address on label			
❏ B1-81537	Lou Donaldson Quartet/ Quintet/Sextet	1989	$30
— Reissue of 1537			
❏ BLP-5021 [10]	Lou Donaldson Quintet/ Quartet	1953	$500
❏ BLP-5055 [10]	Lou Donaldson Sextet, Volume 2	1955	$500
❏ BLP-1591 [M]	Lou Takes Off	1958	$850
— Deep groove" version; W. 63rd St. address on label			
❏ BLP-1591 [M]	Lou Takes Off	1958	$300
— Regular version with W. 63rd St. address on label			
❏ BLP-1591 [M]	Lou Takes Off	1963	$140
— With New York, USA address on label			
❏ BST-1591 [S]	Lou Takes Off	1959	$300
— Deep groove" version; W. 63rd St. address on label			
❏ BST-1591 [S]	Lou Takes Off	1959	$300
— Regular version with W. 63rd St. address on label			
❏ BST-1591 [S]	Lou Takes Off	1963	$250
— With New York, USA address on label			
❏ BST-81591 [S]	Lou Takes Off	1966	$50
— With "A Division of Liberty Records" on label			
❏ BST-84254	Lush Life	1986	$35
— The Finest in Jazz Since 1939" label; first issue of this LP			
❏ BST-84280	Midnight Creeper	1968	$120
— A Division of Liberty Records" on label			
❏ LT-1028	Midnight Sun	1980	$75
❏ BLP-4271 [M]	Mr. Shing-a-Ling	1968	$250
❏ BST-84271 [S]	Mr. Shing-a-Ling	1968	$150
— With "A Division of Liberty Records" on label			
❏ B1-89794	Pretty Thing	1993	$35
— Reissue of 84359			
❏ BST-84359	Pretty Things	1970	$35
❏ BN-LA109-H2	Sassy Soul Strut	1973	$75
❏ BST-84299	Say It Loud!	1969	$150
— With "A Division of Liberty Records" on label			
❏ BN-LA024-H2	Sophisticated Lou	1972	$75
❏ BLP-4036 [M]	Sunny Side Up	1960	$400
— Deep groove" version; W. 63rd St. address on label			
❏ BLP-4036 [M]	Sunny Side Up	1960	$250
— Regular version with W. 63rd St. address on label			
❏ BLP-4036 [M]	Sunny Side Up	1963	$100
— With New York, USA address on label			
❏ BST-84036 [S]	Sunny Side Up	1960	$200
— With W. 63rd St. address on label			
❏ BST-84036 [S]	Sunny Side Up	1963	$150
— With New York, USA address on label			
❏ B1-32095	Sunny Side Up	1995	$35
— Reissue of 84036			
❏ BN-LA259-H2	Sweet Lou	1974	$75
❏ 4254/84254	Sweet Slumber	1967	$0
— Canceled			
❏ BLP-1566 [M]	Swing and Soul	1957	$300
— Deep groove" version; W. 63rd St. address on label			
❏ BLP-1566 [M]	Swing and Soul	1957	$175
— Regular version with W. 63rd St. address on label			
❏ BLP-1566 [M]	Swing and Soul	1963	$100
— With New York, USA address on label			
❏ BST-1566 [S]	Swing and Soul	1959	$175
— Deep groove" version; W. 63rd St. address on label			
❏ BST-1566 [S]	Swing and Soul	1959	$200
— Regular version with W. 63rd St. address on label			
❏ BST-1566 [S]	Swing and Soul	1963	$75
— With New York, USA address on label			
❏ BLP-4108 [M]	The Natural Soul	1963	$175
❏ BST-84108 [S]	The Natural Soul	1963	$120
— With "New York, USA" on label			
❏ BST-84108 [S]	The Natural Soul	1967	$50
— With "A Division of Liberty Records" on label			
❏ BST-84108	The Natural Soul	1987	$30
— The Finest in Jazz Since 1939" reissue			
❏ B1-31876	The Scorpion: Live at the Cadillac Club	1995	$35
❏ BLP-4025 [M]	The Time Is Right	1960	$800
— Deep groove" version (deep indentation under label on both sides)			
❏ BLP-4025 [M]	The Time Is Right	1960	$175
— Regular version with W. 63rd St. address on label			
❏ BLP-4025 [M]	The Time Is Right	1963	$150
— With New York, USA address on label			
❏ BST-84025 [S]	The Time Is Right	1960	$200
— With W. 63rd St. address on label			
❏ BST-84025 [S]	The Time Is Right	1963	$150
— With New York, USA address on label			
❏ BLP-1545 [M]	Wailing with Lou	1957	$1250
— Deep groove" version; W. 63rd St. address on label			
❏ BLP-1545 [M]	Wailing with Lou	1957	$300
— Regular version with W. 63rd St. address on label			
❏ BLP-1545 [M]	Wailing with Lou	1963	$140
— With New York, USA address on label			

Number	Title	Yr	NM
CADET			
❏ LP-789 [M]	Blowin' in the Wind	1967	$75
❏ LPS-789 [S]	Blowin' in the Wind	1967	$50
❏ LP-747 [M]	Cole Slaw	1966	$50
— Reissue of Argo 747			
❏ LPS-747 [S]	Cole Slaw	1966	$35
— Reissue of Argo 747			
❏ LPS-842	Fried Buzzard -- Lou Donaldson Live	1970	$50
❏ LPS-815	Lou Donaldson At His Best	1969	$50
❏ LP-759 [M]	Musty Rusty	1966	$75
❏ LPS-759 [S]	Musty Rusty	1966	$75
❏ LP-734 [M]	Possum Head	1966	$50
— Reissue of Argo 734			
❏ LPS-734 [S]	Possum Head	1966	$35
— Reissue of Argo 734			
❏ LP-768 [M]	Rough House Blues	1966	$75
❏ LPS-768 [S]	Rough House Blues	1966	$75
❏ LP-724 [M]	Signifyin'	1966	$50
— Reissue of Argo 724			
❏ LPS-724 [S]	Signifyin'	1966	$35
— Reissue of Argo 724			
CHESS			
❏ 2CA60007	Ha' Mercy	1972	$30
COTILLION			
❏ SD9905	A Different Scene	1976	$35
❏ SD9915	Color As a Way of Life	1977	$35
MUSE			
❏ MR-5292	Back Street	1983	$30
❏ MR-5247	Sweet Poppa Lou	1982	$30
SUNSET			
❏ SUS-5258	Down Home	1969	$30
❏ SUS-5318	I Won't Cry Anymore	1970	$30
TIMELESS			
❏ SJP-153	Forgotten Man	198?	$25
DONALDSON, WALTER			
MONMOUTH-EVERGREEN			
❏ 7059	The Greatest Song Hits	197?	$30
DONATO, JOAO			
BLUE THUMB			
❏ BT-21	A Bad Donato	1972	$35
— Distributed by Famous Music			
❏ BT-8821	A Bad Donato	1970	$25
— Distributed by Capitol			
MUSE			
❏ MR-5017	Joao Donato	197?	$30
RCA VICTOR			
❏ LPM-3473 [M]	The New Sound of Brazil	1966	$35
❏ LSP-3473 [S]	The New Sound of Brazil	1966	$25
DONEGAN, DOROTHY			
AUDIOPHILE			
❏ AP-209	The Explosive Dorothy Donegan	198?	$25
CAPITOL			
❏ T1226 [M]	Donnybrook with Dorothy	1960	$75
❏ ST1226 [S]	Donnybrook with Dorothy	1960	$75
❏ T1135 [M]	Dorothy Donegan Live!	1959	$75
❏ ST1135 [S]	Dorothy Donegan Live!	1959	$75
FORUM			
❏ F-9003 [M]	Dorothy Donegan at the Embers	196?	$35
— Reissue of Roulette R-25010			
❏ SF-9003 [R]	Dorothy Donegan at the Embers	196?	$30
JUBILEE			
❏ LP-11 [10]	Dorothy Donegan Trio	1955	$100
❏ JLP-1013 [M]	September Song	1956	$75
MGM			
❏ E-278 [10]	Dorothy Donegan Piano	1954	$100
PROGRESSIVE			
❏ PRO-7056	The Explosive Dorothy Donegan	198?	$30
ROULETTE			
❏ R-25010 [M]	Dorothy Donegan at the Embers	1957	$50
❏ R-25154 [M]	It Happened One Night	1961	$30
❏ SR-25154 [S]	It Happened One Night	1961	$40
DONEGAN, LONNIE			
UK skiffle king.			
ABC-PARAMOUNT			
❏ 433 [M]	Sing Hallelujah	1963	$25
❏ S-433 [S]	Sing Hallelujah	1963	$30
ATLANTIC			
❏ 8038 [M]	Skiffle Folk Songs	1960	$40
❏ SD8038 [S]	Skiffle Folk Songs	1960	$50
DOT			
❏ DLP-3159 [M]	Lonnie Donegan	1959	$40

Number	Title	Yr	NM
MERCURY			
❏ MG-20229 [M]	An Englishman Sings American Folk Songs	1957	$50
UNITED ARTISTS			
❏ UA-LA827-?	Puttin' On the Style	1977	$12
DONELIAN, ARMEN			
SUNNYSIDE			
❏ SSC-1019	A Reverie	1987	$25
❏ SSC-1031	Secrets	1988	$25
DONNAS, THE			
LOOKOUT!			
❏ LK-191	American Teenage Rock 'n' Roll Machine	1998	$12
❏ LK-225	Get Skintight	1999	$12

Number	Title	Yr	NM
❏ LK-288 [B]	Spend the Night	2002	$12
❏ LK-255	Turn 21	2001	$12
SUPER*TEEM			
❏ SUP3301	The Donnas	1996	$40
DONNER, RAL			
GONE			
❏ LP-5012 [M]	Takin' Care of Business	1961	$300
STARFIRE			
❏ 1004	An Evening with Ral Donner	1982	$18
— All copies on multi-color vinyl			
DONNER, RAL/RAY SMITH/BOBBY DALE			
CROWN			
❏ CLP-5335 [M]	Ral Donner, Ray Smith and Bobby Dale	1963	$40
❏ CST-335 [R]	Ral Donner, Ray Smith and Bobby Dale	1963	$25
DONNIE AND THE DELCHORDS			
TAURUS			
❏ 1000	Sing with Triple Stereo	1967	$300
DONOVAN			
ALLEGIANCE			
❏ AV-437	Lady of the Stars	1983	$12
ARISTA			
❏ AB4143	Donovan	1980	$12
BELL			
❏ 1135	Early Treasures	1973	$12
COLUMBIA LIMITED EDITION			
❏ LE10184	Mellow Yellow	197?	$12
EPIC			
❏ PE33245	7-Tease	1974	$15
❏ L2N6071 [M]	A Gift from a Flower to a Garden	1967	$175
— Boxed set of two LPs with portfolio of lyrics and drawings. The two records also were issued separately as Epic 24349 and 24350.			
❏ B2N171 [S]	A Gift from a Flower to a Garden	1967	$30
— Boxed set of two LPs with portfolio of lyrics and drawings. The two records also were issued separately as Epic 26349 and 26350.			
❏ E2171	A Gift from a Flower to a Garden	1979	$18
— Blue label			
❏ BN26481 [B]	Barabajagal	1969	$30
❏ PE26481	Barabajagal	1987	$10
— Blue label, new prefix			
❏ KE32156	Cosmic Wheels	1973	$18
— With enclosed poster			
❏ BN26386 [B]	Donovan in Concert	1968	$25
❏ EG33734	Donovan in Concert/ Sunshine Superman	1975	$18

Number	Title	Yr	NM
❏ BXN26439 [P]	Donovan's Greatest Hits	1969	$15

—Yellow label; "Mellow Yellow" is rechanneled; "Sunshine Superman" is the full-length version in stereo; "Catch the Wind" and "Colours" were re-recorded

❏ BXN26439 [P]	Donovan's Greatest Hits	1973	$12

—Orange label

❏ PE26439	Donovan's Greatest Hits	1979	$10

—Blue label

❏ KE32800	Essence to Essence	1974	$15
❏ LN24350 [M]	For Little Ones	1967	$25

—Part of Epic 6071, issued simultaneously

❏ BN26350 [S]	For Little Ones	1967	$18

—Part of Epic 171, issued simultaneously

❏ BN26420 [S]	Hurdy Gurdy Man	1968	$15
❏ PE26420	Hurdy Gurdy Man	1986	$10

—Blue label, new prefix

❏ BN26420 [M]	Hurdy Gurdy Man	1968	$175

—Mono is white label promo only; "Mono" sticker on stereo front cover

❏ EG33731	Hurdy Gurdy Man/Barabajagal	1975	$18
❏ LN24239 [M]	Mellow Yellow	1967	$30
❏ BN26239 [R]	Mellow Yellow	1967	$18
❏ E30125	Open Road	1970	$15
❏ PE33945	Slow Down World	1976	$15
❏ LN24217 [M]	Sunshine Superman	1966	$30

—Contains the single version of "Sunshine Superman"

❏ BN26217 [R]	Sunshine Superman	1966	$18

—Contains the single version of "Sunshine Superman" (rechanneled)

❏ KEG31210	The World of Donovan	1972	$15
❏ LN24349 [M]	Wear Your Love Like Heaven	1967	$18

—Part of Epic 6071, issued simultaneously

❏ BN26349 [S]	Wear Your Love Like Heaven	1967	$18

—Part of Epic 171, issued simultaneously

HICKORY

❏ LPM-123 [M]	Catch the Wind	1965	$30

—Most pressings have Donovan facing left, so he is correctly strumming his guitar with his right hand

❏ LPS-123 [R]	Catch the Wind	1965	$30
❏ LPM-123 [M]	Catch the Wind	1965	$40

—First pressings have Donovan facing right, so it appears as if he's strumming his guitar with his left hand

❏ LPM-127 [M]	Fairy Tale	1965	$25
❏ LPS-127 [P]	Fairy Tale	1965	$30

—Colours" is rechanneled

❏ LPS-143 [P]	Like It Is, Was and Evermore Shall Be	1968	$25
❏ LPS-149 [P]	The Best of Donovan	1969	$25
❏ LPM-135 [M]	The Real Donovan	1966	$25
❏ LPS-135 [P]	The Real Donovan	1966	$30

—Half stereo, including "Colours," the rest rechanneled.

JANUS

❏ 3022	Donovan P. Leitch	1970	$12
❏ 3025	Hear Me Now	1971	$12

KORY

❏ 3012	Early Treasures	1977	$10

PYE

❏ 502	Donovan	1975	$12

SUNDAZED

❏ LP5430 [B]	Mellow Yellow	2013	$30
❏ LP5432 [B]	The Hurdy Gurdy Man	2013	$30
❏ LP5431 [B]	Wear Your Love Like Heaven	2013	$30

DOOBIE BROTHERS, THE
Also see MICHAEL McDONALD; PATRICK SIMMONS.

CAPITOL

❏ C1-594623	Brotherhood	1991	$25

—U.S. vinyl version available only through Columbia House

❏ C1-90371	Cycles	1989	$15

DCC COMPACT CLASSICS

❏ LPZ-2053	Best of the Doobies	1998	$40

—Audiophile vinyl

MOBILE FIDELITY

❏ 1-122	Takin' It to the Streets	1983	$40

—Audiophile vinyl

NAUTILUS

❏ NR-18	Minute by Minute	1981	$30

—Audiophile vinyl

❏ NR-5	The Captain and Me	1980	$40

—Audiophile vinyl

PICKWICK

❏ SPC-3721	Introducing the Doobie Brothers	1980	$40

—Pre-Warner Bros. recordings; withdrawn shortly after release

TPM/RHINO EXCLUSIVE

❏ 9000	Minute by Minute	2008	$25

WARNER BROS.

❏ BS2978	Best of the Doobies	1976	$15
❏ BSK3112	Best of the Doobies	1978	$12

—Burbank" label

❏ BSK3112	Best of the Doobies	1979	$10

—Cream label

❏ BSK3612	Best of the Doobies, Volume 2	1981	$12
❏ 23772	Farewell Tour	1983	$18
❏ BSK3045	Livin' on the Fault Line	1977	$12

—Burbank" label

❏ BSK3045	Livin' on the Fault Line	1977	$10

—Cream label

❏ BSK3193	Minute by Minute	1978	$12
❏ HS3452	One Step Closer	1980	$12
❏ BS2835	Stampede	1975	$12

—Burbank" label

❏ BS2835	Stampede	1979	$10

—Cream label

❏ BS42835 [Q]	Stampede	1975	$40
❏ BS2899	Takin' It to the Streets	1976	$12

—Burbank" label

❏ BS2899	Takin' It to the Streets	1979	$10

—Cream label

❏ BS2694	The Captain and Me	1973	$15

—Burbank" label

❏ BS42694 [Q]	The Captain and Me	1974	$40
❏ BS2694 [B]	The Captain and Me	1979	$10

—Cream label

❏ BS2694	The Captain and Me	1973	$25

—Green label

❏ WS1919	The Doobie Brothers	1971	$18

—Green label original

❏ WS1919	The Doobie Brothers	1973	$12

—Burbank" label

❏ BS2634	Toulouse Street	1972	$18

—Green label original

❏ BS2634	Toulouse Street	1973	$12

—Burbank" label

❏ BS42634 [Q]	Toulouse Street	1975	$40
❏ W2750	What Were Once Vices Are Now Habits	1974	$12

—Burbank" label

❏ W2750	What Were Once Vices Are Now Habits	1979	$10

—Cream label

❏ W42750 [Q]	What Were Once Vices Are Now Habits	1974	$40

DOONICAN, VAL
DECCA

❏ DL4962 [M]	If the Whole World Stopped Lovin'	1968	$18
❏ DL74962 [S]	If the Whole World Stopped Lovin'	1968	$15

LONDON

❏ LL3515 [M]	The Many Shades of Val Doonican	1967	$15
❏ PS515 [S]	The Many Shades of Val Doonican	1967	$18

DOORS, THE
Also see BUTTS BAND; RAY MANZAREK.
DCC COMPACT CLASSICS

❏ LPZ-2050	L.A. Woman	1998	$175

—Audiophile vinyl

❏ LPZ-2045	Strange Days	1997	$100

—Audiophile vinyl

❏ LPZ-2046	The Doors	1997	$175

—Audiophile vinyl

❏ LPZ-2049	Waiting for the Sun	1998	$120

—Audiophile vinyl

ELEKTRA

❏ EKS-74079 [DJ]	13	1970	$40

—White label promo

❏ EKS-74079	13	1970	$18

—Butterfly labels

❏ EKS-74079	13	1980	$12

—Red labels with Warner Communications logo in lower right

❏ EKS-74079	13	1983	$10

—Red and black labels

❏ EKS-9002 [DJ]	Absolutely Live	1970	$100

—White label promo

❏ EKS-9002	Absolutely Live	1970	$30

—Butterfly labels

❏ EKS-9002	Absolutely Live	1980	$18

—Red labels with Warner Communications logo in lower right

❏ EKS-9002	Absolutely Live	1983	$15

—Red and black labels

❏ 60269	Alive, She Cried	1984	$15
❏ 5E-502	An American Prayer	1978	$15

—Butterfly labels

❏ 5E-502	An American Prayer	1980	$12

—Red labels with Warner Communications logo in lower right

❏ 5E-502	An American Prayer	1983	$10

—Red and black labels

❏ 61812	An American Prayer	1995	$18

—Remastered and lengthened version of 5E-502

❏ 5E-502SP DJ [DJ]	An American Prayer	1978	$75

—White label; with sticker on cover "This album has been edited for broadcast from..."; only six tracks are on Side One rather than the eight on stock copies

❏ EQ-5035 [Q]	Best of the Doors	1973	$40

—Butterfly labels

❏ EQ-5035 [Q]	Best of the Doors	1980	$20

—Red labels with Warner Communications logo in lower right

❏ EQ-5035 [Q]	Best of the Doors	1983	$20

—Red and black labels

❏ 6E-5035 [S]	Best of the Doors	1977	$25

—Columbia Record Club edition in stereo with the quad markings blacked out on the cover; note different prefix

❏ 60417	Classics	1986	$15
❏ EKS-75038	Full Circle	1972	$18
❏ 5E-515	Greatest Hits	1980	$12

—Red labels with Warner Communications logo in lower right

❏ 5E-515	Greatest Hits	1983	$10

—Red and black labels

❏ EKS-75011 [DJ]	L.A. Woman	1971	$150

—White label promo

❏ EKS-75011	L.A. Woman	1971	$50

—With see-through window on cover and yellow innersleeve with photo of Jim Morrison on a cross

❏ EKS-75011	L.A. Woman	197?	$15

—Butterfly label, standard cover

❏ EKS-75011	L.A. Woman	1980	$12

—Red labels with Warner Communications logo in lower right

❏ EKS-75011	L.A. Woman	1983	$10

—Red and black labels

❏ R1528723 [B]	L.A. Woman: The Workshop Sessions	2012	$40
❏ R1532513 [B]	Live at the Bowl '68	2012	$40
❏ 60741 [EP]	Live at the Hollywood Bowl	1988	$15
❏ EKS-75007	Morrison Hotel	1970	$30

—Red labels with large stylized "E

❏ EKS-75007 [DJ]	Morrison Hotel	1970	$150

—White label promo

❏ EKS-75007	Morrison Hotel	1971	$15

—Butterfly labels

❏ EKS-75007	Morrison Hotel	1980	$12

—Red labels with Warner Communications logo in lower right

❏ EKS-75007	Morrison Hotel	1983	$10

—Red and black labels

❏ EKS-75007	Morrison Hotel	1970	$75

—Brown or tan labels

❏ EKS-75017	Other Voices	1971	$18
❏ EKL-4014 [M]	Strange Days	1967	$600

—Value assumes the record is mono. There are two different covers for this; some copies have mono numbers on the two covers and the stereo number on the spine, and others have the mono number on the spine and stereo number on front and back covers.

❏ EKS-74014 [S]	Strange Days	1967	$40

—Brown labels

❏ EKS-74014 [S]	Strange Days	1969	$18

—Red labels with large stylized "E

❏ EKS-74014 [S]	Strange Days	1971	$15

—Butterfly labels

❏ EKS-74014 [S]	Strange Days	1980	$12

—Red labels with Warner Communications logo in lower right

❏ EKS-74014 [S]	Strange Days	1983	$10

—Red and black labels

❏ 60345	The Best of the Doors	1985	$18
❏ 60345	The Best of the Doors	1985	$40

—White label promo on audiophile vinyl

❏ EKL-4007 [M]	The Doors	1967	$250
❏ EKS-74007 [S]	The Doors	1967	$50

—Brown labels

❏ EKS-74007 [S]	The Doors	1969	$18

—Red labels with large stylized "E

❏ EKS-74007 [S]	The Doors	1971	$15

—Butterfly labels

❏ EKS-74007 [S]	The Doors	1980	$12

Number	Title	Yr	NM
— Red labels with Warner Communications logo in lower right			
❏ EKS-74007 [S]	The Doors	1983	$10
— Red and black labels			
❏ E1-61047	The Doors	1991	$150
— Soundtrack from the movie; only available on US vinyl from Columbia House			
❏ EKS-75005	The Soft Parade	1969	$50
— Brown or tan labels			
❏ EKS-75005	The Soft Parade	1969	$25
— Red labels with large stylized "E			
❏ EKS-75005	The Soft Parade	1971	$15
— Butterfly labels			
❏ EKS-75005	The Soft Parade	1980	$12
— Red labels with Warner Communications logo in lower right			
❏ EKS-75005	The Soft Parade	1983	$10
— Red and black labels			
❏ EKL-4024 [M]	Waiting for the Sun	1968	$1500
❏ EKS-74024 [S]	Waiting for the Sun	1968	$175
— White label promo			
❏ EKS-74024 [S]	Waiting for the Sun	1968	$30
— Brown labels			
❏ EKS-74024 [S]	Waiting for the Sun	1969	$18
— Red labels with large stylized "E			
❏ EKS-74024 [S]	Waiting for the Sun	1971	$15
— Butterfly labels			
❏ EKS-74024 [S]	Waiting for the Sun	1980	$12
— Red labels with Warner Communications logo in lower right			

Number	Title	Yr	NM
❏ EKS-74024 [S]	Waiting for the Sun	1983	$10
— Red and black labels			
❏ 8E-6001	Weird Scenes Inside the Gold Mine	1972	$25
— Butterfly labels			
❏ 8E-6001	Weird Scenes Inside the Gold Mine	1980	$15
— Red labels with Warner Communications logo in lower right			
❏ 8E-6001	Weird Scenes Inside the Gold Mine	1983	$12
— Red and black labels			
MOBILE FIDELITY			
❏ Jan-0051	The Doors	1980	$150
— Audiophile vinyl			
RHINO			
❏ R1537456 [B]	Curated By Record Store Day	2013	$50
❏ R14014 [B]	Strange Days	2015	$20
— Record Store Day			
❏ R16001 [B]	Weird Scenes Inside The Gold Mine	2014	$85

DORFMAN, ANIA

RCA VICTOR RED SEAL

❏ LSC-2207 [S]	Schumann: Carnaval	1959	$30
— Original with "shaded dog" label			

DORGE, PIERRE, AND WALT DICKERSON

STEEPLECHASE

❏ SCS-1115	Landscape with Open Door	1978	$30

DORGE, PIERRE

STEEPLECHASE

❏ SCS-1132	Ballad Round Left Corner	1979	$30
❏ SCS-1188	Brikama	198?	$25
❏ SCS-1208	Even the Moon Is Dancing	198?	$25
❏ SCS-1228	Johnny Lives	198?	$25
❏ SCS-1162	Pierre Dorge and the New Jungle Orchestra	1982	$30

DORHAM, KENNY

ABC-PARAMOUNT

❏ ABC-122 [M]	Kenny Dorham and the Jazz Prophets	1956	$1000

Number	Title	Yr	NM
BAINBRIDGE			
❏ 1048	Kenny Dorham	198?	$25
❏ 1043	Show Boat	198?	$25
BLUE NOTE			
❏ BLP-5055 [10]	Afro-Cuban Holiday	1955	$2000
❏ BLP-1535 [M]	Kenny Dorham Octet/Sextet	1956	$3000
— Deep groove" version (deep indentation under label on both sides)			
❏ BLP-1535 [M]	Kenny Dorham Octet/Sextet	1956	$175
— Regular version with Lexington Ave. address on label			
❏ BLP-1535 [M]	Kenny Dorham Octet/Sextet	1963	$3500
— New York, USA" address on label			
❏ BLP-1524 [M]	'Round About Midnight at the Café Bohemia	1956	$1000
— Deep groove" version (deep indentation under label on both sides)			
❏ BLP-1524 [M]	'Round About Midnight at the Café Bohemia	1956	$750
— Regular version with Lexington Ave. address on label			
❏ BLP-1524 [M]	'Round About Midnight at the Café Bohemia	1963	$75
— New York, USA" address on label			
❏ BLP-4181 [M]	Trompeta Toccata	1964	$75
— New York, USA" address on label			
❏ BST-84181 [S]	Trompeta Toccata	1964	$40
— New York, USA" address on label			
❏ BST-84181 [S]	Trompeta Toccata	1966	$35
— A Division of Liberty Records" on label			
❏ BST-84181	Trompeta Toccata	1985	$25
— The Finest in Jazz Since 1939" reissue			
❏ BLP-4127 [M]	Una Mas	1963	$75
— New York, USA" address on label			
❏ BST-84127 [S]	Una Mas	1963	$40
— New York, USA" address on label			
❏ BST-84127 [S]	Una Mas	1966	$35
— A Division of Liberty Records" on label			
❏ BST-84127 [S]	Una Mas	197?	$30
— United Artists" on label			
❏ BLP-4063 [M]	Whistle Stop	1961	$175
— W. 63rd St. address on label			
❏ BLP-4063 [M]	Whistle Stop	1963	$150
— New York, USA" address on label			
❏ BST-84063 [S]	Whistle Stop	1961	$120
— W. 63rd St. address on label			
❏ BST-84063 [S]	Whistle Stop	1963	$75
— New York, USA" address on label			
❏ BST-84063 [S]	Whistle Stop	1966	$35
— A Division of Liberty Records" on label			
❏ BST-84063 [S]	Whistle Stop	197?	$30
— United Artists" on label			
❏ B1-28978	Whistle Stop	1994	$35
DEBUT			
❏ DLP-9 [10]	Kenny Dorham Quintet	1954	$1000
FANTASY			
❏ OJC-463	2 Horns 2 Rhythm	1990	$30
— Reissue of Riverside 255			
❏ OJC-134	Blue Spring	198?	$25
❏ OJC-028	Jazz Contrasts	198?	$25
❏ OJC-113	Kenny Dorham Quintet	198?	$25
— Reissue of Debut 9			
❏ OJC-250	Quiet Kenny	1987	$25
— Reissue of New Jazz 8225			
JARO			
❏ JAM-5007 [M]	The Arrival of Kenny Dorham	1960	$400
❏ JAS-8007 [S]	The Arrival of Kenny Dorham	1960	$400
JAZZLAND			
❏ JLP-14 [M]	Kenny Dorham and Friends	1960	$40
❏ JLP-914 [S]	Kenny Dorham and Friends	1960	$50
❏ JLP-82 [M]	Kenny Dorham and Friends	1962	$25
❏ JLP-982 [S]	Kenny Dorham and Friends	1962	$30
❏ JLP-3 [M]	The Swingers	1960	$40
❏ JLP-903 [S]	The Swingers	1960	$50
MILESTONE			
❏ 47036	But Beautiful	197?	$35
MUSE			
❏ MR-5053	Ease It	1974	$35
NEW JAZZ			
❏ NJLP-8225 [M]	Quiet Kenny	1959	$2000
— Purple label			
❏ NJLP-8225 [M]	Quiet Kenny	1965	$175
— Blue label, trident logo at right			
PACIFIC JAZZ			
❏ PJ-41 [M]	Inta Somethin' – Recorded Live at the Jazz Workshop	1962	$700
❏ ST-41 [S]	Inta Somethin' – Recorded Live at the Jazz Workshop	1962	$40
PRESTIGE			
❏ PRST-7754	Kenny Dorham 1959	1970	$25
RIVERSIDE			
❏ RLP 12-255 [M]	2 Horns 2 Rhythm	1957	$300
❏ RLP 12-297 [M]	Blue Spring	1959	$300
❏ RLP-1139 [S]	Blue Spring	1959	$300

Number	Title	Yr	NM
❏ RLP 12-239 [M]	Jazz Contrasts	1957	$400
— White label, blue print			
❏ RLP 12-239 [M]	Jazz Contrasts	1959	$300
— Blue label, microphone logo			
❏ RLP-1105 [S]	Jazz Contrasts	1959	$300
— Black label, microphone logo			
❏ 6075	Jazz Contrasts	197?	$35
❏ RLP 12-275 [M]	This Is the Moment!	1958	$300
STEEPLECHASE			
❏ SCC-6011	Scandia Skies	198?	$30
❏ SCC-6010	Short Story	198?	$30
TIME			
❏ 52004 [M]	Jazz Contemporary	1960	$300
❏ S-2004 [S]	Jazz Contemporary	1960	$300
❏ 52024 [M]	Show Boat	1960	$40
❏ S-2024 [S]	Show Boat	1960	$50
UNITED ARTISTS			
❏ UAJ-14007 [M]	Matador	1962	$30
❏ UAJS-15007 [S]	Matador	1962	$40
❏ UAS-5631	Matador	1971	$25
— Reissue of 15007			
XANADU			
❏ 125	Memorial Album	197?	$35

DORHAM, KENNY/CLARK TERRY

JAZZLAND

❏ JLP-10 [M]	Top Trumpets	1960	$40
❏ JLP-910 [S]	Top Trumpets	1960	$50

DOROUGH, BOB

BETHLEHEM

❏ BCP-11 [M]	Devil May Care	1955	$300
❏ BCP-6023	Yardbird Suite	197?	$50
— Reissue of 11, distributed by RCA Victor			

CLASSIC JAZZ

❏ 18	An Excursion Through Oliver	197?	$35
❏ 19	The Medieval Jazz Quartet Plus 3	197?	$35

FOCUS

❏ FL-336 [M]	Better Than Anything	1967	$30
❏ FS-336 [S]	Better Than Anything	1967	$25

INNER CITY

❏ IC-1023	Just About Everything	197?	$35

LAISSEZ-FAIRE

❏ 02	Beginning to See the Light	1976	$25

MUSIC MINUS ONE

❏ 225 [M]	Oliver	1963	$30

DORS, DIANA

COLUMBIA

❏ CL1436 [M]	Swingin' Dors	1960	$100
❏ CS8232 [S]	Swingin' Dors	1960	$150

DORSEY, JIMMY

ATLANTIC

❏ 81801	Dorsey, Then and Now	1988	$25

CIRCLE

❏ 30	Jimmy Dorsey and His Orchestra 1939-40	198?	$25
❏ 46	Jimmy Dorsey and His Orchestra Mostly 1940	198?	$25

COLUMBIA

❏ CL6095 [10]	Dixie by Dorsey	1950	$150
❏ CL608 [M]	Dixie by Dorsey	1955	$50
— Maroon label with gold print			
❏ CL608 [M]	Dixie by Dorsey	1955	$85
— Red and black label with six "eye" logos			
❏ CL6114 [10]	Dorseyland Band	1950	$150

CORAL

❏ CRL56004 [10]	Contrasting Music, Volume 1	1950	$50
❏ CRL56008 [10]	Contrasting Music, Volume 2	1950	$50
❏ CRL56033 [10]	Gershwin Music	1950	$50

DECCA

❏ DL4853 [M]	Jimmy Dorsey's Greatest Hits	1967	$25
❏ DL74853 [R]	Jimmy Dorsey's Greatest Hits	1967	$30
❏ DL5091 [10]	Latin American Favorites	1950	$175
❏ DL8153 [M]	Latin American Favorites	1955	$175
— Black label, silver print			
❏ DL8609 [M]	The Great Jimmy Dorsey	1957	$120
— Black label, silver print			

DOT

❏ DLP-3437 [M]	So Rare	1962	$85
— Reissue of Fraternity LP			
❏ DLP-25437 [R]	So Rare	196?	$85

FRATERNITY

❏ F-1008 [M]	Fabulous Jimmy Dorsey	1957	$30

HINDSIGHT

❏ HSR-101	Jimmy Dorsey and His Orchestra 1939-40	198?	$25
❏ HSR-153	Jimmy Dorsey and His Orchestra 1942-44	198?	$25

DORSEY, JIMMY

Number	Title	Yr	NM
❏ HSR-203	Jimmy Dorsey and His Orchestra 1948	198?	$25
❏ HSR-165	Jimmy Dorsey and His Orchestra 1949, 1951	198?	$25
❏ HSR-178	Jimmy Dorsey and His Orchestra 1950	198?	$25

INSIGHT

❏ 210	Jimmy Dorsey and His Orchestra 1939-42	198?	$25

LION

❏ L-70063 [M]	Jimmy Dorsey and His Orchestra	1958	$50

MCA

❏ 252	Jimmy Dorsey's Greatest Hits	197?	$30

— Reissue of Decca 74853; black label with rainbow

❏ 252	Jimmy Dorsey's Greatest Hits	198?	$20

— Reissue; blue label with rainbow

❏ 4073	The Best of Jimmy Dorsey	1975	$30

— Original edition has a gatefold cover and black labels with rainbow

POWER PAK

❏ 244	Jimmy Dorsey Plays His Biggest Hits	197?	$25

TIME-LIFE

❏ STBB-10	Big Bands: Jimmy Dorsey	1984	$35

TRIP

❏ 5815	So Rare!	197?	$25

DORSEY, LEE

AMY

❏ 8010 [M]	Ride Your Pony	1966	$30
❏ 8010-S [S]	Ride Your Pony	1966	$40
❏ 8011 [M]	The New Lee Dorsey/Working in the Coal Mine-Holy Cow	1966	$30
❏ 8011-S [S]	The New Lee Dorsey/Working in the Coal Mine-Holy Cow	1966	$30

ARISTA

❏ AL8387	Holy Cow! The Best of Lee Dorsey	1985	$12

FURY

❏ 1002 [M]	Ya Ya	1962	$300

POLYDOR

❏ 24-4024	Yes We Can	1970	$15

SPHERE SOUND

❏ SR-7003 [M]	Ya Ya	196?	$150

— Reissue of Fury 1002

❏ SSR-7003 [R]	Ya Ya	196?	$50

— Rechanneled reissue of Fury 1002

DORSEY, TOMMY, ORCHESTRA (WARREN COVINGTON, DIRECTOR)

DECCA

❏ DL8904 [M]	Dance and Romance	1959	$100
❏ DL78904 [S]	Dance and Romance	1959	$100
❏ DL4120 [M]	Dance to the Songs Everybody Knows	1960	$35
❏ DL74120 [S]	Dance to the Songs Everybody Knows	1960	$25
❏ DL8996 [M]	It Takes Two to Bunny Hop..	1960	$35
❏ DL78996 [S]	It Takes Two to Bunny Hop..	1960	$25
❏ DL8980 [M]	It Takes Two to Cha-Cha…	1959	$100
❏ DL78980 [S]	It Takes Two to Cha-Cha…	1959	$100
❏ DL8943 [M]	More Tea for Two Cha Chas	1959	$100
❏ DL78943 [S]	More Tea for Two Cha Chas	1959	$100
❏ DL8842 [M]	Tea for Two Cha Chas	1958	$150
❏ DL78842 [S]	Tea for Two Cha Chas	1958	$150
❏ DL8802 [M]	The Fabulous Arrangements of Tommy Dorsey	1958	$120
❏ DL78802 [S]	The Fabulous Arrangements of Tommy Dorsey	1958	$120

Number	Title	Yr	NM
❏ DL4130 [M]	Tricky Trombones	1961	$35
❏ DL74130 [S]	Tricky Trombones	1961	$25

MCA

❏ 185	It Takes Two to Bunny Hop..	197?	$25
❏ 534	It Takes Two to Cha-Cha…	197?	$25

— Reissue of Decca 78996

❏ 180	More Tea for Two Cha Chas	197?	$25

— Reissue of Decca 78943

❏ 178	Tea for Two Cha Chas	197?	$25

— Reissue of Decca 78842

DORSEY, TOMMY

On albums with asterisks (*) after them, some of the tracks feature FRANK SINATRA as lead vocalist.

20TH CENTURY FOX

❏ TFM-3157 [M]	This Is Tommy Dorsey and His Greatest Band, Vol. 1	196?	$25
❏ TFS-4157 [R]	This Is Tommy Dorsey and His Greatest Band, Vol. 1	196?	$30
❏ TFM-3158 [M]	This Is Tommy Dorsey and His Greatest Band, Vol. 2	196?	$25
❏ TFS-4158 [R]	This Is Tommy Dorsey and His Greatest Band, Vol. 2	196?	$30
❏ FOX1005 [M]	Tommy Dorsey and His Orchestra: His Greatest Arrangements -- His Greatest Band	196?	$25

— Million Seller Hits" reissue series

❏ TCF101/102 [M]	Tommy Dorsey's Greatest Band	1959	$30

BLUEBIRD

❏ AXM2-5521	The Complete Tommy Dorsey, Volume 1	197?	$35
❏ AXM2-5549	The Complete Tommy Dorsey, Volume 2	197?	$35
❏ AXM2-5560	The Complete Tommy Dorsey, Volume 3	197?	$35
❏ AXM2-5564	The Complete Tommy Dorsey, Volume 4	197?	$35
❏ AXM2-5573	The Complete Tommy Dorsey, Volume 5	197?	$35
❏ AXM2-5578	The Complete Tommy Dorsey, Volume 6	197?	$35
❏ AXM2-5582	The Complete Tommy Dorsey, Volume 7	197?	$35
❏ AXM2-5586	The Complete Tommy Dorsey, Volume 8	197?	$35
❏ 9987-1-RB	Yes, Indeed!	1990	$35

COLPIX

❏ CP401 [M]	The Great T.D.	1958	$50
❏ CP436 [M]	Tommy Dorsey & His Orchestra Volume 4	1962	$50
❏ CP498 [M]	Tommy Dorsey -- A Man and His Trombone	196?	$50

DECCA

❏ DL5448 [10]	In a Sentimental Mood	1952	$175
❏ DL5449 [10]	Tenderly	1952	$175
❏ DL5317 [10]	Tommy Dorsey Plays Howard Dietz	1951	$250
❏ DL5452 [10]	Your Invitation to Dance	1952	$175

HARMONY

❏ HL7334 [M]	On the Sentimental Side	196?	$35
❏ KH32014	The Beat of the Big Bands	1972	$25

MCA

❏ 732	Sentimental	198?	$20
❏ 4074	The Best of Tommy Dorsey	197?	$30

MOVIETONE

❏ MTM-1019 [M]	The Tommy Dorsey Years	1967	$35
❏ MTS-72019 [R]	The Tommy Dorsey Years	1967	$30
❏ MTM-1004 [M]	Tommy Dorsey's Hullaballoo	196?	$35
❏ MTS-72004 [R]	Tommy Dorsey's Hullaballoo	196?	$30

PICKWICK

❏ PTP-2035	I'm Getting Sentimental*	197?	$30

RCA CAMDEN

❏ CAL-800 [M]	Dedicated to You*	1964	$35
❏ CAS-800(e) [R]	Dedicated to You*	1964	$25
❏ ADL2-0178	I'll See You in My Dreams*	1973	$35
❏ CXS-9027	I'm Getting Sentimental*	1972	$35
❏ CAL-650 [M]	The One and Only Tommy Dorsey*	1961	$35
❏ CAS-650(e) [R]	The One and Only Tommy Dorsey*	196?	$25

RCA VICTOR

❏ ALPT-15 [M]	All Time Hits*	1951	$100
❏ LPT-10 [M]	Getting Sentimental with Tommy Dorsey*	1951	$100
❏ LPM-1643 [M]	Having a Wonderful Time*	1958	$40
❏ ANL1-2162(e)	On the Sunny Side of the Street	1977	$25
❏ ANL1-1586	Pure Gold*	1976	$25
❏ LPM-6003 [M]	That Sentimental Gentleman*	1957	$100

— Box set

❏ LPM-3674 [M]	The Best of Tommy Dorsey*	1966	$25
❏ LSP-3674 [R]	The Best of Tommy Dorsey*	1966	$30
❏ ANL1-1087	The Best of Tommy Dorsey	1976	$25
❏ LPT-3005 [M]	This Is Tommy Dorsey*	1952	$100
❏ VPM-6038	This Is Tommy Dorsey*	1971	$30
❏ LPT-3018 [10]	This Is Tommy Dorsey*	1952	$50
❏ VPM-6064	This Is Tommy Dorsey, Volume 2*	197?	$30
❏ VPM-6087	This Is Tommy Dorsey and His Clambake Seven	1973	$25

— Orange labels

❏ VPM-6087	This Is Tommy Dorsey and His Clambake Seven	1977	$20

— Black labels, dog near top

❏ LPM-1425 [M]	Tommy Dorsey Plays Cole Porter and Jerome Kern	1956	$30
❏ LPM-22 [10]	Tommy Dorsey Plays Cole Porter for Dancing	1951	$50
❏ LPM-1432 [M]	Tribute to Dorsey, Volume 1*	1956	$40
❏ LPM-1433 [M]	Tribute to Dorsey, Volume 2*	1956	$40
❏ LPM-1229 [M]	Yes Indeed*	1956	$150

SUNBEAM

❏ 201	Tommy Dorsey and His Orchestra 1935-39	197?	$25
❏ 220	Tommy Dorsey and His Orchestra 1944-46	197?	$25

TIME-LIFE

❏ STBB-19	Big Bands: Sentimental Gerntleman*	1985	$25
❏ STBB-02	Big Bands: Tommy Dorsey*	1983	$25

VOCALION

❏ VL3613 [M]	Dance Party	196?	$35
❏ VL73613 [R]	Dance Party	196?	$25

DORSEY BROTHERS, THE

CIRCLE

❏ 20	The Dorsey Brothers Orchestra 1935	198?	$25

COLUMBIA

❏ CL1240 [M]	Sentimental and Swinging	1958	$30

— Red and black label with six "eye" logos

❏ C2L8	The Fabulous Dorseys in Hi-Fi	1958	$40

— Red and black labels with six "eye" logos

❏ CL1190 [M]	The Fabulous Dorseys in Hi Fi, Volume I	1957	$30

— Red and black labels with six "eye" logos

DECCA

❏ DL8631 [M]	Dixieland Jazz	1958	$120

— Black label, silver print

❏ DL8631 [M]	Dixieland Jazz	1961	$35

— Black label with color bars

❏ DL8654 [M]	The Swinging Dorseys	1958	$150

— Black label, silver print

❏ DL8654 [M]	The Swinging Dorseys	1961	$35

— Black label with color bars

DESIGN

❏ DLP-20 [M]	Their Shining Hour	196?	$30
❏ DLPS-20 [R]	Their Shining Hour	196?	$25

MCA

❏ 1505	The 1934-35 Decca Sessions	198?	$25

RIVERSIDE

❏ RLP 12-811 [M]	A Backward Glance	1958	$300
❏ RLP-1008 [10]	Jazz of the Roaring Twenties	1953	$300
❏ RLP-1051 [10]	The Dorsey Brothers with the California Ramblers	1955	$300

SUNBEAM

❏ 301	The Dorsey Brothers 1934	197?	$25
❏ 210	The Fabulous Dorsey Brothers	197?	$25
❏ 224	The Fabulous Dorsey Brothers, Volume 2	197?	$25

DOTTSY

RCA VICTOR

❏ APL1-1358	The Sweetest Thing	1976	$15
❏ AHL1-3380	Tryin' to Satisfy You	1979	$15

DOUBLE IMAGE

CELESTIAL HARMONIES

❏ CEL-015	In Lands I Never Saw	1986	$25

ECM

❏ 1146	Dawn	1978	$30

ENJA

❏ 2096	Double Image	198?	$30

INNER CITY

❏ IC-3013	Double Image	1978	$35

DOUBLE SIX OF PARIS, THE

CAPITOL

❏ T10259 [M]	The Double Six of Paris	1961	$300
❏ ST10259 [S]	The Double Six of Paris	1961	$300

PHILIPS

❏ PHM200026 [M]	Swingin' Singin'	1962	$40
❏ PHS600026 [S]	Swingin' Singin'	1962	$120
❏ PHM200141 [M]	The Double Six of Paris Sings Ray Charles	1964	$200
❏ PHS600141 [S]	The Double Six of Paris Sings Ray Charles	1964	$175

DOUG AND THE SLUGS

AVION

❏ AVF4603	Doug and the Slugs	1987	$15

Number	Title	Yr	NM
RCA VICTOR			
❏ AFL1-3887	Cognac and Bologna	1981	$14
❏ AFL1-4432	Music for the Hard of Thinking	1983	$14
❏ AFL1-4261	Wrap It	1982	$14
DOUGHERTY, TOMMY			
GUINNESS			
❏ GNS36010 [B]	Tommy Dougherty	1977	$50
DOUGLAS, CARL			
20TH CENTURY			
❏ T-464	Kung Fu Fighting and Other Great Love Songs	1974	$15
DOUGLAS, CAROL			
MIDLAND INT'L.			
❏ BKL1-2222	Full Bloom	1977	$12
❏ BKL1-1798	Midnight Love Affair	1976	$12
❏ BKL1-0931	The Carol Douglas Album	1975	$12
MIDSONG INT'L.			
❏ 3048	Burnin'	1978	$12
❏ W36852	The Best of Carol Douglas	1980	$12
DOUGLAS, GLENN			
DECCA			
❏ DL8748 [M]	Heartbreak Alley	1958	$50
DOUGLAS, K.C.			
BLUESVILLE			
❏ BVLP-1050 [M]	Big Road Blues	1962	$100
— *Blue label, silver print*			
❏ BVLP-1050 [M]	Big Road Blues	1964	$30
— *Blue label, trident logo at right*			
❏ BVLP-1023 [M]	K.C.'s Blues	1961	$100
— *Blue label, silver print*			
❏ BVLP-1023 [M]	K.C.'s Blues	1964	$30
— *Blue label, trident logo at right*			
COOK ROAD			
❏ 5002 [M]	A Dead Beat Guitar and the Mississippi Blues	1956	$500
DOUGLAS, LEW			
CARLTON			
❏ LP 12-126 [M]	Themes from Motion Pictures and TV	1960	$30
DOUGLAS, MIKE			
ATLANTIC			
❏ SD18168	Mike Douglas Sings It All	1976	$12
EPIC			
❏ LN24205 [M]	Dear Mike, Please Sing	1966	$15
❏ BN26205 [S]	Dear Mike, Please Sing	1966	$18
❏ LN24169 [M]	It's Time for Mike Douglas	1965	$15
❏ BN26169 [S]	It's Time for Mike Douglas	1965	$18
❏ LN24322 [M]	My Kind of Christmas	1967	$15
❏ BN26322 [S]	My Kind of Christmas	1967	$15
❏ LN24186 [M]	The Men in My Little Girl's Life	1966	$15
❏ BN26186 [S]	The Men in My Little Girl's Life	1966	$18
❏ LN24179 [M]	You Don't Have to Be Irish	1965	$15
❏ BN26179 [S]	You Don't Have to Be Irish	1965	$18
HARMONY			
❏ HS11263	Young at Heart	1968	$15
WORD			
❏ 8815	Christmas Album	198?	$12
❏ WR-8791	I'll Sing This Song for You	197?	$12
DOUGLAS, STEVE			
CROWN			
❏ CLP-5251 [M]	Twist with Steve Douglas and the Rebel Rousers	1962	$25
MERCURY			
❏ SR-61217	Reflections in a Golden Horn	1969	$30
DOUGLAS, TONY			
DOT			
❏ DLP-26009	Thank You for Touching My Life	1973	$18
PAULA			
❏ LP2198	Heart	1967	$25
DOVAL, JIM, AND THE GAUCHOS			
ABC-PARAMOUNT			
❏ ABC-506 [M]	The Gauchos Featuring Jim Doval	1965	$30
❏ ABCS-506 [S]	The Gauchos Featuring Jim Doval	1965	$40
DOVE, RONNIE			
DIAMOND			
❏ D5007 [M]	Cry	1967	$18
❏ DS5007 [S]	Cry	1967	$25

Number	Title	Yr	NM
❏ D5004 [M]	I'll Make All Your Dreams Come True	1965	$25
❏ DS5004 [S]	I'll Make All Your Dreams Come True	1965	$30
❏ D5003 [M]	One Kiss for Old Times' Sake	1965	$25
❏ DS5003 [S]	One Kiss for Old Times' Sake	1965	$30
❏ D5002 [M]	Right or Wrong	1964	$25
❏ DS5002 [S]	Right or Wrong	1964	$30
❏ D5006 [M]	Ronnie Dove Sings the Hits for You	1966	$18
❏ DS5006 [S]	Ronnie Dove Sings the Hits for You	1966	$25
❏ D5005 [M]	The Best of Ronnie Dove	1966	$18
❏ DS5005 [S]	The Best of Ronnie Dove	1966	$25
❏ D-5008 [M]	The Best of Ronnie Dove -- Vol. 2	1968	$30
❏ SD-5008 [S]	The Best of Ronnie Dove -- Vol. 2	1968	$18
POWER PAK			
❏ 286	Greatest Hits	1975	$15
DOVELLS, THE			
CAMEO			
❏ C-1082 [M]	Len Barry Sings with the Dovells	1965	$30
❏ SC-1082 [S]	Len Barry Sings with the Dovells	1965	$50
PARKWAY			
❏ P7010 [M]	All the Hits of the Teen Groups	1962	$100
❏ P7021 [M]	For Your Hully Gully Party	1962	$50
❏ P7006 [M]	The Bristol Stomp	1961	$150
— *Light orange label*			
❏ P7006 [M]	The Bristol Stomp	1962	$50
— *Dark orange and yellow label*			
❏ P7025 [M]	You Can't Sit Down	1963	$50
WYNCOTE			

Number	Title	Yr	NM
❏ W9052 [M]	Discotheque	1965	$25
❏ SW9052 [R]	Discotheque	1965	$18
❏ W9114 [M]	The Dovells' Biggest Hits	1965	$25
❏ SW9114 [R]	The Dovells' Biggest Hits	1965	$18
DOWELL, JOE			
SMASH			
❏ MGS-27011 [M]	German American Hits	1962	$30
❏ SRS-67011 [S]	German American Hits	1962	$30
❏ MGS-27000 [M]	Wooden Heart	1961	$40
❏ SRS-67000 [S]	Wooden Heart	1961	$50
WING			
❏ MGW-12328 [M]	Wooden Heart	196?	$25
❏ SRW-16328 [S]	Wooden Heart	196?	$25
DOWLING, CHET, AND BILL MINKIN			
COLUMBIA			
❏ CL2776 [M]	Senator Bobby's Christmas Party	1967	$25
❏ CS9576 [S]	Senator Bobby's Christmas Party	1967	$25
DOWN HOME JAZZ BAND, THE			
STOMP OFF			
❏ SOS-1171	Hambone Kelly's Favorites	1987	$25
❏ SOS-1217	The Down Home Jazz Band in New Orleans	1990	$25
❏ SOS-1199	The San Francisco Jazz Tradition	1989	$25
❏ SOS-1190	Yerba Buena Style	1988	$25
DOWNEY, MORTON, JR.			
ARTISTS OF AMERICA			
❏ AOA-5005	You'll Never Ask Me If I Love You	1976	$15
COMPOSE			
❏ 9901	Morton Downey Jr. Sings!	1989	$18

Number	Title	Yr	NM
DOWNING, BIG AL			
TEAM			
❏ 2001	Big Al Downing	1982	$15
DOWNS, HUGH			
EPIC			
❏ LN3597 [M]	An Evening with Hugh Downs	1961	$30
❏ BN541 [S]	An Evening with Hugh Downs	1961	$30
DOYLE, ARTHUR			
AUDIBLE HISS			
❏ AHS-004	Arthur Doyle Plays and Sings from the Songbook, Volume One	1995	$30
ECSTATIC PEACE			
❏ 29	Arthur Doyle Plays More Alabama Feeling	1990	$30
DOYLE, BOBBY, THREE			
KENNY ROGERS was in this group.			
COLUMBIA			
❏ CL1858 [M]	In a Most Unusual Way	1962	$40
❏ CS8658 [S]	In a Most Unusual Way	1962	$50
DOYLE, MIKE			
FLEETWOOD			
❏ FLP-3018 [M]	The Secrets of Surfing	1963	$120
DOZIER, GENE, AND THE BROTHERHOOD			
MINIT			
❏ 40010 [M]	Blues Power	1967	$30
❏ 24010 [S]	Blues Power	1967	$30
DOZIER, LAMONT			
ABC			
❏ D-839	Black Bach	1974	$12
❏ D-804	Out Here on My Own	1973	$12
INVICTUS			
❏ KZ33134	Love and Beauty	1974	$15
WARNER BROS.			
❏ BSK3282	Bittersweet	1979	$12
❏ BS3039	Peddlin'	1977	$12
❏ BS2929	Right There	1976	$12
DR. BUZZARD'S ORIGINAL SAVANNAH BAND			
ELEKTRA			
❏ 6E-218	James Monroe H.S. Presents Dr. Buzzard's Original Savannah Band Goes to Washington	1979	$12
PASSPORT			
❏ 6013	Calling All Beatniks	1986	$12
RCA VICTOR			
❏ APL1-1504	Dr. Buzzard's Original Savannah Band	1976	$18
— *Original copies have tan labels*			
❏ AYL1-3767	Dr. Buzzard's Original Savannah Band	1980	$10
— *Reissue*			
❏ APL1-1504	Dr. Buzzard's Original Savannah Band	1976	$12
— *Reissue on black label with "Nipper" logo*			
❏ AFL1-2402	Dr. Buzzard's Original Savannah Band Meets King Pennet	1978	$15
DR. DRE			
AFTERMATH			
❏ 490486	2001	1999	$18
❏ 490571	2001: Instrumentals	2000	$25
DEATH ROW			
❏ P1-50611	The Chronic	1993	$18
DR. FEELGOOD AND THE INTERNS			
OKEH			
❏ OKM12101 [M]	Dr. Feelgood and the Interns	1962	$150
❏ OKS14101 [S]	Dr. Feelgood and the Interns	1962	$250
DR. HOOK			
CAPITOL			
❏ ST-11522	A Little Bit More	1976	$12
❏ SN-16180	A Little Bit More	198?	$10
— *Budget-line reissue*			
❏ ST-11397	Bankrupt	1975	$12
❏ SN-16179	Bankrupt	198?	$10
— *Budget-line reissue*			
❏ SOO-12122	Dr. Hook/Greatest Hits	1980	$12
❏ SN-16325	Dr. Hook/Greatest Hits	198?	$10
— *Budget-line reissue*			
❏ ST-12114	Live	1981	$12
❏ ST-11632	Makin' Love and Music	1977	$12
❏ SN-16228	Makin' Love and Music	198?	$10

Number	Title	Yr	NM
—Budget-line reissue			
❏ SW-11859	Pleasure and Pain	1978	$12
❏ SN-16181	Pleasure and Pain	198?	$10
—Budget-line reissue			
❏ ST-12018	Sometimes You Win...	1979	$12
❏ SN-16229	Sometimes You Win...	198?	$10
—Budget-line reissue			
❏ SOO-12023	Sometimes You Win...	1979	$12
—Other than the prefix and the number, we don't know if there are any differences between this and 12018, but both do exist			
❏ ST-12325	The Rest of Dr. Hook	1984	$10
CASABLANCA			
❏ NBLP-7264	Players in the Dark	1982	$12
❏ NBLP-7251	Rising	1980	$12
COLUMBIA			
❏ KC32270	Belly Up!	1973	$18
❏ KC30898	Dr. Hook & The Medicine Show	1972	$18
❏ PC30898	Dr. Hook & The Medicine Show	198?	$10
—Budget-line reissue			
❏ C34147	Dr. Hook and the Medicine Show Revisited	1976	$12
❏ PC34147	Dr. Hook and the Medicine Show Revisited	198?	$10
—Budget-line reissue			
❏ KC31622	Sloppy Seconds	1972	$18
❏ PC31622	Sloppy Seconds	198?	$10
—Budget-line reissue			
MERCURY			
❏ 800054-1	Players in the Dark	1983	$10
— Reissue of Casablanca 7264			

DR. JOHN

Number	Title	Yr	NM
ACCORD			
❏ SN-7118	Love Potion	1982	$12
ALLIGATOR			
❏ AL-3901	Dr. John's Gumbo	1986	$12
— Reissue of Atco 7006			
❏ AL-3904	Gris-Gris	1987	$12
— Reissue of Atco 33-234			
ATCO			
❏ SD 33-270	Babylon	1969	$18
❏ SD7043	Desitively Bonaroo	1974	$15

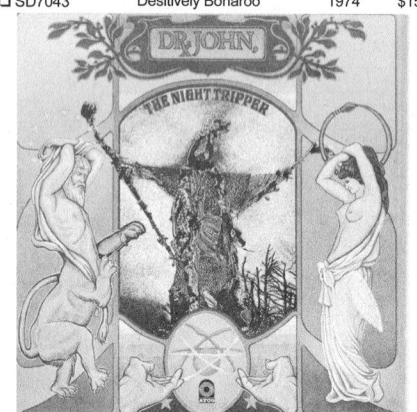

Number	Title	Yr	NM
❏ SD 33-362 [B]	Dr. John, The Night Tripper (The Sun, Moon & Herbs)	1971	$18
❏ SD7006	Dr. John's Gumbo	1972	$15
❏ SD 33-234	Gris-Gris	1968	$30
— Purple and brown label			
❏ SD 33-234	Gris-Gris	1968	$18
— Yellow label			
❏ SD7018	In the Right Place	1973	$15
❏ 0349791111 [B]	In the Right Place	2015	$25
❏ SD 33-316	Remedies	1970	$18
CLEAN CUTS			
❏ 705	Dr. John Plays Mac Rebennack	1982	$12
❏ 707	The Brightest Smile in Town	1984	$12
HORIZON			
❏ SP-732	City Lights	1978	$12
❏ SP-740	Tango Palace	1979	$12
KARATE			
❏ 5404	One Night Late	1978	$12
TRIP			
❏ TLX-350	Superpak	1975	$15
UNITED ARTISTS			
❏ UA-LA552-G	Hollywood Be Thy Name	1975	$15
WARNER BROS.			
❏ 25889	In a Sentimental Mood	1989	$15

DR. JOHN AND CHRIS BARBER

Number	Title	Yr	NM
GREAT SOUTHERN			
❏ GS-11024	On a Mardi Gras Day	1991	$15

DR. WEST'S MEDICINE SHOW AND JUG BAND
Also see NORMAN GREENBAUM.

Number	Title	Yr	NM
GO GO			
❏ 22-17-002 [S]	The Eggplant That Ate Chicago	1967	$30
❏ 22-17-001 [M]	The Eggplant That Ate Chicago	1967	$50
GREGAR			
❏ GG-101	Norman Greenbaum with Dr. West's Medicine Show and Jug Band	1970	$25

DRAGONFLY

Number	Title	Yr	NM
MEGAPHONE			
❏ MS-1202	Dragonfly	1970	$300

DRAGSTERS, THE

Number	Title	Yr	NM
WING			
❏ MGW-12269 [M]	Hey Little Cobra/Drag City	1964	$100
❏ SRW-16269 [S]	Hey Little Cobra/Drag City	1964	$150

DRAKE, DONNA

Number	Title	Yr	NM
LUXOR			
❏ LP-1 [M]	The Wynton Kelly Trio Introduces Donna Drake -- Donna Sings Dinah	1968	$30
❏ LPS-1 [S]	The Wynton Kelly Trio Introduces Donna Drake -- Donna Sings Dinah	1968	$25

DRAKE, GUY

Number	Title	Yr	NM
ROYAL AMERICAN			
❏ 1001	Welfare Cadillac	1970	$30

DRAKE, NICK

Number	Title	Yr	NM
ANTILLES			
❏ AN-7028	Bryter Layter	1977	$100
—Released in England in 1970			
❏ AN-7010	Five Leaves Left	1976	$125
—Released in England in 1969			
HANNIBAL			
❏ HNBX-5302 [B]	Fruit Tree	1986	$250
❏ HNBL-1318 [B]	Time of No Reply	1987	$60
ISLAND			
❏ SMAS-9307 [B]	Nick Drake	1971	$150
—U.S.-only compilation of selected songs from his first two British LPs			
❏ SMAS-9318	Pink Moon	1972	$150
UNIVERSAL			
❏ 3732604 [B]	Nick Drake	2013	$40

DRAKE, PETE

Number	Title	Yr	NM
CANAAN			
❏ 4640 [M]	Steel Away	1967	$18
❏ 9640 [S]	Steel Away	1967	$25
CUMBERLAND			
❏ MGC-29053 [M]	Country Steel Guitar	1963	$25
❏ SRC-69053 [S]	Country Steel Guitar	1963	$30
HILLTOP			
❏ 6052 [M]	Are You Sincere	1967	$15
❏ S-6052 [S]	Are You Sincere	1967	$15
SMASH			
❏ MGS-27053 [M]	Forever	1964	$18
❏ SRS-67053 [S]	Forever	1964	$25
❏ MGS-27064 [M]	Talking Steel and Singing Strings	1965	$18
❏ SRS-67064 [S]	Talking Steel and Singing Strings	1965	$25
❏ MGS-27060 [M]	Talking Steel Guitar	1965	$18
❏ SRS-67060 [S]	Talking Steel Guitar	1965	$25
STARDAY			
❏ SLP-319 [M]	The Amazing Incredible Pete Drake	1964	$30
❏ SLP-180 [M]	The Fabulous Steel Guitar of Pete Drake	1962	$40
STOP			
❏ 1011	The Pete Drake Show	1970	$15

DRAMATICS, THE

Number	Title	Yr	NM
ABC			
❏ AA-1125	Anytime, Anyplace	1979	$18
❏ AA-1072	Do What You Wanna Do	1978	$18
❏ D-916	Drama V	1975	$18
❏ D-955	Joy Ride	1976	$18
❏ AB-1010	Shake It Well	1977	$18
❏ D-867	The Dramatic Jackpot	1975	$18
CAPITOL			
❏ ST-12205	New Dimension	1982	$12
FANTASY			
❏ 9642	Somewhere in Time: A Dramatic Reunion	1986	$15
MCA			
❏ 3196	10 1/2	1980	$12
❏ 762	10 1/2	198?	$10

Number	Title	Yr	NM
—Reissue of 3196			
❏ AA-1125	Anytime, Anyplace	1979	$15
— Reissue of ABC 1125			
❏ 5149	Dramatic Way	1981	$12
❏ 761	Dramatic Way	198?	$10
— Reissue of 5149			
STAX			
❏ STX-4131	A Dramatic Experience	1979	$15
— Reissue of Volt 6019			
❏ MPS-8523	Dramatically Yours	198?	$10
— Reissue of Volt 9501			
❏ MPS-8526	The Best of the Dramatics	198?	$12
❏ MPS-8545	The Dramatics Live	1988	$12
❏ STX-4111	Whatcha See Is Whatcha Get	1978	$15
— Reissue of Volt 6018			
VOLT			
❏ VOS-6019	A Dramatic Experience	1973	$30
❏ VOS-9501	Dramatically Yours	1974	$30
❏ V-3402	Positive State of Mind	1989	$12
❏ V-3407	Stone Cold	1990	$12
❏ VOS-6018	Whatcha See Is Whatcha Get	1972	$30

DRAPER, RAY

Number	Title	Yr	NM
JOSIE			
❏ JOZ-3004 [M]	Tuba Jazz	1963	$30
❏ JLPS-3004 [S]	Tuba Jazz	1963	$25
JUBILEE			
❏ JLP-1090 [M]	Tuba Jazz	1959	$50
NEW JAZZ			
❏ NJLP-8228 [M]	Ray Draper Quintet Featuring John Coltrane	1958	$150
—Purple label			
❏ NJLP-8228 [M]	Ray Draper Quintet Featuring John Coltrane	1965	$175
— Blue label, trident logo at right			
PRESTIGE			
❏ PRLP-7096 [M]	Tuba Sounds	1957	$250

DRAPER, RUSTY

Number	Title	Yr	NM
GOLDEN CREST			
❏ 31029	The Rusty Draper Show	1973	$15
❏ 31030	Tour the USA	1973	$15
MERCURY			
❏ MG-20657 [M]	Country and Western Golden Greats	1961	$30
❏ SR-60657 [S]	Country and Western Golden Greats	1961	$40
❏ MG-20117 [M]	Encores	1957	$30
❏ MG-20499 [M]	Hits That Sold a Million	1960	$30
❏ SR-60176 [S]	Hits That Sold a Million	1960	$40
❏ MG-20068 [M]	Music for a Rainy Night	1956	$30
❏ MG-20118 [M]	Rusty Draper Sings	1957	$30
❏ MG-20173 [M]	Rusty Meets Hoagy	1957	$30
MONUMENT			
❏ MLP-8005 [M]	Greatest Hits	1964	$18
❏ SLP-18005 [S]	Greatest Hits	1964	$25
❏ 6638	Greatest Hits	1977	$15
❏ MLP-8018 [M]	Night Life	1964	$18
❏ SLP-18018 [S]	Night Life	1964	$25
❏ MLP-8026 [M]	Rusty Draper Plays Guitar	1965	$18
❏ SLP-18026 [S]	Rusty Draper Plays Guitar	1965	$25
❏ SLP-18105	Something Old, Something New	1969	$18
❏ ZG33870	Swingin' Country/Something Old, Something New	1976	$18
PLAYCRAFT			
❏ PLP-1302 [M]	Sing-a-Long with Rusty Draper	1958	$30
WING			
❏ MGW-12274 [M]	Country Classics	196?	$18
❏ SRW-16274 [S]	Country Classics	196?	$18
❏ MGW-12243 [M]	Hits That Sold a Million	196?	$18
❏ SRW-16243 [S]	Hits That Sold a Million	196?	$18

DREAD ZEPPELIN
LED ZEPPELIN tribute band with a reggae beat.

Number	Title	Yr	NM
I.R.S.			
❏ X1-13048	Un-Led-Ed	1990	$25
—All copies on gold vinyl			

DREAM 6
With Johnette Napolitano, later of CONCRETE BLONDE.

Number	Title	Yr	NM
HAPPY HERMIT			
❏ 1983 [EP]	Dream 6	1983	$40

DREAM ACADEMY, THE

Number	Title	Yr	NM
REPRISE			
❏ 25625	Remembrance Days	1987	$10
WARNER BROS.			
❏ R154271	The Dream Academy	1986	$12
—RCA Music Service edition			
❏ 25625	The Dream Academy	1985	$10
❏ WBMS-133 [DJ]	The Warner Bros. Music Show	1986	$18
—Promo-only interview; one side is the Dream Academy, one			

Number	Title	Yr	NM

side is Lloyd Cole and the Commotions

DREAM SYNDICATE, THE
4 MEN WITH BEARDS

Number	Title	Yr	NM
4M520LP [B]	The Days of Wine and Roses		$25

A&M

SP-12511	This Is Not the New Dream Syndicate Album...Live	1984	$15

BIG TIME

10022	Out of the Grey	1985	$12

DOWN THERE

2 [EP]	Sure Thing + 3	1982	$25

ENIGMA

73341	Ghost Stories	1988	$10

RUBY

807 [B]	The Days of Wine and Roses	1982	$30

SLASH

23844 [B]	The Days of Wine and Roses	1982	$25

DREAMLOVERS, THE
COLLECTABLES

Number	Title	Yr	NM
COL-5004	The Best of the Dreamlovers	198?	$15
COL-5005	The Best of the Dreamlovers, Volume Two	198?	$15

COLUMBIA

CL2020 [M]	The Bird and Other Golden Dancing Grooves	1963	$40
CS8820 [S]	The Bird and Other Golden Dancing Grooves	1963	$50

DREAMS
COLUMBIA

C30225	Dreams	1970	$35
C30960	Imagine My Surprise	1971	$18

DREAMS AND ILLUSIONS
VERVE FORECAST

FTS-3040	Dreams and Illusions	1968	$25

DREAMS SO REAL
ARISTA

AL8618	Gloryline	1990	$12
8555	Rough Night in Jericho	1988	$12

DREW, DAN
See BOOTS BROWN.

DREW, DORIS
MODE

MOD-126 [M]	The Delightful Doris Drew	1957	$100

DREW, KENNY, AND NIELS-HENNING ORSTED PEDERSEN
INNER CITY

IC-2002	Duo	1973	$35
IC-2010	Duo 2	1974	$35
IC-2031	Duo Live in Concert	1974	$35
SCS-1031	Duo Live in Concert	198?	$30

—Reissue of Inner City 2031

STEEPLECHASE

SCS-1002	Duo	198?	$30

—Reissue of Inner City 2002

SCS-1010	Duo 2	198?	$30

—Reissue of Inner City 2010

DREW, KENNY; DONALD BYRD; HANK MOBLEY
JAZZLAND

JLP-6 [M]	Hard Bop	1960	$50

—Reissue of Riverside 236

JLP-906 [S]	Hard Bop	1960	$40

DREW, KENNY; PAUL CHAMBERS; PHILLY JOE JONES
JAZZLAND

JLP-909 [S]	The Tough Piano Trio	1960	$40
JLP-9 [M]	The Tough Piano Trio	1960	$250

—Reissue of Riverside 224

DREW, KENNY
BLUE NOTE

BLP-5023 [10]	Introducing the Kenny Drew Trio	1953	$400
BLP-4059 [M]	Undercurrent	1961	$400

—W. 63rd St." address on label

BLP-4059 [M]	Undercurrent	1964	$75

—New York, USA" address on label

BST-84059 [S]	Undercurrent	1961	$100

—W. 63rd St." address on label

BST-84059 [S]	Undercurrent	1964	$30

—New York, USA" address on label

BST-84059 [S]	Undercurrent	1966	$35

—A Division of Liberty Records" on label

FANTASY

OJC-065	Kenny Drew Trio	198?	$25
OJC-6007	Kenny Drew Trio/Quartet/Quintet	198?	$30
OJC-483	This Is New	1991	$30

INNER CITY

IC-2007	Everything I Love	1973	$35
IC-2034	If You Could See Me Now	1974	$35
IC-2048	Morning	1975	$35

JAZZ WEST

JWLP-4 [M]	Talkin' and Walkin' with the Kenny Drew Quartet	1955	$700

JUDSON

L-3005 [M]	Harold Arlen Showcase	1957	$50
L-3004 [M]	Harry Warren Showcase	1957	$50

NORGRAN

MGN-1002 [M]	Progressive Piano	1954	$250
MGN-29 [10]	The Ideation of Kenny Drew	1954	$400
MGN-1066 [M]	The Modernity of Kenny Drew	1956	$250

RIVERSIDE

RLP 12-811 [M]	I Love Jerome Kern	1956	$300
RLP 12-224 [M]	Kenny Drew Trio	1956	$2000

—White label, blue print

RLP 12-224 [M]	Kenny Drew Trio	195?	$50

—Blue labe, microphone logo at top

6037	Kenny Drew Trio	197?	$30
RLP 12-249 [M]	Pal Joey	1957	$350
RLP-1112 [S]	Pal Joey	1959	$300
6106	Pal Joey	197?	$30
RLP 12-236 [M]	This Is New	1957	$300

—White label, blue print

RLP 12-236 [M]	This Is New	195?	$50

—Blue labe, microphone logo at top

6066	This Is New	197?	$30

SOUL NOTE

SN-1040	It Might As Well Be Spring	1981	$30
SN-1081	Kenny Drew and Far Away	1983	$30
121081	Kenny Drew and Far Away	198?	$25

—Reissue of 1081

SN-1031	Your Soft Eyes	1980	$30
121031	Your Soft Eyes	198?	$25

—Reissue of 1031

STEEPLECHASE

SCS-1016	Dark Beauty	198?	$30
SCS-1007	Everything I Love	198?	$30

—Reissue of Inner City 2007

SCS-1034	If You Could See Me Now	198?	$30

—Reissue of Inner City 2034

SCS-1106	In Concert	198?	$30
SCS-1077	Lite Flite	198?	$30
SCS-1048	Morning	198?	$30
SCS-1129	Ruby, My Dear	1977	$30

VERVE

MGV-8156 [M]	The Modernity of Kenny Drew	1957	$0

—Canceled?

XANADU

167	For Sure	197?	$30
166	Home Is Where the Soul Is	197?	$30

DREW, PATTI
CAPITOL

ST-156	I've Been Here All the Time	1969	$25
T2804 [M]	Tell Him	1968	$30
ST2804 [S]	Tell Him	1968	$30
ST-408	Wild Is Love	1970	$25

DRIFTERS, THE
ARISTA

AB4140	Every Night Is Saturday Night	1976	$15

ATCO

SD 33-375 [R]	Their Greatest Recordings -- The Early Years	1971	$15

ATLANTIC

81931	All-Time Greatest Hits and More: 1959-1965	1989	$18
8003 [M]	Clyde McPhatter and the Drifters	1956	$500

—Black label

8003 [M]	Clyde McPhatter and the Drifters	1959	$75

—Red and purple label, white "fan" logo at right

8003 [M]	Clyde McPhatter and the Drifters	1963	$40

—Red and purple label, black "fan" logo at right

8113 [M]	I'll Take You Where the Music's Playing	1965	$40
SD8113 [S]	I'll Take You Where the Music's Playing	1965	$50
81927	Let the Boogie-Woogie Roll: Greatest Hits 1953-1958	1989	$18
8093 [M]	Our Biggest Hits	1964	$75

—Red and purple label, white "fan" logo at right

SD8093 [S]	Our Biggest Hits	1964	$100

—Mostly red label, black "fan" logo

8022 [M]	Rockin' and Driftin'	1958	$600

—Black label

8022 [M]	Rockin' and Driftin'	1958	$500

—White "bullseye" label

8022 [M]	Rockin' and Driftin'	1959	$75

—Red and purple label, white "fan" logo at right

8022 [M]	Rockin' and Driftin'	1963	$40

—Red and purple label, black "fan" logo at right

8059 [M]	Save the Last Dance for Me	1962	$120

—Red and purple label, white "fan" logo at right

SD8059 [S]	Save the Last Dance for Me	1962	$250

—Green and blue label, white "fan" logo at right

8059 [M]	Save the Last Dance for Me	1963	$75

—Red and purple label, black "fan" logo at right

SD8059 [S]	Save the Last Dance for Me	1963	$150

—Green and blue label, black "fan" logo at right

SD8059 [S]	Save the Last Dance for Me	1969	$30

—Red and green label, white horizontal stripe through center hole

8153 [M]	The Drifters' Golden Hits	1968	$30
SD8153 [P]	The Drifters' Golden Hits	1968	$30

—Green and blue label

SD8153 [P]	The Drifters' Golden Hits	1969	$18

—Red and green label

8041 [M]	The Drifters' Greatest Hits	1960	$600

—Black label

8041 [M]	The Drifters' Greatest Hits	1960	$150

—Red and purple label, white "fan" logo at right

8041 [M]	The Drifters' Greatest Hits	1963	$50

—Red and purple label, black "fan" logo at right

8103 [M]	The Good Life with the Drifters	1965	$40
SD8103 [S]	The Good Life with the Drifters	1965	$50
8099 [M]	Under the Boardwalk	1964	$100

—Black and white photo of group on cover

8099 [M]	Under the Boardwalk	1964	$50

—Color photo of group on cover

SD8099 [S]	Under the Boardwalk	1964	$120

—Black and white photo of group on cover

SD8099 [S]	Under the Boardwalk	1964	$75

—Color photo of group on cover

8073 [M]	Up on the Roof -- The Best of the Drifters	1963	$150

—Red and purple label, black "fan" logo at right

SD8073 [S]	Up on the Roof -- The Best of the Drifters	1963	$175

—Green and blue label, black "fan" logo at right

CLARION

608 [M]	The Drifters	1964	$25
SD608 [P]	The Drifters	1964	$30

GUSTO

0063	Greatest Hits -- The Drifters	1980	$12

TRIP

TOP-16-6	16 Greatest Hits -- The Drifters	1976	$12

DRIFTIN' SLIM
MILESTONE

MLS-93004	Driftin' Slim and His Blues Band	1968	$30

DRIFTING COWBOYS, THE
MGM

SE-4626	We Remember Hank Williams	1968	$25

DRIFTWOOD, JIMMIE
MONUMENT

MLP-8019 [M]	Down in the Arkansas	1965	$25
SLP-18019 [S]	Down in the Arkansas	1965	$30
MLP-8006 [M]	Voice of the People	1963	$25
SLP-18006 [S]	Voice of the People	1963	$30

RCA VICTOR

LPM-2443 [M]	Driftwood at Sea	1962	$30
LSP-2443 [S]	Driftwood at Sea	1962	$40
LPM-1994 [M]	Jimmie Driftwood and the Wilderness Road	1959	$30
LSP-1994 [S]	Jimmie Driftwood and the Wilderness Road	1959	$40
LPM-1635 [M]	Newly Discovered Early American Folk Songs	1958	$50
LPM-2316 [M]	Songs of Billy Yank and Johnny Reb	1961	$30
LSP-2316 [S]	Songs of Billy Yank and Johnny Reb	1961	$40
LPM-2228 [M]	Tall Tales in Song	1960	$30
LSP-2228 [S]	Tall Tales in Song	1960	$40
LPM-2171 [M]	The Westward Movement	1960	$30
LSP-2171 [S]	The Westward Movement	1960	$40

DRISCOLL, JULIE, BRIAN AUGER & THE TRINITY
ATCO

SD 33-258 [S]	Open	1968	$30
33-258 [M]	Open	1968	$300

Number	Title	Yr	NM

— White label promo; no stock copies were issued in mono

❏ SD 2-701 [B]	Streetnoise	1969	$100

CAPITOL
| ❏ DT-136 [R] | Jools & Brian | 1969 | $15 |

— American issue of pre-Atco material

DRISCOLL, JULIE
SPRINGBOARD
| ❏ SPB4043 [B] | Julie Driscoll | | $25 |

DRIVE-BY TRUCKERS
LOST HIGHWAY
| ❏ 088170308-1 | Southern Rock Opera | 2003 | $25 |

D'RIVERA, PAQUITO
COLUMBIA
❏ FC44077	Celebration	1988	$25
❏ FC40156	Explosion	1985	$25
❏ FC38899	Live at the Keystone Korner	1983	$25
❏ FC40583	Manhattan Burn	1987	$25
❏ FC38177	Mariel	1982	$25
❏ FC37374	Paquito Blowin'	1981	$25
❏ FC39584	Why Not!	1984	$25

D'RONE, FRANK
CADET
| ❏ LPS-806 | Brand New Morning | 1968 | $35 |

MERCURY
❏ MG-20586 [M]	After the Ball	1960	$150
❏ SR-60246 [S]	After the Ball	1960	$175
❏ SR-60721 [S]	Frank D'Rone In Person	196?	$150
❏ MG-20721 [M]	Frank D'Rone In Person	196?	$150
❏ MG-20418 [M]	Frank D'Rone Sings	1959	$150
❏ SR-90064 [S]	Frank D'Rone Sings	1959	$150

DRU HILL
ISLAND BLACK MUSIC
| ❏ PRLP-7317 [DJ] | 97 -- The Year of the Dru | 1997 | $18 |

— Promo-only edition of their debut album, "Dru Hill

DRUIDS OF STONEHENGE, THE
UNI
| ❏ 3004 [M] | Creation | 1967 | $175 |
| ❏ 73004 [S] | Creation | 1967 | $175 |

DRUSKY, ROY, AND PRISCILLA MITCHELL
MERCURY
| ❏ MG-21078 [M] | Together Again | 1966 | $25 |
| ❏ SR-61078 [S] | Together Again | 1966 | $30 |

DRUSKY, ROY
DECCA
❏ DL4160 [M]	Anymore with Roy Drusky	1961	$30
❏ DL74160 [S]	Anymore with Roy Drusky	1961	$30
❏ DL4340 [M]	It's My Way	1962	$25
❏ DL74340 [S]	It's My Way	1962	$30

MERCURY
❏ SR-61306	All My Hard Times	1970	$25
❏ MG-21006 [M]	Country Music All Around the World	1965	$25
❏ SR-61006 [S]	Country Music All Around the World	1965	$30
❏ MG-21097 [M]	If the Whole World Stopped Lovin'	1966	$25
❏ SR-61097 [S]	If the Whole World Stopped Lovin'	1966	$30
❏ SR-61260	I'll Make Amends	1970	$25
❏ SR-61336	I Love the Way That You've Been Lovin' Me	1971	$25
❏ MG-21083 [M]	In a New Dimension	1966	$25
❏ SR-61083 [S]	In a New Dimension	1966	$30
❏ SR-61173	Jody and the Kid	1968	$25
❏ SR-61233	My Grass Is Green	1969	$25
❏ MG-21118 [M]	Now Is a Lonely Time	1967	$30
❏ SR-61118 [S]	Now Is a Lonely Time	1967	$25
❏ SR-61206	Portrait of Roy Drusky	1969	$25
❏ MG-21052 [M]	Roy Drusky's Greatest Hits	1965	$25
❏ SR-61052 [S]	Roy Drusky's Greatest Hits	1965	$30
❏ SR-61145 [S]	Roy Drusky's Greatest Hits Vol. 2	1968	$25
❏ MG-21145 [M]	Roy Drusky's Greatest Hits Vol. 2	1968	$40

— Mono is white label promo only

❏ MG-20883 [M]	Songs of the Cities	1963	$25
❏ SR-60883 [S]	Songs of the Cities	1963	$30
❏ SR-61266	The Best of Roy Drusky	1970	$25
❏ MG-20973 [M]	The Pick of the Country	1964	$25
❏ SR-60973 [S]	The Pick of the Country	1964	$30
❏ MG-20919 [M]	Yesterday's Gone	1964	$25
❏ SR-60919 [S]	Yesterday's Gone	1964	$30

DRY CITY SCAT BAND, THE
ELEKTRA
| ❏ EKL-292 [M] | The Dry City Scat Band | 1965 | $30 |
| ❏ EKS-7292 [S] | The Dry City Scat Band | 1965 | $30 |

DRY JACK
INNER CITY
| ❏ IC-1063 | Magical Elements | 1978 | $35 |

| ❏ IC-1075 | Whale City | 1979 | $35 |

DRY THROAT FIVE, THE
STOMP OFF
| ❏ SOS-1151 | My Melancholy Baby | 1989 | $25 |
| ❏ SOS-1114 | Who's Blue? | 1986 | $25 |

DUALS, THE
SUE
| ❏ LP-2002 [M] | Stick Shift | 1961 | $400 |
— Cartoon cover
| ❏ LP-2002 [M] | Stick Shift | 1964 | $250 |
— Photo cover

DUBS, THE
CANDELITE
| ❏ 1004 | The Best of the Dubs | 197? | $15 |
| ❏ 1003 | You've Got to Be Good to Make It in New York City | 197? | $15 |

DUBS, THE / THE SHELLS
Also see each artist's individual listings.
JOSIE
| ❏ JM-4001 [M] | The Dubs Meet the Shells | 1962 | $300 |
| ❏ JSS-4001 [S] | The Dubs Meet the Shells | 1962 | $600 |

DUCKS DELUXE
MOTORS related.
RCA VICTOR
| ❏ AFL1-3025 | Don't Mind Rockin' Tonight | 1978 | $12 |
| ❏ LPL1-5008 | Ducks Deluxe | 1973 | $18 |

DUDLEY, DAVE
GOLDEN RING
| ❏ GR110 [M] | Dave Dudley Sings Six Days on the Road | 1963 | $100 |

MERCURY
❏ MG-21133 [M]	Dave Dudley Country	1967	$30
❏ SR-61133 [S]	Dave Dudley Country	1967	$25
❏ MG-21046 [M]	Dave Dudley's Greatest Hits	1965	$25
❏ SR-61046 [S]	Dave Dudley's Greatest Hits	1965	$30
❏ SR-61315	Dave Dudley Sings "Listen Betty, I'm Singing Your Song	1971	$18
❏ MG-21098 [M]	Free and Easy	1966	$25
❏ SR-61098 [S]	Free and Easy	1966	$25
❏ MG-21144 [M]	Greatest Hits Vol. 2	1968	$30
❏ SR-61144 [S]	Greatest Hits Vol. 2	1968	$25
❏ SRM-1-669	Keep On Truckin'	1973	$18
❏ MG-21074 [M]	Lonelyville	1966	$25
❏ SR-61074 [S]	Lonelyville	1966	$30
❏ SR-61215	One More Mile	1969	$25
❏ MG-20999 [M]	Rural Route #1	1965	$25
❏ SR-60999 [S]	Rural Route #1	1965	$30
❏ MG-20899 [M]	Songs About the Working Man	1964	$25
❏ SR-60899 [S]	Songs About the Working Man	1964	$30
❏ MG-20970 [M]	Talk of the Town	1964	$25
❏ SR-60970 [S]	Talk of the Town	1964	$30
❏ SR-61172	Thanks for All the Miles	1968	$25
❏ SR-61268	The Best of Dave Dudley	1970	$18
❏ SR-61365	The Original Traveling Man	1972	$18
❏ SR-61276	The Pool Shark	1970	$18
❏ MG-21057 [M]	There's a Star Spangled Banner Waving Somewhere	1966	$25
❏ SR-61057 [S]	There's a Star Spangled Banner Waving Somewhere	1966	$30
❏ MG-20927 [M]	Travelin' with Dave Dudley	1964	$25
❏ SR-60927 [S]	Travelin' with Dave Dudley	1964	$30
❏ MG-21028 [M]	Truck Drivin' Son-of-a-Gun	1965	$25
❏ SR-61028 [S]	Truck Drivin' Son-of-a-Gun	1965	$30
❏ SR-61351	Will the Real Dave Dudley Please Sing	1971	$18

UNITED ARTISTS
| ❏ UA-LA512-G | Uncommonly Good Country | 1975 | $15 |

DUDZIAK, URSZULA
ARISTA
| ❏ AL4132 | Midnight Rain | 1976 | $35 |
| ❏ AL4065 | Urszula | 1975 | $35 |

COLUMBIA
| ❏ KC32902 | Newborn Light | 1972 | $25 |

INNER CITY
| ❏ IC-1066 | Future Talk | 1979 | $35 |

DUFFY
MERCURY
| ❏ 1082201 | Rockferry | 2008 | $25 |

DUGGAN, LAR
PHILO
| ❏ PH-9002 | From the Lake Studies | 198? | $30 |

DUKE, DOUGLAS
HERALD
| ❏ HLP-0102 [M] | Sounds Impossible | 1956 | $50 |

REGENT
| ❏ MG-6013 [M] | Jazz Organist | 196? | $30 |

DUKE, GEORGE
ELEKTRA
❏ 60480	George Duke	1986	$30
❏ 60778	Night After Night	1989	$30
❏ 60398	Thief in the Night	1985	$35

EPIC
❏ FE38208	1976 Solo Keyboard Album	1983	$150
❏ FE36483	A Brazilian Love Affair	1980	$35
❏ JE35366	Don't Let Go	1978	$75
❏ PE35366	Don't Let Go	198?	$20
— Budget-line reissue with new prefix and bar code
❏ FE37532	Dream On	1982	$75
❏ JE35701	Follow the Rainbow	1979	$85
❏ PE34469	From Me to You	1977	$75
— Orange label, no bar code on cover
| ❏ PE34469 | From Me to You | 198? | $20 |
— Budget-line reissue; dark blue label, bar code on cover
❏ FE38513	Guardian of the Light	1983	$75
❏ JE36263	Master of the Game	1979	$85
❏ PE36263	Master of the Game	198?	$25
— Budget-line reissue with new prefix
| ❏ JE34883 | Reach For It | 1977 | $85 |
— Orange label; no bar code on cover
| ❏ PE34883 | Reach For It | 198? | $20 |
— Budget-line reissue; dark blue label, bar code on back
| ❏ FE39262 | Rendezvous | 1984 | $85 |

LIBERTY
| ❏ ST-11004 | Save the Country | 1970 | $75 |
— Original issue

MPS/BASF
❏ 22018	Faces in Reflection	1974	$35
❏ 25355	Feel	1974	$50
❏ 25671	I Love the Blues, She Heard My Cry	1975	$50
❏ 22835	Liberated Fantasies	1976	$35
❏ 25613	The Aura Will Prevail	1975	$50

PACIFIC JAZZ
| ❏ PJ-LA891-H | George Duke | 1978 | $35 |
| ❏ LN-10127 | Save the Country | 198? | $30 |
— Reissue

PAUSA
| ❏ PR7070 | I Love the Blues | 1980 | $25 |
| ❏ PR7042 | The Aura Will Prevail | 198? | $25 |
— Reissue of MPS/BASF 25613

PICKWICK
| ❏ SPC-3588 | Save the Country | 1978 | $35 |
— Reissue of Liberty 11004

VERVE/MPS
| ❏ 821665-1 | Feel | 1984 | $25 |
— Reissue of MPS/BASF 25355
| ❏ 821837-1 | The Aura Will Prevail | 1984 | $25 |
— Reissue of Pausa 7042

DUKE, KENO
STRATA-EAST
| ❏ SES-7416 | Sense of Values | 1974 | $30 |

TRIDENT
| ❏ 501 | Crest of the Wave | 197? | $25 |

DUKE, PATTY, WITH NORMAN VINCENT PEALE
GUIDEPOSTS
| ❏ GP-101 [M] | Guideposts for Christmas | 1963 | $100 |

DUKE, PATTY
UNART
| ❏ 20005 [M] | TV's Teen Star | 1967 | $15 |
| ❏ S20005 [S] | TV's Teen Star | 1967 | $18 |

UNITED ARTISTS
❏ UAL-3452 [M]	Don't Just Stand There	1965	$30
❏ UAS-6452 [S]	Don't Just Stand There	1965	$30
❏ UAL-3492 [M]	Patty	1966	$30
❏ UAS-6492 [S]	Patty	1966	$30
❏ UAL-3535 [M]	Patty Duke's Greatest Hits	1966	$18
❏ UAS-6535 [S]	Patty Duke's Greatest Hits	1966	$30
❏ UAS-6623	Songs from the Valley of the Dolls	1968	$30

DUKE, VERNON
ATLANTIC
| ❏ 407 [10] | Vernon Duke Plays Vernon Duke | 1954 | $150 |

DUKE OF IRON, THE
PRESTIGE
| ❏ PRLP-13068 [M] | Limbo, Limbo, Limbo | 1963 | $30 |

DUKE OF PADUCAH, THE
STARDAY
| ❏ SLP-148 [M] | Button Shoes, Belly Laughs and Monkey Business | 1961 | $40 |

DUKES, JOE, AND JACK MCDUFF
PRESTIGE
| ❏ PRLP-7324 [M] | Soulful Drums | 1964 | $30 |
| ❏ PRST-7324 [S] | Soulful Drums | 1964 | $30 |

Number	Title	Yr	NM

DUKE'S MEN, THE
EPIC
❑ LN3237 [M]	Ellington's Sidekicks	1956	$150
❑ LG3108 [M]	The Duke's Men	1955	$150

DUKES OF DIXIELAND, THE
AUDIO FIDELITY
❑ AFLP-1918 [M]	Carnegie Hall Concert	1959	$35
❑ AFSD-5918 [S]	Carnegie Hall Concert	1959	$35
❑ AFLP-1924 [M]	Louie and the Dukes of Dixieland	1960	$35
❑ AFSD-5924 [S]	Louie and the Dukes of Dixieland	1960	$35
❑ AFLP-1851 [M]	Marching Along with the Dukes of Dixieland, Vol. 3	1957	$35
❑ AFSD-5851 [S]	Marching Along with the Dukes of Dixieland, Vol. 3	1958	$50
❑ AFLP-1862 [M]	Mardi Gras Time	1958	$35
❑ AFSD-5862 [S]	Mardi Gras Time	1958	$50
❑ AFLP-1861 [M]	Minstrel Time with the Phenomenal Dukes of Dixieland, Volume 5	1957	$35
❑ AFSD-5861 [S]	Minstrel Time with the Phenomenal Dukes of Dixieland, Volume 5	1958	$50
❑ AFLP-1976 [M]	More of the Best of the Dukes of Dixieland	1962	$35
❑ AFSD-5976 [S]	More of the Best of the Dukes of Dixieland	1962	$35
❑ AFLP-1928 [M]	Piano Ragtime (Vol. 11)	1960	$35
❑ AFSD-5928 [S]	Piano Ragtime (Vol. 11)	1960	$35
❑ AFSD-6172	Tailgating	1967	$30
❑ AFLP-1956 [M]	The Best of the Dukes of Dixieland	1961	$35
❑ AFSD-5956 [S]	The Best of the Dukes of Dixieland	1961	$35
❑ AFLP-1860 [M]	The Dukes of Dixieland On Bourbon Street, Vol. 4	1958	$35
❑ AFSD-5860 [S]	The Dukes of Dixieland On Bourbon Street, Vol. 4	1958	$50
❑ AFLP-1891 [M]	The Dukes of Dixieland On Campus	1959	$35
❑ AFSD-5891 [S]	The Dukes of Dixieland On Campus	1959	$50
❑ AFSD-6174	The Dukes of Dixieland On Parade	1967	$30
❑ AFLP-1892 [M]	Up the Mississippi	1959	$35
❑ AFSD-5892 [S]	Up the Mississippi	1959	$50
❑ AFLP-1823 [M]	You Have to Hear It to Believe It -- The Dukes of Dixieland, Vol. 1	1956	$35
❑ AFSD-5823 [S]	You Have to Hear It to Believe It -- The Dukes of Dixieland, Vol. 1	196?	$50
❑ AFLP-1840 [M]	You Have to Hear It to Believe It -- The Dukes of Dixieland, Vol. 2	1957	$35
❑ AFSD-5840 [S]	You Have to Hear It to Believe It -- The Dukes of Dixieland, Vol. 2	196?	$50

COLUMBIA
❑ CL1728 [M]	Breakin' It Up on Broadway	1962	$30
❑ CS8528 [S]	Breakin' It Up on Broadway	1962	$35
❑ CL1871 [M]	Dixieland Hootenanny!	1963	$30
❑ CS8671 [S]	Dixieland Hootenanny!	1963	$35
❑ CL2194 [M]	Struttin' at the World's Fair	1964	$30
❑ CS8994 [S]	Struttin' at the World's Fair	1964	$35
❑ CL1966 [M]	The Dukes at Disneyland, Volume 1	1963	$30
❑ CS8766 [S]	The Dukes at Disneyland, Volume 1	1963	$35

DECCA
❑ DL4708 [M]	Come On and Hear	1966	$30
❑ DL74708 [S]	Come On and Hear	1966	$35
❑ DL4863 [M]	Come to the Cabaret	1967	$35
❑ DL74863 [S]	Come to the Cabaret	1967	$30
❑ DL74975	Dixieland's Greatest Hits	1968	$30
❑ DL4653 [M]	Live" At Bourbon Street, Chicago	1965	$30
❑ DL74653 [S]	Live" At Bourbon Street, Chicago	1965	$35
❑ DL4807 [M]	Sunrise, Sunset	1966	$30
❑ DL74807 [S]	Sunrise, Sunset	1966	$35
❑ DL4864 [M]	Thoroughly Modern Millie	1967	$35
❑ DL74864 [S]	Thoroughly Modern Millie	1967	$30

HARMONY
❑ HL7349 [M]	Best of the Dukes of Dixieland	1965	$30
❑ HS11149 [S]	Best of the Dukes of Dixieland	1965	$30

MCA
❑ 268	Dixieland's Greatest Hits	1973	$25

— *Reissue of Decca 74975*

RCA VICTOR
❑ LPM-2097 [M]	The Dukes of Dixieland at the Jazz Band Ball	1960	$30
❑ LSP-2097(e) [R]	The Dukes of Dixieland at the Jazz Band Ball	1960	$35

ROULETTE
❑ R-25029 [M]	Curtain Going Up	1958	$50

VIK
❑ LX-1025 [M]	The Dukes of Dixieland at the Jazz Band Ball	1956	$75

VOCALION
❑ VL73846	Hello, Dolly!	1968	$25

DUNBAR, AYNSLEY
BLUE THUMB
❑ BTS-6 [B]	Doctor Dunbar's Prescription	1969	$35
❑ BTS-4 [B]	The Aynsley Dunbar Retaliation	1968	$40
❑ BTS-16 [B]	To Mum From Aynsley and the Boys	1970	$30

DUNCAN, BILL
KING
❑ 825 [M]	A Scene Near My Country Home	1962	$30

DUNCAN, DANNY
X
❑ LVA-3040 [10]	Ragtime Jamboree	1955	$75

DUNCAN, JOHNNY, AND JANIE FRICKE
COLUMBIA
❑ JC36780	Nice 'N' Easy	1980	$12

DUNCAN, JOHNNY, AND JUNE STEARNS
COLUMBIA
❑ CS9910	Back to Back	1969	$18

DUNCAN, JOHNNY
COLUMBIA
❑ KC35039	Come a Little Bit Closer	1977	$15
❑ KC35628	Greatest Hits	1978	$15
❑ JC36508	In My Dreams	1980	$12
❑ PC34442	Johnny Duncan	1977	$15
❑ CS9824	Johnny One Time	1969	$25
❑ KC35775	See You When the Sun Goes Down	1979	$15
❑ JC36260	Straight from Texas	1980	$12
❑ KC32440	Sweet Country Woman	1973	$18
❑ KC35451	The Best Is Yet to Come	1978	$15
❑ KC34243	The Best of Johnny Duncan	1976	$15
❑ C30618	There's Something About a Lady	1971	$18
❑ JC36829	You're On My Mind	1981	$12

HARMONY
❑ KH32477	You're Gonna Need a Man	1973	$15

DUNCAN, SAMMY
JAZZOLOGY
❑ J-77	Jazz and Blues	1979	$25
❑ J-64	Sammy Duncan and His Underground All Stars	197?	$25
❑ J-84	Swingin' Jazz	1980	$25
❑ J-118	When the Saints Go Marching In	1987	$25
❑ J-119	When You're Swingin'	1987	$25

NATIONAL RECORDING CO.
❑ NRC-LPA1	Cool Dixieland Jazz from Out of the South	197?	$30

DUNHAM, KATHERINE
AUDIO FIDELITY
❑ AFLP-1803 [M]	The Singing Gods-Drum Rhythms of Cuba, Haiti, Brazil	1957	$40

DECCA
❑ DL5251 [10]	Afro-Caribbean Songs and Rhythms	1951	$75

DUNN, HOLLY
MTM
❑ ST-71070	Across the Rio Grande	1988	$15
❑ ST-71063	Cornerstone	1987	$15
❑ ST-71052	Holly Dunn	1986	$15

WARNER BROS.
❑ PRO-A-3692 [DJ]	Blue Rose of Texas Radio Special	1989	$30

— *Promo-only interview record*

❑ 25939	The Blue Rose of Texas	1989	$12

DUNSTEDTER, EDDIE
CAPITOL
❑ T2395 [M]	Christmas Candy	1965	$15
❑ ST2395 [S]	Christmas Candy	1965	$18
❑ T1264 [M]	The Bells of Christmas	1959	$15
❑ ST1264 [S]	The Bells of Christmas	1959	$18
❑ T1968 [M]	The Bells of Christmas Chime Again	1963	$15
❑ ST1968 [S]	The Bells of Christmas Chime Again	1963	$18

DUPRE, MARCEL
MERCURY LIVING PRESENCE
❑ SR90227 [S]	Dupre at Saint-Sulpice, Vol. 1	196?	$40

—*Maroon label, no "Vendor: Mercury Record Corporation*

❑ SR90229 [S]	Dupre at Saint-Sulpice, Vol. 2	196?	$100

—*Maroon label, no "Vendor: Mercury Record Corporation*

❑ SR90229 [S]	Dupre at Saint-Sulpice, Vol. 2	196?	$50

—*Maroon label, with "Vendor: Mercury Record Corporation*

❑ SR90228 [S]	Dupre at Saint-Sulpice, Vol. 3	196?	$40

—*Maroon label, no "Vendor: Mercury Record Corporation*

❑ SR90228 [S]	Dupre at Saint-Sulpice, Vol. 3	196?	$25

—*Maroon label, with "Vendor: Mercury Record Corporation*

❑ SR90230 [S]	Dupre at Saint-Sulpice, Vol. 4	196?	$100

—*Maroon label, no "Vendor: Mercury Record Corporation*

❑ SR90230 [S]	Dupre at Saint-Sulpice, Vol. 4	196?	$25

—*Maroon label, with "Vendor: Mercury Record Corporation*

❑ SR90231 [S]	Dupre at Saint-Sulpice, Vol. 5	196?	$75

—*Maroon label, no "Vendor: Mercury Record Corporation*

❑ SR90231 [S]	Dupre at Saint-Sulpice, Vol. 5	196?	$30

—*Maroon label, with "Vendor: Mercury Record Corporation*

❑ SR90168 [S]	Franck: Piece Heroique; 3 Chorales	196?	$50

—*Maroon label, no "Vendor: Mercury Record Corporation*

❑ SR90168 [S]	Franck: Piece Heroique; 3 Chorales	196?	$30

—*Maroon label, with "Vendor: Mercury Record Corporation*

❑ SR90168 [S]	Franck: Piece Heroique; 3 Chorales	196?	$25

—*Third edition: Dark red (not maroon) label*

❑ SR90169 [S]	Organ Recital	196?	$250

—*Maroon label, no "Vendor: Mercury Record Corporation*

❑ SR90169 [S]	Organ Recital	196?	$250

—*Maroon label, with "Vendor: Mercury Record Corporation*

DUPREE, CHAMPION JACK, AND JIMMY RUSHING
AUDIO LAB
❑ AL-1512 [M]	Two Shades of Blue	1958	$250

DUPREE, CHAMPION JACK, AND MICKEY BAKER
Also see each artist's individual listings.
SIRE
❑ SES-97010	In Heavy Blues	1969	$30

DUPREE, CHAMPION JACK
ATLANTIC
❑ 8019 [M]	Blues from the Gutter	1959	$175

— *Black label*

❑ 8019 [M]	Blues from the Gutter	1960	$50

— *White "fan" logo at right of label*

❑ 8019 [M]	Blues from the Gutter	1963	$25

— *Black "fan" logo at right of label*

❑ SD8019 [S]	Blues from the Gutter	1959	$250

— *Green label*

❑ SD8019 [S]	Blues from the Gutter	1960	$75

— *Green and blue label, white "fan" logo at right of label*

❑ SD8019 [S]	Blues from the Gutter	1963	$30

— *Green and blue label, black "fan" logo at right of label*

❑ SD8255	Blues from the Gutter	1970	$18
❑ 8056 [M]	Champion of the Blues	1961	$50

— *White "fan" logo at right of label*

❑ 8056 [M]	Champion of the Blues	1963	$25

— *Black "fan" logo at right of label*

❑ SD8056 [R]	Champion of the Blues	196?	$18
❑ 8045 [M]	Natural and Soulful Blues	1961	$50

— *White "fan" logo at right of label*

❑ 8045 [M]	Natural and Soulful Blues	1963	$25

— *Black "fan" logo at right of label*

❑ SD8045 [S]	Natural and Soulful Blues	1961	$75

— *Green and blue label, white "fan" logo at right of label*

❑ SD8045 [S]	Natural and Soulful Blues	1963	$30

— *Green and blue label, black "fan" logo at right of label*

BLUE HORIZON
❑ 7702	When You Feel the Feeling	1969	$30

BULLSEYE
❑ BB-9502	Back Home In New Orleans	1990	$15

CONTINENTAL
❑ CLP-16002 [M]	Low Down Blues	1961	$300

EVEREST ARCHIVE OF FOLK & JAZZ
❑ 217	Champion Jack Dupree	197?	$12

FOLKWAYS
❑ FS-3825 [M]	Women Blues of Champion Jack Dupree	1961	$30

GNP CRESCENDO
❑ GNPS-10005	Happy to Be Free	1974	$15
❑ GNPS-10013	Legacy of Blues 3	197?	$15
❑ GNPS-10001	Tricks	1974	$15

JAZZ MAN
❑ BLZ-5501	Champion Jack Dupree	1982	$12

KING
❑ 735 [M]	Champion Jack Dupree Sings the Blues	1961	$300
❑ KS-1084	Walking the Blues	1970	$18

Number	Title	Yr	NM

LONDON

| ❏ PS553 | From New Orleans to Chicago | 1969 | $25 |

OKEH

| ❏ OKM12103 [M] | Cabbage Greens | 1963 | $30 |

STORYVILLE

| ❏ 4010 | Best of the Blues | 1982 | $12 |
| ❏ 4040 | I'm Growing Older Every Day | 198? | $12 |

DUPREE, CORNELL

ANTILLES

| ❏ 90984 | Coast to Coast | 1988 | $25 |

ATLANTIC

| ❏ SD7311 | Teasin' | 1975 | $30 |

DUPREE, SIMON, AND THE BIG SOUND

TOWER

| ❏ ST-5097 [S] | Without Reservations | 1968 | $40 |
| ❏ T-5097 [M] | Without Reservations | 1968 | $150 |

DUPREES, THE

COED

| ❏ LPC-906 [M] | Have You Heard | 1963 | $250 |
| ❏ LPC-905 [M] | You Belong to Me | 1962 | $300 |

COLLECTABLES

| ❏ COL-5008 | The Best of the Duprees | 198? | $15 |

COLOSSUS

| ❏ 5000 | Duprees Gold | 1970 | $30 |
| —As "The Italian Asphalt & Pavement Co." | | | |

HERITAGE

❏ HT-35002 [M]	Total Recall	1968	$150
—Mono is promo only; in stereo cover with "DJ Monaural" sticker on front			
❏ HTS-35002 [S]	Total Recall	1968	$30

POST

| ❏ 1000 | The Duprees Sing | 196? | $30 |

DUPRI, JERMAINE

SO SO DEF

| ❏ C285830 | Instructions | 2001 | $18 |
| ❏ C269087 | Jermaine Dupri Presents Life in 1472 -- The Original Soundtrack | 1998 | $15 |

DURAN, EDDIE

CONCORD JAZZ

| ❏ CJ-94 | Ginza | 1979 | $30 |
| ❏ CJ-271 | One By One | 1985 | $25 |

FANTASY

❏ 3247 [M]	Jazz Guitarist	1957	$100
—Red vinyl			
❏ 3247 [M]	Jazz Guitarist	195?	$40
—Black vinyl			
❏ OJC-120	Jazz Guitarist	198?	$25

DURAN DURAN

CAPITOL

❏ R140395	Arena	1984	$15
—RCA Music Service edition			
❏ SWAV-12374	Arena	1984	$12
—With booklet (deduct 25% if cut out or if booklet is missing)			
❏ R100682	Big Thing	1988	$15
—BMG Direct Marketing edition			
❏ C1-90958	Big Thing	1988	$12
—Deduct 25% for cut-outs			
❏ R173573	Decade	1989	$15
—BMG Direct Marketing edition			
❏ C1-93178	Decade	1989	$15
❏ R134452	Duran Duran	1983	$15
—RCA Music Service edition; with "Is There Something I Should Know?"			
❏ ST-12158	Duran Duran	1983	$12
—Reissue of Harvest 12158 with new cover and 9 tracks, adding "Is There Something I Should Know"			
❏ SPRO-79097/8 [EP]	Duran Goes Dutch	1987	$100
—Promo-only five-song EP recorded live in Rotterdam			
❏ R163458	Liberty	1990	$18
—BMG Direct Marketing edition			
❏ C1-94292	Liberty	1990	$18
❏ R114794	Notorious	1987	$15
—RCA Music Service edition			
❏ PJ-12540	Notorious	1986	$10
❏ R163452	Rio	1983	$18
—RCA Music Service edition; contains Harvest Version 1 of the album			
❏ ST-12211	Rio	1983	$10
—Version 4: Capitol logo replaces Harvest logo on back cover, otherwise it's the same as Harvest Version 3, with the same trail-off markings			

❏ ST-512211 [B]	Rio	1983	$12
—Columbia House edition; otherwise the same as Version 4			
❏ ST-12310 [B]	Seven and the Ragged Tiger	1983	$10

EPIC

| ❏ E292900 | Astronaut | 2004 | $18 |

HARVEST

❏ MLP-15006 [EP]	Carnival	1982	$25
❏ ST-12158	Duran Duran	1982	$18
—Original US issue with yellow label and 8 songs			
❏ ST-12211	Rio	1982	$25
—Version 1: Harvest logo on lower back cover, contains the same versions of the songs as the original UK release; trail-off wax number on Side 1 is "ST-1-12211 Z1			
❏ ST-12211	Rio	1982	$18
—Version 2: Harvest logo on lower back cover, with five songs remixed by David Kershenbaum; Side 1 trail-off wax number is "ST-1-12211-Z13-RE1 #1			
❏ ST-12211	Rio	1982	$15
—Version 3: Harvest logo on lower back cover, with five songs remixed by David Kershenbaum, but with a different mix of "Hungry Like the Wolf" than Version 2; Side 1 trail-off wax number is "ST-1-12211-Z18			

MOBILE FIDELITY

| ❏ 1-182 | Seven and the Ragged Tiger | 1985 | $50 |
| —Audiophile vinyl | | | |

DURANTE, JIMMY

DECCA

❏ DL9049 [M]	Club Durant	195?	$30
❏ DL5116 [10]	Jimmy Durante	195?	$50
❏ DL8884 [M]	Jimmy Durante at the Piano	1959	$18
❏ DL78884 [S]	Jimmy Durante at the Piano	1959	$25

LION

| ❏ L-70053 [M] | Jimmy Durante in Person | 195? | $30 |

MGM

❏ E-3242 [M]	Jimmy Durante in Person	1955	$30
❏ E-4207 [M]	The Very Best of Jimmy Durante	1964	$15
❏ SE-4207 [S]	The Very Best of Jimmy Durante	1964	$18

ROULETTE

| ❏ R-25123 [M] | Jimmy Durante at the Copacabana | 1961 | $25 |
| ❏ SR-25123 [S] | Jimmy Durante at the Copacabana | 1961 | $30 |

WARNER BROS.

❏ W1531 [M]	Hello Young Lovers	1964	$18
❏ WS1531 [S]	Hello Young Lovers	1964	$25
❏ W1577 [M]	Jimmy Durante's Way of Life	1965	$18
❏ WS1577 [S]	Jimmy Durante's Way of Life	1965	$25
❏ W1655 [M]	One of Those Songs	1966	$18
❏ WS1655 [S]	One of Those Songs	1966	$25
❏ W1506 [M]	September Song	1963	$18
❏ WS1506 [S]	September Song	1963	$25
❏ W1713 [M]	Songs for Sunday	1967	$18
❏ WS1713 [S]	Songs for Sunday	1967	$25

DURBIN, DEANNA

DECCA

| ❏ DL8785 [M] | Deanna Durbin | 1958 | $50 |

DURHAM, BOBBY

HIGHTONE

| ❏ 8010 | Where I Grew Up | 1987 | $12 |

DURUTTI COLUMN

4 MEN WITH BEARDS

| ❏ 4M522LP [B] | LC | | $25 |
| ❏ 4M521LP [B] | The Return of the Durutti Column | | $25 |

DURY, IAN, AND THE BLOCKHEADS

POLYDOR

| ❏ PD1-6337 [B] | Lord Upminster | 1981 | $18 |

STIFF

| ❏ STF 0002 [B] | New Boots and Panties | 1978 | $35 |

STIFF AMERICA

❏ USE17	Juke Box Dury	1981	$25
❏ USE 02 [B]	New Boots and Panties	1980	$18
—Reissue of Stiff 0002			

STIFF/EPIC

| ❏ JE36104 [B] | Do It Yourself | 1979 | $30 |
| ❏ JE36998 [B] | Laughter | 1980 | $25 |

DUSHON, JEAN

ARGO

| ❏ LP-4039 [M] | Make Way for Jean DuShon | 1964 | $30 |
| ❏ LPS-4039 [S] | Make Way for Jean DuShon | 1964 | $30 |

DUST
Also see RAMONES, RICK DERRINGER.

KAMA SUTRA

❏ KSBS-2041	Dust	1971	$30
—Pink label			
❏ KSBS-2059	Hard Attack	1972	$30
—Pink label			

DUTCH SWING COLLEGE BAND, THE

EPIC

| ❏ LN3211 [M] | Dixieland Goes Dutch | 1955 | $100 |

EVEREST ARCHIVE OF FOLK & JAZZ

| ❏ 341 | The Dutch Swing College Band | 1979 | $25 |

PHILIPS

| ❏ PHM200010 [M] | Dixie Goes Dutch | 1962 | $35 |
| ❏ PHS600010 [S] | Dixie Goes Dutch | 1962 | $25 |

TIMELESS

| ❏ 525 | The Dutch Swing College Band | 198? | $25 |
| ❏ 516 | The Dutch Swing College Band At Its Best | 198? | $25 |

DUVAL, DENISE / GEORGES PRETRE

RCA VICTOR RED SEAL

| ❏ LDS-2385 [S] | Poulenc: La Voix Humana | 1960 | $75 |
| —Original with "shaded dog" label; also includes booklet | | | |

DUVALL, HUELYN

SUNDAZED

| ❏ LP-5019 | Is You Is Or Is You Ain't? | 199? | $12 |
| —Original with "shaded dog" label; also includes booklet | | | |

DWARVES

SUB POP

❏ 67	Blood, Guts and Pussy	1990	$25
—First 1,000 on red vinyl			
❏ 67 [B]	Blood, Guts and Pussy	1990	$35
❏ 197 [B]	Sugar Fix	1993	$35
❏ 126 [B]	Thank Heaven for Little Girls	1991	$30

DYANI, JOHNNY; OKAY TEMIZ; MONGEZI FEZA

ANTILLES

| ❏ AN-7035 | Music for Xaba | 197? | $30 |

DYANI, JOHNNY

STEEPLECHASE

❏ SCS-1186	Afrika	198?	$30
❏ SCS-1209	Angolan City	198?	$30
❏ SCS-1163	Mbizo	1982	$30
❏ SCS-1109	Song for Biko	1978	$30
❏ SCS-1098	Witchdoctor's Son	197?	$30

DYKE AND THE BLAZERS

ORIGINAL SOUND

❏ LPS8877	Dyke's Greatest Hits	1968	$85
❏ LP8876 [M]	The Funky Broadway	1967	$50
❏ LPS8876 [S]	The Funky Broadway	1967	$85

DYLAN, BOB, AND ALAN J. WEBERMAN

FOLKWAYS

| ❏ FB-5322 [M] | Bob Dylan Vs. A.J. Weberman | 1977 | $600 |
| —A tape-recorded phone conversation; quickly withdrawn from the market | | | |

DYLAN, BOB

ASYLUM

❏ AB-201 [DJ]	Before the Flood	1974	$50
—White label promo			
❏ AB-201	Before the Flood	1974	$25
❏ 7E-1003 [DJ]	Ceremonies of the Horsemen	1974	$3000
—Original title of "Planet Waves"; no records were pressed with this title, but never-glued covers exist, of which 3 or 4 are			

Number	Title	Yr	NM

known. Value is for one of these covers; VG value 1500; VG+ value 2250

❏ 7E-1003   Planet Waves   1974 $18
— Without wraparound (olive green) second cover
❏ 7E-1003   Planet Waves   1974 $25
— With wraparound (olive green) second cover
❏ 7E-1003 [DJ]   Planet Waves   1974 $50
— White label promo
❏ EQ-1003 [Q]   Planet Waves   1974 $150

COLUMBIA
❏ 88883 73489   Another Self Portrait   2013 $50
1 [B]
❏ CL2193 [M]   Another Side of Bob Dylan   1964 $400
— White label promo
❏ CL2193 [M]   Another Side of Bob Dylan   1964 $50
— Guaranteed High Fidelity" on label
❏ CL2193 [M]   Another Side of Bob Dylan   1965 $30
— Mono" on label
❏ CS8993 [S]   Another Side of Bob Dylan   1964 $40
— 360 Sound Stereo" in black on label
❏ CS8993 [S]   Another Side of Bob Dylan   1965 $30
— 360 Sound Stereo" in white on label
❏ CS8993 [S]   Another Side of Bob Dylan   1970 $15
— Orange label
❏ KCS8993 [S]   Another Side of Bob Dylan   197? $12
❏ PC8993 [S]   Another Side of Bob Dylan   198? $10
— Budget-line reissue
❏ PC8993 [S]   Another Side of Bob Dylan   2001 $15
— Reissue on 180-gram vinyl (sealed copies have a sticker indicating this)
❏ CG37661   Before the Flood   1983 $15
— Reissue of Asylum AB-201
❏ C5X38830   Biograph   1985 $30
❏ C2L41 [M]   Blonde on Blonde   1966 $4000
— White label promo
❏ C2L41 [M]   Blonde on Blonde   1966 $1000
— Female photos" inner gatefold with two women pictured
❏ C2L41 [M]   Blonde on Blonde   1968 $600
— No photos of women inside gatefold
❏ C2S841 [S]   Blonde on Blonde   1966 $75
— Female photos" inner gatefold with two women pictured
❏ C2S841 [S]   Blonde on Blonde   1968 $30
— No photos of women inside gatefold; "360 Sound Stereo" on label
❏ C2S841 [S]   Blonde on Blonde   1970 $18
— Orange label
❏ CG841 [S]   Blonde on Blonde   198? $15
❏ PC33235 [DJ]   Blood on the Tracks   1975 $5000
— Test pressing with radically different versions of five songs including "Idiot Wind" and "Tangled Up in Blue"; VG value 2500; VG+ value 3750
❏ PC33235 [DJ]   Blood on the Tracks   1975 $30
— Regular white label promo
❏ PC33235   Blood on the Tracks   1979 $10
— With bar code on back cover
❏ PC33235   Blood on the Tracks   1975 $15
— First editions have liner notes on the back cover in black print
❏ PC33235   Blood on the Tracks   1975 $18
— With drawing on back cover and no liner notes. Actually a second pressing, but available only for a short time
❏ HC43235   Blood on the Tracks   198? $50
— Half-speed mastered edition
❏ PC33235   Blood on the Tracks   2001 $15
— Reissue on 180-gram vinyl (sealed copies have a sticker indicating this)
❏ PC33235   Blood on the Tracks   1975 $12
— Third editions have liner notes restored (after they won a Grammy), but in white print
❏ PC33235   Blood on the Tracks   1975 $2000
— First edition cover; with the original rejected version of Side 2, though Side 1 is the standard version; the master number in the trail-off wax on Side 2 is "-1A"; one copy known, but others may exist
❏ PC33235 [B]   Blood on the Tracks   1974 $1500
— mispressed promo (216 copies known) with the Buckinghams on side A
❏ CL1779 [M]   Bob Dylan   1962 $3500
— Six "eye" logos on label; "A New Star on Columbia" sticker on cover and promo stamp on label
❏ CL1779 [M]   Bob Dylan   1962 $300
— Black and red (not orange) label with six white "eye" logos, three at 9 o'clock, three at 3 o'clock; stock copy
❏ CL1779 [M]   Bob Dylan   1963 $40
— Guaranteed High Fidelity" on label
❏ CL1779 [M]   Bob Dylan   1966 $30
— Mono" on label
❏ CS8579 [S]   Bob Dylan   1962 $1500
— Six "eye" logos on label; "A New Star on Columbia" sticker on cover and promo stamp on label
❏ CS8579 [S]   Bob Dylan   1962 $400
— Red and black label with six white "eye" logos, three together at the left, three together at the right, with "Stereo Fidelity" at the top of the label and "Columbia" at the bottom; stock copy
❏ CS8579 [S]   Bob Dylan   1963 $40

— 360 Sound Stereo" in black on label
❏ CS8579 [S]   Bob Dylan   1965 $30
— 360 Sound Stereo" in white on label
❏ CS8579 [S]   Bob Dylan   1970 $15
— Orange label
❏ KCS8579 [S]   Bob Dylan   197? $12
❏ PC8579 [S]   Bob Dylan   198? $10
— Budget-line reissue
❏ JC8579 [S]   Bob Dylan   197? $10
— Some copies of this pressing of the above album may have the song "You're No Good" listed on the label as "She's No Good." No extra premium has been attached to this error as yet.
❏ PC8579 [S]   Bob Dylan   2001 $15
— Reissue on 180-gram vinyl (sealed copies have a sticker indicating this)
❏ PC236067   Bob Dylan at Budokan   1979 $18
❏ PC236067 [DJ]   Bob Dylan at Budokan   1979 $30
— White label promo
❏ CG36067   Bob Dylan at Budokan   198? $15
❏ CL2302/CS 9102   Bob Dylan In Concert   1965 $4000
— Never pressed; value is for a cover slick, some of which were printed; VG value 2000; VG+ value 3000
❏ KCL2663 [M]   Bob Dylan's Greatest Hits   1967 $85
❏ KCS9463 [S]   Bob Dylan's Greatest Hits   1967 $18
— 360 Sound Stereo" label
❏ KCS9463 [S]   Bob Dylan's Greatest Hits   1970 $15
— Orange label
❏ JC9463 [S]   Bob Dylan's Greatest Hits   197? $12
❏ JC9463 [S]   Bob Dylan's Greatest Hits   2001 $15
— Reissue on 180-gram vinyl (sealed copies have a sticker indicating this)
❏ KG31120   Bob Dylan's Greatest Hits, Vol. II   1971 $18
❏ PG31120   Bob Dylan's Greatest Hits, Vol. II   197? $15
❏ CG31120   Bob Dylan's Greatest Hits, Vol. II   198? $12
❏ 2663/9463   Bob Dylan's Greatest Hits Poster   1967 $4
— Almost every copy into the late 1970s came with a poster
❏ 474000 [B]   Bob Dylan -- The 30th Anniversary Concert Celebration   1993 $40
— Albums pressed in US for export to Europe; some stayed here
❏ CL2328 [M]   Bringing It All Back Home   1965 $300
— White label promo
❏ CL2328 [M]   Bringing It All Back Home   1965 $50
— Guaranteed High Fidelity" on label
❏ CL2328 [M]   Bringing It All Back Home   1965 $30
— Mono" on label
❏ CS9128 [S]   Bringing It All Back Home   1965 $40
— 360 Sound Stereo" in black on label
❏ CS9128 [S]   Bringing It All Back Home   1965 $30
— 360 Sound Stereo" in white on label
❏ CS9128 [S]   Bringing It All Back Home   1970 $15
— Orange label
❏ KCS9128 [S]   Bringing It All Back Home   197? $12
❏ JC9128 [S]   Bringing It All Back Home   197? $12
❏ PC9128 [S]   Bringing It All Back Home   198? $10
— Budget-line reissue
❏ PC9128 [S]   Bringing It All Back Home   2001 $15
— Reissue on 180-gram vinyl (sealed copies have a sticker indicating this)
❏ PC33893   Desire   1976 $15
❏ PC33893 [DJ]   Desire   1976 $30
— White label promo
❏ PCQ33893 [Q]   Desire   1976 $150
❏ JC33893   Desire   1977 $12
— No bar code on back cover
❏ JC33893   Desire   1979 $10
— With bar code on back cover
❏ OC40957   Down in the Groove   1988 $12
❏ PC32747   Dylan   1973 $18
— No bar code on cover
❏ PC32747   Dylan   1979 $10
— With bar code on back cover
❏ OC45056   Dylan and the Dead   1989 $15
— With backing by The Grateful Dead
❏ AS1471 [DJ]   Electric Lunch   1982 $30
— Promo-only sampler
❏ FC40110   Empire Burlesque   1985 $12
❏ 88985316001 [B]   Fallen Angels   2016 $25
❏ C53200 [B]   Good As I Been to You   1992 $80
❏ PC34349   Hard Rain   1976 $15
— No bar code on back cover
❏ PC34349 [DJ]   Hard Rain   1976 $30
— White label promo
❏ JC34349   Hard Rain   1977 $12
❏ PC34349   Hard Rain   198? $10
— With bar code on back cover
❏ CL2389 [M]   Highway 61 Revisited   1965 $700
❏ CL2389 [M]   Highway 61 Revisited   1965 $1000
— White label promo with poster)
❏ CS9189 [S]   Highway 61 Revisited   1965 $300
— With alternate take of "From a Buick 6." Matrix number on Side 1 will end in "--1" plus a letter

❏ CS9189 [S]   Highway 61 Revisited   1965 $30
— With "regular" take of "From a Buick 6." Matrix number on Side 1 will end in "--2" or higher, plus a letter; "360 Sound Stereo" on label
❏ CS9189 [S]   Highway 61 Revisited   1970 $15
— Orange label
❏ KCS9189 [S]   Highway 61 Revisited   197? $12
❏ JC9189 [S]   Highway 61 Revisited   197? $12
❏ PC9189 [S]   Highway 61 Revisited   198? $10
— Budget-line reissue
❏ PC9189 [S]   Highway 61 Revisited   2001 $15
— Reissue on 180-gram vinyl (sealed copies have a sticker indicating this)
❏ AS1770 [DJ]   Infidels   1983 $25
— Promo-only sampler
❏ QC38819   Infidels   1983 $12
❏ PC38819   Infidels   1986 $10
— Budget-line reissue
❏ CL2804 [M]   John Wesley Harding   1968 $300
❏ CS9604 [S]   John Wesley Harding   1968 $25
— 360 Sound Stereo" label
❏ CS9604 [S]   John Wesley Harding   1970 $15
— Orange label
❏ KCS9604 [S]   John Wesley Harding   197? $12
❏ JC9604 [S]   John Wesley Harding   197? $12
❏ PC9604 [S]   John Wesley Harding   198? $10
— Budget-line reissue
❏ PC9604 [S]   John Wesley Harding   2001 $15
— Reissue on 180-gram vinyl (sealed copies have a sticker indicating this)
❏ OC40439   Knocked Out Loaded   1986 $12
❏ C285975   Love and Theft   2001 $18
❏ 82876-87606-1   Modern Times   2006 $18
❏ C267000 [B]   MTV Unplugged   1995 $30
❏ KCS9825   Nashville Skyline   1969 $30
— 360 Sound Stereo" label
❏ KCS9825   Nashville Skyline   1970 $15
— Orange label
❏ JC9825   Nashville Skyline   197? $12
❏ PC9825   Nashville Skyline   198? $10
— Budget-line reissue
❏ KCQ32825 [Q]   Nashville Skyline   1973 $50
❏ HC49825   Nashville Skyline   198? $75
— Half-speed mastered edition
❏ KC30290   New Morning   1970 $18
❏ PC30290   New Morning   197? $10
❏ PC30290   New Morning   2001 $15
— Reissue on 180-gram vinyl (sealed copies have a sticker indicating this)
❏ OC45281   Oh Mercy   1989 $15
❏ KC32460   Pat Garrett and Billy the Kid   1973 $18
❏ PC32460   Pat Garrett and Billy the Kid   197? $10
❏ PC37637   Planet Waves   1981 $12
— Reissue of Asylum 7E-1003
❏ FC39944   Real Live   1984 $12
❏ AS422 [DJ]   Renaldo and Clara   1976 $50
— Promo-only sampler from the movie. Authentic copies have a sticker on a white cover; counterfeits have the title printed on the cover
❏ FC36553   Saved   1980 $12
❏ AS798 [DJ]   Saved   1980 $30
— Promo sampler from LP
❏ PC36553   Saved   198? $10
— Budget-line reissue with new cover
❏ C2X30050   Self Portrait   1970 $175
— 360 Sound Stereo" labels
❏ C2X30050   Self Portrait   1970 $25
— Orange labels
❏ P2X30050   Self Portrait   197? $18
❏ CG30050   Self Portrait   198? $15
❏ TC37496   Shot of Love   1981 $12
❏ PC37496   Shot of Love   198? $10
— Budget-line reissue
❏ 88883772551 [B]   Side Tracks   2013 $40
❏ FC36120   Slow Train Coming   1979 $12
❏ FC36120 [DJ]   Slow Train Coming   1979 $30
— White label promo
❏ PC36120   Slow Train Coming   198? $10
— Budget-line reissue
❏ JC35453   Street Legal   1978 $15
❏ JC35453 [DJ]   Street Legal   1978 $30
— White label promo
❏ PC35453   Street Legal   198? $10
❏ 88725457601 [B]   Tempest   2012 $40
❏ PC233682 [DJ]   The Basement Tapes   1975 $40
— White label promo
❏ PC233682   The Basement Tapes   1975 $25
❏ CG33682   The Basement Tapes   198? $15
❏ CK2-65759-1 [B]   The Bootleg Series Vol. 4: Bob Dylan Live 1966, The "Royal Albert Hall" Concert   1999 $120
— Classic Records box set with 12x12 booklet and two records individually packaged in cardboard jackets and sleeves
❏ C2K-87047-1   The Bootleg Series Vol. 5: Rolling Thunder Revue Starring Bob Dylan   2003 $150
— Classic Records box set with 12x12 booklet, three 200-gram 12-inch records individually packaged in cardboard

Number	Title	Yr	NM

jackets and sleeves, a blue vinyl 7-inch single in a picture sleeve, a poster, a souvenir handbill and facsimile tickets to the show

| ❏ C2K-87047-1 | The Bootleg Series Vol. 5: Rolling Thunder Revue Starring Bob Dylan | 2003 | $50 |

—Similar to the other package, but records are pressed on 140-gram vinyl and come in plain paper (rather than lined) sleeves

❏ AS1259 [DJ]	The Dylan London Interview, July 1981	1981	$30
❏ 88985309551 [B]	The Essential Bob Dylan	2016	$40
❏ CL1986 [M]	The Freewheelin' Bob Dylan	1963	$12000

—Guaranteed High Fidelity" on label; plays "Let Me Die in My Footsteps," "Rocks and Gravel," "Talkin' John Birch Blues" and "Gamblin' Willie's Dead Man's Hand." Label does NOT list these. In dead wax, matrix number ends in "--1" followed by a letter; VG value 4000; VG+ value 8000

| ❏ CL1986 [M] | The Freewheelin' Bob Dylan | 1963 | $3000 |

—White label promo; label and timing strip list the deleted tracks but record plays the "correct" tracks; VG value 1000; VG+ value 2000

| ❏ CL1986 [M] | The Freewheelin' Bob Dylan | 1963 | $2000 |

—White label promo; label lists deleted tracks; timing strip lists, and record plays, "correct" tracks

| ❏ CL1986 [M] | The Freewheelin' Bob Dylan | 1966 | $30 |

—"Mono" on label

| ❏ CS8786 [S] | The Freewheelin' Bob Dylan | 1963 | $50 |

—360 Sound Stereo" in black on label (no arrows)

| ❏ CL1986 [M] | The Freewheelin' Bob Dylan | 1963 | $800 |

—White label promo; timing strip lists deleted tracks; label lists, and record plays, "correct" tracks

| ❏ CL1986 [M] | The Freewheelin' Bob Dylan | 1963 | $500 |

—White label promo; label AND timing strip list, and record plays, "correct" tracks

| ❏ CL1986 [M] | The Freewheelin' Bob Dylan | 1963 | $40 |

—Guaranteed High Fidelity" on label; corrected version (record plays what label says)

| ❏ CS8786 [S] | The Freewheelin' Bob Dylan | 1963 | $30000 |

—360 Sound Stereo" in black on label (no arrows); record plays, and label lists, "Let Me Die in My Footsteps," "Rocks and Gravel," "Talkin' John Birch Blues" and "Gamblin' Willie's Dead Man's Hand." No known stereo copies play these without listing them, but just in case, check the trail-off for the numbers "XSM-58719-1A" and "XSM-58720-1A." If the number after the dash is "2" or higher, it's the standard version; VG value 15000; VG+ value 22500

| ❏ CS8786 [S] | The Freewheelin' Bob Dylan | 1964 | $40 |

—360 Sound Stereo" in black on label (with arrows)

| ❏ CS8786 [S] | The Freewheelin' Bob Dylan | 1965 | $30 |

—360 Sound Stereo" in white on label

| ❏ CS8786 [S] | The Freewheelin' Bob Dylan | 1970 | $15 |

—Orange label

| ❏ KCS8786 [S] | The Freewheelin' Bob Dylan | 197? | $12 |
| ❏ PC8786 [S] | The Freewheelin' Bob Dylan | 198? | $10 |

—Budget-line reissue

| ❏ CS8786 [S] | The Freewheelin' Bob Dylan | 197? | $1000 |

—Orange label; unauthorized red vinyl pressing

| ❏ CS8786 [S] | The Freewheelin' Bob Dylan | 1963 | $400 |

—Canadian pressing with the deleted tracks listed on the front cover. The label lists, and the record plays, the "correct" tracks.

| ❏ PC8786 [S] | The Freewheelin' Bob Dylan | 2001 | $15 |

—Reissue on 180-gram vinyl (sealed copies have a sticker indicating this)

| ❏ CL2105 [M] | The Times They Are a-Changin' | 1964 | $1200 |

—White label promo

| ❏ CL2105 [M] | The Times They Are a-Changin' | 1964 | $40 |

—Guaranteed High Fidelity" on label

| ❏ CL2105 [M] | The Times They Are a-Changin' | 1965 | $30 |

—"Mono" on label

Number	Title	Yr	NM

| ❏ CS8905 [S] | The Times They Are a-Changin' | 1964 | $40 |

—360 Sound Stereo" in black on label

| ❏ CS8905 [S] | The Times They Are a-Changin' | 1965 | $30 |

—360 Sound Stereo" in white on label

| ❏ CS8905 [S] | The Times They Are a-Changin' | 1970 | $15 |

—Orange label

| ❏ KCS8905 [S] | The Times They Are a-Changin' | 197? | $12 |
| ❏ PC8905 [S] | The Times They Are a-Changin' | 198? | $10 |

—Budget-line reissue

| ❏ PC8905 [S] | The Times They Are a-Changin' | 2001 | $15 |

—Reissue on 180-gram vinyl (sealed copies have a sticker indicating this)

| ❏ C268556 | Time Out of Mind | 1998 | $18 |
| ❏ CAS2222 [DJ] | Time Passes Slowly | 1985 | $30 |

—Promo-only sampler from Biograph box set

| ❏ C46794 | Under the Red Sky | 1990 | $15 |

ISLAND
| ❏ AB-201 | Before the Flood | 1974 | $40 |

—Error pressing with wrong labels (should be Asylum)

MOBILE FIDELITY
❏ MFSL2-379 [B]	Another Side Of Bob Dylan	2012	$75
❏ MFSL2-426 [B]	Before the Flood	2014	$100
❏ MFSL3-45009 [B]	Blonde On Blonde	2013	$125
❏ MFSL1-381 [B]	Blood On The Tracks	2013	$40
❏ MFSL2-380 [B]	Bringing It All Back Home	2012	$75
❏ MFSL2-416 [B]	Desire	2014	$50
❏ MFSL2-422 [B]	Highway 61 Revisited	2014	$50
❏ MFSL2-423 [B]	John Wesley Harding	2015	$75

—limited edition, 45rpm, remastered

❏ MFSL1-425 [B]	New Morning	2014	$40
❏ MFSL2-382 [B]	The Basement Tapes	2012	$50
❏ MFSL2-378 [B]	The Freewheelin' Bob Dylan	2012	$75
❏ MFSL2-421 [B]	The Times They Are A-Changin'	2014	$75
❏ 1-114	The Times They Are a-Changin'	1982	$85

—Audiophile vinyl

SUNDAZED
| ❏ LP5121 [M] | Another Side of Bob Dylan | 2002 | $18 |

—180-gram reissue of the original mono mix

| ❏ LP5110 [M] | Blonde on Blonde | 2002 | $30 |

—180-gram reissue of the original mono mix

| ❏ LP5120 [M] | Bob Dylan | 2004 | $18 |

—180-gram reissue of the original mono mix

| ❏ LP5156 [M] | Bob Dylan's Greatest Hits | 2003 | $18 |

—180-gram reissue of the original mono mix

| ❏ LP5070 [M] | Bringing It All Back Home | 2001 | $18 |

—180-gram reissue of the original mono mix

| ❏ LP5071 [M] | Highway 61 Revisited | 2001 | $18 |

—180-gram reissue of the original mono mix

| ❏ LP5123 [M] | John Wesley Harding | 2003 | $18 |

—180-gram reissue of the original mono mix

| ❏ LP5115 [M] | The Freewheelin' Bob Dylan | 2001 | $18 |

—180-gram reissue of the original mono mix

| ❏ LP5108 [M] | The Times They Are a-Changin' | 2001 | $18 |

—180-gram reissue of the original mono mix

WARNER BROS./7 ARTS MUSIC
| ❏ XTV221567 [DJ] | Bob Dylan | 1969 | $1500 |

—One-sided publisher's demo with 8 Dylan performances of then-unreleased songs from the "Basement Tapes" era; add $500 if includes sheet music.

DYNAMIC SUPERIORS
MOTOWN
❏ M6-822	Dynamic Superiors	1974	$15
❏ M6-879	Give and Take	1977	$15
❏ M6-841	Pure Pleasure	1975	$15
❏ M6-875	You Name It	1976	$15

DYNAMICS, THE (1)
BLACK GOLD
| ❏ 5001 | What a Shame | 1973 | $15 |

COTILLION
| ❏ SD9009 | First Landing | 1969 | $18 |

DYNAMICS, THE (2)
BOLO
| ❏ BLP-8001 [M] | The Dynamics with Jimmy Hanna | 1964 | $150 |

DYNATONES, THE (1)
HANNA-BARBERA
| ❏ HLP-8509 [M] | The Fife Piper | 1966 | $25 |
| ❏ HST-8509 [S] | The Fife Piper | 1966 | $30 |

DYNATONES, THE (2)
WARNER BROS.
| ❏ 25672 | Shameless | 1988 | $12 |

Number	Title	Yr	NM

DYSON, RONNIE
COLUMBIA
❏ KC31305	Back Home	1972	$15
❏ C30223	(If You Let Me Make Love to You Then) Why Can't I Touch You?	1970	$15
❏ PC34866	Love in All Flavors	1977	$12
❏ KC32211	One Man Band	1973	$15
❏ PC34350	The More You Do	1976	$12

COTILLION
| ❏ 90119 | Brand New Day | 1982 | $12 |

E

E.S.G. (EMERALD, SAPPHIRE AND GOLD)
99 RECORDS
| ❏ 03LP [B] | Come Away With E.S.G. | 1983 | $20 |

E-TYPES, THE
BEAT ROCKET
| ❏ BR103 | Live at the Rainbow Ballroom | 199? | $15 |

E.W.B.
PAID
| ❏ 2007 | We Could Go On Forever | 1981 | $15 |

EAGER, ALLAN
SAVOY
| ❏ MG-9015 [10] | New Trends in Modern Music, Volume 2 | 1952 | $300 |
| ❏ MG-15044 [10] | Tenor Sax | 1954 | $250 |

EAGLE
Also see THE BEACON STREET UNION.
JANUS
| ❏ JLS-3011 | Come Under Nancy's Tent | 1970 | $75 |

EAGLE BRASS BAND, THE
GHB
| ❏ GHB-60 | The Eagle Brass Band | 1978 | $25 |
| ❏ GHB-170 | The Last of the Line | 1986 | $25 |

EAGLES
Popular 1970s California band. Few of its records used the article "The" before the name. Its members had previously been in THE FLYING BURRITO BROTHERS; THE JAMES GANG; LONGBRANCH PENNYWHISTLE; POCO; and SHILOH, among others. Also see DON FELDER; GLENN FREY; DON HENLEY; RANDY MEISNER; TIMOTHY B. SCHMIT; JOE WALSH.

ASYLUM
| ❏ SD5068 | Desperado | 1973 | $15 |

—Clouds label

| ❏ SD5054 | Eagles | 1972 | $18 |

—Gatefold cover; white label with door-in-a-circle logo at top

| ❏ SD5054 | Eagles | 1973 | $15 |

—Regular cover; clouds label

| ❏ 5054 [M] | Eagles | 1972 | $175 |

—Promo only; white label with "d/j copy monaural" sticker on cover

❏ 60205	Eagles Greatest Hits, Volume 2	1982	$12
❏ BB-705	Eagles Live	1980	$15
❏ 7E-1052	Eagles -- Their Greatest Hits 1971-1975	1976	$12
❏ 6E-105	Eagles -- Their Greatest Hits 1971-1975	1977	$10
❏ 7E-1084	Hotel California	1976	$12

| ❏ 6E-103 [B] | Hotel California | 1977 | $10 |

Number	Title	Yr	NM
❑ 7E-1039	One of These Nights	1975	$12
—Clouds label			
❑ EQ1039 [Q]	One of These Nights	1975	$50
❑ 7E-1004	On the Border	1974	$15
—Clouds label			
❑ EQ1004 [Q]	On the Border	1974	$50
❑ 5E-508	The Long Run	1979	$10

DCC COMPACT CLASSICS

❑ LPZ-2051	Eagles -- Their Greatest Hits 1971-1975	1998	$150
—Audiophile vinyl			
❑ LPZ-2043	Hotel California	1997	$120
—Audiophile vinyl			

ELEKTRA

❑ 60422	Anthology of the Eagles	1985	$0
—Canceled			

MOBILE FIDELITY

❑ 1-126	Hotel California	1984	$250
—Audiophile vinyl			

RHINO

❑ RRM1536271 [B]	The Studio Albums 1972-1979	2013	$120

EAGLES OF DEATH METAL
Includes Josh Homme from KYUSS and QUEENS OF THE STONE AGE.

IPECAC

❑ IPC111	Heart On	2009	$25

EAGLIN, SNOOKS

ARHOOLIE

❑ 2014	Possum Up a Simmon Tree	198?	$12

BLACK TOP

❑ BT-1037	Baby, You Can Get Your Gun	1987	$12
❑ BT-1046	Out of Nowhere	198?	$12

BLUESVILLE

❑ BVLP-1046 [M]	That's All Right	1962	$75
—Blue label, silver print			
❑ BVLP-1046 [M]	That's All Right	1964	$30
—Blue label, trident logo at right			

FOLKWAYS

❑ FA-2476 [M]	New Orleans Street Singer	1959	$40

GNP CRECENDO

❑ 10023	Down Yonder	1979	$12

EANES, JIM

JESSUP

❑ 152	Statesman of Bluegrass Music	1977	$18

LEATHER

❑ 7703	Where the Cool Waters Flow	1978	$25

REBEL

❑ 1643	Bluegrass Ballads	198?	$18
❑ 1673	Let Him Lead You	1989	$18
❑ 1653	Reminiscing	1987	$18

ROUNDER

❑ 1016	The Early Days of Bluegrass. Volume 4	1978	$18

RURAL RHYTHM

❑ 221	Jim Eanes	1969	$18
❑ 197	Jim Eanes with Red Smiley and the Bluegrass Cutups	1968	$18

WEBCO

❑ WLPS 0110	Shenandoah Grass, Yesterday and Today	1983	$18

EARDLEY, JON

FANTASY

❑ OJC-1746	From Hollywood to New York	1988	$25
❑ OJC-123	Jon Eardley Seven	198?	$25

NEW JAZZ

❑ NJLP-1105 [10]	Jon Eardley in Hollywood	1954	$300

PRESTIGE

❑ PRLP-207 [10]	Hey There	1955	$250
❑ PRLP-205 [10]	Jon Eardley in Hollywood	1955	$400
❑ PRLP-7033 [M]	Jon Eardley Seven	1956	$500

EARLAND, CHARLES

COLUMBIA

❑ JC36449	Coming to You Live	1980	$25
❑ FC37573	Earland's Jam	1982	$25
❑ FC38547	Earland's Street Themes	1983	$25

FANTASY

❑ OJC-335	Black Talk!	1988	$25
—Reissue of Prestige 7758			

MERCURY

❑ SRM-1-1049	Odyssey	1976	$25
❑ SRM-1-3720	Perception	1978	$25
❑ SRM-1-1149	Revelation	1977	$25

❑ SRM-1-1139	The Great Pyramid	1976	$25

MILESTONE

❑ M-9165	Front Burner	1988	$25
❑ M-9175	Third Degree Burn	1989	$25

MUSE

❑ MR-5181	Infant Eyes	1980	$25
❑ MR-5240	In the Pocket	1984	$25
❑ MR-5156	Mama Roots	1979	$25
❑ MR-5201	Pleasant Afternoon	1981	$25
❑ MR-5126	Smokin'	1978	$25

PRESTIGE

❑ PRST-7815	Black Drops	1970	$35
❑ 10029	Black Drops	1971	$25
—Reissue of 7815			
❑ PRST-7758	Black Talk!	1970	$50
❑ 10024	Black Talk!	1971	$25
—Reissue of 7758			
❑ 2501	Burners	1982	$25
❑ 10061	Charles III	1973	$30
❑ 10041	Intensity	1972	$30
❑ 10095	Kharma	1975	$30
❑ 66002	Leaving This Planet	1974	$35
❑ 10051	Live at the Lighthouse	1972	$30
❑ 10009	Living Black!	1971	$30
❑ 10018	Soul Story	1971	$30

TRIP

❑ 5004	Charles Earland	1974	$25

EARLE, STEVE

EPIC

❑ FE39226	Early Tracks	1987	$14

MCA

❑ R143506	Exit 0	1987	$15
—BMG Direct Marketing edition			
❑ 5998	Exit 0	1987	$12
❑ R154072	Guitar Town	1986	$15
—RCA Music Service edition			
❑ 5713	Guitar Town	1986	$12

UNI

❑ R100679	Copperhead Road	1988	$15
—BMG Direct Marketing edition			
❑ 7	Copperhead Road	1988	$12

EARLS, THE (1)

CHANCE

❑ 1001	The Earls Today	1983	$15

OLD TOWN

❑ LP-104 [M]	Remember Me Baby	1963	$500
—Counterfeit identification: Counterfeits have more than 1-inch trailoffs or as little as 1/2 inch trailoffs; legitimate copies have 5/8- to 3/4-inch trailoff			

WOODBURY

❑ 104	Remember Me Baby	1976	$18

EARTH, WIND, AND FIRE

ARC

❑ KC236795	Faces	1980	$15
❑ FC35730	I Am	1979	$12
❑ HC45730	I Am	1981	$30
—Half-speed mastered edition			
❑ PC35730	I Am	1984	$10
—Budget-line reissue			
❑ TC37548	Raise!	1981	$12
❑ HC47548	Raise!	1982	$30
—Half-speed mastered edition			
❑ PC37548	Raise!	1984	$10
—Budget-line reissue			
❑ FC35647	The Best of Earth, Wind & Fire, Vol. 1	1978	$12
❑ HC45647	The Best of Earth, Wind & Fire, Vol. 1	1981	$30
—Half-speed mastered edition			

COLUMBIA

❑ JC34905	All 'N All	1977	$15
❑ PC34905	All 'N All	198?	$10
—Budget-line reissue			
❑ QC38980	Electric Universe	1983	$12
❑ PG33694	Gratitude	1975	$18
—No bar code			
❑ PG33694	Gratitude	198?	$12
—Budget-line reissue with bar code			
❑ KC32194	Head to the Sky	1973	$15
❑ CQ32194 [Q]	Head to the Sky	1973	$30
❑ PC32194	Head to the Sky	197?	$10
—Reissue			
❑ C45268	Heritage	1990	$18
❑ KC31702	Last Days and Time	1972	$18
❑ PC31702	Last Days and Time	197?	$10
—Reissue			
❑ KC32712	Open Our Eyes	1974	$15
❑ CQ32712 [Q]	Open Our Eyes	1974	$30

❑ PC32712 [B]	Open Our Eyes	197?	$10
—Reissue			
❑ TC38367	Powerlight	1983	$12
❑ HC48367	Powerlight	1983	$40
—Half-speed mastered edition			
❑ PC38367	Powerlight	1984	$10
—Budget-line reissue			
❑ PC34241	Spirit	1976	$15
—No bar code			
❑ PCQ34241 [Q]	Spirit	1976	$40
❑ PC34241	Spirit	198?	$10
—Budget-line reissue with bar code			
❑ PC33280	That's the Way of the World	1975	$15
—No bar code			
❑ PC33280	That's the Way of the World	198?	$10
—Budget-line reissue with bar code			
❑ PCQ33280 [Q]	That's the Way of the World	1975	$30
❑ OC45013	The Best of Earth, Wind & Fire, Vol. II	1988	$12
❑ FC40596	Touch the World	1987	$12

MOBILE FIDELITY

❑ 1-159	That's the Way of the World	198?	$30
—Audiophile vinyl			

PAIR

❑ PDL2-1064	Beat It to Life	1986	$15

WARNER BROS.

❑ 2WS2798	Another Time	1974	$25
—Burbank" palm trees labels			
❑ WS1905	Earth, Wind, and Fire	1971	$25
—Green label			
❑ WS1958	The Need of Love	1971	$25
—Green label			

EARTH AND FIRE

RED BULLET

❑ RBLP-3000	Earth and Fire	197?	$18

EARTH ISLAND

PHILPS

❑ PHS600340	We Must Survive	1970	$30

EARTH OPERA

ELEKTRA

❑ EKS-74016 [B]	Earth Opera	1968	$30
❑ EKS-74038	The Great American Eagle Tragedy	1969	$25

EARTH QUAKE

A&M

❑ SP-4308	Earth Quake	1971	$18
❑ SP-4337	Why Don't You Try Me?	1972	$18

BESERKLEY

❑ 0047	8.5	1976	$15
❑ PZ34754	8.5	1977	$12
—Reissue of 0047			
❑ 0054	Leveled	1977	$15
❑ PZ34801	Leveled	1977	$12
—Reissue of 0054			
❑ 0045	Rockin' the World	1975	$15
❑ PZ34752	Rockin' the World	1977	$12
—Reissue of 0045			
❑ BZ-10065	Two Years in a Padded Cell	1979	$12

EARTHEN VESSEL

NRS

❑ 2587 [B]	Hard Rock / Everlasting Life	1968	$2000

EARWOOD, MUNDO

EXCELSIOR

❑ 88006	Mundo Earwood	1981	$12

Number	Title	Yr	NM

EASLEY, BILL
SUNNYSIDE
| ❑ SSC-1022 | Wind Inventions | 1988 | $25 |

EASON, GERALD, AND ROBERT KNOTT
BARONET
| ❑ BS1003 [S] | Organ and Chimes for Christmas | 1961 | $18 |

— *Textured silvery cover*

EAST
CAPITOL
| ❑ ST-11083 | East | 1972 | $30 |

EAST NEW YORK ENSEMBLE DE PARIS, THE
FOLKWAYS
| ❑ F-33867 | At the Helm | 1974 | $40 |

EAST OF EDEN
DERAM
| ❑ DES18023 | Mercator Projected | 1969 | $25 |
| ❑ DES18043 | Snafu | 1970 | $25 |
HARVEST
| ❑ SW-806 | East of Eden | 1971 | $25 |

EAST SIDE KIDS, THE
UNI
| ❑ 73032 | The Tiger and the Lamb | 1968 | $30 |

EASTERN REBELLION
TIMELESS
| ❑ 306 | Eastern Rebellion | 1976 | $35 |
| ❑ 318 | Eastern Rebellion II | 1977 | $35 |

EASTMAN-ROCHESTER "POPS" ORCHESTRA (FREDERICK FENNELL, CONDUCTOR)
MERCURY LIVING PRESENCE
| ❑ SR90219 [S] | Grainger: Country Gardens | 196? | $50 |

— *Maroon label, no "Vendor: Mercury Record Corporation*
| ❑ SR90144 [S] | Hi-Fi A La Espanola | 196? | $1000 |

— *Maroon label, no "Vendor: Mercury Record Corporation*
| ❑ SR90144 [S] | Hi-Fi A La Espanola | 199? | $30 |

— *Classic Records reissue*
| ❑ SR90271 [S] | Marches for Orchestra | 196? | $40 |

— *Maroon label, no "Vendor: Mercury Record Corporation*
| ❑ SR90271 [S] | Marches for Orchestra | 196? | $30 |

— *Maroon label, with "Vendor: Mercury Record Corporation*
| ❑ SR90043 [S] | Music of Leroy Anderson, Vol. 2 | 1959 | $30 |

— *Maroon label, no "Vendor: Mercury Record Corporation*
| ❑ SR90043 [S] | Music of Leroy Anderson, Vol. 2 | 196? | $25 |

— *Maroon label, with "Vendor: Mercury Record Corporation*
| ❑ SR90400 [S] | Music of Leroy Anderson, Volume 3 | 196? | $100 |

— *Maroon label, no "Vendor: Mercury Record Corporation*
| ❑ SR90400 [S] | Music of Leroy Anderson, Volume 3 | 196? | $50 |

— *Maroon label, with "Vendor: Mercury Record Corporation*
| ❑ SR90222 [S] | Popovers | 196? | $25 |

— *Maroon label, no "Vendor: Mercury Record Corporation*

EASTMAN-ROCHESTER ORCHESTRA (HOWARD HANSON, CONDUCTOR)
MERCURY LIVING PRESENCE
| ❑ SR90224 [S] | Barber: Medea; Capricorn Concerto | 196? | $25 |

— *Maroon label, no "Vendor: Mercury Record Corporation*
| ❑ SR90223 [S] | Bloch: Concerti Grossi No. 1 and 2 | 196? | $30 |

— *Maroon label, no "Vendor: Mercury Record Corporation*
| ❑ SR90223 [S] | Bloch: Concerti Grossi No. 1 and 2 | 196? | $40 |

— *Maroon label, with "Vendor: Mercury Record Corporation";* *a rare instance where the second edition is more sought-after than the first*
| ❑ SR90223 [S] | Bloch: Concerti Grossi No. 1 and 2 | 196? | $25 |

— *Third edition: Dark red (not maroon) label*
| ❑ SR90286 [S] | Bloch: Schelomo; Herbert: Cello Concerto No. 2 | 196? | $50 |

— *Maroon label, no "Vendor: Mercury Record Corporation*
| ❑ SR90136 [S] | Carpenter: Adventures in a Perambulator; Phillips: Selections from McGuffey's Readers | 1960 | $150 |

— *Maroon label, no "Vendor: Mercury Record Corporation*
| ❑ SR90018 [S] | Chadwick: Symphonic Sketches | 1959 | $30 |

— *Maroon label, no "Vendor: Mercury Record Corporation*
| ❑ SR90134 [S] | Fiesta in Hi-Fi | 1960 | $150 |

— *Maroon label, no "Vendor: Mercury Record Corporation*
| ❑ SR90257 [S] | Ginastera: Overture to a Creole "Faust"; Guarnieri: Three Dances; Still: Sahdji Ballet | 196? | $250 |

— *Maroon label, no "Vendor: Mercury Record Corporation*
| ❑ SR90263 [S] | Gould, Morton: Fall River Legend; Spirituals | 196? | $40 |

— *Maroon label, no "Vendor: Mercury Record Corporation*
| ❑ SR90263 [S] | Gould, Morton: Fall River Legend; Spirituals | 196? | $25 |

— *Maroon label, with "Vendor: Mercury Record Corporation*
| ❑ SR90049 [S] | Grofe: Grand Canyon Suite; Mississippi Suite | 1959 | $30 |

— *Maroon label, no "Vendor: Mercury Record Corporation*
| ❑ SR90150 [S] | Hanson: Elegy in Memory of Koussevitzky; Song of Democracy; Lane: 4 Songs | 196? | $150 |

— *Maroon label, no "Vendor: Mercury Record Corporation*
| ❑ SR90150 [S] | Hanson: Elegy in Memory of Koussevitzky; Song of Democracy; Lane: 4 Songs | 196? | $50 |

— *Maroon label, with "Vendor: Mercury Record Corporation*
| ❑ SR90430 [S] | Hanson: Piano Concerto; Mosaics; LaMontaine: Birds of Paradise | 1965 | $25 |

— *Maroon label, no "Vendor: Mercury Record Corporation*
| ❑ SR90430 [S] | Hanson: Piano Concerto; Mosaics; LaMontaine: Birds of Paradise | 196? | $25 |

— *Maroon label, with "Vendor: Mercury Record Corporation*
| ❑ SR90165 [S] | Hanson: Symphony No. 1 "Nordic"; Fantasy Variations on a Theme of Youth | 196? | $40 |

— *Maroon label, no "Vendor: Mercury Record Corporation*
| ❑ SR90165 [S] | Hanson: Symphony No. 1 "Nordic"; Fantasy Variations on a Theme of Youth | 196? | $25 |

— *Maroon label, with "Vendor: Mercury Record Corporation*
| ❑ SR90192 [S] | Hanson: Symphony No. 2 "Romantic"; Lament for Beowulf | 196? | $30 |

— *Maroon label, no "Vendor: Mercury Record Corporation*
| ❑ SR90192 [S] | Hanson: Symphony No. 2 "Romantic"; Lament for Beowulf | 196? | $25 |

— *Maroon label, with "Vendor: Mercury Record Corporation*
| ❑ SR90449 [S] | Hanson: Symphony No. 3; MacDowell: Symphony No. 1 | 1965 | $40 |

— *Maroon label, no "Vendor: Mercury Record Corporation*
| ❑ SR90163 [S] | Herbert: Cello Concerto; Peter: Sinfonia in G | 196? | $40 |

— *Maroon label, no "Vendor: Mercury Record Corporation*
| ❑ SR90149 [S] | Ives: Three Places in New England; Symphony No. 3 | 196? | $40 |

— *Maroon label, no "Vendor: Mercury Record Corporation*
| ❑ SR90149 [S] | Ives: Three Places in New England; Symphony No. 3 | 196? | $25 |

— *Maroon label, with "Vendor: Mercury Record Corporation*
| ❑ SR90147 [S] | Kennan: Three Pieces; Rogers: Once Upon a Time; Bergama: Gold and the Senor Commandante | 196? | $250 |

— *Maroon label, no "Vendor: Mercury Record Corporation*
| ❑ SR90277 [S] | Loeffler: Deux Rapsodies; Barlow: Night Song; McCauley: Five Miniatures | 196? | $250 |

— *Maroon label, no "Vendor: Mercury Record Corporation*
| ❑ SR90103 [S] | McPhee: Tabuh-Tauhan; Sessions: The Black Maskers | 196? | $300 |

— *Maroon label, no "Vendor: Mercury Record Corporation*
| ❑ SR90053 [S] | Music for Quiet Listening | 1959 | $75 |

— *Maroon label, no "Vendor: Mercury Record Corporation*
| ❑ SR90053 [S] | Music for Quiet Listening | 196? | $50 |

— *Maroon label, with "Vendor: Mercury Record Corporation*
| ❑ SR90206 [S] | Piston: The Incredible Flutist; Moore: Pageant of P.T. Barnum | 196? | $40 |

— *Maroon label, no "Vendor: Mercury Record Corporation*
| ❑ SR90206 [S] | Piston: The Incredible Flutist; Moore: Pageant of P.T. Barnum | 196? | $25 |

— *Maroon label, with "Vendor: Mercury Record Corporation*
| ❑ SR90379 [S] | Schuman: New England Triptych; Mennin: Symphony No. 5; Griffes: Poem for Flute and Orchestra | 196? | $50 |

— *Maroon label, no "Vendor: Mercury Record Corporation*
| ❑ SR90379 [S] | Schuman: New England Triptych; Mennin: Symphony No. 5; Griffes: Poem for Flute and Orchestra | 196? | $25 |

— *Maroon label, with "Vendor: Mercury Record Corporation*
| ❑ SR90175 [S] | The Composer and His Orchestra | 196? | $30 |

— *Maroon label, no "Vendor: Mercury Record Corporation*
| ❑ SR90175 [S] | The Composer and His Orchestra | 196? | $25 |

— *Maroon label, with "Vendor: Mercury Record Corporation*
| ❑ SR90267 [S] | The Composer and His Orchestra, Volume 2 | 196? | $30 |

— *Maroon label, no "Vendor: Mercury Record Corporation*
| ❑ SR90267 [S] | The Composer and His Orchestra, Volume 2 | 196? | $25 |

— *Maroon label, with "Vendor: Mercury Record Corporation*
| ❑ SR90429 [S] | Thomson: Symphony on a Hymn Tune; The Feast of Love; Hanson: Four Psalms | 196? | $40 |

— *Maroon label, no "Vendor: Mercury Record Corporation*
| ❑ SR90429 [S] | Thomson: Symphony on a Hymn Tune; The Feast of Love; Hanson: Four Psalms | 196? | $25 |

— *Maroon label, with "Vendor: Mercury Record Corporation*
| ❑ SR90429 [S] | Thomson: Symphony on a Hymn Tune; The Feast of Love; Hanson: Four Psalms | 196? | $25 |

— *Third edition: Dark red (not maroon) label*

EASTMAN-ROCHESTER PHILHARMONIA (HOWARD HANSON, CONDUCTOR)
MERCURY LIVING PRESENCE
| ❑ SR90299 [S] | Musical Diplomats USA | 196? | $30 |

— *Maroon label, no "Vendor: Mercury Record Corporation*
| ❑ SR90357 [S] | The Composer and His Orchestra, Volume 3 | 196? | $25 |

— *Maroon label, no "Vendor: Mercury Record Corporation*

EASTMAN-ROCHESTER WIND ENSEMBLE (A. CLYDE ROLLER, CONDUCTOR)
MERCURY LIVING PRESENCE
| ❑ SR90366 [S] | Hovhaness: Symphony No. 4; Giannini: Symphony No. 3 | 196? | $100 |

— *Maroon label, no "Vendor: Mercury Record Corporation*
| ❑ SR90366 [S] | Hovhaness: Symphony No. 4; Giannini: Symphony No. 3 | 196? | $40 |

— *Maroon label, with "Vendor: Mercury Record Corporation*
| ❑ SR90366 [S] | Hovhaness: Symphony No. 4; Giannini: Symphony No. 3 | 196? | $25 |

— *Third edition: Dark red (not maroon) label*

EASTMAN-ROCHESTER WIND ENSEMBLE (FREDERICK FENNELL, CONDUCTOR)
MERCURY LIVING PRESENCE
| ❑ SR90256 [S] | Ballet for Band | 196? | $180 |

— *Maroon label, no "Vendor: Mercury Record Corporation*
| ❑ SR90256 [S] | Ballet for Band | 196? | $100 |

— *Maroon label, with "Vendor: Mercury Record Corporation*
| ❑ SR90197 [S] | British Band Classics, Vol. 2 | 196? | $175 |

— *Maroon label, no "Vendor: Mercury Record Corporation*
| ❑ SR90197 [S] | British Band Classics, Vol. 2 | 196? | $40 |

— *Maroon label, no "Vendor: Mercury Record Corporation*
| ❑ SR90197 [S] | British Band Classics, Vol. 2 | 196? | $25 |

— *Third edition: Dark red (not maroon) label*
| ❑ SR90390 [S] | Broadway Marches | 196? | $25 |

— *Maroon label, no "Vendor: Mercury Record Corporation*
| ❑ SR90221 [S] | Diverse Winds | 196? | $120 |

— *Maroon label, no "Vendor: Mercury Record Corporation*
| ❑ SR90245 [S] | Gabrieli Music for Wind Instruments | 196? | $25 |

— *Maroon label, no "Vendor: Mercury Record Corporation*
| ❑ SR90220 [S] | Gould: West Point Symphony; Bennett: Songs; Williams: Fanfare and Allegro; Work: Autumn Walk | 196? | $80 |

— *Maroon label, no "Vendor: Mercury Record Corporation*
| ❑ SR90220 [S] | Gould: West Point Symphony; Bennett: Songs; Williams: Fanfare and Allegro; Work: Autumn Walk | 196? | $50 |

— *Maroon label, with "Vendor: Mercury Record Corporation*
| ❑ SR90207 [S] | Hands Across the Sea | 196? | $50 |

— *Maroon label, no "Vendor: Mercury Record Corporation*
| ❑ SR90143 [S] | Hindemith: Symphony in B-flat; Schoenberg: Theme and Variations; Stravinsky: Symphony of Wind Instru | 196? | $75 |

— *Maroon label, no "Vendor: Mercury Record Corporation*
| ❑ SR90143 [S] | Hindemith: Symphony in B-flat; Schoenberg: Theme and Variations; Stravinsky: Symphony of Wind Instru | 196? | $30 |

— *Maroon label, with "Vendor: Mercury Record Corporation*
| ❑ SR90105 [S] | Marching Along | 1960 | $25 |

— *Maroon label, no "Vendor: Mercury Record Corporation*
| ❑ SR90105 [S] | Marching Along | 196? | $40 |

— *Maroon label, with "Vendor: Mercury Record Corporation";* *a rare instance where the second edition is more sought-after than the first*
| ❑ SR90170 [S] | March Time | 196? | $25 |

— *Maroon label, no "Vendor: Mercury Record Corporation*
| ❑ SR90176 [S] | Mozart: Serenade No. 10 in E-flat | 196? | $50 |

— *Maroon label, no "Vendor: Mercury Record Corporation*
| ❑ SR90176 [S] | Mozart: Serenade No. 10 in E-flat | 196? | $30 |

— *Maroon label, no "Vendor: Mercury Record Corporation*
| ❑ SR90112 [S] | Ruffles and Flourishes | 1960 | $30 |

— *Maroon label, no "Vendor: Mercury Record Corporation*
| ❑ SR90314 [S] | Screamers (Circus Marches) | 196? | $40 |

— *Maroon label, no "Vendor: Mercury Record Corporation*
| ❑ SR90314 [S] | Screamers (Circus Marches) | 196? | $30 |

— *Maroon label, with "Vendor: Mercury Record Corporation*
| ❑ SR90284 [S] | Sousa on Review | 196? | $30 |

— *Maroon label, no "Vendor: Mercury Record Corporation*
| ❑ SR90284 [S] | Sousa on Review | 196? | $100 |

— *Maroon label, with "Vendor: Mercury Record Corporation";*

Number	Title	Yr	NM

a rare instance where the second edition is more sought-after than the first

| ❑ SR90264 [S] | Sousa Sound Off | 196? | $30 |

—Maroon label, no "Vendor: Mercury Record Corporation"

| ❑ SR90111 [S] | Spirit of '76: Music for Fifes and Drums | 1960 | $40 |

—Maroon label, no "Vendor: Mercury Record Corporation"

| ❑ SR90276 [S] | Wagner for Band | 196? | $80 |

—Maroon label, no "Vendor: Mercury Record Corporation"

| ❑ SR90276 [S] | Wagner for Band | 196? | $50 |

—Maroon label, with "Vendor: Mercury Record Corporation" (second edition is more sought after than the first)

| ❑ SR90276 [S] | Wagner for Band | 196? | $40 |

—Third edition: Dark red (not maroon) label

| ❑ SR90173 [S] | Winds in Hi-Fi | 196? | $100 |

—Maroon label, no "Vendor: Mercury Record Corporation"

| ❑ SR90173 [S] | Winds in Hi-Fi | 196? | $50 |

—Maroon label, with "Vendor: Mercury Record Corporation"

| ❑ SR90173 [S] | Winds in Hi-Fi | 196? | $25 |

—Third edition: Dark red (not maroon) label

EASTON, ELLIOT
ELEKTRA

| ❑ 60393 | Change No Change | 1985 | $12 |

EASTON, SHEENA
EMI

| ❑ E1-593338 | The Sheena Easton Collection | 1989 | $18 |

— Columbia House edition

EMI AMERICA

| ❑ ST-17132 | A Private Heaven | 1984 | $10 |
| ❑ R144428 | A Private Heaven | 1984 | $12 |

— RCA Music Service edition

| ❑ ST-517132 | A Private Heaven | 1984 | $12 |

— Columbia House edition

| ❑ ST-17101 | Best Kept Secret | 1983 | $10 |
| ❑ ST-517101 | Best Kept Secret | 1983 | $12 |

— Columbia House edition

| ❑ R163514 | Best Kept Secret | 1983 | $12 |

— RCA Music Service edition

❑ SJ-17173	Do You	1985	$10
❑ ST-17080	Madness, Money and Music	1982	$10
❑ R114422	Madness, Money and Music	1982	$12

— RCA Music Service edition

| ❑ ST-17049 | Sheena Easton | 1981 | $10 |
| ❑ ST-517049 | Sheena Easton | 1981 | $12 |

— Columbia House edition

| ❑ R133902 | Sheena Easton | 1981 | $12 |

— RCA Music Service edition

| ❑ SW-17061 | You Could Have Been with Me | 1981 | $10 |
| ❑ SW-517061 | You Could Have Been with Me | 1981 | $12 |

— Columbia House version

MCA

| ❑ 42249 | The Lover in Me | 1988 | $12 |
| ❑ 10131 | What Comes Naturally | 1991 | $15 |

EASTON, TED
CIRCLE

| ❑ 12 | A Salute to Satchmo | 198? | $25 |

EASTWOOD, CLINT
CAMEO

| ❑ C-1056 [M] | Clint Eastwood Sings Cowboy Favorites | 1963 | $150 |
| ❑ SC-1056 [S] | Clint Eastwood Sings Cowboy Favorites | 1963 | $175 |

EASY RIDERS, THE
See TERRY GILKYSON.

EASY RIDERS JAZZ BAND, THE
JAZZ CRUSADE

| ❑ 1002 | My Life Will Be Sweeter Someday | 1963 | $40 |

EASYBEATS, THE
RARE EARTH

| ❑ 517 | Easy Ridin' | 1970 | $0 |

—Canceled

RHINO

| ❑ RNLP-124 | The Best of the Easybeats | 1985 | $10 |

UNITED ARTISTS

| ❑ UAS6667 [P] | Falling Off the Edge of the World | 1968 | $40 |

—Women" is rechanneled.

| ❑ UAL3588 [M] | Friday on My Mind | 1967 | $40 |

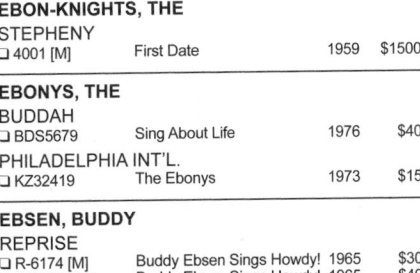

| ❑ UAS6588 [P] | Friday on My Mind | 1967 | $50 |

—Make You Feel Alright" is rechanneled.

VARESE SARABANDE

| ❑ 302 067 418 1 [M] | Good Friday | 2016 | $25 |

— 180g

EATON, CLEVELAND
GAMBLE

| ❑ KZ32077 [B] | Half and Half | 1973 | $75 |

OVATION

| ❑ OV-1703 | Instant Hip | 1974 | $25 |
| ❑ OV-1742 | Keep Love Alive | 197? | $35 |

EATON, CONNIE, AND DAVE PEEL
CHART

| ❑ 1034 | Hit the Road Jack | 1970 | $18 |

EATON, JOHN
CHIAROSCURO

| ❑ CH-174 | Like Old Times | 1977 | $30 |
| ❑ CH-137 | Solo Piano | 1975 | $30 |

EATON, JOHNNY
COLUMBIA

| ❑ CL737 [M] | College Jazz: Modern | 1956 | $40 |
| ❑ CL996 [M] | Far Out, Far In | 1957 | $40 |

EAVES, HUBERT
INNER CITY

| ❑ IC-6012 | Esteric Funk | 1976 | $25 |

EBON-KNIGHTS, THE
STEPHENY

| ❑ 4001 [M] | First Date | 1959 | $1500 |

EBONYS, THE
BUDDAH

| ❑ BDS5679 | Sing About Life | 1976 | $40 |

PHILADELPHIA INT'L.

| ❑ KZ32419 | The Ebonys | 1973 | $15 |

EBSEN, BUDDY
REPRISE

| ❑ R-6174 [M] | Buddy Ebsen Sings Howdy! | 1965 | $30 |
| ❑ RS-6174 [S] | Buddy Ebsen Sings Howdy! | 1965 | $40 |

ECHO AND THE BUNNYMEN
SIRE

| ❑ SRK6096 [B] | Crocodiles | 1980 | $18 |
| ❑ 25597 [B] | Echo and the Bunnymen | 1987 | $15 |

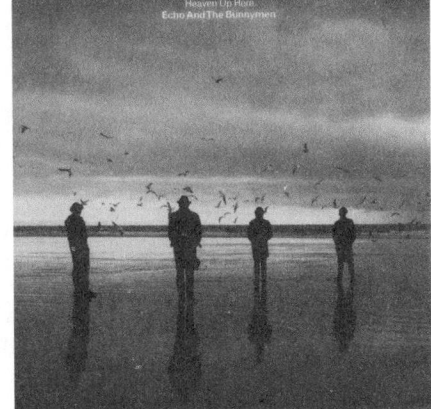

❑ SRK3569 [B]	Heaven Up Here	1981	$18
❑ 25084 [B]	Ocean Rain	1984	$18
❑ 23770 [B]	Porcupine	1983	$18
❑ 25360	Songs to Learn and Sing	1986	$15
❑ 23987 [EP]	The Echo	1983	$12

ECHOES OF HARLEM
ROYALE

| ❑ LP-18128 [10] | Echoes of Harlem | 195? | $100 |

ECKSTINE, BILLY
AUDIO LAB

| ❑ AL-1549 [M] | Mr. B | 1960 | $250 |

DELUXE

| ❑ FA-2010 [M] | Billy Eckstine and His Orchestra | 195? | $100 |

EMARCY

❑ MG-36129 [M]	Billy Eckstine's Imagination	1958	$250
❑ MG-26025 [10]	Blues for Sale	1954	$300
❑ MG-36029 [M]	Blues for Sale	1955	$350
❑ MG-36010 [M]	I Surrender, Dear	1955	$300
❑ MG-26027 [10]	The Love Songs of Mr. B	1954	$300
❑ MG-36030 [M]	The Love Songs of Mr. B	1955	$250

ENTERPRISE

❑ ENS-1017	Feel the Warm	1971	$35
❑ ENS-5004	Senior Soul	1972	$35
❑ ENS-1013	Stormy	1971	$35

FORUM

| ❑ F-9027 [M] | Once More with Feeling | 196? | $35 |
| ❑ SF-9027 [S] | Once More with Feeling | 196? | $35 |

KING

| ❑ 295-12 [10] | The Great Mr. B | 1953 | $300 |

LION

| ❑ L-70057 [M] | The Best of Billy Eckstine | 1958 | $75 |

MERCURY

❑ MG-20674 [M]	Billy Eckstine and Quincy Jones at Basin St. East	1962	$150
❑ SR-60674 [S]	Billy Eckstine and Quincy Jones at Basin St. East	1962	$150
❑ MG-20333 [M]	Billy's Best	1958	$150
❑ SR-60086 [S]	Billy's Best	1958	$175
❑ MG-20637 [M]	Broadway, Bongos and Mr. B	1961	$150
❑ SR-60637 [S]	Broadway, Bongos and Mr. B	1961	$150
❑ MG-20736 [M]	Don't Worry 'Bout Me	1962	$150
❑ SR-60736 [S]	Don't Worry 'Bout Me	1962	$150
❑ MG-20796 [M]	The Golden Hits of Billy Eckstine	1963	$150
❑ SR-60796 [S]	The Golden Hits of Billy Eckstine	1963	$150

METRO

| ❑ M-537 [M] | Everything I Have Is Yours | 1965 | $300 |
| ❑ MS-537 [R] | Everything I Have Is Yours | 1965 | $175 |

MGM

❑ E-153 [10]	Billy Eckstine Sings Rodgers & Hammerstein	1952	$300
❑ E-548 [10]	Favorites	1951	$160
❑ E-257 [10]	I Let a Song Go Out of My Heart	1954	$175
❑ E-3176 [M]	Mr. B with a Beat	1955	$150
❑ E-3209 [M]	Rendezvous	1955	$150
❑ E-523 [10]	Songs by Billy Eckstine	1951	$160
❑ E-219 [10]	Tenderly	1953	$300
❑ E-3275 [M]	That Old Feeling	1956	$150

MOTOWN

❑ MS677	For Love of Ivy	1969	$75
❑ M646 [M]	My Way	1966	$50
❑ MS646 [S]	My Way	1966	$75
❑ M632 [M]	Prime of My Life	1965	$50
❑ MS632 [S]	Prime of My Life	1965	$75

NATIONAL

| ❑ NLP-2001 [10] | Billy Eckstine Sings | 1949 | $250 |

REGENT

❑ MG-6054 [M]	My Deep Blue Dream	1957	$150
❑ MG-6052 [M]	Prisoner of Love	1957	$150
❑ MG-6053 [M]	The Duke, the Blues and Me	1957	$150
❑ MG-6058 [M]	You Call It Madness	1957	$150

ROULETTE

❑ R-25052 [M]	No Cover, No Minimum	1961	$75
❑ SR-25052 [S]	No Cover, No Minimum	1961	$75
❑ R-25104 [M]	Once More with Feeling	1962	$75
❑ SR-25104 [S]	Once More with Feeling	1962	$75

SAVOY

| ❑ 1127 | Billy Eckstine Sings | 1979 | $30 |
| ❑ SJL-2214 | Mr. B and the Band/The Savoy Sessions | 1976 | $35 |

TRIP

| ❑ 5567 | The Modern Sound of Mr. B | 197? | $25 |

VERVE

| ❑ 819442-1 | Everything I Have Is Yours: The MGM Years | 1986 | $35 |

XANADU

| ❑ 207 | I Want to Talk About You | 1987 | $25 |

Number	Title	Yr	NM

ECSTASY, PASSION AND PAIN
ROULETTE
| ❏ SR-3013 | Ecstasy, Passion and Pain | 1974 | $18 |

EDDIE AND BETTY
WARNER BROS.
| ❏ W1350 [M] | Nightlife for Daydreamers | 1959 | $75 |
| ❏ WS1350 [S] | Nightlife for Daydreamers | 1959 | $75 |

EDDIE AND THE SUBTITLES
13TH STORY
| ❏ MR3301 | Dead Drunks Don't Dance | 1983 | $30 |
(NO LABEL)
| ❏ 0(no cat #) | Skeletons in the Closet | 1981 | $40 |

EDDY, DUANE
CAPITOL
| ❏ ST-12567 | Duane Eddy | 1987 | $15 |
COLPIX
❏ CP-490 [M]	Duane A-Go-Go	1965	$30
❏ CPS-490 [S]	Duane A-Go-Go	1965	$40
❏ CPL-494 [M]	Duane Eddy Does Bob Dylan	1965	$30
❏ SCP-494 [S]	Duane Eddy Does Bob Dylan	1965	$40
JAMIE
❏ JLPM-3014 [M]	$1,000,000.00 Worth of Twang	1960	$40
❏ JLPS-3014 [S]	$1,000,000.00 Worth of Twang	1960	$80
—All but one song -- "Up and Down" -- is in true stereo			
❏ JLPM-3021 [M]	$1,000,000.00 Worth of Twang, Volume 2	1962	$40
❏ JLPS-3021 [R]	$1,000,000.00 Worth of Twang, Volume 2	1962	$30
❏ JLPM-3026 [M]	16 Greatest Hits	1964	$40
❏ JLPS-3026 [R]	16 Greatest Hits	1964	$30
❏ JLPM-3025 [M]	Duane Eddy & the Rebels -- In Person	1963	$30
❏ JLPS-3025 [S]	Duane Eddy & the Rebels -- In Person	1963	$40
❏ T-90663 [M]	Duane Eddy & the Rebels -- In Person	1965	$40
—Capitol Record Club edition			
❏ ST-90663 [S]	Duane Eddy & the Rebels -- In Person	1965	$50
—Capitol Record Club edition			
❏ JLPM-3006 [M]	Especially for You...	1959	$75
❏ JLPS-3006 [S]	Especially for You...	1959	$100
❏ JLPM-3019 [M]	Girls! Girls! Girls!	1961	$40
❏ JLPS-3019 [R]	Girls! Girls! Girls!	1961	$30
❏ JLP-3000 [M]	Have "Twangy" Guitar -- Will Travel	1958	$175
—Duane sitting with guitar case, title on cover in white (1st)			
❏ JLP-3000 [M]	Have "Twangy" Guitar -- Will Travel	1959	$150
—Duane sitting with guitar case, title on cover in green and red (2nd)			
❏ JLP-3000 [M]	Have "Twangy" Guitar -- Will Travel	1959	$50
—Duane standing with guitar (3rd)			
❏ JLPS-3000 [S]	Have "Twangy" Guitar -- Will Travel	1958	$400
—Duane sitting with guitar case, title on cover in white (1st)			
❏ JLPS-3000 [S]	Have "Twangy" Guitar -- Will Travel	1959	$300
—Duane sitting with guitar case, title on cover in green and red (2nd)			
❏ JLPS-3000 [S]	Have "Twangy" Guitar -- Will Travel	1959	$150
—Duane standing with guitar (3rd), album plays true stereo			
❏ JLPS-3000 [R]	Have "Twangy" Guitar -- Will Travel	196?	$50
—Duane standing with guitar (3rd), album plays fake stereo			
❏ T-90682 [M]	Have "Twangy" Guitar -- Will Travel	1965	$75
—Capitol Record Club edition			
❏ ST-90682 [S]	Have "Twangy" Guitar -- Will Travel	1965	$100
—Capitol Record Club edition			
❏ JLPM-3011 [M]	Songs of Our Heritage	1960	$100
—Gatefold cover			
❏ JLPM-3011 [M]	Songs of Our Heritage	196?	$30
—Regular cover			
❏ JLPS-3011 [S]	Songs of Our Heritage	1960	$150
—Gatefold cover			
❏ JLPS-3011 [S]	Songs of Our Heritage	1960	$500
—Gatefold cover, red vinyl			
❏ JLPS-3011 [S]	Songs of Our Heritage	1960	$500
—Gatefold cover, blue vinyl			
❏ JLPS-3011 [S]	Songs of Our Heritage	196?	$40
—Regular cover			
❏ JLPM-3024 [M]	Surfin'	1963	$50
❏ JLPS-3024 [S]	Surfin'	1963	$100
❏ JLPM-3009 [M]	The "Twangs" The "Thang	1959	$40
❏ JLPS-3009 [S]	The "Twangs" The "Thang	1959	$75
❏ T-91301 [M]	The "Twangs" The "Thang	1966	$75
—Capitol Record Club edition			
❏ ST-91301 [S]	The "Twangs" The "Thang	1966	$75
—Capitol Record Club edition			

Number	Title	Yr	NM

| ❏ JLPM-3022 [M] | Twistin' with Duane Eddy | 1962 | $40 |
| ❏ JLPS-3022 [P] | Twistin' with Duane Eddy | 1962 | $40 |
RCA VICTOR
❏ LPM-2648 [M]	Dance with the Guitar Man	1962	$30
❏ LSP-2648 [S]	Dance with the Guitar Man	1962	$40
❏ LPM-2798 [M]	Lonely Guitar	1964	$25
❏ LSP-2798 [S]	Lonely Guitar	1964	$30
❏ ANL1-2671	Pure Gold	1978	$12
❏ LPM-3477 [M]	The Best of Duane Eddy	1965	$25
❏ LSP-3477 [P]	The Best of Duane Eddy	1965	$30
—Black "Stereo" label			
❏ LSP-3477 [P]	The Best of Duane Eddy	1969	$18
—Orange label			
❏ LPM-2681 [M]	Twang a Country Song	1963	$30
❏ LSP-2681 [S]	Twang a Country Song	1963	$40
❏ LPM-2993 [M]	Twangin' the Golden Hits	1965	$25
❏ LSP-2993 [S]	Twangin' the Golden Hits	1965	$30
❏ LPM-2700 [M]	Twangin' " Up a Storm!	1963	$30
❏ LSP-2700 [S]	Twangin' " Up a Storm!	1963	$40
❏ LPM-3432 [M]	Twangsville	1965	$25
❏ LSP-3432 [S]	Twangsville	1965	$30
❏ LPM-2576 [M]	Twangy Guitar -- Silky Strings	1962	$30
❏ LSP-2576 [S]	Twangy Guitar -- Silky Strings	1962	$40
❏ LPM-2525 [M]	Twistin' 'N' Twangin'	1962	$30
❏ LSP-2525 [S]	Twistin' 'N' Twangin'	1962	$40
❏ LPM-2918 [M]	Water Skiing	1964	$25
❏ LSP-2918 [S]	Water Skiing	1964	$30
REPRISE
❏ R-6218 [M]	The Biggest Twang of Them All	1966	$30
❏ RS-6218 [S]	The Biggest Twang of Them All	1966	$40
❏ R-6240 [M]	The Roaring Twangies	1967	$30
❏ RS-6240 [S]	The Roaring Twangies	1967	$40
SIRE
| ❏ SASH-3707-2 | The Vintage Years | 1975 | $30 |

EDDY, NELSON
COLUMBIA MASTERWORKS
| ❏ ML4442 [M] | Songs for Christmas | 195? | $40 |
HARMONY
| ❏ HL7201 [M] | Nelson Eddy Sings the Best Loved Carols of Christmas | 195? | $25 |

EDELMAN, RANDY
20TH CENTURY
| ❏ T-494 | Farewell Fairbanks | 1975 | $15 |
| ❏ T-443 | Prime Cuts | 1974 | $18 |
ARISTA
| ❏ AB4139 | If Love Is Real | 1977 | $15 |
| ❏ AB4210 | You're the One | 1979 | $15 |
LION
| ❏ LN-1013 | The Laughter and the Tears | 1972 | $18 |
SUNFLOWER
| ❏ SNF-5005 | Randy Edelman | 1971 | $18 |

EDEN, BARBARA
DOT
| ❏ DLP-3795 [M] | Miss Barbara Eden | 1967 | $40 |
| ❏ DLP-25795 [S] | Miss Barbara Eden | 1967 | $50 |

EDEN'S CHILDREN
ABC
❏ 624 [M]	Eden's Children	1968	$40
❏ S-624 [S]	Eden's Children	1968	$30
❏ S-652	Sure Looks Real	1968	$25

EDGE, GRAEME
LONDON
| ❏ PS686 | Paradise Ballroom | 1977 | $15 |
THRESHOLD
| ❏ THS15 | Kick Off Your Muddy Boots | 1975 | $18 |

EDGE, THE
NOSE
| ❏ NRS-48003 [B] | The Edge | 1970 | $50 |

EDISON, HARRY "SWEETS
AMERICAN RECORDING SOCIETY
| ❏ G-430 [M] | Sweets | 1957 | $40 |
CLEF
| ❏ MGC-717 [M] | Sweets | 1956 | $300 |
LIBERTY
| ❏ LRP-3484 [M] | When Lights Are Low | 1966 | $50 |
| ❏ LST-7484 [S] | When Lights Are Low | 1966 | $75 |
PABLO
❏ 2310934	For My Pals	198?	$30
❏ 2310780	Lights	1976	$35
❏ 2310806	Simply Sweets	1977	$35
PABLO LIVE
| ❏ 2308237 | 'S Wonderful | 198? | $30 |

Number	Title	Yr	NM

PACIFIC JAZZ
| ❏ PJLP-4 [10] | Harry Edison Quartet | 1953 | $175 |
| ❏ PJ-11 [M] | The Inventive Harry Edison | 1960 | $50 |
ROULETTE
❏ R-52041 [M]	Patented by Edison	1960	$30
❏ SR-52041 [S]	Patented by Edison	1960	$40
❏ R-52023 [M]	Sweetenings	1960	$40
❏ SR-52023 [S]	Sweetenings	1960	$40
SUE
| ❏ LP-1030 [M] | Sweets for the Sweet | 1964 | $40 |
| ❏ STLP-1030 [S] | Sweets for the Sweet | 1964 | $50 |
VEE JAY
❏ LP-1104 [M]	For the Sweet Taste of Love	1964	$30
❏ LPS-1104 [S]	For the Sweet Taste of Love	1964	$40
❏ VJS-3065	Home with Sweets	1975	$25
VERVE
❏ MGV-8211 [M]	Gee Baby, Ain't I Good to You?	1958	$175
❏ V-8211 [M]	Gee Baby, Ain't I Good to You?	1961	$25
❏ MGV-8293 [M]	Harry Edison Swings Buck Clayton, And Vice Versa	1958	$150
❏ V-8293 [M]	Harry Edison Swings Buck Clayton, And Vice Versa	1961	$25
❏ MGVS-6016 [S]	Harry Edison Swings Buck Clayton, And Vice Versa	1959	$150
❏ V6-8293 [S]	Harry Edison Swings Buck Clayton, And Vice Versa	1961	$25
❏ MGV-8353 [M]	Mr. Swing	1959	$150
❏ V-8353 [M]	Mr. Swing	1961	$25
❏ MGVS-6118 [S]	Mr. Swing	1960	$150
❏ V6-8358 [S]	Mr. Swing	1961	$25
❏ MGV-8097 [M]	Sweets	1957	$175
❏ V-8097 [M]	Sweets	1961	$25
❏ MGV-8295 [M]	The Swinger	1959	$150
❏ V-8295 [M]	The Swinger	1961	$25
❏ MGVS-6037 [S]	The Swinger	1960	$100
❏ V6-8295 [S]	The Swinger	1961	$25

EDISON ELECTRIC BAND, THE
COTILLION
| ❏ SD9022 | Bless You, Dr. Woodward | 1970 | $25 |

EDMONSON, TRAVIS
Also see BUD AND TRAVIS.
HORIZON
| ❏ WP-1606 [M] | Travis On Cue | 1962 | $25 |
| ❏ WPS-1606 [S] | Travis On Cue | 1962 | $30 |
REPRISE
| ❏ R-6035 [M] | Travis On His Own | 1962 | $30 |
| ❏ R9-6035 [S] | Travis On His Own | 1962 | $30 |

EDMUNDS, DAVE
Also see LOVE SCULPTURE; ROCKPILE.
ATLANTIC
| ❏ PR320 [DJ] | College Network | 1978 | $50 |
| *—Promo-only interview album* | | | |
CAPITOL
| ❏ C1-90372 | Closer to the Flame | 1990 | $18 |
COLUMBIA
❏ FC37930	D.E. 7th	1982	$15
❏ PC37930	D.E. 7th	198?	$10
—Budget-line reissue ("02" added to bar code on back cover)			
❏ FC40603	I Hear You Rockin'	1987	$12
❏ PC40603	I Hear You Rockin'	198?	$10
—Budget-line reissue ("02" added to bar code on back cover)			
❏ FC38651	Information	1983	$15
❏ PC38651	Information	198?	$10
—Budget-line reissue ("02" added to bar code on back cover)			
❏ FC39273	Riff Raff	1984	$12
MAM
| ❏ 3 [B] | Rockpile | 1972 | $50 |
RCA VICTOR
❏ LPL1-5003 [B]	Subtle as a Flying Mallet	1975	$25
❏ AYL1-4238	Subtle as a Flying Mallet	1982	$12
—Reissue (black label, dog near top)			
SWAN SONG
❏ SS8418	Get It	1977	$18
❏ SS8507	Repeat When Necessary	1979	$18
❏ SS8510	The Best of Dave Edmunds	1981	$15
❏ SS8505	Trax on Wax 4	1978	$18
❏ SD16034	Twangin'	1981	$15

EDWARD BEAR
CAPITOL
❏ SKAO-426 [B]	Bearings	1970	$25
❏ ST-11192 [B]	Close Your Eyes	1973	$18
❏ ST-580 [B]	Eclipse	1971	$25
❏ ST-11157 [B]	Edward Bear	1972	$18

EDWARDS, EDDIE
COMMODORE
| ❏ FL-20003 [10] | Eddie Edwards' Original Dixieland Jazz Band | 1950 | $75 |

Number	Title	Yr	NM

EDWARDS, JONATHAN
ATCO
| ❑ SD7036 | Have a Good Time for Me | 1973 | $15 |
| ❑ 7015 [M] | Honky-Tonk Stardust Cowboy | 1972 | $30 |

—Mono is promo only; white label, "dj copy monaural" sticker on stereo cover

| ❑ SD7015 [S] | Honky-Tonk Stardust Cowboy | 1972 | $15 |
| ❑ SD 36-104 | Lucky Day | 1974 | $15 |

CAPRICORN
| ❑ SD862 | Jonathan Edwards | 1971 | $15 |

—Original has green label

| ❑ SD862 | Jonathan Edwards | 198? | $10 |

—Reissue with tan label

CHRONIC
| ❑ 1001 | Live! | 1982 | $15 |

MCA CURB
| ❑ 42256 | The Natural Thing | 1989 | $12 |

REPRISE
| ❑ MS2238 | Rockin' Chair | 1976 | $12 |

SUGAR HILL
| ❑ SH-3747 | Blue Ridge | 1985 | $12 |

—With the Seldom Scene

WARNER BROS.
| ❑ BS3020 | Sailboat | 1977 | $12 |

EDWARDS, JONATHAN AND DARLENE
Actually JO STAFFORD and PAUL WESTON as a comedy team.
COLUMBIA
❑ CL1513 [M]	Jonathan and Darlene Edwards In Paris	1960	$30
❑ CS8313 [S]	Jonathan and Darlene Edwards In Paris	1960	$30
❑ CL1024 [M]	The Piano Artistry of Jonathan Edwards	1955	$50

CORINTHIAN
❑ 103	Jonathan and Darlene Edwards In Paris	198?	$12
❑ 120	Sing Along with Jonathan and Darlene	198?	$12
❑ 122	Songs for Sheiks and Flappers	1986	$12
❑ 104	The Original Piano Artistry of Jonathan Edwards	198?	$12

DOT
| ❑ DLP-3792 [M] | Songs for Sheiks and Flappers | 1967 | $18 |
| ❑ DLP-25792 [S] | Songs for Sheiks and Flappers | 1967 | $25 |

RCA VICTOR
| ❑ LPM-2495 [M] | Sing Along with Jonathan and Darlene | 1962 | $25 |
| ❑ LSP-2495 [S] | Sing Along with Jonathan and Darlene | 1962 | $30 |

EDWARDS, KATHLEEN
ROUNDER
| ❑ 1431151 | Asking for Flowers | 2008 | $25 |

EDWARDS, STONEY
CAPITOL
❑ ST-11499	Blackbird	1976	$25
❑ ST-741	Country Singer	1970	$30
❑ ST-834	Down Home in the Country	1971	$25
❑ ST-11401	Mississippi on My Mind	1975	$25
❑ ST-11173	She's My Rock	1973	$25
❑ ST-11090	Stoney Edwards	1972	$25

EDWARDS, TEDDY
CONTEMPORARY
❑ M-3592 [M]	Good Gravy	1961	$300
❑ S-7592 [S]	Good Gravy	1961	$250
❑ M-3606 [M]	Heart and Soul	1962	$50
❑ S-7606 [S]	Heart and Soul	1962	$250
❑ M-3583 [M]	Teddy's Ready	1960	$250
❑ S-7583 [S]	Teddy's Ready	1960	$250
❑ M-3588 [M]	Together Again	1961	$80
❑ S-7588 [S]	Together Again	1961	$250

FANTASY
| ❑ OJC-177 | Heart and Soul | 198? | $25 |
| ❑ OJC-424 | Together Again | 1990 | $30 |

MUSE
| ❑ MR-5045 | Feelin's | 1974 | $30 |

PACIFIC JAZZ
❑ PJ-6 [M]	It's About Time	1960	$50
❑ ST-6 [S]	It's About Time	1960	$40
❑ PJ-14 [M]	Sunset Eyes	1961	$250

PRESTIGE
❑ PRLP-7522 [M]	It's Alright	1967	$30
❑ PRST-7522 [S]	It's Alright	1967	$30
❑ PRLP-7518 [M]	Nothin' But the Truth	1967	$30
❑ PRST-7518 [S]	Nothin' But the Truth	1967	$30

STEEPLECHASE
| ❑ SCS-1147 | Out of This World | 1980 | $30 |

XANADU
| ❑ 134 | Inimitable | 1976 | $30 |

EDWARDS, TOMMY
LION
| ❑ L-70120 [M] | Tommy Edwards | 1959 | $30 |

METRO
| ❑ M-511 [M] | Tommy Edwards | 1965 | $15 |
| ❑ MS-511 [S] | Tommy Edwards | 1965 | $18 |

MGM
| ❑ E-3760 [M] | For Young Lovers | 1959 | $30 |

—Yellow label

| ❑ SE-3760 [S] | For Young Lovers | 1959 | $40 |

—Yellow label

| ❑ E-3760 [M] | For Young Lovers | 1960 | $25 |

—Black label

| ❑ SE-3760 [S] | For Young Lovers | 1960 | $30 |

—Black label

❑ E-3959 [M]	Golden Coutnry Hits	1961	$25
❑ SE-3959 [S]	Golden Coutnry Hits	1961	$30
❑ E-3732 [M]	It's All in the Game	1958	$30

—Yellow label

| ❑ SE-3732 [S] | It's All in the Game | 1959 | $40 |

—Yellow label

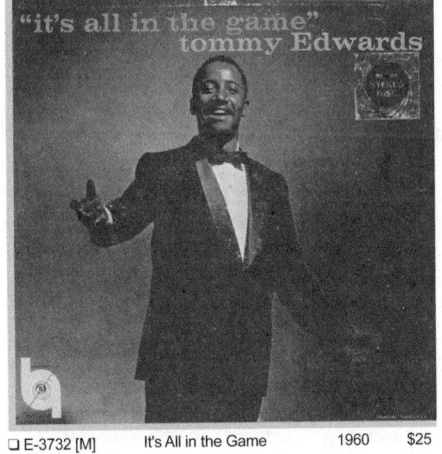

| ❑ E-3732 [M] | It's All in the Game | 1960 | $25 |

—Black label

| ❑ SE-3732 [S] | It's All in the Game | 1960 | $30 |

—Black label

❑ E-4060 [M]	Soft Strings and Two Guitars	1962	$25
❑ SE-4060 [S]	Soft Strings and Two Guitars	1962	$30
❑ E-4020 [M]	Stardust	1962	$25
❑ SE-4020 [S]	Stardust	1962	$30
❑ E-3822 [M]	Step Out Singing	1960	$25
❑ SE-3822 [S]	Step Out Singing	1960	$30
❑ E-4141 [M]	The Very Best of Tommy Edwards	1963	$18
❑ SE-4141 [S]	The Very Best of Tommy Edwards	1963	$25
❑ GAS-123	Tommy Edwards (Golden Archive Series)	1970	$18
❑ E-3884 [M]	Tommy Edwards' Greatest Hits	1961	$25
❑ SE-3884 [S]	Tommy Edwards' Greatest Hits	1961	$30
❑ E-3838 [M]	Tommy Edwards in Hawaii	1960	$25
❑ SE-3838 [S]	Tommy Edwards in Hawaii	1960	$30
❑ E-3805 [M]	You Started Me Dreaming	1960	$25
❑ SE-3805 [S]	You Started Me Dreaming	1960	$30

REGENT
| ❑ MG-6096 [M] | Tommy Edwards Sings | 1958 | $75 |

EDWARDS, VINCENT
DECCA
❑ DL4399 [M]	In Person at the Riviera	1963	$25
❑ DL74399 [M]	In Person at the Riviera	1963	$30
❑ DL4336 [M]	Sometimes I'm Happy... Sometimes I'm Blue	1962	$25
❑ DL74336 [M]	Sometimes I'm Happy... Sometimes I'm Blue	1962	$30
❑ DL4311 [M]	Vincent Edwards Sings	1962	$25
❑ DL74311 [M]	Vincent Edwards Sings	1962	$30

VOCALION
| ❑ VL3852 [M] | Here's Vincent Edwards | 1967 | $15 |
| ❑ VL73852 [S] | Here's Vincent Edwards | 1967 | $15 |

EELS
BONG LOAD
| ❑ BL47 | Daisies of the Galaxy | 2000 | $150 |

DREAMWORKS
| ❑ DRM2-50052 [10] | Electro-shock Blues | 1998 | $50 |

SPINART
| ❑ 128 | Shootenanny! | 2003 | $30 |

EGAN, MARK
GRP
| ❑ GR-9572 | A Touch of Light | 1988 | $25 |

HIPPOCKET
| ❑ HP-104 | Mosaic | 1985 | $25 |

WINDHAM HILL
| ❑ WH-0104 | Mosaic | 1987 | $25 |

—Reissue of HipPocket 104

EGAN, WALTER
BACKSTREET
| ❑ 5400 | Wild Exhibitions | 1983 | $10 |

COLUMBIA
❑ PC34679	Fundamental Roll	1977	$12
❑ JC35796	Hi Fi	1979	$12
❑ JC35077	Not Shy	1978	$12
❑ JC36513	The Last Stroll	1981	$12

EGGS OVER EASY
SQUISH
| ❑ NSFA001 [B] | Fear of Frying | 1981 | $100 |

A&M
| ❑ SP4366 [B] | Good'n'Cheap | 1972 | $60 |

YEP ROC
| ❑ YEP2402 [B] | Good 'n' Cheap: The Eggs Over Easy Story | 2016 | $40 |

EGILSSON, ARNI
INNER CITY
| ❑ IC-1103 | Bassus Erectus | 1981 | $30 |

EIGHT MINUTES, THE
PERCEPTION
| ❑ 27 | An American Family | 1973 | $50 |

8TH DAY, THE
A&M
| ❑ SP-4942 | The 8th Day | 1983 | $12 |

INVICTUS
| ❑ ST-9809 | I Gotta Get Home | 1973 | $15 |
| ❑ ST-7306 | The 8th Day | 1971 | $15 |

KAPP
| ❑ KS3554 | On the Eighth Day | 1968 | $18 |

EIRE APPARENT, THE
BUDDAH
| ❑ BDS-5031 [B] | Sunrise | 1969 | $50 |

EITHER/ORCHESTRA, THE
ACCURATE
| ❑ AC-2222 | Dial "E" for Either/Orchestra | 1987 | $30 |
| ❑ AC-3232 | Radium | 1989 | $30 |

EL CAMPO JADES, THE
GOLD EAGLE
| ❑ LP-101 [M] | The El Campo Jades | 1966 | $50 |

EL CHICANO
KAPP
❑ KS-3663	Celebration	1972	$15
❑ KS-3640	Revolucion	1971	$15
❑ KS-3632	Viva Tirado	1970	$15

MCA
❑ 401	Cinco	1974	$12
❑ 312	El Chicano	1973	$12
❑ 2150	Pyramid of Love	1975	$12
❑ 69	Revolucion	1973	$12

—Reissue of Kapp 3640

| ❑ 437 | The Best of Everything | 1975 | $12 |
| ❑ 548 | Viva Tirado | 197? | $12 |

—Reissue of Kapp 3632

SHADY BROOK
| ❑ SB 33-005 | This Is El Chicano | 1977 | $18 |

EL DORADOS
LOST-NITE
| ❑ LLP-20 [10] | The El Dorados | 1981 | $15 |

—Red vinyl

SOLID SMOKE
| ❑ 8025 | Low Mileage/High Octane | 1984 | $12 |

VEE JAY
| ❑ LP-1001 [M] | Crazy Little Mama | 1959 | $800 |

—Maroon label, thick silver band

| ❑ LP-1001 [M] | Crazy Little Mama | 1960 | $400 |

—Maroon label, thin silver band

| ❑ LP-1001 [M] | Crazy Little Mama | 1962 | $300 |

—Black label with colorband

| ❑ VJLP-1001 [M] | Crazy Little Mama | 198? | $12 |

—Authorized reissue

Number	Title	Yr	NM

ELASTICA

DGC

| ❏ 24728 | Elastica | 1995 | $12 |

GEFFEN

| ❏ B0020112-01 [B] | Elastica | 2014 | $30 |

ELBERT, DONNIE

ALL PLATINUM

| ❏ 3019 | Dancin' the Night Away | 1977 | $30 |
| ❏ 3007 | Where Did Our Love Go | 1971 | $30 |

DELUXE

| ❏ 12003 | Have I Sinned | 1971 | $30 |

KING

| ❏ 629 [M] | The Sensational Donnie Elbert Sings | 1959 | $400 |

SUGAR HILL

| ❏ 256 | From the Git Go | 1981 | $15 |

TRIP

| ❏ 9514 | Donnie Elbert Sings | 197? | $18 |
| ❏ 9524 | Stop in the Name of Love | 197? | $18 |

ELDRIDGE, ROY, AND BENNY CARTER

AMERICAN RECORDING SOCIETY

| ❏ G-413 [M] | The Urbane Jazz of Roy Eldridge and Benny Carter | 1957 | $40 |

VERVE

| ❏ MGV-8202 [M] | The Urbane Jazz of Roy Eldridge and Benny Carter | 1957 | $150 |
| ❏ V-8202 [M] | The Urbane Jazz of Roy Eldridge and Benny Carter | 1961 | $25 |

ELDRIDGE, ROY, AND DIZZY GILLESPIE

CLEF

❏ MGC-641 [M]	Roy and Diz	1955	$300
❏ MGC-671 [M]	Roy and Diz, Volume 2	1955	$300
❏ MGC-731 [M]	The Trumpet Kings	1956	$300
❏ MGC-730 [M]	Trumpet Battle	1956	$300

PABLO

| ❏ 2310816 | Jazz Maturity | 1977 | $35 |

VERVE

❏ VSP-28 [M]	Soul Mates	1966	$35
❏ VSPS-28 [R]	Soul Mates	1966	$30
❏ MGV-8110 [M]	The Trumpet Kings	1957	$150
❏ V-8110 [M]	The Trumpet Kings	1961	$25
❏ MGV-8109 [M]	Trumpet Battle	1957	$150
❏ V-8109 [M]	Trumpet Battle	1961	$25

ELDRIDGE, ROY; DIZZY GILLESPIE; HARRY "SWEETS" EDISON

VERVE

| ❏ MGV-8212 [M] | Tour de Force | 1958 | $175 |
| ❏ V-8212 [M] | Tour de Force | 1961 | $25 |

ELDRIDGE, ROY

AMERICAN RECORDING SOCIETY

| ❏ G-420 [M] | Swing Goes Dixie | 1956 | $40 |

CLEF

❏ MGC-705 [M]	Dale's Wail	1956	$300
❏ MGC-683 [M]	Little Jazz	1956	$300
❏ MGC-716 [M]	Mr. Jazz	1956	$0
—Canceled			
❏ MGC-704 [M]	Rockin' Chair	1956	$300
❏ MGC-113 [10]	Roy Eldridge Collates	1953	$300
❏ MGC-150 [10]	The Roy Eldridge Quintet	1954	$300
❏ MGC-162 [10]	The Strolling Mr. Eldridge	1954	$300

COLUMBIA

| ❏ C238033 | Early Years | 1983 | $30 |

DIAL

| ❏ LP-304 [10] | Little Jazz Four: Trumpet Fantasy | 1953 | $400 |

DISCOVERY

| ❏ DL-2009 [10] | Roy Eldridge with Zoot Sims | 1954 | $300 |

EMARCY

| ❏ MG-36084 [M] | Roy's Got Rhythm | 1956 | $100 |

FANTASY

| ❏ OJC-628 | Happy Time | 1991 | $30 |
| ❏ OJC-373 | Montreux '77 | 1989 | $30 |

GNP CRESCENDO

| ❏ GNP-9009 | Roy Eldridge | 197? | $30 |

JAZZ ARCHIVES

| ❏ JA-14 | Arcadia Shuffle | 198? | $25 |

LONDON

| ❏ PB375 [10] | Roy Eldridge Quartet | 1954 | $120 |

MASTER JAZZ

| ❏ 8110 | The Nifty Cat | 1970 | $25 |
| ❏ 8121 | The Nifty Cat Strikes West | 197? | $25 |

MCA

| ❏ 1355 | All the Cats Join In | 198? | $25 |

MERCURY

| ❏ MGC-113 [10] | Roy Eldridge Collates | 1952 | $300 |

METRO

| ❏ M-513 [M] | Roy Eldridge | 1965 | $175 |
| ❏ MS-513 [R] | Roy Eldridge | 1965 | $175 |

PABLO

❏ 2310746	Happy Time	1975	$35
❏ 2310869	Little Jazz	198?	$30
❏ 2310928	Loose Walk	198?	$25
❏ 2405413	The Best of Roy Eldridge	198?	$25
❏ 2310766	What It's All About	1976	$35

PABLO LIVE

| ❏ 2308203 | Montreux '77 | 1978 | $30 |

PRESTIGE

| ❏ PRLP-114 [10] | Roy Eldridge in Sweden | 1951 | $300 |

VERVE

❏ MGV-8089 [M]	Dale's Wail	1957	$300
—Reissue of Clef 705			
❏ V-8089 [M]	Dale's Wail	1961	$300
❏ VE-2-2531	Dale's Wail	198?	$35
❏ MGV-8068 [M]	Little Jazz	1957	$300
—Reissue of Clef 683			
❏ V-8068 [M]	Little Jazz	1961	$25
❏ MGV-8088 [M]	Rockin' Chair	1957	$250
—Reissue of Clef 704			
❏ V-8088 [M]	Rockin' Chair	1961	$25
❏ UMV-2686	Rockin' Chair	198?	$25

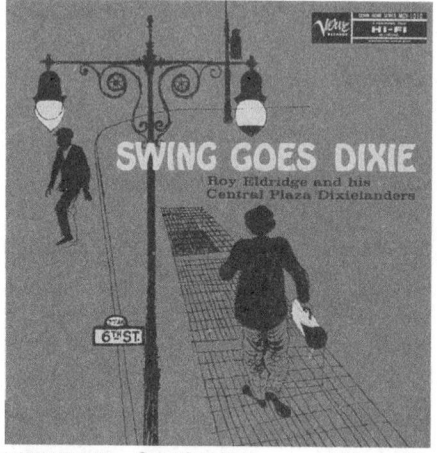

❏ MGV-1010 [M]	Swing Goes Dixie	1957	$50
❏ V-1010 [M]	Swing Goes Dixie	1961	$25
❏ MGV-8389 [M]	Swingin' on the Town	1960	$100
❏ V-8389 [M]	Swingin' on the Town	1961	$25

XANADU

| ❏ 140 | Roy Eldridge at Jerry Newman's | 198? | $25 |

ELDRIDGE, ROY/SAMMY PRICE

BRUNSWICK

| ❏ BL58045 [10] | Battle of Jazz, Volume 7 | 1953 | $75 |

ELECTRAS, THE

John Kerry, senator from Massachusetts and presidential candidate, played bass on this album.

ELECTRA

| ❏ ELT-201 | The Electras | 1961 | $450 |

ELECTRIC FLAG, THE

ATLANTIC

| ❏ SD18112 | The Band Kept Playing | 1974 | $12 |

COLUMBIA

❏ CS9597 [B]	A Long Time Comin'	1968	$25
—360 Sound" label			
❏ CS9597	A Long Time Comin'	1970	$12
—Orange label			
❏ PC9597	A Long Time Comin'	198?	$10
—Budget-line reissue			
❏ C30422	The Best of the Electric Flag	1971	$12
❏ CS9714	The Electric Flag	1968	$18
—360 Sound" label			
❏ CS9714	The Electric Flag	1970	$12
—Orange label			

ELECTRIC INDIAN, THE

UNITED ARTISTS

| ❏ UAS6728 | Keem-O-Sabe | 1969 | $18 |

ELECTRIC LIGHT ORCHESTRA

Evolved from THE MOVE. Also see JEFF LYNNE; ROY WOOD.

CBS ASSOCIATED

| ❏ FZ40048 | Balance of Power | 1986 | $12 |

EPIC

| ❏ 88985312351 [B] | All Over The World - The Very Best Of | 2016 | $25 |
| —180g | | | |

JET

❏ Z4X36966	A Box of Their Best	1980	$30
❏ JZ35529	A New World Record	1978	$12
❏ PZ35529	A New World Record	1981	$10
❏ FZ35769	Discovery	1979	$12
❏ HZ45789	Discovery	1980	$30
—Half-speed mastered edition			
❏ PZ35769	Discovery	1987	$10
❏ JZ35526	Eldorado	1978	$12
❏ PZ35526	Eldorado	198?	$10
❏ JZ35533	Electric Light Orchestra II	1978	$12
❏ PZ35533	Electric Light Orchestra II	1981	$10
❏ FZ36310	ELO's Greatest Hits	1979	$12
❏ PZ36310	ELO's Greatest Hits	1987	$10
❏ HZ36310	ELO's Greatest Hits	1981	$40
—Half-speed mastered edition			
❏ JZ35527	Face the Music	1978	$12
❏ PZ35527 [B]	Face the Music	1981	$10
❏ JZ35524	No Answer	1978	$12
❏ PZ35524	No Answer	1981	$10
❏ JZ35528	Ole Elo	1978	$12

❏ PZ35528 [B]	Ole Elo	1981	$10
❏ JZ35525	On the Third Day	1978	$12
❏ PZ35525	On the Third Day	1981	$10
❏ JT-LA823-L2 [DJ]	Out of the Blue	1977	$30
—Promo only on blue vinyl			
❏ JT-LA823-L2	Out of the Blue	1977	$18
—Originals include poster and die-cut cardboard "spaceship"			
❏ KZ235530	Out of the Blue	1978	$15
❏ QZ38490	Secret Messages	1983	$12
❏ HZ48490	Secret Messages	1983	$30
—Half-speed mastered edition			
❏ PZ38490	Secret Messages	1987	$10
❏ FZ37371	Time	1981	$12
❏ HZ47371	Time	1982	$30
—Half-speed mastered edition			
❏ PZ37371	Time	1987	$10

UNITED ARTISTS

❏ UA-LA679-G	A New World Record	1976	$15
—All copies have custom labels			
❏ UA-LA339-G	Eldorado	1974	$15
—Tan label			
❏ UA-LA339-G	Eldorado	1977	$12
—Sunrise label			
❏ UA-LA040-F	Electric Light Orchestra II	1973	$18
—Tan label			
❏ UA-LA040-F	Electric Light Orchestra II	1978	$12
—Sunrise label			
❏ UA-LA546-G	Face the Music	1975	$15
—Tan label			
❏ UA-LA546-G	Face the Music	1978	$12
—Sunrise label			
❏ UA-LA546-DJ [DJ]	Face the Music	1975	$30
—Promo only, banded for airplay			
❏ UAS-5573	No Answer	1972	$18
—Tan label			
❏ UAS-5573	No Answer	1978	$12
—Sunrise label			
❏ SP-123 [DJ]	Ole Elo	1976	$150
—Gold vinyl, cover similar to the released version except for the single line "Ole Elo" (no "Electric Light Orchestra" underneath) at the top of the front cover			
❏ SP-123 [DJ]	Ole Elo	1976	$100
—Red, blue or white vinyl promos with generic cover			
❏ SP-123 [DJ]	Ole Elo	1976	$50
—Gold vinyl promo with generic cover			
❏ UA-LA630-G	Ole Elo	1976	$15
—Tan label			
❏ UA-LA630-G	Ole Elo	1978	$12

Number	Title	Yr	NM
— Sunrise label			
❑ UA-LA188-F	On the Third Day	1973	$18
— Tan label			
❑ UA-LA188-F	On the Third Day	1978	$12
— Sunrise label			
❑ UA-LA318-F	The Night the Light Went On in Long Beach	1974	$0
— Canceled			
WARNER BROS.			
❑ K56058	The Night the Light Went On in Long Beach	1974	$30
— Import otherwise unavailable in U.S.			

ELECTRIC PRUNES, THE
REPRISE

Number	Title	Yr	NM
❑ RS-6342	Just Good Rock 'n Roll	1969	$30
❑ R-6275 [M]	Mass in F Minor	1967	$250
❑ RS-6275 [S]	Mass in F Minor	1967	$75
❑ RS-6316	Release of an Oath	1968	$30
❑ R-6248 [M]	The Electric Prunes	1967	$175
❑ RS-6248 [S]	The Electric Prunes	1967	$75
❑ R-6262 [M]	Underground	1967	$100
❑ RS-6262 [S]	Underground	1967	$75

ELECTRIC TOILET, THE
NASCO

❑ 9004	In the Hands of Karma	1968	$400

ELECTRIC UNDERGROUND, THE
PREMIER

❑ P-9060 [M]	Guitar Explosion	1967	$100
❑ PS-9060 [S]	Guitar Explosion	1967	$50

ELECTRONIC CONCEPT ORCHESTRA
LIMELIGHT

❑ 86072	Electric Love	1969	$12
❑ 86070	Moog Groove	1969	$12

MERCURY

❑ SR-61279	Cinemoog	1970	$12

ELECTROSONICS, THE
PHILIPS

❑ PHM200047 [M]	Electronic Music	1962	$80
❑ PHS600047 [S]	Electronic Music	1962	$125

ELEGANTS, THE
MURRAY HILL

❑ 210	Little Star	1986	$12

ELEMENTS
ANTILLES

❑ AN-1021	Forward Motion	198?	$25
❑ AN-1017	The Elements	198?	$25
— Reissue of Philo album			

NOVUS

❑ 3031-1-N	Illumination	1988	$25
❑ 3058-1-N	Liberal Arts	1989	$30

PHILO

❑ 9011	The Elements	198?	$35

ELEPHANTS MEMORY
APPLE

❑ SMAS-3389 [B]	Elephants Memory	1972	$35

BUDDAH

❑ BDS-5033	Elephants Memory	1969	$18
❑ BDS-5038	Songs from Midnight Cowboy	1970	$18

METROMEDIA

❑ MD-1035	Take It to the Streets	1970	$25

RCA VICTOR

❑ APL1-0569	Angela Forever	1974	$18

ELEVENTH HOUR, THE
20TH CENTURY

❑ T-435	Greatest Hits	1974	$15
❑ T-511	Hollywood Hot	1975	$18

ELEVENTH HOUSE, THE
See LARRY CORYELL.
See LARRY CORYELL. (JZ)

ELEVENTH HOUSE, THE (WITH LARRY CORYELL)
ARISTA

❑ AL4077	Aspects	1976	$12
❑ AL4052	Level One	1975	$12

VANGUARD

❑ VSQ-40036 [Q]	Introducing the Eleventh House with Larry Coryell	1974	$40
❑ VSD-79342	Introducing the Eleventh House with Larry Coryell	1974	$15

ELF
Also see RAINBOW; DIO; RONNIE DIO; BLACK SABBATH.

EPIC

Number	Title	Yr	NM
❑ KE31789	Elf	1972	$30
— Yellow label			
❑ KE31789	Elf	1973	$25
— Orange label			

MGM

❑ M3G4974	L.A. 59	1974	$25
❑ M3G4994	Trying to Burn the Sun	1975	$25

ELFMAN, DANNY
MCA

❑ 5535	So-Lo	1984	$12

ELGART, BILL
MARK LEVINSON

❑ 3	A Life	1980	$30

ELGART, CHARLIE
NOVUS

❑ 3068-1-N	Balance	1989	$30
❑ 3045-1-N	Signs of Life	1988	$25

ELGART, LARRY
BRUNSWICK

❑ BL58054 [10]	Impressions of Outer Space	1954	$120

DECCA

❑ DL8034 [M]	Music for Barefoot Ballerinas	1955	$175
❑ DL5526 [10]	The Larry Elgart Band with Strings	1954	$200

MGM

❑ E-4080 [M]	More Music in Motion!	1962	$35
❑ SE-4080 [S]	More Music in Motion!	1962	$50
❑ E-4028 [M]	Music in Motion!	1962	$35
❑ SE-4028 [S]	Music in Motion!	1962	$50
❑ E-3891 [M]	Sophisticated Sixties	1960	$35
❑ SE-3891 [S]	Sophisticated Sixties	1960	$50
❑ E-4007 [M]	The City	1961	$35
❑ SE-4007 [S]	The City	1961	$50
❑ E-3896 [M]	The Shape of Sounds to Come	1961	$35
❑ SE-3896 [S]	The Shape of Sounds to Come	1961	$50
❑ E-3961 [M]	Visions	1961	$35
❑ SE-3961 [S]	Visions	1961	$50

PROJECT 3

❑ PR5102	The Larry Elgart Dance Band	1979	$25

RCA CAMDEN

❑ CAL-575 [M]	Easy Goin' Swing	1960	$30
❑ CAS-575 [S]	Easy Goin' Swing	1960	$35
❑ CXS-9036	That Old Feeling	1972	$30

RCA VICTOR

❑ AFL1-4095	Flight of the Condor	1981	$25
❑ AFL1-4343	Hooked on Swing	1982	$25
❑ AYL1-5025	Hooked on Swing	1984	$20
— Budget-line reissue			
❑ AFL1-4589	Hooked on Swing, Volume 2	1983	$25
❑ AYL1-5026	Hooked on Swing, Volume 2	1984	$20
— Budget-line reissue			
❑ AFL1-4850	Larry Elgart and His Manhattan Swing Orchestra	1984	$25
❑ LPM-1961 [M]	Larry Elgart and His Orchestra	1959	$35
❑ LSP-1961 [S]	Larry Elgart and His Orchestra	1959	$50
❑ LPM-2045 [M]	New Sounds at the Roosevelt	1959	$35
❑ LSP-2045 [S]	New Sounds at the Roosevelt	1959	$50
❑ LPM-2166 [M]	Saratoga	1960	$35
❑ LSP-2166 [S]	Saratoga	1960	$50
❑ AYL1-7178	(The Theme from) La Cage Aux Folles	1986	$20

ELGART, LES
CIRCLE

❑ CLP-126	Les Elgart and His Orchestra	198?	$25

COLUMBIA

❑ CS8690 [S]	Best Band on Campus	1963	$30
❑ CL1890 [M]	Best Band on Campus	1963	$25
❑ CL2578 [10]	Campus Hop	1955	$50
❑ CL1500 [M]	Designs for Dancing	1960	$25
❑ CS8291 [S]	Designs for Dancing	1960	$30
❑ CL1008 [M]	For Dancers Also	1957	$30
❑ CL803 [M]	For Dancers Only	1956	$30
❑ CL1567 [M]	Half Satin - Half Latin	1961	$25
❑ CS8367 [S]	Half Satin - Half Latin	1961	$30
❑ CL1659 [M]	It's De-Lovely	1961	$25
❑ CS8459 [S]	It's De-Lovely	1961	$30
❑ CL6287 [10]	Just One More Dance	195?	$40
❑ CL594 [M]	Just One More Dance	1954	$40
— Maroon label, gold print			
❑ CL594 [M]	Just One More Dance	1955	$40
— Red and black label with six "eye" logos			
❑ CL1052 [M]	Les and Larry Elgart and Their Orchestra	1957	$30
❑ CS8092 [S]	Les and Larry Elgart and Their Orchestra	1959	$30
❑ CL1291 [M]	Les Elgart On Tour	1959	$25
❑ CS8103 [S]	Les Elgart On Tour	1959	$30

Number	Title	Yr	NM
❑ CL2590 [10]	More of Les	1955	$50
❑ CL2503 [10]	Prom Date	1954	$40
❑ CL536 [M]	Sophisticated Swing	1953	$40
— Maroon label, gold print			
❑ CS8002 [S]	Sound Ideas	1958	$30
❑ CL619 [M]	The Band of the Year	1955	$50
— Maroon label, gold print; first LP appearance of "Bandstand Boogie"			
❑ CS8245 [S]	The Band with That Sound	1960	$30
❑ CL1450 [M]	The Band with That Sound	1960	$25
❑ CL684 [M]	The Dancing Sound	1955	$40
❑ CL875 [M]	The Elgart Touch	1956	$30
— Red and black label, six "eye" logos			
❑ CL1350 [M]	The Great Sound of Les Elgart	1959	$25
❑ CS8159 [S]	The Great Sound of Les Elgart	1959	$30
❑ CS8585 [S]	The Twist Goes to College	1962	$30
❑ CL1785 [M]	The Twist Goes to College	1962	$25

COLUMBIA SPECIAL PRODUCTS

❑ P13168	The Greatest Dance Band in the Land	197?	$25

HARMONY

❑ HL7374 [M]	The Greatest Dance Band in the Land	196?	$30
❑ HS11174 [R]	The Greatest Dance Band in the Land	196?	$25

SUTTON

❑ SU283 [M]	Les Elgart and Blazing Brass	196?	$25

ELGART, LES AND LARRY
COLUMBIA

❑ CL2112 [M]	Big Band Hootenanny	1963	$35
❑ CS8912 [S]	Big Band Hootenanny	1963	$25
❑ CL2221 [M]	Command Performance! Les & Larry Elgart Play the Great Dance Hits	1964	$35
❑ CS9021 [S]	Command Performance! Les & Larry Elgart Play the Great Dance Hits	1964	$25
❑ CL2355 [M]	Elgart Au-Go-Go	1965	$35
❑ CS9155 [S]	Elgart Au-Go-Go	1965	$25
❑ CL2633 [M]	Girl Watchers	1967	$25
❑ CS9433 [S]	Girl Watchers	1967	$35
❑ CS9722	Les & Larry Elgart's Greatest Hits	1968	$35
❑ CL1123 [M]	Sound Ideas	1958	$30
❑ CL2511 [M]	Sound of the Times	1966	$35
❑ CS9311 [S]	Sound of the Times	1966	$25
❑ PC38341	Swingtime	1982	$25
❑ CL2301 [M]	The New Elgart Touch	1965	$35
❑ CS9101 [S]	The New Elgart Touch	1965	$25
❑ CL2780 [M]	The Wonderful World of Today's Hits	1968	$30
❑ CS9580 [S]	The Wonderful World of Today's Hits	1968	$35
❑ CL2591 [M]	Warm and Sensuous	1966	$35
❑ CS9391 [S]	Warm and Sensuous	1966	$25

HARMONY

❑ KH32053	Wonderful World	1972	$25

SWAMPFIRE

❑ 207	Bridge Over Troubled Water	1971	$30
❑ 202	Nashville Country Brass	196?	$30
❑ 203	Nashville Country Guitars	196?	$30
❑ 201	Nashville Country Piano	196?	$30

ELGINS, THE (1)
V.I.P.

❑ 400 [M]	Darling Baby	1966	$80
❑ S-400 [S]	Darling Baby	1966	$150

ELIAS, ELIANE
BLUE NOTE

❑ B1-48785	Cross Currents	1988	$25
❑ BST-46994	Illusions	1987	$25
❑ B1-91411	So Far So Close	1989	$30

ELIAS, ROSALIND, AND GIORGIO TOZZI
RCA VICTOR RED SEAL

❑ LSC-2350 [S]	A Yuletide Song Fest	1959	$40
— Original with "shaded dog" label			

ELIGIBLES, THE
CAPITOL

❑ T1310 [M]	Along the Trail	1960	$30
❑ ST1310 [S]	Along the Trail	1960	$30
❑ T1411 [M]	Love Is a Gamble	1960	$30
❑ ST1411 [S]	Love Is a Gamble	1960	$30

ELIMINATORS, THE
LIBERTY

❑ LRP-3365 [M]	Liverpool! Dragsters! Cycles! Surfing!	1964	$100
❑ LST-7365 [S]	Liverpool! Dragsters! Cycles! Surfing!	1964	$150

ELIOVSON, STEVE
ECM

❑ 1198	Dawn Dance	198?	$25

Number	Title	Yr	NM

ELIZABETH
VANGUARD
| ❏ VSD-6501 | Elizabeth | 1968 | $150 |

—*Gold label*

ELLIAS, RODDY
INNER CITY
| ❏ IC-1081 | A Night for Stars | 1980 | $25 |

ELLIE POP
MAINSTREAM
| ❏ S-6115 | Ellie Pop | 1968 | $150 |

ELLIMAN, YVONNE
DECCA
| ❏ DL75341 | Yvonne Elliman | 1972 | $18 |
MCA
| ❏ 356 | Food of Love | 1973 | $15 |
RSO
❏ RS-1-3018	Love Me	1977	$12
❏ RS-1-3031	Night Flight	1978	$12
❏ RS-1-3038	Yvonne	1979	$12

ELLINGSON, PAUL
IVY JAZZ
| ❏ IJ1-E-1-2 | Solo Piano Jazz | 198? | $35 |

ELLINGTON, DUKE, ORCHESTRA (MERCER ELLINGTON, DIRECTOR)
DOCTOR JAZZ
| ❏ FW40029 | Hot and Bothered: A Re-Creation | 1986 | $25 |
| ❏ FW40359 | New Mood Indigo | 1987 | $25 |
FANTASY
| ❏ F-9481 | Continuum | 1975 | $30 |
GRP
| ❏ GR-1038 | Digital Duke | 1987 | $25 |
HOLIDAY
| ❏ HDY1916 | Take the Holiday Train | 1980 | $20 |

ELLINGTON, DUKE
AAMCO
| ❏ ALP-301 [M] | The Royal Concert of Duke Ellington, Vol. 1 | 196? | $75 |

—*Reissue of Bethlehem material*

| ❏ ALP-313 [M] | The Royal Concert of Duke Ellington, Vol. 2 | 196? | $75 |

—*Reissue of Bethlehem material*

ABC IMPULSE!
❏ 9285	Ellingtonia, Volume 2	1974	$35
❏ 9256	Ellingtonia: Reevaluations, The Impulse Years	1973	$35
❏ IA-9350	Great Tenor Encounters	1978	$35
AIRCHECK
| ❏ 4 | Duke on the Air | 197? | $25 |
| ❏ 29 | Duke on the Air, Vol. 2 | 198? | $25 |
ALLEGRO
❏ 3082 [M]	Duke Ellington	1953	$150
❏ 1591 [M]	Duke Ellington and His Orchestra Play	1955	$150
❏ 4014 [10]	Duke Ellington and His Orchestra Play	1954	$200
❏ 4038 [10]	Duke Ellington and His Orchestra Play	1954	$200
ATLANTIC
❏ SD1688	Jazz Violin Session	1976	$30
❏ SD1580	New Orleans Suite	1971	$30
❏ QD1580 [Q]	New Orleans Suite	1974	$40
❏ SD1665	Recollections of the Big Band Era	1974	$30
❏ 90043	Recollections of the Big Band Era	1982	$25
❏ SD 2-304	The Great Paris Concert	1972	$35
BASF
| ❏ 21704 | Collages | 1973 | $30 |
BETHLEHEM
❏ BCP-6005 [M]	Duke Ellington Presents	1956	$300
❏ BCP-60 [M]	Historically Speaking, The Duke	1956	$300
❏ 6013	The Bethlehem Years, Vol. 1	197?	$25
BIOGRAPH
| ❏ M-2 | Band Shorts (1929-1935) | 1978 | $25 |
BLUEBIRD
| ❏ 6287-1-RB | And His Mother Called Him Bill | 1987 | $20 |

—*Reissue of RCA Victor 3906*

❏ 6641-1-RB	Black, Brown and Beige	1988	$75
❏ 5659-1-RB	Duke Ellington: The Blanton-Webster Band	1986	$75
❏ 6852-1-RB	Early Ellington	1989	$25
BLUE NOTE
| ❏ BT-85129 | Money Jungle | 1986 | $25 |

—*Reissue of United Artists 15017*

BOOK-OF-THE-MONTH
| ❏ 30-5622 | At Fargo, 1940 | 1978 | $50 |
BRIGHT ORANGE
| ❏ 709 | The Stereophonic Sound of Duke Ellington | 1973 | $30 |
BRUNSWICK
❏ BL54007 [M]	Early Ellington	1954	$150
❏ BL58002 [10]	Ellingtonia, Volume 1	1950	$200
❏ BL58012 [10]	Ellingtonia, Volume 2	1950	$200
BULLDOG
| ❏ BDL-2021 | 20 Golden Pieces of Duke Ellington | 198? | $25 |
CAPITOL
| ❏ T637 [M] | Dance to the Duke | 1955 | $85 |

—*Turquoise label*

| ❏ T637 [M] | Dance to the Duke | 1958 | $100 |

—*Black label with colorband, logo at left*

| ❏ T521 [M] | Ellington '55 | 1955 | $85 |

—*Turquoise label*

| ❏ T521 [M] | Ellington '55 | 1958 | $100 |

—*Black label with colorband, logo at left*

| ❏ M-11674 | Ellington '55 | 1977 | $25 |
| ❏ T679 [M] | Ellington Showcase | 1956 | $75 |

—*Turquoise label*

| ❏ T679 [M] | Ellington Showcase | 1958 | $100 |

—*Black label with colorband, logo at left*

❏ M-11058	Piano Reflections	1972	$30
❏ H440 [10]	Premiered by Ellington	1953	$300
❏ T1602 [M]	The Best of Duke Ellington	1961	$100
❏ DT1602 [R]	The Best of Duke Ellington	1961	$75
❏ SM-1602	The Best of Duke Ellington	197?	$25

—*Reissue with new prefix*

| ❏ N-16172 | The Best of Duke Ellington | 198? | $20 |

—*Budget-line reissue*

| ❏ H477 [10] | The Duke Plays Ellington | 1954 | $300 |
| ❏ T477 [M] | The Duke Plays Ellington | 1954 | $75 |

—*Turquoise label*

| ❏ T477 [M] | The Duke Plays Ellington | 1958 | $100 |

—*Black label with colorband, logo at left*

CIRCLE
❏ CLP-101	Duke Ellington World Broadcasting Series, Vol. 1	1986	$25
❏ CLP-102	Duke Ellington World Broadcasting Series, Vol. 2	1986	$25
❏ CLP-103	Duke Ellington World Broadcasting Series, Vol. 3	1986	$25
❏ CLP-104	Duke Ellington World Broadcasting Series, Vol. 4	199?	$25
❏ CLP-105	Duke Ellington World Broadcasting Series, Vol. 5 (1943)	199?	$25
❏ CLP-106	Duke Ellington World Broadcasting Series, Vol. 6 (1945)	1988	$25
❏ CLP-108	Duke Ellington World Broadcasting Series, Vol. 8 (1945)	1988	$25
❏ CLP-109	Duke Ellington World Broadcasting Series, Vol. 9 (1945)	1988	$25
COLUMBIA
❏ CL951 [M]	A Drum Is a Woman	1957	$40
❏ CL2593 [10]	Al Hibbler with the Duke	1956	$175
❏ CL1790 [M]	All American	1962	$50
❏ CS8590 [S]	All American	1962	$75
❏ CL663 [M]	Blue Light	1955	$50
❏ CL1445 [M]	Blues in Orbit	1960	$75

❏ CS8241 [S]	Blues in Orbit	1960	$30
❏ CL1162 [M]	Brown, Black and Beige	1958	$75
❏ CS8015 [S]	Brown, Black and Beige	1958	$75
❏ CL1282 [M]	Duke Ellington at the Bal Masque	1959	$75
❏ CS8098 [S]	Duke Ellington at the Bal Masque	1959	$75
❏ CL1323 [M]	Duke Ellington Jazz Party	1959	$75
❏ CS8127 [S]	Duke Ellington Jazz Party	1959	$75

❏ KG32064	Duke Ellington Presents Ivie Anderson	1973	$35
❏ CS9629	Duke Ellington's Greatest Hits	1969	$35
❏ CL2522 [10]	Duke's Mixture	1955	$175
❏ CS8648 [R]	Ellington at Newport	1963	$30
❏ PC8648	Ellington at Newport	198?	$20

—*Budget-line reissue*

| ❏ CL934 [M] | Ellington at Newport '56 | 1957 | $40 |

—*Red and black label with six "eye" logos*

| ❏ CL934 [M] | Ellington at Newport '56 | 1963 | $35 |

—*Red label with "Guaranteed High Fidelity" or "360 Sound Mono*

| ❏ CL1085 [M] | Ellington Indigos | 1958 | $75 |
| ❏ CS8053 [S] | Ellington Indigos | 1958 | $75 |

—*Red and black label with six "eye" logos*

| ❏ CL1085 [M] | Ellington Indigos | 1963 | $35 |

—*Red label with "Guaranteed High Fidelity" or "360 Sound Mono*

| ❏ CS8053 [S] | Ellington Indigos | 1963 | $35 |

—*Red label with "360 Sound Stereo*

| ❏ PC8053 | Ellington Indigos | 198? | $20 |

—*Budget-line reissue*

❏ CL1400 [M]	Festival Session	1960	$75
❏ CL1715 [M]	First Time	1962	$75
❏ CS8515 [S]	First Time	1962	$75
❏ CL2562 [10]	Here's the Duke	1955	$175
❏ CL830 [M]	Hi-Fi Ellington Uptown	1956	$40
❏ CL830 [M]	Hi-Fi Ellington Uptown	1963	$35

—*Red label with "Guaranteed High Fidelity" or "360 Sound Mono*

| ❏ PC37340 | It Don't Mean a Thing | 1981 | $20 |

—*Reissue*

❏ C32471	Jazz at the Plaza -- Vol. II	1973	$30
❏ CL6073 [10]	Liberian Suite	1949	$200
❏ CL848 [M]	Liberian Suite	1956	$40

—*Reissue of Columbia 6073*

| ❏ CL825 [M] | Masterpieces by Ellington | 1956 | $40 |

—*Reissue of Columbia Masterworks 4418*

| ❏ CL825 [M] | Masterpieces by Ellington | 1963 | $35 |

—*Red label with "Guaranteed High Fidelity" or "360 Sound Mono*

❏ CL1907 [M]	Midnight in Paris	1963	$50
❏ CS8829 [S]	Midnight in Paris	1963	$75
❏ CL6024 [10]	Mood Ellington	1949	$200
❏ CL1245 [M]	Newport 1958	1959	$75
❏ CS8072 [S]	Newport 1958	1959	$75
❏ CL1597 [M]	Peer Gynt Suite/Suite Thursday	1961	$75
❏ CS8397 [S]	Peer Gynt Suite/Suite Thursday	1961	$75
❏ CL1546 [M]	Piano in the Background	1960	$75
❏ CS8346 [S]	Piano in the Background	1960	$40
❏ CL1546 [M]	Piano in the Background	1963	$35

—*Red label with "Guaranteed High Fidelity" or "360 Sound Mono*

| ❏ CS8346 [S] | Piano in the Background | 1963 | $35 |

—*Red label with "360 Sound Stereo*

❏ CL1033 [M]	Such Sweet Thunder	1957	$40
❏ CL1198 [M]	The Cosmic Scene	1959	$175
❏ C3L27 [M]	The Ellington Era, Vol. 1	1963	$40
❏ C3L39 [M]	The Ellington Era, Vol. 2	1964	$40
❏ FC38028	The Girl's Suite & Perfume Suite	1982	$25
❏ CL558 [M]	The Music of Duke Ellington	1954	$150

—*Maroon label with gold print*

| ❏ CL558 [M] | The Music of Duke Ellington | 1956 | $40 |

—*Red and black label with six "eye" logos*

| ❏ CL558 [M] | The Music of Duke Ellington | 1963 | $35 |

—*Red label with "Guaranteed High Fidelity" or "360 Sound Mono*

❏ CL1541 [M]	The Nutcracker Suite	1960	$75
❏ CS8341 [S]	The Nutcracker Suite	1960	$40
❏ G32564	The World of Duke Ellington	1974	$35
❏ KG33341	The World of Duke Ellington, Volume 2	1975	$35
❏ CG33961	The World of Duke Ellington, Volume 3	1975	$35

COLUMBIA JAZZ MASTERPIECES
| ❏ CJ44051 | Blues in Orbit | 1988 | $25 |

—*Reissue of Columbia 8241*

| ❏ CJ40712 | Duke Ellington Jazz Party | 1987 | $25 |

—*Reissue of Columbia 8127*

| ❏ CJ40587 | Ellington at Newport | 1987 | $25 |

—*Reissue of Columbia 934*

| ❏ CJ44444 | Ellington Indigos | 1989 | $25 |

—*Reissue of Columbia 8053*

| ❏ CJ40586 | First Time | 1987 | $25 |

—*Reissue of Columbia 8515*

| ❏ CJ40836 | Uptown | 1987 | $25 |

COLUMBIA JAZZ ODYSSEY
| ❏ PC36979 | The Festival Session | 1981 | $25 |

COLUMBIA MASTERWORKS
| ❏ ML4639 [M] | Ellington Uptown | 1951 | $200 |

—*Blue or green label, gold print*

| ❏ ML4639 [M] | Ellington Uptown | 195? | $50 |

—*Oddly, this exists as a reissue on the red and black "6 eye" label*

| ❏ ML4418 [M] | Masterpieces by Ellington | 1951 | $200 |

Number	Title	Yr	NM
COLUMBIA SPECIAL PRODUCTS			
❑ P13291	Duke Ellington's Greatest Hits (Recorded Live in Concert)	1976	$25
❑ P13500	Festival Session	1976	$25
❑ P14359	Suite Thursday/ Controversial Suite/Harlem Suite	198?	$25
DAYBREAK			
❑ DR2017	The Symphonic Ellington	1973	$30
DECCA			
❑ DL9224 [M]	Duke Ellington, Volume 1 -- In the Beginning	1958	$120
— Black label, silver print			
❑ DL9224 [M]	Duke Ellington, Volume 1 -- In the Beginning	1961	$75
— Black label with color bars			
❑ DL79224 [R]	Duke Ellington, Volume 1 -- In the Beginning	1958	$120
— Black label, silver print			
❑ DL79224 [R]	Duke Ellington, Volume 1 -- In the Beginning	1961	$35
— Black label with color bars			
❑ DL9241 [M]	Duke Ellington, Volume 2 -- Hot in Harlem	1959	$100
— Black label, silver print			
❑ DL9241 [M]	Duke Ellington, Volume 2 -- Hot in Harlem	1961	$75
— Black label with color bars			
❑ DL79241 [R]	Duke Ellington, Volume 2 -- Hot in Harlem	1959	$100
— Black label, silver print			
❑ DL79241 [R]	Duke Ellington, Volume 2 -- Hot in Harlem	1961	$35
— Black label with color bars			
❑ DL9247 [M]	Duke Ellington, Volume 3 -- Rockin' in Rhythm	1959	$100
— Black label, silver print			
❑ DL9247 [M]	Duke Ellington, Volume 3 -- Rockin' in Rhythm	1961	$75
— Black label with color bars			
❑ DL79247 [R]	Duke Ellington, Volume 3 -- Rockin' in Rhythm	1959	$100
— Black label, silver print			
❑ DL79247 [R]	Duke Ellington, Volume 3 -- Rockin' in Rhythm	1961	$35
— Black label with color bars			
❑ DL75069	Duke Ellington in Canada	1969	$35
DISCOVERY			
❑ 871	Afro Bossa	198?	$25
— Reissue of Reprise 6069			
❑ 841	Concert in the Virgin Islands	198?	$25
— Reissue of Reprise 6185			
DOCTOR JAZZ			
❑ W2X39137	All-Star Road Band	1984	$30
❑ W2X40012	All-Star Road Band, Vol. 2	1985	$30
❑ FW40030	Happy Reunion	1985	$25
❑ FW40359	New Mood Indigo	1986	$25
DO YOU LIKE JAZZ			
❑ P13293	Monologue	1973	$30
EVEREST ARCHIVE OF FOLK & JAZZ			
❑ 327	Duke Ellington at Carnegie Hall	197?	$30
❑ 221	Early Duke Ellington	1968	$30
❑ 249	Early Duke Ellington Vol. 2	1970	$30
❑ 266	Early Duke Ellington Vol. 3	1972	$30
FANTASY			
❑ F-9498	Afro-American Eclipse	1976	$30
❑ F-9636	Duke Ellington Featuring Paul Gonsalves	198?	$25
❑ OJC-623	Duke Ellington Featuring Paul Gonsalves	1991	$30
— Reissue of 9636			
❑ F-8407/8	Duke Ellington's Second Sacred Concert	1971	$35
❑ OJC-108	Great Times!	198?	$25
— Reissue of Riverside 9475			
❑ F-8419	Latin American Suite	1971	$30
❑ OJC-469	Latin American Suite	1990	$25
— Reissue of 8419			
❑ OJC-645	The Afro-Eurasian Eclipse	1991	$30
— Reissue of 9498			
❑ OJC-446	The Ellington Suites	1990	$25
— Reissue of Pablo 2310 762			
❑ F-9640	The Intimacy of the Blues	1986	$25
❑ OJC-624	The Intimacy of the Blues	1991	$30
— Reissue of 9640			
❑ F-9462	The Pianist	1974	$30
❑ OJC-633	Up in Duke's Workshop	1991	$30
— Reissue of Pablo 2310 815			
❑ F-9433	Yale Concert	1974	$30
FLYING DUTCHMAN			
❑ 10166	It Don't Mean a Thing	1973	$30
❑ BXL1-2832	It Don't Mean a Thing	1978	$25
— Reissue			
❑ 10112	My People	1969	$35

Number	Title	Yr	NM
FOLKWAYS			
❑ FJ-2968	First Annual Tour of the Pacific Northwest, Spring, 1952	198?	$40
GALAXY			
❑ 4807	Duke Ellington and His Famous Orchestra and Soloists	197?	$35
GNP CRESCENDO			
❑ GNP-9045	The 1953 Pasadena Concert	1986	$25
❑ GNP-9049	The 1954 Los Angeles Concert	1987	$25
HALL OF FAME			
❑ 625/6/7	The Immortal Duke Ellington	197?	$50
HARMONY			
❑ H30566	Duke Ellington's Greatest Hits Live	1971	$30
❑ HL7436 [M]	Fantasies	1967	$75
❑ HS11236 [R]	Fantasies	1967	$30
❑ HS11323	In My Solitude	1969	$30
HINDSIGHT			
❑ HSR-125	Duke Ellington 1946	198?	$25
❑ HSR-126	Duke Ellington 1946, Volume 2	198?	$25
❑ HSR-127	Duke Ellington 1946, Volume 3	198?	$25
❑ HSR-128	Duke Ellington 1947	198?	$25
❑ HSR-129	Duke Ellington 1947, Volume 2	198?	$25
IAJRC			
❑ LP-45	Fairfield, Connecticut Jazz Fest 1956	198?	$20
INTERMEDIA			
❑ QS-5021	Do Nothin' Till You Hear from Me	198?	$25
❑ QS-5020	Lullaby of Birdland	198?	$25
❑ QS-5063	Satin Doll	198?	$25
❑ QS-5002	Sophisticated Duke	198?	$25
JAZZBIRD			
❑ 2009	Meadowbrook to Manhattan	1980	$25
JAZZ ODYSSEY			
❑ 32160252	Nutcracker and Peer Gynt Suites	196?	$30
JAZZ PANORAMA			
❑ 1802 [10]	Duke Ellington -- Vol. 1	1951	$200
❑ 1811 [10]	Duke Ellington -- Vol. 2	1951	$200
❑ 1816 [10]	Duke Ellington -- Vol. 3	1951	$200
LONDON			
❑ AL-3551 [10]	The Duke -- 1926	195?	$150
MCA			
❑ 1374	Brunswick-Vocalion Rarities	198?	$25
❑ 2075	Duke Ellington, Volume 1 -- In the Beginning	197?	$25
— Reissue of Decca 79224			
❑ 1358	Duke Ellington, Volume 1 -- In the Beginning	198?	$20
— Reissue of 2075			
❑ 2076	Duke Ellington, Volume 2 -- Hot in Harlem	197?	$25
— Reissue of Decca 79241			
❑ 1359	Duke Ellington, Volume 2 -- Hot in Harlem	198?	$20
— Reissue of 2076			
❑ 2077	Duke Ellington, Volume 3 -- Rockin' in Rhythm	197?	$25
— Reissue of Decca 79247			
❑ 1360	Duke Ellington, Volume 3 -- Rockin' in Rhythm	198?	$20
— Reissue of 2077			
❑ 4142	Great Tenor Encounters	198?	$30
— Reissue of Impulse! 9350			
❑ 42325	The Brunswick Era, Vol. 1	1990	$30
MOBILE FIDELITY			
❑ 1-214	Anatomy of a Murder	1995	$120
— Audiophile vinyl			
MOSAIC			
❑ MQ8-160	The Complete Capitol Recordings of Duke Ellington	199?	$300
MUSICRAFT			
❑ 2002	Carnegie Hall Concert	1986	$25
PABLO			
❑ 2310703	Duke's Big 4	1974	$30
❑ 2310787	Intimate	197?	$30
❑ 2405401	The Best of Duke Ellington	198?	$25
❑ 2310762	The Ellington Suites	197?	$30
❑ 2310721	This One's for Blanton	197?	$30
❑ 2310815	Up in Duke's Workshop	1980	$25
PABLO LIVE			
❑ 2308245	Harlem	198?	$25
❑ 2308247	In the Uncommon Market	198?	$25
PAIR			
❑ PDL2-1011	Original Recordings by Duke Ellington	1986	$30
PICCADILLY			
❑ 3524	Classic Ellington	198?	$25

Number	Title	Yr	NM
PICKWICK			
❑ SPC-3390	We Love You Madly	197?	$25
PRESTIGE			
❑ 24045	Duke Ellington's Second Sacred Concert	1974	$30
— Reissue of Fantasy 8407/8			
❑ 24073	The Carnegie Hall Concerts: December 1944	1977	$35
❑ 24075	The Carnegie Hall Concerts: December 1947	1977	$35
❑ 34003	The Carnegie Hall Concerts: January 1943	197?	$50
❑ 24074	The Carnegie Hall Concerts: January 1946	1977	$35
❑ 24029	The Golden Duke	1973	$35
RCA CAMDEN			
❑ CAL-394 [M]	Duke Ellington at Tanglewood	1958	$50
❑ CAL-459 [M]	Duke Ellington at the Cotton Club	1959	$50
❑ ACL2-0152	Mood Indigo	1973	$35
❑ ACL-7052	The Duke at Tanglewood	197?	$25
— Reissue of RCA Red Seal LSC-2857			
RCA VICTOR			
❑ LPM-3906 [M]	And His Mother Called Him Bill	1968	$150
❑ LSP-3906 [S]	And His Mother Called Him Bill	1968	$35
❑ LPM-3582 [M]	Concert of Sacred Music	1966	$35
❑ LSP-3582 [S]	Concert of Sacred Music	1966	$50
❑ LPV-506 [M]	Daybreak Express	1964	$50
❑ LPM-1092 [M]	Duke and His Men	1955	$50
❑ WPT-11 [10]	Duke Ellington	1951	$200
❑ LPM-1715 [M]	Duke Ellington at His Very Best	1958	$40
❑ LPT-3067 [10]	Duke Ellington Plays the Blues	1952	$200
❑ APL1-1023	Eastbourne Performance	1974	$30
❑ LPT-1004 [M]	Ellington's Greatest	1954	$40
❑ LPM-3782 [M]	Far East Suite	1967	$75
❑ LSP-3782 [S]	Far East Suite	1967	$35
❑ LPV-568 [M]	Flaming Youth	1969	$50
❑ LPM-1364 [M]	In a Mellotone	1957	$40
— Black label, dog at top, "Long Play" at bottom			
❑ LPM-1364 [M]	In a Mellotone	196?	$75
— Black label, dog at top, "Mono" at bottom			
❑ LPM-1364 [M]	In a Mellotone	1969	$50
— Orange label			
❑ LPV-541 [M]	Johnny Come Lately	1967	$175
❑ LPV-517 [M]	Jumpin' Punkins	1965	$50
❑ LPV-553 [M]	Pretty Woman	1968	$50
❑ ANL1-2811	Pure Gold	1978	$25
❑ LJM-1002 [M]	Seattle Concert	1954	$150
❑ CPL2-4098	Sophisticated Ellington	1983	$30
❑ SP-33-394 [M]	The Duke at Tanglewood	1966	$75
— Special Interview Recording for Radio Station Programming			
❑ LPM-6009 [M]	The Indispensible Duke Ellington	1961	$150
❑ LPM-3576 [M]	The Popular Duke Ellington	1966	$35
❑ LSP-3576 [S]	The Popular Duke Ellington	1966	$50
❑ VPM-6042	This Is Duke Ellington	1972	$35
❑ LPT-3017 [10]	This Is Duke Ellington and His Orchestra	1952	$200
RCA VICTOR RED SEAL			
❑ LM-2857 [M]	The Duke at Tanglewood	1966	$35
❑ LSC-2857 [S]	The Duke at Tanglewood	1966	$50
REPRISE			
❑ R-6069 [M]	Afro-Bossa	1962	$50
❑ R9-6069 [S]	Afro-Bossa	1962	$50
❑ R-6185 [M]	Concert in the Virgin Islands	1965	$50
❑ RS-6185 [S]	Concert in the Virgin Islands	1965	$35
❑ R-6234 [M]	Duke Ellington's Greatest Hits	1967	$50
❑ RS-6234 [S]	Duke Ellington's Greatest Hits	1967	$35
❑ R-6122 [M]	Ellington '65: Hits of the '60s/ This Time by Ellington	1964	$50
❑ RS-6122 [S]	Ellington '65: Hits of the '60s/ This Time by Ellington	1964	$50
❑ R-6154 [M]	Ellington '66	1965	$50
❑ RS-6154 [S]	Ellington '66	1965	$35
❑ R-6141 [M]	Mary Poppins	1964	$50
❑ RS-6141 [S]	Mary Poppins	1964	$50
❑ R-6097 [M]	The Symphonic Ellington	1963	$50
❑ R9-6097 [S]	The Symphonic Ellington	1963	$50
❑ R-6168 [M]	Will Big Bands Ever Come Back?	1965	$50
❑ RS-6168 [S]	Will Big Bands Ever Come Back?	1965	$35
RIVERSIDE			
❑ RLP 12-129 [M]	Birth of Big Band Jazz	1956	$350
— White label, blue print			
❑ RLP 12-129 [M]	Birth of Big Band Jazz	195?	$30
— Blue label with mike logo			
❑ RLP-475 [M]	Great Times!	1963	$175
❑ RS-9475 [S]	Great Times!	1963	$175
RONDO-LETTE			
❑ A-7 [M]	Duke Ellington and Orchestra	1958	$75
ROULETTE			
❑ 108	Echoes of an Era	1971	$35

Number	Title	Yr	NM

ROYALE

Number	Title	Yr	NM
❏ 18143 [10]	Duke Ellington and His Orchestra	195?	$50
❏ 18152 [10]	Duke Ellington Plays Ellington	195?	$50

SMITHSONIAN COLLECTION

| ❏ P6-15079 | An Explosion of Genius 1938-1940 | 1976 | $150 |

—Produced in association with Columbia Special Products

SOLID STATE

| ❏ SS-19000 | 75th Birthday | 1970 | $50 |
| ❏ SM-18022 | Money Jungle | 1968 | $35 |

—Reissue of United Artists 15017

STANYAN

| ❏ 10105 | For Always | 197? | $30 |

STARDUST

| ❏ SD-124 [M] | Duke | 196? | $30 |
| ❏ SDS-124 [R] | Duke | 196? | $30 |

STORYVILLE

| ❏ SLP-4003 | Duke Ellington and His Orchestra | 198? | $25 |

SUPER MAJESTIC

| ❏ 2000 | Duke Ellington | 197? | $30 |

SUTTON

| ❏ SU-276 [M] | Duke Meets Leonard Feather | 196? | $30 |

TIME-LIFE

❏ STBB-16	Big Bands: Cotton Club Nights	1983	$35
❏ STBB-05	Big Bands: Duke Ellington	1983	$35
❏ STL-J-02	Giants of Jazz	1978	$50

TREND

| ❏ 2004 | Carnegie Hall Concert | 198? | $25 |
| ❏ 529 | The Symphonic Ellington | 1982 | $50 |

UNITED ARTISTS

❏ UAJ-14017 [M]	Money Jungle	1962	$40
❏ UAJS-15017 [S]	Money Jungle	1962	$40
❏ UAS-5632	Money Jungle	1972	$30

—Reissue

| ❏ UXS-92 | Togo Bravo Suite | 1972 | $35 |

VEE JAY

| ❏ VJS-3061 | Love You Madly | 198? | $25 |

VERVE

| ❏ V-8701 [M] | Soul Call | 1967 | $35 |
| ❏ V6-8701 [S] | Soul Call | 1967 | $30 |

X

| ❏ LVA-3037 [10] | Duke Ellington Plays | 1955 | $200 |

ELLINGTON, HARVEY

STEPHENY

| ❏ MF-4010 [M] | I Can't Hide the Blues | 1959 | $150 |

ELLINGTON, MERCER

CORAL

❏ CRL0 (# unknown) [M]	Black and Tan Fantasy	1958	$30
❏ CRL0 (# unknown) [S]	Black and Tan Fantasy	1958	$40
❏ CRL57293 [M]	Colors in Rhythm	1959	$30
❏ CRL757293 [S]	Colors in Rhythm	1959	$40
❏ CRL57225 [M]	Stepping Into Swing Society	1958	$30
❏ CRL757225 [S]	Stepping Into Swing Society	1958	$40

MCA

| ❏ 349 | Black and Tan Fantasy | 197? | $30 |

ELLINGTONIANS, THE

MERCER

| ❏ LP-1004 [10] | The Ellingtonians with Al Hibbler | 1951 | $300 |

ELLIOT, CASS

Also see THE BIG THREE; THE MAMAS AND THE PAPAS; DAVE MASON; THE MUGWUMPS.

ABC DUNHILL

Number	Title	Yr	NM
❏ DS-50055 [B]	Bubble Gum, Lemonade &... Something for Mama	1969	$25
❏ DS-50040	Dream a Little Dream	1968	$25
❏ DS-50071	Make Your Own Kind of Music	1969	$18

—Reissue of 50055 with new title and one added song

| ❏ DS-50093 | Mama's Big Ones | 1970 | $18 |

MCA

| ❏ 719 | Mama's Big Ones | 1980 | $10 |

RCA VICTOR

❏ LSP-4619	Cass Elliot	1971	$18
❏ APL1-0303	Don't Call Me Mama Anymore	1973	$18
❏ LSP-4753	The Road Is No Place for a Lady	1972	$18

ELLIOT, MIKE

ASI

❏ 5003	Atrio	197?	$25
❏ 5007	City Traffic	197?	$25
❏ 5001	Natural Life	197?	$25

PAUSA

| ❏ 7139 | Diffusion | 1981 | $25 |

ELLIOT, RICHARD

INTIMA

| ❏ SJE-73283 | Initial Approach | 1987 | $25 |

—Reissue of ITI album

❏ D1-73348	Take to the Skies	1989	$30
❏ D1-73321	The Power of Suggestion	1988	$30
❏ SJ-73233	Trolltown	1987	$30

ITI

| ❏ JL-030 | Initial Approach | 198? | $35 |

ELLIOTT, DEAN

CAPITOL

❏ T1864 [M]	Heartstrings	1962	$25
❏ ST1864 [S]	Heartstrings	1962	$30
❏ T1834 [M]	Zounds! What Sounds!	1962	$40
❏ ST1834 [S]	Zounds! What Sounds!	1962	$50

ELLIOTT, DON

ABC-PARAMOUNT

❏ ABC-142 [M]	Don Elliott at the Modern Jazz Room	1956	$40
❏ ABC-228 [M]	Jamaica Jazz	1958	$40
❏ ABCS-228 [S]	Jamaica Jazz	1959	$30
❏ ABC-106 [M]	Musical Offering	1956	$40
❏ ABC-190 [M]	The Voices of Don Elliott	1957	$50

BETHLEHEM

| ❏ BCP-15 [M] | Don Elliott Sings | 1955 | $300 |
| ❏ BCP-12 [M] | Mellophone | 1955 | $300 |

COLUMBIA

| ❏ PC33799 | Rejuvenation | 1975 | $30 |

DECCA

| ❏ DL9208 [M] | The Mello Sound | 1958 | $150 |
| ❏ DL79208 [S] | The Mello Sound | 1958 | $150 |

DESIGN

| ❏ DLP-69 [M] | Music for the Sensational 60's | 196? | $35 |
| ❏ DLPS-69 [S] | Music for the Sensational 60's | 196? | $30 |

HALLMARK

| ❏ 317 [M] | Pal Joey | 1957 | $50 |

JAZZLAND

| ❏ JLP-15 [M] | Double Trumpet Doings | 1960 | $40 |
| ❏ JLP-915 [S] | Double Trumpet Doings | 1960 | $30 |

RCA VICTOR

| ❏ LJM-1007 [M] | Don Elliott Quintet | 1954 | $75 |

RIVERSIDE

| ❏ RLP 12-218 [M] | Counterpoint for Six Valves | 1956 | $300 |

—White label, blue print

| ❏ RLP 12-218 [M] | Counterpoint for Six Valves | 195? | $40 |

—Blue label, microphone logo

| ❏ RLP-2517 [10] | Six Valves | 1955 | $300 |

SAVOY

| ❏ MG-9033 [10] | The Versatile Don Elliott | 1953 | $120 |

VANGUARD

| ❏ VRS-8016 [10] | Doubles in Brass | 1954 | $150 |

ELLIOTT, DON/SAM MOST

JAZZTONE

| ❏ J-1256 [M] | Doubles in Jazz | 1957 | $40 |

VANGUARD

| ❏ VRS-8522 [M] | Doubles in Jazz | 1957 | $150 |

—Partial reissue of 8016 and 8014

ELLIOTT, RAMBLIN' JACK

FOLKLORE

❏ FL14029 [M]	Country Style	1964	$25
❏ FL14019 [M]	Hootenanny with Jack Elliott	1964	$25
❏ FL14014 [M]	Ramblin'	1964	$25

Number	Title	Yr	NM
❏ FL14011 [M]	The Songs of Woody Guthrie	1964	$25

MONITOR

❏ MF-380 [M]	Jack Elliott Sings Woody Guthrie and Jimmie Rodgers	1962	$30
❏ MS-380 [S]	Jack Elliott Sings Woody Guthrie and Jimmie Rodgers	1962	$30
❏ MF-379 [M]	Ramblin' Cowboy	1962	$30

PRESTIGE

❏ PRLP-13045 [M]	Country Style	1962	$30
❏ PRLP-13065 [M]	Jack Elliott at the Second Fret	1962	$30
❏ PRLP-13033 [M]	Ramblin'	1961	$30
❏ PRLP-13016 [M]	The Songs of Woody Guthrie	1961	$30

TOPIC

| ❏ T-15 [10] | Jack Takes the Floor | 195? | $40 |

VANGUARD

| ❏ VRS-9151 [M] | Jack Elliott | 1964 | $30 |
| ❏ VSD-79151 [S] | Jack Elliott | 1964 | $40 |

ELLIOTT, RON

WARNER BROS.

| ❏ WS1833 | Candlestickmaker | 1969 | $18 |

ELLIOTT, WALTER & BENNETT

JAM

| ❏ 104/105 | Elliott, Walter & Bennett | 197? | $25 |
| ❏ (# unknown) | Save a Piece of the World | 1975 | $50 |

—As "Elliott and Walter

| ❏ 106 | Zeti Reticuli | 197? | $100 |

ELLIS, ANITA

ELEKTRA

| ❏ EKL-179 [M] | The World in My Arms | 1959 | $40 |

EPIC

| ❏ LN3419 [M] | Him | 1958 | $100 |
| ❏ LN3280 [M] | I Wonder What Became of Me | 1956 | $100 |

ELLIS, DON

ATLANTIC

| ❏ SD19178 | Live at Montreux | 1977 | $30 |
| ❏ SD18227 | Survival/Music from Other Galaxies and Planets | 1977 | $30 |

BARNABY

| ❏ BR-5020 | How Time Passes | 197? | $30 |

—Reissue of Candid LP

BASF

| ❏ 25341 | Haiku | 1974 | $35 |
| ❏ 25123 | Soaring | 1973 | $35 |

CANDID

| ❏ CJM-8004 [M] | How Time Passes | 1961 | $50 |
| ❏ CJS-9004 [S] | How Time Passes | 1961 | $75 |

COLUMBIA

❏ CS9721	Autumn	1969	$35
❏ KC31766	Connection	1972	$35
❏ G30243	Don Ellis at the Fillmore	1970	$25
❏ CG30243	Don Ellis at the Fillmore	197?	$35

—Reissue with new prefix

❏ CL2785 [M]	Electric Bath	1968	$30
❏ CS9585 [S]	Electric Bath	1968	$35
❏ CS9668	Shock Treatment	1968	$35
❏ G30927	Tears of Joy	1971	$25
❏ CG30927	Tears of Joy	197?	$35

—Reissue with new prefix

| ❏ CS9889 | The New Don Ellis Band Goes Underground | 1969 | $25 |

FANTASY

| ❏ OJC-431 | New Ideas | 1990 | $30 |

NEW JAZZ

| ❏ NJLP-8257 [M] | New Ideas | 1961 | $175 |

—Purple label

| ❏ NJLP-8257 [M] | New Ideas | 1965 | $175 |

—Blue label, trident logo at right

PACIFIC JAZZ

❏ PJ-10112 [M]	Don Ellis "Live" At Monterey	1967	$25
❏ ST-20112 [S]	Don Ellis "Live" At Monterey	1967	$35
❏ PJ-55 [M]	Essence	1962	$30
❏ ST-55 [S]	Essence	1962	$40
❏ PJ-10123 [M]	Live in 3/2 3/4 Time	1967	$25
❏ ST-20123 [S]	Live in 3/2 3/4 Time	1967	$35

PAUSA

| ❏ 7028 | Soaring | 1979 | $25 |

—Reissue of BASF 25123

PRESTIGE

| ❏ PRST-7607 | New Ideas | 1969 | $35 |

ELLIS, HERB, AND JOE PASS

CONCORD JAZZ

| ❏ CJ-1 | Jazz/Concord | 197? | $35 |
| ❏ CJ-2 | Seven Come Eleven | 197? | $35 |

PABLO

| ❏ 2310714 | Two for the Road | 1974 | $35 |

Number	Title	Yr	NM

ELLIS, HERB, AND RAY BROWN
CONCORD JAZZ
❑ CJ-6	After You've Gone	197?	$30
❑ CJ-12	Hot Tracks	1977	$30
❑ CJ-10	Rhythm Willie	197?	$30
❑ CJ-3	Soft Shoe	197?	$30

ELLIS, HERB, AND RED MITCHELL
CONCORD JAZZ
| ❑ CJ-372 | Doggin' Around | 1989 | $30 |

ELLIS, HERB, AND REMO PALMIER
CONCORD JAZZ
| ❑ CJ-56 | Windflower | 1978 | $30 |

ELLIS, HERB, AND ROSS TOMPKINS
CONCORD JAZZ
| ❑ CJ-17 | A Pair to Draw On | 1977 | $30 |

ELLIS, HERB
COLUMBIA
| ❑ CL2330 [M] | Herb Ellis Guitar | 1965 | $35 |
| ❑ CS9130 [S] | Herb Ellis Guitar | 1965 | $25 |
CONCORD JAZZ
❑ CJ-116	Herb Ellis at Montreux, Summer 1979	1980	$25
❑ CJ-181	Herb Mix	1982	$25
❑ CJ-77	Soft and Mellow	1979	$25
DOT
❑ DLP-3678 [M]	The Man with the Guitar	1965	$85
❑ DLP-25678 [S]	The Man with the Guitar	1965	$85
EPIC
❑ LA16039 [M]	Herb Ellis and "Stuff" Smith Together	1963	$50
❑ BA17039 [S]	Herb Ellis and "Stuff" Smith Together	1963	$75
❑ LA16034 [M]	The Midnight Roll	1962	$75
❑ BA17034 [S]	The Midnight Roll	1962	$75
❑ LA16036 [M]	Three Guitars in Bossa Nova Time	1963	$50
❑ BA17036 [S]	Three Guitars in Bossa Nova Time	1963	$75
NORGRAN
❑ MGN-1081 [M]	Ellis in Wonderland	1956	$250
VERVE
❑ MGV-8171 [M]	Ellis in Wonderland	1957	$250
— Reissue of Norgran 1081
| ❑ V-8171 [M] | Ellis in Wonderland | 1961 | $25 |
| ❑ MGV-8278 [M] | Herb Ellis | 1958 | $0 |
— Canceled
❑ MGV-8311 [M]	Herb Ellis Meets Jimmy Giuffre	1959	$100
❑ MGVS-6045 [S]	Herb Ellis Meets Jimmy Giuffre	1960	$150
❑ V-8311 [M]	Herb Ellis Meets Jimmy Giuffre	1961	$25
❑ V6-8311 [S]	Herb Ellis Meets Jimmy Giuffre	1961	$25
❑ MGV-8252 [M]	Nothing But the Blues	1958	$100
❑ V-8252 [M]	Nothing But the Blues	1961	$25
❑ V-8448 [M]	Softly...But With That Feeling	1962	$25
❑ V6-8448 [S]	Softly...But With That Feeling	1962	$30
❑ MGV-8381 [M]	Thank You, Charlie Christian	1960	$100
❑ MGVS-6164 [S]	Thank You, Charlie Christian	1960	$100
❑ V-8381 [M]	Thank You, Charlie Christian	1961	$25
❑ V6-8381 [S]	Thank You, Charlie Christian	1961	$25

ELLIS, JIMMY
BOBLO
| ❑ 78-829 | By Request Jimmy Sings Elvis | 1978 | $150 |

ELLIS, LLOYD
CARLTON
| ❑ LP 12-104 [M] | Fastest Guitar in the World | 1958 | $150 |
FAMOUS DOOR
| ❑ HL-100 | Las Vegas 3 AM | 197? | $30 |
TREY
| ❑ TLP-902 [M] | So Tall, So Cool, So There! | 1960 | $75 |

ELLIS, MATTHEW
WARNER BROS.
| ❑ BS2610 | Matthew Ellis | 1972 | $18 |

ELLIS, PEE WEE
SAVOY
| ❑ SJL-3301 | Home in the Country | 1976 | $25 |

ELLIS, RAY
ATCO
| ❑ 33-187 [M] | Big Hits for Swingers | 1966 | $15 |
| ❑ SD 33-187 [S] | Big Hits for Swingers | 1966 | $18 |
COLUMBIA
| ❑ CL1122 [M] | Dancing with Gigi | 1958 | $18 |

Number	Title	Yr	NM
❑ CL993 [M]	Ellis in Wonderland	1957	$18
❑ CL1097 [M]	Let's Get Away from It All	1957	$18
HARMONY			
❑ HS11003 [S]	Gigi	1959	$18
❑ HL7183 [M]	Gigi	1959	$15
MGM			
❑ E-3911 [M]	Carnival in Sound	1961	$0
— Canceled
| ❑ SE-3911 [M] | Carnival in Sound | 1961 | $0 |
— Canceled
❑ E-3779 [M]	I'm in the Mood for Strings	1959	$15
❑ SE-3779 [S]	I'm in the Mood for Strings	1959	$18
❑ E-3820 [M]	I'm in the Mood to Swing	1960	$15
❑ SE-3820 [S]	I'm in the Mood to Swing	1960	$18
❑ E-3813 [M]	The Best of Peter Gunn	1960	$15
❑ E-3842 [M]	The Big Voices, The Big Bands, The Big Songs, The Big Sounds	1960	$15
❑ SE-3842 [S]	The Big Voices, The Big Bands, The Big Songs, The Big Sounds	1960	$18
RCA VICTOR			
❑ LPM-2493 [M]	How to Succeed in Business Without Really Trying	1961	$15
❑ LSP-2493 [S]	How to Succeed in Business Without Really Trying	1961	$18
❑ LPM-2410 [M]	La Dolce Vita	1961	$15
❑ LSP-2410 [S]	La Dolce Vita	1961	$18
❑ LPM-2615 [M]	Our Man on Broadway	1963	$15
❑ LSP-2615 [S]	Our Man on Broadway	1963	$18
❑ LPM-2400 [M]	Ray Ellis Plays the Top 20	1961	$15
❑ LSP-2400 [S]	Ray Ellis Plays the Top 20	1961	$18

ELLIS, RED
STARDAY
❑ SLP-168 [M]	Holy Cry from the Cross	1962	$30
❑ SLP-273 [M]	Old Time Religion Bluegrass Style	1963	$30
❑ SLP-203 [M]	The Sacred Sound of Bluegrass Music	1962	$30

ELLIS, SHIRLEY
COLUMBIA
| ❑ CL2679 [M] | Sugar, Let's Shing-a-Ling | 1967 | $25 |
| ❑ CS9479 [S] | Sugar, Let's Shing-a-Ling | 1967 | $30 |
CONGRESS
❑ CGL-3002 [M]	Shirley Ellis In Action	1964	$30
❑ CGS-3002 [S]	Shirley Ellis In Action	1964	$30
❑ CGL-3003 [M]	The Name Game	1965	$30
❑ CGS-3003 [S]	The Name Game	1965	$30

ELLIS, STEVE, AND THE STARFIRES
I.G.L.
| ❑ 105 | The Steve Ellis Songbook | 1967 | $500 |

ELLISON, LORRAINE
WARNER BROS.
❑ W1674 [M]	Heart and Soul	1967	$40
❑ WS1674 [S]	Heart and Soul	1967	$30
❑ BS2780 [S]	Lorraine Ellison	1974	$18
❑ WS1821	Stay with Me	1969	$40

ELMAN, ZIGGY
CIRCLE
| ❑ 70 | Ziggy Elman and His Orchestra 1947 | 198? | $25 |
MGM
❑ E-163 [10]	Dancing with Zig	1952	$50
❑ E-3389 [10]	Sentimental Trumpet	1956	$40
❑ E-535 [10]	Ziggy Elman and His Orchestra	195?	$150
SUNBEAM
❑ 202	Angels Sing 1938-39	198?	$25

ELMER GANTRY'S VELVET OPERA
EPIC
| ❑ BN26415 | Elmer Gantry's Velvet Opera | 1968 | $85 |

ELMO AND PATSY
EPIC
| ❑ PE39931 | Grandma Got Run Over by a Reindeer | 1985 | $10 |
— reissue of 5E 39931
| ❑ 5E39931 | Grandma Got Run Over by a Reindeer | 1984 | $12 |

ELMORE, ROBERT
MERCURY LIVING PRESENCE
| ❑ SR90127 [S] | Bach on the Biggest | 1960 | $30 |
— Maroon label, no "Vendor: Mercury Record Corporation
| ❑ SR90109 [S] | Boardwalk Pipes | 196? | $150 |
— Maroon label, no "Vendor: Mercury Record Corporation

ELSTAK, NEDLEY
ESP-DISK'
| ❑ 1076 | The Machine | 1969 | $150 |

Number	Title	Yr	NM

ELVIS BROTHERS, THE
PORTRAIT
| ❑ BFR38865 | Movin' Up | 1983 | $15 |

ELY, CHET
GHB
| ❑ 67 | Til Times Get Better | 197? | $25 |

ELY, JOE
HIGHTONE
| ❑ 8015 | Dig All Night | 1988 | $12 |
| ❑ 8008 | Lord of the Highway | 1987 | $12 |
MCA
| ❑ 3080 | Down on the Drag | 1979 | $16 |
— Originals have a gatefold sleeve
❑ 5480	Hi-Res	1984	$15
❑ 2333	Honky Tonk Masquerade	1978	$16
❑ 2242	Joe Ely	1977	$16
❑ R124826	Live at Liberty Lunch	1990	$18
— BMG Music Service edition
| ❑ 5262 | Live Shots | 1981 | $15 |
SOUTHCOAST
| ❑ 5183 | Musta Notta Gotta Lotta | 1981 | $15 |

EMANUELE, VITTORIO
RCA VICTOR RED SEAL
| ❑ LSC-2424 [S] | Vivaldi: The Four Seasons | 1960 | $25 |
— With the Societa Corelli; original with "shaded dog" label

EMBERS, THE
EEE
| ❑ 1069 [M] | Burn You a New One | 1967 | $250 |
JCP
| ❑ 2009 [M] | Just for the Birds | 1966 | $250 |
| ❑ 2006 [M] | The Embers Roll Eleven | 1965 | $250 |

EMERSON, KEITH
Also see EMERSON, LAKE AND PALMER.

EMERSON
| ❑ KEITH LP-1 | The Christmas Album | 1993 | $25 |
— British import only

EMERSON, LAKE AND PALMER
RAZOR & TIE
| ❑ 7930183398-1 [B] | The First Five: Picture Disc Collection | 2013 | $150 |

EMERSON, LAKE AND PALMER
Also see GREG LAKE; ASIA.

ATLANTIC
❑ SD19124	Brain Salad Surgery	1977	$10
❑ SD19120	Emerson, Lake and Palmer	1977	$10
❑ SD19255	Emerson, Lake and Palmer In Concert	1979	$12
❑ SD19211	Love Beach	1978	$12
❑ PR281 [DJ]	On Tour with Emerson, Lake and Palmer	1977	$40
❑ SD19122	Pictures at an Exhibition	1977	$10
❑ SD19121	Tarkus	1977	$10
❑ SD19283	The Best of Emerson, Lake and Palmer	1980	$12
❑ SD19123	Trilogy	1977	$10
❑ SD7000	Works Volume 1	1977	$18
❑ PR277 [DJ]	Works Volume 1	1977	$18
— Promo-only sampler
| ❑ SD19147 | Works Volume 2 | 1977 | $12 |
COTILLION
❑ SD9040	Emerson, Lake and Palmer	1971	$15
❑ ELP66666	Pictures at an Exhibition	1971	$15
❑ SD9900	Tarkus	1971	$15
❑ SD9903	Trilogy	1972	$15
❑ SMAS-94773	Trilogy	1972	$18
— Capitol Record Club edition
MANTICORE
| ❑ ELP66669 | Brain Salad Surgery | 1973 | $15 |
| ❑ SD 3-200 | Welcome Back, My Friends, to the Show That Never Ends, Ladies and Gentlemen | 1974 | $25 |
MOBILE FIDELITY
| ❑ Jan-0031 | Pictures at an Exhibition | 1980 | $50 |
— Audiophile vinyl
| ❑ 1-203 | Tarkus | 1994 | $75 |
— Audiophile vinyl
| ❑ 1-218 | Trilogy | 1994 | $100 |
— Audiophile vinyl

EMERSON, LAKE AND POWELL
That's Cozy Powell of RAINBOW, BLACK SABBATH and MSG fame.

POLYDOR
| ❑ 829297-1 | Emerson, Lake and Powell | 1986 | $12 |

Number	Title	Yr	NM

EMERSON'S OLD-TIMEY CUSTARD-SUCKIN' BAND
ESP-DISK'
| ❏ 2006 | Emerson's Old-Timey Custard-Suckin' Band | 1970 | $75 |

EMF
EMI
| ❏ E1-96238 | Schubert Dip | 1991 | $30 |

EMINEM
AFTERMATH
❏ 1286301 [B]	Relapse	2008	$30
❏ 493290-1	The Eminem Show	2002	$25
❏ 490629-1	The Marshall Mathers LP	2000	$25
❏ 4906291	The Marshall Mathers LP	2008	$30

| ❏ 90287 [B] | The Slim Shady LP | 1999 | $30 |

EMMONS, BOBBY
HI
| ❏ HL-32024 [M] | Blues with a Beat | 1965 | $30 |
| ❏ SHL-32024 [S] | Blues with a Beat | 1965 | $30 |

EMMONS, BUDDY, AND SHOT JACKSON
STARDAY
| ❏ SLP-230 [M] | Singing Strings of Steel and Dobro | 196? | $40 |

EMMONS, BUDDY
MERCURY
| ❏ MG-20843 [M] | Steel Guitar Jazz | 1963 | $175 |
| ❏ SR-60843 [S] | Steel Guitar Jazz | 1963 | $175 |
STEP ONE
| ❏ SOR-0024 | Christmas Sounds of the Steel Guitar | 198? | $15 |

EMOTIONS, THE (1)
ARC
| ❏ JC36149 | Come Into Our World | 1979 | $12 |
| ❏ FC37456 | New Affair | 1981 | $12 |
COLUMBIA
❏ PC34163	Flowers	1976	$12
—No bar code on cover			
❏ PC34163	Flowers	198?	$10
—With bar code on cover			
❏ PC34762	Rejoice	1977	$12
—No bar code on cover			
❏ PC34762	Rejoice	198?	$10
—With bar code on cover			
❏ JC35385	Sunbeam	1978	$12
MOTOWN
| ❏ 6136ML | If I Only Knew | 1985 | $10 |
RED LABEL
| ❏ 001 | Sincerely | 1984 | $12 |
STAX
❏ STX-4121	Chronicle	1979	$12
❏ STX-4110	So I Can Love You	1978	$12
—Reissue of Volt 6008			
❏ STX-4100	Sunshine	1977	$12
❏ STX-4112	Untouched	1978	$12
—Reissue of Volt 6015			
VOLT
| ❏ VOS-6008 | So I Can Love You | 1971 | $30 |
| ❏ VOS-6015 | Untouched | 1972 | $30 |

EN VOGUE
ATLANTIC
| ❏ 82084 [B] | Born to Sing | 1990 | $25 |

END, THE
LONDON
| ❏ PS560 | Introspection | 1969 | $50 |

ENESCU, GEORGE
CONTINENTAL
❏ CLP104 [M]	Bach: Six Sonatas and Partitas for Unaccompanied Violin	1949	$10000
—In original box			
❏ CLP106 [M]	Bach: Sonatas 5 and 6	1949	$4000

ENEVOLDSEN, BOB
LIBERTY
| ❏ LJH-6008 [M] | Smorgasboard | 1956 | $50 |
NOCTURNE
| ❏ NLP-6 [M] | Bob Enevoldsen Quintet | 1954 | $175 |
TAMPA
❏ TP-14 [M]	Reflections in Jazz	1957	$250
—Colored vinyl			
❏ TP-14 [M]	Reflections in Jazz	1958	$175
—Black vinyl			

ENGLAND DAN AND JOHN FORD COLEY
A&M
❏ SP-4305	England Dan and John Ford Coley	1971	$18
❏ SP-4350	Fables	1972	$18
❏ SP-4613	I Hear Music	1976	$15
BIG TREE
❏ BT76018	Best of England Dan & John Ford Coley	1980	$12
❏ BT76000	Dowdy Ferry Road	1977	$12
❏ BT76015	Dr. Heckle & Mr. Jive	1979	$12
❏ BT89517	Nights Are Forever	1976	$12
❏ BT76006	Some Things Don't Come Easy	1978	$12

ENGLISH BEAT, THE
I.R.S.
❏ SP-70606	I Just Can't Stop It	1983	$12
—Reissue of Sire album of the same name			
❏ SP-70032	Special Beat Service	1982	$12
❏ SP-70607	Wha'ppen?	1983	$12
—Reissue of Sire album of the same name			
❏ SP-70040	What Is Beat?	1983	$12
SIRE
| ❏ SRK-6091 | I Just Can't Stop It | 1980 | $18 |
| ❏ SRK-3567 | Wha'ppen | 1981 | $18 |

ENGLISH CONGREGATION, THE
SIGNPOST
| ❏ SP8405 | Jesahel | 1972 | $15 |
| ❏ SP7217 | Softly Whispering I Love You | 1972 | $15 |

ENNIS, ETHEL
BASF
| ❏ 25121 | 10 Sides of Ethel Ennis | 1973 | $35 |
CAPITOL
| ❏ T941 | Change of Scenery | 1957 | $75 |
| ❏ T1078 [M] | Have You Forgotten? | 1959 | $85 |
JUBILEE
❏ JLP-5024 [M]	Ethel Ennis Sings	1963	$25
❏ SJLP-5024 [S]	Ethel Ennis Sings	1963	$30
❏ JLP-1021 [M]	Lullabies for Losers	1956	$50
PICKWICK
| ❏ PC-3021 [M] | Ethel Ennis | 196? | $30 |
| ❏ SPC-3021 [S] | Ethel Ennis | 196? | $30 |
RCA CAMDEN
| ❏ ACL1-0157 | God Bless the Child | 1973 | $25 |
RCA VICTOR
❏ LPM-2984 [M]	Eyes for You	1964	$25
❏ LSP-2984 [S]	Eyes for You	1964	$30
❏ LSP-2862 [S]	Once Again, Ethel Ennis	1964	$30
❏ LPM-2862 [M]	Once Again, Ethel Ennis	1964	$25
❏ LPM-2786 [M]	This Is Ethel Ennis	1964	$25
❏ LSP-2786 [S]	This Is Ethel Ennis	1964	$30

ENNIS, SKINNAY
HINDSIGHT
| ❏ HSR-164 | Skinnay Ennis 1947-48 | 198? | $25 |

ENO, BRIAN
Also see ROXY MUSIC.
ANTILLES
❏ AN-7030	Discreet Music	1975	$30
❏ AN-7018 [B]	Evening Star	1975	$35
—By Robert Fripp and Eno			
❏ AN-7070	Music for Films	1978	$35
❏ AN-7001 [B]	No Pussyfooting	1973	$60
—By Robert Fripp and Eno			

EDITIONS EG
❏ EGS-201	Ambient #1 -- Music for Airports	1982	$25
—Reissue			
❏ EGS-202 [B]	Ambient 2 -- The Plateaux of Mirrors	1982	$70
—By Harold Budd and Brian Eno			
❏ EGED-20 [B]	Ambient 4 -- On Land	1982	$25
❏ ENO-3	Another Green World	1982	$25
—Reissue			
❏ ENO-5 [B]	Apollo: Atmospheres and Soundtracks	1983	$30
❏ ENO-4	Before and After Science	1982	$25
—Reissue			
❏ EGS-303	Discreet Music	1983	$30
—Reissue			
❏ EGS-103	Evening Star	1982	$25
—By Robert Fripp and Eno; reissue			
❏ EGS-107	Fourth World Volume 1: Possible Musics	1980	$30
—With Jon Hassell			
❏ ENO-1	Here Come the Warm Jets	1982	$25
—Reissue			
❏ EGS-105	Music for Films	1982	$25
—Reissue			

FRIPP & ENO
(NO PUSSYFOOTING)

❏ EGS-102 [B]	No Pussyfooting	1982	$25
—By Robert Fripp and Eno; reissue			
❏ EGS-301	Pavilion of Dreams	1982	$75
—By Harold Budd and Brian Eno			
❏ ENO-2	Taking Tiger Mountain (By Strategy)	1982	$40
—Reissue			
❏ EGED-37	The Pearl	1984	$75
—By Harold Budd and Brian Eno			
❏ EGBS-2	Working Backwards: 1983-1973	1984	$350
—Boxed set of nine albums plus Music For Films II and Rarities 12			
ISLAND
❏ ILPS9351 [B]	Another Green World	1975	$40
❏ ILPS9478 [B]	Before and After Science	1977	$40
—Double the value if four lithographs are included with the package.			
❏ ILPS9268 [B]	Here Come the Warm Jets	1973	$50
❏ ILPS9309 [B]	Taking Tiger Mountain (By Strategy)	1974	$60
JEM
| ❏ ENO DJ [DJ] | Music for Airplay | 1981 | $75 |
| *—Promo-only 10-track sampler* | | | |
OPAL/WARNER BROS.
❏ 25769	Music for Films, Vol. III	1988	$25
❏ 26421	Wrong Way Up	1990	$30
—With John Cale			
PVC
| ❏ 7908 [B] | Ambient #1 -- Music for Airports | 1979 | $40 |

ENO/MOEBIUS/ROEDELIUS
4 MEN WITH BEARDS
| ❏ 4M163LP [B] | After The Heat | | $25 |

ENRIQUEZ, BOBBY
GNP CRESCENDO
❏ GNPS-2155	Espana	1983	$25
❏ GNPS-2179	Live at Concerts by the Sea	1985	$20
❏ GNPS-2183	Live at Concerts by the Sea, Volume II	1986	$20
❏ GNPS-2161	Live in Tokyo	198?	$20
❏ GNPS-2168	Live in Tokyo, Volume II	198?	$20
❏ GNPS-2151	Prodigious Piano	198?	$20
❏ GNPS-2144	The Wildman	198?	$20
❏ GNPS-2148	The Wildman Meets the Madman	198?	$20

Number	Title	Yr	NM
PORTRAIT			
❏ FR44160	Wild Piano	1988	$30
ENSEMBLE AL-SALAAM, THE			
STRATA-EAST			
❏ SES-7418	The Sojourner	1974	$40
ENSEMBLE FOR EARLY MUSIC			
NONESUCH			
❏ H-71315	Christmeas in Anglia: Early English Music for Christmastide	1979	$15

— Frederick Renz, director

Number	Title	Yr	NM
ENTWISTLE, JOHN Also see THE WHO.			
ATCO			
❏ SD 38-142	Too Late the Hero	1981	$12
DECCA			
❏ DL79183 [B]	Smash Your Head Against the Wall	1971	$30
MCA			
❏ 2024	Smash Your Head Against the Wall	1973	$15

— Reissue of Decca 79183

Number	Title	Yr	NM
TRACK			
❏ MCA-2129	Mad Dog	1975	$18
❏ MCA-321 [B]	Rigor Mortis Sets In	1973	$30
❏ DL79190	Whistle Rymes	1972	$30
❏ L33-1926 [DJ]	Who's Ox	1975	$150

— Promo-only sampler

Number	Title	Yr	NM
ENYA			
GEFFEN			
❏ GHS24233	Watermark	1988	$18
ENYARD, RON, AND PAULA OWEN			
CADENCE JAZZ			
❏ CJR-1031	Red, Green and Blues (In Living Black and White)	1987	$25
EPIC CHOIR, THE			
EPIC			
❏ LC3144 [M]	The Story of Christmas	1954	$30

— Gatefold cover with bound-in booklet

Number	Title	Yr	NM
EPPS, PRESTON			
ORIGINAL SOUND			
❏ LPM-5002 [M]	Bongo, Bongo, Bongo	1960	$50
❏ LPS-8851 [S]	Bongo, Bongo, Bongo	1960	$100
❏ LPM-5009 [M]	Surfin' Bongos	1963	$40
❏ LPS-8872 [S]	Surfin' Bongos	1963	$50
TOP RANK			
❏ RM-349 [M]	Bongola	1961	$40
❏ RS-349 [S]	Bongola	1961	$50
EQUALS, THE			
LAURIE			
❏ LLP-2045 [M]	Unequalled	1967	$30
❏ SLP-2045 [S]	Unequalled	1967	$30
PRESIDENT			
❏ PTL-1015	Equal Sensation	1968	$30
❏ PTL-1025	Equals Supreme	1968	$30
❏ PTL-1030	Strikeback	1969	$30
❏ PTL-1020	The Sensational Equals	1968	$30
RCA VICTOR			
❏ LSP-4078	Baby Come Back	1968	$30
EQUITABLE CHIMES, THE			
(NO LABEL)			
❏ CTV-84282/3 [10]	The Equitable Chimes Play Ten of the World's Best-Loved Christmas Carols	1962	$18
ERASURE			
MUTE			
❏ 9198	Other People's Songs	2003	$15
MUTE/ELEKTRA			
❏ ED5621 [EP]	Abba-esque	1992	$30

— Promo-only vinyl; remixes of 4-song EP; no special jacket

Number	Title	Yr	NM
SIRE			
❏ 25904 [EP]	Crackers International	1989	$10
❏ 25554	The Circus	1987	$12
❏ R101009	The Innocents	1988	$15

— BMG Music Service edition

Number	Title	Yr	NM
❏ 25730	The Innocents	1988	$12
❏ 25667	The Two Ring Circus	1988	$18
❏ 26026	Wild!	1989	$15
❏ 25354	Wonderland	1987	$12
ERICA			
ESP-DISK'			
❏ 1099	You Used to Think	1968	$400

Number	Title	Yr	NM
ERICKSON, ROKY			
LIGHT IN THE ATTIC			
❏ LITA098 [B]	Don't Slander Me	2013	$35
❏ LITA099 [B]	Gremlins Have Pictures	2013	$30
❏ LITA097 [B]	The Evil One	2013	$30
ERICSON, ROLF			
EMARCY			
❏ MG-36106 [M]	Rolf Ericson and His All American Stars	1957	$250
ERIK			
VANGUARD			
❏ VRS-9267 [M]	Look Where I Am	1967	$30
❏ VSD-79267 [S]	Look Where I Am	1967	$30
ERIK AND THE VIKINGS			
KARATE			
❏ KLP-1401 [M]	Sing A-Long Rock 'n Roll	1965	$250
ERNEY, DEWEY			
DISCOVERY			
❏ DS-881	A Beautiful Friendship	1982	$25
ERSKINE, PETER			
CONTEMPORARY			
❏ C-14010	Peter Erskine	1983	$30
FANTASY			
❏ OJC-610	Peter Erskine	1991	$30
PASSPORT			
❏ 88032	Transition	198?	$25
ERVIN, BOOKER			
BARNABY			
❏ Z30560	That's It!	1971	$35

— Reissue of Candid 9014

Number	Title	Yr	NM
BETHLEHEM			
❏ BCP-6048 [M]	The Book Cooks	1961	$300
❏ BCP-6025	The Book Cooks	197?	$35

— Reissue with RCA Victor distrbution

Number	Title	Yr	NM
BLUE NOTE			
❏ 4134/84134	Back from the Gig	1963	$0

— Canceled

Number	Title	Yr	NM
❏ BN-LA488-H2	Back from the Gig	1975	$25
❏ BST-84314	Booker Ervin	1969	$0

— Canceled

Number	Title	Yr	NM
❏ BST-84283	The In Between	1969	$30
CANDID			
❏ CJM-8014 [M]	That's It!	1961	$175
❏ CJS-9014 [S]	That's It!	1961	$50
PACIFIC JAZZ			
❏ PJ-10199 [M]	Structurally Sound	1968	$40
❏ ST-20199 [S]	Structurally Sound	1968	$25
PRESTIGE			
❏ PRLP-7293 [M]	Exultation!	1964	$150
❏ PRST-7293 [S]	Exultation!	1964	$30
❏ PRST-7844	Exultation!	197?	$35

— Reissue of 7293

Number	Title	Yr	NM
❏ 24091	Freedom and the Space Sessions	1979	$35
❏ PRLP-7417 [M]	Groovin' High	1966	$35
❏ PRST-7417 [S]	Groovin' High	1966	$30
❏ PRLP-7499 [M]	Heavy!	1968	$50
❏ PRST-7499 [S]	Heavy!	1968	$25
❏ PRLP-7435 [M]	Settin' the Pace	1967	$30
❏ PRST-7435 [S]	Settin' the Pace	1967	$25
❏ PRLP-7340 [M]	The Blues Book	1965	$150
❏ PRST-7340 [S]	The Blues Book	1965	$30
❏ PRLP-7295 [M]	The Freedom Book	1964	$85
❏ PRST-7295 [S]	The Freedom Book	1964	$30
❏ PRLP-7318 [M]	The Song Book	1964	$700
❏ PRST-7318 [S]	The Song Book	1964	$30
❏ PRLP-7386 [M]	The Space Book	1965	$30
❏ PRST-7386 [S]	The Space Book	1965	$30
❏ PRLP-7462 [M]	The Trance	1967	$50
❏ PRST-7462 [S]	The Trance	1967	$25
SAVOY			
❏ MG-12154 [M]	Cookin'	1960	$50
SAVOY JAZZ			
❏ SJL-1119	Down in the Dumps	198?	$25
ERVIN, BOOKER/HORACE PARLAN			
INNER CITY			
❏ IC-3006	Lament	1977	$35
ERVIN, SENATOR SAM			
COLUMBIA			
❏ KC32756	Senator Sam at Home	1973	$30
ERWIN, PEE WEE			
BRUNSWICK			
❏ BL54011 [M]	The Land of Dixie	1956	$40

Number	Title	Yr	NM
CADENCE			
❏ CLP-1011 [M]	Dixieland at Grandview Inn	1956	$40
JAZZOLOGY			
❏ J-80	Swingin' That Music	1981	$25
STRAND			
❏ SL-1001 [M]	Peter Meets the Wolf in Dixieland	1959	$50
❏ SLS-1001 [S]	Peter Meets the Wolf in Dixieland	1959	$75
URANIA			
❏ UJLP-1202 [M]	Accent on Dixieland	1955	$300
ESCAPE CLUB, THE			
ATLANTIC			
❏ 81871	Wild, Wild West	1988	$10
EMI AMERICA			
❏ ST-17215	White Fields	1986	$12
ESCHETE, RON			
BAINBRIDGE			
❏ BT-6267	Christmas Impressions	1986	$25
❏ BT-6264	Stump Jumper	1986	$25
MUSE			
❏ MR-5246	Line-Up	1980	$30
❏ MR-5186	To Let You Know I Care	1979	$30
MUSIC IS MEDICINE			
❏ 9055	Christmas Impressions	1982	$35
ESCORTS, THE (1)			
ALITHIA			
❏ 9104	All We Need Is One More Chance	1973	$18
❏ 9106	Three Down and Four to Go	1974	$18
ESCORTS, THE (4)			
TEO			
❏ LPM-5000 [M]	The Escorts Bring Down the House	1966	$250
ESCOVEDO, PETE			
CROSSOVER			
❏ CR-5005	Mister E.	1988	$30
❏ CR-5002	Yesterday's Memories, Tomorrow's Dreams	1987	$30
ESCOVEDO, PETE AND SHEILA			
FANTASY			
❏ F-9545	Happy Together	1977	$35
❏ F-9524	Solo Two	1976	$35
ESHELMAN, DAVE, JAZZ GARDEN BIG BAND			
SEA BREEZE			
❏ SB-2039	Deep Voices	1989	$30
ESP			
DREAM			
❏ DRE187301	The Future Is Now	1986	$50
ESQUERITA			
CAPITOL			
❏ T1186 [M]	Esquerita	1959	$1000
ESQUIRES, THE (1)			
BUNKY			
❏ 300	Get On Up and Get Away	1968	$35
ESQUIVEL			
BAR NONE			
❏ LP-056	Music for a Sparkling Planet	1995	$15
❏ LP-043	Space Age Bachelor Pad Music	1994	$15
RCA VICTOR			
❏ LPM-1978 [M]	Exploring New Sounds in Hi-Fi	1959	$30
❏ LSP-1978 [S]	Exploring New Sounds in Hi-Fi	1959	$75
❏ LPM-1749 [M]	Four Corners of the World	1958	$30
❏ LSP-1749 [S]	Four Corners of the World	1958	$50
❏ LPM-2225 [M]	Infinity in Sound	1960	$30
❏ LSP-2225 [S]	Infinity in Sound	1960	$75
❏ LPM-2296 [M]	Infinity in Sound, Vol. 2	1961	$30
❏ LSP-2296 [S]	Infinity in Sound, Vol. 2	1961	$75
❏ LPM-2418 [M]	Latin-esque	1962	$25
❏ LSP-2418 [S]	Latin-esque	1962	$75

— Die-cut cover that reveals inner sleeve

Number	Title	Yr	NM
❏ LSP-2418 [S]	Latin-esque	1962	$40

— Standard cover

Number	Title	Yr	NM
❏ LPM-1753 [M]	Other Worlds, Other Sounds	1959	$30

Number	Title	Yr	NM

Number	Title	Yr	NM
❏ LSP-1753 [S]	Other Worlds, Other Sounds	1959	$50
❏ LPM-1988 [M]	Strings Aflame	1959	$30
❏ LSP-1988 [S]	Strings Aflame	1959	$50
❏ LPM-3502 [M]	The Best of Esquivel	1966	$25
❏ LSP-3502 [S]	The Best of Esquivel	1966	$30
❏ LPM-3697 [M]	The Genius of Esquivel	1967	$25
❏ LSP-3697 [S]	The Genius of Esquivel	1967	$30
❏ LPM-1345 [M]	To Love Again	1957	$50
REPRISE			
❏ R-6046 [M]	More of Other World, Other Sounds	1962	$30
❏ P9-6046 [S]	More of Other World, Other Sounds	1962	$30

ESSEX, DAVID

COLUMBIA

❏ PC33813	All the Fun of the Fair	1975	$18
❏ KC33289	David Essex	1974	$18
❏ KC32560	Rock On	1974	$25
❏ CQ32560 [Q]	Rock On	1974	$40

MERCURY

| ❏ 812936-1 | David Essex | 1983 | $18 |

ESSEX, THE

ROULETTE

❏ R-25235 [M]	A Walkin' Miracle	1963	$40
❏ SR-25235 [S]	A Walkin' Miracle	1963	$50
❏ R-25234 [M]	Easier Said Than Done	1963	$40
❏ SR-25234 [S]	Easier Said Than Done	1963	$50
❏ R-25246 [M]	Young and Lively	1964	$40
❏ SR-25246 [S]	Young and Lively	1964	$50

ESTEFAN, GLORIA

CBS INTERNATIONAL

| ❏ DFL80432 | Exitos De Gloria Estefan | 1990 | $30 |

EPIC

❏ OE45217	Cuts Both Ways	1989	$12
❏ E69200	Gloria!	1998	$25
❏ E46988	Into the Light	1991	$15
❏ OE40769	Let It Loose	1987	$10

ETC.

WINDI

| ❏ WLPS-1011 | Etc. Is the Name of the Band! | 1976 | $30 |

ETERNITY'S CHILDREN

TOWER

❏ ST-5123 [S]	Eternity's Children	1968	$150
❏ T-5123 [M]	Eternity's Children	1968	$300
❏ ST-5144	Timeless	1969	$400
—Canada only release, but sold into the US.			

ETHEL AND THE SHAMELESS HUSSIES

MCA

| ❏ 42191 | Born to Burn | 1988 | $12 |

ETHERIDGE, MELISSA

ISLAND

❏ 91285	Brave and Crazy	1989	$15
❏ 546591	Breakdown	1999	$18
—With bonus 7-inch single			
❏ 90875	Melissa Etheridge	1988	$12

ETHNIC HERITAGE ENSEMBLE, THE

RED

| ❏ VPA-156 | Impressions | 198? | $35 |

SILKHEART

| ❏ SH-108 | Ancestral Song | 198? | $30 |

Number	Title	Yr	NM

ETHRIDGE, KELLIS

INNER CITY

| ❏ IC-1109 | Tomorrow Sky | 1980 | $25 |

ETZEL, ROY

MGM

| ❏ E-4330 [M] | The Silence (Il Silenzio) | 1965 | $15 |
| ❏ SE-4330 [S] | The Silence (Il Silenzio) | 1965 | $18 |

EUBANKS, JACK

MONUMENT

| ❏ LP-8044 [M] | Guitar Sounds of the South | 1966 | $18 |
| ❏ SLP-18044 [S] | Guitar Sounds of the South | 1966 | $25 |

EUBANKS, KEVIN

ELEKTRA/MUSICIAN

| ❏ 60213 | Guitarist | 1983 | $35 |

GRP

❏ GR-1029	Face to Face	1985	$25
❏ GR-1041	Heat of Heat	1986	$25
❏ GR-1031	Opening Night	1985	$25
❏ GR-1054	Shadow Prophets	1988	$25
❏ GR-1008	Sundance	1984	$25
❏ GR-9580	The Searcher	1989	$30

EUBANKS, ROBIN

JMT

| ❏ 834433-1 | Dedication | 1989 | $30 |
| ❏ 834424-1 | Different Perspectives | 1988 | $25 |

EUPHONIOUS WAIL

KAPP

| ❏ KS-3668 | Euphonious Wail | 1973 | $40 |

EUPHORIA (2)

HERITAGE

| ❏ HTS35005 | Euphoria | 1971 | $30 |

EUPHORIA (3)

CAPITOL

| ❏ SKAO-363 | A Gift from Euphoria | 1969 | $250 |

EUPHORIA (4)

RAINBOW

| ❏ 1003 | Lost in a Trance | 1973 | $300 |

EUREKA BRASS BAND, THE

ATLANTIC

❏ 1408 [M]	The Eureka Brass Band	1963	$50
❏ SD1408 [S]	The Eureka Brass Band	1963	$50
—Multicolor label with black "fan" logo at right			
❏ SD1408 [S]	The Eureka Brass Band	1969	$25
—Red and green label with "1841 Broadway" address			
❏ SD1408 [S]	The Eureka Brass Band	1975	$20
—Red and green label with "75 Rockefeller Plaza" address and "W" logo in perimeter print			

FOLKWAYS

| ❏ FA-2642 [M] | Music of New Orleans | 195? | $50 |

PAX

| ❏ LP-9001 [10] | New Orleans Parade | 1954 | $75 |

EUROGLIDERS

COLUMBIA

| ❏ BFC40269 | Absolutely | 1986 | $12 |
| ❏ BFC39588 | This Island | 1984 | $12 |

EUROPEAN CLASSIC JAZZ BAND, THE

STOMP OFF

| ❏ SOS-1070 | Whip Me with Plenty of Love | 1984 | $25 |

EUROPEAN CLASSIC JAZZ TRIO, THE

STOMP OFF

| ❏ SOS-1142 | That's Like It Ought to Be | 1988 | $25 |

EUROPEAN JAZZ QUARTET, THE

PULSE

| ❏ 3001 [M] | New Jazz from the Old World | 1957 | $50 |

EURYTHMICS

ARISTA

| ❏ AL8606 | We Too Are One | 1989 | $15 |

RCA

❏ 5707-1-RDAA [EP]	Rough and Tough at the Roxy	1986	$35
—Promo-only 4-song live album			
❏ 6794-1-R	Savage	1987	$15

RCA VICTOR

❏ ABL1-5371	1984 (For the Love of Big Brother)	1984	$15
❏ AJL1-5429	Be Yourself Tonight	1985	$15
❏ AJL1-5847	Revenge	1986	$15

Number	Title	Yr	NM
❏ AFL1-4681	Sweet Dreams (Are Made of This)	1983	$12

| ❏ AFL1-4917 [B] | Touch | 1984 | $15 |
| ❏ CPL1-5086 [EP] | Touch Dance | 1983 | $15 |

EVANS, BILL (1), AND JIM HALL

BLUE NOTE

| ❏ B1-90583 | Undercurrent | 1988 | $25 |

SOLID STATE

| ❏ SS-18018 | Undercurrent | 1968 | $25 |

UNITED ARTISTS

❏ UAJ-14003 [M]	Undercurrent	1962	$40
❏ UAJS-15003 [S]	Undercurrent	1962	$50
❏ UAS-5640	Undercurrent	197?	$35

EVANS, BILL (1)

COLUMBIA

❏ KC31490	Living Time: Events I-VIII	1972	$35
❏ C30855	The Bill Evans Album	1971	$35
❏ PC30855	The Bill Evans Album	198?	$20
—Budget-line reissue			
❏ CG33672	The Bill Evans Album/Living Time	1976	$35

CTI

| ❏ 6004 | Montreux II | 1971 | $35 |

ELEKTRA/MUSICIAN

| ❏ 60164 | The Paris Concert, Volume 1 | 1984 | $30 |
| ❏ 60311 | The Paris Concert, Volume 2 | 1986 | $30 |

FANTASY

❏ F-9542	Alone (Again)	1977	$30
❏ OJC-263	Bill Evans at Shelly's Manne-Hole	1987	$25
❏ F-9568	Crosscurrents	1978	$30
❏ F-9618	Eloquence	1982	$25
❏ OJC-068	Everybody Digs Bill Evans	198?	$25
❏ OJC-037	Explorations	198?	$25
❏ F-9630	From the 70s	198?	$25
❏ OJC-369	How My Heart Sings	198?	$25
❏ OJC-308	Interplay	198?	$25
❏ F-9475	Intuition	1975	$30
❏ OJC-470	Intuition	1990	$30
❏ F-9593	I Will Say Goodbye	1980	$30
❏ OJC-434	Moonbeams	1990	$30
❏ F-9510	Montreux III	1976	$30
❏ OJC-025	New Jazz Conceptions	1982	$25
❏ OJC-088	Portrait in Jazz	198?	$25
❏ F-9529	Quintessence	1976	$30
❏ F-9608	Re: The Person I Knew	198?	$25
❏ F-9501	Since We Met	1975	$30
❏ OJC-622	Since We Met	1991	$30
❏ OJC-140	Sunday at the Village Vanguard	198?	$25
❏ F-9457	The Tokyo Concert	1974	$30
❏ OJC-345	The Tokyo Concert	1990	$30
❏ OJC-210	Waltz for Debby	198?	$25

MGM

| ❏ SE-4723 | From Left to Right | 1970 | $35 |

MILESTONE

❏ 47063	Conception	198?	$35
❏ 9151	Jazzhouse	1988	$25
❏ 9125	More from the Vanguard	198?	$25
❏ 47024	Peace Piece & Others	197?	$35
❏ 47034	Spring Leaves	197?	$35
❏ 47066	The Interplay Sessions	198?	$30
❏ 47046	The Second Trio	197?	$35
❏ 9170	The Solo Sessions, Volume 1	1989	$30
❏ 47002	The Village Vanguard Sessions	197?	$35
❏ 47068	Time Remembered	198?	$30
❏ 9164	You're Gonna Hear from Me	198?	$25

MOSAIC

| ❏ MQ10-171 | The Final Village Vanguard Sessions -- June 1980 | 1996 | $250 |

PAUSA

| ❏ 7050 | Symbiosis | 1979 | $25 |

Number	Title	Yr	NM
RIVERSIDE			
❏ 6197	Bill Evans at Shelly's Manne-Hole	198?	$25
❏ RLP-487 [M]	Bill Evans at Shelly's Manne-Hole, Hollywood, California	1965	$175
❏ RS-9487 [S]	Bill Evans at Shelly's Manne-Hole, Hollywood, California	1965	$175
❏ RLP 12-291 [M]	Everybody Digs Bill Evans	1958	$175
— blue label			
❏ RLP1129 [S]	Everybody Digs Bill Evans	1959	$300
❏ 6090	Everybody Digs Bill Evans	197?	$30
❏ RLP-351 [M]	Explorations	1960	$300
— blue label			
❏ RS-9351 [S]	Explorations	1960	$300
— black label			
❏ 6038	Explorations	197?	$30
❏ RLP-473 [M]	How My Heart Sings!	1964	$175
❏ RS-9473 [S]	How My Heart Sings!	1964	$175
❏ RLP-445 [M]	Interplay	1963	$150
❏ RS-9445 [S]	Interplay	1963	$175
❏ RS-3013	Live at Shelly's Manne-Hole	1968	$150
❏ RM-3006 [M]	Live at the Village Vanguard	1967	$150
❏ RS-3006 [S]	Live at the Village Vanguard	1967	$150
❏ RLP-428 [M]	Moonbeams	1962	$175
❏ RS-9428 [S]	Moonbeams	1962	$175
❏ 6175	Moonbeams	198?	$25
❏ RLP 12-223 [M]	New Jazz Conceptions	1956	$1200
— Photo on cover, label is white with blue print			
❏ RLP 12-223 [M]	New Jazz Conceptions	1958	$300
— New cover, label is blue with microphone logo at top			
❏ RS-3042	Peace Pieces	1969	$150
❏ RM-3001 [M]	Polka Dots and Moonbeams	1967	$150
❏ RS-3001 [S]	Polka Dots and Moonbeams	1967	$150
❏ RLP 12-315 [M]	Portrait in Jazz	1959	$400
— deep groove pressing with small reel logos on the label			
❏ RLP1162 [S]	Portrait in Jazz	1959	$300
❏ RLP-376 [M]	Sunday at the Village Vanguard	1961	$50
❏ RS-9376 [S]	Sunday at the Village Vanguard	1961	$250
❏ R-018	The Complete Riverside Recordings	1985	$250
❏ RLP-399 [M]	Waltz for Debby	1961	$1500
— blue label			
❏ RS-9399 [S]	Waltz for Debby	1961	$250
— black label			
❏ 6118	Waltz for Debby	197?	$30
TIMELESS			
❏ LPSJP-331	Consecration I	1990	$35
❏ LPSJP-332	Consecration II	1990	$35
VERVE			
❏ V-8675 [M]	A Simple Matter of Conviction	1966	$35
❏ V6-8675 [S]	A Simple Matter of Conviction	1966	$25
❏ UMV-2107	A Simple Matter of Conviction	198?	$25
❏ V6-8792	Bill Evans Alone	1969	$35
❏ V6-8762	Bill Evans at the Montreux Jazz Festival	1968	$35
❏ 827844-1	Bill Evans at the Montreux Jazz Festival	1986	$25
❏ V6-8762	Bill Evans at the Montreux Jazz Festival	199?	$30
— Classic Records reissue on audiophile vinyl			
❏ V-8683 [M]	Bill Evans at Town Hall	1966	$35
❏ V6-8683 [S]	Bill Evans at Town Hall	1966	$25
❏ V-8578 [M]	Bill Evans Trio '64	1964	$35
❏ V6-8578 [S]	Bill Evans Trio '64	1964	$25
❏ V-8613 [M]	Bill Evans Trio '65	1965	$35
❏ V6-8613 [S]	Bill Evans Trio '65	1965	$25
❏ V-8640 [M]	Bill Evans Trio with Symphony Orchestra	1965	$35
❏ V6-8640 [S]	Bill Evans Trio with Symphony Orchestra	1965	$25
❏ VE-2-2545	California Here I Come	198?	$30
❏ V-8526 [M]	Conversations with Myself	1963	$25
❏ V6-8526 [S]	Conversations with Myself	1963	$30
❏ V-8497 [M]	Empathy	1962	$30
❏ V6-8497 [S]	Empathy	1962	$30
❏ V-8727 [M]	Further Conversations with Myself	1967	$25
❏ V6-8727 [S]	Further Conversations with Myself	1967	$35
❏ V-8655 [M]	Intermodulation	1966	$200
❏ V6-8655 [S]	Intermodulation	1966	$25
❏ UMV-2106	Intermodulation	198?	$25
❏ V3HB-8841	Return Engagement	1973	$25
❏ V-8747 [M]	The Best of Bill Evans	1967	$25
❏ V6-8747 [S]	The Best of Bill Evans	1967	$35
❏ UMV-2053	The Bill Evans Trio at Town Hall	198?	$25
❏ VE-2-2509	Trios and Duos	197?	$35
❏ V6-8777	What's New	1968	$35
WARNER BROS.			
❏ BSK3293	Affinity	1978	$30
❏ BSK3177	New Conversations	1977	$30
❏ HS3411	We Will Meet Again	1979	$30
❏ HS3504	You Must Believe in Spring	1981	$30

EVANS, BILL (2)

Number	Title	Yr	NM
BLUE NOTE			
❏ BT-85111	The Alternative Man	1985	$25
ELEKTRA/MUSICIAN			
❏ 60349	Living in the Crest of a Wave	1986	$25

EVANS, DALE

Number	Title	Yr	NM
ALLEGRO ELITE			
❏ 4116 [10]	Dale Evans Sings	195?	$40
CAPITOL			
❏ ST-399	Get to Know the Lord	1970	$18
❏ T2772 [M]	It's Real	1967	$30
❏ ST2772 [S]	It's Real	1967	$30
EVON			
❏ 336 [M]	Dale Evans Sings Western Favorites/Johnny 'O Calls Western Dances	195?	$30
— Only Side 1 is by Dale Evans			
MANNA			
❏ MS-2075	Reflections of Life	1981	$15
SACRED			
❏ LPS-4507	Favorite Gospel Songs	197?	$15
— Reissue of Word WST-8546			
WORD			
❏ WST-8661	Country Dale	1976	$15
❏ WST-8566	Faith, Hope and Charity	1972	$18
❏ WST-8658 [B]	Heart of the Country	1975	$18
❏ WST-8546	It's Real	1971	$18
❏ WST-8803	Totally Free	1979	$15

EVANS, DAME EDITH

Number	Title	Yr	NM
GOLDEN			
❏ GW245 [M]	The First Christmas	196?	$15

EVANS, DOC

Number	Title	Yr	NM
AUDIOPHILE			
❏ AP-50 [M]	Classics of the 20's	195?	$40
— Red vinyl			
❏ AP-29 [M]	Dixieland Session	195?	$40
❏ AP-11 [M]	Doc Evans and His Band, Volume 1	195?	$40
❏ AP-12 [M]	Doc Evans and His Band, Volume 2	195?	$40
❏ AP-95	Doc Evans at the Gas Light	1989	$25
— Reissue with same number			
❏ AP-95 [M]	Doc Evans at the Gas Light	196?	$25
❏ AS-95 [S]	Doc Evans at the Gas Light	196?	$30
❏ AP-4	Down in Jungle Town	1987	$25
❏ APS-5968	Reminiscing in Dixieland	196?	$30
— Red vinyl			
❏ AP-31 [M]	The Cornet Artistry of Doc Evans	195?	$40
❏ AP-34 [M]	Traditional Jazz	195?	$40
— Red vinyl			
❏ AP-44 [M]	Traditional Jazz	195?	$40
— Red vinyl			
❏ AP-45 [M]	Traditional Jazz	195?	$40
— Red vinyl			
❏ AP-33 [M]	Traditional Jazz	195?	$40
— Red vinyl			
❏ XL-328 [M]	Traditional Jazz	195?	$40
❏ XL-329 [M]	Traditional Jazz	195?	$40
CONCERT DISC			
❏ CS-47	Doc Evans + 4 = Dixie	1961	$30
❏ CS-48	Muskrat Ramble	196?	$30
FOLKWAYS			
❏ FA-2855	Doc Evans and His Dixieland Jazz Band	195?	$30
JAZZOLOGY			
❏ J-86	Blues in Dixieland	197?	$25
❏ J-87	Command Performance	197?	$25
❏ J-85	Jazz Heritage, Volume 1	197?	$25
SOMA			
❏ MG-1201 [M]	Classic Jazz at Carleton	1954	$40
❏ MG-100 [M]	Dixieland Concert	1953	$50
❏ MG-101 [10]	Dixieland Concert	1953	$50

EVANS, GIL

Number	Title	Yr	NM
ABC IMPULSE!			
❏ AS-9 [S]	Into the Hot	1968	$35
❏ AS-4 [S]	Out of the Cool	1968	$35
❏ IA-9340	The Great Arrangers	1978	$35
AMPEX			
❏ A-10102	Gil Evans	1971	$35
ANTILLES			
❏ AN-1010	Priestess	198?	$25
ARTISTS HOUSE			
❏ 14	Where Flamingoes Fly	198?	$25
ATLANTIC			
❏ SD1643	Svengali	1973	$30
❏ QD1643 [Q]	Svengali	1973	$30
❏ 90048	Svengali	1983	$20
BLUE NOTE			
❏ BN-LA461-H2	Pacific Standard Time	1975	$35
EMARCY			
❏ 836401-1	Rhythm-A-Ning	1989	$30
FANTASY			
❏ OJC-346	Gil Evans Plus Ten	198?	$25
IMPULSE!			
❏ A-9 [M]	Into the Hot	1962	$120
❏ AS-9 [S]	Into the Hot	1962	$120
❏ A-4 [M]	Out of the Cool	1961	$120
❏ AS-4 [S]	Out of the Cool	1961	$120
INNER CITY			
❏ IC-1110	Little Wing	198?	$30
MCA			
❏ 29034	Into the Hot	198?	$20
❏ 29033	Out of the Cool	198?	$20
❏ 4143	The Great Arrangers	198?	$25
MCA IMPULSE!			
❏ 5653	Out of the Cool	1986	$25
NEW JAZZ			
❏ NJLP-8215 [M]	Big Stuff	1959	$175
— Purple label			
❏ NJLP-8215 [M]	Big Stuff	1965	$175
— Blue label, trident logo at right			
PACIFIC JAZZ			
❏ PJ-28 [M]	America's #1 Arranger	1961	$30
❏ PJ-40 [M]	Cannonball Adderley/Gil Evans	1962	$30
❏ ST-40 [S]	Cannonball Adderley/Gil Evans	1962	$30
PRESTIGE			
❏ 24049	An Arranger's Touch	197?	$35
❏ PRST-7756	Big Stuff	1970	$35
❏ PRLP-7120 [M]	Gil Evans Plus Ten	1957	$175
RCA VICTOR			
❏ CPL1-0667	Gil Evans Plays Jimi Hendrix	1974	$25
❏ LPM-1057 [M]	There Comes a Time	1955	$100
❏ APL1-1057	There Comes a Time	1976	$30
VERVE			
❏ V6-8838	Previously Unreleased Recordings	1974	$30
❏ V-8555 [M]	The Individualism of Gil Evans	1963	$25
❏ V6-8555 [S]	The Individualism of Gil Evans	1963	$25
WORLD PACIFIC			
❏ WP-1270 [M]	Great Jazz Standards	1959	$175
❏ ST-1027 [S]	Great Jazz Standards	1959	$175
❏ WP-1246 [M]	New Bottle, Old Wine	1958	$175
❏ ST-1011 [S]	New Bottle, Old Wine	1959	$175

EVANS, JOHN

Number	Title	Yr	NM
OMEGA			
❏ OL-49 [M]	Mainstream Jazz Piano	1960	$25
❏ OSL-49 [S]	Mainstream Jazz Piano	1960	$25

EVANS, LEE

Number	Title	Yr	NM
CAPITOL			
❏ T1625 [M]	Big Piano/Big Band/Big Sound	1962	$85
❏ ST1625 [S]	Big Piano/Big Band/Big Sound	1962	$40
❏ T1847 [M]	The Lee Evans Trio	1963	$85
❏ ST1847 [S]	The Lee Evans Trio	1963	$40

EVANS, PAUL

Number	Title	Yr	NM
CARLTON			
❏ TLP-130 [M]	Folk Songs of Many Lands	1961	$40
❏ STLP-130 [S]	Folk Songs of Many Lands	1961	$75
❏ TLP-129 [M]	Hear Paul Evans in Your Home Tonight	1961	$40
❏ STLP-129 [S]	Hear Paul Evans in Your Home Tonight	1961	$75
GUARANTEED			
❏ GUL-1000 [M]	Fabulous Teens	1960	$80
❏ GUS-1000 [S]	Fabulous Teens	1960	$100
KAPP			
❏ KL-1346 [M]	21 Years in a Tennessee Jail	1964	$30
❏ KS-3346 [S]	21 Years in a Tennessee Jail	1964	$40
❏ KL-1475 [M]	Another Town, Another Jail	1966	$30
❏ KS-3475 [S]	Another Town, Another Jail	1966	$30

EVANS, RICHARD

Number	Title	Yr	NM
ARGO			
❏ LP-675 [M]	Home Cookin'	1961	$30
❏ LPS-675 [S]	Home Cookin'	1961	$30
❏ LP-658 [M]	Richard's Almanac	1960	$30
❏ LPS-658 [S]	Richard's Almanac	1960	$40

EVANS, SARA

Number	Title	Yr	NM
RCA			
❏ 66995-1 [DJ]	Three Chords and the Truth	1997	$18
— Vinyl is promo only			

EVEN DOZEN JUG BAND, THE

Among the members of the group were John Sebastian and Maria D'Amato (later Muldaur).

Number	Title	Yr	NM
ELEKTRA			
❏ EKL-246 [M]	The Even Dozen Jug Band	1964	$30

Number	Title	Yr	NM
❑ EKS-7246 [S]	The Even Dozen Jug Band	1964	$50

EVERCLEAR
CAPITOL
| ❑ C1-36503 | So Much for the Afterglow | 1997 | $25 |

— *Blue vinyl*

CAPITOL/TIMKERR
| ❑ C130929 | Sparkle and Fade | 1995 | $40 |

— *Price includes bonus 45 "Live on the Radio"; deduct 25 percent if missing*

EVERETT, BETTY, AND JERRY BUTLER
BUDDAH
| ❑ BDS-7505 | Together | 1969 | $18 |
| ❑ BDS-7505 | Together | 1969 | $18 |

TRADITION
| ❑ 2073 | Starring Betty Everett with Jerry Butler | 197? | $15 |

VEE JAY
❑ LP-1099 [M]	Delicious Together	1964	$25
❑ VJS-1099 [S]	Delicious Together	1964	$30
❑ VJLP-1099	Delicious Together	198?	$12

— *Reissue of original 1099; has softer vinyl*
❑ LP1099 [M]	Delicious Together	1964	$25
❑ VJS1099 [S]	Delicious Together	1964	$30
❑ VJLP1099	Delicious Together	198?	$15

— *Authorized reissue*

EVERETT, BETTY
FANTASY
| ❑ 9480 | Happy Endings | 1975 | $15 |
| ❑ 9447 | Love Rhymes | 1974 | $15 |

SUNSET
| ❑ SUS-5220 | I Need You So | 1968 | $18 |

UNI
| ❑ 73048 | There'll Come a Time | 1969 | $30 |

VEE JAY
❑ LP1077 [M]	It's In His Kiss	1964	$30
❑ SR1077 [S]	It's In His Kiss	1964	$50
❑ LP1122 [M]	The Very Best of Betty Everett	1965	$40
❑ VJS1122 [S]	The Very Best of Betty Everett	1965	$50
❑ VJLP1122	The Very Best of Betty Everett	198?	$12

— *Authorized reissue*
| ❑ LP1077 [M] | You're No Good | 1964 | $40 |
| ❑ SR1077 [S] | You're No Good | 1964 | $80 |

EVERETTE, LEON
MERCURY
| ❑ 824309-1 | Where's the Fire | 1985 | $10 |

ORLANDO
| ❑ 1101 | I Don't Want to Lose | 1980 | $15 |

RCA VICTOR
❑ MHL1-8513 [EP]	Doin' What I Feel	1984	$10
❑ AHL1-4152	Hurricane	1981	$12
❑ AHL1-3916	If I Keep On Going Crazy	1981	$12
❑ MHL1-8600 [EP]	Leon Everette	1983	$10

TRUE
| ❑ 1002 | Goodbye King of Rock and Roll | 1977 | $30 |

— *Deduct 40% if poster of Elvis Presley is missing*

EVERGREEN BLUES, THE
ABC
| ❑ S-669 | Comin' On | 1969 | $18 |

MERCURY
| ❑ SR-61157 [S] | 7 Do 11 | 1968 | $25 |
| ❑ MG-21157 [M] | 7 Do 11 | 1968 | $50 |

— *Mono is white label promo only*

EVERGREEN CLASSIC JAZZ BAND
STOMP OFF
| ❑ SOS-1202 | Trust Me… I'm a Musician | 1991 | $25 |

EVERLAST
Also see HOUSE OF PAIN.

TOMMY BOY
| ❑ TBLP1411 | Eat at Whitey's | 2000 | $25 |

WARNER BROS.
| ❑ 26007 | Forever Everlasting | 1990 | $25 |

EVERLY, DON
ABC HICKORY
| ❑ AH-44003 | Brother Juke-Box | 1977 | $15 |

ODE
| ❑ SP-77005 | Don Everly | 1970 | $18 |
| ❑ SP-77023 | Sunset Towers | 1974 | $18 |

EVERLY, PHIL
ELEKTRA
| ❑ 6E-213 | Living Alone | 1979 | $12 |

PYE
| ❑ 12121 | Mystic Line | 1976 | $15 |
| ❑ 12104 | Phil's Diner | 1975 | $15 |

RCA VICTOR
| ❑ APL1-0092 | Star Spangled Springer | 1973 | $18 |

EVERLY BROTHERS, THE
ARISTA
| ❑ AL9-8207 | 24 Original Classics | 1985 | $18 |

BARNABY
❑ ZG30260	End of an Era	1971	$18
❑ 4004	Greatest Hits, Vol. 1	1977	$12
❑ 4005	Greatest Hits, Vol. 2	1977	$12
❑ 4006	Greatest Hits, Vol. 3	1977	$12
❑ BR-15008	History of the Everly Brothers	1973	$18
❑ BR-6006	The Everly Brothers' Greatest Hits	1974	$18
❑ BGP-350	The Everly Brothers' Original Golden Hits	1970	$25

CADENCE
❑ CLP-3062 [M]	15 Everly Hits 15	1963	$40
❑ CLP-25062 [P]	15 Everly Hits 15	1963	$50
❑ CLP-3059 [M]	Folk Songs of the Everly Brothers	1963	$50

— *Reissue of 3016*
| ❑ CLP-25059 [R] | Folk Songs of the Everly Brothers | 1963 | $40 |
| ❑ CLP-3016 [M] | Songs Our Daddy Taught Us | 1958 | $150 |

— *Maroon label with metronome logo*
| ❑ CLP-3016 [M] | Songs Our Daddy Taught Us | 1962 | $75 |

— *Red label with black border*
| ❑ CLP-3003 [M] | The Everly Brothers | 1958 | $150 |

— *Maroon label with metronome logo*
| ❑ CLP-3003 [M] | The Everly Brothers | 1962 | $75 |

— *Red label with black border*
| ❑ CLP-3025 [M] | The Everly Brothers' Best | 1959 | $125 |

— *Maroon label with metronome logo*
| ❑ CLP-3025 [M] | The Everly Brothers' Best | 1962 | $75 |

— *Red label with black border*
| ❑ CLP-3040 [M] | The Fabulous Style of the Everly Brothers | 1960 | $100 |

— *Maroon label with metronome logo*
| ❑ CLP-25040 [P] | The Fabulous Style of the Everly Brothers | 1960 | $120 |

— *Maroon label with metronome logo*
| ❑ CLP-3040 [M] | The Fabulous Style of the Everly Brothers | 1962 | $50 |

— *Red label with black border*
| ❑ CLP-25040 [P] | The Fabulous Style of the Everly Brothers | 1962 | $75 |

— *Red label with black border*

HARMONY
❑ KH11388	Chained to a Memory	1970	$15
❑ HS11350	Christmas with the Everly Brothers and the Boys Town Choir	1969	$25
❑ HS11304	Wake Up Little Susie	1969	$15

MERCURY
❑ 826142-1	Born Yesterday	1986	$12
❑ 822431-1	EB 84	1984	$12
❑ 832520-1	Some Hearts	1989	$15

PAIR
| ❑ PDL1-1063 | Living Legends | 1986 | $15 |

PASSPORT
| ❑ 11001 | The Everly Brothers Reunion Concert | 1984 | $18 |

RCA VICTOR
❑ AFL1-5401	Home Again	1985	$12
❑ LSP-4781	Pass the Chicken and Listen	1972	$18
❑ LSP-4620	Stories We Could Tell	1972	$18

RHINO
❑ RNLP-214	All They Had to Do Was Dream	1985	$12
❑ RNDF-258 [PD]	Heartaches and Harmonies	1985	$25
❑ R11752 [B]	Roots	2014	$25
❑ RNLP-212	Songs Our Daddy Taught Us	1985	$12
❑ RNLP-70173	The Best of the Everly Brothers (Golden Archive Series)	1987	$12
❑ RNLP-211	The Everly Brothers	1985	$12
❑ RNLP-213	The Fabulous Style of the Everly Brothers	1985	$12

TIME-LIFE
| ❑ SRNR-09 | The Everly Brothers: 1957-1962 | 1986 | $25 |

— *Part of "The Rock 'n' Roll Era" series; box set with insert*

WARNER BROS.
| ❑ W1395 [M] | A Date with the Everly Brothers | 1960 | $50 |

— *Gatefold edition with poster and wallet-size photos*
| ❑ WS1395 [S] | A Date with the Everly Brothers | 1960 | $85 |

— *Gatefold edition with poster and wallet-size photos*
| ❑ W1395 [M] | A Date with the Everly Brothers | 1960 | $40 |

— *Gatefold edition without poster or photos*
| ❑ WS1395 [S] | A Date with the Everly Brothers | 1960 | $50 |

— *Gatefold edition without poster or photos*
| ❑ W1395 [M] | A Date with the Everly Brothers | 1961 | $30 |

— *Regular edition*
| ❑ WS1395 [S] | A Date with the Everly Brothers | 1961 | $40 |

— *Regular edition*
❑ W1605 [M]	Beat & Soul	1965	$40
❑ WS1605 [S]	Beat & Soul	1965	$50
❑ W1418 [M]	Both Sides of an Evening	1961	$30
❑ WS1418 [S]	Both Sides of an Evening	1961	$40
❑ W1483 [M]	Christmas with the Everly Brothers and the Boys Town Choir	1962	$40
❑ WS1483 [S]	Christmas with the Everly Brothers and the Boys Town Choir	1962	$50
❑ W1585 [M]	Gone, Gone, Gone	1965	$40
❑ WS1585 [S]	Gone, Gone, Gone	1965	$50
❑ W1513 [M]	Great Country Hits	1963	$40
❑ WS1513 [S]	Great Country Hits	1963	$50
❑ W1620 [M]	In Our Image	1966	$40
❑ WS1620 [S]	In Our Image	1966	$50
❑ W1430 [M]	Instant Party!	1962	$30
❑ WS1430 [S]	Instant Party!	1962	$40
❑ PRO134 [10]	It's Everly Time!	1960	$600

— *Promo "souvenir sampler" from their debut on WB*
❑ W1381 [M]	It's Everly Time!	1960	$30
❑ WS1381 [S]	It's Everly Time!	1960	$40
❑ W1578 [M]	Rock & Soul	1964	$40
❑ WS1578 [S]	Rock & Soul	1964	$50
❑ WS1752	Roots	1968	$40
❑ ST-91601	Roots	1968	$50

— *Capitol Record Club edition*
| ❑ WS1858 | The Everly Brothers Show | 1970 | $30 |
| ❑ STAO-93286 | The Everly Brothers Show | 1970 | $40 |

— *Capitol Record Club edition*
❑ W1708 [M]	The Everly Brothers Sing	1967	$50
❑ WS1708 [S]	The Everly Brothers Sing	1967	$40
❑ W1471 [M]	The Golden Hits of the Everly Brothers	1962	$30
❑ WS1471 [S]	The Golden Hits of the Everly Brothers	1962	$40

— *Gold label*
| ❑ WS1471 | The Golden Hits of the Everly Brothers | 1967 | $25 |

— *Green "W7" label*
| ❑ WS1471 | The Golden Hits of the Everly Brothers | 1970 | $18 |

— *Green "WB" label*
| ❑ WS1471 | The Golden Hits of the Everly Brothers | 1973 | $15 |

— *Burbank" palm-tree label*
| ❑ WS1471 [B] | The Golden Hits of the Everly Brothers | 1979 | $12 |

— *White or tan label*
❑ W1676 [M]	The Hit Sound of the Everly Brothers	1967	$50
❑ WS1676 [S]	The Hit Sound of the Everly Brothers	1967	$40
❑ W1554 [M]	The Very Best of the Everly Brothers	1964	$30

— *Originals have yellow covers*
| ❑ W1554 [M] | The Very Best of the Everly Brothers | 1965 | $25 |

— *Later pressings have white covers*
| ❑ WS1554 [S] | The Very Best of the Everly Brothers | 1964 | $40 |

— *Originals have yellow covers*
| ❑ WS1554 [S] | The Very Best of the Everly Brothers | 1965 | $30 |

— *White cover; gold label*
| ❑ ST-91343 [S] | The Very Best of the Everly Brothers | 1967 | $40 |

— *Capitol Record Club edition*
| ❑ WS1554 | The Very Best of the Everly Brothers | 1967 | $25 |

— *Green "W7" label*
| ❑ WS1554 | The Very Best of the Everly Brothers | 1970 | $18 |

— *Green "WB" label*
| ❑ WS1554 | The Very Best of the Everly Brothers | 1973 | $15 |

— *Burbank" palm-tree label*
| ❑ WS1554 | The Very Best of the Everly Brothers | 1979 | $12 |

— *White or tan label*
| ❑ W1646 [M] | Two Yanks in England | 1966 | $40 |
| ❑ WS1646 [S] | Two Yanks in England | 1966 | $50 |

EVERPRESENT FULLNESS, THE
WHITE WHALE
| ❑ 7132 | The Everpresent Fullness | 1970 | $85 |

Number	Title	Yr	NM

EVERY MOTHERS' SON
MGM

❑ E-4471 [M]	Every Mothers' Son	1967	$30
❑ SE-4471 [S]	Every Mothers' Son	1967	$25
❑ E-4504 [M]	Every Mothers' Son's Back	1967	$30
❑ SE-4504 [S]	Every Mothers' Son's Back	1967	$25

EVERYMAN BAND
ECM
| ❑ 1234 | Everyman Band | 1983 | $30 |
| ❑ 1290 | Without Warning | 1985 | $25 |

EVERYTHING BUT THE GIRL
ATLANTIC
| ❑ 83214 | Temperamental | 1999 | $18 |
| ❑ 82057 | The Language of Life | 1990 | $15 |
SIRE
❑ 25494	Baby, the Stars Shine Bright	1986	$12
❑ 25214	Everything But The Girl	1984	$12
❑ 25721	Idlewild	1988	$12
❑ 25274	Love Not Money	1985	$12

EVERYTHING IS EVERYTHING
VANGUARD
| ❑ VSD-6512 | Everything Is Everything | 1969 | $30 |

EVIE
WORD
| ❑ 7-01-895210-7 | Christmas, A Happy Time | 1984 | $12 |
| ❑ 8770 | Come On, Ring Those Bells | 1977 | $15 |

EWELL, DON
ANALOGUE PRODUCTIONS
| ❑ APJ-19 | Yellow Dog Blues | 199? | $75 |
| —Audiophile reissue on red vinyl | | | |
AUDIOPHILE
| ❑ APS-5966 | Yellow Dog Blues | 196? | $50 |
CHIAROSCURO
❑ 130	Don Ewell	1974	$35
❑ 106	Jazz Portrait of the Artist	1972	$35
❑ 127	Take It in Stride	1973	$35
GHB
| ❑ 30 | Don Ewell in New Orleans | 196? | $25 |
GOOD TIME JAZZ
❑ L-12046 [M]	Free 'N Easy	1956	$40
❑ S-10046 [S]	Free 'N Easy	1960	$30
❑ L-12021 [M]	Music to Listen to Don Ewell By	1955	$50
❑ L-12043 [M]	The Man Here Plays Fine Piano	1956	$40
❑ S-10043 [S]	The Man Here Plays Fine Piano	1960	$30
JAZZOLOGY
❑ JCE-84	Don Ewell and Bob Greene Together!	198?	$25
❑ J-29	Don Ewell and the All-Stars	197?	$25
❑ J-69	Don Ewell Quintet	198?	$25
NEW ORLEANS
| ❑ NOR-7209 | Don Ewell and Herb Hall in New Orleans | 198? | $25 |
STOMP OFF
| ❑ SOS-1077 | Chicago '57 | 198? | $25 |
WINDIN' BALL
❑ LP-101 [10]	Don Ewell	1953	$50
❑ LP-102 [10]	Don Ewell and Mama Yancey	1953	$50
❑ LP-103 [10]	Don Ewell Plays Tunes Played by the King Oliver Band	1953	$50
❑ LP-103 [M]	Don Ewell Plays Tunes Played by the King Oliver Band	195?	$30

EWING, SKIP
MCA
| ❑ 42128 | The Coast of Colorado | 1988 | $12 |
| ❑ 42301 | The Will to Love | 1989 | $12 |

EXCITERS, THE
RCA VICTOR
| ❑ LSP-4211 | Caviar and Chitlins | 1969 | $30 |
ROULETTE
| ❑ R25326 [M] | The Exciters | 1966 | $30 |
| ❑ SR25326 [S] | The Exciters | 1966 | $40 |
TODAY
| ❑ 1001 [B] | Black Beauty | 1971 | $25 |
UNITED ARTISTS
| ❑ UAL-3264 [M] | Tell Him | 1963 | $80 |
| ❑ UAS-6264 [S] | Tell Him | 1963 | $175 |

EXILE
ARISTA
| ❑ AL-9624 | Still Standing | 1990 | $18 |
EPIC
❑ B6E39154	Exile	1983	$10
❑ FE40401	Greatest Hits	1986	$10
❑ BFE40000	Hang On to Your Heart	1985	$10
❑ FE39424	Kentucky Hearts	1984	$10
❑ FE40901	Shelter from the Night	1987	$10
MCA CURB
❑ 946	All There Is	1986	$10
❑ 5581	Best of Exile	1985	$10
❑ 964	Don't Leave Me This Way	1986	$10
❑ 947	Heart and Soul	1986	$10
❑ 963	Mixed Emotions	1986	$10
❑ 1456	More of the Best of Exile	1986	$10
RCA VICTOR
| ❑ AFL1-3086 | Exile | 1978 | $15 |
| ❑ AFL1-3087 | Stage Pass | 1978 | $15 |
WARNER BROS.
❑ BSK3323	All There Is	1979	$12
❑ BSK3437	Don't Leave Me This Way	1980	$12
❑ BSK3588	Heart and Soul	1981	$12
❑ BSK3205	Mixed Emotions	1978	$12
WOODEN NICKEL
| ❑ BWL1-0120 | Exile | 1973 | $18 |

EXOTIC GUITARS
RANWOOD
❑ 8171	300 Watt Music Box	1975	$12
❑ 8090	All the Guitar Hits	1971	$12
❑ 8080	Country Music	1970	$12
❑ 8061	Everybody's Talkin'	1970	$12
❑ 8073	Holly Holy	1970	$12
❑ 8085	I Can't Stop Loving You	1971	$12
❑ 8051	Indian Love Call	1969	$15
❑ 8002	The Exotic Guitars	1968	$15
❑ 8040	Those Were the Days	1968	$15

EXPLOITED, THE
CLEOPATRA
| ❑ 7318 [B] | Punk At Leeds '83 | | $25 |

EXPOSE
ARISTA
| ❑ AL-8441 | Exposure | 1987 | $10 |
| ❑ AL-8532 | What You Don't Know | 1989 | $12 |

EYEBALL
CMP
| ❑ CMP-11-ST | Eyeball | 198? | $30 |

EYERMANN, TIM, AND EAST COAST OFFERING
BLUEMOON
| ❑ R1-79151 | Jazz on L | 1989 | $30 |
| ❑ R1-79163 | Outside/Inside | 1990 | $30 |
INNER CITY
| ❑ IC-1095 | Aloha | 198? | $30 |
MCA
| ❑ 5494 | East Coast Offering | 1985 | $25 |
| ❑ 5589 | Walkin' With You | 1986 | $25 |

EYES OF BLUE
MERCURY
| ❑ SR-61184 | Crossroads of Time | 1968 | $30 |
| ❑ SR-61220 | In Fields of Ardath | 1969 | $30 |

EYGES, DAVID
MUSIC UNLIMITED
| ❑ 7432 | Crossroads | 1982 | $30 |
| ❑ 7431 | The Arrow | 1981 | $30 |

EZELL, WILLIAM
RIVERSIDE
| ❑ RLP-1043 [10] | Gin Mill Jazz | 1954 | $100 |

F

FABARES, SHELLEY
COLPIX
| ❑ CP-426 [M] | Shelley! | 1962 | $175 |
| ❑ SCP-426 [S] | Shelley! | 1962 | $600 |

| ❑ CP-431 [M] | The Things We Did Last Summer | 1962 | $150 |
| ❑ SCP-431 [S] | The Things We Did Last Summer | 1962 | $400 |

FABIAN
ABC
| ❑ X-806 | 16 Greatest Hits | 1973 | $15 |
CHANCELLOR
❑ CHL-5024 [M]	Fabian's 16 Fabulous Hits	1962	$85
❑ CHL-5005 [M]	Fabulous Fabian	1959	$50
❑ CHLS-5005 [S]	Fabulous Fabian	1959	$85
❑ CHL-5003 [M]	Hold That Tiger!	1959	$150
—Pink label			

❑ CHL-5003 [M]	Hold That Tiger!	1959	$50
—Black label			
❑ CHLS-5003 [S]	Hold That Tiger!	1959	$175
—Pink label			
❑ CHLS-5003 [S]	Hold That Tiger!	1959	$85
—Black label			
❑ CHL-5019 [M]	Rockin' Hot	1961	$85
❑ CHL-69802 [M]	The Fabian Facade: Young and Wonderful	1960	$100
—Felt gatefold cover with die-cut window			
❑ CHL-5012 [M]	The Good Old Summertime	1960	$50
❑ CHLS-5012 [S]	The Good Old Summertime	1960	$85
MCA
| ❑ 27095 | The Best of Fabian | 1985 | $10 |
UNITED ARTISTS
| ❑ UA-LA449-E | The Very Best of Fabian | 1975 | $15 |

FABIAN / FRANKIE AVALON
CHANCELLOR
| ❑ CHL-5009 [M] | The Hit Makers | 1960 | $150 |

FABRIC, BENT
ATCO
❑ 33-148 [M]	Alley Cat	1962	$35
❑ SD 33-148 [S]	Alley Cat	1962	$50
❑ 33-185 [M]	Never Tease Tigers	1966	$30
❑ SD 33-185 [S]	Never Tease Tigers	1966	$35
❑ 33-202 [M]	Operation Lovebirds	1967	$30

Number	Title	Yr	NM
❏ SD 33-202 [S]	Operation Lovebirds	1967	$35
❏ 33-164 [M]	Organ Grinder's Swing	1964	$30
❏ SD 33-164 [S]	Organ Grinder's Swing	1964	$35
❏ 33-221 [M]	Relax	1967	$35
❏ SD 33-221 [S]	Relax	1967	$30
❏ 33-173 [M]	The Drunken Penguin	1965	$30
❏ SD 33-173 [S]	The Drunken Penguin	1965	$35
❏ 33-155 [M]	The Happy Puppy	1963	$30
❏ SD 33-155 [S]	The Happy Puppy	1963	$35

FABULOUS COUNTS, THE
COTILLION
❏ SD9011	Jan Jan	1969	$150
❏ SD9011	Jan Jan	199?	$15
— Reissue; superficially almost identical to original

FABULOUS FLIPPERS, THE
VERITAS
❏ VS-2570	Something Tangible	1970	$30

FABULOUS JOKERS, THE
MONUMENT
❏ MLP-8059 [M]	Guitars Extraordinaire	1966	$150
❏ SLP-18059 [S]	Guitars Extraordinaire	1966	$175

FABULOUS POODLES
EPIC
❏ JE35666 [B]	Mirror Stars	1978	$15
❏ JE35666 [DJ]	Mirror Stars	1978	$25
— White label promo on pink vinyl
❏ JE36256	Think Pink	1979	$12

FABULOUS RHINESTONES, THE
JUST SUNSHINE
❏ 9	Freewheelin'	1973	$15
❏ 1	The Fabulous Rhinestones	1972	$15

FABULOUS THUNDERBIRDS, THE
CBS ASSOCIATED
❏ FZ40818	Hot Number	1987	$10
❏ OZ45094	Powerful Stuff	1989	$12
❏ BFZ40304	Tuff Enuff	1986	$12
❏ FZ40304 [B]	Tuff Enuff	1986	$10
— Reissue with new prefix
CHRYSALIS
❏ CHR1319	Butt Rockin'	1981	$15
❏ PV41319	Butt Rockin'	198?	$10
— Reissue of 1319
❏ CHR1395	T-Bird Rhythm	1982	$15
❏ FV41395	T-Bird Rhythm	1983	$12
— Reissue of 1395
❏ PV41395	T-Bird Rhythm	198?	$10
— Reissue with new prefix
❏ PV41250	The Fabulous Thunderbirds	198?	$12
— Reissue of Takoma 7068
❏ CHR1287	What's the Word	1980	$15
❏ PV41287	What's the Word	198?	$10
— Reissue of 1287
TAKOMA
❏ TAK7068	The Fabulous Thunderbirds	1979	$15

FACE TO FACE (1)
EPIC
❏ BFE39999	Confrontation	1985	$10
❏ BFE38857	Face to Face	1984	$10
MERCURY
❏ 834376-1	One Big Day	1988	$10

FACE TO FACE (2)
FAT WRECK CHORDS
❏ FATLP-515 [B]	Don't Turn Away	1992	$30
VAGRANT
❏ VR328	Face to Face	199?	$12
— Vinyl issue of album first issued on CD by A&M
❏ VRLP366	How to Ruin Everything	2002	$12
❏ VR344	Reactionary	2000	$12

FACENDA, JOHN (NARRATOR)
MANUSCRIPT
❏ MLP-571 [M]	The Nativity	1957	$40
— Original Philadelphia-area issue; gatefold with 12-page booklet
RCA VICTOR
❏ LOP-1504 [M]	The Nativity	1958	$30
— National reissue of Manuscript LP; very similar to original issue

FACES
Also see SMALL FACES; ROD STEWART; RONNIE WOOD.

4 MEN WITH BEARDS
❏ 4M215LP [B]	First Step		$25

WARNER BROS.
❏ BS2574	A Nod Is As Good As a Wink...To a Blind Horse	1971	$18
— Green label
❏ BS2574	A Nod Is As Good As a Wink...To a Blind Horse	1973	$15
— Burbank" palm trees label
❏ WS1851	First Step	1970	$25
— First pressings have "small faces." on front cover
❏ WS1851 [B]	First Step	1970	$15
— Later pressings have "faces." on front cover
❏ WS1892	Long Player	1971	$18
❏ ST-93718	Long Player	1971	$25
— Capitol Record Club edition
❏ BS2665	Ooh La La	1973	$18
— Green label
❏ BS2665	Ooh La La	1973	$15
— Burbank" palm trees label
❏ BS2897	Snakes and Ladders: The Best of Faces	1976	$15

FACHIN, ERIA
CRITIQUE
❏ 90936	My Name Is Eria Fachin	1988	$10

FACTS OF LIFE
KAYVETTE
❏ KAY-803	Matter of Fact	1978	$18
❏ LPK-802	Sometimes	1977	$18

FADDIS, JON
BUDDAH
❏ BDS-5727	Good and Plenty	1979	$30
CONCORD JAZZ
❏ CJ-291	Legacy	1986	$25
EPIC
❏ OE45266	Into the FaddisPhere	1989	$85
PABLO
❏ 2310765	Youngblood	1977	$35

FAGAN, SCOTT
ATCO
❏ SD 33-267	South Atlantic Blues	1968	$25
RCA VICTOR
❏ APL1-1185	Many Sunny Places	1976	$18

FAGEN, DONALD
Also see STEELY DAN.
MOBILE FIDELITY
❏ 1-120	The Nightfly	1982	$40
— Audiophile vinyl
WARNER BROS.
❏ 23696 [B]	The Nightfly	1982	$10

FAGERQUIST, DON
MODE
❏ LP-124 [M]	Music to Fill a Void	1957	$150

FAHEY, JOHN
4 MEN WITH BEARDS
❏ 4M117LP [B]	America		$30
❏ 4M600LP [B]	The Transcendental Waterfall: Guitar Excursions 1962-1967		$175
— The Transcendental Waterfall: Guitar Excursions 1962-1967 is a 6-LP box set drawing from John Fahey's best, and most influential, period. Included in the set are Blind Joe Death, Death Chants, Breakdowns, And Military Waltzes, The Dance Of Death And Other Plantation Favorites, The Great San Bernardino Birthday Party, The Transfiguration Of Blind Joe Death, and Days Have Gone By, all reissued on 180 gram vinyl with deluxe tip-on jackets. Also included are a t-shirt (size L only), a poster, and a postcard, all of which are housed in a deluxe box. An amazing package featuring some of the most important guitar solo recordings of the 20th century. Limited to 2,000 numbered copies.
❏ 4M219LP [B]	The Voice of the Turtle		$30
❏ 4m201 [B]	Volume 1 Blind Joe Death	2015	$20
❏ 4m202 [B]	Volume 2 - Death Chants, Breakdowns and Military Waltzes	2015	$20
❏ 4m203 [B]	Volume 3 - Dance of Death and Other Plantation Favorites	2015	$20
— 180g
❏ 4M205 [B]	Volume 5 - The Transfiguration Of Blind Joe Death	2013	$40
❏ C1014 [B]	Volume 6 - Days Have Gone By	2015	$25
— 180g
REPRISE
❏ MS2145	After the Ball	1973	$35
❏ MS2089	Of Rivers and Religions	1972	$30

RIVERBOAT
❏ RB-1 [M]	The Transfiguration of Blind Joe Death	1967	$150
— Green cover with booklet; "Volume 5" added to back cover
❏ RB-1 [M]	The Transfiguration of Blind Joe Death	1965	$300
— Original issue of 50 copies with booklet, hand-written labels and no "Volume 5" anywhere on the cover
SHANACHIE
❏ 97006	God, Time and Causality	1990	$20
TABLE OF THE ELEMENTS
❏ 38	Georgia Stomps, Atlanta Struts, and Other Contemporary Dance Favorites	1999	$30
TAKOMA
❏ C-1030	America	1972	$30
— With gatefold jacket and booklet
❏ C-1030	America	197?	$18
— Later pressings with no gatefold
❏ C-1002	Blind Joe Death	1964	$50
— White cover, similar to first edition, except it has a Berkeley, Caifornia address on cover; six tracks were re-recorded for this edition
❏ TAK-7002	Blind Joe Death	1979	$15
— Reissue of 1002
❏ (# unknown) [B]	Blind Joe Death	1959	$350
— Original edition of 1,000 has a white cover with "Blind Joe Death" on one side and "John Fahey" on the other; possibly pressed by RCA Victor Custom Division; no Berkeley, California address on cover
❏ C1002 [B]	Blind Joe Death	1967	$40
— reissue
❏ C-1045	Christmas with John Fahey, Vol. 2	1975	$25
❏ TAK-7045	Christmas with John Fahey, Vol. 2	198?	$15
— Reissue of 1045
❏ C-1004	Dance of Death & Other Plantation Favorites/John Fahey Vol. 3	1964	$75
— White cover with block lettering
❏ C1004 [B]	Dance of Death & Other Plantation Favorites/John Fahey Vol. 3	1967	$20
— reissue
❏ TAK-7004	Dance of Death and Other Plantation Favorites	198?	$15
— Reissue of 1004
❏ C-1014	Days Have Gone By Volume 6	1967	$30
— With booklet
❏ C-1014	Days Have Gone By Volume 6	1968	$15
— Without booklet
❏ C-1003	Death Chants, Break Downs & Military Waltzes	1964	$75
— First cover is white with block print with title on cover as above
❏ C1003 [B]	Death Chants, Break Downs & Military Waltzes	1967	$40
— reissue
❏ TAK-7003	Death Chants, Breakdowns and Military Waltzes	198?	$15
— Reissue of 1003
❏ C-1003 [B]	Death Chants, Breakdowns and Military Waltzes Vol. II	1965	$75
— Second cover is white with what looks like handwritten print; title is as listed above and "Vol. II" is added to the lower left corner
❏ C-1035	Fare Forward Voyagers	1973	$25
❏ TAK-7035	Fare Forward Voyagers	198?	$15
— Reissue of 1035
❏ TAK-7069	John Fahey Visits Washington, D.C.	1979	$25
❏ TAK-7089	Live in Tasmania	198?	$25
❏ C-1043	Old Fashioned Love	1975	$20
❏ TAK-7043	Old Fashioned Love	198?	$15
— Reissue of 1043
❏ TAK-7102	Railroads I	1981	$15
❏ C-1058	The Best of John Fahey 1959-1977	1977	$20
❏ TAK-7058	The Best of John Fahey 1959-1977	198?	$15
— Reissue of 1058
❏ C-1020	The New Possibility: John Fahey's Guitar Soli Christmas Album	1968	$30
— Originals with back cover liner notes
❏ C-1020	The New Possibility: John Fahey's Guitar Soli Christmas Album	197?	$20
— Later pressings with no liner notes
❏ TAK-7020	The New Possibility: John Fahey's Guitar Soli Christmas Album	198?	$15
— Reissue of 1020
❏ R-9015	The Transfiguration of Blind Joe Death	1969	$25
— Reissue of Riverboat RB-1; logo added to lower right front cover, and the drawing in the center is much more green than

Number	Title	Yr	NM
	on 1967 Riverboat covers		
❏ TAK-7015	The Transfiguration of Blind Joe Death	198?	$15
	—Reissue of 9015		
❏ C-1019	The Voice of the Turtle	1971	$35
	— With gatefold jacket and booklet		
❏ C-1019	The Voice of the Turtle	197?	$18
	— Later pressings with no gatefold		
❏ C-1008	Vol. 4: The Great San Bernardino Birthday Party	1966	$30
	— First pressings have a discography on the back cover		
❏ C-1008	Vol. 4: The Great San Bernardino Birthday Party	1968	$15
	— Without discography on back cover		
❏ C-1002	Volume 1: Blind Joe Death	1967	$40
	— Psychedelic gold and blue cover; the entire album was re-recorded for this edition, including the six songs re-recorded for the first Berkeley edition and one song not on the white-cover editions, "I'm Gonna Do All I Can For My Lord"		
❏ C-1002	Volume 1: Blind Joe Death	1968	$18
	— Blue and white cover with "Stereo" added to upper left		
❏ C-1003	Volume 2: Death Chants, Breakdowns & Military Waltzes	1967	$40
	— Psychedelic gold and orange cover; most of the album was re-recorded for this edition		
❏ C-1003	Volume 2: Death Chants, Breakdowns & Military Waltzes	1968	$18
	— Orange and white cover with orange lettering		
❏ C-1004	Volume 3: The Dance of Death & Other Plantation Favorites	1967	$40
	— Psychedelic gold and brown cover		
❏ C-1004	Volume 3: The Dance of Death & Other Plantation Favorites	1968	$18
	— Brown and white cover		
❏ TAK-7085	Yes! Jesus Loves Me	1980	$15
TERRA			
❏ T-2	Requia	1985	$20
	— Reissue of Vanguard 79259		
VANGUARD			
❏ VSD55/56	Essential John Fahey	1974	$35
❏ VRS-9259 [M]	Requia	1968	$100
❏ VSD-79259 [S]	Requia	1968	$40
❏ VSD-79293	The Yellow Princess	1969	$30
VARRICK			
❏ VR-028	I Remember Blind Joe Death	1987	$20
❏ VR-002	John Fahey Christmas Guitar, Volume 1	1982	$20
❏ VR-008	Let Go	1983	$20
❏ VR-012	Popular Songs of Christmas and New Year's	1983	$20
❏ VR-019	Rain Forests, Oceans & Other Themes	1985	$20

FAIR, YVONNE
MOTOWN

| ❏ M6-832S1 [B] | The Bitch Is Black | 1975 | $35 |

FAIRCHILD, BARBARA
COLUMBIA

❏ KC31720	A Sweeter Love	1973	$15
❏ PC34868	Free & Easy	1977	$15
❏ KC35311	Greatest Hits	1978	$15
❏ KC32711	Kid Stuff	1974	$15
❏ KC32960	Love Is a Gentle Thing	1974	$15
❏ C31092	Love's Old Song	1971	$15
❏ PC34307	Mississippi	1976	$15
❏ C30123	Someone Special	1970	$18
❏ KC33058	Standing in Yoru Line	1974	$15
❏ KC35536	This Is Me	1978	$15

FAIRGROUND ATTRACTION
RCA

| ❏ 8596-1-R | The First of a Million Kisses | 1988 | $12 |

FAIRPORT CONVENTION
4 MEN WITH BEARDS

❏ 4M159LP [B]	Liege & Lief		$25
❏ 4M158LP [B]	Unhalfbricking		$25
❏ 4M157LP [B]	What We Did On Our Holidays		$25

A&M

❏ SP-4316 [B]	Angel Delight	1971	$30
❏ SP-4333 [B]	Babbacombe" Lee	1972	$30
❏ SP-4185 [B]	Fairport Convention	1969	$25
	—Not a reissue of Cotillion LP, but the US issue of the second UK LP "What We Did on Our Holidays"		
❏ SP-4407	Fairport Nine	1973	$18
❏ SP-3603 [B]	Fairport Nine	1974	$15
	— Early reissue of 4407		
❏ SP-4265 [B]	Full House	1970	$30
❏ SP-4257 [B]	Liege and Lief	1970	$30
❏ SP-4383	Rosie	1973	$18
❏ SP-3530	The Fairport Chronicles	1976	$18
❏ SP-6016	The Fairport Chronicles	198?	$15
	— Reissue of 3530		

Number	Title	Yr	NM
❏ SP-4206 [B]	Unhalfbricking	1969	$25
ANTILLES			
❏ 7054	Gottle O' Geer	1976	$15
CARTHAGE			
❏ CGLP-4417	Full House	198?	$12
	—Reissue of A&M 4265		
❏ CGLP-4418	Unhalfbricking	198?	$12
	—Reissue of A&M 4206		
❏ CGLP-4430	What We Did on Our Holidays	198?	$12
	—Reissue of A&M 4185 with UK title restored		
COTILLION			
❏ 9024 [M]	Fairport Convention	1968	$500
	—Mono is white label promo only; "DJ Copy Monaural" sticker on front cover		
❏ SD9024 [S]	Fairport Convention	1968	$30
HANNIBAL			
❏ HNBL-1329	Heyday	1987	$12
❏ HNBL-1319	House Full	1986	$12
ISLAND			
❏ ILPS-9285	Fairport Live/A Movable Feast	1974	$15
❏ 90678	In Real Time -- Live '87	1987	$12
❏ ILPS-9313	Rising for the Moon	1975	$15
VARRICK			
❏ VR-029 [B]	Expletive Delighted!	1987	$15
❏ VR-023	Gladys' Leap	1986	$12

FAITH, ADAM
AMY

| ❏ 8005 [M] | Adam Faith | 1965 | $30 |
| ❏ S-8005 [S] | Adam Faith | 1965 | $30 |

MGM

| ❏ E-3951 [M] | England's Top Singer | 1961 | $40 |
| ❏ SE-3951 [S] | England's Top Singer | 1961 | $50 |

FAITH, PERCY
COLUMBIA

❏ CL1010 [M]	Adventure in the Sun	1957	$25
❏ KG31588	All-Time Greatest Hits	1972	$15
❏ PG31588	All-Time Greatest Hits	198?	$12
	— Budget-line reissue		
❏ CL1957 [M]	American Serenade	1963	$15
❏ CS8757 [S]	American Serenade	1963	$15
❏ KC32803	A New Thing	1974	$12
❏ CQ32803 [Q]	A New Thing	1974	$20
❏ CL2906 [M]	Angel of the Morning (Hit Themes for Young Lovers)	1968	$25
❏ CS9706 [S]	Angel of the Morning (Hit Themes for Young Lovers)	1968	$15
❏ CL1386 [M]	A Night with Jerome Kern	1959	$18
❏ CS8181 [S]	A Night with Jerome Kern	1959	$25
❏ CL1302 [M]	A Night with Sigmund Romberg	1959	$18
❏ CS8108 [S]	A Night with Sigmund Romberg	1959	$25
❏ G30330	A Time for Love	1971	$18
❏ CL2529 [M]	Bim Bam Boom	1966	$15
❏ CS9329 [S]	Bim Bam Boom	1966	$15
❏ C30800	Black Magic Woman	1971	$12
❏ CL1417 [M]	Bon Voyage!	1960	$18
❏ CS8214 [S]	Bon Voyage!	1960	$18
❏ CL1322 [M]	Bouquet	1959	$18
❏ CS8124 [S]	Bouquet	1959	$18
❏ CL1681 [M]	Bouquet of Love	1962	$15
❏ CS8481 [S]	Bouquet of Love	1962	$18
❏ CL2356 [M]	Broadway Bouquet	1965	$15
❏ CS9156 [S]	Broadway Bouquet	1965	$15
❏ CL1570 [M]	Camelot	1960	$15
❏ CS8370 [S]	Camelot	1960	$18
❏ KC33244	Chinatown (Featuring "The Entertainer")	1974	$12
❏ CQ33244 [Q]	Chinatown (Featuring "The Entertainer")	1974	$20
❏ CS9377 [S]	Christmas Is…	1966	$15
❏ CL2577 [M]	Christmas Is…	1966	$18
❏ 3C9377	Christmas Is…	198?	$10
	— Budget-line reissue		
❏ PC39471	Christmas Melodies	1984	$10
	— Repackage of previously released material		
❏ KC32164	Clair	1973	$12
❏ CQ32164 [Q]	Clair	1973	$20
❏ CL525 [M]	Continental Music	1955	$25
❏ KC32124	Corazon	1974	$12
❏ KC33142	Country Bouquet	1975	$12
❏ KC31627	Day By Day	1972	$12
❏ CQ31627 [Q]	Day By Day	1972	$20
❏ CL681 [M]	Delicado	1956	$25
❏ KC33549	Disco Party	1975	$12
❏ CL2317 [M]	Do I Hear a Waltz	1965	$15
❏ CS9117 [S]	Do I Hear a Waltz	1965	$15
❏ CL1902 [M]	Exotic Strings	1963	$15
❏ CS8702 [S]	Exotic Strings	1963	$15
❏ CL6148 [10]	Football Songs	1950	$40
❏ GP1	Forever Young	1968	$18
❏ CL2810 [M]	For Those in Love	1968	$25
❏ CS9610 [S]	For Those in Love	1968	$18
❏ CL2108 [M]	Great Folk Themes	1964	$15
❏ CS8908 [S]	Great Folk Themes	1964	$15
❏ CG33895	Great Moments of Percy Faith	1976	$15

Number	Title	Yr	NM
❏ CL1187 [M]	Hallelujah!	1957	$25
❏ CS8033 [S]	Hallelujah!	1958	$30
❏ CS1019	Held Over! Today's Great Movie Themes	1970	$15
❏ CL1783 [M]	Hollywood's Great Themes	1962	$15
❏ CS8583 [S]	Hollywood's Great Themes	1962	$18
❏ CL640 [M]	House of Flowers	1956	$25
❏ C30502	I Think I Love You	1971	$12
❏ CQ30502 [Q]	I Think I Love You	1971	$20
❏ CL1501 [M]	Jealousy	1960	$15
❏ CS8292 [S]	Jealousy	1960	$18
❏ C31042	Jesus Christ Superstar	1971	$12
❏ C31301	Joy	1972	$12
❏ CQ31301 [Q]	Joy	1972	$20
❏ CL1188 [M]	Jubliation!	1957	$25

❏ CL550 [M]	Kismet	1955	$25
❏ CS8642 [R]	Kismet	1963	$12
❏ CL2279 [M]	Latin Themes for Young Lovers	1966	$15
❏ CS9079 [S]	Latin Themes for Young Lovers	1965	$15
❏ CS9983	Leaving on a Jet Plane	1970	$15
❏ CL955 [M]	L'il Abner	1957	$25
❏ CL2209 [M]	Love Goddess	1966	$15
❏ CS9009 [S]	Love Goddess	1964	$15
❏ CS9906	Love Theme from "Romeo & Juliet"	1969	$15
❏ CQ31004 [Q]	Love Theme from "Romeo & Juliet"	1971	$20
❏ CL1267 [M]	Malaguena	1958	$25
❏ CS8081 [S]	Malaguena	1958	$30
❏ CL2167 [M]	More Themes for Young Lovers	1964	$15
❏ CS8967 [S]	More Themes for Young Lovers	1964	$15
❏ CL1639 [M]	Mucho Gusto! More Music of Brazil	1961	$15
❏ CS8439 [S]	Mucho Gusto! More Music of Brazil	1961	$18
❏ CL705 [M]	Music for Her	1956	$25
❏ CL577 [M]	Music from Hollywood	1955	$25
❏ CL1381 [M]	Music of Christmas	1959	$25
	—Re-recorded version of CL 588 with same track order		
❏ CS8176 [S]	Music of Christmas	1959	$18
❏ PC38302	Music of Christmas	1983	$10
❏ CL588 [M]	Music of Christmas	1955	$30
❏ CL2405 [M]	Music of Christmas, Volume 2	1965	$15
❏ CS9205 [S]	Music of Christmas, Volume 2	1965	$15
❏ CS9004 [R]	My Fair Lady	1964	$15
❏ CL895 [M]	My Fair Lady	1957	$25
❏ KC32380	My Love	1973	$12
❏ CL880 [M]	Passport to Romance	1956	$25
❏ CL1493 [M]	Percy Faith's Greatest Hits	1960	$18
❏ CS8637 [R]	Percy Faith's Greatest Hits	1963	$12
❏ PC8637 [R]	Percy Faith's Greatest Hits	198?	$10
	— Budget-line reissue		
❏ CS8105 [S]	Porgy and Bess	1959	$25
❏ CL1298 [M]	Porgy and Bess	1959	$18
❏ C32585	Remembering the Hits of the 60's	1973	$12
❏ CL2024 [M]	Shangri-La!	1963	$15
❏ CS8824 [S]	Shangri-La!	1963	$15
❏ CL1105 [M]	South Pacific	1957	$18
❏ CS8005 [S]	South Pacific	1958	$30
❏ KC33915	Summer of '76	1976	$12
❏ CL1627 [M]	Tara's Theme from "Gone with the Wind" and Other Themes	1961	$15
❏ CS8427 [S]	Tara's Theme from "Gone with the Wind" and Other Themes	1961	$18
❏ CL2650 [M]	The Academy Award Winner and Other Great Movie Themes	1967	$18
❏ CS9450 [S]	The Academy Award Winner and Other Great Movie Themes	1967	$15
❏ C30097	The Beatles Album	1970	$15
❏ C2L15 [M]	The Columbia Album of Christmas Music	1958	$30
	—Combines CL 588 and CL 1187 into one gatefold package		

Number	Title	Yr	NM
❑ PCQ33006 [Q]	The Entertainer	1974	$20
❑ CL2441 [M]	Themes for the "In" Crowd	1966	$15
❑ CS9241 [S]	Themes for the "In" Crowd	1966	$15
❑ CL2023 [M]	Themes for Young Lovers	1963	$15
❑ CS8823 [S]	Themes for Young Lovers	1963	$15
❑ CL1822 [M]	The Music of Brazil!	1962	$15
❑ CS8622 [S]	The Music of Brazil!	1962	$18
❑ CL1418 [M]	The Sound of Music	1960	$18
❑ CS8215 [S]	The Sound of Music	1960	$18
❑ CS9762	Those Were the Days	1969	$15
❑ CL2704 [M]	Today's Themes for Young Lovers	1967	$18
❑ CS9504 [S]	Today's Themes for Young Lovers	1967	$15
❑ CL1182 [M]	Touchdown!	1957	$25
❑ CL1075 [M]	Viva!	1957	$25
❑ CS8038 [S]	Viva!	1958	$30
❑ CG33606	Viva!/Mucho Gusto!	1975	$15
❑ CS9835	Windmills of Your Mind	1969	$15

COLUMBIA LIMITED EDITION

❑ LE10042	Bouquet	197?	$12
❑ LE10095	Great Folk Themes	197?	$12
❑ LE10350	Hallelujah!	197?	$12
❑ LE10131	Jealousy	197?	$12
❑ LE10082	Music of Christmas	197?	$12

—Brown label "Limited Edition" series; same contents as CS 8176

❑ LE10088	Music of Christmas, Volume 2	197?	$12
❑ LE10004	Tara's Theme from "Gone with the Wind" and Other Themes	197?	$12
❑ LE10041	Themes for the "In" Crowd	197?	$12
❑ LE10185	Those Were the Days	197?	$12
❑ LE10015	Windmills of Your Mind	197?	$12

COLUMBIA SPECIAL PRODUCTS

❑ P13827	American Serenade	197?	$10
❑ P13091	Broadway Bouquet	197?	$10
❑ P13277	Leaving on a Jet Plane	197?	$10
❑ P213719	The Columbia Album of George Gershwin	197?	$15

HARMONY

❑ KH30607	A Summer Place	1971	$12
❑ KH31777	Every Night at the Movies	1972	$12
❑ KH30977	Raindrops Keep Fallin'	1971	$12
❑ HS11348	Sounds of Music	1969	$12
❑ H30020	Younger Than Springtime	1970	$12

VOCALION

❑ VL3600 [M]	North and South of the Border	1958	$18

FAITH BAND

MERCURY

❑ SRM-1-3770	Face to Face	1979	$15
❑ SRM-1-3759	Rock'n Romance	1978	$15
❑ SRM-1-3807	Vital Signs	1979	$12

VILLAGE

❑ VR7703	Excuse Me ... I Just Cut an Album	1977	$25
❑ VR7805	Rock'n Romance	1978	$25

FAITH HOPE & CHARITY

RCA VICTOR

❑ APL1-1100	Faith, Hope & Charity	1975	$15
❑ APL1-1827	Life Goes	1976	$15

SUSSEX

❑ SXSB-7019	Heavy Love	1972	$18

FAITH NO MORE
MR. BUNGLE and FANTOMAS related.

MORDAM

❑ FNM1	We Care a Lot	1985	$30

SLASH

❑ 25559	Introduce Yourself	1987	$18
❑ 45723	King for a Day/Fool for a Lifetime	1995	$30
❑ 25878	The Real Thing	1989	$25

TPM/RHINO EXCLUSIVE

❑ 2310	Angel Dust	2008	$40

FAITHFULL, MARIANNE

ABKCO

❑ 75471	Greatest Hits	1988	$12

—Reissue of London PS 547

ISLAND

❑ 90066	A Child's Adventure	1983	$12
❑ 90066 [DJ]	A Child's Adventure	1983	$35

—Promo-only Quiex II audiophile pressing

❑ PRO794 [EP]	Blazing Away Sampler	1990	$25

—Promo-only sampler for radio

❑ ILPS9570	Broken English	1979	$12
❑ 90039	Broken English	1983	$10

—Reissue

❑ ILPS9570 [B]	Broken English	1979	$18
❑ ILPS9648	Dangerous Acquaintances	1981	$12
❑ 90613	Strange Weather	1987	$12

LONDON

❑ LL3482 [M]	Faithfull Forever	1966	$18

Number	Title	Yr	NM
❑ PS482 [S]	Faithfull Forever	1966	$25
❑ LL3482 [B]	Faithfull Forever	1966	$18
❑ LL3452 [M]	Go Away from My World	1965	$30

—No Oldham credit.

❑ PS452 [S]	Go Away from My World	1965	$25
❑ LL3452 [M]	Go Away from My World	1965	$30

—With Oldham credit.

❑ PS547	Greatest Hits	1969	$18

❑ LL3423 [M]	Marianne Faithfull	1965	$25
❑ PS423 [R]	Marianne Faithfull	1965	$18
❑ LL3423 [B]	Marianne Faithfull	1965	$25
❑ PS547 [B]	Marianne Faithfull's Greatest Hits	1969	$18

MOBILE FIDELITY

❑ 1-235	Broken English	1995	$75

—Audiophile vinyl

FALCO

A&M

❑ SP-6-4951	Einzelhaft	1982	$12
❑ SP-5105	Falco 3	1985	$10
❑ SP-4993	Junge Roemer	1985	$12

SIRE

❑ 25522	Emotional	1986	$12
❑ 25690	Wiener Blut	1988	$12

FALCON, BILLY

MANHATTAN

❑ MR-LA832-G	Billy Falcon's Burning Rose	1977	$15

MCA

❑ 3238	Falcon Around	1980	$18

UNITED ARTISTS

❑ UA-LA967-H	Billy Falcon	1979	$12

FALCONS, THE (1)

RELIC

❑ 8006	I Found a Love (The Falcons' Story Part Two: 1960-1964)	1987	$15
❑ 8005	You're So Fine (The Falcons' Story Part One: 1956-1959)	1987	$15

FALL, THE
Featuring Mark E. Smith.

BEGGARS BANQUET

❑ 2430-1-H	458489	1990	$12
❑ 9582-1-H	I Am Kurious Oranj	1988	$12
❑ 9807-1-H	Seminal Live	1989	$12
❑ 6897-1-H	The Frenz Experiment	1988	$12
❑ BBQLP2134 [B]	This Nation's Saving Grace	2015	$25

I.R.S.

❑ SP-003	Live at the Witch Trials	1979	$25

I.R.S./FAULTY

❑ COPE-2	Early Years 77-79	1981	$18

MATADOR

❑ OLE95-1	Middle Class Revolt	1994	$12
❑ OLE55-1	The Infotainment Scan	1993	$12

PVC

❑ 8932	The Wonderful and Frightening World of The Fall	1984	$16
❑ 8940	This Nation's Saving Grace	1985	$18

ROUGH TRADE

❑ ROUGH US-8	Grotesque (After the Gramme)	1981	$18
❑ TRADE3/10 [10]	Slates	1981	$15

—10-inch EP

SUPERIOR VIADUCT

❑ SV112 [B]	Dragnet	2016	$30
❑ SV111 [B]	Live at the Witch Trials	2016	$30

FALL OUT BOY

ISLAND

Number	Title	Yr	NM
❑ 1219601	Folie a Deux	2008	$30

FALLEN ANGELS, THE

ROULETTE

❑ SR42011	It's a Long Way Down	1968	$400
❑ R25358 [M]	The Fallen Angels	1967	$30
❑ SR25358 [S]	The Fallen Angels	1967	$40

FALLENROCK

CAPRICORN

❑ CP 0143	Watch for Fallenrock	1974	$12

FALTERMEYER, HAROLD

MCA

❑ 42165	Harold F	1988	$12

FALTSKOG, AGNETHA

ATLANTIC

❑ 81820	I Stand Alone	1988	$18

POLYDOR

❑ 813242-1	Wrap Your Arms Around Me	1983	$12

FAME, GEORGIE, AND ANNIE ROSS

DRG

❑ 5197	Georgie Fame and Annie Ross in Hoagland	198?	$30

FAME, GEORGIE

EPIC

❑ BN26563	Shorty Featuring Georgie Fame	1968	$150
❑ BN26368	The Ballad of Bonnie and Clyde	1968	$150

IMPERIAL

❑ LP-9331 [M]	Get Away	1966	$200
❑ LP-12331 [R]	Get Away	1966	$175
❑ LP-9282 [M]	Yeh, Yeh	1965	$200
❑ LP-12282 [P]	Yeh, Yeh	1965	$200

—Entire album is stereo except "Yeh, Yeh" (rechanneled)

ISLAND

❑ ILPS9293	Georgie Fame	1975	$25

FAME GANG, THE

FAME

❑ SKAO-4200	Solid Gold from Muscle Shoals	1969	$30

FAMILY, THE

PAISLEY PARK

❑ 25322	The Family	1985	$12

FAMILY

REPRISE

❑ RS-6384	A Song for Me	1970	$18
❑ RS-6340	Family Entertainment	1969	$18
❑ RS-6313 [B]	Music in a Doll's House	1968	$30

UNITED ARTISTS

❑ UAS-5527	Anyway	1971	$18
❑ UAS-5644	Bandstand	1972	$18
❑ UAS-5562	Fearless	1972	$18
❑ UA-LA181-F	It's Only a Movie	1974	$15

FAMILY BROWN

UNITED ARTISTS

❑ UA-LA828-G	Imaginary World	1978	$15

FAMILY DOGG

BUDDAH

❑ BDS-5100	The View from Rowland's Head	1972	$30

FAMILY TREE, THE

RCA VICTOR

❑ LSP-3955	Miss Butters	1968	$18

FAMOUS CASTLE JAZZ BAND, THE

GOOD TIME JAZZ

❑ L-12030 [M]	The Famous Castle Jazz Band in Hi-Fi	1957	$40
❑ S-7021 [S]	The Famous Castle Jazz Band in Stereo	1959	$30
❑ S-10030 [S]	The Famous Castle Jazz Band in Stereo	197?	$25
❑ L-12037 [M]	The Famous Castle Jazz Band Plays the Five Pennies	1959	$40
❑ S-10037 [S]	The Famous Castle Jazz Band Plays the Five Pennies	1959	$30

STEREO RECORDS

❑ S-7021 [S]	The Famous Castle Jazz Band in Stereo	1958	$40

Number	Title	Yr	NM
FANCY (1)			
BIG TREE			
❏ BT89502	Wild Thing	1974	$15
RCA VICTOR			
❏ APL1-1482	Fancy Turns You On	1976	$15
FANCY (2)			
POISON RING			
❏ PRR-2238	Meeting You Here	1971	$100
FANKHAUSER, MERRIL			
Also see FAPARDOKLY.			
MAUI			
❏ 101	Merrill Fankhauser	1976	$150
SHAMLEY			
❏ SS-701	Things Going Round in My Mind	1968	$150
FANNY			
CASABLANCA			
❏ NBLP7007	Rock & Roll Survivors	1974	$15
REPRISE			
❏ RS-6456	Charity Ball	1971	$18
❏ RS-6416	Fanny	1970	$18
❏ MS-2058	Fanny Hill	1972	$18
❏ MS-2137	Mother's Pride	1973	$18
FANTASTIC BAGGYS, THE			
IMPERIAL			
❏ LP-9270 [M]	Tell 'Em I'm Surfin'	1964	$175
❏ LP-12270 [S]	Tell 'Em I'm Surfin'	1964	$300
LIBERTY			
❏ LN-10192	Tell 'Em I'm Surfin'	1982	$12
FANTASTIC DEE JAYS, THE			
STONE			
❏ SLP-4003	The Fantastic Dee Jays	1966	$1000
FANTASTIC FOUR, THE			
SOUL			
❏ SS-722	How Sweet He Is	1970	$0
—Canceled			
❏ SS-717	The Best of the Fantastic Four	1969	$40
WESTBOUND			
❏ W201	Alvin Stone (The Birth and Death of a Gangster)	1975	$18
❏ WT6108	BYOF (Bring Your Own Funk)	1978	$18
❏ WT306	Got to Have Your Love	1977	$18
❏ W226	Night People	1976	$18
FANTASTIC JOHNNY C, THE			
PHIL-LA OF SOUL			
❏ 4000	Boogaloo Down Broadway	1968	$100
FANTASY			
LIBERTY			
❏ LSP-7643	Fantasy	1970	$25
FAPARDOKLY			
Also see MERRILL FANKHAUSER.			
U.I.P.			
❏ 2250	Fapardokly	1967	$500
FAR CORPORATION			
ATCO			
❏ 90543	Division One	1986	$10
FAR CRY			
VANGUARD APOSTOLIC			
❏ VSD-6510	Far Cry	1968	$85
FARAGHER BROTHERS, THE			
ABC			
❏ AB-1009	Family Ties	1977	$12
❏ ABCD-941	The Faragher Brothers	1976	$12
POLYDOR			
❏ PD-1-6167	Open Your Eyes	1979	$12
❏ PD-1-6232	The Faraghers	1980	$12
FARDON, DON			
DECCA			
❏ DL75225	I've Paid My Dues	1970	$18
GNP CRESCENDO			
❏ GNPS-2044	Indian Reservation	1968	$25
FARGO, DONNA			
ABC/DOT			
❏ DOSD-2002	Miss Donna Fargo	1974	$15
❏ DO-2075	The Best of Donna Fargo	1977	$15

Number	Title	Yr	NM
❏ DOSD-2029	Whatever I Say Means I Love You	1975	$15
DOT			
❏ DOS-26019	All About a Feeling	1973	$15
❏ DOS-26006	My Second Album	1973	$15
❏ DOS-26000	The Happiest Girl in the Whole U.S.A.	1972	$15
MCA			
❏ 37108	The Best of Donna Fargo	198?	$10
—Budget-line reissue			
❏ 667	The Happiest Girl in the Whole U.S.A.	198?	$10
—Budget-line reissue			
MERCURY			
❏ 830236-1	Winners	1986	$15
❏ 832507-1	Winners	1987	$10
—Reissue with two songs deleted and one added from above			
PICKWICK			
❏ SPC-6187	Superman	197?	$10
SONGBIRD			
❏ 5203	Brotherly Love	1982	$12
WARNER BROS.			
❏ BSK3191	Dark Eyed Lady	1978	$12
❏ BS2996	Donna Fargo Country	1977	$12
❏ BSK3470	Fargo	1980	$12
❏ BSK3377	Just for You	1979	$12
❏ BS2926	On the Move	1976	$12
❏ BS3099	Shame on Me	1977	$12
FARINA, DICK AND VON SCHMIDT, ERIC			
FOLKLORE			
❏ F-LEUT7 [M]	Dick Farina and Eric Von Schmidt	1963	$175
—see also Richard and Mimi Farina, Eric Von Schmidt			
FARINA, RICHARD AND MIMI			
VANGUARD			
❏ VSD79174 [S]	Celebrations for a Grey Day	1965	$15
❏ VRS9174 [M]	Celebrations for a Grey Day	1965	$20
❏ VSD79263 [B]	Memories	1968	$15
❏ VSD79204 [S]	Reflections In A Crystal Wind	1965	$15
—First stereo pressing with "Stereolab" label.			
FARLOW, TAL			
AMERICAN RECORDING SOCIETY			
❏ G-418 [M]	The Swinging Guitar of Tal Farlow	1957	$40
BLUE NOTE			
❏ BLP-5042 [10]	Tal Farlow Quartet	1954	$300
CONCORD JAZZ			
❏ CJ-154	Chromatic Palette	1981	$30
❏ CJ-204	Cookin' on All Burners	1982	$30
❏ CJ-26	Sign of the Times	1976	$30
❏ CJ-57	Tal Farlow '78	1978	$30
❏ CJ-266	The Legendary Tal Farlow	1986	$25
FANTASY			
❏ OJC-356	The Return of Tal Farlow/1969	198?	$25
INNER CITY			
❏ IC-1099	Trilogy	197?	$30
NORGRAN			
❏ MGN-1030 [M]	A Recital by Tal Farlow	1955	$700
❏ MGN-1097 [M]	Autumn in New York	1956	$250
❏ MGN-1101 [M]	Fascinating Rhythm	1956	$250
❏ MGN-1102 [M]	Tal	1956	$150
❏ MGN-1014 [M]	The Artistry of Tal Farlow	1955	$300
❏ MGN-1027 [M]	The Interpretations of Tal Farlow	1955	$700
❏ MGN-19 [10]	The Tal Farlow Album	1954	$175
❏ MGN-1047 [M]	The Tal Farlow Album	1955	$150
PRESTIGE			
❏ 24042	Guitar Player	197?	$25
❏ PRST-7732	The Return of Tal Farlow/1969	1969	$25
VERVE			
❏ MGV-8123 [M]	A Recital by Tal Farlow	1957	$50
—Reissue of Norgran 1030			
❏ V-8123 [M]	A Recital by Tal Farlow	1961	$25
❏ MGV-8184 [M]	Autumn in New York	1957	$250
—Reissue of Norgran 1097			
❏ V-8184 [M]	Autumn in New York	1961	$75
❏ 815236-1	Poppin' and Burnin'	198?	$30
❏ MGV-8021 [M]	Tal	1957	$50
—Reissue of Norgran 1102			
❏ V-8021 [M]	Tal	1961	$25
❏ UMV-2565	Tal	198?	$25
❏ MGV-8371 [M]	Tal Farlow Plays the Music of Harold Arlen	1960	$100
❏ MGVS-6144 [S]	Tal Farlow Plays the Music of Harold Arlen	1960	$0
—Canceled			
❏ V-8371 [M]	Tal Farlow Plays the Music of Harold Arlen	1961	$25
❏ MGV-8370 [M]	The Guitar Artistry of Tal Farlow	1960	$150

Number	Title	Yr	NM
❏ MGVS-6143 [S]	The Guitar Artistry of Tal Farlow	1960	$150
❏ V-8370 [M]	The Guitar Artistry of Tal Farlow	1961	$25
❏ V6-8370 [S]	The Guitar Artistry of Tal Farlow	1961	$35
❏ MGV-8011 [M]	The Interpretations of Tal Farlow	1957	$300
—Reissue of Norgran 1027			
❏ V-8011 [M]	The Interpretations of Tal Farlow	1961	$25
❏ MGV-8201 [M]	The Swinging Guitar of Tal Farlow	1957	$150

Number	Title	Yr	NM
❏ V-8201 [M]	The Swinging Guitar of Tal Farlow	1961	$25
❏ MGV-8138 [M]	The Tal Farlow Album	1957	$150
—Reissue of Norgran 1047			
❏ V-8138 [M]	The Tal Farlow Album	1961	$25
❏ UMV-2584	The Tal Farlow Album	198?	$25
❏ MGV-8289 [M]	This Is Tal Farlow	1958	$175
❏ V-8289 [M]	This Is Tal Farlow	1961	$25
XANADU			
❏ 109	The Fuerst Set	197?	$30
❏ 119	The Second Set	197?	$30
FARLOWE, CHRIS			
COLUMBIA			
❏ CL2593 [M]	The Fabulous Chris Farlowe	1966	$40
❏ CS9393 [R]	The Fabulous Chris Farlowe	1966	$30
IMMEDIATE			
❏ Z1252010 [B]	Paint It Farlowe	1968	$30
POLYDOR			
❏ 24-4041	From Here to Mama Rosa with the Hill	1970	$15
FARM BAND, THE			
MANTRA			
❏ 777	The Farm Band	1972	$85
—With poster			
FARMER, ART			
ABC-PARAMOUNT			
❏ ABC-200 [M]	Last Night When We Were Young	1958	$75
ARGO			
❏ LP-678 [M]	Art	1961	$30
❏ LPS-678 [S]	Art	1961	$30
❏ LP-738 [M]	Perception	1964	$30
❏ LPS-738 [S]	Perception	1964	$30
ATLANTIC			
❏ 1412 [M]	Interaction	1963	$50
❏ SD1412 [S]	Interaction	1963	$50
❏ 1421 [M]	Live at the Half Note	1964	$30
❏ SD1421 [S]	Live at the Half Note	1964	$30
❏ 1442 [M]	Sing Me Softly of the Blues	1965	$25
❏ SD1442 [S]	Sing Me Softly of the Blues	1965	$30
❏ 1430 [M]	To Sweden with Love	1964	$25
❏ SD1430 [S]	To Sweden with Love	1964	$30
COLUMBIA			
❏ CL2746 [M]	Art Farmer Plays the Great Jazz Hits	1967	$30
❏ CS9546 [S]	Art Farmer Plays the Great Jazz Hits	1967	$25
❏ CL2588 [M]	Baroque Sketches	1966	$25
❏ CS9388 [S]	Baroque Sketches	1966	$25
❏ CL2649 [M]	The Time and the Place	1967	$30
❏ CS9449 [S]	The Time and the Place	1967	$25
❏ C238232	Time and Place	198?	$30
COLUMBIA JAZZ ODYSSEY			
❏ PC36826	Art Farmer Plays the Great Jazz Hits	1980	$25
CONCORD JAZZ			
❏ CJ-212	Warm Valley	1982	$30
❏ CJ-179	Work of Art	198?	$30

Number	Title	Yr	NM
CONTEMPORARY			
❏ C-14042	Blame It on My Youth	198?	$25
❏ S-7636	On the Road	197?	$35
❏ C-14055	Ph. D.	1989	$30
❏ C-3554 [M]	Portrait of Art Farmer	1958	$300
❏ S-7027 [S]	Portrait of Art Farmer	1959	$300
❏ S-7554	Portrait of Art Farmer	197?	$35
❏ C-14029	Something to Live For: The Music of Billy Strayhorn	1987	$25
CTI			
❏ 7083	Big Blues	1978	$35
❏ 7073	Crawl	1977	$35
❏ 7080	Something You Got	1977	$35
❏ 9000	Yama	198?	$30
FANTASY			
❏ OJC-241	Art Farmer Quintet	1987	$25
❏ OJC-398	Farmer's Market	1989	$30
❏ OJC-478	On the Road	1990	$30
❏ OJC-166	Portrait of Art	198?	$25
❏ OJC-054	The Art Farmer Septet	198?	$25
❏ OJC-018	Two Trumpets	198?	$25
❏ OJC-072	When Farmer Met Gryce	198?	$25
INNER CITY			
❏ IC-6024	Live at Boomer's	197?	$35
❏ IC-6004	The Summer Knows	197?	$35
❏ IC-6014	To Duke with Love	197?	$35
MAINSTREAM			
❏ MRL-371	Gentle Eyes	1972	$25
❏ MRL-332	Homecoming	1971	$25
MERCURY			
❏ MG-20786 [M]	Listen to Art Farmer and the Orchestra	1963	$150
❏ SR-60786 [S]	Listen to Art Farmer and the Orchestra	1963	$150
MOON			
❏ MLP-014	Art Worker	199?	$35
NEW JAZZ			
❏ NJLP-8258 [M]	Early Art	1961	$175
—*Purple label*			
❏ NJLP-8258 [M]	Early Art	1965	$175
—*Blue label, trident logo at right*			
❏ NJLP-8289 [M]	Evening in Casablanca	1962	$175
—*Purple label*			
❏ NJLP-8289 [M]	Evening in Casablanca	1965	$175
—*Blue label, trident logo at right*			
❏ NJLP-8203 [M]	Farmer's Market	1958	$175
—*Yellow label*			
❏ NJLP-8203 [M]	Farmer's Market	1958	$175
—*Purple label*			
❏ NJLP-8203 [M]	Farmer's Market	1965	$175
—*Blue label, trident logo at right*			
❏ NJLP-8278 [M]	Work of Art	1962	$175
—*Purple label*			
❏ NJLP-8278 [M]	Work of Art	1965	$175
—*Blue label, trident logo at right*			
PAUSA			
❏ 7133	From Vienna with Art	198?	$30
❏ 9025	Modern Art	198?	$25
PRESTIGE			
❏ PRLP-193 [10]	Art Farmer Quartet	1954	$300
❏ PRLP-181 [10]	Art Farmer Quintet	1954	$300
❏ PRLP-209 [10]	Art Farmer Quintet	1955	$300
❏ PRLP-7017 [M]	Art Farmer Quintet Featuring Gigi Gryce	1956	$300
—*Yellow label with W. 50th St. address*			
❏ PRLP-177 [10]	Art Farmer Quintet Featuring Sonny Rollins	1954	$400
❏ PRLP-162 [10]	Art Farmer Septet	1953	$300
❏ PRLP-7031 [M]	Art Farmer Septet	1956	$300
—*Yellow label with W. 50th St. address*			
❏ PRST-7665	Early Art	1969	$35
❏ 24032	Farmer's Market	197?	$35
❏ PRLP-7092 [M]	Three Trumpets	1957	$400
❏ PRLP-7344 [M]	Trumpets All Out	1964	$50
❏ PRST-7344 [R]	Trumpets All Out	1964	$30
❏ PRLP-7062 [M]	Two Trumpets	1956	$250
❏ PRLP-7085 [M]	When Farmer Met Gryce	1957	$500
SCEPTER			
❏ S-521 [M]	The Many Faces of Art Farmer	1964	$25
❏ SS-521 [S]	The Many Faces of Art Farmer	1964	$30
SOUL NOTE			
❏ SN-1026	I'll Take Manhattan	198?	$30
❏ SN-1046	Mirage	1983	$30
❏ SN-1076	You Make Me Smile	1985	$30
STEREO RECORDS			
❏ S-7027 [S]	Portrait of Art Farmer	1958	$40
UNITED ARTISTS			
❏ UAL-4062 [M]	Aztec Suite	1959	$50
❏ UAS-5062 [S]	Aztec Suite	1959	$40
❏ UAL-4047 [M]	Brass Shout	1959	$50
❏ UAS-5047 [S]	Brass Shout	1959	$40
❏ UAL-4007 [M]	Modern Art	1958	$300
❏ UAS-5007 [S]	Modern Art	1959	$300

Number	Title	Yr	NM
FARMER, ART/ART TAYLOR			
PRESTIGE			
❏ PRLP-7342 [M]	Hard Cookin'	1964	$50
❏ PRST-7342 [R]	Hard Cookin'	1964	$30
FARNER, MARK, AND DON BREWER			
Both later of GRAND FUNK RAILROAD.			
QUADICO			
❏ 7401	Monumental Funk	1977	$12
❏ 7401 [PD]	Monumental Funk	1977	$25
—*Picture disc*			
FARNER, MARK			
ATLANTIC			
❏ SD18232	Mark Farner	1977	$12
❏ SD19196	No Frills	1978	$12
FARNHAM, JOHN			
RCA			
❏ 9687-1-R	Age of Reason	1988	$12
❏ 6300-1-R	Whispering Jack	1986	$12
FARQUAHR			
ELEKTRA			
❏ EKS-74083	Farquahr	1970	$15
VERVE FORECAST			
❏ FTS-3053	Fabulous Farquahr	1969	$15
FARR, JIMMY			
CIRCLE			
❏ CLP-26	Best by Farr	197?	$25
FARRAH, SHAMEK			
STRATA-EAST			
❏ SES-7412	First Impressions	1974	$40
FARRELL, JOE; FLORA PURIM; AIRTO MOREIRA			
REFERENCE RECORDINGS			
❏ RR-24	Three-Way Mirror	1989	$25
FARRELL, JOE			
CONTEMPORARY			
❏ C-14002	Sonic Text	1980	$30
CTI			
❏ 6053	Canned Funk	1975	$35
❏ 6003	Joe Farrell Quartet	1970	$25
❏ 6023	Moon Germs	1972	$25
❏ 8003	Moon Germs	197?	$25
—*Reissue of 6023*			
❏ 6014	Outback	1971	$25
❏ 8005	Outback	197?	$25
—*Reissue of 6014*			
❏ 6034	Penny Arcade	1973	$35
❏ 6065	Song of the Wind	1976	$35
❏ 6042	Upon This Rock	1974	$35
JAZZ A LA CARTE			
❏ 4	Farrell's Inferno	1979	$35
WARNER BROS.			
❏ BS3121	La Cathedral y El Toro	1977	$30
❏ BSK3225	Night Dancing	1978	$30
XANADU			
❏ 174	Skateboard Park	1979	$35
FARRELL, RICHARD			
MERCURY LIVING PRESENCE			
❏ SR90126 [S]	Lizst: Piano Concerto No. 1; Grieg: Piano Concerto in A	1960	$30
—*Maroon label, no "Vendor: Mercury Record Corporation*			
FARROW, CEE			
ROCSHIRE			
❏ 22006	Red and Blue	1983	$18
FASCIANI, GUY			
INNER CITY			
❏ IC-1161	The Stairway Caper	198?	$35
FASOLI, CLAUDIO			
SOUL NOTE			
❏ SN-1071	Lido	1983	$35
FASTER PUSSYCAT			
ELEKTRA			
❏ 60730	Faster Pussycat	1987	$10
❏ 60883	Wake Me When It's Over	1989	$12
FAT BOYS			
SUTRA			
❏ SUS1017	Big and Beautiful	1986	$12
❏ SUS1015	Fat Boys	1984	$12
❏ SUS1018	The Best Part of the Fat Boys	1987	$18

Number	Title	Yr	NM
❏ SUS1016	The Fat Boys Are Back	1985	$12
TIN PAN APPLE			
❏ 835809-1	Coming Back Hard Again	1988	$10
❏ 831948-1	Crushin'	1987	$10
❏ 838867-1	On and On	1989	$12
FAT CITY			
ABC PROBE			
❏ 4508	Reincarnation	1969	$25
PARAMOUNT			
❏ PAS-6028	Welcome to Fat City	1972	$18
FAT JOE			
ATLANTIC			
❏ 83472	J.O.S.E. (Jealous Ones Still Envy)	2001	$18
BIG BEAT			
❏ 92805	Don Cartagena	1998	$18
RELATIVITY			
❏ 1239	Jealous One's Envy	1995	$15
❏ 1175	Represent	1993	$15
FAT MATTRESS			
ATCO			
❏ 33-309 [M]	Fat Mattress	1969	$75
—*White label promo only; "DJ Copy Monaural" sticker on cover*			
❏ SD 33-309 [S]	Fat Mattress	1969	$25
❏ SD 33-347 [S]	Fat Mattress II	1970	$18
❏ 33-347 [M]	Fat Mattress II	1970	$100
—*White label promo only; "DJ Copy Monaural" sticker on cover*			
FATBACK			
COTILLION			
❏ 90168	Phoenix	1984	$10
❏ 90253	So Delicious	1985	$10
EVENT			
❏ 6902	Keep On Steppin'	1974	$18
—*As "The Fatback Band*			
❏ 6905	Raising Hell	1976	$18
—*As "The Fatback Band*			
❏ 6904	Yum Yum	1975	$18
—*As "The Fatback Band*			
SPRING			
❏ 6729	14 Karat	1980	$12
❏ 6721	Bright Lites, Big City	1979	$12
❏ 6723	Fatback XII	1979	$12
❏ 6718	Fired Up 'N' Kickin'	1978	$12
❏ 6734	Gigolo	1981	$12
❏ 6726	Hot Box	1980	$12
❏ 6717	Man with a Plan	1978	$15
—*As "The Fatback Band*			
❏ 6711	Night Fever	1976	$15
—*As "The Fatback Band*			
❏ 6714	NYCNYUSA	1977	$15
—*As "The Fatback Band*			
❏ 6736	On the Floor	1982	$12
❏ 6731	Tasty Jam	1981	$12
FATBOY SLIM			
ASTRALWERKS			
❏ ASW6203 [B]	Better Living Through Chemistry	1997	$25
❏ 50460 [B]	Halfway Between the Gutter and the Stars	2000	$25
❏ ASW6221 [EP]	The Beat Burger	1997	$10
❏ ASW6247 [B]	You've Come a Long Way, Baby	1998	$25
FATHER M.C.			
UPTOWN			
❏ 10542	Close to You	1992	$25
❏ 10061	Father's Day	1990	$18
❏ 10937	Sex Is Law	1993	$25
—*As "Father*			
FATHER YOD AND THE SPIRIT OF '76			
See YA HO WA 13.			
FATOOL, NICK			
JAZZOLOGY			
❏ J-158	Nick Fatool's Jazz Band -- Spring of '87	1987	$25
FATTBURGER			
INTIMA			
❏ SJ-73287	Good News	1987	$25
❏ D1-73334	Living in Paradise	1988	$25
❏ D1-73503	Time Will Tell	1989	$30
OPTIMISM			
❏ OP-2001	One of a Kind	198?	$30

Number	Title	Yr	NM

FAUN
Members of JOURNEY.
GREGAR
☐ 7000 | Faun | 1969 | $150

FAUST
TABLE OF THE ELEMENTS
☐ CR24 [B] | Rien | 1994 | $60
4 MEN WITH BEARDS
☐ 4M174LP [B] | So Far | | $25
SUPERIOR VIADUCT
☐ SV048 [B] | Outside the Dream Syndicate | 2016 | $30
—with Tony Conrad
VIRGIN
☐ V2004 [B] | Faust IV | 2009 | $30

FAVERO, ALBERTO
CATALYST
☐ 7914 | Suite Trane | 197? | $30

FAVRE, PIERRE
ECM
☐ 1274 | Singing Drums | 1985 | $30

FAWKES, WALLY
STOMP OFF
☐ SOS-1060 | That's the Blues, Old Man | 198? | $25
☐ SOS-1144 | Whatever Next! | 1988 | $25

FAY, FRANK
BALLY
☐ BAL-10215 [M] | Be Frank with Fay | 1957 | $40

FAYE, FRANCES
BETHLEHEM
☐ BCP-6006 | Bad, Bad, Frances Faye | 1976 | $35
— Reissue of 23, distributed by RCA Victor
☐ BCP-6017 [M] | Frances Faye Sings Folk Songs | 1957 | $300
☐ BCP-23 [M] | I'm Wild Again | 1955 | $300
☐ BCP-62 [M] | Relaxin' with Frances Faye | 1957 | $300
CAPITOL
☐ H512 [10] | No Reservations | 1954 | $175
☐ T512 [M] | No Reservations | 1955 | $100
— Turquoise or gray label
☐ T512 [M] | No Reservations | 1958 | $75
— Black label with colorband, logo at left
GENE NORMAN
☐ GNP-41 [M] | Caught in the Act | 1958 | $40
☐ GNP-92 [M] | Caught in the Act, Volume 2 | 1959 | $40
GNP CRESCENDO
☐ GNP-41 [M] | Caught in the Act | 196? | $35
☐ GNPS-41 [S] | Caught in the Act | 196? | $30
☐ GNP-92 [M] | Caught in the Act, Volume 2 | 196? | $35
☐ GNPS-92 [S] | Caught in the Act, Volume 2 | 196? | $30
IMPERIAL
☐ LP-9063 [M] | Frances Faye | 1959 | $0
— Canceled
☐ LP-9158 [M] | Frances Faye Sings the Blues | 1961 | $175
☐ LP-9059 [M] | Frances Faye Swings Fats Domino | 1958 | $175
☐ LP-12007 [S] | Frances Faye Swings Fats Domino | 1959 | $175
REGINA
☐ R-315 [M] | You Gotta Go! Go! Go! | 1964 | $75
☐ RS-315 [S] | You Gotta Go! Go! Go! | 1964 | $75
VERVE
☐ MGV-2147 [M] | Frances Faye in Frenzy | 1961 | $40
☐ V-2147 [M] | Frances Faye in Frenzy | 1961 | $25
☐ V-8434 [M] | Swinging All the Way with Frances Faye | 1962 | $25
☐ V6-8434 [S] | Swinging All the Way with Frances Faye | 1962 | $30

FAZOLA, IRVING
MERCURY
☐ MG-25016 [10] | Irving Fazola and His Dixielanders | 1950 | $150

FAZOLA, IRVING/GEORGE HARTMANN
EMARCY
☐ MG-36022 [M] | New Orleans Express | 1954 | $250

FEAR
RESTLESS
☐ 72039 | More Beer | 1985 | $18
SLASH
☐ SR111 [B] | The Record | 1982 | $40
☐ 23933 [B] | The Record | 1982 | $30

FEAR ITSELF
DOT
☐ DLP-25942 | Fear Itself | 1969 | $30

FEATHER, LEONARD
ABC-PARAMOUNT
☐ ABC-110 [M] | Swingin' on the Vibories | 1956 | $75
INTERLUDE
☐ MO-511 [M] | Leonard Feather Presents 52nd Street | 1959 | $40
☐ ST-1011 [S] | Leonard Feather Presents 52nd Street | 1959 | $30
MAINSTREAM
☐ MRL-388 | Freedom Jazz Dance | 1974 | $25
☐ MRL-348 | Night Blooming Jazzmen | 1972 | $25
MGM
☐ E-3494 [M] | Hi-Fi Suite | 1957 | $50
☐ E-3650 [M] | Oh, Captain! | 1958 | $50
☐ E-270 [10] | Winter Sequence | 1954 | $250
MODE
☐ LP-127 [M] | Leonard Feather Presents Bop | 1957 | $75

FEATHER, LORRAINE
CONCORD JAZZ
☐ CJ-78 | Sweet Lorraine | 1979 | $30

FEATHER
COLUMBIA
☐ C30137 | Friends by Feather | 1970 | $18

FEATHER (2)
DISCOVERY
☐ DS-867 | ChenYu Lips | 198? | $25
☐ DS-821 | Goin' Through Changes | 198? | $25
☐ DS-903 | Zanzibar | 1986 | $25

FEDERAL DUCK
MUSICOR
☐ MS-3162 | Federal Duck | 1968 | $50

FEELIES, THE
A&M
☐ SP-5214 | Only Life | 1988 | $18
☐ 750217403-1 [DJ] | Paint It Black + 5 | 1990 | $25
— Promo-only 6-song sampler
☐ 750215344-1 | Time for a Witness | 1991 | $18
COYOTE/TWINTONE
☐ TTC8673 | The Good Earth | 1986 | $18
STIFF
☐ USE-4 | Crazy Rhythms | 1980 | $50
— Price is for an actual U.S. pressing. Most copies sold in U.S. were U.K. copies with stickers.

FELDER, DON
Also see EAGLES.
ASYLUM
☐ 60295 | Airborne | 1983 | $12

FELDER, WILTON
ABC
☐ AA-1109 | We All Have a Star | 1978 | $35
MCA
☐ 5406 | Gentle Fire | 1983 | $25
☐ 5144 | Inherit the Wind | 1980 | $25
☐ 27031 | Inherit the Wind | 198? | $20
— Reissue
☐ 42096 | Love Is a Rush | 1987 | $25
☐ 5510 | Secrets | 1985 | $25
☐ AA-1109 | We All Have a Star | 1979 | $25
— Reissue of ABC 1109
☐ 700 | We All Have a Star | 198? | $20
— Budget-line reissue of MCA 1109
WORLD PACIFIC
☐ ST-20152 | Bullitt | 196? | $175

FELDMAN, VICTOR
AVA
☐ A-19 [M] | Soviet Jazz Themes | 1963 | $75
☐ AS-19 [S] | Soviet Jazz Themes | 1963 | $75
CHOICE
☐ CRS1005 [M] | Your Smile | 1974 | $35
COHEARANT
☐ CSR1001 | In My Pocket | 1977 | $40
CONCORD JAZZ
☐ CJ-38 | The Artful Dodger | 1977 | $30
CONTEMPORARY
☐ M-5005 [M] | Latinsville | 1960 | $350
☐ S-9005 [S] | Latinsville | 1960 | $300
☐ C-3541 [M] | Suite Sixteen | 1957 | $40
☐ S-7541 [S] | Suite Sixteen | 1959 | $300
☐ C-3549 [M] | The Arrival of Victor Feldman | 1958 | $300
☐ S-7549 [S] | The Arrival of Victor Feldman | 1959 | $300
FANTASY
☐ OJC-402 | Merry Olde Soul | 1989 | $30
☐ OJC-268 | The Arrival of Victor Feldman | 1987 | $25
INFINITY
☐ 5000 [M] | A Taste of Honey and a Taste of Bossa Nova | 1962 | $75
INTERLUDE
☐ MO-510 [M] | With Mallets Aforethought | 1959 | $40
— Reissue of Mode LP
MODE
☐ LP-120 [M] | Victor Feldman on Vibes | 1957 | $120
NAUTILUS
☐ NR-50 | The Secret of the Andes | 1982 | $50
— Audiophile vinyl
PACIFIC JAZZ
☐ ST-20128 [S] | Venezuela Joropo | 196? | $75
☐ PJ-20128 [M] | Venezuela Joropo | 196? | $75
☐ PJ-10121 [M] | Victor Feldman Plays Everything in Sight | 196? | $50
☐ ST-20121 [S] | Victor Feldman Plays Everything in Sight | 196? | $75
PALO ALTO
☐ PA-8066 | Fiesta | 1984 | $25
☐ PA-8053 | The Secret of the Andes | 1982 | $25
☐ PA-8056 | To Chopin with Love | 1983 | $25
RIVERSIDE
☐ RLP-366 [M] | Merry Ole Soul | 1961 | $250
☐ RS-9366 [S] | Merry Ole Soul | 1961 | $250
VEE JAY
☐ LP-2507 [M] | It's a Wonderful World | 1965 | $50
☐ LP-1096 [M] | Love Me with All Your Heart | 1964 | $75
WORLD PACIFIC
☐ WP-1807 [M] | Stop the World, I Want to Get Off | 1962 | $150
☐ ST-1807 [S] | Stop the World, I Want to Get Off | 1962 | $175
— Black vinyl
☐ ST-1807 [S] | Stop the World, I Want to Get Off | 1962 | $250
— Yellow vinyl

FELICE, DEE
BETHLEHEM
☐ B-10000 | In Heat | 1969 | $50
— Produced by JAMES BROWN.

FELICE, ERNICE
CAPITOL
☐ H192 [10] | Ernice Felice Quartet | 1950 | $150

FELICIANO, JOSE
MOTOWN
☐ 6018ML | Escenas de Amor | 1982 | $12
☐ M8-953 | Jose Feliciano | 1981 | $12
☐ 6035ML | Romance in the Night | 1983 | $12
PAIR
☐ PDL2-1091 | His Hits and Other Classics | 1986 | $15
PRIVATE STOCK
☐ PS-2010 | Angela | 1976 | $12
☐ PS-2022 | Sweet Soul | 1977 | $12
RCA CAMDEN
☐ CAS-2563 | Jose Feliciano Sings | 1972 | $12
RCA VICTOR
☐ LSP-6021 | Alive Alive-O! | 1969 | $18
☐ CPL1-0407 | And the Feeling's Good | 1974 | $12
☐ AFL1-0407 | And the Feeling's Good | 1977 | $10
— Reissue with new prefix
☐ LPM-3503 [M] | Bag Full of Soul (Folk, Rock and Blues) | 1966 | $18
☐ LSP-3503 [S] | Bag Full of Soul (Folk, Rock and Blues) | 1966 | $25
☐ APD1-0141 [Q] | Compartments | 1973 | $40
— All copies are quadraphonic
☐ LSPX-1005 | Encore! Jose Feliciano's Finest Performances | 1971 | $15
☐ AFL1-2824 | Encore! Jose Feliciano's Finest Performances | 1978 | $12
— Reissue of LSPX-1005
☐ FSP-277 | En Mi Soldead | 1971 | $25
☐ LPM-3581 [M] | Fantastic Feliciano | 1966 | $18
☐ LSP-3581 [S] | Fantastic Feliciano | 1966 | $25
☐ FSP-253 | Fantastico | 1970 | $25
☐ LPM-3957 [M] | Feliciano! | 1968 | $30
☐ LSP-3957 [S] | Feliciano! | 1968 | $18
☐ AFL1-3957 | Feliciano! | 1977 | $10
— Reissue with new prefix
☐ LSP-4185 | Feliciano/10 to 23 | 1969 | $18
☐ AFL1-4185 | Feliciano/10 to 23 | 1977 | $10
— Reissue with new prefix
☐ LSP-4370 | Fireworks | 1970 | $15
☐ AFL1-4370 | Fireworks | 1977 | $10

Number	Title	Yr	NM
— Reissue with new prefix			
❑ APL1-0266	For My Love...Mother Music	1974	$12
❑ AFL1-0266	For My Love...Mother Music	1977	$10
— Reissue with new prefix			
❑ LSP-4421	Jose Feliciano	1970	$18
❑ APL1-1005	Just Wanna Rock 'n' Roll	1975	$12
❑ AFL1-1005	Just Wanna Rock 'n' Roll	1977	$10
— Reissue with new prefix			
❑ LSP-4656	Memphis Menu	1972	$15
❑ LSP-4045	Souled	1968	$18
❑ LSP-4573	That the Spirit Needs	1971	$15
❑ LPM-3358 [M]	The Voice and Guitar of Jose Feliciano	1965	$18
❑ LSP-3358 [S]	The Voice and Guitar of Jose Feliciano	1965	$25

FELLER, DICK
ASYLUM
| ❑ CM-1 | No Word on Me | 1974 | $15 |
| ❑ 7E-1044 | Some Days Are Diamonds | 1975 | $12 |
UNITED ARTISTS
| ❑ UA-LA349-R | Dick Feller Wrote | 1974 | $12 |

FELLINI, SUZANNE
CASABLANCA
| ❑ NBLP7205 | Fellini | 1980 | $12 |

FELONY
ROCK 'N' ROLL
| ❑ BFZ38425 | The Fanatic | 1983 | $10 |

FELT
NASCO
| ❑ 9006 | Felt | 1971 | $500 |

FEMININE COMPLEX, THE
ATHENA
| ❑ 6001 | Livin' Love | 1969 | $85 |

FENDER, FREDDY
ABC
| ❑ AA-1062 | Swamp Gold | 1978 | $12 |
| ❑ AA-1132 | Tex-Mex | 1979 | $15 |
ABC/DOT
❑ DOSD-2044	Are You Ready for Freddy	1975	$15
❑ DOSD-2020	Before the Next Teardrop Falls	1975	$15
❑ DP-2090	If You Don't Love Me	1977	$15
❑ DOSD-2061	If You're Ever in Texas	1976	$15
❑ DO-2101	Merry Christmas -- Feliz Navidad	1977	$15
❑ DOSD-2050	Rock 'n Country	1976	$15
❑ DO-2079	The Best of Freddy Fender	1977	$15
ACCORD
| ❑ SN-7121 | Since I Met You Baby | 1981 | $12 |
GRT
| ❑ 8005 | Since I Met You Baby | 1975 | $15 |
INTERMEDIA
| ❑ QS-5035 | Before the Next Teardrop Falls | 198? | $10 |
MCA
❑ 639	Are You Ready for Freddy	1980	$10
— Reissue of ABC/Dot 2044			
❑ 37110	Before the Next Teardrop Falls	1980	$10
— Reissue of ABC/Dot 2020			
❑ 15037	Christmas Time in the Valley	198?	$12
❑ 669	If You Don't Love Me	1980	$10
— Reissue of ABC/Dot 2090			
❑ 15025	Merry Christmas	198?	$10
❑ 668	Swamp Gold	1980	$10
— Reissue of ABC 1062			
❑ AA-1132	Tex-Mex	1979	$12
— Reissue of ABC 1132			
❑ 37109	Tex-Mex	1980	$10
— Reissue of MCA 1132			
❑ 835	The Best of Freddy Fender	198?	$10
— Reissue of MCA 3285			
❑ 3285	The Best of Freddy Fender	1979	$12
— Reissue of ABC/Dot 2079			
PICCADILLY
| ❑ 3589 | Enter My Heart | 1981 | $12 |
PICKWICK
| ❑ JS-6178 | Freddy Fender | 1975 | $12 |
POWER PAK
| ❑ PO-280 | Recorded Inside Louisiana State Prison | 1975 | $12 |
STARFLITE
| ❑ JZ36073 | Balladeer | 1980 | $12 |
| ❑ JZ36284 | Together We Drifted Apart | 1980 | $12 |

FENDERMEN, THE
BEAT ROCKET
| ❑ BR116 | Mule Skinner Blues | 2000 | $18 |

KOALA
| ❑ 14565 | Poison Ivy | 1980 | $50 |
SOMA
| ❑ MG-1240 [M] | Mule Skinner Blues | 1960 | $4000 |
| *— Deep blue vinyl* | | | |

| ❑ MG-1240 [M] | Mule Skinner Blues | 1960 | $1200 |
| *— Black vinyl* | | | |

FENIX JAZZ BAND OF ARGENTINA, THE
STOMP OFF
| ❑ SOS-1129 | Grandpa's Spells | 1987 | $25 |

FERGUSON, ALLYN
AVA
| ❑ A-32 [M] | Pictures at an Exhibition Framed in Jazz | 1963 | $30 |
| ❑ AS-32 [S] | Pictures at an Exhibition Framed in Jazz | 1963 | $30 |
DISCOVERY
| ❑ DS-810 | Pictures at an Exhibition Framed in Jazz | 1980 | $30 |
| *— Reissue of AS-32* | | | |

FERGUSON, JAY
ASYLUM
❑ 7E-1063	All Alone in the End Zone	1976	$12
❑ 6E-158	Real Life Ain't This Way	1979	$12
❑ 7E-1115	Thunder Island	1978	$12
CAPITOL
| ❑ ST-12083 | Terms and Conditions | 1980 | $12 |
| ❑ ST-12196 | White Noise | 1982 | $12 |

FERGUSON, MAYNARD
BASF
| ❑ 20662 | Trumpet Rhapsody | 1973 | $30 |
BLACK HAWK
| ❑ BKH-50101 | Body and Soul | 1986 | $25 |
BLUEBIRD
| ❑ 6455-1-RB | The Bluebird Dreamband | 1987 | $25 |
CAMEO
❑ C-1066 [M]	Come Blow Your Horn	1964	$50
❑ SC-1066 [S]	Come Blow Your Horn	1964	$75
❑ C-1046 [M]	The New Sounds of Maynard Ferguson	1963	$50
❑ SC-1046 [S]	The New Sounds of Maynard Ferguson	1963	$75
COLUMBIA
❑ C31117	Alive and Well in London	1972	$30
❑ PC31117	Alive and Well in London	198?	$20
— Budget-line reissue			
❑ JC35480	Carnival	1978	$25
❑ PC35480	Carnival	1980	$20
— Budget-line reissue			
❑ KC33007	Chameleon	1974	$30
❑ PC33007	Chameleon	1975	$25
— Early reissue of KC 33007; no bar code			
❑ PC33007	Chameleon	1980	$20
— Budget-line reissue with bar code			
❑ PC34457	Conquistador	1977	$25
— No bar code			
❑ PCQ34457 [Q]	Conquistador	1977	$75
❑ PC34457	Conquistador	1980	$20
— Budget-line reissue with bar code			
❑ HC44457	Conquistador	1982	$150
— Half-speed mastered edition			
❑ FC37713	Hollywood	1982	$25
❑ JC36124	Hot	1979	$25
❑ JC36766	It's My Time	1980	$25
❑ PC36978	Maynard Ferguson	1981	$25
❑ C30466	M.F. Horn	1971	$30
❑ PC30466	M.F. Horn	198?	$20
— Budget-line reissue			

Number	Title	Yr	NM
❑ KC32403	M.F. Horn/3	1973	$30
❑ PC32403	M.F. Horn/3	198?	$20
— Budget-line reissue			
❑ KG32732	M.F. Horn 4 & 5/Live at Jimmy's	1973	$35
❑ PG32732	M.F. Horn 4 & 5/Live at Jimmy's	198?	$25
— Budget-line reissue			
❑ CG33660	M.F. Horn/M.F. Horn Two	1975	$35
❑ KC31709	M.F. Horn Two	1972	$30
❑ PC31709	M.F. Horn Two	198?	$20
— Budget-line reissue			
❑ JC34971	New Vintage	1977	$25
❑ PC33953	Primal Scream	1976	$25
— No bar code			
❑ JC36361	The Best of Maynard Ferguson	1980	$25
❑ PC36361	The Best of Maynard Ferguson	1986	$20
— Budget-line reissue			
EMARCY
❑ MG-36076 [M]	Around the Horn with Maynard Ferguson	1956	$250
❑ MG-36114 [M]	Boy with Lots of Brass	1957	$250
❑ MG-26024 [10]	Dimensions	1954	$300
❑ MG-36044 [M]	Dimensions	1956	$250
❑ MG-36009 [M]	Jam Session Featuring Maynard Ferguson	1955	$300
❑ MG-36021 [M]	Maynard Ferguson Octet	1955	$250
❑ MG-26017 [10]	Maynard Ferguson's Hollywood Party	1954	$300
❑ MG-36046 [M]	Maynard Ferguson's Hollywood Party	1956	$250
❑ EMS-2-406	Stratospheric	1976	$30
EMUS
| ❑ ES-12024 [S] | Maynard | 197? | $25 |
| *— Reissue of Roulette material* | | | |
ENTERPRISE
| ❑ S-13-101 | Ridin' High | 1968 | $35 |
FORUM
| ❑ F-9035 [M] | Jazz for Dancing | 196? | $30 |
| ❑ SF-9035 [S] | Jazz for Dancing | 196? | $35 |
INTIMA
| ❑ D1-73390 | Big Bop Nouveau | 1990 | $30 |
| ❑ SJ-73279 | High Voltage | 1987 | $30 |
MAINSTREAM
❑ MRL-372	6 By 6	1973	$30
❑ 805	Big "F"	1974	$35
❑ 56031 [M]	Color Him Wild	1965	$35
❑ S-6031 [S]	Color Him Wild	1965	$50
❑ MRL-359	Dues	1972	$30
❑ 56060 [M]	Maynard Ferguson Sextet	1966	$35
❑ S-6060 [S]	Maynard Ferguson Sextet	1966	$50
❑ MRL-316	Screamin' Blue	1971	$30
❑ 56045 [M]	The Blues Roar	1965	$35
❑ S-6045 [S]	The Blues Roar	1965	$50
MERCURY
| ❑ MG-20556 [M] | Boy with Lots of Brass | 1960 | $150 |
| ❑ SR-60124 [S] | Boy with Lots of Brass | 1960 | $150 |
MOSAIC
| ❑ MQ14-156 | The Complete Roulette Recordings of the Maynard Ferguson Orchestra | 1994 | $300 |
NAUTILUS
| ❑ NR-57 | Storm | 1983 | $40 |
| *— Audiophile vinyl* | | | |
PALO ALTO
| ❑ PA-8077 | Live from San Francisco | 1985 | $25 |
| ❑ PA-8052 | Storm | 1983 | $25 |
PAUSA
| ❑ 7037 | Trumpet Rhapsody | 1980 | $25 |
| *— Reissue of BASF LP* | | | |
PRESTIGE
| ❑ PRLP-7636 | Maynard Ferguson 1969 | 1969 | $35 |
ROULETTE
❑ R52027 [M]	A Message from Birdland	1959	$75
❑ SR52027 [S]	A Message from Birdland	1959	$75
❑ R52012 [M]	A Message from Newport	1958	$75
❑ SR52012 [S]	A Message from Newport	1958	$75
❑ RE-116	A Message from Newport/ Newport Suite	1972	$35
— Reissue of 52012 and 52047 in one package			
❑ R52055 [M]	Let's Face the Music and Dance	1960	$75
❑ SR52055 [S]	Let's Face the Music and Dance	1960	$75
❑ R52064 [M]	Maynard '61	1961	$75
❑ SR52064 [S]	Maynard '61	1961	$75
❑ RE-122	Maynard '61/Si! Si! M.F.	1973	$35
— Reissue of 52064 and 52084 in one package			
❑ R52083 [M]	Maynard '62	1962	$35
❑ SR52083 [S]	Maynard '62	1962	$50
❑ R52097 [M]	Maynard '63	1963	$35
❑ SR52097 [S]	Maynard '63	1963	$50
❑ R52107 [M]	Maynard '64	1964	$35
❑ SR52107 [S]	Maynard '64	1964	$50
❑ R52038 [M]	Maynard Ferguson Plays Jazz for Dancing	1959	$75

Number	Title	Yr	NM
SR52038 [S]	Maynard Ferguson Plays Jazz for Dancing	1959	$75
R52047 [M]	Newport Suite	1960	$75
SR52047 [S]	Newport Suite	1960	$75
R52084 [M]	Si! Si! M.F.	1962	$35
SR52084 [S]	Si! Si! M.F.	1962	$50
R52058 [M]	Swingin' My Way Through College	1960	$75
SR52058 [S]	Swingin' My Way Through College	1960	$75
SK-101	The Ferguson Years	197?	$35
R52110 [M]	The World of Maynard Ferguson	1964	$35
SR52110 [S]	The World of Maynard Ferguson	1964	$50

TRIP

Number	Title	Yr	NM
5558	Around the Horn with Maynard Ferguson	197?	$20
5507	Dimensions	197?	$20
5525	Jam Session Featuring Maynard Ferguson	197?	$20

VIK

Number	Title	Yr	NM
LX-1070 [M]	Birdland Dream Band, Vol. 1	1957	$85
LX-1077 [M]	Birdland Dream Band, Vol. 2	1957	$85

FERKO STRING BAND

ABC-PARAMOUNT

Number	Title	Yr	NM
ABC440 [M]	The World Renowned Ferko String Band	1963	$15
ABCS440 [S]	The World Renowned Ferko String Band	1963	$18

ESSEX

Number	Title	Yr	NM
ESLP-209 [M]	Happy Days Are Here Again!	1956	$25

FERKO

Number	Title	Yr	NM
LP3301 [10]	Favorites	195?	$25

REGENT

Number	Title	Yr	NM
MG-6007 [M]	Ferko String Band	195?	$18
MG-6008 [M]	Ferko String Band, Vol. 2	195?	$18

SOMERSET

Number	Title	Yr	NM
P12700 [M]	Happy Days Are Here Again!	196?	$12
P3700 [M]	The Happiest Music in the World	196?	$12

STEREO-FIDELITY

Number	Title	Yr	NM
SF12700 [S]	Happy Days Are Here Again!	196?	$15

SURE

Number	Title	Yr	NM
Vol.42	Before the Parade Passes By	197?	$12
Vol.8	Ferko String Band On Broadway	196?	$12
SM-7 [M]	The World Renowned Ferko String Band	1963	$18

TRANS-WORLD

Number	Title	Yr	NM
TWLP-209 [M]	Happy Days Are Here Again!	1956	$18

FERLINGHETTI, LAWRENCE

FANTASY

Number	Title	Yr	NM
7004 [M]	The Impeachment of Eisenhower	1958	$250
— Red vinyl			
7004 [M]	The Impeachment of Eisenhower	1958	$175
— Black vinyl			

FERRANTE AND TEICHER

ABC

Number	Title	Yr	NM
558 [M]	Autumn Leaves	1966	$12
S-558 [S]	Autumn Leaves	1966	$15
560 [M]	Bolero	1966	$12
S-560 [S]	Bolero	1966	$15
555 [M]	Heaven Sounds	1966	$12
S-555 [S]	Heaven Sounds	1966	$15
554 [M]	Memories	1966	$12
S-554 [S]	Memories	1966	$15
561 [M]	Temptation	1966	$12
S-561 [S]	Temptation	1966	$15
557 [M]	Twin Piano Magic, Vol. 1	1966	$12
S-557 [S]	Twin Piano Magic, Vol. 1	1966	$15
559 [M]	Twin Piano Magic, Vol. 2	1966	$12
S-559 [S]	Twin Piano Magic, Vol. 2	1966	$15
556 [M]	We've Got Rhythm	1966	$12
S-556 [S]	We've Got Rhythm	1966	$15
553 [M]	World's Greatest Semi-Classical Favorites	1966	$12
S-553 [S]	World's Greatest Semi-Classical Favorites	1966	$15

ABC-PARAMOUNT

Number	Title	Yr	NM
285 [M]	Ferrante and Teicher Blast Off	1959	$18
S-285 [S]	Ferrante and Teicher Blast Off	1959	$25
313 [M]	Ferrante and Teicher Play Light Classics	1960	$18
S-313 [S]	Ferrante and Teicher Play Light Classics	1960	$25
248 [M]	Ferrante and Teicher with Percussion	1958	$18
S-248 [S]	Ferrante and Teicher with Percussion	1958	$25
221 [M]	Heavenly Sounds in Hi-Fi	1958	$18
S-221 [S]	Heavenly Sounds in Hi-Fi	1958	$25
437 [M]	Popular Classics	1962	$15
S-437 [S]	Popular Classics	1962	$18
430 [M]	Postcards from Paris	1962	$15
S-430 [S]	Postcards from Paris	1962	$18
ST-90467 [S]	Postcards from Paris	196?	$18
— Capitol Record Club edition			
454 [M]	The Artistry of Ferrante and Teicher	1963	$15
S-454 [S]	The Artistry of Ferrante and Teicher	1963	$18
336 [M]	Themes from Broadway Shows	1960	$18
S-336 [S]	Themes from Broadway Shows	1960	$25

BAINBRIDGE

Number	Title	Yr	NM
BT-6263	A Few of Our Favorites on Stage	1986	$12
BT-6266	American Fantasy	1987	$12

COLUMBIA

Number	Title	Yr	NM
CL573 [M]	Hi-Fire Works	1955	$30

GRAND AWARD

Number	Title	Yr	NM
GA-263	Themes from Broadway Shows	1962	$15

HARMONY

Number	Title	Yr	NM
HS11411	Encore	1970	$12
HL7427 [M]	Fireworks	1967	$15
HS11227 [R]	Fireworks	1967	$12
HL7325 [M]	Twin Piano Magic	1965	$15
HS11125 [R]	Twin Piano Magic	1965	$12

LIBERTY

Number	Title	Yr	NM
LWB-70	10th Anniversary -- Golden Piano Hits	198?	$12
— Reissue of United Artists 70			
LT-980	Classical Disco	198?	$10
— Reissue of United Artists 980			
LN-10198	Classic Lites	1983	$10
LN-10158	Concert for Lovers	1981	$10
— Budget-line reissue of United Artists 6315			
LW-662	Feelings	198?	$10
— Reissue of United Artists 662			
LN-10242	Ferrante and Teicher Superpak	1984	$12
LKDL-831	For You with Love	198?	$25
— Reissue of United Artists 831			
LM-1016	Midnight Cowboy	1981	$10
— Reissue of United Artists 1016			
LT-782	Rocky and Other Knockouts	198?	$10
— Reissue of United Artists 782			
LN-10175	Showstoppers	1983	$10
LN-10142	Snowbound	1981	$10
— Budget-line reissue of United Artists 6233			
LN-10113	Star Wars	198?	$10
— Reissue of United Artists 855			
LN-10112	Supermen	198?	$10
— Reissue of United Artists 941			
LWB-73	The Best of Ferrante and Teicher	198?	$12
— Reissue of United Artists 73			
LN-10176	The Movie Theme Team	1983	$10
LN-10210	The Movie Theme Team II	1984	$10
LN-10141	The People's Choice	1981	$10
— Budget-line reissue of United Artists 6385			
LT-908	You Light Up My Life	198?	$10
— Reissue of United Artists 908			

PICKWICK

Number	Title	Yr	NM
PC-3003 [M]	Excitement	196?	$12
SPC-3003 [S]	Excitement	196?	$12
SPC-3612	Fabulous Favorites	197?	$10
SPC-3586	Getting Together	1978	$10
SPC-3397	How High the Moon	197?	$10
PC-3077 [M]	In Love	196?	$12
SPC-3077 [S]	In Love	196?	$12

SUNSET

Number	Title	Yr	NM
SUS-5235	Incomparable Piano	1969	$10
SUS-5313	Love Is a Rainbow	1971	$10
SUS-5277	Midnight Memories	1970	$10

UNITED ARTISTS

Number	Title	Yr	NM
UXS-70	10th Anniversary -- Golden Piano Hits	1969	$15
UAL3343 [M]	50 Fabulous Piano Favorites	1964	$15
UAS6343 [S]	50 Fabulous Piano Favorites	1964	$18
UAS6659	A Bouquet of Hits	1968	$12
UAL3572 [M]	A Man and a Woman & Other Motion Picture Themes	1967	$12
UAS6572 [S]	A Man and a Woman & Other Motion Picture Themes	1967	$15
UA-LA681-G	Around	1977	$12
UAL3416 [M]	By Popular Demand	1965	$12
UAS6416 [S]	By Popular Demand	1965	$15
LT-980	Classical Disco	1979	$12
UAL3315 [M]	Concert for Lovers	1964	$15
UAS6315 [S]	Concert for Lovers	1964	$18
UA-LA195-G	Dial M for Music	1974	$12
WW7504 [M]	Dynamic Twin Pianos	1961	$15
UAL3340 [M]	Exotic Love Themes	1964	$15
UAS6340 [S]	Exotic Love Themes	1964	$18
UA-LA662-G	Feelings	1976	$12
UAS5588	Ferrante and Teicher Play Hit Themes	1972	$12
UAS5645	Ferrante and Teicher Salute Nashville	1972	$12
UXS-77	Ferrante and Teicher Superpak	1972	$15
UAS5552	Fiddler on the Roof	1971	$12
UAL3483 [M]	For Lovers of All Ages	1966	$12
UAS6483 [S]	For Lovers of All Ages	1966	$15
UA-LA831-P	For You with Love	1978	$25
UAS5501	Getting Together	1970	$12
WW7505 [M]	Golden Piano Hits	1961	$15
WWS8505 [S]	Golden Piano Hits	1961	$18
UAL3269 [M]	Golden Piano Hits	1963	$12
— Reissue of 7505			
UAS6269 [S]	Golden Piano Hits	1963	$15
— Reissue of 8505			
UAL3210 [M]	Golden Themes from Motion Pictures	1962	$15
UAS6210 [S]	Golden Themes from Motion Pictures	1962	$18
UA-LA101-G2	Greatest Love Themes of the Twentieth Century	1973	$15
UA-LA018-F	Hear & Now	1972	$12
UAL3298 [M]	Holiday for Pianos	1963	$12
UAS6298 [S]	Holiday for Pianos	1963	$15
UA-LA227-G	In a Soulful Mood	1974	$12
UAS5531	It's Too Late	1971	$12
UAL3284 [M]	Keyboard Kapers	1963	$12
UAS6284 [S]	Keyboard Kapers	1963	$15
UAL3247 [M]	Keys to Her Apartment	1963	$15
UAS6247 [S]	Keys to Her Apartment	1963	$18
UA-LA118-G	Killing Me Softly	1973	$12
UAL3135 [M]	Latin Pianos	1960	$15
UAS6135 [S]	Latin Pianos	1960	$18
UAS6701	Listen to the Movies	1969	$12
UAS6771	Love Is a Soft Touch	1970	$12
WW7514 [M]	Love Themes	1961	$15
WWS8514 [S]	Love Themes	1961	$18
UAL3282 [M]	Love Themes	1963	$12
— Reissue of 7514			
UAS6282 [S]	Love Themes	1963	$15
— Reissue of 8514			
UAL3290 [M]	Love Themes from Cleopatra	1963	$15
UAS6290 [S]	Love Themes from Cleopatra	1963	$18
UAS6725	Midnight Cowboy	1969	$12
LM-1016	Midnight Cowboy	1980	$10
— Reissue of 6725			
UAL3361 [M]	My Fair Lady	1964	$12
UAS6361 [S]	My Fair Lady	1964	$15
UAL3434 [M]	Only the Best	1965	$12
UAS6434 [S]	Only the Best	1965	$15
UAL3556 [M]	Our Golden Favorites	1967	$15
UAS6556 [S]	Our Golden Favorites	1967	$12
UA-LA585-G	Piano Portraits	1976	$12
UAL3230 [M]	Pianos in Paradise	1962	$15
UAS6230 [S]	Pianos in Paradise	1962	$18
UA-LA782-G	Rocky and Other Knockouts	1977	$12
UAL3233 [M]	Snowbound	1962	$15
UAS6233 [S]	Snowbound	1962	$18
UA-LA573-G	Spirit of 1976	1975	$12
UAL3406 [M]	Springtime	1965	$12
UAS6406 [S]	Springtime	1965	$15
UA-LA855-G	Star Wars	1978	$15
UA-LA941-H	Supermen	1979	$12
UXS-73	The Best of Ferrante and Teicher	1971	$15
UA-LA490-G	The Carpenters Songbook	1975	$12
UAL3375 [M]	The Enchanted World of Ferrante and Teicher	1964	$15
UAS6375 [S]	The Enchanted World of Ferrante and Teicher	1964	$18
UAL3444 [M]	The Ferrante and Teicher Concert	1965	$12
UAS6444 [S]	The Ferrante and Teicher Concert	1965	$15
UAL3475 [M]	The Ferrante and Teicher Concert, Part 2	1966	$12
UAS6475 [S]	The Ferrante and Teicher Concert, Part 2	1966	$15
UAL3211 [M]	The Many Moods of Ferrante & Teicher	1962	$15
UAS6211 [S]	The Many Moods of Ferrante & Teicher	1962	$18
UAS6792	The Music Lovers	1971	$12
UAL3385 [M]	The People's Choice	1964	$12
UAS6385 [S]	The People's Choice	1964	$15
UA-LA072-G	The Roaring 20's	1973	$12
UA-LA236-G	The Very Best of Ferrante and Teicher	1974	$12
UAL3121 [M]	The World's Greatest Themes	1960	$15
UAS6121 [S]	The World's Greatest Themes	1960	$18
UAL3171 [M]	Tonight	1962	$15
UAS6171 [S]	Tonight	1962	$15
UAL3166 [M]	West Side Story & Other Motion Picture & Broadway Hits	1961	$15
UAS6166 [S]	West Side Story & Other Motion Picture & Broadway Hits	1961	$18
UAL3536 [M]	We Wish You a Merry Christmas	1966	$18
UAS6536 [S]	We Wish You a Merry Christmas	1966	$15
UAS6536 [S]	We Wish You a Merry Christmas	1972	$10
— Tan label (may also exist on late-1960s UA labels)			
UAL3526 [M]	You Asked For It!	1966	$12
UAS6526 [S]	You Asked For It!	1966	$15
ST-90931 [S]	You Asked For It!	1966	$18

Number	Title	Yr	NM
— Capitol Record Club edition			
❏ UA-LA908-H	You Light Up My Life	1978	$12
URANIA			
❏ 8011	Rhapsody	196?	$15
WESTMINSTER			
❏ WP6021 [M]	Adventure in Carols	195?	$25
❏ WL3044 [M]	Christmas Hi-Fi Favorites	195?	$25
❏ SW1048 [S]	Latin American Adventure	195?	$30
❏ WP6001 [M]	Postcards from Paris	195?	$25
❏ SW1045 [S]	Soundproof	195?	$30

FERRARI, LARRY
SURE

Number	Title	Yr	NM
❏ SM703 [M]	I Wish You the Merriest	1966	$12
❏ SS703 [S]	I Wish You the Merriest	1966	$15
❏ SM701 [M]	Merry Christmas Carols	196?	$12
❏ SS701 [S]	Merry Christmas Carols	196?	$15

FERRE, BOULOU
4 CORNERS OF THE WORLD

Number	Title	Yr	NM
❏ FCL-4211 [M]	Boulou with the Paris All Stars	1966	$25
❏ FCS-4211 [S]	Boulou with the Paris All Stars	1966	$30
❏ FCL-4234 [M]	Jazz/Left Bank	1967	$30
❏ FCS-4234 [S]	Jazz/Left Bank	1967	$25
— As "Boulou with the Paris All Stars			

STEEPLECHASE

Number	Title	Yr	NM
❏ SCS-1222	Nuages	198?	$30
❏ SCS-1210	Relax and Enjoy	198?	$30

FERRE, BOULOU AND ELOIS
STEEPLECHASE

Number	Title	Yr	NM
❏ SCS-1140	Gypsy Dreams	198?	$30
❏ SCS-1120	Pour Django	198?	$30

FERRE, BOULOU/NIELS-HENNING ORSTED PEDERSEN/ELOIS FERRE
STEEPLECHASE

Number	Title	Yr	NM
❏ SCS-1171	Trinity	1982	$30

FERRE, CLIFF
KEM

Number	Title	Yr	NM
❏ LP-100 [M]	Looks Like Fun	195?	$30

FERREIRA, SKY
CAPITOL

Number	Title	Yr	NM
❏ B001875701 [B]	Night Time. My Time	2014	$40
— RSD Picture Disc			

FERRY, BRYAN
Also see ROXY MUSIC.
ATLANTIC

Number	Title	Yr	NM
❏ SD18113	Another Time, Another Place	1974	$18
❏ SD18216	In Your Mind	1977	$15
❏ SD18187	Let's Stick Together	1976	$15
❏ SD19205	The Bride Stripped Bare	1978	$15

BRYAN FERRY

Number	Title	Yr	NM
❏ SD7304 [B]	These Foolish Things	1973	$18
REPRISE			
❏ 25598	Bete Noire	1988	$15
WARNER BROS.			
❏ 25082	Boys and Girls	1985	$15

FESTIVAL
RSO

Number	Title	Yr	NM
❏ RS-1-3061	Evita	1980	$12

FESTIVAL CHAMBER ORCHESTRA (ANTAL DORATI, CONDUCTOR)
MERCURY LIVING PRESENCE

Number	Title	Yr	NM
❏ SR90436 [S]	Haydn: Symphonies No. 59 and 81	1965	$25
— Maroon label, with "Vendor: Mercury Record Corporation			
❏ SR90438 [S]	Mozart: Marches; Lucio Silva Overture; Menuet; German Dances	1965	$30
— Maroon label, with "Vendor: Mercury Record Corporation			

FESTIVAL QUARTET
RCA VICTOR RED SEAL

Number	Title	Yr	NM
❏ LSC-2517 [S]	Brahms: Piano Quartet in A	1961	$250
— Originals with "shaded dog" label			
❏ LSC-2330 [S]	Brahms: Piano Quartet in C	1959	$250
— Original with "shaded dog" label			
❏ LM-2473 [M]	Brahms: Piano Quartet in G	1961	$25
— Originals with "shaded dog" label; a rare instance when even the mono version is sought after			
❏ LSC-2473 [S]	Brahms: Piano Quartet in G	1961	$120
— Originals with "shaded dog" label			
❏ LSC-2735 [S]	Faure: Piano Quartet in G	1963	$75
— Original with "shaded dog" label			
❏ LSC-2147 [S]	Schubert: Trout Quintet	1958	$180
— Original with "shaded dog" label			
❏ LSC-2147 [S]	Schubert: Trout Quintet	1964	$120
— Second edition with "white dog" label			

FETTIG, MARY
CONCORD JAZZ

Number	Title	Yr	NM
❏ CJ-273	In Good Company	1985	$25

FEVER TREE
AMPEX

Number	Title	Yr	NM
❏ A-10113	For Sale	1970	$30
MCA			
❏ 551	Fever Tree	197?	$12
UNI			
❏ 73040	Another Time, Another Place	1968	$30
❏ 73067	Creation	1970	$30
❏ 73024	Fever Tree	1968	$30

FIELD, SALLY
COLGEMS

Number	Title	Yr	NM
❏ COM-106 [M]	The Flying Nun	1967	$30
❏ COS-106 [S]	The Flying Nun	1967	$30

FIELDING, JANE
JAZZ WEST

Number	Title	Yr	NM
❏ LP-5 [M]	Embers Glow	1956	$300
❏ LP-3 [M]	Jazz Trio for Voice, Piano and Bass	1955	$300

FIELDING, JERRY
ABC-PARAMOUNT

Number	Title	Yr	NM
❏ ABC-542 [M]	Hollywood Brass	1966	$35
❏ ABCS-542 [S]	Hollywood Brass	1966	$25
COMMAND			
❏ RS 33-921 [M]	Near East Brass	1967	$30
❏ RS921SD [S]	Near East Brass	1967	$35
DECCA			
❏ DL8450 [M]	Fielding's Formula	1957	$120
❏ DL8669 [M]	Hollywood Wind Jazztet	1958	$120
❏ DL8100 [M]	Sweet with a Beat	1955	$175
❏ DL8371 [M]	Swingin' in Hi-Fi	1956	$175
KAPP			
❏ KL-1026 [M]	Dance Concert	1956	$50
SIGNATURE			
❏ SM-1028 [M]	Favorite Christmas Music	1960	$25
❏ SS-1028 [S]	Favorite Christmas Music	1960	$30
TIME			
❏ 52059 [M]	A Bit of Ireland	196?	$35
❏ S-2059 [S]	A Bit of Ireland	196?	$25
❏ 52042 [M]	Magnificence in Brass	196?	$35
❏ S-2042 [S]	Magnificence in Brass	196?	$25
❏ 52119 [M]	We Like Brass	196?	$35
❏ S-2119 [S]	We Like Brass	196?	$25
TREND			
❏ TL-1000 [10]	Jerry Fielding and His Great New Orchestra	1953	$120
❏ TL-1004 [10]	Jerry Fielding Plays a Dance Concert	1954	$150

FIELDS, BRANDON
NOVA

Number	Title	Yr	NM
❏ 8602	The Other Side of the Story	1986	$25
❏ 8811	The Traveler	1988	$25

FIELDS, ERNIE
RENDEZVOUS

Number	Title	Yr	NM
❏ 1309 [M]	In the Mood	1960	$75

FIELDS, GRACIE
LIBERTY

Number	Title	Yr	NM
❏ LRP-3059 [M]	Our Gracie	1957	$40

FIELDS, HERBIE
DECCA

Number	Title	Yr	NM
❏ DL8130 [M]	Blow Hot -- Blow Cool	1956	$175
FRATERNITY			
❏ F-1011 [M]	Fields in Clover	1959	$75
RKO UNIQUE			
❏ ULP-146 [M]	A Night at Kitty's	1957	$50

FIELDS, IRVING
ABC-PARAMOUNT

Number	Title	Yr	NM
❏ ABC-187 [M]	Irving Fields at the St. Moritz	1956	$30
DECCA			
❏ DL8901 [M]	At the Emerald Room, Hotel Astor	1959	$25
❏ DL78901 [S]	At the Emerald Room, Hotel Astor	1959	$30
❏ DL8856 [M]	Bagels and Bongos	1959	$25
❏ DL78856 [S]	Bagels and Bongos	1959	$30
❏ DL4323 [M]	Bikinis and Bongos	1962	$25
❏ DL74323 [S]	Bikinis and Bongos	1962	$30
❏ DL4238 [M]	Champagne and Bongos	1962	$25
❏ DL74238 [S]	Champagne and Bongos	1962	$30

More Bagels and Bongos
IRVING FIELDS TRIO
DECCA RECORDS

Number	Title	Yr	NM
❏ DL4114 [M]	More Bagels and Bongos	1961	$25
❏ DL74114 [S]	More Bagels and Bongos	1961	$30
❏ DL4174 [M]	Pizzas and Bongos	1961	$25
❏ DL74174 [S]	Pizzas and Bongos	1961	$30
EVEREST			
❏ LPBR-5134 [M]	Twisting	1962	$25
❏ SDBR-1134 [S]	Twisting	1962	$30
FIESTA			
❏ FLP-1228 [M]	Fabulous Fingers	195?	$30
GONE			
❏ LP-5003 [M]	Fabulous Touch	1959	$30
KING			
❏ 724 [M]	Classics Go Latin	1960	$25
❏ 724-S [S]	Classics Go Latin	1960	$30
❏ 703 [M]	Irving Fields Favorites	1960	$30
❏ 709 [M]	Live It Up	1960	$30
❏ 742 [M]	Lox, Latin and Bongos	1960	$25
❏ 742-S [S]	Lox, Latin and Bongos	1960	$30
RCA VICTOR			
❏ LPT-38 [10]	Fields Favorites	195?	$50
TOPS			
❏ L-1562 [M]	Irving Fields Plays Irving Berlin	1957	$30

FIELDS, RICHARD "DIMPLES"
BOARDWALK

Number	Title	Yr	NM
❏ NB1-33232	Dimples	1981	$12
❏ NB1-33258	Give Everybody Some	1982	$12
❏ NB1-33249	Mr. Look So Good!	1982	$12
COLUMBIA			
❏ BFC40859	Tellin' It Like It Is	1987	$12
— As "Dimples			
RCA VICTOR			
❏ AFL1-5482	Dark Gable	1984	$12
— As "Dimples			
❏ AFL1-5169	Mmm...	1984	$12

FIELDS, SHEP
CIRCLE

Number	Title	Yr	NM
❏ 133	Shep Fields and His Orchestra 1947-51	199?	$25
❏ 38	Shep Fields and His Rippling Rhythm Orchestra 1947-50	198?	$25

Number	Title	Yr	NM
DOT			
❏ DLP-3348 [M]	The Rippling Rhythm of Shep Fields	1960	$85
❏ DLP-25348 [S]	The Rippling Rhythm of Shep Fields	1960	$85
GOLDEN CREST			
❏ S-3037 [R]	Rippling Rhythms	196?	$30
❏ 3037 [M]	Rippling Rhythms	196?	$25
❏ S-3061 [R]	Shep Fields at the Shamrock Hilton	196?	$30
❏ 3061 [M]	Shep Fields at the Shamrock Hilton	196?	$25
HINDSIGHT			
❏ HSR-179	Shep Fields and His Orchestra 1942	198?	$25
❏ HSR-160	Shep Fields' New Music, 1942-44	198?	$25
JUBILEE			
❏ JLP-1056 [M]	Cocktails, Dinner and Dancing	1958	$30
SUNBEAM			
❏ 316	Shep Fields and His Rippling Rhythm Orchestra 1936-38	198?	$25

FIELDS, THE

Number	Title	Yr	NM
UNI			
❏ 73050	Fields	1969	$50

FIFTH DIMENSION, THE

Number	Title	Yr	NM
ABC			
❏ D-897	Earthbound	1975	$12
ARISTA			
❏ ABM-1106	Greatest Hits on Earth	1975	$10
— *Reissue of Bell 1106*			
❏ AL8335	Greatest Hits on Earth	198?	$10
— *Reissue of Arista 1106*			
BELL			
❏ 1106	Greatest Hits on Earth	1972	$12
❏ 6073	Individually & Collectively	1972	$12
❏ 1116 [B]	Living Together, Growing Together	1973	$12
❏ 6060	Love's Lines, Angles and Rhymes	1971	$15
❏ 6045	Portrait	1970	$15
❏ 6065	Reflections	1971	$12
❏ 1315	Soul and Inspiration	1974	$12
❏ 9000	The 5th Dimension/Live!!	1971	$15
MOTOWN			
❏ M7-896	Star	1978	$12
PAIR			
❏ PDL2-1108	The Glory Days	1986	$15
RHINO			
❏ RNDA-71104	The 5th Dimension Anthology	1986	$15
SOUL CITY			
❏ SCS-92002	Stoned Soul Picnic	1968	$18
❏ SCS-33900	The 5th Dimension/Greatest Hits	1970	$15

❏ SCS-92005 [B]	The Age of Aquarius	1969	$18
❏ SCS-33901	The July 5th Album	1970	$15
❏ SCM-91001 [M]	The Magic Garden	1967	$25
❏ SCS-92001 [S]	The Magic Garden	1967	$18
❏ SCM-91000 [M]	Up, Up and Away	1967	$25
❏ SCS-92000 [S]	Up, Up and Away	1967	$18

FIFTH ESTATE, THE

Number	Title	Yr	NM
JUBILEE			
❏ JGM-8005 [M]	Ding Dong! The Witch Is Dead	1967	$40
❏ JGS-8005 [S]	Ding Dong! The Witch Is Dead	1967	$50

FIFTY FOOT HOSE

Number	Title	Yr	NM
LIMELIGHT			
❏ 86062	Cauldron	1968	$250

50 GUITARS, THE

Number	Title	Yr	NM
MISTLETOE			
❏ MLP-1229	Christmas with the 50 Guitars	1977	$12

FIGURES ON A BEACH

Number	Title	Yr	NM
METRO AMERICA			
❏ MA-1002 [EP]	Swimming	1983	$25
SIRE			
❏ 25804	Figures on a Beach	1989	$12
❏ 25596	Standing on Ceremony	1987	$12

FILETS OF SOUL

Number	Title	Yr	NM
SQUID			
❏ 4857	Freedom	1968	$250

FILTER

Number	Title	Yr	NM
REPRISE			
❏ 45864	Short Bus	1995	$18

FINCHLEY BOYS, THE

Number	Title	Yr	NM
GOLDEN THROAT			
❏ 200-19	Everlasting Tribute	1972	$150

FINE, MILO

Number	Title	Yr	NM
FUSETRON			
❏ 010	Another Outbreak of Iconoclasm (Two Eggs, Slightly Beaten)	1995	$35
HAT ART			
❏ 2033	Old Eyes	1983	$30
HAT HUT			
❏ 0E	Hah!	1977	$35
❏ 0S/T	MFG in Minnesota	1978	$25
❏ 1RO-1	Old Eyes	1980	$35
❏ 0H	The Constant Extension of Inescapable Tradition	1978	$35
SHIH SHIH WU AI			
❏ 3	Against the Betrayers	1980	$25
❏ 6	April/October 1991	1992	$35
❏ 5	Get Down! Shove It! It's Tango Time!	1986	$25
❏ 2	Improvisations (Being Free)	1975	$25
❏ 4	Lucid Anarchists (Meat with Two Potatoes)	1981	$25

FINE YOUNG CANNIBALS

Number	Title	Yr	NM
I.R.S.			
❏ R143927	Fine Young Cannibals	1986	$15
— *BMG Direct Marketing edition*			
❏ 5683	Fine Young Cannibals	1986	$12
❏ R101068	The Raw and the Cooked	1989	$12
— *BMG Direct Marketing edition*			
❏ 6273	The Raw and the Cooked	1989	$12
❏ 10125	The Raw and the Remix	1990	$15

FINN, TIM

Number	Title	Yr	NM
A&M			
❏ SP-4972	Escapade	1983	$12
CAPITOL			
❏ C1-48735	Tim Finn	1989	$12
VIRGIN			
❏ 90879	Big Canoe	1988	$12

FINNEY, ALBERT

Number	Title	Yr	NM
MOTOWN			
❏ M6-889	The Albert Finney Album	1977	$25

FIONA

Number	Title	Yr	NM
ATLANTIC			
❏ 81639	Beyond the Pale	1986	$12
❏ 81242	Fiona	1985	$12
❏ 81903	Heart Like a Gun	1989	$15

FIRE & ICE LTD.

Number	Title	Yr	NM
CAPITOL			
❏ T2577 [M]	The Happening	1966	$30
❏ ST2577 [S]	The Happening	1966	$40

FIRE

Number	Title	Yr	NM
ABC			
❏ ABCS-661 [B]	Fire	1969	$30

FIRE AND RAIN

Number	Title	Yr	NM
MERCURY			
❏ SRM-1-654	Fire and Rain	1973	$18

FIRE ESCAPE, THE

Number	Title	Yr	NM
GNP CRESCENDO			
❏ GNP-2034 [M]	Psychotic Reaction	1967	$40
— *Mono pressings are all original first pressings.*			
❏ GNPS-2034 [S]	Psychotic Reaction	1967	$30
— *Stereo pressings in circulation are various re-pressings.*			

FIREBALLET

Number	Title	Yr	NM
PASSPORT			
❏ 98010	Night on Bald Mountain	1975	$15
❏ 98016	Two, Too…	1976	$15

FIREBALLS, THE

Number	Title	Yr	NM
ATCO			
❏ SD 33-239 [S]	Bottle of Wine	1968	$30
❏ 33-239 [M]	Bottle of Wine	1968	$40
❏ SD 33-275	Come On, React!	1969	$30
CROWN			
❏ CLP-5376 [M]	Jimmy Gilmer and the Fireballs & The Sugar Shackers	1963	$30
❏ CST-376 [R]	Jimmy Gilmer and the Fireballs & The Sugar Shackers	1963	$30
❏ CLP-5387 [M]	The Sensational Jimmy Gilmer & The Fireballs	1964	$30
❏ CST-387 [R]	The Sensational Jimmy Gilmer & The Fireballs	1964	$30
DOT			
❏ DLP-3577 [M]	Buddy's Buddy	1964	$50
— *Jimmy Gilmer and the Fireballs*			
❏ DLP-25577 [S]	Buddy's Buddy	1964	$100
— *Jimmy Gilmer and the Fireballs*			
❏ DLP-3709 [M]	Campusology	1966	$30
❏ DLP-25709 [S]	Campusology	1966	$40
❏ DLP-25856 [S]	Firewater	1968	$30
❏ DLP-3856 [M]	Firewater	1968	$50
— *Stereo cover with "Monaural" and "Promotional Copy Not for Sale" stickers, but the record is stock mono*			
❏ DLP-3668 [M]	Folkbeat	1965	$30
❏ DLP-25668 [S]	Folkbeat	1965	$40
❏ DLP-3643 [M]	Lucky 'Leven	1965	$30
❏ DLP-25643 [S]	Lucky 'Leven	1965	$40
❏ DLP-3545 [M]	Sugar Shack	1963	$40
— *Jimmy Gilmer and the Fireballs*			
❏ DLP-25545 [S]	Sugar Shack	1963	$75
— *Jimmy Gilmer and the Fireballs*			
❏ DLP-3512 [M]	Torquay	1963	$50
❏ DLP-25512 [S]	Torquay	1963	$100
SUNDAZED			
❏ LP-5018	Gunshot!	1995	$12
❏ LP-5016	The Fireballs	1995	$12
❏ LP-5017	Torquay	1995	$12
TOP RANK			
❏ RM-324 [M]	The Fireballs	1960	$175
❏ RM-343 [M]	Vaquero	1960	$175
❏ RS-643 [S]	Vaquero	1960	$250
WARWICK			
❏ W-2042 [M]	Here Are the Fireballs	1961	$175
❏ WST-2042 [S]	Here Are the Fireballs	1961	$300

FIREBIRDS, THE

Number	Title	Yr	NM
CROWN			
❏ CST-589	Light My Fire	1968	$80

FIREFALL

Number	Title	Yr	NM
ATLANTIC			
❏ 80017	Break of Dawn	1983	$12
❏ SD16024	Clouds Across the Sun	1980	$12
❏ SD19183	Elan	1978	$12
❏ SD18174	Firefall	1976	$12
❏ SD19125	Firefall	1977	$10
— *Reissue of 18174*			
❏ SD19101	Luna Sea	1977	$12
❏ 80120	Mirror of the World	1983	$12
❏ SD19316	The Best of Firefall	1981	$12
❏ SD16006	Undertow	1980	$12

FIREFLIES, THE

Number	Title	Yr	NM
TAURUS			
❏ 1002 [M]	You Were Mine	196?	$150
❏ S-1002 [S]	You Were Mine	196?	$300

FIREHOSE
Also see MINUTEMEN.

Number	Title	Yr	NM
COLUMBIA			
❏ C47839	Flyin' the Flannel	1991	$15
SST			
❏ 235	fROMOHIO	1989	$15
❏ 115	If'n	1987	$15
❏ 079	Ragin' Full-On	1986	$15
❏ 131 [EP]	Sometimes	1988	$10

Number	Title	Yr	NM

FIREHOUSE FIVE PLUS TWO, THE
GOOD TIME JAZZ

L-12044 [M]	Around the World	1961	$30
S-10044 [S]	Around the World	1961	$30
L-12040 [M]	Dixieland Favorites	1960	$30
S-10040 [S]	Dixieland Favorites	1960	$30
L-1 [10]	The Firehouse Five Plus Two, Volume 1	1953	$50
L-2 [10]	The Firehouse Five Plus Two, Volume 2	1953	$50
L-6 [10]	The Firehouse Five Plus Two, Volume 3	1953	$50
L-16 [10]	The Firehouse Five Plus Two, Volume 4	1953	$50
L-12049 [M]	The Firehouse Five Plus Two at Disneyland	1962	$30
S-10049 [S]	The Firehouse Five Plus Two at Disneyland	1962	$30
L-12038 [M]	The Firehouse Five Plus Two Crashes a Party	1960	$30
S-10038 [S]	The Firehouse Five Plus Two Crashes a Party	1960	$30
L-12018 [M]	The Firehouse Five Plus Two Goes South!	1955	$40
L-23 [10]	The Firehouse Five Plus Two Goes South!, Volume 5	1954	$75
L-12052 [M]	The Firehouse Five Plus Two Goes to a Fire	1964	$30
S-10052 [S]	The Firehouse Five Plus Two Goes to a Fire	1964	$30
L-12028 [M]	The Firehouse Five Plus Two Goes to Sea	1957	$30
S-10028 [S]	The Firehouse Five Plus Two Goes to Sea	1960	$30
L-12014 [M]	The Firehouse Five Plus Two Plays for Lovers	1955	$40
L-12010 [M]	The Firehouse Five Story, Volume 1	1955	$40
L-12011 [M]	The Firehouse Five Story, Volume 2	1955	$40
L-12012 [M]	The Firehouse Five Story, Volume 3	1955	$40
L-12054 [M]	Twenty Years Later	196?	$30
S-10054 [S]	Twenty Years Later	1969	$30

STEREO RECORDS

| S-7005 [S] | The Firehouse Five Plus Two Goes to Sea | 1959 | $40 |

FIRESIGN THEATRE, THE
BUTTERFLY

| 001 | Jost Folks...A Firesign Chat | 1977 | $12 |

COLUMBIA

| KC32411 | David Ossman's How Time Flys | 1973 | $15 |
| KG31099 [B] | Dear Friends | 1972 | $25 |

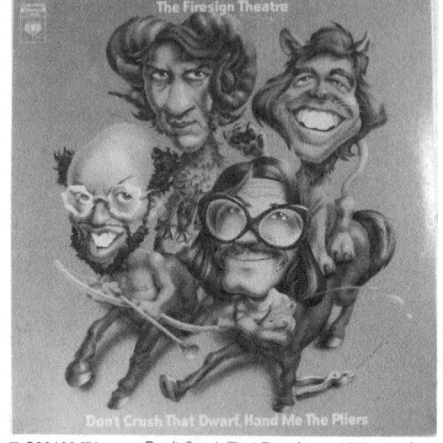

C30102 [B]	Don't Crush That Dwarf, Hand Me the Pliers	1970	$18
KC33141	Everything You Know Is Wrong	1974	$15
CQ33141 [Q]	Everything You Know Is Wrong	1974	$30
PG34391	Forward Into the Past (An Anthology)	1977	$18
CS9884	How Can You Be in Two Places at Once When You're Not Anywhere at All	1969	$18
—360 Sound" label			
PC33475	In the Next World You're On Your Own	1975	$15
C30737	I Think We're All Bozos on This Bus	1971	$18
CQ30737 [Q]	I Think We're All Bozos on This Bus	1972	$30
KC31585	Not Insane or Anything You Want To	1972	$18
KC32730	The Tale of the Giant Rat of Sumatra	1974	$15
CL2718 [M]	Waiting for the Electrician or Someone Like Him	1968	$30
CS9518 [S]	Waiting for the Electrician or Someone Like Him	1968	$18
—360 Sound" label			

Number	Title	Yr	NM

MERCURY

| 826452-1 | Eat or Be Eaten | 1985 | $12 |

RHINO

RNLP-018	Fighting Clowns	1979	$15
RNLP-806	Lawyer's Hospital	1981	$15
RNEP-506 [EP]	Nick Danger, Third Eye	1983	$12
RNLP-812	Nick Danger In: The Three Faces of Al	1984	$15
RNLP-904	Reagan/Carter	1980	$15
RNLP-807	Shakespeare's Lost Comedie	1982	$15

FIRM, THE
Supergroup featuring Jimmy Page of LED ZEPPELIN and Paul Rodgers of BAD COMPANY.

ATLANTIC

81628	Mean Business	1986	$10
PR883 [DJ]	Talks Business	1985	$25
—Promo-only music and interview album			
81239	The Firm	1985	$10

FIRST CHOICE
GOLD MIND

GA9505	Breakaway	1980	$30
7501	Delusions	1977	$18
GA9502	Hold Your Horses	1979	$25

PHILLY GROOVE

| 1400 | Armed and Extremely Dangerous | 1973 | $18 |
| 1502 | The Player | 1974 | $25 |

WARNER BROS.

| BS2934 | So Let Us Entertain You | 1976 | $18 |

FIRST CLASS (1)
UK

| 53108 | The First Class | 1974 | $18 |

FIRST EDITION, THE
JOLLY ROGERS

5001	Backroads	1973	$18
5004	Monumental	1974	$18
—All the above as "Kenny Rogers and the First Edition"			
5003	Rollin'	1974	$18

MCA

913	Country Songs	1984	$10
1460	Greatest Hits	1985	$10
—Reissue of Reprise 6437			
942	Hits and Pieces	1985	$10
912	Love Songs	1984	$10
944	Pieces of Calico Silver	1985	$10
943	The 60's Revisited	1985	$10

REPRISE

RS-6437	Greatest Hits	1971	$25
RS-6352	Ruby, Don't Take Your Love to Town	1969	$25
—Starting above, as "Kenny Rogers and the First Edition"			
ST-92060	Ruby, Don't Take Your Love to Town	1969	$30
—Capitol Record Club edition			
RS-6385	Something's Burning	1970	$25
RS-6412	Tell It All Brother	1970	$25
2XS6476	The Ballad of Calico	1972	$30
R-6276 [M]	The First Edition	1967	$30
RS-6276 [S]	The First Edition	1967	$30
RS-6328	The First Edition '69	1969	$30
RS-6302	The First Edition's Second	1968	$30
MS2039	Transition	1971	$25
—As "Kenny Rogers and the First Edition"			

WARNER SPECIAL PRODUCTS

| OP-2514 | Kenny Rogers and the First Edition | 1979 | $18 |
| *—Manufactured for Lakeshore Music* | | | |

FIRST HOUSE
ECM

| 1393 | Cantilena | 1990 | $30 |
| 1307 | Erendira | 1987 | $25 |

FIRST JAZZ PIANO QUARTET, THE
WARNER BROS.

| W1274 [M] | The First Jazz Piano Quartet | 1959 | $30 |
| WS1274 [S] | The First Jazz Piano Quartet | 1959 | $30 |

FISCHER, CLARE
ATLANTIC

| SD1520 | Thesaurus | 1969 | $35 |

COLUMBIA

| CL2691 [M] | Songs for Rainy Day Lovers | 1967 | $30 |
| CS9491 [S] | Songs for Rainy Day Lovers | 1967 | $35 |

DISCOVERY

DS-820	Alone Together	198?	$25
DS-786	America	1978	$30
DS-934	By and With Himself	1987	$25
DS-852	Clare Fischer and the Sometimes Voices	1982	$25

Number	Title	Yr	NM

DS-914	Crazy Bird	1984	$25
DS-807	Duality	1979	$30
DS-921	Free Fall	1986	$25
DS-835	Machacha	198?	$25
DS-817	Salsa Picante	1979	$30
DS-798	'Twas Only Yesterday	1978	$30

LIGHT

| 5544 | Love Is Surrender | 197? | $30 |

PACIFIC JAZZ

PJ-77 [M]	Extension	1963	$30
ST-77 [S]	Extension	1963	$30
PJ-52 [M]	First Time Out	1962	$30
ST-52 [S]	First Time Out	1962	$30
PJ-10096 [M]	Manteca	1966	$35
ST-20096 [S]	Manteca	1966	$25
PJ-67 [M]	Surging Ahead	1963	$30
ST-67 [S]	Surging Ahead	1963	$30

PAUSA

| 7086 | 2 Plus 2 | 198? | $25 |

REVELATION

REV-2	Easy Living	1968	$35
REV-37	Head, Heart and Hands	198?	$25
REV-31	Jazz Song	1979	$30
REV-6	One to Get Ready, Four to Go	1968	$35
REV-15	Reclamation Act of 1972	1972	$35
REV-23	T'Da-a-a!	1976	$35
REV-13	The Great White Hope	1969	$35
REV-26	The State of His Art	1976	$30

WORLD PACIFIC

| WP-1830 [M] | So Danco Samba | 1964 | $150 |
| ST-21830 [S] | So Danco Samba | 1964 | $150 |

FISCHER, LOU
SEA BREEZE

| SB-2012 | Royal St. | 198? | $25 |

FISCHER, WILD MAN
REPRISE

| 2XS6332 [B] | An Evening with Wild Man Fischer | 1969 | $100 |

RHINO

RNLP-022	Nothing Scary	1981	$15
RNLP-021	Pronounced Normal	1981	$12
RNLP-001	Wildmania	1978	$18

FISCHER, WILLIAM S.
EMBRYO

| 529 | Circles | 1970 | $30 |

FISCHOFF, GEORGE
MMG

| 1140 | Pretty Kitty: The Piano Magic of George Fischoff | 1982 | $25 |

FISELE, JERRY
DELMAR

| DL-101 [10] | Jerry Fisele and the Fabulous Windy City Six | 1954 | $50 |

FISHBONE
COLUMBIA

B6C40032 [EP]	Fishbone	1985	$15
CAS1416 [DJ]	Interchords	198?	$30
—Promo-only music and interviews			
BFC40333	In Your Face	1986	$15
4C44097 [EP]	It's a Wonderful Life (Gonna Have a Good Time)	1987	$12
CAS2235 [EP]	New and Improved Bonin'	1990	$15
—Promo-only five-song sampler			
C46142	The Reality of My Surroundings	1991	$18
FC40891	Truth and Soul	1988	$15

FISHER, AL, AND LOU MARKS
CAMEO

| C-1081 [M] | Rome on the Range | 1964 | $25 |

SWAN

| SLP-514 [M] | It's a Beatle (Coo-Coo) World | 1964 | $40 |

FISHER, CHIP
RCA VICTOR

| LPM-1797 [M] | Chipper at the Sugar Bowl | 1958 | $40 |
| LSP-1797 [S] | Chipper at the Sugar Bowl | 1958 | $50 |

FISHER, EDDIE, QUINTET
CADET

| CA-848 | The Next Hundred Years | 1971 | $35 |
| LPS-828 | The Third Cup | 1969 | $35 |

STANG

| 1032 | Hot Lunch | 1977 | $35 |

Number	Title	Yr	NM

FISHER, EDDIE
DOT
❏ DLP-3631 [M]	Eddie Fisher Today!	1965	$15
❏ DLP-25361 [S]	Eddie Fisher Today!	1965	$18
❏ DLP-3785 [M]	His Greatest Hits	1967	$15
❏ DLP-25785 [S]	His Greatest Hits	1967	$18
❏ DLP-3658 [M]	Mary Christmas	1965	$18
❏ DLP-25658 [S]	Mary Christmas	1965	$25
❏ DLP-3648 [M]	When I Was Young	1965	$15
❏ DLP-25648 [S]	When I Was Young	1965	$18
❏ DLP-3670 [M]	Young and Foolish	1966	$15
❏ DLP-25670 [S]	Young and Foolish	1966	$18

MCA
❏ 1549	The Best of Eddie Fisher	1983	$10

PICKWICK
❏ SPC-3141	Oh My Papa	196?	$15

RAMROD
❏ RR-1 [M]	Eddie Fisher at the Winter Garden	1963	$18
❏ RRS-1 [S]	Eddie Fisher at the Winter Garden	1963	$25

RCA CAMDEN
❏ CAL-789 [M]	Bring Back the Thrill	196?	$15
❏ CAS-789 [R]	Bring Back the Thrill	196?	$12

RCA VICTOR
❏ LOC-1024 [M]	Academy Award Winners	1955	$40
❏ LPM-1647 [M]	As Long As There's Music	1958	$30
❏ LSP-1647 [S]	As Long As There's Music	1958	$50
❏ LPM-1399 [M]	Bundle of Joy	1957	$30
❏ LPM-3065 [10]	Christmas with Eddie Fisher	1952	$50
❏ LPM-2504 [M]	Eddie Fisher's Greatest Hits	1962	$18
❏ LSP-2504 [S]	Eddie Fisher's Greatest Hits	1962	$25
❏ ANL1-1138	Eddie Fisher's Greatest Hits	1975	$10
❏ LPM-3025 [10]	Fisher Sings	1952	$50
❏ LPM-3726 [M]	Games That Lovers Play	1966	$18
❏ LSP-3726 [S]	Games That Lovers Play	1966	$18
❏ LPM-1097 [M]	I Love You	1955	$30
❏ LPM-3058 [10]	I'm in the Mood for Love	1952	$50
❏ LPM-1180 [M]	I'm in the Mood for Love	1955	$30
❏ LPM-3122 [10]	Irving Berlin Favorites	1953	$50
❏ LPM-3185 [10]	May I Sing to You?	1953	$50
❏ LPM-1181 [M]	May I Sing to You?	1955	$30
❏ LPM-3820 [M]	People Like You	1967	$25
❏ LSP-3820 [S]	People Like You	1967	$15
❏ LPM-3375 [M]	The Best of Eddie Fisher	1965	$18
❏ LSP-3375 [R]	The Best of Eddie Fisher	1965	$15
❏ LPM-1548 [M]	Thinking of You	1957	$30
❏ LSP-3914	You Ain't Heard Nothin' Yet	1968	$15

FISHER, ELLIOT
DOBRE
❏ 1003	In the Land of Make Believe	1976	$50

FISHER, KING
JAZZOLOGY
❏ J-13	King Fisher and His All Stars	196?	$30

FISHER, TONI
SIGNET
❏ WP-509 [S]	The Big Hurt	1960	$50
— Issued in "Stereomonic"			

FITCH, MAL
EMARCY
❏ MG-36041 [M]	Mal Fitch	1956	$250

FITE, BUDDY
BELL
❏ 6058	Buddy Fite and Friend	1970	$35

CYCLONE
❏ CY4100	Buddy Fite	1971	$30
❏ CY4110	Changes	1972	$30

DIFFERENT DRUMMER
❏ 1001	Buddy Fite Plays for Satin Dolls	1975	$35

FITZGERALD, ELLA, AND BILLIE HOLIDAY
Also see each artist's individual listings.
AMERICAN RECORDING SOCIETY
❏ G-433 [M]	Ella Fitzgerald and Billie Holiday at Newport	1957	$40

VERVE
❏ MGV-8234 [M]	Ella Fitzgerald and Billie Holiday at Newport	1958	$175
❏ MGVS-6022 [S]	Ella Fitzgerald and Billie Holiday at Newport	1960	$150
❏ V-8234 [M]	Ella Fitzgerald and Billie Holiday at Newport	1961	$50
❏ V6-8234 [S]	Ella Fitzgerald and Billie Holiday at Newport	1961	$50
❏ V-8826	Newport Years	1973	$30

FITZGERALD, ELLA, AND COUNT BASIE
PABLO TODAY
❏ 2312110	A Perfect Match	1980	$30
— Red vinyl			

Number	Title	Yr	NM

VERVE
❏ V-4061 [M]	Ella and Basie!	1963	$75
❏ V6-4061 [S]	Ella and Basie!	1963	$75
❏ ST-90028 [S]	Ella and Basie!	1964	$150
— Capitol Record Club edition			
❏ T-90028 [M]	Ella and Basie!	1964	$150
— Capitol Record Club edition			

FITZGERALD, ELLA, AND DUKE ELLINGTON
PABLO LIVE
❏ 2308242	The Stockholm Concert 1966	1984	$25

FITZGERALD, ELLA, AND LOUIS ARMSTRONG
Also see each artist's individual listings.
METRO
❏ M-601 [M]	Louis and Ella	1967	$175
❏ MS-601 [S]	Louis and Ella	1967	$175

MOBILE FIDELITY
❏ 2-248	Ella and Louis Again	1996	$175
— Audiophile vinyl			

VERVE
❏ MGV-4003 [M]	Ella and Louis	1956	$175
— orange label			
❏ V-4003 [M]	Ella and Louis	1961	$50
❏ V6-8811	Ella and Louis	1972	$35
❏ MGV-4006-2 [M]	Ella and Louis Again	1956	$175
❏ V-4006-2 [M]	Ella and Louis Again	1961	$75
❏ MGV-4017 [M]	Ella and Louis Again, Vol. 1	1958	$175
❏ V-4017 [M]	Ella and Louis Again, Vol. 1	1961	$50
❏ MGV-4018 [M]	Ella and Louis Again, Vol. 2	1958	$175
❏ V-4018 [M]	Ella and Louis Again, Vol. 2	1961	$50
❏ MGV-4011-2 [M]	Porgy and Bess	1957	$300
❏ MGVS-6040-2 [S]	Porgy and Bess	1960	$120
❏ V-4011-2 [M]	Porgy and Bess	1961	$75
❏ V6-4011-2 [S]	Porgy and Bess	1961	$75
❏ VE-1-2507	Porgy and Bess	197?	$25
❏ 827475-1	Porgy and Bess	198?	$30

FITZGERALD, ELLA
AMERICAN RECORDING SOCIETY
❏ G-433 [M]	Ella Fitzgerald At Newport	195?	$40

ATLANTIC
❏ SD1631	Ella Loves Cole	1972	$30

BAINBRIDGE
❏ 6223	Things Ain't What They Used to Be	1982	$25
— Reissue of Reprise 6432			

BASF
❏ 20712	Watch What Happens	1972	$30

CAPITOL
❏ T2685 [M]	Brighten the Corner	1967	$100
❏ ST2685 [S]	Brighten the Corner	1967	$85
❏ SM-11793	Brighten the Corner	1978	$25
❏ T2805 [M]	Ella Fitzgerald's Christmas	1967	$100
❏ ST2805 [S]	Ella Fitzgerald's Christmas	1967	$75
— Same as above, but in stereo			
❏ ST2888	Misty Blue	1968	$85
❏ ST2960	Thirty by Ella	1968	$50
❏ SN-16276	Thirty by Ella	1983	$25
— Budget-line reissue			

CLASSICS RECORD LIBRARY/VERVE
❏ 80-55713	Ella Fitzgerald Sings the George and Ira Gershwin Songbook	1978	$40
— Reissue of the entire set for Book-of-the-Month Club			

COLUMBIA
❏ KG32557	Carnegie Hall & Newport Jazz Festival 1973	1973	$35

DECCA
❏ DL4447 [M]	Early Ella	1964	$35
❏ DL74447 [R]	Early Ella	1964	$30
❏ DL8477 [M]	Ella and Her Fellas	1957	$175
❏ DL5300 [10]	Ella Fitzgerald Sings Gershwin Songs	1951	$250
❏ DL8378 [M]	Ella Sings Gershwin	1957	$175
❏ DL4451 [M]	Ella Sings Gershwin	1964	$35
❏ DL74451 [R]	Ella Sings Gershwin	1964	$30
❏ DL8832 [M]	For Sentimental Reasons	1958	$120
❏ DL4129 [M]	Golden Favorites	1961	$50
❏ DL74129 [R]	Golden Favorites	1961	$30
❏ DL8149 [M]	Lullabies of Birdland	1955	$175
❏ DL8696 [M]	Miss Ella Fitzgerald and Mr. Nelson Riddle Invite You to Listen and Relax	1958	$150
❏ DL4887 [M]	Smooth Sailing	1967	$35
❏ DL74887 [R]	Smooth Sailing	1967	$30
❏ DL8068 [M]	Songs in a Mellow Mood	1954	$175
❏ DL5084 [10]	Souvenir Album	1950	$300
❏ DL4446 [M]	Stairway to the Stars	1964	$35
❏ DL74446 [R]	Stairway to the Stars	1964	$30
❏ DL8155 [M]	Sweet and Hot	1955	$150
❏ DXB156 [M]	The Best of Ella	1959	$250
— Black labels, silver print			
❏ DXB156 [M]	The Best of Ella	1961	$75
— Black labels with color bars			
❏ DXSB7156 [R]	The Best of Ella	196?	$50
❏ DL8695 [M]	The First Lady of Song	1958	$120

Number	Title	Yr	NM

EVEREST ARCHIVE OF FOLK & JAZZ
❏ 276	Ella Fitzgerald	1973	$30

FANTASY
❏ OJC-442	Ella & Nice	1990	$30
— Reissue of Pablo Live 2308 234			
❏ OJC-376	Montreux '77	1989	$30
— Reissue of Pablo Live 2308 206			

INTERMEDIA
❏ QS-5049	Ella by Starlight	198?	$25

MCA
❏ 215	Ella Sings Gershwin	1973	$25
❏ 734	Memories	198?	$25
❏ 4047	The Best of Ella	197?	$35
❏ 4016	The Best of Ella Fitzgerald, Vol. II	1973	$35

METRO
❏ M-500 [M]	Ella Fitzgerald	1965	$175
❏ MS-500 [S]	Ella Fitzgerald	1965	$175
❏ M-567 [M]	The World of Ella Fitzgerald	1966	$175
❏ MS-567 [S]	The World of Ella Fitzgerald	1966	$175

MGM
❏ GAS-130	Ella Fitzgerald (Golden Archive Series)	1970	$35

PABLO
❏ 2310772	Again	1977	$30
❏ 2310938	All That Jazz	1990	$30
❏ 2310814	Dream Dancing	1978	$30
❏ 2310921	Easy Living	1987	$25
❏ 2310759	Ella and Oscar	1976	$30
❏ 2310711	Ella in London	1974	$30
❏ 2310829	Fine and Mellow	1979	$30
❏ 2310825	Lady Time	1978	$30
❏ 2310751	Montreux '75	1976	$30
❏ 2310888	Speak Love	1983	$25
❏ 2310702	Take Love Easy	1974	$30
❏ 24405421	The Best of Ella Fitzgerald	198?	$25

PABLO LIVE
❏ 2308234	Ella & Nice	197?	$35
❏ 2308206	Montreux '77	1978	$30

PABLO TODAY
❏ 2312132	A Classy Pair	1983	$25
❏ 2630201	Ella Abraca Jobim: Ella Fitzgerald Sings the Antonio Carlos Jobim Song Book	1981	$35
❏ 2312140	Nice Work If You Can Get It	198?	$25
❏ 2312138	The Best Is Yet to Come	1982	$25

PAUSA
❏ 7130	Love You Madly	198?	$25

PICKWICK
❏ SPC-3259	Misty Blues	1974	$25

PRESTIGE
❏ PRLP-7685	Sunshine of Your Love	1970	$35

REPRISE
❏ RS-6354	Ella	1969	$35
❏ RS-6432	Things Ain't What They Used to Be	1971	$30

SUNBEAM
❏ 205	Ella Fitzgerald and Her Orchestra, 1940	197?	$25

TIME-LIFE
❏ SLGD-03	Legendary Singers: Ella Fitzgerald	1985	$35

VERVE
❏ V-4066 [M]	A Tribute to Cole Porter	1964	$75
❏ V6-4066 [M]	A Tribute to Cole Porter	1964	$75
❏ V-4053 [M]	Clap Hands, Here Comes Charley	1962	$40
❏ V6-4053 [S]	Clap Hands, Here Comes Charley	1962	$300
❏ V-4072 [M]	Ella & Duke at Cote d'Azur	1967	$40
❏ V6-4072 [S]	Ella & Duke at Cote d'Azur	1967	$75
❏ V-4070 [M]	Ella at Duke's Place	1966	$50
❏ V6-4070 [S]	Ella at Duke's Place	1966	$50
❏ SMAS-90644 [S]	Ella at Duke's Place	1966	$150
— Capitol Record Club edition			
❏ V-4065 [M]	Ella at Juan Les Pins	1964	$75
❏ V6-4065 [S]	Ella at Juan Les Pins	1964	$75
❏ MGV-8264 [M]	Ella Fitzgerald at the Opera House	1958	$175
❏ MGVS-6026 [S]	Ella Fitzgerald at the Opera House	1960	$150
❏ V-8264 [M]	Ella Fitzgerald at the Opera House	1961	$50
❏ V6-8264 [S]	Ella Fitzgerald at the Opera House	1961	$50
❏ MGV-4049 [M]	Ella Fitzgerald Sings Cole Porter	1961	$40
❏ V-4049 [M]	Ella Fitzgerald Sings Cole Porter	1961	$50
❏ MGV-4050 [M]	Ella Fitzgerald Sings More Cole Porter	1961	$40
❏ V-4050 [M]	Ella Fitzgerald Sings More Cole Porter	1961	$50
❏ MGV-4001-2 [M]	Ella Fitzgerald Sings the Cole Porter Song Book	1956	$175
❏ V-4001-2 [M]	Ella Fitzgerald Sings the Cole Porter Song Book	1961	$75
❏ MGV-4010-4 [M]	Ella Fitzgerald Sings the Duke Ellington Song Book	1957	$175
— Combines 4008 and 4009 into one package			

Number	Title	Yr	NM
❑ V-10-4 [M]	Ella Fitzgerald Sings the Duke Ellington Song Book	196?	$150
❑ MGV-4008-2 [M]	Ella Fitzgerald Sings the Duke Ellington Song Book, Vol. 1	1957	$175
❑ V-4008-2 [M]	Ella Fitzgerald Sings the Duke Ellington Song Book, Vol. 1	1961	$75
❑ MGV-4009-2 [M]	Ella Fitzgerald Sings the Duke Ellington Song Book, Vol. 2	1957	$175
❑ V-4009-2 [M]	Ella Fitzgerald Sings the Duke Ellington Song Book, Vol. 2	1961	$75
❑ MGV-4029-5 [M]	Ella Fitzgerald Sings the George and Ira Gershwin Song Book	1959	$300

—Box set with 4024 through 4028 plus bonus 10-inch LP

Number	Title	Yr	NM
❑ MGV-4029-5 [M]	Ella Fitzgerald Sings the George and Ira Gershwin Song Book	1959	$500

—Box set with 4024 through 4028 plus bonus 10-inch LP, all in walnut box with leather pockets

Number	Title	Yr	NM
❑ MGVS-6082-5 [S]	Ella Fitzgerald Sings the George and Ira Gershwin Song Book	1960	$250

—Box set with 6077 through 6081 plus bonus 10-inch LP

Number	Title	Yr	NM
❑ V-29-5 [M]	Ella Fitzgerald Sings the George and Ira Gershwin Song Book	196?	$200

— Reissue of MGV-4029

Number	Title	Yr	NM
❑ V6-29-5 [S]	Ella Fitzgerald Sings the George and Ira Gershwin Song Book	196?	$200

— Reissue of MGVS-6082

Number	Title	Yr	NM
❑ MGV-4024 [M]	Ella Fitzgerald Sings the George and Ira Gershwin Song Book, Vol. 1	1959	$150
❑ MGVS-6077 [S]	Ella Fitzgerald Sings the George and Ira Gershwin Song Book, Vol. 1	1960	$150
❑ V-4024 [M]	Ella Fitzgerald Sings the George and Ira Gershwin Song Book, Vol. 1	1961	$50
❑ V6-4024 [S]	Ella Fitzgerald Sings the George and Ira Gershwin Song Book, Vol. 1	1961	$50
❑ MGV-4025 [M]	Ella Fitzgerald Sings the George and Ira Gershwin Song Book, Vol. 2	1959	$150
❑ MGVS-6078 [S]	Ella Fitzgerald Sings the George and Ira Gershwin Song Book, Vol. 2	1960	$150
❑ V-4025 [M]	Ella Fitzgerald Sings the George and Ira Gershwin Song Book, Vol. 2	1961	$50
❑ V6-4025 [S]	Ella Fitzgerald Sings the George and Ira Gershwin Song Book, Vol. 2	1961	$50
❑ MGV-4026 [M]	Ella Fitzgerald Sings the George and Ira Gershwin Song Book, Vol. 3	1959	$150
❑ MGVS-6079 [S]	Ella Fitzgerald Sings the George and Ira Gershwin Song Book, Vol. 3	1960	$150
❑ V-4026 [M]	Ella Fitzgerald Sings the George and Ira Gershwin Song Book, Vol. 3	1961	$50
❑ V6-4026 [S]	Ella Fitzgerald Sings the George and Ira Gershwin Song Book, Vol. 3	1961	$50
❑ MGV-4027 [M]	Ella Fitzgerald Sings the George and Ira Gershwin Song Book, Vol. 4	1959	$150
❑ MGVS-6080 [S]	Ella Fitzgerald Sings the George and Ira Gershwin Song Book, Vol. 4	1960	$150
❑ V-4027 [M]	Ella Fitzgerald Sings the George and Ira Gershwin Song Book, Vol. 4	1961	$50
❑ V6-4027 [S]	Ella Fitzgerald Sings the George and Ira Gershwin Song Book, Vol. 4	1961	$50
❑ MGV-4028 [M]	Ella Fitzgerald Sings the George and Ira Gershwin Song Book, Vol. 5	1959	$150
❑ MGVS-6081 [S]	Ella Fitzgerald Sings the George and Ira Gershwin Song Book, Vol. 5	1960	$150
❑ V-4028 [M]	Ella Fitzgerald Sings the George and Ira Gershwin Song Book, Vol. 5	1961	$50
❑ V6-4028 [S]	Ella Fitzgerald Sings the George and Ira Gershwin Song Book, Vol. 5	1961	$50
❑ MGV-4013 [M]	Ella Fitzgerald Sings the Gershwin Song Book	1957	$150
❑ MGVS-7000 [S]	Ella Fitzgerald Sings the Gershwin Song Book	1959	$150
❑ MGV-4046-2 [M]	Ella Fitzgerald Sings the Harold Arlen Song Book	1961	$120
❑ V-4057 [M]	Ella Fitzgerald Sings the Harold Arlen Song Book, Vol. 1	1962	$75
❑ V6-4057 [S]	Ella Fitzgerald Sings the Harold Arlen Song Book, Vol. 1	1962	$75
❑ V-4058 [M]	Ella Fitzgerald Sings the Harold Arlen Song Book, Vol. 2	1962	$75
❑ V6-4058 [S]	Ella Fitzgerald Sings the Harold Arlen Song Book, Vol. 2	1962	$75

Number	Title	Yr	NM
❑ MGV-4019-2 [M]	Ella Fitzgerald Sings the Irving Berlin Song Book	1958	$300
❑ MGVS-6005-2 [S]	Ella Fitzgerald Sings the Irving Berlin Song Book	1960	$120
❑ V-4019-2 [M]	Ella Fitzgerald Sings the Irving Berlin Song Book	1961	$75
❑ V6-4019-2 [S]	Ella Fitzgerald Sings the Irving Berlin Song Book	1961	$75
❑ MGV-4030 [M]	Ella Fitzgerald Sings the Irving Berlin Song Book, Vol. 1	1959	$150
❑ MGVS-6052 [S]	Ella Fitzgerald Sings the Irving Berlin Song Book, Vol. 1	1960	$120
❑ V-4030 [M]	Ella Fitzgerald Sings the Irving Berlin Song Book, Vol. 1	1961	$50
❑ V6-4030 [S]	Ella Fitzgerald Sings the Irving Berlin Song Book, Vol. 1	1961	$50
❑ MGV-4031 [M]	Ella Fitzgerald Sings the Irving Berlin Song Book, Vol. 2	1959	$150
❑ MGVS-6053 [S]	Ella Fitzgerald Sings the Irving Berlin Song Book, Vol. 2	1960	$120
❑ V-4031 [M]	Ella Fitzgerald Sings the Irving Berlin Song Book, Vol. 2	1961	$50
❑ V6-4031 [S]	Ella Fitzgerald Sings the Irving Berlin Song Book, Vol. 2	1961	$50
❑ V-4060 [M]	Ella Fitzgerald Sings the Jerome Kern Song Book	1963	$75
❑ V6-4060 [S]	Ella Fitzgerald Sings the Jerome Kern Song Book	1963	$75
❑ V-8670 [M]	Ella Fitzgerald Sings the Jerome Kern Song Book	1967	$0

—Canceled reissue

Number	Title	Yr	NM
❑ V-4067 [M]	Ella Fitzgerald Sings the Johnny Mercer Song Book	1965	$50
❑ V6-4067 [S]	Ella Fitzgerald Sings the Johnny Mercer Song Book	1965	$50
❑ MGV-4002-2 [M]	Ella Fitzgerald Sings the Rodgers & Hart Song Book	1956	$175
❑ MGV-4022 [M]	Ella Fitzgerald Sings the Rodgers & Hart Song Book, Vol. 1	1959	$150
❑ MGVS-6009 [S]	Ella Fitzgerald Sings the Rodgers & Hart Song Book, Vol. 1	1960	$150
❑ V-4022 [M]	Ella Fitzgerald Sings the Rodgers & Hart Song Book, Vol. 1	1961	$50
❑ V6-4022 [S]	Ella Fitzgerald Sings the Rodgers & Hart Song Book, Vol. 1	1961	$50
❑ MGV-4023 [M]	Ella Fitzgerald Sings the Rodgers & Hart Song Book, Vol. 2	1959	$150
❑ MGVS-6010 [S]	Ella Fitzgerald Sings the Rodgers & Hart Song Book, Vol. 2	1960	$150
❑ V-4023 [M]	Ella Fitzgerald Sings the Rodgers & Hart Song Book, Vol. 2	1961	$50
❑ V6-4023 [S]	Ella Fitzgerald Sings the Rodgers & Hart Song Book, Vol. 2	1961	$50
❑ V-4002-2 [M]	Ella Fitzgerald Sings the Rodgers and Hart Song Book	1961	$75
❑ V-4069 [M]	Ella in Hamburg	1966	$50
❑ V6-4069 [S]	Ella in Hamburg	1966	$50
❑ MGV-4052 [M]	Ella in Hollywood	1961	$40
❑ V-4052 [M]	Ella in Hollywood	1961	$50
❑ 835454-1	Ella in Rome: The Birthday Concert	1988	$25
❑ V-8745 [M]	Ella "Live"	1968	$75
❑ V6-8745 [S]	Ella "Live"	1968	$35
❑ V-4059 [M]	Ella Sings Broadway	1963	$75
❑ V6-4059 [S]	Ella Sings Broadway	1963	$75
❑ V-4054 [M]	Ella Swings Brightly with Nelson	1962	$75
❑ V6-4054 [S]	Ella Swings Brightly with Nelson	1962	$75
❑ V-4055 [M]	Ella Swings Gently with Nelson	1962	$75
❑ V6-4055 [S]	Ella Swings Gently with Nelson	1962	$75
❑ MGV-4021 [M]	Ella Swings Lightly	1958	$175
❑ MGVS-6019 [S]	Ella Swings Lightly	1960	$150
❑ V-4021 [M]	Ella Swings Lightly	1961	$50
❑ V6-4021 [S]	Ella Swings Lightly	1961	$50
❑ MGV-4042 [M]	Ella Wishes You a Swinging Christmas	1960	$150
❑ MGVS-64042 [S]	Ella Wishes You a Swinging Christmas	1960	$120
❑ V-4042 [M]	Ella Wishes You a Swinging Christmas	1961	$40
❑ V6-4042 [S]	Ella Wishes You a Swinging Christmas	1961	$150
❑ VE-1-2539	Ella Wishes You a Swinging Christmas	198?	$30

—Reissue

Number	Title	Yr	NM
❑ 827150-1	Ella Wishes You a Swinging Christmas	198?	$25
❑ MGV-4036 [M]	Get Happy!	1960	$150
❑ MGVS-6102 [S]	Get Happy!	1960	$150

Number	Title	Yr	NM
❑ V-4036 [M]	Get Happy!	1961	$25
❑ V6-4036 [S]	Get Happy!	1961	$50
❑ V-4064 [M]	Hello, Dolly!	1964	$75
❑ V6-4064 [S]	Hello, Dolly!	1964	$75
❑ MGV-4034 [M]	Hello, Love	1959	$150
❑ MGVS-6100 [S]	Hello, Love	1960	$150
❑ V-4034 [M]	Hello, Love	1961	$50
❑ V6-4034 [S]	Hello, Love	1961	$50
❑ V6-8817	History	1973	$35
❑ 825098-1	Lady Be Good	1985	$25
❑ MGV-4043 [M]	Let No Man Write My Epitaph	1961	$40
❑ V-4043 [M]	Let No Man Write My Epitaph	1961	$50
❑ V6-4043 [S]	Let No Man Write My Epitaph	1961	$50
❑ MGV-4004 [M]	Like Someone in Love	1957	$175
❑ MGVS-6000 [S]	Like Someone in Love	1960	$150
❑ V-4004 [M]	Like Someone in Love	1961	$50
❑ V6-4004 [S]	Like Someone in Love	1961	$50
❑ MGV-4041 [M]	Mack the Knife -- Ella in Berlin	1960	$40
❑ MGVS-6163 [S]	Mack the Knife -- Ella in Berlin	1960	$150
❑ V-4041 [M]	Mack the Knife -- Ella in Berlin	1961	$50
❑ V6-4041 [S]	Mack the Knife -- Ella in Berlin	1961	$50
❑ 825670-1	Mack the Knife -- Ella in Berlin	1985	$25
❑ MGVS-64041 [S]	Mack the Knife -- Ella in Berlin	1960	$150
❑ MGV-8288 [M]	One O'Clock Jump	1958	$150
❑ V-8288 [M]	One O'Clock Jump	1961	$50
❑ V-4068 [M]	Porgy & Bess	1965	$50
❑ V6-4068 [S]	Porgy & Bess	1965	$50
❑ V-4056 [M]	Rhythm Is My Business	1962	$75
❑ V6-4056 [S]	Rhythm Is My Business	1962	$75
❑ MGV-4032 [M]	Sweet Songs for Swingers	1959	$150
❑ MGVS-6072 [S]	Sweet Songs for Swingers	1960	$100
❑ V-4032 [M]	Sweet Songs for Swingers	1961	$50
❑ V6-4032 [S]	Sweet Songs for Swingers	1961	$50
❑ V-4063 [M]	The Best of Ella Fitzgerald	1964	$35
❑ V6-4063 [S]	The Best of Ella Fitzgerald	1964	$35
❑ V-8720 [M]	The Best of Ella Fitzgerald	1967	$35
❑ V6-8720 [S]	The Best of Ella Fitzgerald	1967	$30
❑ V6-8795	The Best of Ella Fitzgerald, Vol. 2	1969	$30
❑ VE-2-2511	The Cole Porter Song Book	197?	$35
❑ 823278-1	The Cole Porter Song Book	198?	$30
❑ VE-2-2535	The Duke Ellington Song Book	1979	$35
❑ 827163-1	The Duke Ellington Song Book, Vol. 1	198?	$30
❑ VE-2-2540	The Duke Ellington Song Book, Vol. 2	1982	$35
❑ 827169-1	The Duke Ellington Song Book, Vol. 2	198?	$30
❑ 825024-1	The George and Ira Gershwin Songbook (Complete)	198?	$75
❑ 823279-1	The George and Ira Gershwin Songbook (Highlights)	198?	$30
❑ VE-2-2525	The George Gershwin Song Book	1978	$35
❑ 817526-1	The Harold Arlen Song Book	1984	$35
❑ 829533-1	The Irving Berlin Song Book	1988	$30
❑ 825669-1	The Jerome Kern Song Book	1985	$25
❑ 823247-1	The Johnny Mercer Song Book	1985	$25
❑ VE-2-2519	The Rodgers and Hart Song Book	197?	$35
❑ 821693-1	The Rodgers and Hart Song Book	198?	$30
❑ V-4062 [M]	These Are the Blues	1963	$75
❑ V6-4062 [S]	These Are the Blues	1963	$75
❑ V-4071 [M]	Whisper Not	1966	$50
❑ V6-4071 [S]	Whisper Not	1966	$50

VOCALION

Number	Title	Yr	NM
❑ VL3797 [M]	Ella Fitzgerald	1967	$30
❑ VL73797 [R]	Ella Fitzgerald	1967	$30

Number	Title	Yr	NM

FIVE, THE
RCA VICTOR
☐ LPM-1121 [M] — The Five — 1955 — $100

FIVE-A-SLIDE
AUDIOPHILE
☐ AP-180 — Five-a-Slide — 198? — $30

FIVE AMERICANS, THE
ABNAK
☐ ABST-2071 — Now and Then — 1968 — $30
☐ AB-1969 [M] — Progressions — 1967 — $40
☐ ABST-2069 [S] — Progressions — 1967 — $75
☐ AB-1967 [M] — Western Union/Sound of Love — 1967 — $30
☐ ABST-2067 [S] — Western Union/Sound of Love — 1967 — $30

HANNA-BARBERA
☐ HST-9503 [S] — I See the Light — 1966 — $85
☐ HLP-8503 [M] — I See the Light — 1966 — $40

FIVE BROTHERS
TAMPA
☐ TP-25 [M] — Five Brothers — 1957 — $300
—Red vinyl
☐ TP-25 [M] — Five Brothers — 1958 — $175
—Black vinyl

FIVE BY FIVE
PAULA
☐ LPS-2202 — Next Exit — 1969 — $40

FIVE DISCS, THE
CRYSTAL BALL
☐ 119 — Unchained — 1978 — $18
MAGIC CARPET
☐ 1002 — The Five Discs Sing Again — 1991 — $25
—Dark blue cover

FIVE EMPREES, THE
FREEPORT
☐ 4001 [S] — Little Miss Sad — 1966 — $150
—Same LP, new title
☐ 3001 [M] — Little Miss Sad — 1966 — $175
—Same LP, new title
☐ 3001 [M] — The Five Emprees — 1965 — $175
☐ 3001 [S] — The Five Emprees — 1965 — $150

FIVE KEYS, THE
ALADDIN
☐ LP-806 [M] — The Best of the Five Keys — 1956 — $2000
—Copies of Aladdin 806 entitled "On the Town" are bootlegs made in the 1970s; VG value 1000; VG+ value 1500
CAPITOL
☐ T1769 [M] — The Fantastic Five Keys — 1962 — $300
☐ M-1769 — The Fantastic Five Keys — 1977 — $25
—Reissue with new prefix
☐ T828 [M] — The Five Keys On Stage! — 1957 — $500
—On cover, the far left singer's "offending" thumb is airbrushed out
☐ T828 [M] — The Five Keys On Stage! — 1957 — $300
—On cover, the far left singer has his thumb sticking out (inadvertently?) in a phallic way
HARLEM HIT PARADE
☐ 5004 — The Five Keys — 1972 — $18
KING
☐ 5013 — 14 Hits — 1978 — $15
☐ 692 [M] — Rhythm and Blues Hits, Past and Present — 1960 — $600
☐ 688 [M] — The Five Keys — 1960 — $800
SCORE
☐ LP-4003 [M] — The Five Keys On the Town — 1957 — $800
—Reissue of Aladdin 806.

FIVE MAN ELECTRICAL BAND
CAPITOL
☐ ST-165 — Five Man Electrical Band — 1969 — $25
LION
☐ LN-1009 [B] — Sweet Paradise — 1973 — $25
LIONEL
☐ LRS-1101 — Coming of Age — 1971 — $25
☐ LRS-1100 — Good-Byes & Butterflies — 1970 — $30
MGM
☐ SE-4725 — Good-Byes & Butterflies — 1970 — $50
PICKWICK
☐ SPC-3289 — Five Man Electrical Band — 1973 — $12
—Reissue of Capitol material

FIVE ROYALES, THE
APOLLO
☐ LP-488 [M] — The Rockin' 5 Royales — 1956 — $4000

—Purple label; VG value 2000; VG+ value 3000
☐ LP-488 [M] — The Rockin' 5 Royales — 1956 — $2000
—Green label; VG value 1000; VG+ value 1500
☐ LP-488 [M] — The Rockin' 5 Royales — 1956 — $1000
—Yellow label
KING
☐ 5014 — 17 Hits — 197? — $15
☐ 955 [M] — 24 All Time Hits — 1966 — $150
☐ 580 [M] — Dedicated to You — 1957 — $500
☐ 616 [M] — The 5 Royales Sing for You — 1959 — $400
☐ 678 [M] — The Five Royales — 1960 — $300

FIVE SATINS, THE
BUDDAH
☐ BDS-5654 — Black Satin — 1976 — $18
—As "Black Satin
CELEBRITY SHOWCASE
☐ JB-7671 — The Best of the Five Satins — 1970 — $25
COLLECTABLES
☐ COL-5017 — The Five Satins Sing Their Greatest Hits — 198? — $12
ELEKTRA
☐ 60152 — Fred Parris and the Satins — 1982 — $25
EMBER
☐ ELP-401 [M] — The Five Satins Encore — 1960 — $250
—Mostly white "logs" label
☐ ELP-401 [M] — The Five Satins Encore — 1961 — $150
—Black label
☐ ELP-100 [M] — The Five Satins Sing — 1957 — $2000
—Red label; group pictured on front cover; blue vinyl; VG value 1000; VG+ value 1500
☐ ELP-100 [M] — The Five Satins Sing — 1957 — $600
—Red label; group pictured on front cover; black vinyl
☐ ELP-100 [M] — The Five Satins Sing — 1959 — $300
—Mostly white "logs" label; group pictured on front cover
☐ ELP-100 [M] — The Five Satins Sing — 1959 — $250
—Mostly white "logs" label; no picture on cover
☐ ELP-100 [M] — The Five Satins Sing — 1961 — $150
—Black label; no picture on cover
LOST-NITE
☐ LLP-8 [10] — The Five Satins — 1981 — $12
—Red vinyl
☐ LLP-9 [10] — The Five Satins — 1981 — $12
—Red vinyl
MOUNT VERNON
☐ 108 — The Five Satins Sing — 196? — $30
RELIC
☐ 5008 — The Five Satins' Greatest Hits (1956-1959), Volume 1 — 198? — $12
☐ 5013 — The Five Satins' Greatest Hits (1956-1959), Volume 2 — 198? — $12
☐ 5024 — The Five Satins' Greatest Hits (1956-1959), Volume 3 — 198? — $12

FIVE SPECIAL
ELEKTRA
☐ 6E-206 — Five Special — 1979 — $18
☐ 6E-270 — Something Special — 1980 — $18
☐ 5E-553 — Trak'n — 1981 — $25

FIVE STAIRSTEPS, THE
BUDDAH
☐ BDS-5008 — Our Family Portrait — 1967 — $25
☐ BDS-5061 — Stairsteps — 1970 — $18
—As "Stairsteps
☐ BDS-5068 — Step by Step by Step — 1970 — $18
—As "Stairsteps
COLLECTABLES
☐ COL-5023 — Greatest Hits — 1985 — $12
CURTOM
☐ 8002 — Love's Happening — 1969 — $25
WINDY C
☐ 6000 [M] — The Five Stairsteps — 1967 — $30
☐ S-6000 [S] — The Five Stairsteps — 1967 — $30

FIVE STAR
EPIC
☐ E46768 — Five Star — 1990 — $15
RCA
☐ 6635-1-R — Between the Lines — 1987 — $12
☐ NFL1-8052 — Luxury of Life — 1985 — $12
—Original issue
☐ AFL1-9506 — Luxury of Life — 1986 — $10
—Reissue
☐ AFL1-5901 — Silk and Steel — 1986 — $12

FIXX, THE
IMPACT
☐ 10205 — Ink — 1991 — $15
MCA
☐ 42316 — Greatest Hits — 1989 — $18

☐ R153353 — Phantoms — 1984 — $12
—RCA Music Service edition
☐ 5507 — Phantoms — 1984 — $10
☐ L33-1213 [DJ] — Phantoms — 1984 — $15
—Advance version; no interviews
☐ L33-1212 [DJ] — Phantoms — 1984 — $18
—Promo sampler; contains three complete songs, "Are We Ourselves?", "Sunshine in the Shade" and "Less Cities, More Morving People," plus spoken introductions for all the songs on the album

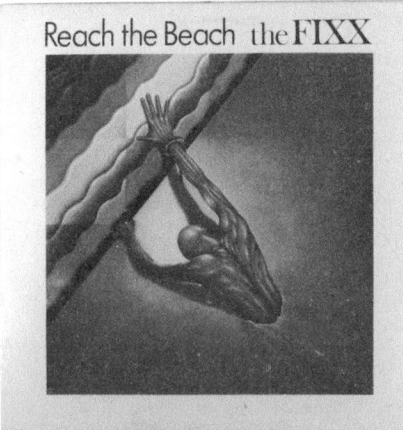

☐ 39001 [B] — Reach the Beach — 1983 — $15
—Original issue
☐ 5417 — Reach the Beach — 1983 — $10
—Reissue
☐ R164166 — React — 1987 — $12
—BMG Direct Marketing edition
☐ 42008 — React — 1987 — $12
☐ 5345 — Shuttered Room — 1982 — $12
☐ R164380 — Walkabout — 1986 — $12
—RCA Music Service edition
☐ 5705 — Walkabout — 1986 — $10
RCA
☐ 8566-1-R — Calm Animals — 1989 — $12

FLACK, ROBERTA, AND DONNY HATHAWAY
ATLANTIC
☐ SD7216 — Roberta Flack and Donny Hathaway — 1972 — $12

FLACK, ROBERTA
ATLANTIC
☐ SD19149 — Blue Lights in the Basement — 1977 — $12
☐ SD1569 — Chapter Two — 1970 — $12
☐ SD18131 — Feel Like Makin' Love — 1974 — $12
☐ SD8230 — First Take — 1969 — $12
—Red and green label (second edition)
☐ SW-94346 — First Take — 1972 — $18
—Capitol Record Club edition
☐ SD8230 — First Take — 1969 — $25
—Brown and purple label (first edition)
☐ SD19354 — I'm the One — 1982 — $12
☐ SD7271 — Killing Me Softly — 1973 — $12
☐ SD19154 — Killing Me Softly — 1978 — $10
—Reissue of 7271
☐ QD7271 [Q] — Killing Me Softly — 1973 — $30
☐ 81916 — Oasis — 1988 — $12
☐ SD1594 — Quiet Fire — 1971 — $12
☐ SD19186 — Roberta Flack — 1978 — $12
☐ SD16013 — Roberta Flack Featuring Donny Hathaway — 1980 — $12
—Only two tracks feature Mr. Hathaway
☐ SD19317 — The Best of Roberta Flack — 1981 — $12
MCA
☐ 5141 — Bustin' Loose — 1981 — $12

FLAGG, FANNIE
RCA VICTOR
☐ LPM-3856 [M] — Rally 'Round the Flagg — 1967 — $25
☐ LSP-3856 [S] — Rally 'Round the Flagg — 1967 — $18

FLAHIVE, LARRY
SEA BREEZE
☐ SB-2020 — Standard Flay — 1983 — $25

FLAIRS, THE (1)
CROWN
☐ CLP-5356 [M] — The Flairs — 1963 — $150

FLAME, THE
BROTHER
☐ BR-2500 — The Flame — 1970 — $30
—Deduct 1/3 if poster is missing

Number	Title	Yr	NM

FLAMIN' GROOVIES, THE

4 MEN WITH BEARDS

Number	Title	Yr	NM
❏ 4M537 [B]	Jumpin' In The Night	2014	$25
❏ 4M536 [B]	Now!	2013	$25
❏ 4M535 [B]	Shake Some Action	2013	$25

BUDDAH

| ❏ BDS-5683 | Shill Shakin' | 1977 | $18 |

EPIC

| ❏ BN26487 | Supersnazz | 1969 | $50 |

KAMA SUTRA

| ❏ KSBS-2021 [B] | Flamingo | 1970 | $40 |

—Pink label

| ❏ KSBS-2021 [B] | Flamingo | 1972 | $25 |

—Blue label

| ❏ KSBS-2031 [B] | Teenage Head | 1971 | $40 |

—Pink label

| ❏ KSBS-2031 [B] | Teenage Head | 1972 | $25 |

—Blue label

SIRE

❏ SRK6067	Jumpin' in the Night	1979	$15
❏ SASD-7521	Shake Some Action	1976	$18
❏ SRK6059	The Flamin' Groovies Now	1978	$18

—Originals have 12 tracks

| ❏ SRK6059 | The Flamin' Groovies Now | 1978 | $15 |

—Reissues have 14 tracks

SNAZZ

| ❏ R-2371 [10] | Sneekers | 1969 | $300 |

—Beware - this album has been counterfeited.

FLAMING EMBER, THE

HOT WAX

| ❏ HA-705 | Sunshine | 1971 | $18 |
| ❏ HA-702 | Westbound #9 | 1970 | $18 |

FLAMING LIPS, THE

ATAVISTIC

| ❏ ALP-04 [EP] | Unconsciously Screamin' | 1991 | $35 |

LOVELY SORTS OF DEATH

| ❏ 0(# unknown) [EP] | The Flaming Lips (Bag Full of Thoughts) | 1984 | $120 |

—Green vinyl; dark brown background on jacket

| ❏ 0(# unknown) [EP] | The Flaming Lips (Bag Full of Thoughts) | 1984 | $100 |

—Red vinyl; black background on jacket

PINK DUST

| ❏ 72173 | Hear It Is | 1986 | $40 |

—Originals on white vinyl

| ❏ 72188 [EP] | The Flaming Lips | 1985 | $40 |

—Originals on lavender vinyl; reissue of Lovely Sorts of Death EP

PLAIN

| ❏ 111 | Hear It Is | 2006 | $18 |

—Reissue on white vinyl

| ❏ 114 | In a Priest Driven Ambulance | 2006 | $18 |

—Reissue on pink vinyl

| ❏ 112 | Oh My Gawd!!!... The Flaming Lips | 2006 | $18 |

—Reissue on clear vinyl

| ❏ 113 | Telepathic Surgery | 2006 | $18 |

—Reissue on blue vinyl

RESTLESS

| ❏ 72359 | In a Priest Driven Ambulance | 1990 | $30 |

—Pink vinyl

| ❏ 72207 | Oh My Gawd, The Flaming Lips | 1987 | $40 |

—Clear vinyl

| ❏ 72350 | Telepathic Surgery | 1989 | $30 |

WARNER BROS.

| ❏ 542236-1 [B] | 7 Skies H3 | 2014 | $30 |
| ❏ 1-44250 | At War with the Mystics | 2006 | $30 |

—180-gram edition on black vinyl

| ❏ 1-49966 | At War with the Mystics | 2006 | $30 |

—150-gram edition; one record is on orange vinyl, the other is on turquoise vinyl

❏ 45911	Clouds Taste Metallic	1995	$18
❏ 45334	Transmissions from the Satellite Heart	1993	$25
❏ 48141	Yoshimi Battles the Pink Robots	2002	$25

FLAMING YOUTH

Phil Collins was in this group.

UNI

| ❏ 73075 [B] | Ark 2 | 1969 | $75 |

FLAMINGO, JOHNNY

DIADON

| ❏ 201 [M] | Johnny Flamingo Sings In the Wee Small Hours | 1961 | $150 |

FLAMINGOS, THE, AND THE MOONGLOWS

VEE JAY

Number	Title	Yr	NM
❏ LP-1052 [M]	The Flamingos Meet the Moonglows on the Dusty Road of Hits	1962	$175
❏ VJLP-1052 [M]	The Flamingos Meet the Moonglows on the Dusty Road of Hits	198?	$18

—Authorized reissue

FLAMINGOS, THE

CHECKER

| ❏ LP-1433 [M] | The Flamingos | 1959 | $400 |

—Black label

| ❏ LP-1433 [M] | The Flamingos | 196? | $175 |

—Blue label

| ❏ LPS-3005 [R] | The Flamingos | 1966 | $30 |

—Rechanneled reissue of 1433

CONSTELLATION

| ❏ CS-3 [M] | Collectors Showcase: The Flamingos | 1964 | $150 |

—With hot pink lettering on cover

| ❏ CS-3 [M] | Collectors Showcase: The Flamingos | 1964 | $50 |

—With more restrained pink lettering on cover

END

❏ LP-307 [M]	Flamingo Favorites	1960	$150
❏ LPS-307 [R]	Flamingo Favorites	1960	$80
❏ LP-304 [M]	Flamingo Serenade	1959	$250

—Gray label with dog

| ❏ LPS-304 [S] | Flamingo Serenade | 1959 | $500 |

—Cover says "Stereo"

| ❏ LPS-304 [S] | Flamingo Serenade | 196? | $250 |

—Cover says "Rechanneled Stereo" (only one track is)

| ❏ LP-304 [M] | Flamingo Serenade | 1959 | $400 |

—Black label with shadow print logo

❏ LP-308 [M]	Requestfully Yours	1960	$150
❏ LPS-308 [R]	Requestfully Yours	1960	$80
❏ LP-316 [M]	The Sound of the Flamingos	1962	$150
❏ LPS-316 [S]	The Sound of the Flamingos	1962	$250

—"Stereo" at upper right corner of front cover

| ❏ LPS-316 [R] | The Sound of the Flamingos | 1962 | $80 |

LOST-NITE

| ❏ LLP-7 [10] | The Flamingos | 1981 | $12 |

—Red vinyl

PHILIPS

| ❏ PHM200206 [M] | Their Hits -- Then and Now | 1966 | $30 |
| ❏ PHS600206 [S] | Their Hits -- Then and Now | 1966 | $30 |

RONZE

| ❏ RLP-1001 | The Flamingos Today | 1972 | $18 |

SOLID SMOKE

| ❏ 8018 | Golden Teardrops | 198? | $12 |

FLANAGAN, TOMMY, AND HANK JONES

GALAXY

| ❏ 5152 | More Delights | 1985 | $25 |
| ❏ 5113 | Our Delights | 1978 | $30 |

FLANAGAN, TOMMY

ENJA

| ❏ 4014 | Confirmation | 1982 | $30 |
| ❏ 4022 | Giant Steps | 1983 | $30 |

FANTASY

❏ OJC-372	Montreux '77	1989	$30
❏ OJC-473	Something Borrowed, Something Blue	1990	$30
❏ OJC-182	The Tommy Flanagan Trio	198?	$25

GALAXY

| ❏ 5110 | Something Borrowed, Something Blue | 1978 | $30 |

INNER CITY

Number	Title	Yr	NM
❏ IC-3029	Ballads and Blues	1979	$35
❏ IC-3009	Eclypso	1977	$35
❏ IC-1071	Tommy Flanagan Plays the Music of Harold Arlen	1980	$30
❏ IC-1084	Trinity	198?	$25

MOODSVILLE

| ❏ MVLP-9 [M] | The Tommy Flanagan Trio | 1960 | $50 |

—Green label

| ❏ MVLP-9 [M] | The Tommy Flanagan Trio | 1965 | $30 |

—Blue label, trident logo at right

NEW JAZZ

| ❏ 8217 [B] | The Cats | 1959 | $300 |

—purple label

ONYX

| ❏ 206 | The Tommy Flanagan Trio and Sextet | 197? | $35 |

PABLO

| ❏ 2405410 | The Best of Tommy Flanagan | 198? | $25 |
| ❏ 2310724 | Tokyo Recital | 1975 | $35 |

PABLO LIVE

| ❏ 2308202 | Montreux '77 | 1978 | $35 |

PRESTIGE

| ❏ PRLP-7134 [M] | Overseas | 1958 | $3500 |
| ❏ PRST-7632 | Overseas | 1969 | $35 |

REGENT

| ❏ MG-6055 [M] | Jazz... It's Magic | 1958 | $100 |

SAVOY JAZZ

| ❏ SJL-1158 | Jazz... It's Magic | 1986 | $25 |

STATIRAS

| ❏ SLP-8073 | The Magnificent | 1985 | $25 |

TIMELESS

| ❏ SJP-301 | Jazz Poet | 1990 | $30 |

FLANDERS, TOMMY

VERVE FORECAST

| ❏ FTS-3075 | Moonstone | 1969 | $25 |

FLANDERS AND SWANN

ANGEL

| ❏ 65042 [M] | At the Drop of a Hat | 1959 | $30 |

—Original issue

❏ 35797 [M]	At the Drop of a Hat	196?	$25
❏ S35797 [S]	At the Drop of a Hat	196?	$30
❏ 36388 [M]	At the Drop of Another Hat	1966	$25
❏ S36388 [S]	At the Drop of Another Hat	1966	$30
❏ 36112 [M]	The Bestiary of Flanders and Swann	196?	$25
❏ S36112 [S]	The Bestiary of Flanders and Swann	196?	$30

FLARES, THE

PRESS

| ❏ PR73001 [M] | Encore of Foot Stompin' Hits | 196? | $100 |
| ❏ PRS83001 [S] | Encore of Foot Stompin' Hits | 196? | $120 |

FLASH

Also see YES.

SOVEREIGN/CAPITOL

❏ SMAS-11040	Flash	1972	$15
❏ SMAS-11115	Flash in the Can	1972	$15
❏ SMAS-11218	Out of Our Hands	1973	$15

FLASH AND THE PAN

EPIC

❏ BFE39618	Early Morning Wake-Up Call	1984	$12
❏ JE36018	Flash And The Pan	1979	$12
❏ ARE37725	Headlines	1982	$15
❏ JE36432	Lights in the Night	1980	$12

FLASH CADILLAC AND THE CONTINENTAL KIDS

EPIC

| ❏ KE31787 | Flash Cadillac and the Continental Kids | 1972 | $18 |

—Yellow label

| ❏ KE31787 | Flash Cadillac and the Continental Kids | 1973 | $15 |

—Orange label

| ❏ KE32488 | There's No Face Like Chrome | 1974 | $15 |

PRIVATE STOCK

| ❏ PS2003 [B] | Sons of Beaches | 1975 | $18 |

FLAT EARTH SOCIETY, THE

FLEETWOOD

| ❏ 3027 | Waleeco | 1968 | $400 |

FLATT, LESTER, AND MAC WISEMAN

RCA VICTOR

| ❏ LSP-4547 | Lester 'n' Mac | 1971 | $25 |
| ❏ LSP-4688 | On the South Bound | 1972 | $25 |

Number	Title	Yr	NM

FLATT, LESTER

COLUMBIA
❏ CS1006	Flatt Out	1970	$25

NUGGET
❏ 104	The One and Only	1971	$25

RCA VICTOR
❏ APL1-0131	Country Boy	1973	$18
❏ LSP-4789	Foggy Mountain Breakdown	1972	$25
❏ LSP-4633	Kentucky Ridgerunner	1972	$25
❏ LSP-4495	Lester Flatt on Victor	1971	$25

FLATT AND SCRUGGS

COLUMBIA
❏ GP30	20 All-Time Great Recordings	1970	$25
❏ C32244	A Boy Named Sue	1973	$15
❏ C30347	Breaking Out	1971	$15
❏ CS9596 [S]	Changin' Times Featuring Foggy Mountain Breakdown	1968	$25

—Red "360 Sound" label
❏ CS9596	Changin' Times Featuring Foggy Mountain Breakdown	1970	$15

—Orange label with six "Columbia"s along edge
❏ CL2796 [M]	Changin' Times Featuring Foggy Mountain Breakdown	1968	$40
❏ CS9945	Final Fling	1970	$18
❏ CL2045 [M]	Flatt and Scruggs at Carnegie Hall	1963	$25
❏ CS8845 [S]	Flatt and Scruggs at Carnegie Hall	1963	$30
❏ PC8845	Flatt and Scruggs at Carnegie Hall	198?	$10

—Budget-line reissue
❏ CL2570 [M]	Flatt and Scruggs' Greatest Hits	1966	$18
❏ CS9370 [S]	Flatt and Scruggs' Greatest Hits	1966	$25
❏ PC9370	Flatt and Scruggs' Greatest Hits	198?	$10

—Budget-line reissue
❏ CL1564 [M]	Foggy Mountain Banjo	1961	$25
❏ CS8364 [S]	Foggy Mountain Banjo	1961	$30
❏ CL1019 [M]	Foggy Mountain Jamboree	1957	$50
❏ CL1830 [M]	Folk Songs of Our Land	1962	$25
❏ CS8630 [S]	Folk Songs of Our Land	1962	$30
❏ CL1951 [M]	Hard Travelin' Featuring The Ballad of Jed Clampett	1963	$25
❏ CS8751 [S]	Hard Travelin' Featuring The Ballad of Jed Clampett	1963	$30
❏ CL2686 [M]	Hear the Whistle Blow	1967	$25
❏ CS9486 [S]	Hear the Whistle Blow	1967	$25
❏ FC37469	Lester Flatt & Earl Scruggs	1981	$12
❏ CS9741	Nashville Airplane	1969	$25
❏ CL2354 [M]	Pickin' Strummin' and Singin'	1965	$18
❏ CS9154 [S]	Pickin' Strummin' and Singin'	1965	$25
❏ CL2134 [M]	Recorded Live at Vanderbilt University	1964	$25
❏ CS8934 [S]	Recorded Live at Vanderbilt University	1964	$30
❏ CL1424 [M]	Songs of Glory	1960	$25
❏ CS8221 [S]	Songs of Glory	1960	$30
❏ CL1664 [M]	Songs of the Famous Carter Family	1961	$25
❏ CS8464 [S]	Songs of the Famous Carter Family	1961	$30
❏ CL2643 [M]	Strictly Instrumental	1967	$25
❏ CS9443 [S]	Strictly Instrumental	1967	$25
❏ CL2255 [M]	The Fabulous Sound of Flatt & Scruggs	1964	$25
❏ CS9055 [S]	The Fabulous Sound of Flatt & Scruggs	1964	$30
❏ CS9649 [S]	The Story of Bonnie & Clyde	1968	$25
❏ CS9649 [M]	The Story of Bonnie & Clyde	1968	$40

—White label promo with "Special Mono Radio Station Copy" sticker and timing strip on front cover
❏ CG31964	The World of Flatt and Scruggs	1972	$18
❏ CL2443 [M]	Town and Country	1966	$18
❏ CS9243 [S]	Town and Country	1966	$25
❏ CL2513 [M]	When the Saints Go Marching In	1966	$18
❏ CS9313 [S]	When the Saints Go Marching In	1966	$25

COLUMBIA LIMITED EDITION
❏ LE10149	Breaking Out	197?	$12

COLUMBIA MUSICAL TREASURY
❏ DS493	Detroit City	1969	$18

COUNTY
❏ CCS-111	You Can Feel It in Your Soul	1988	$12

EVEREST ARCHIVE OF FOLK & JAZZ
❏ 259	Lester Flatt & Earl Scruggs	197?	$12

HARMONY
❏ HS11401	Foggy Mountain Chimes	1970	$15
❏ HL7340 [M]	Great Original Recordings	1965	$18
❏ HL7250 [M]	Lester Flatt & Earl Scruggs	1960	$18
❏ HL7402 [M]	Sacred Songs	1967	$18
❏ HS11202 [S]	Sacred Songs	1967	$15
❏ HL7465 [M]	Songs to Cherish	1968	$18
❏ HS11265 [S]	Songs to Cherish	1968	$15
❏ H30932	Wabash Cannonball	197?	$12

MERCURY
❏ MG-20358 [M]	Country Music	1958	$40
❏ MG-20542 [M]	Lester Flatt & Earl Scruggs	1959	$40
❏ SR-61162	Original Theme from Bonnie & Clyde	1968	$25
❏ MG-20773 [M]	The Original Sound of Flatt & Scruggs	1963	$30
❏ SR-60773 [R]	The Original Sound of Flatt & Scruggs	1963	$18

NASHVILLE
❏ 2087	The Best of Flatt and Scruggs	1970	$15

PICKWICK
❏ 6140	Blue Grass Banjos	197?	$12
❏ 6093	Foggy Mountain Breakdown	197?	$15

POWER PAK
❏ 297	Golden Hits	197?	$12

ROUNDER
❏ SS-08	Don't Get Above Your Raisin'	198?	$12
❏ SS-05	The Golden Era	198?	$12
❏ SS-18	The Mercury Sessions, Volume 1	1985	$12
❏ SS-19	The Mercury Sessions, Volume 2	1985	$12

STARDAY
❏ SLP-365 [M]	Stars of the Grand Ol' Opry	1966	$30

—With Jim and Jesse

WING
❏ SRW-16376	The Original Foggy Mountain Breakdown	1968	$15

FLAVOR

JU-PAR
❏ JP6-1002S1	In Good Taste	1976	$25

FLEETWOOD, MICK

RCA VICTOR
❏ AFL1-4652	I'm Not Me	1983	$10
❏ AFL1-4080	The Visitor	1981	$10
❏ DJL1-4106 [EP]	The Visitor	1981	$10

—Four-song promo sampler from LP

FLEETWOOD MAC
Also see LINDSEY BUCKINGHAM; BUCKINGHAM NICKS; BILLY BURNETTE; MICK FLEETWOOD; DANNY KIRWAN; DAVE MASON; CHRISTINE McVIE; STEVIE NICKS; JEREMY SPENCER; BOB WELCH.

BLUE HORIZON
❏ BH-4802	Blues Jam in Chicago, Vol. 1	1970	$18
❏ BH-4803	Blues Jam in Chicago, Vol. 2	1970	$18
❏ BH-3801	Fleetwood Mac in Chicago	1970	$30

EPIC
❏ KE30632	Black Magic Woman	1971	$25
❏ LN24446 [M]	English Rose	1969	$150

—White label promo only
❏ BN26446 [S]	English Rose	1969	$30
❏ LN24402 [M]	Fleetwood Mac	1968	$250

—White label promo only
❏ BN26402 [S]	Fleetwood Mac	1968	$30
❏ KE33740	Fleetwood Mac/English Rose	1974	$18

MOBILE FIDELITY
❏ Jan-0012 [B]	Fleetwood Mac	1980	$85

—Audiophile vinyl
❏ 1-119 [B]	Mirage	1984	$50

—Audiophile vinyl

NAUTILUS
❏ NR-8 [B]	Rumours	1980	$75

—Audiophile vinyl

REPRISE
❏ MS2080	Bare Trees	1972	$15

—With brown line near all four edges of the front cover
❏ MSK2278	Bare Trees	1977	$10

—Reissue; no brown line on the front cover
❏ MS2080	Bare Trees	197?	$18

—Without brown line on front cover; uncommon with the MS 2080 number
❏ MS2225	Fleetwood Mac	1975	$12
❏ MSK2281	Fleetwood Mac	1977	$10
❏ RS6465	Future Games	1971	$30

—Originals have a pale yellow cover
❏ RS6465	Future Games	1972	$18

—Later pressings have a pale green cover
❏ R16465 [B]	Future Games	2015	$20
❏ MS2196	Heroes Are Hard to Find	1974	$15
❏ RS6408	Kiln House	1970	$18
❏ MS2158	Mystery to Me	1973	$25

—With "Good Things (Come to Those Who Wait)" listed on the album cover; it was replaced at the last minute by "For Your Love"
❏ MS2158	Mystery to Me	1973	$15

—With "For Your Love" listed correctly on the back cover
❏ MSK2279	Mystery to Me	1977	$10

❏ MS2138 [B]	Penguin	1973	$18
❏ RS6368	Then Play On	1969	$30

—First pressings include "When You Say" and "My Dream"
❏ RS6368	Then Play On	1970	$18

—Later pressings replace above two tracks with "Oh Well (Parts 1 and 2).

SIRE
❏ SASH-3715	Fleetwood Mac in Chicago	1975	$18

—Reissue of Blue Horizon 3801
❏ 2XS-6009	Fleetwood Mac in Chicago	1977	$15
❏ 2XS-6045	The Original Fleetwood Mac	1977	$15
❏ SASH-3706	Vintage Years	1975	$18
❏ 2XS-6006	Vintage Years	1977	$15

VARRICK
❏ VR-020	Jumping at Shadows	1985	$15

WARNER BROS.
❏ 26111	Behind the Mask	1990	$18
❏ 2WB3500	Fleetwood Mac Live	1980	$15
❏ R125801 [B]	Greatest Hits	2014	$25
❏ 25801	Greatest Hits	1989	$12
❏ R1553403 [B]	In Concert	2016	$50
❏ 23607 [DJ]	Mirage	1982	$40

—Promo on Quiex II vinyl
❏ 23607	Mirage	1982	$12
❏ BSK3010	Rumours	1977	$12

—With short version (2:02) of "Never Going Back Again"; we do not yet know how to identify these without playing them
❏ BSK3010	Rumours	1977	$10

—With long version (2:16) of "Never Going Back Again"; we do not yet know how to identify these without playing them
❏ BSK3010	Rumours	1979	$10

—White label reissue
❏ 25471	Tango in the Night	1987	$12
❏ 2HS3350	Tusk	1979	$18
❏ PRO-A-866 [DJ]	Tusk Remix	1979	$25

—Promo-only EP

FLEETWOODS, THE

DOLTON
❏ BLP-2030 [M]	Before and After	1965	$75
❏ BST-8030 [S]	Before and After	1965	$40
❏ BLP-2007 [M]	Deep in a Dream	1961	$100

—Pale blue label with dolphins on top
❏ BST-8007 [S]	Deep in a Dream	1961	$50

—Pale blue label with dolphins on top
❏ BLP-2007 [M]	Deep in a Dream	1963	$50

—Dark label, logo on left
❏ BST-8007 [S]	Deep in a Dream	1963	$30

—Dark label, logo on left
❏ BLP-2039 [M]	Folk Rock	1965	$75
❏ BST-8039 [S]	Folk Rock	1965	$40
❏ BLP-2025 [M]	Goodnight My Love	1963	$75
❏ BST-8025 [S]	Goodnight My Love	1963	$40
❏ BLP-2001 [M]	Mr. Blue	1959	$175

—Pale blue label with dolphins on top
❏ BST-8001 [S]	Mr. Blue	1959	$150

—Pale blue label with dolphins on top
❏ BLP-2001 [M]	Mr. Blue	1963	$75

—Dark label, logo on left
❏ BST-8001 [S]	Mr. Blue	1963	$30

—Dark label, logo on left
❏ BLP-2005 [M]	Softly	1961	$150

—Pale blue label with dolphins on top
❏ BST-8005 [S]	Softly	1961	$80

—Pale blue label with dolphins on top
❏ BLP-2005 [M]	Softly	1963	$75

—Dark label, logo on left
❏ BST-8005 [S]	Softly	1963	$30

—Dark label, logo on left
❏ BLP-2011 [M]	The Best of the Oldies	1962	$100

—Pale blue label with dolphins on top
❏ BST-8011 [S]	The Best of the Oldies	1962	$50

Number	Title	Yr	NM
—Pale blue label with dolphins on top			
☐ BLP-2011 [M]	The Best of the Oldies	1963	$50
—Dark label, logo on left			
☐ BST-8011 [S]	The Best of the Oldies	1963	$30
—Dark label, logo on left			
☐ BLP-2002 [M]	The Fleetwoods	1960	$150
—Pale blue label with dolphins on top			
☐ BST-8002 [S]	The Fleetwoods	1960	$80
—Pale blue label with dolphins on top			
☐ BLP-2002 [M]	The Fleetwoods	1963	$50
—Dark label, logo on left			
☐ BST-8002 [S]	The Fleetwoods	1963	$30
—Dark label, logo on left			
☐ BLP-2018 [M]	The Fleetwoods' Greatest Hits	1962	$75
☐ BST-8018 [S]	The Fleetwoods' Greatest Hits	1962	$30
☐ BLP-2020 [M]	The Fleetwoods Sings for Lovers by Night	1963	$75
☐ BST-8020 [S]	The Fleetwoods Sings for Lovers by Night	1963	$40
LIBERTY			
☐ LN-10199	Buried Treasure	1983	$10
☐ LN-10160	The Best Goodies of the Oldies	1982	$10
☐ LN-10159	The Fleetwoods' Greatest Hits	1982	$10
SUNSET			
☐ SUM-1131 [M]	In a Mellow Mood	1966	$15
☐ SUS-5131 [S]	In a Mellow Mood	1966	$18
UNITED ARTISTS			
☐ UA-LA334-E	The Very Best of the Fleetwoods	1975	$15

FLEMING, KING

ARGO

Number	Title	Yr	NM
☐ LP-4004 [M]	Misty Night	1961	$30
☐ LPS-4004 [S]	Misty Night	1961	$30
☐ LP-4019 [M]	Stand By!	1962	$30
☐ LPS-4019 [S]	Stand By!	1962	$30
CADET			
☐ LP-4053 [M]	Weary Traveler	1966	$35
☐ LPS-4053 [S]	Weary Traveler	1966	$25

FLEMING, RHONDA

COLUMBIA

Number	Title	Yr	NM
☐ CL1080 [M]	Rhonda	1958	$75

FLEMONS, WADE

VEE JAY

Number	Title	Yr	NM
☐ LP-1011 [M]	Wade Flemons	1959	$175
—Maroon label			
☐ LP-1011 [M]	Wade Flemons	196?	$100
—Black label			

FLESH FOR LULU

CAPITOL

Number	Title	Yr	NM
☐ SPRO79992/3 [DJ]	Final Vinyl (And Live Flesh)	1990	$25
—Red vinyl; sticker on generic cover			
☐ CLT-48217	Long Live the New Flesh	1987	$15
☐ C1-90232	Plastic Fantastic	1989	$15

FLESHEATERS

HOMESTEAD

Number	Title	Yr	NM
☐ 124-1	Live	1988	$12
☐ 0(# unknown)	Prehistoric Hits Vol. 1	198?	$15
RUBY			
☐ JRR-101	A Minute to Pray, a Second to Die	1981	$25
☐ JRR805	Forever Came Today	1982	$25
SST			
☐ 094	Destroyed by Fire/Greatest Hits	1991	$12
—Reissue with new name			
☐ 273	Dragstrip Riot	1991	$15
☐ 094	Greatest Hits	1986	$15
☐ 264	Prehistoric Fits	1990	$15
UPSETTER			
☐ UP56	A Hard Road to Follow	1983	$30
☐ UPCJ-34	No Questions Asked	1980	$40

FLETCHER, SAM

VAULT

Number	Title	Yr	NM
☐ LP-116 [M]	The Look of Love, the Sound of Soul	1967	$30
☐ VS-116 [S]	The Look of Love, the Sound of Soul	1967	$30
VEE JAY			
☐ LP-1094 [M]	Sam Fletcher Sings	1964	$40

FLINT, SHELBY

MAD SATYR

Number	Title	Yr	NM
☐ MSR-101	You've Been On My Mind	1982	$75

Number	Title	Yr	NM
VALIANT			
☐ VL-5003 [M]	Cast Your Fate to the Wind	1966	$30
☐ VLS-25003 [S]	Cast Your Fate to the Wind	1966	$30
☐ LP-403 [M]	Shelby Flint Sings Folk	1962	$50
☐ LPS-403 [S]	Shelby Flint Sings Folk	1962	$50
☐ LP-401 [M]	Shelby Flint – The Quiet Girl	1961	$50

FLIPPER

4 MEN WITH BEARDS

Number	Title	Yr	NM
☐ 4M513LP [B]	Generic Flipper		$25
☐ 4M514LP [B]	Gone Fishin'		$25
☐ 4M515LP [B]	Public Flipper Limited: Live 1980-1985		$30
☐ 4M516LP [B]	Sex Bomb Baby!		$25
SUBTERRANEAN			
☐ SUB25 [B]	Generic Flipper	1981	$35
☐ SUB42 [B]	Gone Fishin'	1982	$35

Number	Title	Yr	NM
☐ SUB53 [B]	Public Flipper Ltd.	1985	$35

FLIRTATIONS, THE (1)

DERAM

Number	Title	Yr	NM
☐ DES-18028	Nothing But a Heartache	1969	$25

FLIRTS, THE

CBS ASSOCIATED

Number	Title	Yr	NM
☐ BFZ40197	Blondes, Brunettes and Redheads	1985	$12
☐ BFZ40419	Questions of the Heart	1986	$12
O			
☐ 1	10 Cents a Dance	1982	$18
PREPPY			
☐ 1217 [EP]	Heartbreak USA	1984	$15
TELEFON			
☐ 8001	Made in America	1984	$15

FLO AND EDDIE

Also see THE TURTLES.

COLUMBIA

Number	Title	Yr	NM
☐ PC33554 [B]	Illegal, Immoral and Fattening	1975	$18
☐ PC34262 [B]	Moving Targets	1976	$18
EPIPHANY			
☐ ELP-4010 [B]	Rock Steady with Flo & Eddie	1981	$30
REPRISE			
☐ MS2141 [B]	Flo and Eddie	1973	$30
☐ MS2099 [B]	The Phlorescent Leech and Eddie	1972	$30
RHINO			
☐ RNTA-1999 [B]	History of Flo & Eddie	198?	$40

FLOATERS, THE

ABC

Number	Title	Yr	NM
☐ AB-1030	Floaters	1977	$12
☐ AA-1047	Magic	1978	$12
FEE			
☐ WW-711	Get Ready for the Floaters and Shu-Ga	1981	$30
MCA			
☐ 3093	Into the Future	1979	$12

FLOATING BRIDGE, THE

VAULT

Number	Title	Yr	NM
☐ VS-124	The Floating Bridge	1969	$150

FLOCK, THE

COLUMBIA

Number	Title	Yr	NM
☐ C30007	Dinosaur Swamps	1970	$25
—360 Sound" label			
☐ C30007	Dinosaur Swamps	1970	$18
—Orange label			

Number	Title	Yr	NM
☐ CS9911	The Flock	1969	$25
—360 Sound" label			
☐ CS9911	The Flock	1970	$18
—Orange label			
MERCURY			
☐ SRM-1-1035	Inside Out	1975	$18

FLOCK OF SEAGULLS, A

JIVE

Number	Title	Yr	NM
☐ 1009-1-J	A Dream Come True	1986	$10
—Reissue			
☐ JL8-8411	A Dream Come True	1986	$12
☐ VA66000	A Flock of Seagulls	1982	$15
—Original issue			
☐ 1007-1-J	A Flock of Seagulls	1986	$10
—Reissue			
☐ VA33003	A Flock of Seagulls	1983	$12
—Second edition			
☐ JL8-8013	Listen	1983	$12
—Early reissue of 33004			
☐ 1008-1-J	Listen	1986	$10
—Reissue			
☐ VA33004	Listen	1983	$18
—Original issue			
☐ 1034-1-J	The Best of A Flock of Seagulls	1987	$15
☐ JL8-8250	The Story of a Young Heart	1984	$12

FLORA, JIM

RCA VICTOR

Number	Title	Yr	NM
☐ LPM1063 [B]	Mambo for Cats	1955	$175

— nominally a various artists collection of Latin-style standards, the album's value is attreibyted to the cover art by Jim Flora, hence its listing under the artist's name, not "various artists." Perez Prado and his Orchestra, Noro Morales and his Orchestra, the Tony Martinez Quintet and the Al Romero Quintet are among the performers.

FLORENCE, BOB

CARLTON

Number	Title	Yr	NM
☐ LP 12-115 [M]	Name Band: 1959	1959	$40
☐ STLP 12-115 [S]	Name Band: 1959	1959	$75
DISCOVERY			
☐ DS-832	Westlake	1982	$25
ERA			
☐ EL-20003 [M]	Bob Florence and Trio	1956	$150
TREND			
☐ TR-523	Live at Concerts by the Sea	1980	$25
☐ TR-536	Magic Time	1984	$25
☐ TR-545	Trash Can City	1987	$25
WORLD PACIFIC			
☐ WPS-21860 [S]	Pet Project: The Bob Florence Big Band Plays Petula Clark Hits	196?	$150
☐ WP-1860 [M]	Pet Project: The Bob Florence Big Band Plays Petula Clark Hits	196?	$150

FLORE S, CHUCK

CONCORD JAZZ

Number	Title	Yr	NM
☐ CJ-49	Drum Flower	1978	$30
DONRE			
☐ 1001	Flores Azules	1976	$30

FLORES, ROSIE

REPRISE

Number	Title	Yr	NM
☐ 25626	Rosie Flores	1987	$10

FLORY, MED

JOSIE

Number	Title	Yr	NM
☐ JOZ-3506 [M]	Med Flory Big Band	1963	$30
☐ JJS-3506 [S]	Med Flory Big Band	1963	$25
JUBILEE			
☐ JLP-1066 [M]	Jazzwave	1958	$50
☐ SDJLP-1066 [S]	Jazzwave	1959	$40

FLOW

CTI

Number	Title	Yr	NM
☐ 1003 [B]	Flow	1970	$30

FLOWERS, PHIL

GUEST STAR

Number	Title	Yr	NM
☐ G-1456 [M]	I Am the Greatest	1964	$30
☐ GS-1456 [S]	I Am the Greatest	1964	$40
☐ G-1457 [M]	Phil Flowers Sings a Tribute	1964	$30
☐ GS-1457 [S]	Phil Flowers Sings a Tribute	1964	$40
MOUNT VERNON			
☐ 154 [M]	Rhythm and Blues	196?	$30

FLOYD, EDDIE

MALACO

Number	Title	Yr	NM
☐ 6352	Experience	1977	$15

Number	Title	Yr	NM

STAX

Number	Title	Yr	NM
❑ STS-3016	Baby Lay Your Head Down	1973	$30
❑ STS-2029	California Girl	1970	$30
❑ STX-4122	Chronicle	1979	$15
❑ STS-2041 [B]	Down to Earth	1971	$30
❑ STS-2002	I've Never Found a Girl	1968	$30
❑ 714 [M]	Knock on Wood	1967	$150
❑ ST714 [S]	Knock on Wood	1967	$80
❑ STS-2011	Rare Stamps	1969	$30
❑ STS-5512	Soul Street	1974	$30
❑ MPS-8527	Soul Street	198?	$12
❑ STS-2017	You've Got to Have Eddie	1969	$30

FLOYD, KING

CHIMNEYVILLE

❑ SD9047	King Floyd	1971	$18

PULSAR

❑ 10602	A Man in Love	1969	$25

V.I.P.

❑ 407	The Heart of the Matter	1970	$40

FLYING BURRITO BROTHERS, THE

4 MEN WITH BEARDS

❑ 4M153LP [B]	Burrito Deluxe		$25
❑ 4M135LP [B]	The Gilded Palace of Sin		$25

A&M

❑ SP-4258	Burrito Deluxe	1970	$18
—Brown label			
❑ SP-4258	Burrito Deluxe	1974	$15
—Silvery label			
❑ SP-3631 [B]	Close Up the Honky-Tonks	1974	$30
❑ SP-6510	Close Up the Honky-Tonks	198?	$15
—Reissue of 3631			
❑ SP-8070 [DJ]	Hot Burrito	1975	$40
—Promo-only issue with poster			
❑ SP-4343	Last of the Red Hot Burritos	1972	$18
—Brown label			
❑ SP-4343	Last of the Red Hot Burritos	1974	$15
—Silvery label			
❑ SP-4578	Sleepless Nights	1976	$15
—As "Gram Parsons/The Flying Burrito Bros.			
❑ SP-4295	The Flying Burrito Bros.	1971	$18
—Brown label			
❑ SP-4295	The Flying Burrito Bros.	1974	$15
—Silvery label			
❑ SP-4175	The Gilded Palace of Sin	1969	$25
—Brown label			
❑ SP-4175	The Gilded Palace of Sin	1974	$15
—Silvery label			
❑ SP-3122	The Gilded Palace of Sin	198?	$10
—Budget-line reissue			

COLUMBIA

❑ PC34222	Airborne	1976	$15
❑ PC33817	Flying Again	1975	$15

CURB

❑ JZ37004	Hearts on the Line	1981	$12
—As "Burrito Brothers			
❑ FZ37705	Sunset Sundown	1982	$12
—As "Burrito Brothers			

REGENCY

❑ REG-79001	Live from Tokyo	1980	$12

FLYING ISLAND

VANGUARD

❑ VSD-79368	Another Kind of Space	197?	$35
❑ VSD-79359	Flying Island	197?	$35

FLYING LIZARDS, THE

VIRGIN

❑ VA13137	The Flying Lizards	1980	$15

FLYING MACHINE, THE

JANUS

❑ JLS-3007	The Flying Machine	1969	$25

FOCUS

ATCO

❑ SD 36-100	Hamburger Concerto	1974	$15
❑ SD 36-117	Mother Focus	1975	$15

HARVEST

❑ ST-11721	Focus Con Proby	1978	$15
—With P.J. Proby			

MERCURY

❑ 824524-1	Focus: Jan Akkerman and Thijs Van Leer	1986	$15

SIRE

❑ SASD-7505	Dutch Masters -- A Selection of Their Finest Recordings 1969-1973	1975	$15
❑ SAS-3901	Focus 3	1973	$18
❑ SES-97027	In and Out of Focus	1970	$25
—Original issue			
❑ SAS-7404	In and Out of Focus	1973	$15

—Reissue of 97027			
❑ SAS-7408	Live at the Rainbow	1973	$15
❑ SAS-7401	Moving Waves	1972	$15
❑ SASD-7531	Ship of Memories	1977	$15

FOGEL, MARTY

CMP

❑ CMP-37-ST	Many Bobbing Heads, At Last	1990	$30

FOGELBERG, DAN, AND TIM WEISBERG

FULL MOON/EPIC

❑ JE35339	Twin Sons of Different Mothers	1978	$12
❑ PE35339	Twin Sons of Different Mothers	198?	$10
—Budget-line reissue			
❑ HE45339	Twin Sons of Different Mothers	198?	$30
—Half-speed mastered edition			

FOGELBERG, DAN

COLUMBIA

❑ KC31751	Home Free	1972	$15
❑ PC31751	Home Free	197?	$10
—Reissue with new prefix			

FULL MOON/EPIC

❑ PE33499	Captured Angel	1975	$12
—No bar code on cover			
❑ PE33499	Captured Angel	198?	$10
—With bar code on cover			
❑ PEQ33499 [Q]	Captured Angel	1975	$30
❑ QE38308	Dan Fogelberg/Greatest Hits	1982	$12
❑ HE48308	Dan Fogelberg/Greatest Hits	1983	$30
—Half-speed mastered edition			
❑ OE40271	Exiles	1987	$12
❑ FE39616	High Country Snows	1985	$12
❑ A2S1335 [DJ]	Interchords	1982	$30
—Promo-only release			
❑ PE34185	Nether Lands	1977	$12
—No bar code on cover			
❑ PE34185	Nether Lands	198?	$10
—With bar code on cover			
❑ FE35634	Phoenix	1979	$12
❑ HE45634	Phoenix	1981	$30
—Half-speed mastered edition			
❑ PE35364	Phoenix	198?	$10
—Budget-line reissue			
❑ KE33137	Souvenirs	1974	$15
—First pressings have orange Epic label with small Full Moon logo			
❑ KE33137	Souvenirs	1975	$12
—Second pressings have dark blue/black Full Moon label			
❑ PE33137	Souvenirs	197?	$10
—Reissue with new prefix			
❑ KE237393	The Innocent Age	1981	$15
❑ AS1284 [DJ]	The Innocent Age Sampler	1982	$15
—Promo only; 6 songs			
❑ QE39004	Windows and Walls	1984	$12

FOGERTY, JOHN
Includes records as "The Blue Ridge Rangers." Also see CREEDENCE CLEARWATER REVIVAL; TOMMY FOGERTY AND THE BLUE VELVETS; THE GOLLIWOGS.

ASYLUM

❑ 7E-1081	Hoodoo	1976	$0
—Canceled; poor quality bootleg cassettes exist			
❑ 7E-1046	John Fogerty	1975	$15

FANTASY

❑ MPF-4502	John Fogerty: The Blue Ridge Rangers	1981	$12
—Reissues prominently place John Fogerty's name on the cover			
❑ FLP-30523	Revival	2007	$18
❑ F-9415	The Blue Ridge Rangers	1973	$18
—As "The Blue Ridge Rangers			

WARNER BROS.

❑ 25203	Centerfield	1985	$18
—Originals have the last song on side 2 as "Zanz Kant Danz			
❑ 25203	Centerfield	1986	$12
—Later editions have the last song on side 2 re-recorded and listed as "Vanz Kant Danz			
❑ 25203 [DJ]	Centerfield	1985	$30
—Promo versions on Quiex II audiophile vinyl			
❑ 25449	Eye of the Zombie	1986	$12

FOGERTY, TOM
Also see CREEDENCE CLEARWATER REVIVAL; TOMMY FOGERTY AND THE BLUE VELVETS; THE GOLLIWOGS.

FANTASY

❑ 9611	Deal It Out	1981	$12
❑ 9413	Excalibur	1972	$18
❑ 9469	Myopia	1974	$15
❑ 9407	Tom Fogerty	1972	$18
❑ 9448	Zephyr National	1974	$15

FOGHAT
Also see SAVOY BROWN.

BEARSVILLE

❑ BHS6990	Boogie Motel	1979	$12
❑ BR6950	Energized	1974	$12
❑ BR2077	Foghat	1972	$15
❑ BR2136	Foghat	1973	$15
❑ BRK6971	Foghat Live	1977	$12
❑ BR6959	Fool for the City	1975	$12
❑ BRK6980	Fool for the City	1978	$10
—Reissue of 6959			
❑ BRK3578	Girls to Chat & Boys to Bounce	1981	$12
❑ 23747	In the Mood for Something Rude	1982	$12
❑ BR6962	Night Shift	1976	$12
❑ BR6956	Rock and Roll Outlaws	1974	$12
❑ BRK6977	Stone Blue	1978	$12
❑ BHS6999	Tight Shoes	1980	$12
❑ 23888	Zig-Zag Walk	1983	$12

RHINO

❑ RNLP-70883	Energized	1988	$10
—Reissue of Bearsville 6950			
❑ RNLP-70887	Foghat	1988	$10
—Reissue of Bearsville 2077			
❑ R1-70890	Foghat	1988	$10
—Reissue of Bearsville 2136			
❑ RNLP-70884	Foghat Live	1988	$10
—Reissue of Bearsville 6971			
❑ RNLP-70882	Fool for the City	1987	$10
—Reissue of Bearsville 6980			
❑ RNLP-70888	Night Shift	1988	$10
—Reissue of Bearsville 6962			
❑ R1-70889	Rock and Roll Outlaws	1988	$10
—Reissue of Bearsville 6956			
❑ RNLP-70881	Stone Blue	1987	$10
—Reissue of Bearsville 6977			
❑ R1-70088	The Best of Foghat	1989	$12

TPM/RHINO EXCLUSIVE

❑ 295	Fool for the City	2008	$25

FOL, RAYMOND

PHILIPS

❑ PHM200198 [M]	Vivaldi's Four Seasons in Jazz	1966	$30
❑ PHS600198 [S]	Vivaldi's Four Seasons in Jazz	1966	$35

FOLDS, BEN, F IVE

Includes Ben Folds solo.

550 MUSIC

❑ B68809	Fear of Pop Volume 1	1998	$18
—By Ben Folds with numerous guests			
❑ B69808	The Unauthorized Biography of Reinhold Messner	1999	$18
❑ B67762	Whatever and Ever, Amen	1997	$40

EPIC

❑ E261610	Rockin' the Suburbs	2001	$30

SUNDAZED

❑ LP5164	Ben Folds Live	2003	$25

FOLEY, ELLEN

EPIC

❑ BFE38459	Another Breath	1983	$12
❑ JE36052 [B]	Nightout	1979	$20
—features Mick Ronson, Ian Hunter			
❑ NJE36974	Spirit of St. Louis	1981	$12

FOLEY, GEORGE

STOMP OFF

❑ SOS-1085	I Like It	1985	$25
❑ SOS-1187	Smiles and Kisses	1991	$30

FOLEY, LORD ADRIAN

MGM

❑ E-3358 [M]	Lord Adrian Foley at the Piano	1955	$40

FOLEY, RED

DECCA

❑ DL8296 [M]	Beyond the Sunset	1956	$50
❑ DL4140 [M]	Company's Comin'	1961	$25
❑ DL74140 [S]	Company's Comin'	1961	$30
❑ DL4290 [M]	Dear Hearts and Gentle People	1962	$25
❑ DL74290 [S]	Dear Hearts and Gentle People	1962	$30
❑ DL38068 [M]	Gratefully	1958	$150
—Special-products issue for Dickies clothing			
❑ DL8767 [M]	He Walks with Thee	1958	$50
❑ DL8903 [M]	Let's All Sing to Him	1959	$40
❑ DL78903 [S]	Let's All Sing to Him	1959	$50
❑ DL8847 [M]	Let's All Sing with Red Foley	1959	$40
❑ DL78847 [S]	Let's All Sing with Red Foley	1959	$50
❑ DL5338 [10]	Lift Up Your Voice	1952	$100
❑ DL8806 [M]	My Keepsake Album	1958	$50
❑ DL4107 [M]	Red Foley's Golden Favorites	1961	$25

Number	Title	Yr	NM

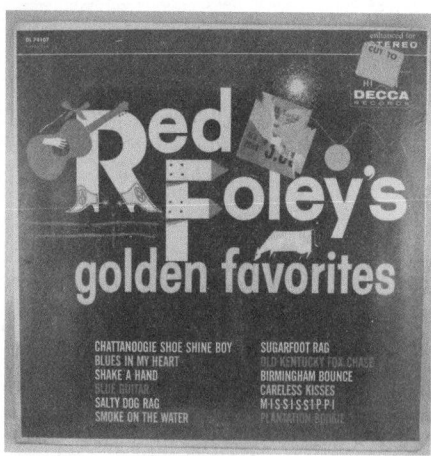

❏ DL74107 [S]	Red Foley's Golden Favorites	1961	$30
❏ DL5003 [M]	Red Foley's Greatest Hits	1968	$50
—White label promo; mono copies may only exist as promos			
❏ DL75003 [S]	Red Foley's Greatest Hits	1968	$18
❏ DL5303 [10]	Red Foley Souvenir Album	1951	$100
❏ DL8294 [M]	Red Foley Souvenir Album	1956	$50
❏ DL4603 [M]	Songs Everybody Knows	1965	$25
❏ DL74603 [S]	Songs Everybody Knows	1965	$30
❏ DL4849 [M]	Songs for the Soul	1967	$30
❏ DL74849 [S]	Songs for the Soul	1967	$25
❏ DL4198 [M]	Songs of Devotion	1961	$25
❏ DL74198 [S]	Songs of Devotion	1961	$30
❏ DL4341 [M]	The Red Foley Show	1963	$25
❏ DL74341 [S]	The Red Foley Show	1963	$30
❏ DXB177 [M]	The Red Foley Story	1964	$30
❏ DXSB7177 [S]	The Red Foley Story	1964	$30

FOLK IMPLOSION, THE
COMMUNION

| ❏ COMM45 | Dare to Be Surprised | 1997 | $12 |
| ❏ COMM32 | Take a Look Inside... | 1994 | $12 |

FOLK SINGERS, THE
ELEKTRA

| ❏ EKL-157 [M] | The Folk Singers | 1958 | $30 |

FOLKNIKS, THE
HIFI-LIFE SERIES

| ❏ L-1017 [M] | The Sound of Twelve-String Guitar and Banjo | 1964 | $25 |
| ❏ SL-1017 [S] | The Sound of Twelve-String Guitar and Banjo | 1964 | $30 |

FOLKSWINGERS, THE
WORLD PACIFIC

❏ WP-1812 [M]	12 String Guitar!	1963	$30
❏ ST-1812 [S]	12 String Guitar!	1963	$30
—Black vinyl			
❏ ST-1812 [S]	12 String Guitar!	1963	$75
—Red vinyl			
❏ WP-1814 [M]	12 String Guitar, Volume 2	1963	$30
❏ ST-1814 [S]	12 String Guitar, Volume 2	1963	$30
❏ WP-1846 [M]	Raga Rock	1966	$85
❏ ST-1846 [S]	Raga Rock	1966	$85

FONDA, HENRY
CORAL

| ❏ CRL57308 [M] | Voices of the 20th Century | 1958 | $75 |

FONTAINE, FRANK
ABC-PARAMOUNT

❏ 541 [M]	All Time Great Hits	1966	$18
❏ S-541 [S]	All Time Great Hits	1966	$25
❏ 470 [M]	How Sweet It Is	1964	$18
❏ S-470 [S]	How Sweet It Is	1964	$25
❏ 514 [M]	I'm Counting on You	1965	$18
❏ S-514 [S]	I'm Counting on You	1965	$25
❏ 490 [M]	More Songs I Sing on the Jackie Gleason Show	1964	$18
❏ S-490 [S]	More Songs I Sing on the Jackie Gleason Show	1964	$25
❏ 460 [M]	Sings Like Crazy	1963	$18
❏ S-460 [S]	Sings Like Crazy	1963	$25
❏ 442 [M]	Songs I Sing on the Jackie Gleason Show	1963	$18
❏ S-442 [S]	Songs I Sing on the Jackie Gleason Show	1963	$25
❏ T-90121 [M]	Songs I Sing on the Jackie Gleason Show	1964	$25
—Capitol Record Club edition			

MGM

| ❏ E-4470 [M] | Frank Fontaine's Ireland | 1967 | $15 |
| ❏ SE-4470 [S] | Frank Fontaine's Ireland | 1967 | $18 |

FONTANA, WAYNE, AND THE MINDBENDERS
Also see WAYNE FONTANA; THE MINDBENDERS.
FONTANA

| ❏ MGF-27542 [M] | The Game of Love | 1965 | $30 |
| ❏ SRF-67542 [R] | The Game of Love | 1965 | $30 |

FONTANA, WAYNE
Also see WAYNE FONTANA AND THE MINDBENDERS.
MGM

| ❏ E-4459 [M] | Wayne Fontana | 1967 | $35 |
| ❏ SE-4459 [S] | Wayne Fontana | 1967 | $30 |

FONTANE SISTERS, THE
DOT

❏ DLP-3042 [M]	A Visit with the Fontane Sisters	1957	$30
❏ DLP-104 [10]	The Fontane Sisters	1955	$50
❏ DLP-3004 [M]	The Fontanes Sing	1956	$40
—Maroon label			
❏ DLP-3004 [M]	The Fontanes Sing	1957	$30
—Black label			
❏ DLP-3531 [M]	The Tips of My Fingers	1963	$18
❏ DLP-25531 [S]	The Tips of My Fingers	1963	$25

FOO FIGHTERS
With Dave Grohl, formerly of NIRVANA.
ROSWELL/CAPITOL

| ❏ C1-34027 | Foo Fighters | 1995 | $30 |
| ❏ 55832 | The Colour and the Shape | 1997 | $75 |

ROSWELL/RCA

❏ 82876-68038-1	In Your Honor	2005	$40
—Box set; all four records play at 45 rpm			
❏ 07863-68008-1 [10]	One By One	2002	$25
❏ 07863-67892-1 [B]	There Is Nothing Left to Lose	1999	$30

FOOD
CAPITOL

| ❏ ST-304 | Forever Is a Dream | 1969 | $140 |

FOOL, THE
MERCURY

| ❏ SR-61178 | The Fool | 1968 | $30 |

FOOLS, THE
EMI AMERICA

❏ SW-17046	Heavy Mental	1981	$15
❏ SW-17024	Sold Out	1980	$15
❏ SPRO-9393/4 [DJ]	The First Annual Official Unofficial April Fools Day Live Bootleg...	1980	$25

PVC

❏ 8962	Wake Up... It's Alive	1987	$18
❏ 8962	Wake Up ... It's Alive!!!	1987	$18
❏ 8930	World Dance Party	1985	$18

FOOLS GOLD
COLUMBIA

| ❏ PC34828 | Mr. Lucky | 1977 | $15 |

MORNING SKY

| ❏ ML5500 | Fools Gold | 1976 | $15 |

FORBERT, STEVE
GEFFEN

| ❏ GHS24194 | Streets of This Town | 1988 | $12 |

NEMPEROR

❏ JZ35538	Alive on Arrival	1978	$12
—Original prefix			
❏ PZ35538	Alive on Arrival	1980	$10
—Budget-line reissue with new prefix			
❏ JZ36191	Jackrabbit Slim	1979	$12
❏ JZ36595	Little Stevie Orbit	1980	$12
❏ ARZ37434	Steve Forbert	1982	$12

FORBES, GRAHAM
PHILLIPS INTERNATIONAL

| ❏ PLP-1955 [M] | The Martini Set | 1959 | $800 |

FORCE M.D.'S
TOMMY BOY

❏ TBLP1010	Chillin'	1985	$12
❏ TBLP1003	Love Letters	1984	$15
❏ 25893	Step to Me	1990	$18
❏ 25631	Touch and Go	1987	$12

FORCE OF NATURE
PHILADELPHIA INT'L.

| ❏ PZ34123 [B] | Unemployment Blues | 1976 | $30 |

FORD, FRANKIE
ACE

| ❏ LP1005 [M] | Let's Take a Sea Cruise | 1959 | $300 |

BRIARMEADE

| ❏ BR-5002 | Frankie Ford | 1976 | $15 |

FORD, LITA
Also see THE RUNAWAYS.
MERCURY

❏ 818864-1	Dancin' on the Edge	1984	$12
❏ 810331-1	Out for Blood	1984	$30
—Original cover has Lita holding a bloody, gored guitar			
❏ 810331-1	Out for Blood	1984	$10
—Reissue cover has a different photo of Lita holding a non-bloody guitar			

RCA

| ❏ 6397-1-R [B] | Lita | 1988 | $12 |
| ❏ 2090-1-R | Stiletto | 1990 | $12 |

FORD, MARY
Also see LES PAUL AND MARY FORD.
CHALLENGE

| ❏ CHL-623 [M] | A Brand New Ford | 1966 | $30 |
| ❏ CHS-2623 [S] | A Brand New Ford | 1966 | $30 |

FORD, NEAL, AND THE FANATICS
HICKORY

| ❏ LPS-141 | Neal Ford and the Fanatics | 1968 | $35 |

FORD, RICKY
MUSE

❏ MR-5227	Flying Colors	1981	$25
❏ MR-5296	Future's Gold	198?	$25
❏ MR-5275	Interpretations	198?	$25
❏ MR-5322	Looking Ahead	1987	$25
❏ MR-5188	Manhattan Plaza	1979	$30
❏ MR-5349	Saxotic Stomp	1988	$25
❏ MR-5314	Shorter Ideas	1985	$25
❏ MR-5250	Tenor for the Times	1982	$25

NEW WORLD

| ❏ 204 | Loxodonta Africana | 1977 | $35 |

FORD, RITA
COLUMBIA

❏ CL1698 [M]	A Music Box Christmas	1961	$25
—Black and red label with six "eye" logos			
❏ CS8498 [R]	A Music Box Christmas	1961	$18
❏ CS9738	The Story of Christmas	1968	$15

EPIC

| ❏ LN24022 [M] | Music Box Wonderland Christmas with Rita Ford's Music Boxes | 1962 | $25 |
| ❏ BN26022 [R] | Music Box Wonderland Christmas with Rita Ford's Music Boxes | 1962 | $18 |

HARMONY

| ❏ KH31577 | Christmas with Rita Ford's Music Boxes | 1972 | $15 |
| —Reissue of Epic BN 26022 | | | |

FORD, ROCKY BILLY
AUDIO LAB

| ❏ AL-1561 [M] | A New Singing Star | 1960 | $175 |

FORD, TENNESSEE ERNIE
CAPITOL

❏ SVBB-11326	25th Anniversary/Hymns & Gospel	1974	$15
❏ SVBB-11325	25th Anniversary/Yesterday and Today	1974	$15
❏ ST-730	Abide with Me	1971	$15
❏ T1272 [M]	A Friend We Have	1959	$18
❏ ST1272 [S]	A Friend We Have	1959	$25
❏ T2681 [M]	Aloha from Tennessee Ernie Ford	1967	$18
❏ ST2681 [S]	Aloha from Tennessee Ernie Ford	1967	$15
❏ STAO-412	America the Beautiful	1970	$15
❏ SM-412	America the Beautiful	197?	$10
—Reissue with new prefix			
❏ SKAO2949	Best Hymns	1968	$15
❏ T1794 [M]	Book of Favorite Hymns	1962	$18
❏ ST1794 [S]	Book of Favorite Hymns	1962	$25
❏ SM-12033	Book of Favorite Hymns	1980	$12
❏ ST-831 [S]	C-H-R-I-S-T-M-A-S	1971	$15
❏ STBB-485	Christmas Special	1970	$18
❏ T1539 [M]	Civil War Songs of the North	1961	$18
❏ ST1539 [S]	Civil War Songs of the North	1961	$25
❏ T1540 [M]	Civil War Songs of the South	1961	$18
❏ ST1540 [S]	Civil War Songs of the South	1961	$25
❏ T2097 [M]	Country Hits...Feelin' Blue	1964	$15
❏ ST2097 [S]	Country Hits...Feelin' Blue	1964	$18
❏ SM-2097	Country Hits...Feelin' Blue	197?	$10
—Reissue with new prefix			
❏ ST-583	Everything Is Beautiful	1971	$15
❏ T2761 [M]	Faith of Our Fathers	1967	$30
❏ ST2761 [S]	Faith of Our Fathers	1967	$15
❏ SM-2761	Faith of Our Fathers	197?	$10
—Reissue with new prefix			
❏ T1227 [M]	Gather 'Round	1959	$18
❏ ST1227 [S]	Gather 'Round	1959	$25

Number	Title	Yr	NM
❏ T2618 [M]	God Lives	1966	$15
❏ ST2618 [S]	God Lives	1966	$18
❏ SN-16042	Gospel	1981	$10
❏ T2026 [M]	Great Gospel Songs	1964	$15
❏ ST2026 [S]	Great Gospel Songs	1964	$18
❏ SM-2026	Great Gospel Songs	197?	$10
—Reissue with new prefix			
❏ T1684 [M]	Here Comes the Mississippi Showboat	1962	$15
❏ ST1684 [S]	Here Comes the Mississippi Showboat	1962	$18
❏ ST-334	Holy, Holy, Holy	1969	$15
❏ T756 [M]	Hymns	1956	$30
—Turquoise label			
❏ T756 [M]	Hymns	1959	$25
—Black label with colorband, logo at left			
❏ T756 [M]	Hymns	1962	$18
—Black label with colorband, logo at top			
❏ ST756 [S]	Hymns	1962	$18
—Re-recording of the original mono LP			
❏ SN-16043	Hymns	1981	$10
❏ SN-16173	Hymns	1981	$10
❏ T1694 [M]	Hymns at Home	1962	$15
❏ ST1694 [S]	Hymns at Home	1962	$18
❏ T1751 [M]	I Love to Tell the Story	1962	$15
❏ ST1751 [S]	I Love to Tell the Story	1962	$18
❏ ST-11092	It's Tennessee Ernie Ford	1973	$12
❏ T2296 [M]	Let Me Walk with Thee	1965	$15
❏ ST2296 [S]	Let Me Walk with Thee	1965	$18
❏ SF-8-0508	Let Me Walk with Thee	1970	$18
—Capitol Record Club edition			
❏ T1875 [M]	Long Long Ago	1963	$15
❏ ST1875 [S]	Long Long Ago	1963	$18
❏ ST-11290	Make a Joyful Noise	1974	$12
❏ ST-11001	Mr. Words and Music	1972	$12
❏ T2444 [M]	My Favorite Things	1966	$15
❏ ST2444 [S]	My Favorite Things	1966	$18
❏ T1005 [M]	Nearer the Cross	1958	$25
—Black label with colorband, logo at left			
❏ T1005 [M]	Nearer the Cross	1962	$18
—Black label with colorband, logo at top			
❏ ST1005 [S]	Nearer the Cross	1959	$30
—Black label with colorband, logo at left			
❏ ST1005 [S]	Nearer the Cross	1962	$25
—Black label with colorband, logo at top			
❏ ST2968	O Come All Ye Faithful	1968	$15
❏ T888 [M]	Ol' Rockin' Ern	1957	$50
—Turquoise or gray label			
❏ T2845 [M]	Our Garden of Hymns	1968	$25
❏ ST2845 [S]	Our Garden of Hymns	1968	$15
❏ SVBB-11382	Precious Memories	1975	$15
❏ TAO1332 [M]	Sing a Hymn with Me	1960	$25
—With hymnal			
❏ STAO1332 [S]	Sing a Hymn with Me	1960	$30
—With hymnal			
❏ T1679 [M]	Sing a Hymn with Me	1962	$15
—Reissue of 1332 with standard cover?			
❏ ST1679 [S]	Sing a Hymn with Me	1962	$18
—Reissue of 1332 with standard cover?			
❏ T1680 [M]	Sing a Spiritual with Me	1962	$15
❏ ST1680 [S]	Sing a Spiritual with Me	1962	$18
❏ T2394 [M]	Sing We Now of Christmas	1965	$15
❏ ST2394 [S]	Sing We Now of Christmas	1965	$18
—Same as above, but in stereo			
❏ T1380 [M]	Sixteen Tons	1960	$18
❏ DT1380 [R]	Sixteen Tons	196?	$15
❏ ST-127	Songs I Like to Sing	1969	$15
❏ T818 [M]	Spirituals	1957	$30
—Turquoise label			
❏ T818 [M]	Spirituals	1959	$25
—Black label with colorband, logo at left			
❏ T818 [M]	Spirituals	1962	$18
—Black label with colorband, logo at top			
❏ ST818 [S]	Spirituals	1962	$18
—Re-recording of the original mono LP			
❏ SN-16174	Spirituals	1981	$10
❏ SF-8-0507	Sweet Hour of Prayer	1970	$18
—Capitol Record Club edition			
❏ STBB-506	Sweet Hour of Prayer/Let Me Walk with Thee	1971	$18
❏ T841 [M]	Tennessee Ernie Ford Favorites	1958	$25
—Black label with colorband, logo at left			
❏ T841 [M]	Tennessee Ernie Ford Favorites	1962	$18
—Black label with colorband, logo at top			
❏ DT841 [R]	Tennessee Ernie Ford Favorites	196?	$15
❏ T841 [M]	Tennessee Ernie Ford Favorites	1957	$30
—Turquoise label			
❏ ST-11232	Tennessee Ernie Ford Sings About Jesus	1973	$12
❏ ST-11495	Tennessee Ernie Ford Sings His Great Love Songs	1975	$12
❏ ST-833	The Folk Album	1971	$15
❏ T1071 [M]	The Star Carol	1958	$30
—Black labels with colorband, "Capitol" logo on left			
❏ ST1071 [S]	The Star Carol	1958	$30
—Black labels with colorband, Capitol logo on left			
❏ T1071 [M]	The Star Carol	1962	$18

Number	Title	Yr	NM
—Black label with colorband, logo on top			
❏ ST1071 [S]	The Star Carol	1962	$25
—Black label with colorband, "Capitol" logo on top. This was also reissued on later Capitol labels into the 1970s with values no more than half the above.			
❏ SN-16289	The Star Carol	1982	$10
—Budget-line reissue			
❏ T1994 [M]	The Story of Christmas	1963	$18
—With the Roger Wagner Chorale			
❏ ST1994 [S]	The Story of Christmas	1963	$25
❏ STCL2942	The Tennessee Ernie Ford Deluxe Set	1968	$25
❏ ST2896	The World of Pop and Country Hits	1968	$15
❏ TBL2183 [M]	The World's Best Loved Hymns	1964	$25
❏ STBL2183 [S]	The World's Best Loved Hymns	1964	$30
❏ T700 [M]	This Lusty Land	1956	$30
—Turquoise label			
❏ T700 [M]	This Lusty Land	1959	$25
—Black label with colorband, logo at left			
❏ T700 [M]	This Lusty Land!	1963	$18
—Black label with colorband, logo at top			
❏ DT700 [R]	This Lusty Land!	196?	$15
❏ T1937 [M]	We Gather Together	1963	$15
❏ ST1937 [S]	We Gather Together	1963	$18
❏ T2557 [M]	Wonderful Peace	1966	$15
❏ ST2557 [S]	Wonderful Peace	1966	$18
❏ SN-16040	Yesterday	1981	$10

EVEREST ARCHIVE OF FOLK & JAZZ

❏ 279	Tennessee Ernie Ford	197?	$12

PICKWICK

❏ SPC-3308	Amazing Grace	197?	$12
❏ SPC-3047	Bless Your Pea-Pickin' Heart	196?	$15
❏ PTP-2050	Hymns	197?	$15
❏ SPC-3066	I Love You So Much	196?	$15
❏ SPC-3273	Jesus Loves Me	197?	$12
❏ SPC-3353	Rock of Ages	197?	$12
❏ SPC-3268	Sixteen Tons	197?	$12
❏ PTP-2016	Tennessee Ernie Ford	197?	$15
❏ SPC-3222	The Need for Prayer	197?	$12

RANWOOD

❏ RLP-7026	Tennessee Ernie Ford Sings 22 Favorite Hymns	198?	$15

WORD

❏ 8764	He Touched Me	1978	$12
❏ 8798	Swing Wide Your Golden Gate	198?	$12
❏ 8841	Tell Me the Old Story	1979	$12
❏ 8841	Tell Me the Old Story	198?	$12
❏ 8858	There's a Song in My Heart	198?	$12

FORD THEATRE, THE

ABC

❏ S-681	Time Changes	1969	$25
❏ S-658	Trilogy	1968	$85

FORDHAM, JULIA

VIRGIN

❏ 90955	Julia Fordham	1988	$12
❏ 91325	Porcelain	1989	$15

FOREFRONT, THE

AFI

❏ 21557	Incantation	197?	$25

FOREIGNER
Also see BLACK SHEEP; SPOOKY TOOTH; MICK JONES; LOU GRAMM.

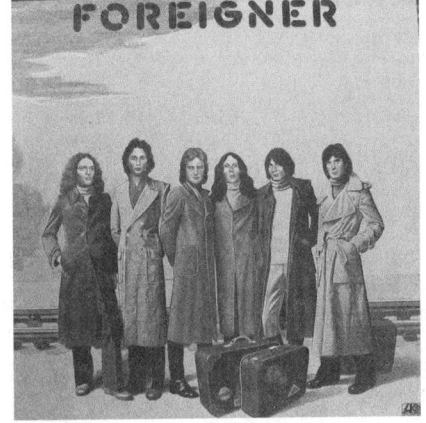

ATLANTIC

❏ SD16999	4	1981	$12
—First pressings have a hologram sticker on the upper back cover			
❏ SD16999 [B]	4	1982	$10
—No hologram sticker on back cover			

Number	Title	Yr	NM
❏ 81999	Agent Provocateur	1984	$10
❏ SD19999	Double Vision	1978	$15
—Original cover is mostly brown with the words "Double Vision" barely visible along the bottom edge of front cover			
❏ SD19999	Double Vision	1979	$10
—Third cover is the same as the second cover, but has a red tint			
❏ SD19999	Double Vision	1978	$12
—Second cover has a blue tint with the words "Double Vision" right under the band name			
❏ SD19109 [B]	Foreigner	1977	$10
—Reissue of 18215			
❏ SD18215	Foreigner	1977	$12
❏ SD29999	Head Games	1979	$12
❏ 81808	Inside Information	1988	$10
❏ 80999	Records	1982	$12
❏ A1-82299	Unusual Heat	1990	$30
—U.S. vinyl available only through Columbia House			

MOBILE FIDELITY

❏ Jan-0052	Double Vision	1981	$50
—Audiophile vinyl			

FOREST

HARVEST

❏ SKAO-419 [B]	Forest	1970	$100

FORESTER SISTERS, THE

WARNER BROS.

❏ 25623	A Christmas Card	1987	$12
❏ 25897	Greatest Hits	1989	$12
❏ 25411	Perfume, Ribbons & Pearls	1986	$12
❏ 25746	Sincerely	1988	$12
❏ R110671	Talkin' About Men	1991	$25
—BMG Direct Marketing edition (no regular vinyl version)			
❏ 25314	The Forester Sisters	1985	$12
❏ 25571	You Again	1987	$12

FORETICH, HERMAN

AUDIOPHILE

❏ AP-124	Herman Foretich and His Atlanta Swing Quartet	196?	$35

JAZZOLOGY

❏ J-144	The Foretich Four	1987	$25

FOREVER MORE

RCA VICTOR

❏ LSP-4425	Words on Black Plastic	1971	$18
❏ LSP-4272	Yours Forever More	1970	$18

FORGOTTEN CHILD

BLUE LAMPION

❏ BLM10001	Forgotten Child	1986	$75

FORMAN, BRUCE, AND GEORGE CABLES

CONCORD JAZZ

❏ CJ-279	Dynamics	1985	$25

FORMAN, BRUCE

CHOICE

❏ 1026	Coast to Coast	1980	$30

CONCORD JAZZ

❏ CJ-251	Full Circle	1984	$25
❏ CJ-368	Pardon Me!	1989	$30
❏ CJ-332	There Are Times	1988	$25

MUSE

❏ MR-5273	20/20	1982	$25
❏ MR-5299	In Transit	1982	$25
❏ MR-5251	River Journey	1981	$25
❏ MR-5315	The Bash	1985	$25

FORMAN, MITCHELL

MAGENTA

❏ MA-0201	Train of Thought	198?	$30

SOUL NOTE

❏ SN-1050	Childhood Dreams	198?	$30
❏ SN-1070	Only a Memory	198?	$30

FORMULA 1

GUINNESS

❏ GNS36003 [B]	Hold On	1977	$300

FORMULA V

BURLINGUEN

❏ 0(# unknown)	Formula V	197?	$30

MIAMI

❏ 6076	Formula V	197?	$30

FORREST, EUGENE "FLIP

SAVOY

❏ MG-14392	I Heard It on the Radio	197?	$25

Number	Title	Yr	NM

FORREST, HELEN, AND DICK HAYMES
MCA
| ❑ 1546 | Long Ago and Far Away | 198? | $30 |

FORREST, HELEN
AUDIOPHILE
| ❑ AP-47 | On the Sunny Side of the Street | 1958 | $75 |

CAPITOL
| ❑ T704 [M] | Voice of the Name Bands | 1956 | $100 |
| *— Turquoise label* | | | |

JOYCE
❑ 6008	Big Bands' Greatest Vocalists, Vol. 2	197?	$20
❑ 6012	Big Bands' Greatest Vocalists, Vol. 4	197?	$20
❑ 6019	Big Bands' Greatest Vocalists, Vol. 7	197?	$20
❑ 6021	Big Bands' Greatest Vocalists, Vol. 8	197?	$20

STASH
| ❑ ST-225 | Now and Forever | 198? | $35 |

FORREST, JIMMY, AND MILES DAVIS
PRESTIGE
| ❑ PRST-7858 | Live at the Barrel | 197? | $35 |
| ❑ PRST-7860 | Live at the Barrel, Volume 2 | 197? | $35 |

FORREST, JIMMY
DELMARK
❑ DL-404	All the Gin Is Gone	196?	$50
❑ DL-427	Black Forrest	1972	$35
❑ DL-435	Night Train	197?	$35

FANTASY
❑ OJC-199	Forrest Fire	1985	$30
❑ OJC-350	Most Much!	198?	$30
❑ OJC-097	Out of the Forrest	198?	$30

NEW JAZZ
❑ NJLP-8250 [M]	Forrest Fire	1960	$250
— Purple label			
❑ NJLP-8250 [M]	Forrest Fire	1965	$175
— Blue label with trident logo at right			
❑ NJLP-8293 [M]	Soul Street	1962	$250
— Purple label			
❑ NJLP-8293 [M]	Soul Street	1965	$175
— Blue label with trident logo at right			

PALO ALTO
| ❑ 8021 | Heart of the Forrest | 1982 | $30 |

PRESTIGE
❑ PRLP-7218 [M]	Most Much!	1961	$250
— Yellow label			
❑ PRLP-7218 [M]	Most Much!	1965	$40
— Blue label with trident logo at right			
❑ PRLP-7202 [M]	Out of the Forrest	1961	$250
— Yellow label			
❑ PRLP-7202 [M]	Out of the Forrest	1965	$40
— Blue label with trident logo at right			
❑ PRLP-7235 [M]	Sit Down and Relax with Jimmy Forrest	1962	$175
— Yellow label			
❑ PRLP-7235 [M]	Sit Down and Relax with Jimmy Forrest	1965	$40
— Blue label with trident logo at right			
❑ PRST-7235 [S]	Sit Down and Relax with Jimmy Forrest	1962	$175
— Silver label			
❑ PRST-7235 [S]	Sit Down and Relax with Jimmy Forrest	1965	$50
— Blue label with trident logo at right			
❑ PRST-7235 [S]	Sit Down and Relax with Jimmy Forrest	1973	$30
— Green label reissue			
❑ PRST-7712	The Best of Jimmy Forrest	196?	$30

UNITED
| ❑ 02 [10] | Night Train | 1955 | $120 |

FORRESTER, BOBBY
DOBRE
| ❑ 1012 | Organist | 197? | $30 |

FORRESTER, HOWDY
CUB
| ❑ 8008 [M] | Fancy Fiddlin' Country Style | 1960 | $40 |

MGM
| ❑ E-4035 [M] | Fancy Fiddlin' Country Style | 1962 | $30 |
| *— Reissue of Cub LP* | | | |

UNITED ARTISTS
| ❑ UAL-3295 [M] | Fiddlin' Country Style | 1963 | $25 |
| ❑ UAS-6295 [S] | Fiddlin' Country Style | 1963 | $30 |

FORRESTER, MAUREEN
RCA VICTOR RED SEAL
| ❑ LSC-2275 [S] | Brahms, Schumann: Lieder | 1959 | $25 |
| *— Original with "shaded dog" label* | | | |

FORT MUDGE MEMORIAL DUMP, THE
MERCURY
| ❑ SR-61256 | The Fort Mudge Memorial Dump | 1970 | $50 |

FORTE, JOHN
RUFFHOUSE
❑ C268639	Poly Sci	1998	$15
❑ C2S41073 [DJ]	Poly Sci	1998	$18
— Promo version of LP			

FORTUNE, JOHNNY
PARK AVENUE
| ❑ P-1301 [M] | Soul Surfer | 1963 | $250 |
| ❑ S-401 [S] | Soul Surfer | 1963 | $300 |

FORTUNE, SONNY
ATLANTIC
❑ SD19187	Infinity Is	1978	$30
❑ SD18225	Serengeti Minstrel	1977	$30
❑ SD19239	With Sound Reason	1979	$30

HORIZON
| ❑ 704 | Awakening | 1975 | $35 |
| ❑ 711 | Waves | 1976 | $35 |

STRATA-EAST
| ❑ SES-7423 | Long Before Our Mothers Cried | 1974 | $25 |

FORTUNE (1)
MCA CAMEL
| ❑ 5673 | Fortune | 1985 | $12 |

FORTUNE (2)
WARNER BROS.
| ❑ BSK3246 | Fortune | 1978 | $12 |

FORTUNES, THE (1)
CAPITOL
❑ ST-647	Freedom	1971	$0
— Canceled			
❑ ST-809	Here Comes That Rainy Day Feeling Again	1971	$25
❑ ST-11041	Storm in a Teacup	1972	$18
— Contains the canceled "Freedom" LP with one track deleted, plus the title song added			

COCA-COLA
| ❑ 0(no cat #) [DJ] | It's the Real Thing | 1969 | $75 |

PRESS
| ❑ PR73002 [M] | The Fortunes | 1965 | $35 |
| ❑ PRS83002 [S] | The Fortunes | 1965 | $50 |

WORLD PACIFIC
| ❑ WPS-21904 | That Same Old Feeling | 1970 | $18 |

49ERS
4TH & B'WAY
| ❑ 444021-1 | 49ers | 1990 | $15 |

49TH PARALLEL, THE
MAVERICK
| ❑ MAS-7001 | The 49th Parallel | 1969 | $300 |

FORUM, THE
MIRA
| ❑ MLP-301 [M] | The River Is Wide | 1967 | $18 |
| ❑ MLPS-301 [S] | The River Is Wide | 1967 | $25 |

FOSTER, BRUCE
MILLENNIUM
| ❑ MNLP8000 | After the Show | 1977 | $15 |

FOSTER, CHUCK
CIRCLE
| ❑ 68 | Chuck Foster and His Orchestra 1945-46 | 198? | $25 |

HINDSIGHT
| ❑ HSR-171 | Chuck Foster and His Orchestra 1938-39 | 198? | $25 |
| ❑ HSR-115 | Chuck Foster and His Orchestra 1940 | 198? | $25 |

PHILLIPS INTERNATIONAL
| ❑ PLP-1965 [M] | Chuck Foster at the Hotel Peabody | 1961 | $250 |

SEA BREEZE
| ❑ SB-2023 | Long Overdue | 1985 | $25 |

FOSTER, DAVID
ATLANTIC
| ❑ 81642 | David Foster | 1986 | $10 |
| ❑ 81799 | The Symphony Sessions | 1988 | $10 |

MOBILE FIDELITY
| ❑ 1-123 | The Best of Me | 1982 | $30 |
| *— Audiophile vinyl* | | | |

FOSTER, FRANK, AND FRANK WESS
CONCORD JAZZ
| ❑ CJ-276 | Frankly Speaking | 1986 | $25 |

PABLO
| ❑ 2310905 | Two for the Blues | 198? | $30 |

SAVOY JAZZ
| ❑ SJL-2249 | Two Franks Please! | 198? | $30 |

FOSTER, FRANK
ARGO
| ❑ LP-717 [M] | Basie Is Our Boss | 1963 | $30 |
| ❑ LPS-717 [S] | Basie Is Our Boss | 1963 | $30 |

BLUE NOTE
❑ BST-84316	Frank Foster	1969	$0
— Canceled			
❑ BLP-5043 [10]	Frank Foster Quintet	1954	$400
❑ BST-84278	Manhattan Fever	1968	$30

MAINSTREAM
| ❑ MRL-349 | The Loud Minority | 1972 | $25 |

PRESTIGE
❑ PRLP-7461 [M]	Fearless	1966	$30
❑ PRST-7461 [S]	Fearless	1966	$30
❑ PRLP-7479 [M]	Soul Outing!	1967	$30
❑ PRST-7479 [S]	Soul Outing!	1967	$30

STEEPLECHASE
| ❑ SCS-1170 | A House That Love Built | 1982 | $30 |

FOSTER, GARY
REVELATION
| ❑ REV-19 | Grand Clu Classe | 197? | $25 |
| ❑ REV-5 | Subconsciously | 1968 | $25 |

FOSTER, HERMAN
ARGO
| ❑ LP-727 [M] | Ready and Willing | 1964 | $50 |
| ❑ LPS-727 [S] | Ready and Willing | 1964 | $30 |

EPIC
❑ LA16010 [M]	Have You Heard?	1960	$50
❑ BA17010 [S]	Have You Heard?	1960	$75
❑ LA16016 [M]	The Explosive Piano of Herman Foster	1961	$250
❑ BA17016 [S]	The Explosive Piano of Herman Foster	1961	$75

FOSTER, PAT
COUNTERPOINT
| ❑ CPT-560 [M] | Documentary Talking Blues | 195? | $40 |

RIVERSIDE
| ❑ RLP-12-654 [M] | Gold Rush Songs | 195? | $40 |

FOSTER, RONNIE
BLUE NOTE
❑ BN-LA425-H2	Cheshire Cat	1975	$35
❑ BN-LA261-H2	On the Avenue	1974	$35
❑ BN-LA098-H2	Sweet Revival	1973	$35
❑ BST-84382	Two Headed Freap	1972	$25
❑ B1-32082	Two Headed Freap	1995	$35
— Reissue of 84382			

COLUMBIA
| ❑ JC36019 | Delight | 1979 | $30 |
| ❑ JC35373 | Love Satellite | 1978 | $30 |

FOSTER AND LLOYD
RCA
| ❑ 9587-1-R | Faster & Llouder | 1989 | $12 |
| ❑ 6372-1-R | Foster and Lloyd | 1987 | $10 |

FOTHERINGAY
A&M
| ❑ SP-4289 | Faotheringay | 1970 | $18 |

FOTOMAKER
ATLANTIC
❑ SD19165	Fotomaker	1978	$12
❑ SD19246	Transfer Station	1979	$15
❑ SD19208	Vis-a-Vis	1978	$12

FOUGERAT, TONY
GHB
| ❑ GHB-89 | Every Man a King | 197? | $25 |
| ❑ GHB-147 | Live at the Maple Leaf Bar | 198? | $25 |

FOUL DOGS, THE
RHYTHM SOUND
| ❑ GA-481 | No. 1 | 1966 | $400 |

FOUNDATIONS, THE
UNI
❑ 73016	Baby Now That I've Found You	1968	$30
❑ 73043	Build Me Up Buttercup	1969	$30
❑ 73058	Digging the Foundations	1969	$30

FOUNTAIN, PETE, AND "BIG" TINY LITTLE

CORAL

Number	Title	Yr	NM
CRL57334 [M]	Mr. New Orleans Meets Mr. Honky Tonk	1961	$35
CRL757334 [S]	Mr. New Orleans Meets Mr. Honky Tonk	1961	$50

FOUNTAIN, PETE, AND AL HIRT

CORAL

Number	Title	Yr	NM
CRL57389 [M]	Bourbon Street	1962	$35
CRL757389 [S]	Bourbon Street	1962	$50

MGM

Number	Title	Yr	NM
E-4216 [M]	The Very Best of Al Hirt and Pete Fountain	1964	$30
SE-4216 [S]	The Very Best of Al Hirt and Pete Fountain	1964	$35

MONUMENT

Number	Title	Yr	NM
8602	Super I	1975	$25

FOUNTAIN, PETE

CAPITOL

Number	Title	Yr	NM
SN-16224	Pete Fountain and Friends	1982	$20
SN-16225	Way Down Yonder in New Orleans	1982	$20

CORAL

Number	Title	Yr	NM
CRL57486 [M]	A Taste of Honey	1966	$30
CRL757486 [S]	A Taste of Honey	1966	$35
CRL757507	Both Sides Now	1969	$30
CRL57487 [M]	Candy Clarinet -- Merry Christmas from Pete Fountain	1966	$30
CRL757487 [S]	Candy Clarinet -- Merry Christmas from Pete Fountain	1966	$35
CRL757513	Dr. Fountain's Magical Licorice Stick	1971	$30
CRL757511	Golden Favorites	1970	$30
CRL57378 [M]	I Love Paris	1961	$35
CRL757378 [S]	I Love Paris	1961	$50
CRL57488 [M]	I've Got You Under My Skin	1967	$30
CRL757488 [S]	I've Got You Under My Skin	1967	$35
CRL57200 [M]	Lawrence Welk Presents Pete Fountain	1958	$50
CRL57460 [M]	Licorice Stick	1964	$30
CRL757460 [S]	Licorice Stick	1964	$35
CRL757510	Make Your Own Kind of Music	1970	$30
CRL57484 [M]	Mood Indigo	1966	$30
CRL757484 [S]	Mood Indigo	1966	$35
CRL57473 [M]	Mr. Stick Man	1965	$30
CRL757473 [S]	Mr. Stick Man	1965	$35
CRL57496 [M]	Music to Turn You On	1967	$35
CRL757496 [S]	Music to Turn You On	1967	$30
CRL57429 [M]	New Orleans at Midnight	1964	$30
CRL757429 [S]	New Orleans at Midnight	1964	$35
CRL57419 [M]	New Orleans Scene	1963	$35
CRL757419 [S]	New Orleans Scene	1963	$50
CRL757517	New Orleans Tennessee	1971	$30
CRL57314 [M]	Pete Fountain at the Bateau Lounge	1960	$35
CRL757314 [S]	Pete Fountain at the Bateau Lounge	1960	$50
CRL57313 [M]	Pete Fountain Day	1960	$35
CRL757313 [S]	Pete Fountain Day	1960	$50
CRL57357 [M]	Pete Fountain On Tour	1961	$35
CRL757357 [S]	Pete Fountain On Tour	1961	$50
CRL57499 [M]	Pete Fountain Plays Bert Kaempfert	1968	$35
CRL757499 [S]	Pete Fountain Plays Bert Kaempfert	1968	$30
CRL57333 [M]	Pete Fountain Salutes the Great Clarinetists	1960	$35
CRL757333 [S]	Pete Fountain Salutes the Great Clarinetists	1960	$50
CRL57359 [M]	Pete Fountain's French Quarter	1961	$35
CRL757359 [S]	Pete Fountain's French Quarter	1961	$50
CRL57401 [M]	Pete Fountain's Music from Dixie	1962	$35
CRL757401 [S]	Pete Fountain's Music from Dixie	1962	$50
CRL57282 [M]	Pete Fountain's New Orleans	1959	$35
CRL757282 [S]	Pete Fountain's New Orleans	1959	$50
CRL57453 [M]	Pete's Place	1964	$30
CRL757453 [S]	Pete's Place	1964	$35
CRL57424 [M]	Plenty of Pete	1963	$35
CRL757424 [S]	Plenty of Pete	1963	$35
CRL757516	Something/Misty	1971	$30
CRL57440 [M]	South Rampart Street Parade	1963	$30
CRL757440 [S]	South Rampart Street Parade	1963	$35
CRL57474 [M]	Standing Room Only	1965	$30
CRL757474 [S]	Standing Room Only	1965	$35
CRL57394 [M]	Swing Low Sweet Chariot	1962	$35
CRL757394 [S]	Swing Low Sweet Chariot	1962	$50
CXS-710	The Best of Pete Fountain	1969	$35
CRL57284 [M]	The Blues	1959	$35
CRL757284 [S]	The Blues	1959	$50
CRL757505	Those Were the Days	1969	$30
CRL757503	Walking Through New Orleans	1968	$30

DECCA

Number	Title	Yr	NM
DL75378	Dr. Fountain's Magical Licorice Stick	1972	$25
— Reissue of Coral 757513			
DL75377	Mr. New Orleans	1972	$30
DL75380	New Orleans Tennessee	1972	$30
— Reissue of Coral 757517			
DL75374	Pete Fountain's New Orleans	1972	$30
— Reissue of Coral 757282			
DL75379	Something/Misty	1972	$25
— Reissue of Coral 757516			
DL75375	The Blues	1972	$30
— Reissue of Coral 757284			

EVEREST ARCHIVE OF FOLK & JAZZ

Number	Title	Yr	NM
257	New Orleans All-Stars	197?	$25

FIRST AMERICAN

Number	Title	Yr	NM
7706	New Orleans Jazz	1978	$25

INTERMEDIA

Number	Title	Yr	NM
QS-5038	Down on Rampart Street	198?	$20

JUCU

Number	Title	Yr	NM
JMK-12S	Pete Fountain's Jazz Reunion	1976	$30

MCA

Number	Title	Yr	NM
336	Crescent City	1974	$25
507	Dr. Fountain's Magical Licorice Stick	1974	$25
— Reissue of Decca 75378			
165	Mr. New Orleans	1973	$25
— Reissue of Decca 75377			
508	New Orleans Tennessee	1974	$25
— Reissue of Decca 75380			
505	Pete Fountain's New Orleans	1974	$25
— Reissue of Decca 75374			
176	Something/Misty	1973	$25
— Reissue of Decca 75379			
2-4032	The Best of Pete Fountain	1974	$30
— Reissue of Coral 710			
2-4095	The Best of Pete Fountain, Vol. 2	1976	$30
— Black labels with rainbow			
2-4095	The Best of Pete Fountain, Vol. 2	1977	$25
— Tan labels			
506	The Blues	1974	$25
— Reissue of Decca 75375			

PICKWICK

Number	Title	Yr	NM
SPC-3201	High Society	1971	$25
SPC-3024	Pete Fountain	196?	$30

RCA CAMDEN

Number	Title	Yr	NM
CAL-727 [M]	Dixieland	1962	$30
CAS-727 [R]	Dixieland	1962	$25

RCA VICTOR

Number	Title	Yr	NM
LPM-2097 [M]	Pete Fountain at the Jazz Band Ball	1960	$35
LSP-2097 [S]	Pete Fountain at the Jazz Band Ball	1960	$50

VOCALION

Number	Title	Yr	NM
VL3803 [M]	And the Angels Sing	1967	$30
VL73803 [S]	And the Angels Sing	1967	$30

FOUR ACES

DECCA

Number	Title	Yr	NM
DL8944 [M]	Beyond the Blue Horizon	1959	$40
— All-black label, silver print			
DL78944 [S]	Beyond the Blue Horizon	1959	$50
— All-black label, silver print			
DL8944 [M]	Beyond the Blue Horizon	196?	$25
— Black label with color bars			
DL78944 [S]	Beyond the Blue Horizon	196?	$30
— Black label with color bars			
DL8228 [M]	Heart and Soul	1956	$50
— All-black label, silver print			
DL8228 [M]	Heart and Soul	196?	$25
— Black label with color bars			
DL8855 [M]	Hits from Broadway	1959	$40
— All-black label, silver print			
DL78855 [S]	Hits from Broadway	1959	$50
— All-black label, silver print			
DL8855 [M]	Hits from Broadway	196?	$25
— Black label with color bars			
DL78855 [S]	Hits from Broadway	196?	$30
— Black label with color bars			
DL8693 [M]	Hits from Hollywood	1958	$50
— All-black label, silver print			
DL8693 [M]	Hits from Hollywood	196?	$25
— Black label with color bars			
DL8191 [M]	Merry Christmas	1956	$50
DL8227 [M]	Sentimental Souvenirs	1956	$50
— All-black label, silver print			
DL8227 [M]	Sentimental Souvenirs	196?	$25
— Black label with color bars			
DL8312 [M]	She Sees All the Hollywood Hits	1957	$50
DL8567 [M]	Shuffling Along	1957	$50
— All-black label, silver print			
DL8567 [M]	Shuffling Along	196?	$25
— Black label with color bars			
DL5429 [10]	The Four Aces	1952	$100
DL4013 [M]	The Golden Hits of the Four Aces	1960	$25
DL74013 [S]	The Golden Hits of the Four Aces	1960	$30
DL8122 [M]	The Mood for Love	1955	$50
— All-black label, silver print			
DL8122 [M]	The Mood for Love	196?	$25
— Black label with color bars			
DL8766 [M]	The Swingin' Aces	1958	$40
— All-black label, silver print			
DL78766 [S]	The Swingin' Aces	1958	$50
— All-black label, silver print			
DL8766 [M]	The Swingin' Aces	196?	$25
— Black label with color bars			
DL78766 [S]	The Swingin' Aces	196?	$30
— Black label with color bars			

MCA

Number	Title	Yr	NM
4033	The Best of the Four Aces	197?	$18

PICKWICK

Number	Title	Yr	NM
SPC-3527	Love Is a Many-Splendored Thing	197?	$12

UNITED ARTISTS

Number	Title	Yr	NM
UAL-3337 [M]	Record Oldies	1963	$25
UAS-6337 [S]	Record Oldies	1963	$30

VOCALION

Number	Title	Yr	NM
VL3604 [M]	The Four Aces Sing	196?	$18
VL73881	There Goes My Heart	1969	$15
VL73902	Written on the Wind	1970	$15

FOUR BROTHERS, THE

VIK

Number	Title	Yr	NM
LX-1096 [M]	The Four Brothers -- Together Again	1957	$100

4 BY FOUR

CAPITOL

Number	Title	Yr	NM
ST-12560	4 By Four	1987	$10

FOUR COINS, THE

EPIC

Number	Title	Yr	NM
LN1104 [M]	The Four Coins	1955	$50
LN3445 [M]	The Four Coins in Shangri-La	1958	$30

MGM

Number	Title	Yr	NM
E-3944 [M]	Greek Songs	1961	$18
SE-3944 [S]	Greek Songs	1961	$25

ROULETTE

Number	Title	Yr	NM
R-25288 [M]	Greek Songs Mama Never Taught Me	1965	$18
SR-25288 [S]	Greek Songs Mama Never Taught Me	1965	$25

FOUR FRESHMEN, THE

CAPITOL

Number	Title	Yr	NM
T763 [M]	4 Freshmen and 5 Trumpets	1957	$75
SM-11965	Best of the Four Freshmen	1978	$25
T1378 [M]	First Affair	1960	$100
ST1378 [S]	First Affair	1960	$150
T844 [M]	Four Freshmen and Five Saxes	1957	$75
T683 [M]	Four Freshmen and Five Trombones	1956	$75
SM-11639	Four Freshmen and Five Trombones	1977	$25
T743 [M]	Freshmen Favorites	1956	$75
DT743 [R]	Freshmen Favorites	196?	$75
SM-743	Freshmen Favorites	197?	$25
T1103 [M]	Freshmen Favorites, Vol. 2	1959	$100
ST1103 [S]	Freshmen Favorites, Vol. 2	1959	$150
T1485 [M]	Freshmen Year	1961	$100
ST1485 [S]	Freshmen Year	1961	$150
T2067 [M]	Funny How Time Slips Away	1964	$85
ST2067 [S]	Funny How Time Slips Away	1964	$100
T1950 [M]	Got That Feelin'	1963	$85
ST1950 [S]	Got That Feelin'	1963	$100
T1189 [M]	Love Lost	1959	$100
ST1189 [S]	Love Lost	1959	$150
T2168 [M]	More Four Freshmen and Five Trombones	1964	$85
ST2168 [S]	More Four Freshmen and Five Trombones	1964	$100
T1682 [M]	Stars in Our Eyes	1962	$100
ST1682 [S]	Stars in Our Eyes	1962	$150
T1753 [M]	Swingers	1963	$50
ST1753 [S]	Swingers	1963	$100
T1640 [M]	The Best of the Four Freshmen	1962	$100
ST1640 [S]	The Best of the Four Freshmen	1962	$150
T1255 [M]	The Four Freshmen and Five Guitars	1959	$100
ST1255 [S]	The Four Freshmen and Five Guitars	1959	$150
T1008 [M]	The Four Freshmen In Person	1958	$150
ST1008 [S]	The Four Freshmen In Person	1958	$75
T1860 [M]	The Four Freshmen In Person, Volume 2	1963	$85
ST1860 [S]	The Four Freshmen In Person, Volume 2	1963	$100

Number	Title	Yr	NM
❏ T1295 [M]	Voices and Brass	1960	$100
❏ ST1295 [S]	Voices and Brass	1960	$150
❏ T1543 [M]	Voices in Fun	1961	$100
❏ ST1543 [S]	Voices in Fun	1961	$150
❏ T992 [M]	Voices in Latin	1958	$150
❏ T1074 [M]	Voices in Love	1958	$100
❏ ST1074 [S]	Voices in Love	1958	$150
❏ H522 [10]	Voices in Modern	1955	$175
❏ T522 [M]	Voices in Modern	1955	$85

CREATIVE WORLD

❏ ST-1059	Stan Kenton and the Four Freshmen at Butler University	1972	$50

LIBERTY

❏ LST-7630	Different Strokes	1969	$35
❏ LST-7590	In a Class By Themselves	1969	$35
❏ LN-10181	In a Class By Themselves	198?	$20
❏ LST-7563	Today Is Tomorrow	1968	$35

PAUSA

❏ PR-9040	4 Freshmen and 5 Trumpets	1985	$25
❏ PR-7193	Fresh!	1986	$25
❏ PR-9029	The Four Freshmen and Five Guitars	198?	$25

PICKWICK

❏ SPC-3563	A Taste of Honey	1977	$25
❏ SPC-3080	The Fabulous Four Freshmen	196?	$30

SUNSET

❏ SUS-5289	My Special Angel	1970	$30

FOUR GIRLS, THE

CORAL

❏ CRL57158 [M]	Make a Joyful Noise Unto the Lord	1957	$75

FOUR JACKS AND A JILL (1)

RCA VICTOR

❏ LSP-4103	Fables	1968	$18
❏ LPM-4019 [M]	Master Jack	1968	$30
❏ LSP-4019 [S]	Master Jack	1968	$18

FOUR KNIGHTS, THE

CAPITOL

❏ H346 [10]	Spotlight Songs	1953	$250
❏ T346 [M]	Spotlight Songs	1956	$175

CORAL

❏ CRL57309 [M]	Million Dollar Baby	1960	$75
❏ CRL757309 [S]	Million Dollar Baby	1960	$100
❏ CRL57221 [M]	The Four Knights	1959	$150

FOUR LADS, THE

COLUMBIA

❏ CL1223 [M]	Breezin' Along	1958	$30
❏ CS8035 [S]	Breezin' Along	1958	$30
❏ CL1550 [M]	Everything Goes	1960	$18
❏ CS8350 [S]	Everything Goes	1960	$25
❏ CL1111 [M]	Four on the Aisle	1958	$30
❏ CS8047 [S]	Four on the Aisle	1958	$30
❏ CL1407 [M]	High Spirits!	1959	$30
❏ CS8203 [S]	High Spirits!	1959	$30
❏ CL1502 [M]	Love Affair	1960	$18
❏ CS8293 [S]	Love Affair	1960	$25
❏ CL912 [M]	On the Sunny Side	1956	$40
❏ CL6329 [10]	Stage Show	1954	$50
❏ CL2577 [10]	Stage Show	1956	$50
❏ CL1235 [M]	The Four Lads' Greatest Hits	1958	$30
❏ CL2545 [10]	The Four Lads Sing Frank Loesser	1956	$50
❏ CL1045 [M]	The Four Lads Sing Frank Loesser	1957	$40
❏ CL1299 [M]	The Four Lads Swing Along	1959	$30
❏ CS8106 [S]	The Four Lads Swing Along	1959	$30
❏ CL861 [M]	The Four Lads with Frankie Laine	1956	$40

DOT

❏ DLP-3438 [M]	Hits of the 60's	1962	$18
❏ DLP-25438 [S]	Hits of the 60's	1962	$25
❏ DLP-3533 [M]	Oh Happy Day	1963	$18
❏ DLP-25533 [S]	Oh Happy Day	1963	$25

HARMONY

❏ HS11369	Moments to Remember	1970	$15

KAPP

❏ KL-1254 [M]	Dixieland Doin's	1961	$18
❏ KS-3254 [S]	Dixieland Doin's	1961	$25
❏ KL-1224 [M]	Twelve Hits	1961	$18
❏ KS-3224 [S]	Twelve Hits	1961	$25

UNITED ARTISTS

❏ UAL-3399 [M]	Songs of World War I	1964	$18
❏ UAS-6399 [S]	Songs of World War I	1964	$25
❏ UAL-3356 [M]	This Year's Top Movie Hits	1964	$18
❏ UAS-6356 [S]	This Year's Top Movie Hits	1964	$25

FOUR LOVERS, THE

RCA VICTOR

❏ LPM-1317 [M]	Joyride	1956	$700

FOUR MOST, THE

DAWN

Number	Title	Yr	NM
❏ DLP-1111 [M]	The Four Most	1956	$100

4 OUT OF 5 DOCTORS

NEMPEROR

❏ JZ36575	4 Out of 5 Doctors	1981	$15
❏ ARZ37700	Second Opinion	1982	$12

FOUR PREPS, THE

CAPITOL

❏ T1814 [M]	Campus Confidential	1963	$18
❏ ST1814 [S]	Campus Confidential	1963	$25
❏ T1647 [M]	Campus Encore	1962	$25
❏ ST1647 [S]	Campus Encore	1962	$30
❏ T1216 [M]	Dancing and Dreaming	1959	$25
❏ ST1216 [S]	Dancing and Dreaming	1959	$30
❏ T1291 [M]	Early in the Morning	1960	$30
❏ DT1291 [R]	Early in the Morning	1960	$15
❏ T2169 [M]	How to Succeed in Love	1964	$18
❏ ST2169 [S]	How to Succeed in Love	1964	$25
❏ T1976 [M]	Songs for a Campus Party	1963	$18
❏ ST1976 [S]	Songs for a Campus Party	1963	$25
❏ T2708 [M]	The Best of the Four Preps	1967	$18
❏ ST2708 [S]	The Best of the Four Preps	1967	$15
❏ T994 [M]	The Four Preps	1958	$30
❏ T1566 [M]	The Four Preps on Campus	1961	$25
❏ ST1566 [S]	The Four Preps on Campus	1961	$30
❏ T1090 [M]	The Things We Did Last Summer	1958	$30

FOUR SEASONS, THE

MCA/CURB

❏ 5632	Starfighter	1985	$12

MOTOWN

❏ 788	Inside Out	1973	$0
—Canceled			

MOWEST

❏ MW108L	Chameleon	1972	$15

PHILIPS

❏ PHM200221 [M]	2nd Vault of Golden Hits	1966	$18
❏ PHS600221 [S]	2nd Vault of Golden Hits	1966	$25
❏ PHM200150 [M]	All the Song Hits of the Four Seasons	1964	$25
❏ PHS600150 [S]	All the Song Hits of the Four Seasons	1964	$30
❏ PHM200193 [M]	Big Hits by Burt Bacharach... Hal David...Bob Dylan	1965	$25
—Open book" cover			
❏ PHM200193 [M]	Big Hits by Burt Bacharach... Hal David...Bob Dylan	1966	$30
—Group photos on cover			
❏ PHS600193 [S]	Big Hits by Burt Bacharach... Hal David...Bob Dylan	1965	$30
—Open book" cover			
❏ PHS600193 [S]	Big Hits by Burt Bacharach... Hal David...Bob Dylan	1966	$40
—Group photos on cover			
❏ PHM200129 [M]	Born to Wander	1964	$25

❏ PHS600129 [S]	Born to Wander	1964	$30
❏ PHM200124 [M]	Dawn (Go Away) and 11 Other Great Songs	1964	$25
❏ PHS600124 [S]	Dawn (Go Away) and 11 Other Great Songs	1964	$30
❏ PHS-2-6501	Edizione d'Oro	1968	$30
—Number "4" on cover is red on gold foil			
❏ PHS-2-6501	Edizione d'Oro	1968	$30
—Number "4" on cover is white on gold foil			
❏ PHS-2-6501	Edizione d'Oro	1969	$30
—Number "4" on cover is white on gold board			
❏ PHS600341	Half & Half	1970	$25
❏ PHM200222 [M]	Lookin' Back	1966	$25
❏ PHS600222 [S]	Lookin' Back	1966	$30
❏ PHM200243 [M]	New Gold Hits	1967	$25
❏ PHS600243 [S]	New Gold Hits	1967	$30
❏ PHM200146 [M]	Rag Doll	1964	$25

Number	Title	Yr	NM
—Without yellow seal noting presence of "Save It For Me"			
❏ PHM200146 [M]	Rag Doll	1964	$25
—With yellow seal noting presence of "Save It For Me"			
❏ PHS600146 [S]	Rag Doll	1964	$30
—Without yellow seal noting presence of "Save It For Me"			
❏ PHS600146 [S]	Rag Doll	1964	$30
—With yellow seal noting presence of "Save It For Me"			
❏ PHM200164 [M]	The 4 Seasons Entertain You	1965	$25
—With orange seal noting presence of "Bye Bye Baby"			
❏ PHM200164 [M]	The 4 Seasons Entertain You	1965	$25
—With orange seal noting presence of "Bye Bye Baby" and "Toy Soldier			
❏ PHM200164 [M]	The 4 Seasons Entertain You	1965	$18
—With blue seal noting presence of "Bye Bye Baby" and "Toy Soldier			
❏ PHS600164 [S]	The 4 Seasons Entertain You	1965	$30
—With orange seal noting presence of "Bye Bye Baby"			
❏ PHS600164 [S]	The 4 Seasons Entertain You	1965	$25
—With blue seal noting presence of "Bye Bye Baby" and "Toy Soldier			
❏ PHS600164 [S]	The 4 Seasons Entertain	1965	$30
—With orange seal noting presence of "Bye Bye Baby" and "Toy Soldier			
❏ PHM200196 [M]	The 4 Seasons' Gold Vault of Hits	1965	$25
—Title in red print with no border			
❏ PHM200196 [M]	The 4 Seasons' Gold Vault of Hits	1965	$18
—Title in red print with black border			
❏ PHM200196 [M]	The 4 Seasons' Gold Vault of Hits	196?	$15
—Title in all-black print			
❏ PHS600196 [S]	The 4 Seasons' Gold Vault of Hits	1965	$30
—Title in red print with no border			
❏ PHS600196 [S]	The 4 Seasons' Gold Vault of Hits	1965	$25
—Title in red print with black border			
❏ PHS600196 [S]	The 4 Seasons' Gold Vault of Hits	196?	$18
—Title in all-black print			
❏ PHM200223 [M]	The Four Seasons' Christmas Album	1966	$30
—Reissue of Vee Jay album (same contents and order) with new cover			
❏ PHS600223 [S]	The Four Seasons' Christmas Album	1966	$30
❏ PHS600290	The Genuine Imitation Life Gazette	1969	$30
—Yellow newspaper			
❏ PHS600290	The Genuine Imitation Life Gazette	1969	$18
—White newspaper			
❏ PHM200201 [M]	Working My Way Back to You	1966	$25
❏ PHS600201 [S]	Working My Way Back to You	1966	$30

PICKWICK

❏ SPC-3223	Brotherhood of Man	1970	$15
—Mass-market version of Sears 609			

PRIVATE STOCK

❏ PS-7000	The Four Seasons Story	1975	$18

RHINO

❏ RNRP-72998	25th Anniversary Collection	1987	$30
❏ R1-71490	Anthology	1988	$15
❏ R1-71248	Big Hits by Burt Bacharach... Hal David...Bob Dylan	1988	$12
—Reissue of Philips 600-193			
❏ RNLP70234	The Four Seasons' Christmas Album	1987	$15
—Reissue of Philips album (same contents and order)			
❏ R1-70249	The Genuine Imitation Life Gazette	1988	$12
—Reissue of Philips 600-290			
❏ R1-70247	Working My Way Back to You	1988	$12
—Reissue of Philips 600-201			

SEARS

❏ SPS-609	Brotherhood of Man	1970	$30

VEE JAY

❏ LP-1059 [M]	Ain't That a Shame and 11 Others	1963	$30
❏ SR-1059 [S]	Ain't That a Shame and 11 Others	1963	$40
❏ LP-1056 [M]	Big Girls Don't Cry and Twelve Others	1963	$30
❏ SR-1056 [S]	Big Girls Don't Cry and Twelve Others	1963	$40
❏ LP-1082 [M]	Folk-Nanny	1964	$30
❏ SR-1082 [S]	Folk-Nanny	1964	$40
❏ LP-1065 [M]	Golden Hits of the Four Seasons	1963	$30
❏ SR-1065 [S]	Golden Hits of the Four Seasons	1963	$40
❏ LP-1088 [M]	More Golden Hits by the Four Seasons	1964	$30

Number	Title	Yr	NM
—With "Long Lonely Nights" on record			
❏ LP-1088 [M]	More Golden Hits by the Four Seasons	1964	$25
—With "Apple of My Eye" on record			
❏ SR-1088 [S]	More Golden Hits by the Four Seasons	1964	$40
—With "Long Lonely Nights" on record			
❏ SR-1088 [S]	More Golden Hits by the Four Seasons	1964	$30
—With "Apple of My Eye" on record			
❏ LP-1154 [M]	Recorded Live on Stage	1965	$30
❏ LPS-1154 [S]	Recorded Live on Stage	1965	$40
❏ LP-1053 [M]	Sherry & 11 Others	1962	$40
❏ SR-1053 [S]	Sherry & 11 Others	1962	$75
❏ LP-1082 [M]	Stay & Other Great Hits	1964	$30
—Retitled version of Folk-Nanny			
❏ SR-1082 [S]	Stay & Other Great Hits	1964	$30
—Retitled version of Folk-Nanny			
❏ LP1055 [M]	The Four Seasons Greetings	1962	$30
❏ SR1055 [S]	The Four Seasons Greetings	1962	$40
❏ LP-1121 [M]	We Love Girls	1965	$30
❏ LPS-1121 [S]	We Love Girls	1965	$40
WARNER BROS.			
❏ BS3016	Helicon	1977	$15
❏ 2WB3497	Reunited Live	1980	$18
❏ BS2900	Who Loves You	1975	$15

FOUR TOPS, THE

Number	Title	Yr	NM
ABC			
❏ AA-1092	At the Top	1978	$15
❏ D-968	Catfish	1976	$15
❏ D-862	Night Lights Harmony	1975	$15
❏ D-1014	The Show Must Go On	1977	$15
ABC DUNHILL			
❏ DSX-50129	Keeper of the Castle	1972	$15
❏ DSX-50188	Live & In Concert	1974	$15
❏ DSX-50144	Main Street People	1973	$15
❏ DSX-50166	Meeting of the Minds	1974	$15
ARISTA			
❏ AL-8492	Indestructible	1988	$10
CASABLANCA			
❏ NBLP7266	One More Mountain	1982	$12
❏ NBLP7258	Tonight!	1981	$12
COMMAND			
❏ CQD-40011 [Q]	Keeper of the Castle	1974	$30
❏ CQD-40012 [Q]	Main Street People	1974	$30
MCA			
❏ 27019	Greatest Hits	198?	$12
MOTOWN			

Number	Title	Yr	NM
❏ 657 [M]	4 Tops on Broadway	1967	$30
❏ MS-657 [S]	4 Tops on Broadway	1967	$30
❏ 647 [M]	4 Tops On Top	1966	$30
❏ MS-647 [S]	4 Tops On Top	1966	$30
❏ M9-809A3	Anthology	1974	$25
❏ 6066ML	Back Where I Belong	1983	$12
❏ MS-721	Changing Times	1970	$25
❏ 622 [M]	Four Tops	1964	$30
❏ MS-622 [S]	Four Tops	1964	$40
❏ M5-122V1	Four Tops	1981	$10
—Reissue of 622			
❏ M-740L	Four Tops Greatest Hits, Vol. 2	1971	$25
❏ 654 [M]	Four Tops Live!	1966	$30
❏ MS-654 [S]	Four Tops Live!	1966	$30
❏ 5258ML	Four Tops Live!	1983	$10
—Reissue of 654			
❏ MS-675	Four Tops Now!	1969	$25
❏ 660 [M]	Four Tops Reach Out	1967	$30
❏ MS-660 [S]	Four Tops Reach Out	1967	$30
❏ M5-149V1	Four Tops Reach Out	1981	$10
—Reissue of 660			
❏ 634 [M]	Four Tops Second Album	1965	$30
❏ MS-634 [S]	Four Tops Second Album	1965	$30
❏ 5314ML	Great Songs	1983	$12

Number	Title	Yr	NM
❏ 6130ML	Magic	1985	$12
❏ M-748L	Nature Planned It	1972	$25
❏ MS-695	Soul Spin	1969	$25
❏ MS-704	Still Waters Run Deep	1970	$25
❏ 5224ML	Still Waters Run Deep	1982	$10
—Reissue of 704			
❏ M5-114V1	Superstar Series, Vol. 14	1981	$12
❏ M-764D	The Best of the 4 Tops	1973	$18
❏ 662 [M]	The Four Tops Greatest Hits	1967	$30
❏ MS-662 [S]	The Four Tops Greatest Hits	1967	$25
❏ M5-209V1	The Four Tops' Greatest Hits	1981	$10
—Reissue of 662			
❏ 669 [M]	Yesterday's Dreams	1968	$30
❏ MS-669 [S]	Yesterday's Dreams	1968	$25
UNIVERSAL MOTOWN			
❏ 5315998 [S]	Four Tops Reach Out	2009	$25
WORKSHOP JAZZ			
❏ 217 [M]	Breakin' Through	1962	$0
—This album is pictured on some early Motown inner sleeves, but is not known to exist			

FOUR TUNES, THE

Number	Title	Yr	NM
JUBILEE			
❏ LP-1039 [M]	12 x 4	1957	$300

FOURTH CEKCION, THE

Number	Title	Yr	NM
SOLAR			
❏ 110	The Fourth Cekcion	1970	$75

FOURTH WAY, THE

Number	Title	Yr	NM
CAPITOL			
❏ ST-317	The Fourth Way	1969	$150
HARVEST			
❏ SKAO-423	The Sun and Moon Have Come Together	1970	$50
❏ ST-666	Werewolf	1971	$50

FOWLER, WALLY

Number	Title	Yr	NM
DECCA			
❏ DL8560 [M]	Call of the Cross	1958	$40
DOVE			
❏ 1000	A Tribute to Elvis Presley	1977	$25
KING			
❏ 702 [M]	Gospel Song Festival	1960	$150
STARDAY			
❏ SLP-301 [M]	All Nite Singing Concert	1964	$30
❏ SLP-112 [M]	All Nite Singing Gospel Concert	1960	$40

FOWLEY, KIM
Instrumental in the career of THE RUNAWAYS.

Number	Title	Yr	NM
ANTILLES			
❏ AN-7075	Snake Document Masquerade	1979	$15
CAPITOL			
❏ ST-11248	Automatic	1974	$25
❏ ST-11075	I'm Bad	1972	$25
❏ ST-11159	International Heroes	1973	$25
GNP CRESCENDO			
❏ GNPS-2132 [B]	Hollywood Confidential	197?	$25
IMPERIAL			
❏ LP-12413	Born to Be Wild	1968	$40
❏ LP-12443	Good Clean Fun	1969	$40
❏ LP-12423	Outrageous	1969	$40
PVC			
❏ 7906 [B]	Sunset Boulevard	1978	$25
TOWER			
❏ T5080 [M]	Love Is Alive and Well	1967	$100
❏ ST5080 [S]	Love Is Alive and Well	1967	$40

FOX, CURLY

Number	Title	Yr	NM
HARMONY			
❏ HL7302 [M]	Traveling Blues	1963	$25
STARDAY			
❏ SLP-235 [M]	Curly Fox and Texas Ruby	1963	$30

FOX, SAMANTHA

Number	Title	Yr	NM
JIVE			
❏ 1150-1-J	I Wanna Have Some Fun	1988	$12
❏ 1357-1-J	Just One Night	1991	$15
❏ 1061-1-J	Samantha Fox	1987	$12
❏ 1012-1-J	Touch Me	1986	$12

FOX, VIRGIL

Number	Title	Yr	NM
CAPITOL			
❏ P8531 [M]	Hark! The Herald Angels	196?	$15
❏ SP8531 [S]	Hark! The Herald Angels	196?	$18

FOX

Number	Title	Yr	NM
ARIOLA AMERICA			
❏ ST-50001	Fox	1975	$15

FOXX, INEZ (AND CHARLIE)

Number	Title	Yr	NM
DYNAMO			
❏ DM-7000 [M]	Come By Here	1967	$30
❏ DS-8000 [S]	Come By Here	1967	$40
❏ DM-7002 [M]	Inez and Charlie Foxx's Greatest Hits	1967	$30
❏ DS-8002 [S]	Inez and Charlie Foxx's Greatest Hits	1967	$40
❏ DS-8003	Swingin' Mockin' Band	1968	$30
SUE			
❏ LP-1027 [M]	Mockingbird	1966	$150
SYMBOL			
❏ SYM-4400 [M]	Mockingbird	1963	$175
VOLT			
❏ VOS-6022	Inez Foxx at Memphis	1973	$18

FOXY

Number	Title	Yr	NM
DASH			
❏ D30001	Foxy	1976	$15
❏ D30005	Get Off	1978	$12
❏ D30010	Hot Number	1979	$12
❏ D30016	Live	1980	$15
❏ D30015	Party Boys	1980	$15

FRACTION

Number	Title	Yr	NM
ANGELUS			
❏ 571 [B]	Moon Blood	1971	$4000
—VG value 1000; VG+ value 1500			

FRAGER, MALCOLM

Number	Title	Yr	NM
RCA VICTOR RED SEAL			
❏ LSC-2465 [S]	Prokofiev: Piano Concerto No. 2	1961	$150
—Originals with "shaded dog" label			

FRAMPTON, PETER
Also see THE HERD; HUMBLE PIE.

Number	Title	Yr	NM
A&M			
❏ SP-3722	Breaking All the Rules	1981	$12
❏ SP-4512	Frampton	1975	$12
❏ SP-3703	Frampton Comes Alive!	1976	$15
❏ SP-6505	Frampton Comes Alive!	198?	$12
—Budget-line reissue			
❏ PR-3703 [B]	Frampton Comes Alive!	1976	$35
—Single-record picture disc of highlights			
❏ SP-4389	Frampton's Camel	1973	$15
—Brown label			
❏ SP-4389	Frampton's Camel	1974	$12
—Silvery label			
❏ SP-4704	I'm In You	1977	$12
❏ SP-4704 [DJ]	I'm In You	1977	$40
—Promo-only picture disc			
❏ SP-17100 [DJ]	Peter Frampton Radio Special	1979	$25
—Promo-only interview record			
❏ SP-3619	Somethin's Happening	1974	$15
❏ SP-4905	The Art of Control	1982	$12
❏ SP-3710	Where I Should Be	1979	$12
❏ SP-4348	Wind of Change	1972	$15
—Brown label			
❏ SP-4348	Wind of Change	1974	$12
—Silvery label			
❏ SP-3133	Wind of Change	198?	$10
—Budget-line reissue			
ATLANTIC			
❏ PR848 [DJ]	Frampton Is Alive!	1986	$25
—Promo-only interview record			
❏ PR3093 [DJ]	Perfect Fit: A Candid Interview	1989	$25
—Promo-only album			
❏ 81290 [B]	Premonition	1986	$10
❏ 82030	Where All the Pieces Fit	1989	$10
MOBILE FIDELITY			
❏ 2-262	Frampton Comes Alive!	1996	$50
—Audiophile vinyl			
SWEET THUNDER			
❏ 6	Frampton Comes Alive!	198?	$150
—Audiophile edition			

FRANCHI, SERGIO

Number	Title	Yr	NM
4 CORNERS OF THE WORLD			
❏ FCL4223 [M]	Buon Natale	196?	$15
❏ FCS4223 [S]	Buon Natale	196?	$18
❏ FCL-4228 [M]	Il Fantastico	196?	$15
❏ FCS-4228 [S]	Il Fantastico	196?	$18
❏ FCL-4221 [M]	La Bella Italia	196?	$15
❏ FCS-4221 [S]	La Bella Italia	196?	$18
METROMEDIA			
❏ MD1047	Sergio Franchi	1971	$12
RCA VICTOR			
❏ LPM-3654 [M]	From Sergio -- With Love	1966	$12
❏ LSP-3654 [S]	From Sergio -- With Love	1966	$15
❏ LPM-3933 [M]	I'm a Fool to Want You	1968	$18
❏ LSP-3933 [S]	I'm a Fool to Want You	1968	$15
❏ LPM-3500 [M]	La Dolce Italy	1966	$12

Number	Title	Yr	NM
❏ LSP-3500 [S]	La Dolce Italy	1966	$15
❏ LPM-3310 [M]	Live at the Cocoanut Grove	1965	$12
❏ LSP-3310 [S]	Live at the Cocoanut Grove	1965	$15
❏ LPM-3365 [M]	Songs of Richard Rodgers	1965	$12
❏ LSP-3365 [S]	Songs of Richard Rodgers	1965	$15
❏ ANL1-2643	Songs of Richard Rodgers	1977	$10
— Reissue of LSP-3365			
❏ ANL1-1070	The Best of Sergio Franchi	1975	$12
❏ LPM-2943 [M]	The Exciting Voice of Sergio Franchi	1964	$15
❏ LSP-2943 [S]	The Exciting Voice of Sergio Franchi	1964	$18
❏ LPM-3437 [M]	The Heart of Christmas (Cuor' di Natale)	1965	$15
❏ LSP-3437 [S]	The Heart of Christmas (Cuor' di Natale)	1965	$18
❏ LPM-3810 [M]	There Goes My Heart	1967	$12
❏ LSP-3810 [S]	There Goes My Heart	1967	$15
❏ VPS-6082	This Is Sergio Franchi	1972	$15
❏ APL1-2132	Volare	1976	$12
❏ LSP-4018 [S]	Wine and Song	1968	$15
❏ LPM-4018 [M]	Wine and Song	1968	$25
❏ AFL1-4018	Wine and Song	1977	$10
— Reissue of LSP-4018			

RCA VICTOR RED SEAL

Number	Title	Yr	NM
❏ LM-2674 [M]	Broadway...I Love You	1963	$15
❏ LSC-2674 [S]	Broadway...I Love You	1963	$18
❏ LM-2657 [M]	Our Man from Italy	1963	$15
❏ LSC-2657 [S]	Our Man from Italy	1963	$18
❏ LM-2640 [M]	Romantic Italian Songs	1962	$15
❏ LSC-2640 [S]	Romantic Italian Songs	1962	$18
❏ LM-2675 [M]	The Dream Duet	1963	$15
— With Anna Moffo			
❏ LSC-2675 [S]	The Dream Duet	1963	$18
— With Anna Moffo			
❏ LM-2696 [M]	The Women in My Life	1964	$15
❏ LSC-2696 [S]	The Women in My Life	1964	$18

UNITED ARTISTS

Number	Title	Yr	NM
❏ UAS-6727	Within Me	1970	$12

FRANCIS, CONNIE, AND HANK WILLIAMS, JR.

Also see each artist's individual listings.

MGM

Number	Title	Yr	NM
❏ E-4251 [M]	Connie Francis & Hank Williams, Jr. Sing Great Country Favorites	1964	$30
❏ SE-4251 [S]	Connie Francis & Hank Williams, Jr. Sing Great Country Favorites	1964	$40

FRANCIS, CONNIE

LEO

Number	Title	Yr	NM
❏ LE-903 [M]	Connie Francis and the Kids Next Door	1967	$50
❏ LES-903 [S]	Connie Francis and the Kids Next Door	1967	$75

MATI-MOR

Number	Title	Yr	NM
❏ 8002 [M]	Sing Along wth Connie Francis	1961	$40
— Made for Brylcreem			

METRO

Number	Title	Yr	NM
❏ M-519 [M]	Connie Francis	1964	$25
❏ MS-519 [S]	Connie Francis	1964	$30
❏ M-538 [M]	Folk Favorites	1965	$25
❏ MS-538 [S]	Folk Favorites	1965	$30
❏ M-571 [M]	Songs of Love	1966	$25
❏ MS-571 [S]	Songs of Love	1966	$30
❏ M-603 [M]	The Incomparable Connie Francis	1967	$25
❏ MS-603 [S]	The Incomparable Connie Francis	1967	$30

MGM

Number	Title	Yr	NM
❏ E-4298 [M]	All Time International Hits	1965	$30
❏ SE-4298 [S]	All Time International Hits	1965	$30
❏ E-4253 [M]	A New Kind of Connie	1964	$30
❏ SE-4253 [S]	A New Kind of Connie	1964	$30
❏ T-90068 [M]	A New Kind of Connie	1964	$30
— Capitol Record Club issue			
❏ ST-90068 [S]	A New Kind of Connie	1964	$35
— Capitol Record Club issue			
❏ E-4048 [M]	Award Winning Motion Picture Hits	1963	$30
❏ SE-4048 [S]	Award Winning Motion Picture Hits	1963	$30
❏ T-90027 [M]	Award Winning Motion Picture Hits	196?	$30
— Capitol Record Club edition			
❏ ST-90027 [S]	Award Winning Motion Picture Hits	196?	$30
— Capitol Record Club edition			
❏ E-3792 [M]	Christmas in My Heart	1959	$30
❏ SE-3792 [S]	Christmas in My Heart	1959	$40
— Same as above, but in stereo			
❏ SE-4573 [S]	Connie & Clyde	1968	$30
❏ E-4573 [M]	Connie & Clyde	1968	$175
— Yellow label "Special Disc Jockey Record" in stereo cover with "Mono" sticker			
❏ E-3913 [M]	Connie Francis at the Copa	1961	$30
❏ SE-3913 [S]	Connie Francis at the Copa	1961	$40
❏ E-4472 [M]	Connie Francis On Broadway Today	1967	$30
❏ SE-4472 [S]	Connie Francis On Broadway Today	1967	$30

Number	Title	Yr	NM
❏ SE-4585	Connie Francis Sings Bacharach & David	1968	$30
❏ E-4294 [M]	Connie Francis Sings For Mama	1965	$30
❏ SE-4294 [S]	Connie Francis Sings For Mama	1965	$30
❏ E-4049 [M]	Connie Francis Sings Second Hand Love and Other Hits	1962	$30
❏ SE-4049 [S]	Connie Francis Sings Second Hand Love and Other Hits	1962	$30
❏ E-4399 [M]	Connie's Christmas	1966	$30
❏ SE-4399 [S]	Connie's Christmas	1966	$30
❏ E-3793 [M]	Connie's Greatest Hits	1960	$30
❏ E-3795 [M]	Country and Western Golden Hits	1960	$30
❏ SE-3795 [S]	Country and Western Golden Hits	1960	$40
❏ E-4079 [M]	Country Music Connie Style	1962	$30
❏ SE-4079 [S]	Country Music Connie Style	1962	$30
❏ E-4022 [M]	Dance Party	196?	$30
— Retitled version of "Do the Twist"			
❏ SE-4022 [S]	Dance Party	196?	$30
— Retitled version of "Do the Twist"			
❏ E-4022 [M]	Do the Twist	1962	$30
❏ SE-4022 [S]	Do the Twist	1962	$40
❏ E-3969 [M]	Folk Song Favorites	1961	$30
❏ SE-3969 [S]	Folk Song Favorites	1961	$40
❏ E-4123 [M]	Follow the Boys	1963	$30
❏ SE-4123 [S]	Follow the Boys	1963	$30
❏ E-4023 [M]	Fun Songs for Children	1962	$50
❏ E-4124 [M]	German Favorites	1963	$30
❏ SE-4124 [S]	German Favorites	1963	$30
❏ E-4474 [M]	Grandes Exitos del Cine de los Anos 60	1967	$30
❏ SE-4474 [S]	Grandes Exitos del Cine de los Anos 60	1967	$30
❏ E-4145 [M]	Greatest American Waltzes	1963	$30
❏ SE-4145 [S]	Greatest American Waltzes	1963	$30
❏ GAS-109	Greatest Golden Groovie Goodies (Golden Archive Series)	1970	$30
❏ MG-1-5410	Greatest Hits	198?	$15
❏ MG-1-5411	Greatest Jewish Hits	198?	$15
❏ E-4522 [M]	Hawaii: Connie	1968	$150
❏ SE-4522 [S]	Hawaii: Connie	1968	$30
❏ MG-1-5406	I'm Me Again	198?	$15
❏ E-4210 [M]	In the Summer of His Years	1964	$30
❏ SE-4210 [S]	In the Summer of His Years	1964	$30
❏ E-4013 [M]	Irish Favorites	1962	$30
❏ SE-4013 [S]	Irish Favorites	1962	$40
❏ E-3791 [M]	Italian Favorites	1959	$30
❏ SE-3791 [S]	Italian Favorites	1959	$40
❏ E-4355 [M]	Jealous Heart	1966	$30
❏ SE-4355 [S]	Jealous Heart	1966	$30
❏ E-3869 [M]	Jewish Favorites	1961	$30
❏ SE-3869 [S]	Jewish Favorites	1961	$40
❏ E-4411 [M]	Live at the Sahara in Las Vegas	1967	$30
❏ SE-4411 [S]	Live at the Sahara in Las Vegas	1967	$30
❏ E-4229 [M]	Looking for Love	1964	$30
❏ SE-4229 [S]	Looking for Love	1964	$30
❏ E-4448 [M]	Love, Italian Style	1967	$30
❏ SE-4448 [S]	Love, Italian Style	1967	$30
❏ E-4161 [M]	Mala Femmena & Connie's Big Hits from Italy	1963	$30
❏ SE-4161 [S]	Mala Femmena & Connie's Big Hits from Italy	1963	$30
❏ E-4102 [M]	Modern Italian Hits	1963	$30
❏ SE-4102 [S]	Modern Italian Hits	1963	$30
❏ E-3942 [M]	More Greatest Hits	1961	$30
❏ SE-3942 [S]	More Greatest Hits	1961	$40
❏ E-3871 [M]	More Italian Favorites	1960	$30
❏ SE-3871 [S]	More Italian Favorites	1960	$40
❏ E-4382 [M]	Movie Greats of the 60's	1966	$30
❏ SE-4382 [S]	Movie Greats of the 60's	1966	$30
❏ ST-91145	My Best to You	1968	$30
— Capitol Record Club			
❏ E-4487 [M]	My Heart Cries for You	1967	$30
❏ SE-4487 [S]	My Heart Cries for You	1967	$30
❏ E-3776 [M]	My Thanks to You	1959	$30
❏ SE-3776 [S]	My Thanks to You	1959	$40
❏ E-3965 [M]	Never on Sunday and Other Title Songs from Motion Pictures	1961	$30
❏ SE-3965 [S]	Never on Sunday and Other Title Songs from Motion Pictures	1961	$40
❏ ST-90592 [S]	Never on Sunday and Other Title Songs from Motion Pictures	1965	$30
— Capitol Record Club edition			
❏ E-3794 [M]	Rock 'N' Roll Million Sellers	1960	$30
❏ SE-3794 [S]	Rock 'N' Roll Million Sellers	1960	$40
❏ E-3893 [M]	Songs to a Swinging Band	1961	$30
❏ SE-3893 [S]	Songs to a Swinging Band	1961	$40
❏ E-3853 [M]	Spanish and Latin American Favorites	1960	$30
❏ SE-3853 [S]	Spanish and Latin American Favorites	1960	$40
❏ E-3761 [M]	The Exciting Connie Francis	1959	$100
— Yellow label			
❏ SE-3761 [S]	The Exciting Connie Francis	1959	$150
— Yellow label			
❏ E-3761 [M]	The Exciting Connie Francis	1959	$30
— Black label			
❏ SE-3761 [S]	The Exciting Connie Francis	1959	$40

Number	Title	Yr	NM
— Black label			
❏ SE-4655	The Songs of Les Reed	1969	$30
❏ T90510 [M]	The Very Best of Connie Francis	1965	$40
— Capitol Record Club edition			
❏ ST90510 [S]	The Very Best of Connie Francis	1965	$40
— Capitol Record Club edition			
❏ E-4167 [M]	The Very Best of Connie Francis	1963	$30
❏ SE-4167 [S]	The Very Best of Connie Francis	1963	$30
❏ SE-4637	The Wedding Cake	1969	$30
❏ E-3686 [M]	Who's Sorry Now?	1958	$150
— Yellow label			

Number	Title	Yr	NM
❏ E-3686 [M]	Who's Sorry Now?	1960	$40
— Black label			

POLYDOR

Number	Title	Yr	NM
❏ 839923-1	12 Exitos De Connie Francis	198?	$12
❏ 827582-1	Greatest Hits	1985	$12
❏ 827584-1	Greatest Jewish Hits	1985	$12
❏ 839922-1	Lo Mejor De Su Repertorio	198?	$12
❏ 827569-1	The Very Best of Connie Francis	1985	$12

FRANCIS, EDMUND, THE ORGAN AND CHIMES OF

IMPERIAL

Number	Title	Yr	NM
❏ LP-9250 [M]	Merry Christmas	1964	$15
❏ LP-12250 [S]	Merry Christmas	1964	$18

FRANCIS, PANAMA

20TH CENTURY FOX

Number	Title	Yr	NM
❏ TFS-6101 [S]	Tough Talk	196?	$30
❏ TFM-6101 [M]	Tough Talk	196?	$30

CLASSIC JAZZ

Number	Title	Yr	NM
❏ 149	Panama Francis and His Savoy Sultans, Volume 1	197?	$25
❏ 150	Panama Francis and His Savoy Sultans, Volume 2	197?	$25

EPIC

Number	Title	Yr	NM
❏ LN3839 [M]	Exploding Drums	1959	$75
❏ BN629 [S]	Exploding Drums	1959	$75

STASH

Number	Title	Yr	NM
❏ ST-223	Everything Swings	198?	$25
❏ ST-218	Grooving	198?	$25

FRANKE AND THE KNOCKOUTS

MCA

Number	Title	Yr	NM
❏ 5473	Makin' the Point	1984	$12

MILLENNIUM

Number	Title	Yr	NM
❏ BXL1-7763	Below the Belt	1982	$10
❏ DJL1-7764 [EP]	Below the Belt Sampler	1982	$25
— Promo-only three-song sampler; contains live version of "I Need Love (The Knockout Shuffle)" that was not issued on LP			
❏ BXL1-7755	Franke and the Knockouts	1981	$10
❏ DJL1-4015 [DJ]	Special Radio Series Volume X	1981	$25
— Promo-only music and interview disc			

FRANKIE AND JOHNNY

WARNER BROS.

Number	Title	Yr	NM
❏ BS2675	The Sweetheart Sampler	1973	$25

FRANKIE GOES TO HOLLYWOOD

ATLANTIC

Number	Title	Yr	NM
❏ 82587	Bang...The Greatest Hits of Frankie Goes to Hollywood	1994	$18

ISLAND

Number	Title	Yr	NM
❏ R120202	Liverpool	1986	$12
— RCA Music Service edition			
❏ 90546	Liverpool	1986	$10
❏ 90232	Welcome to the Pleasuredome	1985	$18

Number	Title	Yr	NM

FRANKLIN, ALAN, EXPLOSION
ALADDIN
| ❏ 104049 | Come Home Baby | 1969 | $100 |

HORNE
| ❏ 0 | Climax | 1970 | $300 |

— Pre-release or demo versions of tracks from The Blues Climax.
| ❏ JC-888 | The Blues Climax | 1970 | $150 |

FRANKLIN, ARETHA
4 MEN WITH BEARDS
| ❏ 4M115 | Aretha Live at Fillmore West | 2003 | $18 |

— Reissue on 180-gram vinyl
| ❏ 4M131 | Aretha Now | 2006 | $18 |

— Reissue on 180-gram vinyl
| ❏ 4M101 | I Never Loved a Man the Way I Love You | 2001 | $18 |

— Reissue on 180-gram vinyl
| ❏ 4M130 | Lady Soul | 2006 | $18 |

— Reissue on 180-gram vinyl
| ❏ 4M111 | Soul '69 | 2002 | $18 |

— Reissue on 180-gram vinyl
| ❏ 4M114 | • Spirit in the Dark | 2003 | $18 |

— Reissue on 180-gram vinyl

ARISTA
| ❏ AL-9538 | Aretha | 1980 | $12 |
| ❏ AL-8442 | Aretha | 1986 | $12 |

— Different album than 9538
❏ AL8-8019	Get It Right	1983	$12
❏ AL-9602	Jump To It	1982	$12
❏ AL-8344	Jump To It	1985	$10

— Budget-line reissue
| ❏ AL-9552 | Love All the Hurt Away | 1981 | $12 |
| ❏ AL-8368 | Love All the Hurt Away | 1985 | $10 |

— Budget-line reissue
❏ A2L-8497	One Lord, One Faith, One Baptism	1987	$25
❏ AL-8572	Through the Storm	1989	$12
❏ AL8-8286	Who's Zoomin' Who	1985	$12

ATLANTIC
❏ 81668	30 Greatest Hits	1986	$18
❏ SD19161	Almighty Fire	1978	$15
❏ SD 2-906	Amazing Grace	1972	$25
❏ 8176 [M]	Aretha: Lady Soul	1968	$30
❏ SD8176 [S]	Aretha: Lady Soul	1968	$25

— Green and blue label
| ❏ SD8176 | Aretha: Lady Soul | 1969 | $15 |

— Green and red label
| ❏ 8150 [M] | Aretha Arrives | 1967 | $30 |
| ❏ SD8150 [S] | Aretha Arrives | 1967 | $25 |

— Green and blue label
| ❏ SD8150 | Aretha Arrives | 1969 | $15 |

— Green and red label
| ❏ 8212 [M] | Aretha Franklin: Soul '69 | 1969 | $50 |

— White label promo; no stock copies in mono
❏ SD8212 [S]	Aretha Franklin: Soul '69	1969	$18
❏ SD8207	Aretha in Paris	1968	$18
❏ QD7205 [Q]	Aretha Live at Fillmore West	1973	$40
❏ SD7205 [S]	Aretha Live at Fillmore West	1971	$18
❏ 7205 [M]	Aretha Live at Fillmore West	1971	$40

— Mono is white label promo only with "d/j copy monaural" sticker on front cover
| ❏ SD8186 | Aretha Now | 1968 | $25 |

— Green and blue label
| ❏ SD8186 | Aretha Now | 1969 | $15 |

— Green and red label
❏ SD8227	Aretha's Gold	1969	$18
❏ SD8295 [S]	Aretha's Greatest Hits	1971	$18
❏ 8295 [M]	Aretha's Greatest Hits	1971	$40

— Mono is white label promo only in stereo cover with "d/j monaural" sticker
❏ 81230	Aretha's Jazz	1984	$12
❏ SD7265	Hey Now Hey (The Other Side of the Sky)	1973	$15
❏ STAO-95151	Hey Now Hey (The Other Side of the Sky)	1973	$18

— Capitol Record Club edition
| ❏ 8139 [M] | I Never Loved a Man the Way I Love You | 1967 | $30 |
| ❏ SD8139 [S] | I Never Loved a Man the Way I Love You | 1967 | $25 |

— Green and blue label
| ❏ SD8139 | I Never Loved a Man the Way I Love You | 1969 | $15 |

— Green and red label
❏ SD19248	La Diva	1979	$15
❏ SD7292	Let Me in Your Life	1974	$15
❏ SD18176	Sparkle	1976	$15
❏ SD8265 [S]	Spirit in the Dark	1970	$18
❏ 8265 [M]	Spirit in the Dark	1970	$40

— Mono is white label promo only in stereo cover with "d/j monaural" sticker
❏ SD19102	Sweet Passion	1977	$15
❏ SD18204	Ten Years of Gold	1976	$15
❏ QD8305 [Q]	The Best of Aretha Franklin	1974	$30
❏ 81280	The Best of Aretha Franklin	1985	$12
❏ SD8248 [S]	This Girl's in Love with You	1970	$18
❏ 8248 [M]	This Girl's in Love with You	1970	$40

Number	Title	Yr	NM

— Mono is white label promo only; cover has "d/j copy monaural" sticker on front
❏ SD18116	With Everything I Feel in Me	1974	$15
❏ SD18151	You	1975	$15
❏ SD7213 [S]	Young, Gifted & Black	1972	$18
❏ 7213 [M]	Young, Gifted & Black	1972	$40

— Mono is promo only; "d/j copy monaural" sticker on front cover

CHECKER
| ❏ 10009 [M] | Gospel Soul | 1967 | $25 |

— Reissue with new title and cover
| ❏ 10009 [M] | Songs of Faith | 1965 | $500 |

— Original issue of this album; cover has Aretha sitting at a piano

COLUMBIA
| ❏ CL1612 [M] | Aretha | 1961 | $150 |

— Red and black label with six "eye" logos
| ❏ CL1612 [M] | Aretha | 1963 | $50 |

— Guaranteed High Fidelity" on label
| ❏ CL1612 [M] | Aretha | 1965 | $35 |

— 360 Sound Mono" on label
| ❏ CS8412 [S] | Aretha | 1961 | $175 |

— Red and black label with six "eye" logos
| ❏ CS8412 [S] | Aretha | 1963 | $75 |

— 360 Sound Stereo" on label
❏ FC40708	Aretha After Hours	1987	$25
❏ CL2673 [M]	Aretha Franklin's Greatest Hits	1967	$75
❏ CS9473 [S]	Aretha Franklin's Greatest Hits	1967	$50

— 360 Sound Stereo" on label
| ❏ CS9601 | Aretha Franklin's Greatest Hits, Volume 2 | 1968 | $50 |

— 360 Sound Stereo" on label
❏ FC40105	Aretha Franklin Sings the Blues	1985	$25
❏ KG31355	In the Beginning/The World of Aretha Franklin 1960-1967	1972	$50
❏ CL2079 [M]	Laughing on the Outside	1963	$50

— Guaranteed High Fidelity" on label
| ❏ CL2079 [M] | Laughing on the Outside | 1965 | $35 |

— 360 Sound Mono" on label
| ❏ CS8879 [S] | Laughing on the Outside | 1963 | $75 |

— 360 Sound Stereo" on label
| ❏ CL2281 [M] | Runnin' Out of Fools | 1964 | $50 |

— Guaranteed High Fidelity" on label
| ❏ CL2281 [M] | Runnin' Out of Fools | 1965 | $35 |

— 360 Sound Mono" on label
| ❏ CS9081 [S] | Runnin' Out of Fools | 1964 | $75 |

— 360 Sound Stereo" on label
| ❏ CS9776 | Soft and Beautiful | 1969 | $50 |

— 360 Sound Stereo" on label
| ❏ CL2521 [M] | Soul Sister | 1966 | $50 |
| ❏ CS9321 [S] | Soul Sister | 1966 | $75 |

— 360 Sound Stereo" on label
❏ PC38042	Sweet Bitter Love	1982	$25
❏ CL2754 [M]	Take a Look	1967	$75
❏ CS9554 [S]	Take a Look	1967	$50

— 360 Sound Stereo" on label
| ❏ CL2629 [M] | Take It Like You Give It | 1967 | $75 |
| ❏ CS9429 [S] | Take It Like You Give It | 1967 | $50 |

— 360 Sound Stereo" on label
| ❏ CL1761 [M] | The Electrifying Aretha Franklin | 1962 | $40 |

— Red and black label with six "eye" logos
| ❏ CL1761 [M] | The Electrifying Aretha Franklin | 1963 | $50 |

— Guaranteed High Fidelity" on label
| ❏ CL1761 [M] | The Electrifying Aretha Franklin | 1965 | $35 |

— 360 Sound Mono" on label
| ❏ CS8561 [S] | The Electrifying Aretha Franklin | 1962 | $150 |

— Red and black label with six "eye" logos

Number	Title	Yr	NM
❏ CS8561 [S]	The Electrifying Aretha Franklin	1963	$30

— 360 Sound Stereo" on label
❏ KC31953	The First 12 Sides	1973	$30
❏ C237377	The Legendary Queen of Soul	1981	$30
❏ CL1876 [M]	The Tender, The Moving, The Swinging Aretha Franklin	1962	$40

— Red and black label with six "eye" logos
| ❏ CL1876 [M] | The Tender, The Moving, The Swinging Aretha Franklin | 1963 | $50 |

— Guaranteed High Fidelity" on label
| ❏ CL1876 [M] | The Tender, The Moving, The Swinging Aretha Franklin | 1965 | $35 |

— 360 Sound Mono" on label
| ❏ CS8676 [S] | The Tender, The Moving, The Swinging Aretha Franklin | 1963 | $75 |

— 360 Sound Stereo" on label
| ❏ CS8676 [S] | The Tender, The Moving, The Swinging Aretha Franklin | 1962 | $150 |

— Red and black label with six "eye" logos
| ❏ CS9956 | Today I Sing the Blues | 1970 | $35 |

— 360 Sound Stereo" on label
| ❏ GP4 | Two All-Time Great Albums in One Great Package | 196? | $75 |

— Contains CS 9081 and CS 9429
| ❏ CL2163 [M] | Unforgettable | 1964 | $50 |

— Guaranteed High Fidelity" on label
| ❏ CL2163 [M] | Unforgettable | 1965 | $35 |

— 360 Sound Mono" on label
| ❏ CS8963 [S] | Unforgettable | 1964 | $75 |

— 360 Sound Stereo" on label
| ❏ CL2351 [M] | Yeah!!! | 1965 | $50 |

— Guaranteed High Fidelity" on label
| ❏ CL2351 [M] | Yeah!!! | 1966 | $35 |

— 360 Sound Mono" on label
| ❏ CS9151 [S] | Yeah!!! | 1965 | $75 |

— 360 Sound Stereo" on label

COLUMBIA SPECIAL PRODUCTS
| ❏ C11282 | Runnin' Out of Fools | 1972 | $30 |
| ❏ C10589 | Take a Look | 1971 | $30 |

HARMONY
❏ KH30606	Greatest Hits 1960-1965	1971	$30
❏ KH30606	Greatest Hits 1960-1966	1972	$30
❏ HS11349	Once in a Lifetime	1969	$30
❏ HS11418	Two Sides of Love	1970	$30

FRANKLIN, CAROLYN
RCA VICTOR
❏ LSP-4160	Baby Dynamite	1969	$25
❏ LSP-4317	Chain Reaction	1970	$25
❏ LSP-4411	I'd Rather Be Lonely	1973	$25

FRANKLIN, ERMA
BRUNSWICK
| ❏ BL754147 | Soul Sister | 1969 | $25 |

EPIC
| ❏ LN3824 [M] | Her Name Is Erma | 1962 | $30 |
| ❏ BN619 [S] | Her Name Is Erma | 1962 | $40 |

FRANKLIN, HENRY
BLACK JAZZ
| ❏ QD-7 | The Skipper | 1972 | $25 |
| ❏ QD-17 | The Skipper At Home | 1974 | $25 |

CATALYST
| ❏ 7618 | Tribal Dance | 1976 | $30 |

OVATION
| ❏ OV-1801 | Blue Lights | 197? | $35 |

FRANKLIN, RODNEY
COLUMBIA
❏ FC37154	Endless Flight	1982	$25
❏ JC35558	In the Center	1978	$25
❏ FC40307	It Takes Two	1986	$25
❏ FC38198	Learning to Love	1983	$25
❏ FC38953	Marathon	1984	$25
❏ JC36747	Rodney Franklin	1980	$25
❏ FC39962	Sky Dance	1985	$25
❏ JC36122	You'll Never Know	1979	$25

NOVUS
| ❏ 3038-1-N | King of Diamonds | 1988 | $25 |

FRANKS, MICHAEL
BRUT
| ❏ 6005 | Michael Franks | 1973 | $50 |

DIRECT DISK
| ❏ SD-16611 | Tiger in the Rain | 1980 | $75 |

— Audiophile vinyl

DRG
| ❏ SL-5210 | Previously Unavailable | 1989 | $30 |

— Reissue of John Hammond LP

Number	Title	Yr	NM

JOHN HAMMOND
| ❑ BFW38664 | Previously Unavailable | 1983 | $35 |

REPRISE
| ❑ 26183 | Blue Pacific | 1990 | $15 |
| ❑ MS2230 | The Art of Tea | 1975 | $25 |

WARNER BROS.
❑ BSK3167	Burchfield Nines	1978	$25
❑ BSK3648	Objects of Desire	1981	$25
❑ BSK3427	One Bad Habit	1980	$25
❑ 23962	Passion Fruit	1983	$20
❑ 25275	Skin Dive	1985	$20
❑ BS3004	Sleeping Gypsy	1977	$25
❑ 25570	The Camera Never Lies	1987	$20
❑ BSK3294	Tiger in the Rain	1979	$25

FRANKS, TILLMAN, SINGERS
HILLTOP
| ❑ JM-6019 | The Hank Williams Songbook | 196? | $15 |

FRANTIC
LIZARD
| ❑ 20103 | Conception | 1971 | $30 |

FRANZETTI, CARLOS
GUINNESS
| ❑ GNS36076 [B] | Grafitti | 1977 | $250 |

INNER CITY
| ❑ IC-1113 | Galaxy Dust | 1980 | $30 |

PROGRESSIVE
| ❑ PRO-7030 | Prometheus | 198? | $30 |

FRASER, ANDY
Also see FREE.
ISLAND
| ❑ 90153 | Fine Fine Line | 1984 | $12 |

FRASER, HUGH
JAZZIMAGE
| ❑ JZ-115 | Looking Up | 1988 | $25 |

FRATERNITY OF MAN, THE
ABC
| ❑ S-647 | The Fraternity of Man | 1968 | $30 |
DOT
| ❑ DLP-25955 | Get It On | 1969 | $30 |

FRAWLEY, WILLIAM
DOT
| ❑ DLP-3061 [M] | William Frawley Sings the Old Ones | 1958 | $40 |

FRAZIER, CAESAR
Some of these may spell his first name "Ceasar."
Organist and male singer. Some of these may spell his first name "Ceasar."
EASTBOUND
| ❑ 9009 | Caesar Frazier '74 | 1974 | $40 |
| ❑ 9002 | Hail Caesar! | 1973 | $50 |
WESTBOUND
| ❑ WT6103 | Another Life | 1978 | $30 |
| ❑ 206 | Caesar Frazier '75 | 1975 | $30 |

FRAZIER, DALLAS
CAPITOL
❑ T2552 [M]	Elvira	1966	$25
❑ ST2552 [S]	Elvira	1966	$30
❑ T2764 [M]	Tell It Like It Is	1967	$30
❑ ST2764 [S]	Tell It Like It Is	1967	$25

FREAK SCENE, THE
COLUMBIA
| ❑ CL2656 [M] | Psychedelic Psoul | 1967 | $80 |
| ❑ CS9456 [S] | Psychedelic Psoul | 1967 | $150 |

FREBERG, STAN
CAPITOL
| ❑ T777 [M] | A Child's Garden of Freberg | 1957 | $50 |
—Turquoise label
❑ T1694 [M]	Face the Funnies	1962	$30
❑ T1816 [M]	Madison Ave. Werewolf	1962	$30
❑ W1573 [M]	Stan Freberg Presents the United States of America	1961	$30
❑ SW1573 [S]	Stan Freberg Presents the United States of America	1961	$30
❑ T1242 [M]	Stan Freberg with the Original Cast	1959	$30
❑ SM-1242 [R]	Stan Freberg with the Original Cast	197?	$12
❑ T2020 [M]	The Best of Stan Freberg	1964	$30
❑ SM-2020 [R]	The Best of Stan Freberg	197?	$12
❑ WBO1035 [M]	The Best of the Stan Freberg Shows	1958	$75
❑ SM-11765	The Best of the Stan Freberg Shows	197?	$15

Number	Title	Yr	NM
❑ T2551 [M]	The Stan Freberg Underground Show #1	1966	$25
❑ ST2551 [S]	The Stan Freberg Underground Show #1	1966	$30
❑ SM-2551 [S]	The Stan Freberg Underground Show #1	197?	$12

FRED, JOHN, AND HIS PLAYBOY BAND
GUINNESS
| ❑ GNS36022 | Juke Box | 1977 | $40 |
JIN
| ❑ 9027 | The Best of John Fred and His Playboys | 198? | $12 |
PAULA
❑ LP-2193 [M]	34:40 of John Fred and His Playboys	1967	$25
❑ LPS-2193 [S]	34:40 of John Fred and His Playboys	1967	$35
❑ LP-2197 [M]	Agnes English	1967	$30
❑ LPS-2197 [S]	Agnes English	1967	$35
❑ LP-2191 [M]	John Fred and His Playboys	1966	$25
❑ LPS-2191 [S]	John Fred and His Playboys	1966	$35
❑ LPS-2197 [S]	Judy in Disguise with Glasses	1968	$25
—Retitled version of "Agnes English"
| ❑ LPS-2201 | Permanently Stated | 1969 | $35 |
UNI
| ❑ 73077 | Love in My Soul | 1970 | $30 |

FREDDIE AND THE DREAMERS
CAPITOL
| ❑ SM-11896 [B] | The Best of Freddie and the Dreamers | 1976 | $12 |
—"I'm Telling You Now," "You Were Made for Me," "I Just Don't Understand," "A Little You" and "Over You" are in stereo, the rest are mono.
MERCURY
❑ MG-21026 [M]	Do the Freddie	1965	$25
❑ SR-61026 [S]	Do the Freddie	1965	$30
❑ MG-21053 [M]	Frantic Freddie	1965	$18
❑ SR-61053 [S]	Frantic Freddie	1965	$25
❑ MG-21017 [M]	Freddie and the Dreamers	1965	$30
❑ SR-61017 [R]	Freddie and the Dreamers	1965	$25
❑ MG-21061 [M]	Fun Lovin' Freddie	1966	$18
❑ SR-61061 [S]	Fun Lovin' Freddie	1966	$25
❑ MG-21031 [M]	Seaside Swingers	1965	$25
❑ SR-61031 [S]	Seaside Swingers	1965	$30
TOWER
| ❑ T5003 [M] | I'm Telling You Now | 1965 | $30 |
—Contains only two Freddie and the Dreamers songs, but the group's picture is on the cover. Also includes Four Just Men (2), Heinz (2), Linda Laine and the Sinners (2), Mike Rabin and the Demons (2) and The Toggery Five (2)
| ❑ DT5003 [R] | I'm Telling You Now | 1965 | $25 |
—Contains only two Freddie and the Dreamers songs, but the group's picture is on the cover. Also includes Four Just Men (2), Heinz (2), Linda Laine and the Sinners (2), Mike Rabin and the Demons (2) and The Toggery Five (2)

FREDRIC
FORTE
| ❑ 80461 | Phases and Faces | 1968 | $800 |

FREE
Also see PAUL KOSSOFF; BAD COMPANY; THE FIRM.
A&M
❑ SP-3663	Best of Free	1975	$15
❑ SP-4268	Fire and Water	1970	$18
❑ SP-3126	Fire and Water	198?	$10
—Budget-line reissue
❑ 5318185	Fire and Water	2009	$25
❑ SP-4204	Free	1969	$18
❑ SP-4349	Free at Last	1972	$18
❑ SP-4306	Free Live!	1971	$18
❑ SP-4287	Highway	1971	$18
❑ SP-4198	Tons of Sobs	1969	$18
ISLAND
| ❑ SW-9324 | Heartbreaker | 1973 | $15 |
—Original U.S. number, distributed by Capitol
| ❑ ILPS9217 | Heartbreaker | 1975 | $12 |
—U.S. reissue with same number as original U.K. issue
| ❑ ILSD4 [B] | The Free Story | 1975 | $30 |
PICKWICK
| ❑ SPC-3706 | Free at Last | 197? | $12 |

FREE BAND, THE
VANGUARD
| ❑ VSD-6507 | The Free Band | 1969 | $25 |

FREE DESIGN, THE
AMBROTYPE
| ❑ 1016 | There Is a Song | 1972 | $175 |
PROJECT 3
❑ PR-5037SD	Heaven/Earth	1969	$30
❑ PR-5019SD	Kites Are Fun	1967	$30
❑ PR-5019QD [Q]	Kites Are Fun	197?	$50

Number	Title	Yr	NM
❑ PR-5061SD	One By One	1971	$30
❑ PR-5045SD	Stars/Times/Bubbles/Love	1971	$30
❑ PR4006SD	The Free Design Sing for Very Important People	1970	$30
❑ PR-5031SD	You Could Be Born Again	1968	$30

FREE FLIGHT
ARABESQUE
| ❑ 8130 | Free Flight | 1981 | $30 |
CBS
| ❑ BFM42143 | Illumination | 1986 | $25 |
PALO ALTO
❑ PA-8075	Beyond the Clouds	1984	$25
❑ PA-8050	Soaring	1983	$25
❑ PA-8024	The Jazz/Classical Union	1982	$25
VOSS
| ❑ VLP1-42932 | Free Flight | 1988 | $25 |
—Reissue of Arabesque LP

FREE MOVEMENT, THE
COLUMBIA
| ❑ KC31136 | I've Found Someone of My Own | 1972 | $18 |

FREE MUSIC QUARTET, THE
ESP-DISK'
| ❑ 1083 | Free Music One and Two | 1969 | $150 |

FREE WILL
GUINNESS
| ❑ GNS36041 [B] | Here's Free Will | 1977 | $300 |

FREEBORNE
MONITOR
| ❑ MPS-607 | Peak Impressions | 1967 | $175 |

FREED, ALAN
BRUNSWICK
| ❑ BL54043 [M] | The Alan Freed Rock 'n' Roll Show | 1959 | $175 |
CORAL
❑ CRL57216 [M]	Alan Freed Presents the King's Henchmen	1958	$175
❑ CRL57063 [M]	Alan Freed's Rock 'n' Roll Dance Party, Vol. 1	1956	$175
❑ CRL57115 [M]	Alan Freed's Rock 'n' Roll Dance Party, Vol. 2	1957	$175
❑ CRL57177 [M]	Go Go Go -- Alan Freed's TV Record Hop	1957	$175
❑ CRL57213 [M]	Rock Around the Block	1958	$175
MGM
| ❑ E-293 [10] | The Big Beat | 195? | $250 |

FREEDMAN, BOB
COBBLESTONE
| ❑ 9009 | Journeys of Odysseus | 1972 | $25 |
SAVOY
| ❑ MG-15040 [10] | Piano Moods | 1954 | $50 |

FREEMAN, BOBBY
AUTUMN
| ❑ LP102 [M] | C'mon and S-W-I-M | 1964 | $50 |
JOSIE
| ❑ JM-4007 [M] | Get In the Swim with Bobby Freeman | 1965 | $30 |
| ❑ JS-4007 [R] | Get In the Swim with Bobby Freeman | 1965 | $30 |
JUBILEE
❑ JLP-1086 [M]	Do You Wanna Dance?	1959	$140
❑ JLPS-1086 [S]	Do You Wanna Dance?	1959	$250
❑ JGM-5010 [M]	Twist with Bobby Freeman	1962	$150
KING
| ❑ 930 [M] | The Lovable Style of Bobby Freeman | 1965 | $300 |

FREEMAN, BUD, AND BUDDY TATE
CIRCLE
| ❑ 69 | Two Beautiful | 198? | $25 |

FREEMAN, BUD
BETHLEHEM
| ❑ BCP-29 [M] | Newport News | 1955 | $300 |
| ❑ BCP-6033 | Test of Time | 197? | $30 |
—Reissue, distributed by RCA Victor
CAPITOL
| ❑ H625 [10] | Classics in Jazz | 1955 | $175 |
| ❑ T625 [M] | Classics in Jazz | 1955 | $100 |
CHIAROSCURO
| ❑ 135 | The Joy of Sax | 1975 | $35 |
CIRCLE
| ❑ 10 | Bud Freeman and Jimmy McPartland Meet the Ted Easton Jazz Band | 198? | $25 |

Number	Title	Yr	NM
COLUMBIA			
❏ CL6107 [10]	Comes Jazz	1950	$150
❏ CL2558 [10]	Jazz -- Chicago Style	1955	$100
COMMODORE			
❏ XFL-14941	Three's No Crowd	198?	$30
DECCA			
❏ DL5213 [10]	Wolverine Jazz	1950	$250
DOT			
❏ DLP-3166 [M]	Bud Freeman and His Summa Cum Laude Trio	1959	$100
❏ DLP-25166 [S]	Bud Freeman and His Summa Cum Laude Trio	1959	$85
❏ DLP-3254 [M]	Midnight Session	1960	$85
❏ DLP-25254 [S]	Midnight Session	1960	$100
EMARCY			
❏ MG-36013 [M]	Midnight at Eddie Condon's	1955	$250
FANTASY			
❏ OJC-183	Bud Freeman All Stars	198?	$25
—Reissue of Swingville 2012			
HALO			
❏ 50275 [M]	Bud Freeman	195?	$35
HARMONY			
❏ HL7046 [M]	Bud Freeman and His All-Star Jazz	1957	$30
IAJRC			
❏ LP-53	See What the Boys in the Back Room Will Have	198?	$25
JAZZ ARCHIVES			
❏ JA-38	Summer Concert 1960	198?	$25
JAZZOLOGY			
❏ J-165	The Compleat Bud Freeman	198?	$25
MONMOUTH-EVERGREEN			
❏ 7022	The Compleat Bud Freeman	1970	$25
PARAMOUNT			
❏ CJS-105 [10]	Bud Freeman and the Chicagoans	195?	$100
PROMENADE			
❏ 2134 [M]	Dixieland U.S.A.	196?	$30
RCA VICTOR			
❏ LPM-1508 [M]	Chicago Austin High School Jazz in Hi-Fi	1957	$50
SWINGVILLE			
❏ SVLP-2012 [M]	Bud Freeman All Stars	1960	$50
—Purple label			
❏ SVLP-2012 [M]	Bud Freeman All Stars	1965	$30
—Blue label with trident logo at right			
TRIP			
❏ 5529	Midnight at Eddie Condon's	197?	$25
UNITED ARTISTS			
❏ UAJ-14033 [M]	Something Tender -- Bud Freeman and Two Guitars	1963	$40
❏ UAJS-15033 [S]	Something Tender -- Bud Freeman and Two Guitars	1963	$50

FREEMAN, CHICO

Number	Title	Yr	NM
BLACKHAWK			
❏ BKH-50801	The Pied Piper	1986	$25
BLACK SAINT			
❏ BSR-0036	No Time Left	1977	$30
CONTEMPORARY			
❏ C-7640	Beyond the Rain	1978	$30
❏ C-14008	Destiny's Dance	1981	$30
❏ C-14005	Peaceful Heart, Gentle Spirit	1980	$30
ELEKTRA/MUSICIAN			
❏ 60361	Tangents	1984	$25
❏ 60163	Tradition in Transition	1983	$25
FANTASY			
❏ OJC-479	Beyond the Rain	1991	$25
INDIA NAVIGATION			
❏ IN-1031	Chico	1977	$35
❏ IN-1035	Kings of Mali	1978	$35
❏ IN-1063	Morning Prayer	198?	$30
❏ IN-1045	Spirit Sensitive	1979	$35
❏ IN-1042	The Outside Within	1981	$30
❏ IN-1059	The Search	1981	$30

FREEMAN, ERNIE

Number	Title	Yr	NM
DUNHILL			
❏ D50026 [M]	Hitmaker	1967	$15
❏ DS50026 [S]	Hitmaker	1967	$18
IMPERIAL			
❏ LP-9133 [M]	Dark at the Top of the Stairs	1959	$30
❏ LP-12067 [S]	Dark at the Top of the Stairs	1959	$40
❏ LP-9057 [M]	Ernie Freeman	1958	$50
❏ LP-9022 [M]	Ernie Freeman Plays Irving Berlin	1957	$50
❏ LP-9030 [M]	Jivin' Around	1957	$50
❏ LP-9148 [M]	Raunchy	1960	$50
❏ LP-9193 [M]	The Stripper	1962	$25
❏ LP-12193 [S]	The Stripper	1962	$30
❏ LP-9157 [M]	Twistin' Time	1961	$30
❏ LP-12081 [S]	Twistin' Time	1961	$40

Number	Title	Yr	NM
LIBERTY			
❏ LRP-3331 [M]	Comin' Home Baby	1963	$25
❏ LST-7331 [S]	Comin' Home Baby	1963	$30
❏ LRP-3264 [M]	Ernie Freeman's Soulful Sounds of Country Classics	1962	$25
❏ LST-7264 [S]	Ernie Freeman's Soulful Sounds of Country Classics	1962	$30
❏ LRP-3283 [M]	Limbo Dance Party	1962	$25
❏ LST-7283 [S]	Limbo Dance Party	1962	$30

FREEMAN, EVELYN

Number	Title	Yr	NM
IMPERIAL			
❏ LP-9101 [M]	Sky High	1960	$25
❏ LP-12043 [S]	Sky High	1960	$30
UNITED ARTISTS			
❏ UAL-3178 [M]	Didn't It Rain	1962	$25
❏ UAS-6178 [S]	Didn't It Rain	1962	$30

FREEMAN, GEORGE

Number	Title	Yr	NM
DELMARK			
❏ DS-424	Birth Sign	197?	$30
GROOVE MERCHANT			
❏ 3305	Man and Woman	1975	$35
❏ 519	New Improved Funk	1973	$35

FREEMAN, RUSS

Number	Title	Yr	NM
PACIFIC JAZZ			
❏ PJ-1232 [M]	Quartet: Russ Freeman/Chet Baker	1957	$250
—Label says Pacific Jazz, but cover is on World Pacific			
❏ PJLP-8 [10]	The Russ Freeman Trio	1953	$120
❏ PJ-1212 [M]	Trio: Russ Freeman/Richard Twardzik	1956	$150
WORLD PACIFIC			
❏ WP-1232 [M]	Quartet: Russ Freeman/Chet Baker	1958	$175
—Both label and cover are on World Pacific			
❏ WP-1212 [M]	Trio: Russ Freeman/Richard Twardzik	1958	$175

FREEMAN, STAN

Number	Title	Yr	NM
AUDIOPHILE			
❏ AP-202	Not a Care in the World	1986	$25
COLUMBIA			
❏ CL6193 [10]	Come On-a Stan's House	1951	$75
❏ CL6158 [10]	Piano Moods	1951	$50
❏ CL1120 [M]	Stan Freeman Swings "The Music Man	1958	$30
HARMONY			
❏ HL7067 [M]	Stan Freeman Plays 30 All-Time Hits	195?	$25

FREEMAN, VON

Number	Title	Yr	NM
ATLANTIC			
❏ SD1628	Doin' It Right Now	1972	$30
NESSA			
❏ 6	Have No Fear	1975	$35
❏ 11	Serenade and Blues	197?	$35

FREEPORT

Number	Title	Yr	NM
MAINSTREAM			
❏ S-6130	Freeport	1970	$50

FREES, PAUL

Number	Title	Yr	NM
MGM			
❏ SE-4735	Paul Frees and the Poster People	1969	$30

FREHLEY, ACE
Also see KISS; includes albums as FREHLEY'S COMET.

Number	Title	Yr	NM
CASABLANCA			
❏ NBPIX-7121 [PD]	Ace Frehley	1978	$50

Number	Title	Yr	NM
❏ NBLP-7121 [B]	Ace Frehley	1978	$25

Number	Title	Yr	NM
EONE			
❏ EOMLP5483 [B]	Origins Vol 1	2016	$50
MEGAFORCE/ATLANTIC			
❏ 81749 [B]	Frehley's Comet	1987	$10
❏ 81826	Live + 1	1988	$10
❏ 81862	Second Sighting	1988	$10
❏ 82042	Trouble Walkin'	1989	$14

FRENCH, ALBERT "PAPA

Number	Title	Yr	NM
NOBILITY			
❏ LP-702 [M]	A Night at Dixieland Hall	195?	$40

FRENCH MARKET JAZZ BAND, THE

Number	Title	Yr	NM
FLYING DUTCHMAN			
❏ BDL1-1239	The French Market Jazz Band	1976	$25

FRESH, DOUG E., AND THE GET FRESH CREW

Number	Title	Yr	NM
GEE STREET			
❏ 444069-1	Play	1993	$18
REALITY			
❏ 9649	Oh, My God!	1986	$40
❏ 9658	The World's Greatest Entertainer	1988	$30

FREY, GLENN
Also see EAGLES.

Number	Title	Yr	NM
ASYLUM			
❏ E1-60129	No Fun Aloud	1982	$12
MCA			
❏ 6239	Soul Searchin'	1988	$12
❏ 5501 [B]	The Allnighter	1984	$18
—Quiex II vinyl promo			

FRIAR TUCK

Number	Title	Yr	NM
MERCURY			
❏ MG-21111 [M]	Friar Tuck and His Psychedelic Guitar	1967	$40
❏ SR-61111 [S]	Friar Tuck and His Psychedelic Guitar	1967	$50

FRICKE, JANIE

Number	Title	Yr	NM
COLUMBIA			
❏ FC40666	After Midnight	1987	$12
❏ FC40383	Black & White	1986	$12
❏ C240684	Celebration	1987	$15
❏ JC36268	From the Heart	1980	$15
❏ FC38310	Greatest Hits	1982	$12
❏ JC36820	I'll Need Someone to Hold Me When I Cry	1980	$12
❏ PC36820	I'll Need Someone to Hold Me When I Cry	198?	$10
—Budget-line reissue with new prefix			
❏ FC38214	It Ain't Easy	1982	$12
❏ AS991535 [DJ]	Janie Fricke On Tour	1982	$75
—Promo-only picture disc			
❏ FC45087	Labor of Love	1989	$15
❏ FC38730	Love Lies	1983	$12
❏ PC38730	Love Lies	1985	$10
—Budget-line reissue with new prefix			
❏ KC35774	Love Notes	1979	$15
❏ PC35774	Love Notes	198?	$10
—Budget-line reissue with new prefix			
❏ FC44143	Saddle the Wind	1988	$12
❏ KC35315	Singer of Songs	1978	$15
❏ PC35315	Singer of Songs	198?	$10
—Budget-line reissue with new prefix			
❏ FC37535	Sleeping with Your Memory	1981	$12
❏ PC37535	Sleeping with Your Memory	198?	$10
—Budget-line reissue with new prefix			
❏ FC39975	Somebody Else's Fire	1985	$12
❏ FC39338	The First Word in Memory	1984	$12
❏ FC40165	The Very Best of Janie	1985	$12

FRIDA

Number	Title	Yr	NM
ATLANTIC			
❏ 80018	Something's Goin' On	1982	$12

FRIEDMAN, DAVID

Number	Title	Yr	NM
ENJA			
❏ 3089	Of the Wind's Eye	1982	$30
INNER CITY			
❏ IC-3004	Futures Passed	1976	$30
❏ IC-6005	Winter Love April Joy	1979	$30

FRIEDMAN, DEAN

Number	Title	Yr	NM
LIFESONG			
❏ LS6008	Dean Friedman	1977	$15
❏ JZ35361	Well, Well, Said the Rocking Chair	1978	$18

FRIEDMAN, DON

Number	Title	Yr	NM
PRESTIGE			
❏ PRLP-7488 [M]	Metamorphosis	1966	$30
❏ PRST-7488 [S]	Metamorphosis	1966	$30

Number	Title	Yr	NM
PROGRESSIVE			
❏ PRO-7036	Hot Knepper and Pepper	198?	$30
RIVERSIDE			
❏ RLP-384 [M]	A Day in the City	1961	$250
❏ RS-9384 [S]	A Day in the City	1961	$250
❏ RLP-431 [M]	Circle Waltz	1962	$250
❏ RS-9431 [S]	Circle Waltz	1962	$250
❏ 6082	Circle Waltz	197?	$35
— Reissue of 9431			
❏ RLP-485 [M]	Dreams and Explorations	1965	$175
❏ RS-9485 [S]	Dreams and Explorations	1965	$175
❏ RLP-463 [M]	Flashback	1963	$175
❏ RS-9463 [S]	Flashback	1963	$175
❏ 6094	Flashback	197?	$35
— Reissue of 9463			
FRIEDMAN, ERICK			
RCA VICTOR RED SEAL			
❏ LSC-2610 [S]	Paganini: Violin Concerto No. 1; Saint-Saens: Intro and Rondo Capriccioso	1962	$40
— Original with "shaded dog" label			
❏ LSC-2610 [S]	Paganini: Violin Concerto No. 1; Saint-Saens: Intro and Rondo Capriccioso	1964	$25
— Second edition with "white dog" label			
FRIEDMAN, KINKY			
ABC			
❏ X-829	Kinky Friedman	1974	$12
EPIC			
❏ PE34304	Lasso from El Paso	1976	$12
VANGUARD			
❏ VSD-79333	Sold American	1973	$15
FRIEND AND LOVER			
VERVE FORECAST			
❏ FTS-3055	Reach Out of the Darkness	1968	$25
FRIENDS, THE			
MGM			
❏ SE-4901	The Friends	1973	$15
FRIENDS			
OBLIVION			
❏ OD-3	Friends	1974	$25
— Jazz-rock band with John Abercrombie and Marc Cohen			
FRIENDS OF DISTINCTION, THE			
RCA VICTOR			
❏ LSP-4492	Friends & People	1971	$18
❏ LSP-4149	Grazin'	1969	$18
❏ LSP-4819	Greatest Hits	1972	$15
❏ APD1-0276 [Q]	Greatest Hits	1973	$40
❏ LSP-4212	Highly Distinct	1969	$18
❏ LSP-4829	Love Can Make It Easier	1973	$15
❏ LSP-4313	Real Friends	1970	$18
❏ LSP-4408	Whatever	1970	$18
FRIESEN, DAVID, AND JOHN STOWELL			
INNER CITY			
❏ IC-1061	Through the Listening Glass	1979	$30
FRIESEN, DAVID			
GLOBAL PACIFIC			
❏ OW40718	Inner Voices	1987	$25
INNER CITY			
❏ IC-1086	Other Mansions	1980	$30
❏ IC-1019	Star Dance	1977	$30
❏ IC-1027	Waterfall Rainbow	1978	$30
MUSE			
❏ MR-5109	Color Pool	197?	$30
❏ MR-5255	Storyteller	1981	$25
STEEPLECHASE			
❏ SCS-1138	Paths Beyond Tracing	1980	$30
FRIESEN, EUGENE			
LIVING MUSIC			
❏ LM-0007	New Friend	1986	$25
FRIGO, JOHNNY			
MERCURY			
❏ MG-20285 [M]	I Love Johnny Frigo, He Swings	1957	$150
FRIJID PINK			
FANTASY			
❏ 9464	All Pink Inside	1974	$18
LION			
❏ LN-1004	Earth Omen	1972	$25
PARROT			
❏ PAS71041	Defrosted	1970	$30
❏ PAS71033	Frijid Pink	1970	$30

Number	Title	Yr	NM
FRIPP AND ENO			
ANTILLES			
❏ AN-7018 [B]	Evening Star	25.00	$
❏ AN-7001 [B]	No Pussyfooting	1976	$35
FRISELL, BILL, AND VERNON REID			
MINOR MUSIC			
❏ MM-005	Smash and Scatteration	1984	$35
FRISELL, BILL			
ECM			
❏ 1241	In Line	198?	$25
❏ 25026	Rambler	1985	$25
ELEKTRA/MUSICIAN			
❏ 60843	Before We Were Born	1988	$25
FRITH, FRED & KAISER, HENRY			
METALANGUAGE			
❏ ML123 [B]	Who Needs Enemies	1983	$25
❏ ML107 [B]	With Friends Like These	1979	$30
FRITH, FRED			
RALPH			
❏ FF8057L [B]	Gravity	1980	$25
❏ FF8106 [B]	Speechless	1981	$18
T.E.C. TONES			
❏ FF8057 [B]	Gravity	1990	$18
❏ FF8106 [B]	Speechless	1990	$18
FRIZZELL, DAVID, AND SHELLY WEST			
VIVA			
❏ 25148	Golden Duets (The Best of Frizzell & West)	1984	$10
❏ 23907	In Session	1984	$10
WARNER BROS.			
❏ BSK3555	Carryin' On the Family Names	1981	$12
❏ 23754	Our Best to You	1983	$12
❏ BSK3643	The David Frizzell & Shelly West Album	1982	$12
FRIZZELL, DAVID			
MCA			
❏ 27093	David Frizzell	1983	$10
VIVA			
❏ 23907	On My Own Again	1983	$10
❏ 25112	Solo	1984	$10
WARNER BROS.			
❏ 23688	The Family's Fine, But This One's All Mine	1982	$10
FRIZZELL, LEFTY			
ABC			
❏ ABCX-799	Lefty	1974	$30
— Original title			
❏ AC-30035	The ABC Collection	1976	$25
❏ ABCX-799	The Legendary Lefty Frizzell	1974	$25
— Revised title			
COLUMBIA			
❏ CL2488 [M]	Lefty Frizzell's Greatest Hits	1966	$30
❏ CS9288 [S]	Lefty Frizzell's Greatest Hits	1966	$40
— Red label, "360 Sound Stereo" at bottom			
❏ CL9019 [10]	Lefty Frizzell Sings the Songs of Jimmie Rodgers	1951	$300
❏ C32249	Lefty Frizzell Sings the Songs of Jimmie Rodgers	1973	$25
❏ CL9021 [10]	Listen to Lefty	1952	$300
❏ CL2772 [M]	Puttin' On	1967	$50
❏ CS9572 [S]	Puttin' On	1967	$40
❏ PC33882	Remembering…The Greatest Hits of Lefty Frizzell	1975	$25
❏ CL2169 [M]	Saginaw, Michigan	1964	$30
❏ CS8969 [S]	Saginaw, Michigan	1964	$40

Number	Title	Yr	NM
❏ CL1342 [M]	The One and Only Lefty Frizzell	1959	$120
❏ CL2386 [M]	The Sad Side of Love	1965	$30
❏ CS9186 [S]	The Sad Side of Love	1965	$40
COLUMBIA LIMITED EDITION			
❏ LE10027	Saginaw, Michigan	197?	$12
HARMONY			
❏ HL7241 [M]	Lefty Frizzell Sings the Songs of Jimmie Rodgers	1960	$30
❏ HS11186 [R]	The Great Sound of "Lefty" Frizzell	196?	$25
FROEBA, FRANK			
DECCA			
❏ DL5043 [10]	Back Room Piano	1950	$175
❏ DL5048 [10]	Old Time Piano	1950	$175
ROYALE			
❏ 1818 [10]	Old Time Piano	1954	$40
VARSITY			
❏ 6031 [10]	Boys in the Backroom	1950	$50
FROGGIE BEAVER			
FROGGIE BEAVER			
❏ 7301 [10]	From the Pond	1973	$75
FROLK HAVEN			
Stewart Copeland is a member.			
LRS			
❏ RT-6023	At the Apex of High	1972	$180
FROM THE OTHER SIDE JAZZ BAND			
SOUL NOTE			
❏ 121106	From the Other Side	1990	$30
FROMAN, JANE			
CAPITOL			
❏ T726 [M]	Faith	1956	$30
❏ T889 [M]	Songs at Sunset	1957	$30
❏ H354 [10]	Yours Alone	1952	$40
DECCA			
❏ DL6021 [10]	Souvenirs	1952	$40
RCA VICTOR			
❏ LPT-3055 [10]	Gems from Gershwin	1952	$40
FRONTIERE, DOMINIC			
COLUMBIA			
❏ CL1427 [M]	Love Eyes: The Moods of Romance	1960	$30
❏ CS8224 [S]	Love Eyes: The Moods of Romance	1960	$40
❏ CL1273 [M]	Pagan Festival	1958	$40
LIBERTY			
❏ LRP-3032 [M]	Dom Frontiere Plays the Classics	1957	$40
❏ LRP-3015 [M]	Fabulous!	1956	$40
❏ LST-7008 [S]	Mr. Accordion	1958	$40
— Evidently not issued in mono			
❏ LJH-6002 [M]	The Dom Frontiere Sextet	1956	$50
FROST, FRANK			
EARWIG			
❏ 4914	Midnight Prowler	1990	$12
❏ 4901	Rockin' the Juke Joint Down	1986	$12
JEWEL			
❏ LPS-5013	Frank Frost	1973	$18
PHILLIPS INTERNATIONAL			
❏ PLP-1975 [M]	Hey Boss Man!	1962	$3000
— VG value 1500; VG+ value 2250			
FROST, MAX, AND THE TROOPERS			
TOWER			
❏ ST-5147	Shape of Things to Come	1968	$50
FROST, THE			
Featuring Dick Wagner.			
VANGUARD			
❏ VSD-79392	Early Frost	1978	$18
❏ VSD-6520	Frost Music	1969	$50
❏ VSD-6541	Rock and Roll Music	1969	$40
❏ VSD-6556	Through the Eyes of Love	1970	$25
FROST, THOMAS AND RICHARD			
UNI			
❏ 73124	Thomas and Richard Frost	1972	$18
FROZEN GHOST			
ATLANTIC			
❏ 81736	Frozen Ghost	1987	$10
❏ 81875	Nice Place to Visit	1988	$10
FRUMMOX			
PROBE			
❏ 4511	From Here to There	1970	$18

FRUSCELLA, TONY

ATLANTIC

Number	Title	Yr	NM
1220 [M]	Tony Fruscella	1955	$500

FRUT

TRASH

Number	Title	Yr	NM
0(# unknown)	Keep On Truckin'	1971	$100

—Originals on yellow vinyl

WESTBOUND

Number	Title	Yr	NM
WB-2005	Keep On Truckin'	1971	$30

—Reissue of Trash LP

Number	Title	Yr	NM
WB-2008	Spoiled Rotten	1972	$30

FRYE, DAVID

BUDDAH

Number	Title	Yr	NM
1600	Richard Nixon: A Fantasy	1973	$15
BDS-5097	Richard Nixon: Superstar	1971	$15

ELEKTRA

Number	Title	Yr	NM
EKS-75006	I Am the President	1969	$15
EKS-74085	Radio Free Nixon	1971	$15

FRYE

Number	Title	Yr	NM
DFP-80	The Great Debate	1980	$18

FU-SCHNICKENS

JIVE

Number	Title	Yr	NM
41519	Nervous Breakdown	1994	$18

FUEL

550 MUSIC

Number	Title	Yr	NM
B68554	Sunburn	1998	$15

FUGAZI

DISCHORD

Number	Title	Yr	NM
30 [EP]	Fugazi	1988	$40
70 [B]	In On the Kill Taker	1993	$30
35 [B]	Margin Walker	1989	$40
90-V [B]	Red Medicine	1995	$30
44 [B]	Repeater	1990	$30
60 [B]	Steady Diet of Nothing	1991	$30

FUGEES

RUFFHOUSE

Number	Title	Yr	NM
C67904	Bootleg Versions	1996	$18
C267147	The Score	1995	$18

FUGITIVES, THE, AND OTHERS

WESTCHESTER

Number	Title	Yr	NM
1005 [M]	Friday at the Cage A-Go-Go	1965	$1500

FUGITIVES, THE

HIDEOUT

Number	Title	Yr	NM
1001 [M]	The Fugitives at Dave's Hideout	1965	$1200

JUSTICE

Number	Title	Yr	NM
JLP-141	The Fugitives On the Run	1967	$300

—Different group from "Hideout" FUGITIVES.

FUGS, THE

4 MEN WITH BEARDS

Number	Title	Yr	NM
4M148LP [B]	It Crawled Into My Hand, Honest		$25
4M147LP [B]	Tenderness Junction		$25

BROADSIDE

Number	Title	Yr	NM
304 [M]	The Village Fugs Sing Ballads of Contemporary Protest, Point of View, and General Dissatisfaction	1965	$500

—With insert

Number	Title	Yr	NM
304 [M]	The Village Fugs Sing Ballads of Contemporary Protest, Point of View, and General Dissatisfaction	1965	$400

—Without insert

ESP-DISK

Number	Title	Yr	NM
2018	Fugs 4, Rounders Score	196?	$160
1028 [S]	The Fugs	1966	$50

—Black and white cover, back cover photos staggered

Number	Title	Yr	NM
1028 [S]	The Fugs	1966	$30

—Black and white cover, back cover photos aligned

Number	Title	Yr	NM
1028 [S]	The Fugs	1966	$100

—Psychedelic color shield on cover

Number	Title	Yr	NM
1018 [M]	The Fugs First Album	1966	$40

—Reissue of Broadside 304 on cover

Number	Title	Yr	NM
1018 [M]	The Fugs First Album	1966	$400

—Turquoise and black cover, different from all other versions

Number	Title	Yr	NM
1018 [M]	The Fugs First Album	1967	$30

—No reference to reissue on cover

Number	Title	Yr	NM
1038 [S]	Virgin Fugs	1967	$300

—"For Adult Minds" sticker on cover; with poster, book and stickers

Number	Title	Yr	NM
1038 [S]	Virgin Fugs	1967	$150

—"For Adult Minds" sticker, no inserts

Number	Title	Yr	NM
1038 [S]	Virgin Fugs	1967	$150

—"For Adult Minds" stamped on cover

Number	Title	Yr	NM
1038 [S]	Virgin Fugs	1967	$150

—"For Adult Minds" printed on cover

PVC

Number	Title	Yr	NM
8914	Proto Punk: The Fugs Greatest Hits, Vol. 1	1982	$18

REPRISE

Number	Title	Yr	NM
RS-6359 [B]	Belle of Avenue A	1969	$35
RS-6396	Golden Fifth	1970	$30
RS-6305 [B]	It Crawled Into My Hand, Honest	1968	$40
R-6280 [M]	Tenderness Junction	1968	$175
RS-6280 [S]	Tenderness Junction	1968	$30

FUHRMAN, MICKI

CANAAN

Number	Title	Yr	NM
CAS9855	Angels Watching Over Me	1979	$12

DAYSPRING

Number	Title	Yr	NM
DST-4021	Look Again	1981	$12

FUKUMURA, HIROSHI

INNER CITY

Number	Title	Yr	NM
IC-6067	Hunt Up Wind	198?	$30

FULL CIRCLE

COLUMBIA

Number	Title	Yr	NM
FC40966	Full Circle	1988	$25
FC44474	Myth America	1989	$30

FULL FAITH AND CREDIT BIG BAND, THE

PALO ALTO

Number	Title	Yr	NM
PA-8001	Debut	198?	$25
PA-8003	JazzFaire	198?	$25

FULL FORCE

COLUMBIA

Number	Title	Yr	NM
BFC40117	Full Force	1985	$12
BFC40395	Full Force Get Busy 1 Time!	1986	$12
FC40894	Guess Who's Comin' to the Crib?	1987	$12
FC45216	Smoove	1989	$15

FULL MOON

DOUGLAS

Number	Title	Yr	NM
KZ31904	Full Moon	1972	$35

FULL SWING

CYPRESS

Number	Title	Yr	NM
YL 0109	In Full Swing	1988	$25
YL 0128	The End of the Sky	1989	$30

PLANET

Number	Title	Yr	NM
BXL1-4426	Good Times Are Back!	1982	$25

FULLER, BOBBY, FOUR

MUSTANG

Number	Title	Yr	NM
M-901 [M]	I Fought the Law	1966	$150
MS-901 [S]	I Fought the Law	1966	$250
M-900 [M]	KRLA King of the Wheels	1965	$250
MS-900 [S]	KRLA King of the Wheels	1965	$300

RHINO

Number	Title	Yr	NM
RNDF-201	The Best of the Bobby Fuller Four	1981	$15
RNLP70174	The Best of the Bobby Fuller Four (Golden Archive Series)	1987	$12
RNLP-057 [B]	The Bobby Fuller Tapes, Vol. 1	1983	$15

VOXX

Number	Title	Yr	NM
VXS200028 [B]	The Bobby Fuller Tapes, Vol. 2	1984	$18

FULLER, CURTIS

ABC IMPULSE!

Number	Title	Yr	NM
AS-22 [S]	Cabin in the Sky	1968	$30

BEE HIVE

Number	Title	Yr	NM
BH-7007	Fire and Filigree	197?	$30

BLUE NOTE

Number	Title	Yr	NM
BLP-1572 [M]	Bone and Bari	1957	$350

—Deep groove" version (deep indentation under label on both sides)

Number	Title	Yr	NM
BLP-1572 [M]	Bone and Bari	1957	$250

—Regular version with W. 63rd St. address on label

Number	Title	Yr	NM
BLP-1572 [M]	Bone and Bari	1963	$130

—New York, USA" address on label

Number	Title	Yr	NM
BST-1572 [S]	Bone and Bari	1959	$500

—Deep groove" version (deep indentation under label on both sides)

Number	Title	Yr	NM
BST-1572 [S]	Bone and Bari	1959	$175

—Regular version with W. 63rd St. address on label

Number	Title	Yr	NM
BST-1572 [S]	Bone and Bari	1963	$150

—New York, USA" address on label

Number	Title	Yr	NM
BST-81572 [S]	Bone and Bari	1967	$35

—A Division of Liberty Records" on label

Number	Title	Yr	NM
BLP-1583 [M]	Curtis Fuller, Volume 3	1958	$900

—Deep groove" version (deep indentation under label on both sides)

Number	Title	Yr	NM
BLP-1583 [M]	Curtis Fuller, Volume 3	1958	$180

—Regular version with W. 63rd St. address on label

Number	Title	Yr	NM
BLP-1583 [M]	Curtis Fuller, Volume 3	1963	$250

—New York, USA" address on label

Number	Title	Yr	NM
BST-1583 [S]	Curtis Fuller, Volume 3	1959	$300

—Deep groove" version (deep indentation under label on both sides)

Number	Title	Yr	NM
BST-1583 [S]	Curtis Fuller, Volume 3	1959	$175

—Regular version with W. 63rd St. address on label

Number	Title	Yr	NM
BST-1583 [S]	Curtis Fuller, Volume 3	1963	$150

—New York, USA" address on label

Number	Title	Yr	NM
BST-81583 [S]	Curtis Fuller, Volume 3	1967	$35

—A Division of Liberty Records" on label

Number	Title	Yr	NM
BLP-1567 [M]	The Opener	1957	$3000

—Deep groove" version (deep indentation under label on both sides)

Number	Title	Yr	NM
BLP-1567 [M]	The Opener	1957	$175

—Regular version with W. 63rd St. address on label

Number	Title	Yr	NM
BLP-1567 [M]	The Opener	1963	$75

—New York, USA" address on label

Number	Title	Yr	NM
BST-1567 [S]	The Opener	1959	$500

—Deep groove" version (deep indentation under label on both sides)

Number	Title	Yr	NM
BST-1567 [S]	The Opener	1959	$50

—Regular version with W. 63rd St. address on label

Number	Title	Yr	NM
BST-1567 [S]	The Opener	1963	$25

—New York, USA" address on label

Number	Title	Yr	NM
BST-81567 [S]	The Opener	1967	$35

—A Division of Liberty Records" on label

EPIC

Number	Title	Yr	NM
LA16020 [M]	South American Cookin'	1961	$300
BA17020 [S]	South American Cookin'	1961	$150
LA16013 [M]	The Magnificent Trombone	1961	$75
BA17013 [S]	The Magnificent Trombone	1961	$100

FANTASY

Number	Title	Yr	NM
OJC-077	New Trombone	198?	$25

IMPULSE!

Number	Title	Yr	NM
A-22 [M]	Cabin in the Sky	1962	$120
AS-22 [S]	Cabin in the Sky	1962	$120
A-13 [M]	Soul Trombone	1962	$120
AS-13 [S]	Soul Trombone	1962	$120

MAINSTREAM

Number	Title	Yr	NM
MRL-333	Crankin'	1971	$25
MRL-370	Smokin'	1972	$25

NEW JAZZ

Number	Title	Yr	NM
NJLP-8305 [M]	Curtis Fuller and Hampton Hawes with French Horns	1963	$0

—Canceled; re-assigned to Status label

Number	Title	Yr	NM
NJLP-8277 [M]	Curtis Fuller with Red Garland	1962	$175

—Purple label

Number	Title	Yr	NM
NJLP-8277 [M]	Curtis Fuller with Red Garland	1965	$175

—Blue label, trident logo at right

PRESTIGE

Number	Title	Yr	NM
PRLP-7107 [M]	New Trombone	1957	$800

REGENT

Number	Title	Yr	NM
MG-6055 [M]	Jazz...It's Magic	1957	$100

SAVOY

Number	Title	Yr	NM
MG-12141 [M]	Blues-Ette	1959	$50
ST-13006 [S]	Blues-Ette	1959	$40
MG-12151 [M]	Curtis Fuller	1960	$40
MG-12164 [M]	Images of Curts Fuller	1960	$40
MG-12144 [M]	Imagination	1959	$40
MG-12209 [M]	Jazz...It's Magic	196?	$25
MG-12143 [M]	The Curtis Fuller Jazztet with Benny Golson	1959	$40

SAVOY JAZZ

Number	Title	Yr	NM
SJL-2239	All-Star Sextets	197?	$30
SJL-1135	Blues-Ette	198?	$25

SMASH

Number	Title	Yr	NM
MGS-27034 [M]	Jazz Conference Abroad	1962	$30
SRS-67034 [S]	Jazz Conference Abroad	1962	$30

STATUS

Number	Title	Yr	NM
ST-8305 [M]	Curtis Fuller and Hampton Hawes with French Horns	1965	$40

UNITED ARTISTS

Number	Title	Yr	NM
UAL-4051 [M]	Sliding Easy	1959	$300
UAS-5051 [S]	Sliding Easy	1959	$40

WARWICK

Number	Title	Yr	NM
W-2038 [M]	Boss of the Soul Stream Trombone	1961	$50
W-2038ST [S]	Boss of the Soul Stream Trombone	1961	$50

FULLER, GIL

PACIFIC JAZZ

Number	Title	Yr	NM
PJ-93 [M]	Gil Fuller and the Monterey Jazz Orchestra with Dizzy Gillespie	1965	$30
ST-93 [S]	Gil Fuller and the Monterey Jazz Orchestra with Dizzy Gillespie	1965	$30

Number	Title	Yr	NM
❏ LN-10060	Gil Fuller and the Monterey Jazz Orchestra with Dizzy Gillespie	198?	$20

— Budget-line reissue

Number	Title	Yr	NM
❏ PJ-10101 [M]	Night Flight	1966	$25
❏ ST-20101 [S]	Night Flight	1966	$30
❏ LN-10128	Night Flight	198?	$20

— Budget-line reissue

FULLER, JERRY
Also see THE FLEAS; THE FULLER BROTHERS.

LIN
❏ 100 [M]	Teenage Love	1960	$300

MCA
❏ 3170	My Turn Now	1979	$15

FULLER, JERRY (2)
Jazz clarinetist.
Clarinetist. (JZ)

ANDEX
❏ A-3008 [M]	Clarinet Portrait	1958	$40
❏ AS-3008 [S]	Clarinet Portrait	1959	$30

FULSON, LOWELL

ARHOOLIE
❏ R-2003	Early Recordings	1962	$30

BIG TOWN
❏ 1008	Lovemaker	1978	$15

CHESS
❏ 408	Hung Down Head	197?	$18

GRANITE
❏ 1006	Ol' Blues Singer	1976	$18

JEWEL
❏ LPS-5003	In a Heavy Bag	1970	$18
❏ LPS-5009	I've Got the Blues	1973	$18

KENT
❏ KLP-5016 [M]	Lowell Fulsom	1965	$30
❏ KST-516 [S]	Lowell Fulsom	1965	$40
❏ KST-531	Lowell Fulsom Now	1969	$30
❏ KLP-5020 [M]	Tramp	1967	$30
❏ KST-520 [S]	Tramp	1967	$40

ROUNDER
❏ 2088	It's a Good Day	198?	$15

FUN AND GAMES

UNI
❏ 73042	Elephant Candy	1968	$30

FUN BOY THREE

CHRYSALIS
❏ CHS1383	Fun Boy Three	1982	$15
❏ PV41383	Fun Boy Three	1984	$10

— Reissue

❏ B6V41417	Waiting	1983	$12
❏ PV41417	Waiting	1986	$10

— Reissue

FUN LOVIN' CRIMINALS

VIRGIN
❏ 23140	100% Colombian	1998	$15

FUNK INC.

PRESTIGE
❏ 10043	Chicken Lickin'	1972	$35
❏ 10031	Funk Inc.	1971	$35
❏ 10059	Hangin' Out	1973	$35
❏ 10087	Priced to Sell	1974	$35
❏ 10071	Superfunk	1973	$35

FUNKADELIC
Also see PARLIAMENT.

4 MEN WITH BEARDS
❏ 4M179LP [B]	America Eats Its Young		$25
❏ 4M173LP [B]	Cosmic Slop		$25
❏ 4M172LP [B]	Free Your Mind... And Your Ass Will Follow		$25
❏ 4M160LP [B]	Funkadelic		$25
❏ 4M160 [B]	Funkadelic	2014	$30
❏ 4M207LP [B]	Let's Take It To the Stage		$25
❏ 4M161LP [B]	Maggot Brain		$25
❏ 4M180LP [B]	Standing On The Verge Of Getting It On		$25
❏ 4M208LP [B]	Tales Of Kidd Funkadelic		$25

SCARFACE/PRIORITY
❏ 53873	Hardcore Jollies	1993	$18

— Limited-edition reissue of Warner Bros. 2973

❏ 53872	One Nation Under a Groove	1993	$18

— Limited-edition reissue of Warner Bros. 3209

❏ 53874	The Electric Spanking of War Babies	1993	$18

— Limited-edition reissue of Warner Bros. 3482

❏ 53875	Uncle Jam Wants You	1993	$18

— Limited-edition reissue of Warner Bros. 3371

WARNER BROS.
❏ BS2973	Hardcore Jollies	1976	$30
❏ BS3209 [B]	One Nation Under a Groove	1978	$30

— Includes bonus 7-inch single with small hole (deduct 20% if missing)

❏ BSK3482	The Electric Spanking of War Babies	1981	$30
❏ BSK3371	Uncle Jam Wants You	1979	$30

WESTBOUND
❏ 2020	America Eats Its Young	1972	$75
❏ 221	America Eats Its Young	1976	$30

— Reissue of Westbound 2020

❏ 2020	America Eats Its Young	1991	$25

— Reissue with bar code

❏ 303	Best of the Early Years	197?	$40
❏ 2022	Cosmic Slop	1973	$50
❏ 223	Cosmic Slop	1976	$30

— Reissue of Westbound 2022

❏ 2022	Cosmic Slop	1991	$18

— Reissue with bar code

❏ 2001	Free Your Mind...And Your Ass Will Follow	1970	$50
❏ 2001	Free Your Mind...And Your Ass Will Follow	1990	$18

— Reissue with bar code

❏ 217	Free Your Mind...And Your Ass Will Follow	1975	$30

— Reissue of Westbound 2001

❏ 2000	Funkadelic	1970	$50
❏ 216	Funkadelic	1975	$30

— Reissue of Westbound 2000

❏ 2000	Funkadelic	1990	$18

— Reissue with bar code

❏ 1004	Funkadelic's Greatest Hits	1975	$50
❏ 215	Let's Take It to the Stage	1975	$50
❏ 215	Let's Take It to the Stage	1992	$18

— Reissue with bar code

❏ 2007	Maggot Brain	1971	$50
❏ 218	Maggot Brain	1975	$30

— Reissue of Westbound 2007

❏ 2007 [B]	Maggot Brain	1990	$18

— Reissue with bar code

❏ 1001	Standing on the Verge of Getting It On	1974	$50
❏ 208	Standing on the Verge of Getting It On	1975	$30

— Reissue of Westbound 1001

❏ 1001	Standing on the Verge of Getting It On	1991	$18

— Reissue with bar code

❏ 227	Tales of Kidd Funkadelic	1976	$50
❏ 227	Tales of Kidd Funkadelic	1992	$18

— Reissue with bar code

FUNKADELIC (2)

LAX
❏ FW37087	Connections and Disconnections	1981	$12

FUNKDOOBIEST

IMMORTAL
❏ E64195	Brothas Doobie	1995	$15

FUNKMASTER FLEX

DEF JAM
❏ 538258-1	The Tunnel	1999	$18

— With Big Kap

LOUD
❏ 1961-1	60 Minutes of Funk, Volume IV: The Mixtape	2000	$18
❏ 67472	Funkmaster Flex: The Mix Tape Volume II	1997	$18
❏ 67647	Funkmaster Flex: The Mix Tape Volume III	1998	$18
❏ 66805	Funkmaster Flex Presents the Mix Tape Volume 1	1995	$18

FUNKY COMMUNICATIONS COMMITTEE

FREE FLIGHT
❏ AHL1-3406	Baby I Want You	1979	$18

RCA VICTOR
❏ AHL1-3583	Do You Believe in Magic	1980	$18

FUNKY GREEN DOGS

TWISTED
❏ 11511	Get Fired Up!	1997	$18

FUNKY KINGS

ARISTA
❏ AL4078	Funky Kings	1976	$15

FUNT, ALLEN

BLOOPERS
❏ CM 0001 [M]	The Best of Allen Funt's Candid Mike	196?	$25

OLUMBIA MASTERWORKS
❏ ML4344 [M]	Allen Funt's Candid Microphone	1950	$40

— Green label

❏ ML4449 [M]	Allen Funt's Candid Microphone, Vol. 2	1951	$40

— Green label

❏ ML4450 [M]	Allen Funt's Candid Microphone, Vol. 3	1951	$40

HARMONY
❏ HL7243 [M]	Allen Funt's Candid Microphone	195?	$25

JUBILEE
❏ KS-2 [M]	Candid Camera	196?	$25

RCA VICTOR
❏ LPM-3679 [M]	Allen Funt and Candid Kids	1967	$40
❏ LSP-3679 [S]	Allen Funt and Candid Kids	1967	$30

FURAY, RICHIE

ASYLUM
❏ 6E-115	Dance a Little Light	1978	$12
❏ 6E-231	I Still Have Dreams	1979	$12
❏ 7E-1067	I've Got a Reason	1976	$18

MYRRH
❏ MSB-6672	I've Got a Reason	1981	$25

— Christian-market reissue of Asylum 7E-1067

❏ MSB-6695	Seasons of Change	1982	$12

FUSE
Early version of Cheap Trick.

EPIC
❏ BN26502	Fuse	1970	$100

FUSE ONE

CTI
❏ 9003	Fuse One	1980	$30
❏ 9006	Silk	1981	$30

FUTTERMAN, JOEL

SILKHEART
❏ SH-125	Vision in Time	1991	$30

FUTURE, THE

SHAMLEY
❏ 703	Down the Country Road	1969	$25

FUTURE PROSPECT

OPTIMISM
❏ OP-7001	Future Prospect	198?	$12

FUTURES, THE

BUDDAH
❏ BDS-5630	Castles in the Sky	1975	$150

PHILADELPHIA INT'L.
❏ JZ36414	Greetings of Peace	1980	$75
❏ JZ35458	Past, Present and the Futures	1979	$50

FUZZ, THE

CALLA
❏ SD2001	The Fuzz	1971	$18

FUZZTONES, THE

CLEOPATRA
❏ 3746 [B]	Lysergic Legacy		$25

SUNDAZED
❏ LP5044	Flashbacks	199?	$18

G

G.B.H.

CLEOPATRA
❏ 7926 [B]	Punked In The O.C. - Live At The Celebrity Theater 1988		$25

G.T.O.'S, THE (2)

REPRISE
❏ RS6390 [B]	Permanent Damage	1970	$80

— Without booklet

❏ RS6390	Permanent Damage	1970	$80

— With booklet

Number	Title	Yr	NM

CSTRAIGHT

❏ STS-1059 [B]	Permanent Damage	1969	$150
—Without booklet			
❏ STS-1059 [B]	Permanent Damage	1969	$175
—With booklet			

GABRIEL, PETER
Also see GENESIS.
ATCO

❏ SD 36-147 [B]	Peter Gabriel	1977	$25
—(The "Solsbury Hill" album) -- Original pressing has yellow labels			
❏ SD 36-147	Peter Gabriel	1980	$12
—(The "Solsbury Hill" album) -- Other than yellow labels			

ATLANTIC

❏ SD-19181	Peter Gabriel	1978	$25
—(The "D.I.Y." album)			

DIRECT DISK

❏ SD-16615	Peter Gabriel	1980	$150
—The "Solsbury Hill" album; contains a long version of "Slowburn" not available elsewhere			

GEFFEN

❏ GHS24070	Birdy (Soundtrack)	1985	$12
❏ GHS24206	Passion: Music for "The Last Temptation of Christ	1989	$40
❏ GHSP2035	Peter Gabriel	1983	$12
—Reissue of Mercury album			
❏ R153801	Peter Gabriel (Security)	1982	$25
—RCA Music Service edition			
❏ GHS2011	Peter Gabriel (Security)	1982	$12
❏ GHS2011 [DJ]	Peter Gabriel (Security)	1982	$40
—Promo-only Quiex II audiophile pressing			
❏ R243372	Plays Live	1983	$30
—RCA Music Service edition			
❏ 2GHS4012	Plays Live	1983	$20
❏ R114764	So	1986	$15
—BMG Direct Marketing edition			
❏ GHS24088	So	1986	$12

MERCURY

❏ SRM-1-3848	Peter Gabriel	1980	$25
—(The "Games Without Frontiers" album)			

REAL WORLD

❏ PGDLP-6	Birdy (Soundtrack)	2004	$30
—Classic Records reissue on 200-gram vinyl			
❏ PGDLP-8	Passion: Music for "The Last Temptation of Christ	2004	$30
—Classic Records reissue on 200-gram vinyl			
❏ PGDLP-1	Peter Gabriel	2002	$30
—(The "Solsbury Hill" album) -- Classic Records audiophile issue			
❏ PGDLP-2	Peter Gabriel	2002	$30
—(The "D.I.Y." album) -- Classic Records audiophile issue			
❏ PGDLP-3	Peter Gabriel	2003	$30
—(The "Games Without Frontiers" album) -- Classic Records audiophile issue			
❏ PGDLP-4	Peter Gabriel (Security)	2003	$30
—Classic Records audiophile edition			
❏ PGDLP5	Plays Live	2004	$40
—Classic Records audiophile issue			
❏ PGDLP-7	So	2003	$30
—Classic Records audiophile edition			
❏ PGDLP11	Up	2002	$40
—Classic Records audiophile issue; includes bonus 45 in picture sleeve			
❏ PGDLP-9	Us	2004	$40
—Classic Records edition on 200-gram vinyl			

GABRIEL BONDAGE
DHARMA

❏ D-804 [B]	Angel Dust	1975	$50
❏ D-808	Another Trip to Earth	1977	$25
—Exists on white, red, or blue vinyl; each of similar value			

Number	Title	Yr	NM

GADD GANG, THE
COLUMBIA

❏ FC44327	Here and Now	1988	$30
❏ FC40864	The Gadd Gang	1987	$25

GAFA, AL
PABLO

❏ 2310782	Leblon Beach	1976	$30

GAILLARD, SLIM
ALLEGRO ELITE

❏ 4050 [10]	Slim Gaillard Plays	195?	$30

CLEF

❏ MGC-126 [10]	Mish Mash	1953	$300
❏ MGC-138 [10]	Slim Cavorts	1953	$300

DISC

❏ DLP-505 [10]	Opera in Vout	195?	$250

DOT

❏ DLP-25190 [S]	Slim Gaillard Rides Again	1959	$100
❏ DLP-3190 [M]	Slim Gaillard Rides Again	1959	$85

KING

❏ 295-80 [10]	Slim Gaillard/Boogie	195?	$150

MCA

❏ 1508	The Dot Sessions	198?	$85

MERCURY

❏ MGC-126 [10]	Mish Mash	1953	$0
—Canceled; reassigned to Clef 126			

NORGRAN

❏ MGN-13 [10]	Slim Gaillard and His Musical Aggregation Wherever They May Be	1954	$150

VERVE

❏ MGV-2013 [M]	Smorgasbord, Help Yourself	1956	$250
❏ V-2013 [M]	Smorgasbord, Help Yourself	1961	$25

GAILLARD, SLIM/DIZZY GILLESPIE
ULTRAPHONIC

❏ ULP-50273 [M]	Gaillard and Gillespie	1958	$40

GAILLARD, SLIM/MEADE LUX LEWIS
CLEF

❏ MGC-506 [10]	Boogie Woogie at the Philharmonic	1954	$300

MERCURY

❏ MGC-506 [10]	Boogie Woogie at the Philharmonic	1951	$300

GAINEN, MAURY
DISCOVERY

❏ DS-855	Jazz Sunrise	198?	$25

GAINSBOURG, SERGE
4 MEN WITH BEARDS

❏ 4M171LP [B]	Aux Armes Et Caetera		$25
❏ 4M195LP [B]	Gainsbourg Percussions		$25
❏ 4M196LP [B]	Initials B.B.		$25
❏ 4M170LP [B]	L'Homme A Tete De Chou		$25

GAITHER, BILL, TRIO
HEART WARMING

❏ R3197	Christmas…Back Home in Indiana	1972	$25

WORD

❏ 8825	Christmas…Back Home in Indiana	198?	$15
—Reissue of Heart Warming 3197			
❏ WSB-8886	He Started the Whole World Singing	1982	$15

GALAHADS, THE
LIBERTY

❏ LRP-3371 [M]	Hello, Galahads	1964	$30
❏ LST-7371 [S]	Hello, Galahads	1964	$35

GALASSO, MICHAEL
ECM

❏ 1245	Scenes	198?	$30

GALAXY ALL-STARS, THE
GALAXY

❏ GXY-95001	Live Under the Sky	1979	$35

GALBRAITH, BARRY
DECCA

❏ DL9200 [M]	Guitar and the Wind	1958	$120
❏ DL79200 [S]	Guitar and the Wind	1959	$100

GALBRAITH, ROB
COLUMBIA

❏ CS1057	Nashville Dirt	1970	$25

Number	Title	Yr	NM

GALE, EDDIE
BLUE NOTE

❏ BST-84320	Black Rhythm Happening	1969	$30
❏ BST-84294	Eddie Gale's Ghetto Music	1968	$30

GALE, ERIC
COLUMBIA

❏ PC34421	Ginseng	1977	$25
—Original edition with no bar code			
❏ JC34938	Multiplication	1978	$25
❏ JC35715	Part of You	1979	$25
❏ JC36363	The Best of Eric Gale	1980	$25
❏ JC36570	Touch of Silk	1981	$25

ELEKTRA/MUSICIAN

❏ 60022	Blue Horizon	1982	$25
❏ 60198	Island Breeze	1984	$25

EMARCY

❏ 836369-1	In a Jazz Tradition	1989	$30

KUDU

❏ 11	Forecast	1973	$35

GALE, SUNNY
CANADIAN AMERICAN

❏ CALP-1015 [M]	Goldies by the Girls	1964	$30

RCA VICTOR

❏ LPM-1277 [M]	Sunny and Blue	1956	$40

ROYALE

❏ 18123 [10]	Sunny Gale and Jazz Orchestra	1954	$50

THIMBLE

❏ TLP-10 [B]	Sunny Sings Dixieland and Blues	1974	$25

WARWICK

❏ W-2018 [M]	Sunny	1960	$30

GALLAGHER, BRIAN
CYPRESS

❏ 0126	Coming Home	1989	$30

GALLAGHER, RORY
Also see TASTE.
ATCO

❏ SD7004 [B]	Deuce	1971	$25
❏ SD 33-368 [B]	Rory Gallagher	1971	$25

CHRYSALIS

❏ CHR1098 [B]	Against the Grain	1975	$18
❏ CHR1124 [B]	Calling Card	1976	$18
❏ CHR1170 [B]	Photo-Finish	1978	$18
❏ CHR1198 [B]	Stage Struck	1980	$18
❏ CHR1235 [B]	Top Priority	1979	$18

MERCURY

❏ SRM-1-4051 [B]	Jinx	1982	$18

POLYDOR

❏ PD-5522 [B]	Blueprint	1973	$25
❏ PD-9501 [B]	Irish Tour '74	1974	$30
❏ PD-5513 [B]	Rory Gallagher/Live!	1972	$25
❏ PD-1-6510 [B]	Sinner...And Saint	1975	$25
❏ PD-5539 [B]	Tattoo	1973	$25
❏ PD-1-6519 [B]	The Story So Far	1975	$25

SPRINGBOARD

❏ SPB-4056 [B]	Take It Easy Baby	1976	$18

GALLERY
SUSSEX

❏ SUX-7026	Jim Gold and Gallery	1973	$15
❏ SUX-7017	Nice to Be with You	1972	$15

GALLERY (2)
ECM

❏ 1206	Gallery	1982	$30

GALLODORO, AL
ARCO

❏ AL-3 [10]	Al Gallodoro Concert	1950	$50

COLUMBIA

❏ CL6188 [10]	Al Gallodoro	1951	$50

GALLOP, FRANK
MUSICOR

❏ MM-2110 [M]	Frank Gallop Sings	1966	$18
❏ MS-3110 [S]	Frank Gallop Sings	1966	$25

GALLOWAY, JIM
SACKVILLE

❏ 4002	The Metro Stompers	198?	$175
❏ 4011	Thou Swell	198?	$25
❏ 2007	Three Is Company	198?	$25

Number	Title	Yr	NM

GALPER, HAL
BLACKHAWK
| ❏ BKH529 | Naturally | 1987 | $35 |

CENTURY
| ❏ 1120 | Speak with a Single Voice | 1978 | $35 |

CONCORD JAZZ
| ❏ CJ-383 | Portrait | 1988 | $25 |

ENJA
| ❏ 4006 | Speak with a Single Voice | 198? | $30 |

INNER CITY
| ❏ IC-3012 | Now Hear This | 1977 | $35 |
| ❏ IC-2067 | Reach Out | 1978 | $35 |

MAINSTREAM

❏ MRL-398 [B]	Inner Journey	1974	$25
❏ MRL-337	The Guerrilla Band	1971	$25
❏ MRL-354	Wild Bird	1972	$50

STEEPLECHASE
| ❏ SCS-1067 | Reach Out | 198? | $30 |
—Reissue of Inner City 2067

GALS & PALS
FONTANA
❏ MGF-27557 [M]	Gals & Pals Sing Something for Everybody	1966	$18
❏ SRF-67557 [S]	Gals & Pals Sing Something for Everybody	1966	$25
❏ MGF-27538 [M]	Gals & Pals (The Exciting Vocal Sounds of Europe's Newest "In" Group)	1965	$18
❏ SRF-67538 [S]	Gals & Pals (The Exciting Vocal Sounds of Europe's Newest "In" Group)	1965	$25

GALWAY, JAMES
RCA RED SEAL
| ❏ HRC1-5888 | James Galway's Christmas Carol | 1986 | $12 |

GAMALON
AMHERST
| ❏ AMH-3318 | Gamalon | 1988 | $35 |

GAMBLE FOLK, THE
EDIFY PRODUCTIONS
| ❏ ED1012 | Christmas Boy | 1977 | $12 |

GAMBRELL, FREDDIE, AND PAUL HORN
WORLD PACIFIC
| ❏ WP-1262 [M] | Mikado | 1959 | $175 |
| ❏ ST-1023 [S] | Mikado | 1959 | $150 |

GAMBRELL, FREDDIE
WORLD PACIFIC
| ❏ WP-1256 [M] | Freddie Gambrell | 1959 | $175 |

GAME
EVOLUTION
| ❏ 2021 | Game | 1970 | $15 |
| ❏ 3008 | Long Hot Summer | 1971 | $15 |

FAITHFUL VIRTUE
| ❏ 2003 | Game | 1969 | $25 |

GAMMA
Also see MONTROSE; ROBIN TROWER.

ELEKTRA
❏ E219	1	1979	$14
❏ E288	2	1980	$14
❏ E160034	3	1982	$12

GANDALF
CAPITOL
| ❏ ST-121 [B] | Gandalf | 1969 | $300 |

GANDALF THE GREY
G.W.R.
| ❏ 7 [B] | The Grey Wizard Am I | 1972 | $700 |

GANDELMAN, LEO
VERVE FORECAST
| ❏ 836424-1 | Western World | 1989 | $30 |

GANELIN TRIO, THE
HAT ART
| ❏ 2027 | Non Troppo | 1986 | $35 |

GANG OF FOUR
WARNER BROS.
❏ MINI3646 [EP]	Another Day, Another Dollar	1982	$12
❏ BSK3446	Entertainment!	1980	$14
❏ BSK3494	Gang of Four	1980	$12
❏ 23936	Hard	1983	$12
❏ BSK3565	Solid Gold	1981	$12
❏ 23683	Songs of the Free	1982	$12

GANG STARR
CHRYSALIS
❏ F1-21910	Daily Operation	1992	$20
❏ F1-28435	Hard to Earn	1994	$20
❏ F1-21798	Step In the Arena	1991	$20
VIRGIN
| ❏ 47279 | Full Clip -- A Decade of Gang Starr | 1999 | $25 |
| ❏ 45585 | Moment of Truth | 1998 | $20 |
WILD PITCH
| ❏ E1-98709 | No More Mr. Nice Guy | 1992 | $15 |
| ❏ 2001 | No More Mr. Nice Guy | 1989 | $20 |

GANNON, JIM
CATALYST
| ❏ 7605 | Gannon's Back in Town | 1976 | $35 |

GANT, CECIL
KING
| ❏ 671 [M] | Cecil Gant | 1960 | $100 |
RED MILL
| ❏ 0(no cat #) [M] | Cecil Gant | 1956 | $500 |
—Red vinyl
SOUND
| ❏ 601 [M] | The Incomparable Cecil Gant | 1958 | $150 |

GANTS, THE
LIBERTY
❏ LRP-3432 [M]	Road Runner	1965	$40
❏ LST-7432 [S]	Road Runner	1965	$40
❏ LRP-3473 [M]	The Gants Again	1966	$40
❏ LST-7473 [S]	The Gants Again	1966	$40
❏ LRP-3455 [M]	The Gants Galore	1966	$40
❏ LST-7455 [S]	The Gants Galore	1966	$40

GAP BAND, THE
CAPITOL
| ❏ C1-90799 | Round Trip | 1989 | $12 |
MERCURY
❏ 826808-1	The 12" Collection	1986	$10
❏ SRM-1-3758	The Gap Band	1979	$12
❏ SRM-1-3804	The Gap Band II	1979	$12
❏ SRM-1-4003	The Gap Band III	1980	$12
❏ 822788-1	The Gap Band III	198?	$10
—Reissue
PASSPORT
| ❏ PB-6026 | Strike a Groove | 1983 | $12 |
SHELTER
| ❏ 2111 | Magicians' Holiday | 1974 | $18 |
TATTOO
| ❏ BJL1-2168 | The Gap Band | 1977 | $18 |
TOTAL EXPERIENCE
❏ 2700-1-T	Gap Band 8	1986	$10
❏ TE-3001	Gap Band IV	1982	$10
❏ 822794-1	Gap Band IV	198?	$10
—Reissue
❏ TEL8-5705	Gap Band VI	1984	$10
❏ TEL8-5714	Gap Band VII	1986	$10
❏ TE-1-3004	Gap Band V -- Jammin'	1983	$10
❏ 812186-1	Gap Band V -- Jammin'	198?	$10
—Reissue
| ❏ 824343-1 | Gap Gold/Best of the Gap Band | 1985 | $10 |
| ❏ 2710-1-T | Straight from the Heart | 1987 | $10 |

GARAGIOLA, JOE
UNITED ARTISTS
| ❏ UAL-3032 [M] | That Holler Guy! | 1959 | $40 |
| ❏ UAS-6032 [S] | That Holler Guy! | 1959 | $50 |

GARBAGE
ALMO SOUNDS
| ❏ 80004 [B] | Garbage | 1995 | $25 |

GARBAREK, JAN, AND BOBO STENSON
ECM
| ❏ 1075 | Dansere | 1976 | $30 |
| ❏ 1041 | Witchi-Tai-To | 1973 | $30 |

GARBAREK, JAN, AND KJELL JOHNSEN
ECM
| ❏ 1169 | Aftenland | 1980 | $25 |

GARBAREK, JAN, AND TERJE RYPDAL
ARISTA FREEDOM
| ❏ AL1031 | Esoteric | 197? | $30 |

GARBAREK, JAN
ECM
❏ 1093	Dis	1977	$30
❏ 1200	Eventyr	1981	$25
❏ 25033	It's OK to Listen to the Gray Voice	1985	$25
❏ 1151	Magico	1979	$25
❏ 1223	Paths, Prints	1982	$25
❏ 1135	Photo With…	1978	$25
❏ 1118	Places	1978	$25
❏ 23798	Wayfarer	1984	$25
FLYING DUTCHMAN
| ❏ FD-10125 | The Esoteric Circle | 1971 | $25 |

GARBER, JAN
DECCA
| ❏ DL8932 [M] | Christmas Dance Party | 1959 | $18 |
—Black label, silver print
| ❏ DL78932 [S] | Christmas Dance Party | 1959 | $25 |
—Black label, silver print
| ❏ DL8482 [M] | Dance at Home | 195? | $25 |
—Black label, silver print
| ❏ DL8484 [M] | Designed for Dancing | 195? | $25 |
—Black label, silver print
| ❏ DL8483 [M] | In a Dancing Mood | 195? | $25 |
—Black label, silver print
| ❏ DL8867 [M] | Jan Garber in Danceland | 195? | $18 |
—Black label, silver print
| ❏ DL78867 [S] | Jan Garber in Danceland | 195? | $25 |
—Black label, silver print
| ❏ DL8793 [M] | Music from the Blue Room, Roosevelt Hotel, New Orleans | 195? | $18 |
—Black label, silver print
| ❏ DL78793 [S] | Music from the Blue Room, Roosevelt Hotel, New Orleans | 195? | $25 |
—Black label, silver print
| ❏ DL8824 [M] | Waltzes | 195? | $18 |
—Black label, silver print
| ❏ DL78824 [S] | Waltzes | 195? | $25 |
—Black label, silver print

GARBO, GRETA
MGM
| ❏ E-4201 [M] | Garbo | 1964 | $40 |

GARCED, JORGE
CAYTRONICS
| ❏ CYZ6011 | Recuerdos | 1981 | $15 |

GARCIA, DICK
DAWN
| ❏ DLP-1106 [M] | A Message from Dick Garcia | 1956 | $150 |
SEECO
| ❏ SLP-428 [M] | A Message from Dick Garcia | 1958 | $175 |

GARCIA, JERRY
Also see THE GRATEFUL DEAD; NEW RIDERS OF THE PURPLE SAGE; OLD & IN THE WAY.
ARISTA
❏ AB4160	Cats Under the Stars	1978	$15
❏ AL9603	Run for the Roses	1982	$15
❏ AL8364	Run for the Roses	198?	$10
—Reissue of 9603
MOBILE FIDELITY
| ❏ MFSL2-430 [B] | Jerry Garcia / David Grisman | 2014 | $75 |
ROUND
❏ RX-102	Garcia	1974	$30
❏ JGFRR1005 [B]	Garcia	2014	$30
❏ RX-107	Reflections	1975	$30

Number	Title	Yr	NM
❑ RN-LA565-G	Reflections	1976	$25

—Reissue of Round 107 with United Artists distribution

WARNER BROS.

Number	Title	Yr	NM
❑ BS2582	Garcia	1972	$40

—Green label with "WB" logo

GARCIA, RUSS, AND MARTY PAICH

BETHLEHEM

Number	Title	Yr	NM
❑ BCP-6039 [M]	Jazz Music for Birds and Hep Cats	1960	$300
❑ SBCP-6039 [S]	Jazz Music for Birds and Hep Cats	1960	$300

GARCIA, RUSS

ABC-PARAMOUNT

Number	Title	Yr	NM
❑ ABC-147 [M]	The Johnny Evergreens	1956	$50

BETHLEHEM

Number	Title	Yr	NM
❑ BCP-46 [M]	Four Horns and a Lush Life	1956	$300
❑ BCP-6044	I'll Never Forget What's Her Name	1978	$30

—Reissue, distributed by RCA Victor

Number	Title	Yr	NM
❑ BCP-1040 [10]	Wigville	1955	$300

DISCOVERY

Number	Title	Yr	NM
❑ DS-814	I Lead a Charmed Life	1980	$30

KAPP

Number	Title	Yr	NM
❑ KL-1050 [M]	Listen to the Music of Russell Garcia	1957	$50

LIBERTY

Number	Title	Yr	NM
❑ LRP-3062 [M]	Enchantment (The Music of Joe Greene)	1958	$30
❑ LRP-3084 [M]	Fantastica	1958	$30

Number	Title	Yr	NM
❑ LST-7005 [S]	Fantastica	1958	$40

VERVE

Number	Title	Yr	NM
❑ MGV-2088 [M]	The Warm Feeling	1957	$150
❑ V-2088 [M]	The Warm Feeling	1961	$25

GARDNER, BROTHER DAVE

4 STAR

Number	Title	Yr	NM
❑ 4S75003	Brother Dave Gardner's New Comedy Album	1976	$25

CAPITOL

Number	Title	Yr	NM
❑ T1867 [M]	It Don't Make No Difference	1963	$25
❑ ST1867 [S]	It Don't Make No Difference	1963	$30
❑ T2055 [M]	It's All in How You Look at It	1964	$25
❑ ST2055 [S]	It's All in How You Look at It	1964	$30

RCA VICTOR

Number	Title	Yr	NM
❑ LPM-2335 [M]	Ain't That Weird?	1961	$25
❑ LSP-2335 [S]	Ain't That Weird?	1961	$30
❑ LPM-2628 [M]	All Seriousness Aside	1963	$25
❑ LSP-2628 [S]	All Seriousness Aside	1963	$30
❑ LPM-2852 [M]	Best of Dave Gardner	1964	$25
❑ LSP-2852 [S]	Best of Dave Gardner	1964	$30
❑ LPM-2498 [M]	Did You Ever?	1962	$25
❑ LSP-2498 [S]	Did You Ever?	1962	$30
❑ LPM-2761 [M]	It's Bigger Than Both of Us	1963	$25
❑ LSP-2761 [S]	It's Bigger Than Both of Us	1963	$30
❑ LPM-2239 [M]	Kick Thy Own Self	1960	$25
❑ LSP-2239(e) [S]	Kick Thy Own Self	196?	$30
❑ LPM-2083 [M]	Rejoice, Dear Hearts!	1960	$25
❑ LSP-2083(e) [S]	Rejoice, Dear Hearts!	196?	$30

TONKA

Number	Title	Yr	NM
❑ TLP713	Out Front	1969	$25

TOWER

Number	Title	Yr	NM
❑ T5050 [M]	Hip-ocracy	1966	$18
❑ ST5050 [S]	Hip-ocracy	1966	$25
❑ T5075 [M]	It Don't Make No Self	1967	$30
❑ ST5075 [S]	It Don't Make No Difference	1967	$25

GARDNER, DON, AND DEE DEE FORD

COLLECTABLES

Number	Title	Yr	NM
❑ COL-5155	Golden Classics: Need Your Lovin'	198?	$15

FIRE

Number	Title	Yr	NM
❑ LP-105 [M]	Need Your Lovin'	1962	$400

SUE

Number	Title	Yr	NM
❑ LP-1044 [M]	Don Gardner and Dee Dee Ford In Sweden	1965	$120

GARDNER, FREDDY, AND AL GALLODORO

COLUMBIA

Number	Title	Yr	NM
❑ CL623 [M]	The Immortal Freddy Gardner and Al Gallodoro	1954	$40

—Maroon label, gold print

GARDNER, FREDDY

COLUMBIA

Number	Title	Yr	NM
❑ CL6187 [10]	Freddy Gardner	195?	$50

GARDNERS, THE

PRESTIGE INT'L.

Number	Title	Yr	NM
❑ PRLP-13062 [M]	Folk Songs Far and Near	1962	$40

GARDONY, LASZLO

ANTILLES

Number	Title	Yr	NM
❑ 91250	The Legend of Tsumi	1989	$30
❑ 90694	The Secret	1988	$30

GARFUNKEL, ART
Also see SIMON AND GARFUNKEL.

COLUMBIA

Number	Title	Yr	NM
❑ KC31474 [M]	Angel Clare	1973	$15
❑ CQ31474 [Q]	Angel Clare	1973	$50
❑ PC31474	Angel Clare	197?	$10

—Reissue

Number	Title	Yr	NM
❑ PC33700 [B]	Breakaway	1975	$15

—Originals have no bar code

Number	Title	Yr	NM
❑ PCQ33700 [Q]	Breakaway	1975	$100
❑ PC33700	Breakaway	197?	$10

—With bar code on cover

Number	Title	Yr	NM
❑ JC35780	Fate for Breakfast	1979	$15

—With six different covers, each illustrating Art Garfunkel at a different stage of eating breakfast. No difference in value.

Number	Title	Yr	NM
❑ OC45008	Garfunkel	1989	$12
❑ FC40942	Lefty	1988	$10
❑ FC37392	Scissors Cut	1981	$12
❑ FC40212	The Animals' Christmas By Jimmy Webb	1986	$12

—With Amy Grant

Number	Title	Yr	NM
❑ JC34975 [DJ]	Watermark	1978	$75

—Test pressing or white label promo with "Fingerpaint" on side 2

Number	Title	Yr	NM
❑ JC34975	Watermark	1978	$150

—Stock copy with "Fingerpaint" on side 2

Number	Title	Yr	NM
❑ JC34975	Watermark	1978	$15

—Stock copy with "(What a) Wonderful World" on side 2

Number	Title	Yr	NM
❑ PC34975	Watermark	198?	$10

—Reissue

GARI, RALPH

EMARCY

Number	Title	Yr	NM
❑ MG-36019 [M]	Ralph Gari	1955	$250

GARLAND, HANK

COLUMBIA

Number	Title	Yr	NM
❑ CL1572 [M]	Jazz Winds from a New Direction	1961	$30
❑ CS8372 [S]	Jazz Winds from a New Direction	1961	$40
❑ CL1913 [M]	The Unforgettable Guitar of Hank Garland	1962	$30
❑ CS8713 [S]	The Unforgettable Guitar of Hank Garland	1962	$40

HARMONY

Number	Title	Yr	NM
❑ HL7231 [M]	Velvet Guitar	196?	$25
❑ HS11028 [S]	Velvet Guitar	196?	$30

SESAC

Number	Title	Yr	NM
❑ SN-2301/2 [M]	Subtle Swing	196?	$150

GARLAND, JUDY, AND LIZA MINNELLI

CAPITOL

Number	Title	Yr	NM
❑ WBO2295 [M]	Live" at the London Palladium	1965	$30
❑ SWBO2295 [S]	Live" at the London Palladium	1965	$30
❑ ST-11191	Live" at the London Palladium	1973	$15

—Condensation of above 2-record set

MOBILE FIDELITY

Number	Title	Yr	NM
❑ Jan-0048	Live" at the London Palladium	1981	$40

—Audiophile vinyl

GARLAND, JUDY

ABC

Number	Title	Yr	NM
❑ 620 [M]	Judy Garland At Home at the Palace -- Opening Night	1967	$25
❑ S-620 [S]	Judy Garland At Home at the Palace -- Opening Night	1967	$30
❑ AC-30007	The ABC Collection	1976	$18

A.E.I.

Number	Title	Yr	NM
❑ 2108	Judy Garland Vol. 1: Born in a Trunk	198?	$12
❑ 2109 [M]	Judy Garland Vol. 2: Stardom 1940-45	1980	$12
❑ 2110	Judy Garland Vol. 3: Superstar 1945-50	198?	$12

CAPITOL

Number	Title	Yr	NM
❑ T835 [M]	Alone	1957	$40
❑ DT835 [R]	Alone	1963	$18
❑ SM-11763	Alone	1978	$12

—Edited reissue of 835

Number	Title	Yr	NM
❑ T1118 [M]	Garland at the Grove	1959	$30
❑ ST1118 [S]	Garland at the Grove	1959	$40
❑ W1861 [M]	I Could Go On Singing	1963	$40
❑ SW1861 [P]	I Could Go On Singing	1963	$75

—I Am the Monarch of the Sea" and "It Never Was You" are rechanneled

Number	Title	Yr	NM
❑ T734 [M]	Judy	1956	$40
❑ DT734 [R]	Judy	1963	$18
❑ WBO1569 [M]	Judy at Carnegie Hall	1961	$40
❑ SWBO1569 [S]	Judy at Carnegie Hall	1961	$50
❑ T1036 [M]	Judy in Love	1958	$30
❑ ST1036 [S]	Judy in Love	1959	$40
❑ T1467 [M]	Judy -- That's Entertainment	1960	$30

—Black rainbow label, Capitol logo at left

Number	Title	Yr	NM
❑ ST1467 [S]	Judy -- That's Entertainment	1960	$40

—Black rainbow label, Capitol logo at left

Number	Title	Yr	NM
❑ SM-11876	Judy -- That's Entertainment	1978	$12

—Edited reissue

Number	Title	Yr	NM
❑ T1467 [M]	Judy -- That's Entertainment	196?	$18

—Black rainbow label, Capitol logo at top

Number	Title	Yr	NM
❑ ST1467 [S]	Judy -- That's Entertainment	196?	$25

—Black rainbow label, Capitol logo at top

Number	Title	Yr	NM
❑ W2062 [M]	Just for Openers	1964	$25
❑ DW2062 [R]	Just for Openers	1964	$18
❑ M-12034	Just for Openers	1979	$12

—Edited reissue

Number	Title	Yr	NM
❑ W676 [M]	Miss Show Business	1955	$40
❑ DW676 [R]	Miss Show Business	1963	$15
❑ T1941 [M]	Our Love Letter	1963	$25

—Reissue of T 1188

Number	Title	Yr	NM
❑ ST1941 [S]	Our Love Letter	1963	$30

—Reissue of ST 1188

Number	Title	Yr	NM
❑ W1710 [M]	The Garland Touch	1962	$25
❑ SW1710 [S]	The Garland Touch	1962	$30
❑ T1999 [M]	The Hits of Judy Garland	1964	$25
❑ ST1999 [P]	The Hits of Judy Garland	1964	$30

—Over the Rainbow," "Come Rain or Come Shine" and "April Showers" are rechanneled

Number	Title	Yr	NM
❑ SM-1999	The Hits of Judy Garland	197?	$12

—Reissue

Number	Title	Yr	NM
❑ SN-16175	The Hits of Judy Garland	198?	$10

—Budget-line reissue

Number	Title	Yr	NM
❑ STCL2988	The Judy Garland Deluxe Set	1968	$40
❑ T1188 [M]	The Letter	1959	$30

—Add 80% if letter is on cover

Number	Title	Yr	NM
❑ ST1188 [S]	The Letter	1959	$40

—Add 80% if letter is on cover

Number	Title	Yr	NM
❑ DNFR-7632	The Magic of Judy Garland	196?	$40

—Box set with 4-page insert; 20 of the 60 tracks are rechanneled

DECCA

Number	Title	Yr	NM
❑ DL6020 [10]	Judy at the Palace	1952	$150
❑ DL75150 [R]	Judy Garland's Greatest Hits	1969	$15
❑ DL8190 [M]	Judy Garland's Greatest Performances	1955	$40

—Black label, silver print

Number	Title	Yr	NM
❑ DL8190 [M]	Judy Garland's Greatest Performances	196?	$30

—Black label with color bars

Number	Title	Yr	NM
❑ DXB172 [M]	The Best of Judy Garland	1963	$25
❑ DXSB7172 [R]	The Best of Judy Garland	1963	$25
❑ DL4199 [M]	The Magic of Judy Garland	1961	$30

DRG

Number	Title	Yr	NM
❑ SL-5187	The Beginning	1979	$18
❑ SL5179	The Wit and the Wonder of Judy Garland	1977	$18

LONGINES SYMPHONETTE

Number	Title	Yr	NM
❑ SY5217	The Magic of Judy Garland	197?	$30

MARK 56

Number	Title	Yr	NM
❑ 632 [PD]	In Concert: San Francisco	1978	$75

MCA

Number	Title	Yr	NM
❑ 4046	Collector's Items (1936-45)	197?	$15
❑ 907	From the Decca Vaults	1984	$12
❑ 4003	The Best of Judy Garland	1973	$18

—Black label with rainbow

Number	Title	Yr	NM
❑ 4003	The Best of Judy Garland	1980	$12

—Blue label with rainbow

Number	Title	Yr	NM
❑ 25165	The Best of Judy Garland from MGM Classic Films	1988	$15

METRO

Number	Title	Yr	NM
❑ M-505 [M]	Judy Garland	1965	$18
❑ MS-505 [S]	Judy Garland	1965	$25
❑ M-581 [M]	Judy Garland in Song	1966	$18
❑ MS-581 [S]	Judy Garland in Song	1966	$25

GARLAND, JUDY

Number	Title	Yr	NM
MGM			
□ PX102	Forever Judy	1969	$30

— White label "Limited Edition" with poster

Number	Title	Yr	NM
□ SDP-1	Golden Years at MGM	1969	$30
□ E-3149 [M]	If You Feel Like Singing, Sing	1955	$75
□ E-82 [10]	Judy Garland Sings	1951	$150
□ E-3989 [M]	The Judy Garland Story Vol. 1: The Star Years	1961	$30
□ E-4005 [M]	The Judy Garland Story Vol. 2: The Hollywood Years	1962	$30
□ E-4204 [M]	The Very Best of Judy Garland	1964	$30
□ SE-4204 [R]	The Very Best of Judy Garland	1964	$18

— Black label

□ SE-4204 [R]	The Very Best of Judy Garland	1964	$12

— Blue and gold label

MINERVA			
□ LP-6JG-FNJ	Judy Garland and Friends	1982	$12
□ LP-6JG-FST	The Judy Garland Show: Mutual Admiration Society	1982	$12
PAIR			
□ PDL2-1030	Golden Memories	1986	$15
□ PDL2-1127	The Legendary Judy Garland	1986	$15
PICKWICK			
□ PTP-2010	Her Greatest Hits	197?	$15
□ SPC-3053	I Feel a Song Coming On	197?	$15
SPRINGBOARD			
□ SPB-4054	Over the Rainbow	197?	$10
STANYAN			
□ 10095	More Than a Memory	1974	$12
□ POW-3001	More Than a Memory	198?	$12

— Reissue of 10095

TIME-LIFE			
□ SLGD-12	Legendary Singers: Judy Garland	1986	$25
TROPHY			
□ TR-7-2145	Judy Garland Concert	1974	$18

GARLAND, RED

Number	Title	Yr	NM
FANTASY			
□ OJC-126	A Garland of Red	198?	$25

— Reissue of Prestige 7064

□ OJC-193	All Kinds of Weather	1985	$25

— Reissue of Prestige 7148

□ OJC-293	All Morning Long	1988	$25

— Reissue of Prestige 7130

□ OJC-265	Bright and Breezy	1987	$25

— Reissue of Jazzland 948

□ OJC-472	Crossings	1990	$30

— Reissue of Galaxy 5106

□ OJC-392	Dig It!	1989	$30

— Reissue of Prestige 7229

□ OJC-061	Groovy	198?	$25

— Reissue of Prestige 7113

□ OJC-349	High Pressure	198?	$25

— Reissue of Prestige 7209

□ OJC-428	Manteca	1990	$30

— Reissue of Prestige 7139

□ OJC-647	Red Alert	1991	$30

— Reissue of Galaxy 5109

□ OJC-360	Red Garland & Eddie "Lockjaw" Davis	198?	$25

— Reissue of Moodsville 1

□ OJC-073	Red Garland's Piano	198?	$25

— Reissue of Prestige 7086

□ OJC-295	Red in Bluesville	198?	$25

— Reissue of Prestige 7157

□ OJC-481	Soul Junction	1991	$30

— Reissue of Prestige 7181

□ OJC-224	The Red Garland Trio	198?	$25

— Reissue of Moodsville 6

GALAXY			
□ 5106	Crossings	1978	$30
□ 5115	Equinox	1979	$30
□ 5109	Red Alert	1978	$30
□ 5129	Stepping Out	198?	$25
□ 5135	Strike Up the Band	198?	$25
JAZZLAND			
□ JLP-48 [M]	Bright and Breezy	1961	$150
□ JLP-948 [S]	Bright and Breezy	1961	$120
□ JLP-87 [M]	Red's Good Groove!	1963	$120
□ JLP-987 [S]	Red's Good Groove!	1963	$120
□ JLP-73 [M]	Solar	1962	$150
□ JLP-973 [S]	Solar	1962	$120
□ JLP-62 [M]	The Nearness of You -- Ballads Played by Red Garland	1962	$150
□ JLP-962 [S]	The Nearness of You -- Ballads Played by Red Garland	1962	$120
MOODSVILLE			
□ MVLP-10 [M]	Alone with the Blues	1960	$150

— Green label

□ MVLP-10 [M]	Alone with the Blues	1965	$50

— Blue label, trident logo at right

□ MVLP-3 [M]	Red Alone -- Vol. 3	1960	$150

— Green label

□ MVLP-3 [M]	Red Alone -- Vol. 3	1965	$50

— Blue label, trident logo at right

□ MVLP-1 [M]	Red Garland & Eddie "Lockjaw' Davis	1960	$150

— Green label

□ MVLP-1 [M]	Red Garland & Eddie "Lockjaw' Davis	1965	$50

— Blue label, trident logo at right

□ MVLP-6 [M]	The Red Garland Trio	1960	$150

— Green label

□ MVLP-6 [M]	The Red Garland Trio	1965	$50

— Blue label, trident logo at right

MUSE			
□ MR-5130	Feelin' Red	1980	$30
□ MR-5311	I Left My Heart	1985	$25
NEW JAZZ			
□ NJLP-8325 [M]	High Pressure	1963	$0

— Canceled; reassigned to Status

□ NJLP-8314 [M]	Li'l Darlin'	1963	$0

— Canceled; reassigned to Status

□ NJLP-8326 [M]	Red Garland Live!	1963	$0

— Canceled; reassigned to Status

PRESTIGE			
□ PRLP-7064 [M]	A Garland of Red	1956	$300

— Yellow label, W. 50th St., New York address on label

□ PRLP-7064 [M]	A Garland of Red	1958	$300

— Yellow label with Bergenfield, N.J. address

□ PRLP-7148 [M]	All Kinds of Weather	1958	$400

— Yellow label with Bergenfield, N.J. address

□ PRLP-7130 [M]	All Morning Long	1958	$500

— Yellow label, W. 50th St., New York address on label

□ PRLP-7130 [M]	All Morning Long	1958	$300

— Yellow label with Bergenfield, N.J. address

□ PRLP-7276 [M]	Can't See for Lookin'	1963	$75
□ PRST-7276 [S]	Can't See for Lookin'	1963	$75
□ PRLP-7229 [M]	Dig It!	1962	$175
□ PRST-7229 [S]	Dig It!	1962	$175
□ PRLP-7113 [M]	Groovy	1957	$500

— Yellow label, W. 50th St., New York address on label

□ PRLP-7113 [M]	Groovy	1958	$300

— Yellow label with Bergenfield, N.J. address

□ PRLP-7288 [M]	Halleloo-Y'all	1964	$75
□ PRST-7288 [S]	Halleloo-Y'all	1964	$100
□ PRLP-7209 [M]	High Pressure	1961	$250

— Yellow label with Bergenfield, N.J. address

□ PRST-7838	It's a Blue World	1971	$50
□ 24023	Jazz Junction	1972	$35
□ PRLP-7139 [M]	Manteca	1958	$300

— Yellow label with Bergenfield, N.J. address

□ PRLP-7139 [M]	Manteca	1958	$250

— Yellow label, W. 50th St. NYC address on label

□ PRST-7752	P.C. Blues	1970	$50
□ PRLP-7170 [M]	Red Garland at the Prelude	1959	$250

— Yellow label with Bergenfield, N.J. address

□ PRST-7658	Red Garland Revisited!	1969	$50
□ PRLP-7086 [M]	Red Garland's Piano	1957	$300

— Yellow label, W. 50th St., New York address on label

□ PRLP-7086 [M]	Red Garland's Piano	1958	$250

— Yellow label with Bergenfield, N.J. address

□ PRLP-7157 [M]	Red in Bluesville	1959	$250

— Yellow label with Bergenfield, N.J. address

□ 24078	Rediscovered Masters	1979	$35
□ PRLP-7193 [M]	Rojo	1961	$250

— Yellow label with Bergenfield, N.J. address

□ 24090	Saying Something	1980	$35
□ PRLP-7307 [M]	Soul Burnin'	1964	$50
□ PRST-7307 [S]	Soul Burnin'	1964	$75
□ PRLP-7181 [M]	Soul Junction	1960	$250

— Yellow label with Bergenfield, N.J. address

□ PRLP-7258 [M]	When There Are Grey Skies	1963	$300
□ PRST-7258 [S]	When There Are Grey Skies	1963	$120
RIVERSIDE			
□ 6099	Bright and Breezy	197?	$35
STATUS			
□ ST-8325 [M]	High Pressure	1965	$75
□ ST-8314 [M]	Li'l Darlin'	1965	$75
□ ST-8326 [M]	Red Garland Live!	1965	$75

GARNER, ERROLL

Number	Title	Yr	NM
ABC-PARAMOUNT			
□ 395 [M]	Closeup in Swing	1961	$50
□ S-395 [S]	Closeup in Swing	1961	$75
□ 365 [M]	Dreamstreet	1961	$50
□ S-365 [S]	Dreamstreet	1961	$75
ATLANTIC			
□ ALR-112 [10]	Erroll Garner at the Piano	1951	$300
□ ALR-128 [10]	Passport to Fame	1952	$350
□ 1315 [M]	Perpetual Motion	1959	$300

— Black label

□ ALR-135 [10]	Piano Solos, Volume 2	1952	$350
□ ALR-109 [10]	Rhapsody	1950	$300
□ 1227 [M]	The Greatest Garner	1956	$300

— Black label

□ 1227 [M]	The Greatest Garner	1961	$175

— Multi-color label with white "fan" logo

□ 1227 [M]	The Greatest Garner	196?	$30

— Multi-color label with black "fan" logo

BARONET			
□ B-109 [M]	Informal Piano Improvisations	1962	$30
□ BS-109 [R]	Informal Piano Improvisations	1962	$25
BLUE NOTE			
□ BLP-5007 [10]	Overture to Dawn, Volume 1	1952	$500
□ BLP-5008 [10]	Overture to Dawn, Volume 2	1952	$500
□ BLP-5014 [10]	Overture to Dawn, Volume 3	1953	$500
□ BLP-5015 [10]	Overture to Dawn, Volume 4	1953	$500
□ BLP-5016 [10]	Overture to Dawn, Volume 5	1953	$500
CLARION			
□ 610 [M]	Serenade in Blue	1966	$30
□ SD610 [S]	Serenade in Blue	1966	$30
COLUMBIA			
□ CL883 [M]	Concert by the Sea	1956	$75
□ CS9821 [R]	Concert by the Sea	1970	$30
□ CL1141 [M]	Encores in Hi-Fi	1958	$75
□ CL535 [M]	Erroll Garner	1953	$120

— Red label with gold print

□ CL535 [M]	Erroll Garner	1956	$75

— Red and black label with six "eye" logos

□ CL6259 [10]	Erroll Garner Plays for Dancing	1953	$175
□ CL667 [M]	Erroll Garner Plays for Dancing	1956	$75
□ CL2540 [10]	Garnerland	1955	$120
□ CL6173 [10]	Gems	1951	$175
□ CL583 [M]	Gems	1954	$120

— Red label with gold print

□ CL583 [M]	Gems	1956	$75

— Red and black label with six "eye" logos

□ CL617 [M]	Gone Garner Gonest	1955	$120

— Red label with gold print

□ CL617 [M]	Gone Garner Gonest	1956	$75

— Red and black label with six "eye" logos

□ CL2606 [10]	He's Here! He's Gone! He's Garner!	1956	$120
□ CL1014 [M]	Other Voices	1957	$75

— Red and black label wirh six "eye" logos

□ CS9820 [R]	Other Voices	1970	$30
□ C2L9 [M]	Paris Impressions	1958	$40
□ CL1216 [M]	Paris Impressions, Volume 1	1958	$50
□ CS8131 [S]	Paris Impressions, Volume 1	1958	$75
□ CL1217 [M]	Paris Impressions, Volume 2	1958	$50
□ CL6139 [10]	Piano Moods	1950	$175
□ PG33424	Play It Again, Erroll!	1975	$30
□ CL1060 [M]	Soliloquy	1957	$75
□ CL6209 [10]	Solo Flight	1952	$175
□ CL1512 [M]	Swinging Solos	1960	$50
□ CS8312 [S]	Swinging Solos	1960	$75
□ CL939 [M]	The Most Happy Piano	1957	$75
□ CL1452 [M]	The One and Only Erroll Garner	1960	$50
□ CS8252 [S]	The One and Only Erroll Garner	1960	$75
□ CL1587 [M]	The Provocative Erroll Garner	1961	$50
□ CS8387 [S]	The Provocative Erroll Garner	1961	$75
COLUMBIA JAZZ MASTERPIECES			
□ CJ40863	Long Ago and Far Away	1987	$30
COLUMBIA SPECIAL PRODUCTS			
□ P14386	Dreamy	1978	$25
DIAL			
□ LP-205 [10]	Erroll Garner, Volume 1	1950	$250
□ LP-902 [M]	Free Piano Improvisations Recorded by Baron Timme Rosenkranz at One of His Famous Gaslight Jazz Sessions	1949	$300
EMARCY			
□ MG-36001 [M]	Contrasts	1955	$30
□ MG-36069 [M]	Erroll!	1956	$250
□ 826224-1	Erroll Garner Plays Gershwin and Kern	1986	$25
□ MG-26016 [M]	Garnering	1954	$250
□ MG-36026 [M]	Garnering	1955	$250
□ MG-26042 [10]	Gone with Garner	1954	$250
□ 832994-1	The Erroll Garner Collection Vol. 1: Easy to Love	1988	$25
□ 834935-1	The Erroll Garner Collection Vol. 2: Dancing on the Ceiling	1989	$25
EVEREST ARCHIVE OF FOLK & JAZZ			
□ 245	Erroll Garner	1970	$25
GUEST STAR			
□ G1403 [M]	Piano Greats	196?	$30

— With tracks by Art Tatum and Mike Di Napoli

□ GS1403 [S]	Piano Greats	196?	$25

— With tracks by Art Tatum and Mike Di Napoli

HALL OF FAME			
□ 610	Early Erroll	198?	$25

Number	Title	Yr	NM

HARMONY
| HS11268 | One More Time | 1968 | $30 |

JAZZTONE
| J-1269 [M] | Early Erroll | 1957 | $40 |

KING
| 295-17 [10] | Piano Stylist | 1952 | $175 |
| 395-540 [S] | Piano Variations | 1958 | $175 |

LONDON
| XPS617 | Gemini | 1972 | $30 |
| APS640 | Magician | 1973 | $30 |

MERCURY
MG-20090 [M]	Afternoon of an Elf	1955	$175
826457-1	Afternoon of an Elf	1986	$25
—Reissue			
MG-25117 [10]	Erroll Garner at the Piano	1951	$300
MG-20009 [M]	Erroll Garner at the Piano	1953	$175
MG-20662 [M]	Erroll Garner Plays Misty	1962	$150
SR-60662 [S]	Erroll Garner Plays Misty	1962	$150
—Black label, all-silver print			
SR-60662 [S]	Erroll Garner Plays Misty	1965	$175
—Red label, "MERCURY" in all caps at top			
SR-60662	Erroll Garner Plays Misty	1975	$25
—Chicago skyline label			
SR-60662	Erroll Garner Plays Misty	1983	$20
—Black label, neon-style "mercury" logo			
MG-21308 [M]	Feeling Is Believing	1964	$150
SR-61308 [S]	Feeling Is Believing	1964	$150
SR-61308 [S]	Feeling Is Believing	1970	$30
—Newer Mercury logo on cover			
MG-25157 [10]	Gone with Garner	1951	$300
MG-20055 [M]	Mambo Moves Garner	1954	$175
MG-20859 [M]	New Kind of Love	1963	$150
SR-60859 [S]	New Kind of Love	1963	$150
MG-20063 [M]	Solitaire	1954	$175
MG-20803 [M]	The Best of Erroll Garner	1963	$150
SR-60803 [S]	The Best of Erroll Garner	1963	$150

MGM
E-4361 [M]	Campus Concert	1966	$30
SE-4361 [S]	Campus Concert	1966	$35
E-4335 [M]	Now Playing: Erroll Garner	1966	$30
SE-4335 [S]	Now Playing: Erroll Garner	1966	$35
E-4463 [M]	That's My Kick	1967	$35
SE-4463 [S]	That's My Kick	1967	$30
E-4520 [M]	Up in Erroll's Room	1967	$35
SE-4520 [S]	Up in Erroll's Room	1967	$30

PICKWICK
| SPC-3254 | Deep Purple | 197? | $25 |

REPRISE
R6080 [M]	One World Concert	1963	$50
RS6080 [S]	One World Concert	1963	$75
R6080 [DJ]	One World Concert	1963	$40
—Six-song sampler -- three on each side -- on a 12-inch record that plays at 45 rpm. This comes in a different cover than the stock copy; this is clearly marked "Special 45 RPM Preview Record" on the top front.			

RONDO-LETTE
| A-15 [M] | Erroll Garner | 1958 | $75 |

SAVOY
SJL-2207	Elf	198?	$30
MG-15026 [10]	Erroll Garner at the Piano	1953	$175
MG-15000 [10]	Erroll Garner Plays Piano Solos	1950	$175
MG-15001 [10]	Erroll Garner Plays Piano Solos, Volume 2	1950	$175
MG-15002 [10]	Erroll Garner Plays Piano Solos, Volume 3	1950	$175
MG-15003 [10]	Erroll Garner Plays Piano Solos, Volume 4	1950	$175
MG-12002 [M]	Penthouse Serenade	1955	$85
SJC-411	Penthouse Serenade	1985	$25
MG-12003 [M]	Serenade to "Laura"	1955	$85
SJL-1118	Yesterdays	198?	$25

TRIP
| 5519 | Garnering | 197? | $25 |

WING
| MGW12134 | Erroll Garner Moods | 196? | $30 |

GARNER, ERROLL/BILLY TAYLOR
SAVOY
| MG-12008 [M] | Erroll Garner/Billy Taylor | 1955 | $150 |

GARNER, ERROLL/OSCAR PETERSON/ART TATUM
RCA CAMDEN
| CAL-882 [M] | Great Jazz Pianists of Our Time | 196? | $35 |
| CAS-882 [R] | Great Jazz Pianists of Our Time | 196? | $30 |

GARNER, ERROLL/PETE JOHNSON
GRAND AWARD
GA 33-321 [M]	Jazz Piano	1956	$150
—With removable David Stone Martin cover still attached			
GA 33-321 [M]	Jazz Piano	1956	$75
—Without removable cover			

GARNER, MORRIS
THUNDERBIRD
| TH-1958 [M] | The Worst of Morris Garner | 196? | $30 |

GARNETT, CARLOS
MUSE
MR-5040	Black Love	1973	$35
MR-5104	Cosmos Nucleus	1976	$40
MR-5057	Journey to Enlightenment	1974	$25
MR-5079	Let the Melody Ring On	1975	$30
MR-5133	New Love	1977	$40

GARNETT, GALE
COLUMBIA
CL2825 [M]	An Audience with the King of Wands	1968	$30
CS9625 [S]	An Audience with the King of Wands	1968	$18
CS9625 [M]	An Audience with the King of Wands	1968	$30
—White label promo with stereo number and "Mono" on label; "Special Mono Radio Station Copy" sticker and timing strip on front cover			
CS9760	Sausalito Heliport	1969	$18

RCA VICTOR
LPM-3747 [M]	Gale Garnett Sings About Flying & Rainbows & Love & Other Groovy Things	1967	$30
LSP-3747 [S]	Gale Garnett Sings About Flying & Rainbows & Love & Other Groovy Things	1967	$25
LPM-3305 [M]	Lovin' Place	1965	$18
LSP-3305 [S]	Lovin' Place	1965	$25
LPM-2833 [M]	My Kind of Folk Songs	1964	$40
—Black and white/blueish cover			
LPM-2833 [M]	My Kind of Folk Songs	1965	$18
—Color photo on cover			
LSP-2833 [S]	My Kind of Folk Songs	1964	$50
—Black and white/blueish cover			
LSP-2833 [S]	My Kind of Folk Songs	1965	$25
—Color photo on cover			
LPM-3586 [M]	New Adventures	1966	$18
LSP-3586 [S]	New Adventures	1966	$25
LPM-3325 [M]	The Many Faces of Gale Garnett	1965	$18
LSP-3325 [S]	The Many Faces of Gale Garnett	1965	$25
LPM-3493 [M]	Variety Is the Spice of Gale Garnett	1966	$18
LSP-3493 [S]	Variety Is the Spice of Gale Garnett	1966	$25

GARRETT, KENNY
ATLANTIC
| 82046 | Prisoner of Love | 1989 | $30 |

GARRETT, LEIF
ATLANTIC
| SD19152 | Leif Garrett | 1977 | $15 |
| —With poster | | | |

SCOTTI BROTHERS
SB7111	Can't Explain	1980	$15
SB7100	Feel the Need	1978	$15
—With photo insert			
FZ37625	My Movie of You	1981	$12
SB16008	Same Goes for You	1979	$15

GARRETT, SNUFF, 'S TEXAS OPERA COMPANY
RANWOOD
| 8158 | Classical Country | 1976 | $12 |

GARRETT, TOMMY, 50 GUITARS OF
LIBERTY
LMM-13025 [M]	50 Guitars Go Country	1963	$15
LSS-14025 [S]	50 Guitars Go Country	1963	$18
LMM-13028 [M]	50 Guitars Go Italiano	1964	$15
LSS-14028 [S]	50 Guitars Go Italiano	1964	$18
LMM-13005 [M]	50 Guitars Go South of the Border	1961	$15
LSS-14005 [S]	50 Guitars Go South of the Border	1961	$18
LMM-13016 [M]	50 Guitars Go South of the Border, Volume 2	1962	$15
LSS-14016 [S]	50 Guitars Go South of the Border, Volume 2	1962	$18
LMM-13037 [M]	50 Guitars in Love	1966	$15
LSS-14037 [S]	50 Guitars in Love	1966	$18
LMM-13022 [M]	50 Guitars Visit Hawaii	1962	$15
LSS-14022 [S]	50 Guitars Visit Hawaii	1962	$18
LMM-13031 [M]	Bordertown Bandito	1964	$15
LSS-14031 [S]	Bordertown Bandito	1964	$18
LMM-13032 [M]	Espana	1964	$15
LSS-14032 [S]	Espana	1964	$18
LSS-14047	For Midnight Lovers	1970	$15
L-5507 [M]	Limited Edition	196?	$15
S-6607 [S]	Limited Edition	196?	$18
LMM-13035 [M]	Love Songs from South of the Border	1965	$15
LSS-14035 [S]	Love Songs from South of the Border	1965	$18
LMM-13030 [M]	Maria Elena	1963	$15
LSS-14030 [S]	Maria Elena	1963	$18
LSS-14046	Mexican Leather	1969	$15
LMM-13039 [M]	More 50 Guitars in Love	1967	$15
LSS-14039 [S]	More 50 Guitars in Love	1967	$15
LMM-13033 [M]	Return to Paradise	1965	$15
LSS-14033 [S]	Return to Paradise	1965	$18
LSS-14045	The Best of the 50 Guitars of Tommy Garrett	1969	$15
LSS-35001	The Best of the 50 Guitars of Tommy Garrett, Volumes 2 & 3	1970	$18
LMM-13036 [M]	Viva Mexico	1966	$15
LSS-14036 [S]	Viva Mexico	1966	$18

MUSICOR
| 4606 | The Best of the 50 Guitars of Tommy Garrett | 1976 | $15 |

PICKWICK
| SPC-3615 | Brazilian Mood | 197? | $10 |
| SPC-3585 | In Love | 197? | $10 |

SUNSET
| SUS-5282 | The Fabulous 50 Guitars of Tommy Garrett | 197? | $12 |

UNITED ARTISTS
UAS-5528	50 Guitars Go South of the Border, Volume 3	1971	$12
UAS-5569	The Way of Love	1972	$12
UXS-79	Tommy Garrett Superpak	1972	$15
UA-LA039-F	You're a Lady	1973	$12

GARRISON, GLEN
IMPERIAL
LP-9346 [M]	Country Country	1967	$18
LP-12346 [S]	Country Country	1967	$18
LP-12378	If I Lived Here	1968	$18

GARROWAY, DAVE
CAMEO
| C-1001 [M] | An Adventure in Hi-Fi Music | 1958 | $40 |
| —Black label, brown print, cameo figure at top | | | |

GARSON, GREER
LION
| L-70102 [M] | Greer Garson Babysits with Stories and Songs | 1958 | $30 |

GARSON, MIKE, AND JIM WALKER
REFERENCE RECORDINGS
| RR-18 | Reflections | 1987 | $35 |

GARSON, MIKE
CONTEMPORARY
| C-14003 [B] | Avant Garson | 1979 | $18 |

JAZZ HOUNDS
| 05 | Jazzical | 1982 | $30 |

REFERENCE RECORDINGS
RR-20	Serendipity	1987	$35
RR-37	The Oxnard Sessions	1991	$50
RR-53	The Oxnard Sessions, Volume Two	1993	$75

GARVIN, REX, AND THE MIGHTY CRAVERS
TOWER
| ST5130 | Raw Funky Earth | 1968 | $30 |

GARY, JOHN
CHURCHILL
| 67236 | In a Class By Himself | 1977 | $12 |

LA BREA
| 8010 [M] | John Gary | 1961 | $30 |
| S-8010 [S] | John Gary | 1961 | $30 |

METRO
| M-522 [M] | John Gary | 1966 | $12 |
| MS-522 [S] | John Gary | 1966 | $15 |

PICKWICK
| SPC-3025 | John Gary | 197? | $12 |

RCA CAMDEN
| CAL-983 [M] | The One and Only John Gary | 1966 | $12 |
| CAS-983 [S] | The One and Only John Gary | 1966 | $15 |

RCA VICTOR
LPM-3666 [M]	A Heart Filled with Song	1966	$15
LSP-3666 [S]	A Heart Filled with Song	1966	$18
LPM-2994 [M]	A Little Bit of Heaven	1965	$15
LSP-2994 [S]	A Little Bit of Heaven	1965	$18
ANL1-2672	A Little Bit of Heaven	1978	$12
—Reissue of LSP-2994			
LPM-2745 [M]	Catch a Rising Star	1963	$18
LSP-2745 [S]	Catch a Rising Star	1963	$25
LPM-3501 [M]	Choice	1966	$15
LSP-3501 [S]	Choice	1966	$18
LPM-2804 [M]	Encore	1964	$18
LSP-2804 [S]	Encore	1964	$25
LPM-3695 [M]	Especially for You	1967	$18
LSP-3695 [S]	Especially for You	1967	$15
LSP-4075	Holding Your Mind	1969	$15
LPM-3928 [M]	John Gary On Broadway	1968	$25

Number	Title	Yr	NM
❏ LSP-3928 [S]	John Gary On Broadway	1968	$15
❏ LPM-3992 [M]	John Gary Sings/John Gary Swings	1968	$25
❏ LSP-3992 [S]	John Gary Sings/John Gary Swings	1968	$15
❏ LSP-4134	Love of a Gentle Woman	1970	$15
❏ ANL1-2342	Pure Gold	1977	$12
❏ LPM-2922 [M]	So Tenderly	1964	$18
❏ LSP-2922 [S]	So Tenderly	1964	$25
❏ LPM-3785 [M]	Spanish Moonlight	1967	$18
❏ LSP-3785 [S]	Spanish Moonlight	1967	$15
❏ LSP-4233	That's the Way It Was	1971	$15
❏ LPM-3730 [M]	The Best of John Gary	1967	$18
❏ LSP-3730 [S]	The Best of John Gary	1967	$15
❏ LOC-1139 [M]	The John Gary Carnegie Hall Concert	1967	$25
❏ LSO-1139 [S]	The John Gary Carnegie Hall Concert	1967	$15
❏ LPM-2940 [M]	The John Gary Christmas Album	1964	$18
❏ LSP-2940 [S]	The John Gary Christmas Album	1964	$25
❏ LPM-3349 [M]	The Nearness of You	1965	$15
❏ LSP-3349 [S]	The Nearness of You	1965	$18
❏ VPS-6041	This Is John Gary	1971	$18
❏ LPM-3570 [M]	Your All-Time Country Favorites	1966	$15
❏ LSP-3570 [S]	Your All-Time Country Favorites	1966	$18
❏ LPM-3411 [M]	Your All-Time Favorite Songs	1965	$15
❏ LSP-3411 [S]	Your All-Time Favorite Songs	1965	$18

GARY, SAM
TRANSITION
Number	Title	Yr	NM
❏ TRLP-F-1 [M]	Spirituals and Work Songs	1958	$30

GAS MASK
TONSIL
| ❏ 4001 [B] | Gas Mask | 1970 | $30 |

GASCA, LUIS
ATLANTIC
| ❏ SD1527 | Little Giants | 1970 | $75 |
BLUE THUMB
| ❏ BTS-37 | Luis Gasca | 1972 | $75 |
FANTASY
❏ F-9461	Born to Love You	1974	$75
❏ F-9504	Collage	1976	$75
—Brown label (original)			

GASKIN, LEONARD
SWINGVILLE
❏ SVLP-2033 [M]	At the Darktown Strutters' Ball	1962	$40
—Purple label			
❏ SVLP-2033 [M]	At the Darktown Strutters' Ball	1965	$25
—Blue label, trident logo at right			
❏ SVST-2033 [S]	At the Darktown Strutters' Ball	1962	$50
—Red label			
❏ SVST-2033 [S]	At the Darktown Strutters' Ball	1965	$30
—Blue label, trident logo at right			
❏ SVLP-2031 [M]	At the Jazz Band Ball	1962	$40
—Purple label			
❏ SVLP-2031 [M]	At the Jazz Band Ball	1965	$25
—Blue label, trident logo at right			
❏ SVST-2031 [S]	At the Jazz Band Ball	1962	$50
—Red label			
❏ SVST-2031 [S]	At the Jazz Band Ball	1965	$30
—Blue label, trident logo at right			

GASLINI, GIORGIO
SOUL NOTE
❏ 121270	Ayler's Wings	1991	$30
❏ SN-1020	Gaslini Plays Monk	1981	$30
❏ 121020	Gaslini Plays Monk	199?	$25
—Reissue of 1020			
❏ 121220	Multipli	199?	$30
❏ SN-1120	Schumann Reflections	1984	$30
❏ 121120	Schumann Reflections	199?	$25
—Reissue of 1120			

GATES, DAVID
ARISTA
| ❏ AL9563 | Take Me Now | 1981 | $12 |
ELEKTRA
❏ 6E-251	Falling in Love Again	1980	$12
❏ EKS-75066	First	1973	$15
❏ EQ-5066 [Q]	First	1973	$30
❏ 6E-148	Goodbye Girl	1978	$15
❏ 7E-1028	Never Let Her Go	1975	$15
❏ EQ-1028 [Q]	Never Let Her Go	1975	$30

GATES, HEN
MASTERSEAL
| ❏ MLP-700 [M] | Let's All Dance to Rock and Roll | 1956 | $150 |
PALACE
❏ P-700 [M]	Let's All Dance to Rock and Roll	1958	$75
—Reissue of Masterseal 700			
❏ PST-700 [S]	Let's All Dance to Rock and Roll	1958	$100
—Labeled stereo, but plays in mono			
PARIS
| ❏ 101 [M] | Rock and Roll Festival | 1957 | $75 |
PLYMOUTH
| ❏ R12-144 [M] | Rock and Roll | 1956 | $75 |

| ❏ R12-149 [M] | Rock and Roll, No. 2 | 1957 | $75 |

GATEWAY SINGERS, THE
DECCA
❏ DL8413 [M]	Puttin' On the Style	1956	$40
❏ DL8671 [M]	The Gateway Singers at the Hungry I	1958	$30
❏ DL8742 [M]	The Gateway Singers in Hi-Fi	1958	$30
MGM
❏ E-3905 [M]	Down in the Valley	1961	$25
❏ SE-3905 [S]	Down in the Valley	1961	$30
❏ E-4154 [M]	Hootenanny	1963	$25
❏ SE-4154 [S]	Hootenanny	1963	$30
WARNER BROS.
❏ W1295 [M]	The Gateway Singers on the Lot	1959	$30
❏ WS1295 [S]	The Gateway Singers on the Lot	1959	$30
❏ W1334 [M]	Wagons West	1960	$30
❏ WS1334 [S]	Wagons West	1960	$30

GATEWAY TRIO, THE
CAPITOL
❏ T2184 [M]	The Gateway Trio	1964	$18
❏ ST2184 [S]	The Gateway Trio	1964	$30
❏ T1868 [M]	The Mad, Mad, Mad Gateway Trio	1963	$18
❏ ST1868 [S]	The Mad, Mad, Mad Gateway Trio	1963	$30

GATLIN, LARRY, AND THE GATLIN BROTHERS BAND
COLUMBIA
❏ FC38183	A Gatlin Family Christmas	1982	$15
❏ PC38183	A Gatlin Family Christmas	198?	$10
—Budget-line reissue			
❏ FC40905	Alive and Well…Living in the Land of Dreams	1988	$12
❏ JC36582	Help Yourself	1980	$12
❏ PC36582	Help Yourself	198?	$10
—Budget-line reissue			
❏ PC36582	Help Yourself	198?	$10
—Budget-line reissue			
❏ PC38338	High Time	1982	$10
—Reissue of Monument 6644			
❏ FC39291	Houston to Denver	1984	$12
❏ JC36488	Larry Gatlin's Greatest Hits, Volume 1	1980	$10
—Reissue of Monument 7628			
❏ FC38923	Larry Gatlin's Greatest Hits, Volume 2	1983	$12
❏ PC38337	Larry Gatlin with Family and Friends	1982	$10
—Reissue of Monument 6634			
❏ PC38336	Love Is Just a Game	1982	$10
—Reissue of Monument 7616			
❏ FC37464	Not Guilty	1981	$12
❏ PC37464	Not Guilty	198?	$10

Number	Title	Yr	NM
—Budget-line reissue			
❏ PC38340	Oh! Brother	1982	$10
—Reissue of Monmnet 7626			
❏ FC40431	Partners	1986	$12
❏ PC38339	Rain-Rainbow	1982	$10
—Reissue of Monmnet 6633			
❏ FC40068	Smile!	1985	$12
❏ JC36250	Straight Ahead	1979	$12
❏ FC38135	Sure Feels Like Love	1982	$12
❏ PC38135	Sure Feels Like Love	198?	$10
—Budget-line reissue			
❏ HC48135	Sure Feels Like Love	1982	$300
—Half-speed mastered edition			
❏ FC44471	The Gatlin Brothers' Biggest Hits (1984-88)	1989	$12
❏ PC36541	The Pilgrim	1980	$10
—Reissue of Monument 6632			

MONUMENT
❏ 6644	High Time	1977	$15
❏ MG7628	Larry Gatlin's Greatest Hits	1978	$15
❏ KZ34042	Larry Gatlin with Family & Friends	1975	$18
❏ 6634	Larry Gatlin with Family and Friends	1976	$15
—Reissue of KZ 34042			
❏ MG7616	Love Is Just a Game	1978	$15
❏ MG7626	Oh! Brother	1978	$15
❏ KZ33069	Rain-Rainbow	1974	$18
❏ 6633	Rain-Rainbow	1976	$15
—Reissue of KZ 33069			
❏ KZ32571	The Pilgrim	1974	$18
❏ 6632	The Pilgrim	1976	$15
—Reissue of KZ 32571			

SWORD & SHIELD
| ❏ 9009 [M] | The Old Country Church | 1961 | $150 |
| —As "The Gatlin Quartet" (with sister La Donna joining Larry, Rudy and Steve) | | | |

GATOR CREEK
MERCURY
| ❏ SR-61311 | Gator Creek | 1970 | $15 |

GAUCHOS, THE
See JIM DOVAL AND THE GAUCHOS.

GAULT, BILLY
INNER CITY
| ❏ IC-2027 | When Destiny Calls | 197? | $35 |
STEEPLECHASE
| ❏ SCS-1027 | When Destiny Calls | 198? | $25 |

GAULT, JONNA, AND HER SYMPHONOPOP SCENE
RCA VICTOR
| ❏ LSP-4081 | Watch Me | 1968 | $30 |

GAUTHE, JACQUES
GHB
| ❏ GHB-179 | Riz A La Creole | 1987 | $25 |
STOMP OFF
| ❏ SOS-1170 | Cassoulet Stomp | 1989 | $25 |

GAVIN, KEVIN
CHARLIE PARKER
| ❏ PLP-810 [M] | Hey! This Is Kevin Gavin | 1962 | $30 |
| ❏ PLP-810S [S] | Hey! This Is Kevin Gavin | 1962 | $40 |

GAYE, MARVIN, AND KIM WESTON
TAMLA
❏ T/TS260	Side by Side	1965	$0
—Canceled			
❏ T270 [M]	Take Two	1966	$30
❏ TS270 [S]	Take Two	1966	$40

GAYE, MARVIN, AND MARY WELLS
MOTOWN
| ❏ M613 [M] | Together | 1964 | $50 |
| ❏ 5260ML | Together | 1982 | $12 |

GAYE, MARVIN, AND TAMMI TERRELL
MOTOWN
❏ M5-102V1	Motown Superstar Series, Vol. 2	1981	$12
❏ M5-200V1	United	1981	$12
—Reissue of Tamla 277			
❏ M5-142V1	You're All I Need	1981	$12
—Reissue of Tamla 284			
TAMLA
❏ TS294	Easy	1969	$25
❏ TS302	Marvin Gaye & Tammi Terrell/Greatest Hits	1970	$25
❏ TAMLA270 [B]	Take Two	2016	$25
❏ T277 [M]	United	1967	$40
❏ TS277 [S]	United	1967	$30

Number	Title	Yr	NM
❏ T284 [M]	You're All I Need	1968	$50
❏ TS284 [S]	You're All I Need	1968	$25

GAYE, MARVIN
CLEOPATRA
❏ 8222 [B]	Live		$30

—picture disc

COLUMBIA
❏ FC39916	Dream of a Lifetime	1985	$12
❏ 9C940133 [PD]	Dream of a Lifetime	1985	$25
❏ FC38197	Midnight Love	1982	$12
❏ HC48197	Midnight Love	1984	$40

—Half-speed mastered edition
❏ PC38197	Midnight Love	1986	$10

—Budget-line reissue
❏ FC40208	Romantically Yours	1986	$12

MOTOWN
❏ 6255ML	A Musical Testament 1964-1984	1988	$15
❏ M9-791A3	Anthology	1974	$25
❏ M5-216V1	A Tribute to the Great Nat King Cole	1981	$12

—Reissue of Tamla 261
❏ 6058ML	Every Great Motown Hit of Marvin Gaye	1983	$12
❏ 952921	I Want You	2008	$25
❏ M5-192V1	Let's Get It On	1981	$12

—Reissue of Tamla 329
❏ M5-181V1	Marvin Gaye Live!	1981	$12

—Reissue of Tamla 333
❏ 5259ML	Marvin Gaye Live at the London Palladium	1983	$15

—Reissue of Tamla 352
❏ M5-191V1	Marvin Gaye's Greatest Hits	1981	$12

—Reissue of Tamla 348
❏ M5-115V1	Motown Superstar Series, Vol. 15	1981	$12
❏ M5-125V1	M.P.G.	1981	$12

—Reissue of Tamla 292
❏ 5306ML	Super Hits	198?	$12
❏ M5-218V1	That Stubborn Kinda' Fellow	1981	$12

—Reissue of Tamla 239
❏ 374631296-1 [DJ]	The Master 1961-1984	1995	$25

—Vinyl is promo only; 8-song sampler from box set

❏ 5339ML [B]	What's Going On	198?	$12

—Reissue of Tamla 322

NATURAL RESOURCES
❏ NR4007T1	The Soulful Moods of Marvin Gaye	1978	$15

—Reissue of Tamla 221

TAMLA
❏ T261 [M]	A Tribute to the Great Nat King Cole	1965	$50
❏ TS261 [S]	A Tribute to the Great Nat King Cole	1965	$50
❏ T259 [M]	Hello Broadway, This Is Marvin	1965	$50
❏ TS259 [S]	Hello Broadway, This Is Marvin	1965	$50
❏ T13-364	Here, My Dear	1978	$18
❏ T258 [M]	How Sweet It Is to Be Loved by You	1965	$50
❏ TS258 [S]	How Sweet It Is to Be Loved by You	1965	$50
❏ TS285 [S]	I Heard It Through the Grapevine	1969	$25

—Retitled version of "In the Groove"
❏ T8-374	In Our Lifetime	1981	$12
❏ T285 [M]	In the Groove	1968	$50
❏ TS285 [S]	In the Groove	1968	$30
❏ T6-342	I Want You	1976	$18
❏ T6-329	Let's Get It On	1973	$18
❏ TS293	Marvin Gaye and His Girls	1969	$25

—Includes duets with Tammi Terrell, Mary Wells, Kim Weston

Number	Title	Yr	NM
❏ T252 [M]	Marvin Gaye/Greatest Hits	1964	$50
❏ TS252 [S]	Marvin Gaye/Greatest Hits	1964	$40
❏ T278 [M]	Marvin Gaye/Greatest Hits, Vol. 2	1967	$30
❏ TS278 [S]	Marvin Gaye/Greatest Hits, Vol. 2	1967	$25
❏ T6-333	Marvin Gaye Live!	1974	$18
❏ T7-352	Marvin Gaye Live at the London Palladium	1977	$18
❏ T6-348	Marvin Gaye's Greatest Hits	1976	$18
❏ TS300	Marvin Gaye Super Hits	1970	$25
❏ T266 [M]	Moods of Marvin Gaye	1966	$40
❏ TS266 [S]	Moods of Marvin Gaye	1966	$50
❏ 6172TL	Motown Remembers Marvin Gaye	1986	$12
❏ TS292	M.P.G.	1969	$25
❏ T242 [M]	Recorded Live -- Marvin Gaye on Stage	1963	$300
❏ TS299	That's the Way Love Is	1969	$25
❏ T239 [M]	That Stubborn Kinda' Fella	1963	$600
❏ TM221 [M]	The Soulful Moods of Marvin Gaye	1961	$1000
❏ T5-322	Trouble Man	1972	$18
❏ T5-310	What's Going On	1971	$18
❏ 5300221 [B]	What's Going On	2015	$25

—yellow vinyl
❏ T251 [M]	When I'm Alone I Cry	1964	$300

UNIVERSAL MOTOWN
❏ 5300221	What's Going On	2008	$25

GAYE, CHARLES
SILKHEART
❏ SH-115	Always Born	1988	$25
❏ SH-116	Homeless	1988	$25
❏ SH-117	Spirits Before	1988	$25

GAYLE, CRYSTAL, AND GARY MORRIS
WARNER BROS.
❏ 25507	What If We Fell in Love?	1987	$12

GAYLE, CRYSTAL
COLUMBIA
❏ FC38803	Crystal Gayle's Greatest Hits	1983	$12
❏ FC37438	Hollywood, Tennessee	1981	$12
❏ PC37438	Hollywood, Tennessee	198?	$10

—Budget-line reissue
❏ JC36203	Miss the Mississippi	1979	$12
❏ PC36203	Miss the Mississippi	198?	$10

—Budget-line reissue
❏ JC36512	These Days	1980	$12
❏ PC36512	These Days	198?	$10

—Budget-line reissue

ELEKTRA
❏ 60200	True Love	1982	$12

LIBERTY
❏ LOO-1080	A Woman's Heart	1981	$12
❏ LN-10150	Classic Crystal	1982	$10

—Budget-line reissue of UA 982
❏ LN-10004	Crystal	1981	$10

—Budget-line reissue of UA 614
❏ LN-10002	Crystal Gayle	1981	$10
❏ LOO-1034	Favorites	1981	$10

—Reissue of UA 1034
❏ LN-10229	Favorites	1984	$10

—Budget-line reissue
❏ LN-10003	Somebody Loves You	1981	$10

—Budget-line reissue of UA 543
❏ LN-10005	We Must Believe in Magic	1981	$10

—Budget-line reissue of UA 771
❏ LN-10006	We Should Be Together	1980	$10

—Budget-line reissue
❏ LMAS-858	When I Dream	1981	$10

—Reissue of UA 858
❏ LN-10227	When I Dream	1984	$10

—Budget-line reissue

MCA
❏ 2334	I've Cried the Blue Right Out of My Eyes	1977	$12

—Reissue of Decca material
❏ 37077	I've Cried the Blue Right Out of My Eyes	198?	$10

—Budget-line reissue

MOBILE FIDELITY
❏ Jan-0043	We Must Believe in Magic	1981	$25

—Audiophile vinyl

NAUTILUS
❏ NR-36	When I Dream	198?	$30

—Audiophile vinyl

PAIR
❏ PDL2-1083	Country Pure	1986	$15
❏ PDL2-1126	Musical Jewels	1986	$15

UNITED ARTISTS
❏ LOO-982	Classic Crystal	1979	$12
❏ UA-LA614-G	Crystal	1976	$15
❏ LOO-1034	Favorites	1980	$12
❏ UA-LA543-G	Somebody Loves You	1975	$15
❏ UA-LA771-G	We Must Believe in Magic	1977	$12

Number	Title	Yr	NM
❏ UA-LA969-H	We Should Be Together	1979	$12
❏ UA-LA858-H	When I Dream	1978	$12

WARNER BROS.
❏ 25508	A Crystal Christmas	1986	$18

—Original cover has decorated Christmas tree on front
❏ 25508	A Crystal Christmas	1987	$12

—Reissue cover has photo of Crystal Gayle on front
❏ 23958	Cage the Songbird	1983	$12
❏ 25706	Nobody's Angel	1988	$12
❏ 25154	Nobody Wants to Be Alone	1984	$12
❏ 25405	Straight to the Heart	1986	$12
❏ 25622	The Best of Crystal Gayle	1987	$12
❏ 60200	True Love	1983	$10

—Reissue of Elektra 60200

GAYLE, ROZELLE
MERCURY
❏ MG-20374 [M]	Like, Be My Guest	1958	$150

GAYLORDS, THE
MERCURY
❏ MG-20620 [M]	American Hits in Italian	1961	$25
❏ SR-60620 [S]	American Hits in Italian	1961	$30
❏ MG-25198 [10]	By Request	1955	$50
❏ MG-20213 [M]	Collection of Golden Hits	1957	$30
❏ MG-20186 [M]	Italia	1957	$30
❏ MG-20356 [M]	Let's Have a Pizza Party	1958	$25
❏ SR-60075 [S]	Let's Have a Pizza Party	1959	$30
❏ MG-20742 [M]	Party Style	1963	$25
❏ SR-60742 [S]	Party Style	1963	$30
❏ MG-20430 [M]	That's Amore	1959	$25
❏ SR-60102 [S]	That's Amore	1959	$30
❏ MG-20695 [M]	The Gaylords at the Shamrock	1962	$25
❏ SR-60695 [S]	The Gaylords at the Shamrock	1962	$30

TIME
❏ 52127 [M]	Bella Italia	196?	$18
❏ S-2127 [S]	Bella Italia	196?	$25
❏ 52109 [M]	Live at Lake Tahoe	196?	$18
❏ S-2109 [S]	Live at Lake Tahoe	196?	$25

WING
❏ MGW-12139 [M]	Italiano Favorites	196?	$15
❏ SRW-16139 [S]	Italiano Favorites	196?	$15
❏ MGW-12278 [M]	Let's Have a Pizza Party	196?	$15
❏ SRW-16278 [S]	Let's Have a Pizza Party	196?	$15

GAYNOR, GLORIA
ATLANTIC
❏ 80033	Gloria Gaynor	1982	$12

MGM
❏ M3G-4997	Experience Gloria Gaynor	1975	$12
❏ M3G-4982	Never Can Say Goodbye	1975	$12

POLYDOR
❏ PD-1-6139	Gloria Gaynor's Park Avenue Sound	1978	$12
❏ PD-1-6095	Glorious	1977	$12
❏ PD-1-6231	I Have a Right	1979	$12
❏ PD-1-6063	I've Got You	1976	$12
❏ PD-1-6184	Love Tracks	1978	$12
❏ PD-1-6274	Stories	1980	$12

GAYNOR, MITZI
VERVE
❏ MGV-2110 [M]	Mitzi	1959	$30
❏ MGVS-6014 [S]	Mitzi	1959	$40
❏ MGV-2115 [M]	Mitzi Gaynor Sings the Lyrics of Ira Gershwin	1959	$30
❏ MGVS-6049 [S]	Mitzi Gaynor Sings the Lyrics of Ira Gershwin	1959	$40

GEARS, THE
PLAYGEMS
❏ GS6471	Rockin' at Ground Zero	1980	$30

GEDDES, DAVID
BIG TREE
❏ BT89511	Run Joey Run	1975	$15

GEE, MATTHEW
RIVERSIDE
❏ RLP 12-221 [M]	Jazz by Gee!	1956	$300

—White label, blue print
❏ RLP 12-221 [M]	Jazz by Gee!	1958	$300

—Blue label, microphone logo at top

GEEZINSLAW BROTHERS, THE
CAPITOL
❏ T2570 [M]	Can You Believe...The Geezinslaw Brothers!	1966	$25
❏ ST2570 [S]	Can You Believe...The Geezinslaw Brothers!	1966	$30
❏ T2771 [M]	My Dirty, Lowdown, Rotten, Cotton-Pickin' Little Darlin'	1967	$25
❏ ST2771 [S]	My Dirty, Lowdown, Rotten, Cotton-Pickin' Little Darlin'	1967	$30
❏ ST2885 [S]	The Geezinslaw Brothers & "Chubby	1968	$30

Number	Title	Yr	NM
❏ T2885 [M]	The Geezinslaw Brothers & "Chubby	1968	$40
❏ ST-130	The Geezinslaw Brothers Are Alive	1969	$25
COLUMBIA			
❏ CL2100 [M]	The Kooky World of the Geezinslaw Brothers	1963	$30
❏ CS8900 [S]	The Kooky World of the Geezinslaw Brothers	1963	$30

GEILS, J., BAND
Featuring Peter Wolf.

Number	Title	Yr	NM
ATLANTIC			
❏ SD19234	Best of the J. Geils Band	1979	$12
❏ SD19284	Best of the J. Geils Band -- 2	1980	$12
❏ SD7260	Bloodshot	1973	$25
—Red vinyl			
❏ SD7260	Bloodshot	1973	$15
—Black vinyl			
❏ QD7260 [Q]	Bloodshot	1973	$50
❏ SD7260 [B]	Bloodshot	2015	$20
❏ SD18147	Hotline	1975	$15
❏ SD7286	Ladies Invited	1973	$15
❏ QD7286 [Q]	Ladies Invited	1973	$0
—Not released			
❏ SD 2-507	Live -- Blow Your Face Out	1976	$18
❏ SD7241	Live" -- Full House	1972	$15
❏ SD19103	Monkey Island	1977	$15
—As "Geils			
❏ SD18107	Nightmares and Other Tales from the Vinyl Jungle	1974	$15
❏ QD18107 [Q]	Nightmares and Other Tales from the Vinyl Jungle	1974	$50
❏ 8275 [M]	The J. Geils Band	1970	$80
—Mono is white label promo only; stereo cover with "dj copy monaural" sticker			
❏ SD8275 [S]	The J. Geils Band	1970	$18
❏ SD8297 [S]	The Morning After	1971	$15
❏ 8297 [M]	The Morning After	1971	$300
—Mono version is white label promo only with "d/j copy monaural" stucker on front cover			
EMI AMERICA			
❏ ST-17174	Flashback -- The Best of the J. Geils Band	1985	$10
❏ SOO-17062	Freeze-Frame	1981	$12
❏ SN-16374	Freeze-Frame	1986	$10
—Reissue			
❏ SOO-17016	Love Stinks	1980	$12
❏ SN-16375	Love Stinks	1986	$10
—Reissue			
❏ SO-17006	Sanctuary	1978	$12
❏ SN-16316	Sanctuary	1985	$10
—Reissue			
❏ SO-17087	Showtime!	1982	$12
❏ SN-16373	Showtime!	1986	$10
—Reissue			
❏ SJ-17137	You're Gettin' Even While I'm Gettin' Odd	1984	$10
NAUTILUS			
❏ NR-25	Love Stinks	1982	$25
—Audiophile vinyl			

GEISSMAN, GRANT

Number	Title	Yr	NM
BLUEMOON			
❏ R1-79152	Take Another Look	1990	$30
CONCORD JAZZ			
❏ CJ-62	Good Stuff	1978	$30
PAUSA			
❏ 7150	Put Away Childish Toys	198?	$30
TBA			
❏ TB-241	All My Tomorrows	1989	$30
❏ TB-217	Drinkin' from the Money River	198?	$30
❏ TB-224	Snapshots	198?	$30

GELB, LARRY

Number	Title	Yr	NM
CADENCE JAZZ			
❏ 1012	The Language of Blue	198?	$25

GELDOF, BOB

Number	Title	Yr	NM
ATLANTIC			
❏ 81687	Deep in the Heart of Nowhere	1986	$12
❏ 1010 [DJ]	Questions and Answers (Interview)	1987	$12
❏ 1010 [DJ]	Questions and Answers (Interview)	1987	$12

GELLER, HERB

Number	Title	Yr	NM
ATCO			
❏ 33-109 [M]	Gypsy	1959	$40
ATLANTIC			
❏ SD1681	Rhyme and Reason	1975	$30
EMARCY			
❏ MG-26045 [10]	Herb Geller Plays	1954	$250

Number	Title	Yr	NM
❏ MG-36045 [M]	Herb Geller Plays	1955	$100
❏ MG-36024 [M]	The Gellers	1955	$300
❏ MG-36040 [M]	The Herb Geller Sextette	1955	$300
JOSIE			
❏ JOZ-3502 [M]	Alto Saxophone	1962	$30
❏ JLPS-3502 [S]	Alto Saxophone	1962	$25
JUBILEE			
❏ JLP-1044 [M]	Fire in the West	1957	$50
❏ SDJLP-1044 [S]	Fire in the West	1959	$40
❏ JG-1094 [M]	Stax of Sax	1959	$50

GELLER, LORRAINE

Number	Title	Yr	NM
DOT			
❏ DLP-3174 [M]	Lorraine Geller at the Piano	1959	$1500

GENE AND BOBBY

Number	Title	Yr	NM
GUINNESS			
❏ GNS36008 [B]	Gene and Bobby Strike Again	1977	$50

GENE AND DEBBE

Number	Title	Yr	NM
TRX			
❏ 1001	Here and Now	1968	$30

GENE LOVES JEZEBEL

Number	Title	Yr	NM
GEFFEN			
❏ GHS24118	Discover	1986	$12
❏ 141 [DJ]	Discover Interview	1986	$30
❏ GHS24260 [B]	Kiss of Life	1990	$35
❏ GHS24165	Promise	1988	$12
—First American issue of 1983 U.K. debut			
❏ 4192 [EP]	Remix Sampler	1990	$25
—Promo-only collection			
❏ GHS24171	The House of Dolls	1988	$12
RELATIVITY			
❏ EMC8075 [EP]	Desire	1985	$15
❏ EMC8036 [B]	Immigrant	1985	$15
WARNER BROS.			
❏ WBMS-141 [DJ]	Discover Interview	1986	$25
—Part of "The Warner Bros. Music Show" series; in die-cut cover			

GENERAL PUBLIC

Number	Title	Yr	NM
I.R.S.			
❏ SP70046	...All the Rage	1984	$12
❏ R142295	Hand to Mouth	1986	$15
—RCA Music Service edition			
❏ 5782	Hand to Mouth	1986	$12

GENERATION BAND, THE

Number	Title	Yr	NM
NAUTILUS			
❏ NR-62	Soft Shoulder	198?	$40
—Audiophile vinyl			
PALO ALTO			
❏ PA-8054	Soft Shoulder	198?	$30
TBA			
❏ TB-202	Call of the Wild	198?	$25
❏ TB-208	High Visibility	1985	$25

GENERATION X
Also see BILLY IDOL.

Number	Title	Yr	NM
CHRYSALIS			
❏ CHR1169	Generation X	1978	$30
❏ PV41169	Generation X	1984	$18
—Reissue			
❏ CHR1327	Kiss Me Deadly	1981	$30
❏ PV41327	Kiss Me Deadly	1985	$18
—Reissue			
❏ CHR1193	Valley of the Dolls	1979	$30

Number	Title	Yr	NM
❏ PV41193	Valley of the Dolls	1984	$25
—Reissue			

GENESIS
Popular British group with Phil Collins, Peter Gabriel, Tony Banks and Mike Rutherford, among others.

Number	Title	Yr	NM
ABC			
❏ ABCX-816 [B]	Trespass	1971	$30
—Reissue of Impulse album; black label			
❏ ABCX-816	Trespass	1974	$15
—Reissue; concentric yellow/orange/purple "target" label			
ABC IMPULSE!			
❏ ASD-9205	Trespass	1971	$120
ATCO			
❏ SD 36-129	A Trick of the Tail	1976	$15
❏ SD 38-101	A Trick of the Tail	1978	$15
—Reissue of SD 36-129			
❏ SD 2-401 [S]	The Lamb Lies Down on Broadway	1974	$40
—Originals have yellow labels (other labels worth less)			
❏ SD 36-144	Wind & Wuthering	1977	$15
❏ SD 38-100	Wind & Wuthering	1978	$15
—Reissue of SD 36-144			
ATLANTIC			
❏ SD19313	Abacab	1981	$15
—Released with four different covers, lettered "A" through "D" on the upper part of the spine; no difference in value			
❏ SD19173	...And Then There Were Three	1978	$15
❏ SD16014	Duke	1980	$15
❏ 81848	Foxtrot	1988	$15
—Reissue of Charisma LP of the same name			
❏ 80116	Genesis	1983	$10
❏ 81855	Genesis Live	1988	$15
—Reissue of Charisma LP of the same name			
❏ 81641	Invisible Touch	1986	$10
❏ 80030	Nursery Cryme	1982	$10
—Reissue of Charisma LP of same name			
❏ SD 2-9002	Seconds Out	1977	$15
❏ SD19277	Selling England by the Pound	1981	$10
—Reissue of Charisma LP of same name			
❏ SD 2-2000	Three Sides Live	1982	$15
❏ PR965 [DJ]	Tonight, Tonight, Tonight -- Exclusive Candid Interview	1986	$30
—Promo-only music and interviews; came with cover letter and cue sheet (deduct 1/3 if missing)			
ATLANTIC/RHINO			
❏ R1188156 [B]	Abacab	2015	$30
❏ R1188284 [B]	And Then There Were Three...	2015	$30
—Half speed remaster from 2008 remix			
❏ R1187964 [B]	A Trick of the Tail	2015	$30
❏ R1188412 [B]	Duke	2015	$30
—half speed remaster			
❏ R1516778 [B]	Foxtrot	2015	$30
❏ R1516780 [B]	Nursery Cryme	2015	$30
❏ R1516781 [B]	Selling England by the Pound	2015	$30
❏ R1188668 [B]	Wind and Wuthering	2015	$30
BUDDAH			
❏ BDS-5659	The Best ... Genesis	1976	$25
—Reissue of "Nursery Cryme" and "Foxtrot" in one set			
CHARISMA			
❏ CAS-1058 [B]	Foxtrot	1972	$40
❏ CAS-1058	Foxtrot	2001	$30
—Classic Records reissue on 180-gram vinyl			
❏ CAS-1666 [B]	Genesis Live	1974	$30
❏ CAS-1666	Genesis Live	2001	$30
—Classic Records reissue on 180-gram vinyl			
❏ CAS-1052 [B]	Nursery Cryme	1971	$40
❏ CAS-1052	Nursery Cryme	2000	$30
—Classic Records reissue on 180-gram vinyl			
❏ CA2-2701 [B]	Nursery Cryme/Foxtrot	1976	$35
—Repackage of the individual albums of these names			
❏ FC-6060 [B]	Selling England by the Pound	1973	$30
❏ FC-6060	Selling England by the Pound	2001	$30
—Classic Records reissue on 180-gram vinyl			
LONDON			
❏ PS643	From Genesis to Revelation	1974	$30
—First US release of debut album			
❏ LC-50006	In the Beginning	1977	$15
❏ 820322-1	In the Beginning	198?	$15
—Reissue of London 50006			
MCA			
❏ ABCX-816	Trespass	1979	$15
—Reissue of ABC ABCX-816			
❏ 37151	Trespass	198?	$10
—Reissue of MCA 816			
MOBILE FIDELITY			
❏ Jan-0062 [B]	A Trick of the Tail	1981	$100
—Audiophile vinyl			

Number	Title	Yr	NM

GENESIS (3)
MERCURY

❏ SR61175	In the Beginning	1968	$150

— First pressing is textured cover, red label.

❏ SR61175	In the Beginning	197?	$25

— Second pressing is non-textured cover, skyline label.

GENTLE GIANT
CAPITOL

❏ ST-11428	Free Hand	1975	$12
❏ SN-16048	Free Hand	1980	$10

— Budget-line reissue

❏ SW-11813	Giant for a Day	1978	$12
❏ SN-16045	Giant for a Day	1980	$10

— Budget-line reissue

❏ ST-11532	Interview	1976	$12
❏ SN-16047	Interview	1980	$10

— Budget-line reissue

❏ ST-11696	The Missing Piece	1977	$12
❏ SN-16046	The Missing Piece	1980	$10

— Budget-line reissue

❏ SKBB-11592	The Official "Live" Gentle Giant -- Playing the Fool	1977	$15
❏ ST-11337	The Power and the Glory	1974	$12
❏ SN-16044	The Power and the Glory	1980	$10

— Budget-line reissue

COLUMBIA

❏ JC36341	Civilian	1980	$12
❏ KC32022	Octopus	1973	$15
❏ PC32022	Octopus	197?	$10

— Reissue

❏ KC31649	Three Friends	1972	$15
❏ PC31649	Three Friends	197?	$10

— Reissue

VERTIGO

❏ VE-1005	Acquiring the Taste	1971	$40

GENTLE SOUL, THE
EPIC

❏ BN26374	The Gentle Soul	1969	$250

— Reproductions exist

GENTRY, BOBBIE
CAPITOL

❏ SKAO-381	Bobbie Gentry's Greatest!	1969	$18
❏ SM-381	Bobbie Gentry's Greatest!	197?	$10
❏ ST-428	Fancy	1970	$18
❏ T2830 [M]	Ode to Billie Joe	1967	$25
❏ ST2830 [S]	Ode to Billie Joe	1967	$18
❏ SM-2830	Ode to Billie Joe	197?	$10
❏ ST-494	Patchwork	1970	$18
❏ STBB-704	Sittin' Pretty/Tobacco Road	1971	$18
❏ ST2842 [S]	The Delta Sweete	1968	$18
❏ T2842 [M]	The Delta Sweete	1968	$30
❏ ST2964	The Local Gentry	1968	$18
❏ ST-155	Touch 'Em with Love	1969	$18

GENTRYS, THE
MGM

❏ E-4346 [M]	Gentry Time	1966	$25
❏ SE-4346 [S]	Gentry Time	1966	$30
❏ E-4336 [M]	Keep On Dancing	1965	$30
❏ SE-4336 [P]	Keep On Dancing	1965	$30
❏ GAS-127	The Gentrys (Golden Archive Series)	1970	$25

SUN

❏ LP-117	The Gentrys	1970	$30

GEORDIE
Includes Brian Johnson, later of AC/DC.
MGM

❏ SE-4903	Hope You Like It	1973	$30

GEORGE, BARBARA
A.F.O.

❏ LP5001 [M]	I Know (You Don't Love Me No More)	1962	$300

GEORGE, LOWELL
Also see LITTLE FEAT.
WARNER BROS.

❏ 3194	Thanks I'll Eat it Here	1979	$18

GEORGIA GRINDERS, THE
STOMP OFF

❏ SOS-1068	A Tribute to Roy Palmer	1984	$25

GEORGIA SATELLITES, THE
ELEKTRA

❏ 60496	Georgia Satellites	1986	$12
❏ 60887	In the Land of Salvation and Sin	1989	$15
❏ 60793	Open All Night	1988	$12

Number	Title	Yr	NM

GERARD, DANYEL
MGM VERVE

❏ MV5081	Danyel Gerard	1972	$15

GERHARD, RAMONA
SOMA

❏ MG1202	Christmas in Hi-Fi with Ramona Gerhard	195?	$25

— Red vinyl

GERMS, THE
CLEOPATRA

❏ 8088 [B]	I Fu*#ed Your Mom - Live '78-'79		$25
❏ 2908 [B]	The Whisky / The Hong Kong Cafe		$25

MOHAWK

❏ SCALP-001	Recorded Live at the Whiskey, June, 1977	1981	$25

— Second edition: Un-numbered edition, with sticker

❏ SCALP-001 [B]	Recorded Live at the Whiskey, June, 1977	1981	$75

— First edition: Numbered edition, with sticker

RHINO

❏ R178602 [B]	GI	2015	$25
❏ R1-78602	(GI)	2005	$18

— Reissue on 180-gram vinyl

SLASH

❏ 23932 [B]	(GI)	1983	$15

— Reissue

❏ SR-103 [B]	(GI)	1981	$30
❏ SREP108	What We Do Is Secret	1981	$18

GERONIMO BLACK
Also see FRANK ZAPPA, as this band included members of the Mothers of Invention.

UNI

❏ 73132	Geronimo Black	1972	$30

GERRARD, DONNY
FREQUENCY

❏ PR505023 [EP]	The Romantic Sampler	2000	$15

— Six-song promo-only vinyl sampler from the CD "The Romantic

GREEDY

❏ G-1002	Donny Gerrard	1976	$18

GERRY AND THE PACEMAKERS
CAPITOL

❏ SM-11898 [B]	The Best of Gerry and the Pacemakers	1979	$10

— All stereo except "I Like It," "Away from You" and "I'm the One," which are mono.

LAURIE

❏ LLP-2024 [M]	Don't Let the Sun Catch You Crying	1964	$30
❏ SLP-2024 [R]	Don't Let the Sun Catch You Crying	1964	$30
❏ T90555 [M]	Don't Let the Sun Catch You Crying	1964	$40

— Capitol Record Club edition

❏ DT90555 [R]	Don't Let the Sun Catch You Crying	1964	$30

— Capitol Record Club edition

❏ LLP-2027 [M]	Gerry and the Pacemakers' Second Album	1964	$30
❏ SLP-2027 [R]	Gerry and the Pacemakers' Second Album	1964	$30
❏ LLP-2037 [M]	Girl on a Swing	1966	$30
❏ SLP-2037 [S]	Girl on a Swing	1966	$25
❏ LLP-2031 [M]	Greatest Hits	1965	$30
❏ SLP-2031 [R]	Greatest Hits	1965	$18
❏ T90384 [M]	Greatest Hits	1965	$30

— Capitol Record Club edition

❏ DT90384 [R]	Greatest Hits	1965	$30

— Capitol Record Club edition

❏ LLP-2030 [M]	I'll Be There	1964	$30
❏ SLP-2030 [R]	I'll Be There	1964	$30

UNITED ARTISTS

❏ UAL3387 [M]	Ferry Cross the Mersey	1965	$30

— Also contains incidental music by George Martin

❏ UAS6387 [S]	Ferry Cross the Mersey	1965	$40
❏ T90812 [M]	Ferry Cross the Mersey	1965	$40

— Capitol Record Club edition

❏ ST90812 [S]	Ferry Cross the Mersey	1965	$50

— Capitol Record Club edition

GESTURES, THE
SUNDAZED

❏ LP-5021	The Gestures	199?	$12

GETZ, EDDIE
MGM

❏ E-3462 [M]	The Eddie Getz Quintette	1957	$50

Number	Title	Yr	NM

GETZ, STAN, AND ALBERT DAILEY
ELEKTRA/MUSICIAN

❏ 60370	Poetry	1985	$25

GETZ, STAN, AND BILL EVANS
VERVE

❏ V3G-8833	Previously Unreleased Recordings	1974	$30

GETZ, STAN, AND BOB BROOKMEYER
VERVE

❏ V-8418 [M]	Stan Getz and Bob Brookmeyer (Recorded Fall 1961)	1961	$50
❏ V6-8418 [S]	Stan Getz and Bob Brookmeyer (Recorded Fall 1961)	1961	$50

GETZ, STAN, AND CHARLIE BYRD
DCC COMPACT CLASSICS

❏ LPZ-2011	Jazz Samba	1995	$75

— Audiophile vinyl

VERVE

❏ V-8432 [M]	Jazz Samba	1962	$50
❏ V6-8432 [S]	Jazz Samba	1962	$75

— With "MGM Records" on label print

❏ UMJ-3158	Jazz Samba	198?	$25
❏ 810061-1	Jazz Samba	198?	$25

— Reissue

❏ V6-8432 [S]	Jazz Samba	1976	$30

— Manufactured and Marketed by Polydor Incorporated" on label

GETZ, STAN, AND CHET BAKER
STORYVILLE

❏ 4090	Line for Lyons	1984	$25

GETZ, STAN, AND GERRY MULLIGAN
MAINSTREAM

❏ MRL364	Yesterday	1972	$35

GETZ, STAN, AND HORACE SILVER
BARONET

❏ B-102 [M]	A Pair of Kings	1962	$35
❏ BS-102 [R]	A Pair of Kings	196?	$25

GETZ, STAN, AND J.J. JOHNSON
VERVE

❏ MGV-8405 [M]	Stan Getz and J.J. Johnson	1961	$0

— Unreleased

❏ MGV-8265 [M]	Stan Getz and J.J. Johnson at the Opera House	1958	$150
❏ MGVS-6027 [S]	Stan Getz and J.J. Johnson at the Opera House	1960	$100
❏ V-8265 [M]	Stan Getz and J.J. Johnson at the Opera House	1961	$50
❏ V6-8265 [S]	Stan Getz and J.J. Johnson at the Opera House	1961	$35
❏ V6-8490 [S]	Stan Getz and J.J. Johnson at the Opera House	1962	$35
❏ V-8490 [M]	Stan Getz and J.J. Johnson at the Opera House	1962	$35

GETZ, STAN, AND JOAO GILBERTO
MOBILE FIDELITY

❏ 1-208	Getz/Gilberto	1994	$150

— Audiophile vinyl

VERVE

❏ V-8623 [M]	Getz/Gilberto #2	1965	$35
❏ V6-8623 [S]	Getz/Gilberto #2	1965	$50
❏ V-8545 [M]	Getz/Gilberto	1964	$35
❏ V6-8545 [S]	Getz/Gilberto	1964	$50
❏ UMV-2099	Getz/Gilberto	198?	$25

— Reissue

❏ 810048-1	Getz/Gilberto	198?	$25

— Reissue

GETZ, STAN, AND LAURINDO ALMEIDA
VERVE

❏ V-8665 [M]	Stan Getz with Guest Artist Laurindo Almeida	1965	$35
❏ V6-8665 [S]	Stan Getz with Guest Artist Laurindo Almeida	1965	$50

GETZ, STAN, AND OSCAR PETERSON
VERVE

❏ MGV-8251 [M]	Stan Getz and the Oscar Peterson Trio	1958	$150
❏ V-8251 [M]	Stan Getz and the Oscar Peterson Trio	1961	$50

— Reissue of MGV-8251

❏ V6-8251 [R]	Stan Getz and the Oscar Peterson Trio	196?	$30
❏ UMV-2665	Stan Getz and the Oscar Peterson Trio	198?	$25

— Reissue

Number	Title	Yr	NM
❏ MGV-8348 [M]	Stan Getz with Gerry Mulligan and the Oscar Peterson Trio	1959	$150
❏ V-8348 [M]	Stan Getz with Gerry Mulligan and the Oscar Peterson Trio	1961	$50
—Reissue of MGV-8348			
❏ V6-8348 [R]	Stan Getz with Gerry Mulligan and the Oscar Peterson Trio	1961	$30

GETZ, STAN, AND WARDELL GRAY
DAWN
❏ DLP-1126 [M]	Tenors Anyone?	1958	$250

SEECO
❏ SLP-7 [10]	Highlights in Modern Jazz	1954	$300

GETZ, STAN, AND ZOOT SIMS
FANTASY
❏ OJC-008	The Brothers	1982	$30

PRESTIGE
❏ PRLP-7022 [M]	The Brothers	1956	$400
—Yellow label with W. 50th St. address			
❏ PRLP-7252 [M]	The Brothers	1963	$200
—Yellow label with Bergenfield, N.J. address			

GETZ, STAN; DIZZY GILLESPIE; SONNY STITT
VERVE
❏ MGV-8198 [M]	For Musicians Only	1958	$175
❏ V-8198 [M]	For Musicians Only	1961	$75

GETZ, STAN
A&M
❏ SP-5297	Apasionado	1990	$35

AMERICAN RECORDING SOCIETY
❏ G-407 [M]	Cool Jazz of Stan Getz	1956	$40
❏ G-428 [M]	Intimate Portrait	1957	$40
❏ G-443 [M]	Stan Getz '57	1957	$40

BLACKHAWK
❏ BKH-51101	Voyage	1986	$25

BLUE RIBBON
❏ BR-8012 [M]	Rhythms	1961	$50
❏ BS-8012 [R]	Rhythms	1961	$25

CLEF
❏ MGC-137 [10]	Stan Getz Plays	1953	$350
❏ MGC-143 [10]	The Artistry of Stan Getz	1953	$350

COLUMBIA
❏ PC33703	Best of Two Worlds	1975	$35
❏ PC32706	Captain Marvel	1974	$35
❏ JC35992	Children of the World	1979	$30
❏ JC36403	The Best of Stan Getz	1980	$30
❏ CJ44047	The Lyrical Stan Getz	1988	$30
❏ FC38272	The Master	1983	$25
❏ JC34873	The Peacocks	1977	$30

CONCORD JAZZ
❏ CJ-188	Pure Getz	1983	$30
❏ CJ-158	The Dolphin	198?	$30

CROWN
❏ CLP-5002 [M]	Groovin' High	1957	$40
—Reissue of Modern 1202			

❏ CLP-5284 [M]	Groovin' High	196?	$25
—Reissue of 5002			

DALE
❏ 21 [10]	In Retrospect	1951	$400

EMARCY
❏ 838771-1	Billy Highstreet Samba	1990	$30

FANTASY
❏ OJC-121	Stan Getz Quartets	198?	$25
—Reissue of Prestige 7002			

HALL OF FAME
❏ 606	Stan Getz and His Tenor Sax	197?	$30

INNER CITY
❏ 1040	Gold	1977	$30

INTERMEDIA
❏ QS-5057	Stella by Starlight	198?	$25

JAZZ MAN
❏ 5014	Forrest Eyes	1982	$30

JAZZTONE
❏ J-1230 [M]	Stan Getz	1956	$40
❏ J-1240 [M]	Stan Getz '57	1957	$40

METRO
❏ M-501 [M]	The Melodic Stan Getz	1965	$175
❏ MS-501 [S]	The Melodic Stan Getz	1965	$300

METRONOME
❏ BLP-6 [M]	The Sound	1956	$250

MGM
❏ SE-4696	Marrakesh Express	1970	$35

MODERN
❏ MLP-1202 [M]	Groovin' High	1956	$175

MOSAIC
❏ MR4-131	The Complete Recordings of the Stan Getz Quintet with Jimmy Raney	199?	$120

NEW JAZZ
❏ NJLP-8214 [M]	Long Island Sound	1959	$300
—Reissue of Prestige 7002; purple label			
❏ NJLP-8214 [M]	Long Island Sound	1965	$175
—Blue label with trident logo on right			

NORGRAN
❏ MGN-1008 [M]	Interpretations by the Stan Getz Quintet #2	1954	$300
❏ MGN-1029 [M]	Interpretations by the Stan Getz Quintet #3	1955	$300
❏ MGN-1000 [M]	Interpretations by the Stan Getz Quintet	1954	$300
❏ MGN-1088 [M]	More West Coast Jazz with Stan Getz	1956	$300
❏ MGN-1087 [M]	Stan Getz '56	1956	$200
❏ MGN-2000-2 [M]	Stan Getz at the Shrine	1955	$300
—Boxed set with booklet			
❏ MGN-1042 [M]	Stan Getz Plays	1955	$700
—Reissue of Clef 137 and 143 on one 12-inch LP			
❏ MGN-1032 [M]	West Coast Jazz	1955	$300

PICKWICK
❏ SPC-3031	Stan Getz In Concert	197?	$25

PRESTIGE
❏ 24088	Early Getz	197?	$30
❏ PRLP-7255 [M]	Early Stan	1963	$40
❏ PRST-7255 [R]	Early Stan	1963	$50
❏ PRLP-7434 [M]	Getz Plays Jazz Classics	1967	$75
—Reissue of PRLP 7255			
❏ PRST-7434 [R]	Getz Plays Jazz Classics	1967	$35
—Reissue of PRST 7255			
❏ PRLP-7516 [M]	Preservation	1967	$75
❏ PRST-7516 [R]	Preservation	1967	$35
❏ 24019	Stan Getz	197?	$35
❏ PRLP-104 [10]	Stan Getz, Volume 2	1951	$300
❏ PRLP-102 [10]	Stan Getz and the Tenor Sax Stars	1951	$300
❏ PRLP-7256 [M]	Stan Getz' Greatest Hits	1963	$40
❏ PRST-7256 [R]	Stan Getz' Greatest Hits	1963	$50
❏ PRLP-7337 [M]	Stan Getz' Greatest Hits	1967	$75
—Reissue of PRLP 7256			
❏ PRST-7337 [R]	Stan Getz' Greatest Hits	1967	$35
—Reissue of PRST 7256			
❏ PRLP-108 [10]	Stan Getz-Lee Konitz	1951	$300
❏ PRLP-7002 [M]	Stan Getz Quartets	1955	$300

ROOST
❏ R-417 [10]	Chamber Music	1953	$300
❏ LP-2258 [M]	Getz Age	1963	$75
❏ SLP-2258 [R]	Getz Age	1963	$35
❏ R-407 [10]	Jazz at Storyville	1952	$175
❏ R-411 [10]	Jazz at Storyville, Volume 2	1952	$175
❏ R-420 [10]	Jazz at Storyville, Volume 3	1954	$175
❏ LP-2255 [M]	Modern World	1963	$175
❏ SLP-2255 [R]	Modern World	1963	$175
❏ LP-2251 [M]	Moonlight in Vermont	1963	$75
❏ SLP-2251 [R]	Moonlight in Vermont	1963	$35
❏ R-423 [10]	Split Kick	1954	$175
❏ R-402 [10]	Stan Getz	1950	$250
❏ R-404 [10]	Stan Getz and the Swedish All Stars	1951	$250
❏ LP-2209 [M]	Storyville	1956	$175
—Reissue of R-407 and half of R-411			
❏ LP-2225 [M]	Storyville, Volume 2	1957	$175
—Reissue of R-423 and the other half of R-411			
❏ LP-2249 [M]	The Greatest of Stan Getz	1963	$75
❏ SLP-2249 [R]	The Greatest of Stan Getz	1963	$18
❏ LP-2207 [M]	The Sounds of Stan Getz	1956	$175
—Reissue of R-402			
❏ RK-103 [M]	The Stan Getz Years	1964	$40
❏ SRK-103 [R]	The Stan Getz Years	1964	$75

ROULETTE
❏ RE-123	Stan Getz/Sonny Stitt	1973	$35
❏ RE-119	The Best of Stan Getz	1972	$35

SAVOY
❏ MG-9004 [10]	New Sounds in Modern Music	1951	$300
❏ SJL-1105	Opus de Bop	1977	$30

STEEPLECHASE
❏ SCS-1073/4	Live at Montmartre	1986	$30

VERVE
❏ VS-200 [M]	An Introduction to the World of Stan Getz	1964	$35
❏ V6S-200 [S]	An Introduction to the World of Stan Getz	1964	$50
—Sampler of material from five LPs plus one single-only track			
❏ VSP-22 [M]	Another Time, Another Place	1966	$35
❏ VSPS-22 [R]	Another Time, Another Place	1966	$25
❏ MGV-8296 [M]	Award Winner	1959	$175
❏ V-8296 [M]	Award Winner	1961	$50
—Reissue of MGV-8296			
❏ V6-8296 [R]	Award Winner	196?	$30
❏ V-8494 [M]	Big Band Bossa Nova	1962	$50
❏ V6-8494 [S]	Big Band Bossa Nova	1962	$75
❏ V6-8807	Communications '72	1972	$35
❏ MGV-8379 [M]	Cool Velvet -- Stan Getz and Strings	1960	$150
❏ MGVS-6160 [S]	Cool Velvet -- Stan Getz and Strings	1960	$0
—Unreleased			
❏ V-8379 [M]	Cool Velvet -- Stan Getz and Strings	1961	$50
—Reissue of MGV-8379			
❏ V6-8379 [S]	Cool Velvet -- Stan Getz and Strings	1961	$50
❏ MGVS-68379 [S]	Cool Velvet -- Stan Getz and Strings	1960	$150
❏ V6-8780	Didn't We	1969	$35
❏ V6-8802-2	Dynasty	1971	$50
❏ VSP-2 [M]	Eloquence	1966	$35
❏ VSPS-2 [R]	Eloquence	1966	$25
❏ V-8412 [M]	Focus	1961	$75
❏ V6-8412 [S]	Focus	1961	$50
❏ VR-1-2528	Focus	1977	$25
—Reissue of 8412			
❏ UMV-2071	Focus	198?	$25
—Reissue			
❏ V-8600 [M]	Getz Au Go Go	1964	$35
❏ V6-8600 [S]	Getz Au Go Go	1964	$50
❏ UMV-2075	Getz Au Go Go	198?	$25
—Reissue			
❏ 821725-1	Getz Au Go Go	198?	$25
—Reissue			
❏ V6-8815-2	History of Stan Getz	1973	$35
❏ MGV-8331 [M]	Imported from Europe	1959	$175
❏ V-8331 [M]	Imported from Europe	1961	$50
—Reissue of MGV-8331			
❏ V6-8331 [R]	Imported from Europe	196?	$30
❏ MGV-8122 [M]	Interpretations by the Stan Getz Quintet #3	1957	$300
—Reissue of Norgran 1029			
❏ V-8122 [M]	Interpretations by the Stan Getz Quintet #3	1961	$50
—Reissue of MGV-8122			
❏ UMV-2100	Jazz Samba Encore	198?	$25
—Reissue			
❏ 823613-1	Jazz Samba Encore	198?	$25
—Reissue			
❏ V-8523 [M]	Jazz Samba Encore!	1963	$50
—With Luiz Bonfa			
❏ V6-8523 [S]	Jazz Samba Encore!	1963	$75
—With Luiz Bonfa			
❏ MGV-8177 [M]	More West Coast Jazz with Stan Getz	1957	$300
—Reissue of Norgran 1088			
❏ V-8177 [M]	More West Coast Jazz with Stan Getz	1961	$50
—Reissue of MGV-8177			
❏ V6-8177 [R]	More West Coast Jazz with Stan Getz	196?	$30
❏ V-8554 [M]	Reflections	1964	$35
❏ V6-8554 [S]	Reflections	1964	$50
❏ V3HB-8844	Return Engagement	1974	$35
❏ MGV-8029 [M]	Stan Getz '57	1957	$150
—Reissue of Norgran 1087 with revised title			
❏ V-8029 [M]	Stan Getz '57	1961	$50
—Reissue of MGV-8029			
❏ MGV-8200 [M]	Stan Getz and the Cool Sounds	1957	$150
—Reissue of American Recording Society 407 with new name			
❏ V-8200 [M]	Stan Getz and the Cool Sounds	1961	$50
—Reissue of MGV-8200			
❏ V6-8200 [R]	Stan Getz and the Cool Sounds	196?	$30
❏ MGV-8393-2 [M]	Stan Getz At Large	1960	$120
❏ V-8393-2 [M]	Stan Getz At Large	1961	$75
—Reissue of MGV-8393-2			
❏ V6-8393-2 [R]	Stan Getz At Large	1961	$35
❏ MGV-8401 [M]	Stan Getz At Large, Volume 1	1960	$0
—Unreleased			
❏ MGV-8402 [M]	Stan Getz At Large, Volume 2	1960	$0
—Unreleased			
❏ MGV-8188-2 [M]	Stan Getz at the Shrine	1957	$200

Number	Title	Yr	NM
—Reissue of Norgran 2000-2			
❏ V-8188-2 [M]	Stan Getz at the Shrine	1961	$75
—Reissue of MGV-8188-2			
❏ V6-8188-2 [R]	Stan Getz at the Shrine	196?	$35
❏ MGV-8213 [M]	Stan Getz in Stockholm	1958	$150
—Reissue of American Recording Society 428 with new name			
❏ V-8213 [M]	Stan Getz in Stockholm	1961	$50
—Reissue of MGV-8213			
❏ V6-8213 [R]	Stan Getz in Stockholm	196?	$30
❏ UMV-2614	Stan Getz in Stockholm	198?	$25
—Reissue			
❏ MGV-8133 [M]	Stan Getz Plays	1957	$150
—Reissue of Norgran 1042			
❏ V-8133 [M]	Stan Getz Plays	1961	$50
—Reissue of MGV-8133			
❏ V6-8133 [R]	Stan Getz Plays	196?	$30
❏ VSP-31 [M]	Stan Getz Plays Blues	1966	$35
❏ VSPS-31 [R]	Stan Getz Plays Blues	1966	$25
❏ MGV-8356 [M]	Stan Getz Quintet	1960	$0
—Unreleased			
❏ MGV-8263 [M]	Stan Meets Chet	1958	$120
—With Chet Baker			
❏ V-8263 [M]	Stan Meets Chet	1961	$50
—Reissue of MGV-8263			
❏ V6-8263 [R]	Stan Meets Chet	196?	$30
❏ 815239-1	Stan the Man	1983	$25
❏ V-8693 [M]	Sweet Rain	1967	$75
❏ V6-8693 [S]	Sweet Rain	1967	$35
❏ V-8719 [M]	The Best of Stan Getz	1967	$75
❏ V6-8719 [S]	The Best of Stan Getz	1967	$35
❏ VE-2-2510	The Corea/Evans Sessions	1976	$35
❏ 823242-1	The Corea/Evans Sessions	198?	$30
—Reissue			
❏ 823611-1	The Girl from Ipanema: The Bossa Nova Years	1984	$150
❏ MGV-8321 [M]	The Soft Swing	1959	$150
❏ V-8321 [M]	The Soft Swing	1961	$50
—Reissue of MGV-8321			
❏ V6-8321 [R]	The Soft Swing	196?	$30
❏ MGV-8294 [M]	The Steamer	1959	$150
❏ V-8294 [M]	The Steamer	1961	$50
—Reissue of MGV-8294			
❏ V6-8294 [R]	The Steamer	196?	$30
❏ V-8707 [M]	Voices	1967	$75
❏ V6-8707 [S]	Voices	1967	$35
❏ MGV-8028 [M]	West Coast Jazz	1957	$250
—Reissue of Norgran 1032			
❏ V-8028 [M]	West Coast Jazz	1961	$50
—Reissue of MGV-8028			
❏ V6-8028 [R]	West Coast Jazz	196?	$30
❏ V-8752 [M]	What the World Needs Now -- Stan Getz Plays Bacharach and David	1968	$75
❏ V6-8752 [S]	What the World Needs Now -- Stan Getz Plays Bacharach and David	1968	$35

GHIGLIONI, TIZIANA
SOUL NOTE

Number	Title	Yr	NM
❏ 121156	Somebody Special	198?	$30
❏ SN-1056	Sounds of Love	1984	$30
❏ 121056	Sounds of Love	198?	$25

GHOULS, THE
CAPITOL

| ❏ T2215 [M] | Dracula's Deuce | 1965 | $120 |
| ❏ ST2215 [S] | Dracula's Deuce | 1965 | $175 |

GIANT CRAB, THE
UNI

| ❏ 73037 | A Giant Crab Comes Forth | 1968 | $30 |
| ❏ 73057 | Cool It, Helios | 1969 | $30 |

GIBB, ANDY
RSO

❏ RS-1-3069	After Dark	1980	$12
❏ RS-1-3091	Andy Gibb's Greatest Hits	1980	$12
❏ RS-1-3019	Flowing Rivers	1977	$12
❏ RS-1-3034	Shadow Dancing	1978	$12

GIBB, BARRY
MCA

| ❏ 5506 | Now Voyager | 1984 | $12 |

GIBB, ROBIN
Also see BEE GEES.
ATCO

| ❏ SD 33-323 | Robin's Reign | 1969 | $40 |

MIRAGE

| ❏ 90170 | Secret Agent | 1984 | $10 |

POLYDOR

| ❏ 810896-1 | How Old Are You? | 1983 | $12 |

GIBBONS, SHANNON
SOUL NOTE

| ❏ 121163 | Shannon Gibbons | 1987 | $30 |

GIBBS, GEORGIA
BELL

Number	Title	Yr	NM
❏ 6000 [M]	Call Me Georgia Gibbs	1966	$18
❏ 6000S [S]	Call Me Georgia Gibbs	1966	$25

CORAL

| ❏ CRL56037 [10] | Ballin' the Jack | 1951 | $50 |

| ❏ CRL57183 [M] | Her Nibs | 1957 | $40 |

EMARCY

| ❏ MG-36103 [M] | Swingin' with Gibbs | 1957 | $250 |

EPIC

| ❏ LN24059 [M] | Georgia Gibbs' Greatest Hits | 1963 | $40 |
| ❏ BN26059 [S] | Georgia Gibbs' Greatest Hits | 1963 | $40 |

GOLDEN TONE

❏ 14093 [R]	Her Nibs!! Miss Georgia Gibbs	1962	$12
—Cover misspells it "Nibbs"			
❏ 4093 [M]	Her Nibs!! Miss Georgia Gibbs	1962	$15

IMPERIAL

| ❏ LP-9107 [M] | Something's Gotta Give | 1960 | $175 |
| ❏ LP-12064 [S] | Something's Gotta Give | 1960 | $175 |

MERCURY

❏ MG-25175 [10]	Georgia Gibbs Sings Oldies	1953	$150
❏ MG-20071 [M]	Music and Memories	1955	$150
❏ MG-20114 [M]	Song Favorites	1956	$150
❏ MG-20170 [M]	Swingin' with Her Nibs	1956	$150
❏ MG-25199 [10]	The Man That Got Away	1954	$150

ROYALE

| ❏ 18126 [10] | Georgia Gibbs and Orchestra | 195? | $40 |

SUNSET

| ❏ SUM-1113 [M] | Her Nibs, Miss Georgia Gibbs | 196? | $20 |
| ❏ SUS-5113 [S] | Her Nibs, Miss Georgia Gibbs | 196? | $20 |

GIBBS, MICHAEL, AND GARY BURTON
POLYDOR

| ❏ PD-6503 | In the Public Interest | 197? | $35 |

GIBBS, MICHAEL
DERAM

| ❏ DES18048 | Michael Gibbs | 1970 | $25 |

GIBBS, TERRI
CANAAN

| ❏ 80398 | Comfort the People | 198? | $15 |

HORIZON

| ❏ SP759 | Turn Around | 1987 | $12 |

MCA

❏ 5255	I'm a Lady	1981	$12
❏ 5443	Over Easy	1983	$10
❏ 5173	Somebody's Knockin'	1981	$12
❏ 37178	Somebody's Knockin'	198?	$10
—Budget-line reissue of 5173			
❏ 5315	Some Days It Rains All Night Long	1982	$10
❏ 1575	The Best of Terri Gibbs	198?	$10

WARNER BROS.

| ❏ 25309 | Old Friends | 1985 | $10 |

GIBBS, TERRY, AND BILL HARRIS
MODE

| ❏ LP-129 [M] | The Ex-Hermanites | 1957 | $100 |

PREMIER

| ❏ PM-2006 [M] | Woodchoppers' Ball | 1963 | $35 |
| ❏ PS-2006 [R] | Woodchoppers' Ball | 1963 | $25 |

GIBBS, TERRY, AND BUDDY DEFRANCO
CONTEMPORARY

| ❏ C-14056 | Air Mail Special | 1990 | $30 |

Number	Title	Yr	NM
❏ C-14036	Chicago Fire	1987	$25

PALO ALTO

| ❏ PA-8011 | Jazz Party -- First Time Together | 1982 | $25 |

GIBBS, TERRY
ABC IMPULSE!

| ❏ AS-58 [S] | Take It from Me | 1968 | $35 |

BRUNSWICK

| ❏ BL54009 [M] | Terry | 1955 | $75 |
| ❏ BL56055 [10] | Terry Gibbs Quartet | 1954 | $150 |

CONTEMPORARY

❏ C-7647	Dream Band	1986	$25
❏ C-14022	The Latin Connection	1986	$25
❏ C-7652	Volume 2: The Sundown Sessions	1987	$25
❏ C-7654	Volume 3: Flying Home	1988	$25
❏ C-7656	Volume 4: Main Stem	1990	$30

DOT

| ❏ DLP-3726 [M] | Reza | 1966 | $85 |
| ❏ DLP-25726 [S] | Reza | 1966 | $85 |

EMARCY

❏ MG-36075 [M]	Mallets A-Plenty	1956	$250
❏ MG-36148 [M]	More Vibes on Velvet	1959	$250
❏ MG-36138 [M]	Steve Allen's All Stars	1958	$250
❏ SR-80004 [S]	Steve Allen's All Stars	1959	$250
❏ MG-36103 [M]	Swingin' Terry Gibbs	1957	$50
❏ MG-36047 [M]	Terry Gibbs	1956	$250
❏ MG-36128 [M]	Terry Plays the Duke	1958	$250
❏ MG-36064 [M]	Vibes on Velvet	1956	$250

IMPULSE!

| ❏ A-58 [M] | Take It from Me | 1964 | $120 |
| ❏ AS-58 [S] | Take It from Me | 1964 | $120 |

INTERLUDE

| ❏ MO-506 [M] | Vibrations | 1959 | $40 |
| ❏ ST-1006 [S] | Vibrations | 1959 | $30 |

JAZZ A LA CARTE

| ❏ 1 | Live at the Lord | 1978 | $35 |
| ❏ 2 | Smoke 'Em Up | 1978 | $30 |

LIMELIGHT

| ❏ LM-82005 [M] | El Nutto | 1964 | $25 |
| ❏ LS-86005 [S] | El Nutto | 1964 | $30 |

MAINSTREAM

| ❏ 56048 [M] | It's Time We Met | 1965 | $35 |
| ❏ S-6048 [S] | It's Time We Met | 1965 | $25 |

MCA

| ❏ 29035 | Take It from Me | 198? | $20 |

MERCURY

❏ MG-20704 [M]	Explosion!	1962	$150
❏ SR-60704 [S]	Explosion!	1962	$150
❏ MG-20812 [M]	Jewish Melodies in Jazztime	1963	$300
❏ SR-60812 [S]	Jewish Melodies in Jazztime	1963	$300
❏ MG-20440 [M]	Launching a New Sound in Music	1959	$150
❏ SR-60112 [S]	Launching a New Sound in Music	1959	$150
❏ MG-20518 [M]	Steve Allen's All Stars	1960	$150
❏ SR-60195 [S]	Steve Allen's All Stars	1960	$150

MODE

| ❏ LP-123 [M] | A Jazz Band Ball | 1957 | $100 |

ROOST

| ❏ LP-2260 [M] | El Latino | 1965 | $35 |
| ❏ RS-2260 [S] | Latino | 1965 | $25 |

TIME

❏ 52105 [M]	Hootenanny My Way	1963	$30
❏ S-2105 [S]	Hootenanny My Way	1963	$30
❏ 52120 [M]	Terry Gibbs with Sal Nistico	196?	$25
❏ S-2120 [S]	Terry Gibbs with Sal Nistico	196?	$30

TRIP

| ❏ 5545 | Launching a New Band | 197? | $25 |

VERVE

❏ MGV-2136 [M]	Music from Cole Porter's "Can-Can	1960	$150
❏ V-2136 [M]	Music from Cole Porter's "Can-Can	1961	$25
❏ MGVS-6145 [S]	Music from Cole Porter's "Can-Can	1960	$150
❏ V6-2136 [S]	Music from Cole Porter's "Can-Can	1961	$25
❏ V-8496 [M]	Straight Ahead	1962	$25
❏ V6-8496 [S]	Straight Ahead	1962	$30
❏ MGV-2134 [M]	Swing Is Here!	1960	$100
❏ V-2134 [M]	Swing Is Here!	1961	$25
❏ MGVS-6140 [S]	Swing Is Here!	1960	$100
❏ V6-2134 [S]	Swing Is Here!	1961	$25
❏ V-8447 [M]	That Swing Thing	1962	$25
❏ V6-8447 [S]	That Swing Thing	1962	$30
❏ MGV-2151 [M]	The Exciting Terry Gibbs Big Band	1960	$120
❏ V-2151 [M]	The Exciting Terry Gibbs Big Band	1961	$25
❏ V6-2151 [S]	The Exciting Terry Gibbs Big Band	1961	$30

WING

| ❏ MGW-12255 [M] | Terry Plays the Duke | 196? | $35 |
| ❏ SRW-16255 [R] | Terry Plays the Duke | 196? | $25 |

Number	Title	Yr	NM
XANADU			
❏ 210	Bopstacle Course	198?	$25
GIBSON, ALTHEA			
DOT			
❏ DLP-3105 [M]	Althea Gibson Sings	1959	$40
❏ DLP-25105 [S]	Althea Gibson Sings	1959	$50
GIBSON, BOB, AND BOB CAMP			
ELEKTRA			
❏ EKL-207 [M]	Gibson and Camp at the Gate of Horn	1961	$40
❏ EKS-7207 [S]	Gibson and Camp at the Gate of Horn	1961	$50
MOUNTAIN RAILROAD			
❏ 52781 [S]	Homemade Music	1978	$18
GIBSON, BOB			
ELEKTRA			
❏ EKL-177 [M]	Ski Songs	1959	$30
❏ EKS-7177 [S]	Ski Songs	1959	$30
❏ EKL-239 [M]	Where I'm Bound	1964	$25
❏ EKS-7239 [S]	Where I'm Bound	1964	$30
❏ EKL-197 [M]	Yes I See	1961	$25
❏ EKS-7197 [S]	Yes I See	1961	$30
RIVERSIDE			
❏ RLP 12-816 [M]	Carnegie Concert	1958	$40
❏ RM7542 [M]	Hootenanny at Carnegie	1963	$25
—Reissue of 12-816 with slightly altered lineup			
❏ RLP 12-806 [M]	I Come For to Sing	1957	$40
❏ RLP 12-802 [M]	Offbeat Folk Songs	1956	$40

Number	Title	Yr	NM
❏ RLP 12-830 [M]	There's a Meetin' Here Tonight	1958	$40
❏ RLP-1111 [S]	There's a Meetin' Here Tonight	1959	$50
STINSON			
❏ SLP-76 [10]	Folksongs of Ohio	1954	$50
GIBSON, DEBBIE			
ATLANTIC			
❏ 81932	Electric Youth	1989	$12
❏ 81780	Out of the Blue	1987	$12
GIBSON, DON, AND SUE THOMPSON			
HICKORY/MGM			
❏ H3G-4520	Oh How Love Changes	1975	$15
GIBSON, DON			
ABC HICKORY			
❏ AH-44007	If You Ever	1977	$15
❏ AH-44001	I'm All Wrapped Up in You	1976	$15
❏ AH-44014	Look Who's Blue	1978	$15
❏ AH-44010	Starting All Over	1978	$15
HARMONY			
❏ KH31765	Sample Kisses	1972	$12
❏ HL7358 [M]	The Fabulous Don Gibson Sings	196?	$18
❏ HS11158 [R]	The Fabulous Don Gibson Sings	196?	$15
HICKORY			
❏ LPS-160	Country Green	1971	$18
❏ LPS-157	Don Gibson Sings Hank Williams	1971	$18
❏ LPS-153	Hits, The Don Gibson Way	1970	$18
❏ LPS-155	Perfect Mountain	1971	$18
❏ LPS-166	Woman (Sensuous Woman)	1972	$18
❏ ST-94817	Woman (Sensuous Woman)	1972	$25
—Capitol Record Club edition			
HICKORY/MGM			
❏ H3G-4516	Bring Back Your Love to Me	1974	$15
❏ H3G-4519	I'm the Loneliest Man	1975	$15
❏ H3F-4509	Snap Your Fingers	1974	$18
❏ H3G-4502	The Very Best of Don Gibson	1974	$18

Number	Title	Yr	NM
❏ HR-4501	Touch the Morning/That's What I'll Do	1973	$18
LION			
❏ L-70069 [M]	Songs by Don Gibson	1958	$100
METRO			
❏ M-529 [M]	Don Gibson	1965	$15
❏ MS-529 [R]	Don Gibson	1965	$12
MGM			
❏ GAS-138	Don Gibson (Golden Archive Series)	1970	$18
RCA CAMDEN			
❏ CAL-852 [M]	A Blue Million Tears	196?	$15
❏ CAS-852 [P]	A Blue Million Tears	196?	$15
—All tracks are rechanneled except "I Let Her Get Lonely" and "I May Never Get to Heaven," which are true stereo			
❏ CAS-2592	Am I That Easy to Forget	1972	$15
❏ CAL-2101 [M]	Hurtin' Inside	1966	$15
❏ CAS-2101 [S]	Hurtin' Inside	1966	$18
❏ CAS-2246	I Love You So Much	1968	$15
❏ CAS-2502	I Walk Alone	1971	$15
❏ ACL1-0328	Just Call Me Lonesome	1973	$12
❏ ACL1-0758	Just One Time	1974	$12
❏ CAS-2392	Lovin' Lies	1970	$15
❏ CAS-2317	My God Is Real	1969	$15
RCA VICTOR			
❏ LPM-3843 [M]	All My Love	1967	$25
❏ LSP-3843 [S]	All My Love	1967	$30
❏ LSP-4169	All-Time Country Gold	1969	$18
❏ CPL1-7052	Collector's Series	1985	$12
❏ LPM-3594 [M]	Don Gibson with Spanish Guitars	1966	$25
❏ LSP-3594 [S]	Don Gibson with Spanish Guitars	1966	$30
❏ LPM-2361 [M]	Girls, Guitars and Gibson	1961	$30
❏ LSP-2361 [S]	Girls, Guitars and Gibson	1961	$40
❏ LPM-2878 [M]	God Walks These Hills	1964	$25
❏ LSP-2878 [S]	God Walks These Hills	1964	$30
❏ LPM-3680 [M]	Great Country Songs	1966	$25
❏ LSP-3680 [S]	Great Country Songs	1966	$30
❏ LPM-2702 [M]	I Wrote a Song	1963	$30
❏ LSP-2702 [S]	I Wrote a Song	1963	$40
❏ LPM-2184 [M]	Look Who's Blue	1960	$30
❏ LSP-2184 [S]	Look Who's Blue	1960	$40
❏ LSP-4053	More Country Soul	1968	$25
❏ LPM-1918 [M]	No One Stands Alone	1959	$30
❏ LSP-1918 [S]	No One Stands Alone	1959	$40
❏ LPM-1743 [S]	Oh Lonesome Me	1958	$50
❏ LPM-2448 [M]	Some Favorites of Mine	1962	$30
❏ LSP-2448 [S]	Some Favorites of Mine	1962	$40
❏ LPM-2269 [M]	Sweet Dreams	1960	$30
❏ LSP-2269 [S]	Sweet Dreams	1960	$40
❏ LPM-2038 [M]	That Gibson Boy	1959	$30
❏ LSP-2038 [S]	That Gibson Boy	1959	$40
❏ LPM-3376 [M]	The Best of Don Gibson	1965	$25
❏ LSP-3376 [S]	The Best of Don Gibson	1965	$30
❏ LSP-4281	The Best of Don Gibson, Vol. 2	1970	$18
❏ LPM-3974 [M]	The King of Country Soul	1968	$50
❏ LSP-3974 [S]	The King of Country Soul	1968	$25
❏ LPM-3470 [M]	Too Much Hurt	1965	$25
❏ LSP-3470 [S]	Too Much Hurt	1965	$30
GIBSON, DON (2)			
JAZZOLOGY			
❏ J-40	The Al Capone Memorial Jazz Band	197?	$30
GIBSON, GERALD, AND HIS SING-A-LONGERS			
INTERNATIONAL AWARD SERIES			
❏ AK-0	Christmas Sing-a-Long	196?	$15
GIBSON, JON			
CHATHAM SQUARE PRODUCTIONS			
❏ LP24 [B]	Two Solo Pieces	1977	$60
❏ LP12 [B]	Visitations	1973	$60
SUPERIOR VIADUCT			
❏ SV068 [B]	Visitations	2015	$25
GIBSON, STEVE, AND THE RED CAPS			
MERCURY			
❏ MG-25116 [10]	Blueberry Hill (Singing & Swinging)	1952	$400
❏ MG-25115 [10]	You're Driving Me Crazy (Harmony Time)	1952	$400
GIFFORD, KATHIE LEE			
HEARTLAND			
❏ HL-3046	Christmas with Kathie Lee Gifford	1993	$25
GIFFORD, WALT			
DELMARK			
❏ DS-204 [M]	Walt Gifford's New Yorkers	1959	$30
GIL, GILBERTO			
BRAZILOID			
❏ BR-4009	Ao Vivo Em Toquio	1989	$30
❏ BR-4000	Soy Loco Por Ti America	1988	$30

Number	Title	Yr	NM
ELEKTRA			
❏ 6E-167	Nightingale	1979	$30
PHILIPS			
❏ 832216-1	Gilberto Gil	1988	$25
GILBERT, ANN			
GROOVE			
❏ LG-1004 [M]	The Many Moods of Ann	1956	$50
GILBERT, RONNIE			
Also see THE WEAVERS.			
MERCURY			
❏ MG-20917 [M]	Alone with Ronnie Gilbert	1964	$25
❏ SR-60917 [S]	Alone with Ronnie Gilbert	1964	$30
RCA VICTOR			
❏ LPM-1591 [M]	In Hi-Fi, The Legend of Bessie Smith	1958	$40
GILBERT & SULLIVAN JAZZ WORKSHOP, THE			
ANDEX			
❏ A-27101 [M]	The Coolest Mikado	1961	$25
❏ AS-27101 [S]	The Coolest Mikado	1961	$30
GILBERTO, ASTRUD			
CTI			
❏ CTS-6008	Astrud Gilberto with Stanley Turrentine	1970	$30
ELEKTRA/MUSICIAN			
❏ 60760	Live in Montreux	1988	$25
PERCEPTION			
❏ 29	Now	1973	$25
VERVE			
❏ V6-8793	17-Sep-69	1969	$30
❏ V-8673 [M]	A Certain Smile, A Certain Sadness	1966	$30
❏ V6-8673 [S]	A Certain Smile, A Certain Sadness	1966	$35
❏ V-8708 [M]	Beach Samba	1967	$30
❏ V6-8708 [S]	Beach Samba	1967	$35
❏ V6-8776	I Haven't Got Anything Better to Do	1969	$30
❏ V-8643 [M]	Look to the Rainbow	1966	$30
❏ V6-8643 [S]	Look to the Rainbow	1966	$35
❏ 821566-1	Look to the Rainbow	1986	$25
—Reissue of V6-8643			
❏ V-8608 [M]	The Astrud Gilberto Album	1965	$30
❏ V6-8608 [S]	The Astrud Gilberto Album	1965	$35
❏ V-8629 [M]	The Shadow of Your Smile	1965	$30
❏ V6-8629 [S]	The Shadow of Your Smile	1965	$35
❏ SW-90649 [S]	The Shadow of Your Smile	1965	$100
—Capitol Record Club edition			
❏ V6-8754	Windy	1968	$30
GILBERTO, JOAO			
ATLANTIC			
❏ 8070 [M]	The Boss of the Bossa Nova	1963	$50
❏ SD8070 [S]	The Boss of the Bossa Nova	1963	$50
❏ 8076 [M]	The Warm World of Joao Gilberto	1964	$35
❏ SD8076 [S]	The Warm World of Joao Gilberto	1964	$25
CAPITOL			
❏ T2160 [M]	Joao Gilberto and Antonio Carlos Jobim	1964	$85
❏ ST2160 [S]	Joao Gilberto and Antonio Carlos Jobim	1964	$40
❏ ST2160 [S]	Joao Gilberto and Antonio Carlos Jobim	1978	$12
—Purple label, large Capitol logo			
❏ T10280 [M]	Pops in Portuguese	196?	$50
❏ ST10280 [S]	Pops in Portuguese	196?	$75
WARNER BROS.			
❏ BS3053	Amoroso	1978	$25
❏ BSK3613	Brasel	1981	$25
GILDER, NICK			
CASABLANCA			
❏ NBLP7259	Body Talk Muzik	1982	$18
❏ NBLP7243	Rock America	1980	$12
CHRYSALIS			
❏ CHR1202	City Nights	1978	$12
❏ CHR1219	Frequency	1979	$12
❏ CHR1147	You Know Who You Are	1977	$15
RCA VICTOR			
❏ NFL1-8051	Nick Gilder	1985	$12
GILELS, EMIL			
RCA VICTOR RED SEAL			
❏ LSC-2219 [S]	Brahms: Piano Concerto No. 2	1959	$100
—With Fritz Reiner/Chicago Symphony Orchestra; original with "shaded dog" label			
❏ LSC-2493 [S]	Schubert: Piano Sonata, op. 53	1961	$50
—Original with "shaded dog" label			

Number	Title	Yr	NM

GILES, GILES & FRIPP
Also see KING CRIMSON.

DERAM
| ❏ DES18019 [B] | The Cheerful Insanity of Giles, Giles & Fripp | 1968 | $400 |

GILES, RANDY

GUINNESS
| ❏ GNS36030 [B] | Seal It Together | 1977 | $20 |
—DJ copies only

GILKYSON, TERRY

COLUMBIA
❏ CL1103 [M]	Blue Mountain	1958	$40
❏ CL990 [M]	Marianne and Other Songs	1957	$50
❏ CL1302 [M]	Wanderin' Folk Songs	1959	$30

DECCA
| ❏ DL5263 [10] | Folk Songs | 1950 | $50 |
| ❏ DL5457 [10] | Golden Minutes of Folk Music | 1952 | $50 |

KAPP
❏ KL1196 [M]	Rollin'	1960	$18
❏ KS3196 [S]	Rollin'	1960	$25
❏ KL1327 [M]	The Cry of the Wild Goose	1963	$18
❏ KS3327 [S]	The Cry of the Wild Goose	1963	$25

GILL, JOHN

STOMP OFF
❏ SOS-1157	Big City Blues	1988	$25
❏ SOS-1126	Down Home Blues	1987	$25
❏ SOS-1066	Finger Buster	1984	$25
❏ SOS-1094	I Lost My Heart in Dixie Land	1986	$25
❏ SOS-1156	Some Sweet Day	1988	$25

GILL, JOHNNY

COTILLION
| ❏ 90250 | Chemistry | 1985 | $12 |
| ❏ 90103 | Johnny Gill | 1983 | $12 |

MOTOWN
| ❏ 6283 | Johnny Gill | 1990 | $15 |

GILL, VINCE

MCA
| ❏ R173599 | Pocket Full of Gold | 1991 | $25 |
—Only released on vinyl through BMG Direct Marketing
| ❏ 42321 | When I Call Your Name | 1989 | $25 |

RCA
| ❏ 5923-1-R | The Way Back Home | 1987 | $18 |

RCA VICTOR
| ❏ CPL1-5348 | The Things That Matter | 1985 | $18 |
| ❏ MHL1-8517 [EP] | Turn Me Loose | 1984 | $12 |

GILLAN, IAN, & ROGER GLOVER
Also see DEEP PURPLE.

VIRGIN
| ❏ 90953 | Accidentally on Purpose | 1988 | $15 |

GILLAN
Also see BLACK SABBATH; DEEP PURPLE; IAN GILLAN BAND.

VIRGIN
| ❏ 2196 [B] | Future Shock | 1981 | $18 |
| ❏ 13146 [B] | Glory Road | 1980 | $18 |

GILLAN BAND, IAN
Also see BLACK SABBATH, DEEP PURPLE, GILLAN.

ISLAND
| ❏ ILPS9500 [B] | Clear Air Turbulence | 1977 | $25 |
| ❏ ILPS9511 | Scarabus | 1978 | $18 |
—Different cover from UK issue

OYSTER
| ❏ OY11602 [B] | Child In Time | 1976 | $30 |

GILLEN, THEODORE

THE LITURGICAL PRESS
| ❏ 8146-7131-4 | The Nativity of the Lord | 1980 | $12 |

GILLESPIE, DANA

LONDON
| ❏ PS540 [B] | Foolish Seasons | 1968 | $50 |

GILLESPIE, DARLENE

DISNEYLAND
| ❏ WDL-3010 [M] | Darlene of the Teens | 1957 | $100 |
| ❏ DQ-1228 [M] | Sleeping Beauty | 1962 | $25 |
—Cover is black and white; later pressings, which go for less, are shaded blue on the back
| ❏ WDL-3010 [M] | Top Tunes of the '50's -- Darlene Gillespie Sings TV Favorites | 1958 | $50 |
—Reissue with new title and cover

| ❏ WDL-1010 [M] | Top Tunes of the '50's -- Darlene Gillespie Sings TV Favorites | 1959 | $40 |
—Reissue of 3010

MICKEY MOUSE CLUB
| ❏ MM-32 [M] | Sleeping Beauty | 1959 | $40 |

GILLESPIE, DIZZY, AND CHARLIE PARKER

ROOST
| ❏ LP-2234 [M] | Diz 'n' Bird In Concert | 1959 | $100 |
| ❏ SK-106 [M] | The Beginning: Diz and Bird | 1960 | $150 |

GILLESPIE, DIZZY, AND DJANGO REINHARDT

CLEF
| ❏ MGC-747 [M] | Jazz from Paris | 1956 | $350 |
—Canceled; reassigned to Verve

VERVE
| ❏ MGV-8015 [M] | Jazz from Paris | 1957 | $175 |
| ❏ V-8015 [M] | Jazz from Paris | 1961 | $30 |

GILLESPIE, DIZZY, AND STAN GETZ

NORGRAN
❏ MGN-1050 [M]	Diz and Getz	1956	$250
❏ MGN-2 [10]	The Dizzy Gillespie-Stan Getz Sextet #1	1954	$300
❏ MGN-18 [10]	The Dizzy Gillespie-Stan Getz Sextet #2	1954	$300

VERVE
| ❏ MGV-8141 [M] | Diz and Getz | 1957 | $175 |
—Reissue of Norgran 1050
| ❏ V-1041 [M] | Diz and Getz | 1961 | $75 |
| ❏ VE-2-2521 | Diz and Getz | 197? | $35 |

GILLESPIE, DIZZY

ALLEGRO
❏ 3083 [M]	Dizzy Gillespie	195?	$120
❏ 4023 [10]	Dizzy Gillespie	195?	$250
❏ 3017 [M]	Dizzy Gillespie Plays	195?	$120
❏ 4108 [10]	Dizzy Gillespie Plays	195?	$250

AMERICAN RECORDING SOCIETY
| ❏ G-423 [M] | Big Band Jazz | 1955 | $150 |
| ❏ G-405 [M] | Jazz Creations/Dizzy Gillespie | 1955 | $150 |

ATLANTIC
| ❏ 81646 | Closer to the Source | 1986 | $25 |
| ❏ 1257 [M] | Dizzy at Home and Abroad | 1957 | $300 |
—Black label
| ❏ 1257 [M] | Dizzy at Home and Abroad | 1961 | $175 |
—Multi-color label with white "fan" logo
| ❏ ALR-138 [10] | Dizzy Gillespie | 1952 | $400 |
| ❏ ALR-142 [10] | Dizzy Gillespie, Vol. 2 | 1952 | $400 |

BANDSTAND
| ❏ BDLP-1513 | Groovin' High | 1992 | $35 |

BARONET
| ❏ 105 [M] | A Handful of Modern Jazz | 1961 | $40 |

BLUEBIRD
| ❏ 5785-1-RB | Dizziest | 1987 | $35 |

BLUE NOTE
| ❏ BLP-5017 [10] | Horn of Plenty | 1953 | $300 |

BULLDOG
| ❏ BDL-2006 | 20 Golden Pieces of Dizzy Gillespie | 198? | $25 |

CLEF
| ❏ MGC-136 [10] | Dizzy Gillespie with Strings | 1953 | $350 |

CONTEMPORARY
| ❏ C-2504 [10] | Dizzy in Paris | 1953 | $300 |

COUNTERPOINT
| ❏ C-5548 | Dizzy Gillespie, 1941 | 197? | $30 |

DEE GEE
| ❏ LP-1000 [10] | Dizzy Gillespie | 1950 | $300 |

DIAL
| ❏ 212 [10] | Modern Trumpets | 1952 | $400 |

DISCOVERY
| ❏ DL-3013 [10] | Dizzy Gillespie Plays, Johnny Richards Conducts | 1950 | $300 |

ELEKTRA/MUSICIAN
| ❏ 60300 | One Night in Washington | 1984 | $25 |

EMARCY
| ❏ EMS-2-410 | Composer's Concepts | 197? | $35 |

EVEREST ARCHIVE OF FOLK & JAZZ
❏ 237	Dizzy Gillespie	1970	$25
❏ 272	Dizzy Gillespie, Volume 2	197?	$25
❏ 301	Dizzy Gillespie, Volume 3	197?	$25
❏ 346	The King of Bop	198?	$25

FANTASY
❏ OJC-447	Afro-Cuban Jazz Moods	1990	$30
❏ OJC-381	Dizzy Gillespie Jam: Montreux '77	1989	$25
❏ OJC-443	Dizzy's Big Four	1990	$25

GATEWAY
| ❏ 7025 | Sweet Soul | 198? | $30 |

GENE NORMAN
| ❏ GNP-23 [M] | Dizzy Gillespie and His Big Band | 1957 | $100 |
| ❏ GNP-4 [10] | Dizzy Gillespie with His Original Big Band | 195? | $250 |

GNP CRESCENDO
❏ GNP-9028	Dizzy!	197?	$25
❏ GNP-23 [M]	Dizzy Gillespie and His Big Band	196?	$25
❏ GNPS-23 [R]	Dizzy Gillespie and His Big Band	196?	$30
❏ GNP-9006	Paris Concert	197?	$25

GRP
| ❏ GR-1012 | New Faces | 198? | $25 |

GWP
| ❏ 2023 | Souled Out | 197? | $35 |

IMPULSE!
| ❏ AS-9149 | Swing Low, Sweet Cadillac! | 1967 | $250 |

INTERMEDIA
| ❏ QS-5033 | Body & Soul Featuring Sarah Vaughan | 198? | $25 |

JAZZ MAN
| ❏ 5017 | The Giant | 198? | $30 |
| ❏ 5021 | The Source | 198? | $30 |

LIMELIGHT
❏ LM-82007 [M]	Jambo Caribe	1964	$25
❏ LS-86007 [S]	Jambo Caribe	1964	$30
❏ LM-82042 [M]	The Melody Lingers On	1967	$25
❏ LS-86042 [S]	The Melody Lingers On	1967	$30
❏ LM-82022 [M]	The New Continent	1965	$25
❏ LS-86022 [S]	The New Continent	1965	$30

MAINSTREAM
| ❏ MRL-325 | Dizzy Gillespie with the Mitchell-Ruff Duo | 1972 | $35 |

MCA
| ❏ 29036 | Swing Low, Sweet Cadillac | 198? | $20 |

MOON
| ❏ MLP-035 | Angel City | 1992 | $35 |

MUSICRAFT
| ❏ MVS-2009 | Groovin' High | 1986 | $25 |
| ❏ MVS-2010 | One Bass Hit | 1986 | $25 |

NORGRAN
❏ MGN-1003 [M]	Afro Dizzy	1954	$400
❏ MGN-1090 [M]	Diz Big Band	1956	$300
❏ MGN-1023 [M]	Dizzy and Strings	1955	$300
❏ MGN-1083 [M]	Jazz Recital	1956	$300
❏ MGN-1084 [M]	World Statesman	1956	$250

PABLO
❏ 2310771	Afro-Cuban Jazz Moods	1976	$30
❏ 2625708	Bahiana	1976	$35
❏ 2310719	Dizzy's Big Four	1975	$30
❏ 2310749	Dizzy's Big Seven: Montreux '75	1976	$30
❏ 2310794	Free Ride	1977	$30
❏ 2310889	In Helsinki: To a Finland Station	198?	$25
❏ 2310784	Party	1977	$30
❏ 2312136	The Alternate Blues	198?	$25
❏ 2310885	The Best of Dizzy Gillespie	198?	$25
❏ 2405411	The Best of Dizzy Gillespie	198?	$25

PABLO LIVE
❏ 2308226	Digital Dizzy at Montreux 1980	1980	$30
❏ 2308211	Dizzy Gillespie Jam: Montreux '77	1977	$30
❏ 2308229	Sumemrtime	1980	$30

PERCEPTION
| ❏ 13 | Portrait of Jenny | 1971 | $35 |
| ❏ 2 | The Real Thing | 197? | $35 |

PHILIPS
❏ PHM200048 [M]	Dizzy at the French Riviera	1962	$25
❏ PHS600048 [S]	Dizzy at the French Riviera	1962	$30
❏ PHM200106 [M]	Dizzy Gillespie and the Double Six of Paris	1963	$150
❏ PHS600106 [S]	Dizzy Gillespie and the Double Six of Paris	1963	$175
❏ PHM200123 [M]	Dizzy Gillespie Goes Hollywood	1964	$25
❏ PHS600123 [S]	Dizzy Gillespie Goes Hollywood	1964	$30
❏ 822897-1	Dizzy Gillespie on the Frence Riviera	1986	$25
❏ PHM200070 [M]	New Wave!	1962	$25
❏ PHS600070 [S]	New Wave!	1962	$30
❏ PHM200091 [M]	Something Old, Something New	1963	$25
❏ PHS600091 [S]	Something Old, Something New	1963	$30
❏ PHM200138 [M]	The Cool World	1964	$150
❏ PHS600138 [S]	The Cool World	1964	$175

PHOENIX
| ❏ 4 | The Big Bands | 197? | $25 |
| ❏ 2 | The Small Groups | 197? | $25 |

PRESTIGE
❏ PRST-7818	Dizzy Gillespie at Salle Plevel '48	1970	$30
❏ 24030	In the Beginning	197?	$35
❏ P-24047	The Giant	1975	$35

Number	Title	Yr	NM

RCA VICTOR
- LJM-1009 [M] — Dizzier and Dizzier — 1954 — $120
- LPV-530 [M] — Dizzy Gillespie — 1966 — $30
- LPM-2398 [M] — The Greatest of Dizzy Gillespie — 1961 — $50

—"Long Play" on label

REGENT
- MG-6043 [M] — School Days — 1957 — $150

REPRISE
- R-6072 [M] — Dateline: Europe — 1963 — $25
- R9-6072 [S] — Dateline: Europe — 1963 — $30

RONDO-LETTE
- A-11 [M] — Dizzy Gillespie — 195? — $30

ROOST
- LP-2214 [M] — Concert in Paris — 1957 — $120
- R-414 [10] — Dizzy Over Paris — 1953 — $300

SAVOY
- MG-12020 [M] — Groovin' High — 1955 — $85
- MG-12047 [M] — The Champ — 1956 — $75
- MG-12110 [M] — The Dizzy Gillespie Story — 1957 — $75

SAVOY JAZZ
- SJL-2209 — Dee Gee Days — 197? — $35
- SJC-402 — The Dizzy Gillespie Story — 1985 — $25

SOLID STATE
- SS-18061 — Cornucopia — 1969 — $25
- SS-18034 — Live at the Village Vanguard — 1968 — $75
- SS-18054 — My Way — 1969 — $25

SUTTON
- SU-287 [M] — Featuring Dizzy Gillespie — 196? — $20
- SSU-287 [S] — Featuring Dizzy Gillespie — 196? — $15

TIMELESS
- LPSJP-250 — Dizzy Gillespie Meets the Phil Woods Quintet — 1990 — $30

TRIP
- 5566 — Something Old, Something New — 197? — $25

VERNON
- 506 [M] — The Everlivin' "Diz — 196? — $35
- 506 [S] — The Everlivin' "Diz — 196? — $30

VERVE
- MGV-8191 [M] — Afro Dizzy — 1957 — $250
- V-8401 [M] — An Electrifying Evening with the Dizzy Gillespie Quintet — 1961 — $25
- V6-8401 [S] — An Electrifying Evening with the Dizzy Gillespie Quintet — 1961 — $30
- UMV-2605 — An Electrifying Evening with the Dizzy Gillespie Quintet — 198? — $25
- V-8423 [M] — Carnegie Hall Concert — 1962 — $25
- V6-8423 [S] — Carnegie Hall Concert — 1962 — $30
- VE-2-2524 — Diz and Roy — 197? — $35
- MGV-8178 [M] — Diz Big Band — 1957 — $150
- V-8178 [M] — Diz Big Band — 1961 — $30
- V-8477 [M] — Dizzy, Rollins & Stitt — 1962 — $25

—Reissue of MGV-8260

- V6-8477 [S] — Dizzy, Rollins & Stitt — 1962 — $30
- V-8560 [M] — Dizzy at Newport — 1964 — $25
- V6-8560 [S] — Dizzy at Newport — 1964 — $30
- MGV-8214 [M] — Dizzy Gillespie and Stuff Smith — 1958 — $175
- V-8214 [M] — Dizzy Gillespie and Stuff Smith — 1961 — $30
- MGV-8242 [M] — Dizzy Gillespie at Newport — 1958 — $175
- V-8242 [M] — Dizzy Gillespie at Newport — 1961 — $30
- MGVS-6023 [S] — Dizzy Gillespie at Newport — 1960 — $150
- V6-8242 [S] — Dizzy Gillespie at Newport — 1961 — $30
- MGV-8017 [M] — Dizzy in Greece — 1957 — $150
- V-8017 [M] — Dizzy in Greece — 1961 — $30
- MGV-8260 [M] — Duets — 1958 — $175

—With Sonny Rollins and Sonny Stitt

- MGV-8394 [M] — Gillespiana — 1960 — $150
- V-8394 [M] — Gillespiana — 1961 — $30
- V6-8394 [S] — Gillespiana — 1961 — $30
- MGV-8352 [M] — Greatest Trumpet of Them All — 1959 — $150
- V6-8352 [S] — Greatest Trumpet of Them All — 1961 — $30
- V-8352 [M] — Greatest Trumpet of Them All — 1961 — $30
- MGVS-6117 [S] — Greatest Trumpet of Them All — 1960 — $150
- MGV-8313 [M] — Have Trumpet, Will Excite — 1959 — $150
- V-8313 [M] — Have Trumpet, Will Excite — 1961 — $30
- MGVS-6047 [S] — Have Trumpet, Will Excite — 1960 — $150
- V6-8313 [S] — Have Trumpet, Will Excite — 1961 — $30
- UMV-2692 — Have Trumpet, Will Excite — 198? — $25
- MGV-8173 [M] — Jazz Recital — 1957 — $175
- V-8173 [M] — Jazz Recital — 1961 — $30
- MGV-8208 [M] — Manteca — 1958 — $120
- V-8208 [M] — Manteca — 1961 — $30
- VSP-7 [M] — Night in Tunisia — 1966 — $35
- VSPS-7 [S] — Night in Tunisia — 1966 — $35
- V-8411 [M] — Perceptions — 1961 — $25
- V6-8411 [S] — Perceptions — 1961 — $30
- MGV-8386 [M] — Portrait of Duke — 1960 — $175
- V-8386 [M] — Portrait of Duke — 1961 — $30
- MGV-8328 [M] — The Ebullient Mr. Gillespie — 1959 — $150
- V6-8328 [S] — The Ebullient Mr. Gillespie — 1961 — $30
- V-8328 [M] — The Ebullient Mr. Gillespie — 1961 — $30
- MGVS-6068 [S] — The Ebullient Mr. Gillespie — 1960 — $150

Number	Title	Yr	NM

- V-8566 [M] — The Essential Dizzy Gillespie — 1964 — $25
- V6-8566 [S] — The Essential Dizzy Gillespie — 1964 — $30
- V6-8830 — The Newport Years — 197? — $30
- 821662-1 — The Reunion Big Band — 198? — $25
- VE-2-2505 — The Sonny Rollins/Sonny Stitt Sessions — 1976 — $35
- MGV-8174 [M] — World Statesman — 1957 — $120
- V-8174 [M] — World Statesman — 1961 — $75

WING
- MGW-12318 [M] — The New Wave! — 1966 — $30
- SRW-16318 [S] — The New Wave! — 1966 — $30

GILLESPIE, DIZZY/JIMMY McPARTLAND

MGM
- E-3286 [M] — Hot vs. Cool — 1955 — $100

GILLETTE, STEVE

REGENCY
- REG-79002 — A Little Warmth — 1979 — $12

GILLEY, MICKEY

ACCORD
- SN-7151 — Suburban Cowboy — 1981 — $12

ASTRO
- 101 [M] — Lonely Wine — 1964 — $300

COLUMBIA SPECIAL PRODUCTS
- P16198 — All My Best — 1982 — $12

EPIC
- PE37595 — Christmas at Gilley's — 1981 — $12

—Some labels have "FE" prefix

- JE36851 — Encore — 1981 — $12
- PE34776 — First Class — 198? — $10

—Budget-line reissue

- FE38583 — Fool for Your Love — 1983 — $12
- PE38583 — Fool for Your Love — 1985 — $10

—Budget-line reissue

- FE40115 — I Feel Good (About Lovin' You) — 1985 — $12
- FE39900 — Live at Gilley's — 1984 — $12
- JE36201 — Mickey Gilley — 1980 — $12
- FE38320 — Mickey Gilley's Biggest Hits — 1982 — $12
- FE38082 — Put Your Dreams Away — 1982 — $12
- PE38082 — Put Your Dreams Away — 198? — $10

—Budget-line reissue

- PE34736 — Room Full of Roses — 198? — $10

—Budget-line reissue

- PE34749 — Smokin' — 198? — $10

—Budget-line reissue

- KE35174 — Songs We Made Love To — 1979 — $12
- KE239867 — Ten Years of Hits — 1984 — $15
- JE36492 — That's All That Matters to Me — 1980 — $12
- PE36492 — That's All That Matters to Me — 198? — $10

—Budget-line reissue

- FE40353 — The One and Only — 1986 — $12
- FE39324 — Too Good to Stop Now — 1983 — $12
- FE37416 — You Don't Know Me — 1981 — $12
- PE37416 — You Don't Know Me — 198? — $10

—Budget-line reissue

- FE39000 — You've Really Got a Hold on Me — 1983 — $12

INTERMEDIA
- QS-5024 — With Love from Pasadena, Texas — 198? — $12

J.M.
- 8127 — Norwegian Wood — 1981 — $15

PAIR
- PDL2-1072 — The Best of Mickey Gilley — 1986 — $15

PAULA
- LP-2195 [M] — Down the Line — 1967 — $40
- LPS-2195 [S] — Down the Line — 1967 — $40
- LPS-2234 — Mickey Gilley — 1978 — $15
- LPS-2224 — Mickey Gilley at His Best — 1974 — $18

PICKWICK
- SPC-6180 — Wild Side of Life — 1975 — $12

PLAYBOY
- PB-403 — City Lights — 1974 — $25
- PZ34776 — First Class — 1977 — $15
- KZ35099 — Flyin' High — 1977 — $15
- KZ34881 — Gilley's Greatest Hits, Vol. 2 — 1977 — $15
- PB-409 — Gilley's Greatest Hits Vol. 1 — 1976 — $18
- PZ34743 — Gilley's Greatest Hits Vol. 1 — 1977 — $12

—Reissue of 409

- PZ34749 — Gilley's Smokin' — 1977 — $15

—Reissue of 415

- PB-415 — Gilley's Smokin' — 1976 — $18
- PB-405 [B] — Mickey's Movin' On — 1975 — $18
- PB-408 — Overnight Sensation — 1976 — $18
- PZ34742 — Overnight Sensation — 1977 — $12

—Reissue of 408

- PB-128 — Room Full of Roses — 1974 — $25
- PZ34736 — Room Full of Roses — 1977 — $12

—Reissue of 128

Number	Title	Yr	NM

GILMER, JULIA ANN

ABC-PARAMOUNT
- ABC-168 [M] — Cads, Blackguards and False True-Loves — 1956 — $30

GILMORE, JIMMIE DALE

HIGHTONE
- HT-8011 — Fair and Square — 1988 — $12
- HT-8018 — Jimmie Dale Gilmore — 1989 — $12

GILSTRAP, JIM

ROXBURY
- 105 — Love Talk — 1976 — $12
- 102 — Swing Your Daddy — 1975 — $12

GIN BLOSSOMS

A&M
- 7502153691 [EP] — Up and Crumbling — 1991 — $18

SAN JACINTO
- DRAM 019 — Dusted — 1989 — $25

—With picture insert and biographical material

GINGOLD, HERMIONE

DOLPHIN
- D-7 [M] — La Gingold — 195? — $18

DRG
- MRS-902 — La Gingold — 197? — $12

GINNY AND THE GALLIONS

DOWNEY
- D-1003 [M] — Two Sides of Ginny and the Gallions — 1964 — $30
- DS-1003 [S] — Two Sides of Ginny and the Gallions — 1964 — $40

GINSBERG, ALLEN

ATLANTIC
- 4001 [M] — Allen Ginsburg Reads Kaddish — 1966 — $75

FANTASY
- F-7006 [M] — Howl and Other Poems — 1959 — $500

—Red vinyl

- F-7006 [M] — Howl and Other Poems — 1959 — $300

—Black non-flexible vinyl

GIOVANNI, NIKKI

NIKTOM
- NK4200 — Like a Ripple on a Pond — 1973 — $12
- NK4201 — The Way I Feel — 1975 — $12

RIGHT-ON
- 5001 — Truth Is On Its Way — 1971 — $12

GIRARD, GEORGE

VIK
- LX-1058 [M] — Jam Session on Bourbon Street — 1957 — $40
- LX-1063 [M] — Stompin' at the Famous Door — 1957 — $40

GIRLS NEXT DOOR

MTM
- D1-71071 — Love and Other Fairy Tales — 1988 — $0

—Canceled?

- ST-71053 — The Girls Next Door — 1986 — $12
- ST-71062 — What a Girl Next Door Could Do — 1987 — $12

GISMONTI, EGBERTO, AND NANA VASCONCELOS

ECM
- 25015 — Duas Vozes — 1985 — $25

GISMONTI, EGBERTO

ECM
- 1089 — Danca Das Cabecas — 1976 — $30
- 1203 — Sanfona — 1981 — $35
- 1116 — Sol Do Meio Dia — 1978 — $30
- 1136 — Solo — 1979 — $25

GITS, THE

BROKEN REKIDS
- SKIP44 [B] — Kings & Queens — 1995 — $30
- SKIP87 — Seafish Louisville — 2000 — $18

C/Z
- 051 [B] — Frenching the Bully — 1992 — $40

—Originals on red vinyl

GIUFFRE, JIMMY, AND MARTY PAICH

GNP CRESCENDO
- GNPS-9040 — Tenors West — 197? — $30

GIUFFRE, JIMMY

ATLANTIC
- 1295 [M] — Four Brothers Sound — 1959 — $300

Number	Title	Yr	NM
—Black label			
❑ 1295 [M]	Four Brothers Sound	1960	$300
—Multicolor label, white "fan" logo at right			
❑ SD1295 [S]	Four Brothers Sound	1959	$300
—Green label			
❑ SD1295 [S]	Four Brothers Sound	1960	$300
—Multicolor label, white "fan" logo at right			
❑ 90144	Jimmy Giuffre Clarinet	198?	$25
❑ 1276 [M]	Music Man	1958	$300
—Black label			
❑ 1276 [M]	Music Man	1960	$300
—Multicolor label, white "fan" logo at right			
❑ 1276 [M]	Music Man	1963	$35
—Multicolor label, black "fan" logo at right			
❑ SD1276 [S]	Music Man	1959	$300
—Green label			
❑ SD1276 [S]	Music Man	1960	$300
—Multicolor label, white "fan" logo at right			
❑ SD1276 [S]	Music Man	1963	$35
—Multicolor label, black "fan" logo at right			
❑ 1238 [M]	The Jimmy Giuffre Clarinet	1956	$300
—Black label			
❑ 1238 [M]	The Jimmy Giuffre Clarinet	1960	$300
—Multicolor label, white "fan" logo at right			
❑ 1238 [M]	The Jimmy Giuffre Clarinet	1963	$50
—Multicolor label, black "fan" logo at right			
❑ 1254 [M]	The Jimmy Giuffre Three	1957	$300
—Black label			
❑ 1254 [M]	The Jimmy Giuffre Three	1960	$300
—Multicolor label, white "fan" logo at right			

Number	Title	Yr	NM
❑ 1254 [M]	The Jimmy Giuffre Three	1963	$50
—Multicolor label, black "fan" logo at right			
❑ 1282 [M]	Trav'lin' Light	1958	$300
—Black label			
❑ 1282 [M]	Trav'lin' Light	1960	$300
—Multicolor label, white "fan" logo at right			
❑ 1282 [M]	Trav'lin' Light	1963	$35
—Multicolor label, black "fan" logo at right			
❑ SD1282 [S]	Trav'lin' Light	1959	$300
—Green label			
❑ SD1282 [S]	Trav'lin' Light	1960	$300
—Multicolor label, white "fan" logo at right			
❑ SD1282 [S]	Trav'lin' Light	1963	$35
—Multicolor label, black "fan" logo at right			
❑ 1330 [M]	Western Suite	1960	$50
—Multicolor label, white "fan" logo at right			
❑ 1330 [M]	Western Suite	1963	$35
—Multicolor label, black "fan" logo at right			
❑ SD1330 [S]	Western Suite	1960	$50
—Multicolor label, white "fan" logo at right			
❑ SD1330 [S]	Western Suite	1963	$35
—Multicolor label, black "fan" logo at right			

CAPITOL
❑ H549 [10]	Jimmy Giuffre	1954	$300
❑ T549 [M]	Jimmy Giuffre	1955	$250
❑ T634 [M]	Tangents in Jazz	1955	$250

CHOICE
❑ 1001	Music for People, Birds, Butterflies and Mosquitos	1974	$50
❑ 1011	River Chant	1975	$50

COLUMBIA
❑ CL1964 [M]	Free Fall	1963	$35
❑ CS8764 [S]	Free Fall	1963	$25

IAI
❑ 373859	Jimmy Giuffre at the IAI Festival	1978	$30

MOSAIC
❑ MQ10-176	The Complete Capitol & Atlantic Recordings of Jimmy Giuffre	1998	$300
—Limited edition of 5,000			

SOUL NOTE
Number	Title	Yr	NM
❑ SN-1058	Dragonfly	1983	$35
❑ 121058	Dragonfly	199?	$30
❑ 121158	Liquid Dancers	1991	$35
❑ SN-1108	Quasar	1986	$50
❑ 121108	Quasar	199?	$30

VERVE
❑ MGV-8361 [M]	Ad Lib	1960	$175
❑ V-8361 [M]	Ad Lib	1961	$75
❑ MGVS-6130 [S]	Ad Lib	1960	$175
❑ V6-8361 [S]	Ad Lib	1961	$75
❑ MGV-8397 [M]	Fusion	1961	$40
❑ V-8397 [M]	Fusion	1961	$25
❑ V6-8397 [S]	Fusion	1961	$30
❑ MGV-8395 [M]	Piece for Clarinet and String Orchestra	1961	$40
❑ V-8395 [M]	Piece for Clarinet and String Orchestra	1961	$25
❑ V6-8395 [S]	Piece for Clarinet and String Orchestra	1961	$30
❑ MGV-8307 [M]	Seven Pieces	1959	$150
❑ V-8307 [M]	Seven Pieces	1961	$25
❑ MGVS-6039 [S]	Seven Pieces	1960	$150
❑ V6-8307 [S]	Seven Pieces	1961	$35
❑ MGV-8337 [M]	The Easy Way	1960	$150
❑ V-8337 [M]	The Easy Way	1961	$25
❑ MGVS-6095 [S]	The Easy Way	1960	$150
❑ V6-8337 [S]	The Easy Way	1961	$35
❑ MGV-8387 [M]	The Jimmy Giuffre Quartet In Person	1961	$40
❑ V-8387 [M]	The Jimmy Giuffre Quartet In Person	1961	$25
❑ V6-8387 [S]	The Jimmy Giuffre Quartet In Person	1961	$30
❑ MGV-8402 [M]	Thesis	1961	$40
❑ V-8402 [M]	Thesis	1961	$25
❑ V6-8402 [S]	Thesis	1961	$30

GLACIERS, THE
MERCURY
❑ MG-20895 [M]	From Sea to Ski	1964	$50
❑ SR-60895 [S]	From Sea to Ski	1964	$75

GLAD, THE
ABC
❑ S-655	Feelin' Glad	1969	$30

GLADSTONE
ABC
❑ ABCX-751	From Down Home in Tyler, Texas, U.S.A.	1972	$15
❑ ABCX-778	Lookin' for a Smile	1973	$15

GLAHE, WILL
LONDON
❑ LL1710 [M]	Beer Garden Music	195?	$25
❑ LL3021 [M]	Beer Garden Musik	195?	$18
❑ LB311 [10]	Beer Garden Rhythms	195?	$30
❑ PS344 [S]	Big Polka Band Hits	196?	$18
❑ LL3344 [M]	Big Polka Band Hits	196?	$15
❑ TW91225 [M]	Cafe International	195?	$18
❑ PS146 [S]	Christmas Greetings from Germany	195?	$25
❑ TW91223 [M]	Christmas Greetings from Germany	195?	$18
❑ SW99009 [S]	German Sing-a-Long	195?	$18
❑ LL3397 [M]	Happy Days Are Here Again	196?	$18
❑ PS397 [S]	Happy Days Are Here Again	196?	$18
❑ SW99419 [S]	More German Sing-a-Long	196?	$15
❑ LL3099 [M]	Old Heidelberg	196?	$18
❑ PS150 [S]	Old Heidelberg	196?	$18
❑ TW91227 [M]	Old Heidelberg	196?	$15
❑ SW99227 [S]	Old Heidelberg	196?	$15
❑ LL3046 [M]	The Polka King	195?	$18

LONDON PHASE 4
❑ SP-44257	Bavarian Merry-Go-Round	1976	$18
❑ SP-44069	New Beer Barrel Polka	196?	$18
❑ SP-44145	Oktoberfest!	1970	$18
❑ SP-44122	Strictly Oompah	1969	$18
❑ SP-44224	The Polka King, Volume 1	197?	$18
❑ SP-44226	The Polka King, Volume 2	197?	$18

RICHMOND
❑ B20016 [M]	Polka Hits	196?	$15

GLASEL, JOHN
ABC-PARAMOUNT
❑ ABC-165 [M]	Jazz Session	1957	$50

GOLDEN CREST
❑ 1002 [M]	Jazz Unlimited	1960	$30

GLASER, JIM
MCA
❑ 5723	Everybody Knows I'm Yours	1986	$10
❑ 5612	Past the Point of No Return	1985	$10

NOBLE VISION
❑ 2001	The Man in the Mirror	1983	$12

STARDAY
❑ SLP-158 [M]	Just Looking for a Home	1961	$75
❑ SLP-149 [M]	Old Time Christmas Singing	1960	$80

GLASER, TOMPALL
ABC
Number	Title	Yr	NM
❑ AB-1036	The Wonder of It All	1977	$12
❑ AB-978	Tompall Glaser and His Outlaw Band	1977	$12

MGM
❑ M3G-5014	The Great Tompall and His Outlaw Band	1976	$15
❑ M3G-4977	Tompall	1974	$15

GLASS, PHILIP
ANTILLES
❑ 906261 [B]	Koyaanisqatsi	1983	$15

CBS
❑ FM39539 [B]	DancePieces	1987	$30
❑ PM37265 [B]	Glassworks	1982	$15
❑ I3M39672 [B]	Satyagraha	1985	$50
❑ FM45576 [B]	Solo Piano	1989	$250
❑ FM39564 [B]	Songs From Liquid Days	15.00	$
❑ FM45580 [B]	Songs From The Trilogy	1989	$20
❑ FM37849 [B]	The Photographer	1983	$15

CHATHAM SQUARE PRODUCTIONS
❑ LP1003 [B]	Music In Similar Motion / Music In Fifths	1973	$75
❑ LP1001/2 [B]	Music With Changing Parts	1971	$125

ELEKTRA/NONESUCH
❑ 791921 [B]	Powaqqatsi	1988	$25

NONESUCH
❑ 9791131F [B]	Mishima	1985	$20
❑ 9792091 [B]	The Thin Blue Line	1988	$15

ORANGE MOUNTAIN MUSIC
❑ OMM8001 [B]	How Now / Strung Out	2014	$30

TOMATO
❑ TOM8029 [B]	Dance Nos. 1 And 3	1980	$40

VIRGIN
❑ 7910651 [B]	1000 Airplanes On The Roof	1989	$20
❑ 910131 [B]	North Star	1988	$25
❑ PZ34669 [B]	North Star	1977	$20

GLASS, PHILIP AND WILSON, ROBERT
TOMATO
❑ TOM 42901 [B]	Einstein On The Beach	1979	$100

GLASS BOTTLE, THE
AVCO
❑ 33012	The Glass Bottle	1971	$18

GLASS HARP
DECCA
❑ DL75261	Glass Harp	1971	$30
❑ DL75358	It Makes Me Glad	1972	$30
❑ DL75306	Synergy	1971	$30

MCA
❑ 293	Glass Harp	1974	$12
—Reissue of Decca 75261			

GLASS HOUSE, THE
INVICTUS
❑ ST-7305	Inside the Glass House	1971	$15
❑ ST-9810	Thanks I Needed That	1972	$15

GLASS PRISM, THE
RCA VICTOR
❑ LSP-4270 [B]	On Joy and Sorrow	1970	$18
❑ LSP-4201 [B]	Poe Through the Glass Prism	1969	$18

GLASS TIGER
EMI MANHATTAN
❑ E1-48684	Diamond Sun	1988	$12

Number	Title	Yr	NM

MANHATTAN

Number	Title	Yr	NM
❏ ST-53034	The Thin Red Line	1986	$12

GLAZER, TOM

KAPP

| ❏ KL1331 [M] | On Top of Spaghetti | 1963 | $15 |
| ❏ KS3331 [S] | On Top of Spaghetti | 1963 | $18 |

UNITED ARTISTS

| ❏ UAL3540 [M] | Tom Glazer Sings the Ballad of Namu the Killer Whale and Other Ballads of Adventure | 1966 | $30 |
| ❏ UAS6540 [S] | Tom Glazer Sings the Ballad of Namu the Killer Whale and Other Ballads of Adventure | 1966 | $30 |

WASHINGTON

| ❏ WC-301 [M] | The Tom Glazer Concert For and With Children | 1959 | $30 |

GLEASON, JACKIE

CAPITOL

❏ STBB-346	All I Want for Christmas	1969	$18
❏ WBO1619 [M]	A Lover's Portfolio	1962	$25
❏ SWBO1619 [S]	A Lover's Portfolio	1962	$30
❏ W1979 [M]	A Lover's Portfolio, Vol. 1 (Music for Sippin' and Dancin')	1963	$15
❏ SW1979 [S]	A Lover's Portfolio, Vol. 1 (Music for Sippin' and Dancin')	1963	$18
❏ W1980 [M]	A Lover's Portfolio, Vol. 2 (Music for Listenin' and Lovin')	1963	$15
❏ SW1980 [S]	A Lover's Portfolio, Vol. 2 (Music for Listenin' and Lovin')	1963	$18
❏ H511 [10]	And Awaaay We Go!	1954	$100
❏ W511 [M]	And Awaaay We Go!	1955	$40
❏ W1250 [M]	Aphrodisia	1960	$25
❏ SW1250 [S]	Aphrodisia	1960	$30
❏ W2684 [M]	A Taste of Brass For Lovers Only	1967	$15
❏ SW2684 [S]	A Taste of Brass For Lovers Only	1967	$18
❏ W1830 [M]	Champagne, Candlelight & Kisses	1963	$15
❏ SW1830 [S]	Champagne, Candlelight & Kisses	1963	$18
❏ SWBB-256	Close-Up	1969	$18

— Reissue of Capitol DW 352 and DW 509 in one package

❏ ST-480	Come Saturday Morning	1970	$15
❏ SW2880	Doublin' in Brass	1968	$18
❏ W2582 [M]	How Sweet It Is For Lovers Only	1966	$15
❏ SW2582 [S]	How Sweet It Is For Lovers Only	1966	$18
❏ SW-106	Irving Berlin's Music	1968	$15
❏ W568 [M]	Jackie Gleason Plays Romantic Jazz	1955	$30
❏ W905 [M]	Jackie Gleason Presents "Oooo!	1957	$30
❏ SW905 [S]	Jackie Gleason Presents "Oooo!	1959	$30

— We haven't confirmed if this is in true stereo or not.

❏ W2144 [M]	Last Dance For Lovers Only	1964	$15
❏ SW2144 [S]	Last Dance For Lovers Only	1964	$18
❏ W1439 [M]	Lazy Lively Love	1961	$25
❏ SW1439 [S]	Lazy Lively Love	1961	$30
❏ H627 [10]	Lonesome Echo	1955	$30
❏ W627 [M]	Lonesome Echo	1955	$30
❏ DW627 [R]	Lonesome Echo	196?	$12
❏ W1689 [M]	Love, Embers and Flame	1962	$18
❏ SW1689 [S]	Love, Embers and Flame	1962	$25
❏ H366 [10]	Lover's Rhapsody	1953	$30
❏ W758 [M]	Merry Christmas	1956	$30
❏ DW758 [R]	Merry Christmas	196?	$12
❏ W1877 [M]	Movie Themes -- For Lovers Only	1963	$15
❏ SW1877 [S]	Movie Themes -- For Lovers Only	1963	$18
❏ W509 [M]	Music, Martini and Memories	1954	$30
❏ SW509 [S]	Music, Martini and Memories	196?	$18

— Re-recorded for stereo

| ❏ SM-509 | Music, Martini and Memories | 197? | $12 |

— Reissue

❏ H1-509 [10]	Music, Martini and Memories Part 1	1954	$30
❏ H2-509 [10]	Music, Martini and Memories Part 2	1954	$30
❏ W2471 [M]	Music Around the World -- For Lovers Only	1966	$15
❏ SW2471 [S]	Music Around the World -- For Lovers Only	1966	$18
❏ H352 [10]	Music for Lovers Only	1952	$30
❏ W352 [M]	Music for Lovers Only	1953	$30
❏ SW352 [S]	Music for Lovers Only	1963	$12

— Re-recorded version; black rainbow label, Capitol logo at top

| ❏ SM-352 | Music for Lovers Only | 197? | $12 |

— Reissue

| ❏ SW352 [S] | Music for Lovers Only | 1959 | $18 |

— Re-recorded version of W 352; black rainbow label, Capitol logo at left

Number	Title	Yr	NM
❏ WAO475 [M]	Music for Lovers Only/Music to Make You Misty	1954	$40
❏ W816 [M]	Music for the Love Hours	1957	$30
❏ DW816 [R]	Music for the Love Hours	196?	$12
❏ W632 [M]	Music to Change Her Mind	1956	$30
❏ DW632 [R]	Music to Change Her Mind	196?	$12
❏ H455 [10]	Music to Make You Misty	1954	$30
❏ W455 [M]	Music to Make You Misty	1954	$30
❏ DW455 [R]	Music to Make You Misty	196?	$12
❏ SM-455	Music to Make You Misty	197?	$12

— Reissue

❏ W570 [M]	Music to Remember Her	1955	$30
❏ DW570 [R]	Music to Remember Her	196?	$12
❏ W717 [M]	Night Winds	1956	$30
❏ DW717 [R]	Night Winds	196?	$12
❏ W1315 [M]	Opiate D'Amour	1960	$18
❏ SW1315 [S]	Opiate D'Amour	1960	$25
❏ W1075 [M]	Rebound	1959	$25
❏ SW1075 [S]	Rebound	1959	$30
❏ W1020 [M]	Riff Jazz	1958	$50
❏ SW1020 [S]	Riff Jazz	1959	$75
❏ ST-398	Romeo and Juliet	1970	$15
❏ W2409 [M]	Silk 'N' Brass	1966	$15
❏ SW2409 [S]	Silk 'N' Brass	1966	$18
❏ L471 [10]	Tawny	1954	$30
❏ W471 [M]	Tawny	1954	$30
❏ STBB-510	Tenderly/Laura	1971	$18
❏ W1147 [M]	That Moment	1959	$25
❏ SW1147 [S]	That Moment	1959	$30
❏ W2796 [M]	The Best of Jackie Gleason	1967	$18
❏ SW2796 [S]	The Best of Jackie Gleason	1967	$18
❏ SM-2796	The Best of Jackie Gleason	197?	$12

— Reissue

❏ SKAO-146	The Best of Jackie Gleason (Vol. 2)	1968	$15
❏ W1519 [M]	The Gentle Touch	1961	$25
❏ SW1519 [S]	The Gentle Touch	1961	$30
❏ TCL2816 [M]	The Jackie Gleason Deluxe Set	1968	$30
❏ STCL2816 [S]	The Jackie Gleason Deluxe Set	1968	$30

— Reissue of three complete LPs (titles unknown)

❏ SW2935	The Now Sound ... For Today's Lovers	1968	$18
❏ W961 [M]	The Torch with Blue Flame	1958	$25
❏ SW961 [S]	The Torch with Blue Flame	1959	$30
❏ ST2791 [S]	'Tis the Season	1967	$18
❏ T2791 [M]	'Tis the Season	1967	$25
❏ W1978 [M]	Today's Romantic Hits/For Lovers Only	1963	$15
❏ SW1978 [S]	Today's Romantic Hits/For Lovers Only	1963	$18
❏ W2056 [M]	Today's Romantic Hits/For Lovers Only, Vol. 2	1964	$15
❏ SW2056 [S]	Today's Romantic Hits/For Lovers Only, Vol. 2	1964	$18
❏ SQBO91546	Velvet & Gold: For Lovers Only	196?	$25

— Capitol Record Club exclusive

| ❏ W859 [M] | Velvet Brass | 1957 | $30 |
| ❏ SW859 [S] | Velvet Brass | 1959 | $30 |

— We haven't confirmed if this is in true stereo or not.

| ❏ SM-859 | Velvet Brass | 197? | $12 |

— Reissue

| ❏ ST-693 | Words of Love | 1971 | $15 |

PAIR

| ❏ PDL2-1069 | Lush Moods | 1986 | $15 |

PICKWICK

❏ SPC-3064	Plays Pretty for the People	196?	$12
❏ SPC-2004	Romantic Moods	197?	$12
❏ SPC-3218	Shangri-La	197?	$12
❏ SPC-2029	The More I See You	197?	$12
❏ SPC-1008	White Christmas	197?	$12

— Abridged version of Capitol ST 2791

GLENN, DARRELL

NRC

| ❏ LPA-5 [M] | Crying in the Chapel | 1959 | $30 |
| ❏ SLPA-5 [S] | Crying in the Chapel | 1959 | $30 |

GLENN, LLOYD

ALADDIN

| ❏ LP-808 [M] | Chica-Boo | 1956 | $2000 |

— Red vinyl; VG value 1000; VG+ value 1500

| ❏ LP-808 [M] | Chica-Boo | 1956 | $1000 |

— Black vinyl

BLACK & BLUE

| ❏ 33077 | Old Time Shuffle | 1977 | $15 |

IMPERIAL

❏ LP-9175 [M]	After Hours	1962	$175
❏ LP-12175 [S]	After Hours	1962	$250
❏ LP-9174 [M]	Chica-Boo	1962	$175
❏ LP-12174 [S]	Chica-Boo	1962	$250

SCORE

| ❏ SLP-4020 [M] | After Hours | 1958 | $1000 |
| ❏ SLP-4006 [M] | Lloyd Glenn | 1957 | $1000 |

SWING TIME

| ❏ 1901 [10] | Lloyd Glenn Presents All Time Favorites | 1954 | $3000 |

— VG value 1500; VG+ value 2250

Number	Title	Yr	NM

GLENN, ROGER

FANTASY

| ❏ F-9516 | Reachin' | 197? | $30 |

GLENN, TYREE

ROULETTE

❏ R-25115 [M]	Let's Have a Ball	1960	$30
❏ SR-25115 [S]	Let's Have a Ball	1960	$30
❏ R-25184 [M]	The Trombone Artistry of Tyree Glenn	1962	$25
❏ SR-25184 [S]	The Trombone Artistry of Tyree Glenn	1962	$30
❏ R-25075 [M]	Try a Little Tenderness	1959	$40
❏ SR-25075 [S]	Try a Little Tenderness	1959	$30
❏ R-25138 [M]	Tyree Glenn at London House in Chicago	1961	$25
❏ SR-25138 [S]	Tyree Glenn at London House in Chicago	1961	$30
❏ R-25009 [M]	Tyree Glenn at the Embers	1957	$40
❏ R-25050 [M]	Tyree Glenn at the Roundtable	1959	$40
❏ SR-25050 [S]	Tyree Glenn at the Roundtable	1959	$30

GLITTER, GARY

BELL

| ❏ 6082 | Gary Glitter | 1973 | $18 |
| ❏ 1108 [B] | Glitter | 1972 | $25 |

EPIC

| ❏ PE39299 | The Leader | 1984 | $18 |

EPIC/NU-DISK

| ❏ 3E36848 [10] | Glitter & Gold | 1981 | $18 |

GLITTERHOUSE

DYNOVOICE

| ❏ 31905 | Color Bland | 1968 | $25 |

GLOBETROTTERS, THE

KIRSHNER

| ❏ KES-108 | The Globetrotters | 1970 | $25 |

GLORY (1)

AVALANCHE

| ❏ AV-LA148-F | Glory | 1973 | $18 |

GLORY (2)

TEXAS REVOLUTION

| ❏ CFS-2531 | A Meat Music Sampler | 1969 | $150 |

GO-GO'S, THE

RCA VICTOR

| ❏ LPM-2930 [M] | Swim with the Go-Go's | 1964 | $30 |
| ❏ LSP-2930 [S] | Swim with the Go-Go's | 1964 | $30 |

GO-GO'S

I.R.S.

| ❏ SP70021 | Beauty and the Beat | 1981 | $15 |

— First pressings with peach-colored cover and light label

| ❏ SP70021 | Beauty and the Beat | 1981 | $10 |

— Second pressings with dark blue cover and darker label

| ❏ R151667 | Talk Show | 1984 | $12 |

— RCA Music Service edition

| ❏ SP70041 | Talk Show | 1984 | $10 |
| ❏ SP70031 | Vacation | 1982 | $10 |

GO WEST

CHRYSALIS

❏ BFV41550	Dancing on the Couch	1987	$12
❏ BFV41495	Go West	1985	$15
❏ FV41495	Go West	1987	$10

— Reissue with new prefix

GODCHAUX, KEITH AND DONNA

See KEITH AND DONNA.

GODFREY, ARTHUR

RCA CAMDEN

| ❏ CAS-1092 [S] | All I Want for Christmas Is My Two Front Teeth | 1967 | $0 |

GODLEY AND CREME

MERCURY

| ❏ SRM-31700 [B] | Consequences | 1977 | $75 |

— with booklet. LP credit to Lol Creme/Kevin Godley

MIRAGE

| ❏ WTG19341 | Snack Attack | 1981 | $15 |

POLYDOR

❏ PD-1-6257	Freeze Frame	1979	$15
❏ 835348-1	Goodbye Blue Sky	1988	$12
❏ PD-1-6177	L	1978	$15
❏ 825981-1 [B]	The History Mix Volume 1	1985	$15

GODZ, THE
ESP-DISK'

Number	Title	Yr	NM
❑ 1037 [M]	Contact High with the Godz	1967	$175
❑ S-1037 [S]	Contact High with the Godz	1967	$150
❑ 1047	Godz 2	1968	$150
❑ 2017	Godzundheit	1970	$150
❑ 1077	Third Testament	1969	$150

GOGGLES, THE
AUDIO FIDELITY

Number	Title	Yr	NM
❑ AFSD-6244	The Goggles	1971	$18

GOLD, ANDREW
ASYLUM

Number	Title	Yr	NM
❑ 6E-116 [B]	All This and Heaven Too	1978	$15
❑ 7E-1047 [B]	Andrew Gold	1975	$15
❑ 7E-1086 [B]	What's Wrong with This Picture?	1977	$15
❑ 6E-264 [B]	Whirlwind	1979	$15

GOLD, MARTY
KAPP

Number	Title	Yr	NM
❑ KL-1125 [M]	By the Waters of the Minnetonka	1959	$18

PICKWICK

Number	Title	Yr	NM
❑ ACL-9003	Songs from "How the Grinch Stole Christmas" and Other Children's Christmas Songs	197?	$10

RCA VICTOR

Number	Title	Yr	NM
❑ LSP-2290 [S]	It's Magic	1961	$18
❑ LPM-2290 [M]	It's Magic	1961	$15
❑ LSP-3599 [S]	Soundaroundus	1966	$15
❑ LPM-2620 [M]	Soundpower!	1963	$15
❑ LSP-2620 [S]	Soundpower!	1963	$18
❑ LSP-2381 [S]	Stereo Action Goes Hollywood	1962	$15

VIK

Number	Title	Yr	NM
❑ LX-1069 [M]	Organized for Hi-Fi	1957	$18

GOLD, SANFORD
PRESTIGE

Number	Title	Yr	NM
❑ PRLP-7019 [M]	Piano d'Or	1956	$300

GOLDBERG, BARRY
ATCO

Number	Title	Yr	NM
❑ SD7040	Barry Goldberg	1974	$15

BUDDAH

Number	Title	Yr	NM
❑ BDS-5081	Blast from My Past	1974	$18
❑ BDS-5051	Street Man	1970	$18
❑ BDM-1012 [M]	The Barry Goldberg Reunion	1968	$50

— White-label promo in stereo cover with "mono" sticker

Number	Title	Yr	NM
❑ BDS-5012 [S]	The Barry Goldberg Reunion	1968	$30
❑ BDS-5029	Two Jews Blues	1969	$30

EPIC

Number	Title	Yr	NM
❑ LN24199 [M]	Blowing My Mind	1966	$30
❑ BN26199 [S]	Blowing My Mind	1966	$40

RECORD MAN

Number	Title	Yr	NM
❑ CR5015	Barry Goldberg and Friends	1972	$18

GOLDBERG, STU
PAUSA

Number	Title	Yr	NM
❑ 7123	Eye of the Beholder	1981	$25
❑ 7036	Solos, Duos, Trio	1978	$25
❑ 7095	Variations by Goldberg	1980	$25

GOLDDIGGERS, THE
METROMEDIA

Number	Title	Yr	NM
❑ MD1009	The Golddiggers	1969	$15
❑ MD1012	We Need a Little Christmas	1969	$18

RCA VICTOR

Number	Title	Yr	NM
❑ LSP-4643	The Golddiggers Today!	1972	$15

GOLDEBRIARS, THE
EPIC

Number	Title	Yr	NM
❑ LN24114 [M]	Straight Ahead	1964	$18
❑ BN26114 [S]	Straight Ahead	1964	$25
❑ LN24087 [M]	The Goldebriars	1964	$18
❑ BN26087 [S]	The Goldebriars	1964	$25

GOLDEN, WILLIAM LEE
MCA

Number	Title	Yr	NM
❑ 5749	American Vagabond	1986	$10

GOLDEN AGE JAZZ BAND
ARHOOLIE

Number	Title	Yr	NM
❑ 4007	Golden Age Jazz Band	197?	$35

GOLDEN DAWN
INTERNATIONAL ARTISTS

Number	Title	Yr	NM
❑ 4	Power Plant	1968	$300
❑ 4	Power Plant	1979	$18

— Reissue with "Masterfonics" in trail-off wax

GOLDEN EARRING
21 RECORDS

Number	Title	Yr	NM
❑ T1-1-9004	Cut	1982	$12
❑ 817585-1	Cut	1985	$10

— Reissue

Number	Title	Yr	NM
❑ T1-1-9008	N.E.W.S.	1984	$12
❑ 823717-1 [B]	Something Heavy Going Down -- Live from the Twilight Zone	1984	$18
❑ 90514	The Hole	1986	$12

ATLANTIC

Number	Title	Yr	NM
❑ SD8244 [B]	Eight Miles High	1970	$40

CAPITOL

Number	Title	Yr	NM
❑ ST-164 [B]	Miracle Mirror	1969	$75
❑ ST-11315	The Golden Earring	1974	$15
❑ T2823 [M]	Winter Harvest	1967	$300
❑ ST2823 [S]	Winter Harvest	1967	$175

DWARF

Number	Title	Yr	NM
❑ 2000 [B]	Golden Earring	1971	$40

MCA

Number	Title	Yr	NM
❑ 8009	Golden Earring Live!	1977	$18
❑ 6004	Golden Earring Live!	198?	$12

— Reissue of 8009

Number	Title	Yr	NM
❑ 3057	Grab It For a Second	1978	$15
❑ 703	Grab It For a Second	198?	$10

— Reissue of 3057

Number	Title	Yr	NM
❑ 2254	Mad Love	1977	$15
❑ 2352	Moontan	1978	$12

— Reissue of Track 396

Number	Title	Yr	NM
❑ 37172	Moontan	198?	$10

— Reissue of 2352

Number	Title	Yr	NM
❑ 2139 [B]	Switch	197?	$12

— Reissue of Track 2139

Number	Title	Yr	NM
❑ 827	Switch	198?	$10

— Reissue of 2139

Number	Title	Yr	NM
❑ 2183	To the Hilt	1976	$15

POLYDOR

Number	Title	Yr	NM
❑ PD-1-6303	Long Blond Animal	1980	$15
❑ PD-1-6223	No Promises...No Debts	1979	$15

TRACK

Number	Title	Yr	NM
❑ 396 [B]	Moontan	1974	$30

— Original cover with nude dancer

Number	Title	Yr	NM
❑ 396	Moontan	1974	$18

— Reissue cover with close-up of earring in ear

Number	Title	Yr	NM
❑ 2139 [B]	Switch	1975	$25

GOLDEN GATE QUARTET, THE
COLUMBIA

Number	Title	Yr	NM
❑ CL6102 [10]	Golden Gate Spirituals	1950	$175

HARMONY

Number	Title	Yr	NM
❑ HL7018 [M]	The Golden Chariot	1957	$100

— Original pressing has maroon labels

Number	Title	Yr	NM
❑ HL7018 [M]	The Golden Chariot	195?	$30

— Second pressing has black labels

MERCURY

Number	Title	Yr	NM
❑ MG-25063 [10]	Spirituals	1951	$175

RCA CAMDEN

Number	Title	Yr	NM
❑ CAL-308 [M]	The Golden Gate Quartet	1956	$100

GOLDEN STATE JAZZ BAND
STOMP OFF

Number	Title	Yr	NM
❑ SOS-1006	Alive and At Bay	1983	$25

GOLDEN STRINGS
SOUND 80

Number	Title	Yr	NM
❑ S80-173-1812S	Holiday Request Album	1974	$12

— Jacket has Side 1 and Side 2 reversed; this is as they appear on the record

GOLDENROD
CHARTMAKER

Number	Title	Yr	NM
❑ CSG-1101	Goldenrod	1968	$400

GOLDIE, DON
ARGO

Number	Title	Yr	NM
❑ LP-4010 [M]	Brilliant!	1961	$30
❑ LPS-4010 [S]	Brilliant!	1961	$30
❑ LP-708 [M]	Trumpet Caliente	1963	$30
❑ LPS-708 [S]	Trumpet Caliente	1963	$30

JAZZOLOGY

Number	Title	Yr	NM
❑ J-135	Don Goldie's Jazz Express	1986	$25

VERVE

Number	Title	Yr	NM
❑ V-8475 [M]	Trumpet Exodus	1962	$30
❑ V6-8475 [S]	Trumpet Exodus	1962	$30

GOLDKETTE, JEAN
X

Number	Title	Yr	NM
❑ LVA-3017 [10]	Jean Goldkette and His Orchestra Featuring Bix Beiderbecke	1954	$75

GOLDSBORO, BOBBY
CURB

Number	Title	Yr	NM
❑ JZ36822	Bobby Goldsboro	1980	$15
❑ FZ37734	Round-Up Saloon	1982	$12

EPIC

Number	Title	Yr	NM
❑ PE34703	Goldsboro	1977	$15

LIBERTY

Number	Title	Yr	NM
❑ LN-10007	Bobby Goldsboro's 10th Anniversary Album, Volume 1	1981	$10
❑ LN-10047	Bobby Goldsboro's 10th Anniversary Album, Volume 2	1981	$10
❑ LMAS-5502	Bobby Goldsboro's Greatest Hits	1981	$10

— Reissue of United Artists 5502

Number	Title	Yr	NM
❑ LN-10114	The Best of Bobby Goldsboro	1981	$10

SUNSET

Number	Title	Yr	NM
❑ SUS-5313	Autumn of My Life	1971	$15
❑ SUS-5284	Pledge of Love	1970	$15
❑ SUS-5236	This Is Bobby Goldsboro	1969	$15

UNITED ARTISTS

Number	Title	Yr	NM
❑ UAL3552 [M]	Blue Autumn	1967	$25
❑ UAS6552 [S]	Blue Autumn	1967	$30
❑ UA-LA311-H2	Bobby Goldsboro's 10th Anniversary Album	1974	$25
❑ UAS5502	Bobby Goldsboro's Greatest Hits	1970	$25
❑ UA-LA019-F	Brand New Kind of Love	1972	$18
❑ UAL3471 [M]	Broomstick Cowboy	1966	$25
❑ UAS6471 [S]	Broomstick Cowboy	1966	$30
❑ UA-LA639-G	Butterfly for Bucky	1976	$15
❑ UAS-5578	California Wine	1972	$18
❑ UAS5516	Come Back Home	1971	$18
❑ UAS6642 [S]	Honey	1968	$25

— Later copies have the correct title "Honey" on the label

Number	Title	Yr	NM
❑ ST-91460	Honey	1968	$30

— Capitol Record Club edition

Number	Title	Yr	NM
❑ UAL3642 [M]	Honey	1968	$40

— Some, if not all, copies of this have the title "Pledge of Love" on the label

Number	Title	Yr	NM
❑ UAL6642 [S]	Honey	1968	$30

— Early copies of this have the title "Pledge of Love" on the label

Number	Title	Yr	NM
❑ UAL3381 [M]	I Can't Stop Loving You	1964	$25
❑ UAS6358 [S]	I Can't Stop Loving You	1964	$30
❑ UAL3486 [M]	It's Too Late	1966	$25
❑ UAS6486 [S]	It's Too Late	1966	$30
❑ UAL3425 [M]	Little Things	1965	$25
❑ UAS6425 [S]	Little Things	1965	$30
❑ UAL6735	Muddy Mississippi Line	1969	$25
❑ UAL3599 [M]	Romantic, Soulful, Wacky	1967	$25
❑ UAS6599 [S]	Romantic, Soulful, Wacky	1967	$25
❑ UAL3561 [M]	Sold Goldsboro/Bobby Goldsboro's Greatest Hits	1967	$25
❑ UAS6561 [S]	Sold Goldsboro/Bobby Goldsboro's Greatest Hits	1967	$25
❑ UA-LA124-F	Summer (The First Time)	1973	$18
❑ UAL3358 [M]	The Bobby Goldsbob Album	1964	$25
❑ UAS6358 [S]	The Bobby Goldsbob Album	1964	$30
❑ SP-58 [DJ]	The Bobby Goldsboro Family Album	1971	$50

— Promo-only compilation

Number	Title	Yr	NM
❑ UA-LA424-G	Through the Eyes of a Man	1975	$15
❑ UAS6704	Today	1969	$25

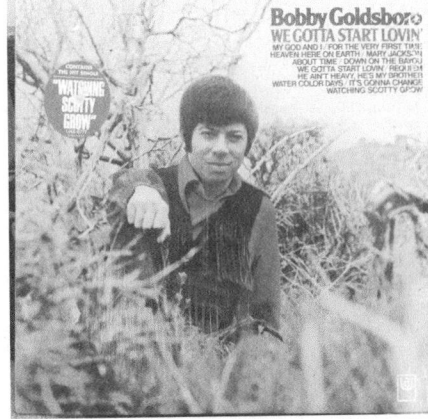

Number	Title	Yr	NM
❑ UAS6777 [B]	Watching Scotty Grow	1971	$18

— Retitled version of above

Number	Title	Yr	NM
❑ UAS6777	We Gotta Start Lovin'	1970	$25
❑ UAS6657	Word Pictures Featuring Autumn of My Life	1968	$25
❑ SKAO-91543 [B]	Word Pictures Featuring Autumn of My Life	1968	$30

— Capitol Record Club edition

Number	Title	Yr	NM

GOLDSBURY, MACK
MUSE
| ❏ MR-5194 | Anthropo-logic | 1979 | $25 |

GOLDSTEIN, GIL
CHIAROSCURO
| ❏ 201 | Pure As Rain | 1978 | $30 |
MUSE
| ❏ MR-5229 | Wrapped in a Cloud | 1980 | $25 |

GOLDTONES, THE
LABREA
| ❏ L-8011 [M] | The Goldtones | 1961 | $40 |
| ❏ LS-8011 [S] | The Goldtones | 1961 | $50 |

GOLIA, VINNY
NINE WINDS
❏ NW 0110	Compositions for Large Ensemble	1984	$25
❏ NW 0120	Facts of Their Own Lives	1986	$35
❏ NW 0117	Goin' Ahead	1985	$30
❏ NW 0103	... In the Right Order ...	1979	$35
❏ NW 0102	Openhearted	1978	$30
❏ NW 0127	Out for Blood	1989	$30
❏ NW 0108	Slice of Life	1981	$30
❏ NW 0104	Solo	1980	$30
❏ NW 0101	Spirits in Fellowship	1977	$30
❏ NW 0109	The Gift of Fury	1982	$30

GOLLIWOGS, THE
Early CREEDENCE CLEARWATER REVIVAL. Also see TOMMY FOGERTY AND THE BLUE VELVETS.
FANTASY
| ❏ F-9474 | Pre-Creedence | 1975 | $30 |
— Reissue of Fantasy and Scorpio sides

GOLSON, BENNY
ARGO
❏ LP-716 [M]	Free	1963	$50
❏ LPS-716 [S]	Free	1963	$75
❏ LP-681 [M]	Take a Number from 1 to 10	1961	$30
❏ LPS-681 [S]	Take a Number from 1 to 10	1961	$40
AUDIO FIDELITY
❏ AFLP-2150 [M]	Just Jazz	1966	$75
❏ AFSD-6150 [S]	Just Jazz	1966	$40
❏ AFLP-1978 [M]	Pop + Jazz = Swing	1962	$75
❏ AFSD-5978 [S]	Pop + Jazz = Swing	1962	$40
COLUMBIA
| ❏ JC35359 | I'm Always Dancin' to the Music | 1978 | $50 |
| ❏ PC34678 | Killer Joe | 1977 | $50 |
CONTEMPORARY
| ❏ C-3552 [M] | Benny Golson's New York Scene | 1958 | $300 |
FANTASY
| ❏ OJC-164 | Benny Golson's New York Scene | 198? | $30 |
— Reissue of Contemporary 3552
| ❏ OJC-226 | Groovin' with Golson | 198? | $30 |
— Reissue of New Jazz 8220
| ❏ OJC-1750 | The Other Side of Benny Golson | 1990 | $35 |
— Reissue of Riverside 290
JAZZLAND
| ❏ JLP-85 [M] | Reunion | 1962 | $75 |
| ❏ JLP-985 [S] | Reunion | 1962 | $50 |
MERCURY
| ❏ MG-20801 [M] | Turning Point | 1963 | $150 |
| ❏ SR-60801 [S] | Turning Point | 1963 | $150 |
MILESTONE
| ❏ M-47048 | Blues On Down | 1978 | $50 |
NEW JAZZ
| ❏ NJLP-8248 [M] | Gettin' With It | 1960 | $250 |
— Purple label
| ❏ NJLP-8248 [M] | Gettin' With It | 1965 | $175 |
— Blue label, trident logo at right
| ❏ NJLP-8235 [M] | Gone with Golson | 1960 | $400 |
— Purple label
| ❏ NJLP-8235 [M] | Gone with Golson | 1965 | $175 |
— Blue label, trident logo at right
| ❏ NJLP-8220 [M] | Groovin' with Golson | 1959 | $250 |
— Purple label
| ❏ NJLP-8220 [M] | Groovin' with Golson | 1965 | $175 |
— Blue label, trident logo at right
PRESTIGE
| ❏ PRLP-7361 [M] | Stockholm Sojourn | 1965 | $30 |
| ❏ PRST-7361 [S] | Stockholm Sojourn | 1965 | $40 |
RIVERSIDE
❏ 6070	The Modern Touch	197?	$30
❏ RLP 12-256 [M]	The Modern Touch of Benny Golson	1957	$300
❏ RLP 12-290 [M]	The Other Side of Benny Golson	1958	$300

SWING
| ❏ SW-8418 | Benny Golson in Paris | 1987 | $30 |
TIMELESS
| ❏ LPSJP-177 | California Message | 1980 | $35 |
| ❏ LPSJP-235 | This Is for You, John | 1983 | $35 |
UNITED ARTISTS
| ❏ UAL-4020 [M] | Benny Golson and the Philadelphians | 1959 | $150 |
| ❏ UAS-5020 [S] | Benny Golson and the Philadelphians | 1959 | $100 |
VERVE
| ❏ V-8710 [M] | Tune In, Turn On | 1967 | $40 |
| ❏ V6-8710 [S] | Tune In, Turn On | 1967 | $75 |

GOMEZ, EDDIE
COLUMBIA
| ❏ FC44214 | Power Play | 1988 | $25 |

GOMEZ, VICENTE
DECCA
❏ DL4088 [M]	Concerto Flamenco	1960	$18
❏ DL74088 [S]	Concerto Flamenco	1960	$25
❏ DL4312 [M]	Guitar Extraordinary	1962	$18
❏ DL74312 [S]	Guitar Extraordinary	1962	$25
❏ DL4156 [M]	Rio Flamenco	1961	$18
❏ DL74156 [S]	Rio Flamenco	1961	$25
❏ DL8439 [M]	Romantic Guitar	1957	$30
— Black label, silver print

| ❏ DL8017 [M] | Spanish Guitar Recital | 195? | $30 |
— Black label, silver print
| ❏ DL8965 [M] | The Artistry of Vicente Gomez | 1959 | $25 |
— Black label, silver print
| ❏ DL78965 [S] | The Artistry of Vicente Gomez | 1959 | $30 |
— Maroon or black label
| ❏ DL8918 [M] | Vicente Gomez | 1959 | $25 |
— Black label, silver print
| ❏ DL78918 [S] | Vicente Gomez | 1959 | $30 |
— Maroon or black label

GOMM, IAN
STIFF/EPIC
| ❏ JE36103 | Gomm with the Wind | 1979 | $25 |
| ❏ JE36433 | What a Blow | 1980 | $20 |

GONG
VIRGIN
| ❏ PZ34428 [B] | Expresso | 1976 | $20 |
— released elsewhere as Gazeuse!
| ❏ PZ34156 [B] | Shamal | 1975 | $40 |
| ❏ VR13-113 [B] | You | 1974 | $40 |

GONN
BEAT ROCKET
| ❏ BR108 | The Loudest Band in Town | 1999 | $15 |

GONSALVES, PAUL, AND ROY ELDREDGE
FANTASY
| ❏ F-9646 | Mexican Bandit Meets Pittsburgh Pirate | 1986 | $25 |

GONSALVES, PAUL
ABC IMPULSE!
❏ AS-41 [S]	Cleopatra Feelin' Jazzy	1967	$35
❏ AS-52 [S]	Salt and Pepper	1967	$35
❏ AS-55 [S]	Tell It the Way It Is	1967	$35
ARGO
| ❏ LP-626 [M] | Cookin' | 1958 | $300 |
| ❏ LPS-626 [S] | Cookin' | 1959 | $40 |
BLACK LION
| ❏ 191 | Just a Sittin' and a Rockin' | 197? | $35 |

CATALYST
| ❏ 7913 | Buenos Aires | 197? | $35 |
FANTASY
| ❏ OJC-203 | Gettin' Together | 198? | $25 |
IMPULSE!
❏ A-41 [M]	Cleopatra Feelin' Jazzy	1963	$120
❏ AS-41 [S]	Cleopatra Feelin' Jazzy	1963	$120
❏ A-52 [M]	Salt and Pepper	1963	$120
❏ AS-52 [S]	Salt and Pepper	1963	$120
❏ A-55 [M]	Tell It the Way It Is	1963	$120
❏ AS-55 [S]	Tell It the Way It Is	1963	$120
JAZZLAND
| ❏ JLP-36 [M] | Gettin' Together | 1961 | $120 |
| ❏ JLP-936 [S] | Gettin' Together | 1961 | $75 |

GONSALVES, VIRGIL
LIBERTY
| ❏ LJH-6010 [M] | Jazz San Francisco Style | 1956 | $50 |
NOCTURNE
| ❏ NLP-8 [10] | Virgil Gonsalves | 1954 | $100 |
OMEGA
| ❏ OML-1047 [M] | Jazz at Monterey | 1959 | $40 |

GONZALES, BABS
CHIAROSCURO
| ❏ 2025 | Live at Small's Paradise | 197? | $35 |
DAUNTLESS
| ❏ DM-4311 [M] | Sunday Afternoon at Small's Paradise | 1963 | $40 |
| ❏ DS-6311 [S] | Sunday Afternoon at Small's Paradise | 1963 | $50 |
HOPE
| ❏ 01 [M] | Voila! | 1958 | $175 |
JARO
| ❏ JAM-5000 [M] | Cool Philosophy | 1959 | $175 |
| ❏ JAS-8000 [S] | Cool Philosophy | 1959 | $150 |

GONZALES, JERRY
AMERICAN CLAVE
| ❏ 1001 | Ya Yo Me Cure | 198? | $30 |
ENJA
| ❏ R1-79609 | Obatala | 1990 | $30 |
| ❏ 4040 | The River Is Deep | 1982 | $30 |

GONZALES, NITOY
CAPITOL
| ❏ T10305 [M] | Christmas in the Philippines | 196? | $15 |
| ❏ ST10305 [S] | Christmas in the Philippines | 196? | $18 |

GOO GOO DOLLS
ENIGMA
| ❏ 773406-1 | JED | 1989 | $25 |
MERCENARY
| ❏ MER-2102 | Goo Goo Dolls | 1987 | $85 |

GOOD AND PLENTY
SENATE
| ❏ LP-21001 [M] | The World of Good and Plenty | 1967 | $30 |
| ❏ LPS-21001 [S] | The World of Good and Plenty | 1967 | $30 |

GOOD GUYS, THE
GNP CRESCENDO
| ❏ GNP-2001 [M] | Sidewalk Surfing | 1964 | $30 |
| ❏ GNPS-2001 [S] | Sidewalk Surfing | 1964 | $40 |
UNITED ARTISTS
| ❏ UAL-3370 [M] | The Good Guys Sing | 1964 | $18 |
| ❏ UAS-6370 [S] | The Good Guys Sing | 1964 | $25 |

GOOD RATS, THE
KAPP
| ❏ KS-3580 | The Good Rats | 1969 | $40 |
PASSPORT
❏ PB-9830	Birth Comes to Us All	1978	$15
❏ PB-9825	From Rats to Riches	1978	$15
❏ SP-20 [DJ]	Rats the Way You Like It (Live)	1978	$50
RAT CITY
❏ RCR-8003	Great American Music	1981	$15
❏ 998	Live at Last	1979	$18
❏ RCR-8001	Rat City in Blue	1975	$25
❏ RCR-8002	Tasty	1978	$15
RAT CITY/GEMM
| ❏ RCR-8004 | Rat City in Blue | 1976 | $25 |
— Reissue with extra track
WARNER BROS.
| ❏ BS2813 | Tasty | 1974 | $30 |

GOOD TIMES, THE
KAMA SUTRA
| ❏ KLP-8052 [M] | The Good Times | 1966 | $18 |

Number	Title	Yr	NM
❏ KSLP-8052 [S]	The Good Times	1966	$25

GOODE, BRAD

DELMARK

❏ DS-440	Shock of the New	1989	$30

GOODEES, THE

HIP

❏ HIS-7002	Candy Coated Goodees	1969	$30

GOODMAN, BENNY

ABC

❏ AC-30014	The ABC Collection	1976	$30

AIRCHECK

❏ 16	Benny Goodman and His Orchestra	197?	$30
❏ 16	Benny Goodman and His Orchestra On the Air, Vol. 1	1986	$25

—*Reissue of above with revised title*

❏ 32	Benny Goodman and His Orchestra On the Air, Vol. 2	1986	$25
❏ 34	Benny Goodman and His Orchestra On the Air, Vol. 3	1986	$25

BIOGRAPH

❏ C-1	Great Soloists 1929-33	1972	$25

BLUEBIRD

❏ AXM2-5505	The Complete Benny Goodman, Vol. 1 (1935)	197?	$30
❏ AXM2-5515	The Complete Benny Goodman, Vol. 2 (1935-36)	197?	$30
❏ AXM2-5532	The Complete Benny Goodman, Vol. 3 (1936)	197?	$30
❏ AXM2-5537	The Complete Benny Goodman, Vol. 4 (1936-37)	197?	$30
❏ AXM2-5557	The Complete Benny Goodman, Vol. 5 (1937-38)	197?	$30
❏ AXM2-5566	The Complete Benny Goodman, Vol. 6 (1938)	197?	$30
❏ AXM2-5567	The Complete Benny Goodman, Vol. 7 (1938-39)	197?	$30
❏ AXM2-5568	The Complete Benny Goodman, Vol. 8 (1936-39)	197?	$30

BRUNSWICK

❏ BL54010 [M]	Benny Goodman 1927-34	1954	$40
❏ BL58015 [10]	Chicago Jazz Classics	1950	$50

CAPITOL

❏ T669 [M]	Benny Goodman Combos	1956	$75

—*Turquoise label*

❏ T669 [M]	Benny Goodman Combos	1958	$40

—*Black label with colorband, Capitol logo on left*

❏ W565 [M]	B.G. in Hi-Fi	1955	$85

—*Gray label*

❏ W565 [M]	B.G. in Hi-Fi	1958	$30

—*Black label with colorband, Capitol logo on left*

❏ H1-565 [10]	B.G. in Hi-Fi (Volume 1)	1955	$85
❏ H2-565 [10]	B.G. in Hi-Fi (Volume 2)	1955	$85
❏ H295 [10]	Easy Does It	1952	$100
❏ T2157 [M]	Hello Benny!	1964	$75
❏ ST2157 [S]	Hello Benny!	1964	$85
❏ T2282 [M]	Made in Japan	1965	$75
❏ ST2282 [S]	Made in Japan	1965	$85
❏ T668 [M]	Mostly Sextets	1956	$75

—*Turquoise label*

❏ T668 [M]	Mostly Sextets	1958	$40

—*Black label with colorband, Capitol logo on left*

❏ S706 [M]	Selections Featured in "The Benny Goodman Story	1956	$75

—*Turquoise label*

❏ S706 [M]	Selections Featured in "The Benny Goodman Story	1958	$50

—*Black label with colorband, Capitol logo on left*

❏ SM-706	Selections Featured in "The Benny Goodman Story	197?	$25

—*Reissue of S 706*

❏ H202 [10]	Session for Six	1950	$100
❏ T395 [M]	Session for Six	1953	$85

—*Turquoise label*

❏ T395 [M]	Session for Six	1958	$50

—*Black label with colorband, Capitol logo on left*

❏ H479 [10]	Small Combo 1947	1954	$100
❏ H409 [10]	The Benny Goodman Band	1953	$100
❏ T409 [M]	The Benny Goodman Band	1953	$75

—*Turquoise label*

❏ T409 [M]	The Benny Goodman Band	1958	$40

—*Black label with colorband, Capitol logo on left*

❏ H343 [10]	The Benny Goodman Trio	1952	$100
❏ H441 [10]	The Goodman Touch	1953	$100
❏ T441 [M]	The Goodman Touch	1953	$75

—*Turquoise label*

❏ T441 [M]	The Goodman Touch	1958	$50

—*Black label with colorband, Capitol logo on left*

❏ T1514 [M]	The Hits of Benny Goodman	1961	$50

—*Black label with colorband, Capitol logo on left*

❏ T1514 [M]	The Hits of Benny Goodman	1963	$85

—*Black label with colorband, Capitol logo on top*

❏ DT1514 [R]	The Hits of Benny Goodman	1961	$75
❏ SM-1514	The Hits of Benny Goodman	197?	$25

—*Reissue of DT 1514*

CBS MASTERWORKS

❏ OSL160 [M]	The Famous 1938 Carnegie Hall Jazz Concert	198?	$35

—*Late reissue; grayish labels with "CBS Masterworks" circling the edge*

CENTURY

❏ 1150	The King of Swing Direct to Disc	1979	$30

—*Direct-to-disc audiophile recording*

CHESS

❏ LP-1440 [DJ]	Benny Rides Again	1960	$150

—*Multi-color swirl vinyl*

❏ LP-1440 [M]	Benny Rides Again	1960	$50
❏ LPS-1440 [S]	Benny Rides Again	1960	$30
❏ CH-9161	Benny Rides Again	1984	$25

—*Reissue*

CLASSICS RECORD LIBRARY

❏ RL-7673 [M]	An Album of Swing Classics	1967	$50
❏ SRL-7673 [S]	An Album of Swing Classics	1967	$40

—*Above two were compiled for Book-of-the-Month Club*

COLUMBIA

❏ CL2533 [10]	Benny at the Ballroom	1955	$50

—*Retitled reissue of 6100*

❏ CL534 [M]	Benny Goodman and His Orchestra	1953	$40

—*Maroon label with gold print*

❏ CL534 [M]	Benny Goodman and His Orchestra	1955	$40

—*Red and black label with six "eye" logos*

❏ CL6033 [10]	Benny Goodman and Peggy Lee	1949	$100
❏ CL523 [M]	Benny Goodman Presents Eddie Sauter Arrangements	1953	$40

—*Maroon label with gold print*

❏ CL523 [M]	Benny Goodman Presents Eddie Sauter Arrangements	1955	$40

—*Red and black label with six "eye" logos*

❏ GL523 [M]	Benny Goodman Presents Eddie Sauter Arrangements	1953	$50

—*Black label, silver print*

❏ CL524 [M]	Benny Goodman Presents Fletcher Henderson Arrangements	1954	$40

—*Maroon label with gold print*

❏ CL524 [M]	Benny Goodman Presents Fletcher Henderson Arrangements	1953	$40

—*Red and black label with six "eye" logos*

❏ GL524 [M]	Benny Goodman Presents Fletcher Henderson Arrangements	1953	$50

—*Black label, silver print*

❏ CL2483 [M]	Benny Goodman's Greatest Hits	1966	$35
❏ CS9283 [S]	Benny Goodman's Greatest Hits	1966	$30

—*360 Sound Stereo" on label*

❏ PC9283	Benny Goodman's Greatest Hits	198?	$20

—*Reissue*

❏ CL1579 [M]	Benny Goodman Swings Again	1960	$30
❏ CS8379 [S]	Benny Goodman Swings Again	1960	$30
❏ C2L16 [M]	Benny in Brussels	195?	$40

—*Red and black label with six white "eye" logos*

❏ CL1247 [M]	Benny in Brussels, Vol. I	1958	$30
❏ CS8075 [S]	Benny in Brussels, Vol. I	1959	$40
❏ CL1248 [M]	Benny in Brussels, Vol. II	1958	$30
❏ CS8076 [S]	Benny in Brussels, Vol. II	1959	$40
❏ CL814 [M]	Carnegie Hall Jazz Concert, Volume 1	1956	$30

—*Red and black label with six "eye" logos*

❏ CL814 [M]	Carnegie Hall Jazz Concert, Volume 1	1963	$25

—*Red label with "Guaranteed High Fidelity" or "Mono" at bottom*

❏ CL815 [M]	Carnegie Hall Jazz Concert, Volume 2	1956	$30

—*Red and black label with six "eye" logos*

❏ CL815 [M]	Carnegie Hall Jazz Concert, Volume 2	1963	$25

—*Red label with "Guaranteed High Fidelity" or "Mono" at bottom*

❏ CL815 [M]	Carnegie Hall Jazz Concert, Volume 2	197?	$15

—*Orange label with "Mono" under "CL 815" at left*

❏ CL816 [M]	Carnegie Hall Jazz Concert, Volume 3	1956	$30

—*Red and black label with six "eye" logos*

❏ CL816 [M]	Carnegie Hall Jazz Concert, Volume 3	1963	$25

—*Red label with "Guaranteed High Fidelity" or "Mono" at bottom*

❏ CL500 [M]	Combos	1952	$40

—*Maroon label with gold print*

❏ CL500 [M]	Combos	1955	$40

—*Red and black label with six "eye" logos*

❏ GL500 [M]	Combos	1951	$50

—*Black label, silver print*

❏ CL6048 [10]	Dance Parade	1949	$50
❏ CL6100 [10]	Dance Parade, Volume 2	1950	$50
❏ CL6052 [10]	Goodman Sextet Session	1949	$50
❏ GL102 [10]	Let's Hear the Melody	1950	$75
❏ CL6302 [10]	Let's Hear the Melody	1951	$50

—*Reissue of GL 102*

❏ FC38265	Seven Come Eleven	1983	$25
❏ PG33405	Solid Gold Instrumental Hits	1975	$30

❏ XTV28995/6 [M]	Swing Into Spring	1959	$25

—*Special item made for Texaco service stations*

❏ KG31547	The All-Time Greatest Hits of Benny Goodman	1972	$35
❏ PG31547	The All-Time Greatest Hits of Benny Goodman	197?	$30

—*Reissue*

❏ CL652 [M]	The Benny Goodman Sextet and Orchestra with Charlie Christian	1955	$40

—*Red and black label with six "eye" logos*

❏ CL652 [M]	The Benny Goodman Sextet and Orchestra with Charlie Christian	1963	$25

—*Red label with "Guaranteed High Fidelity" or "Mono" at bottom*

❏ CL516 [M]	The Benny Goodman Trio Plays for the Fletcher Henderson Fund	1953	$40

—*Maroon label with gold print*

❏ CL516 [M]	The Benny Goodman Trio Plays for the Fletcher Henderson Fund	1955	$40

—*Red and black label with six "eye" logos*

❏ GL516 [M]	The Benny Goodman Trio Plays for the Fletcher Henderson Fund	1952	$50

—*Reissue of Martin Block 1000; black label, silver print*

❏ CL2564 [10]	The B.G. Six	1955	$50

—*Retitled reissue of 6052*

❏ CL501 [M]	The Golden Era Series Presents Benny Goodman and His Orchestra	1952	$40

—*Maroon label with gold print*

❏ CL501 [M]	The Golden Era Series Presents Benny Goodman and His Orchestra	1955	$40

—*Red and black label with six "eye" logos*

❏ GL501 [M]	The Golden Era Series Presents Benny Goodman and His Orchestra	1951	$50

—*Black label, silver print*

❏ CL820 [M]	The Great Benny Goodman	1956	$30

—*Red and black label with six "eye" logos*

❏ CL820 [M]	The Great Benny Goodman	1963	$25

—*Red label with "Guaranteed High Fidelity" or "Mono" at bottom*

❏ CS8643 [R]	The Great Benny Goodman	1962	$30

—*Red label, "360 Sound Stereo" at bottom*

❏ PC8643	The Great Benny Goodman	198?	$20

—*Reissue*

❏ CS8643 [R]	The Great Benny Goodman	1970	$25

—*Orange label*

❏ CL1324 [M]	The Happy Session	1959	$30
❏ CS8129 [S]	The Happy Session	1959	$30
❏ CL817 [M]	The King of Swing, Volume 1	1956	$30
❏ CL818 [M]	The King of Swing, Volume 2	1956	$30
❏ CL819 [M]	The King of Swing, Volume 3	1956	$30
❏ CL552 [M]	The New Benny Goodman Sextet	1954	$40

—*Maroon label with gold print*

❏ CL552 [M]	The New Benny Goodman Sextet	1955	$40

—*Red and black label with six "eye" logos*

❏ CL821 [M]	Vintage Goodman	1956	$30

COLUMBIA JAZZ MASTERPIECES

❏ CJ44292	Slipped Disc, 1945-1946	1988	$25

COLUMBIA MASTERWORKS

Number	Title	Yr	NM
SL180 [M]	1937-38 Jazz Concert No. 2	1950	$175
ML4590 [M]	1937-38 Jazz Concert No. 2, Volume 1	1950	$40
ML4591 [M]	1937-38 Jazz Concert No. 2, Volume 2	1950	$40
ML4358 [M]	Carnegie Hall Jazz Concert, Volume 1	1950	$40
ML4359 [M]	Carnegie Hall Jazz Concert, Volume 2	1950	$40
SL176 [M]	King of Swing	1950	$175
ML4613 [M]	King of Swing, Volume 1	1950	$40
ML4614 [M]	King of Swing, Volume 2	1950	$40
ML6205 [M]	Meeting at the Summit	1961	$35

— With the Columbia Jazz Combo and the Columbia Orchestra

Number	Title	Yr	NM
MS6805 [S]	Meeting at the Summit	1961	$25

— With the Columbia Jazz Combo and the Columbia Orchestra

Number	Title	Yr	NM
SL160 [M]	The Famous 1938 Carnegie Hall Jazz Concert	1950	$150

— Green labels

Number	Title	Yr	NM
OSL160 [M]	The Famous 1938 Carnegie Hall Jazz Concert	1963	$40

— Gray labels with "Columbia" at top

Number	Title	Yr	NM
OSL160 [M]	The Famous 1938 Carnegie Hall Jazz Concert	1956	$175

— Gray and black labels with six "eye" logos

Number	Title	Yr	NM
OSL160 [M]	The Famous 1938 Carnegie Hall Jazz Concert	1970	$25

— Olive labels with "Columbia" circling edge

Number	Title	Yr	NM
OSL180 [M]	The King of Swing	1956	$175

— Gray and black labels with six "eye" logos

Number	Title	Yr	NM
OSL180 [M]	The King of Swing	1963	$40

— Gray labels with "Columbia" at top

COLUMBIA MUSICAL TREASURY

Number	Title	Yr	NM
P4M5678	The Best of Benny Goodman	197?	$30

— Issued by Columbia House

COMMAND

Number	Title	Yr	NM
RS-921	Benny Goodman & Paris: Listen to the Magic	1967	$35

DECCA

Number	Title	Yr	NM
DXB188 [M]	The Benny Goodman Story	1956	$300

— Black label, silver print

Number	Title	Yr	NM
DXB188 [M]	The Benny Goodman Story	1961	$40

— Black label with color bars

Number	Title	Yr	NM
DXSB7188 [R]	The Benny Goodman Story	196?	$35
DL8252 [M]	The Benny Goodman Story, Volume 1	1956	$300

— Black label, silver print

Number	Title	Yr	NM
DL8252 [M]	The Benny Goodman Story, Volume 1	1961	$25

— Black label with color bars

Number	Title	Yr	NM
DL78252 [R]	The Benny Goodman Story, Volume 1	1961	$25
DL8253 [M]	The Benny Goodman Story, Volume 2	1956	$300

— Black label, silver print

Number	Title	Yr	NM
DL8253 [M]	The Benny Goodman Story, Volume 2	1961	$25

— Black label with color bars

Number	Title	Yr	NM
DL78253 [R]	The Benny Goodman Story, Volume 2	1961	$25

DOCTOR JAZZ

Number	Title	Yr	NM
W2X40350	Airplay	1986	$30

EVEREST ARCHIVE OF FOLK & JAZZ

Number	Title	Yr	NM
277	Benny Goodman	1973	$30

GIANTS OF JAZZ

Number	Title	Yr	NM
1030	The Benny Goodman Caravans -- Big Band Broadcasts Vol. 1: Ciribiribin	1983	$25
1033	The Benny Goodman Caravans -- Big Band Broadcasts Vol. 2: Swingin' Down the Lane	1985	$25
1036	The Benny Goodman Caravans -- Big Band Broadcasts Vol. 3: One O'Clock Jump	1985	$25
1039	The Benny Goodman Caravans -- Big Band Broadcasts Vol. 4: Sing, Sing, Sing	1985	$25
1034	The Benny Goodman Caravans -- The Small Groups, Vol. 1	1985	$25

HARMONY

Number	Title	Yr	NM
HL7005 [M]	Peggy Lee Sings with Benny Goodman	1957	$30
HS11271 [R]	Sing, Sing, Sing	1968	$25
HL7278 [M]	Swingin' Benny Goodman Sextet	196?	$35
HL7225 [M]	Swing Time	196?	$35
HL7190 [M]	Swing with Benny Goodman in High Fidelity	196?	$35
HS11090 [R]	Swing with Benny Goodman in High Fidelity	196?	$25

INTERMEDIA

Number	Title	Yr	NM
QS-5046	All the Cats Join In	198?	$25

LONDON

Number	Title	Yr	NM
PS918/9	Live at Carnegie Hall 1978	1979	$35

LONDON PHASE 4

Number	Title	Yr	NM
SP-44182/83	Benny Goodman On Stage	1972	$35
SPB-21	Benny Goodman Today	1971	$35

MARTIN BLOCK

Number	Title	Yr	NM
MB-1000 [M]	The Benny Goodman Trio Plays for the Fletcher Henderson Fund	1951	$75

MCA

Number	Title	Yr	NM
4018	Jazz Holiday	197?	$30

MEGA

Number	Title	Yr	NM
51-5002	Let's Dance Again	1971	$30
606	Let's Dance Again	1974	$25

— Reissue of 51-5002

MGM

Number	Title	Yr	NM
E-3788 [M]	Performance Recordings, Volume 1	1959	$30
E-3789 [M]	Performance Recordings, Volume 2	1959	$30
E-3790 [M]	Performance Recordings, Volume 3	1959	$30
3E-9 [M]	The Benny Goodman Treasure Chest	1959	$175
E-3788 [M]	The Benny Goodman Treasure Chest, Volume 1	198?	$20

— Reissue on blue and gold label

Number	Title	Yr	NM
E-3789 [M]	The Benny Goodman Treasure Chest, Volume 2	198?	$20

— Reissue on blue and gold label

Number	Title	Yr	NM
E-3790 [M]	The Benny Goodman Treasure Chest, Volume 3	198?	$20

— Reissue on blue and gold label

Number	Title	Yr	NM
E-3810 [M]	The Sound of Music	1960	$25
SE-3810 [S]	The Sound of Music	1960	$30

MOSAIC

Number	Title	Yr	NM
MQ6-148	The Complete Capitol Small Group Recordings of Benny Goodman 1944-1955	199?	$175

MUSICMASTERS

Number	Title	Yr	NM
MM-20102Z	Let's Dance	1986	$25

— From the PBS TV special of 1985

PAIR

Number	Title	Yr	NM
PDL2-1014	Original Recordings by Benny Goodman	1986	$30
PDL2-1054	Original Recordings by Benny Goodman, Volume 2	1986	$30
PDL2-1093	Original Recordings by Benny Goodman, Volume 3	1986	$30

PAUSA

Number	Title	Yr	NM
9031	The Benny Goodman Trios (and One Duet)	198?	$25

PICKWICK

Number	Title	Yr	NM
SPC-3529	Francaise	197?	$25
SPC-3270	Let's Dance	197?	$25

PRESTIGE

Number	Title	Yr	NM
PRST-7644	Benny Goodman and the Giants of Swing	1969	$35

RCA CAMDEN

Number	Title	Yr	NM
CAL-872 [M]	Benny Goodman and His Orchestra Featuring Great Vocalists of Our Times	1965	$35
CAS-872 [S]	Benny Goodman and His Orchestra Featuring Great Vocalists of Our Times	1965	$30
CAL-624 [M]	Swing, Swing, Swing	1960	$35
CAS-624(e) [R]	Swing, Swing, Swing	1960	$25

RCA VICTOR

Number	Title	Yr	NM
CPL1-2470	A Legendary Performer	1977	$25
LPT-17 [10]	A Treasury of Immortal Performances	1951	$50
WPT12 [10]	Benny Goodman	1951	$50
LPT-1005 [M]	Benny Goodman	1954	$40
LOC-6008 [M]	Benny Goodman in Moscow	1962	$25
LSO-6008 [S]	Benny Goodman in Moscow	1962	$30
LPT-3004 [10]	Benny Goodman Quintet	1952	$50
LPV-521 [M]	B.G. The Small Groups	1965	$35
WPT26 [10]	Immortal Performances	1952	$50
ANL1-0973(e)	Pure Gold	1974	$25

— Reissue of LSP-4005(e)

Number	Title	Yr	NM
LPM-1226 [M]	The Benny Goodman Trio/Quartet/Quintet	1956	$40
LSP-4005(e)	The Best of Benny Goodman	1968	$35
AFL1-4005(e)	The Best of Benny Goodman	1977	$25

— Reissue of LSP-4005

Number	Title	Yr	NM
LPM-1099 [M]	The Golden Age of Benny Goodman	1956	$40
LPT-6703 [M]	The Golden Age of Swing	1956	$600

— Five-record set in white vinyl binder with bound-in booklet

Number	Title	Yr	NM
LPM-2247 [M]	The Kingdom of Swing	1960	$25
LSP-2247 [S]	The Kingdom of Swing	1960	$30
LPM-1239 [M]	This Is Benny Goodman	1956	$40
VPM-6040 [PS]	This Is Benny Goodman	1971	$35
VPM-6063	This Is Benny Goodman, Vol. 2	1972	$35
LPT-3056 [10]	This Is Benny Goodman and His Orchestra	1954	$50
LPM-2698 [M]	Together Again	1964	$35
LSP-2698 [S]	Together Again	1964	$25

SUNBEAM

Number	Title	Yr	NM
126	At the Madhattan Room Dec. 18, 1937	197?	$30
123	At the Madhattan Room Nov. 4, 1937	197?	$30
116	At the Madhattan Room Oct. 13, 1937	197?	$15
117	At the Madhattan Room Oct. 16, 1937	197?	$30
118	At the Madhattan Room Oct. 20, 1937	197?	$30
133	Benny Goodman 1933	197?	$25
148	Benny Goodman 1934	197?	$25
158	Benny Goodman 1941-42	1984	$25
154	Benny Goodman 1946	197?	$25
111	Benny Goodman Accompanies Girls 1931-33	197?	$25
138	Benny Goodman and His Orchestra 1931-33, Volume 1	197?	$25
139	Benny Goodman and His Orchestra 1931-33, Volume 2	197?	$25
140	Benny Goodman and His Orchestra 1931-33, Volume 3	197?	$25
152	Benny Goodman and His Orchestra 1937-38	197?	$30
135	Benny Goodman and the Modernists 1934-35	197?	$25
106	Benny Goodman In a Mellotone Manner 1930-31	197?	$25
105	Benny Goodman On the Air 1935-36, Volume 1	197?	$25
153	Benny Goodman On the Air 1935-36, Volume 2	197?	$25
107	Benny Goodman On the Side 1929-31	197?	$25
142	Benny Goodman On V-Disc 1939-48, Volume 1	197?	$25
143	Benny Goodman On V-Disc 1939-48, Volume 2	197?	$25
144	Benny Goodman On V-Disc 1939-48, Volume 3	197?	$25
156	Broadcasts from Hollywood 1946-47	197?	$25
146	Camel Caravan 1937, Volume 1	197?	$25
147	Camel Caravan 1937, Volume 2	197?	$25
145	Fitch Bandwagon 1945	197?	$25
128/32	From the Congress Hotel, Chicago, 1935-36	197?	$30
149	Jam Session 1935-37	197?	$25
112	Rare Benny Goodman 1927-29	197?	$25
141	The Benny Goodman Boys 1928-29	197?	$25
151	The Benny Goodman Show 1946	197?	$25
113	The Hotsy Totsy Gang 1928-29	197?	$25
100	The Let's Dance Broadcasts 1934-35, Volume 1	197?	$25
104	The Let's Dance Broadcasts 1934-35, Volume 2	197?	$25
150	The Let's Dance Broadcasts 1934-35, Volume 3	197?	$25
114	Whoopee Makers 1928-29	197?	$25

TIME-LIFE

Number	Title	Yr	NM
STBB-03	Big Bands: Benny Goodman	1983	$35
STBB-23	Big Bands: King of Swing	1986	$35
STL-J-05	Giants of Jazz	1979	$50

VERVE

Number	Title	Yr	NM
V-8582 [M]	The Essential Benny Goodman	1964	$35
V6-8582 [S]	The Essential Benny Goodman	1964	$35
MGV-4015-2 [M]	The Superlative Goodman	1958	$0

— Canceled

Number	Title	Yr	NM
MGV-4013 [M]	The Superlative Goodman, Volume 1	1958	$0

— Canceled

Number	Title	Yr	NM
MGV-4014 [M]	The Superlative Goodman, Volume 2	1958	$0

— Canceled

WESTINGHOUSE

Number	Title	Yr	NM
XTV27713/4 [M]	Benny Goodman Plays World Favorites in High Fidelity	1958	$30

— No number on cover or label; these numbers come from the trail-off wax

Number	Title	Yr	NM
0(no cat #) [M]	Benny in Brussels	1958	$150

GOODMAN, BENNY/CHARLIE BARNET

CAPITOL

Number	Title	Yr	NM
M-11061	BeBop Spoken Here	197?	$30

GOODMAN, DICKIE

CASH

Number	Title	Yr	NM
CR6000	Mr. Jaws and Other Fables	1975	$30

COMET

Number	Title	Yr	NM
69	My Son, the Joke	1963	$40

IX CHAINS

Number	Title	Yr	NM
NCS9000	The Original Flying Saucers	1973	$40

Number	Title	Yr	NM

RHINO
- RNLP-811 · Dickie Goodman's Greatest Hits · 1983 · $18

RORI
- 3301 · The Many Heads of Dickie Goodman · 1962 · $100

GOODMAN, DODY
CORAL
- CRL57196 [M] · Dody Goodman Sings? · 1958 · $30

GOODMAN, JERRY, AND JAN HAMMER
NEMPEROR
- SD430 · Like Children · 1975 · $25

GOODMAN, STEVE
ASYLUM
- 6E-174 · High and Outside · 1979 · $15
- 6E-297 · Hot Spot · 1980 · $15
- 7E-1037 · Jessie's Jig & Other Favorites · 1975 · $15
- 7E-1118 · Say It in Private · 1977 · $15
- 7E-1061 · Words We Can Dance To · 1976 · $15

BUDDAH
- BDS5121 · Somebody Else's Troubles · 1972 · $18
- BDS5096 · Steve Goodman · 1971 · $18
- BDS5665 · The Essential Steve Goodman · 1976 · $18

RED PAJAMAS
- RPJ-002 · Affordable Art · 1983 · $15
- RPJ-001 · Artistic Hair · 1982 · $15
- RPJ-006 · Best of the Asylum Years, Vol. 1 · 198? · $15
- RPJ-007 · Best of the Asylum Years, Vol. 2 · 198? · $15
- RPJ-003 · Santa Ana Winds · 1984 · $15
- RPJ-005 · Unfinished Business · 1985 · $15

GOODRICH, ALEXANDER
DIPLOMAT
- X-1711 [M] · Organ and Chimes at Christmas · 1965 · $15
- SX-1711 [S] · Organ and Chimes at Christmas · 1965 · $15
— *Same as above, but in stereo*

GOODRICK, MICK
ECM
- 1139 · In Pas(s)ing · 1979 · $30

GOODWIN, BILL
OMNISOUND
- 1029 · Bill Goodwin's Solar Energy · 1981 · $25
- 1050 · Network · 1983 · $25

GOODWIN, RON
CAPITOL
- T10078 [M] · It Can't Be Wrong · 1957 · $25
- SP-10560 · Jet Flight to Beirut · 196? · $25
- T10251 [M] · Music for an Arabian Night · 1959 · $30
- ST10251 [S] · Music for an Arabian Night · 1959 · $30
- T10188 [M] · Music in Orbit · 1958 · $30
- ST10188 [S] · Music in Orbit · 1958 · $40
- ST-11012 · Ron Goodwin Plays Someone Named Burt Bacharach · 1972 · $12
- T10177 [M] · Swinging Sweethearts · 1958 · $25

GOOSE CREEK SYMPHONY
CAPITOL
- SM-444 · Goose Creek Symphony · 197? · $12
— *Reissue*
- ST-444 · Goose Creek Symphony · 1970 · $18
- ST-690 [B] · Welcome to Goose Creek · 1971 · $18
- ST-11044 · Words of Earnest · 1972 · $18

COLUMBIA
- KC32918 · Do Your Thing But Don't Touch Mine · 1974 · $15

GORDIAN KNOT, THE
VERVE
- V-5062 [M] · Tones · 1968 · $30
— *White label promo only (no stock copies were issued in mono)*
- V6-5062 [S] · Tones · 1968 · $18

GORDON, BARRY
CAPITOL
- ST-805 · Pieces of Time · 1971 · $15

UNITED ARTISTS
- UAL3491 [M] · Yes Sir, That's My Baby · 1966 · $18
- UAS6491 [S] · Yes Sir, That's My Baby · 1966 · $25

GORDON, BOB
PACIFIC JAZZ
- PJLP-12 [10] · Meet Mr. Gordon · 1954 · $250

TAMPA
- TP-26 [M] · Jazz Impressions · 1957 · $300
— *Red vinyl*
- TP-26 [M] · Jazz Impressions · 1958 · $175
— *Black vinyl*

GORDON, BOBBY
DECCA
- DL4726 [M] · The Lamp Is Low · 1966 · $30
- DL74726 [S] · The Lamp Is Low · 1966 · $35
- DL4394 [M] · Warm and Sentimental · 1963 · $30
- DL74394 [S] · Warm and Sentimental · 1963 · $35
- DL4507 [M] · Young Man's Fancy · 1964 · $30
- DL74507 [S] · Young Man's Fancy · 1964 · $35

GORDON, BOB/CLIFFORD BROWN
PACIFIC JAZZ
- PJ-3 [M] · Jazz Immortal · 1960 · $50
- PJ-1214 [M] · The Bob Gordon Quintet/The Clifford Brown Ensemble · 1956 · $150

GORDON, DEXTER
BASF
- 20698 · A Day in Copenhagen · 197? · $35

BETHLEHEM
- BCP-36 [M] · Daddy Plays the Horn · 1956 · $1400
- BCP-6008 · The Bethlehem Years · 197? · $30
— *Reissue, distributed by RCA Victor*

BLACK LION
- 108 · The Montmartre Collection · 197? · $35

BLUE NOTE
- BLP-4133 [M] · A Swingin' Affair · 1963 · $120
— *With "New York, USA" address on label*
- BST-84133 [S] · A Swingin' Affair · 1963 · $175
— *With "New York, USA" address on label*
- BST-84133 [S] · A Swingin' Affair · 1967 · $40
— *With "A Division of Liberty Records" on label*
- BST-84133 · A Swingin' Affair · 199? · $30
— *Classic Records 180-gram audiophile reissue*
- LT-989 · Clubhouse · 1980 · $30
- BLP-4083 [M] · Dexter Calling · 1961 · $250
— *With W. 63rd St. address on label*
- BLP-4083 [M] · Dexter Calling · 1963 · $175
— *With "New York, USA" address on label*
- BST-84083 [S] · Dexter Calling · 1961 · $250
— *With W. 63rd St. address on label*
- BST-84083 [S] · Dexter Calling · 1963 · $175
— *With "New York, USA" address on label*
- BST-84083 [S] · Dexter Calling · 1967 · $40
— *With "A Division of Liberty Records" on label*
- BN-LA393-H2 · Dexter Gordon · 1975 · $75
- BLP-4077 [M] · Doin' Allright · 1961 · $300
— *With W. 63rd St. addresss on label*
- BLP-4077 [M] · Doin' Allright · 1963 · $175
— *With "New York, USA" address on label*
- BST-84077 [S] · Doin' Allright · 1961 · $300
— *With W. 63rd St. addresss on label*
- BST-84077 [S] · Doin' Allright · 1963 · $250
— *With "New York, USA" address on label*
- BST-84077 [S] · Doin' Allright · 1967 · $40
— *With "A Division of Liberty Records" on label*
- BST-84077 · Doin' Allright · 1985 · $30
— *The Finest in Jazz Since 1939" reissue*
- BST-84077 [S] · Doin' Allright · 1970 · $75
— *Mostly black label with "Liberty/UA" at bottom*
- BLP-4204 [M] · Gettin' Around · 1965 · $7000
— *With "New York, USA" address on label*
- BST-84204 [S] · Gettin' Around · 1965 · $100
— *With "New York, USA" address on label*
- BST-84204 [S] · Gettin' Around · 1967 · $75
— *With "A Division of Liberty Records" on label*
- BLP-4112 [M] · Go · 1962 · $175
— *With "New York, USA" address on label*
- BST-84112 [S] · Go · 1962 · $120
— *With "New York, USA" address on label*
- BST-84112 [S] · Go · 1967 · $40
— *With "A Division of Liberty Records" on label*
- BST-84112 [B] · Go · 1985 · $30
— *The Finest in Jazz Since 1939" reissue*
- LT-1051 · Landslide · 1980 · $30
- BABB-85112 · Nights at the Keystone · 198? · $30
- BLP-4176 [M] · One Flight Up · 1964 · $175
— *With "New York, USA" address on label*
- BST-84176 [S] · One Flight Up · 1964 · $100
— *With "New York, USA" address on label*
- BST-84176 [S] · One Flight Up · 1967 · $75
— *With "A Division of Liberty Records" on label*
- BST-84176 · One Flight Up · 1986 · $30
— *The Finest in Jazz Since 1939" reissue*
- BLP-4146 [M] · Our Man in Paris · 1963 · $175
— *With "New York, USA" address on label*
- BST-84146 [S] · Our Man in Paris · 1963 · $150
— *With "New York, USA" address on label*
- BST-84146 [S] · Our Man in Paris · 1967 · $75
— *With "A Division of Liberty Records" on label*
- BST-84146 · Our Man in Paris · 1987 · $30
— *The Finest in Jazz Since 1939" reissue*
- B1-91139 · The Best of Dexter Gordon · 1988 · $30
- BT-85135 · The Other Side of 'Round Midnight · 1986 · $30

BOPLICITY
- BOP-6 · Dexter Blows Hot and Cool · 198? · $25

COLUMBIA
- JC36853 · Gotham City · 1981 · $25
- JC36853 · Gotham City · 2000 · $30
— *180-gram reissue*
- JC35987 · Great Encounters · 1979 · $25
- PG34650 · Homecoming · 1977 · $35
- JC35608 · Manhattan Symphonie · 1978 · $30
- PC35608 · Manhattan Symphonie · 198? · $20
— *Budget-line reissue*
- JC34989 · Sophisticated Giant · 1977 · $30
- JC36356 · The Best of Dexter Gordon · 1979 · $25

DIAL
- LP-204 [10] · Dexter Gordon Quintet · 1950 · $400

DISCOVERY
- 79005 · American Classic · 1995 · $35

DOOTO
- DL-207 [M] · Dexter Blows Hot and Cool · 196? · $400
— *Maroon label with "Dooto*

DOOTONE
- DL-207 [M] · Dexter Blows Hot and Cool · 1956 · $3000
— *Red vinyl*
- DL-207 [M] · Dexter Blows Hot and Cool · 1957 · $1200
— *Black vinyl; "Dootone" label with no zip code*
- DL-207 [M] · Dexter Blows Hot and Cool · 197? · $150
— *Maroon label with zip code*

ELEKTRA/MUSICIAN
- 60126 · American Classic · 1983 · $25

FANTASY
- OJC-299 · Tower of Power · 198? · $25

INNER CITY
- IC-2080 · Biting the Apple · 1977 · $30
- IC-2060 · Bouncin' · 197? · $35
- IC-2030 · More Than You Know · 197? · $35
- IC-2040 · Stable Mable · 1975 · $35
- IC-2050 · Swiss Nights · 1975 · $35
- IC-2025 · The Apartment · 197? · $35
- IC-2006 · The Meeting · 1973 · $35
- IC-2020 · The Source · 1973 · $35

JAZZLAND
- JLP-29 [M] · The Resurgence of Dexter Gordon · 1960 · $50
- JLP-929 [S] · The Resurgence of Dexter Gordon · 1960 · $75

JAZZ MAN
- 5023 · Dexter Gordon at Montmartre · 198? · $25

PAUSA
- 7058 · A Day in Copenhagen · 1980 · $25

PRESTIGE
- PRST-7763 · A Day in Copenhagen · 1970 · $25
- 10079 · Blues A La Suisse · 1973 · $35
- 10051 · Ca' Purange · 197? · $35
- 10069 · Generation · 197? · $35
- 10020 · Jumpin' Blues · 197? · $35
- PRST-7680 · More Power · 1969 · $25
- PRST-7829 · Panther! · 1971 · $25
- 2511 · Resurgence · 198? · $25
- 10091 · Tangerine · 197? · $25
- 2502 · The Ballad Album · 198? · $25
- PRST-7623 · The Tower of Power · 1969 · $25

SAVOY
- MG-9003 [10] · All Star Series -- Dexter Gordon · 1951 · $300
- MG-12130 [M] · Dexter Rides Again · 1958 · $150

Number	Title	Yr	NM
❏ MG-9016 [10]	New Trends in Modern Jazz, Volume 3	1952	$300

SAVOY JAZZ
❏ SJC-407	Jazz Concert, West Coast	1985	$25
❏ SJL-2211	Long Tall Dexter	197?	$35
❏ SJL-1154	Master Takes: The Savoy Recordings	198?	$25
❏ SJL-2222	The Hunt	197?	$35

STEEPLECHASE
❏ SCC-6028	Billie's Bounce	198?	$30
❏ SCC-1080	Biting the Apple	198?	$25
❏ SCS-1060	Bouncin'	198?	$25
❏ SCC-6008	Cheese Cake	198?	$30
❏ SCC-6004	Cry Me a River	198?	$30
❏ SCC-6022	It's You or No One	198?	$30
❏ SCC-6015	I Want More	198?	$30
❏ SCS-1156	Lullaby for a Monster	198?	$25
❏ SCS-1030	More Than You Know	198?	$25
❏ SCS-1136	Something Different	1980	$30
❏ SCS-1040	Stable Mable	198?	$25
❏ SCS-1145	Strings & Things	198?	$30
❏ SCS-1050	Swiss Nights, Volume 1	198?	$35
❏ SCS-1090	Swiss Nights, Volume 2	198?	$25
❏ SCS-1110	Swiss Nights, Volume 3	198?	$25
❏ SCS-1025	The Apartment	198?	$25
❏ SCS-1206	The Shadow of Your Smile	198?	$30

WHO'S WHO IN JAZZ
❏ 21011	Who's Who Presents Dexter Gordon and Lionel Hampton	1977	$30

GORDON, DEXTER/HOWARD MCGHEE
JAZZTONE
❏ J-1235 [M]	The Chase	1956	$40

GORDON, FRANK
SOUL NOTE
❏ SN-1096	Clarion Echoes	1986	$25

GORDON, GRAY
HINDSIGHT
❏ HSR-206	Gray Gordon and His Tic Toc Rhythm 1939	198?	$25

GORDON, HONI
PRESTIGE
❏ PRLP-7230 [M]	Honi Gordon Sings	1962	$175
❏ PRST-7230 [S]	Honi Gordon Sings	1962	$175

GORDON, JOE
CONTEMPORARY
❏ M-3597 [M]	Lookin' Good	1961	$250
❏ S-7597 [S]	Lookin' Good	1961	$250

EMARCY
❏ MG-26046 [10]	Introducing Joe Gordon	1954	$250
❏ MG-36025 [M]	Introducing Joe Gordon	1955	$300

FANTASY
❏ OJC-174	Lookin' Good	198?	$25

TRIP
❏ 5535	Introducing Joe Gordon	197?	$25

GORDON, JOHN
STRATA-EAST
❏ SES-19760	Step by Step	197?	$25

GORDON, JON
GEMINI TAURUS
❏ TRLP-827	Beginning and Endings	1989	$30

TIGER LILY
❏ TL14008 [B]	Jon Gordon	1976	$300

GORDON, JUSTIN
DOT
❏ DLP-3214 [M]	Justin Gordon Swings	1959	$40

GORDON, KELLY
CAPITOL
❏ ST-201	Defunked	1969	$25

GORDON, ROBERT
PRIVATE STOCK
❏ PS-7008 [B]	Fresh Fish Special	1978	$16
❏ PS-2030 [B]	Robert Gordon with Link Wray	1977	$25
— Formerly with Tuff Darts			

RCA VICTOR
❏ AFL1-3773	Are You Gonna Be the One	1981	$15
❏ AFL1-3523	Bad Boy	1980	$15
❏ DJL1-3411 [DJ]	Essential Robert Gordon	1979	$30
— Promo-only live album with tracks from Tuff Darts			
❏ DJL1-3411 [DJ]	Essential Robert Gordon	1979	$30
— Promo-only live album with tracks from Tuff Darts			
❏ AFL1-3299	Fresh Fish Special	1979	$15
— Reissue			

Number	Title	Yr	NM
❏ AFL1-3296	Robert Gordon with Link Wray	1979	$15
— Reissue			
❏ AFL1-3294	Rock Billy Boogie	1979	$25
— Original pressing on white vinyl			
❏ AFL1-3294	Rock Billy Boogie	1979	$15
❏ AFL1-4380	Too Fast to Live, Too Young to Die	1982	$15

GORDON 'N ROGERS' INTER-URBAN ELECTRIC A&E PIT CREW & RHYTHM BAND
CAPITOL
❏ STAO-276	Bug In!	1969	$25

GORE, CHARLIE
AUDIO LAB
❏ AL-1526 [M]	The Country Gentleman	1959	$250

GORE, LESLEY
A&M
❏ SP-4564	Love Me by Name	1975	$18

MERCURY
❏ MG21066 [M]	All About Love	1966	$30
❏ SR61066 [S]	All About Love	1966	$40
— Stereo version has a different cover and liner notes than the mono version			
❏ MG20901 [M]	Boys, Boys, Boys	1964	$30
❏ SR60901 [S]	Boys, Boys, Boys	1964	$40
❏ MG21120 [M]	California Nights	1967	$30
❏ SR61120 [S]	California Nights	1967	$40
❏ MG20943 [M]	Girl Talk	1964	$30
❏ SR60943 [S]	Girl Talk	1964	$40
❏ SR61185	Golden Hits Vol. 2	1968	$40
❏ MG20805 [M]	I'll Cry If I Want To	1963	$30
— With no blurb for "It's My Party"			
❏ MG20805 [M]	I'll Cry If I Want To	1964	$25
— With blurb for "It's My Party"			
❏ SR60805 [S]	I'll Cry If I Want To	1963	$40
— With no blurb for "It's My Party"			
❏ SR60805 [S]	I'll Cry If I Want To	1964	$30
— With blurb for "It's My Party"			
❏ ML-8016	I'll Cry If I Want To	1980	$12
— Reissue of 60805			
❏ MG20849 [M]	Lesley Gore Sings of Mixed-Up Hearts	1963	$30
❏ SR60849 [S]	Lesley Gore Sings of Mixed-Up Hearts	1963	$40
❏ MG21042 [M]	My Town, My Guy & Me	1965	$30
❏ SR61042 [S]	My Town, My Guy & Me	1965	$40
❏ MG21024 [M]	The Golden Hits of Lesley Gore	1965	$30
❏ SR61024 [S]	The Golden Hits of Lesley Gore	1965	$40
— Originals have 12 tracks			
❏ SR61024 [S]	The Golden Hits of Lesley Gore	196?	$18
— Reissues have 10 tracks			
❏ 810370-1	The Golden Hits of Lesley Gore	1983	$12
— Reissue of 61024			

MOWEST
❏ MW117L	Someplace Else Now	1972	$18

RHINO
❏ RNFP-71496	The Lesley Gore Anthology (1963-1968)	1986	$18

WING
❏ SRW-16350	Girl Talk	1968	$18
❏ SRW-16382	Love, Love, Love	1968	$18
❏ PRW-2-119	The Sound of Young Love	1969	$25

GORE, MARTIN
SIRE
❏ 25980 [EP]	Counterfeit	1989	$12

GORILLA
THRILL JOCKEY
❏ 003	Deal With It	1993	$12

GORME, EYDIE
ABC-PARAMOUNT
❏ 150 [M]	Eydie Gorme	1957	$30
❏ 218 [M]	Eydie Gorme Vamps the Roaring 20's	1958	$30
❏ S-218 [S]	Eydie Gorme Vamps the Roaring 20's	196?	$15
❏ 343 [M]	Eydie in Dixieland	1960	$30
❏ S-343 [S]	Eydie in Dixieland	1960	$30
❏ 246 [M]	Eydie in Love	1958	$30
❏ S-246 [S]	Eydie in Love	196?	$15
❏ 192 [M]	Eydie Swings the Blues	1957	$30
❏ 273 [M]	Love Is a Season	1959	$30
❏ S-273 [S]	Love Is a Season	1959	$30
❏ 307 [M]	On Stage	1959	$30
❏ S-307 [S]	On Stage	1959	$30
❏ 254 [M]	Show Stoppers	1959	$30
❏ S-254 [S]	Show Stoppers	1959	$30
❏ 512 [M]	The Best of Romance, Ballads, Blues, Dixieland, Roaring 20's, Showstoppers	1965	$18

Number	Title	Yr	NM
❏ S-512 [S]	The Best of Romance, Ballads, Blues, Dixieland, Roaring 20's, Showstoppers	1965	$25

COLUMBIA
❏ CL2203 [M]	Amor	1964	$18
❏ CS9003 [S]	Amor	1964	$25
❏ PC9003	Amor	198?	$10
— Budget-line reissue			
❏ CL2012 [M]	Blame It on the Bossa Nova	1963	$18
❏ CS8812 [S]	Blame It on the Bossa Nova	1963	$25
❏ CL2476 [M]	Don't Go to Strangers	1966	$18
❏ CS9276 [S]	Don't Go to Strangers	1966	$25
❏ CL2764 [M]	Eydie Gorme's Greatest Hits	1967	$25
❏ CS9564 [S]	Eydie Gorme's Greatest Hits	1967	$18
❏ PC9564	Eydie Gorme's Greatest Hits	198?	$10
— Budget-line reissue			
❏ CL2120 [M]	Gorme Country Style	1964	$18
❏ CS8920 [S]	Gorme Country Style	1964	$25
❏ CL2065 [M]	Let the Good Times Roll	1963	$18
❏ CS8865 [S]	Let the Good Times Roll	1963	$25
❏ CL2376 [M]	More Amor	1965	$18
❏ CS9176 [S]	More Amor	1965	$25
❏ CL2557 [M]	Navidad Means Christmas	1966	$18
— With Trio Los Panchos			
❏ CS9357 [S]	Navidad Means Christmas	1966	$25
— With Trio Los Panchos			
❏ CL2594 [M]	Softly, As I Leave You	1967	$18
❏ CS9394 [S]	Softly, As I Leave You	1967	$25
❏ CS9652 [M]	The Look of Love	1968	$30
— White label promo; "Special Mono Radio Station Copy" sticker on front of stereo jacket			
❏ CS9652 [S]	The Look of Love	1968	$18
❏ CL2300 [M]	The Sound of Music (And Other Broadway Hits)	1965	$18
❏ CS9100 [S]	The Sound of Music (And Other Broadway Hits)	1965	$25

CORAL
❏ CRL57109 [M]	Delight	1957	$40

HARMONY
❏ KH30319	If He Walked Into My Life	1971	$12
❏ HS11361	Yes Indeed!	1970	$12

MGM
❏ SE-4780	It Was a Good Time	1971	$15

RCA VICTOR
❏ LSP-4093	Eydie	1968	$15
❏ LSP-4303	Tonight I'll Say a Prayer	1970	$15

UNITED ARTISTS
❏ UAL3143 [M]	Come Sing with Me	1961	$25
❏ UAS6143 [S]	Come Sing with Me	1961	$30
❏ UAL3152 [M]	I Feel So Spanish	1961	$25
❏ UAS6152 [S]	I Feel So Spanish	1961	$30
❏ UAL3189 [M]	The Very Best of Eydie	1962	$25
❏ UAS6189 [S]	The Very Best of Eydie	1962	$30

VOCALION
❏ VL3708 [M]	Here's Eydie Gorme	196?	$18
❏ VL73708 [R]	Here's Eydie Gorme	196?	$15

GORRILL, LIZ, AND ANDY FITE
NEW ARTISTS
❏ NA-1004	Phantasmagoria	1988	$25

GORRILL, LIZ
JAZZ RECORDS
❏ JR-2	I Feel Like I'm Home	198?	$35
❏ JR-7	True Fun	198?	$30

GOSDIN, VERN
AMI
❏ 1502	Today My World Slipped Away	1983	$15

COLUMBIA
❏ 1P8037	10 Years of Greatest Hits – Newly Recorded	1990	$25
— Columbia House vinyl edition (only U.S. version)			
❏ FC45104	Alone	1989	$15
❏ FC40982	Chiseled in Stone	1988	$10

COMPLEAT
❏ 671022	Greatest Hits	1986	$12
❏ 1004	If You're Gonna Do Me Wrong (Do It Right)	1983	$12
❏ 1008	There Is a Season	1984	$12
❏ 671012	Time Stood Still	1984	$12

ELEKTRA
❏ 6E-124	Never My Love	1978	$12
❏ 6E-228	The Best of Vern Gosdin	1979	$12
❏ 7E-1112	Till the End	1977	$12
❏ 6E-180	You've Got Somebody	1979	$12

GOSDIN BROTHERS, THE
Also see REX GOSDIN; VERN GOSDIN.
CAPITOL
❏ ST2852	Sounds of Goodbye	1968	$30

GOSPEL STARS, THE
TAMLA
❏ TM-222 [M]	The Great Gospel Stars	1961	$3000
— VG value 1000; VG+ value 2000			

Number	Title	Yr	NM

GOSSETT, LOU
B.T. PUPPY
❏ BTS-1013	From Me to You	1970	$40

GOSSEZ, PIERRE
VANGUARD CARDINAL
❏ C-10061	Bach Takes a Trip	1969	$25

GOTTLIEB, DANNY
ATLANTIC
❏ 81806	Aquamarine	1988	$25
❏ 81958	Whirlwind	1989	$30

GOULD, CHUCK
VIK
❏ LX-1123 [M]	Chuck Gould Plays A La Fletcher Henderson	1957	$50

GOULD, MORTON
COLUMBIA MASTERWORKS
❏ ML2065 [10]	Christmas Music for Orchestra	1949	$40
RCA VICTOR RED SEAL
❏ LSC-2217 [S]	Baton and Bows	1959	$30
— Original with "shaded dog" label			
❏ LSC-2437 [S]	Bizet: Carmen for Orchestra	1960	$40
— Original with "shaded dog" label			
❏ LSC-2104 [S]	Blues in the Night	1958	$30
— Original with "shaded dog" label			
❏ LSC-2080 [S]	Brass and Percussion	1958	$25
— Original with "shaded dog" label			
❏ LSC-2195 [S]	Copland: Billy the Kid; Rodeo	1959	$40
— Original with "shaded dog" label			
❏ LSC-2195 [S]	Copland: Billy the Kid; Rodeo	1964	$30
— Second edition with "white dog" label			
❏ LSC-2308 [S]	Doubling in Brass	1959	$50
— Original with "shaded dog" label			
❏ LSC-2532 [S]	Fall River Legend	1961	$30
— Original with "shaded dog" label			
❏ LSC-2559 [S]	Jerome Kern and Cole Porter Favorites	1961	$25
— Original with "shaded dog" label			

❏ LSC-1994 [S]	Jungle Drums	1958	$30
— Original with "shaded dog" label			
❏ LSC-2317 [S]	Living Strings	1959	$30
— Original with "shaded dog" label			
❏ LSC-2232 [S]	Moon, Wind and Stars	1959	$25
— Original with "shaded dog" label			
❏ LSC-2579 [S]	Piano Favorites	1962	$50
— Original with "shaded dog" label			
❏ LSC-2686 [S]	Spirituals for Strings	1962	$30
— Original with "shaded dog" label			
❏ LSC-2345 [S]	Tchaikovsky: 1812 Overture; Ravel: Bolero	1960	$25
— Original with "shaded dog" label			
❏ LSC-2224 [S]	Where's the Melody?	1959	$25
— Original with "shaded dog" label			

GOULDMAN, GRAHAM
RCA VICTOR
❏ LPM-3954 [M]	The Graham Gouldman Thing	1968	$300
❏ LSP-3954 [S]	The Graham Gouldman Thing	1968	$75

GOULET, ROBERT
COLUMBIA
❏ CL1676 [M]	Always You	1962	$15
❏ CS8476 [S]	Always You	1962	$18
❏ CL2342 [M]	Begin to Love	1965	$15
❏ CS9142 [S]	Begin to Love	1965	$18
❏ CS9763	Both Sides Now	1969	$15
❏ CL2727 [M]	Hollywood Mon Amour (Great Songs from the Movies)	1967	$18
❏ CS9527 [S]	Hollywood Mon Amour (Great Songs from the Movies)	1967	$15
❏ CL2482 [M]	I Remember You	1966	$15
❏ CS9282 [S]	I Remember You	1966	$18
❏ CG30011	I Wish You Love	1970	$18
❏ CS9096 [S]	My Love, Forgive Me	1964	$18
❏ CL2296 [M]	My Love Forgive Me	1964	$15
❏ CL2088 [M]	Robert Goulet in Person	1963	$15
❏ CS8888 [S]	Robert Goulet in Person	1963	$18
❏ CL2418 [M]	Robert Goulet on Broadway	1965	$15
❏ CS9218 [S]	Robert Goulet on Broadway	1965	$18
❏ CL2586 [M]	Robert Goulet on Broadway, Volume 2	1967	$15
❏ CS9386 [S]	Robert Goulet on Broadway, Volume 2	1967	$18
❏ CS9815	Robert Goulet's Greatest Hits	1969	$15
❏ PC9815	Robert Goulet's Greatest Hits	197?	$10
— Reissue with new prefix			
❏ CS9734	Robert Goulet's Wonderful World of Christmas	1968	$15
❏ CL1931 [M]	Sincerely Yours	1962	$15
❏ CS8731 [S]	Sincerely Yours	1962	$18
❏ CS9874	Souvenir d'Italie	1969	$15
❏ CL2380 [M]	Summer Sounds	1965	$15
❏ CS9180 [S]	Summer Sounds	1965	$18
❏ CL1993 [M]	The Wonderful World of Love	1963	$15
❏ CS8793 [S]	The Wonderful World of Love	1963	$18
❏ CL2076 [M]	This Christmas I Spend with You	1963	$15
❏ CS8876 [S]	This Christmas I Spend with You	1963	$18
❏ C1051	Today's Greatest Hits	1970	$15
❏ CS1051	Today's Greatest Hits	1970	$15
❏ PC1051	Today's Greatest Hits	198?	$10
— Budget-line reissue			
❏ CL2541 [M]	Traveling On	1966	$15
❏ CS9341 [S]	Traveling On	1966	$18
❏ CL1826 [M]	Two of Us	1962	$15
❏ CS8626 [S]	Two of Us	1962	$18
❏ CL2200 [M]	Without You	1964	$15
❏ CS9000 [S]	Without You	1964	$18
❏ CS9695	Woman, Woman	1968	$15
COLUMBIA SPECIAL PRODUCTS
❏ P13345	Robert Goulet's Wonderful World of Christmas	1976	$15
— Same as CS 9734, but "Exclusively distributed by Sutton Distributors, Inc.			
HARMONY
❏ KH31107	Bridge Over Troubled Water	1972	$12
❏ KH30507	Raindrops Keep Fallin' on My Head	1971	$12
MERLIN
❏ 2001	I Never Did As I Was Told	1971	$15

GOWANS, BRAD
RCA VICTOR
❏ LJM-3000 [10]	Brad Gowans' New York Nine	1954	$50

GOYKOVICH, DUSKO
ENJA
❏ 2020	After Hours	197?	$30

GOZZO, CONRAD
RCA VICTOR
❏ LPM-1124 [M]	Goz the Great	1955	$75

GRAAS, JOHN
ANDEX
❏ A-3003 [M]	Premiere in Jazz	1958	$50
❏ AS-3003 [S]	Premiere in Jazz	1959	$40
DECCA
❏ DL8343 [M]	Jazz Lab 1	1956	$175
❏ DL8478 [M]	Jazz Lab 2	1957	$120
❏ DL8677 [M]	Jazzmantics	1958	$120
❏ DL8079 [M]	Jazz Studio 2	1954	$175
❏ DL8104 [M]	Jazz Studio 3	1955	$175
EMARCY
❏ MG-36117 [M]	Coup de Graas	1958	$250
KAPP
❏ KL-1046 [M]	French Horn Jazz	1957	$50
MERCURY
❏ SR-80020 [S]	Coup de Graas	1959	$150
TREND
❏ TL-1005 [10]	French Horn Jazz	1954	$120

GRACEN, THELMA
EMARCY
❏ MG-36096 [M]	Thelma Gracen	1956	$350
WING
❏ MGW-60005 [M]	Thelma Gracen	1956	$175

GRACES, THE
A&M
❏ SP-5265	Perfect View	1989	$12

GRACIOUS
PAUL DAVIS was in this group.
CAPITOL
❏ ST-602	Gracious	1970	$40

GRADY, DON
ELEKTRA
❏ EKS-75057	Homegrown	1973	$18
—As "Don Agrati			

GRAFFITI
ABC
❏ S-663	Graffiti	1968	$75

GRAFFMAN, GARY
RCA VICTOR RED SEAL
❏ LSC-2396 [S]	Beethoven: Piano Concerto No. 3	1960	$300
— Original with "shaded dog" label			
❏ LSC-2274 [S]	Brahms: Piano Concerto No. 1	1959	$30
— With Charles Munch/Boston Symphony Orchestra; original with "shaded dog" label			
❏ LSC-2304 [S]	Chopin: Ballades	1959	$25
— Original with "shaded dog" label			
❏ LSC-2468 [S]	Chopin: Concerto No. 1; Mendelssohn: Capriccio Brilliant	1961	$150
— Original with "shaded dog" label			

GRAHAM, DAVY
LONDON
❏ PS552 [B]	Large As Life and Twice As Natural	1968	$30

GRAHAM, ED
M&K REALTIME
❏ 106	Hot Stix	1980	$40
—Direct-to-disc recording; plays at 45 rpm			

GRAHAM CENTRAL STATION
WARNER BROS.
❏ BS2876	Ain't No 'Bout-a-Doubt It	1975	$12
❏ BS42876 [Q]	Ain't No 'Bout-a-Doubt It	1975	$20
❏ BS2763	Graham Central Station	1974	$12
❏ BS42763 [Q]	Graham Central Station	1974	$20
❏ BS2937	Mirror	1976	$12
❏ BSK3175	My Radio Sure Sounds Good to Me	1978	$12
— As "Larry Graham and Graham Central Station			
❏ BS3041	Now Do U Wanta Dance	1977	$12
❏ BS2814	Release Yourself	1974	$12
❏ BSK3322	Star Walk	1979	$12
— As "Larry Graham and Graham Central Station			

GRAMERCY SIX, THE
EDISON INTERNATIONAL
❏ P-502 [M]	Great Swinging Sounds Vol. 1	1959	$30

GRAMMER, BILLY
DECCA
❏ DL4642 [M]	Country Guitar	1965	$15
❏ DL74642 [S]	Country Guitar	1965	$18
❏ DL4460 [M]	Golden Gospel Favorites	1964	$15
❏ DL74460 [S]	Golden Gospel Favorites	1964	$18
❏ DL4212 [M]	Gospel Guitar	1962	$18
❏ DL74212 [S]	Gospel Guitar	1962	$25
❏ DL4542 [M]	Gotta Travel On	1965	$15
❏ DL74542 [S]	Gotta Travel On	1965	$18
EPIC
❏ LN24233 [M]	Sunday Guitar	1967	$18
❏ BN26233 [S]	Sunday Guitar	1967	$18
MONUMENT
❏ MLP-4000 [M]	Travelin' On	1959	$40
❏ MLP-8039 [M]	Travelin' On	1965	$30
❏ SLP-18039 [P]	Travelin' On	1965	$30
VOCALION
❏ VL73826	Favorites	1968	$15

GRANATA, ROCCO
LAURIE
❏ LLP-2003 [M]	Marina and Other Italian Favorites	1960	$30

Number	Title	Yr	NM

GRAND DOMINION JAZZ BAND

GHB
❏ GHB-174	Grand Dominion Jazz Band	1984	$25

STOMP OFF
❏ SOS-1189	Ain't Nobody Got the Blues Like Me	1988	$25
❏ SOS-1139	Don't Give Up the Ship	1987	$25

GRAND FUNK RAILROAD
Includes records as "Grand Funk." Also see MARK FARNER; MARK FARNER AND DON BREWER; TERRY KNIGHT AND THE PACK.

CAPITOL
❏ SO-11356	All the Girls in the World Beware!!!	1974	$18

— With poster (deduct 33% if missing)
❏ ST-11482	Born to Die	1976	$12
❏ SABB-11445	Caught in the Act	1975	$12
❏ SKAO-471	Closer to Home	1970	$18
❏ SN-16176	Closer to Home	1981	$10
❏ SW-853 [B]	E Pluribus Funk	1971	$50

— Round cover designed like a coin; price reflects rarity in NM condition
❏ SKAO-406	Grand Funk	1970	$18
❏ SN-16177	Grand Funk	1981	$10
❏ ST-11579	Grand Funk Hits	1976	$12
❏ SN-16138	Grand Funk Hits	1981	$10
❏ SWBB-633	Live Album	1970	$18

— Includes poster
❏ SABB-11042 [B]	Mark, Don and Mel 1969-71	1972	$25
❏ ST-307 [B]	On Time	1969	$30
❏ SN-16178	On Time	1981	$10
❏ SMAS-11099	Phoenix	1972	$15
❏ SWAE-11278	Shinin' On	1974	$30

— With 3-D glasses attached to cover and with 3-D poster
❏ SWAE-11278	Shinin' On	1974	$10

— With 3-D glasses missing and no poster
❏ SW-764	Survival	1971	$18

— Lime-green label; add $5 if individual photos of the band members are included
❏ SW-764 [B]	Survival	1971	$18

— Red "target" label; add $5 if individual photos of the band members are included
❏ SW-764	Survival	1973	$12

— Orange label, "Capitol" at bottom
❏ SMAS-11207	We're An American Band	1973	$30

— Gold vinyl with sheet of four stickers
❏ SMAS-11207	We're An American Band	1973	$12

— Black vinyl
❏ SMAS-11207	We're An American Band	1973	$25

— Gold vinyl without sheet of four stickers
❏ 21692	We're An American Band	1999	$30

— Limited-edition reissue on 180-gram gold vinyl with original 1973 packaging

FULL MOON
❏ HS3625	Grand Funk Lives	1981	$12
❏ 23750	What's Funk	1983	$12

MCA
❏ 2216	Good Singin' Good Playin'	1976	$15

— Produced by Frank Zappa

GRANDMA'S ROCKERS

FREDLO
❏ 6727	Homemade Apple Pie	1967	$1500

— VG value 500; VG+ value 1000

GRANDMASTER FLASH

ELEKTRA
❏ 60723	Ba-Dop-Boom-Bang	1987	$12
❏ 60769	On the Strength	1988	$15
❏ 60389	They Said It Couldn't Be Done	1985	$15

SUGAR HILL
❏ SH9121	Greatest Messages	1984	$25

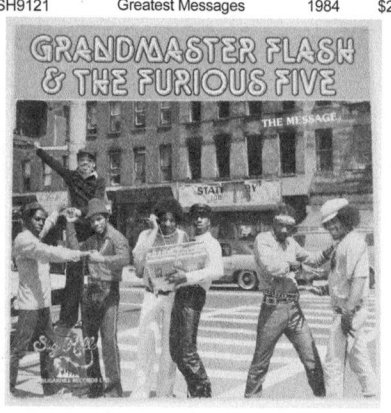

❏ SH268 [B]	The Message	1982	$25

— Note: This album has been reissued to look like the original

GRANDMASTER MELLE MEL

NEW DAY
❏ ND222	Piano	1989	$12

SUGAR HILL
❏ SH9205	Grandmaster Melle Mel and the Furious Five	1984	$18

GRANT, AMY

A&M
❏ SP-5057	A Christmas Album	1985	$12

— Reissue of Myrrh 6768
❏ SP-5056	Age to Age	1985	$10

— Reissue of Myrrh 6697
❏ SP-5051	Amy Grant	1985	$10

— Reissue of Myrrh 6586 with new cover
❏ SP-5054	Amy Grant In Concert	1985	$10

— Reissue of Myrrh 6668
❏ SP-5055	Amy Grant In Concert, Volume Two	1985	$10

— Reissue of Myrrh 6677
❏ 7502153211	Heart in Motion	1991	$18
❏ SP-5199	Lead Me On	1988	$10

— Issued simultaneously with Myrrh 687106
❏ SP-5052	My Father's Eyes	1985	$10

— Reissue of Myrrh 6625
❏ SP-5053	Never Alone	1985	$10

— Reissue of Myrrh 6645
❏ SP-5058	Straight Ahead	1985	$10

— Reissue of Myrrh 675706
❏ SP-3900	The Collection	1986	$10

— Issued simultaneously with Myrrh 684306
❏ SP-5060	Unguarded	1985	$10

— Issued simultaneously with Myrrh 680606, and with four different covers; "W" on spine
❏ SP-5060	Unguarded	1985	$10

— Issued simultaneously with Myrrh 680606, and with four different covers; "O" on spine
❏ SP-5060	Unguarded	1985	$10

— Issued simultaneously with Myrrh 680606, and with four different covers; "R" on spine
❏ SP-5060	Unguarded	1985	$10

— Issued simultaneously with Myrrh 680606, and with four different covers; "D" on spine

MYRRH
❏ MSB-6768	A Christmas Album	1983	$15
❏ 901-611135-2 [DJ]	A Christmas Album	1983	$100

— Promo-only picture disc in die-cut sleeve
❏ MSB-6697	Age to Age	1982	$15
❏ MSB-6586 [B]	Amy Grant	1977	$25

— With colorized "ugly cover" of Amy's head and shoulders; "Amy Grant" at upper left
❏ MSB-6586	Amy Grant	198?	$12

— With new cover of Amy in natural color; "Amy Grant" at upper right
❏ MSB-6668	Amy Grant In Concert	1981	$15
❏ MSB-6677	Amy Grant In Concert, Volume Two	1981	$15
❏ 701-687106-1	Lead Me On	1988	$12

— Issued simultaneously with A&M 5199
❏ MSB-6625	My Father's Eyes	1979	$15
❏ MSB-6645	Never Alone	1980	$15
❏ 701-675706-4	Straight Ahead	1984	$12
❏ 901-622335-5 [DJ]	Straight Ahead	1984	$150

— Promo-only music and interview album for Christian radio stations
❏ 701-684306-8	The Collection	1986	$12

— Issued simultaneously with A&M 3900
❏ 701-680606-5	Unguarded	1985	$12

— Issued simultaneously with A&M 5060, and with four different covers; "W" on spine
❏ 701-680606-5	Unguarded	1985	$12

— Issued simultaneously with A&M 5060, and with four different covers; "O" on spine
❏ 701-680606-5	Unguarded	1985	$12

— Issued simultaneously with A&M 5060, and with four different covers; "R" on spine
❏ 701-680606-5	Unguarded	1985	$12

— Issued simultaneously with A&M 5060, and with four different covers; "D" on spine

GRANT, EARL

DECCA
❏ DL75158	A Time for Us	1970	$15
❏ DL4806 [M]	Bali Ha'i	1967	$15
❏ DL74806 [S]	Bali Ha'i	1967	$18
❏ DL4231 [M]	Beyond the Reef	1962	$15
❏ DL74231 [S]	Beyond the Reef	1962	$18
❏ DL4188 [M]	Earl After Dark	1961	$15
❏ DL74188 [S]	Earl After Dark	1961	$18
❏ DL75223	Earl Grant	1970	$15

❏ DL4299 [M]	Earl Grant at Basin Street East	1962	$15
❏ DL74299 [S]	Earl Grant at Basin Street East	1962	$18
❏ DL4813 [M]	Earl Grant's Greatest Hits	1967	$18
❏ DL74813 [S]	Earl Grant's Greatest Hits	1967	$18
❏ DL4165 [M]	Ebb Tide	1961	$15
❏ DL74165 [S]	Ebb Tide	1961	$18
❏ DL4454 [M]	Fly Me to the Moon	1963	$15
❏ DL74454 [S]	Fly Me to the Moon	1963	$18
❏ DL4937 [M]	Gently Swingin'	1968	$25
❏ DL74937 [S]	Gently Swingin'	1968	$18
❏ DL8905 [M]	Grant Takes Rhythm	1959	$18
❏ DL78905 [S]	Grant Takes Rhythm	1959	$25
❏ DL75052	In Motion	1969	$18
❏ DL4811 [M]	Just a Closer Walk with Thee	1967	$18
❏ DL74811 [S]	Just a Closer Walk with Thee	1967	$18
❏ DL4506 [M]	Just for a Thrill	1964	$15
❏ DL74506 [S]	Just for a Thrill	1964	$18
❏ DL4576 [M]	Just One More Time	1964	$15
❏ DL74576 [S]	Just One More Time	1964	$18
❏ DL4338 [M]	Midnight Sun	1963	$15
❏ DL74338 [S]	Midnight Sun	1963	$18
❏ DL8916 [M]	Nothing But the Blues	1960	$18
❏ DL78916 [S]	Nothing But the Blues	1960	$25
❏ DL8935 [M]	Paris Is My Beat	1960	$18
❏ DL78935 [S]	Paris Is My Beat	1960	$25
❏ DL4729 [M]	Songs Made Famous by Nat Cole	1966	$15
❏ DL74729 [S]	Songs Made Famous by Nat Cole	1966	$18
❏ DL4974 [M]	Spanish Eyes	1968	$30
❏ DL74974 [S]	Spanish Eyes	1968	$18
❏ DL4624 [M]	Spotlight on Earl Grant	1965	$15
❏ DL74624 [S]	Spotlight on Earl Grant	1965	$18
❏ DL4738 [M]	Stand By Me	1966	$15
❏ DL74738 [S]	Stand By Me	1966	$18
❏ DXS7204	The Best of Earl Grant	1969	$25
❏ DL8830 [M]	The End	1959	$18
❏ DL78830 [S]	The End	1959	$25
❏ DL4044 [M]	The Magic of Earl Grant	1960	$15
❏ DL74044 [S]	The Magic of Earl Grant	1960	$18
❏ DL8672 [M]	The Versatile Earl Grant	1958	$25
❏ DL75108	This Magic Moment	1970	$18
❏ DL4623 [M]	Trade Winds	1965	$15
❏ DL74623 [S]	Trade Winds	1965	$18
❏ DL4677 [M]	Winter Wonderland	1965	$15
❏ DL74677 [S]	Winter Wonderland	1965	$18
❏ DL4405 [M]	Yes Sirree	1963	$15
❏ DL74405 [S]	Yes Sirree	1963	$18

VOCALION
❏ VL3793 [M]	It's So Good	1967	$15
❏ VL73793 [S]	It's So Good	1967	$15
❏ VL73893	One for My Baby	1969	$15
❏ VL73860	Send for Me	1969	$15

GRANT, EDDY

EPIC
❏ JE36522	My Turn to Love You	1980	$15
❏ JE36244	Walking on Sunshine	1979	$15

PORTRAIT
❏ BFR40284	Born Tuff	1986	$12
❏ FR39261	Going for Broke	1984	$12
❏ B6R38554	Killer on the Rampage	1983	$12

— Original prefix
❏ FR38554	Killer on the Rampage	1983	$10

— Reissue prefix after LP became popular

GRANT, GOGI

ERA
❏ 20001 [M]	Suddenly There's Gogi Grant	1956	$150

— Red vinyl

❏ 20001 [M]	Suddenly There's Gogi Grant	1956	$75

— Black vinyl
❏ EL-106 [M]	The Wayward Wind	196?	$30

Number	Title	Yr	NM
LIBERTY			
LRP-3144 [M]	If You Want to Get to Heaven, Shout	1960	$30
LST-7144 [S]	If You Want to Get to Heaven, Shout	1960	$40
PETE			
S-1101	Gogi Grant	1968	$18
S-1111	The Way a Woman Feels	1970	$18
RCA VICTOR			
LPM-2000 [M]	Granted… It's Gogi	1960	$30
LSP-2000 [S]	Granted… It's Gogi	1960	$40
LOC-1030 [M]	The Helen Morgan Story	1957	$75
LPM-1940 [M]	Torch Time	1959	$30
LSP-1940 [S]	Torch Time	1959	$40
LPM-1717 [M]	Welcome to My Heart	1958	$40

GRANT, TOM

Number	Title	Yr	NM
CMG			
CML-8007	Heart of the City	198?	$20
CML-8009	Just the Right Moment	198?	$20
CML-8010	Take Me to Your Dream	198?	$20
CML-8008	Tom Grant	198?	$20
PAUSA			
7174	Just the Right Moment	1985	$25
7199	Take Me to Your Dream	1986	$25
7145	Tom Grant	198?	$25

GRAPEFRUIT

Number	Title	Yr	NM
ABC DUNHILL			
DS-50050 [B]	Around Grapefruit	1968	$75
RCA VICTOR			
LSP-4215	Deep Water	1969	$30

GRAPPELLI, STEPHANE, AND BARNEY KESSEL

Number	Title	Yr	NM
BLACK LION			
105	I Remember Django	197?	$35
JAZZ MAN			
5008	I Remember Django	198?	$25
MOBILE FIDELITY			
1-111	I Remember Django	1984	$50

—Audiophile vinyl

GRAPPELLI, STEPHANE, AND DAVID GRISMAN

Number	Title	Yr	NM
WARNER BROS.			
BSK3550	Live	1981	$25

GRAPPELLI, STEPHANE, AND GEORGE SHEARING

Number	Title	Yr	NM
VERVE			
821868-1	The Reunion	1985	$25

GRAPPELLI, STEPHANE, AND HANK JONES

Number	Title	Yr	NM
MUSE			
MR-5287	A Two-fer	198?	$25

GRAPPELLI, STEPHANE, AND JEAN-LUC PONTY

Number	Title	Yr	NM
EVEREST ARCHIVE OF FOLK & JAZZ			
FS-355	Violin Summit	1979	$25
PAUSA			
7074	Giants	1979	$25

GRAPPELLI, STEPHANE, AND MCCOY TYNER

Number	Title	Yr	NM
MILESTONE			
M-9181	One on One	1990	$30

GRAPPELLI, STEPHANE, AND TERESA BREWER

Number	Title	Yr	NM
DOCTOR JAZZ			
FW38448	On the Road Again	1983	$25

GRAPPELLI, STEPHANE, AND VASSAR CLEMENTS

Number	Title	Yr	NM
FLYING FISH			
FF-421	Together at Last	1987	$25

GRAPPELLI, STEPHANE, AND YO-YO MA

Number	Title	Yr	NM
CBS			
FM45574	Anything Goes: The Music of Cole Porter	1989	$30

GRAPPELLI, STEPHANE

Number	Title	Yr	NM
ANGEL			
DS-37790	Brandenberg Boogie (Music of Bach)	1980	$30
DS-38063	Just One of Those Things	198?	$30
DS-37886	We've Got the World on a String	198?	$30
ARSITA FREEDOM			
AL1033	The Parisian	197?	$30
ATLANTIC			
1391 [M]	Feeling + Finesse = Jazz	1962	$175
SD1391 [S]	Feeling + Finesse = Jazz	1962	$175
90140	Feeling + Finesse = Jazz	198?	$25
82095	Olympia '88	1990	$30

Number	Title	Yr	NM
BARCLAY			
820007	Music to Pass the Time	196?	$25
BASF			
20876	Afternoon in Paris	1972	$35
BLACK LION			
047	I Got Rhythm	1974	$25
211	Just One of the Things	1974	$35
313	Talk of the Town	1975	$30
CLASSIC JAZZ			
23	Homage to Django	197?	$25
24	Stephane Grappelli and Bill Coleman	197?	$35
COLUMBIA			
JC35415	Uptown Dance	1978	$25
CONCORD JAZZ			
CJ-139	Stephane Grappelli at the Winery	1980	$25
CJ-225	Stephanova	1983	$25
CJ-169	Vintage 1981	1981	$25
DOCTOR JAZZ			
FW38727	Live at Carnegie Hall	1983	$25
EMARCY			
MG-36120 [M]	Improvisations	1957	$250
EVEREST ARCHIVE OF FOLK & JAZZ			
311	Stephane Grappelli	197?	$30
FANTASY			
OJC-441	Tivoli Gardens	1990	$25
GRP			
GR-1032	Stephane Grappelli Plays Jerome Kern	1987	$25
PABLO LIVE			
2308220	Tivoli Gardens	1979	$30
PAUSA			
7071	Afternoon in Paris	1979	$25
7098	Violinspiration	198?	$25
7041	Young Django	1979	$25
VANGUARD			
VSD-81/82	Satin Doll	197?	$35
VMS-73130	Satin Doll, Volume 1	198?	$25
VERVE			
MGV-20001 [M]	Musique Pour Arreter Le Temps (Music to Stop the Clock By)	195?	$75

—As "Stephane Grappelly"

Number	Title	Yr	NM
815672-1	Young Django	198?	$25

GRASS ROOTS, THE

Number	Title	Yr	NM
ABC			
PRO-40013	Midnight Confessions/Sooner or Later/Where Were You When I Needed You//Temptation Eyes/Wait a Million Years/Heaven Knows	1974	$25

—Quadraphonic jukebox issue; small hole, plays at 33 1/3 rpm

Number	Title	Yr	NM
PRO-40013 [PS]	Their 16 Greatest Hits	1974	$25

—Has the same sleeve as ABC-Dunhill PRO-50107, except for a sticker "4 Channel - Quadraphonic" on front

Number	Title	Yr	NM
AC-30003	The ABC Collection	1976	$18
ABC DUNHILL			
DSX-50137	A Lotta Mileage	1973	$18
DS-50027	Feelings	1968	$18

—Reissue with ABC logo

Number	Title	Yr	NM
DS-50047	Golden Grass	1968	$25
DS-50067	Leaving It All Behind	1969	$25
DS-50052	Lovin' Things	1969	$25
DS-50087	More Golden Grass	1970	$25
DSX-50112	Move Along	1972	$18
DSX-50107	Their 16 Greatest Hits	1971	$25
COMMAND			
QD-40013 [Q]	Their 16 Greatest Hits	1974	$40
DUNHILL			

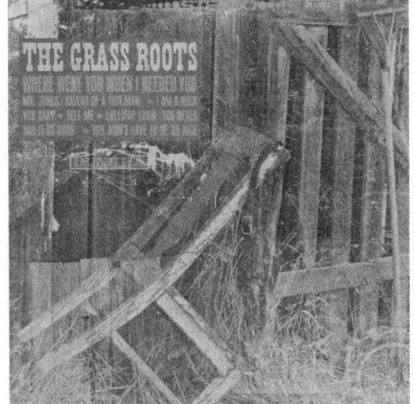

Number	Title	Yr	NM
D-50027 [M]	Feelings	1968	$30
DS-50027 [S]	Feelings	1968	$25
D-50020 [M]	Let's Live for Today	1967	$30
DS-50020 [S]	Let's Live for Today	1967	$30
D-50011 [M]	Where Were You When I Needed You	1966	$85
DS-50011 [S]	Where Were You When I Needed You	1966	$150
HAVEN			
ST-9204	The Grass Roots	1975	$18
MCA			
5331	Powers of the Night	1982	$15
37154	Their 16 Greatest Hits	198?	$10

—Budget-line reissue of ABC Dunhill 50107

GRATEFUL DEAD, THE

Also see JERRY GARCIA; MICKEY HART; KEITH AND DONNA; BOB WEIR.

Number	Title	Yr	NM
ARISTA			
AL8575	Built to Last	1989	$18
A2L8606	Dead Set	1981	$18
AL8112	Dead Set	198?	$35

—Budget-line reissue of 8606

Number	Title	Yr	NM
AL9508	Go to Heaven	1980	$15
AL8332	Go to Heaven	198?	$12

—Budget-line reissue of 9508

Number	Title	Yr	NM
SP-35 [DJ]	Grateful Dead Sampler	1978	$75
AL8452	In the Dark	1987	$18
A2L8604	Reckoning	1981	$18
AB4198 [B]	Shakedown Street	1978	$18
AL8321	Shakedown Street	198?	$12

—Budget-line reissue of 4198

Number	Title	Yr	NM
AL7001	Terrapin Station	1977	$18
AL7001 [DJ]	Terrapin Station	1977	$75

—Radio station promos are banded for airplay

Number	Title	Yr	NM
AL8329	Terrapin Station	198?	$12

—Budget-line reissue of 7001

Number	Title	Yr	NM
AL38634	Without a Net	1990	$35
DIRECT DISK			
SD-16619	Terrapin Station	1980	$150

—Audiophile vinyl

Number	Title	Yr	NM
GRATEFUL DEAD			
GD-LA494-G [B]	Blues for Allah	1975	$35
GD-102	Grateful Dead from the Mars Hotel	1974	$35

—Without United Artists distribution

Number	Title	Yr	NM
GD-102	Grateful Dead from the Mars Hotel	1975	$18

—With United Artists distribution and "Grateful Dead" label

Number	Title	Yr	NM
GD-LA620-27690 [B]	Steal Your Face	1976	$35
GD-01 [DJ]	Wake of the Flood	1973	$500

—Green vinyl meant for fan-club members; ironically, most copies were damaged in a flood before distribution

Number	Title	Yr	NM
GD-01 [B]	Wake of the Flood	1973	$35

—With no contributing artists on back cover

Number	Title	Yr	NM
GD-01	Wake of the Flood	1975	$18

—With contributing artists on back cover and United Artists distribution

Number	Title	Yr	NM
MOBILE FIDELITY			
Jan-0014	American Beauty	1980	$150

—Audiophile vinyl

Number	Title	Yr	NM
1-172 [B]	Grateful Dead from the Mars Hotel	1984	$150

—Audiophile vinyl

Number	Title	Yr	NM
PAIR			
PDL2-1053	For the Faithful...	1986	$15
PRIDE			
PRD 0016	The History of the Grateful Dead	1972	$35

—Reissue of material from Sunflower LPs

Number	Title	Yr	NM

RHINO

Number	Title	Yr	NM
❏ R1-74397	American Beauty	2003	$30

— Reissue on 180-gram vinyl

❏ R1537164 [B]	Family Dog At The Great Highway, San Francisco, CA, April 18, 1970	2013	$45
❏ R1541159 [B]	Hampton '79	2014	$50
❏ R1-74395	Live/Dead	2003	$35

— Reissue on 180-gram vinyl

❏ R1534703 [B]	Rare Cuts & Oddities 1966	2013	$45
❏ R1552660 [B]	Shrine Exposition Hall, Los Angeles, CA 11/10/1967	2016	$60
❏ R1536031 [B]	Veneta, Oregon 8/27/72 (Sunshine Daydream)	2013	$150
❏ R1544279 [B]	Wake Up To Find Out	2015	$100

— Record Store Day

| ❏ R1-74396 | Workingman's Dead | 2003 | $30 |

— Reissue on 180-gram vinyl

SUNFLOWER

| ❏ SNF-5004 | Historic Dead | 1971 | $50 |
| ❏ SUN-5001 | Vintage Dead | 1970 | $45 |

— Album has been counterfeited, but bogus covers are 1/4" shorter than normal LP cover

UNITED ARTISTS

| ❏ GD-102 | Grateful Dead from the Mars Hotel | 1978 | $18 |

— With United Artists "sunrise" label

WARNER BROS,

| ❏ WS1869 [B] | Workingman's Dead | 2015 | $85 |

— 180 gram, swirled gold and brown vinyl

WARNER BROS.

| ❏ WS1893 | American Beauty | 1970 | $35 |

— Green label with "WB" logo

| ❏ WS1893 | American Beauty | 1973 | $15 |

— Burbank" palm-trees label

| ❏ WS1893 | American Beauty | 1979 | $10 |

— White or tan label

| ❏ ST-93416 | American Beauty | 1970 | $75 |

— Capitol Record Club edition; green label with "W7" logo

| ❏ WS1749 | Anthem of the Sun | 1968 | $50 |

— Green label with "W7" logo

| ❏ WS1749 | Anthem of the Sun | 1970 | $18 |

— Green label with "WB" logo, purple cover

| ❏ WS1749 | Anthem of the Sun | 197? | $50 |

— Green label with "WB" logo, white background on cover with radically remixed version of LP

| ❏ WS1749 | Anthem of the Sun | 1973 | $15 |

— Burbank" palm-trees label

| ❏ WS1749 | Anthem of the Sun | 1979 | $10 |

— White or tan label

| ❏ WS1790 | Aoxomoxoa | 1969 | $45 |

— Green label with "W7" logo

| ❏ WS1790 | Aoxomoxoa | 1970 | $18 |

— Green label with "WB" logo

| ❏ WS1790 | Aoxomoxoa | 1973 | $15 |

— Burbank" palm-trees label

| ❏ WS1790 | Aoxomoxoa | 1979 | $10 |

— White or tan label

| ❏ 3WX2668 | Europe '72 | 1972 | $50 |

— Green labels with "WB" logo

| ❏ 3WX2668 | Europe '72 | 1973 | $35 |

— Burbank" palm-trees labels

| ❏ 3WX2668 | Europe '72 | 1979 | $15 |

— White or tan labels

| ❏ 2WS1935 | Grateful Dead | 1971 | $45 |

— Green labels with "WB" logo

| ❏ 2WS1935 | Grateful Dead | 1973 | $18 |

— Burbank" palm-trees labels

| ❏ 2WS1935 | Grateful Dead | 1979 | $12 |

— White or tan labels

| ❏ BS2721 | History of the Grateful Dead, Vol. 1 (Bear's Choice) | 1973 | $35 |

— Burbank" palm-trees labels

| ❏ BS2721 | History of the Grateful Dead, Vol. 1 (Bear's Choice) | 1978 | $10 |

— White or tan labels

| ❏ 2WS1830 | Live/Dead | 1969 | $75 |

— Green labels with "W7" logo

| ❏ 2WS1830 | Live/Dead | 1970 | $35 |

— Green labels with "WB" logo

| ❏ 2WS1830 | Live/Dead | 1973 | $18 |

— Burbank" palm-trees labels

| ❏ 2WS1830 | Live/Dead | 1979 | $12 |

— White or tan labels

| ❏ W2764 | The Best of/Skeletons from the Closet | 1974 | $35 |

— Burbank" palm-trees labels

| ❏ W2764 | The Best of/Skeletons from the Closet | 1979 | $10 |

— White or tan labels

| ❏ W1689 [M] | The Grateful Dead | 1967 | $400 |
| ❏ WS1689 [S] | The Grateful Dead | 1967 | $150 |

— Gold label

| ❏ WS1689 [S] | The Grateful Dead | 1968 | $45 |

— Green label with "W7" logo

| ❏ WS1689 [S] | The Grateful Dead | 1970 | $18 |

— Green label with "WB" logo

| ❏ WS1689 [S] | The Grateful Dead | 1973 | $15 |

— Burbank" palm-trees label

| ❏ WS1689 [S] | The Grateful Dead | 1979 | $10 |

— White or tan label

| ❏ 2WS3091 | What a Long Strange Trip It's Been: The Best of the Grateful Dead | 1977 | $35 |

— Burbank" palm-trees labels

| ❏ 2WS3091 | What a Long Strange Trip It's Been: The Best of the Grateful Dead | 1979 | $12 |

— White or tan labels

| ❏ WS1869 | Workingman's Dead | 1970 | $35 |

— Green label with "WB" logo; textured cover with back cover slick upside down

| ❏ WS1869 | Workingman's Dead | 1973 | $15 |

— Burbank" palm-trees label; standard cover with back cover right side up

| ❏ WS1869 | Workingman's Dead | 1979 | $10 |

— White or tan label

GRAVEDIGGAZ

GEE STREET

| ❏ 32501-1 | The Pick, the Sickle and the Shovel | 1997 | $15 |

GRAVENITES, NICK

COLUMBIA

| ❏ CS9899 [B] | My Labors | 1969 | $25 |

GRAVES, CONLEY

DECCA

❏ DL8220 [M]	Genius at Work	1956	$175
❏ DL8412 [M]	Piano Dynamics	1957	$120
❏ DL8475 [M]	Rendezvous in Paris	1957	$120

LIBERTY

| ❏ LRP-3007 [M] | V.I.P. (Very Important Pianist) | 1956 | $40 |

NOCTURNE

| ❏ NLP-4 [10] | Piano Artistry | 1954 | $150 |

GRAVES, JOE

CAPITOL

| ❏ T1977 [M] | The Great New Swingers | 1963 | $75 |
| ❏ ST1977 [S] | The Great New Swingers | 1963 | $75 |

GRAVES, MILFORD

ESP-DISK'

| ❏ 1015 [M] | Milford Graves Percussion Ensemble | 1966 | $150 |
| ❏ S-1015 [S] | Milford Graves Percussion Ensemble | 1966 | $150 |

IPS

| ❏ 04 | Babi | 197? | $35 |
| ❏ 290 | Nommo | 197? | $35 |

GRAVES, TERESA

KIRSHNER

| ❏ KOS-104 | Teresa Graves | 1970 | $30 |

GRAVINE, ANITA

STASH

| ❏ ST-256 | I Always Knew | 1985 | $25 |

GRAVITY ADJUSTERS EXPANSION BAND

NOCTURNE

| ❏ NRS-302 | One | 1973 | $300 |

GRAY, BILLY

DECCA

| ❏ DL5567 [10] | Dance-O-Rama | 1956 | $250 |

GRAY, CLAUDE

DECCA

❏ DL4882 [M]	Claude Gray Sings	1967	$30
❏ DL74882 [S]	Claude Gray Sings	1967	$25
❏ DL74963	The Easy Way of Claude Gray	1968	$25

HILLTOP

| ❏ JM-6051 [M] | Treasure of Love | 1967 | $18 |
| ❏ JS-6051 [S] | Treasure of Love | 1967 | $15 |

MERCURY

❏ MG-20718 [M]	Country Goes to Town	1962	$25
❏ SR-60718 [S]	Country Goes to Town	1962	$30
❏ SR-60658 [S]	Songs of Broken Love Affairs	1962	$30
❏ MG-20658 [M]	Songs of Broken Love Affairs	1962	$25

GRAY, DOBIE

CAPITOL

| ❏ ST-12489 | From Where I Stand | 1986 | $12 |

CAPRICORN

| ❏ CP 0163 | New Ray of Sunshine | 1976 | $12 |

CHARGER

| ❏ CHR-M-2002 [M] | Dobie Gray Sings for "In" Crowders That Go "Go Go | 1965 | $40 |
| ❏ CHR-S-2002 [S] | Dobie Gray Sings for "In" Crowders That Go "Go Go | 1965 | $120 |

DECCA

| ❏ DL75397 | Drift Away | 1973 | $15 |

INFINITY

| ❏ INF-9001 | Midnight Diamond | 1979 | $12 |

MCA

| ❏ 515 | Drift Away | 1974 | $12 |

— Reissue of Decca 75397

| ❏ 449 | Hey Dixie | 1974 | $12 |
| ❏ 371 | Loving Arms | 1973 | $12 |

ROBOX

| ❏ RBX8102 | Welcome Home | 1981 | $12 |

STRIPE

| ❏ LPM2001 [M] | Look -- Dobie Gray | 1963 | $150 |

TIGER LILY

| ❏ TL14022 [B] | Dobie Gray | 1976 | $300 |

GRAY, DOLORES

CAPITOL

| ❏ T897 [M] | Warm Brandy | 1957 | $30 |

GRAY, GLEN

CAPITOL

| ❏ T856 [M] | Casa Loma Caravan | 1957 | $100 |

— Turquoise label

❏ W747 [M]	Casa Loma in Hi-Fi!	1956	$150
❏ T1506 [M]	Please Mr. Gray…More Sounds of the Great Bands	1961	$75
❏ ST1506 [S]	Please Mr. Gray…More Sounds of the Great Bands	1961	$50
❏ T1615 [M]	Shall We Swing?	1961	$75
❏ ST1615 [S]	Shall We Swing?	1961	$50
❏ T1234 [M]	Solo Spotlight	1960	$75
❏ ST1234 [S]	Solo Spotlight	1960	$50
❏ W1022 [M]	Sounds of the Great Bands!	1959	$75
❏ SW1022 [S]	Sounds of the Great Bands!	1959	$50
❏ SM-1022	Sounds of the Great Bands!	197?	$25

— Reissue

❏ T2131 [M]	Sounds of the Great Bands in Latin	1964	$50
❏ ST2131 [S]	Sounds of the Great Bands in Latin	1964	$75
❏ T1067 [M]	Sounds of the Great Bands Volume 2	1959	$75
❏ ST1067 [S]	Sounds of the Great Bands Volume 2	1959	$50
❏ SM-1067	Sounds of the Great Bands Volume 2	197?	$25

— Reissue

❏ T1739 [M]	Sounds of the Great Bands Volume 5: They All Swung the Blues	1962	$75
❏ ST1739 [S]	Sounds of the Great Bands Volume 5: They All Swung the Blues	1962	$50
❏ T1938 [M]	Sounds of the Great Bands Volume 7: Today's Best	1963	$50
❏ ST1938 [S]	Sounds of the Great Bands Volume 7: Today's Best	1963	$75
❏ T2014 [M]	Sounds of the Great Bands Volume 8: More of Today's Best	1964	$50
❏ ST2014 [S]	Sounds of the Great Bands Volume 8: More of Today's Best	1964	$75
❏ T1588 [M]	Sounds of the Great Casa Loma Band	1961	$50
❏ DT1588 [R]	Sounds of the Great Casa Loma Band	1961	$75
❏ SM-1588	Sounds of the Great Casa Loma Band	197?	$25

— Reissue

❏ T1289 [M]	Swingin' Decade	1960	$75
❏ ST1289 [S]	Swingin' Decade	1960	$50
❏ T1400 [M]	Swingin' Southern Style	1961	$75
❏ ST1400 [S]	Swingin' Southern Style	1961	$50
❏ T1812 [M]	Themes of the Great Bands	1963	$75
❏ ST1812 [S]	Themes of the Great Bands	1963	$50
❏ SM-1812	Themes of the Great Bands	197?	$25

— Reissue

CIRCLE

| ❏ 16 | Glen Gray and the Casa Loma Orchestra | 198? | $25 |

CORAL

| ❏ CRL56009 [10] | Glen Gray Souvenirs | 1950 | $150 |
| ❏ CRL56006 [10] | Hoagy Carmichael Songs | 1950 | $150 |

CREATIVE WORLD

| ❏ ST-1055 | Shall We Swing? | 197? | $25 |

DECCA

❏ DL75016 [R]	Greatest Hits	1968	$30
❏ DL5089 [10]	Musical Smoke Rings	1950	$120
❏ DL5397 [10]	No-Name Jive	1953	$175
❏ DL8570 [M]	Smoke Rings	1957	$120

Number	Title	Yr	NM
HARMONY			
❏ HL7045 [M]	The Great Recordings of Glen Gray	1957	$50
HINDSIGHT			
❏ HSR-104	Glen Gray and the Casa Loma Orchestra, 1939-1940	198?	$25
❏ HSR-120	Glen Gray and the Casa Loma Orchestra, 1943-1946	198?	$25
INSIGHT			
❏ 214	Glen Gray and the Casa Loma Orchestra, 1939-1946	198?	$25
MCA			
❏ 122	Greatest Hits	1973	$25
— Reissue of Decca 75016			
❏ 20199	Smoke Rings	198?	$20
❏ 4076	The Best of Glen Gray	197?	$30

GRAY, JERRY
Number	Title	Yr	NM
CRAFTSMAN			
❏ 8035 [M]	More Miller Hits	195?	$25
DECCA			
❏ DL5375 [10]	A Tribute to Glenn Miller	1951	$250
❏ DL5478 [10]	Dance Time	1952	$175
❏ DL5266 [10]	Dance to the Music of Gray	1950	$175
❏ DL5312 [10]	In the Mood ...	1951	$250
❏ DL8101 [M]	Jerry Gray and His Orchestra	1955	$175
DOT			
❏ DLP-3741 [M]	This Is Jerry Gray	1966	$85
❏ DLP-25741 [S]	This Is Jerry Gray	1966	$85
GOLDEN TONE			
❏ C-4005 [M]	Glenn Miller Favorites	196?	$30
HINDSIGHT			
❏ HSR-212	Jerry Gray and His Orchestra 1952	198?	$25
LIBERTY			
❏ LRP-3038 [M]	Hi-Fi Shades of Gray	1956	$40
❏ LST-7002 [S]	Hi-Fi Shades of Gray	1958	$40
❏ LRP-3089 [M]	Jerry Gray at the Hollywood Palladium	1958	$40
❏ LST-7013 [S]	Jerry Gray at the Hollywood Palladium	1958	$40
TOPS			
❏ L-1627 [M]	A Salute to Glenn Miller	1958	$30
❏ L-1640 [M]	Glenn Miller Greats	1958	$30
VOCALION			
❏ VL3602 [M]	A Tribute to Glenn Miller	196?	$25
WARNER BROS.			
❏ W1446 [M]	Singin' and Swingin'	1962	$25
❏ WS1446 [S]	Singin' and Swingin'	1962	$30

GRAY, MACY
Number	Title	Yr	NM
EPIC			
❏ E69490	On How Life Is	1999	$15
❏ E85200	The Id	2001	$15

GRAY, MARK
Number	Title	Yr	NM
COLUMBIA			
❏ FC39143	Magic	1984	$10
❏ PC39143	Magic	1985	$10
— Budget-line reissue with new prefix			
❏ FC40126	That Feeling Inside	1986	$10
❏ FC39518	This Ol' Piano	1984	$10
❏ PC39518	This Ol' Piano	1986	$10
— Budget-line reissue with new prefix			

GRAY, WARDELL, AND DEXTER GORDON
Number	Title	Yr	NM
DECCA			
❏ DL7025 [10]	The Chase and the Steeple Chase	1952	$300
JAZZTONE			
❏ J-1235 [M]	The Chase and the Steeple Chase	1956	$50
MCA			
❏ 1336	The Chase and the Steeple Chase	198?	$25

GRAY, WARDELL
Number	Title	Yr	NM
CROWN			
❏ CLP-5293 [M]	Wardell Gray	196?	$35
— Gray label			
❏ CST-293 [R]	Wardell Gray	196?	$30
❏ CLP-5004 [M]	Way Out Wardell	1957	$40
— Originals have a black label with the word "crown" in small letters at top			
❏ CLP-5278 [M]	Way Out Wardell	1962	$25
❏ CST-278 [R]	Way Out Wardell	1962	$15
CUSTOM			
❏ CS-1060 [R]	Shades of Gray	196?	$30
❏ CM-2060 [M]	Shades of Gray	196?	$35
FANTASY			
❏ OJC-050	Wardell Gray Memorial, Volume 1	1982	$25
— Reissue of Prestige 7008			

Number	Title	Yr	NM
❏ OJC-051	Wardell Gray Memorial, Volume 2	1982	$25
— Reissue of Prestige 7009			
MODERN			
❏ MLP-1204 [M]	Way Out Wardell	1956	$300
PHILOLOGY/SPHERE			
❏ W-14	Light Gray, Vol. 1	198?	$25
❏ W-36	Light Gray, Vol. 2	198?	$25
PRESTIGE			
❏ P-24062	Central Ave.	1976	$50
❏ PRLP-128 [10]	Jazz Concert	1952	$300
❏ PRLP-7008 [M]	Wardell Gray Memorial, Volume 1	1955	$300
❏ PRLP-7009 [M]	Wardell Gray Memorial, Volume 2	1955	$300
❏ PRLP-7343 [M]	Wardell Gray Memorial Album	1964	$50
❏ PRST-7343 [R]	Wardell Gray Memorial Album	1964	$30
❏ PRLP-147 [10]	Wardell Gray's Los Angeles Stars	1953	$350
❏ PRLP-115 [10]	Wardell Gray Tenor Sax	1951	$350
UNITED			
❏ US-7722 [R]	Shades of Gray	197?	$30
XANADU			
❏ 146	Live in Hollywood	197?	$35

GRAYE, TONY
Number	Title	Yr	NM
FUTURA			
❏ 55514	Let's Swing Away	197?	$35
❏ 55515	The Blue Horn of Tony Graye	197?	$35
ZIM			
❏ ZMS-2001	Oh Gee!	1975	$35

GRAYSON, JACK
Number	Title	Yr	NM
JOE-WES			
❏ 8100	Jack Grayson Sings	1982	$15
KOALA			
❏ 15751	When a Man Loves a Woman	1981	$15

GREAN, CHARLES RANDOLPH
Number	Title	Yr	NM
HARMONY			
❏ KH31389	Volume 2	1972	$12
RANWOOD			
❏ 8105	Masterpiece	1972	$15
❏ 8055	Quentin's Theme	1969	$15
❏ 8075	The Charles Randolph Grean Sounde	1970	$15

GREASE BAND
Number	Title	Yr	NM
SHELTER			
❏ SW-8904 [B]	Grease Band	1971	$18

GREAT BUILDINGS
Number	Title	Yr	NM
COLUMBIA			
❏ NJC36920	Great Buildings	1980	$18

GREAT EXCELSIOR JAZZ BAND
Number	Title	Yr	NM
VOYAGER			
❏ VRLP-202	Hot Jazz from the Territory	198?	$25
❏ VRLP-204	Remembering Joe	198?	$25
❏ VRLP-203	Roast Chestnuts	198?	$25

GREAT JAZZ TRIO, THE
Number	Title	Yr	NM
EAST WIND			
❏ 10005	Direct from L.A.	1978	$75
— Direct-to-disc recording			
INNER CITY			
❏ IC-6023	Kindness, Joy, Love and Happiness	1978	$30
❏ IC-6003	Love for Sale	1976	$30
❏ IC-6030	Milestones	1979	$30
❏ IC-6013	The Great Jazz Trio at the Village Vanguard	1977	$30

GREAT SCOTS, THE
Number	Title	Yr	NM
BEAT ROCKET			
❏ BR101	The Great Scots ... Arrive!	199?	$12
SUNDAZED			
❏ LP5052	The Great Lost Great Scots Album!	199?	$12

GREAT SOCIETY, THE
Number	Title	Yr	NM
COLUMBIA			
❏ CS9627 [M]	Conspicuous Only In Its Absence	1968	$75
— White label promo only; "Special Mono Radio Station Copy" sticker on front; same number as stereo version			
❏ CS9627 [S]	Conspicuous Only In Its Absence	1968	$30
— Red label, "360 Sound Stereo"			

Number	Title	Yr	NM
❏ CS9702 [B]	How It Was	1968	$30
— Red label, "360 Sound Stereo			
❏ G30459	The Great Society Collectors Item	1971	$18
HARMONY			
❏ KH30391	Somebody to Love	1970	$15

GREAT SPECKLED BIRD
Number	Title	Yr	NM
AMPEX			
❏ A-10103 [B]	Great Speckled Bird	1970	$30

GREAVES, R.B.
Number	Title	Yr	NM
ATCO			
❏ SD 33-311	R.B. Greaves	1969	$25
INTERMEDIA			
❏ QS-5032	Rock and Roll	198?	$12

GRECH, RIC
Number	Title	Yr	NM
RSO			
❏ SO876 [B]	The Last Five Years	1973	$18
— Compiles his work with such groups as Family, Traffic, Blind Faith, Ginger Baker's Air Force and KGB			

GRECO, BUDDY
Number	Title	Yr	NM
APPLAUSE			
❏ APLP-1004	Hot Nights	1982	$25
BAINBRIDGE			
❏ 8004	Greatest Hits	198?	$35
CORAL			
❏ CRL57022 [M]	Buddy Greco at Mister Kelly's	1956	$75
EPIC			
❏ LN24010 [M]	Buddy and Soul	1962	$75
❏ BN26010 [S]	Buddy and Soul	1962	$85
❏ LN24043 [M]	Buddy Greco's Greatest Hits	1963	$75
❏ BN26043 [S]	Buddy Greco's Greatest Hits	1963	$85
❏ LN24057 [M]	Buddy Greco Sings for Intimate Moments	1963	$75
❏ BN26057 [S]	Buddy Greco Sings for Intimate Moments	1963	$85
❏ LN3771 [M]	Buddy's Back in Town	1961	$75
❏ BN593 [S]	Buddy's Back in Town	1961	$85
❏ LN24181 [M]	From the Wrists Down	1965	$75
❏ BN26181 [S]	From the Wrists Down	1965	$85
❏ LN3793 [M]	I Like It Swinging	1961	$75
❏ BN602 [S]	I Like It Swinging	1961	$85
❏ LN3820 [M]	Let's Love	1961	$75
❏ BN615 [S]	Let's Love	1961	$85
❏ LN24130 [M]	Modern Sounds of Hank Williams	1965	$75
❏ BN26130 [S]	Modern Sounds of Hank Williams	1965	$85
❏ LN3660 [M]	My Buddy	1960	$75
❏ BN557 [S]	My Buddy	1960	$85
❏ LN24088 [M]	My Last Night in Rome	1964	$75
❏ BN26088 [S]	My Last Night in Rome	1964	$85
❏ LN24116 [M]	On Stage	1964	$75
❏ BN26116 [S]	On Stage	1964	$85
❏ LN24032 [M]	Soft and Gentle	1962	$75
❏ BN26032 [S]	Soft and Gentle	1962	$85
❏ LN3746 [M]	Songs for Swinging Losers	1960	$75
❏ BN585 [S]	Songs for Swinging Losers	1960	$85
HARMONY			
❏ HL7448 [M]	You're Something Else	196?	$25
❏ HS11248 [S]	You're Something Else	196?	$30
KAPP			
❏ KL-1033 [M]	Broadway Melodies	1956	$50
❏ KL-1107 [M]	Buddy	1958	$50
❏ KL-1231 [M]	The Best of Buddy Greco	1961	$35
PROJECT 3			
❏ PR5105	For Once in My Life: In Concert	1980	$25
REPRISE			
❏ RS-6256 [S]	Away We Go!	1967	$30

Number	Title	Yr	NM
❏ R-6256 [M]	Away We Go!	1967	$35
❏ R-6220 [M]	Big Band and Ballads	1966	$30
❏ RS-6220 [S]	Big Band and Ballads	1966	$35
❏ RS-6230 [S]	Buddy's in a Brand New Bag	1966	$35
❏ R-6230 [M]	Buddy's in a Brand New Bag	1966	$30

SCEPTER

Number	Title	Yr	NM
❏ SPS-579	Let the Sunshine In	1969	$30

SUTTON

Number	Title	Yr	NM
❏ SSU282 [M]	All Time Favorites Featuring Buddy Greco	196?	$25

VOCALION

Number	Title	Yr	NM
❏ VL3706 [M]	Here's Buddy Greco	1964	$30
❏ VL73706 [R]	Here's Buddy Greco	1964	$25

GRECO, JULIETTE

COLUMBIA

Number	Title	Yr	NM
❏ CL569 [M]	St. Germain-des-Pres	1954	$30

— *Maroon label, gold print*

GREEK FOUNTAIN RIVER FRONT BAND, THE

MONTEL

Number	Title	Yr	NM
❏ 110 [M]	The Greek Fountain River Band Takes Requests	1965	$120

GREELEY, GEORGE

CAPITOL

Number	Title	Yr	NM
❏ H438 [10]	Piano Demitasse	1954	$30

REPRISE

Number	Title	Yr	NM
❏ R6092 [M]	Piano Rhapsodies of Love	1964	$12
❏ RS6092 [S]	Piano Rhapsodies of Love	1964	$15

WARNER BROS.

Number	Title	Yr	NM
❏ WS1338 [S]	22 Best Loved Christmas Piano Concertos	1959	$25
❏ W1503 [M]	A Classic Affair	1963	$15
❏ WS1503 [S]	A Classic Affair	1963	$18
❏ W1560 [M]	Best Loved Christmas Piano Concertos	1965	$15
❏ WS1560 [S]	Best Loved Christmas Piano Concertos	1965	$18
❏ W1427 [M]	Famous Film Themes	1961	$15
❏ WS1427 [S]	Famous Film Themes	1961	$18
❏ W1451 [M]	George Greeley Plays George Gershwin	1962	$15
❏ WS1451 [S]	George Greeley Plays George Gershwin	1962	$18
❏ W1415 [M]	Great Broadway Musicals	1961	$15
❏ WS1415 [S]	Great Broadway Musicals	1961	$18
❏ W1402 [M]	Piano Italiano	1961	$15
❏ WS1402 [S]	Piano Italiano	1961	$18
❏ W1410 [M]	The Best of the Popular Piano Concertos	1961	$15
❏ WS1410 [S]	The Best of the Popular Piano Concertos	1961	$18
❏ W1319 [M]	The Greatest Motion Picture Piano Concertos	1959	$18
❏ WS1319 [S]	The Greatest Motion Picture Piano Concertos	1959	$25
❏ W1476 [M]	Themes from Mutiny on the Bounty and Other Great Films	1962	$15
❏ WS1476 [S]	Themes from Mutiny on the Bounty and Other Great Films	1962	$18
❏ W1366 [M]	The Most Beautiful Music of Hawaii	1960	$15
❏ WS1366 [S]	The Most Beautiful Music of Hawaii	1960	$18
❏ W1387 [M]	The World's Greatest Love Themes	1960	$15
❏ WS1387 [S]	The World's Greatest Love Themes	1960	$18
❏ W1249 [M]	The World's Greatest Popular Piano Concertos	1958	$18
❏ WS1249 [S]	The World's Greatest Popular Piano Concertos	1959	$25
❏ W1291 [M]	World Renowned Popular Piano Concertos	1959	$18
❏ WS1291 [S]	World Renowned Popular Piano Concertos	1959	$25

GREEN, AL

A&M

Number	Title	Yr	NM
❏ SP-5228	I Get Joy	1989	$12
❏ SP-5150	Soul Survivor	1987	$12

BELL

Number	Title	Yr	NM
❏ 6076	Al Green	1972	$25

— *Reissue of Hot Line LP*

BLUE NOTE

Number	Title	Yr	NM
❏ BTE74584	Everything's OK	2005	$18
❏ 93556	I Can't Stop	2003	$18

DCC COMPACT CLASSICS

Number	Title	Yr	NM
❏ LPZ-2058	Greatest Hits	1998	$30

— *Audiophile vinyl*

HI

Number	Title	Yr	NM
❏ SHL-32087	Al Green Explores Your Mind	1974	$18
❏ SHL-32062	Al Green Gets Next to You	1971	$18
❏ 8001	Al Green Gets Next to You	1977	$15
❏ SHL-32089	Al Green/Greatest Hits	1975	$18
❏ SHL-32092	Al Green Is Love	1975	$18
❏ SHL-32105	Al Green's Greatest Hits, Volume II	1977	$18
❏ SHL-32077	Call Me	1973	$18
❏ SHL32087 [B]	Explores Your Mind	2015	$25
❏ SHL-32097	Full of Fire	1976	$18
❏ SHL-32055	Green Is Blues	1969	$18
❏ SHL-32103	Have a Good Time	1976	$18
❏ SHL-32074	I'm Still in Love with You	1972	$18
❏ SHL-32070	Let's Stay Together	1972	$18
❏ 8007	Let's Stay Together	1977	$15
❏ SHL-32082	Livin' for You	1973	$18
❏ 6004	The Belle Album	1977	$15
❏ 8000	Tired of Being Alone	1977	$15
❏ 6009	Truth 'N' Time	1978	$15

HOT LINE

Number	Title	Yr	NM
❏ 1500 [M]	Back Up Train	1967	$50

— *As "Al Greene"*

Number	Title	Yr	NM
❏ S-1500 [S]	Back Up Train	1967	$100

— *As "Al Greene"*

KORY

Number	Title	Yr	NM
❏ 1005	Al Green	1977	$12

— *Reissue of Bell LP*

MCA

Number	Title	Yr	NM
❏ 42308	Love Ritual	1988	$12

MOTOWN

Number	Title	Yr	NM
❏ 5283ML	Al Green/Greatest Hits	198?	$12

— *Reissue of Hi 32089*

Number	Title	Yr	NM
❏ 5291ML	Al Green's Greatest Hits, Volume II	198?	$12

— *Reissue of Hi 32105*

Number	Title	Yr	NM
❏ 5284ML	I'm Still in Love with You	198?	$12

— *Reissue of Hi 32074*

Number	Title	Yr	NM
❏ 5290ML	Let's Stay Together	198?	$12

— *Reissue of Hi 32070*

Number	Title	Yr	NM
❏ 5317ML	Truth N' Time	198?	$12

MYRRH

Number	Title	Yr	NM
❏ MSB-6774	Al Green and the Full Gospel Tabernacle Choir	1984	$12
❏ WR-8209	Al Green and the Full Gospel Tabernacle Choir	1986	$10

— *Reissue with new number and A&M logo*

Number	Title	Yr	NM
❏ MSB-6671	Higher Plane	1981	$12
❏ WR-8114	Higher Plane	1985	$10

— *Reissue with new number and A&M logo*

Number	Title	Yr	NM
❏ MSB-6747	I'll Rise Again	1982	$12
❏ WR-8116	I'll Rise Again	1985	$10

— *Reissue with new number and A&M logo*

Number	Title	Yr	NM
❏ MSB-6702	Precious Lord	1981	$12
❏ WR-8115	Precious Lord	1985	$10

— *Reissue with new number and A&M logo*

Number	Title	Yr	NM
❏ MSB-6661	The Lord Will Make a Way	1980	$12
❏ WR-8113	The Lord Will Make a Way	1985	$10

— *Reissue with new number and A&M logo*

Number	Title	Yr	NM
❏ WR-8118	Trust in God	1985	$10

— *Reissue with new number and A&M logo*

Number	Title	Yr	NM
❏ 7-01-678306-?	Trust in God	1984	$12
❏ WR-8117	White Christmas	1985	$12

— *Reissue with new number and A&M logo*

Number	Title	Yr	NM
❏ 7-01-678006-6	White Christmas	1984	$15

THE RIGHT STUFF

Number	Title	Yr	NM
❏ T1-27627	I'm Still in Love with You	1995	$18

— *Green vinyl reissue*

Number	Title	Yr	NM
❏ T1-27121	Let's Stay Together	1995	$18

— *Green vinyl reissue*

WORD

Number	Title	Yr	NM
❏ E77000	One in a Million	1991	$15

GREEN, BENNIE

BAINBRIDGE

Number	Title	Yr	NM
❏ 1048	Bennie Green	198?	$25

BARBARY

Number	Title	Yr	NM
❏ M33015 [M]	Play More Than You Can Stand	196?	$30

BETHLEHEM

Number	Title	Yr	NM
❏ BCP-6018	Cat Walk	197?	$35

— *Reissue of 6054, distributed by RCA Victor*

Number	Title	Yr	NM
❏ BCP-6054 [M]	Hornful of Soul	1961	$300
❏ BCP-4019 [M]	Hornful of Soul	196?	$25

— *Reissue of 6054*

BLUE NOTE

Number	Title	Yr	NM
❏ BLP-1587 [M]	Back on the Scene	1958	$300

— *Deep groove" version (deep indentation under label on both sides)*

Number	Title	Yr	NM
❏ BLP-1587 [M]	Back on the Scene	1958	$250

— *Regular version with W. 63rd St. addresss on label*

Number	Title	Yr	NM
❏ BLP-1587 [M]	Back on the Scene	1963	$175

— *With "New York, USA" address on label*

Number	Title	Yr	NM
❏ BST-1587 [S]	Back on the Scene	1959	$350

— *Deep groove" version (deep indentation under label on both sides)*

Number	Title	Yr	NM
❏ BST-1587 [S]	Back on the Scene	1959	$150

— *Regular version with W. 63rd St. addresss on label*

Number	Title	Yr	NM
❏ BST-81587 [S]	Back on the Scene	1963	$25

— *With "New York, USA" address on label*

Number	Title	Yr	NM
❏ BST-81587 [S]	Back on the Scene	1967	$35

— *With "A Division of Liberty Records" on label*

Number	Title	Yr	NM
❏ BLP-1599 [M]	Soul Stirrin'	1958	$120

— *Deep groove" version (deep indentation under label on both sides)*

Number	Title	Yr	NM
❏ BLP-1599 [M]	Soul Stirrin'	1958	$175

— *Regular version with W. 63rd St. addresss on label*

Number	Title	Yr	NM
❏ BLP-1599 [M]	Soul Stirrin'	1963	$75

— *With "New York, USA" address on label*

Number	Title	Yr	NM
❏ BST-1599 [S]	Soul Stirrin'	1959	$100

— *Deep groove" version (deep indentation under label on both sides)*

Number	Title	Yr	NM
❏ BST-1599 [S]	Soul Stirrin'	1959	$75

— *Regular version with W. 63rd St. addresss on label*

Number	Title	Yr	NM
❏ BST-81599 [S]	Soul Stirrin'	1963	$25

— *With "New York, USA" address on label*

Number	Title	Yr	NM
❏ BST-81599 [S]	Soul Stirrin'	1967	$35

— *With "A Division of Liberty Records" on label*

Number	Title	Yr	NM
❏ BLP-4010 [M]	Walkin' and Talkin'	1959	$300

— *Deep groove" version (deep indentation under label on both sides)*

Number	Title	Yr	NM
❏ BLP-4010 [M]	Walkin' and Talkin'	1959	$175

— *Regular version with W. 63rd St. addresss on label*

Number	Title	Yr	NM
❏ BLP-4010 [M]	Walkin' and Talkin'	1963	$75

— *With "New York, USA" address on label*

Number	Title	Yr	NM
❏ BST-4010 [S]	Walkin' and Talkin'	1959	$300

— *Deep groove" version (deep indentation under label on both sides)*

Number	Title	Yr	NM
❏ BST-4010 [S]	Walkin' and Talkin'	1959	$75

— *Regular version with W. 63rd St. addresss on label*

Number	Title	Yr	NM
❏ BST-84010 [S]	Walkin' and Talkin'	1963	$25

— *With "New York, USA" address on label*

Number	Title	Yr	NM
❏ BST-84010 [S]	Walkin' and Talkin'	1967	$35

— *With "A Division of Liberty Records" on label*

ENRICA

Number	Title	Yr	NM
❏ 2002 [M]	Bennie Green Swings the Blues	1960	$30
❏ S-2002 [S]	Bennie Green Swings the Blues	1960	$40

FANTASY

Number	Title	Yr	NM
❏ OJC-1728	Bennie Green Blows His Horn	198?	$25
❏ OJC-1752	Walkin' Down	198?	$25

JAZZLAND

Number	Title	Yr	NM
❏ JLP-43 [M]	Glidin' Along	1961	$30
❏ JLP-943 [S]	Glidin' Along	1961	$30

PRESTIGE

Number	Title	Yr	NM
❏ PRLP-210 [10]	Bennie Blows His Horn	1955	$300
❏ PRLP-7041 [M]	Bennie Green and Art Farmer	1956	$400
❏ PRLP-7052 [M]	Bennie Green Blows His Horn	1956	$300
❏ PRLP-7160 [M]	Bennie Green Blows His Horn	1959	$250
❏ PRST-7776	The Best of Bennie Green	1970	$35
❏ PRLP-7049 [M]	Walking Down	1956	$300

RCA VICTOR

Number	Title	Yr	NM
❏ LPM-2376 [M]	Futura	1961	$30
❏ LSP-2376 [S]	Futura	1961	$30

TIME

Number	Title	Yr	NM
❏ 52021 [M]	Bennie Green	1960	$40
❏ S-2021 [S]	Bennie Green	1960	$50

VEE JAY

Number	Title	Yr	NM
❏ LP-1005 [M]	The Swingin'est	1959	$50
❏ SR-1005 [S]	The Swingin'est	1959	$50

— *This LP was reissued as "Juggin' Around" by GENE AMMONS on Vee Jay 3024*

Number	Title	Yr	NM
❏ VJS-1005 [S]	The Swingin'est	198?	$25

— *Reissue on thinner vinyl*

GREEN, BENNIE/PAUL QUINICHETTE

DECCA

Number	Title	Yr	NM
❏ DL8176 [M]	Blow Your Horn	1955	$175

GREEN, BERNIE

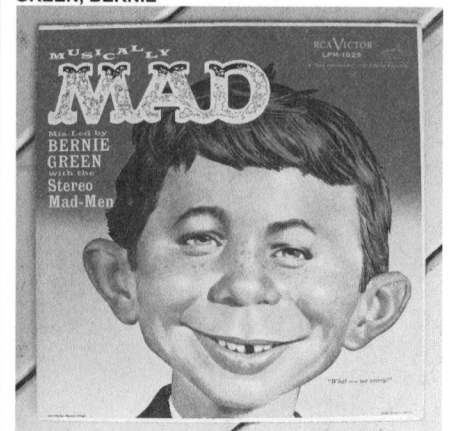

Number	Title	Yr	NM

BARBARY COAST
| ❏ 33015-S [S] | Bernie Green Plays More Than You Can Stand in Hi-Fi | 1958 | $150 |

RCA VICTOR
❏ LSA-2376 [S]	Futura	1961	$150
❏ LPM-1929 [M]	Musically Mad	1959	$75
❏ LSP-1929 [S]	Musically Mad	1959	$200

SAN FRANCISCO
| ❏ M-33015 [M] | Bernie Green Plays More Than You Can Stand in Hi-Fi | 1957 | $150 |

GREEN, BUNKY

ARGO
| ❏ LP-753 [M] | Testifyin' Time | 1965 | $30 |
| ❏ LPS-753 [S] | Testifyin' Time | 1965 | $30 |

CADET
❏ LP-766 [M]	Playin' for Keeps	1966	$30
❏ LPS-766 [S]	Playin' for Keeps	1966	$30
❏ LP-753 [M]	Testifyin' Time	1966	$35
❏ LPS-753 [S]	Testifyin' Time	1966	$25
❏ LP-780 [M]	The Latinization of Bunky Green	1967	$30
❏ LPS-780 [S]	The Latinization of Bunky Green	1967	$30

VANGUARD
❏ VSD-79425	Places We've Never Been	1979	$30
❏ VSD-79387	Transformations	197?	$30
❏ VSD-79413	Visions	1978	$30

GREEN, BYRDIE

PRESTIGE
❏ PRLP-7509 [M]	I Got It Bad	1967	$25
❏ PRST-7509 [S]	I Got It Bad	1967	$35
❏ PRST-7574	Sister Byrdie	1968	$35
❏ PRLP-7503 [M]	The Golden Thrush Speaks	1967	$25
❏ PRST-7503 [S]	The Golden Thrush Speaks	1967	$35

GREEN, FREDDIE

RCA VICTOR
| ❏ LPM-1210 [M] | Mr. Rhythm | 1956 | $50 |

GREEN, GARLAND

RCA VICTOR
| ❏ APL1-2351 | Love Is What We Came Here For | 1977 | $15 |

UNI
| ❏ 73073 | Jealous Kind of Fellow | 1969 | $25 |

GREEN, GRANT

BLUE NOTE
| ❏ BLP-84360 | Alive! | 1970 | $120 |
—We're not sure what the original label is; it could be the blue and white label with "A Division of Liberty Records," the mostly black label with "Liberty/UA," or the blue and white label with "A Division of United Artists Records"
| ❏ BLP-84360 | Alive! | 1973 | $150 |
—Dark blue label with black stylized "b" at upper right
| ❏ BLP-4139 [M] | Am I Blue | 1963 | $200 |
—With "New York, USA" on label
| ❏ BLP-84139 [S] | Am I Blue | 1963 | $200 |
—With New York, USA address on label
| ❏ BLP-84139 [S] | Am I Blue | 1968 | $150 |
—With "A Division of Liberty Records" on label
| ❏ BLP-84432 | Born to Be Blue | 1985 | $250 |
| ❏ BLP-84327 | Carryin' On | 1969 | $200 |
—A Division of Liberty Records" on label
| ❏ BLP-4132 [M] | Feelin' the Spirit | 1963 | $100 |
| ❏ BLP-84132 [S] | Feelin' the Spirit | 1963 | $200 |
—With New York, USA address on label
| ❏ BLP-84132 [S] | Feelin' the Spirit | 1968 | $150 |
—With "A Division of Liberty Records" on label
| ❏ BLP-84310 | Goin' West | 1969 | $200 |
—A Division of Liberty Records" on label
| ❏ BLP-4064 [M] | Grant's First Stand | 1961 | $250 |
—With W. 63rd St. addresss on label
| ❏ BLP-4064 [M] | Grant's First Stand | 1963 | $250 |
—With New York, USA address on label
| ❏ BLP-84064 [S] | Grant's First Stand | 1961 | $175 |
—With W. 63rd St. addresss on label
| ❏ BLP-84064 [S] | Grant's First Stand | 1963 | $175 |
—With New York, USA address on label
| ❏ BLP-84064 [S] | Grant's First Stand | 1968 | $150 |
—With "A Division of Liberty Records" on label
| ❏ BLP-4086 [M] | Grant Stand | 1962 | $250 |
—With W. 63rd St. address on label
| ❏ BLP-4086 [M] | Grant Stand | 1963 | $200 |
—With New York, USA address on label
| ❏ BLP-84086 [S] | Grant Stand | 1962 | $175 |
—With W. 63rd St. addresss on label
| ❏ BLP-84086 [S] | Grant Stand | 1963 | $200 |
—With New York, USA address on label
| ❏ BLP-84086 [S] | Grant Stand | 1968 | $150 |
—With "A Division of Liberty Records" on label
| ❏ BLP-84086 [S] | Grant Stand | 197? | $150 |
—Dark blue label with white stylized "b" at upper right

Number	Title	Yr	NM
❏ BLP-84342	Green Is Beautiful	1970	$120
—A Division of Liberty Records" on label
| ❏ BLP-4071 [M] | Green Street | 1961 | $250 |
—With W. 63rd St. addresss on label
| ❏ BLP-4071 [M] | Green Street | 1963 | $120 |
—With New York, USA address on label
| ❏ BLP-84071 [S] | Green Street | 1961 | $175 |
—With W. 63rd St. addresss on label
| ❏ BLP-84071 [S] | Green Street | 1963 | $120 |
—With New York, USA address on label
| ❏ BLP-84071 [S] | Green Street | 1968 | $150 |
—With "A Division of Liberty Records" on label
| ❏ BLP-4154 [M] | Idle Moments | 1964 | $800 |
| ❏ BLP-84154 [S] | Idle Moments | 1964 | $200 |
—With New York, USA address on label
| ❏ BLP-84154 [S] | Idle Moments | 1968 | $150 |
—With "A Division of Liberty Records" on label
| ❏ BLP-4202 [M] | I Want to Hold Your Hand | 1964 | $100 |
| ❏ BLP-84202 [S] | I Want to Hold Your Hand | 1964 | $200 |
—With New York, USA address on label
| ❏ BLP-84202 [S] | I Want to Hold Your Hand | 1968 | $150 |
—With "A Division of Liberty Records" on label
❏ BN-LA037-G2	Live at the Lighthouse	1973	$150
❏ LT-1032	Nigeria	1980	$150
❏ BLP-84413	Shades of Green	1972	$175
—A Division of United Artists Records" on blue and white label
| ❏ LT-990 | Solid | 1980 | $40 |
| ❏ BLP-4253 [M] | Street of Dreams | 1967 | $200 |
—A Division of Liberty Records" on label
| ❏ BLP-84253 [S] | Street of Dreams | 1967 | $175 |
—A Division of Liberty Records" on label
| ❏ BLP-4099 [M] | Sunday Mornin' | 1962 | $250 |
—With W. 63rd St. address on label
| ❏ BLP-4099 [M] | Sunday Mornin' | 1963 | $175 |
—With New York, USA address on label
| ❏ BLP-84099 [S] | Sunday Mornin' | 1962 | $175 |
—With W. 63rd St. address on label
| ❏ BLP-84099 [S] | Sunday Mornin' | 1963 | $250 |
—With New York, USA address on label
| ❏ BLP-84099 [S] | Sunday Mornin' | 1968 | $150 |
—With "A Division of Liberty Records" on label
| ❏ BLP-84183 [M] | Talkin' About! | 1964 | $100 |
| ❏ BLP-84183 [S] | Talkin' About! | 1964 | $200 |
—With New York, USA address on label
| ❏ BLP-84183 [S] | Talkin' About! | 1968 | $150 |
—With "A Division of Liberty Records" on label
| ❏ BLP-84415 | The Final Comedown | 1972 | $175 |
—A Division of United Artists Records" on blue and white label
| ❏ BLP-4111 [M] | The Latin Bit | 1962 | $200 |
—With "New York, USA" on label
| ❏ BLP-84111 [S] | The Latin Bit | 1962 | $200 |
—With New York, USA address on label; reproductions exist
| ❏ BLP-84111 [S] | The Latin Bit | 1968 | $150 |
—With "A Division of Liberty Records" on label
| ❏ BLP-84373 | Visions | 1971 | $175 |

COBBLESTONE
| ❏ CST-9002 | Iron City | 1972 | $200 |
—Reproductions exist

DELMARK
❏ DL-404 [M]	All the Gin Is Gone	1966	$75
❏ DS-404 [S]	All the Gin Is Gone	1966	$75
❏ DL-427 [M]	Black Forrest	1966	$75
❏ DS-427 [S]	Black Forrest	1966	$75

KUDU
| ❏ KU-29 | The Main Attraction | 1976 | $75 |

MOSAIC
| ❏ MR5-133 | The Complete Blue Note Recordings of Grant Green with Sonny Clark | 199? | $300 |

MUSE
| ❏ MR-5014 | Green Blues | 1973 | $75 |
| ❏ MR-5120 | Iron City | 197? | $75 |

VERSATILE
| ❏ MSG-6002 | Easy | 1978 | $50 |

VERVE
| ❏ V-8627 [M] | His Majesty, King Funk | 1965 | $200 |
| ❏ V6-8627 [S] | His Majesty, King Funk | 1965 | $120 |

GREEN, KEITH

PRETTY GOOD
| ❏ PGR-1 | So You Wanna Go Back to Egypt | 1980 | $15 |

SPARROW
| ❏ SP-9901 | For Him Who Has Ears to Hear | 198? | $10 |
—Reissue of 1015
| ❏ SPR-1015 | For Him Who Has Ears to Hear | 1977 | $15 |
| ❏ SP-9904 | No Compromise | 198? | $10 |
—Reissue of 1024
| ❏ SPR-1024 | No Compromise | 1978 | $15 |
| ❏ SP-9927 | The Collection | 198? | $12 |

Number	Title	Yr	NM

GREEN, LLOYD

CHART
❏ CHS-1010	Cool Steel Man	1969	$30
❏ 1024	Moody River	1970	$30
❏ CHM-1006 [M]	Mr. Nashville Sound	1968	$50
❏ CHS-1006 [S]	Mr. Nashville Sound	1968	$30

GRT
| ❏ 8018 | Feelings | 1977 | $15 |

LITTLE DARLIN'
| ❏ LD-4002 | Day for Decision | 196? | $30 |
| ❏ LD4005 | The Hit Sounds of Lloyd Green | 196? | $30 |

MONUMENT
| ❏ KZ32532 | Shades of Steel | 1973 | $18 |
| ❏ KZ33368 | Steel Rides | 1975 | $18 |

TIME
| ❏ T-2152 [M] | Big Steel Guitar | 1964 | $30 |
| ❏ ST-2152 [S] | Big Steel Guitar | 1964 | $40 |

GREEN, PETER
Also see FLEETWOOD MAC.

REPRISE
| ❏ RS6436 [B] | The End of the Game | 1970 | $30 |

SAIL
| ❏ 0110 [B] | In the Skies | 1979 | $15 |
| ❏ 0112 [B] | Little Dreamer | 1980 | $15 |

GREEN, PHIL

LONDON
| ❏ LPB-17 [10] | Rhythm on Reeds | 1950 | $50 |

GREEN, URBIE

ABC-PARAMOUNT
| ❏ ABC-137 [M] | All About Urbie Green | 1956 | $50 |
| ❏ ABC-101 [M] | Blues and Other Shades of Green | 1955 | $85 |

BETHLEHEM
| ❏ BCP-14 [M] | East Coast Jazz, Volume 6 | 1955 | $300 |
| ❏ BCP-6041 | The Lyrical Language of Urbie Green | 197? | $30 |
—Reissue of 14, distributed by RCA Victor

BLUE NOTE
| ❏ BLP-5036 [10] | Urbie Green Septet | 1954 | $300 |

COMMAND
❏ RS 33-815 [M]	The Persuasive Trombone of Urbie Green	1960	$30
❏ RS815SD [S]	The Persuasive Trombone of Urbie Green	1960	$35
❏ RS 33-838 [M]	The Persuasive Trombone of Urbie Green, Volume 2	1962	$30
❏ RS838SD [S]	The Persuasive Trombone of Urbie Green, Volume 2	1962	$35
❏ RS 33-857 [M]	Urbie Green and His 6-Tet	1963	$30
❏ RS857SD [S]	Urbie Green and His 6-Tet	1963	$35

CTI
| ❏ 7079 | Senor Blues | 1977 | $30 |
| ❏ 7070 | The Fox | 1976 | $30 |

PROJECT 3
❏ PR5014SD	21 Trombones	1967	$30
❏ PR5024SD	21 Trombones, Volume 2	1968	$30
❏ PR5066SD	Bein' Green	1972	$30
❏ PR5087SD	Big Beautiful Band	1974	$25
❏ PR5052SD	Green Power	1970	$30

RCA VICTOR
❏ LPM-1969 [M]	Best of the New Broadway Show Hits	1959	$40
❏ LSP-1969 [S]	Best of the New Broadway Show Hits	1959	$40
❏ LPM-1741 [M]	Jimmy McHugh in Hi-Fi	1958	$50
❏ LSP-1741 [S]	Jimmy McHugh in Hi-Fi	1958	$75
❏ LPM-1667 [M]	Let's Face the Music and Dance	1958	$40
❏ LSP-1667 [S]	Let's Face the Music and Dance	1958	$40

VANGUARD
| ❏ VRS-8010 [10] | Urbie Green and His Band | 1954 | $120 |

X
| ❏ LXA-3026 [10] | A Cool Yuletide | 1954 | $120 |

GREEN, URBIE/VIC DICKENSON

JAZZTONE
| ❏ J-1259 [M] | Urbie Green Octet/Slidin' Swing | 1957 | $40 |

GREEN, WILLIAM

EVEREST
| ❏ LPBR-5213 [M] | Shades of Green | 1963 | $35 |
| ❏ SDBR-1213 [S] | Shades of Green | 1963 | $25 |

GREEN

ATCO
| ❏ SD 33-282 | Green | 1969 | $18 |
| ❏ SD 33-366 | To Help Somebody | 1971 | $15 |

Number	Title	Yr	NM

GREEN BULLFROG
DECCA
❑ DL75269 [B]	Green Bullfrog	1971	$40

GREEN DAY
ADELINE
❑ AR033-1	American Idiot	2006	$30
❑ 012-1	Warning:	2000	$25

LOOKOUT!
❑ 22 [B]	39/Smooth	1990	$30
❑ 46 [B]	Kerplunk	1992	$30

REPRISE
❑ 541860-1 [B]	Demolicious	2014	$30
❑ 45529	Dookie	1994	$25
— Original stock issue on black vinyl			
❑ 45529 [B]	Dookie	1995	$30
— Reissue on pink vinyl			
❑ 45529 [DJ]	Dookie	1994	$35
— Promo version on clear green vinyl in plain white cover			
❑ 45529 [DJ]	Dookie	1994	$30
— Promo version on milky pale-green vinyl			
❑ 46046 [B]	Insomniac	1995	$30
❑ 47613-1 [B]	Warning	2014	$25

GREEN RIVER
Members of this band later joined MOTHER LOVE BONE, MUDHONEY and PEARL JAM.
HOMESTEAD
❑ 031 [B]	Come On Down	1985	$50
— Originals do not have a UPC code (deduct 25% if UPC is there)			

SUB POP
❑ 11 [EP]	Dry as a Bone	1987	$100
— First 2,000 copies have yellow inserts			
❑ 11 [EP]	Dry as a Bone	1987	$50
— Later copies have pink inserts			
❑ 15 [EP]	Rehab Doll	1988	$50
— First 1,000 copies on green vinyl			
❑ 15 [EP]	Rehab Doll	1988	$35

GREENBAUM, NORMAN
Also see DR. WEST'S MEDICINE SHOW AND JUG BAND.
REPRISE
❑ RS6422	Back Home Again	1970	$18
❑ MS2048	Petaluma	1972	$30
❑ RS6365	Spirit in the Sky	1969	$18

VARESE SARABANDE
❑ 3020662291 [B]	Spirit in the Sky	2014	$30

GREENBRIAR BOYS, THE
ELEKTRA
❑ EKL-233 [M]	Dian and the Greenbriar Boys	1963	$30
❑ EKS-7233 [S]	Dian and the Greenbriar Boys	1963	$30

VANGUARD
❑ VRS-9233 [M]	Better Late Than Never	1966	$25
❑ VSD-79233 [S]	Better Late Than Never	1966	$30
❑ VRS-9159 [M]	Ragged But Right	1964	$25
❑ VSD-79159 [S]	Ragged But Right	1964	$30
❑ VRS-9104 [M]	The Greenbriar Boys	1962	$30

GREENE, BOB
RCA VICTOR
❑ ARL1-0504	The World of Jelly Roll Morton	1974	$15

GREENE, BURTON, AND ALAN SILVA
HAT HUT
❑ 15	Ongoing Strings	198?	$35

GREENE, BURTON
COLUMBIA
❑ CS9784	Presenting Burton Greene	1969	$35

ESP-DISK'
❑ 1024 [M]	Burton Greene	1966	$150
❑ S-1024 [S]	Burton Greene	1966	$150
❑ S-1074	Burton Greene Concert Tour	1968	$150

GREENE, DODO
BLUE NOTE
❑ BLP-9001 [M]	My Hour of Need	1962	$150
— With W. 63rd St. addresss on label			
❑ BLP-9001 [M]	My Hour of Need	1963	$75
— With "New York, USA" address on label			
❑ BST-89001 [S]	My Hour of Need	1967	$25
— With "A Division of Liberty Records" on label			

GREENE, JACK, AND JEANNIE SEELY
DECCA
❑ DL75171	Jack Greene and Jeannie Seely	1970	$18
❑ DL75392	Two for the Show	1972	$18

MCA
❑ 77	Two for the Show	1973	$15
— Reissue of Decca 75392			

GREENE, JACK
DECCA
❑ DL4904 [M]	All the Time	1967	$25
❑ DL74904 [S]	All the Time	1967	$18
❑ DL75156	Back in the Arms of Love	1969	$18
❑ DL75208	Greatest Hits	1970	$18
❑ DL75308	Greene Country	1972	$18
❑ DL75080	I Am Not Alone	1969	$18
❑ DL75188	Lord Is That Me	1970	$18
❑ DL75124	Statue of a Fool	1969	$18
❑ DL4845 [M]	There Goes My Everything	1967	$25
❑ DL74845 [S]	There Goes My Everything	1967	$18
❑ DL75283	There's a Whole Lot About a Woman	1971	$18
❑ DL4939 [M]	What Locks the Door	1968	$30
❑ DL74939 [S]	What Locks the Door	1968	$18
❑ T-91433 [M]	What Locks the Door	1968	$40
— Capitol Record Club edition			
❑ ST-91433 [S]	What Locks the Door	1968	$25
— Capitol Record Club edition			
❑ DL4979 [M]	You Are My Treasure	1968	$30
❑ DL74979 [S]	You Are My Treasure	1968	$18

MCA
❑ 291	Greatest Hits	1973	$15
— Reissue of Decca 75208			
❑ 295	Greene Country	1973	$15
— Reissue of Decca 75308			

PICKWICK
❑ SPC-6173	I Never Had It So Good	197?	$12

GREENE, LORNE; MICHAEL LANDON; DAN BLOCKER
RCA VICTOR
❑ LPM-2583 [M]	Bonanza -- Ponderosa Party Time!	1962	$30
❑ LSP-2583 [S]	Bonanza -- Ponderosa Party Time!	1962	$40
❑ LPM-2757 [M]	Christmas on the Ponderosa	1963	$30
❑ LSP-2757 [S]	Christmas on the Ponderosa	1963	$30

GREENE, LORNE
RCA CAMDEN
❑ CAS-2391	Five Card Stud	1970	$30

RCA VICTOR
❑ LPM-3410 [M]	Have a Happy Holiday	1965	$30
❑ LSP-3410 [S]	Have a Happy Holiday	1965	$30
❑ LPM-3409 [M]	Lorne Greene's American West	1965	$30
❑ LSP-3409 [S]	Lorne Greene's American West	1965	$30
❑ SP327 [DJ]	Palaver with The Man	1965	$50
— Promo-only interview record with script			
❑ SP-33-327 [DJ]	Palaver with The Man	1965	$50
— Promo-only interview record with script			
❑ LPM-3678 [M]	Portrait of the West	1966	$30
❑ LSP-3678 [S]	Portrait of the West	1966	$30
❑ LPM-3302 [M]	The Man	1965	$30
❑ LSP-3302 [S]	The Man	1965	$30
❑ LPM-2843 [M]	Welcome to the Ponderosa	1964	$30
❑ LSP-2843 [S]	Welcome to the Ponderosa	1964	$30
❑ LPM-2661 [M]	Young at Heart	1963	$30
❑ LSP-2661 [S]	Young at Heart	1963	$30

RCA VICTOR RED SEAL
❑ LM-2783 [M]	Peter and the Wolf	1964	$30
❑ LSC-2783 [S]	Peter and the Wolf	1964	$30
— Above with the London Symphony Orchestra			

GREENIDGE, ROBERT, AND MICHAEL UTLEY
MCA MASTER SERIES
❑ 6258	Heat	1989	$30
❑ 42045	Jubilee	1987	$25
❑ 5695	Mad Music	1985	$25

GREENSLADE
CLEOPATRA
❑ CLP0988 [B]	Live In Stockholm, March 10, 1975	2013	$30

MERCURY
❑ SRM-1-1015	Spy Guest	1974	$16
❑ SRM-1-1025	Time and Tide	1975	$16

WARNER BROS.
❑ BS2698 [B]	Greenslade	1973	$25

GREENSLEEVES, EDDIE
CAMEO
❑ C-1031 [M]	Humorous Folk Songs	1963	$25
❑ SC-1031 [S]	Humorous Folk Songs	1963	$30

GREENWICH, ELLIE
Also see THE RAINDROPS.
UNITED ARTISTS
❑ UAS-6648	Ellie Greenwich Composes, Produces and Sings	1968	$50

VERVE
❑ V6-5091	Let It Be Written, Let It Be Sung	1973	$30

GREENWICH, SONNY
PM
❑ PMR-016	Evol-ution: Love's Opposite	1978	$35

GREENWOOD, LEE
MCA
❑ 5623	Christmas to Christmas	1985	$12
❑ 5582	Greatest Hits	1985	$10
❑ 42219	Greatest Hits -- Volume Two	1988	$10
❑ 42300	If Only for One Night	1989	$12
❑ 5999	If There's Any Justice	1987	$10
❑ 5305	Inside and Out	1982	$15
— Original title			
❑ 5305	Inside Out	1982	$10
— Corrected title			
❑ 1452	Inside Out	1985	$10
— Reissue of second version of 5305			
❑ 5770	Love Will Find Its Way to You	1986	$10
❑ 5403	Somebody's Gonna Love You	1983	$10
❑ 1573	Somebody's Gonna Love You	1986	$10
— Reissue of 5488			
❑ 5622	Streamline	1985	$10
❑ 42167	This Is My Country	1988	$10
❑ 5488	You've Got a Good Love Comin'	1984	$10
❑ 1451	You've Got a Good Love Comin'	1985	$10
— Reissue of 5488			

GREENWOOD COUNTY SINGERS, THE
KAPP
❑ KL1448 [M]	Ballad of Cat Ballou	1965	$15
❑ KS3448 [S]	Ballad of Cat Ballou	1965	$18
❑ KL1422 [M]	Have You Heard	1965	$15
❑ KS3422 [S]	Have You Heard	1965	$18
❑ KL1487 [M]	Tear Down the Walls	1966	$15
— As "The Greenwood Singers			
❑ KS3487 [S]	Tear Down the Walls	1966	$18
— As "The Greenwood Singers			
❑ KL1362 [M]	The First Recordings by the Joyful Greenwood County Singers	1964	$18
— Original title			
❑ KS3362 [S]	The First Recordings by the Joyful Greenwood County Singers	1964	$25
— Original title			
❑ KL1362 [M]	The New Frankie and Johnny Song	1964	$15
❑ KS3362 [S]	The New Frankie and Johnny Song	1964	$18

RCA VICTOR
❑ LSP-4384	Return to Greenwood County	1970	$18

GREENWOODS, THE
DECCA
❑ DL4496 [M]	Folk Instrumentals	1964	$15
❑ DL74496 [S]	Folk Instrumentals	1964	$18

GREER, PAULA
WORKSHOP JAZZ
❑ WSJ203 [M]	Introducing Miss Paula Greer	1963	$300

GREGG, BOBBY
EPIC
❑ LN24051 [M]	Let's Stomp and Wild Weekend	1963	$30
❑ BN26051 [S]	Let's Stomp and Wild Weekend	1963	$40

GREGORY, DICK
COLPIX
❑ CP420 [M]	East and West	1961	$30
❑ CP417 [M]	In Living Black and White	1961	$30
❑ CP480 [M]	We All Have Problems	1964	$30

GATEWAY
❑ GLP9007 [M]	My Brother's Keeper	1963	$40

POPPY
❑ PP-LA176-G2	Caught in the Act	1973	$18
❑ PYS60005	Dick Gregory at Kent State	1971	$18
❑ PYS40011	Dick Gregory at the Village Gate	1972	$18
❑ PYS40008	Dick Gregory On...	1970	$18
❑ PYS60004	Frankenstein	1970	$18
❑ PYS60001	The Light Side: The Dark Side	1969	$25

TOMATO
❑ 9001	The Best of Dick Gregory	1978	$25

VEE JAY
❑ LP4001 [M]	Dick Gregory Talks Turkey	1962	$30

Number	Title	Yr	NM

GREGORY, DICK

Number	Title	Yr	NM
❏ LP1093 [M]	Running for President	1964	$30
❏ LP4005 [M]	Two Sides of Dick Gregory	1963	$30

GREGORY, TERRY

HANDSHAKE
❏ FW37907	From the Heart	1982	$10
❏ FW37131	Just Like Me	1981	$10
— Reissue of 12196			
❏ 12196	Just Like Me	1981	$12

GRENFELL, JOYCE

ELEKTRA
| ❏ EKL-184 [M] | Presenting Joyce Grenfell | 1960 | $35 |

GREY, AL, AND WILD BILL DAVIS

CLASSIC JAZZ
| ❏ 103 | Keybone | 197? | $35 |

GREY, AL

ARGO
❏ LP-689 [M]	Al Grey and the Billy Mitchell Sextet	1962	$25
❏ LPS-689 [S]	Al Grey and the Billy Mitchell Sextet	1962	$30
❏ LP-731 [M]	Boss Bones	1964	$25
❏ LPS-731 [S]	Boss Bones	1964	$30
❏ LP-718 [M]	Having a Ball	1963	$25
❏ LPS-718 [S]	Having a Ball	1963	$30
❏ LP-711 [M]	Night Song	1963	$25
❏ LPS-711 [S]	Night Song	1963	$30
❏ LP-700 [M]	Snap Your Fingers	1962	$25
❏ LPS-700 [S]	Snap Your Fingers	1962	$30
❏ LP-653 [M]	The Last of the Big Plungers	1960	$30
❏ LPS-653 [S]	The Last of the Big Plungers	1960	$30
❏ LP-677 [M]	The Thinking Man's Trombone	1961	$25
❏ LPS-677 [S]	The Thinking Man's Trombone	1961	$30

CHESS
| ❏ 2-ACMJ-409 | Basic Grey | 1976 | $35 |

CLASSIC JAZZ
| ❏ 118 | Grey's Mood | 197? | $35 |

COLUMBIA
| ❏ FC38505 | Struttin' and Shoutin' | 1983 | $25 |

TANGERINE
| ❏ TRC-1504 [M] | Shades of Grey | 1965 | $35 |
| ❏ TRCS-1504 [S] | Shades of Grey | 1965 | $25 |

GRICE, JANET

OPTIMISM
| ❏ OP-3203 | Song for Andy | 1988 | $25 |

GRIER, JIMMY

HINDSIGHT
| ❏ HSR-177 | Jimmy Grier and His Orchestra 1935-36 | 198? | $25 |

GRIER, ROOSEVELT

RIC
| ❏ M-1008 [M] | Soul City | 1964 | $25 |
| ❏ S-1008 [S] | Soul City | 1964 | $30 |

WORD
| ❏ WR-8342 | Committed | 1986 | $15 |

GRIFF, RAY

ABC DOT
| ❏ DOSD-2011 | Expressions | 1974 | $15 |

CAPITOL
❏ ST-11486	Ray Griff	1976	$12
❏ ST-11718	Raymond's Place	1977	$12
❏ ST-11566	The Last of the Winfield Amateurs	1976	$12

DOT
| ❏ DLP-25868 | A Ray of Sunshine | 1968 | $25 |
| ❏ DOS-26013 | Songs for Everyone | 1973 | $18 |

ROYAL AMERICAN
| ❏ RAS1007 | Ray Griff Sings | 1972 | $18 |

GRIFFIN, DELLA

DOBRE
| ❏ 1009 | Della Griffin Sings | 1978 | $30 |

GRIFFIN, DICK

STRATA-EAST
| ❏ SES-19747 | The Eighth Wonder | 1975 | $25 |

GRIFFIN, JIMMY

POLYDOR
| ❏ PD6018 | James Griffin and Co. | 1973 | $18 |

REPRISE
| ❏ R-6091 [M] | Summer Holiday | 1963 | $50 |
| ❏ R9-6091 [S] | Summer Holiday | 1963 | $75 |

GRIFFIN, JOHNNY, AND MATTHEW GEE

ATLANTIC
| ❏ 1431 | Soul Groove | 1965 | $25 |
| ❏ SD1431 [S] | Soul Groove | 1965 | $30 |

GRIFFIN, JOHNNY

ARGO
| ❏ LP-624 [M] | Johnny Griffin Quartet | 1958 | $50 |

BLACK LION
| ❏ 304 | You Leave Me Breathless | 197? | $35 |

BLUE NOTE
❏ BLP-1559 [M]	A Blowing Session	1957	$300
—Deep groove" version (deep indentation under label on both sides)			
❏ BLP-1559 [M]	A Blowing Session	1957	$1000
— Regular version, "W. 63rd St." address on label			
❏ BLP-1559 [M]	A Blowing Session	1963	$130
— With "New York, USA" address on label			
❏ BST-85133	Introducing Johnny Griffin	1985	$25
— The Finest in Jazz Since 1939" reissue			
❏ BT-46536	Introducing Johnny Griffin	198?	$25
— Another "The Finest in Jazz Since 1939" reissue			
❏ BLP-1533 [M]	Introducing Johnny Griffin	1956	$3000
—Deep groove" version (deep indentation under label on both sides)			
❏ BLP-1533 [M]	Introducing Johnny Griffin	1956	$500
— Regular version, Lexington Ave. address on label			
❏ BLP-1533 [M]	Introducing Johnny Griffin	1957	$250
— With "W. 63rd St." address on label			
❏ BLP-1533 [M]	Introducing Johnny Griffin	1963	$150
— With "New York, USA" address on label			
❏ BST-81580 [S]	The Congregation	1967	$35
— With "A Division of Liberty Records" on label			
❏ B1-89383	The Congregation	1994	$35
— The Finest in Jazz Since 1939" reissue			
❏ BLP-1580 [M]	The Congregation	1958	$1000
—Deep groove" version (deep indentation under label on both sides). Andy Warhol cover			
❏ BLP-1580 [M]	The Congregation	1958	$500
— Regular version, "W. 63rd St." address on label. Andy Warhol cover			
❏ BLP-1580 [M]	The Congregation	1963	$150
— With "New York, USA" address on label. Andy Warhol cover			
❏ BST-1580 [S]	The Congregation	1959	$600
—Deep groove" version (deep indentation under label on both sides). Andy Warhol cover			
❏ BST-1580 [S]	The Congregation	1959	$300
— Regular version, "W. 63rd St." address on label. Andy Warhol cover			
❏ BST-1580 [S]	The Congregation	1963	$150
— With "New York, USA" address on label. Andy Warhol cover			

EMARCY
| ❏ MG-26001 [M] | Night Lady | 1967 | $150 |
| ❏ SR-66001 [S] | Night Lady | 1967 | $150 |

FANTASY
| ❏ OJC-485 | The Big Soul-Band | 1990 | $30 |
| ❏ OJC-136 | The Little Giant | 198? | $25 |

GALAXY
❏ 5126	Bush Dance	1979	$30
❏ 5146	Call It Whatchawaana	1984	$30
❏ 5132	NYC Underground	1980	$30
❏ 5117	Return of the Griffin	1979	$30
❏ 5139	To the Ladies	1981	$30

INNER CITY
| ❏ IC-2004 | Blues for Harvey | 1973 | $35 |
| ❏ IC-6042 | Live Tokyo | 197? | $25 |

JAZZLAND
| ❏ JLP-93 [M] | The Little Giant | 1961 | $40 |
| ❏ JLP-993 [S] | The Little Giant | 1961 | $30 |

MILESTONE
| ❏ 47014 | Big Soul | 197? | $25 |
| ❏ 47054 | Little Giant | 197? | $35 |

MOON
| ❏ MLP-004 | Body and Soul | 1992 | $35 |

RIVERSIDE
❏ RLP-368 [M]	Change of Pace	1961	$250
❏ RS-9368 [S]	Change of Pace	1961	$250
❏ RLP-462 [M]	Do Nothing 'Til You Hear from Me	1963	$175
❏ RS-9462 [S]	Do Nothing 'Til You Hear from Me	1963	$175
❏ RLP-437 [M]	Grab This!	1962	$175
❏ RS-9437 [S]	Grab This!	1962	$175
❏ RLP 12-264 [M]	Johnny Griffin Sextet	1958	$350
❏ 6145	Studio Jazz Party	198?	$30
❏ RLP-338 [M]	Studio Jazz Party	1960	$250
❏ RS-9338 [S]	Studio Jazz Party	1960	$250
❏ RLP 12-331 [M]	The Big Soul-Band	1960	$250
❏ RLP-1171 [S]	The Big Soul-Band	1960	$250
❏ RLP-420 [M]	The Kerry Dancers	1962	$350
❏ RS-9420 [S]	The Kerry Dancers	1962	$175
❏ RLP 12-304 [M]	The Little Giant	1959	$300
❏ RLP-1149 [S]	The Little Giant	1959	$300
❏ RLP-479 [M]	Wade in the Water	1964	$175
❏ RS-9479 [S]	Wade in the Water	1964	$175
❏ RLP 12-274 [M]	Way Out!	1958	$300
❏ RLP-387 [M]	White Gardenia	1961	$250
❏ RS-9387 [S]	White Gardenia	1961	$250

STEEPLECHASE
| ❏ SCS-1004 | Blues for Harvey | 198? | $30 |

TIMELESS
❏ 311	The Jamfs Are Coming	198?	$30
❏ LPSJP-121	The Jamfs Are Coming	1990	$25
— Reissue of 311			

GRIFFIN, KEN

COLUMBIA
❏ CL6130 [10]	Christmas Carols by Ken Griffin	1950	$30
❏ CS8760 [S]	The Organ Plays at Christmas	1963	$15
❏ CL692 [M]	The Organ Plays at Christmas	1955	$30
— Red and black label with six "eye" logos			

GRIFFIN, MERV

51 WEST
| ❏ Q16281 | P.S. I Love You | 198? | $10 |

CAMEO
| ❏ C-1060 [M] | My Favorite Songs | 1964 | $25 |
| ❏ SC-1060 [S] | My Favorite Songs | 1964 | $30 |

CARLTON
| ❏ LP-12-134 [M] | Merv Griffin's Dance Party | 1961 | $30 |
| ❏ STLP-12-134 [S] | Merv Griffin's Dance Party | 1961 | $40 |

GRIFFIN
| ❏ G3G-1501 | As Time Goes By | 1973 | $15 |

METROMEDIA
| ❏ MD1023 | Appearing Nightly | 1969 | $15 |

MGM
❏ E-4381 [M]	'Alf and 'Alf: Songs of the British Music Hall	1966	$18
— With Arthur Treacher			
❏ SE-4381 [S]	'Alf and 'Alf: Songs of the British Music Hall	1966	$25
— With Arthur Treacher			
❏ E-4401 [M]	And a Sled .... And a Catcher's Mitt ... And a Puppy ... And a Popgun ... And a Big Christmas Album from Merv Griffin and His TV Family	1966	$25
❏ SE-4401 [S]	And a Sled .... And a Catcher's Mitt ... And a Puppy ... And a Popgun ... And a Big Christmas Album from Merv Griffin and His TV Family	1966	$30
❏ E-4326 [M]	A Tinkling Piano in the Next Apartment	1965	$15
❏ SE-4326 [S]	A Tinkling Piano in the Next Apartment	1965	$18
❏ SE-4562 [S]	Irving Berlin Songs	1968	$0
— Canceled			

GRIFFITH, ANDY

CAPITOL
❏ T2066 [M]	Andy and Cleopatra	1964	$25
❏ ST2066 [S]	Andy and Cleopatra	1964	$30
❏ T1105 [M]	Andy Griffith Shouts the Blues and Old Timey Songs	1959	$40
❏ ST1105 [S]	Andy Griffith Shouts the Blues and Old Timey Songs	1959	$50
❏ T962 [M]	Just for Laughs	1958	$40
❏ T1611 [M]	Songs, Themes and Laughs from The Andy Griffith Show	1961	$100
❏ ST1611 [S]	Songs, Themes and Laughs from The Andy Griffith Show	1961	$120
❏ T1215 [M]	This Here Andy Griffith	1959	$30
❏ ST1215 [S]	This Here Andy Griffith	1959	$40

Number	Title	Yr	NM

GRIFFITH, JOHNNY, TRIO
WORKSHOP JAZZ
❑ WSJ205 [M]	Jazz	1963	$250

GRIFFITH, NANCI
B.F. DEAL
| ❑ BFD9 | There's a Light Beyond These Woods | 1978 | $50 |

ELEKTRA
| ❑ 62015 | Blue Roses from the Moons | 1997 | $15 |

FEATHERBED
| ❑ FB902 | Poet in My Window | 1982 | $25 |
| ❑ FB903 | There's a Light Beyond These Woods | 1982 | $25 |

MCA
❑ 42102	Little Love Affairs	1988	$10
❑ 5927	Lone Star State of Mind	1987	$10
❑ 42255	One Fair Summer Evening	1988	$10
❑ 6319	Storms	1989	$12

PHILO
❑ PH-1109	Last of the True Believers	1986	$15
❑ PH-1096	Once in a Very Blue Moon	1984	$15
❑ PH-1098	Poet in My Window	1986	$15
❑ PH-1097	There's a Light Beyond These Woods	1986	$15

GRIFFITH, SHIRLEY
BLUESVILLE
❑ BVLP-1087 [M]	The Blues of Shirley Griffith	1964	$50
—Blue label, silver print			
❑ BVLP-1087 [M]	The Blues of Shirley Griffith	1964	$30
—Blue label, trident logo at right			

GRIMES, GARY
DIRECT DISK
| ❑ SD-16630 | Starhand Visions | 198? | $30 |
| —Audiophile vinyl | | | |

GRIMES, HENRY
ESP-DISK'
| ❑ 1027 [M] | Henry Grimes Trio | 1966 | $150 |
| ❑ S-1027 [S] | Henry Grimes Trio | 1966 | $150 |

GRIMES, TINY
CLASSIC JAZZ
| ❑ 114 | Some Groovy Fours | 197? | $30 |

COLLECTABLES
❑ COL-5321	Tiny Grimes and Friends	198?	$25
❑ COL-5317	Tiny Grimes and His Rocking Highlanders, Volume 2	198?	$25
❑ COL-5304	Tiny Grimes Featuring Screamin' Jay Hawkins	198?	$25

FANTASY
| ❑ OJC-191 | Callin' the Blues | 1985 | $25 |

MUSE
| ❑ MR-5012 | Profoundly Blue | 1974 | $30 |

PRESTIGE
❑ PRLP-7138 [M]	Blues Grooves	1958	$300
— Yellow label			
❑ PRLP-7144 [M]	Callin' the Blues	1958	$250

SWINGVILLE
❑ SVLP-2004 [M]	Callin' the Blues	1960	$50
—Purple label			
❑ SVLP-2004 [M]	Callin' the Blues	1965	$30
—Blue label, trident logo at right			
❑ SVLP-2002 [M]	Tiny in Swingville	1960	$50
—Purple label			
❑ SVLP-2002 [M]	Tiny in Swingville	1965	$30
—Blue label, trident logo at right			

UNITED ARTISTS
| ❑ UAL-3232 [M] | Big Time Guitar | 1962 | $30 |
| ❑ UAS-6232 [S] | Big Time Guitar | 1962 | $30 |

GRIN
Features NILS LOFGREN.
A&M
| ❑ SP-4415 | Gone Crazy | 1973 | $12 |

COLUMBIA LIMITED EDITION
| ❑ LE10265 | All Out | 197? | $12 |
| —Remixed version on Columbia's brown-label "Limited Edition" series | | | |

EPIC
❑ PE34247	The Best of Grin	1976	$12
—Without bar code on back			
❑ PE34247	The Best of Grin	198?	$10
—With bar code on back			

SPINDIZZY
❑ Z31038	1 + 1	1972	$15
❑ KZ31701	All Out	1973	$15
❑ Z30321 [B]	Grin	1971	$15

GRISMAN, DAVID
Mandolin player. Also see STEPHANE GRAPPELLI; GRATEFUL DEAD related.

HORIZON
| ❑ SP-731 | Hot Dawg | 1979 | $16 |

ROUNDER
❑ 0190	Acoustic Christmas	1983	$30
❑ 0169	Here Today	198?	$25
❑ 0251/2	Home Is Where the Heart Is	1988	$30
❑ 0069	The Rounder Album	1976	$16

SUGAR HILL
| ❑ SH-3713 | Early Dawg | 1980 | $25 |

WARNER BROS.
❑ BSK3469	David Grisman Quintet '80	1980	$25
❑ 23804	Dawg Jazz	1983	$25
❑ BSK3618	Mondo Mando	1982	$25

ZEBRA/ACOUSTIC
| ❑ ZEA-6153 | Acousticity | 1986 | $25 |

GRISMAN QUINTET, DAVID
KALEIDOSCOPE
| ❑ 5 | David Grisman Quintet | 1977 | $25 |

GRISSOM, JIMMY
ARGO
| ❑ LP-729 [M] | World of Trouble | 1963 | $75 |
| ❑ LPS-729 [S] | World of Trouble | 1963 | $75 |

GROCE, LARRY
DAYBREAK
| ❑ 2010 | Crescentville | 1972 | $15 |
| ❑ 2000 | The Wheat Lies Low | 1971 | $15 |

DISNEYLAND
❑ 1V-8120	Disney's Children's Favorites Volume I	1979	$18
—Part of Realm Records numbering system; probably Columbia House record club edition			
❑ 2505	Disney's Children's Favorites Volume I	1979	$18
❑ 1V-8121	Disney's Children's Favorites Volume II	1979	$18
—Part of Realm Records numbering system; probably Columbia House record club edition			
❑ 2508	Disney's Children's Favorites Volume II	1979	$18
❑ 2525	Disney's Children's Favorites Volume III	1986	$18

WARNER BROS.
| ❑ BS2933 | Junkfood Junkie | 1976 | $12 |

GRODECK WHIPPERJENNY
Grodeck Whipperjenny is actually the title of the album - by David Matthews. But it's commonly refered to as a group name.
PEOPLE
| ❑ 3000 | Grodeck Whipperjenny | 1969 | $250 |

GROLNICK, DON, AND MICHAEL BRECKER
HIPPOCKET
| ❑ HP-106 | Hearts and Numbers | 1985 | $30 |

WINDHAM HILL
| ❑ WH-0106 | Hearts and Numbers | 1987 | $25 |
| —Reissue of HipPocket 106 | | | |

GROOTNA
COLUMBIA
| ❑ C31033 | Grootna | 1971 | $25 |

GROOV-U
GATEWAY
| ❑ GLP-3010 | Groov-U On Campus | 196? | $40 |

GROOVE, MAX
OPTIMISM
| ❑ OP-3108 | Center of Gravity | 198? | $25 |

GROOVE COLLECTIVE, THE
REPRISE
| ❑ 45541 | The Groove Collective | 1994 | $25 |

GROOVIE GOOLIES, THE
RCA VICTOR
| ❑ LSP-4420 | The Groovie Goolies | 1970 | $30 |

GROSS, HENRY
A&M
| ❑ SP-4416 | Henry Gross | 1973 | $15 |
| ❑ SP-4502 | Plug Me Into Something | 1974 | $15 |

ABC
| ❑ X-747 | Henry Gross | 1971 | $18 |

CAPITOL
| ❑ ST12113 | What's in a Name | 1980 | $12 |

LIFESONG
❑ JZ35280	Love Is the Stuff	1978	$12
❑ LS6002	Release	1976	$12
❑ PZ34995	Release	1978	$10
—Reissue of 6002			
❑ LS6010	Show Me to the Stage	1977	$12
❑ PZ35002	Show Me to the Stage	1978	$10
—Reissue of 6010			

GROSSMAN, STEVE
ATLANTIC
| ❑ SD19230 | Perspective | 1979 | $25 |

PM
| ❑ PMR-002 | Some Shapes to Come | 1974 | $30 |
| ❑ PMR-012 | Terra Firma | 1977 | $30 |

RED
| ❑ VPA189 | Love Is the Thing | 1986 | $30 |
| ❑ VPA176 | Way Out East | 1985 | $30 |

GROSZ, MARTY
RIVERSIDE
| ❑ RLP 12-268 [M] | Hurrah for Bix | 1958 | $300 |
| ❑ RLP-1109 [S] | Hurrah for Bix | 1959 | $300 |

STOMP OFF
| ❑ SOS-1158 | Marty Grosz and the Keepers of the Flame | 1988 | $25 |
| ❑ SOS-1214 | Unsaturated Fats | 1991 | $25 |

GROUNDHOGS, THE
Featuring Tony McPhee.
CLEVE
| ❑ CH-82871 | The Groundhogs with John Lee Hooker and John Mayall | 196? | $150 |

IMPERIAL
| ❑ LP-12452 | Blues Obituary | 1969 | $40 |

LIBERTY
| ❑ LST-7644 [B] | Thank Christ for the Bomb | 1970 | $30 |

UNITED ARTISTS
❑ UA-LA680-G	Black Diamond	1976	$25
❑ UA-LA603-G	Crosscut Saw	1976	$25
❑ UA-LA008-F	Hogwash	1973	$25
❑ UAS-5513	The Groundhogs Split	1971	$25
❑ UAS-5570	Who Will Save the World	1972	$25

WORLD PACIFIC
| ❑ WPS-21892 | Scratching the Surface | 1968 | $40 |

GROUP, THE
BELL
| ❑ 6038 | The Group | 1970 | $25 |

RCA VICTOR
| ❑ LPM-2663 [M] | The Group | 1963 | $50 |
| ❑ LSP-2663 [S] | The Group | 1963 | $75 |

GROUP IMAGE, THE
COMMUNITY
| ❑ A-101 | A Mouth in the Clouds | 1968 | $30 |

GROUP ONE
RCA VICTOR
| ❑ LPM-3524 [M] | Brothers Go to Mothers and Others | 1966 | $18 |
| ❑ LSP-3524 [S] | Brothers Go to Mothers and Others | 1966 | $25 |

GROUP THERAPY
PHILIPS
| ❑ PHS600303 | 37 Minutes of Group Therapy | 1969 | $18 |

RCA VICTOR
| ❑ LPM-3976 [M] | People Get Ready for Group Therapy | 1968 | $40 |
| ❑ LSP-3976 [S] | People Get Ready for Group Therapy | 1968 | $25 |

GROVE, BOBBY
KING
| ❑ 831 [M] | It Was for You | 1963 | $40 |

GROVE, DICK
PACIFIC JAZZ
| ❑ PJ-74 [M] | Little Bird Suite | 1963 | $25 |
| ❑ ST-74 [S] | Little Bird Suite | 1963 | $30 |

GROWING CONCERN, THE
MAINSTREAM
| ❑ 56108 [M] | The Growing Concern | 1968 | $100 |
| ❑ S-6108 [S] | The Growing Concern | 1968 | $300 |

GROWL
DISCREET
| ❑ DS2209 | Growl | 1974 | $250 |

Number	Title	Yr	NM

GRUNING, TOM
INNER CITY
| ❑ IC-1119 | Midnight Lullaby | 198? | $30 |

GRUNTZ, GEORGE
PHILIPS
| ❑ PHM200162 [M] | Bach Humbug | 1964 | $35 |
| ❑ PHS600162 [S] | Bach Humbug | 1964 | $25 |

GRUSIN, DAVE, AND LEE RITENOUR
GRP
| ❑ GRPA-1015 | Harlequin | 1985 | $25 |

GRUSIN, DAVE
COLUMBIA
| ❑ CL2344 [M] | Kaleidoscope | 1965 | $25 |
| ❑ CS9144 [S] | Kaleidoscope | 1965 | $30 |
EPIC
❑ LN24023 [M]	Piano Strings and Moonlight	1962	$100
❑ BN26023 [S]	Piano Strings and Moonlight	1962	$150
❑ LN3829 [M]	Subways Are for Sleeping	1962	$100
❑ BN622 [S]	Subways Are for Sleeping	1962	$150
GRP
❑ GR-1037	Cinemagic	1987	$25
❑ GRP-A-1001	Dave Grusin and the NY/LA Dream Band	1982	$25
❑ GR-9592	Migration	1989	$30
❑ GRP-A-1018	Mountain Dance	198?	$20
—Another reissue of GRP/Arista 5010
❑ GRP-A-1006	Night-Lines	1984	$25
❑ GR-1011	One of a Kind	198?	$25
❑ GR-1051	Sticks and Stones	1988	$25
❑ GR-9579	The Dave Grusin Collection	1989	$30
GRP/ARISTA
❑ GL5506	Live in Japan	1981	$25
❑ GRP-5010	Mountain Dance	1980	$25
❑ GL8-8058	Mountain Dance	198?	$20
—Budget-line reissue
❑ GRP-5900	Mountain Dance	1981	$25
—Limiteed edition special pressing
❑ GRP-5510	Out of the Shadows	1982	$25
❑ GL8-8139	Out of the Shadows	198?	$20
—Budget-line reissue
POLYDOR
| ❑ PD-1-6118 | One of a Kind | 1977 | $35 |
SHEFFIELD LABS
| ❑ SL-5 | Discovered Again! | 1976 | $30 |
| —Direct-to-disc recording |
SHEFFIELD TREASURY
| ❑ ST-500 | Discovered Again! | 198? | $25 |
| —Reissue of Sheffield Labs 5 |
VERSATILE
| ❑ NED1135 | Don't Touch | 1977 | $25 |

GRYCE, GIGI, AND CLIFFORD BROWN
BLUE NOTE
| ❑ BLP-5048 [10] | Gigi Gryce-Clifford Brown Sextet | 1954 | $400 |

GRYCE, GIGI
BLUE NOTE
❑ BLP-5050 [10]	Gigi Gryce and His Little Band, Volume 2	1954	$300
❑ BLP-5051 [10]	Gigi Gryce Qunitet/Sextet, Volume 3	1954	$300
❑ BLP-5049 [10]	Gigi Gryce's Jazztime Paris	1954	$300
FANTASY
| ❑ OJC-081 | The Rat Race Blues | 198? | $25 |
MERCURY
| ❑ MG-20628 [M] | Reminiscin' | 1961 | $150 |
| ❑ SR-60628 [S] | Reminiscin' | 1961 | $150 |
METROJAZZ
| ❑ E-1006 [M] | Gigi Gryce | 1958 | $350 |
| ❑ SE-1006 [S] | Gigi Gryce | 1959 | $350 |
NEW JAZZ
| ❑ NJLP-8230 [M] | Sayin' Somethin'! | 1959 | $175 |
| —Purple label |
| ❑ NJLP-8230 [M] | Sayin' Somethin'! | 1965 | $175 |
| —Blue label, trident logo at right |
| ❑ NJLP-8246 [M] | The Hap'nin's | 1960 | $150 |
| —Purple label |
| ❑ NJLP-8246 [M] | The Hap'nin's | 1965 | $175 |
| —Blue label, trident logo at right |
| ❑ NJLP-8262 [M] | The Rat Race Blues | 1961 | $175 |
| —Purple label |
| ❑ NJLP-8262 [M] | The Rat Race Blues | 1965 | $175 |
| —Blue label, trident logo at right |
SAVOY
| ❑ MG-12137 [M] | Nica's Tempo | 1958 | $100 |
SIGNAL
| ❑ S-1201 [M] | Gigi Gryce Quartet | 1955 | $300 |

GRYPHON
BELL
| ❑ 1316 | Red Queen to Gryphon Three | 1974 | $25 |
(NO LABEL)
| ❑ 12497 | Gryphon | 1973 | $100 |

GTR
Also see YES; GENESIS.
ARISTA
| ❑ AL8-8400 | GTR | 1986 | $10 |

GUADALCANAL DIARY
DB
| ❑ 73 | Walking in the Shadow of the Big Man | 1984 | $18 |
ELEKTRA
| ❑ 60752 | 2X4 | 1987 | $12 |
| ❑ 60848 [DJ] | Flip-Flop | 1989 | $12 |
| —Promo-only white label audiophile vinyl |
| ❑ 60848 | Flip-Flop | 1989 | $12 |
| ❑ 60848 [DJ] | Flip-Flop | 1989 | $15 |
| —Promo-only white label audiophile vinyl |
| ❑ 60478 | Jamboree | 1986 | $12 |

| ❑ 60429 [B] | Walking in the Shadow of the Big Man | 1985 | $12 |
ENTERTAINMENT ON DISC
| ❑ EOD102 [EP] | Watusi Rodeo | 1983 | $30 |

GUARALDI, VINCE
FANTASY
| ❑ 85017 [B] | A Boy Named Charlie Brown -- Jazz Impressions | 196? | $30 |
| ❑ 8430 [B] | A Boy Named Charlie Brown -- Jazz Impressions | 1971 | $25 |
| —Reissue of 85017 |
| ❑ 8431 | A Charlie Brown Christmas | 1971 | $30 |
| —Reissue of 85019; dark blue label |
| ❑ 8431 | A Charlie Brown Christmas | 1988 | $35 |
| —Remastered version with "1988" on back cover. Lighter blue label. Also has a bonus track! |
| ❑ 5019 [M] | A Charlie Brown Christmas | 1964 | $30 |

| ❑ 85019 [S] | A Charlie Brown Christmas | 1964 | $40 |
| ❑ 3257 [M] | A Flower Is a Lovesome Thing | 1958 | $40 |
| —Red vinyl |
| ❑ 3257 [M] | A Flower Is a Lovesome Thing | 195? | $30 |
| —Black vinyl, red label, non-flexible vinyl |

| ❑ 3257 [M] | A Flower Is a Lovesome Thing | 196? | $35 |
| —Black vinyl, red label, flexible vinyl |
| ❑ OJC-235 | A Flower Is a Lovesome Thing | 198? | $25 |
| —Reissue of 3257 |
❑ 3362 [M]	From All Sides	1966	$25
❑ 8362 [S]	From All Sides	1966	$25
❑ 3359 [M]	Jazz Impressions	1965	$30
❑ 8359 [S]	Jazz Impressions	1965	$30
❑ OJC-287	Jazz Impressions	1987	$25
—Reissue of 8359
❑ 3337 [M]	Jazz Impressions of Black Orpheus (Cast Your Fate to the Wind)	1962	$40
—Red vinyl
❑ 3337 [M]	Jazz Impressions of Black Orpheus (Cast Your Fate to the Wind)	1962	$30
—Black vinyl, red label, non-flexible vinyl
❑ 3337 [M]	Jazz Impressions of Black Orpheus (Cast Your Fate to the Wind)	1962	$35
—Black vinyl, red label, flexible vinyl
❑ 8089 [S]	Jazz Impressions of Black Orpheus (Cast Your Fate to the Wind)	1962	$40
—Blue vinyl
❑ 8089 [S]	Jazz Impressions of Black Orpheus (Cast Your Fate to the Wind)	1962	$35
—Black vinyl, blue label, flexible vinyl
❑ 8089 [S]	Jazz Impressions of Black Orpheus (Cast Your Fate to the Wind)	1962	$30
—Black vinyl, blue label, non-flexible vinyl
❑ OJC-437	Jazz Impressions of Black Orpheus (Cast Your Fate to the Wind)	198?	$25
—Reissue of 8089
❑ 3371 [M]	Live at the El Matador	1967	$25
❑ 8371 [S]	Live at the El Matador	1967	$25
❑ OJC-289	Live at the El Matador	1987	$25
—Reissue of 8371
❑ 8377	Live-Live-Live	1968	$25
❑ 3213 [M]	Modern Music from San Francisco	1956	$250
—Red vinyl
❑ 3213 [M]	Modern Music from San Francisco	195?	$30
—Black vinyl, red label, non-flexible vinyl
❑ OJC-272	Modern Music from San Francisco	1987	$25
—Reissue of 3213
❑ 3360 [M]	The Latin Side of Vince Guaraldi	1965	$30
❑ 8360 [S]	The Latin Side of Vince Guaraldi	1965	$30
❑ 3358 [M]	Tour de Force	1964	$30
❑ 8358 [S]	Tour de Force	1964	$30
❑ 3356 [M]	Vince Guaraldi and Bola Sete and Friends	1964	$30
❑ 8356 [S]	Vince Guaraldi and Bola Sete and Friends	1964	$30
❑ 3367 [M]	Vince Guaraldi at Grace Cathedral	1967	$25
❑ 8367 [S]	Vince Guaraldi at Grace Cathedral	1967	$25
❑ 3352 [M]	Vince Guaraldi in Person	1963	$30
❑ 8352 [S]	Vince Guaraldi in Person	1963	$75
❑ MPF-4505	Vince Guaraldi's Greatest Hits	1981	$30
❑ 3225 [M]	Vince Guaraldi Trio	1956	$50
—Red vinyl
❑ 3225 [M]	Vince Guaraldi Trio	195?	$30
—Black vinyl, red label, non-flexible vinyl
❑ 3225 [M]	Vince Guaraldi Trio	196?	$35
—Black vinyl, red label, flexible vinyl
❑ OJC-149	Vince Guaraldi Trio	198?	$25
—Reissue of 3225
MOBILE FIDELITY
| ❑ 1-112 | Jazz Impressions of Black Orpheus (Cast Your Fate to the Wind) | 1983 | $50 |
| —Audiophile vinyl |
WARNER BROS.
❑ WS1828	Alma-Ville	1970	$35
❑ WS1775	Eclectic	1969	$35
❑ WS1747	Oh Good Grief!	1968	$25

GUARALDI, VINCE/CONTE CANDOLI
CROWN
| ❑ CLP-5417 [M] | Vince Guaraldi and the Conte Candoli All Stars | 1963 | $30 |
| ❑ CST-417 [R] | Vince Guaraldi and the Conte Candoli All Stars | 1963 | $25 |
PREMIER
| ❑ PM-2009 [M] | Vince Guaraldi-Conte Candoli Quartet | 1963 | $30 |
| ❑ PS-2009 [R] | Vince Guaraldi-Conte Candoli Quartet | 1963 | $25 |

Number	Title	Yr	NM

GUARALDI, VINCE/FRANK ROSOLINO
PREMIER
❏ PM-2014 [M]	Vince Guaraldi-Frank Rosolino Quintet	1963	$30
❏ PS-2014 [R]	Vince Guaraldi-Frank Rosolino Quintet	1963	$25

GUARD, DAVE, AND THE WHISKEYHILL SINGERS
CAPITOL
❏ T1728 [M]	Dave Guard and the Whiskeyhill Singers	1962	$25
❏ ST1728 [S]	Dave Guard and the Whiskeyhill Singers	1962	$30

GUARNIERI, JOHNNY
CLASSIC JAZZ
❏ 105	Gliss Me Again	197?	$30

CORAL
❏ CRL57085 [M]	Songs of Hudson and DeLange	1957	$40
❏ CRL57086 [M]	The Duke Again	1957	$40

DOBRE
❏ 1017	Johnny Guarnieri Plays Walter Donaldson	197?	$30

DOT
❏ DLP-3647 [M]	Piano Dimensions	1965	$85
❏ DLP-25647 [S]	Piano Dimensions	1965	$85

GOLDEN CREST
❏ GC-3020 [M]	Johnny Guarnieri Plays Johnny Guarnieri	1958	$40

JIM TAYLOR PRESENTS
❏ 102	Johnny Guarnieri Plays Harry Warren	197?	$30

RCA CAMDEN
❏ CAL-345 [M]	Cheerful Little Earful	1958	$35
❏ CAL-391 [M]	Side by Side	1958	$35

ROYALE
❏ 1296 [M]	An Hour of Modern Music	1952	$40
❏ VLP6047 [10]	Johnny Guarnieri/Tony Mottola/Bob Haggart/Cozy Cole	195?	$50

SAVOY
❏ MG-15007 [10]	Hot Piano	1951	$100

SOUNDS GREAT
❏ SG-5001	Echoes of Ellington	198?	$25

TAZ-JAZ
❏ 1002	Stealin' Apples	1977	$30
❏ 1001	Superstride	1976	$30

GUESNON, GEORGE
JAZZ CRUSADE
❏ 2011	Echoes from New Orleans	196?	$35

JAZZOLOGY
❏ JCE-11	Creole Blues	1967	$35

GUESS WHO, THE
Also see CHAD ALLAN; RANDY BACHMAN; BURTON CUMMINGS.

COMPLEAT
❏ 672012-1	The Best of the Gues Who, Live	1986	$25

HILLTAK
❏ HT19227	All This for a Song	1979	$15

MGM
❏ SE-4645	The Guess Who	1969	$18
—Compilation of pre-RCA Victor recordings			

PICKWICK
❏ SPC-3246	Wild One	1970	$15
—Available in two different covers - "bike" cover and "girl on car" cover; both same price			

P.I.P.
❏ 6806	The Guess Who Play Pure Guess Who	197?	$15

PRIDE
❏ PRD 0012	The History of the Guess Who	197?	$15

RCA
❏ 7622-1-R	The Greatest of the Guess Who	1987	$12
—Late reissue			

RCA VICTOR
❏ APL1-0130	#10	1973	$18
❏ APD1-0130 [Q]	#10	1974	$40
❏ LSP-4266	American Woman	1970	$25
—Orange label, non-flexible vinyl			
❏ LSP-4266	American Woman	1971	$15
—Orange label, flexible vinyl			
❏ AFL1-4266	American Woman	1977	$12
—Reissue with new prefix			
❏ AYL1-3673	American Woman	1979	$10
—Best Buy Series" reissue			
❏ LSP-4830	Artificial Paradise	1973	$18

—Add 1/3 if paper bag is with package			
❏ LSP-4157	Canned Wheat Packed By the Guess Who	1969	$25
—Orange label, non-flexible vinyl			
❏ LSP-4157	Canned Wheat Packed By the Guess Who	1971	$15
—Orange label, flexible vinyl			
❏ ANL1-0983	Canned Wheat Packed By the Guess Who	1975	$12
—Reissue of LSP-4157			
❏ CPL1-0636	Flavours	1975	$18
❏ CPD1-0636 [Q]	Flavours	1975	$40
❏ LSP-4779	Live at the Paramount (Seattle)	1972	$30
❏ APL1-0995	Power in the Music	1975	$18
❏ APD1-0995 [Q]	Power in the Music	1975	$40
❏ APL1-0405	Road Food	1974	$18
❏ APD1-0405 [Q]	Road Food	1974	$40
❏ LSP-4602	Rockin'	1972	$18
❏ LSP-4359	Share the Land	1970	$25
—Orange label, non-flexible vinyl			
❏ LSP-4359	Share the Land	1971	$15
—Orange label, flexible vinyl			
❏ LSP-4574	So Long, Bannatyne	1971	$18
❏ LSPX-1004	The Best of the Guess Who	1971	$18
❏ AYL1-3662	The Best of the Guess Who	1979	$10
—Best Buy Series" reissue			
❏ AFL1-2594	The Best of the Guess Who	1978	$12
—Reissue of LSPX-1004			
❏ APL1-0269	The Best of the Guess Who, Volume II	1973	$18
❏ APD1-0269 [Q]	The Best of the Guess Who, Volume II	1974	$40
❏ AFL1-0269	The Best of the Guess Who, Volume II	1977	$12
—Reissue with new prefix			
❏ APL1-2253	The Greatest of the Guess Who	1977	$18
❏ AYL1-3746	The Greatest of the Guess Who	1980	$10
—Best Buy Series" reissue			
❏ APL1-1778	The Way They Were	1976	$18
❏ LSP-4141	Wheatfield Soul	1969	$25
—Orange label, non-flexible vinyl			
❏ LSP-4141	Wheatfield Soul	1971	$15
—Orange label, flexible vinyl			
❏ ANL1-1117	Wheatfield Soul	1975	$12
—Reissue of LSP-4141			

SCEPTER
❏ SP-533 [M]	Shakin' All Over	1966	$40
❏ SPS-533 [P]	Shakin' All Over	1966	$30
—The above lists the artist as "The Guess Who's Chad Allan & The Expressions" on the cover			

SPRINGBOARD
❏ SPB-4022	Shakin' All Over	1972	$12

SUNDAZED
❏ LP5113	Shakin' All Over	2001	$18

WAND
❏ WDS-691 [P]	Born in Canada	1969	$18
—Reissue of Scepter LP; three tracks are rechanneled			

GUIDED BY VOICES
E RECORDS
❏ GBV 0001	Devil Between My Toes	1987	$300

HALO
❏ 1 [B]	Sandbox	1987	$150
❏ 2	Self Inflicted Aerial Nostalgia	1989	$175

I WANNA
❏ 0(no cat #) [EP]	Forever Since Breakfast	1986	$175

MATADOR
❏ OLE-123 [B]	Alien Lanes	1995	$18
❏ OLE-241	Mag Earwhig!	1997	$12
❏ OLE-185 [EP]	Sunfish Holy Breakfast	1996	$12
❏ OLE-161	Under the Bushes, Under the Stars	1996	$15
—One side of Record 2 is blank			

ROCKATHON
❏ 0(no cat #)	Propeller	1992	$1000
—Hand-colored cover with nature-book paste-on; signed and numbered			
❏ 02	Tonics & Twisted Chasers	1997	$15
—1,000 copies were pressed on various colors of vinyl			

ROCKATHON/FADING CAPTAIN SERIES
❏ 10	Daredevil Stamp Collector: Do the Collapse B-Sides	2001	$15
—1,000 copies were pressed			
❏ 7	Suitcase Abridged: Drinks and Deliveries	2000	$15
—500 copies were pressed			

ROCKET #9
❏ 0(no cat #) [B]	Same Place the Fly Got Smashed	1990	$75

SCAT
❏ 35 [B]	Bee Thousand	1994	$18
❏ 40	Box	1994	$75
❏ 31 [B]	Vampire on Titus	1993	$30

TVT
❏ 1980	Do the Collapse	1999	$12
❏ 2160	Isolation Drills	2001	$12

GUITAR, BONNIE
DOT
❏ DLP-25947	Affair!	1969	$25
❏ DLP-3793 [M]	Award Winner	1967	$25
❏ DLP-25793 [S]	Award Winner	1967	$25
❏ DLP-25840	Bonnie Guitar	1968	$25
❏ DLP-3335 [M]	Dark Moon	1961	$30
❏ DLP-25335 [R]	Dark Moon	196?	$18
❏ DLP-25892	Leaves Are the Tears of Autumn	1968	$25
❏ DLP-3746 [M]	Merry Christmas from Bonnie Guitar	1966	$25
❏ DLP-25746 [S]	Merry Christmas from Bonnie Guitar	1966	$30
❏ DLP-3737 [M]	Miss Bonnie Guitar	1966	$25
❏ DLP-25737 [S]	Miss Bonnie Guitar	1966	$30
❏ DLP-3069 [M]	Moonlight and Shadows	1957	$50
❏ DLP-25069 [R]	Moonlight and Shadows	196?	$18
❏ DLP-3696 [M]	Two Worlds	1966	$25
❏ DLP-25696 [S]	Two Worlds	1966	$30
❏ DLP-3151 [M]	Whispering Hope	1958	$40
❏ DLP-25151 [S]	Whispering Hope	1958	$50

PARAMOUNT
❏ PAS-5018	Allegheny	1970	$18

PICKWICK
❏ SPC-3086	Favorite Lady of Song	196?	$15
❏ SPC-3144	Green, Green Grass of Home	196?	$15

RCA CAMDEN
❏ CAS-2339	Night Train to Memphis	1969	$18

GUITAR RAMBLERS, THE
COLUMBIA
❏ CL2067 [M]	The Happy, Youthful New Sounds of the Guitar Ramblers	1964	$30
❏ CS8867 [S]	The Happy, Youthful New Sounds of the Guitar Ramblers	1964	$30

GUITAR SLIM
ATLANTIC
❏ 81760	The Atco Sessions	1987	$12

SPECIALTY
❏ SP-2130	Things That I Used to Do	1969	$25

GULDA, FRIEDRICH
COLUMBIA
❏ CL2251 [M]	From Vienna with Jazz	1964	$30
❏ CS9051 [S]	From Vienna with Jazz	1964	$35
❏ CL2346 [M]	The Ineffable Friedrich Gulda	1965	$30
❏ CS9146 [S]	The Ineffable Friedrich Gulda	1965	$35

RCA VICTOR
❏ LPM-1355 [M]	Friedrich Gulda at Birdland	1957	$50

GULLIN, LARS
ATLANTIC
❏ 1246 [M]	Baritone Sax	1956	$300
—Black label			
❏ 1246 [M]	Baritone Sax	1960	$300
—Multicolor label, white "fan" logo at right			

CONTEMPORARY
❏ C-2505 [10]	Modern Sounds	1953	$300

EASTWEST
❏ 4003 [M]	Lars Gullin Swings	196?	$75

EMARCY
❏ MG-26044 [10]	Gullin's Garden	1954	$300

Number	Title	Yr	NM
❏ MG-36012 [M]	Lars Gullin	1955	$120
❏ MG-26041 [10]	Lars Gullin Quartet	1954	$300
❏ MG-36059 [M]	Lars Gullin with the Moretone Singers	1955	$250
PRESTIGE			
❏ PRLP-144 [10]	New Sounds from Sweden, Volume 5	1953	$300
❏ PRLP-151 [10]	New Sounds from Sweden, Volume 7	1953	$300

GULLIVER
With Daryl Hall. John Oates joined later, but is not on these records.

ELEKTRA

❏ EKS-74070	Gulliver	1970	$25

GULLY LOW JAZZ BAND

GHB

❏ GHB-163	In Dreamland	1984	$25

GUMBS, ONAJE ALLAN

STEEPLECHASE

❏ SCS-1069	Onaje	198?	$30
ZEBRA/MCA			
❏ ZEB-42120	That Special Part of Me	1988	$25

GUN

EPIC

❏ BN26468 [B]	Gun	1969	$30
❏ BN26551	Gunsight	1970	$30

GUNHILL ROAD

KAMA SUTRA

❏ KLS-2061	Gunhill Road	1972	$15
MERCURY			
❏ SR-61341	Gun Hill Road	1971	$15

GUNS & BUTTER

COTILLION

❏ SD9901	Guns & Butter	1972	$25

GUNS N' ROSES
Also see VELVET REVOLVER.

GEFFEN

❏ R170348	Appetite for Destruction	1987	$15
—BMG Direct Marketing edition			
❏ GHS24148	Appetite for Destruction	1987	$18
❏ XXXG24148 [B]	Appetite for Destruction	1987	$75
—Original "rape cover"; the XXXG prefix is on the cover only; all copies of the record use the GHS prefix			
❏ GHS24148	Appetite for Destruction	2008	$25
❏ R100805	G N' R Lies	1988	$15
—BMG Direct Marketing edition			
❏ GHS24198	G N' R Lies	1988	$15
❏ 490514-1	Live Era '87-'93	1999	$120
❏ GEF24617 [B]	The Spaghetti Incident?	1993	$40
—Orange vinyl			
❏ GEF24415	Use Your Illusion I	1991	$30
❏ GEF24420	Use Your Illusion II	1991	$30
UZI SUICIDE			
❏ USR 001 [EP]	Live ?!*@ Like a Suicide	1986	$300

GUNTER, ARTHUR

EXCELLO

❏ LPS-8017	Black and Blues	1971	$30

GURU

CHRYSALIS

❏ F1-21998	Jazzmatazz Vol. 1	1993	$25
❏ F1-34290	Jazzmatazz Vol. 2: The New Reality	1995	$20
VIRGIN			
❏ 50188	Jazzmatazz Vol. 3: Streetsoul	2000	$20

GUSTAFSSON, RUNE

ATLANTIC

❏ SD8234	Rune at the Top	1969	$30
GNP CRESCENDO			
❏ GNPS-2118	Move	1976	$25
PABLO TODAY			
❏ 2312106	The Sweetest Sounds	1979	$30

GUTHRIE, ARLO

REPRISE

❏ R6267 [M]	Alice's Restaurant	1967	$50
❏ RS6267 [S]	Alice's Restaurant	1967	$18
—Pink, green and gold label			
❏ RS6267 [S]	Alice's Restaurant	1968	$15
—With "W7" and "r:" logos on two-tone orange label			
❏ RS6267 [S]	Alice's Restaurant	1970	$12
—With only "r:" logo on all-orange (tan) label			
❏ MS2239	Amigo	1976	$15

Number	Title	Yr	NM
❏ RS6299	Arlo	1968	$18
—With "W7" and "r:" logos on two-tone orange label			
❏ RS6299	Arlo	1970	$12
—With only "r:" logo on all-orange (tan) label			
❏ MS2183	Arlo Guthrie	1974	$15
❏ MS2060	Hobo's Lullaby	1972	$15
❏ MS2142	Last of the Brooklyn Cowboys	1973	$15
❏ MS42142 [Q]	Last of the Brooklyn Cowboys	1973	$30
❏ RS6346	Running Down the Road	1969	$18
—With "W7" and "r:" logos on two-tone orange label			
❏ RS6346	Running Down the Road	1970	$12
—With only "r:" logo on all-orange (tan) label			
❏ RS6411	Washington County	1970	$15
WARNER BROS.			
❏ BSK3232	One Night	1978	$12
❏ BSK3336	Outlasting the Blues	1979	$12
❏ BSK3558	Power of Love	1981	$12
❏ BSK3117	The Best of Arlo Guthrie	1977	$12
—Burbank" palm trees label			
❏ BSK3117	The Best of Arlo Guthrie	1979	$10
—White or tan label			

GUTHRIE, JACK

CAPITOL

❏ T2456 [M]	Jack Guthrie's Greatest Songs	1966	$30

GUTHRIE, WOODY, AND CISCO HOUSTON

STINSON

❏ SLP-32 [10]	Cowboy Songs	1951	$300
❏ SLP-44 [10]	Folk Songs, Vol. 1	1952	$250
—Red vinyl			
❏ SLP-53 [10]	More Songs	1953	$250

GUTHRIE, WOODY; SONNY TERRY; ALEX STEWART

STINSON

❏ SLP-7 [10]	Chain Gang, Vol. 1	1950	$350
❏ SLP-8 [10]	Chain Gang, Vol. 2	1950	$350

GUTHRIE, WOODY

COLLECTABLES

❏ COL-5095	Golden Classics Vol. 1: Worried Man Blues	198?	$15
❏ COL-5098	Golden Classics Vol. 2: Immortal	198?	$15
ELEKTRA			
❏ EKL-271/2 [M]	The Library of Congress Recordings	1964	$40
—Original pressing has "guitar player" labels			
EVEREST ARCHIVE OF FOLK & JAZZ			
❏ 204	Woody Guthrie	1966	$15
FOLKWAYS			
❏ FH-5485 [M]	Ballads of Sacco and Vanzetti	196?	$35
❏ FA-2481 [M]	Bound for Glory: Songs and Stories of Woody Guthrie	1956	$75
❏ FP-11 [10]	Dust Bowl Ballads	1950	$200
❏ FA-2011 [10]	Dust Bowl Ballads	195?	$150
—Reissue of FP-11			
❏ FH-5212 [M]	Dust Bowl Ballads	1964	$40
❏ FC-7005 [10]	Songs to Grow On	1950	$600
❏ FP-715 [10]	Songs to Grow On For Mother and Child	195?	$250
❏ FC-7015 [10]	Songs to Grow On For Mother and Child	1953	$250
—Reissue of FP-715			
❏ FC-7027 [10]	Songs to Grow On Vol. 3	1951	$250
❏ FA-2485 [M]	Struggle	1964	$75
❏ 31001 [R]	This Land Is Your Land	196?	$20
❏ FA-2483 [M]	Woody Guthrie Sings Folk Songs	1964	$50
❏ FA-2484 [M]	Woody Guthrie Sings Folk Songs, Vol. 2	1964	$50
RCA VICTOR			
❏ LPV-502 [M]	Dust Bowl Ballads	1964	$30
ROUNDER			
❏ 1036	Columbia River Collection	1987	$12
❏ 1040	Dust Bowl Ballads	1988	$12
❏ 1041/2/3	The Library of Congress Recordings	1988	$25
SMITHSONIAN FOLKWAYS			
❏ SF-40025	Struggle	1989	$15
❏ SF-40007	Woody Guthrie Sings Folk Songs	1989	$15
VERVE FOLKWAYS			
❏ FV-9007 [M]	Bed on the Floor	1965	$50
❏ FVS-9007 [R]	Bed on the Floor	1965	$30
❏ FV-9036 [M]	Bonneville Dam & Other Columbia River Songs	1965	$40
❏ FVS-9036 [R]	Bonneville Dam & Other Columbia River Songs	1965	$30

Number	Title	Yr	NM
GUY, BUDDY			
BLUE THUMB			
❏ BTS20	Buddy and the Juniors	1970	$30
❏ BTS20 [B]	Buddy and the Juniors	1970	$150
—black and white marbled vinyl			
CHESS			
❏ CH-9115	Buddy Guy	1984	$10
❏ LP-1527 [M]	I Left My Blues in San Francisco	1968	$30
❏ LP-409	I Was Walking Through the Woods	1970	$25
MCA			
❏ 11165	I Was Walking Through the Woods	1995	$30
—Heavy Vinyl" audiophile reissue			
VANGUARD			
❏ VSD-79272	A Man and the Blues	1968	$30
❏ VSD-79323	Hold That Plane!	1972	$25

❏ VSD-79290 [B]	This Is Buddy Guy	1969	$30

GUY, CHARLES

CAPITOL

❏ T1920 [M]	Prisoner's Dream	1963	$25
❏ ST1920 [S]	Prisoner's Dream	1963	$30

GUY & RALNA

RANWOOD

❏ 8110	Country Songs We Love to Sing	1973	$12
❏ 8120	Give Me That Old Time Religion	1974	$12
❏ 8148	How Great Thou Art	1975	$12

GWALTNEY, TOMMY

RIVERSIDE

❏ RLP-353 [M]	Goin' to Kansas City	1960	$250
❏ RS-9353 [S]	Goin' to Kansas City	1960	$40

GYPSY

METROMEDIA

❏ MD-1031 [B]	Gypsy	1970	$30
❏ MD1044 [B]	In the Garden	1971	$25
RCA VICTOR			
❏ LSP-4775	Antithesis	1972	$18
❏ APL1-0093	Unlock the Gates	1973	$18

H

H.P. LOVECRAFT

CADABRA

❏ CADABR002 [B]	The Hound and Music of Erich Zann	2016	$25
❏ CADABR002 [B]	The Lurking Fear	2016	$30
MERCURY			
❏ SRM-1-1041	We Love You	1975	$25
PHILIPS			
❏ PHM200252 [M]	H.P. Lovecraft	1967	$100

Number	Title	Yr	NM

H.P. LOVECRAFT

Number	Title	Yr	NM
❏ PHS600252 [S]	H.P. Lovecraft	1967	$30
❏ PHS600279	Lovecraft II	1968	$30
REPRISE			
❏ RS6419	Valley of the Moon	1970	$30
SUNDAZED			
❏ LP-5004 [B]	Live May 11, 1968	1991	$25

H.Y. SLEDGE
SSS INTERNATIONAL

| ❏ 22 | Bootleg Music | 1971 | $25 |

HACKAMORE BRICK
KAMA SUTRA

| ❏ KSBS-2025 | One Kiss Leads to Another | 1971 | $15 |

HACKETT, BOBBY, AND BILLY BUTTERFIELD
VERVE

| ❏ V-8723 [M] | Bobby/Billy/Brazil | 1967 | $35 |
| ❏ V6-8723 [S] | Bobby/Billy/Brazil | 1967 | $30 |

HACKETT, BOBBY
BRUNSWICK

❏ BL56014 [10]	Trumpet Solos	1950	$50
CAPITOL			
❏ T1172 [M]	Blues with a Kick	1959	$75
❏ ST1172 [S]	Blues with a Kick	1959	$75
❏ T1077 [M]	Bobby Hackett at the Embers	1958	$75
—Black colorband label, logo at left			
❏ ST1077 [S]	Bobby Hackett at the Embers	1958	$75
—Black colorband label, logo at left			
❏ T1077 [M]	Bobby Hackett at the Embers	1962	$40
—Black colorband label, logo at top			
❏ ST1077 [S]	Bobby Hackett at the Embers	1962	$40
—Black colorband label, logo at top			
❏ T1235 [M]	Bobby Hackett Quartet	1959	$75
❏ ST1235 [S]	Bobby Hackett Quartet	1959	$75
❏ T692 [M]	Coast Concert	1956	$75
—Turquoise or gray label			
❏ T692 [M]	Coast Concert	1956	$30
—Black colorband label, logo at left			
❏ T1002 [M]	Don't Take Your Love from Me	1958	$75
—Turquoise or gray label			
❏ T1002 [M]	Don't Take Your Love from Me	1958	$75
—Black colorband label, logo at left			
❏ T1413 [M]	Easy Beat	1960	$50
❏ ST1413 [S]	Easy Beat	1960	$75
❏ T857 [M]	Gotham Jazz Scene	1957	$75
—Turquoise or gray label			
❏ T857 [M]	Gotham Jazz Scene	1957	$75
—Black colorband label, logo at left			
❏ T575 [M]	In a Mellow Mood	1955	$85
—Turquoise or gray label			
❏ T575 [M]	In a Mellow Mood	1955	$85
—Black colorband label, logo at left			
❏ T933 [M]	Jazz Ultimate	1958	$85
—Turquoise or gray label			
❏ T933 [M]	Jazz Ultimate	1958	$75
—Black colorband label, logo at left			
❏ ST933 [S]	Jazz Ultimate	1959	$75
—Black colorband label, logo at left			
❏ SM-933	Jazz Ultimate	1976	$25
—Reissue with new prefix			
❏ T719 [M]	Rendezvous	1956	$85
—Turquoise or gray label			

❏ T719 [M]	Rendezvous	1956	$75
—Black colorband label, logo at left			
❏ H458 [10]	Soft Lights	1954	$100
❏ T458 [M]	Soft Lights	1955	$85
—Turquoise or gray label			
❏ T458 [M]	Soft Lights	1955	$85
—Black colorband label, logo at left			
CHIAROSCURO			
❏ 105	Live at Roosevelt Grill	1972	$30
❏ 138	Live at Roosevelt Grill, Volume 2	197?	$30
❏ 161	Live at Roosevelt Grill, Volume 3	197?	$30
COLUMBIA			
❏ CL1602 [M]	Dream Awhile	1961	$25
❏ CS8402 [S]	Dream Awhile	1961	$30
❏ CL6156 [10]	Jazz Session	1951	$50
❏ CL1895 [M]	Night Love	1962	$35
❏ CS8695 [S]	Night Love	1962	$25
❏ CL2566 [10]	The Bobby Hackett Horn	1955	$75
❏ CL1729 [M]	The Most Beautiful Horn in the World	1962	$25
❏ CS8529 [S]	The Most Beautiful Horn in the World	1962	$30
COMMODORE			
❏ FL-20016 [10]	Horn A Plenty	1951	$50
DOBRE			
❏ 1004	Thanks Bobby	197?	$25
ENCORE			
❏ EE22003 [M]	The Bobby Hackett Horn	1968	$30
EPIC			
❏ LN24174 [M]	A String of Pearls	1966	$75
❏ BN26174 [S]	A String of Pearls	1966	$85
❏ LN24099 [M]	Hello, Louis!	1964	$75
❏ BN26099 [S]	Hello, Louis!	1964	$85
❏ LA16037 [M]	Oliver!	1963	$75
❏ BA17037 [S]	Oliver!	1963	$85
❏ LN3106 [M]	The Hackett Horn	1956	$100
❏ LN24080 [M]	The Music of Bert Kaempfert	1964	$75
❏ BN26080 [S]	The Music of Bert Kaempfert	1964	$85
❏ LN24061 [M]	The Music of Mancini	1963	$75
❏ BN26061 [S]	The Music of Mancini	1963	$85
❏ FLM13107 [M]	The Swingin'est Gals in Town	196?	$85
❏ FLS15107 [S]	The Swingin'est Gals in Town	196?	$25
❏ LN24155 [M]	The Trumpet's Greatest Hits	1965	$75
❏ BN26155 [S]	The Trumpet's Greatest Hits	1965	$85
❏ LN24220 [M]	Tony Bennett's Greatest Hits	1966	$75
❏ BN26220 [S]	Tony Bennett's Greatest Hits	1966	$85
FLYING DUTCHMAN			
❏ BDL1-0829	Strike Up the Band	1975	$30
❏ FD-10159	What a Wonderful World	1973	$30
JAZZOLOGY			
❏ J-111	Bobby Hackett and His Orchestra, 1943	198?	$25
❏ JCE-76	Live from Manassas	1979	$25
PAUSA			
❏ 9038	Coast Concert	198?	$25
PICKWICK			
❏ PC-3012 [M]	Bobby Hackett with Strings	1966	$30
❏ SPC-3012 [S]	Bobby Hackett with Strings	1966	$25
PROJECT 3			
❏ PR5016SD	A Time for Love	1968	$30
❏ PR26033	Memorable and Mellow	1979	$30
❏ PR5006SD	That Midnight Touch	1967	$30
❏ PR5034SD	This Is My Bag	1969	$30
SEAGULL			
❏ LG-8201	Goodnight My Love	198?	$25
SESAC			
❏ N-4105 [M]	Candlelight and Romance	1960	$30
❏ SN-4105 [S]	Candlelight and Romance	1960	$30
❏ N-4101 [M]	The Spirit Swings Me	1960	$30
❏ SN-4101 [S]	The Spirit Swings Me	1960	$30
STORYVILLE			
❏ 4059	Sextet Recordings	198?	$25
VERVE			
❏ V-8698 [M]	Creole Cookin'	1967	$40
❏ V6-8698 [S]	Creole Cookin'	1967	$30

HACKETT, BOBBY/MAX KAMINSKY
BRUNSWICK

| ❏ BL58043 [10] | Battle of Jazz, Vol. 5 | 1953 | $50 |

HADEN, CHARLIE, AND HAMPTON HAWES
ARTISTS HOUSE

| ❏ 4 | As Long As There's Music | 1979 | $30 |

HADEN, CHARLIE; JAN GARBAREK; EGBERTO GISMONTI
ECM

| ❏ 1170 | Folk Songs | 1979 | $30 |

HADEN, CHARLIE
ABC IMPULSE!

| ❏ AS-9183 | Liberation Music Orchestra | 1973 | $250 |

ECM			
❏ 23794	Ballad of the Fallen	1982	$25
HORIZON			
❏ SP-710	Closeness	197?	$35
❏ SP-727	The Golden Number	1978	$35
SOUL NOTE			
❏ 121172	Silence	1990	$30
VERVE			
❏ 831673-1	Quartet West	1987	$25
❏ 837031-1	Quartet West in Angel City	1988	$25

HAGAR, ERNIE
SAGE AND SAND

| ❏ C-42 [M] | Swinging Steel Guitar | 1965 | $30 |

HAGAR, SAMMY
Also see MONTROSE; VAN HALEN; CHICKENFOOT.

CAPITOL

❏ SMAS-11812	All Night Long	1978	$15
❏ SN-16326	All Night Long	198?	$10
—Budget-line reissue of 11812			
❏ ST-12069	Danger Zone	1980	$15
—With poster (deduct if missing)			
❏ SK-12299	Live 1980	1983	$12
❏ SN-16376	Live 1980	1986	$10
—Budget-line reissue of 12299			
❏ ST-11706	Musical Chairs	1977	$15
❏ SN-16051	Musical Chairs	1979	$10
—Budget-line reissue of 11706			

❏ ST-11489 [B]	Nine on a Ten Scale	1976	$15
❏ SN-16049	Nine on a Ten Scale	1979	$10
—Budget-line reissue of 11489			
❏ ST-12238	Rematch	1982	$12
❏ SN-16336	Rematch	198?	$10
—Budget-line reissue of 12238			
❏ ST-11599	Sammy Hagar	1977	$15
❏ SN-16050	Sammy Hagar	1979	$10
—Budget-line reissue of 11599			
❏ ST-11983	Street Machine	1979	$15
❏ SN-16340	Street Machine	198?	$10
—Budget-line reissue of 11983			
GEFFEN			
❏ GHS24144	Sammy Hagar	1987	$12
❏ GHS2006	Standing Hampton	1982	$12
❏ GHS2021	Three Lock Box	1982	$12
❏ GHS24043	VOA	1984	$12

HAGEN, NINA
COLUMBIA

❏ ARC38008	Nunsexmonkrock	1982	$15
❏ PC38008	Nunsexmonkrock	198?	$12
—Reissue with new prefix			
❏ 3C36817 [10]	TV Glotzer	1980	$15

HAGERS, THE
BARNABY

❏ BR15002	Music on the Countryside	1972	$18
CAPITOL			
❏ ST-783	Apple Pie, Motherhood and the Flag	1971	$18
❏ ST-438	The Hagers	1970	$18
❏ ST-553	Two Hagers Are Better Than One	1970	$18
ELEKTRA			
❏ 7E-1021	The Hagers	1974	$15

HAGGARD, MERLE, AND BONNIE OWENS
CAPITOL

| ❏ T2453 [M] | Just Between the Two of Us | 1966 | $30 |
| ❏ ST2453 [S] | Just Between the Two of Us | 1966 | $30 |

Number	Title	Yr	NM

HAGGARD, MERLE, AND GEORGE JONES
EPIC
| ❏ FE38203 | A Taste of Yesterday's Wine | 1982 | $12 |

HAGGARD, MERLE, AND LEONA WILLIAMS
MERCURY
| ❏ 812183-1 | Heart to Heart | 1983 | $12 |

HAGGARD, MERLE, AND WILLIE NELSON
EPIC
| ❏ FE37958 | Pancho and Lefty | 1983 | $12 |

—Reissue corrects spelling of LP title
| ❏ FE37958 | Pancho and Lefty | 1983 | $18 |

—Note misspelled LP title
| ❏ FE40293 | Seashores of Old Mexico | 1987 | $12 |

HAGGARD, MERLE
CAPITOL
❏ ST-319	A Portrait of Merle Haggard	1969	$25
❏ ST-638	A Tribute to the Best Damn Fiddle Player in the World (Or, My Salute to Bob Wills)	1970	$30
❏ SN-16279	A Tribute to the Best Damn Fiddle Player in the World (Or, My Salute to Bob Wills)	1982	$10

—Budget-line reissue
❏ ST-11693	A Working Man Can't Get Nowhere Today	1977	$15
❏ T2789 [M]	Branded Man	1967	$30
❏ ST2789 [S]	Branded Man	1967	$30
❏ SWBB-259	Close-Up	1969	$30

—Reissue in one package of "Strangers" and "Swinging Doors"
| ❏ ST-11745 | Eleven Winners | 1977 | $15 |
| ❏ SN-16303 | Eleven Winners | 1984 | $10 |

—Budget-line reissue
| ❏ ST-735 | Hag | 1971 | $18 |
| ❏ SN-16053 | High on a Hilltop | 1979 | $10 |

—Budget-line reissue
❏ ST-11276	If We Make It Through December	1974	$15
❏ ST-11200	I Love Dixie Blues...So I Recorded "Live" in New Orleans	1973	$15
❏ T2702 [M]	I'm a Lonesome Fugitive	1967	$30
❏ ST2702 [S]	I'm a Lonesome Fugitive	1967	$30
❏ SM-2702	I'm a Lonesome Fugitive	197?	$12

—Reissue with new prefix
| ❏ SM-12036 | It's All in the Movies | 1979 | $12 |

—Reissue
❏ ST-11483	It's All in the Movies	1975	$15
❏ ST-11127	It's Not Love	1972	$15
❏ ST-11365	Keep Movin' On	1975	$15
❏ ST-882	Let Me Tell You About a Song	1972	$25
❏ ST2972	Mama Tried	1968	$30
❏ ST-11331	Merle Haggard Presents His 30th Album	1974	$15
❏ ST-11230	Merle Haggard's Christmas Present (Something Old, Something New)	1973	$15
❏ SM-11823	My Love Affair with Trains	1978	$12

—Reissue
❏ ST-11544	My Love Affair with Trains	1976	$15
❏ ST-384	Okie from Muskogee	1970	$25
❏ SN-16277	Okie from Muskogee	1982	$10

—Budget-line reissue
| ❏ SKAO-168 | Pride In What I Am | 1969 | $30 |
| ❏ SM-168 | Pride In What I Am | 197? | $12 |

—Reissue with new prefix
| ❏ SWBB-223 | Same Train, A Different Time | 1969 | $30 |
| ❏ SN-16052 | Sing a Sad Song | 1979 | $10 |

—Budget-line reissue
❏ STBB-707	Sing a Sad Song/High on a Hilltop	1971	$30
❏ T2848 [M]	Sing Me Back Home	1968	$30
❏ ST2848 [S]	Sing Me Back Home	1968	$30
❏ ST-835	Someday We'll Look Back	1971	$25
❏ SABB-11531	Songs I'll Always Sing	1976	$18
❏ T2373 [M]	Strangers	1965	$30
❏ ST2373 [S]	Strangers	1965	$30
❏ T2585 [M]	Swinging Doors	1966	$30
❏ ST2585 [S]	Swinging Doors	1966	$30
❏ SM-2585	Swinging Doors	197?	$12

—Reissue with new prefix
| ❏ SKAO2951 | The Best of Merle Haggard | 1968 | $30 |
| ❏ SN-16054 | The Best of Merle Haggard | 1979 | $10 |

—Budget-line reissue
❏ ST-11082	The Best of the Best of Merle Haggard	1972	$18
❏ ST-451	The Fightin' Side of Me	1970	$25
❏ SN-16278	The Fightin' Side of Me	1982	$10

—Budget-line reissue
❏ SWBO-803	The Land of Many Churches	1971	$75
❏ ST2912	The Legend of Bonnie and Clyde	1968	$30
❏ ST-11586	The Roots of My Raising	1976	$15
❏ SW-11839	The Way It Was	1978	$15
❏ ST-11141	Totally Instrumental with One Exception	1973	$18
❏ ST-823	Truly the Best of Merle Haggard	1971	$40

CAPITOL SPECIAL MARKETS
| ❏ SLB-8137 | Merle Haggard Salutes the Greats | 1980 | $18 |
| ❏ SL-8086 | Songs I'll Always Sing | 1977 | $25 |

EPIC
❏ FE44283	5:01 Blues	1989	$12
❏ FE40286	A Friend in California	1986	$12
❏ FE40224	Amber Waves of Grain	1985	$12
❏ FE37593	Big City	1981	$12
❏ PE37593	Big City	1985	$10
❏ FE40986	Chill Factor	1988	$12
❏ FE38092	Going Where the Lonely Go	1982	$12
❏ PE38092	Going Where the Lonely Go	1985	$10

—Budget-line reissue
❏ PE38307	Goin' Home for Christmas	1982	$12
❏ FE39545	His Epic Hits: The First 11	1985	$12
❏ FE39364	It's All in the Game	1984	$12
❏ FE39602	Kern River	1985	$12
❏ FE40107	Out Among the Stars	1986	$12
❏ PE40107	Out Among the Stars	1986	$10

—Budget-line reissue
❏ FE38815	That's the Way Love Goes	1983	$12
❏ FE39159	The Epic Collection	1983	$12
❏ PE39159	The Epic Collection	1985	$10

—Budget-line reissue
MCA
❏ 5139	Back to the Barrooms	1980	$15
❏ 5386	Greatest Hits	1982	$15
❏ 5573	His Best	1985	$12
❏ 2375	I'm Always on a Mountain	1978	$15
❏ 37140	I'm Always on a Mountain	1980	$10

—Budget-line reissue
| ❏ 2314 | My Farewell to Elvis | 1977 | $18 |
| ❏ 37139 | My Farewell to Elvis | 1980 | $10 |

—Budget-line reissue
| ❏ 37138 | Ramblin' Fever | 1980 | $10 |

—Budget-line reissue
❏ 2267	Ramblin' Fever	1977	$15
❏ 3089	Serving 190 Proof	1979	$15
❏ 37141	Serving 190 Proof	1980	$10

—Budget-line reissue
❏ 5250 [B]	Songs for the Mamma That Tried	1981	$15
❏ 3229	The Way I Am	1980	$15
❏ 37207	The Way I Am	1982	$10

—Budget-line reissue

HAGGART, BOB
COMMAND
| ❏ RS 33-849 [M] | Big Noise from Winnetka | 1963 | $30 |
| ❏ RS849SD [S] | Big Noise from Winnetka | 1963 | $35 |

JAZZOLOGY
❏ J-149	A Portrait of Bix	1986	$25
❏ J-94	Bob Haggart Enjoys Carolina in the Morning	1982	$25
❏ J-74	Sentimental Journey	1980	$25

HAHN, JERRY
ARHOOLIE
| ❏ 8006 | Jerry Hahn Quintet | 197? | $35 |

CHANGES
| ❏ LP-7001 | Arabein | 1968 | $25 |

FANTASY
| ❏ F-9426 | Moses | 1974 | $35 |

HAIG, AL, AND JIMMY RANEY
CHOICE
| ❏ 1010 | Strings Attached | 197? | $30 |

HAIG, AL
COUNTERPOINT
| ❏ C-551 [M] | Jazz Will o' the Wisp | 1957 | $150 |

ESOTERIC
| ❏ ESJ-7 [10] | Al Haig Trio | 1954 | $250 |

EVEREST ARCHIVE OF FOLK & JAZZ
| ❏ 293 | Jazz Will o' the Wisp | 197? | $25 |

INNER CITY
| ❏ IC-1073 | Al Haig Plays Music of Jerome Kern | 197? | $30 |

INTERPLAY
| ❏ 7707 | Portrait of Bud Powell | 1978 | $30 |
| ❏ 7713 | Serendipity | 1978 | $30 |

MINT
| ❏ AL-711 [M] | Al Haig Today | 1964 | $175 |

PACIFIC JAZZ
| ❏ PJLP-18 [10] | Al Haig Trio | 1955 | $175 |

PERIOD
| ❏ SPL-1104 [10] | Al Haig Quartet | 1954 | $175 |

PRESTIGE
| ❏ PRST-7841 | Al Haig Trio and Quartet | 1970 | $35 |

SEABREEZE
| ❏ 1005 | Interplay | 1977 | $30 |
| ❏ 1008 | Manhattan Memories | 1978 | $30 |

| ❏ 1001 | Piano Interpretation | 1976 | $30 |
| ❏ 1006 | Piano Time | 1977 | $30 |

SEECO
| ❏ SLP-7 [10] | Highlights in Modern Jazz | 195? | $300 |

XANADU
| ❏ 206 | Live in Hollywood | 198? | $25 |

HAIG, AL/MARY LOU WILLIAMS
PRESTIGE
| ❏ PRLP-175 [10] | Piano Moderns | 1953 | $300 |

HAINES, CONNIE
CORAL
| ❏ CRL56055 [10] | Connie Haines Sings | 1955 | $120 |

RCA VICTOR
| ❏ LPM-2264 [M] | Faith, Hope and Charity | 1961 | $25 |
| ❏ LSP-2264 [S] | Faith, Hope and Charity | 1961 | $30 |

TOPS
| ❏ L-1606 [M] | Connie Haines Sings Helen Morgan | 1959 | $30 |

HAIRCUT ONE HUNDRED
ARISTA
| ❏ AL6600 | Pelican West | 1982 | $18 |
| ❏ ALB6-8330 | Pelican West | 198? | $15 |

—Reissue

HAISLEY, LINDSAY
ARMADILLO
| ❏ ARLP82-1 | Christmas on the Autoharp | 1982 | $12 |

HAKIM, OMAR
GRP
| ❏ GR-9585 | Rhythm Deep | 1989 | $30 |

HAKIM, SADIK
STEEPLECHASE
| ❏ SCS-1091 | Witches, Goblins | 198? | $30 |

HALE, CORKY
GENE NORMAN
| ❏ GNP-17 [M] | Corky Hale | 1956 | $50 |

GNP CRESCENDO
| ❏ GNP-17 [M] | Corky Hale | 196? | $35 |
| ❏ GNP-9035 | Corky Hale Plays Gershwin and Duke | 197? | $30 |

STASH
| ❏ ST-245 | Harp Beat | 198? | $30 |

HALEN, CARL
EMPIRICAL
| ❏ LP-101 [10] | Gin Bottle Seven | 1957 | $50 |

RIVERSIDE
| ❏ RLP 12-231 [M] | Gin Bottle Jazz | 1958 | $300 |

—White label, blue print
| ❏ RLP 12-231 [M] | Gin Bottle Jazz | 1959 | $300 |

—Blue label, microphone logo at top
| ❏ RLP 12-261 [M] | Whoopee Makers' Jazz | 1958 | $300 |
| ❏ RLP-1103 [S] | Whoopee Makers' Jazz | 1958 | $300 |

HALEY, BILL, AND HIS COMETS
51 WEST
| ❏ Q16120 | Live in New York/Greatest Hits | 1981 | $12 |

—All selections under license from Buddah Records
ACCORD
| ❏ SN-7125 | Rockin' and Rollin' | 1981 | $12 |

DECCA
❏ DL8821 [M]	Bill Haley's Chicks	1959	$150
❏ DL78821 [S]	Bill Haley's Chicks	1959	$250
❏ DXSE-7211	Bill Haley's Golden Hits	1972	$18
❏ DL75027	Bill Haley's Greatest Hits	1968	$18
❏ DL8315 [M]	Music for the Boyfriend	1956	$175
❏ DL8225 [M]	Rock Around the Clock	1955	$300

—All-black label with silver print
| ❏ DL8225 [M] | Rock Around the Clock | 1960 | $50 |

—Black label with colorband, no mention of MCA on label
| ❏ DL8225 [M] | Rock Around the Clock | 1967 | $30 |

—Black label with colorband, "A Division of MCA" on label
| ❏ DL78225 [R] | Rock Around the Clock | 1959 | $150 |

—All-black label with silver print
| ❏ DL78225 [R] | Rock Around the Clock | 1960 | $30 |

—Black label with colorband, no mention of MCA on label
| ❏ DL78225 [R] | Rock Around the Clock | 1967 | $18 |

—Black label with colorband, "A Division of MCA" on label
| ❏ DL8692 [M] | Rockin' Around the World | 1958 | $175 |
| ❏ DL8775 [M] | Rockin' the Joint | 1958 | $175 |

Number	Title	Yr	NM

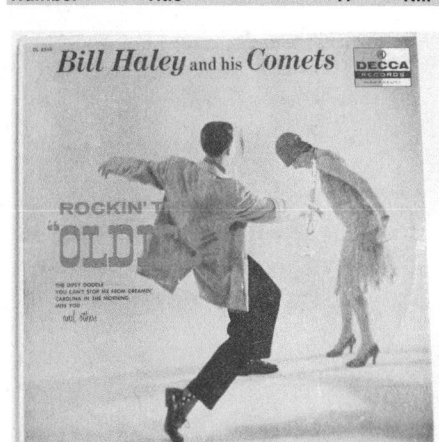

BILL HALEY and his Comets
DECCA RECORDS
ROCKIN' "OLDI..."

Number	Title	Yr	NM
❏ DL8569 [M]	Rockin' the Oldies	1957	$175
❏ DL8345 [M]	Rock 'n Roll Stage Show	1956	$175
❏ DL5560 [10]	Shake, Rattle and Roll	1955	$1000
❏ DL8964 [M]	Strictly Instrumental	1960	$150
❏ DL78964 [S]	Strictly Instrumental	1960	$175

ESSEX
| ❏ LP202 [M] | Rock with Bill Haley and the Comets | 1955 | $500 |

GNP CRESCENDO
| ❏ GNPS-2097 | Rock Around the Country | 1976 | $15 |
| ❏ GNPS-2077 | Rock 'N' Roll | 1973 | $15 |

GREAT NORTHWEST
| ❏ GNW4015 | Interviewed by Red Robinson | 1981 | $15 |

JANUS
| ❏ 7003 | Razzle-Dazzle | 1972 | $18 |
| ❏ 3035 | Travelin' Band | 1972 | $30 |

KAMA SUTRA
| ❏ KLPS-2014 | Scrapbook | 1970 | $30 |

MCA
❏ 4010	Bill Haley's Golden Hits	1973	$15
—Reissue of Decca 7211			
❏ 161	Bill Haley's Greatest Hits	1973	$12
—Reissue of Decca 75027			
❏ 5539	From the Original Master Tapes	1987	$15

PAIR
| ❏ MSM2-35069 | Rock and Roll Giant | 1986 | $15 |

PICCADILLY
| ❏ PIC-3408 | Greatest Hits | 1980 | $12 |

PICKWICK
❏ SPC-3256	Bill Haley and the Comets	1970	$12
❏ PTP-2077	Rock 'N' Roll	197?	$15
❏ SPC-3280	Rock 'N' Roll Revival	197?	$12

ROULETTE
| ❏ R25174 [M] | Twistin' Knights at the Roundtable | 1962 | $100 |
| ❏ SR25174 [S] | Twistin' Knights at the Roundtable | 1962 | $150 |

SOMERSET
| ❏ P-4600 [M] | Rock with Bill Haley and the Comets | 1958 | $175 |

TRANS WORLD
| ❏ LP202 [M] | Rock with Bill Haley and the Comets | 1956 | $300 |

VOCALION
| ❏ VL3696 [M] | Bill Haley and the Comets | 1963 | $30 |

WARNER BROS.
❏ W1378 [M]	Bill Haley and His Comets	1959	$50
❏ WS1378 [S]	Bill Haley and His Comets	1959	$80
❏ W1391 [M]	Bill Haley's Jukebox	1960	$50
❏ WS1391 [S]	Bill Haley's Jukebox	1960	$80
❏ WS1831	Rock 'N' Roll Revival	1970	$18
❏ ST-93103	Rock 'N' Roll Revival	1970	$30
—Capitol Record Club edition			

HALFNELSON
See SPARKS.

BEARSVILLE
| ❏ BV208 [B] | Halfnelson | 1971 | $75 |

HALIFAX THREE, THE
COLUMBIA SPECIAL PRODUCTS
| ❏ CSRP26038 [S] | The Halifax Three | 196? | $12 |
| —"Special Archive Series" sticker on cover | | | |

EPIC
❏ LN24060 [M]	San Francisco Bay Blues	1963	$15
❏ BN26060 [S]	San Francisco Bay Blues	1963	$18
❏ LN24038 [M]	The Halifax Three	1962	$15
❏ BN26038 [S]	The Halifax Three	1962	$18

HALL, ADELAIDE
MONMOUTH-EVERGREEN
| ❏ 7080 | That Wonderful... | 1970 | $25 |

HALL, BECKY
AAMCO
| ❏ ALP-324 [M] | A Tribute to Bessie Smith | 1958 | $30 |

HALL, CONNIE
DECCA
| ❏ DL4217 [M] | Connie Hall | 1962 | $30 |
| ❏ DL74217 [S] | Connie Hall | 1962 | $30 |

VOCALION
❏ VL73752 [S]	Country Songs	1965	$30
❏ VL3752 [M]	Country Songs	1965	$25
❏ VL3801 [M]	Country Style	1968	$25
❏ VL73801 [S]	Country Style	1968	$25

HALL, DARYL, AND JOHN OATES
ALLEGIANCE
| ❏ AV-5014 | Nucleus | 198? | $10 |

ARISTA
| ❏ AL-8614 | Change of Season | 1989 | $15 |
| ❏ AL-8539 | Ooh Yeah! | 1988 | $12 |

ATLANTIC
❏ SD7269 [B]	Abandoned Luncheonette	1973	$15
❏ SD19139	Abandoned Luncheonette	1977	$10
❏ SD18213	No Goodbyes	1977	$12
❏ SD18109	War Babies	1974	$15
❏ SD7242	Whole Oats	1972	$15
❏ 7242 [M]	Whole Oats	1972	$100
—White label promo only with "d/j copy monaural" sticker on cover			

CHELSEA
| ❏ CHL-547 | Past Times Behind | 1976 | $15 |

INTERMEDIA
| ❏ QS-5040 | The Early Years | 198? | $10 |

JEM
| ❏ 55002 | Early Years | 198? | $10 |

MOBILE FIDELITY
❏ Jan-0069 [B]	Abandoned Luncheonette	1982	$50
—Audiophile vinyl			
❏ MFSL1-413 [B]	H2O	2014	$40
❏ MFSL1-412 [B]	Private Eyes	2014	$40
❏ MFSL1-411 [B]	Voices	2014	$35

RCA VICTOR
❏ AFL1-2804	Along the Red Ledge	1978	$12
❏ AYL1-4231	Along the Red Ledge	1981	$10
❏ AFL1-2804	Along the Red Ledge	1978	$18
—Red vinyl			
❏ AFL1-2300	Beauty on a Back Street	1977	$12
❏ AYL1-4230	Beauty on a Back Street	1981	$10
❏ AJL1-5336	Big Bam Boom	1984	$12
❏ AFL1-5309	Big Bam Boom	1984	$15

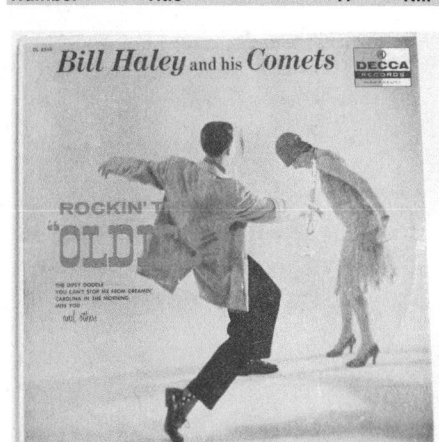

BIGGER THAN BOTH OF US — DARYL JOHN HALL OATES

❏ APL1-1467 [B]	Bigger Than Both of Us	1976	$12
❏ AYL1-3866	Bigger Than Both of Us	1980	$10
❏ APL1-1144	Daryl Hall & John Oates	1976	$12
❏ ANL1-3463	Daryl Hall & John Oates	1979	$10
❏ AYL1-3836	Daryl Hall & John Oates	1980	$10
❏ AFL1-4383	H2O	1982	$12
❏ AFL1-7035	Live at the Apollo	1985	$12
❏ AFL1-2802	Livetime!	1978	$12
❏ AYL1-4722	Livetime!	1983	$10
❏ DJL1-3512 [DJ]	Post Static	1979	$25
—Promo-only one-sided 4-song sampler			
❏ AFL1-4028	Private Eyes	1981	$12
❏ DJL1-3832 [B]	RCA Radio Special Interview Series	1980	$30
❏ CPL1-4858	Rock 'n Soul Part 1	1983	$15
—Original cover: back cover says "Plus Two New Songs (Recorded September 1983)" WITHOUT mentioning what the songs are			

❏ CPL1-4858	Rock 'n Soul Part 1	1983	$12
—"RE" on lower left back: back cover says "Plus Two New Songs (Recorded September 1983)," then mentions "Say It Isn't So" and "Adult Education"			
❏ CPL1-4858	Rock 'n Soul Part 1	1983	$10
—"RE 2" on lower left back: Variation unknown			
❏ DJL1-4179	Special Radio Series	1981	$18
❏ AQL1-3646	Voices	1980	$15
—No "RE" of any type on back cover: Embossed lettering and sound waves, Hall's head almost touches the word "Voices" on front			
❏ AQL1-3646	Voices	1980	$15
—"RE" on back cover: Variation unknown			
❏ AQL1-3646	Voices	1980	$15
—"RE 3" on back cover: Cover lettering in black			
❏ AQL1-3646	Voices	1980	$12
—"RE 2" on back cover: Cover not embossed; Hall's head 3 inches-plus below "Voices" on front cover			
❏ AQL1-3646	Voices	1980	$10
—"RE 4" on back cover: Color photo of Hall and Oates on each side			
❏ AQL1-3646	Voices	1981	$10
—"RE 5" on back cover: Variation unknown			
❏ AQL1-3646	Voices	1981	$10
—"RE 6" on back cover: Bar code on upper left back cover			
❏ AFL1-3494	X-Static	1979	$12
❏ AYL1-4303	X-Static	1982	$10

HALL, DARYL
RCA VICTOR
| ❏ AFL1-3573 | Sacred Songs | 1980 | $12 |
| ❏ AJL1-7196 | Three Hearts in the Happy Ending Machine | 1986 | $10 |

HALL, DICKSON
EPIC
| ❏ LN3427 [M] | 25 All-Time Country and Western Hits | 1958 | $30 |

KAPP
❏ KS-3464 [S]	24 Fabulous Country Hits	1966	$30
❏ KL-1464 [M]	24 Fabulous Country Hits	1966	$25
❏ KL-1067 [M]	Fabulous Country Hits Way Out West	1957	$30

MGM
| ❏ E-329 [10] | Outlaws of the Old West | 1954 | $75 |
| ❏ E-3263 [M] | Outlaws of the Old West | 1956 | $40 |

PERFECT
| ❏ P-14016 [M] | Country & Western Million Sellers | 1960 | $25 |
| ❏ PS-14016 [S] | Country & Western Million Sellers | 1960 | $30 |

HALL, EDMOND
BLUE NOTE
| ❏ B-6505 [M] | Celestial Express | 1969 | $25 |

CIRCLE
| ❏ C-52 | Rompin' in '44 | 198? | $25 |

MOSAIC
| ❏ MR6-109 | The Complete Edmond Hall/ James P. Johnson/Sidney De Paris/Vic Dickenson Blue Note Sessions | 199? | $150 |

MOUNT VERNON
| ❏ MVM-124 | Rumpus on Rampart St. | 197? | $30 |

STORYVILLE
| ❏ 4009 | Live at Club Hangover, Volume 4 | 198? | $25 |

UNITED ARTISTS
| ❏ UAL-4028 [M] | Petite Fleur | 1959 | $40 |
| ❏ UAS-5028 [S] | Petite Fleur | 1959 | $30 |

HALL, EDMOND/ART HODES
BLUE NOTE
| ❏ B-6504 [M] | Original Blue Note Jazz, Volume 1 | 1969 | $25 |

HALL, EDMOND/SIDNEY DEPARIS
BLUE NOTE
| ❏ BLP-7007 [10] | Jamming in Jazz Hall | 1951 | $250 |

HALL, GEORGE
BLUEBIRD
| ❏ AXM2-5504 | George Hall and His Taft Hotel Orchestra (1933-1937) | 1975 | $35 |

HINDSIGHT
| ❏ HSR-144 | George Hall and His Orchestra 1937 | 198? | $25 |

HALL, HERB
BIOGRAPH
| ❏ 3003 | Herb Hall Quartet | 196? | $35 |

Number	Title	Yr	NM

HALL, JIM, AND RED MITCHELL
ARTISTS HOUSE

| ❏ 5 | Jim Hall and Red Mitchell | 1979 | $30 |

HALL, JIM, AND RON CARTER
FANTASY

| ❏ OJC-467 | Alone Together | 1990 | $30 |

MILESTONE

| ❏ 9045 | Alone Together | 1974 | $35 |

HALL, JIM
BASF

| ❏ 20708 | It's Nice to Be with You | 1972 | $35 |

CONCORD JAZZ

❏ CJ-384	All Across the City	1989	$30
❏ CJ-161	Circles	1982	$25
❏ CJ-298	Jim Hall's Three	1986	$25

CTI

| ❏ 6060 | Concierto | 1977 | $30 |

FANTASY

| ❏ OJC-649 | Where Would I Be | 1991 | $30 |

HORIZON

| ❏ SP-715 | Commitment | 1976 | $30 |
| ❏ SP-705 | Live | 1975 | $30 |

MILESTONE

| ❏ 9037 | Where Would I Be | 1973 | $35 |

PACIFIC JAZZ

| ❏ PJ-10 [M] | Good Friday Blues | 1960 | $40 |

JAZZ GUITAR: JIM HALL PACIFIC JAZZ 1227

❏ PJ-1227 [M]	Jazz Guitar	1957	$175
❏ PJ-79 [M]	Jazz Guitar	1963	$30
❏ ST-79 [S]	Jazz Guitar	1963	$30

PAUSA

| ❏ 7112 | In a Sentimental Mood | 198? | $25 |

WORLD PACIFIC

| ❏ WP-1227 [M] | Jazz Guitar | 1958 | $175 |

HALL, JOANIE
SAGE AND SAND

| ❏ C-34 [M] | Western Meets Country | 1962 | $12 |

HALL, JUANITA
COUNTERPOINT

| ❏ 558 [S] | Juanita Hall Sings the Blues | 1959 | $175 |

HALL, LARRY
STRAND

| ❏ SL-1005 [M] | Sandy | 1960 | $175 |
| ❏ SLS-1005 [S] | Sandy | 1960 | $250 |

HALL, TOM T., AND EARL SCRUGGS
COLUMBIA

| ❏ FC37953 | Storyteller and Banjo Man | 1982 | $12 |

HALL, TOM T.
MERCURY

❏ SR-61307	100 Children	1970	$16
❏ SRM-1-1139	About Love	1977	$10
❏ SR-61211	Ballad of Forty Dollars and His Other Great Songs	1969	$16
❏ SRM-1-1009	Country Is	1974	$10
❏ 834779-1	Country Songs for Children	1988	$10
—Reissue			
❏ SRM-1-1076	Faster Horses	1976	$10
❏ SRM-1-687	For the People in the Last Hard Town	1974	$10
❏ SR-61369	Greatest Hits	1972	$12
❏ 824143-1	Greatest Hits	1985	$10
—Reissue			
❏ SRM-1-1044	Greatest Hits, Volume 2	1975	$10
❏ 824144-1	Greatest Hits, Volume 2	1985	$10
—Reissue			

❏ SRM-1-5008	Greatest Hits, Volume 3	1978	$10
❏ 824145-1	Greatest Hits, Volume 3	1985	$10
—Reissue			
❏ SR-61247	Homecoming	1969	$16
❏ SR-61350	In Search of a Song	1971	$12
❏ 822500-1	In Search of a Song	1987	$10
❏ SRM-1-1033 [B]	I Wrote A Song About It	1975	$10
❏ 814025-1	Jesus to Jack Daniels	1983	$10
❏ SRM-1-1111	Magnificent Music	1977	$10
❏ 822425-1	Natural Dreams	1984	$10
❏ 824508-1	Song in a Seashell	1985	$10
❏ SRM-1-500	Songs of Fox Hollow	1975	$10
❏ 832350-1	Songs of Fox Hollow	1987	$10
—Reissue			
❏ SRM-1-668	The Rhymer and Other Five and Dimers	1973	$10
❏ SR-61362	We All Got Together And…	1972	$12
❏ SR-61277	Witness Life	1970	$16

PICCADILLY

| ❏ 3558 | I Like Beer | 198? | $10 |

RCA VICTOR

❏ AHL1-4749	In Concert: Recorded Live at the Grand Ole Opry	1983	$12
❏ AYL1-5432	In Concert: Recorded Live at the Grand Ole Opry	1985	$10
—Best Buy Series" reissue			
❏ AHL1-2622	New Train	1978	$12
❏ AHL1-3018	Places I've Been	1979	$12
❏ AHL1-3685	Soldier of Fortune	1980	$12
❏ AHL1-3495	T's in Town	1979	$12

HALL BROTHERS JAZZ BAND, THE
GHB

❏ GHBS-11 [S]	Hall Brothers Jazz Band	1964	$18
❏ GHB-11 [M]	Hall Brothers Jazz Band	1964	$15
❏ GHBS-46 [S]	Sweet Like This	196?	$18
❏ GHB-46 [M]	Sweet Like This	196?	$15

STOMP OFF

| ❏ SOS-1062 | Fizz Water | 198? | $12 |
| ❏ SOS-1013 | Waiting at the End of the Road | 198? | $12 |

HALLBERG, BENGT
EPIC

| ❏ LN3375 [M] | Bengt Hallberg | 1957 | $300 |

PRESTIGE

| ❏ PRLP-176 [10] | Bengt Hallberg's Swedish All-Stars | 1953 | $350 |

HALLBERG, BENGT/ARNE DOMNERUS
PRESTIGE

| ❏ PRLP-145 [10] | New Sounds from Sweden, Volume 6 | 1953 | $400 |

HALLBERG, BENGT/LARS GULLIN
PRESTIGE

| ❏ PRLP-121 [10] | New Sounds from Sweden, Volume 2 | 1952 | $400 |

HALLE ORCHESTRA (GEORGE WELDON, CONDUCTOR)
MERCURY LIVING PRESENCE

| ❏ SR90137 [S] | Khachaturian: Gayne Ballet Suite; Mussorgsky: Night on Bare Mountain | 196? | $30 |
| —Maroon label, no "Vendor: Mercury Record Corporation | | | |

HALLE ORCHESTRA (JOHN BARBIROLLI, CONDUCTOR)
MERCURY LIVING PRESENCE

❏ SR90125 [S]	Elgar: Enigma Variations; Purcell: Suite for Strings	1960	$25
—Maroon label, no "Vendor: Mercury Record Corporation			
❏ SR90161 [S]	Encore Please, Sir John!	196?	$250
—Maroon label, no "Vendor: Mercury Record Corporation			
❏ SR90164 [S]	Grieg: Peer Gynt Suite; Symphonic Dances; Elegiac Melodies	196?	$100
—Maroon label, no "Vendor: Mercury Record Corporation			
❏ SR90160 [S]	Suppe: Overtures	196?	$50
—Maroon label, no "Vendor: Mercury Record Corporation			
❏ SR90124 [S]	Viennese Night at the Proms	1960	$30
—Maroon label, no "Vendor: Mercury Record Corporation			
❏ SR90115 [S]	Williams, Vaughan: Symphony No. 8; Bax: Garden of Fand; Butterworth: Shropshire Lad	1960	$30
—Maroon label, no "Vendor: Mercury Record Corporation			

HALLEY, PAUL
GRAMAVISION

| ❏ 7704 | Nightwatch | 198? | $25 |

LIVING MUSIC

| ❏ LM-0009 | Pianosong | 1986 | $25 |

HALLYDAY, JOHNNY
PHILIPS

| ❏ PHM200019 [M] | America's Rockin' Hits | 1962 | $150 |
| ❏ PHS600019 [S] | America's Rockin' Hits | 1962 | $120 |

HALOS, THE
WARWICK

| ❏ W-2046 [M] | The Halos | 1962 | $400 |

HAMBLEN, STUART
COLUMBIA

❏ CL1769 [M]	Of God I Sing	1962	$25
❏ CS8569 [S]	Of God I Sing	1962	$30
❏ CL1588 [M]	The Spell of the Yukon	1961	$25
❏ CS8388 [S]	The Spell of the Yukon	1961	$30

CORAL

| ❏ CRL57254 [M] | Remember Me | 1960 | $30 |

HARMONY

| ❏ HL7009 [M] | Hymns | 1957 | $30 |

RCA CAMDEN

| ❏ CAL-537 [M] | Beyond the Sun | 1959 | $30 |

RCA VICTOR

❏ LPM-1436 [M]	Grand Old Hymns	1957	$40
❏ LPM-3265 [10]	It Is No Secret	1954	$75
❏ LPM-1253 [M]	It Is No Secret	1956	$40

HAMBRO, LENNY
COLUMBIA

| ❏ CL757 [M] | Message from Hambro | 1956 | $40 |

EPIC

| ❏ LN3361 [M] | The Nature of Things | 1956 | $100 |

SAVOY

| ❏ MG-15031 [10] | Mambo Hambro | 1954 | $50 |

HAMILTON, CHICO
ABC IMPULSE!

❏ AS-82 [S]	Chi Chi Chico	1968	$35
❏ AS-9102 [S]	El Chico	1968	$35
❏ AS-9213	His Great Hits	1971	$250
❏ AS-59 [S]	Man from Two Worlds	1968	$35
❏ AS-29 [S]	Passin' Thru	1968	$35
❏ AS-9174	The Best of Chico Hamilton	1969	$35
❏ AS-9130 [S]	The Dealer	1968	$35
❏ AS-9114 [S]	The Further Adventures of El Chico	1968	$35

BLUE NOTE

| ❏ BN-LA622-G | Chico Hamilton & Players | 1976 | $30 |
| ❏ BN-LA520-G | Peregrinations | 1975 | $30 |

COLUMBIA

❏ CL1619 [M]	Chico Hamilton Special	1961	$30
❏ CS8419 [S]	Chico Hamilton Special	1961	$75
❏ CL1807 [M]	Drumfusion	1962	$30
❏ CS8607 [S]	Drumfusion	1962	$75
❏ CL1590 [M]	Selections from "Bye Bye Birdie	1961	$30
❏ CS8390 [S]	Selections from "Bye Bye Birdie	1961	$30

DECCA

| ❏ DL8614 [M] | Jazz from the Sweet Smell of Success | 1957 | $120 |

DISCOVERY

| ❏ 831 | Gongs East | 1981 | $25 |
| —Reissue of Warner Bros. 1271 | | | |

ELEKTRA

| ❏ 6E-257 | Nomad | 1980 | $25 |

ENTERPRISE

| ❏ SD7501 | The Master | 1974 | $30 |

FLYING DUTCHMAN

| ❏ 10135 | Exigente | 1971 | $35 |

Number	Title	Yr	NM
IMPULSE!			
❑ A-82 [M]	Chi Chi Chico	1965	$250
❑ AS-82 [S]	Chi Chi Chico	1965	$250
❑ A-9102 [M]	El Chico	1965	$250
❑ AS-9102 [S]	El Chico	1965	$120
❑ A-59 [M]	Man from Two Worlds	1964	$250
❑ AS-59 [S]	Man from Two Worlds	1964	$250
❑ A-29 [M]	Passin' Thru	1963	$250
❑ AS-29 [S]	Passin' Thru	1963	$250
❑ A-9130 [M]	The Dealer	1966	$250
❑ SMAS-91138 [S]	The Dealer	1966	$300
— Capitol Record Club edition			
❑ A-9114 [M]	The Further Adventures of El Chico	1966	$250
❑ AS-9114 [S]	The Further Adventures of El Chico	1966	$250
JAZZTONE			
❑ J-1264 [M]	Delightfully Modern	1957	$40
MCA			
❑ 638	El Chico	198?	$20
— Reissue of Impulse! 9102			
❑ 637	Man from Two Worlds	198?	$20
— Reissue of Impulse! 59			
❑ 29037	Passin' Thru	198?	$25
— Reissue of Impulse! 29			
❑ 29038	The Best of Chico Hamilton	198?	$25
— Reissue of Impulse! 9174			
MERCURY			
❑ SRM-1-1163	Catwalk	1977	$30
NAUTILUS			
❑ NR-13	Reaching for the Top	1981	$75
— Audiophile vinyl			
PACIFIC JAZZ			
❑ PJ-1231 [M]	Chico Hamilton Plays the Music of Fred Katz	1957	$175
❑ PJ-1209 [M]	Chico Hamilton Quintet	1955	$175
❑ PJ-1225 [M]	Chico Hamilton Quintet	1957	$175
❑ PJ-1216 [M]	Chico Hamilton Quintet In Hi-Fi	1956	$175
❑ PJLP-17 [10]	Chico Hamilton Trio	1955	$200
❑ PJ-1220 [M]	Chico Hamilton Trio	1956	$175
❑ PJ-39 [M]	Spectacular	1962	$75
— Reissue of 1209			
REPRISE			
❑ R-6078 [M]	A Different Journey	1963	$75
❑ R9-6078 [S]	A Different Journey	1963	$40
SOLID STATE			
❑ SS-18050	Headhunters	1969	$35
❑ SS-18043	The Gamut	1969	$35
SOUL NOTE			
❑ 121191	Reunion	1989	$30
SUNSET			
❑ SUS-5215	Easy Livin'	196?	$30
WARNER BROS.			
❑ W1245 [M]	Chico Hamilton Quintet with Strings Attached	1958	$150
❑ WS1245 [S]	Chico Hamilton Quintet with Strings Attached	1958	$120

Number	Title	Yr	NM
❑ W1271 [M]	Gongs East	1958	$50
❑ WS1271 [S]	Gongs East	1958	$120
❑ W1344 [M]	The Three Faces of Chico	1959	$175
❑ WS1344 [S]	The Three Faces of Chico	1959	$100
WORLD PACIFIC			
❑ WP-1231 [M]	Chico Hamilton Plays the Music of Fred Katz	1958	$250
❑ WP-1225 [M]	Chico Hamilton Quintet	1958	$250
❑ ST-1005 [S]	Chico Hamilton Quintet	1958	$175
❑ WP-1216 [M]	Chico Hamilton Quintet In Hi-Fi	1958	$250
❑ WP-1258 [M]	Ellington Suite	1959	$250
❑ ST-1016 [S]	Ellington Suite	1959	$175
❑ PJ-1238 [M]	South Pacific in Hi-Fi	1957	$250
❑ WP-1238 [M]	South Pacific in Hi-Fi	1958	$175
❑ ST-1003 [S]	South Pacific in Hi-Fi	1958	$175

Number	Title	Yr	NM
❑ PJ-1242 [M]	The Chico Hamilton Trio Featuring Freddie Gambrell	1957	$250
❑ WP-1242 [M]	The Chico Hamilton Trio Featuring Freddie Gambrell	1958	$175
❑ ST-1008 [S]	The Chico Hamilton Trio Featuring Freddie Gambrell	1958	$175
❑ WP-1287 [M]	The Original Hamilton Quintet	1960	$250

HAMILTON, DAVE

WORKSHOP JAZZ

Number	Title	Yr	NM
❑ WSJ-206 [M]	Blue Vibrations	1963	$100

HAMILTON, GEORGE, IV

ABC

Number	Title	Yr	NM
❑ X-750	16 Greatest Hits	1972	$12
❑ AC-30032	The ABC Collection	1975	$15
ABC/DOT			
❑ DO-2081	Fine Lace	1977	$12
ABC-PARAMOUNT			
❑ 461 [M]	George Hamilton IV's Big 15	1963	$30
❑ S-461 [P]	George Hamilton IV's Big 15	1963	$40

Number	Title	Yr	NM
❑ 220 [M]	On Campus	1958	$40
❑ S-220 [S]	On Campus	1958	$50
❑ 251 [M]	Sing Me a Sad Song (A Tribute to Hank Williams)	1958	$40
❑ S-251 [S]	Sing Me a Sad Song (A Tribute to Hank Williams)	1958	$50
DOT			
❑ 39033	George Hamilton IV	1985	$12
HARMONY			
❑ HS11379	Your Cheatin' Heart	1970	$12
LAMB AND LION			
❑ 1015	Bluegrass Gospel	1974	$15
MCA			
❑ 3206	Forever Young	1980	$12
❑ 705	Forever Young	198?	$10
— Reissue of 3206			
RCA CAMDEN			
❑ CAL-2200 [M]	A Rose and a Baby Ruth	1967	$18
❑ CAS-2200 [S]	A Rose and a Baby Ruth	1967	$12
❑ CAS-2468	Early Morning Rain	1971	$12
❑ ACL1-0242	Singin' on the Mountains	1973	$12
RCA VICTOR			
❑ LPM-2778 [M]	Abilene	1963	$30
❑ LSP-2778 [S]	Abilene	1963	$30
❑ LSP-4342	Back Where It's At	1970	$18
❑ LSP-4164	Canadian Pacific	1969	$18
❑ LPM-3510 [M]	Coast Country	1966	$30
❑ LSP-3510 [S]	Coast Country	1966	$30
❑ LSP-4700	Country Music in My Soul	1972	$15
❑ LSP-4435	Down Home in the Country	1971	$18
❑ LPM-3752 [M]	Folk Country Classics	1967	$30
❑ LSP-3752 [S]	Folk Country Classics	1967	$25
❑ LPM-3854 [M]	Folksy	1967	$30
❑ LSP-3854 [S]	Folksy	1967	$25
❑ LPM-2972 [M]	Fort Worth, Dallas or Houston	1964	$30
❑ LSP-2972 [S]	Fort Worth, Dallas or Houston	1964	$30
❑ APL1-0455	Greatest Hits	1974	$15
❑ LSP-4826	International Ambassador	1973	$15
❑ LSP-4066	In the 4th Dimension	1968	$25
❑ LPM-3371 [M]	Mister Sincerity... A Tribute to Ernest Tubb	1965	$30
❑ LSP-3371 [S]	Mister Sincerity... A Tribute to Ernest Tubb	1965	$30
❑ LSP-4517	North Country	1971	$18
❑ LPM-3601 [M]	Steel Rail Blues	1966	$25
❑ LSP-3601 [S]	Steel Rail Blues	1966	$25
❑ LSP-4265	The Best of George Hamilton IV	1970	$18
❑ LPM-3962 [M]	The Gentle Country Sound of George Hamilton IV	1968	$40
❑ LSP-3962 [S]	The Gentle Country Sound of George Hamilton IV	1968	$25

Number	Title	Yr	NM
❑ LPM-2373 [M]	To You and Yours from Me and Mine	1961	$30
❑ LSP-2373 [S]	To You and Yours from Me and Mine	1961	$30
❑ LSP-4772	Travelin' Light	1972	$15
❑ LSP-4609	West Texas Highway	1971	$18

HAMILTON, GEORGE, V

MTM

Number	Title	Yr	NM
❑ ST-71061	House of Tears	1987	$12
— As "Hege V"			

HAMILTON, GEORGE

ABC-PARAMOUNT

Number	Title	Yr	NM
❑ 535 [M]	By George	1966	$12
❑ S-535 [S]	By George	1966	$15

HAMILTON, JEFF

CONCORD JAZZ

Number	Title	Yr	NM
❑ CJ-187	Indiana	1982	$25

HAMILTON, JIMMY

EVEREST

Number	Title	Yr	NM
❑ LPBR-5100 [M]	Swing Low, Sweet Chariot	1960	$30
❑ SDBR-1100 [S]	Swing Low, Sweet Chariot	1960	$30
SWINGVILLE			
❑ SVLP-2028 [M]	Can't Help Swingin'	1961	$50
— Purple label			
❑ SVLP-2028 [M]	Can't Help Swingin'	1965	$30
— Blue label, trident logo at right			
❑ SVLP-2022 [M]	It's About Time	1961	$75
— Purple label			
❑ SVLP-2022 [M]	It's About Time	1965	$35
— Blue label, trident logo at right			
URANIA			
❑ UJLP-1204 [M]	Accent on Clarinet	1955	$300
❑ UJLP-1003 [10]	Clarinet in Hi-Fi	1954	$350
❑ UJLP-1208 [M]	Clarinet in Hi-Fi	1955	$175

HAMILTON, JOE FRANK & REYNOLDS

ABC DUNHILL

Number	Title	Yr	NM
❑ DSX-50113	Hallway Symphony	1972	$12
❑ DS-50103	Hamilton, Joe Frank & Reynolds	1971	$12
❑ SKAO-93823	Hamilton, Joe Frank & Reynolds	1971	$18
— Capitol Record Club edition; label has the old-style "Dunhill" label without the "ABC" in the logo			
PLAYBOY			
❑ PB-407	Fallin' in Love	1975	$12
❑ PZ34741	Fallin' in Love	1977	$10
— Reissue of 107			

HAMILTON, ROY

EPIC

Number	Title	Yr	NM
❑ LN3561 [M]	Come Out Swingin'	1959	$30
❑ BN530 [S]	Come Out Swingin'	1959	$30
❑ LN3364 [M]	Golden Boy	1957	$50
❑ LN3580 [M]	Have Blues, Must Travel	1959	$30
❑ BN535 [S]	Have Blues, Must Travel	1959	$30
❑ LN24000 [M]	Mr. Rock and Soul	1962	$30
❑ BN26000 [S]	Mr. Rock and Soul	1962	$30
❑ LN3807 [M]	Only You	1961	$30
❑ BN610 [S]	Only You	1961	$30
❑ LN3176 [M]	Roy Hamilton	1955	$75
❑ LN3628 [M]	Roy Hamilton At His Best	1960	$40
❑ LN24009 [M]	Roy Hamilton's Greatest Hits	1962	$25
❑ BN26009 [S]	Roy Hamilton's Greatest Hits	1962	$30
❑ LN24316 [M]	Roy Hamilton's Greatest Hits, Vol. 2	1967	$25
❑ BN26316 [S]	Roy Hamilton's Greatest Hits, Vol. 2	1967	$30
❑ LN3717 [M]	Soft 'n Warm	1960	$30
❑ BN578 [S]	Soft 'n Warm	1960	$30
❑ LN3654 [M]	Spirituals	1960	$30
❑ BN551 [S]	Spirituals	1960	$30
❑ LN1103 [10]	The Voice of Roy Hamilton	1954	$250
❑ LN3545 [M]	Why Fight The Feeling?	1959	$30
❑ BN525 [S]	Why Fight The Feeling?	1959	$30
❑ LN3519 [M]	With All My Love	1958	$30
❑ BN518 [S]	With All My Love	1958	$40
❑ LN3775 [M]	You Can Have Her	1961	$30
❑ BN595 [S]	You Can Have Her	1961	$40
❑ LN1023 [10]	You'll Never Walk Alone	1954	$250
❑ LN3294 [M]	You'll Never Walk Alone	1956	$80
❑ BN632 [R]	You'll Never Walk Alone	1962	$25
MGM			
❑ E-4233 [M]	Sentimental, Lonely & Blue	1964	$18
❑ SE-4233 [S]	Sentimental, Lonely & Blue	1964	$25
❑ E-4139 [M]	Warm and Soul	1963	$18
❑ SE-4139 [S]	Warm and Soul	1963	$25
RCA VICTOR			
❑ LPM-3552 [M]	The Impossible Dream	1966	$18
❑ LSP-3552 [S]	The Impossible Dream	1966	$25

HAMILTON, RUSS

KAPP

Number	Title	Yr	NM
❑ KL-1076 [M]	Rainbow	1957	$100

Number	Title	Yr	NM

HAMILTON, SCOTT, AND BUDDY TATE
CONCORD JAZZ
| ❑ CJ-85 | Back to Back | 1979 | $30 |
| ❑ CJ-148 | Scott's Buddy | 1981 | $25 |

HAMILTON, SCOTT, AND WARREN VACHE
CONCORD JAZZ
| ❑ CJ-111 | Skyscrapers | 1980 | $25 |
| ❑ CJ-70 | With Scott's Band in New York | 1978 | $30 |

HAMILTON, SCOTT; JAKE HANNA; DAVE MCKENNA
CONCORD JAZZ
| ❑ CJ-305 | Major League | 1986 | $25 |

HAMILTON, SCOTT
CONCORD JAZZ
❑ CJ-165	Apples and Oranges	1981	$25
❑ CJ-197	Close Up	1982	$25
❑ CJ-233	In Concert	1984	$25
❑ CJ-61	Scott Hamilton 2	1978	$30
❑ CJ-42	Scott Hamilton Is a Good Wind Who Is Blowing Us No III	1977	$30
❑ CJ-127	Tenorshoes	1980	$25
❑ CJ-311	The Right Time	1987	$25
❑ CJ-254	The Second Set	1984	$25

FAMOUS DOOR
| ❑ 119 | The Swinging Young Scott | 197? | $25 |

PROGRESSIVE
| ❑ 7026 | Grand Appearance | 1979 | $25 |

HAMILTON STREETCAR
DOT
| ❑ DLP-25939 [B] | Hamilton Streetcar | 1969 | $18 |

HAMLIN, JOHNNY
ARGO
| ❑ LP-4001 [M] | Johnny Hamiln Quintet | 1961 | $30 |
| ❑ LPS-4001 [S] | Johnny Hamiln Quintet | 1961 | $30 |

HAMLISCH, MARVIN
MCA
❑ 2115	The Entertainer	1974	$12
❑ 390 [B]	The Sting	1973	$15
❑ 37091	The Sting	198?	$10
— Budget-line reissue

HAMMACK, BOBBY
LIBERTY
| ❑ LRP-3016 [M] | Power House | 1956 | $40 |

HAMMER, ATLE
GEMINI TAURUS
| ❑ GMLP-65 | Arizona Blue | 1991 | $35 |

HAMMER, BOB
ABC-PARAMOUNT
| ❑ ABC-497 [M] | Beatle Jazz | 1964 | $30 |
| ❑ ABCS-497 [S] | Beatle Jazz | 1964 | $40 |

HAMMER, JACK
WARWICK
| ❑ W-2014 [M] | Rebellion: Jack Hammer Sings and Reads Songs and Poems of the Beat Generation | 1960 | $100 |

HAMMER, JAN
ASYLUM
| ❑ 6E-173 | Black Sheep | 1979 | $12 |
| ❑ 6E-232 | Hammer | 1979 | $12 |

BASF
| ❑ MC20688 | Make Love | 1976 | $15 |
— Recorded in 1968

MCA
| ❑ 42103 | Escape from Television | 1988 | $12 |

NEMPEROR
| ❑ JZ35003 | Melodies | 1977 | $12 |
| ❑ PZ35003 | Melodies | 198? | $10 |
— Budget-line reissue
❑ NE437	Oh, Yeah?	1976	$20
❑ BZ40382	The Early Years (1974-1977)	1986	$12
❑ NE432	The First Seven Days	1975	$15
❑ AS424 [DJ]	The Jan Hammer Group Live	1978	$30
— Promo-only album

PASSPORT
| ❑ PB6051 | City Slicker | 1985 | $15 |
— With James Young

HAMMER, MC
BUSTIN'
| ❑ BR-LP-001 | Feel My Power | 1987 | $30 |

CAPITOL
| ❑ SPRO-79080 [EP] | A Bit Legit | 1991 | $10 |
— Promo-only three-track sampler
❑ C1-90924	Let's Get It Started	1988	$12
❑ C1-92857	Please Hammer Don't Hurt 'Em	1990	$18
❑ C1-98151	Too Legit to Quit	1991	$18

GIANT
| ❑ PRO-A-6798 [DJ] | The Funky Headhunter | 1994 | $25 |
— Vinyl version is promo only

HAMMER
SAN FRANCISCO
| ❑ SD203 | Hammer | 1970 | $18 |

HAMMILL, PETER
Also see VAN DER GRAAF GENERATOR.
CHARISMA
❑ CAS-1037 [B]	Fool's Mate	1972	$30
❑ CH-1-2205 [B]	PH 7	1979	$18
❑ CH-1-2202 [B]	The Future Now	1978	$18

ENIGMA
| ❑ ST-73246 [B] | And Close As This | 1987 | $18 |
| ❑ ST-73206 [B] | Skin | 1986 | $15 |

PVC
| ❑ 8902 | Sitting Targets | 1981 | $15 |

RESTLESS
| ❑ 772337-1 [B] | In A Foreign Town | 1988 | $15 |

VISA
| ❑ IMP016 [B] | Vision | 1978 | $18 |

HAMMOND, ALBERT
COLUMBIA
| ❑ FC38181 | Somewhere in America | 1982 | $12 |
| ❑ JC36964 | Your World and My World | 1981 | $12 |

EPIC
| ❑ JE35049 | When I Need You | 1977 | $12 |

MUMS
❑ KZ32834	Albert Hammond	1974	$12
❑ KZ31905	It Never Rains in Southern California	1972	$12
❑ KZ32267	The Free Electric Band	1973	$12

HAMMOND, JOHN
ATLANTIC
❑ 8152 [M]	I Can Tell	1967	$25
❑ SD8152 [S]	I Can Tell	1967	$25
❑ SD8206	Sooner or Later	1968	$18
❑ SD8251	Southern Fried	1969	$18

CAPRICORN
| ❑ CP 0153 | Can't Beat the Kid | 1975 | $15 |

COLUMBIA
| ❑ KC31318 | I'm Satisfied | 1972 | $15 |
| ❑ C30458 | Source Point | 1971 | $15 |

FLYING FISH
| ❑ FF-502 | Nobody But You | 1988 | $12 |

ROUNDER
❑ 3060	Frogs for Snakes	1982	$12
❑ 3074	John Hammond Live	1984	$12
❑ 3042	Mileage	1980	$12

VANGUARD
| ❑ VRS-9153 [M] | Big City Blues | 1964 | $75 |

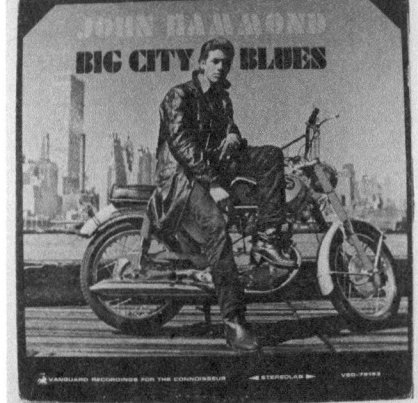

❑ VSD-79153 [S]	Big City Blues	1964	$75
❑ VRS-9198 [M]	Country Blues	1966	$50
❑ VSD-79198 [S]	Country Blues	1966	$50
❑ VSD-79400	Footwork	1978	$12
❑ VSD-79424	Hot Tracks	1979	$12
❑ VRS-9132 [M]	John Hammond	1964	$75
❑ VSD-2148 [S]	John Hammond	1964	$75
❑ VRS-9245 [M]	Mirrors	1967	$30
❑ VSD-79245 [S]	Mirrors	1967	$30
❑ VSD-79380 [B]	Solo	1976	$12
❑ VRS-9178 [M]	So Many Roads	1965	$50
❑ VSD-79178 [S]	So Many Roads	1965	$50
❑ VSD11/12 [B]	The Best of John Hammond	1970	$25

HAMMOND, JOHNNY
KUDU
❑ 01	Breakout	1971	$30
❑ 16	Higher Ground	1974	$30
❑ KSQX-16 [Q]	Higher Ground	1974	$75
❑ 10	The Prophet	1973	$30
❑ 04	Wild Horses/Rock Steady	1972	$30

MILESTONE
❑ 9083	Don't Let the System Get You	1978	$35
❑ 9068	Forever Taurus	1976	$35
❑ 9062	Gears	1975	$35
❑ 9076	Storm Warning	1977	$35

NEW JAZZ
| ❑ NJLP-8221 [M] | All Soul | 1959 | $250 |
— Purple label
| ❑ NJLP-8221 [M] | All Soul | 1965 | $175 |
— Blue label with trident logo
| ❑ NJLP-8288 [M] | Look Out! | 1962 | $250 |
— Purple label
| ❑ NJLP-8288 [M] | Look Out! | 1965 | $175 |
— Blue label with trident logo
| ❑ NJLP-8241 [M] | Talk That Talk | 1960 | $250 |
— Purple label
| ❑ NJLP-8241 [M] | Talk That Talk | 1965 | $175 |
— Blue label with trident logo
| ❑ NJLP-8229 [M] | That Good Feelin' | 1959 | $250 |
— Purple label
| ❑ NJLP-8229 [M] | That Good Feelin' | 1965 | $175 |
— Blue label with trident logo

PRESTIGE
❑ PRST-7777	Best for Lovers	1970	$35
❑ PRST-7736	Black Feeling	1969	$35
❑ PRST-7564	Dirty Grape	1968	$50
❑ PRLP-7494 [M]	Ebb Tide	1967	$75
❑ PRST-7494 [S]	Ebb Tide	1967	$50
❑ PRLP-7217 [M]	Gettin' the Message	1961	$250
— Yellow label
| ❑ PRLP-7217 [M] | Gettin' the Message | 1965 | $75 |
— Blue label with trident logo
❑ PRST-7846	Good 'Nuff	1970	$35
❑ 10002	Here It 'Tis	1971	$35
❑ PRLP-7482 [M]	Love Potion #9	1967	$75
❑ PRST-7482 [S]	Love Potion #9	1967	$50
❑ PRST-7588	Nasty	1968	$50
❑ PRLP-7420 [M]	Opus de Funk	1966	$50
❑ PRST-7420 [S]	Opus de Funk	1966	$75
❑ PRST-7549	Soul Flowers	1968	$50
❑ PRST-7681	Soul Talk	1969	$50
❑ PRLP-7203 [M]	Stimulation	1961	$50
— Yellow label
| ❑ PRLP-7203 [M] | Stimulation | 1965 | $75 |
— Blue label with trident logo
❑ PRST-7786	Stimulation	1970	$35
❑ PRST-7705	The Best of Johnny "Hammond" Smith	1969	$35
❑ PRLP-7408 [M]	The Stinger	1965	$50
❑ PRST-7408 [S]	The Stinger	1965	$75
❑ PRLP-7464 [M]	The Stinger Meets the Golden Thrush	1966	$50
❑ PRST-7464 [S]	The Stinger Meets the Golden Thrush	1966	$75
❑ 10015	What's Going On	1971	$35

RIVERSIDE
❑ RLP-496 [M]	A Little Taste	1965	$175
❑ RS-9496 [S]	A Little Taste	1965	$175
❑ RLP-442 [M]	Black Coffee	1963	$175
❑ RS-9442 [S]	Black Coffee	1963	$175
❑ RLP-466 [M]	Mr. Wonderful	1963	$175
❑ RS-9466 [S]	Mr. Wonderful	1963	$175
❑ RLP-482 [M]	Open House!	1965	$175
❑ RS-9482 [S]	Open House!	1965	$175

SALVATION
| ❑ 702 | A Gambler's Life | 1974 | $30 |

HAMPEL, GUNTER, AND BOULOU FERRE
BIRTH
| ❑ 006 | Espace | 1970 | $30 |

HAMPEL, GUNTER
BIRTH
❑ 0028	All Is Real	1978	$25
❑ 0031	All the Things You Could Be If Charles Mingus Was Your Daddy	1980	$25
❑ 009	Angel	1972	$25
❑ 0032	A Place to Be with Us	1981	$25
❑ 0011	Broadway/Folksong	1972	$25
❑ 0034	Cavana	1982	$25
❑ 0021/0022	Celebrations	1974	$30

Number	Title	Yr	NM
❏ 0036	Companion	1983	$25
❏ 0024	Cosmic Dancer	1975	$25
❏ 002	Dances	1970	$30
❏ 0025	Enfant Terrible	1976	$25
❏ 008	Familie	1972	$25
❏ 0030	Freedom of the Universe	1978	$25
❏ 0039	Fresh Heat	1985	$25
❏ 0035	Generator	1982	$25
❏ 0012	I Love Being with You	1972	$25
❏ 0017	Journey to the Song Within	1974	$25
❏ 0038	Jubilation	1984	$25
❏ 0033	Life on This Planet 1981	1981	$25
❏ 0016	Out from Under	1974	$25
❏ 005	People Symphony	1970	$30
❏ 0023	Ruomi	1975	$25
❏ 007	Spirits	1971	$25
❏ 003	Symphony No. 5 and 6	1970	$30
❏ 0027	That Came Down on Me	1978	$25
❏ 001	The 8th of July, 1969	1969	$40
❏ 0026	Transformation	1976	$25
❏ 0013	Unity Dance	1973	$25
❏ 0029	Vogelfrei	1978	$25
❏ 0010	Waltz for 3 Universes in a Corridor	1972	$25

ESP-DISK'

❏ 1042 [M]	Music from Europe	1967	$150
❏ S-1042 [S]	Music from Europe	1967	$150

FLYING DUTCHMAN

❏ 126	The 8th of July, 1969	1970	$40
❏ FD-10126	The 8th of July, 1969	1971	$25

FMP

❏ 0770	Wellen/Waves	1980	$35

HORO

❏ 33/34	Oasis	1978	$30

KHARMA

❏ PK8	Flying Carpet	1978	$30

HAMPTON, LIONEL, AND CHARLIE TEAGARDEN

CORAL

❏ CRL57438 [M]	The Great Hamp and Little T.	1963	$15
❏ CRL757438 [S]	The Great Hamp and Little T.	1963	$25

HAMPTON, LIONEL, AND STAN GETZ

NORGRAN

❏ MGN-1037 [M]	Hamp and Getz	1955	$1002

VERVE

❏ MGV-8128 [M]	Hamp and Getz	1957	$175
❏ V-8128 [M]	Hamp and Getz	1961	$25

HAMPTON, LIONEL, AND SVEND ASMUSSEN

SONET

❏ 779	As Time Goes By	1979	$30

HAMPTON, LIONEL; ART TATUM; BUDDY RICH

CLEF

❏ MGC-709 [M]	The Hampton-Tatum-Rich Trio	1956	$250

VERVE

❏ MGV-8093 [M]	The Hampton-Tatum-Rich Trio	1957	$175
❏ V-8093 [M]	The Hampton-Tatum-Rich Trio	1961	$25

HAMPTON, LIONEL

ABC IMPULSE!

❏ AS-78 [S]	You Better Know It	1968	$35

AMERICAN RECORDING SOCIETY

❏ G-403 [M]	The Swinging Jazz of Lionel Hampton	1956	$40

ATLANTIC

❏ 81644	Sentimental Journey	1986	$25

AUDIO FIDELITY

❏ AFLP-1913 [M]	Hamp's Big Band	1958	$30
❏ AFSD-5913 [S]	Hamp's Big Band	1958	$40

❏ AFLP-1849 [M]	Lionel	1957	$30

Number	Title	Yr	NM
❏ AFSD-5849 [S]	Lionel	1958	$40

BLUEBIRD

❏ 6458-1RB	Hot Mallets	1987	$25
❏ AXM6-5536	The Complete Lionel Hampton 1937-1941	1976	$50

BLUE NOTE

❏ BLP-5046 [10]	Rockin' and Groovin'	1954	$300

BRUNSWICK

❏ BL754213	Off Into a Black Thing	1977	$30
❏ BL754190	Please Sunrise	1973	$35
❏ BL754203	Stop! I Don't Need No Sympathy	1974	$35
❏ BL754182	Them Changes	1972	$35
❏ BL754198	There It Is!	1974	$35

CLASSIC JAZZ

❏ 136	Jazz Giants '77	198?	$25

CLEF

❏ MGC-727 [M]	Air Mail Special	1956	$300
❏ MGC-735 [M]	Flying Home	1956	$300
❏ MGC-738 [M]	Hamp!	1956	$300
❏ MGC-737 [M]	Hamp Roars Again	1956	$0
—Canceled			
❏ MGC-744 [M]	Hamp's Big Four	1956	$300
❏ MGC-726 [M]	King of the Vibes	1956	$300
❏ MGC-670 [M]	Lionel Hampton Big Band	1955	$300
❏ MGC-714 [M]	Lionel Hampton Plays Love Songs	1956	$300
❏ MGC-736 [M]	Swingin' with Hamp	1956	$300
❏ MGC-142 [10]	The Lionel Hampton Quartet	1953	$300
❏ MGC-611 [M]	The Lionel Hampton Quartet	1954	$250
❏ MGC-673 [M]	The Lionel Hampton Quartet	1955	$250
❏ MGC-667 [M]	The Lionel Hampton Quartet and Quintet	1955	$300
❏ MGC-628 [M]	The Lionel Hampton Quintet	1954	$250
❏ MGC-642 [M]	The Lionel Hampton Quintet, Volume 2	1955	$300

COLUMBIA

❏ CL1304 [M]	Golden Vibes	1959	$30
❏ CS8110 [S]	Golden Vibes	1959	$25
❏ CL1486 [M]	Silver Vibes	1960	$30
❏ CS8277 [S]	Silver Vibes	1960	$25
❏ CL1661 [M]	Soft Vibes	1961	$25
❏ CS8461 [S]	Soft Vibes	1961	$25
❏ CL711 [M]	Wailin' at the Trianon	1956	$40

CONTEMPORARY

❏ C-3502 [M]	Hampton in Paris	1955	$250

CORONET

❏ CX-159 [M]	Lionel Hampton	196?	$15
❏ CXS-159 [S]	Lionel Hampton	196?	$15

DECCA

❏ DL8088 [M]	All American Award Concert at Carnegie Hall	1955	$175
—Black label, silver print			
❏ DL8088 [M]	All American Award Concert at Carnegie Hall	196?	$25
—Black label with color bars			
❏ DL5230 [10]	Boogie Woogie	1950	$175
❏ DL4296 [M]	Hamp's Golden Favorites	1962	$35
❏ DL74296 [S]	Hamp's Golden Favorites	1962	$25
❏ DL7013 [10]	Just Jazz	1962	$100
❏ DL9055 [M]	Just Jazz	1958	$120
❏ DL5297 [10]	Moonglow	1951	$250
❏ DL8230 [M]	Moonglow	1956	$120
—Black label, silver print			
❏ DL8230 [M]	Moonglow	196?	$25
—Black label with color bars			
❏ DL79244 [R]	Stepping Out Volume 1 1942-1945	197?	$15
❏ DL4194 [M]	The Original Star Dust	1962	$35
❏ DL74194 [S]	The Original Star Dust	1962	$25

EMARCY

❏ MG-27538 [10]	Crazy Hamp	1954	$300
❏ MG-36034 [M]	Crazy Rhythm	1955	$250
❏ MG-27537 [10]	Hamp in Paris	1954	$250
❏ MG-36032 [M]	Hamp in Paris	1955	$300
❏ MG-36035 [M]	Jam Session in Paris	1955	$300

EPIC

❏ LN3190 [M]	Apollo Hall Concert 1954	1955	$150
❏ LA16027 [M]	Many Splendored Vibes	1962	$50
❏ BA17027 [S]	Many Splendored Vibes	1962	$75

EVEREST ARCHIVE OF FOLK & JAZZ

❏ 348	Hamp in Paris	197?	$25

FOLKWAYS

❏ FJ-2871	A Jazz Man for All Seasons	196?	$50

GATEWAY

❏ 7020	Jazz Showcase	197?	$30

GENE NORMAN

❏ GNP-15 [M]	Lionel Hampton with the Just Jazz All-Stars	1956	$50

GLAD HAMP

❏ GH-3050 [M]	All That Twistin' Jazz	1962	$30
❏ GHS-3050 [S]	All That Twistin' Jazz	1962	$30
❏ GH-1024	Ambassador at Large	198?	$25
❏ GH-1009 [M]	A Taste of Hamp	1965	$25
❏ GHS-1009 [S]	A Taste of Hamp	1965	$25
❏ GH-1004 [M]	Bossa Nova Jazz	1963	$25
❏ GHS-1004 [S]	Bossa Nova Jazz	1963	$25
❏ GH-1021	Chameleon	198?	$25

Number	Title	Yr	NM
❏ GH-1007 [M]	East Meets West	1965	$175
❏ GHS-1007 [S]	East Meets West	1965	$175
❏ GH-1006 [M]	Hamp in Japan	1964	$25
❏ GHS-1006 [S]	Hamp in Japan	1964	$25
❏ GHS-1011	Hamp Stamps	1967	$35
❏ GH-1005 [M]	Lionel Hampton on Tour	1963	$25
❏ GHS-1005 [S]	Lionel Hampton on Tour	1963	$25
❏ GH-1020	Lionel Hampton's Big Band Live	198?	$25
❏ GH-1023	Made in Japan	198?	$25
❏ GH-1026	One of a Kind	1988	$25
❏ GH-1022	Outrageous	198?	$25
❏ GH-1003 [M]	The Exciting Hamp in Europe	1962	$25
❏ GHS-1003 [S]	The Exciting Hamp in Europe	1962	$25
❏ GH-1001 [M]	The Many Sides of Lionel Hampton	1961	$25
❏ GHS-1001 [S]	The Many Sides of Lionel Hampton	1961	$25

GNP CRESCENDO

❏ GNP-15 [M]	Lionel Hampton with the Just Jazz All-Stars	196?	$25
❏ GNPS-15 [R]	Lionel Hampton with the Just Jazz All-Stars	196?	$30

GROOVE MERCHANT

❏ 4400	The Works!	197?	$35

HARMONY

❏ KH32165	Good Vibes	1972	$25
❏ HL7115 [M]	Hamp in Hi-Fi	1958	$30
❏ HL7281 [M]	The One and Only Lionel Hampton	1961	$25

HINDSIGHT

❏ HSR-237	Lionel Hampton Septet 1962	1988	$25

IMPULSE!

❏ A-78 [M]	You Better Know It	1965	$250
❏ AS-78 [S]	You Better Know It	1965	$250

JAZZ MAN

❏ 5011	Lionel Hampton and His Giants	198?	$25

JAZZTONE

❏ J-1246 [M]	Lionel Hampton's All Star Groups	1957	$40
❏ J-1238 [M]	The Fabulous Lionel Hampton and His All-Stars	1957	$40
❏ J-1040 [10]	Visit on a Skyscraper	195?	$50

LION

❏ L-70064 [M]	Lionel Hampton and His Orchestra	1958	$30

MCA

❏ 42329	Gene Norman Presents Just Jazz	1990	$30
❏ 204	Golden Favorites	197?	$25
❏ 1351	Rarities	198?	$25
❏ 1315	Steppin' Out	198?	$25
❏ 1331	Sweatin' with Hamp	198?	$25
❏ 4057	The Best of Lionel Hampton	197?	$30

MGM

❏ E-285 [10]	Oh, Rock	1954	$120
❏ E-3386 [M]	Oh, Rock	1956	$50

NORGRAN

❏ MGN-1080 [M]	Lionel Hampton and His Giants	1956	$250

PERFECT

❏ 12002 [M]	Lionel Hampton Swings	1959	$30
❏ 14002 [S]	Lionel Hampton Swings	1959	$40

QUINTESSENCE

❏ 25031	Flyin'	197?	$30

RCA CAMDEN

❏ CAL-402 [M]	Jivin' the Vibes	1958	$30
❏ CAL-317 [M]	Open House	1957	$30

RCA VICTOR

❏ LPT-18 [10]	A Treasury of Immortal Performances	1951	$150
❏ LJM-1000 [M]	Hot Mallets	1954	$50
❏ LPM-1422 [M]	Jazz Flamenco	1957	$50
❏ LPM-3917 [M]	Lionel Hampton Plays Bert Kaempfert	1968	$30
❏ LSP-3917 [S]	Lionel Hampton Plays Bert Kaempfert	1968	$35
❏ LPM-2318 [M]	Swing Classics	1961	$30
❏ LSP-2318 [R]	Swing Classics	196?	$35

SPIN-O-RAMA

❏ M-3077 [M]	Lionel Hampton at the Vibes	196?	$30

SWING

❏ SW-8415	Lionel Hampton in Paris	1987	$25

TIMELESS

❏ LPSJP-142	Lionel Hampton's All Star Band at Newport '78	1990	$30
❏ 303	Live in Emmen, Holland	197?	$30

TIME-LIFE

❏ STBB-24	Big Bands: Lionel Hampton	1986	$35

UPFRONT

❏ UPF-153	Jammin'	197?	$30

VERVE

❏ MGV-8106 [M]	Air Mail Special	1957	$250
❏ V-8106 [M]	Air Mail Special	1961	$75
❏ MGV-8112 [M]	Flying Home	1957	$175

Number	Title	Yr	NM
❏ V-8112 [M]	Flying Home	1961	$25
❏ MGV-8226 [M]	Hallelujah Hamp	1958	$150
❏ V-8226 [M]	Hallelujah Hamp	1961	$25
❏ MGV-8114 [M]	Hamp!	1957	$175
❏ V-8114 [M]	Hamp!	1961	$25
❏ MGV-8117 [M]	Hamp's Big Four	1957	$175
❏ V-8117 [M]	Hamp's Big Four	1961	$25
❏ MGV-8105 [M]	King of the Vibes	1957	$175
❏ V-8105 [M]	King of the Vibes	1961	$25
❏ MGV-8275 [M]	Lionel Hampton	1958	$0
—Canceled			
❏ MGV-8223 [M]	Lionel Hampton '58	1958	$120
❏ V-8223 [M]	Lionel Hampton '58	1961	$25
❏ MGV-8170 [M]	Lionel Hampton and His Giants	1957	$175
❏ V-8170 [M]	Lionel Hampton and His Giants	1961	$25
❏ MGV-2018 [M]	Lionel Hampton Plays Love Songs	1957	$175
❏ V-2018 [M]	Lionel Hampton Plays Love Songs	1961	$25
❏ MGV-8113 [M]	Swingin' with Hamp	1957	$175
❏ V-8113 [M]	Swingin' with Hamp	1961	$25
❏ VE-2-2543	The Blues Ain't News to Me	1982	$35
❏ MGV-8215 [M]	The Genius of Lionel Hampton	1958	$150
❏ V-8215 [M]	The Genius of Lionel Hampton	1961	$25
❏ MGV-8228 [M]	The High and the Mighty	1958	$175
❏ V-8228 [M]	The High and the Mighty	1961	$25
❏ MGV-8019 [M]	Travelin' Band	1957	$150
❏ V-8019 [M]	Travelin' Band	1961	$25

WHO'S WHO IN JAZZ
| ❏ 21017 | Blackout | 1978 | $30 |
| ❏ 21008 | Who's Who Presents Lionel Hampton | 1977 | $30 |

HAMPTON, SLIDE
ATLANTIC
| ❏ 1396 [M] | Explosion! | 1962 | $175 |
| ❏ SD1396 [S] | Explosion! | 1962 | $175 |

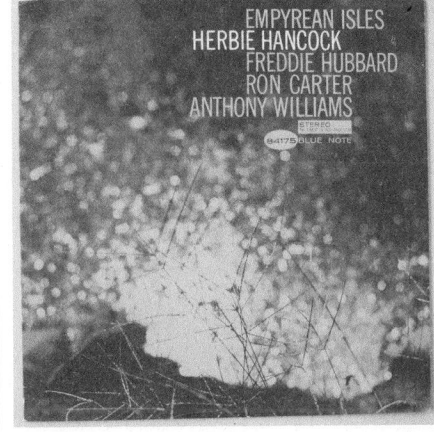

❏ 1379 [M]	Jazz with a Twist	1962	$30
❏ SD1379 [S]	Jazz with a Twist	1962	$175
❏ 1339 [M]	Sister Salvation	1960	$300
—Multicolor label, white "fan" logo at right			
❏ 1339 [M]	Sister Salvation	1962	$175
—Multicolor label, black "fan" logo at right			
❏ SD1339 [S]	Sister Salvation	1960	$300
—Multicolor label, white "fan" logo at right			
❏ SD1339 [S]	Sister Salvation	1962	$175
—Multicolor label, black "fan" logo at right			
❏ 1362 [M]	Somethin' Sanctified	1961	$175
—Multicolor label, white "fan" logo at right			
❏ 1362 [M]	Somethin' Sanctified	1962	$175
—Multicolor label, black "fan" logo at right			
❏ SD1362 [S]	Somethin' Sanctified	1961	$175
—Multicolor label, white "fan" logo at right			
❏ SD1362 [S]	Somethin' Sanctified	1962	$175
—Multicolor label, black "fan" logo at right			

CHARLIE PARKER
| ❏ PLP-803 [M] | Two Sides of Slide | 1962 | $30 |
| ❏ PLP-803S [S] | Two Sides of Slide | 1962 | $30 |

EPIC
| ❏ LA16030 [M] | Drum Suite | 1963 | $40 |
| ❏ BA17030 [S] | Drum Suite | 1963 | $75 |

STRAND
| ❏ SL-1006 [M] | Slide Hampton and His Horn of Plenty | 1959 | $40 |
| ❏ SLS-1006 [S] | Slide Hampton and His Horn of Plenty | 1959 | $40 |

HAMPTON STRING QUARTET
RCA RED SEAL
| ❏ 5621-1-RC | What If Mozart Wrote "Have Yourself a Merry Little Christmas | 1986 | $12 |

Number	Title	Yr	NM

HANCOCK, HERBIE, AND CHICK COREA
COLUMBIA
| ❏ PC235663 | An Evening with Herbie Hancock and Chick Corea | 1979 | $30 |

POLYDOR
| ❏ PD-2-6238 | An Evening with Chick Corea and Herbie Hancock | 1979 | $35 |

HANCOCK, HERBIE
BLUE NOTE

❏ BLP-4175 [M]	Empyrean Isles	1964	$150
❏ BST-84175 [S]	Empyrean Isles	1964	$150
—With New York, USA address on label			
❏ BST-84175 [S]	Empyrean Isles	1967	$35
—With "A Division of Liberty Records" on label			
❏ BST-84175	Empyrean Isles	1985	$25
—The Finest in Jazz Since 1939" reissue			
❏ BN-LA399-H2	Herbie Hancock	1975	$35
❏ BLP-4147 [M]	Inventions and Dimensions	1963	$80
❏ BST-84147 [S]	Inventions and Dimensions	1963	$50
—With New York, USA address on label			
❏ BST-84147 [S]	Inventions and Dimensions	1967	$35
—With "A Division of Liberty Records" on label			
❏ BST-84147	Inventions and Dimensions	1987	$25
—The Finest in Jazz Since 1939" reissue			
❏ BLP-4195 [M]	Maiden Voyage	1965	$175
❏ BST-84195 [S]	Maiden Voyage	1965	$300
—With New York, USA address on label			
❏ BST-84195 [S]	Maiden Voyage	1967	$35
—With "A Division of Liberty Records" on label			
❏ BST-84195 [S]	Maiden Voyage	197?	$30
—A Division of United Artists" on label			
❏ B1-46339	Maiden Voyage	1997	$50
—Audiophile reissue			
❏ BST-84195 [S]	Maiden Voyage	1985	$25
—The Finest in Jazz Since 1939" reissue			
❏ ST84105 [B]	Maiden Voyage	2015	$20
❏ BLP-4126 [M]	My Point of View	1963	$150
❏ BST-84126 [S]	My Point of View	1963	$150
—With New York, USA address on label			
❏ BST-84126 [S]	My Point of View	1967	$35
—With "A Division of Liberty Records" on label			
❏ BST-84126	My Point of View	1987	$25
—The Finest in Jazz Since 1939" reissue			
❏ BST-84279	Speak Like a Child	1968	$35
❏ BST-84279	Speak Like a Child	1986	$25
—The Finest in Jazz Since 1939" reissue			
❏ BN-LA152-F	Succotash	1974	$30
❏ BLP-4109 [M]	Takin' Off	1962	$250
❏ BST-84109 [S]	Takin' Off	1962	$175
—With New York, USA address on label			
❏ BST-84109 [S]	Takin' Off	1967	$35
—With "A Division of Liberty Records" on label			
❏ BST-84109	Takin' Off	1987	$25
—The Finest in Jazz Since 1939" reissue			
❏ BST-84407	The Best of Herbie Hancock	1971	$35
❏ B1-91142	The Best of Herbie Hancock	1988	$25
❏ BST-84321	The Prisoner	1969	$35
❏ BST-84321	The Prisoner	1987	$25
—The Finest in Jazz Since 1939" reissue			

COLUMBIA
❏ JC35764	Feets Don't Fail Me Now	1979	$30
❏ PC35764	Feets Don't Fail Me Now	198?	$20
—Budget-line reissue			
❏ FC38814	Future Shock	1983	$25
❏ 8C839913 [EP]	Hardrock	1984	$30
—Picture disc			
❏ KC32371	Head Hunters	1973	$30
❏ CQ32371 [Q]	Head Hunters	1973	$40
❏ PC32371	Head Hunters	197?	$20
—Reissue (with or without bar code)			
❏ FC37928	Lite Me Up	1982	$25
❏ PC37928	Lite Me Up	198?	$20

Number	Title	Yr	NM
—Budget-line reissue			
❏ FC37387	Magic Windows	1981	$25
❏ PC37387	Magic Windows	198?	$20
—Budget-line reissue			
❏ PC33812	Man-Child	1975	$30
—No bar code on cover			
❏ PC33812	Man-Child	198?	$20
—Budget-line reissue with bar code			
❏ JC36415	Monster	1980	$25
❏ PC36415	Monster	198?	$20
—Budget-line reissue			
❏ JC36578	Mr. Hands	1980	$25
❏ PC36578	Mr. Hands	198?	$20
—Budget-line reissue			
❏ FC40025	Perfect Machine	1988	$25
❏ SC40464	'Round Midnight	1986	$25
❏ PC34280	Secrets	1976	$30
—No bar code on cover			
❏ PCQ34280 [Q]	Secrets	1976	$40
❏ PC34280	Secrets	198?	$20
—Budget-line reissue with bar code			
❏ KC32212	Sextant	1973	$30
❏ PC32212	Sextant	198?	$20
—Budget-line reissue			
❏ PCQ32212 [Q]	Sextant	197?	$75
❏ FC39478	Sound-System	1984	$25
❏ PC39478	Sound-System	1985	$20
—Budget-line reissue			
❏ JC34907	Sunlight	1978	$30
❏ JC36309	The Best of Herbie Hancock	1979	$30
❏ PC32965	Thrust	1974	$30
—No bar code on cover			
❏ PCQ32965 [Q]	Thrust	1974	$40
❏ PC32965	Thrust	198?	$20
—Budget-line reissue with bar code			
❏ FC39870	Village Life	1985	$25
❏ PG34688	V.S.O.P.	1977	$35
❏ C234976	V.S.O.P. Quintet	1978	$35

MGM
❏ E-4447 [M]	Blow-Up	1967	$40
❏ SE-4447 [S]	Blow-Up	1967	$150
—Also includes one track by the Yardbirds			

PAUSA
| ❏ 9002 | Succotash | 198? | $25 |

TRIP
| ❏ UPF-194 | Traces | 197? | $30 |

WARNER BROS.
❏ BS2617	Crossings	1972	$35
❏ WS1834	Fat Albert Rotunda	1970	$35
❏ WS1898	Mwandishi	1971	$35
❏ 2WS2807	Treasure Chest	1974	$35

HANDSOME BOY MODELING SCHOOL
ELEKTRA
| ❏ 62941 | White People | 2004 | $18 |

TOMMY BOY
| ❏ TB1258 | So...How's Your Girl? | 1999 | $30 |

HANDY, CAP'N JOHN
GHB
❏ GHBS-41	All Aboard, Volume 1	1967	$50
❏ GHBS-42	All Aboard, Volume 2	1967	$50
❏ GHBS-43	All Aboard, Volume 3	1967	$50
❏ GHB-166	Cap'n John Handy with Geoff Bull and Bary Martyn's Band	1986	$25
❏ GHB-38	Everybody's Talking	1967	$50

RCA VICTOR
❏ LPM-3762 [M]	Introducing Cap'n John Handy	1967	$30
❏ LSP-3762 [S]	Introducing Cap'n John Handy	1967	$35
❏ LSP-3929	New Orleans and the Blues	1968	$50

HANDY, GEORGE
X
| ❏ LXA-1032 [M] | By George! Handy, Of Course | 1954 | $100 |
| ❏ LXA-1004 [M] | Handyland, U.S.A. | 1954 | $150 |

HANDY, JOHN
ABC IMPULSE!
| ❏ AS-9324 | Carnival | 1977 | $25 |
| ❏ ASD-9314 | Hard Work | 1976 | $35 |

COLUMBIA
❏ CL2697 [M]	New View	1967	$75
❏ CS9497 [S]	New View	1967	$75
❏ CS9689	Projections	1968	$75
❏ CL2462 [M]	Recorded Live at the Monterey Jazz Festival	1966	$35
❏ CS9262 [S]	Recorded Live at the Monterey Jazz Festival	1966	$50
❏ CL2567 [M]	The Second John Handy Album	1966	$50
❏ CS9367 [S]	The Second John Handy Album	1966	$75

Number	Title	Yr	NM
MILESTONE			
❏ M-9173	Centerpiece: John Handy with Class	1989	$30
QUARTET			
❏ Q-1005	Excursion in Blue	1988	$75
ROULETTE			
❏ RE-132	In the Vernacular	197?	$50
— Compilation of earlier material			
❏ R52042 [M]	In the Ver-nac'-u-lar	1960	$50
❏ SR52042 [S]	In the Ver-nac'-u-lar	1960	$50
❏ R52121 [M]	John Handy Jazz	1964	$50
❏ SR52121 [S]	John Handy Jazz	1964	$75
❏ R52088 [M]	No Coast Jazz	1962	$50
❏ SR52088 [S]	No Coast Jazz	1962	$75
❏ R52124 [M]	Quote, Unquote	1964	$50
❏ SR52124 [S]	Quote, Unquote	1964	$75
WARNER BROS.			
❏ BSK3242	Handy Dandy Man	1978	$30
❏ BSK3170	Where Go the Boats	1978	$30
HANDY, W.C.			
DRG			
❏ SL-5192	Father of the Blues	1980	$25
HERITAGE			
❏ 0052 [10]	Blues Revisited	195?	$120
HANGMEN, THE			
MONUMENT			
❏ MLP-8077 [M]	Bitter Sweet	1967	$80
❏ SLP-18077 [S]	Bitter Sweet	1967	$40
HANKINS, ESCO			
AUDIO LAB			
❏ AL-1547 [M]	Country Style	1961	$250
HANNA, JAKE			
CONCORD JAZZ			
❏ CJ-11	Jake Hanna and Carl Fontana Live	1975	$30
❏ CJ-35	Jake Hanna Takes Manhattan	1977	$30
❏ CJ-22	Kansas City Express	1976	$30
HANNA, KEN			
CAPITOL			
❏ T6512 [M]	Jazz for Dancers	1955	$85
HANNA, ROLAND, AND GEORGE MRAZ			
CHOICE			
❏ 1018	Sir Elf Plus One	1978	$35
HANNA, ROLAND			
ARISTA FREEDOM			
❏ AL1010	Perugia	1975	$30
ATCO			
❏ 33-108 [M]	Destry Rides Again	1959	$40
❏ SD 33-108 [S]	Destry Rides Again	1959	$40
❏ 33-121 [M]	Easy to Love	1960	$30
❏ SD 33-121 [S]	Easy to Love	1960	$40
AUDIOPHILE			
❏ AP-157	This Must Be Love	198?	$25
BASF			
❏ 20875	Child of Gemini	1972	$30
BEE HIVE			
❏ BH-7013	Roland Hanna and the New York Jazz Quartet in Chicago	198?	$25
CHOICE			
❏ 1003	Sir Elf	1974	$35
INNER CITY			
❏ IC-1072	Roland Hanna Plays Music of Alec Wilder	197?	$30
PROGRESSIVE			
❏ 7012	Time for the Dancers	1978	$30
STORYVILLE			
❏ 4018	Swing Me No Waltzes	198?	$25
WEST 54TH			
❏ 8003	A Gift from the Magi	1979	$30
HANNIBAL			
ATLANTIC			
❏ 81973	Visions of a New World	1989	$30
HANRAHAN, KIP			
AMERICAN CLAVE			
❏ 1011 [EP]	A Few Short Notes at the End of the Run	1987	$30
❏ 1007	Coup De Tete	198?	$30
❏ 1008/9	Desire Develops an Edge	1984	$35
❏ 1010	Vertical's Currency	1985	$30
PANGAEA			
❏ 42137	Days & Nights of Blue Luck Inverted	1988	$12

Number	Title	Yr	NM
HANSON			
MANTICORE			
❏ MC66672 [B]	Magic Dragon	1974	$15
❏ MC66670	Now Hear This	1973	$15
HANSSON, BO			
CHARISMA			
❏ CAS-1059 [B]	Lord of the Rings	1973	$35
❏ FC6062	Magician's Hat	1974	$15
SIRE			
❏ SASD-7525	Attic Thoughts	1976	$12
❏ SR6044	Music Inspired by Watership Down	1977	$12
HA'PENNYS, THE			
FERSCH			
❏ FL-1110	Love Is Not the Same	1968	$250
HAPPENINGS, THE			
B.T. PUPPY			
❏ BTP-1003 [M]	Psycle	1967	$30
❏ BTPS-1003 [S]	Psycle	1967	$30
❏ BTP-1001 [M]	The Happenings (Bye-Bye, So Long, Farewell…See You in September)	1966	$40
❏ BTS-1001 [S]	The Happenings (Bye-Bye, So Long, Farewell…See You in September)	1966	$30
❏ BTS-1004	The Happenings Golden Hits!	1968	$40
JUBILEE			
❏ JGS-8028	Piece of Mind	1969	$30
❏ JGS-8030	The Happenings' Greatest Hits	1969	$30
HAPPY CHIPMUNKS, THE			
HOLIDAY			
❏ HDY-1950	Merry Christmas from the Happy Chipmunks	1982	$30
—Record quickly pulled from market because of unauthorized use of the name "Chipmunks"			
HAPPY CRICKETS, THE			
GRAND PRIX			
❏ KX-9	Christmas with the Happy Crickets	1959	$18
HAPPY DRAGON BAND, THE			
FIDDLER'S MUSIC			
❏ 1157	The Happy Dragon Band	1977	$100
HAPPY JAZZ BAND, THE			
AUDIOPHILE			
❏ AP-114	College Street Caper	196?	$30
❏ AP-96 [M]	Goose Pimples	196?	$30
❏ APS-96 [S]	Goose Pimples	196?	$35
❏ AP-200	High Society	196?	$30
❏ AP-86 [M]	Jazz from the San Antonio River	196?	$30
❏ APS-86 [S]	Jazz from the San Antonio River	196?	$35
❏ AP-93 [M]	Jim Cullum's Happy Jazz Band	196?	$30
❏ APS-93 [S]	Jim Cullum's Happy Jazz Band	196?	$35
❏ AP-87 [M]	Real Stuff	196?	$30
❏ APS-87 [S]	Real Stuff	196?	$35
HAPPY JAZZ			
❏ HJ-202	We've Had Mighty Good Weather	1970	$30
❏ HJ-201	Zacatecas	1969	$30
—Cliff Brewton, piano; Benny Valfre,banjo; Harvey Kindervater,drums; Willson Davis, sousaphone; Gene McKinney, trombone; Jim Cullum Jr.,cornet; Jim Cullum Sr., clarinet.			
HAPPY MONDAYS			
ELEKTRA			
❏ 60854	Bummed	1989	$12
RHINO			
❏ R160986 [B]	Pills 'N' Thrills and Bellyaches	2015	$20
—Record Store Day			
HAPSHASH AND THE COLOURED COAT			
IMPERIAL			
❏ LP-9377 [M]	Hapshash and the Coloured Coat	1968	$150
❏ LP-12377 [S]	Hapshash and the Coloured Coat	1968	$40
❏ LP-12430	Western Flyer	1969	$40
HAQUE, FAREED			
PANGAEA			
❏ 82012	Manresa	1989	$30
❏ 42156	Voices Rising	1988	$25

Number	Title	Yr	NM
HARD MEAT			
WARNER BROS.			
❏ WS1852	Hard Meat	1969	$18
❏ WS1879	Through a Window	1970	$18
HARD TIMES, THE			
WORLD PACIFIC			
❏ WP-1867 [M]	Blew Mind	1968	$30
❏ WPS-21867 [S]	Blew Mind	1968	$30
HARDAWAY, BOB			
BETHLEHEM			
❏ BCP-1028 [10]	Bob Hardaway	1955	$400
HARDEN, ARLENE			
COLUMBIA			
❏ CS9633 [S]	Sing Me Back Home	1967	$25
❏ CL2833 [M]	Sing Me Back Home	1967	$30
❏ CS9674	What Can I Say	1968	$25
HARDEN, BOBBY			
STARDAY			
❏ SLP-443	Nashville Sensation	1969	$18
HARDEN, WILBUR			
SAVOY			
❏ MG-12131 [M]	Jazz Way Out	1958	$50
❏ SST-13004 [S]	Jazz Way Out	1959	$40
❏ MG-12127 [M]	Mainstream 1958/The East Coast Jazz Scene Featuring John Coltrane	1958	$75
❏ MG-12136 [M]	Tanganyika Suite	1958	$50
❏ SST-13005 [S]	Tanganyika Suite	1959	$40
❏ MG-12134 [M]	The King and I	1958	$50
❏ SST-13002 [S]	The King and I	1959	$40
HARDEN TRIO, THE			
COLUMBIA			
❏ CL2506 [M]	Tippy Toeing	1966	$25
❏ CS9306 [S]	Tippy Toeing	1966	$30
HARDIMAN, DAVID			
THERESA			
❏ 104	It'll Be Alright	197?	$25
HARDIN, GUS			
RCA VICTOR			
❏ CPL1-4937	Fallen Angel	1984	$10
❏ MHL1-8603 [EP]	Gus Hardin	1983	$10
❏ CPL1-5358	Wall of Tears	1985	$10
❏ CPL1-7033	Wall of Tears	1985	$10
HARDIN, TIM			
ANTILLES			
❏ 7023	Nine	1974	$12
ATCO			
❏ 33-210 [M]	This Is Tim Hardin	1967	$75
❏ SD 33-210 [R]	This Is Tim Hardin	1967	$18
COLUMBIA			
❏ C30551	Bird on a Wire	1971	$25
❏ KC31764	Painted Head	1972	$25
❏ CS9787 [B]	Suite for Susan Moore and Damion -- We Are -- One, One, All in One	1969	$30
— 360 Sound" label			
❏ PC37164	The Shock of Grace	1981	$15
MGM			
❏ M3G-4952	Archetypes	1974	$12
❏ GAS-104	Tim Hardin (Golden Archive Series)	1970	$15
POLYDOR			
❏ PD-1-6333	Memorial Album	1981	$15
VERVE FOLKWAYS			
❏ FT-3004 [M]	Tim Hardin/1	1966	$75
❏ FTS-3004 [S]	Tim Hardin/1	1966	$40
VERVE FORECAST			
❏ FTS-3078	The Best of Tim Hardin	1970	$25
❏ FT-3004 [M]	Tim Hardin/1	1967	$80
❏ FTS-3004 [S]	Tim Hardin/1	1967	$25
❏ FTS-3022	Tim Hardin/2	1967	$30
❏ FTS-3049	Tim Hardin/3 -- Live in Concert	1968	$30
❏ FTS-3064	Tim Hardin/4	1969	$30
HARDING, ELLERINE			
MAINSTREAM			
❏ MRL-377	Ellerine Harding	1972	$25
HARDMAN, BILL			
MUSE			
❏ MR-5259	Focus	198?	$25
❏ MR-5152	Home	1978	$30
❏ MR-5184	Politely	1981	$30

Number	Title	Yr	NM

SAVOY
| MG-12170 [M] | Bill Hardman Quintet | 1961 | $175 |

SAVOY JAZZ
| SJL-1164 | Saying Something | 1986 | $25 |

HARDWATER
CAPITOL
| ST-2954 | Hardwater | 1968 | $40 |

HARDY, FRANCOISE
4 CORNERS OF THE WORLD
FCL-4231 [M]	Francoise...	1968	$150
FCS-4231 [S]	Francoise...	1968	$35
FCL-4238 [M]	Je Vous Aime	1969	$150
FCS-4238 [S]	Je Vous Aime	1969	$35
FCL-4219 [M]	Maid in Paris	1967	$75
FCS-4219 [S]	Maid in Paris	1967	$50
FCS-4255 [S]	The Best of Francoise Hardy	1969	$30
FCL-4208 [M]	The "Yeh Yeh" Girl from Paris!	1965	$75
FCS-4208 [S]	The "Yeh Yeh" Girl from Paris!	1965	$50

4 MEN WITH BEARDS
| FMN2051LP [B] | La Question | 2016 | $30 |

REPRISE
RS6290	Francoise Hardy	1968	$30
RS6318	Loving	1969	$30
RS6345	Mon Amour, Adieu	1969	$30

HARDY, HAGOOD
CAPITOL
ST-11552	Maybe Tomorrow	1976	$25
ST-11488	The Homecoming	1975	$25
SN-16300	The Homecoming	198?	$20
— Budget-line reissue

HARDY BOYS, THE
RCA VICTOR
| LSP-4217 | Here Come the Hardy Boys | 1969 | $25 |
| LSP-4315 | Wheels | 1970 | $25 |

HARGROVE, LINDA
CAPITOL
ST-11685	Impressions	1977	$15
ST-11564	Just Like You	1976	$15
ST-11463	Love, You're the Teacher	1975	$15

ELEKTRA
| 7E-1013 | Blue Jean Country Queen | 1974 | $15 |
| EKS-75063 | Music Is Your Mistress | 1973 | $18 |

HARGROVE, ROY
NOVUS
| 3082-1-N | Diamond in the Rough | 1990 | $30 |

HARIAN, KENT
CARAVAN
| LP-15611 [M] | Echoes of Joy | 1956 | $300 |

HARLEY, RUFUS
ATLANTIC
SD3001 [S]	Bagpipe Blues	1967	$35
3001 [M]	Bagpipe Blues	1967	$25
SD1539	King/Queens	1970	$35
SD3006	Scotch & Soul	1968	$35
SD1504	Tribute to Courage	1969	$35

HARMONAIRES MALE QUINTET, THE
VARSITY
| 6915 [10] | Spirituals | 195? | $100 |

HARMONICA FRANK
PURITAN
| 3003 | The Great Original Recordings of Harmonica Frank | 197? | $18 |

HARMONY BLAZERS, THE
HARMONY
HL7126 [M]	Rock & Roll Vol. II	1959	$40
HL7103 [M]	Ten Big Hits	1959	$40
HL7200 [M]	The Big Ten	1959	$40

HARMONY CHORISTERS, THE
HARMONY
| HL7073 [M] | Christmas Hymns and Carols | 195? | $18 |

HARNELL, JOE
CAPITOL
| ST-11657 | Harnell | 1977 | $15 |

COLUMBIA
CL2699 [M]	Bossa Now	1967	$18
CS9499 [S]	Bossa Now	1967	$15
CL2466 [M]	Golden Piano Hits	1966	$15
CS9266 [S]	Golden Piano Hits	1966	$18

Number	Title	Yr	NM

EPIC
| BN573 [S] | I Want to Be Happy | 1960 | $25 |
| LN0(# unknown) [M] | I Want to Be Happy | 1960 | $18 |

JUBILEE
| JGM-5020 [M] | Joe Harnell and His Trio | 1963 | $35 |
— Reissue of 1015
| JLP-1015 [M] | Piano Inventions of Jo Harnell | 1956 | $150 |

KAPP
KL1318 [M]	Fly Me to the Moon and the Bossa Nova Pops	1962	$18
KS3318 [S]	Fly Me to the Moon and the Bossa Nova Pops	1962	$25
KL1339 [M]	Joe Harnell	1963	$18
KS3339 [S]	Joe Harnell	1963	$25
KL1325 [M]	More Joe Harnell, More Bossa Nova Pops	1963	$18
KS3325 [S]	More Joe Harnell, More Bossa Nova Pops	1963	$25
KL1480 [M]	The Best of Joe Harnell	1966	$15
KS3480 [S]	The Best of Joe Harnell	1966	$18
KL1416 [M]	The Rhythm and the Fire	1965	$15
KS3416 [S]	The Rhythm and the Fire	1965	$18

MOTOWN
| MS-698 | Moving On!! | 1969 | $40 |

HARP, FELIX
GUINNESS
| GNS36053 [B] | Dear | 1977 | $20 |
| GNS36054 [B] | Time To Give | 1977 | $30 |

HARPER, BEN
CARDAS
| CR5818 | Pleasure and Pain | 1992 | $500 |
— With Tom Freund

VIRGIN
| 48151 | Burn to Shine | 1999 | $50 |
— As "Ben Harper and the Innocent Criminals
| 83003 | Diamonds on the Inside | 2003 | $25 |
| 10079 | Live from Mars | 2001 | $150 |
— As "Ben Harper and the Innocent Criminals
| 71206 | There Will Be a Light | 2005 | $25 |
— With the Blind Boys of Alabama

HARPER, BILLY
BLACK SAINT
| BSR-0001 | Black Saint | 198? | $18 |

SOUL NOTE
| SN-1001 | Billy Harper In Europe | 198? | $18 |

STRATA-EAST
| SES-19739 | Capra Black | 1973 | $40 |

HARPER, HERBIE
BETHLEHEM

| BCP-1025 [10] | Herbie Harper | 1955 | $120 |

LIBERTY
| LRP-6003 [M] | Herbie Harper | 1956 | $100 |

MODE
| LP-100 [M] | Herbie Harper Sextet | 1957 | $150 |

NOCTURNE
| NLP-7 [10] | Herbie Harper | 1954 | $175 |
| NLP-1 [10] | Herbie Harper Quintet | 1954 | $175 |

SEABREEZE
| SBD-101 | Herbie Harper Revisited | 1981 | $30 |

TAMPA
| TP-11 [M] | Herbie Harper Quintet | 1957 | $250 |
— Red vinyl
| TP-11 [M] | Herbie Harper Quintet | 1958 | $175 |
— Black vinyl

Number	Title	Yr	NM

HARPER, JANICE
CAPITOL
| T1337 [M] | Embers of Love | 1960 | $25 |
| ST1337 [S] | Embers of Love | 1960 | $30 |

HARPER, ROY
CHRYSALIS
| CH21164 | Flashes from the Archives of Oblivion | 1978 | $18 |
— Released in the UK in 1974
| CHR1160 | Flat Baroque and Berserk | 1978 | $18 |
— Reissue of Harvest LP
PRO-620 [DJ]	Introduction to Roy Harper	1976	$40
PRO-620 [DJ]	Introduction to Roy Harper	1976	$30
CHR1162	Lifemask	1978	$15
— Released in the UK in 1973
| CHR1139 | One of Those Days in England | 1977 | $18 |
| CHR1161 | Stormcock | 1978 | $15 |
— Released in the UK in 1971
| CHR1163 | Valentine | 1978 | $15 |
— Released in the UK in 1974
| CHR1105 | When An Old Cricketer Leaves the Crease | 1976 | $18 |

HARVEST
| SKAO-418 | Flat Baroque and Berserk | 1970 | $30 |

PVC
| 8937 [B] | Whatever Happened to Jugula | 198? | $15 |
— featuring Jimmy Page

WORLD PACIFIC
| WPS-21888 | Folkjokeopus | 1969 | $30 |

HARPER, TONI
RCA VICTOR
LPM-2092 [M]	Lady Lonely	1960	$30
LSP-2092 [S]	Lady Lonely	1960	$40
LPM-2253 [M]	Night Mood	1960	$30
LSP-2253 [S]	Night Mood	1960	$40

VERVE
| MGV-2001 [M] | Toni Harper Sings | 1956 | $250 |
| V-2001 [M] | Toni Harper Sings | 1961 | $50 |

HARPER, WALT
GATEWAY
7005 [M]	Harper's Ferry	1964	$35
7016 [M]	On the Road	1966	$25
S-7016 [M]	On the Road	1966	$35

HARPER BROTHERS, THE
VERVE
| 837033-1 | The Harper Brothers | 1988 | $25 |

HARPERS BIZARRE
FOREST BAY
| 7545 | As Time Goes By | 1976 | $18 |

WARNER BROS.
| WS1716 | Anything Goes | 1967 | $25 |
| ST-91351 | Anything Goes | 1968 | $25 |
— Capitol Record Club edition
| W1693 [M] | Feelin' Groovy | 1967 | $25 |
| WS1693 [S] | Feelin' Groovy | 1967 | $14 |
— Gold label
| WS1693 [S] | Feelin' Groovy | 1968 | $18 |
— Green "W7" label
| WS1784 | Harpers Bizarre Four | 1969 | $16 |
| WS1739 | The Secret Life of Harpers Bizarre | 1968 | $16 |

HARPO, SLIM
EXCELLO

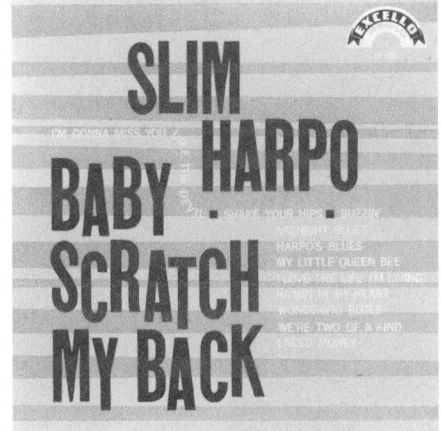

Number	Title	Yr	NM
❏ LP-8005 [M]	Baby Scratch My Back	1966	$250
—Orange and blue label			
❏ LPS-8005 [M]	Baby Scratch My Back	196?	$150
—All-blue label			
❏ LP-8003 [M]	Raining in My Heart	1961	$300
—Orange and blue label			
❏ LPS-8003 [M]	Raining in My Heart	196?	$150
—All-blue label			
❏ LPS-8013 [M]	Slim Harpo Knew the Blues	1970	$50
❏ LPS-8010 [M]	The Best of Slim Harpo	1969	$50
❏ LPS-8008 [M]	Tip On In	1968	$50
RHINO			
❏ R1-70169	Scratch My Back: The Best of Slim Harpo	1989	$15
❏ RNLP-106	The Best of Slim Harpo	198?	$18

HARPTONES, THE
AMBIENT SOUND

❏ FZ37718	Love Needs	1982	$15
HARLEM HIT PARADE			
❏ 5006	The Harptones	197?	$18
RELIC			
❏ LP-5001	The Greatest Hits of the Harptones, Vol. 1	197?	$15
❏ LP-5003	The Greatest Hits of the Harptones, Vol. 2	197?	$15

HARRELL, TOM
BLACKHAWK

❏ BKH-50901	The Play of Light	1986	$25
CONTEMPORARY			
❏ C-14059	Form	1990	$30
❏ C-14054	Sail Away	1989	$30
❏ C-14043	Stories	1988	$25

HARRIOTT, JOE
ATLANTIC

❏ 1482 [M]	Indo-Jazz Fusions	1967	$35
❏ SD1482 [S]	Indo-Jazz Fusions	1967	$30
❏ 1465 [M]	Indo-Jazz Suite	1966	$30
❏ SD1465 [S]	Indo-Jazz Suite	1966	$35
CAPITOL			
❏ T10351 [M]	Abstract	1962	$50
❏ DT10351 [R]	Abstract	1962	$50
JAZZLAND			
❏ JLP-49 [M]	Free Form	1961	$30
❏ JLP-949 [S]	Free Form	1961	$30
❏ JLP-37 [M]	Southern Horizons	1961	$30
❏ JLP-937 [S]	Southern Horizons	1961	$30

HARRIS, ART, AND MITCH LEIGH
EPIC

❏ LG1010 [10]	Modern Woodwind Expressions	1954	$150
❏ LN3200 [M]	New Jazz in Hi-Fi	1956	$100
KAPP			
❏ KL-1011 [M]	Baroque Band and Brass Choir -- Jazz 1775	1956	$40

HARRIS, ART
KAPP

❏ KL-1015 [M]	Jazz Goes to Post-Graduate School	1956	$40

HARRIS, BARRY
ARGO

❏ LP-644 [M]	Breakin' It Up	1959	$40
❏ LPS-644 [S]	Breakin' It Up	1959	$30
CADET			
❏ LP-644 [M]	Breakin' It Up	1966	$25
❏ LPS-644 [S]	Breakin' It Up	1966	$35
FANTASY			
❏ OJC-208	Barry Harris at the Jazz Workshop	1986	$25
❏ OJC-486	Preminado	1991	$30
MILESTONE			
❏ 47050	Stay Right With It	197?	$35
PRESTIGE			
❏ PRST-7600	Bull's Eye	1969	$25
❏ PRLP-7498 [M]	Luminescence	1967	$30
❏ PRST-7498 [S]	Luminescence	1967	$25
❏ PRST-7733	Magnificent!	1970	$25
RIVERSIDE			
❏ RLP 12-326 [M]	Barry Harris at the Jazz Workshop	1960	$300
❏ RLP-1177 [S]	Barry Harris at the Jazz Workshop	1960	$250
❏ 6123	Barry Harris at the Jazz Workshop	197?	$30
❏ RLP-435 [M]	Chasin' the Bird	1962	$250
❏ RS-9435 [S]	Chasin' the Bird	1962	$250
❏ RLP-392 [M]	Listen to Barry Harris	1961	$250
❏ RS-9392 [S]	Listen to Barry Harris	1961	$250
❏ RLP-413 [M]	Newer Than New	1962	$175
❏ RS-9413 [S]	Newer Than New	1962	$175
❏ RLP-354 [M]	Preminado	1961	$140

Number	Title	Yr	NM
❏ RS-9354 [S]	Preminado	1961	$250
❏ 6047	Preminado	197?	$30
XANADU			
❏ 154	Barry Harris Plays Barry Harris	1978	$30
❏ 113	Barry Harris Plays Tadd Dameron	1975	$30
❏ 130	Live in Tokyo	1976	$30
❏ 213	The Bird of Red and Gold	1990	$35
❏ 177	Tokyo: 1976	1980	$30

HARRIS, BEAVER, AND DON PULLEN
HANNIBAL

❏ HNBL-2701	A Well Kept Secret	198?	$25

HARRIS, BEAVER
BLACK SAINT

❏ BSR-0006/7	In-Sanity	198?	$50
CADENCE JAZZ			
❏ 1002	Live at Nyon	198?	$30
❏ 1003	Negcaumongus	198?	$25
RED			
❏ VPA-146	360 Degree Aeutopia	198?	$30
❏ VPA-151	Safe	198?	$30
SOUL NOTE			
❏ SN-1002	Beautiful Africa	198?	$35

HARRIS, BILL (1), AND CHARLIE VENTURA
PHOENIX

❏ 14	Aces	197?	$25
❏ 11	Live at the Three Deuces	197?	$25

HARRIS, BILL (1)
CLEF

❏ MGC-125 [10]	Bill Harris Collates	1953	$300
FANTASY			
❏ 3263 [M]	Bill Harris and Friends	1958	$40
—Red vinyl			
❏ 3263 [M]	Bill Harris and Friends	1959	$30
—Black vinyl			
❏ OJC-083	Bill Harris and Friends	198?	$25
MERCURY			
❏ MGC-125 [10]	Bill Harris Collates	1953	$0
—Canceled			
NORGRAN			
❏ MGN-1062 [M]	The Bill Harris Herd	1956	$250
VERVE			
❏ MGV-8152 [M]	The Bill Harris Herd	1957	$175
XANADU			
❏ 191	Memorial Album	198?	$30

HARRIS, BILL (2)
EMARCY

❏ MG-36097 [M]	Bill Harris	1956	$250
❏ MG-36113 [M]	The Harris Touch	1957	$250
MERCURY			
❏ MG-20552 [M]	The Harris Touch	1960	$150
❏ SR-60552 [S]	The Harris Touch	1960	$150
WING			
❏ MGW-12220 [M]	Great Guitar Sounds	1963	$25
❏ SRW-16220 [S]	Great Guitar Sounds	1963	$35

HARRIS, CRAIG
INDIA NAVIGATION

❏ IN-1060	Aboriginal Affairs	198?	$30
JMT			
❏ 834415-1	Blackout in the Square Root of Soul	1988	$30
❏ 834408-1	Shelter	1987	$30
SOUL NOTE			
❏ SN-1055	Black Bone	198?	$30

HARRIS, DAVE
DECCA

❏ DL4113 [M]	Dinner Music for a Pack of Hungry Cannibals	1961	$25
❏ DL74113 [S]	Dinner Music for a Pack of Hungry Cannibals	1961	$30

HARRIS, DON "SUGARCANE"
BASF

❏ 21792	Cup Full of Dreams	1973	$35
❏ 20878	Fiddler on the Rock	1972	$35
❏ 21912	I'm On Your Case	1974	$35
❏ 21293	Sugarcane's Got the Blues	1972	$35
EPIC			
❏ E30027	Sugarcane	1971	$85

HARRIS, EDDIE
ANGELACO

❏ AN3002	Sounds Incredible	1980	$30

Number	Title	Yr	NM
ATLANTIC			
❏ SD1675	Bad Luck Is All I Have	1975	$30
❏ SD1554	Come On Down!	1970	$35
❏ SD1595	Eddie Harris Live at Newport	1971	$30
❏ SD1625	Eddie Harris Sings the Blues	1973	$30
❏ SD1647	E.H. in the U.K.	1974	$30
❏ SD 2-311	Excursions	1973	$35
❏ SD1573	Free Speech	1971	$35
❏ SD1529	High Voltage	1969	$35
❏ SD1698	How Can You Live Like That	1977	$30
❏ SD1669	I Need Some Money	1975	$30
❏ SD1611	Instant Death	1972	$30
❏ SW-94771	Instant Death	1972	$35
—Capitol Record Club edition			
❏ SD1659	Is It In	1974	$30
❏ 1453 [M]	Mean Greens	1966	$30
❏ SD1453 [S]	Mean Greens	1966	$35
❏ SD1506	Plug Me In	1968	$35
❏ SD1517	Silver Cycles	1969	$35
❏ SD1545	The Best of Eddie Harris	1970	$35
❏ 1545 [M]	The Best of Eddie Harris	1970	$75
—Promo-only white label mono pressing			
❏ SD1495	The Electrifying Eddie Harris	1968	$35
❏ 1448 [M]	The In Sound	1966	$30
❏ SD1448 [S]	The In Sound	1966	$35
❏ 1478 [M]	The Tender Storm	1967	$35
❏ SD1478 [S]	The Tender Storm	1967	$35
❏ SD8807	The Versatile Eddie Harris	1982	$25
❏ SD1683	Why You're Overweight	1976	$30
BUDDAH			
❏ BDS4004	Sculpture	1969	$30
COLUMBIA			
❏ CL2168 [M]	Cool Sax, Warm Heart	1964	$35
❏ CS8968 [S]	Cool Sax, Warm Heart	1964	$50
❏ CL2295 [M]	Cool Sax from Hollywood to Broadway	1965	$35
❏ CS9095 [S]	Cool Sax from Hollywood to Broadway	1965	$50
❏ CS9681 [S]	Here Comes the Judge	1968	$35
❏ CS9681 [M]	Here Comes the Judge	1968	$75
—Mono copies are promo only			
EXODUS			
❏ EX-6002 [M]	For Bird and Bags	1966	$35
GNP CRESCENDO			
❏ GNPS-2073	Black Sax	1973	$35
JANUS			
❏ 3020	Smokin'	1970	$30
MUTT & JEFF			
❏ 5018	The Real Electrifying Eddie Harris	1982	$30
RCA VICTOR			
❏ APL1-2942	I'm Tired	1978	$25
❏ AFL1-3402	Playin' With Myself	1980	$25
STEEPLECHASE			
❏ 1151	Eddie Harris Steps Up	1981	$25
SUNSET			
❏ SUS-5234	The Explosive Eddie Harris	1969	$30
TRADITION			
❏ 2067	Genius	1969	$30
TRIP			
❏ 5005	Shades of Eddie Harris	1974	$30
UPFRONT			
❏ UPF-106	The Soul of Eddie Harris	197?	$25
VEE JAY			
❏ LP3028 [M]	A Study in Jazz	1962	$50
❏ SR3028 [S]	A Study in Jazz	1962	$75
❏ LP3034 [M]	Bossa Nova	1963	$50

❏ SR3034 [S]	Bossa Nova	1963	$30
❏ LP3031 [M]	Eddie Harris Goes to the Movies	1962	$50
❏ SR3031 [S]	Eddie Harris Goes to the Movies	1962	$75
❏ LP3016 [M]	Exodus to Jazz	1961	$75
❏ SR3016 [S]	Exodus to Jazz	1961	$40

Number	Title	Yr	NM
❏ VJS-3016	Exodus to Jazz	198?	$25

—Reissue with thinner vinyl

Number	Title	Yr	NM
❏ VJS-3058	For Bird and Bags	198?	$25
❏ LP3037 [M]	Half and Half	1963	$75
❏ SR3037 [S]	Half and Half	1963	$75
❏ LP3027 [M]	Jazz for "Breakfast at Tiffany's	1961	$75
❏ SR3027 [S]	Jazz for "Breakfast at Tiffany's	1961	$40
❏ LP3025 [M]	Mighty Like a Rose	1961	$75
❏ SR3025 [S]	Mighty Like a Rose	1961	$40
❏ VJLP1081 [M]	The Theme from Exodus and Other Film Spectaculars	1964	$35
❏ VJLPS1081 [S]	The Theme from Exodus and Other Film Spectaculars	1964	$50

HARRIS, EMMYLOU
JUBILEE
Number	Title	Yr	NM
❏ JGS-8031 [B]	Gliding Bird	1969	$250

—Originals have color covers; counterfeit covers are black and white

MOBILE FIDELITY
❏ Jan-0015	Quarter Moon in a Ten Cent Town	1979	$40

—Audiophile vinyl

NONESUCH
❏ 541970-1 [B]	Wrecking Ball	2015	$50

—Deluxe Edition, Limited Edition

REPRISE
❏ 25776	Bluebird	1989	$15
❏ MS2236	Elite Hotel	1976	$12
❏ MSK2286 [B]	Elite Hotel	1977	$10

—Reissue of 2236

❏ MS2213	Pieces of the Sky	1975	$12
❏ MSK2284	Pieces of the Sky	1977	$10

—Reissue of 2213

WARNER BROS.
❏ 25585	Angel Band	1987	$12
❏ BSK3318	Blue Kentucky Girl	1979	$12
❏ BSK3603	Cimarron	1981	$12
❏ BSK3508	Evangeline	1981	$12
❏ 23740	Last Date	1982	$12
❏ BSK3484	Light of the Stable: The Christmas Album	1980	$12
❏ BSK3115	Luxury Liner	1977	$12

—Reissue of 2998

❏ BS2998	Luxury Liner	1977	$15
❏ BSK3258	Profile/Best of Emmylou Harris	1978	$12
❏ 25161	Profile II -- The Best of Emmylou Harris	1984	$12
❏ BSK3141	Quarter Moon in a Ten Cent Town	1978	$12
❏ BSK3422	Roses in the Snow	1980	$12
❏ 25205	The Ballad of Sally Rose	1985	$12
❏ 25352	Thirteen	1986	$12
❏ 23961	White Shoes	1983	$12

HARRIS, GENE
BLUE NOTE
❏ BN-LA313-G	Astral Signal	1974	$25
❏ BST-84423	Gene Harris of the Three Sounds	1972	$25
❏ BN-LA519-G	Nexus	1975	$35
❏ BN-LA634-G	Special Way	1976	$35
❏ BST-84378	The Three Sounds	1971	$25
❏ BN-LA760-G	Tone Tantrum	1977	$35
❏ BN-LA141-G	Yesterday, Today and Tomorrow	1973	$75

CONCORD JAZZ
❏ CJ-303	The Gene Harris Trio Plus One	1986	$25

JAM
❏ 08	Hot Lips	198?	$30

JUBILEE
❏ JGM-1115 [M]	Genie in My Soul	1959	$40
❏ JLP-1005 [M]	Our Love Is Here to Stay	1955	$75

HARRIS, HAROLD
VEE JAY
❏ LP-3036 [M]	Harold Harris at the Playboy Club	1963	$30
❏ SR-3036 [S]	Harold Harris at the Playboy Club	1963	$30
❏ LP-3018 [M]	Here's Harold	1962	$30
❏ SR-3018 [S]	Here's Harold	1962	$30

HARRIS, MAJOR
ATLANTIC
❏ SD18160	Jealousy	1976	$18
❏ SD18119	My Way	1974	$18

RCA VICTOR
❏ APL1-2803	How Do You Take Your Love	1978	$15

WMOT
❏ 627	Mellow Major	1977	$15
❏ PW37067	The Best of Major Harris, Now and Then	1981	$12

HARRIS, PEPPERMINT
TIME
❏ 5 [M]	Peppermint Harris	1962	$250

HARRIS, PHIL
MEGA
❏ MLPS-608	Southern Comfort ... The Best of Phil Harris	1974	$18

RCA CAMDEN
❏ CAL-456 [M]	That's What I Like About the South	1963	$18
❏ CAS-456(e) [R]	That's What I Like About the South	1963	$12

RCA VICTOR
❏ LPM-3037 [10]	Phil Harris On the Record	1952	$40
❏ LPM-1985 [M]	The South Shall Rise Again	1959	$30
❏ LSP-1985 [S]	The South Shall Rise Again	1959	$30

SUNBEAM
❏ HB302	Broadcasts from the Cocoanut Grove, L.A., 1932	198?	$12

HARRIS, RICHARD
ABC DUNHILL
❏ DS-50032 [B]	A Tramp Shining	1968	$25
❏ DSX-50159	I, In the Membership	1974	$10
❏ DSX-50160	Jonathan Livingston Seagull	1973	$10

—Spoken-word recording

❏ DSX-50116	My Boy	1971	$10
❏ DSX-50133	Slides	1972	$10
❏ DSX-50139	The Great Performances	1973	$10
❏ DS-50074 [B]	The Love Album	1970	$15
❏ DS-50042 [B]	The Yard Went On Forever	1968	$25

ATLANTIC
❏ SD18120	The Prophet by Kahlil Gibran	1974	$10

—Spoken-word recording

❏ QD18120 [Q]	The Prophet by Kahlil Gibran	1974	$40

—Spoken-word recording

MCA
❏ 27016	A Tramp Shining	198?	$10

—Budget-line reissue

PICKWICK
❏ SPC-3626	A Tramp Shining	1978	$12

HARRIS, ROLF
EPIC
❏ LN24110 [M]	Join Rolf Harris Singing The Count of King Caractacus (And Other Fun Songs)	1964	$18
❏ BN26110 [S]	Join Rolf Harris Singing The Count of King Caractacus (And Other Fun Songs)	1964	$15
❏ LN24053 [M]	Tie Me Kangaroo Down, Sport & Sun Arise	1963	$18
❏ BN26053 [S]	Tie Me Kangaroo Down, Sport & Sun Arise	1963	$15

HARRIS, SHAUN
Also see THE WEST COAST POP ART EXPERIMENTAL BAND.

CAPITOL
❏ ST-11168	Shaun Harris	1973	$30

HARRIS, WYNONIE
KING
❏ KS-1086	Good Rockin' Blues	1970	$30

HARRISON, CASS
MGM
❏ E-3388 [M]	The Duke and I	1956	$40
❏ E-3495 [M]	Wrappin' It Up	1957	$40

HARRISON, GEORGE, AND FRIENDS
The "Friends" include BADFINGER; ERIC CLAPTON; BOB DYLAN; BILLY PRESTON; LEON RUSSELL; RAVI SHANKAR; RINGO STARR.

APPLE
❏ STCX-3385	The Concert for Bangla Desh	1971	$40

—With 64-page booklet and custom innersleeves

❏ STCX-3385	The Concert for Bangla Desh	1975	$50

—As above, but with "All Rights Reserved" on labels

CAPITOL
❏ SABB-12248	The Concert for Bangla Desh	1982	$300

—Scheduled reissue that was never officially released, though a few copies got out by mistake

HARRISON, GEORGE
Also see THE BEATLES; TRAVELING WILBURYS.

APPLE
❏ STCH-639 [B]	All Things Must Pass	1970	$75

—Apple labels on first two records and "Apple Jam" labels on third; includes poster and lyric innersleeves

❏ SMAS-3418	Dark Horse	1974	$18
❏ SW-3420	Extra Texture (Read All About It)	1975	$18
❏ SMAS-3410	Living in the Material World	1973	$18
❏ ST-3350 [B]	Wonderwall Music	1968	$150

—With "Mfd. by Apple" on label

❏ ST-3350	Wonderwall Music	1968	$175

—With Capitol logo on Side 2 bottom

❏ ST-3350	Wonderwall Music Bonus Photo	1968	$10

CAPITOL
❏ STCH-639	All Things Must Pass	1976	$30

—Orange labels with poster and lyric innersleeves

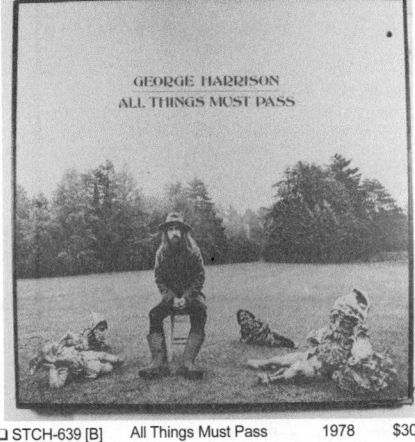

❏ STCH-639 [B]	All Things Must Pass	1978	$30

—Purple labels with poster and lyric innersleeves

❏ STCH-639	All Things Must Pass	1983	$150

—Black labels, print in colorband, with poster and lyric innersleeves

❏ SN-16055	Dark Horse	1980	$18

—Budget-line reissue; reverses front and back covers

❏ SN-16217	Extra Texture (Read All About It)	1980	$30

—Budget-line reissue

❏ SN-16216	Living in the Material World	1980	$25

—Budget-line reissue

❏ ST-11578	The Best of George Harrison	1976	$18

—Custom label, no bar code on back

❏ ST-11578	The Best of George Harrison	1976	$180

—Orange label

❏ ST-11578	The Best of George Harrison	1978	$12

—Purple label, large Capitol logo

❏ ST-11578	The Best of George Harrison	1983	$30

—Black label, print in colorband

❏ ST-11578	The Best of George Harrison	1988	$30

—Odd reissue with custom label; large stand-alone "S" in trail-off area; bar code on cover

❏ ST-11578	The Best of George Harrison	1989	$100

—Purple label, small Capitol logo

CAPITOL/APPLE
❏ STCH-639	All Things Must Pass	1988	$100

—Odd pressing with Apple labels and Capitol cover (look for stand-alone "S" in trail-off wax); with large sticker on back cover

DARK HORSE
❏ PRO649 [DJ]	A Personal Music Dialogue at Thirty Three and 1/3	1976	$50
❏ PRO649 [DJ]	A Personal Music Dialogue at Thirty Three and 1/3	1976	$40
❏ 25726	Best of Dark Horse 1976-1989	1989	$30
❏ W1-25726	Best of Dark Horse 1976-1989	1989	$18

—Columbia House edition

❏ R180307	Best of Dark Horse 1976-1989	1989	$18

—BMG Direct Marketing edition

❏ 25643	Cloud Nine	1987	$12
❏ W1-25643	Cloud Nine	1987	$15

—Columbia House edition

❏ R174328	Cloud Nine	1987	$18

—BMG Direct Marketing edition

❏ 0(no cat #) [DJ]	Dark Horse Radio Special	1974	$400

—Promo-only; George Harrison introduces his new record label and artists

❏ 0(no cat #) [DJ]	Dark Horse Radio Special	1974	$400

—Promo-only; George Harrison introduces his new record label and artists

❏ DHK3255	George Harrison	1979	$12

—Deduct 30% for cut-outs

❏ DHK3255	George Harrison	1979	$40

Number	Title	Yr	NM

— Columbia House edition (back cover says "Manufactured by Columbia House Under License

| ❏ 23724 [DJ] | Gone Troppo | 1982 | $30 |

— Promo on Quiex II vinyl

| ❏ 23724 [B] | Gone Troppo | 1982 | $12 |

— Deduct 30% for cut-outs

| ❏ 23724 [DJ] | Gone Troppo | 1982 | $30 |

— Promo on Quiex II vinyl

| ❏ DHK3492 | Somewhere in England | 1981 | $12 |

— Deduct 30% for cut-outs

| ❏ DH3005 | Thirty Three and 1/3 | 1976 | $12 |

—Deduct 30% for cut-outs

ZAPPLE

| ❏ ST-3358 [B] | Electronic Sound | 1969 | $150 |

HARRISON, JERRY
SIRE

❏ 25663	Casual Gods	1988	$12
❏ SRK3631	The Red and the Black	1981	$12
❏ 25943	Walk on Water	1990	$12

HARRISON, NOEL
LONDON

| ❏ LL3459 [M] | Noel Harrison | 1966 | $25 |
| ❏ PS459 [S] | Noel Harrison | 1966 | $30 |

REPRISE

❏ R-6263 [M]	Collage	1967	$18
❏ RS-6263 [S]	Collage	1967	$25
❏ RS-6295 [S]	Santa Monica Pier	1968	$18
❏ R-6295 [M]	Santa Monica Pier	1968	$40

— White label promo only

| ❏ RS-6321 | The Great Electric Experiment Is Over | 1969 | $18 |

HARRISON, WENDELL
REBIRTH

❏ WHR-140	Birth of a Fossil	1986	$25
❏ WHR-160	Carnivorous Lady	1988	$30
❏ WHR-015	Dreams of a Love Supreme	1985	$25
❏ WHR-016	Organic Dream	1985	$25
❏ WHR-040	Reawakening	1985	$25
❏ WHR-150	Wait" Broke the Wagon Down	1987	$25

TRIBE

| ❏ PRSD-2212 | Evening with the Devil | 197? | $150 |
| ❏ PRSD-4002 | Message from the Tribe, Vol. 3 | 197? | $150 |

WENHA

| ❏ 015 | Dreams of a Love Supreme | 198? | $50 |
| ❏ 2212 | Evening with the Devil | 198? | $25 |

— Reissue of Tribe 2212

| ❏ 4002 | Message from the Tribe | 198? | $25 |

— Reissue of Tribe 4002

| ❏ 016 | Organic Dream | 198? | $40 |

HARRISON, WES
PHILIPS

| ❏ PHM200103 [M] | You Won't Believe Your Ears | 1963 | $25 |
| ❏ PHS600103 [S] | You Won't Believe Your Ears | 1963 | $30 |

HARRISON, WILBERT
BUDDAH

| ❏ BDS-5002 | Wilbert Harrison | 1971 | $30 |

CHELSEA

| ❏ CH523 | Wilbert Harrison | 1977 | $25 |

JUGGERNAUT

| ❏ ST-8803 [B] | Shoot You Full of Love | 1971 | $50 |

SAVOY JAZZ

| ❏ SJL-1182 | Listen to My Song | 1987 | $15 |

SPHERE SOUND

| ❏ SSR-7000 [M] | Kansas City | 1965 | $300 |
| ❏ SSSR-7000 [R] | Kansas City | 1965 | $250 |

SUE

| ❏ SSLP-8801 | Let's Work Together | 1970 | $50 |

WET SOUL

| ❏ 1001 | Anything You Want | 197? | $50 |

HARROW, NANCY
ATLANTIC

| ❏ 8075 [M] | You Never Know | 1963 | $75 |
| ❏ SD8075 [S] | You Never Know | 1963 | $75 |

AUDIOPHILE

| ❏ AP-142 | Anything Goes | 1979 | $30 |

CANDID

| ❏ CD-8008 [M] | Wild Women Don't Have the Blues | 1962 | $75 |
| ❏ CD-9008 [S] | Wild Women Don't Have the Blues | 1962 | $40 |

HARRY, DEBBIE
CHRYSALIS

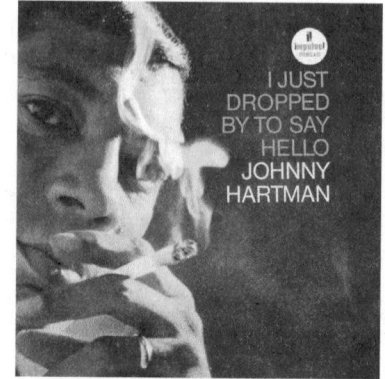

| ❏ FV41347 [B] | Koo Koo | 1983 | $12 |

—Reissue

| ❏ CHR1347 | Koo Koo | 1981 | $12 |

GEFFEN

| ❏ R124347 | Rockbird | 1986 | $15 |

—RCA Music Service edition

| ❏ GHS24123 | Rockbird | 1986 | $12 |

SIRE

| ❏ 25938 | Def, Dumb & Blonde | 1989 | $15 |

HART, BILLY
GRAMAVISION

| ❏ 18-8502 | Oshumare | 1986 | $30 |

HORIZON

| ❏ SP-725 | Enchance | 1978 | $30 |

HART, CLAY
METROMEDIA

| ❏ 1008 | Spring | 1969 | $18 |

RANWOOD

| ❏ 8122 | Most Requested Country Favorites | 1973 | $12 |
| ❏ 8135 | Travelin' Minstrel Man | 1974 | $12 |

HART, FREDDIE
CAPITOL

❏ ST-11073	Bless Your Heart	1972	$15
❏ ST-593	California Grapevine	1970	$15
❏ ST-11353	Country Heart 'N' Soul	1975	$15
❏ ST-838	Easy Loving	1971	$15
❏ ST-11107	Got the All-Overs	1972	$15
❏ ST-11374	Greatest Hits	1975	$15
❏ ST-11296	Hang In There Girl	1974	$15
❏ ST-11252	If You Can't Feel It	1974	$15
❏ ST-11014	My Hang-Up Is You	1972	$15
❏ ST-469	New Sounds	1970	$15
❏ ST-11724	Only You	1978	$12
❏ ST-11504	People Put to Music	1976	$12
❏ ST-11156	Super Kind of Woman	1973	$15
❏ ST-11568	That Look in Her Eyes	1976	$12
❏ ST-11449	The First Time	1975	$12
❏ ST-11626	The Pleasure's Been All Mine	1977	$12
❏ ST-11197	Trip to Heaven	1973	$15

COLUMBIA

| ❏ CL1792 [M] | The Spirited Freddie Hart | 1962 | $40 |
| ❏ G31550 | The World of Freddie Hart | 1972 | $18 |

HARMONY

❏ KH31165	Lonesome Love	1972	$12
❏ HL7412 [M]	The Best of Freddie Hart	1967	$15
❏ HS11212 [S]	The Best of Freddie Hart	1967	$15
❏ KH32467	You Are My World	1973	$12

HILLTOP

| ❏ 6117 | From Canada to Tennessee | 1972 | $12 |

KAPP

❏ KS-3568	Born a Fool	1968	$25
❏ KS-3592	Greatest Hits	1969	$18
❏ KL-1513 [M]	Hurtin' Man	1967	$25
❏ KS-3513 [S]	Hurtin' Man	1967	$25
❏ KL-1492 [M]	Straight from the Heart	1966	$18
❏ KS-3492 [S]	Straight from the Heart	1966	$25
❏ KL-1456 [M]	The Hart of Country Music	1966	$18
❏ KS-3456 [S]	The Hart of Country Music	1966	$25
❏ KL-1539 [M]	The Neon and the Rain	1967	$25
❏ KS-3539 [S]	The Neon and the Rain	1967	$25
❏ KS-3546	Togetherness	1968	$25

MCA

| ❏ 4088 | The Best of Freddie Hart | 1975 | $18 |

SUNBIRD

| ❏ ST-50100 | Sure Thing | 1980 | $15 |

HART, JOHN
BLUE NOTE

| ❏ B1-93476 | One Down | 1990 | $35 |

HART, MICKEY, AIRTO, FLORA PURIM, BATUCAJE
REFERENCE RECORDINGS

| ❏ RR-12 | Dafos | 1985 | $18 |

HART, MICKEY
Also see THE GRATEFUL DEAD.

RELIX

| ❏ 2026 [B] | Rolling Thunder | 1987 | $15 |

WARNER BROS.

| ❏ BS2635 | Rolling Thunder | 1972 | $25 |

HART, ROD
PLANTATION

| ❏ 500 | Breakeroo! | 1976 | $15 |

HARTFORD, JOHN
FLYING FISH

❏ FF-044	All in the Name of Love	1983	$12
❏ FF-259	Catalogue	1982	$12
❏ FF-289	Gum Tree Canoe	1984	$12
❏ FF-063	Headin' Down Into the Mystery Below	1978	$12
❏ FF-020	Mark Twang	1976	$12
❏ FF-440	Me Oh My, How Time Flies	1987	$12
❏ FF-028	Nobody Knows What You Do	1977	$12
❏ FF-095	Slumberin' on the Cumberland	1979	$12

— With Pat Burton and Benny Martin

| ❏ FF-228 | You and Me at Home | 1980 | $12 |

MCA

| ❏ 5861 | Annual Waltz | 1987 | $10 |

RCA VICTOR

❏ LPM-3796 [M]	Earthwords and Music	1967	$30
❏ LSP-3796 [S]	Earthwords and Music	1967	$18
❏ LSP-4068	Gentle on My Mind and Other Originals	1968	$18
❏ LPM-3998 [M]	Housing Project	1968	$50
❏ LSP-3998 [S]	Housing Project	1968	$18
❏ LSP-4337	Iron Mountain Depot	1970	$18
❏ LSP-4156	John Hartford	1969	$18
❏ LPM-3687 [M]	John Hartford Looks at Life	1966	$25
❏ LSP-3687 [S]	John Hartford Looks at Life	1966	$18
❏ LPM-3884 [M]	The Love Album	1967	$30
❏ LSP-3884 [S]	The Love Album	1967	$18

WARNER BROS.

| ❏ WS1916 | Aereo-Plain | 1971 | $15 |
| ❏ BS2651 | Morning Bugle | 1972 | $15 |

HARTH, ALFRED
ECM

| ❏ 1264 | This Earth | 198? | $25 |

HARTLEY, KEEF
DERAM

❏ DES18024 [B]	Halfbreed	1969	$25
❏ XDES18070	Lancashire Hustler	1973	$18
❏ DES18057	Overdog	1971	$18
❏ XDES18065	The 72nd Brave	1972	$18
❏ DES18035	The Battle of North West Six	1970	$18
❏ DES18047	The Time Is Near	1970	$18

HARTMAN, DAN
BLUE SKY

| ❏ JZ35641 | Instant Replay | 1978 | $15 |
| ❏ JZ36302 | Relight My Fire | 1980 | $15 |

MCA

| ❏ 5525 | I Can Dream About You | 1984 | $12 |

HARTMAN, JOHNNY
ABC IMPULSE!

Number	Title	Yr	NM
❑ AS-57 [S]	I Just Dropped By to Say Hello	1968	$30
❑ AS-74 [S]	The Voice That Is	1968	$30
ABC-PARAMOUNT			
❑ ABC-574 [M]	The Unforgettable Johnny Hartman	1966	$30
❑ ABCS-574 [S]	The Unforgettable Johnny Hartman	1966	$40
AUDIOPHILE			
❑ AP-181	This One's for Tedi	1981	$30
BEE HIVE			
❑ BH-7012	Once in Every Life	198?	$25
BETHLEHEM			
❑ BCP-6045	All of Me	197?	$30
— Reissue, distributed by RCA Victor			
❑ BCP-6014 [M]	All of Me: The Debonair Mr. Hartman	1957	$300
❑ BCP-43 [M]	Songs from the Heart	1956	$300
IMPULSE!			
❑ A-57 [M]	I Just Dropped By to Say Hello	1964	$250
❑ AS-57 [S]	I Just Dropped By to Say Hello	1964	$250
❑ A-74 [M]	The Voice That Is	1965	$250
❑ AS-74 [S]	The Voice That Is	1965	$250
MCA			
❑ 29039	I Just Dropped By to Say Hello	1980	$25
❑ 29040	The Voice That Is	1980	$25
MUSICOR			
❑ 2502	Johnny Hartman, Johnny Hartman	1976	$30
PERCEPTION			
❑ PLP-41	I've Been There	1973	$35
REGENT			
❑ MG-6014 [M]	Just You, Just Me	1956	$100
SAVOY JAZZ			
❑ SJL-1134	First, Lasting and Always	198?	$25

HARTMAN, LISA

Number	Title	Yr	NM
KIRSHNER			
❑ JZ35609	Hold On	1978	$30
❑ PZ34109	Lisa Hartman	1976	$30

HARUMI

Number	Title	Yr	NM
VERVE FORECAST			
❑ FTS-3030 [B]	Harumi	1968	$30

HARVEY, ALEX (1)

Number	Title	Yr	NM
ATLANTIC			
❑ SD18248 [B]	Live	1975	$18
VERTIGO			
❑ VEL-1017 [B]	Next	1973	$75
❑ VEL-2000 [B]	The Impossible Dream	1974	$40
❑ VEL-2004 [B]	Tomorrow Belongs to Me	1975	$40

HARVEY, ALEX (2)

Number	Title	Yr	NM
CAPITOL			
❑ ST-789	Alex Harvey	1972	$15
❑ ST-11128	Souvenirs	1973	$15

HARVEY, LAURENCE

Number	Title	Yr	NM
ATLANTIC			
❑ 1367 [M]	This Is My Beloved	1962	$175
❑ SD1367 [S]	This Is My Beloved	1962	$175

HARVEY, PJ

Number	Title	Yr	NM
ISLAND			
❑ 524085-1	To Bring You My Love	1995	$18

HASHIM, MICHAEL

Number	Title	Yr	NM
STASH			
❑ 227	Peacocks	1983	$25

HASKELL, JACK

Number	Title	Yr	NM
STRAND			
❑ SL-1020 [M]	Jack Haskell Swings for Jack Paar	1961	$25
❑ SLS-1020 [S]	Jack Haskell Swings for Jack Paar	1961	$30

HASKELL, JIMMIE

Number	Title	Yr	NM
IMPERIAL			
❑ LP-9068 [M]	Countdown	1959	$30
❑ LP-12015 [S]	Countdown	1959	$50

HASKILL, CLARA

Number	Title	Yr	NM
MERCURY LIVING PRESENCE			
❑ SR90413 [S]	Mozart: Piano Concertos No. 20 and 23; Rondo in A	196?	$30
— Maroon label, no "Vendor: Mercury Record Corporation"			
❑ SR90413 [S]	Mozart: Piano Concertos No. 20 and 23; Rondo in A	196?	$100
— Maroon label, with "Vendor: Mercury Record Corporation" (second edition is more sought after than the first)			

HASSELBACH, MARK

Number	Title	Yr	NM
JAZZIMAGE			
❑ JZ-104	Hasselblast	198?	$30

HASSELL, JON

Number	Title	Yr	NM
ECM			
❑ 1327	Power Spot	1987	$30
INTUITION			
❑ C1-91186	Flash of the Spirit	1989	$30
❑ C1-46880	The Surgeon of the Nightsky Restores Dead Things by the Power of Sound	1988	$30
LOVELY			
❑ 1021	Vernal Equinox	1978	$35
OPAL/WARNER BROS.			
❑ 26153	City: Works of Fiction	1990	$35
TOMATO			
❑ TOM-7019	Earthquake Island	1979	$35

HASSLES, THE
BILLY JOEL was in this group.

Number	Title	Yr	NM
LIBERTY			
❑ LN-10139	Hour of the Wolf	1981	$15
❑ LN-10138	The Hassles	1981	$15
UNITED ARTISTS			
❑ UAS-6699	Hour of the Wolf	1969	$30
❑ UAS-6631 [B]	The Hassles	1968	$30

HASTINGS ST JAZZ EXPERIENCE

Number	Title	Yr	NM
MIDNITE			
❑ MR1976 [B]	The Detroit Jazz Composers Ltd	1976	$600

HATCHER, ROGER

Number	Title	Yr	NM
GUINNESS			
❑ GNS36033 [B]	R & Better	1977	$300

HATFIELD, BOBBY

Number	Title	Yr	NM
MGM			
❑ SE-4727	Messin' in Muscle Shoals	1971	$15

HATHAWAY, DONNY

Number	Title	Yr	NM
ATCO			
❑ SD 33-360	Donny Hathaway	1971	$15
❑ SD 33-386	Donny Hathaway Live	1972	$15
❑ SD 33-332	Everything Is Everything	1970	$15
❑ SD7029	Extension of a Man	1973	$12
❑ QD7029 [Q]	Extension of a Man	1974	$30
❑ SD 38-107	The Best of Donny Hathaway	1978	$12
ATLANTIC			
❑ SD19278	In Performance	1980	$12
RHINO			
❑ R1541097 [B]	Live at the Bitter End, 1971	2014	$30

HATZA, GREG

Number	Title	Yr	NM
CORAL			
❑ CRL57495 [M]	Organized Jazz	1963	$35
❑ CRL757495 [S]	Organized Jazz	1963	$25
❑ CRL57493 [M]	The Wizardry of Greg Hatza	1962	$30
❑ CRL757493 [S]	The Wizardry of Greg Hatza	1962	$35

HAUSER, FRITZ

Number	Title	Yr	NM
HAT ART			
❑ 2023	Solodrumming	1986	$35

HAVENS, BOB

Number	Title	Yr	NM
GHB			
❑ GHB-143 [M]	Bob Havens' New Orleans All-Stars	1969	$150
SOUTHLAND			
❑ 226 [M]	Bob Havens in New Orleans	1961	$35
❑ 243 [M]	Bob Havens' New Orleans All-Stars	1966	$30

HAVENS, RICHIE

Number	Title	Yr	NM
A&M			
❑ SP-4641	Mirage	1977	$12
❑ SP-4598	The End of the Beginning	1976	$12
DOUGLAS			
❑ D-780 [M]	Electric Havens	1966	$25
❑ SD-780 [S]	Electric Havens	1966	$18
❑ D-779 [M]	Richie Havens' Record	1966	$25
❑ SD-779 [S]	Richie Havens' Record	1966	$16
ELEKTRA			
❑ 6E-242	Connections	1980	$12
MGM			
❑ SE-4698	Mixed Bag	1970	$18
— Reissue of Verve Forecast 3006			
❑ SE-4700	Richard P. Havens, 1963	1970	$25
— Reissue of Verve Forecast 3047			
❑ SE-4699	Something Else Again	1970	$18
— Reissue of Verve Forecast 3034			

Number	Title	Yr	NM
RBI			
❑ 400	Simple Things	1987	$12
STORMY FOREST			
❑ SFS-6005	Alarm Clock	1970	$15
❑ SFS-6201	Mixed Bag II	1974	$15
❑ SFS-6013	Portfolio	1973	$15
❑ SFS-6012 [B]	Richie Havens On Stage	1972	$25
❑ SFS-6001	Stonehenge	1969	$18
❑ SFS-6010	The Great Blind Degree	1971	$15
SUNDAZED			
❑ LP5476 [M]	Mixed Bag	2015	$20
VERVE FOLKWAYS			
❑ FT-3006 [M]	Mixed Bag	1967	$30
❑ FTS-3006 [S]	Mixed Bag	1967	$25
VERVE FORECAST			
❑ FTS-3006	Mixed Bag	1968	$18
❑ FTS-3047	Richard P. Havens, 1983	1968	$30
❑ FTS-3061	Richie Havens	1969	$0
— Canceled			
❑ FT-3034 [M]	Something Else Again	1968	$50

Number	Title	Yr	NM
❑ FTS-3034 [S]	Something Else Again	1968	$25

HAWES, HAMPTON

Number	Title	Yr	NM
ARISTA FREEDOM			
❑ AL1043	Copenhagen Night Music	1977	$50
❑ AL1020	Live at the Montmartre	1976	$50
BLACK LION			
❑ 122	Spanish Steps	197?	$50
CONCORD JAZZ			
❑ CJ-222	Recorded Live at the Great American Music Hall	198?	$35
CONTEMPORARY			
❑ C-3545 [M]	All Night Session! Volume 1	1958	$300
❑ S-7545 [S]	All Night Session! Volume 1	1960	$300
❑ C-3546 [M]	All Night Session! Volume 2	1958	$300
❑ S-7546 [S]	All Night Session! Volume 2	1960	$300
❑ C-3547 [M]	All Night Session! Volume 3	1958	$300
❑ S-7547 [S]	All Night Session! Volume 3	1960	$300
❑ C-3523 [M]	Everybody Likes Hampton Hawes	1956	$250
❑ M-3589 [M]	For Real!	1959	$300
❑ S-7589 [S]	For Real!	1959	$300
❑ C-3553 [M]	Four! Hampton Hawes!!!	1958	$300
❑ S-7553 [S]	Four! Hampton Hawes!!!	1960	$300
❑ C-3505 [M]	Hampton Hawes	1955	$250
❑ M-3616 [M]	Here and Now	1965	$175
❑ S-7616 [S]	Here and Now	1965	$175
❑ M-3631 [M]	I'm All Smiles	1967	$175
❑ S-7631 [S]	I'm All Smiles	1967	$175
❑ M-3614 [M]	The Green Leaves of Summer	1964	$250
❑ S-7614 [S]	The Green Leaves of Summer	1964	$250
❑ M-3621 [M]	The Seance	1966	$175
❑ S-7621 [S]	The Seance	1966	$175
❑ C-3515 [M]	This Is Hampton Hawes	1956	$250
ENJA			
❑ 3099	Live at Jazz Showcase in Chicago, Vol. 1	198?	$35
FANTASY			
❑ OJC-638	All Night Session! Volume 1	1991	$35
❑ OJC-639	All Night Session! Volume 2	1991	$35
❑ OJC-640	All Night Session! Volume 3	1991	$35
❑ OJC-421	Everybody Likes Hampton Hawes	1990	$35
❑ OJC-165	Four! Hampton Hawes!!!	198?	$30
❑ OJC-316	Hampton Hawes	198?	$30
❑ OJC-178	I'm All Smiles	198?	$30
❑ OJC-455	Seance	1990	$35
❑ OJC-476	The Green Leaves of Summer	1991	$35
❑ OJC-318	This Is Hampton Hawes	198?	$30
JAS			
❑ JAS-4002	Hampton Hawes Trio at Montreux	1976	$35
❑ JAS-4004	The Two Sides of Hampton Hawes	1977	$50

Richie Havens — Something Else Again

HAWES, HAMPTON

Number	Title	Yr	NM
JAZZ MAN			
5022	Spanish Steps	198?	$25
MOON			
MLP-005	Autumn Leaves in Paris	1990	$75
PRESTIGE			
PR-10060	Blues for Walls	1973	$75
PRST-7695	Hampton Hawes in Europe	1969	$75
PRLP-212 [10]	Hampton Hawes Quartet	1955	$300
10088	Northern Windows	1974	$40
P-10077	Playin' in the Yard	1974	$75
PR-10046	The Universe	1972	$75
RCA VICTOR			
JPL1-1508	Challenge	1976	$50
STEREO RECORDS			
S-7026 [S]	Four! Hampton Hawes!!!	1959	$150
VANTAGE			
VLP-1 [10]	Hamp Hawes	1954	$300
VAULT			
LPS-9009	Hampton Hawes Plays Movie Musicals	1969	$25
LPS-9010	High in the Sky	1970	$30
XANADU			
161	Memorial Album	198?	$35

HAWES, HAMPTON/PAUL CHAMBERS

Number	Title	Yr	NM
XANADU			
104	The East/West Controversy	1975	$75

HAWKINS, COLEMAN, AND BENNY CARTER

Number	Title	Yr	NM
MOON			
MLP-001	Jammin' the Blues	199?	$35
SWING			
8403	Coleman Hawkins and Benny Carter	1985	$25

HAWKINS, COLEMAN, AND BUD POWELL

Number	Title	Yr	NM
BLACK LION			
159	Hawk in Germany	197?	$30

HAWKINS, COLEMAN, AND CLARK TERRY

Number	Title	Yr	NM
COLUMBIA			
CL1991 [M]	Back in Bean's Bag	1963	$35
CS8791 [S]	Back in Bean's Bag	1963	$25
CS8791 [S]	Back in Bean's Bag	1999	$30
— *Classic Records reissue on audiophile vinyl*			

HAWKINS, COLEMAN, AND FRANK HUNTER

Number	Title	Yr	NM
MIRA			
M-3003 [M]	The Hawk and the Hunter	1965	$25
MS-3003 [S]	The Hawk and the Hunter	1965	$30

HAWKINS, COLEMAN, AND LESTER YOUNG

Number	Title	Yr	NM
DOCTOR JAZZ			
FW38446	Classic Tenors	1983	$25
FLYING DUTCHMAN			
BXM1-2823	Classic Tenors	1978	$30
ZIM			
1000	Coleman Hawkins and Lester Young	197?	$25

HAWKINS, COLEMAN, AND PEE WEE RUSSELL

Number	Title	Yr	NM
CANDID			
CD-8020 [M]	Jazz Reunion	1960	$40
CS-9020 [S]	Jazz Reunion	1960	$40

HAWKINS, COLEMAN, AND ROY ELDREDGE

Number	Title	Yr	NM
PHOENIX			
3	Coleman Hawkins and Roy Eldredge 1939	197?	$25
VERVE			
MGV-8266 [M]	At the Opera House	1958	$175
V-8266 [M]	At the Opera House	1961	$75
MGVS-6028 [S]	At the Opera House	1960	$175
V6-8266 [S]	At the Opera House	1961	$75

HAWKINS, COLEMAN; ROY ELDREDGE; JOHNNY HODGES

Number	Title	Yr	NM
VERVE			
V-8509 [M]	Alive at the Village Gate	1963	$25
V6-8509 [S]	Alive at the Village Gate	1963	$30
V6-8509 [S]	Alive at the Village Gate	199?	$30
— *Classic Records reissue on audiophile vinyl*			

HAWKINS, COLEMAN; ROY ELDREDGE; PETE BROWN; JO JONES

Number	Title	Yr	NM
VERVE			
MGV-8240 [M]	All Stars at Newport	1958	$175
V-8240 [M]	All Stars at Newport	1961	$75

HAWKINS, COLEMAN

Number	Title	Yr	NM
ABC IMPULSE!			
AS-28 [S]	Desafinado	1968	$35
AS-26 [S]	Duke Ellington Meets Coleman Hawkins	1968	$35
AS-9258	Reevaluations: The Impulse Years	197?	$35
AS-34 [S]	Today and Now	1968	$35
AS-87 [S]	Wrapped Tight	1968	$35
ADVANCE			
LSP-9 [10]	Coleman Hawkins Favorites	1951	$300
AMERICAN RECORDING SOCIETY			
G-316 [M]	Coleman Hawkins and His Orchestra	1956	$50
APOLLO			
LAP-101 [10]	Coleman Hawkins All Stars	1951	$300
BLUEBIRD			
5658-1-RB	Body and Soul	1986	$35
BRUNSWICK			
BL58030 [10]	Tenor Sax	1952	$250
CAPITOL			
H327 [10]	Classics in Jazz	1952	$300
T819 [M]	Gilded Hawk	1957	$175
M-11030	Hollywood Stampede	1973	$35
COMMODORE			
XFL-14936	Coleman Hawkins	198?	$25
FL-20025 [10]	King of the Tenor Sax	1952	$300
CONCERT HALL JAZZ			
J-1201 [M]	Improvisations Unlimited	1955	$85
CONTINENTAL			
16006 [M]	On the Bean	1962	$30
S-16006 [S]	On the Bean	1962	$30
CROWN			
CLP-5181 [M]	Coleman Hawkins and His Orchestra	1960	$25
CST-206 [R]	Coleman Hawkins and His Orchestra	196?	$25
CLP-5207 [M]	The Hawk Swing	1961	$25
CST-224 [R]	The Hawk Swing	196?	$25
DECCA			
DL4081 [M]	The Hawk Blows at Midnight	1961	$30
DL74081 [S]	The Hawk Blows at Midnight	1961	$40
DL8127 [M]	The Hawk Talks	1955	$175
EMARCY			
MG-26013 [10]	The Bean	1954	$300
EVEREST ARCHIVE OF FOLK & JAZZ			
252	Coleman Hawkins	197?	$25
FANTASY			
OJC-181	At Ease with Coleman Hawkins	1985	$25
OJC-418	Coleman Hawkins Plus the Red Garland Trio	1990	$30
OJC-294	Hawk Eyes	1988	$25
OJC-6001	In a Mellow Tone	1988	$25
OJC-420	Night Hawk	1990	$30
OJC-096	Soul	198?	$25
OJC-225	The Coleman Hawkins All Stars	198?	$25
OJC-027	The Hawk Flies High	1982	$25
FELSTED			
FAJ-7005 [M]	The High and Mighty Hawk	1959	$75
SJA-2005 [S]	The High and Mighty Hawk	1959	$100
GNP CRESCENDO			
GNP-9003	Coleman Hawkins in Holland	197?	$25
GRP IMPULSE!			
227 [S]	Desafinado	199?	$35
— *Reissue on audiophile vinyl*			
IMPULSE!			
A-28 [M]	Desafinado	1963	$120
AS-28 [S]	Desafinado	1963	$120
A-26 [M]	Duke Ellington Meets Coleman Hawkins	1962	$120
AS-26 [S]	Duke Ellington Meets Coleman Hawkins	1962	$120
A-34 [M]	Today and Now	1963	$120
AS-34 [S]	Today and Now	1963	$120
A-87 [M]	Wrapped Tight	1965	$250
AS-87 [S]	Wrapped Tight	1965	$250
JAZZ MAN			
5042	Jazz Reunion	198?	$25
JAZZTONE			
J-1201 [M]	Timeless Jazz	1955	$75
— *Reissue of Concert Hall Jazz 1201*			
MAINSTREAM			
56037 [M]	Meditations	1965	$30
S-6037 [R]	Meditations	1965	$35
MASTER JAZZ			
8115	The High and Mighty Hawk	197?	$30
MILESTONE			
M-47015	The Hawk Flies	1973	$35
MOODSVILLE			
MVLP-7 [M]	At Ease with Coleman Hawkins	1960	$50
— *Green label*			
MVLP-7 [M]	At Ease with Coleman Hawkins	1965	$30
— *Blue label, trident logo at right*			
MVLP-23 [M]	Good Old Broadway	1962	$40
— *Gren label*			
MVLP-23 [M]	Good Old Broadway	1965	$25
— *Blue label, trident logo at right*			
MVST-23 [S]	Good Old Broadway	1962	$50
— *Green label*			
MVST-23 [S]	Good Old Broadway	1965	$30
— *Blue label, trident logo at right*			
MVLP-31 [M]	Make Someone Happy	1963	$40
— *Green label*			
MVLP-31 [M]	Make Someone Happy	1965	$25
— *Blue label, trident logo at right*			
MVST-31 [S]	Make Someone Happy	1963	$50
— *Green label*			
MVST-31 [S]	Make Someone Happy	1965	$30
— *Blue label, trident logo at right*			
MVLP-15 [M]	The Hawk Relaxes	1961	$50
— *Green label*			
MVLP-15 [M]	The Hawk Relaxes	1965	$30
— *Blue label, trident logo at right*			
MVLP-25 [M]	The Jazz Version of No Strings	1962	$40
— *Green label*			
MVLP-25 [M]	The Jazz Version of No Strings	1965	$25
— *Blue label, trident logo at right*			
MVST-25 [S]	The Jazz Version of No Strings	1962	$50
— *Green label*			
MVST-25 [S]	The Jazz Version of No Strings	1965	$30
— *Blue label, trident logo at right*			
MOON			
MLP-018	Coleman Hawkins Vs. Oscar Peterson	199?	$35
PABLO			
2310933	Bean Stalkin'	198?	$30
2310707	Sirius	197?	$35
PHILIPS			
PHM200022 [M]	Jazz at the Metropole	1962	$25
PHS600022 [S]	Jazz at the Metropole	1962	$30
PHOENIX			
13	Centerpiece	197?	$25
8	In Concert	197?	$25
PRESTIGE			
PRST-7824	Bean and the Boys	1970	$35
PRST-7753	Blues Groove	1970	$35
PRST-7824	Coleman Hawkins and the Boys	1971	$30
PRLP-7156 [M]	Hawk Eyes	1958	$300
PRST-7857	Hawk Eyes!	1971	$35
24051	Jam Session in Swingville	198?	$30
P-24106	Moonglow	1981	$30
PRST-7671	Night Hawk	1969	$35
PRST-7647	Pioneers	1969	$35
PRLP-7149 [M]	Soul	1958	$250
24083	The Real Thing	198?	$30
QUINTESSENCE			
25371	Golden Hawk	1979	$25
RCA VICTOR			
LPV-501 [M]	Body and Soul	1965	$25
LJM-1017 [M]	Hawk In Flight	1955	$100

THE HAWK IN HI FI — COLEMAN HAWKINS WITH BILLY BYERS AND HIS ORCHESTRA — RCA VICTOR LPM-1281

Number	Title	Yr	NM
LPM-1281 [M]	Hawk in Hi-Fi	1956	$100
RIVERSIDE			
RLP 12-117/8 [M]	Coleman Hawkins: A Documentary	1956	$300
RLP 12-233 [M]	The Hawk Flies High	1957	$250
— *White label, blue print*			
RLP 12-233 [M]	The Hawk Flies High	1959	$300
— *Blue label, microphone logo at top*			
3049	Think Deep	1970	$150

Number	Title	Yr	NM

SAVOY
| MG-12013 [M] | The Hawk Returns | 1955 | $120 |
| MG-15039 [10] | The Hawk Talks | 1954 | $250 |

SAVOY JAZZ
| SJL-1123 | Coleman Hawkins Meets the Big Sax Section | 1979 | $25 |

STINSON
| SLP-22 [10] | Originals with Hawkins | 1950 | $300 |
| SLP-22 [M] | Originals with Hawkins | 195? | $40 |

SUNBEAM
| 204 | Coleman Hawkins at the Savoy 1940 | 197? | $25 |

SWINGVILLE
SVLP-2035 [M]	Blues Groove	1962	$50
—Purple label			
SVLP-2035 [M]	Blues Groove	1965	$30
—Blue label, trident logo at right			
SVST-2035 [S]	Blues Groove	1962	$40
—Red label			
SVST-2035 [S]	Blues Groove	1965	$25
—Blue label, trident logo at right			
SVLP-2001 [M]	Coleman Hawkins Plus the Red Garland Trio	1960	$50
—Purple label			
SVLP-2001 [M]	Coleman Hawkins Plus the Red Garland Trio	1965	$30
—Blue label, trident logo at right			
SVLP-2039 [M]	Hawk Eyes	1962	$50
—Purple label			
SVLP-2039 [M]	Hawk Eyes	1965	$30
—Blue label, trident logo at right			
SVST-2039 [S]	Hawk Eyes	1962	$40
—Red label			
SVST-2039 [S]	Hawk Eyes	1965	$25
—Blue label, trident logo at right			
SVLP-2016 [M]	Night Hawk	1961	$50
—Purple label			
SVLP-2016 [M]	Night Hawk	1965	$30
—Blue label, trident logo at right			
SVLP-2038 [M]	Soul	1962	$50
—Purple label			
SVLP-2038 [M]	Soul	1965	$30
—Blue label, trident logo at right			
SVST-2038 [S]	Soul	1962	$40
—Red label			
SVST-2038 [S]	Soul	1965	$25
—Blue label, trident logo at right			
SVLP-2005 [M]	The Coleman Hawkins All Stars	1960	$50
—Purple label			
SVLP-2005 [M]	The Coleman Hawkins All Stars	1965	$30
—Blue label, trident logo at right			
SVLP-2024 [M]	Things Ain't What They Used to Be	1961	$40
—Purple label			
SVLP-2024 [M]	Things Ain't What They Used to Be	1965	$25
—Blue label, trident logo at right			
SVST-2024 [S]	Things Ain't What They Used to Be	1961	$50
—Red label			
SVST-2024 [S]	Things Ain't What They Used to Be	1965	$30
—Blue label, trident logo at right			
SVLP-2025 [M]	Years Ago	1961	$40
—Purple label			
SVLP-2025 [M]	Years Ago	1965	$50
—Blue label, trident logo at right			
SVST-2025 [S]	Years Ago	1961	$150
—Red label			
SVST-2025 [S]	Years Ago	1965	$75
—Blue label, trident logo at right			

TIME-LIFE
| STL-J-06 | Giants of Jazz | 1979 | $50 |

TRIP
| 5515 | Coleman Hawkins and the Trumpet Kings | 197? | $25 |

URANIA
| UJLP-1201 [M] | Accent on Tenor Sax | 1955 | $150 |
| UJLP-41201 [R] | Accent on Tenor Sax | 196? | $175 |

VERVE
MGV-8346 [M]	Coleman Hawkins and His Confreres with the Oscar Peterson Trio	1959	$175
MGVS-6110 [S]	Coleman Hawkins and His Confreres with the Oscar Peterson Trio	1960	$150
V-8346 [M]	Coleman Hawkins and His Confreres with the Oscar Peterson Trio	1961	$30
V6-8346 [S]	Coleman Hawkins and His Confreres with the Oscar Peterson Trio	1961	$25
UMV-2623	Coleman Hawkins at Newport	198?	$25
MGV-8327 [M]	Coleman Hawkins Encounters Ben Webster	1959	$175

MGVS-6066 [S]	Coleman Hawkins Encounters Ben Webster	1960	$150
V-8327 [M]	Coleman Hawkins Encounters Ben Webster	1961	$30
V6-8327 [S]	Coleman Hawkins Encounters Ben Webster	1961	$25
UMV-2532	Coleman Hawkins Encounters Ben Webster	198?	$25
MGVS-6066 [S]	Coleman Hawkins Encounters Ben Webster	199?	$30
—Classic Records reissue on audiophile vinyl			
V-8509 [M]	Hawkins! Alive! At the Village Gate	1963	$30
V6-8509 [S]	Hawkins! Alive! At the Village Gate	1963	$30
V-8568 [M]	The Essential Coleman Hawkins	1964	$25
V6-8568 [S]	The Essential Coleman Hawkins	1964	$30
MGV-8261 [M]	The Genius of Coleman Hawkins	1958	$150
MGVS-6033 [S]	The Genius of Coleman Hawkins	1960	$175
V-8261 [M]	The Genius of Coleman Hawkins	1961	$30
V6-8261 [S]	The Genius of Coleman Hawkins	1961	$25
825673-1	The Genius of Coleman Hawkins	1986	$25
V6-8829	The Newport Years	197?	$35

VIK
| LX-1059 [M] | The Hawk in Paris | 1957 | $100 |

WORLD WIDE
| MGS-20001 [S] | Coleman Hawkins with the Basie Saxophone Section | 1958 | $50 |

XANADU
189	Dutch Treat	198?	$25
195	Jazz Tones	198?	$25
111	Thanks for the Memory	198?	$25

HAWKINS, COLEMAN/BEN WEBSTER

BRUNSWICK
| BL54016 [M] | The Big Sounds of Coleman Hawkins and Ben Webster | 1956 | $100 |

HAWKINS, COLEMAN/GEORGIE AULD

GRAND AWARD
GA 33-316 [M]	Jazz Concert	1955	$150
—With wrap-around cover intact			
GA 33-316 [M]	Jazz Concert	1955	$75
—Without wrap-around cover			

HAWKINS, DALE

BELL
| 6036 | L.A., Memphis and Tyler, Texas | 1969 | $40 |

CHESS
ACRR-706	Dale Hawkins	1976	$18
LP-1429 [M]	Oh! Susie-Q	1958	$1500
—VG value 500; VG+ value 1000			

ROULETTE
| R25175 [M] | Let's All Twist at the Miami Beach Peppermint Lounge | 1962 | $250 |
| SR25175 [S] | Let's All Twist at the Miami Beach Peppermint Lounge | 1962 | $300 |

HAWKINS, DOLORES

EPIC
| LN3250 [M] | Dolores | 1957 | $40 |
| LN1119 [M] | Meet Dolores Hawkins | 1955 | $40 |

HAWKINS, EDWIN

ACCORD
| SN-7120 | The Genius of Edwin Hawkins | 1981 | $12 |

BIRTHRIGHT
ST-70202	Angels Will Be Singing	1987	$10
WR-8119	Edwin Hawkins Live	198?	$12
ST-70300	Give Us Peace	1987	$10
ST-70201	Have Mercy	1987	$10
D1-70208	Live with the Oakland Symphony, Vol. 1	1988	$10
—Reissue of Myrrh 6691			
D1-70210	Live with the Oakland Symphony, Vol. 2	1988	$10
—Reissue of Myrrh 6700			
4020	The Comforter	197?	$15
LS5904	The Edwin Hawkins Christmas Album	1985	$18
ST-70200	The Edwin Hawkins Christmas Album	1987	$10
—Reissue			
D1-70315	The Name	1988	$12

BUDDAH
BDS-5086	Children (Get Together)	1971	$18
BDS-5101	I'd Like to Teach the World to Sing	1972	$18
BDS-5064	More Happy Days	1970	$18
BDS-5070	Oh Happy Day	1970	$15
—Reissue of Pavilion LP			
BDS-5054	Peace Is Blowin' in the Wind	1969	$18

| BDS-5606 | The Edwin Hawkins Singers – Live | 1974 | $18 |

LECTION
| 501 | Imagine Heaven | 1982 | $12 |
| 810639-1 | The Edwin Hawkins Mass Choir | 198? | $12 |

MYRRH
| 6691 | Live with the Oakland Symphony, Vol. 1 | 198? | $12 |
| 6700 | Live with the Oakland Symphony, Vol. 2 | 198? | $12 |

PAVILION
| BPS-10002 | He's a Friend of Mine | 1969 | $18 |
| BPS-10001 | Let Us Go Into the House of the Lord | 1969 | $18 |

SAVOY
| 7077 | The Best of the Edwin Hawkins Singers | 198? | $15 |

HAWKINS, ERSKINE

CORAL
| CRL56051 [10] | After Hours | 1954 | $120 |

DECCA
| DL4081 [M] | The Hawk Blows at Midnight | 1960 | $30 |
| DL74081 [S] | The Hawk Blows at Midnight | 1960 | $40 |

IMPERIAL
LP-9191 [M]	25 Golden Years of Jazz, Volume 1	1962	$175
LP-12191 [S]	25 Golden Years of Jazz, Volume 1	1962	$175
LP-9197 [M]	25 Golden Years of Jazz, Volume 2	1962	$175
LP-12197 [S]	25 Golden Years of Jazz, Volume 2	1962	$175

MCA
| 1361 | Tuxedo Junction | 198? | $25 |

RCA VICTOR
| LPM-2227 [M] | After Hours | 1960 | $40 |

HAWKINS, HAWKSHAW

GLADWYNNE
| G-2006 [M] | Country Western Cavalcade with Hawkshaw Hawkins | 195? | $120 |

HARMONY
| HL7301 [M] | The Great Hawkshaw Hawkins | 1963 | $25 |
| HS11044 [R] | The Great Hawkshaw Hawkins | 1963 | $18 |

KING
592 [M]	Grand Ole Opry Favorites	1958	$150
587 [M]	Hawkshaw Hawkins	1958	$150
599 [M]	Hawkshaw Hawkins	1959	$150
858 [M]	Taken From Our Vaults, Volume 1	1963	$40
870 [M]	Taken From Our Vaults, Volume 2	1963	$40
873 [M]	Taken From Our Vaults, Volume 3	1964	$40
808 [M]	The All New Hawkshaw Hawkins	1963	$100
KS-808 [S]	The All New Hawkshaw Hawkins	1963	$150

LABREA
| 8020 [M] | Hawkshaw Hawkins | 195? | $150 |

RCA CAMDEN
CAL-808 [M]	Hawkshaw Hawkins Sings	1964	$25
CAS-808 [R]	Hawkshaw Hawkins Sings	1964	$18
CAL-931 [M]	The Country Gentleman	1966	$25
CAS-931 [R]	The Country Gentleman	1966	$18

HAWKINS, JENNELL

AMAZON
| 1002 [M] | Moments to Remember | 1962 | $175 |
| 1001 [M] | The Many Moods of Jenny | 1961 | $175 |

HAWKINS, RONNIE

ACCORD
| SN-7213 | Premonition | 1983 | $12 |

COTILLION
| SD9019 | Ronnie Hawkins | 1970 | $18 |
| SD9039 | The Hawk | 1971 | $18 |

MONUMENT
KZ31330	Rock and Roll Resurrection	1972	$15
ZG33855	Rock and Roll Resurrection/ The Ghost of Rock and Roll	1976	$18
KZ32940	The Giant of Rock 'n' Roll	1974	$15

ROULETTE
R25102 [M]	Mr. Dynamo	1960	$175
SR25102 [S]	Mr. Dynamo	1960	$250
—Black vinyl			
SR25102 [S]	Mr. Dynamo	1960	$600
—Red vinyl			
R25078 [M]	Ronnie Hawkins	1959	$175
—White label with spokes			
SR25078 [S]	Ronnie Hawkins	1959	$250
—White label with spokes; black vinyl			
SR25078 [S]	Ronnie Hawkins	1959	$600
—White label with spokes; red vinyl			

Number	Title	Yr	NM
❏ R25078 [M]	Ronnie Hawkins	1964	$80
—Orange/yellow label			
❏ SR25078 [S]	Ronnie Hawkins	1964	$75
—Orange/yellow label			
❏ R25137 [M]	Ronnie Hawkins Sings the Songs of Hank Williams	1960	$150
❏ SR25137 [S]	Ronnie Hawkins Sings the Songs of Hank Williams	1960	$175
❏ SR42045	The Best of Ronnie Hawkins and His Band	1970	$30
❏ R25120 [M]	The Folk Ballads of Ronnie Hawkins	1960	$150
❏ SR25120 [S]	The Folk Ballads of Ronnie Hawkins	1960	$175
UNITED ARTISTS			
❏ UA-LA968-H	The Hawk	1979	$12

HAWKINS, SCREAMIN' JAY
EPIC

Number	Title	Yr	NM
❏ LN3448 [M]	At Home with Screamin' Jay Hawkins	1958	$800
❏ LN3457 [M]	I Put a Spell on You	1958	$800
❏ BN26457 [R]	I Put a Spell on You	1969	$150
PHILIPS			
❏ PHS600336	Screamin' Jay Hawkins	1970	$40
❏ PHS600319	What That Is	1969	$40
SOUNDS OF HAWAII			
❏ 5015	A Night at Forbidden City	196?	$50

HAWKS, BILLY
PRESTIGE

Number	Title	Yr	NM
❏ PRST-7556	More Heavy Soul	1968	$25
❏ PRLP-7501 [M]	New Genius of the Blues	1967	$30
❏ PRST-7501 [S]	New Genius of the Blues	1967	$25

HAWKWIND
Also see HIGH TIDE; MOTORHEAD.

4 MEN WITH BEARDS

Number	Title	Yr	NM
❏ 4M185LP [B]	Hawkwind		$25
ATCO			
❏ SD 36-115 [B]	Warrior on the Edge of Time	1975	$30
GWR			
❏ 1237 [B]	Live Chronicles	1986	$30
LIBERTY			
❏ LW-5567 [B]	In Search of Space	1981	$25
—Reissue of United Artists 5567			
❏ LWB-120 [B]	Space Ritual/Alive in Liverpool and London	1981	$30
—Reissue of United Artists 120			
SIRE			
❏ SRK6047 [B]	Quark Strangeness and Charm	1978	$50
UNITED ARTISTS			
❏ UA-LA001-F [B]	Doremi Fasol Latido	1973	$100
❏ UA-LA328-G [B]	Hall of the Mountain Grill	1974	$85
❏ UAS-5519 [B]	Hawkwind	1971	$150
❏ UAS-5567 [B]	In Search of Space	1972	$100
❏ UA-LA120-H [B]	Space Ritual/Alive in Liverpool and London	1973	$175

HAWN, GOLDIE
REPRISE

Number	Title	Yr	NM
❏ MS2061 [B]	Goldie	1972	$18

HAY, COLIN JAMES
COLUMBIA

Number	Title	Yr	NM
❏ FC40611	Looking for Jack	1987	$12
MCA			
❏ 6346	Wayfaring Sons	1990	$12
—As "Colin Hay Band"			

HAYDEN, WILLIE
DOOTO

Number	Title	Yr	NM
❏ DTL-293 [M]	Blame It on the Blues	1960	$500
—Maroon label			
❏ DTL-293 [M]	Blame It on the Blues	196?	$250
—Multi-color label			

HAYES, ALVIN
PALO ALTO/TBA

Number	Title	Yr	NM
❏ TBA-221	Star Gaze	1987	$25

HAYES, BILL
ABC-PARAMOUNT

Number	Title	Yr	NM
❏ 194 [M]	Bill Hayes Sings the Best of Disney	1957	$40
DAYBREAK			
❏ DR-2020	The Look of Love	1972	$30
KAPP			
❏ KL-1106 [M]	Jimmy Crack Corn	1958	$30

HAYES, CLANCY
DELMARK

Number	Title	Yr	NM
❏ DS-210 [M]	Oh By Jingo	1965	$25
❏ DS-9210 [S]	Oh By Jingo	1965	$30
DOWN HOME			
❏ MGD-3 [M]	Clancy Hayes Sings	1956	$75
GOOD TIME JAZZ			
❏ L-12050 [M]	Swingin' Minstrel	1963	$25
❏ S-10050 [S]	Swingin' Minstrel	1963	$30
VERVE			
❏ MGV-1003 [M]	Clancy Hayes Sings	1957	$175

HAYES, ISAAC, AND DIONNE WARWICK
ABC/HBS

Number	Title	Yr	NM
❏ D-996	A Man and a Woman	1977	$18
MCA			
❏ 10012	A Man and a Woman	198?	$15
—Reissue of ABC/HBS 996			

HAYES, ISAAC
ABC/HBS

Number	Title	Yr	NM
❏ D-874 [B]	Chocolate Chip	1975	$18
❏ D-923	Disco Connection	1975	$15
❏ D-925	Groove-a-Thon	1976	$15
❏ D-953 [B]	Juicy Fruit (Disco Freak)	1976	$15
ATLANTIC			
❏ SD1599	In the Beginning	1972	$18
—Reissue of Enterprise 100			
COLUMBIA			
❏ FC40941	Love Attack	1988	$12
❏ FC40316	U-Turn	1986	$12
ENTERPRISE			
❏ ENS-5003	Black Moses	1971	$25
❏ ENS-1001	Hot Buttered Soul	1969	$25
❏ ENS-5007 [B]	Joy	1973	$15
❏ EQS-5007 [Q]	Joy	1973	$50
❏ ENS-5005	Live at the Sahara Tahoe	1973	$18
❏ XQS-5005 [Q]	Live at the Sahara Tahoe	1973	$100
❏ E-100 [M]	Presenting Isaac Hayes	1968	$150
❏ ES-100 [S]	Presenting Isaac Hayes	1968	$40
❏ ENS-5002	Shaft	1971	$25
❏ EQS-2-5002 [Q]	Shaft	1971	$150
❏ ENS-7510	The Best of Isaac Hayes	1975	$15
❏ ENS-1010	The Isaac Hayes Movement	1970	$25
❏ ENS-1014	To Be Continued	1970	$25
❏ ENS-7504	Tough Guys	1974	$15
❏ EQS-7504 [Q]	Tough Guys	1974	$50
❏ ENS-7507	Truck Turner	1974	$18
MOBILE FIDELITY			
❏ MFSL 1-273	Hot Buttered Soul	2003	$75
—Original Master Recording" at top of front cover			
POINTBLANK			
❏ SPRO-12787 [DJ]	Funky Junky	1995	$18
—Vinyl is promo only			
POLYDOR			
❏ PD-1-6269	And Once Again	1980	$12
❏ PD-1-6224	Don't Let Go	1979	$12
❏ PD-1-6164	For the Sake of Love	1978	$12
❏ PD-1-6120	New Horizon	1977	$12
STAX			
❏ STX-88003	Enterprise: His Greatest Hits	1980	$15
❏ MPS-8509	Excerpts from Black Moses	1981	$12
❏ MPS-8515	His Greatest Hit Singles	1982	$12
❏ STX-4102 [B]	Hotbed	197?	$15
❏ STX-4114 [B]	Hot Buttered Soul	1978	$15
—Reissue of Enterprise 1001			
❏ MPS-8530	Joy	1984	$12
—Reissue of Enterprise 5007			
❏ STX-88004	Live at the Sahara Tahoe	198?	$15
—Reissue of Enterprise 5005			
❏ STX-88002	Shaft	1979	$15
—Reissue of Enterprise 5002			
❏ STX-4129	The Isaac Hayes Movement	197?	$12
—Reissue of Enterprise 1010			
❏ STX-4133	To Be Continued	197?	$12
—Reissue of Enterprise 1014			

HAYES, LOUIS, AND JUNIOR COOK
TIMELESS

Number	Title	Yr	NM
❏ 307	Ichi-Ban	1979	$50

HAYES, LOUIS
GRYPHON

Number	Title	Yr	NM
❏ G-787	Variety Is the Spice of Life	1979	$50
MUSE			
❏ MR-5052	Breath of Life	1974	$75
❏ MR-5125	Real Thing	1977	$35
VEE JAY			
❏ LP-3010 [M]	Louis Hayes	1960	$100
❏ SR-3010 [S]	Louis Hayes	1960	$175

HAYES, MARTHA
JUBILEE

Number	Title	Yr	NM
❏ JLP-1023 [M]	A Hayes Named Martha	1956	$50

HAYES, RICHARD
ABC-PARAMOUNT

Number	Title	Yr	NM
❏ ABC-131 [M]	Richard Hayes	1956	$40
MALA			
❏ MLP-25 [M]	Love on the Rocks	1959	$30

HAYES, ROLAND
VANGUARD

Number	Title	Yr	NM
❏ VRS-7016 [10]	Christmas Carols of the Nations	195?	$50
❏ VRS-494 [M]	My Songs, Aframerican Religious Folk Songs	1955	$75
❏ VRS-462 [M]	The Life of Christ in Folk Song	1954	$30

HAYES, TUBBY
EPIC

Number	Title	Yr	NM
❏ LA16019 [M]	Introducing Tubby	1961	$100
❏ BA17019 [S]	Introducing Tubby	1961	$150
❏ LA16023 [M]	Tubby the Tenor	1962	$100
❏ BA17023 [S]	Tubby the Tenor	1962	$150
❏ BA17023 [S]	Tubby the Tenor	199?	$75
—Classic Records reissue on audiophile vinyl			

IMPERIAL

Number	Title	Yr	NM
❏ LP-9046 [M]	Little Giant of Jazz	1957	$100
SMASH			
❏ MGS-27026 [M]	Tubby's Back in Town	1963	$40
❏ SRS-67026 [S]	Tubby's Back in Town	1963	$50

HAYMARKET SQUARE
CHAPARRAL

Number	Title	Yr	NM
❏ 201	Magic Lantern	1968	$1500

HAYMES, DICK
AUDIOPHILE

Number	Title	Yr	NM
❏ AP-130	For You, For Me, Forevermore	197?	$15
❏ AP-79	Imagination	1978	$15
❏ AP-200	Keep It Simple	198?	$15
BALLAD			
❏ DHS-6	As Time Goes By	1978	$18
❏ DHS-7	Last Goodbye	1980	$18
❏ DHS-8	Rare Dick Haymes	198?	$18
CAPITOL			
❏ T787 [M]	Moondreams	1956	$30
—Turquoise label			
❏ T713 [M]	Rain or Shine	1956	$30
—Turquoise label			
DAYBREAK			
❏ DR2016	Dick Haymes Comes Home	1973	$18
DECCA			
❏ DL5022 [10]	Christmas Songs	1949	$50
❏ DL5023 [10]	Dick Haymes Sings Irving Berlin	1949	$50
❏ DL5243 [10]	Dick Haymes Sings with Helen Forrest, Volume 1	195?	$50
❏ DL5038 [10]	Little Shamrocks	1950	$50
❏ DL8773 [M]	Little White Lies	1959	$40
❏ DL5291 [10]	Sentimental Songs	195?	$50
❏ DL5012 [10]	Souvenir Album	1949	$50
❏ DL5335 [10]	Sweethearts	195?	$50
MCA			
❏ 2-4097	The Best of Dick Haymes	1976	$18
—Black labels with rainbow			
MCA CORAL			
❏ CB-20016	Easy	1973	$12

Number	Title	Yr	NM
VOCALION			
❏ VL3616 [M]	Dick Haymes	196?	$18
WARWICK			
❏ W-2023 [M]	Richard the Lion-Hearted	1960	$30

HAYNES, GRAHAM

MUSE			
❏ MR-5402	What Time It Be!	1991	$30

HAYNES, ROY; PHINEAS NEWBORN; PAUL CHAMBERS

FANTASY			
❏ OJC-196	We Three	1986	$25
NEW JAZZ			
❏ NJLP-8210 [M]	We Three	1958	$250

HAYNES, ROY

ABC IMPULSE!			
❏ AS-23	Out of the Afternoon	1968	$250
—Black label with red ring			
EMARCY			
❏ MG-26048 [10]	Bushman's Holiday	1954	$300
GALAXY			
❏ 5103	Thank You	1978	$30
❏ 5116	Vistalite	1979	$30
IMPULSE!			

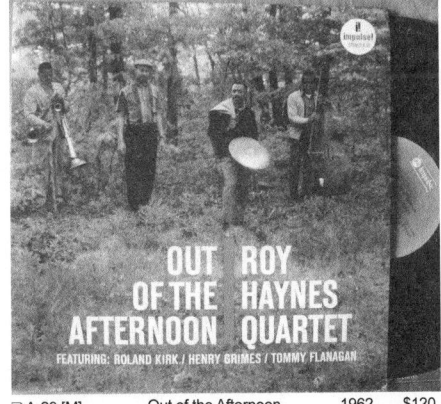

❏ A-23 [M]	Out of the Afternoon	1962	$120
❏ AS-23 [S]	Out of the Afternoon	1962	$160
MAINSTREAM			
❏ MRL-313	Hip Ensemble	1971	$25
❏ MRL-351	Senyah	1972	$25
MCA			
❏ 639	Out of the Afternoon	1980	$25
NEW JAZZ			
❏ NJLP-8286 [M]	Cracklin'	1962	$175
—Purple label			
❏ NJLP-8286 [M]	Cracklin'	1965	$175
—Blue label, trident logo at right			
❏ NJLP-8287 [M]	Cymbalism	1962	$175
—Purple label			
❏ NJLP-8287 [M]	Cymbalism	1965	$175
—Blue label, trident logo at right			
❏ NJLP-8245 [M]	Just Us	1960	$250
—Purple label			
❏ NJLP-8245 [M]	Just Us	1965	$175
—Blue label, trident logo at right			
PACIFIC JAZZ			
❏ PJ-82 [M]	People	1964	$30
❏ ST-82 [S]	People	1964	$40
PRESTIGE			
❏ 2504	Bad News	198?	$30

HAYNES, ROY/QUINCY JONES

EMARCY			
❏ MG-36083 [M]	Jazz Abroad	1956	$250

HAYWARD, JUSTIN, AND JOHN LODGE
Also see JUSTIN HAYWARD; THE MOODY BLUES.

THRESHOLD			
❏ THS14 [B]	Blue Jays	1975	$18
❏ THSX101 [DJ]	Blue Jays	1975	$30
—Open-end interview with script; used to promote the LP of the same name			

HAYWARD, JUSTIN

DERAM			
❏ DRL4801	Night Flight	1980	$15
❏ DES18073	Songwriter	1977	$18

HAYWOOD, LEON

20TH CENTURY			
❏ T-411 [B]	Back to Stay	1973	$15
❏ T-476	Come and Get Yourself Some	1975	$12
❏ T-440 [B]	Keep It in the Family	1974	$15
❏ T-613	Naturally	1980	$12
COLUMBIA			
❏ PC34363	Intimate	1976	$12
DECCA			
❏ DL74949	It's Got to Be Mellow	1969	$25
FAT FISH			
❏ LP2525	Soul Cargo	1966	$75
GALAXY			
❏ 8206	Mellow, Mellow	196?	$25
MCA			
❏ 2322	Double My Pleasure	1978	$12
❏ 3090	Energy	1979	$12

HAYZI FANTAYZEE

RCA			
❏ AFL1-4823 [B]	Battle Hymns for Children Singing	1983	$18

HAZARD, DONNA

EXCELSIOR			
❏ 88008	My Turn	1981	$12

HAZEL, EDDIE
Member of PARLIAMENT/FUNKADELIC.

WARNER BROS.			
❏ BSK3058	Games, Dames and Guitar Thangs	1977	$50

HAZEL, MONK

SOUTHLAND			
❏ SLP-217 [M]	Monk Hazel	1956	$40

HAZELL, EDDIE

AUDIOPHILE			
❏ AP-179	Live at Gulliver's -- I Go for That!	1984	$25
❏ AP-137	Sugar, Don't You Know	1979	$30
MONMOUTH-EVERGREEN			
❏ 7075	Take Your Shoes Off, Baby	197?	$30

HAZILLA, JON

CADENCE JAZZ			
❏ CJR-1035	Chicplacity	1988	$25

HAZLEWOOD, LEE
Also see ANN-MARGRET; SUZI JANE HOKUM; NANCY SINATRA.

CAPITOL			
❏ ST-11171	Poet, Fool or Bum	1973	$40
HARMONY			
❏ HS11290 [S]	Houston	196?	$25
—Reissue of Reprise 6163			
LHI			
❏ S-12009	Forty	1969	$40
❏ S-12006	Trouble Is a Lonesome Town	1969	$25
—Reissue of Mercury 60860			
LIGHT IN THE ATTIC			
❏ LITA096 [B]	Trouble is a Lonesome Town	2013	$30
MERCURY			
❏ MG-20860 [M]	Trouble Is a Lonesome Town	1964	$40
❏ SR-60860 [S]	Trouble Is a Lonesome Town	1964	$40
MGM			
❏ E-4403 [M]	Lee Hazlewoodism - Its Cause and Cure	1966	$30
❏ SE-4403 [S]	Lee Hazlewoodism - Its Cause and Cure	1966	$40
❏ E-4362 [M]	The Very Special World of Lee Hazlewood	1966	$30
❏ SE-4362 [S]	The Very Special World of Lee Hazlewood	1966	$30
REPRISE			
❏ RS-6163 [S]	Friday's Child	1965	$40
❏ R-6163 [M]	Friday's Child	1965	$40
❏ RS-6297 [B]	Love and Other Crimes	1968	$40
❏ R-6133 [M]	The N.S.V.I.P.'s	1965	$30
❏ RS-6133 [S]	The N.S.V.I.P.'s	1965	$40
SMELLS LIKE			
❏ SLR-40	13	2000	$18
❏ SLR-30	Cowboy in Sweden	1999	$18
❏ SLR-38	Requiem for an Almost Lady	1999	$18
❏ SLR-37	Trouble Is a Lonesome Town	1999	$18

HEAD, JIM, AND HIS DEL RAYS

HP			
❏ 22893 [M]	Jim Head and His Del Rays	1963	$300

HEAD, MURRAY

A&M			
❏ SP-4558	Say It Ain't So	1976	$15

HEAD, ROY

ABC			
❏ AB-1054	Tonight's the Night	1978	$12
ABC DOT			
❏ DO-2066	A Head of His Time	1977	$15
❏ DO-2051	Head First	1976	$15
ABC DUNHILL			
❏ DS-50080 [B]	Same People	1970	$25
ELEKTRA			
❏ 6E-234	In Our Room	1979	$12
❏ 6E-298	The Many Sides of Roy Head	1980	$12
MCA			
❏ 796	Tonight's the Night	1980	$10
—Reissue of ABC album			
SCEPTER			
❏ S-532 [M]	Treat Me Right	1965	$30
❏ SS-532 [S]	Treat Me Right	1965	$40
TMI			
❏ 1000	Dismal Prisoner	1972	$18
TNT			
❏ 101 [M]	Roy Head and the Traits	1965	$175
—Counterfeit alert: Authentics do NOT contain the hit "Treat Her Right.			

HEAD EAST

A&M			
❏ SP-4795	A Different Kind of Crazy	1979	$12

❏ SP-4537 [B]	Flat as a Pancake	1975	$12
❏ SP-3196 [B]	Flat as a Pancake	198?	$10
—Budget-line reissue			
❏ SP-4624	Gettin' Lucky	1977	$12
❏ SP-4579	Get Yourself Up	1976	$12
❏ SP-3162	Get Yourself Up	198?	$10
—Budget-line reissue			
❏ SP-4680	Head East	1978	$12
❏ SP-6007	Head East Live!	1979	$15
❏ SP-4826	U.S. 1	1980	$12
ALLEGIANCE			
❏ AV-432	Onward and Upward	1986	$10
PYRAMID			
❏ 0(no cat #)	Flat as a Pancake	1974	$250
—Original issue; 5,000 were pressed; has a different cover than the A&M version of the same album, plus the A and B sides are opposite the reissue			

HEAD OVER HEELS

CAPITOL			
❏ ST-797	Head Over Heels	1971	$30

HEAD SHOP, THE

EPIC			
❏ BN26476 [B]	The Head Shop	1969	$100

HEADHUNTERS

ARISTA			
❏ AB4146	Straight from the Gate	1978	$40
❏ AL4038	Survival of the Fittest	1975	$120
—Reproductions exist			

HEADS, HANDS AND FEET

ATCO			
❏ SD7025	Old Soldiers Never Die	1973	$18
CAPITOL			
❏ SVBB-680	Heads, Hands and Feet	1971	$25
❏ ST-11051	Tracks	1972	$18

Number	Title	Yr	NM

HEADS, THE
LIBERTY
❏ LST-7581	Heads Up	1968	$30

HEADSTONE
STARR
❏ 0 (# unknown)	Still Looking	1974	$175

HEALY, PAT
WORLD PACIFIC
❏ WP-409 [M]	Just Before Dawn	1958	$175

HEARD, J.C.
ARGO
❏ LP-633 [M]	This Is Me, J.C.	1958	$40
❏ LPS-633 [S]	This Is Me, J.C.	1959	$30

HEART
Well-known Pacific Northwest-based group featuring the Wilson sisters, Ann and Nancy. Also see BORDERSONG; ANN WILSON; ANN AND NANCY WILSON.

CAPITOL
❏ PJ-12546	Bad Animals	1987	$10
❏ PJ-512546	Bad Animals	1987	$12
—Columbia House edition			
❏ R153552	Bad Animals	1987	$12
—BMG Direct Marketing edition			
❏ C1-91820	Brigade	1990	$15
❏ C1-591820	Brigade	1990	$15
—Columbia House edition			
❏ SQ-12500	Dreamboat Annie	1986	$10
❏ 72435-21184-1	Dreamboat Annie	1999	$18
—180-gram audiophile reissue			
❏ ST-12410	Heart	1985	$18
—With original mix of "Never			
❏ ST-12410	Heart	1985	$12
—With remix of "Never." Side one trail-off wax has an "RE-1			
❏ ST-512410	Heart	1985	$18
—Columbia House edition; has original mix of "Never			
❏ SQ-12501	Magazine	1986	$10

EPIC
❏ FE36371	Bebe Le Strange	1980	$12
❏ KE236888	Greatest Hits/Live	1980	$15
❏ AS884 [DJ]	Heart	1980	$25
—Promo-only sampler from "Greatest Hits/Live			
❏ AS884 [DJ]	Heart	1980	$25
—Promo-only sampler from "Greatest Hits/Live			
❏ QE38800	Passionworks	1983	$12
❏ PE38800	Passionworks	1985	$10
❏ FE38049	Private Audition	1982	$12
❏ PE38049 [B]	Private Audition	1985	$10

MUSHROOM
❏ MRS-5005 [B]	Dreamboat Annie	1976	$12

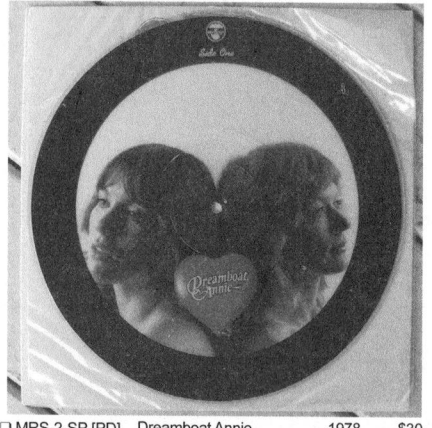

❏ MRS-2-SP [PD]	Dreamboat Annie	1978	$30
❏ MRS-5008 [B]	Magazine	1977	$100

—Original issue, quickly recalled; "Magazine" is the last song on side 1; Side 2, Track 3 is "Blues Medley (Mother Earth) (You Shook Me Babe)"; at the bottom of the back cover is "Mushroom Records regrets that a contractual dispute has made it necessary to complete this record without the cooperation or endorsement of the group Heart, who have expressly disclaimed artistic involvement in completing this record.

❏ MRS-5008	Magazine	1978	$12

—Authorized edition; Side 2, Track 3 is "Mother Earth Blues

❏ MRS-1-SP [PD]	Magazine	1978	$25

NAUTILUS
❏ NR-3 [B]	Dreamboat Annie	1980	$50

—Audiophile pressing

PORTRAIT
❏ FR35555	Dog and Butterfly	1978	$12
❏ PR35555	Dog and Butterfly	1981	$10
❏ JR34799	Little Queen	1977	$12

❏ HR44799	Little Queen	1981	$50
—Half-speed mastered edition			
❏ PR34799 [B]	Little Queen	1984	$10

HEART (3)
LOOK
❏ LLP-11000	Heart	1969	$15

HEART (U)
KING
❏ KS-1119	Have a Heart	1970	$15

NATURAL RESOURCES
❏ NR-102	Heart	1972	$15

HEARTBEATS, THE
EMUS
❏ ES-12033	A Thousand Miles Away	1979	$30

ROULETTE
❏ R25107 [M]	A Thousand Miles Away	1960	$400

HEARTBEATS, THE /SHEP AND THE LIMELITES
ROULETTE
❏ RE-115 [B]	Echoes of a Rock Era: The Groups	1972	$25

HEARTS, THE
ZELLA
❏ 337 [M]	I Feel Good	1963	$400

HEARTS AND FLOWERS
CAPITOL
❏ T2762 [M]	Now Is the Time for Hearts and Flowers	1967	$40
❏ ST2762 [S]	Now Is the Time for Hearts and Flowers	1967	$40
❏ ST2868 [B]	Of Horses, Kids and Forgotten Women	1968	$50

HEARTS OF STONE
V.I.P.
❏ VIPS-404	Stop the World... We Wanna Get On	1970	$40

HEARTSFIELD
COLUMBIA
❏ PC34456	Collector's Item	1976	$12

MERCURY
❏ SRM-1-1034	Foolish Pleasures	1975	$12
❏ SRM-1-688	Heartsfield	1973	$12
❏ SRM-1-1003	The Wonder of It All	1974	$12

HEATH, ALBERT
MUSE
❏ MR-5031	Kwanza (The First)	1974	$25

O'BE
❏ LP-301	Kawaida	1969	$40

TRIP
❏ 5032	Kawaida	1974	$30
—As "Kuumba Toudie Heath			

HEATH, JIMMY
COBBLESTONE
❏ CST-9012	The Gap Sealer	197?	$35

FANTASY
❏ OJC-6006	Nice People	198?	$25

LANDMARK
❏ LLP-1506	New Picture	1986	$25
❏ LLP-1514	Peer Pleasure	1987	$25

MILESTONE
❏ 47025	Fast Company	197?	$35

MUSE
❏ MR-5138	Jimmy	197?	$35
❏ MR-5028	Love and Understanding	1974	$35

RIVERSIDE
❏ RLP-486 [M]	On the Trail	1965	$175
❏ RS-9486 [S]	On the Trail	1965	$175
❏ RLP 12-333 [M]	Really Big	1960	$250
❏ RLP-1188 [S]	Really Big	1960	$40
❏ 6060	Swamp Seed	197?	$30
❏ RLP-465 [M]	Swamp Soul	1963	$175
❏ RS-9465 [S]	Swamp Soul	1963	$175
❏ RLP-372 [M]	The Quota	1961	$250
❏ RS-9372 [S]	The Quota	1961	$250
❏ RLP 12-314 [M]	The Thumper	1960	$250
❏ RLP-1160 [S]	The Thumper	1960	$250
❏ RLP-400 [M]	Triple Threat	1962	$175
❏ RS-9400 [S]	Triple Threat	1962	$175

XANADU
❏ 118	Picture of Heath	1976	$30

HEATH, TED, BAND
LONDON PHASE 4
❏ SP44186	A Salute to Glenn Miller	1972	$25
❏ SP44148	Beatles, Bach and Bacharach	1971	$35
❏ SP44177	Big Band Themes Revisited	197?	$25
❏ SP44178	Big Band Themes Revisited, Volume 2	197?	$25
❏ SP44140	Big Ones	1970	$30
❏ SP44284	Coast to Coast	1977	$25
❏ SP44104	Swing Is King	1968	$30
❏ SP44113	Swing Is King, Volume 2	1969	$30
❏ SP44220	The Ted Heath Band Salutes the Duke	197?	$25
❏ SP44228	The Ted Heath Band Salutes Tommy Dorsey	197?	$25
❏ SP44164	Those Were the Days	1971	$30

HEATH, TED
EVEREST ARCHIVE OF FOLK & JAZZ
❏ 215	Ted Heath's Big Band	1970	$25

LONDON
❏ PS535	21st Anniversary Album	1968	$30
❏ LL1716 [M]	All Time Top Twelve	1957	$50
❏ PS117 [S]	All Time Top Twelve	1958	$75
—Re-recorded version of LL 1716			
❏ LL1676 [M]	A Yank in Europe	1956	$50
❏ LL3125 [M]	Big Band Blues	1959	$50
❏ PS172 [S]	Big Band Blues	1959	$75
❏ LL3325 [M]	Big Band Spirituals	1963	$30
❏ LB-732 [10]	Black and White Magic	195?	$40
❏ LL1217 [M]	Gershwin for Moderns	1956	$50
❏ LL3106 [M]	Great Film Hits	1959	$50
❏ PS159 [S]	Great Film Hits	1959	$75
❏ LL3057 [M]	Hits I Missed	1958	$50
❏ PS116 [S]	Hits I Missed	1958	$75
❏ LL1211 [M]	Jazz Concert at the London Palladium, Vol. 3	1955	$75
❏ LL1379 [M]	Jazz Concert at the London Palladium, Vol. 4	1956	$50
❏ LL1279 [M]	Kern for Moderns	1956	$50
❏ LL3195 [M]	Latin Swingers	1961	$35
❏ PS219 [S]	Latin Swingers	1961	$25
❏ LB-511 [10]	Listen to My Music	195?	$40
❏ LL3127 [M]	My Very Good Friends The Bandleaders	1959	$50
❏ PS174 [S]	My Very Good Friends The Bandleaders	1959	$75
❏ LL3367 [M]	New Palladium Performances	1964	$30
❏ LL3058 [M]	Old English	1958	$50
❏ LL3124 [M]	Pop Hits from the Classics	1959	$50
❏ PS171 [S]	Pop Hits from the Classics	1959	$75
❏ LL1749 [M]	Rhapsody in Blue	1957	$50
❏ LL1500 [M]	Rodgers for Moderns	1956	$50
❏ LL3062 [M]	Shall We Dance	1959	$50
❏ PS148 [S]	Shall We Dance	1959	$75
❏ LL3146 [M]	Songs for the Young at Heart	1960	$35
❏ PS190 [S]	Songs for the Young at Heart	1960	$50
❏ LL1721 [M]	Spotlight on Sidemen	1957	$50
❏ PS138 [S]	Swing Session	1958	$75
—New stereo recordings of the same material as appears on LL 802			
❏ LPB-374 [10]	Ted Heath and His Orchestra	195?	$40
❏ LL1566 [M]	Ted Heath at Carnegie Hall	1956	$50
❏ LL802 [M]	Ted Heath at the London Palladium	1953	$50
❏ LL3143 [M]	Ted Heath in Concert	1960	$35
❏ PS187 [S]	Ted Heath in Concert	1960	$50
❏ LL978 [M]	Ted Heath Plays the Music of Fats Waller	1954	$50
❏ LL1564 [M]	Ted Heath's First American Tour	1956	$50
❏ LL750 [M]	Ted Heath Strikes Up the Band	1953	$50
❏ LL1475 [M]	Ted Heath Swings in Hi-Fi	1956	$25
❏ PS140 [S]	Ted Heath Swings in High Stereo	1958	$75
❏ LPB-340 [10]	Tempo for Dancing	195?	$40
❏ LL1000 [M]	The 100th London Palladium Concert	1955	$25
❏ LL3138 [M]	The Big Band Dixie Sound	1960	$35
❏ PS184 [S]	The Big Band Dixie Sound	1960	$50
❏ LL3192 [M]	The Hits of the Thirties	1961	$35
❏ PS216 [S]	The Hits of the Thirties	1961	$50
❏ LL3128 [M]	The Hits of the Twenties	1960	$35
❏ PS175 [S]	The Hits of the Twenties	1960	$50
❏ LL3047 [M]	Things to Come	1958	$50
❏ LL1743 [M]	Tribute to the Fabulous Dorseys	1957	$50

LONDON PHASE 4
❏ SP44017	Big Band Bash	1962	$35
❏ P54002 [M]	Big Band Percussion	1961	$30
❏ SP44002 [S]	Big Band Percussion	1961	$35
❏ SP44036 [S]	Big Band Spirituals	1963	$35
❏ SP44074	Chartbusters	1966	$30
❏ SP44046 [S]	New Palladium Performances	1964	$30
❏ SP44079	Pow!	1966	$30
❏ SP44023	Satin Strings and Bouncing Brass	1963	$35
❏ SP44038	Swing vs. Latin	1964	$35
❏ SP44063	The Sound of Music	1965	$30

Number	Title	Yr	NM

RICHMOND
❏ B20034 [M]	Big Band Beat	196?	$30
❏ B20096 [M]	Big Band Gershwin	196?	$30
❏ B20097 [M]	Big Band Kern	196?	$30
❏ B20098 [M]	Big Band Rodgers	196?	$30
❏ B20037 [M]	Ted Heath Plays Gershwin	196?	$30
❏ B20082 [M]	Ted Heath Plays the Music of Fats Waller	196?	$30

HEATH BROTHERS, THE
ANTILLES
| ❏ AN-1003 | Brotherly Love | 1982 | $30 |
| ❏ AN-1016 | Brothers and Others | 198? | $30 |
COLUMBIA
❏ FC37126	Expressions of Life	1981	$30
❏ JC35816	In Motion: The Heath Brothers and Brass Choir	1979	$30
❏ FC36374	Live at the Public Theatre	1980	$30
❏ JC35573	Passin' Thru	1978	$30
STRATA-EAST
❏ SES-19766 [B]	Marchin' On	1975	$100

HEATHER BLACK
AMERICAN PLAYBOY
| ❏ 1001 | Heather Black Live | 197? | $75 |
| ❏ 1001 | Heather Black Live | 197? | $175 |
— Evidently, some copies of this were 2-record sets
DOUBLE BAYOU
| ❏ 2000 | Heather Black | 197? | $30 |

HEATHERTON, JOEY
MGM
| ❏ SE-4858 | The Joey Heatherton Album | 1972 | $18 |

HEATS, THE
ALBATROSS
| ❏ 1001 | The Heats | 1980 | $30 |

HEATWAVE
EPIC
| ❏ FE36873 | Candles | 1980 | $12 |
| ❏ JE35260 | Central Heating | 1978 | $12 |
— Originals have orange labels
❏ FE38065	Current	1982	$12
❏ FE39279	Greatest Hits	1984	$12
❏ PE39279	Greatest Hits	198?	$10
— Budget-line reissue
| ❏ FE35970 | Hot Property | 1979 | $12 |
| ❏ PE34761 [B] | Too Hot to Handle | 1977 | $15 |
— Originals have orange labels

HEAVEN & HELL
Also see BLACK SABBATH; DIO; RICK DERRINGER; ELF; RAINBOW.
WARNER BROS./RHINO
| ❏ 519252 [B] | The Devil You Know | 2009 | $25 |

HEAVEN 17
ARISTA
| ❏ AL6606 | Heaven 17 | 1982 | $15 |
| ❏ AL8-8007 | Heaven 17 | 1983 | $12 |
— Reissue
| ❏ AL8-8259 | How Men Are | 198? | $12 |
| ❏ AL8-8020 | Luxury Gap | 1983 | $12 |
CAROLINE
| ❏ 1393 | Teddy Bear Duke & Psycho | 1988 | $12 |
VIRGIN
| ❏ 90569 | Pleasure One | 1986 | $12 |

HEAVY BALLOON, THE
ELEPHANT

| ❏ EVS-104 [B] | 32,000 Lbs. | 1969 | $150 |

HEBB, BOBBY
EPIC
| ❏ BN26523 [B] | Love Games | 1970 | $15 |

Number	Title	Yr	NM

PHILIPS
| ❏ PHM200212 [M] | Sunny | 1966 | $30 |
— With "200-212" in trail-off; this record is mono
| ❏ PHS600212 [S] | Sunny | 1966 | $30 |
| ❏ PHM200212 [S] | Sunny | 1966 | $30 |
— With "2/600-212" in trail-off; this record plays stereo, though labeled mono

HECKMAN, DON
ICTUS
| ❏ 101 | Summerlin Improvisational Jazz Workshop | 1967 | $75 |

HEDGE & DONNA
CAPITOL
| ❏ ST-107 | 2 | 1969 | $18 |
— Black label with rainbow ring
| ❏ ST-279 | All the Friendly Colours | 1969 | $18 |
— Lime green label
| ❏ ST-2869 | Hedge & Donna | 1968 | $18 |
— The label calls this LP "Love"
| ❏ ST-447 | Special Circumstances | 1970 | $18 |
JANUS
| ❏ JLS-3045 | Capers & Carson | 1973 | $15 |
POLYDOR
| ❏ 24-4063 | Revolution | 1971 | $15 |

HEE
BUDDAH
| ❏ BDS-5062 | Head | 1970 | $30 |
— With coloring book (deduct 1/3 if missing)

HEFTI, NEAL
COLUMBIA
| ❏ CL1516 [M] | Light and Right | 1960 | $25 |
| ❏ CS8316 [S] | Light and Right | 1960 | $30 |
CORAL
❏ CX2 [M]	Hollywood Song Book	1959	$40
❏ 7CX2 [S]	Hollywood Song Book	1959	$75
❏ CRL57241 [M]	Hollywood Song Book, Volume 1	1958	$30
❏ CRL757241 [S]	Hollywood Song Book, Volume 1	1959	$30
❏ CRL57242 [M]	Hollywood Song Book, Volume 2	1958	$30
❏ CRL757242 [S]	Hollywood Song Book, Volume 2	1959	$30
❏ CRL57256 [M]	Music U.S.A.	1959	$25
❏ CRL757256 [S]	Music U.S.A.	1959	$30
❏ CRL56083 [10]	Swingin' on a Coral Reef	1953	$50
EPIC
❏ LN3481 [M]	Pardon My Do-Wah	1958	$75
❏ LN3113 [M]	Singing Instrumentals	1956	$150
❏ LN3440 [M]	Singing Instrumentals	1958	$30
❏ LG1013 [10]	Singing Instrumentals	1955	$150
RCA VICTOR
❏ LPM-3573 [M]	Batman Theme (and 11 Other Bat-Songs)	1966	$50
❏ LSP-3573 [S]	Batman Theme (and 11 Other Bat-Songs)	1966	$75
❏ LPM-3621 [M]	Hefti in Gotham City	1966	$50
❏ LSP-3621 [S]	Hefti in Gotham City	1966	$75
REPRISE
❏ R-6039 [M]	Jazz Pops	1962	$25
❏ R9-6039 [S]	Jazz Pops	1962	$30
❏ R-6018 [M]	Themes from TV's Top 12	1962	$30
❏ R9-6018 [S]	Themes from TV's Top 12	1962	$30
VIK
❏ LX-1092 [M]	Concert Miniatures	1957	$75
X
❏ LXA-3021 [10]	Music of Rudolf Frimi	1954	$50

HEIDT, HORACE
HINDSIGHT
| ❏ HSR-194 | Horace Heidt and His Musical Knights 1939 | 198? | $25 |
| ❏ HSR-202 | The Uncollected Horace Heidt and His Orchestra Vol. 2 | 1984 | $25 |
SUNBEAM
| ❏ 4 | Horace Heidt and His Orchestra 1927-29 | 198? | $25 |

HEIFETZ, JASCHA, AND GREGOR PIATIGORSKI
RCA VICTOR RED SEAL
| ❏ LDS-2513 [S] | Brahms: Double Concerto | 1961 | $40 |
— Originals with "shaded dog" label

HEIFETZ, JASCHA; WILLIAM PRIMROSE; GREGOR PIATIGORSKI
RCA VICTOR RED SEAL
| ❏ LSC-2550 [S] | Beethoven: Serenade, op. 8; Kodaly: Duo | 1961 | $40 |
— Originals with "shaded dog" label

Number	Title	Yr	NM

| ❏ LSC-2563 [S] | Beethoven: Trio in D; Bach: Three Sinfonias; Schubert: Trio No. 2 | 1961 | $40 |
— Original with "shaded dog" label

HEIFETZ, JASCHA
RCA VICTOR RED SEAL
| ❏ LSC-2577 [S] | Bach: Concerto for Two Violins; Beethoven: Kreutzer Sonata | 1962 | $80 |
— Original with "shaded dog" label
| ❏ LSC-1992 [S] | Beethoven: Violin Concerto in D | 1958 | $50 |
— With Charles Munch/Boston Symphony Orchestra
| ❏ LSC-1903 [S] | Brahms: Violin Concerto | 1958 | $50 |
— With Fritz Reiner/Chicago Symphony Orchestra; original with "shaded dog" label
| ❏ LSC-2603 [S] | Bruch: Scottish Fantasy; Vieuxtemps: Violin Concerto No. 5 | 1962 | $50 |
— Original with "shaded dog" label
| ❏ LSC-2652 [S] | Bruch: Violin Concerto No. 1 in G; Mozart: Violin Concerto No. 4 in D | 1962 | $75 |
— Original with "shaded dog" label
| ❏ LSC-2734 [S] | Glazunov: Violin Concerto; Mozart: Sinfonia Concertante | 1963 | $150 |
— Original with "shaded dog" label
| ❏ LSC-2314 [S] | Mendelssohn: Violin Concerto in E; Prokofiev: Violin Concerton in G | 1959 | $30 |
— With Charles Munch/Boston Symphony Orchestra
| ❏ LSC-2435 [S] | Sibelius: Violin Concerto | 1960 | $40 |
— Originals with "shaded dog" label
| ❏ LSC-2129 [S] | Tchaikovsky: Violin Concerto | 1958 | $40 |
— With Fritz Reiner/Chicago Symphony Orchestra; original with "shaded dog" label
| ❏ LSC-2129 [S] | Tchaikovsky: Violin Concerto | 1999 | $30 |
— Classic Records reissue

HEINDORF, RAY
DCC COMPACT CLASSICS
| ❏ LPZ-2023 | For Whom the Bell Tolls | 1996 | $30 |
— Audiophile vinyl
WARNER BROS.
| ❏ B1201 [M] | For Whom the Bell Tolls | 1958 | $30 |
— Re-recording of 1943 movie score; the first LP on Warner Bros. Records
| ❏ BS1201 [S] | For Whom the Bell Tolls | 1959 | $40 |
— Gold label
| ❏ W1213 [M] | Spellbound | 1958 | $30 |
— Re-recording of 1945 movie score
| ❏ WS1213 [S] | Spellbound | 1959 | $40 |
— Gold label

HEINTJE
MGM
| ❏ SE-4772 | Best of All | 1971 | $15 |
| ❏ SE-4739 | Mama | 1970 | $15 |

HELIOCENTRIC
DISCOVERY
| ❏ 806 | Heliocentric | 1979 | $30 |

HELL, RICHARD, AND THE VOIDOIDS
Early member of TELEVISION.
RED STAR
| ❏ RED801 | Destiny Street | 1982 | $25 |
— Richard Hell solo
SIRE
| ❏ SRK6037 | Blank Generation | 1977 | $30 |
| ❏ SR6037 [B] | Blank Generation | 2015 | $25 |

HELLBORG, JONAS
DAY EIGHT
❏ DEM 002	All Our Steps	1983	$35
❏ DEM 006	Axis	1986	$30
❏ DEM 009	Bass	1988	$30
❏ DEM 004	Elegant Punk	1984	$30
❏ DEM0(# unknown)	Jonas Hellborg Group	1988	$30
❏ DEM 001	The Bassic Thing	1982	$50

HELLERS, THE
COMMAND
| ❏ RS934SD | Singers, Talkers, Players, Swingers and Doers | 1968 | $25 |

HELLO PEOPLE, THE
ABC
| ❏ D-882 | Bricks | 1975 | $12 |
ABC DUNHILL
| ❏ DS-50184 | The Handsome Devils | 1974 | $12 |

Number	Title	Yr	NM
MEDIARTS			
❑ 41-8	Have You Seen the Light	1970	$15
PHILIPS			
❑ PHS600276	Fusion	1969	$18
❑ PHS600265 [S]	The Hello People	1968	$18
❑ PHS200265 [M]	The Hello People	1968	$40
—*Possibly white label promo only*			
UNITED ARTISTS			
❑ UAS5524	Have You Seen the Light	1971	$12
—*Reissue of Mediarts LP*			

HELM, BOB
RIVERSIDE			
❑ RLP-2510 [10]	Bob Helm	1954	$300

HELM, BOB/LU WATTERS
RIVERSIDE			
❑ RLP 12-213 [M]	San Francisco Style	1956	$300

HELMS, BOBBY
COLUMBIA			
❑ CL2060 [M]	The Best of Bobby Helms	1963	$30
❑ CS8860 [S]	The Best of Bobby Helms	1963	$30
DECCA			
❑ DL8638 [M]	Bobby Helms Sings to My Special Angel	1957	$120
HARMONY			
❑ HL7409 [M]	Fraulein	1967	$25
❑ HS11209 [S]	Fraulein	1967	$18
KAPP			
❑ KL1463 [M]	I'm the Man	1966	$18
❑ KS3463 [S]	I'm the Man	1966	$25
❑ KL1505 [M]	Sorry My Name Isn't Fred	1966	$18
❑ KS3505 [S]	Sorry My Name Isn't Fred	1966	$25
LITTLE DARLIN'			
❑ 8088	All New Just for You	1968	$30
MISTLETOE			
❑ MLP-1206 [B]	Jingle Bell Rock	197?	$15
POWER PAK			
❑ 283	Greatest Hits	197?	$12
VOCALION			
❑ VL73874	My Special Angel	1969	$15
❑ VL3743 [M]	Someone Already There	1965	$18
❑ VL73743 [R]	Someone Already There	1965	$15

HELMS, DON
SMASH			
❑ MGS-27019 [M]	Don Helms' Steel Guitar	1962	$25
❑ SRS-67019 [S]	Don Helms' Steel Guitar	1962	$30
❑ MGS-27001 [M]	The Steel Guitar Sounds of Hank Williams	1962	$25
❑ SRS-67001 [S]	The Steel Guitar Sounds of Hank Williams	1962	$30

HELP
DECCA			
❑ DL75257	Help	1970	$30
❑ DL75304	Second Coming	1971	$30

HEMPHILL, JULIUS
ARISTA FREEDOM			
❑ AL1012 [B]	'Coon Bid'ness	1975	$25
❑ AL1028 [B]	Dogon A.D.	1976	$30
BLACK SAINT			
❑ BSR-0040	Flat-Out Jump Suite	198?	$35
❑ BSR-0015	Raw Material and Residuals	197?	$35
ELEKTRA/MUSICIAN			
❑ 60831	Julius Hemphill's Big Band	1988	$25
MBARI			
❑ 0(# unknown)	Blue Boye	1977	$75
❑ 0(# unknown)	'Coon Bid'ness	1974	$40
❑ 5001	Dogon A.D.	1972	$50
MINOR MUSIC			
❑ MM-003	Georgia Blue	1985	$30
RED			
❑ VPA-138	Live in New York	1976	$35
SACKVILLE			
❑ 3018	Buster Bee	198?	$30

HENDERSON, BILL
DISCOVERY			
❑ 779	Live at the Times	1978	$30
❑ 802	Street of Dreams	1979	$30
❑ 846	Tribute to Johnny Mercer	1982	$30
MGM			
❑ E-4128 [M]	Bill Henderson with the Oscar Peterson Trio	1963	$30
❑ SE-4128 [S]	Bill Henderson with the Oscar Peterson Trio	1963	$30
VEE JAY			
❑ LP-1031 [M]	Bill Henderson	1961	$30
❑ SR-1031 [S]	Bill Henderson	1961	$40

Number	Title	Yr	NM
❑ LP-1015 [M]	Bill Henderson Sings	1959	$30
❑ SR-1015 [S]	Bill Henderson Sings	1959	$40
VERVE			
❑ V-8619 [M]	When My Dreamboat Comes Home	1965	$50
❑ V6-8619 [S]	When My Dreamboat Comes Home	1965	$75

HENDERSON, BOBBY
CHIAROSCURO

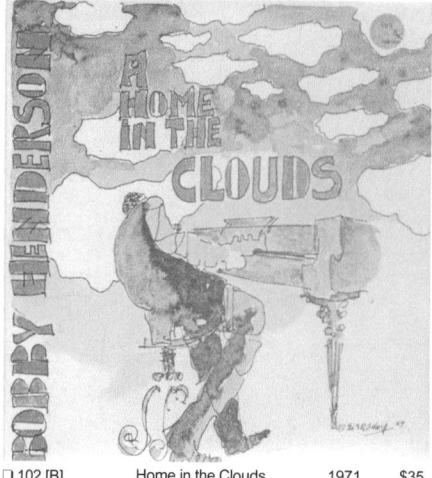

❑ 102 [B]	Home in the Clouds	1971	$35
—*Reissue of Halcyon 102*			
❑ 122	Last Recordings	1973	$35
HALCYON			
❑ 102	Home in the Clouds	1970	$25
VANGUARD			
❑ VRS-8511 [M]	Handful of Keys	1955	$100

HENDERSON, BUGS
ARMADILLO			
❑ LP-78-1 [B]	The Bugs Henderson Group At Last	1978	$40

HENDERSON, EDDIE
BLUE NOTE			
❑ BN-LA636-G	Heritage	1976	$25
❑ BN-LA46-G	Sunburst	1975	$25
CAPITOL			
❑ ST-11761	Comin' Through	1977	$35
❑ SW-11846	Mahal	1978	$30
❑ ST-11984	Runnin' To Your Love	1979	$30
CAPRICORN			
❑ CP 0122	Inside Out	1974	$35
❑ CP 0118	Realization	1973	$35

HENDERSON, FLETCHER
BIOGRAPH			
❑ 12039	Fletcher Henderson 1923-27	197?	$30
❑ C-12	Fletcher Henderson 1924-41	197?	$30
BLUEBIRD			
❑ AXM2-5507	The Complete Fletcher Henderson	197?	$35
COLUMBIA			
❑ C4L19 [M]	The Fletcher Henderson Story	1961	$150
—*Box set with booklet; red and black labels with six "eye" logos*			
❑ C4L19 [M]	The Fletcher Henderson Story	1963	$50
—*Red "Guaranteed High Fidelity" labels*			
❑ C4L19 [M]	The Fletcher Henderson Story	1966	$30
—*Red "360 Sound Mono" labels*			
DECCA			
❑ DL9227 [M]	Fletcher Henderson: First Impression (Vol. 1 1924-1931)	1958	$120
—*Black label, silver print*			
❑ DL9227 [M]	Fletcher Henderson: First Impression (Vol. 1 1924-1931)	1961	$30
—*Black label with color bars*			
❑ DL79227 [R]	Fletcher Henderson: First Impression (Vol. 1 1924-1931)	196?	$35
❑ DL9228 [M]	Fletcher Henderson: The Swing's the Thing (Vol. 2 1931-1934)	1958	$120
—*Black label, silver print*			
❑ DL9228 [M]	Fletcher Henderson: The Swing's the Thing (Vol. 2 1931-1934)	1961	$30

Number	Title	Yr	NM
—*Black label with color bars*			
❑ DL79228 [R]	Fletcher Henderson: The Swing's the Thing (Vol. 2 1931-1934)	196?	$35
❑ DL6025 [10]	Fletcher Henderson Memorial Album	1952	$175
HISTORICAL			
❑ 13	Fletcher Henderson 1923-24	1967	$25
❑ 18	Fletcher Henderson Volume 2: 1923-25	1967	$25
JAZZTONE			
❑ J-1285 [M]	The Big Reunion	1958	$30
MCA			
❑ 1310	First Impressions	198?	$25
❑ 1346	The Rarest Fletcher	198?	$25
❑ 1318	The Swing's the Thing	198?	$25
MILESTONE			
❑ M-2005	The Immortal Fletcher Henderson	196?	$30
RIVERSIDE			
❑ RLP-1055 [10]	Fletcher Henderson	1954	$300
SAVOY JAZZ			
❑ SJL-1152	The Crown King of Swing	198?	$25
SUTTON			
❑ SSL-286 [M]	Fletcher Henderson with Slam Stewart	195?	$30
SWING			
❑ SW-8445/6	Fletcher Henderson and His Dixie Stompers 1925-1928	198?	$35
X			
❑ LVA-3013 [10]	Fletcher Henderson and His Connie's Inn Orchestra	1954	$175

HENDERSON, JOE
BLUE NOTE			
❑ BLP-4189 [M]	Inner Urge	1965	$175
❑ BST-84189 [S]	Inner Urge	1965	$250
—*New York, USA" address on label*			
❑ BST-84189 [S]	Inner Urge	1967	$35
—*A Division of Liberty Records" on label*			
❑ BLP-4166 [M]	In 'n Out	1964	$300
❑ BST-84166 [S]	In 'n Out	1964	$150
—*New York, USA" address on label*			
❑ BST-84166 [S]	In 'n Out	1967	$35
—*A Division of Liberty Records" on label*			
❑ BLP-4227 [M]	Mode for Joe	1966	$150
❑ BST-84227 [S]	Mode for Joe	1966	$100
—*New York, USA" address on label*			
❑ BST-84227 [S]	Mode for Joe	1967	$35
—*A Division of Liberty Records" on label*			
❑ BLP-4152 [M]	Our Thing	1963	$150
❑ BST-84152 [S]	Our Thing	1963	$150
—*New York, USA" address on label*			
❑ BST-84152 [S]	Our Thing	1967	$35
—*A Division of Liberty Records" on label*			
❑ BLP-4140 [M]	Page One	1963	$250
❑ BST-84140 [S]	Page One	1963	$150
—*New York, USA" address on label*			
❑ BST-84140 [S]	Page One	1967	$35
—*A Division of Liberty Records" on label*			
❑ BT-85123	State of the Tenor	1987	$25
❑ BT-85126	State of the Tenor Vol. 2: Live at the Village Vanguard	1987	$25
CONTEMPORARY			
❑ C-14006	Relaxin' at Camarillo	198?	$30
FANTASY			
❑ OJC-465	The Kicker	1990	$30
FONTANA			
❑ SRF-67590	Hits, Hits, Hits!	1969	$75
MILESTONE			
❑ M-9040	Black Is the Color	1972	$25
❑ M-9066	Black Miracle	1976	$35
❑ M-9071	Black Narcissus	1976	$35
❑ M-9057	Canyon Lady	1974	$35
❑ M-9053	Elements	1974	$35
❑ 47058	Foresight	198?	$35
❑ M-9028	If You're Not Part	1970	$25
❑ M-9034	In Pursuit of Blackness	1971	$25
❑ M-9047	Joe Henderson In Japan	1972	$35
❑ M-9050	Multiple	1973	$35
❑ M-9024 [B]	Power to the People	1970	$25
❑ M-9017 [B]	Tetragon	1969	$25
❑ M-9008	The Kicker	1968	$25
PAUSA			
❑ 7075	Mirror, Mirror	1980	$25
TODD			
❑ MT-2701 [M]	Snap Your Fingers	1962	$150
❑ ST-2701 [S]	Snap Your Fingers	1962	$140

HENDERSON, MICHAEL
BUDDAH			
❑ BDS5719	Do It All	1979	$18
❑ BDS6004	Fickle	1983	$18
❑ BDS5693	Goin' Places	1977	$15
❑ BDS5712	In the Night-Time	1978	$18

Number	Title	Yr	NM
❏ BDS6002	Slingshot	1981	$15
❏ BDS5662	Solid	1976	$18
❏ BDS6001	Wide Receiver	1980	$15

EMI AMERICA

❏ ST-17181	Bedtime Stories	1986	$12

HENDERSON, SKITCH

CAPITOL

❏ H110 [10]	Keyboard Sketches	1950	$50

HENDERSON, WAYNE

ABC

❏ AB-1020	Big Daddy's Place	1977	$25

POLYDOR

❏ PD-1-6227	Emphasized	1980	$25
❏ PD-1-6145	Living on a Dream	1978	$25

HENDRICKS, JON

COLUMBIA

❏ CL1583 [M]	Evolution of the Blues	1961	$30
❏ CS8383 [S]	Evolution of the Blues	1961	$40
❏ CL1805 [M]	Fast Livin' Blues	1962	$30
❏ CS8605 [S]	Fast Livin' Blues	1962	$40

ENJA

❏ 4032	Cloudburst	198?	$30

MUSE

❏ MR-5258	Love	1982	$25

REPRISE

❏ R-6089 [M]	Salud!	1964	$30
❏ R9-6089 [S]	Salud!	1964	$30

SMASH

❏ MGS-27069 [M]	Recorded In Person at the Trident	1963	$30
❏ SRS-67069 [S]	Recorded In Person at the Trident	1963	$30

STANYAN

❏ 10132	September Songs	197?	$30

WORLD PACIFIC

❏ WP-1283 [M]	A Good Git-Together	1959	$175

HENDRICKS, MICHELE

MUSE

❏ MR-5336	Carryin' On	1988	$25
❏ MR-5363	Keepin' Me Satisfied	1989	$30

HENDRIX, JIMI, AND LITTLE RICHARD

EVEREST ARCHIVE OF FOLK & JAZZ

❏ 296	Roots of Rock	1974	$15

PICKWICK

❏ SPC-3347	Jimi Hendrix and Little Richard Together	1973	$15

HENDRIX, JIMI, AND LONNIE YOUNGBLOOD

MAPLE

❏ 6004	Two Great Experiences Together	1971	$50

HENDRIX, JIMI

ACCORD

❏ SN-7112	Before London	1981	$12
❏ SN-7139	Cosmic Feeling	1981	$12
❏ SN-7101	Kaleidoscope	1981	$12

CAPITOL

❏ STAO-472	Band of Gypsys	1970	$25
❏ SN-16319	Band of Gypsys	1985	$12
— Budget-line reissue			
❏ C1-96414 [B]	Band of Gypsys	1995	$25
— Numbered reissue			
❏ SJ-12416	Band of Gypsys 2	1986	$12
— Side 2 lists, and plays, three songs			
❏ SJ-12416	Band of Gypsys 2	1986	$175
— Side 2 lists three songs, but plays four completely different songs. Four bands are visible on the record.			
❏ T2894 [M]	Flashing	1968	$175
❏ ST2894 [S]	Flashing	1968	$40
❏ T2856 [M]	Get That Feeling	1967	$175
❏ ST2856 [S]	Get That Feeling	1967	$40
❏ SWBB-659	Get That Feeling/Flashing	1971	$30
❏ MLP-15022 [EP]	Johnny B. Goode	1986	$10

EXPERIENCE HENDRIX

❏ 88875099781 [B]	Freedom: Atlanta Pop Festival	2015	$40
❏ 88843042031 [B]	Live at Monterey	2014	$40

EXPERIENCE HENDRIX/CAPITOL

❏ ST-472	Band of Gypsys	1997	$30
— Limited edition on "heavy vinyl" with booklet; distributed by Classic Records			

EXPERIENCE HENDRIX/CLASSIC

❏ RTH2006	Blues	2002	$75
— Limited edition on 200-gram blue vinyl			
❏ RTH2006	Blues	2003	$40
— Limited edition on 200-gram black vinyl			

Number	Title	Yr	NM
❏ B0000698-01	Martin Scorsese Presents the Blues: Jimi Hendrix	2004	$50
— Limited edition of 1,000 on blue vinyl			
❏ B0000698-01	Martin Scorsese Presents the Blues: Jimi Hendrix	2004	$40
— Regular edition on black vinyl			
❏ RTH-2016	Voodoo Child: The Jimi Hendrix Collection	2005	$40
— Box set; red vinyl			
❏ RTH-2016	Voodoo Child: The Jimi Hendrix Collection	2005	$100
— Black 200-gram vinyl			

EXPERIENCE HENDRIX/MCA

❏ 11602	Are You Experienced?	1997	$50
— Limited edition on "heavy vinyl" with booklet			
❏ 11608	Are You Experienced?	1997	$40
— Limited edition on "heavy vinyl" with booklet; pressed in U.S. for export to Europe; has different cover than US version			
❏ 11601	Axis: Bold As Love	1997	$50
— Limited edition on "heavy vinyl" with booklet			
❏ 11607	Band of Gypsys	1997	$30
— Limited edition on "heavy vinyl" with booklet; pressed in U.S. for export to Europe			
❏ 11742 [B]	BBC Sessions	1998	$35
❏ 113086-1	Blue Wild Angel: Jimi Hendrix Live at the Isle of Wight	2002	$40
❏ 11600	Electric Ladyland	1997	$40
— Limited edition on "heavy vinyl" with booklet			
❏ 11671	Experience Hendrix: The Best of Jimi Hendrix	1998	$30
— Despite lower number, was released after South Saturn Delta			
❏ 11599 [B]	First Rays of the New Rising Sun	1997	$75
— Limited edition on "heavy vinyl" with booklet			
❏ B0001159-01	Live at Berkeley	2003	$30
❏ 11931	Live at the Fillmore East	1999	$30
❏ 11987	Live at Woodstock	1999	$40
❏ 311987	Live at Woodstock	2009	$40
❏ 311987	Live at Woodstock	2009	$40
❏ 112984	Smash Hits	2002	$18
— Limited edition on "heavy vinyl			
❏ 11684 [B]	South Saturn Delta	1997	$35
— Numbered, limited edition on "heavy vinyl			
❏ 112316	The Jimi Hendrix Experience	2000	$150
— Limited edition of 5,000 in purple felt box			

EXPERIENCE HENDRIX/UME

❏ B0009845-01	The Jimi Hendrix Experience Live at Monterey	2007	$18

NUTMEG

❏ 1002	Cosmic Turnaround	1981	$15
❏ 1001	High, Live 'N' Dirty	1978	$30
— Red vinyl			
❏ 1001	High, Live 'N' Dirty	1978	$30
— Black vinyl			

PHOENIX 10

❏ PHX320	Rare Hendrix	1981	$10
❏ PHX324	Roots of Hendrix	1981	$10

PICKWICK

❏ SPC-3528	Jimi	197?	$12

REPRISE

❏ R6261 [M]	Are You Experienced?	1967	$350
❏ RS6261 [S]	Are You Experienced?	1967	$100
— Pink, gold and green label			
❏ RS6261 [S]	Are You Experienced?	1968	$30
— With "W7" and "r." logos on two-tone orange label			
❏ RS6261 [S]	Are You Experienced?	1970	$15
— With only "r." logo on all-orange (tan) label			
❏ RS6261 [S]	Are You Experienced?	198?	$10
— Red and black label or gold and light blue label			
❏ R6281 [M]	Axis: Bold As Love	1968	$5000
❏ RS6281 [S]	Axis: Bold As Love	1968	$100
— Pink, gold and green label			
❏ RS6281 [S]	Axis: Bold As Love	1968	$30
— With "W7" and "r." logos on two-tone orange label			
❏ RS6281 [S]	Axis: Bold As Love	1970	$15
— With only "r." logo on all-orange (tan) label			
❏ RS6281 [S]	Axis: Bold As Love	198?	$10
— Red and black label or gold and light blue label			
❏ SKAO-91441	Axis: Bold As Love	1968	$40
— Capitol Record Club edition; two-tone orange label with "W7" and "r." at top			
❏ MS2204	Crash Landing	1975	$18
❏ 2R6307 [M]	Electric Ladyland	1968	$6000
— Mono is promo only; VG value 2000; VG+ value 3000			
❏ 2RS6307 [S]	Electric Ladyland	1968	$150
— With "W7" and "r." logos on two-tone orange label			
❏ 2RS6307 [S]	Electric Ladyland	1970	$18
— With only "r." logo on all-orange (tan) label			
❏ 2RS6307 [S]	Electric Ladyland	198?	$15
— Red and black label or gold and light blue label			
❏ STBO-91568	Electric Ladyland	1968	$175
— Capitol Record Club edition			
❏ MS2049 [B]	Hendrix in the West	1972	$30

Number	Title	Yr	NM
❏ MS2029	Historic Performances As Recorded at the Monterey International Pop Festival	1970	$25
— Side 1: Jimi Hendrix; Side 2: Otis Redding; with only "r." logo on all-orange (tan) label			
❏ MS2029	Historic Performances As Recorded at the Monterey International Pop Festival	1970	$250
— Side 1: Jimi Hendrix; Side 2: Otis Redding; with "W7" and "r." logos on two-tone orange label			
❏ 25358	Jimi Plays Monterey	1986	$12
❏ 25119	Kiss the Sky	1984	$12
❏ MS2229	Midnight Lightning	1975	$18
❏ HS2299	Nine to the Universe	1980	$12
❏ MS2040	Rainbow Bridge	1971	$25
❏ SMAS-93972	Rainbow Bridge	1971	$50
— Capitol Record Club edition			
❏ MS2025	Smash Hits	1969	$40
— With "W7" and "r." logos on two-tone orange label			
❏ MS2025	Smash Hits	1970	$15
— With only "r." logo on all-orange (tan) label			
❏ MS2025	Smash Hits	198?	$10
— Red and black label or gold and light blue label			
❏ MSK2276	Smash Hits	1977	$12
— Reissue			
❏ MS2025	Smash Hits Bonus Poster	1969	$40
❏ 2RS6481	Soundtrack Recordings from the Film Jimi Hendrix	1973	$30
❏ MS2034	The Cry of Love	1971	$500
— With "W7" and "r." logos on two-tone orange label			
❏ MS2034	The Cry of Love	1971	$18
— With only "r." logo on all-orange (tan) label			
❏ SMAS-93467	The Cry of Love	1971	$75
— Capitol Record Club edition			
❏ 2RS2245	The Essential Jimi Hendrix	1978	$25
❏ HS2293	The Essential Jimi Hendrix Volume Two	1979	$18
— Add 100% if bonus single of "Gloria" with picture sleeve is enclosed			
❏ 22306	The Jimi Hendrix Concerts	1982	$15
❏ MS2103	War Heroes	1972	$25

RHINO

❏ RNDF-254 [PD]	The Jimi Hendrix Interview	1982	$30

RYKO ANALOGUE

❏ RALP-0038 [B]	Live at Winterland	1988	$75
❏ RALP-0078 [B]	Radio One	1988	$85
— Clear vinyl			

SPRINGBOARD

❏ SPB-4010	Jimi Hendrix	197?	$12

TRACK

❏ 612003 [M]	Axis: Bold As Love	2000	$30
— Classic Records issue of the original U.K. mono mix, on a reproduction of the original British label			

TRIP

❏ TLP-9512	Moods	1973	$15
❏ TLP-9500	Rare Hendrix	1972	$18
❏ TLP-9501	Roots of Hendrix	1972	$15
❏ 3509	Superpak	197?	$18
❏ TLP-9523	The Genius of Jimi Hendrix	1973	$15

UNITED ARTISTS

❏ UA-LA505-E	The Very Best of Jimi Hendrix	1975	$15

WARNER BROS.

❏ HS2299	Nine to the Universe	1980	$18
— Reprise cover, Warner Bros. tan "pinstripe" label; possibly Columbia House edition?			

HENKE, MEL

CONTEMPORARY

❏ C-5001 [M]	Dig Mel Henke	1955	$250
❏ C-5003 [M]	Now Spin This	1956	$250

DOBRE

❏ 1031	Love Touch	197?	$30

WARNER BROS.

❏ WS1472 [S]	La Dolce Henke	1962	$50
❏ W1472 [M]	La Dolce Henke	1962	$40

HENLEY, DON
Also see EAGLES; STEVIE NICKS.

ASYLUM

❏ E1-60048 [B]	I Can't Stand Still	1982	$12

GEFFEN

❏ GHS24026	Building the Perfect Beast	1984	$12
❏ GHS24217	The End of the Innocence	1989	$15

HENRIQUE, LUIZ

FONTANA

❏ MGF-27553 [M]	Listen to Me	1966	$25
❏ SRF-67553 [S]	Listen to Me	1966	$30

VERVE

❏ V-8697 [M]	Barra Limpa	1967	$30
❏ V6-8697 [S]	Barra Limpa	1967	$25

Number	Title	Yr	NM
HENRY, CLARENCE			
ARGO			
❏ LP-4009 [M]	You Always Hurt the One You Love	1961	$175
CADET			
❏ LP-4009 [M]	You Always Hurt the One You Love	1966	$50
—Includes copies of Cadet LP in Argo sleeves			
ROULETTE			
❏ SR42039	Alive and Well and Living in New Orleans	1969	$30
HENRY, ERNIE			
FANTASY			
❏ OJC-086	Last Chorus	198?	$25
❏ OJC-102	Presenting Ernie Henry	198?	$30
❏ OJC-1722	Seven Standards and a Blues	198?	$30
RIVERSIDE			
❏ RLP 12-266 [M]	Last Chorus	1958	$300
❏ RLP 12-222 [M]	Presenting Ernie Henry	1956	$500
❏ 6040	Presenting Ernie Henry	197?	$75
❏ RLP 12-248 [M]	Seven Standards and a Blues	1957	$500
HENRY COW			
INTERZONE			
❏ IZ1001 [B]	Western Culture	1980	$30
RED			
❏ RED003 [B]	In Praise Of Learning	1979	$30
❏ RED001 [B]	The Henry Cow Legend	1973	$40
❏ RED002 [B]	Unrest	1979	$30
HENRY TREE			
MAINSTREAM			
❏ S-6129	Electric Holy Man	1968	$30
HENRY'S BOOTBLACKS			
STOMP OFF			
❏ SOS-1149	Hullabaloo	1988	$25
HENSKE, JUDY, AND JERRY YESTER			
REPRISE			
❏ RS-6388	Farewell Aldebaran	1969	$25
STRAIGHT			
❏ STS-1052	Farewell Aldebaran	1968	$50
HENSKE, JUDY			
ELEKTRA			
❏ EKL-241 [M]	High Flying Bird	1964	$25
❏ EKL-7241 [S]	High Flying Bird	1964	$30
❏ EKL-231 [M]	Judy Henske	1963	$25
❏ EKS-7231 [S]	Judy Henske	1963	$30
MERCURY			
❏ MG-21010 [M]	Little Bit of Sunshine…Little Bit of Rain	1965	$25
❏ SR-61010 [S]	Little Bit of Sunshine…Little Bit of Rain	1965	$30
REPRISE			
❏ R-6203 [M]	The Death Defying Judy Henske: The First Concert Album	1966	$25
❏ RS-6203 [S]	The Death Defying Judy Henske: The First Concert Album	1966	$30
HENSLEY, KEN			
Also see URIAH HEEP; BLACKFOOT.			
MERCURY			
❏ SRM-1-661	Proud Words on a Dusty Shelf	1973	$15
WARNER BROS.			
❏ BS2863	Eager to Please	1975	$12
HENSLEY, WALTER			
CAPITOL			
❏ T2149 [M]	The Five-String Banjo Today	1964	$18
❏ ST2149 [S]	The Five-String Banjo Today	1964	$25
HENSON-CONANT, DEBORAH			
GRP			
❏ GR-9578	On the Rise	1989	$20
HERBECK, RAY			
CIRCLE			
❏ CLP-78	Modern Music with Romance	198?	$25
GLENDALE			
❏ 6025	Live and Romantic	1985	$25
HERBERT, MORT			
SAVOY			
❏ MG-12073 [M]	Night People	1956	$40

Number	Title	Yr	NM
HERBIG, GARY			
HEADFIRST			
❏ A-723	Gary Herbig	198?	$25
HERD, THE			
FONTANA			
❏ SRF-67579	Lookin' Thru You	1968	$30
HERDSMEN, THE			
FANTASY			
❏ 3201 [M]	The Herdsmen Play Paris	1955	$100
—Green vinyl			
❏ 3201 [M]	The Herdsmen Play Paris	1955	$40
—Black vinyl			
HERMAN, JERRY			
UNITED ARTISTS			
❏ UAL-3432 [M]	Hello, Jerry!	1965	$25
❏ UAS-6432 [S]	Hello, Jerry!	1965	$30
HERMAN, WOODY			
ACCORD			
❏ SN-7185	All Star Session	1981	$25
AMERICAN RECORDING SOCIETY			
❏ G-410 [M]	The Progressive Big Band Sound	1956	$40
ATLANTIC			
❏ 1328 [M]	Woody Herman at the Monterey Jazz Festival	1960	$300
❏ SD1328 [S]	Woody Herman at the Monterey Jazz Festival	1960	$300
❏ 90044	Woody Herman at the Monterey Jazz Festival	1982	$25
—Reissue of 1328			
BRUNSWICK			
❏ BL54024 [M]	The Swinging Herman Herd	1957	$40
BULLDOG			
❏ 2005	20 Golden Pieces of Woody Herman	198?	$25
CADET			
❏ LPS-835	Heavy Exposure	1969	$30
❏ LPS-819	Light My Fire	1969	$30
❏ LPS-845	Woody	1970	$30
CAPITOL			
❏ T784 [M]	Blues Groove	1956	$75
❏ H324 [10]	Classics in Jazz	1952	$300
❏ T324 [M]	Classics in Jazz	1955	$85
❏ M-11034	Early Autumn	1972	$25
❏ T748 [M]	Jackpot!	1956	$40
❏ T658 [M]	Road Band	1955	$85
❏ T1554 [M]	The Hits of Woody Herman	1961	$100
❏ DT1554 [R]	The Hits of Woody Herman	1961	$75
❏ SM-1554	The Hits of Woody Herman	197?	$20
❏ T560 [M]	The Woody Herman Band	1955	$85
CENTURY			
❏ CR-1110	Chick, Donald, Walter and Woodrow	1978	$30
❏ CRDD-1080	Road Father	1979	$75
—Direct-to-disc recording			
CHESS			
❏ 402	Double Exposure	197?	$35
CLEF			
❏ MGC-745 [M]	Jazz, the Utmost!	1956	$300
COLUMBIA			
❏ CL6049 [10]	Dance Parade	1949	$140
❏ C32530	Jazz Hoot	1974	$30
❏ CL651 [M]	Music for Tired Lovers	1955	$50
❏ CL2357 [M]	My Kind of Broadway	1965	$30
❏ CS9157 [S]	My Kind of Broadway	1965	$35
❏ CL2509 [10]	Ridin' Herd	1955	$120
❏ CL6026 [10]	Sequence in Jazz	1949	$140
❏ CL2552 [M]	The Jazz S(w)inger	1966	$30
❏ CS9352 [S]	The Jazz S(w)inger	1966	$35
❏ CL592 [M]	The Three Herds	1955	$150
—Maroon label with gold print			
❏ CL592 [M]	The Three Herds	1956	$75
—Red and black label with six "eye" logos			
❏ C3L25 [M]	The Thundering Herds	1963	$150
❏ CL683 [M]	Twelve Shades of Blue	1956	$75
❏ CL2563 [10]	Woody!	1955	$120
❏ CL6092 [10]	Woody Herman and His Woodchoppers	1950	$140
❏ CL2491 [M]	Woody Herman's Greatest Hits	1966	$30
❏ CS9291 [S]	Woody Herman's Greatest Hits	1966	$35
❏ PC9291	Woody Herman's Greatest Hits	198?	$20
—Reissue with new prefix			
❏ CL2693 [M]	Woody Live – East & West	1967	$300
❏ CS9493 [S]	Woody Live – East & West	1967	$300
❏ CL2436 [M]	Woody's Winners	1965	$30
❏ CS9236 [S]	Woody's Winners	1965	$35
CONCORD JAZZ			
❏ CJ-302	50th Anniversary Tour	1986	$30
❏ CJ-191	Live at the Concord Jazz Festival	1982	$30

Number	Title	Yr	NM
❏ CJ-170	Woody Herman and Friends at the Monterey Jazz Festival 1979	198?	$30
❏ CJ-330	Woody's Gold Star	1987	$30
❏ CJ-240	World Class	1983	$30
CORAL			
❏ CRL56005 [10]	Blue Prelude	1950	$140
❏ CRL56010 [10]	Woody Herman Souvenirs	1950	$140
❏ CRL56090 [10]	Woody's Best	1953	$140
CROWN			
❏ CLP5180 [M]	The New Swingin' Herman Band	1960	$50
❏ CST205 [S]	The New Swingin' Herman Herd	1960	$50
DECCA			
❏ DL9229 [M]	The Turning Point – 1943-44	1967	$35
❏ DL79229 [R]	The Turning Point – 1943-44	1967	$25
❏ DL8133 [M]	Woodchopper's Ball	1955	$175
❏ DL4484 [M]	Woody Herman's Golden Hits	1964	$35
❏ DL74484 [R]	Woody Herman's Golden Hits	1964	$25
DIAL			
❏ LP-210 [10]	Swinging with the Woodchoppers	1950	$175
DISCOVERY			
❏ 815	The Third Herd	198?	$25
❏ 845	The Third Herd, Volume 2	198?	$25
EVEREST			
❏ SDBR-1032 [S]	Moody Woody	1958	$40
❏ LPBR-5032 [M]	Moody Woody	1958	$75
❏ EV-1222 [M]	The Best of Woody Herman	1963	$35
❏ EV-5222 [S]	The Best of Woody Herman	1963	$50
❏ LPBR-5003 [M]	The Herd Rides Again	1958	$75
❏ SDBR-1003 [S]	The Herd Rides Again… In Stereo	1958	$40
EVEREST ARCHIVE OF FOLK & JAZZ			
❏ 281	Woody Herman	197?	$25
❏ 316	Woody Herman, Vol. 2	197?	$25
❏ 338	Woody Herman, Vol. 3	197?	$25
FANTASY			
❏ 8414	Brand New	1971	$30
❏ F-9477	Children of Lima	1975	$30
❏ FPM-4003 [Q]	Children of Lima	1975	$75
❏ F-9609	Feelin' So Blue	1982	$25
❏ F-9432	Giant Steps	1973	$30
❏ OJC-344	Giant Steps	198?	$25
—Reissue of 9432			
❏ F-9499	King Cobra	1976	$30
❏ F-9470	The Herd at Montreux	1974	$30
❏ 9416	The Raven Speaks	1972	$30
❏ F-9452	The Thundering Herd	1973	$30
FORUM			
❏ F-9016 [M]	Woody Herman Sextet at the Round Table	196?	$50
❏ FS-9016 [S]	Woody Herman Sextet at the Round Table	196?	$75
HARMONY			
❏ HL7013 [M]	Bijou	1957	$50
❏ HL7093 [M]	Summer Sequence	1957	$50
HINDSIGHT			
❏ HSR-116	Woody Herman and His Orchestra 1937	198?	$25
❏ HSR-134	Woody Herman and His Orchestra 1944	198?	$25
INSIGHT			
❏ 208	Woody Herman and His Orchestra 1937-44	198?	$25
JAZZLAND			
❏ JLP-17 [M]	The Fourth Herd	1960	$75
❏ JLP-917 [S]	The Fourth Herd	1960	$75
LION			
❏ L-70059 [M]	The Herman Herd at Carnegie Hall	1958	$75
MARS			
❏ MRX-1 [10]	Dance Date on Mars	1952	$300
❏ MRX-2 [10]	Woody Herman Goes Native	1953	$300
MCA			
❏ 219	Golden Favorites	1973	$25
❏ 4077	The Best of Woody Herman	197?	$35
METRO			
❏ M-514 [M]	Woody Herman	1966	$300
❏ MS-514 [R]	Woody Herman	1966	$175
MGM			
❏ E-284 [10]	Blue Flame	1955	$140
❏ E-3043 [M]	Carnegie Hall 1946	1953	$150
—Compiles 158 and 159 on one 12-inch LP			
❏ E-3385 [M]	Hi-Fi-ing Herd	1956	$50
❏ E-192 [10]	The Third Herd	1953	$140
❏ E-158 [10]	Woody Herman at Carnegie Hall, Vol. 1	1952	$140
❏ E-159 [10]	Woody Herman at Carnegie Hall, 1946, Vol. 2	1952	$140
MOBILE FIDELITY			
❏ 1-219	The Fourth Herd	1994	$75
—Audiophile vinyl			

Number	Title	Yr	NM
PHILIPS			
❑ PHM200092 [M]	Encore: Woody Herman 1963	1963	$35
❑ PHS600092 [S]	Encore: Woody Herman 1963	1963	$50
❑ PHM200004 [M]	Swing Low, Sweet Chariot	1962	$35
❑ PHS600004 [S]	Swing Low, Sweet Chariot	1962	$50
❑ PHM200131 [M]	The Swinging Herman Herd Recorded Live	1964	$35
❑ PHS600131 [S]	The Swinging Herman Herd Recorded Live	1964	$50
❑ PHM200118 [M]	Woody Herman: 1964	1964	$35
❑ PHS600118 [S]	Woody Herman: 1964	1964	$50
❑ PHM200065 [M]	Woody Herman 1963	1963	$35
❑ PHS600065 [S]	Woody Herman 1963	1963	$50
❑ PHM200171 [M]	Woody's Big Band Goodies	1965	$35
❑ PHS600171 [S]	Woody's Big Band Goodies	1965	$50
PICCADILY			
❑ 3333	It's Coolin' Time	198?	$25
PICKWICK			
❑ SPC-3591	Blowin' Up a Storm	1978	$25
RCA VICTOR			
❑ BGL2-2203	40th Anniversary Carnegie Hall Concert	1977	$35
ROULETTE			
❑ R25067 [M]	Woody Herman Sextet at the Round Table	1959	$75
❑ SR25067 [S]	Woody Herman Sextet at the Round Table	1959	$40
SUNBEAM			
❑ 206	Woody Herman and His Orchestra 1936	198?	$25
SUNSET			
❑ SUM-1139 [M]	Blowin' Up a Storm	1966	$25
❑ SUS-5139 [S]	Blowin' Up a Storm	1966	$30
TIME-LIFE			
❑ STBB-09	Big Bands: Woody Herman	1984	$35
TRIP			
❑ 5547	Woody 1963	1974	$25
VERVE			
❑ V6-8764	Concerto for Herd	1968	$50
❑ MGV-2030 [M]	Early Autumn	1957	$150
❑ V-2030 [M]	Early Autumn	1963	$35
❑ V-8558 [M]	Hey! Heard the Herd?	1963	$50
—Reissue of Verve 8216			
❑ V6-8558 [S]	Hey! Heard the Herd?	1963	$35
❑ MGV-8014 [M]	Jazz, the Utmost!	1957	$300
—Reissue of Clef LP			
❑ V-8014 [M]	Jazz, the Utmost!	1963	$35
❑ MGV-2096 [M]	Love Is the Sweetest Thing – Sometimes	1958	$120
❑ V-2096 [M]	Love Is the Sweetest Thing – Sometimes	1963	$35
❑ MGV-8216 [M]	Men from Mars	1958	$120
❑ MGV-2069 [M]	Songs for Hip Lovers	1957	$175
❑ V-2069 [M]	Songs for Hip Lovers	1963	$35
❑ VSP-1 [M]	The First Herd at Carnegie Hall	1966	$35
❑ VSPS-1 [R]	The First Herd at Carnegie Hall	1966	$25
❑ MGV-8255 [M]	Woody Herman '58	1958	$175
❑ V-8255 [M]	Woody Herman '58	1963	$35
❑ VSP-26 [M]	Woody Herman's Woodchoppers & The First Herd Live at Carnegie Hall	1966	$35
❑ VSPS-26 [R]	Woody Herman's Woodchoppers & The First Herd Live at Carnegie Hall	1966	$25
WHO'S WHO IN JAZZ			
❑ 21013	Lionel Hampton Presents Woody Herman	1979	$30
WING			
❑ MGW-12329 [M]	Woody's Big Band Goodies	1966	$25
❑ SRW-16329 [S]	Woody's Big Band Goodies	1966	$30
HERMAN, WOODY/TITO PUENTE			
EVEREST			
❑ LPBR-5010 [M]	Herman's Beat of Puente	1958	$40
❑ SDBR-1010 [S]	Herman's Beat of Puente	1958	$40
HERMAN'S HERMITS			
ABKCO			
❑ 4227-1	Their Greatest Hits	1988	$10
—Abridged version of AB 4227			
❑ AB-4227	XX (Greatest Hits)	1973	$15
MGM			
❑ E-4478 [M]	Blaze	1967	$30
❑ SE-4478 [S]	Blaze	1967	$12
❑ T-91286 [M]	Blaze	1967	$30
—Capitol Record Club edition			
❑ ST-91286 [S]	Blaze	1967	$25
—Capitol Record Club edition			
❑ E-4386 [M]	Both Sides of Herman's Hermits	1966	$12
❑ SE-4386 [R]	Both Sides of Herman's Hermits	1966	$10
❑ E-4295 [M]	Herman's Hermits On Tour	1965	$15
❑ SE-4295 [R]	Herman's Hermits On Tour	1965	$12
❑ ST-90421 [R]	Herman's Hermits On Tour	1965	$25
—Capitol Record Club edition			
❑ T-90421 [M]	Herman's Hermits On Tour	1965	$30
—Capitol Record Club edition			
❑ E-4342 [M]	Hold On!	1966	$18
❑ SE-4342 [P]	Hold On!	1966	$15
❑ T-90646 [M]	Hold On!	1966	$30
—Capitol Record Club edition			
❑ ST-90646 [R]	Hold On!	1966	$25
—Capitol Record Club edition			
❑ E-4282 [M]	Introducing Herman's Hermits	1965	$30
—Version 1: With "Including Their Hit Single 'I'm Into Something Good' " on front cover			
❑ SE-4282 [R]	Introducing Herman's Hermits	1965	$25
—Version 1: With "Including Their Hit Single 'I'm Into Something Good' " on front cover			
❑ E-4282 [M]	Introducing Herman's Hermits	1965	$25
—Version 2: Same as above, but with a sticker that says "Featuring "Mrs. Brown You Have a Lovely Daughter".			
❑ SE-4282 [R]	Introducing Herman's Hermits	1965	$18
—Version 2: Same as above, but with a sticker that says "Featuring "Mrs. Brown You Have a Lovely Daughter".			
❑ E-4282 [M]	Introducing Herman's Hermits	1965	$18
—Version 3: With "Including 'Mrs. Brown You've Got a Lovely Daughter' " on front cover			
❑ SE-4282 [R]	Introducing Herman's Hermits	1965	$12
—Version 3: With "Including 'Mrs. Brown You've Got a Lovely Daughter' " on front cover			
❑ T-90416 [M]	Introducing Herman's Hermits	1965	$30
—Capitol Record Club edition			
❑ ST-90416 [R]	Introducing Herman's Hermits	1965	$25
—Capitol Record Club edition			
❑ SE-4548 [P]	Mrs. Brown You've Got a Lovely Daughter	1968	$12
—"Mrs. Brown You've Got a Lovely Daughter" and "There's a Kind of Hush" are rechanneled			
❑ E-4315 [M]	The Best of Herman's Hermits	1965	$15

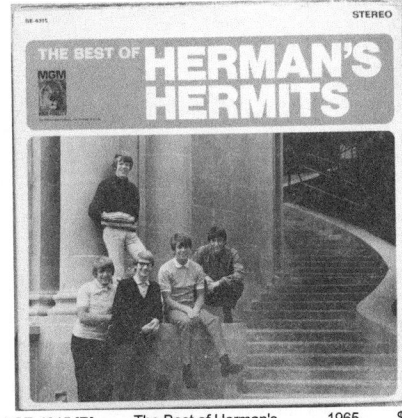

Number	Title	Yr	NM
❑ SE-4315 [R]	The Best of Herman's Hermits	1965	$12
❑ KAO-90613 [M]	The Best of Herman's Hermits	1966	$18
—Capitol Record Club edition			
❑ E-4416 [M]	The Best of Herman's Hermits, Volume 2	1966	$15
❑ SE-4416 [P]	The Best of Herman's Hermits, Volume 2	1966	$12
—Add 50% if bonus photo of Herman is included. "Hold On" and "Leaning on the Lamp Post" are in true stereo.			
❑ E-4505 [M]	The Best of Herman's Hermits, Volume 3	1967	$25
❑ SE-4505 [P]	The Best of Herman's Hermits, Volume 3	1967	$12
—"Don't Go Out Into the Rain," "Museum," "Last Bus Home" and "Mum and Dad" are in true stereo.			
❑ E-4438 [M]	There's a Kind of Hush All Over the World	1967	$25
❑ SE-4438 [R]	There's a Kind of Hush All Over the World	1967	$10
HERMETO			
MUSE			
❑ MR-5086	Hermeto	197?	$30
WARNER BROS.			
❑ BS2980	Slaves Mass	1976	$35
HERNANDEZ, PATRICK			
COLUMBIA			
❑ JC36100	Born to Be Alive	1979	$15

Number	Title	Yr	NM
HERON, MIKE			
ELEKTRA			
❑ EKS-74093 [B]	Smiling Men with Bad Reputations	1971	$30
HERRICK, CHRISTOPHER			
MUSICAL HERITAGE SOCIETY			
❑ MHS7005	Christmas Organ Music from Westmister Abbey	1984	$12
—Recorded in 1979			
HERRMANN, BERNARD			
MOBILE FIDELITY			
❑ 1-240	The Fantasy Film World of Bernard Herrmann	1996	$30
—Audiophile vinyl			
❑ 1-255	The Four Faces of Jazz	1996	$30
—Audiophile vinyl			
HERSCH, FRED			
CHESKY			
❑ 90	Dancing in the Dark	1993	$25
CONCORD JAZZ			
❑ CJ-267	Horizons	1985	$25
HERSEY, BAIRD			
ARISTA NOVUS			
❑ AN3016	Have You Heard	1979	$30
❑ AN3004	Lookin' for That Groove	1977	$30
HERSHEY, MARLENE			
BALDWIN SOUND			
❑ CS7386	Merry Christmas Melodies	196?	$15
HERWIG, CONRAD			
SEA BREEZE			
❑ SB-2034	With Every Breath	1987	$25
HESITATIONS, THE			
KAPP			
❑ KS-3574	Solid Gold	1969	$30
❑ KL-1525 [M]	Soul Superman	1967	$30
❑ KS-3525 [S]	Soul Superman	1967	$30
❑ KS-3548	The New Born Free	1968	$30
❑ KS-3561	Where We're At	1968	$30
HESS, CHUCK			
STRAND			
❑ SL-1084 [M]	Country & Western Favorites	1960	$25
❑ SLS-1084 [S]	Country & Western Favorites	1960	$30
HESTER, CAROLYN			
COLUMBIA			
❑ CL1796 [M]	Carolyn Hester	1962	$100
—With Bob Dylan on harmonica on three tracks; black and red label with six "eye" logos			
❑ CS8596 [S]	Carolyn Hester	1962	$100
—With Bob Dylan on harmonica on three tracks; black and red label with six "eye" logos			
❑ CL1796 [M]	Carolyn Hester	1963	$75
—Red label with "Guaranteed High Fidelity			
❑ CS8596 [S]	Carolyn Hester	1963	$50
—Red label, "360 Sound Stereo" in black			
❑ CL2032 [M]	This Life I'm Living	1963	$40
❑ CS8832 [S]	This Life I'm Living	1963	$50
CORAL			

Number	Title	Yr	NM
❑ CRL57143 [M]	Scarlet Ribbons	1957	$50

Number	Title	Yr	NM

DOT
❏ DLP-3638 [M]	Carolyn Hester at Town Hall One	1965	$18
❏ DLP-25638 [S]	Carolyn Hester at Town Hall One	1965	$25
❏ DLP-3649 [M]	Carolyn Hester at Town Hall Two	1965	$18
❏ DLP-25649 [S]	Carolyn Hester at Town Hall Two	1965	$25
❏ DLP-3604 [M]	That's My Song	1964	$18
❏ DLP-25604 [S]	That's My Song	1964	$25

FOLK ODYSSEY
❏ 32160264	Simply Carolyn Hester	196?	$25

METROMEDIA
❏ MD-1022	Magazine	1970	$75
❏ MD-1001	The Carolyn Hester Coalition	1969	$25

RCA VICTOR
❏ APD1-0086 [Q]	Carolyn Hester	1973	$30

— *Only released in quadraphonic*

TRADITION
❏ TLP-1043 [M]	Carolyn Hester	1961	$40

HEYWARD, NICK

ARISTA
❏ AL8-8106	North of a Miracle	1983	$12

REPRISE
❏ 25758	I Love You Avenue	1988	$12
❏ PRO-A-3384 [DJ]	Words and Music	1988	$25

— *Promo-only interview record*

HEYWOOD, EDDIE

BRUNSWICK
❏ BL58036 [10]	Eddie Heywood '45	1953	$150

CAPITOL
❏ ST-163	Soft Summer Breeze	1969	$75
❏ ST2833	With Love and Strings	1968	$75

COLUMBIA
❏ CL6157 [10]	Piano Moods	1951	$150

COMMODORE
❏ FL-20007 [10]	Eight Selections	1950	$175
❏ XFL-15876	The Biggest Little Band of the Forties	198?	$30

CORAL
❏ CRL57095 [M]	Featuring Eddie Heywood	1957	$40

DECCA
❏ DL8202 [M]	Lightly and Politely	1956	$120
❏ DL8270 [M]	Swing Low Sweet Heywood	1956	$175

EMARCY
❏ MG-36042 [M]	Eddie Heywood	1955	$250

EPIC
❏ LN3327 [M]	Eddie Heywood at Twilight	1956	$150

LIBERTY
❏ LRP-3313 [M]	Canadian Sunset Bossa Nova	1963	$30
❏ LST-7313 [S]	Canadian Sunset Bossa Nova	1963	$35
❏ LRP-3250 [M]	Eddie Heywood's Golden Encores	1962	$30
❏ LST-7250 [S]	Eddie Heywood's Golden Encores	1962	$35
❏ LST-7279 [S]	Manhattan Beat	1963	$35
❏ LRP-3279 [M]	Manhattan Beat	1963	$30

MAINSTREAM
❏ S-6001 [S]	Begin the Beguine	1964	$35
❏ 96001 [M]	Begin the Beguine	1964	$30

MERCURY
❏ MG-20445 [M]	Breezin' Along with the Breeze	1959	$150
❏ SR-60115 [S]	Breezin' Along with the Breeze	1959	$150
❏ MG-20590 [M]	Eddie Heywood at the Piano	1960	$150
❏ SR-60248 [S]	Eddie Heywood at the Piano	1960	$150
❏ MG-20632 [M]	One for My Baby	1960	$150
❏ SR-60632 [S]	One for My Baby	1960	$150

MGM
❏ E-3260 [M]	Eddie Heywood	1956	$40
❏ E-135 [10]	It's Easy to Remember	1952	$150
❏ E-3093 [M]	Pianorama	1955	$50

RCA VICTOR
❏ LPM-1529 [M]	Canadian Sunset	1957	$75
❏ LSP-1529 [S]	Canadian Sunset	1958	$40
❏ LPM-1900 [M]	The Keys and I	1958	$75
❏ LPM-1466 [M]	The Touch of Eddie Heywood	1957	$75

SUNSET
❏ SUM-1121 [M]	An Affair to Remember	196?	$30
❏ SUS-5121 [S]	An Affair to Remember	196?	$30

VOCALION
❏ VL3748 [M]	The Piano Stylings of Eddie Heywood	1966	$35
❏ VL73748 [R]	The Piano Stylings of Eddie Heywood	1966	$30

WING
❏ MGW-12287 [M]	Breezin' Along	196?	$35
❏ SRW-16287 [S]	Breezin' Along	196?	$30

❏ MGW-12137 [M]	Eddie Heywood	196?	$35
❏ SRW-16137 [S]	Eddie Heywood	196?	$30

HI-LITES, THE (2)

DANDEE
❏ DLP-206 [M]	For Your Precious Love	1961	$2000

HI-LO'S, THE

COLUMBIA
❏ CL1509 [M]	All Over the Place	1960	$30
❏ CS8300 [S]	All Over the Place	1960	$75
❏ CL1416 [M]	Broadway Playbill	1959	$75
❏ CS8213 [S]	Broadway Playbill	1959	$40
❏ CS8057 [S]	Love Nest	1958	$40
❏ CL1023 [M]	Now Hear This	1957	$75
❏ CL952 [M]	Suddenly It's the Hi-Lo's	1957	$75
❏ CL1259 [M]	The Hi-Lo's and All That Jazz	1958	$75
❏ CS8077 [S]	The Hi-Lo's and All That Jazz	1958	$40
❏ CL1723 [M]	This Time It's Love	1962	$75
❏ CS8523 [S]	This Time It's Love	1962	$75

COLUMBIA SPECIAL PRODUCTS
❏ P14387	Harmony in Jazz	1978	$30

DRG
❏ SL5184	Clap Yo' Hands	198?	$30

KAPP
❏ KL1194 [M]	On Hand	1960	$75

— *Reissue of Starlite 7008*

❏ KL1027 [M]	The Hi-Lo's and the Jerry Fielding Band	1956	$75
❏ KL1184 [M]	Under Glass	1959	$75

— *Reissue of Starlite 7005*

MCA
❏ 4171	The Hi-Lo's Collection	197?	$35

OMEGA
❏ OSL-11 [S]	The Hi-Lo's in Stereo	195?	$30

PAUSA
❏ 7040	Back Again	198?	$30
❏ 7093	Now	198?	$30

REPRISE
❏ R-6066 [M]	The Hi-Lo's Happen to Bossa Nova	1963	$50
❏ R9-6066 [S]	The Hi-Lo's Happen to Bossa Nova	1963	$75

STARLITE
❏ 6004 [10]	Listen!	1955	$120
❏ 7006 [M]	Listen!	1956	$40

— *Reissue of 6004*

❏ 7008 [M]	On Hand	1956	$40
❏ 6005 [10]	The Hi-Lo's, I Presume	1955	$120
❏ 7007 [M]	The Hi-Lo's. I Presume	1956	$40

— *Reissue of 6005*

❏ 7005 [M]	Under Glass	1956	$40

HI-TONES, THE

HI
❏ HL-31011 [M]	Raunchy Sounds	1963	$25
❏ SHL-32011 [S]	Raunchy Sounds	1963	$30

L&M
❏ 223	I'm So Sorry	196?	$250

HIATT, JOHN

A&M
❏ SP-5158	Bring the Family	1987	$12
❏ SP-5206	Slow Turning	1988	$12
❏ 7502153101	Stolen Moments	1990	$15

EPIC
❏ KE32688	Hangin' Around the Observatory	1974	$12
❏ KE33190	Overcoats	1975	$12
❏ PE33190	Overcoats	198?	$10

— *Budget-line reissue*

GEFFEN
❏ GHS2009	All of a Sudden	1982	$12
❏ GHS4017	Riding with the King	1983	$12
❏ GHS24055	Warming Up to the Ice Age	1984	$12

MCA
❏ 3088	Slug Line	1979	$15
❏ 747	Slug Line	198?	$10

— *Reissue*

❏ 5123	Two-Bit Monster	1980	$15
❏ 741	Two-Bit Monster	198?	$10

— *Reissue*

MOBILE FIDELITY
❏ 1-210	Bring the Family	1994	$50

— *Audiophile vinyl*

HIBBLER, AL

ARGO
❏ LP-601 [M]	Melodies by Al Hibbler	1956	$40

— *Reissue of Marterry LP*

ATLANTIC
❏ 1251 [M]	After the Lights Go Down Low	1957	$300

— *Black label*

❏ 1251 [M]	After the Lights Go Down Low	1961	$300

— *Mostly red label, white fan logo*

❏ 1251 [M]	After the Lights Go Down Low	1963	$175

— *Mostly red label, black fan logo*

BRUNSWICK
❏ BL54036 [M]	Al Hibbler with the Ellingtonians	1957	$50

DECCA
❏ DL8862 [M]	Al Hibbler Remembers the Big Songs of the Big Bands	1959	$150
❏ DL78862 [S]	Al Hibbler Remembers the Big Songs of the Big Bands	1959	$150
❏ DL8420 [M]	Here's Hibbler	1957	$120
❏ DL8757 [M]	Hits by Hibbler	1958	$120
❏ DL8328 [M]	Starring Al Hibbler	1956	$175
❏ DL8697 [M]	Torchy and Blue	1958	$150

DISCOVERY
❏ 842	It's Monday Every Day	198?	$15

— *Reissue of Reprise LP*

LMI
❏ 10001 [M]	Early One Morning	1964	$30

MARTERRY
❏ LP-601 [M]	Melodies by Al Hibbler	1956	$150

MCA
❏ 4098	The Best of Al Hibbler	197?	$20

NORGRAN
❏ MGN-4 [10]	Al Hibbler Favorites	1954	$300
❏ MGN-15 [10]	Al Hibbler Sings Duke Ellington	1954	$300

OPEN SKY
❏ OSR-3126	For Sentimental Reasons	1986	$15

REPRISE
❏ R-2005 [M]	It's Monday Every Day	1961	$30
❏ R9-2005 [S]	It's Monday Every Day	1961	$40

SCORE
❏ SLP-4013 [M]	I Surrender, Dear	1957	$150

VERVE
❏ MGV-4000 [M]	Al Hibbler Sings Love Songs	1956	$175
❏ V-4000 [M]	Al Hibbler Sings Love Songs	1961	$75

HICKEY, ERSEL

BACK-TRAC
❏ P18750	The Rockin' Bluebird	1985	$75

— *Allegedly, only 200 copies of this were pressed*

HICKMAN, DWAYNE

CAPITOL
❏ T1441 [M]	Dobie!	1960	$40
❏ ST1441 [S]	Dobie!	1960	$50

HICKS, DAN, AND HIS HOT LICKS

BLUE THUMB
❏ BTS-51	Last Train to Hicksville...The Home of Happy Feet	1973	$15
❏ BTS-36	Striking It Rich!	1972	$15
❏ BTS-29	Where's the Money?	1971	$15

EPIC
❏ BN26464	Original Recordings	1969	$18

— *Yellow label*

❏ BN26464	Original Recordings	1973	$12

— *Orange label*

❏ PE26464	Original Recordings	198?	$10

— *Reissue with new prefix*

MCA
❏ 671	Last Train to Hicksville...The Home of Happy Feet	198?	$10

— *Reissue*

❏ 670	Striking It Rich!	198?	$10

— *Reissue*

WARNER BROS.
❏ BSK3158	It Happened One Bite	1978	$12

HICKS, JOHN

STRATA-EAST
❏ SES-8002	Hells Bells	1979	$35

THERESA
❏ TR-119	John Hicks	1986	$30
❏ TR-123	John Hicks In Concert	1987	$30
❏ TR-115	Some Other Time	1983	$30

WEST 54TH
❏ 8004	After the Morning	1980	$30

HIGGINBOTHAM, J.C.

JAZZOLOGY
❏ J-28	J.C. Higginbotham Comes Home!	1968	$30

Number	Title	Yr	NM

HIGGINS, BERTIE
KAT FAMILY
| ❏ FZ37901 | Just Another Day in Paradise | 1982 | $12 |
| ❏ PZ37901 | Just Another Day in Paradise | 198? | $10 |

—*Budget-line reissue with new prefix*
| ❏ FZ38587 | Pirates and Poets | 1983 | $12 |

HIGGINS, BILLY
CONTEMPORARY
| ❏ C-14024 | Bridgework | 1987 | $25 |
RED
| ❏ VPA-164 | Once More | 198? | $30 |
| ❏ VPA-141 | Soweto | 1979 | $30 |

HIGGINS, CHUCK
COMBO
| ❏ LP-300 [M] | Pachuko Hop | 195? | $800 |

—*"Naked woman" cover (well, she's wearing a scarf)*
| ❏ LP-300 [M] | Pachuko Hop | 195? | $40 |

—*Chuck Higgins on cover, fully clothed*

HIGGINS, EDDIE
ATLANTIC
| ❏ 1446 [M] | Soulero | 1966 | $35 |
| ❏ SD1446 [S] | Soulero | 1966 | $25 |
VEE JAY
| ❏ LP-3017 [M] | Eddie Higgins | 1961 | $30 |
| ❏ SR-3017 [S] | Eddie Higgins | 1961 | $40 |

HIGH INERGY
GORDY
❏ G7-989R1	Frenzy	1979	$15
❏ 6041GL	Groove Patrol	1983	$12
❏ G8-1005M1	High Inergy	1981	$15
❏ G8-996M1	Hold On	1980	$15
❏ 6006GL	So Right	1982	$12
❏ G7-982R1	Steppin' Out	1978	$15
❏ G6-978S1	Turnin' On	1977	$15

HIGH SOCIETY JAZZ BAND, THE
STOMP OFF
| ❏ SOS-1166 | 'Lasses Candy | 1989 | $25 |
| ❏ SOS-1010 | Shake It and Break It | 1981 | $30 |

HIGH TIDE
Includes Simon House of HAWKWIND.
LIBERTY
| ❏ LST-7638 [B] | Sea Shanties | 1969 | $100 |

HIGH TREASON
ABBOTT
| ❏ ABS-1209 [B] | High Treason | 1968 | $100 |

HIGHER PRIMATES
GM
| ❏ 3003 | Environmental Impressions | 1985 | $25 |

HIGHFILL, GEORGE
WARNER BROS.
| ❏ 25618 | Waitin' Up | 1987 | $15 |

HIGHTOWER, DEAN
ABC-PARAMOUNT
| ❏ ABC-312 [M] | Twangy Guitar with a Beat | 1959 | $30 |
| ❏ ABCS-312 [S] | Twangy Guitar with a Beat | 1959 | $30 |

HIGHTOWER, DONNA
CAPITOL
❏ T1273 [M]	Gee Baby…Ain't I Good to You	1959	$75
❏ ST1273 [S]	Gee Baby…Ain't I Good to You	1959	$100
❏ T1133 [M]	Take One	1959	$85
❏ ST1133 [S]	Take One	1959	$100

HIGHTOWER, WILLIE
CAPITOL
| ❏ ST-367 | If I Had a Hammer | 1969 | $150 |
COLLECTABLES
| ❏ COL-5170 | Golden Classics | 198? | $12 |

HIGHWAY 101
WARNER BROS.
| ❏ 25742 | 101 (2) | 1988 | $10 |
| ❏ 1P8076 | Greatest Hits | 1990 | $18 |

—*Columbia House edition (no regular vinyl version)*
| ❏ R183480 | Greatest Hits | 1990 | $25 |

—*BMG Direct Marketing edition (no regular vinyl version)*
| ❏ 25608 | Highway 101 | 1987 | $10 |
| ❏ 25992 | Paint the Town | 1989 | $12 |

HIGHWAYMEN, THE
ABC-PARAMOUNT
| ❏ 522 [M] | On a New Road | 1965 | $12 |
| ❏ S-522 [S] | On a New Road | 1965 | $15 |
UNITED ARTISTS

❏ UAL3225 [M]	Encore!	1962	$15
❏ UAS6225 [S]	Encore!	1962	$18
❏ UAL3348 [M]	Homecoming	1964	$15
❏ UAS6348 [S]	Homecoming	1964	$18
❏ UAL3294 [M]	Hootenanny with the Highwaymen	1963	$15
❏ UAS6294 [S]	Hootenanny with the Highwaymen	1963	$18
❏ UAL3245 [M]	March On, Brothers	1963	$15
❏ UAS6245 [S]	March On, Brothers	1963	$18
❏ UAL3323 [M]	One More Time	1964	$12
❏ UAS6323 [S]	One More Time	1964	$18
❏ UAL3168 [M]	Standing Room Only!	1962	$15
❏ UAS6168 [S]	Standing Room Only!	1962	$18
❏ UAL3125 [M]	The Highwaymen	1961	$12
❏ UAS6125 [S]	The Highwaymen	1961	$18

HILDEBRAND, RAY
WORD
| ❏ WST-8411 | He's Everything to Me | 196? | $15 |
| ❏ WST-8465 | I Need You Every Hour | 1971 | $15 |

HILDEGARDE
DECCA
| ❏ DL8656 [M] | Souvenir Album | 1958 | $30 |

—*Black label, silver print*

HILDINGER, DAVE
BATON
| ❏ 1204 [M] | The Young Moderns | 1957 | $40 |

HILL, ANDREW
ARISTA FREEDOM
| ❏ AL1023 | Montreux | 1976 | $35 |
| ❏ AL1007 | Spiral | 1975 | $35 |
ARTISTS HOUSE
| ❏ 9 | From California with Love | 1979 | $30 |
BLUE NOTE
| ❏ BLP4203 [M] | Andrew!!! -- The Music of Andrew Hill | 1965 | $0 |

—*not known to exist*
| ❏ BST-84203 [S] | Andrew!!! -- The Music of Andrew Hill | 1967 | $85 |

—*With "A Division of Liberty Records" on label; version with "New York, USA" on label not known to exist*
| ❏ BLP-4151 [M] | Black Fire | 1963 | $300 |
| ❏ BST-84151 [S] | Black Fire | 1963 | $150 |
—*With "New York, USA" address on label*
| ❏ BST-84151 [S] | Black Fire | 1967 | $35 |
—*With "A Division of Liberty Records" on label*
| ❏ BLP-4217 [M] | Compulsion | 1965 | $75 |
| ❏ BST-84217 [S] | Compulsion | 1965 | $30 |
—*With "New York, USA" on label*
| ❏ BST-84217 [S] | Compulsion | 1967 | $35 |
—*With "A Division of Liberty Records" on label*
❏ LN-1030	Dance with Andrew Hill	1980	$30
❏ BST-84303	Grass Roots	1968	$25
❏ B1-92051	Internal Spirit	198?	$25
❏ BLP-4159 [M]	Judgment!	1964	$150
❏ BST-84159 [S]	Judgment!	1964	$40
—*With "New York, USA" on label*
| ❏ BST-84159 [S] | Judgment! | 1967 | $35 |
—*With "A Division of Liberty Records" on label*
❏ B1-28981	Judgment!	1994	$35
❏ BST-84330	Lift Every Voice	1969	$25
❏ BLP-4233 [M]	One for One	1966	$0

—*Canceled*
| ❏ BST-84233 [S] | One for One | 1966 | $0 |

—*Canceled*
❏ BN-LA459-H2	One for One	1975	$25
❏ BLP-4167 [M]	Point of Departure	1964	$75
❏ BST-84167 [S]	Point of Departure	1964	$40
—*With "New York, USA" address on label*
| ❏ BST-84167 [S] | Point of Departure | 1967 | $35 |
—*With "A Division of Liberty Records" on label*
❏ B1-32097	Smokestack	1995	$35
❏ BLP-4160 [M]	Smoke Stack	1964	$150
❏ BST-84160 [S]	Smoke Stack	1964	$40
—*With "New York, USA" address on label*
| ❏ BST-84160 [S] | Smoke Stack | 1967 | $35 |
—*With "A Division of Liberty Records" on label*
INNER CITY
❏ IC-2044	Divine Revelation	1976	$35
❏ IC-2026	Invitation	1975	$35
❏ IC-6022	Nefertiti	1977	$35
MOSAIC
| ❏ MQ10-161 [B] | The Complete Andrew Hill Blue Note Sessions | 199? | $400 |
SOUL NOTE
❏ SN-1010	Faces of Hope	198?	$30
❏ 121113	Shades	199?	$30
❏ SN-1013	Strange Serenade	198?	$30
❏ 121110	Verona Rag	199?	$30
STEEPLECHASE
| ❏ SCS-1044 | Divine Revelation | 198? | $30 |
| ❏ SCS-1026 | Invitation | 198? | $30 |
WARWICK
| ❏ W-2002 [M] | So in Love | 1960 | $75 |
| ❏ W-2002ST [S] | So in Love | 1960 | $100 |

HILL, BENNY
CAPITOL
| ❏ SN-12049 | Words and Music | 1979 | $18 |

HILL, BUCK
MUSE
| ❏ MR-5384 | Capital Hill | 198? | $12 |
STEEPLECHASE
❏ SCS-1160	Easy to Love	198?	$35
❏ SCS-1173	Impressions	198?	$35
❏ SCS-1123	Scope	1980	$35
❏ SCS-1095	This Is Buck Hill	1979	$35

HILL, GOLDIE
DECCA
❏ DL4219 [M]	According to My Heart	1962	$25
❏ DL74219 [S]	According to My Heart	1962	$30
❏ DL4492 [M]	Country Hit Parade	1964	$25
❏ DL74492 [S]	Country Hit Parade	1964	$30
❏ DL4034 [M]	Goldie Hill	1960	$30
❏ DL74034 [S]	Goldie Hill	1960	$30
❏ DL4148 [M]	Lonely Heartaches	1961	$25
❏ DL74148 [S]	Lonely Heartaches	1961	$30
VOCALION
| ❏ VL73800 | Country Songs | 196? | $15 |

HILL, LAURYN
RUFFHOUSE
| ❏ C269035 | The Miseducation of Lauryn Hill | 1998 | $18 |

HILL, TINY
HINDSIGHT
| ❏ HSR-159 | The Uncollected Tiny Hill and His Orchestra, 1944 | 1980 | $12 |
MERCURY
❏ MG-20630 [M]	Dancin' and Singin' with Tiny Hill	195?	$175
❏ MG-20631 [M]	Golden Hits	195?	$30
❏ SR-60631 [R]	Golden Hits	196?	$20
❏ MG-25126 [10]	Tiny Hill	1952	$150

HILL, VINCE
TOWER
| ❏ T5064 [M] | At the Club | 1966 | $30 |

HILL, VINSON
SAVOY
| ❏ MG-12187 [M] | The Vinson Hill Trio | 1966 | $30 |

HILL, Z.Z.
COLUMBIA
| ❏ JC35030 | Let's Make a Deal | 1978 | $15 |
| ❏ JC36125 | The Mark of Z.Z. | 1979 | $15 |
KENT
| ❏ KST-528 | A Whole Lot of Soul | 1969 | $18 |
| ❏ KST-560 | Dues Paid in Full | 1971 | $18 |
MALACO
| ❏ 7415 | I'm a Blues Man | 1984 | $12 |
| ❏ 7411 | The Rhyhtm & The Blues | 1983 | $12 |
MANKIND
| ❏ 201 | The Brand New Z.Z. Hill | 1971 | $18 |

Number	Title	Yr	NM

UNITED ARTISTS

❏ UA-LA417-G	Keep On Lovin' You	1975	$15
❏ UAS5589	The Best Thing That's Ever Happened to Me	1972	$15

HILLAGE, STEVE

ATLANTIC

❏ SD18205 [B]	L	1976	$18
❏ SD19144 [B]	Motivation Radio	1977	$18

VIRGIN

❏ VR13-118 [B]	Fish Rising	1975	$35

HILLMAN, CHRIS

ASYLUM

❏ 7E-1104	Clear Sailin'	1977	$15
❏ 7E-1062	Slippin' Away	1976	$15

SUGAR HILL

❏ SH3743	Desert Rose	1984	$15
❏ SH3729	Morning Sky	1982	$15

HILLMEN, THE

TOGETHER

❏ STT-1012	The Hillmen	1970	$100

HILLOW HAMMET

HOUSE OF FOX

❏ 2	Hammer	1968	$175

HILLSIDE SINGERS, THE

METROMEDIA

❏ MD1051	I'd Like to Teach the World to Sing	1971	$15

HILLTOPPERS, THE

DOT

❏ DLP-3073 [M]	Love in Bloom	1958	$30
❏ DLP-105 [10]	The Hilltoppers	1954	$75
❏ DLP-106 [10]	The Hilltoppers	1954	$75
❏ DLP-3003 [M]	The Hilltoppers Present Tops in Pops	1955	$50

—Cartoon of female fan on cover

❏ DLP-3003 [M]	The Hilltoppers Present Tops in Pops	1956	$30

—Four caps with "W" on them on cover

❏ DLP-3029 [M]	The Towering Hilltoppers	1957	$30

HIMBER, RICHARD

CIRCLE

❏ 7	Richard Himber and His Orchestra: 1939-1940	198?	$25

HINDU LOVE GODS

GIANT

❏ 24406	Hindu Love Gods	1990	$18

HINES, EARL "FATHA," AND BUDD JOHNSON

CLASSIC JAZZ

❏ 129	Linger Awhile	197?	$30

HINES, EARL "FATHA," AND COLEMAN HAWKINS

LIMELIGHT

❏ LM-82020 [M]	The Grand Reunion	1965	$25
❏ LS-86020 [S]	The Grand Reunion	1965	$30

TRIP

❏ 5557	The Grand Reunion	197?	$25

HINES, EARL "FATHA," AND JAKI BYARD

VERVE/MPS

❏ 825195-1	Duet	1985	$25

HINES, EARL "FATHA," AND MARVA JOSIE

CATALYST

❏ 7622	His Old Lady and Me	197?	$30

HINES, EARL "FATHA," AND MAXINE SULLIVAN

CHIAROSCURO

❏ 107	Live at the Overseas Press Club	1971	$35

HINES, EARL "FATHA," AND PAUL GONSALVES

BLACK LION

❏ 306	It Don't Mean a Thing	197?	$30

HINES, EARL "FATHA," AND ROY ELDRIDGE

LIMELIGHT

❏ LM-82028 [M]	The Grand Reunion, Volume 2	1965	$25
❏ LS-86028 [S]	The Grand Reunion, Volume 2	1965	$30

XANADU

❏ 106	At the Village Vanguard	197?	$30

Number	Title	Yr	NM

HINES, EARL "FATHA," AND TERESA BREWER

DOCTOR JAZZ

❏ FW38810	We Love You Fats	1983	$25

HINES, EARL "FATHA

ABC IMPULSE!

❏ AS-9108 [S]	Once Upon a Time	1968	$35

ADVANCE

❏ 4 [10]	Fats Waller Memorial Set	1951	$175

ATLANTIC

❏ ALS-120 [10]	Earl Hines: QRS Solos	1952	$350

AUDIOPHILE

❏ APS-112	Earl Hines Comes In Handy	197?	$35
❏ APS-113	Hines Does Hoagy	197?	$35
❏ APS-111	My Tribute to Louis	1971	$35

BASF

❏ 20742	Fatha and His Flock On Tour	1972	$35

BIOGRAPH

❏ 12056	Earl Hines in New Orleans	197?	$25
❏ 12055	Solo Walk in Tokyo	197?	$25

BLACK LION

❏ 112	Tea for Two	1973	$30
❏ 200	Tour de Force	1974	$30

BLUEBIRD

❏ AXM2-5508	Fatha Jumps	197?	$35

BRAVO

❏ K-134	Earl Fatha Hines and His Orchestra	196?	$25

BRUNSWICK

❏ BL58035 [10]	Earl Hines Plays Fats Waller	1953	$120

CAPITOL

❏ T1971 [M]	Earl "Fatha" Hines	1963	$75
❏ ST1971 [S]	Earl "Fatha" Hines	1963	$75

CHIAROSCURO

❏ 116	An Evening with Hines	1972	$25
❏ 200	Earl Hines in New Orleans	1978	$30
❏ 157	Live at the New School	1974	$30
❏ 180	Live at the New School, Volume 2	1977	$30
❏ 131	Quintessential 1974	1974	$35
❏ 120	Quintessential Continued	1973	$35
❏ 101	Quintessential Recording Session	1971	$35

—Reissue of Halcyon 101

CLASSIC JAZZ

❏ 144	Earl Hines at Sundown	198?	$30
❏ 31	Earl Hines Plays Gershwin	1974	$35

COLUMBIA

❏ CL6171 [10]	Piano Moods	1951	$120
❏ CL2320 [M]	The New Earl Hines Trio	1965	$25
❏ CS9120 [S]	The New Earl Hines Trio	1965	$30

COLUMBIA JAZZ MASTERPIECES

❏ CJ44197	Live at the Village Vanguard	1988	$25

CONTACT

❏ 2 [M]	Spontaneous Explorations	1964	$30
❏ S-2 [S]	Spontaneous Explorations	1964	$30

CRAFTSMEN

❏ 8041 [M]	Swingin' and Singin'	1960	$30

DECCA

❏ DL79235 [R]	Earl Hines at the Apex Club	1968	$30
❏ DL9235 [M]	Earl Hines at the Apex Club	1968	$30
❏ DL75048	Fatha Blows Best	1969	$35
❏ DL9221 [M]	Southside Swing (1934-35)	1967	$30
❏ DL79221 [R]	Southside Swing (1934-35)	1967	$30

DELMARK

❏ DS-212	Earl Hines At Home	1969	$30

DIAL

❏ LP-306 [10]	Earl Hines All Stars	1953	$300
❏ LP-303 [10]	Earl Hines Trio	1952	$300

ENSIGN

❏ 22021	Earl Hines Rhythm	1969	$25

EPIC

❏ LN3501 [M]	Earl "Fatha" Hines	1958	$150
❏ LN3223 [M]	Oh, Fatha!	1956	$150

EVEREST ARCHIVE OF FOLK & JAZZ

❏ 246	Earl "Fatha" Hines	1970	$30
❏ 322	Earl "Fatha" Hines, Volume 2	197?	$25

FANTASY

❏ OJC-1740	A Monday Date	198?	$25
❏ 3238 [M]	Earl "Fatha" Hines Solo	1956	$150

—Red vinyl

❏ 3238 [M]	Earl "Fatha" Hines Solo	195?	$50

—Black vinyl

❏ 3217 [M]	Fatha" Plays "Fats	1956	$150

—Red vinyl

❏ 3217 [M]	Fatha" Plays "Fats	195?	$50

—Black vinyl

❏ 8381	Incomparable	1968	$30

Number	Title	Yr	NM

FLYING DUTCHMAN

❏ FD-10147	The Mighty Fatha	1973	$35

FOCUS

❏ FM-335 [M]	The Real Earl Hines In Concert	1965	$30
❏ FS-335 [S]	The Real Earl Hines In Concert	1965	$30

GNP CRESCENDO

❏ GNP-9042	Earl "Fatha" Hines All-Stars	197?	$25
❏ GNP-9043	Earl "Fatha" Hines All-Stars, Vol. 2	197?	$25
❏ GNP-9010	Earl "Fatha" Hines in Paris	197?	$25
❏ GNPS-9054	Live at the Crescendo	1992	$30

HALCYON

❏ 101	The Quintessential Recording Session	196?	$25

HALL OF FAME

❏ 609	Earl "Fatha" Hines All-Stars	197?	$25

IMPROV

❏ 7114	Live at the Downtown Club	1976	$30

IMPULSE!

❏ A-9108 [M]	Once Upon a Time	1966	$120
❏ AS-9108 [S]	Once Upon a Time	1966	$120

INNER CITY

❏ IC-1142	Paris Session	198?	$30

JAZZ PANORAMA

❏ 7 [M]	All Stars	1961	$40

M&K

❏ 105	Fatha	1979	$30

—Direct-to-disc recording

MASTER JAZZ

❏ 8101	Blues and Things	1970	$35
❏ 8114	Earl Hines Plays Duke Ellington	1971	$35
❏ 8132	Earl Hines Plays Duke Ellington, Volume 4	1975	$30
❏ 8126	Earl Hines Plays Duke Ellington, Volumes 2 and 3	1973	$25
❏ 8109	Hines '65	1971	$35

MCA

❏ 29070	Once Upon a Time	198?	$25
❏ 1373	Rhythm Sundae	198?	$25
❏ 1311	South Side Swing	198?	$25

MERCURY

❏ MG-25018 [10]	Earl Hines and the All Stars	1950	$300

MGM

❏ E-3832 [M]	Earl's Pearls	1960	$30
❏ SE-3832 [S]	Earl's Pearls	1960	$30

MILESTONE

❏ 2012	Monday Date 1928	197?	$30

MUSE

❏ MR-2001/2	The Legendary Little Theatre Concert of 1964	198?	$35
❏ DE-602	The Legendary Little Theatre Concert of 1964, Volume 1	198?	$25

NOCTURNE

❏ NLP-5 [10]	Earl "Fatha" Hines	1954	$175

PRESTIGE

❏ 24043	Another Monday Date	197?	$35
❏ 2515	Boogie Woogie on St. Louis Blues	198?	$30

QUICKSILVER

❏ QS-9001	Fatha	198?	$25
❏ QS-9000	Live and in Living Jazz	198?	$25

RCA VICTOR

❏ LPT-20 [10]	Earl Hines with Billy Eckstine	1953	$120
❏ LPV-512 [M]	The Grand Terrace Band	1965	$30
❏ LPM-3380 [M]	Up to Date	1965	$25
❏ LSP-3380 [S]	Up to Date	1965	$30

RIVERSIDE

❏ RLP-398 [M]	A Monday Date	1961	$250
❏ RS-9398 [R]	A Monday Date	196?	$25

ROYALE

❏ 18166 [10]	Eal "Fatha" Hines -- Great Piano Solos	195?	$120

STORYVILLE

❏ 4063	Earl Hines at the Club Hangover	198?	$25

TIARA

❏ TMT-7524 [M]	Earl "Fatha" Hines with Buck Clayton	195?	$25

TIME-LIFE

❏ STL-J-11	Giants of Jazz	1980	$75

TOPS

❏ L-1599 [M]	Fatha	195?	$30

TRIP

❏ J-3	All-Star Session	1970	$30

VERVE

❏ VSP-35 [M]	Life with Fatha	1966	$25
❏ VSPS-35 [R]	Life with Fatha	1966	$30

Number	Title	Yr	NM
WHO'S WHO IN JAZZ			
❏ 21004	Lionel Hampton Presents Earl Hines	1978	$30
X			
❏ LVA-3023 [10]	Piano Solos	1954	$120
XANADU			
❏ 203	Varieties!	1985	$25
HINES, ERNIE			
WE PRODUCE			
❏ 1902	Electrified	1972	$50
HINES, HINES & DAD			
COLUMBIA			
❏ CS9679	Pandemonium	1968	$25
HINES, MIMI			
DECCA			
❏ DL4834 [M]	Mimi Hines Is a Happening	1967	$30
❏ DL74834 [S]	Mimi Hines Is a Happening	1967	$25
❏ DL4709 [S]	Mimi Hines Sings	1966	$25
❏ DL74709 [S]	Mimi Hines Sings	1966	$30
HINO, TERUMASA			
CATALYST			
❏ 7910	At the Berlin Jazz Festival '71	197?	$30
❏ 7901	Fuji	197?	$30
EMJA			
❏ 2028	Taro's Mood	197?	$35
INNER CITY			
❏ IC-6068	City Connection	198?	$30
❏ IC-6069	Daydream	198?	$30
❏ IC-6065	May Dance	197?	$30
❏ IC-6027	Speak to Loneliness	197?	$30
HINSON, DON, AND THE RIGAMORTICIANS			
CAPITOL			
❏ T2219 [M]	Monster Dance Party	1964	$50
❏ ST2219 [S]	Monster Dance Party	1964	$50
HINTON, JOE			
BACK BEAT			
❏ B-60 [M]	Funny (How Time Slips Away)	1965	$50
❏ BS-60 [S]	Funny (How Time Slips Away)	1965	$80
DUKE			
❏ DLPS-91	Duke-Peacock Remembers Joe Hinton	1969	$25
HINTON, MILT; WENDELL MARSHALL; BULL RUTHER			
RCA VICTOR			
❏ LPM-1107 [M]	Basses Loaded!	1955	$100
HINTON, MILT			
BETHLEHEM			
❏ BCP-10 [M]	East Coast Jazz Series #5	1957	$300
❏ BCP-1020 [10]	Milt Hinton Quartet	1955	$300
CHIAROSCURO			
❏ 188	Trio	1978	$30
EPIC			
❏ LN3271 [M]	The Rhythm Section	1956	$150
EXPOSURE			
❏ 6231910	The Judge's Decision	198?	$30
FAMOUS DOOR			
❏ 104	Here Swings The Judge	197?	$35
HINTON, SAM			
DECCA			
❏ DL8418 [M]	A Family Tree of Folk Songs	1957	$30
❏ DL8108 [M]	Singing Across the Land	1955	$40
HINZE, CHRIS			
ATLANTIC			
❏ SD19185	Bamboo	1978	$30
COLUMBIA			
❏ KC33363	Sister Slick	1975	$30
HIPP, JUTTA			
BLUE NOTE			
❏ BLP-1515 [M]	Jutta Hipp at the Hickory House, Volume 1	1956	$1000
—Deep groove" version, Lexington Ave. address on label			
❏ BLP-1515 [M]	Jutta Hipp at the Hickory House, Volume 1	1956	$800
—Deep groove" version, W. 63rd St. address on label			
❏ BLP-1515 [M]	Jutta Hipp at the Hickory House, Volume 1	1963	$250
—With "New York, USA" address on label			
❏ BLP-1516 [M]	Jutta Hipp at the Hickory House, Volume 2	1956	$1500

Number	Title	Yr	NM
—Deep groove" version, Lexington Ave. address on label			
❏ BLP-1516 [M]	Jutta Hipp at the Hickory House, Volume 2	1956	$800
—Deep groove" version, W. 63rd St. address on label			
❏ BLP-1516 [M]	Jutta Hipp at the Hickory House, Volume 2	1963	$175
—With "New York, USA" address on label			
❏ BLP-1516 [B]	Jutta Hipp at the Hickory House, Volume 2	1956	$1000
—Lexington Ave address			
❏ BLP-1530 [M]	Jutta Hipp with Zoot Sims	1956	$5000
—Deep groove" version; Lexington Ave. address on label			
❏ BLP-1530 [M]	Jutta Hipp with Zoot Sims	1956	$2000
—Deep groove" version, W. 63sr St. address on label			
❏ BLP-1530 [M]	Jutta Hipp with Zoot Sims	1963	$175
—With "New York, USA" address on label			

Number	Title	Yr	NM
❏ BLP-1530 [M]	Jutta Hipp with Zoot Sims	1971	$75
—A Division of United Artists" on label			
❏ BLP-1530 [M]	Jutta Hipp with Zoot Sims	2003	$150
—200-gram reissue; distributed by Classic Records			
❏ BLP-5056 [10]	Jutta -- New Faces, New Sounds from Germany	1955	$800
MGM			
❏ E-3157 [M]	Cool Europe	1955	$175
HIPSWAY			
COLUMBIA			
❏ BFC40522	Hipsway	1986	$12
HIROTA, JOJI			
INNER CITY			
❏ IC-1127	Wheel of Fortune	198?	$30
HIRT, AL, AND ANN-MARGRET			
RCA VICTOR			
❏ LPM-2690 [M]	Beauty and the Beard	1964	$25
❏ LSP-2690 [S]	Beauty and the Beard	1964	$25
HIRT, AL			
ACCORD			
❏ SN-7187	Java	1981	$10
ALLEGIANCE			
❏ AV-5032	Blues Line	1986	$10
❏ AV-5018	Showtime	1985	$10
AUDIO FIDELITY			
❏ AF-6282	Hirt...So Good!	1978	$25
❏ AFLP-1878 [M]	Swingin' Dixie	1959	$35
❏ AFSD-5878 [S]	Swingin' Dixie	1959	$25
❏ AFLP-1877 [M]	Swingin' Dixie (At Dan's Pier 600 in New Orleans)	1959	$35
❏ AFSD-5877 [S]	Swingin' Dixie (At Dan's Pier 600 in New Orleans)	1959	$25
❏ AFLP-1926 [M]	Swingin' Dixie (Vol. 3)	1961	$35
❏ AFSD-5926 [S]	Swingin' Dixie (Vol. 3)	1961	$25
❏ T-90284 [M]	Swingin' Dixie (Vol. 3)	196?	$100
—Capitol Record Club edition			
❏ ST-90284 [S]	Swingin' Dixie (Vol. 3)	196?	$100
—Capitol Record Club edition			
❏ AFLP-1927 [M]	Swingin' Dixie (Vol. 4)	1961	$35
❏ AFSD-5927 [S]	Swingin' Dixie (Vol. 4)	1961	$25
CORAL			
❏ CRL57402 [M]	Al Hirt in New Orleans	1962	$30
❏ CRL757402 [S]	Al Hirt in New Orleans	1962	$35
CROWN			
❏ CLP-5457 [M]	The Dawn Busters	196?	$30
❏ CST-457 [S]	The Dawn Busters	196?	$30
GHB			
❏ 107	Mardi Gras Parade Music	197?	$25
GWP			
❏ 2005	Al Hirt Country	1971	$25
❏ 2004	Al Hirt Gold	1971	$25
❏ 2002	Paint Your Wagon	1970	$25

Number	Title	Yr	NM
LONGINES SYMPHONETTE			
❏ LWCP1	The Best of Dixieland Jazz	196?	$30
METRO			
❏ M-517 [M]	Al Hirt	1965	$175
❏ MS-517 [S]	Al Hirt	1965	$175
MONUMENT			
❏ 7603	Jumbo's Gumbo	1977	$10
—Reissue of 33885			
❏ PZ33885	Jumbo's Gumbo	1975	$25
❏ KZ32913	Raw Sugar/Sweet Sauce/ Banana Puddin'	1974	$25
❏ 6642	Raw Sugar/Sweet Sauce/ Banana Puddin'	1976	$10
—Reissue of 32913			
PAIR			
❏ PDL2-1048	New Orleans By Night	1986	$15
RCA CAMDEN			
❏ CXS-9015	Al Hirt Blows His Own Horn	1972	$30
❏ CAS-2316	Al's Place	1970	$25
❏ CAS-2573	Have a Merry Little	1971	$25
❏ CAL-2138 [M]	Struttin' Down Royal Street	1967	$30
❏ CAS-2138 [S]	Struttin' Down Royal Street	1967	$25
RCA VICTOR			
❏ LPM-2354 [M]	Al (He's the King) Hirt and His Band	1961	$30
❏ LSP-2354 [S]	Al (He's the King) Hirt and His Band	1961	$35
❏ LSP-4247	Al Hirt	1970	$30
❏ LPM-2497 [M]	Al Hirt at the Mardi Gras	1962	$30
❏ LSP-2497 [S]	Al Hirt at the Mardi Gras	1962	$35
❏ LSP-4101	Al Hirt Now	1969	$30
❏ LPM-3917 [M]	Al Hirt Plays Bert Kaempfert	1968	$20
❏ LSP-3917 [S]	Al Hirt Plays Bert Kaempfert	1968	$35
❏ LPM-2917 [M]	Cotton Candy	1964	$30
❏ LSP-2917 [S]	Cotton Candy	1964	$35
❏ LSP-4161	Here in My Heart	1969	$30
❏ LPM-2733 [M]	Honey in the Horn	1963	$30
❏ LSP-2733 [S]	Honey in the Horn	1963	$35
❏ LPM-2446 [M]	Horn A-Plenty	1962	$30
❏ LSP-2446 [S]	Horn A-Plenty	1962	$35
❏ LSP-4020	In Love with You	1968	$30
❏ LPM-3653 [M]	Latin in the Horn	1966	$30
❏ LSP-3653 [S]	Latin in the Horn	1966	$35
❏ LPM-3416 [M]	Live at Carnegie Hall	1965	$30
❏ LSP-3416 [S]	Live at Carnegie Hall	1965	$35
❏ LPM-3773 [M]	Music to Watch Girls By	1967	$35
❏ LSP-3773 [S]	Music to Watch Girls By	1967	$35
❏ LPM-2607 [M]	Our Man in New Orleans	1963	$30
❏ LSP-2607 [S]	Our Man in New Orleans	1963	$35
❏ LM-2729 [M]	Pops" Goes the Trumpet	1964	$35
❏ LSC-2729 [S]	Pops" Goes the Trumpet	1964	$25
—With the Boston Pops Orchestra conducted by Arthur Fiedler			
❏ LPM-3878 [M]	Soul in the Horn	1967	$35
❏ LSP-3878 [S]	Soul in the Horn	1967	$35
❏ LPM-2965 [M]	Sugar Lips	1964	$30
❏ LSP-2965 [S]	Sugar Lips	1964	$35
❏ LPM-3337 [M]	That Honey Horn Sound	1965	$30
❏ LSP-3337 [S]	That Honey Horn Sound	1965	$35
❏ LPM-3309 [M]	The Best of Al Hirt	1965	$30
❏ LSP-3309 [S]	The Best of Al Hirt	1965	$35
❏ ANL1-1034	The Best of Al Hirt	1975	$25
❏ LPM-3556 [M]	The Best of Al Hirt, Volume 2	1966	$30
❏ LSP-3556 [S]	The Best of Al Hirt, Volume 2	1966	$35
❏ LPM-2366 [M]	The Greatest Horn in the World	1961	$30
❏ LSP-2366 [S]	The Greatest Horn in the World	1961	$35
❏ LPM-3579 [M]	The Happy Trumpet	1966	$30
❏ LSP-3579 [S]	The Happy Trumpet	1966	$35
❏ LPM-3716 [M]	The Horn Meets the Hornet	1967	$30
❏ LSP-3716 [S]	The Horn Meets the Hornet	1967	$35
❏ LPM-3417 [M]	The Sound of Christmas	1965	$25
❏ LSP-3417 [S]	The Sound of Christmas	1965	$30
❏ LPM-3492 [M]	They're Playing Our Song	1966	$30
❏ LSP-3492 [S]	They're Playing Our Song	1966	$35
❏ VPS-6025	This Is Al Hirt	1970	$35
❏ VPS-6057	This Is Al Hirt, Volume 2	1972	$35
❏ LPM-2584 [M]	Trumpet and Strings	1962	$30
❏ LSP-2584 [S]	Trumpet and Strings	1962	$35
❏ LPM-3979 [M]	Unforgettable	1968	$20
❏ LSP-3979 [S]	Unforgettable	1968	$30
VERVE			
❏ MGV-1027 [M]	Blockbustin' Dixie!	195?	$25
❏ V-1027 [M]	Blockbustin' Dixie!	1961	$25
❏ MGV-1012 [M]	Swinging Dixie from Dan's Pier 600	1957	$175
VOCALION			
❏ VL73907	Floatin' Down to Cotton Town	1970	$25
WYNCOTE			
❏ 9089	The Dawn Busters	196?	$25

Number	Title	Yr	NM

HITCHCOCK, ROBYN, AND THE EGYPTIANS
A&M

❑ SP-5182 [B]	Globe of Frogs	1988	$15
❑ 7502153681 [B]	Perspex Island	1991	$30
❑ SP-5241	Queen Elvis	1989	$15

RELATIVITY
❑ 88561-8088-1	Black Snake Diamond Role	1986	$15

— First U.S. issue of U.K. album
❑ 88561-8130-1	Element of Light	1987	$15
❑ 8074 [EP]	Exploding in Silence	1986	$30

— Picture disc
❑ EMC8056	Gotta Let This Hen Out	1985	$15
❑ 88561-8083-1	Groovy Decoy	1986	$15

— First U.S. issue of U.K. album
❑ 88561-8089-1	Invisible Hitchcock	1986	$15
❑ 88561-8082-1	I Often Dream of Trains	1986	$15

— First U.S. issue of U.K. album

SLASH
❑ 25316	Fegmania!	1985	$15

TWIN/TONE
❑ TTR89175	Eye	1990	$15

WARNER BROS.
❑ 46399	Mossy Liquor	1996	$30

— Collection of demos; released only on vinyl
❑ 47147	Storefront Hitchcock	1998	$25

HITCHCOCK, STAN
AUDIOGRAPH
❑ 6004	Stan Hitchcock	1982	$12

CINNAMON
❑ CIN5001	Stan Hitchcock Country	1973	$18

EPIC
❑ BN26530	Honey, I'm Home	1969	$18
❑ BN26408 [M]	I'm Easy to Love	1968	$40

— White label promo with stereo number; "Epic Mono" sticker on front cover
❑ BN26408 [S]	I'm Easy to Love	1968	$25
❑ LN24138 [M]	Just Call Me Lonesome	1965	$25
❑ BN26138 [S]	Just Call Me Lonesome	1965	$30
❑ BN26438	Softly and Tenderly	1969	$25

GRT
❑ 20001	Dixie Belle	1970	$18

HITTMAN, JEFF, AND YOSHITAKA UEMATSU
SOUL NOTE
❑ 121137	Mosaic	1990	$35

HIVES, THE
GEARHEAD
❑ RPM30	Barely Legal	2000	$15
❑ RPM30	Barely Legal	2000	$18
❑ RPM40	Veni Vidi Vicious	2001	$15

INTERSCOPE
❑ B0002756-01	Tyrannosaurus Hives	2004	$25

HO, DON
REPRISE
❑ R-6186 [M]	Don Ho…Again!	1966	$12
❑ RS-6186 [S]	Don Ho…Again!	1966	$15
❑ RS-6461	Don Ho at the Polynesian Palace	1970	$12
❑ RS-6357	Don Ho -- Greatest Hits!	1969	$15
❑ R-6244 [M]	East Coast/West Coast	1967	$15
❑ RS-6244 [S]	East Coast/West Coast	1967	$15
❑ RS-6303	Hawaii-Ho!	1968	$15
❑ RS-6418	Hawaii's Greatest Hits	1970	$12
❑ RS-6283	Instant Happy	1968	$15
❑ RS-6331	Suck 'Em Up	1969	$15
❑ R-6161 [M]	The Don Ho Show	1965	$15
❑ RS-6161 [S]	The Don Ho Show	1965	$18
❑ RS-6367	The Don Ho TV Show	1969	$15

❑ R-6232 [M]	Tiny Bubbles	1966	$12
❑ RS-6232 [S]	Tiny Bubbles	1966	$15
❑ R-6219 [M]	You're Gonna Hear From Me	1966	$12
❑ RS-6219 [S]	You're Gonna Hear From Me	1966	$15

HOBBITS, THE
DECCA
❑ DL4920 [M]	Down to Middle-Earth	1967	$100
❑ DL74920 [S]	Down to Middle-Earth	1967	$50
❑ DL75009 [S]	Men and Doors	1968	$30
❑ DL5009 [M]	Men and Doors	1968	$150

HOBBS, BECKY
MCA
❑ 434	Becky Hobbs	1974	$18

MTM
❑ D1-71067	All Keyed Up	1988	$12

TATTOO
❑ BJL1-2169	Everyday	1977	$15
❑ BJL1-1673	Heartland	1976	$15

HODEIR, ANDRE
EMARCY
❑ SR-66005	Plain Old Blues	1967	$150

JAZZOLOGY
❑ J-7	Summit Meeting	1965	$35

PHILIPS
❑ PHM200073 [M]	Jazz Et Al	1963	$30
❑ PHS600073 [S]	Jazz Et Al	1963	$30

SAVOY
❑ MG-12104 [M]	American Jazzmen Play Andre Hodeir	1957	$40
❑ MG-12113 [M]	Andre Hodeir Presents the Paris Scene	1957	$40

SAVOY JAZZ
❑ SJL-1194	Essais	198?	$25

HODES, ART
AUDIOPHILE
❑ AP-54	Mostly Blues	196?	$35
❑ AP-54	Some Legendary Art	1986	$25

— Retitled reissue
BLUE NOTE
❑ BLP-7005 [10]	Art Hodes' Hot Five	1950	$500
❑ BLP-7015 [10]	Dixieland Clambake	1951	$500
❑ BLP-7006 [10]	Dixieland Jubilee	1950	$500
❑ BLP-7021 [10]	Out of the Backroom	1952	$500
❑ B-6508 [M]	Sittin' In	1969	$30
❑ BLP-7004 [10]	The Best in Two-Beat	1950	$500
❑ B-6502 [M]	The Funky Piano of Art Hodes	1969	$30

— A Division of Liberty Records" on label
CAPITOL
❑ M-11030	Hollywood Stampede	1973	$100

DELMARK
❑ DS-215	Friar's Inn Revisited	197?	$35
❑ DS-213	Hodes' Art	197?	$35
❑ DS-211	My Bucket's Got a Hole In It	1969	$50

DOTTED EIGHTH
❑ 1000 [M]	Art for Art's Sake	195?	$50

EMARCY
❑ MG-26104 [10]	Jazz Chicago Style	1954	$250
❑ SRE-66005	Plain Old Blues	196?	$25

EUPHONIC
❑ 1213	I Remember Bessie	198?	$25
❑ 1207	The Art of Hodes	198?	$25
❑ 1218	When Music Was Music	198?	$25

GHB
❑ 171	Art Hodes and the Magolia Jazz Band, Vol. 1	1984	$35
❑ 172	Art Hodes and the Magolia Jazz Band, Vol. 2	1984	$35

JAZZOLOGY
❑ J-20	Andre Hodeir with the All-Star Stompers	1966	$50
❑ J-104	Apex Blues	198?	$30
❑ J-155	Art Hodes and His Blues Six-Blues Groove	198?	$30
❑ J-74	Down Home Blues	197?	$30
❑ J-79	Echoes of Chicago	1979	$35
❑ J-46 [M]	For Art's Sake	196?	$25
❑ J-58	Home Cookin'	1974	$35
❑ J-83	The Jazz Record Story, Vol. 2	1979	$30
❑ J-113	The Trios	198?	$30

MERCURY
❑ MG-20185 [M]	Chicago Style Jazz	1957	$150

MOSAIC
❑ MR5-114	The Complete Art Hodes Blue Note Sessions	199?	$250

— Limited edition of 7,500
MUSE
❑ MR-5279	Just the Two of Us	1982	$25
❑ MR-5252	Someone to Watch Over Me	1981	$25

PARAMOUNT
❑ LP-113 [M]	The Trios	1955	$175

PRESTIGE
❑ 24083	The Real Thing	198?	$35

RIVERSIDE
❑ RLP-1012 [10]	Chicago Rhythm Kings	1953	$300

SACKVILLE
❑ 3039	Blues in the Night	198?	$25

STOMP OFF
❑ SOS-1184	The Music of Lovie Austin	1988	$25

STORYVILLE
❑ 4057	Selections from the Gutter	198?	$25

HODGES, JOHNNY, AND EARL "FATHA" HINES
VERVE
❑ V-8647 [M]	Stride Right	1966	$25
❑ V6-8647 [S]	Stride Right	1966	$30
❑ V-8732 [M]	Swing's Our Thing	1967	$30
❑ V6-8732 [S]	Swing's Our Thing	1967	$35

HODGES, JOHNNY, AND WILD BILL DAVIS
RCA VICTOR
❑ LPM-3393 [M]	Con-Soul and Sax	1965	$25
❑ LSP-3393 [S]	Con-Soul and Sax	1965	$30
❑ LPM-3706 [M]	Eddie Hodges and Wild Bill Davis In Atlantic City	1966	$35
❑ LSP-3706 [S]	Eddie Hodges and Wild Bill Davis In Atlantic City	1966	$25

VERVE
❑ V-8570 [M]	A Mess of Blues	1964	$25
❑ V6-8570 [S]	A Mess of Blues	1964	$30
❑ V-8406 [M]	Blue Hodges	1961	$25
❑ V6-8406 [S]	Blue Hodges	1961	$30
❑ V-8635 [M]	Blue Pyramid	1965	$25
❑ V6-8635 [S]	Blue Pyramid	1965	$30
❑ V-8599 [M]	Blue Rabbit	1964	$25
❑ V6-8599 [S]	Blue Rabbit	1964	$30
❑ V-8617 [M]	Joe's Blues	1965	$25
❑ V6-8617 [S]	Joe's Blues	1965	$30
❑ V-8630 [M]	Wings and Things	1965	$50
❑ V6-8630 [S]	Wings and Things	1965	$75

HODGES, JOHNNY
ABC IMPULSE!
❑ AS-61 [S]	Everybody Knows	1968	$35

AMERICAN RECORDING SOCIETY
❑ G-421 [M]	Johnny Hodges and the Ellington All-Stars	195?	$40

BLUEBIRD
❑ 5903-1-RB	Triple Play	1987	$25

CLEF
❑ MGC-128 [10]	Johnny Hodges Collates #2	1953	$350
❑ MGC-111 [10]	Johnny Hodges Collates	1953	$300
❑ MGC-151 [10]	Swing with Johnny Hodges	1954	$0

— Canceled; reassigned to Norgran
DOT
❑ DLP-3682 [M]	Johnny Hodges with Lawrence Welk's Orchestra	1966	$85
❑ DLP-25682 [S]	Johnny Hodges with Lawrence Welk's Orchestra	1966	$150

ENCORE
❑ EE-22001 [M]	Hodge Podge	1968	$35

EPIC
❑ LN3105 [M]	Hodge Podge	1955	$150

FLYING DUTCHMAN
❑ FD-10120	Three Shades of Blue	1972	$35
❑ 120	Three Shades of Blue	1971	$25

IMPULSE!
❑ A-61 [M]	Everybody Knows	1964	$120
❑ AS-61 [S]	Everybody Knows	1964	$120

JAZZ PANORAMA
❑ 1806 [10]	Johnny Hodges	1951	$175

MASTER JAZZ
❑ 8107	Memory	1970	$35

MCA
❑ 29071	Everybody Knows	198?	$25

MERCER
❑ LP-1000 [10]	Johnny Hodges, Vol. 1	1951	$175
❑ LP-1006 [10]	Johnny Hodges, Vol. 2	1951	$175

MERCURY
❑ MGC-128 [10]	Johnny Hodges Collates #2	1953	$0

— Canceled; reassigned to Clef
❑ MGC-111 [10]	Johnny Hodges Collates	1952	$350

MGM
❑ SE-4715	Tribute	1970	$35

MOSAIC
❑ MR6-126	The Complete Johnny Hodges Sessions 1951-1955	199?	$175

NORGRAN
❑ MGN-1048 [M]	Castle Rock	1955	$250
❑ MGN-1045 [M]	Creamy	1955	$300
❑ MGN-1055 [M]	Ellingtonia '56	1956	$250

Number	Title	Yr	NM
❏ MGN-1092 [M]	In a Mellow Tone	1956	$250
❏ MGN-1059 [M]	In a Tender Mood	1956	$250
❏ MGN-1024 [M]	Johnny Hodges Dance Bash	1955	$300
❏ MGN-1004 [M]	Memories of Ellington	1954	$300
❏ MGN-1009 [M]	More of Johnny Hodges	1954	$300
❏ MGN-1091 [M]	Perdido	1956	$250
❏ MGN-1 [10]	Swing with Johnny Hodges	1954	$250
❏ MGN-1061 [M]	The Blues	1956	$100
❏ MGN-1060 [M]	Used to Be Duke	1956	$250

ONYX
| ❏ 216 | Ellingtonia | 197? | $30 |

PABLO LIVE
| ❏ 2620102 | Sportpalast, Berlin | 1978 | $35 |

PRESTIGE
| ❏ 24103 | Caravan | 198? | $35 |

RCA VICTOR
❏ LPT-3000 [10]	Alto Sax	1952	$175
❏ LPV-533 [M]	Things Ain't What They Used to Be	1966	$25
❏ LPM-3867 [M]	Triple Play	1967	$30
❏ LSP-3867 [S]	Triple Play	1967	$25

STORYVILLE
| ❏ 4073 | A Man and His Music | 198? | $30 |

TIME-LIFE
| ❏ STL-J-19 | Giants of Jazz | 1981 | $50 |

VERVE
❏ VSP-20 [M]	Alto Blues	1966	$30
❏ VSPS-20 [R]	Alto Blues	1966	$25
❏ MGV-8317 [M]	Back to Back -- Duke Ellington and Johnny Hodges Play the Blues	1959	$175
❏ MGVS-6055 [S]	Back to Back -- Duke Ellington and Johnny Hodges Play the Blues	1960	$175
❏ V-8317 [M]	Back to Back -- Duke Ellington and Johnny Hodges Play the Blues	1961	$25
❏ V6-8317 [S]	Back to Back -- Duke Ellington and Johnny Hodges Play the Blues	1961	$25
❏ V-8680 [M]	Blue Notes	1966	$75
❏ V6-8680 [S]	Blue Notes	1966	$40
❏ MGV-8358 [M]	Blues-a-Plenty	1960	$175
❏ MGVS-6123 [S]	Blues-a-Plenty	1960	$0
— Unreleased			
❏ V-8358 [M]	Blues-a-Plenty	1961	$25
❏ V6-8358 [S]	Blues-a-Plenty	1961	$25
❏ V6-8358 [S]	Blues-a-Plenty	199?	$30
— Classic Records reissue on audiophile vinyl			
❏ MGV-8139 [M]	Castle Rock	1957	$250
— Reissue of Norgran 1048			
❏ V-8139 [M]	Castle Rock	1961	$25
❏ 827758-1	Castle Rock	1986	$25
❏ MGV-8136 [M]	Creamy	1957	$250
— Reissue of Norgran 1045			
❏ V-8136 [M]	Creamy	1961	$25
❏ V-8726 [M]	Don't Sleep in the Subway	1967	$25
❏ V6-8726 [S]	Don't Sleep in the Subway	1967	$35
❏ MGV-8203 [M]	Duke's in Bed	1957	$150
❏ V-8203 [M]	Duke's in Bed	1961	$25
❏ MGV-8145 [M]	Ellingtonia '56	1957	$250
— Reissue of Norgran 1055			
❏ V-8145 [M]	Ellingtonia '56	1961	$25
❏ MGV-8180 [M]	In a Mellow Tone	1957	$300
— Reissue of Norgran 1092			
❏ V-8180 [M]	In a Mellow Tone	1961	$25
❏ MGV-8149 [M]	In a Tender Mood	1957	$300
— Reissue of Norgran 1059			
❏ V-8149 [M]	In a Tender Mood	1961	$25
❏ MGV-8391 [M]	Johnny Hodges	1961	$0
— Canceled			
❏ V/V6-8546	Johnny Hodges	1963	$0
— Canceled			
❏ VSP-3 [M]	Johnny Hodges and All the Duke's Men	1966	$30
❏ VSPS-3 [R]	Johnny Hodges and All the Duke's Men	1966	$25
❏ V-8452 [M]	Johnny Hodges with Billy Strayhorn	1962	$30
❏ V6-8452 [S]	Johnny Hodges with Billy Strayhorn	1962	$30
❏ MGV-8355 [M]	Not So Dukish	1960	$175
❏ MGVS-6120 [S]	Not So Dukish	1960	$0
— Canceled			
❏ V-8355 [M]	Not So Dukish	1961	$25
❏ MGV-8179 [M]	Perdido	1957	$175
— Reissue of Norgran 1091			
❏ V-8179 [M]	Perdido	1961	$25
❏ V6-8834	Previously Unreleased Recordings	1973	$35
❏ V6-8753	Rippin' and Runnin'	1968	$35
❏ V-8561 [M]	Sandy's Gone	1963	$30
❏ V6-8561 [S]	Sandy's Gone	1963	$30
❏ MGV-8345 [M]	Side by Side	1959	$150
❏ MGVS-6109 [S]	Side by Side	1960	$150
❏ V-8345 [M]	Side by Side	1961	$25
❏ V6-8345 [S]	Side by Side	1961	$25
❏ MGVS-6109 [S]	Side by Side	199?	$30
— Classic Records reissue on audiophile vinyl			
❏ MGV-8271 [M]	The Big Sound	1958	$175
❏ MGVS-6017 [S]	The Big Sound	1960	$175
❏ V-8271 [M]	The Big Sound	1961	$25

Number	Title	Yr	NM
❏ V6-8271 [S]	The Big Sound	1961	$25
❏ UMV-2525	The Big Sound	198?	$25
❏ MGV-8151 [M]	The Blues	1957	$50
— Reissue of Norgran 1061			
❏ V-8151 [M]	The Blues	1961	$25
❏ V-8492 [M]	The Eleventh Hour	1962	$30
❏ V6-8492 [M]	The Eleventh Hour	1962	$30
❏ MGV-8314 [M]	The Prettiest Gershwin	1959	$150
❏ MGVS-6048 [S]	The Prettiest Gershwin	1960	$150
❏ V-8314 [M]	The Prettiest Gershwin	1961	$25
❏ V6-8314 [S]	The Prettiest Gershwin	1961	$25
❏ MGV-8350 [M]	The Smooth One	1960	$0
— Canceled			
❏ MGVS-6115 [S]	The Smooth One	1960	$0
— Canceled			
❏ VE2-2532	The Smooth One	1979	$35
❏ MGV-8150 [M]	Used to Be Duke	1957	$250
— Reissue of Norgran 1060			
❏ V-8150 [M]	Used to Be Duke	1961	$25

HODGES, YVONNE
GUINNESS
| ❏ GNS36032 [B] | You Never Wanted Me | 1977 | $85 |

HOFFMAN, ABBIE
BIG TOE
| ❏ 1 [B] | Wake Up, America! | 196? | $75 |

HOFMANN, HOLLY
CAPRI
| ❏ 74011 | Take Note | 1989 | $30 |

HOFNER, ADOLPH
COLUMBIA
| ❏ CL9017 [10] | Dude Ranch Dances | 1951 | $250 |
DECCA
| ❏ DL5564 [10] | Dance-O-Rama | 1955 | $400 |

HOG HEAVEN
The Shondells after Tommy James went solo.
ROULETTE
| ❏ SR42057 | Hog Heaven | 1971 | $25 |

HOGAN, CLAIRE
MGM
| ❏ E-4501 [M] | Boozers and Losers | 1967 | $25 |
| ❏ SE-4501 [S] | Boozers and Losers | 1967 | $30 |

HOGAN, SILAS
EXCELLO
| ❏ LPS-8019 | Trouble at Home | 1972 | $25 |

HOGG, SMOKEY
CROWN

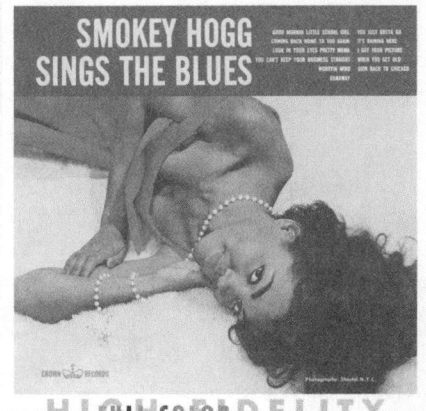

| ❏ CLP-5226 [M] | Smokey Hogg Sings the Blues | 1962 | $50 |
TIME
| ❏ 6 [M] | Smokey Hogg | 1962 | $100 |
UNITED
| ❏ US-7745 | Smokey Hogg | 1970 | $15 |

HOGGARD, JAY
CONTEMPORARY
| ❏ C-14007 | Rain Forest | 1980 | $30 |
GRAMAVISION
| ❏ GR-8204 | Love Survives | 1983 | $25 |
GRP/ARISTA
| ❏ GL5004 | Days Like These | 1979 | $30 |

Number	Title	Yr	NM
INDIA NAVIGATION			
❏ IN-1049	Mystic Winds, Tropic Breezes	1981	$30
❏ IN-1068	Riverside Dance	1985	$30
❏ IN-1040	Solo Vibes Concert	1979	$35
MUSE			
❏ MR-5383	Overview	1989	$30
❏ MR-5410	The Little Tiger	1991	$35

HOLDEN, RANDY
Also see BLUE CHEER.
HOBBIT
| ❏ 5002 | Population II | 1968 | $250 |

HOLDEN, RON
DONNA
| ❏ DLP-2111 [M] | I Love You So | 1960 | $300 |
| ❏ DLPS-2111 [S] | I Love You So | 1960 | $300 |
— Stereo records not known to exist; this is for a mono record in a stereo cover

HOLDSWORTH, ALLAN
Guitarist of BRUFORD and UK fame.
CTI
| ❏ 6068 | Velvet | 197? | $18 |
ENIGMA
| ❏ ST-73203 | Atavachron | 1986 | $15 |
| ❏ 72031-1 | I.O.U. | 1985 | $18 |
— Reissue
LUNA CRACK
| ❏ AH-100 | I.O.U. | 1982 | $25 |

HOLIDAY, BILLIE, AND STAN GETZ
DALE
| ❏ 25 [10] | Billie and Stan | 1951 | $400 |

HOLIDAY, BILLIE
AMERICAN RECORDING SOCIETY
| ❏ G-409 [M] | Billie Holiday Sings | 1956 | $300 |
— Reissue of Clef 713
| ❏ G-431 [M] | Lady Sings the Blues | 1957 | $300 |
— Reissue of Clef 721
ATLANTIC
| ❏ 1614 | Strange Fruit | 1972 | $35 |
BLACKHAWK
| ❏ BKH-50701 | Billie Holiday at Monterey | 1986 | $25 |
BOOK-OF-THE-MONTH CLUB
| ❏ 90-5652 | Ain't Nobody's Business If I Do | 1975 | $75 |
— Box set with booklet; pressed on CSP labels; alternate number is "P4 12969
BULLDOG
| ❏ 1007 | Billie's Blues | 198? | $25 |
CLEF
| ❏ MGC-144 [10] | An Evening with Billie Holiday | 1954 | $250 |
| ❏ MGC-686 [M] | A Recital by Billie Holiday | 1956 | $350 |
— Reissue of 144 and 161 as one 12-inch LP
❏ MGC-169 [10]	Billie Holiday at Jazz at the Philharmonic	1955	$600
❏ MGC-161 [10]	Billie Holiday Favorites	1954	$350
❏ MGC-118 [10]	Billie Holiday Sings	1953	$250
❏ MGC-721 [M]	Lady Sings the Blues	1956	$350
❏ MGC-669 [M]	Music for Torching	1955	$175
❏ MGC-690 [M]	Solitude -- Songs by Billie Holiday	1956	$350
— Reissue of 118
| ❏ MGC-713 [M] | Velvet Mood | 1956 | $120 |
CLEOPATRA
| ❏ 8768 [B] | Lady Day - The Ultimate Collection | | $30 |
— picture disc
| ❏ 5365 [B] | The Essential Rare Collection | | $25 |
COLLECTABLES
| ❏ COL-5142 | Fine and Mellow | 198? | $30 |
COLUMBIA
❏ CL6163 [10]	Billie Holiday Favorites	1951	$250
❏ CL2666 [M]	Billie Holiday's Greatest Hits	1967	$35
❏ CL6129 [10]	Billie Holiday Sings	1950	$250
❏ C32080	Billie's Blues/The Original Recordings by Billie Holiday	1973	$35
❏ PC32080	Billie's Blues/The Original Recordings by Billie Holiday	198?	$20
— Reissue of Harmony LP
| ❏ G30782 | God Bless the Child | 1972 | $50 |
| ❏ CL637 [M] | Lady Day | 1954 | $140 |
— Maroon label, gold print
| ❏ CL637 [M] | Lady Day | 1956 | $40 |
— Red and black label with six "eye" logos
| ❏ CL637 [M] | Lady Day | 1962 | $35 |
— Red "Guaranteed High Fidelity" or "360 Sound" label
| ❏ CL637 [M] | Lady Day | 197? | $30 |
— Orange label

Number	Title	Yr	NM
❑ CL1157 [M]	Lady in Satin	1958	$40
—Red and black label with six "eye" logos			
❑ CS8048 [S]	Lady in Satin	1958	$40
—Red and black label with six "eye" logos			
❑ CL1157 [M]	Lady in Satin	1962	$35
—Red "Guaranteed High Fidelity" or "360 Sound" label			
❑ CS8048 [S]	Lady in Satin	1962	$35
—Red "Guaranteed High Fidelity" or "360 Sound" label			
❑ CS8048 [S]	Lady in Satin	1999	$75
— Classic Records reissue on audiophile vinyl			
❑ CG32121	The Billie Holiday Story, Volume 1	1973	$35
❑ CG32124	The Billie Holiday Story, Volume 2	1973	$35
❑ CG32127	The Billie Holiday Story, Volume 3	1973	$35
❑ C3L21 [M]	The Golden Years	1962	$150
—Red and black label with six "eye" logos			
❑ C3L21 [M]	The Golden Years	1963	$75
—Red "Guaranteed High Fidelity" or "360 Sound" label			
❑ C3L40 [M]	The Golden Years, Volume 2	1966	$75
—Red label, "Mono" at bottom			
❑ C3L40 [M]	The Golden Years, Volume 2	197?	$50
— Orange labels			
COLUMBIA JAZZ MASTERPIECES			
❑ CJ40247	Lady in Satin	1987	$25
❑ CJ40646	The Quintessential Billie Holiday, Vol. 1	1987	$25
❑ CJ40790	The Quintessential Billie Holiday, Vol. 2	1987	$25
❑ CJ44048	The Quintessential Billie Holiday, Vol. 3	1988	$25
❑ CJ44252	The Quintessential Billie Holiday, Vol. 4	1988	$25
❑ CJ44423	The Quintessential Billie Holiday, Vol. 5	1989	$25
❑ C45449	The Quintessential Billie Holiday, Vol. 6	1990	$25
❑ C46180	The Quintessential Billie Holiday, Vol. 7	1990	$25
COLUMBIA MUSICAL TREASURY			
❑ P3M5869	The Golden Years	197?	$50
COLUMBIA SPECIAL PRODUCTS			
❑ P14338	Swing, Brother, Swing	198?	$25
COMMODORE			
❑ FL-30008 [M]	Billie Holiday	1959	$150
— Reissue of 20006			
❑ FL-20005 [10]	Billie Holiday, Volume 1	1950	$300
❑ FL-20006 [10]	Billie Holiday, Volume 2	1950	$300
❑ FL-30011 [M]	Billie Holiday with Eddie Heywood and His Orchestra	1959	$150
— Reissue of 20005			
CROWN			
❑ CLP-5380 [M]	Billie Holiday & Vivian Fears	196?	$50
❑ CST-380 [R]	Billie Holiday & Vivian Fears	196?	$30
DECCA			
❑ DL75040 [R]	Billie Holiday's Greatest Hits	1968	$30
❑ DL5040 [M]	Billie Holiday's Greatest Hits	1968	$75
— Mono is white label promo only; "Monaural" sticker covers the word "Stereo" on cover			
❑ DL5345 [10]	Lover Man	1951	$250
❑ DL8702 [M]	Lover Man	1958	$120
❑ DXB-161 [M]	The Billie Holiday Story	1959	$250
❑ DXSB-7161 [R]	The Billie Holiday Story	1959	$250
❑ DL8701 [M]	The Blues Are Brewin'	1958	$120
❑ DL8215 [M]	The Lady Sings	1956	$120
ESP-DISK'			
❑ 3002	The Lady Lives, Vol. 1	1973	$150
❑ 3003	The Lady Lives, Vol. 2	1973	$150
EVEREST ARCHIVE OF FOLK & JAZZ			
❑ 265	Billie Holiday	197?	$30
❑ FS-310	Billie Holiday, Vol. 2	1976	$30
HALL			
❑ 622	I've Gotta Right to Sing	197?	$30
HARMONY			
❑ KH32080	Billie's Blues	1973	$25
INTERMEDIA			
❑ QS-5076	Billie Holiday Talks and Sings	198?	$25
JAZZ MAN			
❑ 5005	Billie Holiday at Storyville	198?	$25
JAZZTONE			
❑ J-1209 [M]	Billie Holiday Sings	1955	$150
— Reissue of Commodore 20005			
JOLLY ROGER			
❑ 5020 [10]	Billie Holiday, Volume 1	1954	$200
❑ 5021 [10]	Billie Holiday, Volume 2	1954	$200
❑ 5022 [10]	Billie Holiday, Volume 3	1954	$200
KENT GOSPEL			
❑ KST600	Billie Holiday Sings	197?	$35
MAINSTREAM			
❑ 56022 [M]	Once Upon a Time	1965	$75
❑ S-6022 [R]	Once Upon a Time	1965	$30
❑ 56000 [M]	The Commodore Recordings	1965	$75

Number	Title	Yr	NM
❑ S-6000 [R]	The Commodore Recordings	1965	$30
MCA			
❑ 275	Billie Holiday's Greatest Hits	1973	$25
— Reissue of Decca 75040			
❑ 4006	The Billie Holiday Story	1973	$30
— Reissue of Decca 7161			
METRO			
❑ M-515 [M]	Billie Holiday	1965	$300
❑ MS-515 [R]	Billie Holiday	1965	$175
MGM			
❑ M3G-4948	Archetypes	1974	$30
❑ E-3764 [M]	Billie Holiday	1959	$40
❑ SE-3764 [S]	Billie Holiday	1959	$150
❑ GAS-122	Billie Holiday (Golden Archive Series)	1970	$30
MOBILE FIDELITY			
❑ 1-247	Body and Soul	1996	$250
— Audiophile vinyl			
MONMOUTH/EVERGREEN			
❑ 7046	Gallant Lady	1973	$30
PARAMOUNT			
❑ PA-6059	Songs and Conversations	1973	$30
PHOENIX 10			
❑ PHX-312	Billie Holiday Live	1981	$20
PICKWICK			
❑ PC-3335	Billie Holiday Sings the Blues	197?	$25
RIC			
❑ M-2001 [M]	Rare Live Recording	1964	$75
SCORE			
❑ SLP-4014 [M]	Billie Holiday Sings the Blues	1957	$250
SOLID STATE			
❑ SS-18040	Lady Love	1969	$30
SUNSET			
❑ SUM-1147 [M]	Shades of Blue	1967	$30
❑ SUS-5147 [R]	Shades of Blue	1967	$25
TIME-LIFE			
❑ STL-J-03	Giants of Jazz	1979	$75
—Alternate number is Columbia Special Products P3 14786			
TOTEM			
❑ 1037	Billie Holiday On the Air	198?	$25
TRIP			
❑ 5024	Billie Holiday Live	1974	$25
UNITED ARTISTS			
❑ UAJ-14014 [M]	Lady Love	1962	$40
❑ UASJ-15014 [S]	Lady Love	1962	$150
❑ UAS-5625	Lady Love	1972	$25
— Reissue of 15014			
VERVE			
❑ MGV-8329 [M]	All or Nothing at All	1959	$175
❑ V-8329 [M]	All or Nothing at All	1959	$175
❑ V6-8329 [R]	All or Nothing at All	196?	$30
❑ VE-2-2529	All or Nothing at All	198?	$35
❑ 827160-1	All or Nothing at All	1987	$25
❑ MGV-8027 [M]	A Recital by Billie Holiday	1957	$250
— Reissue of Clef 686			
❑ V-8027 [M]	A Recital by Billie Holiday	1961	$50
❑ MGV-8197 [M]	Body and Soul	1957	$175
❑ V-8197 [M]	Body and Soul	1961	$50
❑ 817359-1	Embraceable You	198?	$30
❑ 2V6S-8816	History of the Real Billie Holiday	1973	$35
❑ 823233-1	History of the Real Billie Holiday	198?	$30
❑ VSP-5 [M]	Lady	1966	$35
❑ VSPS-5 [R]	Lady	1966	$30
❑ MGV-8099 [M]	Lady Sings the Blues	1957	$300
— Reissue of Clef 721			
❑ V-8099 [M]	Lady Sings the Blues	1957	$50
❑ MGV-8026 [M]	Music for Torching	1957	$300
— Reissue of Clef 669			
❑ V-8026 [M]	Music for Torching	1961	$50
❑ MGV-8074 [M]	Solitude -- Songs by Billie Holiday	1957	$250
— Reissue of Clef 690			
❑ V-8074 [M]	Solitude – Songs by Billie Holiday	1961	$50
❑ V6-8074 [R]	Solitude – Songs by Billie Holiday	196?	$30
❑ MGV-8257 [M]	Songs for Distingue Lovers	1958	$120
❑ MGVS-6021 [S]	Songs for Distingue Lovers	1960	$120
❑ V-8257 [M]	Songs for Distingue Lovers	1961	$50
❑ V6-8257 [S]	Songs for Distingue Lovers	1961	$75
❑ MGVS-6021-45 [S]	Songs for Distingue Lovers	1999	$50
—Classic Records reissue on two 12-inch 45-rpm records			
❑ MGVS-6021 [S]	Songs for Distingue Lovers	199?	$75
—Classic Records reissue on audiophile vinyl			
❑ MGV-8302 [M]	Stay with Me	1959	$150
❑ V-8302 [M]	Stay with Me	1961	$50
❑ VE-2-2515	Stormy Blues	1976	$35
❑ 823230-1	Stormy Blues	198?	$30
❑ V6-8808 [R]	The Best of Billie Holiday	1973	$25
❑ 823246-1	The Billie Holiday Songbook	198?	$25

Number	Title	Yr	NM
❑ V-8410 [M]	The Essential Billie Holiday	1961	$50
❑ V6-8410 [R]	The Essential Billie Holiday	1961	$30
❑ V-8505 [M]	The Essential Jazz Vocals	1963	$50
❑ V6-8505 [R]	The Essential Jazz Vocals	1963	$30
❑ VE-2-2503	The First Verve Sessions	1976	$35
❑ MGV-8338-2 [M]	The Unforgettable Lady Day	1959	$175
❑ V-8338-2 [M]	The Unforgettable Lady Day	1961	$75

❑ MGV-8096 [M]	Velvet Mood	1957	$40
— Reissue of Clef 713			
❑ V-8096 [M]	Velvet Mood	1961	$25

HOLIDAY, BILLIE/AL HIBBLER
IMPERIAL

❑ LP-9185 [M]	Billie Holiday, Al Hibbler and the Blues	1962	$250
❑ LP-12185 [R]	Billie Holiday, Al Hibbler and the Blues	196?	$200

HOLIDAY, JIMMY
MINIT

❑ LP-24005 [M]	Turning Point	1966	$30
❑ LP-40005 [S]	Turning Point	1966	$40

HOLIDAY, JOE
DECCA

❑ DL8487 [M]	Holiday for Jazz	1957	$120

PRESTIGE

❑ PRLP-131 [10]	Joe Holiday	1952	$300

HOLIDAY, JOE/BILLY TAYLOR
PRESTIGE

❑ PRLP-171 [10]	Mambo Jazz	1953	$350

HOLIDAY BELLS, THE
KAPP

❑ KL-1155 [M]	Ring the Bells on Christmas Day	1959	$18

HOLIDAY STRINGS, THE
DIPLOMAT

❑ X1717 [M]	Silent Night	196?	$15
❑ SX1717 [S]	Silent Night	196?	$18
—Same as above, but in stereo			

HOLLAND, DAVE
ECM

❑ 1027	Conference of the Birds	1974	$35
—As "David Holland"			
❑ 1109	Emerald Tears	1978	$30
❑ 25001	Jumpin' In	1984	$25
❑ 23787	Life Cycle	1983	$25
❑ 25032	Seeds of Time	1985	$25

HOLLAND, EDDIE
MOTOWN

❑ 604 [M]	Eddie Holland	1963	$400

HOLLIDAY, JUDY, AND GERRY MULLIGAN
DRG

❑ SL-5191	Holliday with Mulligan	1979	$30

HOLLIDAY, JUDY
COLUMBIA

❑ CL1153 [M]	Trouble Is a Man	1958	$30
❑ CS8041 [S]	Trouble Is a Man	1959	$40

DRG

❑ MRS-602	Trouble Is a Man	198?	$25

HOLLIES, THE
ATLANTIC

❑ 80076	What Goes Around	1983	$12

Number	Title	Yr	NM
CAPITOL			
❏ N-16056	Hollies' Greatest	1980	$10
COLUMBIA LIMITED EDITION			
❏ LE10178	He Ain't Heavy, He's My Brother	1976	$15
EMI AMERICA			
❏ SN-16397	More Great Hits (1963-1968)	1986	$10
EPIC			
❏ JE35334	A Crazy Steal	1978	$12
❏ PE33387	Another Night	1975	$12
❏ PE34714	Clarke, Hicks, Sylvester, Calvert & Elliot	1977	$12
❏ LN24344 [M]	Dear Eloise/King Midas in Reverse	1967	$30
❏ BN26344 [S]	Dear Eloise/King Midas in Reverse	1967	$30
❏ KE30958	Distant Light	1972	$18
— Yellow label			
❏ KE30958	Distant Light	1974	$12
— Orange label			
❏ PE30958	Distant Light	1986	$10
— Blue label			
❏ AS138 [DJ]	Everything You Always Wanted to Hear by the Hollies But Were Afraid to Ask For	1976	$25
— Promo-only sampler album			
❏ LN24315 [M]	Evolution	1967	$35
❏ BN26315 [S]	Evolution	1967	$30
❏ BN26538	He Ain't Heavy, He's My Brother	1970	$25
❏ KE32574	Hollies	1974	$12
❏ E30255	Moving Finger	1971	$25
❏ KE31992	Romany	1972	$15
— Yellow label			
❏ KE31992	Romany	1974	$12
— Orange label			
❏ KE32061	The Hollies' Greatest Hits	1973	$15
— Yellow label			
❏ KE32061	The Hollies' Greatest Hits	1974	$12
— Orange label			
❏ PE32061	The Hollies' Greatest Hits	1979	$10
— Blue label			
❏ BN26447	Words and Music by Bob Dylan	1969	$18
— Yellow label			
❏ BN26447	Words and Music by Bob Dylan	1973	$12
— Orange label			
IMPERIAL			
❏ LP-9330 [M]	Bus Stop	1966	$30
— Black and pink label			

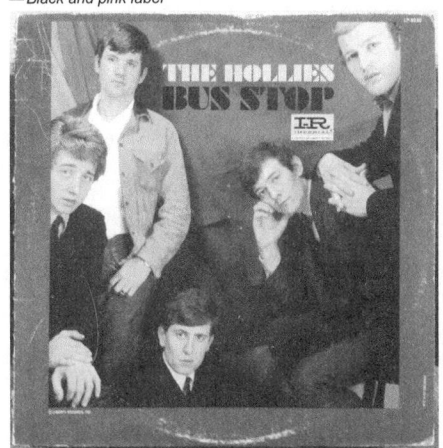

Number	Title	Yr	NM
❏ LP-9330 [M]	Bus Stop	1966	$30
— Black and green label			
❏ LP-12330 [R]	Bus Stop	1966	$30
— Black and pink label			
❏ LP-12330 [R]	Bus Stop	1966	$25
— Black and green label			
❏ LP-9299 [M]	Hear! Here!	1965	$50
❏ LP-12299 [R]	Hear! Here!	1965	$30
❏ LP-9265 [M]	Here I Go Again	1964	$175
— Black label with stars			
❏ LP-9265 [M]	Here I Go Again	1964	$50
— Black label with stars			
❏ LP-12265 [R]	Here I Go Again	1964	$150
— Black label with silver print			
❏ LP-12265 [R]	Here I Go Again	1964	$30
— Black and pink label			
❏ LP-9339 [M]	Stop! Stop! Stop!	1966	$30
❏ LP-12339 [S]	Stop! Stop! Stop!	1966	$30
❏ LP-9312 [M]	The Hollies -- Beat Group	1966	$30
❏ LP-12312 [S]	The Hollies -- Beat Group	1966	$40
❏ LP-9350 [M]	The Hollies' Greatest Hits	1967	$25
❏ LP-12350 [P]	The Hollies' Greatest Hits	1967	$30

Number	Title	Yr	NM
LIBERTY			
❏ LN-10216	Pay You Back with Interest	1982	$10
PAIR			
❏ PDL2-1041	Hottest Hits	1986	$18
REALM			
❏ 2V-8026	The Hollies, Volume 1	1976	$18
— Two-record TV package			
❏ 1V-8027	The Hollies, Volume 2	1976	$15
— TV package sold with Realm 8026			
UNITED ARTISTS			
❏ UA-LA329-E	The Very Best of the Hollies	1975	$12

HOLLOWAY, BRENDA

Number	Title	Yr	NM
MOTOWN			
❏ 5242ML	Every Little Bit Hurts	1982	$15
TAMLA			
❏ T257 [M]	Every Little Bit Hurts	1964	$250
❏ TS257 [R]	Every Little Bit Hurts	1964	$175

HOLLOWAY, LOLEATTA

Number	Title	Yr	NM
GOLD MIND			
❏ 7500	Loleatta	1977	$25
❏ GA-9506	Love Sensation	1979	$25
❏ A-9501 [B]	Queen of the Night	1978	$25

HOLLOWAY, RED, AND CLARK TERRY

Number	Title	Yr	NM
CONCORD JAZZ			
❏ CJ-390	Locksmith Blues	1989	$30

HOLLOWAY, RED

Number	Title	Yr	NM
CONCORD JAZZ			
❏ CJ-322	Red Holloway & Company	1987	$25
FANTASY			
❏ OJC-327	Cookin' Together	1988	$25
JAM			
❏ 014	Hittin' the Road Again	198?	$30
PRESTIGE			
❏ PRST-7778	Best of the Soul Organ Giants	1970	$35
❏ PRLP-7299 [M]	Burner	1964	$50
— Yellow label, Bergenfield, N.J. address			
❏ PRLP-7299 [M]	Burner	1965	$30
— Blue label, trident logo at right			
❏ PRST-7299 [S]	Burner	1964	$50
— Yellow label, Bergenfield, N.J. address			
❏ PRST-7299 [S]	Burner	1965	$30
— Blue label, trident logo at right			
❏ PRLP-7325 [M]	Cookin' Together	1964	$30
❏ PRST-7325 [S]	Cookin' Together	1964	$40
❏ PRLP-7473 [M]	Red Soul	1966	$25
❏ PRST-7473 [S]	Red Soul	1966	$30
❏ PRLP-7390 [M]	Sax, Strings and Soul	1965	$25
❏ PRST-7390 [S]	Sax, Strings and Soul	1965	$30
STEEPLECHASE			
❏ SCS-1192	Nica's Dream	198?	$30

HOLLY, BUDDY

Number	Title	Yr	NM
CORAL			
❏ CRL57210 [M]	Buddy Holly	1958	$400
— Maroon label			
❏ CRL57210 [M]	Buddy Holly	1964	$150
— Black label with color bars			
❏ CRL57405 [M]	Buddy Holly and the Crickets	1962	$175
— Reissue of the Crickets LP on Brunswick 54038			
❏ CRL757405 [R]	Buddy Holly and the Crickets	1963	$40
❏ CRL57492 [M]	Buddy Holly's Greatest Hits	1967	$100
❏ CRL757492 [P]	Buddy Holly's Greatest Hits	1967	$50
❏ CRL57450 [M]	Buddy Holly Showcase	1964	$150
❏ CRL757450 [R]	Buddy Holly Showcase	1964	$100
❏ CRL757504 [S]	Giant	1969	$50
❏ CRL57463 [M]	Holly in the Hills	1965	$120

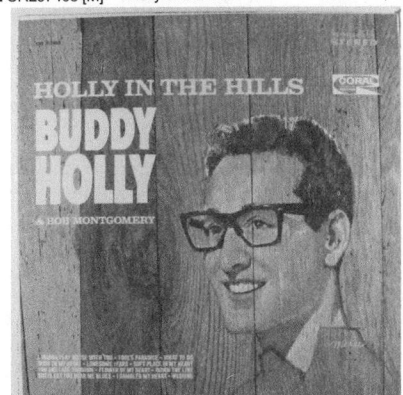

Number	Title	Yr	NM
❏ CRL757463 [R]	Holly in the Hills	1965	$150
❏ CRL57426 [M]	Reminiscing	1963	$250
— Maroon label			
❏ CRL57426 [M]	Reminiscing	1964	$100
— Black label with color bars			
❏ CRL757426 [R]	Reminiscing	1964	$40
❏ CXB8 [M]	The Best of Buddy Holly	1966	$100
❏ CXSB8 [R]	The Best of Buddy Holly	1966	$50
❏ CRL57279 [M]	The Buddy Holly Story	1959	$300
— Maroon label; back color print in black and red			
❏ CRL57279 [M]	The Buddy Holly Story	1959	$175
— Maroon label; back color print in all black			
❏ CRL57279 [M]	The Buddy Holly Story	1963	$100
— Black label with color bars			
❏ CRL757279 [R]	The Buddy Holly Story	1963	$40
❏ CRL57326 [M]	The Buddy Holly Story, Vol. 2	1959	$250
— Maroon label			
❏ CRL57326 [M]	The Buddy Holly Story, Vol. 2	1963	$100
— Black label with color bars			
❏ CRL757326 [R]	The Buddy Holly Story, Vol. 2	1963	$40
CRICKET			
❏ C001000	Buddy Holly Live -- Volume 1	197?	$25
❏ C001001	Buddy Holly Live -- Volume 1	197?	$25
DECCA			
❏ DXSE7207	A Rock 'n' Roll Collection	1972	$40
❏ DL8707 [M]	That'll Be the Day	1958	$1500
— Black label with silver print			
❏ DL8707 [M]	That'll Be the Day	1961	$300
— Black label with color bars			
GREAT NORTHWEST			
❏ GNW-4014	Visions of Buddy	197?	$12
— Interview album			
MCA			
❏ 4009	A Rock 'n' Roll Collection	1973	$25
— Black labels with rainbow			
❏ 4009	A Rock 'n' Roll Collection	1978	$15
— Later pressings on tan or blue/rainbow labels			
❏ 25239	Buddy Holly	1989	$15
— Reissue of Coral 57210			
❏ 11161	Buddy Holly	1995	$40
— Audiophile "Heavy Vinyl" reissue with gatefold cover			
❏ 3040	Buddy Holly/The Crickets 20 Golden Greats	1978	$18
❏ 1484	Buddy Holly/The Crickets 20 Golden Greats	198?	$10
— Reissue of 3040			
❏ 27059	For the First Time Anywhere	1983	$12
❏ 5540	From the Original Master Tapes	1986	$30
❏ 4184	Legend	1985	$25
❏ 80000	The Complete Buddy Holly	1981	$100
— Box set with booklet and custom innersleeves			
❏ 737	The Great Buddy Holly	197?	$12
— Reissue of MCA Coral LP			
MCA CORAL			
❏ CD-20101	The Great Buddy Holly	1973	$15
VOCALION			
❏ VL73923	Good Rockin'	1971	$120
❏ VL3811 [M]	The Great Buddy Holly	1967	$100
❏ VL73811 [R]	The Great Buddy Holly	1967	$50

HOLLY, DOYLE

Number	Title	Yr	NM
BARNABY			
❏ BR-15010	Doyle Holly	1973	$18
❏ BR-15011	Just Another Cowboy Song	1973	$18

HOLLYRIDGE STRINGS, THE

Number	Title	Yr	NM
CAPITOL			
❏ T2404 [M]	Christmas Favorites by the Hollyridge Strings	1965	$15
❏ ST2404 [S]	Christmas Favorites by the Hollyridge Strings	1965	$18
❏ SM-11830	Christmas Favorites by the Hollyridge Strings	1978	$12
— Abridged reissue of ST 2404			
❏ T2221 [M]	Hits Made Famous by Elvis Presley	1965	$18
❏ ST2221 [S]	Hits Made Famous by Elvis Presley	1965	$25
❏ ST2998	Hits Made Famous by Simon and Garfunkel	1968	$18
❏ T2199 [M]	Hits Made Famous by the Four Seasons	1965	$18
❏ ST2199 [S]	Hits Made Famous by the Four Seasons	1965	$25
❏ ST-883 [B]	Hits of the 70's	1971	$15
❏ T2564 [M]	Oldies But Goldies	1966	$18
❏ ST2564 [S]	Oldies But Goldies	1966	$25
❏ T2611 [M]	Skyscraper	1966	$18
❏ ST2611 [S]	Skyscraper	1966	$25
❏ T2156 [M]	The Beach Boys Song Book	1964	$18
❏ ST2156 [S]	The Beach Boys Song Book	1964	$25
❏ SM-2156	The Beach Boys Song Book	197?	$12
❏ T2749 [M]	The Beach Boys Song Book, Vol. 2	1967	$25
❏ ST2749 [S]	The Beach Boys Song Book, Vol. 2	1967	$18

Number	Title	Yr	NM
❏ T2116 [M]	The Beatles Song Book	1964	$18
❏ ST2116 [S]	The Beatles Song Book	1964	$25
❏ SM-2116	The Beatles Song Book	197?	$12
❏ T2202 [M]	The Beatles Song Book, Vol. 2	1965	$18
❏ ST2202 [S]	The Beatles Song Book, Vol. 2	1965	$25
❏ T2656 [M]	The Beatles Song Book, Vol. 4	1967	$25
❏ ST2656 [S]	The Beatles Song Book, Vol. 4	1967	$18
❏ T2310 [M]	The Nat King Cole Song Book	1965	$18
❏ ST2310 [S]	The Nat King Cole Song Book	1965	$25
❏ T2429 [M]	The New Beatles Song Book	1966	$18
❏ ST2429 [S]	The New Beatles Song Book	1966	$25
❏ SM-2429	The New Beatles Song Book	197?	$12

HOLLYWOOD ARGYLES, THE
LUTE
❏ L-9001 [M]	The Hollywood Argyles (Alley Oop)	1960	$700

HOLLYWOOD BOWL SYMPHONY ORCHESTRA
CAPITOL
❏ STBB-489	Great Orchestral Music of Christmas	1970	$18
❏ P8393 [M]	The Music of Christmas	195?	$18

HOLLYWOOD JAZZ QUINTET, THE
GATEWAY
❏ 7018	Neon	1979	$30
❏ 7019	Nuances	1980	$30

HOLLYWOOD PERSUADERS, THE
ORIGINAL SOUND
❏ LPM-5013 [M]	Drums a-Go-Go	1965	$50
❏ LPS-8874 [S]	Drums a-Go-Go	1965	$75

HOLLYWOOD ROSE
CLEOPATRA
❏ 8144 [B]	The Roots Of Guns N' Roses		$30

—*picture disc*

HOLLYWOOD SAXOPHONE QUARTET, THE
LIBERTY
❏ LRP-3047 [M]	Gold Rush Suite	1957	$40
❏ LRP-3080 [M]	Sax Appeal	1958	$30
❏ LRP-6005 [M]	The Hollywood Saxophone Quartet	1955	$50

HOLMAN, BILL
ANDEX
❏ A-3004 [M]	In a Jazz Orbit	1958	$40
❏ AS-3004 [S]	In a Jazz Orbit	1959	$30
❏ A-3005 [M]	Jive for Five	1958	$40
❏ AS-3005 [S]	Jive for Five	1959	$30
CAPITOL
❏ T1464 [M]	Great Big Band	1960	$75
❏ ST1464 [S]	Great Big Band	1960	$75
❏ H6500 [10]	The Bill Holman Octet	1954	$250
CORAL
❏ CRL57188 [M]	The Fabulous Bill Holman	1958	$100
CREATIVE WORLD
❏ ST-1053	Great Big Band	197?	$35

HOLMAN, EDDIE
ABC
❏ S-701	I Love You	1970	$30
SALSOUL
❏ 5511	A Night to Remember	1977	$12

HOLMBERG, JIM
ESP-DISK'
❏ 1098	MIJ	196?	$25

HOLMES, CARL, AND THE COMMANDERS
ATLANTIC
❏ 8060 [M]	Twist Party at the Roundtable	1962	$40
❏ SD8060 [S]	Twist Party at the Roundtable	1962	$50

HOLMES, CECIL'S, SOULFUL SOUNDS
BUDDAH
❏ BDS-5139	Music for Soulful Lovers	1973	$15
❏ BDS-5129	The Black Motion Picture Experience	1973	$15

HOLMES, CLINT
EPIC
❏ KE32269	Playground in My Mind	1973	$12

HOLMES, JAKE
COLUMBIA
❏ C30996	Jake Holmes	1972	$15
POLYDOR
❏ 24-4007	Jake Holmes	1969	$15
❏ 24-4034	So Close, So Very Far to Go	1970	$15
TOWER
❏ T5079 [M]	Above Ground	1967	$25
❏ DT5079 [R]	Above Ground	1967	$18
❏ ST5127	Letter to Katherine December	1968	$18

HOLMES, MARVIN
BROWN DOOR
❏ MH-6581	Honor Thy Father	1975	$50
❏ MH-6573	Summer of '73	1973	$50
UNI
❏ 73046	Ooh, Ooh, The Dragon And Other Monsters	1969	$150

—*Reproductions exist*

HOLMES, RICHARD "GROOVE"
BLUE NOTE
❏ BST-84372	Comin' On Home	1971	$30
FANTASY
❏ OJC-329	Soul Message	1988	$25

—*Reissue of Prestige 7435*

FLYING DUTCHMAN
❏ BDL1-1537	I'm in the Mood for Love	1976	$30
GROOVE MERCHANT
❏ 505	American Pie	1972	$30
❏ 4402 [B]	Hunk-A-Funk	1975	$25
❏ 527	New Groove	1973	$30
❏ 512	Night Glider	1972	$30
MUSE
❏ 5358	Blues All Day Long	1989	$25
❏ 5239	Broadway	1981	$25
❏ 5167	Good Vibrations	1979	$25
❏ 5134	Shippin' Out	1978	$25
PACIFIC JAZZ
❏ PJ-59 [M]	After Hours	1962	$50
❏ ST-59 [S]	After Hours	1962	$75
❏ ST-20171	Come Together	1970	$35
❏ PJ-32 [M]	Groovin' with Jug	1961	$75
❏ ST-32 [S]	Groovin' with Jug	1961	$40
❏ LN-10130	Groovin' with Jug	198?	$20

—*Busget-line reissue*

❏ PJ-23 [M]	Richard "Groove" Holmes	1961	$75
❏ ST-23 [S]	Richard "Groove" Holmes	1961	$75
❏ PJ-51 [M]	Somethin' Special	1962	$50
❏ ST-51 [S]	Somethin' Special	1962	$75
❏ PJ-10105 [M]	Tell It Like It Tis	1966	$35
❏ ST-20105 [S]	Tell It Like It Tis	1966	$50
❏ ST-20153	Workin' on a Groovy Thing	1969	$35
❏ ST-20163	X-77	1969	$35
PRESTIGE
❏ PRLP-7514 [M]	Get Up and Get It	1967	$30
❏ PRST-7514 [S]	Get Up and Get It	1967	$35
❏ PRLP-7468 [M]	Living Soul	1966	$35
❏ PRST-7468 [S]	Living Soul	1966	$50
❏ PRLP-7485 [M]	Misty	1966	$35
❏ PRST-7485 [S]	Misty	1966	$50
❏ PRLP-7435 [M]	Soul Message	1966	$35
❏ PRST-7435 [S]	Soul Message	1966	$50
❏ PRST-7741	Soul Mist	1970	$35
❏ PRST-7543	Soul Power	1968	$35
❏ PRLP-7493 [M]	Spicy	1967	$50
❏ PRST-7493 [S]	Spicy	1967	$35
❏ PRLP-7497 [M]	Super Cool	1967	$50
❏ PRST-7497 [S]	Super Cool	1967	$35
❏ PRST-7601	That Healin' Feelin'	1969	$35
❏ PRST-7768	The Best for Beautiful People	1971	$35
❏ PRST-7700	The Best of Richard "Groove" Holmes	1969	$35
❏ PRST-7778	The Best of Soul Organ Giants	1972	$30
❏ PRST-7570	The Groover	1968	$35
VERSATILE
❏ MSG6003	Dancing in the Sun	1977	$35
WARNER BROS.
❏ W1553 [M]	Book of the Blues	1964	$50
❏ WS1553 [S]	Book of the Blues	1964	$75
WORLD PACIFIC
❏ ST-20147	Welcome Home	1968	$175

HOLMES, RUPERT
ELEKTRA
❏ 5E-560	Full Circle	1982	$12
EPIC
❏ KE33443	Rupert Holmes	1975	$15
❏ PE34288	Singles	1976	$15
❏ KE32864	Widescreen	1974	$15
EXCELSIOR
❏ XMP-6000	Rupert Holmes	1980	$12
❏ XMP-6022	She Lets Her Hair Down	1981	$12

INFINITY
❏ 9020	Partners in Crime	1979	$12
MCA
❏ 5129	Adventure	1980	$12
❏ 9020	Partners in Crime	1980	$10

—*Reissue of Infinity LP*

❏ 37166	Pursuit of Happiness	198?	$10

—*Reissue of Private Stock LP*

PRIVATE STOCK
❏ PS-7006	Pursuit of Happiness	1978	$15

HOLT, RED
ARGO
❏ LP-696 [M]	Look Out! Look Out!	1962	$25
❏ LPS-696 [S]	Look Out! Look Out!	1962	$30
PAULA
❏ 4006	Isaac, Isaac, Isaac	197?	$35
❏ 4007	The Other Side of the Moon	197?	$35

HOLY MACKEREL, THE
REPRISE
❏ RS-6311	The Holy Mackerel	1968	$30

HOLY MODAL ROUNDERS, THE
4 MEN WITH BEARDS
❏ 4M184LP [B]	2		$25
❏ 4M183LP [B]	The Holy Modal Rounders		$25
ADELPHIA
❏ 1030	Last Round	198?	$12
ELEKTRA
❏ EKS-74026 [B]	The Moray Eels Eat the Holy Modal Rounders	1968	$30
ESP-DISK'
❏ 1068 [M]	Indian War Whoop	1967	$150
❏ 1068-S [S]	Indian War Whoop	1967	$40
FANTASY
❏ F-24711	Stampfel and Weber	1972	$25
FOLKLORE
❏ FRLP-14031 [M]	The Holy Modal Rounders	1964	$100
METROMEDIA
❏ MD-1039	Good Taste Is Timeless	1970	$30
PRESTIGE
❏ PRLP-7451 [M]	The Holy Modal Rounders	1966	$40

—*Reissue of Folklore LP*

❏ PR-7720	The Holy Modal Rounders	1969	$30
❏ PRLP-7410 [M]	The Holy Modal Rounders 2	1965	$40
ROUNDER
❏ 3004	Alleged in Their Own Time	198?	$12
SUNDAZED
❏ LP5126	The Moray Eels Eat the Holy Modal Rounders	2002	$15

—*Reissue on 180-gram vinyl*

HOMBRES, THE
VERVE FORECAST
❏ FT-3036 [M]	Let It Out (Let It All Hang Out)	1967	$30
❏ FTS-3036 [S]	Let It Out (Let It All Hang Out)	1967	$30
❏ FTS-3068	The Hombres	1968	$0

—*Canceled*

HOMER
UNITED
❏ HS-101	Grown in U.S.A.	1970	$300

HOMER AND JETHRO
AUDIO LAB
❏ AL-1513 [M]	Musical Madness	1958	$150
KING
❏ KS-1005	24 Great Songs in the Homer & Jethro Style	1967	$25
❏ 848 [M]	Cornier Than Corn	1963	$80
❏ 639 [M]	They Sure Are Corny	1959	$150
RCA CAMDEN
❏ CAL-707 [M]	Homer and Jethro Strike Back	1961	$18
RCA VICTOR
❏ LPM-3538 [M]	Any News from Nashville?	1966	$30
❏ LSP-3538 [S]	Any News from Nashville?	1966	$30
❏ LPM-1412 [M]	Barefoot Ballads	1957	$50
❏ LSP-4001	Cool, Crazy Christmas	1968	$25
❏ LPM-2928 [M]	Cornfucius Say	1964	$30
❏ LSP-2928 [S]	Cornfucius Say	1964	$30
❏ LPM-2954 [M]	Fractured Folk Songs	1964	$30
❏ LSP-2954 [S]	Fractured Folk Songs	1964	$30
❏ LPM-3112 [10]	Homer & Jethro Fracture Frank Loesser	1953	$175
❏ LPM-2492 [M]	Homer and Jethro at the Convention	1962	$30
❏ LSP-2492 [S]	Homer and Jethro at the Convention	1962	$30
❏ LPM-2181 [M]	Homer and Jethro at the Country Club	1960	$30

Number	Title	Yr	NM
❏ LSP-2181 [S]	Homer and Jethro at the Country Club	1960	$40
❏ LSP-4024	Homer and Jethro at Vanderbilt U.	1969	$25
❏ LPM-2674 [M]	Homer and Jethro Go West	1963	$30
❏ LSP-2674 [S]	Homer and Jethro Go West	1963	$30
❏ LPM-3357 [M]	Homer and Jethro Sing Tenderly	1965	$30
❏ LSP-3357 [S]	Homer and Jethro Sing Tenderly	1965	$30
❏ LSP-4148	Homer and Jethro's Next Album	1969	$25
❏ LPM-3701 [M]	It Ain't Necessarily Square	1967	$30
❏ LSP-3701 [S]	It Ain't Necessarily Square	1967	$30
❏ LPM-1880 [M]	Life Can Be Miserable	1958	$30
❏ LSP-1880 [S]	Life Can Be Miserable	1958	$50
❏ LPM-3822 [M]	Nashville Cats	1967	$40
❏ LSP-3822 [S]	Nashville Cats	1967	$30
❏ LPM-2743 [M]	Ooh, That's Corny	1963	$30
❏ LSP-2743 [S]	Ooh, That's Corny	1963	$30
❏ LPM-2459 [M]	Playing It Straight	1962	$30
❏ LSP-2459 [S]	Playing It Straight	1962	$30
❏ LPM-3877 [M]	Somethin' Stupid	1967	$50
❏ LSP-3877 [S]	Somethin' Stupid	1967	$30
❏ LPM-2286 [M]	Songs My Mother Never Sang	1961	$30
❏ LSP-2286 [S]	Songs My Mother Never Sang	1961	$30
❏ LPM-3474 [M]	The Best of Homer and Jethro	1966	$30
❏ LSP-3474 [S]	The Best of Homer and Jethro	1966	$30
❏ LPM-3462 [M]	The Old Crusty Minstrels	1965	$30
❏ LSP-3462 [S]	The Old Crusty Minstrels	1965	$30
❏ LPM-3973 [M]	There's Nothing Like an Old Hippie	1968	$150
❏ LSP-3973 [S]	There's Nothing Like an Old Hippie	1968	$30
❏ LPM-1560 [M]	The Worst of Homer & Jethro	1958	$50
❏ LPM-3673 [M]	Wanted for Murder	1966	$30
❏ LSP-3673 [S]	Wanted for Murder	1966	$30
❏ LPM-2455 [M]	Zany Songs of the '30s	1962	$30
❏ LSP-2455 [S]	Zany Songs of the '30s	1962	$30

HOMESICK JAMES

PRESTIGE
❏ PRLP-7388 [M]	Homesick James	1965	$30

HOMI & JARVIS

GRP
❏ GR-1005	Friend of a Friend	198?	$25

HONDELLS, THE

MERCURY
❏ MG-20940 [M]	Go Little Honda	1964	$40
❏ SR-60940 [S]	Go Little Honda	1964	$75
❏ MG-20982 [M]	The Hondells	1965	$50
❏ SR-60982 [S]	The Hondells	1965	$100

HONEY AND THE BEES

JOSIE
❏ JOS-4013	Love	1970	$25

HONEY CONE, THE

HOT WAX
❏ HA-713	Love, Peace & Soul	1972	$15
❏ HA-707	Soulful Tapestry	1971	$15
❏ HA-706	Sweet Replies	1971	$15
❏ HA-701	Take Me With You	1970	$15

HONEY DREAMERS, THE

FANTASY
❏ 3207 [M]	The Honey Dreamers Sing Gershwin	1956	$100
—Red vinyl			
❏ 3207 [M]	The Honey Dreamers Sing Gershwin	195?	$40
—Black vinyl			

HONEY LTD

LIGHT IN THE ATTIC
❏ LITA102 [M]	The Complete LHI Recordings	2013	$30

HONEYCOMBS, THE

INTERPHON
❏ IN-88001 [M]	Here Are the Honeycombs	1964	$50
❏ IN-88001 [R]	Here Are the Honeycombs	1964	$50

VEE JAY
❏ IN-88001 [M]	Here Are the Honeycombs	1964	$75
❏ IN-88001 [R]	Here Are the Honeycombs	1964	$75

HONEYDRIPPERS, THE

ES PARANZA
❏ 90220 [EP]	The Honeydrippers, Volume One	1984	$10

HONEYMOON SUITE

WARNER BROS.
❏ 25098	Honeymoon Suite	1984	$12

Number	Title	Yr	NM
❏ R162140	Racing After Midnight	1988	$15
—BMG Direct Marketing edition			
❏ 25652	Racing After Midnight	1988	$12
❏ R144489	The Big Prize	1986	$15
—RCA Music Service edition			
❏ 25293	The Big Prize	1986	$12

HONEYTREE

BIRDWING
❏ BWR2029	Merry Christmas	1981	$15

HONK

20TH CENTURY
❏ T-406	Honk	1973	$15

EPIC
❏ KE33094	Honk	1974	$15

GRANITE
❏ GR7720	Five Summer Stories	1972	$18

HOODOO GURUS

A&M
❏ SP5012	Stone Age Romeos	1983	$15

BIG TIME
❏ 009 [B]	Mars Needs Guitars	1985	$18

ELEKTRA
❏ 60728	Blow Your Cool	1987	$12
❏ 60485	Mars Needs Guitars	1986	$12
—Reissue of Big Time LP			

RCA
❏ 9781-1-R	Magnum Cum Louder	1989	$12

HOODOO RHYTHM DEVILS, THE

CAPITOL
❏ ST-842	The Hoodoo Rhythm Devils	1971	$25

HOOK, THE

UNI
❏ 73038	Hooked	1969	$18
❏ 73023	The Hook Will Grab You	1968	$18

HOOKER, EARL

ARHOOLIE
❏ LP1044	2 Bugs and a Roach	1968	$30
❏ LP1066	His First and Last Recordings	1970	$30
❏ LP1051	Hooker and Steve	1969	$30

BLUES ON BLUES
❏ 10002	The Last of the Great Earl Hooker	197?	$25

BLUESWAY
❏ BLS-6032	Don't Have to Worry	1969	$30
❏ BLS-6072	Do You Remember the Great Earl Hooker	1973	$18
❏ BLS-6038	If You Miss Him	1970	$30

BLUE THUMB
❏ BTS12	Sweet Black Angel	1969	$30

CUCA
❏ 3400 [M]	The Genius of Earl Hooker	1965	$300

HOOKER, JOHN LEE, AND CANNED HEAT

LIBERTY
❏ 35002	Hooker 'n' Heat	1971	$25

RHINO
❏ RNDA-71105	Infinite Boogie	1987	$15
❏ RNLP-801	Recorded Live at the Fox Venice Theatre	1985	$15

HOOKER, JOHN LEE

ABC
❏ X-768	Born in Mississippi, Raised Up in Tennessee	1973	$25
❏ XQ-768 [Q]	Born in Mississippi, Raised Up in Tennessee	1974	$40
❏ S-720	Endless Boogie	1971	$25
❏ X-838	Free Beer and Chicken	1974	$18
❏ XQ-838 [Q]	Free Beer and Chicken	1974	$40
❏ X-761	Live at Soledad Prison	1972	$25
❏ XQ-761 [Q]	Live at Soledad Prison	1974	$40
❏ X-736	Never Get Out of These Blues Alive	1972	$25
❏ XQ-736 [Q]	Never Get Out of These Blues Alive	1974	$40

ATCO
❏ 33-151 [M]	Don't Turn Me From Your Door	1963	$150
❏ SD 33-151 [R]	Don't Turn Me From Your Door	1967	$50

ATLANTIC
❏ SD7228	Detroit Special	1972	$25

BATTLE
❏ BLP-6114 [M]	How Long Blues	196?	$175
❏ BLP-6113 [M]	John Lee Hooker	196?	$175

BLUESWAY
❏ BLS-6038	If You Miss 'Em	1969	$25
❏ BL-6002 [M]	Live at Café A-Go-Go	1967	$30
❏ BLS-6002 [S]	Live at Café A-Go-Go	1967	$25
❏ BLS-6052	Live at Kabuki-Wuki	1973	$18
❏ BLQ-6052 [Q]	Live at Kabuki-Wuki	1974	$40
❏ BLS-6023	Simply the Truth	1968	$25
❏ BL-6012 [M]	Urban Blues	1967	$30
❏ BLS-6012 [S]	Urban Blues	1967	$25

BUDDAH
❏ BDS-7506	Big Band Blues	1970	$18
❏ BDS-4002	The Very Best of John Lee Hooker	1970	$18

CHAMELEON
❏ D1-74808	The Healer	1989	$12
❏ D1-74794	The Hook	1989	$12

CHESS
❏ LP-1438 [M]	House of the Blues	1960	$300
—Black label			
❏ LP-1438 [M]	House of the Blues	1966	$50
—Blue and white label			
❏ CH-9258	House of the Blues	1987	$10
❏ LP-1454 [M]	John Lee Hooker Plays and Sings the Blues	1961	$300
—Black label			
❏ LP-1454 [M]	John Lee Hooker Plays and Sings the Blues	1966	$50
—Blue and white label			
❏ CH-9199	John Lee Hooker Plays and Sings the Blues	1986	$10
—Reissue			
❏ 60011	Mad Man Blues	1973	$25
❏ CH2-92507	Mad Man Blues	198?	$15
❏ LP-1508 [M]	Real Folk Blues	1966	$50
❏ LPS-1508 [R]	Real Folk Blues	1966	$30
❏ CH-9271	The Real Folk Blues	1988	$10

CLEOPATRA
❏ 3479 [B]	Blues On Fire		$25
❏ 8836 [B]	Electric Blues		$40
—picture disc			

COLLECTABLES
❏ COL-5151	Golden Classics	198?	$15

CROWN
❏ CLP-5295 [M]	Folk Blues	1962	$30
—Gray label			
❏ CLP-5295 [M]	Folk Blues	1962	$15
—Black label with multi-color "Crown			
❏ CLP-5232 [M]	John Lee Hooker Sings the Blues	1962	$150
—Black label with silver "Crown			
❏ CLP-5232 [M]	John Lee Hooker Sings the Blues	1962	$30
—Gray label			
❏ CLP-5232 [M]	John Lee Hooker Sings the Blues	196?	$15
—Black label with multi-color "Crown			
❏ CLP-5157 [M]	The Blues	1960	$150
—Black label with silver "Crown			
❏ CLP-5157 [M]	The Blues	1962	$30
—Gray label			
❏ CLP-5157 [M]	The Blues	196?	$15
—Black label with multi-color "Crown			
❏ CLP-5353 [M]	The Great John Lee Hooker	1963	$30
—Gray label			
❏ CLP-5353 [M]	The Great John Lee Hooker	1963	$15
—Black label with multi-color "Crown			

EVEREST ARCHIVE OF FOLK & JAZZ
❏ 347	Hooked On Blues	1980	$15
❏ 222	John Lee Hooker	1968	$15

EXODUS
❏ 325 [M]	Is He the World's Greatest Blues Singer?	1966	$30

FANTASY
❏ 24722	Black Snake	197?	$18
❏ 24706	Boogie Chillun	1972	$18

GALAXY
❏ 201 [M]	I'm John Lee Hooker	1961	$300
❏ 205 [M]	Live at Sugar Hill	1962	$300
❏ 8205 [S]	Live at Sugar Hill	1962	$300

GNP CRESCENDO
❏ GNPS-10007	The Best of John Lee Hooker	1974	$18

GREENE BOTTLE
❏ 3130	Johnny Lee	1972	$18

IMPULSE!
❏ A-9103 [M]	It Serves You Right to Suffer	1966	$120
❏ AS-9103 [S]	It Serves You Right to Suffer	1966	$160

JEWEL
❏ 5005	I Feel Good	1971	$18

KING
❏ 727 [M]	John Lee Hooker Sings the Blues	1960	$500
❏ KLP-727	John Lee Hooker Sings the Blues	1988	$10
—Reissue of earlier 727			

Number	Title	Yr	NM
❏ KS-1085	Moanin' and Stompin' Blues	1970	$30
LABOR			
❏ 4	Alone	1982	$12
MUSE			
❏ 5205	Sittin' Here Thinkin'	1980	$15
PAUSA			
❏ PR-7197	Jealous	1986	$12
RIVERSIDE			
❏ RLP 12-321 [M]	That's My Story	1960	$150
❏ RLP 12-838 [M]	The Country Blues of John Lee Hooker	1959	$150
SPECIALTY			
❏ SPS-2125	Alone	1970	$30
❏ SPS-2127	Going Down Highway 51	1970	$30
STAX			
❏ STS-2013	That's Where It's At	1970	$18
❏ STX-4134	That's Where It's At	1979	$12
—Reissue of 2013			
TOMATO			
❏ 7009	The Cream	1978	$18
TRADITION			
❏ 2089	Real Blues	1970	$18
UNITED ARTISTS			
❏ UAS-5512	Coast to Coast Blues Band	1971	$18
❏ UA-LA127-J	John Lee Hooker's Detroit	1974	$30
VEE JAY			
❏ LP-1043 [M]	Burnin'	1962	$50
❏ SR-1043 [S]	Burnin'	1962	$175
❏ LP-1078 [M]	Concert at Newport	1964	$50
❏ SR-1078 [S]	Concert at Newport	1964	$175
❏ VJLP-1078 [B]	Concert at Newport	1986	$10
—Reissue of original on flimsier vinyl			
❏ LP-1007 [M]	I'm John Lee Hooker	1959	$300
—Maroon label			
❏ LP-1007 [M]	I'm John Lee Hooker	1960	$100
—Black label with colorband			
❏ VJLP-1007	I'm John Lee Hooker	1986	$10
—Reissue of original on flimsier vinyl			
❏ LP-8502 [M]	Is He the World's Greatest Blues Singer?	1965	$40
—This is the title on the cover; the label calls it "Is He Really the World's Greatest Blues Singer?"			
❏ VJLP-8502	Is He the World's Greatest Blues Singer?	1986	$10
—Reissue of original on flimsier vinyl; this is the title on the cover; the label calls it "Is He Really the World's Greatest Blues Singer?"			
❏ DY-7301	John Lee Hooker In Person	198?	$10
❏ LP-1066 [M]	John Lee Hooker On Campus	1963	$50
❏ SR-1066 [S]	John Lee Hooker On Campus	1963	$175
❏ LP-1049 [M]	The Best of John Lee Hooker	1962	$50
❏ SR-1049 [P]	The Best of John Lee Hooker	1962	$100
❏ VJLP-1049	The Best of John Lee Hooker	1986	$10
—Reissue of original on flimsier vinyl			
❏ LP-1058 [M]	The Big Soul of John Lee Hooker	1963	$50
❏ SR-1058 [S]	The Big Soul of John Lee Hooker	1963	$175
❏ VJLP-1058	The Big Soul of John Lee Hooker	1986	$10
—Reissue of original on flimsier vinyl			
❏ LP-1033 [M]	The Folk Lore of John Lee Hooker	1961	$50
❏ SR-1033 [S]	The Folk Lore of John Lee Hooker	1961	$100
❏ LP-1023 [M]	Travelin'	1960	$100
VERVE FOLKWAYS			
❏ FT-3003 [M]	John Lee Hooker and Seven Nights	1965	$40
❏ FTS-3003 [S]	John Lee Hooker and Seven Nights	1965	$40
WAND			
❏ WDS-689	On the Waterfront	1972	$18

HOOPER, LES

Number	Title	Yr	NM
CHURCHILL			
❏ 67234	Dorian Blue	1977	$30
❏ 67235	Hoopla	1978	$30
CREATIVE WORLD			
❏ ST-3002	Look What They've Done	197?	$35
JAZZ HOUNDS			
❏ 04	Raisin' the Roof	1982	$30
PAUSA			
❏ 7185	Hoopla	1986	$25

HOOPER, STIX

Number	Title	Yr	NM
ARTFUL BALANCE			
❏ ABI-7214	Lay It on the Line	1989	$15
MCA			
❏ 3180	The World Within	1980	$12
❏ 5374	Touch the Feeling	1982	$12

HOOPES, RONNIE

Number	Title	Yr	NM
REVELATION			
❏ 21	Respect for a Great Tradition	197?	$35

HOOTCH

Number	Title	Yr	NM
PROGRESS			
❏ PRS-4844	Hootch	1974	$600

HOOTERS

Number	Title	Yr	NM
ANTENNA			
❏ HOO83	Amore	1983	$25
COLUMBIA			
❏ BFC39912	Nervous Night	1985	$15
❏ FC39912	Nervous Night	1985	$12
—Reissue with new prefix			
❏ OC40659	One Way Home	1987	$12
❏ C45058	Zig Zag	1989	$12

HOOTIE & THE BLOWFISH

Number	Title	Yr	NM
ATLANTIC			
❏ 82613	Cracked Rear View	1995	$75
—Red vinyl			
❏ 82886	Fairweather Johnson	1996	$25
❏ 83136	Musical Chairs	1998	$18

HOPE, BOB

Number	Title	Yr	NM
CADET			
❏ LP-4046 [B]	On the Road to Vietnam	1965	$18
CAPITOL			
❏ ST-11538 [B]	America Is 200 Years Old ... And There's Still Hope!	1976	$15
DECCA			
❏ DL4396 [M]	Hope in Russia and One Other Place	1963	$25
❏ DL74396 [S]	Hope in Russia and One Other Place	1963	$30
MCA			
❏ 906	Bob Hope in Hollywood	1984	$15
RADIOLA			
❏ MR-1060	The Bob Hope Radio Show	197?	$12
—Includes two radio shows: October 23, 1945 and December 18, 1945			
RCA VICTOR			
❏ LOC-1055 [M]	Not So Long Ago: NBC Project Twenty	1960	$25
❏ LSO-1055 [S]	Not So Long Ago: NBC Project Twenty	1960	$30
SPEAR			
❏ 4700	Holidays	1973	$18

HOPE, ELMO

Number	Title	Yr	NM
AUDIO FIDELITY			
❏ AFLP-2119 [M]	Sounds from Riker's Island	1963	$150
❏ AFSD-6119 [S]	Sounds from Riker's Island	1963	$100
BEACON			
❏ B-401 [M]	High Hopes	1961	$350
❏ BS-401 [S]	High Hopes	1961	$350
BLUE NOTE			
❏ BLP-5044 [10]	Elmo Hope Quintet	1954	$300
❏ BLP-5029 [10]	Elmo Hope Trio	1953	$300
CELEBRITY			
❏ 209 [M]	Elmo Hope Trio	1962	$30
❏ S-209 [S]	Elmo Hope Trio	1962	$30
CONTEMPORARY			
❏ M-3620 [M]	The Elmo Hope Trio	1966	$175
❏ S-7620 [S]	The Elmo Hope Trio	1966	$30
FANTASY			
❏ OJC-477	Elmo Hope Trio	1991	$30
❏ OJC-1703	Hope Meets Foster	1985	$25
❏ OJC-1751	Meditations	198?	$25
HIFI			
❏ J-616 [M]	Elmo Hope	1960	$40
❏ JS-616 [S]	Elmo Hope	1960	$50
INNER CITY			
❏ IC-1018	Last Sessions	197?	$35
❏ IC-1037	Last Sessions, Volume 2	1978	$35
MILESTONE			
❏ 47037	All Star Sessions	197?	$35
PRESTIGE			
❏ PRST-7675	Elmo Hope Memorial Album	1969	$35
❏ PRLP-7021 [M]	Hope Meets Foster	1956	$600
❏ PRLP-7043 [M]	Informal Jazz	1956	$1500
❏ PRLP-7010 [M]	Meditations	1956	$600
❏ PRLP-7021 [M]	Wail, Frank, Wail	1957	$300
—Retitled reissue of above album			
RIVERSIDE			
❏ RLP-381 [M]	Homecoming!	1961	$250
❏ RS-9381 [S]	Homecoming!	1961	$250
❏ 6161	Homecoming!	198?	$30
❏ RLP-408 [M]	Hope-Full	1962	$175
❏ RS-9408 [S]	Hope-Full	1962	$175

HOPE, LYNN

Number	Title	Yr	NM
ALADDIN			
❏ LP-707 [10]	Lynn Hope and His Tenor Sax	1953	$600
❏ LP-805 [M]	Lynn Hope and His Tenor Sax	1955	$500
IMPERIAL			
❏ LP-9177-A [M]	Tenderly	1962	$40
❏ LP-12177-A [S]	Tenderly	1962	$75
KING			
❏ 717 [M]	Maharajah of the Saxophone	1961	$120
SCORE			
❏ SLP-4015 [M]	Tenderly	1957	$250

HOPE, STAN

Number	Title	Yr	NM
MAINSTREAM			
❏ MRL-327	Stan Hope	1972	$35

HOPKIN, MARY

Number	Title	Yr	NM
APPLE			
❏ SMAS-3381	Earth Song/Ocean Song	1970	$18
❏ ST-3351 [B]	Post Card	1969	$18
❏ ST-5-3351	Post Card	1969	$25
—Capitol Record Club edition			
❏ SW-3395 [B]	Those Were the Days	1972	$30

HOPKINS, CLAUDE

Number	Title	Yr	NM
CHIAROSCURO			
❏ 114	Crazy Fingers	1972	$35
DESIGN			
❏ DLP-30 [M]	Golden Era of Dixieland Jazz 1887-1937	1957	$30
JAZZ ARCHIVES			
❏ JA-27	Singin' in the Rain	198?	$25
SWINGVILLE			
❏ SVLP-2020 [M]	Let's Jam	1961	$50
—Purple label			
❏ SVLP-2020 [M]	Let's Jam	1965	$30
—Blue label, trident logo at right			
❏ SVLP-2041 [M]	Swing Time	1962	$50
—Purple label			
❏ SVLP-2041 [M]	Swing Time	1965	$30
—Blue label, trident logo at right			
❏ SVLP-2009 [M]	Yes Indeed	1960	$150
—Purple label			
❏ SVLP-2009 [M]	Yes Indeed	1965	$75
—Blue label, trident logo at right			

HOPKINS, KENYON

Number	Title	Yr	NM
VERVE			
❏ V-8694 [M]	Dream Songs	1967	$25
❏ V6-8694 [S]	Dream Songs	1967	$30

HOPKINS, LIGHTNIN'

Number	Title	Yr	NM
ANALOGUE PRODUCTIONS			
❏ AAPB-014	Goin' Away	199?	$40
—Audiophile reissue			
ARHOOLIE			
❏ 1030	Blues Festival	196?	$18
❏ 2007	Early Recordings	197?	$18
❏ 2010	Early Recordings Volume 2	197?	$18
❏ 1022	Lightnin' Hopkins, His Brother and Barbara Dane	196?	$25
❏ 1011	Lightnin' Hopkins and His Guitar	196?	$25
❏ 1063	Lightnin' Hopkins in Berkeley	1969	$18
❏ 1087	Poor Lightnin'	1970	$18
❏ 1034	Texas Blues Man	1968	$18
BARNABY			
❏ Z30247	Lightnin' Hopkins in New York	1970	$18
BLUES CLASSICS			
❏ 30	Historic Recordings 1952-1953	1986	$15
BLUESVILLE			
❏ BVLP-1045 [M]	Blues in My Bottle	1962	$150
—Blue label, silver print			
❏ BVLP-1045 [M]	Blues in My Bottle	1964	$30
—Blue label, trident logo on right			
❏ BVLP-1086 [M]	Down Home Blues	1964	$30
❏ BVLP-1073 [M]	Goin' Away	1963	$150
—Blue label, silver print			
❏ BVLP-1073 [M]	Goin' Away	1964	$30
—Blue label, trident logo on right			
❏ BVLP-1081 [M]	Gotta Move Your Baby	1964	$30
—Blue label, trident logo on right			
❏ BVLP-1029 [M]	Last Night Blues	1961	$150
—Blue label, silver print			
❏ BVLP-1061 [M]	Lightnin' & Co.	1963	$150
—Blue label, silver print			
❏ BVLP-1061 [M]	Lightnin' & Co.	1964	$30

Number	Title	Yr	NM

— Blue label, trident logo on right

| ❏ BVLP-1019 [M] | Lightnin' | 1961 | $150 |

— Blue label, silver print

| ❏ BVLP-1019 [M] | Lightnin' | 1964 | $30 |

— Blue label, trident logo on right

| ❏ BVLP-1084 [M] | Lightnin' Hopkins' Greatest Hits | 1964 | $40 |
| ❏ BVLP-1070 [M] | Smokes Like Lightnin' | 1963 | $150 |

— Blue label, silver print

| ❏ BVLP-1070 [M] | Smokes Like Lightnin' | 1964 | $30 |

— Blue label, trident logo on right

| ❏ BVLP-1057 [M] | Walkin' This Street | 1962 | $150 |

— Blue label, silver print

| ❏ BVLP-1057 [M] | Walkin' This Street | 1964 | $30 |

— Blue label, trident logo on right

BLUESWAY

| ❏ S-6039 | If You Miss 'Im | 1969 | $25 |

BULLDOG

| ❏ 1010 | The Texas Bluesman | 1965 | $18 |

CANDID

| ❏ CM-8010 [M] | Lightnin' in New York | 1961 | $120 |
| ❏ CS-9010 [S] | Lightnin' in New York | 1961 | $175 |

COLLECTABLES

❏ COL-5143	Golden Classics, Part 1: Drinkin' the Blues	198?	$12
❏ COL-5144	Golden Classics, Part 2: Prison Blues	198?	$12
❏ COL-5145	Golden Classics, Part 3: Mama and Papa Hopkins	198?	$12
❏ COL-5146	Golden Classics, Part 4: Nothin' But the Blues	198?	$12
❏ COL-5111	Golden Classics -- Mojo Hand	198?	$12
❏ COL-5121	The Herald Recordings/1954	198?	$12
❏ COL-5203	The Lost Texas Tapes, Vol. 1	198?	$12
❏ COL-5204	The Lost Texas Tapes, Vol. 2	198?	$12
❏ COL-5205	The Lost Texas Tapes, Vol. 3	198?	$12
❏ COL-5206	The Lost Texas Tapes, Vol. 4	198?	$12
❏ COL-5207	The Lost Texas Tapes, Vol. 5	198?	$12

CROWN

| ❏ CLP-5224 [M] | Lightnin' Hopkins Sings the Blues | 1962 | $150 |

— Black label, silver "Crown"

| ❏ CLP-5224 [M] | Lightnin' Hopkins Sings the Blues | 1962 | $50 |

— Gray label

| ❏ CLP-5224 [M] | Lightnin' Hopkins Sings the Blues | 196? | $30 |

— Black label, multi-color logo

DART

| ❏ D-8000 [M] | Blues Underground | 196? | $250 |

— Retitled version of above

| ❏ D-8000 [M] | Lightning Strikes Again | 1960 | $400 |

DCC COMPACT CLASSICS

| ❏ LPZ-2007 | Blues Hoot | 1996 | $50 |

— Audiophile vinyl

EVEREST ARCHIVE OF FOLK & JAZZ

❏ 342	Autobiography in Blues	1979	$15
❏ 241	Lightnin' Hopkins	1969	$18
❏ 313	Lightnin' Hopkins, Vol. 2	197?	$18

FANTASY

❏ OBC-506	Blues in My Bottle	198?	$15
❏ 24702	Double Blues	1972	$25
❏ OBC-522	Goin' Away	1988	$15
❏ 24725	How Many More Years	1981	$18
❏ OBC-532	Lightnin'	1990	$15

FIRE

| ❏ FLP104 [M] | Mojo Hand | 1960 | $1500 |

FOLKLORE

| ❏ FRLP-14021 [M] | Hootin' the Blues | 1964 | $75 |
| ❏ FRST-14021 [S] | Hootin' the Blues | 1964 | $80 |

FOLKWAYS

| ❏ FS-3822 [M] | Lightnin' Hopkins | 1962 | $40 |
| ❏ 31011 | Roots | 196? | $20 |

GNP CRESCENDO

| ❏ 10022 | Legacy of the Blues, Volume 12 | 1978 | $15 |

GUEST STAR

| ❏ G-1459 [M] | Live" at the Bird Lounge, Houston, Texas | 1964 | $30 |
| ❏ GS-1459 [R] | Live" at the Bird Lounge, Houston, Texas | 1964 | $25 |

HERALD

| ❏ LP1012 [M] | Lightnin' and the Blues | 1959 | $1500 |

— Black label; VG value 750; VG+ value 1125

| ❏ LP1012 [M] | Lightnin' and the Blues | 1959 | $800 |

— Yellow label

| ❏ LP1012 [M] | Lightnin' and the Blues | 196? | $500 |

— Multi-color label

IMPERIAL

❏ LP-9211 [M]	Lightnin' Hopkins and the Blues	1963	$250
❏ LP-12211 [R]	Lightnin' Hopkins and the Blues	1963	$150
❏ LP-9180 [M]	Lightnin' Hopkins On Stage	1962	$300
❏ LP-9186 [M]	Lightnin' Hopkins Sings the Blues	1962	$300

INTERNATIONAL ARTISTS

| ❏ IA-6 | Free Form Patterns | 1968 | $250 |

— With photo on cover

| ❏ IA-6 | Free Form Patterns | 1968 | $50 |

— With psychedelic art on cover

JAZZ MAN

| ❏ BLZ-5502 | Lightnin' in New York | 1982 | $12 |

JEWEL

❏ 5000	Blue Lightnin'	1967	$18
❏ 5015	Great Electric Show and Dance	1970	$18
❏ 5001	Talkin' Some Sense	1968	$18

KING

| ❏ KS-1085 | Moanin' Blues | 1969 | $18 |

MAINSTREAM

❏ S-6040 [S]	Blues	196?	$30
❏ 56040 [M]	Blues	196?	$30
❏ 326	Dirty Blues	197?	$18
❏ 405	Low Down Dirty Blues	1974	$18
❏ 311	The Blues	1971	$18

MOUNT VERNON

| ❏ 104 [M] | Nothin' But the Blues | 196? | $30 |

OLYMPIC GOLD MEDAL

| ❏ 7110 | Blues Giant | 1974 | $15 |

POPPY

| ❏ 60002 | Lightnin'! | 1969 | $30 |

PRESTIGE

❏ PRST-7831	Gotta Move Your Baby	1970	$18
❏ PRST-7806	Hootin' the Blues	1969	$18
❏ PRST-7592	Lightnin' Hopkins' Greatest Hits	1969	$18
❏ PRLPT-7370 [M]	My Life with the Blues	1965	$75
❏ PRST-7370 [S]	My Life with the Blues	1965	$80
❏ PRLP-7377 [M]	Soul Blues	1966	$50
❏ PRST-7377 [S]	Soul Blues	1966	$75
❏ PRST-7714	The Best of Lightnin' Hopkins & His Texas Blues Band	1969	$18
❏ PRST-7811	The Blues of Lightnin' Hopkins	1969	$18

RHINO

| ❏ RNLP103 | Los Angeles Blues | 1982 | $12 |

SCORE

| ❏ SLP-4022 [M] | Lightnin' Hopkins Strums the Blues | 1958 | $1200 |

SMITHSONIAN FOLKWAYS

| ❏ SF-40019 | Lightnin' Hopkins | 1990 | $15 |

SPHERE SOUND

| ❏ SSR-7001 [M] | Lightnin' Hopkins | 1964 | $400 |
| ❏ SSSR-7001 [R] | Lightnin' Hopkins | 1964 | $300 |

TIME

❏ 1 [M]	Blues/Folk	1960	$120
❏ 2 [M]	Blues/Folk Volume 2	1960	$120
❏ T-70004 [M]	Last of the Great Blues Singers	1962	$120
❏ ST-70004 [S]	Last of the Great Blues Singers	1962	$120

TOMATO

| ❏ 7004 | Lightnin'! | 1977 | $18 |

TRADITION

| ❏ TLP-1040 [M] | Autobiography in Blues | 1961 | $30 |
| ❏ TLP-1035 [M] | Country Blues | 1960 | $30 |

| ❏ TLP-2103 [M] | Lightnin' Strikes | 1972 | $18 |
| ❏ TLP-2056 [M] | The Best of Lightnin' Hopkins | 1967 | $25 |

TRIP

| ❏ TLP-8015 | Lightnin' Hopkins | 1971 | $15 |

UNITED

❏ US-7785	A Legend in His Time	196?	$18
❏ US-7713	Lightnin' Hopkins Sings the Blues	196?	$18
❏ US-7744	Original Folk Blues	196?	$18

UNITED ARTISTS

| ❏ UAS-5512 | Coast to Coast Blues Band | 197? | $18 |

UP FRONT

| ❏ 158 | Lightnin' Blues | 1973 | $15 |

VAULT

| ❏ 129 | California Mudslide | 1969 | $30 |

VEE JAY

| ❏ LP1044 [M] | Lightnin' Strikes | 1962 | $50 |

VERVE

| ❏ V-8453 [M] | Fast Life Woman | 1962 | $40 |

VERVE FOLKWAYS

❏ FV-9022 [M]	Lightnin' Strikes	1965	$35
❏ FVS-9022 [S]	Lightnin' Strikes	1965	$35
❏ FV-9000 [M]	The Roots of Lightnin' Hopkins	1965	$30
❏ FVS-9000 [S]	The Roots of Lightnin' Hopkins	1965	$35

VERVE FORECAST

❏ FTS-3031	Lightnin' Strikes	1968	$25
❏ FT-3013 [M]	Something Blue	1967	$25
❏ FTS-3013 [S]	Something Blue	1967	$30

WORLD PACIFIC

| ❏ WP-1817 [M] | First Meetin' | 1963 | $30 |
| ❏ ST-1817 [S] | First Meetin' | 1963 | $100 |

— Red vinyl

| ❏ ST-1817 [S] | First Meetin' | 1963 | $40 |

— Black vinyl

HOPKINS, NICKY

COLUMBIA

| ❏ KC32074 [B] | The Tin Man Was a Dreamer | 1973 | $30 |

MERCURY

| ❏ SRM-1-1028 [B] | No More Changes | 1975 | $30 |

HOPNEY

ILLUSION

❏ CM-1034	Cosmic Rockout	1977	$500
❏ CM-1032	Ends and Means	1979	$300
❏ CM-1033	Perils of Love	1978	$300

HORENSTEIN, STEPHEN

SOUL NOTE

| ❏ SN-1099 | Collages: Jerusalem '85 | 1986 | $30 |

HORN, PAUL

ABC IMPULSE!

| ❏ IA-9356 | Plenty of Horn | 1978 | $35 |

BLUE NOTE

| ❏ BN-LA529-H2 | Paul Horn in India | 1975 | $35 |

COLUMBIA

❏ CL2050 [M]	Impressions of "Cleopatra	1963	$35
❏ CS8850 [S]	Impressions of "Cleopatra	1963	$15
❏ CL1922 [M]	Profile of a Jazz Musician	1962	$30
❏ CS8722 [S]	Profile of a Jazz Musician	1962	$15
❏ CL1677 [M]	The Sound of Paul Horn	1961	$12
❏ CS8477 [S]	The Sound of Paul Horn	1961	$30

DOT

❏ DLP-3091 [M]	House of Horn	1957	$150
❏ DLP-9002 [M]	Plenty of Horn	1958	$150
❏ DLP-29002 [S]	Plenty of Horn	1959	$100

EPIC

❏ PE34231	Altura do Sol	1976	$75
❏ BXN26466	Inside	1969	$85
❏ PE26466	Inside	198?	$20

— Budget-line reissue with new prefix

❏ KE31600	Inside II	1971	$85
❏ KE33561	Paul Horn + Nexus	1975	$75
❏ KE32837	Visions	1973	$75

EVEREST ARCHIVE OF FOLK & JAZZ

| ❏ 308 | Paul Horn | 197? | $25 |

HIFI

| ❏ J-615 [M] | Something Blue | 1960 | $30 |
| ❏ JS-615 [S] | Something Blue | 1960 | $40 |

ISLAND

| ❏ ILSD6 | Special Edition | 197? | $15 |

KUCKUCK

❏ 11075	Inside the Cathedral	198?	$30
❏ KU-060/061	Inside the Great Pyramid	198?	$25
❏ 12060	Inside the Great Pyramid	198?	$35

— Reissue with new number

| ❏ 11062 | Inside the Taj Mahal | 198? | $30 |
| ❏ 11083 | The Peace Album | 1988 | $30 |

Number	Title	Yr	NM
LOST LAKE			
❏ LL-0091	Sketches: A Collection	1986	$30
MCA			
❏ 4144	Plenty of Horn	198?	$30
OVATION			
❏ OV-1405	Concert Ensemble	1970	$35
RCA VICTOR			
❏ LPM-3386 [M]	Cycle	1965	$25
❏ LSP-3386 [S]	Cycle	1965	$12
❏ LPM-3519 [M]	Here's That Rainy Day	1966	$35
❏ LSP-3519 [S]	Here's That Rainy Day	1966	$25
❏ LPM-3414 [M]	Jazz Suite on the Mass Texts	1965	$25
❏ LSP-3414 [S]	Jazz Suite on the Mass Texts	1965	$12
❏ LPM-3613 [M]	Monday, Monday	1966	$25
❏ LSP-3613 [S]	Monday, Monday	1966	$25
WORLD PACIFIC			
❏ WP-1266 [M]	Impressions	1959	$175

HORN, SHIRLEY

Number	Title	Yr	NM
ABC-PARAMOUNT			
❏ ABC-538 [M]	Travelin' Light	1965	$40
❏ ABCS-538 [S]	Travelin' Light	1965	$50
MERCURY			
❏ MG-20761 [M]	Loads of Love	1963	$150

Number	Title	Yr	NM
❏ SR-60761 [S]	Loads of Love	1963	$75
❏ MG-20835 [M]	Shirley Horn with Horns	1963	$150
❏ SR-60835 [S]	Shirley Horn with Horns	1963	$150
❏ SR-60835 [S]	Shirley Horn with Horns	199?	$30
—Classic Records reissue on audiophile vinyl			
STEEPLECHASE			
❏ SCS-1111	A Lazy Afternoon	1979	$30
❏ SCS-1157	All Night Long	1981	$30
❏ SCS-1023	Garden of the Blues	198?	$30
❏ SCS-1164	Violets for Your Furs	1982	$30
STEREO-CRAFT			
❏ RTN-16 [M]	Embers and Ashes	1961	$75
❏ RTS-16 [S]	Embers and Ashes	1961	$100
VERVE			
❏ 837933-1	Close Enough for Love	1989	$30
❏ 832235-1	I Thought About You	1987	$25

HORNE, JIMMY "BO"

Number	Title	Yr	NM
SUNSHINE SOUND			
❏ SSE-7801	Dance Across the Floor	1978	$25
❏ SSE-7805	Goin' Home for Love	1979	$18

HORNE, LENA, AND HARRY BELAFONTE

Number	Title	Yr	NM
RCA VICTOR			
❏ LOC-1507 [M]	Porgy and Bess	1959	$75
❏ LSO-1507 [S]	Porgy and Bess	1959	$40

HORNE, LENA

Number	Title	Yr	NM
20TH CENTURY FOX			
❏ TF-4115 [M]	Here's Lena Now	1964	$35
❏ TFS-4115 [S]	Here's Lena Now	1964	$50
ACCORD			
❏ SN-7190	Standing Room Only	198?	$25
BLUEBIRD			
❏ 9985-1-RB	Stormy Weather: The Legendary Lena	1990	$30
BUDDAH			
❏ BDS-5084	Nature's Baby	1971	$30
❏ BDS-5669	The Essential Lena Horne	197?	$30
BULLDOG			
❏ BDL-2000	20 Golden Pieces of Lena Horne	198?	$25
CHARTER			
❏ CLP-101 [M]	Lena Sings Your Requests	1963	$35
❏ CLS-101 [S]	Lena Sings Your Requests	1963	$50

Number	Title	Yr	NM
❏ CLP-106 [M]	Like Latin	1964	$35
❏ CLS-106 [S]	Like Latin	1964	$50
DRG			
❏ MRS-510	Lena Goes Latin	1986	$25
❏ MRS-501	Lena Horne With Lennie Hayton & the Marty Paich Orchestra	1985	$25
JAZZTONE			
❏ J-1262 [M]	Lena and Ivie	1957	$150
LIBERTY			
❏ LN-10194	Lena in Hollywood	198?	$20
LION			
❏ L-70050 [M]	I Feel So Smoochie	1959	$50
MGM			
❏ E-545 [10]	Lena Horne Sings	1952	$150
❏ M3G-5409	The One and Only	197?	$25
MOBILE FIDELITY			
❏ Feb-0094	Lena Horne: The Lady and Her Music	1982	$150
—Audiophile vinyl			
MOVIETONE			
❏ MTM71005 [M]	Once in a Lifetime	196?	$35
❏ MTS72005 [S]	Once in a Lifetime	196?	$50
PAIR			
❏ PDL2-1055	Lena	1986	$30
QWEST			
❏ 2QW3597	Lena Horne: The Lady and Her Music	1981	$30
RCA VICTOR			
❏ LPM-1879 [M]	Give the Lady What She Wants	1958	$75
❏ LSP-1879 [S]	Give the Lady What She Wants	1958	$40
❏ LPM-1148 [M]	It's Love	1955	$150
❏ BGL1-1799	Lena	1976	$30
❏ AYL1-4389	Lena, A New Album	1983	$20
—"Best Buy Series" reissue			
❏ BGL1-1026	Lena and Michel	1975	$30
—With Michel Legrand			
❏ LPM-2364 [M]	Lena Horne at the Sands	1961	$75
❏ LSP-2364 [S]	Lena Horne at the Sands	1961	$75

Number	Title	Yr	NM
❏ LOC-1028 [M]	Lena Horne at the Waldorf Astoria	1957	$30
❏ LSO-1028 [S]	Lena Horne at the Waldorf Astoria	1957	$40
❏ LPM-2587 [M]	Lena…Lovely and Alive	1963	$75
❏ LSP-2587 [S]	Lena…Lovely and Alive	1963	$75
❏ LPM-2465 [M]	Lena on the Blue Side	1962	$75
❏ LSP-2465 [S]	Lena on the Blue Side	1962	$75
❏ LPM-1895 [M]	Songs of Burke and Van Heusen	1959	$75
❏ LSP-1895 [S]	Songs of Burke and Van Heusen	1959	$40
❏ LPM-1375 [M]	Stormy Weather	1956	$150
❏ LPT-3061 [10]	This Is Lena Horne	1952	$150
SKYE			
❏ 15	Lena & Gabor	1970	$35
—With Gabor Szabo			
STANYAN			
❏ POW-3006	Stormy Weather	198?	$25
—Reissue of 10126			
❏ 10126	Stormy Weather	197?	$30
SUNBEAM			
❏ 212	A Date with Lena Horne	198?	$25
—With Fletcher Henderson and His Orchestra			
THREE CHERRIES			
❏ TC-44411	The Men in My Life	1989	$25
TIME-LIFE			
❏ SLGD-05	Legendary Singers: Lena Horne	1985	$35
TOPS			
❏ L-1502 [M]	Lena Horne	1958	$50

Number	Title	Yr	NM
❏ L-931 [10]	Lena Horne Sings	195?	$40
❏ L-910 [10]	Moanin' Low	195?	$40
UNITED ARTISTS			
❏ UAL3433 [M]	Feelin' Good	1965	$35
❏ UAS6433 [S]	Feelin' Good	1965	$50
❏ UAL3470 [M]	Lena in Hollywood	1966	$35
❏ UAS6470 [S]	Lena in Hollywood	1966	$50
❏ UAL3546 [M]	Merry from Lena	1966	$35
❏ UAS6546 [S]	Merry from Lena	1966	$50
—Black label, "United Artists" in rounded box at top			
❏ UAS6546 [S]	Merry from Lena	1972	$30
—Tan label			
❏ UAL3496 [M]	Soul	1966	$35
❏ UAS6496 [S]	Soul	1966	$50

HORNETS, THE

Number	Title	Yr	NM
LIBERTY			
❏ LRP-3364 [M]	Big Drag Boats U.S.A.	1964	$50
❏ LST-7364 [S]	Big Drag Boats U.S.A.	1964	$75
❏ LRP-3348 [M]	Motorcycles U.S.A.	1963	$40
❏ LST-7348 [S]	Motorcycles U.S.A.	1963	$50

HORNSBY, BRUCE, AND THE RANGE

Number	Title	Yr	NM
RCA			
❏ 2041-1-R	A Night on the Town	1990	$15
❏ 6275-1-R [DJ]	Live The Way It Is Tour 1986-87	1987	$50
—Promo-only release			
❏ 6686-1-R	Scenes from the Southside	1988	$10
RCA VICTOR			
❏ NFL1-8058	The Way It Is	1986	$18
—Original edition; cover is light brown with blurry picture of Hornsby in the middle			
❏ 5904-1-RX	The Way It Is	1986	$10
—Revised cover and altered catalog number			
❏ AFL1-5904	The Way It Is	1986	$12
—Revised edition; cover is dark with a photo of the whole band; "AFL1" prefix			

HOROWITZ, VLADIMIR

Number	Title	Yr	NM
RCA VICTOR RED SEAL			
❏ LSC-2366 [S]	Beethoven: Piano Sonata in D "Appassionata	1960	$25
—Originals with "shaded dog" label			

HORSES

Don Johnson of "Miami Vice" and "Nash Bridges" fame was supposedly in this band.

Number	Title	Yr	NM
WHITE WHALE			
❏ WWS-7121	Horses	1970	$40

HORSLIPS

Number	Title	Yr	NM
ATCO			
❏ SD7030	Happy to Meet, Sorry to Part	1973	$15
❏ SD7039	The Tain	1974	$15
DJM			
❏ 16	Aliens	1978	$12
❏ 10	Book of Invasions	1977	$12
❏ 20	The Man Who Built America	1979	$12
HORSLIPS			
❏ M 009	Drive the Cold Winter Away	1975	$25
—U.K./Ireland import			
MERCURY			
❏ SRM-1-3842	Belfast Gigs	1980	$12
❏ SRM-1-3809	Short Stories/Tall Tales	1979	$12
RCA VICTOR			
❏ CPL1-0709	Dancehall Sweethearts	1974	$15

HORTA, TONINHO

Number	Title	Yr	NM
VERVE FORECAST			
❏ 835183-1	Diamond Land	1988	$25
❏ 839734-1	Moonstone	1989	$30

HORTON, JOHNNY

Number	Title	Yr	NM
BRIAR			
❏ 104 [M]	Done Rovin'	196?	$175
COLUMBIA			
❏ CL1721 [M]	Honky-Tonk Man	1962	$30
❏ CS8779 [R]	Honky-Tonk Man	1962	$18
❏ CL2299 [M]	I Can't Forget You	1965	$30
❏ CS9099 [R]	I Can't Forget You	1965	$18
❏ CL1478 [M]	Johnny Horton Makes History	1960	$30
❏ CS8269 [S]	Johnny Horton Makes History	1960	$40
❏ CL2566 [M]	Johnny Horton on Stage at the Louisiana Hayride	1966	$25
❏ CS9366 [S]	Johnny Horton on Stage at the Louisiana Hayride	1966	$30
❏ CS9940	Johnny Horton On the Road	1969	$18
❏ CL1596 [M]	Johnny Horton's Greatest Hits	1961	$30
❏ CS8396 [S]	Johnny Horton's Greatest Hits	1961	$30
❏ PC8396	Johnny Horton's Greatest Hits	198?	$10

Number	Title	Yr	NM
—Budget-line reissue			
❏ 1596/8396	Johnny Horton's Greatest Hits Bonus Photo	1961	$12
❏ CL1362 [M]	The Spectacular Johnny Horton	1959	$30
❏ CS8167 [S]	The Spectacular Johnny Horton	1959	$40
❏ G30884	The World of Johnny Horton	1971	$18
DOT			
❏ DLP3221 [M]	Johnny Horton	1962	$30
❏ DLP25221 [R]	Johnny Horton	1962	$18
HARMONY			
❏ KH30394	The Battle of New Orleans	1971	$15
❏ HS11384	The Legendary Johnny Horton	1970	$15
❏ HS11291 [R]	The Unforgettable Johnny Horton	196?	$15
HILLTOP			
❏ JS-6060	All for the Love of a Girl	196?	$15
❏ 6012	The Voice of Johnny Horton	196?	$15
MERCURY			
❏ MG-20478 [M]	The Fantastic Johnny Horton	1959	$50
SESAC			
❏ 1201 [M]	Free and Easy Songs	1959	$175

HORTON, ROBERT
COLUMBIA

Number	Title	Yr	NM
❏ CL2408 [M]	A Man Called Shenandoah	1966	$30
❏ CS9208 [S]	A Man Called Shenandoah	1966	$30
❏ CL2202 [M]	The Very Thought of You	1964	$30
❏ CS9002 [S]	The Very Thought of You	1964	$30

HORTON, STEVEN WAYNE
CAPITOL

Number	Title	Yr	NM
❏ C1-91983	Steven Wayne Horton	1989	$15

HORTON, WALTER "SHAKEY
ARGO

Number	Title	Yr	NM
❏ LP-4037 [M]	The Soul of Blues Harmonica	1964	$175
❏ LPS-4037 [S]	The Soul of Blues Harmonica	1964	$300

HORVITZ, WAYNE
BLACK SAINT

Number	Title	Yr	NM
❏ BSR-0059	Some Order, Long Understood	1982	$30
ELEKTRA/MUSICIAN			
❏ 60759	This New Generation	1988	$25

HOSFORD, LARRY
SHELTER

Number	Title	Yr	NM
❏ 2132	A.K.A. Lorenzo	1975	$18
❏ SRL-52003	Crosswords	1976	$15

HOT ANTIC JAZZ BAND, THE
STOMP OFF

Number	Title	Yr	NM
❏ SOS-1044	I Got the Stinger	1982	$25
❏ SOS-1099	Jazz Battle	1985	$25
❏ SOS-1154	Puttin' On the Ritz	1988	$25
❏ SOS-1058	We Love You Jabbo	1983	$25

HOT BUTTER
MUSICOR

Number	Title	Yr	NM
❏ MS-3242	Popcorn	1972	$25
—Die-cut cover			
❏ MS-3242	Popcorn	1972	$15
—Regular cover			

HOT CHOCOLATE
BIG TREE

Number	Title	Yr	NM
❏ BT76002	10 Greatest Hits	1977	$12
❏ BT89503	Cicero Park	1975	$12
❏ BT89512	Hot Chocolate	1975	$12
❏ BT89519	Man to Man	1976	$12
EMI AMERICA			
❏ ST-17077	Mystery	1982	$12
INFINITY			
❏ INF-9002	Every 1's a Winner	1978	$12
❏ INF-9010	Going Through the Motions	1979	$12

HOT COTTON JAZZ BAND, THE
GHB

Number	Title	Yr	NM
❏ 168	Stompin' Room Only, Vol. 1	1984	$25
❏ 169	Stompin' Room Only, Vol. 2	1984	$25
❏ 188	Take Your Tomorrow	1986	$25

HOT DOG
GUINNESS

Number	Title	Yr	NM
❏ GNS36082 [B]	Hot Dog	1977	$150

HOT DOGGERS, THE
EPIC

Number	Title	Yr	NM
❏ LN24054 [M]	Surfin' U.S.A.	1963	$175

Number	Title	Yr	NM
❏ BN26054 [S]	Surfin' U.S.A.	1963	$250

HOT JAZZ ORCHESTRA
REVELATION

Number	Title	Yr	NM
❏ 28	Hot Jazz Orchestra	1979	$25

HOT POOP
HOT POOP

Number	Title	Yr	NM
❏ 3072	Hot Poop Does Their Own Thing	1971	$300

HOT RODDERS, THE
CROWN

Number	Title	Yr	NM
❏ CLP-5378 [M]	Big Hot Rod	1963	$25
❏ CST-378 [S]	Big Hot Rod	1963	$30

HOT TUNA
Offshoot of JEFFERSON AIRPLANE.
GRUNT

Number	Title	Yr	NM
❏ BFL1-0820	America's Choice	1975	$18
❏ BFD1-0820 [Q]	America's Choice	1975	$40
❏ FTR-1004	Burgers	1972	$18
❏ BXL1-2591	Burgers	1978	$15
—Reissue of 1004			
❏ CYL2-2545	Double Dose	1978	$25
❏ BXL1-3357	Final Vinyl	1979	$15
❏ BFL1-1920	Hoppkorv	1976	$18
❏ DJL1-2852 [DJ]	The Last Interview? A Live Hot Tuna Radio Classic	1978	$30
❏ BFL1-0348	The Phosphorescent Rat	1974	$18
❏ BFL1-1238	Yellow Fever	1975	$18
❏ BFD1-1238 [Q]	Yellow Fever	1975	$40
RCA VICTOR			
❏ AYL1-3951	Burgers	1981	$10
—Best Buy Series" reissue			
❏ LSP-4550	First Pull Up Then Pull Down	1971	$18
❏ AYL1-3865	First Pull Up Then Pull Down	1981	$10
—Best Buy Series" reissue			
❏ LSP-4353	Hot Tuna	1970	$18
❏ AYL1-3864	Hot Tuna	1981	$10
—Best Buy Series" reissue			

HOTEL EDISON ROOF ORCHESTRA, THE
STOMP OFF

Number	Title	Yr	NM
❏ SOS-1169	Breakaway	1988	$25

HOTGUN
GUINNESS

Number	Title	Yr	NM
❏ GNS36014 [B]	Hotgun	1977	$50

HOTHOUSE FLOWERS
LONDON

Number	Title	Yr	NM
❏ 85 [DJ]	Conversation and Music with Hothouse Flowers	1988	$18
❏ 085 [DJ]	Conversation and Music with Hothouse Flowers	1988	$18
❏ PRO884-1 [DJ]	Live	1990	$30
—Six-song promo-only live EP			
❏ 828101-1	People	1988	$15

HOTLEGS
Early incarnation of 10CC. Also see GRAHAM GOULDMAN.
CAPITOL

Number	Title	Yr	NM
❏ ST-587 [B]	Hotlegs Thinks: School Stinks	1970	$40

HOUGHTON, STEVE
SEABREEZE

Number	Title	Yr	NM
❏ SB-2018	The Steve Houghton Album	198?	$25

HOUK, RALPH
CARLTON

Number	Title	Yr	NM
❏ HH-16 [M]	Hear How to Play Better Baseball	1961	$40

HOUN, FRED, AND THE AFRO-ASIAN MUSIC ENSEMBLE
SOUL NOTE

Number	Title	Yr	NM
❏ SN-1117	Tomorrow Is Now!	1986	$30
❏ 121117	Tomorrow Is Now!	198?	$30
—Reissue of 1117			
❏ 121167	We Refuse to Be Used and Abused	1990	$35

HOUR GLASS, THE
LIBERTY

Number	Title	Yr	NM
❏ LRP-3536 [M]	The Hour Glass	1967	$75
❏ LST-7536 [S]	The Hour Glass	1967	$30
❏ LST-7555	The Power of Love	1968	$30
SPRINGBOARD			
❏ SPB-4016	Duane and Gregg Allman with the Hour Glass	1976	$12
UNITED ARTISTS			
❏ UA-LA013-G2 [B]	The Hour Glass	1973	$18

HOUSE, SON, AND J.D. SHORT
VERVE FOLKWAYS

Number	Title	Yr	NM
❏ FV-9035 [M]	Blues from the Mississippi Delta	1966	$50
❏ FVS-9035 [R]	Blues from the Mississippi Delta	1966	$30

HOUSE, SON
COLUMBIA

Number	Title	Yr	NM
❏ CL2417 [M]	Father of the Folk Blues	1965	$25
❏ CS9217 [S]	Father of the Folk Blues	1965	$30
—Red "360 Sound" label			

HOUSE OF PAIN
Also see EVERLAST.
TOMMY BOY

Number	Title	Yr	NM
❏ TB1056	House of Pain (Fine Malt Lyrics)	1992	$40
❏ TB1161	Truth Crushed to Earth Shall Rise Again	1996	$30

HOUSE OF SCHOCK
CAPITOL

Number	Title	Yr	NM
❏ C1-46925	House of Schock	1988	$12

HOUSEMARTINS, THE
ELEKTRA

Number	Title	Yr	NM
❏ 60501	London 0 Hull 4	1986	$12
❏ 60761 [DJ]	The People Who Grinned Themselves to Death	1987	$15
—Promo-only audiophile pressing			
❏ 60761	The People Who Grinned Themselves to Death	1987	$12
❏ 60761 [DJ]	The People Who Grinned Themselves to Death	1987	$18
—Promo-only white label audiophile pressing			

HOUSTON, CISSY
COLUMBIA

Number	Title	Yr	NM
❏ JC36193	Step Aside for a Lady	1980	$12
❏ JC36112	Warning Danger	1979	$12
COMMONWEALTH UNITED			
❏ 6008	Cissy Houston	1970	$0
—Canceled?			
JANUS			
❏ 3001	Cissy Houston	1970	$18
PRIVATE STOCK			
❏ PS2031	Cissy Houston	1977	$15
❏ PS7015	Think It Over	1978	$15

HOUSTON, DAVID, AND BARBARA MANDRELL
EPIC

Number	Title	Yr	NM
❏ KE31705	A Perfect Match	1972	$15
❏ KE32915	The Best of David Houston and Barbara Mandrell	1974	$15

HOUSTON, DAVID, AND TAMMY WYNETTE
EPIC

Number	Title	Yr	NM
❏ LN24325 [M]	My Elusive Dreams	1967	$25
❏ BN26325 [S]	My Elusive Dreams	1967	$18

HOUSTON, DAVID
EPIC

Number	Title	Yr	NM
❏ LN24156 [M]	12 Great Country Hits	1965	$18
❏ BN26156 [S]	12 Great Country Hits	1965	$25
❏ LN24213 [M]	Almost Persuaded	1966	$18
❏ BN26213 [S]	Almost Persuaded	1966	$25
❏ LN24303 [M]	A Loser's Cathedral	1967	$25
❏ BN26303 [S]	A Loser's Cathedral	1967	$18
❏ BN26391	Already It's Heaven	1968	$18
❏ KE33350	A Man Needs Love	1975	$15
❏ E30657	A Woman Always Knows	1971	$18
❏ BN26539	Baby, Baby	1970	$18
❏ BN26482	David	1969	$18
❏ LN24342 [M]	David Houston's Greatest Hits	1968	$30
❏ BN26342 [S]	David Houston's Greatest Hits	1968	$18
❏ E30602	David Houston's Greatest Hits, Volume 2	1971	$18
❏ LN24320 [M]	Golden Hymns	1967	$25
❏ BN26320 [S]	Golden Hymns	1967	$18
❏ KE32189	Good Things	1973	$15
❏ LN24112 [M]	New Voice from Nashville	1964	$18
❏ BN26112 [S]	New Voice from Nashville	1964	$25
❏ E30437	Sweet Lovin'	1971	$18
❏ KE31385	The Day Love Walked In	1972	$15
❏ EGP502	The World of David Houston	1970	$25
❏ KE33948	What a Night	1976	$15
❏ BN26432	Where Love Used to Live	1969	$18
❏ E30108	Wonders of the Wine	1970	$18
❏ LN24338 [M]	You Mean the World to Me	1967	$25
❏ BN26338 [S]	You Mean the World to Me	1967	$18
GUSTO			
❏ 0012	The Best of David Houston	1978	$12
HARMONY			
❏ HS11412	David Houston	1970	$12
❏ KH32287	Old Time Religion	1973	$12

Number	Title	Yr	NM
❏ KH31778	The Many Sides of David Houston	1972	$12

RCA CAMDEN

❏ CAL-2126 [M]	David Houston Sings	1966	$18
❏ CAS-2126 [R]	David Houston Sings	1966	$12

STARDAY

❏ 990	David Houston	1978	$12

HOUSTON, JOE

COMBO

❏ LP-100 [M]	Joe Houston	195?	$400

— Color photo of Joe Houston on cover

❏ LP-100 [M]	Joe Houston	195?	$400

— Silver cover with "J" in the shape of a saxophone

❏ LP-400 [M]	Rockin' at the Drive In	195?	$300

— Black ink on front and back covers

❏ LP-400 [M]	Rockin' at the Drive In	195?	$250

— Blue ink on front and back covers

CROWN

❏ CLP-5246 [M]	Doin' the Twist	1962	$40
❏ CLP-5006 [M]	Joe Houston Rock and Rolls All Night Long	195?	$150

— Black label, gold print

❏ CLP-5006 [M]	Joe Houston Rock and Rolls All Night Long	196?	$40

— Gray label, black print

❏ CLP-5319 [M]	Limbo	1963	$40
❏ CST-319 [R]	Limbo	1963	$30
❏ CLP-5313 [M]	Surf Rockin'	1963	$40
❏ CST-313 [R]	Surf Rockin'	1963	$30
❏ CLP-5203 [M]	Wild Man of the Tenor Sax	1962	$40

MODERN

❏ LMP-1206 [M]	Joe Houston Blows All Night Long	1956	$300

TOPS

❏ L-1518 [M]	Rock and Roll	195?	$100

HOUSTON, THELMA, AND JERRY BUTLER

MOTOWN

❏ M6-887	Thelma and Jerry	1977	$12
❏ M7-903	Two to One	1978	$12

HOUSTON, THELMA

ABC DUNHILL

❏ DS-50054	Sun Shower	1969	$30

MCA

❏ 5527	Qualifying Heat	1984	$12
❏ 5395	Thelma Houston	1983	$12

MOTOWN

❏ M5-226V1 [B]	Any Way You Like It	1982	$12
❏ M5-127V1	Sunshower	1981	$10
❏ M5-120V1	Superstar Series, Vol. 20	1981	$12

MOWEST

❏ MW-102	Thelma Houston	1972	$25

RCA VICTOR

❏ AFL1-3500	Breakwater Cat	1980	$12
❏ AFL1-3842	Never Gonna Be Another One	1981	$12

REPRISE

❏ 26234	Throw You Down	1990	$18

SHEFFIELD LABS

❏ 2	I've Got the Music In Me	1975	$40

SHEFFIELD TREASURY

❏ ST-200	I've Got the Music In Me	1983	$25

— Reissue of Sheffield Labs 2

TAMLA

❏ T6-345R1	Any Way You Like It	1976	$15
❏ T7-361R1	Ready to Roll	1978	$12
❏ T7-358R1	The Devil in Me	1977	$12

HOUSTON, WHITNEY

ARISTA

❏ AL18616 [B]	I'm Your Baby Tonight	1990	$18
❏ 19037	My Love Is Your Love	1998	$15
❏ 14652	The Unreleased Mixes	2000	$25

— Box set of 12-inch single remixes

❏ AL8405 [B]	Whitney	1987	$15
❏ AL8212 [B]	Whitney Houston	1985	$15

HOUSTON FEARLESS

IMPERIAL

❏ LP-12421	Houston Fearless	1969	$25

HOWARD, CHUCK

BRYLEN

❏ BN4478	The Fire Behind His Eyes	198?	$12

HOWARD, DAVE

CHOREO

❏ C-5 [M]	I Love Everybody	1961	$30
❏ CS-5 [S]	I Love Everybody	1961	$30

HOWARD, EDDY

CIRCLE

❏ 29 [B]	Eddy Howard 1949-1952	198?	$18
❏ 79 [B]	Eddy Howard 1949-1953	1985	$18

COLUMBIA

❏ CL6067 [10]	Eddy Howard	1949	$120

HINDSIGHT

❏ HSR-156	Eddy Howard 1945-1948	198?	$25
❏ HSR-119	Eddy Howard 1946-1951	198?	$25
❏ HSR-405	Eddy Howard and His Orchestra Play 22 Original Big Band Favorites	198?	$30

INSIGHT

❏ 205	Eddy Howard and His Orchestra 1945-1951	198?	$25

MERCURY

❏ MG-20562 [M]	Eddy Howard's Golden Hits	1961	$150
❏ SR-60562 [S]	Eddy Howard's Golden Hits	1961	$150
❏ MG-20817 [M]	Eddy Howard Sings and Plays the Great Band Hits	196?	$150
❏ SR-60817 [S]	Eddy Howard Sings and Plays the Great Band Hits	196?	$150
❏ MG-20665 [M]	Eddy Howard Sings and Plays the Great Old Waltzes	1962	$150
❏ SR-60665 [S]	Eddy Howard Sings and Plays the Great Old Waltzes	1962	$150
❏ MG-20432 [M]	Great for Dancing	1958	$150
❏ SR-60104 [S]	Great for Dancing	1959	$150
❏ MG-20910 [M]	Intimately Yours	1965	$150
❏ SR-60910 [S]	Intimately Yours	1965	$150
❏ MG-20593 [M]	More Eddy Howard's Golden Hits	1962	$150
❏ SR-60593 [S]	More Eddy Howard's Golden Hits	1962	$150
❏ MG-20312 [M]	Paradise Isle	195?	$150
❏ MG-25011 [10]	Selected Song Favorites	1949	$175

— Title appears only on label; cover simply states "Eddy Howard and His Orchestra

❏ MG-20112 [M]	Singing in the Rain	195?	$150
❏ MG-21014 [M]	Softly and Sincerely	196?	$150
❏ SR-61014 [S]	Softly and Sincerely	196?	$150

WING

❏ MGW-12171 [M]	Eddy Howard Sings Words of Love	196?	$30
❏ SRW-16171 [S]	Eddy Howard Sings Words of Love	196?	$30
❏ MGW-12104 [M]	Saturday Night Dance Date	196?	$30
❏ SRW-16104 [S]	Saturday Night Dance Date	196?	$30
❏ MGW-12194 [M]	Sleepy Serenade	196?	$30
❏ SRW-16194 [S]	Sleepy Serenade	196?	$30
❏ MGW-12249 [M]	The Velvet Voice	196?	$30
❏ SRW-16249 [S]	The Velvet Voice	196?	$30
❏ MGW-12171 [M]	Words of Love	196?	$30
❏ SRW-16171 [S]	Words of Love	196?	$30

HOWARD, GEORGE

GRP

❏ GR-9629	Love and Understanding	1991	$35

MCA

❏ 5855	A Nice Place to Be	1987	$25
❏ 6335	Personal	1990	$30
❏ 42145	Reflections	1988	$25

PALO ALTO

❏ PA-8035	Asphalt Garden	1982	$30
❏ TB-205	Dancing in the Sun	198?	$25
❏ TB-210	Love Will Follow	1987	$25
❏ TB-201	Steppin' Out	198?	$25

HOWARD, HARLAN

CAPITOL

❏ T1631 [M]	Harlan Howard Sings Harlan Howard	1961	$30
❏ ST1631 [S]	Harlan Howard Sings Harlan Howard	1961	$40

MONUMENT

❏ MLP-8038 [M]	All-Time Favorite Country Songwriter	1965	$30
❏ SLP-18038 [S]	All-Time Favorite Country Songwriter	1965	$30

RCA VICTOR

❏ LPM-3886 [M]	Down to Earth	1968	$50
❏ LSP-3886 [S]	Down to Earth	1968	$25
❏ LPM-3729 [M]	Mr. Songwriter	1967	$30
❏ LSP-3729 [S]	Mr. Songwriter	1967	$25

HOWARD, JAN

CAPITOL

❏ T1779 [M]	Sweet and Sentimental	1962	$25
❏ ST1779 [S]	Sweet and Sentimental	1962	$30

DECCA

❏ DL4832 [M]	Bad Seed	1966	$18
❏ DL74832 [S]	Bad Seed	1966	$25
❏ DL5012 [M]	Count Your Blessings, Woman	1968	$40

— White label promo only

❏ DL75012 [M]	Count Your Blessings, Woman	1968	$25
❏ DL75166	For God and Country	1969	$30
❏ DL75130	Jan Howard	1969	$25
❏ DL4793 [M]	Jan Howard Sings Evil on Your Mind	1966	$18
❏ DL74793 [S]	Jan Howard Sings Evil on Your Mind	1966	$25
❏ DL75293	Love Is Like a Spinning Wheel	1972	$25
❏ DL75207	Rock Me Back to Little Rock	1970	$25
❏ DL4931 [M]	This Is Jan Howard Country	1967	$30
❏ DL74931 [S]	This Is Jan Howard Country	1967	$25

PICKWICK

❏ JS6174	Rock Me Back to Little Rock!	197?	$12

TOWER

❏ T5068 [M]	Lonely Country	1967	$25
❏ ST5068 [S]	Lonely Country	1967	$25
❏ DT5119 [R]	The Real Me	1968	$18

WRANGLER

❏ 1005 [M]	Jan Howard	1962	$30
❏ S-1005 [S]	Jan Howard	1962	$30

HOWARD, JIM

SEABREEZE

❏ SB-2005	No Compromise	1983	$25

HOWARD, JOE

KING

❏ 661 [M]	The Golden Sound	1959	$50

SUNSET

❏ SU-3001 [M]	Patterns for Trombone	1955	$50

HOWARD, KID

GHB

❏ 23	Kid Howard at San Jacinto Hall	1966	$30

JAZZOLOGY

❏ JCE-14	Kid Howard and the Vida Jazz Band	1967	$30
❏ JCE-18	Kid Howard's Olympia Band	1967	$30

HOWARD, NOAH

ALTOSAX

❏ 1001	Patterns	197?	$35
❏ 25055	Quartetto	197?	$35

CHIAROSCURO

❏ 2016	Oie	1979	$30

ESP-DISK'

❏ S-1064 [S]	Live at Judson Hall	1969	$150
❏ 1073	Noah Howard	1968	$0

— Canceled

❏ 1031 [M]	Noah Howard Quartet	1966	$175
❏ S-1031 [S]	Noah Howard Quartet	1966	$175

HOWARD, RANDY

ATLANTIC AMERICA

❏ 90679	Randy Howard	1987	$12

WARNER BROS.

❏ 23820	All-American Redneck	1983	$10

HOWE, STEVE
Also see YES.

ATLANTIC

❏ SD18154	Beginnings	1975	$15
❏ SD19243	The Steve Howe Album	1980	$15

HOWELL, MICHAEL

CATALYST

❏ 7615	Alone	1976	$30

MILESTONE

❏ M-9054	In the Silence	1974	$30
❏ M-9048	Looking Glass	1973	$30

Number	Title	Yr	NM

HOWELL, REUBEN
MOTOWN

Number	Title	Yr	NM
❏ M771L	Reuben Howell	1973	$50
❏ M6-799S1	Rings	1974	$18

HOWL THE GOOD
RARE EARTH

❏ RS-537 [B]	Howl the Good	1972	$35

HOWLIN' WOLF
CADET

❏ LPS-319	This Is Howlin' Wolf's New Album	1969	$30

CHESS

❏ CH-50045	Back Door Wolf	1974	$25
❏ CH-93001	Change My Way	198?	$12
❏ CH-9182	Chicago -- 26 Golden Years	1985	$12
❏ LP-1540	Evil	1969	$30
❏ CH-9107	His Greatest Sides, Vol. 1	1985	$12
❏ LP-1469 [M]	Howlin' Wolf	1962	$600
❏ 201	Howlin' Wolf	1976	$18
❏ CH-60016	Howlin' Wolk, AKA Chester Burnett	1972	$30
❏ CH-50015	Live and Cookin'	1972	$25
❏ CH-50002	Message to the Young	1971	$25
❏ LP-1434 [M]	Moanin' in the Moonlight	1958	$600
❏ CH-9195	Moanin' in the Moonlight	1986	$10
—Reissue of 1434			
❏ LP-1512 [M]	More Real Folk Blues	1966	$175
❏ CH-9279	More Real Folk Blues	1988	$12
—Reissue of 1512			
❏ CH5-9332	The Chess Box	1991	$40
❏ CH-60008	The London Howlin' Wolf Sessions	1971	$25
❏ CH-9297	The London Howlin' Wolf Sessions	1989	$12
—Reissue of 60008			
❏ LP-1502 [M]	The Real Folk Blues	1966	$175
❏ CH-9273	The Real Folk Blues	1988	$12
—Reissue of 1502			

CLEOPATRA

❏ 6796 [B]	Killing Floor - Blues Essentials		$25

CROWN

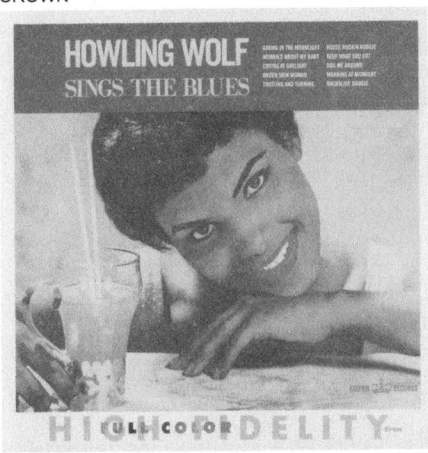

❏ CLP-5240 [M]	Howlin' Wolf Sings the Blues	1962	$30

CUSTOM

❏ CM-2055 [M]	Big City Blues	196?	$40
❏ CS-2055 [R]	Big City Blues	196?	$25

KENT

❏ KST-527	Howlin' Wolf's 20 Greatest R&B Hits	1968	$15
❏ KLP-526 [M]	Original Folk Blues	1967	$18
❏ KST-526 [R]	Original Folk Blues	1967	$15
❏ KST-535	Underground Blues	1968	$15

ROUNDER

❏ SS-28	Cadillac Daddy: Memphis Recordings, 1952	1989	$15

HUBBARD, DAVE
MAINSTREAM

❏ MRL-317	Dave Hubbard	1971	$35

HUBBARD, FREDDIE, AND OSCAR PETERSON
PABLO

❏ 2310876	Face to Face	198?	$25

HUBBARD, FREDDIE, AND STANLEY TURRENTINE
CTI

❏ CTS-6044	In Concert, Volume 1	1974	$25
❏ CTS-6049	In Concert, Volume 2	1975	$25

HUBBARD, FREDDIE
ABC IMPULSE!

Number	Title	Yr	NM
❏ AS-9237	Re-Evaluation: The Impulse Years	1973	$35
❏ AS-27 [S]	The Artistry of Freddie Hubbard	1968	$30
❏ AS-38 [S]	The Body and Soul of Freddie Hubbard	1968	$30

ATLANTIC

❏ 1477 [M]	Backlash	1967	$75
❏ SD1477 [S]	Backlash	1967	$35
❏ 90466	Backlash	1986	$20
—Reissue of SD 1477			
❏ SD1549	Black Angel	1971	$30
❏ SD1501	High Pressure Blues	1969	$35
❏ SD1526	Soul Experiment	1970	$30
❏ 80108	Sweet Return	1983	$25
❏ SD 2-314	The Art of Freddie Hubbard	1974	$35

BASF

❏ 10726	The Hub of Hubbard	1972	$30

BLUE NOTE

❏ BLP-4196 [M]	Blue Spirits	1965	$150
❏ BST-84196 [S]	Blue Spirits	1965	$100
— With New York, USA address on label			
❏ BST-84196 [S]	Blue Spirits	1967	$35
— With "A Division of Liberty Records" on label			
❏ BST-84196	Blue Spirits	1987	$25
— The Finest in Jazz Since 1939" reissue			
❏ BLP-4172 [M]	Breaking Point	1964	$150
❏ BST-84172 [S]	Breaking Point	1964	$100
— With New York, USA address on label			
❏ BST-84172 [S]	Breaking Point	1967	$35
— With "A Division of Liberty Records" on label			
❏ B1-85121	Doubletake	1987	$25
❏ BN-LA356-H [(2)]	Freddie Hubbard	1975	$35
❏ BLP-4056 [M]	Goin' Up	1960	$700
— With W. 63rd St. address on label			
❏ BLP-4056 [M]	Goin' Up	1963	$150
— With New York, USA address on label			
❏ BST-84056 [S]	Goin' Up	1960	$175
— With W. 63rd St. addresss on label			
❏ BST-84056 [S]	Goin' Up	1963	$75
— With New York, USA address on label			
❏ BST-84056 [S]	Goin' Up	1967	$35
— With "A Division of Liberty Records" on label			
❏ 4135/84135	Here to Stay	1963	$0
— Scheduled, but unreleased until 1985			
❏ BST-84135	Here to Stay	1985	$30
❏ BLP-4073 [M]	Hub Cap	1961	$250
— With W. 63rd St. address on label			

HUB CAP/FREDDIE HUBBARD
julian priester|jimmy heath|cedar walton|larry ridley|philly joe jones

❏ BLP-4073 [M]	Hub Cap	1963	$75
— With New York, USA address on label			
❏ BST-84073 [S]	Hub Cap	1961	$150
— With W. 63rd St. addresss on label			
❏ BST-84073 [S]	Hub Cap	1963	$75
— With New York, USA address on label			
❏ BST-84073 [S]	Hub Cap	1967	$35
— With "A Division of Liberty Records" on label			
❏ BST-84073	Hub Cap	198?	$25
— The Finest in Jazz Since 1939" reissue			
❏ BLP-4115 [M]	Hub Tones	1962	$175
❏ BST-84115 [S]	Hub-Tones	1962	$75
— With New York, USA address on label			
❏ BST-84115 [S]	Hub-Tones	1967	$35
— With "A Division of Liberty Records" on label			
❏ BST-84115	Hub-Tones	1985	$25
— The Finest in Jazz Since 1939" reissue			
❏ B1-85139	Life-Flight	1987	$25
❏ BLP-4040 [M]	Open Sesame	1960	$1200
— Deep groove" version (deep indentation under label on both sides)			
❏ BLP-4040 [M]	Open Sesame	1960	$300
— Regular version with W. 63rd St. address on label			

Number	Title	Yr	NM
❏ BLP-4040 [M]	Open Sesame	1963	$150
— With New York, USA address on label			
❏ BST-84040 [S]	Open Sesame	1960	$120
— With W. 63rd St. addresss on label			
❏ BST-84040 [S]	Open Sesame	1963	$75
— With New York, USA address on label			
❏ BST-84040 [S]	Open Sesame	1967	$35
— With "A Division of Liberty Records" on label			
❏ BST-84040	Open Sesame	1989	$25
— The Finest in Jazz Since 1939" reissue			
❏ BST-84040 [S]	Open Sesame	199?	$75
— Classic Records reissue on audiophile vinyl			
❏ BLP-4085 [M]	Ready for Freddie	1961	$175
— With 61st St. address on label			
❏ BLP-4085 [M]	Ready for Freddie	1963	$150
— With New York, USA address on label			
❏ BST-84085 [S]	Ready for Freddie	1961	$150
— With 61st St. addresss on label			
❏ BST-84085 [S]	Ready for Freddie	1963	$75
— With New York, USA address on label			
❏ BST-84085 [S]	Ready for Freddie	1967	$35
— With "A Division of Liberty Records" on label			
❏ B1-32094	Ready for Freddie	1995	$30
— The Finest in Jazz Since 1939" reissue			
❏ B1-93202	The Best of Freddie Hubbard	1989	$30
❏ BJT-48017	The Eternal Triangle	1988	$30
❏ BLP-4207	The Night of the Cookers -- Live at Club Le Marchal, Vol. 1	1965	$150
❏ BST-84207 [S]	The Night of the Cookers -- Live at Club Le Marchal, Vol. 1	1965	$75
— With New York, USA address on label			
❏ BST-84207 [S]	The Night of the Cookers -- Live at Club Le Marchal, Vol. 1	1967	$35
— With "A Division of Liberty Records" on label			
❏ BLP-4208 [M]	The Night of the Cookers -- Live at Club Le Marchal, Vol. 2	1965	$150
❏ BST-84208 [S]	The Night of the Cookers -- Live at Club Le Marchal, Vol. 2	1965	$75
— With New York, USA address on label			
❏ BST-84208 [S]	The Night of the Cookers -- Live at Club Le Marchal, Vol. 2	1967	$35
— With "A Division of Liberty Records" on label			
❏ B1-90905	Times 'R Changin'	1989	$30

COLUMBIA

❏ PC34902	Bundle of Joy	1977	$25
❏ KC33048	High Energy	1974	$25
❏ PC33556	Liquid Love	1975	$25
❏ JC36015	Love Connection	1979	$25
❏ FC36418	Skagly	1980	$25
❏ JC35386	Super Blue	1978	$25
❏ JC36358	The Best of Freddie Hubbard	1979	$25
❏ PC34166	Windjammer	1976	$25

CTI

❏ CTS-6013	First Light	1972	$30
❏ 8017	First Light	198?	$20
—Reissue of 6013			
❏ CTS-6044	Freddie Hubbard In Concert	1974	$25
❏ CTS-6036	Keep Your Soul Together	1974	$25
❏ CTS-6056	Polar AC	1975	$25
❏ CTS-6001	Red Clay	1970	$30
❏ 8016	Red Clay	198?	$20
—Reissue of 6001			
❏ CTS-6018	Sky Dive	1973	$25
❏ CTS-6047	The Baddest Hubbard	1974	$25
❏ CTS-6007	The Straight Life	1971	$30
❏ 8022	The Straight Life	198?	$20
—Reissue of 6007			

CTI/CBS ASSOCIATED

❏ FZ40687	First Light	1987	$25

ELEKTRA/MUSICIAN

❏ 60029	Ride Like the Wind	1982	$25

ENJA

❏ 3095	Outpost	1981	$25

FANTASY

❏ 9626	A Little Night Music	1983	$25
❏ 9635	Classics	1984	$25
❏ 9615	Keystone Bop	1982	$25
❏ 9610	Splash	1981	$25

IMPULSE!

❏ A-27 [M]	The Artistry of Freddie Hubbard	1962	$250
❏ AS-27 [S]	The Artistry of Freddie Hubbard	1962	$250
❏ A-38 [M]	The Body and Soul of Freddie Hubbard	1963	$250
❏ AS-38 [S]	The Body and Soul of Freddie Hubbard	1963	$250

LIBERTY

❏ LT-1110	Mistral	1981	$25

PABLO

❏ 2312134 [B]	Born to Be Blue	1976	$25

Number	Title	Yr	NM
—red vinyl add 25%			
❏ 2310884	The Best of Freddie Hubbard	1983	$25
PABLO LIVE			
❏ 2620113	Live at the Northsea Jazz Festival, The Hague, 1980	1983	$30
PABLO TODAY			
❏ 2312134	Born to Be Blue	198?	$25
PAUSA			
❏ 7122	Rollin'	1982	$25
PHOENIX 10			
❏ PHX318	Extended	1981	$20
PICCADILLY			
❏ 3467	Intrepid Fox	198?	$25
QUINTESSENCE			
❏ 25161	Skylark	1978	$25
REAL TIME			
❏ 305	Back to Birdland	198?	$25

HUBBELL, FRANK
PHILIPS

Number	Title	Yr	NM
❏ PHS600293	Frank Hubbell and the Stompers	1969	$35

HUBNER, ABBI, AND HIS LOW DOWN WIZARDS
STOMP OFF

Number	Title	Yr	NM
❏ SOS-1093	Twenty Years, Live in Concert	1986	$25

HUCKO, PEANUTS, AND RALPH SUTTON
CHIAROSCURO

Number	Title	Yr	NM
❏ 167	Live at Condon's	1978	$30

HUCKO, PEANUTS
CIRCLE

Number	Title	Yr	NM
❏ C-21	Peanuts	198?	$25
GRAND AWARD			
❏ GA 33-331 [M]	Tribute to Benny Goodman	1956	$40
WALDORF MUSIC HALL			
❏ MH 33-153 [10]	A Tribute to Benny Goodman	1956	$30

HUCKO, PEANUTS/RAY MCKINLEY
GRAND AWARD

Number	Title	Yr	NM
❏ GA 33-333 [M]	The Swingin' 30s	1956	$40

HUDSON, DEAN
CIRCLE

Number	Title	Yr	NM
❏ C-13	Dean Hudson and His Orchestra 1942-1948	198?	$25
❏ CLP-136	Dean Hudson and His Orchestra 1943-1944	198?	$25
❏ C-40	Dean Hudson and His Orchestra -- Now!	1982	$25
❏ C-86	More Dean Hudson and His Orchestra 1941 and 1948`	198?	$25

HUDSON, ROCK
STANYAN

Number	Title	Yr	NM
❏ SR-10014 [B]	Rock Gently	1971	$30

HUDSON AND LANDRY
DORE

Number	Title	Yr	NM
❏ 324	Hanging In There	1971	$25
❏ 326	Losing Their Heads	1971	$25
❏ 329	Right-Off!	1972	$25
❏ 333	The Best of Hudson and Landry	1974	$18
❏ 334	The Best of Hudson and Landry 2	1975	$18
❏ 331	Weird Kingdom	1973	$25

HUDSON BROTHERS, THE
ARISTA

Number	Title	Yr	NM
❏ AB4199	The Truth About Us	1978	$12
CASABLANCA			
❏ NBLP-7004	Hollywood Situation	1974	$12
ELEKTRA			
❏ 6E-299	Damn Those Kids	1980	$12
—As "Hudson"			
FIRST AMERICAN			
❏ 7708	The Hudson Brothers	1980	$12
PLAYBOY			
❏ 102	Hudson	1972	$18
ROCKET			
❏ PIG-2169	Ba-Fa	1975	$12
❏ PIG-460	Totally Out of Control	1974	$12

HUEBNER, LOUISE
HI HORSE

Number	Title	Yr	NM
❏ 18190 [B]	Seduction Through Witchcraft	2009	$35

Number	Title	Yr	NM
—reissue			
WARNER BROS./7 ARTS MUSIC			
❏ WS1819 [B]	Seduction Through Witchcraft	1969	$175

HUES CORPORATION, THE
RCA VICTOR

Number	Title	Yr	NM
❏ APL1-0323	Freedom for the Stallion	1973	$12
❏ APL1-0938	Love Corporation	1975	$12
❏ APD1-0938 [Q]	Love Corporation	1975	$20
❏ APL1-0755	Rockin' Soul	1974	$12
❏ APD1-0755 [Q]	Rockin' Soul	1974	$20
❏ ANL1-2147	Rock the Boat	1976	$10
❏ APL1-2408	The Best of the Hues Corporation	1977	$12
WARNER BROS.			
❏ BS3043	I Caught Your Act	1977	$12
❏ BSK3196	Your Place or Mine	1978	$12

HUG, ARMAND
CIRCLE

Number	Title	Yr	NM
❏ L-411 [10]	New Orleans 88	1951	$75
GHB			
❏ 144	Armand Hug	1988	$25
GOLDEN CREST			
❏ GC-3045 [M]	New Orleans Piano	196?	$35
❏ GC-3064	Rags and Blues	196?	$35
JAZZOLOGY			
❏ J-83	Armand Hug Plays Bix	197?	$30
LAND O' JAZZ			
❏ 3475	Autobiography in Jazz	197?	$30
PARAMOUNT			
❏ LP-114 [10]	Armand Hug Plays Armand Piron	1954	$50
SOUTHLAND			
❏ 228 [M]	Dixieland	1961	$35
❏ 244 [M]	Piano in New Orleans	196?	$35

HUG, ARMAND/EDDIE MILLER
GHB

Number	Title	Yr	NM
❏ 121	Armand Hug and His New Orleans Dixielanders/Eddie Miller and His New Orleans Rhythm Pals	198?	$25
LAND O' JAZZ			
❏ 5876	Just Friends	198?	$25

HUGHES, FRED
BRUNSWICK

Number	Title	Yr	NM
❏ BL754147 [B]	Baby Boy	1970	$25

HUGHES, FREDDIE
WAND

Number	Title	Yr	NM
❏ WDS-664	Send My Baby Back	1968	$30

—The numbering system suggests this would have been issued in 1965, but the singles from this LP were issued in 1968, thus we use the later date.

HUGHES, JIMMY
ATCO

Number	Title	Yr	NM
❏ 33-209 [M]	Why Not Tonight	1967	$25
❏ SD 33-209 [S]	Why Not Tonight	1967	$25
VEE JAY			
❏ VJ-1102 [M]	Steal Away	1965	$30
❏ VJS-1102 [R]	Steal Away	1965	$30
VOLT			
❏ VOS-6003	Something Special	1969	$25

HUGHES, LANGSTON
FOLKWAYS

Number	Title	Yr	NM
❏ FA-7312 [10]	The Story of Jazz for Children	1954	$175
—With booklet			
MGM			
❏ E-3697 [M]	The Weary Blues	1958	$175
—Yellow label			
VERVE			
❏ VSP-36 [M]	The Weary Blues	1966	$25
❏ VSPS-36 [R]	The Weary Blues	1966	$15

HUGHES, RHETA
COLUMBIA

Number	Title	Yr	NM
❏ CL2385 [M]	Introducing An Electrifying New Star	1965	$30
❏ CS9185 [S]	Introducing An Electrifying New Star	1965	$40

HUGO AND LUIGI
RCA VICTOR

Number	Title	Yr	NM
❏ LPM-2717 [M]	Let's Fall in Love	1963	$12
❏ LSP-2717 [S]	Let's Fall in Love	1963	$15
❏ LSP-4083	Maggie Flynn	1968	$12
❏ LPM-2641 [M]	The Cascading Voices of the Hugo & Luigi Chorus	1963	$12
❏ LSP-2641 [S]	The Cascading Voices of the Hugo & Luigi Chorus	1963	$15
❏ LPM-2789 [M]	The Cascading Voices of the Hugo & Luigi Chorus -- With Brass	1964	$12
❏ LSP-2789 [S]	The Cascading Voices of the Hugo & Luigi Chorus -- With Brass	1964	$15
❏ LPM-2863 [M]	The Cascading Voices of the Hugo & Luigi Chorus -- With Strings	1964	$12
❏ LSP-2863 [S]	The Cascading Voices of the Hugo & Luigi Chorus -- With Strings	1964	$15
❏ LPM-2254 [M]	The Sound of Children at Christmas	1960	$18
❏ LSP-2254 [S]	The Sound of Children at Christmas	1960	$25
ROULETTE			
❏ R-25283 [M]	Cascading Voices	1965	$15
❏ SR-25283 [S]	Cascading Voices	1965	$18
❏ R-25044 [M]	When Good Fellows Get Together	1959	$25
WING			
❏ MGW12207 [M]	Sing Along by the Fireside	195?	$15

HULLABALLOOS, THE
ROULETTE

Number	Title	Yr	NM
❏ R-25297 [M]	England's Newest Singing Sensations	1965	$50
❏ SR-25297 [P]	England's Newest Singing Sensations	1965	$85
❏ R-25310 [M]	The Hullabaloos on Hullabaloo	1965	$50
❏ SR-25310 [P]	The Hullabaloos on Hullabaloo	1965	$85

HULLABALOO SINGERS AND ORCHESTRA, THE
COLUMBIA

Number	Title	Yr	NM
❏ CL2410 [M]	The Hullabaloo Show	1965	$30
❏ CS9210 [S]	The Hullabaloo Show	1965	$35

HUMAN ARTS ENSEMBLE
ARISTA FREEDOM

Number	Title	Yr	NM
❏ AF1022	Under the Sun	1975	$30
❏ AF1039	Whisper of Dharma	1977	$30

HUMAN BEINZ, THE
CAPITOL

Number	Title	Yr	NM
❏ ST2926	Evolutions	1968	$40
❏ ST2906	Nobody But Me	1968	$30
GATEWAY			
❏ GLP-3012	Nobody But Me	1968	$40
—With added tracks by The Mammals			

HUMAN LEAGUE
A&M

Number	Title	Yr	NM
❏ R162455	Crash	1986	$15
—RCA Music Service edition			
❏ SP-5129	Crash	1986	$12
❏ SP-6-4892	Dare	1981	$12
❏ SP-12501 [EP]	Fascination!	1983	$12
❏ R100837	Greatest Hits	1989	$18
—BMG Direct Marketing edition			
❏ SP-5227	Greatest Hits	1989	$18
❏ SP-4923	Hysteria	1984	$12
❏ SP-3209	Love and Dancing	1982	$12
—As "The League Unlimited Orchestra"; instrumental versions			
❏ 7502153061	Romantic?	1990	$15
VIRGIN			
❏ 90881	Reproduction	1988	$12
—First issue of early U.K. album			
❏ 90880	Travelogue	1988	$12
—Reissue of early U.K. album			
VIRGIN INTERNATIONAL			
❏ VI2160	Travelogue	1980	$18

—U.S. pressings have "VI" prefix; imports, which go for less, have simply a "V" prefix.

HUMANS, THE
I.R.S.

Number	Title	Yr	NM
❏ SP-17900 [EP]	The Humans	1980	$12
—Promo-only 12-inch with die-cut sleeve			
❏ SP-70025	The Humans (Happy Hour)	1981	$12

HUMBARD, REX, AND THE CATHEDRAL OF TOMORROW STAFF
CATHEDRAL OF TOMORROW

Number	Title	Yr	NM
❏ ARC700910	Seasons Greetings from Rex Humbard and the Cathedral of Tomorrow Staff	19??	$15

—Album cover also serves as mailer for LP

Number	Title	Yr	NM

HUMBARD FAMILY SINGERS, THE
IMPACT
| ❑ 0 | Christmas with the Humbards | 1979 | $12 |

HUMBLE PIE
Also see PETER FRAMPTON; STEVE MARRIOTT.
A&M
❑ SP-3701 [B]	Eat It	1973	$25
❑ SP-6503	Eat It	1981	$12
— Budget-line reissue			
❑ SP-4270	Humble Pie	1970	$15
❑ SP-3127	Humble Pie	1981	$10
— Budget-line reissue			
❑ SP-3513 [B]	Lost and Found	1972	$25
❑ SP-6009	Lost and Found	1981	$12
— Budget-line reissue			
❑ SP-3506 [B]	Performance -- Rockin' the Fillmore	1971	$25
❑ SP-6008	Performance -- Rockin' the Fillmore	1981	$12
— Budget-line reissue			
❑ SP-4301	Rock On	1971	$15
❑ SP-4342	Smokin'	1972	$15
❑ SP-3132	Smokin'	1981	$10
— Budget-line reissue			
❑ SP-4514	Street Rats	1975	$15
❑ SP-3208	The Best of Humble Pie	1982	$12
❑ SP-3611 [B]	Thunderbox	1974	$15
ACCORD
| ❑ SN-7192 | Recaptured | 1981 | $12 |
ATCO
| ❑ SD 38-131 | Go for the Throat | 1981 | $12 |
| ❑ SD 38-122 | On to Victory | 1980 | $12 |
CLEOPATRA
| ❑ 7546 [B] | California '81 | | $25 |
| ❑ 5128 [B] | Live At Winterland | | $40 |
COMPLEAT
| ❑ 672009-1 | A Slice of Humble Pie | 1985 | $15 |
IMMEDIATE
| ❑ IMOCS-101 | As Safe As Yesterday Is | 1969 | $30 |

HUMBLEBUMS, THE
GERRY RAFFERTY was in this group.
LIBERTY
| ❑ LST-7656 | Open Up the Door | 1970 | $30 |
| ❑ LST-7636 | The Humblebums | 1969 | $25 |

HUMES, HELEN
AUDIOPHILE
| ❑ AP-107 | Helen Humes | 1980 | $50 |
CLASSIC JAZZ
| ❑ 120 | Let the Good Times Roll | 197? | $30 |
| ❑ 110 | Sneakin' Around | 197? | $30 |
COLUMBIA
| ❑ PC33488 | The Talk of the Town | 1975 | $35 |
CONTEMPORARY
❑ M-3582 [M]	Songs I Like to Sing	1960	$250
❑ S-7582 [S]	Songs I Like to Sing	1960	$250
❑ M-3598 [M]	Swingin' with Humes	1961	$250
❑ S-7598 [S]	Swingin' with Humes	1961	$250
❑ M-3571 [M]	'Tain't Nobody's Biz-Ness If I Do	1960	$250
❑ S-7571 [S]	'Tain't Nobody's Biz-Ness If I Do	1960	$250
FANTASY
❑ OJC-171	Songs I Like to Sing	198?	$30
❑ OJC-608	Swingin' with Humes	1991	$35
❑ OJC-453	'Tain't Nobody's Biz-Ness If I Do	1990	$35
JAZZ MAN
| ❑ 5003 | On the Sunny Side of the Street | 1981 | $35 |
JAZZOLOGY
| ❑ J-55 | Incomparable | 197? | $30 |
MUSE
| ❑ MR-5233 | Helen | 1980 | $30 |
| ❑ MR-5217 | Helen Humes with the Muse All Stars | 197? | $30 |
SAVOY JAZZ
| ❑ SJL-1159 | E-Baba-Le-Ba": The Rhythm & Blues Years | 1986 | $30 |

HUMPERDINCK, ENGELBERT
EPIC
❑ PE34381	After the Lovin'	1976	$12
— Orange label			
❑ PE34381	After the Lovin'	1979	$10
— Dark blue label; back cover does not yet have bar code			
❑ PE34381 [B]	After the Lovin'	198?	$10
— Dark blue label; back cover has bar code			
❑ E2X36782	All of Me/Live in Concert	1980	$15
❑ PE36765	A Merry Christmas with Engelbert Humperdinck	1980	$12
— Some copies of the record have a "JE" prefix			

Number	Title	Yr	NM
❑ PE35031	Christmas Tyme	1977	$15
❑ FE37128	Don't You Love Me Anymore	1981	$12
❑ PE37128	Don't You Love Me Anymore	1983	$10
— Budget-line reissue			
❑ E34719	Golden Love Songs	1977	$12
— Orange label			
❑ PE34719	Golden Love Songs	198?	$10
— Reissue with bar code; dark blue label			
❑ JE35020	Last of the Romantics	1978	$12
— Orange label			
❑ (no #) [PD]	Last of the Romantics	1978	$30
❑ PE35020	Last of the Romantics	198?	$10
— Reissue with bar code; dark blue label			
❑ JE36431	Love's Only Love	1980	$12
❑ PE34730	Miracles	1977	$12
— Orange label			
❑ PE34730	Miracles	198?	$10
— Reissue with bar code; dark blue label			
❑ E34436	The Ultimate	1977	$12
— Orange label			
❑ PE34436	The Ultimate	198?	$10
— Reissue with bar code; dark blue label			
❑ JE35791	This Moment in Time	1979	$12
❑ PE35791	This Moment in Time	198?	$10
— Budget-line reissue			
❑ PE39469	White Christmas	1984	$12
❑ FE38087	You and Your Lover	1983	$12
LONDON
| ❑ BP688/9 | Engelbert Humperdinck Sings for You | 1977 | $18 |
| ❑ PS709 | Love Letters | 1978 | $12 |
PARROT
❑ PAS71022	A Man Without Love	1968	$18
❑ XPAS71048	Another Time, Another Place	1971	$18
❑ PAS71026	Engelbert	1969	$18
❑ XPAS71030	Engelbert Humperdinck	1969	$18
❑ PAS71067	His Greatest Hits	1974	$18
❑ XPAS71056	In Time	1972	$18
❑ XPAS71061	King of Hearts	1973	$18
❑ XPAS71051	Live at the Riviera, Las Vegas	1971	$18
❑ APAS71065	My Love	1974	$18
❑ PA61012 [M]	Release Me	1967	$25
❑ PAS71012 [S]	Release Me	1967	$18
❑ XPAS71043	Sweetheart	1971	$18
❑ PA61015 [M]	The Last Waltz	1967	$25
❑ PAS71015 [S]	The Last Waltz	1967	$18
❑ XPAS71038	We Made It Happen	1970	$18
❑ SW-93216	We Made It Happen	1970	$25
— Capitol Record Club edition			
SILVER EAGLE
| ❑ SE1034 | A Lovely Way to Spend an Evening | 1985 | $18 |
| — Mail-order offer | | | |

HUMPHREY, BOBBI
BLUE NOTE
❑ BN-LA142-G	Blacks and Blues	1974	$25
❑ BST-84421	Dig This	1972	$30
❑ BN-LA550-G	Fancy Dancer	1975	$25
❑ BST-84379	Flute-In	1971	$30
❑ BN-LA344-G	Satin Doll	1974	$25
❑ BN-LA699-G	The Best of Bobbi Humphrey	1976	$25
EPIC
❑ JE35338	Freestyle	1978	$25
❑ PE34704	Tailor Made	1977	$25
❑ JE36368	The Best of Bobbi Humphrey	1980	$25
❑ JE35607	The Good Life	1979	$25

HUMPHREY, EARL
BIOGRAPH
| ❑ CEN-11 | Earl Humphrey and His Footwarmers | 197? | $30 |

HUMPHREY, PAUL
BLUE THUMB
| ❑ BTS66 | America, Wake Up! | 1974 | $30 |
| ❑ BTS47 | Supermellow | 1973 | $30 |
DISCOVERY
| ❑ DS-850 | Paul Humphrey Sextet | 1981 | $25 |
LIZARD
| ❑ 20106 | Paul Humphrey & the Cool Aid Chemists | 1971 | $35 |

HUMPHREY, PERCY
BIOGRAPH
| ❑ CEN-13 | Percy Humphrey at Manny's Tavern | 197? | $30 |
GHB
| ❑ 85 | Percy Humphrey and the Crescent City Joymakers | 197? | $25 |
JAZZOLOGY
| ❑ JCE-26 | Percy Humphrey and the Crescent City Joymakers | 197? | $30 |

Number	Title	Yr	NM
PEARL
| ❑ PS-3 | Climax Rag | 197? | $35 |
RIVERSIDE
| ❑ RLP-378 [M] | Percy Humphrey's Crescent City Joymakers | 1961 | $250 |
| ❑ RS-9378 [R] | Percy Humphrey's Crescent City Joymakers | 196? | $35 |

HUMPHREY, WILLIE
GHB
| ❑ 248 | New Orleans Jazz from Willie Humphrey | 198? | $25 |

HUNDLEY, CRAIG
WORLD PACIFIC
❑ WPS-21880	Arrival of a Young Giant	1968	$18
❑ WPS-21900	Rhapsody in Blue	1970	$150
❑ WPS-21896	The Craig Hundley Trio Plays with the Big Boys	1969	$150

HUNGER
PUBLIC
| ❑ 1006 | Strictly from Hunger | 1969 | $600 |

HUNLEY, CON
MCA
| ❑ 5423 | Once You Get the Feel of It | 1983 | $18 |
WARNER BROS.
❑ BSK3617	Ask Any Woman	1981	$12
❑ BSK3285	Con Hunley	1979	$12
— With this title on both cover and label			
❑ BSK3474	Don't It Break Your Heart	1980	$12
❑ BSK3378	I Don't Want to Lose You	1980	$12
❑ BSK3285	No Limit	1979	$18
— Same cover as "Con Hunley," but the above title is on the label			
❑ BSK3693	Oh Girl	1982	$12

HUNT, PEE WEE
ALLEGRO
| ❑ 1633 [M] | Dixieland | 1956 | $30 |
CAPITOL
❑ T984 [M]	Cole Porter Ala Dixie	1957	$75
— Turquoise label			
❑ T573 [M]	Dixieland Classics	1955	$30
❑ H312 [10]	Dixieland Detour	1952	$100
❑ T1265 [M]	Dixieland Kickoff	1959	$75
❑ ST1265 [S]	Dixieland Kickoff	1959	$30
❑ T783 [M]	Pee Wee and Fingers	1956	$75
❑ T1362 [M]	Pee Wee Hunt's Dance Party	1960	$40
❑ ST1362 [S]	Pee Wee Hunt's Dance Party	1960	$100
❑ H203 [10]	Straight from Dixie	1950	$85
❑ T203 [M]	Straight from Dixie	195?	$75
❑ H492 [10]	Swingin' Down Dixie	1954	$85
❑ T1853 [M]	The Best of Pee Wee Hunt	1962	$85
❑ DT1853 [R]	The Best of Pee Wee Hunt	1962	$75
❑ T1144 [M]	The Blues A La Dixie	1958	$75
ROYALE
| ❑ 18153 [10] | Pee Wee Hunt and His Dixieland Band | 195? | $40 |
SOLITAIRE
| ❑ 507 [10] | Dixieland Capers | 195? | $30 |

HUNT, PEE WEE/PEE WEE RUSSELL
RONDO-LETTE
| ❑ A2 [M] | Dixieland: Pee Wee Hunt and Pee Wee Russell | 195? | $30 |

HUNT, TOMMY
DYNAMO
| ❑ D-7001 [M] | Tommy Hunt's Greatest Hits | 1967 | $25 |
| ❑ DS-8001 [S] | Tommy Hunt's Greatest Hits | 1967 | $30 |
SCEPTER
| ❑ 506 [M] | I Just Don't Know What to Do with Myself | 1962 | $50 |
| ❑ SS-506 [S] | I Just Don't Know What to Do with Myself | 1962 | $75 |

HUNTER, ALBERTA
COLUMBIA
❑ JC36430	Amtrak Blues	1980	$25
❑ FC38970	Look for the Silver Lining	1983	$25
❑ FC37691	The Glory of Alberta Hunter	1982	$30
❑ PC37691	The Glory of Alberta Hunter	1985	$20
— Budget-line reissue			
DRG
| ❑ SL-5195 | Legendary Alberta Hunter | 198? | $25 |
FANTASY
| ❑ OBC-510 | Alberta Hunter with Lovie Austin's Blues Serenaders | 198? | $25 |
RIVERSIDE
| ❑ RLP-418 [M] | Alberta Hunter with Lovie Austin's Blues Serenaders | 1962 | $250 |

Number	Title	Yr	NM
❏ RS-9418 [R]	Alberta Hunter with Lovie Austin's Blues Serenaders	196?	$35

STASH

Number	Title	Yr	NM
❏ ST-115	Classic Alberta Hunter: The Thirties	1978	$25
❏ ST-123	Young Alberta Hunter: The Twenties	1984	$25

HUNTER, FRANK
JUBILEE

Number	Title	Yr	NM
❏ JLP-1020 [M]	Sounds of Hunter	1956	$50

HUNTER, IAN, AND MICK RONSON
MERCURY

Number	Title	Yr	NM
❏ 838973-1	Y U I Orta	1989	$15

HUNTER, IAN
Also see MOTT THE HOOPLE.
CHRYSALIS

Number	Title	Yr	NM
❏ 2CHS1269 [B]	Ian Hunter Live/Welcome to the Club	1980	$25
❏ CHS1326	Short Back N' Sides	1981	$12
❏ PV41326	Short Back N' Sides	1982	$10
— Budget-line reissue			
❏ CHR1214 [B]	You're Never Alone with a Schizophrenic	1979	$18
❏ PV41214 [B]	You're Never Alone with a Schizophrenic	1982	$10
— Budget-line reissue			

COLUMBIA

Number	Title	Yr	NM
❏ PC34142 [B]	All American Alien Boy	1976	$18
— No bar code on cover			
❏ PC34142	All American Alien Boy	198?	$10
— Budget-line reissue with bar code			
❏ FC38628	All of the Good Ones Are Taken	1983	$12
❏ PC33480 [B]	Ian Hunter	1975	$18
— No bar code on cover			
❏ PC33480	Ian Hunter	198?	$10
— Budget-line reissue with bar code			
❏ PC34721 [B]	Overnight Angels	1977	$25
— No bar code on cover			
❏ C236251 [B]	Shades of Ian Hunter	1980	$18

HUNTER, IVORY JOE
ATLANTIC

Number	Title	Yr	NM
❏ 8008 [M]	Ivory Joe Hunter	1957	$250
— Black label			
❏ 8008 [M]	Ivory Joe Hunter	1960	$150
— Purple and red label			
❏ 8015 [M]	The Old and the New	1958	$250
— Black label			
❏ 8015 [M]	The Old and the New	1960	$150
— Purple and red label			

DOT

Number	Title	Yr	NM
❏ DLP-3569 [M]	This Is Ivory Joe Hunter	1964	$40
❏ DLP-25569 [S]	This Is Ivory Joe Hunter	1964	$50

EPIC

Number	Title	Yr	NM
❏ E30348	The Return of Ivory Joe Hunter	1971	$25

EVEREST ARCHIVE OF FOLK & JAZZ

Number	Title	Yr	NM
❏ 289	Ivory Joe Hunter	1974	$15

GOLDISC

Number	Title	Yr	NM
❏ 403 [M]	The Fabulous Ivory Joe Hunter	1961	$75

HOME COOKING

Number	Title	Yr	NM
❏ 112	I'm Coming Down with the Blues	1989	$15

KING

Number	Title	Yr	NM
❏ 605 [M]	16 of His Greatest Hits	1958	$400

LION

Number	Title	Yr	NM
❏ L-70068 [M]	I Need You So	1959	$75

MGM

Number	Title	Yr	NM
❏ E-3488 [M]	I Get That Lonesome Feeling	1957	$300

PARAMOUNT

Number	Title	Yr	NM
❏ PAS-6080	I've Always Been Country	1974	$15

POLYDOR

Number	Title	Yr	NM
❏ 830897-1	Since I Met You Baby	1987	$15

SMASH

Number	Title	Yr	NM
❏ MGS-27037 [M]	Ivory Joe Hunter's Golden Hits	1963	$40
❏ SRS-67037 [S]	Ivory Joe Hunter's Golden Hits	1963	$50

SOUND

Number	Title	Yr	NM
❏ M-603 [M]	Ivory Joe Hunter	1959	$175

STRAND

Number	Title	Yr	NM
❏ SL-1123 [M]	The Artistry of Ivory Joe Hunter	196?	$40
❏ SLS-1123 [S]	The Artistry of Ivory Joe Hunter	196?	$50

HUNTER, LURLEAN
ATLANTIC

Number	Title	Yr	NM
❏ 1344 [M]	Blue and Sentimental	1960	$300
❏ SD1344 [S]	Blue and Sentimental	1960	$300

RCA VICTOR

Number	Title	Yr	NM
❏ LPM-1151 [M]	Lonesome Gal	1955	$150

VIK

Number	Title	Yr	NM
❏ LX-1061 [M]	Night Life	1956	$100
❏ LX-1116 [M]	Stepping Out	1957	$100

HUNTER, ROBERT
GRATEFUL DEAD lyricist.
RELIX

Number	Title	Yr	NM
❏ 2002 [PD]	Promontory Rider	1982	$25
— Limited edition of 1,000 picture discs			

ROUND

Number	Title	Yr	NM
❏ RX-101	Tales of the Great Rum Runners	1974	$25
❏ RX-105	Tiger Rose	1975	$25

HUNTER, STAN, AND SONNY FORTUNE
PRESTIGE

Number	Title	Yr	NM
❏ PRLP-7458 [M]	Trip on the Strip	1967	$30
❏ PRST-7458 [S]	Trip on the Strip	1967	$25

HUNTER, TAB
DOT

Number	Title	Yr	NM
❏ DLP-3370 [M]	Young Love	1961	$25
❏ DLP-25370 [S]	Young Love	1961	$25

WARNER BROS.

Number	Title	Yr	NM
❏ W1367 [M]	R.F.D. Tab Hunter	1960	$25
❏ WS1367 [S]	R.F.D. Tab Hunter	1960	$30
❏ W1221 [M]	Tab Hunter	1958	$25
❏ WS1221 [S]	Tab Hunter	1958	$30
❏ W1292 [M]	When I Fall in Love	1959	$25
❏ WS1292 [S]	When I Fall in Love	1959	$30

HUNTER MUSKETT
BRADLEY

Number	Title	Yr	NM
❏ 1003	Hunter Muskett	1973	$100

HURT, CINDY
CHURCHILL

Number	Title	Yr	NM
❏ 9422	Talk to Me	1982	$12

HURT, MISSISSIPPI JOHN
BIOGRAPH

Number	Title	Yr	NM
❏ C-4 [M]	1928: His First Recordings	1972	$25

PIEDMONT

Number	Title	Yr	NM
❏ PLP-13157 [M]	Folk Songs and Blues	1963	$100
❏ PLP-13181 [M]	Worried Blues	1964	$100

VANGUARD

Number	Title	Yr	NM
❏ VRS-9145 [M]	Blues at Newport	1965	$30
❏ VSD-79145 [S]	Blues at Newport	1965	$30
❏ VRS-9220 [M]	Mississippi John Hurt/Today	1966	$30
❏ VSD-79220 [S]	Mississippi John Hurt/Today	1966	$30
❏ VSD-19/20	The Best of Mississippi John Hurt	197?	$30
❏ VRS-9248 [M]	The Immortal Mississippi John Hurt	1967	$30
❏ VSD-79248 [S]	The Immortal Mississippi John Hurt	1967	$30
❏ VSD-79327	The Last Session	1972	$25

HURVITZ, SANDY
VERVE

Number	Title	Yr	NM
❏ V6-5064	Sandy's Album Is Here at Last	1968	$30
— Produced by FRANK ZAPPA			

HUSKER DU
Also see BOB MOULD; SUGAR.
NEW ALLIANCE

Number	Title	Yr	NM
❏ 007 [B]	Land Speed Record	1982	$30
— No reference to SST on cover			
❏ 007	Land Speed Record	1982	$15
— Second pressing, "Marketed by SST" on cover			

REFLEX

Number	Title	Yr	NM
❏ #D0	Everything Falls Apart	1982	$40

RHINO

Number	Title	Yr	NM
❏ R125385 [B]	Candy Apple Grey	2014	$30

SST

Number	Title	Yr	NM
❏ PSST E-27 [DJ]	Eight Miles High/6 from Zen Arcade	1984	$30
— Promo sampler, etched design on side 1, sticker cover			
❏ 915 [10]	Eight Miles High/Makes No Sense at All	199?	$12
❏ 055	Flip Your Wig	1985	$18
❏ 195	Land Speed Record	198?	$15
— Reissue of New Alliance 007			
❏ 020 [EP]	Metal Circus	1983	$15
❏ 908 [10]	Metal Circus	199?	$10
❏ 031	New Day Rising	1985	$18

Number	Title	Yr	NM
❏ 027 [B]	Zen Arcade	1984	$18

WARNER BROS.

Number	Title	Yr	NM
❏ 25385	Candy Apple Grey	1986	$15
❏ WBMS-145 [DJ]	The Warehouse Interview	1987	$30
— Promo only, part of the Warner Bros. Music Show series			
❏ PRO02719 [DJ]	Warehouse: Songs and Stories	1987	$10
— Promo-only four-song sampler			
❏ 25544	Warehouse: Songs and Stories	1987	$18
❏ PRO-A-2719 [DJ]	Warehouse: Songs and Stories	1987	$18
— Promo-only four-song sampler			

HUSKY, FERLIN
ABC

Number	Title	Yr	NM
❏ X-849	Champagne Ladies and Blue Ribbon Babies	1974	$15
❏ X-818	Freckles and Polliwog Days	1974	$15
❏ X-803	Sweet Honky Tonk	1974	$15
❏ X-884	The Foster-Rice Songbook	1975	$15
❏ X-776	True True Lovin'	1973	$15

CAPITOL

Number	Title	Yr	NM
❏ T1204 [M]	Born to Lose	1959	$40
— Black colorband label, Capitol logo at left			
❏ T1204 [M]	Born to Lose	1962	$30
— Black colorband label, Capitol logo at top			
❏ T880 [M]	Boulevard of Broken Dreams	1957	$75
— Turquoise label			
❏ T880 [M]	Boulevard of Broken Dreams	1958	$40
— Black colorband label, Capitol logo at left			
❏ T2101 [M]	By Request	1964	$18
❏ ST2101 [S]	By Request	1964	$25
❏ T2793 [M]	Christmas All Year Long	1967	$18
❏ ST2793 [S]	Christmas All Year Long	1967	$18
❏ T2439 [M]	Ferlin Husky Sings the Songs of Music City, U.S.A.	1966	$18
❏ ST2439 [S]	Ferlin Husky Sings the Songs of Music City, U.S.A.	1966	$25
❏ T1280 [M]	Ferlin's Favorites	1960	$40
— Black colorband label, Capitol logo at left			
❏ T1280 [M]	Ferlin's Favorites	1962	$30
— Black colorband label, Capitol logo at top			
❏ T1383 [M]	Gone	1960	$40
— Black colorband label, Capitol logo at left			
❏ T1383 [M]	Gone	1962	$30
— Black colorband label, Capitol logo at top			
❏ DT1383 [R]	Gone	196?	$15
❏ T1383 [M]	Gone	196?	$25
— Gold "The Star Line" label; "The Star Line" logo on cover			
❏ T2548 [M]	I Could Sing All Night	1966	$18
❏ ST2548 [S]	I Could Sing All Night	1966	$25
❏ T2870 [M]	Just for You	1968	$30
❏ ST2870 [S]	Just for You	1968	$18
❏ ST-11069	Just Plain Lonely	1972	$18
❏ T1633 [M]	Memories of Home	1961	$30
— Black colorband label, Capitol logo at left			
❏ T1633 [M]	Memories of Home	1962	$18
— Black colorband label, Capitol logo at top			
❏ ST1633 [S]	Memories of Home	1961	$30
— Black colorband label, Capitol logo at left			
❏ ST1633 [S]	Memories of Home	1962	$25
— Black colorband label, Capitol logo at top			
❏ ST-768	One More Time	1971	$18
❏ T976 [M]	Sittin' On a Rainbow	1958	$75
— Turquoise label			
❏ T1720 [M]	Some of My Favorites	1962	$18
❏ ST1720 [S]	Some of My Favorites	1962	$25
❏ T718 [M]	Songs of the Home and Heart	1956	$75
— Turquoise label			

Number	Title	Yr	NM
❏ T718 [M]	Songs of the Home and Heart	1959	$40
—Black colorband label, Capitol logo at left			
❏ T718 [M]	Songs of the Home and Heart	1962	$30
—Black colorband label, Capitol logo at top			
❏ ST-239	That's Why I Love You So Much	1969	$18
❏ SKAO-143	The Best of Ferlin Husky	1969	$18
❏ SM-143	The Best of Ferlin Husky	197?	$12
—Reissue with new prefix			
❏ T1885 [M]	The Heart and Soul of Ferlin Husky	1963	$18
❏ ST1885 [S]	The Heart and Soul of Ferlin Husky	1963	$25
❏ T1991 [M]	The Hits of Ferlin Husky	1963	$18
❏ DT1991 [R]	The Hits of Ferlin Husky	1963	$15
❏ T2305 [M]	True, True Lovin'	1965	$18
❏ ST2305 [S]	True, True Lovin'	1965	$25
❏ T1546 [M]	Walkin' and Hummin'	1961	$30
—Black colorband label, Capitol logo at left			
❏ T1546 [M]	Walkin' and Hummin'	1962	$18
—Black colorband label, Capitol logo at top			
❏ ST1546 [S]	Walkin' and Hummin'	1961	$30
—Black colorband label, Capitol logo at left			
❏ ST1546 [S]	Walkin' and Hummin'	1962	$25
—Black colorband label, Capitol logo at top			
❏ T2705 [M]	What Am I Gonna Do Now?	1967	$25
❏ ST2705 [S]	What Am I Gonna Do Now?	1967	$18
❏ ST2913	Where No One Stands Alone	1968	$18
❏ ST-115	White Fences and Evergreen Trees	1968	$18
❏ ST-433	Your Love Is Heavenly Sunshine	1970	$18
❏ ST-591	Your Sweet Love Lifted Me	1970	$18

HILLTOP

Number	Title	Yr	NM
❏ 6086	Green, Green Grass of Home	1970	$15
❏ 6005	Ole Opry Favorites	196?	$15
❏ 6099	Wings of a Dove	197?	$15

KING

Number	Title	Yr	NM
❏ 647 [M]	Country Tunes Sung from the Heart	1959	$80
❏ 728 [M]	Easy Livin'	1960	$80

STARDAY

Number	Title	Yr	NM
❏ 3018	Greatest Hits	197?	$15

HUSSAIN, ZAKIR

ECM

Number	Title	Yr	NM
❏ 1349	Making Music	1987	$25

HUSTAD, DON, AND TEDD SMITH

WORD

Number	Title	Yr	NM
❏ WST-8319	Christmastime with Don Hustad and Tedd Smith	196?	$15

HUSTLER

A&M

Number	Title	Yr	NM
❏ SP4504	High Street	1974	$18
❏ SP4556	Play Loud	1975	$18

HUTCH, WILLIE

MOTOWN

Number	Title	Yr	NM
❏ M6-871	Color Her...	1977	$15
❏ M6-854	Concert in Blues	1976	$15
❏ M6-811	Foxy Brown	1974	$15
❏ M784	Fully Exposed	1973	$15
❏ M6-874	Havin' a House Party	1977	$15
❏ M6-815	Mark of the Beast	1974	$15
❏ M6-838	Ode to My Lady	1975	$15
❏ M766	The Mack	1973	$15
❏ 5281ML	The Mack	1983	$10
—Reissue of 766			

RCA VICTOR

Number	Title	Yr	NM
❏ LSP-4213	Soul Portrait: Willie Hutch	1969	$18

WHITFIELD

Number	Title	Yr	NM
❏ BSK3226	In Tune	1978	$12
❏ BSK3352	Midnight Dancer	1979	$12

HUTCHERSON, BOBBY

BLUE NOTE

Number	Title	Yr	NM
❏ BST-84333	Bobby Hutcherson Now	1969	$25
—With "A Division of Liberty Records" on label			
❏ BN-LA257-G	Cirrus	1973	$30
❏ BLP-4213 [M]	Components	1966	$150
❏ BST-84213 [S]	Components	1966	$75
—With "New York, USA" address on label			
❏ BST-84213 [S]	Components	1967	$35
—With "A Division of Liberty Records" on label			
❏ B1-29027	Components	1994	$35
—Reissue			
❏ BLP-4198 [M]	Dialogue	1965	$150
❏ BST-84198 [S]	Dialogue	1965	$80
—With "New York, USA" address on label			
❏ BST-84198 [S]	Dialogue	1967	$35
—With "A Division of Liberty Records" on label			
❏ BST-84198	Dialogue	198?	$25

Number	Title	Yr	NM
—The Finest in Jazz Since 1939" reissue			
❏ BLP-4231 [M]	Happenings	1967	$150
❏ BST-84231 [S]	Happenings	1967	$100
—With "New York, USA" address on label			
❏ BST-84231 [S]	Happenings	1967	$75
—With "A Division of Liberty Records" on label			
❏ BST-84376	Head On	1971	$35
❏ BN-LA789-H	Knucklebean	1977	$30
❏ BN-LA396-G	Linger Lane	1974	$30
❏ LT-1086	Medina	1980	$25
❏ BN-LA551-G	Montara	1975	$30
❏ BST-84416	Natural Illusions	1972	$35
❏ LT-1044	Patterns	1980	$25
❏ B1-33583	Patterns	1995	$35
—Reissue			
❏ BST-84362	San Francisco	1970	$25
❏ B1-28268	San Francisco	1994	$35
—Reissue			
❏ LT-996	Spiral	1979	$25
❏ BLP-4244 [M]	Stick-Up!	1968	$300
—Scheduled for release in mono, but evidently never came out			
❏ BST-84244 [S]	Stick-Up!	1968	$25
—With "A Division of Liberty Records" on label			
❏ BST-84291	Total Eclipse	1969	$25
—With "A Division of Liberty Records" on label			
❏ BST-84291	Total Eclipse	1985	$25
—The Finest in Jazz Since 1939" reissue			
❏ BN-LA710-G	View from Inside	1977	$30
❏ BN-LA615-G	Waiting	1976	$30

COLUMBIA

Number	Title	Yr	NM
❏ JC35814	Conception: The Gift of Love	1979	$25
❏ JC35550	Highway 1	1978	$25
❏ FC36402	Un Poco Loco	1980	$25

CONTEMPORARY

Number	Title	Yr	NM
❏ C-14009	Solo/Quartet	1982	$30

FANTASY

Number	Title	Yr	NM
❏ OJC-425	Solo/Quartet	1990	$30

LANDMARK

Number	Title	Yr	NM
❏ LLP-1522	Ambos Mundos	1989	$35
❏ LLP-1508	Color Schemes	1986	$30
❏ LLP-1517	Cruisin' the 'Bird	1988	$30
❏ LLP-501	Good Bait	1985	$30
❏ LLP-1513	In the Vanguard	1987	$30

THERESA

Number	Title	Yr	NM
❏ TR-124	Farewell Keystone	1989	$30

HUTTON, BETTY

CAPITOL

Number	Title	Yr	NM
❏ H256 [10]	Square in the Social Circle	1950	$75

WARNER BROS.

Number	Title	Yr	NM
❏ W1267 [M]	Betty Hutton at the Saints and Sinners Ball	1959	$25
❏ WS1267 [S]	Betty Hutton at the Saints and Sinners Ball	1959	$30

HUTTON, DANNY

Also see THREE DOG NIGHT.

MGM

Number	Title	Yr	NM
❏ SE-4664	Pre-Dog Night	1970	$25

HYLAND, BRIAN

ABC-PARAMOUNT

Number	Title	Yr	NM
❏ 463 [M]	Country Meets Folk	1964	$30
❏ S-463 [S]	Country Meets Folk	1964	$40
❏ 400 [M]	Let Me Belong to You	1961	$30
❏ S-400 [S]	Let Me Belong to You	1961	$40
❏ 431 [M]	Sealed with a Kiss	1962	$30

SEALED WITH A KISS
BRIAN HYLAND

Number	Title	Yr	NM
❏ S-431 [S]	Sealed with a Kiss	1962	$40

DOT

Number	Title	Yr	NM
❏ DLP25954	Stay and Love Me All Summer	1969	$18
❏ DLP25926	Tragedy/A Million to One	1969	$18

KAPP

Number	Title	Yr	NM
❏ KL1202 [M]	The Bashful Blonde	1960	$50
❏ KS3202 [S]	The Bashful Blonde	1960	$100

PHILIPS

Number	Title	Yr	NM
❏ PHM200136 [M]	Here's to Our Love	1964	$25
❏ PHS600136 [S]	Here's to Our Love	1964	$30
❏ PHM200158 [M]	Rockin' Folk	1965	$25
❏ PHS600158 [S]	Rockin' Folk	1965	$30
❏ PHM200217 [M]	Run, Run, Look and See/ The Joker Went Wild	1966	$25
—With "200-217" in trail-off; this record plays mono			
❏ PHS600217 [S]	Run, Run, Look and See/ The Joker Went Wild	1966	$30
❏ PHM200217 [S]	Run, Run, Look and See/ The Joker Went Wild	1966	$25
—With "2/600-217" in trail-off; this record plays stereo, though labeled mono			

PICKWICK

Number	Title	Yr	NM
❏ SPC-3261	Young Years	197?	$12

PRIVATE STOCK

Number	Title	Yr	NM
❏ PS-7003	In a State of Bayou	1977	$15

RHINO

Number	Title	Yr	NM
❏ RNLP-70226	Greatest Hits	1987	$12

UNI

Number	Title	Yr	NM
❏ 73097	Brian Hyland	1970	$18
—The album is listed as "stereo," but "Gypsy Woman" is rechanneled			

WING

Number	Title	Yr	NM
❏ MGW-12341 [M]	Here's to Our Love	1967	$15
❏ SRW-16341 [S]	Here's to Our Love	1967	$15

HYLTON, JACK

FLAPPER

Number	Title	Yr	NM
❏ 702	Jack Hylton and His Orchestra 1925-28: Light Music from the Variety Stage	198?	$25

HYMAN, DICK

ATLANTIC

Number	Title	Yr	NM
❏ SD1671	Satchmo Remembered	1975	$25

CHIAROSCURO

Number	Title	Yr	NM
❏ 198	Themes and Variations on "A Child Is Born"	1978	$25

COLUMBIA MASTERWORKS

Number	Title	Yr	NM
❏ M32587	Ferdinand "Jelly Roll" Morton -- Transcriptions for Orchestra	1974	$30

COMMAND

Number	Title	Yr	NM
❏ RS 33-911 [M]	Brazilian Impressions	1966	$35
❏ RS911SD [S]	Brazilian Impressions	1966	$50
❏ RS951SD	Concerto Electro	1970	$75
❏ RS 33-856 [M]	Electrodynamics	1963	$35
❏ RS856SD [S]	Electrodynamics	1963	$50
❏ RS 33-862 [M]	Fabulous	1963	$35
❏ RS862SD [S]	Fabulous	1963	$50
❏ RS 33-899 [M]	Happening!	1966	$35
❏ RS899SD [S]	Happening!	1966	$50
❏ RS 33-875 [M]	Keyboard Kaleidoscope	1964	$35
❏ RS875SD [S]	Keyboard Kaleidoscope	1964	$50
❏ RS924SD	Mirrors	1967	$50
❏ RS938SD	Moog -- The Electric Eclectics of Dick Hyman	1968	$75
❏ RSSD980/2	Organ Antics	1974	$50
❏ RS 33-811 [M]	Provocative Piano	1960	$35
❏ RS811SD [S]	Provocative Piano	1960	$50
❏ RS 33-824 [M]	Provocative Piano Volume 2	1961	$35
❏ RS824SD [S]	Provocative Piano Volume 2	1961	$50
❏ RS933SD	Sweet Sweet Soul	1968	$75
❏ RS946SD [B]	The Age of Electronicus	1969	$40
❏ RS 33-832 [M]	The Dick Hyman Trio	1961	$35
❏ RS832SD [S]	The Dick Hyman Trio	1961	$25
❏ RSSD973/2	The Kaleidoscopic Keyboard	1974	$50
❏ RS 33-891 [M]	The Man from O.R.G.A.N.	1965	$40
❏ RS891SD [S]	The Man from O.R.G.A.N.	1965	$150
❏ RSSD968/2	The Synthesizer	1973	$40
—Reissue of "Electric Eclectics" and "Age of Electronicus			

GRAPEVINE

Number	Title	Yr	NM
❏ 3309	Waltz Dressed in Blue	1978	$30

LION

Number	Title	Yr	NM
❏ L-70067 [M]	Swingin' Double Date	1958	$35

MGM

Number	Title	Yr	NM
❏ E-3535 [M]	60 Great All-Time Songs, Vol. 1	1957	$50
—Yellow label			
❏ E-3536 [M]	60 Great All-Time Songs, Vol. 2	1957	$50
—Yellow label			
❏ E-3537 [M]	60 Great All-Time Songs, Vol. 3	1957	$50
—Yellow label			
❏ E-3586 [M]	60 Great All-Time Songs, Vol. 4	1958	$50
—Yellow label			
❏ E-3587 [M]	60 Great All-Time Songs, Vol. 5	1958	$50
—Yellow label			

Number	Title	Yr	NM
❏ E-3588 [M]	60 Great All-Time Songs, Vol. 6	1958	$50
— Yellow label			
❏ E-3726 [M]	60 Great Continental and Classical Favorites	1959	$50
❏ E-3725 [M]	60 Great Songs from Broadway Musicals	1959	$50
— Yellow label			
❏ E-3724 [M]	60 Great Songs That Say "I Love You	1959	$50
— Yellow label			
❏ E-3821 [M]	After Six	1960	$50
❏ SE-3821 [S]	After Six	1960	$75
❏ E-3379 [M]	Behind a Shady Nook	1956	$75
— Yellow label			
❏ E-3606 [M]	Dick Hyman and Harpsichord in Hi-Fi	1958	$50
— Yellow label			
❏ E-3642 [M]	Gigi	1958	$50
— Yellow label			
❏ E-3494 [M]	Hi-Fi Suite	1957	$75
— Yellow label			
❏ E-4119 [M]	Moon Gas	1963	$50
❏ SE-4119 [S]	Moon Gas	1963	$75
❏ E-3483 [M]	Red Sails in the Sunset	1957	$75
— Yellow label			
❏ E-3553 [M]	Rockin' Sax and Rollin' Organ	1958	$75
— Yellow label			
❏ SE-4649	Space Reflex	1969	$35
❏ E-3808 [M]	Strictly Organic	1960	$50
❏ SE-3808 [S]	Strictly Organic	1960	$75
❏ E-3280 [M]	The Dick Hyman Trio Swings	1954	$75
— Yellow label			
❏ E-3329 [M]	The "Unforgettable" Sound of the Dick Hyman Trio	1955	$85
— Yellow label			
❏ E-289 [10]	The "Unforgettable" Sound of the Dick Hyman Trio	1955	$50
❏ E-3747 [M]	Whoop-Up!	1959	$50
— Yellow label			
❏ SE-3747 [S]	Whoop-Up!	1959	$75
MONMOUTH-EVERGREEN			
❏ MES7065	Genius at Play	1974	$35
MUSICAL HERITAGE SOCIETY			
❏ MHS912213K	Face the Music: Irving Berlin	198?	$25
PROJECT 3			
❏ PR5057SD	Fantomfingers	1971	$75
❏ PR5070SD	Piano Solos	1972	$35
❏ PR5054SD	The Sensuous Piano of "D	1970	$35
❏ PR5080SD	Traditional Jazz Piano	1973	$35
RCA VICTOR GOLD SEAL			
❏ AGL1-3651	Scott Joplin: 16 Classic Rags	1980	$20
— Reissue			
RCA VICTOR RED SEAL			
❏ XRL1-4746	Kitten on the Keys: Music of Zez Confrey	1983	$25
❏ ARL1-1257	Scott Joplin: 16 Classic Rags	1976	$25
REFERENCE RECORDINGS			
❏ RR-33	Dick Hyman Plays Fats Waller	1991	$75
SEAGULL			
❏ LG-8209	Love Story	198?	$25
STOMP OFF			
❏ SOS-1141	Gulf Coast Blues: The Music of Clarence Williams	1987	$25
SUNSET			
❏ SUM-1140 [M]	I'll Never Be the Same	1966	$30
❏ SUS-5140 [S]	I'll Never Be the Same	1966	$35

I

IAN, JANIS

ANALOGUE PRODUCTIONS

Number	Title	Yr	NM
❏ AAP 027	Breaking Silence	1995	$30
— Audiophile vinyl			
CAPITOL			
❏ SKAO-683	Present Company	1971	$18
❏ SN-683	Present Company	1975	$12
COLUMBIA			
❏ PC33919	Aftertones	1976	$12
— No bar code on cover			
❏ PCQ33919 [Q]	Aftertones	1976	$20
❏ PC33919	Aftertones	1979	$10
— With bar code on cover			
❏ PC33394	Between the Lines	1975	$12
— No bar code on cover			
❏ PCQ33394 [Q]	Between the Lines	1975	$20
❏ PC33394 [B]	Between the Lines	1979	$10
— With bar code on cover			

Number	Title	Yr	NM
❏ JC35325	Janis Ian	1978	$12
❏ JC34440	Miracle Row	1977	$12
❏ JC36139	Night Rains	1979	$12
❏ PC36139	Night Rains	198?	$10
❏ FC37360	Restless Eyes	1981	$12
❏ KC32857	Stars	1974	$12
❏ PC32857 [B]	Stars	197?	$10
MGM			
❏ GAS-121	Janis Ian (Golden Archive Series)	1970	$30
POLYDOR			
❏ PD-6058	Janis Ian	1976	$12
VERVE			
❏ V/VS-5027	Janis Ian	1967	$0
— Scheduled, possibly not released; same LP is Verve Forecast 3017			
VERVE FOLKWAYS			
❏ FT-3017 [M]	Janis Ian	1967	$35
❏ FTS-3017 [S]	Janis Ian	1967	$35
VERVE FORECAST			
❏ FT-3024 [M]	For All the Seasons of Your Mind	1967	$50
❏ FTS-3024 [S]	For All the Seasons of Your Mind	1967	$18
❏ FT-3017 [M]	Janis Ian	1967	$30
❏ FTS-3017 [S]	Janis Ian	1967	$18
❏ FTS-3048	The Secret Life of J. Eddy Fink	1968	$18
❏ FTS-3063	Who Really Cares?	1969	$18

IAN AND SYLVIA

Number	Title	Yr	NM
AMPEX			
❏ A-10103	Great Speckled Bird	1970	$25
COLUMBIA			
❏ C30736	Ian and Sylvia	1971	$15
❏ G32516	The Best of Ian and Sylvia	1973	$18
❏ KC31337	You Were On My Mind	1972	$15
MGM			
❏ SE-4550 [S]	Full Circle	1968	$25
❏ E-4550 [M]	Full Circle	1968	$50
— Mono is yellow label promo only; cover has "DJ Monaural" sticker on front			
❏ GAS-115	Ian and Sylvia (Golden Archive Series)	1970	$18
❏ E-4388 [M]	Lovin' Sound	1967	$40
❏ SE-4388 [S]	Lovin' Sound	1967	$18
VANGUARD			
❏ VRS-9175 [M]	Early Morning Rain	1965	$30
❏ VSD-79175 [S]	Early Morning Rain	1965	$35
❏ VRS-9133 [M]	Four Strong Winds	1963	$25
❏ VSD-2149 [S]	Four Strong Winds	1963	$30
❏ VSD-73114	Greatest Hits	1985	$12
❏ VRS-9109 [M]	Ian and Sylvia	1963	$30
❏ VSD-2113 [S]	Ian and Sylvia	1963	$30
❏ VSD-5/6	Ian and Sylvia's Greatest Hits	1969	$18
❏ VSD-23/24	Ian and Sylvia's Greatest Hits, Vol. 2	1970	$18
❏ VSD-79284	Nashville	1968	$18
❏ VRS-9154 [M]	Northern Journey	1964	$25
❏ VSD-79154 [S]	Northern Journey	1964	$30
❏ VRS-9215 [M]	Play One More	1966	$25
❏ VSD-79215 [S]	Play One More	1966	$30
❏ VRS-9241 [M]	So Much for Dreaming	1967	$25
❏ VSD-79241 [S]	So Much for Dreaming	1967	$30
❏ VSD-79269	The Best of Ian & Sylvia	1968	$18

IAN AND THE ZODIACS

PHILIPS

Number	Title	Yr	NM
❏ PHM200176 [M]	Ian and the Zodiacs	1965	$40
❏ PHS600176 [S]	Ian and the Zodiacs	1965	$50

IBRAHIM, ABDULLAH

Originally recorded as "Dollar Brand," which is the name on these records.
Pianist, male singer, cellist, flutist and soprano saxophone player.
Originally recorded under the name "Dollar Brand"; those albums are also listed below.

Number	Title	Yr	NM
BLACKHAWK			
❏ BKH-50207	Water from an Ancient Well	1986	$25
BLACK LION			
❏ 192	This Is Dollar Brand	197?	$30
CHIAROSCURO			
❏ 2004	Cape Town Fringe	197?	$30
❏ 187	Journey	1978	$30
❏ 2012	Soweto	197?	$30
DENON			
❏ 7537	Anthems for the New Nations	1978	$30
ELEKTRA			
❏ 6E-252	African Marketplace	1980	$25
ENJA			
❏ R1-79617	African River	1990	$35
❏ 2026	African Sketchbook	197?	$35
❏ 2032	African Space Program	197?	$35
❏ 2048	Good News from Africa	1976	$35
❏ R1-79601	Mindif (Original Soundtrack Recording for the Film "Chocolat")	1989	$35
INNER CITY			
❏ IC-3003	Children of Africa	197?	$30
❏ IC-6049	Ode to Duke Ellington	198?	$25
❏ IC-3031	Tears and Laughter	1979	$30
REPRISE			
❏ R-6111 [M]	Duke Ellington Presents the Dollar Brand Trio	1965	$25
❏ RS-6111 [S]	Duke Ellington Presents the Dollar Brand Trio	1965	$30
SACKVILLE			
❏ 3009	African Portraits	198?	$25
WEST 54			
❏ 8011	Memories	1979	$30

ICE-T

Number	Title	Yr	NM
ATOMIC POP			
❏ AP 0011	Greatest Hits: The Evidence	2000	$25
RHYME SYNDICATE			
❏ 53858 [B]	Home Invasion	1993	$25
SIRE			
❏ PRO-A-4959 [DJ]	O.G. Original Gangster	1991	$30
— Promo-only radio-ready version of album otherwise unavailable on U.S. vinyl			
❏ 25765	Power	1988	$18
❏ 25602	Rhyme Pays	1987	$18
❏ 26028	The Iceberg/Freedom of Speech...Just Watch What You Say	1989	$18

ICE CUBE

Number	Title	Yr	NM
BEST SIDE			
❏ 50700	War & Peace Vol. 1 (The War Disc)	1998	$18
❏ 50015	War & Peace Vol. 2 (The Peace Disc)	2000	$18
PRIORITY			
❏ 57120	AmeriKKKa's Most Wanted	1990	$18
❏ P1-53921	Bootlegs & B-Sides	1994	$18
❏ 57155	Death Certificate	1991	$18
❏ 29091	Greatest Hits	2001	$18
❏ 7230 [EP]	Kill at Will	1990	$15
❏ P1-53876	Lethal Injection	1993	$18
❏ 57185	The Predator	1992	$18

ICEHOUSE

Number	Title	Yr	NM
CHRYSALIS			
❏ 5V41436 [EP]	Fresco	1983	$12
— Five-track LP, with same songs on both sides			
❏ R100935	Great Southern Land	1989	$18
— BMG Direct Marketing edition			
❏ F1-21680	Great Southern Land	1989	$18
❏ CHR1350	Icehouse	1981	$15
❏ FV41350	Icehouse	1983	$10
— Reissue of CHS 1350			
❏ R143633	Man of Colours	1987	$15
— BMG Direct Marketing edition			
❏ OV41592	Man of Colours	1987	$12
❏ R144571	Measure for Measure	1986	$15
— RCA Music Service edition			
❏ BFV41527	Measure for Measure	1986	$12
❏ CHR1390	Primitive Man	1982	$15
❏ FV41390	Primitive Man	1983	$12
— Reissue of CHR 1390			
❏ PV41390	Primitive Man	198?	$10
— Reissue with new prefix			
❏ FV41458	Sidewalk	1983	$12

ICICLE WORKS

Number	Title	Yr	NM
ARISTA			
❏ AL6-8202	Icicle Works	1984	$12

Number	Title	Yr	NM

BEGGARS BANQUET
| ❏ 6447-1-H | If You Want to Defeat Your Enemy, Sing His Song | 1987 | $15 |

ID, THE
Two different groups.

AURA
| ❏ 1000 | Where Are We Going? | 1976 | $50 |

RCA VICTOR
| ❏ LPM-3805 [M] | The Inner Sounds of the Id | 1967 | $75 |
| ❏ LSP-3805 [S] | The Inner Sounds of the Id | 1967 | $40 |

IDES OF MARCH, THE

RCA VICTOR
| ❏ APL1-0143 | Midnight Oil | 1973 | $18 |
| ❏ LSP-4812 [B] | World Woven | 1972 | $18 |

SUNDAZED
| ❏ LP-5032 | Ideology | 199? | $15 |

WARNER BROS.
❏ WS1896	Common Bond	1971	$18
❏ WS1863	Vehicle	1970	$25
— Green "W7" label			
❏ WS1863 [B]	Vehicle	1970	$25
— Green "WB" label			

IDLE RACE, THE
Jeff Lynne, later of THE MOVE and ELECTRIC LIGHT ORCHESTRA, was in this group.

LIBERTY
| ❏ LST-7603 [B] | Birthday Party | 1969 | $50 |
| ❏ LST7603 [B] | Birthday Party | 1969 | $75 |

PARLOPHONE
| ❏ 825646335374 [B] | The Birthday Party | 2014 | $40 |

IDOL, BILLY
Also see GENERATION X.

CHRYSALIS
❏ R104806	Billy Idol	1982	$15
— RCA Music Service edition			
❏ CHR1377	Billy Idol	1982	$15
❏ FV41377	Billy Idol	1983	$12
— Reissue of Chrysalis CHR 1377			
❏ VAS2610 [DJ]	Billy Idol Interview	1983	$30
❏ R162264	Charmed Life	1990	$14
— BMG Direct Marketing edition			

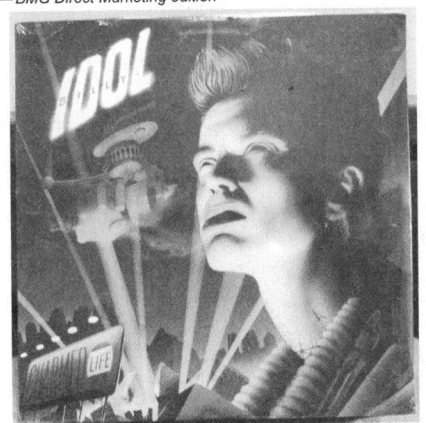

❏ F1-21735 [B]	Charmed Life	1990	$15
❏ R153899 [B]	Don't Stop	1981	$15
— RCA Music Service edition			
❏ CEP4000 [EP]	Don't Stop	1981	$15
❏ 5V44000 [EP]	Don't Stop	1983	$10
— Reissue of CEP 4000			
❏ PV44000 [EP]	Don't Stop	198?	$10
— Reissue with new prefix			
❏ R124674	Rebel Yell	1984	$15
— RCA Music Service edition			
❏ FV41450	Rebel Yell	1983	$12
❏ R154038	Vital Idol	1987	$15
— BMG Direct Marketing edition			
❏ OV41620	Vital Idol	1987	$12
❏ R154108	Whiplash Smile	1986	$15
— RCA Music Service edition			
❏ OV41514	Whiplash Smile	1986	$12

IF

CAPITOL
❏ ST-539 [B]	If	1970	$18
❏ SW-676	If2	1971	$18
❏ SMAS-820	If3	1971	$18
❏ ST-11299 [B]	Not Just Another Bunch of Pretty Faces	1974	$18
❏ ST-11344	Tea Break Over -- Back On Your 'Eads!	1974	$15

METROMEDIA
| ❏ BML1-0174 | Double Diamond | 1973 | $15 |
| ❏ KMD-1057 | Waterfall | 1972 | $15 |

IFIELD, FRANK

CAPITOL
| ❏ T10356 [M] | I'm Confessin' | 1963 | $25 |
| ❏ ST10356 [S] | I'm Confessin' | 1963 | $30 |

HICKORY
❏ LPM-136 [M]	Tale of Two Cities	1967	$18
❏ LPS-136 [S]	Tale of Two Cities	1967	$25
❏ LPM-132 [M]	The Best of Frank Ifield	1966	$25
❏ LPS-132 [P]	The Best of Frank Ifield	1966	$25
❏ T-90753 [M]	The Best of Frank Ifield	1966	$30
— Capitol Record Club edition			
❏ ST-90753 [S]	The Best of Frank Ifield	1966	$30
— Capitol Record Club edition			

VEE JAY
| ❏ LP1054 [M] | I Remember You | 1962 | $30 |
| ❏ SR1054 [S] | I Remember You | 1962 | $50 |

IGGY AND THE STOOGES
Also see IGGY POP.

BOMP!
| ❏ 1018 [B] | Kill City | 1978 | $430 |
| *— By "Iggy Pop and James Williamson"* | | | |

CLEOPATRA
❏ 8614 [B]	I Wanna Be Your Dog		$30
— picture disc			
❏ 4588 [B]	I Wanna be Your Dog		$25
❏ 9051 [B]	Jesus Loves The Stooges		$25
❏ 3687 [B]	More Power		$25

COLUMBIA
❏ KC32111 [B]	Raw Power	1973	$150
❏ 88691959351 [B]	Raw Power	2012	$40
— double album includes original mix and later Iggy remix			

IMPORT/BOMP!
❏ 1018 [B]	Kill City	1978	$50
— By "Iggy Pop and James Williamson"; original issue on green vinyl			
❏ 1015	Metallic K.O.	1977	$40

SUNDAZED
| ❏ LP5149 | The Stooges | 2002 | $20 |
| *— By "The Stooges"; reissue on 180-gram vinyl* | | | |

IGGY POP
Also see IGGY AND THE STOOGES.

4 MEN WITH BEARDS
| ❏ 4M525LP [B] | Lust For Life | | $25 |
| ❏ 4M524LP [B] | The Idiot | | $25 |

A&M
❏ R134099	Blah Blah Blah	1986	$15
— RCA Music Service edition			
❏ SP-5145 [B]	Blah Blah Blah	1986	$12
❏ SP-5198	Instinct	1988	$12
❏ SP-17641 [DJ]	Live at the Channel 7/19/88	1988	$40
— Numbered, rubber-stamped promo-only edition			

ANIMAL
❏ 6000 [B]	Zombie Birdhouse	1982	$18
❏ FV41399	Zombie Birdhouse	1983	$10
— Reissue			

ARISTA
❏ AL4237 [B]	New Values	1979	$30
❏ AL9572 [B]	Party	1981	$18
❏ AL5-8189	Party	198?	$10
— Reissue			
❏ AB4259 [B]	Soldier	1980	$25
❏ AL5-8172	Soldier	198?	$10
— Reissue			
❏ SP-115 [EP]	Special Rock Club Versions	1981	$25
— Promo-only remixes of 4 songs from the "Party" LP			

CLEOPATRA
| ❏ 3738 [B] | Iggy & Ziggy - Cleveland '77 | | $25 |

LOMA VISTA
| ❏ LVR3908801 [B] | Post Pop Depression | 2016 | $30 |

PAIR
| ❏ PDL2-1051 | Iggy Pop | 1986 | $15 |
| *— Compilation of RCA Victor material* | | | |

RCA VICTOR
❏ AFL1-4957	Choice Cuts	1984	$18
❏ AFL1-2488 [B]	Lust for Life	1977	$40
❏ APL1-2275 [B]	The Idiot	1977	$40
❏ AFL1-2796 [B]	TV Eye -- 1977 Live	1978	$35

SUNDAZED
❏ LP5039	New Values	200?	$15
— Reissue on 180-gram vinyl			
❏ LP5041	Soldier	200?	$15
— Reissue on 180-gram vinyl			

VIRGIN
| ❏ 91381 | Brick by Brick | 1990 | $14 |

IGLESIAS, JULIO

COLUMBIA
| ❏ FC38640 | Julio | 1984 | $10 |

IKETTES, THE

MODERN
| ❏ M-102 [M] | Soul Hits | 1965 | $50 |
| ❏ MST-102 [S] | Soul Hits | 1965 | $40 |

UNITED ARTISTS
| ❏ UA-LA190-F [B] | (G)Old and New | 1973 | $15 |

ILL WIND, THE

ABC
| ❏ S-641 [B] | Flashes | 1968 | $150 |

ILLINOIS SPEED PRESS, THE

COLUMBIA
| ❏ CS9976 | Duet | 1970 | $18 |
| ❏ CS9792 | The Illinois Speed Press | 1969 | $18 |

ILLUSION, THE

STEED
❏ ST-37006	If It's So	1970	$18
❏ ST-37003	The Illusion	1969	$25
❏ ST-37005	Together (As a Way of Life)	1969	$18

ILLUSTRATION

JANUS
| ❏ JLP-3010 [B] | Illustration | 1969 | $30 |

ILMO SMOKEHOUSE

BEAUTIFUL SOUND
| ❏ 3002 [B] | Ilmo Smokehouse | 1971 | $50 |

ROULETTE
| ❏ RS-3002 | Ilmo Smokehouse | 1971 | $25 |

ILORI, SOLOMON

BLUE NOTE
❏ BLP-4136 [M]	African High Life	1963	$150
❏ BST-84136 [S]	African High Life	1963	$100
— With "New York, USA" address on label			
❏ BST-84136 [S]	African High Life	1967	$30
— With "A Division of Liberty Records" on label			

IMAGINATIONS, THE (1)

RELIC
| ❏ LP-5058 | The Imaginations (1961-1962) | 198? | $12 |

IMPACS, THE

KING
❏ 916 [M]	A Weekend with the Impacs	1964	$250
❏ KS-916 [S]	A Weekend with the Impacs	1964	$300
❏ 886 [M]	Impact!	1964	$250
❏ KS-886 [S]	Impact!	1964	$300

IMPACTS, THE

DEL-FI
❏ DFLP-1234 [M]	Wipe Out	1963	$75
❏ DFS-1234 [S]	Wipe Out	1963	$100
❏ DLF-1234 [B]	Wipe Out	199?	$15
— Reissue with bar code			

IMPALA SYNDROME, THE

PARALLAX
| ❏ 4002 [B] | The Impala Syndrome | 1970 | $175 |

IMPALAS, THE

CUB
| ❏ 8003 [M] | Sorry (I Ran All the Way Home) | 1959 | $400 |
| ❏ S-8003 [S] | Sorry (I Ran All the Way Home) | 1959 | $600 |

IMPERIALS, THE

DAYSPRING
| ❏ DST-4020 | Christmas with the Imperials | 1980 | $15 |

WORD
| ❏ 8237 | Christmas with the Imperials | 198? | $12 |
| *— Reissue of Dayspring LP* | | | |

IMPRESSIONS, THE
Also see JERRY BUTLER; CURTIS MAYFIELD.

ABC
❏ S-727	16 Greatest Hits	1971	$15
❏ D-780	Curtis Mayfield/His Early Years with the Impressions	1973	$25
❏ S-654	The Best of the Impressions	1968	$18
❏ ST-91540	The Best of the Impressions	1968	$25
— Capitol Record Club edition			
❏ 606 [M]	The Fabulous Impressions	1967	$40
❏ S-606 [S]	The Fabulous Impressions	1967	$30
❏ S-668 [B]	The Versatile Impressions	1969	$18

Number	Title	Yr	NM
❏ S-635	We're a Winner	1968	$18

ABC-PARAMOUNT

Number	Title	Yr	NM
❏ 493 [M]	Keep On Pushing	1964	$30
❏ S-493 [S]	Keep On Pushing	1964	$40
❏ ST-90106 [S]	Keep On Pushing	1965	$50
— Capitol Record Club edition			
❏ 523 [M]	One By One	1965	$25
❏ S-523 [S]	One By One	1965	$30
❏ T-90520 [M]	One By One	1965	$30
— Capitol Record Club edition			
❏ ST-90520 [S]	One By One	1965	$30
— Capitol Record Club edition			
❏ 505 [M]	People Get Ready	1965	$30
❏ S-505 [S]	People Get Ready	1965	$40
❏ ST-90097 [S]	People Get Ready	1965	$50
— Capitol Record Club edition			
❏ 545 [M]	Ridin' High	1966	$25
❏ S-545 [S]	Ridin' High	1966	$30
❏ 450 [M]	The Impressions	1963	$30
❏ S-450 [S]	The Impressions	1963	$40
❏ T-90472 [M]	The Impressions	1965	$40
— Capitol Record Club edition			
❏ 515 [M]	The Impressions' Greatest Hits	1965	$25
❏ S-515 [S]	The Impressions' Greatest Hits	1965	$30
❏ 468 [M]	The Never Ending Impressions	1964	$30
❏ S-468 [S]	The Never Ending Impressions	1964	$40
❏ ST-90492 [S]	The Never Ending Impressions	1965	$50
— Capitol Record Club edition			

CHI-SOUND

Number	Title	Yr	NM
❏ T-596	Come to My Party	1979	$12
❏ T-624	Fan the Fire	1981	$12

COTILLION

Number	Title	Yr	NM
❏ SD9912	It's About Time	1976	$15

CURTOM

Number	Title	Yr	NM
❏ CRS-8004	Best Impressions -- Curtis, Sam, Dave	1969	$18
❏ CRS-8006	Check Out Your Mind	1970	$18
❏ CRS-8019	Finally Got Myself Together	1974	$18
❏ CU5003	First Impressions	1975	$15
❏ CUR-2006	Lasting Impressions	198?	$12
❏ CU5009	Loving Power	1976	$15
❏ CRS-8016	Preacher Man	1973	$18
❏ CRS-8003	The Young Mods' Forgotten Story	1969	$18
❏ CRS-8001	This Is My Country	1968	$18
❏ CRS-8012	Times Have Changed	1972	$18

LOST-NITE

Number	Title	Yr	NM
❏ LLP-22 [10]	Jerry Butler and the Impressions	1981	$18
— Red vinyl			

MCA

Number	Title	Yr	NM
❏ 5373	In the Heat of the Night	1982	$12
❏ 1500	The Impressions Greatest Hits	1982	$10

PICKWICK

Number	Title	Yr	NM
❏ SPC-3602	The Impressions	1978	$10

SCEPTER CITATION

Number	Title	Yr	NM
❏ CTN-18018	The Best of Curtis Mayfield and the Impressions	1972	$12

SIRE

Number	Title	Yr	NM
❏ SASH-3717	The Vintage Years	1977	$18
— Includes solo hits by Jerry Butler and Curtis Mayfield			

IMPROVISATION CHAMBER ENSEMBLE

RCA VICTOR RED SEAL

Number	Title	Yr	NM
❏ LSC-2558 [S]	Studies in Improvisation	1961	$30
— Original with "shaded dog" label			

IMUS, DON

BANG

Number	Title	Yr	NM
❏ 407	This Honky's Nuts	1974	$30

RCA VICTOR

Number	Title	Yr	NM
❏ LSP-4699	1200 Hamburgers to Go	1972	$30
— As "Imus in the Morning"			
❏ LSP-4819	One Sacred Chicken to Go	1973	$30

IN-SECT, THE

RCA CAMDEN

Number	Title	Yr	NM
❏ CAL-909 [M]	Introducing the In-Sect Direct from England	1964	$40
❏ CAS-909 [S]	Introducing the In-Sect Direct from England	1964	$50

IN GROUP, THE

IN

Number	Title	Yr	NM
❏ I-1002 [M]	Swinging 12 String	1964	$25
❏ IS-1002 [S]	Swinging 12 String	1964	$30

IN PURSUIT

MTM

Number	Title	Yr	NM
❏ ST-71057	Standing in Your Shadow	1986	$12

Number	Title	Yr	NM
❏ MLP-72150 [EP]	When Darkness Falls	1986	$10

INCREDIBLE BONGO BAND, THE

PRIDE

Number	Title	Yr	NM
❏ 028	Bongo Rock	1973	$100
— Note: This album has been reissued to look like the original			
❏ 6010	The Return of the Incredible Bongo Band	1974	$25

INCREDIBLE STRING BAND, THE

4 MEN WITH BEARDS

Number	Title	Yr	NM
❏ 4M210LP [B]	The Big Huge		$25
❏ 4M209LP [B]	Wee Tam		$25

CARTHAGE

Number	Title	Yr	NM
❏ CGLP-4421	The Hangman's Beautiful Daughter	198?	$15

ELEKTRA

Number	Title	Yr	NM
❏ EKS-74057 [B]	Changing Horses	1969	$30
— Red label, large stylized "E"			
❏ EKS-74057	Changing Horses	1971	$15
— Butterfly label			
❏ EKS-74061 [B]	I Looked Up	1970	$30
— Red label, large stylized "E"			
❏ EKS-74061	I Looked Up	1971	$15
— Butterfly label			
❏ EKS-74112 [B]	Liquid Acrobat As Regards the Air	1972	$30
— Butterfly label			
❏ 7E-2004 [B]	Relics of the Incredible String Band	1971	$30
— Butterfly label			
❏ EKM-4010 [M]	The 5,000 Spirits	1967	$150
❏ EKS-74010 [S]	The 5,000 Spirits	1967	$30
— Brown label			
❏ EKS-74010	The 5,000 Spirits	1969	$18
— Red label, large stylized "E"			
❏ EKS-74010 [B]	The 5,000 Spirits	1971	$18
— Butterfly label			
❏ EKS-74037 [B]	The Big Huge	1969	$30
— Brown label			
❏ EKS-74037	The Big Huge	1969	$18
— Red label, large stylized "E"			
❏ EKS-74037	The Big Huge	1971	$15
— Butterfly label			
❏ EKS-74021 [B]	The Hangman's Beautiful Daughter	1968	$30
— Brown label			
❏ EKS-74021	The Hangman's Beautiful Daughter	1969	$18
— Red label, large stylized "E"			
❏ EKS-74021	The Hangman's Beautiful Daughter	1971	$15
— Butterfly label			
❏ EKM-322 [M]	The Incredible String Band	1967	$30
❏ EKS-7322 [S]	The Incredible String Band	1967	$25
— Brown label			
❏ EKS-7322	The Incredible String Band	1969	$18
— Red label, large stylized "E"			
❏ EKS-7322	The Incredible String Band	1971	$15
— Butterfly label			
❏ 7E-2002	'U'	1971	$30
— Butterfly label			
❏ EKS-74036 [B]	Wee Tam	1969	$30
— Brown label			
❏ EKS-74036	Wee Tam	1969	$18
— Red label, large stylized "E"			
❏ EKS-74036	Wee Tam	1971	$15
— Butterfly label			

REPRISE

Number	Title	Yr	NM
❏ MS2122 [B]	Earthspan	1973	$18
❏ MS2198 [B]	Hard Rope and Silver Twine	1974	$18
❏ MS2139 [B]	No Ruinous Feud	1973	$18

SUNDAZED

Number	Title	Yr	NM
❏ LP5128 [S]	The 5,000 Spirits	2003	$15
— Reissue on 180-gram vinyl			
❏ LP5129 [S]	The Hangman's Beautiful Daughter	2003	$15
— Reissue on 180-gram vinyl			
❏ LP5127 [S]	The Incredible String Band	2003	$15
— Reissue on 180-gram vinyl			

INCREDIBLES, THE

AUDIO ARTS

Number	Title	Yr	NM
❏ AAS-7000	Heart and Soul	1970	$25

IND, PETER

WAVE

Number	Title	Yr	NM
❏ W-1 [M]	Looking Out	1961	$30
❏ WS-1 [S]	Looking Out	1961	$30

INDEEP

BECKET

Number	Title	Yr	NM
❏ BKS-016	Pajama Party Time	1984	$15

SOUND OF NEW YORK

Number	Title	Yr	NM
❏ SNY-1201	Last Night a D.J. Saved My Life	1983	$15

INDEPENDENTS, THE

WAND

Number	Title	Yr	NM
❏ WDS-699	Discs of Gold	1974	$25
❏ WDS-694	The First Time We Met	1973	$25
❏ WDS-696	The Independents	1973	$25

INDEX

DC

Number	Title	Yr	NM
❏ 71	The Index	1968	$3000
— Black label; issued with black and white jacket; number is from deal wax; VG value 1500; VG+ value 2250			
❏ 4736	The Index	1968	$2000
— Red label; issued with generic white jacket, though sometimes found in first LP's jacket; number in dead wax; VG value 1000; VG+ value 1500			

INDIA.ARIE

MOTOWN

Number	Title	Yr	NM
❏ 440 013770-1	Acoustic Soul	2001	$18

INDIAN SUMMER

RCA/NEON

Number	Title	Yr	NM
❏ NE-3	Indian Summer	1971	$30

INDIGO GIRLS

DRAGON PATH

Number	Title	Yr	NM
❏ 0LMM-I [EP]	Indigo Girls	1986	$250
— Blue or clear vinyl (each of equal value)			
❏ 0LMM-I [EP]	Indigo Girls	1986	$175
— Black vinyl			

EPIC

Number	Title	Yr	NM
❏ FE45044	Indigo Girls	1989	$18
❏ EAS4020 [DJ]	Indigo Girls Live	1991	$40
— Promo-only version of "Back on the Bus Y'All"			
❏ EAS1481 [EP]	Indigo Girls Sampler	1989	$18
— Promo-only item with tour-dates sticker on white cardboard cover; includes Kid Fears/Closer to Fine/Center Stage/Prince of Darkness			
❏ EAS1861 [EP]	Land of Canaan Plus Five Live	1989	$30
— Promo-only item with five live tracks on B-side			
❏ E46820	Nomads*Indians*Saints	1990	$25
❏ EAS2201 [DJ]	Shades of Indigo: An Interview by Shawn Colvin	1990	$80
❏ FE45427	Strange Fire	1989	$18
— Reissue of Indigo release			
❏ E57621	Swamp Ophelia	1994	$40
— Black vinyl; all copies autographed on the label by the Indigo Girls			
❏ E57621	Swamp Ophelia	1994	$40
— Green vinyl; all copies autographed on the label by the Indigo Girls			

INDIGO

Number	Title	Yr	NM
❏ 0LMM-II	Strange Fire	1987	$175
— Black vinyl			
❏ 0LMM-II	Strange Fire	1987	$250
— Blue, clear or red vinyl (each of equal value)			

INFLUENCE

ABC

Number	Title	Yr	NM
❏ ABCS-630	Influence	1968	$30

INGMANN, JORGEN

ATCO

Number	Title	Yr	NM
❏ 33-130 [M]	Apache	1961	$40
❏ 33-139 [M]	The Many Guitars of Jorgen Ingmann	1962	$40

MERCURY

Number	Title	Yr	NM
❏ MG-20200 [M]	Swinging Guitar	1956	$75
❏ MG-20292 [M]	Swing Softly	1956	$75

UNITED ARTISTS

Number	Title	Yr	NM
❏ UAS-6785	El Condor Pasa	1970	$25

INGRAM, JAMES

QWEST

Number	Title	Yr	NM
❏ 23970	It's Your Night	1983	$10
❏ 23970 [DJ]	It's Your Night	1983	$18
— Promo version on "Quiex II" vinyl			
❏ 25424	Never Felt So Good	1986	$10

WARNER BROS.

Number	Title	Yr	NM
❏ 25924	It's Real	1989	$15

INGRAM, LUTHER

KOKO

Number	Title	Yr	NM
❏ KOS-2202	If Loving You Is Wrong I Don't Want to Be Right	1972	$18
❏ KOS-2201	I've Been Here All the Time	1971	$18

Number	Title	Yr	NM

INK SPOTS

COLORTONE
❏ 4901 [M]	The Ink Spots	1958	$75
❏ 4947 [M]	The Ink Spots, Vol. 2	1959	$75

CROWN
❏ CLP5221 [M]	More Ink Spots	196?	$18
❏ CLP-5142 [M]	The Ink Spots	1961	$25
❏ CST-175 [S]	The Ink Spots	1961	$30
—Black vinyl			
❏ CST-175 [S]	The Ink Spots	1961	$50
—Red vinyl			
❏ CLP-5112 [M]	The Ink Spots' Greatest Hits	1959	$25
❏ CST-144 [S]	The Ink Spots' Greatest Hits	1959	$30
—Black vinyl			
❏ CST-144 [S]	The Ink Spots' Greatest Hits	1959	$50
—Red vinyl			
❏ CLP-5187 [M]	The Sensational Ink Spots	1962	$25
❏ CST-217 [S]	The Sensational Ink Spots	1962	$30
—Black vinyl			
❏ CST-217 [S]	The Sensational Ink Spots	1962	$50
—Red vinyl			

DECCA
❏ DL4297 [M]	Our Golden Favorites	1962	$30
❏ DL74297 [S]	Our Golden Favorites	1962	$25
❏ DL5333 [10]	Precious Memories	1951	$50
❏ DL5541 [10]	Street of Dreams	1954	$50
❏ DL8154 [M]	The Best of the Ink Spots	1955	$40
—Black label, silver print			
❏ DXB182 [M]	The Best of the Ink Spots	1965	$30
❏ DXSB7182 [P]	The Best of the Ink Spots	1965	$25
❏ DL5056 [10]	The Ink Spots	1950	$50
❏ DL5071 [10]	The Ink Spots, Vol. 2	1950	$50
❏ DL8232 [M]	Time Our for Tears	1956	$40
—Black label, silver print			
❏ DL8768 [M]	Torch Time	1958	$40
—Black label, silver print			

EVEREST ARCHIVE OF FOLK & JAZZ
| ❏ 350 | The Ink Spots in London | 197? | $12 |

GOLDEN TONE
| ❏ C4037 | Ink Spots Vol. II | 195? | $15 |
| ❏ C4024 | The Fabulous Ink Spots | 195? | $15 |

GRAND AWARD
❏ GA 33-328 [M]	The Ink Spots' Greatest, Volume 1	1958	$30
❏ GA 33-354 [M]	The Ink Spots' Greatest, Volume 2	1958	$30
❏ GA 33-396 [M]	The Ink Spots' Greatest, Volume 3	1959	$30
❏ GA232SD [S]	The Ink Spots' Greatest, Volume 3	1959	$40

KING
❏ 5001	18 Hits by the Ink Spots	197?	$12
❏ 535 [M]	Something Old, Something New	1956	$400
❏ 642 [M]	Songs That Will Live Forever	1959	$300
—Reissue of 535			

LONGINES SYMPHONETTE
| ❏ SYS5830 | 10 of the Best Ink Spots Hits | 197? | $12 |
| —Label calls this "The Best of the Ink Spots"; also on label is "New Premiun for Mills Bros. V&R Offer | | | |

MCA
| ❏ MSM2-35253 | The Beautiful Music Company Presents the Ink Spots | 1991 | $25 |
| ❏ 4005 | The Best of the Ink Spots | 197? | $15 |

OPEN SKY
| ❏ 3125 | Just Like Old Times | 198? | $12 |

PAULA
| ❏ 2212 | The Ink Spots Sing Country | 1972 | $12 |

RONDO
❏ RS-2010 [S]	The Ink Spots in the Spotlite	1963	$18
—Title on label is "The Ink Spots			
❏ R-2010 [M]	The Ink Spots in the Spotlite	1963	$15

TOPS
| ❏ L-1561 [M] | The Ink Spots | 1957 | $40 |
| ❏ L-1668 [M] | The Ink Spots, Vol. 2 | 1959 | $40 |

VERVE
| ❏ MGV-2124 [M] | The Ink Spots' Favorites | 1959 | $30 |
| ❏ MGVS-6096 [S] | The Ink Spots' Favorites | 1959 | $40 |

VOCALION
❏ VL3725 [M]	Lost in a Dream	1965	$15
❏ VL73725 [R]	Lost in a Dream	1965	$12
❏ VL3606 [M]	Sincerely Yours	196?	$15
❏ VL73606 [R]	Sincerely Yours	196?	$12

WALDORF MUSIC HALL
| ❏ MH 33-144 [10] | Songs of the South Seas | 195? | $100 |
| ❏ MH 33-152 [10] | The Ink Spots Quartet | 195? | $100 |

INMAN, AUTRY

EPIC
| ❏ BN26428 | Ballad of Two Brothers | 1968 | $25 |

JUBILEE
❏ JGM-2056 [M]	New Year's Eve with Autry Inman	1964	$25
❏ JGS-2056 [S]	New Year's Eve with Autry Inman	1964	$30
❏ JGM-2055 [M]	Riscotheque Saturday Night	1964	$25
❏ JGS-2055 [S]	Riscotheque Saturday Night	1964	$30

MOUNTAIN DEW
| ❏ 7022 [M] | Autry Inman | 1963 | $25 |
| ❏ S-7022 [S] | Autry Inman | 1963 | $30 |

SIMS
| ❏ 107 [M] | Autry Inman at the Frontier Club | 1964 | $25 |
| ❏ S-107 [S] | Autry Inman at the Frontier Club | 1964 | $30 |

INMAN, JERRY

COLUMBIA
| ❏ CL2793 [M] | Lennon-McCartney Country Style R.F.D. | 1967 | $30 |
| ❏ CS9593 [S] | Lennon-McCartney Country Style R.F.D. | 1967 | $25 |

ELEKTRA
| ❏ 7E-1068 | You Betchum! | 1976 | $15 |

INMATES, THE

POLYDOR
| ❏ PD1-6241 | First Offence | 1979 | $15 |
| ❏ PD1-6302 | Shot in the Dark | 1980 | $15 |

INNOCENCE, THE
KAMA SUTRA

| ❏ KLP-8059 [M] | The Innocence | 1967 | $25 |
| ❏ KLPS-8059 [S] | The Innocence | 1967 | $30 |

INNOCENT, THE
With Trent Reznor, pre-NINE INCH NAILS.

RED LABEL
| ❏ 7300 [B] | Livin' in the Street | 1985 | $100 |

INNOCENTS, THE

INDIGO
❏ 503 [M]	Inocently Yours	1961	$500
—Plain white cover; promo only			
❏ 503 [M]	Inocently Yours	1961	$100

INSECT TRUST, THE

ATCO
| ❏ SD 33-313 [B] | Hoboken Saturday Night | 1970 | $75 |

CAPITOL
| ❏ SKAO-109 | The Insect Trust | 1968 | $50 |

INSIDE OUT

FREDLO
| ❏ 6834 | Bringing It All Back | 1968 | $250 |

INSTANT COMPOSERS POOL (ICP ORCHESTRA)

ICP
❏ 022	Live Soncino	1980	$30
❏ 020	Tetterettet	1977	$30
❏ 026	The ICP Orchestra Performs Nichols-Monk	1987	$35

INTERNATIONAL JAZZ BAND

GHB
| ❏ 20 | International Jazz Band Volume 1 | 1966 | $35 |
| ❏ 21 | International Jazz Band Volume 2 | 1966 | $35 |

INTERNATIONAL JAZZ GROUP

SWING
| ❏ SW-8407 | International Jazz Group, Volume 1 | 198? | $25 |
| ❏ SW-8416 | International Jazz Group, Volume 2 | 1987 | $25 |

INTERNATIONAL POP ORCHESTRA

CAMEO
❏ C-4001 [M]	An Exciting Evening at Home	1962	$15
❏ SC-4001 [S]	An Exciting Evening at Home	1962	$18
❏ C-2001 [M]	International Pop Orchestra -- 110 Men	1962	$15
❏ SC-2001 [S]	International Pop Orchestra -- 110 Men	1962	$18
❏ SC-1039 [S]	Musical Jewels	1963	$18
❏ C-1039 [M]	Musical Jewels	1963	$15
❏ C-1037 [M]	Songs That Will Live Forever	1963	$15
❏ SC-1037 [S]	Songs That Will Live Forever	1963	$18
❏ SC-2003 [S]	The 12 Greatest Songs Ever Written	1962	$18

WYNCOTE
❏ W-9005 [M]	110 Musicians (Fascination)	1964	$15
❏ SW-9005 [S]	110 Musicians (Fascination)	1964	$18
❏ SW-9185 [S]	110 Musicians Play "That's Life	1967	$15
❏ W-9185 [M]	110 Musicians Play "That's Life	1967	$18
❏ W-9117 [M]	Christmas Favorites	1965	$15
❏ SW-9117 [S]	Christmas Favorites	1965	$18
❏ W-9063 [M]	Cole Porter Favorites	1964	$15
❏ SW-9063 [S]	Cole Porter Favorites	1964	$18
❏ W-9135 [M]	Fascination and Other All-Time Favorites	1966	$15
❏ SW-9135 [S]	Fascination and Other All-Time Favorites	1966	$18
❏ SW-9165 [S]	For Lovers Everywhere	1967	$15
❏ W-9165 [M]	For Lovers Everywhere	1967	$18
❏ SW-9102 [S]	George Gershwin Favorites	1965	$18
❏ W-9102 [M]	George Gershwin Favorites	1965	$15
❏ SW-9090 [S]	Lerner and Loewe Favorites	1965	$18
❏ W-9090 [M]	Lerner and Loewe Favorites	1965	$15
❏ SW-9193 [S]	Let's Fall in Love	1967	$15
❏ W-9193 [M]	Let's Fall in Love	1967	$18
❏ SW-9040 [S]	Love Themes from the Classics	1964	$18
❏ W-9040 [M]	Love Themes from the Classics	1964	$15
❏ SW-9120 [S]	Musical Jewels	1965	$18
❏ W-9120 [M]	Musical Jewels	1965	$15
❏ SW-9123 [S]	Reminiscing	1966	$18
❏ W-9123 [M]	Reminiscing	1966	$15
❏ W-9084 [M]	Rhapsody in Blue/Slaughter on Tenth Avenue	1965	$15
❏ SW-9084 [S]	Rhapsody in Blue/Slaughter on Tenth Avenue	1965	$18
❏ W-9071 [M]	Richard Rodgers Favorites	1964	$15
❏ SW-9071 [S]	Richard Rodgers Favorites	1964	$18
❏ SW-9059 [S]	Stardust	1964	$18
❏ W-9059 [M]	Stardust	1964	$15
❏ SW-9021 [S]	The International Pop Orchestra Plays for Lovers Only	1964	$18
❏ W-9021 [M]	The International Pop Orchestra Plays for Lovers Only	1964	$15
❏ W-9014 [M]	The International Pop Orchestra Visits the World's Fair	1964	$15
❏ SW-9014 [S]	The International Pop Orchestra Visits the World's Fair	1964	$18
❏ SW-9076 [S]	The Sound of Music	1965	$18
❏ W-9076 [M]	The Sound of Music	1965	$15
❏ SW-9124 [S]	When Lights Are Low	1966	$18
❏ W-9124 [M]	When Lights Are Low	1966	$15

INTERNATIONAL SUBMARINE BAND, THE
Also see GRAM PARSONS.

LHI
| ❏ 12001 [B] | Safe at Home | 1968 | $175 |
| —Counterfeits have white labels, legitimate copies have multi-color labels | | | |

RHINO
| ❏ RNLP 069 | Safe at Home | 1985 | $30 |

SUNDAZED
| ❏ LP5112 | Safe at Home | 2001 | $15 |
| —Reissue on 180-gram vinyl | | | |

INTERPRETERS, THE

CADET
| ❏ LP-762 [M] | The Knack | 1966 | $18 |
| ❏ LPS-762 [S] | The Knack | 1966 | $25 |

INTRIGUES, THE

YEW
| ❏ YS-777 | In a Moment | 1970 | $30 |

INTRUDERS, THE (1)

GAMBLE
❏ GS-5004 [B]	Cowboys to Girls	1968	$50
❏ KZ31991	Save the Children	1973	$25
❏ KZ32131	Super Hits	1973	$25
❏ G-5001 [M]	The Intruders Are Together	1967	$40
❏ GS-5001 [S]	The Intruders Are Together	1967	$50
❏ GS-5005	The Intruders Greatest Hits	1969	$40

Number	Title	Yr	NM
❑ GS-5008	When We Get Married	1970	$50
PHILADELPHIA INT'L.			
❑ PZ32131	Super Hits	198?	$10
—Reissue of Gamble 32131			
TSOP			
❑ KZ33149	Energy of Love	1974	$18

INVADERS, THE
JUSTICE
❑ JLP-125	On the Right Track	196?	$300

INVICTAS, THE
20TH CENTURY FOX
❑ TCF-3152 [M]	The Invictas	1964	$40
INVICTAS			
❑ M80P-5816/7 [M]	The Invictas	196?	$300
SAHARA			
❑ 101 [M]	The Invictas A-Go-Go	1965	$120

INVISIBLE MAN'S BAND, THE
Successor to THE FIVE STAIRSTEPS.
BOARDWALK
❑ NB1-33238	Really Wanna See Ya	1981	$25

INXS
ATCO
❑ 90115 [EP]	Dekadance	1983	$15
❑ 90184	INXS	1984	$12
—U.S. issue of 1980 Australian album			
❑ 90072	Shabooh Shoobah	1983	$12
❑ 90160	The Swing	1984	$12
❑ 90185	Underneath the Colours	1984	$15
—U.S. issue of 1981 Australian album			
ATLANTIC			
❑ R153606	Kick	1987	$15
—BMG Direct Marketing edition			
❑ 81796	Kick	1987	$12
❑ R114468	Listen Like Thieves	1985	$15
—RCA Music Service edition			
❑ 81277	Listen Like Thieves	1985	$12
❑ A1-82294	Live Baby Live	1991	$30
—Columbia House version (only U.S. vinyl pressing)			
❑ R164378	X	1990	$15
—BMG Direct Marketing edition			
❑ 82140	X	1990	$12

IRAKERE
COLUMBIA
❑ JC35655	Irakere	1979	$30
❑ JC36107	Irakere II	1980	$30
MILESTONE			
❑ M-9103	Chekere Son	198?	$30
❑ M-9111	El Coco	198?	$30

IRIS, DONNIE
HME
❑ BFW39949	No Muss... No Fuss	1985	$12
MCA			
❑ 3272	Back on the Streets	1980	$15
❑ 5179	Back on the Streets	1981	$10
—Reissue of 3272			
❑ 5427	Fortune 410	1983	$12
❑ 5237	King Cool	1981	$12
❑ 5358	The High and the Mighty	1982	$12

IRISH ROVERS, THE
DECCA
❑ DL75037	All Hung Up	1968	$18
❑ DL4835 [M]	First	1967	$25
❑ DL74835 [S]	First	1967	$18
❑ DL75157	Life of the Rover	1969	$18
❑ DL75302	On the Shores of Americay	1971	$18
❑ DL75081	Tales to Warm Your Mind	1969	$18
❑ DL4951 [M]	The Unicorn	1968	$30
❑ DL74951 [S]	The Unicorn	1968	$18
MCA			
❑ 249	First	1973	$12
—Reissue of Decca 74835			
❑ 4066	Greatest Hits	1976	$18
❑ 284	Life of the Rover	1973	$12
—Reissue of Decca 75157			
❑ 175	On the Shores of Americay	1973	$12
—Reissue of Decca 75302			
❑ 15	The Unicorn	1973	$12
—Reissue of Decca 74951			

IRON BUTTERFLY
Also see CAPTAIN BEYOND.
ATCO
❑ SD 33-280	Ball	1969	$18
❑ 33-227 [M]	Heavy	1967	$150
❑ SD 33-227 [S]	Heavy	1967	$30

Number	Title	Yr	NM
—Brown and purple label			
❑ SD 33-227 [S]	Heavy	1969	$18
—Yellow label			
❑ 33-250 [M]	In-A-Gadda-Da-Vida	1968	$175
❑ SD 33-250 [S]	In-A-Gadda-Da-Vida	1968	$30
—Brown and purple label			
❑ SD 33-250 [S]	In-A-Gadda-Da-Vida	1969	$18
—Yellow label			
❑ SD 33-250 [S]	In-A-Gadda-Da-Vida	197?	$12
—Any later Atco label; LP was in print into the late 1980s			
❑ SD 33-318	Iron Butterfly Live	1970	$18
—Yellow label			
❑ SD 33-318	Iron Butterfly Live	197?	$12
—Any later Atco label; LP was in print into the late 1980s			
❑ SD 33-339	Metamorphosis	1970	$18
❑ SD 33-369	The Best of Iron Butterfly/ Evolution	1971	$18
CLEOPATRA			
❑ CLP1762 [B]	Live at the Galaxy 1967	2014	$30
MCA			
❑ 465	Scorching Beauty	1975	$15
❑ 2164	Sun and Steel	1976	$15
PAIR			
❑ PDL2-1065	Rare Flight	1986	$18

IRON MAIDEN
CAPITOL
❑ 53185	Best of the Beast	1996	$100
—Box set with booklet; probably a UK pressing stickered with US bar code			
❑ ST-12094	Iron Maiden	198?	$15
—Reissue of Harvest 12094			
❑ ST-12141	Killers	198?	$15
—Reissue of Harvest 12141			
❑ SABB-12441	Live After Death	1985	$25
❑ SQ-15017 [EP]	Maiden Japan	198?	$12
—Reissue of Harvest 15000			
❑ SEAX-12306 [PD]	Piece of Mind	1983	$75
❑ ST-12274	Piece of Mind	1983	$15
❑ SJ-12321	Powerslave	1984	$15
❑ C1-90258	Seventh Son of a Seventh Son	1988	$12
❑ SJ-12524	Somewhere in Time	1986	$15
❑ SEAX-12219 [PD]	The Number of the Beast	1982	$50
❑ ST-12202	The Number of the Beast	1982	$15
EPIC			
❑ E46905	No Prayer for the Dying	1990	$30
—Red vinyl			
HARVEST			

❑ ST-12094 [B]	Iron Maiden	1980	$18
❑ ST-12141	Killers	1981	$18
❑ MLP-15000 [EP]	Maiden Japan	1981	$12
PARLOPHONE			
❑ 0825646507832 [B]	Empire of the Clouds	2016	$30
—Limited Edition, Picture Disc			

IRVIN, TINY
EARWIG
❑ LPS-4903	You Don't Know What Love Is	1986	$30

IRVINE, WELDON
BMG SPECIAL PRODUCTS
❑ DRL1-1794	Cosmic Vortex	199?	$20
—Reissue			
❑ DRL1-1795	Sinbad	199?	$20
—Reissue			
❑ DRL1-1796	Spirit Man	199?	$20
—Reissue			
NODLEW			
❑ 1001	Liberated Brother	1972	$300

Number	Title	Yr	NM
❑ 1002	Time Capsule	1973	$300
—Reproductions exist			
RCA VICTOR			
❑ APL1-0703	Cosmic Vortex	1974	$120
❑ APL1-1363	Sinbad	1976	$175
❑ APL1-0909	Spirit Man	1975	$120
STRATA-EAST			
❑ SES-19479	In Harmony	1974	$120

ISAACS, IKE
RGB
❑ 2000	Ike Isaccs at the Pied Piper	197?	$30

ISAAK, CHRIS
REPRISE
❑ 25837	Heart Shaped World	1989	$15
WARNER BROS.			
❑ 25336	Chris Isaak	1987	$12
❑ 25156	Silvertone	1985	$12

ISHAM, MARK
VIRGIN
❑ 90900	Castalia	1988	$25
WINDHAM HILL			
❑ WH-1041	Film Music of Mark Isham	1985	$25
❑ WH-1080	Tibet	1989	$30
❑ WH-1027	Vapor Drawings	1983	$25

ISLEY BROTHERS, THE
BUDDAH
❑ BDS-5652	The Best of the Isley Brothers	1976	$18
COLLECTABLES			
❑ COL-5103	Shout!	198?	$12
DEF SOUL			
❑ B0004812-01	Baby Makin' Music	2006	$18
ISLAND			
❑ 7243 [DJ]	Mission to Please	1996	$25
—Promo-only vinyl in generic cover			
MOTOWN			
❑ M5-143V1	Doin' Their Thing (Best of the Isley Brothers)	1981	$10
—Reissue of Tamla 287			
❑ M5-106V1	Motown Superstar Series, Volume 6	1981	$10
❑ M5-128V1	This Old Heart of Mine	1981	$10
—Reissue of Tamla 269			
PICKWICK			
❑ SPC-3331	Soul Shout!	197?	$12
RCA CAMDEN			
❑ ACL1-0861	Rock Around the Clock	1975	$15
❑ ACL1-0126	Rock On Brother	1973	$15
RCA VICTOR			
❑ LPM-2156 [M]	Shout!	1959	$120
—Long Play" label			
❑ LSP-2156 [S]	Shout!	1959	$250
—Living Stereo" label			
SCEPTER			
❑ SC-552 [M]	Take Some Time Out for the Isley Brothers	1966	$30
❑ SCS-552 [S]	Take Some Time Out for the Isley Brothers	1966	$40
SUNSET			
❑ SUS-5257	The Isley Brothers Do Their Thing	1969	$18
TAMLA			
❑ TS-287	Doin' Their Thing (Best of the Isley Brothers)	1969	$25
❑ T-275 [M]	Soul on the Rocks	1967	$30
❑ TS-275 [S]	Soul on the Rocks	1967	$30
❑ T-269 [M]	This Old Heart of Mine	1966	$30
❑ TS-269 [S]	This Old Heart of Mine	1966	$30
T-NECK			
❑ KZ32453	3 + 3	1973	$15
❑ ZQ32453 [Q]	3 + 3	1974	$30
❑ PZ32453	3 + 3	197?	$10
—Reissue with new prefix			
❑ FZ38674	Between the Sheets	1983	$12
❑ PZ38674	Between the Sheets	1985	$10
—Budget-line reissue			
❑ TNS-3009	Brother, Brother, Brother	1972	$18
❑ ASZ137 [DJ]	Everything You Always Wanted to Hear by the Isley Brothers But Were Afraid to Ask For	1976	$25
—Promo-only compilation			
❑ PZ34452	Forever Gold	1977	$12
❑ TNS-3006	Get Into Something	1970	$18
❑ TNS-3008	Givin' It Back	1971	$18
❑ FZ36305	Go All the Way	1980	$12
❑ PZ36305	Go All the Way	198?	$10
—Budget-line reissue			
❑ PZ34432	Go for Your Guns	1977	$15

Number	Title	Yr	NM
—No bar code on cover			
❏ PZQ34432 [Q]	Go for Your Guns	1977	$30
❏ PZ34432	Go for Your Guns	198?	$10
—Budget-line reissue with bar code			
❏ FZ37080	Grand Slam	1981	$12
❏ PZ37080	Grand Slam	198?	$10
—Budget-line reissue			
❏ FZ39240	Greatest Hits, Vol. 1	1984	$12
❏ PZ39240	Greatest Hits, Vol. 1	1985	$10
—Budget-line reissue			
❏ PZ33809	Harvest for the World	1976	$15
—No bar code on cover			
❏ PZQ33809 [Q]	Harvest for the World	1976	$30
❏ FZ37533	Inside You	1981	$12
❏ TNS-3007	In the Beginning (With Jimi Hendrix)	1970	$25
❏ TNS-3011	Isleys' Greatest Hits	1973	$18
❏ TNS-3001	It's Our Thing	1969	$25
❏ PZ33070	Live It Up	1974	$15
—No bar code on cover			
❏ PZQ33070 [Q]	Live It Up	1974	$30
❏ JZ34930	Showdown	1978	$12
❏ PZ34930	Showdown	198?	$10
—Budget-line reissue			
❏ TNS-3002	The Brothers: Isley	1969	$25
❏ PZ33536	The Heat Is On	1975	$15
—No bar code on cover			
❏ PZ33536	The Heat Is On	198?	$10
—Budget-line reissue with bar code			
❏ TNS-3010	The Isleys Live	1973	$25
❏ FZ38047	The Real Deal	1982	$12
❏ KZ235650	Timeless	1978	$15
❏ PZ236077	Winner Takes All	1979	$15
UNITED ARTISTS			
❏ UAL-3313 [M]	The Famous Isley Brothers	1963	$50
❏ UAS-6313 [S]	The Famous Isley Brothers	1963	$75
❏ UA-LA500-E	The Very Best of the Isley Brothers	1975	$12
WAND			
❏ WD-653 [M]	Twist & Shout	1962	$100
❏ WDS-653 [S]	Twist & Shout	1962	$150
WARNER BROS.			
❏ 25347	Masterpiece	1985	$12
❏ 25586	Smooth Sailin'	1987	$12
❏ 25940	Spend the Night	1989	$12

ITOH, KIMIKO

COLUMBIA

Number	Title	Yr	NM
❏ FC45214	Follow Me	1989	$30
❏ FC44203	For Lovers Only	1988	$25

IT'S A BEAUTIFUL DAY

COLUMBIA

Number	Title	Yr	NM
❏ KC32660 [DJ]	A Thousand and One Nights	1973	$50
—Canceled before commercial release?			
❏ C30734	Choice Quality Stuff/Anytime	1971	$18
❏ CS9768 [B]	It's A Beautiful Day	1969	$35
—Red "360 Sound" label			
❏ CS9768	It's A Beautiful Day	1970	$25
—Orange label			
❏ KC31338	It's a Beautiful Day at Carnegie Hall	1972	$18
❏ KC32181	It's a Beautiful Day...Today	1973	$18
❏ CS1058	Marrying Maiden	1970	$30
—Red "360 Sound" label			
❏ CS1058 [B]	Marrying Maiden	1970	$25
—Orange label			
❏ KC32181 [B]	Today	1973	$30
SAN FRANCISCO SOUND			
❏ 11790	It's A Beautiful Day	1985	$30
—Limited reissue			

IVERS, PETER

EPIC

Number	Title	Yr	NM
❏ BN26500	Knight of the Blue Communion	1970	$40

WARNER BROS.

Number	Title	Yr	NM
❏ BS2930	Peter Ivers	1976	$15
❏ BS2804	Terminal Love	1974	$15

IVES, BURL

BELL

Number	Title	Yr	NM
❏ 6055	Time	1971	$12

COLUMBIA

Number	Title	Yr	NM
❏ CS9728	Burl Ives Christmas Album	1968	$15
❏ CL980 [M]	Burl Ives Sings Songs for All Ages	1956	$30
❏ CL2570 [10]	Children's Favorites	1955	$40
—"House Party Series" issue			
❏ CL6144 [10]	More Folk Songs	1950	$50
❏ CL1459 [M]	Return of the Wayfaring Stranger	1960	$30

Number	Title	Yr	NM
❏ CS9925 [B]	Softly and Tenderly	1969	$15
❏ CL6058 [10]	The Return of the Wayfaring Stranger	1949	$50
❏ CS9675	The Times They Are a-Changin'	1969	$15
❏ CL6109 [10]	The Wayfaring Stranger	1950	$50
❏ CL628 [M]	The Wayfaring Stranger	1955	$30
❏ CS9041 [R]	The Wayfaring Stranger	1964	$15
DECCA			
❏ DL5080 [10]	A Collection of Ballads and Folk Songs, Volume One	1949	$50
❏ DL8749 [M]	Australian Folk Songs	1959	$30
❏ DL5093 [10]	Ballads, Folk and Country Songs	1949	$50
❏ DL5013 [10]	Ballads and Folk Songs, Volume II	1949	$50
❏ DL4972 [M]	Big Country Hits	1968	$18
❏ DL74972 [S]	Big Country Hits	1968	$15
❏ DL4876 [M]	Broadway	1967	$18
❏ DL74876 [S]	Broadway	1967	$15
❏ DL4361 [M]	Burl	1963	$18
❏ DL74361 [S]	Burl	1963	$25
❏ DL4850 [M]	Burl Ives' Greatest Hits	1967	$18
❏ DL74850 [S]	Burl Ives' Greatest Hits	1967	$15
❏ DL8248 [M]	Burl Ives Sings for Fun	1956	$30
❏ DL4734 [M]	Burl's Choice	1966	$15
❏ DL74734 [S]	Burl's Choice	1966	$18
❏ DL8587 [M]	Captain Burl Ives' Ark	1958	$30
❏ DL8886 [M]	Cheers	1959	$30
❏ DL78886 [S]	Cheers	1959	$30
❏ DL5428 [10]	Christmas Day in the Morning	1952	$50
❏ DL8391 [M]	Christmas Eve	1957	$30
❏ DL78391 [R]	Christmas Eve	196?	$12
❏ DL8080 [M]	Coronation Concert	1953	$40
❏ DL8245 [M]	Down to the Sea in Ships	1956	$30
❏ DL5467 [10]	Folk Songs Dramatic and Dangerous	1953	$50
❏ DL4689 [M]	Have a Holly Jolly Christmas	1965	$15
❏ DL74689 [S]	Have a Holly Jolly Christmas	1965	$18
❏ DL8247 [M]	In the Quiet of Night	1956	$30
❏ DL4279 [M]	It's Just My Funny Way of Laughin'	1962	$18
❏ DL74279 [S]	It's Just My Funny Way of Laughin'	1962	$25
❏ DL8125 [M]	Men	1956	$30
❏ DL4606 [M]	My Gal Sal	1965	$15
❏ DL74606 [S]	My Gal Sal	1965	$18
❏ DL8637 [M]	Old Time Varieties	1958	$30
❏ DL4668 [M]	On the Beach at Waikiki	1965	$15
❏ DL74668 [S]	On the Beach at Waikiki	1965	$18
❏ DL4578 [M]	Pearly Shells	1964	$18
❏ DL74578 [S]	Pearly Shells	1964	$25
❏ DL4433 [M]	Singin' Easy	1964	$18
❏ DL74433 [S]	Singin' Easy	1964	$25
❏ DL4304 [M]	Sing Out, Sweet Land	1962	$18
❏ DL74304 [S]	Sing Out, Sweet Land	1962	$25
❏ DL4789 [M]	Something Special	1966	$15
❏ DL74789 [S]	Something Special	1966	$18
❏ DL8444 [M]	Songs of Ireland	1958	$30
❏ DL4179 [M]	Songs of the West	1961	$18
❏ DL74179 [S]	Songs of the West	1961	$25
❏ DL4320 [M]	Sunshine in My Soul	1962	$18
❏ DL74320 [S]	Sunshine in My Soul	1962	$25
❏ DXSB7167 [S]	The Best of Burl Ives	1961	$30
❏ DXB167 [M]	The Best of Burl Ives	1961	$30
❏ DL4390 [M]	The Best of Burl's for Boys and Girls	1963	$18
❏ DL74390 [S]	The Best of Burl's for Boys and Girls	1963	$25
❏ DL4152 [M]	The Versatile Burl Ives	1961	$18
❏ DL74152 [S]	The Versatile Burl Ives	1961	$25
❏ DL8107 [M]	The Wild Side of Life	1955	$30
❏ DL4533 [M]	True Love	1964	$18
❏ DL74533 [S]	True Love	1964	$25
❏ DL8246 [M]	Women	1956	$30
❏ DL5490 [10]	Women: Folk Songs About the Fair Sex	1954	$50
DISNEYLAND			
❏ ST-3927 [M]	Chim Chim Chiree and Other Children's Choices	1964	$18
❏ STER-3927 [S]	Chim Chim Chiree and Other Children's Choices	1964	$25

Number	Title	Yr	NM
EVEREST ARCHIVE OF FOLK & JAZZ			
❏ 340	Burl Ives Live	1978	$12
HARMONY			
❏ HS11275	Got the World by the Tail	196?	$12
❏ HL9507 [M]	The Little White Duck	196?	$18
❏ HL9551 [M]	The Lollipop Tree	196?	$18
MCA			
❏ 114	Burl Ives' Greatest Hits	1973	$12
—Reissue of Decca 74850			
❏ 15002	Have a Holly Jolly Christmas	1973	$15
—Reissue of Decca 74689; black label with rainbow			
❏ 15002	Have a Holly Jolly Christmas	1980	$10
—Blue label with rainbow			
❏ 318	Paying My Dues Again	1973	$12
❏ 15030	Santa Claus Is Coming to Town	198?	$12
❏ 4034	The Best of Burl Ives	197?	$15
❏ 4089	The Best of Burl Ives Volume 2	197?	$15
NATIONAL GEOGRAPHIC			
❏ 07806	We Americans	1978	$15
PICKWICK			
❏ SPC-1018	Twelve Days of Christmas	197?	$12
STINSON			
❏ SLP-1 [10]	The Wayfaring Stranger	1949	$75
SUNSET			
❏ SUS-5280	Favorites	1970	$12
UNITED ARTISTS			
❏ UAL3060 [M]	Ballads	1959	$18
❏ UAS6060 [S]	Ballads	1959	$25
WORD			
❏ 3259 [M]	Faith and Joy	196?	$18
❏ 8140 [S]	Faith and Joy	196?	$25
❏ 8537	How Great Thou Art	1971	$15
❏ 3391 [M]	I Do Believe	1967	$15
❏ 8391 [S]	I Do Believe	1967	$18
❏ 3339 [M]	Shall We Gather at the River	1966	$15
❏ 8339 [S]	Shall We Gather at the River	1966	$18

IVORY, JACKIE

ATCO

Number	Title	Yr	NM
❏ 33-178 [M]	Soul Discovery	1965	$25
❏ SD 33-178 [S]	Soul Discovery	1965	$30

IVORY

PLAYBOY

Number	Title	Yr	NM
❏ 115	Ivory	1973	$15

TETRAGRAMMATON

Number	Title	Yr	NM
❏ T-104 [B]	Ivory	1968	$25

IVY LEAGUE, THE

CAMEO

Number	Title	Yr	NM
❏ C2000 [M]	Tossing and Turning	1965	$30
❏ CS2000 [R]	Tossing and Turning	1965	$30

IVY LEAGUE TRIO, THE

CORAL

Number	Title	Yr	NM
❏ CRL757399 [S]	On and Off Campus	1962	$25
❏ CRL57399 [M]	On and Off Campus	1962	$18
❏ CRL757404 [S]	Rare and Well Done	1962	$25
❏ CRL57404 [M]	Rare and Well Done	1962	$18
REPRISE			
❏ R9-6087 [R]	Folk Ballads from the World of Edgar Allan Poe	1963	$30
❏ R-6087 [M]	Folk Ballads from the World of Edgar Allan Poe	1963	$25

J

J.B.'S, THE

See FRED WESLEY.

J.F.K. QUINTET, THE

RIVERSIDE

Number	Title	Yr	NM
❏ RLP-396 [M]	New Frontiers from Washington	1961	$250
❏ RS-9396 [S]	New Frontiers from Washington	1961	$250
❏ RLP-424 [M]	Young Ideas	1962	$175
❏ RS-9424 [S]	Young Ideas	1962	$175

J.K. AND COMPANY

BEAT ROCKET

Number	Title	Yr	NM
❏ BR-126	Suddenly One Summer	2000	$15
—Reissue on 180-gram vinyl			

WHITE WHALE

Number	Title	Yr	NM
❏ WWS-7117 [B]	Suddenly One Summer	1969	$150

JACINTHA

GROOVE NOTE

Number	Title	Yr	NM
❏ 2001	Here's to Ben	1999	$30
—Audiophile vinyl			

Number	Title	Yr	NM

JACK PINE SAVAGES, THE
JIM TAYLOR PRESENTS
| ❏ 104 | The Beiderbecke Legend Is Alive and Well | 197? | $35 |

JACKIE AND ROY
See JACKIE CAIN AND ROY KRAL.

JACKS, TERRY
BELL
| ❏ 1307 [B] | Seasons in the Sun | 1974 | $15 |

JACKS, THE
CROWN

❏ CLP-5021 [M]	Jumpin' with the Jacks	1960	$250
❏ CLP-5372 [M]	Jumpin' with the Jacks	1962	$150
❏ CST-372 [R]	Jumpin' with the Jacks	1962	$50
RELIC			
❏ 5023	The Jacks' Greatest Hits	198?	$12
RPM			
❏ LRP-3006 [M]	Jumpin' with the Jacks	1956	$2000
—VG value 1000; VG+ value 1500
| **UNITED** | | | |
| ❏ US-7797 | Rock 'n' Roll Hits of the 50's | 197? | $18 |

JACKSON, ALAN
ARISTA
| ❏ AL8681 | Don't Rock the Jukebox | 1991 | $30 |
—Columbia House vinyl edition
| ❏ R143877 | Don't Rock the Jukebox | 1991 | $30 |
—BMG Direct Marketing vinyl version
| ❏ AL8623 | Here in the Real World | 1990 | $25 |

JACKSON, BULL MOOSE
AUDIO LAB
❏ AL-1524 [M]	Bull Moose Jackson	1959	$600
BOGUS			
❏ 6-0214851	Moosemania!	1985	$12

JACKSON, CALVIN
COLUMBIA
❏ CL756 [M]	Calvin Jackson and the All Stars Quartet	1956	$50
❏ CL824 [M]	Rave Notice	1956	$50
LIBERTY			
❏ LRP-3071 [M]	Jazz Variations	1957	$40
X			
❏ LXA-1005 [M]	Calvin Jackson at the Plaza	1954	$50

JACKSON, CHUBBY, AND BILL HARRIS
EMARCY
❏ MG-26012 [M]	Out of the Herd	1965	$150
❏ SR-66012 [R]	Out of the Herd	1965	$150
❏ MG-26003 [10]	The Small Herd	1954	$250
MERCURY			
❏ MG-25076 [10]	Jazz Journey	1950	$300

JACKSON, CHUBBY
ARGO
❏ LP-614 [M]	Chubby's Back	1957	$100
❏ LPS-614 [S]	Chubby's Back	1959	$150
❏ LP-625 [M]	I'm Entitled to You	1958	$100
EVEREST			
❏ LPBR-5009 [M]	Chubby Takes Over	1959	$30
❏ SDBR-1009 [S]	Chubby Takes Over	1959	$40
❏ LPBR-5041 [M]	Jazz Then Till Now	1960	$30
❏ SDBR-1041 [S]	Jazz Then Till Now	1960	$40
❏ LPBR-5029 [M]	The Big Three	1959	$30
❏ SDBR-1029 [S]	The Big Three	1959	$40
LAURIE			
❏ LLP-2011 [M]	Twist Calling	1962	$30
NEW JAZZ			
❏ NJLP-105 [10]	Chubby Jackson and His All Star Band	1950	$800

Number	Title	Yr	NM

—Original; reissued as Prestige 105
PRESTIGE
❏ PRLP-105 [10]	Chubby Jackson and His All Star Band	1951	$600
❏ PRST-7641	Chubby Jackson Sextet and Big Band	1969	$25
RAINBOW			
❏ 708 [10]	Chubby Jackson	1951	$400
STEREO-CRAFT			
❏ RTN-108 [M]	The Big Three	195?	$50
❏ RTS-108 [S]	The Big Three	195?	$50

JACKSON, CHUCK, AND MAXINE BROWN
Also see each artist's individual listings.
WAND
❏ WD-678 [M]	Hold On, We're Coming	1966	$30
❏ WDS-678 [S]	Hold On, We're Coming	1966	$40
❏ WD-669 [M]	Say Something	1965	$30
❏ WDS-669 [S]	Say Something	1965	$40

JACKSON, CHUCK, AND TAMMI TERRELL
Also see each artist's individual listings.
WAND
| ❏ WD-682 [M] | The Early Show | 1967 | $30 |
| ❏ WDS-682 [S] | The Early Show | 1967 | $30 |

JACKSON, CHUCK
ABC
❏ X-798	Through All Times	1973	$18
ALL PLATINUM			
❏ 3014	Needing You, Wanting You	1976	$18
COLLECTABLES			
❏ COL-5115	Golden Classics	198?	$12
EMI AMERICA			
❏ SW-17031	I Wanna Give You Some Love	1980	$12
GUEST STAR			
❏ GS-1912 [M]	Chuck Jackson	196?	$25
❏ GSS-1912 [R]	Chuck Jackson	196?	$15
MOTOWN			
❏ M-667 [M]	Chuck Jackson Arrives!	1967	$40
❏ MS-667 [S]	Chuck Jackson Arrives!	1967	$30
❏ MS-687	Goin' Back to Chuck Jackson	1969	$30
SCEPTER			
❏ 5100	A Tribute to Burt Bacharach	1972	$18
SPIN-O-RAMA			
❏ 123 [M]	Starring Chuck Jackson	196?	$25
❏ S-123 [R]	Starring Chuck Jackson	196?	$15
STRAND			
❏ SL-1125 [M]	The Great Chuck Jackson	196?	$30
❏ SLS-1125 [S]	The Great Chuck Jackson	196?	$30
UNITED ARTISTS			
❏ UA-LA499-E	The Very Best of Chuck Jackson	1974	$12
V.I.P.			
❏ 403	Teardrops Keep Fallin' on My Heart	1970	$40
WAND			
❏ LP-654 [M]	Any Day Now	1962	$40
❏ WD-673 [M]	A Tribute to Rhythm and Blues	1966	$30
❏ WDS-673 [S]	A Tribute to Rhythm and Blues	1966	$40
❏ WD-676 [M]	A Tribute to Rhythm and Blues, Volume 2	1966	$30
❏ WDS-676 [S]	A Tribute to Rhythm and Blues, Volume 2	1966	$40
❏ WD-658 [M]	Chuck Jackson On Tour	1964	$40
❏ WD-683 [M]	Chuck Jackson's Greatest Hits	1967	$25
❏ WDS-683 [S]	Chuck Jackson's Greatest Hits	1967	$30
❏ WD-680 [M]	Dedicated to the King!!	1966	$40
❏ WDS-680 [S]	Dedicated to the King!!	1966	$50
❏ WD-655 [M]	Encore	1963	$40
❏ LP-650 [M]	I Don't Want to Cry	1961	$40
❏ WDM-667 [M]	Mr. Everything	1965	$30
❏ WDS-667 [S]	Mr. Everything	1965	$40

JACKSON, DEON
ATCO
❏ 33-188 [M]	Love Makes the World Go Round	1966	$30
❏ SD 33-188 [S]	Love Makes the World Go Round	1966	$40
COLLECTABLES			
❏ COL-5106	Golden Classics	198?	$12

JACKSON, FRANZ
PINNACLE
❏ 109 [M]	Franz Jackson	1966	$25
❏ S-104 [S]	Night at Red Arrow	196?	$25
❏ 104 [M]	Night at Red Arrow	196?	$35
❏ 102 [M]	No Saints	1961	$25

Number	Title	Yr	NM

RIVERSIDE
| ❏ RLP-406 [M] | Franz Jackson and the Original Jass All-Stars | 1962 | $250 |
| ❏ RS-9406 [R] | Franz Jackson and the Original Jass All-Stars | 196? | $35 |

JACKSON, FRED
BLUE NOTE
| ❏ BLP-4094 [M] | Hootin' 'N Tootin' | 1962 | $300 |
—With 61st St. address on label
| ❏ BLP-4094 [M] | Hootin' 'N Tootin' | 1963 | $250 |
—With "New York, USA" address on label
| ❏ BST-84094 [S] | Hootin' 'N Tootin' | 1962 | $175 |
—With 61st St. address on label
| ❏ BST-84094 [S] | Hootin' 'N Tootin' | 1963 | $150 |
—With "New York, USA" address on label
| ❏ BST-84094 [S] | Hootin' 'N Tootin' | 1967 | $25 |
—With "A Division of Liberty Records" on label

JACKSON, FREDDIE
CAPITOL
❏ C1-92217	Do Me Again	1990	$15
❏ C1-48987	Don't Let Love Slip Away	1988	$10
❏ ST-12495	Just Like the First Time	1986	$10
❏ ST-12404	Rock Me Tonight	1985	$10

JACKSON, J.J.
CALLA
❏ C-1101 [M]	But It's Alright/I Dig Girls	1967	$25
❏ CS-1101 [S]	But It's Alright/I Dig Girls	1967	$30
CONGRESS			
❏ CS-7000	The Greatest Little Soul Band in the World	1968	$30
PERCEPTION			
❏ 3	J.J. Jackson's Dilemma	1970	$18
WARNER BROS.			
❏ WS1797	The Great J.J. Jackson	1969	$25

JACKSON, JACKIE
MOTOWN
❏ M785V1	Jackie Jackson	1973	$18
POLYDOR			
❏ 837766-1	Be the One	1989	$12

JACKSON, JANET
A&M
| ❏ SP-3905 | Control | 1986 | $10 |
—Second issue; most have a black label
| ❏ SP-5106 | Control | 1986 | $12 |
—Original issue; silver label with fading A&M logo
❏ 31454 03991	Design of a Decade 1986/1996	1995	$18
❏ SP-4962	Dream Street	1984	$15
❏ SP-6-4907	Janet Jackson	1982	$15
❏ SP-3920	Janet Jackson's Rhythm Nation 1814	1989	$18
VIRGIN			
❏ 10144	All for You	2001	$18
❏ 84404	Damita Jo	2004	$18

JACKSON, JERMAINE
ARISTA
❏ AL-8493	Don't Take It Personal	1989	$12
❏ AL8-8203	Jermaine Jackson	1984	$12
❏ AL-8421	Jermaine Jackson	1986	$10
—Budget-line reissue
❏ AL8-8277	Precious Moments	1986	$12
MOTOWN			
❏ M-775L	Come Into My Life	1973	$12
❏ M6-888S1	Feel the Fire	1977	$12
❏ M7-898R1	Frontiers	1978	$12

Number	Title	Yr	NM
❑ M8-952M1	I Like Your Style	1981	$12
❑ M-752L	Jermaine	1972	$12
❑ M8-948M1	Jermaine	1980	$12
❑ 6017ML	Let Me Tickle Your Fancy	1982	$12
❑ M7-928R1	Let's Get Serious	1980	$12
❑ M5-117V1	Motown Superstar Series, Vol. 17	1981	$12
❑ M6-842S1	My Name Is Jermaine	1976	$12

JACKSON, JOE

A&M

Number	Title	Yr	NM
❑ SP-3241	Beat Crazy	198?	$10
—Reissue of SP-4837			
❑ SP-4837	Beat Crazy	1980	$12
❑ R244331	Big World	1986	$18
—RCA Music Service edition			
❑ SP-6021	Big World	1986	$18
❑ R101141	Blaze of Glory	1989	$15
—BMG Direct Marketing edition			
❑ SP-5249	Blaze of Glory	1989	$12
❑ SP-5000	Body and Soul	1984	$12
❑ SP-3286	Body and Soul	1986	$10
—Reissue of SP-5000			
❑ SP-3221	I'm the Man	198?	$10
—Reissue of SP-4794			
❑ SP-4794	I'm the Man	1979	$12
❑ SP-3271	Joe Jackson's Jumpin' Jive	198?	$10
—Reissue of SP-4871			
❑ SP-4871	Joe Jackson's Jumpin' Jive	1981	$12
❑ SP-6706	Live: 1980-1986	1988	$18
❑ R209597	Live 1980-1986	1987	$18
—BMG Direct Marketing edition			
❑ SP-3187	Look Sharp!	198?	$10
—Reissue of SP-4743			
❑ SP-4743	Look Sharp!	1979	$15
❑ SP-3666	Look Sharp!	1979	$25
—Two 10-inch records in gatefold sleeve with button			
❑ SP-4931	Mike's Murder [Soundtrack]	1983	$15
❑ SP-4906	Night and Day	1982	$12
❑ SP-3908	Will Power	1987	$15

MOBILE FIDELITY

Number	Title	Yr	NM
❑ Jan-0080	Night and Day	1982	$50
—Audiophile vinyl			

RYKODISC

Number	Title	Yr	NM
❑ 310921	Rain	2008	$18

JACKSON, LIL' SON

ARHOOLIE

Number	Title	Yr	NM
❑ 1004 [M]	Lil' Son Jackson	1960	$30

IMPERIAL

Number	Title	Yr	NM
❑ LP-9142 [M]	Rockin' and Rollin'	1961	$400

JACKSON, MAHALIA

APOLLO

Number	Title	Yr	NM
❑ 1001/2 [M]	Command Performance	1961	$30
❑ 499 [M]	Mahalia Jackson	1962	$30
❑ 482 [M]	No Matter How You Pray	1959	$30
❑ 201/202 [M]	Spirituals	1954	$30

COLUMBIA

Number	Title	Yr	NM
❑ CG30744	America's Favorite Hymns	1971	$18
❑ CS9659	A Mighty Fortress	1968	$15
❑ CL899 [M]	Bless This House	1956	$30
❑ CS8761 [R]	Bless This House	1963	$15
❑ PC8761	Bless This House	198?	$10
—Budget-line reissue			
❑ CS9727	Christmas with Mahalia	1968	$15
❑ CL1428 [M]	Come On Children, Let's Sing	1960	$25
❑ CS8225 [S]	Come On Children, Let's Sing	1960	$30
❑ CL1643 [M]	Every Time I Feel the Spirit	1961	$18
❑ CS8443 [S]	Every Time I Feel the Spirit	1961	$25
❑ CL2546 [M]	Garden of Prayer	1967	$25
❑ CS9346 [S]	Garden of Prayer	1967	$15
❑ CL1824 [M]	Great Songs of Love and Faith	1962	$18
❑ CS8624 [S]	Great Songs of Love and Faith	1962	$25
❑ KC34073	How I Got Over	1976	$12
❑ CL1549 [M]	I Believe	1960	$18
❑ CS8349 [S]	I Believe	1960	$25
❑ CL2130 [M]	Let's Pray Together	1964	$15
❑ CS8930 [S]	Let's Pray Together	1964	$18
❑ CL644 [M]	Mahalia Jackson	1955	$40
❑ CS8759 [R]	Mahalia Jackson	1963	$15
❑ CL2690 [M]	Mahalia Jackson In Concert, Easter Sunday 1967	1967	$18
❑ CS9490 [S]	Mahalia Jackson In Concert, Easter Sunday 1967	1967	$15
❑ CL2004 [M]	Mahalia Jackson's Greatest Hits	1963	$15
❑ CS8804 [S]	Mahalia Jackson's Greatest Hits	1963	$18
❑ PC37710	Mahalia Jackson's Greatest Hits	198?	$10
❑ CL2452 [M]	Mahalia Sings	1966	$15
❑ CS9252 [S]	Mahalia Sings	1966	$18
❑ CL1936 [M]	Make a Joyful Noise Unto the Lord	1962	$18
❑ CS8736 [S]	Make a Joyful Noise Unto the Lord	1962	$25
❑ CL2605 [M]	My Faith	1967	$18

Number	Title	Yr	NM
❑ CS9405 [S]	My Faith	1967	$15
❑ CL1244 [M]	Newport 1958	1959	$25
❑ CS8071 [S]	Newport 1958	1959	$30
❑ CL1726 [M]	Recorded in Europe During Her Latest Concert Tour	1962	$18
❑ CS8526 [S]	Recorded in Europe During Her Latest Concert Tour	1962	$25
❑ CS9813	Right Out of the Church	1969	$15
❑ CL1903 [M]	Silent Night	1962	$18
❑ CS8703 [S]	Silent Night	1962	$25
❑ 3C38304	Silent Night	1982	$10
—Reissue			
❑ CL702 [M]	Sweet Little Jesus Boy	1955	$40
❑ CL1343 [M]	That Great Gettin' Up Morning	1959	$25
❑ CS8153 [S]	That Great Gettin' Up Morning	1959	$30
❑ CS9686	The Best-Loved Hymns of Dr. Martin Luther King Jr.	1968	$18
❑ PC9686	The Best-Loved Hymns of Dr. Martin Luther King Jr.	198?	$10
—Budget-line reissue			
❑ KG31379	The Great Mahalia Jackson	1972	$18
❑ CL1473 [M]	The Power and the Glory	1960	$25
❑ CS8264 [S]	The Power and the Glory	1960	$30
❑ CS9950	What the World Needs Now	1970	$15
❑ CL2552 [10]	You'll Never Walk Alone	1955	$50

COLUMBIA SPECIAL PRODUCTS

Number	Title	Yr	NM
❑ P213200	(HRB Music Proudly Presents) The Best of Mahalia Jackson: Hymns, Spirituals & Songs of Inspiration	1976	$18

FOLKWAYS

Number	Title	Yr	NM
❑ 31101	I Sing Because I'm Happy, Volume 1	198?	$15
❑ 31102	I Sing Because I'm Happy, Volume 2	198?	$15

GRAND AWARD

Number	Title	Yr	NM
❑ GA265SD	I Believe	1966	$18
—Reissue of 326			
❑ GA 33-326 [M]	Mahalia Jackson	1955	$30
❑ GA 33-390 [M]	Mahalia Jackson	195?	$30

HARMONY

Number	Title	Yr	NM
❑ HS11372	Abide with Me	1970	$12
❑ KH31111	Lord Don't Let Me Fall	1972	$12
❑ H30019	Sunrise, Sunset	1970	$12
❑ HS11279	You'll Never Walk Alone	196?	$12

KENWOOD

Number	Title	Yr	NM
❑ 1001/2	Command Performance	196?	$25
❑ 501	I Lift My Voice	196?	$18
❑ 474	In the Upper Room	196?	$18
❑ 479	Just As I Am	196?	$18
❑ 486	Mahalia	196?	$18
❑ 489	Mahalia Jackson With the Greatest Spiritual Singers	196?	$18
❑ 482	No Matter How You Pray	196?	$18
❑ 502	Sing Out	196?	$18
❑ 500	The Best of Mahalia Jackson	196?	$18

PICKWICK

Number	Title	Yr	NM
❑ SPC-3510	I Believe	197?	$12

PRIORITY

Number	Title	Yr	NM
❑ PU37710	Mahalia Jackson's Greatest Hits	1981	$12

JACKSON, MARLON

CAPITOL

Number	Title	Yr	NM
❑ CLT-46942	Baby Tonight	1987	$12

JACKSON, MARY ANNE

HANOVER

Number	Title	Yr	NM
❑ HM-8009 [M]	The Wild Piano of Mary Anne Jackson	1959	$100

JACKSON, MICHAEL

Also see THE JACKSONS or JACKSON 5; MICHAEL JACKSON AND PAUL McCARTNEY.

EPIC

Number	Title	Yr	NM
❑ OE40600 [B]	Bad	1987	$18
❑ 9E944043 [PD]	Bad	1987	$35
❑ E268000 [B]	Blood on the Dance Floor: HIStory in the Mix	1997	$75
❑ E245400 [B]	Dangerous	1991	$30
❑ E359000	HIStory: Past, Present and Future -- Book I	1995	$30
—Box set with 12x12 booklet			
❑ E269400	Invincible	2001	$30
❑ FE35745 [B]	Off the Wall	1979	$25
❑ HE47545 [B]	Off the Wall	1982	$100
—Half-speed mastered edition			
❑ QE38112 [B]	Thriller	1982	$30
❑ HE48112 [B]	Thriller	1982	$150
—Half-speed mastered edition			

Number	Title	Yr	NM
❑ 8.00E+0838867 [PD]	Thriller	1983	$150

MOTOWN

Number	Title	Yr	NM
❑ M755 [B]	Ben	1972	$30
—With only Michael Jackson on front cover			
❑ M5-153V1 [B]	Ben	1981	$25
—Reissue of Motown 755			
❑ M755	Ben	1972	$75
—With Michael Jackson on top half of cover, rats on the bottom half			
❑ 6101ML [B]	Farewell My Summer Love 1984	1984	$30
❑ M6-825S [B]	Forever, Michael	1975	$30
❑ M747	Got to Be There	1972	$25
❑ M5-130V1	Got to Be There	1981	$15
—Reissue of Motown 747			
❑ 6099ML	Michael Jackson and The Jackson 5 – 14 Greatest Hits	1984	$15
—Picture disc packaged with one glove			
❑ M5-107V1	Motown Superstar Series, Vol. 7	1981	$12
❑ M767 [B]	Music and Me	1973	$30
❑ M8-956M1	One Day in Your Life	1981	$15
❑ M6-851S	The Best of Michael Jackson	1975	$15
❑ M5-194V1	The Best of Michael Jackson	1981	$12
—Reissue of Motown 851			

JACKSON, MICHAEL GREGORY

ARISTA/NOVUS

Number	Title	Yr	NM
❑ AN3015	Heart & Center	1979	$35

BIJA

Number	Title	Yr	NM
❑ 1000	Clarity	1976	$30

ENJA

Number	Title	Yr	NM
❑ 4026	Cowboys, Cartoons and Assorted Candy	1982	$35

IAI

Number	Title	Yr	NM
❑ 373857	Karmonic Suite	1978	$25

JACKSON, MILLIE, AND ISAAC HAYES

POLYDOR

Number	Title	Yr	NM
❑ PD-1-6229	Royal Rappin's	1979	$12

JACKSON, MILLIE

JIVE

Number	Title	Yr	NM
❑ 1016-1-J	An Imitation of Love	1986	$10
❑ 1186-1-J	Back to the Shit	1989	$12
❑ 1103-1-J	The Tide Is Turning	1988	$10
❑ 1447-1-J	Young Man, Older Woman	1991	$15

SPRING

Number	Title	Yr	NM
❑ SP-1-6722	A Moment's Pleasure	1979	$12
❑ SPR-6703	Caught Up	1974	$12
❑ SP-6715	Feelin' Bitchy	1977	$12
❑ SP-1-6727	For Men Only	1980	$12
❑ SP-1-6719	Get It Out'cha System	1978	$12
❑ SP-1-6737	Hard Times	1983	$12
❑ SP-1-6730	I Had to Say It	1981	$12
❑ SPR-5706	It Hurts So Good	1973	$15
❑ SP-2-6725	Live & Uncensored	1979	$15
❑ SP-1-6735	Live and Outrageous (Rated XXX)	1982	$12
❑ SP-6712	Lovingly Yours	1976	$12
❑ SPR-6701	Millie	1974	$12
❑ SPR-5703	Millie Jackson	1972	$15
❑ SPR-6708	Still Caught Up	1975	$12

JACKSON, MILT, AND JOHN COLTRANE

Also see each artist's individual listings.

ATLANTIC

Number	Title	Yr	NM
❑ 1368 [M]	Bags and Trane	1961	$250
—Multicolor label, white "fan" logo at right			
❑ 1368 [M]	Bags and Trane	1963	$50
—Multicolor label, black "fan" logo at right			
❑ SD1368 [S]	Bags and Trane	1961	$300
—Multicolor label, white "fan" logo at right			
❑ SD1368 [S]	Bags and Trane	1963	$100
—Multicolor label, black "fan" logo at right			

Number	Title	Yr	NM

JACKSON, MILT, AND MONTY ALEXANDER
PABLO
❑ 2310804	Soul Fusion	1978	$30

JACKSON, MILT, AND WES MONTGOMERY
Also see each artist's individual listings.
FANTASY
❑ OJC-234	Bags Meets Wes	198?	$25

RIVERSIDE
❑ RLP-407 [M]	Bags Meets Wes	1962	$250
❑ RS-9407 [S]	Bags Meets Wes	1962	$250
❑ 6058	Bags Meets Wes	197?	$30

JACKSON, MILT
ABC IMPULSE!
❑ AS-70 [S]	Jazz n' Samba	1968	$35
❑ AS-9193	Memphis Jackson	1969	$250
❑ AS-9230	Milt Jackson Quartet	1973	$30
❑ AS-14 [S]	Statements	1968	$35
❑ AS-9189	That's the Way It Is	1969	$250
❑ AS-9282	The Impulse Years	1974	$35

ATLANTIC
❑ 1294 [M]	Bags & Flutes	1958	$300
—Black label			
❑ 1294 [M]	Bags & Flutes	1961	$300
—Multicolor label, white "fan" logo at right			
❑ 1294 [M]	Bags & Flutes	1963	$50
—Multicolor label, black "fan" logo at right			
❑ SD1294 [S]	Bags & Flutes	1959	$300
—Green label			
❑ SD1294 [S]	Bags & Flutes	1961	$300
—Multicolor label, white "fan" logo at right			
❑ SD1294 [S]	Bags & Flutes	1963	$50
—Multicolor label, black "fan" logo at right			
❑ 1342 [M]	Ballad Artistry	1960	$300
—Multicolor label, white "fan" logo at right			
❑ 1342 [M]	Ballad Artistry	1963	$50
—Multicolor label, black "fan" logo at right			
❑ SD1342 [S]	Ballad Artistry	1960	$300
—Multicolor label, white "fan" logo at right			
❑ SD1342 [S]	Ballad Artistry	1963	$50
—Multicolor label, black "fan" logo at right			
❑ 1242 [M]	Ballads and Blues	1956	$300
—Black label			
❑ 1242 [M]	Ballads and Blues	1961	$300
—Multicolor label, white "fan" logo at right			
❑ 1242 [M]	Ballads and Blues	1963	$50
—Multicolor label, black "fan" logo at right			
❑ 1316 [M]	Bean Bags	1959	$300
—Black label			
❑ 1316 [M]	Bean Bags	1961	$300
—Multicolor label, white "fan" logo at right			
❑ 1316 [M]	Bean Bags	1963	$50
—Multicolor label, black "fan" logo at right			
❑ SD1316 [S]	Bean Bags	1959	$300
—Green label			
❑ SD1316 [S]	Bean Bags	1961	$300
—Multicolor label, white "fan" logo at right			
❑ SD1316 [S]	Bean Bags	1963	$50
—Multicolor label, black "fan" logo at right			
❑ 90465	Bean Bags	1986	$25
❑ 1269 [M]	Plenty, Plenty Soul	1957	$300
—Black label			
❑ SD1269 [S]	Plenty, Plenty Soul	1959	$300
—Green label			
❑ 1269 [M]	Plenty, Plenty Soul	1961	$175
—Multicolor label, white "fan" logo at right			
❑ 1269 [M]	Plenty, Plenty Soul	1963	$35
—Multicolor label, black "fan" logo at right			
❑ SD1269 [S]	Plenty, Plenty Soul	1961	$175
—Multicolor label, white "fan" logo at right			
❑ SD1269 [S]	Plenty, Plenty Soul	1963	$35
—Multicolor label, black "fan" logo at right			
❑ SD8811	Plenty, Plenty Soul	198?	$25
❑ SD 2-319	The Art of Milt Jackson	197?	$35
❑ 1417 [M]	Vibrations	1964	$35
❑ SD1417 [S]	Vibrations	1964	$25

BLUE NOTE
❑ BN-LA590-1-n [B]	All Star Bags	1976	$35
❑ BLP-1509 [M]	Milt Jackson	1956	$500
—Deep groove" version (deep indentation under label on both sides)			
❑ BLP-1509 [M]	Milt Jackson	1956	$250
—Regular version with Lexington Ave. address on label			
❑ BLP-1509 [M]	Milt Jackson	1963	$75
—With "New York, USA" address on label			
❑ BST-81509 [R]	Milt Jackson	196?	$35
—With "A Division of Liberty Records" on label			
❑ B1-81509	Milt Jackson	1987	$25
—The Finest in Jazz Since 1939" reissue			
❑ BLP-5011 [10]	Wizard of the Vibes	1952	$300

CTI
❑ 6038	Goodbye	1974	$35
❑ 6046	Olinga	1974	$35

❑ 6024	Sunflower	1973	$35
❑ 8004	Sunflower	197?	$25
—Reissue of 6024			

DEE GEE
❑ 1002 [10]	Milt Jackson	1952	$300

EASTWEST
❑ 90991	Bebop	1988	$30

FANTASY
❑ OJC-366	Big Bags	198?	$25
❑ OJC-448	Feelings	1990	$25
❑ OJC-404	For Someone I Love	1989	$30
❑ OJC-260	Invitation	1987	$25
❑ OJC-601	It Don't Mean a Thing If You Can't Tap Your Foot to It	1991	$35
❑ OJC-309	Live" at the Village Gate	1988	$25
❑ OJC-001	Milt Jackson Quartet	1982	$35
❑ OJC-375	Montreux '77	198?	$25

GNP CRESCENDO
❑ GNP-9007	Milt Jackson	197?	$25

IMPULSE!
❑ A-70 [M]	Jazz n' Samba	1964	$120
❑ AS-70 [S]	Jazz n' Samba	1964	$120
❑ A-14 [M]	Statements	1962	$120
❑ AS-14 [S]	Statements	1962	$120

LIMELIGHT
❑ LM-82024 [M]	At the Museum of Modern Art	1965	$25
❑ LS-86024 [S]	At the Museum of Modern Art	1965	$30
❑ LM-82045 [M]	Born Free	1966	$25
❑ LS-86045 [S]	Born Free	1966	$30
❑ LM-82006 [M]	In a New Setting	1964	$25
❑ LS-86006 [S]	In a New Setting	1964	$30

MILESTONE
❑ 47006	Big Band Bags	1972	$35

PABLO
❑ 2310873	Ain't But a Few of Us Left	198?	$30
❑ 2310932	A London Bridge	1988	$30
❑ 2310842	Bag's Bag	1979	$30
❑ 2310867	Big Mouth	198?	$30
❑ 2310916	Brother Jim	1987	$25
❑ 2310774	Feelings	1976	$30
❑ 2310909	It Don't Mean a Thing If You Can't Tap Your Foot to It	1986	$35
❑ 2310897	Milt Jackson & Co.	198?	$30
❑ 2310822	Milt Jackson with Count Basie and the Big Band, Volume 1	1978	$30
❑ 2310823	Milt Jackson with Count Basie and the Big Band, Volume 2	1978	$30
❑ 2310832	Soul Believer	1979	$30
❑ 2405405	The Best of Milt Jackson	198?	$25
❑ 2310757	The Big 3	1976	$30
❑ 2310753	The Big 4 at Montreux '75	1976	$30

PABLO LIVE
❑ 2620103	Kosei Nenkin	197?	$35
❑ 2308235	Live in London: Memories of Thelonious Monk	198?	$30
❑ 2308205	Montreux '77	1977	$30

PABLO TODAY
❑ 2312124	Nightmist	198?	$30

PRESTIGE
❑ PRLP-7003 [M]	Milt Jackson	1955	$350
❑ PRLP-183 [10]	Milt Jackson Quintet	1954	$300
❑ 24048	Opus de Funk	197?	$35
❑ PRLP-7224 [M]	Soul Pioneers	1962	$175
❑ PRST-7655	The Complete Milt Jackson	1969	$35

QUINTESSENCE
❑ 25391	Milt Jackson (1961-69)	1980	$25

RIVERSIDE
❑ 3021	Bags and Brass	1968	$150
❑ RLP-429 [M]	Big Bags	1962	$250
❑ RS-9429 [S]	Big Bags	1962	$250
❑ RLP-478 [M]	For Someone I Love	1966	$150
❑ RS-9478 [S]	For Someone I Love	1966	$150
❑ RLP-446 [M]	Invitation	1963	$175
❑ RS-9446 [S]	Invitation	1963	$175
❑ RLP-495 [M]	Live" at the Village Gate	1967	$150
❑ RS-9495 [S]	Live" at the Village Gate	1967	$150

SAVOY
❑ MG-12080 [M]	Jackson's Ville	1956	$50
❑ MG-12070 [M]	Jazz Skyline	1956	$50
❑ MG-12061 [M]	Meet Milt	1956	$50
❑ MG-15058 [10]	Milt Jackson	1954	$175
❑ MG-12046 [M]	Milt Jackson Quartette	1955	$75
❑ MG-12042 [M]	Roll 'Em Bags	1955	$75

SAVOY JAZZ
❑ SJL-1130	Bluesology	198?	$25
❑ SJL-2204	Second Nature	197?	$30
❑ SJL-1106	The First Q	197?	$25
❑ SJC-410	The Jazz Skyline	1985	$25

TRIP
❑ 5553	At the Museum of Modern Art	197?	$25

UNITED ARTISTS
❑ UAL-4022 [M]	Bags' Opus	1959	$40
❑ UAS-5022 [S]	Bags' Opus	1959	$30

VERVE
❑ V6-8761	Milt Jackson and the Hip String Quartet	1969	$35

JACKSON, MUNYUNGO
VITAL MUSIC
❑ VTL-002	Munyungo	199?	$35

JACKSON, PAUL, JR.
ATLANTIC
❑ 81841	I Came to Play	1988	$25
❑ 82065	Out of the Shadows	1990	$30

JACKSON, RANDY
A&M
❑ SP-5191	Randy and the Gypsys	1989	$15
—As "Randy and the Gypsys			

JACKSON, REBBIE
COLUMBIA
❑ BFC39238	Centipede	1984	$12

JACKSON, RONALD SHANNON
ABOUT TIME
❑ AT-1003	Eye on You	1980	$25

ANTILLES
❑ AN-1015	Barbeque Dog	1983	$35
❑ AN-1008	Man Dance	1982	$35

CARAVAN OF DREAMS
❑ 85005	Live at the Caravan of Dreams	1986	$35
❑ 012	Texas	1988	$35
❑ 09	When Colors Play	1987	$35

ISLAND
❑ 90247	Decode Yourself	1985	$25

MOERS
❑ 01086	Nasty	1981	$25
❑ 01081	Street Priest	1981	$25

OAO/CELLULOID
❑ 5011	Pulse	1984	$35

JACKSON, SAMMY
ARVEE
❑ A-434 [M]	Ladies Man	1962	$50
❑ SA-434 [S]	Ladies Man	1962	$75

JACKSON, SHOT
CUMBERLAND
❑ MGC-29513 [M]	Bluegrass Dobro	1965	$25
❑ SRC-69513 [S]	Bluegrass Dobro	1965	$30

STARDAY
❑ SLP-230 [M]	The Singing Strings of Steel Guitar and Dobro	1962	$30

JACKSON, STONEWALL
COLUMBIA
❑ CL2509 [M]	All's Fair in Love 'n' War	1966	$18
❑ CS9309 [S]	All's Fair in Love 'n' War	1966	$25
❑ CL2674 [M]	Help Stamp Out Loneliness	1967	$30
❑ CS9474 [S]	Help Stamp Out Loneliness	1967	$25
❑ CL2059 [M]	I Love a Song	1963	$25
❑ CS8859 [S]	I Love a Song	1963	$30
❑ CS9669	Nothing Takes the Place of Loving You	1968	$25
❑ CL1770 [M]	Sadness in a Song	1962	$25
❑ CS8570 [S]	Sadness in a Song	1962	$30
❑ CL2762 [M]	Stonewall Jackson Country	1967	$30
❑ CS9562 [S]	Stonewall Jackson Country	1967	$25
❑ CL2377 [M]	Stonewall Jackson's Greatest Hits	1965	$18
❑ CS9177 [S]	Stonewall Jackson's Greatest Hits	1965	$25
❑ CL1391 [M]	The Dynamic Stonewall Jackson	1959	$30
❑ CS8186 [S]	The Dynamic Stonewall Jackson	1959	$30
❑ CS9708	The Great Old Songs	1968	$25
❑ CS9754	The Old Country Church	1969	$30
❑ C30254	The Real Thing	1971	$18
❑ CS9880	Tribute to Hank Williams	1969	$25
❑ CL2278 [M]	Trouble & Me	1964	$18
❑ CS9078 [S]	Trouble & Me	1964	$25

HARMONY
❑ HS11187	The Exciting Stonewall Jackson	196?	$15

JACKSON, TOMMY
DECCA
❑ DL8950 [M]	Square Dances Without Calls	1959	$25
❑ DL78950 [S]	Square Dances Without Calls	1959	$30

DOT
❑ DLP-3163 [M]	Do-Si-Do	1959	$25
❑ DLP-3471 [M]	Greatest Bluegrass Hits	1962	$25
❑ DLP-25471 [S]	Greatest Bluegrass Hits	1962	$30

Number	Title	Yr	NM
DLP-3015 [M]	Popular Square Dance Music	1957	$30
DLP-3330 [M]	Square Dance Festival, Vol. 1	1960	$25
DLP-3331 [M]	Square Dance Festival, Vol. 2	1960	$25
DLP-3532 [M]	Square Dance Festival, Vol. 3	1961	$25
DLP-3580 [M]	Square Dances	1963	$18
DLP-25380 [S]	Square Dances	1963	$25
DLP-3085 [M]	Square Dance Tonight!	1958	$30
DLP-3454 [M]	Swing Your Partner	1962	$18
DLP-25454 [S]	Swing Your Partner	1962	$25

MERCURY

Number	Title	Yr	NM
MG-20346 [M]	Square Dance Fiddle Favorites	1958	$30

JACKSON, WALTER
CHI-SOUND

Number	Title	Yr	NM
CS-LA656-G	Feeling Good	1976	$15
CS-LA844-G	Good to See You	1978	$15
CS-LA733-G	I Want to Come Back As A Song	1977	$15

COLUMBIA

FC37132	Tell Me Where It Hurts	1981	$12

EPIC

E34657	Greatest Hits	1977	$12
PE40434	Greatest Hits	1987	$10

OKEH

OKM12107 [M]	It's All Over	1965	$30
OKS14107 [S]	It's All Over	1965	$30
OKM12120 [M]	Speak Her Name	1967	$30
OKS14120 [S]	Speak Her Name	1967	$30
OKS14128	Walter Jackson's Greatest Hits	1969	$18
OKM12108 [M]	Welcome Home	1966	$30
OKS14108 [S]	Welcome Home	1966	$30

JACKSON, WANDA
CAPITOL

ST-554	A Woman Lives for Love	1970	$18
T2306 [M]	Blues in My Heart	1965	$30
ST2306 [S]	Blues in My Heart	1965	$30
ST-11161	Country Keepsakes	1973	$18
ST2976	Cream of the Crop	1968	$18
ST-669	I've Gotta Sing!	1971	$18
ST-11096	I Wouldn't Want You Any Other Way	1972	$18
T1911 [M]	Love Me Forever	1963	$30
ST1911 [S]	Love Me Forever	1963	$30
ST-11023	Praise the Lord	1972	$18
T2704 [M]	Reckless Love Affair	1967	$25
ST2704 [S]	Reckless Love Affair	1967	$18
T1596 [M]	Right or Wrong	1961	$40

— Black colorband label, Capitol logo at left

T1596 [M]	Right or Wrong	1962	$25

— Black colorband label, Capitol logo at top

ST1596 [S]	Right or Wrong	1961	$50

— Black colorband label, Capitol logo at left

ST1596 [S]	Right or Wrong	1962	$30

— Black colorband label, Capitol logo at top

T1384 [M]	Rockin' with Wanda	1960	$400

— Black colorband label, Capitol logo at left

T1384 [M]	Rockin' with Wanda	1962	$300

— Gold "Star Line" label

T1384 [M]	Rockin' with Wanda	1963	$175

— Black "Star Line" label

ST2883 [S]	The Best of Wanda Jackson	1968	$18
T2883 [M]	The Best of Wanda Jackson	1968	$40

— Red and white "Starline" label

ST-238 [B]	The Happy Side of Wanda Jackson	1969	$18
ST-129	The Many Moods of Wanda Jackson	1969	$18
T1511 [M]	There's a Party Goin' On	1961	$300

— Black colorband label, Capitol logo at left

ST1511 [S]	There's a Party Goin' On	1961	$400

— Black colorband label, Capitol logo at left

Number	Title	Yr	NM
T2030 [M]	Two Sides of Wanda	1964	$30
ST2030 [S]	Two Sides of Wanda	1964	$30
T1041 [M]	Wanda Jackson	1958	$300

— Black colorband label, Capitol logo at left

T1041 [M]	Wanda Jackson	1962	$150

— Black colorband label, Capitol logo at top

ST-434	Wanda Jackson Country!	1970	$18
ST-345	Wanda Jackson In Person	1970	$18
ST 8-0345	Wanda Jackson In Person	1970	$25

— Capitol Record Club edition

T2606 [M]	Wanda Jackson Salutes the Country Music Hall of Fame	1966	$18
ST2606 [S]	Wanda Jackson Salutes the Country Music Hall of Fame	1966	$25
T2438 [M]	Wanda Jackson Sings Country Songs	1965	$30
ST2438 [S]	Wanda Jackson Sings Country Songs	1965	$30
T1776 [M]	Wonderful Wanda	1962	$30
ST1776 [S]	Wonderful Wanda	1962	$30
T2812 [M]	You'll Always Have My Love	1967	$25
ST2812 [S]	You'll Always Have My Love	1967	$18

CLEOPATRA

6795 [B]	The Queen Of Rockabilly Salutes The King Of Rock N' Roll		$25

DECCA

DL4224 [M]	Lovin' Country Style	1962	$50

GUSTO

GT 0057	Greatest Hits	1980	$12

HILLTOP

6123	By the Time I Get to Phoenix	1973	$12
6074	Leave My Baby Alone	1969	$15
6058	Please Help Me I'm Falling	1968	$12
6182	Tears at the Grand Ole Opry	1974	$12
6116	We'll Sing in the Sunshine	1972	$15

MYRRH

MSB-6556	Make Me Like a Child Again	1976	$15
MSB-6533	Now I Have Everything	1975	$15
MSB-6513	When It's Time to Fall in Love Again	1974	$15

PICKWICK

PTP-2053	Wanda Jackson	1974	$15

SYMPATHY FOR THE RECORD INDUSTRY

SFTRI-724	Heart Trouble	2003	$15

VARRICK

VR-025	Rock 'n' Roll Away Your Blues	1987	$15

VOCALION

VL73861 [R]	Nobody's Darlin'	1968	$15

WORD

WST-8781	Closer to Jesus	1977	$15
WST-8614	Country Gospel	1973	$15

JACKSON, WILLIS
ATLANTIC

SD18145	The Way We Were	1975	$30

CADET

LP-763 [M]	Smoking with Willis	1966	$35
LPS-763 [S]	Smoking with Willis	1966	$50

COTILLION

SD9908	Willis Jackson Plays with Feeling	1977	$35

CTI

6024	Sunflower	1972	$35

FANTASY

OJC-220	Cool Gator	198?	$25
OJC-321	Please, Mr. Jackson	1988	$25

MOODSVILLE

MVLP-17 [M]	In My Solitude	1961	$150

— Green label

MVLP-17 [M]	In My Solitude	1965	$75

— Blue label, trident logo at right

MUSE

MR-5162	Bar Wars	1978	$30
MR-5048	Headed and Gutted	1975	$30
MR-5100	In the Valley	1976	$30
MR-5200	Lockin' Horns	1979	$30
MR-5294	Nothing Butt	198?	$25
MR-5146	The Gator Horn	1978	$30
MR-5036	West Africa	1974	$30
MR-5316	Ya Understand Me?	198?	$25

PRESTIGE

PRLP-7183 [M]	Blue Gator	1960	$250
PRST-7850	Blue Gator	197?	$35
PRLP-7260 [M]	Bossa Nova Plus	1962	$175
PRST-7260 [S]	Bossa Nova Plus	1962	$175
PRLP-7329 [M]	Boss Shoutin'	1964	$75
PRST-7329 [S]	Boss Shoutin'	1964	$75
PRLP-7211 [M]	Cookin' Sherry	1961	$250
PRST-7211 [S]	Cookin' Sherry	1961	$250
PRLP-7172 [M]	Cool Gator	1959	$250
2516	Gatorade	198?	$30
PRST-7648	Gator's Groove	1969	$50
PRLP-7285 [M]	Grease 'n' Gravy	1963	$75
PRST-7285 [S]	Grease 'n' Gravy	1963	$40
PRST-7830	Keep On a-Blowing	1971	$50
PRLP-7380 [M]	Live! Action	1965	$75
PRST-7380 [S]	Live! Action	1965	$75
PRLP-7348 [M]	Live! Jackson's Action	1965	$75
PRST-7348 [S]	Live! Jackson's Action	1965	$75
PRLP-7273 [M]	Loose...	1963	$75
PRST-7273 [S]	Loose...	1963	$40
PRLP-7317 [M]	More Gravy	1964	$75
PRST-7317 [S]	More Gravy	1964	$40
PRLP-7264 [M]	Neapolitan Nights	1963	$75
PRST-7264 [S]	Neapolitan Nights	1963	$40
PRLP-7162 [M]	Please, Mr. Jackson	1959	$250
PRST-7783	Please Mr. Jackson	1970	$50
PRLP-7196 [M]	Really Groovin'	1961	$250
PRST-7551	Soul Grabber	1968	$50
PRLP-7396 [M]	Soul Night -- Live!	1965	$75
PRST-7396 [S]	Soul Night -- Live!	1965	$75
PRST-7571	Star Bag	1968	$50
PRST-7602	Swivel Hips	1969	$50
PRLP-7412 [M]	Tell It...	1966	$50
PRST-7412 [S]	Tell It...	1966	$75
PRST-7702	The Best of Willis Jackson with Brother Jack McDuff	1969	$35
PRLP-7770	The Best -- Soul Stompin'	1971	$35
PRLP-7296 [M]	The Good Life	1964	$75
PRST-7296 [S]	The Good Life	1964	$40
PRLP-7232 [M]	Thunderbird	1962	$175
PRST-7232 [S]	Thunderbird	1962	$175
PRLP-7364 [M]	Together Again	1965	$75
PRST-7364 [S]	Together Again	1965	$75
PRLP-7428 [M]	Together Again...Again	1966	$50
PRST-7428 [S]	Together Again...Again	1966	$75

TRIP

5028	Funky Reggae	197?	$25
5007	Mellow Blues	197?	$30
5030	Willis Jackson Plays Around with the Hits	197?	$25

VERVE

V-8589 [M]	'Gator Tails	1964	$35
V6-8589 [S]	'Gator Tails	1964	$50
V6-8782	Willis Jackson	1969	$35

JACKSON HEIGHTS
MERCURY

SR-61331	King Progress	1970	$30

VERVE

V6-5089	Jackson Heights	1973	$25

JACKSON SISTERS
TIGER LILY

TL14061 [B]	Jackson Sisters	1976	$1,500.00

JACKSONS, THE
Includes records as "The Jackson Five." Also see JACKIE JACKSON; JERMAINE JACKSON; MICHAEL JACKSON.

EPIC

OE40911	2300 Jackson Street	1989	$10
JE35552	Destiny	1978	$15

— Orange label

JE35552	Destiny	1979	$10

— Dark blue label

JE34835	Goin' Places	1977	$14

— Orange label

PE34835	Goin' Places	198?	$10

— Budget-line reissue

KE237545	Jacksons Live	1981	$15
PE34229 [PD]	The Jacksons	1976	$2000

— Picture disc promo

PE34229 [B]	The Jacksons	1976	$10

— Orange label. Deduct 50% for budget-line reissue with bar code and dark blue label

FE36424	Triumph	1980	$10
HE46424	Triumph	1982	$75

— Half-speed mastered edition

QE38946	Victory	1984	$10
8E839576 [PD]	Victory	1984	$18

MOTOWN

MS709 [B]	ABC	1970	$30
M5-152V1	ABC	1981	$12
M7-868	Anthology	1976	$25
MS713 [B]	Christmas Album	1970	$30
5250ML	Christmas Album	1982	$10

— Reissue of Motown 713

M6-780	Dancing Machine	1974	$18
MS700 [B]	Diana Ross Presents the Jackson 5	1969	$40
M5-129V1	Diana Ross Presents the Jackson Five	1981	$12
M6-783	Get It Together	1973	$18
M-742	Goin' Back to Indiana	1971	$25
M-741	Jackson 5 Greatest Hits	1971	$25
M5-201V1	Jackson 5 Greatest Hits	1981	$12
M6-865	Joyful Jukebox Music	1976	$18
M-750	Lookin' Through the Windows	1972	$25
M-735	Maybe Tomorrow	1971	$25
5228ML	Maybe Tomorrow	1982	$12
M5-112V1	Motown Superstar Series, Vol. 12	1981	$15
M6-829	Moving Violation	1975	$18
M-761	Skywriter	1973	$18
374631294-1 [DJ]	Soulsation!	1995	$25

Number	Title	Yr	NM

—Vinyl is promo only; 4-song sampler from box set

| ❏ MS718 [B] | Third Album | 1970 | $25 |
| ❏ M5-157V1 | Third Album | 1981 | $12 |

UNIVERSAL MOTOWN

| ❏ 5316421 | ABC | 2009 | $25 |

JACOBI, LOU
CAPITOL

| ❏ T2596 [M] | Al Tijuana and His Jewish Brass | 1966 | $18 |
| ❏ ST2596 [S] | Al Tijuana and His Jewish Brass | 1966 | $25 |

JACOBS, DICK
CORAL

| ❏ CRL57381 [M] | The Electro-Sonic Orchestra Presenting a New Concept in Sound | 1958 | $25 |
| ❏ CRL757381 [S] | The Electro-Sonic Orchestra Presenting a New Concept in Sound | 1958 | $30 |

JACOBS, FREDDIE
WESTMINSTER

| ❏ WP-6087 [M] | Swingin' Folk Tunes | 195? | $30 |

JACOBS, HANK
SUE

| ❏ LP-1023 [M] | So Far Away | 1964 | $100 |

JACOBY, DON
DECCA

| ❏ DL4241 [M] | The Swinging Big Sound | 1963 | $35 |
| ❏ DL74241 [S] | The Swinging Big Sound | 1963 | $25 |

JACQUET, ILLINOIS, AND BEN WEBSTER
CLEF

| ❏ MGC-680 [M] | The Kid" and "The Brute | 1955 | $350 |

VERVE

| ❏ MGV-8065 [M] | The Kid" and "The Brute | 1957 | $300 |

—Reissue of Clef 680

| ❏ V-8065 [M] | The Kid" and "The Brute | 1961 | $25 |

JACQUET, ILLINOIS, AND LESTER YOUNG
ALADDIN

| ❏ LP-701 [10] | Battle of the Saxes | 1953 | $1200 |

JACQUET, ILLINOIS
ALADDIN

| ❏ LP-708 [10] | Illinois Jacquet and His Tenor Sax | 1954 | $500 |
| ❏ LP-803 [M] | Illinois Jacquet and His Tenor Sax | 1956 | $300 |

APOLLO

| ❏ LP-104 [10] | Illinois Jacquet Jam Session | 1951 | $600 |

ARGO

❏ LP-746 [M]	Bosses of the Ballad	1964	$40
❏ LP-735 [M]	Desert Winds	1964	$40
❏ LPS-735 [S]	Desert Winds	1964	$50
❏ LPS-746 [S]	Illinois Jacquet Plays Cole Porter	1964	$50
❏ LP-722 [M]	The Message	1963	$40
❏ LPS-722 [S]	The Message	1963	$50

ATLANTIC

| ❏ 81816 | Jacquet's Got It! | 1988 | $30 |

BLACK LION

| ❏ 146 | Genius at Work | 197? | $50 |

CADET

| ❏ LP-746 [M] | Bosses of the Ballad | 1966 | $50 |

—Reissue of Argo 746; fading blue label

| ❏ LPS-746 [S] | Bosses of the Ballad | 1966 | $30 |

—Reissue of Argo 746; fading blue label

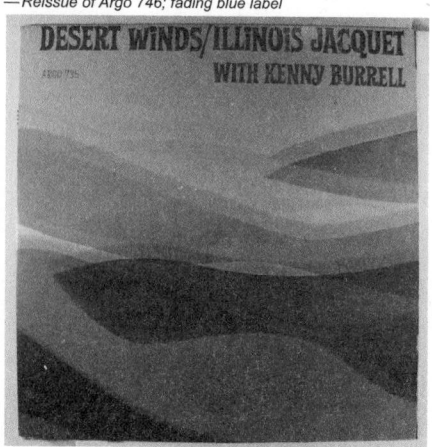

| ❏ LP-735 [M] | Desert Winds | 1966 | $50 |

—Reissue of Argo 735; fading blue label

| ❏ LPS-735 [S] | Desert Winds | 1966 | $30 |

—Reissue of Argo 735; fading blue label

❏ LP-773 [M]	Go Power!	1966	$40
❏ LPS-773 [S]	Go Power!	1966	$50
❏ LP-754 [M]	Spectrum	1965	$40
❏ LPS-754 [S]	Spectrum	1965	$50
❏ LP-722 [M]	The Message	1966	$50

—Reissue of Argo 722; fading blue label

| ❏ LPS-722 [S] | The Message | 1966 | $30 |

—Reissue of Argo 722; fading blue label

| ❏ CA-722 [M] | The Message | 197? | $25 |

—Yellow and red label

CHESS

| ❏ CH-91554 | The Message | 1984 | $25 |

—Reissue

CLASSIC JAZZ

| ❏ 112 | Illinois Jacquet with Wild Bill Davis | 1978 | $50 |
| ❏ 146 | Jacquet's Street | 1981 | $50 |

CLEF

❏ MGC-702 [M]	Groovin' with Jacquet	1956	$350
❏ MGC-129 [10]	Illinois Jacquet Collates #2	1953	$350
❏ MGC-112 [10]	Illinois Jacquet Collates	1953	$350
❏ MGC-676 [M]	Illinois Jacquet Septet	1955	$350
❏ MGC-167 [10]	Jazz by Jacquet	1954	$350
❏ MGC-622 [M]	Jazz Moods	1955	$350
❏ MGC-700 [M]	Jazz Moods by Illinois Jacquet	1956	$300
❏ MGC-701 [M]	Port of Rico	1956	$300
❏ MGC-750 [M]	Swing's the Thing	1956	$300

EPIC

❏ LA16033 [M]	Illinois Jacquet	1963	$100
❏ BA17033 [S]	Illinois Jacquet	1963	$150
❏ BA17033 [S]	Illinois Jacquet	199?	$30

—Classic Records reissue on audiophile vinyl

FANTASY

| ❏ OJC-417 | Bottoms Up! | 1990 | $30 |
| ❏ OJC-614 | The Blues -- That's Me | 1991 | $35 |

GROOVE NOTE

| ❏ 2003 | Birthday Party | 1999 | $50 |

—Audiophile vinyl; one record has the entire album, the other has two tracks at 45 rpm

IMPERIAL

| ❏ LP-9184 [M] | Flying Home | 1962 | $175 |
| ❏ LP-12184 [S] | Flying Home | 1962 | $175 |

JAZZ MAN

| ❏ 5034 | Genius at Work | 198? | $30 |

JRC

| ❏ 11434 | Birthday Party | 197? | $75 |

MERCURY

| ❏ MGC-129 [10] | Illinois Jacquet Collates #2 | 1953 | $0 |

—Canceled; issued on Clef

| ❏ MGC-112 [10] | Illinois Jacquet Collates | 1952 | $500 |

MOSAIC

| ❏ MQ6-165 | The Complete Illinois Jacquet Sessions 1945-50 | 199? | $150 |

PRESTIGE

❏ PRST-7575	Bottoms Up!	1968	$40
❏ P-24057	How High the Moon	1975	$75
❏ PRST-7731	The Blues -- That's Me	1969	$40
❏ PRST-7597	The King!	1968	$40
❏ PRST-7629	The Soul Explosion	1969	$40

RCA VICTOR

| ❏ LPM-3236 [10] | Black Velvet | 1954 | $500 |

ROULETTE

| ❏ R-52035 [M] | Illinois Jacquet Flies Again | 1959 | $150 |
| ❏ SR-52035 [S] | Illinois Jacquet Flies Again | 1959 | $75 |

SAVOY

| ❏ MG-15024 [10] | Tenor Sax | 1953 | $400 |

VERVE

| ❏ MGV-8086 [M] | Groovin' with Jacquet | 1957 | $300 |

—Reissue of Clef 702

| ❏ V-8086 [M] | Groovin' with Jacquet | 1961 | $30 |
| ❏ MGV-8061 [M] | Illinois Jacquet and His Orchestra | 1957 | $300 |

—Reissue of Clef 676

| ❏ V-8061 [M] | Illinois Jacquet and His Orchestra | 1961 | $30 |
| ❏ MGV-8084 [M] | Jazz Moods by Illinois Jacquet | 1957 | $300 |

—Reissue of Clef 700

| ❏ V-8084 [M] | Jazz Moods by Illinois Jacquet | 1961 | $30 |
| ❏ MGV-8085 [M] | Port of Rico | 1957 | $250 |

—Reissue of Clef 701

| ❏ V-8085 [M] | Port of Rico | 1961 | $30 |
| ❏ MGV-8023 [M] | Swing's the Thing | 1957 | $250 |

—Reissue of Clef 750

| ❏ V-8023 [M] | Swing's the Thing | 1961 | $30 |
| ❏ VE-2-2544 | The Cool Rage | 198? | $50 |

JACQUET, RUSSELL
KING

| ❏ 295-81 [10] | Russell Jacquet and His All Stars | 1954 | $300 |

JADE, FAINE
RSVP

| ❏ 8002 | Introspection: A Faine Jade Recital | 1968 | $400 |

JADE
GENERAL AMERICAN

| ❏ 11311 | The Faces of Jade | 1968 | $100 |

JADE WARRIOR
ANTILLES

| ❏ AN-7045 | Floating World | 198? | $10 |

—Reissue of Island 9290

| ❏ AN-7056 | Kites | 198? | $10 |

—Reissue of Island 9393

| ❏ AN-7048 | Waves | 198? | $10 |

—Reissue of Island 9318

| ❏ AN-7068 | Way of the Sun | 1978 | $12 |

ISLAND

❏ ILPS9290	Floating World	1974	$12
❏ ILPS9393	Kites	1976	$12
❏ ILPS9318	Waves	1975	$12

VERTIGO

❏ VEL-1007	Jade Warrior	1971	$85
❏ VEL-1012	Last Autumn's Dream	1972	$75
❏ VEL-1009	Released	1972	$50

JADES, THE
JARRETT

| ❏ 21517 [M] | Live at the Disco a-Go-Go | 1965 | $120 |

JAFFE, ANDY
STASH

| ❏ ST-247 | Manhattan Projections | 1985 | $25 |

JAG PANZER
AZRA IRON WORKS

| ❏ 1001 [PD] | Ample Destruction | 1985 | $30 |

—Allegedly, 250 were pressed as picture discs

JAGGER, CHRIS
ASYLUM

| ❏ SD5069 | Chris Jagger | 1973 | $15 |
| ❏ 7E-1009 | The Adventures of Valentine Vox the Ventriloquist | 1974 | $15 |

JAGGER, MICK
COLUMBIA

| ❏ OC40919 | Primitive Cool | 1987 | $10 |
| ❏ FC39940 | She's the Boss | 1985 | $12 |

JAGGERZ, THE
GAMBLE

| ❏ GS-5006 | Introducing the Jaggerz | 1969 | $25 |

KAMA SUTRA

| ❏ KSBS-2017 | We Went to Different Schools Together | 1970 | $18 |

WOODEN NICKEL

| ❏ BWL1-0772 | Come Again | 1975 | $15 |

JAIM
ETHEREAL

| ❏ 1001 | Prophecy Fulfilled | 1970 | $50 |

JAKUS, JEAN
LONDON

| ❏ SW99018 | German Christmas Singalong | 195? | $18 |

JALOPY FIVE, THE
MODERN SOUND

| ❏ M-561 [M] | I Love That West Coast Sound | 1965 | $50 |
| ❏ MS-561 [S] | I Love That West Coast Sound | 1965 | $50 |

JAM, THE
Paul Weller next's band was THE STYLE COUNCIL.

POLYDOR

❏ PD1-6188 [B]	All Mod Cons	1979	$30
❏ 810751-1 [EP]	Beat Surrender	1982	$18
❏ PD1-6365 [B]	Dig the New Breed	1982	$25
❏ PD1-6110 [B]	In the City	1977	$30
❏ 817124-1	In the City	198?	$12

—Reissue

❏ PD1-6249 [B]	Setting Sons	1980	$18
❏ 815537-1 [B]	Snap!	1983	$30
❏ PD1-6315 [B]	Sound Affects	1981	$18
❏ PX1-506 [EP]	The Bitterest Pill	1982	$12

Number	Title	Yr	NM
❑ PD1-6349 [B]	The Gift	1982	$18
❑ PX1-503 [EP]	The Jam	1982	$12
❑ PD1-6129 [B]	This Is the Modern World	1978	$30
❑ 823281-1 [B]	This Is the Modern World	198?	$15

— Reissue

JAM FACTORY
EPIC
Number	Title	Yr	NM
❑ BN26521	Sittin' in the Trap	1970	$30

JAMAL, AHMAD
20TH CENTURY
Number	Title	Yr	NM
❑ T-417	Ahmad Jamal '73	1973	$25
❑ T-600	Genetic Walk	1980	$25
❑ T-631	Greatest Hits	1981	$25
❑ T-622	Intervals	1980	$25
❑ T-432	Jamaica	1974	$25
❑ T-459	Jamal Plays Jamal	1975	$25
❑ T-555	One	1978	$25
❑ T-515	Steppin' Out with a Dream	1977	$25

ABC
Number	Title	Yr	NM
❑ S-660	Tranquility	1968	$30

ABC IMPULSE!
Number	Title	Yr	NM
❑ AS-9176	At the Top -- Poinciana Revisited	1969	$35
❑ SMAS-92005	At the Top -- Poinciana Revisited	1969	$175

— Capitol Record Club edition

Number	Title	Yr	NM
❑ AS-9217	Freeflight	1971	$30
❑ AS-9226	Outertimeinnerspace	1972	$30
❑ AS-9260	Re-evaluations: The Impulse Years	1975	$30
❑ AS-9194	The Awakening	1970	$35
❑ AS-9238	Tranquility	1973	$30

ARGO
Number	Title	Yr	NM
❑ LP-636 [M]	Ahmad Jamal, Volume IV	1958	$75
❑ LPS-636 [S]	Ahmad Jamal, Volume IV	1958	$40
❑ LP-703 [M]	Ahmad Jamal at the Blackhawk	1962	$50
❑ LPS-703 [S]	Ahmad Jamal at the Blackhawk	1962	$75
❑ LP-667 [M]	Ahmad Jamal at the Pershing Volume 2	1961	$50
❑ LPS-667 [S]	Ahmad Jamal at the Pershing Volume 2	1961	$75
❑ LP-685 [M]	Alhambra	1961	$50
❑ LPS-685 [S]	Alhambra	1961	$75
❑ LP-691 [M]	All of You	1962	$50
❑ LPS-691 [S]	All of You	1962	$75
❑ LP-628 [M]	But Not for Me/Ahmad Jamal at the Pershing	1958	$75
❑ LPS-628 [S]	But Not for Me/Ahmad Jamal at the Pershing	1958	$40
❑ LP-602 [M]	Chamber Music of the New Jazz	1956	$150

— With "Creative Hi-Fidelity Modern Music" on cover; "ship" label; reissue of Parrot LP

Number	Title	Yr	NM
❑ LP-602 [M]	Chamber Music of the New Jazz	1956	$75

— Dark green label, gold or silver print

Number	Title	Yr	NM
❑ LP-610 [M]	Count 'Em 88	1957	$75
❑ LP-758 [M]	Extensions	1965	$50
❑ LPS-758 [S]	Extensions	1965	$75
❑ LP-662 [M]	Happy Moods	1960	$50
❑ LPS-662 [S]	Happy Moods	1960	$75
❑ LP-646 [M]	Jamal at the Penthouse	1959	$75
❑ LPS-646 [S]	Jamal at the Penthouse	1959	$40
❑ LP-673 [M]	Listen to Ahmad Jamal	1961	$50
❑ LPS-673 [S]	Listen to Ahmad Jamal	1961	$75
❑ LP-712 [M]	Macanudo	1963	$50
❑ LPS-712 [S]	Macanudo	1963	$75
❑ LP-733 [M]	Naked City" Theme	1964	$50
❑ LPS-733 [S]	Naked City" Theme	1964	$75
❑ LP-719 [M]	Poin'-ci-an'a	1963	$50
❑ LPS-719 [S]	Poin'-ci-an'a	1963	$75
❑ LP-2638 [M]	Portfolio of Ahmad Jamal	1959	$40

— Textured cover with raised image of Jamal; limited, numbered edition

Number	Title	Yr	NM
❑ LPS-2638 [S]	Portfolio of Ahmad Jamal	1959	$150
❑ LP-751 [M]	The Roar of the Greasepaint	1965	$50
❑ LPS-751 [S]	The Roar of the Greasepaint	1965	$75

ATLANTIC
Number	Title	Yr	NM
❑ 81793	Crystal	1987	$25
❑ 81258	Digital Works	1985	$30
❑ 81699	Live at the Montreal Jazz Festival 1985	1986	$30
❑ 81645	Rossiter Road	1986	$25

CADET
Number	Title	Yr	NM
❑ LP-636 [M]	Ahmad Jamal, Volume IV	1966	$30
❑ LPS-636 [S]	Ahmad Jamal, Volume IV	1966	$35
❑ LP-703 [M]	Ahmad Jamal at the Blackhawk	1966	$30
❑ LPS-703 [S]	Ahmad Jamal at the Blackhawk	1966	$35
❑ LP-667 [M]	Ahmad Jamal at the Pershing Volume 2	1966	$30
❑ LPS-667 [S]	Ahmad Jamal at the Pershing Volume 2	1966	$35
❑ LP-685 [M]	Alhambra	1966	$30
❑ LPS-685 [S]	Alhambra	1966	$35
❑ LP-691 [M]	All of You	1966	$30
❑ LPS-691 [S]	All of You	1966	$35
❑ LP-628 [M]	But Not for Me/Ahmad Jamal at the Pershing	1966	$30

Number	Title	Yr	NM
❑ LPS-628 [S]	But Not for Me/Ahmad Jamal at the Pershing	1966	$35
❑ LP-792 [M]	Cry Young	1967	$50
❑ LPS-792 [S]	Cry Young	1967	$35
❑ LP-758 [M]	Extensions	1966	$30
❑ LPS-758 [S]	Extensions	1965	$35
❑ CA-758 [S]	Extensions	197?	$30

— Reissue; yellow and red label with "A Division of All Platinum Record Group" on label

Number	Title	Yr	NM
❑ LP-662 [M]	Happy Moods	1966	$30
❑ LPS-662 [S]	Happy Moods	1966	$35
❑ LP-777 [M]	Heat Wave	1966	$35
❑ LPS-777 [S]	Heat Wave	1966	$50

— Original with fading blue label

Number	Title	Yr	NM
❑ LPS-777 [S]	Heat Wave	1977	$30

— Reissue, "a division of All Platinum Record Group" on back cover

Number	Title	Yr	NM
❑ 50035	Inspiration	1974	$35
❑ LP-646 [M]	Jamal at the Penthouse	1966	$30
❑ LPS-646 [S]	Jamal at the Penthouse	1966	$35
❑ LP-673 [M]	Listen to Ahmad Jamal	1966	$30
❑ LPS-673 [M]	Listen to Ahmad Jamal	1966	$35
❑ LP-712 [M]	Macanudo	1966	$30
❑ LPS-712 [S]	Macanudo	1966	$35
❑ LP-733 [M]	Naked City" Theme	1966	$30
❑ LPS-733 [S]	Naked City" Theme	1966	$35
❑ LP-719 [M]	Poin'-ci-an'a	1966	$30
❑ LPS-719 [S]	Poin'-ci-an'a	1966	$35
❑ LP-2638 [M]	Portfolio of Ahmad Jamal	1966	$40

— Cadet issues generally did not have embossed covers

Number	Title	Yr	NM
❑ LPS-2638 [S]	Portfolio of Ahmad Jamal	1966	$50

— Cadet issues generally did not have embossed covers

Number	Title	Yr	NM
❑ LP-764 [M]	Rhapsody	1966	$35
❑ LPS-764 [S]	Rhapsody	1966	$50
❑ LP-786 [M]	Standard Eyes	1967	$35
❑ LPS-786 [S]	Standard Eyes	1967	$50
❑ LPS-807	The Bright, the Blue and the Beautiful	1968	$35
❑ LP-751 [M]	The Roar of the Greasepaint	1966	$30
❑ LPS-751 [S]	The Roar of the Greasepaint	1966	$35

CATALYST
Number	Title	Yr	NM
❑ 7606	Live at Oil Can Harry's	1978	$30

CHESS
Number	Title	Yr	NM
❑ CH-91553	Poinciana	198?	$25
❑ CH-2-9223	Sun Set	1984	$30

EPIC
Number	Title	Yr	NM
❑ LN3212 [M]	Ahmad Jamal Trio	1956	$300

— Yellow label with lines around rim

Number	Title	Yr	NM
❑ BN627 [R]	Ahmad Jamal Trio	196?	$150
❑ LN3212 [M]	Ahmad Jamal Trio	1963	$300

— Yellow label, no lines around rim

Number	Title	Yr	NM
❑ LN3631 [M]	The Piano Scene of Ahmad Jamal	1959	$150
❑ BN634 [S]	The Piano Scene of Ahmad Jamal	1959	$150

GRP/IMPULSE!
Number	Title	Yr	NM
❑ 226	The Awakening	199?	$35

— Reissue on audiophile vinyl

MCA
Number	Title	Yr	NM
❑ 29041	At the Top -- Poinciana Revisited	198?	$20

— Reissue of Impulse! 9178

Number	Title	Yr	NM
❑ 29043	Freelight	198?	$20

— Reissue of Impulse! 9217

Number	Title	Yr	NM
❑ 29042	The Awakening	198?	$20

— Reissue of Impulse! 9194

MCA/IMPULSE!
Number	Title	Yr	NM
❑ 5644	The Awakening	1986	$25

— Another reissue of Impulse! 9194

MOTOWN
Number	Title	Yr	NM
❑ M8-945	Night Song	1981	$25

PARROT
Number	Title	Yr	NM
❑ 55-245/6 [M]	Ahmad Jamal Plays	1955	$1500

— VG value 500; VG+ value 1000

JAMAL, KHAN
DOGTOWN
Number	Title	Yr	NM
❑ no number [B]	Drum Dance to the Motherland		$1500

STASH
Number	Title	Yr	NM
❑ ST-278	Infinity	1988	$25

STEEPLECHASE
Number	Title	Yr	NM
❑ SCS-1196	Dark Warrior	198?	$30

JAMES, BOB, AND DAVID SANBORN
WARNER BROS.
Number	Title	Yr	NM
❑ 25393	Double Vision	1986	$25

JAMES, BOB, AND EARL KLUGH
CAPITOL
Number	Title	Yr	NM
❑ SMAS-12244	Two of a Kind	1982	$30

MOBILE FIDELITY
Number	Title	Yr	NM
❑ 1-124	Two of a Kind	1984	$40

— Original Master Recording" banner across top of front cover

Number	Title	Yr	NM

TAPPAN ZEE
Number	Title	Yr	NM
❑ HC46241	One on One	198?	$75

— Half-speed mastered edition

Number	Title	Yr	NM
❑ FC36241	One on One	1979	$25

JAMES, BOB
CBS MASTERWORKS
Number	Title	Yr	NM
❑ IM39540	Rameau	1985	$30

COLUMBIA
Number	Title	Yr	NM
❑ FC38678	The Genie (Themes & Variations from the TV Series "Taxi")	1983	$25

CTI
Number	Title	Yr	NM
❑ 7074	BJ4	1977	$35
❑ CTS-6043	One	1974	$50
❑ CTS-6063	Three	1976	$35
❑ CTS-6057	Two	1975	$75

ESP-DISK'
Number	Title	Yr	NM
❑ 1009 [M]	Explosions	1965	$175
❑ S-1009 [S]	Explosions	1965	$200

MERCURY
Number	Title	Yr	NM
❑ MG-20768 [M]	Bold Conceptions	1963	$150
❑ SR-60768 [S]	Bold Conceptions	1963	$175

TAPPAN ZEE
Number	Title	Yr	NM
❑ FC39580	12	1985	$25
❑ C2X36786	All Around the Town	1981	$30
❑ FC36838	BJ4	1981	$25

— Reissue of CTI 7074

Number	Title	Yr	NM
❑ PC36838	BJ4	1985	$10

— Budget-line reissue

Number	Title	Yr	NM
❑ AS1299 [DJ]	Bob James/Dave Herman Interview	1981	$35

— Promo-only radio program

Number	Title	Yr	NM
❑ FC38801	Foxie	1983	$25
❑ JC36422	H	1980	$25
❑ FC38067	Hands Down	1982	$25
❑ JC34896	Heads	1977	$25
❑ PC34896	Heads	1985	$10

— Budget-line reissue

Number	Title	Yr	NM
❑ JC36056	Lucky Seven	1979	$25
❑ PC36056	Lucky Seven	1985	$10

— Budget-line reissue

Number	Title	Yr	NM
❑ AS699 [DJ]	Lucky Seven/One on One Sampler	1979	$75

— Edited selections from both of the above albums; promo only

Number	Title	Yr	NM
❑ FC36835	One	1981	$25

— Reissue of CTI 6043

Number	Title	Yr	NM
❑ PC36835	One	1985	$10

— Budget-line reissue

Number	Title	Yr	NM
❑ FC37495	Sign of the Times	1981	$25
❑ HC47495	Sign of the Times	1982	$75

— Half-speed mastered edition

Number	Title	Yr	NM
❑ FC36837	Three	1981	$30

— Reissue of CTI 6063

Number	Title	Yr	NM
❑ PC36837	Three	1985	$10

— Budget-line reissue

Number	Title	Yr	NM
❑ JC35594	Touchdown	1978	$25
❑ HC45594	Touchdown	1982	$75

— Half-speed mastered edition

Number	Title	Yr	NM
❑ PC35594	Touchdown	1985	$10

— Budget-line reissue

Number	Title	Yr	NM
❑ FC36836	Two	1981	$30

— Reissue of CTI 6057

Number	Title	Yr	NM
❑ PC36836	Two	1985	$20

— Budget-line reissue

WARNER BROS.
Number	Title	Yr	NM
❑ 26256	Grand Piano Canyon	1990	$35
❑ 25757	Ivory Coast	1988	$25
❑ 25495	Obsession	1986	$25

JAMES, DENNIS
KAPP
Number	Title	Yr	NM
❑ KL-1009 [M]	Let's All Sing a Song for Christmas	1955	$30

JAMES, DWIGHT
CADENCE JAZZ
Number	Title	Yr	NM
❑ CJ-1014	Inner Heat	198?	$25

JAMES, ELMORE
BELL
Number	Title	Yr	NM
❑ 6037	Elmore James	1969	$30

CHESS
Number	Title	Yr	NM
❑ LP-1537	Whose Muddy Shoes	1969	$30

COLLECTABLES
Number	Title	Yr	NM
❑ COL-5112	Golden Classics	198?	$15
❑ COL-5184	The Complete Fire and Enjoy Sessions, Part 1	198?	$12
❑ COL-5185	The Complete Fire and Enjoy Sessions, Part 2	198?	$12
❑ COL-5186	The Complete Fire and Enjoy Sessions, Part 3	198?	$12
❑ COL-5187	The Complete Fire and Enjoy Sessions, Part 4	198?	$12

Number	Title	Yr	NM

CROWN

Number	Title	Yr	NM
❏ CLP-5168 [M]	Blues After Hours	1961	$300

— Black label, silver "Crown

| ❏ CLP-5168 [M] | Blues After Hours | 1962 | $50 |

— Gray label

INTERMEDIA

| ❏ QS-5034 | Red Hot Blues | 198? | $12 |

KENT

❏ KLP-9001	Anthology of the Blues Legend	196?	$30
❏ KLP-5022 [M]	Original Folk Blues	1964	$40
❏ KST-522 [R]	Original Folk Blues	1964	$30
❏ KLP-9010	The Resurrection of Elmore James	196?	$30

SPHERE SOUND

❏ SR-7008 [M]	I Need You	1966	$175
❏ SSR-7008 [R]	I Need You	1966	$120
❏ SR-7002 [M]	The Sky Is Crying	1965	$180
❏ SSR-7002 [R]	The Sky Is Crying	1965	$120

UP FRONT

| ❏ UP-122 | The Great Elmore James | 1970 | $15 |

JAMES, ETTA

ARGO

❏ LP-4003 [M]	At Last!	1961	$75
❏ LPS-4003 [S]	At Last!	1961	$100
❏ LP-4013 [M]	Etta James	1962	$30
❏ LPS-4013 [P]	Etta James	1962	$40

— Two duets with Harvey Fuqua are rechanneled

❏ LP-4032 [M]	Etta James Rocks the House	1964	$150
❏ LPS-4032 [S]	Etta James Rocks the House	1964	$175
❏ LP-4018 [M]	Etta James Sings for Lovers	1962	$30
❏ LPS-4018 [S]	Etta James Sings for Lovers	1962	$40
❏ LP-4025 [M]	Etta James Top Ten	1963	$30
❏ LPS-4025 [S]	Etta James Top Ten	1963	$40
❏ LP-4040 [M]	The Queen of Soul	1965	$30
❏ LPS-4040 [S]	The Queen of Soul	1965	$40
❏ LP-4011 [M]	The Second Time Around	1961	$30
❏ LPS-4011 [S]	The Second Time Around	1961	$40

CADET

❏ LP-4003 [M]	At Last!	1966	$15
❏ LPS-4003 [S]	At Last!	1966	$18
❏ LP-4055 [M]	Call My Name	1967	$18
❏ LPS-4055 [S]	Call My Name	1967	$25
❏ LP-4013 [M]	Etta James	1966	$15
❏ LPS-4013 [S]	Etta James	1966	$18
❏ LP-4018 [M]	Etta James Sings for Lovers	1966	$15
❏ LPS-4018 [S]	Etta James Sings for Lovers	1966	$18
❏ LPS-832	Etta James Sings Funk	1969	$25
❏ LP-4025 [M]	Etta James Top Ten	1966	$15
❏ LPS-4025 [S]	Etta James Top Ten	1966	$18
❏ LPS-847	Losers Weepers	1970	$18
❏ LP-802 [M]	Tell Mama	1968	$30

❏ LPS-802 [S]	Tell Mama	1968	$25
❏ LP-4040 [M]	The Queen of Soul	1966	$15
❏ LPS-4040 [S]	The Queen of Soul	1966	$18
❏ LP-4011 [M]	The Second Time Around	1966	$15
❏ LPS-4011 [S]	The Second Time Around	1966	$18

CHESS

| ❏ CH-9266 | At Last! | 1987 | $10 |

—Reissue

| ❏ CH-60029 | Come a Little Closer | 1974 | $18 |
| ❏ CH-91509 | Come a Little Closer | 198? | $10 |

— Reissue

❏ ACH-19003	Etta Is Betta Than Evvah!	1976	$18
❏ CH-50042	Etta James	1973	$18
❏ CH-9184	Etta James Rocks the House	1986	$10

— Reissue

❏ CH-9110	Her Greatest Sides, Vol. 1	1984	$12
❏ 2CH-60004	Peaches	1971	$25
❏ CH-9269	Tell Mama	1987	$10

— Reissue

| ❏ CH-9287 | The Second Time Around | 1989 | $10 |

— Reissue

| ❏ CH2-6028 | The Sweetest Peaches | 1989 | $15 |

CROWN

| ❏ CLP-5360 [M] | Etta James | 1963 | $30 |

— With Etta smiling on cover

| ❏ CLP-5360 [M] | Etta James | 1963 | $30 |

— With Etta somber on cover

| ❏ CST-360 [R] | Etta James | 1963 | $25 |

— With Etta smiling on cover

| ❏ CST-360 [R] | Etta James | 1963 | $25 |

— With Etta somber on cover

| ❏ CLP-5209 [M] | Miss Etta James | 1961 | $150 |

— First edition, with framed picture on cover

| ❏ CLP-5209 [M] | Miss Etta James | 1962 | $75 |

— Second edition, all-white cover with "Miss Etta James

| ❏ CLP-5234 [M] | The Best of Etta James | 1962 | $75 |

— Black label

| ❏ CLP-5234 [M] | The Best of Etta James | 1963 | $30 |

— Gray label

| ❏ CLP-5250 [M] | Twist with Etta James | 1962 | $75 |

— Black label

| ❏ CLP-5250 [M] | Twist with Etta James | 1963 | $30 |

— Gray label

INTERMEDIA

| ❏ QS-5014 | Etta, Red Hot 'N' Live! | 198? | $12 |

ISLAND

| ❏ 91018 | Seven Year Itch | 1988 | $12 |
| ❏ 842926-1 | Sticking to My Guns | 1990 | $15 |

KENT

| ❏ KLP-5000 [M] | Miss Etta James | 1964 | $30 |
| ❏ KST-500 [R] | Miss Etta James | 1964 | $100 |

— Red vinyl

| ❏ KST-500 [R] | Miss Etta James | 1964 | $30 |

— Black vinyl

UNITED

| ❏ US7712 | Etta James Sings | 197? | $12 |

WARNER BROS.

| ❏ BSK3156 | Deep in the Night | 1978 | $15 |

JAMES, GREGORY

INNER CITY

| ❏ IC-1050 | Alicia | 1978 | $35 |

JAMES, HARRY

Trumpeter and bandleader. Items with an asterisk (*) feature at least one track with FRANK SINATRA on vocals.

AIRCHECK

| ❏ 18 | Harry James On the Air | 197? | $25 |
| ❏ 33 | Harry James On the Air, Vol. 2 | 1986 | $25 |

BAINBRIDGE

| ❏ BT-6252 | Ciribiribin | 1982 | $25 |

CAPITOL

❏ W654 [M]	Harry James in Hi-Fi	1955	$85
❏ T1093 [M]	Harry's Choice	1958	$75
❏ W712 [M]	More Harry James in Hi-Fi	1956	$75
❏ T1515 [M]	The Hits of Harry James	1961	$50

— Black colorband label, logo at left

| ❏ DT1515 [R] | The Hits of Harry James | 1961 | $75 |
| ❏ T1515 [M] | The Hits of Harry James | 1962 | $85 |

— Black colorband label, logo at top

| ❏ M-1515 | The Hits of Harry James | 197? | $30 |

— Mono reissue

| ❏ T1037 [M] | The New James | 1958 | $75 |
| ❏ T874 [M] | Wild About Harry | 1957 | $150 |

CIRCLE

| ❏ 39 | Harry James and His Orchestra 1954 | 198? | $25 |
| ❏ 5 | Harry James and His Orchestra with Dick Haymes | 198? | $25 |

COLUMBIA

| ❏ CL655 [M] | *All Time Favorites | 1955 | $50 |

— Maroon label, gold print

❏ CL6009 [10]	*All Time Favorites	1949	$150
❏ CL2630 [M]	*Harry James' Greatest Hits	1967	$50
❏ CS9430 [R]	*Harry James' Greatest Hits	1967	$30

— Red "360 Sound" label

| ❏ CS9430 [R] | *Harry James' Greatest Hits | 1970 | $25 |

— Orange label

| ❏ PC9430 | *Harry James' Greatest Hits | 198? | $20 |

— Budget-line reissue

| ❏ CL6088 [10] | Dance Parade | 1950 | $50 |
| ❏ CL562 [M] | Dancing in Person with Harry James at the Hollywood Palladium | 1954 | $40 |

— Maroon label, gold print

| ❏ CL669 [M] | Jazz Session | 1955 | $50 |
| ❏ CL615 [M] | Juke Box Jamboree | 1955 | $50 |

— Maroon label, gold print

| ❏ GL522 [M] | One Night Stand | 1953 | $50 |

— Black label, silver print

| ❏ CL522 [M] | One Night Stand | 1953 | $40 |

— Maroon label, gold print

| ❏ CL581 [M] | Soft Lights, Sweet Trumpet | 1954 | $40 |

— Maroon label, gold print

❏ CL6207 [10]	Soft Lights, Sweet Trumpet	1952	$50
❏ CL2527 [10]	The Man with the Horn	1955	$75
❏ CL553 [M]	Trumpet After Midnight	1954	$40

— Maroon label, gold print

| ❏ CL6044 [10] | Trumpet Time | 1950 | $50 |
| ❏ CL6138 [10] | Your Dance Date | 1951 | $150 |

DOT

❏ DLP-3735 [M]	Harry James and His Western Friends	1966	$85
❏ DLP-25735 [S]	Harry James and His Western Friends	1966	$85
❏ DLP-3728 [M]	Live at the Riverboat	1966	$85
❏ DLP-25728 [S]	Live at the Riverboat	1966	$85
❏ DLP-3801 [M]	Our Leader	1967	$85
❏ DLP-25801 [S]	Our Leader	1967	$85

HARMONY

❏ KH32018	Best of the Big Bands	1972	$25
❏ HL7159 [M]	Harry James and His Great Vocalists	196?	$35
❏ HL7191 [M]	Harry James Plays the Songs That Sold a Million	196?	$35
❏ HS11245 [R]	Harry James Plays the Songs That Sold a Million	196?	$25
❏ HL7162 [M]	Harry James Plays Trumpet Rhapsody	196?	$35
❏ HS11326	Laura	1969	$25
❏ HL7269 [M]	Strictly Instrumental	196?	$35

HINDSIGHT

❏ HSR-102	Harry James and His Orchestra 1943-46	198?	$25
❏ HSR-123	Harry James and His Orchestra 1943-46	198?	$25
❏ HSR-141	Harry James and His Orchestra 1943-46, Vol. 4	198?	$25
❏ HSR-142	Harry James and His Orchestra 1943-53	198?	$25
❏ HSR-150	Harry James and His Orchestra 1947-49	198?	$25
❏ HSR-135	Harry James and His Orchestra 1948-49	198?	$25
❏ HSR-406	Harry James and His Orchestra Play 22 Original Big Band Recordings	198?	$30

INSIGHT

| ❏ 203 | Harry James and His Orchestra 1943-53 | 198? | $25 |

JAZZ ARCHIVES

| ❏ JA-31 | Young Harry James | 198? | $25 |

LONDON PHASE 4

| ❏ SP-44109 | Golden Trumpet | 1968 | $35 |

LONGINES SYMPHONETTE

| ❏ LS-217 | Harry James Dance Band Spectacular | 196? | $30 |

METRO

| ❏ M-536 [M] | Harry Not Jesse | 1966 | $175 |
| ❏ MS-536 [S] | Harry Not Jesse | 1966 | $175 |

MGM

❏ E-4214 [M]	25th Anniversary Album	1964	$30
❏ SE-4214 [S]	25th Anniversary Album	1964	$35
❏ E-4137 [M]	Double Dixie	1963	$35
❏ SE-4137 [S]	Double Dixie	1963	$25
❏ E-3778 [M]	Harry James and His New Swingin' Band	1959	$25
❏ SE-3778 [S]	Harry James and His New Swingin' Band	1959	$30
❏ E-3848 [M]	Harry James Today	1960	$25
❏ SE-3848 [S]	Harry James Today	1960	$30
❏ E-4274 [M]	In a Relaxed Mood	1965	$30
❏ SE-4274 [S]	In a Relaxed Mood	1965	$35
❏ E-4265 [M]	New Versions of Down Beat Favorites	1965	$30
❏ SE-4265 [S]	New Versions of Down Beat Favorites	1965	$35
❏ E-4003 [M]	Requests on the Road	1961	$25
❏ SE-4003 [S]	Requests on the Road	1961	$30
❏ E-4058 [M]	The Solid Gold Trumpet	1962	$35
❏ SE-4058 [S]	The Solid Gold Trumpet	1962	$25

PAIR

| ❏ PDL2-1158 | Big Band Favorites | 1986 | $30 |

PAUSA

| ❏ 9037 | More Harry James in Hi-Fi | 198? | $25 |

PICKWICK

❏ PC-3006 [M]	Mr. Trumpet	196?	$35
❏ SPC-3006 [R]	Mr. Trumpet	196?	$25
❏ SPC-3126	The Shadow of Your Smile	196?	$25
❏ PC-3044 [M]	You Made Me Love You	196?	$35
❏ SPC-3044 [R]	You Made Me Love You	196?	$25

SAVOY JAZZ

| ❏ SJL-2262 | First Team Player on the Jazz Varsity | 198? | $30 |

SHEFFIELD LABS

| ❏ 6 | Comin' From a Good Place | 1978 | $35 |

— Direct-to-disc recording

| ❏ 11 | Still Harry After All These Years | 1979 | $25 |

— Direct-to-disc recording; comes in box with booklet

| ❏ 3 | The King James Version | 1976 | $35 |

— Direct-to-disc recording

Number	Title	Yr	NM
SUNBEAM			
❏ 203	Harry James and His Orchestra 1940	197?	$25
❏ 217	Harry James and His Orchestra 1954	197?	$25
TIME-LIFE			
❏ STBB-04	Big Bands: Harry James	1983	$35

JAMES, JIMMY, AND THE VAGABONDS

Number	Title	Yr	NM
ATCO			
❏ 33-222 [M]	The New Religion	1967	$40
❏ SD 33-222 [S]	The New Religion	1967	$25
PYE			
❏ 12111	You Don't Stand a Chance If You Can't Dance	1975	$12

JAMES, JONI

Number	Title	Yr	NM
MGM			
❏ E-3755 [M]	100 Strings and Joni	1959	$100
— Yellow label			
❏ E-3755 [M]	100 Strings and Joni	1960	$40
— Black label			
❏ SE-3755 [S]	100 Strings and Joni	1959	$120
— Yellow label			
❏ SE-3755 [S]	100 Strings and Joni	1960	$50
— Black label			
❏ E-3840 [M]	100 Strings and Joni In Hollywood	1960	$75
❏ SE-3840 [S]	100 Strings and Joni In Hollywood	1960	$80
❏ E-3839 [M]	100 Strings and Joni On Broadway	1960	$75
❏ SE-3839 [S]	100 Strings and Joni On Broadway	1960	$80
❏ E-3892 [M]	100 Voices, 100 Strings	1960	$50
❏ SE-3892 [S]	100 Voices, 100 Strings	1960	$75
❏ E-4008 [M]	After Hours	1962	$50
❏ SE-4008 [S]	After Hours	1962	$75
❏ E-3602 [M]	Among My Souvenirs	1958	$100
— Yellow label			
❏ E-3602 [M]	Among My Souvenirs	1960	$40
— Black label			
❏ E-234 [10]	Award Winning Album	1954	$250
❏ E-3346 [M]	Award Winning Album	1956	$100
— Yellow label			
❏ E-3346 [M]	Award Winning Album	1960	$40
— Black label			
❏ E-3706 [M]	Award Winning Album, Volume 2	1958	$100
— Yellow label			
❏ E-3706 [M]	Award Winning Album, Volume 2	1960	$40
— Black label			
❏ E-4263 [M]	Beyond the Reef	1964	$40
❏ SE-4263 [S]	Beyond the Reef	1964	$50
❏ E-4286 [M]	Bossa Nova Style	1965	$40
❏ SE-4286 [S]	Bossa Nova Style	1965	$50
❏ E-4101 [M]	Country Girl Style	1962	$50
❏ SE-4101 [S]	Country Girl Style	1962	$75
❏ E-3958 [M]	Folk Songs by Joni James	1961	$50
❏ SE-3958 [S]	Folk Songs by Joni James	1961	$75
❏ E-3528 [M]	Give Us This Day	1957	$100
— Yellow label			
❏ E-3528 [M]	Give Us This Day	1960	$40
— Black label			
❏ E-4053 [M]	I Feel a Song Comin' On	1962	$50
❏ SE-4053 [S]	I Feel a Song Comin' On	1962	$75
❏ E-3837 [M]	I'm in the Mood for Love	1960	$75
❏ SE-3837 [S]	I'm in the Mood for Love	1960	$100
❏ E-4054 [M]	I'm Your Girl	1962	$50
❏ SE-4054 [S]	I'm Your Girl	1962	$75
❏ E-3328 [M]	In the Still of the Night	1956	$100
— Yellow label			
❏ E-3328 [M]	In the Still of the Night	1960	$40
— Black label			
❏ E-3749 [M]	Irish Favorites	1959	$100
— Yellow label			
❏ E-3749 [M]	Irish Favorites	1960	$40
— Black label			
❏ SE-3749 [S]	Irish Favorites	1959	$120
— Yellow label			
❏ SE-3749 [S]	Irish Favorites	1960	$50
— Black label			
❏ E-4208 [M]	Italianissime!	1963	$40
❏ SE-4208 [S]	Italianissime!	1963	$50
❏ E-3718 [M]	Je T'aime (I Love You)	1958	$100
— Yellow label			
❏ E-3718 [M]	Je T'aime (I Love You)	1960	$40
— Black label			
❏ SE-3718 [S]	Je T'aime (I Love You)	1958	$120
— Yellow label			
❏ SE-3718 [S]	Je T'aime (I Love You)	1960	$50
— Black label			
❏ E-3800 [M]	Joni James at Carnegie Hall	1959	$75
❏ SE-3800 [S]	Joni James at Carnegie Hall	1959	$100
❏ E-4255 [M]	Joni James Sings the Gershwins	1964	$40
❏ SE-4255 [S]	Joni James Sings the Gershwins	1964	$50
❏ E-3772 [M]	Joni James Swings Sweet	1959	$75

Number	Title	Yr	NM
❏ SE-3772 [S]	Joni James Swings Sweet	1959	$100
❏ E-222 [10]	Let There Be Love	1953	$250
❏ E-3348 [M]	Let There Be Love	1956	$100
— Yellow label			
❏ E-3348 [M]	Let There Be Love	1960	$40
— Black label			
❏ E-272 [10]	Little Girl Blue	1955	$250
❏ E-3347 [M]	Little Girl Blue	1956	$100
— Yellow label			
❏ E-3347 [M]	Little Girl Blue	1960	$40
— Black label			
❏ E-3468 [M]	Merry Christmas from Joni	1956	$120
— Yellow label original			
❏ E-3468 [M]	Merry Christmas from Joni	1960	$75
— Black label reissue			
❏ E-3885 [M]	More Joni Hits	1960	$50
❏ SE-3885 [S]	More Joni Hits	1960	$75
❏ E-4200 [M]	My Favorite Things	1963	$40
❏ SE-4200 [S]	My Favorite Things	1963	$50
❏ E-4248 [M]	Put On a Happy Face	1964	$40
❏ SE-4248 [S]	Put On a Happy Face	1964	$50
❏ E-4158 [M]	Something for the Boys	1963	$40
❏ SE-4158 [S]	Something for the Boys	1963	$50
❏ E-3533 [M]	Songs by Jerome Kern and Harry Warren	1957	$100
— Yellow label			
❏ E-3533 [M]	Songs by Jerome Kern and Harry Warren	1960	$40
— Black label			
❏ E-3449 [M]	Songs by Victor Young and Frank Loesser	1956	$100
— Yellow label			
❏ E-3449 [M]	Songs by Victor Young and Frank Loesser	1960	$40
— Black label			
❏ E-3739 [M]	Songs of Hank Williams	1959	$100
— Yellow label			
❏ E-3739 [M]	Songs of Hank Williams	1960	$40
— Black label			
❏ SE-3739 [S]	Songs of Hank Williams	1959	$120
— Yellow label			
❏ SE-3739 [S]	Songs of Hank Williams	1960	$50
— Black label			
❏ E-3991 [M]	The Mood Is Blue	1961	$50
❏ SE-3991 [S]	The Mood Is Blue	1961	$75
❏ E-3990 [M]	The Mood Is Romance	1961	$50
❏ SE-3990 [S]	The Mood Is Romance	1961	$75
❏ E-3987 [M]	The Mood Is Swinging	1961	$50
❏ SE-3987 [S]	The Mood Is Swinging	1961	$75
❏ E-4151 [M]	The Very Best of Joni James	1963	$40
❏ SE-4151 [S]	The Very Best of Joni James	1963	$50
❏ E-4182 [M]	Three O'Clock in the Morning	1963	$40
❏ SE-4182 [S]	Three O'Clock in the Morning	1963	$50
❏ E-3623 [M]	Ti Voglio Bene	1958	$100
— Yellow label			
❏ E-3623 [M]	Ti Voglio Bene	1960	$40
— Black label			
❏ E-3240 [M]	When I Fall in Love	1955	$100
— Yellow label			
❏ E-3240 [M]	When I Fall in Love	1960	$40
— Black label			

JAMES, LEONARD

Number	Title	Yr	NM
DECCA			
❏ DL8772 [M]	Boppin' and a-Strollin'	1958	$50

JAMES, RICK

Number	Title	Yr	NM
GORDY			
❏ G7-984 [B]	Bustin' Out of L. Seven	1979	$15
❏ 6043GL	Cold Blooded	1983	$10
❏ G7-981 [B]	Come Get It!	1978	$15
❏ G8-990 [B]	Fire It Up	1979	$15
❏ G8-995	Garden of Love	1980	$12
❏ 6135GL	Glow	1985	$10
❏ 6095GL	Reflections	1984	$10
❏ G8-1002	Street Songs	1981	$10
❏ 6005GL	Throwin' Down	1982	$10
MOTOWN			
❏ 5263ML	Come Get It!	198?	$10
❏ 5382ML	Greatest Hits	1986	$10
❏ MOT-5405	Street Songs	1987	$10
REPRISE			
❏ 25659	Wonderful	1988	$12
UNIVERSAL MOTOWN			
❏ 5316010	Street Songs	2009	$25

JAMES, SKIP

Number	Title	Yr	NM
VANGUARD			
❏ VSD-79273	Devil Got My Woman	1968	$30
❏ VRS-9219 [M]	Skip James Today!	1966	$30
❏ VSD-79219 [S]	Skip James Today!	1966	$30

JAMES, SONNY

Number	Title	Yr	NM
ABC			
❏ AC-30027	The ABC Collection	1976	$15

Number	Title	Yr	NM
CAPITOL			
❏ ST-629	#1	1970	$18
❏ T2884 [M]	A World of Our Own	1968	$30
❏ ST2884 [S]	A World of Our Own	1968	$18
❏ T2415 [M]	Behind the Tear	1965	$25
❏ ST2415 [S]	Behind the Tear	1965	$30
❏ ST-111	Born to Be with You	1968	$18
❏ SWBB-258	Close-Up	1969	$25
— Combines ST 2500 and ST 2788 in one package			
❏ ST-734	Empty Arms	1971	$18
❏ ST2937	Heaven Says Hello	1968	$18
❏ ST-849	Here Comes Honey Again	1971	$18
❏ T988 [M]	Honey	1958	$50
— Turquoise label			
❏ T988 [M]	Honey	1964	$25
— Black label with colorband, logo on top			
❏ T2317 [M]	I'll Keep Holding On	1965	$25
❏ ST2317 [S]	I'll Keep Holding On	1965	$30
❏ T2788 [M]	I'll Never Find Another You	1967	$25
❏ ST2788 [S]	I'll Never Find Another You	1967	$18
❏ ST-432	It's Just a Matter of Time	1970	$18
❏ ST 8-0432	It's Just a Matter of Time	1970	$25
— Capitol Record Club edition			
❏ T2589 [M]	My Christmas Dream	1966	$25
❏ ST2589 [S]	My Christmas Dream	1966	$30
❏ ST-478	My Love/Don't Keep Me Hangin' On	1970	$18
❏ T2703 [M]	Need You	1967	$25
❏ ST2703 [S]	Need You	1967	$18
❏ ST-193	Only the Lonely	1969	$18
❏ ST 8-0193	Only the Lonely	1969	$25
— Capitol Record Club edition			
❏ T867 [M]	Sonny	1957	$50
— Turquoise label			
❏ T867 [M]	Sonny	1964	$25
— Black label with colorband, logo on top			
❏ SQBO-91357	That Special Country Feeling	196?	$30
— Capitol Record Club exclusive			
❏ ST-11067	That's Why I Love You Like I Do	1972	$18
❏ ST-320	The Astrodome Presents In Person Sonny James	1969	$18
❏ T2615 [M]	The Best of Sonny James	1966	$18
❏ ST2615 [S]	The Best of Sonny James	1966	$25
— Black Starline label			
❏ SM-2615	The Best of Sonny James	197?	$12
❏ SKAO-144	The Best of Sonny James Vol. 2	1969	$18
❏ ST-11013	The Biggest Hits of Sonny James	1972	$18
❏ SM-11013	The Biggest Hits of Sonny James	197?	$12
❏ ST-11144	The Gentleman from the South	1973	$15
❏ T2017 [M]	The Minute You're Gone	1964	$25
❏ ST2017 [S]	The Minute You're Gone	1964	$30
❏ ST-804	The Sensational Sonny James	1971	$18
❏ T779 [M]	The Southern Gentleman	1957	$50
— Turquoise label			
❏ T779 [M]	The Southern Gentleman	1964	$25
— Black label with colorband, logo on top			
❏ T1178 [M]	This Is Sonny James	1959	$40
— Black label with colorband, logo at left			
❏ T1178 [M]	This Is Sonny James	1964	$25
— Black label with colorband, logo on top			
❏ T2561 [M]	Till the Last Leaf Shall Fall	1966	$25
❏ ST2561 [S]	Till the Last Leaf Shall Fall	1966	$30
❏ ST-11108	Traces	1972	$15
❏ T2500 [M]	True Love's a Blessing	1966	$25
❏ ST2500 [S]	True Love's a Blessing	1966	$30
❏ ST-11196	Young Love	1973	$15
❏ T2209 [M]	You're the Only World I Know	1965	$25
❏ ST2209 [S]	You're the Only World I Know	1965	$30
❏ STBB-535	You're the Only World I Know/I'll Never Find Another You	1970	$25
— Combines the two listed albums in one package			
COLUMBIA			
❏ PC34035	200 Years of Country Music	1976	$15
❏ KC33428	A Little Bit South of Saskatoon/Little Band of Gold	1975	$15
❏ KC33056	A Mi Esposa Con Amor (To My Wife with Love)	1974	$15
❏ PC33846	Country Male Artist of the Decade	1975	$15
❏ KC32291	If She Just Helps Me Get Over You	1973	$15
❏ KC32805	Is It Wrong	1974	$15
❏ KC35626	Sonny James' Greatest Hits	1978	$15
❏ PC34706	Sonny James In Prison, In Person	1977	$15
❏ KC32028	Sonny James Sings the Greatest Country Hits of '72	1973	$15
❏ KC33477	The Guitars of Sonny James	1975	$15
❏ KC35379	This Is the Love	1978	$15
❏ PC34309	When Something Is Wrong with My Baby	1976	$15
❏ KC31646	When the Snow Is on the Roses	1972	$15
❏ CG33627	When the Snow Is on the Roses/If She Just Helps Me Get Over You	1975	$18

Number	Title	Yr	NM
❏ PC34472	You're Free to Go	1977	$15
DOT			
❏ DLP3462 [M]	Young Love	1962	$40
❏ DLP25462 [S]	Young Love	1962	$50
DOT/MCA			
❏ 39087	Sonny James	198?	$12
HILLTOP			
❏ 6067	Invisible Tears	1969	$12
❏ 6079	Timberline	1969	$12
PICKWICK			
❏ SPC-3594	Young Love	1977	$10
RCA CAMDEN			
❏ CAL-2140 [M]	Young Love	1967	$18
❏ CAS-2140 [S]	Young Love	1967	$15

JAMES, STAFFORD
RED RECORD

Number	Title	Yr	NM
❏ VPA-142	Stafford James Ensemble	198?	$15

JAMES, TOMMY, AND THE SHONDELLS
RHINO

Number	Title	Yr	NM
❏ R1-70920	Anthology	1989	$18
ROULETTE			
❏ SR42030	Cellophane Symphony	1969	$25
❏ SR42023	Crimson and Clover	1969	$25
❏ SR25357 [S]	Gettin' Together	1968	$30
❏ R25357 [M]	Gettin' Together	1968	$40
❏ R25336 [M]	Hanky Panky	1966	$30
❏ SR25336 [P]	Hanky Panky	1966	$30
—*Hanky Panky" is rechanneled*			
❏ R25353 [M]	I Think We're Alone Now	1967	$40
❏ R25353 [P]	I Think We're Alone Now	1967	$30
—*Footprints cover; "I Think We're Alone Now" is rechanneled*			
❏ SR25353 [P]	I Think We're Alone Now	1967	$18
—*Photo cover*			
❏ R25344 [M]	It's Only Love	1967	$40
❏ SR25344 [S]	It's Only Love	1967	$30

Number	Title	Yr	NM
❏ SR42012 [B]	Mony Mony	1968	$25
❏ R25355 [M]	Something Special! The Best of Tommy James & The Shondells	1968	$100
❏ SR42005	Something Special! The Best of Tommy James & The Shondells	1968	$18
❏ SR25355 [S]	Something Special! The Best of Tommy James & The Shondells	1968	$30
❏ SR42040	The Best of Tommy James & The Shondells	1969	$25
—*Original versions are in a Unipak (gatefold must be opened to remove record)*			
❏ SR42040	The Best of Tommy James & The Shondells	197?	$18
—*Later versions have gatefold covers, but record can be removed without opening it*			
❏ SR42044	Travelin'	1970	$18
SCEPTER CITATION			
❏ CTN-18025	The Best of Tommy James and the Shondells	1973	$12

JAMES, TOMMY
FANTASY

Number	Title	Yr	NM
❏ 9509	In Touch	1976	$15
❏ 9532	Midnight Rider	1977	$15
MILLENNIUM			
❏ BXL1-7758	Easy to Love	1981	$12
❏ BXL1-7748	Three Times in Love	1980	$12
ROULETTE			
❏ SR-3001	Christian of the World	1971	$18
❏ SR-3007	My Head, My Bed, My Red Guitar	1972	$18
❏ SR-42061	Tommy James	1970	$18

JAMES, WOODY; SHELLY MANNE; FRANK STRAZZARI
PAUSA

Number	Title	Yr	NM
❏ 7020	Crystallizations	198?	$25

JAMES, WOODY
SEA BREEZE

Number	Title	Yr	NM
❏ SB-2011	Hardcore Jazz	198?	$25
❏ SB-2015	Zinger	1985	$25

JAMES
SIRE

Number	Title	Yr	NM
❏ 25437	Stutter	1986	$12

JAMES GANG, THE (1)
Also see TOMMY BOLIN; JOE WALSH; THE EAGLES.
ABC

Number	Title	Yr	NM
❏ X-801	16 Greatest Hits	1973	$18
❏ X-733	James Gang Live in Concert	1971	$15
❏ S-711 [B]	James Gang Rides Again	1970	$30
—*First pressing with a short version of Ravel's "Bolero" as part of the song "The Bomber"; exists on both promos and early stock copies; no "RE-1" in trail-off wax*			
❏ S-711	James Gang Rides Again	1970	$15
—*Standard pressing without "Bolero" as part of "The Bomber"; "RE-1" in trail-off wax*			
❏ X-760	Passin' Thru	1972	$15
❏ X-741	Straight Shooter	1972	$15
❏ ABCX-774	The Best of the James Gang Featuring Joe Walsh	1973	$15
—*Most copies of this LP contain the edited version of "The Bomber." The full title of the LP is on the spine, and the record's trail-off wax has the number "ABCX-774-A-RE-1".*			
❏ ABCX-774	The Best of the James Gang Featuring Joe Walsh	1973	$25
—*A few copies of this LP contain the full version of "The Bomber" with the "Bolero" excerpt. The words "The Best Of" do NOT appear on the spine, and the record's trail-off wax has the number "ABCX-774-A".*			
❏ X-721	Thirds	1971	$15
❏ S-688	Yer' Album	1970	$15
ATCO			
❏ SD7037	Bang	1973	$12
❏ SD 36-141	Jesse Come Home	1976	$12
❏ SD 36-102	Miami	1974	$12
❏ SD 36-112	Newborn	1975	$12
BLUESWAY			
❏ BLS-6034 [B]	Yer' Album	1969	$30
MCA			
❏ 6012	16 Greatest Hits	1980	$12
—*Reissue*			
❏ 37111	James Gang Rides Again	1980	$10
—*Reissue*			
❏ 37112	The Best of the James Gang Featuring Joe Walsh	1980	$10
—*Reissue*			

JAMME
ABC DUNHILL

Number	Title	Yr	NM
❏ DS-50072	Jamme	1970	$25

JAN AND DEAN
COLUMBIA

Number	Title	Yr	NM
❏ CL2661 [M]	Save for a Rainy Day	1967	$0
—*Canceled*			
❏ CS9461 [S]	Save for a Rainy Day	1967	$4000
—*LP not known to exist, but an acetate does, and possibly an import on this label and number; VG value 2000; VG+ value 3000*			

DEADMAN'S CURVE

Number	Title	Yr	NM
❏ 0(no cat #)	Live at the Keystone Berkeley	1981	$50
—*Plain jacket with front and back cover inserts*			
❏ 0(no cat #)	Live at the Keystone Berkeley	1981	$30
—*With front and back covers pasted on*			

DORE

Number	Title	Yr	NM
❏ LP-101 [M]	Jan and Dean	1960	$400
—*Original with blue label*			
❏ LP-101	Jan and Dean	197?	$18
—*Reissue with black label*			
❏ LP-101	Jan and Dean Bonus Photo	1960	$120

J&D

Number	Title	Yr	NM
❏ 101 [M]	Save for a Rainy Day	1967	$300
—*Private pressing by Dean Torrence of unreleased Columbia album*			

LIBERTY

Number	Title	Yr	NM
❏ LRP-3403 [M]	Command Performance/Live in Person	1965	$30
❏ LST-7403 [S]	Command Performance/Live in Person	1965	$40
❏ LN-10011	Dead Man's Curve	1980	$10
—*Budget-line reissue*			

Number	Title	Yr	NM
❏ LRP-3361 [M]	Dead Man's Curve/The New Girl in School	1964	$75
—*Black and white cover with pink tint*			
❏ LRP-3361 [M]	Dead Man's Curve/The New Girl in School	1964	$40
—*Full-color cover*			
❏ LST-7361 [S]	Dead Man's Curve/The New Girl in School	1964	$50
—*Black and white cover with pink tint*			
❏ LST-7361 [S]	Dead Man's Curve/The New Girl in School	1964	$40
—*Full-color cover*			

Number	Title	Yr	NM
❏ LRP-3339 [M]	Drag City	1963	$40
❏ LST-7339 [S]	Drag City	1963	$50
❏ LRP-3441 [M]	Filet of Soul	1966	$30
❏ LST-7441 [S]	Filet of Soul	1966	$40
❏ LRP-3431 [M]	Folk 'N' Roll	1965	$30
❏ LST-7431 [S]	Folk 'N' Roll	1965	$40
❏ LRP-3444 [M]	Jan and Dean Meet Batman	1966	$50
❏ LST-7444 [S]	Jan and Dean Meet Batman	1966	$80
❏ LRP-3248 [M]	Jan and Dean's Golden Hits	1962	$30
❏ LST-7248 [S]	Jan and Dean's Golden Hits	1962	$40
❏ LRP-3417 [M]	Jan and Dean's Golden Hits, Volume 2	1965	$30
❏ LST-7417 [S]	Jan and Dean's Golden Hits, Volume 2	1965	$30
❏ LRP-3460 [M]	Jan and Dean's Golden Hits, Volume 3	1966	$30
❏ LST-7460 [S]	Jan and Dean's Golden Hits, Volume 3	1966	$30
❏ LRP-3294 [M]	Jan and Dean Take Linda Surfin'	1963	$50
—*With correct title on LP spine*			
❏ LST-7294 [S]	Jan and Dean Take Linda Surfin'	1963	$100
—*With correct title on LP spine*			
❏ LRP-3294 [M]	Jan and Dean Take Linda Surfin'	1963	$75
—*With title on spine "Mr. Bass Man Takes Linda Surfin'*			
❏ LST-7294 [S]	Jan and Dean Take Linda Surfin'	1963	$150
—*With title on spine "Mr. Bass Man Takes Linda Surfin'*			
❏ LRP-3458 [M]	Popsicle	1966	$30
❏ LST-7458 [S]	Popsicle	1966	$40
❏ LRP-3368 [M]	Ride the Wild Surf	1964	$30
❏ LST-7368 [S]	Ride the Wild Surf	1964	$40
❏ LRP-3314 [M]	Surf City and Other Swingin' Cities	1963	$40
❏ LST-7314 [S]	Surf City and Other Swingin' Cities	1963	$50
❏ LN-10115	The Best of Jan and Dean	1981	$10
❏ LRP-3377 [M]	The Little Old Lady from Pasadena	1964	$30
❏ LST-7377 [S]	The Little Old Lady from Pasadena	1964	$40
❏ LN-10151	The Little Old Lady from Pasadena	1982	$10
—*Budget-line reissue*			
❏ LRP-3361 [M]	The New Girl in School/ Dead Man's Curve	1964	$25
—*Reissue with reversed title*			
❏ LST-7361 [S]	The New Girl in School/ Dead Man's Curve	1964	$30
—*Reissue with reversed title*			
PAIR			
❏ PDL2-1071	California Gold	1986	$15
RHINO			
❏ RNDA1498	One Summer Night -- Live	1982	$25
SUNDAZED			
❏ LP5040	Jan and Dean (The Dore Album)	1996	$12
—*Reissue of Dore LP on colored vinyl with extra tracks and poster*			
❏ LP5022	Save for a Rainy Day	1996	$18
—*First release to the general public; colored vinyl*			
SUNSET			
❏ SUM-1156 [M]	Jan and Dean	1967	$30
❏ SUS-5156 [S]	Jan and Dean	1967	$18

Number	Title	Yr	NM

UNITED ARTISTS
☐ UAS-9961	Anthology (Legendary Masters Series, Vol. 3)	1971	$30
☐ UA-LA341-H2	Gotta Take That One Last Ride	1974	$18
☐ UA-LA443-E	The Very Best of Jan and Dean	1975	$12
☐ UA-LA515-E	The Very Best of Jan and Dean, Volume 2	1975	$12

JAN AND KJELD
KAPP
| ☐ KL-1190 [M] | Banjo Boy | 1960 | $30 |

JAN AND LORRAINE
ABC
| ☐ S-691 | Gypsy People | 1969 | $30 |

JANE'S ADDICTION
PORNO FOR PYROS and RED HOT CHILI PEPPERS related.

TRIPLE X
| ☐ 51004 [B] | Jane's Addiction | 1987 | $35 |

WARNER BROS.
| ☐ 25727 | Nothing's Shocking | 1988 | $15 |
| ☐ 25993 [B] | Ritual de lo Habitual | 1990 | $30 |
— *First cover, with drawing*
| ☐ 26223 | Ritual de lo Habitual | 1990 | $15 |
— *Second cover, all white with text of First Amendment*
| ☐ PRO-A-3369 [DJ] | Words and Music | 1988 | $40 |
— *Promo-only interview album*

JANIGRO, ANTONIO
RCA VICTOR RED SEAL
| ☐ LSC-2460 [S] | Bach: Suite No. 2 in B; Brandenburg Concerto No. 5 | 1961 | $25 |
— *Original with "shaded dog" label*
| ☐ LSC-2365 [S] | Cello Concertos | 1960 | $30 |
— *Original with "shaded dog" label*
| ☐ LSC-2653 [S] | Music for Strings | 1962 | $40 |
— *Original with "shaded dog" label*

JANIS, BYRON
MERCURY LIVING PRSENSCE
| ☐ SR90305 [S] | Encore | 196? | $175 |
— *Maroon label, no "Vendor: Mercury Record Corporation*
| ☐ SR90329 [S] | Liszt: Piano Concertos No. 1 and 2 | 196? | $50 |
— *Maroon label, no "Vendor: Mercury Record Corporation*
| ☐ SR90300 [S] | Prokofiev: Piano Concerto No. 2; Rachmaninoff: Piano Concerto No. 1 | 196? | $40 |
— *Maroon label, no "Vendor: Mercury Record Corporation*
| ☐ SR90300 [S] | Prokofiev: Piano Concerto No. 2; Rachmaninoff: Piano Concerto No. 1 | 196? | $30 |
— *Maroon label, with "Vendor: Mercury Record Corporation*
| ☐ SR90300 [S] | Prokofiev: Piano Concerto No. 2; Rachmaninoff: Piano Concerto No. 1 | 196? | $25 |
— *Third edition: Dark red (not maroon) label*
| ☐ SR90260 [S] | Rachmaninoff: Piano Concerto No. 2; Preludes in C# and E-flat | 196? | $75 |
— *With Antal Dorati/Minneapolis Symphony Orchestra; maroon label, no "Vendor: Mercury Record Corporation*
| ☐ SR90260 [S] | Rachmaninoff: Piano Concerto No. 2; Preludes in C# and E-flat | 196? | $30 |
— *With Antal Dorati/Minneapolis Symphony Orchestra; maroon label, with "Vendor: Mercury Record Corporation*
| ☐ SR90283 [S] | Rachmaninoff: Piano Concerto No. 3 | 196? | $150 |
— *With Antal Dorati/London Symphony Orchestra; maroon label, no "Vendor: Mercury Record Corporation*
| ☐ SR90283 [S] | Rachmaninoff: Piano Concerto No. 3 | 196? | $40 |
— *With Antal Dorati/London Symphony Orchestra; maroon label, with "Vendor: Mercury Record Corporation*
| ☐ SR90383 [S] | Schumann: Piano Concerto; Arabesque; Wieck Variations | 196? | $30 |
— *With Stanislaw Skrowaczewski/London Symphony Orchestra; maroon label, no "Vendor: Mercury Record Corporation*
| ☐ SR90266 [S] | Tchaikovsky: Piano Concerto No. 1 | 196? | $50 |
— *With Herbert Menges/London Symphony Orchestra; maroon label, no "Vendor: Mercury Record Corporation*
| ☐ SR90266 [S] | Tchaikovsky: Piano Concerto No. 1 | 196? | $30 |
— *With Herbert Menges/London Symphony Orchestra; maroon label, with "Vendor: Mercury Record Corporation*

RCA VICTOR RED SEAL
| ☐ LSC-2541 [S] | Liszt: Todtentanz; Rachmaninoff: Piano Concerto No. 1 | 1961 | $150 |
— *With Fritz Reiner/Chicago Symphony Orch.; originals with "shaded dog" label*

| ☐ LSC-2541 [S] | Liszt: Todtentanz; Rachmaninoff: Piano Concerto No. 1 | 1961 | $30 |
— *With Fritz Reiner/Chicago Symphony Orch.; Classic Records reissue*
| ☐ LSC-2237 [S] | Rachmaninoff: Piano Concerto No. 3 | 1959 | $250 |
— *With Charles Munch/Boston Symphony Orchestra; original with "shaded dog" label*

JANIS, CONRAD
CIRCLE
| ☐ L-404 [10] | Conrad Janis' Tailgate Jazz Band | 1951 | $50 |
JUBILEE
| ☐ JLP-1010 [M] | Conrad Janis and His Tailgate Five | 1955 | $50 |
| ☐ JLP-7 [10] | Conrad Janis and His Tailgaters | 1954 | $50 |
RIVERSIDE
| ☐ RLP 12-215 [M] | Dixieland Jam Session | 1956 | $300 |
— *White label, blue print*
| ☐ RLP 12-215 [M] | Dixieland Jam Session | 1959 | $30 |
— *Blue label, microphone label at top*

JANIS, JOHNNY
ABC-PARAMOUNT
| ☐ ABC-140 [M] | For the First Time | 1956 | $75 |
COLUMBIA
| ☐ CL1674 [M] | The Start of Something Big | 1961 | $30 |
| ☐ CS8474 [S] | The Start of Something Big | 1961 | $30 |
MONUMENT
| ☐ MLP-8036 [M] | Once in a Blue Moon | 1965 | $18 |
| ☐ SLP-18036 [S] | Once in a Blue Moon | 1965 | $25 |

JANKOWSKI, HORST
MERCURY
☐ SR-61160	And We Got Love	1968	$15
☐ SR-61232	A Walk in the Evergreens	1970	$15
☐ MG-21106 [M]	Baby But Grand	1967	$15
☐ SR-61106 [S]	Baby But Grand	1967	$18
☐ SR-61219	Jankowski Plays Jankowski	1969	$15
☐ MG-21054 [M]	More Genius of Jankowski	1965	$15
☐ SR-61054 [S]	More Genius of Jankowski	1965	$18
☐ SR-61195	Piano Affairs	1968	$15
☐ MG-21093 [M]	So What's New?	1966	$15
☐ SR-61093 [S]	So What's New?	1966	$18
☐ MG-21076 [M]	Still More Genius of Jankowski	1966	$15
☐ SR-61076 [S]	Still More Genius of Jankowski	1966	$18
☐ MG-20993 [M]	The Genius of Jankowski	1965	$15
☐ SR-60993 [S]	The Genius of Jankowski	1965	$18
☐ MG-21125 [M]	With Love	1967	$15
☐ SR-61125 [S]	With Love	1967	$18

JANSE, DON, CHORALE
DESIGN
| ☐ SDLPX-25 | Hark! The Herald Angels Sing | 196? | $15 |
— *Reissue of International Award Series LP with same contents*
| ☐ SDLP-X-13 [S] | The Little Drummer Boy | 196? | $15 |
GRAND PRIX
| ☐ KX-5 | Christmas Chorale | 196? | $18 |
INTERNATIONAL AWARD SERIES
| ☐ AX-0 | Christmas Chorale | 196? | $18 |

JANSSEN, DAVID
EPIC
| ☐ LN24150 [M] | Hidden Island | 1965 | $25 |
| ☐ BN26150 [S] | Hidden Island | 1965 | $30 |

JAPAN
ARIOLA AMERICA
| ☐ SW-50037 | Adolescent Sex | 1978 | $25 |
| ☐ SW-50047 [EP] | Obscure Alternatives | 1979 | $18 |
VIRGIN/EPIC
| ☐ ARE37914 | Japan | 1982 | $12 |

JARMAN, JOSEPH, AND DON MOYE
BLACK SAINT
| ☐ BSR-0042 | Black Paladins | 198? | $30 |
| ☐ BSR-0052 | Earth Passage | 198? | $30 |
INDIA NAVIGATION
| ☐ IN-1033 | Egwu-Anwu | 1978 | $25 |

JARMAN, JOSEPH
AECO
| ☐ 02 | Sunbound | 1979 | $35 |
DELMARK
| ☐ DS-417 | As If It Were the Seasons | 1969 | $25 |
| ☐ DS-410 | Song for | 1968 | $25 |

JARMELS, THE
COLLECTABLES
| ☐ COL-5044 | Golden Classics | 198? | $12 |

JAROSLAV
COLUMBIA
| ☐ JC35537 | Checkin' In | 1978 | $30 |

JARRE, JEAN-MICHEL
DREYFUS/POLYDOR
☐ 833170-1	Concerts Houston/Lyon	1987	$25
☐ 829456-1	Equinoxe	1987	$20
☐ 829457-1	Magnetic Fields	1987	$20
☐ 827885-1	Oxygene	1987	$20
☐ 829125-1	Rendez-Vous	1986	$20
☐ 811551-1	The Concerts in China	1983	$30
☐ 823763-1	Zoolook	1984	$20
MOBILE FIDELITY
| ☐ 1-227 | Equinoxe | 1995 | $50 |
— *Audiophile vinyl*
| ☐ 1-212 | Oxygene | 1995 | $50 |
— *Audiophile vinyl*
POLYDOR
☐ PD-1-6175	Equinoxe	1979	$25
☐ PD-1-6225	Magnetic Fields	1981	$25
☐ PD-1-6112	Oxygene	1977	$25

JARREAU, AL
BAINBRIDGE
| ☐ BT-6237 | Al Jarreau 1965 | 1982 | $10 |
MOBILE FIDELITY
| ☐ Jan-0019 | All Fly Home | 1980 | $40 |
— *Audiophile vinyl*
REPRISE
☐ MS2248	Glow	1976	$12
☐ 25778	Heart's Horizon	1988	$12
☐ MS2224	We Got By	1975	$12
WARNER BROS.
☐ 25331	Al Jarreau in London	1985	$10
☐ BSK3229	All Fly Home	1978	$12
☐ BSK3576	Breakin' Away	1981	$10
☐ 25106	High Crime	1984	$10
☐ 23801	Jarreau	1983	$10
☐ 25477	L Is for Lover	1986	$10
☐ 2WS3052	Look to the Rainbow/Live in Europe	1977	$15
☐ BSK3434	This Time	1980	$10

JARRETT, KEITH, AND JACK DEJOHNETTE
ECM
| ☐ 1021ST | Ruta & Daitya | 1973 | $35 |
— *Original issue; made in Germany?*
| ☐ ECM-1-1021 | Ruta & Daitya | 197? | $30 |
— *Manufactured by Polydor*

JARRETT, KEITH
ABC IMPULSE!
☐ ASH-9305	Backhand	1975	$250
☐ IA-9334	Bop-Be	1977	$30
☐ AS-9305	Byablue	1977	$30
☐ ASD-9301	Death and the Flower	1974	$35
☐ AS-9240	Fort Yawuh	1973	$35
☐ ASD-9315	Mysteries	1976	$30
☐ ASD-9322	Shades	1976	$30
☐ IA-9348	The Best of Keith Jarrett	1978	$25
☐ AS-9274	Treasure Island	1974	$35
ATLANTIC
☐ SD1612	Birth	1972	$35
☐ SD1673	El Juicio (The Judgment)	1975	$30
☐ SD1596	Mourning of a Star	1971	$50
☐ SD8808	Somewhere Before	1981	$30
— *Reissue of Vortex 2012*
COLUMBIA
| ☐ KG31580 | Expectations | 1972 | $50 |
— *Original edition*
| ☐ PG31580 | Expectations | 198? | $30 |
— *Reissue with new prefix; some with bar code on cover*
ECM
| ☐ ECM-1-1070 | Arbour Zena | 1976 | $30 |
— *Distributed by Polydor*
| ☐ ECM-1-1070 | Arbour Zena | 197? | $25 |
— *Distributed by Warner Bros. (reissue)*
| ☐ 1050ST | Belonging | 1974 | $35 |
— *Original, made in Germany*
| ☐ 1344/5 | Book of Ways | 1986 | $30 |
— *Made in Germany*
| ☐ ECM1-1175 | Celestial Hawk | 1981 | $25 |
— *Distributed by Warner Bros.*
| ☐ 1392 | Changeless | 1990 | $75 |
— *Made in Germany*
| ☐ 25007 | Changes | 1984 | $25 |
— *Distributed by Warner Bros.*
| ☐ 1276 | Changes | 1984 | $35 |
— *Made in Germany (U.S. version issued on 25007)*

Number	Title	Yr	NM
❏ ECM1-1228	Concerts	1982	$25
—Abridged version of 1227; distributed by Warner Bros.			
❏ ECM3-1227	Concerts	1982	$50
—Distributed by Warner Bros.; box set			
❏ 1379	Dark Intervals	1988	$35
—Made in Germany			
❏ ECM-T-1150	Eyes of the Heart	1979	$35
—Distributed by Warner Bros.			
❏ 1017ST	Facing You	1973	$35
—Original edition, made in Germany?			
❏ ECM 1-1017	Facing You	197?	$30
—U.S. pressing, distributed by Polydor			
❏ ECM1-1174	G.I. Gurdjieff Sacred Hymns	1981	$25
—Distributed by Warner Bros.			
❏ ECM-2-1086	Hymns/Spheres	1977	$35
—Distributed by Polydor			
❏ 1033/4 ST	In the Light	1976	$50
—Original edition			
❏ ECM 2-1033	In the Light	197?	$35
—Reissue with new prefix, distributed by Polydor			
❏ ECM-D-1201	Invocations/The Moth and the Flame	1981	$30
—Distributed by Warner Bros.			
❏ 1049ST	Luminessence	1974	$35
—Original, made in Germany			
❏ ECM1-1049	Luminessence	197?	$30
—Distributed by Warner Bros.			
❏ ECM1-1115	My Song	1978	$30
—Distributed by Warner Bros.			
❏ ECM2-1171	Nude Ants	1980	$35
—Distributed by Warner Bros.			
❏ 1382	Personal Mountains	1989	$35
—Made in Germany			
❏ 1035/6/7 ST	Solo Concerts	1974	$75
—Original issue, made in Germany?			
❏ ECM-3-1035	Solo Concerts	197?	$50
—Distributed by Polydor			
❏ 1333/4	Spirits	1986	$50
—Made in Germany			
❏ ECM-2-1090	Staircase	1977	$35
—Distributed by Polydor			
❏ 23793	Standards, Volume 1	1983	$30
—Distributed by Warner Bros.			
❏ 1255	Standards, Volume 1	1983	$35
—Made in Germany			
❏ 25023	Standards, Volume 2	1985	$30
—Distributed by Warner Bros.			
❏ 1289	Standards, Volume 2	1985	$35
—Made in Germany			
❏ 25041	Standards Live	1986	$30
—Distributed by Warner Bros.			
❏ 1317	Standards Live	1986	$35
—Made in Germany			
❏ 1360/1	Still Live	1988	$75
—Made in Germany			
❏ ECM-1-1085	Survivors' Suite	1977	$30
—Distributed by Polydor			
❏ ECM-2-1064	The Koln Concert	1976	$35
—Distributed by Polydor			
❏ 1100	The Sun Bear Concerts	1977	$175
—Made in Germany			

MCA

Number	Title	Yr	NM
❏ 29048	Bop-Be	1980	$25
—Reissue of Impulse 9334			
❏ 29047	Byablue	1980	$25
—Reissue of Impulse 9331			
❏ 29046	Death and the Flower	1980	$25
—Reissue of Impulse 9301			
❏ 29044	Fort Yawuh	1980	$25
—Reissue of Impulse 9240			
❏ 2-4125	Great Moments with Keith Jarrett	1981	$50
❏ 29045	Treasure Island	1980	$25
—Reissue of Impulse 9274			
❏ 39106	Treasure Island	198?	$250
—Another reissue of Impulse 9274			

VORTEX

Number	Title	Yr	NM
❏ 2006	Life Between the Exit Signs	1969	$75
❏ 2008	Restoration Ruin	1969	$75
❏ 2012	Somewhere Before	1970	$75

JARRETT, KEITH/MCCOY TYNER

AT EASE

Number	Title	Yr	NM
❏ MD-11119	Masters of the Piano	1978	$50
—Record made for sale at military bases			

JARRETT, SCOTT

GRP/ARISTA

Number	Title	Yr	NM
❏ GL5007	Without Rhyme or Reason	1979	$30

JARS OF CLAY

ESSENTIAL/SILVERTONE

Number	Title	Yr	NM
❏ 83061-0088-1	Much Afraid	1997	$18

JARVIS, JOHN

CRYSTAL CLEAR

Number	Title	Yr	NM
❏ 8004	Evolutions	1980	$50
—Direct-to-disc recording			

MCA

Number	Title	Yr	NM
❏ 5690	So Far So Good	1986	$25
❏ 5963	Something Constructive	1987	$25
❏ 6263	Whatever Works	1988	$25

JASEN, DAVE

BLUE GOOSE

Number	Title	Yr	NM
❏ 3001	Fingerbustin' Ragtime	197?	$30
❏ 3002	Rompin', Stompin' Ragtime	197?	$30

EUPHONIC

Number	Title	Yr	NM
❏ 1206	Creative Ragtime	196?	$30

FOLKWAYS

Number	Title	Yr	NM
❏ FC-3561	Rip-Roarin' Ragtime	1977	$25

JASMINE

GUINNESS

Number	Title	Yr	NM
❏ GNS36075 [B]	Jasmine	1977	$250

WEST 54

Number	Title	Yr	NM
❏ 8007	Jasmine	1980	$30

JASPAR, BOBBY

EMARCY

Number	Title	Yr	NM
❏ MG-36105 [M]	Bobby Jaspar and His All Stars	1957	$250

RIVERSIDE

Number	Title	Yr	NM
❏ RLP 12-240 [M]	Bobby Jaspar	1957	$300
—White label, blue print			
❏ RLP 12-240 [M]	Bobby Jaspar	1959	$300
—Blue label, microphone label at top			
❏ 6156	Tenor and Flute	198?	$30

SWING

Number	Title	Yr	NM
❏ SW-8413	Bobby Jaspar In Paris	1986	$25

JASPER WRATH

SUNFLOWER

Number	Title	Yr	NM
❏ SNF-5003 [B]	Jasper Wrath	1971	$50

JAUME, ANDRE, AND JOE MCPHEE

HAT HUT

Number	Title	Yr	NM
❏ 12	Tales and Prophecies	1980	$50

JAUME, ANDRE

HAT ART

Number	Title	Yr	NM
❏ 2003	Musique Pour 3 & 8: Errance	1986	$35

HAT HUT

Number	Title	Yr	NM
❏ 1989/90	Musique Pour 8: L'oc	1981	$50
❏ 0R	Saxanimalier	1979	$30

JAY AND THE AMERICANS

LIBERTY

Number	Title	Yr	NM
❏ LM-1010	Jay and the Americans Greatest Hits	1981	$10
—Another reissue			

RHINO

Number	Title	Yr	NM
❏ RNLP70224 [B]	All-Time Greatest Hits	1986	$15

SUNSET

Number	Title	Yr	NM
❏ SUS-5278	Early American Hits	1969	$18

Number	Title	Yr	NM
❏ SUS-5252 [B]	Jay and the Americans!!	1968	$15

UNART

Number	Title	Yr	NM
❏ M-20018 [M]	Jay and the Americans!!	196?	$15
❏ MS-21018 [S]	Jay and the Americans!!	196?	$15

UNITED ARTISTS

Number	Title	Yr	NM
❏ UAL-3300 [M]	At the Café Wha?	1963	$50
❏ UAS-6300 [S]	At the Café Wha?	1963	$150
❏ UAL-3417 [M]	Blockbusters	1965	$30
❏ UAS-6417 [S]	Blockbusters	1965	$30
❏ UAS-6762	Capture the Moment	1970	$25
❏ UAL-3407 [M]	Come a Little Bit Closer	1964	$30
❏ UAS-6407 [S]	Come a Little Bit Closer	1964	$30

Number	Title	Yr	NM
❏ UAL-3453 [M]	Jay and the Americans Greatest Hits	1965	$25
❏ UAS-6453 [S]	Jay and the Americans Greatest Hits	1965	$30
❏ ST-90814 [S]	Jay and the Americans Greatest Hits	1966	$30
—Capitol Record Club edition			
❏ LM-1010	Jay and the Americans Greatest Hits	1980	$12
—Reissue			
❏ UAL-3555 [M]	Jay and the Americans Greatest Hits, Volume 2	1966	$25
❏ UAS-6555 [S]	Jay and the Americans Greatest Hits, Volume 2	1966	$25
❏ ST-90815 [S]	Jay and the Americans Greatest Hits, Volume 2	1966	$30
—Capitol Record Club edition			
❏ UAL-3534 [M]	Livin' Above Your Head	1966	$25
❏ UAS-6534 [S]	Livin' Above Your Head	1966	$30
❏ UAS-6671	Sands of Time	1969	$25
❏ UAL-3222 [M]	She Cried	1962	$50
❏ UAS-6222 [S]	She Cried	1962	$150
❏ UAL-3474 [M]	Sunday and Me	1966	$25
❏ UAS-6474 [S]	Sunday and Me	1966	$30
❏ UA-LA357-E	The Very Best of Jay and the Americans	1975	$15
❏ UAL-3562 [M]	Try Some of This!	1967	$25
❏ UAS-6562 [S]	Try Some of This!	1967	$40
❏ UAS-6719	Wax Museum	1970	$25
❏ UAS-6751	Wax Museum, Volume 2	1970	$25

JAY AND THE TECHNIQUES

SMASH

Number	Title	Yr	NM
❏ MGS-27095 [M]	Apples, Peaches, Pumpkin Pie	1967	$50
❏ SRS-67095 [S]	Apples, Peaches, Pumpkin Pie	1967	$30
—First cover with "live" photo of the band			
❏ SRS-67095 [S]	Apples, Peaches, Pumpkin Pie	1968	$25
—Second cover with "posed" photo of the band			
❏ SRS-67102 [S]	Love Lost and Found	1968	$30
❏ MGS-27102 [M]	Love Lost and Found	1968	$100
—Mono may be white-label promo only			

JAYE, JERRY

HI

Number	Title	Yr	NM
❏ SHL-32102	Honky Tonk Women Love Redneck Men	1976	$15
❏ HL-12038 [M]	My Girl Josephine	1967	$25
❏ SHL-32038 [S]	My Girl Josephine	1967	$25

JAYHAWKS, THE

This is the alt-country group, not the '50s vocal group.

AMERICAN

Number	Title	Yr	NM
❏ 43114	Sound of Lies	1997	$25
❏ 43006	Tomorrow the Green Grass	1995	$25

BUNKHOUSE

Number	Title	Yr	NM
❏ 7001	The Jayhawks	1986	$100

TWIN/TONE

Number	Title	Yr	NM
❏ TTR89151	Blue Earth	1989	$18

JAYNETTS, THE

TUFF

Number	Title	Yr	NM
❏ LP13 [M]	Sally Go 'Round the Roses	1963	$300

JAZZ ARTISTS GUILD, THE

CANDID

Number	Title	Yr	NM
❏ CD-8022 [M]	Newport Rebels	1960	$40
❏ CS-9022 [S]	Newport Rebels	1960	$50

JAZZ BROTHERS, THE

RIVERSIDE

Number	Title	Yr	NM
❏ RLP-371 [M]	Hey, Baby!	1961	$250
❏ RS-9371 [S]	Hey, Baby!	1961	$250
❏ RLP-335 [M]	Jazz Brothers	1960	$250
❏ RS-9335 [S]	Jazz Brothers	1960	$250
❏ RLP-405 [M]	Spring Fever	1962	$175
❏ RS-9405 [S]	Spring Fever	1962	$175

JAZZ CITY

RAHMP

Number	Title	Yr	NM
❏ 2	Jazz City	197?	$25

JAZZ CITY ALL-STARS, THE

BETHLEHEM

Number	Title	Yr	NM
❏ BCP-79 [M]	Jazz City Presents the Jazz City All-Stars	1957	$300

JAZZ COMPOSERS ORCHESTRA

JCOA

Number	Title	Yr	NM
❏ LP-1001/2	Jazz Composers Orchestra	1968	$40

JAZZ CONTEMPORARIES

STRATA-EAST

Number	Title	Yr	NM
❏ SES1972-2	Reasons in Tonality	1972	$35

Number	Title	Yr	NM

JAZZ CORPS, THE
PACIFIC JAZZ
PJ-10116 [M]	The Jazz Corps Under the Direction of Tommy Peltier	1967	$30
ST-20116 [S]	The Jazz Corps Under the Direction of Tommy Peltier	1967	$35
LN-10131	The Jazz Corps Under the Direction of Tommy Peltier	198?	$25

—Budget-line reissue

JAZZ COURIERS, THE
CARLTON
| LP 12-116 [M] | The Couriers of Jazz | 1959 | $50 |
| ST 12-116 [S] | The Couriers of Jazz | 1959 | $40 |
JAZZLAND
| JLP-34 [M] | Message from Britain | 1961 | $30 |
| JLP-934 [S] | Message from Britain | 1961 | $30 |
WHIPPET
| WLP-700 [M] | The Jazz Couriers | 1956 | $120 |

JAZZ CRUSADERS, THE
See THE CRUSADERS.

JAZZ EXPONENTS, THE
ARGO
| LP-622 [M] | The Jazz Exponents | 1958 | $40 |

JAZZ FIVE, THE
RIVERSIDE
| RLP-361 [M] | The Hooter | 1961 | $250 |
| RS-9361 [S] | The Hooter | 1961 | $250 |

JAZZ INTERACTIONS ORCHESTRA, THE
VERVE
| V-8731 [M] | Jazzhattan Suite | 1967 | $25 |
| V6-8731 [S] | Jazzhattan Suite | 1967 | $30 |

JAZZ LAB, THE
COLUMBIA
| CL998 [M] | Jazz Lab | 1957 | $175 |
| CL998 [M] | Jazz Lab | 199? | $30 |

—180-gram reissue

| CL1058 [M] | Modern Jazz Perspective/ Jazz Lab, Volume 2 | 1957 | $300 |
JAZZLAND
| JLP-1 [M] | Jazz Lab | 1960 | $50 |
| JLP-901 [S] | Jazz Lab | 1960 | $75 |
JOSIE
| JOZ-3500 [M] | Gigi Gryce and Donald Byrd | 1962 | $40 |

—Reissue of Jubilee album

| JS-3500 [R] | Gigi Gryce and Donald Byrd | 196? | $25 |
JUBILEE
| JLP-1059 [M] | Jazz Lab | 1958 | $150 |
RIVERSIDE
| RLP 12-229 [M] | Gigi Gryce and the Jazz Lab Quintet | 1957 | $300 |

— White label, blue print

| RLP 12-229 [M] | Gigi Gryce and the Jazz Lab Quintet | 1959 | $300 |

— Blue label, microphone logo at top

| RLP-1110 [S] | Gigi Gryce and the Jazz Lab Quintet | 1959 | $300 |

JAZZ MEMBERS BIG BAND
SEA BREEZE
| SB-2028 | Live at Fitzgerald | 1986 | $25 |
| SB-2014 | May Day | 1985 | $25 |

JAZZ MESSENGERS, THE
See ART BLAKEY.

JAZZ O'MANIACS, THE
STOMP OFF
| SOS-1046 | Have You Ever Felt This Way | 198? | $25 |
| SOS-1071 | Sweet Mumtaz | 1984 | $25 |

JAZZ PIANO QUARTET, THE
RCA VICTOR
| CPL1-0680 | Let It Happen | 1974 | $35 |

JAZZ SYMPHONICS
RENFRO
| LP-12369 | The Beginning | 1968 | $75 |

JAZZ WARRIORS
ANTILLES
| 90681 | Out of Many, One People | 1987 | $25 |

JAZZMOBILE ALL-STARS, THE
TAYLOR-MADE
| TL-1003 | The Jazzmobile All Stars | 1989 | $30 |

Number	Title	Yr	NM

JAZZPICKERS, THE
EMARCY
| MG-36123 [M] | Command Performance | 1958 | $250 |
| MG-36111 [M] | The Jazzpickers | 1957 | $250 |
MERCURY
| SR-80013 [S] | For Moderns Only | 1959 | $150 |

JAZZTET, THE
ARGO
LP-672 [M]	Big City Sounds	1961	$40
LPS-672 [S]	Big City Sounds	1961	$50
LP-664 [M]	Meet the Jazztet	1960	$50
LPS-664 [S]	Meet the Jazztet	1960	$75
LP-684 [M]	The Jazztet and John Lewis	1961	$40
LPS-684 [S]	The Jazztet and John Lewis	1961	$50
LP-688 [M]	The Jazztet at Birdhouse	1961	$40
LPS-688 [S]	The Jazztet at Birdhouse	1961	$50
CADET
| LP-664 [M] | Meet the Jazztet | 1966 | $75 |
| LPS-664 [S] | Meet the Jazztet | 1966 | $30 |

—Fading blue label

| CA-664 [S] | Meet the Jazztet | 197? | $25 |

— Yellow and red label

CHESS
| CH-9159 | Meet the Jazztet | 198? | $15 |

—Reissue

CONTEMPORARY
| C-14020 | Back to the City | 1987 | $30 |
| C-14034 | Real Time | 1988 | $30 |
MERCURY
MG-20737 [M]	Another Git-Together	1962	$150
SR-60737 [S]	Another Git-Together	1962	$150
MG-20698 [M]	Here and Now	1962	$150
SR-60698 [S]	Here and Now	1962	$150
SOUL NOTE
| SN-1066 | Moment to Moment | 1984 | $35 |

JAZZY JEFF AND FRESH PRINCE
JIVE
| 1188-1-J | And in This Corner... | 1989 | $12 |
| 41489-1 | Code Red | 1993 | $15 |

—LP in generic black cover with center hole and sticker

| 1091-1-J | He's the D.J., I'm the Rapper | 1988 | $15 |

— Without "Nightmare on My Street" disclaimer on cover

| 1091-1-J RE | He's the D.J., I'm the Rapper | 1988 | $16 |

— With "Nightmare on My Street" disclaimer on cover (much scarcer than original)

1392-1-J	Homebase	1991	$15
JL6-8399	On Fire	1985	$15
1026-1-J	Rock the House	1986	$12

— Reissued in 1989 with same catalog number and one new track

RAPSTER
| RR 008LP | The Magnificent | 2002 | $18 |

— By "DJ Jazzy Jeff"; full-length version with different cover than EP

| RR 008EP [EP] | The Magnificent EP | 2002 | $10 |

— By "DJ Jazzy Jeff"

WORD UP
| WDLP-0001 | Rock the House | 1985 | $30 |

JEANNEAU, FRANCOIS
INNER CITY
| IC-1022 | Techniques Douces | 197? | $35 |

JEFFERSON, BLIND LEMON
MILESTONE
MLP-2013 [M]	Black Snake Moan	1970	$100
MLP-2004 [M]	The Immortal Blind Lemon Jefferson	1968	$30
MLP-2007 [M]	The Immortal Blind Lemon Jefferson, Vol. 2	1969	$30
RIVERSIDE
RLP 12-136 [M]	Blind Lemon Jefferson, Volume 2	1958	$120
RLP 12-125 [M]	Blind Lemon Jefferson -- Classic Folk Blues	1957	$120
1053 [10]	Penitentiary Blues	1955	$300
1014 [10]	The Folk Blues of Blind Lemon Jefferson	1953	$300

JEFFERSON, CARTER
TIMELESS
| 309 | The Rise of Atlantis | 1979 | $30 |

JEFFERSON, EDDIE
FANTASY
OJC-396	Body and Soul	1989	$30
OJC-613	Come Along with Me	1991	$30
OJC-307	Letter from Home	1988	$25
INNER CITY
| IC-1016 | Jazz Singer | 197? | $35 |
| IC-1033 | Main Man | 1978 | $35 |
MUSE
| MR-5063 | Still On the Planet | 1976 | $30 |

Number	Title	Yr	NM

| MR-5127 | The Live-Liest | 197? | $30 |
| MR-5043 | Things Are Getting Better | 1974 | $30 |
PRESTIGE
PRST-7619	Body and Soul	1969	$25
PRST-7698	Come Along with Me	1969	$25
24095	There I Go Again	198?	$35
RIVERSIDE
| RLP-411 [M] | Letter from Home | 1962 | $175 |
| RS-9411 [S] | Letter from Home | 1962 | $175 |

JEFFERSON, RON
CATALYST
| 7601 | Vous Etes Swing | 1976 | $30 |
PACIFIC JAZZ
| PJ-36 [M] | Love Lifted Me | 1962 | $30 |
| ST-36 [S] | Love Lifted Me | 1962 | $40 |

JEFFERSON
JANUS
| JLS-3006 | Jefferson | 1969 | $18 |

JEFFERSON AIRPLANE
Also see MARTY BALIN; PAPA JOHN CREACH; HOT TUNA; JEFFERSON STARSHIP; PAUL KANTNER; JORMA KAUKONEN; GRACE SLICK.
DCC COMPACT CLASSICS
| LPZ-2033 | Surrealistic Pillow | 1997 | $85 |

—Audiophile vinyl

EPIC
| OE45271 | Jefferson Airplane | 1989 | $18 |
GRUNT
| FTR-1001 [B] | Bark | 1971 | $30 |

—With brown paper bag

| FTR-1001 | Bark | 1971 | $12 |

—Without brown paper bag

AYL1-4386	Bark	1981	$10
APL1-0437	Early Flight	1974	$15
CYL2-1255	Flight Log 1966-1976	1977	$15
FTR-1007	Long John Silver	1972	$15
BFL1-0147	Thirty Seconds Over Winterland	1973	$15
AYL1-4391	Thirty Seconds Over Winterland	1981	$10
MOBILE FIDELITY
| 1-148 [B] | Crown of Creation | 1984 | $80 |

—Audiophile vinyl

PAIR
| PDL2-1090 | Time Machine | 1986 | $15 |
RCA
| 5724-1-R [B] | 2400 Fulton Street: An Anthology | 1987 | $35 |
RCA VICTOR
| LOP-1511 [M] | After Bathing at Baxter's | 1967 | $250 |
| LSO-1511 [S] | After Bathing at Baxter's | 1967 | $25 |

— Black label, dog on top

| LSO-1511 [S] | After Bathing at Baxter's | 1969 | $15 |

— Orange label

| LSO-1511 [S] | After Bathing at Baxter's | 1975 | $12 |

— Tan label

AFL1-4545	After Bathing at Baxter's	1981	$10
AYL1-4718	After Bathing at Baxter's	1983	$10
LSP-4133	Bless Its Pointed Little Head	1969	$15

— Orange label

| LSP-4133 | Bless Its Pointed Little Head | 1975 | $12 |

— Tan label

| AYL1-3798 | Bless Its Pointed Little Head | 1980 | $10 |
| LSP-4058 | Crown of Creation | 1968 | $30 |

— Black label, dog on top

| LSP-4058 | Crown of Creation | 1969 | $15 |

— Orange label

| LSP-4058 | Crown of Creation | 1975 | $12 |

— Tan label

| AYL1-3797 | Crown of Creation | 1980 | $10 |
| LSP-3584 [S] | Jefferson Airplane Takes Off! | 1966 | $5000 |

— Version 1: See Version 1 note under mono version; VG value 2000; VG+ value 3500

| LPM-3584 [M] | Jefferson Airplane Takes Off! | 1966 | $3500 |

— Version 1: With "Runnin' 'Round This World" as last song on side 1. Count the number of bands on Side 1 of the record; don't rely on the cover listing, as some jackets list the title. when it's not on the record. Matrix numbers are: Side 1, TPRM-0171-12S; Side 2, TPRM-01772-3S. VG value 2000; VG+ value 2500

| LPM-3584 [M] | Jefferson Airplane Takes Off! | 1966 | $1000 |

— Version 2: No "Runnin' 'Round This World", but "questionable" lyrics remain in "Let Me In" ("Don't tell me you want money") and "Run Around" ("That sway as you lay under me"). Until the exact matrix numbers are known, it must be heard to confirm.

| LSP-3584 [S] | Jefferson Airplane Takes Off! | 1966 | $1800 |

— Version 2: See Version 2 note under mono version

| LPM-3584 [M] | Jefferson Airplane Takes Off! | 1966 | $100 |

— Version 3: No "Runnin' 'Round This World", altered lyrics to "Let Me In" ("Don't tell me it's so funny") and "Run Around

Number	Title	Yr	NM

("That sway as you stay here by me"). All later versions confirm to Version 3.

Number	Title	Yr	NM
❏ LSP-3584 [S]	Jefferson Airplane Takes Off!	1966	$30
—Version 3: See Version 3 note under mono version			
❏ LSP-3584 [S]	Jefferson Airplane Takes Off!	1969	$15
—Orange label			
❏ LSP-3584 [S]	Jefferson Airplane Takes Off!	1975	$12
—Tan label			
❏ AYL1-3739	Jefferson Airplane Takes Off!	1980	$10
❏ LPM-3766 [M]	Surrealistic Pillow	1967	$100
❏ LSP-3766 [S]	Surrealistic Pillow	1967	$30
—Black label, dog on top			
❏ LSP-3766 [S]	Surrealistic Pillow	1969	$15
—Orange label			
❏ LSP-3766 [S]	Surrealistic Pillow	1975	$12
— Tan label			
❏ AYL1-3738	Surrealistic Pillow	1980	$10
❏ LSP-4459	The Worst of Jefferson Airplane	1970	$15
❏ AYL1-3661	The Worst of Jefferson Airplane	1980	$10
❏ LSP-4238	Volunteers	1969	$15
—Orange label			
❏ LSP-4238	Volunteers	1975	$12
—Tan label			
❏ APD1-0320 [Q]	Volunteers	1973	$175
— Yellow/orange label			
❏ APD1-0320 [Q]	Volunteers	1975	$100
—Tan label			
❏ AYL1-3867	Volunteers	1980	$10

SUNDAZED

❏ LP5187 [M]	After Bathing at Baxter's	2005	$18
—Reissue on 180-gram vinyl			
❏ LP5186 [M]	Jefferson Airplane Takes Off	2005	$18
—Reissue on 180-gram vinyl			
❏ LP5186 [B]	Takes Off	2015	$25
—mono			

JEFFERSON STARSHIP
See cross-references under JEFFERSON AIRPLANE.

DCC COMPACT CLASSICS

❏ LPZ-2036	Red Octopus	1997	$40
—Audiophile vinyl			

GRUNT

❏ BFL1-0717	Dragon Fly	1974	$12
❏ BFD1-0717 [Q]	Dragon Fly	1974	$40
❏ AYL1-3796	Dragon Fly	1980	$10
❏ BXL1-2515	Earth	1978	$12
❏ AYL1-4172	Earth	1981	$10
❏ BZL1-3452	Freedom at Point Zero	1979	$12
❏ AYL1-5161	Freedom at Point Zero	1984	$10
❏ BZL1-3247	Gold	1978	$12
❏ DJL1-3363 [PD]	Gold	1978	$30
— Promo-only picture disc			
❏ BZL1-3848	Modern Times	1981	$12
❏ BXL1-4921	Nuclear Furniture	1984	$12
❏ BFL1-0999	Red Octopus	1975	$12
❏ BFD1-0999 [Q]	Red Octopus	1975	$40
❏ AYL1-3660	Red Octopus	1980	$10
❏ BFL1-1557	Spitfire	1976	$12
❏ BFD1-1557 [Q]	Spitfire	1976	$40
❏ AYL1-3953	Spitfire	1981	$10
❏ BXL1-4372	Winds of Change	1982	$12

JEFFREY, JOE, GROUP

WAND

❏ WDS-686	My Pledge of Love	1969	$30

JEFFREY, PAUL

MAINSTREAM

❏ MRL-376	Family	1972	$35
❏ MRL-406	Paul Jeffrey	1973	$35
❏ MRL-390	Watershed	1973	$35

SAVOY

❏ MG-12192 [M]	Electrifying Sounds	1968	$25

JEFFREYS, GARLAND

A&M

❏ SP-4778	American Boy and Girl	1979	$12
❏ SP-4629	Ghost Writer	1977	$15
❏ SP-4681	One-Eyed Jack	1978	$12

ATLANTIC

❏ SD7253	Garland Jeffreys	1973	$18

EPIC

❏ PE36983	Escape Artist	1981	$12
❏ ARE38190	Guts for Love	1983	$12
❏ FE37436	Rock 'N' Roll Adult	1981	$12

JEFFRIES, FRAN

MONUMENT

❏ MLP-8069 [M]	This Is Fran Jeffries	1967	$25
❏ SLP-18069 [S]	This Is Fran Jeffries	1967	$25

WARWICK

❏ W-2020 [M]	Fran Can Really Hang You Up the Most	1960	$25

JEFFRIES, HERB

BETHLEHEM

❏ BCP-72 [M]	Say It Isn't So	1957	$300

CORAL

❏ CRL56066 [10]	Herb Jeffries Sings Flamingo and Other Songs in a Mellow Mood	1952	$250
❏ CRL56044 [10]	Time on My Hands	1951	$200

DOBRE

❏ DR-1047	I Remember the Bing	1978	$35

GOLDEN TONE

❏ 14066 [S]	The Devil Is a Woman	196?	$30
❏ C-4066 [M]	The Devil Is a Woman	196?	$30

HARMONY

❏ HL7048 [M]	Herb Jeffries	195?	$20

MERCURY

❏ MG-25090 [10]	Herb Jeffries Sings	1950	$300
❏ MG-25091 [10]	Just Jeffries	1950	$300
❏ MG-25089 [10]	Magenta Moods	1950	$300

RCA VICTOR

❏ LPM-1608 [M]	Senor Flamingo	1957	$40

RKO UNIQUE

❏ ULP-128 [M]	Jamaica	1956	$75

JELLY BEAN BANDITS, THE

MAINSTREAM

❏ 56103 [M]	The Jelly Bean Bandits	1967	$150
❏ S-6103 [S]	The Jelly Bean Bandits	1967	$175

JELLYBREAD

BLUE HORIZON

❏ BH-4801 [B]	First Slice	1970	$75

JELVING, AKE

CAPITOL

❏ T10079 [M]	Christmas in Sweden	195?	$25
— Black label with colorband, logo on left			
❏ T10079 [M]	Christmas in Sweden	196?	$18
— Black label with colorband, logo on top			
❏ SP-10079 [R]	Christmas in Sweden	1969	$12
— Reissue with new label and prefix			
❏ SM-10079 [R]	Christmas in Sweden	197?	$10
— Reissue with new label and prefix			
❏ DT10079 [R]	Christmas in Sweden	196?	$15
❏ T10079 [M]	Christmas in Sweden	1957	$30
— Turquoise label			

JENKINS, FLORENCE FOSTER

RCA VICTOR

❏ LRT-7001 [10]	A Florence! Foster!! Jenkins!!! Recital!!!!	195?	$50
❏ LM-2597 [M]	The Glory (????) of the Human Voice	1961	$25

JENKINS, GORDON

BAINBRIDGE

❏ BT-1022 [S]	Soul of a People	1980	$12

CAPITOL

❏ T1023 [M]	Dream Dust	1958	$30
❏ T781 [M]	Night Dreams	1956	$30
— Turquoise label			
❏ T884 [M]	Stolen Hours	1956	$30
— Turquoise label			
❏ ST884 [S]	Stolen Hours	1959	$30
❏ T766 [M]	The Complete Manhattan Tower	1956	$30
— Turquoise label			
❏ DT766 [R]	The Complete Manhattan Tower	196?	$15
❏ T1048 [M]	Tropicana Holiday	1958	$30
❏ ST1048 [S]	Tropicana Holiday	1958	$30

COLUMBIA

❏ CL1764 [M]	Hawaiian Wedding Songs	1962	$15
❏ CS8564 [S]	Hawaiian Wedding Songs	1962	$18
❏ CL2009 [M]	In a Tender Mood	1963	$15
❏ CS8809 [S]	In a Tender Mood	1963	$18
❏ CL1882 [M]	The Magic World of Gordon Jenkins	1962	$15
❏ CS8682 [S]	The Magic World of Gordon Jenkins	1962	$18

DECCA

❏ DL5307 [10]	For You	195?	$40
❏ DL8116 [M]	Heartbeats	195?	$30
❏ DL8313 [M]	He Likes to Go Dancing: Music for Her Boy Friend	195?	$30
❏ DL8077 [M]	In the Still of the Night	195?	$30
❏ DL8011 [M]	Manhattan Tower/California (The Golden State)	1951	$30
— Black label, gold print			
❏ DL78011 [R]	Manhattan Tower/California (The Golden State)	196?	$15
❏ DL5469 [10]	Me and Juliet/Can-Can	1953	$40
❏ DL4714 [M]	My Heart Sings	1966	$15
❏ DL74714 [S]	My Heart Sings	1966	$18
❏ DL5275 [10]	Playing His Compositions	195?	$40
❏ DL8109 [M]	P.S. I Love You	195?	$30

DOT

❏ DLP-3752 [M]	Soft Soul	1966	$15
❏ DLP-25752 [S]	Soft Soul	1966	$18

GWP

❏ 2035	Way Back Now	1971	$12

KAPP

❏ KL1361 [M]	I Live Alone	196?	$15
❏ KS3361 [S]	I Live Alone	196?	$18

MAINSTREAM

❏ S-6093 [S]	Soul of a People	196?	$15
— Reissue of Time S-2050			
❏ 56093 [M]	Soul of a People	196?	$12
— Reissue of Time 52050			

MCA

❏ 166	Manhattan Tower/California (The Golden State)	1973	$12
— Black label with rainbow			

MCA CORAL

❏ CB-20030	Romance	1973	$12

PICKWICK

❏ PC-3005 [M]	Yours -- The Magic of Gordon Jenkins	196?	$15
❏ SPC-3005 [S]	Yours -- The Magic of Gordon Jenkins	196?	$15

SEARS

❏ SPS-403 [S]	The Romantic Moods of Gordon Jenkins	196?	$18

SUNSET

❏ SUM-1149 [M]	Blue Prelude	196?	$18
❏ SUS-5149 [S]	Blue Prelude	196?	$15

TIME

❏ S-2061 [S]	France	196?	$18
❏ 52061 [M]	France	196?	$15
❏ 52130 [M]	Paris, I Wish You Love	196?	$15
❏ S-2130 [S]	Paris, I Wish You Love	196?	$18
❏ S-2050 [S]	Soul of a People	196?	$18
❏ 52050 [M]	Soul of a People	196?	$15

VEE JAY

❏ VJLP-1089 [M]	The Great Movie Themes of the 30s, 40s and 50s	1964	$15
❏ VJLPS-1089 [S]	The Great Movie Themes of the 30s, 40s and 50s	1964	$25

VOCALION

❏ VL3615 [M]	Dreamer's Holiday	196?	$18

WARNER BROS.

❏ W1464 [M]	Let's Duet	1963	$15
❏ WS1464 [S]	Let's Duet	1963	$18

JENKINS, JOHN; CLIFF JORDAN; BOBBY TIMMONS

FANTASY

❏ OJC-251	Jenkins, Jordan & Timmons	1987	$30

NEW JAZZ

❏ NJLP-8232 [M]	Jenkins, Jordan and Timmons	1960	$250
—Purple label			
❏ NJLP-8232 [M]	Jenkins, Jordan and Timmons	1965	$175
— Blue label with trident logo			

JENKINS, JOHN

BLUE NOTE

❏ BLP-1573 [M]	John Jenkins with Kenny Burrell	1958	$1500
— Deep groove version; W. 63rd St. address on label			
❏ BLP-1573 [M]	John Jenkins with Kenny Burrell	1958	$1000
— Regular version with W. 63rd St., New York address on label			
❏ BLP-1573 [M]	John Jenkins with Kenny Burrell	1963	$140
— With "New York, USA" address on label			
❏ BST-1573 [S]	John Jenkins with Kenny Burrell	1959	$1500
— Deep groove" version; W. 63rd St. address on label			
❏ BST-1573 [S]	John Jenkins with Kenny Burrell	1959	$300
— Regular version with W. 63rd St., New York address on label			
❏ BST-1573 [S]	John Jenkins with Kenny Burrell	1963	$140
— With "New York, USA" address on label			
❏ BST-81573 [S]	John Jenkins with Kenny Burrell	1967	$75
— With "A Division of Liberty Records" on label			

REGENT

❏ MG-6056 [M]	Jazz Eyes	1957	$175

SAVOY

❏ MG-12201 [M]	Jazz Eyes	196?	$40

JENKINS, LEROY, AND MUHAL RICHARD ABRAMS

BLACK SAINT

❏ BSR-0033	Duo	198?	$30

Number	Title	Yr	NM
JENKINS, LEROY			
BLACK SAINT			
❏ BSR-0060	Mixed Quartet	198?	$30
❏ BSR-0022	The Legend of Ai Glatson	198?	$30
❏ BSR-0083	Urban Blues	1985	$30
INDIA NAVIGATION			
❏ IN-1028	Solo Concert	1977	$30
JCOA			
❏ LP-1010	For Players Only	1975	$35
TOMATO			
❏ TOM-8001	Space Minds, New Worlds	1979	$35
JENKINS, MARV			
OROVOX			
❏ 1001 [M]	Marv Jenkins Arrives	196?	$40
❏ S-1001 [S]	Marv Jenkins Arrives	196?	$40
REPRISE			
❏ R-6077 [M]	Good Little Man at the Rubaiyat Room	1963	$25
❏ R9-6077 [S]	Good Little Man at the Rubaiyat Room	1963	$30
JENKS, GLENN			
STOMP OFF			
❏ SOS-1179	Ragtime Alchemy	1989	$25
JENNEY, JACK			
COLUMBIA			
❏ GL100 [10]	The Golden Era	1949	$50
COLUMBIA MASTERWORKS			
❏ ML4803 [M]	Jack Jenney	195?	$100
JENNINGS, BILL			
AUDIO LAB			
❏ AL-1514 [M]	Guitar/Vibes	1959	$150
KING			
❏ 398-527 [M]	Billy in the Lion's Den	1956	$700
❏ 295-105 [10]	Jazz Interlude	195?	$400
❏ 398-508 [M]	Mood Indigo	1955	$150
❏ 295-106 [10]	The Fabulous Guitar of Bill Jennings	195?	$300
PRESTIGE			
❏ PRST-7788	Enough Said	1970	$30
❏ PRLP-7164 [M]	Enough Said!	1959	$175
❏ PRLP-7177 [M]	Glide On	1960	$250
❏ PRST-7836	Glide On	1971	$30
JENNINGS, WAYLON; WILLIE NELSON; JESSI COLTER; TOMPALL GLASER			
RCA VICTOR			
❏ APL1-1321	Wanted! The Outlaws	1976	$15
— Tan label			
❏ APL1-1321	Wanted! The Outlaws	1976	$12
— Black label, dog near top			
❏ AAL1-1321	Wanted! The Outlaws	198?	$10
— Reissue			
JENNINGS, WAYLON			
A&M			
❏ SP-4238	Don't Think Twice	1969	$40
BAT			
❏ 1001 [M]	Waylon Jennings at JD's	1964	$700
— Approximately 500 copies pressed			
COLUMBIA			
❏ FC40056	Highwayman	1985	$12
— Waylon Jennings/Willie Nelson/Johnny Cash/Kris Kristofferson			
❏ C45240	Highwayman 2	1990	$18
— Waylon Jennings/Willie Nelson/Johnny Cash/Kris Kristofferson			
❏ 1P-8030	The Eagle	1990	$30
— Vinyl released only through Columbia House			
MCA			
❏ 42038	A Man Called Hoss	1987	$12
❏ 42038 [DJ]	A Man Called Hoss	1987	$75
— Promo-only edition with letter and 48-page book			
❏ 42222	Full Circle	1988	$12
❏ 5911	Hangin' Tough	1987	$12
❏ 42287	New Classic Waylon	1989	$12
❏ 731	Waylon Jennings	198?	$15
— Reissue of Vocalion LP			
❏ 5688	Will the Wolf Survive	1986	$12
MCA CORAL			
❏ VL73873	Waylon Jennings	197?	$15
— Reissue of Vocalion 73873; cover still says "Vocalion" but label is "MCA Coral			
PAIR			
❏ PDL1-1033	A Couple More Years	1986	$15
❏ PDL1-1110	Honly Tonk Hero	1986	$15
❏ PDL1-1005	Waylon!	1986	$15

Number	Title	Yr	NM
PICKWICK			
❏ CAS-2556	Heartaches by the Number	197?	$10
— Reissue of RCA Camden CAS-2556			
❏ ACL-0306	Only Daddy That'll Walk the Line	197?	$10
— Reissue of RCA Camden LP			
❏ ACL-7019 [S]	The Dark Side of Fame	1976	$12
— Reissue of RCA Camden CAS-2183			
RCA			
❏ 5620-1-RB	The Best of Waylon	1987	$12
❏ 9561-1-R	The Early Years (1965-1969)	1989	$12
RCA CAMDEN			
❏ CAS-2556	Heartaches by the Number	1972	$15
❏ ACL-0306	Only Daddy That'll Walk the Line	1973	$12
❏ CAS-2608	Ruby, Don't Take Your Love to Town	1972	$15
❏ CAS-2183 [S]	The One and Only Waylon Jennings	1967	$15
❏ CAL-2183 [M]	The One and Only Waylon Jennings	1967	$18
RCA VICTOR			
❏ APL1-1816	Are You Ready for the Country	1976	$12
❏ AYL1-3663	Are You Ready for the Country	1980	$10
— Budget-line reissue			
❏ AFL1-1816	Are You Ready for the Country	1977	$10
— Black label, dog near side; new prefix			
❏ AHL1-4247	Black On Black	1982	$12
❏ LSP-4567	Cedartown, Georgia	1971	$25
❏ AHL1-5473	Collector's Series	1985	$12
❏ LSP-4180	Country-Folk	1969	$30
❏ APL1-1062	Dreaming My Dreams	1975	$12
❏ AYL1-4072	Dreaming My Dreams	1981	$10
— Budget-line reissue			
❏ LPM-3523 [M]	Folk-Country	1966	$30

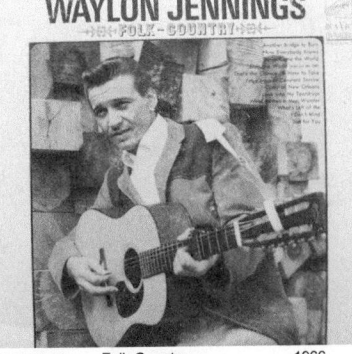

Number	Title	Yr	NM
❏ LSP-3523 [S]	Folk-Country	1966	$40
❏ LSP-4647	Good Hearted Woman	1972	$25
❏ AHL1-3378	Greatest Hits	1979	$12
❏ LPM-3918 [M]	Hangin' On	1968	$150
❏ LSP-3918 [S]	Hangin' On	1968	$30
❏ APL1-0240	Honky Tonk Heroes	1973	$18
❏ AYL1-3897	Honky Tonk Heroes	1980	$10
— Budget-line reissue			
❏ AHL1-4673	It's Only Rock & Roll	1983	$12
❏ AFL1-2979	I've Always Been Crazy	1978	$12
❏ AYL1-4164	I've Always Been Crazy	1981	$10
— Budget-line reissue			
❏ LSP-4085	Jewels	1968	$30
❏ LSP-4137	Just to Satisfy You	1969	$30
❏ LSP-4751	Ladies Love Outlaws	1972	$25
❏ LPM-3620 [M]	Leavin' Town	1966	$30
❏ LSP-3620 [S]	Leavin' Town	1966	$40
❏ LSP-4854	Lonesome, On'ry and Mean	1973	$18
— Original issue; orange label			
❏ AFL1-4854	Lonesome, On'ry and Mean	197?	$12
— Reissue with new prefix			
❏ LPM-3825 [M]	Love of the Common People	1967	$30
❏ LSP-3825 [S]	Love of the Common People	1967	$30
❏ AHL1-3602	Music Man	1980	$12
❏ AYL1-4250	Music Man	1982	$10
— Budget-line reissue			
❏ LPM-3736 [M]	Nashville Rebel	1967	$40
❏ LSP-3736 [S]	Nashville Rebel	1967	$50
❏ AHL1-5017	Never Could Toe the Mark	1984	$12
❏ AYL1-7046	Never Could Toe the Mark	1985	$10
— Budget-line reissue			
❏ APL1-2317	Ol' Waylon	1977	$12
❏ AAL1-2317	Ol' Waylon	198?	$10
— Reissue			
❏ AYL1-5126	Ol' Waylon	1984	$10
— Budget-line reissue			
❏ LPM-4023 [M]	Only the Greatest	1968	$175
❏ LSP-4023 [S]	Only the Greatest	1968	$30
❏ LSP-4418	Singer of Sad Songs	1970	$25
❏ AHL1-7184	Sweet Mother Texas	1986	$12
❏ LSP-4341	The Best of Waylon Jennings	1970	$25

Number	Title	Yr	NM
❏ AYL1-4828	The Best of Waylon Jennings	1983	$10
— Budget-line reissue			
❏ APL1-0734	The Ramblin' Man	1974	$15
— Original issue; tan label			
❏ AYL1-4073	The Ramblin' Man	1981	$10
— Budget-line reissue			
❏ AFL1-0734	The Ramblin' Man	197?	$12
— Reissue with new prefix			
❏ LSP-4487	The Taker/Tulsa	1971	$25
❏ APL1-0539	This Time	1974	$15
❏ AHL1-5428	Turn the Page	1985	$12
❏ LSP-4260	Waylon	1970	$25
❏ AHL1-4826	Waylon and Company	1983	$12
❏ AYL1-5433	Waylon and Company	1985	$10
— Budget-line reissue			
❏ APL1-1108	Waylon Live	1976	$12
❏ AYL1-4163	Waylon Live	1981	$10
— Budget-line reissue			
❏ AHL1-5325	Waylon's Greatest Hits, Vol. 2	1984	$12
❏ LPM-3660 [M]	Waylon Sings Ol' Harlan	1967	$30
❏ LSP-3660 [S]	Waylon Sings Ol' Harlan	1967	$40
❏ AHL1-3493	What Goes Around Comes Around	1979	$12
SOUNDS			
❏ 1001 [M]	Waylon Jennings at JD's	1964	$500
— Approximately 500 copies pressed; reissue of Bat 1001			
TIME-LIFE			
❏ STW-102	Country Music	1981	$12
JENSEN, DICK			
PHILADELPHIA INT'L.			
❏ KZ31794 [B]	Dick Jensen	1973	$35
JENSEN, KRIS			
HICKORY			
❏ LP110 [M]	Torture	1963	$100
JENSEN, KURT			
HOLLYWOOD			
❏ LPH-137 [M]	An Evening with Jayne	195?	$75
— Collectible for its "cheesecake" cover of Jayne Mansfield			
JEREMY AND THE SATYRS			
REPRISE			
❏ R-6282 [M]	Jeremy and the Satyrs	1968	$40
— Mono is white label promo only			
❏ RS-6282 [S]	Jeremy and the Satyrs	1968	$25
JEREMY'S FRIENDS			
WARWICK			
❏ W-2019 [M]	Jeremy's Friends	1960	$50
JERICHO			
AMPEX			
❏ A-10112	Jericho	1971	$30
JERNIGAN, DOUG, AND BUCKY PIZZARELLI			
FLYING FISH			
❏ 043	Doug and Bucky	1977	$30
JESSE J. AND THE BANDITS			
RECAR			
❏ 2011 [M]	Top Teen Hits	1965	$150
JESTERS, THE			
COLLECTABLES			
❏ COL-5036	The Best of the Jesters	198?	$12
JESUS AND MARY CHAIN, THE			
REPRISE			
❏ 25383	Psychocandy	1985	$15
WARNER BROS.			
❏ 26015	Automatic	1989	$14
❏ 25729	Barbed Wire Kisses	1988	$15
❏ 25656	Darklands	1987	$15
JESUS JONES			
SBK			
❏ SPRO-05348/9 [DJ]	A Conversation with Jesus	1990	$25
— Generic cover with sticker			
❏ K1-94480	Liquidizer	1989	$18
JETHRO TULL			
Featuring flutist Ian Anderson. Also BLODWYN PIG related.			
CHRYSALIS			
❏ V5X41653	20 Years of Jethro Tull	1988	$100
❏ VX241655	20 Years of Jethro Tull	1989	$30
— Abridged version of Chrysalis 41653			
❏ CHR1301	A	1980	$12
❏ PV41301	A	1983	$10
❏ CHR1040 [B]	A Passion Play	1973	$20

Number	Title	Yr	NM
— Green label, "3300 Warner Blvd." address			
❑ CHR1040	A Passion Play	1977	$12
— Blue label, New York address			
❑ PV41040	A Passion Play	1983	$10
❑ CHR1044	Aqualung	1973	$15
— Green label, "3300 Warner Blvd." address			
❑ CHR1044	Aqualung	1977	$12
— Blue label, New York address			
❑ CH41044 [Q]	Aqualung	1974	$100
❑ FV41044	Aqualung	1983	$10
❑ CHR1043	Benefit	1973	$15
— Green label, "3300 Warner Blvd." address			
❑ CHR1043	Benefit	1977	$12
— Blue label, New York address			
❑ PV41043	Benefit	1983	$10
❑ FV41590	Crest of a Knave	1987	$12
❑ CHR1175	Heavy Horses	1978	$12
❑ PV41175	Heavy Horses	1983	$10
❑ CHR21201	Jethro Tull Live -- Bursting Out	1978	$15
❑ V2X41201	Jethro Tull Live -- Bursting Out	1983	$15
❑ RP1171187 [B]	Live at Carnegie Hall 1970	2015	$50
❑ 2CH1035 [B]	Living in the Past	1972	$30
— Two-record set with booklet; green labels			
❑ CHR1035 [B]	Living in the Past	1977	$25
— Blue label, New York address			
❑ KV241035	Living in the Past	1983	$15
❑ CHR1082	Minstrel in the Gallery	1975	$15
— Green label, "3300 Warner Blvd." address			
❑ CHR1082	Minstrel in the Gallery	1977	$12
— Blue label, New York address			
❑ PV41082	Minstrel in the Gallery	1983	$10
❑ CHR1078	M.U. -- The Best of Jethro Tull	1975	$15
— Green label, "3300 Warner Blvd." address			
❑ CHR1078	M.U. -- The Best of Jethro Tull	1977	$12
— Blue label, New York address			
❑ FV41078	M.U. -- The Best of Jethro Tull	1983	$10
❑ FV41515	Original Masters	1985	$12
❑ CHR1135	Repeat -- The Best of Jethro Tull, Vol. II	1977	$12
❑ FV41135	Repeat -- The Best of Jethro Tull, Vol. II	1983	$10
❑ PV41135	Repeat -- The Best of Jethro Tull, Vol. II	1986	$10
❑ F1-21708	Rock Island	1989	$12
❑ CHR1132	Songs from the Wood	1977	$12
❑ PV41132	Songs from the Wood	1983	$10
❑ CHR1042	Stand Up	1973	$15
— Green label, "3300 Warner Blvd." address			
❑ CHR1042	Stand Up	1977	$12
— Blue label, New York address			
❑ PV41042	Stand Up	1983	$10
❑ CHR1238	Stormwatch	1979	$12
❑ PV41238	Stormwatch	1983	$10
❑ CHR1380	The Broadsword and the Beast	1982	$12
❑ FV41380	The Broadsword and the Beast	1983	$10
❑ PV41380	The Broadsword and the Beast	1986	$10
❑ PRO623 [DJ]	The Jethro Tull Radio Show	1975	$75
❑ CHR1003	Thick as a Brick	1973	$15
— Green label, "3300 Warner Blvd." address			
❑ CHR1003	Thick as a Brick	1977	$12
— Blue label, New York address			
❑ FV41003	Thick as a Brick	1983	$10
❑ PV41003	Thick as a Brick	1986	$10
❑ CHR1041	This Was	1973	$15
— Green label, "3300 Warner Blvd." address			
❑ CHR1041	This Was	1977	$12
— Blue label, New York address			
❑ PV41041	This Was	1983	$10
❑ 0825646020478 [B]	Too Old To Rock 'n' Roll: Too Young To Die - The TV Special Edition	2016	$25
❑ CHR1111	Too Old to Rock 'N' Roll; Too Young to Die!	1976	$15
— Green label, "3300 Warner Blvd." address			
❑ CHR1111	Too Old to Rock 'N' Roll; Too Young to Die!	1977	$12
— Blue label, New York address			
❑ PV41111	Too Old to Rock 'N' Roll; Too Young to Die!	1983	$10
❑ FV41461	Under Wraps	1984	$12
❑ PV41461	Under Wraps	1986	$10
❑ CHR1067	War Child	1974	$15
— Green label, "3300 Warner Blvd." address			
❑ CHR1067	War Child	1974	$12
— Blue label, New York address			
❑ CH41067 [Q]	War Child	1974	$100
❑ PV41067	War Child	1983	$10

DCC COMPACT CLASSICS

Number	Title	Yr	NM
❑ LPZ2033	Aqualung	1997	$150
— Audiophile vinyl			
❑ LPZ-2059	Original Masters	1998	$40
— Audiophile vinyl			

MOBILE FIDELITY

Number	Title	Yr	NM
❑ Jan-0061 [B]	Aqualung	1980	$150

Number	Title	Yr	NM
— Audiophile vinyl			
❑ Jan-0092 [B]	The Broadsword and the Beast	1982	$75
— Audiophile vinyl			
❑ 1-187 [B]	Thick as a Brick	1985	$100
— Audiophile vinyl			

REPRISE

Number	Title	Yr	NM
❑ MS2035	Aqualung	1971	$18
❑ RS6400	Benefit	1970	$25
— Two-tone orange label with "r:" and "W7" logos on label			
❑ RS6400	Benefit	1970	$18
— All-one-color (orange/brown) label with no "W7" on label			
❑ R1536858 [B]	Benefit	2013	$30
❑ 2MS2106 [B]	Living in the Past	1972	$30
— Two-record set with booklet; original edition, rather than using cardboard outer sleeve for the records, has record sleeves attached to enclosed booklet, and thus is difficult to find intact			
❑ RS6360	Stand Up	1969	$25
— Two-tone orange label with "r:" and "W7" logos on label; band "stands up" when gatefold is opened			
❑ RS6360 [B]	Stand Up	1970	$18
— All-one-color (orange/brown) label with no "W7" on label			
❑ MS2072	Thick as a Brick	1972	$18
❑ RS6336	This Was	1969	$25
— Two-tone orange label with "r:" and "W7" logos on label			
❑ RS6336	This Was	1970	$18
— All-one-color (orange/brown) label with no "W7" on label			

JETS, THE

MCA

Number	Title	Yr	NM
❑ 5856	Christmas with the Jets	1986	$12

JETSTREAM

PALO ALTO

Number	Title	Yr	NM
❑ TB-211	Around the World	198?	$25

JETT, JOAN, AND THE BLACKHEARTS

Also see THE RUNAWAYS.

BLACKHEART

Number	Title	Yr	NM
❑ 48337 53161 [B]	Glorious Results Of A Misspent Youth	2014	$30
❑ BFZ40544	Good Music	1986	$15
❑ JJ707 [B]	Joan Jett	1980	$100
❑ Z47488	Notorious	1991	$30
❑ Z45473	The Hit List	1990	$18
❑ FZ44146	Up Your Alley	1988	$12

BOARDWALK

Number	Title	Yr	NM
❑ FW37065	Bad Reputation	1981	$15
— Essentially a reissue of Blackheart JJ 707			
❑ NB1-33251	Bad Reputation	1982	$12
— Reissue of FW 37065			
❑ NB1-33243 [B]	I Love Rock-n-Roll	1982	$18
— First pressing contains "Little Drummer Boy," which was replaced on second pressings			
❑ NB1-33243	I Love Rock-n-Roll	1982	$15
— Second pressing, with "Oh Woe Is Me"			

MCA

Number	Title	Yr	NM
❑ 5437	Album	1983	$15
❑ R163731	Glorious Results of a Misspent Youth	1984	$16
— RCA Music Service edition			
❑ 5476	Glorious Results of a Misspent Youth	1984	$15

REPRISE

Number	Title	Yr	NM
❑ 45567	Pure and Simple	1994	$25

JEWEL

ATLANTIC

Number	Title	Yr	NM
❑ 82700	Pieces of You	1997	$30
— Contains five songs not on the 1995 CD of the same name			
❑ 82950	Spirit	1998	$30
❑ 83519-1	This Way	2001	$50

JEWKES, NOEL

REVELATION

Number	Title	Yr	NM
❑ 30	Just Passin' Thru	1980	$30

JIM & JESSE

COLUMBIA LIMITED EDITION

Number	Title	Yr	NM
❑ LE10542	All-Time Great Country Instrumentals	197?	$12

EPIC

Number	Title	Yr	NM
❑ BN26394	All-Time Great Country Instrumentals	1968	$25
❑ BN26176 [S]	Berry Pickin' the Country	1965	$30
❑ LN24176 [M]	Berry Pickin' the Country	1965	$25
❑ LN24074 [M]	Bluegrass Classics	1963	$25
❑ BN26074 [S]	Bluegrass Classics	1963	$30
❑ LN24031 [M]	Bluegrass Special	1963	$25
❑ BN26031 [S]	Bluegrass Special	1963	$30
❑ LN24314 [M]	Diesel on My Tail	1967	$25
❑ BN26314 [S]	Diesel on My Tail	1967	$30
❑ BN26465	Saluting the Louvin Brothers	1969	$25
❑ LN24204 [M]	Sing Unto Him	1966	$25
❑ BN26204 [S]	Sing Unto Him	1966	$30

Number	Title	Yr	NM
❑ LN24107 [M]	The Old Country Church	1964	$25
❑ BN26107 [S]	The Old Country Church	1964	$30
❑ LN24144 [M]	Y'All Come	1964	$25
❑ BN26144 [S]	Y'All Come	1964	$30

JIMENEZ, JOSE

A&M

Number	Title	Yr	NM
❑ SP-4144 [B]	Mashuganishi Yogi	1968	$25

CAPITOL

Number	Title	Yr	NM
❑ ST-464 [B]	Hoo Ha! Direct from Noshville	1970	$25

KAPP

Number	Title	Yr	NM
❑ KL-1402 [M]	Bill Dana in Las Vegas	1964	$25
❑ KL1238 [M]	Jose Jimenez at the Hungry I	196?	$18
— Reissue with new title			
❑ KS3238 [S]	Jose Jimenez at the Hungry I	196?	$18
— Reissue with new title			
❑ KL-1332 [M]	Jose Jimenez in Jollywood	1963	$25
❑ KS-3332 [S]	Jose Jimenez in Jollywood	1963	$30
❑ KL-1257 [M]	Jose Jimenez in Orbit -- Bill Dana on Earth	1961	$25
❑ KS-3257 [S]	Jose Jimenez in Orbit -- Bill Dana on Earth	1961	$30
❑ KL-1320 [M]	Jose Jimenez -- Our Secret Weapon	1963	$25
❑ KL1304 [M]	Jose Jimenez Talks to Teenagers of All Ages	1962	$25
❑ KS3304 [S]	Jose Jimenez Talks to Teenagers of All Ages	1962	$30
❑ KL1238 [M]	Jose Jimenez -- The Astronaut (The First Man in Space)	1961	$25
❑ KS3238 [S]	Jose Jimenez -- The Astronaut (The First Man in Space)	1961	$30
❑ KL1215 [M]	Jose Jimenez the Submarine Officer	1961	$30
— Original title			
❑ KL1215 [M]	More Jose Jimenez	1961	$25

ROULETTE

Number	Title	Yr	NM
❑ R25161 [M]	My Name…Jose Jimenez	1961	$25
— Reissue of Signature LP			

SIGNATURE

Number	Title	Yr	NM
❑ SM1013 [M]	My Name…Jose Jimenez	1960	$30

JIMMIE DALE AND THE FLATLANDERS

PLANTATION

Number	Title	Yr	NM
❑ 22	One Road More	1972	$0
— May exist only as an 8-track tape. Should an LP exist, its value would be in the hundreds.			

ROUNDER

Number	Title	Yr	NM
❑ SS-34	More a Legend Than a Band	1990	$15
— As "The Flatlanders"; reissue of Plantation material			

JIVE FIVE, THE

AMBIENT SOUND

Number	Title	Yr	NM
❑ FZ37717	Here We Are	1982	$18

AMBIENT SOUND/ROUNDER

Number	Title	Yr	NM
❑ ASR-801	Way Back	1985	$15

COLLECTABLES

Number	Title	Yr	NM
❑ COL-5022	Greatest Hits	198?	$12

RELIC

Number	Title	Yr	NM
❑ 5020	The Jive Five's Greatest Hits (1961-1963)	198?	$12

UNITED ARTISTS

Number	Title	Yr	NM
❑ UAL-3455 [M]	The Jive Five	1965	$50
❑ UAS-6455 [S]	The Jive Five	1965	$85

JO JO GUNNE

Featuring Jay Ferguson.

ASYLUM

Number	Title	Yr	NM
❑ SD5065	Bite Down Hard	1973	$18
❑ SD5053	Jo Jo Gunne	1972	$18
❑ SD5071 [B]	Jumpin' the Gunne	1973	$25
— Gatefold cover			
❑ SD5071	Jumpin' the Gunne	1974	$12
— Regular cover			
❑ 7E-1022	So…Where's the Show?	1974	$12

JO JO ZEP AND THE FALCONS

A&M

Number	Title	Yr	NM
❑ SP-4968	Cha	1983	$10

COLUMBIA

Number	Title	Yr	NM
❑ JC36642	Screaming Targets	1980	$15
❑ NFC37047	Step Lively	1981	$12

JOBIM, ANTONIO CARLOS

A&M

Number	Title	Yr	NM
❑ SP-3031	Tide	1970	$35
❑ SP9-3031	Tide	1984	$50
— Audio Master Plus" reissue			
❑ SP-3002	Wave	1968	$35
❑ SP9-3002	Wave	1983	$50
— Audio Master Plus" reissue			

Number	Title	Yr	NM

CTI
| ❏ 6002 | Stone Flower | 1973 | $30 |

DISCOVERY
| ❏ DS-848 | A Certain Mr. Jobim | 198? | $25 |

PHILIPS
| ❏ 832766-1 | Personalidade Series | 1988 | $25 |

VERSATILE
| ❏ NED1132 | Jobim | 1977 | $30 |

VERVE
❏ 833234-1	Passarim	1988	$25
❏ V-8547 [M]	The Composer of "Desafinado" Plays	1963	$30
❏ V6-8547 [S]	The Composer of "Desafinado" Plays	1963	$35

WARNER BROS.
❏ W1636 [M]	Love, Strings	1966	$25
❏ WS1636 [S]	Love, Strings	1966	$25
— Gold label			
❏ 2BS3409	Terra Brasilis	1981	$30
❏ W1611 [M]	The Wonderful World of Antonio Carlos Jobim	1966	$25
❏ WS1611 [S]	The Wonderful World of Antonio Carlos Jobim	1966	$25
❏ BS2928	Urubu	1976	$25

JOE & EDDIE

GNP CRESCENDO
❏ GNP-96 [M]	Coast to Coast	1964	$25
❏ GNPS-96 [S]	Coast to Coast	1964	$30
❏ GNP-75 [M]	Joe & Eddie	1963	$25
❏ GNP-99 [M]	Joe & Eddie, Volume 4	1964	$25
❏ GNPS-99 [S]	Joe & Eddie, Volume 4	1964	$30
❏ GNP-2007 [M]	Joe & Eddie Live in Hollywood	1965	$18
❏ GNPS-2007 [S]	Joe & Eddie Live in Hollywood	1965	$25
❏ GNP-2005 [M]	Tear Down the Walls	1965	$18
❏ GNPS-2005 [S]	Tear Down the Walls	1965	$25
❏ GNP-2032 [M]	The Best of Joe & Eddie	1966	$18
❏ GNPS-2032 [S]	The Best of Joe & Eddie	1966	$25
❏ GNP-2021 [M]	The Magic of Their Singing	1966	$18
❏ GNPS-2021 [S]	The Magic of Their Singing	1966	$25
❏ GNP-86 [M]	There's a Meetin' Here Tonite	1963	$25
❏ GNP-2014 [M]	Walkin' Down the Line	1965	$18
❏ GNPS-2014 [S]	Walkin' Down the Line	1965	$25

JOEL, BILLY

COLUMBIA
❏ FC35609	52nd Street	1978	$12
❏ PC35609	52nd Street	1985	$10
❏ HC45609	52nd Street	1982	$30
— Half-speed mastered edition			
❏ QC38837	An Innocent Man	1983	$12
❏ HC48837	An Innocent Man	1983	$30
— Half-speed mastered edition			
❏ AS1343 [DJ]	Billy Joel Interview	1982	$25
❏ PC38984	Cold Spring Harbor	1983	$10
— Remixed, remastered version of Family Productions album			
❏ FC36384	Glass Houses	1980	$12
❏ PC36384	Glass Houses	1986	$10
❏ C240121	Greatest Hits, Volumes 1 and 2	1985	$15
❏ AS402 [DJ]	Inter Chords/Billy Joel Interview	1977	$25
— Promo-only interview album			
❏ C240996	KOHUEPT	1987	$18
❏ KC32544	Piano Man	1973	$15
— Some copies have the first song spelled "Travelin' Prayer," others have it "Travellin' Prayer." No difference in value.			
❏ PC32544	Piano Man	1976	$12
— No bar code on back cover			
❏ PC32544	Piano Man	1979	$10
— With bar code on back cover			
❏ CQ32544 [Q]	Piano Man	1974	$30
❏ TC37461	Songs in the Attic	1981	$12
❏ PC37461	Songs in the Attic	1984	$10
❏ HC47461	Songs in the Attic	1982	$80
— Half-speed mastered edition			
❏ AS326 [DJ]	Souvenir	1976	$25
— Promo-only LP with one side live, one side a compilation of studio tracks			
❏ OC44366	Storm Front	1989	$15
❏ PC33146	Streetlife Serenade	1975	$12
— No bar code on back cover			
❏ PCQ33146 [Q]	Streetlife Serenade	1975	$30
❏ PC33146	Streetlife Serenade	1979	$10
— With bar code on back cover			
❏ OC40402	The Bridge	1986	$12
❏ QC38200	The Nylon Curtain	1982	$12
❏ JC34987	The Stranger	1977	$12
❏ PC34987	The Stranger	1979	$10
❏ HC34987	The Stranger	1981	$30
— Original pressing of half-speed mastered edition			
❏ HC44987	The Stranger	1982	$30
— Half-speed mastered edition (reissue)			
❏ PC33848	Turnstiles	1976	$12
— No bar code on back cover			
❏ PC33848	Turnstiles	1976	$10
— With bar code on back cover			
❏ PCQ33848 [Q]	Turnstiles	1976	$30

FAMILY PRODUCTIONS
| ❏ FPS-2700 | Cold Spring Harbor | 1971 | $40 |
| *— Authentic copies have mostly dark blue labels; when reissued on Columbia, the entire LP was remixed and remastered, and "You Can Make Me Free" was shortened by three minutes* | | | |

MOBILE FIDELITY
❏ MFSL2-384 [B]	52nd Street	2013	$75
❏ MFSL2-388 [B]	An Innocent Man	2013	$75
❏ MFSL2-385 [B]	Glass Houses	2013	$75
❏ MFSL2-386 [B]	Songs in the Attic	2014	$40
❏ MFSL2-387 [B]	The Nylon Curtain	2014	$40
❏ MFSL2-383 [B]	The Stranger	2013	$75

JOHANSEN, DAVID
Also see NEW YORK DOLLS.

BLUE SKY
❏ JZ34926	David Johansen	1978	$12
❏ FZ36589	Here Comes the Night	1981	$12
❏ JZ36082	In Style	1979	$12
❏ AS1281 [DJ]	Live and Sampler	1981	$15
— Promo-only four-song sampler			
❏ ARZ38004	Live It Up	1982	$12
❏ AS519 [DJ]	The David Johansen Group Live	1978	$30

PASSPORT
| ❏ PB-6043 | Sweet Revenge | 1984 | $12 |

JOHANSSON, JAN

DOT
| ❏ DLP-3416 [M] | Sweden Non-Stop | 1962 | $85 |
| ❏ DLP-25416 [S] | Sweden Non-Stop | 1962 | $85 |

JOHANSSON, LASSE

KICKING MULE
| ❏ KM-170 | King Porter Stomp -- The Music of Jelly Roll Morton | 198? | $30 |

JOHN, ELTON

COLUMBIA SPECIAL PRODUCTS
❏ P16196	The Best of Elton John, Volume One	1981	$15
❏ P16197	The Best of Elton John, Volume Two	1981	$15
— Both of the above "Distributed Exclusively by Scott Distributing Corp.			

DCC COMPACT CLASSICS
❏ LPZ-2013	Elton John's Greatest Hits	1995	$150
— Audiophile vinyl			
❏ LPZ-2020	Elton John's Greatest Hits, Volume 2	1996	$0
— Canceled			
❏ LPZ-2004	Madman Across the Water	1994	$120
— Audiophile vinyl			

DIRECT DISC
| ❏ SD-16614 | Goodbye Yellow Brick Road | 1980 | $50 |
| *— Audiophile vinyl* | | | |

GEFFEN
| ❏ GHS24031 [DJ] | Breaking Hearts | 1984 | $30 |
| *— Promo pressing on Quiex II vinyl* | | | |

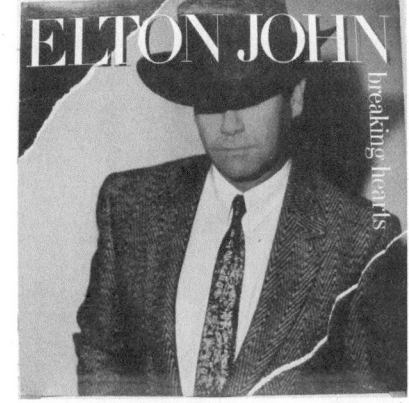

❏ GHS24031 [B]	Breaking Hearts	1984	$12
❏ GHS24153	Elton John's Greatest Hits, Vol. 3, 1979-1987	1987	$12
❏ GHS24077	Ice on Fire	1985	$12
❏ GHS2013	Jump Up!	1982	$12
❏ GHS24114	Leather Jackets	1986	$12
❏ PRO-A-2176 [DJ]	Sasson Presents Elton John	1983	$30
— One-sided promo with four tracks on A-side and an etched facsimile autograph on B-side			
❏ GHS2002	The Fox	1981	$12
❏ GHS4006	Too Low for Zero	1983	$12

ISLAND
| ❏ B0024337-01 [B] | Wonderful Crazy Night | 2016 | $25 |

MCA
❏ 5121	21 at 33	1980	$12
— Originals have custom labels			
❏ 772	21 at 33	1981	$10
❏ 619	11/17/1970	1979	$10
❏ 2015	11/17/1970	1973	$12
❏ 3065	A Single Man	1978	$12
❏ 14951 [PD]	A Single Man	1978	$25
— Stock picture disc			
❏ L33-1995 [PD]	A Single Man	1978	$40
— Promo picture disc			
❏ 37068	A Single Man	1979	$10
❏ 6011	Blue Moves	1979	$12
❏ 2142	Captain Fantastic and the Brown Dirt Cowboy	1975	$15
— With custom label, two booklets and poster			
❏ 2142 [DJ]	Captain Fantastic and the Brown Dirt Cowboy	1975	$300
— Brown vinyl promo, autographed by Elton John and Bernie Taupin			
❏ 37066	Captain Fantastic and the Brown Dirt Cowboy	1979	$10
❏ 2116	Caribou	1974	$12
❏ 37065	Caribou	1979	$10
❏ 2100	Don't Shoot Me, I'm Only the Piano Player	1973	$25
— With all-black label (no rainbow) and booklet			
❏ 2100	Don't Shoot Me, I'm Only the Piano Player	1973	$12
— With black rainbow label and booklet			
❏ 37113	Don't Shoot Me, I'm Only the Piano Player	1979	$10
❏ 2012	Elton John	1973	$12
❏ 37067	Elton John	1979	$10
❏ 2128	Elton John's Greatest Hits	1974	$12
❏ 5224	Elton John's Greatest Hits	1981	$10
❏ 37215	Elton John's Greatest Hits	1983	$10
❏ 37216	Elton John's Greatest Hits	1983	$10
❏ 1689	Elton John's Greatest Hits	198?	$10
❏ 3027	Elton John's Greatest Hits, Volume 2	1977	$12
❏ 5225	Elton John's Greatest Hits, Volume 2	1981	$10
❏ 2130	Empty Sky	1975	$12
— First American issue of his 1969 debut			
❏ 620	Empty Sky	1979	$10
❏ 2-10003	Goodbye Yellow Brick Road	1973	$18
❏ 6894	Goodbye Yellow Brick Road	1980	$12
❏ R231711	Greatest Hits Volumes One and Two	198?	$18
— RCA Music Service exclusive; combines both MCA greatest-hits sets			
❏ 2197	Here and There	1976	$12
❏ 622	Here and There	1979	$10
❏ 2017	Honky Chateau	1973	$12
❏ 37064	Honky Chateau	1979	$10
❏ 8022	Live in Australia with the Melbourne Symphony Orchestra	1987	$18
❏ 2016	Madman Across the Water	1973	$12
— With booklet			
❏ 3003	Madman Across the Water	1977	$10
❏ 37200	Madman Across the Water	1982	$10
❏ 6240	Reg Strikes Back	1988	$12
❏ 2163	Rock of the Westies	1975	$12
❏ 621	Rock of the Westies	1979	$10
❏ 6321	Sleeping with the Past	1989	$12
❏ 39115	The Complete Thom Bell Sessions	1989	$30
❏ 13921 [EP]	The Thom Bell Sessions	1979	$10
❏ 2014	Tumbleweed Connection	1973	$12
— With booklet			
❏ 3001	Tumbleweed Connection	1977	$10
❏ 37199	Tumbleweed Connection	1982	$10
❏ 5104	Victim of Love	1979	$12
❏ 771	Victim of Love	1981	$10
❏ 4L33-1848 [DJ]	Victim of Love	1979	$150
— Promo-only collection of the entire album as four 12-inch singles			
❏ 37266	Your Songs	1986	$12

MERCURY
| ❏ 5310374 | Goodbye Yellow Brick Road | 2008 | $30 |

MOBILE FIDELITY
| ❏ 2-160 | Goodbye Yellow Brick Road | 1984 | $75 |
| *— Audiophile vinyl* | | | |

NAUTILUS
| ❏ NR-42 | Elton John's Greatest Hits | 198? | $150 |
| *— Audiophile vinyl* | | | |

PARAMOUNT
❏ PAS6004 [B]	Friends (Soundtrack)	1971	$30
— Whitish gray label original			
❏ PAS6004 [B]	Friends (Soundtrack)	1975	$40
— Dark blue label with "Paramount" logo at top and ABC Records reference along edge; much rarer than the original			

ROCKET
| ❏ 2-11004 | Blue Moves | 1976 | $18 |
| *— Originals have light blue labels with a train at the top of the label* | | | |

Number	Title	Yr	NM
❑ L33-1173/4 [DJ]	Get Up and Dance	1977	$150

—*Promo-only sampler from "Blue Moves" LP; blue vinyl*

❑ 526915-1	Made in England	1995	$25

—*U.S. version is on 180-gram vinyl, distributed by Classic Records*

UNI

❑ 93105	11/17/1970	1971	$18
❑ 73090 [B]	Elton John	1970	$25
❑ 93090	Elton John	1971	$15
❑ 93135	Honky Chateau	1972	$25

—*With "(P) 1972 MCA Records, Inc." on label*

❑ 93135	Honky Chateau	1972	$18

—*With "(P) 1972 This Record Co., Ltd." on label*

❑ 93120	Madman Across the Water	1971	$18

—*With booklet*

❑ 73096 [B]	Tumbleweed Connection	1971	$25

—*With booklet*

❑ 93096	Tumbleweed Connection	1971	$15

—*With booklet*

JOHN, LITTLE WILLIE

BLUESWAY

❑ BLS-6069	Free at Last	1973	$30

KING

❑ 802 [M]	Come On and Join Little Willie John	1962	$120
❑ 395-564 [M]	Fever	1956	$1000

—*"Nurse with thermometer" cover*

❑ 564 [M]	Fever	1957	$600

—*White cover with "Fever" in large colorful letters*

❑ KS-1081	Free at Last	1970	$40
❑ 691 [M]	Little Willie John In Action	1960	$300
❑ 949 [M]	Little Willie Sings All Originals	1966	$150
❑ KS-949 [S]	Little Willie Sings All Originals	1966	$175
❑ 603 [M]	Mister Little Willie John	1958	$300
❑ 739 [M]	Sure Things	1961	$175
❑ 596 [M]	Talk to Me	1958	$300
❑ 895 [M]	These Are My Favorite Songs	1964	$150
❑ 767 [M]	The Sweet, the Hot, the Teenage Beat	1961	$175

JOHN, ROBERT

COLUMBIA

❑ CS9687 [S]	If You Don't Want My Love	1968	$25
❑ CS9687 [M]	If You Don't Want My Love	1968	$50

—*Mono is white label promo only with stereo number; "Special Mono Radio Station Copy" sticker is on front cover*

EMI AMERICA

❑ SW-17027	Back on the Street	1980	$12
❑ SW-17007	Robert John	1979	$12

GUINNESS

❑ GNS36047 [B]	A Place to Live	1977	$150

HARMONY

❑ KH31353	On the Way Up	1972	$15

JOHNNIE AND JACK

DECCA

❑ DL4308 [M]	Smiles and Tears	1962	$25
❑ DL74308 [S]	Smiles and Tears	1962	$30

RCA CAMDEN

❑ CAL-747 [M]	Johnny & Jack Sing "Poison Love" and Other Country Favorites	1963	$30
❑ CAS-747 [R]	Johnny & Jack Sing "Poison Love" and Other Country Favorites	1963	$15
❑ CAL-822 [M]	Sincerely	1964	$30
❑ CAS-822 [R]	Sincerely	1964	$15

RCA VICTOR

❑ VPM-6022	All the Best of Johnnie & Jack	1970	$30
❑ LPM-2017 [M]	Hits by Johnnie & Jack	1959	$30
❑ LSP-2017 [R]	Hits by Johnnie & Jack	1959	$25

❑ LPM-1587 [M]	The Tennessee Mountain Boys	1957	$40

JOHNNIE AND JOE

AMBIENT SOUND

❑ FZ38345	Kingdom of Love	1982	$15

JOHNNY AND THE BLUE BEATS

WINSOR

❑ 1001	Smile	196?	$40

JOHNNY AND THE HURRICANES

ATILA

❑ 1030 [M]	Live at the Star-Club	1964	$300

BIG TOP

❑ 12-1302 [M]	The Big Sound of Johnny and the Hurricanes	1960	$300
❑ ST 12-1302 [S]	The Big Sound of Johnny and the Hurricanes	1960	$300

WARWICK

❑ W-2007 [M]	Johnny and the Hurricanes	1959	$175
❑ W-2007ST [S]	Johnny and the Hurricanes	1959	$300
❑ W-2010 [M]	Stormsville	1960	$175
❑ W-2010ST [S]	Stormsville	1960	$300

JOHNNY HATES JAZZ

VIRGIN

❑ 90860	Turn Back the Clock	1988	$12

JOHNS, SAMMY

GRC

❑ 5003	Sammy Johns	1975	$15

JOHN'S CHILDREN

WHITE WHALE

❑ WWS7128 [B]	Orgasm	1970	$350

JOHNSON, ALPHONSO

EPIC

❑ PE34118	Moonshadows	1975	$25
❑ JE34869	Spellbound	1977	$25
❑ JE36521	The Best of Alphonso Johnson	1979	$25
❑ PE34364	Yesterday's Dreams	1976	$25

JOHNSON, ARNOLD

CIRCLE

❑ 32	Swinging the Classics	198?	$25

JOHNSON, BETTY

ATLANTIC

❑ 8017 [M]	Betty Johnson	1958	$50
❑ 8027 [M]	The Song You Heard When You Fell in Love	1959	$50

—*Black label*

❑ SD8027 [S]	The Song You Heard When You Fell in Love	1959	$100

—*Green label*

❑ 8027 [M]	The Song You Heard When You Fell in Love	1960	$25

—*White "fan" logo on right*

❑ SD8027 [S]	The Song You Heard When You Fell in Love	1960	$30

—*White "fan" logo on right*

JOHNSON, BLIND WILLIE

FOLKWAYS

❑ FG-3585 [M]	Blind Willie Johnson: His Story	1957	$120

RBF

❑ 10 [M]	Blind Willie Johnson 1927-1930	1965	$80

JOHNSON, BOB, AND THE LONESOME TRAVELERS

PARKWAY

❑ P-7017 [M]	12 Shades of Bluegrass	1962	$50

JOHNSON, BUBBER

KING

❑ 624 [M]	Bubber Johnson Sings Sweet Love Songs	1959	$175
❑ 569 [M]	Come Home	1957	$250

JOHNSON, BUDD

ARGO

❑ LP-721 [M]	French Cookin'	1963	$30
❑ LPS-721 [S]	French Cookin'	1963	$30
❑ LP-748 [M]	Off the Wall	1965	$30
❑ LPS-748 [S]	Off the Wall	1965	$30
❑ LP-736 [M]	Ya! Ya!	1964	$75
❑ LPS-736 [S]	Ya! Ya!	1964	$75

FANTASY

❑ OJC-209	Budd Johnson and the Four Brass Giants	1985	$25
❑ OJC-1720	Let's Swing	198?	$25

FELSTED

❑ FAJ-7007 [M]	Blues A La Mode	1959	$75

❑ SJA-2007 [S]	Blues A La Mode	1959	$100

MASTER JAZZ

❑ 8119	Blues A La Mode	197?	$30

RIVERSIDE

❑ RLP-343 [M]	Budd Johnson and the Four Brass Giants	1960	$250
❑ RS-9343 [S]	Budd Johnson and the Four Brass Giants	1960	$250

SWINGVILLE

❑ SVLP-2015 [M]	Let's Swing	1961	$50

—*Purple label*

❑ SVLP-2015 [M]	Let's Swing	1965	$30

—*Blue label, trident logo at right*

JOHNSON, BUDDY & ELLA

MERCURY

❑ MG-20347 [M]	Swing Me	195?	$175

ROULETTE

❑ R25085 [M]	Go Ahead and Rock and Roll	1959	$175
❑ SR25085 [S]	Go Ahead and Rock and Roll	1959	$250

JOHNSON, BUDDY

MCA

❑ 1356	Fine Brown Frame	198?	$25

MERCURY

❑ MG-20330 [M]	Buddy Johnson Wails	195?	$175
❑ SR-60072 [S]	Buddy Johnson Wails	195?	$175
❑ MG-20209 [M]	Rock 'N' Roll	195?	$175
❑ MG-20347 [M]	Swing Me	195?	$175
❑ MG-20322 [M]	Walkin'	195?	$175

WING

❑ MGW-12234 [M]	Buddy Johnson Wails	196?	$75
❑ MGW-12005 [M]	Rock 'N' Roll	1956	$175
❑ MGW-12111 [M]	Rock 'n' Roll Stage Show	1963	$40

JOHNSON, BUNK, AND LU WATTERS

GOOD TIME JAZZ

❑ L-12024 [M]	Bunk and Lu	195?	$40

JOHNSON, BUNK

AMERICAN MUSIC

❑ 644 [10]	Bunk Johnson Talking	1952	$75
❑ 638 [10]	Bunk Plays the Blues -- The Spirituals	1951	$75

COLUMBIA

❑ CL829 [M]	Bunk Johnson	1955	$50

—*Red and black label with six "eye" logos*

❑ GL520 [M]	Bunk Johnson and His Band	1952	$75

—*Black label, silver print*

❑ CL520 [M]	Bunk Johnson and His Band	1953	$50

—*Maroon label, gold print*

❑ CL520 [M]	Bunk Johnson and His Band	1955	$50

—*Red and black label with six "eye" logos*

COLUMBIA MASTERWORKS

❑ ML4802 [M]	The Last Testament of a Great New Orleans Jazzman	1950	$100

COMMODORE

❑ DL-30007 [M]	The Bunk Johnson Band	1952	$50

FOLKLYRIC

❑ 9047	Bunk Johnson and His New Orleans Jazz Band	1986	$25

GHB

❑ 101	Spicy Advice	198?	$25

GOOD TIME JAZZ

❑ L-12048 [M]	Bunk Johnson and His Superior Jazz Band	1962	$30
❑ L-17 [10]	Bunk Johnson and the Yerba Buena Jazz Band	1953	$50

MAINSTREAM

❑ 56039 [M]	Bunk Johnson -- A Legend	1965	$25
❑ S-6039 [R]	Bunk Johnson -- A Legend	1965	$30

TRIP

❑ J-2	Bunk Johnson	1970	$30

JOHNSON, CANDY

CANJO

❑ LP-1002 [M]	Bikini Beach	1964	$40
❑ LP-1001 [M]	The Candy Johnson Show	1964	$40

JOHNSON, CHARLIE

X

❑ LVA-3026 [10]	Harlem in the Twenties, Vol. 2	1954	$75

JOHNSON, DAVID EARLE; JAN HAMMER; JOHN ABERCROMBIE

PLUG

❑ 1	The Midweek Blues	1986	$30

JOHNSON, DAVID EARLE

CMP
Number	Title	Yr	NM
❏ CMP-14-ST	Hip Address	1980	$30
❏ CMP-20-ST	Skin Deep -- Yeah!	1981	$30

VANGUARD
Number	Title	Yr	NM
❏ VSD-79401	Time Free	197?	$25

JOHNSON, DEREK,'S VOCAL ORCHESTRA

IMPACT
Number	Title	Yr	NM
❏ R3427	The ReGeneration: Christmas in Velvet	197?	$18

— With velvet-like cover

JOHNSON, DICK

CONCORD JAZZ
Number	Title	Yr	NM
❏ CJ-107	Dick Johnson Plays Alto Sax & Flute & Soprano Sax & Clarinet	1979	$30
❏ CJ-146	Piano Mover	1980	$30
❏ CJ-135	Spider's Blues	1980	$30
❏ CJ-167	Swing Shift	1981	$30

EMARCY
Number	Title	Yr	NM
❏ MG-36081 [M]	Music for Swinging Moderns	1956	$250

RIVERSIDE

Number	Title	Yr	NM
❏ RLP 12-253 [M]	Most Likely...	1957	$100

JOHNSON, EDDIE

NESSA
Number	Title	Yr	NM
❏ N-22	Indian Summer	1981	$30

JOHNSON, ERNIE

RONN
Number	Title	Yr	NM
❏ LPS-8001	Just in Time	1985	$18

JOHNSON, HENRY

MCA
Number	Title	Yr	NM
❏ 6329	Never Too Much	1990	$30

JOHNSON, HOLLY

UNI
Number	Title	Yr	NM
❏ 603	Blast	1988	$12

JOHNSON, J.J., AND JOE PASS

PABLO
Number	Title	Yr	NM
❏ 2310911	We'll Be Together Again	198?	$25

JOHNSON, J.J., AND KAI WINDING

A&M
Number	Title	Yr	NM
❏ SP-3016	Betwixt and Between	1969	$25

— As "J & K

Number	Title	Yr	NM
❏ SP-3008	Israel	1968	$25

— As "K. & J.J.

Number	Title	Yr	NM
❏ SP9-3008	Israel	1983	$20

— As "K. & J.J."; "Audio Master Plus" reissue

Number	Title	Yr	NM
❏ SP-3027	Stonebone	1970	$0

— Canceled

ABC IMPULSE!
Number	Title	Yr	NM
❏ AS-1 [S]	The Great Kai & J.J.	1968	$30

BETHLEHEM
Number	Title	Yr	NM
❏ BCP-6001 [M]	K + J.J. (East Coast Jazz/7)	1955	$300

— With the number "BCP 13" on the upper right corner of the front cover and "BCP 6001" stickers on the back cover and "BCP 6001" on the labels

Number	Title	Yr	NM
❏ BCP-13 [M]	K + J.J. (East Coast Jazz/7)	1955	$300

— With "BCP 13" on the label as well as the cover

Number	Title	Yr	NM
❏ BCP-6001 [M]	The Finest Kai Winding and J.J. Johnson	197?	$30

— Reissue with new title, distributed by RCA Victor

COLUMBIA
Number	Title	Yr	NM
❏ CL973 [M]	Jay and Kai	1957	$50

— Red and black label with six "eye" logos

Number	Title	Yr	NM
❏ CL973 [M]	Jay and Kai	1963	$25

— Red label with "Guaranteed High Fidelity" or "360 Sound Mono" at bottom

Number	Title	Yr	NM
❏ CL892 [M]	J.J. Johnson, Kai Winding + 6	1956	$50

— Red and black "6-eye" label

Number	Title	Yr	NM
❏ CL892 [M]	J.J. Johnson, Kai Winding + 6	1963	$25

— Red label with "Guaranteed High Fidelity" or "360 Sound Mono" at bottom

Number	Title	Yr	NM
❏ CL2573 [10]	Kai + J.J.	1955	$100
❏ CL742 [M]	Trombone for Two	1956	$50

— Red label with "360 Sound Stereo" in black or white at bottom

Number	Title	Yr	NM
❏ CL742 [M]	Trombone for Two	1963	$25

— Red label with "Guaranteed High Fidelity" or "360 Sound Mono" at bottom

COLUMBIA JAZZ ODYSSEY
Number	Title	Yr	NM
❏ PC37001 [M]	J.J. Johnson, Kai Winding + 6	198?	$25

IMPULSE!
Number	Title	Yr	NM
❏ A-1 [M]	The Great Kai & J.J.	1961	$160
❏ AS-1 [S]	The Great Kai & J.J.	1961	$250

MCA
Number	Title	Yr	NM
❏ 29061	The Great Kai & J.J.	1980	$25

PRESTIGE
Number	Title	Yr	NM
❏ PRLP-195 [10]	Jay and Kai	1954	$300
❏ PRLP-7253 [M]	Looking Back	1963	$50
❏ PRST-7253 [R]	Looking Back	1963	$30
❏ PRLP-109 [10]	Modern Jazz Trombones	1951	$300

SAVOY
Number	Title	Yr	NM
❏ MG-15038 [10]	Jay and Kai	1954	$120
❏ MG-12010 [10]	Jay and Kai	1955	$100
❏ MG-15048 [10]	Jay and Kai, Volume 2	1955	$150
❏ MG-15049 [10]	Jay and Kai, Volume 3	1955	$150
❏ MG-12106 [M]	J.J. Johnson's Jazz Quintets	1957	$100

X
Number	Title	Yr	NM
❏ LXA-1040 [M]	An Afternoon at Birdland	1956	$100

JOHNSON, J.J., AND NAT ADDERLEY

PABLO LIVE
Number	Title	Yr	NM
❏ 2620109	Yokohama Concert	1977	$35

JOHNSON, J.J.; KAI WINDING; BENNIE GREEN

DEBUT
Number	Title	Yr	NM
❏ DEB-126 [M]	Four Trombones	1958	$175
❏ DLP-5 [10]	Jazz Workshop, Volume 1	1953	$300
❏ DLP-14 [10]	Jazz Workshop, Volume 2	1955	$300

FANTASY
Number	Title	Yr	NM
❏ 6005 [M]	Four Trombones	1963	$50

— Red vinyl

Number	Title	Yr	NM
❏ 6005 [M]	Four Trombones	1963	$30

— Black vinyl

Number	Title	Yr	NM
❏ 86005 [R]	Four Trombones	1963	$40

— Blue vinyl

Number	Title	Yr	NM
❏ 86005 [R]	Four Trombones	1963	$25

— Black vinyl

Number	Title	Yr	NM
❏ OJC-091	Trombones by Three	198?	$25

PRESTIGE
Number	Title	Yr	NM
❏ PRLP-7030 [M]	J.J. Johnson, Kai Winding, Bennie Green	1956	$350

— Yellow label with W. 50th St. address

Number	Title	Yr	NM
❏ PRLP-7023 [M]	Trombone by Three	1956	$750

— Yellow label with W. 50th St. address. Andy Warhol cover.

Number	Title	Yr	NM
❏ 16-4 [M]	Trombone by Three	1956	$2000

— This album plays at 16 2/3 rpm and is marked as such; white label

JOHNSON, J.J.

ABC IMPULSE!
Number	Title	Yr	NM
❏ AS-68 [S]	Proof Positive	1968	$250

— Black label with red ring

Number	Title	Yr	NM
❏ AS-68 [S]	Proof Positive	1975	$30

— Green, blue, purple "target" label

BLUE NOTE
Number	Title	Yr	NM
❏ BLP-5057 [10]	Jay Jay Johnson, Volume 2	1955	$700
❏ BLP-5070 [10]	Jay Jay Johnson, Volume 3	1955	$700
❏ BLP-5028 [10]	Jay Jay Johnson All Stars	1953	$700
❏ BLP-1505 [M]	The Eminent Jay Jay Johnson, Volume 1	1955	$1000

— Deep groove" version; Lexington Ave. address on label

Number	Title	Yr	NM
❏ BLP-1505 [M]	The Eminent Jay Jay Johnson, Volume 1	1958	$1000

— Deep groove" version, W. 63rd St. address on label

Number	Title	Yr	NM
❏ BLP-1505 [M]	The Eminent Jay Jay Johnson, Volume 1	1963	$150

— New York, USA" address on label

Number	Title	Yr	NM
❏ BST-81505 [R]	The Eminent Jay Jay Johnson, Volume 1	1967	$50

— A Division of Liberty Records" on label

Number	Title	Yr	NM
❏ BLP-1506 [M]	The Eminent Jay Jay Johnson, Volume 2	1958	$1500

— Deep groove" version, W. 63rd St. address on label

Number	Title	Yr	NM
❏ BLP-1506 [M]	The Eminent Jay Jay Johnson, Volume 2	1955	$1500

— Deep groove" version; Lexington Ave. address on label

Number	Title	Yr	NM
❏ BLP-1506 [M]	The Eminent Jay Jay Johnson, Volume 2	1963	$150

— New York, USA" address on label

Number	Title	Yr	NM
❏ BST-81506 [R]	The Eminent Jay Jay Johnson, Volume 2	1967	$50

— A Division of Liberty Records" on label

Number	Title	Yr	NM
❏ B1-81505	The Eminent J.J. Johnson, Volume 1	1989	$35

— The Finest in Jazz Since 1939" reissue

Number	Title	Yr	NM
❏ B1-81506	The Eminent J.J. Johnson, Volume 2	1989	$35

— The Finest in Jazz Since 1939" reissue

COLUMBIA
Number	Title	Yr	NM
❏ CL1737 [M]	A Touch of Satin	1962	$40

— Red and black label with six "eye" logos

Number	Title	Yr	NM
❏ CL1737 [M]	A Touch of Satin	1963	$35

— Red label with "Guaranteed High Fidelity" or "360 Sound Mono" at bottom

Number	Title	Yr	NM
❏ CS8537 [S]	A Touch of Satin	1962	$50

— Red and black label with six "eye" logos

Number	Title	Yr	NM
❏ CS8537 [S]	A Touch of Satin	1963	$25

— Red label with "360 Sound Stereo" in black or white at bottom

Number	Title	Yr	NM
❏ CL1303 [M]	Blue Trombone	1959	$40

— Red and black label with six "eye" logos

Number	Title	Yr	NM
❏ CL1303 [M]	Blue Trombone	1963	$30

— Red label with "Guaranteed High Fidelity" or "360 Sound Mono" at bottom

Number	Title	Yr	NM
❏ CS8109 [S]	Blue Trombone	1959	$50

— Red and black label with six "eye" logos

Number	Title	Yr	NM
❏ CS8109 [S]	Blue Trombone	1963	$35

— Red label with "360 Sound Stereo" in black or white at bottom

Number	Title	Yr	NM
❏ CL1084 [M]	Dial J.J. 5	1957	$50

— Red and black label with six "eye" logos

Number	Title	Yr	NM
❏ CL1084 [M]	Dial J.J. 5	1963	$35

— Red label with "Guaranteed High Fidelity" or "360 Sound Mono" at bottom

Number	Title	Yr	NM
❏ CL1030 [M]	First Place	1957	$50

— Red and black label with six "eye" logos

Number	Title	Yr	NM
❏ CL1030 [M]	First Place	1963	$35

— Red label with "Guaranteed High Fidelity" or "360 Sound Mono" at bottom

Number	Title	Yr	NM
❏ CL935 [M]	"J" Is for Jazz	1956	$50

— Red and black label with six "eye" logos

Number	Title	Yr	NM
❏ CL935 [M]	"J" Is for Jazz	1963	$35

— Red label with "Guaranteed High Fidelity" or "360 Sound Mono" at bottom

Number	Title	Yr	NM
❏ CL1606 [M]	J.J. Inc	1961	$30

— Red and black label with six "eye" logos

Number	Title	Yr	NM
❏ CL1606 [M]	J.J. Inc	1963	$30

— Red label with "Guaranteed High Fidelity" or "360 Sound Mono" at bottom

Number	Title	Yr	NM
❏ CS8406 [S]	J.J. Inc	1961	$40

— Red and black label with six "eye" logos

Number	Title	Yr	NM
❏ CS8406 [S]	J.J. Inc	1963	$35

— Red label with "360 Sound Stereo" in black or white at bottom

Number	Title	Yr	NM
❏ CL1161 [M]	J.J. In Person	1958	$50

— Red and black label with six "eye" logos

Number	Title	Yr	NM
❏ CL1161 [M]	J.J. In Person	1963	$35

— Red label with "Guaranteed High Fidelity" or "360 Sound Mono" at bottom

Number	Title	Yr	NM
❏ CS8009 [S]	J.J. In Person	1959	$40

— Red and black label with six "eye" logos

Number	Title	Yr	NM
❏ CS8009 [S]	J.J. In Person	1963	$30

— Red label with "360 Sound Stereo" in black or white at bottom

Number	Title	Yr	NM
❏ CL1383 [M]	Really Livin'	1959	$40

— Red and black label with six "eye" logos

Number	Title	Yr	NM
❏ CL1383 [M]	Really Livin'	1963	$30

— Red label with "Guaranteed High Fidelity" or "360 Sound Mono" at bottom

Number	Title	Yr	NM
❏ CS8178 [S]	Really Livin'	1959	$50

— Red and black label with six "eye" logos

Number	Title	Yr	NM
❏ CS8178 [S]	Really Livin'	1963	$35

— Red label with "360 Sound Stereo" in black or white at bottom

Number	Title	Yr	NM
❏ CL1547 [M]	Trombones and Voices	1960	$30

— Red and black label with six "eye" logos

Number	Title	Yr	NM
❏ CL1547 [M]	Trombones and Voices	1963	$30

— Red label with "Guaranteed High Fidelity" or "360 Sound Mono" at bottom

Number	Title	Yr	NM
❏ CS8347 [S]	Trombones and Voices	1960	$40

— Red and black label with six "eye" logos

Number	Title	Yr	NM
❏ CS8347 [S]	Trombones and Voices	1963	$35

— Red label with "360 Sound Stereo" in black or white at bottom

COLUMBIA JAZZ ODYSSEY
Number	Title	Yr	NM
❏ PC36808	J.J. Inc.	1979	$25

IMPULSE!
Number	Title	Yr	NM
❏ A-68 [M]	Proof Positive	1965	$160

Number	Title	Yr	NM
❏ AS-68 [S]	Proof Positive	1965	$250
MCA			
❏ 29072	Proof Positive	1980	$25
MILESTONE			
❏ M-9093	Pinnacles	1979	$30
MOSAIC			
❏ MQ11-169	The Complete Columbia J.J. Johnson Small Group Sessions	199?	$300
PABLO TODAY			
❏ 2312123	Concepts in Blue	1980	$30
PRESTIGE			
❏ 24067	Early Bones	197?	$35
RCA VICTOR			
❏ LPM-3544 [M]	Broadway Express	1966	$25
❏ LSP-3544 [S]	Broadway Express	1966	$30
❏ LPM-3458 [M]	Goodies	1965	$25
❏ LSP-3458 [S]	Goodies	1965	$30
❏ LPM-3350 [M]	J.J.!	1965	$25
❏ LSP-3350 [S]	J.J.!	1965	$30
❏ LPM-3833 [M]	The Total J.J. Johnson	1967	$30
❏ LSP-3833 [S]	The Total J.J. Johnson	1967	$25
REGENT			
❏ MG-6001 [M]	Jazz South Pacific	1956	$50
SAVOY			
❏ MG-12205 [M]	Jazz South Pacific	196?	$50
—Reissue of Regent 6001			
SAVOY JAZZ			
❏ SJL-2232	Mad Bebop	198?	$30
VERVE			
❏ V-8530 [M]	J.J.'s Broadway	1963	$25
❏ V6-8530 [S]	J.J.'s Broadway	1963	$30

JOHNSON, J.J./BENNIE GREEN

Number	Title	Yr	NM
PRESTIGE			
❏ PRLP-123 [10]	Modern Jazz Trombones, Volume 2	1952	$300

JOHNSON, JACK

Number	Title	Yr	NM
UNIVERSAL REPUBLIC			
❏ 1058001	Sleep Through the Static	2008	$30

JOHNSON, JAMES P.

Number	Title	Yr	NM
BIOGRAPH			
❏ 1003	Rare Piano Rolls	1972	$30
❏ 1009	Rare Piano Rolls, Volume 2	1972	$30
BLUE NOTE			
❏ BLP-7012 [10]	Jazz Band Ball	1951	$300
❏ BLP-7011 [10]	Stomps, Rags and Blues	1951	$300
COLUMBIA			
❏ CL1780 [M]	Father of the Stride Piano	1961	$30
—Red and black label with six "eye" logos			
❏ CL1780 [M]	Father of the Stride Piano	1963	$35
—All-red label, "Guaranteed High Fidelity" or "360 Sound Mono" at bottom			
DECCA			
❏ DL5228 [10]	James P. Johnson Plays Fats Waller Favorites	1951	$250
❏ DL5190 [10]	The Daddy of the Piano	1950	$175
FOLKWAYS			
❏ FJ-2816	Striding in Dixieland	196?	$25
❏ FJ-2850	The Original James P. Johnson	196?	$30
❏ FJ-2842 [M]	Yamekraw	1962	$75
RIVERSIDE			
❏ RLP 12-151 [M]	Backwater Blues	1955	$300
—White label, blue print			
❏ RLP 12-151 [M]	Backwater Blues	1959	$300
—Blue label, microphone logo at top			
❏ RLP-1046 [10]	Early Harlem Piano, Vol. 2	1954	$300
❏ RLP-1056 [10]	Harlem Rent Party	1955	$300
❏ RLP 12-105 [M]	Rediscovered Early Solos	1955	$300
—White label, blue print			
❏ RLP 12-105 [M]	Rediscovered Early Solos	1959	$300
—Blue label, microphone logo at top			
❏ RLP-1011 [10]	Rent Party	1953	$300
SOUNDS			
❏ 1204	Father of the Stride Piano	196?	$35
STINSON			
❏ SLP-21 [10]	New York Jazz	1950	$120
❏ SLP-21 [M]	New York Jazz	195?	$50
TIME-LIFE			
❏ STL-J-18	Giants of Jazz	1981	$50

JOHNSON, JIMMY

Number	Title	Yr	NM
DELMARK			
❏ DS-644	Johnson Whacks	1979	$12

JOHNSON, KEITH

Number	Title	Yr	NM
REFERENCE RECORDINGS			
❏ RR-7	Prof. Johnson's Astounding Sound Show	198?	$25
—Plays at 45 rpm			

JOHNSON, LAMONT

Number	Title	Yr	NM
MAINSTREAM			
❏ MRL-328	Sun, Moon and Stars	1972	$35

JOHNSON, LAURIE

Number	Title	Yr	NM
COLPIX			
❏ CP471 [M]	England's New Big Band	1964	$25

JOHNSON, LOIS

Number	Title	Yr	NM
20TH CENTURY			
❏ T-465	Lois Johnson	1975	$15

JOHNSON, LONNIE, AND VICTORIA SPIVEY

Number	Title	Yr	NM
BLUESVILLE			
❏ BVLP-1044 [M]	Idle Hours	1962	$175
—Blue label, silver print			
❏ BVLP-1044 [M]	Idle Hours	1964	$50
—Blue label with trident logo at right			
❏ BVLP-1054 [M]	Woman Blues	1962	$175
—Blue label, silver print			
❏ BVLP-1054 [M]	Woman Blues	1964	$50
—Blue label with trident logo at right			
FANTASY			
❏ OBC-518	Idle Hours	198?	$15

JOHNSON, LONNIE

Number	Title	Yr	NM
BLUESVILLE			
❏ BVLP-1062 [M]	Another Night to Cry	1963	$250
—Blue label, silver print			
❏ BVLP-1062 [M]	Another Night to Cry	1964	$75
—Blue label with trident logo at right			
❏ BVLP-1011 [M]	Blues and Ballads	1960	$250
—Blue label, silver print			
❏ BVLP-1011 [M]	Blues and Ballads	1964	$75
—Blue label with trident logo at right			
❏ BVLP-1007 [M]	Blues by Lonnie	1960	$250
—Blue label, silver print			
❏ BVLP-1007 [M]	Blues by Lonnie	1964	$75
—Blue label with trident logo at right			
❏ BVLP-1024 [M]	Losing Game	1961	$250
—Blue label, silver print			
❏ BVLP-1024 [M]	Losing Game	1964	$75
—Blue label with trident logo at right			
COLUMBIA			
❏ C46221	Steppin' On the Blues	1990	$25
FANTASY			
❏ OBC-531	Blues and Ballads	1990	$15
❏ OBC-502	Blues by Lonnie	198?	$15
KING			
❏ 520 [M]	Lonesome Road	1958	$2000
—VG value 750; VG+ value 1375			
❏ 958 [M]	Lonnie Johnson 24 Twelve-Bar Blues	1966	$75
❏ KS-958 [R]	Lonnie Johnson 24 Twelve-Bar Blues	1966	$75
❏ KS-1083	Tomorrow Night	1970	$30
PRESTIGE			
❏ PRST-7724	The Blues of Lonnie Johnson	1970	$25

JOHNSON, MARC

Number	Title	Yr	NM
ECM			
❏ 25040	Bass Desires	1986	$25

JOHNSON, MARV

Number	Title	Yr	NM
UNITED ARTISTS			
❏ UAL3187 [M]	I Believe	1962	$175
❏ UAS6187 [S]	I Believe	1962	$250
❏ UAL3081 [M]	Marvelous Marv Johnson	1960	$175
❏ UAS6081 [S]	Marvelous Marv Johnson	1960	$250
❏ UAL3118 [M]	More Marv Johnson	1961	$175
❏ UAS6118 [S]	More Marv Johnson	1961	$250

JOHNSON, MICHAEL

Number	Title	Yr	NM
ATCO			
❏ SD7028	There Is a Breeze	1973	$18
EMI AMERICA			
❏ SW-17035	Call Me Blue	1980	$12
❏ SW-17010	Dialogue	1979	$12
❏ SW-17057	Home Free	1981	$12
❏ SW-17104	Lifetime Guarantee	1983	$12
❏ SW-17002	The Michael Johnson Album	1978	$12
RCA			
❏ 6715-1-R	That's That	1988	$10
RCA VICTOR			
❏ AEL1-9501	Wings	1986	$10

(continued)
SANSKRIT

Number	Title	Yr	NM
❏ (# unknown)	There Is a Breeze	1973	$50

JOHNSON, OSIE

Number	Title	Yr	NM
BETHLEHEM			
❏ BCP-66 [M]	The Happy Jazz of Osie Johnson	1957	$300
PERIOD			
❏ SPL-1112 [10]	Johnson's Whacks	1955	$100
❏ SPL-1108 [10]	Osie's Oasis	1955	$100
RCA VICTOR			
❏ LPM-1369 [M]	A Bit of the Blues	1957	$40

JOHNSON, PETE

Number	Title	Yr	NM
BLUE NOTE			
❏ BLP-7019 [10]	Boogie Woogie Blues and Skiffle	1952	$300
BRUNSWICK			
❏ BL58041 [10]	Boogie Woogie Mood	1953	$100
MCA			
❏ 1333	Boogie Woogie Mood	198?	$25
MOSAIC			
❏ MR1-119 [B]	The Pete Johnson/Earl Hines/Teddy Bunn Blue Note Sessions	199?	$25
RIVERSIDE			
❏ RLP-1056 [10]	Jumpin' with Pete Johnson	1955	$300
SAVOY			
❏ MG-14018 [M]	Pete's Blues	1958	$120
SAVOY JAZZ			
❏ SJL-414	Pete's Blues	1985	$25

JOHNSON, PETE/HADDA BROOKS

Number	Title	Yr	NM
CROWN			
❏ CLP-5058 [M]	Boogie	195?	$25

JOHNSON, PLAS

Number	Title	Yr	NM
CAPITOL			
❏ T1503 [M]	Mood for the Blues	1961	$75
❏ ST1503 [S]	Mood for the Blues	1961	$75
❏ T1281 [M]	This Must be the Plas!	1960	$75
❏ ST1281 [S]	This Must be the Plas!	1960	$75
CONCORD JAZZ			
❏ CJ-15	Blues	1975	$25
❏ CJ-24	Positively	1976	$25
TAMPA			
❏ TP-24 [M]	Bop Me, Daddy	1957	$250
—Colored vinyl			
❏ TP-24 [M]	Bop Me, Daddy	1958	$175
—Black vinyl			

JOHNSON, ROBERT

Number	Title	Yr	NM
COLUMBIA			
❏ CL1654 [M]	King of the Delta Blues Singers	1961	$500
—Red and black label with six "eye" logos			
❏ CL1654 [M]	King of the Delta Blues Singers	1963	$50
—Guaranteed High Fidelity" label			
❏ CL1654 [M]	King of the Delta Blues Singers	1965	$30
—360 Sound Mono" label			
❏ CL1654 [M]	King of the Delta Blues Singers	1970	$15
—Orange label with "Columbia" circling the edge			
❏ CL1654 [M]	King of the Delta Blues Singers	1998	$12
—Red label, "Columbia" in white at top, "Sony Music" under side numbers			
❏ CL1654 [M]	King of the Delta Blues Singers	2001	$18
—Reissue on 180-gram vinyl (sealed copies have a sticker indicating this)			
❏ C30034 [M]	King of the Delta Blues Singers, Volume 2	1970	$25
❏ PC30034 [M]	King of the Delta Blues Singers, Volume 2	1979	$12
❏ C346222	Robert Johnson -- The Complete Recordings	1990	$50

JOHNSON, RUDOLPH

Number	Title	Yr	NM
BLACK JAZZ			
❏ 11	Second Coming	1972	$30
❏ 4	Spring Rain	1971	$30
OVATION			
❏ OV-1805	Time and Space	1977	$35

JOHNSON, SYL

Number	Title	Yr	NM
TWINIGHT			
❏ LPS-1002	Is It Because I'm Black?	1968	$75

JOHNSON, WAYNE

Number	Title	Yr	NM
INNER CITY			
❏ IC-1098	Arrowhead	198?	$30

Number	Title	Yr	NM
ZEBRA			
❏ ZR-5003	Everybody's Painting Pictures	1984	$30
ZEBRA/MCA			
❏ 42228	Spirit of the Dancer	1988	$25

JOHNSON AND DRAKE
OVATION

| ❏ OVQD-1434 [Q] | Carry It On | 1973 | $30 |

JOHNSON FAMILY SINGERS, THE
RCA VICTOR

| ❏ LPM-1128 [M] | Old Time Religion | 1955 | $30 |

JOHNSTON, BRUCE
COLUMBIA

❏ PC34459	Going Public	1976	$18
❏ CL2057 [M]	Surfin' 'Round the World	1963	$250
❏ CS8857 [S]	Surfin' 'Round the World	1963	$300

DEL-FI

| ❏ DFLP-1228 [M] | Surfers' Pajama Party | 1963 | $250 |
| ❏ DFST-1228 [S] | Surfers' Pajama Party | 1963 | $300 |

JOHNSTON, COLONEL JUBILATION B., AND THE MYSTIC KNIGHTS BAND AND STREET SINGERS
COLUMBIA

| ❏ CL2532 [M] | Moldy Goldies | 1966 | $30 |
| ❏ CS9332 [S] | Moldy Goldies | 1966 | $30 |

JOHNSTON, TOM
WARNER BROS.

| ❏ BSK3304 | Everything You've Heard Is True | 1979 | $12 |
| ❏ BSK3527 | Still Feels Good | 1981 | $12 |

JOLLY, PETE
A&M

❏ SP-4184	Give a Damn	1970	$30
❏ SP-4145	Herb Alpert Presents Pete Jolly	1968	$30
❏ SP-3033	Seasons	1969	$30

AVA

❏ A-51 [M]	Hello Jolly	1964	$50
❏ AS-51 [S]	Hello Jolly	1964	$75
❏ A-22 [M]	Little Bird	1963	$50
❏ AS-22 [S]	Little Bird	1963	$75
❏ A-39 [M]	Sweet September	1963	$50
❏ AS-39 [S]	Sweet September	1963	$75

CHARLIE PARKER

| ❏ PLP-825 [M] | Pete Jolly Gasses Everybody | 1962 | $50 |
| ❏ PLP-825S [S] | Pete Jolly Gasses Everybody | 1962 | $75 |

COLUMBIA

| ❏ CL2397 [M] | Too Much, Baby | 1965 | $50 |
| ❏ CS9197 [S] | Too Much, Baby | 1965 | $75 |

MAINSTREAM

| ❏ S-6114 | The Best of Pete Jolly | 196? | $35 |

METROJAZZ

| ❏ E-1014 [M] | Impossible | 1958 | $300 |
| ❏ SE-1014 [S] | Impossible | 1958 | $300 |

MGM

| ❏ E-4127 [M] | 5 O'Clock Shadows | 1963 | $50 |
| ❏ SE-4127 [S] | 5 O'Clock Shadows | 1963 | $75 |

RCA VICTOR

❏ LPM-1125 [M]	Duo, Trio, Quartet	1955	$150
❏ LPM-1105 [M]	Jolly Jumps In	1955	$150
❏ LPM-1367 [M]	When Lights Are Low	1957	$150

STEREO FIDELITY

| ❏ SFS-11000 [S] | Continental Jazz | 1960 | $75 |

TRIP

| ❏ TLP-5817 | A Touch of Jazz | 197? | $25 |

JOLSON, AL
DECCA

❏ DLP5030 [10]	Al Jolson, Vol. III	1949	$30
❏ DLP5026 [10]	Al Jolson In Songs He Made Famous	1949	$30
❏ DL9095 [M]	Al Jolson with Oscar Levant at the Piano	1961	$30
❏ DL79095 [R]	Al Jolson with Oscar Levant at the Piano	196?	$15
❏ DL9050 [M]	Among My Souvenirs	1957	$30
—Black label, silver print			
❏ DL9050 [M]	Among My Souvenirs	196?	$18
—Black label with color bars			
❏ DL79050 [R]	Among My Souvenirs	196?	$15
❏ DL9099 [M]	Jolie	196?	$30
—Black label, silver print			
❏ DLP5006 [10]	Jolson Sings Again	1949	$30
❏ DL9038 [M]	Memories	1957	$30
—Black label, silver print			
❏ DL9038 [M]	Memories	1957	$18
—Black label with color bars			
❏ DL79038 [R]	Memories	196?	$15

❏ DL9070 [M]	Overseas	1959	$30
—Black label, silver print			
❏ DL9070 [M]	Overseas	196?	$18
—Black label with color bars			
❏ DL79070 [R]	Overseas	196?	$15
❏ DL9036 [M]	Rainbow 'Round My Shoulder	1957	$30
—Black label, silver print			
❏ DL9036 [M]	Rainbow 'Round My Shoulder	196?	$18
—Black label with color bars			
❏ DL79036 [R]	Rainbow 'Round My Shoulder	196?	$15
❏ DL9035 [M]	Rock-a-Bye Your Baby	1957	$30
—Black label, silver print			
❏ DL9035 [M]	Rock-a-Bye Your Baby	196?	$18
—Black label with color bars			
❏ DL79035 [R]	Rock-a-Bye Your Baby	196?	$15
❏ DLP5029 [10]	Souvenir Album, Vol. II	1949	$30
❏ DLP5031 [10]	Souvenir Album, Vol. IV	1949	$30
❏ DL5314 [10]	Souvenir Album, Vol. V	1951	$30
❏ DL5315 [10]	Souvenir Album, Vol. VI	1951	$30
❏ DL5308 [10]	Stephen Foster Songs	1950	$150
❏ DXA169 [M]	The Best of Jolson	196?	$30
❏ DXSA7169 [R]	The Best of Jolson	196?	$18
❏ DL9063 [M]	The Immortal Al Jolson	1958	$30
—Maroon label, silver print			
❏ DL9063 [M]	The Immortal Al Jolson	196?	$18
—Black label with color bars			
❏ DL9074 [M]	The World's Greatest Entertainer	1959	$30
—Black label, silver print			
❏ DL9074 [M]	The World's Greatest Entertainer	196?	$18
—Black label with color bars			

❏ DL79074 [R]	The World's Greatest Entertainer	196?	$15
❏ DL9037 [M]	You Ain't Heard Nothin' Yet!	1957	$30
—Black label, silver print			
❏ DL9037 [M]	You Ain't Heard Nothin' Yet!	1957	$18
—Black label with color bars			
❏ DL79037 [R]	You Ain't Heard Nothin' Yet!	196?	$15
❏ DL9034 [M]	You Made Me Love You	1957	$30
—Black label, silver print			
❏ DL9034 [M]	You Made Me Love You	196?	$18
—Black label with color bars			
❏ DL79034 [R]	You Made Me Love You	196?	$15

MCA

❏ 2064	Among My Souvenirs	197?	$12
❏ 2061	Memories	197?	$12
❏ 27055	Memories	198?	$10
❏ 2059	Rainbow 'Round My Shoulder	197?	$12
❏ 27053	Rainbow 'Round My Shoulder	198?	$10
❏ 2058	Rock-a-Bye Your Baby	197?	$12
❏ 27052	Rock-a-Bye Your Baby	198?	$10
❏ 10002	The Best of Jolson	1973	$15
❏ 2066	The Immortal Al Jolson	197?	$12
❏ 27057	The Immortal Al Jolson	198?	$10
❏ 2067	The World's Greatest Entertainer	197?	$12
❏ 27058	The World's Greatest Entertainer	198?	$10
❏ 2060	You Ain't Heard Nothin' Yet!	197?	$12
❏ 27054	You Ain't Heard Nothin' Yet!	198?	$10
❏ 2057	You Made Me Love You	197?	$12
❏ 27051	You Made Me Love You	198?	$10

SUNBEAM

| ❏ 505 | California, Here I Come | 197? | $12 |
| ❏ 503 | Steppin' Out | 197? | $12 |

TOTEM

| ❏ 1006 [B] | Al Jolson On the Air, Volume 1 | 197? | $15 |
| ❏ 1012 [B] | Al Jolson On the Air, Volume 2 | 197? | $15 |

❏ 1019 [B]	Al Jolson On the Air, Volume 3	197?	$15
❏ 1030 [B]	Al Jolson On the Air, Volume 4	197?	$15
❏ 1040 [B]	Al Jolson On the Air, Volume 5	197?	$15

JON AND ROBIN AND THE IN CROWD
ABNAK

❏ ABST-2070	Elastic Event	1968	$25
❏ ABM-2068 [M]	Soul of a Boy and Girl	1967	$50
❏ ABST-2068 [S]	Soul of a Boy and Girl	1967	$25

JONES, ANN, AND HER AMERICAN SWEETHEARTS
AUDIO LAB

| ❏ AL-1521 [M] | Ann Jones and Her American Sweethearts | 1959 | $175 |
| ❏ AL-1556 [M] | Hit and Run | 1960 | $175 |

JONES, ANTHONY ARMSTRONG
CHART

❏ 1047	Greatest Hits, Vol. 1	1971	$18
❏ 1019	Proud Mary	1969	$18
❏ 1036	Sugar in the Flowers	1970	$18
❏ 1027	Take a Letter Maria	1970	$18

JONES, BOBBY
ENJA

| ❏ 2046 | Hill Country Suite | 1975 | $35 |

JONES, BOOGALOO JOE
PRESTIGE

❏ 10072	Black Whip	1973	$30
❏ PRST-7697	Boogaloo Joe	1969	$25
❏ PRST-7557	Mind Bender	1968	$25
❏ PRST-7617	My Fire! More of the Psychedelic Soul Jazz Guitar of Joe Jones	1968	$25
—As "Joe Jones"			
❏ 10004	No Way!	1971	$30
❏ PRST-7766	Right On Brother!	1970	$25
❏ 10056	Snake Rhythm Rock	1972	$30
❏ 10035	What It Is	1971	$30

JONES, BRIAN
ROLLING STONES

| ❏ COC49100 [B] | Brian Jones Presents the Pipes of Pan at Joujouka | 1971 | $150 |

JONES, CARMELL
PACIFIC JAZZ

❏ PJ-53 [M]	Business Meetin'	1962	$40
❏ ST-53 [S]	Business Meetin'	1962	$50
—Black vinyl			
❏ ST-53 [S]	Business Meetin'	1962	$100
—Yellow vinyl			
❏ PJ-29 [M]	The Remarkable Carmell Jones	1961	$40
❏ ST-29 [S]	The Remarkable Carmell Jones	1961	$50

PRESTIGE

❏ PRST-7669	Carmell Jones in Europe	1969	$25
❏ PRLP-7401 [M]	Jay Hawk Talk	1965	$30
❏ PRST-7401 [S]	Jay Hawk Talk	1965	$40

JONES, CONNIE
JAZZOLOGY

| ❏ J-49 | Connie Jones with the Crescent City Jazz Band | 197? | $25 |

JONES, CURTIS
BLUESVILLE

❏ BVLP-1022 [M]	Trouble Blues	1961	$100
—Blue label, silver print			
❏ BVLP-1022 [M]	Trouble Blues	1964	$30
—Blue label, trident logo at right			

DELMARK

| ❏ DL-605 [M] | Lonesome Bedroom Blues | 1963 | $40 |

JONES, DALINE
TBA

| ❏ TBA-220 | Secret Fantasy | 1986 | $30 |
| ❏ TBA-231 | Share the Love | 1987 | $30 |

JONES, DAVID LYNN
MERCURY

| ❏ 832518-1 | Hard Times on Easy Street | 1987 | $10 |

JONES, DAVY
Also see DOLENZ, JONES & TORK; DOLENZ, JONES, BOYCE & HART; THE MONKEES.

BELL

| ❏ 6067 [B] | Davy Jones | 1971 | $30 |

Number	Title	Yr	NM
COLPIX			
❑ CP493 [M]	David Jones	1965	$30
❑ CPS493 [S]	David Jones	1965	$50
— *This album charted in 1967 thanks to the singer's membership in The Monkees*			
FRIDAY MUSIC			
❑ FRM493 [B]	David Jones	2016	$25

JONES, DEAN

VALIANT			
❑ VLM-407 [M]	Introducing Dean Jones	196?	$25
❑ VLS-407 [S]	Introducing Dean Jones	196?	$25

JONES, DILL

CHIAROSCURO			
❑ 112	The Music of Bix Beiderbecke	197?	$35
PALO ALTO			
❑ PA-8016	Earth Jones	1982	$30

JONES, ELVIN, AND THE JIMMY GARRISON SEXTETTE

IMPULSE!			
❑ A-49 [M]	Illumination	1963	$120
❑ AS-49 [S]	Illumination	1963	$120

JONES, ELVIN

ABC IMPULSE!			
❑ AS-88 [S]	Dear John C.	1968	$35
❑ AS-9160	Heavy Sounds	1968	$250
❑ AS-9283	The Impulse Years	197?	$35
ATLANTIC			
❑ 1443 [M]	And Then Again	1965	$25
❑ SD1443 [S]	And Then Again	1965	$30
❑ 1485 [M]	Midnight Walk	1967	$25
❑ SD1485 [S]	Midnight Walk	1967	$30
BLUE NOTE			
❑ BST-84361	Coalition	1970	$30
❑ BST-84414	Elvin Jones	1972	$25
❑ BST-84369	Genesis	1971	$25
❑ BN-LA015-G [(2)]	Live at the Lighthouse	1973	$25
❑ BN-LA110-F	Mr. Jones	1973	$35
❑ BST-84331	Poly-Currents	1969	$30
❑ BST-84331	Poly-Currents	1986	$25
— *The Finest in Jazz Since 1939" reissue*			
❑ BN-LA506-H2	Prime Element	1976	$25
❑ BST-84282	Puttin' It Together	1968	$30
❑ BST-84305	The Ultimate Elvin Jones	1969	$30
ENJA			
❑ 2036	Live at the Vanguard	1974	$35
FANTASY			
❑ OJC-259	Elvin!	1987	$25
IMPULSE!			
❑ A-88 [M]	Dear John C.	1965	$120
❑ AS-88 [S]	Dear John C.	1965	$120
MCA			
❑ 29068	Dear John C.	1980	$25
PAUSA			
❑ 7052	Remembrance	1979	$25
PM			
❑ 04	Live at Town Hall	197?	$35
❑ 05	On the Mountain	197?	$35
QUICKSILVER			
❑ QS-4001	Brother John	198?	$25
RIVERSIDE			
❑ RLP-409 [M]	Elvin!	1962	$250
❑ RS-9409 [S]	Elvin!	1962	$250
❑ 6192	Elvin!	198?	$30
VANGUARD			
❑ VSD-79372	Main Force	1976	$35
❑ VSD-79362	New Agenda	1975	$35
❑ VSD-79389	Time Capsule	1977	$35

JONES, ETTA

FANTASY			
❑ OJC-298	Don't Go to Strangers	198?	$25
❑ OJC-221	Something Nice	198?	$25
KING			
❑ 707 [M]	Etta Jones Sings	1960	$100
❑ 544 [M]	The Jones Girl...Etta	1956	$175
MUSE			
❑ MR-5411	Christmas with Etta Jones	1989	$30
❑ MR-5333	Fine and Mellow	1987	$25
❑ MR-5175	If You Could See Me Now	1979	$30
❑ MR-5351	I'll Be Seeing You	1989	$30
❑ MR-5262	Love Me with All of Your Heart	198?	$25
❑ MR-5145	Mother's Eyes	1977	$30
❑ MR-5099	Ms. Jones to You	197?	$30
❑ MR-5214	Save Your Love for Me	1981	$25
❑ MR-5379	Sugar	1989	$30
PRESTIGE			
❑ PRLP-7186 [M]	Don't Go to Strangers	1960	$250

Number	Title	Yr	NM
— *Yellow label*			
❑ PRLP-7186 [M]	Don't Go to Strangers	1964	$25
— *Blue label, trident logo at right*			
❑ PRST-7186 [S]	Don't Go to Strangers	1960	$250
— *Silver label*			
❑ PRST-7186 [S]	Don't Go to Strangers	1964	$30
— *Blue label, trident logo at right*			
❑ PRLP-7443 [M]	Etta Jones' Greatest Hits	1967	$30
❑ PRST-7443 [S]	Etta Jones' Greatest Hits	1967	$25
❑ PRLP-7214 [M]	From the Heart	1961	$250
— *Yellow label*			
❑ PRLP-7214 [M]	From the Heart	1964	$25
— *Blue label, trident logo at right*			
❑ PRST-7214 [S]	From the Heart	1961	$250
— *Silver label*			
❑ PRST-7214 [S]	From the Heart	1964	$30
— *Blue label, trident logo at right*			
❑ PRLP-7284 [M]	Holler!	1963	$40
— *Yellow label*			
❑ PRLP-7284 [M]	Holler!	1964	$25
— *Blue label, trident logo at right*			
❑ PRST-7284 [S]	Holler!	1963	$50
— *Silver label*			
❑ PRST-7284 [S]	Holler!	1964	$30
— *Blue label, trident logo at right*			
❑ PRLP-7241 [M]	Lonely and Blue	1962	$175
— *Yellow label*			
❑ PRLP-7241 [M]	Lonely and Blue	1964	$25
— *Blue label, trident logo at right*			
❑ PRST-7241 [S]	Lonely and Blue	1962	$175
— *Silver label*			
❑ PRST-7241 [S]	Lonely and Blue	1964	$30
— *Blue label, trident logo at right*			
❑ PRLP-7272 [M]	Love Shout	1963	$40
— *Yellow label*			
❑ PRLP-7272 [M]	Love Shout	1964	$25
— *Blue label, trident logo at right*			
❑ PRST-7272 [S]	Love Shout	1963	$50
— *Silver label*			
❑ PRST-7272 [S]	Love Shout	1964	$30
— *Blue label, trident logo at right*			
❑ PRLP-7194 [M]	Something Nice	1961	$250
— *Yellow label*			
❑ PRLP-7194 [M]	Something Nice	1964	$30
— *Blue label, trident logo at right*			
❑ PRLP-7204 [M]	So Warm -- Etta Jones and Strings	1961	$250
— *Yellow label*			
❑ PRLP-7204 [M]	So Warm -- Etta Jones and Strings	1964	$25
— *Blue label, trident logo at right*			
❑ PRST-7204 [S]	So Warm -- Etta Jones and Strings	1961	$250
— *Silver label*			
❑ PRST-7204 [S]	So Warm -- Etta Jones and Strings	1964	$30
— *Blue label, trident logo at right*			
ROULETTE			
❑ R-25329 [M]	Etta Jones Sings	1965	$25
❑ SR-25329 [S]	Etta Jones Sings	1965	$30
WESTBOUND			
❑ 203	Etta Jones '75	1975	$25

JONES, GEORGE, AND JOHNNY PAYCHECK

EPIC			
❑ JE35783	Double Trouble	1980	$12

JONES, GEORGE, AND MARGIE SINGLETON

MERCURY			
❑ MG-20747 [M]	Duets Country Style	1962	$30
❑ SR-60747 [S]	Duets Country Style	1962	$40

JONES, GEORGE, AND MELBA MONTGOMERY

GUEST STAR			
❑ GS1465 [M]	George Jones and Melba Montgomery	196?	$15
— *Contains two solo records by each artist (no duets!) and assorted stuff by others*			
LIBERTY			
❑ LN-10169	Singing What's In Our Hearts	1981	$10
MUSICOR			
❑ MM-2109 [M]	Close Together (As You and Me)	1966	$25
❑ MS-3109 [S]	Close Together (As You and Me)	1966	$30
❑ MM-2127 [M]	Let's Get Together/Boy Meets Girl	1967	$30
❑ MS-3127 [S]	Let's Get Together/Boy Meets Girl	1967	$25
❑ MM-2127 [M]	Party Pickin'	1967	$30
— *Alternate title*			
❑ MS-3127 [S]	Party Pickin'	1967	$25
— *Alternate title*			

Number	Title	Yr	NM
UNITED ARTISTS			
❑ UAL-3352 [M]	Bluegrass Hootenanny	1964	$30
❑ UAS-6352 [S]	Bluegrass Hootenanny	1964	$30
❑ UAL-3472 [M]	Blue Moon of Kentucky	1966	$25
❑ UAS-6472 [S]	Blue Moon of Kentucky	1966	$30
❑ T-90832 [M]	Blue Moon of Kentucky	1966	$30
— *Capitol Record Club edition*			
❑ UAL-3301	Singing What's In Our Hearts	1963	$30
❑ UAS-6301 [S]	Singing What's In Our Hearts	1963	$30

JONES, GEORGE, AND TAMMY WYNETTE

EPIC			
❑ FE37348	Encore	1981	$12
❑ PE37348	Encore	198?	$10
— *Budget-line reissue*			
❑ KE33351	George & Tammy & Tina	1975	$18
❑ KE34291	Golden Ring	1976	$15
— *Orange label*			
❑ PE34291	Golden Ring	198?	$10
— *Dark blue label*			
❑ KE34716	Greatest Hits	1977	$15
❑ PE34716	Greatest Hits	198?	$10
— *Budget-line reissue*			
❑ KE32113	Let's Build a World Together	1973	$18
❑ KE31554	Me and the First Lady	1972	$18
— *Yellow label*			
❑ KE31554	Me and the First Lady	1973	$15
— *Orange label*			
❑ JE36764	Together Again	1980	$12
❑ PE36764	Together Again	198?	$10
— *Budget-line reissue*			
❑ KE30802	We Go Together	1971	$18
❑ EQ30802 [Q]	We Go Together	1971	$40
❑ BG33752	We Go Together/Me and the First Lady	1976	$18
❑ KE31719	We Love to Sing About Jesus	1972	$18
— *Yellow label*			
❑ KE31719	We Love to Sing About Jesus	1973	$15
— *Orange label*			
❑ KE32757	We're Gonna Hold On	1973	$18

JONES, GEORGE; MELBA MONTGOMERY; GENE PITNEY

MUSICOR			
❑ MM-2079 [M]	Famous Country Duets	1965	$25
❑ MS-3079 [S]	Famous Country Duets	1965	$30

JONES, GEORGE; MELBA MONTGOMERY; JUDY LYNN

UNITED ARTISTS			
❑ UAL-3367 [M]	A King and Two Queens	1964	$25
❑ UAS-6367 [S]	A King and Two Queens	1964	$30

JONES, GEORGE

ACCORD			
❑ SN-7201	Tender Years	1982	$12
ALLEGIANCE			
❑ AV-5015	Cold Cold Heart	198?	$12
BULLDOG			
❑ BDL-2009	20 Golden Pieces of George Jones	198?	$12
EPIC			
❑ PE34692	All-Time Greatest Hits Volume 1	1977	$15
— *Orange label*			
❑ PE34692	All-Time Greatest Hits Volume 1	198?	$10
— *Dark blue label*			
❑ KE34290	Alone Again	1976	$15
❑ KE238323	Anniversary -- 10 Years of Hits	1982	$15
❑ KE31718	A Picture of Me (Without You)	1972	$18
— *Yellow label*			
❑ KE31718	A Picture of Me (Without You)	1973	$15
— *Orange label*			
❑ KE35414	Bartender's Blues	1978	$15
❑ PE35414	Bartender's Blues	198?	$10
— *Budget-line reissue*			
❑ FE39546	By Request	1984	$12
❑ FE37346	Encore	1981	$12
❑ FE39899	First Time Live!	1985	$12
❑ KE31321	George Jones	1972	$18
— *Yellow label*			
❑ KE31321	George Jones	1973	$15
— *Orange label*			
❑ BG33749	George Jones/A Picture of Me (Without You)	1976	$18
❑ JE36586	I Am What I Am	1980	$15
❑ KE32563	In a Gospel Way	1974	$18
❑ PE34717	I Wanta Sing	1977	$15
— *Orange label*			
❑ PE34717	I Wanta Sing	198?	$10
— *Dark blue label*			

Number	Title	Yr	NM
❑ FE38978	Jones Country	1983	$12
❑ PE38978	Jones Country	1985	$10
—Budget-line reissue			
❑ FE39272	Ladies' Choice	1984	$12
❑ KE33547	Memories of Us	1975	$18
❑ JE35544	My Very Special Guests	1979	$15
❑ PE35544	My Very Special Guests	198?	$10
—Budget-line reissue			
❑ KE32412	Nothing Ever Hurt Me (Half As Bad As Losing You)	1973	$18
❑ FE44078	One Woman Man	1989	$12
❑ FE38406	Shine On	1983	$12
❑ PE38406	Shine On	198?	$10
—Budget-line reissue			
❑ FE37106	Still the Same Old Me	1981	$12
❑ PE37106	Still the Same Ole Me	198?	$10
—Budget-line reissue			
❑ FE40776	Super Hits	1987	$12
❑ KE34034	The Battle	1976	$15
❑ KE33352	The Best of George Jones	1975	$18
❑ PE33352	The Best of George Jones	1981	$10
—Budget-line reissue			
❑ KE33083	The Grand Tour	1974	$18
❑ FE40781	Too Wild Too Long	1988	$12
❑ FE39598	Who's Gonna Fill Their Shoes	1985	$12
❑ FE40413	Wine Colored Roses	1986	$12
❑ FE39002	You've Still Got a Place in My Heart	1984	$12

EVEREST ARCHIVE OF FOLK & JAZZ

Number	Title	Yr	NM
❑ 353	George Jones Sings Country Hits	198?	$12

HILLTOP

❑ 6092	Heartaches by the Number	1969	$18
❑ 6133	Oh Lonesome Me	1970	$18
❑ 6048	You're In My Heart	1968	$18

INTERMEDIA

❑ QS-5061	How I Love These Old Songs	198?	$12
❑ QS-5044	I Can't Change Overnight	198?	$12

LIBERTY

❑ LN-10168	I Get Lonely in a Hurry	1981	$10
❑ LN-10167	Trouble in Mind	1981	$10

MCA

❑ 10398	And Along Came Jones	1991	$25
—Vinyl issued only through Columbia House			

MERCURY

❑ MG-20306 [M]	14 Country Favorites	1957	$175
❑ MG-20906 [M]	Blue and Lonesome	1964	$30
❑ SR-60906 [S]	Blue and Lonesome	1964	$30
❑ MG-20624 [M]	Country and Western Hits	1961	$40
❑ SR-60624 [P]	Country and Western Hits	1961	$50
❑ MG-20937 [M]	Country and Western No. 1 Male Singer	1964	$30
❑ SR-60937 [S]	Country and Western No. 1 Male Singer	1964	$30
❑ MG-20462 [M]	Country Church Time	1959	$250
❑ MG-20621 [M]	George Jones' Greatest Hits	1961	$40
❑ SR-60621 [P]	George Jones' Greatest Hits	1961	$50
❑ MG-21048 [M]	George Jones' Greatest Hits Volume 2	1965	$30
❑ SR-61048 [S]	George Jones' Greatest Hits Volume 2	1965	$30
❑ MG-20596 [M]	George Jones Salutes Hank Williams	1960	$100
❑ SR-60257 [S]	George Jones Salutes Hank Williams	1960	$150
❑ 822646-1	George Jones Salutes Hank Williams	1985	$12
❑ MG-20694 [M]	George Jones Sings From the Heart	1962	$40
❑ SR-60694 [S]	George Jones Sings From the Heart	1962	$50
❑ MG-20477 [M]	George Jones Sings White Lightning and Other Favorites	1959	$175
❑ ML-8014	Greatest Hits	1980	$15
❑ 826248-1	Greatest Hits	1986	$12
❑ MG-20990 [M]	Heartaches and Tears	1965	$30
❑ SR-60990 [S]	Heartaches and Tears	1965	$30
❑ MG-20282 [M]	Hillbilly Hit Parade, Volume 1	1957	$175
—Five tracks by George Jones, one by George Jones with Benny Barnes, and four by other artists			
❑ 826095-1	Rockin' the Country	1985	$12
❑ MG-21029 [M]	Singing the Blues	1965	$30
❑ SR-61029 [S]	Singing the Blues	1965	$30
❑ MG-20836 [M]	The Ballad Side of George Jones	1963	$40
❑ SR-60836 [S]	The Ballad Side of George Jones	1963	$50
❑ MG-20793 [M]	The Novelty Side of George Jones	1963	$100
❑ SR-60793 [S]	The Novelty Side of George Jones	1963	$150

MUSICOR

❑ MM-2124 [M]	Cup of Loneliness	1967	$30
❑ MS-3124 [S]	Cup of Loneliness	1967	$25
❑ MM-2116 [M]	George Jones' Greatest Hits	1967	$30
❑ MS-3116 [S]	George Jones' Greatest Hits	1967	$30
❑ MS-3194	George Jones With Love	1971	$25
❑ MM-2128 [M]	Hits by George	1967	$30
❑ MS-3128 [S]	Hits by George	1967	$25
❑ MS-3158	If My Heart Had Windows	1968	$25
❑ MS-3177	I'll Share My World with You	1969	$25
❑ MM-2099 [M]	I'm a People	1966	$30

Number	Title	Yr	NM
❑ MS-3099 [S]	I'm a People	1966	$30
❑ MM-2088 [M]	Love Bug	1966	$30
❑ MS-3088 [S]	Love Bug	1966	$40
❑ MM-2046 [M]	Mr. Country and Western Music	1965	$30
❑ MS-3046 [S]	Mr. Country and Western Music	1965	$40
❑ M2S-3169	My Country	1969	$30
❑ MM-2060 [M]	New Country Hits	1965	$30
❑ MS-3060 [S]	New Country Hits	1965	$40
❑ MM-2061 [M]	Old Brush Arbors	1966	$30
❑ MS-3061 [S]	Old Brush Arbors	1966	$40
❑ MS-3191	The Best of George Jones	1970	$25
❑ MS-3203	The Best of Sacred Music	1971	$25

❑ M2S-3159 [B]	The George Jones Story: The Musical Loves, Life and Sorrows of America's Great Country Star	1968	$30
❑ MS-3204	The Great Songs of Leon Payne	1971	$25
❑ MS-3149	The Songs of Dallas Frazier	1968	$25
❑ MM-2119 [M]	Walk Through This World with Me	1967	$30
❑ MS-3119 [S]	Walk Through This World with Me	1967	$25
❑ MM-2106 [M]	We Found Heaven Right Here on Earth	1966	$30
❑ MS-3106 [S]	We Found Heaven Right Here on Earth	1966	$30
❑ MS-3181	Where Grass Won't Grow	1969	$25
❑ MS-3188	Will You Visit Me on Sunday?	1970	$25

NASHVILLE

❑ 2076	Seasons of My Heart	1970	$18

PAIR

❑ PDL2-1080	Country, By George!	1986	$15
❑ PDL2-1074	The Best of George Jones	1986	$15

POWER PAK

❑ 271	The Crown Prince of Country Music	197?	$12

QUICKSILVER

❑ QS-1011	Frozen in Time	198?	$12
❑ QS-1012	If My Heart Had Windows	198?	$12

RCA CAMDEN

❑ CAS-2591	Flowers for Mama	1973	$15
❑ ACL1-0377	The Race Is On	1973	$15

RCA VICTOR

❑ LSP-4716	Best of George Jones Vol. I	1972	$18
❑ APL1-0316	Best of George Jones Vol. II	1973	$18
❑ LSP-4727	Country Singer	1972	$18
❑ LSP-4672	First in the Hearts of Country Music Lovers	1972	$18
❑ LSP-4785	Four-O Thirty-Three	1972	$18
❑ LSP-4733	George Jones And Friends	1972	$18
❑ APL1-0612	His Songs	1974	$18
❑ APL1-0815	I Can Love You Enough	1974	$18
❑ LSP-4847	I Can Still See Him	1973	$18
❑ LSP-4726	I Made Leaving (Easy for You)	1972	$18
❑ LSP-4725	Poor Man's Riches	1972	$18
❑ LSP-4787	Take Me	1972	$18
❑ LSP-4786	Tender Years	1972	$18
❑ APL1-1113	The Best of the Best	1975	$18
❑ LSP-4801	Wrapped Around Her Finger	1973	$18
❑ APL1-0486	You Gotta Be My Baby	1974	$18

ROUNDER

❑ SS-15	Burn the Honky Tonk Down	198?	$12
❑ SS-17	Heartaches & Hangovers	198?	$12

SEARS

❑ SPS-125	Maybe, Little Baby	196?	$25

STARDAY

❑ 3021	16 Greatest Hits	197?	$12
❑ SLP335 [M]	George Jones	1965	$40
❑ SLP150 [M]	George Jones Sings His Greatest Hits	1962	$50
❑ DT-90080 [R]	George Jones Sings His Greatest Hits	1964	$100
—Capitol Record Club edition			

Number	Title	Yr	NM
❑ SLP344 [M]	Long Live King George	1965	$40
❑ DT-90611 [R]	The Crown Prince of Country Music	196?	$40
—Capitol Record Club edition			
❑ SLP125 [M]	The Crown Prince of Country Music	1960	$160
❑ SLP151 [M]	The Fabulous Country Music Sound of George Jones	1962	$50
❑ SLP401	The George Jones Song Book & Picture Album	1967	$30
—Without book			
❑ SLP401	The George Jones Song Book & Picture Album	1967	$50
—With book			
❑ SLP366 [M]	The George Jones Story	1966	$30
❑ SLP366	The George Jones Story Bonus Photo	1966	$25
❑ SLP440 [M]	The Golden Country Hits of George Jones	1969	$30
❑ SLP101 [M]	The Grand Ole Opry's New Star	1958	$1200

TIME-LIFE

❑ STW-103	Country Music	1981	$12

UNITED ARTISTS

❑ UAL-3532 [M]	George Jones' Golden Hits, Volume 1	1966	$25
❑ UAS-6532 [S]	George Jones' Golden Hits, Volume 1	1966	$30
❑ UAL-3566 [M]	George Jones' Golden Hits, Volume 2	1967	$30
❑ UAS-6566 [S]	George Jones' Golden Hits, Volume 2	1967	$25
❑ UAS-6696	George Jones' Golden Hits, Volume 3	1968	$25
❑ UAL-3221 [M]	George Jones Sings Bob Wills	1962	$40
❑ UAS-6221 [S]	George Jones Sings Bob Wills	1962	$50
❑ UAL-3364 [M]	George Jones Sings Like the Dickens	1964	$40
❑ UAS-6364 [S]	George Jones Sings Like the Dickens	1964	$50
❑ UAL-3218 [M]	George Jones Sings the Hits of His Country Cousins	1962	$30
❑ UAS-6218 [S]	George Jones Sings the Hits of His Country Cousins	1962	$40
❑ UXS-85	George Jones Superpak	1972	$25
❑ UAL-3219 [M]	Homecoming in Heaven	1962	$30
❑ UAS-6219 [S]	Homecoming in Heaven	1962	$40
❑ UAL-3388 [M]	I Get Lonely in a Hurry	1964	$30
❑ UAS-6388 [S]	I Get Lonely in a Hurry	1964	$40
❑ UAL-3270 [M]	I Wish the Night Would Never End	1963	$30
❑ UAS-6270 [S]	I Wish the Night Would Never End	1963	$30
❑ UAL-3442 [M]	King of Broken Hearts	1965	$30
❑ UAS-6442 [S]	King of Broken Hearts	1965	$40
❑ UAL-3338 [M]	More New Favorites	1964	$30
❑ UAS-6328 [S]	More New Favorites	1964	$30
❑ UAL-3220 [M]	My Favorites of Hank Williams	1962	$30
❑ UAS-6220 [S]	My Favorites of Hank Williams	1962	$40
❑ UAL-3291 [M]	The Best of George Jones	1963	$30
❑ UAS-6291 [S]	The Best of George Jones	1963	$30
❑ UAL-3457 [M]	The Great George Jones	1966	$30
❑ UAS-6457 [S]	The Great George Jones	1966	$40
❑ UAL-3193 [M]	The New Favorites of George Jones	1962	$30
❑ UAS-6193 [S]	The New Favorites of George Jones	1962	$40
❑ UAL-3422 [M]	The Race Is On	1965	$30
—With photo of George Jones on front			
❑ UAL-3422 [M]	The Race Is On	1965	$25
—With cartoon on front			
❑ UAS-6422 [S]	The Race Is On	1965	$40
—With photo of George Jones on front			
❑ UAS-6422 [S]	The Race Is On	1965	$30
—With cartoon on front			
❑ T-90829 [M]	The Race Is On	1965	$30
—Capitol Record Club edition; photo on front			
❑ ST-90829 [S]	The Race Is On	1965	$40
—Capitol Record Club edition; photo on front			
❑ UAL-3558 [M]	The Young George Jones	1967	$30
❑ UAS-6558 [S]	The Young George Jones	1967	$25
❑ UAL-3408 [M]	Trouble in Mind	1965	$30
❑ UAS-6408 [S]	Trouble in Mind	1965	$40

WING

❑ MGW-12266 [M]	The Great George Jones	196?	$18
❑ SRW-16266 [S]	The Great George Jones	196?	$18

JONES, GRANDPA

DECCA

❑ DL4364 [M]	An Evening with Grandpa Jones	1963	$30
❑ DL74364 [S]	An Evening with Grandpa Jones	1963	$30

KING

❑ 822 [M]	16 Sacred Gospel Songs	1963	$75
❑ 845 [M]	Do You Remember?	1963	$75
❑ 554 [M]	Grandpa Jones Sings His Biggest Hits	1958	$150
❑ 809 [M]	Rollin' Along with Grandpa Jones	1963	$75
❑ 625 [M]	Strictly Country Tunes	1959	$150
❑ KS-1042	The Living Legend of Country Music	1969	$25

Number	Title	Yr	NM
❏ 888 [M]	The Other Side of Grandpa Jones	1964	$75

MONUMENT

Number	Title	Yr	NM
❏ SLP-18083	Everybody's Grandpa	1968	$25
❏ MLP-4006 [M]	Grandpa Jones Makes the Rafters Ring	1962	$30
❏ SLP-14006 [S]	Grandpa Jones Makes the Rafters Ring	1962	$30
❏ MLP-8041 [M]	Grandpa Jones Remembers the Brown's Ferry Four	1966	$30
❏ SLP-18041 [S]	Grandpa Jones Remembers the Brown's Ferry Four	1966	$30
❏ SLP-18131	Grandpa Jones Sings Hits from Hee Haw	1969	$25
❏ MLP-8021 [M]	Real Folk Songs	1964	$25
❏ SLP-18021 [S]	Real Folk Songs	1964	$30
❏ MLP-8001 [M]	Yodeling Hits	1963	$25
❏ SLP-18001 [S]	Yodeling Hits	1963	$30

JONES, HANK, AND RED MITCHELL

TIMELESS

Number	Title	Yr	NM
❏ SJP-283	Duo	1990	$35

JONES, HANK; RAY BROWN; JIMMIE SMITH

CONCORD JAZZ

Number	Title	Yr	NM
❏ CJ-32	Hank Jones/Ray Brown/ Jimmie Smith	197?	$30

JONES, HANK

ABC-PARAMOUNT

Number	Title	Yr	NM
❏ ABC-496 [M]	This Is Ragtime Now	1964	$25
❏ ABCS-496 [S]	This Is Ragtime Now	1964	$30

ARGO

| ❏ LP-728 [M] | Here's Love | 1963 | $25 |
| ❏ LPS-728 [S] | Here's Love | 1963 | $30 |

CAPITOL

❏ T1175 [M]	Porgy and Bess	1959	$85
❏ ST1175 [S]	Porgy and Bess	1959	$75
❏ T1044 [M]	The Talented Touch of Hank Jones	1958	$85
❏ ST1044 [S]	The Talented Touch of Hank Jones	1958	$75

CLEF

| ❏ MGC-100 [10] | Hank Jones Piano | 1953 | $300 |
| ❏ MGC-707 [M] | Urbanity -- Piano Solos by Hank Jones | 1956 | $300 |

CONCORD JAZZ

| ❏ CJ-391 | Lazy Afternoon | 1989 | $30 |

FANTASY

| ❏ OJC-471 | Just for Fun | 1990 | $30 |

GALAXY

❏ 5123	Ain't Misbehavin'	1979	$30
❏ 5105	Just for	1977	$30
❏ 5108	Tiptoe Tapdance	1978	$30

GOLDEN CREST

❏ GC-3042 [M]	Hank Jones Swings "Gigi	1958	$50
❏ GC-5002 [S]	Hank Jones Swings "Gigi	1959	$40
❏ GCS-3042 [S]	Hank Jones Swings "Gigi	196?	$25

INNER CITY

| ❏ IC-6020 | Hanky Panky | 197? | $30 |

MERCURY

❏ MG-25022 [10]	Hank Jones Piano	1950	$300
❏ MG-35014 [10]	Hank Jones Piano	1950	$300
❏ MGC-100 [10]	Hank Jones Piano	195?	$300

MUSE

| ❏ MR-5123 | Bop Redux | 1977 | $30 |
| ❏ MR-5169 | Grovin' High | 1979 | $30 |

PAUSA

| ❏ 7051 | Have You Met This Jones? | 1979 | $25 |

PROGRESSIVE

| ❏ 7004 | Arigato | 1976 | $30 |

RCA VICTOR

| ❏ LPM-2570 [M] | Arrival Time | 1962 | $30 |
| ❏ LSP-2570 [S] | Arrival Time | 1962 | $30 |

SAVOY

❏ MG-12037 [M]	Hank Jones Quartet-Quintet	1955	$100
❏ MG-12087 [M]	Hank Jones Trio	1956	$100
❏ MG-12084 [M]	Have You Met Hank Jones	1956	$100
❏ MG-12053 [M]	The Trio	1956	$100

SAVOY JAZZ

❏ SJL-1193	Bluebird	198?	$25
❏ SJL-1124	Hank Jones	198?	$25
❏ SJL-1138	Relaxin' at Camarillo	198?	$25

VERVE

| ❏ MGV-8091 [M] | Urbanity -- Piano Solos by Hank Jones | 1957 | $150 |
| ❏ V-8091 [M] | Urbanity -- Piano Solos by Hank Jones | 1961 | $30 |

JONES, HOWARD

ELEKTRA

❏ R133246 [EP]	Action Replay	1986	$10
—RCA Music Service edition			
❏ 60466 [EP]	Action Replay	1986	$10
❏ 60794	Cross That Line	1989	$12
❏ 60794 [DJ]	Cross That Line	1989	$15

Number	Title	Yr	NM
—Promo-only white label audiophile vinyl			
❏ R143992	Dream into Action	1985	$12
—RCA Music Service edition			
❏ 60390	Dream into Action	1985	$10
❏ 60346	Human's Lib	1984	$10
❏ R134013	One to One	1986	$12
—RCA Music Service edition			
❏ 60499	One to One	1986	$12

JONES, ISHAM

RCA VICTOR

Number	Title	Yr	NM
❏ LPV-504 [M]	The Great Isham Jones and His Orchestra	1966	$25

JONES, JACK

CAPITOL

❏ T2100 [M]	In Love	1964	$18
❏ ST2100 [S]	In Love	1964	$25
—Reissue of 1274			
❏ T1274 [M]	This Love of Mine	1959	$30
❏ ST1274 [S]	This Love of Mine	1959	$30

KAPP

❏ KL-1365 [M]	Bewitched	1964	$15
❏ KS-3365 [S]	Bewitched	1964	$18
❏ KL-1328 [M]	Call Me Irresponsible	1963	$15
❏ KS-3328 [S]	Call Me Irresponsible	1963	$18
❏ KS-3566	Curtain Time	1968	$15
❏ KL-1415 [M]	Dear Heart	1964	$15
❏ KS-3415 [S]	Dear Heart	1964	$18
❏ KL-1465 [M]	For the "In" Crowd	1966	$15
❏ KS-3465 [S]	For the "In" Crowd	1966	$18
❏ KS-3559	Greatest Hits	1968	$15
❏ KL-1559 [M]	Greatest Hits	1968	$25
—May exist only as a white label promo; covers are stereo with a "Mono" sticker			
❏ KS-3602	Greatest Hits Vol. 2	1970	$15
❏ KL-1265 [M]	I've Got a Lot of Livin' to Do	1962	$15
❏ KS-3265 [S]	I've Got a Lot of Livin' to Do	1962	$18
❏ KS-3590	Jack Jones in Hollywood	1969	$15
❏ KL-1500 [M]	Jack Jones Sings	1966	$15
❏ KS-3500 [S]	Jack Jones Sings	1966	$18
❏ KL-1511 [M]	Lady	1967	$18
❏ KS-3511 [S]	Lady	1967	$15
❏ KL-1259 [M]	Lollipops and Roses	196?	$15
—Revised title			
❏ KS-3259 [S]	Lollipops and Roses	196?	$18
—Revised title			
❏ KL-1433 [M]	My Kind of Town	1965	$15
❏ KS-3433 [S]	My Kind of Town	1965	$18
❏ KL-1531 [M]	Our Song	1967	$18
❏ KS-3531 [S]	Our Song	1967	$15
❏ KL-1228 [M]	Shall We Dance	1961	$15
❏ KS-3228 [S]	Shall We Dance	1961	$18
❏ KL-1337 [M]	She Loves Me	1963	$15
❏ KS-3337 [S]	She Loves Me	1963	$18
❏ KXS-5009	The Best of Jack Jones	196?	$18
❏ KL-1486 [M]	The Impossible Dream	1966	$15
❏ KS-3486 [S]	The Impossible Dream	1966	$18
❏ KL1399 [M]	The Jack Jones Christmas Album	1964	$15
❏ KS3399 [S]	The Jack Jones Christmas Album	1964	$18
❏ KL-1435 [M]	There's Love & There's Love & There's Love	1965	$15
❏ KS-3435 [S]	There's Love & There's Love & There's Love	1965	$18
❏ KL-1259 [M]	This Was My Love	1962	$25
—Original title			
❏ KS-3259 [S]	This Was My Love	1962	$30
—Original title			
❏ KS-3551 [S]	What the World Needs Now Is Love!	1968	$15
❏ KL-1551 [M]	What the World Needs Now Is Love!	1968	$25
—May only exist as a white label promo; covers are stereo with "Mono" sticker			
❏ KL-1396 [M]	Where Love Has Gone	1964	$15
❏ KS-3396 [S]	Where Love Has Gone	1964	$18
❏ KL-1352 [M]	Wives and Lovers	1963	$15
❏ KS-3352 [S]	Wives and Lovers	1963	$18

MCA

❏ 4115	The Best of Jack Jones	197?	$15
—Reissue of Kapp KXS-5009			
❏ 15014	The Jack Jones Christmas Album	197?	$12
—Reissue			
❏ 15036	White Christmas	198?	$10

MGM

| ❏ MG-1-5024 | Don't Stop Now | 1980 | $12 |
| ❏ MG-1-5023 | Nobody Does It Better | 1979 | $12 |

PICKWICK

❏ SPC-3041	A Very Precious Love	196?	$12
❏ PC-3001 [M]	This Love of Mine	196?	$15
❏ SPC-3001 [S]	This Love of Mine	196?	$15

RCA CAMDEN

| ❏ ACL1-0255 | Christmas with Jack Jones | 1973 | $15 |
| *—Reissue of RCA Victor LSP-4234* | | | |

RCA VICTOR

| ❏ LSP-4234 | A Jack Jones Christmas | 1969 | $18 |
| ❏ LSP-4613 | A Song for You | 1971 | $15 |

Number	Title	Yr	NM
❏ LSP-4209	A Time for Us	1969	$15
❏ LSP-4692	Bread Winners	1972	$12
❏ APL1-0408	Harbour	1974	$12
❏ LPM-3969 [M]	If You Ever Leave Me	1968	$25
❏ LSP-3969 [S]	If You Ever Leave Me	1968	$15
❏ LSP-4413	In Person at the Sands, Las Vegas	1970	$15
❏ LSP-4480	Jack Jones Sings Michel Legrand	1970	$15
❏ ANL1-1081	Jack Jones Sings Michel Legrand	1975	$10
—Reissue			
❏ LSP-4108	L.A. Break Down	1969	$15
❏ APL1-2067	The Full Life	1976	$12
❏ APL1-0139	Together	1973	$12
❏ APL1-1111	What I Did for Love	1975	$12
❏ LSP-4048	Where Is Love	1968	$15
❏ APL1-2361	With One More Look at You	1977	$12
❏ LPM-3911 [M]	Without Her	1967	$25
❏ LSP-3911 [S]	Without Her	1967	$15
❏ APL1-0773	Write Me a Love Song, Charlie	1975	$12

VOCALION

| ❏ VL73913 | Jack Jones Showcase | 1970 | $12 |

JONES, JIMMY

JEN JILLUS

Number	Title	Yr	NM
❏ 1001	The Handy Man's Back in Town	1977	$15

MGM

| ❏ E-3847 [M] | Good Timin' | 1960 | $120 |
| ❏ SE-3847 [S] | Good Timin' | 1960 | $160 |

JONES, JO

EVEREST

Number	Title	Yr	NM
❏ LPBR-5023 [M]	Jo Jones Trio	1959	$30
❏ SDBR-1023 [S]	Jo Jones Trio	1959	$30
❏ LPBR-5110 [M]	Percussion and Bass	1960	$30
❏ SDBR-1110 [S]	Percussion and Bass	1960	$30
❏ LPBR-5099 [M]	Vamp Till Ready	1960	$30
❏ SDBR-1099 [S]	Vamp Till Ready	1960	$30

EVEREST ARCHIVE OF FOLK & JAZZ

| ❏ 329 | Jo Jones | 197? | $25 |

JAZZTONE

| ❏ J-1242 [M] | Jo Jones Special | 1956 | $50 |

PABLO

| ❏ 2310799 | Main Man | 1976 | $35 |

VANGUARD

❏ VRS-8525 [M]	Jo Jones Plus Two	1959	$75
❏ VSD-2031 [S]	Jo Jones Plus Two	1959	$50
❏ VRS-8503 [M]	Jo Jones Special	1955	$150

JONES, JOE

ROULETTE

| ❏ R25143 [M] | You Talk Too Much | 1961 | $175 |
| ❏ SR25143 [R] | You Talk Too Much | 1961 | $150 |

JONES, JOHN PAUL

Also see LED ZEPPELIN.

COLUMBIA

| ❏ KC32047 | John Paul Jones | 1973 | $25 |

JONES, JONAH, AND EARL "FATHA" HINES

CHIAROSCURO

| ❏ 118 | Back on the Street | 1973 | $30 |

JONES, JONAH

ANGEL

| ❏ ANG.60005 [10] | Jonah Wails -- 1st Blast | 1954 | $175 |
| ❏ ANG.60006 [10] | Jonah Wails -- 2nd Blast | 1954 | $175 |

BETHLEHEM

| ❏ BCP-1014 [10] | Jonah Jones Sextet | 1954 | $300 |

Number	Title	Yr	NM
CAPITOL			
❏ T1948 [M]	And Now, In Person -- Jonah Jones	1963	$85
❏ ST1948 [S]	And Now, In Person -- Jonah Jones	1963	$100
❏ T1405 [M]	A Touch of Blue	1960	$100
❏ ST1405 [S]	A Touch of Blue	1960	$150
❏ T2087 [M]	Blowin' Up a Storm	1964	$85
❏ ST2087 [S]	Blowin' Up a Storm	1964	$100
❏ T1641 [M]	Broadway Swings Again	1961	$100
❏ ST1641 [S]	Broadway Swings Again	1961	$150
❏ T1557 [M]	Great Instrumental Hits Styled by Jonah Jones	1961	$100
❏ ST1557 [S]	Great Instrumental Hits Styled by Jonah Jones	1961	$150
❏ T1375 [M]	Hit Me Again!	1960	$100
❏ ST1375 [S]	Hit Me Again!	1960	$150
❏ T1193 [M]	I Dig Chicks	1959	$100
❏ ST1193 [S]	I Dig Chicks	1959	$150
❏ T1773 [M]	Jazz Bonus	1962	$85
❏ ST1773 [S]	Jazz Bonus	1962	$100
❏ T1660 [M]	Jonah Jones/Glenn Gray	1961	$100
❏ ST1660 [S]	Jonah Jones/Glenn Gray	1961	$150
❏ SM-1660	Jonah Jones/Glenn Gray	197?	$25
❏ T1115 [M]	Jonah Jumps Again	1959	$150
❏ ST1115 [S]	Jonah Jumps Again	1959	$150
❏ T1404 [M]	Jumpin' with a Shuffle	1960	$100
❏ ST1404 [S]	Jumpin' with a Shuffle	1960	$150
❏ T1039 [M]	Jumpin' with Jonah	1958	$150
❏ ST1039 [S]	Jumpin' with Jonah	1958	$150
❏ T839 [M]	Muted Jazz	1957	$85
❏ T1083 [M]	Swingin' at the Cinema	1958	$150
❏ ST1083 [S]	Swingin' at the Cinema	1958	$150
❏ T963 [M]	Swingin' On Broadway	1958	$85
❏ T1237 [M]	Swingin' 'Round the World	1959	$100
❏ ST1237 [S]	Swingin' 'Round the World	1959	$150
❏ T2594 [M]	The Best of Jonah Jones	1966	$85
❏ ST2594 [S]	The Best of Jonah Jones	1966	$75
❏ T1532 [M]	The Unsinkable Molly Brown	1961	$100
❏ ST1532 [S]	The Unsinkable Molly Brown	1961	$150
CIRCLE			
❏ CLP-83	1944: Butterflies in the Rain	198?	$25
DECCA			
❏ DL4638 [M]	Hello Broadway	1965	$30
❏ DL74638 [S]	Hello Broadway	1965	$35
❏ DL74918	Jazz Tropical!	1968	$30
❏ DL4688 [M]	On the Sunny Side of the Street	1966	$30
❏ DL74688 [S]	On the Sunny Side of the Street	1966	$35
❏ DL4800 [M]	Sweet with a Beat	1967	$35
❏ DL74800 [S]	Sweet with a Beat	1967	$30
❏ DL4765 [M]	Tijuana Taxi	1966	$30
❏ DL74765 [S]	Tijuana Taxi	1966	$35
GROOVE			
❏ LG-1001 [M]	Jonah Jones at the Embers	1956	$150
HALL OF FAME			
❏ 613	After Hours Jazz	198?	$25
JAZZ MAN			
❏ 5009	Confessin'	1981	$25
MOTOWN			
❏ M-683	Along Came Jonah	1969	$40
❏ M-690	Little Dis, Little Dat	1970	$40
PICKWICK			
❏ SPC-3008	Swing Along	196?	$30
RCA CAMDEN			
❏ CAS-2328	Jonah Jones Quartet	1969	$30
RCA VICTOR			
❏ LPM-2004 [M]	Jonah Jones at the Embers	1959	$40
— Reissue of Groove and Vik LP			
SWING			
❏ 8408	Paris 1954	198?	$25
VIK			
❏ LXA-1135 [M]	Jonah Jones at the Embers	1958	$40
— Reissue of Groove LP			

JONES, JONAH/CHARLIE SHAVERS

Number	Title	Yr	NM
BETHLEHEM			
❏ BCP-6034 [M]	Sounds of the Trumpets	1959	$250

JONES, LINDA

Number	Title	Yr	NM
LOMA			
❏ 5907	Hypnotized	1967	$30
TURBO			
❏ 7007	Your Precious Love	1972	$25

JONES, NORAH

Number	Title	Yr	NM
BLUE NOTE			
❏ BTE32088	Come Away with Me	2004	$20
— Standard-weight issue with lyrics on back cover; "Manufactured by Caroline Distribution" on back			
❏ BTE84800	Feels Like Home	2004	$20
— Standard-weight edition; "Manufactured by Caroline Distribution" on back cover			
CLASSICRECORDS.COM			
❏ JP-5004	Come Away with Me	2002	$30
— Audiophile pressing; heavyweight vinyl with gatefold cover			

JONES, ORAN "JUICE

Number	Title	Yr	NM
COLUMBIA			
❏ FC45321	To Be Immortal	1989	$12
DEF JAM			
❏ FC40955	G.T.O. Gangsters Takin' Over	1987	$18
❏ BFC40367	Juice	1986	$15

JONES, PAUL

Original lead singer for MANFRED MANN.

Number	Title	Yr	NM
CAPITOL			
❏ T2795 [M]	Paul Jones Sings Songs from the Film "Privilege" and Others	1967	$75
❏ ST2795 [S]	Paul Jones Sings Songs from the Film "Privilege" and Others	1967	$30
LONDON			
❏ XPS605	Crucifix in a Horseshoe	1971	$15

JONES, PHILLY JOE, AND ELVIN JONES

Number	Title	Yr	NM
ATLANTIC			
❏ 1428 [M]	Together	1964	$30
❏ SD1428 [S]	Together	1964	$30

JONES, PHILLY JOE

Number	Title	Yr	NM
ATLANTIC			
❏ 1340 [M]	Philly Joe's Beat	1960	$300
— Multicolor label, white "fan" logo on right			
❏ 1340 [M]	Philly Joe's Beat	1963	$35
— Multicolor label, black "fan" logo on right			
❏ SD1340 [S]	Philly Joe's Beat	1960	$300
— Multicolor label, white "fan" logo on right			
❏ SD1340 [S]	Philly Joe's Beat	1963	$35
— Multicolor label, black "fan" logo on right			
BLACK LION			
❏ 142	Trailways Express	197?	$30
FANTASY			
❏ OJC-230	Blues for Dracula	198?	$25
❏ OJC-484	Showcase	1991	$30
GALAXY			
❏ 5122	Advance!	1980	$30
❏ 5153	Drum Song	1985	$25
❏ 5112	Philly Mignon	1978	$30
RIVERSIDE			
❏ RLP 12-282 [M]	Blues for Dracula	1958	$300
❏ 6055	Blues for Dracula	197?	$35
❏ RLP 12-302 [M]	Drums Around the World	1959	$300
❏ RLP-1147 [S]	Drums Around the World	1959	$300
❏ RLP 12-313 [M]	Showcase	1959	$300
❏ RLP-1159 [S]	Showcase	1959	$300
❏ 6193	Showcase	198?	$30
UPTOWN			
❏ 2715	Look, Stop, Listen	198?	$30
❏ 2711	To Tadd with Love	198?	$30

JONES, QUINCY

Number	Title	Yr	NM
A&M			
❏ SP-3617	Body Heat	1974	$25
❏ QU-53617 [Q]	Body Heat	1974	$30
❏ SP-3191	Body Heat	1982	$20
— Budget-line reissue			
❏ SP-3030	Gula Matari	1970	$30
❏ SP-3705	I Heard That!!	1976	$30
❏ SP-6507	I Heard That!!	198?	$25
— Budget-line reissue			
❏ SP-4526	Mellow Madness	1975	$25
❏ QU-54526 [Q]	Mellow Madness	1975	$30
❏ SP-4626	Roots	1977	$25
❏ SP-3037	Smackwater Jack	1971	$30
❏ SP-4685	Sounds…And Stuff Like That!	1978	$25
❏ SP-3249	Sounds…And Stuff Like That!	198?	$20
— Budget-line reissue			
❏ SP-3200	The Best	1982	$20
❏ SP-3278	The Best, Vol. 2	1985	$20
❏ SP-3721	The Dude	1981	$25
❏ SP-3248	The Dude	198?	$20
— Budget-line reissue			
❏ SP-3023	Walking in Space	1969	$30
❏ SP-3041	You've Got It Bad Girl	1973	$30
❏ QU-53041 [Q]	You've Got It Bad Girl	1974	$30
ABC			
❏ D-782	Mode	1973	$30
ABC IMPULSE!			
❏ IA-9342	Quintessential Charts	1978	$30
❏ AS-11 [S]	The Quintessence	1968	$35
ABC-PARAMOUNT			
❏ 186 [M]	Go West, Man!	1957	$200
❏ 149 [M]	This Is How I Feel About Jazz	1956	$200
CHESS			
❏ CH-91562	The Music of Quincy Jones	198?	$25

Number	Title	Yr	NM
COLGEMS			
❏ COM-107 [M]	In Cold Blood	1967	$50
❏ COS-107 [S]	In Cold Blood	1967	$30
EMARCY			
❏ MG-36083 [M]	Jazz Abroad	1956	$250
❏ 818177-1	The Birth of a Band	1984	$30
GRP/IMPULSE!			
❏ 222	The Quintessence	199?	$35
— Reissue on audiophile vinyl			
IMPULSE!			
❏ A-11 [M]	The Quintessence	1962	$250
❏ AS-11 [S]	The Quintessence	1962	$250
LIBERTY			
❏ LOM-16004 [M]	Enter Laughing	1967	$75
❏ LOS-17004 [S]	Enter Laughing	1967	$75
MCA			
❏ 4145	Quintessential Charts	198?	$25
— Reissue of ABC Impulse 9342			
❏ 5578	The Slugger's Wife	1985	$30
MCA/IMPULSE!			
❏ 5728	The Quintessence	1986	$20
MERCURY			
❏ PPS-2014 [M]	Around the World	1961	$150
❏ PPS-6014 [S]	Around the World	1961	$150
❏ MG-20751 [M]	Big Band Bossa Nova	1962	$150
❏ SR-60751 [S]	Big Band Bossa Nova	1962	$150
❏ MG-20444 [M]	Birth of a Band	1959	$175
❏ SR-60129 [S]	Birth of a Band	1959	$250
❏ MG-20938 [M]	Golden Boy	1964	$150
❏ SR-60938 [S]	Golden Boy	1964	$150
❏ MG-20612 [M]	I Dig Dancers	1960	$150
❏ SR-60612 [S]	I Dig Dancers	1960	$175
❏ MG-21025 [M]	Mirage	1965	$150
❏ SR-61025 [S]	Mirage	1965	$150
❏ SRM-2-623	Nenda	1972	$35
❏ MG-20653 [M]	Quincy Jones at Newport '61	1961	$150
❏ SR-60653 [S]	Quincy Jones at Newport '61	1961	$150
❏ MG-20863 [M]	Quincy Jones Explores the Music of Henry Mancini	1964	$150
❏ SR-60863 [S]	Quincy Jones Explores the Music of Henry Mancini	1964	$150
❏ MG-21050 [M]	Quincy Jones Plays for Pussycats	1965	$150
❏ SR-61050 [S]	Quincy Jones Plays for Pussycats	1965	$150
❏ MG-20799 [M]	Quincy Jones Plays Hip Hits	1963	$150
❏ SR-60799 [S]	Quincy Jones Plays Hip Hits	1963	$150
❏ MG-21063 [M]	Quincy's Got a Brand New Bag	1965	$150
❏ SR-61063 [S]	Quincy's Got a Brand New Bag	1965	$150
❏ MG-21070 [M]	Slender Thread	1966	$150
❏ SR-61070 [S]	Slender Thread	1966	$150
❏ MG-20561 [M]	The Great, Wide World of Quincy Jones	1960	$175
❏ SR-60221 [S]	The Great, Wide World of Quincy Jones	1960	$250
❏ MG-21011 [M]	The Pawnbroker	1964	$150
❏ SR-61011 [S]	The Pawnbroker	1964	$150
MOBILE FIDELITY			
❏ Jan-0078	You've Got It Bad Girl	1981	$75
— Audiophile vinyl			
NAUTILUS			
❏ NR-52	The Dude	198?	$40
— Audiophile vinyl			
PRESTIGE			
❏ PRLP-172 [10]	Quincy Jones with the Swedish-American All Stars	1953	$300
QWEST			
❏ 26020	Back on the Block	1989	$30
❏ 25356	The Color Purple	1985	$50
— Boxed set on purple vinyl			
❏ 25389	The Color Purple	1985	$35
— Gatefold package on purple vinyl			
TRIP			
❏ 5554	Live at Newport '61	197?	$20
❏ 5514	The Great Wide World of Quincy Jones	1974	$20
UNITED ARTISTS			
❏ UAS-5214	They Call Me Mister Tibbs	1970	$75
WING			
❏ SRW-16398	Around the World	1969	$30

JONES, RICHARD

Number	Title	Yr	NM
PAX			
❏ 6010 [10]	New Orleans Style	1954	$100
RIVERSIDE			
❏ RLP-1017 [10]	Richard P. Jones and Clarence Williams	1953	$100

JONES, RICHARD M.

Number	Title	Yr	NM
FOLKWAYS			
❏ FJ-2817	Chicago Dixieland in the Forties	198?	$30

Number	Title	Yr	NM

JONES, RICKIE LEE
GEFFEN
| ❏ GHS24246 | Flying Cowboys | 1989 | $12 |

MOBILE FIDELITY
| ❏ Jan-0089 | Rickie Lee Jones | 1982 | $250 |

—Audiophile vinyl
| ❏ MFSL2-45010 [B] | Rickie Lee Jones | 2013 | $75 |

WARNER BROS.
| ❏ 23805 [10] | Girl at Her Volcano | 1983 | $10 |
| ❏ 23805 [10] | Girl at Her Volcano | 1983 | $18 |

—Promo-only version on Quiex II vinyl
❏ BSK3432	Pirates	1981	$10
❏ BSK3296	Rickie Lee Jones	1979	$10
❏ 25117	The Magazine	1984	$10

JONES, RODNEY
TIMELESS
| ❏ 323 | Articulation | 1979 | $30 |

JONES, RUFUS
CAMEO
| ❏ C-1076 [M] | Five on Eight | 1964 | $30 |
| ❏ SC-1076 [S] | Five on Eight | 1964 | $30 |

JONES, SAM
FANTASY
| ❏ OJC-6008 | Right Down in Front | 198? | $25 |

INTERPLAY
| ❏ 7720 | The Bassist | 1979 | $30 |

MUSE
| ❏ MR-5149 | Something in Common | 1977 | $35 |

RIVERSIDE
❏ RLP-432 [M]	Down Home	1962	$250
❏ RS-9432 [S]	Down Home	1962	$250
❏ 6079	Soul Society	197?	$35
❏ RLP-358 [M]	The Chant!	1961	$250
❏ RS-9358 [S]	The Chant!	1961	$250
❏ RLP 12-324 [M]	The Soul Society	1960	$250
❏ RLP-1172 [S]	The Soul Society	1960	$250

SEA BREEZE
| ❏ 2004 | Something New | 1979 | $30 |

STEEPLECHASE
| ❏ SCS-1097 | Visitation | 198? | $30 |

XANADU
| ❏ 129 | Cello Again | 197? | $30 |
| ❏ 150 | Changes and Things | 1978 | $30 |

JONES, SPIKE, AND THE CITY SLICKERS
CORNOGRAPHIC
| ❏ 1001 | King of Corn | 197? | $25 |

GOLDBERG & O'REILY
| ❏ MF205/4 | The Craziest Show on Earth | 1977 | $50 |

—Collection of radio show performances

HINDSIGHT
| ❏ HSR-185 | The Uncollected Spike Jones 1946 | 198? | $25 |

LIBERTY
❏ LRP-3154 [M]	60 Years of Music America Hates Best	1960	$150
❏ LST-7154 [S]	60 Years of Music America Hates Best	1960	$175
❏ LRP-3370 [M]	My Man	1964	$50
❏ LST-7370 [S]	My Man	1964	$75
❏ LRP-3140 [M]	Omnibust	1959	$150
❏ LST-7140 [S]	Omnibust	1959	$175

—Black vinyl
| ❏ LST-7140 [S] | Omnibust | 1959 | $175 |

—Red vinyl
❏ LRP-3349 [M]	Spike Jones' New Band	1964	$75
❏ LST-7349 [S]	Spike Jones' New Band	1964	$40
❏ LRP-3401 [M]	Spike Jones Plays Hank Williams Hits	1965	$50
❏ LST-7401 [S]	Spike Jones Plays Hank Williams Hits	1965	$75
❏ LRP-3338 [M]	Washington Square	1963	$50
❏ LST-7338 [S]	Washington Square	1963	$75

RCA GOLD SEAL
| ❏ AGL1-4142 | Spike Jones Is Murdering the Classics! | 1982 | $20 |

—Reissue

RCA RED SEAL
| ❏ LSC-3235 [R] | Spike Jones Is Murdering the Classics! | 1971 | $50 |

RCA VICTOR
❏ LPM-3054 [10]	Bottoms Up	1952	$250
❏ LPM-3128 [10]	Spike Jones Murders Carmen and Kids the Classics	1953	$250
❏ LPT-18 [10]	Spike Jones Plays the Charleston	1952	$250
❏ LPM-2224 [M]	Thank You Music Lovers	1960	$150

—"RCA Victor" in silver above dog, "Long 33 1/3 Play" at bottom of label
| ❏ LPM-2224 [M] | Thank You Music Lovers | 1965 | $75 |

—"RCA Victor" in white above dog, "Monaural" at bottom of

❏ LPM-3849 [M]	The Best of Spike Jones	1967	$75
❏ LSP-3849 [R]	The Best of Spike Jones	1967	$50
❏ ANL1-1035	The Best of Spike Jones	1975	$25

—Reissue
| ❏ AYL1-3748 | The Best of Spike Jones, Volume 1 | 1980 | $20 |

—Best Buy Series" reissue
| ❏ AYL1-3870 | The Best of Spike Jones, Volume 2 | 1981 | $20 |

—Best Buy Series" reissue
| ❏ ANL1-2312 | The Best of Spike Jones, Volume 2 | 1977 | $25 |

—Reissue

RHINO
| ❏ R170261 | Dinner Music...For People Who Aren't Very Hungry | 1988 | $30 |
| ❏ R170196 | It's a Spike Jones Christmas | 1988 | $30 |

UNITED ARTISTS
| ❏ UA-LA439-E | The Very Best of Spike Jones | 1975 | $30 |

VERVE
❏ MGV-4005 [M]	Dinner Music...For People Who Aren't Very Hungry	1957	$175
❏ V-4005 [M]	Dinner Music...For People Who Aren't Very Hungry	1961	$75
❏ MGV-2021 [M]	Let's Sing a Song for Christmas	1956	$250
❏ V-2021 [M]	Let's Sing a Song for Christmas	1961	$75

WARNER BROS.
| ❏ W1332 [M] | Spike Jones in Hi-Fi | 1959 | $40 |
| ❏ WS1332 [S] | Spike Jones in Hi-Fi | 1959 | $150 |

— This is the title on the front of the LP cover, but the spine says "Spike Jones in Stereo

JONES, STAN
BUENA VISTA
| ❏ BV-3306 [M] | Ghost Riders in the Sky | 1961 | $30 |

—Reissue of Disneyland WDL-3015

DISNEYLAND
| ❏ WDL-3015 [M] | Creakin' Leather | 1958 | $40 |
| ❏ WDL-1005 [M] | Songs of the National Parks | 1958 | $40 |

— Sold only at national parks
| ❏ WDL-3033 [M] | This Was the West – The Story and the Songs | 1958 | $40 |

JONES, TAMIKO
A&M
| ❏ SP-3011 | I'll Be Anything for You | 1969 | $75 |

ARISTA
| ❏ AL-4040 | Love Trip | 1975 | $75 |

DECEMBER
| ❏ DR-8500 | Tamiko | 1968 | $75 |

METROMEDIA
| ❏ MD1030 | Tamiko Jones in Muscle Shoals | 1970 | $75 |

JONES, THAD, AND MEL LEWIS
ARTISTS HOUSE
| ❏ 3 | Quartet | 1980 | $30 |

BLUE NOTE
❏ BST-84346	Consummation	1970	$30
❏ BN-LA392-H [(2)]	Thad Jones/Mel Lewis	1975	$35
❏ BST-89905	The Jazz Wave Ltd. On Tour (Volume 1)	1970	$30

HORIZON
❏ SP-724	Live in Munich	1978	$30
❏ SP-707	New Life	1976	$30
❏ SP-701	Suite for Pops	1975	$30

MOSAIC
| ❏ MQ7-151 | The Complete Solid State Recordings of the Thad Jones-Mel Lewis Orchestra | 199? | $175 |

PAUSA
| ❏ 7012 | Thad Jones-Mel Lewis Orchestra and Manuel De Sica | 198? | $25 |

PHILADELPHIA INT'L.
| ❏ KZ33152 [B] | Potpourri | 1974 | $175 |

RCA VICTOR
| ❏ AFL1-3423 | Thad Jones/Mel Lewis and Umo | 1980 | $50 |

SOLID STATE
❏ SS-18058	Central Park North	1969	$35
❏ SM-17016 [M]	Live at the Village Vanguard	1967	$40
❏ SS-18016 [S]	Live at the Village Vanguard	1967	$40
❏ SS-18048	Monday Night	1969	$35
❏ SM-17003 [M]	Presenting Thad Jones, Mel Lewis and the Jazz Orchestra	1966	$25
❏ SS-18003 [S]	Presenting Thad Jones, Mel Lewis and the Jazz Orchestra	1966	$25
❏ SS-18041	Thad Jones and Mel Lewis Featuring Miss Ruth Brown	1968	$35

JONES, THAD, AND PEPPER ADAMS
MILESTONE
| ❏ MLP-1001 [M] | Mean What You Say | 1966 | $175 |
| ❏ MSP-9001 [S] | Mean What You Say | 1966 | $75 |

JONES, THAD
BIOGRAPH
| ❏ 12059 | Greetings and Salutations | 197? | $30 |

BLUE NOTE
| ❏ BLP-1513 [M] | Detroit-New York Junction | 1956 | $1500 |

—Deep groove" version; Lexington Ave. address on label
| ❏ BLP-1513 [M] | Detroit-New York Junction | 1958 | $1500 |

—Deep groove" version, W. 63rd St. address on label
| ❏ BLP-1513 [M] | Detroit-New York Junction | 1963 | $500 |

— With "New York, USA" address on label
| ❏ BST-81513 [R] | Detroit-New York Junction | 1967 | $50 |

— With "A Division of Liberty Records" on label
| ❏ BLP-1527 [M] | The Magnificent Thad Jones | 1956 | $1000 |

—Deep groove" version; Lexington Ave. address on label
| ❏ BLP-1527 [M] | The Magnificent Thad Jones | 1956 | $750 |

—Deep groove" version, W. 63rd St. address on label
| ❏ BLP-1527 [M] | The Magnificent Thad Jones | 1963 | $150 |

— With "New York, USA" address on label
| ❏ BST-81527 [R] | The Magnificent Thad Jones | 1967 | $50 |

— With "A Division of Liberty Records" on label
| ❏ BLP-1546 [M] | The Magnificent Thad Jones, Volume 3 | 1957 | $800 |

—Deep groove" version; W. 63rd St. address on label
| ❏ BLP-1546 [M] | The Magnificent Thad Jones, Volume 3 | 1957 | $400 |

—Regular version, W. 63rd St., NY address on label
| ❏ BLP-1546 [M] | The Magnificent Thad Jones, Volume 3 | 1963 | $175 |

— With "New York, USA" address on label
| ❏ BST-81546 [R] | The Magnificent Thad Jones, Volume 3 | 1967 | $50 |

— With "A Division of Liberty Records" on label

DEBUT
❏ DLP-17 [10]	Jazz Collaborations	1954	$600
❏ DEB-127 [M]	Thad Jones	1958	$400
❏ DLP-12 [10]	The Fabulous Thad Jones	1954	$600

FANTASY
| ❏ 6004 [M] | The Fabulous Thad Jones | 1962 | $50 |

—Red vinyl
| ❏ 6004 [M] | The Fabulous Thad Jones | 1962 | $30 |

—Black vinyl
| ❏ 86004 [R] | The Fabulous Thad Jones | 1962 | $30 |

—Blue vinyl
| ❏ 86004 [R] | The Fabulous Thad Jones | 1962 | $35 |

—Black vinyl
| ❏ OJC-625 | The Fabulous Thad Jones | 1991 | $35 |

MOSAIC
| ❏ MQ5-172 | The Complete Blue Note/ UA/Roulette Recordings of Thad Jones | 199? | $150 |

PERIOD
| ❏ SPL-1208 [M] | Mad Thad | 1956 | $650 |

PRESTIGE
| ❏ PRLP-7118 [M] | After Hours | 1957 | $400 |

— Yellow label with W. 50th St. address
| ❏ P-24017 | After Hours | 197? | $50 |
| ❏ MPP-2506 | Thad Jones and Charles Mingus | 1980 | $35 |

STEEPLECHASE
| ❏ SCS-1197 | Three and One | 198? | $30 |

UNITED ARTISTS
| ❏ UAL-4025 [M] | Motor City Scene | 1959 | $500 |

—red label
| ❏ UAS-5025 [S] | Motor City Scene | 1959 | $75 |

JONES, TOM
EPIC
❏ PE34383	Classic Tom Jones	1976	$15
❏ PE34468	Say You'll Stay Until Tomorrow	1977	$15
❏ PE34720	Tom Is Love	1977	$12
❏ JE35023	What a Night	1978	$12

JIVE
| ❏ 1214-1-J | Move Closer | 1989 | $15 |

LONDON
❏ PS717	The Country Side of Tom Jones	1978	$12
❏ 820234-1	This Is Tom Jones	1985	$10
❏ LC-50002	Tom Jones' Greatest Hits	1977	$15
❏ 820319-1	Tom Jones' Greatest Hits	1985	$12

MCA
| ❏ 37114 | Rescue Me | 1980 | $10 |
| ❏ 3182 | Tom Jones | 1979 | $12 |

MERCURY
❏ SRM-1-4010	Darlin'	1981	$12
❏ 814448-1	Don't Let Our Dreams Die Young	1983	$12
❏ 822701-1	Love Is on the Radio	1984	$12
❏ 826140-1	Tender Loving Care	1985	$12

Number	Title	Yr	NM
❏ 830409-1	Things That Matter Most to Me	1987	$12
❏ SRM-1-4062	Tom Jones Country	1982	$12

PARROT

Number	Title	Yr	NM
❏ PA61007 [M]	A-Tom-Ic Jones	1966	$18
❏ PAS71007 [S]	A-Tom-Ic Jones	1966	$18
❏ XPAS71055	Close Up	1972	$15
❏ PA61011 [M]	Funny Familiar Forgotten Feelings	1967	$25
❏ PAS71011 [S]	Funny Familiar Forgotten Feelings	1967	$18
❏ PA61009 [M]	Green, Green Grass of Home	1967	$18
❏ PAS71009 [S]	Green, Green Grass of Home	1967	$18
❏ PAS71025	Help Yourself	1969	$15
❏ PA61004 [M]	It's Not Unusual	1965	$18
❏ PAS71004 [S]	It's Not Unusual	1965	$18
❏ PAS71039	I (Who Have Nothing)	1970	$15
❏ 2XPAS71049/50	Live at Caesar's Palace	1971	$15
❏ PAS71031	Live in Las Vegas	1969	$15
❏ PAS71068	Memories Don't Leave Like People Do	197?	$15
❏ PAS71046	She's a Lady	1971	$15
❏ PAS71066	Somethin' 'Bout You Baby I Like	1974	$15
❏ XPAS-1 [DJ]	Special Tom Jones Interview	1970	$150
—Promo-only open-end interview with gatefold cover and script			
❏ XPAS71060	The Body and Soul of Tom Jones	197?	$15
❏ PAS71019	The Tom Jones Fever Zone	1968	$15
❏ PAS71028	This Is Tom Jones	1969	$15
❏ ST-92025	This Is Tom Jones	1969	$18
—Capitol Record Club edition			
❏ PAS71037	Tom	1970	$15
❏ SW-93186	Tom	197?	$18
—Capitol Record Club edition			
❏ XPAS71062	Tom Jones' Greatest Hits	1973	$15
❏ PAS71014 [S]	Tom Jones Live	1967	$18
❏ PA61014 [M]	Tom Jones Live	1967	$18
❏ PA61006 [M]	What's New Pussycat?	1965	$18

Number	Title	Yr	NM
❏ PAS71006 [S]	What's New Pussycat?	1965	$18

JONES BOYS, THE

MUSICOR

Number	Title	Yr	NM
❏ MM-2017 [M]	Country and Western Songbook	1964	$30
❏ MS-3017 [S]	Country and Western Songbook	1964	$30
❏ MS-3182	My Boys, the Jones Boys	1970	$25

JONES BOYS, THE (2)
A collaboration of unrelated musicians, all with the last name of Jones: Eddie, Jimmy, Jo, Quincy, Renauld and Thad.

PERIOD

Number	Title	Yr	NM
❏ SPL-1210 [M]	The Jones Bash	1954	$100

JONES BROTHERS, THE

METROJAZZ

Number	Title	Yr	NM
❏ E-1003 [M]	Keepin' Up with the Joneses	1958	$120
❏ SE-1003 [S]	Keepin' Up with the Joneses	1958	$120

JOOK, THE

SING SING

Number	Title	Yr	NM
❏ SING053 [B]	The Jook	2013	$25
—featuring members of John's Children, Sparks, Jet			

JOPLIN, JANIS
Also see BIG BROTHER AND THE HOLDING COMPANY.

COLUMBIA

Number	Title	Yr	NM
❏ AS1377 [DJ]	A Collection	1982	$25
❏ PC37569	Farewell Song	1982	$12
❏ KCS9913 [B]	I Got Dem Ol' Kozmik Blues Again Mama!	1969	$30
—360 Sound Stereo" on label			
❏ KCS9913	I Got Dem Ol' Kozmik Blues Again Mama!	1970	$15
—Orange label			
❏ PC9913	I Got Dem Ol' Kozmik Blues Again Mama!	198?	$10
—Budget-line reissue			
❏ PG33345 [B]	Janis	1975	$18
❏ CG33345	Janis	198?	$15
❏ KC32168	Janis Joplin's Greatest Hits	1973	$18
❏ PC32168	Janis Joplin's Greatest Hits	197?	$10
❏ C2X31160 [B]	Joplin in Concert	1972	$30
❏ CG31160	Joplin in Concert	198?	$15
❏ KC30322	Pearl	1971	$18
❏ PC30322	Pearl	1975	$15
—Reissue without bar code			
❏ CQ30322 [Q]	Pearl	1974	$50
❏ PC30322	Pearl	198?	$10
—Reissue with bar code			

COLUMBIA SPECIAL PRODUCTS

Number	Title	Yr	NM
❏ 2P13792	The Greatest Hits of Janis Joplin	1977	$25

JOPLIN, SCOTT

BIOGRAPH

Number	Title	Yr	NM
❏ 1008	Ragtime, Vol. 2	197?	$25
❏ 1010	Ragtime, Vol. 3	197?	$25
❏ 1006	Scott Joplin 1916: Classic Solos	197?	$25

JORDAN, CLIFFORD

ATLANTIC

Number	Title	Yr	NM
❏ 1444 [M]	These Are My Roots	1965	$30
❏ SD1444 [S]	These Are My Roots	1965	$30

BEE HIVE

Number	Title	Yr	NM
❏ BH-7018	Dr. Chicago	1986	$25

BLUE NOTE

Number	Title	Yr	NM
❏ BLP-1549 [M]	Blowing In from Chicago	1957	$250
—Deep groove" version (deep indentation under label on both sides)			
❏ BLP-1549 [M]	Blowing In from Chicago	1957	$800
—Regular version, W. 63rd St., NY address on label			
❏ BLP-1549 [M]	Blowing In from Chicago	1963	$175
—With "New York, USA" address on label			
❏ BST-81549 [R]	Blowing In from Chicago	1967	$30
—With "A Division of Liberty Records" on label			
❏ BLP-1582 [M]	Cliff Craft	1958	$3000
—Deep groove" version (deep indentation under label on both sides)			
❏ BLP-1582 [M]	Cliff Craft	1958	$600
—Regular version, W. 63rd St., NY address on label			
❏ BLP-1582 [M]	Cliff Craft	1963	$175
—With "New York, USA" address on label			
❏ BST-1582 [S]	Cliff Craft	1959	$350
—Deep groove" version (deep indentation under label on both sides)			
❏ BST-1582 [S]	Cliff Craft	1959	$250
—Regular version, W. 63rd St., NY address on label			
❏ BST-1582 [S]	Cliff Craft	1963	$150
—With "New York, USA" address on label			
❏ BST-81582 [S]	Cliff Craft	1967	$35
—With "A Division of Liberty Records" on label			
❏ BST-81582 [S]	Cliff Craft	199?	$30
—Classic Records reissue on audiophile vinyl			
❏ BLP-1565 [M]	Clifford Jordan	1957	$800
—Deep groove" version (deep indentation under label on both sides)			
❏ BLP-1565 [M]	Clifford Jordan	1957	$175
—Regular version, W. 63rd St., NY address on label			
❏ BLP-1565 [M]	Clifford Jordan	1963	$75
—With "New York, USA" address on label			
❏ BST-1565 [S]	Clifford Jordan	1959	$800
—Deep groove" version (deep indentation under label on both sides)			
❏ BST-1565 [S]	Clifford Jordan	1959	$75
—Regular version, W. 63rd St., NY address on label			
❏ BST-1565 [S]	Clifford Jordan	1963	$25
—With "New York, USA" address on label			
❏ BST-81565 [S]	Clifford Jordan	1967	$35
—With "A Division of Liberty Records" on label			

FANTASY

Number	Title	Yr	NM
❏ OJC-494	Bearcat	1991	$35
❏ OJC-147	Starting Time	198?	$25

INNER CITY

Number	Title	Yr	NM
❏ IC-2033	Firm Roots	197?	$35
❏ IC-2047	The Highest Mountain	197?	$35

JAZZLAND

Number	Title	Yr	NM
❏ JLP-40 [M]	A Story Tale	1961	$30
❏ JLP-940 [S]	A Story Tale	1961	$40
❏ JLP-69 [M]	Bearcat	1962	$30
❏ JLP-969 [S]	Bearcat	1962	$40
❏ JLP-52 [M]	Starting Time	1961	$30
❏ JLP-952 [S]	Starting Time	1961	$40

MUSE

Number	Title	Yr	NM
❏ MR-5128	Inward Fire	197?	$30
❏ MR-5076	Night of the Mark VII	197?	$30

Number	Title	Yr	NM
❏ MR-5105	Remembering Me-Me	197?	$30
❏ MR-5163	The Adventurer	197?	$30

RIVERSIDE

Number	Title	Yr	NM
❏ RLP-340 [M]	Spellbound	1960	$250
❏ RS-9340 [S]	Spellbound	1960	$250

SOUL NOTE

Number	Title	Yr	NM
❏ SN-1084	Repetition	1984	$30

STEEPLECHASE

Number	Title	Yr	NM
❏ SCS-1033	Film Roots	198?	$30
❏ SCS-1198	Half Note	198?	$30
❏ SCS-1071	On Stage, Volume 1	197?	$30
❏ SCS-1092	On Stage, Volume 2	198?	$30
❏ SCS-1104	On Stage, Volume 3	198?	$30
❏ SCS-1047	The Highest Mountain	198?	$30

STRATA-EAST

Number	Title	Yr	NM
❏ SES19737/8	Glass Bead Games	1974	$30
❏ SES1972-1	In the World	1972	$25

VORTEX

Number	Title	Yr	NM
❏ 2010	Soul Fountain	1970	$25

JORDAN, DUKE

BLUE NOTE

Number	Title	Yr	NM
❏ BLP-4046 [M]	Flight to Jordan	1960	$500
—With W. 63rd St., NY address on label			
❏ BLP-4046 [M]	Flight to Jordan	1963	$75
—With "New York, USA" address on label			
❏ BST-84046 [S]	Flight to Jordan	1960	$75
—With W. 63rd St., NY address on label			
❏ BST-84046 [S]	Flight to Jordan	1963	$25
—With "New York, USA" address on label			
❏ BST-84046 [S]	Flight to Jordan	1967	$35
—With "A Division of Liberty Records" on label			

CHARLIE PARKER

Number	Title	Yr	NM
❏ PLP-805 [M]	East and West of Jazz	1962	$250
❏ PLP-805S [S]	East and West of Jazz	1962	$250

INNER CITY

Number	Title	Yr	NM
❏ IC-2046	Duke's Delight	197?	$35
❏ IC-2011	Flight to Denmark	197?	$35
❏ IC-2024	Two Loves	197?	$35

NEW JAZZ

Number	Title	Yr	NM
❏ NJ-810 [10]	Jordu	195?	$250

PRESTIGE

Number	Title	Yr	NM
❏ PRST-7849	Jordu	1970	$30

SAVOY

Number	Title	Yr	NM
❏ MG-12149 [M]	Duke Jordan	1959	$100

SAVOY JAZZ

Number	Title	Yr	NM
❏ SJL-1169	Flight to Jordan	1986	$25

SIGNAL

Number	Title	Yr	NM
❏ S-1202 [M]	Duke Jordan	1955	$300

STEEPLECHASE

Number	Title	Yr	NM
❏ SCS-1135	Change of Pace	1979	$30
❏ SCS-1103	Duke's Artistry	1978	$30
❏ SCS-1046	Duke's Delight	198?	$30
❏ SCS-1011	Flight to Denmark	198?	$30
❏ SCS-1088	Flight to Japan	198?	$30
❏ SCS-1150	Great Session	198?	$30
❏ SCS-1063/4	Live in Japan	198?	$35
❏ SCS-1127	Lover Man	198?	$30
❏ SCS-1143	Midnight Moonlight	198?	$30
❏ SCS-1053	Misty Thursday	198?	$30
❏ SCS-1165	Thinking of You	198?	$30
❏ SCS-1189	Tivol One	198?	$30
❏ SCS-1193	Tivol Two	198?	$30
❏ SCS-1175	Truth	198?	$30
❏ SCS-1024	Two Loves	198?	$30
❏ SCS-1211	Wait and See	198?	$30

JORDAN, DUKE/HALL OVERTON

SAVOY

Number	Title	Yr	NM
❏ MG-12145 [M]	Do It Yourself Jazz	1959	$150
❏ MG-12146 [M]	Jazz Laboratory Series	1959	$150

SIGNAL

Number	Title	Yr	NM
❏ S-101/2 [M]	Jazz Laboratory Series	1955	$300
—Deduct 20 percent if book is missing			

JORDAN, JERRY

MCA

Number	Title	Yr	NM
❏ 2174	Don't Call Me... I'll Call You	1976	$12
❏ 473	Phone Call from God	1975	$12

JORDAN, KENT

COLUMBIA

Number	Title	Yr	NM
❏ FC39325	No Question About It	1984	$25

JORDAN, KING

CORAL

Number	Title	Yr	NM
❏ CRL57372 [M]	Phantom Guitar	1962	$25
❏ CRL757372 [S]	Phantom Guitar	1962	$30

JORDAN, LOUIS

CIRCLE

Number	Title	Yr	NM
❏ 53	Louis Jordan and the Tympany Five: 1944-45	198?	$12

Number	Title	Yr	NM
❑ 97	More Louis Jordan and His Tympany Five	198?	$12
CLASSIC JAZZ			
❑ 148	I Believe in Music	198?	$15
DECCA			
❑ DL5035 [M]	Greatest Hits	1968	$30
❑ DL7035 [R]	Greatest Hits	1968	$20
❑ DL8551 [M]	Let the Good Times Roll	1958	$150
—Black label, silver print			
MCA			
❑ 274	Greatest Hits	197?	$12
❑ 1337	Greatest Hits, Vol. 2	1980	$12
❑ 4079	The Best of Louis Jordan	197?	$15
MERCURY			
❑ MG-20331 [M]	Man, We're Wailin'	1958	$250
❑ MG-20242 [M]	Somebody Up There Digs Me	1957	$250
SCORE			
❑ SLP-4007 [M]	Go Blow Your Horn	1957	$250
TANGERINE			
❑ 1503 [M]	Hallelujah	1964	$25
❑ S-1503 [S]	Hallelujah	1964	$30
WING			
❑ MGW-12126 [M]	Somebody Up There Digs Me	1962	$30

JORDAN, SHEILA

Number	Title	Yr	NM
BLACKHAWK			
❑ BKH-50501	The Crossing	1986	$25
BLUE NOTE			
❑ BLP-9002 [M]	Portrait of Sheila Jordan	1962	$175
—With W. 63rd St., NY address on label			
❑ BLP-9002 [M]	Portrait of Sheila Jordan	1963	$75
—With "New York, USA" address on label			
❑ BST-89002 [R]	Portrait of Sheila Jordan	1967	$30
—With "A Division of Liberty Records" on label			
MUSE			
❑ MR-5390	Lost and Found	1990	$35
❑ MR-5366	Old Time Feeling	1989	$30
PALO ALTO			
❑ PA-8038	Old Time Feeling	1982	$30
STEEPLECHASE			
❑ SCS-1081	Sheila	1978	$30
WAVE			
❑ W-1 [M]	Looking Out	1961	$75
❑ WS-1 [S]	Looking Out	1961	$100

JORDAN, STANLEY

Number	Title	Yr	NM
BLUE NOTE			
❑ B1-92356	Cornucopia	1990	$35
❑ BT-85101	Magic Touch	1985	$25
❑ BT-85130	Standards Volume 1	1986	$25
❑ SPRO-9434/5 [DJ]	Stanley Jordan	1985	$50
—Promo-only live recordings			
EMI MANHATTAN			
❑ E1-48682	Flying Home	1988	$25
TANGENT			
❑ 1001	Touch Sensitive	1982	$200

JORDAN, TAFT

Number	Title	Yr	NM
MERCURY			
❑ MG-20429 [M]	The Moods of Taft Jordan	1959	$150
❑ SR-60101 [S]	The Moods of Taft Jordan	1959	$150
MOODSVILLE			
❑ MVLP-21 [M]	Mood Indigo -- Taft Jordan Plays Duke Ellington	1961	$50
—Green label			
❑ MVLP-21 [M]	Mood Indigo -- Taft Jordan Plays Duke Ellington	1965	$30
—Blue label, trident logo at right			
STATUS			
❑ 21 [M]	Mood Indigo -- Taft Jordan Plays Duke Ellington	196?	$30
—Reissue of Moodsville 21			

JORDAN BROTHERS, THE

Number	Title	Yr	NM
JBP			
❑ ASM-416	Today's Yesterdays Volume 1	1980	$30

JORDANAIRES, THE

Number	Title	Yr	NM
CAPITOL			
❑ T1167 [M]	Gloryland	1959	$75
❑ T1011 [M]	Heavenly Spirit	1958	$75
❑ T1311 [M]	Land of Jordan	1960	$75
❑ ST1311 [S]	Land of Jordan	1960	$75
❑ T1742 [M]	Spotlight on the Jordanaires	1962	$50
❑ ST1742 [S]	Spotlight on the Jordanaires	1962	$50
❑ T1559 [M]	To God Be the Glory	1961	$50
❑ ST1559 [S]	To God Be the Glory	1961	$50

Number	Title	Yr	NM
CLASSIC			
❑ CCR1935	Christmas to Elvis from the Jordanaires	1978	$15
COLUMBIA			
❑ CL2458 [M]	The Big Country Hits	1966	$25
❑ CS9258 [S]	The Big Country Hits	1966	$30
❑ CL2214 [M]	This Land	1964	$25
❑ CS9014 [S]	This Land	1964	$30
DECCA			
❑ DL8681 [M]	Peace in the Valley	1957	$50
RCA VICTOR			
❑ LPM-3081 [10]	Beautiful City	1953	$150
SESAC			
❑ 1401/2 [M]	Of Rivers and Plains	195?	$100

JORGENSMANN, THEO

Number	Title	Yr	NM
CMP			
❑ CMP-4-ST	Go Ahead Clarinet	198?	$25
❑ CMP-19-ST	Laterna Magica	198?	$25
❑ CMP-15-ST	Next Adventure	198?	$25
❑ CMP-6-ST	Song of BoWaGe	198?	$25

JORGENSON, CHRISTINE

Number	Title	Yr	NM
J RECORDS			
❑ J-1 [M]	Christine Jorgenson Reveals	1958	$50

JOSEFUS

Number	Title	Yr	NM
HOOKAH			
❑ 330	Dead Man	1969	$300
MAINSTREAM			
❑ S-6127	Josefus	1970	$150

JOSEPH, MARGIE

Number	Title	Yr	NM
ATLANTIC			
❑ SD19182	Feeling My Way	1978	$25
❑ SD18126	Margie	1975	$25
❑ SD7248	Margie Joseph	1973	$30
❑ SD7277	Sweet Surrender	1974	$25
COTILLION			
❑ SD9906	Hear the Words, Feel the Feeling	1976	$30
❑ 90158	Ready for the Night	1984	$18
H.C.R.C.			
❑ HLP-20009	Knockout	1983	$15
ICHIBAN			
❑ 1027	Stay	1988	$18
VOLT			
❑ VOS-6012	Margie Joseph Makes a New Impression	1971	$30
❑ VOS-6016	Phase II	1971	$30

JOSEPH

Number	Title	Yr	NM
SCEPTER			
❑ SRS-674 [B]	Stoned Age Man	1970	$150

JOSHUA FOX

Number	Title	Yr	NM
TETRAGRAMMATON			
❑ T-125	Joshua Fox	1969	$30

JOSIE AND THE PUSSYCATS

Number	Title	Yr	NM
CAPITOL			
❑ ST-665	Josie and the Pussycats	1970	$250

JOURNEY

Original lead singer Gregg Rolie was also the original lead singer of SANTANA.
Also see STEVE PERRY.

Number	Title	Yr	NM
COLUMBIA			
❑ AS1606 [DJ]	A Candid Conversation with Journey	1983	$30
—Promo-only interview and songs LP			
❑ KC237016 [B]	Captured	1981	$15
❑ FC36339	Departure	1980	$10
❑ HC46339 [B]	Departure	1980	$30
—Half-speed mastered edition			
❑ HC47998 [B]	Dream After Dream	1982	$35
—Half-speed mastered edition			
❑ FC37998	Dream After Dream	1982	$15
❑ PC37998	Dream After Dream	1986	$10
—Budget-line reissue			
❑ TC37408	Escape	1981	$10
❑ HC47408 [B]	Escape	1982	$30
—Half-speed mastered edition			
❑ FC35797	Evolution	1979	$10
❑ PC35797	Evolution	1985	$10
—Budget-line reissue			
❑ QC38504	Frontiers	1983	$10
❑ HC48504 [B]	Frontiers	1983	$35
—Half-speed mastered edition			
❑ OC44493	Greatest Hits	1988	$12
❑ JC34912	Infinity	1978	$12
—No bar code on cover			
❑ HC44912 [B]	Infinity	1982	$35

Number	Title	Yr	NM
—Half-speed mastered edition			
❑ JC34912	Infinity	1979	$10
—With bar code on cover			
❑ C236324 [B]	In the Beginning	1979	$15
❑ PC33388	Journey	1975	$12
—No bar code on cover			
❑ PC33388	Journey	198?	$10
—With bar code on cover			
❑ AS914 [DJ]	Journey	1981	$25
—Promo-only four-song sampler			
❑ PC33904	Look Into the Future	1976	$12
—No bar code on cover			
❑ PC33904	Look Into the Future	198?	$10
—With bar code on cover			
❑ PCQ33904 [Q]	Look Into the Future	1976	$0
—Not released			
❑ PC34311	Next	1977	$12
—No bar code on cover			
❑ PC34311	Next	198?	$10
—With bar code on cover			
❑ OC39936	Raised on Radio	1986	$10
MOBILE FIDELITY			
❑ 1-144	Escape	1984	$250
—Audiophile vinyl			

JOURNEYMEN, THE (1)

Number	Title	Yr	NM
CAPITOL			
❑ T1770 [M]	Coming Attraction -- Live!	1962	$30
❑ ST1770 [S]	Coming Attraction -- Live!	1962	$30
❑ T1951 [M]	New Directions in Folk Music	1963	$30
❑ ST1951 [S]	New Directions in Folk Music	1963	$30
❑ T1629 [M]	The Journeymen	1961	$30
❑ ST1629 [S]	The Journeymen	1961	$30

JOY DIVISION

Also see NEW ORDER.

Number	Title	Yr	NM
FACTORY			
❑ FACT US6 [B]	Closer	1980	$100
—Purple tint vinyl			
❑ FACT US6 [B]	Closer	1980	$75
—Red tint vinyl			
❑ FACT US1 [B]	Unknown Pleasures	1979	$50
QWEST			
❑ 25841 [B]	Closer	1989	$18
—Reissue of FACT US 6			
❑ 25747	Substance	1988	$30
❑ 25840	Unknown Pleasures	1989	$18
—Reissue of FACT US 1			
RHINO			
❑ R156282 [B]	Closer	2015	$25

JOY OF COOKING

Number	Title	Yr	NM
CAPITOL			
❑ ST-11050	Castles	1972	$15
❑ SMAS-828	Closer to the Ground	1971	$18
❑ ST-661	Joy of Cooking	1971	$18

JOY STRINGS, THE

Number	Title	Yr	NM
EPIC			
❑ LN24321 [M]	Well Seasoned	1967	$25
❑ BN26321 [S]	Well Seasoned	1967	$25

JOY UNLIMITED

Number	Title	Yr	NM
BASF			
❑ 21090	Butterflies	1972	$30
MERCURY			
❑ SR-61283	Joy Unlimited	1970	$30

JOYCE, JIMMY

Number	Title	Yr	NM
WARNER BROS.			
❑ W1237 [M]	A Christmas to Remember	1958	$18
❑ WS1237 [S]	A Christmas to Remember	1959	$25
❑ W1566 [M]	This Is Christmas: A Complete Collection of the Alfred S. Burt Carols	1964	$18
❑ WS1566 [S]	This Is Christmas: A Complete Collection of the Alfred S. Burt Carols	1964	$25

JOYOUS NOISE

Number	Title	Yr	NM
CAPITOL			
❑ SMAS-844	Joyous Noise	1971	$18

JOYRIDE

Number	Title	Yr	NM
NOVA			
❑ 8705	Joyride	1987	$25

Number	Title	Yr	NM

JPJ QUARTET, THE
MASTER JAZZ
| ☐ 8111 | Montreux '71 | 1972 | $35 |

J'S WITH JAMIE, THE
COLUMBIA
☐ CL2005 [M]	Hey, Look Us Over!	1963	$30
☐ CS8805 [S]	Hey, Look Us Over!	1963	$40
☐ CS8949 [S]	The Remarkable J's with Jamie	1964	$40
☐ CL2149 [M]	The Remarkable J's with Jamie	1964	$30

JUDAS PRIEST
FIGHT, TWO, HALFORD, TRAPEZE, RACER X, WINTERS BANE related.
COLUMBIA
☐ JC36443	British Steel	1980	$12
☐ FC38219	Defenders of the Faith	1984	$10
☐ 9C939926 [PD]	Great Vinyl and Concert Hits	1984	$75
☐ JC35706	Hell Bent for Leather	1979	$12
☐ FC37052	Point of Entry	1981	$10
☐ C240794	Priest ... Live!	1987	$12
☐ FC44244	Ram It Down	1988	$10
☐ AS991543 [DJ]	Screaming for Vengeance	1982	$30

— Promo-only "world tour" picture disc; plays the correct LP
| ☐ AS991543 [DJ] | Screaming for Vengeance | 1982 | $30 |

— Promo-only "world tour" picture disc; plays Neil Diamond's "Heartlight" LP in error
| ☐ FC38160 | Screaming for Vengeance | 1982 | $10 |
| ☐ PC34787 | Sin After Sin | 1977 | $15 |

— Originals have no bar code on back cover
| ☐ PC34787 | Sin After Sin | 198? | $10 |

— Reissue; bar code on back cover
| ☐ JC35296 | Stained Class | 1978 | $12 |
| ☐ PC35296 | Stained Class | 198? | $10 |

— Budget-line reissue
☐ OC40158	Turbo	1986	$10
☐ JC36179	Unleashed in the East (Live in Japan)	1979	$10
☐ PC36179	Unleashed in the East (Live in Japan)	1985	$10

— Budget-line reissue with new prefix
GULL
| ☐ GU6-403S1 | Rocka-Rolla | 1975 | $0 |

— Canceled
JANUS
| ☐ JXS-7019 | Sad Wings of Destiny | 1976 | $25 |
| ☐ JXS-7019 [DJ] | Sad Wings of Destiny | 1976 | $30 |

— Promo version, with "Specially faded for easier programming" sticker on cover
MOBILE FIDELITY
☐ MOFI1-036 [B]	Killing Machine	2014	$30
☐ MOFI1-038 [B]	Screaming for Vengeance	2014	$35
☐ MOFI1-037 [B]	Stained Class	2014	$35
OVATION
☐ OV-1751	Sad Wings of Destiny	1980	$18
RCA VICTOR
☐ CYL1-5399	Hero, Hero	1985	$25
☐ AYL1-5041	Rocka-Rolla	1984	$12

— Reissue of Visa 7001 with new cover
| ☐ AYL1-4747 | Sad Wings of Destiny | 1983 | $12 |

— Reissue of Ovation LP
| ☐ AYL1-4933 | The Best of Judas Priest | 1984 | $10 |
VISA
| ☐ IMP-7001 | Rocka Rolla | 1979 | $18 |

— First U.S. issue of unreleased Gull LP; front cover has a bottle-cap motif

JUDD, WYNONNA
MCA
| ☐ 1P-8201 | Wynonna | 1992 | $30 |

— Only released on vinyl through Columbia House; label misspells her name as "Wyonna"!

JUDDS, THE
HEARTLAND
| ☐ HL-2041 | Classic Gold | 1992 | $25 |
RCA
☐ 6422-1-R	Christmas Time with the Judds	1987	$12
☐ 8318-1-R	Greatest Hits	1988	$12
☐ 5916-1-R	Heartland	1987	$12
☐ 9595-1-R	River of Time	1989	$15
RCA VICTOR
☐ AHL1-7042	Rockin' with the Rhythm	1985	$12
☐ MHL1-8515 [EP]	The Judds	1984	$10
☐ AHL1-5319	Why Not Me	1984	$12

JULIAN'S TREATMENT
DECCA
| ☐ DL75224 [B] | A Time Before This | 1970 | $30 |

JULLIARD STRING QUARTET
RCA VICTOR RED SEAL
| ☐ LSC-2626 [S] | Beethoven: String Quartet in C# Minor | 1962 | $30 |

— Original with "shaded dog" label
| ☐ LSC-2626 [S] | Beethoven: String Quartet in C# Minor | 1964 | $50 |

— Second edition with "white dog" label; a rare instance where the later pressing is more sought after than the original
| ☐ LSC-2632 [S] | Beethoven: String Quartet in F, Op. 95; String Quartet in F, Op. 135 | 1962 | $75 |

— Original with "shaded dog" label
| ☐ LSC-2531 [S] | Berg: Lyric Suite; Webern: 5 Pieces; Six Bagatelles | 1961 | $50 |

— Originals with "shaded dog" label
| ☐ LSC-2481 [S] | Carter: String Quartet No. 2; Schuman: String Quartet No. 3 | 1961 | $40 |

— Original with "shaded dog" label
| ☐ LSC-2413 [S] | Debussy: String Quartet in G; Ravel: String Quartet in F | 1960 | $175 |

— Original with "shaded dog" label
| ☐ LSC-2524 [S] | Dvorak: String Quartet in C; Wolf: Italian Serenade | 1961 | $30 |

— Originals with "shaded dog" label
| ☐ LSC-2378 [S] | Schubert: String Quartet No. 14 "Death and the Maiden" | 1960 | $100 |

— Original with "shaded dog" label

JULY
EPIC
| ☐ BN26416 | July | 1969 | $250 |

JULY
PARLOPHONE
| ☐ 825646335329 [B] | July | 2014 | $50 |

JUNGLE CRAWLERS, THE
STOMP OFF
| ☐ SOS-1084 | Stompin' On Down | 1985 | $25 |

JUNIOR'S EYES
A&M
| ☐ SP-4189 [B] | Junior's Eyes | 1970 | $50 |

JURGENS, DICK
HINDSIGHT
☐ HSR-138	Dick Jurgens and His Orchestra 1937-38	198?	$25
☐ HSR-111	Dick Jurgens and His Orchestra 1937-39	198?	$25
☐ HSR-191	Dick Jurgens and His Orchestra 1938	198?	$25

JURIS, VIC
MUSE
☐ MR-5265	Bleecker Street	1982	$30
☐ MR-5206	Horizon Drive	1979	$35
☐ MR-5150	Road Song	1978	$35

JUST IV
LIBERTY
| ☐ LRP-3340 [M] | First Twelve Sides | 1964 | $25 |
| ☐ LST-7340 [S] | First Twelve Sides | 1964 | $30 |

JUST US
KAPP
| ☐ KL-1502 [M] | I Can't Grow Peaches on a Cherry Tree | 1966 | $25 |
| ☐ KS-3502 [S] | I Can't Grow Peaches on a Cherry Tree | 1966 | $30 |

JUSTICE, JIMMY
KAPP
| ☐ KL-1308 [M] | Justice for All | 1963 | $30 |
| ☐ KS-3308 [S] | Justice for All | 1963 | $40 |

JUSTIS, BILL
HARMONY
| ☐ KH31189 | Enchanted Sea | 1972 | $15 |
MONUMENT
| ☐ MLP8078 [M] | The Eternal Sea | 1967 | $18 |
| ☐ SLP18078 [S] | The Eternal Sea | 1967 | $18 |
PHILLIPS INTERNATIONAL
| ☐ PLP-1950 [M] | Cloud Nine | 1959 | $400 |
SMASH
☐ MGS-27021 [M]	Bill Justis Plays 12 Big Instrumental Hits (Alley Cat/ Green Onions)	1962	$18
☐ SRS-67021 [S]	Bill Justis Plays 12 Big Instrumental Hits (Alley Cat/ Green Onions)	1962	$25
☐ MGS-27030 [M]	Bill Justis Plays 12 More Big Instrumental Hits (Telstar/ The Lonely Bull)	1963	$18
☐ SRS-67030 [S]	Bill Justis Plays 12 More Big Instrumental Hits (Telstar/ The Lonely Bull)	1963	$25
☐ MGS-27043 [M]	Bill Justis Plays 12 Other Instrumental Hits	1964	$18
☐ SRS-67043 [S]	Bill Justis Plays 12 Other Instrumental Hits	1964	$25
☐ MGS-27031 [M]	Bill Justis Plays 12 Smash Instrumental Hits	1963	$18
☐ SRS-67031 [S]	Bill Justis Plays 12 Smash Instrumental Hits	1963	$25
☐ MGS-27036 [M]	Bill Justis Plays 12 Top Tunes	1963	$18
☐ SRS-67036 [S]	Bill Justis Plays 12 Top Tunes	1963	$25
☐ MGS-27047 [M]	Dixieland Folk Style	1964	$18
☐ SRS-67047 [S]	Dixieland Folk Style	1964	$25
☐ MGS-27065 [M]	More Instrumental Hits	1965	$18
☐ SRS-67065 [S]	More Instrumental Hits	1965	$25
☐ 830898-1	Raunchy	1987	$12
☐ MGS-27077 [M]	Taste of Honey/The "In" Crowd	1966	$18
☐ SRS-67077 [S]	Taste of Honey/The "In" Crowd	1966	$25
SUN
☐ LP-109	Raunchy	1969	$15

K

K.C. AND THE SUNSHINE BAND
EPIC
| ☐ FE38073 | All in a Night's Work | 1982 | $12 |
| ☐ PE38073 [B] | All in a Night's Work | 1984 | $10 |

— Budget-line reissue
| ☐ FE37490 | The Painter | 1981 | $12 |
| ☐ PE37490 | The Painter | 1982 | $10 |

— Budget-line reissue
MECA
| ☐ 8301 | KC Ten | 1984 | $12 |
SUNSHINE SOUND
| ☐ 614 | Space Cadet/Solo Flight | 1981 | $12 |
T.K.
☐ 500	Do It Good	1974	$15
☐ 611	Do You Wanna Go Party	1979	$12
☐ 612	Greatest Hits	1980	$12
☐ 603	K.C. and the Sunshine Band	1975	$12
☐ 605	Part 3	1976	$12

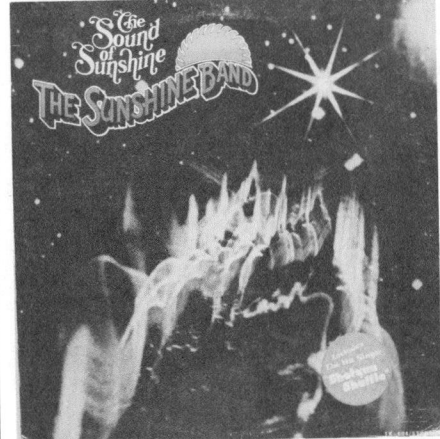

| ☐ 604 [B] | The Sound of Sunshine | 1975 | $12 |

— By "The Sunshine Band" (all instrumental)
| ☐ 607 | Who Do Ya (Love) | 1978 | $12 |

K-CI AND JOJO
MCA
☐ 113069	Emotional	2002	$18
☐ 11937	It's Real	1999	$15
☐ 11613	Love Always	1997	$15

K-DOE, ERNIE
JANUS
| ☐ JLS-3030 [B] | Ernie K-Doe | 1971 | $30 |
MINIT
| ☐ LP-0002 [M] | Mother-in-Law | 1961 | $300 |

— Orange label
| ☐ LP-24002 [R] | Mother-in-Law | 196? | $175 |

— Black label, not issued until after Imperial bought Minit

Number	Title	Yr	NM

KAEMPFERT, BERT
DECCA
Number	Title	Yr	NM
❑ DL4273 [M]	Afrikaan Beat and Other Favorites	1962	$15
❑ DL74273 [S]	Afrikaan Beat and Other Favorites	1962	$18
❑ DL8881 [M]	April in Portugal	1959	$18
❑ DL78881 [S]	April in Portugal	1959	$25
❑ DL75305	Bert Kaempfert Now!	1971	$18
❑ DL734485 [S]	Bert Kaempfert's Best	1966	$25

— Special Decca Custom Division edition
| ❑ DL34485 [M] | Bert Kaempfert's Best | 1966 | $18 |

— Special Decca Custom Division edition
❑ DL4810 [M]	Bert Kaempfert's Greatest Hits	1966	$15
❑ DL74810 [S]	Bert Kaempfert's Greatest Hits	1966	$18
❑ DL75367	Bert Kaempfert's Greatest Hits, Volume 2	1972	$18
❑ DL4569 [M]	Blue Midnight	1965	$15
❑ DL74569 [S]	Blue Midnight	1965	$18
❑ ST-91165	Blue Midnight	196?	$25

— Capitol Record Club edition
❑ DL4693 [M]	Bye Bye Blues	1966	$15
❑ DL74693 [S]	Bye Bye Blues	1966	$18
❑ DL4441 [M]	Christmas Wonderland	1963	$18
❑ DL74441 [S]	Christmas Wonderland	1963	$16

— Same as above, but in stereo
❑ DL4161 [M]	Dancing in Wonderland	1961	$18
❑ DL74161 [S]	Dancing in Wonderland	1961	$25
❑ DL75234	Free and Easy	1970	$18
❑ DL4860 [M]	Hold Me	1967	$15
❑ DL74860 [S]	Hold Me	1967	$18
❑ DL4265 [M]	Lights Out, Sweet Dreams	1963	$15
❑ DL74265 [S]	Lights Out, Sweet Dreams	1963	$18
❑ DL4374 [M]	Living It Up!	1963	$15
❑ DL74374 [S]	Living It Up!	1963	$18
❑ DL4986 [M]	Love That	1968	$25
❑ DL74986 [S]	Love That	1968	$18
❑ ST-91502	Love That	1968	$25

— Capitol Record Club edition
❑ DL75059	My Way of Life	1968	$18
❑ DL75256	Orange Colored Sky	1971	$18
❑ ST-93495	Orange Colored Sky	1971	$25

— Capitol Record Club edition
❑ DL75322	Six Plus Six	1972	$18
❑ DL4795 [M]	Strangers in the Night	1966	$15
❑ DL74795 [S]	Strangers in the Night	1966	$18
❑ T-90995 [M]	Strangers in the Night	1966	$18

— Capitol Record Club edition
❑ DL4305 [M]	That Happy Feeling	1962	$15
❑ DL74305 [S]	That Happy Feeling	1962	$18
❑ DL4490 [M]	That Latin Feeling	1964	$15
❑ DL74490 [S]	That Latin Feeling	1964	$18
❑ DXS7200	The Best of Bert Kaempfert	197?	$25
❑ DL75175	The Kaempfert Touch	1970	$18
❑ DL4616 [M]	The Magic Music of Far Away Places	1965	$15
❑ DL74616 [S]	The Magic Music of Far Away Places	1965	$18
❑ DL4117 [M]	The Wonderland of Bert Kaempfert	1961	$18
❑ DL74117 [S]	The Wonderland of Bert Kaempfert	1961	$25
❑ DL4925 [M]	The World We Knew	1967	$25
❑ DL74925 [S]	The World We Knew	1967	$18
❑ DL4670 [M]	Three O'Clock in the Morning	1965	$15
❑ DL74670 [S]	Three O'Clock in the Morning	1965	$18
❑ DL75140	Traces of Love	1969	$18
❑ DL75089	Warm and Wonderful	1969	$18
❑ DL4228 [M]	With a "Sound" in My Heart	1962	$15
❑ DL74228 [S]	With a "Sound" in My Heart	1962	$18
❑ DL4101 [M]	Wonderland by Night	1960	$18
❑ DL74101 [S]	Wonderland by Night	1960	$25

LONGINES SYMPHONETTE
| ❑ LWS299/300/1/2/3 | Strangers in the Night | 196? | $30 |
| ❑ LWS304 | Sweet and Gentle | 196? | $12 |

MCA
| ❑ 11 | Bert Kaempfert's Greatest Hits | 1973 | $12 |

— Reissue of Decca 74810
| ❑ 15020 | Christmas Wonderland | 197? | $12 |

— Reissue; black label with rainbow
| ❑ 15020 | Christmas Wonderland | 198? | $10 |

— Reissue; blue label with rainbow
| ❑ 214 | Christmas Wonderland | 1973 | $15 |

— First MCA reissue of Decca 74441
❑ 447	Gallery	1974	$15
❑ 466	Golden Memories	1974	$15
❑ 489	Moon Over Miami	1975	$15
❑ 4043	The Best of Bert Kaempfert	197?	$18

— Reissue of Decca 7200; black label with rainbow
| ❑ 4100 | The Best of Bert Kaempfert, Volume 2 | 197? | $18 |

— Black label with rainbow
❑ 314	The Fabulous Fifties	1973	$15
❑ 402	The Most Beautiful Girl	1974	$15
❑ 368	To the Good Life	1973	$15

POLYDOR
| ❑ SPH37556 | Afrikaan Beat and Other Favorites | 1967 | $15 |

— Columbia Record Club edition
| ❑ SPH37598 | Lights Out, Sweet Dreams | 1967 | $15 |

— Columbia Record Club edition
| ❑ SPH37599 | Living It Up! | 1967 | $15 |

— Columbia Record Club exclusive
| ❑ K2S5052 [S] | The Happy Wonderland of Bert Kaempfert | 1966 | $18 |

— Columbia Record Club exclusive
| ❑ K2M5051 [M] | The Happy Wonderland of Bert Kaempfert | 1966 | $18 |

— Columbia Record Club exclusive
| ❑ SPH37580 | With a "Sound" in My Heart | 1967 | $15 |

— Columbia Record Club edition
| ❑ SPH37553 | Wonderland by Night | 1967 | $15 |

— Columbia Record Club edition

KAJAGOOGOO
EMI AMERICA
Number	Title	Yr	NM
❑ ST-17169	Crazy People's Right to Speak	1985	$12

— As "Kaja"
| ❑ MLP-19012 [EP] | Extra Play | 1984 | $15 |

— Original issue
| ❑ ST-17157 [EP] | Extra Play | 1984 | $12 |

— Reissue of 19012
| ❑ ST-17094 | White Feathers | 1983 | $15 |

KAK
EPIC
| ❑ BN26429 | Kak | 1969 | $300 |

— Beware -- a reissue that looks almost identical to the original and sells for around $12 appeared in stores in 2000-2001

KALABASH CORP., THE
UNCLE BILL
| ❑ KB-3114 | The Kalabash Corp. | 1970 | $100 |

KALEIDOSCOPE, THE
EPIC
❑ LN24333 [M]	Beacon from Mars	1967	$75
❑ BN26333 [S]	Beacon from Mars	1967	$150
❑ BN26508	Bernice	1970	$30
❑ BN26467	Incredible Kaleidoscope	1969	$30
❑ LN24304 [M]	Side Trips	1967	$30
❑ BN26304 [S]	Side Trips	1967	$40

PACIFIC ARTS
| ❑ 102 | When Scopes Collide | 1978 | $15 |

KALIN TWINS, THE
DECCA
| ❑ DL8812 [M] | The Kalin Twins | 1959 | $150 |

VOCALION
| ❑ VL3771 [M] | When | 1966 | $18 |
| ❑ VL73771 [R] | When | 1966 | $15 |

KALLAO, ALEX
BATON
| ❑ BL-1205 [M] | Alex Kallao in Concert, University of Ottawa | 1957 | $75 |

RCA VICTOR
| ❑ LJM-1011 [M] | Evening at the Embers | 1954 | $50 |

KALLEN, KITTY
COLUMBIA
❑ CL1662 [M]	Honky Tonk Angel	1961	$25
❑ CS8462 [S]	Honky Tonk Angel	1961	$30
❑ CL1404 [M]	If I Give My Heart to You	1960	$25
❑ CS8204 [S]	If I Give My Heart to You	1960	$30

DECCA
| ❑ DL8397 [M] | It's a Lonesome Old Town | 1958 | $40 |

MERCURY
| ❑ MG25206 [10] | Pretty Kitty Kallen Sings | 1955 | $50 |

MOVIETONE
| ❑ S-72026 [S] | Delightfully | 1967 | $18 |
| ❑ 71026 [M] | Delightfully | 1967 | $18 |

RCA VICTOR
| ❑ LPM-2640 [M] | My Coloring Book | 1963 | $25 |
| ❑ LSP-2640 [S] | My Coloring Book | 1963 | $30 |

VOCALION
| ❑ VL3679 [M] | Little Things Mean a Lot | 1959 | $30 |

WING
| ❑ MGW-12241 [M] | Kitty Kallen Sings | 196? | $18 |
| ❑ SRW-16241 [R] | Kitty Kallen Sings | 196? | $15 |

KALLMAN, DICK
RCA VICTOR
| ❑ LPM-3485 [M] | Dick Kallman Drops In as Hank | 1966 | $25 |
| ❑ LSP-3485 [S] | Dick Kallman Drops In as Hank | 1966 | $30 |

KALLMANN, GUNTER, CHORUS
4 CORNERS OF THE WORLD
Number	Title	Yr	NM
❑ FCS-4248	Live for Love	1968	$15
❑ FCS-4256	Love Is Blue	1968	$15
❑ FCL-4218 [M]	Serenade for a Lady in Love	1965	$15
❑ FCS-4218 [S]	Serenade for a Lady in Love	1965	$18
❑ FCL-4209 [M]	Serenade for Elisabeth	1965	$15
❑ FCS-4209 [S]	Serenade for Elisabeth	1965	$18
❑ FCL-4226 [M]	Songs for My Love	1966	$15
❑ FCS-4226 [S]	Songs for My Love	1966	$18
❑ FCL-4235 [M]	Wish Me a Rainbow	1966	$15
❑ FCS-4235 [S]	Wish Me a Rainbow	1966	$18
❑ FCL-4237 [M]	With All My Heart	1967	$15
❑ FCS-4237 [S]	With All My Heart	1967	$18

POLYDOR
| ❑ 24-4506 | Early in the Morning | 1970 | $12 |
| ❑ 24-6003 | Once in Each Life | 1969 | $12 |

KAMINSKY, MAX
CHIAROSCURO
| ❑ 176 | When Summer Is Gone | 1977 | $30 |

COMMODORE
| ❑ FL-20019 [10] | Max Kaminsky | 1952 | $50 |

CONCERT HALL JAZZ
| ❑ 1009 [10] | Windy City Jazz | 1955 | $150 |

JAZZTONE
| ❑ J-1208 [M] | Chicago Style | 1955 | $40 |

MGM
| ❑ E-261 [10] | When the Saints Go Marching In | 1954 | $150 |

RCA VICTOR
| ❑ LJM-3003 [10] | Jazz on the Campus, Ltd. | 1954 | $50 |

UNITED ARTISTS
| ❑ UAL-3174 [M] | Max Goes East | 1961 | $25 |
| ❑ UAS-6174 [S] | Max Goes East | 1961 | $30 |

KAMON, KAREN
ATCO
| ❑ 90575 | Voices | 1987 | $12 |

COLUMBIA
| ❑ BFC39407 | Heart of You | 1984 | $12 |

MOZE, INI
COLUMBIA
| ❑ C67056 | Here Comes the Hotstepper | 1994 | $12 |

EASTWEST
| ❑ 61764 | Lyrical Gangsta | 1995 | $12 |

MANGO
❑ MMA-101 [EP]	Ini Kamoze	1983	$10
❑ MNLP-9801	Pirate	1986	$12
❑ MNLP-9800	Statement	1984	$12

RAS
| ❑ 3036 | Shocking Out | 1988 | $12 |

KAMUCA, RICHIE
CONCORD JAZZ
❑ CJ-96	Charlie	1979	$75
❑ CJ-39	Drop Me Off in Harlem	1977	$35
❑ CJ-41	Richie	1977	$50

FANTASY
| ❑ OJC-1760 | West Coast Jazz in Hi-Fi | 198? | $30 |

HIFI
❑ R-604 [M]	Jazz Erotica	1957	$250
❑ J-609 [M]	West Coast Jazz in Hi-Fi	1959	$75
❑ JS-609 [S]	West Coast Jazz in Hi-Fi	1959	$50

JAZZZ
| ❑ 104 | Richie Kamuca 1976 | 1976 | $30 |

MODE

| ❑ LP-102 [M] | Richie Kamuka Quartet | 1957 | $250 |

Number	Title	Yr	NM

KAKANE, BIG DADDY

COLD CHILLIN'

Number	Title	Yr	NM
❏ 25941	It's a Big Daddy Thing	1989	$30
❏ 25731	Long Live the Kane	1988	$40
❏ PRO-A-5205 [DJ]	Prince of Darkness	1991	$30

— *Vinyl is promo only*

| ❏ 26303 | Taste of Chocolate | 1990 | $25 |

LABEL

| ❏ 371801-1 | Veteranz Day | 1998 | $18 |

MCA

| ❏ 11102 [DJ] | Daddy's Home | 1994 | $18 |

KANE, KIERAN

ELEKTRA

| ❏ E1-60004 | Kieran Kane | 1982 | $12 |

KANE, MADLEEN

CHALET

| ❏ CH 0702 | Don't Wanna Lose You | 1981 | $12 |
| ❏ CH 0701 | Sounds of Love | 1980 | $12 |

WARNER BROS.

| ❏ BSK3315 | Cheri | 1979 | $15 |
| ❏ BSK3188 | Rough Diamond | 1978 | $15 |

KANE GANG, THE

CAPITOL

| ❏ CLX-48176 | Mracle | 1987 | $10 |

LONDON

| ❏ 820215-1 | Lowdown | 1984 | $12 |

KANE'S COUSINS

SHOVE LOVE

| ❏ 9827 | Undergum Bubbleground | 1969 | $40 |

KANGAROO

MGM

| ❏ SE-4586 [B] | Kangaroo | 1968 | $35 |

KANNIBAL KOMIX

COLOSSUS

| ❏ 1004 | Kannibal Komix | 1970 | $25 |

KANO

EMERGENCY

| ❏ EMLP7505 | Kano | 1980 | $15 |

MIRAGE

| ❏ WTG19327 | New York Cake | 1981 | $12 |

KANSAS

Vocalist Steve Walsh was also in STREETS. Chief writer Kerry Livgren's solo album included a Ronnie James Dio cameo.

CBS ASSOCIATED

| ❏ QZ38733 | Drastic Measures | 1983 | $10 |
| ❏ QZ39283 | The Best of Kansas | 1984 | $10 |

KIRSHNER

| ❏ FZ36588 | Audio-Visions | 1980 | $12 |
| ❏ PZ36588 | Audio-Visions | 198? | $10 |

— *Budget-line reissue*

| ❏ KZ32817 | Kansas | 1974 | $15 |
| ❏ PZ32817 | Kansas | 197? | $10 |

— *Reissue*

| ❏ JZ34224 [B] | Leftoverture | 1976 | $12 |
| ❏ HZ44224 | Leftoverture | 1982 | $40 |

— *Half-speed mastered edition*

| ❏ PZ34224 | Leftoverture | 198? | $10 |

— *Budget-line reissue*

| ❏ PZ33806 | Masque | 1975 | $15 |

— *Without bar code on cover*

Number	Title	Yr	NM
❏ PZ33806	Masque	198?	$10

— *With bar code on cover*

| ❏ FZ36008 | Monolith | 1979 | $12 |
| ❏ HZ46008 | Monolith | 1982 | $50 |

— *Half-speed mastered edition*

| ❏ PZ36008 | Monolith | 198? | $10 |

— *Budget-line reissue*

| ❏ JZ34929 | Point of Know Return | 1977 | $12 |
| ❏ HZ44929 | Point of Know Return | 1982 | $40 |

— *Half-speed mastered edition*

| ❏ PZ33385 [B] | Song for America | 1975 | $15 |

— *Without bar code on cover*

| ❏ PZ33385 | Song for America | 198? | $10 |

— *With bar code on cover*

| ❏ PZ235660 | Two for the Show | 1978 | $18 |
| ❏ AS555 [DJ] | Two for the Show (Sampler) | 1978 | $25 |

— *Promo-only single disc of selections from 35660*

| ❏ FZ38002 | Vinyl Confessions | 1982 | $12 |
| ❏ HZ48002 | Vinyl Confessions | 1982 | $150 |

— *Half-speed mastered edition*

| ❏ PZ38002 | Vinyl Confessions | 198? | $10 |

— *Budget-line reissue*

MCA

| ❏ 6254 | In the Spirit of Things | 1988 | $10 |
| ❏ 5838 | Power | 1986 | $10 |

KANTNER, PAUL, AND GRACE SLICK

GRUNT

| ❏ BXL1-0148 [B] | Baron Von Tollbooth and the Chrome Nun | 1973 | $25 |

— *Original prefix*

| ❏ AYL1-3799 | Baron Von Tollbooth and the Chrome Nun | 1980 | $10 |

— *Budget-line reissue*

| ❏ BFL1-0148 | Baron Von Tollbooth and the Chrome Nun | 1977 | $12 |

— *Reissue with new prefix*

| ❏ FTR-1002 | Sunfighter | 1971 | $18 |

— *With booklet (deduct 33% if missing)*

KANTNER, PAUL

RCA VICTOR

| ❏ AFL1-4320 [B] | The Planet Earth Rock and Roll Orchestra | 1983 | $12 |

— *clear vinyl add 25%*

KANTNER, PAUL/JEFFERSON STARSHIP

RCA VICTOR

| ❏ LSP-4448 [B] | Blows Against the Empire | 1970 | $25 |
| ❏ LSP-4448 [DJ] | Blows Against the Empire | 1970 | $150 |

— *Clear vinyl promo*

| ❏ AYL1-3868 | Blows Against the Empire | 1981 | $10 |

— *Budget-line reissue*

| ❏ AFL1-4448 | Blows Against the Empire | 1977 | $12 |

— *Reissue of LSP-4448*

KAPLAN, ARTIE

HOPI

| ❏ VHS901 | Confessions of a Male Chauvinist Pig | 1971 | $30 |

KAPLAN, GABRIEL

ABC

| ❏ ABCD-905 | Holes and Mello-Rolls | 1976 | $15 |

— *Reissue with photo of the "Welcome Back, Kotter" cast on cover*

| ❏ ABCD-815 | Holes and Mellow Rolls | 1974 | $18 |

— *Original release with painting of ice-cream bars on cover*

| ❏ ABC-102 [10] | Holes and Mellow Rolls | 1974 | $18 |

— *Promo-only 10-inch sampler*

KAPLAN, LEIGH

CAMBRIA

| ❏ C-1019 | Dizzy Fingers | 1987 | $25 |
| ❏ C-1016 | Shades of Dring | 198? | $25 |

KARAS, ANTON

COLUMBIA

| ❏ CL2576 [M] | Rendezvous in Vienna | 1967 | $15 |
| ❏ CS9376 [S] | Rendezvous in Vienna | 1967 | $18 |

DESIGN

| ❏ DLP-120 [M] | The Viennese Strings of Anton Karas | 1959 | $18 |

LONDON

❏ LL1560 [M]	The Third Man" Theme	1959	$30
❏ PS319 [S]	Vienna, City of Dreams	1963	$18
❏ LL3319 [M]	Vienna, City of Dreams	1963	$15

PERIOD

| ❏ SPL-1917 | Viennese Bonbons | 196? | $12 |
| ❏ SPL-1918 | Viennese Bonbons Volume II | 196? | $12 |

SURREY

| ❏ S-1001 [M] | Zither Magic | 196? | $15 |
| ❏ SS-1001 [S] | Zither Magic | 196? | $15 |

Number	Title	Yr	NM

VOX

| ❏ VX-25180 [10] | Movie Cocktails | 1954 | $30 |

KARLOFF, BORIS

CAEDMON

❏ TC-1221 [M]	Aesop's Fables	1967	$50
❏ TC-1038 [M]	Just So Stories and Other Tales	195?	$30
❏ TC-1100 [M]	Kipling's Jungle Books: How Fear Came	196?	$30
❏ TC-1176 [M]	Kipling's Jungle Books: Toomai of the Elephants	196?	$30
❏ TC-1088 [M]	More of Kipling's Just So Stories	196?	$30
❏ TC-1139 [M]	The Cat That Walked By Herself	196?	$30
❏ TC-1117 [M]	The Little Match Girl and Other Tales	196?	$30
❏ TC-1075 [M]	The Pied Piper; The Hunting of the Snarks	196?	$30
❏ TC-1074 [M]	The Reluctant Dragon	196?	$30
❏ TC-1129 [M]	The Three Bears, Henny Penny and Other Fairy Tales	1962	$30
❏ TC-1109 [M]	The Ugly Duckling and Other Tales	196?	$30

DECCA

| ❏ DL4833 [M] | An Evening with Boris Karloff and His Friends | 1967 | $25 |
| ❏ DL74833 [S] | An Evening with Boris Karloff and His Friends | 1967 | $30 |

MERCURY

❏ MG-20815 [M]	Tales of the Frightened, Volume 1	1963	$40
❏ SR-60815 [S]	Tales of the Frightened, Volume 1	1963	$50
❏ MG-20816 [M]	Tales of the Frightened, Volume 2	1963	$40
❏ SR-60816 [S]	Tales of the Frightened, Volume 2	1963	$50

KARMA

HORIZON

| ❏ SP-713 | Celebration | 1976 | $35 |
| ❏ SP-723 | For Everybody | 1977 | $35 |

KARMEN, STEVE

JUBILEE

| ❏ JGM-2048 [M] | This Is a City? | 1963 | $25 |

STRUTTIN'

| ❏ STR-104 | Reconnecting | 1977 | $15 |

KARUKAS

OPTIMISM

| ❏ OP-3101 | The Nightowl | 1988 | $25 |

KASAI, KIMIKO

CATALYST

| ❏ 7900 | One for the Lady | 1977 | $30 |

KASANDRA

CAPITOL

| ❏ ST-157 | A Higher Plateau | 1969 | $18 |
| ❏ ST-2957 | John W. Anderson Presents KaSandra | 1968 | $18 |

RESPECT

❏ TAS-2603	Beautiful New World	1972	$18
❏ TAS-2602	Color Me Human	1972	$18
❏ TAS-2605	The Mod Messiah	1974	$18
❏ TAS-2604	True Genius	1972	$18

KASENETZ-KATZ SINGING ORCHESTRAL CIRCUS

BUDDAH

| ❏ BDS-5020 [S] | Kasenetz-Katz Singing Orchestral Circus | 1968 | $18 |
| ❏ BDM-1020 [M] | Kasenetz-Katz Singing Orchestral Circus | 1968 | $175 |

— *Mono is promo only; in stereo cover with "Mono" sticker*

| ❏ BDS-5028 | Kasenetz-Katz Super Circus | 1969 | $18 |

KASHIF

ARISTA

❏ AL8-8385	Condition of the Heart	1985	$10
❏ AL-9620	Kashif	1983	$10
❏ AL-8595	Kashif	1989	$12

— *Different album from 9620*

| ❏ AL-8001 | Kashif | 198? | $10 |

— *Reissue of 9620*

| ❏ AL-8447 | Love Changes | 1987 | $10 |
| ❏ ADP-9662 [DJ] | Love Changes In Store Sampler | 1987 | $15 |

— *All 10 songs with interview and preview segments*

| ❏ AL8-8205 | Send Me Your Love | 1984 | $10 |

KASSEL, ART

HINDSIGHT

| ❏ HSR-162 | Kassels In The Air Orchestra 1944 | 198? | $25 |
| ❏ HSR-170 | Kassels In The Air Orchestra 1945 | 198? | $25 |

Number	Title	Yr	NM

KAPP
| ❏ KL-1248 [M] | Dance to the Music of Art Kassel | 1962 | $25 |
| ❏ KS-3248 [S] | Dance to the Music of Art Kassel | 1962 | $30 |

KAT MANDU
MARLIN
| ❏ 2233 | Kat Mandu | 1979 | $25 |

KATALINA
THUMP
| ❏ 9958 | Sonic Groove | 1996 | $18 |

KATINDIG, BOY
PAUSA
| ❏ 7137 | Midnight Lady | 198? | $25 |

KATMANDU
MAINSTREAM
| ❏ S-6131 | Katmandu | 1971 | $40 |

KATRINA AND THE WAVES
CAPITOL
| ❏ ST-12400 | Katrina and the Waves | 1985 | $12 |
| ❏ ST-12478 | Waves | 1986 | $12 |
SBK
| ❏ K1-92649 | Break of Hearts | 1989 | $15 |

KATZ, BRUCE
AUDIOQUEST
| ❏ AQ-1012 | Crescent Crawl | 199? | $30 |
| ❏ AQ-1026 | Transformation | 1994 | $30 |

KATZ, DICK; DEREK SMITH; RENE URTREGER
ATLANTIC
❏ 1287 [M]	John Lewis Presents Jazz Piano International	1958	$300
—Black label			
❏ 1287 [M]	John Lewis Presents Jazz Piano International	1961	$175
—Multicolor label, white "fan" logo at right			

KATZ, DICK
ATLANTIC
❏ 1314 [M]	Piano and Pin	1959	$300
—Black label			
❏ 1314 [M]	Piano and Pin	1961	$175
—Multicolor label, white "fan" logo at right			
❏ SD1314 [S]	Piano and Pin	1959	$300
—Green label			
❏ SD1314 [S]	Piano and Pin	1961	$175
—Multicolor label, white "fan" logo at right			

KATZ, FRED
DECCA
❏ DL9213 [M]	4-5-6 Trio	1958	$120
❏ DL79213 [S]	4-5-6 Trio	1958	$120
❏ DL9217 [M]	Fred Katz and Jammers	1958	$120

❏ DL79217 [S]	Fred Katz and Jammers	1958	$30
❏ DL9202 [M]	Soulo Cello	1958	$150
❏ DL79202 [S]	Soulo Cello	1958	$150
WARNER BROS.
| ❏ W1277 [M] | Folk Songs for Far Out Folks | 1959 | $30 |
| ❏ WS1277 [S] | Folk Songs for Far Out Folks | 1959 | $30 |

KATZ, MICKEY
CAPITOL
❏ T1603 [M]	At the U.N.	1961	$25
—Black colorband label, logo at left			
❏ ST1603 [S]	At the U.N.	1961	$30

Number	Title	Yr	NM

—Black colorband label, logo at left			
❏ W1307 [M]	Comin' Round the Katzkills	1959	$30
—Black colorband label, logo at left			
❏ W1257 [M]	Katz Pajamas	1959	$30
—Black colorband label, logo at left			
❏ T1021 [M]	Katz Plays Music for Weddings, Bar Mitzvahs and Brisses	1958	$30
—Turquoise or gray label			
❏ T934 [M]	Katz Puts On the Dog	1958	$30
—Turquoise or gray label			
❏ H298 [10]	Mickey Katz: The Star of Broadway's Borschtcapades	195?	$40
❏ T799 [M]	Mish Mosh	1957	$30
—Turquoise or gray label			
❏ T1744 [M]	Sing Along with Mickele	1962	$25
❏ ST1744 [S]	Sing Along with Mickele	1962	$30
❏ T1445 [M]	The Borscht Jester	1960	$25
—Black colorband label, logo at left			
❏ ST1445 [S]	The Borscht Jester	1960	$30
—Black colorband label, logo at left			
❏ H457 [10]	The Family Danced	195?	$40
❏ T1102 [M]	The Most Mishige	1959	$30
—Black colorband label, logo at left			
❏ T298 [M]	The Very Best of Mickey Katz	195?	$30
—Turquoise or gray label			
RCA VICTOR
| ❏ LPM-3193 [10] | Borscht | 1954 | $40 |

KAUFMANN, BOB
LHI
| ❏ 12002 | Trip Through a Blown Mind | 1967 | $75 |

KAUKONEN, JORMA
GRUNT
❏ BFL1-0209 [B]	Quah	1973	$18
❏ BXL1-0209	Quah	197?	$12
—Reissue with new prefix			
❏ AYL1-3747	Quah	1981	$10
—Best Buy Series" reissue			
❏ BRK240 [B]	Quah	2014	$30
RCA VICTOR
| ❏ AFL1-3725 | Barbecue King | 1981 | $12 |
| ❏ AFL1-3446 | Jorma | 1979 | $12 |

KAUKONEN, PETER
GRUNT
| ❏ FTR1006 [B] | Black Kangaroo | 1972 | $25 |

KAWAGUCHI, GEORGE, AND ART BLAKEY
STORYVILLE
| ❏ 4100 | Killer Joe | 1982 | $30 |

KAWASAKI, RYO
INNER CITY
| ❏ IC-6006 | Eight Mile Road | 197? | $35 |
| ❏ IC-6016 | Prism | 197? | $35 |
RCA VICTOR
| ❏ APL1-1855 | Juice | 1977 | $35 |

KAY, JOHN, AND SPARROW
See SPARROW.

KAY, JOHN, AND STEPPENWOLF
See STEPPENWOLF.

KAY, JOHN
ABC DUNHILL
| ❏ DSX-50120 | Forgotten Songs & Unsung Heroes | 1972 | $12 |
| ❏ DSX-50147 | My Sportin' Life | 1973 | $12 |
MERCURY
| ❏ SRM-1-3715 | All in Good Time | 1978 | $12 |

KAY, JOHNNY
PROMENADE
| ❏ 2122 | Johnny Kay Sings Season's Greeetings | 196? | $15 |
SPINORAMA
| ❏ 4009 | White Christmas | 196? | $15 |

KAY-GEES, THE
DE-LITE
| ❏ 9510 | Burn Me Up | 1979 | $12 |
| ❏ 9505 | Kilowatt | 1978 | $12 |
GANG
| ❏ 102 | Find a Friend | 1975 | $12 |
| ❏ 101 | Keep On Bumpin' & Masterplan | 1975 | $12 |

KAYAK
HARVEST
| ❏ ST-11305 | See See the Sun | 1973 | $18 |

Number	Title	Yr	NM

JANUS
❏ NXS-7039 [B]	Phantom of the Night	1979	$12
❏ 0(no cat #) [PD]	Phantom of the Night	1979	$30
—Numbered limited edition of 3,000			
❏ NXS-7023	Royal Bed Bouncer	1975	$12
❏ NXS-7034	Starlight Dancer	1978	$12
MERCURY
| ❏ SRM-1-3824 | Periscope Life | 1980 | $12 |

KAYE, DANNY
CAPITOL
| ❏ T937 [M] | Mommy Gimme a Drinka Water | 1958 | $40 |

COLUMBIA
| ❏ CL6023 [10] | Danny Kaye | 1949 | $50 |
| ❏ CL6249 [10] | Danny Kaye Entertains | 195? | $50 |
DECCA
| ❏ DL8461 [M] | Danny at the Palace | 1957 | $50 |
| *—Black label, silver print* | | | |

❏ DL8461 [M]	Danny at the Palace	1960	$30
—Black label with color bars			
❏ DLP5033 [10]	Danny Kaye	1950	$50
❏ DL8726 [M]	Danny Kaye for Children	1959	$30
—Black label, silver print			
❏ DL8726 [M]	Danny Kaye for Children	1960	$30
—Black label with color bars			
❏ DL5094 [10]	Gilbert and Sullivan and Danny Kaye	1950	$50
❏ DXB175 [M]	The Best of Danny Kaye	1965	$30
❏ DSXB175 [R]	The Best of Danny Kaye	1965	$18
❏ DL8212 [M]	The Court Jester	1955	$50
—Black label, silver print			

KAYE, MARY, TRIO
20TH CENTURY FOX
| ❏ TFM-3117 [M] | Night Life | 1964 | $15 |
| ❏ TFS-4117 [S] | Night Life | 1964 | $18 |
COLUMBIA
| ❏ CL1910 [M] | Our Hawaii | 1962 | $18 |
| ❏ CS8710 [S] | Our Hawaii | 1962 | $25 |
DECCA
❏ DL8434 [M]	Music on a Silver Platter	1957	$30
❏ DL8238 [M]	The Mary Kaye Trio	1956	$30
❏ DL8650 [M]	You Don't Know What Love Is	1958	$30
MOVIETONE
| ❏ S72027 [S] | Just Us | 1967 | $15 |
| ❏ 71027 [M] | Just Us | 1967 | $15 |
VERVE
❏ V-8446 [M]	For the Record	1962	$25
❏ V6-8446 [S]	For the Record	1962	$30
❏ MGV-2142 [M]	Up Front!	1960	$40
WARNER BROS.
❏ W1263 [M]	Jackpot	1959	$25
❏ WS1263 [S]	Jackpot	1959	$30
❏ W1342 [M]	The Mary Kaye Trio on the Sunset Strip	1959	$25
❏ WS1342 [S]	The Mary Kaye Trio on the Sunset Strip	1959	$30
❏ B1222 [M]	Too Much!	1958	$25

KAYE, MILTON
GOLDEN CREST
❏ GC-31032	Ragtime at the Rosebud	197?	$30
❏ CRS-4127	The Classic Rags of Joe Lamb	197?	$30
—Single-sided LP in gatefold sleeve (B-side is blank)			

KAYE, SAMMY
COLUMBIA
| ❏ CL2541 [10] | Christmas Serenade | 1955 | $50 |
| *—House Party Series" issue* | | | |

Number	Title	Yr	NM
CL1571 [M]	Dancing on a Silken Cloud	1960	$35
CS8371 [S]	Dancing on a Silken Cloud	1960	$50
CL668 [M]	Music, Maestro, Please!	195?	$30
CL885 [M]	My Fair Lady (For Dancing)	1956	$50
CL1018 [M]	Popular American Waltzes	1957	$50
CL1236 [M]	Strauss Waltzes for Dancing	1959	$35
CL6155 [10]	Sunday Serenade	1953	$40
CL964 [M]	Sunday Serenade	1957	$50
CL561 [M]	Swing and Sway with Sammy Kaye	195?	$30
CL891 [M]	What Makes Sammy Swing and Sway	1956	$25

DECCA

Number	Title	Yr	NM
DL4070 [M]	Christmas Day with Sammy Kaye	1960	$30
DL74070 [S]	Christmas Day with Sammy Kaye	1960	$35
DL4502 [M]	Come Dance to the Hits	1964	$30
DL74502 [S]	Come Dance to the Hits	1964	$35
DL4357 [M]	Come Dance with Me	1963	$30
DL74357 [S]	Come Dance with Me	1963	$35
DL4590 [M]	Come Dance with Me (Vol. 2)	1965	$30
DL74590 [S]	Come Dance with Me (Vol. 2)	1965	$35
DL4924 [M]	Dance and Be Happy	1967	$35
DL74924 [S]	Dance and Be Happy	1967	$30
DL4655 [M]	Dancetime	1965	$30
DL74655 [S]	Dancetime	1965	$35
DL4121 [M]	Dance to My Golden Favorites	1961	$30
DL74121 [S]	Dance to My Golden Favorites	1961	$35
DL4424 [M]	Dreamy Serenades	1963	$30
DL74424 [S]	Dreamy Serenades	1963	$35
DL4306 [M]	For Your Dancing Pleasure	1962	$30
DL74306 [S]	For Your Dancing Pleasure	1962	$35
DL4970 [M]	Glory of Love	1967	$35
DL74970 [S]	Glory of Love	1967	$30
DL4823 [M]	Let's Face the Music	1967	$30
DL74823 [S]	Let's Face the Music	1967	$35
DL4247 [M]	New Twists on Old Favorites	1962	$30
DL74247 [S]	New Twists on Old Favorites	1962	$35
DL4215 [M]	Sexy Strings and Subtle Saxes	1962	$30
DL74215 [S]	Sexy Strings and Subtle Saxes	1962	$35
DL4754 [M]	Shall We Dance	1966	$30
DL74754 [S]	Shall We Dance	1966	$35
DL4071 [M]	Sing and Sway with Sammy Kaye	1960	$30
DL74071 [S]	Sing and Sway with Sammy Kaye	1960	$35
DL4154 [M]	Songs I Wish I Had Played…The First Time Around	1961	$30
DL74154 [S]	Songs I Wish I Had Played…The First Time Around	1961	$35
DL4862 [M]	Swing & Sway in Hawaii	1967	$35
DL74862 [S]	Swing & Sway in Hawaii	1967	$30
DL4687 [M]	Swing and Sway Au-Go-Go	1965	$35
DL74687 [S]	Swing and Sway Au-Go-Go	1965	$30
DL75106	The 30's Are Here to Stay	1968	$30

HARMONY

Number	Title	Yr	NM
HS11261	All-Time Waltz Favorites	1968	$30
HL7357 [M]	Beautiful Waltzes for Dancing	196?	$35
HS11157 [R]	Beautiful Waltzes for Dancing	196?	$30
KH32013	Best of the Big Bands	1971	$25
HL7187 [M]	Dancing with Sammy Kaye in Hi-Fi	196?	$35
HS11087 [R]	Dancing with Sammy Kaye in Hi-Fi	196?	$30
HS11377	Harbor Lights	1970	$25
HL7230 [M]	In a Dancing Mood	196?	$35
HS11121 [R]	My Fair Lady	1964	$30
HL7321 [M]	My Fair Lady	1964	$35

HINDSIGHT

Number	Title	Yr	NM
HSR-402	22 Original Big Band Recordings	198?	$30
HSR-158	1940-41	198?	$25
HSR-163	1942-43	198?	$25
HSR-207	1944-46	198?	$25

MCA

Number	Title	Yr	NM
191	Dance to My Golden Favorites	1973	$25

—*Reissue of Decca 74121*

Number	Title	Yr	NM
205	Plays Swing & Sway	1973	$25

—*Reissue of Decca 74306*

Number	Title	Yr	NM
278	The 30's Are Here to Stay	197?	$25

—*Reissue of Decca material*

Number	Title	Yr	NM
4027	The Best of Sammy Kaye	197?	$30

PROJECT 3

Number	Title	Yr	NM
PR-5065SD	If You've Got the Time	1972	$25
PR-5065QD [Q]	If You've Got the Time	1972	$30

RCA CAMDEN

Number	Title	Yr	NM
CAL-261 [M]	Music for Dancing	1956	$50
CAL-355 [M]	Swing and Sway with Sammy Kaye	1957	$50

RCA VICTOR

Number	Title	Yr	NM
LPM15 [10]	Sammy Kaye Plays Irving Berlin for Dancing	1950	$150
LPM-3966 [M]	The Best of Sammy Kaye	1967	$50
LSP-3966 [R]	The Best of Sammy Kaye	1967	$30
VPM-6070	This Is Sammy Kaye	1972	$30

VOCALION

Number	Title	Yr	NM
VL73919	Theme from "Love Story"	1971	$25

KAZ, FRED

ATLANTIC

Number	Title	Yr	NM
1335 [M]	Eastern Exposure	1960	$300

—*Multicolor label, white "fan" logo at right*

Number	Title	Yr	NM
SD1335 [S]	Eastern Exposure	1960	$300

—*Multicolor label, white "fan" logo at right*

KAZAN, LAINIE

MGM

Number	Title	Yr	NM
E-4385 [M]	Lainie Kazan	1966	$25
SE-4385 [S]	Lainie Kazan	1966	$30
SE-4496	Love Is	1968	$25
E-4340 [M]	Right Now	1966	$25
SE-4340 [S]	Right Now	1966	$30
SE-4631	The Best of Lainie Kazan	1969	$25
E-4451 [M]	The Love Album	1967	$30
SE-4451 [S]	The Love Album	1967	$25

KBC BAND

ARISTA

Number	Title	Yr	NM
AL8440	KBC Band	1986	$10

KEANE BROTHERS, THE

20TH CENTURY

Number	Title	Yr	NM
T-536	The Keane Brothers	1977	$18

ABC

Number	Title	Yr	NM
AA-1122	Taking Off	1979	$18

KEARNEY, RAMSEY

NASHCO

Number	Title	Yr	NM
646	Broken Heart	1986	$18
616	God Made Them All	1981	$18
613	I Write the Words	1981	$18
611	Lots to Look Back On	198?	$18
654	Red White and Blue USA	1987	$18
615	Reflections of You	1981	$18
608	Together in a Song	198?	$18

KEATING, JOHNNY

BALLY

Number	Title	Yr	NM
BAL-12001 [M]	English Jazz	1956	$50

DOT

Number	Title	Yr	NM
DLP-3066 [M]	Swinging Scots	1957	$100

KEENE, BOB

ANDEX

Number	Title	Yr	NM
S-4001 [M]	Solo for 7	1958	$50

DEL-FI

Number	Title	Yr	NM
DFLP-1222 [M]	Twist to Radio KRLA	1962	$30
DFLP-1202 [M]	Unforgettable Love Songs of the 50's	1959	$40

GENE NORMAN

Number	Title	Yr	NM
GNP-149 [10]	Bob Keene	1954	$50

KEISER TWINS, THE

CBS

Number	Title	Yr	NM
FM44737	The Keiser Twins	1988	$25

KEITH

MERCURY

Number	Title	Yr	NM
MG-21102 [M]	98.6/Ain't Gonna Lie	1967	$30
SR-61102 [S]	98.6/Ain't Gonna Lie	1967	$25
MG-21129 [M]	Out of Crank	1967	$30
SR-61129 [S]	Out of Crank	1967	$25

RCA VICTOR

Number	Title	Yr	NM
LSP-4143	The Adventures of Keith	1969	$25

KEITH AND DONNA
Also see THE GRATEFUL DEAD.

ROUND

Number	Title	Yr	NM
RX-104	Keith and Donna	1975	$30

KELLAWAY, ROGER, AND RED MITCHELL

STASH

Number	Title	Yr	NM
ST-271	Fifty/Fifty	1988	$25

KELLAWAY, ROGER

A&M

Number	Title	Yr	NM
SP-3034	Cello Quartet	1970	$30
SP-3040	Center of the Circle	1972	$35
SP-3618	Come to the Meadow	1974	$25

CHOICE

Number	Title	Yr	NM
CRS-6833	Ain't Misbehavin'	1989	$25

DISCWASHER

Number	Title	Yr	NM
003	Nostalgia Suite	1979	$25

DOBRE

Number	Title	Yr	NM
1045	Say That Again	1978	$25

PACIFIC JAZZ

Number	Title	Yr	NM
PJ-10122 [M]	Spirit Feel	196?	$25

Number	Title	Yr	NM
ST-20122 [S]	Spirit Feel	196?	$35
LN-10070	Spirit Feel	198?	$20

—*Budget-line reissue*

PRESTIGE

Number	Title	Yr	NM
PRLP-7399 [M]	The Roger Kellaway Trio	1965	$30
PRST-7399 [S]	The Roger Kellaway Trio	1965	$30

REGINA

Number	Title	Yr	NM
R-298 [M]	Portraits	1964	$25
RS-298 [S]	Portraits	1964	$30

VOSS

Number	Title	Yr	NM
VLP1-42935	Nostalgia Suite	1988	$25

WORLD PACIFIC

Number	Title	Yr	NM
WP-21861 [M]	Stride	1967	$150
WPS-21861 [S]	Stride	1967	$150

KELLEM, MANNY

EPIC

Number	Title	Yr	NM
BN26367	Love Is Blue	1968	$12

KELLER, ALLEN

CHARLIE PARKER

Number	Title	Yr	NM
PLP-817 [M]	A New Look at the World	1962	$30
PLP-817S [S]	A New Look at the World	1962	$30

KELLER, HAL

SAND

Number	Title	Yr	NM
7 [M]	Hal Keller Debut	1957	$175

SOUND

Number	Title	Yr	NM
602 [M]	Hal Keller Debut	1959	$175

KELLER, JERRY

KAPP

Number	Title	Yr	NM
KL-1178 [M]	Here Comes Jerry Keller	1959	$40
KS-3178 [S]	Here Comes Jerry Keller	1959	$50

KELLERMAN, SALLY

DECCA

Number	Title	Yr	NM
DL75359 [B]	Roll with the Feelin'	1972	$25

KELLEY, PAT

NOVA

Number	Title	Yr	NM
8704-1	Views of the Future	1988	$25

KELLEY, PECK

COMMODORE

Number	Title	Yr	NM
XF2-17017	Peck Kelley Jam	198?	$30

KELLIN, MIKE

VERVE FORECAST

Number	Title	Yr	NM
FT-3028 [M]	Mike Kellin	1967	$30
FTS-3028 [S]	Mike Kellin	1967	$30

KELLIN, ORANGE

BIOGRAPH

Number	Title	Yr	NM
CEN-7	Orange Kellin in New Orleans	197?	$25

KELLUM, MURRY

PLANTATION

Number	Title	Yr	NM
531	Country Comedy	1978	$15

KELLY, BEVERLY

AUDIO FIDELITY

Number	Title	Yr	NM
AFLP-1874 [M]	Beverly Kelly Sings	1958	$30
AFSD-5874 [S]	Beverly Kelly Sings	1958	$40

RIVERSIDE

Number	Title	Yr	NM
RLP-345 [M]	Bev Kelly In Person	1960	$30
RS-9345 [S]	Bev Kelly In Person	1960	$250
6042	Bev Kelly In Person	197?	$30
RLP-328 [M]	Love Locked Out	1960	$250
RS-9328 [S]	Love Locked Out	1960	$250
6052	Love Locked Out	197?	$30

KELLY, CASEY

ELEKTRA

Number	Title	Yr	NM
EKS-75040	Casey Kelly	1972	$18
EKS-75072	For Sale	1974	$18

KELLY, ED

THERESA

Number	Title	Yr	NM
106	Ed Kelly and Friend	197?	$35
103	Music from the Black Museum	197?	$30

KELLY, EMMETT

ROULETTE

Number	Title	Yr	NM
R-25130 [M]	Sing Along with Emmett Kelly	1962	$30
SR-25130 [S]	Sing Along with Emmett Kelly	1962	$30

Number	Title	Yr	NM

KELLY, GEORGE
STASH
❏ 240	George Kelly Plays Music of Don Redman	198?	$25

KELLY, JACK
JUBILEE
| ❏ JLP-21 [10] | Jack Kelly's Badinage | 1955 | $75 |

KELLY, JOE
BLACKBIRD
| ❏ 4001 | Blackbird Presents Joe Kelly | 197? | $30 |

KELLY, JULIE, AND TOM GARVIN
CMG
| ❏ CML-8017 | Some Other Time | 1989 | $30 |

KELLY, JULIE
PAUSA
| ❏ 7186 | Never Let Me Go | 1986 | $25 |
| ❏ 7154 | We're On Our Way | 198? | $25 |

KELLY, MONTY
ALSHIRE
| ❏ SAS610 | Passport to Romance | 196? | $12 |
CARLTON
❏ LP 12-111 [M]	Porgy and Bess	1959	$25
❏ STLP 12-111 [S]	Porgy and Bess	1959	$30
❏ LP 12-123 [M]	Summer Set	1960	$25
❏ STLP 12-123 [S]	Summer Set	1960	$30
ESSEX
❏ ESLP-106 [10]	I Love	1954	$30
❏ ESLP-108 [10]	Monty Kelly Takes Me to Far Away Places	1954	$30
❏ ESLP-203 [M]	Tropicana	1955	$30
SOMERSET
| ❏ P7300 [M] | Tropicana | 196? | $12 |
| —Reissue of Trans World 203 | | | |
TRANS WORLD
| ❏ TWLP-203 [M] | Tropicana | 1956 | $25 |
| —Reissue of Essex 203 | | | |

KELLY, NANCY
AMHERST
| ❏ AMH-3317 | Live Jazz | 1988 | $25 |

KELLY, PAUL
HAPPY TIGER
| ❏ 1015 | Stealing in the Name of the Lord | 1970 | $18 |
WARNER BROS.
❏ BS2605	Dirt	1972	$15
❏ BS2689	Don't Burn Me	1973	$15
❏ BS2812	Hooked, Hogtied & Collared	1974	$15
❏ BS3026	Stand on the Positive Side	1976	$15

KELLY, R.
JIVE
❏ 41625	R.	1998	$25
❏ 41579	R. Kelly	1995	$18
❏ 41748	TP-2.com	2000	$18

KELLY, WYNTON
BLUE NOTE
| ❏ BLP-5025 [10] | Piano Interpretations by Wynton Kelly | 1953 | $400 |
DELMARK
| ❏ DS-441 | The Last Trio Session | 1989 | $50 |
EPITAPH
| ❏ E-4007 | Wynton Kelly 1931-1971 | 1975 | $50 |
FANTASY
| ❏ OJC-033 | Kelly Blue | 198? | $30 |
| ❏ OJC-401 | Wynton Kelly Piano | 1989 | $35 |
JAZZLAND
| ❏ JLP-83 [M] | Whisper Not | 1962 | $40 |
| ❏ JLP-983 [S] | Whisper Not | 1962 | $150 |
MILESTONE
| ❏ MSP-9004 | Full View | 1968 | $75 |
| ❏ M-47026 | Keep It Moving | 1975 | $75 |
RIVERSIDE
❏ RLP 12-298 [M]	Kelly Blue	1959	$400
❏ RLP-1142 [S]	Kelly Blue	1959	$300
❏ 6114	Kelly Blue	197?	$35
❏ 6043	Whisper Not	197?	$35

| ❏ RLP 12-254 [M] | Wynton Kelly Piano | 1957 | $350 |
TRIP
| ❏ TLX-5010 | Smokin' | 197? | $35 |
VEE JAY
❏ VJ-1086 [M]	Best of Wynton Kelly	1964	$40
❏ VJS-1086 [S]	Best of Wynton Kelly	1964	$50
❏ VJS-3072-2	Final Notes	1977	$30
❏ LP-3011 [M]	Kelly at Midnite	1960	$100
❏ SR-3011 [S]	Kelly at Midnite	1960	$500
❏ LP-1016 [M]	Kelly Great	1960	$100
❏ SR-1016 [S]	Kelly Great	1960	$150
❏ LP-3004 [M]	Kelly Great	1960	$75
—Reissue of LP-1016			
❏ SR-3004 [S]	Kelly Great	1960	$100
—Reissue of SR-1016			
❏ VJS-3038	Someday My Prince Will Come	1977	$50
❏ LP-3022 [M]	Wynton Kelly	1961	$150
❏ SR-3022 [S]	Wynton Kelly	1961	$120
❏ VJS-3071	Wynton Kelly In Concert	1977	$50
VERVE
❏ V-8576 [M]	Comin' in the Back Door	1964	$75
❏ V6-8576 [S]	Comin' in the Back Door	1964	$40
❏ V-8588 [M]	It's All Right	1964	$75
❏ V6-8588 [S]	It's All Right	1964	$30
❏ V-8633 [M]	Smokin' at the Half Note	1965	$50
❏ V6-8633 [S]	Smokin' at the Half Note	1965	$30
❏ V-8622 [M]	Undiluted	1965	$40
❏ V6-8622 [S]	Undiluted	1965	$50
XANADU
| ❏ 198 | Blues On Purpose | 198? | $25 |

KELLY BROTHERS, THE
EXCELLO
| ❏ LPS-8007 | Sweet Soul | 1968 | $50 |
KING
| ❏ 810 [M] | The Kelly Brothers Sing a Page of Songs from the Good Book | 1962 | $150 |

KEMP, HAL
CIRCLE
| ❏ C-25 | Hal Kemp and His Orchestra 1934 | 198? | $25 |
HINDSIGHT
❏ HSR-143	Hal Kemp and His Orchestra 1934	198?	$25
❏ HSR-161	Hal Kemp and His Orchestra 1934, Volume 2	198?	$25
❏ HSR-222	Hal Kemp and His Orchestra 1936	198?	$25

KEMP, JOHNNY
COLUMBIA
| ❏ BFC40192 | Johnny Kemp | 1986 | $12 |
| ❏ BFC40770 | Secrets of Flying | 1988 | $12 |

KEMP, WAYNE
DECCA
| ❏ DL75290 | Wayne Kemp | 1971 | $18 |
MCA
| ❏ 369 | Kentucky Sunshine | 1973 | $15 |

KENDALL, CHARLES S.
DOT
| ❏ DLP3083 [M] | Christmas Chimes | 1958 | $18 |

KENDALLS, THE
DOT
| ❏ DLP-26001 | Two Divided by Love | 1972 | $18 |
EPIC
| ❏ E245249 | 20 Favorites | 1989 | $18 |

GUSTO
| ❏ GT 0001 | 1978 Grammy Award Winners -- Best Country Duo | 1978 | $12 |
MCA
| ❏ 27021 | Never Ending Song of Love | 198? | $12 |
MCA CURB
| ❏ 5724 | Fire at First Sight | 1986 | $10 |
MERCURY
❏ SRM-1-6005	Lettin' You In on a Feelin'	1981	$12
❏ 812779-1	Movin' Train	1983	$10
❏ SRM-1-4046	Stickin' Together	1982	$12
❏ 826307-1	Thank God for the Radio... And All the Hits	1986	$10
❏ 824250-1	Two Heart Harmony	1985	$10
OVATION
❏ 1746	Heart of the Matter	1979	$15
❏ 1719	Heaven's Just a Sin Away	1977	$15
❏ 1739 [B]	Just Like Real People	1979	$15
❏ 1733 [B]	Old Fashioned Love	1978	$15
❏ 1756	The Best of the Kendalls	1980	$15
POWER PAK
| ❏ PO-216 | Leavin' on a Jet Plane | 197? | $12 |
STEP ONE
| ❏ 0023 | Break the Routine | 1987 | $12 |
STOP
| ❏ 1020 | Meet the Kendalls | 1970 | $25 |

KENDRICKS, EDDIE
ARISTA
| ❏ AB4250 | Something More | 1979 | $12 |
| ❏ AB4170 | Vintage '78 | 1978 | $12 |
ATLANTIC
| ❏ SD19294 | Love Keys | 1981 | $12 |
MOTOWN
❏ M5-151V1	Eddie Kendricks	1981	$10
—Reissue of Tamla 327			
❏ M5-196V1	He's a Friend	1981	$10
—Reissue of Tamla 343			
TAMLA
❏ T-309	All By Myself	1971	$12
❏ T330V1	Boogie Down!	1974	$12
❏ T327L	Eddie Kendricks	1973	$12
❏ T7-354	Eddie Kendricks at His Best	1977	$12
❏ T6-335	For You	1974	$12
❏ T6-346	Goin' Up in Smoke	1976	$12
❏ T6-343	He's a Friend	1976	$12
❏ T315L	People...Hold On	1972	$12
❏ T8-356	Slick	1978	$12
❏ T6-338	The Hit Man	1975	$12

KENIA
ZEBRA
| ❏ ZEB-42149 | Distant Horizon: Rio/New York | 1988 | $30 |
| ❏ ZEB-5967 | Initial Thrill | 1987 | $30 |

KENNEDY, DAVE
COULEE
| ❏ 1001 [M] | Breaking Up Is Hard to Do | 1964 | $50 |

KENNEDY, GENE, AND KAREN JEGLUM
DOOR KNOB
| ❏ 1004 | Gene Kennedy and Karen Jeglum | 1981 | $15 |

KENNEDY, HARRISON
INVICTUS
| ❏ ST9806 [B] | Hypnotic Music | 1972 | $75 |

KENNEDY, JERRY
Also see TOM AND JERRY
SMASH
❏ MGS-27004 [M]	Dancing Guitars Rock Elvis' Hits	1962	$30
❏ SRS-67004 [S]	Dancing Guitars Rock Elvis' Hits	1962	$40
❏ MGS-27066 [M]	From Nashville to Soulville	1965	$25
❏ SRS-67066 [S]	From Nashville to Soulville	1965	$30
❏ MGS-27024 [M]	Jerry Kennedy's Guitars and Strings Play the Golden Standards	1963	$25
❏ SRS-67024 [S]	Jerry Kennedy's Guitars and Strings Play the Golden Standards	1963	$30

KENNEDY, JOHN FITZGERALD
Various tribute records, most of which were released in the immediate aftermath of his assassination in 1963.
20TH CENTURY
| ❏ TCF3127 [M] | The Presidential Years 1960-1963 | 1963 | $25 |
| —Narrated by David Teig | | | |
CAEDMON
| ❏ TC-2021 | Self-Portrait | 196? | $25 |

Number	Title	Yr	NM
CAPITOL			
☐ ST2486 [S]	Years of Lightning, Day of Drums	1966	$30
☐ T2486 [M]	Years of Lightning, Day of Drums	1966	$25

— Narrated by Gregory Peck; U.S. Information Agency movie soundtrack

COLPIX			
☐ CP2500 [M]	Four Days That Shocked the World	1964	$50

— Narrated by Reid Collins; covers Nov. 22-25, 1963

DECCA			
☐ DL9116 [M]	That Was The Week That Was	1963	$25

— BBC show's tribute to JFK, broadcast Nov. 23, 1963

DIPLOMAT			
☐ 10000 [M]	John F. Kennedy -- A Memorial Album	1963	$18
DOCUMENTARIES UNLIMITED			
☐ 0(no cat #) [M]	JFK The Man, The President	1963	$25

— Narrated by Barry Gray

HARMONICA			
☐ HLP-3005 [M]	Kennedy Speaks	1963	$25
LEGACY			
☐ L2L1017 [M]	John Fitzgerald Kennedy... As We Remember Him	1965	$30

— Narrated by Charles Kuralt; with 240-page book

PICKWICK			
☐ 169 [M]	The Presidential Years (1960-1963)	1963	$18
PREMIER			
☐ 2099 [M]	A Memorial Album	1963	$25

— From WMCA Radio, New York, Nov. 22, 1963

RCA VICTOR			
☐ VDM-101 [M]	The Kennedy Wit	1964	$18

— Narrated by David Brinkley with introduction by Adlai E. Stevenson

SOMERSET			
☐ 16100 [M]	Actual Speeches of Franklin D. Roosevelt and John F. Kennedy	1963	$18

— One side has FDR speeches, the other, JFK speeches

KENNEDY, JOYCE

Number	Title	Yr	NM
A&M			
☐ SP-4996	Lookin' for Trouble	1984	$12
☐ SP-5073	Wanna Play Your Game!	1985	$12

KENNEDY, MIKE
Also see LOS BRAVOS.

Number	Title	Yr	NM
ABC			
☐ ABCX-754	Louisianna	1972	$25

KENNEDY, RAY (1)

Number	Title	Yr	NM
ARC			
☐ NJC36395	Ray Kennedy	1980	$15
CREAM			
☐ CR9001	Raymond Louis Kennedy	1972	$18

KENNEDY, ROBERT FRANCIS
Tribute album released shortly after his death.

Number	Title	Yr	NM
COLUMBIA			
☐ C2S792	A Memorial	1968	$25

KENNER, CHRIS

Number	Title	Yr	NM
ATLANTIC			
☐ 8117 [M]	Land of 1,000 Dances	1965	$50
COLLECTABLES			
☐ COL-5116	Golden Classics: I Like It Like That	198?	$15

KENNEY, BEVERLY
DECCA

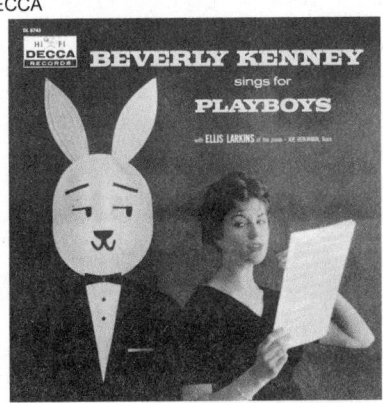

Number	Title	Yr	NM
☐ DL8743 [M]	Beverly Kenney Sings for Playboys	1958	$400
☐ DL8850 [M]	Born to Be Blue	1959	$300
☐ DL8948 [M]	Like Yesterday	1960	$250
☐ DL78948 [S]	Like Yesterday	1960	$300
ROOST			
☐ RST-2206 [M]	Beverly Kenney Sings for Johnny Smith	1956	$300
☐ RST-2218 [M]	Beverly Kenney with Jimmy Jones and the Basie-ites	1957	$300
☐ RST-2212 [M]	Come Swing with Me	1956	$300

KENNY, BILL

Number	Title	Yr	NM
WARWICK			
☐ W-2021 [M]	Mr. Ink Spot	1960	$30

KENNY AND THE KASUALS

Number	Title	Yr	NM
MARK			
☐ 7000 [S]	Garage Kings	1979	$30
☐ 6000 [M]	Teen Dreams	1978	$300

— Red vinyl; numbered, signed limited edition

☐ 5000 [M]	The Impact Sound of Kenny and the Kasuals Live at the Studio Club	1966	$1000
☐ 5000 [M]	The Impact Sound of Kenny and the Kasuals Live at the Studio Club	1977	$30

— Reissue, 1977" appears on cover

KENNY G

Number	Title	Yr	NM
ARISTA			
☐ AL8-8427	Duotones	1986	$20
☐ AL8-8192	G Force	1984	$20
☐ AL8-8282	Gravity	1985	$20
☐ AL9608	Kenny G	1982	$25
☐ ALB6-8299	Kenny G	1985	$20

— Reissue of 9608

☐ A2L-8613	Kenny G Live	1989	$30
☐ AL-8457	Silhouette	1988	$20

KENSINGTON MARKET

Number	Title	Yr	NM
WARNER BROS.			
☐ WS1780	Aardvark	1969	$25
☐ WS1754	Avenue Road	1968	$25

KENT, GEORGE

Number	Title	Yr	NM
SHANNON			
☐ 1003	George Kent	1974	$25

KENT, MARSHALL

Number	Title	Yr	NM
HERWIN			
☐ 301	Pallet on the Floor	197?	$35

KENTON, STAN, AND TEX RITTER
Also see each artist's individual listings.

Number	Title	Yr	NM
CAPITOL			
☐ T1757 [M]	Stan Kenton/Tex Ritter	1962	$250
☐ ST1757 [S]	Stan Kenton/Tex Ritter	1962	$300

KENTON, STAN

Number	Title	Yr	NM
CAPITOL			
☐ T1985 [M]	Adventures in Blues	1963	$50

— Black label with colorband, Capitol logo at top

☐ ST1985 [S]	Adventures in Blues	1963	$85

— Black label with colorband, Capitol logo at top

☐ T1796 [M]	Adventures in Jazz	1962	$50

— Black label with colorband, Capitol logo at top

☐ ST1796 [S]	Adventures in Jazz	1962	$85

— Black label with colorband, Capitol logo at top

☐ T1844 [M]	Adventures in Time	1963	$50

— Black label with colorband, Capitol logo at top

☐ ST1844 [S]	Adventures in Time	1963	$85

— Black label with colorband, Capitol logo at top

☐ T1621 [M]	A Merry Christmas	1961	$85
☐ ST1621 [S]	A Merry Christmas	1961	$100
☐ H172 [10]	A Presentation of Progressive Jazz	1950	$250
☐ T172 [M]	A Presentation of Progressive Jazz	195?	$85
☐ T1931 [M]	Artistry in Bossa Nova	1963	$75
☐ ST1931 [S]	Artistry in Bossa Nova	1963	$85
☐ M-11027	Artistry in Jazz	1972	$25
☐ H167 [10]	Artistry in Rhythm	1950	$250
☐ T167 [M]	Artistry in Rhythm	195?	$75

— Turquoise label

☐ T167 [M]	Artistry in Rhythm	1959	$85

— Black label with colorband, Capitol logo at left

☐ T167 [M]	Artistry in Rhythm	1962	$75

— Black label with colorband, Capitol logo at top

☐ DT167 [R]	Artistry in Rhythm	1969	$40
☐ SM-167 [R]	Artistry in Rhythm	1975	$20

— Reissue with new prefix

☐ T2132 [M]	Artistry in Voices and Brass	1964	$75

— Black label with colorband, Capitol logo at top

☐ ST2132 [S]	Artistry in Voices and Brass	1964	$85

— Black label with colorband, Capitol logo at top

☐ T995 [M]	Back to Balboa	1958	$75

Number	Title	Yr	NM
— Turquoise label			
☐ H353 [10]	City of Glass	1952	$250
☐ T736 [M]	City of Glass/This Modern World	1956	$75

— Combination of 353 and 460 onto one 12-inch LP, turquoise label

☐ H358 [10]	Classics	1952	$250
☐ T358 [M]	Classics	195?	$75
— Turquoise label			
☐ T666 [M]	Contemporary Concepts	1955	$250
— Turquoise label			
☐ T731 [M]	Cuban Fire!	1956	$75
— Turquoise label			
☐ T731 [M]	Cuban Fire!	1959	$100

— Black label with colorband, Capitol logo at left

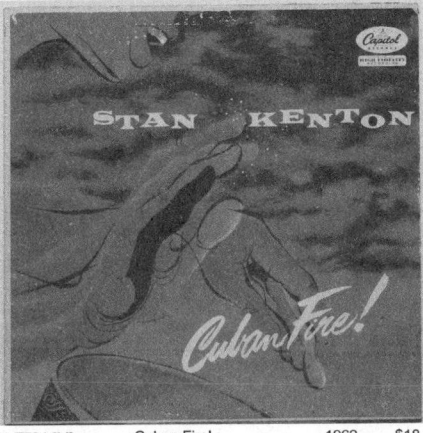

☐ T731 [M]	Cuban Fire!	1962	$18

— Black label with colorband, Capitol logo at top

☐ SM-11794 [M]	Cuban Fire!	1978	$25

— Reissue of Capitol T 731

☐ T656 [M]	Duet	1955	$85

— With June Christy; turquoise label

☐ H155 [10]	Encores	1950	$250
☐ T155 [M]	Encores	195?	$75
— Turquoise label			
☐ ST2974	Finian's Rainbow	1968	$75
☐ P189 [10]	Innovations in Modern Music	1950	$250
☐ ST2932	Jazz Compositions of Dee Barton	1968	$75
☐ T1460 [M]	Kenton at the Las Vegas Tropicana	1961	$150

— Black label with colorband, Capitol logo at left

☐ ST1460 [S]	Kenton at the Las Vegas Tropicana	1961	$100

— Black label with colorband, Capitol logo at left

☐ W724 [M]	Kenton in Hi-Fi	1956	$85

— Gray label

☐ W724 [M]	Kenton in Hi-Fi	1959	$100

— Black label with colorband, logo at left

☐ SW724 [S]	Kenton in Hi-Fi	1959	$175

— Black label with colorband, logo at left; one fewer track than mono version

☐ SW724 [S]	Kenton in Hi-Fi	1962	$150

— Black label with colorband, logo at top; one fewer track than mono version

☐ T2655 [M]	Kenton Plays for Today	1966	$75

— Black label with colorband, Capitol logo at top

☐ ST2655 [S]	Kenton Plays for Today	1966	$85

— Black label with colorband, Capitol logo at top

☐ TAO2217 [M]	Kenton Plays Wagner	1964	$75

— Black label with colorband, Capitol logo at top

☐ STAO2217 [S]	Kenton Plays Wagner	1964	$85

— Black label with colorband, Capitol logo at top

☐ W524 [M]	Kenton Showcase	1954	$85
☐ H526 [10]	Kenton Showcase -- The Music of Bill Holman	1954	$250
☐ H525 [10]	Kenton Showcase -- The Music of Bill Russo	1954	$250
☐ T1609 [M]	Kenton's West Side Story	1961	$150

— Black label with colorband, Capitol logo at left

☐ ST1609 [S]	Kenton's West Side Story	1961	$100

— Black label with colorband, Capitol logo at left

☐ T1609 [M]	Kenton's West Side Story	1961	$85

— Black label with colorband, Capitol logo at top

☐ ST1609 [S]	Kenton's West Side Story	1961	$75

— Black label with colorband, Capitol logo at top

☐ SM-12037	Kenton's West Side Story	1979	$25

— Reissue of Capitol ST 1609

☐ T810 [M]	Kenton with Voices	1957	$85
— Turquoise label			
☐ T1130 [M]	Lush Interlude	1959	$150

— Black label with colorband, Capitol logo at top

☐ ST1130 [S]	Lush Interlude	1959	$100

— Black label with colorband, Capitol logo at left

☐ H190 [10]	Milestones	1950	$250
☐ T190 [M]	Milestones	195?	$85

Number	Title	Yr	NM
— Turquoise label			
❏ T190 [M]	Milestones	196?	$150
— Black colorband label, logo at left			
❏ ST-305	Music from "Hair"	1969	$50
❏ H383 [10]	New Concepts of Artistry in Rhythm	1953	$250
❏ T383 [M]	New Concepts of Artistry in Rhythm	195?	$85
— Turquoise label			
❏ H421 [10]	Popular Favorites	1953	$250
❏ T421 [M]	Popular Favorites	195?	$85
— Turquoise label			
❏ H462 [10]	Portraits on Standards	1953	$250
❏ T462 [M]	Portraits on Standards	195?	$85
— Turquoise label			
❏ T462 [M]	Portraits on Standards	196?	$150
— Black colorband label, logo at left			
❏ H386 [10]	Prologue: This Is an Orchestra	1953	$250
❏ T932 [M]	Rendezvous with Kenton	1957	$85
— Turquoise label			
❏ TBO1327 [M]	Road Show	1960	$85
— Black label with colorband, Capitol logo at left			
❏ STBO1327 [S]	Road Show	1960	$150
— Black label with colorband, Capitol logo at left			
❏ TBO1327 [M]	Road Show	1962	$100
— Black label with colorband, Capitol logo at left			
❏ STBO1327 [S]	Road Show	1962	$50
— Black label with colorband, Capitol logo at top			
❏ H426 [10]	Sketches on Standards	1953	$250
❏ T426 [M]	Sketches on Standards	195?	$85
— Turquoise label			
❏ T1394 [M]	Standards in Silhouette	1960	$150
— Black label with colorband, Capitol logo at left			
❏ ST1394 [S]	Standards in Silhouette	1960	$100
— Black label with colorband, Capitol logo at left			
❏ T1394 [M]	Standards in Silhouette	1962	$50
— Black label with colorband, Capitol logo at top			
❏ ST1394 [S]	Standards in Silhouette	1962	$75
— Black label with colorband, Capitol logo at top			
❏ STCL-575	Stan Kenton	1970	$100
❏ MAS2424 [M]	Stan Kenton Conducts the Los Angeles Neophonic Orchestra	1966	$75
— Black label with colorband, Capitol logo at top			
❏ SMAS2424 [S]	Stan Kenton Conducts the Los Angeles Neophonic Orchestra	1966	$50
— Black label with colorband, Capitol logo at top			
❏ L248 [10]	Stan Kenton Presents	1951	$250
❏ T248 [M]	Stan Kenton Presents	195?	$85
— Turquoise label			
❏ T248 [M]	Stan Kenton Presents	196?	$150
— Black colorband label, logo at left			
❏ T248 [M]	Stan Kenton Presents	196?	$50
— Black colorband label, logo at top			
❏ T2327 [M]	Stan Kenton's Greatest Hits	1965	$75
— Black label with colorband, Capitol logo at top			
❏ DT2327 [R]	Stan Kenton's Greatest Hits	1965	$50
— Black label with colorband, Capitol logo at top			
❏ SM-2327	Stan Kenton's Greatest Hits	197?	$20
— Reissue with new prefix			
❏ N-16182	Stan Kenton's Greatest Hits	1984	$20
— Budget-line reissue			
❏ T1068 [M]	The Ballad Style of Stan Kenton	1959	$150
— Black label with colorband, Capitol logo at left			
❏ ST1068 [S]	The Ballad Style of Stan Kenton	1959	$100
— Black label with colorband, Capitol logo at left			
❏ T1068 [M]	The Ballad Style of Stan Kenton	1962	$85
— Black label with colorband, Capitol logo at top			
❏ ST1068 [S]	The Ballad Style of Stan Kenton	1962	$75
— Black label with colorband, Capitol logo at top			
❏ STB-12016	The Comprehensive Kenton	1979	$35
❏ TDB569 [M]	The Kenton Era	1955	$300
— Box set with 44-page book			
❏ WDX569 [M]	The Kenton Era	196?	$300
— Box set with 44-page book; limited edition reissue with black label, Capitol logo at left			
❏ PRO-206/7 [DJ]	The Kenton Era (Excerpts)	1955	$85
❏ T1276 [M]	The Kenton Touch	1960	$150
— Black label with colorband, Capitol logo at left			
❏ ST1276 [S]	The Kenton Touch	1960	$100
❏ T1533 [M]	The Romantic Approach	1961	$150
— Black label with colorband, Capitol logo at left			
❏ ST1533 [S]	The Romantic Approach	1961	$100
— Black label with colorband, Capitol logo at left			
❏ T1533 [M]	The Romantic Approach	1961	$50
— Black label with colorband, Capitol logo at top			
❏ ST1533 [S]	The Romantic Approach	1961	$75
— Black label with colorband, Capitol logo at top			
❏ T1674 [M]	The Sophisticated Approach	1962	$75
— Black label with colorband, Capitol logo at top			
❏ ST1674 [S]	The Sophisticated Approach	1962	$50

Number	Title	Yr	NM
— Black label with colorband, Capitol logo at top			
❏ T1166 [M]	The Stage Door Swings	1959	$150
— Black label with colorband, Capitol logo at left			
❏ ST1166 [S]	The Stage Door Swings	1959	$100
— Black label with colorband, Capitol logo at left			
❏ STCL2989	The Stan Kenton Deluxe Set	1968	$100
❏ ST2810	The World We Know	1968	$75
❏ H460 [10]	This Modern World	1953	$250
❏ W1305 [M]	Viva Kenton!	1960	$150
— Black label with colorband, Capitol logo at left			
❏ SW1305 [S]	Viva Kenton!	1960	$100
— Black label with colorband, Capitol logo at left			
CREATIVE WORLD			
❏ ST1070	7.5 on the Richter Scale	1973	$25
❏ ST1037 [R]	A Concert in Progressive Jazz	197?	$20
— Reissue of Capitol T 172			
❏ ST1012	Adventures in Blues	197?	$25
— Reissue of Capitol ST 1985			
❏ ST1010	Adventures in Jazz	197?	$25
— Reissue of Capitol ST 1796			
❏ ST1025	Adventures in Standards	197?	$25
❏ ST1011	Adventures in Time	197?	$25
— Reissue of Capitol ST 1844			
❏ ST1045	Artistry in Bossa Nova	197?	$25
❏ ST1043 [R]	Artistry in Rhythm	197?	$20
— Reissue of Capitol DT 167			
❏ ST1038	Artistry in Voices and Brass	197?	$25
— Reissue of Capitol ST 2132			
❏ ST1031	Back to Balboa	197?	$25
— Reissue of Capitol T 995			
❏ ST1065	Birthday in Britain	1973	$25
❏ ST1006 [R]	City of Glass/This Modern World	197?	$20
— Reissue of Capitol T 736			
❏ ST1027 [R]	Collector's Choice	197?	$20
❏ ST1003 [R]	Contemporary Concepts	197?	$20
— Reissue of Capitol T 666			
❏ ST1008 [R]	Cuban Fire!	197?	$20
— Reissue of Capitol T 731			
❏ ST1048 [R]	Duet	197?	$20
— Reissue of Capitol T 656			
❏ ST1034 [R]	Encores	197?	$20
— Reissue of Capitol T 155			
❏ ST1073	Fire, Fury and Fun	1974	$25
❏ ST1074	Hits in Concert	197?	$25
❏ ST1009 [R]	Innovations in Modern Music	197?	$20
— Reissue of Capitol P 189			
❏ ST1022	Jazz Compositions of Dee Barton	197?	$25
— Reissue of Capitol ST 2932			
❏ ST1077	Journey Into Capricorn	1977	$25
❏ ST1076	Kenton '76	1976	$25
❏ ST1032	Kenton at the Las Vegas Tropicana	197?	$25
— Reissue of Capitol ST 1460			
❏ ST1036 [R]	Kenton By Request, Vol. I	197?	$20
❏ ST1040 [R]	Kenton By Request, Vol. II	197?	$20
❏ ST1062 [R]	Kenton By Request, Vol. III	197?	$20
❏ ST1064 [R]	Kenton By Request, Vol. IV	197?	$20
❏ ST1066 [R]	Kenton By Request, Vol. V	197?	$20
❏ ST1069 [R]	Kenton By Request, Vol. VI	197?	$25
❏ ST1004 [R]	Kenton in Stereo	197?	$25
— Reissue of Capitol W 724			
❏ ST1072	Kenton Plays Chicago	1974	$25
❏ ST1024	Kenton Plays Wagner	197?	$25
— Reissue of Capitol STAO 2217			
❏ ST1001	Kenton's Christmas	1970	$30
❏ ST1026 [R]	Kenton Showcase	197?	$20
— Reissue of Capitol W 524			
❏ ST1007	Kenton's West Side Story	197?	$25
— Reissue of Capitol ST 1609			
❏ ST1039 [Q]	Live at Brigham Young	1971	$40
❏ ST1058 [Q]	Live at Butler University	1972	$75
❏ ST1015	Live at Redlands University	1971	$25
❏ ST1005	Lush Interlude	197?	$25
— Reissue of Capitol ST 1130			
❏ ST1047 [R]	Milestones	197?	$20
— Reissue of Capitol T 190			
❏ ST1060 [Q]	National Anthems of the World	1972	$75
❏ ST1002 [R]	New Concepts of Artistry in Rhythm	197?	$25
— Reissue of Capitol T 383			
❏ ST1042 [R]	Portraits on Standards	197?	$20
— Reissue of Capitol T 462			
❏ ST1057	Rendezvous with Kenton	197?	$25
— Reissue of Capitol T 932			
❏ ST1019	Road Show, Volume 1	197?	$25
— Partial reissue of Capitol STBO 1327			
❏ ST1020	Road Show, Volume 2	197?	$25
— Partial reissue of Capitol STBO 1327			
❏ ST1041 [R]	Sketches on Standards	197?	$20
— Reissue of Capitol T 426			
❏ ST1071	Solo	1973	$25
❏ ST1029 [R]	Some Women I've Known	197?	$20
❏ ST1049	Standards in Silhouette	197?	$25
— Reissue of Capitol ST 1394			

Number	Title	Yr	NM
❏ ST1013	Stan Kenton Conducts the Los Angeles Neophonic Orchestra	197?	$25
— Reissue of Capitol SMAS 2424			
❏ ST1061 [R]	Stan Kenton -- Formative Years	197?	$20
— Reissue of Decca DL 8259			
❏ ST1023 [R]	Stan Kenton Presents	197?	$20
— Reissue of Capitol T 248			
❏ CW-3005	Stan Kenton Presents Gabe Baltazar	1979	$25
❏ ST1046	Stan Kenton with Jean Turner	197?	$25
❏ ST1059 [Q]	Stan Kenton with the Four Freshmen at Butler University	1972	$75
❏ ST1079	Street of Dreams	197?	$25
❏ ST1068	The Ballad Style of Stan Kenton	197?	$20
— Reissue of Capitol ST 1068			
❏ ST1035 [R]	The Christy Years	197?	$20
❏ ST1080	The Exciting Stan Kenton	197?	$25
❏ ST1028 [R]	The Fabulous Alumni of Stan Kenton	197?	$20
❏ ST1078 [R]	The Jazz Compositions of Stan Kenton	197?	$20
❏ ST1030 [R]	The Kenton Era	197?	$100
— Reissue of Capitol TDB 569			
❏ ST1033	The Kenton Touch	197?	$25
— Reissue of Capitol ST 1276			
❏ ST1050 [R]	The Lighter Side of Stan Kenton	197?	$20
❏ ST1017	The Romantic Approach	197?	$20
— Reissue of Capitol ST 1533			
❏ ST1018	The Sophisticated Approach	197?	$25
— Reissue of Capitol ST 1674			
❏ ST1044	The Stage Door Swings	197?	$25
— Reissue of Capitol ST 1166			
❏ ST1067	Too Much	197?	$25
❏ ST1063	Viva Kenton!	197?	$25
— Reissue of Capitol SW 1305			
DECCA			
❏ DL8259 [M]	Stan Kenton -- Formative Years	195?	$30
— All-black label with silver print			
❏ DL8259 [M]	Stan Kenton -- Formative Years	1960	$35
— Black label with color bars			
HINDSIGHT			
❏ HSR-118	Stan Kenton 1941	1984	$20
❏ HSR-124	Stan Kenton 1941, Volume 2	1984	$20
❏ HSR-136	Stan Kenton 1943-44	1984	$20
❏ HSR-147	Stan Kenton 1944-45	1984	$20
❏ HSR-157	Stan Kenton 1945-47	1984	$20
❏ HSR-195	Stan Kenton 1962	1984	$20
INSIGHT			
❏ 206	Stan Kenton and His Orchestra, Volume 1	197?	$25
❏ 217	Stan Kenton and His Orchestra, Volume 2	197?	$25
LONDON PHASE 4			
❏ ST-44276	Live in Europe	1976	$25
❏ BP44179/80	Stan Kenton Today	1972	$40
MOBILE FIDELITY			
❏ Jan-0091	Kenton Plays Wagner	1982	$75
— Audiophile vinyl			
MOSAIC			
❏ MR6-136	The Complete Capitol Recordings of the Holman and Russo Charts	199?	$300
❏ MQ10-163	The Complete Capitol Studio Recordings of Stan Kenton 1943-47	199?	$300
SUNBEAM			
❏ 213	Artistry in Rhythm, 1944-45	197?	$25
TIME-LIFE			
❏ STBB-13	Big Bands: Stan Kenton	1984	$35

KENTON, STAN/JUNE CHRISTY/THE FOUR FRESHMEN

CAPITOL

❏ STCL-575	Stan Kenton/June Christy/The Four Freshmen	1970	$150

— Reissue of an album by each artist in a 3-LP box -- ST 1796 (Kenton), ST 516 (Christy), ST 1008 (Four Freshmen)

KENTUCKY COLONELS, THE

BRIAR

❏ BT-7202	Livin' in the Past	1975	$30
❏ 109	The New Sounds of Bluegrass America	1976	$40

WORLD PACIFIC

❏ T1821 [M]	Appalachian Swing	1964	$50
❏ ST1821 [S]	Appalachian Swing	1964	$75

KENTUCKY HEADHUNTERS, THE

MERCURY

❏ 838744-1	Pickin' on Nashville	1989	$18

Number	Title	Yr	NM

KENYATTA, ROBIN
ATLANTIC
❏ SD1633	Gypsy Man	1972	$25
❏ SD1656	Stompin' at the Savoy	1974	$35
❏ SD1644	Terra Nova	1973	$35

ECM
❏ 1008 [B]	The Girl from Martinique	197?	$25

MUSE
❏ MR-5095	Beggars	1979	$30
❏ MR-5062	Nomusa	1975	$30

VORTEX
❏ 2005	Until	1969	$25

KEPPARD, FREDDIE
HERWIN
❏ 101	Freddie Keppard 1926	197?	$30

MILESTONE
❏ 2014	Freddie Keppard and Tommy Ladnier	197?	$30

KEROUAC, JACK
DOT
❏ DLP-3154 [M]	Poetry for the Beat Generation	1959	$10000

—*Acknowledged to be extremely rare; approximately 130 copies were distributed and only a small handful are known to exist today; the same performance is on Hanover 5000; VG value 5000; VG+ value 7500*

HANOVER
❏ HML-5006 [M]	Blues and Haikus	1959	$300

—*AL COHN and ZOOT SIMS play saxophones behind Kerouac on this album*

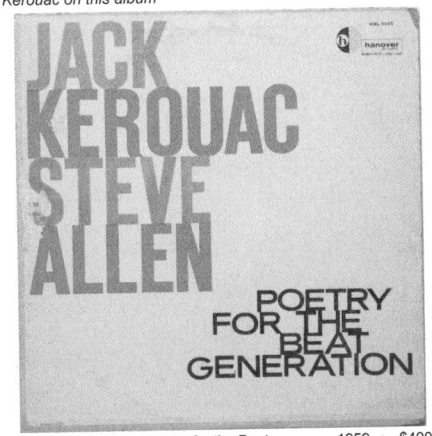

❏ HML-5000 [M]	Poetry for the Beat Generation	1959	$400

—*Reissue of Dot LP with new cover; STEVE ALLEN plays piano on this record*

RHINO
❏ R1-70939	The Jack Kerouac Collection	1990	$120

—*Box set compiling the Hanover and Verve LPs plus an LP of unreleased material*

VERVE
❏ MGV-15005 [M]	Readings on the Beat Generation	1960	$300

KERR, ANITA, SINGERS
AMPEX
❏ A-10142	A Christmas Story	1971	$15

—*With the Royal Philharmonic Orchestra*
❏ A-10136	Grow to Know Me	1971	$12

BAINBRIDGE
❏ 6226	I Sang with Jim Reeves	1981	$12
❏ 6228	'Round Midnight	1981	$12
❏ 6224	Slightly Baroque	1981	$12
❏ 6227	The Simon and Garfunkel Songbook	1981	$12

CENTURY
❏ 1160	Anita Kerr Performs Wonder's	1979	$12

DECCA
❏ DL4061 [M]	For You, For Me, Forevermore	1960	$18
❏ DL74061 [S]	For You, For Me, Forevermore	1960	$25
❏ DL8647 [M]	Quartet Voices in Hi-Fi	1958	$18
❏ DL75159	Till the End of Time	1970	$12

DOT
❏ DLP25944	Precious Teresa	1969	$12
❏ DLP25906	The Anita Kerr Singers Reflect on the Hits of Burt Bacharach & Hal David	1969	$12
❏ DLP25970	Touchlove	1970	$12
❏ DLP25961 [B]	Velvet Voices and Bold Brass	1969	$12

RCA CAMDEN
❏ CAS-2209 [B]	Georgia on My Mind	1968	$12

RCA VICTOR
❏ APL1-2298	Anite Kerr and the French Connection	1977	$12
❏ LPM-2480 [M]	From Nashville…The Hit Sound	1962	$15
❏ LSP-2480 [S]	From Nashville…The Hit Sound	1962	$18
❏ LPM-3322 [M]	Mellow Moods of Love	1965	$15
❏ LSP-3322 [S]	Mellow Moods of Love	1965	$18
❏ LPM-3485 [M]	Sunday Serenade	1966	$15
❏ LSP-3485 [S]	Sunday Serenade	1966	$18
❏ LPM-2679 [M]	Tender Words	1963	$15
❏ LSP-2679 [S]	Tender Words	1963	$18
❏ APL1-1166	The Anita Kerr Singers	1975	$12
❏ LPM-2581 [M]	The Genius" In Harmony	1962	$15
❏ LSP-2581 [S]	The Genius" In Harmony	1962	$18
❏ LPM-3428 [M]	We Dig Mancini	1965	$15
❏ LSP-3428 [S]	We Dig Mancini	1965	$18

VOCALION
❏ VL73899	For You	1969	$12

WARNER BROS.
❏ W1724 [M]	All You Need Is Love	1967	$18
❏ WS1724 [M]	All You Need Is Love	1967	$15
❏ W1707 [M]	Bert Kaempfert Turns Us On!	1967	$18
❏ WS1707 [S]	Bert Kaempfert Turns Us On!	1967	$15
❏ W1665 [M]	Slightly Baroque	1966	$15
❏ WS1665 [S]	Slightly Baroque	1966	$18

WORD
❏ 8647	Hallelujah Brass	197?	$12
❏ 8707	Hallelujah Guitars	197?	$12
❏ 8808	Hallelujah Voices	197?	$12
❏ 8741	Hallelujah Woodwinds	197?	$12
❏ 8692	Hymns	197?	$12

—*With Kurt Kaiser*
❏ 8706	Precious Memories	1977	$12
❏ 8696	Walk a Little Slower	197?	$12

KERR, BROOKS, AND PAUL QUINICHETTE
FAMOUS DOOR
❏ 106	Preview	197?	$35

KERR, BROOKS
CHIAROSCURO
❏ 2001	Soda Fountain Rag	197?	$30

KERSHAW, DOUG
SCOTTI BROTHERS
❏ SB7115	Instant Hero	1981	$15
❏ FZ37428	Instant Hero	1981	$12

WARNER BROS.
❏ BS2851	Alive & Pickin'	1975	$15
❏ WS1820	Cajun Way	1969	$25

—*Green label, "W7" box logo at top*
❏ WS1820	Cajun Way	1970	$18

—*Green label, "WB" shield logo at top*
❏ BS2649	Devil's Elbow	1973	$18
❏ WS1906	Doug Kershaw	1971	$18

—*Green label*
❏ BS2725	Douglas James Kershaw	1973	$18
❏ BS3025	Flip, Flop & Fly	1977	$15
❏ BSK3166	Louisiana Man	1978	$15
❏ BS2793	Mama Kershaw's Boy	1974	$18
❏ BS2910	Ragin' Cajun	1976	$15
❏ WS1861	Spanish Moss	1970	$18

—*Green label*
❏ BS2581	Swamp Grass	1972	$18

—*Green label*

KERSHAW, NIK
MCA
❏ 39020	Human Racing	1984	$12
❏ 5930	Radio Musicola	1986	$15

—*May only exist as a Canadian pressing*
❏ 5548	The Riddle	1985	$12

KERSHAW, RUSTY AND DOUG
HICKORY
❏ LPM-103 [M]	Rusty and Doug Sing Louisiana Man	1960	$120

HICKORY/MGM
❏ H3G-4506	Louisiana Man	1974	$25

KESEY, KEN
SOUND CITY
❏ 27690 [M]	The Acid Test	1967	$1000

—*THE GRATEFUL DEAD appear on this LP*

KESL, LENNIE
REVELATION
❏ 29	Walkin' On Air	1978	$30

KESNER, DICK
BRUNSWICK
❏ BL54051 [M]	Dick Kesner and His Magic Stradivarius	1959	$18
❏ BL754051 [S]	Dick Kesner and His Magic Stradivarius	1959	$25
❏ BL54054 [M]	Intermezzo	1960	$18
❏ BL754054 [S]	Intermezzo	1960	$25
❏ BL54044 [M]	Lawrence Welk Presents Dick Kesner	1958	$25
❏ BL754044 [S]	Lawrence Welk Presents Dick Kesner	1959	$30

CORAL
❏ CRL57393 [M]	Amor Latino	1962	$15
❏ CRL757393 [S]	Amor Latino	1962	$18
❏ CRL57360 [M]	A "New" Old Refrain	1961	$15
❏ CRL757360 [S]	A "New" Old Refrain	1961	$18
❏ CRL57435 [M]	Golden Favorites	1964	$15
❏ CRL757435 [S]	Golden Favorites	1964	$18
❏ CRL57352 [M]	Music of Hawaii	1960	$15
❏ CRL757352 [S]	Music of Hawaii	1960	$18
❏ CRL57376 [M]	The Sound of Gypsy Music	1961	$15
❏ CRL757376 [S]	The Sound of Gypsy Music	1961	$18

VOCALION
❏ VL3777 [M]	Latin Favorites	196?	$15
❏ VL73777 [S]	Latin Favorites	196?	$18

KESSEL, BARNEY, AND HERB ELLIS
CONCORD JAZZ
❏ CJ-34	Butterfly	1976	$30

KESSEL, BARNEY, AND RED MITCHELL
JAZZ MAN
❏ 5025	Two Way Conversation	198?	$25

KESSEL, BARNEY, AND STEPHANE GRAPPELLI
BLACK LION
❏ 173	Limehouse Blues	197?	$35

KESSEL, BARNEY
BLACK LION
❏ 310	Blue Soul	197?	$35
❏ 210	Summertime in Montreux	197?	$30
❏ 130	Swinging Easy	197?	$30

CONCORD JAZZ
❏ CJ-9	Barney Plays Kessel	197?	$30
❏ CJ-164	Jellybeans	1981	$25
❏ CJ-33	Soaring	1976	$30
❏ CJ-221	Solo	1982	$25

CONTEMPORARY
❏ C-2508 [10]	Barney Kessel, Volume 1	1953	$300
❏ C-2514 [10]	Barney Kessel, Volume 2	1954	$300
❏ M-3563 [M]	Barney Kessel Plays "Carmen"	1959	$300
❏ S-7563 [S]	Barney Kessel Plays "Carmen"	1959	$300
❏ C-3511 [M]	Easy Like	1956	$250
❏ M-3618 [M]	Feeling Free	1965	$175
❏ S-7618 [S]	Feeling Free	1965	$175
❏ C-3512 [M]	Kessel Plays Standards	1956	$250
❏ M-3603 [M]	Let's Cook!	1962	$250
❏ S-7603 [S]	Let's Cook!	1962	$250
❏ C-3521 [M]	Music to Listen to Barney Kessel By	1956	$250
❏ S-7521 [S]	Music to Listen to Barney Kessel By	1959	$300
❏ C-14044	Red Hot and Blues	198?	$25
❏ M-3565 [M]	Some Like It Hot	1959	$300
❏ S-7565 [S]	Some Like It Hot	1959	$300
❏ C-14033	Spontaneous Combustion	1987	$25
❏ M-3613 [M]	Swingin' Party	1963	$250
❏ S-7613 [S]	Swingin' Party	1963	$250
❏ C-3513 [M]	To Swing or Not to Swing	1956	$250
❏ M-3585 [M]	Workin' Out!	1960	$250
❏ S-7585 [S]	Workin' Out!	1960	$250

EMERALD
❏ 1401 [M]	On Fire	1965	$35
❏ 2401 [S]	On Fire	1965	$25

FANTASY
❏ OJC-269	Barney Kessel Plays "Carmen"	198?	$25
❏ OJC-153	Easy Like	198?	$25
❏ OJC-179	Feeling Free	198?	$25
❏ OJC-238	Kessel Plays Standards	198?	$25
❏ OJC-168	Some Like It Hot	198?	$25
❏ OJC-317	To Swing or Not to Swing	1987	$25

RCA CAMDEN
❏ CAS-2404	Guitarra	1970	$25

REPRISE
❏ R-6049 [M]	Bossa Nova	1962	$35
❏ R9-6049 [S]	Bossa Nova	1962	$25
❏ R-6019 [M]	Breakfast at Tiffany's	1961	$35

Number	Title	Yr	NM
❏ R9-6019 [S]	Breakfast at Tiffany's	1961	$25
❏ R-6073 [M]	Kessel/Jazz	1963	$35
❏ R9-6073 [S]	Kessel/Jazz	1963	$25

STEREO RECORDS
| ❏ S-7001 [S] | Music to Listen to Barney Kessel By | 1958 | $50 |

KESSLER, SIEGFRIED, AND DAUNIK LAZRO
HAT HUT
| ❏ 3502 | Aeros | 1982 | $30 |

KEYMEN, THE
ABC-PARAMOUNT
❏ 258 [M]	Dance with Dick Clark	1958	$30
❏ S-258 [S]	Dance with Dick Clark	1958	$50
❏ 288 [M]	Dance with Dick Clark, Volume 2	1959	$30
❏ S-288 [S]	Dance with Dick Clark, Volume 2	1959	$50

CORAL
| ❏ CRL57112 [M] | Vocal Sounds of the Keymen | 1957 | $30 |

GOLDUST
| ❏ LPS-153 [M] | The Keymen Live | 196? | $50 |

KEYS, CALVIN
BLACK JAZZ
| ❏ 5 [B] | Shawn-neeq | 1972 | $30 |
OVATION
| ❏ OV-1804 | Criss Cross | 1978 | $30 |

KGB
MCA
| ❏ 2166 | KGB | 1976 | $12 |
| ❏ 2221 | Motion | 1976 | $12 |

KHAN, CHAKA
REPRISE
| ❏ PRO-A-8478 [DJ] | Epiphany: The Best of Chaka Khan Sampler | 1996 | $18 |
| —Promo-only six-song sampler | | | |

WARNER BROS.
❏ BSK3245 [B]	Chaka	1978	$12
❏ 23729	Chaka Khan	1982	$12
❏ 25707	C.K.	1988	$12
❏ 25425	Destiny	1986	$12
❏ 25162	I Feel for You	1984	$12
❏ 25946	Life Is a Dance: The Remix Project	1989	$18
❏ BSK3385	Naughty	1980	$12
❏ HS3526	What Cha' Gonna Do for Me	1981	$12

KHAN, STEVE
ANTILLES
| ❏ AN-1020 | Casa Loco | 198? | $25 |
| ❏ AN-1018 | Eyewitness | 198? | $25 |
ARISTA/NOVUS
| ❏ AN3023 | Evidence | 1980 | $30 |
COLUMBIA
❏ JC36129	Arrows	1979	$25
❏ JC36406	The Best of Steve Khan	1980	$25
❏ JC35539	The Blue Man	1978	$25
❏ JC34857	Tightrope	1977	$25

KHAN
PVC
| ❏ 7902 [B] | Space Shanty | 1978 | $30 |
| —first US release for rare 1972 prog album | | | |

KHAZAD DOOM
LPL
| ❏ 892 | Level 6 1/2 | 1970 | $1000 |

KIARA
ARISTA
| ❏ AL-8617 | Civilized Rogue | 1990 | $15 |
| ❏ AL-8533 | To Change And/Or Make a Difference | 1988 | $12 |

KICKLIGHTER, RICHY
ICHIBAN
| ❏ ICH-1051 | In the Night | 198? | $25 |
| ❏ ICH-1019 | Just for Kicks | 198? | $25 |

KICKSTANDS, THE
CAPITOL
❏ T2078 [M]	Black Boots and Bikes	1964	$120
❏ ST2078 [S]	Black Boots and Bikes	1964	$175
❏ T/ST2078	Black Boots and Bikes Bonus Fold-Out	1964	$50

KID CASHMERE
GUINNESS
| ❏ GNS36081 [B] | Kid Cashmere | 1977 | $50 |

KID CREOLE AND THE COCONUTS
ANTILLES
| ❏ AN7078 | Off the Coast of Me | 1980 | $15 |
SIRE
❏ 23977	Doppelganger	1983	$12
❏ SRK3534	Fresh Fruit in Foreign Places	1981	$12
❏ 25579	I, Too, Have Seen the Woods	1987	$12
❏ 25298	In Praise of Older Women and Other Crimes	1985	$12
❏ SRK3681	Wise Guy	1982	$12

KID FROST
VIRGIN
| ❏ 91377 | Hispanic Causing Panic | 1990 | $18 |

KID 'N PLAY
SELECT
❏ 21628	2 Hype	1988	$15
❏ 61206	Face the Nation	1991	$15
❏ 21638	Kid 'N Play's Funhouse	1990	$15

KID ROCK
ATLANTIC
❏ 83482	Cocky	2001	$25
❏ 83119	Devil Without a Cause	1999	$25
❏ 83685	Kid Rock	2003	$18
❏ 83314	The History of Rock	2000	$25
JIVE
| ❏ 1409-1 | Grits Sandwiches for Breakfast | 1990 | $25 |

KID STUFF REPERTORY COMPANY, THE
KID STUFF
| ❏ KS 090 | A Christmas Carol | 1978 | $15 |

KID THOMAS
AMERICAN MUSIC
| ❏ 642 [10] | Kid Thomas | 1952 | $50 |
ARHOOLIE
| ❏ 1016 | New Orleans Jazz | 1967 | $30 |
GHB
❏ GHB-80	Kid Thomas and His Algiers Stompers	197?	$30
❏ GHB-291	Kid Thomas in England	198?	$25
❏ GHB-24 [M]	Kid Thomas + The Hall Brothers Jazz Band	196?	$25
JAZZOLOGY
| ❏ JCE-13 | Sonnets from Algiers | 1967 | $30 |
NEW ORLEANS
| ❏ NOR7201 | Kid Thomas at Kohlman's Tavern | 1972 | $30 |
| —Label calls this "Thomas Valentine at Kohlman's Tavern" | | | |
RIVERSIDE
❏ RLP-365 [M]	Kid Thomas and His Algiers Stompers	1961	$250
❏ RS-9365 [R]	Kid Thomas and His Algiers Stompers	1961	$250
❏ RLP-386 [M]	Kid Thomas and His Algiers Stompers	1961	$250
❏ RS-9386 [R]	Kid Thomas and His Algiers Stompers	1961	$250

KIHN, GREG, BAND
BESERKLEY
❏ JBZ 0052	Again	1978	$12
—Third issue, distributed by Janus			
❏ PZ34779	Again	1977	$18
—Second issue, distributed by CBS			
❏ 60117	Again	1982	$10
—Reissue			
❏ BZ 0052	Again	1977	$15
—First issue, distributed by Playboy			

❏ BZ10068	Glass House Rock	1980	$12
❏ JBZ 0046	Greg Kihn Band	1978	$12
—Third issue, distributed by Janus			
❏ BZ 0046 [B]	Greg Kihn Band	1976	$25
—First issue, distributed by Playboy			
❏ PZ34753	Greg Kihn Band	1977	$0
—Second issue; never issued with this number?			
❏ BZ10069	Greg Rockihnroll Band	1981	$10
❏ 60224	Kihnspiracy	1983	$10
❏ 60354	Kihntagious	1984	$10
❏ 60101	Kihntinued	1982	$10
❏ JBZ 0056	Next of Kihn	1978	$12
—Original issue, distributed by Janus			
❏ 60116	Next of Kihn	1982	$10
—Reissue			
❏ BZ10063	With the Naked Eye	1979	$12
EMI AMERICA
| ❏ SJ-17152 | Citizen Kihn | 1985 | $10 |
| ❏ ST-17180 | Love and Rock and Roll | 1986 | $10 |
RHINO
| ❏ R1-70900 | Kihnsolidation: The Best of Greg Kihn | 1989 | $15 |

KIKUCHI, MASABUMI
CATALYST
| ❏ 7916 | Matrix | 197? | $30 |
INNER CITY
| ❏ IC-6021 | Wishes/Kochi | 1979 | $35 |

KILGORE, MERLE
STARDAY
| ❏ SLP-251 [M] | There's Gold in Them Thar Hills | 1963 | $30 |
WING
| ❏ MGW-12316 [M] | Tall Texan | 196? | $18 |
| ❏ SRW-16316 [S] | Tall Texan | 196? | $15 |

KILIMANJARO
PHILO
| ❏ 9001 | Kilimanjaro | 1979 | $30 |
| ❏ 9005 | Kilimanjaro 2 | 1981 | $30 |

KILLING FLOOR
SIRE
| ❏ SES-97019 [B] | Killing Floor | 1970 | $85 |

KIM, ANDY
ABC DUNHILL
| ❏ DSDP-50193 | Andy Kim's Greatest Hits | 1974 | $15 |
| —Reissue of Steed 37008 | | | |
CAPITOL
| ❏ ST-11318 | Andy Kim | 1974 | $15 |
| ❏ ST-11368 | The Pilot | 1975 | $15 |
STEED
❏ ST37008	Andy Kim's Greatest Hits	1970	$18
❏ ST37004	Baby I Love You	1969	$18
❏ ST-7001 [M]	How Did We Ever Get This Way?	1968	$40
—In stereo cover with "Monaural" sticker			
❏ STS-37001 [S]	How Did We Ever Get This Way?	1968	$18
❏ STS-37002	Rainbow Ride	1969	$18
UNI
| ❏ 73137 | Andy Kim | 1972 | $15 |

KIMBALL, JEANETTE
NEW ORLEANS
| ❏ 7208 | Sophisticated Lady | 198? | $25 |

KIMBERLYS, THE
HAPPY TIGER
| ❏ HT-1014 | New Horizon | 1970 | $18 |
| ❏ HT-1006 | The Kimberlys | 1970 | $18 |

KIME, WARREN, AND HIS BRASS IMPACT ORCHESTRA
COMMAND
❏ 33-910 [M]	Brass Impact	1967	$12
❏ SD-910 [S]	Brass Impact	1967	$15
❏ 33-919 [M]	Explosive Brass Impact	1967	$12
❏ SD-919 [S]	Explosive Brass Impact	1967	$15

KIMURA, YOSHIKO
INNER CITY
| ❏ IC-6043 | Memories | 1978 | $35 |

KINCAID, BRADLEY
VARSITY
| ❏ 6988 [10] | American Ballads | 1955 | $75 |

Number	Title	Yr	NM

LP 34 AMERICAN BALLADS AND FOLK SONGS - BRADLEY KINCAID

AMERICAN BALLADS AND FOLK SONGS

BLUE TAIL FLY
FOOTPRINTS IN THE SNOW
THE FATAL DERBY DAY
THE MINERS SONG
HUMMING BIRD SPECIAL
RED LIGHT AHEAD
THOSE PRECIOUS LOVE LETTERS
THE LEGEND OF
THE ROBIN RED BREAST

BRADLEY KINCAID

Number	Title	Yr	NM
❏ 34 [M]	Bradley Kincaid Sings American Ballads and Folk Songs	1957	$40

KINCAIDE, DEAN
WEATHERS
| ❏ 5610 [M] | Arranged for You | 1954 | $50 |

KINES, TOM
ELEKTRA
| ❏ EKL-137 [M] | Of Maids and Mistresses | 1958 | $30 |

KINESIS
HEADFIRST
| ❏ 9705 | New Life | 198? | $25 |

KING, ALBERT
ATLANTIC
| ❏ SD8213 | King of the Blues Guitar | 1969 | $30 |
FANTASY
| ❏ 9633 | I'm in a Phone Booth, Baby | 1984 | $12 |
| ❏ 9627 | San Francisco '83 | 1983 | $12 |
KING
| ❏ 852 [M] | Big Blues | 1963 | $500 |
| ❏ KS-1060 | Travelin' to California | 1969 | $30 |
MODERN BLUES
| ❏ MBLP-723 | Let's Have a Natural Ball | 198? | $12 |
STAX
❏ MPS-8546	Blues at Sunrise	1988	$12
❏ MPS-8504	Blues for Elvis	1981	$12
—Retitled reissue of 2015			
❏ ST-723 [M]	Born Under a Bad Sign	1967	$100
❏ STS-723 [S]	Born Under a Bad Sign	1967	$120
❏ STS-3009	I'll Play the Blues for You	1972	$25
❏ MPS-8513	I'll Play the Blues for You	1981	$12
—Reissue of 3309			
❏ STS-5505	I Wanna Get Funky	1974	$18
❏ MPS-8536	I Wanna Get Funky	1987	$12
—Reissue of 5505			
❏ STS-2015	King Does the King's Thing	1969	$30
❏ STS-2003	Live Wire/Blues Power	1968	$50
❏ STX-4128 [B]	Live Wire/Blues Power	1979	$12
—Reissue of 2003			
❏ STS-2040	Lovejoy	1971	$25
❏ MPS-8517	Lovejoy	1981	$12
—Reissue of 2040			
❏ STS-5520	Montreux Festival	1975	$18
❏ STX-4132	Montreux Festival	1980	$12
—Retitled reissue of 5520			
❏ MPS-8534	The Lost Session	1986	$12
❏ STX-4101	The Pinch	1977	$15
❏ MPS-8557	Tuesday Night in San Francisco	1990	$12
❏ MPS-8556	Wednesday Night in San Francisco	1990	$12
❏ STS-2010	Years Gone By	1969	$30
❏ MPS-8522	Years Gone By	1982	$12
—Reissue of 2010			
SUNDAZED
❏ LP5031	Born Under a Bad Sign	1999	$18
—Reissue on 180-gram vinyl			
❏ 5429 [B]	The Big Blues		$30
TOMATO
❏ TOM-6002	King Albert	1978	$15
❏ TOM-7022	New Orleans Heat	1979	$15
UTOPIA
❏ BUL1-1731	Albert	1976	$15
❏ CUL2-2205	Albert Live	1977	$18
❏ BUL1-1387	Truckload of Lovin'	1976	$15

KING, ALBERT/LITTLE MILTON
STAX
| ❏ STX-4123 | Chronicle | 1979 | $15 |
| —One side devoted to each artist | | | |

KING, ALBERT/OTIS RUSH
CHESS
❏ LPS1538	Door to Door	1969	$30
❏ CH-9322	Door to Door	1990	$12
—Reissue			

KING, ALBERT/STEVE CROPPER/POP STAPLES
STAX
❏ STS-2020	Jammed Together	1969	$30
❏ MPS-8544	Jammed Together	1988	$12
—Reissue			

KING, ANNA
SMASH
| ❏ MGS-27059 [M] | Back to Soul | 1964 | $150 |
| ❏ SRS-67059 [S] | Back to Soul | 1964 | $120 |

KING, B.B.
CLEOPATRA
❏ 2849 [B]	King of the Blues		$25
❏ 8143 [B]	King of the Blues		$30
—picture disc			

KING, B.B.
ABC
❏ D-878	Back in the Alley	1975	$15
—Reissue of BluesWay 6050			
❏ D-730	B.B. King in London	1971	$15
❏ D-704	Blues Is King	1970	$15
—Reissue of BluesWay 6001			
❏ D-709	Blues on Top of Blues	1970	$15
—Reissue of BluesWay 6011			
❏ D-868	Completely Well	1975	$15
—Reissue of BluesWay 6037			
❏ D-825	Friends	1974	$15
❏ X-759	Guess Who	1972	$15
❏ D-813	His Best/The Electric B.B. King	1974	$15
—Reissue of BluesWay 6022			
❏ D-713	Indianola Mississippi Seeds	1970	$15
❏ AB-977	King Size	1977	$15
❏ D-743	L.A. Midnight	1972	$15
❏ D-819	Live and Well	1974	$15
—Reissue of BluesWay 6031			
❏ D-724	Live at the Regal	1971	$15
—Reissue of ABC-Paramount 509			
❏ D-723	Live in Cook County Jail	1971	$15
❏ D-712	Lucille	1970	$15
—Reissue of BluesWay 6016			
❏ D-898	Lucille Talks Back	1975	$15
❏ AA-1061	Midnight Believer	1978	$15
❏ X-767	The Best of B.B. King	1973	$15
❏ X-794	To Know You Is to Love You	1973	$15
ABC-PARAMOUNT
❏ 528 [M]	Confessin' the Blues	1965	$30
❏ S-528 [S]	Confessin' the Blues	1965	$40
❏ 509 [M]	Live at the Regal	1965	$40
❏ S-509 [S]	Live at the Regal	1965	$50
❏ 456 [M]	Mr. Blues	1963	$30
❏ S-456 [S]	Mr. Blues	1963	$40
BLUESWAY
❏ BLS-6050 [B]	Back in the Alley	1970	$25
❏ BL-6001 [M]	Blues Is King	1967	$40
❏ BLS-6001 [S]	Blues Is King	1967	$30

STEREO BLS 6011
BLUESWAY
B.B. KING
...ON TOP OF BLUES...

❏ BLS-6011 [S]	Blues on Top of Blues	1968	$30
❏ BL-6011 [M]	Blues on Top of Blues	1968	$50
—Mono is white label promo only			

❏ BLS-6037	Completely Well	1969	$25
❏ BLS-6022	His Best/The Electric B.B. King	1969	$25
❏ BLS-6031 [B]	Live and Well	1969	$25
❏ BLS-6016	Lucille	1968	$30
COMMAND
❏ CQD-40022 [Q]	Friends	1974	$30
CROWN
❏ CLP-5359 [M]	B.B. King	1963	$40
—Gray label, black "Crown			
❏ CLP-5359 [M]	B.B. King	196?	$15
—Black label, multi-color "Crown			
❏ CST-359 [P]	B.B. King	1963	$15
—Half of the album is in stereo, half is rechanneled			
❏ CLP-5119 [M]	B.B. King Sings Spirituals	1960	$75
—Gray label, black "Crown			
❏ CLP-5119 [M]	B.B. King Sings Spirituals	196?	$15
—Black label, multi-color "Crown			
❏ CST-152 [R]	B.B. King Sings Spirituals	1960	$15
—Black vinyl			
❏ CST-152 [R]	B.B. King Sings Spirituals	1960	$150
—Red vinyl			
❏ CLP-5115 [M]	B.B. King Wails	1959	$100
—Black label, silver "Crown			
❏ CLP-5115 [M]	B.B. King Wails	1963	$25
—Gray label, black "Crown			
❏ CLP-5115 [M]	B.B. King Wails	196?	$15
—Black label, multi-color "Crown			
❏ CST-147 [R]	B.B. King Wails	1960	$15
—Black vinyl			
❏ CST-147 [R]	B.B. King Wails	1960	$150
—Red vinyl			
❏ CLP-5309 [M]	Blues in My Heart	1963	$40
—Gray label, black "Crown			
❏ CLP-5309 [M]	Blues in My Heart	196?	$15
—Black label, multi-color "Crown			
❏ CST-309 [R]	Blues in My Heart	1963	$15
❏ CLP-5286 [M]	Easy Listening Blues	1962	$75
—Gray label, black "Crown			
❏ CLP-5286 [M]	Easy Listening Blues	196?	$15
—Black label, multi-color "Crown			
❏ CLP-5167 [M]	King of the Blues	1961	$75
—Gray label, black "Crown			
❏ CLP-5167 [M]	King of the Blues	196?	$15
—Black label, multi-color "Crown			
❏ CST-195 [S]	King of the Blues	1961	$25
—Black vinyl; this album is in true stereo, contrary to prior reports			
❏ CST-195 [S]	King of the Blues	1961	$120
—Red vinyl; this album is in true stereo, contrary to prior reports			
❏ CLP-5230 [M]	More B.B. King	1962	$75
—Gray label, black "Crown			
❏ CLP-5230 [M]	More B.B. King	196?	$15
—Black label, multi-color "Crown			
❏ CLP-5188 [M]	My Kind of Blues	1961	$75
—Gray label, black "Crown			
❏ CLP-5188 [M]	My Kind of Blues	196?	$15
—Black label, multi-color "Crown			
❏ CLP-5020 [M]	Singin' the Blues	1957	$150
—Black label, silver "Crown			
❏ CLP-5020 [M]	Singin' the Blues	1963	$25
—Gray label, black "Crown			
❏ CLP-5020 [M]	Singin' the Blues	196?	$15
—Black label, multi-color "Crown			
❏ CLP-5063 [M]	The Blues	1958	$100
—Black label, silver "Crown			
❏ CLP-5063 [M]	The Blues	1963	$25
—Gray label, black "Crown			
❏ CLP-5063 [M]	The Blues	196?	$15
—Black label, multi-color "Crown			
❏ CLP-5143 [M]	The Great B.B. King	1961	$75
—Gray label, black "Crown			
❏ CLP-5143 [M]	The Great B.B. King	196?	$15
—Black label, multi-color "Crown			
❏ CLP-5248 [M]	Twist with B.B. King	1962	$75
—Gray label, black "Crown			
❏ CLP-5248 [M]	Twist with B.B. King	196?	$15
—Black label, multi-color "Crown			
CRUSADERS
❏ 16013	Live in London	1982	$30
—Part of MCA's "Audiophile Series			
CUSTOM
❏ CM-2046 [M]	Blues for Me	196?	$15
❏ CM-2049 [M]	I Love You So	196?	$15
❏ CM-2052 [M]	The Soul of B.B. King	196?	$15
DIRECT DISK
❏ SD-16616	Midnight Believer	1980	$50
—Audiophile vinyl			
GALAXY
❏ 202 [M]	16 Greatest Hits	1963	$75
❏ 8202 [S]	16 Greatest Hits	1963	$100

Number	Title	Yr	NM
GRP			
❏ GR-9637	Live at the Apollo	1991	$18
KENT			
❏ KST-565	B.B. King Live	1972	$18
❏ KLP-5015 [M]	B.B. King Live on Stage	1965	$25
❏ KST-515 [R]	B.B. King Live on Stage	1965	$18
❏ KST-561	Better Than Ever	1971	$18
❏ KLP-5029 [M]	Boss of the Blues	1968	$25
❏ KST-529 [R]	Boss of the Blues	1968	$18
❏ KST-563	Doing My Thing, Lord	1971	$18
❏ KST-533 [B]	From the Beginning	1969	$25
❏ KST-552	Greatest Hits, Volume 1	1971	$18
❏ KLP-2008	Incredible Soul of B.B. King	1987	$15
❏ KLP-5013 [M]	Let Me Love You	1965	$25
❏ KST-513 [R]	Let Me Love You	1965	$18
❏ KLP-5017 [M]	Pure Soul	1966	$25
❏ KST-517 [R]	Pure Soul	1966	$18
❏ KLP-5012 [M]	Rock Me Baby	1964	$25
❏ KST-512 [R]	Rock Me Baby	1964	$18
❏ KST-539	The Incredible Soul of B.B. King	1970	$18
❏ KLP-5021 [M]	The Jungle	1967	$25
❏ KST-521 [R]	The Jungle	1967	$18
❏ KST-568	The Original Sweet Sixteen	1972	$18
❏ KLP-5016 [M]	The Soul of B.B. King	1966	$25
❏ KST-516 [R]	The Soul of B.B. King	1966	$18
❏ KST-548	Turn On to B.B. King	1970	$18
❏ KST-535	Underground Blues	1969	$18
MCA			
❏ 27010	Back in the Alley	1980	$10
— Reissue of ABC 878			
❏ 5413	Blues 'N' Jazz	1983	$12
❏ 27009	Completely Well	1980	$10
— Reissue of ABC 868			
❏ 27007	His Best/The Electric B.B. King	1980	$10
— Reissue of ABC 813			
❏ 27008	Live and Well	1980	$10
— Reissue of ABC 819			
❏ 6455	Live at San Quentin	1990	$15
❏ 27006	Live at the Regal	1980	$10
— Reissue of ABC 724			
❏ 27005	Live in Cook County Jail	1980	$10
— Reissue of ABC 723			
❏ 5307	Love Me Tender	1982	$12
❏ 27011	Midnight Believer	1980	$10
— Reissue of ABC 1061			
❏ 2-8016	Now Appearing" at Ole Miss	1980	$15
❏ 5616	Six Silver Strings	1985	$12
❏ 3151	Take It Home	1979	$12
❏ 27028	Take It Home	1981	$10
— Reissue of MCA 3151			
❏ 27074	The Best of B.B. King	1984	$10
— Reissue of ABC 767			
❏ 42183	The King of the Blues: 1989	1989	$12
❏ 5162	There Must Be a Better World Somewhere	1981	$12
❏ 27034	There Must Be a Better World Somewhere	1983	$10
— Reissue of MCA 5162			
MCA IMPULSE!			
❏ MCA2-4124	Great Moments with B.B. King	1981	$15
MOBILE FIDELITY			
❏ 1-235	Lucille	1995	$50
— Audiophile vinyl			
PICKWICK			
❏ SPC-3593	Live at the Regal	197?	$10
❏ SPC-3654	Live in Cook County Jail	197?	$10
STAX			
❏ ORS-4508	16 Original Big Hits	198?	$10
UNITED			
❏ US-7788	9 x 9	197?	$10
❏ US-7736	B.B. King Live on Stage	197?	$10
— Reissue of Kent 515			
❏ US-7708	Blues for Me	197?	$10
— Reissue of Custom 2046			
❏ US-7750	Boss of the Blues	197?	$10
— Reissue of Kent 529			
❏ US-7705	Easy Listening Blues	197?	$10
— Reissue of Crown 5286			
❏ US-7766	Greatest Hits, Volume 1	197?	$10
— Reissue of Kent 552			
❏ US-7703	Heart Full of Blues	197?	$10
❏ US-7711	I Love You So	197?	$10
— Reissue of Custom 2049			
❏ US-7734	Let Me Love You	197?	$10
— Reissue of Kent 513			
❏ US-7724	My Kind of Blues	197?	$10
— Reissue of Crown 5188			
❏ US-7733	Rock Me, Baby	197?	$10
— Reissue of Kent 5012			
❏ US-7726	Singin' the Blues	197?	$10
— Reissue of Crown 5020			
❏ US-7721	Swing Low	197?	$10
❏ US-7732	The Blues	197?	$10
— Reissue of Crown 5063			
❏ US-7728	The Great B.B. King	197?	$10

Number	Title	Yr	NM
— Reissue of Crown 5143			
❏ US-7756	The Incredible Soul of B.B. King	197?	$10
— Reissue of Kent 539			
❏ US-7742	The Jungle	197?	$10
— Reissue of Kent 521			
❏ US-7773	The Original Sweet Sixteen	197?	$10
— Reissue of Kent 568			
❏ US-7714	The Soul of B.B. King	197?	$10
— Reissue of Custom 2052			
❏ US-7763	Turn On with B.B. King	197?	$10
— Reissue of Kent 548			

KING, BEN E.
Also see AVERAGE WHITE BAND; THE DRIFTERS.

Number	Title	Yr	NM
ATCO			
❏ 33-165 [M]	Ben E. King's Greatest Hits	1964	$30
❏ SD 33-165 [S]	Ben E. King's Greatest Hits	1964	$40
— Purple and brown label			
❏ SD 33-165 [S]	Ben E. King's Greatest Hits	1969	$15
— Yellow label			
❏ SD 33-165 [S]	Ben E. King's Greatest Hits	197?	$10
— Any other color label			
❏ 33-137 [M]	Ben E. King Sings for Soulful Lovers	1962	$40
❏ SD 33-137 [S]	Ben E. King Sings for Soulful Lovers	1962	$75
❏ 33-142 [M]	Don't Play That Song	1962	$40
❏ SD 33-142 [S]	Don't Play That Song	1962	$75
❏ 33-174 [M]	Seven Letters	1965	$40
❏ SD 33-174 [S]	Seven Letters	1965	$50
❏ 33-133 [M]	Spanish Harlem	1961	$150
— Yellow label with harp			
❏ 33-133 [M]	Spanish Harlem	1962	$85
— Gold and gray label			
❏ SD 33-133 [S]	Spanish Harlem	1961	$175
— Yellow label with harp			
❏ SD 33-133 [S]	Spanish Harlem	1962	$50
— Purple and brown label			
ATLANTIC			
❏ SD18169	I Have a Love	1976	$15
❏ SD19200	Let Me Live in Your Life	1978	$15
❏ SD19269	Music Trance	1980	$12
❏ SD18191	Rhapsody	1976	$15
❏ 81716	Stand By Me: The Best of Ben E. King	1987	$10
— Includes seven Ben E. King tracks and three by the Drifters			
❏ SD19300	Street Tough	1981	$12

Number	Title	Yr	NM
❏ SD18132 [B]	Supernatural	1975	$15
CLARION			
❏ 606 [M]	Young Boy Blues	1966	$30
❏ SD606 [S]	Young Boy Blues	1966	$30
MANDALA			
❏ MLP-3008 [DJ]	Audio Biography	1972	$30
— Promo-only interview by Richard Robinson			
❏ MLP3007	The Beginning of It All for Ben E. King	1972	$25
MAXWELL			
❏ ML-88001	Rough Edges	1969	$25

KING, CAROLE

Number	Title	Yr	NM
ATLANTIC			
❏ SD19344	One to One	1982	$12
❏ 80118	Speeding Time	1983	$12
CAPITOL			
❏ C1-90885	City Streets	1989	$15
❏ SOO-12073	Pearls -- Songs of Goffin and King	1980	$12
❏ SMAS-11667 [B]	Simple Things	1977	$12
❏ SN-16057	Simple Things	1980	$10
— Budget-line reissue			
❏ SWAK-11963	Touch the Sky	1979	$12
❏ SN-16059	Touch the Sky	1980	$10
— Budget-line reissue			
❏ ST-11953	Touch the Sky	1979	$12

Number	Title	Yr	NM
❏ SPRO-9103/4 [EP]	Touch the Sky Sampler	1979	$18
— Promo-only four-song excerpt from "Touch the Sky			
❏ SW-11785	Welcome Home	1978	$12
❏ SN-16058	Welcome Home	1980	$10
— Budget-line reissue			
❏ SW-11785	Welcome Home	1978	$12
MOBILE FIDELITY			
❏ MFSL1-414 [B]	Tapestry	2013	$75
ODE			
❏ PE34944	Carole King: Writer	1977	$12
— Reissue of 77006			
❏ SP-77018 [B]	Fantasy	1973	$18
❏ PE34962	Fantasy	1977	$12
— Reissue of 77018			
❏ JE34967	Her Greatest Hits	1978	$12
❏ SP-77013 [B]	Music	1971	$25
❏ QU-88013 [Q]	Music	1974	$75
❏ PE34949	Music	1977	$12
— Reissue of 77013			
❏ SP-77027	Really Rosie	1975	$15
❏ PE34955 [B]	Really Rosie	1977	$12
— Reissue of 77027			
❏ SP-77016 [B]	Rhymes and Reasons	1972	$18
❏ PE34950	Rhymes and Reasons	1977	$12
— Reissue of 77016			
❏ SP-77009	Tapestry	1971	$15
❏ PE34946	Tapestry	1977	$12
— Reissue of 77009			
❏ HE44946	Tapestry	1980	$50
— Half-speed mastered edition			
❏ FE34946	Tapestry	1979	$50
— Reissue with new prefix			
❏ SP-77034	Thoroughbred	1976	$15
❏ PE34963	Thoroughbred	1977	$12
— Reissue of 77034			
❏ SP-77024	Wrap Around Joy	1974	$15
❏ PE34953	Wrap Around Joy	1977	$12
— Reissue of 77024			
❏ SP-77006	Writer: Carole King	1970	$15

KING, CLAUDE

Number	Title	Yr	NM
COLUMBIA			
❏ C30804	Chip 'n' Dale's Place	1971	$18
❏ CS1024	Friend, Lover, Woman, Wife	1970	$18
❏ CS9789	I Remember Johnny Horton	1968	$18
— 360 Sound Stereo" on red label			
❏ CL1810 [M]	Meet Claude King	1962	$30
— Six "eye" logos on label			
❏ CS8610 [S]	Meet Claude King	1962	$40
— Six "eye" logos on label			
❏ CL1810 [M]	Meet Claude King	1963	$18
— Guaranteed High Fidelity" or "Mono" on red label			
❏ CS8610 [S]	Meet Claude King	1963	$25
— 360 Sound Stereo" on red label			
❏ CL2415 [M]	Tiger Woman	1965	$25
❏ CS9215 [S]	Tiger Woman	1965	$30
— 360 Sound Stereo" on red label			
HARMONY			
❏ HS11300	The Best of Claude King	1969	$15

KING, CLYDE

Number	Title	Yr	NM
TIGER LILY			
❏ TL14037 [B]	Rushing to Meet You	1976	$20

KING, CLYDIE

Number	Title	Yr	NM
LIZARD			
❏ A-20104	Direct Me	1971	$15

KING, DON

Number	Title	Yr	NM
CON BRIO			
❏ 052	Dreams 'n Things	1977	$15
❏ 053	The Feelin's So Right	1978	$15

KING, EVELYN "CHAMPAGNE

Number	Title	Yr	NM
EMI			
❏ E-92049	The Girl Next Door	1989	$15
EMI MANHATTAN			
❏ E1-46968	Flirt	1988	$10
RCA VICTOR			
❏ AFL1-7015	A Long Time Coming (A Change Is Gonna Come)	1985	$12
❏ AFL1-3543	Call On Me	1980	$12
❏ AFL1-4725	Face to Face	1983	$10
❏ AFL1-4337	Get Loose	1982	$10
— As "Evelyn King			
❏ AFL1-3962	I'm in Love	1981	$12
— As "Evelyn King			
❏ AFL1-3033	Music Box	1979	$12
❏ APL1-2466	Smooth Talk	1978	$12
❏ AFL1-5308	So Romantic	1984	$10

Number	Title	Yr	NM
KING, FREDDIE			
COTILLION			
❏ SD9004	Freddie King Is a Blues Master	1969	$30
❏ SD9016	My Feeling for the Blues	1970	$30
KING			
❏ 964 [M]	24 Vocals and Instrumentals	1966	$30

FREDDY KING... gives you a BONANZA of instrumentals

Number	Title	Yr	NM
❏ 928 [M]	A Bonanza of Instrumentals	1965	$50
❏ KS-928 [S]	A Bonanza of Instrumentals	1965	$75
❏ 821 [M]	Bossa Nova and Blues	1962	$175
❏ 856 [M]	Freddie King Goes Surfin'	1963	$100
❏ KS-856 [S]	Freddie King Goes Surfin'	1963	$120
❏ 762 [M]	Freddie King Sings the Blues	1961	$300
❏ KS-1059	Hide Away	1969	$18
❏ 773 [M]	Let's Hide Away and Dance Away	1961	$300
MCA			
❏ 690	The Best of Freddie King	1979	$10
— Reissue of Shelter 52021			
MODERN BLUES			
❏ MBLP-722	Freddie King Sings	198?	$12
❏ MB2LP-721	Just Pickin'	198?	$18
RSO			
❏ SD4803	Burglar	1974	$15
❏ RS-1-3025	Freddie King 1934-1976	1977	$15
❏ SD4811	Larger Than Life	1975	$15
SHELTER			
❏ SW-8905	Getting Ready	1971	$18
❏ SW-8913	Texas Cannonball	1972	$18
❏ 2140	The Best of Freddie King	1975	$18
— Original with MCA distribution			
❏ SRL52021	The Best of Freddie King	1977	$15
— Second edition with ABC distribution			
❏ SW-8919	Woman Across the River	1973	$18
STARDAY/GUSTO			
❏ 5012	17 Original Hits	1977	$12
❏ 5033	Hide Away	1978	$12
KING, FREDDIE/LULA REED/BOBBY THOMPSON			
KING			
❏ 777 [M]	Boy-Girl-Boy	1962	$300
KING, JEAN			
HANNA-BARBERA			
❏ HLP-8505 [M]	Jean King Sings for the In Crowd	1966	$25
KING, JONATHAN			
PARROT			
❏ PA61013 [M]	Jonathan King Or Then Again....	1967	$150
❏ PAS71013 [P]	Jonathan King Or Then Again....	1967	$75
— Only "Where the Sun Has Never Shown" is rechanneled.			
U.K.			
❏ 53101 [B]	Bubble Rock Is Here to Stay	1972	$50
❏ 53104 [B]	Pandora's Box	1973	$30
KING, MORGANA			
ASCOT			
❏ AM13020 [M]	Everybody Loves Saturday Night	1965	$30
❏ AS16020 [S]	Everybody Loves Saturday Night	1965	$75
❏ AM13025 [M]	More Morgana	1965	$75
❏ AS16025 [S]	More Morgana	1965	$75
❏ AM13019 [M]	The End of a Love Affair	1965	$75
— Reissue of United Artists 30020			
❏ AS16019 [S]	The End of a Love Affair	1965	$30
— Reissue of United Artists 40020			
❏ AM13014 [M]	The Winter of My Discontent	1964	$75
❏ AS16014 [S]	The Winter of My Discontent	1964	$75

Number	Title	Yr	NM
EMARCY			
❏ MG-36079 [M]	For You, For Me, For Evermore	1956	$250
MAINSTREAM			
❏ MRL-355	Cuore di Mama	1974	$35
❏ 56052 [M]	Miss Morgana King	1965	$50
❏ S-6052 [S]	Miss Morgana King	1965	$75
❏ MRL-321	Taste of Honey	1972	$35
❏ 56015 [M]	With a Taste of Honey	1964	$50

MORGANA KING with a taste of honey

Number	Title	Yr	NM
❏ S-6015 [S]	With a Taste of Honey	1964	$75
MERCURY			
❏ MG-20231 [M]	Morgana King Sings the Blues	1958	$300
MUSE			
❏ MR-5339	Another Time, Another Space	1988	$25
❏ MR-5190	Everything Must Change	1978	$25
❏ MR-5224	Higher Ground	1979	$25
❏ MR-5257	Looking Through the Eyes of Love	1981	$25
❏ MR-5301	Portraits	1983	$25
❏ MR-5326	Simply Eloquent	1986	$25
❏ MR-5166	Stretchin' Out	1977	$25
PARAMOUNT			
❏ PAS-6067	New Beginnings	1973	$30
RCA CAMDEN			
❏ CAL-543 [M]	The Greatest Songs Ever Swung	1959	$50
❏ CAS-543 [S]	The Greatest Songs Ever Swung	1959	$75
REPRISE			
❏ R6257 [M]	Gemini Changes	1967	$50
❏ RS6257 [S]	Gemini Changes	1967	$75
❏ R6192 [M]	It's a Quiet Thing	1966	$50
❏ RS6192 [S]	It's a Quiet Thing	1966	$75
❏ R6205 [M]	Wild Is Love	1966	$50
❏ RS6205 [S]	Wild Is Love	1966	$75
TRIP			
❏ 5533	Morgana King Sings	197?	$25
UNITED ARTISTS			
❏ UAL3028 [M]	Folk Songs A La King	1960	$175
❏ UAS6028 [S]	Folk Songs A La King	1960	$200
❏ UAL30020 [M]	Let Me Love You	1960	$200
❏ UAS30020-S [S]	Let Me Love You	1960	$120
VERVE			
❏ V-5061 [M]	I Know How It Feels	1968	$75
❏ V6-5061 [S]	I Know How It Feels	1968	$75
WING			
❏ MGW-12307 [M]	More Morgana King	1965	$35
❏ SRW-16307 [S]	More Morgana King	1965	$50
KING, PEE WEE			
BRIAR			
❏ 102	Golden Olde Tyme Dances	1975	$75
LONGHORN			
❏ 1236 [M]	The Legendary Pee Wee King	1967	$30
RCA CAMDEN			
❏ CAL-876 [M]	Country Barn Dance	1965	$25
❏ CAS-876 [R]	Country Barn Dance	1965	$15
RCA VICTOR			
❏ LPM-3028 [10]	Pee Wee King	195?	$100
❏ LPM-3280 [10]	Swing West	195?	$100
❏ LPM-1237 [M]	Swing West	1956	$40
❏ LPM-3109 [10]	Waltzes	195?	$100
❏ LPM-3071 [10]	Western Hits	195?	$100
STARDAY			
❏ SLP-284 [M]	Back Again with the Songs That Made Them Famous	1964	$30
KING, PEGGY			
COLUMBIA			
❏ CL2549 [10]	Wish Upon a Star	1955	$50

Number	Title	Yr	NM
IMPERIAL			
❏ LP-9078 [M]	Lazy Afternoon	1959	$25
❏ LP-12026 [S]	Lazy Afternoon	1959	$30
STASH			
❏ 246	Peggy King Sings Jerome Kern: Till the Clouds Roll By	198?	$10
KING, PETE, CHORALE			
KAPP			
❏ KL1214 [M]	Christmas Time	1960	$18
KING, REV. MARTIN LUTHER			
The 1968 releases are posthumous tributes.			
20TH CENTURY			
❏ TCF-3110 [M]	Freedom March on Washington	1963	$30
❏ S-3201	The Rev. Dr. Martin Luther King, Jr.	1968	$25
BUDDAH			
❏ BDS-2002	Man of Love	1968	$25
CREED			
❏ 3201 [M]	I Have a Dream	1968	$25
DOOTO			
❏ DTL-831 [M]	Martin Luther King at Zion Hill	1962	$30
❏ DTL-841 [B]	The American Dream	1968	$25
GORDY			
❏ G-929	...Free at Last	1968	$30
— Original with gatefold cover			
❏ G-908 [M]	The Great March on Washington	1963	$40
— Gordy" in script at top of label			
❏ G-908 [M]	The Great March on Washington	1968	$18
— Later pressings			
❏ G-906 [M]	The Great March to Freedom	1963	$40
— Gordy" in script at top of label			
❏ G-906 [M]	The Great March to Freedom	1968	$18
— Later pressings			
MERCURY			
❏ SR-61170	In Search of Freedom	1968	$25
MR. MAESTRO			
❏ 1000 [M]	The March on Washington	1963	$30
SUNSET			
❏ 21033	The Struggle for Freedom	1968	$18
UNART			
❏ S21033	In the Struggle for Freedom and Human Dignity	1968	$25
KING, SANDRA			
AUDIOPHILE			
❏ AP-197	Songs by Vernon Duke	1984	$30
KING, TEDDI, AND DAVE MCKENNA			
INNER CITY			
❏ IC-1044	This Is New	1977	$50
KING, TEDDI			
AUDIOPHILE			
❏ AP-117	Lovers and Losers	1976	$35
❏ AP-150	Someone to Light Up Your Life	1979	$30
CORAL			
❏ CRL57278 [M]	All the King's Songs	1959	$75
❏ CRL757278 [S]	All the King's Songs	1959	$175
RCA VICTOR			
❏ LPM-1454 [M]	A Girl and Her Songs	1957	$175
❏ LPM-1147 [M]	Bidin' My Time	1956	$175
❏ LPM-1313 [M]	To You from Teddi King	1957	$200
STORYVILLE			
❏ STLP-903 [M]	Now In Vogue	1956	$175
❏ STLP-302 [10]	'Round Midnight	1954	$300
❏ STLP-314 [10]	Storyville Presents Teddi King	1954	$250
KING, WAYNE			
DECCA			
❏ DL4438 [M]	Have Yourself a Merry Little Christmas	1963	$18
❏ DL74438 [S]	Have Yourself a Merry Little Christmas	1963	$16
KING BISCUIT BOY			
EPIC			
❏ KE32891	King Biscuit Boy	1974	$15
PARAMOUNT			
❏ PAS-6023 [B]	Gooduns	1972	$18
❏ PAS-5030	Official Music	1970	$18
— As "King Biscuit Boy with Crowbar"			

KING CRIMSON
Also see YES; ADRIAN BELEW; PETER GABRIEL; URIAH HEEP.

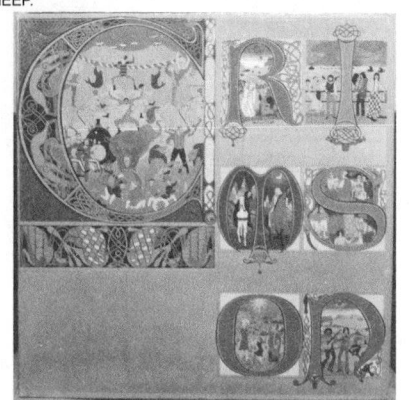

ATLANTIC

Number	Title	Yr	NM
8245 [M]	In the Court of the Crimson King – An Observation by King Crimson	1969	$500

—Mono is white label promo only; comes in stereo cover with "DJ Copy Monaural" sticker on front

| SD19155 | In the Court of the Crimson King – An Observation by King Crimson | 1978 | $30 |

—Reissue of Atlantic 8245

SD8245 [B]	In the Court of the Crimson King – An Observation by King Crimson	1969	$50
SD8266 [B]	In the Wake of Poseidon	1970	$60
SD7212 [B]	Islands	1972	$60
SD7263 [B]	Larks' Tongues in Aspic	1973	$50
SD8278 [B]	Lizard	1971	$50
SD18110 [B]	Red	1974	$50
SD7298 [B]	Starless and Bible Black	1974	$50
SD18136 [B]	USA	1975	$40

EDITIONS EG

| EGKC-1 | In the Court of the Crimson King – An Observation by King Crimson | 1985 | $30 |

—Reissue of Atlantic 19155

| EGKC-2 | In the Wake of Poseidon | 1985 | $30 |

—Reissue of Atlantic 8266

| EGKC-4 | Islands | 1985 | $30 |

—Reissue of Atlantic 7212

| EGKC-6 | Lark's Tongue in Aspic | 1985 | $30 |

—Reissue of Atlantic 7263

| EGKC-3 | Lizard | 1985 | $30 |

—Reissue of Atlantic 8278

| EGKC-8 | Red | 1985 | $30 |

—Reissue of Atlantic 18110

| EGKC-7 | Starless and Bible Black | 1985 | $30 |

—Reissue of Atlantic 7298

| EGKC-10 [B] | The Young Person's Guide to King Crimson | 1985 | $50 |
| EGKC-9 | USA | 1985 | $30 |

—Reissue of Atlantic 18135

MOBILE FIDELITY

| Jan-0075 | In the Court of the Crimson King – An Observation by King Crimson | 1981 | $200 |

—Audiophile vinyl

WARNER BROS.

23692	Beat	1982	$25
BSK3629	Discipline	1981	$25
WBMS-119 [DJ]	The Return of King Crimson	1981	$50

—Promo-only interview and music show

| 25071 | Three of a Perfect Pair | 1984 | $25 |

KING CURTIS

ATLANTIC

Number	Title	Yr	NM
SD 7-33-338 [PS]	Get Ready	197?	$30

—Part of "Little LP" series (#217)

| SD 7-33-338 | Let It Be/Get Ready/ Something//Sugar Foot/ Soulin'/Someday We'll Be Together | 197? | $20 |

—Stereo jukebox issue; small hole, plays at 33 1/3 rpm

ATCO

SD 33-385	Everybody's Talkin'	1972	$50
SD 33-338	Get Ready	1970	$50
33-113 [M]	Have Tenor Sax, Will Blow	1959	$40
SD 33-113 [S]	Have Tenor Sax, Will Blow	1959	$120
SD 33-293	Instant Groove	1969	$50
33-231 [M]	King Size Soul	1967	$75
SD 33-231 [S]	King Size Soul	1967	$50
SD 33-359	Live at Fillmore West	1971	$50
33-198 [M]	Live at Small's Paradise	1966	$50
SD 33-198 [S]	Live at Small's Paradise	1966	$75
33-247 [M]	Sweet Soul	1968	$75
SD 33-247 [S]	Sweet Soul	1968	$50

Number	Title	Yr	NM
33-189 [M]	That Lovin' Feeling	1966	$50
SD 33-189 [S]	That Lovin' Feeling	1966	$75
SD 33-266	The Best of King Curtis	1968	$50
33-211 [M]	The Great Memphis Hits	1967	$50
SD 33-211 [S]	The Great Memphis Hits	1967	$75

ATLANTIC

| SD1637 | Blues Montreux | 1973 | $30 |

CAPITOL

T1756 [M]	Country Soul	1963	$150
ST1756 [S]	Country Soul	1963	$75
T2341 [M]	King Curtis Plays the Hits Made Famous by Sam Cooke	1965	$150
ST2341 [S]	King Curtis Plays the Hits Made Famous by Sam Cooke	1965	$150
T2095 [M]	Soul Serenade	1964	$150
ST2095 [S]	Soul Serenade	1964	$150
SM-11798	Soul Serenade	1978	$25

—Reissue

| T2858 [M] | The Best of King Curtis | 1968 | $175 |

—Red and white "Starline" label; may be promo only

| SM-11963 | The Best of King Curtis | 1979 | $25 |

—Reissue

| ST2858 [S] | The Best of King Curtis | 1968 | $150 |

CLARION

| 615 [M] | The Great "K" Curtis | 1966 | $50 |
| SD615 [S] | The Great "K" Curtis | 1966 | $75 |

COLLECTABLES

| COL-5156 | Golden Classics: Enjoy… The Best of King Curtis | 198? | $25 |
| COL-5119 | Soul Twist | 198? | $25 |

ENJOY

| ENLP-2001 [M] | Soul Twist | 1962 | $50 |

EVEREST

| LPBR-5121 [M] | Azure | 1961 | $150 |
| SDBR-1121 [S] | Azure | 1961 | $85 |

FANTASY

| OJC-198 | The New Scene of King Curtis | 1985 | $25 |

—Reissue of New Jazz 8237

| OBC-512 | Trouble in Mind | 1988 | $25 |

—Reissue of Tru-Sound 15001

NEW JAZZ

| NJLP-8237 [M] | The New Scene of King Curtis | 1960 | $250 |

—Purple label

| NJLP-8237 [M] | The New Scene of King Curtis | 1965 | $175 |

—Blue label with trident logo on right

PRESTIGE

24033	Jazz Groove	198?	$35
PRST-7789	King Soul	1970	$35
PRLP-7222 [M]	Soul Meeting	1962	$175
PRST-7222 [M]	Soul Meeting	1962	$175
PRST-7833	Soul Meeting	1971	$35

—Reissue of 7222

| PRST-7709 | The Best of King Curtis | 1969 | $35 |
| PRST-7775 | The Best of King Curtis -- One More Time | 1970 | $35 |

RCA CAMDEN

| CAS-2242 | Sax in Motion | 1968 | $35 |

RCA VICTOR

| LPM-2494 [M] | Arthur Murray's Music for Dancing: The Twist! | 1962 | $75 |
| LSP-2494 [S] | Arthur Murray's Music for Dancing: The Twist! | 1962 | $75 |

TRU-SOUND

TS-15009 [M]	Doin' the Dixie Twist	1962	$150
TS-15008 [M]	It's Party Time	1962	$150
TS-15001 [M]	Trouble in Mind	1961	$150

KING FAMILY, THE

CAPITOL

| T2352 [M] | Love at Home | 1965 | $18 |

Number	Title	Yr	NM
DT2352 [R]	Love at Home	1965	$15

FANNY FARMER/FLEETWOOD

| FCLP3039 | Fanny Farmer Presents The King Family Christmas Album | 196? | $15 |

HARMONY

| HS11293 | The Wonderful King Family | 196? | $12 |

WARNER BROS.

W1627 [M]	Christmas with the King Family	1965	$15
WS1627 [S]	Christmas with the King Family	1965	$18
W1633 [M]	Sunday with the King Family	1966	$15
WS1633 [S]	Sunday with the King Family	1966	$18
W1613 [M]	The King Family Album	1965	$15
WS1613 [S]	The King Family Album	1965	$18
W1601 [M]	The King Family Show!	1965	$15
WS1601 [S]	The King Family Show!	1965	$18

KING HARVEST

A&M

| SP-4540 | King Harvest | 1975 | $12 |

PERCEPTION

| 36 | Dancing in the Moonlight | 1973 | $15 |

KING PINS, THE (1)

KING

| 865 [M] | It Won't Be This Way Always | 1963 | $300 |

KING PLEASURE

EVEREST ARCHIVE OF FOLK AND JAZZ

| FS-262 [M] | King Pleasure | 197? | $15 |

FANTASY

| OJC-1771 [S] | Golden Days | 1991 | $20 |

HIFI

| J-425 [M] | Golden Days | 1960 | $40 |
| JS-425 [S] | Golden Days | 1960 | $50 |

PRESTIGE

PRLP-208 [10]	King Pleasure Sings	1955	$500
PRLP-7586	Original Moody's Mood	1968	$30
PR-24017	The Source	1972	$30

SOLID STATE

| SS-18021 [S] | Mr. Jazz | 1968 | $30 |

—Reissue of United Artists 15031

UNITED ARTISTS

UAS-5634 [S]	Moody's Mood for Love	1972	$25
UAJ-14031 [M]	Mr. Jazz	1962	$40
UAJS-15031 [S]	Mr. Jazz	1962	$50

KING PLEASURE/ANNIE ROSS

FANTASY

| OJC-217 [M] | King Pleasure Sings/Annie Ross Sings | 198? | $15 |

PRESTIGE

| PRLP-7128 [M] | King Pleasure Sings/Annie Ross Sings | 1957 | $300 |

—Yellow label, W. 50th Street address on label

| PRLP-7128 [M] | King Pleasure Sings/Annie Ross Sings | 1958 | $300 |

—Yellow label, Bergenfield, N.J. address on label

| PRLP-7128 [M] | King Pleasure Sings/Annie Ross Sings | 1965 | $40 |

—Blue label, trident logo at right

KING RICHARD'S FLUEGEL KNIGHTS

MTA

5001 [B]	A Sign of the Times	1966	$18
5014 [B]	One of Those Songs	1969	$18
5005 [B]	Something Super	1967	$18
5005 [B]	Something Super!	1968	$18

KING SISTERS, THE

CAPITOL

| T808 [M] | Aloha | 1957 | $30 |

—Turquoise or gray label

| T919 [M] | Imagination | 1958 | $30 |

—Turquoise or gray label

| T1205 [M] | Warm and Wonderful | 1959 | $25 |

—Black colorband label, logo at left

| ST1205 [S] | Warm and Wonderful | 1959 | $30 |

—Black colorband label, logo at left

KINGBEES, THE

RSO

| RS1-3097 | The Big Rock | 1981 | $18 |
| RS1-3075 | The Kingbees | 1980 | $18 |

KINGDOM

SPECIALTY

| SPS-2135 | Kingdom | 1970 | $75 |

KINGFISH
With Bob Weir of THE GRATEFUL DEAD.

Number	Title	Yr	NM

ROUND
| ❏ RX-108 | Kingfish | 1976 | $16 |

KINGS, THE
ELEKTRA
| ❏ 5E-543 | Amazon Beach | 1981 | $15 |
| ❏ 6E-277 | The Kings Are Here | 1980 | $30 |

KING'S MEN FIVE, THE
CUCA
| ❏ 1130 [M] | The King's Men Five | 1965 | $25 |

KING'S ROAD
PICKWICK
❏ SPC-3537	A Million or More! '75	1975	$12
❏ SPC-3547	A Million or More! '75, Vol. 2	1975	$12
❏ SPC-3513	A Million or More in '74	1975	$12
❏ SPC-3560	A Million or More in '76	1976	$12
❏ SPC-3516	Elton John Rock Hits	197?	$12
❏ SPC-3509	Lucy in the Sky with Diamonds	197?	$12
❏ SPC-3135	Plays Today's Pops	197?	$12
❏ SPC-3507	Song Hits of Neil Diamond	1976	$12
❏ SPC-3904	Super Hits, Vol. 3	197?	$12
❏ SPC-3905	Super Hits, Vol. 4	197?	$12
❏ SPC-3906	Super Hits, Vol. 5	197?	$12
❏ SPC-3907	Super Hits, Vol. 6	197?	$12
❏ SPC-3908	Super Hits, Vol. 7	197?	$12
❏ SPC-3909	Super Hits, Vol. 8	197?	$12
❏ SPC-3910	Super Hits, Vol. 9	197?	$12
❏ PTP-2062	The Beatles 1962-1970	1973	$18
❏ SPC-3506	The Hits of Simon and Garfunkel	1976	$12
❏ SPC-3239	The Long and Winding Road	197?	$12
❏ SPC-3557	The Neil Sedaka Songbook	197?	$12
❏ SPC-3551	Today's T.V. Hits	1976	$12
❏ SPC-3355	Watkins Glen	1973	$12

KING'S SINGERS, THE
MMG
❏ 1126	Christmas With the King's Singers	197?	$15
❏ 1108	Deck the Hall -- Songs for Christmas	1973	$15
—Produced by George Martin!			

KINGS VERSES
BEAT ROCKET
| ❏ BR-105 | Kings Verses | 199? | $15 |

KINGSLEY, GERSHON
Also see PERREY-KINGSLEY.
AUDIO FIDELITY
| ❏ AFSD-6222 | Music to Moog By | 1969 | $40 |

KINGSMEN, THE (1)
RHINO
| ❏ RNLP-126 | The Best of the Kingsmen | 1985 | $12 |
SCEPTER
| ❏ CTN-18002 | The Best of the Kingsmen | 1972 | $12 |
WAND
❏ WDM-674 [M]	15 Great Hits	1966	$25
❏ WDS-674 [P]	15 Great Hits	1966	$30
❏ WDM-662 [M]	The Kingsmen, Volume 3	1965	$30
❏ WDS-662 [S]	The Kingsmen, Volume 3	1965	$30
❏ WDM-659 [M]	The Kingsmen, Volume II	1964	$30
— With "Death of an Angel"			
❏ WDM-659 [M]	The Kingsmen, Volume II	1964	$40
—Without "Death of an Angel" (replaced by untitled instrumental)			
❏ WDS-659 [S]	The Kingsmen, Volume II	1964	$40
— With "Death of an Angel"			
❏ WDS-659 [S]	The Kingsmen, Volume II	1964	$50
—Without "Death of an Angel" (replaced by untitled instrumental)			

| ❏ WDM-657 [M] | The Kingsmen In Person | 1964 | $30 |

Number	Title	Yr	NM

❏ WDS-657 [P]	The Kingsmen In Person	1964	$40
❏ WDM-670 [M]	The Kingsmen On Campus	1965	$30
❏ WDS-670 [S]	The Kingsmen On Campus	1965	$30
❏ WDM-681 [M]	The Kingsmen's Greatest Hits	1967	$18
❏ WDS-681 [S]	The Kingsmen's Greatest Hits	1967	$25
❏ WDM-675 [M]	Up and Away	1966	$25
❏ WDS-675 [S]	Up and Away	1966	$30
❏ ST-91011 [S]	Up and Away	1966	$30
—Capitol Record Club edition			

KINGSTON TRIO, THE
Also see DAVE GUARD AND THE WHISKEYHILL SINGERS; BOB SHANE; JOHN STEWART.
CAPITOL
❏ T2081 [M]	Back in Town	1964	$18
❏ ST2081 [S]	Back in Town	1964	$25
❏ T1642 [M]	Close-Up	1961	$30
—Black label with colorband, Capitol logo at left			
❏ T1642 [M]	Close-Up	1962	$18
—Black label with colorband, Capitol logo at top			
❏ ST1642 [S]	Close-Up	1961	$40
—Black label with colorband, Capitol logo at left			
❏ ST1642 [S]	Close-Up	1962	$25
—Black label with colorband, Capitol logo at top			
❏ T1658 [M]	College Concert	1962	$25
❏ ST1658 [S]	College Concert	1962	$30
❏ T1612 [M]	Encores	1961	$30
—Black label with colorband, Capitol logo at left			
❏ T1612 [M]	Encores	1962	$18
—Black label with colorband, Capitol logo at top			
❏ DT1612 [R]	Encores	1961	$25
—Black label with colorband, Capitol logo at left			
❏ DT1612 [R]	Encores	1962	$12
—Black label with colorband, Capitol logo at top			
❏ T1107 [M]	From the Hungry I	1959	$40
—Black label with colorband, Capitol logo at left			
❏ T1107 [M]	From the Hungry I	1962	$25
—Black label with colorband, Capitol logo at top			
❏ M-11968	From the Hungry I	1979	$12
❏ T1564 [M]	Goin' Places	1961	$30
—Black label with colorband, Capitol logo at left			
❏ T1564 [M]	Goin' Places	1962	$18
—Black label with colorband, Capitol logo at top			
❏ ST1564 [S]	Goin' Places	1961	$40
—Black label with colorband, Capitol logo at left			
❏ ST1564 [S]	Goin' Places	1962	$25
—Black label with colorband, Capitol logo at top			
❏ T1258 [M]	Here We Go Again!	1959	$30
—Black label with colorband, Capitol logo at left			
❏ T1258 [M]	Here We Go Again!	1962	$18
—Black label with colorband, Capitol logo at top			
❏ ST1258 [S]	Here We Go Again!	1959	$40
—Black label with colorband, Capitol logo at left			
❏ ST1258 [S]	Here We Go Again!	1962	$25
—Black label with colorband, Capitol logo at top			
❏ T1474 [M]	Make Way!	1961	$30
—Black label with colorband, Capitol logo at left			
❏ T1474 [M]	Make Way!	1962	$18
—Black label with colorband, Capitol logo at top			
❏ ST1474 [S]	Make Way!	1961	$40
—Black label with colorband, Capitol logo at left			
❏ ST1474 [S]	Make Way!	1962	$25
—Black label with colorband, Capitol logo at top			
❏ T1809 [M]	New Frontier	1962	$25
❏ ST1809 [S]	New Frontier	1962	$30
❏ SN-16186	Scarlet Ribbons	1981	$10
❏ KAO2005 [M]	Sing a Song with the Kingston Trio	1963	$30
❏ SKAO2005 [S]	Sing a Song with the Kingston Trio	1963	$30
❏ T1352 [M]	Sold Out	1960	$30
—Black label with colorband, Capitol logo at left			
❏ T1352 [M]	Sold Out	1962	$18
—Black label with colorband, Capitol logo at top			
❏ ST1352 [S]	Sold Out	1960	$40
—Black label with colorband, Capitol logo at left			
❏ ST1352 [S]	Sold Out	1962	$25
—Black label with colorband, Capitol logo at top			
❏ T1747 [M]	Something Special	1962	$25
❏ T1747 [S]	Something Special	1962	$30
❏ ST1183 [S]	Stereo Concert	1959	$50
—Black label with colorband, Capitol logo at left			
❏ ST1183 [S]	Stereo Concert	1962	$30
—Black label with colorband, Capitol logo at top			
❏ T1407 [M]	String Along	1960	$30
—Black label with colorband, Capitol logo at left			
❏ T1407 [M]	String Along	1962	$18
—Black label with colorband, Capitol logo at left			
❏ ST1407 [S]	String Along	1960	$40
—Black label with colorband, Capitol logo at left			
❏ ST1407 [S]	String Along	1962	$25
—Black label with colorband, Capitol logo at top			
❏ T1935 [M]	Sunny Side!	1963	$25
❏ ST1935 [S]	Sunny Side!	1963	$30
❏ T1705 [M]	The Best of the Kingston Trio	1962	$25

Number	Title	Yr	NM

❏ ST1705 [P]	The Best of the Kingston Trio	1962	$25
❏ SM-1705	The Best of the Kingston Trio	197?	$12
❏ SN-16183	The Best of the Kingston Trio	1981	$10
—Budget-line reissue			
❏ T2280 [M]	The Best of the Kingston Trio, Volume 2	1965	$18
❏ ST2280 [S]	The Best of the Kingston Trio, Volume 2	1965	$25
❏ SM-2280	The Best of the Kingston Trio, Volume 2	197?	$12
❏ SN-16184	The Best of the Kingston Trio, Volume 2	1981	$10
—Budget-line reissue			
❏ T2614 [M]	The Best of the Kingston Trio, Volume 3	1966	$18
❏ ST2614 [S]	The Best of the Kingston Trio, Volume 3	1966	$25
❏ SM-2614	The Best of the Kingston Trio, Volume 3	197?	$12
❏ TCL2180 [M]	The Folk Era	1964	$40
—Box set with booklet			
❏ STCL2180 [S]	The Folk Era	1964	$50
—Box set with booklet			
❏ T1871 [M]	The Kingston Trio #16	1963	$25
❏ ST1871 [S]	The Kingston Trio #16	1963	$30
❏ T996 [M]	The Kingston Trio	1958	$50
—Turquoise label			
❏ T996 [M]	The Kingston Trio	1958	$40
—Black label with colorband, Capitol logo at left			
❏ T996 [M]	The Kingston Trio	1962	$25
—Black label with colorband, Capitol logo at top			
❏ M-11577	The Kingston Trio	1976	$12
❏ DT996 [R]	The Kingston Trio	196?	$15
❏ T1199 [M]	The Kingston Trio at Large	1959	$30
—Black label with colorband, Capitol logo at left, "Long Playing High-Fidelity			
❏ T1199 [M]	The Kingston Trio at Large	1962	$18
—Black label with colorband, Capitol logo at top			
❏ ST1199 [S]	The Kingston Trio at Large	1959	$40
—Black label with colorband, Capitol logo at left			
❏ ST1199 [S]	The Kingston Trio at Large	1962	$25
—Black label with colorband, Capitol logo at top			
❏ T1199 [M]	The Kingston Trio at Large	1960	$30
—Black label with colorband, Capitol logo at left, white line replaces "Long Playing High-Fidelity			
❏ T1446 [M]	The Last Month of the Year	1960	$30
❏ ST1446 [S]	The Last Month of the Year	1960	$40
—Same as above, but in stereo			
❏ T2011 [M]	Time to Think	1964	$18
❏ ST2011 [S]	Time to Think	1964	$25
❏ N-16185	Tom Dooley	1981	$10
❏ STBB-513	Tom Dooley/Scarlet Ribbons	1970	$25
DECCA
❏ DL4758 [M]	Children of the Morning	1966	$30
❏ DL74758 [S]	Children of the Morning	1966	$30
❏ DL4694 [M]	Somethin' Else	1965	$30
❏ DL74694 [S]	Somethin' Else	1965	$30
❏ DL4656 [M]	Stay Awhile	1965	$30
❏ DL74656 [S]	Stay Awhile	1965	$30
❏ DL4613 [M]	The Kingston Trio (Nick-Bob-John)	1965	$30
❏ DL74613 [S]	The Kingston Trio (Nick-Bob-John)	1965	$30
FOLK ERA
| ❏ FE-2036 | Hidden Treasures | 198? | $12 |
| ❏ FE-2001 | Rediscover the Kingston Trio | 198? | $12 |
NAUTILUS
| ❏ NR-2 | Aspen Gold | 1979 | $40 |
| *—Audiophile vinyl* | | | |
PAIR
| ❏ PDL2-1067 | Early American Heroes | 1986 | $15 |
PICKWICK
| ❏ SPC-3260 | Tom Dooley | 196? | $15 |
TETRAGRAMMATON
| ❏ T-5101 | Once Upon a Time | 1969 | $30 |
XERES
| ❏ 1-10001 | 25 Years Non-Stop | 1982 | $15 |

KINKS, THE
Also see DAVE DAVIES.
4 MEN WITH BEARDS
| ❏ 4M801LP [B] | Kinda Kinks | | $25 |
ARISTA
❏ SP-85 [EP]	A Fistful of Kinks	1980	$30
—Promo-only four-song sampler from "One for the Road			
❏ AL118428	Come Dancing with the Kinks	1986	$15
❏ AL9567	Give the People What They Want	1981	$12
❏ ALB68328	Give the People What They Want	1985	$10
—Budget-line reissue			
❏ AB4240	Low Budget	1979	$12
❏ ALB68300	Low Budget	1985	$10
—Budget-line reissue			
❏ SP-69 [DJ]	Low Budget Radio Interview	1979	$30

Number	Title	Yr	NM

—Promo-only radio show featuring Ray Davies
| ❏ AL4167 [DJ] | Misfits | 1978 | $30 |

— White label promo
| ❏ AL4167 [B] | Misfits | 1978 | $12 |
| ❏ ALB68377 | Misfits | 1985 | $10 |

— Budget-line reissue
| ❏ AL138041 | One for the Road | 1983 | $12 |

— Reissue of 8609
| ❏ A2L8401 | One for the Road | 1980 | $18 |

— Original edition has this number
| ❏ A2L8609 | One for the Road | 198? | $15 |

— Second edition of 8401
| ❏ AL4106 [DJ] | Sleepwalker | 1977 | $30 |

— White label promo

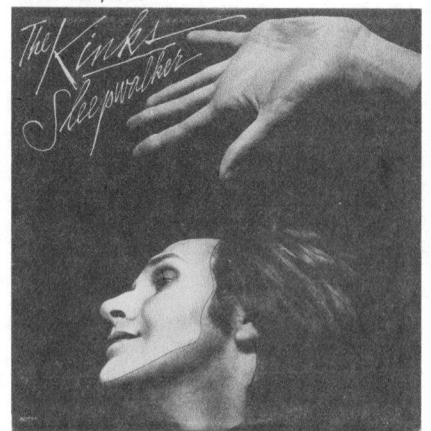

| ❏ AL4106 [B] | Sleepwalker | 1977 | $12 |
| ❏ ALB68375 | Sleepwalker | 1985 | $10 |

— Budget-line reissue
| ❏ AL 8-8018 | State of Confusion | 1983 | $12 |
| ❏ AL8264 | Word of Mouth | 1984 | $12 |

COMPLEAT
| ❏ CPL2-2003 | 20th Anniversary Edition | 1984 | $15 |
| ❏ CPL2-2001 | A Compleat Collection | 1984 | $15 |

MCA
| ❏ L33-17281 [DJ] | A Look at "Think Visual | 1987 | $30 |

— Promo only in white jacket
❏ 42107	Live: The Road	1988	$12
❏ 5822	Think Visual	1987	$12
❏ 6337	UK Jive	1989	$15

MOBILE FIDELITY
| ❏ Jan-0070 | Misfits | 1981 | $50 |

— Audiophile vinyl

PICKWICK
| ❏ ACL-7072 | Preservation Act 1 | 197? | $15 |

— Reissue of RCA Victor LPL1-5002

PYE
| ❏ 505 | The Kinks | 1975 | $15 |
| ❏ 509 | The Kinks, Vol. 2 | 1976 | $15 |

RCA VICTOR
| ❏ APL1-1743 | Celluloid Heroes (The Kinks' Greatest) | 1976 | $12 |
| ❏ AYL1-3869 | Celluloid Heroes (The Kinks' Greatest) | 1981 | $10 |

— Budget-line reissue
| ❏ VPS-6065 | Everybody's in Showbiz | 1972 | $25 |

— Orange label
| ❏ VPS-6065 | Everybody's in Showbiz | 1975 | $15 |

— Brown label
| ❏ LSP-4644 | Muswell Hillbillies | 1971 | $30 |
| ❏ AYL1-4558 | Muswell Hillbillies | 1982 | $10 |

— Budget-line reissue
❏ LPL1-5002	Preservation Act 1	1973	$18
❏ CPL2-5040	Preservation Act 2	1974	$25
❏ LPL1-5102	Schoolboys in Disgrace	1975	$12
❏ AYL1-3749	Schoolboys in Disgrace	1980	$10

— Budget-line reissue
| ❏ APL1-3520 | Second Time Around | 1980 | $12 |
| ❏ AYL1-4719 | Second Time Around | 1983 | $10 |

— Budget-line reissue
| ❏ LPL1-5081 | Soap Opera | 1975 | $18 |

— Orange label
| ❏ LPL1-5081 | Soap Opera | 1975 | $12 |

— Brown label
| ❏ AYL1-3750 | Soap Opera | 1980 | $10 |

— Budget-line reissue

REPRISE
| ❏ SMAS-93034 | Arthur (Or The Decline and Fall of the British Empire) | 1970 | $40 |

— Capitol Record Club edition
| ❏ RS-6366 | Arthur (Or The Decline and Fall of the British Empire) | 1969 | $30 |

— Two-tone orange label with "r:" and "W7" logos with steamboat

Number	Title	Yr	NM

| ❏ RS-6366 | Arthur (Or The Decline and Fall of the British Empire) | 1971 | $12 |

— Orange label with "r:" and steamboat at top
| ❏ R-6228 [M] | Face to Face | 1967 | $100 |
| ❏ RS-6228 [P] | Face to Face | 1967 | $30 |

— Pink, gold and green label
| ❏ RS-6228 [P] | Face to Face | 1971 | $20 |

— Orange label with "r:" and steamboat at top
| ❏ PRO328 [P] | God Save the Kinks | 1969 | $600 |

— Mail-order box with decal, postcard, bag of grass, two pins, letter, Kinks consumer guide and "Then Now and In Between" LP. Price is for complete package.
| ❏ R-6173 [M] | Kinda Kinks | 1965 | $250 |

— White label promo
❏ R-6173 [M]	Kinda Kinks	1965	$50
❏ RS-6173 [R]	Kinda Kinks	1965	$30
❏ R-6184 [M]	Kinks Kinkdom	1965	$250

— White label promo
❏ R-6184 [M]	Kinks Kinkdom	1965	$75
❏ RS-6184 [R]	Kinks Kinkdom	1965	$30
❏ R-6158 [M]	Kinks-Size	1965	$250

— White label promo
❏ R-6158 [M]	Kinks-Size	1965	$50
❏ RS-6158 [R]	Kinks-Size	1965	$30
❏ RS-6423 [B]	Lola Versus Powerman and the Moneygoround, Part One	1970	$30

— Original pressings have blue printing on a white cover
| ❏ RS-6423 [B] | Lola Versus Powerman and the Moneygoround, Part One | 1971 | $25 |

— Later pressings have black printing on a white cover
| ❏ R-6279 [M] | Something Else by the Kinks | 1968 | $300 |

— White label promo; no stock copies were issued in mono
| ❏ RS-6279 [S] | Something Else by the Kinks | 1968 | $80 |

— Pink, gold and green label
| ❏ RS-6279 [S] | Something Else by the Kinks | 1968 | $50 |

— Two-tone orange label with "r: and "W7" logos with steamboat
| ❏ RS-6279 [S] | Something Else by the Kinks | 1971 | $25 |

— Orange label with "r:" and steamboat at top
| ❏ MS-2127 | The Great Lost Kinks Album | 1973 | $50 |
| ❏ R-6197 [M] | The Kink Kontroversy | 1966 | $250 |

— White label promo
❏ R-6197 [M]	The Kink Kontroversy	1966	$75
❏ RS-6197 [R]	The Kink Kontroversy	1966	$30
❏ 2XS-6454 [B]	The Kink Kronicles	1972	$40
❏ RS-6327	The Kinks Are the Village Green Preservation Society	1969	$30

— Two-tone orange label with "r: and "W7" logos with steamboat
| ❏ RS-6327 [B] | The Kinks Are the Village Green Preservation Society | 1971 | $25 |

— Orange label with "r:" and steamboat at top
| ❏ R-6217 [M] | The Kinks Greatest Hits! | 1966 | $40 |
| ❏ RS-6217 [R] | The Kinks Greatest Hits! | 1966 | $30 |

— Pink, gold and green label
| ❏ RS-6217 [R] | The Kinks Greatest Hits! | 1971 | $20 |

— Orange label with "r:" and steamboat at top
| ❏ R-6260 [M] | The Live Kinks | 1967 | $75 |
| ❏ RS-6260 [S] | The Live Kinks | 1967 | $30 |

— Pink, gold and green label
| ❏ RS-6260 [S] | The Live Kinks | 1971 | $20 |

— Orange label with "r:" and steamboat at top
| ❏ PRO328 [P] | Then Now and In Between | 1969 | $150 |

— Album that came with above box is sometimes found by itself without all the other goodies.
| ❏ R-6143 [M] | You Really Got Me | 1965 | $400 |

— White label promo
| ❏ R-6143 [M] | You Really Got Me | 1965 | $75 |
| ❏ RS-6143 [P] | You Really Got Me | 1965 | $100 |

— Pink, gold and green label
| ❏ RS-6143 [P] | You Really Got Me | 1971 | $25 |

— Orange label with "r:" and steamboat at top

RHINO
❏ R170316	Kinda Kinks	1988	$15
❏ R170318	Kinks Kinkdom	1988	$15
❏ R170317	Kinks-Size	1988	$15
❏ R170086	The Kinks Greatest Hits! Vol. 1	1989	$15
❏ R170315	You Really Got Me	1988	$15

SANCTUARY
| ❏ BMG14049V [B] | Kinda Kinks | 25.00 | $ |

KINSEY, TONY

LONDON
| ❏ LL1672 [M] | Kinsey Come On | 1957 | $50 |

KIRBY, DAVE

DOT
| ❏ DLP-26014 | Singer, Picker, Writer | 1973 | $15 |

KIRBY, FRED

CROWN
| ❏ 5196 [M] | Christmas Favorites | 196? | $15 |

CUSTOM
| ❏ CS4 [S] | Christmas Favorites | 196? | $15 |

— Same as Crown LP, but in stereo

Number	Title	Yr	NM

YULETIDE SERIES
| ❏ YS-214 [S] | Christmas Favorites | 197? | $12 |

— Reissue of Custom LP

KIRBY, GEORGE

ARGO
| ❏ LP-4045 [M] | The Real George Kirby | 1965 | $30 |
| ❏ LPS-4045 [S] | The Real George Kirby | 1965 | $40 |

DOOTO
| ❏ DTL-250 [M] | A Night in Hollywood | 196? | $25 |

KIRBY, JOHN

CIRCLE
| ❏ 14 | John Kirby and His Orchestra 1941 | 198? | $25 |
| ❏ 64 | John Kirby and His Orchestra 1941-42 | 198? | $25 |

CLASSIC JAZZ
| ❏ 22 | The Biggest Little Band in the Land | 197? | $25 |

COLUMBIA
| ❏ CG33557 | Boss of the Bass | 1975 | $35 |
| ❏ GL502 [M] | John Kirby and His Orchestra | 1951 | $50 |

— Black label, silver print
| ❏ CL502 [M] | John Kirby and His Orchestra | 1953 | $40 |

— Maroon label, gold print

COLUMBIA MASTERWORKS
| ❏ ML4801 [10] | John Kirby and His Orchestra | 195? | $75 |

EPITAPH
| ❏ E-4004 | John Kirby 1908-1952 | 1975 | $30 |

HARMONY
| ❏ HL7124 [M] | Intimate Swing | 1958 | $30 |

TRIP
| ❏ 5802 | The Biggest Little Band | 197? | $25 |

KIRCHNER, BILL

SEA BREEZE
| ❏ SB-2017 | Infant Eyes | 1983 | $25 |
| ❏ SB-2010 | What It Is to Be Frank | 1982 | $25 |

KIRK, ANDY

CORAL
| ❏ CRL56019 [10] | Andy Kirk Souvenir Album -- Vol. 1 | 1951 | $150 |

DECCA
| ❏ DL79232 | Instrumentally | 1968 | $35 |

MAINSTREAM
| ❏ MRL-399 | Mar-36 | 1975 | $30 |

MCA
❏ 1308	Instrumentally Speaking	198?	$25
❏ 4105	The Best of Andy Kirk and the Clouds of Joy	197?	$30
❏ 1343	The Lady Who Swings the Band	198?	$25

RCA VICTOR
| ❏ LPM-1302 [M] | A Mellow Bit of Rhythm | 1956 | $40 |

KIRK, RAHSAAN ROLAND

ABC
| ❏ AA-1106 | Cry | 1978 | $30 |

ARGO
| ❏ LP-669 [M] | Introducing Roland Kirk | 1960 | $75 |
| ❏ LPS-669 [S] | Introducing Roland Kirk | 1960 | $100 |

ATLANTIC
| ❏ SD1630 | A Meeting of the Times | 1973 | $35 |

— With Al Hibbler
❏ SD1601	Blacknuss	1972	$35
❏ SD 2-907	Bright Moments	1974	$25
❏ 3007 [M]	Here Comes the Whistle Man	1967	$30
❏ SD3007 [S]	Here Comes the Whistle Man	1967	$35
❏ SD1518	Left and Right	1969	$35
❏ SD1578	Natural Black Inventions	1971	$35
❏ SD1686	Other Folks' Music	1976	$30
❏ SD1640	Prepare Thyself to Deal with a Miracle	1974	$35
❏ SD1575	Rahsaan Rahsaan	1970	$35
❏ SD 2-303	The Art of Rahsaan Roland Kirk	1973	$25
❏ SD1592	The Best of Rahsaan Roland Kirk	1972	$35
❏ SD1674	The Case of the 3-Sided Dream in Audio Color	1975	$35
❏ 1502 [M]	The Inflated Tear	1968	$30
❏ SD1502 [S]	The Inflated Tear	1968	$35
❏ 90045	The Inflated Tear	1983	$25
❏ SD 2-1003	Vibration	1978	$35
❏ SD1534	Volunteered Slavery	1969	$35

BETHLEHEM
| ❏ BCP-6016 | Early Roots | 197? | $50 |

— Reissue of 6064, distributed by RCA Victor
| ❏ BCP-6064 [M] | Third Dimension | 1962 | $300 |

Number	Title	Yr	NM

EMARCY
❏ EMS-2-411	Kirk's Works	1975	$50

FANTASY
❏ OJC-459	Kirk's Work	1990	$35

KING
❏ 539 [M]	Triple Threat	1956	$1750

LIMELIGHT
❏ LM-82008 [M]	I Talk with the Spirits	1964	$120
❏ LS-86008 [S]	I Talk with the Spirits	1964	$175

— *Reproductions exist*
❏ LM-82027 [M]	Rip, Rig and Panic	1965	$150
❏ LS-86027 [S]	Rip, Rig and Panic	1965	$120
❏ LM-82033 [M]	Slightly Latin	1966	$150
❏ LS-86033 [S]	Slightly Latin	1966	$120

MERCURY
❏ MG-20748 [M]	Domino	1962	$150
❏ SR-60748 [S]	Domino	1962	$150
❏ MG-20939 [M]	Gifts and Messages	1964	$150
❏ SR-60939 [S]	Gifts and Messages	1964	$150
❏ MG-20894 [M]	Kirk in Copenhagen	1963	$150
❏ SR-60894 [S]	Kirk in Copenhagen	1963	$150
❏ MG-20800 [M]	Reeds and Deeds	1963	$150
❏ SR-60800 [S]	Reeds and Deeds	1963	$150
❏ MG-20844 [M]	Roland Kirk Meets the Benny Golson Orchestra	1963	$150
❏ SR-60844 [S]	Roland Kirk Meets the Benny Golson Orchestra	1963	$150
❏ MG-20679 [M]	We Free Kings	1962	$150
❏ SR-60679 [S]	We Free Kings	1962	$150
❏ 826455-1	We Free Kings	1986	$30

PRESTIGE
❏ PRLP-7450 [M]	Funk Underneath	1967	$50
❏ PRST-7450 [R]	Funk Underneath	1967	$75
❏ PRLP-7210 [M]	Kirk's Work	1961	$250
❏ 24080	Pre-Rahsaan	1978	$35

TRIP
❏ TLP-5503	Domino	197?	$50
❏ TLP-5512	Kirk in Copenhagen	197?	$50
❏ TLP-5541	We Free Kings	197?	$50

VERVE
❏ V-8709 [M]	Now Please Don't You Cry, Beautiful Edith	1967	$150
❏ V6-8709 [S]	Now Please Don't You Cry, Beautiful Edith	1967	$100

WARNER BROS.
❏ BSK3035	Boogie-Woogie String Along for Real	1977	$25
❏ BS2982	Kirkatron	1977	$25
❏ BS2918	The Return of the 5,000 Pound Man	1976	$25

KIRKLAND, LEROY

IMPERIAL
❏ LP-9198 [M]	Twistin', Mashin' and All That Jazz	1962	$175
❏ LP-12198 [S]	Twistin', Mashin' and All That Jazz	1962	$175

KISS

Also see PETER CRISS; ACE FREHLEY; GENE SIMMONS; PAUL STANLEY (and their simultaneously released solo albums from 1978).

CASABLANCA
❏ NBLP7020	Alive!	1975	$40

— *Dark blue labels; with booklet*
❏ NBLP7020	Alive!	1976	$25

— *Tan labels with desert scene, "Casablanca" label*
❏ NBLP7020	Alive!	1977	$18

— *Tan labels with desert scene, "Casablanca Record and FilmWorks" label*
❏ 822780-1	Alive!	1984	$12

— *Reissue*
❏ NBLP7076	Alive II	1977	$18

— *Without inserts*
❏ NBLP7076 [B]	Alive II	1977	$500

— *With 8-page booklet, tattoo insert and "Combat Gear" order form; back cover lists three tracks -- "Take Me," "Hooligan" and "Do You Love Me" -- that were not included on the record; no records with these tracks were made; perhaps as few as 50 copies of this cover were made*
❏ NBLP7076 [B]	Alive II	1977	$75

— *With 8-page booklet, tattoo insert and "Combat Gear" order form; back cover contents are correct*
❏ 822781-1	Alive II	1984	$12

— *Reissue*
❏ NB20128 [DJ]	A Taste of Platinum	1978	$50

— *Promo-only sampler from Double Platinum*
❏ NBLP7270	Creatures of the Night	1982	$40

— *Original version has band with makeup*
❏ 824154-1	Creatures of the Night	1984	$10

— *Reissue; features band without its makeup on cover*
❏ 824154-1 [B]	Creatures of the Night	1985	$50

— *Reissue; glow-in-the-dark vinyl; gatefold edition; makeup cover restored*
❏ NBLP7025	Destroyer	1976	$30

— *Dark blue label*
❏ NBLP7025	Destroyer	1976	$18

— *Tan label with desert scene, "Casablanca" label*

❏ NBLP7025	Destroyer	1977	$15

— *Tan label with desert scene, "Casablanca Record and FilmWorks" label*
❏ 824149-1	Destroyer	1984	$10

— *Reissue*
❏ NBLP7100	Double Platinum	1978	$40

— *With "platinum award" cardboard insert and "Double Platinum Kiss Gear" order form*
❏ NBLP7100	Double Platinum	1978	$18

— *Without inserts*
❏ 824155-1	Double Platinum	1984	$12

— *Reissue*
❏ NBLP7016	Dressed to Kill	1975	$30

— *Dark blue label*
❏ NBLP7016	Dressed to Kill	1976	$18

— *Tan label with desert scene, "Casablanca" label*
❏ NBLP7016 [B]	Dressed to Kill	1977	$15

— *Tan label with desert scene, "Casablanca Record and FilmWorks" label*
❏ 824148-1	Dressed to Kill	1984	$10

— *Reissue*
❏ NBLP7152	Dynasty	1979	$18

— *With poster and merchandise order form*
❏ NBLP7152	Dynasty	1979	$12

— *With neither poster nor order form*
❏ 812770-1	Dynasty	1983	$10

— *Reissue*
❏ NBLP7006	Hotter Than Hell	1974	$30

— *Dark blue label*
❏ NBLP7006	Hotter Than Hell	1976	$18

— *Tan label with desert scene, "Casablanca" label*
❏ NBLP7006	Hotter Than Hell	1977	$15

— *Tan label with desert scene, "Casablanca Record and FilmWorks" label*
❏ 824147-1	Hotter Than Hell	1984	$10

— *Reissue*
❏ NB9001	Kiss	1974	$100

— *First Warner Bros.-distributed version does NOT have "Kissin' Time"*
❏ NBLP7001	Kiss	1974	$30

— *All renumbered versions have "Kissin' Time"; dark blue label*
❏ NBLP7001	Kiss	1976	$18

— *Tan label with desert scene, "Casablanca" label*
❏ NBLP7001	Kiss	1977	$15

— *Tan label with desert scene, "Casablanca Record and FilmWorks" label*
❏ 824146-1	Kiss	1984	$10

— *Reissue*
❏ NB9001	Kiss	1974	$50

— *Second Warner Bros.-distributed version DOES have "Kissin' Time" on Side 2 (RE-1 on label)*
❏ NBLP7225 [B]	Kiss Unmasked	1980	$25

— *With poster and "Kiss Essential Gear" order form*
❏ NBLP7225	Kiss Unmasked	1980	$12

— *With neither poster nor order form*
❏ NBLP7057	Love Gun	1977	$40

— *with "Hot Goods from the Supply Depot" order form, unpunched-out cardboard gun and "Bang!" sticker. All items must be intact to get top dollar for this.*
❏ NBLP7057	Love Gun	1977	$15

— *Without inserts*
❏ 824151-1	Love Gun	1984	$10

— *Reissue*
❏ NBLP7261	Music from The Elder	1981	$30

— *Various editions have paper or plastic innersleeves, lyric sheets, even incorrect track listings on the back cover; no difference in value is noted between variations*
❏ 824153-1	Music from The Elder	1984	$10

— *Reissue*
❏ NB20137 [DJ]	Peter Criss, Ace Frehley, Gene Simmons, Paul Stanley	1978	$75

— *Promo-only sampler from the band's solo albums*

❏ NBLP7037	Rock and Roll Over	1976	$25

— *Tan label with desert scene, "Casablanca" label; comes with sticker and Kiss Army paraphenalia order form*
❏ NBLP7037	Rock and Roll Over	1977	$15

— *Tan label with desert scene, "Casablanca Record and FilmWorks" label, with inserts*
❏ 824150-1	Rock and Roll Over	1984	$10

— *Reissue*
❏ NBLP737 [DJ]	Rock and Roll Over Special Edition	1977	$120

— *Five-track sampler from the LP*
❏ Kiss '76 [DJ]	Special Kiss Tour Album	1976	$150

— *Special four-track sampler*
❏ NBLP7032 [B]	The Originals	1976	$250

— *Tan label with desert scene, "Casablanca" label; with booklet, six Kiss cards, a Kiss Army sticker*
❏ NBLP7032	The Originals	1976	$150

— *Tan label with desert scene, "Casablanca" label; without extras*
❏ NBLP7032	The Originals	1977	$150

— *Tan label with desert scene, "Casablanca Record and FilmWorks" label; "Second Printing" on cover; with extras listed above*
❏ NBLP7032	The Originals	1977	$50

— *Tan label with desert scene, "Casablanca Record and FilmWorks" label; "Second Printing" on cover; without extras*
❏ 826242-1	Unmasked	1985	$10

— *Reissue*

MERCURY
❏ 8227801	Alive!	2008	$30
❏ 522647-1	Alive III	1994	$30

— *Limited edition black vinyl*
❏ 522647-1	Alive III	1994	$30

— *Limited edition white vinyl*
❏ 522647-1	Alive III	1994	$30

— *Limited edition blue vinyl*
❏ 522647-1	Alive III	1994	$30

— *Limited edition red vinyl*
❏ 822495-1	Animalize	1984	$15
❏ 826099-1	Asylum	1985	$12
❏ 832632-1	Crazy Nights	1987	$12
❏ 832903-1 [PD]	Crazy Nights	1987	$30
❏ 528674-1 [PD]	Creatures of the Night	1995	$35

— *Reissue; picture disc of makeup cover*
❏ 792-1 [DJ]	First Kiss, Last Licks	1990	$150

— *Promo-only sampler*
❏ 838913-1	Hot in the Shade	1989	$12
❏ 814297-1	Lick It Up	1983	$15
❏ 528950-1	MTV Unplugged	1996	$25

— *First editions are on black vinyl*
❏ 528950-1 [B]	MTV Unplugged	1996	$50

— *Second editions are on yellow marbled vinyl*
❏ 836427-1	Smashes, Thrashes and Hits	1988	$12
❏ 836887-1 [PD]	Smashes, Thrashes and Hits	1988	$30
❏ 532741-1	You Wanted the Best, You Got the Best!!	1996	$25

KISSOON, MAC AND KATIE

STATE/MCA
❏ 2192	The Two of Us	1976	$15

KIT KATS, THE

JAMIE
❏ LPM-3029 [M]	It's Just a Matter of Time	1966	$30
❏ LPS-3029 [S]	It's Just a Matter of Time	1966	$30
❏ LPM-3032 [M]	The Kit Kats Do Their Thing -- Live!	1967	$30
❏ LPS-3032 [S]	The Kit Kats Do Their Thing -- Live!	1967	$40
❏ JLPS-3034	To Understand Is to Love	1970	$30

— *As "New Hope"*

KITAEV, ANDREI, AND BILL DOUGLASS

REFERENCE RECORDINGS
❏ RR-6	First Takes	198?	$25

KITAJIMA, OSANU

ARISTA
❏ AL9570	Dragon King	1982	$25

HEADFIRST
❏ HF-9706	Masterless Samurai	1981	$25

KITAMURA, ELJI

CONCORD JAZZ
❏ CJ-217	Seven Stars	198?	$25
❏ CJ-152	Swing Elji	198?	$25

KITCHEN CINQ, THE

LHI
❏ E-12000 [M]	Everything But the Kitchen Cinq	1967	$30
❏ E7-12000 [S]	Everything But the Kitchen Cinq	1967	$40

Number	Title	Yr	NM

KITT, EARTHA

CAEDMON

Number	Title	Yr	NM
❏ TC-1267	Folk Tales of the Tribes of Africa	1969	$25

DECCA

| ❏ DL4635 [M] | Eartha Kitt Sings in Spanish | 1965 | $30 |
| ❏ DL74635 [S] | Eartha Kitt Sings in Spanish | 1965 | $40 |

GNP CRESCENDO

| ❏ GNPS-2008 [S] | At the Plaza | 1965 | $25 |
| ❏ GNP-2008 [M] | At the Plaza | 1965 | $18 |

KAPP

| ❏ KL-1192 [M] | Eartha Kitt Revisited | 1960 | $30 |
| ❏ KS-3192 [S] | Eartha Kitt Revisited | 1960 | $30 |

| ❏ KL-1162 [M] | The Fabulous Eartha Kitt | 1959 | $30 |
| ❏ KS-3046 [S] | The Fabulous Eartha Kitt | 1959 | $30 |

MCA

| ❏ 1554 | The Best of Eartha Kitt | 1983 | $15 |

MGM

| ❏ E-4009 [M] | Bad But Beautiful | 1962 | $30 |
| ❏ SE-4009 [S] | Bad But Beautiful | 1962 | $30 |

RCA VICTOR

❏ LPM-1109 [M]	Down to Eartha	1955	$50
❏ LPM-3062 [10]	RCA Victor Presents Eartha Kitt	1953	$100
❏ LPM-1661 [M]	St. Louis Blues	1958	$40
❏ LSP-1661 [S]	St. Louis Blues	1958	$50
❏ LPM-3187 [10]	That Bad Eartha	1953	$100
❏ LPM-1153 [M]	That Bad Eartha	1955	$50
❏ LPM-1300 [M]	Thursday's Child	1956	$50

STANYAN

| ❏ SR-10037 | Best of All Possible Worlds | 1972 | $18 |
| ❏ SR-10040 | For Always | 1975 | $18 |

SUNNYVIEW

| ❏ SUN-4902 | I Love Men | 1984 | $12 |

KITTRELL, JEAN

GHB

| ❏ 51 | 'Tain't Nobody's Bizness | 197? | $30 |

KITTYHAWK

EMI AMERICA

| ❏ SW-17029 | Kittyhawk | 1980 | $30 |
| ❏ ST-17053 | Race for the Oasis | 1981 | $30 |

ZEBRA

| ❏ ZR-5001 | Fanfare | 198? | $30 |

KITZJIMA, OSAMU

ANTILLES

| ❏ AN7016 [B] | Benzaiten | 1976 | $35 |

KLAATU
Subject of extensive BEATLES hoax.

CAPITOL

| ❏ ST-12080 | Endangered Species | 1980 | $15 |

❏ ST-11633 [B]	Hope	1977	$15
❏ SN-16061	Hope	1980	$10
—Budget-line reissue			
❏ ST-11542	Klaatu	1976	$18
❏ SN-16060	Klaatu	1980	$10
—Budget-line reissue			
❏ SW-11836	Sir Army Suit	1978	$15
❏ SN-16062	Sir Army Suit	1980	$10
—Budget-line reissue			

KLARK KENT
STEWART COPELAND of THE POLICE in disguise.

KRYPTONE/I.R.S.

| ❏ SP70600 [EP] | Music Madness from the Kinetic Kid | 1980 | $25 |
| —Green vinyl 10" in die-cut 12" sleeve | | | |

KLEIN, JOHN

COLUMBIA

| ❏ PC44387 [M] | Caroling on the Carillon | 1987 | $12 |
| —Contains previously released material | | | |

RCA VICTOR

| ❏ LPM-2914 [M] | Let's Ring the Bells All Around the Christmas Tree | 1964 | $15 |
| ❏ LSP-2914 [S] | Let's Ring the Bells All Around the Christmas Tree | 1964 | $18 |

KLEIN, ROBERT

BRUT

| ❏ 6001 | Child of the 50's | 1973 | $15 |
| ❏ 6600 | Mind Over Matter | 1974 | $15 |

CAEDMON

| ❏ TC9100 | The Unauthorized Biography of Howard Who | 1969 | $15 |

EPIC

| ❏ PE33535 | New Teeth | 1975 | $12 |

KLEMMER, JOHN, AND EDDIE HARRIS

CRUSADERS

| ❏ 16015 | Two Tone | 1982 | $75 |
| —Part of MCA's "Audiophile Series" | | | |

KLEMMER, JOHN

ABC

❏ AA-1068	Arabesque	1978	$25
❏ ABCD-950	Barefoot Ballet	1976	$25
❏ AA-1116	Brazilia	1979	$25
❏ AA-1106	Cry	1978	$25
❏ ABCD-836	Fresh Feathers	1974	$35
❏ AB-1007	LifeStyle (Living & Loving)	1977	$25
❏ ABCD-922	Touch	1975	$25

ABC IMPULSE!

❏ AS-9214	Constant Throb	1973	$35
❏ AS-9244	Intensity	1974	$250
❏ AS-9269	Magic and Movement	1974	$250
❏ AS-9220	Waterfalls	1973	$35

ARISTA/NOVUS

| ❏ AN2-3500 | Nexus | 1979 | $35 |

BLUEBIRD

| ❏ 6577-1-RB | Nexus One | 1987 | $25 |

CADET

❏ LPS808	And We Were Lovers	1968	$50
❏ LP797 [M]	Involvement	1967	$40
❏ LPS797 [S]	Involvement	1967	$50
—Fading blue label			
❏ CA-797 [S]	Involvement	197?	$35
—Pink and yellow label reissue			

CADET CONCEPT

❏ LPS326	All the Children Cried	1970	$50
❏ LPS321	Blowin' Gold	1969	$75
❏ LPS330	Eruptions	1971	$50

CHESS

❏ CH2-92501	Blowin' Gold	1984	$30
—Reissue of CH-8300			
❏ CH-8300	Blowin' Gold	1982	$30
—Compilation of tracks from three Cadet Concept LPs			
❏ 2ACMJ-401	Magic Moments	1976	$35

ELEKTRA

❏ 5E-527	Hush	1981	$25
❏ 6E-284	Magnificent Madness	1980	$25
❏ 5E-566	Solo Saxophone II: Life	1982	$25

ELEKTRA/MUSICIAN

| ❏ 60197 | Finesse | 1983 | $25 |

MCA

❏ 37015	Arabesque	1980	$20
—Reissue of ABC 1068			
❏ 1585	Arabesque	198?	$20
—Reissue of MCA 37015			
❏ 37013	Barefoot Ballet	1980	$20
—Reissue of ABC 950			
❏ AA-1116	Brazilia	1979	$20
—Reissue of ABC 1116			
❏ 37115	Brazilia	1980	$20

—Reissue of MCA 1116			
❏ 1639	Brazilia	198?	$20
—Reissue of MCA 37115			
❏ 37017	Constant Throb	1980	$20
—Reissue of ABC Impulse 9214			
❏ 37016	Cry	1980	$20
—Reissue of ABC 1106			
❏ 37012	Fresh Feathers	1980	$25
—Reissue of ABC 836			
❏ 37019	Intensity	1980	$25
—Reissue of ABC Impulse 9244			
❏ 37014	LifeStyle (Living & Loving)	1980	$20
—Reissue of ABC 1007			
❏ 37020	Magic and Movement	1980	$25
—Reissue of ABC Impulse 9269			
❏ 6246	Music	1989	$30
❏ 8014	The Best of John Klemmer, Volume One/Mosaic	1979	$30
❏ 6007	The Best of John Klemmer, Volume One/Mosaic	198?	$25
—Reissue of MCA 8014			
❏ 6017	The Best of John Klemmer, Volume Two/The Impulse Years	1982	$30
❏ 37152	Touch	198?	$20
—Reissue of ABC 922			
❏ 1654	Touch	198?	$20
—Reissue of MCA 37152			
❏ 37018	Waterfalls	1980	$25
—Reissue of ABC Impulse 9220			

MOBILE FIDELITY

| ❏ Jan-006 | Touch | 1979 | $75 |
| —Original Master Recording" at top of front cover; audiophile vinyl | | | |

NAUTILUS

❏ NR-22	Finesse	1981	$175
—SuperDisc" audiophile vinyl			
❏ NR-4	Straight from the Heart	1980	$175
—Super Disc" audiophile vinyl			

KLF, THE

TVT

| ❏ 4040 | History of the JAMS a.k.a. The Timelords | 1988 | $25 |
| —As "The JAMs | | | |

WAX TRAX!

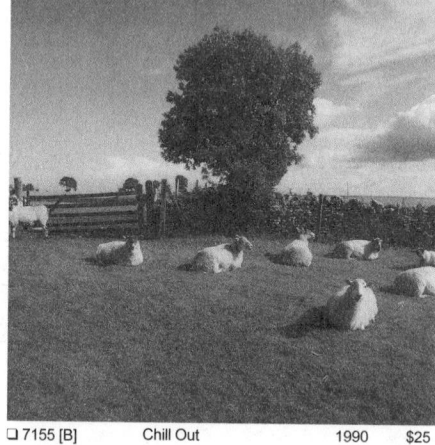

| ❏ 7155 [B] | Chill Out | 1990 | $25 |

KLINK, AL/BOB ALEXANDER

GRAND AWARD

❏ GA 33-525 [M]	Progressive Jazz	1956	$100
—With removable outer cover			
❏ GA 33-525 [M]	Progressive Jazz	1956	$30
—Without removable outer cover			

KLOSS, ERIC, AND BARRY MILES

MUSE

| ❏ MR-5112 | Together | 1976 | $35 |

KLOSS, ERIC, AND GIL GOLDSTEIN

OMNISOUND

| ❏ 1044 | Sharing | 1981 | $30 |

KLOSS, ERIC

COBBLESTONE

| ❏ 9006 | Doors | 1972 | $25 |

MUSE

❏ MR-5077	Bodies' Warmth	1975	$35
❏ MR-5196	Celebration	1979	$30
❏ MR-5291	Doors	198?	$30
—Reissue of Cobblestone 9006			

Number	Title	Yr	NM
❏ MR-5038	Essence	1974	$35
❏ MR-5147	Now	1978	$30
❏ MR-5019	One, Two, Free	1973	$35

PRESTIGE

Number	Title	Yr	NM
❏ PRST-7793	Consciousness!	1970	$35
❏ PRLP-7520 [M]	First Class Kloss	1967	$30
❏ PRST-7520 [S]	First Class Kloss	1967	$25
❏ PRST-7486 [M]	Grits & Gravy	1967	$30
❏ PRST-7486 [S]	Grits & Gravy	1967	$25
❏ PRST-7627	In the Land of the Giants	1969	$35
❏ PRLP-7442 [M]	Introducing Eric Kloss	1966	$25
❏ PRST-7442 [S]	Introducing Eric Kloss	1966	$30
❏ PRST-7535	Life Force	1968	$25
❏ PRLP-7469 [M]	Love and All That Jazz	1966	$25
❏ PRST-7469 [S]	Love and All That Jazz	1966	$30
❏ PRST-7594	Sky Shadows	1969	$35
❏ PRST-7689	To Hear Is to See!	1970	$35
❏ PRST-7565	We're Goin' Up	1968	$35

KLOWNS, THE

RCA VICTOR

Number	Title	Yr	NM
❏ LSP-4438	The Klowns	1970	$12

KLUGH, EARL

BLUE NOTE

Number	Title	Yr	NM
❏ BN-LA596-H2	Earl Klugh	1976	$25
❏ LN-10163	Earl Klugh	198?	$20
—Budget-line reissue			
❏ BN-LA737-H2	Finger Paintings	1977	$25
❏ LO-737	Finger Paintings	198?	$20
—Reissue with new prefix			
❏ BN-LA667-H2	Living Inside Your Love	1976	$25
❏ LO-667	Living Inside Your Love	198?	$20
—Reissue with new prefix			

CAPITOL

Number	Title	Yr	NM
❏ ST-12405	Key Notes (Greatest Hits)	1985	$25
❏ ST-12253	Low Ride	1983	$25
❏ ST-12372	Nightsongs	1984	$25
❏ ST-12323	Wishful Thinking	1984	$25

LIBERTY

Number	Title	Yr	NM
❏ LT-51113	Crazy for You	1981	$25
❏ LN-10308	Crazy for You	1986	$20
—Budget-line reissue			
❏ LN-10257	Finger Paintings	198?	$20
—Budget-line reissue			
❏ LO-942	Heart String	198?	$20
—Reissue of United Artists 942			
❏ LN-10231	Heart String	198?	$20
—Budget-line reissue			
❏ LT-1079	Late Night Guitar	1980	$25
❏ LN-10233	Living Inside Your Love	198?	$20
—Budget-line reissue			
❏ LMAS-877	Magic in Your Eyes	198?	$20
—Reissue of United Artists 877			

MOBILE FIDELITY

Number	Title	Yr	NM
❏ Jan-0025	Finger Paintings	1979	$150
—Audiophile vinyl			
❏ UHQR 1-025	Finger Paintings	1982	$250
—Ultra High Quality" audiophile vinyl in box			
❏ Jan-0076	Late Night Guitar	1981	$150
—Audiophile vinyl			

NAUTILUS

Number	Title	Yr	NM
❏ NR-46 [B]	Crazy for You	198?	$40
—Audiophile vinyl			

UNITED ARTISTS

Number	Title	Yr	NM
❏ LT-1026	Dream Come True	1980	$25
❏ UA-LA942-H	Heart String	1979	$25
❏ UA-LA877-H	Magic in Your Eyes	1978	$25

WARNER BROS.

Number	Title	Yr	NM
❏ 25478	Life Stories	1986	$25
❏ 25262	Soda Fountain Shuffle	1985	$25
❏ 26018	Solo Guitar	1989	$30
❏ 25902	Whispers and Promises	1989	$30

KNACK, THE

CAPITOL

Number	Title	Yr	NM
❏ SOO-12045	...But the Little Girls Understand	1980	$10
❏ SOO-512045	...But the Little Girls Understand	1980	$10
—Columbia House edition			
❏ SO-11948	Get the Knack	1979	$10
❏ R142110	Get the Knack	1979	$10
—RCA Music Service edition			
❏ SO-511948	Get the Knack	1979	$10
—Columbia House edition			
❏ ST-12168	Round Trip	1981	$10

KNAPP, JAMES

ECM

Number	Title	Yr	NM
❏ 1194	First Avenue	198?	$30

KNEE, BERNIE

AUDIOPHILE

Number	Title	Yr	NM
❏ AP-144	Bernie Knee	198?	$30

KNEPPER, JIMMY

BETHLEHEM

Number	Title	Yr	NM
❏ BCP-77 [M]	A Swinging Introduction to Jimmy Knepper	1957	$300
❏ BCP-6031	Idol of the Flies	197?	$30
—Reissue, distributed by RCA Victor			

DEBUT

Number	Title	Yr	NM
❏ DEB-129 [M]	New Faces	1956	$0
—Canceled			

INNER CITY

Number	Title	Yr	NM
❏ IC-6047	Knepper in L.A.	197?	$30

SOUL NOTE

Number	Title	Yr	NM
❏ SN-1092	I Dream Too Much	1984	$30

STEEPLECHASE

Number	Title	Yr	NM
❏ SCS-1061	Cunningbird	1977	$30

KNICKERBOCKERS, THE

CHALLENGE

Number	Title	Yr	NM
❏ CH-621 [M]	Jerk and Twine Time	1965	$400
❏ CH-622 [M]	Lies	1966	$150
❏ CHS-622 [S]	Lies	1966	$250
❏ LP-12664 [M]	Llyod Thaxton Presents the Knickerbockers	1965	$250

SUNDAZED

Number	Title	Yr	NM
❏ LP-5154	Rockin' with the Knickerbockers	2003	$15
❏ LP-5000	The Great Lost Knickerbockers Album	1990	$18
—Blue vinyl			

KNIGHT, BOBBY, AND THE GREAT AMERICAN TROMBONE CO.

SEA BREEZE

Number	Title	Yr	NM
❏ SB-2009	Cream of the Crop	198?	$25

KNIGHT, CHRIS, AND MAUREEN MCCORMICK
Also see each artist's individual listings; THE BRADY BUNCH.

PARAMOUNT

Number	Title	Yr	NM
❏ PAS-6062	Chris Knight and Maureen McCormick	1973	$120

KNIGHT, FREDERICK

STAX

Number	Title	Yr	NM
❏ STS-3011	I've Been Lonely So Long	1973	$25

KNIGHT, GLADYS, AND THE PIPS

ACCORD

Number	Title	Yr	NM
❏ SN-7103	Every Beat of My Heart	1981	$12
❏ SN-7131	I Feel a Song	1981	$12
❏ SN-7188	It's Showtime	1982	$12
❏ SN-7105	Letter Full of Tears	1981	$12

ALLEGIANCE

Number	Title	Yr	NM
❏ AV-5002	Glad to Be...	198?	$12

BELL

Number	Title	Yr	NM
❏ 1323	In the Beginning	1975	$15
❏ 6013	Tastiest Hits	1968	$25

BUDDAH

Number	Title	Yr	NM
❏ BDS-5639	2nd Anniversary	1975	$15
❏ BDS-5602	Claudine	1974	$30
❏ BDS-5612	I Feel a Song	1974	$15
❏ BDS-5141	Imagination	1973	$15
❏ BDS-5714	Miss Gladys Knight	1978	$15
❏ BDS-5676	Pipe Dreams	1976	$15
❏ BDS-5689	Still Together	1977	$15
❏ BDS-5653	The Best of Gladys Knight & The Pips	1976	$15
❏ BDS-5701	The One and Only	1978	$15

CASABLANCA

Number	Title	Yr	NM
❏ NBLP7081	At Last...The Pips	1977	$12
—As "The Pips"			
❏ NBLP7113	Callin'	1978	$12
—As "The Pips"			

COLLECTABLES

Number	Title	Yr	NM
❏ COL-5154	Golden Classics: Letter Full of Tears	198?	$12

COLUMBIA

Number	Title	Yr	NM
❏ JC36387	About Love	1980	$12
❏ PC36387	About Love	198?	$10
—Budget-line reissue			
❏ JC35704	Gladys Knight	1979	$12
❏ PC35704	Gladys Knight	198?	$10
—Budget-line reissue			
❏ FC40376	Greatest Hits	1986	$12
❏ FC39423	Life	1985	$12
❏ PC39423	Life	198?	$10
—Budget-line reissue			
❏ FC38114	That Special Time of Year	1982	$12
❏ PC38114	That Special Time of Year	1983	$10
—Same as above with new prefix			
❏ FC40878	The Best of Gladys Knight and the Pips/The Columbia Years	1988	$12
❏ FC37086	Touch	1981	$12
❏ PC37086	Touch	198?	$10
—Budget-line reissue			

Number	Title	Yr	NM
❏ FC38205	Visions	1983	$12
❏ PC38205	Visions	198?	$10
—Budget-line reissue			

FURY

Number	Title	Yr	NM
❏ 1003 [M]	Letter Full of Tears	1962	$500

LOST-NITE

Number	Title	Yr	NM
❏ LLP-17 [10]	The Best of Gladys Knight and the Pips	1981	$15
—Red vinyl			

MAXX

Number	Title	Yr	NM
❏ 3000 [M]	Gladys Knight and the Pips	1964	$175

MCA

Number	Title	Yr	NM
❏ 42004	All Our Love	1987	$12
❏ 10329	Good Woman	1991	$18

MOTOWN

Number	Title	Yr	NM
❏ MOT5303	All the Great Hits of Gladys Knight and the Pips	198?	$10
❏ M792S2	Anthology	1974	$18
❏ M5-126V1	Everybody Needs Love	1981	$15
—Reissue of Soul 706			
❏ M5-113V	Motown Superstar Series, Vol. 13	1981	$12
❏ M5-193V1	Neither One of Us	1981	$15
—Reissue of Soul 737			
❏ M5-148V1	Nitty Gritty	1981	$15
—Reissue of Soul 713			

NATURAL RESOURCES

Number	Title	Yr	NM
❏ NR4004T1	Silk N' Soul	1978	$12
—Reissue of Soul 711			

PAIR

Number	Title	Yr	NM
❏ PDL2-1198	The Best of Gladys Knight and the Pips	1987	$15

PICKWICK

Number	Title	Yr	NM
❏ SPC-3349	Every Beat of My Heart	197?	$12

SOUL

Number	Title	Yr	NM
❏ S744	A Little Knight Music	1975	$15
❏ SS730	All in a Knight's Work	1970	$18
❏ S739L	All I Need Is Time	1973	$18
❏ S706 [M]	Everybody Needs Love	1967	$30
❏ SS706 [S]	Everybody Needs Love	1967	$30
❏ S707 [M]	Feelin' Bluesy	1968	$40
—Mono copies are white label promo only; cover has "Monaural Record DJ Copy" sticker			
❏ SS707 [S]	Feelin' Bluesy	1968	$30
❏ SS723	Gladys Knight and the Pips Greatest Hits	1970	$18
❏ SS731	If I Were Your Woman	1971	$18
❏ S741	Knight Time	1974	$15

Number	Title	Yr	NM
❏ S737L [B]	Neither One of Us	1973	$18
❏ SS713	Nitty Gritty	1969	$30
❏ SS711	Silk N' Soul	1968	$30
❏ S736L	Standing Ovation	1971	$18

SPHERE SOUND

Number	Title	Yr	NM
❏ SR-7006 [M]	Gladys Knight and the Pips	196?	$250
❏ SSR-7006 [R]	Gladys Knight and the Pips	196?	$120

SPRINGBOARD

Number	Title	Yr	NM
❏ SPB-4035	Early Hits	1972	$12
❏ SPB-4050	How Do You Say Goodbye	1973	$12

TRIP

Number	Title	Yr	NM
❏ TLP-9509	It Hurt Me So Bad	1973	$12

UNITED ARTISTS

Number	Title	Yr	NM
❏ UA-LA503-E	The Very Best of Gladys Knight and the Pips	1975	$15

UPFRONT

Number	Title	Yr	NM
❏ UPF130	Gladys Knight and the Pips	197?	$12
❏ UPF185	Gladys Knight and the Pips	197?	$12

VEE JAY

Number	Title	Yr	NM
❏ D1-74796	Every Beat of My Heart: The Greatest Hits of the Early Years	1989	$18

Number	Title	Yr	NM

KNIGHT, JEAN
COTILLION
| ❏ SD5230 | Jean Knight and Premium | 1981 | $18 |

MIRAGE
| ❏ 90282 | My Toot Toot | 1985 | $12 |

STAX
| ❏ STS-2045 | Mr. Big Stuff | 1971 | $40 |
| ❏ MPS-8554 | Mr. Big Stuff | 198? | $12 |

KNIGHT, ROBERT
RISING SONS
| ❏ RSM-7000 [M] | Everlasting Love | 1967 | $30 |
| ❏ RSS-17000 [S] | Everlasting Love | 1967 | $40 |

KNIGHT, SONNY
AURA
| ❏ AR-3001 [M] | If You Want This Love | 1964 | $30 |
| ❏ AS-3001 [S] | If You Want This Love | 1964 | $35 |

KNIGHT, TED
RANWOOD
| ❏ R-8149 [B] | Hi Guys! | 1976 | $30 |

KNIGHT, TERRY, AND THE PACK
Group evloved into GRAND FUNK RAILROAD.
ABKCO
| ❏ AB-4217 [B] | Mark, Don and Terry 1966-67 | 1972 | $30 |

CAMEO
| ❏ C2007 [M] | Reflections | 1967 | $25 |
— Reissue of Lucky Eleven LE-8001
| ❏ CS2007 [S] | Reflections | 1967 | $30 |
— Reissue of Lucky Eleven LES-8001

LUCKY ELEVEN
❏ LE-8001 [M]	Reflections	1967	$30
❏ LES-8001 [S]	Reflections	1967	$75
❏ LE-8000 [M]	Terry Knight and the Pack	1966	$75
❏ LES-8000 [R]	Terry Knight and the Pack	1966	$30

KNIGHTS, THE
At least three, and perhaps four, different groups.
ACE
❏ 200854	Across the Board	1966	$400
❏ 4763	Cold Days, Hot Knights	196?	$400
❏ 201302	The Knights 1967	1967	$400

CAPITOL
| ❏ T2189 [M] | Hot Rod High | 1964 | $400 |
| ❏ DT2189 [R] | Hot Rod High | 1964 | $400 |

JUSTICE
| ❏ JLP-156 | On the Move | 196? | $300 |

KNIGHTS OF DIXIELAND, THE
JAZZOLOGY
| ❏ J-4 [M] | A Night with the Knights of Dixieland | 1964 | $35 |

KNIGHTSBRIDGE STRINGS, THE
MONUMENT
❏ MAM-3001 [M]	3/4 Time	1966	$12
❏ MAS-13001 [S]	3/4 Time	1966	$15
❏ MAM-3002 [M]	Cinema	1966	$12
❏ MAS-13002 [S]	Cinema	1966	$15
❏ MAM-3000 [M]	Espana	1966	$12
❏ MAS-13000 [S]	Espana	1966	$15
❏ MAS-13006 [S]	Gilbert and Sullivan	1967	$15
❏ MAM-3006 [M]	Gilbert and Sullivan	1967	$15
❏ MAS-13005 [S]	Hawaii	1967	$15
❏ MAM-3005 [M]	Hawaii	1967	$15
❏ MAS-13007	Marching Strings	1969	$12
❏ MAS-13008	Nashville	1969	$12
❏ MAS-13004 [S]	Reverie	1966	$15
❏ MAM-3004 [M]	Reverie	1966	$12
❏ MAM-3003 [M]	The Knightsbridge Strings Go Pop	1966	$12
❏ MAS-13003 [S]	The Knightsbridge Strings Go Pop	1966	$15

PURIST
| ❏ SR-9 | Nostalgic Swing Mood | 196? | $15 |
| ❏ SR-3 | Spanish Mood | 196? | $15 |

RIVERSIDE
❏ RS-97533 [S]	Big Beat	196?	$15
❏ RM-7533 [M]	Big Beat	196?	$12
❏ RS-97518 [S]	Strings on the March	196?	$15
❏ RM-7518 [M]	Strings on the March	196?	$12
❏ RS-97532 [S]	Waltzing Strings	196?	$15
❏ RM-7532 [M]	Waltzing Strings	196?	$12

SESAC
| ❏ C-1701/2 [M] | Songs of America Vol. 1 | 195? | $18 |
| ❏ C-1703/4 [M] | Songs of America Vol. 2 | 195? | $18 |

TOP RANK
❏ RM-315 [M]	Latin Cameos	1960	$15
❏ RS-615 [S]	Latin Cameos	1960	$18
❏ RM-325 [M]	More Swinging Strings	1960	$15
❏ RS-625 [S]	More Swinging Strings	1960	$18
❏ RM-341 [M]	Soft Swaying Strings	1960	$15

— Title on label is "More Swaying Strings
| ❏ RS-641 [S] | Soft Swaying Strings | 1960 | $18 |
— Title on label is "More Swaying Strings
❏ RM-303 [M]	The Strings Sing	1959	$15
❏ RS-603 [S]	The Strings Sing	1959	$18
❏ RM-308 [M]	The Strings Swing	1959	$15
❏ RS-608 [S]	The Strings Swing	1959	$18

KNITTERS, THE
SLASH
| ❏ 25310 | Poor Little Critter in the Road | 1985 | $15 |
— With members of X and The Blasters

KNOBLOCK, FRED
SCOTTI BROTHERS
| ❏ SB7109 | Why Not Me | 1980 | $12 |

KNOCKOUTS, THE (1)
TRIBUTE
| ❏ 1202 [M] | Go Ape with the Knockouts | 1964 | $250 |

KNOPF, PAUL
PLAYBACK
❏ PLP-502 [M]	And the Walls Came Tumbling Down	1960	$40
❏ PLP-502ST [S]	And the Walls Came Tumbling Down	1960	$50
❏ PLP-501 [M]	Enigma of a Day	1959	$40
❏ PLP-501ST [S]	Enigma of a Day	1959	$50
❏ PLP-600 [M]	Music from the Morgue	1961	$40
❏ PLP-600ST [S]	Music from the Morgue	1961	$50
❏ PLP-503 [M]	Paul Knoft Trio	1960	$40
❏ PLP-503ST [S]	Paul Knoft Trio	1960	$50
❏ PLP-500 [M]	The Outcat	1959	$40
❏ PLP-500ST [S]	The Outcat	1959	$50

KNOWBODY ELSE
Members were later in BLACK OAK ARKANSAS.
HIP
| ❏ HIS-7003 | Knowbody Else | 1969 | $40 |

KNOX, BUDDY
ACCORD
| ❏ SN-7218 | Party Doll and Other Hits | 1981 | $12 |
LIBERTY
| ❏ LRP-3251 [M] | Buddy Knox's Golden Hits | 1962 | $30 |
| ❏ LST-7251 [S] | Buddy Knox's Golden Hits | 1962 | $50 |
ROULETTE
| ❏ R25003 [M] | Buddy Knox | 1957 | $250 |
— Black label, all silver print (original)
| ❏ R25003 [M] | Buddy Knox | 1957 | $175 |
— Black label, red and silver print

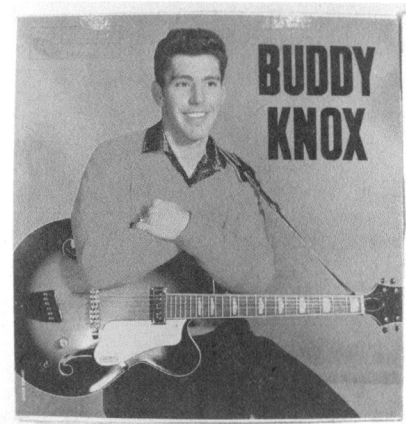

| ❏ R25003 [M] | Buddy Knox | 1959 | $150 |
— White label with colored spokes
| ❏ R25048 [M] | Buddy Knox and Jimmy Bowen | 1959 | $250 |
— Black label, red and silver print
| ❏ R25048 [M] | Buddy Knox and Jimmy Bowen | 1959 | $150 |
— White label with colored spokes

UNITED ARTISTS
| ❏ UAS6689 | Gypsy Man | 1969 | $30 |

KOALA, THE
CAPITOL
| ❏ SKAO-176 | The Koala | 1969 | $75 |

KOCH, MERLE
AUDIOPHILE
| ❏ AP-135 | Merle Koch and Eddie Miller at Michele's | 1979 | $25 |
| ❏ AP-126 | The Polite Jazz Quartet | 1978 | $25 |

JAZZOLOGY
| ❏ J-80 | Jazz Piano | 197? | $25 |

KODAKS, THE / THE STARLITES
SPHERE SOUND
| ❏ SSR-7005 [M] | The Kodaks Vs. the Starlites | 1965 | $250 |

KOERNER, RAY AND GLOVER
AUDIOPHILE
| ❏ AP-78 [M] | Blues, Rags and Hollers | 1963 | $50 |
— Includes four songs not on the Elektra reissue
ELEKTRA
| ❏ EKL-240 [M] | Blues, Rags and Hollers | 1963 | $30 |
— Not issued in stereo on Elektra
❏ EKL-267 [M]	Lots More Blues, Rags and Hollers	1964	$25
❏ EKS-7267 [S]	Lots More Blues, Rags and Hollers	1964	$30
❏ EKL-305 [M]	The Return of Koerner, Ray and Glover	1965	$25
❏ EKS-7305 [S]	The Return of Koerner, Ray and Glover	1965	$30

KOERNER, SPIDER JOHN, AND WILLIE MURPHY
ELEKTRA
| ❏ EKS-74041 | Running, Jumping, Standing Still | 1969 | $25 |

KOERNER, SPIDER JOHN
ELEKTRA
| ❏ EKL-290 [M] | Spider Blues | 1965 | $25 |
| ❏ EKS-7290 [S] | Spider Blues | 1965 | $30 |
SWEET JANE
| ❏ SJL-5872 | Music Is Just a Bunch of Notes | 1972 | $150 |
— With Willie and the Bumblebees and BONNIE RAITT
| ❏ SJL-1074 | Some American Folksongs Like They Used To | 1974 | $30 |

KOFFMAN, MOE
ASCOT
| ❏ AM13001 [M] | Moe Koffman Plays for the Teens | 1962 | $50 |
| ❏ AS16001 [S] | Moe Koffman Plays for the Teens | 1962 | $30 |
JANUS
| ❏ 7037 | Museum Pieces | 1978 | $25 |
JUBILEE
❏ JLP-1037 [M]	Cool and Hot Sax	1957	$40
❏ JGS-8009	Moe Koffman Goes Electric	1968	$75
❏ JLP-1074 [M]	The Shepherd Swings Again	1958	$40
❏ JGS-8016	Turned On	1968	$75
KAMA SUTRA
| ❏ KSBS-2018 [B] | Moe's Curried Soul | 1970 | $18 |
SOUNDWINGS/DUKE STREET
| ❏ SW2108 | Oop-Pop-A-Da | 1988 | $30 |
— With Dizzy Gillespie
UNITED ARTISTS
| ❏ UAJ-14029 [M] | Tales of Koffman | 1963 | $75 |
| ❏ UAJS-15029 [S] | Tales of Koffman | 1963 | $75 |

KOFI
ATLANTIC
| ❏ DMD2182 [DJ] | A Very Reggae Christmas | 1994 | $18 |
— Promo only on green vinyl; generic white cover with custom sticker

KOHANNA, DEE
ROCK CREEK
| ❏ 01 | Eclipse | 1979 | $35 |

KOHLMAN, FREDDIE
MGM
| ❏ E-297 [10] | New Orleans Now -- New Orleans Then | 1955 | $100 |

KOINONIA
BREAKER
| ❏ 9970 | Celebration | 1984 | $25 |
| ❏ 9946 | More Than a Feeling | 1983 | $25 |

KOKI, SAM, AND THE PARADISE ISLANDERS
KAPP
| ❏ KL-1321 [M] | Surfin' at Waikiki | 1963 | $18 |
| ❏ KS-3321 [S] | Surfin' at Waikiki | 1963 | $25 |

KOKOMO (1)
FELSTED
| ❏ FL7513 [M] | Asia Minor | 1961 | $40 |
| ❏ FS17513 [S] | Asia Minor | 1961 | $50 |

Number	Title	Yr	NM
KOKOMO (2)			
COLUMBIA			
❏ PC33442 [B]	Kokomo	1975	$18
❏ PC34031 [B]	Rise and Shine!	1976	$18
KOLBY, DIANE			
COLUMBIA			
❏ KC31386	Diane Kolby	1972	$18
KOLE, JERRY, AND THE STRINGERS			
CROWN			
❏ CLP-5385 [M]	Hot Rod Alley	1963	$30
❏ CST-385 [S]	Hot Rod Alley	1963	$40
KOLLER, HANS			
DISCOVERY			
❏ DL-2005 [10]	Hans Koller	1954	$300
VANGUARD			
❏ VRS-8509 [M]	Hans Across the Sea	1956	$150
KOLOC, BONNIE			
OVATION			
❏ OVQD 14-21 [Q]	After All This Time	1971	$20
❏ OVQD 14-29 [Q]	Bonnie Koloc	1973	$20
❏ OVQD 14-26 [Q]	Hold On to Me	1972	$20
❏ OVQD 14-38 [Q]	You're Gonna Love Yourself in the Morning	1974	$20
KOMACK, JAMES			
RCA VICTOR			
❏ LPM-1501 [M]	Inside Me	1957	$30
KON KAN			
ATLANTIC			
❏ 81984	Move to Move	1989	$15
KONGOS, JOHN			
ELEKTRA			
❏ EKS-75019 [B]	Kongos	1971	$18
JANUS			
❏ JLS3032 [B]	Confusions About a Goldfish	1970	$30
KONITZ, LEE, AND HAL GALPER			
INNER CITY			
❏ IC-2057	Windows	1976	$35
STEEPLECHASE			
❏ SCS-1057	Windows	198?	$30
KONITZ, LEE, AND MARTIAL SOLAI			
PAUSA			
❏ 7138	Duo: Live at Berlin Jazz Days 1980	198?	$25
KONITZ, LEE, AND RED MITCHELL			
INNER CITY			
❏ IC-2018	I Concentrate on You	1975	$35
STEEPLECHASE			
❏ SCS-1018	I Concentrate on You	198?	$30
KONITZ, LEE			
ATLANTIC			
❏ SD8235	Duets	1969	$35
❏ 1258 [M]	Inside Hi-Fi	1957	$300
—Black label			
❏ 1258 [M]	Inside Hi-Fi	1961	$175
—Multicolor label, white "fan" logo at right			
❏ SD1258 [S]	Inside Hi-Fi	1958	$300
—Green label			
❏ SD1258 [S]	Inside Hi-Fi	1961	$175
—Multicolor label, white "fan" logo at right			
❏ 1217 [M]	Lee Konitz with Warne Marsh	1955	$300
—Black label			
❏ 1217 [M]	Lee Konitz with Warne Marsh	1961	$175
—Multicolor label, white "fan" logo at right			
❏ 90050	Lee Konitz with Warne Marsh	198?	$25
❏ 1273 [M]	The Real Lee Konitz	1958	$300
—Black label			
❏ 1273 [M]	The Real Lee Konitz	1961	$175
—Multicolor label, white "fan" logo at right			
CHIAROSCURO			
❏ 186	The Nonet	1977	$30
❏ 166	The Quartet	1976	$30
CHOICE			
❏ 1019	Tenorlee	1977	$30
FANTASY			
❏ OJC-466	Duets	1990	$30
❏ OJC-186	Subconscious-Lee	198?	$25
GROOVE MERCHANT			
❏ GM-3306 [B]	Chicago 'n All That Jazz!	1975	$25

Number	Title	Yr	NM
IAI			
❏ 373845	Pyramid	1977	$35
INNER CITY			
❏ IC-2035	Lone-Lee	1975	$35
JAZZTONE			
❏ J-1275 [M]	Jazz at Storyville Jazz at Storyville	1957	$40
MILESTONE			
❏ MSP-9025	Peacemeal	1968	$25
❏ MSP-9060	Satori	1975	$25
❏ MSP-9038	Spirits	1969	$25
❏ MSP-9013	The Lee Konitz Duets	1968	$25
PAUSA			
❏ 7019	Lee Konitz Meets Warne Marsh Again	198?	$25
PRESTIGE			
❏ 24081	First Sessions 1949-50	198?	$35
❏ PRLP-7004 [M]	Lee Konitz Groups	1955	$350
❏ PRLP-116 [10]	Lee Konitz -- The New Sounds	1951	$400
❏ PRLP-7250 [M]	Subconscious-Lee	1962	$175
PROGRESSIVE			
❏ 7003	Figure and Spirit	1977	$35
ROOST			
❏ LP-416 [10]	Originalee	1953	$250
ROULETTE			
❏ SR-5006	The Nonet	1976	$35
SOUL NOTE			
❏ 121119	Ideal Scene	198?	$30
❏ SN-1069	Live at Laren	198?	$30
❏ 121169	The New York Album	1990	$30
STEEPLECHASE			
❏ SCS-1072	Jazz & Juan	198?	$30
❏ SCS-1035	Lone-Lee	198?	$30
❏ SCS-1119	Yes, Yes Nonet	1979	$30
STORYVILLE			
❏ STLP-313 [10]	Konitz	1954	$300
❏ STLP-304 [10]	Lee Konitz at Storyville	1954	$300
❏ STLP-901 [M]	Lee Konitz at Storyville	1956	$120
❏ STLP-323 [10]	Lee Konitz in Harvard Square	1955	$250
SUNNYSIDE			
❏ SSC-1003	Dovetail	1985	$25
VERVE			
❏ MGV-8286 [M]	An Image -- Lee Konitz with Strings	1958	$120
❏ V-8286 [M]	An Image -- Lee Konitz with Strings	1961	$30
❏ MGVS-6035 [S]	An Image -- Lee Konitz with Strings	1959	$175
❏ V6-8286 [S]	An Image -- Lee Konitz with Strings	1961	$25
❏ MGV-8335 [M]	Lee Konitz Meets Jimmy Giuffre	1959	$150
❏ V-8335 [M]	Lee Konitz Meets Jimmy Giuffre	1961	$25
❏ MGVS-6073 [S]	Lee Konitz Meets Jimmy Giuffre	1959	$150
❏ V6-8335 [S]	Lee Konitz Meets Jimmy Giuffre	1961	$35
❏ V-8399 [M]	Motion	1961	$25
❏ V6-8399 [S]	Motion	1961	$30
❏ UMV-2563	Motion	198?	$25
❏ MGV-8281 [M]	Tranquility	1958	$175
❏ V-8281 [M]	Tranquility	1961	$30
❏ MGV-8209 [M]	Very Cool	1958	$175
❏ V-8209 [M]	Very Cool	1961	$30
❏ MGV-8362 [M]	You and Lee	1960	$75
❏ V-8362 [M]	You and Lee	1961	$50
❏ MGVS-6131 [S]	You and Lee	1960	$75
❏ V6-8362 [S]	You and Lee	1961	$35
KONITZ, LEE/MILES DAVIS/TEDDY CHARLES			
NEW JAZZ			
❏ NJLP-8295 [M]	Ezz-Thetic	1962	$175
—Purple label			
❏ NJLP-8295 [M]	Ezz-Thetic	1965	$175
—Blue label, trident logo at right			
PRESTIGE			
❏ PRST-7827	Ezz-Thetic	1970	$30
KONRAD, BERNT			
HAT HUT			
❏ 3509	Traumtanzer	198?	$30
KOOL AND THE GANG			
DE-LITE			
❏ 8505	As One	1982	$12
❏ 822535-1	As One	1984	$10
—Reissue			
❏ 9518	Celebrate!	1980	$12
❏ 822538-1	Celebrate!	1984	$10
—Reissue			
❏ 822943-1	Emergency	1984	$10
❏ 9509	Everybody's Dancin'	1979	$12
❏ 2012	Good Times	1973	$15
❏ MK-48 [DJ]	History of Kool and the Gang	1979	$18

Number	Title	Yr	NM
❏ 8508	In the Heart	1983	$12
❏ 814351-1	In the Heart	1984	$10
—Reissue			
❏ 2015	Kool & The Gang Greatest Hits!	1975	$12
❏ 9507	Kool & The Gang Spin Their Top Ten Hits	1978	$12
❏ 822536-1	Kool & The Gang Spin Their Top Ten Hits	1984	$10
—Reissue			
❏ 2003	Kool and the Gang	1969	$30
❏ 4001	Kool Jazz	1973	$12

Number	Title	Yr	NM
❏ 9513 [B]	Ladies Night	1979	$12
❏ 822537-1	Ladies Night	1984	$10
—Reissue			
❏ 2014	Light of Worlds	1974	$12
❏ 2010	Live at PJ's	1971	$18
❏ 2008	Live at the Sex Machine	1971	$18
❏ 2018	Love and Understanding	1976	$12
❏ 2011	Music Is the Message	1972	$15
❏ 2023	Open Sesame	1976	$12
❏ 8502	Something Special	1981	$12
❏ 822534-1	Something Special	1984	$10
—Reissue			
❏ 2016	Spirit of the Boogie	1975	$12
❏ 2009	The Best of Kool and the Gang	1971	$18
❏ 9501	The Force	1978	$12
❏ 2013	Wild and Peaceful	1973	$12
MERCURY			
❏ 834780-1	Everything's Kool & the Gang: Greatest Hits & More	1988	$10
❏ 830398-1	Forever	1986	$10
❏ 838233-1	Sweat	1989	$10
KOONSE, DAVE AND LARRY			
DOBRE			
❏ 1035	Father and Son	197?	$30
KOOPER, AL			
Also see BLOOD, SWEAT AND TEARS; MIKE BLOOMFIELD; THE BLUES PROJECT.			
COLUMBIA			
❏ KC31159	A Possible Projection of the Future/Childhood's End	1972	$18
❏ FC38137	Championship Wrestling	1982	$12
❏ G30031	Easy Does It	1970	$25
❏ CS9718 [B]	I Stand Alone	1969	$25
—360 Sound" label			
❏ CS9718	I Stand Alone	1970	$12
—Orange label			
❏ CS9951	Kooper Session	1970	$18
—With Shuggie Otis; "360 Sound" label			
❏ CS9951	Kooper Session	1970	$12
—With Shuggie Otis; orange label			
❏ KC31723	Naked Songs	1973	$18
❏ KC30506	New York City (You're a Woman)	1971	$18
❏ PG33169	Unclaimed Freight (Al's Big Deal)	1975	$18
❏ CS9855 [B]	You Never Know Who Your Friends Are	1969	$25
—360 Sound" label			
❏ CS9855	You Never Know Who Your Friends Are	1970	$12
—Orange label			
UNITED ARTISTS			
❏ UA-LA702-G	Act Like Nothing's Wrong	1976	$15
KORNER, ALEXIS			
COLUMBIA			
❏ PC33427	Get Off of My Cloud	1975	$18
JUST SUNSHINE			
❏ 13 [B]	All Star Blues Incorporated	1974	$18
MOBILE FIDELITY			
❏ 1-265	Blues at the Marquee	1996	$40

Number	Title	Yr	NM

—Audiophile vinyl

WARNER BROS.

| ❏ BS2647 | Accidentally Borne in New Orleans | 1972 | $18 |
| ❏ 2XS1966 | Bootleg Him | 1972 | $30 |

KORVEN, MARK

MILAN

| ❏ SEL109 [B] | The Witch (Original Motion Picture Soundtrack) | 2016 | $40 |

KOSSOFF, PAUL

DJM

| ❏ 2300 | Koss | 1977 | $18 |

ISLAND

| ❏ ILPS9264 | Back Street Crawler | 1975 | $12 |

KOSTELANETZ, ANDRE

COLUMBIA

❏ CS9740	Andre Kostelanetz' Greatest Hits	1969	$12
❏ KG31491	Andre Kostelanetz Plays Cole Porter	1972	$18
❏ KG32825	Andre Kostelanetz Plays Gershwin	1974	$15
❏ KC32580	Andre Kostelanetz Plays Legrand's Greatest Hits	1974	$12
❏ CQ32147 [Q]	A Quadraphonic Concert	1972	$20
❏ CL864 [M]	Beautiful Dreamer	1956	$25

—Red and black label with six "eye" logos

| ❏ CL758 [M] | Bravo! | 1956 | $25 |

—Red and black label with six "eye" logos

| ❏ CL863 [M] | Café Continental | 1956 | $25 |

—Red and black label with six "eye" logos

| ❏ CL811 [M] | Calendar Girl | 1956 | $25 |

—Red and black label with six "eye" logos

❏ CL2688 [M]	Concert in the Park	1967	$12
❏ CS9488 [S]	Concert in the Park	1967	$12
❏ PC34352	Dance with Me	1977	$12
❏ C30037	Everything Is Beautiful	1970	$12
❏ CL2581 [M]	Exotic Nights	1966	$12
❏ CS9381 [S]	Exotic Nights	1966	$15
❏ C30672	For All We Know	1971	$12
❏ CS9691 [S]	For the Young at Heart	1968	$12
❏ CL2891 [M]	For the Young at Heart	1968	$18
❏ CL1495 [M]	Gershwin: Rhapsody in Blue; Previn: Concerto in F	1960	$15
❏ CS8286 [S]	Gershwin: Rhapsody in Blue; Previn: Concerto in F	1960	$18
❏ CL2133 [M]	Gershwin Wonderland	1964	$12
❏ CS8933 [S]	Gershwin Wonderland	1964	$15
❏ CS9973	Greatest Hits of the 60's	1970	$12
❏ CL1431 [M]	Gypsy Passion	1960	$15
❏ CS8228 [S]	Gypsy Passion	1960	$18
❏ CS9724	Hits from Funny Girl, Finian's Rainbow, and Star!	1968	$12
❏ CS9998	I'll Never Fall in Love Again	1970	$12
❏ KC34157	I'm Easy and Other Themes	1976	$12
❏ CL2185 [M]	I Wish You Love	1964	$12
❏ CS8985 [S]	I Wish You Love	1964	$15
❏ CL1528 [M]	Joy to the World: Music for Christmas	1959	$18
❏ CS8328 [S]	Joy to the World: Music for Christmas	1959	$25

—Red and black label with six "eye" logos

❏ CL2078 [M]	Kostelanetz in Wonderland	1964	$12
❏ CS8878 [S]	Kostelanetz in Wonderland	1964	$15
❏ C31002	Kostelanetz Plays Chicago	1971	$12
❏ KC32451	Kostelanetz Plays Great Hits of Today	1973	$12
❏ CL797 [M]	La Boheme for Orchestra	1956	$25

—Red and black label with six "eye" logos

❏ KC32187	Last Tango in Paris	1973	$12
❏ C30501	Love Story	1971	$12
❏ CL780 [M]	Lure of the Tropics	1956	$25

—Red and black label with six "eye" logos

| ❏ KZ1 [M] | Meet Andre Kostelanetz | 1955 | $25 |

—Red and black label with six "eye" logos

| ❏ CL704 [M] | Mood for Love | 1956 | $25 |

—Red and black label with six "eye" logos

❏ KC33061	Musical Reflections of Broadway and Hollywood	1974	$12
❏ AK1 [M]	Musical Tour of the World	195?	$25
❏ KC33954	Music from A Chorus Line and Treemonisha	1975	$12
❏ PC34660	Music of Charlie Chaplin and Duke Ellington	1977	$12
❏ CL768 [M]	Music of Irving Berlin	1956	$25

—Red and black label with six "eye" logos

❏ C33550	Never Can Say Goodbye	1975	$10
❏ KC33550	Never Can Say Goodbye	1975	$12
❏ CL2250 [M]	New Orleans Wonderland	1965	$12
❏ CS9050 [S]	New Orleans Wonderland	1965	$15
❏ CL2138 [M]	New York Wonderland	1964	$12
❏ CS8938 [S]	New York Wonderland	1964	$15
❏ KC33437	Orient Express	1975	$12
❏ CL720 [M]	Peter and the Wolf; Carnival of the Animals	1956	$25

—Red and black label with six "eye" logos

❏ CQ32856 [Q]	Quadraphonic Pop Concert	1973	$20
❏ CL1220 [M]	Romantic Music of...	1958	$18
❏ CS9623 [S]	Scarborough Fair	1968	$12
❏ CL2823 [M]	Scarborough Fair	1968	$18

| ❏ CL806 [M] | Show Boat/South Pacific/Slaughter on 10th Avenue | 1956 | $25 |

—Red and black label with six "eye" logos

| ❏ GP10 | Sounds of Love | 1969 | $15 |
| ❏ CL781 [M] | Stardust | 1956 | $25 |

—Red and black label with six "eye" logos

❏ CL1718 [M]	Star-Spangled Marches	1962	$15
❏ CS8518 [S]	Star-Spangled Marches	1962	$18
❏ CL1354 [M]	Strauss Waltzes	1959	$15
❏ CS8162 [S]	Strauss Waltzes	1959	$18
❏ KG33065	Strike Up the Band	1974	$15
❏ JC35788	Superman	1979	$10
❏ CL1199 [M]	Theatre Party	1958	$18
❏ CL2609 [M]	The Kostelanetz Sound of Today	1967	$12
❏ CS9409 [S]	The Kostelanetz Sound of Today	1967	$12
❏ CL1335 [M]	The Lure of Paradise	1959	$15
❏ CS8144 [S]	The Lure of Paradise	1959	$18
❏ CL765 [M]	The Music of Victor Herbert	1956	$25

—Red and black label with six "eye" logos

| ❏ CL734 [M] | The Music of Victor Youmans | 1956 | $25 |

—Red and black label with six "eye" logos

| ❏ C2L11 [M] | The Romantic Music of Tchaikovsky | 195? | $30 |

—Red and black label with six "eye" logos

❏ CL2467 [M]	The Shadow of Your Smile and Other Great Movie Themes	1966	$12
❏ CS9267 [S]	The Shadow of Your Smile and Other Great Movie Themes	1966	$12
❏ CL843 [M]	The Very Thought of You	1956	$25

—Red and black label with six "eye" logos

❏ KG32002	The World's Greatest Love Songs	1973	$15
❏ CL2359 [M]	Thunder (The Spectacular Sound of John Philip Sousa)	1965	$12
❏ CS9159 [S]	Thunder (The Spectacular Sound of John Philip Sousa)	1965	$15
❏ CL2534 [M]	Today's Golden Hits	1966	$12
❏ CS9334 [S]	Today's Golden Hits	1966	$15
❏ CL2756 [M]	Today's Greatest Movie Hits	1967	$15
❏ CS9556 [S]	Today's Greatest Movie Hits	1967	$12
❏ CS9823	Traces	1969	$12
❏ JC36382	Various Themes	1980	$10
❏ CL2068 [M]	Wonderland of Christmas	1963	$15
❏ CS8868 [S]	Wonderland of Christmas	1963	$18
❏ CL2039 [M]	Wonderland of Golden Hits	1963	$12
❏ CS8839 [S]	Wonderland of Golden Hits	1963	$15
❏ CL1995 [M]	Wonderland of Opera	1963	$12
❏ CS8795 [S]	Wonderland of Opera	1963	$15
❏ CL1657 [M]	Wonderland of Sound	1961	$15
❏ CS8457 [S]	Wonderland of Sound	1961	$18
❏ CL1827 [M]	Wonderland of Sound (Broadway's Greatest Hits)	1962	$15
❏ CS8627 [S]	Wonderland of Sound (Broadway's Greatest Hits)	1962	$18
❏ CL1898 [M]	Wonderland of Sound (Fire and Jealousy)	1962	$15
❏ CS8698 [S]	Wonderland of Sound (Fire and Jealousy)	1962	$18
❏ CL1938 [M]	Wonderland of Sound (The World's Greatest Waltzes)	1963	$12
❏ CS8738 [S]	Wonderland of Sound (The World's Greatest Waltzes)	1963	$15
❏ JC35328	You Light Up My Life	1978	$12

COLUMBIA LIMITED EDITION

| ❏ LE10083 | Joy to the World: Music for Christmas | 197? | $12 |

—Reissue of CS 8328

| ❏ LE10086 | Wonderland of Christmas | 197? | $12 |

—Reissue of CS 8868

COLUMBIA MASTERWORKS

❏ ML4455 [M]	An American in Paris	195?	$25
❏ MS7108 [S]	Andre Kostelanetz Conducts Great Romantic Ballads	196?	$12
❏ ML4409 [M]	Bizet: L'arlesienne Suites 1 & 2	195?	$25
❏ ML4082 [M]	Carnival Tropicana	195?	$25
❏ ML2056 [10]	Chopin-Kostelanetz	195?	$30
❏ ML4066 [M]	Clair de Lune	195?	$25
❏ MS7427	Extravaganza	1970	$12
❏ ML6226 [M]	Favorite Romantic Concertos	1961	$15
❏ MS6826 [S]	Favorite Romantic Concertos	1961	$18
❏ ML4065 [M]	Favorites	195?	$25
❏ M35114	Festive Overtures	1978	$10
❏ ML4822 [M]	Lure of the Tropics	1956	$25
❏ ML2022 [10]	Motion Picture Favorites	195?	$30
❏ MS7319	Musical Evenings	1969	$12
❏ M30075	Music for Strings	1970	$12
❏ ML4253 [M]	Music of Fritz Kreisler and Sigmund Romberg	195?	$25
❏ ML2007 [10]	Music of Stephen Foster	195?	$30
❏ MS6106 [S]	Offenbach: Gaite Parisienne; Bizet: Carmen (Highlights)	195?	$25
❏ ML6206 [M]	Promenade Favorites	1966	$15
❏ MS6806 [S]	Promenade Favorites	1966	$18
❏ ML6111 [M]	Romantic Strings	1960	$15
❏ MS6711 [S]	Romantic Strings	1960	$18
❏ ML6224 [M]	Romantic Waltzes of Tchaikovsky	1961	$15
❏ MS6824 [S]	Romantic Waltzes of Tchaikovsky	1961	$18
❏ ML6129 [M]	Showstoppers	1960	$15
❏ MS6729 [S]	Showstoppers	1960	$18

❏ ML2014 [10]	Songs of Cole Porter	195?	$30
❏ ML4308 [M]	Swan Lake (Highlights)	195?	$25
❏ MS7087	Vienna, City of Dreams	1968	$15
❏ ML2011 [10]	Waltzes of Johann Strauss	195?	$30
❏ ML6179 [M]	Wishing You a Merry Christmas	1960	$15
❏ MS6779 [S]	Wishing You a Merry Christmas	1960	$18

COLUMBIA SPECIAL PRODUCTS

| ❏ P13286 | Scarborough Fair | 197? | $10 |
| ❏ C10975 | Wishing You a Merry Christmas | 1972 | $12 |

—Reissue of Columbia Masterworks MS 6779

HARMONY

❏ KH31571	Andre Kostelanetz Plays Richard Rogers	1973	$12
❏ H30014	Be My Love	1970	$12
❏ HL7371 [M]	Broadway Theatre Party	196?	$12
❏ HS11171 [S]	Broadway Theatre Party	196?	$12
❏ HL7395 [M]	Grand Canyon Suite	196?	$12
❏ HS11195 [S]	Grand Canyon Suite	196?	$12
❏ KH31414	Greatest Hits of Broadway and Hollywood	1972	$12
❏ HL7432 [M]	Joy to the World: Music for Christmas	1967	$15

—Reissue of Columbia 1528

| ❏ HS11232 [S] | Joy to the World: Music for Christmas | 1967 | $15 |

—Reissue of Columbia 8328

❏ KH31500	Love Theme from "The Godfather"	1972	$12
❏ KH32170	Strike Up the Band	1973	$12
❏ HS11281	The Magic of Music	1968	$12
❏ HL7368 [M]	You and the Night and the Music	196?	$12
❏ HS11168 [S]	You and the Night and the Music	196?	$12

READER'S DIGEST

| ❏ RD-120-A | The Best of Andre Kostelanetz | 197? | $30 |

KOTTKE, LEO

CAPITOL

| ❏ ST-11446 [B] | Chewing Pine | 1975 | $15 |
| ❏ SN-16188 | Chewing Pine | 1980 | $10 |

—Budget-line reissue

| ❏ ST-11335 [B] | Dreams and All That Stuff | 1974 | $15 |
| ❏ SN-16187 | Dreams and All That Stuff | 1980 | $10 |

—Budget-line reissue

| ❏ ST-11000 [B] | Greenhouse | 1972 | $15 |
| ❏ SN-16065 | Greenhouse | 1979 | $10 |

—Budget-line reissue

| ❏ ST-11262 [B] | Ice Water | 1974 | $15 |
| ❏ SN-16064 | Ice Water | 1979 | $10 |

—Budget-line reissue

| ❏ ST-11576 | Leo Kottke 1971-1976 -- Did You Hear Me? | 1976 | $12 |
| ❏ SN-16189 | Leo Kottke 1971-1976 -- Did You Hear Me? | 1980 | $10 |

—Budget-line reissue

| ❏ ST-682 | Mudlark | 1971 | $15 |
| ❏ SN-16063 | Mudlark | 1979 | $10 |

—Budget-line reissue

| ❏ ST-11164 [B] | My Feet Are Smiling | 1973 | $15 |
| ❏ SWBC-11867 | The Best of Leo Kottke | 1979 | $15 |

CHRYSALIS

| ❏ CHR1234 | Balance | 1979 | $12 |
| ❏ PV41234 | Balance | 1985 | $10 |

—Budget-line reissue

| ❏ CHR1191 | Burnt Lips | 1978 | $12 |
| ❏ PV41191 | Burnt Lips | 1985 | $10 |

—Budget-line reissue

| ❏ CHR1328 | Guitar Music | 1981 | $12 |
| ❏ PV41328 | Guitar Music | 1983 | $10 |

—Budget-line reissue

| ❏ CHR1106 | Leo Kottke | 1977 | $12 |
| ❏ PV41106 | Leo Kottke | 1985 | $10 |

—Budget-line reissue

| ❏ FV41411 | Time Step | 1983 | $12 |
| ❏ PV41411 | Time Step | 1986 | $10 |

—Budget-line reissue

OBLIVION

| ❏ S-1 | 12-String Blues/Live at the Scholar Coffee House | 1969 | $30 |

PRIVATE MUSIC

❏ 2007-1-P	A Shout Toward Noon	1986	$12
❏ 2050-1-P	My Father's Face	1989	$12
❏ 2025-1-P	Regards from Chuck Pink	1988	$12

SYMPOSIUM

| ❏ 2001 | Circle Round the Sun | 1970 | $15 |

TAKOMA

| ❏ 1024 | 6 and 12 String Guitar | 1969 | $15 |

KOTTKE, LEO/PETER LANG/JOHN FAHEY

TAKOMA

| ❏ 1040 | Leo Kottke/Peter Lang/John Fahey | 1974 | $15 |

Number	Title	Yr	NM

KRAFTWERK

ASTRALWERKS
☐ ASW60611   Minimum-Maximum   2005 $50
—Box set; each LP is in a cardboard inner sleeve and paper sleeve

CAPITOL
| ☐ ST-11457 | Radio-Activity | 1975 | $25 |
| ☐ SN-16380 | Radio-Activity | 1986 | $12 |

—Reissue
| ☐ SW-11728 | The Man-Machine | 1978 | $25 |
| ☐ SN-16302 | The Man-Machine | 198? | $12 |

—Reissue
| ☐ SW11603 | Trans-Europe Express | 1977 | $25 |
| ☐ SN-16301 | Trans-Europe Express | 198? | $18 |

—Reissue

ELEKTRA
| ☐ 60611 | Autobahn | 1988 | $18 |

—Still another reissue of this album
| ☐ 60789 | Computer World | 1988 | $18 |

—Reissue
| ☐ 60798 | Electric Cafe | 1988 | $18 |

—Reissue
| ☐ 60869 | The Mix | 1991 | $25 |

MERCURY
| ☐ SRM-1-3704 [B] | Autobahn | 1977 | $35 |

—Reissue of Vertigo VEL-2003

MUTE/KLING KLANG
| ☐ STUMM306 [B] | The Man Machine | 2009 | $30 |
| ☐ STUMM305 [B] | Trans Europe Express | 2009 | $30 |

VERTIGO

| ☐ VEL-2003 [B] | Autobahn | 1974 | $40 |
| ☐ VEL-2006 [B] | Ralf & Florian | 1976 | $100 |

—Recorded in 1973

WARNER BROS.
| ☐ 25326 | Autobahn | 1985 | $35 |

—Another reissue of Vertigo VEL-2003
| ☐ HS3549 | Computer World | 1981 | $12 |
| ☐ 25525 | Electric Cafe | 1986 | $15 |

KRAINIA CONSORT

MERCURY LIVING PRESENCE
| ☐ SR90397 [S] | Music in Shakespeare's England | 196? | $75 |

—Maroon label, no "Vendor: Mercury Record Corporation
| ☐ SR90397 [S] | Music in Shakespeare's England | 196? | $25 |

—Maroon label, with "Vendor: Mercury Record Corporation

KRAINIS, BERNARD

MERCURY LIVING PRESENCE
| ☐ SR90443 [S] | Concertos for Recorder and Strings | 1965 | $30 |

—Maroon label, with "Vendor: Mercury Record Corporation

KRAL, IRENE

AVA
| ☐ A-33 [M] | Better Than Anything | 1963 | $40 |
| ☐ AS-33 [S] | Better Than Anything | 1963 | $50 |

CATALYST
| ☐ 7625 | Kral Space | 1977 | $30 |

CHOICE
| ☐ CRS1020 | Gentle Rain | 197? | $30 |
| ☐ CRS1012 | Where Is Love? | 197? | $30 |

DRG
| ☐ MRS-505 | Irene Kral and the Junior Mance Trio | 198? | $25 |

MAINSTREAM
| ☐ 56058 [M] | Wonderful Life | 1965 | $75 |
| ☐ S-6058 [S] | Wonderful Life | 1965 | $40 |

UNITED ARTISTS
☐ UAL-3052 [M]	Steve Irene O!	1959	$120
☐ UAS-6052 [S]	Steve Irene O!	1959	$175
☐ UAL-4016 [M]	The Band and I	1959	$120
☐ UAS-5016 [S]	The Band and I	1959	$175

KRALL, DIANA

VERVE
| ☐ 1243301 | Quiet Nights | 2009 | $25 |

KRAMER, BILLY J., AND THE DAKOTAS

CAPITOL
| ☐ SM-11897 [P] | The Best of Billy J. Kramer and the Dakotas | 1979 | $12 |

IMPERIAL
☐ LP9273 [M]	I'll Keep You Satisfied/From a Window	1964	$30
☐ LP12273 [P]	I'll Keep You Satisfied/From a Window	1964	$40
☐ LP9267 [M]	Little Children	1964	$50

—Black label with stars
| ☐ LP9267 [M] | Little Children | 1964 | $30 |

—Black and pink label
| ☐ LP12267 [P] | Little Children | 1964 | $100 |

—Black label with silver print
| ☐ LP12267 [P] | Little Children | 1964 | $40 |

—Black and pink label
| ☐ LP9291 [M] | Trains and Boats and Planes | 1965 | $30 |
| ☐ LP12921 [R] | Trains and Boats and Planes | 1965 | $30 |

KRAUSS, ALISON, AND UNION STATION

MOBILE FIDELITY
| ☐ MFSL 2-276 | So Long, So Wrong | 2004 | $150 |

—Original Master Recording" at top of cover

ROUNDER
☐ 0275	I've Got That Old Feeling	1990	$18
☐ 0325	Now That I've Found You: A Collection	1995	$18
☐ 0235	Too Late to Cry	1987	$18
☐ 0265	Two Highways	1989	$18

KRAVITZ, LENNY

VIRGIN
| ☐ 39169 | Are You Gonna Go My Way | 1993 | $30 |

—Clear-vinyl LP plus bonus CD with 8 unreleased tracks
| ☐ 91290 | Let Love Rule | 1989 | $15 |

KRAZY KATS, THE

DAMON
| ☐ 12478 [M] | Movin' Out!! With the Krazy Kats | 1964 | $120 |

KREED

VISION OF SOUND
| ☐ 71-56 | Kreed | 1971 | $1200 |

KRESS, CARL

CAPITOL
| ☐ H368 [10] | Classics in Jazz | 1953 | $100 |

KRESTON, JUDY, AND DAVID LAHM

PLUG
| ☐ PLUG-6 | Here In Love Lies the Answer | 1986 | $30 |

KRISTOFFERSON, KRIS, AND RITA COOLIDGE

A&M
☐ SP-4403	Full Moon	1973	$15
☐ SP-4690	Natural Act	1979	$12
☐ PR-4690	Natural Act	1979	$18

—Picture disc

MONUMENT
| ☐ PZ33278 | Breakaway | 1974 | $15 |

KRISTOFFERSON, KRIS

COLUMBIA
| ☐ PZ31302 | Border Lord | 1976 | $10 |

—Reissue
| ☐ JZ35310 | Easter Island | 1978 | $15 |
| ☐ FC40056 | Highwayman | 1985 | $12 |

—Waylon Jennings/Willie Nelson/Johnny Cash/Kris Kristofferson
| ☐ C45240 | Highwayman 2 | 1990 | $18 |

—Waylon Jennings/Willie Nelson/Johnny Cash/Kris Kristofferson
| ☐ PZ31909 | Jesus Was a Capricorn | 1976 | $10 |

—Reissue
| ☐ PZ30817 | Me and Bobby McGee | 1976 | $10 |

—Reissue
☐ JZ36135	Shake Hands with the Devil	1979	$15
☐ PZ34687	Songs of Kristofferson	1977	$15
☐ PZ32914	Spooky Lady's Sideshow	1976	$10

—Reissue
| ☐ PZ30679 | The Silver Tongued Devil and I | 1976 | $10 |

—Reissue
| ☐ JZ36885 | To the Bone | 1980 | $15 |
| ☐ PZ33379 | Who's to Bless…And Who's to Blame | 1976 | $10 |

—Reissue

MERCURY
| ☐ 830406-1 | Repossessed | 1987 | $12 |

MONUMENT
☐ KZ31302	Border Lord	1972	$15
☐ ZQ31302 [Q]	Border Lord	1972	$30
☐ KZ31909	Jesus Was a Capricorn	1972	$15
☐ ZQ31909 [Q]	Jesus Was a Capricorn	1973	$30
☐ SLP-18139	Kristofferson	1970	$30

—Original label is light green with a yellow ring
| ☐ Z30817 | Me and Bobby McGee | 1971 | $15 |

—Reissue of 18139 with new title
| ☐ PW38392 | Songs of Kristofferson | 1982 | $10 |

—Reissue of 34687
☐ PZ32914	Spooky Lady's Sideshow	1974	$15
☐ PZQ32914 [Q]	Spooky Lady's Sideshow	1974	$30
☐ PZ34254	Surreal Thing	1976	$15
☐ Z30679	The Silver Tongued Devil and I	1971	$15
☐ ZQ30679 [Q]	The Silver Tongued Devil and I	1972	$30
☐ PZ33379	Who's to Bless…And Who's to Blame	1975	$15

PAIR
| ☐ PDL2-1078 | My Songs | 1986 | $15 |

KRISTYL

(NO LABEL)
| ☐ 0(no cat #) | Kristyl | 1975 | $250 |

KRIVDA, ERNIE

CADENCE JAZZ
| ☐ CJR-1028 | Tough Tenor Red Hot | 1987 | $25 |

INNER CITY
☐ IC-1043	Alchemist	1978	$35
☐ IC-1083	Glory Strut	198?	$30
☐ IC-1031	Satanic	1977	$35

KROG, KARIN, AND DEXTER GORDON

STORYVILLE
| ☐ 4045 | Some Other Spring | 198? | $30 |

KRONOS QUARTET

LANDMARK
| ☐ LLP-1505 | Monk Suite (Music of Monk & Ellington) | 1985 | $30 |
| ☐ LLP-1510 | Music of Bill Evans | 1986 | $30 |

NONESUCH
| ☐ 979111-1F [B] | Kronos Quartet | 1986 | $18 |

REFERENCE RECORDINGS
| ☐ RR-9 | In Formation | 198? | $30 |

—Audiophile vinyl

KRUPA, GENE, AND CHARLIE VENTURA

COMMODORE
| ☐ FL-20028 [10] | The Krupa-Ventura Trio | 1950 | $150 |

KRUPA, GENE; LIONEL HAMPTON; TEDDY WILSON

CLEF
| ☐ MGC-681 [M] | Selections from "The Benny Goodman Story | 1956 | $250 |

VERVE
| ☐ MGV-8066 [M] | Gene Krupa-Lionel Hampton-Teddy Wilson with Red Callender | 1957 | $300 |

—Reissue of Clef 681 with new title
| ☐ V-8066 [M] | Gene Krupa-Lionel Hampton-Teddy Wilson with Red Callender | 1961 | $30 |

KRUPA, GENE

AIRCHECK
| ☐ 35 | Gene Krupa on the Air, 1944-46 | 198? | $25 |

AMERICAN RECORDING SOCIETY
| ☐ L-427 [M] | Drummer Man | 1957 | $40 |
| ☐ L-411 [M] | Gene Krupa Quartet | 1956 | $40 |

CLEF
| ☐ MGC-703 [M] | Drum Boogie | 1956 | $250 |
| ☐ MGC-607 [M] | Gene Krupa | 1954 | $0 |

—Canceled
☐ MGC-514 [10]	Gene Krupa Trio	1953	$250
☐ MGC-684 [M]	Krupa and Rich	1955	$250
☐ MGC-710 [M]	Krupa's Wail	1956	$0

—Canceled
| ☐ MGC-627 [M] | Sing, Sing, Sing -- The Rocking Mr. Krupa and His Orchestra | 1954 | $250 |
| ☐ MGC-728 [M] | The Driving Gene Krupa Plays with His Sextet | 1956 | $250 |

Number	Title	Yr	NM
❑ MGC-687 [M]	The Exciting Gene Krupa and His Quartet	1956	$250
❑ MGC-668 [M]	The Gene Krupa Quartet	1955	$250
❑ MGC-147 [10]	The Gene Krupa Sextet #1	1954	$250
❑ MGC-152 [10]	The Gene Krupa Sextet #2	1954	$250
❑ MGC-631 [M]	The Gene Krupa Sextet #3	1954	$250
❑ MGC-500 [M]	The Gene Krupa Trio at Jazz at the Philharmonic	1953	$250
❑ MGC-121 [10]	The Gene Krupa Trio Collates	1953	$300

— With either Clef or Mercury cover

COLUMBIA

❑ CL6066 [10]	Dance Parade	1949	$150
❑ CL2515 [10]	Drummin' Man	1955	$75
❑ C2L29 [M]	Drummin' Man	1962	$50

— Red and black labels with six "eye" logos; box set with booklet; deduct 20 percent if book is missing

❑ C2L29 [M]	Drummin' Man	1963	$25

— Red labels, "Guaranteed High Fidelity" or "360 Sound Mono" on label

❑ CL6017 [10]	Gene Krupa	1949	$150
❑ CL735 [M]	Gene Krupa	1956	$30

— Red and black label with six "eye" logos

❑ CL735 [M]	Gene Krupa	1963	$35

— Red label, "Guaranteed High Fidelity" or "360 Sound Mono" on label

❑ KG32663	Gene Krupa, His Orchestra and Anita O'Day	1974	$35
❑ CL641 [M]	Gene Krupa's Sidekicks	1955	$50

— Maroon label, gold print

❑ CL641 [M]	Gene Krupa's Sidekicks	1955	$40

— Red and black label with six "eye" logos

COLUMBIA SPECIAL PRODUCTS

❑ P14379	Krupa Swings	197?	$25

ENCORE

❑ EE22027	That Drummer's Band	196?	$35

HARMONY

❑ HL7252 [M]	The Gene Krupa Story in Music	1960	$35

INTERMEDIA

❑ QS-5050	Hot Drums	198?	$25

MERCURY

❑ MGC-514 [10]	Gene Krupa Trio	1953	$250
❑ MGC-500 [M]	The Gene Krupa Trio at Jazz at the Philharmonic	1953	$175
❑ MGC-121 [10]	The Gene Krupa Trio Collates	1953	$300

— With Mercury cover and Mercury labels

METRO

❑ M-518 [M]	Gene Krupa	1965	$300
❑ MS-518 [R]	Gene Krupa	1965	$175

MGM

❑ GAS-132	Gene Krupa (Golden Archive Series)	1970	$30

RCA CAMDEN

❑ CAL-340 [M]	Mutiny in the Parlor	1958	$30

SUNBEAM

❑ 225	The World's Greatest Drummer	197?	$25

TIME-LIFE

❑ STBB-12	Big Bands: Gene Krupa	1984	$35

VERVE

❑ MGV-8310 [M]	Big Noise from Winnetka -- Gene Krupa at the London House	1959	$50
❑ MGVS-6042 [S]	Big Noise from Winnetka -- Gene Krupa at the London House	1960	$175
❑ V-8310 [M]	Big Noise from Winnetka -- Gene Krupa at the London House	1961	$30
❑ V6-8310 [S]	Big Noise from Winnetka -- Gene Krupa at the London House	1961	$25
❑ V-8450 [M]	Classics in Percussion	1962	$35
❑ V6-8450 [S]	Classics in Percussion	1962	$25
❑ MGV-8087 [M]	Drum Boogie	1957	$150
❑ V-8087 [M]	Drum Boogie	1961	$30
❑ 827843-1	Drummer Man	1986	$25
❑ MGV-2008 [M]	Drummer Man -- Gene Krupa in Highest-Fi	1956	$175

— Orange label

❑ MGV-2008 [M]	Drummer Man -- Gene Krupa in Highest-Fi	1957	$150

— Black label

❑ V-2008 [M]	Drummer Man -- Gene Krupa in Highest-Fi	1961	$30
❑ MGV-8373 [M]	Gene Krupa	1960	$0

— Canceled

❑ MGVS-6148 [S]	Gene Krupa	1960	$0

— Canceled

❑ MGV-8292 [M]	Gene Krupa Plays Gerry Mulligan Arrangements	1958	$175
❑ MGVS-6008 [S]	Gene Krupa Plays Gerry Mulligan Arrangements	1959	$150
❑ V-8292 [M]	Gene Krupa Plays Gerry Mulligan Arrangements	1961	$30
❑ V6-8292 [S]	Gene Krupa Plays Gerry Mulligan Arrangements	1961	$25

❑ MGV-4016 [M]	Gene Krupa Plays the Classics	1958	$0

— Canceled

❑ MGV-8300 [M]	Hey! Here's Gene Krupa	1959	$175
❑ V-8300 [M]	Hey! Here's Gene Krupa	1961	$30
❑ MGV-8069 [M]	Krupa and Rich	1957	$175
❑ V-8069 [M]	Krupa and Rich	1961	$30
❑ V-8400 [M]	Krupa and Rich	1961	$30
❑ V6-8400 [S]	Krupa and Rich	1961	$25
❑ MGV-8276 [M]	Krupa Rocks	1958	$175
❑ V-8276 [M]	Krupa Rocks	1961	$30
❑ V-8571 [M]	Let Me Off Uptown -- The Essential Gene Krupa	1964	$35
❑ V6-8571 [S]	Let Me Off Uptown -- The Essential Gene Krupa	1964	$25
❑ V-8414 [M]	Percussion King	1961	$35
❑ V6-8414 [S]	Percussion King	1961	$25
❑ MGV-8190 [M]	Sing, Sing, Sing	1957	$100
❑ V-8190 [M]	Sing, Sing, Sing	1961	$30
❑ VSP-4 [M]	That Drummer's Band	1966	$35
❑ VSPS-4 [R]	That Drummer's Band	1966	$30
❑ MGV-8107 [M]	The Driving Gene Krupa	1957	$150
❑ V-8107 [M]	The Driving Gene Krupa	1961	$30
❑ MGV-8369 [M]	The Drum Battle	1960	$150
❑ UMV-2594	The Exciting Gene Krupa	198?	$25
❑ MGV-8071 [M]	The Exciting Gene Krupa and His Quartet	1957	$150
❑ V-8071 [M]	The Exciting Gene Krupa and His Quartet	1961	$30
❑ MGV-8031 [M]	The Gene Krupa Trio	1957	$175
❑ V-8031 [M]	The Gene Krupa Trio	1961	$30
❑ V-8584 [M]	The Great New Gene Krupa Quartet Featuring Charlie Ventura	1964	$35
❑ V6-8584 [S]	The Great New Gene Krupa Quartet Featuring Charlie Ventura	1964	$25
❑ MGV-8204 [M]	The Jazz Rhythms of Gene Krupa	1957	$175
❑ V-8204 [M]	The Jazz Rhythms of Gene Krupa	1961	$30
❑ V-8484 [M]	The Original Drum Battle	1962	$35
❑ V6-8484 [R]	The Original Drum Battle	196?	$30
❑ V-8594 [M]	Verve's Choice -- The Best of Gene Krupa	1964	$35
❑ V6-8594 [S]	Verve's Choice -- The Best of Gene Krupa	1964	$30

KUBAN, BOB, AND THE IN-MEN

MUSICLAND U.S.A.

❑ LP-3500 [M]	Look Out for the Cheater	1966	$30
❑ SLP-3500 [S]	Look Out for the Cheater	1966	$40

KUHN, JOACHIM

ATLANTIC

❑ SD1695	Springfever	1976	$30
❑ SD19193	Sunshower	1978	$25

CMP

❑ CMP-26#NAME?	Distance	1987	$25
❑ CMP-22#NAME?	I'm Not Dreaming	1986	$25
❑ CMP-29#NAME?	Wandlungen/Transformations	1987	$25

KUHN, PETER

HAT HUT

❑ 09	Ghost of a Trance	1980	$35

SOUL NOTE

❑ SN-1043	The Kill	1981	$30

KUHN, ROLF

URANIA

❑ US-1220 [M]	Sound of Jazz	1962	$150
❑ US-41220 [M]	Sound of Jazz	1962	$150

VANGUARD

❑ VRS-8510 [M]	Streamline	1955	$150

KUHN, ROLF AND JOACHIM

ABC IMPULSE!

❑ AS-9150	Impressions of New York	1968	$250

KUHN, STEVE, AND SHEILA JORDAN

ECM

❑ 1159	Playground	1979	$30

KUHN, STEVE, AND TOSHIKO AKIYOSHI

DAUNTLESS

❑ DM-4308 [M]	The Country & Western Sound for Jazz Pianos	1963	$25
❑ DS-6308 [S]	The Country & Western Sound for Jazz Pianos	1963	$30

KUHN, STEVE

ABC IMPULSE!

❑ AS-9136 [S]	The October Suite	1968	$30

BUDDAH

❑ BDS-5098	Steve Kuhn	1972	$35

CONTACT

❑ CM-5 [M]	Steve Kuhn Trio Featuring Steve Swallow and Pete LaRoca	1965	$25

❑ CS-5 [S]	Steve Kuhn Trio Featuring Steve Swallow and Pete LaRoca	1965	$30

ECM

❑ ECM-1-1058	Ecstasy	1975	$30
❑ 1213	Last Year's Waltz	1982	$25
❑ 1094	Motility	1977	$30
❑ 1124	Non-Fiction	1978	$30
❑ 1052	Trance	197?	$30

IMPULSE!

❑ A-9136 [M]	The October Suite	1967	$160
❑ AS-9136 [S]	The October Suite	1967	$120

MUSE

❑ MR-5106	Raindrops/Live in New York	1978	$30

PRESTIGE

❑ PRST-7694	Steve Kuhn in Europe	1969	$35

KUSTBANDET

STOMP OFF

❑ SOS-1178	The New Call of the Freaks	1989	$30

KUSTOM KINGS, THE

SMASH

❑ MGS-27051 [M]	Kustom City, U.S.A.	1964	$120
❑ SRS-67051 [S]	Kustom City, U.S.A.	1964	$250

KWESKIN, JIM

MOUNTAIN RAILROAD

❑ MR-52782	Jim Kweskin Lives Again	198?	$12
❑ MR-52672	Jug Band Blues	198?	$12
❑ MR-52790	Side by Side	198?	$12
❑ MR-52793	Swing on a Star	198?	$12

REPRISE

❑ RS6464 [B]	America	1971	$18
❑ R6266 [M]	Garden of Joy	1967	$25
❑ RS6266 [S]	Garden of Joy	1967	$18

VANGUARD

❑ VSD13/14	Greatest Hits	1970	$18
❑ VRS-9139 [M]	Jim Kweskin and the Jug Band	1963	$25
❑ VSD-2158 [S]	Jim Kweskin and the Jug Band	1963	$30
❑ VRS-9163 [M]	Jug Band Music	1965	$50
❑ VSD-79163 [S]	Jug Band Music	1965	$50
❑ VRS-9243 [M]	Jump for Joy	1967	$25
❑ VSD-79243 [S]	Jump for Joy	1967	$30
❑ VRS-9188 [M]	Relax Your Mind	1966	$30
❑ VSD-79188 [S]	Relax Your Mind	1966	$35
❑ VRS-9234 [M]	See Reverse Side for Title	1967	$30
❑ VSD-79234 [S]	See Reverse Side for Title	1967	$30
❑ VRS-9270 [M]	The Best of Jim Kweskin and the Jug Band	1968	$40
❑ VSD-79270 [S]	The Best of Jim Kweskin and the Jug Band	1968	$18

KYNARD, CHARLES

FANTASY

❑ OJC-333	Reelin' with the Feelin'	1988	$25

MAINSTREAM

❑ MRL-331	Charles Kynard	1972	$25
❑ MRL-366 [B]	Woga	1973	$50
❑ MRL-389	Your Mama Don't Dance	1973	$50

PACIFIC JAZZ

❑ PJ-72 [M]	Where It's At!	1963	$75
❑ ST-72 [S]	Where It's At!	1963	$40

PRESTIGE

❑ PRST-7796	Afro-disiac	1970	$25
❑ PRST-7599	Professor Soul	1968	$25
❑ PRST-7688	Reelin' with the Feelin'	1969	$25
❑ PRST-7630	The Soul Brotherhood	1969	$25
❑ 10008	Wa-tu-wa-zui	1971	$25

WORLD PACIFIC

❑ WP-1823 [M]	Warm Winds	1964	$150
❑ ST-1823 [S]	Warm Winds	1964	$150

KYSER, KAY

CAPITOL

❑ T1692 [M]	Kay Kyser's Greatest Hits	196?	$50
❑ ST1692 [S]	Kay Kyser's Greatest Hits	196?	$40

COLUMBIA

❑ CL6012 [10]	Campus Favorites	1948	$100
❑ CG33572	The World of Kay Kyser	1976	$20

HARMONY

❑ HL7136 [M]	Campus Rally	196?	$20

Number	Title	Yr	NM

❏ HL7041 [M]	Kay Kyser	196?	$18
SUNBEAM			
❏ SB-218 [M]	Kay Kyser and His Orchestra 1935-39	198?	$15

L

L.A. 4
CONCORD JAZZ
❏ CJ-215	Executive Suite	1982	$25
❏ CJ-1001 [B]	Just Friends	1980	$150
—Direct-to-disc recording			
❏ CJ-199	Just Friends	1981	$25
—Regular version			
❏ CJ-100	Live at Montreux, 1979	1980	$25
❏ CJ-156	Montage	1981	$25
❏ CJ-8	Scores	197?	$35
❏ CJ-18	The L.A. 4	197?	$30
❏ CJ-63	Watch What Happens	1978	$30
❏ CJ-130	Zaca	1980	$25
EAST WIND
❏ 10004	Going Home	197?	$30
—Audiophile issue			
❏ 10003	Pavanne Pour Une Infante Defunte	197?	$30
—Audiophile issue			

L.A. GUNS
CLEOPATRA
| ❏ 8691 [B] | Hollywood Forever | | $25 |
| ❏ 8796 [B] | Riot On Sunset - The Best Of | | $25 |

L.A. JAZZ CHOIR, THE
MOBILE FIDELITY
| ❏ Jan-0096 | Listen | 1982 | $175 |
| *—Audiophile vinyl* | | | |
PAUSA
| ❏ 7184 | From All Sides | 1986 | $30 |

L.A. JAZZ ENSEMBLE, THE
PBR
| ❏ 8 | Urantia | 197? | $30 |

L.A. JAZZ WORKSHOP, THE
AM-PM
| ❏ 16 | The Shopwork Shuffle | 1986 | $25 |
SEA BREEZE
| ❏ SB-2021 | Stan's Donuts | 198? | $25 |

L.L. COOL J
DEF JAM
❏ C253325	14 Shots to the Dome	1993	$18
❏ 524125-1	All World	1996	$18
❏ FC40793	Bigger and Deffer	1987	$15
❏ 546819-1	G.O.A.T. Featuring James T. Smith the Greatest of All Time	2000	$18
❏ C46888	Mama Said Knock You Out	1990	$18
❏ 523845-1	Mr. Smith	1995	$15
❏ 539186-1	Phenomenon	1997	$18
❏ FC40239	Radio	1985	$15
❏ OC45173	Walking with a Panther	1989	$18

L.T.D.
A&M
❏ SP-4771	Devotion	1979	$12
❏ SP-3660	Gittin' Down	1975	$15
❏ SP-4881	Love Magic	1981	$12

Number	Title	Yr	NM
❏ SP-4589	Love to the World	1976	$12
❏ SP-3146	Love to the World	198?	$10
—Budget-line reissue			
❏ SP-3602	L.T.D.	1974	$15
❏ SP-3119	L.T.D.	198?	$10
—Budget-line reissue			
❏ SP-4819	Shine On	1980	$12
❏ SP-4646	Something to Love	1977	$12
❏ SP-3148	Something to Love	198?	$10
—Budget-line reissue			
❏ SP-4705	Togetherness	1978	$12

L7
EPITAPH
| ❏ 86401 [B] | L7 | 1988 | $75 |
| *—Original press with Donita Sparks' head cut off* | | | |
SLASH
| ❏ 45624 [B] | Hungry for Stink | 1994 | $18 |
SUB POP
❏ 79 [EP]	Smell the Magic	1990	$50
—First 1,000 on purple vinyl			
❏ 79 [EP]	Smell the Magic	1990	$18

LA COSTA
CAPITOL
❏ ST-12090	Changin' All the Time	1980	$15
❏ ST-11345	Get On My Love Train	1974	$15
❏ ST-11713	La Costa	1977	$15
❏ ST-11569	Lovin' Somebody	1975	$15
❏ ST-11391	With All My Love	1975	$15

LA DÜSSELDORF
4 MEN WITH BEARDS
| ❏ 4M166LP [B] | La Düsseldorf | | $25 |
| ❏ 4M167LP [B] | Viva | | $25 |

LA LUPE
ROULETTE
| ❏ SR-42024 | The Queen Does Her Thing | 1969 | $30 |

LABARBERA, PAT
PM
| ❏ 09 | Pass It On | 197? | $30 |

LABEEF, SLEEPY
ROUNDER
❏ 3070	Electricity	198?	$12
❏ 3052	It Ain't What You Eat...	198?	$12
❏ 3072	Nothin' But the Truth	198?	$12
SUN
❏ 130	Bull's Night Out	1974	$15
❏ 1018	Downtown Rockabilly	1978	$15
❏ 1004	Rockabilly 1977	1977	$15
❏ 138	Western Gold	197?	$15

LABELLE, PATTI, AND THE BLUE BELLES
ATLANTIC
❏ 8147 [M]	Dreamer	1967	$75
❏ SD8147 [S]	Dreamer	1967	$50
❏ 8119 [M]	Over the Rainbow	1966	$40
❏ SD8119 [S]	Over the Rainbow	1966	$50
MISTLETOE
| ❏ MLP-1204 | Merry Christmas from LaBelle | 1976 | $25 |
NEWTOWN
| ❏ 632 [M] | Sleigh Bells, Jingle Bells and Blue Bells | 1963 | $300 |
| ❏ 631 [M] | Sweethearts of the Apollo | 1963 | $400 |
PARKWAY
❏ P-7043 [M]	The Bluebelles On Stage	1965	$175
—With bonus single			
❏ P-7043 [M]	The Bluebelles On Stage	1965	$120
—Without bonus single			
TRIP
❏ 9525	Early Hits	197?	$12
❏ 3508	Patti LaBelle and the Bluebelles	197?	$12
❏ 8000	Patti LaBelle and the Bluebelles' Greatest Hits	1971	$12
UNITED ARTISTS
| ❏ UA-LA504-E | The Very Best of Patti LaBelle and the Bluebelles | 1975 | $12 |

LABELLE, PATTI
EPIC
❏ FE36997	Best of Patti LaBelle	1981	$12
❏ PE36997	Best of Patti LaBelle	198?	$10
—Budget-line reissue			
❏ JE35772	It's Alright with Me	1979	$15
❏ PE34847	Patti LaBelle	1977	$18
—Original with no bar code and orange label			
❏ PE34847	Patti LaBelle	1986	$10
—Reissue with bar code and dark blue label			
❏ JE36381	Released	1980	$15

Number	Title	Yr	NM
❏ JE35335	Tasty	1978	$18
MCA			
❏ 6292	Be Yourself	1989	$12
❏ 10439	Burnin'	1991	$15
❏ 5737	Winner in You	1986	$12
PHILADELPHIA INT'L.			
❏ FZ38539	I'm in Love Again	1983	$15
❏ FZ40020	Patti	1985	$15
❏ FZ37380	The Spirit's In It	1981	$15
❏ PZ37380	The Spirit's In It	198?	$10
—Budget-line reissue			

LABELLE
EPIC
❏ PE34189	Chameleon	1976	$12
—Original with no bar code and orange label			
❏ PE34189	Chameleon	198?	$10
—Reissue with bar code and dark blue label			
❏ KE33075	Nightbirds	1974	$15
❏ PE33075	Nightbirds	197?	$10
—Reissue with new prefix			
❏ PEQ33075 [Q]	Nightbirds	1975	$40
❏ PE33579	Phoenix	1975	$12
❏ PEQ33579 [Q]	Phoenix	1975	$40
RCA VICTOR
❏ AYL1-4176	Pressure Cookin'	1982	$10
—Best Buy Series" reissue			
❏ APL1-0205	Pressure Cookin'	1973	$15
WARNER BROS.
| ❏ WS1943 | LaBelle | 1971 | $18 |
| ❏ BS2618 [B] | Moonshadow | 1972 | $18 |

LACEWING
MAINSTREAM
| ❏ S-6132 | Lacewing | 1971 | $50 |

LACY, STEVE, AND MAL WALDRON
HAT ART
| ❏ 2015 | Herbe de L'Oubli & Snake-Out | 1986 | $35 |
HAT HUT
| ❏ 3501 | Snake-Out | 198? | $30 |

LACY, STEVE, AND MICHAEL SMITH
IAI
| ❏ 373847 | Sidelines | 197? | $35 |

LACY, STEVE
ADELPHI
| ❏ 5004 | Raps | 1977 | $30 |
BARNABY
| ❏ BR-5013 | The Straight Horn of Steve Lacy | 1977 | $30 |
BLACK SAINT
| ❏ BSR-0008 | Trickles | 198? | $30 |
| ❏ BSR-0035 | Troubles | 198? | $30 |
CANDID
| ❏ CD-8007 [M] | The Straight Horn of Steve Lacy | 1960 | $40 |
| ❏ CS-9007 [S] | The Straight Horn of Steve Lacy | 1960 | $50 |
EMANEM
❏ 3310	Saxophone Special	1975	$35
❏ 3316	School Days	1975	$35
❏ 301	Steve Lacy Solo	1973	$35
❏ 304	The Crust	1974	$35
ESP-DISK'
| ❏ 1060 [M] | The Forest and the Zoo | 1967 | $250 |
| ❏ S-1060 [S] | The Forest and the Zoo | 1967 | $250 |
FANTASY
❏ OJC-1755	Evidence	198?	$30
❏ OJC-063	Reflections: Steve Lacy Plays Thelonious Monk	198?	$30
❏ OJC-130	Steve Lacy Soprano Sax	198?	$30
HAT ART
❏ 2006	Blinks	1986	$35
❏ 2022	Futurities	1986	$35
❏ 2014	N.Y. Capers	1986	$35
❏ 2029	The Way	1987	$35
HAT HUT
❏ 1982/3	Ballets	1982	$35
❏ 14	Capers	1980	$35
❏ 0F	Clinkers	1977	$35
❏ 2001	Prospectus	198?	$35
❏ 1985/86	Songs	1982	$35
❏ 0K/L	Stamps	1978	$25
❏ 03	The Way	1979	$25
❏ 20	Tips	1980	$30
NEW JAZZ
❏ NJLP-8271 [M]	Evidence	1962	$250
—Purple label			
❏ NJLP-8271 [M]	Evidence	1965	$175
—Blue label, trident logo at right			

LACY, STEVE

Number	Title	Yr	NM
❏ NJLP-8206 [M]	Reflections: Steve Lacy Plays Thelonious Monk	1958	$300
—Purple label			
❏ NJLP-8206 [M]	Reflections: Steve Lacy Plays Thelonious Monk	1965	$175
—Blue label, trident logo at right			
❏ NJLP-8308 [M]	Wynton Kelly with Steve Lacy	1963	$0
—Canceled; issued on Status			
NOVUS			
❏ 3079-1-N	Anthem	1990	$30
❏ 3021-1-N	Momentum	1988	$25
❏ 3049-1-N	The Door	1989	$30
PRESTIGE			
❏ 2505	Evidence	198?	$30
❏ PRLP-7125 [M]	Steve Lacy Soprano Sax	1956	$500
QED			
❏ 997	School Days	197?	$30
RED			
❏ VPA-120	Axieme Vol. 1	198?	$30
❏ VPA-121	Axieme Vol. 2	198?	$30
SILKHEART			
❏ SH-103	One Fell Swoop	198?	$25
❏ SH-102	The Gleam	198?	$25
SOUL NOE			
❏ SN-1035	The Flame	198?	$30
SOUL NOTE			
❏ 121210	More Monk	199?	$35
❏ 121160	Only Monk	199?	$35
❏ 121135	The Condor	1990	$35
❏ 121185	The Window	199?	$35
STATUS			
❏ ST-8308 [M]	Wynton Kelly with Steve Lacy	1965	$120

LADD, CHERYL

Number	Title	Yr	NM
CAPITOL			
❏ SW-11808	Cheryl Ladd	1978	$15
❏ ST-11927	Dance Forever	1979	$15

LADNIER, TOMMY

Number	Title	Yr	NM
RIVERSIDE			
❏ RLP-1026 [10]	Early Ladnier	1954	$300
❏ RLP-1019 [10]	Ida Cox with Tommy Ladnier	1953	$300
❏ RLP-1044 [10]	Tommy Ladnier Plays the Blues	1954	$300
X			
❏ LVA-3027 [M]	Tommy Ladnier	1954	$75

LADY FLASH

Number	Title	Yr	NM
RSO			
❏ RS-1-3002	Beauties in the Night	1976	$15

LAFARGE, PETER

Number	Title	Yr	NM
COLUMBIA			
❏ CL1795 [M]	Ira Hayes and Other Ballads	1962	$25
❏ CS8595 [S]	Ira Hayes and Other Ballads	1962	$30
VERVE FOLKWAYS			
❏ FV-9004 [M]	Peter LaFarge Sings Women Blues	1965	$30
❏ FVS-9004 [S]	Peter LaFarge Sings Women Blues	1965	$30

LAFORGE, JACK

Number	Title	Yr	NM
AUDIO FIDELITY			
❏ AFLP-2161 [M]	Hit the Road Jack	196?	$35
❏ AFSD-6161 [S]	Hit the Road Jack	196?	$25
REGINA			
❏ R-309 [M]	Comin' Home Baby	196?	$25
❏ RS-309 [S]	Comin' Home Baby	196?	$30
❏ R-319 [M]	Goldfinger	1965	$25
❏ RS-319 [S]	Goldfinger	1965	$30
❏ R-716 [M]	Hawaii and I	196?	$25
❏ RS-716 [S]	Hawaii and I	196?	$30
❏ R-282 [M]	I Remember You	196?	$25
❏ RS-282 [S]	I Remember You	196?	$30
❏ R-314 [M]	Jazz Portrait of Jack LaForge	196?	$25
❏ RS-314 [S]	Jazz Portrait of Jack LaForge	196?	$30
❏ R-327 [M]	Our Crazy Affair	196?	$25
❏ RS-327 [S]	Our Crazy Affair	196?	$30
❏ R-313 [M]	Promise Her Anything	196?	$25
❏ RS-313 [S]	Promise Her Anything	196?	$30
❏ R-288 [M]	Unchain My Heart	196?	$25
❏ RS-288 [S]	Unchain My Heart	196?	$30
❏ R-301 [M]	You Fascinate Me So	196?	$50
❏ RS-301 [S]	You Fascinate Me So	196?	$75

LAGGERS, MAX, AND THE STOMPERS

Number	Title	Yr	NM
GHB			
❏ GHB-157	In the New Orleans Tradition	198?	$25

LAGRENE, BIRELI

Number	Title	Yr	NM
ANTILLES			
❏ AN-1009	15	198?	$25
❏ AN-1002	Routes to Django	1981	$30

Number	Title	Yr	NM
BLUE NOTE			
❏ B1-90967	Foreign Affairs	1988	$25
❏ BT-48016	Inferno	1987	$25

LAHM, DAVID

Number	Title	Yr	NM
PALO ALTO			
❏ PA-8027	Real Jazz for Folks Who Feel Jazz	198?	$30
PLUG			
❏ PLUG-7	The Highest Standards	1986	$25

LAINE, CLEO, AND DUDLEY MOORE

Number	Title	Yr	NM
FINESSE			
❏ FW38091	Smilin' Through	1983	$30

LAINE, CLEO, AND JAMES GALWAY

Number	Title	Yr	NM
RCA RED SEAL			
❏ ARL1-3628	Sometimes When We Touch	198?	$25

LAINE, CLEO

Number	Title	Yr	NM
BUDDAH			
❏ BDS-5607	Day By Day	1972	$35
CBS			
❏ FM39211	Let the Music Take You	1984	$25
❏ FM39736	That Old Feeling	1985	$25
DRG			
❏ MR2S-608	An Evening with Cleo Lane and the John Dankworth Quartet	198?	$30
❏ DARC2-2101	Cleo at Carnegie: The 10th Anniversary Concert	198?	$30
❏ MRS-502	Cleo Lane with John Dankworth's Orchestra	198?	$25
❏ SL-5198	One More Day	198?	$25
FONTANA			
❏ MGF-27531 [M]	Shakespeare and All That Jazz	1966	$35
❏ SRF-67531 [S]	Shakespeare and All That Jazz	1966	$35
❏ MGF-27552 [M]	Woman to Woman	1967	$50
❏ SRF-67552 [S]	Woman to Woman	1967	$35
GNP CRESCENDO			
❏ GNPS-9024	Cleo's Choice	197?	$25
JAZZ MAN			
❏ 5033	Live at Wavendon Festival	198?	$25
RCA			
❏ 7702-1-R	Cleo Sings Sondheim	1988	$25
RCA VICTOR			
❏ CPL1-5059	A Beautiful Thing	1974	$35
❏ AFL1-5059	A Beautiful Thing	1978	$25
—Reissue with new prefix			
❏ AYL1-3805	A Beautiful Thing	1980	$20
—Budget-line reissue			
❏ APL1-1937	Best Friends	1976	$30
❏ AFL1-1937	Best Friends	1978	$25
—Reissue with new prefix			
❏ LPL1-5113	Born Friday	197?	$30
❏ AFL1-5113	Born Friday	1978	$25
—Reissue with new prefix			
❏ AFL1-2926	Gonna Get Through	1978	$25
❏ LPL1-5000	I Am a Song	1973	$35
❏ AFL1-5000	I Am a Song	1978	$25
—Reissue with new prefix			
❏ LPL1-5015	Live at Carnegie Hall	1973	$35
❏ AFL1-5015	Live at Carnegie Hall	1978	$25
—Reissue with new prefix			
❏ AYL1-3751	Live at Carnegie Hall	1980	$20
—Budget-line reissue			
❏ APL1-2407	Return to Carnegie Hall	1977	$30
❏ AFL1-2407	Return to Carnegie Hall	1978	$25
—Reissue with new prefix			
STANYAN			
❏ 10067	Day By Day	197?	$30
❏ 10122	Easy Livin'	197?	$30

LAINE, DENNY

Also see THE MOODY BLUES; WINGS.

Number	Title	Yr	NM
CAPITOL			
❏ ST-11588 [B]	Holly Days	1977	$30
REPRISE			
❏ MS2190 [B]	Ah, Laine!	1972	$18
TAKOMA			
❏ 7034 [B]	Japanese Tears	1983	$15

LAINE, FRANKIE

Number	Title	Yr	NM
ABC			
❏ 604 [M]	I'll Take Care of Your Cares	1967	$15
❏ S-604 [S]	I'll Take Care of Your Cares	1967	$18
❏ 608 [M]	I Wanted Someone to Love	1967	$15
❏ S-608 [S]	I Wanted Someone to Love	1967	$18
❏ S-657	Take Me Back to Laine Country	1968	$18
❏ 628 [M]	To Each His Own	1968	$25
❏ S-628 [S]	To Each His Own	1968	$18
❏ S-682	You Gave Me a Mountain	1969	$18

Number	Title	Yr	NM
AMOS			
❏ 7013	Brand New Day	1971	$15
❏ 7009	Frankie Laine's Greatest Hits	1970	$15
BULLDOG			
❏ BDL-1035	All of Me	198?	$12
CAPITOL			
❏ T2277 [M]	I Believe	1965	$15
❏ ST2277 [S]	I Believe	1965	$18
COLUMBIA			
❏ CL1829 [M]	Call of the Wild	1962	$18
❏ CS8629 [S]	Call of the Wild	1962	$25
❏ CL625 [M]	Command Performance	1954	$40
❏ CL1696 [M]	Deuces Wild	1962	$25
—Red and black label with six "eye" logos			
❏ CL1696 [M]	Deuces Wild	1962	$18
—Guaranteed High Fidelity" or "360 Sound Mono" label			
❏ CS8496 [S]	Deuces Wild	1962	$30
—Red and black label with six "eye" logos			
❏ CS8496 [S]	Deuces Wild	1962	$25
—360 Sound Stereo" label			
❏ CL1116 [M]	Foreign Affair	1958	$30
❏ CL1393 [M]	Frankie Laine, Balladeer	1960	$25
❏ CS8188 [S]	Frankie Laine, Balladeer	1960	$30
❏ CL1231 [M]	Frankie Laine's Greatest Hits	1958	$30
—Red and black label with six "eye" logos			
❏ CL1231 [M]	Frankie Laine's Greatest Hits	1962	$18
—Guaranteed High Fidelity" or "360 Sound Mono" label			
❏ CS8636 [R]	Frankie Laine's Greatest Hits	1963	$15
❏ PC8636	Frankie Laine's Greatest Hits	198?	$25
—Reissue with new prefix			
❏ CL1615 [M]	Hell Bent for Leather!	1961	$25
—Red and black label with six "eye" logos			
❏ CL1615 [M]	Hell Bent for Leather!	1962	$18
—Guaranteed High Fidelity" or "360 Sound Mono" label			
❏ CS8415 [S]	Hell Bent for Leather!	1961	$30
—Red and black label with six "eye" logos			
❏ CS8415 [S]	Hell Bent for Leather!	1962	$25
—360 Sound Stereo" label			
❏ CL808 [M]	Jazz Spectacular	1956	$30
❏ CL2504 [10]	Lover's Laine	1955	$40

Number	Title	Yr	NM
❏ CL6278 [10]	Mr. Rhythm	1954	$50
❏ CL6200 [10]	One for My Baby	1952	$50
❏ CL2548 [10]	One for My Baby	1955	$40
❏ CL1277 [M]	Reunion in Rhythm	1959	$25
❏ CS8087 [S]	Reunion in Rhythm	1959	$30
❏ CL975 [M]	Rockin'	1957	$30
❏ CL1176 [M]	Torchin'	1959	$25
❏ CS8024 [S]	Torchin'	1959	$30
❏ CL1962 [M]	Wanderlust	1963	$18
❏ CS8762 [S]	Wanderlust	1963	$25
❏ CL1317 [M]	You Are My Love	1960	$50
❏ CS8119 [S]	You Are My Love	1960	$30
GALAXY SERIES			
❏ 4821 [M]	Frankie Laine Sings	195?	$15
HARMONY			
❏ H30406	High Noon	1971	$15
❏ HS11345	I'm Gonna Live 'Til I Die	1969	$15
❏ HL7425 [M]	Memories	196?	$15
❏ HS11225 [S]	Memories	196?	$15
❏ HL7329 [M]	Roving Gambler	196?	$15
❏ HS11129 [S]	Roving Gambler	196?	$15
❏ HL7382 [M]	That's My Desire	196?	$15
❏ HS11182 [S]	That's My Desire	196?	$15
HINDSIGHT			
❏ HSR-216	Frankie Laine with Carl Fischer and His Orchestra, 1947	1985	$12
MERCURY			
❏ MG-25082 [10]	Christmas Favorites	1951	$50
❏ MG-20085 [M]	Concert Date	1957	$40

Number	Title	Yr	NM
☐ MG-25007 [10]	Favorites	1949	$50
☐ MG-25025 [10]	Frankie Laine	1950	$50
☐ MG-25026 [10]	Frankie Laine	1950	$50
☐ MG-25027 [10]	Frankie Laine	1950	$50
☐ MG-20587 [M]	Frankie Laine's Golden Hits	1960	$30
☐ SR-60587 [R]	Frankie Laine's Golden Hits	196?	$15
☐ MG-20083 [M]	Frankie Laine Sings For Us	1957	$40
☐ MG-25124 [10]	Listen to Laine	1952	$50
☐ MG-25097 [10]	Mr. Rhythm Sings	1951	$50
☐ MG-20069 [M]	Songs by Frankie Laine	1956	$40
☐ MG-25024 [10]	Songs from the Heart	1950	$50
☐ MG-20080 [M]	That's My Desire	1957	$40
☐ PKW-2-111	The Great Years	1969	$18
☐ MG-20105 [M]	With All My Heart	1957	$40
PICKWICK			
☐ SPC-3526	That Lucky Old Sun	197?	$12
☐ SPC-3601	You Gave Me a Mountain	197?	$12
TOWER			
☐ T5092 [M]	Memory Laine	1967	$15
☐ ST5092 [S]	Memory Laine	1967	$18
WING			
☐ MGW12110 [M]	All-Time Favorites	196?	$18
☐ SRW16110 [R]	All-Time Favorites	196?	$15
☐ MGW12158 [M]	Singing the Blues	196?	$18
☐ SRW16158 [R]	Singing the Blues	196?	$15
☐ MGW12202 [M]	That's My Desire	196?	$18
☐ SRW16202 [R]	That's My Desire	196?	$15

LAIRD, RICK
TIMELESS
| ☐ 308 | Soft Focus | 197? | $30 |

LAKE, GREG
CHRYSALIS
| ☐ CHR1357 | Greg Lake | 1981 | $10 |

LAKE, OLIVER
ARISTA/FREEDOM
| ☐ AF1008 | Heavy Spirits | 1975 | $35 |
| ☐ AF1024 | Ntu | 1976 | $35 |
ARISTA/NOVUS
| ☐ AN3010 | Focus | 1979 | $30 |
| ☐ AN3003 | Life Dance Of Is | 1978 | $30 |
BLACK SAINT
| ☐ BSR-0054 | Clevont Fitzhubert | 198? | $30 |
| ☐ BSR-0044 | Prophet | 198? | $30 |
GRAMAVISION
| ☐ 8106 | Oliver Lake & Jump Up | 198? | $25 |
| ☐ 8206 | Plug It | 198? | $25 |

LALA, MIKE
GHB
| ☐ GHB-120 | Mike Lala and His Dixie Six | 198? | $25 |

LAMARCH, SUSAN
STOMP OFF
| ☐ SOS-1032 | Vamp 'Til Ready | 198? | $25 |

LAMARE, NAPPY, AND KID ORY
MODERN
| ☐ 2010 [10] | Modern Records Volume 10 | 195? | $75 |
| —No printing on back cover | | | |

LAMAS, FERNANDO
ROULETTE
| ☐ R-25041 [M] | With Love, Fernando Lamas | 1958 | $40 |

LAMB, JOSEPH
FOLKWAYS
| ☐ FJ-3562 [M] | Classic Ragtime | 1960 | $30 |

LAMB, NATALIE, AND SAMMY PRICE
GHB
| ☐ GHB-84 | Natalie Lamb and Sammy Price and the Blues | 198? | $25 |

LAMB
FILLMORE
| ☐ F30003 | Sign of Change | 1970 | $25 |
WARNER BROS.
| ☐ WS1952 | Bring Out the Sun | 1972 | $25 |
| ☐ WS1920 | Cross Between | 1971 | $25 |

LAMBERT, DAVE
UNITED ARTISTS
| ☐ UAL-3084 [M] | Dave Lambert Sings and Swings Alone | 1959 | $40 |
| ☐ UAS-6084 [S] | Dave Lambert Sings and Swings Alone | 1959 | $50 |

LAMBERT, DONALD
JAZZOLOGY
| ☐ JCE-59 | Giant Stride | 197? | $25 |

LAMBERT, HENDRICKS AND BAVAN
BLUEBIRD
| ☐ 6282-1-RB | Swingin' Til the Girls Come Home | 1987 | $25 |
RCA VICTOR
☐ LPM-2747 [M]	Lambert, Hendricks and Bavan at Newport	1963	$30
☐ LSP-2747 [S]	Lambert, Hendricks and Bavan at Newport	1963	$40
☐ LPM-2861 [M]	Lambert, Hendricks and Bavan at the Village Gate	1964	$30
☐ LSP-2861 [S]	Lambert, Hendricks and Bavan at the Village Gate	1964	$40
☐ LPM-2635 [M]	Live at Basin Street East	1963	$30
☐ LSP-2635 [S]	Live at Basin Street East	1963	$40

LAMBERT, HENDRICKS AND ROSS
ABC IMPULSE!
| ☐ AS-83 [S] | Sing a Song of Basie | 1968 | $35 |
ABC-PARAMOUNT
| ☐ ABC-223 [M] | Sing a Song of Basie | 1958 | $50 |
| ☐ ABCS-223 [S] | Sing a Song of Basie | 1958 | $50 |
COLUMBIA
☐ CL1675 [M]	High Flying	1961	$30
—Black and red label with six "eye" logos			
☐ CS8475 [S]	High Flying	1961	$40
—Black and red label with six "eye" logos			
☐ CL1675 [M]	High Flying	1963	$35
—Red label with "Guaranteed High Fidelity" or "360 Sound Mono" at bottom			
☐ CS8475 [S]	High Flying	1963	$25
—Red label with "360 Sound Stereo" at bottom			
☐ CL1510 [M]	Lambert, Hendricks and Ross Sing Ellington	1960	$30
—Black and red label with six "eye" logos			
☐ CS8310 [S]	Lambert, Hendricks and Ross Sing Ellington	1960	$40
—Black and red label with six "eye" logos			
☐ CL1510 [M]	Lambert, Hendricks and Ross Sing Ellington	1963	$35
—Red label with "Guaranteed High Fidelity" or "360 Sound Mono" at bottom			
☐ CS8310 [S]	Lambert, Hendricks and Ross Sing Ellington	1963	$25
—Red label with "360 Sound Stereo" at bottom			
☐ KC32911	The Best of Lambert, Hendricks and Ross	1974	$35
☐ C32911	The Best of Lambert, Hendricks and Ross	197?	$25
—First reissue with new prefix			
☐ PC32911	The Best of Lambert, Hendricks and Ross	198?	$20
—Second reissue with new prefix and bar code			
☐ CL1403 [M]	The Hottest New Group in Jazz	1959	$30
—Black and red label with six "eye" logos			
☐ CL1403 [M]	The Hottest New Group in Jazz	1963	$35
—Red label with "Guaranteed High Fidelity" or "360 Sound Mono" at bottom			
☐ CS8198 [S]	The Hottest New Group in Jazz	1959	$40
—Black and red label with six "eye" logos			
☐ CS8198 [S]	The Hottest New Group in Jazz	1963	$25
—Red label with "360 Sound Stereo" at bottom			
COLUMBIA JAZZ ODYSSEY
| ☐ PC37020 | Lambert, Hendricks and Ross with the Ike Isaacs Trio | 1983 | $25 |
IMPULSE!
☐ A-83 [M]	Sing a Song of Basie	1965	$120
—Reissue of ABC-Paramount ABC-223			
☐ AS-83 [S]	Sing a Song of Basie	1965	$120
—Reissue of ABC-Paramount ABCS-223			
MCA
| ☐ 29049 | Sing a Song of Basie | 1980 | $20 |
ODYSSEY
| ☐ 32160292 | Way-Out Voices | 1968 | $35 |
ROULETTE
| ☐ R-52018 [M] | Sing Along with Basie | 1959 | $40 |
| ☐ SR-52018 [S] | Sing Along with Basie | 1959 | $50 |
WORLD PACIFIC
| ☐ WP-1264 [M] | The Swingers! | 1959 | $175 |
| ☐ ST-1025 [S] | The Swingers! | 1959 | $175 |

LAMBSON, ROGER
SEA BREEZE
| ☐ SB-2035 | Dreams of Mexico | 198? | $25 |

LAMEGO, DANNY, AND HIS JUMPIN' JACKS
FORGET-ME-NOT
| ☐ 105 [M] | The Big Weekend | 1964 | $150 |

LAMM, ROBERT
COLUMBIA
| ☐ PC33095 | Skinny Boy | 1974 | $15 |

LAMOND, DON
COMMAND
| ☐ RS 33-842 [M] | Off Beat Percussion | 1962 | $35 |
| ☐ RS832SD [S] | Off Beat Percussion | 1962 | $25 |
PROGRESSIVE
| ☐ PRO-7067 | Extraordinary | 198? | $25 |

LAMONT, CHARLES
UNI
| ☐ 73076 | A Legend in His Own Mind | 1970 | $30 |
| —As "Lamont | | | |

LAMOUR, DOROTHY
DECCA
| ☐ DL5115 [10] | Favorite Hawaiian Songs | 1950 | $100 |

LANCASTER, BYARD
VORTEX
| ☐ 2003 | It's Not Up to Us | 1968 | $30 |

LANCE, HERB
CHESS
| ☐ LP-1506 [M] | The Comeback | 1966 | $30 |
| ☐ LPS-1506 [S] | The Comeback | 1966 | $30 |

LANCE, LYNDA K.
ROYAL AMERICAN
| ☐ RA2801 | A Woman's Side of Love | 1969 | $18 |

LANCE, MAJOR
KAT FAMILY
| ☐ FZ38898 | The Major's Back | 1983 | $15 |
OKEH
☐ OKM-12110 [M]	Major's Greatest Hits	1965	$40
☐ OKS-14110 [S]	Major's Greatest Hits	1965	$40
☐ OKM-12105 [M]	The Monkey Time	1963	$75
☐ OKS-14105 [S]	The Monkey Time	1963	$50

| ☐ OKM-12106 [M] | Um, Um, Um, Um, Um, Um | 1964 | $75 |
| ☐ OKS-14106 [S] | Um, Um, Um, Um, Um, Um | 1964 | $50 |
SOUL
| ☐ S7-751 | Now Arriving | 1978 | $15 |

LANCELOT LINK AND THE EVOLUTION REVOLUTION
ABC
| ☐ S-715 | Lancelot Link and the Evolution Revolution | 1970 | $40 |

LANCERS, THE
CORAL
| ☐ CRL57100 [M] | Dixieland Ball | 1957 | $30 |
IMPERIAL
| ☐ LP-9075 [M] | Concert in Contrasts | 1959 | $30 |
| ☐ LP-12023 [S] | Concert in Contrasts | 1959 | $40 |
TREND
| ☐ TL-1009 [10] | The Lancers | 1954 | $40 |

LANCHESTER, ELSA
HIFI
| ☐ 406 [M] | Songs for a Shuttered Parlor | 1958 | $25 |
| ☐ 405 [M] | Songs for a Smoke-Filled Room | 1957 | $25 |
VERVE
| ☐ MGV-15015 [M] | Cockney London | 1960 | $30 |
| ☐ MGV-15024 [M] | Herself | 1962 | $30 |

LAND, HAROLD, AND BLUE MITCHELL
CONCORD JAZZ
| ☐ CJ-44 | Mapenzi | 1977 | $30 |

Number	Title	Yr	NM

LAND, HAROLD
BLUE NOTE
| ❏ LT-1057 | Take Aim | 1980 | $25 |

CADET
| ❏ LPS-813 | The Peace-Maker | 1968 | $35 |

CONTEMPORARY
| ❏ M-3550 [M] | Grooveyard | 1959 | $300 |

—*Reissue with new title*
❏ S-7550 [S]	Grooveyard	1959	$300
❏ C-3550 [M]	Harold in the Land of Hi-Fi	1958	$300
❏ M-3619 [M]	The Fox	1965	$175
❏ S-7619 [S]	The Fox	1965	$175

FANTASY
❏ OJC-493	Eastward Ho! Harold Land in New York	1991	$30
❏ OJC-162 [B]	In the Land of Jazz	1984	$250
❏ OJC-343	The Fox	198?	$25
❏ OJC-146	West Coast Blues!	198?	$25

HIFI
| ❏ J-612 [M] | The Fox | 1960 | $150 |
| ❏ SJ-612 [S] | The Fox | 1960 | $100 |

IMPERIAL
| ❏ LP-9247 [M] | Jazz Impressions of Folk Music | 1963 | $175 |
| ❏ LP-12247 [S] | Jazz Impressions of Folk Music | 1963 | $175 |

JAZZLAND
❏ JLP-33 [M]	Eastward Ho! Harold Land in New York	1961	$40
❏ JLP-933 [S]	Eastward Ho! Harold Land in New York	1961	$50
❏ JLP-20 [M]	West Coast Blues!	1960	$40
❏ JLP-920 [S]	West Coast Blues!	1960	$50

MAINSTREAM
❏ MRL-344	Choma (Burn)	1972	$35
❏ MRL-367	Damisi	1973	$35
❏ MRL-314	New Shade of Blue	1971	$35

MUSE
| ❏ MR-5272 | Xocia's Dance | 198? | $25 |

LANDE, ART, AND JAN GARBAREK
ECM
| ❏ 1038 | Red Lanta | 197? | $35 |

LANDE, ART; DAVE SAMUELA; PAUL McCANDLESS
ECM
| ❏ 1208 | Skylight | 1982 | $30 |

LANDE, ART
1750 ARCH
| ❏ 1769 | The Eccentricities of Earl Dant | 1978 | $35 |
| ❏ 1778 | The Story of Ba-Ku | 1979 | $35 |
ECM
| ❏ 1106 | Desert | 197? | $35 |
| ❏ 1081 | Rubisa Patrol | 197? | $35 |

LANDSLIDE
CAPITOL
| ❏ ST-11006 | Two-Sided Fantasy | 1972 | $40 |

LANE, ABBE
MERCURY
❏ MG-20643 [M]	Abbe Lane with Xavier Cugat and His Orchestra	1961	$30
❏ SR-60643 [S]	Abbe Lane with Xavier Cugat and His Orchestra	1961	$30
❏ SR-60930 [S]	The Many Sides of Abbe Lane	1964	$30
❏ MG-20930 [M]	The Many Sides of Abbe Lane	1964	$25
RCA VICTOR
❏ LPM-1554 [M]	Be Mine Tonight	1957	$30
❏ LSP-1554 [S]	Be Mine Tonight	1958	$40
❏ LPM-1688 [M]	The Lady in Red	1958	$30
❏ LSP-1688 [S]	The Lady in Red	1958	$40

LANE, CRISTY
ARRIVAL
| ❏ NU9640 | One Day at a Time: 14 Songs of Inspiration and Harmony | 1983 | $12 |
LANE
| ❏ LPS-101 | Cristy Lane Salutes the G.I.'s of Vietnam | 197? | $30 |
LIBERTY
| ❏ LT-51117 | Amazing Grace | 1982 | $10 |
| ❏ LN-10239 | Amazing Grace | 198? | $10 |
—*Budget-line reissue*
| ❏ LT-1023 | Ask Me to Dance | 1981 | $10 |
—*Reissue of United Artists 1023*
❏ LN-10226	Christmas with Cristy	198?	$12
❏ LT-51153	Cristy Lane At Her Best	1984	$10
❏ LN-10309	Cristy Lane At Her Best	1986	$10
—*Budget-line reissue*

| ❏ LT-51148 | Footprints in the Sand | 1983 | $10 |
| ❏ LN-10306 | Footprints in the Sand | 1986 | $10 |
—*Budget-line reissue*
❏ LT-51112	Fragile -- Handle with Care	1981	$10
❏ LT-51137	Here's to Us	1982	$10
❏ LT-1083	I Have a Dream	1981	$10
❏ LT-978	Simple Little Words	1981	$10
—*Reissue of United Artists 978*
LS
❏ 1987	Christmas Gold	1987	$12
❏ SLL-8358	Christmas Is the Man from Galilee	1983	$12
❏ 2002	Country Classics Vol. 2	198?	$12
❏ 2003	Country Classics Vol. 3	198?	$12
❏ 8027	Cristy Lane Is the Name	1978	$15
❏ 9227	Cristy Lane Salutes the G.I.'s of Vietnam	198?	$12
❏ 1001	Easy to Love	198?	$12
❏ SLL-8385	Greatest Hits	198?	$12
❏ 8028	Love Lies	1979	$15
❏ SLL-8386	One Day at a Time	198?	$12
❏ SLL-8334	The Sweetest Voice This Side of Heaven	198?	$12
RIVERSONG
❏ 2413	14 Golden Hymns	198?	$12
SUFFOLK MARKETING
❏ SLL-8289	One Day at a Time	198?	$12
UNITED ARTISTS
❏ LT-1023	Ask Me to Dance	1980	$12
❏ UA-LA978-H	Simple Little Words	1979	$12

LANE, JERRY "MAX"
CHART
| ❏ CHS-1025 | Lover's Lane | 1970 | $18 |

LANE, RED
RCA VICTOR
| ❏ LSP-4576 | The World Needs a Melody | 1971 | $18 |

LANE, ROBIN, AND THE CHARTBUSTERS
RERON
| ❏ 77 [EP] | Heart Connection | 1984 | $15 |
—*Robin Lane solo*
WARNER BROS.
❏ MINI3495	Five Live	1980	$18
❏ BSK3537	Imitation Life	1981	$18
❏ BSK3424	Robin Lane and the Chartbusters	1980	$18

LANE, STEVE, AND THE SOUTHERN STOMPERS
STOMP OFF
| ❏ SOS-1040 | Snake Rag | 198? | $25 |

LANEGAN, MARK
Also see SCREAMING TREES.
SUB POP
| ❏ SP419 | Scraps at Midnight | 1998 | $25 |
| ❏ SP61 | The Winding Sheet | 1990 | $30 |
—*First 1,000 on red vinyl*
| ❏ SP61 | The Winding Sheet | 1990 | $12 |
—*Black vinyl. Among the backing musicians are Kurt Cobain and Krist Novoselic of NIRVANA.*
| ❏ SP132 | Whisky for the Holy Ghost | 1994 | $25 |

LANG, EDDIE
YAZOO
| ❏ 1059 | Virtuoso | 198? | $25 |

LANG, K.D.
BUMSTEAD
| ❏ BUM-842 | A Truly Western Experience | 1984 | $35 |
—*Canadian import; first issue*

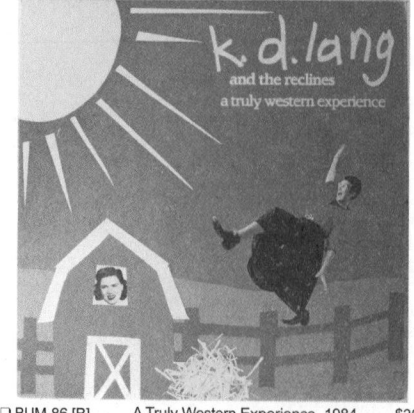

| ❏ BUM-86 [B] | A Truly Western Experience | 1984 | $30 |
—*Canadian import; reissue of Bumstead 842*

SIRE
| ❏ 25877 | Absolute Torch and Twang | 1989 | $15 |
| ❏ R160100 | Angel with a Lariat | 1987 | $15 |
—*BMG Direct Marketing edition*
| ❏ 25441 | Angel with a Lariat | 1987 | $12 |
| ❏ R134567 | Shadowland | 1988 | $15 |
—*BMG Direct Marketing edition*
| ❏ 25724 | Shadowland | 1988 | $12 |
| ❏ PRO-A-3120 [DJ] | The Making of Shadowland | 1988 | $25 |
—*Interview album*
WARNER BROS.
| ❏ 46034 | All You Can Eat | 1995 | $25 |

LANG, RONNIE
TOPS
| ❏ L-1521 [M] | Modern Jazz | 1958 | $300 |

LANGDON, DORY
VERVE
| ❏ MGV-2101 [M] | Leprechauns Are Upon Me | 1957 | $40 |

LANGDON, JIM
CUCA
| ❏ 1100 [M] | Jim Langdon Trio | 1965 | $25 |

LANGFORD, BILL
FANTASY
| ❏ 8396 | Gangbusters and Lollipops | 197? | $25 |

LANGNER SISTERS, THE
STUDIO CITY
| ❏ 9012 | It's the Country Life for Me | 1967 | $30 |
| ❏ 9011 | The Langner Sisters | 1966 | $30 |

LANIN, LESTER
AUDIO FIDELITY
| ❏ AFSD-6180 [S] | Thoroughly Modern | 1968 | $15 |
| ❏ AFLP-2180 [M] | Thoroughly Modern | 1968 | $18 |
EPIC
❏ LN3617 [M]	Christmas Dance Party (Volume 9)	1959	$18
❏ BN547 [S]	Christmas Dance Party (Volume 9)	1959	$25
❏ LN3531 [M]	Cocktail Dancing	1959	$18
❏ BN516 [S]	Cocktail Dancing	1959	$25
❏ LN24317 [M]	Cole Porter's Greatest Hits	1967	$15
❏ BN26317 [S]	Cole Porter's Greatest Hits	1967	$15
❏ LN3656 [M]	Dance to the Lester Lanin Beat	1960	$18
❏ BN556 [S]	Dance to the Lester Lanin Beat	1960	$25
❏ LN3340 [M]	Dance to the Music of Lester Lanin	1957	$18
❏ BN633 [R]	Dance to the Music of Lester Lanin	1962	$15
❏ LN24016 [M]	Dancing Theatre Party	1962	$15
❏ BN26016 [S]	Dancing Theatre Party	1962	$18
❏ LN3525 [M]	Have Band, Will Travel	1958	$18
❏ BN517 [S]	Have Band, Will Travel	1959	$25
❏ LN3699 [M]	High Society	1961	$15
❏ BN570 [S]	High Society	1961	$18
❏ LN3242 [M]	Lester Lanin and His Orchestra	1956	$18
❏ BN628 [R]	Lester Lanin and His Orchestra	1962	$15
❏ LN3410 [M]	Lester Lanin at the Tiffany Ball	1957	$18
❏ BN505 [S]	Lester Lanin at the Tiffany Ball	1959	$25
❏ LN3474 [M]	Lester Lanin Goes to College	1958	$18
❏ BN501 [S]	Lester Lanin Goes to College	1959	$25
❏ LN24105 [M]	Richard Rogers Hits	1964	$15
❏ BN26105 [S]	Richard Rogers Hits	1964	$18
❏ SN6046 [M]	The Dance Album	1964	$18
❏ BSN146 [S]	The Dance Album	1964	$25
❏ LN3825 [M]	Twistin' in High Society!	1961	$15
❏ BN620 [S]	Twistin' in High Society!	1961	$18
HARMONY
❏ HS11262	Everybody Dance	1968	$12
HINDSIGHT
❏ HSR-210	Dance Instrumentals: 1960-1962	198?	$10
METROMEDIA
❏ MD-1006	Narrowing the Generation Gap	1969	$15
PHILIPS
❏ PHM200145 [M]	Dancing at the Discotheque	1964	$12
❏ PHS600145 [S]	Dancing at the Discotheque	1964	$15
❏ PHM200211 [M]	Forty Beatles Hits	1966	$15
❏ PHS600211 [S]	Forty Beatles Hits	1966	$18
❏ PHM200181 [M]	Hits for Dancing	1965	$12
❏ PHS600181 [S]	Hits for Dancing	1965	$15
❏ PHM200165 [M]	I Had a Ball	1965	$12
❏ PHS600165 [S]	I Had a Ball	1965	$15
❏ PHM200192 [M]	Lester Lanin at the Country Club	1966	$12
❏ PHS600192 [S]	Lester Lanin at the Country Club	1966	$15

Number	Title	Yr	NM
❏ PHM200132 [M]	Lester Lanin Plays for Dancing	1964	$12
❏ PHS600132 [S]	Lester Lanin Plays for Dancing	1964	$15

LANZA, MARIO
PAIR
| ❏ PDL2-1059 | The Voice of the Century | 1986 | $15 |

PICKWICK
| ❏ CAS-777(e) [R] | Christmas Hymns and Carols | 1977 | $10 |

— Same contents as RCA Camden CAS-777(e)

RCA CAMDEN
❏ CAL-777 [M]	Christmas Hymns and Carols	196?	$18
❏ CAS-777(e) [R]	Christmas Hymns and Carols	196?	$15
❏ CAL-450 [M]	You Do Something to Me	195?	$18
❏ CAS-450(e) [R]	You Do Something to Me	195?	$15

RCA RED SEAL
❏ CRL1-1750	A Legendary Performer	1976	$12
❏ ARL1-0134	Lanza Sings Caruso	1973	$12
❏ VCS-6192	Mario Lanza's Greatest Hits	1970	$30
❏ VCS-7073	Opera's Greatest Hits	1971	$25
❏ ANL1-2874	Pure Gold	1978	$12
❏ ARL1-4405	The Great Caruso	198?	$10
❏ CRM5-4158	The Mario Lanza Collection	1981	$75

RCA VICTOR RED SEAL
❏ LM-1860 [M]	A Kiss" and Other Love Songs	1955	$40
❏ LSC-1860(e) [R]	A Kiss" and Other Love Songs	196?	$15
❏ LM-2454 [M]	A Mario Lanza Program	1960	$18
❏ LSC-2454 [S]	A Mario Lanza Program	1960	$25
❏ LSC-3289	Be My Love	1972	$15
❏ LM-2090 [M]	Cavalcade of Show Tunes	1957	$30
❏ LSC-2090(e) [R]	Cavalcade of Show Tunes	196?	$15
❏ LM-2422 [M]	Double Feature -- Mario Lanza	1960	$25
❏ LM-2338 [M]	For the First Time	1959	$18
❏ LSC-2338 [S]	For the First Time	1959	$25
❏ LM-2932 [M]	His Favorite Arias	196?	$15
❏ LSC-2932 [S]	His Favorite Arias	196?	$18
❏ LM-2790 [M]	If You Are But a Dream	196?	$15
❏ LSC-2790 [S]	If You Are But a Dream	196?	$18
❏ LM-2720 [M]	I'll See You in My Dreams	1964	$15
❏ LSC-2720 [S]	I'll See You in My Dreams	1964	$18
❏ LM-2607 [M]	I'll Walk with God	1962	$25
❏ LSC-2607(e) [R]	I'll Walk with God	1962	$15
❏ LM-2070 [M]	Lanza on Broadway	1956	$30
❏ LSC-2070(e) [R]	Lanza on Broadway	196?	$15
❏ LSC-2333 [S]	Lanza Sings Christmas Carols	1959	$25

— Original copies have "shaded dog" on labels

❏ LM-2333 [M]	Lanza Sings Christmas Carols	1959	$18
❏ LM-1188 [M]	Love Songs and a Neapolitan Serenade	195?	$40
❏ LSC-1188(e) [R]	Love Songs and a Neapolitan Serenade	196?	$15
❏ LM-1943 [M]	Magic Mario	1955	$40
❏ LM-2331 [M]	Mario	1959	$25
❏ LSC-2331 [S]	Mario!	1959	$30
❏ LSC-3101	Mario Lanza in Opera	1969	$18
❏ LSC-3102	Mario Lanza Memories	1969	$18
❏ LM-2393 [M]	Mario Lanza Sings Caruso Favorites	1960	$18
❏ LSC-2393 [S]	Mario Lanza Sings Caruso Favorites	1960	$25
❏ LM-155 [10]	Mario Lanza Sings Christmas Songs	1951	$50
❏ LM1837 [M]	Mario Lanza Sings the Hit Songs from "The Student Prince" and Other Great Musical Comedies	1955	$40
❏ LSC1837(e) [R]	Mario Lanza Sings the Hit Songs from "The Student Prince" and Other Great Musical Comedies	196?	$15
❏ LSC-3103	Mario Lanza…Speak to Me of Love	1969	$18
❏ LM-1996 [M]	Serenade	1956	$40
❏ LM-2211 [M]	Seven Hills of Rome	1958	$30
❏ LM-2748 [M]	The Best of Mario Lanza	1964	$15
❏ LSC-2748 [S]	The Best of Mario Lanza	1964	$18
❏ LM-2998 [M]	The Best of Mario Lanza, Volume 2	1968	$25
❏ LSC-2998 [S]	The Best of Mario Lanza, Volume 2	1968	$18
❏ LM-2440 [M]	The Desert Song	1960	$18
❏ LSC-2440 [S]	The Desert Song	1960	$25
❏ LM-1127 [M]	The Great Caruso	195?	$40
❏ LSC-1127(e) [R]	The Great Caruso	196?	$15
❏ LM-2339 [M]	The Student Prince	1959	$18
❏ LSC-2339 [S]	The Student Prince	1959	$25
❏ LSC-3216	The Student Prince	1971	$15
❏ LM-1927 [M]	The Touch of Your Hand	1955	$40
❏ LSC-1927(e) [R]	The Touch of Your Hand	196?	$15
❏ LM-2509 [M]	The Vagabond King	1961	$18
❏ LSC-2509 [S]	The Vagabond King	1961	$25
❏ LSC-3049	Younger Than Springtime	1968	$15

LAPORTA, JOHN
DEBUT
| ❏ DLP-10 [10] | The John LaPorta Quintet | 1954 | $400 |
| ❏ DEB-122 [M] | Three Moods | 1955 | $350 |

EVEREST
| ❏ LPBR-5037 [M] | The Most Minor | 1959 | $50 |
| ❏ SDBR-1037 [S] | The Most Minor | 1959 | $75 |

FANTASY
❏ 3228 [M]	Conceptions	1956	$100
—Red vinyl			
❏ 3228 [M]	Conceptions	1956	$40
—Black vinyl			
❏ 3237 [M]	South American Brothers	1956	$100
—Red vinyl			
❏ 3237 [M]	South American Brothers	1956	$40
—Black vinyl			
❏ 3248 [M]	The Clarinet Artistry of John LaPorta	1957	$100
—Red vinyl			
❏ 3248 [M]	The Clarinet Artistry of John LaPorta	1957	$40
—Black vinyl			

MUSIC MINUS ONE
| ❏ 4003 [M] | Eight Men In Search of a Drummer | 1961 | $30 |

LAREDO, JAIME
RCA VICTOR RED SEAL
❏ LSC-2414 [S]	Brahms: Violin Sonata No. 3; Bach: Partita No. 3	1960	$100
—Original with "shaded dog" label			
❏ LSC-2472 [S]	Bruch: Violin Concerto No. 1; Mozart: Violin Concerto No. 3	1961	$40
—Original with "shaded dog" label			
❏ LSC-2373 [S]	Presenting Jaime Laredo	1960	$40
—Original with "shaded dog" label			

LARKIN, BILLY
AURA
❏ AR83003 [M]	Blue Lights	196?	$50
❏ ARS23003 [S]	Blue Lights	196?	$75
❏ 23002 [S]	Pigmy	1964	$30
—As "The Delegates			
❏ 83002 [M]	Pigmy	1964	$25
—As "The Delegates			

BRYAN
| ❏ 105 | Billy Larkin | 1975 | $20 |

SUNBIRD
| ❏ SN50107 | All My Best | 1981 | $12 |

WORLD PACIFIC
❏ WP-1843 [M]	Ain't That a Groove	1966	$150
❏ WPS-21843 [S]	Ain't That a Groove	1966	$150
❏ WP-1863 [M]	Don't Stop!	1967	$150
❏ WPS-21863 [S]	Don't Stop!	1967	$150
❏ WP-1850 [M]	Hold On	1967	$150
❏ WPS-21850 [S]	Hold On	1967	$150
❏ WP-1837 [M]	Hole in the Wall	1966	$150
❏ WPS-21837 [S]	Hole in the Wall	1966	$150
❏ WPS-21883	The Best of Billy Larkin & the Delegates	1968	$150

LARKINS, ELLIS, AND TONY MIDDLETON
CONCORD JAZZ
| ❏ CJ-134 | Swingin' for Hamp | 1979 | $25 |

LARKINS, ELLIS
ANTILLES
| ❏ DGTL-101 | Ellis Larkins | 198? | $35 |

CLASSIC JAZZ
| ❏ 145 | Smooth One | 1977 | $30 |

DECCA
❏ DL9211 [M]	Blue and Sentimental	1958	$120
❏ DL79211 [S]	Blue and Sentimental	1958	$120
❏ DL5391 [10]	Blues in the Night	1952	$250
❏ DL8303 [M]	Manhattan at Midnight	1956	$120
❏ DL9205 [M]	The Soft Touch	1958	$150
❏ DL79205 [S]	The Soft Touch	1958	$150

STANYAN
❏ 10074	Ellis Larkins Plays Bacharach and McKuen	197?	$35
❏ 10011	Hair	1969	$30
❏ 10024	Lost in the Wood	197?	$30

STORYVILLE
| ❏ STLP-913 [M] | Do Nothin' Till You Hear from Me | 1956 | $50 |
| ❏ STLP-316 [10] | Perfume and Rain | 1955 | $100 |

LARKINS, ELLIS/LEE WILEY
STORYVILLE
| ❏ STLP-911 [M] | Duologue | 1956 | $75 |

LARKS, THE (1)
COLLECTABLES
| ❏ COL-5176 | Golden Classics: The Jerk | 198? | $12 |

MONEY
❏ LP-1107 [M]	Soul Kaleidoscope	1966	$40
❏ ST-1107 [S]	Soul Kaleidoscope	1966	$50
❏ LP-1110 [M]	Superslick	1967	$40
❏ ST-1110 [S]	Superslick	1967	$50
❏ LP-1102 [M]	The Jerk	1965	$40
❏ ST-1102 [S]	The Jerk	1965	$50

LAROCA, PETE
BLUE NOTE
❏ B1-32091	Basra	1995	$35
—The Finest in Jazz Since 1939" reissue			
❏ BLP-4205 [M]	Basra	1965	$75
❏ BST-84205 [S]	Basra	1965	$40
—With "New York, USA" address on label			
❏ BST-84205 [S]	Basra	1967	$35
—With "A Division of Liberty Records" on label			

DOUGLAS
| ❏ SD782 | Turkish Woman at the Bath | 1969 | $35 |

MUSE
| ❏ MR-5011 | Bliss | 197? | $30 |

LAROCCA, NICK
SOUTHLAND
| ❏ 230 [M] | Nick LaRocca and His Dixieland Band | 196? | $25 |

LAROSA, JULIUS
AUDIOPHILE
| ❏ AP-190 | It's a Wrap! | 1985 | $15 |

CADENCE
| ❏ CLP1007 [M] | Julius LaRosa (Julie's Best) | 1955 | $40 |

FORUM
| ❏ F-16012 [M] | Just Say I Love Her | 1960 | $18 |
| ❏ FS-16012 [S] | Just Say I Love Her | 1960 | $25 |

KAPP
| ❏ KL-1245 [M] | The New Julie LaRosa | 1961 | $18 |
| ❏ KS-3245 [S] | The New Julie LaRosa | 1961 | $25 |

METROMEDIA
| ❏ MD-1036 | Words | 1971 | $15 |

MGM
❏ E-4437 [M]	Hey Look Me Over	1967	$15
❏ SE-4437 [S]	Hey Look Me Over	1967	$18
❏ E-4398 [M]	You're Gonna Hear From Me	1966	$15
❏ SE-4398 [S]	You're Gonna Hear From Me	1966	$18

RCA VICTOR
| ❏ LPM-1299 [M] | Julius LaRosa | 1956 | $40 |

ROULETTE
❏ R25054 [M]	Love Songs A LaRosa	1959	$25
❏ SR25054 [S]	Love Songs A LaRosa	1959	$30
❏ R25083 [M]	On the Sunny Side	1960	$25
❏ SR25083 [S]	On the Sunny Side	1960	$30

LARRY AND HANK
PRESTIGE
| ❏ PRLP-7472 [M] | The Blues/A New Generation | 1965 | $25 |
| ❏ PRST-7472 [S] | The Blues/A New Generation | 1965 | $30 |

LARRY AND LENORE
REQUEST
| ❏ 10037 [M] | Traveling Guitars | 1959 | $150 |

LARSEN, MORTON G.
STOMP OFF
| ❏ SOS-1009 | Morton G. Larsen Plays Robert Clemente | 198? | $25 |

LARSEN, NEIL
A&M
❏ SP-3117	High Gear	1980	$25
❏ SP-3116	Jungle Fever	1980	$25
—Reissue of Horizon 733			

HORIZON
| ❏ SP-738 | High Gear | 1979 | $35 |
| ❏ SP-733 | Jungle Fever | 1978 | $35 |

LARSON, NICOLETTE
MCA
| ❏ 5719 | Rose of My Heart | 1986 | $10 |
| ❏ 5556 | … Say When | 1985 | $10 |

WARNER BROS.
❏ BSK3678	All Dressed Up & No Place to Go	1982	$12
❏ HS3370	In the Nick of Time	1979	$12
❏ BSK3243	Nicolette	1978	$12
❏ BSK3502	Radioland	1980	$12

LASALLE, DENISE
ABC
❏ D-966	Second Breath	1976	$15
❏ D-1027	The Bitch Is Bad	1977	$15
❏ AA-1087	Under the Influence	1978	$15

MALACO
| ❏ 7412 | A Lady in the Street | 198? | $12 |
| ❏ 7447 | Hittin' Where It Hurts | 198? | $12 |

Number	Title	Yr	NM
❏ 7441	It's Lying Time Again	198?	$12
❏ 7464	Love Me Right	198?	$12
❏ 7422	Love Talkin'	198?	$12
❏ 7434	Rain and Fire	198?	$12
❏ 7417	Right Place, Right Time	1984	$12
❏ 7454	Still Trapped	198?	$12

MCA

❏ 3239	I'm So Hot	1980	$12
❏ 760	I'm So Hot	198?	$10
—Reissue of 3239			
❏ 3089	Unwrapped	1979	$12
❏ 759	Unwrapped	198?	$10
—Reissue of 3089			

WESTBOUND

❏ 209	Here I Am Again	1975	$15
❏ 2016	On the Loose	1973	$18
❏ 2012	Trapped by a Thing Called Love	1972	$18

LASHA, PRINCE

CONTEMPORARY

❏ S-7617	Firebirds	1968	$85
❏ M-3610 [M]	The Cry	1963	$250
❏ S-7610 [S]	The Cry	1963	$250

LASHLEY, BARBARA, AND RAY SKJELBRED

STOMP OFF

❏ SOS-1152	Sweet and Lowdown	1988	$25

LASK, ULRICH

ECM

❏ 1217	Lask	198?	$30
❏ 1268	Sucht und Ordnung	1985	$30

LAST, JAMES

POLYDOR

❏ 24-4505	Classics Up to Date	1970	$15
❏ 24-4509	El Condor Pasa	1971	$15
❏ 24-4512	Good Times	1971	$15
❏ 24-6004	Hair	1969	$15
❏ PD-5512	Love Must Be the Reason	1972	$12
❏ PD-5538	M.O.R.	1973	$12
❏ PD-5505	Music from Across the Way	1972	$12
❏ PD-5534	Non Stop Dancing	1973	$12
❏ PD-1-6283	Seduction	1980	$12
❏ 24-4507	Soft Rock	1970	$15
❏ PD-5506	The Love Album	197?	$12
❏ PD-6040	Well Kept Secret	1975	$12

LAST CALL OF SHILOH, THE

LAST CALL

❏ 5136	The Last Call	196?	$250

LAST EXIT

CELLULOID

❏ CELL-8140	Cassette Recordings '87	1988	$15

ENEMY

❏ 88561-8176-1	Last Exit	1986	$25
❏ 88561-8178-1	The Noise of Trouble	1987	$18

VENTURE

❏ 91015	Iron Path	1988	$15

LAST POETS, THE

BLUE THUMB

❏ BT-52	At Last	1973	$75
❏ BT-39	Chastisement	1972	$75

CASABLANCA

❏ NBLP7051	Delights of the Garden	1977	$75

CELLULOID

❏ 6136	Delights of the Garden	198?	$25
❏ 6108	Oh My People	198?	$25

❏ 6101 [B]	The Last Poets	198?	$12

Number	Title	Yr	NM
❏ 6105 [B]	This Is Madness	198?	$12

COLLECTABLES

❏ COL-6500	Right On!	198?	$25

DOUGLAS

❏ 3 [B]	The Last Poets	1970	$75
❏ Z30811 [B]	The Last Poets	1971	$50
❏ Z30583 [B]	This Is Madness	1971	$75

JUGGERNAUT

❏ 8802	Right On!	1971	$150
—As "The Original Last Poets			

LASWELL, BILL, AND PETER BROTZMANN

CELLULOID

❏ CELL-5016	Low Life	198?	$15

LASWELL, BILL

ELEKTRA/MUSICIAN

❏ 60221	Basslines	1984	$12

VENTURE

❏ 90888	Hear No Evil	1988	$12

LATARSKI, DON

INNER CITY

❏ IC-1114	Haven	198?	$30

PAUSA

❏ 7146	Lifeline	1983	$25

LATEEF, YUSEF

ABC IMPULSE!

❏ AS-84 [S]	1984	1968	$250
❏ AS-9117 [S]	A Flat, G Flat and C	1968	$250
❏ ASD-9310	Club Date	1976	$160
❏ AS-56 [S]	Jazz Around the World	1968	$250
❏ AS-69 [S]	Live at Pep's	1968	$250
❏ AS-92 [S]	Psychicemotus	1968	$250
❏ AS-9259	Re-evaluations: The Impulse Years	1974	$250
❏ AS-9125 [S]	The Golden Flute	1968	$250
❏ IA-9353	The Live Session	1978	$250

ALA

❏ AJ-502	Archives of Jazz, Vol. 2	198?	$25

ARGO

❏ LP-634 [M]	Live at Cranbrook	1959	$175

ATLANTIC

❏ SD 2-1000	10 Years Hence	1977	$75
❏ 81663	Concerto for Yusef Lateef	1988	$30
❏ SD1635	Hush 'n' Thunder	1973	$50
❏ 81977	Nocturnes	1989	$35
❏ SD1650	Part of the Search	1974	$35
❏ SD1563	Suite 16	1970	$75
❏ SD1591	The Best of Yusef Lateef	1971	$50
—1841 Broadway" address on label			
❏ SD1591	The Best of Yusef Lateef	1976	$30
—75 Rockefeller Plaza" address on label			
❏ SD1508	The Blue Lateef	1968	$75
—Blue and green label			
❏ SD1508	The Blue Lateef	1969	$50
—Red and green label			
❏ SD1499	The Complete Lateef	1968	$40
—Blue and green label			
❏ SD1499	The Complete Lateef	1969	$50
—Red and green label			
❏ SD1548	The Diverse Lateef	1970	$75
❏ SD1685	The Doctor Is In... And Out	1976	$50
❏ SD1602	The Gentle Giant	1972	$75
❏ SD1525	Yusef Lateef's Detroit	1969	$200
—Reproductions exist			
❏ 81717	Yusef Lateef's Little Symphony	1987	$35

CADET

❏ LPS-816	Live at Cranbrook	1969	$75
❏ LP-634 [M]	Live at Cranbrook	1966	$40

CHARLIE PARKER

❏ PLP-814 [M]	Lost in Sound	1962	$150
❏ PLP-814S [S]	Lost in Sound	1962	$120

CTI

❏ 7082	Autophysiopsychic	1977	$50
❏ 7088	In a Temple Garden	1979	$50

DELMARK

❏ DL-407 [M]	Yusef!	1965	$40
❏ DS-407 [S]	Yusef!	1965	$150

EVEREST ARCHIVE OF FOLK & JAZZ

❏ FS-285	Yusef Lateef	197?	$25

FANTASY

❏ OJC-482	Cry! Tender	1991	$30
—Reissue of Prestige 7748			
❏ OJC-612	Eastern Sounds	1991	$35
—Reissue of Prestige 7139			
❏ OJC-399	Other Sounds	1989	$25

IMPULSE!

❏ A-84 [M]	1984	1965	$250
❏ AS-84 [S]	1984	1965	$160
❏ A-9117 [M]	A Flat, G Flat and C	1966	$250

Number	Title	Yr	NM
❏ AS-9117 [S]	A Flat, G Flat and C	1966	$250
❏ A-56 [M]	Jazz Around the World	1963	$160
❏ AS-56 [S]	Jazz Around the World	1963	$250
❏ A-69 [M]	Live at Pep's	1964	$250
❏ AS-69 [S]	Live at Pep's	1964	$250
❏ MAS-90216 [M]	Live at Pep's	1964	$300
—Capitol Record Club edition			
❏ A-92 [M]	Psychicemotus	1966	$250
❏ AS-92 [S]	Psychicemotus	1966	$250
❏ A-9125 [M]	The Golden Flute	1966	$250
❏ AS-9125 [S]	The Golden Flute	1966	$250

LANDMARK

❏ LLP-502	Yusef Lateef in Nigeria	1985	$50

MCA

❏ 4146	Live Session	198?	$35
—Reissue of ABC Impulse 9353			

MILESTONE

❏ M-47009	The Many Faces of Yusef Lateef	1973	$75

MOODSVILLE

❏ MVLP-22 [M]	Eastern Sounds	1961	$200
—Green label, silver print			
❏ MVST-22 [S]	Eastern Sounds	1961	$250
—Green label, silver print			

NEW JAZZ

❏ NJLP-8234 [M]	Cry! Tender	1960	$300
—Purple label			
❏ NJLP-8234 [M]	Cry! Tender	1965	$250
—Blue label, trident logo at right			
❏ NJLP-8272 [M]	Into Something	1962	$300
—Purple label			
❏ NJLP-8272 [M]	Into Something	1965	$250
—Blue label, trident logo at right			
❏ NJLP-8218 [M]	Other Sounds	1959	$300
—Purple label			
❏ NJLP-8218 [M]	Other Sounds	1965	$250
—Blue label, trident logo at right			
❏ NJLP-8261 [M]	The Sounds of Yusef	1961	$300
—Reissue of Prestige 7122; purple label			
❏ NJLP-8261 [M]	The Sounds of Yusef	1965	$250
—Blue label, trident logo at right			

PRESTIGE

❏ P-24035	Blues for the Orient	1974	$35
❏ PRST-7748	Cry! Tender	1970	$50
❏ PRLP-7319 [M]	Eastern Sounds	1964	$120
❏ PRLP-7319 [S]	Eastern Sounds	1964	$140
—Reissue of Moodsville 22			
❏ PRST-7653	Expressions	1969	$40
❏ PRST-7832	Imagination	1971	$75
❏ PRST-7637	Into Something	1968	$35
❏ PR-24007	Lateef	1972	$75
❏ PRLP-7122 [M]	The Sounds of Yusef	1957	$250
—Yellow label			
❏ PRLP-7398 [M]	The Sounds of Yusef	1966	$75
❏ PRST-7398 [S]	The Sounds of Yusef Lateef	1966	$40
❏ PRLP-7447 [M]	Yusef Lateef Plays for Lovers	1967	$75
❏ PRST-7447 [S]	Yusef Lateef Plays for Lovers	1967	$75
❏ P-24105	Yusef's Bag	1981	$75

RIVERSIDE

❏ RLP-337 [M]	The Centaur and the Phoenix	1960	$250
❏ RLP-9337 [S]	The Centaur and the Phoenix	1960	$250
❏ RS-3011	This Is Yusef Lateef	1968	$150
❏ RLP 12-325 [M]	Three Faces of Yusef Lateef	1960	$250
❏ RLP-1176 [S]	Three Faces of Yusef Lateef	1960	$300

SAVOY

❏ MG-12120 [M]	Jazz and the Sounds of Nature	1958	$200
❏ MG-12109 [M]	Jazz for the Thinker	1957	$200
❏ MG-12103 [M]	Jazz Mood	1957	$200
❏ MG-12117 [M]	Prayer to the East	1957	$200
❏ MG-12139 [M]	The Dreamer	1958	$200
❏ SR-13007 [S]	The Dreamer	1959	$200
❏ MG-12140 [M]	The Fabric of Jazz	1958	$200
❏ SR-13008 [S]	The Fabric of Jazz	1959	$200

SAVOY JAZZ

❏ SJL-2238	Angel Eyes	1979	$75
❏ SJL-2226	Gong!	1978	$75
❏ SJL-2205	Morning: The Savoy Sessions	1976	$50

TRIP

❏ 5018	Outside Blues	1973	$30

UPFRONT

❏ UPF-183	Dexterity	197?	$25

VERVE

❏ MGV-8217 [M]	Before Dawn	1958	$250
❏ V-8217 [M]	Before Dawn	1961	$40

VJ INTERNATIONAL

❏ VJS-3052 [M]	Contemplation	1974	$150
—Reissue of Vee-Jay 3010, which was originally credited to LOUIS HAYES.			

Number	Title	Yr	NM

LATIMORE

GLADES
❏ 7515	Dig a Little Deeper	1978	$12
❏ 7509	It Ain't Where You Been	1976	$12
❏ 6502	Latimore	1973	$15
❏ 7505	Latimore 3	1975	$15
❏ 6503	More, More, More	1974	$15

MALACO
❏ 7468	Catchin' Up	1993	$15
❏ 7436	Every Way But Wrong	198?	$12
❏ 7423	Good Time Man	198?	$12
❏ 7414	I'll Do Anything for You	198?	$12
❏ 7409	Singing in the Key of Love	198?	$12
❏ 7443	Slow Down	198?	$12
❏ 7456	The Only Way Is Up	198?	$12

LATIN ALL-STARS, THE

CROWN
❏ CLP5159 [M]	Jazz Heat-Bongo Beat	1959	$30

LATIN JAZZ QUINTET, THE

NEW JAZZ
❏ NJLP-8251 [M]	Caribe	1960	$250
—Purple label			
❏ NJLP-8251 [M]	Caribe	1965	$250
—Blue label, trident logo at right			
❏ NJLP-8321 [M]	Latin Soul	1963	$0
—Reassigned to Status			

PRESTIGE
❏ MPP-2503 [B]	Caribe	1980	$25
❏ NJLP8251 [M]	Caribe	1960	$300
—Purple label			

STATUS
❏ ST-8321 [M]	Latin Soul	1965	$85

TRIP
❏ 8008	Oh! Pharoah Speak	197?	$30

TRU-SOUND
❏ TRU-15003 [M]	Hot Sauce	1962	$40
❏ TRU-15012 [M]	The Latin Jazz Quintet	1962	$40

UNITED ARTISTS
❏ UAL-4071 [M]	The Latin Jazz Quintet	1960	$150
❏ UAS-5071 [S]	The Latin Jazz Quintet	1960	$125

LATIN SOULS, THE

KAPP
❏ KL-1524 [M]	Boo-Ga-Loo and Shing-a-Ling	1967	$30
❏ KS-3524 [S]	Boo-Ga-Loo and Shing-a-Ling	1967	$25
❏ KS-3553	Tigar Boo-Ga-Loo	1968	$25

LATTISAW, STACY, AND JOHNNY GILL

COTILLION
❏ 90136	Perfect Combination	1984	$12

LATTISAW, STACY

COTILLION
❏ 90280	I'm Not the Same Girl	1985	$12
❏ SD5219	Let Me Be Your Angel	1980	$12
❏ 90106	Sixteen	1983	$12
❏ 90002	Sneakin' Out	1982	$12
❏ SD16049	With You	1981	$12
❏ SD5214	Young and In Love	1979	$15

MOTOWN
❏ 6247ML	Personal Attention	1988	$10
❏ 6212ML	Take Me All the Way	1986	$10

LAUER, CHRISTOF

CMP
❏ CMP-39-ST	Christof Lauer	1990	$30

LAUGHTON, CHARLES

CAPITOL
❏ TBO1650 [M]	The Story Teller	1962	$30
❏ STBO1650 [S]	The Story Teller	1962	$30

DECCA
❏ DLP8010 [M]	A Christmas Carol/Mr. Pickwick's Christmas	1955	$25
—A-side read by Ronald Colman			
❏ DL8031 [M]	Readings from the Bible	195?	$30

MCA
❏ 15010	A Christmas Carol/Mr. Pickwick's Christmas	1955	$25
—A-side read by Ronald Colman; reissue of Decca LP			

LAUPER, CYNDI
Also see BLUE ANGEL.

EPIC
❏ OE44318	A Night to Remember	1989	$12

PORTRAIT
❏ BFR38930 [B]	She's So Unusual	1983	$15
❏ 9R939610	She's So Unusual	1984	$25
—Picture disc in plastic sleeve with sticker			
❏ FR38930	She's So Unusual	1984	$10
—Reissue with new prefix			
❏ OR40313	True Colors	1986	$12

SIRE
❏ R1554096 [B]	Detour	2016	$25

LAUREN, ROD

RCA VICTOR
❏ LPM-2176 [M]	I'm Rod Lauren	1961	$40
❏ LSP-2176 [S]	I'm Rod Lauren	1961	$50

LAURENCE, BABY

CLASSIC JAZZ
❏ 30	Dancemaster	197?	$25

LAURIE, ANNIE

AUDIO LAB
❏ AL-1510 [M]	It Hurts to Be in Love	1959	$300

LAURIE SISTERS, THE

RCA CAMDEN
❏ CAL-545 [M]	Hits of the Great Girl Groups	1960	$30
❏ CAS-545 [S]	Hits of the Great Girl Groups	1960	$30

LAVERNE, ANDY

STEEPLECHASE
❏ SCS-1086	Another World	198?	$30

LAVETTE, BETTY

ANTI
❏ 86873-1	Scene of the Crime	2007	$18
—As "Bettye LaVette"; comes with a certificate for a free MP3 download of the album			

DBK WORKS
❏ DBK116	I've Got My Own Hell to Raise	2005	$18
—As "Bettye LaVette"			

MOTOWN
❏ 6000ML	Tell Me a Lie	1982	$15
—As "Bettye LaVette"			

SUNDAZED
❏ LP5208	Do Your Duty	2006	$18
—As "Bettye LaVette"; compilation of recordings for Silver Fox and SSS International			

LAVITZ, T.

INTIMA
❏ D1-73512	T. Lavitz and the Bad Habits	1989	$30

LAWRENCE, ARNIE

DOCTOR JAZZ
❏ FW38445	Arnie Lawrence and Treasure Island	1983	$25

EMBRYO
❏ SD525	Inside an Hour Glass	1970	$25

PROJECT 3
❏ PR-5028	Look Toward a Dream	1968	$25
❏ PR-5011	You're Gonna Hear From Me	1967	$50

LAWRENCE, AZAR

PRESTIGE
❏ 10086	Bridge Into a New Age	1973	$35
❏ 10099	People Moving	1976	$35
❏ 10097	Summer Solstice	1975	$35

LAWRENCE, BILL

TOPS
❏ L-1576 [M]	Bill Lawrence Sings I'm in the Mood for Love	1957	$25

LAWRENCE, CAROL

CAMEO
❏ C-1077 [M]	An Evening with Carol Lawrence	1964	$25
❏ SC-1077 [S]	An Evening with Carol Lawrence	1964	$30

CHANCELLOR
❏ CHL-5015 [M]	Tonight at 8:30	1960	$25
❏ CHLS-5015 [S]	Tonight at 8:30	1960	$30

LAWRENCE, EDDIE

CORAL
❏ CRL57155 [M]	Eddie "The Old Philosopher" Lawrence	1957	$30
❏ CRL57411 [M]	Seven Characters In Search of Eddie Lawrence	1962	$30
❏ CRL757411 [S]	Seven Characters In Search of Eddie Lawrence	1962	$40
❏ CRL57203 [M]	The Kingdom of Eddie Lawrence	1958	$30
❏ CRL57103 [M]	The Old Philosopher	1956	$30
❏ CRL57371 [M]	The Side Splitting Personality of Eddie Lawrence	1961	$30

EPIC
❏ LN24149 [M]	Is That What's Bothering You Bunkie?	1965	$30
❏ BN26149 [S]	Is That What's Bothering You Bunkie?	1965	$40

SIGNATURE
❏ SM-1003 [M]	The Garden of Eddie Lawrence	1960	$40

LAWRENCE, ELLIOT

DECCA
❏ DL5274 [10]	College Prom	1950	$175
❏ DL5353 [10]	Moonlight on the Campus	1951	$250

FANTASY
❏ 3290 [M]	Big Band Sound	1959	$40
—Red vinyl			
❏ 3290 [M]	Big Band Sound	1959	$30
—Black vinyl, red label, non-flexible vinyl			
❏ 3290 [M]	Big Band Sound	196?	$35
—Black vinyl, red label, flexible vinyl			
❏ 8031 [S]	Big Band Sound	196?	$30
—Blue vinyl			
❏ 8031 [S]	Big Band Sound	196?	$25
—Black vinyl, blue label, non-flexible vinyl			
❏ 8031 [S]	Big Band Sound	196?	$30
—Black vinyl, blue label, flexible vinyl			
❏ 3226 [M]	Dream	1956	$50
—Red vinyl			
❏ 3226 [M]	Dream	1956	$30
—Black vinyl, red label, non-flexible vinyl			
❏ 3226 [M]	Dream	196?	$25
—Black vinyl, red label, flexible vinyl			
❏ 3261 [M]	Dream On -- Dance On	1958	$40
—Red vinyl			
❏ 3261 [M]	Dream On -- Dance On	1958	$30
—Black vinyl, red label, non-flexible vinyl			
❏ 3261 [M]	Dream On -- Dance On	196?	$35
—Black vinyl, red label, flexible vinyl			
❏ 8002 [S]	Dream On -- Dance On	196?	$30
—Blue vinyl			
❏ 8002 [S]	Dream On -- Dance On	196?	$25
—Black vinyl, blue label, non-flexible vinyl			
❏ 8002 [S]	Dream On -- Dance On	196?	$30
—Black vinyl, blue label, flexible vinyl			
❏ 3246 [M]	Elliot Lawrence Plays for Swinging Dancers	1957	$40
—Red vinyl			
❏ 3246 [M]	Elliot Lawrence Plays for Swinging Dancers	1957	$30
—Black vinyl, red label, non-flexible vinyl			
❏ 3246 [M]	Elliot Lawrence Plays for Swinging Dancers	196?	$35
—Black vinyl, red label, flexible vinyl			
❏ 8021 [S]	Elliot Lawrence Plays for Swinging Dancers	196?	$30
—Blue vinyl			
❏ 8021 [S]	Elliot Lawrence Plays for Swinging Dancers	196?	$25
—Black vinyl, blue label, non-flexible vinyl			
❏ 8021 [S]	Elliot Lawrence Plays for Swinging Dancers	196?	$30
—Black vinyl, blue label, flexible vinyl			
❏ 3206 [M]	Elliot Lawrence Plays Gerry Mulligan Arrangements	1956	$50
—Red vinyl			
❏ 3206 [M]	Elliot Lawrence Plays Gerry Mulligan Arrangements	1956	$30
—Black vinyl, red label, non-flexible vinyl			

Number	Title	Yr	NM
❏ 3206 [M]	Elliot Lawrence Plays Gerry Mulligan Arrangements	196?	$25
— Black vinyl, red label, flexible vinyl			
❏ OJC-117	Elliot Lawrence Plays Gerry Mulligan Arrangements	198?	$25
❏ 3219 [M]	Elliot Lawrence Plays Tiny Kahn and Johnny Mandel Arrangements	1956	$50
— Red vinyl			
❏ 3219 [M]	Elliot Lawrence Plays Tiny Kahn and Johnny Mandel Arrangements	1956	$30
— Black vinyl, red label, non-flexible vinyl			
❏ 3219 [M]	Elliot Lawrence Plays Tiny Kahn and Johnny Mandel Arrangements	196?	$25
— Black vinyl, red label, flexible vinyl			
❏ 3236 [M]	Swinging at the Steel Pier	1956	$50
— Red vinyl			
❏ 3236 [M]	Swinging at the Steel Pier	1956	$30
— Black vinyl, red label, non-flexible vinyl			
❏ 3236 [M]	Swinging at the Steel Pier	196?	$25
— Black vinyl, red label, flexible vinyl			

HINDSIGHT

Number	Title	Yr	NM
❏ HSR-182	Elliot Lawrence and His Orchestra 1946	1982	$25

JAZZTONE

Number	Title	Yr	NM
❏ J-1279 [M]	Big Band Modern	1958	$75

MOBILE FIDELITY

Number	Title	Yr	NM
❏ 2-229	The Music of Elliot Lawrence	1995	$40
— "Original Master Recording" at top of cover			

SESAC

Number	Title	Yr	NM
❏ N-1153 [M]	Jump Steady	1960	$30
❏ SN-1153 [S]	Jump Steady	1960	$40

SURREY

Number	Title	Yr	NM
❏ S-1019 [M]	Winds on Velvet	196?	$30
❏ SS-1019 [S]	Winds on Velvet	196?	$35

TOP RANK

Number	Title	Yr	NM
❏ RM-304 [M]	Music for Trapping (Tender, That Is)	1959	$75

VIK

Number	Title	Yr	NM
❏ LX-1124 [M]	Hi-Fi-ing Winds	1958	$40
❏ LX-1113 [M]	Jazz Goes Broadway	1958	$75

LAWRENCE, GARY

BLUE GOOSE

Number	Title	Yr	NM
❏ 2020	Gary Lawrence and His Sizzling Syncopators	1979	$25

LAWRENCE, GERTRUDE

DECCA

Number	Title	Yr	NM
❏ DL8673 [M]	A Remembrance	1958	$30
— Black label, silver print			
❏ DL5418 [10]	Souvenir Album	1952	$50

LAWRENCE, MIKE

OPTIMISM

Number	Title	Yr	NM
❏ OP-3104	Nightwind	198?	$25

LAWRENCE, STEVE, AND EYDIE GORME
Also see each artist's individual listings.

ABC

Number	Title	Yr	NM
❏ X-764	20 Golden Performances	1974	$15

ABC-PARAMOUNT

Number	Title	Yr	NM
❏ 469 [M]	Our Best to You	1964	$18
❏ S-469 [S]	Our Best to You	1964	$25
❏ 311 [M]	Steve and Eydie Sing the Golden Hits	1960	$25
❏ S-311 [S]	Steve and Eydie Sing the Golden Hits	1960	$30
❏ 300 [M]	We Got Us	1960	$25
❏ S-300 [S]	We Got Us	1960	$30

CALENDAR

Number	Title	Yr	NM
❏ KOM-1001 [M]	Golden Rainbow	1968	$30
❏ KOS-1001 [S]	Golden Rainbow	1968	$40

COLUMBIA

Number	Title	Yr	NM
❏ CL2730 [M]	Bonfa and Brazil	1968	$18
❏ CS9530 [S]	Bonfa and Brazil	1968	$15
❏ CL2021 [M]	Steve and Eydie at the Movies	1964	$15
❏ CS8821 [S]	Steve and Eydie at the Movies	1964	$18
❏ CL2636 [M]	Steve and Eydie Together On Broadway	1967	$15
❏ CS9436 [S]	Steve and Eydie Together On Broadway	1967	$18
❏ CL2262 [M]	That Holiday Feeling	1964	$15
❏ CS9062 [S]	That Holiday Feeling	1964	$18

CORAL

Number	Title	Yr	NM
❏ CRL57336 [M]	Steve and Eydie	1962	$25

HARMONY

Number	Title	Yr	NM
❏ H30292	Something's Gotta Give	1971	$12

MATI-MOR

Number	Title	Yr	NM
❏ 8003	It's Us Again	196?	$25
— Promotional item for Silvikrin shampoo			

MGM

Number	Title	Yr	NM
❏ SE-4881	Feelin'	1973	$12
❏ SE-4803	The World of Steve Lawrence and Eydie Gorme	1972	$12

RCA VICTOR

Number	Title	Yr	NM
❏ LSP-4393	A Man and a Woman	1971	$15
❏ LSP-4107	Real True Lovin'	1969	$15
❏ VPS-6035	This Is Steve Lawrence and Eydie Gorme	1971	$18
❏ VPS-6050	This Is Steve Lawrence and Eydie Gorme, Vol. 2	1972	$18
❏ LSP-4115	What It Was, Was Love	1969	$15

STAGE 2

Number	Title	Yr	NM
❏ 712	Hallelujah	198?	$12

UNITED ARTISTS

Number	Title	Yr	NM
❏ WWL-4509 [M]	Cozy	1961	$25
❏ WWS-8509 [S]	Cozy	1961	$30
❏ UAL-3191 [M]	The Very Best of Eydie and Steve	1962	$25
❏ UAS-6191 [S]	The Very Best of Eydie and Steve	1962	$30
❏ UAL-3268 [M]	Two on the Aisle	1963	$25
❏ UAS-6268 [S]	Two on the Aisle	1963	$30

VOCALION

Number	Title	Yr	NM
❏ VL3825 [M]	Presenting Steve and Eydie	1968	$15
❏ VL73825 [R]	Presenting Steve and Eydie	1968	$12

LAWRENCE, STEVE

ABC-PARAMOUNT

Number	Title	Yr	NM
❏ 290 [M]	Swing Softly with Me	1959	$30
❏ S-290 [S]	Swing Softly with Me	1959	$30
❏ 392 [M]	The Best of Steve Lawrence	1960	$25
❏ S-392 [S]	The Best of Steve Lawrence	1960	$30

APPLAUSE

Number	Title	Yr	NM
❏ 1001	Take It On Home	1981	$12

COLUMBIA

Number	Title	Yr	NM
❏ CL2121 [M]	Academy Award Losers	1964	$15
❏ CS8921 [S]	Academy Award Losers	1964	$18
❏ CL2227 [M]	Everybody Knows	1964	$15
❏ CS9027 [S]	Everybody Knows	1964	$18
❏ PC9565	Greatest Hits	198?	$10
— Reissue with new prefix			
❏ CS9565	Greatest Hits	1968	$15
❏ CL2540 [M]	Of Love and… Sad Young Men	1966	$15
❏ CS9340 [S]	Of Love and… Sad Young Men	1966	$18
❏ CL2419 [M]	The Steve Lawrence Show	1965	$15
❏ CS9219 [S]	The Steve Lawrence Show	1965	$18
❏ CL1953 [M]	Winners!	1963	$15
❏ CS8753 [S]	Winners!	1963	$18

CORAL

Number	Title	Yr	NM
❏ CRL57050 [M]	About That Girl	1956	$40
❏ CRL57268 [M]	All About Love	1959	$30
❏ CRL757268 [S]	All About Love	1959	$40
❏ CRL57204 [M]	Here's Steve Lawrence	1958	$40
❏ CRL57182 [M]	Songs by Steve Lawrence	1957	$40

Number	Title	Yr	NM
❏ CRL57434 [M]	Songs Everybody Knows	1963	$30
❏ CRL757434 [S]	Songs Everybody Knows	1963	$30

HARMONY

Number	Title	Yr	NM
❏ HS11397	Love Me	1970	$12
❏ HS11257	Moon River	196?	$12
❏ HS11327	Ramblin' Rose	1969	$12

KING

Number	Title	Yr	NM
❏ 593 [M]	Steve Lawrence	1959	$100

MGM

Number	Title	Yr	NM
❏ SE-4824	Portrait	1973	$12

RCA VICTOR

Number	Title	Yr	NM
❏ LSP-4167	I've Gotta Be Me	1969	$15
❏ LSP-4347	On a Clear Day	1970	$15

UNITED ARTISTS

Number	Title	Yr	NM
❏ UAL-3265 [M]	People Will Say We're in Love	1963	$25
❏ UAS-6265 [S]	People Will Say We're in Love	1963	$30
❏ UAL-3150 [M]	Portrait of My Love	1961	$25
❏ UAS-6150 [S]	Portrait of My Love	1961	$30
❏ UAL-3368 [M]	Steve Lawrence Conquers Broadway	1964	$18
❏ UAS-6368 [S]	Steve Lawrence Conquers Broadway	1964	$25
❏ UAL-3114 [M]	Steve Lawrence Goes Latin	1960	$25
❏ UAS-6114 [S]	Steve Lawrence Goes Latin	1960	$30
❏ UAL-3098 [M]	The Steve Lawrence Sound	1960	$25
❏ UAS-6098 [S]	The Steve Lawrence Sound	1960	$30
❏ UAL-3190 [M]	The Very Best of Steve Lawrence	1962	$25
❏ UAS-6190 [S]	The Very Best of Steve Lawrence	1962	$30

VOCALION

Number	Title	Yr	NM
❏ VL3775 [M]	Here's Steve Lawrence	196?	$15
❏ VL73775 [R]	Here's Steve Lawrence	196?	$12
❏ VL73886	The More I See You	1970	$12

LAWRENCE, T.J.

EAGLE

Number	Title	Yr	NM
❏ SM-4194	Illuminations	1985	$25

LAWRENCE, VICKI

BELL

Number	Title	Yr	NM
❏ 1120	The Night the Lights Went Out in Georgia	1973	$15

LAWRENCE UNIVERSITY CONCERT CHOIR

(NO LABEL)

Number	Title	Yr	NM
❏ DRS86-630	Christmas at Lawrence	1986	$10

LAWS, HUBERT

ATLANTIC

Number	Title	Yr	NM
❏ 1452 [M]	Flute By-Laws	1966	$50
❏ SD1452 [S]	Flute By-Laws	1966	$50
❏ SD1509	Laws Cause	1970	$75
❏ 1432 [M]	The Laws of Jazz	1965	$50
❏ SD1432 [S]	The Laws of Jazz	1965	$75
— Red and purple label			
❏ SD8813	The Laws of Jazz	1981	$20
— Reissue of 1432			
❏ SD1432 [S]	The Laws of Jazz	1969	$35
— Red and green label			
❏ SD1624	Wild Flower	1973	$35

CBS

Number	Title	Yr	NM
❏ M39858	Blanchard: New Earth Sonata; Telemann: Suite in A; Amazing Grace	1985	$25

COLUMBIA

Number	Title	Yr	NM
❏ JC36396	Family	1980	$35
❏ JC35708	Land of Passion	1979	$25
❏ FC38850	Make It Last	1983	$25
❏ PC34330	Romeo and Juliet	1976	$30
❏ JC35022	Say It with Silence	1978	$25
❏ FC36365	The Best of Hubert Laws	1981	$25

CTI

Number	Title	Yr	NM
❏ 6006	Afro-Classic	1971	$50
❏ 8019	Afro-Classic	198?	$25
— Reissue of 6006			
❏ 6025	Carnegie Hall	1973	$35
❏ 1002	Crying Song	1970	$75
— Original issue			
❏ 6000	Crying Song	1970	$35
— Reissue of 1002			
❏ CTX-33	In the Beginning	1974	$50
❏ 6022	Morning Star	1972	$35
❏ 6012	Rite of Spring	1972	$35
❏ 8020	Rite of Spring	198?	$25
— Reissue of 6012			
❏ 6058	The Chicago Theme	1975	$35
❏ 8015	The Chicago Theme	198?	$25
— Reissue of 6058			
❏ 6065	Then There Was Light, Vol. 1	1976	$30
— Half of "In the Beginning," originally issued as part of CTX 3+3			
❏ 6066	Then There Was Light, Vol. 2	1976	$30
— Half of "In the Beginning," originally issued as part of CTX 3+3			
❏ 7071	The San Francisco Concert	1977	$35

LAWS, RONNIE

BLUE NOTE

Number	Title	Yr	NM
❏ BN-LA628-G	Fever	1976	$30
❏ BN-LA730-H	Friends and Strangers	1977	$25
❏ BN-LA452-G	Pressure Sensitive	1975	$35

CAPITOL

Number	Title	Yr	NM
❏ ST-12375	Classic Masters	1984	$25
❏ ST-512375	Classic Masters	1984	$30
— Columbia House edition			
❏ ST-12261	Mr. Nice Guy	1983	$25

COLUMBIA

Number	Title	Yr	NM
❏ FC40902	All Day Rhythm	1987	$25
❏ BFC40089	Mirror Town	1986	$25

Number	Title	Yr	NM
LIBERTY			
❏ LT-1001	Every Generation	1981	$20
—Reissue of United Artists 1001			
❏ LO-628	Fever	198?	$20
—Reissue of Blue Note 628			
❏ LN-10255	Fever	198?	$20
—Budget-line reissue			
❏ LO-881	Flame	198?	$20
—Reissue of United Artists 881			
❏ LN-10232	Flame	198?	$20
—Budget-line reissue			
❏ LW-730	Friends and Strangers	198?	$20
—Reissue of Blue Note 730			
❏ LN-10164	Pressure Sensitive	198?	$20
—Reissue of Blue Note 452			
❏ LO-51087	Solid Ground	1981	$25
❏ LN-10307	Solid Ground	1986	$20
—Budget-line reissue			
UNITED ARTISTS			
❏ LT-1001	Every Generation	1980	$30
❏ UA-LA881-H	Flame	1978	$25

LAWSON, DEE
ROULETTE

| ❏ R-52017 [M] | 'Round Midnight | 1958 | $30 |
| ❏ SR-52017 [S] | 'Round Midnight | 1958 | $40 |

LAWSON, HUGH
SOUL NOTE

| ❏ SN-1052 | Colour | 1983 | $30 |

STORYVILLE

| ❏ 4078 | Prime Time | 198? | $25 |

LAWSON, JANET
INNER CITY

| ❏ IC-1118 | Janet Lawson Quintet | 1981 | $30 |

OMNISOUND

| ❏ 1052 | Dreams Can Be | 1983 | $30 |

LAWSON, LINDA
CHANCELLOR

| ❏ CHL-5010 [M] | Introducing Linda Lawson | 1960 | $30 |

LAWSON, STELLA
STASH

| ❏ 235 | Goin' For It | 198? | $25 |

LAWSON, YANK, AND BOB HAGGART
ATLANTIC

| ❏ SD1570 | Live at the Roosevelt Grill | 1970 | $35 |
| ❏ SD1582 | What's New? | 1971 | $35 |

DECCA

❏ DL5456 [10]	Blues on the River	1952	$250
❏ DL8196 [M]	Blues on the River	1955	$175
❏ DL8801 [M]	Boppin' at the Hop	1959	$150
❏ DL78801 [S]	Boppin' at the Hop	1959	$150
❏ DL5427 [10]	College Fight Songs	1952	$175
❏ DL8453 [M]	Hold That Tiger	1956	$175
❏ DL5439 [10]	Lawson-Haggart Band	1952	$175
❏ DL5368 [10]	Lawson-Haggart Band Play Jelly Roll's Jazz	1952	$175
❏ DL8182 [M]	Lawson-Haggart Band Play Jelly Roll's Jazz	1955	$175
❏ DL5437 [10]	Lawson-Haggart Band Play King Oliver's Jazz	1952	$175
❏ DL8195 [M]	Lawson-Haggart Band Play King Oliver's Jazz	1955	$175
❏ DL5533 [10]	Louis' Hot Fives and Sevens	1954	$175
❏ DL8200 [M]	Louis' Hot Fives and Sevens	1955	$175
❏ DL5529 [10]	South of the Mason-Dixon Line	1954	$250
❏ DL8197 [M]	South of the Mason-Dixon Line	1955	$250
❏ DL5502 [10]	Windy City Jazz	1953	$175
❏ DL8198 [M]	Windy City Jazz	1955	$175

EVEREST

❏ LPBR-5084 [M]	Dixieland Goes West	1960	$25
❏ SDBR-1084 [S]	Dixieland Goes West	1960	$30
❏ LPBR-5040 [M]	Junior Prom	1959	$30
❏ SDBR-1040 [S]	Junior Prom	1959	$25

PROJECT 3

| ❏ PR-5039 | Extra | 1969 | $25 |
| ❏ PR-5033 | The World's Greatest Jazz Band | 1968 | $25 |

STINSON

| ❏ SLP-59 [10] | Lawson-Haggart with Jerry Jerome and His Orchestra | 1957 | $30 |

LAWSON, YANK
ABC-PARAMOUNT

❏ ABC-518 [M]	Big Yank Is Here	1965	$35
❏ ABCS-518 [S]	Big Yank Is Here	1965	$25
❏ ABC-567 [M]	Ole Dixie	1965	$35
❏ ABCS-567 [S]	Ole Dixie	1965	$25

AUDIOPHILE

| ❏ AP-221 | Yank Lawson Plays Mostly Blues | 1986 | $25 |

Number	Title	Yr	NM
BRUNSWICK			
❏ BL58035 [10]	Yank Lawson	1953	$120
DOCTOR JAZZ			
❏ FW40064	That's a Plenty	1985	$25
RIVERSIDE			
❏ RLP-2509 [10]	Yank Lawson's Dixieland Jazz	1954	$300

LAY, RODNEY
CHURCHILL

| ❏ 9423 | Heartbreak | 1982 | $12 |

SUN

❏ 1022	Rockabilly Nuggets	1979	$15
❏ 1027	Silent Partners	1981	$15
—All copies on yellow vinyl			

LAY, SAM
BLUE THUMB

| ❏ BTS14 | Sam Lay in Bluesland | 1970 | $30 |

LAYTON, EDDIE
EPIC

| ❏ LN24118 [M] | Organ Music for Christmas | 1964 | $15 |
| ❏ BN26118 [S] | Organ Music for Christmas | 1964 | $18 |

LAZAR, SAM
ARGO

❏ LP-4015 [M]	Playback	1962	$30
❏ LPS-4015 [S]	Playback	1962	$40
❏ LP-714 [M]	Soul Merchant	1963	$30
❏ LPS-714 [S]	Soul Merchant	1963	$30
❏ LP-4002 [M]	Space Flight	1961	$30
❏ LPS-4002 [S]	Space Flight	1961	$40

LAZARUS
AMAZON

| ❏ 1001 | Lazarus | 1970 | $25 |

LAZRO, DAUNIK
HAT ART

| ❏ 2010 | Sweet Zee | 1986 | $35 |

HAT HUT

| ❏ 11 | Entrance Gates Tshee Park | 198? | $35 |

LAZY LESTER
EXCELLO

❏ LP-8006 [M]	True Blues	1967	$400
❏ LPS-8006 [M]	True Blues	196?	$75
—Says "Stereo" but plays mono			

LAZY SMOKE
ONYX

| ❏ 6003 | Corridor of Faces | 1967 | $1200 |

LEA, BARBARA, AND BOB DOROUGH
AUDIOPHILE

| ❏ AP-165 | Hoagy's Children | 1981 | $30 |

LEA, BARBARA
AUDIOPHILE

❏ AP-86	A Woman in Love	197?	$30
❏ AP-175	Do It Again	1984	$25
❏ AP-125	Remembering Lee Wiley	197?	$30
❏ AP-119	The Devil Is Afraid of Music	197?	$30

FANTASY

| ❏ OJC-1713 | Barbara Lea | 198? | $25 |
| ❏ OJC-1742 | Lea in Love | 1990 | $30 |

PRESTIGE

| ❏ PRLP-7065 [M] | Barbara Lea | 1956 | $300 |
| ❏ PRLP-7100 [M] | Lea in Love | 1957 | $300 |

RIVERSIDE

| ❏ RLP-2518 [10] | A Woman in Love | 1955 | $300 |

LEA, TERREA
ABC-PARAMOUNT

| ❏ ABC-141 [M] | Terrea Lea and Her Singing Guitar | 1956 | $30 |

HIFI

| ❏ R-404 [M] | Folk Songs and Ballads | 1957 | $30 |

LEACH, CURTIS
LONGHORN

| ❏ 003 | Indescribable | 1965 | $50 |

LEADBELLY
ALLEGRO

| ❏ L-4027 [10] | Sinful Songs | 195? | $300 |

CAPITOL

| ❏ H369 [10] | Classics in Jazz | 1953 | $300 |
| ❏ T1821 [M] | Leadbelly: Huddie Ledbetter's Best | 1962 | $40 |

Number	Title	Yr	NM
CLEOPATRA			
❏ 2068 [B]	Where Did You Sleep Last Night?		$25
ELEKTRA			
❏ EKL-301/2	The Library of Congress Recordings	1966	$30
FOLKWAYS			
❏ FA-3106 [M]	Leadbelly Sings Folk Songs	196?	$40
❏ FP-241 [M]	Leadbelly's Last Sessions, Vol. 1	196?	$40
❏ FP-242 [M]	Leadbelly's Last Sessions, Vol. 2	196?	$40
❏ FA-2941 [M]	Leadbelly's Last Sessions, Vol. 3	196?	$30
❏ FA-2942 [M]	Leadbelly's Last Sessions, Vol. 4	196?	$30
❏ FP-4 [10]	Lead Belly's Legacy, Vol. 1: Take This Hammer	1950	$175
❏ FA-2004 [10]	Lead Belly's Legacy, Vol. 1: Take This Hammer	195?	$50
—Reissue of FP-4			
❏ FP-14 [10]	Lead Belly's Legacy, Vol. 2: Rock Island Line	1951	$175
❏ FA-2014 [10]	Lead Belly's Legacy, Vol. 2: Rock Island Line	195?	$50
—Reissue of FP-14			
❏ FP-24 [10]	Lead Belly's Legacy, Vol. 3: Early Recordings	1951	$175
❏ FA-2024 [10]	Lead Belly's Legacy, Vol. 3: Early Recordings	195?	$50
—Reissue of FP-24			
❏ FP-34 [10]	Lead Belly's Legacy, Vol. 4: Easy Rider	1951	$175
❏ FA-2034 [10]	Lead Belly's Legacy, Vol. 4: Easy Rider	195?	$50
—Reissue of FP-34			
RCA VICTOR			
❏ LPV-505 [M]	Midnight Special	1964	$40
ROYALE			
❏ 18131 [10]	Blues Songs	1954	$120
—As "The Lonesome Blues Singer"			
VERVE FOLKWAYS			

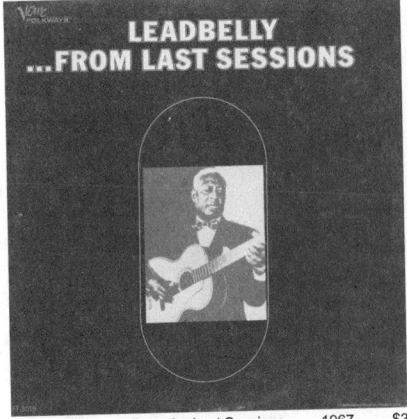

❏ FT-3019 [M]	From the Last Sessions	1967	$35
❏ FTS-3019 [R]	From the Last Sessions	1967	$20
❏ FV-9021 [M]	Keep Your Hands Off Her	1965	$40
❏ FVS-9021 [R]	Keep Your Hands Off Her	1965	$20
❏ FV-9001 [M]	Take This Hammer	1965	$35
❏ FVS-9001 [R]	Take This Hammer	1965	$25

LEADERS, THE
BLACK SAINT

| ❏ 120119 | Out Here Like This | 1989 | $35 |
| ❏ 120129 | Unforeseen Blessings | 1990 | $35 |

LEAHEY, HARRY
OMNISOUND

| ❏ 1042 | Silver Threads | 198? | $25 |
| ❏ 1031 | Still Waters | 198? | $25 |

LEAHY, JOE
TOWER

❏ T5057 [M]	A Taste of Trumpets, A Touch of Voices	1967	$25
❏ ST5057 [S]	A Taste of Trumpets, A Touch of Voices	1967	$30
❏ T5014 [M]	Tabasco and Trumpets	1966	$25
❏ ST5014 [S]	Tabasco and Trumpets	1966	$30

LEAPER, BOB
LONDON

| ❏ LL3391 [M] | Big Band Beatle Songs | 1964 | $75 |
| ❏ SP44056 [S] | Big Band Beatle Songs | 1964 | $40 |

LEAPY LEE
DECCA

| ❏ DL75237 | Leapy Lee | 1970 | $18 |
| ❏ DL75076 | Little Arrows | 1968 | $25 |

Number	Title	Yr	NM

LEARY, DR. TIMOTHY

DOUGLAS

❏ 1 [B]	You Can Be Anyone This Time Around	1969	$175

ESP-DISK'

| ❏ 1027 [M] | Turn On, Tune In, Drop Out | 1966 | $400 |

MERCURY

| ❏ MG-21131 [M] | Turn On, Tune In, Drop Out | 1967 | $150 |
| ❏ SR-61131 [S] | Turn On, Tune In, Drop Out | 1967 | $50 |

PIXIE

| ❏ CA-1069 [M] | L.S.D. | 1966 | $100 |

LEARY, JAMES

VITAL MUSIC

| ❏ VTL-003 | James | 199? | $35 |
| ❏ VTL-005 | James II | 199? | $35 |

LEATHERCOATED MINDS, THE

VIVA

| ❏ V-6003 [M] | Trip Down Sunset Strip | 1967 | $75 |
| ❏ V-36003 [S] | Trip Down Sunset Strip | 1967 | $100 |

LEAVES, THE

CAPITOL

| ❏ T2638 [M] | All the Good That's Happening | 1967 | $75 |
| ❏ ST2638 [S] | All the Good That's Happening | 1967 | $30 |

MIRA

| ❏ LP-3005 [M] | Hey Joe | 1966 | $40 |
| ❏ LPS-3005 [S] | Hey Joe | 1966 | $50 |

SURREY

| ❏ LPS-3005 | Hey Joe | 196? | $175 |

— Issued in Mira jackets

LED ZEPPELIN

Also see JOHN PAUL JONES; JIMMY PAGE; ROBERT PLANT; THE FIRM.

ATLANTIC

| ❏ 83061 | BBC Sessions | 2000 | $75 |

— Classic Records limited edition; each LP is in its own cardboard sleeve inside a box with a sheet of liner notes

❏ 532632R1 [B]	Celebration Day	2013	$100
❏ 83268	Early Days: The Best of Led Zeppelin Vol. 1	1999	$18
❏ 7255 [M]	Houses of the Holy	1973	$3000

— White label promo only

| ❏ SD7255 [S] | Houses of the Holy | 1973 | $18 |

— 1841 Broadway" address on label

| ❏ SD7255 [S] | Houses of the Holy | 1974 | $12 |

— 75 Rockefeller Plaza" address on label

| ❏ SD19130 | Houses of the Holy | 1977 | $10 |
| ❏ SD7255 [S] | Houses of the Holy | 2001 | $175 |

— Classic Records reissue on audiophile vinyl

| ❏ 83278 | Latter Days: The Best of Led Zeppelin Vol. 2 | 2000 | $18 |
| ❏ SD8216 [S] | Led Zeppelin | 1969 | $300 |

— Possible mispress with purple and brown labels

| ❏ 8216 [M] | Led Zeppelin | 1969 | $2000 |

— White label promo only

| ❏ SD8216 [DJ] | Led Zeppelin | 1969 | $250 |

— Stereo white label promo

| ❏ SD8216 [S] | Led Zeppelin | 1969 | $25 |

— 1841 Broadway" address on label

| ❏ SD8216 [S] | Led Zeppelin | 1974 | $12 |

— 75 Rockefeller Plaza" address on label

| ❏ SD19126 | Led Zeppelin | 1977 | $10 |
| ❏ SD8216 [S] | Led Zeppelin | 2000 | $150 |

— Classic Records reissue on audiophile vinyl

| ❏ 82144 [B] | Led Zeppelin (Box Set) | 1990 | $250 |
| ❏ 8236 [M] | Led Zeppelin II | 1969 | $2000 |

— White label promo only

| ❏ SD8236 [DJ] | Led Zeppelin II | 1969 | $300 |

— Stereo white label promo

| ❏ SD8236 [S] | Led Zeppelin II | 1969 | $25 |

— 1841 Broadway" address on label

| ❏ SD8236 [S] | Led Zeppelin II | 1974 | $12 |

— 75 Rockefeller Plaza" address on label

| ❏ SD19127 | Led Zeppelin II | 1977 | $10 |
| ❏ SD8236 [S] | Led Zeppelin II | 2000 | $50 |

— Classic Records reissue on audiophile vinyl

| ❏ 7201 [M] | Led Zeppelin III | 1970 | $1500 |

— White label promo only

| ❏ SD7201 [DJ] | Led Zeppelin III | 1970 | $250 |

— Stereo white label promo

| ❏ SD7201 [S] | Led Zeppelin III | 1970 | $25 |

— Die-cut cover with movable wheel; "1841 Broadway" address on label

| ❏ SD7201 [S] | Led Zeppelin III | 1974 | $12 |

— 75 Rockefeller Plaza" address on label

| ❏ SD19128 | Led Zeppelin III | 1977 | $10 |
| ❏ SD7201 [S] | Led Zeppelin III | 2001 | $150 |

— Classic Records reissue on audiophile vinyl

| ❏ 7208 [M] | Led Zeppelin (IV) (Runes) | 1971 | $300 |

— White label promo only

Number	Title	Yr	NM
❏ SD7208 [DJ]	Led Zeppelin (IV) (Runes)	1971	$175

— Stereo white label promo

| ❏ SD7208 [S] | Led Zeppelin (IV) (Runes) | 1971 | $18 |

— 1841 Broadway" address on label

| ❏ SD7208 [S] | Led Zeppelin (IV) (Runes) | 1974 | $12 |

— 75 Rockefeller Plaza" address on label

| ❏ SD19129 | Led Zeppelin (IV) (Runes) | 1977 | $10 |
| ❏ SMAS-94019 | Led Zeppelin (IV) (Runes) | 1972 | $40 |

— Capitol Record Club edition

| ❏ SD7208 [S] | Led Zeppelin (IV) (Runes) | 2001 | $250 |

— Classic Records reissue on audiophile vinyl

| ❏ R1547434 [B] | Presence | 2015 | $40 |
| ❏ WARB-ATL3905 [B] | The Complete BBC Sessions (Deluxe Edition) | 2016 | $125 |

— 5 LPs 180g

ATLANTIC CATALOGUE GROUP

| ❏ 344700 [B] | Mothership | 2008 | $75 |
| ❏ 371900 [B] | The Song Remains the Same | 2008 | $250 |

ATLANTIC/RHINO

| ❏ R1536123 [B] | Led Zeppelin | 2014 | $40 |
| ❏ R1536180 [B] | Led Zeppelin II | 2014 | $40 |

MOBILE FIDELITY

| ❏ Jan-0065 | Led Zeppelin II | 1981 | $250 |

— Audiophile vinyl

SWAN SONG

| ❏ 90051 | Coda | 1982 | $14 |
| ❏ 90051-1 [B] | Coda | 2001 | $85 |

— Classic Records reissue on audiophile vinyl

| ❏ SS16002 [B] | In Through the Out Door | 1979 | $30 |

— Letter "A" on spine; add 50% if brown paper bag is still with jacket

| ❏ SS16002 [B] | In Through the Out Door | 1979 | $30 |

— Letter "B" on spine; add 50% if brown paper bag is still with jacket

| ❏ SS16002 [B] | In Through the Out Door | 1979 | $30 |

— Letter "C" on spine; add 50% if brown paper bag is still with jacket

| ❏ SS16002 [B] | In Through the Out Door | 1979 | $30 |

— Letter "D" on spine; add 50% if brown paper bag is still with jacket

| ❏ SS16002 [B] | In Through the Out Door | 1979 | $30 |

— Letter "E" on spine; add 50% if brown paper bag is still with jacket

| ❏ SS16002 [B] | In Through the Out Door | 1979 | $30 |

— Letter "F" on spine; add 50% if brown paper bag is still with jacket

| ❏ SS16002 [B] | In Through the Out Door | 2003 | $175 |

— Classic Records reissue on 200-gram vinyl; contains a 12-page insert with all six covers; we don't know if the label actually pressed these with six different covers

| ❏ R1547432 [B] | In Through the Out Door | 2015 | $50 |

— expanded remastered edition

| ❏ SS 2-200 | Physical Graffiti | 1975 | $25 |
| ❏ SS 2-200 | Physical Graffiti | 2002 | $250 |

— Classic Records reissue on audiophile vinyl

| ❏ SS8416 | Presence | 1976 | $18 |
| ❏ SS8416 [B] | Presence | 2002 | $175 |

— Classic Records reissue on audiophile vinyl

| ❏ SS 2-201 | The Song Remains the Same | 1976 | $25 |
| ❏ SS 2-201 | The Song Remains the Same | 2003 | $40 |

— Classic Records edition on 200-gram vinyl

| ❏ SS2-201 [B] | The Song Remains The Same | 2005 | $250 |

— Classic Records reissue on audiophile vinyl

LEDOUX, CHRIS

AMERICAN COWBOY SONGS

❏ ACS23001	Chris LeDoux and the Saddle Boogie Band	198?	$25
❏ ACS20001	Melodies and Memories	1984	$30
❏ ACS17001	Thirty Dollar Cowboy	1983	$30

Number	Title	Yr	NM

LUCKY MAN

❏ NR9175	Chris LeDoux Sings Western Country	1978	$30
❏ LM10193	Paint Me Back Home in Wyoming	1978	$30
❏ NR4249	Rodeo Songs Old and New	1973	$30
❏ ACS5524	Sing Me a Song, Mr. Rodeo Man	197?	$30
❏ NR7648	Songs of the American West	1976	$30
❏ LM10194	Western Tunesmith	1980	$30

LEE, ALVIN

Also see TEN YEARS AFTER.

21 RECORDS

| ❏ 90517 | Detroit Diesel | 1986 | $12 |

ATLANTIC

| ❏ SD19287 | Free Fall | 1980 | $12 |
| ❏ SD19306 | RX5 | 1981 | $12 |

COLUMBIA

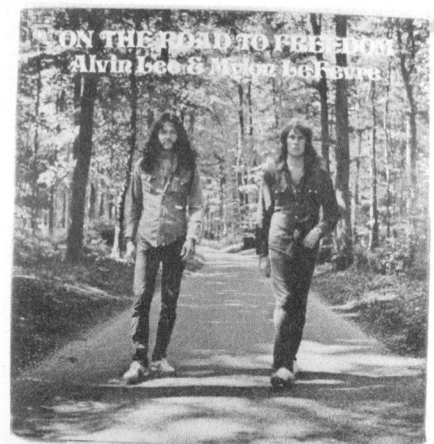

| ❏ PG33187 | In Flight | 1974 | $18 |
| ❏ KC32729 [B] | On the Road to Freedom | 1973 | $15 |

— With Mylon LeFevre

| ❏ PC32729 | On the Road to Freedom | 197? | $10 |

— With Mylon LeFevre; reissue with new prefix

| ❏ PC33796 | Pump Iron! | 1975 | $15 |

RSO

| ❏ RS-1-3049 | Ride On | 1979 | $15 |

— With "Ten Years Later"

| ❏ RS-1-3033 | Rocket Fuel | 1978 | $15 |

— With "Ten Years Later"

LEE, ARTHUR

Also see LOVE.

A&M

| ❏ SP-4356 | Vindicator | 1972 | $30 |

RHINO

| ❏ RNLP 020 | Arthur Lee | 1981 | $12 |

LEE, BRENDA

DECCA

| ❏ DL4757 [M] | 10 Golden Years | 1966 | $30 |

— With gatefold cover

| ❏ DL4757 [M] | 10 Golden Years | 196? | $18 |

— With regular cover

| ❏ DL74757 [S] | 10 Golden Years | 1966 | $30 |

— With gatefold cover

| ❏ DL74757 [S] | 10 Golden Years | 196? | $25 |

— With regular cover

| ❏ ST-90997 [S] | 10 Golden Years | 1966 | $30 |

— Capitol Record Club edition

❏ DL4370 [M]	All Alone Am I	1963	$30
❏ DL74370 [S]	All Alone Am I	1963	$30
❏ DL4176 [M]	All the Way	1961	$30
❏ DL74176 [S]	All the Way	1961	$30
❏ DL4326 [M]	Brenda, That's All	1962	$30
❏ DL74326 [S]	Brenda, That's All	1962	$30
❏ DL4039 [M]	Brenda Lee	1960	$30
❏ DL74039 [S]	Brenda Lee	1960	$30

BRENDA LEE — BYE BYE BLUES (DECCA)

A TASTE OF HONEY / WHAT A DIFFERENCE A DAY MADE / SEPTEMBER IN THE RAIN / REMEMBER WHEN / THE SHADOW OF YOUR SMILE / BYE BYE BLUES / YESTERDAY / THE GOOD LIFE / SOFTLY, AS I LEAVE YOU / FLOWERS ON THE WALL / MAKE THE WORLD GO AWAY / RUSTY BELLS

Number	Title	Yr	NM
DL4755 [M]	Bye Bye Blues	1966	$25
DL74755 [S]	Bye Bye Blues	1966	$30
DL4509 [M]	By Request	1964	$25
DL74509 [S]	By Request	1964	$30
DL4825 [M]	Coming On Strong	1966	$18
DL74825 [S]	Coming On Strong	1966	$25
DL4104 [M]	Emotions	1961	$30
DL74104 [S]	Emotions	1961	$30
DL74955	For the First Time	1968	$18

— With Pete Fountain

Number	Title	Yr	NM
DL8873 [M]	Grandma, What Great Songs You Sang	1960	$40
DL78873 [S]	Grandma, What Great Songs You Sang	1960	$50
DL75111	Johnny One Time	1969	$18
ST-92062	Johnny One Time	1969	$25

— Capitol Record Club edition

Number	Title	Yr	NM
DL4439 [M]	Let Me Sing	1963	$30
DL74439 [S]	Let Me Sing	1963	$30
DL75232	Memphis Portrait	1970	$18
DL4583 [M]	Merry Christmas from Brenda Lee	1964	$25
DL74583 [S]	Merry Christmas from Brenda Lee	1964	$30
R103619 [S]	Merry Christmas from Brenda Lee	1971	$25

— RCA Music Service edition

Number	Title	Yr	NM
DL4941 [M]	Reflections in Blue	1967	$25
DL74941 [S]	Reflections in Blue	1967	$18
DL4216 [M]	Sincerely	1962	$30
DL74216 [S]	Sincerely	1962	$30
DL4661 [M]	The Versatile Brenda Lee	1965	$25
DL74661 [S]	The Versatile Brenda Lee	1965	$30
DL4082 [M]	This Is…Brenda	1960	$30
DL74082 [S]	This Is…Brenda	1960	$30
DL4684 [M]	Too Many Rivers	1965	$25
DL74684 [S]	Too Many Rivers	1965	$30
DL4626 [M]	Top Teen Hits	1965	$25
DL74626 [S]	Top Teen Hits	1965	$30

MCA

Number	Title	Yr	NM
305	Brenda	1973	$18
433	Brenda Lee Now	1974	$15
3211	Even Better	1979	$12
758	Even Better	198?	$10

— Reissue of 3211

Number	Title	Yr	NM
5626	Feels So Right	1985	$12
5342	Greatest Country Hits	1982	$12
2233	L.A. Sessions	1976	$12
232 [S]	Merry Christmas from Brenda Lee	1973	$15
15021 [S]	Merry Christmas from Brenda Lee	197?	$12
373	New Sunrise	1973	$15
5278	Only When I Laugh	1981	$12
824	Only When I Laugh	1982	$10

— Reissue of 5278

Number	Title	Yr	NM
15038	Rockin' Around the Christmas Tree	198?	$12
477	Sincerely, Brenda Lee	1975	$12
5143	Take Me Back	1980	$12
2-4012	The Brenda Lee Story -- Her Greatest Hits	1973	$25

MCA CORAL

Number	Title	Yr	NM
CB-20044	Let It Be Me	197?	$12

VOCALION

Number	Title	Yr	NM
VL3795 [M]	Here's Brenda Lee	1967	$15
VL73795 [S]	Here's Brenda Lee	1967	$15
VL73890	Let It Be Me	1970	$15

LEE, BYRON, AND THE DRAGONAIRES

ATCO

Number	Title	Yr	NM
33-182 [M]	Jump Up	1966	$25
SD 33-182 [S]	Jump Up	1966	$30

BMN

Number	Title	Yr	NM
004	Dance the Ska	196?	$25

JAD

Number	Title	Yr	NM
JS-1004	Byron Lee and the Dragonaires	1968	$25

TOWERS HALL

Number	Title	Yr	NM
006	The Sounds of Jamaica	196?	$25

LEE, DICKEY

MERCURY

Number	Title	Yr	NM
SRM-1-5020	Dickey Lee	1979	$12
SRM-1-5026	Dickey Lee Again	1980	$12

RCA VICTOR

Number	Title	Yr	NM
APL1-1725	Angels, Roses and Rain	1976	$15
LSP-4715	Ashes of Love	1972	$15
LSP-4791	Baby, Bye Bye	1972	$15
LSP-4857	Crying Over You	1973	$15
LSP-4637	Never Ending Song of Love	1971	$15
APL1-1243	Rocky	1975	$15
APL1-0311	Sparklin' Brown Eyes	1974	$15

SMASH

Number	Title	Yr	NM
MGS-27020 [M]	The Tale of Patches	1962	$30
SRS-67020 [S]	The Tale of Patches	1962	$40

TCF HALL

Number	Title	Yr	NM
TCF-8001 [M]	Dickey Lee Sings "Laurie" and "The Girl from Peyton Place"	1965	$25
TCF-9001 [S]	Dickey Lee Sings "Laurie" and "The Girl from Peyton Place"	1965	$30

LEE, EDDIE

GEORGIAN

Number	Title	Yr	NM
GR2001 [M]	Windy City Profile	1958	$40

LEE, JACKIE (1)

MIRWOOD

Number	Title	Yr	NM
MW-7000 [M]	The Duck	1966	$25
SW-7000 [S]	The Duck	1966	$30

LEE, JEANNE, AND RAN BLAKE

BLUEBIRD

Number	Title	Yr	NM
6461-1-RB	The Legendary Duets	1987	$30

RCA VICTOR

Number	Title	Yr	NM
LPM-2500 [M]	The Newest Sound Around	1962	$30
LSP-2500 [S]	The Newest Sound Around	1962	$40

LEE, JEANNE

EARTHFORM RECORDS

Number	Title	Yr	NM
814 [B]	Conspiracy	1975	$350

SEEDS

Number	Title	Yr	NM
no cat [B]	Conspiracy		$500

LEE, JOHN, AND GERRY BROWN

BLUE NOTE

Number	Title	Yr	NM
BN-LA541-G	Mango Sunrise	1976	$30
BN-LA701-G	Still Can't Say Enough	1977	$30

LEE, JOHNNY

ACCORD

Number	Title	Yr	NM
7219	Country Party	1983	$10

ASYLUM

Number	Title	Yr	NM
6E-309	Lookin' for Love	1980	$12

CURB

Number	Title	Yr	NM
10617	New Directions	1989	$12

FULL MOON

Number	Title	Yr	NM
23899	Hey Bartender	1983	$10

FULL MOON/ASYLUM

Number	Title	Yr	NM
5E-541	Bet Your Heart on Me	1981	$10
60147	Sounds Like Love	1982	$10

PLANTATION

Number	Title	Yr	NM
45	Party Time	1981	$12

WARNER BROS.

Number	Title	Yr	NM
23967	Greatest Hits	1983	$10
25210	Keep Me Hangin' On	1985	$10
6E-309	Lookin' for Love	198?	$10

— Reissue of Asylum 6E-309

Number	Title	Yr	NM
25056	'Til the Bars Burn Down	1984	$10
25125	Workin' for a Livin'	1984	$10

LEE, JONI

MCA

Number	Title	Yr	NM
2194	Joni Lee	1976	$15

LEE, JULIA

CAPITOL

Number	Title	Yr	NM
H228 [10]	Party Time	1950	$300
T228 [M]	Party Time	195?	$150

PAUSA

Number	Title	Yr	NM
9020	Julia Lee and Her Boyfriends	198?	$25

LEE, KATIE

HORIZON

Number	Title	Yr	NM
WP-1604 [M]	The Best of Katie Lee	1962	$25
WP-1604Stereo [S]	The Best of Katie Lee	1962	$30

REPRISE

Number	Title	Yr	NM
R-6025 [M]	Songs of Coach and Consultation	1961	$30

SPECIALTY

Number	Title	Yr	NM
SP-5000 [M]	Spicy Songs for Cool Knights	1959	$30

LEE, LAURA

CHESS

Number	Title	Yr	NM
CH-50031	Love More Than Pride	1972	$25

HOT WAX

Number	Title	Yr	NM
HA-714	Laura Lee	1972	$18
HA-715	The Best of Laura Lee	1973	$18
HA-708	Women's Love Rights	1971	$18

INVICTUS

Number	Title	Yr	NM
KZ33133	Laura Lee	1974	$12

LEE, LONDON

PHILIPS

Number	Title	Yr	NM
PHS600322	The Rich Kid	1969	$18

LEE, MICHELE

COLUMBIA

Number	Title	Yr	NM
CL2486 [M]	A Taste of the Fantastic	1966	$18
CS9286 [S]	A Taste of the Fantastic	1966	$25
CS9682	L. David Sloane and Other Hits of Today	1968	$25

LEE, PEGGY

A&M

Number	Title	Yr	NM
SP-4547	Mirrors	1975	$15

ATLANTIC

Number	Title	Yr	NM
SD18108	Let's Love	1974	$15

CAPITOL

Number	Title	Yr	NM
T1366 [M]	All Aglow Again	1960	$50

— Black label with colorband, Capitol logo at left

Number	Title	Yr	NM
T1366 [M]	All Aglow Again	1962	$100

— Black label with colorband, Capitol logo at top

Number	Title	Yr	NM
ST1366 [S]	All Aglow Again	1960	$50

— Black label with colorband, Capitol logo at left

Number	Title	Yr	NM
ST1366 [S]	All Aglow Again	1962	$40

— Black label with colorband, Capitol logo at top

Number	Title	Yr	NM
T1213 [M]	Alright, Okay, You Win	1959	$75
ST1213 [S]	Alright, Okay, You Win	1959	$75
ST-183	A Natural Woman	1969	$40
T1520 [M]	Basin Street East	1961	$40

— Black label with colorband, Capitol logo at left

Number	Title	Yr	NM
T1520 [M]	Basin Street East	1962	$100

— Black label with colorband, Capitol logo at top

Number	Title	Yr	NM
ST1520 [S]	Basin Street East	1961	$75

— Black label with colorband, Capitol logo at left

Number	Title	Yr	NM
ST1520 [S]	Basin Street East	1962	$40

— Black label with colorband, Capitol logo at top

Number	Title	Yr	NM
SM-1520	Basin Street East	1977	$12

— Reissue with new prefix

Number	Title	Yr	NM
T1219 [M]	Beauty and the Beat	1959	$75

— With George Shearing; black label with colorband, Capitol logo at left

Number	Title	Yr	NM
ST1219 [S]	Beauty and the Beat	1959	$75

— With George Shearing; black label with colorband, Capitol logo at left

Number	Title	Yr	NM
T1219 [M]	Beauty and the Beat	1962	$40

— With George Shearing; black label with colorband, Capitol logo at top

Number	Title	Yr	NM
ST1219 [S]	Beauty and the Beat	1962	$40

— With George Shearing; black label with colorband, Capitol logo at top

Number	Title	Yr	NM
T1743 [M]	Bewitching-Lee!	1962	$300

— Black "The Star Line" label

Number	Title	Yr	NM
DT1743 [R]	Bewitching-Lee!	1962	$40
T2475 [M]	Big $pender	1966	$40
ST2475 [S]	Big $pender	1966	$40
T1671 [M]	Blue Cross Country	1962	$40
ST1671 [S]	Blue Cross Country	1962	$75
ST-463	Bridge Over Troubled Water	1970	$15
T1423 [M]	Christmas Carousel	1960	$25
ST1423 [S]	Christmas Carousel	1960	$75
T2732 [M]	Extra Special	1967	$40
ST2732 [S]	Extra Special	1967	$25
STBB-517	Folks Who Live on the Hill/ Broadway Ala Lee	1970	$20
T2469 [M]	Guitars Ala Lee	1966	$40
ST2469 [S]	Guitars Ala Lee	1966	$50
T2390 [M]	Happy Holiday	1965	$50
ST2390 [S]	Happy Holiday	1965	$40
T1630 [M]	If You Go	1962	$50
ST1630 [S]	If You Go	1962	$75
T1131 [M]	I Like Men	1959	$75
ST1131 [S]	I Like Men	1959	$75
T1857 [M]	I'm a Woman	1963	$50
ST1857 [S]	I'm a Woman	1963	$30
SM-1857	I'm a Woman	1977	$12

— Reissue with new prefix

Number	Title	Yr	NM
T1969 [M]	In Love Again	1963	$50
ST1969 [S]	In Love Again	1963	$75
T2096 [M]	In the Name of Love	1964	$40
ST2096 [S]	In the Name of Love	1964	$25

Number	Title	Yr	NM
❏ ST-386	Is That All There Is?	1969	$50
❏ SM-386	Is That All There Is?	197?	$12
— Reissue with new prefix			
❏ T979 [M]	Jump for Joy	1958	$85
— Turquoise or gray label			
❏ T979 [M]	Jump for Joy	1959	$75
— Black label with colorband, Capitol logo at left			
❏ ST979 [S]	Jump for Joy	1959	$75
❏ T1290 [M]	Latin Ala Lee!	1960	$40
— Black label with colorband, Capitol logo at left			
❏ T1290 [M]	Latin Ala Lee!	1962	$50
— Black label with colorband, Capitol logo at top			
❏ ST1290 [S]	Latin Ala Lee!	1960	$75
— Black label with colorband, Capitol logo at left			
❏ ST1290 [S]	Latin Ala Lee!	1962	$40
— Black label with colorband, Capitol logo at top			
❏ SM-1290	Latin Ala Lee!	1977	$12
— Reissue with new prefix			
❏ ST-622	Make It with You	1970	$15
❏ T1850 [M]	Mink Jazz	1963	$40
❏ ST1850 [S]	Mink Jazz	1963	$75
❏ H204 [10]	My Best to You	1952	$175
❏ T204 [M]	My Best to You	1954	$100
— Turquoise or gray label			
❏ T204 [M]	My Best to You	1959	$75
— Black label with colorband, Capitol logo at left			
❏ ST-11077	Norma Deloris Egstrom from Jamestown, North Dakota	1972	$15
❏ T1475 [M]	Ole Ala Lee!	1961	$25
❏ ST1475 [S]	Ole Ala Lee!	1961	$75
❏ T2320 [M]	Pass Me By	1965	$40
❏ ST2320 [S]	Pass Me By	1965	$50
❏ STCL-576	Peggy Lee	1970	$30
❏ DKAO-377	Peggy Lee's Greatest	1969	$15
❏ SN-16140	Peggy Lee Sings Songs of Cy Coleman	198?	$10
❏ T1401 [M]	Pretty Eyes	1960	$50
— Black label with colorband, Capitol logo at left			
❏ T1401 [M]	Pretty Eyes	1962	$40
— Black label with colorband, Capitol logo at top			
❏ ST1401 [S]	Pretty Eyes	1960	$75
— Black label with colorband, Capitol logo at left			
❏ ST1401 [S]	Pretty Eyes	1962	$40
— Black label with colorband, Capitol logo at top			
❏ H151 [10]	Rendezvous with Peggy Lee	1952	$175
❏ T151 [M]	Rendezvous with Peggy Lee	1954	$100
— Turquoise or gray label			
❏ T151 [M]	Rendezvous with Peggy Lee	1959	$75
— Black label with colorband, Capitol logo at left			
❏ ST2781	Somethin' Groovy	1968	$40
❏ T1772 [M]	Sugar 'n' Spice	1962	$50
❏ ST1772 [S]	Sugar 'n' Spice	1962	$75
❏ T2388 [M]	That Was Then, Now Is Now	1965	$40
❏ ST2388 [S]	That Was Then, Now Is Now	1965	$50
❏ ST2887	The Hits of Peggy Lee	1968	$25
❏ T864 [M]	The Man I Love	1957	$100
— Turquoise label			
❏ T864 [M]	The Man I Love	1959	$30
— Black label with colorband, Capitol logo at left			
❏ ST864 [S]	The Man I Love	1959	$75
❏ T1049 [M]	Things Are Swingin'	1958	$75
❏ ST1049 [S]	Things Are Swingin'	1959	$75
❏ ST-105 [B]	Two Shows Nightly	1969	$500

— Withdrawn immediately after release; most of the known copies have the word "FREE" stamped diagonally in the upper right corner of the cover

Number	Title	Yr	NM
❏ ST-810	Where Did They Go	1971	$30
COLUMBIA			
❏ CL6033 [10]	Benny Goodman and Peggy Lee	1949	$75
DECCA			
❏ DL5482 [10]	Black Coffee	1953	$175

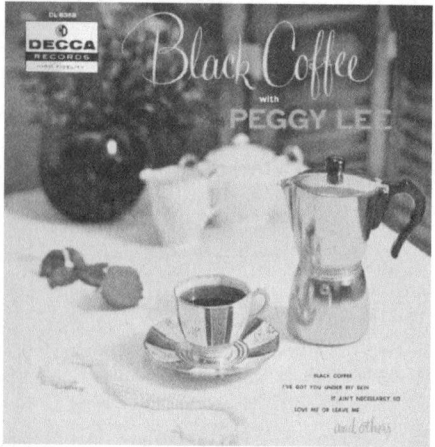

Number	Title	Yr	NM
❏ DL8358 [M]	Black Coffee	1956	$75

Number	Title	Yr	NM
❏ DL8411 [M]	Dream Street	1957	$75
❏ DL4458 [M]	Lover	1964	$30
❏ DL74458 [R]	Lover	1964	$25
❏ DL8816 [M]	Miss Wonderful	1959	$100
❏ DL8591 [M]	Sea Shells	1958	$150
❏ DL5539 [10]	Songs in an Intimate Style	1953	$175
❏ DXB164 [M]	The Best of Peggy Lee	1964	$30
❏ DXSB7164 [R]	The Best of Peggy Lee	1964	$25
❏ DL4461 [M]	The Fabulous Peggy Lee	1964	$30
❏ DL74461 [R]	The Fabulous Peggy Lee	1964	$25
DRG			
❏ SL-5190	Close Enough for Love	1979	$15
EVEREST ARCHIVE OF FOLK & JAZZ			
❏ 294	Peggy Lee	197?	$12
GLENDALE			
❏ 6023	You Can Depend on Me	1982	$25
HARMONY			
❏ H30024	Miss Peggy Lee	1970	$12
❏ HL7005 [M]	Peggy Lee Sings with Benny Goodman	195?	$30
HINDSIGHT			
❏ HSR-220	Peggy Lee with the David Barbour and Billy May Bands, 1948	1985	$12
MCA			
❏ 4049	The Best of Peggy Lee	197?	$15
MERCURY			
❏ SRM-1-1172	Live in London	1977	$15
MUSICMASTERS			
❏ 5005	Peggy Sings the Blues	1988	$15
PAUSA			
❏ PR-9043	Sugar 'n' Spice	1985	$12
PICKWICK			
❏ SPC-3192	I've Got the World	1971	$12
❏ SPC-3090	Once More with Feeling	196?	$12
S&P			
❏ 502	Bewitching-Lee!	2003	$30
— Reissue on 180-gram vinyl			
❏ 504	Latin Ala Lee!	2004	$30
— Reissue on 180-gram vinyl			
TIME-LIFE			
❏ SLGD-07	Legendary Singers: Peggy Lee	1985	$20
VOCALION			
❏ VL73903	Crazy in the Heart	1969	$12
❏ VL3776 [M]	So Blue	1966	$20
❏ VL73776 [R]	So Blue	1966	$12

LEE, PERRY
ROULETTE

Number	Title	Yr	NM
❏ R-52080 [M]	A Night at Count Basie's	1962	$25
❏ SR-52080 [S]	A Night at Count Basie's	1962	$25

LEE, PINKY
DECCA

| ❏ DL8421 [M] | The Surprise Party | 1957 | $40 |

LEE, ROBIN
ATLANTIC AMERICA

| ❏ 90906 | This Old Flame | 1988 | $12 |

DOT

| ❏ DLP-3661 [M] | Robin Lee | 1965 | $30 |

EVERGREEN

| ❏ 1001 | Robin Lee | 1986 | $15 |

LEE, SPANKY AND LEE, JOHNNY
TIGER LILY

| ❏ TL14049DJ [B] | Spanky and Johnny | 1976 | $500 |

LEE, STAN
SAVOY

| ❏ MG-14313 | Humble Yourself | 197? | $15 |

LEE, THOMAS OBOE
GM RECORDINGS

| ❏ GM-3004 | Departed Feathers | 1986 | $25 |

LEEDS, ERIC
PAISLEY PARK

| ❏ 27499 | Times Square | 1991 | $35 |

LEES, GENE, AND ROGER KELLAWAY
CHOICE

| ❏ CRS-6832 | Leaves on the Water | 1986 | $25 |

LEES, GENE
STASH

| ❏ ST-269 | Gene Lees Sings the Gene Lees Songbook | 1987 | $25 |

Number	Title	Yr	NM
LEESE, TIM			
MUSIC IS MEDICINE			
❏ 9036	After Hours	198?	$30
LEFEBVRE, DAVE			
JAZZ HOUNDS			
❏ 01	Marble Dust	198?	$30
LEFEBVRE, GARY			
DISCOVERY			
❏ DS-849	Gary LeFebvre Quartet	1981	$30
LEFEVERE, KAMIEL			
MERCURY LIVING PRESENCE			
❏ SR90189 [S]	The Magic of the Bells	196?	$50
— Maroon label, no "Vendor: Mercury Record Corporation"			
LEFEVRE, RAYMOND			
4 CORNERS OF THE WORLD			
❏ FCS-4250	La La La (He Gives Me Love)	1968	$15
❏ FCL-4239 [M]	Love Me, Please Love Me	1967	$15
❏ FCS-4239 [S]	Love Me, Please Love Me	1967	$15
❏ FCS-4257	Merry Christmas	1968	$15
❏ FCS-4244	Soal Coaxing (Ame Caline)	1968	$15
ATLANTIC			
❏ 8044 [M]	Romantica	1961	$25
❏ SD8044 [S]	Romantica	1961	$30
BUDDAH			
❏ BDS-5109	Oh Happy Day	1972	$12
❏ BDS-5095	Raymond Lefevre	1971	$12
KAPP			
❏ KL-1510 [M]	You Don't Have to Stay	1967	$18
❏ KS-3510 [S]	You Don't Have to Stay	1967	$15
MONUMENT			
❏ MLP-8067 [M]	Paris Cancan	1967	$30
❏ SLP-18067 [S]	Paris Cancan	1967	$15
LEFT BANKE, THE			
RHINO			
❏ RNLP-123	History of the Left Banke	1985	$12
SMASH			
❏ SRS-67113	The Left Banke, Too	1968	$50
❏ MGS-27088 [M]	Walk Away Renee/Pretty Ballerina	1967	$75
❏ SRS-67088 [S]	Walk Away Renee/Pretty Ballerina	1967	$40

THE LEFT BANKE
WALK AWAY RENEE
PRETTY BALLERINA

Number	Title	Yr	NM
❏ SRS-67088 [B]	Walk Away Renee/Pretty Ballerina	198?	$12

— Reissue with thinner vinyl

LEGARDE TWINS, THE			
KOALA			
❏ K10001	Andaleigha Mia	197?	$18
LEGEND			

Probably two different groups.

BELL			
❏ 6027	Legend	1969	$50
MEGAPHONE			
❏ 101	Legend	1970	$100
LEGENDS, THE			
CAPITOL			
❏ T1925 [M]	The Legends Let Loose	1963	$75
❏ ST1925 [S]	The Legends Let Loose	1963	$100
COLUMBIA			
❏ CL1707 [M]	Hit Sounds of Today's Smash Hit Combos	1961	$30
❏ CS8507 [S]	Hit Sounds of Today's Smash Hit Combos	1961	$40

Number	Title	Yr	NM

ERMINE
| ❏ LP-101 [M] | The Legends Let Loose | 1963 | $250 |

LEGGE, WADE
BLUE NOTE
| ❏ BLP-5031 [10] | New Faces New Sounds | 1953 | $600 |

LEGGIO, CARMEN
DREAMSTREET
| ❏ 103 | Aerial View | 1979 | $30 |
FAMOUS DOOR
| ❏ 125 | Tarytown Tenor | 1978 | $30 |
GOLDEN CREST
| ❏ GCS-1000 | Jazz | 196? | $25 |
PROGRESSIVE
| ❏ PRO-7010 | Smile | 1980 | $25 |

LEGRAND, MICHEL
BELL
| ❏ 6071 | Brian's Song Themes & Variations | 1972 | $25 |
| ❏ 4200 | Twenty Songs of the Century | 1974 | $30 |
COLUMBIA
❏ CL888 [M]	Castles in Spain	1956	$75
❏ CL647 [M]	Holiday in Rome	1955	$85
❏ CL555 [M]	I Love Paris	1954	$40
❏ CL1437 [M]	I Love Paris	1960	$75
❏ CS8237 [S]	I Love Paris	1960	$50
❏ PC9237	I Love Paris	1987	$20
— *Reissue with new prefix*
| ❏ CL1139 [M] | Legrand in Rio | 1957 | $75 |
| ❏ CL1250 [M] | Legrand Jazz | 1958 | $40 |
— *Miles Davis appears on this record*
| ❏ CS8079 [S] | Legrand Jazz | 1959 | $40 |
— *Miles Davis appears on this record*
| ❏ CL1115 [M] | Michel Legrand Plays Cole Porter | 1957 | $75 |
| ❏ CL706 [M] | Vienna Holiday | 1955 | $85 |
GRYPHON
| ❏ 786 | Jazz Grand | 1978 | $25 |
HARMONY
❏ KH31549	Cole Porter, Volume I	1972	$25
❏ KH31540	Cole Porter, Volume II	1972	$25
❏ HL7331 [M]	I Love Paris	196?	$30
❏ HS11131 [S]	I Love Paris	196?	$30
MERCURY
| ❏ MG20342 [M] | C'est Magnifique | 1958 | $150 |
MGM
| ❏ SE-4491 | Cinema La Grand | 1967 | $35 |
MOBILE FIDELITY
| ❏ 1-504 | Jazz Grand | 198? | $150 |
— *Audiophile vinyl*
PABLO TODAY
| ❏ 2312139 | After the Rain | 198? | $25 |
PHILIPS
❏ PHM200143 [M]	Michel Legrand Sings	1964	$75
❏ PHS600143 [S]	Michel Legrand Sings	1964	$75
❏ PHM200074 [M]	The Michel Legrand Big Band Plays Richard Rogers	1963	$50
❏ PHS600074 [S]	The Michel Legrand Big Band Plays Richard Rogers	1963	$75
RCA VICTOR
| ❏ BGL1-1028 | Concert | 1976 | $25 |
| ❏ BXL1-1028 | Concert | 1978 | $20 |
— *Reissue with new prefix*
| ❏ BGL1-0850 | Jimmy's | 1975 | $25 |
| ❏ BXL1-0850 | Jimmy's | 1978 | $20 |
— *Reissue with new prefix*
| ❏ BGL1-1392 | Michel Legrand and Friends | 1976 | $25 |
| ❏ BXL1-1392 | Michel Legrand and Friends | 1978 | $20 |
— *Reissue with new prefix*
VERVE
| ❏ V6-8760 | Michel Legrand at Shelly's Mann-Hole | 1969 | $30 |

LEGS DIAMOND
CREAM
| ❏ CR1010 | Fire Power | 1979 | $30 |
MERCURY
| ❏ SRM-1-1191 | A Diamond Is a Hard Rock | 1977 | $30 |
| ❏ SRM-1-1136 | Legs Diamond | 1977 | $30 |

LEHR, ZELLA
COLUMBIA
| ❏ FC37431 | Feedin' the Fire | 1982 | $12 |

LEHRER, TOM
LEHRER
| ❏ TL-202 [M] | An Evening Wasted with Tom Lehrer | 1959 | $30 |
| ❏ TL-202S [S] | An Evening Wasted with Tom Lehrer | 1959 | $40 |

❏ TL-102 [M]	More of Tom Lehrer	1958	$40
❏ TL-102S [S]	More of Tom Lehrer	1959	$40
❏ TLP-1 [10]	Songs by Tom Lehrer	1953	$150
❏ TL-101 [M]	Songs by Tom Lehrer	1959	$40
❏ TL-201 [M]	Tom Lehrer Revisited	1959	$30
REPRISE
| ❏ R6199 [M] | An Evening Wasted with Tom Lehrer | 1966 | $25 |
— *Reissue of Lehrer 202*
| ❏ RS6199 [S] | An Evening Wasted with Tom Lehrer | 1966 | $30 |
— *Reissue of Lehrer 202*
❏ R-6216 [M]	Songs by Tom Lehrer	1966	$25
❏ RS-6216 [S]	Songs by Tom Lehrer	1966	$30
❏ R-6179 [M]	That Was the Year That Was	1965	$25
❏ RS-6179 [S]	That Was the Year That Was	1965	$30
— *Pink, yellow and green label*
| ❏ RS-6179 [S] | That Was the Year That Was | 1968 | $18 |
— *Two-tone orange label with "W7" and "r:" logos*
| ❏ RS-6179 [S] | That Was the Year That Was | 1970 | $12 |
— *Orange/tan label with "r:" logo*

LEIBER, JERRY
KAPP
| ❏ KL-1127 [M] | Scooby-Doo | 1959 | $50 |

LEIBER AND STOLLER BIG BAND, THE
ATLANTIC
| ❏ 8047 [M] | Yakety Yak | 1960 | $75 |
— *White "fan" logo on right side of label*
| ❏ SD8047 [S] | Yakety Yak | 1960 | $75 |
— *White "fan" logo on right side of label*
| ❏ 8047 [M] | Yakety Yak | 1962 | $40 |
— *Black "fan" logo on right side of label*
| ❏ SD8047 [S] | Yakety Yak | 1962 | $40 |
— *Black "fan" logo on right side of label*

LEIBERT, DICK
RCA CAMDEN
| ❏ ADL2-0243 | Christmas at Radio City Music Hall | 1973 | $18 |
RCA VICTOR
| ❏ LPM-2558 [M] | The Sound of Christmas on the Radio City Music Hall Organ | 1962 | $15 |
| ❏ LSP-2558 [S] | The Sound of Christmas on the Radio City Music Hall Organ | 1962 | $18 |
WESTMINSTER
❏ WST15020 [S]	A Merry Wurlitzer Christmas	195?	$25
❏ WST15034 [S]	Leibert Takes a Holiday	195?	$25
❏ WST15006 [S]	Leibert Takes Broadway	195?	$25
❏ WST15009 [S]	Leibert Takes Richmond	195?	$25
❏ WST15043 [S]	Leibert Takes You Dancing	195?	$25
❏ WST15050 [S]	Sing a Song with Leibert	195?	$25

LEIGH, CAROL
GHB
❏ 152	Blame It on the Blues	198?	$30
❏ 167	Go Back Where You Stayed Last Night	198?	$30
❏ GHB-88	Wild Women Don't Have the Blues	197?	$30
❏ 136	You've Got to Give Me Some	1980	$30
STOMP OFF
| ❏ SOS-1064 | If You Don't Know, I Know Who Will | 1983 | $25 |
| ❏ SOS-1087 | I'm Busy and You Can't Come In | 1985 | $25 |

LEIGH, RICHARD
UNITED ARTISTS
| ❏ LT-1036 | Richard Leigh | 1980 | $12 |

LEIGHTON, BERNIE
CAMEO
| ❏ C-1005 [M] | Dizzy Fingers | 1959 | $75 |
COLUMBIA
| ❏ CL6112 [10] | East Side Rendezvous | 1950 | $100 |
MONMOUTH-EVERGREEN
| ❏ 7068 | Bernie Leighton Plays Duke Ellington Live at Jimmy Weston's | 197? | $30 |

LEIGHTON, BERNIE/JOHNNY GUARNIERI
EMARCY
| ❏ MG-26018 [10] | Piano Stylings | 1954 | $300 |

LEITCH, PETER
PAUSA
| ❏ 7132 | Jump Street | 1981 | $25 |

LELLIS, TOM
INNER CITY
| ❏ IC-1090 | And In This Corner | 198? | $35 |

LEMER, PETER
ESP-DISK'
| ❏ 1057 | Local Colour | 1968 | $250 |

LEMMON, JACK
CAPITOL
| ❏ T1943 [M] | Jack Lemmon Plays Piano Selections from Irma La Douce | 1963 | $30 |
| ❏ ST1943 [S] | Jack Lemmon Plays Piano Selections from Irma La Douce | 1963 | $35 |
EPIC
❏ LN3491 [M]	A Twist of Lemmon	1959	$30
❏ BN523 [S]	A Twist of Lemmon	1959	$30
❏ LN3559 [M]	Jack Lemmon Sings and Plays Music from Some Like It Hot	1959	$30
❏ BN528 [S]	Jack Lemmon Sings and Plays Music from Some Like It Hot	1959	$30

LEMON PIPERS, THE
BUDDAH
❏ BDS-5009 [S]	Green Tambourine	1968	$30
❏ BDM-1009 [M]	Green Tambourine	1968	$30
❏ BDS-5016 [S]	Jungle Marmalade	1968	$30
❏ BDM-1016 [M]	Jungle Marmalade	1968	$40
— *Mono is promo only; in stereo cover with "Mono" sticker*

LEMONGELLO, PETER
PRIVATE STOCK
| ❏ PS-2018 | Do I Love You | 1976 | $25 |
RAPP
| ❏ LR8899 | Love '76 | 1976 | $30 |

LEMONHEADS, THE
Featuring Evan Dando.
ATLANTIC
| ❏ SAM1267 [DJ] | Come On Feel the Lemonheads | 1993 | $30 |
— *Promo-only four-song sampler*
| ❏ 82537 | Come On Feel the Lemonheads | 1993 | $30 |
— *5,000 copies pressed, all on green vinyl; imports sell for less*
| ❏ 82137 | Lovey | 1990 | $25 |
— *U.S. edition; imports with a similar number go for less*
TAANG!
| ❏ 23 | Creator | 1988 | $18 |
| ❏ 15 | Hate Your Friends | 1987 | $40 |
— *The first 3,000 were on black vinyl, yellow lettering on sleeve, yellow label*
| ❏ 15 | Hate Your Friends | 1987 | $30 |
— *The second 2,000 are on black vinyl, red lettering on sleeve, yellow label*
| ❏ 15 | Hate Your Friends | 1987 | $30 |
— *Third pressing: Black vinyl, red lettering on sleeve, red label*
| ❏ 15 | Hate Your Friends | 1987 | $30 |
— *Fourth pressing: Black vinyl, red lettering on sleeve, blue and green label*
| ❏ 15 | Hate Your Friends | 1987 | $25 |
— *Fifth pressing: Yellow vinyl, yellow lettering on sleeve, yellow label*
| ❏ 15 | Hate Your Friends | 1987 | $15 |
— *Any edition not listed among the first five pressings above*
| ❏ 32 | Lick | 1989 | $18 |
TAG/ATLANTIC
| ❏ 92726 | Car Button Cloth | 1996 | $25 |
TPM/RHINO EXCLUSIVE
| ❏ 138 | It's a Shame About Ray | 2008 | $18 |

LENNON, JOHN
Includes records as "Plastic Ono Band," "John Ono Lennon," "John Lennon/Plastic Ono Band" and other records he made with Yoko Ono. Also see THE BEATLES.
ADAM VIII
| ❏ A-8018 | John Lennon Sings the Great Rock & Roll Hits (Roots) | 1975 | $1000 |
— *Counterfeits abound. On authentic copies, cover is posterboard (not slicks); labels are normal size (not overly large); printing on cover is sharp, not blurry; the word "Greatest" does NOT appear on the spine. Authentic copies usually have ad sleeve also.*
APPLE
| ❏ SW-3379 [B] | Imagine | 1971 | $40 |
— *With either of two postcard inserts, lyric sleeve, poster*
| ❏ SW-3379 | Imagine | 1975 | $25 |
— *"All Rights Reserved" label*
| ❏ SW-3372 | John Lennon Plastic Ono Band | 1970 | $40 |
| ❏ SW-3362 | Live Peace in Toronto 1969 | 1970 | $25 |
— *By "The Plastic Ono Band" -- without calendar*
| ❏ SW-3362 [B] | Live Peace in Toronto 1969 | 1970 | $40 |
— *By "The Plastic Ono Band"; with calendar*

Number	Title	Yr	NM
❏ SW-3414	Mind Games	1973	$25
❏ SK-3419	Rock 'N' Roll	1975	$30
❏ SW-3421	Shaved Fish	1975	$30
❏ SVBB-3392 [B]	Some Time in New York City	1972	$40

—By John and Yoko; with photo card and petition

| ❏ SVBB-3392 [DJ] | Some Time in New York City | 1972 | $1000 |

—White label promo

| ❏ T-5001 | Two Virgins -- Unfinished Music No. 1 | 1968 | $50 |

—With Yoko Ono; without brown bag

| ❏ T-5001 | Two Virgins -- Unfinished Music No. 1 | 1968 | $175 |

—With Yoko Ono; price with brown bag

| ❏ T-5001 | Two Virgins -- Unfinished Music No. 1 | 1968 | $175 |

—With Yoko Ono; with die-cut bag

| ❏ T-5001 | Two Virgins -- Unfinished Music No. 1 | 1985 | $20 |

—With Yoko Ono; reissue, flat label

| ❏ SW-3416 [B] | Walls and Bridges | 1974 | $50 |

—With fold-open segmented front cover

| ❏ SMAX-3361 | Wedding Album | 1969 | $175 |

—With photo strip, postcard, poster of wedding photos, poster of lithographs, "Bagism" bag, booklet, photo of slice of wedding cake. Missing inserts reduce the value.

CAPITOL

| ❏ C1-91425 | Double Fantasy | 1989 | $25 |

—Very briefly available reissue

| ❏ C1-591425 | Double Fantasy | 1989 | $75 |

—Columbia House edition of reissue

| ❏ SW-3379 | Imagine | 1978 | $12 |

—Purple label, large Capitol logo

| ❏ SW-3379 | Imagine | 1986 | $30 |

—Black label, print in colorband

| ❏ SW-3379 | Imagine | 1987 | $30 |

—Black label, print in colorband; "Digitally Re-Mastered" at top of front cover

| ❏ SW-3379 | Imagine | 1988 | $30 |

—Purple label, small Capitol logo

| ❏ C1-90803 | Imagine: Music from the Motion Picture | 1988 | $25 |
| ❏ SW-3372 | John Lennon Plastic Ono Band | 1978 | $15 |

—Purple label, large Capitol logo

| ❏ SW-3372 | John Lennon Plastic Ono Band | 1982 | $25 |

—Black label, print in colorband

| ❏ SW-3372 | John Lennon Plastic Ono Band | 1988 | $30 |

—Purple label, small Capitol logo

| ❏ SV-12451 | Live in New York City | 1986 | $20 |
| ❏ SV-512451 | Live in New York City | 1986 | $20 |

—Columbia House edition

| ❏ R144497 | Live in New York City | 1986 | $20 |

—RCA Music Service edition

| ❏ ST-12239 | Live Peace in Toronto 1969 | 1983 | $50 |

—By "The Plastic Ono Band"; reissue, black Capitol label

| ❏ ST-12239 | Live Peace in Toronto 1969 | 1982 | $15 |

—By "The Plastic Ono Band"; reissue, purple Capitol label

| ❏ SJ-12533 | Menlove Ave. | 1986 | $20 |
| ❏ R144136 | Menlove Ave. | 1986 | $50 |

—RCA Music Service edition

| ❏ R144136 | Menlove Ave. | 198? | $50 |

—BMG Direct Marketing edition

| ❏ SW-3414 | Mind Games | 1978 | $40 |

—Purple label, large Capitol logo

| ❏ SN-16068 | Mind Games | 1980 | $15 |

—Budget-line reissue

| ❏ SN-16069 | Rock 'N' Roll | 1980 | $15 |

—Budget-line reissue

| ❏ SK-3419 | Rock 'N' Roll | 1978 | $40 |

—Purple label, large Capitol logo

| ❏ SW-3421 | Shaved Fish | 1978 | $15 |

—Purple Capitol label with Apple logo on cover

| ❏ SW-3421 | Shaved Fish | 1978 | $40 |

—Purple Capitol label with Capitol logo on cover

| ❏ SW-3421 | Shaved Fish | 1983 | $25 |

—Black Capitol label with Apple logo on cover

| ❏ SW-3421 | Shaved Fish | 1983 | $40 |

—Black Capitol label with Capitol logo on cover

| ❏ SW-3421 | Shaved Fish | 1989 | $40 |

—Purple Capitol label (small logo) with Capitol logo on cover

| ❏ SVBB-3392 | Some Time in New York City | 197? | $30 |

—By John and Yoko; purple label, large Capitol logo

| ❏ SVBB-3392 | Some Time in New York City | 197? | $150 |

—Both discs in single-pocket gatefold (the other pocket is glued shut)

| ❏ SW-3416 | Walls and Bridges | 1978 | $20 |

—Purple label, large Capitol logo; standard front cover

| ❏ SW-3416 | Walls and Bridges | 1982 | $30 |

—Black label, print in colorband

| ❏ SW-3416 | Walls and Bridges | 1989 | $30 |

—Purple label, small Capitol logo

GEFFEN

| ❏ GHS2001 | Double Fantasy | 1986 | $50 |

—Same as above, but with black Geffen label

Number	Title	Yr	NM
❏ GHS2001	Double Fantasy	1981	$85

—Columbia House edition (all have corrected back cover) with "CH" on label

| ❏ GHS2001 | Double Fantasy | 1980 | $35 |

—Seven tracks by John, seven by Yoko; off-white label; titles on back cover out of order

| ❏ GHS2001 | Double Fantasy | 1981 | $25 |

—Off-white label, titles in order on the back cover

| ❏ GHS2001 | Double Fantasy | 1981 | $15 |

—Columbia House edition (all have corrected back cover) without "CH" on label

| ❏ R104689 | Double Fantasy | 1981 | $40 |

—RCA Music Service edition

| ❏ GHSP2023 [DJ] | The John Lennon Collection | 1982 | $50 |

—Promo only on Quiex II audiophile vinyl

| ❏ GHSP2023 | The John Lennon Collection | 1982 | $25 |
| ❏ GHSP2023 [DJ] | The John Lennon Collection | 1982 | $50 |

—Promo only on Quiex II audiophile vinyl

MOBILE FIDELITY

| ❏ MFSL 1-277 | Imagine | 2004 | $50 |

—Original Master Recording" at top of front cover

| ❏ 1-153 [B] | Imagine | 1984 | $500 |

—Audiophile vinyl

| ❏ MFSL 1-280 | John Lennon Plastic Ono Band | 2004 | $75 |

—Original Master Recording" at top of front cover

NAUTILUS

| ❏ NR-47 | Double Fantasy | 1982 | $100 |

—Half-speed master

| ❏ NR-47 | Double Fantasy | 1982 | $2000 |

—Half-speed master; alternate experimental cover with yellow and red added to black and white front

PARLOPHONE

| ❏ 21954 | Lennon Legend | 1998 | $25 |

—Made in U.S.A." on back cover

POLYDOR

| ❏ 817238-1 | Heart Play (Unfinished Dialogue) | 1983 | $25 |

—Interviews with John Lennon and Yoko Ono

| ❏ 817160-1 | Milk and Honey | 1983 | $12 |

—Six tracks by John, six by Yoko

| ❏ 817160-1 | Milk and Honey | 1984 | $175 |

—Yellow or green vinyl; unauthorized "inside jobs"

SILHOUETTE

| ❏ SM-10012 | Reflections and Poetry | 1984 | $30 |

ZAPPLE

| ❏ ST-3357 | Life with the Lions -- Unfinished Music No. 2 | 1969 | $300 |

—With Yoko Ono

LENNON, JULIAN

ATLANTIC

| ❏ 81928 | Mr. Jordan | 1989 | $12 |
| ❏ PR2693 [DJ] | Mr. Jordan According to Mr. Lennon | 1989 | $18 |

—Promo-only interview album

| ❏ 81640 [B] | The Secret Value of Daydreaming | 1986 | $12 |
| ❏ 81084 [B] | Valotte | 1984 | $12 |

LENNON SISTERS, THE

BRUNSWICK

| ❏ BL54039 [M] | Lawrence Welk Presents the Lennon Sisters | 1958 | $30 |
| ❏ BL54031 [M] | Let's Get Acquainted | 1957 | $30 |

DOT

❏ DLP-3250 [M]	Best-Loved Catholic Hymns	1959	$18
❏ DLP-25250 [S]	Best-Loved Catholic Hymns	1959	$25
❏ DLP-3417 [M]	Can't Help Falling in Love	1962	$15
❏ DLP-25417 [S]	Can't Help Falling in Love	1962	$18

Number	Title	Yr	NM
❏ DLP3343 [M]	Christmas with the Lennon Sisters	1961	$18
❏ DLP25343 [S]	Christmas with the Lennon Sisters	1961	$25
❏ DLP-3557 [M]	Dominique and Other Great Folk Songs	1964	$15
❏ DLP-25557 [S]	Dominique and Other Great Folk Songs	1964	$18
❏ DLP-3589 [M]	No. 1 Hits of the 1960s	1964	$15
❏ DLP-25589 [S]	No. 1 Hits of the 1960s	1964	$18
❏ DLP-3398 [M]	Sad Movies (Make Me Cry)	1961	$18
❏ DLP-25398 [S]	Sad Movies (Make Me Cry)	1961	$25
❏ DLP-3659 [M]	Solos	1965	$15
❏ DLP-25659 [S]	Solos	1965	$18
❏ DLP-3797 [M]	Somethin' Stupid	1967	$18
❏ DLP-25797 [S]	Somethin' Stupid	1967	$15
❏ DLP-3481 [M]	The Lennon Sisters' Favorites	1963	$15
❏ DLP-25481 [S]	The Lennon Sisters' Favorites	1963	$18
❏ DLP-3292 [M]	The Lennon Sisters Sing 12 Great Hits	1960	$18
❏ DLP-25292 [S]	The Lennon Sisters Sing 12 Great Hits	1960	$25
❏ DLP-3622 [M]	Twelve Great Hits, Volume 2	1965	$15
❏ DLP-25622 [S]	Twelve Great Hits, Volume 2	1965	$18

HAMILTON

| ❏ HLP-119 [M] | Melody of Love | 196? | $15 |
| ❏ HLP-12119 [S] | Melody of Love | 196? | $15 |

MERCURY

| ❏ SR-61201 | Pop Country | 1969 | $15 |
| ❏ SR-61164 | The Lennon Sisters Today!! | 1968 | $15 |

PICKWICK

❏ PTP-2014	America's Sweethearts	1973	$15
❏ SPC-3110	Goodnight Sweetheart	197?	$12
❏ SPC-3084	Our Favorite Songs	196?	$12

RANWOOD

❏ 7027	22 Songs of Faith and Inspiration	198?	$12
❏ 8205	Best of the Lennon Sisters	198?	$10
❏ 8212	How Great Thou Art	198?	$10

VOCALION

| ❏ VL73887 | The Lennon Sisters with Lawrence Welk | 1970 | $12 |
| ❏ VL73864 | Too Marvelous for Words | 1969 | $12 |

LENOIR, J.B.

CHESS

| ❏ CH-9323 | Natural Man | 1990 | $15 |
| ❏ LP-410 | Natural Man | 1970 | $40 |

POLYDOR

| ❏ 24-4011 | J.B. Lenoir | 1970 | $18 |

LENYA, LOTTE

COLUMBIA MASTERWORKS

| ❏ ML5056 [M] | Berlin Theater Songs by Kurt Weill | 1957 | $30 |
| ❏ KL5229 [M] | September Song | 1958 | $30 |

LEONARD, HARLAN

RCA VICTOR

| ❏ LPV-531 [M] | Harlan Leonard and His Rockets | 1965 | $30 |

LEONARD, HARVEY

KEYNOTE

| ❏ 1102 [M] | Jazz Ecstasy | 1955 | $75 |

LEONARD, JACK E.

VIK

| ❏ LX-1080 [M] | Rock 'n Roll for People Over Sixteen | 1957 | $50 |

LEONHART, JAY

SUNNYSIDE

| ❏ SSC-1032 | The Double Cross | 1989 | $30 |
| ❏ SSC-1006 | There's Gonna Be Trouble | 1985 | $25 |

LEOPARDS, THE

MOON

| ❏ 0(# unknown) | Kansas City Slickers | 1977 | $30 |

LES DJINNS SINGERS

ABC-PARAMOUNT

| ❏ ABC-397 [M] | Joyeaux Noel | 1961 | $18 |
| ❏ ABCS-397 [S] | Joyeaux Noel | 1961 | $25 |

LES JAZZ MODES

ATLANTIC

| ❏ 1306 [M] | Les Jazz Modes | 1959 | $300 |

—Black label

| ❏ 1306 [M] | Les Jazz Modes | 1961 | $175 |

—Multicolor label, white "fan" logo at right

| ❏ SD-1306 [S] | Les Jazz Modes | 1959 | $300 |

—Green label

| ❏ SD-1306 [S] | Les Jazz Modes | 1961 | $175 |

—Multicolor label, white "fan" logo at right

| ❏ 1280 [M] | The Most Happy Fella | 1958 | $300 |

Number	Title	Yr	NM

—Black label
- ❑ 1280 [M] — The Most Happy Fella — 1961 — $175

—Multicolor label, white "fan" logo at right

DAWN
- ❑ DLP-1101 [M] — Jazzville — 1956 — $150
- ❑ DLP-1108 [M] — Les Jazz Modes — 1956 — $150
- ❑ DLP-1117 [M] — Mood in Scarlet — 1957 — $150

SEECO
- ❑ CELP-466 [M] — Smart Jazz for the Smart Set — 1960 — $150

LESBERG, JACK

FAMOUS DOOR
- ❑ 120 — Hollywood — 1977 — $30

LESLIE, BILL

ARGO
- ❑ LP-710 [M] — Diggin' the Chicks — 1962 — $30
- ❑ LPS-710 [S] — Diggin' the Chicks — 1962 — $30

LESMANA, INDRA

ZEBRA
- ❑ ZEB-5709 — For Earth and Heaven — 1986 — $25
- ❑ ZR-5005 — Indra Lesmana and Nebula — 1984 — $30

LESTER, KETTY

AVI
- ❑ 6116 — A Collection of Her Best — 1982 — $18

ERA
- ❑ EL-108 [M] — Love Letters — 1962 — $40
- ❑ ES-108 [S] — Love Letters — 1962 — $75

PETE
- ❑ 1109 — Ketty Lester — 1969 — $18

RCA VICTOR
- ❑ LPM-2945 [M] — The Soul of Me — 1964 — $30
- ❑ LSP-2945 [S] — The Soul of Me — 1964 — $30
- ❑ LPM-3326 [M] — Where Is Love — 1965 — $30
- ❑ LSP-3326 [S] — Where Is Love — 1965 — $30

SHEFFIELD
- ❑ 15 — Ketty Lester In Concert — 1977 — $18

TOWER

- ❑ T5029 [M] — When a Woman Loves a Man — 1966 — $30
- ❑ ST5029 [S] — When a Woman Loves a Man — 1966 — $30

LETMAN, JOHN

BETHLEHEM
- ❑ BCP-6053 [M] — The Many Angles of John Letman — 1961 — $250
- ❑ SBCP-6053 [S] — The Many Angles of John Letman — 1961 — $250

LET'S ACTIVE

I.R.S.
- ❑ SP-70505 [EP] — Afoot — 1983 — $15
- ❑ 5703 — Big Plans for Everybody — 1986 — $10
- ❑ SP-70648 — Cypress — 1984 — $12

LETTERMEN, THE

APPLAUSE
- ❑ 1006 — Love Is... — 198? — $12

CAPITOL
- ❑ SPRO-4798/9 [DJ] — A Collection of Their Finest Songs — 1969 — $30

—Promo-only collection of excerpts of 20 songs
- ❑ T2013 [M] — A Lettermen Kind of Love — 1964 — $15
- ❑ ST2013 [S] — A Lettermen Kind of Love — 1964 — $18
- ❑ SW-11183 — Alive" Again ... Naturally — 1973 — $12
- ❑ SW-11249 — All-Time Greatest Hits — 1973 — $12
- ❑ SN-16312 — All-Time Greatest Hits — 198? — $10

—Budget-line reissue
- ❑ SN-16191 — And I Love Her — 1981 — $10

—Budget-line reissue
- ❑ T2496 [M] — A New Song for Young Love — 1966 — $15
- ❑ ST2496 [S] — A New Song for Young Love — 1966 — $18
- ❑ T1669 [M] — A Song for Young Love — 1962 — $18
- ❑ ST1669 [S] — A Song for Young Love — 1962 — $25
- ❑ SWBB-251 — Close-Up — 1969 — $18

—Reissue of ST 2013 and ST 2083 in one package
- ❑ T1829 [M] — College Standards — 1963 — $18
- ❑ ST1829 [S] — College Standards — 1963 — $25
- ❑ ST-634 — Everything's Good About You — 1971 — $15
- ❑ SW-781 — Feelings — 1971 — $15
- ❑ T2587 [M] — For Christmas This Year — 1966 — $15
- ❑ ST2587 [S] — For Christmas This Year — 1966 — $18
- ❑ ST-8-2587 [S] — For Christmas This Year — 1966 — $25

—Capitol Record Club edition
- ❑ ST2865 — Goin' Out of My Head — 1968 — $18
- ❑ SM-11970 — Goin' Out of My Head — 1979 — $10

—Reissue of 2865
- ❑ ST-269 — Hurt So Bad — 1969 — $15
- ❑ SM-11678 — Hurt So Bad — 1977 — $10

—Reissue of 269
- ❑ ST 8-0269 — Hurt So Bad — 1969 — $18

—Capitol Record Club edition
- ❑ ST-202 — I Have Dreamed — 1969 — $15
- ❑ T1761 [M] — Jim, Tony and Bob — 1962 — $18
- ❑ ST1761 [S] — Jim, Tony and Bob — 1962 — $25
- ❑ SW-11508 — Kind of Country — 1976 — $12
- ❑ SN-16190 — Let It Be Me — 1981 — $10

—Budget-line reissue
- ❑ STBB-710 — Let It Be Me/And I Love Her — 1971 — $18
- ❑ SW-11010 — Lettermen 1 — 1972 — $12
- ❑ ST-836 — Love Book — 1971 — $15
- ❑ SW-11424 — Make Time — 1975 — $12
- ❑ T2428 [M] — More Hit Sounds of the Lettermen! — 1966 — $15
- ❑ ST2428 [S] — More Hit Sounds of the Lettermen! — 1966 — $18
- ❑ SW-11319 — Now and Forever — 1974 — $12
- ❑ T1711 [M] — Once Upon a Time — 1962 — $18
- ❑ ST1711 [S] — Once Upon a Time — 1962 — $25
- ❑ T2270 [M] — Portrait of My Love — 1965 — $15
- ❑ ST2270 [S] — Portrait of My Love — 1965 — $18
- ❑ ST-147 — Put Your Head on My Shoulder — 1968 — $18
- ❑ SM-147 — Put Your Head on My Shoulder — 1977 — $10

—Reissue with new prefix
- ❑ ST-496 — Reflections — 1970 — $15
- ❑ ST 8-0496 — Reflections — 1970 — $18

—Capitol Record Club edition
- ❑ T2142 [M] — She Cried — 1964 — $15
- ❑ ST2142 [S] — She Cried — 1964 — $18
- ❑ ST2934 — Special Request — 1968 — $18
- ❑ SW-11124 — Spin Away — 1972 — $12
- ❑ T2711 [M] — Spring! — 1967 — $18
- ❑ ST2711 [S] — Spring! — 1967 — $18
- ❑ SM-2711 — Spring! — 1977 — $10

—Reissue with new prefix
- ❑ T2554 [M] — The Best of the Lettermen — 1966 — $15
- ❑ ST2554 [S] — The Best of the Lettermen — 1966 — $18
- ❑ SN-16071 — The Best of the Lettermen — 1980 — $10

—Budget-line reissue
- ❑ SKAO-138 — The Best of the Lettermen, Vol. 2 — 1969 — $15
- ❑ SN-16222 — The Best of the Lettermen, Vol. 2 — 198? — $10

—Budget-line reissue
- ❑ T2359 [M] — The Hit Sounds of the Lettermen — 1965 — $15
- ❑ ST2359 [S] — The Hit Sounds of the Lettermen — 1965 — $18
- ❑ STCL-577 — The Lettermen — 1970 — $30
- ❑ T2758 [M] — The Lettermen!!!... And "Live! — 1967 — $25
- ❑ ST2758 [S] — The Lettermen!!!... And "Live! — 1967 — $18
- ❑ SM-11814 — The Lettermen!!! ... And "Live! — 1978 — $10

—Reissue of 2758
- ❑ T1936 [M] — The Lettermen In Concert — 1963 — $18
- ❑ ST1936 [S] — The Lettermen In Concert — 1963 — $25
- ❑ T2083 [M] — The Lettermen Look at Love — 1964 — $15
- ❑ ST2083 [S] — The Lettermen Look at Love — 1964 — $18
- ❑ SW-11364 — There Is No Greater Love — 1974 — $12
- ❑ SW-11470 — The Time Is Right — 1975 — $12
- ❑ ST-390 — Traces/Memories — 1970 — $15
- ❑ T2633 [M] — Warm — 1967 — $18
- ❑ ST2633 [S] — Warm — 1967 — $18
- ❑ T2213 [M] — You'll Never Walk Alone — 1965 — $15
- ❑ ST2213 [S] — You'll Never Walk Alone — 1965 — $18

LONGINES SYMPHONETTE
- ❑ 220 — A Time for Us — 1972 — $30

PICKWICK
- ❑ SPC-3294 — Soft Hits — 1972 — $12
- ❑ SPC-3565 — With Love — 1978 — $10

LEVEL 42

A&M
- ❑ SP-4995 — Standing in the Light — 1984 — $15

POLYDOR
- ❑ 821935-1 — Level 42 — 1986 — $15

—First U.S. issue of early U.K. LP
- ❑ 841399-1 — Level Best — 1989 — $12
- ❑ R16226 — Running in the Family — 1987 — $14

—BMG Direct Marketing edition
- ❑ 831593-1 — Running in the Family — 1987 — $15
- ❑ 813865-1 — Standing in the Light — 1986 — $10

—Reissue
- ❑ 837247-1 — Staring at the Sun — 1988 — $12
- ❑ PD1-6359 — The Pursuit of Accidents — 1982 — $16
- ❑ 810015-1 — The Pursuit of Accidents — 1986 — $10

—Reissue
- ❑ 823542-1 — True Colours — 1986 — $15
- ❑ 827487-1 — World Machine — 1986 — $15

LEVERT

ATLANTIC
- ❑ 81669 — Bloodline — 1986 — $10
- ❑ 82462 — For Real Tho' — 1993 — $18
- ❑ 81926 — Just Coolin' — 1988 — $10
- ❑ 82164 — Rope a Dope Style — 1990 — $15
- ❑ 81773 — The Big Throwdown — 1987 — $10

TEMPRE
- ❑ TL1234 — I Get Hot — 1985 — $18

LEVEY, STAN

BETHLEHEM
- ❑ BCP-71 [M] — Grand Stan — 1957 — $300
- ❑ BCP-1017 [10] — Stan Levey Plays — 1954 — $300
- ❑ BCP-6030 [M] — Stanley the Steamer — 197? — $35

—Reissue of 37, distributed by RCA Victor
- ❑ BCP-37 [M] — This Time the Dream's On Me — 1956 — $300

MODE
- ❑ LP-101 [M] — Stan Levey Quartet — 1957 — $100

LEVIATHAN

MACH
- ❑ XMA-12501 [B] — Leviathan — 1974 — $40

LEVIEV, MILCHO

DOBRE
- ❑ 1025 — Piano Lesson — 197? — $30

OPTIMISM
- ❑ OP-2004 — Destination — 198? — $25

TREND
- ❑ 530 — Music for Big Band and Symphony Orchestra — 1982 — $25

LEVIN, MARC

SAVOY
- ❑ MG-12190 [M] — The Dragon Suite — 1967 — $30

SWEET DRAGON
- ❑ 1 — Songs, Dances and Prayers — 197? — $25

LEVIN, PETE

GRAMAVISION
- ❑ R1-79456 — Party in the Basement — 1990 — $35

LEVINE, HENRY

RCA CAMDEN
- ❑ CAL-321 [M] — Lower Basin Street — 1958 — $30

RCA VICTOR
- ❑ LPM-1283 [M] — Dixieland Jazz Band — 1956 — $50

LEVINE, MARK

CATALYST
- ❑ 7614 — Up 'Til Now — 1976 — $30

CONCORD JAZZ
- ❑ CJ-234 — Concepts — 1984 — $25
- ❑ CJ-352 — Smiley and Me — 1988 — $25

LEVINSON, MARK

MARK LEVINSON
- ❑ 7 — Jazz at Long Wharf — 1979 — $75

—Audiophile edition pressed at 45 rpm

LEVISTER, ALONZO

DEBUT
- ❑ DEB-125 [M] — Manhattan Moondrama — 1956 — $300

LEVITT, ROD

RCA VICTOR
- ❑ LPM-3615 [M] — 42nd Street — 1966 — $35
- ❑ LSP-3615 [S] — 42nd Street — 1966 — $25
- ❑ LPM-3372 [M] — Insight — 1965 — $35
- ❑ LSP-3372 [S] — Insight — 1965 — $25
- ❑ LPM-3448 [M] — Solid Ground — 1965 — $35
- ❑ LSP-3448 [S] — Solid Ground — 1965 — $25

Number	Title	Yr	NM
RIVERSIDE			
❑ RLP-471 [M]	The Dynamic Sound Patterns of the Rod Levitt Orchestra	1964	$175
❑ RS-9471 [S]	The Dynamic Sound Patterns of the Rod Levitt Orchestra	1964	$175

LEVITTS, THE
Number	Title	Yr	NM
ESP-DISK'			
❑ S-1095	We Are the Levitts	1970	$250

LEVY, LOU
Number	Title	Yr	NM
DOBRE			
❑ 1042	A Touch of Class	1978	$30
INTERPLAY			
❑ 7711	Tempus Fugue It	197?	$25
JUBILEE			
❑ JLP-1101 [M]	Lou Levy Plays Baby Grand Jazz	1959	$40
❑ SDJLP-1101 [S]	Lou Levy Plays Baby Grand Jazz	1959	$40
NOCTURNE			
❑ NLP-10 [10]	Lou Levy Trio	1954	$150
PHILIPS			
❑ PHM200056 [M]	The Hymn	1962	$35
❑ PHS600056 [S]	The Hymn	1962	$25
RCA VICTOR			
❑ LPM-1491 [M]	A Most Musical Fella	1957	$50
❑ LPM-1319 [M]	Jazz in Four Colors	1956	$50
❑ LPM-1267 [M]	Solo Scene	1956	$50

LEVY, LOU/CONTE CANDOLI
Number	Title	Yr	NM
ATLANTIC			
❑ 1268 [M]	West Coast Wailers	1957	$300
—Black label			
❑ 1268 [M]	West Coast Wailers	1961	$175
—Multicolor label, white "fan" logo at right			

LEVY, O'DONEL
Number	Title	Yr	NM
GROOVE MERCHANT			
❑ 501	Black Velvet	1971	$30
❑ 507	Breeding of Mind	1972	$30
❑ 518	Dawn of a New Day	1973	$30
❑ 535	Everything I Do Gonna Be Funky	1975	$30
❑ 4408	Hands of Fire	197?	$30
❑ 526	Simba	1974	$30
❑ 3313	Windows	197?	$50

LEWD
Number	Title	Yr	NM
ICI			
❑ CF200	American Wino	1982	$40

LEWES, WILSON
Number	Title	Yr	NM
DIPLOMAT			
❑ D-2369 [M]	The "In" Crowd	1965	$25
❑ DS-2369 [S]	The "In" Crowd	1965	$30
❑ D-2378 [M]	The Shadow of Your Smile	1966	$25
❑ DS-2378 [S]	The Shadow of Your Smile	1966	$30

LEWIS, BARBARA
Number	Title	Yr	NM
ATLANTIC			
❑ 8110 [M]	Baby, I'm Yours	1965	$40
❑ SD8110 [S]	Baby, I'm Yours	1965	$50
❑ 8086 [M]	Hello Stranger	1963	$40
❑ SD8086 [S]	Hello Stranger	1963	$50
❑ 8118 [M]	It's Magic	1966	$30
❑ SD8118 [S]	It's Magic	1966	$40
❑ 8090 [M]	Snap Your Fingers	1964	$40
❑ SD8090 [S]	Snap Your Fingers	1964	$50
❑ SD8286 [S]	The Best of Barbara Lewis	1971	$25
❑ 8286 [M]	The Best of Barbara Lewis	1971	$40
—Mono is white label promo only; front cover has "d/j copy monaural" sticker			
❑ SD8173	Workin' on a Groovy Thing	1968	$30
COLLECTABLES			
❑ COL-5104	Golden Classics	198?	$12
ENTERPRISE			
❑ ENS-1006	The Many Grooves of Barbara Lewis	1970	$30

LEWIS, BOBBY (1)
R&B singer; not to be confused with the country singer of the same name, who recorded for Ace of Hearts, Capricorn, GRT, HME, RPA and United Artists.

Number	Title	Yr	NM
BELTONE			
❑ 4000 [M]	Tossin' and Turnin'	1961	$250

LEWIS, BOBBY (2)
Country singer. Not to be confused with the R&B singer Bobby Lewis, who had a big pop hit in 1961 with "Tossin' and Turnin'."

Number	Title	Yr	NM
ACE OF HEARTS			
❑ 1002	Too Many Memories	1974	$18

Number	Title	Yr	NM
RPA			
❑ 1002	Portrait in Love	1976	$12
❑ 1013	Soul Full of Music	1977	$12
UNITED ARTISTS			
❑ UAS-6629	An Ordinary Miracle	1968	$25
❑ UAS-6616	A World of Love from Bobby Lewis	1967	$25
❑ UAS-6673	From Heaven to Heartache	1968	$25
❑ UAL-3582 [M]	How Long Has It Been	1967	$30
❑ UAS-6582 [S]	How Long Has It Been	1967	$30
❑ UAS-6717	Thanks for You and I	1969	$25
❑ UAS-6760	The Best of Bobby Lewis, Vol. 1	1970	$18

LEWIS, DAVE
Number	Title	Yr	NM
A&M			
❑ LP-105 [M]	Little Green Thing	1964	$25
❑ SP-4105 [S]	Little Green Thing	1964	$30
JERDEN			
❑ JRL-7006 [M]	Dave Lewis Plays Herb Alpert and the Tijuana Brass	1966	$25
❑ JRLS-7006 [S]	Dave Lewis Plays Herb Alpert and the Tijuana Brass	1966	$30

LEWIS, FURRY
Number	Title	Yr	NM
AMPEX			
❑ A-10140	Live at the Gaslight	1971	$30
BLUESVILLE			
❑ BVLP-1036 [M]	Back on My Feet Again	1961	$150
—Blue label, silver print			
❑ BVLP-1036 [M]	Back on My Feet Again	1964	$30
—Blue label, trident logo at right			
❑ BVLP-1037 [M]	Done Changed My Mind	1961	$150
—Blue label, silver print			
❑ BVLP-1037 [M]	Done Changed My Mind	1964	$30
—Blue label, trident logo at right			

LEWIS, GARY, AND THE PLAYBOYS
Number	Title	Yr	NM
LIBERTY			
❑ LRP-3419 [M]	A Session with Gary Lewis and the Playboys	1965	$25
❑ LST-7419 [S]	A Session with Gary Lewis and the Playboys	1965	$30
❑ LST-7606	Close Cover Before Playing	1969	$18
❑ LRP-3428 [M]	Everybody Loves a Clown	1965	$25
❑ LST-7428 [S]	Everybody Loves a Clown	1965	$30
❑ LST-7568	Gary Lewis Now!	1968	$18
❑ LRP-3468 [M]	Golden Greats	1966	$18
❑ LST-7468 [S]	Golden Greats	1966	$25
—Side 2 plays as listed			
❑ LST-7468 [S]	Golden Greats	1966	$30
—Side 2, Song 2 claims to be "I Won't Make That Mistake Again" but it plays "You've Got to Hide Your Love Away"			
❑ LN-10241	Golden Greats	198?	$10
—Budget-line reissue			
❑ LRP-3452 [M]	Hits Again!	1966	$18
❑ LST-7452 [S]	Hits Again!	1966	$25
❑ LST-7633	I'm On the Right Road Now	1970	$18
❑ LST-7524 [S]	Listen	1967	$18
❑ LRP-3524 [M]	Listen!	1967	$18
❑ LST-7589	More Golden Greats	1968	$18
❑ LRP-3519 [M]	New Directions	1967	$18
❑ LST-7519 [S]	New Directions	1967	$18
❑ LST-7623	Rhythm of the Rain	1969	$18
❑ LRP-3435 [M]	She's Just My Style	1966	$18
❑ LST-7435 [S]	She's Just My Style	1966	$25
❑ LRP-3408 [M]	This Diamond Ring	1965	$25
❑ LST-7408 [S]	This Diamond Ring	1965	$30
❑ LM-1003	This Diamond Ring	1981	$10
—Reissue of United Artists 1008			
❑ LRP-3487 [M]	(You Don't Have to) Paint Me a Picture	1967	$18
—Side 1 plays as listed			
❑ LRP-3487 [M]	(You Don't Have to) Paint Me a Picture	1967	$25
—Side 1, Song 4 claims to be "Tina" but plays "Ice Melts in the Sun"			
❑ LST-7487 [S]	(You Don't Have to) Paint Me a Picture	1967	$25
—Side 1 plays as listed			
❑ LST-7487 [S]	(You Don't Have to) Paint Me a Picture	1967	$30
—Side 1, Song 4 claims to be "Tina" but plays "Ice Melts in the Sun"			
RHINO			
❑ RNLP-163	Greatest Hits (1965-1968)	1985	$12
SUNSET			
❑ SUM-1168 [M]	Gary Lewis and the Playboys	1967	$15
❑ SUS-5168 [S]	Gary Lewis and the Playboys	1967	$15
❑ SUS-5262	Rhythm!	1969	$15
UNITED ARTISTS			
❑ UA-LA430-E	The Very Best of Gary Lewis and the Playboys	1975	$12
❑ LM-1003	This Diamond Ring	1980	$12
—Edited reissue of Liberty 7408			

Number	Title	Yr	NM
LEWIS, GEORGE (1)			
AMERICAN MUSIC			
❑ 645 [10]	George Lewis with Kid Shots Madison	1952	$100
❑ 639 [10]	The George Lewis Band in the French Quarter	1951	$100
ATLANTIC			
❑ 1411 [M]	The George Lewis Band	1963	$50
❑ SD1411 [S]	The George Lewis Band	1963	$50
BIOGRAPH			
❑ CEN-1	George Lewis and His Mustache Stompers	197?	$25
BLUE NOTE			
❑ BLP-1205 [M]	George Lewis and His New Orleans Stompers, Volume 1	1955	$300
—Deep groove" version (deep indentation under label on both sides)			
❑ BLP-1205 [M]	George Lewis and His New Orleans Stompers, Volume 1	1955	$1000
—Regular version, Lexington Ave. address on label			
❑ BLP-1205 [M]	George Lewis and His New Orleans Stompers, Volume 1	1963	$175
—With "New York, USA" address on label			
❑ BST-81205 [R]	George Lewis and His New Orleans Stompers, Volume 1	1967	$30
—With "A Division of Liberty Records" on label			
❑ BLP-1206 [M]	George Lewis and His New Orleans Stompers, Volume 2	1955	$350
—Deep groove" version (deep indentation under label on both sides)			
❑ BLP-1206 [M]	George Lewis and His New Orleans Stompers, Volume 2	1955	$1000
—Regular version, Lexington Ave. address on label			
❑ BLP-1206 [M]	George Lewis and His New Orleans Stompers, Volume 2	1963	$175
—With "New York, USA" address on label			
❑ BST-81206 [R]	George Lewis and His New Orleans Stompers, Volume 2	1967	$30
—With "A Division of Liberty Records" on label			
❑ BLP-1208 [M]	George Lewis Concert!	1955	$450
—Deep groove" version (deep indentation under label on both sides)			
❑ BLP-1208 [M]	George Lewis Concert!	1955	$800
—Regular version, Lexington Ave. address on label			
❑ BLP-1208 [M]	George Lewis Concert!	1963	$150
—With "New York, USA" address on label			
❑ BST-81208 [R]	George Lewis Concert!	1967	$30
—With "A Division of Liberty Records" on label			
❑ BLP-7010 [10]	George Lewis' New Orleans Stompers, Volume 1	1951	$300
❑ BLP-7013 [10]	George Lewis' New Orleans Stompers, Volume 2	1951	$300
❑ BLP-7027 [10]	George Lewis' New Orleans Stompers, Volume 3	1954	$300
❑ BLP-7028 [10]	George Lewis' New Orleans Stompers, Volume 4	1954	$300
CAVALIER			
❑ CVLP-6004 [M]	George Lewis in Hi-Fi	1956	$75
CIRCLE			
❑ L-421 [10]	George Lewis and His New Orleans All-Stars	1951	$100
DELMAR			
❑ DL-201 [M]	Doctor Jazz	195?	$50
❑ DL-202 [M]	On Parade	195?	$50
DELMARK			
❑ DL-203	George Lewis Memorial Album	196?	$25
❑ DL-202	George Lewis' New Orleans Stompers	196?	$30
DISC JOCKEY			
❑ DDL-100 [M]	Jazz at Ohio Union	195?	$1200
—Box set with booklet			
EMPIRICAL			
❑ EM-107 [10]	Spirituals in Ragtime	1956	$100
EVEREST ARCHIVE OF FOLK & JAZZ			
❑ 240	George Lewis	197?	$25
FANTASY			
❑ OJC-1739	George Lewis of New Orleans	198?	$25
❑ OJC-1736	Jazz at Vespers	198?	$25
FOLKLYRIC			
❑ 9030	George Lewis and His New Orleans Ragtime Jazz Band	198?	$25
GHB			
❑ GHB-10	City of a Million Dreams	1964	$30
❑ GHB-29	Easy Riders Jazz Band	1965	$30
❑ GHB-39	Easy Riders Jazz Band	1968	$30
❑ GHB-37	For Dancers Only	1968	$30
❑ GHB-5	George Lewis and His Ragtime Stompers	196?	$30
❑ GHB-14	George Lewis in Japan, Volume 1	1965	$30
❑ GHB-15	George Lewis in Japan, Volume 2	1965	$30
❑ GHB-16	George Lewis in Japan, Volume 3	1965	$30
❑ GHB-68	The Big Four	1970	$30

Number	Title	Yr	NM
JAZZ CRUSADE			
□ 2004	Jazzology Poll	1965	$30
JAZZ MAN			
□ LP-1 [10]	George Lewis' Ragtime Band	1953	$100
—Limited First Pressing Dec. 25, 1953" on label at left			
□ LJ-331 [10]	New Orleans Music	1954	$100
JAZZOLOGY			
□ JCE-19	Endless the Trek	1967	$30
□ JCE-3 [M]	George Lewis and His Ragtime Stompers	196?	$35
□ SJCE-3 [S]	George Lewis and His Ragtime Stompers	196?	$30
□ JCE-27	George Lewis at Congo Square	196?	$30
MOSAIC			
□ MR5-132	The Complete Blue Note Recordings of George Lewis	199?	$150
PARADOX			
□ LP-6001 [10]	George Lewis	1951	$100
RIVERSIDE			
□ RLP-2507 [10]	George Lewis	1954	$300
□ RLP 12-283 [M]	George Lewis of New Orleans	1958	$300
□ RLP-2512 [10]	George Lewis with Guest Artist Red Allen	1955	$300
□ RLP 12-230 [M]	Jazz at Vespers	1957	$300
—White label, blue print			
□ RLP 12-230 [M]	Jazz at Vespers	1959	$300
—Blue label, microphone logo at top			
□ RLP 12-207 [M]	Jazz in the Classic New Orleans Tradition	1956	$300
—White label, blue print			
□ RLP 12-207 [M]	Jazz in the Classic New Orleans Tradition	1959	$300
—Blue label, microphone logo at top			
SOUTHLAND			
□ SLP-208 [10]	George Lewis	1955	$100
STORYVILLE			
□ 4022	George Lewis and His Ragtime Band In Concert	197?	$30
□ 4055	George Lewis at Club Hangover, Volume 1	198?	$25
□ 4061	George Lewis at Club Hangover, Volume 3	198?	$25
□ 4049	Jazz from New Orleans	198?	$25
VERVE			
□ MGV-1019 [M]	Blues from the Bayou	1957	$175
□ V-1019 [M]	Blues from the Bayou	1961	$25
□ MGVS-6113 [S]	Blues from the Bayou	1960	$120
□ V6-1019 [S]	Blues from the Bayou	1961	$35
□ MGV-1021 [M]	Doctor Jazz	1957	$150
□ V-1021 [M]	Doctor Jazz	1961	$25
□ MGVS-6122 [S]	Doctor Jazz	1960	$150
□ V6-1021 [S]	Doctor Jazz	1961	$35
□ MGV-8232 [M]	George Lewis and Turk Murphy at Newport	1958	$150
□ V-8232 [M]	George Lewis and Turk Murphy at Newport	1961	$25
□ MGV-1027 [M]	George Lewis' Dixieland Band	1957	$175
□ V-1027 [M]	George Lewis' Dixieland Band	1961	$25
□ MGV-1024 [M]	Hot Time in the Old Town Tonight	1957	$175
□ V-1024 [M]	Hot Time in the Old Town Tonight	1961	$25
□ V6-1024 [S]	Hot Time in the Old Town Tonight	1961	$25
□ MGV-8325 [M]	Oh, Didn't He Ramble	1959	$150
□ MGVS-6064 [S]	Oh, Didn't He Ramble	1960	$150
□ V-8325 [M]	Oh, Didn't He Ramble	1961	$25
□ V6-8325 [S]	Oh, Didn't He Ramble	1961	$35
□ MGV-8303 [M]	On Stage: George Lewis Concert, Volume 1	1959	$150
□ V-8303 [M]	On Stage: George Lewis Concert, Volume 1	1961	$25
□ MGV-8304 [M]	On Stage: George Lewis Concert, Volume 2	1959	$150
□ V-8304 [M]	On Stage: George Lewis Concert, Volume 2	1961	$25
□ MGV-8277 [M]	The Perennial George Lewis	1958	$150
□ V-8277 [M]	The Perennial George Lewis	1961	$25
□ UMV-2621	Verve at Newport	198?	$30

LEWIS, GEORGE (2), AND DOUGLAS EWART
Number	Title	Yr	NM
BLACK SAINT			
□ BSR-0026	The Imaginary Suite	198?	$30

LEWIS, GEORGE (2)
Number	Title	Yr	NM
BLACK SAINT			
□ BSR-0029	Homage to Charles Parker	198?	$30
□ BSR-0016	Monads	198?	$30
LOVELY			
□ VR-1101	Chicago Slow Dance	198?	$35

LEWIS, HUEY, AND THE NEWS
Number	Title	Yr	NM
CHRYSALIS			
□ 8V842795 [EP]	84 Sports Tour	1984	$18
—Three-song picture disc numbered as if it were a single			
□ OV41534	Fore!	1986	$10
□ CHR1292	Huey Lewis and the News	1980	$15

Number	Title	Yr	NM
□ FV41292	Huey Lewis and the News	1983	$10
—Reissue of 1292			
□ PV41292	Huey Lewis and the News	198?	$10
—Reissue with new prefix			

Number	Title	Yr	NM
□ CHR1340 [B]	Picture This	1982	$12
□ FV41340	Picture This	1983	$10
—Reissue of 1340			
□ OV41622	Small World	1988	$10
□ FV41412	Sports	1983	$10
□ OV41412	Sports	198?	$10
—Reissue with new prefix			
MOBILE FIDELITY			
□ 1-181	Sports	1985	$30
—Original Master Recording" on front cover			

LEWIS, HUGH X.
Number	Title	Yr	NM
KAPP			
□ KS-3563	Country Fever	1968	$30
□ KS-3545	Just a Prayer Away	1968	$30
□ KL-1494 [M]	Just Before Dawn	1966	$25
□ KS-3494 [S]	Just Before Dawn	1966	$30
□ KS-3522 [S]	My Kind of Country	1967	$30
□ KL-1522 [M]	My Kind of Country	1967	$30
□ KL-1462 [M]	The Hugh X. Lewis Album	1966	$25
□ KS-3462 [S]	The Hugh X. Lewis Album	1966	$30

LEWIS, JERRY
Number	Title	Yr	NM
DECCA			
□ DL8936 [M]	Big Songs for Little People	1959	$50
□ DL78936 [S]	Big Songs for Little People	1959	$75
□ DL8410 [M]	Jerry Lewis Just Sings	1956	$75
□ DL8595 [M]	More Jerry Lewis	1957	$75
DOT			
□ DLP3664 [M]	The Jerry Lewis Singers	1964	$18
□ DLP25664 [S]	The Jerry Lewis Singers	1964	$25

LEWIS, JERRY LEE, AND LINDA GAIL LEWIS
Number	Title	Yr	NM
SMASH			
□ SRS-67126	Together	1969	$25

LEWIS, JERRY LEE
Number	Title	Yr	NM
ACCORD			
□ SN-7133	I Walk the Line	1981	$12
DESIGN			
□ DLP-165 [M]	Rockin' with Jerry Lee Lewis	1963	$30
□ DST-165 [R]	Rockin' with Jerry Lee Lewis	1963	$25
ELEKTRA			
□ 6E-184	Jerry Lee Lewis	1979	$15
□ 6E-291	Killer Country	1980	$15
□ 60191	The Best of Jerry Lee Lewis Featuring 39 and Holding	1982	$12
□ 6E-254	When Two Worlds Collide	1980	$15
HILLTOP			
□ 6110	Roll Over Beethoven	1972	$12
□ 6120	Rural Route #1	1972	$12
□ 6102	Sunday After Church	1971	$12
MCA			
□ 5478	I Am What I Am	1984	$12
□ 5387	My Fingers Do the Talkin'	1983	$12
MERCURY			
□ 690 [DJ]	A Jerry Lee Lewis Radio Special	1973	$50
□ SRM-1-1030	Boogie Woogie Country Man	1975	$18
□ SRM-1-1109	Country Class	1976	$18
□ SRM-1-5004	Country Memories	1977	$18
□ 826251-1	Greatest Hits	198?	$12
□ SRM-1-710	I-40 Country	1974	$18
□ SR-61318	In Loving Memories	1970	$30
□ SRM-1-5010	Jerry Lee Lewis Keeps Rockin'	1978	$18
□ 836935-1	Killer: The Mercury Years Volume One, 1963-1968	1989	$15

Number	Title	Yr	NM
□ 836941-1	Killer: The Mercury Years Volume Three, 1973-1977	1989	$15
□ 836938-1	Killer: The Mercury Years Volume Two, 1969-1972	1989	$15
□ SR-61278	Live at the International, Las Vegas	1970	$18
□ SRM-1-1064	Odd Man In	1975	$18
□ SRM-1-677	Sometimes a Memory Ain't Enough	1973	$18
□ SRM-1-690	Southern Roots -- Back Home to Memphis	1973	$18
□ SRM-1-5006 [B]	The Best of Jerry Lee Lewis Volume II	1978	$18
□ 822789-1	The Best of Jerry Lee Lewis Volume II	198?	$12
□ SRM-1-637	The "Killer" Rocks On	1972	$18
□ SR-61323	There Must Be More to Love Than This	1971	$18
□ SRM-2-803	The Session	1973	$25
□ SR-61343	Touching Home	1971	$18
—With photo of Jerry Lee in front of a brick wall			
□ SR-61343	Touching Home	1971	$25
—With drawing on cover and small photo of Jerry Lee			
□ SR-61366	Who's Gonna PlayThis Old Piano… (Think About It Darlin')	1972	$18
□ 830399-1	Would You Take Another Chance on Me	1987	$12
—Reissue of 61346			
□ SR-61346	Would You Take Another Chance on Me?	1971	$18
PAIR			
□ PDL2-1132	Solid Gold	1986	$15
PICKWICK			
□ SPC-3344	Drinking Wine Spo-Dee-O-Dee	1973	$12
□ SPC-3224	High Heel Sneakers	1970	$12
□ PTP-2055	Jerry Lee Lewis	1973	$15
POLYDOR			
□ 839516-1	Great Balls of Fire!	1989	$15
□ 826139-1	I'm on Fire	1985	$12
POWER PAK			
□ 247	From the Vaults of Sun	1974	$12
RHINO			
□ R1-70656	Jerry Lee Lewis	1989	$15
—Reissue of Sun 1230			
□ R1-70657	Jerry Lee's Greatest	1989	$15
—Reissue of Sun 1265			
□ RNDA-1499	Milestones	1985	$18
□ R1-71499	Milestones	1989	$15
—Reissue of 1499			
□ RNDF-255 [PD]	Original Sun Greatest Hits	1983	$18
□ R1-70255	Original Sun Greatest Hits	1989	$12
—Reissue of 255 on black vinyl			
□ R1-70899	Wild One: Rare Tracks from Jerry Lee Lewis	1989	$15
SEARS			
□ SPS-610	Hound Dog	1970	$30
SMASH			
□ SRS-67071	All Country	1969	$18
—Retitled reissue			
□ SRS-67104	Another Place Another Time	1968	$25
□ MGS-27086 [M]	By Request -- More of the Greatest Live Show on Earth	1966	$30
□ SRS-67086 [S]	By Request -- More of the Greatest Live Show on Earth	1966	$40
□ MGS-27071 [M]	Country Songs for City Folks	1965	$30
□ SRS-67071 [S]	Country Songs for City Folks	1965	$30
□ SL-7001	Golden Hits	1980	$15
□ SRS-67117	Jerry Lee Lewis Sings the Country Music Hall of Fame Hits, Vol. 1	1969	$25
□ SRS-67118	Jerry Lee Lewis Sings the Country Music Hall of Fame Hits, Vol. 2	1969	$25
□ MGS-27079 [M]	Memphis Beat	1966	$30
□ SRS-67079 [S]	Memphis Beat	1966	$30

Number	Title	Yr	NM
❏ SRS-67128	She Even Woke Me Up to Say Goodbye	1970	$25
❏ SRS-67112 [B]	She Still Comes Around (To Love What's Left of Me)	1969	$25
❏ MGS-27097 [M]	Soul My Way	1967	$30
❏ SRS-67097 [S]	Soul My Way	1967	$40
❏ SRS-67131	The Best of Jerry Lee Lewis	1970	$25
❏ MGS-27040 [M]	The Golden Hits of Jerry Lee Lewis	1964	$30
❏ SRS-67040 [S]	The Golden Hits of Jerry Lee Lewis	1964	$30
❏ SRS-67040 [S]	The Golden Rock Hits of Jerry Lee Lewis	1969	$18

— *Retitled reissue*

Number	Title	Yr	NM
❏ MGS-27056 [M]	The Greatest Live Show on Earth	1964	$150
❏ SRS-67056 [S]	The Greatest Live Show on Earth	1964	$175
❏ MGS-27063 [M]	The Return of Rock	1965	$30
❏ SRS-67063 [S]	The Return of Rock	1965	$40

SUN

Number	Title	Yr	NM
❏ LP-114 [B]	A Taste of Country	1970	$18
❏ SUN-1011	Duets	1978	$18

— *As "Jerry Lee Lewis and Friends"; gold vinyl*

Number	Title	Yr	NM
❏ SLP-1230 [M]	Jerry Lee Lewis	1958	$250
❏ SLP-1265 [M]	Jerry Lee's Greatest	1961	$300
❏ SLP-1265 [M]	Jerry Lee's Greatest	1961	$800

— *White label promo*

Number	Title	Yr	NM
❏ LP-124	Monsters	1971	$18
❏ LP-121	Ole Tyme Country Music	1971	$18
❏ LP-102	Original Golden Hits – Volume 1	1969	$18
❏ LP-103	Original Golden Hits – Volume 2	1969	$18
❏ LP-128	Original Golden Hits – Volume 3	1972	$18
❏ LP-107	Rockin' Rhythm and Blues	1969	$18
❏ SUN-145	Roots	1982	$15
❏ SUN-108	The Golden Cream of the Country	1969	$18
❏ SUN-108 [M]	The Golden Cream of the Country	1969	$40

— *Mono version is white label promo only; the word "MONO" appears at 9 o'clock on the label*

Number	Title	Yr	NM
❏ 1005	The Original	1978	$15
❏ 1018	Trio +	1979	$15

— *With Carl Perkins, Charlie Rich and (uncredited) Orion*

SUNNYVALE

Number	Title	Yr	NM
❏ 905	The Sun Story, Vol. 5	1977	$12

WING

Number	Title	Yr	NM
❏ SRW-16340	In Demand	1968	$12
❏ PKW2-125	The Legend of Jerry Lee Lewis	1969	$30
❏ MGW-12340 [M]	The Return of Rock	1967	$15
❏ SRW-16340 [S]	The Return of Rock	1967	$15
❏ SRW-16406	Unlimited	1968	$15

LEWIS, JOHN, AND BILL PERKINS

PACIFIC JAZZ

Number	Title	Yr	NM
❏ PJ-1217 [M]	Grand Encounter: 2' East, 3' West	1956	$300
❏ PJ-44 [M]	Grand Encounter: 2' East, 3' West	1962	$75

— *Reissue with new number*

PAUSA

Number	Title	Yr	NM
❏ 9019	Grand Encounter: 2' East, 3' West	198?	$30

WORLD PACIFIC

Number	Title	Yr	NM
❏ WP-1217 [M]	Grand Encounter: 2' East, 3' West	1959	$300

LEWIS, JOHN, AND HANK JONES

LITTLE DAVID

Number	Title	Yr	NM
❏ LD1079	An Evening with Two Grand Pianos	1979	$30

LEWIS, JOHN, AND SACHA DISTEL

ATLANTIC

Number	Title	Yr	NM
❏ 1267 [M]	Afternoon in Paris	1964	$25

— *Multicolor label, black "fan" logo at right*

Number	Title	Yr	NM
❏ 1267 [M]	Afternoon in Paris	1957	$300

— *Black label*

Number	Title	Yr	NM
❏ 1267 [M]	Afternoon in Paris	1961	$300

— *Multicolor label, white "fan" logo at right*

LEWIS, JOHN

ATLANTIC

Number	Title	Yr	NM
❏ 1402 [M]	Animal Dance	1963	$175
❏ SD1402 [S]	Animal Dance	1963	$175
❏ 1425 [M]	Essence	1964	$35
❏ SD1425 [S]	Essence	1964	$25
❏ 1392 [M]	European Encounter	1963	$50
❏ SD1392 [S]	European Encounter	1963	$50
❏ 90533	European Encounter	1986	$25
❏ 1313 [M]	Improvised Meditations and Excursions	1959	$300

— *Black label*

Number	Title	Yr	NM
❏ 1313 [M]	Improvised Meditations and Excursions	1961	$175

— *Multicolor label, white "fan" logo at right*

Number	Title	Yr	NM
❏ 1313 [M]	Improvised Meditations and Excursions	1964	$35

— *Multicolor label, black "fan" logo at right*

Number	Title	Yr	NM
❏ SD1313 [S]	Improvised Meditations and Excursions	1959	$300

— *Green label*

Number	Title	Yr	NM
❏ SD1313 [S]	Improvised Meditations and Excursions	1961	$175

— *Multicolor label, white "fan" logo at right*

Number	Title	Yr	NM
❏ SD1313 [S]	Improvised Meditations and Excursions	1964	$35

— *Multicolor label, black "fan" logo at right*

Number	Title	Yr	NM
❏ 1365 [M]	John Lewis Presents Jazz Abstractions	1961	$175

— *Multicolor label, white "fan" logo at right*

Number	Title	Yr	NM
❏ 1365 [M]	John Lewis Presents Jazz Abstractions	1964	$35

— *Multicolor label, black "fan" logo at right*

Number	Title	Yr	NM
❏ SD1365 [S]	John Lewis Presents Jazz Abstractions	1961	$175

— *Multicolor label, white "fan" logo at right*

Number	Title	Yr	NM
❏ SD1365 [S]	John Lewis Presents Jazz Abstractions	1964	$25

— *Multicolor label, black "fan" logo at right*

Number	Title	Yr	NM
❏ 1370 [M]	Original Sin	1961	$175

— *Multicolor label, white "fan" logo at right*

Number	Title	Yr	NM
❏ 1370 [M]	Original Sin	1964	$35

— *Multicolor label, black "fan" logo at right*

Number	Title	Yr	NM
❏ SD1370 [S]	Original Sin	1961	$175

— *Multicolor label, white "fan" logo at right*

Number	Title	Yr	NM
❏ SD1370 [S]	Original Sin	1964	$25

— *Multicolor label, black "fan" logo at right*

Number	Title	Yr	NM
❏ 1334 [M]	The Golden Striker	1960	$300

— *Multicolor label, white "fan" logo at right*

Number	Title	Yr	NM
❏ 1334 [M]	The Golden Striker	1964	$35

— *Multicolor label, black "fan" logo at right*

Number	Title	Yr	NM
❏ SD1334 [S]	The Golden Striker	1960	$300

— *Multicolor label, white "fan" logo at right*

Number	Title	Yr	NM
❏ SD1334 [S]	The Golden Striker	1964	$50

— *Multicolor label, black "fan" logo at right*

Number	Title	Yr	NM
❏ 1272 [M]	The John Lewis Piano	1958	$300

— *Black label*

Number	Title	Yr	NM
❏ 1272 [M]	The John Lewis Piano	1961	$175

— *Multicolor label, white "fan" logo at right*

Number	Title	Yr	NM
❏ 1272 [M]	The John Lewis Piano	1964	$35

— *Multicolor label, black "fan" logo at right*

Number	Title	Yr	NM
❏ 1375 [M]	The Wonderful World of Jazz	1961	$175

— *Multicolor label, white "fan" logo at right*

Number	Title	Yr	NM
❏ SD1375 [S]	The Wonderful World of Jazz	1961	$175

— *Multicolor label, white "fan" logo at right*

Number	Title	Yr	NM
❏ 1375 [M]	The Wonderful World of Jazz	1964	$35

— *Multicolor label, black "fan" logo at right*

Number	Title	Yr	NM
❏ SD1375 [S]	The Wonderful World of Jazz	1964	$25

— *Multicolor label, black "fan" logo at right*

Number	Title	Yr	NM
❏ 90979	The Wonderful World of Jazz	1989	$30

COLUMBIA

Number	Title	Yr	NM
❏ PC33534	P.O.V.	1976	$25

EMARCY

Number	Title	Yr	NM
❏ 838036-1	Midnight in Paris	1990	$30
❏ 834478-1	The Garden of Delight: Delaunay's Dilemma	1989	$30

FINESSE

Number	Title	Yr	NM
❏ FW37681	Album for Nancy Harrow	1982	$25
❏ FW38187	Kansas City Breaks	1983	$25

PHILIPS

Number	Title	Yr	NM
❏ 836821-1	Bach: Preludes and Fugues, Vol. 3	1989	$30
❏ 824381-1	John Lewis Plays Bach's "Well-Tempered Clavier"	1985	$25
❏ 826698-1	The Bridge Game	1986	$25
❏ 832015-1	The Chess Game	1987	$30
❏ 832588-1	The Chess Game, Volume 2	1988	$30

RCA VICTOR

Number	Title	Yr	NM
❏ LPM-1742 [M]	European Windows	1958	$50

LEWIS, KATHARINE HANDY

FOLKWAYS

Number	Title	Yr	NM
❏ FJ-3540 [M]	W.C. Handy Blues	1958	$30

LEWIS, LINDA GAIL

SMASH

Number	Title	Yr	NM
❏ SRS-67119	Two Sides of Linda Gail Lewis	1969	$30

LEWIS, MEADE LUX, AND LOUIS BELLSON

CLEF

Number	Title	Yr	NM
❏ MGC-632 [M]	Boogie Woogie Piano and Drums	1954	$250

LEWIS, MEADE LUX

ABC-PARAMOUNT

Number	Title	Yr	NM
❏ ABC-164 [M]	Out of the Roaring 20's	1956	$50

ATLANTIC

Number	Title	Yr	NM
❏ ALS-133 [10]	Boogie-Woogie Interpretations	1952	$300

BLUE NOTE

Number	Title	Yr	NM
❏ BLP-7018 [10]	Boogie-Woogie Classics	1952	$600

DISC

Number	Title	Yr	NM
❏ DLP-352 [10]	Meade Lux Lewis at the Philharmonic	195?	$400

DOWN HOME

Number	Title	Yr	NM
❏ MGD-6 [M]	Cat House Piano	1955	$0

— *Canceled*

Number	Title	Yr	NM
❏ MGD-7 [M]	Yancey's Last Ride	1956	$120

FANTASY

Number	Title	Yr	NM
❏ OJC-1759	The Blues Piano Artistry of Meade Lux Lewis	198?	$30

MERCURY

Number	Title	Yr	NM
❏ MG-25158 [10]	Meade Lux Lewis	1951	$300

MUSE

Number	Title	Yr	NM
❏ MR-5063	Still On the Planet	1976	$50

PHILIPS

Number	Title	Yr	NM
❏ PHM200044 [M]	Boogie Woogie House Party	196?	$25
❏ PHS600044 [S]	Boogie Woogie House Party	196?	$30

RIVERSIDE

Number	Title	Yr	NM
❏ RLP-402 [M]	The Blues Piano Artistry of Meade Lux Lewis	1962	$250
❏ RS-9402 [S]	The Blues Piano Artistry of Meade Lux Lewis	1962	$250

STINSON

Number	Title	Yr	NM
❏ 25 [M]	Meade Lux Lewis	196?	$30

TOPS

Number	Title	Yr	NM
❏ L-1533 [M]	Barrelhouse Piano	195?	$40

VERVE

Number	Title	Yr	NM
❏ MGV-1006 [M]	Cat House Piano	1957	$250
❏ V-1006 [M]	Cat House Piano	1961	$40
❏ MGV-1007 [M]	Meade Lux Lewis	1957	$175
❏ V-1007 [M]	Meade Lux Lewis	1961	$30

LEWIS, MEL

ATLANTIC

Number	Title	Yr	NM
❏ 81655	20th Anniversary	1986	$25

FINESSE

Number	Title	Yr	NM
❏ FW37987	Make Me Smile	1984	$25

HORIZON

Number	Title	Yr	NM
❏ SP-716	Mel Lewis and Friends	1976	$30

MODE

Number	Title	Yr	NM
❏ LP-103 [M]	Mel Lewis Sextet	1957	$120

PAUSA

Number	Title	Yr	NM
❏ 7115	Live in Montreux	1981	$25

SAN FRANCISCO

Number	Title	Yr	NM
❏ 2 [M]	Got 'Cha	1957	$175

TELARC

Number	Title	Yr	NM
❏ DG-10044	Naturally	1980	$30

VEE JAY

Number	Title	Yr	NM
❏ VJS-3062	Gettin' Together	1974	$25

LEWIS, RAMSEY, AND JEAN DUSHON

ARGO

Number	Title	Yr	NM
❏ 750 [M]	You Better Believe Me	1965	$75
❏ 750S [S]	You Better Believe Me	1965	$75

LEWIS, RAMSEY, AND NANCY WILSON

COLUMBIA

Number	Title	Yr	NM
❏ FC39326	The Two of Us	1984	$25

LEWIS, RAMSEY

Pianist and keyboard player. Most of his Argo and Chess albums were released under the moniker "Ramsey Lewis Trio." The other two members of the classic trio were ELDEE YOUNG (bass) and RED HOLT (drums), who later formed their own groups.

ARGO

Number	Title	Yr	NM
❏ LP-645 [M]	An Hour with the Ramsey Lewis Trio	1959	$40
❏ LPS-645 [S]	An Hour with the Ramsey Lewis Trio	1959	$150
❏ LP-732 [M]	Bach to the Blues	1964	$75
❏ LPS-732 [S]	Bach to the Blues	1964	$75
❏ LP-723 [M]	Barefoot Sunday Blues	1963	$75
❏ LPS-723 [S]	Barefoot Sunday Blues	1963	$75
❏ LP-705 [M]	Bossa Nova	1962	$75
❏ LPS-705 [S]	Bossa Nova	1962	$75
❏ LP-755 [M]	Choice! The Best of the Ramsey Lewis Trio	1965	$75
❏ LPS-755 [S]	Choice! The Best of the Ramsey Lewis Trio	1965	$40
❏ LP-701 [M]	Country Meets the Blues	1962	$75
❏ LPS-701 [S]	Country Meets the Blues	1962	$75
❏ LP-627 [M]	Gentleman of Jazz	1958	$150
❏ LPS-627 [S]	Gentleman of Jazz	1959	$120
❏ LP-611 [M]	Gentleman of Swing	1958	$150
❏ LPS-611 [S]	Gentleman of Swing	1959	$120
❏ LP-680 [M]	More Music from the Soil	1961	$40
❏ LPS-680 [S]	More Music from the Soil	1961	$150
❏ LP-745 [M]	More Sounds of Christmas	1964	$75
❏ LPS-745 [S]	More Sounds of Christmas	1964	$75
❏ LP-715 [M]	Pot Luck	1963	$75

Number	Title	Yr	NM
❏ LPS-715 [S]	Pot Luck	1963	$75
❏ LP-687 [M]	Sound of Christmas	1961	$40
❏ LPS-687 [S]	Sound of Christmas	1961	$150
❏ LP-665 [M]	Stretching Out	1960	$40
❏ LPS-665 [S]	Stretching Out	1960	$150
❏ LP-757 [M]	The In Crowd	1965	$75
❏ LPS-757 [S]	The In Crowd	1965	$75
❏ LP-741 [M]	The Ramsey Lewis Trio at the Bohemian Caverns	1964	$75
❏ LPS-741 [S]	The Ramsey Lewis Trio at the Bohemian Caverns	1964	$75
❏ LP-671 [M]	The Ramsey Lewis Trio in Chicago	1961	$40
❏ LPS-671 [S]	The Ramsey Lewis Trio in Chicago	1961	$150
❏ LP-642 [M]	The Ramsey Lewis Trio with Lee Winchester	1959	$40
❏ LPS-642 [S]	The Ramsey Lewis Trio with Lee Winchester	1959	$150
❏ LP-693 [M]	The Sound of Spring	1962	$75
❏ LPS-693 [S]	The Sound of Spring	1962	$75
CADET			
❏ LP-645 [M]	An Hour with the Ramsey Lewis Trio	1966	$30
❏ LPS-645 [S]	An Hour with the Ramsey Lewis Trio	1966	$35
❏ LPS-827	Another Voyage	1969	$35
❏ LP-732 [M]	Bach to the Blues	1966	$30
❏ LPS-732 [S]	Bach to the Blues	1966	$35
❏ 60001	Back to the Roots	1971	$30
❏ LP-723 [M]	Barefoot Sunday Blues	1966	$30
❏ LPS-723 [S]	Barefoot Sunday Blues	1966	$35
❏ LP-705 [M]	Bossa Nova	1966	$30
❏ LPS-705 [S]	Bossa Nova	1966	$35
❏ LP-755 [M]	Choice! The Best of the Ramsey Lewis Trio	1965	$35
❏ LPS-755 [S]	Choice! The Best of the Ramsey Lewis Trio	1965	$50
❏ LP-701 [M]	Country Meets the Blues	1966	$30
❏ LPS-701 [S]	Country Meets the Blues	1966	$35
❏ LP-794 [M]	Dancing in the Street	1967	$50
❏ LPS-794 [S]	Dancing in the Street	1967	$35
❏ LP-627 [M]	Gentleman of Jazz	1966	$30
❏ LPS-627 [S]	Gentleman of Jazz	1966	$35
❏ LP-611 [M]	Gentleman of Swing	1966	$30
❏ LPS-611 [S]	Gentleman of Swing	1966	$35
❏ LP-790 [M]	Goin' Latin	1967	$50
❏ LPS-790 [S]	Goin' Latin	1967	$35
❏ 50020	Groover	1973	$30
❏ LP-761 [M]	Hang On Ramsey!	1966	$35
❏ LPS-761 [S]	Hang On Ramsey!	1966	$50
❏ 60018	Inside Ramsey Lewis	1972	$35
❏ LPS-811	Maiden Voyage	1968	$35
❏ LP-680 [M]	More Music from the Soil	1966	$30
❏ LPS-680 [S]	More Music from the Soil	1966	$35
❏ LPS-680 [S]	More Music from the Soil	197?	$30
—Reissue with "A Division of All Platinum Record Group" on label			
❏ LP-745 [M]	More Sounds of Christmas	1966	$35
❏ LPS-745 [S]	More Sounds of Christmas	1966	$50
❏ LPS-821	Mother Nature's Son	1969	$35
❏ LP-715 [M]	Pot Luck	1966	$30
❏ LPS-715 [S]	Pot Luck	1966	$35
❏ LPS-836	Ramsey Lewis, The Piano Player	1970	$35
❏ 50058	Solid Ivory	1974	$35
❏ LP-687X [M]	Sound of Christmas	1966	$50
—Reissue of Argo 687			
❏ LPS-687X [S]	Sound of Christmas	1966	$50
—Reissue of Argo 687-S			
❏ LP-665 [M]	Stretching Out	1966	$30
❏ LPS-665 [S]	Stretching Out	1966	$35
❏ LP-771 [M]	Swingin'	1966	$35
❏ LPS-771 [S]	Swingin'	1966	$50
❏ LPS-839	The Best of Ramsey Lewis	1970	$35
❏ LP-757 [M]	The In Crowd	1965	$30
❏ LPS-757 [S]	The In Crowd	1965	$35
❏ LPS-844	Them Changes	1970	$35
❏ LP-782 [M]	The Movie Album	1967	$50
❏ LPS-782 [S]	The Movie Album	1967	$35
❏ LP-741 [M]	The Ramsey Lewis Trio at the Bohemian Caverns	1966	$30
❏ LPS-741 [S]	The Ramsey Lewis Trio at the Bohemian Caverns	1966	$35
❏ LP-671 [M]	The Ramsey Lewis Trio in Chicago	1966	$30
❏ LPS-671 [S]	The Ramsey Lewis Trio in Chicago	1966	$35
❏ LP-693 [M]	The Sound of Spring	1966	$30
❏ LPS-693 [S]	The Sound of Spring	1966	$35
❏ LPS-799	Up Pops Ramsey Lewis	1968	$35
❏ LP-774 [M]	Wade in the Water	1966	$35
❏ LPS-774 [S]	Wade in the Water	1966	$50
❏ LP-750 [M]	You Better Believe It	1966	$30
❏ LPS-750 [S]	You Better Believe It	1966	$35
CBS			
❏ FM42661	A Classic Encounter	1988	$25
CHESS			
❏ 9001	Solid Ivory	197?	$30
—Reissue of Cadet 50058			
❏ CH9716	Sound of Christmas	1984	$25
—Reissue of Argo 687-S			
COLUMBIA			
❏ FC38294	Chance Encounter	1983	$25
❏ PC33800	Don't It Feel Good	1975	$25
—Originals have no bar code			

Number	Title	Yr	NM
❏ PC33800	Don't It Feel Good	198?	$20
—Budget-line reissue with bar code			
❏ FC40108	Fantasy	1985	$25
❏ KC32030	Funky Serenity	1973	$30
❏ FC40677	Keys to the City	1987	$25
❏ JC35483	Legacy	1978	$25
❏ PC35483	Legacy	198?	$20
—Budget-line reissue			
❏ FC38787	Les Fleurs	1983	$25
❏ FC37687	Live at the Savoy	1982	$25
❏ PC37687	Live at the Savoy	198?	$20
—Budget-line reissue			
❏ HC47687	Live at the Savoy	1982	$175
—Half-speed mastered edition			
❏ PC34696	Love Notes	1977	$25
❏ JC35815	Ramsey	1979	$25
❏ KC32490	Ramsey Lewis' Newly Recorded All-Time, Non-Stop Golden Hits	1973	$30
❏ PC32490	Ramsey Lewis' Newly Recorded All-Time, Non-Stop Golden Hits	197?	$20
—Reissue with new prefix			
❏ FC39158	Reunion	1983	$25
❏ JC36423	Routes	1980	$25
❏ PC36423	Routes	198?	$20
—Budget-line reissue			
❏ PC34173	Salongo	1976	$25
—Originals have no bar code			
❏ PC34173	Salongo	198?	$20
—Budget-line reissue with bar code			
❏ KC32897	Solar Wind	1974	$30
❏ KC33194	Sun Goddess	1974	$25
❏ PC33194	Sun Goddess	197?	$20
—Reissue with new prefix			
❏ HC43194	Sun Goddess	1982	$150
—Half-speed mastered edition			
❏ JC35018	Tequila Mockingbird	1977	$25
❏ FC36364	The Best of Ramsey Lewis	1980	$25
❏ FC37153	Three Piece Suite	1981	$25
❏ KC31096	Upendo Ni Pamoja	1972	$30
❏ CQ31096 [Q]	Upendo Ni Pamoja	1972	$75
❏ CG33663	Upendo Ni Pamoja/Funky Serenity	1975	$30
❏ FC44190	Urban Renewal	1989	$35
COLUMBIA JAZZ ODYSSEY			
❏ PC37019	Blues for the Night Owl	1981	$25
EMARCY			
❏ MG-36150 [M]	Down to Earth	1958	$250
❏ SR-80029 [S]	Down to Earth	1958	$150
MERCURY			
❏ MG-20536 [M]	Down to Earth	1965	$150
❏ SR-60536 [S]	Down to Earth	1965	$150
LEWIS, ROBERT Q.			
ATCO			
❏ 33-212 [M]	I'm Just Wild About Vaudeville	1963	$30
❏ SD 33-212 [S]	I'm Just Wild About Vaudeville	1963	$30
X			
❏ LXA-1033 [M]	Robert Q. Lewis and His Gang	1956	$50
LEWIS, SHARI			
RCA CAMDEN			
❏ CAL-1052 [M]	Jack and the Beanstalk and Other Stories	1964	$30
❏ CAS-1052 [S]	Jack and the Beanstalk and Other Stories	1964	$30
RCA VICTOR			
❏ LBY-1006 [M]	Fun in Shariland	1954	$100
LEWIS, SMILEY			
IMPERIAL			
❏ LP-9141 [M]	I Hear You Knocking	1961	$600
—Black vinyl			
❏ LP-9141 [M]	I Hear You Knocking	1961	$6000
—Green vinyl (one copy known)			
LEWIS, TED			
BIOGRAPH			
❏ C-7	Ted Lewis' Orchestra, Volume 1	198?	$25
❏ C-8	Ted Lewis' Orchestra, Volume 2	198?	$25
COLUMBIA			
❏ CL6127 [10]	Classic Jazz	1950	$50
DECCA			
❏ DL8321 [M]	Is Everybody Happy?	1956	$175
❏ DL5114 [10]	Ted Lewis and His Orchestra	195?	$50
❏ DL4905 [M]	Ted Lewis' Greatest Hits	1967	$30
❏ DL74905 [R]	Ted Lewis' Greatest Hits	1967	$35
❏ DL8322 [M]	The Medicine Man for the Blues	1956	$120
EPIC			
❏ LN3170 [M]	Everybody's Happy!	1955	$100

Number	Title	Yr	NM
MCA			
❏ 2-4101	The Best of Ted Lewis	1976	$35
—Black rainbow labels			
OLYMPIC			
❏ OL-7127	Me and My Shadow	1974	$25
RKO			
❏ ULP-108 [M]	Me and My Shadow	195?	$50
LEWIS, WILLIE			
SWING			
❏ 8400/1	Willie Lewis and His Entertainers	198?	$30
LEWIS AND CLARKE EXPEDITION, THE			
COLGEMS			
❏ COM-105 [M]	The Lewis and Clarke Expedition	1967	$30
❏ COS-105 [S]	The Lewis and Clarke Expedition	1967	$30
LEWIS CONNECTION, THE			
Minneapolis group; PRINCE is featured on one track.			
(NO LABEL)			
❏ 0(no cat #)	The Lewis Connection	1979	$400
LEWIS FAMILY, THE			
STARDAY			
❏ SLP-252 [M]	All Night Singing Convention	1963	$30
❏ SLP-161 [M]	Anniversary Celebration	1962	$30
❏ SLP-433	Did You Ever Go Sailing	1969	$25
❏ SLP-422	Golden Gospel Banjo	1968	$25
❏ SLP-450	Golden Gospel of the Lewis Family	1970	$25
❏ SLP-193 [M]	Gospel Special	1962	$30
❏ SLP-395 [M]	Shall We Gather at the River	1966	$30
❏ SLP-289 [M]	Singin' in My Soul	1964	$30
❏ SLP-121 [M]	Singin' Time Down South	1960	$30
❏ SLP-238 [M]	Sing Me a Gospel Song	1962	$30
❏ SLP-331 [M]	The First Family of Gospel Music	1965	$30
❏ SLP-381 [M]	The Lewis Family Album	1965	$30
❏ SLP-364 [M]	The Lewis Family Sings the Gospel with Carl Story	1965	$30
❏ SLP-408 [M]	Time Is Moving On	1966	$30
LIBBY, JERRY			
SABRINA			
❏ SA-100 [M]	Live? At Wilkins	1964	$25
LIBERACE, GEORGE			
COLUMBIA			
❏ CL587 [M]	A Musical Journey with George Liberace	1954	$40
—Maroon label, gold print			
CROWN			
❏ CST-218 [S]	Hawaiian Paradise	196?	$30
—Black label; red vinyl			
❏ CLP-5218 [M]	Hawaiian Paradise	196?	$18
—Black label			
IMPERIAL			
❏ LP-9039 [M]	George Liberace Goes Teenage	1957	$50
LIBERACE			
ABC			
❏ 4002	16 Great Performances	1974	$15
AVI			
❏ 1023	Candlelight Classics	1973	$15
❏ 1029	The World of Liberace	1974	$15
CBS			
❏ FM42244	Concert Favorites	1986	$12
COLUMBIA			
❏ CL6239 [10]	An Evening with Liberace	1953	$100
❏ CL589 [M]	Christmas at Liberace's	1954	$50
—Maroon label, gold print			
❏ CL6269 [10]	Concertos for You	1953	$100
❏ CL6283 [10]	Concertos for You, Volume 2	1953	$100
❏ CL645 [M]	Hollywood Bowl Encore	1955	$40
❏ CL2592 [10]	Kiddin' on the Keys	1955	$75
❏ CL896 [M]	Liberace at Home	1956	$50
❏ CL600 [M]	Liberace at the Hollywood Bowl	1955	$40
❏ CL6217 [10]	Liberace at the Piano	1952	$100
❏ CL575 [M]	Liberace at the Piano	1954	$40
—Maroon label, gold print			
❏ CL6251 [10]	Liberace by Candlelight	1953	$100
❏ CL661 [M]	Liberace by Candlelight	1955	$40
❏ CL6327 [10]	Liberace Plays Chopin	1954	$100
❏ CL6328 [10]	Liberace Plays Chopin, Volume 2	1954	$100
❏ CS9845	Liberace's Greatest Hits	1969	$15
—Red "360 Sound" label			
❏ CS9845	Liberace's Greatest Hits	1970	$12
—Orange label			
❏ CL2516 [10]	Piano Reverie	1955	$75
❏ CL800 [M]	Sincerely Yours	1956	$50
❏ CL1118 [M]	South Pacific	1957	$30

Number	Title	Yr	NM

CORAL
❑ CRL57392 [M]	As Time Goes By	1962	$15
❑ CRL757392 [S]	As Time Goes By	1962	$18
❑ CRL57452 [M]	Golden Themes from Hollywood	1964	$15
❑ CRL757452 [S]	Golden Themes from Hollywood	1964	$18
❑ CRL57346 [M]	Liberace at the Palladium	1961	$15
❑ CRL757346 [S]	Liberace at the Palladium	1961	$18
❑ CRL57344 [M]	My Inspiration	1961	$15
❑ CRL757344 [S]	My Inspiration	1961	$18
❑ CRL57377 [M]	My Parade of Golden Favorites	1961	$15
❑ CRL757377 [S]	My Parade of Golden Favorites	1961	$18
❑ CRL57292 [M]	Piano Song Book -- Movie Themes	1959	$18
❑ CRL757292 [S]	Piano Song Book -- Movie Themes	1959	$25
❑ CRL57395 [M]	Rhapsody by Candlelight	1962	$15
❑ CRL757395 [S]	Rhapsody by Candlelight	1962	$18
❑ CXB9 [M]	The Best of Liberace	1965	$18
❑ 7CXB9 [S]	The Best of Liberace	1965	$25
❑ CRL57305 [M]	The Magic Pianos of Liberace	1960	$15
❑ CRL757305 [S]	The Magic Pianos of Liberace	1960	$18
❑ CRL57305 [M]	The Magic Pianos of Liberace	1960	$18
❑ CRL757305 [S]	The Magic Pianos of Liberace	1960	$25

DOT
❑ DLP-3550 [M]	A Liberace Christmas	1964	$15
❑ DLP-25550 [S]	A Liberace Christmas	1964	$18
❑ DLP-3595 [M]	Liberace at the Americana, Volume 1	1965	$15
❑ DLP-25595 [S]	Liberace at the Americana, Volume 1	1965	$18
❑ DLP-3596 [M]	Liberace at the Americana, Volume 2	1965	$15
❑ DLP-25596 [S]	Liberace at the Americana, Volume 2	1965	$18
❑ DLP-3816 [M]	Liberace Now!	1967	$18
❑ DLP-25816 [S]	Liberace Now!	1967	$18
❑ DLP-3547 [M]	Mr. Showmanship	1964	$15
❑ DLP-25547 [S]	Mr. Showmanship	1964	$18
❑ DLP-3563 [M]	My Most Requested	1965	$15
❑ DLP-25563 [S]	My Most Requested	1965	$18
❑ DLP-3755 [M]	New Sounds	1966	$15
❑ DLP-25755 [S]	New Sounds	1966	$18
❑ DLP-9502 [M]	Silver Anniversary	1965	$15
❑ DLP-29502 [S]	Silver Anniversary	1965	$18
❑ DLP-25901	Sound of Love	1969	$15
❑ DLP-25858	The Love Album	1968	$15

HARMONY
❑ HL7361 [M]	Concerto by Candlelight	196?	$15
❑ HS11161 [R]	Concerto by Candlelight	196?	$15
❑ HL7237 [M]	Rhapsody in Blue	196?	$15
❑ HL11175 [R]	Rhapsody in Blue	196?	$12
❑ HS11325	Tenderly	1969	$12
❑ HL7154 [M]	The Liberace Show	1959	$18
❑ HS11054 [R]	The Liberace Show	196?	$12
❑ HS11391	The Very Thought of You	1970	$12

MCA
❑ 740	Here's Liberace	198?	$10

— Reissue of Vocalion 73821

❑ 4167	The Artistry of Liberace	198?	$15
❑ 4060	The Best of Liberace	197?	$15

MISTLETOE
❑ MLP-1208	Twas the Night Before Christmas	1974	$12

PARAMOUNT
❑ PAS-1032	Liberace In Concert	1974	$18
❑ PAS-1009	The Best of Liberace	1973	$15

PICKWICK
❑ SPC-3208	By the Time I Get to Phoenix	197?	$12
❑ SPC-3124	Strangers in the Night	196?	$12
❑ SPC-3159	What Now My Love	1969	$12
❑ SPC-3085	You Made Me Love You	196?	$12

VOCALION
❑ VL3821 [M]	Here's Liberace	196?	$15
❑ VL73821 [R]	Here's Liberace	196?	$15

WARNER BROS.
❑ WS1847	A Brand New Me	1969	$15
❑ WS1889	Love and Music Festival "Live	1970	$15

LIBERMAN, JEFFERY
LIBRAH
❑ 1545	Jeffery Liberman	1975	$100
❑ 6969	Solitude Within	1975	$120
❑ 12157	Synergy	1976	$120

LIDSTROM, JACK
WORLD PACIFIC
❑ PJ-1235 [M]	Look, Dad! They're Comin' Down the Street in Hi-Fi	1957	$175

LIEBERMAN, LORI
CAPITOL
❑ ST-11297	A Piece of Time	1974	$15
❑ ST-11203	Becoming	1973	$15
❑ ST-11081	Lori Lieberman	1972	$15

LIEBMAN, DAVE
ARTISTS HOUSE
❑ 8	Pendulum	1978	$30

CMP
❑ CMP-40-ST	Chant	1990	$35
❑ CMP-9-ST	Dedications	198?	$30
❑ CMP-24-ST	The Loneliness of a Long-Distance Runner	1987	$30

COLUMBIA
❑ JC36581	What It Is	1979	$25

ECM
❑ 1046	Drum Ode	1975	$35
❑ 1039	Lookout Farm	197?	$35

— As "David Liebman"

HEADS UP
❑ HUP-3005	The Energy of the Chance	1989	$35

HORIZON
❑ SP-709	Fantasies	1976	$30
❑ SP-721	Light'n Up, Please!	1977	$30
❑ SP-702	Sweet Hands	1976	$30

PM
❑ PMR-022	Memories, Dreams and Reflections	1986	$30
❑ PMR-023	Picture Show	1986	$30

WEST 54
❑ 8012	First Visit	1979	$30

LIFE WITHOUT BUILDINGS
TUGBOAT
❑ TUGS016 [B]	Any Other City	2014	$30

LIFEGUARDS, THE (U)
WYNCOTE
❑ W-9043 [M]	C'mon and Swim	1964	$15
❑ SW-9043 [S]	C'mon and Swim	1964	$18

LIFT
GUINNESS
❑ GNS36021 [B]	Caverns Of Your Brain	1977	$250

LIGGINS, JOE
MERCURY
❑ MG-20731 [M]	Honeydripper	1962	$100
❑ SR-60731 [S]	Honeydripper	1962	$150

LIGHT, ENOCH
COMMAND
❑ SE70SD	I'm Looking Over a Four Leaf Clover/Mary Lou/If I Could Be with You One Hour Tonight/Last Night on the Back Porch (I Loved Her Best of All)/California Here I Come/Sunny Side Up	196?	$10

— Stereo jukebox issue; small hole, plays at 33 1/3 rpm

❑ SE70SD [PS]	The Roaring '20s	196?	$12

ABC WESTMINSTER/GRAND AWARD
❑ 68008	Sing Along with the Original Roaring 20's	1974	$12
❑ 68009	The Flirty 30's	1974	$12
❑ 68012	The Torchy Thirties	1974	$12

COMMAND
❑ 33-854 [M]	1963 -- The Year's Most Popular Themes	1963	$15
❑ 854SD [S]	1963 -- The Year's Most Popular Themes	1963	$18
❑ QD-40002 [Q]	A New Concept	1972	$20
❑ 33-844 [M]	Big Band Bossa Nova	1962	$15
❑ 844SD [S]	Big Band Bossa Nova	1962	$18
❑ 33-818 [M]	Big Bold and Brassy	1961	$15
❑ 818SD [S]	Big Bold and Brassy	1961	$18
❑ 33-868 [M]	Command Performances	1964	$15
❑ 868SD [S]	Command Performances	1964	$18
❑ 915SD	Command Performances, Volume 2	1969	$18
❑ 33-867 [M]	Dimension "3	1964	$15
❑ 867SD [S]	Dimension "3	1964	$18
❑ 873SD [S]	Discotheque Dance... Dance...Dance	1964	$18
❑ 33-873 [M]	Discotheque Dance... Dance…Dance	1964	$15
❑ 882SD [S]	Discotheque Dance... Dance...Dance, Volume 2	1965	$18
❑ 33-882 [M]	Discotheque Dance... Dance…Dance, Volume 2	1965	$15
❑ 33-840 [M]	Enoch Light and His Orchestra At Carnegie Hall Play Irving Berlin	1962	$15
❑ 840SD [S]	Enoch Light and His Orchestra At Carnegie Hall Play Irving Berlin	1962	$18
❑ 33-822 [M]	Far Away Places	1961	$15
❑ 822SD [S]	Far Away Places	1961	$18
❑ 33-850 [M]	Far Away Places, Volume 2	1963	$15
❑ 850SD [S]	Far Away Places, Volume 2	1963	$18
❑ 33-879 [M]	Great Cole Porter Songs	1965	$15
❑ 879SD [S]	Great Cole Porter Songs	1965	$18
❑ 33-835 [M]	Great Themes from Hit Films	1962	$15
❑ 835SD [S]	Great Themes from Hit Films	1962	$18
❑ 33-871 [M]	Great Themes from Hit Films	1964	$15
❑ 871SD [S]	Great Themes from Hit Films	1964	$18
❑ 33-851 [M]	Let's Dance the Bossa Nova	1963	$15
❑ 851SD [S]	Let's Dance the Bossa Nova	1963	$18
❑ 33-887 [M]	Magnificent Movie Themes	1965	$15
❑ 887SD [S]	Magnificent Movie Themes	1965	$18
❑ 33-805 [M]	Paperback Ballet	1960	$15
❑ 805SD [S]	Paperback Ballet	1960	$18
❑ 33-800 [M]	Persuasive Percussion	1960	$15

— By "Terry Snyder and the All-Stars

❑ 800SD [S]	Persuasive Percussion	1960	$18

— By "Terry Snyder and the All-Stars

❑ 33-808 [M]	Persuasive Percussion, Volume 2	1960	$15

— By "Terry Snyder and the All-Stars

❑ 808SD [S]	Persuasive Percussion, Volume 2	1960	$18

— By "Terry Snyder and the All-Stars

❑ 33-817 [M]	Persuasive Percussion, Volume 3	1961	$15

— By "The Command All-Stars

❑ 817SD [S]	Persuasive Percussion, Volume 3	1961	$18

— By "The Command All-Stars

❑ 33-830 [M]	Persuasive Percussion, Volume 4	1962	$15
❑ 830SD [S]	Persuasive Percussion, Volume 4	1962	$18
❑ 33-895 [M]	Persuasive Percussion 1966	1966	$15
❑ 895SD [S]	Persuasive Percussion 1966	1966	$18
❑ 33-814 [M]	Pertinent Percussion Cha-Cha's	1960	$15
❑ 814SD [S]	Pertinent Percussion Cha-Cha's	1960	$18
❑ 33-806 [M]	Provocative Percussion	1960	$15

— By "The Command All-Stars

❑ 806SD [S]	Provocative Percussion	1960	$18

— By "The Command All-Stars

❑ 33-810 [M]	Provocative Percussion, Volume 2	1960	$15
❑ 810SD [S]	Provocative Percussion, Volume 2	1960	$18
❑ 33-821 [M]	Provocative Percussion, Volume 3	1961	$15
❑ 821SD [S]	Provocative Percussion, Volume 3	1961	$18
❑ 33-834 [M]	Provocative Percussion, Volume 4	1962	$15
❑ 834SD [S]	Provocative Percussion, Volume 4	1962	$18
❑ 33-863 [M]	Rome 35/MM	1964	$15
❑ 863SD [S]	Rome 35/MM	1964	$18
❑ 826SD [S]	Stereo 35/MM	1961	$18
❑ 831SD [S]	Stereo 35/MM, Volume Two	1962	$18
❑ 33-804 [M]	The Sound of Strings	1960	$15
❑ 804SD [S]	The Sound of Strings	1960	$18
❑ 33-833 [M]	Vibrations	1962	$15
❑ 833SD [S]	Vibrations	1962	$18

GRAND AWARD
❑ GA 33-399 [M]	All the Things You Are	1959	$25
❑ GA-236SD [S]	All the Things You Are	1959	$30
❑ GA-214SD [S]	Around the World in 80 Days	1958	$30
❑ GA-237SD [S]	Come to Hawaii	1959	$30
❑ GA 33-405 [M]	Come to Hawaii	1959	$25
❑ GA-215SD [S]	Gigi	1958	$30
❑ GA 33-381 [S]	Glenn Miller's Song Hits	1958	$25
❑ GA-207SD [S]	Glenn Miller's Song Hits	1958	$30
❑ GA 33-391 [M]	Happy Cha Cha's, Vol. 2	1959	$25

❑ GA-227SD [S]	Happy Cha Cha's, Vol. 2	1959	$30
❑ GA 33-388 [M]	I Want to Be Happy Cha Cha's	1959	$25
❑ GA-222SD [S]	I Want to Be Happy Cha Cha's	1959	$30
❑ GA-246SD [S]	Just for Kicks	1959	$30
❑ GA-216SD [S]	My Fair Lady	1958	$30
❑ GA-224SD [S]	New World Symphony	1958	$30
❑ GA-217SD [S]	Oklahoma/South Pacific	1958	$30
❑ GA 33-380 [M]	Paris Spectacular	1958	$25

Number	Title	Yr	NM
❏ GA-228SD [S]	Show Spectacular	1959	$30
❏ GA 33-419 [M]	Sing Along with the Original Roaring 20's	1959	$25
❏ GA-251SD [S]	Sing Along with the Original Roaring 20's	1959	$30
❏ GA 33-410 [M]	Something to Remember You By	1959	$25
❏ GA-242SD [S]	Something to Remember You By	1959	$30
❏ GA-202SD [S]	The Flirty Thirties	1958	$30
❏ GA 33-371 [M]	The Flirty Thirties	1958	$25
❏ GA-225SD [S]	The Great Themes of America's Great Bands	1958	$30
❏ GA 33-392 [M]	The Great Themes of America's Great Bands	1958	$25
❏ GA-201SD [S]	The Roaring Twenties	1958	$30
❏ GA 33-327 [M]	The Roaring Twenties	1958	$25
❏ GA-211SD [S]	The Roaring Twenties, Volume 2	1958	$30
❏ GA 33-353 [M]	The Roaring Twenties, Volume 2	1959	$25
❏ GA-229SD [S]	The Roaring Twenties, Volume 3	1959	$30
❏ GA-220SD [S]	The Torchy Thirties	1958	$30
❏ GA-206SD [S]	Tommy Dorsey's Song Hits	1958	$30
❏ GA 33-382 [M]	Tommy Dorsey's Song Hits	1958	$25
❏ GA-372 [M]	Waltzes for Dancing	1958	$25
❏ GA-203SD [S]	Waltzes for Dancing	1958	$30
❏ GA 33-406 [M]	With My Eyes Wide Open I'm Dreaming	1959	$25
❏ GA-238SD [S]	With My Eyes Wide Open I'm Dreaming	1959	$30

PROJECT 3

Number	Title	Yr	NM
❏ PR4C-5068 [Q]	4 Channel Dynamite!	1973	$20
❏ PR-6034	20 Great Movie Themes	1980	$18
❏ PR-5084SD	Beatles Classics	1974	$15
❏ PR4C-5084 [Q]	Beatles Classics	1974	$20
❏ PR-5046SD	Best of the Movie Themes 1970	1970	$15
❏ PR4C-5046 [Q]	Best of the Movie Themes 1970	1973	$20
❏ PR-5056SD	Big Band Hits of the 30's & 40's!	1971	$15
❏ PR4C-5056 [Q]	Big Band Hits of the 30's & 40's!	1973	$20
❏ PR-6005/6	Big Band Hits of the 30's, 40's & 50's	1974	$18
❏ PR4C-6005/6 [Q]	Big Band Hits of the 30's, 40's & 50's	1974	$30
❏ PR-5049SD	Big Band Hits of the 30's	1971	$15
❏ PR4C-5049 [Q]	Big Band Hits of the 30's	1973	$20
❏ PR-5089SD	Big Band Hits of the 30's, Volume 2	1975	$15
❏ PR4C-5089 [Q]	Big Band Hits of the 30's, Volume 2	1975	$20
❏ PR-6013/14	Big Band Hits of the 30's and 40's	197?	$18
❏ PR4C-6013/14 [Q]	Big Band Hits of the 30's and 40's	197?	$30
❏ PR4C-5076 [Q]	Big Band Hits of the 40's & 50's	1973	$20
❏ PR-5059SD	Big Hits of the 20's	1971	$15
❏ PR4C-5059 [Q]	Big Hits of the 20's	1973	$20
❏ PR-6003/4	Big Hits of the Seventies	1974	$18
❏ PR4C-6003/4 [Q]	Big Hits of the Seventies	1974	$30
❏ PR4C-5073 [Q]	Charge!	1973	$20
❏ PR4C-5092 [Q]	Disco Disque	197?	$20
❏ PR-5092SD	Disco Disque	197?	$15
❏ PR-5036SD	Enoch Light and the Brass Menagerie	1969	$15
❏ PR4C-5036 [Q]	Enoch Light and the Brass Menagerie	1973	$20
❏ PR-5042SD	Enoch Light and the Brass Menagerie, Volume 2	1969	$15
❏ PR4C-5042 [Q]	Enoch Light and the Brass Menagerie, Volume 2	1973	$20
❏ PR-5060SD	Enoch Light and the Brass Menagerie 1973	1972	$15
❏ PR4C-5060 [Q]	Enoch Light and the Brass Menagerie 1973	1973	$20
❏ PR-5013SD	Film Fame	1968	$15
❏ PR-5005SD	Film on Film -- Great Movie Themes	1967	$15
❏ PR4C-5077 [Q]	Future Sound Shock	1973	$20
❏ PR-5038SD	Glittering Guitars	1969	$15
❏ PR-5086SD	Great Hits from the Gatsby Era	1974	$15
❏ PR4C-5086 [Q]	Great Hits from the Gatsby Era	1974	$20
❏ PR-5051SD	Hit Movie Themes	1971	$15
❏ PR4C-5051 [Q]	Hit Movie Themes	1973	$20
❏ PR-5004SD	It's Happening	1967	$15
❏ PR-5100	Let It Be	197?	$15
❏ PR-5063SD	Movie Hits!	1972	$15
❏ PR4C-5063 [Q]	Movie Hits!	1973	$20
❏ PR-6011/12	Music Maestro, Please	197?	$18
❏ PR-5048SD	Permissive Polyphonics	1970	$15
❏ PR4C-5048 [Q]	Permissive Polyphonics	1973	$20

Number	Title	Yr	NM
❏ PR-5043SD [B]	Spaced Out	1970	$15
❏ PR4C-5043 [Q]	Spaced Out	1973	$20
❏ PR-5000SD	Spanish Strings	1967	$15
❏ PR4C-5000 [Q]	Spanish Strings	1973	$20
❏ PR-5027SD	The Best of Hollywood '68-'69	1968	$15
❏ PR-5109	The Most Beautiful Music in the World	1981	$15
❏ PR-5021SD	Twelve Smash Hits	1968	$15
❏ PR-5030SD	Whoever You Are, I Love You	1968	$15

SEAGULL

Number	Title	Yr	NM
❏ LG-8204	Blowin' in the Wind	198?	$12
❏ LG-8207	Music from the Movies	198?	$12

LIGHT CRUST DOUGHBOYS, THE

AUDIO LAB

Number	Title	Yr	NM
❏ AL-1525 [M]	The Light Crust Doughboys	1959	$175

LIGHTFOOT, GORDON

LIBERTY

Number	Title	Yr	NM
❏ LN-10040	Back Here on Earth	198?	$10
—Budget-line reissue			
❏ LN-10041	Did She Mention My Name	198?	$10
—Budget-line reissue			
❏ LN-10044	Lightfoot	198?	$10
—Budget-line reissue			
❏ LN-10039	Sunday Concert	198?	$10
—Budget-line reissue			
❏ LN-10038	The Best of Lightfoot	198?	$10
—Budget-line reissue			
❏ LN-10043	The Way I Feel	198?	$10
—Budget-line reissue			

MOBILE FIDELITY

Number	Title	Yr	NM
❏ Jan-0018	Sundown	1979	$40
—Audiophile vinyl			

PAIR

Number	Title	Yr	NM
❏ PDL2-1081	Songbook	1986	$15

REPRISE

Number	Title	Yr	NM
❏ MS2206	Cold on the Shoulder	1975	$15
❏ MS4-2206 [Q]	Cold on the Shoulder	1975	$40
❏ MS2056	Don Quixote	1972	$15
❏ 2RS2237	Gord's Gold	1975	$18
❏ RS6392	If You Could Read My Mind	1971	$12
—Retitled version			
❏ MS2116	Old Dan's Records	1972	$15
❏ RS6392	Sit Down Young Stranger	1970	$18
❏ ST-93228	Sit Down Young Stranger	1970	$25
—Capitol Record Club edition			
❏ MS2037	Summer Side of Life	1971	$15
❏ MS2246	Summertime Dream	1976	$15
❏ MS2177	Sundown	1974	$15
❏ MS4-2177 [Q]	Sundown	1974	$40

UNITED ARTISTS

Number	Title	Yr	NM
❏ UAS-6672	Back Here on Earth	1969	$25
❏ UAS-5510	Classic Lightfoot (The Best of Lightfoot/Volume 2)	1971	$18
❏ UAS-6649 [B]	Did She Mention My Name	1968	$25
❏ UAL-3487 [M]	Lightfoot	1966	$25
❏ UAS-6487 [S]	Lightfoot	1966	$30
❏ UAS-6714	Sunday Concert	1969	$18
❏ UAS-6754	The Best of Gordon Lightfoot	1970	$18
❏ UA-LA243-G	The Very Best of Gordon Lightfoot	1974	$15
❏ UAL-3587 [M]	The Way I Feel	1967	$25
❏ UAS-6587 [S]	The Way I Feel	1967	$30

WARNER BROS.

Number	Title	Yr	NM
❏ HS3426	Dream Street Rose	1980	$12
❏ 25482	East of Midnight	1986	$12
❏ BSK3149	Endless Wire	1978	$12
❏ 25784	Gord's Gold, Volume II	1989	$15
❏ 23901	Salute	1983	$12
❏ BSK3633	Shadows	1982	$12

LIGHTFOOT, PAPA

VAULT

Number	Title	Yr	NM
❏ 130	Natchez Trace	1969	$18
—As "Papa George Lightfoot			

LIGHTHOUSE

EVOLUTION

Number	Title	Yr	NM
❏ 3014	Lighthouse Live!	1972	$25
❏ 3007 [B]	One Fine Morning	1971	$30
❏ 3016	Sunny Days	1973	$18
❏ 3010 [B]	Thoughts of Movin' On	1972	$25

JANUS

Number	Title	Yr	NM
❏ JSX-7025	The Best of Lighthouse	1976	$15

POLYDOR

Number	Title	Yr	NM
❏ PD-5056	Can You Feel It	1973	$15
❏ PD-1-6028	Good Day	1974	$15

RCA VICTOR

Number	Title	Yr	NM
❏ LSP-4173	Lighthouse	1969	$18
❏ LSP-4325	Peacing It All Together	1970	$18
❏ LSP-4241	Suite Feeling	1969	$18

LIGHTNIN' SLIM

EXCELLO

Number	Title	Yr	NM
❏ LPS8018	High and Low Down	1971	$18
❏ LP8004 [M]	Lightnin' Slim's Bell Ringer	1965	$300
❏ LPS8004 [M]	Lightnin' Slim's Bell Ringer	196?	$50
—Thogh labeled "Electronic Stereo," this record is mono			
❏ LPS8023	London Gumbo	1972	$18
❏ LP8000 [M]	Rooster Blues	1960	$800
❏ LPS8000 [M]	Rooster Blues	196?	$50
—Thogh labeled "Electronic Stereo," this record is mono			

INTERMEDIA

Number	Title	Yr	NM
❏ QS-5062	That's All Right	198?	$12

LIGHTNING

P.I.P.

Number	Title	Yr	NM
❏ 6807 [B]	Lightning	1971	$35

LIGHTNING SEEDS, THE

MCA

Number	Title	Yr	NM
❏ 6404	Cloudcuckooland	1990	$18

LIGHTSEY, KIRK

SUNNYSIDE

Number	Title	Yr	NM
❏ SSC-1020	Everything Is Changed	198?	$30
❏ SSC-1002	Lightsey 1	1985	$30
❏ SSC-1005	Lightsey 2	1985	$30
❏ SSC-1014	Lightsey Live	1987	$30

LIGON, BERT

INNER CITY

Number	Title	Yr	NM
❏ IC-1107	The Condor	198?	$30

SEA BREEZE

Number	Title	Yr	NM
❏ SB-3002	Dancing Bare	198?	$30

LIL BOW WOW

SO SO DEF

Number	Title	Yr	NM
❏ C269981	Beware of Dog	2000	$18

LIL' KIM

UNDEAS

Number	Title	Yr	NM
❏ 92733	Hard Core	1996	$25
❏ 92840	The Notorious K.I.M.	2000	$18

LIL' ROMEO

SME/PRIORITY

Number	Title	Yr	NM
❏ 50198	Lil' Romeo	2001	$18

LI'L WALLY

JAY JAY

Number	Title	Yr	NM
❏ 5080 [S]	A Polka Christmas	1966	$15
❏ 1080 [M]	A Polka Christmas	1966	$18
❏ 8003	Christmas from Poland	19??	$15
❏ 5026 [S]	Christmas Time	196?	$15
❏ 1039 [M]	Christmas Time	196?	$18
❏ 5012 [S]	Dance Around the Christmas Tree	196?	$15
❏ 1026 [M]	Dance Around the Christmas Tree	196?	$18
❏ 1023 [M]	Polish Christmas Carols	196?	$18
❏ 5011 [S]	Polish Christmas Carols	196?	$15
❏ 1017 [M]	Polish Christmas Carols	195?	$18

LILLIE, BEATRICE

DECCA

Number	Title	Yr	NM
❏ DL5453 [10]	Souvenir Album	1954	$50

LIBERTY MUSIC SHOP

Number	Title	Yr	NM
❏ 1002 [10]	Thirty Minutes with Bea Lillie	1954	$50

LONDON

Number	Title	Yr	NM
❏ LL1373 [M]	An Evening with Bea Little	1956	$30
❏ 5471 [M]	Auntie Bea	1959	$30

Number	Title	Yr	NM

LILLY BROTHERS, THE
FOLKLORE
❏ FL-14010 [M]	Bluegrass Breakdown	1963	$25
❏ FLS-14010 [S]	Bluegrass Breakdown	1963	$30
❏ FL-14035 [M]	Country Songs	1964	$25
❏ FLS-14035 [S]	Country Songs	1964	$30

FOLKWAYS
❏ FA-2433 [M]	Folk Songs from the Southern Mountains	196?	$30

LIMAHL
EMI AMERICA
❏ ST-17194	Colour All My Days	1986	$12
❏ ST-17142	Don't Suppose	1985	$12

LIMEHOUSE JAZZ BAND, THE
STOMP OFF
❏ SOS-1014	Rhythm Is Our Business	1981	$25

LIMELITERS, THE
Also see GLENN YARBROUGH.
ELEKTRA
❏ EKM-180 [M]	The Limeliters	1960	$25
❏ EKS-7180 [S]	The Limeliters	1960	$30

GNP CRESCENDO
❏ GNPS-2188	Alive! In Concert, Vol. 1	1986	$12
❏ GNPS-2190	Alive! In Concert, Vol. 2	1987	$12

LEGACY
❏ 113	Their First Historic Album	1970	$15

RCA CAMDEN
❏ ACL1-0602	This Train	1974	$12

RCA VICTOR
❏ LPM-2547 [M]	Folk Matinee	1962	$25
❏ LSP-2547 [S]	Folk Matinee	1962	$30
❏ LPM-2671 [M]	Fourteen 14K Folk Songs	1963	$25
❏ LSP-2671 [S]	Fourteen 14K Folk Songs	1963	$30
❏ LPM-2906 [M]	Leave It to the Limeliters	1964	$18
❏ LSP-2906 [S]	Leave It to the Limeliters	1964	$25
❏ LPM-2907 [M]	London Concert	1964	$18
❏ LSP-2907 [S]	London Concert	1964	$25
❏ LPM-2588 [M]	Makin' a Joyful Noise	1963	$25
❏ LSP-2588 [S]	Makin' a Joyful Noise	1963	$30
❏ LPM-2844 [M]	More of Everything!	1964	$18
❏ LSP-2844 [S]	More of Everything!	1964	$25
❏ LPM-2609 [M]	Our Men in San Francisco	1963	$25
❏ LSP-2609 [S]	Our Men in San Francisco	1963	$30
❏ ANL1-2336	Pure Gold	1977	$10
❏ LPM-2445 [M]	Sing Out!	1962	$25
❏ LSP-2445 [S]	Sing Out!	1962	$30
❏ LPM-2889 [M]	The Best of the Limeliters	1964	$18
❏ LSP-2889 [S]	The Best of the Limeliters	1964	$25
❏ LPM-3385 [M]	The Limeliters Look at Love… In Depth	1965	$18
❏ LSP-3385 [S]	The Limeliters Look at Love… In Depth	1965	$25
❏ LSP-4100	The Original "Those Were the Days	1969	$18
❏ LPM-2393 [M]	The Slightly Fabulous Limeliters	1961	$25
❏ LSP-2393 [S]	The Slightly Fabulous Limeliters	1961	$30
❏ LPM-2512 [M]	Through Children's Eyes	1962	$25
❏ LSP-2512 [S]	Through Children's Eyes	1962	$30
❏ LPM-2272 [M]	Tonight: In Person	1961	$25
❏ LSP-2272 [S]	Tonight: In Person	1961	$30

WEST KNOLL
❏ WK-1001	Alive! In Concert, Vol. 1	198?	$12
❏ WK-1002	Alive! In Concert, Vol. 2	198?	$12

LIMOUSINE
GSF
❏ 1002	Limousine	1972	$25

LINCOLN, ABBEY
BARMABY
❏ KZ31037	Straight Ahead	1972	$75

CANDID
❏ CD-8015 [M]	Straight Ahead	1960	$100
❏ CS-9015 [S]	Straight Ahead	1960	$150

ENJA
❏ 4060	Talking to the Sun	1983	$50

FANTASY
❏ OJC-069	Abbey Is Blue	1983	$30
❏ OJC-205	It's Magic	1985	$30
❏ OJC-085	That's Him!	198?	$30

INNER CITY
❏ IC-1117	Golden Lady	198?	$75
❏ IC-6040	The People in Me	1978	$50

JAZZ MAN
❏ 5043	Straight Ahead	198?	$35
—Reissue of Barnaby 31037			

LIBERTY
❏ LRP-3025 [M]	Abbey Lincoln's Affair	1957	$150

RIVERSIDE
❏ RLP 12-308 [M]	Abbey Is Blue	1959	$300
❏ RLP-1153 [S]	Abbey Is Blue	1959	$300

❏ 6088	Abbey Is Blue	197?	$50
❏ RLP 12-277 [M]	It's Magic	1958	$300
❏ RLP 12-251 [M]	That's Him!	1957	$175
❏ RLP-1107 [S]	That's Him!	1958	$300

LINCOLN, PHILAMORE
EPIC
❏ BN26497	North Wind Blew South	1970	$30

LINCOLN STREET EXIT
MAINSTREAM
❏ S-6126	Drive It	1970	$150

LIND, BOB
CAPITOL
❏ ST-780	Since There Were Circles	1971	$18

VERVE FOLKWAYS
❏ FT-3005 [M]	The Elusive Bob Lind	1966	$50
❏ FTS-3005 [S]	The Elusive Bob Lind	1966	$50

WORLD PACIFIC
❏ WP-1841 [M]	Don't Be Concerned	1966	$25
❏ ST-21841 [S]	Don't Be Concerned	1966	$30
❏ WP-1851 [M]	Photographs of Feeling	1966	$25
❏ ST-21851 [S]	Photographs of Feeling	1966	$30

LINDBERG, JOHN
BLACK SAINT
❏ BSR-0062	Dimension 5	1982	$30
❏ BSR-0072	Give and Take	1983	$30
❏ BSR-0082	Trilogy of Works for Eleven Instrumentalists	1985	$30

SOUND ASPECTS
❏ SAS-001	The East Side Suite	1985	$30

LINDBERG, NILS
CAPITOL
❏ T10363 [M]	Trisection	196?	$25
❏ ST10363 [S]	Trisection	196?	$75

LINDE, DENNIS
INTREPID
❏ 4004 [M]	Linde Manor	1966	$25
❏ 74004 [S]	Linde Manor	1966	$30

LINDEN, KATHY
FELSTED
❏ 7501 [M]	That Certain Boy	1959	$75

LINDH, JAYSON
JAS
❏ JAS-4000	Second Carneval	1975	$25

METRONOME
❏ DIX-3001	Cous-Cous	1973	$30
❏ DIX-3000	Ramadan	1972	$30
❏ DIX-3002	Sissel	1974	$30

STORYVILLE
❏ 4132	Atlantis	1983	$30
—As "Bjorn J-Son Lindh"			

VANGUARD
❏ VSD-79434	A Day at the Surface	1979	$30
—As "Bjorn J-Son Lindh"			

LINDISFARNE
ATCO
❏ SD 38-108	Back and Fourth	1978	$15

ELEKTRA
❏ EKS-75043 [B]	Dingly Dell	1972	$20
❏ EKS-75021 [B]	Fog on the Tyne	1972	$25
❏ 7E-1018 [B]	Happy Daze	1975	$18
❏ EKS-74099 [B]	Nicely Out of Tune	1971	$20
❏ EKS-75077	Roll On, Ruby	1974	$18

LINDSAY, MARK
COLUMBIA
❏ CS9986	Arizona	1970	$18
—Red "360 Sound" label			
❏ CS9986	Arizona	1970	$15
—Orange label			
❏ C30111	Silver Bird	1970	$15
❏ C30735	You've Got a Friend	1971	$15

LINDSEY, GEORGE
CAPITOL
❏ ST-230	96 Miles to Bakersfield	1969	$30
❏ ST2965	Goober Sings!	1968	$30

LINDSEY, LAWANDA
CAPITOL
❏ ST-11306	This Is LaWanda Lindsey	1974	$15

CHART
❏ CHS-1048	LaWanda Lindsey's Greatest Hits, Volume 1	1971	$18
❏ CHS-1015	Swingin' and Singin' My Song	1969	$18
❏ CHS-1035	We'll Sing in the Sunshine	1970	$18

LINGLE, PAUL
EUPHONIC
❏ 1217	Dance of the Witch Hazels	198?	$25
❏ 1220	The Legend of Lingle	198?	$25

LINKLETTER, ART
COLUMBIA
❏ CL703 [M]	Howlers, Boners and Shockers	1956	$40

LINN, RAY
DISCOVERY
❏ DS-823	Empty Suit Blues	1981	$25

TREND
❏ 515	Chicago Jazz	1980	$50
—Direct-to-disc recording			

LINN COUNTY
MERCURY
❏ SR-61218	Fever Shot	1969	$25
❏ SR-61181	Proud Flesh Soothseer	1968	$25

PHILIPS
❏ PHS600326	Till the Break of Dawn	1970	$18

LINS, IVAN
PHILIPS
❏ 822672-1	Juntos (Together)	1986	$25

LINSKY, JEFF
CONCORD PICANTE
❏ CJP-363	Up Late	1988	$25

LINTON, SHERWIN
BLACK GOLD
❏ 7116	I'm Not Johnny Cash	1972	$30

BREAKER
❏ BR-4001	Christmas Memories	1987	$15

RE-CAR
❏ 2108	Sherwin Linton and the Cotton Kings	1968	$75

LIPPS, INC.
CASABLANCA
❏ NBLP7262	Designer Music	1981	$12
❏ 811022-1	Four	1983	$12
❏ NBLP7197	Mouth to Mouth	1980	$12
❏ NBLP7242	Pucker Up	1980	$12

LIPSCOMB, MANCE
ARHOOLIE
❏ 1033 [M]	Mance Lipscomb, Vol. 4	1966	$40
❏ 1049	Mance Lipscomb, Vol. 5	1970	$30
❏ 1069	Mance Lipscomb, Vol. 6	1975	$30
❏ 1001 [M]	Texas Sharecropper and Songster	1960	$50
❏ 1023 [M]	Texas Songster, Vol. 2	1963	$40
❏ 1026 [M]	Texas Songster, Vol. 3	1965	$40

REPRISE
❏ R-2012 [M]	Trouble in Mind	1961	$150
❏ R9-2012 [S]	Trouble in Mind	1961	$175
❏ RS-6404	Trouble in Mind	1969	$30

LIPSKIN, MIKE
FLYING DUTCHMAN
❏ FD-10140	California	1972	$35

LIPSKY, HELMUT
JAZZIMAGE
❏ JZ-101	Melosphere	198?	$30

LIPSTIQUE
TOM N JERRY
❏ TJ-4701	At the Discotheque	1978	$25

LIPTON, PEGGY
ODE
❏ Z1244006 [B]	Peggy Lipton	1968	$30

LIQUID SMOKE
AVCO EMBASSY
❏ AVE-33005	Liquid Smoke	1970	$30

LISA LISA AND CULT JAM
COLUMBIA
❏ FC40135	Lisa Lisa and Cult Jam with Full Force	1985	$10
—Second prefix			
❏ BFC40135	Lisa Lisa and Cult Jam with Full Force	1985	$15

Number	Title	Yr	NM
— Original prefix			
❏ FC40477	Spanish Fly	1987	$10
❏ OC44378	Straight to the Sky	1989	$12

LIST, EUGENE
MERCURY LIVING PRESENCE

Number	Title	Yr	NM
❏ SR90290 [S]	Gershwin Favorites	196?	$25
— Maroon label, no "Vendor: Mercury Record Corporation			

LIST, GARRETT
LOVELY

❏ VR-1201	Fire and Ice	198?	$30

LISTEN (2)
INNER CITY

❏ IC-1055	Growing	1978	$35
❏ IC-1025	Listen	1977	$35

LISTENING
VANGUARD

❏ VSD-6504	Listening	1968	$75

LISTON, MELBA
METROJAZZ

❏ E-1013 [M]	Melba Liston and Her Bones	1958	$120
❏ SE-1013 [S]	Melba Liston and Her Bones	1958	$120

LITE STORM, THE
BEVERLY HILLS

❏ 1135	Lite Storm Warning	1973	$75

LITTER
EVA

❏ 12013	Rare Tracks	1983	$18

HEXAGON

❏ 681	$100 Fine	1968	$400

PROBE

❏ 4504	Emerge	1969	$50

WARICK

❏ 671	Distortions	1967	$500

LITTLE, BIG TINY
CORAL

❏ CRL57391 [M]	Christmas with Big Tiny Little	1961	$18
❏ CRL757391 [S]	Christmas with Big Tiny Little	1961	$25

LITTLE, BOOKER, AND BOOKER ERVIN
TCB

❏ 1003	Sounds of Inner City	197?	$40

LITTLE, BOOKER
BAINBRIDGE

❏ BT-1041	Booker Little	1981	$25

BARNABY

❏ BR-5019	Out Front	1977	$35

BETHLEHEM

❏ BCP-6061 [M]	Booker Little and Friends	1962	$350
❏ BCP-6034	Victory and Sorrow	197?	$75
— Reissue of 6061, distributed by RCA Victor			

CANDID

❏ CD-8027 [M]	Out Front	1961	$120
❏ CS-9027 [S]	Out Front	1961	$100

TIME

❏ 52011 [M]	Booker Little	1960	$175
❏ S-2011 [S]	Booker Little	1960	$250

UNITED ARTISTS

❏ UAL-4034 [M]	The Booker Little Four	1959	$120
❏ UAS-5034 [S]	The Booker Little Four	1959	$150

LITTLE, PEGGY
DOT

❏ DLP-25948	A Little Bit of Peggy	1969	$18
❏ DLP-25982	More Than a Little	1971	$18

LITTLE ANTHONY AND THE IMPERIALS
ACCORD

❏ SN-7216	Tears on My Pillow	1983	$12

AVCO

❏ AV-11012	On a New Street	1973	$25

DCP

❏ DCL-3808 [M]	Goin' Out of My Head	1965	$30
❏ DCS-6808 [S]	Goin' Out of My Head	1965	$30
❏ DCL-3801 [M]	I'm On the Outside Looking In	1964	$30
❏ DCS-6801 [S]	I'm On the Outside Looking In	1964	$30
❏ DCL-3809 [M]	The Best of Little Anthony and the Imperials	1965	$25
❏ DCS-6809 [S]	The Best of Little Anthony and the Imperials	1965	$30

END

❏ LP311 [M]	Shades of the 40's	1960	$250

Number	Title	Yr	NM
❏ LP303 [M]	We Are The Imperials Featuring Little Anthony	1959	$300

FORUM

❏ F-9107 [M]	Little Anthony and the Imperials' Greatest Hits	196?	$18
❏ FS-9107 [R]	Little Anthony and the Imperials' Greatest Hits	196?	$15

LIBERTY

❏ LM-1017	Out of Sight, Out of Mind	1981	$10
— Reissue of United Artists 1017			
❏ LN-10133	The Best of Little Anthony and the Imperials	1981	$10
— Budget-line reissue			

PICKWICK

❏ SPC-3029	The Hits of Little Anthony and the Imperials	196?	$15

RHINO

❏ R1-70919	The Best of Little Anthony and the Imperials	1989	$15

ROULETTE

❏ SR-42007	Forever Yours	1968	$18
❏ R-25294 [M]	Little Anthony and the Imperials' Greatest Hits	1965	$30
❏ SR-25294 [R]	Little Anthony and the Imperials' Greatest Hits	1965	$25

SONGBIRD

❏ 3245	Daylight	1980	$12

SUNSET

❏ SUS-5287	Little Anthony and the Imperials	1970	$18

UNITED ARTISTS

❏ UA-LA026-G	Legendary Masters Series	1972	$30
❏ UAS6720	Out of Sight, Out of Mind	1969	$25
❏ LM-1017	Out of Sight, Out of Mind	1980	$12
— Reissue of United Artists 6720			
❏ UA-LA255-G	The Very Best of Little Anthony and the Imperials	1974	$12

VEEP

❏ VP13511 [M]	Goin' Out of My Head	1966	$18
❏ VPS16511 [S]	Goin' Out of My Head	1966	$25
❏ VP13510 [M]	I'm On the Outside Looking In	1966	$18
❏ VPS16510 [S]	I'm On the Outside Looking In	1966	$25
❏ VP13516 [M]	Movie Grabbers	1967	$18
❏ VPS16516 [S]	Movie Grabbers	1967	$25
❏ VP13513 [M]	Payin' Our Dues	1966	$18
❏ VPS16513 [S]	Payin' Our Dues	1966	$25
❏ VP13514 [M]	Reflections	1967	$18
❏ VPS16514 [S]	Reflections	1967	$25
❏ VPS16519	The Best of Little Anthony, Volume 2	1968	$18
❏ VP13512 [M]	The Best of Little Anthony and the Imperials	1966	$18
❏ VPS16512 [S]	The Best of Little Anthony and the Imperials	1966	$25
❏ ST-90840 [S]	The Best of Little Anthony and the Imperials	1966	$30
— Capitol Record Club edition			

LITTLE BILL AND THE BLUENOTES
CAMELOT

❏ 102 [M]	The Fiesta Club Presents Little Bill and the Bluenotes	1960	$400

LITTLE BOY BLUES
FONTANA

❏ SRF-67578	In the Woodland of Weir	1968	$30

LITTLE CAESAR AND THE ROMANS
DEL-FI

❏ DFLP-1218 [M]	Memories of Those Oldies But Goodies	1961	$300

LITTLE ESTHER
See LITTLE ESTHER PHILLIPS.

LITTLE EVA
DIMENSION

❏ DLP-6000 [M]	LLLLLoco-Motion	1962	$175
— Without "Keep Your Hands Off My Baby			
❏ DLP-6000 [M]	LLLLLoco-Motion	1962	$250
— With "Keep Your Hands Off My Baby			
❏ DLPS-6000 [R]	LLLLLoco-Motion	1962	$175
— Without "Keep Your Hands Off My Baby			
❏ DLPS-6000 [R]	LLLLLoco-Motion	1962	$250
— With "Keep Your Hands Off My Baby			

LITTLE FEAT
Also see LOWELL GEORGE.
MOBILE FIDELITY

❏ Jan-0013	Waiting for Columbus	1979	$100
— Audiophile vinyl			

NAUTILUS

❏ NR-24	Time Loves a Hero	198?	$50
— Audiophile vinyl			

TPM/RHINO EXCLUSIVE

❏ 299	Little Feat	2008	$25

Number	Title	Yr	NM
WARNER BROS.			
❏ BS2686	Dixie Chicken	1973	$18
— Burbank" palm trees label			
❏ BS2686	Dixie Chicken	1979	$10
— Tan or white label			
❏ HS3345	Down on the Farm	1979	$12
❏ BS2748	Feats Don't Fail Me Now	1974	$18
— Burbank" palm trees label			
❏ BS2748	Feats Don't Fail Me Now	1979	$10
— Tan or white label			
❏ R12784 [B]	Feats Don't Fail Me Now	2016	$25
❏ 2BSK3538	Hoy-Hoy!	1981	$15
❏ PRO-A-984 [DJ]	Hoy-Hoy!	1981	$25
— Single-album sampler of 2-LP set			
❏ 25750	Let It Roll	1988	$12
❏ WS1890	Little Feat	1971	$25
— Green "WB" label; with photo on back cover			
❏ WS1890	Little Feat	1971	$18
— Green "WB" label; without photo on back cover			
❏ WS1890	Little Feat	1973	$12
— Burbank" palm trees label			
❏ WS1890	Little Feat	1979	$10
— Tan or white label			
❏ 26263	Representing the Mambo	1990	$18
❏ BS2600	Sailin' Shoes	1972	$18
— Green "WB" label			
❏ BS2600	Sailin' Shoes	1973	$12
— Burbank" palm trees label			
❏ BS2600	Sailin' Shoes	1979	$10
— Tan or white label			
❏ 307	Sailin' Shoes	2008	$25
❏ BS2884	The Last Record Album	1975	$18
— Burbank" palm trees label			
❏ BS2884	The Last Record Album	1979	$10
— Tan or white label			
❏ BS3015	Time Loves a Hero	1977	$15
— Burbank" palm trees label			
❏ BS3015	Time Loves a Hero	1979	$10
— Tan or white label			
❏ 2WS3140	Waiting for Columbus	1978	$18
— Burbank" palm trees label			
❏ 2WS3140	Waiting for Columbus	1979	$12
— Tan or white label			
ZOO/CLASSIC			
❏ 11097	Ain't Had Enough Fun	1995	$25
— 180-gram vinyl			
❏ 11097	Ain't Had Enough Fun	1995	$25
— 150-gram vinyl			

LITTLE GIRLS
FTM ENTERPRISES

❏ 0(no cat #) [EP]	Little Girls 1985	1985	$150

— Promo-only three-song EP, with all songs on same side, on clear vinyl in clear plastic sleeve; also contains two black & white photos of the group and three pages of biographical notes and reviews; 100 pressed

PVC

❏ 5904 [EP]	Thank Heaven!	1983	$25

LITTLE JOE
BRUNSWICK

❏ BL754135	Little Joe (Sure Can Sing)	1968	$25

LITTLE MILTON
CHECKER

❏ LP-3011 [B]	Grits Ain't Groceries	1969	$30
❏ LP-3012	If Walls Could Talk	1970	$30
❏ LP-3002 [M]	Little Milton Sings Big Blues	1966	$50
❏ LP-2995 [M]	We're Gonna Make It	1965	$150
— Black label			
❏ LP-2995 [M]	We're Gonna Make It	1966	$80
— Blue label with red and black checkers			
❏ LP-2995 [M]	We're Gonna Make It	196?	$30
— Blue, fading to white, label			

CHESS

❏ CH-9289	If Walls Could Talk	1989	$12
— Reissue of Checker 3012			
❏ 204	Little Milton	1976	$18
❏ CH-50013	Little Milton's Greatest Hits	1972	$18
❏ CH-9265	Little Milton Sings Big Blues	1987	$12
— Reissue of Checker 3002			
❏ CH-9252	We're Gonna Make It	1986	$12
— Reissue of Checker 2995			

GLADES

❏ 7508	Friend of Mine	1976	$15
❏ 7511	Me for You, You for Me	1977	$15

MALACO

❏ 7435	Annie Mae's Café	198?	$15
❏ 7448	Back to Back	198?	$15
❏ 7427	I Will Survive	198?	$15
❏ 7445	Movin' to the Country	198?	$15
❏ 7419	Playin' for Keeps	198?	$15
❏ 7453	Too Much Pain	198?	$15

Number	Title	Yr	NM
MCA			
❏ 5414	Age Ain't Nothin' But a Number	1983	$12
ROUNDER			
❏ SS-35	The Sun Masters	198?	$15
STAX			
❏ 5514	Blues 'n' Soul	1974	$25
❏ MPS-8518	Blues 'n' Soul	1981	$12
—Reissue of 5514			
❏ MPS-8529	Grits Ain't Groceries	198?	$12
—Despite the title, this is NOT a reissue of Checker 3011, but a later live recording			
❏ STS-3012	Waiting for Little Milton	1973	$25
❏ 4117	Waiting for Little Milton	1978	$15
—Reissue of 3012			
❏ MPS-8514	Walking the Back Streets	1981	$12
❏ MPS-8550	What It Is	198?	$12

LITTLE MISS CORNSHUCKS

Number	Title	Yr	NM
CHESS			
❏ LP-1453 [M]	The Loneliest Gal in Town	1961	$250

LITTLE RICHARD

Number	Title	Yr	NM
20TH FOX			
❏ FXG-5010 [M]	Little Richard Sings Gospel	1959	$150
❏ SGM-5010 [S]	Little Richard Sings Gospel	1959	$175
ACCORD			
❏ SN-7123	Tutti Frutti	1981	$12
AUDIO ENCORES			
❏ 1002	Little Richard	1980	$30
BUDDAH			
❏ BDS-7501	Little Richard	1969	$30
CLEOPATRA			
❏ 3427 [B]	Tutti Frutti - Greatest Hits		$25
CORAL			
❏ CRL57446 [M]	Coming Home	1963	$40
❏ CRL757446 [S]	Coming Home	1963	$50
CROWN			
❏ CLP-5362 [M]	Little Richard Sings Freedom Songs	1963	$25
CUSTOM			
❏ 2061 [M]	Little Richard Sings Spirituals	196?	$15
EPIC			
❏ EG30428	Cast a Long Shadow	1971	$25
❏ PE40389	Little Richard's Greatest Hits	1986	$12
❏ PE40390	The Explosive Little Richard	1986	$12
EXACT			
❏ 206	The Best of Little Richard	1980	$12
GNP CRESCENDO			
❏ GNP-9033	The Big Hits	1974	$15
GRT			
❏ 2103	The Original Little Richard	1977	$12
GUEST STAR			
❏ GS-1429 [M]	Little Richard with Sister Rosetta Tharpe	196?	$15
❏ GSS-1429 [R]	Little Richard with Sister Rosetta Tharpe	196?	$15
KAMA SUTRA			
❏ KSBS-2023	Little Richard	1970	$30
MERCURY			
❏ MG-20656 [M]	It's Real	1961	$50
❏ SR-60656 [S]	It's Real	1961	$75
MODERN			
❏ 100 [M]	His Greatest Hits/Recorded Live	1966	$25
❏ 1000 [S]	His Greatest Hits/Recorded Live	1966	$30
❏ 103 [M]	The Explosive Little Richard	1966	$25
❏ 1003 [S]	The Explosive Little Richard	1966	$30
OKEH			
❏ OKM12121 [M]	Little Richard's Greatest Hits	1967	$30
❏ OKS14121 [S]	Little Richard's Greatest Hits	1967	$25
❏ OKS14117 [S]	The Explosive Little Richard	1967	$25
❏ OKM12117 [M]	The Explosive Little Richard	1967	$30
PICKWICK			
❏ SPC-3258	King of the Gospel Singers	197?	$12
RCA CAMDEN			
❏ CAS-2430(e)	Every Hour with Little Richard	1970	$15
❏ CAL-420 [M]	Little Richard	1956	$250
REPRISE			
❏ RS6462	King of Rock and Roll	1972	$25
❏ RS6406	The Rill Thing	1971	$25
❏ MS2107	The Second Coming	1973	$25
RHINO			
❏ R1-70236	Shut Up! A Collection of Rare Tracks, 1951-1964	1988	$15
SCEPTER CITATION			
❏ CTN-18020	The Best of Little Richard	1972	$15
SPECIALTY			
❏ 100 [M]	Here's Little Richard	1957	$700

Number	Title	Yr	NM
❏ SP-2100 [M]	Here's Little Richard	1957	$250
— Thick vinyl			
❏ SP-2103 [M]	Little Richard	1958	$175
—Front cover photo occupies the entire cover			
❏ SP-2103 [M]	Little Richard	196?	$150
—Front cover photo partially obscured by a black triangle at uper right; thick vinyl			
❏ SP-2103 [M]	Little Richard	197?	$25
—Reissue with thinner vinyl			
❏ SP-2111	Little Richard -- His Biggest Hits	1963	$50
❏ SP-2111 [M]	Little Richard -- His Biggest Hits	197?	$25
—Reissue with thinner vinyl			
❏ SP-2113	Little Richard's Grooviest 17 Original Hits	1968	$30
— Thick vinyl			
❏ SP-2104 [M]	The Fabulous Little Richard	1958	$175
— Thick vinyl			
❏ SP-2104 [M]	The Fabulous Little Richard	197?	$25
—Reissue with thinner vinyl			
❏ SP-8508	The Specialty Sessions	1989	$40
❏ SP-2136	Well Alright!	1970	$25
SPIN-O-RAMA			
❏ 119 [M]	Clap Your Hands	196?	$15
TRIP			
❏ 8013	Greatest Hits	1972	$15
UNITED			
❏ US-7775	His Greatest Hits/Recorded Live	197?	$12
❏ US-7777	The Wild and Frantic Little Richard	197?	$12
UNITED ARTISTS			
❏ UA-LA497-E	The Very Best of Little Richard	1975	$12
UPFRONT			
❏ UPF-197	Little Richard Sings Gospel	197?	$12
❏ UPF-123	The Best of Little Richard	197?	$12
VEE JAY			
❏ LP-1107 [M]	Little Richard Is Back!	1964	$50
❏ LPS-1107 [S]	Little Richard Is Back!	1964	$80
❏ VJLP-1107	Little Richard's Back	198?	$12
— Reissue with thin vinyl			
❏ LP-1124 [M]	Little Richard's Greatest Hits	1965	$30
❏ LPS-1124 [S]	Little Richard's Greatest Hits	1965	$40
❏ VJLP-1124	Little Richard's Greatest Hits	198?	$12
— Reissue with thin vinyl			
❏ DY-7304	Talkin' 'Bout Soul	198?	$15
VEE JAY/CHAMELEON			
❏ D1-74797	Rip It Up	1989	$15
WARNER BROS.			
❏ 25529	Lifetime Friend	1986	$15
WING			
❏ MGW-12288 [M]	King of the Gospel Singers	1964	$18
❏ SRW-16288 [S]	King of the Gospel Singers	1964	$25

LITTLE RIVER BAND

Number	Title	Yr	NM
CAPITOL			
❏ SN-16072	After Hours	1979	$12
—First U.S. issue of their second Australian LP			
❏ SWBK-12061	Backstage Pass	1980	$12
❏ SN-16141	Beginnings	1980	$12
❏ SN-16142	Beginnings, Vol. 2	1980	$12
❏ SN-16455	Diamantina Cocktail	1987	$10
❏ SOO-11954	First Under the Wire	1979	$10
❏ SN-16345	First Under the Wire	198?	$10
—Budget-line reissue			
❏ ST-12247	Greatest Hits	1982	$10
❏ SN-16457	Greatest Hits	1987	$10
—Budget-line reissue			
❏ SN-16454	Little River Band	1987	$10
—Budget-line reissue			
❏ ST-12480	No Reins	1986	$10
❏ SJ-12365	Playing to Win	1985	$10
—As "LRB			
❏ SN-16456	Sleeper Catcher	1987	$10
—Budget-line reissue			
❏ ST-12273	The Net	1983	$10
❏ ST-12163	Time Exposure	1981	$10
❏ SN-16346	Time Exposure	198?	$10
—Budget-line reissue			
HARVEST			
❏ SW-11645 [B]	Diamantina Cocktail	1977	$12
❏ ST-11512	Little River Band	1976	$12
❏ SW-11783	Sleeper Catcher	1978	$12
MCA			
❏ 6269	Get Lucky	1990	$15
❏ 42193	Monsoon	1989	$12
MOBILE FIDELITY			
❏ Jan-0036	First Under the Wire	1980	$50
—Audiophile vinyl			

LITTLE SISTERS, THE

Number	Title	Yr	NM
MGM			
❏ E-4116 [M]	The Joys of Love	1963	$30
❏ SE-4116 [S]	The Joys of Love	1963	$30

LITTLE SONNY

Number	Title	Yr	NM
ENTERPRISE			
❏ ENS-1018	Black and Blue	1971	$40
❏ ENS-1036	Hard Goin' Up	1973	$40
❏ ENS-1005	New King of the Blues Harmonica	1970	$40

LITTLE WALTER

Number	Title	Yr	NM
CHECKER			
❏ LP-1428 [M]	The Best of Little Walter	1957	$500
—Black or maroon label			
❏ LP-3004 [M]	The Best of Little Walter	1967	$50
—Reissue of 1428			
CHESS			
❏ 2CH-60014	Boss Blues Harmonica	1972	$25
❏ CHV-416 [M]	Confessin' the Blues	1974	$15
❏ LP-1535 [M]	Hate to See You Go	1969	$30
❏ 2ACMB-202	Little Walter	1976	$25
—Reissue of 60014			

LIVE

Number	Title	Yr	NM
RADIOACTIVE			
❏ RAR2-11590	Secret Samadhi	1997	$18
— White vinyl; includes poster			
❏ RAR2-11590	Secret Samadhi	1997	$18
— Clear vinyl; includes poster			
❏ RAR-10997	Throwing Copper	1994	$50
— Clear vinyl			
❏ RAR-10997	Throwing Copper	1994	$25
— Black vinyl			

LIVELY ONES, THE

Number	Title	Yr	NM
DEL-FI			
❏ DFLP-1237 [M]	Surf City	1963	$40
❏ DFST-1237 [S]	Surf City	1963	$50
❏ DLF1237	Surf City	1997	$15
❏ DFLP-1231 [M]	Surf Drums	1963	$50
❏ DFST-1231 [S]	Surf Drums	1963	$80
❏ DLF1231	Surf Drums	1997	$15
❏ DFLP-1240 [M]	Surfin' South of the Border	1964	$40
❏ DFST-1240 [S]	Surfin' South of the Border	1964	$50
❏ DFLP-1226 [M]	Surf Rider	1963	$150
❏ DFST-1226 [S]	Surf Rider	1963	$175
MGM			
❏ E-4449 [M]	Bugalu Party	1967	$25
❏ SE-4449 [S]	Bugalu Party	1967	$30

LIVERPOOL BEATS, THE

Number	Title	Yr	NM
RONDO			
❏ 2026 [M]	The New Merseyside Sound	1964	$30

LIVERPOOL FIVE, THE

RCA VICTOR

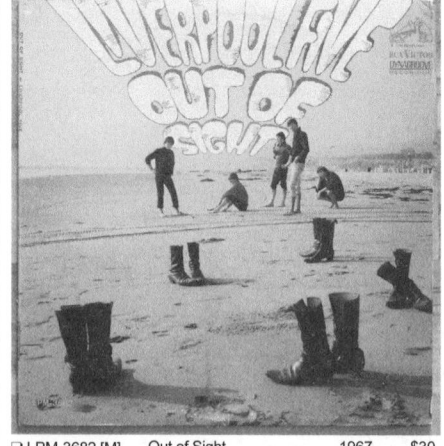

Number	Title	Yr	NM
❏ LPM-3682 [M]	Out of Sight	1967	$30
❏ LSP-3682 [S]	Out of Sight	1967	$30
❏ LPM-3583 [M]	The Liverpool Five Arrive	1966	$30
❏ LSP-3583 [S]	The Liverpool Five Arrive	1966	$30

LIVERPOOL SCENE, THE

Number	Title	Yr	NM
EPIC			
❏ LN24336 [M]	The Incredible New Liverpool Scene	1967	$50
❏ BN26336 [S]	The Incredible New Liverpool Scene	1967	$30

99999999999999999

LIVERPOOLS, THE
WYNCOTE
Number	Title	Yr	NM
W-9001 [M]	Beatle Mania! In the U.S.A.	1964	$30
SW-9001 [S]	Beatle Mania! In the U.S.A.	1964	$40
W-9061 [M]	The Hit Sounds from England	1964	$18
SW-9061 [S]	The Hit Sounds from England	1964	$40

LIVIN' BLUES
DWARF
Number	Title	Yr	NM
2003	Dutch Treat	1971	$30

LIVING COLOUR
EPIC
Number	Title	Yr	NM
E46202	Time's Up	1990	$12
— Yellow vinyl
| FE44099 | Vivid | 1988 | $10 |

LIVING JAZZ
RCA CAMDEN
Number	Title	Yr	NM
CAL-985 [M]	A Lover's Concerto	1966	$25
CAS-985 [S]	A Lover's Concerto	1966	$30
CAL-878 [M]	Dear Heart and Other Favorites	1965	$25
CAS-878 [S]	Dear Heart and Other Favorites	1965	$30
CAS-2298	Fool on the Hill	1969	$25
CAS-2436	Hot Butter and Soul	1970	$25
ACL1-0202	Manha de Carnival	1973	$25
CAL-2196 [M]	Ode to Young Lovers	1968	$30
CAS-2196 [S]	Ode to Young Lovers	1968	$25
CAL-914 [M]	Quiet Nights	1965	$25
CAS-914 [S]	Quiet Nights	1965	$30
CAL-848 [M]	The Girl from Ipanema and Other Hits	1964	$25
CAS-848 [S]	The Girl from Ipanema and Other Hits	1964	$30
CAL-2135 [M]	The Soul of Brazil	1967	$30
CAS-2135 [S]	The Soul of Brazil	1967	$25
RCA VICTOR
| APL1-2386 | Hello Young Lovers | 1977 | $25 |

LIVING STRINGS
PICKWICK
Number	Title	Yr	NM
ACL-9006	The Sound of Christmas	197?	$10
— Reissue of RCA Camden CAS-2426
RCA CAMDEN
CAS-2426	The Sound of Christmas	1970	$15
CAL-783 [M]	The Spirit of Christmas	1963	$12
CAS-783 [S]	The Spirit of Christmas	1963	$15
— Same as above, but in stereo

LIVING STRINGS AND LIVING VOICES
RCA CAMDEN
Number	Title	Yr	NM
CAS2258	White Christmas	1968	$15

LIVING VOICES
PICKWICK
Number	Title	Yr	NM
ACL-9008	Living Voices Sing Christmas Music	1977	$10
— Reissue of RCA Camden CAS-725
RCA CAMDEN
| CAL-725 [M] | Living Strings Sing Christmas Music | 1962 | $12 |
| CAS-725 [S] | Living Strings Sing Christmas Music | 1962 | $15 |
— Same as above, but in stereo
| CAL-911 [M] | The Little Drummer Boy | 1965 | $12 |
| CAS-911 [S] | The Little Drummer Boy | 1965 | $15 |
— Same as above, but in stereo

LIVING WATER
PSALM ONE
Number	Title	Yr	NM
37946	There Lay Love/Living Water Christmas	1980	$12

LLOYD, CHARLES
4 MEN WITH BEARDS
Number	Title	Yr	NM
4M-119	Love-In	2003	$35
— 180-gram audiophile reissue
A&M
| SP-3046 | Geeta | 1973 | $50 |
| SP-3044 | Waves | 1973 | $35 |
ATLANTIC
SD1500	Charles Lloyd in Europe	1969	$50
SD1571	Charles Lloyd in the Soviet Union	1971	$50
1459 [M]	Dream Weaver	1966	$35
SD1459 [S]	Dream Weaver	1966	$50
— Blue and green label
| SD1459 [S] | Dream Weaver | 1969 | $30 |
— Red and green label, white stripe through center hole
SD1586	Flowering of the Original Charles Lloyd Quintet	1972	$50
1473 [M]	Forest Flower	1967	$75
SD1473 [S]	Forest Flower	1967	$75
SD1493	Journey Within	1968	$75
1481 [M]	Love-In	1967	$40
SD1481 [S]	Love-In	1967	$40
SD1519	Soundtrack	1970	$50
SD1556	The Best of Charles Lloyd	1970	$35
BLUE NOTE
| BT-85104 | A Night in Copenhagen | 1985 | $35 |
COLUMBIA
CL2267 [M]	Discovery!	1965	$250
CS9067 [S]	Discovery!	1965	$250
CS9609 [M]	Nirvana	1968	$150
— White label promo; "Special Mono Radio Station Copy" sticker on stereo cover
CS9609 [S]	Nirvana	1968	$75
CL2412 [M]	Of Course, Of Course	1966	$75
CS9212 [S]	Of Course, Of Course	1966	$75
PC36981 [S]	Of Course, Of Course	1980	$25
— Reissue of CS 9212
DESTINY
| 10003 | Autumn in New York Volume 1 | 1979 | $35 |
ECM
| 1398 | Fish Out of Water | 1990 | $50 |
— Made in Germany
ELEKTRA/MUSICIAN
| 60220 | Montreux '82 | 1983 | $30 |
KAPP
| KS-3634 | Moon Man | 1971 | $35 |
| KS-3647 | Warm Waters | 1971 | $75 |
PACIFIC ARTS
| 7-139 | Big Sur Tapestry | 1979 | $30 |
| 7-123 | Weavings | 1978 | $30 |

LLOYD, DAVID
EPIC
Number	Title	Yr	NM
LN24151 [M]	Confidential (Sounds for a Secret Agent)	1965	$25
BN26151 [S]	Confidential (Sounds for a Secret Agent)	1965	$30

LLOYD, HAROLD, JR.
CORAL
Number	Title	Yr	NM
CRL57471 [M]	The Intimate Style of Harold Lloyd, Jr.	1963	$18
CRL757471 [S]	The Intimate Style of Harold Lloyd, Jr.	1963	$25

LOADING ZONE, THE
RCA VICTOR
Number	Title	Yr	NM
LSP-3959	The Loading Zone	1968	$30
UMBRELLA
| US-101 | One for All | 1967 | $100 |

LOBO
BIG TREE
Number	Title	Yr	NM
BT89505	A Cowboy Afraid of Horses	1975	$15
2101	Calumet	1973	$18
2003	Introducing Lobo	1971	$18
2100	Introducing Lobo	1973	$15
— Reissue of 2003 with new cover
BT89501	Just a Singer	1974	$15
2013	Of a Simple Man	1972	$18
BT89513	The Best of Lobo	1976	$15
MCA
| 3194 | Lobo | 1979 | $12 |

LOBO (2)
Jazz guitarist and singer named Edu Lobo. No relation to the 1970s pop singer, whose real name is Kent Lavoie.
A&M
| SP-3035 | Sergio Mendes Presents Lobo | 1970 | $30 |

LOCASCIO, JOE
CMG
Number	Title	Yr	NM
CML-8002	Gliders	1988	$25
CML-8015	Marionette	1989	$30

LOCKE, JOE
CADENCE JAZZ
Number	Title	Yr	NM
CJR-1034	Scenario	1988	$25

LOCKLIN, HANK
DESIGN
Number	Title	Yr	NM
DLP-603 [M]	Hank Locklin	196?	$18
HILLTOP
JM-6003 [M]	Born to Ramble	196?	$18
JS-6003 [R]	Born to Ramble	196?	$15
JM-6041 [M]	Hank Locklin Sings Hank Locklin	196?	$18
JS-6041 [R]	Hank Locklin Sings Hank Locklin	196?	$15
JM-6083	Queen of Hearts	196?	$18
KING
| 738 [M] | Encores | 1961 | $75 |
| 672 [M] | The Best of Hank Locklin | 1961 | $75 |
METRO
| M541 [M] | Down Texas Way | 196? | $18 |
| MS541 [R] | Down Texas Way | 196? | $15 |
RCA CAMDEN
CAL-705 [M]	Hank Locklin	1962	$18
CAL-912 [M]	My Kind of Country Music	196?	$18
CAS-912 [R]	My Kind of Country Music	196?	$15
RCA VICTOR
LPM-2597 [M]	A Tribute to Roy Acuff, the King of Country Music	1962	$30
LSP-2597 [S]	A Tribute to Roy Acuff, the King of Country Music	1962	$30
LPM-3946 [M]	Country Hall of Fame	1968	$150
LSP-3946 [S]	Country Hall of Fame	1968	$25
LPM-1673 [M]	Foreign Love	1958	$75
LPM-3391 [M]	Hank Locklin Sings Eddy Arnold	1965	$25
LSP-3391 [S]	Hank Locklin Sings Eddy Arnold	1965	$30
LPM-2997 [M]	Hank Locklin Sings Hank Williams	1964	$25
LSP-2997 [S]	Hank Locklin Sings Hank Williams	1964	$30
LPM-2464 [M]	Happy Journey	1962	$30
LSP-2464 [S]	Happy Journey	1962	$30
LPM-2801 [M]	Irish Songs, Country Style	1964	$25
LSP-2801 [S]	Irish Songs, Country Style	1964	$30
LSP-4191	Lookin' Back	1969	$18
LSP-4030	My Love Song for You	1968	$25
LPM-3841 [M]	Nashville Women	1967	$30
LSP-3841 [S]	Nashville Women	1967	$25
LPM-3465 [M]	Once Over Lightly	1965	$25
LSP-3465 [S]	Once Over Lightly	1965	$30
LPM-2291 [M]	Please Help Me, I'm Falling	1960	$30
LSP-2291 [S]	Please Help Me, I'm Falling	1960	$40
LPM-3770 [M]	Send Me the Pillow You Dream On	1967	$30
LSP-3770 [S]	Send Me the Pillow You Dream On	1967	$25
LSP-4113	Softly	1969	$25
LPM-3559 [M]	The Best of Hank Locklin	1966	$25
LSP-3559 [S]	The Best of Hank Locklin	1966	$30
LPM-3588 [M]	The Girls Get Prettier	1966	$25
LSP-3588 [S]	The Girls Get Prettier	1966	$30
LPM-3656 [M]	The Gloryland Way	1966	$25
LSP-3656 [S]	The Gloryland Way	1966	$30
LPM-2680 [M]	The Ways of Life	1963	$30
LSP-2680 [S]	The Ways of Life	1963	$30
SEARS
| SPS-104 | Send Me the Pillow You Dream On | 196? | $30 |
STEREO-SPECTRUM
| SDLP-603 [R] | Hank Locklin | 196? | $15 |
— Stereo" version of Design DLP-603
WRANGLER
| 1004 [M] | Hank Locklin | 1962 | $30 |

LOCKWOOD, DIDIER
GRAMAVISION
Number	Title	Yr	NM
18-8412	Didier Lockwood Group	1984	$25
18-8504	Out of the Blue	1985	$25
INNER CITY
| IC-1092 | Surya | 1982 | $30 |
PAUSA
7125	Fasten Seat Belts	1981	$25
7094	Live in Montreux	1981	$25
7046	New World	1979	$25

LOCKWOOD, ROBERT, JR.
TRIX
Number	Title	Yr	NM
3307	Contrasts	197?	$25

LOCO, JOE
FANTASY
Number	Title	Yr	NM
3277 [M]	Cha-Cha-Cha	1958	$30
— Red vinyl
| 3277 [M] | Cha-Cha-Cha | 1958 | $30 |
— Black vinyl, red label, non-flexible vinyl
| 3277 [M] | Cha-Cha-Cha | 196? | $20 |
— Black vinyl, red label, flexible vinyl
| 8022 [S] | Cha-Cha-Cha | 1962 | $30 |
— Blue vinyl
| 8022 [S] | Cha-Cha-Cha | 1962 | $25 |
— Black vinyl, blue label, non-flexible vinyl
| 8022 [S] | Cha-Cha-Cha | 196? | $20 |
— Black vinyl, blue label, flexible vinyl
| 3280 [M] | Going Loco | 1958 | $30 |
— Red vinyl
| 3280 [M] | Going Loco | 1958 | $30 |
— Black vinyl, red label, non-flexible vinyl
| 3280 [M] | Going Loco | 196? | $20 |
— Black vinyl, red label, flexible vinyl
| 8042 [S] | Going Loco | 1962 | $30 |
— Blue vinyl
| 8042 [S] | Going Loco | 1962 | $25 |
— Black vinyl, blue label, non-flexible vinyl

Number	Title	Yr	NM
❏ 8042 [S]	Going Loco	196?	$20
—Black vinyl, blue label, flexible vinyl			
❏ 3215 [M]	Invitation to the Mambo	1956	$30
—Red vinyl			
❏ 3215 [M]	Invitation to the Mambo	1956	$30
—Black vinyl, red label, non-flexible vinyl			
❏ 3215 [M]	Invitation to the Mambo	196?	$20
—Black vinyl, red label, flexible vinyl			
❏ 3294 [M]	Latin Jewels	1959	$30
—Red vinyl			
❏ 3294 [M]	Latin Jewels	1959	$25
—Black vinyl, red label, non-flexible vinyl			
❏ 3294 [M]	Latin Jewels	196?	$25
—Black vinyl, red label, flexible vinyl			
❏ 8041 [S]	Latin Jewels	1962	$30
—Blue vinyl			
❏ 8041 [S]	Latin Jewels	1962	$25
—Black vinyl, blue label, non-flexible vinyl			
❏ 8041 [S]	Latin Jewels	196?	$25
—Black vinyl, blue label, flexible vinyl			
❏ 3285 [M]	Ole, Ole, Ole	1959	$30
—Red vinyl			
❏ 3285 [M]	Ole, Ole, Ole	1959	$25
—Black vinyl, red label, non-flexible vinyl			
❏ 3285 [M]	Ole, Ole, Ole	196?	$25
—Black vinyl, red label, flexible vinyl			
❏ 8028 [S]	Ole, Ole, Ole	1962	$30
—Blue vinyl			
❏ 8028 [S]	Ole, Ole, Ole	1962	$25
—Black vinyl, blue label, non-flexible vinyl			
❏ 8028 [S]	Ole, Ole, Ole	196?	$25
—Black vinyl, blue label, flexible vinyl			
❏ 3321 [M]	Pachanga with Joe Loco	1961	$30
—Red vinyl			
❏ 3321 [M]	Pachanga with Joe Loco	1961	$25
—Black vinyl, red label, non-flexible vinyl			
❏ 3321 [M]	Pachanga with Joe Loco	196?	$25
—Black vinyl, red label, flexible vinyl			
❏ 8064 [S]	Pachanga with Joe Loco	1962	$30
—Blue vinyl			
❏ 8064 [S]	Pachanga with Joe Loco	1962	$25
—Black vinyl, blue label, non-flexible vinyl			
❏ 8064 [S]	Pachanga with Joe Loco	196?	$25
—Black vinyl, blue label, flexible vinyl			
❏ 3303 [M]	The Best of Joe Loco	1960	$30
—Red vinyl			
❏ 3303 [M]	The Best of Joe Loco	1960	$25
—Black vinyl, red label, non-flexible vinyl			
❏ 3303 [M]	The Best of Joe Loco	196?	$20
—Black vinyl, red label, flexible vinyl			
❏ 8048 [S]	The Best of Joe Loco	1962	$30
—Blue vinyl			
❏ 8048 [S]	The Best of Joe Loco	1962	$25
—Black vinyl, blue label, non-flexible vinyl			
❏ 8048 [S]	The Best of Joe Loco	196?	$20
—Black vinyl, blue label, flexible vinyl			
IMPERIAL			
❏ LP-12019 [S]	Happy Go Loco	1959	$175
❏ LP-9073 [M]	Happy Go Loco	1959	$175
❏ LP-12014 [S]	Let's Go Loco	1959	$175
❏ LP-9070 [M]	Let's Go Loco	1959	$175
❏ LP-9166 [M]	Pachanga Twist	1962	$175
❏ LP-12079 [S]	Pachanga Twist	1962	$175
TICO			
❏ LP-132 [10]	Instrumental Mambos (Vol. 7)	1955	$50
❏ LP-1008 [M]	Make Mine Mambo	1955	$30
❏ LP-123 [10]	Mambo Dance Favorites, Vol. 5	195?	$40
❏ LP-1012 [M]	Mambo Fantasy	1956	$30
❏ LP-1006 [M]	Mambo Moods	1955	$40
❏ LP-109 [10]	Mambos, Vol. 1	195?	$40
❏ LP-111 [10]	Mambos, Vol. 2	195?	$40
❏ LP-121 [10]	Mambos, Vol. 3	195?	$40
❏ LP-122 [10]	Mambos, Vol. 4	195?	$40
❏ LP-129 [10]	Mambo U.S.A.	1954	$40
❏ LP-1013 [M]	Viva Mambo!	1956	$30

LODGE, JOHN
LONDON
Number	Title	Yr	NM
❏ PS683	Natural Avenue	1977	$15

LODI
MOWEST
Number	Title	Yr	NM
❏ MW101L [B]	Happiness	1972	$30

LOEB, LISA, AND NINE STORIES
GEFFEN
Number	Title	Yr	NM
❏ GEF24734	Tails	1996	$15
—CD and cassette released in 1995			

LOFGREN, NILS
Also see GRIN. Also was a member of BRUCE SPRINGSTEEN's E Street Band.

Number	Title	Yr	NM
A&M			
❏ SP-8362 [DJ]	Authorized Bootleg	1976	$50
❏ SP-4573	Cry Tough	1976	$12
❏ SP-3145	Cry Tough	198?	$10
—Reissue of 4573			
❏ SP-4628	I Came to Dance	1977	$12
❏ SP-3707	Night After Night	1977	$15
❏ SP-6509	Night After Night	198?	$12
—Reissue of 3707			
❏ SP-4756	Nils	1979	$12
❏ SP-4509	Nils Lofgren	1975	$12
❏ SP-3201	The Best	1982	$12
BACKSTREET			
❏ 5251	Night Fades Away	1981	$12
❏ 5421	Wonderland	1983	$12
COLUMBIA			
❏ BFC39982	Flip	1985	$12

LOFSKY, LORNE
PABLO TODAY
Number	Title	Yr	NM
❏ 2312122	It Could Happen to You	1979	$30

LOFTON, CLARENCE
RIVERSIDE
Number	Title	Yr	NM
❏ RLP-1037 [10]	Honky-Tonk and Boogie-Woogie Piano	1954	$300

LOFTON, TRICKY, AND CARMELL JONES
PACIFIC JAZZ
Number	Title	Yr	NM
❏ PJ-49 [M]	Brass Bag	1962	$40
❏ ST-49 [S]	Brass Bag	1962	$50

LOGAN, GIUSEPPI
ESP-DISK'
Number	Title	Yr	NM
❏ 1007 [M]	Giuseppi Logan Quartet	1965	$250
❏ S-1007 [S]	Giuseppi Logan Quartet	1965	$250
❏ 1013 [M]	More Giuseppi Logan	1965	$250
❏ S-1013 [S]	More Giuseppi Logan	1965	$250

LOGGINS, DAVE
EPIC
Number	Title	Yr	NM
❏ KE32833	Apprentice (In a Musical Workshop)	1974	$12
❏ PE33946	Country Suite	1975	$12
❏ JE35792	David Loggins	1979	$12
❏ PE34713	One Way	1977	$12
VANGUARD			
❏ VSD-6580	Personal Belongings	1972	$18

LOGGINS, KENNY
COLUMBIA
Number	Title	Yr	NM
❏ OC40535	Back to Avalon	1988	$12
❏ PC34655	Celebrate Me Home	1977	$12
—Originals have no bar code			
❏ PC34655	Celebrate Me Home	1979	$10
—Reissues have bar code			
❏ AS946 [DJ]	For Radio Only	1980	$18
—Promo-only four-song sampler from "Kenny Loggins Alive			
❏ TC38127	High Adventure	1982	$12
❏ JC36172	Keep the Fire	1979	$12
❏ PC36172	Keep the Fire	198?	$10
—Budget-line reissue			
❏ C2X36738	Kenny Loggins Alive	1980	$15
❏ AS569 [DJ]	Kenny Loggins Live	1979	$18
—One-sided promo with three otherwise unavailable live recordings			
❏ HC45387	Nightwatch	198?	$80
—Half-speed mastered edition			
❏ JC35387	Nightwatch	1978	$12
—Originals have no bar code			
❏ PC35387	Nightwatch	198?	$10
—Reissue with new prefix			
❏ FC39174	Vox Humana	1985	$10

LOGGINS AND MESSINA
Also see KENNY LOGGINS; JIM MESSINA.

COLUMBIA
Number	Title	Yr	NM
❏ JG34167	Finale	1977	$15
❏ KC32540	Full Sail	1973	$12
❏ CQ32540 [Q]	Full Sail	1973	$40
❏ PC32540	Full Sail	197?	$10
—Reissue with new prefix			
❏ C31044	Kenny Loggins with Jim Messina Sittin' In	1972	$12
❏ PC31044	Kenny Loggins with Jim Messina Sittin' In	197?	$10
—Reissue with new prefix			
❏ KC31748	Loggins and Messina	1972	$12
❏ CQ31748 [Q]	Loggins and Messina	1973	$40
❏ PC31748	Loggins and Messina	197?	$10
—Reissue with new prefix			
❏ PC33175	Mother Lode	1974	$12
—Original with no bar code			
❏ PC33175	Mother Lode	198?	$10
—With bar code			
❏ PC33578	Native Sons	1976	$12
—Original with no bar code			
❏ PCQ33578 [Q]	Native Sons	1976	$40
❏ PC33578	Native Sons	198?	$10
—With bar code			
❏ PG32848	On Stage	1974	$15
—Original with no bar code			
❏ PG32848	On Stage	198?	$12
—With bar code			
❏ PC33810	So Fine	1975	$12
—Original with no bar code			
❏ PC33810	So Fine	198?	$10
—With bar code			
❏ PC34388	The Best of Friends	1976	$12
—Original with no bar code			
❏ HC44388	The Best of Friends	1982	$50
—Half-speed mastered edition			
❏ PC34388	The Best of Friends	198?	$10
—With bar code			
DIRECT DISC			
❏ SD16606	Full Sail	198?	$30
—Audiophile vinyl			
EPIC			
❏ PC34388	The Best of Friends	1976	$25
—Mispressing with wrong label			

LOGSDON, JIMMIE
KING
Number	Title	Yr	NM
❏ 843 [M]	Howdy Neighbors	1963	$75

LOLITA
KAPP
Number	Title	Yr	NM
❏ KL-1219 [M]	Sailor	1961	$30
❏ KS-3219 [S]	Sailor	1961	$30
❏ KL-1229 [M]	Songs You Will Never Forget	1961	$30
❏ KS-3229 [S]	Songs You Will Never Forget	1961	$30

LOLLIPOP SHOPPE, THE
UNI
Number	Title	Yr	NM
❏ 73019	The Lollipop Shoppe	1968	$100

LOLLIPOP SINGERS, THE
PETER PAN
Number	Title	Yr	NM
❏ 8112	The Candy Man Can	197?	$18

LOMAX, JACKIE
APPLE
Number	Title	Yr	NM
❏ ST-3354	Is This What You Want?	1969	$25
CAPITOL			
❏ ST-11668	Did You Ever	1977	$12
❏ ST-11558	Livin' for Lovin'	1976	$12
WARNER BROS.			
❏ PRO520 [DJ]	An Interview with Jackie Lomax	1972	$30
❏ WS1914	Home Is In My Head	1971	$15
❏ BS2591	Three	1972	$15

LOMBARDO, GUY
CAPITOL
Number	Title	Yr	NM
❏ T916 [M]	A Decade on Broadway 1935-45	1958	$100
—Turquoise label			
❏ T916 [M]	A Decade on Broadway 1935-45	1958	$85
—Black colorband label, logo at left			
❏ T916 [M]	A Decade on Broadway 1935-45	1962	$75
—Black colorband label, logo at top			
❏ DT916 [R]	A Decade on Broadway 1935-45	196?	$40
—Black colorband label, logo at top			
❏ T788 [M]	A Decade on Broadway 1946-56	1956	$100
—Turquoise label			
❏ T788 [M]	A Decade on Broadway 1946-56	1958	$85
—Black colorband label, logo at left			
❏ T788 [M]	A Decade on Broadway 1946-56	1962	$75
—Black colorband label, logo at top			
❏ DT788 [R]	A Decade on Broadway 1946-56	196?	$40
—Black colorband label, logo at top			
❏ T2481 [M]	A Wonderful Year	1966	$75
❏ ST2481 [S]	A Wonderful Year	1966	$75
❏ T1019 [M]	Berlin by Lombardo	1958	$100
—Turquoise or gray label			
❏ ST1019 [S]	Berlin by Lombardo	1959	$150
—Black colorband label, logo at left			
❏ T1019 [M]	Berlin by Lombardo	1959	$85
—Black colorband label, logo at left			
❏ T1019 [M]	Berlin by Lombardo	1962	$40
—Black colorband label, logo at top			
❏ ST1019 [S]	Berlin by Lombardo	1962	$75
—Black colorband label, logo at top			
❏ T1121 [M]	Dancing Room Only	1959	$85
—Black colorband label, logo at left			

Number	Title	Yr	NM
❏ ST1121 [S]	Dancing Room Only	1959	$100
—*Black colorband label, logo at left*			
❏ ST1121 [S]	Dancing Room Only	1962	$75
—*Black colorband label, logo at top*			
❏ T1121 [M]	Dancing Room Only	1962	$40
—*Black colorband label, logo at top*			
❏ SN-16192	Dancing Room Only	198?	$20
—*Budget-line reissue*			
❏ T1593 [M]	Drifting and Dreaming	1961	$85
—*Black colorband label, logo at left*			
❏ ST1593 [S]	Drifting and Dreaming	1961	$100
—*Black colorband label, logo at left*			
❏ ST1593 [S]	Drifting and Dreaming	1962	$75
—*Black colorband label, logo at top*			
❏ T1593 [M]	Drifting and Dreaming	1962	$40
—*Black colorband label, logo at top*			
❏ SM-1593	Drifting and Dreaming	1976	$20
—*Reissue with new prefix*			
❏ STCL-578	Guy Lombardo	1970	$150
❏ T2350 [M]	Guy Lombardo and His Royal Canadians Play Songs of Carmen Lombardo	1965	$75
❏ DT2350 [R]	Guy Lombardo and His Royal Canadians Play Songs of Carmen Lombardo	1965	$50
❏ ST1393 [S]	Guy Lombardo at Harrah's Club	1960	$100
❏ T1393 [M]	Guy Lombardo at Harrah's Club	1960	$85
❏ T2298 [M]	Guy Lombardo Presents Kenny Gardner	1965	$75
❏ ST2298 [S]	Guy Lombardo Presents Kenny Gardner	1965	$85
❏ T2559 [M]	Guy Lombardo's Broadway	1966	$75
❏ ST2559 [S]	Guy Lombardo's Broadway	1966	$85
❏ ST-340	Is That All There Is?	1969	$25
❏ SM-340	Is That All There Is?	1976	$20
—*Reissue with new prefix*			
❏ T892 [M]	Lively Guy	1957	$100
—*Turquoise label*			
❏ T892 [M]	Lively Guy	1958	$85
—*Black colorband label, logo at left*			
❏ T892 [M]	Lively Guy	1962	$75
—*Black colorband label, logo at top*			
❏ DT892 [R]	Lively Guy	196?	$25
❏ T2777 [M]	Lombardo Country	1967	$85
❏ ST2777 [S]	Lombardo Country	1967	$75
❏ W738 [M]	Lombardo in Hi-Fi	1956	$100
—*Gray label*			
❏ W738 [M]	Lombardo in Hi-Fi	1958	$85
—*Black colorband label, logo at left*			
❏ W738 [M]	Lombardo in Hi-Fi	1962	$75
—*Black colorband label, logo at top*			
❏ ST2825	Medleys on Parade	1968	$40
❏ KAO1443 [M]	Sing the Songs of Christmas	1960	$50
—*Black colorband label, logo at left*			
❏ SKAO1443 [S]	Sing the Songs of Christmas	1960	$100
—*Black colorband label, logo at left*			
❏ TAO1443 [M]	Sing the Songs of Christmas	1962	$75
—*Black colorband label, logo at left*			
❏ STAO1443 [S]	Sing the Songs of Christmas	1962	$50
—*Black colorband label, logo at top*			
❏ T1461 [M]	The Best of Guy Lombardo	1961	$100
—*Black colorband label, logo at top*			
❏ DT1461 [R]	The Best of Guy Lombardo	1961	$40
—*Black colorband label, logo at top*			
❏ T1461 [M]	The Best of Guy Lombardo	1962	$75
—*Black colorband label, logo at top*			
❏ SKAO2940	The Best of Guy Lombardo, Vol. 2	1968	$25
❏ T2052 [M]	The Lombardo Touch	1964	$75
❏ ST2052 [S]	The Lombardo Touch	1964	$85
❏ TDL2181 [M]	The Lombardo Years	1964	$150
❏ STDL2181 [S]	The Lombardo Years	1964	$150
❏ ST-128	The New Songs -- The New Sounds	1969	$25
❏ T1947 [M]	The Sweetest Medleys This Side of Heaven	1963	$75
❏ DT1947 [R]	The Sweetest Medleys This Side of Heaven	1963	$50
❏ T2639 [M]	The Sweetest Sounds Today	1967	$50
❏ ST2639 [S]	The Sweetest Sounds Today	1967	$75
❏ T1306 [M]	The Sweetest Waltzes This Side of Heaven	1960	$50
—*Black colorband label, logo at left*			
❏ ST1306 [S]	The Sweetest Waltzes This Side of Heaven	1960	$100
—*Black colorband label, logo at left*			
❏ ST1306 [S]	The Sweetest Waltzes This Side of Heaven	1962	$75
—*Black colorband label, logo at top*			
❏ T1306 [M]	The Sweetest Waltzes This Side of Heaven	1962	$50
—*Black colorband label, logo at top*			
❏ SN-16193	The Sweetest Waltzes This Side of Heaven	198?	$20
—*Budget-line reissue*			
❏ ST2829	They're Playing Our Songs	1968	$25
❏ T1738 [M]	Waltzing with Guy Lombardo	1962	$75
❏ ST1738 [S]	Waltzing with Guy Lombardo	1962	$75
❏ T739 [M]	Your Guy Lombardo Medley	1956	$150
—*Turquoise label*			

Number	Title	Yr	NM
❏ T739 [M]	Your Guy Lombardo Medley	1958	$75
—*Black colorband label, logo at left*			
❏ T739 [M]	Your Guy Lombardo Medley	1962	$75
—*Black colorband label, logo at top*			
❏ DT739 [R]	Your Guy Lombardo Medley	196?	$50
❏ SM-739	Your Guy Lombardo Medley	1976	$20
—*Reissue with new prefix*			
❏ T1244 [M]	Your Guy Lombardo Medley, Vol. 2	1960	$75
—*Black colorband label, logo at left*			
❏ ST1244 [S]	Your Guy Lombardo Medley, Vol. 2	1960	$100
—*Black colorband label, logo at left*			
❏ T1244 [M]	Your Guy Lombardo Medley, Vol. 2	1962	$50
—*Black colorband label, logo at top*			
❏ ST1244 [S]	Your Guy Lombardo Medley, Vol. 2	1962	$75
—*Black colorband label, logo at top*			
❏ T1598 [M]	Your Guy Lombardo Medley, Vol. 3	1961	$75
—*Black colorband label, logo at left*			
❏ ST1598 [S]	Your Guy Lombardo Medley, Vol. 3	1961	$100
—*Black colorband label, logo at left*			
❏ ST1598 [S]	Your Guy Lombardo Medley, Vol. 3	1962	$75
—*Black colorband label, logo at top*			
❏ T1598 [M]	Your Guy Lombardo Medley, Vol. 3	1962	$50
—*Black colorband label, logo at top*			

DECCA

Number	Title	Yr	NM
❏ DL8070 [M]	A Night at the Roosevelt	195?	$50
—*Black label, silver print*			
❏ DL8070 [M]	A Night at the Roosevelt	1961	$30
—*Black label with color bars*			
❏ DL4280 [M]	By Special Request	1962	$30
❏ DL74280 [S]	By Special Request	1962	$35
❏ DL4735 [M]	Dance Medley Time	1966	$25
❏ DL74735 [S]	Dance Medley Time	1966	$30
❏ DL4180 [M]	Dance to the Songs Everybody Knows	1961	$30
❏ DL74180 [S]	Dance to the Songs Everybody Knows	1961	$35
❏ DL4288 [M]	Dancing Piano	1962	$30
❏ DL74288 [S]	Dancing Piano	1962	$35
❏ DL8136 [M]	Enjoy Yourself	1955	$175
—*Black label, silver print*			
❏ DL8136 [M]	Enjoy Yourself	1961	$30
—*Black label with color bars*			
❏ DL5329 [10]	Enjoy Yourself	195?	$75
❏ DL8254 [M]	Everybody Dance	1956	$175
—*Black label, silver print*			
❏ DL8254 [M]	Everybody Dance	1961	$30
—*Black label with color bars*			
❏ DL5442 [10]	Everybody Dance, Vol. 2	1952	$175
❏ DL5434 [10]	Everybody Dance to the Music of Guy Lombardo	1952	$175
❏ DL4149 [M]	Far Away Places	1961	$30
❏ DL74149 [S]	Far Away Places	1961	$35
❏ DL4430 [M]	Golden Folk Songs	1964	$25
❏ DL74430 [S]	Golden Folk Songs	1964	$30
❏ DL4593 [M]	Golden Medleys	1965	$25
❏ DL74593 [S]	Golden Medleys	1965	$30
❏ DL4380 [M]	Golden Minstrel Songs for Dancing	1963	$30
❏ DL74380 [S]	Golden Minstrel Songs for Dancing	1963	$35
❏ DL4812 [M]	Guy Lombardo's Greatest Hits	1966	$25
❏ DL74812 [S]	Guy Lombardo's Greatest Hits	1966	$30
❏ DL5156 [10]	Hawaiian Songs	1950	$175
❏ DL8843 [M]	Instrumentally Yours	1959	$100
—*Black label, silver print*			
❏ DL8843 [M]	Instrumentally Yours	1961	$30
—*Black label with color bars*			
❏ DL4516 [M]	Italian Songs Everybody Knows	1964	$25
❏ DL74516 [S]	Italian Songs Everybody Knows	1964	$30
❏ DL8354 [M]	Jingle Bells	1956	$175
—*Black label, silver print*			
❏ DL78354 [R]	Jingle Bells	196?	$25
❏ DL8354 [M]	Jingle Bells	1961	$30
—*Black label with color bars*			
❏ DL5430 [10]	Jingle Bells	1952	$175
❏ DL5127 [10]	Latin Rhythms	195?	$75
❏ DL8249 [M]	Lombardoland	1956	$120
—*Black label, silver print*			
❏ DL8249 [M]	Lombardoland	1961	$30
—*Black label with color bars*			
❏ DL5041 [10]	Lombardoland	1949	$175
❏ DL8097 [M]	Lombardoland, U.S.A.	195?	$50
—*Black label, silver print*			
❏ DL8097 [M]	Lombardoland, U.S.A.	1961	$30
—*Black label with color bars*			
❏ DL5328 [10]	Lombardoland, Vol. 2	195?	$75
❏ DL4177 [M]	New Year's Eve with Guy Lombardo	1961	$30
❏ DL74177 [S]	New Year's Eve with Guy Lombardo	1961	$35
❏ DL8255 [M]	Oh! How We Danced	1956	$120

Number	Title	Yr	NM
—*Black label, silver print*			
❏ DL8255 [M]	Oh! How We Danced	1961	$30
—*Black label with color bars*			
❏ DL4371 [M]	Play a Happy Song	1963	$30
❏ DL74371 [S]	Play a Happy Song	1963	$35
❏ DL5024 [10]	Sidewalks of New York	1949	$175
❏ DL8333 [M]	Silver Jubilee	1956	$175
—*Black label, silver print*			
❏ DL8333 [M]	Silver Jubilee	1961	$30
—*Black label, silver print*			
❏ DL5235 [10]	Silver Jubilee -- 1925-1950	1950	$175
❏ DL4567 [M]	Snuggled on Your Shoulder	1965	$25
❏ DL74567 [S]	Snuggled on Your Shoulder	1965	$30
❏ DL8135 [M]	Soft and Sweet	1955	$175
—*Black label, silver print*			
❏ DL8135 [M]	Soft and Sweet	1961	$30
—*Black label with color bars*			
❏ DL5097 [10]	Song Hits from Broadway Shows	1949	$175
❏ DL5322 [10]	Souvenirs	195?	$75
❏ DL5277 [10]	Square Dances (Without Calls)	195?	$75
❏ DL8208 [M]	The Band Played On	1955	$175
—*Black label, silver print*			
❏ DL8208 [M]	The Band Played On	1961	$30
—*Black label with color bars*			
❏ DXB185 [M]	The Best of Guy Lombardo	1964	$50
❏ DXSB7185 [R]	The Best of Guy Lombardo	1964	$35
❏ DL4268 [M]	The Best Songs Are the Old Songs	1962	$35
❏ DL74268 [R]	The Best Songs Are the Old Songs	196?	$30
❏ DL8894 [M]	The Sidewalks of New York	1959	$100
—*Black label, silver print*			
❏ DL8894 [M]	The Sidewalks of New York	1961	$30
—*Black label with color bars*			
❏ DL5330 [10]	The Sweetest Music This Side of Heaven	195?	$75
❏ DL8962 [M]	The Sweetest Music This Side of Heaven (A Musical Biography 1926-1932)	1960	$35
—*Black label, silver print*			
❏ DL8962 [M]	The Sweetest Music This Side of Heaven (A Musical Biography 1926-1932)	1960	$25
—*Black label with color bars*			
❏ DL78962 [S]	The Sweetest Music This Side of Heaven (A Musical Biography 1926-1932)	1960	$50
—*Black label, silver print*			
❏ DL78962 [S]	The Sweetest Music This Side of Heaven (A Musical Biography 1926-1932)	1960	$30
—*Black label with color bars*			
❏ DL4229 [M]	The Sweetest Music This Side of Heaven (A Musical Biography 1932-1939)	1962	$30
❏ DL74229 [S]	The Sweetest Music This Side of Heaven (A Musical Biography 1932-1939)	1962	$35
❏ DL4328 [M]	The Sweetest Music This Side of Heaven (A Musical Biography 1944-1948)	1962	$30
❏ DL74328 [S]	The Sweetest Music This Side of Heaven (A Musical Biography 1944-1948)	1962	$35
❏ DL4329 [M]	The Sweetest Music This Side of Heaven (A Musical Biography 1949-1954)	1962	$30
❏ DL74329 [S]	The Sweetest Music This Side of Heaven (A Musical Biography 1949-1954)	1962	$35
❏ DL4123 [M]	The Sweetest Pianos This Side of Heaven	1961	$30
❏ DL74123 [S]	The Sweetest Pianos This Side of Heaven	1961	$35
❏ DLP5002 [10]	The Twin Pianos -- Vol. 1	1949	$175
—*Both record and sleeve have "DLP" prefix*			
❏ DL5002 [10]	The Twin Pianos -- Vol. 1	195?	$75
—*Record has "DL" prefix; sleeve may or may not have "DL*			
❏ DLP5003 [10]	The Twin Pianos -- Vol. 2	1949	$175
—*Both record and sleeve have "DLP" prefix*			
❏ DL5003 [10]	The Twin Pianos -- Vol. 2	195?	$75
—*Record has "DL" prefix; sleeve may or may not have "DL*			
❏ DL8251 [M]	Twin Piano Magic	1956	$175
—*Black label, silver print*			
❏ DL8251 [M]	Twin Piano Magic	1961	$30
—*Black label with color bars*			
❏ DL5447 [10]	Twin Piano Magic	195?	$75
❏ DL8119 [M]	Twin Pianos	195?	$50
—*Black label, silver print*			
❏ DL8119 [M]	Twin Pianos	1961	$30
—*Black label with color bars*			
❏ DL5193 [10]	Waltzes	195?	$75
❏ DL8256 [M]	Waltzland	1956	$175
—*Black label, silver print*			
❏ DL8256 [M]	Waltzland	1961	$30
—*Black label with color bars*			
❏ DL5325 [10]	Waltzland	1951	$250
❏ DL8205 [M]	Waltz Time	1955	$175
—*Black label, silver print*			
❏ DL8205 [M]	Waltz Time	1961	$30
—*Black label with color bars*			

Number	Title	Yr	NM

HINDSIGHT
❏ HSR-187 — Guy Lombardo and His Royal Canadians 1950 — 198? — $25

LONDON
❏ XPS904 — Every Night Is New Year's Eve — 1973 — $25

MCA
❏ 15031 — Auld Lang Syne — 198? — $25
❏ 242 — Dance Medley Time — 197? — $20
— *Reissue of Decca 74735*
❏ 197 — Dance to the Songs Everybody Knows — 1973 — $20
— *Reissue of Decca 74180*
❏ 103 — Golden Medleys — 1973 — $20
— *Reissue of Decca 74593*
❏ 245 — Guy Lombardo's Greatest Hits — 197? — $20
— *Reissue of Decca 74812*
❏ 15035 — I Saw Mommy Kissing Santa Claus — 198? — $25
❏ 15012 — Jingle Bells — 197? — $25
— *Reissue of Decca 78354; black rainbow label*
❏ 15012 — Jingle Bells — 1977 — $25
— *Tan label*
❏ 15012 — Jingle Bells — 1980 — $20
— *Blue rainbow label*
❏ 15000 — New Year's Eve with Guy Lombardo — 1974 — $25
— *Reissue of MCA 195; black rainbow label*
❏ 195 — New Year's Eve with Guy Lombardo — 1973 — $30
— *Reissue of Decca 74177*
❏ 15000 — New Year's Eve with Guy Lombardo — 1977 — $20
— *Tan label*
❏ 15000 — New Year's Eve with Guy Lombardo — 1980 — $20
— *Blue rainbow label*
❏ 4041 — The Best of Guy Lombardo — 197? — $30
— *Black rainbow labels*
❏ 4041 — The Best of Guy Lombardo — 1977 — $25
— *Tan labels*
❏ 4041 — The Best of Guy Lombardo — 1980 — $25
— *Blue rainbow labels*
❏ 4082 — The Best of Guy Lombardo, Vol. 2 — 197? — $30
— *Black rainbow labels*
❏ 4082 — The Best of Guy Lombardo, Vol. 2 — 1977 — $25
— *Tan labels*
❏ 4082 — The Best of Guy Lombardo, Vol. 2 — 1980 — $25
— *Blue rainbow labels*
❏ 89 — The Best Songs Are the Old Songs — 1973 — $20
— *Reissue of Decca 74268*
❏ 201 — The Sweetest Music This Side of Heaven — 1973 — $20
— *Reissue of Decca 78962?*

MCA CORAL
❏ CR20105 — Here's Guy Lombardo — 197? — $25

PAIR
❏ PDL2-1046 — Guy Lombardo — 1986 — $30

PICKWICK
❏ SPC-3358 — Alley Cat — 197? — $20
❏ SPC1011 — Deck the Halls — 196? — $25
— *Silver label*
❏ SPC1011 — Deck the Halls — 197? — $20
— *Reissue on black label*
❏ SPC-3193 — Enjoy Yourself — 196? — $25
❏ SPC-3257 — Red Roses for a Blue Lady — 197? — $20
❏ SPC-3530 — Seems Like Old Times — 197? — $20
❏ SPC-3530 — Seems Like Old Times — 197? — $20
❏ SPC-3073 — Sweet and Heavenly — 196? — $25
❏ SPC-3312 — The Impossible Dream — 197? — $20
❏ PTP-2009 — The Sweet Sounds — 197? — $25

RCA CAMDEN
❏ CAL-445 [M] — An Evening with Guy Lombardo — 195? — $35
❏ CAS-445 [R] — An Evening with Guy Lombardo — 196? — $25
❏ CAL-255 [M] — Guy Lombardo Plays — 195? — $35
❏ CAS-255 [R] — Guy Lombardo Plays — 196? — $25
❏ CAL-578 [M] — He's My Guy — 195? — $35

RCA VICTOR
❏ CPL1-2047(e) — A Legendary Performer — 1977 — $25
❏ VPM-6071 — This Is Guy Lombardo — 197? — $30
❏ LPT-3059 [10] — This Is Guy Lombardo and His Orchestra — 1954 — $40

SUNBEAM
❏ 308 — On the Air 1935 — 197? — $25

VOCALION
❏ VL3605 [M] — Dance in the Moonlight — 1958 — $35
❏ VL73605 [R] — Dance in the Moonlight — 196? — $25
❏ VL73833 — Here's Guy Lombardo — 1968 — $25

LONDON, JULIE

LIBERTY
❏ LRP-3043 [M] — About the Blues — 1957 — $40
— *Green label*
❏ LST-7012 [S] — About the Blues — 1958 — $140
— *Black label, silver print*
❏ LRP-3043 [M] — About the Blues — 1960 — $50
— *Black label, colorband and logo at left*
❏ LST-7012 [S] — About the Blues — 1960 — $75
— *Black label, colorband and logo at left*
❏ LRP-3434 [M] — All Through the Night — 1965 — $75
❏ LST-7434 [S] — All Through the Night — 1965 — $75
❏ LRP-3164 [M] — Around Midnight — 1960 — $75
❏ LST-7164 [S] — Around Midnight — 1960 — $40
❏ SCR-1 [S] — By Myself — 196? — $75
— *Columbia Record Club exclusive*
❏ MCR-1 [M] — By Myself — 196? — $75
— *Columbia Record Club exclusive*
❏ SL-9002 [M] — Calendar Girl — 1956 — $200
❏ LST-7546 — Easy Does It — 1968 — $50
❏ LRP-3416 [M] — Feeling Good — 1965 — $75
❏ LST-7416 [S] — Feeling Good — 1965 — $75
❏ LRP-3478 [M] — For the Night People — 1966 — $75
❏ LST-7478 [S] — For the Night People — 1966 — $75
❏ LRP-3096 [M] — Julie — 1957 — $40
— *Green label*
❏ LST-7004 [S] — Julie — 1958 — $140
— *Black label, silver print*
❏ LRP-3152 [M] — Julie…At Home — 1960 — $75
❏ LST-7152 [S] — Julie…At Home — 1960 — $200
— *Blue vinyl*
❏ LST-7152 [S] — Julie…At Home — 1960 — $40
— *Black vinyl*

❏ LRP-3006 [M] — Julie Is Her Name — 1956 — $50
— *Green label*
❏ LST-7027 [S] — Julie Is Her Name — 1958 — $200
— *Blue vinyl*
❏ LST-7027 [S] — Julie Is Her Name — 1958 — $200
— *Red vinyl*
❏ LST-7027 [S] — Julie Is Her Name — 1958 — $40
— *Black label, silver print*
❏ LRP-3006 [M] — Julie Is Her Name — 1960 — $50
— *Black label, colorband and logo at left*
❏ LST-7027 [S] — Julie Is Her Name — 1960 — $75
— *Black label, colorband and logo at left*
❏ LRP-3100 [M] — Julie Is Her Name, Volume 2 — 1958 — $40
— *Green label*
❏ LST-7100 [S] — Julie Is Her Name, Volume 2 — 1958 — $40
— *Black label, silver print*
❏ LRP-3100 [M] — Julie Is Her Name, Volume 2 — 1960 — $50
— *Black label, colorband and logo at left*
❏ LST-7100 [S] — Julie Is Her Name, Volume 2 — 1960 — $75
— *Black label, colorband and logo at left*
❏ LRP-3342 [M] — Julie London — 1964 — $75
❏ LST-7342 [S] — Julie London — 1964 — $75
❏ LRP-3375 [M] — Julie London In Person at the Americana — 1964 — $75
❏ LST-7375 [S] — Julie London In Person at the Americana — 1964 — $75
❏ LRP-3291 [M] — Julie's Golden Greats — 1963 — $75
— *White cover*
❏ LRP-3291 [M] — Julie's Golden Greats — 1963 — $75
— *Black cover*
❏ LST-7291 [S] — Julie's Golden Greats — 1963 — $75
— *White cover*
❏ LST-7291 [S] — Julie's Golden Greats — 1963 — $75
— *Black cover*
❏ LRP-3278 [M] — Latin in a Satin Mood — 1963 — $75
❏ LST-7278 [S] — Latin in a Satin Mood — 1963 — $75
❏ LRP-3105 [M] — London By Night — 1958 — $75
— *Green label*
❏ LST-7105 [S] — London By Night — 1958 — $40
— *Black label, silver print*
❏ LRP-3012 [M] — Lonely Girl — 1956 — $150

— *Green label*
❏ LST-7029 [S] — Lonely Girl — 1958 — $40
— *Black label, silver print*
❏ LRP-3012 [M] — Lonely Girl — 1960 — $50
— *Black label, colorband and logo at left*
❏ LST-7029 [S] — Lonely Girl — 1960 — $75
— *Black label, colorband and logo at left*
❏ LRP-3231 [M] — Love Letters — 1962 — $75
❏ LST-7231 [S] — Love Letters — 1962 — $75
❏ LRP-3249 [M] — Love on the Rocks — 1963 — $75
❏ LST-7249 [S] — Love on the Rocks — 1963 — $75
❏ LRP-3060 [M] — Make Love to Me — 1957 — $40
— *Green label*
❏ LST-7060 [S] — Make Love to Me — 1958 — $40
— *Black label, silver print*
❏ LRP-3060 [M] — Make Love to Me — 1960 — $50
— *Black label, colorband and logo at left*
❏ LST-7060 [S] — Make Love to Me — 1960 — $75
— *Black label, colorband and logo at left*
❏ LRP-3493 [M] — Nice Girls Don't Stay for Breakfast — 1967 — $75
❏ LST-7493 [S] — Nice Girls Don't Stay for Breakfast — 1967 — $75
❏ LRP-3392 [M] — Our Fair Lady — 1965 — $75
❏ LST-7392 [S] — Our Fair Lady — 1965 — $75
❏ LRP-3171 [M] — Send for Me — 1961 — $75
❏ LST-7171 [S] — Send for Me — 1961 — $40
❏ LRP-3203 [M] — Sophisticated Lady — 1962 — $75
❏ LST-7203 [S] — Sophisticated Lady — 1962 — $75
❏ LRP-3119 [M] — Swing Me an Old Song — 1959 — $75
— *Green label*
❏ LST-7119 [S] — Swing Me an Old Song — 1959 — $40
— *Black label, silver print*
❏ L-5501 [M] — The Best of Julie London — 1962 — $30
❏ S-6601 [S] — The Best of Julie London — 1962 — $40
❏ LRP-3300 [M] — The End of the World — 1963 — $75
❏ LST-7300 [S] — The End of the World — 1963 — $75
❏ LRP-3324 [M] — The Wonderful World of Julie London — 1963 — $75
❏ LST-7324 [S] — The Wonderful World of Julie London — 1963 — $75
❏ LRP-3192 [M] — Whatever Julie Wants — 1961 — $75
❏ LST-7192 [S] — Whatever Julie Wants — 1961 — $40
❏ LRP-3514 [M] — With Body and Soul — 1967 — $75
❏ LST-7514 [S] — With Body and Soul — 1967 — $75
❏ LRP-3130 [M] — Your Number Please — 1959 — $75
— *Green label*
❏ LST-7130 [S] — Your Number Please — 1959 — $40
— *Black label, silver print*
❏ LRP-3130 [M] — Your Number Please — 1960 — $50
— *Black label, colorband and logo at left*
❏ LST-7130 [S] — Your Number Please — 1960 — $75
— *Black label, colorband and logo at left*
❏ LST-7609 — Yummy, Yummy, Yummy — 1969 — $50

SUNSET
❏ SUS-5207 — Gone with the Wind — 196? — $30
❏ SUM-1104 [M] — Julie London — 196? — $30
❏ SUS-5104 [S] — Julie London — 196? — $35
❏ SUM-1161 [M] — Soft and Sweet — 196? — $30
❏ SUS-5161 [S] — Soft and Sweet — 196? — $35

UNITED ARTISTS
❏ UA-LA437-E — The Very Best of Julie London — 1975 — $30

LONDON, LAURIE

CAPITOL
❏ T10169 [M] — England's 14 Year Old Singing Sensation -- Laurie London — 1958 — $50

LONDON POPS ORCHESTRA (FREDERICK FENNELL, CONDUCTOR)

MERCURY LIVING PRESENCE
❏ SR90439 [S] — Coates: Three Elizabeths; London Suite; Four Ways Suite — 1965 — $25
— *Maroon label, with "Vendor: Mercury Record Corporation*

LONDON PROMS SYMPHONY ORCHESTRA (CHARLES MACKERRAS, CONDUCTOR)

RCA VICTOR RED SEAL
❏ LSC-2336 [S] — Sibelius: Finlandia — 1960 — $40
— *Original with "shaded dog" label*
❏ LSC-2336 [S] — Sibelius: Finlandia — 199? — $30
— *Classic Records reissue*

LONDON PROMS SYMPHONY ORCHESTRA (RAYMOND AGOULT, CONDUCTOR)

RCA VICTOR RED SEAL
❏ LSC-2326 [S] — Clair de Lune — 1960 — $220
— *Original with "shaded dog" label*
❏ LSC-2326 [S] — Clair de Lune — 199? — $30
— *Classic Records reissue*

LONDON PROMS SYMPHONY ORCHESTRA (ROBERT SHARPLES, CONDUCTOR)

RCA VICTOR RED SEAL
❏ LSC-2299 [S] — Lehar: Waltzes — 1959 — $30

Number	Title	Yr	NM

— Original with "shaded dog" label

LONDON RAGTIME ORCHESTRA, THE
STOMP OFF
| ☐ SOS-1081 | Bouncing Around | 1985 | $25 |

LONDON SOUND 70 ORCHESTRA AND CHORUS
DECCA
| ☐ DEB7-7 | The Sounds of Christmas | 1970 | $30 |

LONDON SYMPHONY ORCHESTRA
HALLMARK
| ☐ 6250 | Hallmark Presents: The Best Loved Christmas Carols | 1985 | $15 |

— Sold only at Hallmark Cards dealers. Also see other "Hallmark Presents:" LPs in the various artists section.

RCA VICTOR
| ☐ XRL1-7067 | A Classic Case: The London Symphony Orchestra Plays Music of Jethro Tull | 1985 | $15 |

— Ian Anderson of Jethro Tull appears

LONDON SYMPHONY ORCHESTRA (ALEXANDER GIBSON, CONDUCTOR)
RCA VICTOR RED SEAL
| ☐ LSC-2405 [S] | Sibelius: Symphony No. 5 | 1960 | $220 |

— Original with "shaded dog" label
| ☐ LSC-2405 [S] | Sibelius: Symphony No. 5 | 199? | $30 |

— Classic Records reissue

LONDON SYMPHONY ORCHESTRA (ANTAL DORATI, CONDUCTOR)
MERCURY LIVING PRESENCE
| ☐ SR90311 [S] | Bartok: Bluebeard's Castle | 196? | $25 |

— Maroon label, no "Vendor: Mercury Record Corporation
| ☐ SR90378 [S] | Bartok: Concerto for Orchestra | 196? | $400 |

— Maroon label, no "Vendor: Mercury Record Corporation
| ☐ SR90426 [S] | Bartok: The Wooden Prince | 196? | $40 |

— Maroon label, no "Vendor: Mercury Record Corporation
| ☐ SR90426 [S] | Bartok: The Wooden Prince | 196? | $25 |

— Maroon label, with "Vendor: Mercury Record Corporation
| ☐ SR90317 [S] | Beethoven: Symphony No. 5; Egmont Overture; Consecration of the House Overture | 196? | $100 |

— Maroon label, no "Vendor: Mercury Record Corporation
| ☐ SR90317 [S] | Beethoven: Symphony No. 5; Egmont Overture; Consecration of the House Overture | 196? | $30 |

— Maroon label, with "Vendor: Mercury Record Corporation
| ☐ SR90278 [S] | Berg: Suites from Lulu and Wozzeck | 196? | $75 |

— Maroon label, no "Vendor: Mercury Record Corporation
| ☐ SR90278 [S] | Berg: Suites from Lulu and Wozzeck | 196? | $30 |

— Maroon label, with "Vendor: Mercury Record Corporation
| ☐ SR90122 [S] | Borodin: Polovetsian Dances; Rimsky-Korsakov: Coq d-Or | 1960 | $30 |

— Maroon label, with "Vendor: Mercury Record Corporation
| ☐ SR90437 [S] | Brahms: 16 Hungarian Dances | 1965 | $25 |

— Maroon label, with "Vendor: Mercury Record Corporation
| ☐ SR90154 [S] | Brahms: Haydn Variations; Hungarian Dances | 196? | $30 |

— Maroon label, no "Vendor: Mercury Record Corporation
| ☐ SR90268 [S] | Brahms: Symphony No. 1 | 196? | $50 |

— Maroon label, no "Vendor: Mercury Record Corporation
| ☐ SR90246 [S] | Copland: Appalachian Spring; Billy the Kid | 196? | $100 |

— Maroon label, no "Vendor: Mercury Record Corporation
| ☐ SR90246 [S] | Copland: Appalachian Spring; Billy the Kid | 196? | $100 |

— Maroon label, with "Vendor: Mercury Record Corporation
| ☐ SR90246 [S] | Copland: Appalachian Spring; Billy the Kid | 196? | $25 |

— Third edition: Dark red (not maroon) label
| ☐ SR90236 [S] | Dvorak: Symphony No. 4 (8) in G; Carnaval Overture | 196? | $120 |

— Maroon label, no "Vendor: Mercury Record Corporation
| ☐ SR90158 [S] | Handel-Harty: Water Music Suite; Royal Fireworks Music | 196? | $50 |

— Maroon label, no "Vendor: Mercury Record Corporation
| ☐ SR90155 [S] | Haydn: Symphonies 100 and 101 | 196? | $150 |

— Maroon label, no "Vendor: Mercury Record Corporation
| ☐ SR90415 [S] | Haydn: Symphony No. 100 in G; Beethoven: Symphony No. 6 in F | 196? | $25 |

— Maroon label, no "Vendor: Mercury Record Corporation
| ☐ SR90209 [S] | Khachaturian: Gayne Ballet Suite; Tchaikovsky: Romeo and Juliet | 196? | $30 |

— Maroon label, no "Vendor: Mercury Record Corporation

Number	Title	Yr	NM

| ☐ SR90209 [S] | Khachaturian: Gayne Ballet Suite; Tchaikovsky: Romeo and Juliet | 196? | $30 |

— Maroon label, with "Vendor: Mercury Record Corporation
| ☐ SR90235 [S] | Liszt: Hungarian Rhapsodies No. 2 and 3; Enescu: Rumanian Rhapsodies No. 1 and 2 | 196? | $75 |

— Maroon label, with "Vendor: Mercury Record Corporation
| ☐ SR90235 [S] | Liszt: Hungarian Rhapsodies No. 2 and 3; Enescu: Rumanian Rhapsodies No. 1 and 2 | 196? | $75 |

— Maroon label, no "Vendor: Mercury Record Corporation
| ☐ SR90235 [S] | Liszt: Hungarian Rhapsodies No. 2 and 3; Enescu: Rumanian Rhapsodies No. 1 and 2 | 196? | $25 |

— Third edition: Dark red (not maroon) label
| ☐ SR90371 [S] | Liszt: Hungarian Rhapsodies Nos. 1, 4, 5 and 6 | 196? | $400 |

— Maroon label, no "Vendor: Mercury Record Corporation
| ☐ SR90371 [S] | Liszt: Hungarian Rhapsodies Nos. 1, 4, 5 and 6 | 196? | $75 |

— Maroon label, with "Vendor: Mercury Record Corporation
| ☐ SR90371 [S] | Liszt: Hungarian Rhapsodies Nos. 1, 4, 5 and 6 | 196? | $30 |

— Third edition: Dark red (not maroon) label
| ☐ SR90214 [S] | Lizst: Les Preludes; Smetana: The Moldau; Mussorgsky: Night on Bald Mountain; Sibelius: Valse Triste | 196? | $40 |

— Maroon label, no "Vendor: Mercury Record Corporation
| ☐ SR90123 [S] | Mendelssohn: Symphony No. 3; Fingel's Cave Overture | 1960 | $40 |

— Maroon label, no "Vendor: Mercury Record Corporation
| ☐ SR90280 [S] | Mozart: Symphony No. 40; Haydn: Symphony No. 45 | 196? | $25 |

— Maroon label, no "Vendor: Mercury Record Corporation
| ☐ SR90435 [S] | Paris 1917-1938 | 1965 | $150 |

— Maroon label, with "Vendor: Mercury Record Corporation
| ☐ SR90435 [S] | Paris 1917-1938 | 196? | $25 |

— Maroon label, oval "Mercury" logo
| ☐ SR90006 [S] | Prokofiev: Love for Three Oranges Suite; Scythian Suite | 195? | $300 |
| ☐ SR90006 [S] | Prokofiev: Love for Three Oranges Suite; Scythian Suite | 199? | $30 |

— Classic Records reissue
| ☐ SR90153 [S] | Respighi: The Birds; Brazilian Impressions | 196? | $250 |

— Maroon label, no "Vendor: Mercury Record Corporation
| ☐ SR90153 [S] | Respighi: The Birds; Brazilian Impressions | 196? | $50 |

— Maroon label, with "Vendor: Mercury Record Corporation
| ☐ SR90265 [S] | Rimsky-Korsakov: Capriccio Espagnol; Russian Easter Overture; Borodin: Prince Igor Overture | 196? | $50 |

— Maroon label, no "Vendor: Mercury Record Corporation
| ☐ SR90226 [S] | Stravinsky: The Firebird | 196? | $300 |

— Maroon label, no "Vendor: Mercury Record Corporation
| ☐ SR90226 [S] | Stravinsky: The Firebird | 196? | $30 |

— Maroon label, with "Vendor: Mercury Record Corporation
| ☐ SR90226 [S] | Stravinsky: The Firebird | 196? | $30 |

— Third edition: Dark red (not maroon) label
| ☐ SR90226 [S] | Stravinsky: The Firebird | 199? | $30 |

— Classic Records reissue
| ☐ SR90387 [S] | Stravnisky: Song of the Nightingale; Fireworks; Scherzo; Four Etudes | 196? | $150 |

— Maroon label, no "Vendor: Mercury Record Corporation
| ☐ SR90387 [S] | Stravinsky: Song of the Nightingale; Fireworks; Scherzo; Four Etudes | 196? | $40 |

— Maroon label, with "Vendor: Mercury Record Corporation
| ☐ SR90409 [S] | Tchaikovsky: Rococo Variations; Saint-Saens: Cello Concerto No. 1 | 196? | $150 |

— Maroon label, no "Vendor: Mercury Record Corporation
| ☐ SR90409 [S] | Tchaikovsky: Rococo Variations; Saint-Saens: Cello Concerto No. 1 | 196? | $40 |

— Maroon label, with "Vendor: Mercury Record Corporation
| ☐ SR90255 [S] | Tchaikovsky: Symphony No. 5 | 196? | $175 |

— Maroon label, no "Vendor: Mercury Record Corporation
| ☐ SR90279 [S] | Tchakivosky: Symphony No. 4 in F | 196? | $300 |

— Maroon label, no "Vendor: Mercury Record Corporation
| ☐ SR90312 [S] | Tchakovsky: Symphony No. 6 | 196? | $50 |

— Maroon label, no "Vendor: Mercury Record Corporation
| ☐ SR90312 [S] | Tchakovsky: Symphony No. 6 | 196? | $50 |

— Maroon label, with "Vendor: Mercury Record Corporation
| ☐ SR90156 [S] | Verdi: Overtures | 196? | $25 |

— Maroon label, no "Vendor: Mercury Record Corporation
| ☐ SR90316 [S] | Vienna 1908-1914 | 196? | $250 |

— Maroon label, no "Vendor: Mercury Record Corporation

Number	Title	Yr	NM

| ☐ SR90316 [S] | Vienna 1908-1914 | 196? | $120 |

— Maroon label, with "Vendor: Mercury Record Corporation
| ☐ SR90287 [S] | Wagner: Mesitersinger Prelude; Tannhauser Overture; Parsifal; Lohengrin Selections | 196? | $40 |

— Maroon label, no "Vendor: Mercury Record Corporation
| ☐ SR90287 [S] | Wagner: Mesitersinger Prelude; Tannhauser Overture; Parsifal; Lohengrin Selections | 196? | $30 |

— Maroon label, with "Vendor: Mercury Record Corporation
| ☐ SR90234 [S] | Wagner: Tristan und Isolde Prelude and Liebestod; Tannhauser Overture; Lohengrin Prelude | 196? | $30 |

— Maroon label, no "Vendor: Mercury Record Corporation

LONDON SYMPHONY ORCHESTRA (ARTHUR BLISS, CONDUCTOR)
RCA VICTOR RED SEAL
| ☐ LSC-2257 [S] | Elgar: Pomp and Circumstance Marches 1-5 | 1959 | $150 |

— Original with "shaded dog" label

LONDON SYMPHONY ORCHESTRA (HANS SCHMIDT-ISSERSTEDT, CONDUCTOR)
MERCURY LIVING PRESENCE
| ☐ SR90184 [S] | Mozart: Symphonies No. 39 and 41 | 196? | $120 |

— Maroon label, no "Vendor: Mercury Record Corporation
| ☐ SR90184 [S] | Mozart: Symphonies No. 39 and 41 | 196? | $30 |

— Maroon label, with "Vendor: Mercury Record Corporation

LONDON SYMPHONY ORCHESTRA (JEAN MARTINON, CONDUCTOR)
RCA VICTOR RED SEAL
| ☐ LSC-2298 [S] | Borodin: Symphony No. 2; Rimsky-Korsakov: Capriccio Espagnole | 1960 | $80 |

— Original with "shaded dog" label
| ☐ LSC-2298 [S] | Borodin: Symphony No. 2; Rimsky-Korsakov: Capriccio Espagnole | 199? | $30 |

— Classic Records reissue
| ☐ LSC-2419 [S] | Dvorak: Slavonic Dances | 1960 | $180 |

— Original with "shaded dog" label
| ☐ LSC-2419 [S] | Dvorak: Slavonic Dances | 199? | $30 |

— Classic Records reissue
| ☐ LSC-2322 [S] | Shostakovich: Symphony No. 1 | 1960 | $150 |

— Original with "shaded dog" label
| ☐ LSC-2322 [S] | Shostakovich: Symphony No. 1 | 199? | $30 |

— Classic Records reissue

LONDON SYMPHONY ORCHESTRA (PIERRE MONTEUX, CONDUCTOR)
RCA VICTOR RED SEAL
| ☐ LSC-2489 [S] | Dvorak: Symphony No. 2 | 196? | $30 |

— Original with "shaded dog" label
| ☐ LSC-2489 [S] | Dvorak: Symphony No. 2 | 199? | $30 |

— Classic Records reissue
| ☐ LSC-2418 [S] | Elgar: Enigma Variations | 1960 | $100 |

— Original with "shaded dog" label
| ☐ LSC-2418 [S] | Elgar: Enigma Variations | 199? | $30 |

— Classic Records reissue
| ☐ LSC-2208 [S] | Rimsky-Korsakov: Scheherazade | 1959 | $30 |

— Original with "shaded dog" label
| ☐ LSC-2342 [S] | Sibelius: Symphony No. 2 | 1960 | $25 |

— Original with "shaded dog" label
| ☐ LSC-2342 [S] | Sibelius: Symphony No. 2 | 199? | $30 |

— Classic Records reissue
| ☐ LSC-2177 [S] | Tchaikovsky: Sleeping Beauty (Excerpts) | 1959 | $30 |

— Original with "shaded dog" label

LONDON SYMPHONY ORCHESTRA (WALTER SUSSKIND, HANS SCHMIDT-ISSERSTEDT, CONDUCTORS)
MERCURY LIVING PRESENCE
| ☐ SR90196 [S] | Schubert: Symphonies No. 4 and 6 | 196? | $25 |

— Maroon label, no "Vendor: Mercury Record Corporation

LONDONBEAT
RADIOACTIVE
| ☐ 10192 | In the Blood | 1991 | $15 |

LONE JUSTICE
GEFFEN
| ☐ GHS24060 | Lone Justice | 1985 | $12 |
| ☐ GHS24122 | Shelter | 1986 | $12 |

Number	Title	Yr	NM

LONE STAR RAMBLERS, THE
LONGHORN
❑ LP-600 [M]	Texas Square Dancing with Red at the 60 Club	196?	$30

LONESOME BLUES SINGER, THE
See LEADBELLY.

LONESOME PINE FIDDLERS, THE
STARDAY
❑ SLP-155 [M]	14 Mountain Songs Featuring 5-String Banjo	1961	$40
❑ SLP-194 [M]	Bluegrass	1962	$40
❑ SLP-222 [M]	More Bluegrass	1963	$40

LONESOME RHODES
RCA VICTOR
❑ LPM-3759 [M]	Lonesome Rhodes	1967	$30
❑ LSP-3759 [S]	Lonesome Rhodes	1967	$25

LONESOME STRANGERS, THE
HIGHTONE
❑ 8016	The Lonesome Strangers	1989	$15

LONESOME SUNDOWN
EXCELLO
❑ LPS-8012	Lonesome Lonely Blues	1970	$30

LONG, BARBARA
SAVOY
❑ MG-12161 [M]	Soul	1961	$30

LONG, DANNY
CAPITOL
❑ T1988 [M]	Jazz Furlough	1963	$85
❑ ST1988 [S]	Jazz Furlough	1963	$50

LONG, JOHNNY
CIRCLE
❑ 56	Johnny Long and His Orchestra 1941-1942	198?	$25

LONG, SHORTY (1)
R&B singer.
SOUL
❑ SS-709 [S]	Here Comes the Judge	1968	$25
❑ SM-709 [M]	Here Comes the Judge	1968	$50
—*Mono is white label promo only; mono sticker on stereo cover*
❑ SS-719 [B]	The Prime of Shorty Long	1969	$18

LONG, SHORTY (2)
C&W singer. Not to be confused with the soul singer who used the same name.
FORD
❑ FXM-712 [M]	Country Jamboree	1963	$25

LONGBRANCH PENNYWHISTLE
AMOS
❑ AAS-7007 [B]	Longbranch Pennywhistle	1969	$75

LONGET, CLAUDINE
A&M
❑ LP-121 [M]	Claudine	1967	$18
❑ SP-4121 [S]	Claudine	1967	$15
❑ SP-4163	Colours	1969	$15
❑ SP-4142	Love Is Blue	1968	$15
❑ SP-4232	Run Wild, Run Free	1970	$15
❑ LP-128 [M]	The Look of Love	1967	$18
❑ SP-4128 [S]	The Look of Love	1967	$15
BARNABY
❑ KZ31383	Let's Spend the Night Together	1972	$15
❑ Z30377	We've Only Just Begun	1971	$15

LONGINES SYMPHONETTE SOCIETY
LONGINES SYMPHONETTE
❑ AV-201	Avon Wishes You a Happy Holiday and a Joyous New Year	1971	$18
—*Give to Avon salespeople; on label: "Avon Presents the Longines Symphonette Society*
❑ LWS192	Home for Christmas	196?	$15
❑ LWSH5/6	Shell's Wonderful World of Music -- Special Christmas Edition	196?	$18
—*Sold only at Shell gas stations*
❑ LWSH7/8	Shell's Wonderful World of Music -- Special Christmas Edition, Volume II	196?	$18
—*Sold only at Shell gas stations*
❑ LWS155 [S]	The Sweet Voices of Christmas	196?	$15
—*Same as above, but in stereo*

❑ LW155 [M]	The Sweet Voices of Christmas	196?	$12
—*With the children's voices from the choirs of Westminster Abbey and St. Paul's Cathedral*

LONGMIRE, WILBERT
COLUMBIA
❑ JC35754	Champagne	1979	$25
❑ JC35365	Sunny Side Up	1978	$25
PACIFIC JAZZ
❑ ST-20161	Revolution	1969	$25

LONGNON, JEAN-LOUP
ATLANTIC
❑ 81829	Jean-Loup Longnon and His New Your Orchestra	1988	$25

LONGO, MIKE
GROOVE MERCHANT
❑ 525	Funkia	1974	$25
MAINSTREAM
❑ MRL-334	Matrix	1972	$35
❑ MRL-357	The Awakening	1972	$35
PABLO
❑ 2310769	Talk with Spirits	197?	$35

LONGO, PAT
TOWN HALL
❑ 33	Billy May for President	198?	$25
❑ 25	Chain Reaction	1980	$25
❑ 30	Crocodile Tears	1981	$25

LONZO AND OSCAR
COLUMBIA
❑ CS9587	Mountain Dew	1968	$25
DECCA
❑ DL4363 [M]	Country Comedy Time	1963	$25
STARDAY
❑ SLP-119 [M]	America's Greatest Country Comedians	1960	$40
❑ SLP-244 [M]	Country Music Time	1963	$40

LOOKING GLASS
EPIC
❑ KE31320	Looking Glass	1972	$18
❑ KE32167	Subway Serenade	1973	$18

LOOKOFSKY, HARRY
ATLANTIC
❑ 1319 [M]	Stringville	1959	$300
—*Black label*
❑ 1319 [M]	Stringville	1961	$175
—*Multicolor label, white "fan" logo at right*
❑ 1319 [M]	Stringville	1964	$35
—*Multicolor label, black "fan" logo at right*
❑ SD1319 [S]	Stringville	1959	$300
—*Green label*
❑ SD1319 [S]	Stringville	1961	$175
—*Multicolor label, white "fan" logo at right*
❑ SD1319 [S]	Stringville	1964	$30
—*Multicolor label, black "fan" logo at right*

LOOSE
NOCTURNE
❑ 906	Freaky Billie, The Wheelie King	1970	$30

LOOSE FUR
DRAG CITY
❑ DC203	Loose Fur	2003	$30

LOPEZ, TRINI
CAPITOL
❑ SK11009	Viva	1972	$12
GUEST STAR
❑ GS-1499 [M]	Trini Lopez and Scott Gregory	1964	$50
—*"Scott Gregory" is said to be a pseudonym for BILL HALEY.*
HARMONY
❑ H30012	Bye Bye Love	1970	$12
KING
❑ 962 [M]	24 Songs by the Great Trini Lopez	1966	$30
❑ 877 [M]	More of Trini Lopez	1964	$75
❑ 863 [M]	Teenage Love Songs	1963	$75
REPRISE
❑ R-6226 [M]	Greatest Hits!	1966	$15
❑ RS-6226 [S]	Greatest Hits!	1966	$18
❑ RS-6285 [S]	It's a Great Life	1968	$15
❑ R-6285 [M]	It's a Great Life	1968	$30
—*Mono is white label promo only*
❑ R-6134 [M]	Live at Basin St. East	1964	$15
❑ RS-6134 [S]	Live at Basin St. East	1964	$18

❑ R-6103 [M]	More Trini Lopez at PJ's	1963	$15
❑ RS-6103 [S]	More Trini Lopez at PJ's	1963	$18
❑ R-6112 [M]	On the Move	1964	$15
❑ RS-6112 [S]	On the Move	1964	$18
❑ R-6147 [M]	The Folk Album	1965	$15
❑ RS-6147 [S]	The Folk Album	1965	$18
❑ R-6125 [M]	The Latin Album	1964	$15
❑ RS-6125 [S]	The Latin Album	1964	$18
❑ R-6165 [M]	The Love Album	1965	$15
❑ RS-6165 [S]	The Love Album	1965	$18
❑ R-6171 [M]	The Rhythm & Blues Album	1965	$15
❑ RS-6171 [S]	The Rhythm & Blues Album	1965	$18
❑ R-6215 [M]	The Second Latin Album	1966	$15
❑ RS-6215 [S]	The Second Latin Album	1966	$18
❑ R-6183 [M]	The Sing-Along World of Trini Lopez	1965	$15
❑ RS-6183 [S]	The Sing-Along World of Trini Lopez	1965	$18
❑ RS-6361	The Trini Lopez Show	1970	$18
❑ RS-6337	The Whole Enchilada	1969	$15
❑ R-6196 [M]	Trini	1966	$15
❑ RS-6196 [S]	Trini	1966	$18
❑ R-6093 [M]	Trini Lopez at PJ's	1963	$15
❑ R9-6093 [S]	Trini Lopez at PJ's	1963	$18
❑ R-6238 [M]	Trini Lopez in London	1967	$18
❑ RS-6238 [S]	Trini Lopez in London	1967	$15
❑ R-6255 [M]	Trini Lopez -- Now!	1967	$18
❑ RS-6255 [S]	Trini Lopez -- Now!	1967	$15
❑ RS-6300	Welcome to Trini Country	1968	$15
ROULETTE
❑ 3020	Transformed by Time	1978	$12

LORBER, JEFF
ARISTA
❑ AL9545	Galaxian	1981	$12
❑ AL8119	Galaxian	198?	$10
—*Reissue of 9545*
❑ AL8-8025	In the Heat of the Night	1984	$12
❑ AL9583	It's a Fact	1982	$12
❑ AL8218	It's a Fact	198?	$10
—*Reissue of 9583*
❑ AL8393	Lift Off	1986	$12
❑ AL8-8269	Step by Step	1985	$12
❑ AB4234	Water Sign	1979	$12
❑ AL8360	Water Sign	198?	$10
—*Reissue of 4234*
❑ AL9516	Wizard Island	1980	$25
❑ AL8340	Wizard Island	198?	$20
—*Reissue of 9516*
INNER CITY
❑ IC-1026	Jeff Lorber Fusion	1977	$18
❑ IC-1056	Soft Space	1978	$18
WARNER BROS.
❑ 25492	Private Passion	1986	$12

LORD, BOBBY
DECCA
❑ DL75246 [B]	Bobby Lord	1970	$18
HARMONY
❑ HL7322 [M]	Bobby Lord's Best	1964	$30
HICKORY
❑ LP-126 [M]	The Bobby Lord Show	1965	$25

LORD, VIVIAN
STASH
❑ ST-241	Love Dance	198?	$25

LORD SITAR
CAPITOL
❑ ST2916 [B]	Lord Sitar	1968	$50

LORDS OF THE NEW CHURCH
DRASTIC PLASTIC
❑ DPRLP57 [B]	Is Nothing Sacred?	2015	$25
❑ DPRLP58 [B]	The Method to our Madness	2015	$25
—*limited numbered edition*
I.R.S.
❑ SP-70039 [B]	Is Nothing Sacred?	1983	$18
❑ 5726 [B]	Killer Lords	1986	$18
❑ SP-70029 [B]	The Lords of the New Church	1982	$25
❑ SP-70049	The Method to Our Madness	1984	$15
—*As "The Lords*

LOREN, DONNA
CAPITOL
❑ T2323 [M]	Beach Blanket Bingo	1965	$40
❑ ST2323 [S]	Beach Blanket Bingo	1965	$50

LORIMER, MICHAEL
DANCING CAT
❑ DC-3002	Remembranza	198?	$30

LORING, GLORIA
ATLANTIC
❑ 81852	Full Moon, No Hesitation	1988	$10
❑ 81679	Gloria Loring	1986	$10

Number	Title	Yr	NM

MGM
❏ SE-4499	Today	1968	$25

LOS ADMIRADORES
COMMAND
| ❏ 809SD [S] | Bongos Bongos Bongos | 1960 | $18 |
| ❏ 812SD [S] | Bongos/Flutes/Guitars | 1960 | $18 |

LOS ANGELES PHILHARMONIC (ZUBIN MEHTA, CONDUCTOR)
MOBILE FIDELITY
| ❏ Jan-008 | Suites from "Star Wars" and "Close Encounters of the Third Kind" | 1979 | $50 |

—*Audiophile vinyl*

LOS BRAVOS
Also see MIKE KENNEDY.
PARROT
| ❏ PAS71021 | Bring a Little Lovin' | 1968 | $100 |

—*Among the other tracks, "Black Is Black" in in true stereo.*

PRESS
| ❏ PR73003 [M] | Black Is Black | 1966 | $75 |
| ❏ PRS83003 [R] | Black Is Black | 1966 | $40 |

LOS INDIOS TABAJARAS
RCA CAMDEN
| ❏ CXS-9031 | Los Indios Tabajaras | 1973 | $18 |
RCA INTERNATIONAL
| ❏ IL5-7367 | Los Grandes Exitos | 198? | $15 |
RCA VICTOR
❏ LPM-2912 [M]	Always in My Heart	1964	$18
❏ LSP-2912 [S]	Always in My Heart	1964	$25
❏ AFL1-2912	Always in My Heart	1977	$12
—*Reissue with new prefix*
❏ AFL1-3990	Beautiful Sounds	1981	$12
❏ LPM-3505 [M]	Casually Classical	1966	$18
❏ LSP-3505 [S]	Casually Classical	1966	$25
❏ AFL1-3505	Casually Classical	1977	$12
—*Reissue with new prefix*
| ❏ CPL1-0668 | Classical Guitars | 1974 | $15 |
| ❏ AFL1-0668 | Classical Guitars | 1977 | $12 |
—*Reissue with new prefix*
❏ LSP-4365	Dreams of Love	1970	$18
❏ LPM-3909 [M]	Fascinating Rhythms of Their Brazil	1968	$25
❏ LSP-3909 [S]	Fascinating Rhythms of Their Brazil	1968	$18
❏ APL1-0210	Favorite Movie Themes	1973	$15
❏ AFL1-0210	Favorite Movie Themes	1977	$12
—*Reissue with new prefix*
❏ AFL1-4649	Guitars on the Go	1983	$12
❏ LSP-4013	In a Sentimental Mood	1968	$18
❏ ANL1-2321	In a Sentimental Mood	1977	$12
❏ LPM-3413 [M]	Many-Splendored Guitars	1965	$18
❏ LSP-3413 [S]	Many-Splendored Guitars	1965	$25
❏ LPM-2822 [M]	Maria Elena	1963	$25
—*Reissue of LPM-1788*
| ❏ LSP-2822 [S] | Maria Elena | 1963 | $30 |
—*Reissue of LSP-1788*
| ❏ FSP-296 | Maria Elena | 1971 | $15 |
| ❏ ANL1-1179 | Maria Elena | 1976 | $12 |
—*Reissue*
❏ AFL1-2526	Masterpieces	1978	$15
❏ APL1-2082	Mellow Nostalgia	1977	$15
❏ AFL1-4273	Music for Romance	1982	$12
❏ AFL1-3535	Rainbows	1980	$12
❏ APL1-1033	Secret Love	1975	$15
❏ AFL1-1033	Secret Love	1977	$12
—*Reissue with new prefix*
❏ FSP-300	Siempre En Mi Corazon	1972	$15
❏ FSP-310	Softly	1972	$15
❏ LSP-4129	Song of the Islands	1969	$18
❏ LPM-1788 [M]	Sweet and Savage	1958	$40
❏ LSP-1788 [S]	Sweet and Savage	1958	$50
❏ LSP-4007	The Best of Los Indios Tabajaras	1968	$18
❏ AFL1-4007	The Best of Los Indios Tabajaras	1977	$12
—*Reissue with new prefix*
❏ LPM-3723 [M]	Their Very Special Touch	1967	$18
❏ LSP-3723 [S]	Their Very Special Touch	1967	$25
❏ LSP-4496	The Very Thought of You	1971	$18
❏ LPM-2959 [M]	Twin Guitar Moods	1964	$18
❏ LSP-2959 [S]	Twin Guitar Moods	1964	$25
❏ LPM-3611 [M]	Twin Guitars -- In a Mood for Lovers	1966	$18
❏ LSP-3611 [S]	Twin Guitars -- In a Mood for Lovers	1966	$25
❏ AFL1-3241	Two Guitars	1979	$12
❏ LSP-4615	What the World Needs Now	1971	$15

LOS LOBOS
NEW VISTAS
| ❏ 1001 | Just Another Band from East L.A. | 1978 | $300 |
SLASH
| ❏ 23963 [EP] | And a Time to Dance | 1983 | $15 |
| ❏ R144507 | By the Light of the Moon | 1987 | $15 |

—*RCA Music Service edition*
❏ 25523	By the Light of the Moon	1987	$12
❏ 25177	How Will the Wolf Survive?	1984	$12
❏ 25790	La Pistola y El Corazon	1988	$18
❏ 26131	The Neighborhood	1990	$25

LOS LOCOS DEL RITMO
DIMSA
| ❏ 8178 | Rock! | 196? | $150 |

LOS SEVEN DAYS
ECO
| ❏ 314 | Sha-La-La | 196? | $50 |

LOST & FOUND
INTERNATIONAL ARTISTS
| ❏ IA-3 | Everybody's Here | 1968 | $150 |
—*Original pressing, no "Masterfonics" in dead wax*
| ❏ IA-3 | Everybody's Here | 1979 | $18 |
—*Reissue with "Masterfonics" in trail-off wax*

LOST NATION, THE
RARE EARTH
| ❏ RS-518 | Paradise Lost | 1970 | $25 |

LOTHAR AND THE HAND PEOPLE
CAPITOL
| ❏ ST2997 [B] | Presenting Lothar and the Hand People | 1968 | $75 |
| ❏ SM-2997 | Presenting Lothar and the Hand People | 1977 | $10 |
—*Reissue with new prefix*

| ❏ ST-247 [B] | Space Hymn | 1969 | $75 |

LOTTRIDGE, RICHARD, AND JOAN WILDMAN
UNIVERSITY OF WISCONSIN
| ❏ UW-102 | Something New: The Unique Sounds of Jazz Bassoon | 1986 | $35 |

LOUDERMILK, JOHN D.
RCA VICTOR
❏ LPM-3497 [M]	A Bizarre Collection of the Most Unusual Songs	1965	$25
❏ LSP-3497 [S]	A Bizarre Collection of the Most Unusual Songs	1965	$30
❏ LSP-4040	Country Love Songs	1968	$25
❏ LPM-2434 [M]	Language of Love	1961	$30
❏ LSP-2434 [S]	Language of Love	1961	$30
❏ LPM-3807 [M]	Suburban Attitudes in Country Music	1967	$30
❏ LSP-3807 [S]	Suburban Attitudes in Country Music	1967	$25
❏ LSP-4097	The Open Mind of John D. Loudermilk	1968	$25
❏ LPM-2539 [M]	Twelve Sides of Loudermilk	1962	$25
❏ LSP-2539 [S]	Twelve Sides of Loudermilk	1962	$30
WARNER BROS.
❏ WS1922	Volume 1, Elloree	1971	$18

LOUDON, DOROTHY
CORAL
| ❏ CRL57265 [M] | At the Blue Angel | 1959 | $25 |
| ❏ CRL757265 [S] | At the Blue Angel | 1959 | $30 |

LOUIE AND THE LOVERS
EPIC
| ❏ E30026 [B] | Rise | 1970 | $30 |

LOUISE, TINA
CONCERT HALL
| ❏ H-1503 [M] | Her Portrait in Hi-Fi | 1958 | $50 |
| ❏ H-1521 [M] | It's Time for Tina | 1958 | $250 |

URANIA
| ❏ USD-2005 [S] | It's Time for Tina | 1959 | $300 |
| ❏ ULM-2005 [M] | It's Time for Tina | 1959 | $250 |

LOUISIANA HONEY DRIPPERS, THE
PRESTIGE
| ❏ PR-13035 [M] | Bluegrass | 1961 | $30 |

LOUISIANA RED
ROULETTE
| ❏ R-25200 [M] | The Lowdown Back Porch Blues | 1963 | $40 |

LOUISIANA REPERTORY JAZZ BAND
STOMP OFF
❏ SOS-1140	Hot and Sweet Sounds of Lost New Orleans	1987	$25
❏ SOS-1029	New Orleans	198?	$25
❏ SOS-1055	Uptown Jazz	198?	$25

LOUNGE LIZARDS, THE
EDITIONS EG
| ❏ EGS-108 | The Lounge Lizards | 1981 | $30 |
EUROPA
| ❏ JP-2012 | Live from the Drunken Boat | 1983 | $35 |
ISLAND
| ❏ 90529 | Live in Tokyo -- Big Heart | 1986 | $25 |
| ❏ 90592 | No Pain for Cakes | 1987 | $25 |

LOUSSIER, JACQUES
LONDON
❏ LL3454/5 [M]	Bach Jazz	1965	$35
❏ PS454/5 [S]	Bach Jazz	1965	$25
❏ 820245-1 [S]	Bach Jazz, Vol. 1	1985	$25
❏ 820246-1 [S]	Bach Jazz, Vol. 2	1985	$25
❏ PS524	Bach Jazz, Vol. 5	1968	$30
❏ LL3144 [M]	Play Bach	196?	$35
❏ LL3287 [M]	Play Bach, Vol. 1	1964	$30
❏ PS287 [S]	Play Bach, Vol. 1	1964	$35
❏ LL3288 [M]	Play Bach, Vol. 2	1964	$30
❏ PS288 [S]	Play Bach, Vol. 2	1964	$35
❏ LL3289 [M]	Play Bach, Vol. 3	1964	$30
❏ PS289 [S]	Play Bach, Vol. 3	1964	$35
❏ LL3365 [M]	Play Bach, Vol. 4	1964	$30
❏ PS365 [S]	Play Bach, Vol. 4	1964	$35

LOUVIN, CHARLIE, AND MELBA MONTGOMERY
CAPITOL
| ❏ ST-808 | Baby, You've Got What It Takes | 1971 | $25 |
| ❏ ST-686 | Somethin' to Brag About | 1971 | $25 |

LOUVIN, CHARLIE
Also see JIM AND JESSE; THE LOUVIN BROTHERS.

CAPITOL
❏ ST-416	Here's a Toast to Mama	1970	$25
❏ ST-142	Hey Daddy	1969	$25
❏ ST-8-0142	Hey Daddy	1969	$30
—*Capitol Record Club edition*
❏ T2787 [M]	I Forgot to Cry	1967	$30
❏ ST2787 [S]	I Forgot to Cry	1967	$25
❏ T2689 [M]	I'll Remember Always	1967	$30
❏ ST2689 [S]	I'll Remember Always	1967	$25
❏ T2208 [M]	Less and Less and I Don't Love You Anymore	1965	$25
❏ ST2208 [S]	Less and Less and I Don't Love You Anymore	1965	$30
❏ T2482 [M]	Lonesome Is Me	1966	$25
❏ ST2482 [S]	Lonesome Is Me	1966	$30
❏ ST-555	Ten Times Charlie	1970	$25
❏ ST-248	The Kind of Man I Am	1969	$25
❏ T2437 [M]	The Many Moods of Charlie Louvin	1966	$25
❏ ST2437 [S]	The Many Moods of Charlie Louvin	1966	$30
❏ ST2958	Will You Visit Me on Sundays	1968	$25
UNITED ARTISTS
❏ UA-LA248-G	It Almost Felt Like Love	1974	$18

LOUVIN, IRA
Also see THE LOUVIN BROTHERS.
CAPITOL
| ❏ T2413 [M] | The Unforgettable Ira Louvin | 1965 | $30 |
| ❏ ST2413 [S] | The Unforgettable Ira Louvin | 1965 | $30 |

LOUVIN BROTHERS, THE
Also see CHARLIE LOUVIN; IRA LOUVIN.
CAPITOL
| ❏ T1449 [M] | A Tribute to the Delmore Brothers | 1960 | $100 |
—*Black colorband label, logo at left*
| ❏ T1449 [M] | A Tribute to the Delmore Brothers | 1962 | $30 |
—*Black colorband label, logo at top*
| ❏ T1616 [M] | Country Christmas | 1961 | $50 |
—*Black rainbow label with "Capitol" at left*
| ❏ ST1616 [S] | Country Christmas | 1961 | $100 |

Number	Title	Yr	NM
—Black rainbow label with "Capitol" at left			
❏ T1616 [M]	Country Christmas	1962	$25
—Black rainbow label with "Capitol" at top			
❏ ST1616 [S]	Country Christmas	1962	$30
—Black rainbow label with "Capitol" at top			
❏ T1106 [M]	Country Love Ballads	1959	$100
—Black colorband label, logo at left			
❏ T1106 [M]	Country Love Ballads	1962	$30
—Black colorband label, logo at top			
❏ T1547 [M]	Encore	1961	$100
—Black colorband label, logo at left			
❏ T1547 [M]	Encore	1962	$30
—Black colorband label, logo at top			
❏ T910 [M]	Ira and Charlie	1958	$150
—Turquoise label			
❏ T910 [M]	Ira and Charlie	1959	$40
—Black colorband label, logo at left			
❏ T910 [M]	Ira and Charlie	1962	$30
—Black colorband label, logo at top			
❏ T1834 [M]	Keep Your Eyes on Jesus	1963	$40
❏ ST1834 [S]	Keep Your Eyes on Jesus	1963	$50
❏ T1385 [M]	My Baby's Gone	1960	$100
—Black colorband label, logo at left			
❏ T1385 [M]	My Baby's Gone	1962	$30
—Black colorband label, logo at top			
❏ T825 [M]	Nearer My God to Thee	1957	$150
— Turquoise label			
❏ T825 [M]	Nearer My God to Thee	1959	$40
—Black colorband label, logo at left			
❏ T825 [M]	Nearer My God to Thee	1962	$30
—Black colorband label, logo at top			
❏ T1277 [M]	Satan Is Real	1960	$100
—Black colorband label, logo at left			
❏ T1277 [M]	Satan Is Real	1962	$30
—Black colorband label, logo at top			
❏ T2331 [M]	Thank God for My Christian Home	1965	$30
❏ ST2331 [S]	Thank God for My Christian Home	1965	$30
❏ T1061 [M]	The Family Who Prays	1958	$100
—Black colorband label, logo at left			
❏ T1061 [M]	The Family Who Prays	1962	$30
—Black colorband label, logo at top			
❏ DT1061 [R]	The Family Who Prays	196?	$25
❏ ST2827 [S]	The Great Roy Acuff Songs	1967	$30
❏ T2827 [M]	The Great Roy Acuff Songs	1967	$40
❏ T2091 [M]	The Louvin Brothers Sing and Play Their Current Hits	1964	$30
❏ ST2091 [S]	The Louvin Brothers Sing and Play Their Current Hits	1964	$30
❏ T769 [M]	Tragic Songs of Life	1956	$150
— Turquoise label			
❏ T769 [M]	Tragic Songs of Life	1959	$40
—Black colorband label, logo at left			

Number	Title	Yr	NM
❏ T769 [M]	Tragic Songs of Life	1962	$30
—Black colorband label, logo at top			
❏ DT769 [R]	Tragic Songs of Life	196?	$25
❏ T1721 [M]	Weapon of Prayer	1962	$40
❏ ST1721 [S]	Weapon of Prayer	1962	$50
METRO			
❏ M-598 [M]	The Louvin Brothers	1966	$30
❏ MS-598 [R]	The Louvin Brothers	1966	$25
MGM			
❏ E-3426 [M]	The Louvin Brothers	1957	$250
SEARS			
❏ SP-119 [M]	Ira & Charles Louvin	196?	$25
❏ SPS-119 [R]	Ira & Charles Louvin	196?	$18
TOWER			
❏ DT5122	Country Heart and Soul	1968	$25
❏ T5038 [M]	Two Different Worlds	1966	$30
❏ DT5038 [R]	Two Different Worlds	1966	$25

Number	Title	Yr	NM
LOVANO, JOE			
SOUL NOTE			
❏ 121132	Tones, Shapes and Colors	1985	$30
❏ 121182	Village Rhythm	1988	$30
LOVE, DARLENE			
COLUMBIA			
❏ FC40605	Paint Another Picture	1988	$15
LOVE, HOLLY			
ACE			
❏ LP-1022 [M]	My Love Confessions	1962	$30
LOVE, PEACE AND HAPPINESS			
RCA VICTOR			
❏ LSP-4721	Here 'Tis	1972	$15
❏ LSP-4535	Love Is Stronger	1971	$15
LOVE, PRESTON			
KENT			
❏ KST-540	Omaha Bar-B-Q	1968	$25
LOVE			
Also see ARTHUR LEE.			
BLUE THUMB			
❏ BTS-8822 [B]	False Start	1970	$30
❏ BTS-9000 [B]	Out Here	1969	$40
ELEKTRA			
❏ EKL-4005 [M]	Da Capo	1967	$500
❏ EKS-74005 [S]	Da Capo	1967	$40
—Brown label			
❏ EKS-74005 [S]	Da Capo	1969	$18
—Red label with large stylized "E			
❏ EKS-74005 [S]	Da Capo	1971	$15
—Butterfly label			
❏ EKL-4013 [M]	Forever Changes	1967	$500
❏ EKL-4013 [M]	Forever Changes	1967	$500
—White label promo			
❏ EKS-74013 [S]	Forever Changes	1967	$30
—Brown label			
❏ EKS-74013 [S]	Forever Changes	1969	$18
—Red label with large stylized "E			
❏ EKS-74013 [S]	Forever Changes	1971	$15
—Butterfly label			
❏ EKS-74013 [S]	Forever Changes	1980	$12
—Red label, small "E," Warner Communications logo on label			
❏ EKS-74013 [S]	Forever Changes	1984	$10
—Red and black label			
❏ EKS-74049 [DJ]	Four Sail	1969	$100
—White label promo			
❏ EKS-74049	Four Sail	1969	$30
—Red label with large stylized "E			
❏ EKS-74049	Four Sail	1971	$15
—Butterfly label			
❏ EKL-4001 [M]	Love	1966	$300
❏ EKL-4001 [M]	Love	1966	$350
—White label promo			
❏ EKS-74001 [S]	Love	1966	$50
—Brown label			
❏ EKS-74001 [S]	Love	1969	$18
—Red label with large stylized "E			
❏ EKS-74001 [S]	Love	1971	$15
—Butterfly label			
❏ EKS-74058	Revisited	1970	$30
—Red label with large stylized "E			
❏ EKS-74058	Revisited	1971	$15
—Butterfly label			
❏ EKS-74058	Revisited	1984	$10
—Red and black label			
❏ EKS-74058	Revisited	198?	$12
—Red label, small "E," Warner Communications logo on label			
MCA			
❏ 27025	Studio/Live	1982	$12
RHINO			
❏ RNLP-800	Best of Love	1980	$12
❏ RNDF-251 [PD]	Love Live	1981	$18
❏ RNLP-70175	The Best of Love (1966-1969) (Golden Archive Series)	1987	$12
RSO			
❏ SO4804	Reel to Real	1974	$18
SUNDAZED			
❏ LP5101	Da Capo	2001	$15
—Reissue on 180-gram vinyl			
❏ LP5102	Forever Changes	2001	$15
—Reissue on 180-gram vinyl			
❏ LP5103	Four Sail	2004	$15
❏ LP5100	Love	2001	$15
—Reissue on 180-gram vinyl			
❏ LP5104	Revisited	2001	$15
—Reissue on 180-gram vinyl			

Number	Title	Yr	NM
LOVE AND ROCKETS			
BAUHAUS related.			
BEGGARS BANQUET			
❏ 9715-1-R [B]	Love and Rockets	1989	$30
BIG TIME/RCA			
❏ 6058-1-B8	Earth.Sun.Moon	1987	$12
❏ 6011-1-B	Express	1986	$15
DRASTIC PLASTIC			
❏ DPRLP61 [B]	Earth Sun Moon	2015	$25
—ltd ed, numbered			
RCA			
❏ 8507-1-R	Seventh Dream of Teenage Heaven	1988	$12
LOVE CHILDS AFRO CUBAN BLUES BAND			
MIDSONG INT'L.			
❏ BKL1-2292	Spandisco	1977	$12
ROULETTE			
❏ 3016	Out Among 'Em	1975	$12
LOVE EXCHANGE, THE			
TOWER			
❏ ST5115 [S]	The Love Exchange	1968	$30
❏ T5115 [M]	The Love Exchange	1968	$75
LOVE GENERATION, THE			
IMPERIAL			
❏ LP-12364	A Generation of Love	1968	$25
❏ LP-12408	Montage	1968	$25
❏ LP-9351 [M]	The Love Generation	1967	$50
❏ LP-12351 [S]	The Love Generation	1967	$25
LOVE PEOPLE			
GUINNESS			
❏ GNS36059 [B]	Sing It Again	1977	$300
LOVE SCULPTURE			
DAVE EDMUNDS was in this group.			
EMI AMERICA			
❏ SQ-17208	Blues Helping	1986	$15
— Reissue of Rare Earth LP			
PARROT			
❏ PAS71035 [B]	Forms and Feelings	1970	$35
RARE EARTH			
❏ RS-505 [B]	Blues Helping	1969	$75
LOVE UNLIMITED			
20TH CENTURY			
❏ T-443	In Heat	1974	$12
❏ T-414	Under the Influence of…	1973	$12
MCA			
❏ 181	Love Unlimited	1973	$15
—Reissue of Uni 73131			
❏ 316	Under the Influence of…	1973	$0
—Canceled; issued on 20th Century 414			
UNI			
❏ 73131	Love Unlimited	1972	$18
UNLIMITED GOLD			
❏ 101	He's All I Got	1977	$12
❏ JZ36130	Love Is Back	1979	$12
LOVE UNLIMITED ORCHESTRA			
20TH CENTURY			
❏ T-582	Movie Themes	1978	$12
❏ T-480	Music Maestro Please	1975	$12
❏ T-554	My Musical Bouquet	1978	$12
❏ T-517	My Sweet Summer Suite	1976	$12
❏ T-433	Rhapsody in White	1974	$12
❏ T-101	Together Brothers	1974	$15
❏ T-458	White Gold	1974	$12
UNLIMITED GOLD			
❏ FZ38366	Rise	1983	$12
❏ FZ37425	Welcome Aboard	1981	$12
LOVECRAFT			
See H.P. LOVECRAFT.			
LOVELESS, PATTY			
MCA			
❏ 42223	Honky Tonk Angel	1988	$12
❏ 42092	If My Heart Had Windows	1988	$12
❏ 5915	Patty Loveless	1987	$12

Number	Title	Yr	NM

LOVELITES, THE
UNI

73081 [B]	The Lovelites	1970	$30

LOVERBOY
Includes members of STREETHEART and MOXY.
COLUMBIA

OC45411	Big Ones	1989	$15
FC37638	Get Lucky	1981	$10
QC38703	Keep It Up	1983	$10
JC36762	Loverboy	1980	$10
A2S1256 [DJ]	Loverboy Live from Dayton, Ohio	1981	$25

—Promo-only release; three sides have music, the fourth side has the band's autographs etched into the record

FC39953	Lovin' Every Minute of It	1985	$10
OC40893	Wildside	1987	$10

LOVETT, LEE
STRAND

SL-1055 [M]	Jazz Dance Party	1962	$50
SLS-1055 [S]	Jazz Dance Party	1962	$75
SL-1059 [M]	Misty	1962	$50
SLS-1059 [S]	Misty	1962	$75

WYNNE

WLP-108 [M]	Jazz Dance Party	195?	$30

LOVETT, LYLE
MCA/CURB

R133603	Lyle Lovett	1986	$15

—RCA Music Service edition

5748	Lyle Lovett	1986	$12
R100932	Lyle Lovett And His Large Band	1989	$15

—BMG Direct Marketing edition

42263	Lyle Lovett And His Large Band	1989	$12
17355 [EP]	Not Exactly Mr. Showbiz	1987	$18

—Promo-only five-song EP with special sleeve

R153258	Pontiac	1988	$15

—BMG Direct Marketing edition

42028	Pontiac	1988	$12

LOVICH, LENE
STIFF/EPIC

JE36308	Flex	1980	$25
5E37452 [EP]	New Toy	1981	$20
ARE38399	No Man's Land	1983	$15
JE36102 [B]	Stateless	1979	$40

—Red vinyl

JE36102 [B]	Stateless	1979	$20

LOVIN' SPOONFUL, THE
Also see JOE BUTLER; JOHN SEBASTIAN; ZALMAN YANOVSKY.
51 WEST

Q16023	... So Nice	1979	$12

ACCORD

SN-7196	Distant Echoes	1981	$12

BUDDAH

BDM-5706	The Best of the Lovin' Spoonful	197?	$15
BLB6-8339	The Best of the Lovin' Spoonful	198?	$12

—Reissue of 5706

KAMA SUTRA

KLPS-750-2	24 Karat Hits	1968	$25
KLP-8051 [M]	Daydream	1966	$40
KLPS-8051 [S]	Daydream	1966	$30
T-90675 [M]	Daydream	1966	$30

—Capitol Record Club edition

ST-90675 [S]	Daydream	1966	$40

—Capitol Record Club edition

KLP-8050 [M]	Do You Believe in Magic	1965	$35

Number	Title	Yr	NM
KLPS-8050 [S]	Do You Believe in Magic	1965	$30
T-90597 [M]	Do You Believe in Magic	1965	$30

—Capitol Record Club edition

ST-90597 [S]	Do You Believe in Magic	1965	$40

—Capitol Record Club edition

KLPS-8061 [S]	Everything Playing	1968	$25
KLP-8061 [M]	Everything Playing	1968	$75
KLP-8054 [M]	Hums of the Lovin' Spoonful	1966	$40
KLPS-8054 [S]	Hums of the Lovin' Spoonful	1966	$30
ST-90988 [S]	Hums of the Lovin' Spoonful	1966	$40

—Capitol Record Club edition

KSBS-2029	Once Upon a Time	1971	$18
KLPS-8073	Revelation: Revolution '69	1969	$30
KSBS-2608	The Best…Lovin' Spoonful	1976	$25
KLP-8056 [M]	The Best of the Lovin' Spoonful	1967	$18

—Came with four bonus photos of the band, which are priced separately

KLPS-8056 [S]	The Best of the Lovin' Spoonful	1967	$18

—Came with four bonus photos of the band, which are priced separately

KAO-91102 [M]	The Best of the Lovin' Spoonful	1967	$30

—Capitol Record Club edition

SKAO-91102 [S]	The Best of the Lovin' Spoonful	1967	$25

—Capitol Record Club edition

KLP-8064 [M]	The Best of the Lovin' Spoonful, Volume 2	1968	$50
KLPS-8064 [S]	The Best of the Lovin' Spoonful, Volume 2	1968	$25
KLP/S-8056	The Best of the Lovin' Spoonful Bonus Photos (4)	1967	$12
KSBS-2011	The John Sebastian Song Book	1970	$18
KSBS-2013	The Very Best of the Lovin' Spoonful	1970	$18
KLP-8053 [M]	What's Up, Tiger Lily?	1966	$40
KLPS-8053 [S]	What's Up, Tiger Lily?	1966	$30
KLP-8058 [M]	You're a Big Boy Now	1967	$75
KLPS-8058 [S]	You're a Big Boy Now	1967	$25
ST-91198 [S]	You're a Big Boy Now	1967	$30

—Capitol Record Club edition

KOALA

KO14221	Day Dream	1979	$12

PAIR

PDL2-1200	The Best of the Lovin' Spoonful	1986	$15

RHINO

RNLP-114	The Best of the Lovin' Spoonful, Vol. 2	1985	$12

SUNDAZED

LP5160	Daydream	2002	$18

—Reissue on 180-gram vinyl

LP5159	Do You Believe in Magic	2002	$18

—Reissue on 180-gram vinyl

LP5166	Hums of the Lovin' Spoonful	2003	$18

—Reissue on 180-gram vinyl

LOW, ANDY FAIRWEATHER
A&M

SP-4602	Be Bop 'n' Holla	1976	$12
SP-4542	La Booga Rooga	1975	$12
SP-3646 [B]	Spider Jiving	1974	$15

WARNER BROS.

BSK3450	Mega-Shebang	1980	$15

LOWE, BERNIE, ORCHESTRA
CAMEO

C-1057 [M]	Encore	1963	$25
C-4005 [M]	If the Big Bands Were Here Today	1962	$25
SC-4005 [S]	If the Big Bands Were Here Today	1962	$30
C-4007 [M]	If the Big Bands Were Here Today, Vol. 2	1962	$25
SC-4007 [S]	If the Big Bands Were Here Today, Vol. 2	1962	$30

LOWE, FRANK, AND EUGENE CHADBOURNE
QED

995	Don't Punk Out	1977	$30

LOWE, FRANK
ARISTA/FREEDOM

AF1015	Fresh	1976	$30

BLACK SAINT

BSR-0005	The Flam	198?	$30

CADENCE JAZZ

CJR-1007	Skizoke	198?	$25

ESP-DISK'

3013	Black Beings	197?	$250

SOUL NOTE

SN-1082	Decision in Paradise	1985	$30
SN-1032	Erotic Heartbreak	198?	$30

Number	Title	Yr	NM

LOWE, JIM
DOT

DLP-3681 [M]	Songs They Sing Behind the Green Door	1965	$30
DLP-25881 [S]	Songs They Sing Behind the Green Door	1965	$30
DLP-3051 [M]	The Green Door	1956	$175
DLP-3114 [M]	Wicked Women	1958	$150

MERCURY

MG-20246 [M]	The Door of Fame	1957	$175

LOWE, MUNDELL
CHARLIE PARKER

PLP-822 [M]	Blues for a Stripper	1962	$40
PLP-822S [S]	Blues for a Stripper	1962	$50

DOBRE

1018	Incomparable	1978	$35

FAMOUS DOOR

HL-102	California Guitar	1974	$30

JAZZLAND

JLP-8 [M]	Low-Down Guitar	1960	$75

OFFBEAT

OLP-3010 [M]	Tacet for Neurotics	1960	$100
OS-93010 [S]	Tacet for Neurotics	1960	$150

PAUSA

7152	Mundell Lowe Presents Transit West	1983	$35

RCA CAMDEN

CAL-490 [M]	Porgy and Bess	1959	$25
CAS-490 [S]	Porgy and Bess	1959	$25
CAL-522 [M]	TV Action Jazz!	1959	$25
CAS-522 [S]	TV Action Jazz!	1959	$25
CAL-627 [M]	TV Action Jazz! -- Volume 2	1960	$30
CAS-627 [S]	TV Action Jazz! -- Volume 2	1960	$30

RCA VICTOR

LJM-3002 [10]	The Mundell Lowe Quintet	1954	$120

RIVERSIDE

RLP 12-238 [M]	A Grand Night for Swinging	1957	$300

—White label, blue print

RLP 12-238 [M]	A Grand Night for Swinging	1959	$300

—Blue label, microphone logo at top

RLP 12-208 [M]	Guitar Moods	1956	$300

—White label, blue print

RLP 12-208 [M]	Guitar Moods	1959	$50

—Blue label, microphone logo at top

6089	Mundell Lowe Quintet	197?	$35
RLP 12-219 [M]	New Music of Alec Wilder	1956	$300

—White label, blue print

RLP 12-219 [M]	New Music of Alec Wilder	1959	$300

—Blue label, microphone logo at top

RLP 12-204 [M]	The Mundell Lowe Quartet	1956	$300

—White label, blue print

RLP 12-204 [M]	The Mundell Lowe Quartet	1959	$300

—Blue label, microphone logo at top

LOWE, NICK
Also see DAVE EDMUNDS; ROCKPILE.
COLUMBIA

AS1400 [DJ]	An Interrogation of Nick Lowe	1990	$30

—Promo-only interview album

AS1400 [DJ]	An Interrogation of Nick Lowe	1990	$30

—Promo-only interview album

JC36087	Labour of Lust	1979	$12
PC36087	Labour of Lust	198?	$10

—Budget-line reissue

FC39371	Nick Lowe and His Cowboy Outfit	1984	$15
PC39371	Nick Lowe and His Cowboy Outfit	1986	$10

—Budget-line reissue

Number	Title	Yr	NM
❏ FC37932	Nick the Knife	1982	$15
❏ PC37932	Nick the Knife	198?	$10
—Budget-line reissue			
❏ FC40381	Pinker and Prouder Than Previous	1988	$14
❏ JC35529	Pure Pop for Now People	1978	$25
❏ PC35529	Pure Pop for Now People	198?	$10
—Budget-line reissue			
❏ FC38589	The Abominable Showman	1983	$15
❏ PC38589	The Abominable Showman	1986	$10
—Budget-line reissue			
❏ FC39958	The Rose of England	1985	$15
REPRISE			
❏ 26132	Party of One	1990	$15

LOWE, SAMMY
RCA VICTOR
| ❏ LPM-2770 [M] | Hitsville U.S.A. | 1963 | $25 |
| ❏ LSP-2770 [S] | Hitsville U.S.A. | 1963 | $30 |

LOWRY, RON
REPUBLIC
| ❏ 1303 | Marry Me | 1970 | $18 |

LRY
CONGRESS OF THE CROW
| ❏ 8031002 | The LRY Record | 1968 | $250 |

LUBOFF, NORMAN, CHOIR
COLUMBIA
❏ CL2545 [10]	Carols for Christmas	1955	$30
—House Party Series			
❏ CL6272 [10]	Christmas Carols	1953	$40
❏ CL545 [M]	Easy to Remember	1954	$25
—Maroon label, gold print			
❏ CL926 [M]	Songs of Christmas	1957	$18
—Six LPs pictured on back cover: "exciting moments from Columbia's treasury of jazz			
❏ CS8846 [R]	Songs of Christmas	1963	$18
❏ CL926 [M]	Songs of Christmas	1957	$18
—Six LPs pictured on back cover: "dazzling performances of music from Hollywood			
RCA VICTOR			
❏ LPM-2941 [M]	Christmas with the Norman Luboff Choir	1964	$15
❏ LSP-2941 [S]	Christmas with the Norman Luboff Choir	1964	$18

LUCAS, BUDDY
UNITED ARTISTS
| ❏ UAL-3482 [M] | Fifty Fabulous Harmonica Favorites | 1966 | $25 |
| ❏ UAS-6482 [S] | Fifty Fabulous Harmonica Favorites | 1966 | $30 |

LUCAS, DOUG
SHADY BROOK
| ❏ SB 33-004 | Niara | 1975 | $30 |

LUCAS, NICK
CAVALIER
❏ CAV-5003 [10]	Tip-Toe Thru the Tulips	195?	$100
—Green vinyl			
DECCA			
❏ DL8653 [M]	Painting the Clouds with Sunshine	1957	$40

LUCAS, REGGIE
INNER CITY
| ❏ IC-6010 | Survival Themes | 197? | $35 |

LUCEY, CHRIS
SURREY
| ❏ SS-1027 [M] | Songs of Protest and Anti-Protest | 197? | $40 |

LUCIE, LAWRENCE
TOY
❏ 1001	Cool and Warm Guitar	197?	$35
❏ 1006	Mixed Emotions	1980	$30
❏ 1003	Sophisticated Lady/After Sundown	1978	$30
❏ 1005	This Is It	1979	$30

LUCRAFT, HOWARD
DECCA
| ❏ DL8679 [M] | Showcase for Modern Jazz | 1958 | $150 |

LUDDEN, ALLEN
RCA VICTOR
| ❏ LPM-2934 [M] | Allen Ludden Sings His Favorite Songs | 1964 | $25 |
| ❏ LSP-2934 [S] | Allen Ludden Sings His Favorite Songs | 1964 | $30 |

LUDI, WERNER
HAT ART
| ❏ 2018 | Lunatico | 1986 | $35 |

LUDWIG, GENE
MUSE
| ❏ MR-5164 | Now's the Time | 1979 | $30 |

LUKE
LIL' JOE
❏ 260	Luke's Booty Calls & Chants	2000	$18
LUKE			
❏ 7694 [DJ]	Changin' the Game	1997	$18
—Vinyl is promo only			
❏ 6996	Freak for Life 6996	1994	$18
—Vinyl may be promo only			
❏ 91830	I Got Shit on My Mind	1992	$18
❏ 91842	I Got Sumthin' on My Mind	1992	$18
—Clean version of 91830			
❏ 200	In the Nude	1993	$15
❏ 201	In the Nude (Edited)	1993	$18

LUTHER CAMPBELL
| ❏ 161000-1 | Uncle Luke | 1996 | $15 |

LULU
ALFA
❏ 10006	Lulu	1981	$15
ATCO			
❏ SD 33-330 [S]	Melody Fair	1970	$15
❏ 33-330 [M]	Melody Fair	1970	$50
—White label promo, "DJ Copy Monaural" on cover; no stock copies were issued in mono			
❏ 33-310 [M]	New Routes	1970	$30
—White label promo; no stock copies were issued in mono			
❏ SD 33-310 [S]	New Routes	1970	$15
CHELSEA			
❏ CHL-518	Heaven and Earth and the Stars	1976	$25
❏ BCL1-0144	Lulu	1973	$15
EPIC			
❏ BN26536	It's Lulu	1970	$15
❏ LN24339 [M]	To Sir with Love	1967	$30
❏ BN26339 [P]	To Sir with Love	1967	$30
HARMONY			
❏ H30249	To Love Somebody	1970	$25
PARROT			
❏ PA61016 [M]	From Lulu with Love	1967	$100
❏ PAS71016 [S]	From Lulu with Love	1967	$100
PICKWICK			
❏ SPC-3237	Lulu	1973	$10
ROCKET			
❏ BXL1-3073	Don't Take Love for Granted	1978	$15

LULU BELLE AND SCOTTY
STARDAY
❏ SLP-285 [M]	Down Memory Lane	1964	$40
❏ SLP-351 [M]	Lulu Belle & Scotty	1965	$40
❏ SLP-206 [M]	The Sweethearts of Country Music	1963	$40
SUPER			
❏ 6201 [M]	Lule Belle & Scotty	1963	$50

LUMAN, BOB
EPIC
❏ BN26393	Ain't Got Time to Be Unhappy	1968	$25
❏ KE34445	Alive and Well!	1976	$15
❏ KE32759	Bob Luman's Greatest Hits	1974	$18
❏ E30923	Chain Don't Take to Me	1972	$25
❏ BN26463 [B]	Come On Home and Sing the Blues	1969	$25
❏ BN26541	Gettin' Back	1970	$25
❏ E30617	Is It Any Wonder	1971	$25
❏ KE31746	Lonely Women Make Good Lovers	1972	$25
❏ KE32192	Neither One of Us	1973	$18
❏ KE33942	Satisfied Mind	1975	$15
❏ KE31375	When You Say Love	1972	$25
HARMONY			
❏ KH32006	Bob Luman	1973	$15
HICKORY			
❏ LPM-124 [M]	Livin' Lovin' Sounds	1965	$30
❏ LPS-124 [S]	Livin' Lovin' Sounds	1965	$30
HICKORY/MGM			
❏ H3G-4508	Still Loving You	1974	$18
POLYDOR			
❏ PD-1-6135	Bob Luman	1978	$15
WARNER BROS.			
❏ W1396 [M]	Let's Think About Livin'	1960	$50
❏ WS1396 [S]	Let's Think About Livin'	1960	$80

LUMLEY, RUFUS
RCA VICTOR
| ❏ LPM-3898 [M] | Rufus Lumley | 1967 | $50 |
| ❏ LSP-3898 [S] | Rufus Lumley | 1967 | $40 |

LUNA
ARHOOLIE
| ❏ ST-8001 | Space Swell | 1968 | $25 |

LUNCEFORD, JIMMIE
AIRCHECK
❏ 8	Victory	197?	$25
ALLEGRO ELITE			
❏ 0(# unknown) [10]	Jimmie Lunceford Plays	195?	$40
CIRCLE			
❏ 11	Jimmie Lunceford and His Orchestra 1940	198?	$25
❏ CLP-92	Jimmie Lunceford and His Orchestra 1944	198?	$25
COLUMBIA			
❏ GL104 [10]	Lunceford Special	1950	$100
❏ CL2715 [M]	Lunceford Special	1967	$30
❏ CS9515 [R]	Lunceford Special	1967	$35
—Red "360 Sound" label			
❏ CL634 [M]	Lunceford Special	1955	$75
—Maroon label, gold print			
❏ CL634 [M]	Lunceford Special	1956	$40
—Red and black label with six "eye" logos			
COLUMBIA MASTERWORKS			
❏ ML4804 [M]	Lunceford Special	195?	$75
DECCA			
❏ DL5393 [10]	For Dancers Only	1952	$175
❏ DL9238 [M]	Harlem Shout	1968	$40
❏ DL79238 [R]	Harlem Shout	1968	$25
❏ DL8050 [M]	Jimmie Lunceford and His Orchestra	1954	$175
❏ DL9237 [M]	Rhythm Is Our Business	1968	$40
❏ DL79237 [R]	Rhythm Is Our Business	1968	$25
MCA			
❏ 1314	Blues in the Night	198?	$25
❏ 1307	For Dancers Only	198?	$25
❏ 1305	Harlem Shout	198?	$25
❏ 1320	Jimmie's Legacy	198?	$25
❏ 1321	Last Sparks	198?	$25
❏ 1302	Rhythm Is Our Business	198?	$25
PICKWICK			
❏ SPC-3531	Blues in the Night	197?	$25
SUNBEAM			
❏ 221	Jimmie Lunceford and Band 1939-42	197?	$25
TIME-LIFE			
❏ STBB-27	Big Bands: Jimmie Lunceford	1986	$35
X			
❏ LX-3002 [M]	Jimmie Lunceford and His Chickasaw Syncopators	1954	$75

LUNCH, LYDIA
RUBY

❏ JRR806 [B]	13.13	1982	$50
ZE/BUDDAH			
❏ 33006 [B]	Queen of Siam	1980	$50

LUND, GARRETT
(NO LABEL)
| ❏ 0(no cat #) | Almost Grown | 1975 | $300 |

LUNDY, PAT
COLUMBIA
| ❏ CS9588 | Soul Ain't Nothin' But the Blues | 1968 | $25 |

LUNN, ROBERT
STARDAY
| ❏ SLP-228 [M] | The Original Talking Blues Man | 1962 | $30 |

Number	Title	Yr	NM

LUNSFORD, MIKE
STARDAY

Number	Title	Yr	NM
❑ SD969X	Mike Lunsford	1977	$15
❑ SD951	Mike Lunsford	1975	$15

LURIE, ELLIOTT
EPIC

❑ PE33337	Elliott Lurie	1975	$12

LURIE, JOHN
ENIGMA

❑ SJ-73213	Stranger Than Paradise	1986	$25

LUSCIOUS JACKSON
GRAND ROYAL

❑ GR 038	Fever In Fever Out	1996	$15
❑ GR 001 [EP]	In Search of Manny	1993	$10
❑ GR 009	Natural Ingredients	1994	$12

LUTCHER, NELLIE
CAPITOL

❑ H232 [10]	Real Gone	1950	$75
❑ T232 [M]	Real Gone	1955	$40

EPIC

❑ LN1108 [10]	Whee! Nellie	1955	$50

LIBERTY

❑ LRP-3014 [M]	Our New Nellie	1956	$40

LUTHERAN BROTHERHOOD SINGERS, THE
LUTHERAN BROTHERHOOD

❑ E-504	Christmas with the Lutheran Brotherhood Singers	197?	$12

LUV'D ONES, THE
SUNDAZED

❑ LP5033	Truth Gotta Stand	199?	$15

LYLE, BOBBY
ATLANTIC

❑ 81938	Ivory Dreams	1989	$30

CAPITOL

❑ ST-11627	Genie	1976	$25
❑ SW-11809	New Warrior	1978	$25

LYMAN, ABE
HINDSIGHT

❑ HSR-184	Abe Lyman and His Orchestra 1941	198?	$25

LYMAN, ARTHUR
GNP CRESCENDO

❑ GNP-607 [M]	Cast Your Fate to the Wind	1965	$18
❑ GNPS-607 [S]	Cast Your Fate to the Wind	1965	$25
❑ GNP-605 [M]	Exotic Sounds	1963	$18
❑ GNPS-605 [S]	Exotic Sounds	1963	$25
❑ GNP-606 [M]	Paradise	1964	$18
❑ GNPS-606 [S]	Paradise	1964	$25
❑ GNPS-2091	Puka Shells	1975	$12

HIFI

❑ R-818 [M]	Arthur Lyman On Broadway	1960	$25
❑ SR-818 [S]	Arthur Lyman On Broadway	1960	$30
❑ R-815 [M]	Bahia	1959	$25
❑ SR-815 [S]	Bahia	1959	$30
❑ R-808 [M]	Bwan-A	1959	$25
❑ SR-808 [S]	Bwan-A	1959	$30
❑ R-807 [M]	Hawaiian Sunset	1959	$25
❑ SR-807 [S]	Hawaiian Sunset	1959	$30
❑ R-607 [M]	Leis of Jazz	1958	$50
❑ SR-607 [S]	Leis of Jazz	1958	$75
❑ R-806 [M]	Taboo	1958	$25
❑ SR-806 [S]	Taboo	1958	$25
❑ R-822 [M]	Taboo (Volume 2)	1960	$25
❑ SR-822 [S]	Taboo (Volume 2)	1960	$30
❑ R-813 [M]	The Legend of Pele	1959	$25
❑ SR-813 [S]	The Legend of Pele	1959	$30

LIFE

❑ L1034 [M]	Aloha, Amigo	1966	$18
❑ SL1034 [S]	Aloha, Amigo	1966	$25
❑ SL1038	Aphrodisia	1968	$18
❑ L1036 [M]	Arthur Lyman at the Port of L.A.	1967	$18
❑ SL1036 [S]	Arthur Lyman at the Port of L.A.	1967	$25
❑ L1014 [M]	Blowin' in the Wind	1963	$25
❑ SL1014 [S]	Blowin' in the Wind	1963	$30
❑ L1024 [M]	Call of the Midnight Sun	1964	$25
❑ SL1024 [S]	Call of the Midnight Sun	1964	$30
❑ L1010 [M]	Cotton Fields	1963	$25
❑ SL1010 [S]	Cotton Fields	1963	$30
❑ L1030 [M]	Greatest Hits	1965	$15
❑ SL1030 [S]	Greatest Hits	1965	$18
❑ L1025 [M]	Hawaiian Sunset, Volume 2	1965	$18
❑ SL1025 [S]	Hawaiian Sunset, Volume 2	1965	$25
❑ SL1035 [S]	Ilikai	1967	$25
❑ L1035 [M]	Ilikai	1967	$18
❑ L1023 [M]	Isle of Enchantment	1964	$25
❑ SL1023 [S]	Isle of Enchantment	1964	$30
❑ L1009 [M]	I Wish You Love	1963	$25
❑ SL1009 [S]	I Wish You Love	1963	$30
❑ SL1037	Latitude 20	1968	$18
❑ L1009 [M]	Love for Sale!	1963	$30
—Alternate title			
❑ SL1009 [S]	Love for Sale!	1963	$30
—Alternate title			
❑ L1031 [M]	Lyman '66	1965	$18
❑ SL1031 [S]	Lyman '66	1965	$25
❑ L1018 [M]	Mele Kalikimaka (Merry Christmas)	1963	$25
❑ SL1018 [S]	Mele Kalikimaka (Merry Christmas)	1963	$30
❑ L1004 [M]	Percussion Spectacular	1961	$30
❑ SL1004 [S]	Percussion Spectacular	1961	$40
❑ L1027 [M]	Polynesia	1965	$18
❑ SL1027 [S]	Polynesia	1965	$25
❑ L1005 [M]	The Colorful Percussions of Arthur Lyman	1962	$25
❑ SL1005 [S]	The Colorful Percussions of Arthur Lyman	1962	$30
❑ L1007 [M]	The Many Moods of Arthur Lyman	1962	$25
❑ SL1007 [S]	The Many Moods of Arthur Lyman	1962	$30
❑ L1033 [M]	The Shadow of Your Smile	1966	$18
❑ SL1033 [S]	The Shadow of Your Smile	1966	$25
❑ SL1040	Today's Greatest Hits	1970	$18
❑ SL1039	Winner's Circle	1969	$18
❑ L1004 [M]	Yellow Bird	1961	$25
—Reissue with new title reflecting the hit single			
❑ SL1004 [S]	Yellow Bird	1961	$30
—Reissue with new title reflecting the hit single			

LYMON, FRANKIE, AND THE TEENAGERS
ACCORD

❑ SN-7203	Why Do Fools Fall in Love	1982	$12

GEE

❑ GLP-701 [M]	The Teenagers Featuring Frankie Lymon	1956	$500
—Red label			
❑ GLP-701 [M]	The Teenagers Featuring Frankie Lymon	1961	$175
—Gray label			
❑ GLP-701 [M]	The Teenagers Featuring Frankie Lymon	197?	$15
—White label on thinner vinyl			

MURRAY HILL

❑ 148	Frankie Lymon and the Teenagers	198?	$80

RHINO

❑ R1-70918	The Best of Frankie Lymon and the Teenagers	1989	$15

LYMON, FRANKIE
GUEST STAR

❑ GS-1406 [M]	Rock & Roll Party Starring Frankie Lymon	196?	$30
—Various-artists compilation; retitled, black and white cover			
❑ GS-1406 [M]	Teen Time Tunes Starring Frankie Lymon	1959	$40
—Various-artists compilation; color cover			

ROULETTE

❑ R-25013 [M]	Frankie Lymon at the London Palladium	1958	$300
❑ R-25250 [M]	Frankie Lymon's Greatest	1964	$30
❑ SR-25250 [R]	Frankie Lymon's Greatest	1964	$30
❑ R-25036 [M]	Rock 'N' Roll	1958	$300

LYMON, LEWIS, AND THE TEENCHORDS
COLLECTABLES

❑ COL-5049	Lewis Lymon and the Teenchords Meet the Kodaks	198?	$12

LOST-NITE

❑ LLP-13 [10]	Lewis Lymon and the Teenchords	1981	$12
—Red vinyl			

LYNN, BARBARA
ATLANTIC

❑ 8171 [M]	Here Is Barbara Lynn	1968	$50
❑ SD8171 [S]	Here Is Barbara Lynn	1968	$40

JAMIE

❑ JLP-3026 [M]	Sister of Soul	1964	$0
—Canceled			
❑ JLPS-3026 [S]	Sister of Soul	1964	$0
—Canceled			
❑ JLP-3023 [M]	You'll Lose a Good Thing	1962	$50
❑ JLPS-3023 [R]	You'll Lose a Good Thing	1962	$50

LYNN, CHERYL
COLUMBIA

❑ JC35486	Cheryl Lynn	1978	$12
—Original issue			
❑ PC35486	Cheryl Lynn	198?	$10
—Budget-line reissue; orange label with six "Columbia"s around outer edge			
❑ JC35486 [DJ]	Cheryl Lynn	1978	$18
—White-label promo only (not a designate promo)			
❑ PC35486	Cheryl Lynn	2001	$12
—Reissue on 180-gram vinyl from original LP master; red label with single white "Columbia" at top			
❑ JC36145	In Love	1979	$12
❑ FC38057	Instant Love	1982	$12
❑ FC37034	In the Night	1981	$12
❑ FC40024	It's Gonna Be Right	1985	$12
❑ FC38961	Preppie	1983	$12

MANHATTAN

❑ ST-53035	Start Over	1987	$10

VIRGIN

❑ 91254	Whatever It Takes	1989	$15

LYNN, DIANA
CAPITOL

❑ H180 [10]	Piano Moods	1950	$75

LYNN, DONNA
CAPITOL

❑ T2085 [M]	Java Jones/My Boyfriend Got a Beatle Haircut	1964	$25
❑ ST2085 [S]	Java Jones/My Boyfriend Got a Beatle Haircut	1964	$30

LYNN, JUDY
AMARET

❑ AST-5014	Naturally	197?	$18
❑ ST-5011	Parts of Love	1971	$18

COLUMBIA

❑ CS9879	Judy Lynn Sings at Caesar's Palace	1968	$18

MUSICOR

❑ MM-2126 [M]	Golden Nuggets	1967	$18
❑ MS-3126 [S]	Golden Nuggets	1967	$18
❑ MM-2112 [M]	Honey Stuff	1966	$18
❑ MS-3112 [S]	Honey Stuff	1966	$25
❑ MS-3096 [S]	The Judy Lynn Show Plays Again	1966	$25
❑ MM-2096 [M]	The Judy Lynn Show Plays Again	1966	$18

UNART

❑ 20009 [M]	Judy Lynn in Las Vegas	1967	$18
❑ 21009 [S]	Judy Lynn in Las Vegas	1967	$15

UNITED ARTISTS

❑ UAL-3342 [M]	America's Number One Most Promising Country and Western Girl Singer	1964	$18
❑ UAS-6342 [S]	America's Number One Most Promising Country and Western Girl Singer	1964	$25
❑ UAL-3288 [M]	Here Is Our Gal, Judy Lynn	1963	$18
❑ UAS-6288 [S]	Here Is Our Gal, Judy Lynn	1963	$25
❑ UAL-3226 [M]	Judy Lynn Sings at the Golden Nugget	1962	$25
❑ UAS-6226 [S]	Judy Lynn Sings at the Golden Nugget	1962	$30
❑ UAL-3461 [M]	The Best of Judy Lynn	1966	$18
❑ UAS-6461 [S]	The Best of Judy Lynn	1966	$25
❑ UAL-3390 [M]	The Judy Lynn Show	1964	$18
❑ UAS-6390 [S]	The Judy Lynn Show	1964	$25
❑ UAL-3443 [M]	The Judy Lynn Show Act 2	1965	$18
❑ UAS-6443 [S]	The Judy Lynn Show Act 2	1965	$25

LYNN, LORETTA, AND CONWAY TWITTY
See CONWAY TWITTY AND LORETTA LYNN.

LYNN, LORETTA, AND ERNEST TUBB
See ERNEST TUBB AND LORETTA LYNN.

LYNN, LORETTA
DECCA

❑ DL4541 [M]	Before I'm Over You	1964	$30
❑ DL74541 [S]	Before I'm Over You	1964	$40
❑ DL4665 [M]	Blue Kentucky Girl	1965	$30
❑ DL74665 [S]	Blue Kentucky Girl	1965	$40
❑ DL75253	Coal Miner's Daughter	1971	$25
❑ DL4817 [M]	Country Christmas	1966	$30
❑ DL74817 [S]	Country Christmas	1966	$30
❑ DL4842 [M]	Don't Come Home a-Drinkin' (With Lovin' on Your Mind)	1967	$30
❑ DL74842 [S]	Don't Come Home a-Drinkin' (With Lovin' on Your Mind)	1967	$30

Number	Title	Yr	NM
❑ DL74997 [S]	Fist City	1968	$30
❑ DL4997 [M]	Fist City	1968	$50

—Mono version appears to exist only as a white label promo

Number	Title	Yr	NM
❑ DL75351	God Bless America Again	1972	$25
❑ DL75381	Here I Am Again	1972	$25
❑ DL4695 [M]	Hymns	1965	$30
❑ DL74695 [S]	Hymns	1965	$40
❑ DL4744 [M]	I Like 'Em Country	1966	$30
❑ DL74744 [S]	I Like 'Em Country	1966	$30
❑ DL75282	I Wanna Be Free	1971	$25
❑ DL75000	Loretta Lynn's Greatest Hits	1968	$30
❑ ST-91604	Loretta Lynn's Greatest Hits	1968	$30

—Capitol Record Club edition

Number	Title	Yr	NM
❑ DL4457 [M]	Loretta Lynn Sings	1963	$75
❑ DL74457 [S]	Loretta Lynn Sings	1963	$100
❑ DL75198	Loretta Lynn Writes 'Em and Sings 'Em	1970	$30
❑ DL75334	One's On the Way	1972	$25
❑ DL4930 [M]	Singin' with Feelin'	1967	$30
❑ DL74930 [S]	Singin' with Feelin'	1967	$30
❑ DL4620 [M]	Songs from My Heart	1965	$30
❑ DL74620 [S]	Songs from My Heart	1965	$40
❑ DL4928 [M]	Who Says God Is Dead!	1967	$40
❑ DL74928 [S]	Who Says God Is Dead!	1967	$30
❑ DL75163	Wings Upon Your Horns	1970	$30
❑ DL75113	Woman of the World/To Make a Man	1969	$30
❑ DL4783 [M]	You Ain't Woman Enough	1966	$30

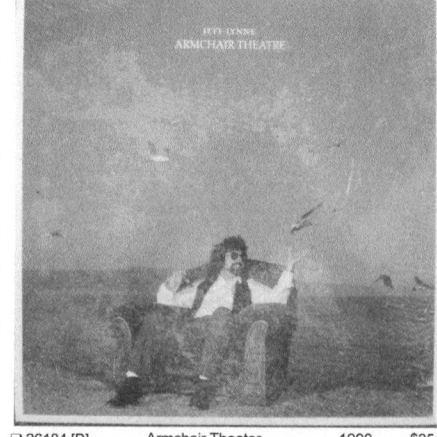

Number	Title	Yr	NM
❑ DL74783 [S]	You Ain't Woman Enough	1966	$30
❑ DL75310	You're Lookin' at Country	1971	$25
❑ DL75084	Your Squaw Is On the Warpath	1969	$40

—First editions had a track called "Barney

Number	Title	Yr	NM
❑ DL75084	Your Squaw Is On the Warpath	1969	$30

—Later editions delete the track "Barney

MCA

Number	Title	Yr	NM
❑ 35013	Allis-Chalmers Presents Loretta Lynn	1978	$40

—Special products compilation

Number	Title	Yr	NM
❑ 735	Alone with You	198?	$12
❑ 471	Back to the Country	1975	$15
❑ 15032	Christmas Without Daddy	198?	$15
❑ 2342	Coal Miner's Daughter	1978	$15

—Reissue

Number	Title	Yr	NM
❑ 37236	Coal Miner's Daughter	198?	$10

—Budget-line reissue

Number	Title	Yr	NM
❑ 15022	Country Christmas	1980	$12

—Blue rainbow label

Number	Title	Yr	NM
❑ 248	Country Christmas	1973	$18

—First reissue of Decca LP

Number	Title	Yr	NM
❑ 15022	Country Christmas	1974	$15

—Second reissue of Decca LP; black rainbow label

Number	Title	Yr	NM
❑ 35018	Crisco Presents Loretta Lynn's Country Classics	1979	$40

—Special products compilation

Number	Title	Yr	NM
❑ 113	Don't Come Home a-Drinkin' (With Lovin' on Your Mind)	1973	$18

—Reissue of Decca 74842

Number	Title	Yr	NM
❑ 300	Entertainer of the Year -- Loretta	1973	$18
❑ 58	Here I Am Again	1973	$18

—Reissue of Decca 75381

Number	Title	Yr	NM
❑ 2146	Home	1975	$15
❑ 5	Hymns	1973	$18

—Reissue of Decca 74695

Number	Title	Yr	NM
❑ 5293	I Lie	1982	$12
❑ 2265	I Remember Patsy	1977	$15
❑ 37080	I Remember Patsy Cline	198?	$10

—Budget-line reissue

Number	Title	Yr	NM
❑ 5613	Just a Woman	1985	$12
❑ 5148	Lookin' Good	1980	$12
❑ 3217	Loretta	1980	$12
❑ 37165	Loretta	198?	$10

—Budget-line reissue

Number	Title	Yr	NM
❑ L33-1934 [DJ]	Loretta Lynn	1974	$40

—Promo-only compilation

Number	Title	Yr	NM
❑ 1	Loretta Lynn's Greatest Hits	1973	$18

—Reissue of Decca 75000

Number	Title	Yr	NM
❑ 2341	Loretta Lynn's Greatest Hits	1978	$15

—Reissue of MCA 1

Number	Title	Yr	NM
❑ 37235	Loretta Lynn's Greatest Hits	198?	$10

—Budget-line reissue

Number	Title	Yr	NM
❑ 420	Loretta Lynn's Greatest Hits Vol. II	1974	$18
❑ 2353	Loretta Lynn's Greatest Hits Vol. II	1978	$15

—Reissue of MCA 420

Number	Title	Yr	NM
❑ 37205	Loretta Lynn's Greatest Hits Vol. II	198?	$10

—Budget-line reissue

Number	Title	Yr	NM
❑ 355	Love Is the Foundation	1973	$18
❑ 5426	Lyin', Cheatin', Woman Chasin', Honky Tonkin', Whiskey Drinkin' You	1983	$12
❑ 2330	Out of My Head and Back in My Bed	1978	$15
❑ 2228	Somebody Somewhere	1976	$15
❑ 630	Somebody Somewhere	198?	$10

—Budget-line reissue

Number	Title	Yr	NM
❑ 444	They Don't Make 'Em Like My Daddy	1974	$18
❑ 3073	We've Come a Long Way, Baby	1979	$15
❑ 721	We've Come a Long Way, Baby	198?	$10

—Budget-line reissue

Number	Title	Yr	NM
❑ 2179	When the Tingle Becomes a Chill	1976	$15
❑ 628	When the Tingle Becomes a Chill	198?	$10

—Budget-line reissue

Number	Title	Yr	NM
❑ 7	Who Says God Is Dead!	1973	$18

—Reissue of Decca 74928

Number	Title	Yr	NM
❑ 42174	Who Was That Stranger	1988	$12
❑ 6	You Ain't Woman Enough	1973	$18

—Reissue of Decca 74783

VOCALION

Number	Title	Yr	NM
❑ VL73853	Here's Loretta Lynn	1968	$18

LYNN, VERA

LONDON

Number	Title	Yr	NM
❑ LL3294 [M]	Golden Hits	196?	$25
❑ LL1510 [M]	If I Am Dreaming	195?	$25
❑ LPB-58 [10]	Sincerely Yours	195?	$75
❑ LB-690 [10]	Sincerely Yours Vol. 2	195?	$75
❑ LL1306 [M]	Vera Lynn Concert	195?	$25
❑ LL3142 [M]	Vera Lynn Sings Songs of the Twenties	196?	$25
❑ PS156 [S]	Vera Lynn Sings Songs of the Twenties	196?	$30
❑ LL3359 [M]	Wonderful Vera	1964	$25
❑ PS359 [S]	Wonderful Vera	1964	$30

MGM

Number	Title	Yr	NM
❑ E-3889 [M]	As Time Goes By	1961	$25
❑ SE-3889 [S]	As Time Goes By	1961	$30
❑ E-3887 [M]	Yours	1961	$25
❑ SE-3887 [S]	Yours	1961	$30

STANYAN

Number	Title	Yr	NM
❑ 10123	Among My Souvenirs	197?	$18
❑ 10080	Vera Lynn Remembers the World at War	197?	$18
❑ 10032	When the Lights Go On Again	197?	$18

SUFFOLK MARKETING

Number	Title	Yr	NM
❑ SMI-1-28	All My Best (Her World Famous Recordings)	198?	$12

UNITED ARTISTS

Number	Title	Yr	NM
❑ UAL-3591 [M]	It Hurts to Say Goodbye	1967	$30
❑ UAS-6591 [S]	It Hurts to Say Goodbye	1967	$18

LYNN, GLORIA

ABC IMPULSE!

Number	Title	Yr	NM
❑ ASD-9311	I Don't Know How to Love Him	1976	$30

CANYON

Number	Title	Yr	NM
❑ 7709	Happy and In Love	1970	$35

COLLECTABLES

Number	Title	Yr	NM
❑ COL-5138	Golden Classics	198?	$25

DESIGN

Number	Title	Yr	NM
❑ D-177 [M]	My Funny Valentine	196?	$25
❑ DS-177 [S]	My Funny Valentine	196?	$30

EVEREST

Number	Title	Yr	NM
❑ EV-5230 [M]	After Hours	1965	$50
❑ EV-1230 [S]	After Hours	1965	$75
❑ LPBR-5101 [M]	Day In, Day Out	1961	$50
❑ SDBR-1101 [S]	Day In, Day Out	1961	$75
❑ EV-5220 [M]	Gloria, Marty & Strings	1963	$50
❑ EV-1220 [S]	Gloria, Marty & Strings	1963	$75
❑ LPBR-5203 [M]	Gloria Blue	1962	$50
❑ SDBR-1203 [S]	Gloria Blue	1962	$75
❑ EV-5238 [M]	Gloria Lynne '66	1966	$35
❑ EV-1238 [S]	Gloria Lynne '66	1966	$50
❑ LPBR-5132 [M]	Gloria Lynne at Basin Street East	1962	$50
❑ SDBR-1132 [S]	Gloria Lynne at Basin Street East	1962	$75

Number	Title	Yr	NM
❑ LPBR-5208 [M]	Gloria Lynne at the Las Vegas Thunderbird	1963	$50
❑ SDBR-1208 [S]	Gloria Lynne at the Las Vegas Thunderbird	1963	$75
❑ E-5001 [M]	Gloria Lynne Live! Take 1	1959	$75
❑ ES-1001 [S]	Gloria Lynne Live! Take 1	1959	$40
❑ EV-5228 [M]	Glorious Gloria Lynne	1964	$50
❑ EV-1228 [S]	Glorious Gloria Lynne	1964	$75
❑ EV-5237 [M]	Go! Go! Go!	1965	$35
❑ EV-1237 [S]	Go! Go! Go!	1965	$50
❑ LPBR-5128 [M]	He Needs Me	1961	$50
❑ SDBR-1128 [S]	He Needs Me	1961	$75
❑ LPBR-5126 [M]	I'm Glad There Is You	1961	$50
❑ SDBR-1126 [S]	I'm Glad There Is You	1961	$75
❑ EV-5226 [M]	I Wish You Love	1964	$50
❑ EV-1226 [S]	I Wish You Love	1964	$75
❑ ST-90057 [M]	I Wish You Love	196?	$150

—Capitol Record Club edition

Number	Title	Yr	NM
❑ LPBR-5063 [M]	Lonely and Sentimental	1960	$50
❑ SDBR-1063 [S]	Lonely and Sentimental	1960	$75
❑ LPBR-5022 [M]	Miss Gloria Lynne	1959	$50
❑ SDBR-1022 [S]	Miss Gloria Lynne	1959	$75
❑ EV-5231 [M]	The Best of Gloria Lynne	1965	$35
❑ EV-1231 [S]	The Best of Gloria Lynne	1965	$50
❑ LPBR-5131 [M]	This Little Boy of Mine	1961	$50
❑ SDBR-1131 [S]	This Little Boy of Mine	1961	$75
❑ LPBR-5090 [M]	Try a Little Tenderness	1960	$50
❑ SDBR-1090 [S]	Try a Little Tenderness	1960	$75

FONTANA

Number	Title	Yr	NM
❑ MGF-27561 [M]	Gloria	1966	$35
❑ SRF-67561 [S]	Gloria	1966	$50
❑ SRF-67577	Here, There and Everywhere	1968	$35
❑ MGF-27528 [M]	Intimate Moments	1964	$35
❑ SRF-67528 [S]	Intimate Moments	1964	$50
❑ MGF-27546 [M]	Love and a Woman	1965	$35
❑ SRF-67546 [S]	Love and a Woman	1965	$50
❑ MGF-27541 [M]	Soul Serenade	1965	$35
❑ SRF-67541 [S]	Soul Serenade	1965	$50
❑ MGF-27571 [M]	The Other Side of Gloria Lynne	1967	$50
❑ SRF-67571 [S]	The Other Side of Gloria Lynne	1967	$35
❑ MGF-27555 [M]	Where It's At	1966	$35
❑ SRF-67555 [S]	Where It's At	1966	$50

HIFI

Number	Title	Yr	NM
❑ SR-441	Greatest Hits	1969	$35
❑ L-440 [M]	The Gloria Lynne Calendar	1966	$35
❑ SL-440 [S]	The Gloria Lynne Calendar	1966	$50

INTERMEDIA

Number	Title	Yr	NM
❑ QS-5069	Classics	198?	$25

MERCURY

Number	Title	Yr	NM
❑ SRM-1-633	A Very Gentle Sound	1972	$35

MUSE

Number	Title	Yr	NM
❑ MR-5381	A Time for Love	198?	$25

SUNSET

Number	Title	Yr	NM
❑ SUM-1145 [M]	Gloria Lynne	1966	$30
❑ SUS-5145 [S]	Gloria Lynne	1966	$30
❑ SUS-5221	Golden Greats	1968	$30
❑ SUM-1171 [M]	I Wish You Love	1967	$30
❑ SUS-5171 [S]	I Wish You Love	1967	$30

UPFRONT

Number	Title	Yr	NM
❑ 146	Gloria Lynne	197?	$30

LYNNE, JEFF
Also see ELECTRIC LIGHT ORCHESTRA.

REPRISE

Number	Title	Yr	NM
❑ 26184 [B]	Armchair Theater	1990	$25

LYNOTT, PHIL
Also see THIN LIZZY.

WARNER BROS.

Number	Title	Yr	NM
❑ BSK3405	Solo in Soho	1980	$25
❑ 23745	The Philip Lynott Album	1982	$25

Number	Title	Yr	NM

LYNYRD SKYNYRD
Also see ROSSINGTON COLLINS BAND; ROSSINGTON, BLACKFOOT, VAN ZANT, JOHNNY VAN ZANT BAND, ALLEN COLLINS, ARTIMUS PYLE BAND, OUTLAWS, DAM YANKEES.

ATLANTIC

| ❏ A1-82258 | Lynyrd Skynyrd 1991 | 1991 | $25 |

— The only U.S. vinyl version was released through Columbia House

GEFFEN

| ❏ MCA1686 | Second Helping | 2008 | $25 |

MCA

| ❏ 5370 | Best of the Rest | 1982 | $12 |

— Original version

❏ 1448	Best of the Rest	1985	$10
❏ 2170	Gimme Back My Bullets	1976	$15
❏ 37069	Gimme Back My Bullets	1980	$10
❏ 3022	Gimme Back My Bullets	1977	$12

— Reissue with new number on black rainbow label

| ❏ 11008 | Gold & Platinum | 1979 | $15 |

— Originals with embossed gatefold cover

| ❏ 6898 | Gold & Platinum | 1985 | $12 |

— Most, if not all, of these pressings have no gatefold

❏ 42084	Legend	1987	$12
❏ 2137	Nuthin' Fancy	1975	$15
❏ 3021	Nuthin' Fancy	1976	$12

— Reissue with new number on black rainbow label

| ❏ 37070 | Nuthin' Fancy | 1980 | $10 |
| ❏ L33-1946 [DJ] | One More From the Road | 1976 | $30 |

— Promo only on black vinyl

| ❏ L33-1946 [DJ] | One More From the Road | 1976 | $50 |

— Promo on blue, gold, purple or red vinyl (each has the same value)

| ❏ 6001 | One More From the Road | 1976 | $18 |

— Originals with black rainbow label and gatefold cover

| ❏ 10014 | One More From the Road | 1980 | $12 |

— Second reissue

| ❏ 6897 | One More From the Road | 1985 | $12 |

— Most, if not all, of these pressings have no gatefold

| ❏ 8011 | One More From the Road | 1977 | $15 |

— First reissue with new number

| ❏ 363 | (pronounced leh-nerd skin-nerd) | 1975 | $15 |

— Reissue on black rainbow label

| ❏ 3019 | (pronounced leh-nerd skin-nerd) | 1976 | $12 |

— Second reissue with new number on black rainbow label

❏ 5221	(pronounced leh-nerd skin-nerd)	1980	$10
❏ 37211	(pronounced leh-nerd skin-nerd)	1985	$10
❏ 413	Second Helping	1975	$15

— Reissue on black rainbow label

| ❏ 3020 | Second Helping | 1976 | $12 |

— Second reissue with new number on black rainbow label

❏ 5222	Second Helping	1980	$10
❏ 37212	Second Helping	1985	$10
❏ L33-1988 [DJ]	Skynyrd's First and…Last	1978	$30

— Promo sampler

| ❏ 3047 | Skynyrd's First and…Last | 1978 | $15 |

— Originals with tan labels and gatefold cover

❏ 37071	Skynyrd's First and…Last	1980	$10
❏ 42293	Skynyrd's Innyrds	1989	$15
❏ 8027	Southern by the Grace of God	1988	$15
❏ 3029	Street Survivors	1977	$30

— Originals with the band in flames on the front cover and a smaller band photo on the back cover

| ❏ 3029 | Street Survivors | 1977 | $12 |

— After the band's plane crash, the "flames" photo was replaced with the back cover photo; the back cover is black with only the song titles

| ❏ 5223 | Street Survivors | 1980 | $10 |
| ❏ 37213 | Street Survivors | 1985 | $10 |

MOBILE FIDELITY

| ❏ MFSL1-400 [B] | (Pronounced 'Lĕh-'nérd 'Skin-'nérd) | 2013 | $40 |

SOUNDS OF THE SOUTH

| ❏ 363 | (pronounced leh-nerd skin-nerd) | 1973 | $25 |
| ❏ 413 | Second Helping | 1974 | $25 |

— Both of the above are original pressings with yellow labels

LYON, JIMMY
FINNADAR

| ❏ 9034 | Johnny Lyon Plays Cole Porter's Steinway and Music | 198? | $35 |

LYONS, JIMMY
BLACK SAINT

| ❏ BSR-0087 | Give It Up | 1986 | $30 |
| ❏ 120125 | Something in Return | 1990 | $35 |

HAT ART

| ❏ 2028 | Jump Up/What to Do About | 1986 | $35 |

— Reissue of Hat Hut 21

HAT HUT

| ❏ 21 | Jump Up/What to Do About | 198? | $25 |
| ❏ 0Y/Z/Z | Push | 1979 | $30 |

| ❏ 3503 | Riffs | 198? | $30 |

LYONS, MARIE
DELUXE

| ❏ 12001 | Soul Fever | 1970 | $30 |

LYTLE, JOHNNY
FANTASY

| ❏ OJC-110 | The Village Caller | 198? | $25 |

JAZZLAND

❏ JLP-22 [M]	Blue Vibes	1960	$30
❏ JLP-922 [S]	Blue Vibes	1960	$30
❏ JLP-44 [M]	Happy Ground	1961	$30
❏ JLP-944 [S]	Happy Ground	1961	$30
❏ JLP-81 [M]	Moon Child	1962	$30
❏ JLP-981 [S]	Moon Child	1962	$30
❏ JLP-67 [M]	Nice and Easy	1962	$30
❏ JLP-967 [S]	Nice and Easy	1962	$30

MILESTONE

| ❏ 9043 | People and Love | 197? | $35 |
| ❏ 9036 | Soulful Rebel | 197? | $35 |

MUSE

❏ MR-5158	Everything Must Change	1978	$30
❏ MR-5185	Fast Hands	1981	$25
❏ MR-5271	Good Vibes	1982	$25
❏ MR-5387	Happy Ground	1991	$35

RIVERSIDE

❏ RM-3003 [M]	A Groove	1967	$150
❏ RS-3003 [S]	A Groove	1967	$150
❏ RLP-456 [M]	Got That Feeling	1963	$175
❏ RS-9456 [S]	Got That Feeling	1963	$175
❏ RLP-470 [M]	Happy Ground	1964	$175
❏ RS-9470 [S]	Happy Ground	1964	$175
❏ RS-3017	Moon Child	1968	$150
❏ RLP-480 [M]	The Village Caller	1965	$150

| ❏ RS-9480 [S] | The Village Caller | 1965 | $30 |

SOLID STATE

❏ SS-18014	A Man and a Woman	1967	$25
❏ SS-18044	Be Proud	1969	$25
❏ SS-18056	Close Enough	1969	$25

LYTTELTON, HUMPHREY
ANGEL

| ❏ ANG.60008 [10] | Some Like It Hot | 1955 | $85 |

BETHLEHEM

| ❏ BCP-6063 [M] | Humph Plays Standards | 1961 | $300 |

LONDON

❏ LL3132 [M]	Humph Dedicates	195?	$30
❏ PS178 [S]	Humph Dedicates	1959	$30
❏ LL3101 [M]	I Play As I Please	195?	$30

SACKVILLE

| ❏ 3033 | Humphrey Lyttelton in Canada | 198? | $30 |

STOMP OFF

| ❏ SOS-1160 | Delving Back and Forth with Humph | 1989 | $25 |
| ❏ SOS-1111 | Scatterbrains | 1986 | $25 |

LYTTLE, KEVIN
ATLANTIC

| ❏ 83699 | Kevin Lyttle | 2004 | $18 |

M

M
SIRE

❏ SRK3672	Famous Last Words	1982	$12
❏ SRK6084	New York-London-Paris-Munich	1979	$15
❏ SRK6099	The Official Secrets Act	1981	$12

MABERN, HAROLD
FANTASY

| ❏ OJC-330 | Rakin' and Scrapin' | 1988 | $25 |

PRESTIGE

❏ PRST-7568 [B]	A Few Miles from Memphis	1968	$80
❏ PRST-7764 [B]	Greasy Kid Stuff	1970	$50
❏ PRST-7624 [B]	Rakin' and Scrapin'	1969	$50
❏ PRST-7687 [B]	Workin' and Wailin'	1969	$150

SACKVILLE

| ❏ 2016 | Live at Café Des Copains | 198? | $30 |

MABLEY, MOMS
CHESS

❏ LP-1479 [M]	I Got Somethin' to Tell You!	1963	$30
❏ LP-1447 [M]	Moms Mabley, Funniest Woman in the World, Onstage	1961	$30
❏ LP-1463 [M]	Moms Mabley at Geneva Conference	1962	$30
❏ LP-1460 [M]	Moms Mabley at the Playboy Club	1961	$30
❏ LP-1452 [M]	Moms Mabley at the "UN	1961	$30
❏ LP-1472 [M]	Moms Mabley Breaks It Up	1962	$30
❏ LPS-1525	Moms Mabley Breaks Up the Network	1968	$25
❏ LPS-1530	Moms Mabley Sings	1969	$25
❏ LP-1486 [M]	Moms Wows	1964	$30
❏ LP-1487 [M]	The Best of Moms	1964	$30
❏ LP-1482 [M]	The Funny Sides of Moms Mabley	1963	$30
❏ LP-1497 [M]	The Man in My Life	1965	$25
❏ LP-1477 [M]	Young Men, Si -- Old Men, No	1962	$30

MERCURY

❏ SR-61235	Abraham, Martin and John	1969	$18
❏ SR-61205	Her Young Thing	1969	$18
❏ SR-61263	Live at Sing Sing	1970	$18
❏ MG-21090 [M]	Moms Mabley at the White House	1966	$18
❏ SR-61090 [S]	Moms Mabley at the White House	1966	$25
❏ MG-20907 [M]	Moms the Word	1964	$18
❏ SR-60907 [S]	Moms the Word	1964	$25
❏ MG-21012 [M]	Now Hear This	1965	$18
❏ SR-61012 [S]	Now Hear This	1965	$25
❏ MG-20889 [M]	Out on a Limb	1964	$18
❏ SR-60889 [S]	Out on a Limb	1964	$25
❏ MG-21139 [M]	The Best of Moms Mabley	1967	$30
❏ SR-61139 [S]	The Best of Moms Mabley	1967	$18
❏ SR-61229 [B]	The Youngest Teenager	1969	$18

MABON, WILLIE
CHESS

| ❏ LP-1439 [M] | Willie Mabon | 1958 | $400 |

— Black label

MACARTHUR, DOUGLAS
ATCO

| ❏ 8095 [M] | The Life of General MacArthur | 1964 | $40 |

MACCOLL, EWAN
FOLKWAYS

| ❏ FW8759 [B] | Bothy Ballads of Scotland | 1961 | $25 |

— accompanied by Peggy Seeger and Alf Edwards

| ❏ FW3044 [B] | Broadside Ballads, Vol.2 (London: 1600 - 1700) - Female Frollicks And Politicke | | $1962 |

— 15.00

| ❏ FW3043 [B] | Broadside Ballads (London: 1600-1700) | 1962 | $20 |
| ❏ FW8736 [B] | Folkways Record Of Contemporary Songs | 1973 | $15 |

— credited to Peggy Seeger and MacColl

| ❏ FS3850 [B] | Musical Score From The Film: Whaler Out Of New Bedford. Based On The Original Panorama of Whaling Voyage Round The World And Other Songs Of The Whaling Era | 1962 | $20 |

— credited to MacColl, AL Lloyd, Peggy Seeger

| ❏ FW8757 [B] | Popular Scottish Songs | 1961 | $25 |

— credited to MacColl with Peggy Seeger

❏ FW8758 [B]	Songs of Robert Burns	1959	$40
❏ FW8756 [B]	Songs Of Two Rebellions - The Jacobite Wars Of 1715 And 1745 In Scotland	1961	$25
❏ FG3509 [B]	The English And Scottish Popular Ballads (Child Ballads)	1961	$25
❏ FG3510 [B]	The English And Scottish Popular Ballads (Child Ballads), Vol. 2	1964	$25
❏ FW8732 [B]	The New Briton Gazette	1960	$30

— credited to MacColl and Peggy Seeger

— 302-286-0206

| ❏ FW8501 [B] | The Singing Streets - Childhood Memories Of Ireland And Scotland | 1964 | $40 |

— credited to MacColl and Dominic Behan

Number	Title	Yr	NM
❏ FW8760 [B]	Traditional Songs And Ballads	1964	$40
— credited to MacColl and Peggy Seeger			
❏ FW8755 [B]	Two Way Trip	1961	$15
— credited to Peggy Seeger and Ewan MacColl			
PRESTIGE INT'L.			
❏ INT13061 [B]	A Lover's Garland	196?	$20
— credited to Peggy Seeger and MacColl			
❏ INT13043 [B]	A Sailor's Garland	1962	$15
— credited to MacColl and AL Lloyd			
❏ INT13004 [B]	The Best of Ewan MacColl	1961	$20
RIVERSIDE			
❏ RLP-12656 [B]	English and Scottish Love Songs	1959	$50
— credited to MacColl and Isla Cameron			
❏ RLP-12637 [B]	Matching Songs of the British Isles and America	1957	$50
— credited to MacColl and Peggy Seeger			
❏ RLP-12605 [B]	Scots Drinking Songs	1956	$50
❏ RLP 12612 [B]	Scots Street Songs	1956	$100
❏ RLP 12635 [B]	Thar She Blows! Whaling Ballads And Songs	196?	$25
— credited to AL Lloyd and MacColl			
ROUNDER			
❏ 4003 [B]	At The Present Moment	1973	$20
— credited to Peggy Seeger and MacColl			
STINSON			
❏ SLP79 [B]	Fourpence A Day And Other British Industrial Folk Songs	1963	$50
— credited to MacColl accompanied by Brian Daly			
TRADITION			
❏ TLP1026 [B]	Blow Boys Blow	1960	$50
— credited to MacColl and AL Lloyd			
❏ TLP1015 [B]	Classic Scots Ballads	1959	$25
— credited to MacColl and Peggy Seeger			
VANGUARD			
❏ VRS9090 [M]	Ewan MacColl Sings British Industrial Ballads	1961	$50
WASHINGTON			
❏ WLP723 [B]	Great Child Ballads Not Included In The Child Collection	197?	$15
— credited to MacColl and AL Lloyd			
❏ WLP733 [B]	Scots Folk Songs	197?	$15
❏ WLP738 [B]	Street Songs Of Scotland	197?	$15
❏ WLP715 [B]	The English And Scottish Popular Ballads (The Child Ballads) Volume 1	197?	$15
— credited to MacColl and AL Lloyd			
❏ WLP716 [B]	The English And Scottish Popular Ballads (The Child Ballads) Volume 2	197?	$15
— credited to MacColl and AL Lloyd			
❏ WLP717 [B]	The English And Scottish Popular Ballads (The Child Ballads) Volume 3	197?	$15
— credited to MacColl and AL Lloyd			
❏ WLP718 [B]	The English And Scottish Popular Ballads (The Child Ballads) Volume 4	197?	$15
— credited to MacColl and AL Lloyd			
❏ WLP719 [B]	The English And Scottish Popular Ballads (The Child Ballads) Volume 5	197?	$15
— credited to MacColl and AL Lloyd			

MACDONALD, JEANETTE, AND NELSON EDDY
RCA VICTOR

Number	Title	Yr	NM
❏ LPM-1738 [M]	Favorites in Hi-Fi	1958	$40
❏ LPV-526 [M]	Rose Marie	1965	$30
❏ LPT-16 [10]	Rose Marie	1952	$75

MACDONALD, KEITH
LANDMARK

Number	Title	Yr	NM
❏ LLP-1503	This Is Keith MacDonald	1985	$25
❏ LLP-1509	Waiting	1986	$25

MACDOWELL, AL
GRAMAVISION

Number	Title	Yr	NM
❏ R1-79450	Time Peace	1990	$30

MACEO AND ALL THE KING'S MEN
EXCELLO

Number	Title	Yr	NM
❏ LPS-8022	Funky Music Machine	1972	$30

HOUSE OF FOX

Number	Title	Yr	NM
❏ LP-1	Doing Their Own Thing	1971	$30

MACEO AND THE MACKS
PEOPLE

Number	Title	Yr	NM
❏ PE-6601	Us	1973	$30

MACERO, TEO
AMERICAN CLAVE

Number	Title	Yr	NM
❏ 1002	Teo	198?	$35

Number	Title	Yr	NM
COLUMBIA			
❏ CL842 [M]	What's New?	1956	$100
— Red and black label with six "eye" logos			
DEBUT			
❏ DLP-6 [10]	Explorations by Teo Macero	1954	$500
DOCTOR JAZZ			
❏ FW40111	Acoustical Suspension	1986	$35
FANTASY			
❏ OJC-1715	Teo – Teo Macero with the Prestige Jazz Quartet	198?	$30
FINNADAR			
❏ SR9024	Time Plus 7	1979	$50
PALO ALTO			
❏ PA-8046	Impressions of Charles Mingus	1984	$50
PRESTIGE			
❏ PRLP-7104 [M]	Teo – Teo Macero with the Prestige Jazz Quartet	1957	$300

MACGREGOR, BYRON
WESTBOUND

Number	Title	Yr	NM
❏ WB-1000	Americans	1974	$12

MACGREGOR, MARY
ARIOLA AMERICA

Number	Title	Yr	NM
❏ SW-50025	In Your Eyes	1978	$15
❏ SMAS-50015	Torn Between Two Lovers	1977	$15

RSO

Number	Title	Yr	NM
❏ RS-1-3083	Mary MacGregor	1979	$15

MACHITO
CLEF

Number	Title	Yr	NM
❏ MGC-505 [10]	Afro-Cuban Jazz	1953	$300
❏ MGC-689 [M]	Afro-Cuban Jazz	1956	$300
❏ MGC-511 [10]	Machito Jazz with Flip and Bird	1953	$300
CORAL			

Number	Title	Yr	NM
❏ CRL57258 [M]	Vacation at the Concord	1959	$40
❏ CRL757258 [S]	Vacation at the Concord	1959	$30
DECCA			
❏ DL5157 [10]	Machito's Afro-Cuban	1950	$300
FORUM			
❏ F-9043 [M]	Asia Minor	196?	$30
— Reissue of Tico 1033			
❏ SF-9043 [S]	Asia Minor	196?	$30
❏ F-9038 [M]	Mi Amigo, Machito	196?	$30
— Reissue of Tico 1053			
❏ SF-9038 [S]	Mi Amigo, Machito	196?	$30
GNP CRESCENDO			
❏ GNPS-58 [R]	Machito at the Crescendo	198?	$20
❏ GNPS-72 [R]	The World's Greatest Latin Band	198?	$20
MERCURY			
❏ MGC-505 [10]	Afro-Cuban Jazz	1951	$300
❏ MG-25009 [10]	Jungle Drums	1950	$300
❏ MGC-511 [10]	Machito Jazz with Flip and Bird	1952	$300
❏ MG-25020 [10]	Rhumbas	1950	$300
RCA VICTOR			
❏ LPM-3944 [M]	Machito Goes Memphis	1968	$40
❏ LSP-3944 [S]	Machito Goes Memphis	1968	$25
ROULETTE			
❏ R-52006 [M]	Kenya	1958	$40
❏ SR-52006 [S]	Kenya	1958	$30
❏ R-52026 [M]	With Flute to Boot	1959	$40
❏ SR-52026 [S]	With Flute to Boot	1959	$75
TICO			
❏ LP-1074 [M]	A Night with Machito	1960	$50
❏ LPS-1074 [S]	A Night with Machito	1960	$75
❏ LP-1029 [M]	Asia Minor Cha Cha Cha	1956	$100
❏ LP-1002 [M]	Cha Cha Cha at the Palladium	1955	$100
❏ LP-138 [10]	El Niche	1956	$175
❏ LP-1045 [M]	Inspired by "The Sun Also Rises"	1957	$100
❏ LP-1062 [M]	Irving Berlin in Latin America	1959	$75
❏ CLP-1314	Latin Soul Plus Jazz	1973	$25
❏ CLP-1328	Lo Mejor De Machito Y Sus AfroCubans Con Graciela	1974	$25

Number	Title	Yr	NM
❏ LP-1053 [M]	Mi Amigo, Machito	1959	$75
❏ LP-1033 [M]	Si Si, No No	1957	$100
❏ LP-1084 [M]	The New Sound of Machito (El Sonido Nuevo de Machito)	1962	$40
❏ LPS-1084 [S]	The New Sound of Machito (El Sonido Nuevo de Machito)	1962	$50
❏ LP-1094 [M]	Tremendo Cumban!	1963	$40
❏ LPS-1094 [S]	Tremendo Cumban!	1963	$50
❏ LP-1090 [M]	Variedades	1963	$40
❏ LPS-1090 [S]	Variedades	1963	$50
TIMELESS			
❏ LPSJP-183	Machito and His Salsa Big Band	1990	$30
VERVE			
❏ MGV-8073 [M]	Afro-Cuban Jazz	1957	$250
❏ V-8073 [M]	Afro-Cuban Jazz	1961	$75
❏ VSP-19 [M]	Soul Source	1966	$25
❏ VSPS-19 [R]	Soul Source	1966	$30

MACK, DAVID
SEREMUS

Number	Title	Yr	NM
❏ SRE-1009 [M]	New Directions	1965	$25
❏ SRS-12009 [S]	New Directions	1965	$30

MACK, LONNIE
ALLIGATOR

Number	Title	Yr	NM
❏ AL-4786	Live!: Attack of the Killer V	1990	$15
❏ AL-4750	Second Sight	1987	$12
❏ AL-4739	Strike Like Lightning	1985	$12
❏ AL-3903	The Wham of That Memphis Man	1987	$12
— Reissue of Fraternity LP			
CAPITOL			
❏ ST-11619	Home at Last	1976	$15
❏ ST-11703	Lonnie Mack and Pismo	1977	$15
ELEKTRA			
❏ EKS-74077	For Collectors Only	1970	$30
❏ EKS-74040	Glad I'm In the Band	1969	$30
❏ EKS-74102	The Hills of Indiana	1971	$30
❏ EKS-74050	Whatever's Right	1969	$30
EPIC			
❏ FE44075	Roadhouses and Dance Halls	1989	$15
FRATERNITY			
❏ SF-1014 [M]	The Wham of That Memphis Man	1963	$120
❏ SSF-1014 [S]	The Wham of That Memphis Man	1963	$300
TRIP			
❏ TLX-9522	The Memphis Sounds of Lonnie Mack	1975	$15

MACK, WARNER
DECCA

Number	Title	Yr	NM
❏ DL4883 [M]	Drifting Apart	1967	$30
❏ DL74883 [S]	Drifting Apart	1967	$25
❏ DL75165	I'll Still Be Missing You	1969	$25
❏ DL4912 [M]	Songs We Sand in Church and Home	1967	$30
❏ DL74912 [S]	Songs We Sand in Church and Home	1967	$25
❏ DL4692 [M]	The Bridge Washed Out	1965	$25
❏ DL74692 [S]	The Bridge Washed Out	1965	$30
❏ DL75092	The Country Beat of Warner Mack	1969	$25
❏ DL4766 [M]	The Country Touch	1966	$25
❏ DL74766 [S]	The Country Touch	1966	$30
❏ DL74995	The Many Country Moods of Warner Mack	1968	$25
KAPP			
❏ KL-1461 [M]	Everybody's Country Favorites	196?	$18
❏ KS-3461 [S]	Everybody's Country Favorites	196?	$25
❏ KL-1255 [M]	Golden Country Hits	1961	$25
❏ KS-3255 [S]	Golden Country Hits	1961	$30
❏ KL-1279 [M]	Golden Country Hits, Vol. 2	1962	$25
❏ KS-3279 [S]	Golden Country Hits, Vol. 2	1962	$30

MACKAY, BRUCE
ORO

Number	Title	Yr	NM
❏ 1	Bruce Mackay	196?	$25

MACKAY, DAVID, AND VICKI HAMILTON
ABC IMPULSE!

Number	Title	Yr	NM
❏ AS-9184	David MacKay and Vicki Hamilton	1969	$250

DISCOVERY

Number	Title	Yr	NM
❏ 868	Hands	1982	$25

MACKENZIE, GISELE
EVEREST

Number	Title	Yr	NM
❏ LPBR-5069 [M]	In Person at the Empire Room	1959	$30
❏ SDBR-1069 [S]	In Person at the Empire Room	1959	$30

Number	Title	Yr	NM
GLENDALE			
❏ GL-6017	Gisele MacKenzie Sings	1978	$15
RCA VICTOR			
❏ LPM-2006 [M]	Christmas with Gisele	1959	$30
❏ LSP-2006 [S]	Christmas with Gisele	1959	$40
❏ LPM-1790 [M]	Gisele	1958	$30
❏ LSP-1790 [S]	Gisele	1958	$40
SUNSET			
❏ SUM-1155 [M]	In Person at the Empire Room	196?	$15
❏ SUS-5155 [S]	In Person at the Empire Room	196?	$18
VIK			
❏ LX-1099 [M]	Christmas with Gisele	1957	$40
❏ LX-1055 [M]	Gisele MacKenzie	1956	$40
❏ LX-1075 [M]	Mam'selle MacKenzie	1956	$40

MACLAINE, SHIRLEY
COLUMBIA

Number	Title	Yr	NM
❏ PC34223	Live at the Palace	1976	$15

MACON, UNCLE DAVE
DECCA

Number	Title	Yr	NM
❏ DL4760 [M]	Uncle Dave Macon	1966	$30

MACPHERSON, FRASER
CONCORD JAZZ

Number	Title	Yr	NM
❏ CJ-224	Indian Summer	1983	$25
❏ CJ-269	Jazz Prose	1985	$25
❏ CJ-92	Live at the Planetarium	1976	$25

MACRAE, GORDON, AND JO STAFFORD
See JO STAFFORD AND GORDON MacRAE.

MACRAE, GORDON
ALLEGRO ROYALE

Number	Title	Yr	NM
❏ 1606 [M]	Gordon MacRae	1952	$25
ANGEL			
❏ S37319	The Desert Song	1973	$12
—Operetta with Dorothy Kirsten; reissue of Capitol SW 1842			
❏ S37320	The New Moon	1973	$12
—Operetta with Dorothy Kirsten; reissue of Capitol SW 1966			
❏ S37318	The Student Prince	1973	$12
—Operetta with Dorothy Kirsten; reissue of Capitol SW 1841			
CAPITOL			
❏ L485 [10]	3 Sailors and a Girl	1953	$75
—With Jane Powell and Gene Nelson			
❏ H422 [10]	By the Light of the Silvery Moon	1953	$40
—With June Hutton; not the soundtrack from the movie because MacRae and movie co-star Doris Day were on different labels			
❏ T834 [M]	Cowboy's Lament	1957	$30
—Turquoise or gray label			
❏ T980 [M]	Gordon MacRae in Concert	1957	$30
—Turquoise or gray label			
❏ ST980 [S]	Gordon MacRae in Concert	1959	$40
—Black colorband label, logo at left			
❏ H231 [10]	Gordon MacRae Sings	1951	$40
❏ T1466 [M]	Hallowed Be Thy Name	1960	$18
—Black colorband label, Capitol logo at left			
❏ ST1466 [S]	Hallowed Be Thy Name	1960	$25
—Black colorband label, Capitol logo at left			
❏ T2578 [M]	If She Walked Into My Life	1966	$15
❏ ST2578 [S]	If She Walked Into My Life	1966	$18
❏ W2022 [M]	Kismet	1964	$15
—Operetta with Dorothy Kirsten			
❏ SW2022 [S]	Kismet	1964	$18
—Operetta with Dorothy Kirsten			
❏ T875 [M]	Motion Picture Soundstage	1957	$30
—Turquoise or gray label			
❏ L468 [10]	Naughty Marietta	1954	$40
—Operetta with Marguerite Piazza			
❏ T551 [M]	Naughty Marietta and The Red Mill	1955	$30
—Turquoise label original			
❏ T219 [M]	New Moon and The Vagabond King	195?	$30
—Operettas with Lucille Norman; turquoise label			
❏ P219 [M]	New Moon and The Vagabond King	1951	$30
—Operettas with Lucille Norman; original			
❏ ST-125	Only Love	1969	$15
❏ T681 [M]	Operetta Favorites	1956	$30
—Turquoise or gray label			
❏ T1353 [M]	Our Love Story	1960	$18
—With Sheila MacRae; black colorband label, Capitol logo at left			
❏ ST1353 [S]	Our Love Story	1960	$25
—With Sheila MacRae; black colorband label, Capitol logo at left			
❏ L334 [10]	Roberta	1952	$40
—Operetta with Lucille Norman and Anne Triola			
❏ T537 [M]	Romantic Ballads	1955	$30
—Turquoise or gray label			
❏ T1251 [M]	Songs for an Evening at Home	1959	$18

Number	Title	Yr	NM
—Black colorband label, Capitol logo at left			
❏ ST1251 [S]	Songs for an Evening at Home	1959	$25
—Black colorband label, Capitol logo at left			
❏ T765 [M]	The Best Things in Life Are Free	1956	$30
—Turquoise or gray label			
❏ L351 [10]	The Desert Song	1953	$40
—Operetta with Lucille Norman and Bob Sands			
❏ W1842 [M]	The Desert Song	1963	$15
—Operetta with Dorothy Kirsten			
❏ SW1842 [S]	The Desert Song	1963	$18
—Operetta with Dorothy Kirsten			
❏ T394 [M]	The Desert Song and Roberta	195?	$30
—Turquoise label original			
❏ L335 [10]	The Merry Widow	1952	$40
—With Lucille Norman			
❏ W1966 [M]	The New Moon	1963	$15
—Operetta with Dorothy Kirsten			
❏ SW1966 [S]	The New Moon	1963	$18
—Operetta with Dorothy Kirsten			
❏ L530 [10]	The Red Mill	1954	$40
—Operetta with Lucille Norman			
❏ T1146 [M]	The Seasons of Love	1959	$18
—Black colorband label, Capitol logo at left			
❏ ST1146 [S]	The Seasons of Love	1959	$25
—Black colorband label, Capitol logo at left			
❏ L407 [10]	The Student Prince	1953	$40
—Operetta with Dorothy Warenskjold and Harry Stanton			
❏ W1841 [M]	The Student Prince	1963	$15
—Operetta with Dorothy Kirsten			
❏ SW1841 [S]	The Student Prince	1963	$18
—Operetta with Dorothy Kirsten			
❏ T437 [M]	The Student Prince and The Merry Widow	195?	$30
—Turquiose label original			
❏ P437 [M]	The Student Prince and The Merry Widow	1953	$40
—Original			
❏ H218 [10]	The Vagabond King	1951	$50
—Operetta with Lucille Norman			
❏ T1050 [M]	This Is Gordon MacRae	1958	$30
—Turquoise label			
COLORTONE			
❏ 4939 [M]	Gordon MacRae Sings	1958	$18
EVON			
❏ 320 [M]	Gordon MacRae Sings	1958	$18
—Reissue of Allegro Royale LP			
GALAXY			
❏ 4805 [M]	Gordon MacRae	1958	$18
—Reissue of Allegro Royale LP			
RONDO-LETTE			
❏ A5 [M]	Gordon MacRae	1958	$18
—Reissue of Allegro Royale LP			
ROYALE			
❏ 18155 [10]	Gordon MacRae and Orchestra	195?	$30
❏ 18106 [10]	Gordon MacRae and Walter Gross Orchestra	195?	$30
SUTTON			
❏ SU292 [M]	Gordon MacRae Sings Broadway's Best!	196?	$12
❏ SSU292 [R]	Gordon MacRae Sings Broadway's Best!	196?	$12

MACRAE, SHEILA
ABC

Number	Title	Yr	NM
❏ ABCS-611	How Sweet She Is	1968	$30

MAD CLIFF
GUINNESS

Number	Title	Yr	NM
❏ GNS36084 [B]	Mad Cliff	1977	$300

MAD LADS, THE
STAX

Number	Title	Yr	NM
❏ MPS-8525	The Best of the Mad Lads	198?	$12
VOLT			
❏ VOS-6020	A New Beginning	1973	$25
❏ VOS-6005	The Mad, Mad, Mad, Mad, Mad Lads	1969	$30
❏ 414 [M]	The Mad Lads In Action	1966	$50
❏ S-414 [S]	The Mad Lads In Action	1966	$75

MAD RIVER
CAPITOL

Number	Title	Yr	NM
❏ ST2985	Mad River	1968	$85
❏ ST-185	Paradise Bar and Grill	1969	$85

MADDOX, JOHNNY
DOT

Number	Title	Yr	NM
❏ DLP-102 [10]	Authentic Ragtime	1952	$40
❏ DLP-3289 [M]	Crazy Otto Piano	1960	$15
❏ DLP-25289 [S]	Crazy Otto Piano	1960	$18

Number	Title	Yr	NM
❏ DLP-3131 [M]	Dieieland Blues	1959	$18
❏ DLP-25131 [S]	Dieieland Blues	1959	$25
❏ DLP-3005 [M]	Johnny Maddox Plays	1956	$30
❏ DLP-3314 [M]	Johnny Maddox Plays More Million Sellers	1960	$15
❏ DLP-25314 [S]	Johnny Maddox Plays More Million Sellers	1960	$18
❏ DLP-3122 [M]	Johnny Maddox Plays the Million Sellers	1958	$18
❏ DLP-25122 [S]	Johnny Maddox Plays the Million Sellers	1959	$25
❏ DLP-3549 [M]	Johnny Maddox Plays the Million Sellers, Volume 3	1963	$15
❏ DLP-25549 [S]	Johnny Maddox Plays the Million Sellers, Volume 3	1963	$18
❏ DLP-3044 [M]	King of Ragtime	1957	$25
❏ DLP-3539 [M]	Memphis	1963	$15
❏ DLP-25539 [S]	Memphis	1963	$18
❏ DLP-3645 [M]	More Ragtime Twenties	1965	$15
❏ DLP-25645 [S]	More Ragtime Twenties	1965	$18
❏ DLP-3067 [M]	My Old Flames	1957	$25
❏ DLP-3334 [M]	Near You	1960	$15
❏ DLP-3198 [M]	Old Fashioned Love	1959	$18
❏ DLP-25198 [S]	Old Fashioned Love	1959	$25

Number	Title	Yr	NM
❏ DLP-3621 [M]	Raggin' the Hits	1965	$15
❏ DLP-25621 [M]	Raggin' the Hits	1965	$18
❏ DLP-3633 [M]	Ragtime by Request	1965	$15
❏ DLP-25633 [S]	Ragtime by Request	1965	$18
❏ DLP-3521 [M]	Ragtime Duets	1963	$15
—With Glenn Rowell			
❏ DLP-25521 [S]	Ragtime Duets	1963	$18
—With Glenn Rowell			
❏ DLP-3000 [M]	Ragtime Melodies	1955	$30
❏ DLP-3724 [M]	Ragtime Memories	1966	$15
❏ DLP-25724 [S]	Ragtime Memories	1966	$18
❏ DLP-3108 [M]	Ragtime Piano 1917-18	1958	$18
❏ DLP-3739 [M]	Ragtime Piano Man	1966	$15
❏ DLP-25739 [S]	Ragtime Piano Man	1966	$18
❏ DLP-3493 [M]	Ragtime Twenties	1963	$15
❏ DLP-25493 [S]	Ragtime Twenties	1963	$18
❏ DLP-3378 [M]	Sabre Dance	1961	$15
❏ DLP-25378 [S]	Sabre Dance	1961	$18
❏ DLP-3817 [M]	Second Hand Rose	1967	$18
❏ DLP-25817 [S]	Second Hand Rose	1967	$18
❏ DLP-3008 [M]	Tap Dance Rhythms	1956	$30
❏ DLP-3063 [M]	The Thirties in Ragtime	1957	$25
❏ DLP-3321 [M]	The World's Greatest Piano Rolls	1960	$15
❏ DLP-25321 [S]	The World's Greatest Piano Rolls	1960	$18
❏ DLP-3476 [M]	World's Greatest Piano Rolls, Volume 2	1962	$15
❏ DLP-25476 [S]	World's Greatest Piano Rolls, Volume 2	1962	$18
❏ DLP-3477 [M]	World's Greatest Piano Rolls, Volume 3	1962	$15
❏ DLP-25477 [S]	World's Greatest Piano Rolls, Volume 3	1962	$15
❏ DLP-3478 [M]	World's Greatest Piano Rolls, Volume 4	1962	$15
❏ DLP-25478 [S]	World's Greatest Piano Rolls, Volume 4	1962	$18
❏ DLP-3720 [M]	World's Greatest Piano Rolls, Volume 5	1966	$15
❏ DLP-25720 [S]	World's Greatest Piano Rolls, Volume 5	1966	$18
❏ DLP-3721 [M]	World's Greatest Piano Rolls, Volume 6	1966	$15
❏ DLP-25721 [S]	World's Greatest Piano Rolls, Volume 6	1966	$18
❏ DLP-3722 [M]	World's Greatest Piano Rolls, Volume 7	1966	$15
❏ DLP-25722 [S]	World's Greatest Piano Rolls, Volume 7	1966	$18
HAMILTON			
❏ HLP-115 [M]	12 Ragtime Greats	1964	$12
❏ HLP-12115 [S]	12 Ragtime Greats	1964	$15
❏ HLP-150 [M]	Great Marches and Waltzes	1964	$12
❏ HLP-12150 [S]	Great Marches and Waltzes	1964	$15
PARAMOUNT			
❏ PAS-2-1029	Piano Roll Greats	1974	$15
PICKWICK			
❏ SPC-3097 [S]	Alley Cat and Other Piano Roll Favorites	196?	$12
❏ PC-3097 [M]	Alley Cat and Other Piano Roll Favorites	196?	$15

Number	Title	Yr	NM

MADDOX, LESTER
LEFEVRE
❏ MLSP-3485	God, Family and Country	197?	$40

MADDOX, ROSE
Also see THE MADDOX BROTHERS AND ROSE; BUCK OWENS.
CAPITOL
❏ T1548 [M]	A Big Bouquet of Roses	1961	$30
❏ ST1548 [S]	A Big Bouquet of Roses	1961	$40
❏ T1993 [M]	Alone with You	1963	$30
❏ ST1993 [S]	Alone with You	1963	$40
❏ T1437 [M]	Glorybound Train	1960	$30
❏ ST1437 [S]	Glorybound Train	1960	$40
❏ T1799 [M]	Rose Maddox Sings Bluegrass	1962	$40
❏ ST1799 [S]	Rose Maddox Sings Bluegrass	1962	$50
❏ T1312 [M]	The One Rose	1960	$30
❏ ST1312 [S]	The One Rose	1960	$40
COLUMBIA
❏ CL1159 [M]	Precious Memories	1958	$40

MADDOX BROTHERS AND ROSE
Also see ROSE MADDOX.
KING
❏ 669 [M]	A Collection of Standard Sacred Songs	1959	$175
❏ 752 [M]	I'll Write Your Name in the Sand	1961	$120
❏ 677 [M]	The Maddox Brothers and Rose	1960	$120
WRANGLER
❏ W-1003 [M]	The Maddox Brothers and Rose	1962	$30
❏ WS-1003 [S]	The Maddox Brothers and Rose	1962	$40

MADIGAN, BETTY
MGM
❏ E-3448 [M]	Am I Blue?	1956	$40

MADISON, AL
GOLDEN CREST
❏ GC-3048 [M]	Meet Al Madison	196?	$30

MADISON, JIMMY
ADELPHI
❏ 5007	Bumps	1978	$30

MADNESS
GEFFEN
❏ GHS4022	Keep Moving	1984	$12
❏ GHS4003	Madness	1983	$12
❏ GHS24079	Mad Not Mad	1985	$12
SIRE
❏ SRK6094	Absolutely	1980	$12
❏ SRK6085	One Step Beyond	1979	$15

MADONNA
MAVERICK
❏ PRO-A-7311 [DJ]	Bedtime Stories	1994	$150
—Promo only on pink vinyl			
❏ PRO-A-5904 [DJ]	Erotica	1992	$75
—Vinyl is promo only			
❏ PRO-A-100871 [DJ]	GHV2 Remixed -- The Best of 1991-2001	2001	$40
—Promo-only remixes of 12 songs from the "GHV2" CD; comes in generic black jacket with hole in center			
❏ PRO-A-100500-A [DJ]	Music	2000	$50
—Vinyl is promo only; generic white die-cut sleeve			
❏ PRO-A-9378 [DJ]	Ray of Light	1998	$75
—Vinyl is promo only; generic cover with sticker			
SIRE
❏ 26209	I'm Breathless	1990	$12
❏ W1-26209	I'm Breathless	1990	$18
—Columbia House edition			
❏ R100572	I'm Breathless	1990	$18
—BMG Direct Marketing edition			
❏ 25844 [B]	Like a Prayer	1989	$18
❏ W1-25844	Like a Prayer	1989	$18
—Columbia House edition			
❏ R101029	Like a Prayer	1989	$18
—BMG Direct Marketing edition			
❏ R125844 [B]	Like a Prayer	2016	$25
❏ R125157 [B]	Like A Virgin	2016	$25
❏ 25157	Like a Virgin	1984	$75
—White vinyl with silver colored spine			
❏ 25157 [B]	Like a Virgin	1984	$75
—White vinyl with cream colored spine			
❏ W1-25157	Like a Virgin	1985	$18
—Columbia House edition			
❏ R161153	Like a Virgin	1985	$18
—RCA Music Service edition			
❏ 25157	Like a Virgin	1984	$12
❏ 23867 [B]	Madonna	1983	$50

—First pressing with 4:48 version of "Burning Up"; this version has only been found on copies with a gold promo stamp on the cover
❏ 23867 [B]	Madonna	1983	$18
—Second pressing with 3:49 version of "Burning Up"			
❏ W1-23867	Madonna	1984	$18
—Columbia House edition			
❏ R164288	Madonna	1984	$18
—RCA Music Service edition			
❏ R123867 [B]	Madonna	2016	$180g
❏ 26440	The Immaculate Collection	1990	$18
❏ W1-26440	The Immaculate Collection	1990	$25
—Columbia House edition			
❏ R254164	The Immaculate Collection	1990	$25
—BMG Direct Marketing edition			
❏ 25442	True Blue	1986	$15
—With poster			
❏ 25442	True Blue	1986	$10
—Without poster			
❏ W1-25442	True Blue	1986	$18
—Columbia House edition; issued with poster			
❏ R143811	True Blue	1986	$18
—RCA Music Service edition; issued with poster			
❏ 25535	You Can Dance	1987	$15
—With gold obi "Madonna and Dancing			
❏ 25535	You Can Dance	1987	$10
—Without gold obi			
❏ PRO-A-2892 [B]	You Can Dance	1987	$50
—Promo-only; contains single edits of the seven songs on the stock editions			
❏ W1-25535	You Can Dance	1987	$18
—Columbia House edition; not issued with obi			
❏ R134536	You Can Dance	1987	$18
—RCA Music Service edition; not issued with obi			
WARNER BROS.
❏ 49460-1	Confessions on a Dance Floor	2005	$40
—All copies on pink vinyl			
❏ 42916-0	Confessions Remixed	2005	$40
—Six remixes of five different songs from "Confessions on a Dance Floor"			

MADRID CONCERT ORCHESTRA AND CHORUS
UNITED ARTISTS
❏ UAL3059 [M]	Christmas in Spain	1959	$18

MADRIGAL
SSS INTERNATIONAL
❏ 18	Madrigal	1971	$30

MADURA
COLUMBIA
❏ G30794	Madura	1971	$25
❏ KC32545	Madura II	1973	$18

MAESTRO, JOHNNY
Also see THE BROOKLYN BRIDGE; THE CRESTS.
BUDDAH
❏ BDS-5091	The Johnny Maestro Story	1971	$40
—With inserts; deduct 40% if missing			

MAGAZINE
Also see BUZZCOCKS.
I.R.S.
❏ SP-70030	After the Fact	1982	$12
❏ SP-70020	Magic, Murder and the Weather	1981	$15
❏ SP-70015	Play	1981	$15
VIRGIN
❏ 90891	Rays & Hail 1978-1981	1987	$18
❏ VA13144	The Correct Use of Soap	1980	$12
VIRGIN INTERNATIONAL
❏ VI-2100	Real Life	1978	$18
❏ VI-2121	Secondhand Daylight	1979	$14

MAGGARD, CLEDUS
MERCURY
❏ SRM-1-1072	The White Knight	1976	$15

MAGI, THE
UNCLE DIRTY
❏ 6102-N13	Win or Lose	1975	$300

MAGIC
May be two different groups.
ARMADILLO
❏ 8031	Enclosed	1970	$400
RARE EARTH
❏ RS-527	Magic	1971	$30

MAGIC FERN, THE
PANORAMA
❏ 108	The Magic Fern	1980	$175

MAGIC LANTERNS
ATLANTIC
❏ SD8217	Shame, Shame	1969	$25

MAGIC ORGAN, THE
RANWOOD
❏ R-8136	A Magic Christmas	1974	$12
❏ R-8092	Street Fair	1972	$12

MAGIC SAM
DELMARK
❏ DL-620	Black Magic	1969	$30
❏ DL-615	West Side Soul	1968	$30

MAGIC SAND
UNI
❏ 73094 [B]	Magic Sand	1971	$30

MAGNIFICENT MEN, THE
CAPITOL
❏ T2678 [M]	The Magnificent Men	1967	$25
❏ ST2678 [S]	The Magnificent Men	1967	$18
❏ T2775 [M]	The Magnificent Men "Live!	1967	$25
❏ ST2775 [S]	The Magnificent Men "Live!	1967	$18
❏ T2846 [M]	World of Soul	1968	$30
❏ ST2846 [S]	World of Soul	1968	$18
MERCURY
❏ SR-61252	Better Than a Ten Cent Movie	1970	$18

MAGNOLIA JAZZ BAND
STOMP OFF
❏ SOS-1016	Red Onion Blues	198?	$25
❏ SOS-1137	Shake That Thing	1987	$25

MAGNUSSON, BOB
DISCOVERY
❏ 804	Revelation	1979	$30
❏ 824	Road Work Ahead	1980	$30
❏ 912	Song for Janet Lee	1984	$25
TREND
❏ 528	Two Generations of Music	1981	$35
—Direct-to-disc recording			

MAGNUSSON, JAKOB
OPTIMISM
❏ OP-2002	Time Zone	198?	$25

MAHAL, TAJ
COLUMBIA
❏ PC34466	Anthology Volume 1	1977	$15
❏ GP18	Giant Step/De Ole Folks at Home	1969	$25
—Red "360 Sound" label			
❏ GP18	Giant Step/De Ole Folks at Home	1971	$18
—Orange label			
❏ CG18	Giant Step/De Ole Folks at Home	198?	$12
—Reissue with new prefix			
❏ C30767	Happy to Be Like I Am	1971	$15
❏ PC30767	Happy to Be Like I Am	198?	$10
—Budget-line reissue			
❏ KC33051	Mo' Roots	1974	$15
❏ PC33051	Mo' Roots	198?	$10
—Budget-line reissue			
❏ PC33801	Music Keeps Me Together	1975	$15
❏ KC32600	Oooh So Good 'N Blues	1973	$15
❏ PC32600	Oooh So Good 'N Blues	198?	$10
—Budget-line reissue			
❏ KC31605	Recycling the Blues & Other Related Stuff	1972	$15
❏ PC31605	Recycling the Blues & Other Related Stuff	198?	$10
—Budget-line reissue			
❏ PC34103	Satisfied & Tickled Too	1976	$15
❏ CL2779 [M]	Taj Mahal	1967	$75
❏ CS9579 [S]	Taj Mahal	1967	$18
—Red "360 Sound" label			
❏ CS9579 [S]	Taj Mahal	1971	$15
—Orange label			
❏ PC9579 [S]	Taj Mahal	198?	$10
—Reissue with new prefix			
❏ FC36528	The Best of Taj Mahal	1981	$12
❏ PC36528	The Best of Taj Mahal	198?	$10
—Budget-line reissue			
❏ 88765494151 [B]	The Hidden Treasures Of Taj Mahal (1969-1973)	2013	$25
❏ CS9698	The Natch'l Blues	1968	$18
—Red "360 Sound" label			
❏ CS9698	The Natch'l Blues	1971	$15
—Orange label			

Number	Title	Yr	NM
❏ PC9698	The Natch'l Blues	198?	$10
— Reissue with new prefix			
❏ 88883700461 [B]	The Natch'l Blues	2013	$25
❏ G30619	The Real Thing	1971	$25
❏ CG30619	The Real Thing	198?	$12
— Reissue with new prefix			

CRYSTAL CLEAR

Number	Title	Yr	NM
❏ 5011 [B]	Live and Direct	1980	$30
— Direct-to-disc recording			

WARNER BROS.

Number	Title	Yr	NM
❏ BS3024	Brothers	1977	$12
❏ BS3094	Evolution (Recent)	1978	$12
❏ BS2994	Music Fuh Ya' (Musica Para Tu)	1977	$12

MAHAN, LARRY
WARNER BROS.

Number	Title	Yr	NM
❏ BS2959	King of the Rodeo	1976	$25

MAHARIS, GEORGE
EPIC

Number	Title	Yr	NM
❏ LN24191 [M]	A New Route: George Maharis	1966	$15
❏ BN26191 [S]	A New Route: George Maharis	1966	$18
❏ LN24001 [M]	George Maharis Sings!	1962	$15
❏ BN26001 [S]	George Maharis Sings!	1962	$18
❏ LN24037 [M]	Just Turn Me Loose!	1963	$15
❏ BN26037 [S]	Just Turn Me Loose!	1963	$18
❏ LN24079 [M]	Make Love to Me	1964	$15
❏ BN26079 [S]	Make Love to Me	1964	$18
❏ LN24021 [M]	Portrait in Music	1962	$15
❏ BN26021 [S]	Portrait in Music	1962	$18
❏ LN24111 [M]	Tonight You Belong to Me	1964	$15
❏ BN26111 [S]	Tonight You Belong to Me	1964	$18
❏ LN24064 [M]	Where Can You Go for a Broken Heart?	1963	$15
❏ BN26064 [S]	Where Can You Go for a Broken Heart?	1963	$18

MAHAVISHNU ORCHESTRA
COLUMBIA

Number	Title	Yr	NM
❏ KC32957	Apocalypse	1974	$35
❏ PC32957	Apocalypse	197?	$20
— Reissue with new prefix			
❏ KC32766	Between Nothingness and Eternity	1973	$35
❏ CQ32766 [Q]	Between Nothingness and Eternity	1973	$50
❏ PC32766	Between Nothingness and Eternity	197?	$20
— Reissue with new prefix; with or without bar code on cover			
❏ KC31996	Birds of Fire	1973	$25
❏ CQ31996 [Q]	Birds of Fire	1973	$75
❏ PC31996	Birds of Fire	197?	$20
— Reissue with new prefix; with or without bar code			
❏ PC33908	Inner Worlds	1976	$25
— Original with no bar code			
❏ PC33908	Inner Worlds	198?	$20
— Reissue with bar code			
❏ JC36394	The Best of Mahavishnu Orchestra	1980	$25
❏ KC31067 [B]	The Inner Mounting Flame	1972	$18
— As "Mahavishnu Orchestra with John McLaughlin			
❏ PC31067	The Inner Mounting Flame	197?	$20
— Reissue with new prefix; with or without bar code			
❏ PC33411	Visions of the Emerald Beyond	1975	$25
— Original with no bar code			
❏ PC33411	Visions of the Emerald Beyond	198?	$20
— Reissue with bar code			

MAHOGANY RUSH
Featuring Frank Marino.

20TH CENTURY

Number	Title	Yr	NM
❏ T-451	Child of the Novelty	1974	$30
❏ T-463	Maxoom	1975	$30
— Reissue of Nine 936			

Number	Title	Yr	NM
❏ T-482 [B]	Strange Universe	1975	$25

COLUMBIA

Number	Title	Yr	NM
❏ JC35257	Frank Marino & Mahogany Rush Live	1978	$18
❏ PC35257	Frank Marino & Mahogany Rush Live	198?	$10
— Budget-line reissue			
❏ PC34190	Mahogany Rush IV	1976	$18
— Original with no bar code			
❏ PC34190	Mahogany Rush IV	198?	$10
— Reissue with bar code			
❏ JC35753	Tales of the Unexpected	1979	$18
❏ PC35753	Tales of the Unexpected	198?	$10
— Budget-line reissue			
❏ JC36204	What's Next	1980	$18
❏ PC36204	What's Next	198?	$10
— Budget-line reissue			
❏ PC34677	World Anthem	1977	$18
— Original with no bar code			
❏ PC34677	World Anthem	198?	$10
— Reissue with bar code			

NINE

Number	Title	Yr	NM
❏ 936	Maxoom	1973	$50

MAHONES, GILDO
NEW JAZZ

Number	Title	Yr	NM
❏ NJLP-8299 [M]	Shooting High	1963	$0
— Canceled			

PRESTIGE

Number	Title	Yr	NM
❏ PRLP-16004 [M]	Shooting High	1964	$40
❏ PRLP-7339 [M]	The Soulful Piano of Gildo Mahones	1964	$30
❏ PRST-7339 [S]	The Soulful Piano of Gildo Mahones	1964	$40

MAIDEN, SIDNEY
BLUESVILLE

Number	Title	Yr	NM
❏ BVLP-1035 [M]	Trouble An' Blues	1961	$100
— Blue label, silver print			
❏ BVLP-1035 [M]	Trouble An' Blues	1964	$25
— Blue label, trident logo at right			

MAIN ATTRACTION, THE
TOWER

Number	Title	Yr	NM
❏ ST-5117 [S]	And Now...The Main Attraction	1968	$30
❏ T-5117 [M]	And Now...The Main Attraction	1968	$50

MAIN INGREDIENT, THE
COLLECTABLES

Number	Title	Yr	NM
❏ COL-5101	Golden Classics	198?	$12

POLYDOR

Number	Title	Yr	NM
❏ 841249-1	I Just Wanna Love You	1989	$15

RCA VICTOR

Number	Title	Yr	NM
❏ LSP-4834	Afrodisiac	1973	$15
❏ LSP-4677	Bitter Sweet	1972	$15
❏ LSP-4483	Black Seeds	1971	$15
❏ APL1-0335	Euphrates River	1974	$15
❏ APD1-0335 [Q]	Euphrates River	1974	$30
❏ APL1-0314	Greatest Hits	1974	$15
❏ AFL1-3963	I Only Have Eyes for You	1981	$12
❏ APL1-1558	Music Maximus	1977	$15
❏ AFL1-3641	Ready for Love	1980	$12
❏ APL1-0644	Rolling Down a Mountainside	1975	$15
❏ ANL1-2667	Rolling Down a Mountainside	1978	$12
— Reissue of APL1-0644			
❏ APL1-1003	Shame On the World	1975	$15
❏ APL1-1858	Super Hits	1977	$15
❏ LSP-4412	Tasteful Soul	1971	$15
❏ LSP-4253	The Main Ingredient L.T.D.	1970	$15

MAINER, J.E.
ARHOOLIE

Number	Title	Yr	NM
❏ F5002	J.E. Mainer's Mountaineers	197?	$15

BLUE JAY

Number	Title	Yr	NM
❏ 101	70th Happy Birthday	1968	$25
❏ 102	Precious Memories	1968	$25

KING

Number	Title	Yr	NM
❏ 666 [M]	Good Ole Mountain Music	1960	$150
❏ 666	Good Ole Mountain Music	197?	$15
— Gusto reissue			
❏ 765 [M]	Variety Album	1961	$150

OLD HOMESTEAD

Number	Title	Yr	NM
❏ 146	J.E. Mainer at Home with Family and Friends, Vol. 1	197?	$18

OLD TIMEY

Number	Title	Yr	NM
❏ 107	J.E. Mainer's Mountaineers, Vol. 2	197?	$15

RURAL RHYTHM

Number	Title	Yr	NM
❏ RRJE-191	More Old Time Mountain Music	198?	$15
❏ RRJE-198	The Legendary J.E. Mainer, Vol. 3	198?	$15
❏ RRJE-225	The Legendary J.E. Mainer, Vol. 7	198?	$15
❏ RRJE-246	The Legendary J.E. Mainer, Vol. 16	198?	$15
❏ RRJE-250	The Legendary J.E. Mainer, Vol. 20	198?	$15
❏ RRJE-185	The Legendary J.E. Mainer and His Mountaineers	198?	$15

MAINER, WADE
KING

Number	Title	Yr	NM
❏ 769 [M]	Soulful Sacred Songs	1961	$150

OLD HOMESTEAD

Number	Title	Yr	NM
❏ 4000	From the Maple to the Hill	1976	$25
❏ 90123	Old Time Songs	1980	$18
❏ 90016	Sacred Songs Mountain Style	197?	$18
❏ 90001	Sacred Songs of Mother and Home	1971	$18

MAINES BROTHERS BAND, THE
MERCURY

Number	Title	Yr	NM
❏ 814985-1	High Rollin'	1984	$10
❏ 826143-1	The Boys Are Back in Town	1986	$10

MAINIERI, MIKE, AND WARREN BERNHARDT
ARISTA/NOVUS

Number	Title	Yr	NM
❏ AN3009	Free	1978	$30

MAINIERI, MIKE
ARGO

Number	Title	Yr	NM
❏ LP-706 [M]	Blues on the Other Side	1963	$30
❏ LPS-706 [S]	Blues on the Other Side	1963	$30

ARISTA

Number	Title	Yr	NM
❏ AL4133	Love	1976	$25

SOLID STATE

Number	Title	Yr	NM
❏ SS-18029	Insight	1968	$20
❏ SS-18049	Journey Thru an Electric Tube	1969	$20

WARNER BROS.

Number	Title	Yr	NM
❏ BSK3586	Wanderlust	1982	$25

MAIZE, JOE
DECCA

Number	Title	Yr	NM
❏ DL8817 [M]	Hawaiian Dreams	1959	$25
❏ DL78817 [S]	Hawaiian Dreams	1959	$30
❏ DL4555 [M]	Isle of Dreams	1965	$25
❏ DL74555 [S]	Isle of Dreams	1965	$30
❏ DL8590 [M]	Presenting Joe Maize and His Cordsmen	1958	$30

MAJIC SHIP, THE
BEL AMI

Number	Title	Yr	NM
❏ BA-711	The Majic Ship	1968	$500

MAJORS, THE (1)
IMPERIAL

Number	Title	Yr	NM
❏ LP-9222 [M]	Meet the Majors	1963	$150
❏ LP-12222 [S]	Meet the Majors	1963	$250

MAKEBA, MIRIAM
KAPP

Number	Title	Yr	NM
❏ KL-1274 [M]	The Many Voices of Miriam Makeba	1962	$25
❏ KS-3274 [S]	The Many Voices of Miriam Makeba	1962	$30

MERCURY

Number	Title	Yr	NM
❏ MG-21095 [M]	All About Miriam	1967	$15
❏ SR-61095 [S]	All About Miriam	1967	$18
❏ MG-21082 [M]	The Magnificent Miriam Makeba	1966	$15
❏ SR-61082 [S]	The Magnificent Miriam Makeba	1966	$18

MERCURY/URBAN AFRICA

Number	Title	Yr	NM
❏ 838208-1	Welela	1989	$15

PETERS INT'L.

Number	Title	Yr	NM
❏ PLD2082	Miriam Makeba in Concert	1977	$15

RCA VICTOR

Number	Title	Yr	NM
❏ LPM-3321 [M]	Makeba Sings	1965	$18
❏ LSP-3321 [S]	Makeba Sings	1965	$25
❏ LPM-2267 [M]	Miriam Makeba	1960	$25
❏ LSP-2267 [S]	Miriam Makeba	1960	$30
❏ LPM-3982 [M]	The Best of Miriam Makeba	1968	$30
❏ LSP-3982 [S]	The Best of Miriam Makeba	1968	$15
❏ LPM-3512 [M]	The Magic of Makeba	1966	$18
❏ LSP-3512 [S]	The Magic of Makeba	1966	$25
❏ LPM-2845 [M]	The Voice of Africa	1964	$18
❏ LSP-2845 [S]	The Voice of Africa	1964	$25
❏ LPM-2750 [M]	The World of Miriam Makeba	1963	$18
❏ LSP-2750 [S]	The World of Miriam Makeba	1963	$25

REPRISE

Number	Title	Yr	NM
❏ RS-6381	Keep Me in Mind	1970	$15
❏ RS-6310	Makeba!	1968	$15
❏ R-6253 [M]	Miriam Makeba In Concert!	1967	$18
❏ RS-6253 [S]	Miriam Makeba In Concert!	1967	$15
❏ R-6274 [M]	Pata Pata	1967	$18

Number	Title	Yr	NM
❏ RS-6274 [S]	Pata Pata	1967	$15
WARNER BROS.			
❏ 25673	Sangoma	1988	$12

MAKEM, TOMMY
TRADITION
| ❏ TLP-1044 [M] | Songs of Tommy Makem | 1961 | $30 |
| ❏ TLPS-1044 [S] | Songs of Tommy Makem | 1961 | $40 |

MAKOWICZ, ADAM, AND GEORGE MRAZ
STASH
| ❏ ST-216 | Classic Jazz Duets | 198? | $25 |

MAKOWICZ, ADAM
CHOICE
| ❏ 1028 | From My Window | 198? | $30 |
COLUMBIA
| ❏ JC35320 | Adam | 1978 | $25 |
NOVUS
| ❏ 3003-1-N | Moonray | 1986 | $25 |
| ❏ 3022-1-N | Naughty Baby | 1988 | $25 |
SHEFFIELD LABS
| ❏ 21 | The Name Is Makowicz (ma-ko-vitch) | 1984 | $50 |
—Audiophile vinyl

MALACHI
VERVE
| ❏ V-5024 [M] | Holy Music | 1967 | $50 |
| ❏ V6-5024 [S] | Holy Music | 1967 | $40 |

MALCHAK, TIM
ALPINE
| ❏ 1001 | Colorado Moon | 1987 | $15 |
UNIVERSAL
| ❏ UVL-76002 | Different Circles | 1989 | $12 |

MALCOLM X
DOUGLAS
❏ Z30743 [M]	By Any Means Necessary	1971	$35
❏ SD797 [B]	His Wit and Wisdom	196?	$35
❏ SD795 [M]	Malcolm X Talks to Young People	1968	$35
PAUL WINLEY
| ❏ 135 | The Ballot or the Bullet | 197? | $25 |
RCA
| ❏ 66132 | Words from the Frontlines: Excerpts from the Great Speeches of Malcolm X | 1992 | $25 |
UPFRONT

❏ UPF-152 [B]	Malcolm X Speaks to the People in Harlem	197?	$18
WARNER BROS.			
❏ BS2619 [B]	Malcolm X	1972	$30
❏ PRO-A-5943 [DJ]	Malcolm X Speaks	1992	$25
❏ PRO-A-5957 [DJ]	Music and Dialog from the Historic 1992 Documentary Film Malcolm X	1992	$25

MALHEIROS, ALEX
MILESTONE
| ❏ M-9131 | Atlantic Forest | 1985 | $25 |

MALINVERNI, PETE
SEA BREEZE
| ❏ SB-2037 | Don't Be Shy | 198? | $25 |

MALLET BUSTERS
JAZZIMAGE
| ❏ JZ-103 | Mallet Busters | 198? | $25 |

MALO
WARNER BROS.
❏ BS2769	Ascencion	1974	$15
❏ BS2652	Dos	1972	$15
❏ BS2702	Evolution	1973	$15
❏ BS2584 [B]	Malo	1972	$18

MALTBY, RICHARD
COLUMBIA
❏ CL1341 [M]	Hello Young Lovers	1959	$25
❏ CS8151 [S]	Hello Young Lovers	1959	$30
❏ CL1271 [M]	Swingin' Down the Lane	1959	$25
❏ CS8083 [S]	Swingin' Down the Lane	1959	$30
RCA CAMDEN
❏ CAL-526 [M]	A Bow to the Big Name Bands	1959	$25
❏ CAL-711 [M]	Most Requested	1961	$25
❏ CAL-600 [M]	Music from Mr. Lucky	1960	$25
ROULETTE
❏ R-25178 [M]	Brilliant Big Band Ballads and Blues	1962	$25
❏ SR-25178 [S]	Brilliant Big Band Ballads and Blues	1962	$30
❏ R-25129 [M]	Richard Maltby Swings for Dancers	1960	$25
❏ R-25148 [M]	Swing Folksongs	1961	$25
❏ SR-25148 [S]	Swing Folksongs	1961	$30
VIK
❏ LX-1051 [M]	Hue-Fi Moods by Maltby	1957	$30
❏ LX-1071 [M]	Maltby with Strings Attached	1958	$30
❏ LX-1068 [M]	Manhattan Bandstand	1957	$30
X
| ❏ LX-1038 [M] | Make Mine Maltby | 1956 | $30 |

MALVIN, ARTIE
WALDORF MUSIC HALL
| ❏ 33-149 [10] | Rock and Roll | 1955 | $120 |

MAMA CASS
See CASS ELLIOT.

MAMA LION
FAMILY PRODUCTIONS
| ❏ FPS-2713 | Give It Everything I've Got | 1973 | $25 |
| ❏ FPS-2702 | Mama Lion | 1972 | $25 |

MAMAS AND THE PAPAS, THE
ABC
| ❏ AC-30005 | The ABC Collection | 1976 | $18 |
ABC DUNHILL
❏ DS-50064	16 of Their Greatest Hits	1969	$18
❏ DSX-50145	20 Golden Hits	1973	$25
❏ DS-50073	A Gathering of Flowers	1970	$30
❏ DS-50025 [B]	Farewell to the First Golden Era	1968	$15
❏ DS-50038	Golden Era, Volume 2	1968	$25
❏ DS-50006	If You Can Believe Your Eyes and Ears	1968	$15
❏ DSX-50100	Monterey International Pop Festival	1970	$18
❏ SMAS-93470	Monterey International Pop Festival	1970	$30

—Capitol Record Club edition; label has the old-style "Dunhill" logo without the "ABC" as part of it
❏ DSX-50106	People Like Us	1971	$15
❏ DS-50010	The Mamas and the Papas	1968	$15
❏ DS-50014	The Mamas and the Papas Deliver	1968	$15
❏ DS-50031 [B]	The Papas and the Mamas	1968	$18
—The five LPs above are reissues of records originally without the ABC logo
DUNHILL
❏ D-50025 [M]	Farewell to the First Golden Era	1967	$30
❏ DS-50025 [S]	Farewell to the First Golden Era	1967	$35
❏ D-50006 [M]	If You Can Believe Your Eyes and Ears	1966	$175
—With toilet completely visible in lower right
| ❏ D-50006 [M] | If You Can Believe Your Eyes and Ears | 1966 | $50 |
—With scroll over toilet
| ❏ DS-50006 [S] | If You Can Believe Your Eyes and Ears | 1966 | $150 |
—With toilet completely visible in lower right
| ❏ DS-50006 [S] | If You Can Believe Your Eyes and Ears | 1966 | $30 |
—With scroll over toilet proclaiming "Includes California Dreamin'
| ❏ DS-50006 [S] | If You Can Believe Your Eyes and Ears | 1966 | $50 |
—Black cover with photo cropped to render toilet invisible
| ❏ ST-90797 [S] | If You Can Believe Your Eyes and Ears | 1966 | $50 |
—Capitol Record Club edition; known copies have scroll

proclaiming "Includes California Dreamin'".
| ❏ DS-50006 [S] | If You Can Believe Your Eyes and Ears | 1966 | $30 |
—With scroll over toilet proclaiming "Includes California Dreamin'... Monday Monday... I Call Your Name
| ❏ D-50006 [M] | If You Can Believe Your Eyes and Ears | 1966 | $75 |
—Black cover with photo cropped to render toilet invisible
| ❏ T-90797 [M] | If You Can Believe Your Eyes and Ears | 1966 | $50 |
—Capitol Record Club edition; known copies have scroll proclaiming "Includes California Dreamin'.
❏ D-50010 [M]	The Mamas and the Papas	1966	$35
❏ DS-50010 [S]	The Mamas and the Papas	1966	$30
❏ T-90924 [M]	The Mamas and the Papas	1966	$35
—Capitol Record Club edition
| ❏ ST-90924 [S] | The Mamas and the Papas | 1966 | $40 |
—Capitol Record Club edition
❏ D-50014 [M]	The Mamas and the Papas Deliver	1967	$35
❏ DS-50014 [S]	The Mamas and the Papas Deliver	1967	$30
❏ DS-50031	The Papas and the Mamas	1968	$30
MCA
❏ 37145	16 of Their Greatest Hits	1980	$10
❏ 709	Farewell to the First Golden Era	1980	$10
❏ 6019	The Best of the Mamas and the Papas	1986	$15
❏ 710	The Papas and the Mamas	1980	$10
PICKWICK
| ❏ SPC-3352 | California Dreaming | 1972 | $15 |
SUNDAZED
| ❏ LP5446 [B] | Deliver | 2013 | $25 |
| ❏ LP5445 [B] | The Mamas and the Papas | 2013 | $25 |

MAN
PHILIPS
| ❏ PHS600313 | Revelation | 1969 | $25 |
—As "Manpower

MANCE, JUNIOR
ATLANTIC
❏ SD1521	At the Top	1969	$35
❏ 1479 [M]	Harlem Lullaby	1967	$25
❏ SD1479 [S]	Harlem Lullaby	1967	$35
❏ 1496 [M]	I Believe to My Soul	1968	$30
❏ SD1496 [S]	I Believe to My Soul	1968	$35
❏ SD1562	With a Lotta Help from My Friends	1970	$35
BEE HIVE
| ❏ BH-7015 | Truckin' and Trakin' | 198? | $30 |
CAPITOL
| ❏ T2092 [M] | Get Ready, Set, Jump! | 1964 | $50 |
| ❏ ST2092 [S] | Get Ready, Set, Jump! | 1964 | $75 |

❏ T2218 [M]	Straight Ahead	1965	$50
❏ ST2218 [S]	Straight Ahead	1965	$50
❏ T2393 [M]	That's Where It Is	1965	$50
❏ ST2393 [S]	That's Where It Is	1965	$50
FANTASY
| ❏ OJC-204 | Junior Mance Trio at the Village Vanguard | 198? | $25 |
INNER CITY
| ❏ IC-6018 | Holy Mama | 197? | $35 |
JAZZLAND
❏ JLP-53 [M]	Big Chief!	1961	$30
❏ JLP-953 [S]	Big Chief!	1961	$30
❏ JLP-77 [M]	Happy Time	1962	$30
❏ JLP-977 [S]	Happy Time	1962	$30
❏ JLP-41 [M]	Junior Mance Trio at the Village Vanguard	1961	$40
❏ JLP-941 [S]	Junior Mance Trio at the Village Vanguard	1961	$40
❏ JLP-63 [M]	The Jazz Soul of Hollywood	1961	$30
❏ JLP-963 [S]	The Jazz Soul of Hollywood	1961	$30
❏ JLP-30 [M]	The Soulful Piano of Junior Mance	1960	$30

Number	Title	Yr	NM
❏ JLP-930 [S]	The Soulful Piano of Junior Mance	1960	$30

MILESTONE
Number	Title	Yr	NM
❏ M-9041	That Lovin' Feelin'	197?	$35

POLYDOR
Number	Title	Yr	NM
❏ PD-5051	Touch	1974	$35

RIVERSIDE
Number	Title	Yr	NM
❏ RLP-447 [M]	Junior's Blues	1963	$175
❏ RS-9447 [S]	Junior's Blues	1963	$175
❏ 6059	Soulful Piano	197?	$30

SACKVILLE
Number	Title	Yr	NM
❏ 3031	For Dancers Only	198?	$25

VERVE
Number	Title	Yr	NM
❏ MGV-8319 [M]	Junior	1959	$150
❏ MGVS-6057 [S]	Junior	1960	$150
❏ V-8319 [M]	Junior	1961	$25
❏ V6-8319 [S]	Junior	1961	$35

MANCHESTER, MELISSA

ARISTA
Number	Title	Yr	NM
❏ AL4067	Better Days & Happy Endings	1976	$12
❏ AQ4067 [Q]	Better Days & Happy Endings	1976	$20
❏ AL4011	Bright Eyes	1975	$12
—Reissue of Bell 1303			
❏ AB4186	Don't Cry Out Loud	1978	$12
❏ AL8373	Don't Cry Out Loud	198?	$10
—Budget-line reissue of 4186			
❏ AL8094	Emergency	1983	$12
❏ AL9533	For the Working Girl	1980	$12
❏ AL9611	Greatest Hits	1983	$12
❏ AL8293	Greatest Hits	198?	$10
—Budget-line reissue of 9611			
❏ AL4095	Help Is On the Way	1976	$12
❏ AL9574	Hey Ricky	1982	$12
❏ AL8350	Hey Ricky	198?	$10
—Budget-line reissue of 9574			
❏ AL4006	Home to Myself	1975	$12
—Reissue of Bell 1123			
❏ AL4031	Melissa	1975	$12
❏ AQ4031 [Q]	Melissa	1975	$20
❏ AL8055	Melissa	1983	$12
—Budget-line reissue of 4031			
❏ AL9506	Melissa Manchester	1979	$12
❏ AL4136	Singin'	1977	$12

BELL
Number	Title	Yr	NM
❏ 1303	Bright Eyes	1974	$15
❏ 1123	Home to Myself	1973	$15

MCA
Number	Title	Yr	NM
❏ 5587	Mathematics	1985	$12

MIKA
Number	Title	Yr	NM
❏ 841273-1	Tribute	1989	$15

MOBILE FIDELITY
Number	Title	Yr	NM
❏ 1-Jan-0028 [B]	Melissa	1980	$30
—Audiophile vinyl			

NAUTILUS
Number	Title	Yr	NM
❏ NR-33	Don't Cry Out Loud	198?	$40
—Audiophile vinyl			

PAIR
Number	Title	Yr	NM
❏ PDL2-1086	The Many Moods of Melissa Manchester	1986	$15

MANCHESTERS, THE (1)

DIPLOMAT
Number	Title	Yr	NM
❏ D-2307 [M]	Beatlerama	1964	$18
—No artist credited on label or cover			
❏ D-2307 [M]	Beatlerama	1964	$18
—With artist credited			
❏ DS-2307 [S]	Beatlerama	1964	$25
—No artist credited on label or cover			
❏ DS-2307 [S]	Beatlerama	1964	$25
—With artist credited			

GUEST STAR
Number	Title	Yr	NM
❏ G-2307 [M]	Beatlerama	1964	$18
❏ GS-2307 [S]	Beatlerama	1964	$25

MANCINI, HENRY

AVCO EMBASSY
Number	Title	Yr	NM
❏ AVE 0110	Sunflower	1970	$18

DECCA
Number	Title	Yr	NM
❏ DL79185	Sometimes a Great Notion	1971	$18

LIBERTY
Number	Title	Yr	NM
❏ LRP-3121 [M]	The Versatile Henry Mancini	1959	$25
❏ LST-7121 [S]	The Versatile Henry Mancini	1959	$30
❏ LT-51135	Trail of the Pink Panther	1982	$25

MCA
Number	Title	Yr	NM
❏ 6222	The Glass Menagerie	1987	$12
❏ 2085	The Great Waldo Pepper	1975	$15

PAIR
Number	Title	Yr	NM
❏ PDL2-1092	The Mancini Collection (Film Music)	1986	$15

PARAMOUNT
Number	Title	Yr	NM
❏ PAS-6000	The Molly Maguires	1970	$25

RCA CAMDEN
Number	Title	Yr	NM
❏ CAS-2510	Dream of You	1971	$12
❏ CXS-9034	Everybody's Favorite	1972	$12
❏ ACL2-0293	Film Music	1973	$15
❏ CXS-9005	Mancini Magic	1971	$15
❏ CAL-2158 [M]	Mancini Plays Mancini and Other Composers	1968	$15
❏ CAS-2158 [S]	Mancini Plays Mancini and Other Composers	1968	$12
❏ CAL-928 [M]	The Second Time Around and Others	1966	$15
❏ CAS-928 [S]	The Second Time Around and Others	1966	$15

RCA SPECIAL PRODUCTS
Number	Title	Yr	NM
❏ DPL1-0678	Taking It Easy	1984	$18
—Manufactured for Abbott Laboratories			

RCA VICTOR
Number	Title	Yr	NM
❏ PRM-175 [M]	Academy Award Songs, Volume Two	1965	$18
—Made for the B.F. Goodrich tire company			
❏ PRS-175 [S]	Academy Award Songs, Volume Two	1965	$25
—Made for the B.F. Goodrich tire company			
❏ CPL1-1843	A Legendary Performer	1976	$12
❏ LPM-3612 [M]	A Merry Mancini Christmas	1966	$12
—Original front cover has a photo of Henry Mancini and family			
❏ LSP-3612 [S]	A Merry Mancini Christmas	1966	$15
—Same as above, but in stereo			
❏ ANL1-1928 [S]	A Merry Mancini Christmas	1976	$10
—Reissue with new number and new front cover			
❏ LPM-3623 [M]	Arabesque	1966	$15
❏ LSP-3623 [S]	Arabesque	1966	$18
❏ LSP-4140	A Warm Shade of Ivory	1969	$18
❏ AFL1-4140	A Warm Shade of Ivory	1977	$10
—Reissue with new prefix			
❏ AYL1-3757	A Warm Shade of Ivory	1980	$10
—Best Buy Series" reissue			
❏ LSP-4630	Big Screen -- Little Screen	1972	$18
❏ APL1-0098	Brass, Ivory and Strings	1973	$15
❏ APD1-0098 [Q]	Brass, Ivory and Strings	1973	$30
❏ LSP-4629	Brass on Ivory	1972	$15
❏ AFL1-4629	Brass on Ivory	1977	$10
—Reissue with new prefix			
❏ AYL1-3756	Brass on Ivory	1980	$10
—Best Buy Series" reissue			
❏ LPM-2362 [M]	Breakfast at Tiffany's	1961	$25
❏ LSP-2362 [S]	Breakfast at Tiffany's	1961	$30
❏ LPM-2755 [M]	Charade	1963	$18
❏ LSP-2755 [S]	Charade	1963	$25
❏ LPM-2258 [M]	Combo!	1960	$50
❏ LSP-2258 [S]	Combo!	1960	$75
❏ APL1-1379	Concert of Film Music	1975	$12
❏ APL1-1896	Cop Show Themes	1976	$12
❏ APL1-0270	Country Gentlemen	1973	$15
❏ AFL1-0270	Country Gentlemen	1977	$12
—Reissue with new prefix			
❏ APD1-0270 [Q]	Country Gentlemen	1973	$30
❏ AYL1-3954	Country Gentlemen	1981	$10
—Best Buy Series" reissue			
❏ LPM-2990 [M]	Dear Heart and Other Songs About Love	1965	$15
❏ LSP-2990 [S]	Dear Heart and Other Songs About Love	1965	$18
❏ LPM-3887 [M]	Encore! More of the Concert Sound of Henry Mancini	1967	$25
❏ LSP-3887 [S]	Encore! More of the Concert Sound of Henry Mancini	1967	$18
❏ LPM-2442 [M]	Experiment in Terror	1962	$30
—Original cover has Lee Remick under attack			
❏ LPM-2442 [M]	Experiment in Terror	1962	$25
—Reissue cover has two mannequins			
❏ LSP-2442 [S]	Experiment in Terror	1962	$40
—Original cover has Lee Remick under attack			
❏ LSP-2442 [S]	Experiment in Terror	1962	$30
—Reissue cover has two mannequins			
❏ LPM-3840 [M]	Gunn	1967	$25
❏ LSP-3840 [S]	Gunn	1967	$30
❏ CPL1-0672	Hangin' Out	1974	$15
❏ AFL1-0672	Hangin' Out	1977	$12
—Reissue with new prefix			
❏ APD1-0672 [Q]	Hangin' Out	1974	$30
❏ LPM-2559 [M]	Hatari!	1962	$25
❏ LSP-2559 [S]	Hatari!	1962	$30
❏ LPM-3694 [M]	Mancini '67	1967	$35
❏ LSP-3694 [S]	Mancini '67	1967	$35
❏ LSP-4542	Mancini Concert	1971	$18
❏ AFL1-4542	Mancini Concert	1977	$12
—Reissue with new prefix			
❏ LSP-4307	Mancini Country	1970	$18
❏ AFL1-4307	Mancini Country	1977	$12
—Reissue with new prefix			
❏ AYL1-3668	Mancini Country	1980	$10
—Best Buy Series" reissue			
❏ LSP-4466	Mancini Plays the Theme from Love Story	1971	$18
❏ ANL1-2484	Mancini Plays the Theme from Love Story	1977	$12
—Reissue of LSP-4466			
❏ APL1-0013	Mancini Salutes Sousa	1972	$15
❏ APD1-0013 [Q]	Mancini Salutes Sousa	1973	$30

Number	Title	Yr	NM
❏ APL1-2290	Mancini's Angels	1977	$12
❏ LPM-2040 [M]	More Music from Peter Gunn	1959	$50
❏ LSP-2040 [S]	More Music from Peter Gunn	1959	$75
❏ LPM-2360 [M]	Mr. Lucky Goes Latin	1961	$50
❏ LSP-2360 [S]	Mr. Lucky Goes Latin	1961	$75
❏ LPM-2198 [M]	Music from Mr. Lucky	1960	$50
❏ LSP-2198 [S]	Music from Mr. Lucky	1960	$75
❏ LPM-3713 [M]	Music of Hawaii	1966	$15
❏ LSP-3713 [S]	Music of Hawaii	1966	$18
❏ AFL1-3713	Music of Hawaii	1977	$12
—Reissue with new prefix			
❏ AYL1-3877	Music of Hawaii	1981	$10
—Best Buy Series" reissue			
❏ APL1-0271	Oklahoma Crude	1973	$15
❏ LPM-2604 [M]	Our Man in Hollywood	1963	$18
❏ LSP-2604 [S]	Our Man in Hollywood	1963	$25
❏ LPM-3997 [M]	Party	1968	$30
❏ LSP-3997 [S]	Party	1968	$18
❏ ANL1-0980	Pure Gold	1975	$12
❏ AYL1-3667	Pure Gold	1980	$10
—Best Buy Series" reissue			
❏ ABL1-0968	Return of the Pink Panther	1975	$30
❏ ABD1-0968 [Q]	Return of the Pink Panther	1975	$75
❏ LSP-4239	Six Hours Past Sunset	1969	$18
❏ APL1-1025	Symphonic Soul	1975	$12
❏ APD1-1025 [Q]	Symphonic Soul	1975	$30
❏ AFL1-1025	Symphonic Soul	1977	$10
❏ LPM-6013 [M]	The Academy Award Songs	1966	$18
❏ LSP-6013 [S]	The Academy Award Songs	1966	$25
❏ LPM-2693 [M]	The Best of Mancini	1964	$15
❏ LSP-2693 [S]	The Best of Mancini	1964	$18
❏ AFL1-2693	The Best of Mancini	1977	$12
—Reissue with new prefix			
❏ AYL1-3822	The Best of Mancini	1981	$10
—Best Buy Series" reissue			
❏ LPM-3557 [M]	The Best of Mancini, Volume 2	1966	$15
❏ LSP-3557 [S]	The Best of Mancini, Volume 2	1966	$18
❏ AFL1-3557	The Best of Mancini, Volume 2	1977	$12
—Reissue with new prefix			
❏ AQL1-3347	The Best of Mancini, Volume 3	1979	$12
❏ LSP-4049	The Big Latin Band of Henry Mancini	1968	$18
❏ LPM-2147 [M]	The Blues and the Beat	1960	$30
❏ LSP-2147 [S]	The Blues and the Beat	1960	$30
❏ LPM-2897 [M]	The Concert Sound of Henry Mancini	1964	$15
❏ LSP-2897 [S]	The Concert Sound of Henry Mancini	1964	$18
❏ LPM-3402 [M]	The Great Race	1965	$15
❏ LSP-3402 [S]	The Great Race	1965	$18
❏ LPM-3356 [M]	The Latin Sound of Henry Mancini	1965	$15
❏ LSP-3356 [S]	The Latin Sound of Henry Mancini	1965	$18
❏ LSP-4689	The Mancini Generation	1972	$15
❏ LPM-3943 [M]	The Mancini Sound	1968	$25
❏ LSP-3943 [S]	The Mancini Sound	1968	$18
❏ LPM-2101 [M]	The Mancini Touch	1959	$25
❏ LSP-2101 [S]	The Mancini Touch	1959	$30
❏ LSP-4350	Theme from "Z" and Other Film Music	1970	$18
❏ LPM-1956 [M]	The Music from Peter Gunn	1959	$40
—Original cover is a "block" design with "Peter Gunn" at top			
❏ LPM-1956 [M]	The Music from Peter Gunn	1959	$50
—First reissue cover is green/blue on front with huge "Peter Gunn" in center; back cover has a figure with a gun and a small photo of Henry Mancini at the lower left positioned so that it appears the gun is aimed at his head; catalog number on back cover is followed by "RE			
❏ LSP-1956 [S]	The Music from Peter Gunn	1959	$150
—Original cover is a "block" design with "Peter Gunn" at top			
❏ LSP-1956 [S]	The Music from Peter Gunn	1959	$75
—First reissue cover is green/blue on front with huge "Peter Gunn" in center; back cover has a figure with a gun and a small photo of Henry Mancini at the lower left positioned so that it appears the gun is aimed at his head; catalog number on back cover is followed by "RE			
❏ LPM-1956 [M]	The Music from Peter Gunn	1959	$30
—Second reissue cover is green/blue on front with huge "Peter Gunn" in center; back cover has a figure with a gun and a large photo of Henry Mancini at the upper left; catalog number on back is followed by "RE 2			
❏ LSP-1956 [S]	The Music from Peter Gunn	1959	$35
—Second reissue cover is green/blue on front with huge "Peter Gunn" in center; back cover has a figure with a gun and a large photo of Henry Mancini at the upper left; catalog number on back is followed by "RE 2			
❏ LPM-2795 [M]	The Pink Panther	1964	$35
❏ LSP-2795 [S]	The Pink Panther	1964	$50
❏ AQL1-3052	The Theme Scene	1978	$12
❏ VPS-6029	This Is Henry Mancini	1970	$25
❏ VPS-6053	This Is Henry Mancini, Volume 2	1972	$25
❏ LPM-3802 [M]	Two for the Road	1967	$25
❏ LSP-3802 [S]	Two for the Road	1967	$18
❏ LPM-2692 [M]	Uniquely Mancini	1963	$18
❏ LSP-2692 [S]	Uniquely Mancini	1963	$25
❏ ABL1-0231	Visions of Eight	1973	$15

Number	Title	Yr	NM
❏ LPM-3648 [M]	What Did You Do in the War, Daddy?	1966	$15
❏ LSP-3648 [S]	What Did You Do in the War, Daddy?	1966	$18
SUNSET			
❏ SUM-1105 [M]	Sounds and Voices	1966	$15
❏ SUS-5105 [S]	Sounds and Voices	1966	$15
UNITED ARTISTS			
❏ UAS-5210	The Hawaiians	1970	$15
❏ SW-93297	The Hawaiians	1970	$25
—Capitol Record Club edition			
❏ UA-LA694-G	The Pink Panther Strikes Again	1976	$20
WARNER BROS.			
❏ BSK3399	10	1979	$18
❏ W1491 [M]	Marches	1963	$18
❏ WS1491 [S]	Marches	1963	$25
❏ W1312 [M]	March Step in Hi-Fi	1959	$25
❏ WS1312 [S]	March Step in Stereo	1959	$30
❏ W1465 [M]	Sousa's Greatest Marches	1962	$18
❏ WS1465 [S]	Sousa's Greatest Marches	1962	$25
❏ BS2700	The Thief Who Came to Dinner	1973	$18

MANCUSO, GUS

Number	Title	Yr	NM
FANTASY			
❏ 3223 [M]	Introducing Gus Mancuso	1956	$75
—Red vinyl			
❏ 3223 [M]	Introducing Gus Mancuso	1956	$40
—Black vinyl			
❏ 3282 [M]	Music from New Faces	1958	$40
—Red vinyl			
❏ 3282 [M]	Music from New Faces	1958	$30
—Black vinyl			
❏ 8025 [S]	Music from New Faces	1960	$30
—Blue vinyl			
❏ 8025 [S]	Music from New Faces	1960	$35
—Black vinyl			

MANDEL, HARVEY

Number	Title	Yr	NM
EDITIONS EG			
❏ CAROL-1535-1	Cristo Redentor	198?	$12
—Reissue of Philips 600-281			
JANUS			
❏ JLS-3017	Baby Batter	1970	$25
❏ JSX-3067	Feel the Sound of Harvey Mandel	1974	$25
❏ JLS-3047	Shangrenade	1973	$25
❏ JXS-7014	The Best of Harvey Mandel	1975	$18
❏ JLS-3037	The Snake	1972	$25
OVATION			
❏ OV-1415	Get Off in Chicago	1971	$18
PHILIPS			
❏ PHS600281	Cristo Redentor	1969	$30
❏ PHS600325	Games Guitars Play	1970	$30
❏ PHS600306	Righteous	1969	$30

MANDEL, MIKE

Number	Title	Yr	NM
VANGUARD			
❏ VSD-79409	Sky Music	1978	$30
❏ VSD-79437	Utopia Parkway	1979	$30

MANDO AND THE CHILI PEPPERS

Number	Title	Yr	NM
GOLDEN CREST			
❏ CR-3023 [M]	On the Road with Rock and Roll	1957	$500

MANDRAKE MEMORIAL

Number	Title	Yr	NM
POPPY			
❏ PYS40002 [B]	Mandrake Memorial	1968	$50
❏ PYS40003	Medium	1969	$40
❏ PYS40006	Puzzle	1970	$40

MANDRELL, BARBARA, AND LEE GREENWOOD

Number	Title	Yr	NM
MCA			
❏ 5477	Meant for Each Other	1984	$10

MANDRELL, BARBARA

Number	Title	Yr	NM
ABC			
❏ AB-1088	Moods	1978	$15
❏ AB-1119	The Best of Barbara Mandrell	1979	$15
ABC DOT			
❏ DO-2076	Lovers, Friends and Strangers	1977	$15
❏ DO-2098	Love's Ups and Downs	1977	$15
❏ DOSD-2067	Midnight Angel	1976	$15
❏ DOSD-2045	This Is Barbara Mandrell	1976	$15
CAPITOL			
❏ C1-90416	I'll Be Your Jukebox Tonight	1988	$12
❏ C1-91977	Morning Sun	1990	$15
COLUMBIA			
❏ FC37437	Looking Back	1982	$12
❏ PC37437	Looking Back	198?	$10
—Budget-line reissue			

Number	Title	Yr	NM
❏ PC34876	The Best of Barbara Mandrell	1977	$15
—No bar code on cover			
❏ PC34876	The Best of Barbara Mandrell	198?	$10
—Reissue with bar code on cover			
❏ KC32743	The Midnight Oil	1973	$18
❏ PC32743	The Midnight Oil	198?	$10
—Budget-line reissue			
❏ KC32959 [B]	This Time I Almost Made It	1974	$18
❏ C30967	Treat Him Right	1971	$25
COLUMBIA LIMITED EDITION			
❏ LE10550	Treat Him Right	197?	$12
EMI AMERICA			
❏ ET-46956	Sure Feels Good	1987	$12
MCA			
❏ 5243	Barbara Mandrell Live	1981	$12
❏ 37224	Barbara Mandrell Live	198?	$10
—Budget-line reissue			
❏ 5519	Christmas at Our House	1984	$15
❏ 5474	Clean Cut	1984	$12
❏ 5619	Get to the Heart	1985	$12
❏ 5566	Greatest Hits	1985	$12
❏ 5330	He Set My Life to Music	1982	$12
❏ 5295	…In Black and White	1982	$12
❏ 3165	Just for the Record	1979	$12
❏ 37173	Just for the Record	198?	$10
—Budget-line reissue			
❏ 5136	Love Is Fair	1980	$12
❏ 673	Lovers, Friends and Strangers	198?	$10
—Reissue of ABC Dot 2076			
❏ 674	Love's Ups and Downs	198?	$10
—Reissue of ABC Dot 2098			
❏ 641	Midnight Angel	198?	$10
—Reissue of ABC Dot 2067			
❏ 3280	Moods	1980	$10
—Reissue of ABC 1088			
❏ 37202	Moods	198?	$10
—Budget-line reissue			
❏ 5377	Spun Gold	1983	$12
❏ 672	This Is Barbara Mandrell	198?	$10
—Reissue of ABC Dot 2045			
PAIR			
❏ PDL1-1079	The Best of Barbara Mandrell	1986	$15
TIME-LIFE			
❏ STW-104	Country Music	1981	$12

MANDRELL, LOUISE, AND R.C. BANNON

Number	Title	Yr	NM
RCA VICTOR			
❏ AHL1-4059	Me and My RC	1982	$12
❏ AHL1-4377	(You're My) Super Woman/ (You're My) Incredible Man	1982	$12

MANDRELL, LOUISE

Number	Title	Yr	NM
EPIC			
❏ FE37242	Louise Mandrell	1981	$12
❏ PE37242	Louise Mandrell	198?	$10
—Budget-line reissue			
RCA			
❏ 5622-1-R	Dreamin'	1987	$12
❏ 6714-1-R	The Best of Louise Mandrell	1988	$10
RCA VICTOR			
❏ MHL1-8601 [EP]	Close Up	1983	$10
❏ AHL1-5015	I'm Not Through Loving You Yet	1984	$12
❏ AHL1-5454	Maybe My Baby	1985	$12
❏ AHL1-4820	Too Hot to Sleep	1983	$12
❏ AYL1-5434	Too Hot to Sleep	1985	$10
—Best Buy Series" reissue			

MANDRILL

Number	Title	Yr	NM
ARISTA			
❏ AL9527	Getting In the Mood	1980	$12
❏ AL4195	New Worlds	1978	$12
❏ AL4144	We Are One	1977	$12
LIBERTY			
❏ LN-10196	Rebirth	1983	$10
MONTAGE			
❏ ST-72008	Energize	1982	$15
POLYDOR			
❏ PD-5043 [B]	Composite Truth	1973	$18
❏ PD-5059 [B]	Just Outside of Town	1973	$18
❏ 24-4060 [B]	Mandrill	1971	$18
❏ PD-2-9002	Mandrilland	1976	$18
❏ PD-5025 [B]	Mandrill Is	1972	$18
❏ PD-1-6047	The Best of Mandrill	1975	$15
UNITED ARTISTS			
❏ UA-LA577-G	Beast from the East	1976	$15
❏ UA-LA408-G	Solid	1975	$15

MANETTA, FESS

Number	Title	Yr	NM
JAZZOLOGY			
❏ JCE-6	Whorehouse Piano	198?	$25

MANGELSDORF, ALBERT

Number	Title	Yr	NM
ENJA			
❏ 2006	Live in Tokyo	1974	$35
PACIFIC JAZZ			
❏ PJ-10095	Now, Jazz Ramwong	1966	$30
❏ ST-20095 [S]	Now, Jazz Ramwong	1966	$35
PAUSA			
❏ 7091	Hamburger Idylle	198?	$25
❏ 7055	Triologue	197?	$25

MANGIONE, CHUCK

Number	Title	Yr	NM
A&M			
❏ SP-4911	70 Miles Young	1982	$25
❏ SP-3237	70 Miles Young	198?	$10
—Budget-line reissue			
❏ SP-6701	An Evening of Magic -- Chuck Mangione Live at the Hollywood Bowl	1979	$30
❏ SP-4557	Bellavia	1975	$25
❏ QU-54557 [Q]	Bellavia	1975	$75
❏ SP-3172	Bellavia	198?	$10
—Budget-line reissue			
❏ SP-4518	Chase the Clouds Away	1975	$25
❏ QU-54518 [Q]	Chase the Clouds Away	1975	$75
❏ SP-3115	Chase the Clouds Away	198?	$10
—Budget-line reissue			
❏ SP-6700	Children of Sanchez	1978	$30
❏ SP-4658	Feels So Good	1977	$25
❏ SP-3219	Feels So Good	198?	$10
—Budget-line reissue			
❏ SP-3715	Fun and Games	1980	$25
❏ SP-3193	Fun and Games	1983	$10
—Budget-line reissue			
❏ SP-4612	Main Squeeze	1976	$25
❏ SP-3220	Main Squeeze	198?	$10
—Budget-line reissue			
❏ SP-6513	Tarantella	1981	$30
❏ SP-3282	The Best of Chuck Mangione	1985	$25
COLUMBIA			
❏ FC39479	Disguise	1984	$25
❏ FC40984	Eyes of the Veiled Temptress	1988	$25
❏ FC38686	Journey to a Rainbow	1983	$25
❏ PC38686	Journey to a Rainbow	1986	$10
—Budget-line reissue			
❏ FC38101	Love Notes	1982	$25
❏ PC38101	Love Notes	198?	$10
—Budget-line reissue			
❏ FC40254	Save Tonight for Me	1986	$25
FANTASY			
❏ OJC-495	Recuerdo	1991	$30
—Reissue of Jazzland 984			
JAZZLAND			
❏ JLP-84 [M]	Recuerdo	1962	$40
❏ JLP-984 [S]	Recuerdo	1962	$150
MERCURY			
❏ SRM-1-650	Alive!	1973	$30
❏ 824301-1	Alive!	198?	$20
—Reissue of 650			
❏ SRM-1-1050	Encore/The Chuck Mangione Concerts	1975	$25
❏ SRM-2-800	Friends & Love – A Chuck Mangione Concert	1971	$35
❏ SRM-1-681	Friends & Love/Highlights	1973	$30
❏ SRM-1-684	Land of Make Believe	1973	$30
❏ SRM-2-8601	The Best of Chuck Mangione	1978	$30
❏ SRM-1-631	The Chuck Mangione Quartet	1972	$30
❏ SRM-2-7501	Together: A New Chuck Mangione Concert	1971	$35
MILESTONE			
❏ 47042	Jazz Brother	1977	$30
—Reissue of material issued by "The Jazz Brothers			
MOBILE FIDELITY			

Number	Title	Yr	NM
❑ Jan-0068 [B]	Feels So Good	1981	$50
—Audiophile vinyl			

MANGIONE, GAP
A&M
Number	Title	Yr	NM
❑ SP-4762	Dancin' Is Makin' Love	1979	$25
❑ SP-4621	Gap Mangione!	197?	$25
❑ SP-3407	She and I	1974	$25
❑ SP-4694	Suite Lady	1978	$25

FEELS SO GOOD
❑ FSG9002	The Boys from Rochester	1987	$30

GRC
❑ 9001	Diana in the Autumn Wind	1968	$30

MERCURY
❑ SRM-1-647	Sing Along Junk	1972	$30

MANHATTAN JAZZ ALL-STARS, THE
COLUMBIA
❑ CL1426 [M]	Swinging Guys and Dolls	1960	$30
❑ CS8223 [S]	Swinging Guys and Dolls	1960	$30

MANHATTAN JAZZ SEPTETTE, THE
CORAL
❑ CRL57090 [M]	The Manhattan Jazz Septette	1956	$100

MANHATTAN RHYTHM KINGS
INNER CITY
❑ IC-1124	Manhattan Rhythm Kings	198?	$30

MANHATTAN TRANSFER
ATLANTIC
❑ 80104	Bodies and Souls	1983	$25
❑ 81233	Bop Doo-Wopp	1984	$30
❑ 81803	Brasil	1987	$25
❑ SD18183	Coming Out	1976	$25
❑ SD19258	Extensions	1979	$25
❑ 81723	Live	1987	$25
❑ SD16036	Mecca for Moderns	1981	$25
❑ SD19163	Pastiche	1978	$25
❑ SD19319	The Best of the Manhattan Transfer	1981	$25
❑ SD18133	The Manhattan Transfer	1975	$25
❑ 81266	Vocalese	1985	$25

CAPITOL
❑ ST-778	Jukin'	1971	$35
—With Gene Pistilli			
❑ ST-11405	Jukin'	1975	$25
—With Gene Pistilli; reissue of 778			
❑ SN-16223	Jukin'	198?	$20
—With Gene Pistilli; budget-line reissue			

COLUMBIA
❑ C47079	The Offbeat of Avenues	1991	$35

MOBILE FIDELITY
❑ 1-199	Extensions	1994	$150
—Audiophile vinyl			
❑ Jan-0022 [B]	Manhattan Transfer Live	1979	$40
—Audiophile vinyl			

MANHATTANS, THE (1)
CARNIVAL
❑ CMLP-201 [M]	Dedicated to You	1966	$300
❑ CSLP-201 [S]	Dedicated to You	1966	$500
❑ CMLP-202 [M]	For You and Yours	1967	$175
❑ CSLP-202 [S]	For You and Yours	1967	$300

COLLECTABLES
❑ COL-5135	Dedicated to You: Golden Carnival Classics, Part One	198?	$12
❑ COL-5136	For You and Yours: Golden Carnival Classics, Part Two	198?	$12

COLUMBIA
❑ JC36411	After Midnight	1980	$15
❑ PC35693	After Midnight	198?	$10
—Budget-line reissue			
❑ FC37156	Black Tie	1981	$12
❑ PC37156	Black Tie	198?	$10
—Budget-line reissue			
❑ FC38600	Forever By Your Side	1983	$12
❑ PC34450	It Feels So Good	1977	$15
—No bar code on back cover			
❑ PCQ34450 [Q]	It Feels So Good	1977	$30
❑ PC34450	It Feels So Good	198?	$10
—With bar code on back cover			
❑ JC35693	Love Talk	1979	$15
❑ JC36861	Manhattans Greatest Hits	1980	$15
❑ KC33064	That's How Much I Love You	1975	$18
❑ PC33820	The Manhattans	1976	$15
—No bar code on back cover			
❑ PC33820	The Manhattans	198?	$10
—With bar code on back cover			
❑ JC35252	There's No Good in Goodbye	1978	$15
❑ KC32444	There's No Me Without You	1973	$18
❑ PC32444	There's No Me Without You	198?	$10
—Budget-line reissue			

Number	Title	Yr	NM
❑ FC39277	Too Hot to Stop It	1985	$12

DELUXE
❑ 12004	A Million to One	1972	$30
❑ 12000	With These Hands	1971	$30

SOLID SMOKE
❑ 8007	Follow Your Heart	1981	$12

VALLEY VUE
❑ D1-72946	Sweet Talk	1989	$15

MANILLA ROAD
ROADSTER
❑ MR1003	Crystal Logic	1983	$50
❑ MR1001	Invasion	1980	$150
❑ MR1002	Metal	1982	$150

MANILOW, BARRY
ARISTA
❑ AL8-8254	2:00 A.M. Paradise Café	1984	$10
❑ AL9537	Barry	1980	$10
❑ AL8-8117	Barry	198?	$10
—Reissue of 9537			
❑ AL-8570	Barry Manilow	1989	$10
❑ AL8-8102	Barry Manilow/Greatest Hits, Vol. II	1983	$10
❑ AL8-8291	Barry Manilow/Greatest Hits, Vol. II	1985	$10
❑ AL4007	Barry Manilow I	1975	$12
—Revised version of Bell 1129 with new cover; "Could It Be Magic" especially is noticeably different between the Bell and Arista versions			
❑ AL8-8372	Barry Manilow I	1985	$10
❑ AB4007	Barry Manilow I	1977	$10
—Reissue of AL 4007 with new prefix			
❑ AL5-8153	Barry Manilow I	198?	$10
—Reissue of 8372			
❑ AL4016	Barry Manilow II	1975	$12
—Reissue of Bell 1314			
❑ AQ4016 [Q]	Barry Manilow II	1975	$20
❑ AL8-8370	Barry Manilow II	1985	$10
❑ AB4016	Barry Manilow II	1977	$10
—Reissue of AL 4016 with new prefix			
❑ AL5-8085	Barry Manilow II	198?	$10
—Reissue of 8370			
❑ AL8500	Barry Manilow/Live	1977	$15
❑ AL13-8049	Barry Manilow/Live	1983	$12
❑ AL-8644	Because It's Christmas	1990	$18
❑ AB4164	Even Now	1978	$10
❑ AL8-8322	Even Now	1985	$10
❑ AL5-8052	Even Now	198?	$10
—Reissue of 8322			
❑ A2L8601	Greatest Hits	1978	$15
❑ A2L8601 [PD]	Greatest Hits	1979	$40
—Entire contents on two picture discs (yes, it has the same number as the regular issue)			
❑ AL13-8039	Greatest Hits	1983	$12
❑ AL-8598	Greatest Hits, Vol. 1	1989	$12
❑ AL-8599	Greatest Hits, Vol. 2	1989	$12
❑ AL-8600	Greatest Hits, Vol. 3	1989	$12
❑ AL9610	Here Comes the Night	1982	$10
❑ AL8-8003	Here Comes the Night	198?	$10
—Reissue of 9610			
❑ AL9573	If I Should Love Again	1981	$10
❑ AL8-8123	If I Should Love Again	198?	$10
—Reissue of 9573			
❑ AL-8638	Live on Broadway	1990	$25
❑ NU9740	Manilow Magic	1982	$15
—Manufactured by K-Tel!			
❑ AB2500 [EP]	Oh, Julie!	1982	$25
❑ AL9505	One Voice	1979	$10
❑ AL5-8046	One Voice	198?	$10
—Reissue of 9505			
❑ AL-8527	Swing Street	1987	$10
❑ AL9-8274	The Manilow Collection -- 20 Classic Hits	1985	$10
❑ AL4090	This One's for You	1976	$12
❑ AL8-8331	This One's for You	1985	$10
❑ AB4090	This One's for You	1977	$10
—Reissue of AL 4090 with new prefix			
❑ AL5-8160	This One's for You	198?	$10
—Reissue of 8331			
❑ AQ4090 [Q]	This One's for You	1976	$30
❑ AL4060	Tryin' to Get the Feeling	1975	$12
❑ AQ4060 [Q]	Tryin' to Get the Feeling	1975	$20
❑ AL8-8336	Tryin' to Get the Feeling	1985	$10
❑ AL5-8070	Tryin' to Get the Feeling	198?	$10
—Reissue of 8336			
❑ AB4060	Tryin' to Get the Feeling	1977	$10
—Reissue of AL 4060 with new prefix			

BELL
❑ 1129	Barry Manilow	1973	$30
❑ 1314	Barry Manilow II	1974	$18

MOBILE FIDELITY
❑ Jan-0097 [B]	Barry Manilow I	1981	$35
—Audiophile vinyl			

RCA VICTOR
❑ AFL1-7044	Manilow	1985	$10

MANN, AIMEE
MOBILE FIDELITY
Number	Title	Yr	NM
❑ MFSL 1-278	Lost in Space	2003	$40
—Original Master Recording" at top of front cover			

MANN, BARRY
ABC-PARAMOUNT
❑ 399 [M]	Who Put the Bomp	1963	$120
❑ S-399 [S]	Who Put the Bomp	1963	$300

CASABLANCA
❑ NBLP7226	Barry Mann	1980	$12

NEW DESIGN
❑ Z30876	Lay It All Out	1971	$15

RCA VICTOR
❑ DJL1-1162 [DJ]	Flo and Eddie Interview Barry Mann	1975	$50
❑ APL1-0860	Survivor	1975	$15

MANN, CARL
PHILLIPS INT'L.
❑ PLP-1960 [M]	Like Mann	1960	$600

MANN, DAVID
ANTILLES
❑ 90628	Games	1988	$25
❑ 91050	Insight	1989	$30

MANN, ED
CMP
❑ CMP-38-ST	Get Up	1988	$25

MANN, HERBIE, AND BUDDY COLLETTE
INTERLUDE
❑ MO-503 [M]	Flute Fraternity	1959	$40
—Reissue of Mode 114			
❑ ST-1103 [S]	Flute Fraternity	1959	$75

MODE
❑ LP-114 [M]	Flute Fraternity	1957	$140

MANN, HERBIE, AND JOAO GILBERTO
ATLANTIC
❑ 8105 [M]	Herbie Mann and Joao Gilberto with Antonio Carlos Jobim	1965	$25
❑ SD8105 [S]	Herbie Mann and Joao Gilberto with Antonio Carlos Jobim	1965	$50

MANN, HERBIE, AND MACHITO
ROULETTE
❑ R-52122 [M]	Afro-Jazziac	1963	$35
❑ SR-52122 [S]	Afro-Jazziac	1963	$50

MANN, HERBIE
A&M
❑ LP-2003 [M]	Glory of Love	1967	$75
❑ SP-3003 [S]	Glory of Love	1967	$35
❑ SP9-3003	Glory of Love	1983	$50
—Audio Master Plus" reissue			

ATLANTIC
❑ 80077	Astral Island	1983	$25
❑ SD18209	Bird in a Silver Cage	1977	$25
❑ SD19169	Brazil -- Once Again	1978	$25
❑ SD1540	Concerto Grosso in D Blues	1969	$30
❑ SD1670	Discotheque	1975	$30
❑ 1397 [M]	Do the Bossa Nova with Herbie Mann	1962	$175
❑ SD1397 [S]	Do the Bossa Nova with Herbie Mann	1962	$175
❑ SD1658	First Light	1974	$30
❑ SD19112	Herbie Mann & Fire Island	1977	$25
❑ 1380 [M]	Herbie Mann at the Village Gate	1962	$175
❑ SD1380 [S]	Herbie Mann at the Village Gate	1962	$175
❑ 1413 [M]	Herbie Mann Live at Newport	1963	$50
❑ SD1413 [S]	Herbie Mann Live at Newport	1963	$50
❑ 1407 [M]	Herbie Mann Returns to the Village Gate	1963	$50
❑ SD1407 [S]	Herbie Mann Returns to the Village Gate	1963	$50
❑ 1454 [M]	Herbie Mann Today	1966	$35
❑ SD1454 [S]	Herbie Mann Today	1966	$50
❑ SD1632	Hold On, I'm Comin'	1973	$30
❑ QD1632 [Q]	Hold On, I'm Comin'	1973	$75
❑ 1475 [M]	Impressions of the Middle East	1967	$50
❑ SD1475 [S]	Impressions of the Middle East	1967	$35
❑ 1422 [M]	Latin Fever	1964	$35
❑ SD1422 [S]	Latin Fever	1964	$50
❑ SD1536	Live at the Whisky A-Go-Go	1969	$30
❑ SD1648	London Underground	1974	$30
❑ 8141 [M]	Mann and a Woman	1967	$50
❑ SD8141 [S]	Mann and a Woman	1967	$35
❑ SD16046	Mellow	1981	$25
❑ SD1522	Memphis Underground	1969	$30

Number	Title	Yr	NM
❏ SD1610	Mississippi Gambler	1972	$30
❏ 1462 [M]	Monday Night at the Village Gate	1966	$35
❏ SD1462 [S]	Monday Night at the Village Gate	1966	$50
❏ 1433 [M]	My Kinda Groove	1965	$35
❏ SD1433 [S]	My Kinda Groove	1965	$50
❏ 1471 [M]	New Mann at Newport	1967	$50
❏ SD1471 [S]	New Mann at Newport	1967	$35
❏ 1426 [M]	Nirvana	1964	$35
❏ SD1426 [S]	Nirvana	1964	$25
❏ 90141	Nirvana	1984	$25
❏ 1464 [M]	Our Mann Flute	1966	$35
❏ SD1464 [S]	Our Mann Flute	1966	$50
❏ SD1655	Reggae	1974	$30
❏ 1384 [M]	Right Now	1962	$175
❏ SD1384 [S]	Right Now	1962	$175
❏ 81285	See Through Spirits	1986	$25
❏ 1445 [M]	Standing Ovation at Newport	1965	$35
❏ SD1445 [S]	Standing Ovation at Newport	1965	$50
❏ SD19221	Super Mann	1979	$25
❏ SD1682	Surprises	1976	$30
❏ 1483 [M]	The Beat Goes On	1967	$50
❏ SD1483 [S]	The Beat Goes On	1967	$35
❏ SD1544	The Best of Herbie Mann	1970	$30
❏ 1343 [M]	The Common Ground	1960	$300
❏ SD1343 [S]	The Common Ground	1960	$300
❏ SD 2-300 [S]	The Evolution of Mann	1972	$35
❏ 2-300 [M]	The Evolution of Mann	1972	$40

—Mono is white label promo only with "d/j copy monaural" sticker on front cover

Number	Title	Yr	NM
❏ 1371 [M]	The Family of Mann	1961	$175
❏ SD1371 [S]	The Family of Mann	1961	$175
❏ 1490 [M]	The Herbie Mann String Album	1968	$75
❏ SD1490 [S]	The Herbie Mann String Album	1968	$35
❏ 1513 [M]	The Inspiration I Feel	1969	$75

—Mono is promo only

Number	Title	Yr	NM
❏ SD1513 [S]	The Inspiration I Feel	1969	$35
❏ 1437 [M]	The Roar of the Greasepaint, The Smell of the Crowd	1965	$35
❏ SD1437 [S]	The Roar of the Greasepaint, The Smell of the Crowd	1965	$50
❏ SD1642	Turtle Bay	1973	$30
❏ SD1497	Wailing Dervishes	1968	$35
❏ SD1676	Waterbed	1975	$30
❏ SD1507	Windows Open	1969	$30
❏ SD19252	Yellow Fever	1980	$25

BETHLEHEM
Number	Title	Yr	NM
❏ BCP-6011	Early Mann	1976	$25

—Reissue of older material; distributed by Caytronics

Number	Title	Yr	NM
❏ BCP-1018 [10]	East Coast Jazz 4	1954	$300
❏ BCP-24 [M]	Flamingo, My Goodness — Four Flutes, Vol. 2	1955	$300
❏ BCP-58 [M]	Herbie Mann Plays	1956	$300
❏ BCP-63 [M]	Love and the Weather	1956	$175
❏ BCP-6067 [M]	The Epitome of Jazz	1963	$250
❏ BCP-40 [M]	The Herbie Mann-Sam Most Quintet	1956	$300
❏ BCP-6020 [M]	The Mann with the Most	1960	$300

COLUMBIA
Number	Title	Yr	NM
❏ CS1068	Big Boss	1970	$30
❏ CL2388 [M]	Latin Mann	1965	$35
❏ CS9188 [S]	Latin Mann	1965	$50

COLUMBIA SPECIAL PRODUCTS
Number	Title	Yr	NM
❏ JCS9188	Latin Mann	197?	$30

—Part of "Jazz Greats" Collectors' Series

EMBRYO
Number	Title	Yr	NM
❏ 531	Memphis Two-Step	1971	$30
❏ 526	Muscle Shoals Nitty Gritty	1970	$30
❏ 532	Push Push	1971	$30
❏ 520	Stone Flute	1970	$30

EPIC
Number	Title	Yr	NM
❏ LN3499 [M]	Herbie Mann with the Ilcken Trio	1958	$300
❏ LN3395 [M]	Salute to the Flute	1957	$300

FINNADAR
Number	Title	Yr	NM
❏ 9014	Gagaku and Beyond	197?	$25

HERBIE MANN MUSIC
Number	Title	Yr	NM
❏ HMM-1	Herbie Mann Music	1981	$75

—Direct-to-disc recording

JAZZLAND
Number	Title	Yr	NM
❏ JLP-5 [M]	Herbie Mann Quintet	1960	$75

—Reissue of Riverside 245

MILESTONE
Number	Title	Yr	NM
❏ 47010	Let Me Tell You	1973	$30

NEW JAZZ
Number	Title	Yr	NM
❏ NJLP-8211 [M]	Just Walkin'	1958	$250

—Purple label

Number	Title	Yr	NM
❏ NJLP-8211 [M]	Just Walkin'	1964	$175

—Blue label with trident logo

PRESTIGE
Number	Title	Yr	NM
❏ PRLP-7124 [M]	Flute Flight	1957	$150
❏ PRLP-7101 [M]	Flute Souffle	1957	$150
❏ PRST-7659	Herbie Mann in Sweden	1969	$30
❏ PRLP-7136 [M]	Mann in the Morning	1958	$300
❏ PRLP-7432 [M]	The Best of Herbie Mann	1965	$35

Number	Title	Yr	NM
❏ PRST-7432 [R]	The Best of Herbie Mann	1965	$30

RIVERSIDE
Number	Title	Yr	NM
❏ RLP 12-245 [M]	Great Ideas of Western Mann	1957	$300
❏ 6084	Great Ideas of Western Mann	197?	$25
❏ S-3029	Moody Mann	1969	$150
❏ RLP 12-234 [M]	Sultry Serenade	1957	$300

—Blue on white label

Number	Title	Yr	NM
❏ RLP 12-234 [M]	Sultry Serenade	1958	$300

—Blue label with reel and microphone logo

SAVOY
Number	Title	Yr	NM
❏ MG-12102 [M]	Flute Suite	1957	$150
❏ MG-12107 [M]	Mann Alone	1957	$150
❏ MG-12108 [M]	Yardbird Suite	1957	$150

SAVOY JAZZ
Number	Title	Yr	NM
❏ SJL-1102	Be Bop Synthesis	197?	$25

SOLID STATE
Number	Title	Yr	NM
❏ SS-18020	Jazz Impressions of Brazil	1968	$30
❏ SS-18023	St. Thomas	1968	$30

SURREY
Number	Title	Yr	NM
❏ S-1015 [M]	Big Band	1965	$35
❏ SS-1015 [S]	Big Band	1965	$50

TRIP
Number	Title	Yr	NM
❏ 5031	Super Mann	1974	$25

UNITED ARTISTS
Number	Title	Yr	NM
❏ UAL-4042 [M]	African Suite	1959	$75
❏ UAS-5042 [S]	African Suite	1959	$40
❏ UAJ-14009 [M]	Brasil, Bossa Nova and Blue	1962	$75
❏ UAJS-15009 [S]	Brasil, Bossa Nova and Blue	1962	$40
❏ UAS-5638	Brazil Blues	1972	$30
❏ UAJ-14022 [M]	St. Thomas	1962	$75
❏ UAJS-15022 [S]	St. Thomas	1962	$40

VERVE
Number	Title	Yr	NM
❏ VSP-19 [M]	Big Band Mann	1966	$35
❏ VSPS-19 [R]	Big Band Mann	1966	$30
❏ VSP-8 [M]	Bongo, Conga and Flute	1966	$35
❏ VSPS-8 [R]	Bongo, Conga and Flute	1966	$30
❏ V6-8821	Et Tu Flute	1973	$35
❏ MGV-8336 [M]	Flautista! -- Herbie Mann Plays Afro-Cuban Jazz	1959	$150
❏ MGVS-6074 [S]	Flautista! -- Herbie Mann Plays Afro-Cuban Jazz	1960	$120
❏ V-8336 [M]	Flautista! -- Herbie Mann Plays Afro-Cuban Jazz	1961	$50
❏ V6-8336 [S]	Flautista! -- Herbie Mann Plays Afro-Cuban Jazz	1961	$35
❏ MGV-8392 [M]	Flute, Brass, Vibes and Percussion	1960	$120
❏ V-8392 [M]	Flute, Brass, Vibes and Percussion	1961	$50
❏ MGV-8247 [M]	The Magic Flute of Herbie Mann	1958	$120
❏ V-8247 [M]	The Magic Flute of Herbie Mann	1961	$50
❏ V-8527 [M]	The Sound of Mann	1963	$50
❏ V6-8527 [S]	The Sound of Mann	1963	$35

MANN, JOHNNY, SINGERS
EPIC
Number	Title	Yr	NM
❏ KE31954	Stand Up and Cheer!	1973	$15

LIBERTY
Number	Title	Yr	NM
❏ LRP-3134 [M]	Alma Mater	1959	$18
❏ LST-7134 [S]	Alma Mater	1959	$25
❏ LRP-3198 [M]	Ballads of the King	1961	$18
❏ LST-7198 [S]	Ballads of the King	1961	$25
❏ LRP-3217 [M]	Ballads of the King, Volume 2	1961	$18
❏ LST-7217 [S]	Ballads of the King, Volume 2	1961	$25
❏ LRP-3447 [M]	Daydream	1966	$15
❏ LST-7447 [S]	Daydream	1966	$18
❏ LST-7629	Golden	1969	$15
❏ LRP-3253 [M]	Golden Folk Song Hits	1963	$15
❏ LST-7253 [S]	Golden Folk Song Hits	1963	$18
❏ LRP-3296 [M]	Golden Folk Song Hits, Volume 2	1963	$15
❏ LST-7296 [S]	Golden Folk Song Hits, Volume 2	1963	$18
❏ LRP-3355 [M]	Golden Folk Song Hits, Volume 3	1964	$15
❏ LST-7355 [S]	Golden Folk Song Hits, Volume 3	1964	$18
❏ LRP-3411 [M]	If I Loved You	1965	$15
❏ LST-7411 [S]	If I Loved You	1965	$18
❏ LRP-3436 [M]	I'll Remember You	1965	$15
❏ LST-7426 [S]	I'll Remember You	1965	$18
❏ LRP-3387 [M]	Invisible Tears	1964	$15
❏ LST-7387 [S]	Invisible Tears	1964	$18
❏ LRP-3149 [M]	Roar Along with the Singing Twenties	1960	$18
❏ LST-7149 [S]	Roar Along with the Singing Twenties	1960	$25
❏ LRP-3156 [M]	Swing Along with the Singing Thirties	1960	$18
❏ LST-7156 [S]	Swing Along with the Singing Thirties	1960	$25
❏ LRP-3391 [M]	The Ballad Sound (Beatle Songs)	1964	$18
❏ LST-7391 [S]	The Ballad Sound (Beatle Songs)	1964	$25
❏ LMM-13017 [M]	The Great Bands with Great Voices Swing the Great Voices of the Great Bands	1962	$18

Number	Title	Yr	NM
❏ LSS-14017 [S]	The Great Bands with Great Voices Swing the Great Voices of the Great Bands	1962	$25
❏ LRP-3523 [M]	We Can Fly! Up-Up and Away	1967	$15
❏ LST-7523 [S]	We Can Fly! Up-Up and Away	1967	$18
❏ LRP-3522 [M]	We Wish You a Merry Christmas	1967	$18
❏ LST-7522 [S]	We Wish You a Merry Christmas	1967	$18

SUNSET
Number	Title	Yr	NM
❏ SUS-5288	At Our Best	1970	$15
❏ SUS-5231	Country Style	1969	$15
❏ SUS-5196	Heart Full of Song	1968	$15
❏ SUM-1115 [M]	The Flowing Voices of the Johnny Mann Singers	196?	$12
❏ SUS-5115 [S]	The Flowing Voices of the Johnny Mann Singers	196?	$15

UNITED ARTISTS
Number	Title	Yr	NM
❏ UXS-87	The Johnny Mann Singers Superpak	1972	$18

MANN, LORENE
RCA VICTOR
Number	Title	Yr	NM
❏ LSP-4243	A Mann Named Lorene	1969	$18

MANN, MANFRED
ASCOT
Number	Title	Yr	NM
❏ AM-13024 [M]	Mann Made	1966	$40
❏ AS-16024 [S]	Mann Made	1966	$50
❏ AM-13021 [M]	My Little Red Book of Winners	1965	$40
❏ AS-16021 [S]	My Little Red Book of Winners	1965	$50
❏ AM-13018 [M]	The Five Faces of Manfred Mann	1965	$50
❏ AS-16018 [P]	The Five Faces of Manfred Mann	1965	$50
❏ AM-13015 [M]	The Manfred Mann Album	1964	$50
❏ AS-16015 [P]	The Manfred Mann Album	1964	$50

CAPITOL
Number	Title	Yr	NM
❏ SM-11688	The Best of Manfred Mann	1977	$12
❏ SN-16073	The Best of Manfred Mann	1980	$10

JANUS
Number	Title	Yr	NM
❏ JXS-3064	The Best of Manfred Mann	1974	$15

MERCURY
Number	Title	Yr	NM
❏ SR-61168	The Mighty Quinn	1968	$30

POLYDOR
Number	Title	Yr	NM
❏ 24-4013	Chapter Three	1970	$18

SUNDAZED
Number	Title	Yr	NM
❏ LP5454 [B]	Mann Made	2013	$30
❏ LP5453 [B]	My Little Red Book Of Winners	2013	$30
❏ LP5455 [B]	Pretty Flamingo	2013	$30
❏ LP5452 [B]	The Five Faces Of Manfred Mann	2013	$30
❏ LP5451 [B]	The Manfred Mann Album	2013	$30

UNITED ARTISTS
Number	Title	Yr	NM
❏ 94 [DJ]	Manfred Mann Interview	1966	$250

—Promotional album in plain white jacket

Number	Title	Yr	NM
❏ UAL3551 [M]	Manfred Mann's Greatest Hits	1966	$30
❏ UAS6551 [P]	Manfred Mann's Greatest Hits	1966	$40

—Do Wah Diddy Diddy," "Sha La La," "I Got You Babe" and "Satisfaction" are rechanneled.

Number	Title	Yr	NM
❏ UAL3549 [M]	Pretty Flamingo	1966	$30
❏ UAS6549 [S]	Pretty Flamingo	1966	$40

MANN, MANFRED'S, EARTH BAND
ARISTA
Number	Title	Yr	NM
❏ AL8194	Somewhere in Afrika	1983	$12

POLYDOR
Number	Title	Yr	NM
❏ PD-5050	Get Your Rocks Off	1973	$18
❏ PD-5031	Glorified, Magnified	1972	$18
❏ PD-5015	Manfred Mann's Earth Band	1971	$18
❏ PD-1-6019	Solar Fire	1974	$18

WARNER BROS.
Number	Title	Yr	NM
❏ BSK3302	Angel Station	1979	$12
❏ BSK3498	Chance	1980	$12
❏ BS2877	Nightingales and Bombers	1975	$15
❏ BS2826	The Good Earth	1974	$15
❏ BS2965	The Roaring Silence	1976	$15

—Orange cover

Number	Title	Yr	NM
❏ BSK3055	The Roaring Silence	1977	$12

—Blue cover; re-recording of "Spirit in the Night" is added

Number	Title	Yr	NM
❏ BSK3157	Watch	1978	$12

MANN, REV. COLUMBUS
TAMLA
Number	Title	Yr	NM
❏ T-227 [M]	They Shall Be Mine	1962	$4000

—VG value 2000; VG+ value 3000

WINGATE
Number	Title	Yr	NM
❏ 701 [M]	He Satisfies Me	196?	$900

Number	Title	Yr	NM

MANN, SHADOW
TOMORROW
| ❏ TPS-69001 | Come Live with Me | 1974 | $75 |

MANNA, CHARLIE
DECCA
❏ DL4213 [M]	Manna Live!!	1962	$30
❏ DL74213 [R]	Manna Live!!	1962	$18
❏ DL4159 [M]	Manna Overboard!!	1961	$30
❏ DL74159 [R]	Manna Overboard!!	1961	$18
VERVE
| ❏ V-15051 [M] | The Rise and Fall of the Great Society | 1966 | $15 |
| ❏ V6-15051 [S] | The Rise and Fall of the Great Society | 1966 | $18 |

MANNE, SHELLY
ABC IMPULSE!
| ❏ AS-20 [S] | 2 3 4 | 1968 | $250 |
— Black label with red ring
ATLANTIC
❏ 1469 [M]	Boss Sounds!	1967	$35
❏ SD1469 [S]	Boss Sounds!	1967	$30
❏ 8157 [M]	Daktari	1968	$30
❏ SD8157 [S]	Daktari	1968	$30
❏ 1487 [M]	Jazz Gunn	1967	$25
❏ SD1487 [S]	Jazz Gunn	1967	$30
CAPITOL
❏ T2313 [M]	Manne, That's Gershwin	1965	$85
❏ ST2313 [S]	Manne, That's Gershwin	1965	$40
❏ T2173 [M]	My Fair Lady" with Un-Original Cast	1964	$50
❏ ST2173 [S]	My Fair Lady" with Un-Original Cast	1964	$40
❏ SM-2173	My Fair Lady" with Un-Original Cast	1976	$25
— Reissue with new prefix
| ❏ T2610 [M] | Shelly Manne Sounds | 1966 | $75 |
| ❏ ST2610 [S] | Shelly Manne Sounds | 1966 | $50 |
CONCORD JAZZ
| ❏ CJ-21 | Perk Up | 1976 | $30 |
CONTEMPORARY
❏ C-3559 [M]	Bells Are Ringing	1958	$300
❏ S-7559 [S]	Bells Are Ringing	1959	$300
❏ M-3599 [M]	Checkmate	1961	$250
❏ S-7599 [S]	Checkmate	1961	$250
❏ C-3536 [M]	Concerto for Clarinet and Combo	1957	$300
❏ C-3533 [M]	Li'l Abner	1957	$300
❏ S-7533 [S]	Li'l Abner	1959	$300
❏ M-3593/4 [M]	Live! Shelly Manne and His Men at the Manne-Hole	1961	$250
❏ S-7593/4 [S]	Live! Shelly Manne and His Men at the Manne-Hole	1961	$250
❏ C-3527 [M]	Modern Jazz Performance of Songs from "My Fair Lady	1957	$300
❏ S-7527 [S]	Modern Jazz Performance of Songs from "My Fair Lady	1959	$350
❏ C-3519 [M]	More Swinging Sounds, Vol. 5	1957	$300
❏ M-3609 [M]	My Son, the Jazz Drummer!	1962	$250
❏ S-7609 [S]	My Son, the Jazz Drummer!	1962	$250
❏ M-3624 [M]	Outside	1966	$175
❏ S-7624 [S]	Outside	1966	$175
❏ C-3525 [M]	Shelly Manne and His Friends	1957	$300
❏ C-2503 [10]	Shelly Manne and His Men	1953	$300
❏ C-2511 [10]	Shelly Manne and His Men, Volume 2	1954	$300
❏ M-3577 [M]	Shelly Manne and His Men at the Black Hawk, Vol. 1	1960	$250
❏ S-7577 [S]	Shelly Manne and His Men at the Black Hawk, Vol. 1	1960	$250
❏ M-3578 [M]	Shelly Manne and His Men at the Black Hawk, Vol. 2	1960	$250
❏ S-7578 [S]	Shelly Manne and His Men at the Black Hawk, Vol. 2	1960	$250
❏ M-3579 [M]	Shelly Manne and His Men at the Black Hawk, Vol. 3	1960	$250
❏ S-7579 [S]	Shelly Manne and His Men at the Black Hawk, Vol. 3	1960	$250
❏ M-3580 [M]	Shelly Manne and His Men at the Black Hawk, Vol. 4	1960	$250
❏ S-7580 [S]	Shelly Manne and His Men at the Black Hawk, Vol. 4	1960	$250
❏ C-14018	Shelly Manne in Zurich	1986	$25
❏ C-3560 [M]	Shelly Manne Plays "Peter Gunn	1958	$300
❏ S-7025 [S]	Shelly Manne Plays "Peter Gunn	1959	$300
❏ M-3566 [M]	Son of Gunn	1959	$300
❏ S-7566 [S]	Son of Gunn	1959	$300
❏ M-5006 [M]	Sounds Unheard Of	1962	$250
❏ S-9006 [S]	Sounds Unheard Of	1962	$250
❏ C-3516 [M]	Swinging Sounds, Vol. 4	1956	$300
❏ S-7519 [S]	Swinging Sounds in Stereo	1959	$300
❏ C-3557 [M]	The Gambit	1958	$300
❏ S-7557 [S]	The Gambit	1959	$300
❏ C-2516 [10]	The Three	1954	$300
❏ M-3584 [M]	The Three and The Two	1960	$250
❏ C-2518 [10]	The Two	1954	$300
❏ C-3507 [M]	The West Coast Sound	1955	$250
DEE GEE
| ❏ 1003 [10] | Here's That Manne | 1952 | $300 |

DISCOVERY
| ❏ 909 | Manne, That's Gershwin! | 1986 | $25 |
— Reissue of Capitol ST 2313
| ❏ 783 | Rex | 1976 | $35 |
DOCTOR JAZZ
| ❏ FW38728 | Shelly Manne and His Friends | 1983 | $25 |
FANTASY
❏ OJC-336	Modern Jazz Performance of Songs from "My Fair Lady	198?	$25
❏ OJC-320	More Swinging Sounds, Vol. 5	198?	$25
❏ OJC-240	Shelly Manne and His Men at the Black Hawk, Vol. 1	198?	$25
❏ OJC-267	Swinging Sounds, Vol. 4	1987	$25
❏ OJC-176	The Three and The Two	198?	$25
❏ OJC-152	The West Coast Sound	198?	$25
FLYING DUTCHMAN
| ❏ FD-10150 | Signature: Shelly Manne & Co. | 1973 | $35 |
— Reissue of 1940s recordings in mono
GALAXY
| ❏ 5101 | Essence | 1978 | $30 |
| ❏ 5124 | French Concert | 1979 | $30 |
IMPULSE!
| ❏ A-20 [M] | 2 3 4 | 1962 | $160 |
| ❏ AS-20 [S] | 2 3 4 | 1962 | $250 |
MAINSTREAM
| ❏ MRL-375 | Mannekind | 1972 | $35 |
MCA
| ❏ 29073 | 2 3 4 | 1980 | $20 |
STEREO RECORDS
❏ S-7019 [S]	Li'l Abner	1958	$50
❏ S-7002 [S]	Modern Jazz Performance of Songs from "My Fair Lady	1958	$300
❏ S-7025 [S]	Shelly Manne Plays "Peter Gunn	1958	$50
❏ S-7007 [S]	Swinging Sounds in Stereo	1958	$100
❏ S-7030 [S]	The Gambit	1958	$50
TREND
❏ 526	Double Piano Jazz Quartet	1980	$30
❏ 527	Double Piano Jazz Quartet, Volume 2	1980	$30
❏ 525	Interpretations of Bach and Mozart	1980	$30

MANNE, SHELLY/BILL RUSSO
SAVOY
| ❏ MG-12045 [M] | Deep Purple | 1955 | $75 |

MANNHEIM STEAMROLLER
AMERICAN GRAMAPHONE
❏ AG-1988	A Fresh Aire Christmas	1988	$18
❏ AG355	Fresh Aire	1975	$12
❏ AG359	Fresh Aire II	1977	$12
❏ AG365	Fresh Aire III	1979	$12
❏ AG373	Fresh Aire Interludes	1981	$15
❏ AG370	Fresh Aire IV	1981	$12
❏ AG385	Fresh Aire V	1983	$12
❏ AG386	Fresh Aire VI	1986	$15
❏ AG-1984	Mannheim Steamroller Christmas	1984	$18
— There are at least two label variations (red and brown) and many cover variations ("American Gramaphone Records" along top edge, no bar code on back cover, bar-code sticker on back cover, bar code as part of the art on the back cover, various stickers on front including "Now Available in Sheet Music" and "Grammy Nominee"); as yet, there's no difference in value we can see between the variations
| ❏ AG2086 | Saving the Wildlife | 1986 | $12 |

MANNING, TERRY
ENTERPRISE
| ❏ ENS-1008 | Home Sweet Home | 1969 | $40 |

MANONE, WINGY
DECCA
| ❏ DL8473 [M] | Trumpet on the Wing | 1957 | $120 |
IMPERIAL
| ❏ LP-9190 [M] | Wingy Manone on the Jazzband Bus | 1962 | $200 |
| ❏ LP-12190 [S] | Wingy Manone on the Jazzband Bus | 1962 | $175 |
MCA
| ❏ 1364 | Jam and Jive | 1983 | $15 |
RCA VICTOR
| ❏ LPV-563 [M] | Wingy Manone, Volume 1 | 1969 | $50 |
STORYVILLE
| ❏ 4066 | Wingy Manone with Papa Bue's Viking Jazzband | 198? | $25 |
X
| ❏ LVA-3014 [10] | Wingy Manone, Vol. 1 | 1954 | $150 |

MANPOWER
See MAN.

MANSFIELD, JAYNE
20TH CENTURY
| ❏ FOX-3049 [M] | Jayne Mansfield Busts Up Las Vegas | 1961 | $250 |
MGM

Jayne Mansfield: Shakespeare, Tchaikovsky & Me

| ❏ E-4202 [M] | Shakespeare, Tchaikovsky and Me | 1964 | $40 |
| ❏ SE-4202 [S] | Shakespeare, Tchaikovsky and Me | 1964 | $75 |

MANSON, CHARLES
AWARENESS
| ❏ LP-2144 | Lie: The Love and Terror Cult | 197? | $40 |
| ❏ 08903-1056 | Lie: The Love and Terror Cult | 1987 | $25 |
ESP-DISK'
| ❏ 2003 [B] | Lie: The Love and Terror Cult | 1970 | $300 |

MANSON, MARILYN
NOTHING
| ❏ 069490790-1 | Holywood | 2000 | $35 |
| ❏ 90273 | Mechanical Animals | 1998 | $35 |
— One record on blue vinyl, the other on red; packaged in two separate cardboard covers in the same shrink wrap

MANTECA
DUKE STREET
| ❏ DSR31038 | Fire Me Up | 1987 | $30 |
— Made in Canada
| ❏ DSR31027 | No Heroes | 1986 | $30 |
— Made in Canada
| ❏ DSR31055 | Perfect Foot | 1989 | $35 |
— Made in Canada
READY
| ❏ LR 017 | Manteca | 198? | $35 |
— Made in Canada
| ❏ LR 050 | Strength in Numbers | 1985 | $35 |
— Made in Canada
SOUNDWINGS/DUKE STREET
| ❏ SW2111 | No Heroes | 1986 | $30 |

MANTILLA, RAY
INNER CITY
| ❏ IC-1052 | Mantilla | 1978 | $35 |
RED RECORD
| ❏ VPA-174 | Hands of Fire | 198? | $30 |

MANTLE, MICKEY
RCA VICTOR
| ❏ LPM-1704 [M] | My Favorite Hits | 1958 | $400 |

MANTLER, MICHAEL
ECM
| ❏ 23786 | Something There | 1984 | $25 |
WATT
| ❏ 3 | 13 & 3/4 | 197? | $25 |
| ❏ 4 [B] | Hapless Child | 1976 | $50 |
— musical settings to Edward Gorey stories
❏ 7	Movies	1978	$35
❏ 2	No Answer	197?	$25
❏ 5	Silence	197?	$25

MANTOVANI
BAINBRIDGE
| ❏ BT-6277 | Mantovani's Italia | 1988 | $10 |
| ❏ 8001 | The Magic of Mantovani: Live at the Royal Festival Hall | 1982 | $15 |
FLEETWOOD
| ❏ FMS1019 | 90 Minutes with Mantovani | 1978 | $15 |
— Side 1: Great Songs of Christmas (reissue of London

Number	Title	Yr	NM

recordings); Side 2: Great Songs for All Seasons

HOLIDAY

Number	Title	Yr	NM
❏ HDY1928	Holy Night	1981	$12

LONDON

Number	Title	Yr	NM
❏ LL3122/3 [M]	All-American Showcase	1959	$25
❏ PS165/6 [S]	All-American Showcase	1959	$30
❏ XPS906	All-Time Greatest Hits, Volume 1	1973	$12
❏ XPS915	American Encores	1976	$12
❏ LL3260 [M]	American Waltzes	1962	$12
❏ PS248 [S]	American Waltzes	1962	$15
❏ LL766 [M]	An Enchanted Evening with Mantovani	1953	$25
❏ XPS902	An Evening with Mantovani	1973	$12
❏ XPS610	Annunzio Paolo Mantovani (25th Anniversary)	1972	$15
❏ LL1502 [M]	Candlelight	195?	$18
❏ LL913 [M]	Christmas Carols	1953	$18
— Original recordings in mono			
❏ PS142 [S]	Christmas Carols	196?	$18
— Reissue with white back cover			
❏ LL913 [M]	Christmas Carols	1959	$15
— Mono versions of stereo re-recordings			
❏ PS142 [S]	Christmas Carols	1959	$25
— Originals have blue back cover, "Stereophonic" on upper left front cover and dark blue "FFSS" labels			
❏ BP720/1	Christmas Favorites	19??	$18
❏ LL3338 [M]	Christmas Greetings from Mantovani	1963	$15
❏ PS338 [S]	Christmas Greetings from Mantovani	1963	$18
❏ LL3269 [M]	Classical Encores	1963	$12
❏ PS269 [S]	Classical Encores	1963	$15
❏ LL3004 [M]	Concert Encores	1958	$18
❏ PS133 [S]	Concert Encores	1959	$25
❏ LL3095 [M]	Continental Encores	1959	$18
❏ PS147 [S]	Continental Encores	1959	$25
❏ PS921	Favorite Melodies from Opera	1978	$12
❏ LL1700 [M]	Film Encores	1957	$25
❏ PS124 [S]	Film Encores	1959	$18
❏ LL3117 [M]	Film Encores, Vol. 2	1959	$18
❏ PS164 [S]	Film Encores, Vol. 2	1959	$25
❏ LL3360 [M]	Folk Songs Around the World	1964	$12
❏ PS360 [S]	Folk Songs Around the World	1964	$15
❏ XPS585/6 [S]	From Monty with Love	1971	$18
❏ LL3032 [M]	Gems Forever	1958	$18
❏ PS106 [S]	Gems Forever	1959	$25
❏ LL1262 [M]	Gershwin: Concerto	1955	$25
❏ LL1262 [M]	Gershwin: Rhapsody in Blue	1955	$25
❏ PS570	Greensleeves	1970	$15
❏ LL570 [M]	Greensleeves (A Selection of Favorite Waltzes)	1952	$25
❏ XPS900	Gypsy Soul	1972	$12
❏ LL3239 [M]	Italia Mia	1961	$15
❏ PS232 [S]	Italia Mia	1961	$18
❏ PM55001 [M]	Kismet	1964	$15
❏ LL3295 [M]	Latin Rendezvous	1963	$12
❏ PS295 [S]	Latin Rendezvous	1963	$15
❏ LL1259 [M]	Lonely Ballerina (Musical Modes)	1956	$25
❏ LL3516 [M]	Mantovani/Hollywood	1967	$15
❏ PS516 [S]	Mantovani/Hollywood	1967	$15
❏ PS578 [S]	Mantovani In Concert	1970	$15
❏ LL3448 [M]	Mantovani Magic	1966	$12
❏ PS448 [S]	Mantovani Magic	1966	$15
❏ LL3328 [M]	Mantovani/Manhattan	1963	$12
❏ PS328 [S]	Mantovani/Manhattan	1963	$15
❏ PS542 [S]	Mantovani…Memories	1968	$15
❏ LL3422 [M]	Mantovani Ole	1965	$12
❏ PS422 [S]	Mantovani Ole	1965	$15
❏ LL3231 [M]	Mantovani Plays Music from Exodus and Other Great Themes	1960	$15
❏ PS224 [S]	Mantovani Plays Music from Exodus and Other Great Themes	1960	$18
❏ LL768 [M]	Mantovani Plays Tangos	1953	$25
❏ LL3483 [M]	Mantovani's Golden Hits	1967	$15
❏ PS483 [S]	Mantovani's Golden Hits	1967	$15
❏ 820085-1	Mantovani's Golden Hits	198?	$10
— Reissue of 483			
❏ SS1 [S]	Mantovani Stereo Showcase	1959	$25
❏ PS532 [S]	Mantovani/Tango	1968	$15
❏ 820333-1	Mantovani/Tango	198?	$10
— Reissue of 532			
❏ PS572 [S]	Mantovani Today	1970	$15
❏ LL3261 [M]	Moon River and Other Great Film Themes	1962	$12
❏ PS249 [S]	Moon River and Other Great Film Themes	1962	$15
❏ XPS914	More Golden Hits	197?	$12
❏ LL3474 [M]	Mr. Music…Mantovani	1966	$12
❏ PS474 [S]	Mr. Music…Mantovani	1966	$15
❏ APS907	Musical Moments	1974	$12
❏ LL1525 [M]	Music from the Ballet	1956	$25
❏ LL1513 [M]	Music from the Films	1956	$25
❏ PS112 [S]	Music from the Films	1959	$18
❏ LL1331 [M]	Operatic Arias	1955	$25
❏ LL3181 [M]	Operetta Memories	1960	$15
❏ PS202 [S]	Operetta Memories	1960	$18
❏ BP910/1	Romantic Hits	197?	$15
❏ LL979 [M]	Romantic Melodies	1954	$25
❏ LL1219 [M]	Song Hits from Theatreland	1955	$25
❏ PS125 [S]	Song Hits from Theatreland	1959	$18
❏ LL3251 [M]	Songs of Praise	1961	$12

Number	Title	Yr	NM
❏ PS245 [S]	Songs of Praise	1961	$15
❏ LL3149 [M]	Songs to Remember	1960	$15
❏ PS193 [S]	Songs to Remember	1960	$18
❏ LL3270 [M]	Stop the World--I Want to Get Off/Oliver	1962	$12
❏ PS270 [S]	Stop the World--I Want to Get Off/Oliver	1962	$15
❏ LL685 [M]	Strauss Waltzes	1953	$25
❏ PS118 [S]	Strauss Waltzes	1959	$25
❏ XPS917	Strictly Mantovani	1977	$12
❏ LL3136 [M]	The American Scene	1960	$15
❏ PS182 [S]	The American Scene	1960	$18
❏ XPS913	The Greatest Gift Is Love	197?	$12
❏ LL3392 [M]	The Incomparable Mantovani	1964	$12
❏ PS392 [S]	The Incomparable Mantovani	1964	$15
❏ 820334-1	The Incomparable Mantovani	198?	$10
— Reissue of 392			
❏ PS548 [S]	The Mantovani Scene	1969	$15
❏ LL3419 [M]	The Mantovani Sound -- Big Hits from Broadway and Hollywood	1965	$12
❏ PS419 [S]	The Mantovani Sound -- Big Hits from Broadway and Hollywood	1965	$15
❏ LL3526 [M]	The Mantovani Touch	1968	$18
❏ PS526 [S]	The Mantovani Touch	1968	$15
❏ LL3250 [M]	Themes from Broadway (Carnival)	1961	$15
❏ PS242 [S]	Themes from Broadway (Carnival)	1961	$18
❏ LL3123 [M]	The Music of Irving Berlin and Rudolf Friml	1959	$18
❏ PS166 [S]	The Music of Irving Berlin and Rudolf Friml	1959	$25
❏ LL1150 [M]	The Music of Rudolf Frimi	1955	$25
❏ LL3122 [M]	The Music of Victor Herbert and Sigmund Romberg	1959	$18
❏ PS165 [S]	The Music of Victor Herbert and Sigmund Romberg	1959	$25
❏ PS565 [S]	The World of Mantovani	1969	$15
❏ LL1748 [M]	The World's Favorite Love Songs	1957	$25
❏ LL3280 [M]	The World's Great Love Songs	1963	$12
❏ PS280 [S]	The World's Great Love Songs	1963	$15
❏ XPS598 [S]	To Lovers Everywhere U.S.A.	1971	$15
❏ PS119 [S]	Waltz Encores	1959	$25
❏ LL1452 [M]	Waltzes of Irving Berlin	1956	$25
❏ LL1094 [M]	Waltz Time	1954	$25

LONDON PHASE 4

Number	Title	Yr	NM
❏ SP-44043 [S]	Kismet	1964	$18
❏ BP44302/3	Million Sellers	1978	$15

MANZAREK, RAY
Also see THE DOORS; RICK AND THE RAVENS.

A&M

Number	Title	Yr	NM
❏ SP-4945	Carmina Burana	1984	$12

MERCURY

Number	Title	Yr	NM
❏ SRM-1-703	The Golden Scarab	1974	$15
❏ SRM-1-1014	The Whole Thing Started with Rock & Roll Now It's Out of Control	1975	$15

MAPHIS, JOE

COLUMBIA

Number	Title	Yr	NM
❏ CL1005 [M]	Fire on the Strings	1957	$150

HARMONY

Number	Title	Yr	NM
❏ HL7180 [M]	Hi-Fi Holiday for Banjo	1959	$30
❏ HS11032 [S]	Hi-Fi Holiday for Banjo	1959	$30

KAPP

Number	Title	Yr	NM
❏ KL-1347 [M]	Hootenanny Star	1964	$25
❏ KS-3347 [S]	Hootenanny Star	1964	$30

MACGREGOR

Number	Title	Yr	NM
❏ MGR-1205 [M]	King of the Strings	196?	$100

MOSRITE

Number	Title	Yr	NM
❏ MA-400 [M]	The New Sound of Joe Maphis	1967	$30
❏ MS-400 [S]	The New Sound of Joe Maphis	1967	$30

STARDAY

Number	Title	Yr	NM
❏ SLP-373 [M]	Country Guitar Goes to the Jimmy Dean Show	1966	$75
— Deduct 1/3 if instruction book is missing			
❏ SLP-316 [M]	King of the Strings	1966	$50

MAPHIS, JOE AND ROSE LEE

CAPITOL

Number	Title	Yr	NM
❏ T1778 [M]	Rose Lee and Joe Maphis	1962	$30
❏ ST1778 [S]	Rose Lee and Joe Maphis	1962	$40

STARDAY

Number	Title	Yr	NM
❏ SLP-322 [M]	Golden Gospel	1966	$30

Number	Title	Yr	NM
❏ SLP-286 [M]	Mr. and Mrs. Country Music	1964	$30

MAPHIS, ROSE LEE

COLUMBIA

Number	Title	Yr	NM
❏ CL1598 [M]	Rose Lee Maphis	1961	$35
❏ CS8398 [S]	Rose Lee Maphis	1961	$40

MAR-KEYS

ATLANTIC

Number	Title	Yr	NM
❏ 8062 [M]	Do the Pop-Eye with the Mar-Keys	1962	$75
❏ SD8062 [R]	Do the Pop-Eye with the Mar-Keys	1966	$40
❏ 8055 [M]	Last Night	1961	$150
— White "fan" logo on right			
❏ 8055 [M]	Last Night	1962	$100
— Black "fan" logo on right			
❏ SD8055 [R]	Last Night	1966	$75

STAX

Number	Title	Yr	NM
❏ STS-2025	Damifiknew	1969	$25
❏ STS-2036	Memphis Experience	1971	$25
❏ ST-707 [M]	The Great Memphis Sound	1966	$75
❏ STS-707 [R]	The Great Memphis Sound	1966	$40

MAR-KEYS/BOOKER T. AND THE MG'S
Also see each artist's individual listings.

STAX

Number	Title	Yr	NM
❏ ST-720 [M]	Back to Back	1967	$30
❏ STS-720 [S]	Back to Back	1967	$50

MARABLE, LAWRENCE

JAZZ WEST

Number	Title	Yr	NM
❏ LP-8 [M]	Tenor Man	1956	$2000
— Deep Groove			

MARAIS, JOSEPH, AND MIRANDA

DECCA

Number	Title	Yr	NM
❏ DL9047 [M]	Africana Suite and Songs of Spirit and Humor	1956	$30
❏ DL5268 [10]	Ballads of Many Lands	1950	$50
❏ DL9030 [M]	Christmas with Joseph and Miranda	1955	$30
❏ DL9026 [M]	Marais and Miranda In Person, Vol. 1	1955	$30
❏ DL9027 [M]	Marais and Miranda In Person, Vol. 2	1955	$30
❏ DL8711 [M]	Sundown Songs	1957	$30

MARAIS, JOSEPH

DECCA

Number	Title	Yr	NM
❏ DL5083 [10]	Songs from the Veld, Vol. 2	1950	$50
❏ DL5106 [10]	Songs of Many Lands	1950	$50
❏ DL5014 [10]	South African Veld	1949	$50

MARANATHA SINGERS, THE

MARANATHA!

Number	Title	Yr	NM
❏ MM 0071A	Emmanuel, A Christmas Praise Album	1980	$12

MARATHONS, THE (1)

ARVEE

Number	Title	Yr	NM
❏ A-428 [M]	Peanut Butter	1961	$180

MARBLE PHROGG, THE

DERRICK

Number	Title	Yr	NM
❏ 8868	The Marble Phrogg	1968	$1000

MARCEAU, MARCEL

GONE

Number	Title	Yr	NM
❏ LP1F	The Best of Marcel Marceau	196?	$50

MGM

Number	Title	Yr	NM
❏ SE-4	The Best of Marcel Marceau	196?	$40
— The above records are identical: 38 minutes of silence and 2 minutes of applause!			

Number	Title	Yr	NM

MARCELS, THE
COLPIX
❏ CP-416 [M] — Blue Moon — 1961 — $350
—Gold label
❏ CP-416 [M] — Blue Moon — 1963 — $120
—Blue label

MARCH, HAL
DOT
❏ DLP-3092 [M] — The Moods of March — 1958 — $30
❏ DLP-25092 [S] — The Moods of March — 1958 — $40
HAMILTON
❏ HLP-101 [M] — Hal March Conducts — 1960 — $18
❏ HLP-12101 [S] — Hal March Conducts — 1960 — $25
—Reissue of Dot LP

MARCH, LITTLE PEGGY
RCA VICTOR
❏ LPM-2732 [M] — I Will Follow Him — 1963 — $75
❏ LSP-2732 [S] — I Will Follow Him — 1963 — $100
❏ LPM-3883 [M] — No Foolin' — 1968 — $40
❏ LSP-3883 [S] — No Foolin' — 1968 — $30

MARCH, LITTLE PEGGY/BENNIE THOMAS
RCA VICTOR
❏ LPM-3408 [M] — In Our Fashion — 1965 — $40
❏ LSP-3408 [S] — In Our Fashion — 1965 — $50

MARCHAN, BOBBY
COLLECTABLES
❏ COL-5113 — Golden Classics — 198? — $12
SPHERE SOUND
❏ SSR-7004 [M] — There's Something on Your Mind — 1964 — $300

MARCUS, LEW
SAVOY
❏ MG-15006 [10] — Back Room Piano — 1951 — $50

MARCUS, STEVE
FLYING DUTCHMAN
❏ BDL1-1461 — Sometime Other Than Now — 1976 — $30
VORTEX
❏ 2009 — The Count's Rock Band — 1969 — $25
❏ 2013 — The Lord's Prayer — 1969 — $25
❏ 2001 — Tomorrow Never Knows — 1968 — $25

MARCUS, WADE
ABC IMPULSE!
❏ AS-9318 — Metamorphosis — 197? — $30

MARDIN, ARIF
ATLANTIC
❏ SD1661 — Journey — 1974 — $30

MARESCA, ERNIE
SEVILLE
❏ SV77001 [M] — Shout! Shout! Knock Yourself Out — 1962 — $120
❏ SV87001 [S] — Shout! Shout! Knock Yourself Out — 1962 — $250

MARGITZA, RICK
BLUE NOTE
❏ B1-92279 — Color — 1989 — $30

MARGOLIN, STUART
WARNER BROS.
❏ BSK3439 — And the Angel Sings — 1980 — $25

MARGULIS, CHARLIE
CARLTON
❏ LP 12-103 [M] — Marvelous Margulis — 1958 — $30
❏ STLP 12-103 [S] — Marvelous Margulis — 1959 — $30

MARIA, TANIA
CAPITOL
❏ C1-90966 — Forbidden Colors — 1988 — $25
CONCORD PICANTE
❏ CJP-200 — Come with Me — 1982 — $25
❏ CJP-230 — Love Explosion — 1984 — $25
❏ CJP-151 — Piquant — 1981 — $25
❏ CJP-175 — Taurus — 1982 — $25
❏ CJP-264 — The Real Tania Maria: Wild! — 1985 — $25
MANHATTAN
❏ ST-53045 — Lady from Barzil — 1986 — $25
❏ ST-53000 — Made in New York — 1985 — $25

MARIACHI BRASS, THE
WORLD PACIFIC
❏ WP-1839 [M] — A Taste of Tequila — 1966 — $150
❏ WPS-21839 [S] — A Taste of Tequila — 1966 — $150

❏ WP-1852 [M] — Double Shot — 1966 — $150
❏ WPS-21852 [S] — Double Shot — 1966 — $150
❏ WP-1842 [M] — Hats Off!!! — 1966 — $150
❏ WPS-21842 [S] — Hats Off!!! — 1966 — $150
❏ WP-1859 [M] — In the Mood — 1967 — $150
❏ WPS-21859 [S] — In the Mood — 1967 — $150

MARIAH
UNITED ARTISTS
❏ UA-LA493-G — Mariah — 1975 — $18

MARIANI
SONOBEAT
❏ HEC411/2 — Perpetuum Mobile — 197? — $2500
—Issued in generic white cover; the band and label names are stamped on the jacket, and each of the 50 copies is numbered and autographed by the members of the band; VG value 1000; VG+ value 1750

MARIANO, CHARLIE, AND JERRY DODGION
WORLD PACIFIC
❏ WP-1245 [M] — Beauties of 1918 — 1958 — $175

MARIANO, CHARLIE
ATLANTIC
❏ SD1608 — The Mirror — 197? — $35
BETHLEHEM
❏ BCP-25 [M] — Alto Sax for Young Moderns — 1956 — $500
❏ BCP-49 [M] — Charlie Mariano Plays Chloe — 1957 — $350
❏ BCP-1022 [10] — Charlie Mariano Sextet — 1955 — $350
CATALYST
❏ 7915 — Reflections — 197? — $35
CMP
❏ CMP-10-ST — Crystal Balls — 198? — $25
❏ CMP-2-ST — October — 198? — $25
ECM
❏ 1256 — Charlie Mariano with the Kamataka College of Percussion — 1985 — $30
FANTASY
❏ OJC-1745 — Charlie Mariano Boston All Stars — 1990 — $30
❏ 3-10 [10] — Charlie Mariano Sextet — 1953 — $180
IMPERIAL
❏ IMP-3006 [10] — Charlie Mariano Quintet Volume 1 — 1955 — $400
❏ IMP-3007 [10] — Charlie Mariano Quintet Volume 2 — 1955 — $250
INNER CITY
❏ IC-1024 — October — 1977 — $35
INTUITION
❏ C1-90787 — Mariano — 1988 — $25
PRESTIGE
❏ PRLP-130 [10] — Charlie Mariano — 1952 — $300
❏ PRLP-153 [10] — Charlie Mariano Boston All Stars — 1953 — $300
REGINA
❏ R-286 [M] — A Jazz Portrait of Charlie Mariano — 1963 — $30
❏ RS-286 [S] — A Jazz Portrait of Charlie Mariano — 1963 — $30

MARIENTHAL, ERIC
GRP
❏ GR-9586 — Round Trip — 1989 — $30
❏ GR-1052 — Voices of the Heart — 1988 — $25

MARINERS, THE
CADENCE
❏ CLP-1008 [M] — The Mariners Sing Spirituals — 1956 — $40
COLUMBIA
❏ CL609 [M] — Hymns — 1955 — $40

MARINO, FRANK, AND MAHOGANY RUSH
See MAHOGANY RUSH.

MARK-ALMOND
ABC
❏ D-945 — To the Heart — 1976 — $25
BLUE THUMB
❏ BTS27 — Mark-Almond — 1971 — $30
—Reissue of 8827
❏ BTS-8827 — Mark-Almond — 1971 — $35
❏ BTS32 — Mark-Almond II — 1971 — $30
❏ BTS50 — The Best of Mark-Almond — 1973 — $30
COLUMBIA
❏ KC32486 — Mark-Almond 73 — 1973 — $30
❏ KC31917 — Rising — 1972 — $30
❏ PC31917 — Rising — 198? — $20
—Budget-line reissue
❏ CG33648 — Rising/Mark-Almond 73 — 1976 — $35
HORIZON
❏ SP-730 — Other People's Rooms — 1978 — $25

MCA
❏ 711 — Mark-Almond II — 198? — $20
—Reissue of Blue Thumb 32
❏ 792 — The Best of Mark-Almond — 198? — $20
—Reissue of Blue Thumb 50
❏ 793 — To the Heart — 198? — $20
—Reissue of ABC 945
PACIFIC ARTS
❏ 7-142 — The Best of the Mark-Almond Band…Live — 1980 — $25

MARK & DIANE, THE HAWAIIANS
TEMPO
❏ R-7126 — Christmas Aloha — 1975 — $12

MARKAY, GRACE
CAPITOL
❏ ST2687 [S] — Grace Markay — 1967 — $18
❏ T2687 [M] — Grace Markay — 1967 — $25
UNITED ARTISTS
❏ UAS-6722 — Please Come Back — 1969 — $25

MARKETTS, THE
LIBERTY
❏ LRP-3226 [M] — Surfer's Stomp — 1962 — $40
—Add 20% if "Surfer's Stomp" instruction sheet is enclosed

❏ LST-7226 [S] — Surfer's Stomp — 1962 — $50
—Add 20% if "Surfer's Stomp" instruction sheet is enclosed
❏ LRP-3226 [M] — The Surfing Scene — 196? — $30
—Retitled version of above
❏ LST-7226 [S] — The Surfing Scene — 196? — $40
—Retitled version of above
MERCURY
❏ SRM-1-679 — AM, FM, Etc. — 1973 — $18
WARNER BROS.
❏ W1537 [M] — Out of Limits! — 1964 — $30
❏ WS1537 [S] — Out of Limits! — 1964 — $40
❏ W1642 [M] — The Batman Theme — 1966 — $40
❏ WS1642 [S] — The Batman Theme — 1966 — $50
❏ W1509 [M] — The Marketts Take to Wheels — 1963 — $40
❏ WS1509 [S] — The Marketts Take to Wheels — 1963 — $50
WORLD PACIFIC
❏ WP-1870 [M] — Sun Power — 1967 — $30
❏ WPS-21870 [S] — Sun Power — 1967 — $25

MARKEWICH, REESE
MODERN AGE
❏ MA-134 [M] — New Designs in Jazz — 1958 — $50

MARKHAM, JOHN
FAMOUS DOOR
❏ 121 — San Francisco Jazz — 1977 — $30

MARKHAM, PIGMEAT
CHESS
❏ LP-1467 [M] — Anything Goes — 1962 — $30
❏ LP-1521 [M] — Backstage — 1968 — $25
❏ LPS-1521 [S] — Backstage — 1968 — $25
❏ LPS-1534 — Bag — 1970 — $18
❏ LPS-1525 — Here Comes the Judge — 1968 — $25
❏ CH-9166 — Here Comes the Judge — 1985 — $12
—Reissue of 1525
❏ LPS-1529 — Hustlers — 1969 — $18
❏ LP-1505 [M] — If You Can't Be Good, Be Careful — 1966 — $18
❏ LPS-1505 [S] — If You Can't Be Good, Be Careful — 1966 — $25
❏ LP-1493 [M] — Mr. Funny Man — 1965 — $30
❏ LP-1515 [M] — Mr. Vaudeville — 1967 — $18
❏ LPS-1515 [S] — Mr. Vaudeville — 1967 — $25

Number	Title	Yr	NM
❑ LP-1484 [M]	Open the Door, Richard	1964	$30
❑ LP-1462 [M]	Pigmeat Markham At the Party	1962	$30
❑ LP-1517 [M]	Save Your Soul, Baby	1967	$25
❑ LPS-1517 [S]	Save Your Soul, Baby	1967	$25
❑ LP-1451 [M]	The Trial	1961	$30
❑ LP-1475 [M]	The World's Greatest Clown	1963	$30
❑ LP-1500 [M]	This'll Kill Ya	1965	$30
❑ LPS-1526	Tune Me In	1968	$18

JEWEL

❑ 5007	Crap-Shootin' Rev	1972	$15
❑ 5012	Will the Real Pigmeat Markham Please Sit Down	1973	$15

MARKIE, BIZ

COLD CHILLIN'

❑ 45261	All Samples Cleared!	1993	$18
❑ CDC5003	Biz's Baddest Beats	1995	$18
❑ CDC9001	Goin' Off	1995	$15

—Reissue of 25675

❑ 25675	Goin' Off	1988	$18
❑ CDC9000	I Need a Haircut	1995	$15

—Reissue with banned track, "Alone Again," deleted

❑ PRO-A-5179 [DJ]	I Need a Haircut	1991	$40

—Promo-only issue on vinyl; includes "Alone Again," which sampled the Gilbert O'Sullivan hit without authorization and resulted in the entire album's withdrawal from sale

❑ CDC9009	The Biz Never Sleeps	1995	$15

—Reissue of 26003

❑ 26003	The Biz Never Sleeps	1989	$18

LANDSPEED

❑ LSR8802	Best of Cold Chillin'	2000	$25

MARKLEY

FORWARD

❑ 1007	A Group	1969	$30

MARKOWITZ, MARKIE

FAMOUS DOOR

❑ 111	Marky's Vibes	197?	$35

MARKS, GUY

ABC

❑ 549 [M]	Hollywood Sings	1966	$18
❑ S-549 [S]	Hollywood Sings	1966	$18
❑ S-648	Loving You Has Made Me Bananas	1968	$25

MARKS, J., AND SHIPEN LEBZELTER

COLUMBIA MASTERWORKS

❑ M30006	First National Nothing	1970	$25
❑ MS7193	Rock and Other Four-Letter Words	1969	$30

MARLEY, BOB, AND THE WAILERS

ACCORD

❑ SN-7211	Jamaican Storm	1982	$12

CALLA

❑ ZX34760	Early Music	1977	$12

—Reissue of Record 2 of Calla 1240

❑ CAS-1240	The Birth of a Legend	1976	$18
❑ ZX34759	The Birth of a Legend	1977	$12

—Reissue of Record 1 of Calla 1240

CLEOPATRA

❑ 3397 [B]	Lee "Scratch" Perry Masters		$25
❑ 8235 [B]	Reggae Classics		$30

—picture disc

❑ 5541 [B]	Soul Rebel		$25
❑ CLP1830 [B]	Soul Revolution Part 2: Dub	2014	$25

COLUMBIA

❑ PZ34760	Early Music	198?	$10

—Budget-line reissue of Calla 34760

❑ PZ34759	The Birth of a Legend	198?	$10

—Budget-line reissue of Calla 34759

COTILLION

❑ SD5228	Chances Are	1981	$12

ISLAND

❑ 90029	Babylon by Bus	1983	$15
❑ ISLD11	Babylon by Bus	1978	$18

—Island distribution

❑ ISLD11	Babylon by Bus	1979	$15

—Warner Bros. distribution

❑ 90031	Burnin'	1983	$10
❑ SMAS-9338	Burnin'	1973	$25

—Capitol distribution

❑ ILPS9256	Burnin'	1974	$18

—Island distribution

❑ ILPS9256	Burnin'	1978	$15

—Warner Bros. distribution

❑ 5488941	Burnin'	2008	$25
❑ 90030	Catch a Fire	1983	$10
❑ SW-9329	Catch a Fire	1973	$150

—Cigarette lighter" cover with flip-open top; Capitol distribution

Number	Title	Yr	NM
❑ 462011	Catch a Fire	2009	$25

—Reissue with standard cover; Island distribution

❑ ILPS9241	Catch a Fire	1978	$15

—Reissue; Warner Bros. distribution

❑ 546404-1 [B]	Chant Down Babylon	1999	$25
❑ 90085	Confrontation	1983	$12
❑ 524419-1	Dreams of Freedom	1997	$15
❑ 90034	Exodus	1983	$10
❑ ILPS9498	Exodus	1977	$15

—Island distribution (all have multicolor labels)

❑ ILPS9498	Exodus	1978	$12

—Warner Bros. distribution

❑ 5318419	Exodus	2009	$25
❑ 90035	Kaya	1983	$10
❑ ILPS9517	Kaya	1978	$15

—Island distribution

❑ ILPS9517	Kaya	1979	$12

—Warner Bros. distribution

❑ 90169	Legend	1984	$12
❑ 5303052	Legend	2009	$25
❑ 90032	Live!	1983	$10
❑ ILPS9376	Live!	1975	$15

—Island distribution

❑ ILPS9376	Live!	1978	$12

—Warner Bros. distribution

❑ 90037	Natty Dread	1983	$10

—90029-90037 are reissues with Atco distribution

❑ ILPS9281	Natty Dread	1974	$18

—Island distribution

❑ ILPS9281	Natty Dread	1978	$15

—Warner Bros. distribution

❑ 90033	Rastaman Vibration	1983	$10
❑ ILPS9383 [DJ]	Rastaman Vibration	1976	$150

—Promotional package with burlap box and press kit

❑ ILPS9383	Rastaman Vibration	1976	$15

—Island distribution

❑ ILPS9383	Rastaman Vibration	1978	$12

—Warner Bros. distribution

❑ 90520	Rebel Music	1986	$12
❑ ILPS9542	Survival	1979	$15
❑ 90036	Uprising	1983	$10
❑ ILPS9596	Uprising	1980	$15

MOBILE FIDELITY

❑ 1-236	Catch a Fire	1995	$175

—Audiophile vinyl

❑ 1-221	Exodus	1995	$150

—Audiophile vinyl

TUFF GONG

❑ 846197-1	Babylon by Bus	1990	$18
❑ 846200-1	Burnin'	1990	$15
❑ 846201-1	Catch a Fire	1990	$15
❑ 846207-1	Confrontation	1990	$15
❑ 846208-1	Exodus	1990	$15
❑ 846209-1	Kaya	1990	$15
❑ 846210-1	Legend	1990	$15
❑ 846203-1	Live!	1990	$15
❑ 846204-1	Natty Dread	1990	$15
❑ 524103-1	Natural Mystic	1995	$18
❑ 846205-1	Rastaman Vibration	1990	$15
❑ 846206-1	Rebel Music	1990	$15
❑ 846202-1	Survival	1990	$15
❑ 848243-1	Talkin' Blues	1991	$15
❑ 846211-1	Uprising	1990	$15

UNIVERSAL

❑ 600753600689 [B]	Catch a Fire	2015	$25

MARLO, MICKI

ABC-PARAMOUNT

❑ 295 [M]	Married I Can Always Get	1959	$25
❑ S-295 [S]	Married I Can Always Get	1959	$30

MARLOW, JANET

CMG

❑ CML-8003	Outside the City	198?	$25

MARLOWE, MARION, AND FRANK PARKER

COLUMBIA

❑ CL576 [M]	Arthur Godfrey's TV Sweethearts	1954	$30

—Maroon label, gold print

MARLOWE, MEXIE

KING

❑ 799 [M]	Meet Mexie Marlowe	1962	$150

MARMALADE, THE

EPIC

❑ BN26553	The Best of the Marmalade	1970	$25

LONDON

❑ PS575 [B]	Reflections of My Life	1970	$30

MARMAROSA, DODO

ARGO

❑ LP-4012 [M]	Dodo's Back	1961	$300

—Deep Groove

Number	Title	Yr	NM
❑ LPS-4012 [S]	Dodo's Back	1961	$30

PHOENIX

❑ 20	Piano Man	197?	$30

SPOTLITE

❑ 108	Dodo Marmarosa Trio	197?	$25

MARMAROSA, DODO/ERROLL GARNER

CONCERT HALL JAZZ

❑ 1001 [10]	Piano Contrasts	1955	$75

DIAL

❑ LP-208 [10]	Piano Contrasts	1950	$300

MAROCCO, FRANK

DISCOVERY

❑ 797	Jazz Accordion	1979	$30
❑ 854	Road to Marocco	198?	$25
❑ 838	The Trio	198?	$25

TREND

❑ 516	New Colors	1980	$35

—Direct-to-disc recording

MAROHNIC, CHUCK

STEEPLECHASE

❑ SCS-4002	Copenhagen Suite	198?	$30
❑ SCS-1155	Permutations	198?	$30

MAROON 5

OCTONE/J

❑ 50001	Songs About Jane	2004	$18

MARR, HANK

KING

❑ KSD-1061	Greasy Spoon	1969	$25
❑ 1011 [M]	Hank Marr Plays 24 Originals	1966	$25
❑ 899 [M]	Live at Club 502	1964	$40
❑ 933 [M]	On and Off Stage	1965	$30
❑ 1025 [M]	Sounds from the Marr-Ket Place	1968	$25
❑ 829 [M]	Teentime Dance Steps	1963	$30

MARROW, ESTHER

FANTASY

❑ 9414	Sister Woman	1972	$35

MARS, CHRIS
Also see THE REPLACEMENTS.

SMASH

❑ 513198-1 [DJ]	Horseshoes and Hand Grenades	1992	$25

—Vinyl is promo only

MARS, SYLVIA

LYRIC

❑ 124	Blues Walk Right In	196?	$75

MARS VOLTA, THE

UNIVERSAL MOTOWN

❑ 1061601	The Bedlam in Gotham	2008	$30

MARSALA, JOE

JAZZOLOGY

❑ J-106	Joe Marsala and His Jazz Band, 1944	198?	$25

MARSALA, JOE/BUD FREEMAN

BRUNSWICK

❑ BL58037 [10]	Battle of Jazz, Vol. 1	1953	$50

MARSALIS, BRANFORD

CBS MASTERWORKS

❑ M42122	Romances for Saxophone	1986	$15

COLUMBIA

❑ OC44055	Random Abstract	1988	$12
❑ FC40711	Renaissance	1987	$12
❑ FC40363	Royal Garden Blues	1986	$12
❑ FC38951	Scenes in the City	1984	$12
❑ CX244199	Trio Jeepy	1989	$20
❑ CAS1628 [DJ]	Trio Jeepy Interchords Special	1989	$20

JAZZ PLANET

❑ JP-5004	The Dark Keys	1996	$30

MARSALIS, ELLIS

SPINDLETOP

❑ ST-105	Homecoming	1986	$12

MARSALIS, WYNTON

CBS

❑ IM42137	Carnaval	1987	$12

Number	Title	Yr	NM
COLUMBIA			
❏ FC40009	Black Codes (From the Underground)	1985	$12
❏ FC45287	Crescent City Christmas Card	1989	$12
❏ FC39530	Hot House Flowers	1984	$12
❏ FC40308	J Mood	1986	$12
❏ PC240675	Live at Blues Alley	1988	$15
❏ FC40461	Marsalis Standard Time	1987	$12
❏ C47346	Standard Time Vol. 2 -- Intimacy Calling	1991	$20
❏ C46143	Standard Time Vol. 3 -- The Resolution of Romance	1990	$15
❏ OC45091	The Majesty of the Blues	1989	$15
❏ FC38641	Think of One	1983	$12
❏ HC47574	Wynton Marsalis	198?	$75
—Half-speed mastered edition			
❏ FC37574	Wynton Marsalis	1982	$25
WHO'S WHO IN JAZZ			
❏ 21024	Wynton Marsalis with Art Blakey and His Jazz Messengers	1981	$35

MARSH, GEORGE, AND JOHN ABERCROMBIE

Number	Title	Yr	NM
1750 ARCH			
❏ 1804	Drum Strum	198?	$30

MARSH, GEORGE

Number	Title	Yr	NM
1750 ARCH			
❏ 1791	Marshland	1982	$30

MARSH, HUGH

Number	Title	Yr	NM
SOUNDWINGS/DUKE STREET			
❏ SW-210	Shaking the Pumpkin	1988	$30

MARSH, MILTON

Number	Title	Yr	NM
STRATA-EAST			
❏ SES-19758	Monism	1975	$25

MARSH, WARNE, AND SAL MOSCA

Number	Title	Yr	NM
INTERPLAY			
❏ 7725	How Deep/How High	1980	$30

MARSH, WARNE; CLARE FISCHER; GARY FOSTER

Number	Title	Yr	NM
REVELATION			
❏ 17	First Symposium on Relaxed Improvisation	197?	$35

MARSH, WARNE

Number	Title	Yr	NM
ATLANTIC			
❏ 1291 [M]	Warne Marsh	1958	$175
—Black label			
❏ 1291 [M]	Warne Marsh	1961	$175
—Multicolor label, white "fan" logo at right			
❏ SD1291 [S]	Warne Marsh	1958	$250
—Green label			
❏ SD1291 [S]	Warne Marsh	1961	$175
—Multicolor label, white "fan" logo at right			
DISCOVERY			
❏ 863	How Deep/How High	198?	$25
IMPERIAL			
❏ LP-9027 [M]	Jazz of Two Cities	1957	$200
❏ LP-12013 [S]	The Winds of Warne Marsh	1959	$200
—Retitled version in stereo?			
INTERPLAY			
❏ 8604	Posthumous	1986	$30
❏ 8602	Two Days in the Life of Warne Marsh	1986	$30
❏ 7709	Warne Out	197?	$30
MODE			
❏ LP-125 [M]	Music for Prancing	1957	$300
NESSA			
❏ N-7	All Music	1977	$30
REVELATION			
❏ R-12	Ne Plus Ultra	1970	$25
❏ 22	The Art of Improvising	197?	$30
❏ 27	The Art of Improvising, Vol. 3	197?	$30
STORYVILLE			
❏ 4001	Jazz Exchange, Vol. 1	197?	$30
❏ 4026	Jazz Exchange, Vol. 2: Live at the Montmartre Club	198?	$30
XANADU			
❏ 151	Live in Hollywood	197?	$30

MARSHALL, CHUCK

Number	Title	Yr	NM
DECCA			
❏ DL4267 [M]	Twist to Songs Everybody Knows	1962	$18
❏ DL74267 [S]	Twist to Songs Everybody Knows	1962	$25

MARSHALL, EDDIE

Number	Title	Yr	NM
TIMELESS			
❏ 315	Dance of the Sun	1977	$30

MARSHALL, JACK

Number	Title	Yr	NM
CAPITOL			
❏ T1108 [M]	18th Century Jazz	1959	$50
❏ ST1108 [S]	18th Century Jazz	1959	$75
❏ T1939 [M]	My Son the Surf Nut	1963	$75
❏ ST1939 [S]	My Son the Surf Nut	1963	$85
❏ T1601 [M]	Songs Without Words	1961	$50
❏ ST1601 [S]	Songs Without Words	1961	$75
❏ T1194 [M]	Soundsville!	1959	$50
❏ ST1194 [S]	Soundsville!	1959	$75
❏ T1351 [M]	The Marshall Swings	1960	$40
❏ ST1351 [S]	The Marshall Swings	1960	$75
❏ T1727 [M]	The Twangy, Shoutin', Fantastic Big-Band Sounds of Tuff Jack	1962	$75
❏ ST1727 [S]	The Twangy, Shoutin', Fantastic Big-Band Sounds of Tuff Jack	1962	$85

MARSHALL, PENNY, AND CINDY WILLIAMS

Number	Title	Yr	NM
ATLANTIC			
❏ SD18203	Laverne and Shirley Sing	1979	$25

MARSHALL, PETER

Number	Title	Yr	NM
DOT			
❏ DLP-25930	For the Love of Pete	1969	$25

MARSHALL TUCKER BAND, THE

Number	Title	Yr	NM
CAPRICORN			
❏ CP 0124	A New Life	1974	$15
❏ CPK 0180	Carolina Dreams	1977	$15
❏ CPN-0214	Greatest Hits	1978	$15
❏ CP 0170	Long Hard Ride	1976	$15
❏ CP 0161 [B]	Searchin' for a Rainbow	1975	$15
❏ CP 0112	The Marshall Tucker Band	1973	$15
❏ CP 0205	Together Forever	1978	$15
❏ 2CP 0145	Where We All Belong	1974	$18
MERCURY			
❏ 832794-1	Still Holdin' On	1988	$12
WARNER BROS.			
❏ BSK3662	A New Life	1982	$12
—Reissue of Capricorn 0124			
❏ BSK3610	Carolina Dreams	1982	$12
—Reissue of Capricorn 0180			
❏ HS3525	Dedicated	1981	$12
❏ BSK3611	Greatest Hits	1982	$12
—Reissue of Capricorn 0214			
❏ 23803	Just Us	1983	$12
❏ BSK3663	Long Hard Ride	1982	$12
—Reissue of Capricorn 0170			
❏ BSK3317	Running Like the Wind	1979	$12
❏ BSK3609	Searchin' for a Rainbow	1982	$12
—Reissue of Capricorn 0161			
❏ HS3410	Tenth	1980	$12
❏ BSK3606	The Marshall Tucker Band	1982	$12
—Reissue of Capricorn 0112			
❏ BSK3664	Together Forever	1982	$12
—Reissue of Capricorn 0205			
❏ BSK3684	Tuckerized	1982	$12
❏ 2WS3608	Where We All Belong	1982	$15
—Reissue of Capricorn 0145			

MARSHMALLOW WAY

Number	Title	Yr	NM
UNITED ARTISTS			
❏ UAS-6708	Marshmallow Way	1969	$25

MARTELL, LINDA

Number	Title	Yr	NM
PLANTATION			
❏ 9	Color Me Country	1970	$18

MARTERIE, RALPH

Number	Title	Yr	NM
AMBASSADOR			
❏ S-98058	Big Band Man/On the Sunny Side of the Street	196?	$12
MERCURY			
❏ MG-20054 [M]	Alone Together	195?	$25
❏ SR-60183 [S]	Big Band Man	1960	$25
❏ MG-20506 [M]	Big Band Man	1960	$18
❏ MG-20294 [M]	College Dance Favorites	1959	$25
—Revised title			
❏ SR-60035 [S]	College Dance Favorites	1959	$30
❏ MG-20066 [M]	Dance Band in Town	195?	$25
❏ MG-20253 [M]	Dance Date	195?	$25
❏ SR-60034 [S]	Dance Party	1959	$30
❏ MG-20395 [M]	Dance Party	195?	$18
❏ MG-25171 [10]	Dancing on the Down Beat	195?	$50
❏ SR-60036 [S]	Hi-Fidelity Concert	1959	$25
❏ MG-20397 [M]	Hi-Fidelity Concert	195?	$18
❏ MG-20336 [M]	Hits That Made Ralph Marterie and His Orchestra Famous	195?	$25
❏ MG-25121 [10]	Junior Prom	195?	$50
❏ MG-20174 [M]	Love Themes from the Classics	195?	$25

Number	Title	Yr	NM
❏ MG-25102 [10]	Moods for Dancing	195?	$50
❏ SR-60109 [S]	Music for a Private Eye	1960	$30
❏ MG-20437 [M]	Music for a Private Eye	1960	$25
❏ SRW-16238 [S]	Music for a Private Eye	196?	$18
❏ MG-20125 [M]	On Bandstand No. 1	195?	$25
❏ MG-25085 [10]	Ralph Marterie and His Orchestra	195?	$40
❏ MG-20128 [M]	Salute to the Aragon Ballroom	195?	$25
❏ MG-20010 [M]	Sweet and Lovely	195?	$25
❏ MG-20124 [M]	Swing Baby	195?	$25
❏ MG-20198 [M]	Young America Dances	195?	$25
MUSICOR			
❏ MS-3011	51 Discotheque Dance Favorites	196?	$12
❏ MS-3049	Motion Picture Hits	196?	$15
UNITED ARTISTS			
❏ UAS-6349 [S]	50 Fabulous Dance Favorites	196?	$18
❏ UAL-3349 [M]	50 Fabulous Dance Favorites	196?	$15
❏ WWS8506 [S]	88 Strings	196?	$18
❏ WWR3506 [M]	88 Strings	196?	$15
❏ UAL-3285 [M]	Dancers Choice	196?	$15
❏ UAS-6285 [S]	Dancers Choice	196?	$18
❏ UAL-3235 [M]	Dance to the Music Man	1962	$15
❏ UAS-6235 [S]	Dance to the Music Man	1962	$18
❏ UAS-6223 [S]	Ralph Marterie Plays Again	196?	$18
❏ UAL-3223 [M]	Ralph Marterie Plays Again	196?	$15
WING			
❏ MGW-12179 [M]	Dance Album	195?	$15
❏ MGW-12117 [M]	Dance Date	195?	$15
❏ MGW-12259 [M]	Dance Party	196?	$15
❏ SRW-16269 [S]	Dance Party	196?	$15
❏ MGW-12160 [M]	Love Themes from the Classics	195?	$15
❏ SRW-12511 [S]	Marvelous Marterie	1959	$18
❏ MGW-12154 [M]	Marvelous Marterie	195?	$15
❏ MGW-12238 [M]	Music for a Private Eye	196?	$15
❏ MGW-12185 [M]	Soft Tender Trumpet	195?	$15
❏ MGW-12155 [M]	Trumpeters Lullaby	195?	$15

MARTHA AND THE MUFFINS

Number	Title	Yr	NM
RCA VICTOR			
❏ AFL1-4664	Danseparc	1983	$12
VIRGIN			
❏ VA13145	Metro Music	1980	$12

MARTHA AND THE VANDELLAS

Number	Title	Yr	NM
GORDY			
❏ GS-958	Black Magic	1972	$25
❏ G-902 [M]	Come and Get These Memories	1963	$400
❏ GS-902 [S]	Come and Get These Memories	1963	$800
❏ G-915 [M]	Dance Party	1965	$50
❏ GS-915 [S]	Dance Party	1965	$75
❏ G-917 [M]	Greatest Hits	1966	$30
❏ GS-917 [S]	Greatest Hits	1966	$30
❏ G-907 [M]	Heat Wave	1963	$175
❏ GS-907 [S]	Heat Wave	1963	$400
—Mono cover with "Stereo" sticker			
❏ GS-907 [R]	Heat Wave	1963	$175
—Stereo" banner pre-printed on cover			
❏ G-925 [M]	Martha and the Vandellas Live!	1967	$30
❏ GS-925 [S]	Martha and the Vandellas Live!	1967	$30
❏ GS-952	Natural Resources	1970	$25
❏ G-926 [M]	Ridin' High	1968	$75
—Mono is promo only			
❏ GS-926 [S]	Ridin' High	1968	$25
❏ GS-944	Sugar 'N Spice	1969	$25
❏ G-920 [M]	Watchout!	1966	$30
❏ GS-920 [S]	Watchout!	1966	$30
MOTOWN			
❏ M7-778	Anthology	1974	$18
❏ M5-204V1	Greatest Hits	1981	$12
—Reissue of Gordy 917			
❏ M5-145V1	Heat Wave	1981	$12
—Reissue of Gordy 907			
❏ M5-111V1	Motown Superstar Series, Vol. 11	1981	$12

MARTIKA

Number	Title	Yr	NM
COLUMBIA			
❏ FC44290	Martika	1988	$12

MARTIN, ARCH

Number	Title	Yr	NM
ZEPHYR			
❏ 12009 [M]	Arch Martin Quintet	1959	$30

MARTIN, BENNY

Number	Title	Yr	NM
STARDAY			
❏ SLP-131 [M]	Country Music's Sensational Entertainer	1961	$50

MARTIN, BOBBI

Number	Title	Yr	NM
BUDDAH			
❏ BDS-5090	Tomorrow	1971	$15

Number	Title	Yr	NM

CORAL

Number	Title	Yr	NM
❏ CRL57472 [M]	Don't Forget I Still Love You	1965	$18
❏ CRL757472 [S]	Don't Forget I Still Love You	1965	$25
❏ CRL57478 [M]	I Love You So	1965	$18
❏ CRL757478 [S]	I Love You So	1965	$25

SUNSET

❏ SUS-5319	Thinking of You	197?	$12

UNITED ARTISTS

❏ UAS-6700	For the Love of Him	1969	$15
❏ UAS-6668	Harper Valley P.T.A.	1968	$15
❏ UAS-6755	With Love	1970	$15

VOCALION

❏ VL73906	Have You Ever Been Lonely	196?	$12

MARTIN, DEAN

CAPITOL

❏ T1285 [M]	A Winter Romance	1959	$25
❏ ST1285 [S]	A Winter Romance	1959	$30
❏ T1702 [M]	Cha Cha De Amor	1962	$25
❏ ST1702 [S]	Cha Cha De Amor	1962	$30
❏ W1580 [M]	Dean Martin	1961	$25
❏ SW1580 [S]	Dean Martin	1961	$30
❏ H401 [10]	Dean Martin Sings	1953	$150
❏ T401 [M]	Dean Martin Sings	1953	$50
❏ T2297 [M]	Dean Martin Sings -- Sinatra Conducts	1965	$18
❏ ST2297 [S]	Dean Martin Sings -- Sinatra Conducts	1965	$25
❏ T2333 [M]	Dean Martin -- Southern Style	1965	$18
❏ DT2333 [R]	Dean Martin -- Southern Style	1965	$15
❏ T1659 [M]	Dino -- Italian Love Songs	1962	$25
❏ ST1659 [S]	Dino -- Italian Love Songs	1962	$30
❏ SM-1659	Dino -- Italian Love Songs	197?	$12

— *Reissue with new prefix*

❏ T2212 [M]	Hey Brother Pour the Wine	1964	$25
❏ DT2212 [R]	Hey Brother Pour the Wine	1964	$15
❏ TT2343 [M]	Holiday Cheer	1965	$18

— *Reissue of 1285 with one fewer track*

❏ STT2343 [S]	Holiday Cheer	1965	$25

— *Some copies of this LP have labels that state the title as "Baby, It's Cold Outside.*

❏ T849 [M]	Pretty Baby	1957	$30
❏ T1150 [M]	Sleep Warm	1959	$30
❏ ST1150 [S]	Sleep Warm	1959	$30
❏ T576 [M]	Swingin' Down Yonder	1955	$30
❏ T2601 [M]	The Best of Dean Martin	1966	$18
❏ DT2601 [R]	The Best of Dean Martin	1966	$15
❏ SM-2601	The Best of Dean Martin	197?	$12

— *Reissue with new prefix*

❏ SKAO-140	The Best of Dean Martin, Vol. 2	1968	$18
❏ TCL2815 [M]	The Dean Martin Deluxe Set	1967	$30
❏ DTCL2815 [R]	The Dean Martin Deluxe Set	1967	$25
❏ T1047 [M]	This Is Dean Martin	1958	$30
❏ DT1047 [R]	This Is Dean Martin	196?	$15
❏ ST1442 [S]	This Time I'm Swingin'	1961	$30

❏ T1442 [M]	This Time I'm Swingin'	1961	$25
❏ STBB-523	You're Nobody 'Til Somebody Loves You/ Return to Me	1970	$25

LONGINES SYMPHONETTE

❏ LS-124A	Memories Are Made of This	197?	$30

— *Records are individually numbered SYS 5230, 5231, 5232, 5233 and 5234.*

PAIR

❏ PDL2-1029	Dreams and Memories	1986	$15

PICKWICK

❏ PTP-2051	Dean Martin	197?	$15
❏ SPC-3283	Deluxe	197?	$12
❏ SPC-3089	I Can't Give You Anything But Love	196?	$12
❏ SPC-3057	You Can't Love 'Em All	196?	$12
❏ SPC-3136	Young and Foolish	196?	$12
❏ SPC-3175	You Were Made for Love	197?	$12

REPRISE

❏ R-6061 [M]	Country Style	1963	$18
❏ R9-6061 [S]	Country Style	1963	$25
❏ R-6146 [M]	Dean Martin Hits Again	1965	$15
❏ RS-6146 [S]	Dean Martin Hits Again	1965	$18
❏ RS-6301	Dean Martin's Greatest Hits! Vol. 1	1968	$18
❏ RS-6320	Dean Martin's Greatest Hits! Vol. 2	1968	$18
❏ R-6085 [M]	Dean "Tex" Martin Rides Again	1963	$18
❏ R9-6085 [S]	Dean "Tex" Martin Rides Again	1963	$25
❏ MS2053	Dino	1972	$18
❏ SW-94345	Dino	1972	$25

— *Capitol Record Club edition*

❏ R-6054 [M]	Dino Latino	1962	$18
❏ R9-6054 [S]	Dino Latino	1962	$25
❏ R-6123 [M]	Dream with Dean	1964	$15
❏ RS-6123 [S]	Dream with Dean	1964	$18
❏ R-6130 [M]	Everybody Loves Somebody	1964	$15
❏ RS-6130 [S]	Everybody Loves Somebody	1964	$18
❏ RS-6428	For the Good Times	1971	$18
❏ R-6021 [M]	French Style	1962	$18
❏ R9-6021 [S]	French Style	1962	$18
❏ RS-6330 [S]	Gentle on My Mind	1968	$18
❏ R-6330 [M]	Gentle on My Mind	1968	$30
❏ R-6242 [M]	Happiness Is Dean Martin	1967	$18
❏ RS-6242 [S]	Happiness Is Dean Martin	1967	$18
❏ R-6181 [M]	Houston	1965	$15
❏ RS-6181 [S]	Houston	1965	$18
❏ RS-6338	I Take a Lot of Pride in What I Am	1969	$18
❏ RS-6403	My Woman, My Woman, My Wife	1970	$18
❏ MS2267	Once in a Lifetime	1978	$15
❏ R-6170 [M]	(Remember Me) I'm the One Who Loves You	1965	$15
❏ RS-6170 [S]	(Remember Me) I'm the One Who Loves You	1965	$18
❏ MS2113	Sittin' on Top of the World	1973	$18
❏ R-6201 [M]	Somewhere There's a Someone	1966	$15
❏ RS-6201 [S]	Somewhere There's a Someone	1966	$18
❏ R6222 [M]	The Dean Martin Christmas Album	1966	$18
❏ RS6222 [S]	The Dean Martin Christmas Album	1966	$25
❏ R-6233 [M]	The Dean Martin TV Show	1966	$15
❏ RS-6233 [S]	The Dean Martin TV Show	1966	$18
❏ R-6140 [M]	The Door Is Still Open to My Heart	1964	$15
❏ RS-6140 [S]	The Door Is Still Open to My Heart	1964	$18
❏ R-6213 [M]	The Hit Sound of Dean Martin	1966	$15
❏ RS-6213 [S]	The Hit Sound of Dean Martin	1966	$18
❏ R-6211 [M]	The Silencers	1966	$25
❏ RS-6211 [S]	The Silencers	1966	$30
❏ R-6250 [M]	Welcome to My World	1967	$18
❏ RS-6250 [S]	Welcome to My World	1967	$18
❏ MS2174	You're the Best Thing That Ever Happened to Me	1973	$18

TOWER

❏ T5036 [M]	Happy in Love	1966	$18
❏ ST5036 [S]	Happy in Love	1966	$25
❏ T5018 [M]	Relaxin'	1966	$25
❏ DT5018 [R]	Relaxin'	1966	$18
❏ T5006 [M]	The Lush Years	1965	$25
❏ DT5006 [R]	The Lush Years	1965	$18

WARNER BROS.

❏ 23870	The Nashville Sessions	1983	$15

MARTIN, DEWEY, AND MEDICINE BALL
Dewey is a former member of BUFFALO SPRINGFIELD.

UNI

❏ 73088	Dewey Martin and Medicine Ball	1970	$30

MARTIN, FREDDY

CAPITOL

❏ T2347 [M]	As Time Goes By	1965	$40
❏ ST2347 [S]	As Time Goes By	1965	$75
❏ T2098 [M]	Best of the New Favorites	1964	$40
❏ ST2098 [S]	Best of the New Favorites	1964	$75
❏ T1269 [M]	C'mon, Let's Dance	1960	$75

— *Black colorband label, logo at left*

❏ T1269 [M]	C'mon, Let's Dance	1962	$40

— *Black colorband label, logo at top*

❏ ST1269 [S]	C'mon, Let's Dance	1960	$85

— *Black colorband label, logo at left*

❏ ST1269 [S]	C'mon, Let's Dance	1962	$75

— *Black colorband label, logo at top*

❏ T2028 [M]	Freddy Martin Plays the Hits	1964	$50
❏ ST2028 [S]	Freddy Martin Plays the Hits	1964	$75
❏ T2163 [M]	Freddy Martin Plays the Hits, Vol, 2	1964	$50
❏ ST2163 [S]	Freddy Martin Plays the Hits, Vol, 2	1964	$75
❏ T1889 [M]	In a Sentimental Mood	1963	$50
❏ ST1889 [S]	In a Sentimental Mood	1963	$75
❏ T1486 [M]	Seems Like Old Times	1961	$75

— *Black colorband label, logo at top*

❏ T1486 [M]	Seems Like Old Times	1962	$50

— *Black colorband label, logo at top*

❏ ST1486 [S]	Seems Like Old Times	1961	$50

— *Black colorband label, logo at left*

❏ ST1486 [S]	Seems Like Old Times	1962	$75

— *Black colorband label, logo at top*

❏ T1582 [M]	The Hits of Freddie Martin	1962	$50
❏ ST1582 [S]	The Hits of Freddie Martin	1962	$75
❏ T2018 [M]	Tonight We Love	1964	$50
❏ ST2018 [S]	Tonight We Love	1964	$75

DECCA

❏ DL74908 [R]	Freddy Martin's Greatest Hits	1967	$25
❏ DL4908 [M]	Freddy Martin's Greatest Hits	1967	$35
❏ DL4839 [M]	The Most Requested	1967	$35
❏ DL74839 [R]	The Most Requested	1967	$25

HINDSIGHT

❏ HSR-151	Freddy Martin and His Orchestra 1940	198?	$25
❏ HSR-169	Freddy Martin and His Orchestra 1944-46	198?	$25
❏ HSR-205	Freddy Martin and His Orchestra 1948, 1952	198?	$25
❏ HSR-190	Freddy Martin and His Orchestra 1952	198?	$25

KAPP

❏ KL-1286 [M]	Dancing Tonight	1963	$30
❏ KS-3286 [S]	Dancing Tonight	1963	$35
❏ KL-1261 [M]	Great Waltzes of the World	1962	$30
❏ KS-3261 [S]	Great Waltzes of the World	1962	$35
❏ KL-1271 [M]	Great Waltzes of the World, Volume 2	1962	$30
❏ KS-3271 [S]	Great Waltzes of the World, Volume 2	1962	$35
❏ KL-1490 [M]	The Most Beautiful Girl in the World	1966	$30
❏ KS-3490 [S]	The Most Beautiful Girl in the World	1966	$35

MCA

❏ 4021	54 Great Waltzes	197?	$30
❏ 258	Freddy Martin's Greatest Hits	197?	$20
❏ 4080	The Best of Freddy Martin	197?	$30

RCA VICTOR

❏ LPM-1414 [M]	Freddy Martin at the Cocoanut Grove	1957	$30
❏ LSP-4044 [R]	The Best of Freddy Martin	1969	$25
❏ VPM-6072	This Is Freddy Martin	197?	$35

SUNBEAM

❏ 313	Music in the Martin Manner 1933-39	197?	$25

MARTIN, GEORGE

UNITED ARTISTS

❏ UAL3383 [M]	A Hard Day's Night	1964	$50
❏ UAS6383 [S]	A Hard Day's Night	1964	$75
❏ UAL3420 [M]	George Martin	1965	$50
❏ UAS6420 [S]	George Martin	1965	$50
❏ UAL3448 [M]	George Martin Plays "Help	1965	$50
❏ UAS6448 [S]	George Martin Plays "Help	1965	$100
❏ UAL3539 [M]	George Martin Salutes the Beatle Girls	1966	$50
❏ UAS6539 [S]	George Martin Salutes the Beatle Girls	1966	$100
❏ UAL3647 [M]	London by George	1967	$30
❏ UAS6647 [S]	London by George	1967	$40
❏ UAL3377 [M]	Off the Beatle Track	1964	$150
❏ UAS6377 [S]	Off the Beatle Track	1964	$150

MARTIN, GRADY

DECCA

❏ DL4072 [M]	Big City Lights	1960	$25
❏ DL74072 [S]	Big City Lights	1960	$30
❏ DL5566 [10]	Dance-O-Rama	1955	$250
❏ DL8883 [M]	Hot Time Tonight	1959	$25
❏ DL78883 [S]	Hot Time Tonight	1959	$30
❏ DL8292 [M]	Juke Box Jamboree	1956	$30
❏ DL8181 [M]	Powerhouse Dance Party	1955	$30
❏ DL4476 [M]	Songs Everybody Knows	1963	$18
❏ DL74476 [S]	Songs Everybody Knows	1963	$25
❏ DL4286 [M]	Swingin' Down the River	1962	$18
❏ DL74286 [S]	Swingin' Down the River	1962	$25
❏ DL8648 [M]	The Roaring Twenties	1957	$30

MARTIN, JIMMY

DECCA

❏ DL4891 [M]	Big and Country Instrumentals	1967	$25
❏ DL74891 [S]	Big and Country Instrumentals	1967	$25
❏ DL4285 [M]	Country Music Time	1962	$30
❏ DL74285 [S]	Country Music Time	1962	$30
❏ DL4016 [M]	Good 'n Country	1960	$30
❏ DL74016 [S]	Good 'n Country	1960	$30
❏ DL4769 [M]	Mr. Good 'n Country Music	1966	$25
❏ DL74769 [S]	Mr. Good 'n Country Music	1966	$30
❏ DL4643 [M]	Sunny Side of the Mountain	1965	$25
❏ DL74643 [S]	Sunny Side of the Mountain	1965	$30
❏ DL74996 [S]	Tennessee	1968	$25
❏ DL4996 [M]	Tennessee	1968	$75

— *Mono is white label promo only*

❏ DL4360 [M]	This World Is Not My Home	1963	$30
❏ DL74360 [S]	This World Is Not My Home	1963	$30
❏ DL4536 [M]	Widow Maker	1964	$25

Number	Title	Yr	NM
❏ DL74536 [S]	Widow Maker	1964	$30

MARTIN, JUAN
NOVUS

Number	Title	Yr	NM
❏ 3005-1-N	Painter in Sound	1986	$25
❏ 3036-1-N	Through the Moving Window	1988	$25

MARTIN, MARILYN
ATLANTIC

Number	Title	Yr	NM
❏ 81292	Marilyn Martin	1986	$10
❏ 81814	This Is Serious	1988	$10

MARTIN, MARY
COLUMBIA MASTERWORKS

Number	Title	Yr	NM
❏ ML2061 [10]	Mary Martin Sings for You	1949	$50

DISNEYLAND

Number	Title	Yr	NM
❏ WD-3038 [M]	Hi-Ho!	1958	$25
❏ STER-3038 [S]	Hi-Ho!	1959	$30
❏ WDL-4016 [M]	Hi-Ho!	1958	$25
❏ STER-4016 [S]	Hi-Ho!	1959	$30
❏ WDL-1038 [M]	Hi-Ho -- Mary Martin Sings and Swings Walt Disney Favorites	1958	$25
❏ WD-3031 [M]	Mary Martin Sings a Musical Love Story	1958	$25
❏ STER-3031 [S]	Mary Martin Sings a Musical Love Story	1959	$30
❏ DQ-1296 [M]	Mary Martin Songs from Rodgers and Hammerstein's The Sound of Music	1966	$18
❏ STER-1296 [M]	Mary Martin Songs from Rodgers and Hammerstein's The Sound of Music	1966	$25
❏ ST-3936 [M]	Mary Martin Songs from Rodgers and Hammerstein's The Sound of Music	1966	$18
❏ STER-3936 [S]	Mary Martin Songs from Rodgers and Hammerstein's The Sound of Music	1966	$25
❏ ST-2002 [M]	The Little Lame Lamb	1958	$50
❏ ST-3911 [M]	The Story of Sleeping Beauty	1958	$30

— Back cover art features Sleeping Beauty and prince

Number	Title	Yr	NM
❏ ST-3911 [M]	The Story of Sleeping Beauty	1969	$25

— Back cover art features pictures from the booklet

MARTIN, MIKE
GUINNESS

Number	Title	Yr	NM
❏ GNS36080 [B]	Thick Tongue Fool	1977	$30

MARTIN, RAY
CAPITOL

Number	Title	Yr	NM
❏ T10101 [M]	Global Hop	195?	$18
❏ T10067 [M]	High Barbaree	195?	$18
❏ T10066 [M]	International Vibrations	195?	$18
❏ T10056 [M]	My London	195?	$18
❏ T10017 [M]	Rainy Night in London	195?	$18

COLUMBIA

Number	Title	Yr	NM
❏ CL529 [M]	Pop Concert	1953	$30

ESSEX

Number	Title	Yr	NM
❏ ESLP-105 [10]	I Love	1954	$30

IMPERIAL

Number	Title	Yr	NM
❏ LP-9085 [M]	Boots and Saddle	1959	$15
❏ LP-12020 [S]	Boots and Saddle	1959	$18
❏ LP-9083 [M]	Love of My Life	1959	$15
❏ LP-12018 [S]	Love of My Life	1959	$18
❏ LP-9087 [M]	Martin Goes Latin	1959	$15
❏ LP-12022 [S]	Martin Goes Latin	1959	$18

JUBILEE

Number	Title	Yr	NM
❏ JLP-1055 [M]	Witchcraft	1958	$18

LONDON PHASE 4

Number	Title	Yr	NM
❏ SP-44040 [S]	The Sound of Sight: Music for an Experiment in Imagination	1964	$25

MONUMENT

Number	Title	Yr	NM
❏ LP8068 [M]	Romance in Vienna	1966	$12
❏ LP18068 [S]	Romance in Vienna	1966	$15

RCA CAMDEN

Number	Title	Yr	NM
❏ CAL-2102 [M]	Comic Strip Favorites	1967	$15
❏ CAS-2102 [S]	Comic Strip Favorites	1967	$12
❏ CAL-913 [M]	Goldfinger and Other Music from James Bond Thrillers	1965	$12
❏ CAS-913 [S]	Goldfinger and Other Music from James Bond Thrillers	1965	$15
❏ CAL-976 [M]	Michelle Going for Baroque	1966	$12
❏ CAS-976 [S]	Michelle Going for Baroque	1966	$15
❏ CAL-927 [M]	Thunderball and Other Thriller Music	1965	$12
❏ CAS-927 [S]	Thunderball and Other Thriller Music	1965	$15
❏ CAL-2181 [M]	Up-Up and Away	1967	$15
❏ CAS-2181 [S]	Up-Up and Away	1967	$12

RCA VICTOR

Number	Title	Yr	NM
❏ LSA-2287 [S]	Dynamica	1961	$18
❏ LPM-2287 [M]	Dynamica	1961	$15
❏ LSA-2422 [S]	Excitement, Incorporated	1961	$18
❏ LPM-2422 [M]	Excitement, Incorporated	1961	$15
❏ LPM-1771 [M]	Pop Goes the Swingin' Marchin' Band	1958	$15

Number	Title	Yr	NM
❏ LSP-1771 [S]	Pop Goes the Swingin' Marchin' Band	1958	$25
❏ LPM-2130 [M]	The Rockin' Strings of Ray Martin	1959	$15
❏ LSP-2130 [S]	The Rockin' Strings of Ray Martin	1959	$18

STRAND

Number	Title	Yr	NM
❏ SL-1037 [M]	Dancing After Dark	1962	$15

MARTIN, RONEE
SOUNDWINGS

Number	Title	Yr	NM
❏ SW-2105	Sensation	1987	$25

MARTIN, SPIDER
IMPROV

Number	Title	Yr	NM
❏ 7118	Absolutely	197?	$30

MARTIN, TONY
20TH CENTURY FOX

Number	Title	Yr	NM
❏ TFM-3138 [M]	Live at Carnegie Hall	1964	$15
❏ TFS-4138 [S]	Live at Carnegie Hall	1964	$18

APPLAUSE

Number	Title	Yr	NM
❏ APLP-1003	I'll See You in My Dreams	1982	$12
❏ R134276	I'll See You in My Dreams	1982	$15

— RCA Music Service edition

AUDIO FIDELITY

Number	Title	Yr	NM
❏ AFSD-6200	Tony Martin	1968	$18

CHART

Number	Title	Yr	NM
❏ CHS-1029	Tony Martin in Nashville	1970	$25

DECCA

Number	Title	Yr	NM
❏ DL8366 [M]	In the Spotlight	195?	$30

— Black label, silver print

Number	Title	Yr	NM
❏ DL8286 [M]	Melody Lane	195?	$30

— Black label, silver print

Number	Title	Yr	NM
❏ DL8287 [M]	Our Love Affair	195?	$30

— Black label, silver print

Number	Title	Yr	NM
❏ DL5189 [10]	Tony Martin Sings, Vol. 1	1950	$40

DOT

Number	Title	Yr	NM
❏ DLP-3360 [M]	His Greatest Hits	1961	$18
❏ DLP-25360 [S]	His Greatest Hits	1961	$25

KOALA

Number	Title	Yr	NM
❏ KO14140	I'm Always Chasing Rainbows	198?	$15

MCA

Number	Title	Yr	NM
❏ 1515 [M]	Tony Martin Collectibles	198?	$15

MCA CORAL

Number	Title	Yr	NM
❏ CB-20019	Melody	1973	$15

MERCURY

Number	Title	Yr	NM
❏ MG-20079 [M]	Dream Music	195?	$30
❏ MG-20644 [M]	Golden Hits by Tony Martin	1961	$18
❏ MG-60644 [S]	Golden Hits by Tony Martin	1961	$18
❏ MG-20075 [M]	Mr. Song Man	195?	$30
❏ MG-25004 [10]	Tony Martin	1950	$40

MOTOWN

Number	Title	Yr	NM
❏ MS-645 [S]	Live! At the Americana	1966	$0

— Canceled

Number	Title	Yr	NM
❏ MT-645 [M]	Live! At the Americana	1966	$0

— Canceled

MOVIETONE

Number	Title	Yr	NM
❏ MTM-1007 [M]	Live at Carnegie Hall	196?	$12

— Reissue of 20th Century Fox 3138

Number	Title	Yr	NM
❏ MTS-2007 [S]	Live at Carnegie Hall	196?	$15

— Reissue of 20th Century Fox 4138

RCA CAMDEN

Number	Title	Yr	NM
❏ CAL-412 [M]	I Get Ideas	195?	$18
❏ CAL-576 [M]	Tonight	195?	$18
❏ CAL-484 [M]	Tony Martin Sings of Love	195?	$18

RCA SPECIAL PRODUCTS

Number	Title	Yr	NM
❏ DML2-0999	The Greatest Singer of Them All!	1991	$18

RCA VICTOR

Number	Title	Yr	NM
❏ LPM-1357 [M]	A Night at the Copacabana with Tony Martin	1956	$30
❏ LPM-2107 [M]	Dream a Little Dream	1960	$25
❏ LSP-2107 [S]	Dream a Little Dream	1960	$30
❏ LPM-3136 [10]	One for My Baby	195?	$40
❏ LPM-1263 [M]	Speak to Me of Love	1956	$30
❏ LPM-1218 [M]	The Night Was Made for Love	1956	$30
❏ LPM-2146 [M]	Tony Martin at the Desert Inn	1960	$25
❏ LSP-2146 [S]	Tony Martin at the Desert Inn	1960	$30
❏ LPM-3126 [10]	World-Wide Favorites	195?	$40

VOCALION

Number	Title	Yr	NM
❏ VL3610 [M]	Tony Martin	196?	$18

WING

Number	Title	Yr	NM
❏ MGW-12115 [M]	It's Just Love	196?	$15
❏ MGW-12203 [M]	Mr. Song Man	196?	$15

MARTIN, TRADE
BUDDAH

Number	Title	Yr	NM
❏ BDS-5126	Let Me Touch You	1972	$18

MARTIN, VINCE, AND FRED NEIL
ELEKTRA

Number	Title	Yr	NM
❏ EKL-248 [M]	Tear Down the Walls	1964	$50
❏ EKS-7248 [S]	Tear Down the Walls	1964	$75

MARTINDALE, WINK
DOT

Number	Title	Yr	NM
❏ DLP-3403 [M]	Big Bad John	1962	$18
❏ DLP-25403 [S]	Big Bad John	1962	$25
❏ DLP-3245 [M]	Deck of Cards	1960	$25
❏ DLP-25245 [S]	Deck of Cards	1960	$30
❏ DLP-3692 [M]	Giddyup Go	1966	$18
❏ DLP-25692 [S]	Giddyup Go	1966	$25
❏ DLP-3571 [M]	My True Love	1964	$18
❏ DLP-25571 [S]	My True Love	1964	$25
❏ DLP-3293 [M]	The Bible Story	1960	$18
❏ DLP-25293 [S]	The Bible Story	1960	$25

MARTINELLI, DINO
HARMONY

Number	Title	Yr	NM
❏ HS11010 [S]	Dino Martinelli Plays Music for Christmas	1959	$18

MARTINEZ, TONY
DEL-FI

Number	Title	Yr	NM
❏ DFLP-1205 [M]	The Many Sides of Pepino	1959	$30
❏ DFLP-1205S [S]	The Many Sides of Pepino	1959	$40

MARTINO, AL
20TH CENTURY FOX

Number	Title	Yr	NM
❏ SF-3025 [M]	Al Martino	1959	$30
❏ SFX-3025 [S]	Al Martino	1959	$30
❏ TF-4168 [M]	Al Martino Sings	196?	$25
❏ TFS-4168 [S]	Al Martino Sings	196?	$30
❏ SF-3032 [M]	Sing Along with Al Martino	1959	$30
❏ SFX-3032 [S]	Sing Along with Al Martino	1959	$30
❏ XG-5009 [M]	When Your Lover Has Gone	1963	$25
❏ SXG-5009 [S]	When Your Lover Has Gone	1963	$30

CAPITOL

Number	Title	Yr	NM
❏ STCL-572	Al Martino	1971	$30
❏ T2165 [M]	A Merry Christmas from Al Martino	1964	$15
❏ ST2165 [S]	A Merry Christmas from Al Martino	1964	$18
❏ ST-405	Can't Help Falling in Love	1970	$15
❏ T2733 [M]	Daddy's Little Girl	1967	$18
❏ ST2733 [S]	Daddy's Little Girl	1967	$18
❏ STBB-526	Here in My Heart/Yesterday	1970	$18
❏ T1914 [M]	I Love You Because	1963	$15
❏ ST1914 [S]	I Love You Because	1963	$18
❏ T2107 [M]	I Love You More and More Every Day/Tears and Roses	1964	$15
❏ ST2107 [S]	I Love You More and More Every Day/Tears and Roses	1964	$18
❏ STBB-713	I Wish You Love/Losing You	1971	$18
❏ ST-11302	I Won't Last a Day Without You	1974	$12
❏ ST-379	Jean	1969	$15
❏ T2040 [M]	Living a Lie	1964	$15
❏ ST2040 [S]	Living a Lie	1964	$18
❏ ST2908	Love Is Blue	1968	$18
❏ ST-11071	Love Theme from "The Godfather"	1972	$12
❏ SM-11071	Love Theme from "The Godfather"	1977	$10

— Reissue with new prefix

Number	Title	Yr	NM
❏ T2780 [M]	Mary in the Morning	1967	$18
❏ ST2780 [S]	Mary in the Morning	1967	$18
❏ T2362 [M]	My Cherie	1965	$15
❏ ST2362 [S]	My Cherie	1965	$18
❏ ST-497	My Heart Sings	1970	$15
❏ T1975 [M]	Painted, Tainted Rose	1963	$15
❏ ST1975 [S]	Painted, Tainted Rose	1963	$18
❏ ST-180	Sausalito	1969	$15
❏ ST-11572	Sing My Love Songs	1976	$12
❏ T2312 [M]	Somebody Else Is Taking My Place	1965	$15
❏ ST2312 [S]	Somebody Else Is Taking My Place	1965	$18
❏ T2435 [M]	Spanish Eyes	1966	$15
❏ ST2435 [S]	Spanish Eyes	1966	$18
❏ ST-793	Summer of '42	1971	$18
❏ SKAO2946	The Best of Al Martino	1968	$18
❏ SM-2946	The Best of Al Martino	197?	$12

— Reissue with new prefix

Number	Title	Yr	NM
❏ SN-16074	The Best of Al Martino	1981	$10

— Budget-line reissue

Number	Title	Yr	NM
❏ T1774 [M]	The Exciting Voice of Al Martino	1962	$18
❏ ST1774 [S]	The Exciting Voice of Al Martino	1962	$25
❏ T1907 [M]	The Italian Voice of Al Martino	1963	$18
❏ ST1907 [S]	The Italian Voice of Al Martino	1963	$25
❏ ST-11741	The Next Hundred Years	1978	$12
❏ SQBO-91280	The Romantic World of Al Martino	196?	$25

— Capitol Record Club exclusive

Number	Title	Yr	NM
❏ T2528 [M]	Think I'll Go Somewhere and Cry Myself to Sleep	1966	$15
❏ ST2528 [S]	Think I'll Go Somewhere and Cry Myself to Sleep	1966	$18
❏ ST2843	This Is Al Martino	1968	$18
❏ T2592 [M]	This Is Love	1966	$15

Number	Title	Yr	NM
❏ ST2592 [S]	This Is Love	1966	$18
❏ T2654 [M]	This Love for You	1967	$18
❏ ST2654 [S]	This Love for You	1967	$18
❏ ST-11366	To the Door of the Sun	1975	$12
❏ SM-11679	To the Door of the Sun	1977	$10
— Reissue of 11366			
❏ ST2983	Wake Up to Me Gentle	1968	$18
❏ T2200 [M]	We Could	1964	$15
❏ ST2200 [S]	We Could	1964	$18

MOVIETONE

❏ MTM2015 [M]	All of Me	1967	$25
❏ MTS72015 [S]	All of Me	1967	$18
❏ MTM2002 [M]	That Old Feeling	196?	$18
❏ MTS72002 [S]	That Old Feeling	196?	$25

PICKWICK

❏ SPC-3049	Don't Go to Strangers	196?	$15
❏ SPC-3276	Mary in the Morning	197?	$12

SPRINGBOARD

❏ 4074	Time After Time	1978	$10

MARTINO, PAT

COBBLESTONE

❏ 9015	The Visit	1972	$25

FANTASY

❏ OJC-355	Baiyina (The Clear Evidence)	198?	$25
❏ OJC-397	Desperado	1989	$30
❏ OJC-248	East!	198?	$25
❏ OJC-195	El Hombre	198?	$25
❏ OJC-223	Strings!	198?	$25

MUSE

❏ MR-5039	Consciousness	1975	$30
❏ MR-5075	Exit	1976	$30
❏ MR-5096	Footprints	1977	$30
❏ MR-5026	Live!	1974	$30
❏ MR-5328	The Return	198?	$25
❏ MR-5090	We'll Be Together Again	1977	$30

PRESTIGE

❏ PRST-7589	Baiyina (The Clear Evidence)	1968	$35
❏ PRST-7795	Desperado	1970	$35
❏ PRST-7562	East!	1968	$35
❏ PRST-7513 [S]	El Hombre	1967	$35
❏ PRLP-7513 [M]	El Hombre	1967	$30
❏ PRLP-7547 [M]	Strings!	1967	$30
❏ PRST-7547 [S]	Strings!	1967	$35

WARNER BROS.

❏ BS2977	Joyous Lake	1977	$25
❏ BS2921	Starbright	1976	$25

MARTYN, JOHN & BEVERLEY

4 MEN WITH BEARDS

❏ 4M803LP [B]	Stormbringer!		$25

MARVELETTES, THE

MOTOWN

❏ M7-827	Anthology	1975	$18
❏ M5-180V1	Greatest Hits	1981	$12
— Reissue of Tamla 253			
❏ 5266ML	Please Mr. Postman	1982	$12
— Reissue of Tamla 228			

TAMLA

❏ T-253 [M]	Greatest Hits	1966	$30
— Yellow cover			
❏ T-253 [M]	Greatest Hits	1967	$50
— Green cover			
❏ TS-253 [S]	Greatest Hits	1966	$40
— Yellow cover			
❏ TS-253 [S]	Greatest Hits	1967	$25
— Green cover			
❏ TS-288	In Full Bloom	1969	$18
❏ T-231 [M]	Playboy	1962	$500
— Yellow label with overlapping record and globe logo			
❏ T-231 [M]	Playboy	1963	$300
— Yellow label with side-by-side globes logo			
❏ T-231 [M]	Playboy	1962	$600
— White label			
❏ T-228 [M]	Please Mr. Postman	1961	$600
— White label			
❏ T-228 [M]	Please Mr. Postman	1963	$300
— Yellow label with globes logo			
❏ T-243 [M]	Recorded Live on Stage	1963	$100
❏ TS-305	Return of the Marvelettes	1970	$18
❏ T-229 [M]	Smash Hits of 62'	1962	$1200
— Title as listed on front cover; large black "M" with song titles in circles; VG value 600; VG+ value 900			
❏ T-286 [M]	Sophisticated Soul	1968	$40
❏ TS-286 [M]	Sophisticated Soul	1968	$25
❏ T-229 [M]	The Marvelettes Sing	1962	$500
— Title as listed on front cover (misspelled); all-black cover with white circles			
❏ T-229 [M]	The Marveletts Sing	1963	$300
— Yellow label with side-by-side globes logo			
❏ T-274 [M]	The Marveletttes	1967	$30
❏ TS-274 [S]	The Marvelettes	1967	$25
❏ T-237 [M]	The Marvelous Marvelettes	1963	$175

MARVELOWS, THE

ABC

❏ S-643	The Mighty Marvelows	1968	$30

MARVIN AND JOHNNY

CROWN

❏ CLP-5381 [M]	Marvin and Johnny	1963	$50
❏ CST-381 [R]	Marvin and Johnny	1963	$15

MARX, BILL

VEE JAY

❏ LP-3032 [M]	Jazz Kaleidoscope	1962	$25
❏ SR-3032 [S]	Jazz Kaleidoscope	1962	$30
❏ LP-3035 [M]	My Son, the Folk Swinger	1963	$25
❏ SR-3035 [S]	My Son, the Folk Swinger	1963	$30

MARX, DICK, AND JOHN FRIGO

BRUNSWICK

❏ BL54006 [M]	Two Much Piano	1955	$50

MARX, DICK

OMEGA

❏ OML-1002 [M]	Marx Makes Broadway	1958	$40
❏ OSL-2 [S]	Marx Makes Broadway	1959	$30
— The front cover of the above LP spells his last name "Marks," though it is spelled correctly on the label and back cover			

MARX, GROUCHO

DECCA

❏ DL5405 [10]	Hooray for Captain Spaulding	1954	$300

MARX, HARPO

MERCURY

❏ MG-20363 [M]	Harpo at Work!	1959	$175
❏ SR-60016 [S]	Harpo at Work!	1959	$175
❏ MG-20232 [M]	Harpo in Hi-Fi	1957	$175

RCA VICTOR

❏ LPM-27 [10]	Harp by Harpo	1952	$300

WING

❏ MGW-12164 [M]	Harpo	1960	$40

MARX, RICHARD

CAPITOL

❏ C1-595874	Rush Street	1992	$30
— Columbia House edition; only U.S. vinyl version			

EMI

❏ E1-90380	Repeat Offender	1989	$10
❏ E1-590380	Repeat Offender	1989	$12
— Columbia House edition			

MANHATTAN

❏ ST-53049	Richard Marx	1987	$10
❏ ST-553049	Richard Marx	1987	$12
— Columbia House edition			
❏ R134073	Richard Marx	1987	$15
— BMG Direct Marketing edition			

MARY BUTTERWORTH

CUSTOM FIDELITY

❏ 2092	Mary Butterworth	1969	$300

MARYLAND JAZZ BAND

GHB

❏ GHB-178	25 Years of Jazz with the Maryland Jazz Band	1987	$25

MAS, JEAN-PIERRE, AND CESARIUS ALVIM

INNER CITY

❏ IC-1014	Lourmel	197?	$35

MASEKELA, HUGH

ABC IMPULSE!

❏ IA-9343	African Connection	1978	$30

BLUE THUMB

❏ BT-6003	Home Is Where the Music Is	1973	$25
❏ BT-6015	I Am Not Afraid	1974	$25
❏ BT-62	Introducing Hedzoleh Sounds	1972	$25

CASABLANCA

❏ NBLP7023	Colonial Man	1976	$25
❏ NBLP7036	Melody Maker	1977	$25
❏ NBLP7017	The Boy's Doin' It	1975	$25
❏ NBLP7079	You Told Your Mama	1978	$25

CHISA

❏ CS-803	Reconstruction	1970	$30
❏ CS-808	Union of South Africa	1971	$30

JIVE

❏ JL-8210	Techno Bush	1984	$25
❏ JL-8382	Waiting for the Rain	1985	$25

MERCURY

❏ SR-61109	Grr	1969	$30

❏ MG-20797 [M]	The Trumpet of Hugh Masekela	1963	$150
❏ SR-60797 [S]	The Trumpet of Hugh Masekela	1963	$150

MGM

❏ GAS-116	Hugh Masekela (Golden Archive Series)	1970	$30
❏ E-4415 [M]	Hugh Masekela's Next Album	1966	$30
❏ SE-4415 [S]	Hugh Masekela's Next Album	1966	$35
❏ E-4372 [M]	The Americanization of Ooga Booga	1966	$30
❏ SE-4372 [S]	The Americanization of Ooga Booga	1966	$35
❏ E-4468 [M]	The Lasting Impression of Hugh Masekela	1967	$35
❏ SE-4468 [S]	The Lasting Impression of Hugh Masekela	1967	$30

NOVUS

❏ 3070-1-R	Uptownship	1990	$30

UNI

❏ 3015 [M]	Hugh Masekela Is Alive and Well at the Whisky	1967	$50
❏ 73015 [S]	Hugh Masekela Is Alive and Well at the Whisky	1967	$30
❏ 3010 [M]	Hugh Masekela's Latest	1967	$35
❏ 73010 [S]	Hugh Masekela's Latest	1967	$30
❏ 73041	Masekela	1969	$30
❏ 73051	Masekela -- Vol. 2	1970	$30
❏ 73028	The Promise of a Future	1968	$30

VERVE

❏ V6-8651	24 Karat Hits	1968	$35

WARNER BROS.

❏ 25566	Tomorrow	1987	$25

MASHMAKHAN

EPIC

❏ E30235	Mashmakhan	1970	$16
❏ E30813	The Family	1971	$16

MASKED MARAUDERS, THE

Fictional supergroup from a Rolling Stone magazine album review, which noted the presence of Bob Dylan, Mick Jagger, John Lennon and Paul McCartney. The below, recorded using the bogus review as a guide, was actually THE CLEANLINESS AND GODLINESS SKIFFLE BAND.

DEITY

❏ RS6378	The Masked Marauders	1969	$18

MASLAK, KESHAVAN

BLACK SAINT

❏ BSR-0079	Blaster Master	198?	$30

MASON, BARBARA, AND BUNNY SIGLER

CURTOM

❏ CU5014	Locked in This Position	1977	$18

MASON, BARBARA

ARCTIC

❏ ALPS-1004	Oh, How It Hurts	1968	$100
❏ ALP-1000 [M]	Yes, I'm Ready	1965	$100

❏ ALPS-1000 [P]	Yes, I'm Ready	1965	$120

BUDDAH

❏ BDS-5117	Give Me Your Love	1972	$18
❏ BDS-5140	Lady Love	1973	$25
❏ BDS-5628	Love's the Thing	1975	$25
❏ BDS-5610	Transition	1974	$25

NATIONAL GENERAL

❏ 2001	If You Knew Him Like I Do	1970	$75

PRELUDE

❏ 12159	I Am Your Woman, She Is Your Wife	1978	$25

Number	Title	Yr	NM

MASON, CHRISTOPHER

OPTIMISM
❏ OP-3218	Something Beautiful	198?	$25

MASON, DAVE, AND CASS ELLIOT
Also see each artist's individual listings.

BLUE THUMB
❏ BTS-8825	Dave Mason and Cass Elliot	1971	$25

MASON, DAVE

BLUE THUMB
❏ BTS-19	All Together	1970	$250

—*Erroneous pressing of "Alone Together"*
❏ BTS-19	Alone Together	1970	$25

—*Originals on multicolored vinyl*
❏ BTS-8819	Alone Together	1971	$50

—*Capitol-distributed black vinyl reissue*
❏ BTS-19	Alone Together	1975	$15

—*Multicolor label with "ABC" logo*
❏ ABCD-880	Dave Mason At His Best	1975	$12
❏ BTS-54	Dave Mason Is Alive!	1973	$18
❏ BTS-34	Headkeeper	1972	$18
❏ BT-6013	The Best of Dave Mason	1974	$12
❏ BT-6032	Very Best of Dave Mason	1978	$12

CHUMLEY
❏ 00101	Some Assembly Required	1987	$12

COLUMBIA
❏ PG34174	Certified Live	1976	$15
❏ PC33096	Dave Mason	1974	$12

—*No bar code on cover*
❏ PCQ33096 [Q]	Dave Mason	1974	$30
❏ PC33096	Dave Mason	198?	$10

—*Budget-line reissue with bar code*
❏ KC31721	It's Like You Never Left	1973	$12
❏ CQ31721 [Q]	It's Like You Never Left	1973	$30
❏ PC31721	It's Like You Never Left	197?	$10

—*Reissue with new prefix*
❏ PC34680	Let It Flow	1977	$12

—*No bar code on cover*
❏ PC34680	Let It Flow	198?	$10

—*Budget-line reissue with bar code*
❏ JC35285	Mariposa de Oro	1978	$12
❏ JC36144	Old Crest on a New Wave	1980	$12
❏ PC33698	Split Coconut	1975	$12
❏ PCQ33698 [Q]	Split Coconut	1975	$30
❏ FC37089	The Best of Dave Mason	1981	$12
❏ PC37089	The Best of Dave Mason	1983	$10

—*Budget-line reissue*

MCA
❏ 27035	Alone Together	198?	$10

—*Reissue of Blue Thumb 19*
❏ 11319	Alone Together	1995	$25

—*"Heavy Vinyl" gatefold reissue*
❏ 714	Dave Mason At His Best	198?	$10

—*Reissue of Blue Thumb 880*
❏ 713	Dave Mason Is Alive	198?	$10

—*Reissue of Blue Thumb 54*
❏ 712	Headkeeper	198?	$10

—*Reissue of Blue Thumb 34*
❏ 800	The Best of Dave Mason	1981	$10

—*Reissue of Blue Thumb 6013*
❏ 42086	Two Hearts	1988	$12
❏ 715	Very Best of Dave Mason	198?	$10

—*Reissue of Blue Thumb 6032*

S&P
❏ 503	It's Like You Never Left	2003	$25

—*Reissue on 180-gram vinyl*

MASON, HARVEY

ARISTA
❏ AL4096	Earthmover	1976	$30
❏ AL4157	Funk in a Mason Jar	1978	$30
❏ AL4054	Marching in the Street	1975	$30

MASON, JACKIE

VERVE
❏ V-15045 [M]	Great Moments in Comedy	1964	$25
❏ V-15033 [M]	I'm the Greatest Comedian in the World Only Nobody Knows It Yet	1962	$25
❏ V-15034 [M]	I Want to Leave You with the Words of a Great Comedian	1963	$25

WARNER BROS.
❏ 25603	The World According to Me!	1987	$12

MASON, JAMES

CHIAROSCURO
❏ 189	Rhythm of Life	1978	$15

MASON DIXON

CAPITOL
❏ C1-90120	Exception to the Rule	1989	$12

MASON PROFFIT

AMPEX
❏ A-10138	Last Night I Had the Strangest Dream	1971	$30

HAPPY TIGER
❏ HT-1019	Movin' Toward Happiness	1971	$25
❏ HT-1009	Wanted! Mason Proffit	1970	$30

WARNER BROS.
❏ BS2704 [B]	Bareback Rider	1973	$25
❏ 2WS2746	Come and Gone	1974	$25
❏ BS2657 [B]	Rockfish Crossing	1972	$25

MASQUERADERS, THE

ABC/HBS
❏ ABCD-921	Everybody Wanna Live On	1975	$18
❏ AB-962	Love Anonymous	1976	$18

BANG
❏ NJZ36321	The Masqueraders	1980	$18

MASSEY, WAYNE

POLYDOR
❏ PD-1-6309	One Life to Live	1980	$15

MASSO, GEORGE

DREAMSTREET
❏ DR-108	Pieces of Eight	1986	$25

FAMOUS DOOR
❏ 129	Choice N.Y.C.	197?	$30
❏ 148	No Frills, Just Music	198?	$25
❏ 138	Swinging Case of Masso-ism	1981	$30

MASTER CYLINDER

INNER CITY
❏ IC-1112	Elsewhere	198?	$30

MASTER FLEET

SUSSEX
❏ SRA-8028	High on the Sea	1974	$40

MASTER P

NO LIMIT/PRIORITY
❏ P150969	The Ghettos Tryin to Kill Me!	1997	$18

—*Generic black sleeve with center hole*

MASTERS, FRANKIE

CIRCLE
❏ 62	Frankie Masters and His Orchestra 1945-46	198?	$25

MASTERS, JOE

COLUMBIA
❏ CS9398 [S]	The Jazz Mass	1967	$25
❏ CL2598 [M]	The Jazz Mass	1967	$30

DISCOVERY
❏ 785	The Jazz Mass	197?	$35

MASTERS, MARK

SEA BREEZE
❏ SB-2022	Early Start	198?	$30
❏ SB-2033	Silver Threads Among the Blues	1987	$30

MASTERSOUNDS, THE

FANTASY
❏ 3316 [M]	A Date with the Mastersounds	1961	$40

—*Red vinyl*
❏ 3316 [M]	A Date with the Mastersounds	1962	$30

—*Black vinyl*
❏ 8062 [S]	A Date with the Mastersounds	1961	$30

—*Blue vinyl*
❏ 8062 [S]	A Date with the Mastersounds	1962	$25

—*Black vinyl*
❏ OJC-282	A Date with the Mastersounds	1987	$25
❏ OJC-280	Swinging with the Mastersounds	1987	$25
❏ 3305 [M]	Swinging' with the Mastersounds	1960	$40

—*Red vinyl*
❏ 3305 [M]	Swinging' with the Mastersounds	1962	$30

—*Black vinyl*
❏ 8050 [S]	Swingin' with the Mastersounds	1961	$30

—*Blue vinyl*
❏ 8050 [S]	Swingin' with the Mastersounds	1962	$25

—*Black vinyl*
❏ 3327 [M]	The Mastersounds on Tour	1961	$40

—*Red vinyl*
❏ 3327 [M]	The Mastersounds on Tour	1962	$30

—*Black vinyl*
❏ 8066 [S]	The Mastersounds on Tour	1961	$30

—*Blue vinyl*
❏ 8066 [S]	The Mastersounds on Tour	1962	$25

—*Black vinyl*

PACIFIC JAZZ
❏ PJM-403 [M]	Introducing the Mastersounds	1957	$50
❏ PJM-405 [M]	The King and I	1958	$50

WORLD PACIFIC
❏ WP-1260 [M]	Ballads and Blues	1959	$175
❏ ST-1019 [S]	Ballads and Blues	1959	$150
❏ WP-1252 [M]	Flower Drum Song	1958	$175
❏ ST-1012 [S]	Flower Drum Song	1958	$150
❏ WP-1280 [M]	Happy Holidays from Many Lands	1959	$175
❏ ST-1030 [S]	Happy Holidays from Many Lands	1959	$150
❏ WP-1271 [M]	Jazz Showcase	1959	$150

—*Reissue of Pacific Jazz 403*
❏ WP-1243 [M]	Kismet	1958	$175
❏ ST-1010 [S]	Kismet	1958	$150
❏ WP-1272 [M]	The King and I	1959	$150

—*Reissue of Pacific Jazz 405*
❏ ST-1017 [S]	The King and I	1959	$150
❏ WP-1269 [M]	The Mastersounds in Concert	1959	$175
❏ ST-1026 [S]	The Mastersounds in Concert	1959	$150
❏ WP-1284 [M]	The Mastersounds Play Horace Silver	1960	$175
❏ ST-1284 [S]	The Mastersounds Play Horace Silver	1960	$150

MATCHBOX 20

LAVA
❏ 92721	Yourself or Someone Like You	1997	$15

MATERIAL

ELEKTRA/MUSICIAN
❏ 60042	Memory Serves	1982	$12
❏ 60206	One Down	1984	$12

MATHEWS, MAT

AUDIOPHILE
❏ AP-219	Mat Mathews and Friends	1987	$25

BRUNSWICK
❏ BL54013 [M]	Bag's Groove	1956	$100

DAWN
❏ DLP-1104 [M]	The Modern Art of Jazz	1956	$300

MATHEWS, RONNIE

BEE HIVE
❏ 7011	Legacy	197?	$30
❏ 7008	Roots, Branches and Dances	197?	$30

PRESTIGE
❏ PRLP-7303 [M]	Doin' the Thang	1964	$30
❏ PRST-7303 [S]	Doin' the Thang	1964	$40

TIMELESS
❏ LPSJP-304	Selena's Dance	1990	$30

MATHIS, COUNTRY JOHNNY
The "original" Johnny Mathis, the "Country" prefix was added to his name after the "other" Johnny Mathis became far more popular. Also see JIMMY AND JOHNNY.

Number	Title	Yr	NM
HILLTOP GOSPEL			
❏ GS-7004	Country Johnny Mathis	1965	$30
LITTLE DARLIN'			
❏ 8007	He Keeps Me Singin'	1967	$25

MATHIS, JOHNNY

COLUMBIA

Number	Title	Yr	NM
❏ FC38718	A Special Part of Me	1984	$12
❏ FC40447	Christmas Eve with Johnny Mathis	1986	$12
❏ 3C38306	Christmas with Johnny Mathis	1982	$10
—Reissue of Columbia LE 10196 with same contents			
❏ C30210	Close to You	1970	$15
❏ JC36505	Different Kinda Different	1980	$12
❏ CL1422 [M]	Faithfully	1959	$25
—Red and black label with six "eye" logos			
❏ CL1422 [M]	Faithfully	1962	$18
—Red label with either "Guaranteed High Fidelity" or "360 Sound Mono			
❏ CS8219 [S]	Faithfully	1959	$30
—Red and black label with six "eye" logos			
❏ CS8219 [S]	Faithfully	1962	$25
—Red "360 Sound" label			
❏ PC33887	Feelings	1975	$12
❏ PC39468	For Christmas	1984	$10
❏ FC37748	Friends in Love	1982	$12
❏ CS9923	Give Me Your Love for Christmas	1969	$15
❏ CL1119 [M]	Good Night, Dear Lord	1958	$30
—Red and black label with six "eye" logos			
❏ CL1119 [M]	Good Night, Dear Lord	1962	$18
—Red label with either "Guaranteed High Fidelity" or "360 Sound Mono			
❏ CS8012 [S]	Good Night, Dear Lord	1958	$40
—Red and black label with six "eye" logos			
❏ CS8012 [S]	Good Night, Dear Lord	1962	$25
—Red "360 Sound" label			
❏ CL1351 [M]	Heavenly	1959	$25
—Red and black label with six "eye" logos			
❏ CL1351 [M]	Heavenly	1962	$18
—Red label with either "Guaranteed High Fidelity" or "360 Sound Mono			
❏ CS8152 [S]	Heavenly	1959	$30
—Red and black label with six "eye" logos			
❏ CS8152 [S]	Heavenly	1962	$25
—Red "360 Sound" label			
❏ PC8152 [S]	Heavenly	198?	$10
—Reissue with new prefix			
❏ CS8152 [S]	Heavenly	1971	$12
—Orange label			
❏ CG33621	Heavenly/Faithfully	1975	$15
❏ PC34872	Hold Me, Thrill Me, Kiss Me	1977	$12
❏ CL1623 [M]	I'll Buy You a Star	1961	$18
—Red and black label with six "eye" logos			
❏ CL1623 [M]	I'll Buy You a Star	1962	$15
—Red label with either "Guaranteed High Fidelity" or "360 Sound Mono			
❏ CS8423 [S]	I'll Buy You a Star	1961	$25
—Red and black label with six "eye" logos			
❏ CS8423 [S]	I'll Buy You a Star	1962	$18
—Red "360 Sound" label			
❏ CL2143 [M]	I'll Search My Heart and Other Great Hits	1964	$15
❏ CS8943 [S]	I'll Search My Heart and Other Great Hits	1964	$18
—Red "360 Sound" label			
❏ KC32435	I'm Coming Home	1973	$12
❏ CQ32435 [Q]	I'm Coming Home	1973	$30
❏ PC32435	I'm Coming Home	198?	$10
—Budget-line reissue			
❏ OC44336	In the Still of the Night	1989	$15
❏ PC34117	I Only Have Eyes for You	1976	$12
❏ CL2044 [M]	Johnny	1963	$15
❏ CS8844 [S]	Johnny	1963	$18
—Red "360 Sound" label			
❏ CL887 [M]	Johnny Mathis	1957	$150
❏ KG31345	Johnny Mathis' All-Time Greatest Hits	1972	$18
❏ PC34667	Johnny Mathis' Greatest Hits	1977	$12
❏ KG30979	Johnny Mathis In Person	1972	$18
❏ 2CQ30979 [Q]	Johnny Mathis In Person	1972	$40
❏ FC38699	Johnny Mathis Live	1983	$12
❏ G30350	Johnny Mathis Sings the Music of Bacharach & Kaempfert	1970	$18
❏ CL1133 [M]	Johnny's Greatest Hits	1958	$30
—Red and black label with six "eye" logos			
❏ CL1133 [M]	Johnny's Greatest Hits	1962	$18
—Red label with either "Guaranteed High Fidelity" or "360 Sound Mono			
❏ CS8634 [R]	Johnny's Greatest Hits	1963	$15
❏ CL1526 [M]	Johnny's Mood	1960	$25
—Red and black label with six "eye" logos			
❏ CL1526 [M]	Johnny's Mood	1962	$18
—Red label with either "Guaranteed High Fidelity" or "360 Sound Mono			
❏ CS8326 [S]	Johnny's Mood	1960	$30
—Red and black label with six "eye" logos			
❏ CS8326 [S]	Johnny's Mood	1962	$25
—Red "360 Sound" label			
❏ CL2016 [M]	Johnny's Newest Hits	1963	$15
❏ CS8816 [S]	Johnny's Newest Hits	1963	$18
—Red "360 Sound" label			
❏ KC32258	Killing Me Softly with Her Song	1973	$12
❏ CL1711 [M]	Live It Up!	1962	$18
—Red and black label with six "eye" logos			
❏ CL1711 [M]	Live It Up!	1962	$15
—Red label with either "Guaranteed High Fidelity" or "360 Sound Mono			
❏ CS8511 [S]	Live It Up!	1962	$25
—Red and black label with six "eye" logos; add 1/3 if portrait is there			
❏ CS8511 [S]	Live It Up!	1962	$18
—Red "360 Sound" label			
❏ CS9637 [S]	Love Is Blue	1968	$18
❏ CL2837 [M]	Love Is Blue	1968	$30
❏ C30499	Love Story	1971	$15
❏ PC30499	Love Story	198?	$10
—Budget-line reissue			
❏ CS9909	Love Theme from "Romeo and Juliet"	1969	$18
—Red "360 Sound" label			
❏ PC9909	Love Theme from "Romeo and Juliet"	198?	$10
—Reissue with new prefix			
❏ CS9909	Love Theme from "Romeo and Juliet"	1971	$12
—Orange label			
❏ PC34441	Mathis Is…	1977	$12
❏ JC36216	Mathis Magic	1979	$12
❏ KC32114	Me and Mrs. Jones	1973	$12
❏ CQ32114 [Q]	Me and Mrs. Jones	1973	$30
❏ CL1195 [M]	Merry Christmas	1958	$40
—Original cover has Johnny standing, holding skis and poles			
❏ CS8021 [S]	Merry Christmas	1959	$30
—Original cover has Johnny standing, holding skis and poles; red and black label with six "eye" logos			
❏ CL1195 [M]	Merry Christmas	196?	$30
—Second cover has Johnny sitting, with skis and poles in snow			
❏ CS8021 [S]	Merry Christmas	196?	$25
—Second cover has Johnny sitting, with skis and poles in snow			
❏ PC8021 [S]	Merry Christmas	198?	$10
—New prefix; original "standing" cover; bar code on back cover with "02" suffix			
❏ CL1344 [M]	More Johnny's Greatest Hits	1959	$30
—Red and black label with six "eye" logos			
❏ CL1344 [M]	More Johnny's Greatest Hits	1962	$18
—Red label with either "Guaranteed High Fidelity" or "360 Sound Mono			
❏ CS8150 [S]	More Johnny's Greatest Hits	1959	$30
—Red and black label with six "eye" logos			
❏ CS8150 [S]	More Johnny's Greatest Hits	1962	$25
—Red "360 Sound" label			
❏ PC8150 [S]	More Johnny's Greatest Hits	198?	$10
—Reissue with new prefix			
❏ CS8150 [S]	More Johnny's Greatest Hits	1971	$12
—Orange label			
❏ OC44156	Once in a While	1988	$12
❏ CL1270 [M]	Open Fire, Two Guitars	1959	$30
—Red and black label with six "eye" logos			
❏ CL1270 [M]	Open Fire, Two Guitars	1962	$18
—Red label with either "Guaranteed High Fidelity" or "360 Sound Mono			
❏ CS8056 [S]	Open Fire, Two Guitars	1959	$40
—Red and black label with six "eye" logos			
❏ CS8056 [S]	Open Fire, Two Guitars	1962	$25
—Red "360 Sound" label			
❏ CS9871	People	1969	$18
❏ CL1644 [M]	Portrait of Johnny	1961	$18
—Red and black label with six "eye" logos; add 1/3 if portrait is there			
❏ CL1644 [M]	Portrait of Johnny	1962	$15
—Red label with either "Guaranteed High Fidelity" or "360 Sound Mono			
❏ CS8444 [S]	Portrait of Johnny	1961	$25
—Red and black label with six "eye" logos; add 1/3 if portrait is there			
❏ CS8444 [S]	Portrait of Johnny	1962	$18
—Red "360 Sound" label			
❏ CS1005	Raindrops Keep Fallin' on My Head	1970	$15
❏ CL1915 [M]	Rapture	1962	$15
❏ CS8715 [S]	Rapture	1962	$18
—Red "360 Sound" label			
❏ FC39601	Right from the Heart	1985	$12
❏ CL2098 [M]	Romantically	1963	$15
❏ CS8898 [S]	Romantically	1963	$18
—Red "360 Sound" label			
❏ C35578	Romantically	1978	$10
❏ KC31626	Song Sung Blue	1972	$15
❏ CQ31626 [Q]	Song Sung Blue	1972	$30
❏ CL1165 [M]	Swing Softly	1958	$30
—Red and black label with six "eye" logos			
❏ CL1165 [M]	Swing Softly	1962	$18
—Red label with either "Guaranteed High Fidelity" or "360 Sound Mono			
❏ CS8023 [S]	Swing Softly	1958	$40
—Red and black label with six "eye" logos			
❏ CL2223 [M]	The Ballads of Broadway	1964	$15
❏ CS9023 [S]	The Ballads of Broadway	1964	$18
—Red "360 Sound" label			
❏ CS9024 [S]	The Ballads of Broadway	1964	$18
—Red "360 Sound" label			
❏ JC35649	The Best Days of My Life	1979	$12
❏ PC35649	The Best Days of My Life	1985	$10
—Budget-line reissue			
❏ JC36871	The Best of Johnny Mathis 1975-1980	1980	$12
❏ C2X37440	The First 25 Years -- The Silver Anniversary Album	1981	$15
❏ KC31342	The First Time Ever (I Saw Your Face)	1972	$15
❏ CQ31342 [Q]	The First Time Ever (I Saw Your Face)	1972	$30
❏ PC31342	The First Time Ever (I Saw Your Face)	198?	$10
—Budget-line reissue			
❏ C2L34 [M]	The Great Years	1964	$18
❏ C2S834 [S]	The Great Years	1964	$25
—Red "360 Sound" label			
❏ KC33251	The Heart of a Woman	1974	$12
❏ FC40372	The Hollywood Musicals	1986	$12
—With Henry Mancini			
❏ CS9872	The Impossible Dream	1969	$18
—Red "360 Sound" label			
❏ PC9872	The Impossible Dream	198?	$10
—Reissue with new prefix			
❏ CS9872	The Impossible Dream	1971	$12
—Orange label			
❏ C2L17 [M]	The Rhythms and Ballads of Broadway	1960	$30
—Red and black label with six "eye" logos			
❏ C2L17 [M]	The Rhythms and Ballads of Broadway	1962	$25
—Red label with either "Guaranteed High Fidelity" or "360 Sound Mono			
❏ C2S803 [S]	The Rhythms and Ballads of Broadway	1960	$30
—Red and black label with six "eye" logos			
❏ C2S803 [S]	The Rhythms and Ballads of Broadway	1962	$30
—Red "360 Sound" label			
❏ CL2224 [M]	The Rhythms of Broadway	1964	$15
❏ CS9705 [S]	Those Were the Days	1968	$18
❏ CL2905 [M]	Those Were the Days	1968	$40
❏ CL2726 [M]	Up, Up and Away	1967	$18
❏ CS9526 [S]	Up, Up and Away	1967	$18
❏ CL1078 [M]	Warm	1957	$30
—Red and black label with six "eye" logos			
❏ CL1078 [M]	Warm	1962	$18
—Red label with either "Guaranteed High Fidelity" or "360 Sound Mono			
❏ CS8039 [S]	Warm	1958	$40
—Red and black label with six "eye" logos			
❏ CS8039 [S]	Warm	1962	$25
—Red "360 Sound" label			
❏ GP2	Warm/Open Fire, Two Guitars	1969	$18
❏ C32963	What'll I Do	1974	$12
❏ PC33420	When Will I See You Again	1975	$12
❏ CL1028 [M]	Wonderful Wonderful	1957	$30
—Red and black label with six "eye" logos			
❏ CL1028 [M]	Wonderful Wonderful	1962	$18
—Red label with either "Guaranteed High Fidelity" or "360 Sound Mono			
❏ CS9046 [R]	Wonderful Wonderful	1964	$15
❏ JC35359	You Light Up My Life	1978	$12
❏ PC35259	You Light Up My Life	1986	$10
—Budget-line reissue			
❏ C30740	You've Got a Friend	1971	$15
❏ CQ30740 [Q]	You've Got a Friend	1972	$30
❏ PC30740	You've Got a Friend	198?	$10
—Budget-line reissue			

COLUMBIA LIMITED EDITION

Number	Title	Yr	NM
❏ LE10196	Christmas with Johnny Mathis	1976	$12
—Reissue of Harmony KH 30684 with same contents			
❏ LE10003	Portrait of Johnny	197?	$12

COLUMBIA MUSICAL TREASURY

Number	Title	Yr	NM
❏ 6P6030	The Johnny Mathis Treasury	197?	$30

COLUMBIA SPECIAL PRODUCTS

Number	Title	Yr	NM
❏ P14658	Holidays at the Fireside	197?	$25
—Bonus album with box set 14628			
❏ P414971	Johnny	197?	$30
❏ C10896	Merry Christmas	1972	$15
—Reissue			
❏ P614628	Misty Memories: The Complete Johnny Mathis Treasury	197?	$30
—Maunfactured for Candelite Music			
❏ P311837	Romantically, Johnny Mathis	197?	$30
❏ P11477	Romantically, Johnny Mathis	197?	$15

Number	Title	Yr	NM
❏ P14908	The Heart of Johnny Mathis	197?	$18

—Bonus album with box set 14628

HARMONY

Number	Title	Yr	NM
❏ KH30684	Christmas with Johnny Mathis	1971	$15

—Reissue of Mercury SR 60837 with two fewer tracks

Number	Title	Yr	NM
❏ KH30017	Johnny Mathis	1970	$12
❏ KH31935	Something for Everyone	1973	$12

MERCURY

Number	Title	Yr	NM
❏ MG-20988 [M]	Johnny Mathis Ole	1965	$15
❏ SR-60988 [S]	Johnny Mathis Ole	1965	$18
❏ MG-21107 [M]	Johnny Mathis Sings	1967	$18
❏ SR-61107 [S]	Johnny Mathis Sings	1967	$18
❏ MG-20991 [M]	Love Is Everything	1965	$15
❏ SR-60991 [S]	Love Is Everything	1965	$18
❏ MG-21093 [M]	So Nice	1966	$15
❏ SR-61093 [S]	So Nice	1966	$18
❏ MG20837 [M]	Sounds of Christmas	1963	$15
❏ SR60837 [S]	Sounds of Christmas	1963	$18
❏ MG-20890 [M]	Tender Is the Night	1964	$15
❏ SR-60890 [S]	Tender Is the Night	1964	$18
❏ MG-21073 [M]	The Shadow of Your Smile	1966	$15
❏ SR-61073 [S]	The Shadow of Your Smile	1966	$18
❏ MG-21041 [M]	The Sweetheart Tree	1965	$15
❏ SR-61041 [S]	The Sweetheart Tree	1965	$18
❏ MG-20913 [M]	The Wonderful World of Make Believe	1964	$15
❏ SR-60913 [S]	The Wonderful World of Make Believe	1964	$18
❏ MG-20942 [M]	This Is Love	1964	$15
❏ SR-60942 [S]	This Is Love	1964	$18

MOBILE FIDELITY

Number	Title	Yr	NM
❏ 1-171	Heavenly	1985	$40

—Audiophile vinyl

READER'S DIGEST

Number	Title	Yr	NM
❏ RB4-097	His Greatest Hits and Finest Performances	198?	$30

TIME-LIFE

Number	Title	Yr	NM
❏ SLGD-08	Legendary Singers: Johnny Mathis	1985	$18

MATHIS, JOHNNY/DENIECE WILLIAMS

COLUMBIA

Number	Title	Yr	NM
❏ JC35435	That's What Friends Are For	1978	$12
❏ PC35435	That's What Friends Are For	198?	$10

—Budget-line reissue

MATLOCK, MATTY

RCA VICTOR

Number	Title	Yr	NM
❏ LPM-1413 [M]	Pete Kelly at Home	1957	$40

WARNER BROS.

Four-Button Dixie — MATTY MATLOCK and the Paducah Patrol

Number	Title	Yr	NM
❏ W1280 [M]	Four Button Dixie	1958	$30
❏ WS1280 [S]	Four Button Dixie	1958	$40

X

Number	Title	Yr	NM
❏ LXA-3035 [10]	Sports Parade	1955	$75

MATRIX

PABLO TODAY

Number	Title	Yr	NM
❏ 2312121	Harvest	1980	$30

MATTEA, KATHY

MERCURY

Number	Title	Yr	NM
❏ R110791	A Collection of Hits	1990	$25

—Only released on vinyl by BMG Direct Marketing

Number	Title	Yr	NM
❏ 824308-1	From My Heart	1985	$12
❏ 818560-1	Kathy Mattea	1984	$12
❏ 832793-1	Untasted Honey	1987	$12
❏ 830405-1	Walk the Way the Wind Blows	1986	$12
❏ 836950-1	Willow in the Wind	1989	$15

MATTHEWS, DAVE, BAND

RCA

Number	Title	Yr	NM
❏ 67660	Before These Crowded Streets	1998	$250

MATTHEWS, DAVID

CTI

Number	Title	Yr	NM
❏ 5005	Dune	1977	$30

GNP CRESCENDO

Number	Title	Yr	NM
❏ GNP-2153	Delta Lady	198?	$25
❏ GNP-2162	Grand Connection	198?	$25
❏ GNP-2157	Grand Cross	198?	$25
❏ GNP-2174	Ice Fuse One	198?	$25
❏ GNP-2185	Speed Demon	1986	$25
❏ GNP-2169	Super Funky Sax	198?	$25

KUDU

Number	Title	Yr	NM
❏ 30	Shoogie Wanna Boogie	1976	$35

MUSE

Number	Title	Yr	NM
❏ MR-5073	David Matthews' Big Band at the 5 Spot	1976	$25
❏ MR-5096	Flight	1977	$25

MATTHEWS, IAN

COLUMBIA

Number	Title	Yr	NM
❏ PC34102	Go for Broke	1976	$12
❏ PC34671	Hit and Run	1977	$12

ELEKTRA

Number	Title	Yr	NM
❏ EKS-75078	Some Days You Eat the Bear	1974	$15
❏ EKS-75051	Valley Hi	1973	$15

MUSHROOM

Number	Title	Yr	NM
❏ MRS-5014	Siamese Friends	1979	$12
❏ MRS-5012	Stealin' Home	1978	$12

RSO

Number	Title	Yr	NM
❏ RS-1-3092	A Spot of Interference	1980	$12

VERTIGO

Number	Title	Yr	NM
❏ VEL-1002 [B]	If You Saw Thro' My Eyes	1971	$50
❏ VEL-1010 [B]	Tigers Will Survive	1972	$50

WINDHAM HILL

Number	Title	Yr	NM
❏ WD-1070	Walking a Changing Line: The Songs of Jules Shear	1987	$12

MATTHEWS, ONZY

CAPITOL

Number	Title	Yr	NM
❏ T2099 [M]	Blues with a Touch of Elegance	1964	$85
❏ ST2099 [S]	Blues with a Touch of Elegance	1964	$40

MATTHEWS, WALT

FRETLESS

Number	Title	Yr	NM
❏ 158	The Dance in Your Eye	198?	$30

MATTHEWS' SOUTHERN COMFORT

DECCA

Number	Title	Yr	NM
❏ DL75264	Later That Same Year	1971	$15
❏ DL75191 [B]	Matthews' Southern Comfort	1970	$18
❏ DL75242	Second Spring	1970	$15

PICKWICK

Number	Title	Yr	NM
❏ SPC-3698	Later That Same Year	197?	$10

MATTSON, PHIL

DOCTOR JAZZ

Number	Title	Yr	NM
❏ FW40349	Setting Standards	1986	$25

MATZ, PETER

PROJECT 3

Number	Title	Yr	NM
❏ PR5007SD	Peter Matz Brings 'Em Back	1967	$35

MAUDS, THE

MERCURY

Number	Title	Yr	NM
❏ MG-21135 [M]	The Mauds Hold On	1967	$25
❏ SR-61135 [S]	The Mauds Hold On	1967	$30

MAULAWI

STRATA-EAST

Number	Title	Yr	NM
❏ SES104-74	Maulawi	1974	$30

MAUPIN, BENNIE

ECM

Number	Title	Yr	NM
❏ 1043	The Jewel in the Lotus	197?	$35

MERCURY

Number	Title	Yr	NM
❏ SRM-1-3717	Moonscapes	1978	$25
❏ SRM-1-1148	Slow Traffic	1976	$25

MAURA AND MARIA

WYNCOTE

Number	Title	Yr	NM
❏ W-9075 [M]	Songs Made Famous by Joan Baez	1965	$12
❏ SW-9075 [S]	Songs Made Famous by Joan Baez	1965	$15

MAURIAT, PAUL

FANTASY

Number	Title	Yr	NM
❏ 8389	Joyeux Noel	1968	$15
❏ 8394	Latin Style	1969	$15
❏ 8380	Paris by Night	1968	$15

MERCURY

Number	Title	Yr	NM
❏ SRM-1-3746	Overseas	1978	$12

MGM

Number	Title	Yr	NM
❏ M3G-4999	Have You Never Been Mellow	1975	$12
❏ SE-4838	Love Theme from "The Godfather"	1972	$12

PHILIPS

Number	Title	Yr	NM
❏ PHM200248 [M]	Blooming Hits	1967	$25
❏ PHS600248 [S]	Blooming Hits	1967	$18

—Original copies have no "blurb" for "Love Is Blue" on front cover

Number	Title	Yr	NM
❏ PHS600248 [S]	Blooming Hits	1968	$15

—With blurb for "Love Is Blue" on front cover

Number	Title	Yr	NM
❏ PHS600292	Doing My Thing	1969	$18
❏ PHS600352	El Condor Pasa	1970	$15
❏ PHS600345	Gone Is Love	1970	$15
❏ PHM200197 [M]	Listen Too	1965	$15
❏ PHS600197 [S]	Listen Too	1965	$18
❏ PHS600320	L-O-V-E	1969	$18
❏ PHS600270	Mauriat Magic	1968	$18
❏ PHS600337	Midnight Cowboy/Let the Sunshine In	1970	$15
❏ PHM200226 [M]	More Mauriat	1967	$18
❏ PHS600226 [S]	More Mauriat	1967	$18
❏ PHM200215 [M]	Of Vodka and Caviar	1966	$15
❏ PHS600215 [S]	Of Vodka and Caviar	1966	$18
❏ PHS600280	Prevailing Airs	1968	$18
❏ PHM200255 [M]	The Christmas Album	1967	$25
❏ PHS600255 [S]	The Christmas Album	1967	$18
❏ PHS600299	The Soul of Paul Mauriat	1969	$18

VERVE

Number	Title	Yr	NM
❏ V6-5087	Theme from "A Summer Place"	1973	$12

MAURO, TURK

STORYVILLE

Number	Title	Yr	NM
❏ 4076	The Underdog	198?	$25

MAVERICKS, THE

MCA

Number	Title	Yr	NM
❏ 11257	Music for All Occasions	1995	$12

MAXIMILLIAN

ABC

Number	Title	Yr	NM
❏ S-696	Maximillian	1969	$40

MAXTED, BILLY

BRUNSWICK

Number	Title	Yr	NM
❏ BL58052 [10]	Honky Tonk Piano	1953	$75

CADENCE

Number	Title	Yr	NM
❏ CLP-1005 [M]	Billy Maxted Plays Hi-Fi Keyboard	1955	$50
❏ CLP-1013 [M]	Dixieland Manhattan Style	1955	$50
❏ CLP-3013 [M]	Dixieland Manhattan Style	1958	$30
❏ CLP-1012 [M]	Jazz at Nick's	1955	$50

LIBERTY

Number	Title	Yr	NM
❏ LRP-3474 [M]	Maxted Makes It	1966	$30
❏ LST-7474 [S]	Maxted Makes It	1966	$35
❏ LRP-3492 [M]	Satin Doll	1967	$35
❏ LST-7492 [S]	Satin Doll	1967	$30

SEECO

Number	Title	Yr	NM
❏ CELP-458 [M]	Art of Jazz	1960	$150
❏ CELP-4580 [S]	Art of Jazz	1960	$150
❏ CELP-438 [M]	Bourbon St. Billy and the Blues	1960	$150
❏ CELP-4380 [S]	Bourbon St. Billy and the Blues	1960	$150

MAXWELL, DIANE

CHALLENGE

Number	Title	Yr	NM
❏ CHL-607 [M]	Almost Seventeen	1959	$40
❏ CHS-2501 [S]	Almost Seventeen	1959	$50

MAXWELL, JIMMIE

CIRCLE

Number	Title	Yr	NM
❏ 50	Let's Fall in Love	198?	$25

MAXWELL, ROBERT

COMMAND

Number	Title	Yr	NM
❏ SD913 [S]	Anytime	1967	$15
❏ 33-913 [M]	Anytime	1967	$18

DECCA

Number	Title	Yr	NM
❏ DL4723 [M]	Let's Get Away from It All	1966	$15
❏ DL74723 [S]	Let's Get Away from It All	1966	$18
❏ DL4563 [M]	Peg o' My Heart	1964	$15
❏ DL74563 [S]	Peg o' My Heart	1964	$18
❏ DL4421 [M]	Shangri-La	1964	$15
❏ DL74421 [S]	Shangri-La	1964	$18
❏ DL4609 [M]	Songs for All Seasons	1965	$15
❏ DL74609 [S]	Songs for All Seasons	1965	$18

MGM

Number	Title	Yr	NM
❏ E-4246 [M]	The Very Best of Robert Maxwell	1964	$15
❏ SE-4246 [S]	The Very Best of Robert Maxwell	1964	$18

MAY, BILLY

Number	Title	Yr	NM
BAINBRIDGE			
❏ ST1001	I Believe in You	197?	$30
CAPITOL			
❏ H349 [10]	A Band Is Born!	1952	$75
❏ T349 [M]	A Band Is Born!	195?	$75
— Turquoise label original			
❏ H374 [10]	Bacchanalia!	1953	$75
❏ T374 [M]	Bacchanalia!	195?	$75
— Turquoise label original			
❏ L329 [10]	Big Band Bash	1952	$75
❏ T329 [M]	Big Band Bash	195?	$75
— Turquoise label original			
❏ T1043 [M]	Big Fat Brass	1958	$100
— Black colorband label, Capitol logo at left			
❏ ST1043 [S]	Big Fat Brass	1958	$150
— Black colorband label, Capitol logo at left			
❏ T1888 [M]	Bill's Bag	1963	$85
❏ ST1888 [S]	Bill's Bag	1963	$100
❏ T771 [M]	Billy May Plays for Fancy Dancin'	1956	$150
— Turquoise label original			
❏ H487 [10]	Billy May's Naughty Operetta!	1953	$75
❏ T487 [M]	Billy May's Naughty Operetta!	195?	$75
— Turquoise label original			
❏ T2560 [M]	Billy May Today	1965	$75

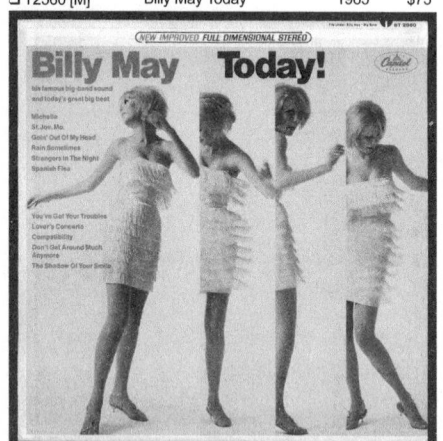

Number	Title	Yr	NM
❏ ST2560 [S]	Billy May Today	1965	$18
❏ ST1329 [S]	Cha Cha!	1959	$150
— Black colorband label, Capitol logo at left			
❏ T1329 [M]	Cha Cha!	1959	$100
— Black colorband label, Capitol logo at left			
❏ T1367 [M]	Cha Cha Mambos	1959	$100
— Black colorband label, logo at left			
❏ TAO924 [M]	Jimmie Lunceford in Hi-Fi: Authentic Re-Creations of the Lunceford Style	1958	$150
— Turquoise label original			
❏ STAO924 [S]	Jimmie Lunceford in Hi-Fi: Authentic Re-Creations of the Lunceford Style	1958	$85
— Black colorband label, Capitol logo at left			
❏ H237 [10]	Join the Band	1951	$85
❏ T1377 [M]	Pow!	1959	$300
— Gold "The Star Line" label			
❏ T677 [M]	Sorta-Dixie!	195?	$75
— Turquoise label original			
❏ M11885 [M]	Sorta-Dixie!	197?	$25
— Reissue of Capitol 677			
❏ T562 [M]	Sorta-May	195?	$75
— Turquoise label original			
❏ M562 [M]	Sorta-May	197?	$25
— Reissue with new prefix			
❏ T1417 [M]	The Girls and Boys on Broadway	1960	$85
— Black colorband label, Capitol logo at left			
❏ ST1417 [S]	The Girls and Boys on Broadway	1960	$100
— Black colorband label, Capitol logo at left			
❏ T1581 [M]	The Great Jimmie Lunceford: Authentic Re-Creations of the Lunceford Style by Billy May	1961	$300
— Gold "The Star Line" label			
❏ ST1581 [S]	The Great Jimmie Lunceford: Authentic Re-Creations of the Lunceford Style by Billy May	1961	$300
— Gold "The Star Line" label			
❏ T1709 [M]	The Sweetest Swingin' Sounds of No Strings	196?	$50
❏ ST1709 [S]	The Sweetest Swingin' Sounds of No Strings	196?	$100
CREATIVE WORLD			
❏ ST-1054	Sorta-Dixie!	197?	$30

Number	Title	Yr	NM
❏ ST-1051 [M]	Sorta-May	197?	$30
IMPERIAL			
❏ LP-9042 [M]	Fuzzy Pink Nightgown	1957	$250
— Movie soundtrack			
PAUSA			
❏ PR9035	A Band Is Born!	198?	$25
— Reissue of Capitol T 349			
PICKWICK			
❏ PC-3010 [M]	Hey It's May	196?	$35
❏ SPC-3010 [R]	Hey It's May	196?	$20
STEREO SOUNDS			
❏ SA-12	Music for Uptight Guys	196?	$35
TIME			
❏ 52064 [M]	Billy May and His Orchestra	1962	$35
❏ S-2064 [S]	Billy May and His Orchestra	1962	$50
TIME-LIFE			
❏ STL-340	The Swing Era: 1930-1936	197?	$50
— Box set with hardcover book; re-creations of original big-band charts, with some contributions by the Glenn Gray Orchestra			
❏ STL-341	The Swing Era: 1936-1937	197?	$50
— Box set with hardcover book; re-creations of original big-band charts, with some contributions by the Glenn Gray Orchestra			
❏ STL-342	The Swing Era: 1937-1938	197?	$50
— Box set with hardcover book; re-creations of original big-band charts, with some contributions by the Glenn Gray Orchestra			
❏ STL-343	The Swing Era: 1938-1939	197?	$50
— Box set with hardcover book; re-creations of original big-band charts, with some contributions by the Glenn Gray Orchestra			
❏ STL-344	The Swing Era: 1939-1940	197?	$50
— Box set with hardcover book; re-creations of original big-band charts, with some contributions by the Glenn Gray Orchestra			
❏ STL-345	The Swing Era: 1940-1941	197?	$50
— Box set with hardcover book; re-creations of original big-band charts, with some contributions by the Glenn Gray Orchestra			
❏ STL-346	The Swing Era: 1941-1942	197?	$50
— Box set with hardcover book; re-creations of original big-band charts, with some contributions by the Glenn Gray Orchestra			
❏ STL-347	The Swing Era: 1942-1944	197?	$50
— Box set with hardcover book; re-creations of original big-band charts, with some contributions by the Glenn Gray Orchestra			
❏ STL-348	The Swing Era: 1944-1945	197?	$50
— Box set with hardcover book; re-creations of original big-band charts, with some contributions by the Glenn Gray Orchestra			
❏ STL-352	The Swing Era: Curtain Call	197?	$50
— Box set with hardcover book; re-creations of original big-band charts, with some contributions by the Glenn Gray Orchestra			
❏ STL-351	The Swing Era: Encore!	197?	$50
— Box set with hardcover book; re-creations of original big-band charts, with some contributions by the Glenn Gray Orchestra			
❏ STL-350	The Swing Era: Into the '50s	197?	$50
— Box set with hardcover book; re-creations of original big-band charts, with some contributions by the Glenn Gray Orchestra			
❏ STL-353	The Swing Era: One More Time	197?	$50
— Box set with hardcover book; re-creations of original big-band charts, with some contributions by the Glenn Gray Orchestra			
❏ STL-349	The Swing Era: The Postwar Years	197?	$50
— Box set with hardcover book; re-creations of original big-band charts, with some contributions by the Glenn Gray Orchestra			

MAY BLITZ

Number	Title	Yr	NM
PARAMOUNT			
❏ PAS-5020	May Blitz	1970	$30

MAYALL, JOHN

Number	Title	Yr	NM
ABC			
❏ D-958	A Banquet in Blues	1976	$12
❏ D-1039	A Hard Core Package	1977	$12
❏ D-1086	Last of the British Blues	1978	$12
❏ D-992	Lots of People	1977	$12
❏ ABCD-926	Notice to Appear	1976	$12
ACCORD			
❏ SN-7209	Roadshow Blues Band	1982	$12
BLUE THUMB			
❏ BTS-6019	New Year, New Band, New Company	1975	$12
DECAL			
❏ LIK-1	Some of My Best Friends Are Blues	1986	$12

Number	Title	Yr	NM
DJM			
❏ 29	No More Interviews	1979	$12
❏ 23	The Bottom Line	1979	$12
GNP CRESCENDO			
❏ 2184	Behind the Iron Curtain	1986	$12
ISLAND			
❏ 842795-1	A Sense of Place	1990	$15
❏ 91005	Chicago Line	1988	$12
LONDON			
❏ LL3502 [M]	A Hard Road	1967	$100
❏ PS502 [S]	A Hard Road	1967	$25
❏ PS537	Bare Wires	1968	$18
❏ LL3492 [M]	Blues Breakers with Eric Clapton	1966	$175
❏ PS492 [S]	Blues Breakers with Eric Clapton	1966	$100
❏ LC-50009	Blues Breakers with Eric Clapton	1977	$12
— Reissue of London PS 492			
❏ 800086-1	Blues Breakers with Eric Clapton	1983	$10
— Reissue of London 50009			
❏ PS545	Blues from Laurel Canyon	1969	$18
❏ LL3529 [M]	Crusade	1967	$50
❏ PS529 [S]	Crusade	1967	$30
❏ 2PS618 [B]	Down the Line	1973	$18
❏ PS589	Live in Europe	1971	$15
❏ PS562	Looking Back	1969	$18
❏ 820331-1	Looking Back	1985	$10
— Reissue of London PS 562			
❏ 820320-1	Primal Solos	1985	$10
❏ PS543	Raw Blues	1968	$18
❏ 820342-1	Raw Blues	1985	$10
— Reissue of London PS 543			
❏ PS534	The Blues Alone	1968	$18
❏ PS570	The Diary of a Band	1970	$15
❏ 2PS600 [B]	Through the Years	1971	$18
MCA			
❏ 795	Hard Core	1980	$10
— Reissue of ABC 1039			
❏ 716	Last of the British Blues	1980	$10
— Reissue of ABC 1086			
MOBILE FIDELITY			
❏ 1-183 [B]	Blues Breakers Featuring Eric Clapton	1985	$100
— Audiophile vinyl			
❏ 1-246	The Blues Alone	1996	$30
— Audiophile vinyl			
POLYDOR			
❏ 837127-1	Archive to the Eighties	1988	$10
❏ 25-3002 [B]	Back to the Roots	1971	$18
❏ 24-4010	Empty Rooms	1970	$12
❏ PD-5027	Jazz-Blues Fusion	1972	$12
❏ PD-5012	Memories	1971	$12
❏ PD-5036	Moving On	1972	$12
❏ PD2-3005 [B]	Ten Years Are Gone	1973	$18
❏ PD2-3006 [B]	The Best of John Mayall	1973	$18
❏ PD-6030	The Latest Edition	1974	$15
❏ 24-4004	The Turning Point	1970	$12
❏ 823305-1	The Turning Point	1985	$10
— Reissue of Polydor 24-4004			
❏ 24-4022	U.S.A. Union	1970	$12
❏ SKAO-93398	U.S.A. Union	1970	$18
— Capitol Record Club edition			

MAYER, JOHN

Number	Title	Yr	NM
COLUMBIA			
❏ C86185	Heavier Things	2003	$15
❏ C85293	Room for Squares	2001	$15

MAYER, NATHANIEL

Number	Title	Yr	NM
FORTUNE			
❏ 8014 [M]	Goin' Back to the Village of Love	1964	$300
— Light blue label			
❏ 8014 [M]	Goin' Back to the Village of Love	196?	$175
— Purple label			
❏ 8014 [M]	Goin' Back to the Village of Love	196?	$75
— Yellow label			
❏ 8014 [M]	Goin' Back to the Village of Love	197?	$18
— Bluish purple label, with much more flexible vinyl than earlier pressings			

MAYERL, BILLY

Number	Title	Yr	NM
FLAPPER			
❏ 704/5	The Versatility of Billy Mayerl	198?	$35

MAYFIELD, CURTIS

Also see FISHBONE; THE IMPRESSIONS.

Number	Title	Yr	NM
BOARDWALK			
❏ NB1-33256	Honesty	1982	$12
❏ NB1-33239	Love Is the Place	1981	$12

Number	Title	Yr	NM
CRC			
❑ 2001	We Come in Peace with a Message of Love	1985	$15
CURTOM			
❑ CRS-8015	Back to the World	1973	$18
❑ CRS-8005	Curtis	1970	$18
❑ CRS-8018	Curtis in Chicago	1973	$18
❑ CRS-8008	Curtis/Live!	1971	$25
❑ CUK5022	Do It All Night	1978	$15
❑ CU5007	Give, Get, Take and Have	1976	$15
❑ CRS-8604	Got to Find a Way	1974	$15
❑ CUR-2902	Greatest Hits of All Time (Classic Collection)	198?	$15
❑ CUR-2901	Live in Europe	198?	$15
❑ CU5013	Never Say You Can't Survive	1977	$15
❑ CRS-8009	Roots	1971	$18
❑ CUR-2005	Something to Believe In	198?	$10
—*Reissue of RSO 3077*			
❑ CRS-8014	Superfly	1972	$25
❑ CRS-8601	Sweet Exorcist	1974	$15
❑ CUR-2008	Take It to the Street	198?	$12
❑ CU5001	There's No Place Like America Today	1975	$15
❑ CUR-2003	There's No Place Like America Today	198?	$10
—*Reissue of 5001*			
RHINO			
❑ 8122796557 [B]	Curtis	2013	$30
RSO			
❑ RS-1-3053	Heartbeat	1979	$12
❑ RS-1-3077	Something to Believe In	1980	$12

MAYFIELD, PERCY
BRUNSWICK
❑ BL754145	Walking on a Tightrope	1968	$25
INTERMEDIA			
❑ QS-5010	Please Send Me Someone to Love	198?	$12
RCA VICTOR			
❑ LSP-4558 [B]	Blues And Then Some	1971	$18
❑ LSP-4269	Percy Mayfield Sings Percy Mayfield	1970	$18
❑ LSP-4444	Weakness Is a Thing Called Man	1970	$18
SPECIALTY			
❑ SP-7001	Poet of the Blues	1990	$18
❑ SPS-2126	The Best of Percy Mayfield	1970	$25
TANGERINE			
❑ TRC-1510 [M]	Bought Blues	1967	$30
❑ TRCS-1510 [S]	Bought Blues	1967	$50
❑ TRC-1505 [M]	My Jug and I	1966	$30

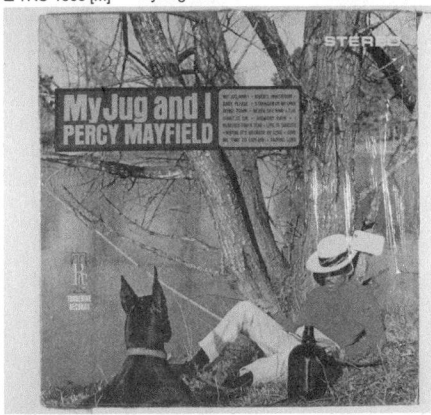

| ❑ TRCS-1505 [S] | My Jug and I | 1966 | $50 |

MAYL, GENE
BLACKBIRD
❑ 12006	A Trip to Waukesha	1969	$35
JAZZOLOGY			
❑ J-6 [M]	Gene Mayl's Dixieland Rhythm Kings	1964	$35

MAYPOLE
COLOSSUS
| ❑ CS-1007 | Maypole | 1971 | $75 |

MAYS, BILL
TREND
| ❑ TR-532 | Tha's Delights | 1984 | $30 |

MAYS, LYLE
GEFFEN
| ❑ GHS24097 | Lyle Mays | 1986 | $25 |
| ❑ GHS24204 | Street Dreams | 1988 | $25 |

Number	Title	Yr	NM
MAZE			
MTA			
❑ 5012	Armageddon	1969	$150
MAZZY STAR			
CAPITOL			
❑ C1-27224	Among My Swan	1996	$100
ROUGH TRADE			
❑ RUS771	She Hangs Brightly	1990	$150
M'BOOM			
COLUMBIA			
❑ JC37066	M'Boom	1981	$30
SOUL NOTE			
❑ SN-1059	Collage	198?	$30
MC5			
ALIVE			
❑ 08 [10]	Ice Pick Slim/Mad Like Eldridge Cleaver	1994	$15
❑ 05 [10]	Power Trip	1994	$15
ATLANTIC			
❑ SD8247	Back in the USA	1970	$100
❑ SD8285	High Time	1971	$100
CLEOPATRA			
❑ 8387 [B]	Kick Out The Jams! 1966-1970		$30
—*picture disc*			
ELEKTRA			
❑ EKS-74042 [B]	Kick Out the Jams	1969	$250
—*Gatefold cover with John Sinclair liner notes in center spread; brownish label*			
❑ EKS-74042	Kick Out the Jams	1969	$40
—*All other editions*			
SUNDAZED			
❑ LP5093	Back in the USA	2002	$25
—*Reissue on 180-gram vinyl*			
❑ LP5094	High Time	2002	$25
—*Reissue on 180-gram vinyl*			
❑ LP5092	Kick Out the Jams	2001	$25
—*Reissue of original Elektra album, complete with uncensored liner notes*			
TOTAL ENERGY			
❑ 2001 [10]	The American Ruse	1994	$15

MCANALLY, MAC
ARIOLA AMERICA
❑ ST-50019	Mac McAnally	1977	$15
❑ SW-50029	No Problem	1978	$15
GEFFEN			
❑ 24191	Finish Lines	1988	$12
❑ GHS2033	Nothing But the Truth	1983	$12
RCA VICTOR			
❑ AFL1-3519	Cuttin' Corners	1980	$15

MCAULIFFE, LEON
ABC-PARAMOUNT
❑ ABC-394 [M]	Cozy Inn	1961	$40
❑ ABCS-394 [S]	Cozy Inn	1961	$75
CAPITOL			
❑ T2148 [M]	Everybody Dance! Everybody Swing!	1964	$30
❑ ST2148 [S]	Everybody Dance! Everybody Swing!	1964	$40
❑ T2016 [M]	The Dancin'est Band Around	1964	$30
❑ ST2016 [S]	The Dancin'est Band Around	1964	$40
CIMARRON			
❑ CLP-2002 [M]	The Swingin' Western Strings of Leon McAuliff	1960	$50
DOT			
❑ DLP-3689 [M]	Golden Country Hits	1966	$40
❑ DLP-25689 [R]	Golden Country Hits	1966	$30
❑ DLP-3139 [M]	Take Off	1958	$75
SESAC			
❑ (# unknown) [M]	Just a Minute	1957	$150
❑ 1601 [M]	Points West	1957	$150
STARDAY			
❑ SLP-171 [M]	Mr. Western Swing	1962	$50
❑ SLP-309 [M]	The Swingin' Western Strings of Leon McAuliff	1964	$40
❑ SLP-280 [M]	The Swingin' West with Leon McAuliff	1964	$40

MCBEE, CECIL
ENJA
❑ 3041	Compassion	198?	$30
INDIA NAVIGATION			
❑ IN-1043	Alternate Spaces	197?	$35
❑ IN-1053	Flying Out	198?	$35
INNER CITY			
❑ IC-3023	Music from the Source	197?	$35

Number	Title	Yr	NM
STRATA-EAST			
❑ SES-7417	Mutima	1975	$30

MCBRIDE, DALE
CON BRIO
| ❑ 051 | The Ordinary Man Album | 1977 | $15 |

MCBROWNE, LENNY
PACIFIC JAZZ
❑ PJ-1 [M]	The Four Souls	1960	$30
❑ ST-1 [S]	The Four Souls	1960	$40
RIVERSIDE			
❑ RLP-346 [M]	Eastern Lights	1960	$250
❑ RS-9346 [S]	Eastern Lights	1960	$250

MCCALL, C.W.
MGM
❑ M3G-5008	Black Bear Road	1975	$12
❑ M3G-4989	Wolf Creek Pass	1975	$12
POLYDOR			
❑ PD-1-6190	C.W. McCall & Co.	1979	$12
❑ PD-1-6156	Greatest Hits	1978	$12
❑ 825793-1	Greatest Hits	198?	$10
—*Reissue of 6156*			
❑ PD-1-6125	Roses for Mama	1978	$12
❑ PD-1-6094	Rubber Duck	1977	$12
❑ PD-1-6069	Wilderness	1976	$12

MCCALL, DARRELL
COLUMBIA
❑ KC34718	Lily Dale	1977	$15
WAYSIDE			
❑ 1030	Meet Darrell McCall	1969	$25

MCCALL, MARY ANN
CORAL
❑ CRL57276 [M]	Melancholy Baby	1959	$75
❑ CRL757276 [S]	Melancholy Baby	1959	$100
DISCOVERY			
❑ 3011 [10]	Mary Ann McCall Sings	1950	$300
JUBILEE			
❑ JLP-1078 [M]	Detour to the Moon	1958	$75
REGENT			

❑ MG-6040 [M]	Easy Living	1957	$100
SAVOY JAZZ			
❑ SJL-1178	Easy Living	198?	$35

MCCALL, TOUSSAINT
RONN
| ❑ 7527 [M] | Nothing Can Take the Place of You | 1967 | $30 |
| ❑ 7527S [S] | Nothing Can Take the Place of You | 1967 | $40 |

MCCALLUM, DAVID
CAPITOL
❑ T2748 [M]	McCallum	1967	$25
❑ ST2748 [S]	McCallum	1967	$18
❑ T2498 [M]	Music: A Bit More of Me	1966	$15
❑ ST2498 [S]	Music: A Bit More of Me	1966	$18
❑ T2651 [M]	Music: It's Happening Now	1967	$18
❑ ST2651 [S]	Music: It's Happening Now	1967	$18
❑ T2432 [M]	Music -- A Part of Me	1966	$15
❑ ST2432 [S]	Music -- A Part of Me	1966	$18

MCCANN, HOOPS
MCA
| ❑ 42202 | The Hoops McCann Band Plays the Music of Steely Dan | 1988 | $25 |

Number	Title	Yr	NM

MCCANN, LES, AND EDDIE HARRIS

ATLANTIC

❏ SD1583	Second Movement	1971	$35
❏ SD1537	Swiss Movement	1969	$35

MCCANN, LES

A&M

❏ SP-4780	Tall, Dark and Handsome	1979	$25
❏ SP-4718	The Man	1978	$25

ABC IMPULSE!

❏ AS-9333	Live at the Roxy	1978	$25
❏ AS-9329	The Music Lets Me Be	1977	$25

ATLANTIC

❏ SD1666	Another Beginning	1974	$30
❏ SD1547	Comment	1970	$35
❏ SD1679	Hustle to Survive	1975	$30
❏ SD1603 [S]	Invitation to Openness	1972	$30
❏ 1603 [M]	Invitation to Openness	1972	$75

— Mono is white label promo only with "d/j copy monaural" sticker on front cover

❏ SD1646	Layers	1973	$30
❏ SD 2-312	Live at Montreux	1974	$35
❏ SD1516	Much Les	1969	$35
❏ SD1690	River High, River Low	1976	$30
❏ SD1619	Talk to the People	1972	$30

JAM

❏ 019	Les McCann's Music Box	1984	$25
❏ 012	The Longer You Wait	1984	$25

LIMELIGHT

❏ LM-82031 [M]	Beaux J. Pooboo	1966	$35
❏ LS-86031 [S]	Beaux J. Pooboo	1966	$50
❏ LM-82043 [M]	Bucket O' Grease	1967	$50
❏ LS-86043 [S]	Bucket O' Grease	1967	$35
❏ LM-82016 [M]	But Not Really	1965	$35
❏ LS-86016 [S]	But Not Really	1965	$50
❏ LM-82041 [M]	Les McCann Plays the Hits	1966	$35
❏ LS-86041 [S]	Les McCann Plays the Hits	1966	$50
❏ LM-82036 [M]	Live at Shelly's Manne-Hole	1966	$35
❏ LS-86036 [S]	Live at Shelly's Manne-Hole	1966	$50
❏ LM-82046 [M]	Live at the Bohemian Caverns, Washington, D.C.	1967	$50
❏ LS-86046 [S]	Live at the Bohemian Caverns, Washington, D.C.	1967	$35
❏ LM-82025 [M]	Poo Boo	1965	$35
❏ LS-86025 [S]	Poo Boo	1965	$50

PACIFIC JAZZ

❏ PJ-10107 [M]	A Bag of Gold	1966	$35
❏ ST-20107 [S]	A Bag of Gold	1966	$50
❏ PJ-81 [M]	Jazz Waltz	1964	$35
❏ ST-81 [S]	Jazz Waltz	1964	$50
❏ PJ-45 [M]	Les McCann in New York	1962	$50
❏ ST-45 [S]	Les McCann in New York	1962	$75
❏ LN-10078	Les McCann in New York	1980	$20

— Budget-line reissue

❏ PJ-16 [M]	Les McCann in San Francisco	1961	$75
❏ ST-16 [S]	Les McCann in San Francisco	1961	$75
❏ LN-10077	Les McCann in San Francisco	1980	$20

— Budget-line reissue

❏ PJ-31 [M]	Les McCann Sings	1961	$50
❏ ST-31 [S]	Les McCann Sings	1961	$75
❏ PJ-84 [M]	McCanna	1964	$35
❏ ST-84 [S]	McCanna	1964	$50
❏ PJ-91 [M]	McCann/Wilson	1965	$35

— With Gerald Wilson

❏ ST-91 [S]	McCann/Wilson	1965	$50

— With Gerald Wilson

❏ PJ-56 [M]	On Time	1962	$40

— Yellow vinyl

❏ PJ-56 [M]	On Time	1962	$50

— Black vinyl

❏ ST-56 [S]	On Time	1962	$150

— Yellow vinyl

❏ ST-56 [S]	On Time	1962	$75

— Black vinyl

❏ PJ-25 [M]	Pretty Lady	1961	$50
❏ ST-25 [S]	Pretty Lady	1961	$75
❏ PJ-63 [M]	Shampoo	1962	$35
❏ ST-63 [S]	Shampoo	1962	$50
❏ PJ-78 [M]	Soul Hits	1963	$35
❏ ST-78 [S]	Soul Hits	1963	$50
❏ LN-10079	Soul Hits	1980	$20

— Budget-line reissue

❏ PJ-10097 [M]	Spanish Onions	1966	$35
❏ ST-20097 [S]	Spanish Onions	1966	$50
❏ PJ-69 [M]	The Gospel Truth	1963	$35
❏ ST-69 [S]	The Gospel Truth	1963	$50
❏ PJ-7 [M]	The Shout	1960	$75
❏ ST-7 [S]	The Shout	1960	$75
❏ LN-10083	The Shout	1980	$20

— Budget-line reissue

❏ PJ-2 [M]	The Truth	1960	$75
❏ ST-2 [S]	The Truth	1960	$75

STONE

❏ 1906	Butterfly	1988	$25

SUNSET

❏ SUS-5214	Django	1969	$25
❏ SUS-5296	Unlimited	1970	$25

WORLD PACIFIC

❏ ST-20173	Les McCann Sings & Plays in the Big City	1970	$150
❏ ST-20166	More Or Les McCann	1969	$150

MCCARTERS, THE

WARNER BROS.

❏ 25737	The Gift	1988	$12

MCCARTHY, JOHN, CHORALE

RCA MUSIC SERVICE

❏ R114285	The Greatest Songs of Christmas	1973	$15

MCCARTNEY, PAUL

Includes duets with Linda McCartney plus his work with Wings. Also see THE BEATLES; MICHAEL JACKSON AND PAUL McCARTNEY.

APPLE

❏ SO-3415	Band on the Run	1973	$25

— Credited to "Paul McCartney and Wings"; with photo innersleeve and poster

❏ SPRO-6210 [DJ]	Brung to Ewe By	1971	$400

— Promo-only radio spots for "Ram"; counterfeits have uneven spacing between tracks

❏ STAO-3363	McCartney	1970	$30

— "McCartney" and "Paul McCartney" on separate lines on label; New York address on back cover

❏ STAO-3363	McCartney	1970	$30

— "McCartney" and "Paul McCartney" on separate lines on label; California address on back cover

❏ STAO-3363	McCartney	1970	$100

— Apple label with small Capitol logo on B-side

❏ STAO-3363	McCartney	1970	$25

— Only "McCartney" on label; back cover does NOT say "An Abkco managed company

❏ STAO-3363	McCartney	1970	$30

— Only "McCartney" on label; back cover says "An Abkco managed company

❏ SMAS-3363	McCartney	197?	$25

— New prefix on label

❏ SMAS-3363	McCartney	1975	$150

— With "All Rights Reserved" on label

❏ MAS-3375 [M]	Ram	1971	$11000

— Credited to "Paul and Linda McCartney"; mono record in stereo cover for radio station use only

❏ SMAS-3375	Ram	1971	$18

— Credited to "Paul and Linda McCartney"; unsliced apple on one label, sliced apple on other

❏ SMAS-3375	Ram	1971	$30

— Credited to "Paul and Linda McCartney"; unsliced apple on both labels

❏ SMAS-3375	Ram	1971	$50

— Credited to "Paul and Linda McCartney"; Apple label with small Capitol logo on B-side

❏ SMAS-3375	Ram	1975	$150

— Credited to "Paul and Linda McCartney"; with "All Rights Reserved" on label

❏ SMAL-3409	Red Rose Speedway	1973	$25

— Credited to "Paul McCartney and Wings"; with bound-in booklet

❏ SW-3386	Wild Life	1971	$18

— Credited to "Wings

CAPITOL

❏ CLW-48287	All the Best!	1987	$25
❏ SO-3415	Band on the Run	1975	$25

— Credited to "Paul McCartney and Wings"; custom label with MPL logo

❏ SO-3415	Band on the Run	197?	$50

— Credited to "Paul McCartney and Wings"; black label, "Manufactured by Capitol Records...

❏ SO-3415	Band on the Run	197?	$25

— Credited to "Paul McCartney and Wings"; black label, "Manufactured by MPL Communications Inc." at top

❏ SEAX-11901 [PD]	Band on the Run	1978	$40

— Credited to "Paul McCartney and Wings"; picture disc

❏ 99176	Band on the Run	1999	$40

— Limited-edition 180-gram reissue with original LP on one record and interviews and "The Making of.." on the second

❏ C1-56500	Flaming Pie	1997	$30
❏ C1-91653	Flowers in the Dirt	1989	$25
❏ SW-11777	London Town	1978	$18

— Credited to "Wings"; custom label with poster

❏ SMAS-3363	McCartney	1976	$30

— Black label, "Manufactured by McCartney Music Inc" at top

❏ SMAS-3363	McCartney	1976	$25

— Black label, "Manufactured by MPL Communications Inc" at top

❏ PJAS-12475	Press to Play	1986	$15
❏ SMAS-3375	Ram	1976	$30

— Credited to "Paul and Linda McCartney"; black label, "Manufactured by McCartney Music Inc" at top

❏ SMAS-3375	Ram	197?	$25

— Credited to "Paul and Linda McCartney"; black label, "Manufactured by MPL Communications Inc" at top

❏ SMAS-3375	Ram	197?	$40

— Credited to "Paul and Linda McCartney"; black label, "Manufactured by Capitol Records…" on label

❏ SMAL-3409	Red Rose Speedway	1976	$30

— Credited to "Paul McCartney and Wings"; black label, "Manufactured by McCartney Music Inc" at top

❏ SMAL-3409	Red Rose Speedway	197?	$30

— Credited to "Paul McCartney and Wings"; black label, "Manufactured by MPL Communications Inc" at top

❏ ST-11642	Thrillington	1977	$150

— Credited to "Percy 'Thrills' Thrillington"; instrumental versions of songs from Ram LP

❏ C1-94778	Tripping the Live Fantastic	1990	$75
❏ C1-595379	Tripping the Live Fantastic -- Highlights!	1990	$30

— Released on vinyl only through Columbia House; with U.S. address on back cover

❏ C1-595379	Tripping the Live Fantastic -- Highlights!	1990	$30

— Released on vinyl only through Columbia House; with Canada address on back cover, this was sold in the U.S. by Columbia House

❏ SMAS-11419	Venus and Mars	1975	$18

— Credited to "Wings"; with two posters and two stickers

❏ SW-3386	Wild Life	1976	$30

— Credited to "Wings"; black label, "Manufactured by McCartney Music Inc" at top

❏ SW-3386	Wild Life	197?	$25

— Credited to "Wings"; black label, "Manufactured by MPL Communications Inc" at top

❏ SW-11525	Wings at the Speed of Sound	1976	$12

— Credited to "Wings"; custom label

❏ SW-11525 [DJ]	Wings at the Speed of Sound	1976	$300

— Credited to "Wings"; white label advance promo

❏ SOO-11905	Wings Greatest	1978	$18

— Credited to "Wings"; custom label with poster

❏ SOO-11905 [DJ]	Wings Greatest	1978	$400

— Credited to "Wings"; white label advance promo/test pressing

❏ SWCO-11593	Wings Over America	1976	$30

— Credited to "Wings"; custom labels with poster

COLUMBIA

❏ FC36057	Back to the Egg	1979	$12

— Credited to "Wings"; custom label

❏ FC36057 [DJ]	Back to the Egg	1979	$40

— Credited to "Wings"; "Demonstration -- Not for Sale" on custom label

❏ PC36057	Back to the Egg	1984	$30

— Credited to "Wings"; "PC" cover with "FC" label

❏ PC36057	Back to the Egg	1984	$40

— Credited to "Wings"; "PC" cover with "PC" label

❏ JC36482	Band on the Run	1980	$18

— Credited to "Paul McCartney and Wings"; custom label

❏ JC36482	Band on the Run	198?	$150

— Credited to "Paul McCartney and Wings"; white "MPL" logo on lower left front cover

❏ PC36482	Band on the Run	198?	$25

— Credited to "Paul McCartney and Wings"; "PC" cover with "JC" label

❏ PC36482	Band on the Run	198?	$30

— Credited to "Paul McCartney and Wings"; "PC" cover with "PC" label

❏ HC46382	Band on the Run	1981	$50

— Credited to "Paul McCartney and Wings"; half-speed mastered edition

❏ SC39613	Give My Regards to Broad Street	1984	$18
❏ JC36478	McCartney	1979	$18
❏ PC36478	McCartney	1984	$18

— Budget-line reissue

❏ FC36511 [DJ]	McCartney II	1980	$30

— White label promo

❏ FC36511	McCartney II	1980	$12

— Add 80% if bonus single of "Coming Up (Live at Glasgow)" (AE7 1204) is with package

❏ PC36511	McCartney II	1984	$30

— PC" cover with "FC" label

❏ PC36511	McCartney II	1984	$150

— PC" cover with "PC" label

❏ QC39169	Pipes of Peace	1983	$15
❏ JC36479	Ram	1980	$18

— Credited to "Paul and Linda McCartney"

❏ PC36479	Ram	1984	$18

— Credited to "Paul and Linda McCartney"; budget-line reissue

❏ JC36481	Red Rose Speedway	1980	$18

— Credited to "Paul McCartney and Wings"; flat or glossy cover

❏ PC36481	Red Rose Speedway	198?	$18

— Credited to "Paul McCartney and Wings"; not issued with booklet

❏ A2S821 [DJ]	The McCartney Interview	1980	$40

— Promo-only set; one LP is the entire interview, the other is banded for airplay; white labels with black print; counterfeits have blank white labels

Number	Title	Yr	NM
☐ PC36987	The McCartney Interview	1980	$15

—Stock release of interview originally intended for promotional use only

☐ TC37462	Tug of War	1982	$12
☐ PC37462	Tug of War	1984	$30

—Custom label; "PC" cover with "TC" label

☐ PC37462	Tug of War	1984	$150

—Regular Columbia label; "PC" cover with "PC" label

☐ JC36801	Venus and Mars	1980	$18

—Credited to "Wings"; with one poster and two stickers

☐ PC36801	Venus and Mars	1982	$18

—Credited to "Wings"; budget-line reissue, not issued with inserts

☐ JC36480	Wild Life	1980	$18

—Credited to "Wings

☐ PC36480	Wild Life	1982	$18

—Credited to "Wings"; budget-line reissue

☐ PC37409	Wings at the Speed of Sound	1982	$18

—Credited to "Wings"; regular Columbia label, budget-line reissue

☐ FC37409	Wings at the Speed of Sound	1981	$18

—Credited to "Wings"; custom label

☐ C3X37990	Wings Over America	1982	$50

—Credited to "Wings"; custom labels, no poster

HEAR MUSIC

☐ HMLP-30383	Memory Almost Full	2007	$18

MPL/PARLOPHONE

☐ 888072348486 [B]	New	2013	$30
☐ HRM33452-01 [M]	Ram	2012	$30

—reissue of 1971 promo

☐ 96413	Unplugged (The Official Bootleg)	1991	$85

—No U.S. pressings; "American" copies were U.K. imports with liner notes in Spanish!

NATIONAL FEATURES CORP.

☐ 2955/6	Band on the Run Radio Interview Special	1973	$1500

—Promo-only interview disc

MCCLAIN, CHARLY

EPIC

☐ JE36090	Alone Too Long	1979	$15
☐ FE40186	Biggest Hits	1985	$10
☐ FE39425	Charly	1984	$10
☐ FE37347	Encore	1981	$12
☐ PE37347	Encore	198?	$10

—Budget-line reissue with new prefix

☐ FE38313	Greatest Hits	1982	$12
☐ PE34447	Here's Charly McClain	1977	$15

—Original with orange label

☐ PE34447	Here's Charly McClain	1979	$10

—Budget-line reissue with dark blue label and bar code

☐ KE35448	Let Me Be Your Baby	1978	$15

—Original with orange label

☐ PE35448	Let Me Be Your Baby	198?	$10

—Budget-line reissue; dark blue label

☐ FE38584	Paradise	1983	$12
☐ PE38584	Paradise	1985	$10

—Budget-line reissue with new prefix

☐ FE39871	Radio Heart	1985	$10
☐ FE40534	Still I Stay	1987	$10
☐ FE37108	Surround Me with Love	1981	$12
☐ PE37108	Surround Me with Love	198?	$10

—Budget-line reissue with new prefix

☐ FE40907	Ten Year Anniversary	1987	$10
☐ FE38979	The Woman in Me	1984	$12
☐ PE38979	The Woman in Me	1986	$10

—Budget-line reissue with new prefix

☐ FE38064	Too Good to Hurry	1982	$12
☐ PE38064	Too Good to Hurry	198?	$10

—Budget-line reissue with new prefix

☐ JE36760	Who's Cheatin' Who	1980	$12
☐ PE36760	Who's Cheatin' Who	198?	$10

—Budget-line reissue with new prefix

☐ JE36408	Women Get Lonely	1980	$12
☐ PE36408	Women Get Lonely	198?	$10

—Budget-line reissue with new prefix

MERCURY

☐ 834998-1	Charly McClain	1988	$10

MCCLINTON, DELBERT

ABC

☐ ABCD-959	Genuine Cowhide	1976	$25

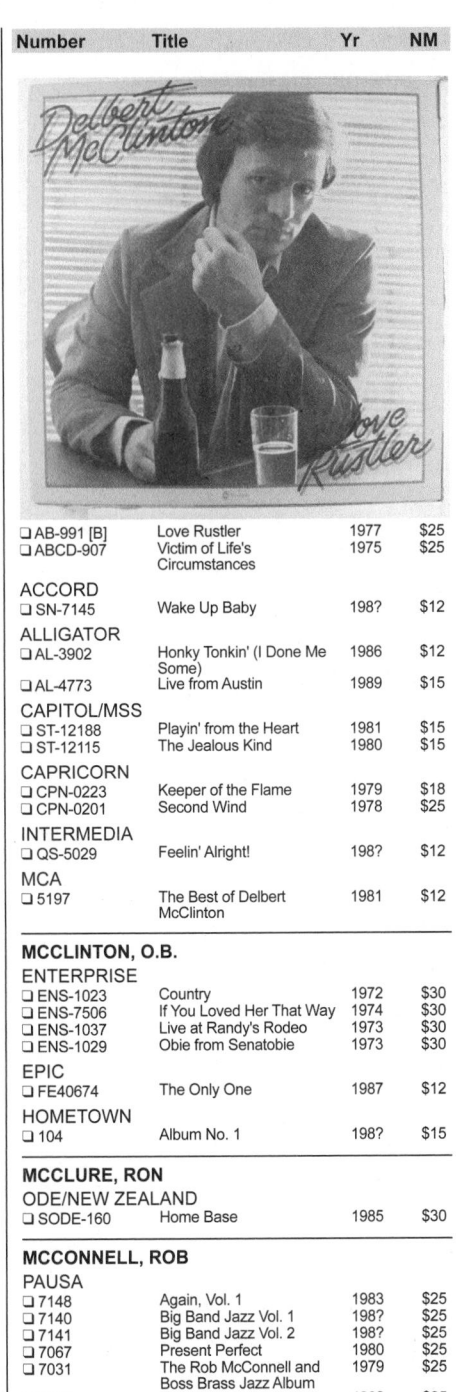

☐ AB-991 [B]	Love Rustler	1977	$25
☐ ABCD-907	Victim of Life's Circumstances	1975	$25

ACCORD

☐ SN-7145	Wake Up Baby	198?	$12

ALLIGATOR

☐ AL-3902	Honky Tonkin' (I Done Me Some)	1986	$12
☐ AL-4773	Live from Austin	1989	$15

CAPITOL/MSS

☐ ST-12188	Playin' from the Heart	1981	$15
☐ ST-12115	The Jealous Kind	1980	$15

CAPRICORN

☐ CPN-0223	Keeper of the Flame	1979	$18
☐ CPN-0201	Second Wind	1978	$25

INTERMEDIA

☐ QS-5029	Feelin' Alright!	198?	$12

MCA

☐ 5197	The Best of Delbert McClinton	1981	$12

MCCLINTON, O.B.

ENTERPRISE

☐ ENS-1023	Country	1972	$30
☐ ENS-7506	If You Loved Her That Way	1974	$30
☐ ENS-1037	Live at Randy's Rodeo	1973	$30
☐ ENS-1029	Obie from Senatobie	1973	$30

EPIC

☐ FE40674	The Only One	1987	$12

HOMETOWN

☐ 104	Album No. 1	198?	$15

MCCLURE, RON

ODE/NEW ZEALAND

☐ SODE-160	Home Base	1985	$30

MCCONNELL, ROB

PAUSA

☐ 7148	Again, Vol. 1	1983	$25
☐ 7140	Big Band Jazz Vol. 1	198?	$25
☐ 7141	Big Band Jazz Vol. 2	198?	$25
☐ 7067	Present Perfect	1980	$25
☐ 7031	The Rob McConnell and Boss Brass Jazz Album	1979	$25
☐ 7106	Trubute	198?	$25

MCCOO, MARILYN, AND BILLY DAVIS, JR.

ABC

☐ ABCD-952	I Hope We Get to Love in Time	1976	$15
☐ AB-1026	The Two of Us	1977	$15

COLUMBIA

☐ JC35603	Marilyn and Billy	1978	$18

MCCOO, MARILYN

RCA VICTOR

☐ AFL1-4863	Solid Gold	1983	$12

MCCORKLE, SUSANNAH

CONCORD JAZZ

☐ CJ-370	No More Blues	1989	$30

INNER CITY

☐ IC-1141	Music of Harry Warren	198?	$30
☐ IC-1151	People You Never Get to Love	1984	$30
☐ IC-1101	Songs of Johnny Mercer	198?	$30
☐ IC-1131	Songs of Yip Harburg	198?	$30

PAUSA

☐ 7195	How Do You Keep the Music Playing?	1986	$25
☐ 7175	Thanks for the Memory	1985	$25

MCCORMICK, GAYLE

ABC DUNHILL

☐ DS-50109	Gayle McCormick	1971	$15

DECCA

☐ DL75364	Flesh and Blood	1972	$15

FANTASY

☐ 9467	One More Hour	1974	$15

MCCORMICK BROTHERS, THE

HICKORY

☐ LP-108 [M]	Authentic Bluegrass Hits	1962	$75
☐ LP-102 [M]	Songs for Home Folks	1961	$100

METROMEDIA

☐ MM-1019	Grass Meets Brass	1969	$25

MCCOY, CHARLIE

CMH

☐ 9030	Flat-Picking Spectacular	1984	$15

MONUMENT

☐ 7632	Appalachian Fever	1979	$12
☐ KZ31910	Charlie McCoy	1972	$15
☐ 6624	Charlie McCoy	1976	$12

—Reissue of 31910

☐ 6628	Charlie My Boy!	1976	$12

—Reissue of 33384

☐ PZ33384	Charlie My Boy!	1975	$15
☐ 7612	Cookin'	1977	$12
☐ KZ32215	Good Time Charlie	1973	$15
☐ 6625	Good Time Charlie	1976	$12

—Reissue of 32215

☐ 7622	Greatest Hits	1978	$12
☐ PZ33802	Harpin' the Blues	1975	$15
☐ 6629	Harpin' the Blues	1976	$12

—Reissue of 33802

☐ 6630	Play It Again Charlie	1976	$12
☐ KZ32749	The Fastest Harp in the South	1974	$15
☐ 6626	The Fastest Harp in the South	1976	$12

—Reissue of 32749

☐ PW38387	The Greatest Hits of Charlie McCoy	1982	$10
☐ KZ32922	The Nashville Hit Man	1974	$15
☐ 6627	The Nashville Hit Man	1976	$12

—Reissue of 32922

☐ Z31329	The Real McCoy	1971	$15
☐ 6623	The Real McCoy	1976	$12

—Reissue of 31329

☐ SLP-18097	The World of Charlie McCoy	1968	$18

MCCOY, CLYDE

CAPITOL

☐ H311 [10]	Sugar Blues	195?	$175
☐ T311 [M]	Sugar Blues	1955	$100

—Turquoise or gray label

☐ T311 [M]	Sugar Blues	1959	$85

—Black colorband label, logo at left

☐ T311 [M]	Sugar Blues	1963	$75

—Black colorband label, logo at top

☐ DT311 [R]	Sugar Blues	196?	$75
☐ SM-311 [R]	Sugar Blues	197?	$25

CIRCLE

☐ CLP-82	Sugar Blues, 1951	198?	$25

DESIGN

☐ DLP-28 [M]	The Golden Era of the Sugar Blues	196?	$30

HINDSIGHT

☐ HSR-180	Clyde McCoy and His Orchestra 1936	198?	$25

MERCURY

☐ MG-20730 [M]	Blue Prelude	1962	$150
☐ SR-60730 [S]	Blue Prelude	1962	$150
☐ MG25141 [10]	Date for Dancing	195?	$30
☐ SR-60677 [S]	Really McCoy	1961	$150
☐ MG-20677 [M]	Really McCoy	1961	$150
☐ MG25034 [10]	Sugar Blues	195?	$40
☐ MG-20110 [M]	The Blues	195?	$150

TODD

☐ MT-5000 [M]	Clyde McCoy and His Waaa Waaa Dixieland Band	196?	$25

TOP RANK

☐ RM-350 [M]	Dixieland's Best Friend	1961	$30
☐ RS-650 [S]	Dixieland's Best Friend	1961	$40

WING

☐ MGW-12260 [M]	Dancing to the Blues	196?	$30
☐ SRW-16260 [S]	Dancing to the Blues	196?	$30

MCCOY, FREDDIE

COBBLESTONE

☐ 9004	Gimme Some	1972	$25

PRESTIGE

☐ PRST-7542	Beans and Greens	1968	$30
☐ PRLP-7470 [M]	Funk Drops	1967	$30
☐ PRST-7470 [S]	Funk Drops	1967	$30
☐ PRST-7582	Listen Here	1968	$30

Number	Title	Yr	NM
❑ PRLP-7395 [M]	Lonely Avenue	1965	$25
❑ PRST-7395 [S]	Lonely Avenue	1965	$30
❑ PRLP-7487 [M]	Peas 'N' Rice	1967	$30
❑ PRST-7487 [S]	Peas 'N' Rice	1967	$30
❑ PRST-7561	Soul Yogi	1968	$30
❑ PRLP-7444 [M]	Spider Man	1966	$50
❑ PRST-7444 [S]	Spider Man	1966	$40
❑ PRST-7706	The Best of Freddie McCoy	1969	$25

MCCOY, VAN

AVCO

Number	Title	Yr	NM
❑ AV-69006	Disco Baby	1975	$12
❑ AV-69002	Love Is the Answer	1974	$12
❑ AV-69009	The Disco Kid	1975	$12

BUDDAH

❑ BDS-5648	From Disco to Love	1975	$12
— Retitled reissue of 5103			
❑ BDS-5103	Soul Improvisations	1971	$18

COLUMBIA

❑ CL2497 [M]	Night Time Is the Lonely Time	1966	$35
❑ CS9297 [S]	Night Time Is the Lonely Time	1966	$30

H&L

❑ HL-69006	Disco Baby	1976	$10
— Reissue of Avco 69006			
❑ HL-69002	Love Is the Answer	1976	$10
— Reissue of Avco 69002			
❑ HL-69014	Rhythms of the World	1976	$12
❑ HL-69009	The Disco Kid	1976	$10
— Reissue of Avco 69009			
❑ HL-69016	The Hustle and Best of Van McCoy	1976	$12
❑ HL-69012	The Real McCoy	1976	$12
❑ HL-69022	Van McCoy and His Magnificent Movie Machine	1977	$12

MCA

❑ 3054	A Woman Called Moses	1978	$12
❑ 3071	Lovely Dancer	1979	$12
❑ 3036	My Favorite Fantasy	1978	$12

MCCOYS, THE
Also see RICK DERRINGER.

BANG

❑ BLP-212 [M]	Hang On Sloopy	1965	$150
❑ BLPS-212 [S]	Hang On Sloopy	1965	$100
❑ BLP-213 [M]	You Make Me Feel So Good	1966	$150
❑ BLPS-213 [S]	You Make Me Feel So Good	1966	$100

MERCURY

❑ SR-61207	Human Ball	1969	$30
❑ SR-61163	Infinite McCoys	1968	$30

MCCRACKLIN, JIMMY

CHESS

❑ LP-1464 [M]	Jimmy McCracklin Sings	1961	$175

CROWN

❑ CLP-5244 [M]	Twist with Jimmy McCracklin	1962	$50
— Black label, silver "Crown"			
❑ CLP-5244 [M]	Twist with Jimmy McCracklin	1962	$30
— Gray label			
❑ CLP-5244 [M]	Twist with Jimmy McCracklin	196?	$18
— Black label, multi-color "Crown"			

EVEJIM

❑ EJR-4013	Same Lovin'	198?	$15

IMPERIAL

❑ LP-9285 [M]	Every Night, Every Day	1965	$30
❑ LP-12285 [S]	Every Night, Every Day	1965	$30
❑ LP-9219 [M]	I Just Gotta Know	1964	$30
❑ LP-12219 [S]	I Just Gotta Know	1964	$30
❑ LP-9306 [M]	My Answer	1966	$30
❑ LP-12306 [S]	My Answer	1966	$30
❑ LP-9316 [M]	The New Soul of Jimmy McCracklin	1966	$30
❑ LP-12316 [S]	The New Soul of Jimmy McCracklin	1966	$30
❑ LP-9297 [M]	Think	1965	$30
❑ LP-12297 [S]	Think	1965	$30

MINIT

❑ LP-24011	Let's Get Together	1968	$30
❑ LP-24017	Stinger Man	1969	$30
❑ LP-4009 [M]	The Best of Jimmy McCracklin	1967	$30
❑ LP-24009 [S]	The Best of Jimmy McCracklin	1967	$30

STAX

❑ MPS-8506	High on the Blues	1980	$12
❑ STS-2047	Yesterday Is Gone	1972	$25

MCCRAE, GEORGE

GOLD MOUNTAIN

❑ GM80008	Own the Night	1984	$12

T.K.

❑ 606	Diamond Touch	1977	$12
❑ 602	George McCrae	1975	$12
❑ 501	Rock Your Baby	1974	$12

MCCRAE, GEORGE AND GWEN

CAT

Number	Title	Yr	NM
❑ 2606	Together	1976	$12

MCCRAE, GWEN

ATLANTIC

❑ 80014	On My Way	1982	$12

CAT

❑ 2603	Gwen McCrae	1974	$12
❑ 2605	Rockin' Chair	1975	$12
❑ 2608	Something So Right	1976	$12

MCCROBY, RON

CONCORD JAZZ

❑ CJ-208	Ron McCroby Plays Puccolo	1982	$25
❑ CJ-257	The Other Whistler	1984	$25

PRO ARTE

❑ PAD-258	Breezin' the Classics	1985	$25

MCCULLOCH, DANNY

CAPITOL

❑ ST-174	Wings of a Man	1969	$25

MCCURDY, ED; JACK ELLIOTT; OSCAR BRAND; DICK WILDER

ELEKTRA

❑ EKL-129 [M]	Badmen, Heroes and Pirate Songs	1957	$25

MCCURDY, ED; JACK ELLIOTT; OSCAR BRAND

ELEKTRA

❑ EKL-14 [10]	Badmen and Heroes	1955	$50

MCCURDY, ED

DAWN

❑ DLP-1127 [M]	The Folk Singer	195?	$30

ELEKTRA

❑ EKL-205 [M]	A Treasure Chest of American Folk Song	1961	$25
❑ EKL-108 [M]	Blood Booze 'n' Bones	1956	$25
❑ EKL-24 [10]	Sin Songs -- Pro and Con	1955	$30
❑ EKL-124 [M]	Sin Songs -- Pro and Con	1957	$25
— Reissue of EKL-24 with extra tracks			
❑ EKL-112 [M]	Songs of the Old West	1956	$25
❑ EKL-170 [M]	Son of Dalliance	1959	$25
❑ EKL-213 [M]	The Best of Dalliance	1961	$25
❑ EKL-110 [M]	When Dalliance Was In Flower 1	1956	$25
❑ EKL-140 [M]	When Dalliance Was In Flower 2	1958	$25
❑ EKL-160 [M]	When Dalliance Was In Flower 3	1959	$25
❑ EKS-7160 [S]	When Dalliance Was In Flower 3	1959	$30

RIVERSIDE

❑ RLP 12-601 [M]	The Ballad Record	195?	$30

TRADITION

❑ TLP-1003 [M]	A Ballad Singer's Choice	195?	$30
❑ TLP-1027 [M]	Children's Songs	195?	$30
❑ TLP-2061 [M]	Songs of the West	196?	$25

MCCURN, GEORGE

A&M

❑ LP-102 [M]	Country Boy Goes to Town!!!!!	1963	$30

MCDANIEL, MEL

CAPITOL

❑ ST-11694	Gentle to Your Senses	1977	$12
❑ ST-12572	Greatest Hits	1987	$10
❑ ST-12116	I'm Countryfied	1980	$12
❑ SN-16307	I'm Countryfied	198?	$10
— Budget-line reissue			
❑ ST-12528	Just Can't Sit Down Music	1986	$10
❑ ST-12402	Let It Roll	1985	$10
❑ ST-11779	Mello	1978	$12
❑ ST-12326	Mel McDaniel with Oklahoma Wind	1984	$10
❑ ST-12265	Naturally Country	1983	$10
❑ C1-48058	Now You're Talkin'	1988	$10
❑ C1-91133	Rock-a-Billy Boy	1989	$15
❑ ST-12437	Stand Up	1985	$10
❑ ST-12208	Take Me to the Country	1982	$12
❑ SN-16381	Take Me to the Country	1986	$10
— Budget-line reissue			

MCDANIEL, WILLARD

CROWN

❑ CLP-5024 [M]	88 A La Carte	1958	$150

MCDANIELS, GENE

ATLANTIC

❑ SD8281	Headless Heroes	1971	$18
❑ SD8259	Outlaw	1970	$18

LIBERTY

❑ LRP-3191 [M]	100 Lbs. of Clay!	1961	$30
❑ LST-7191 [S]	100 Lbs. of Clay!	1961	$40
❑ LRP-3204 [M]	Gene McDaniels Sings Movie Memories	1962	$30
❑ LST-7204 [S]	Gene McDaniels Sings Movie Memories	1962	$40
❑ LRP-3258 [M]	Hit After Hit	1962	$30
❑ LST-7258 [S]	Hit After Hit	1962	$40
❑ LRP-3146 [M]	In Times Like These	1960	$30
❑ LST-7146 [S]	In Times Like These	1960	$250
— Blue vinyl			
❑ LST-7146 [S]	In Times Like These	1960	$40
— Black vinyl			
❑ LRP-3175 [M]	Sometimes I'm Happy, Sometimes I'm Blue	1960	$30
❑ LST-7175 [S]	Sometimes I'm Happy, Sometimes I'm Blue	1960	$40
❑ LRP-3275 [M]	Spanish Lace	1963	$30
❑ LST-7275 [S]	Spanish Lace	1963	$30
❑ LRP-3311 [M]	The Wonderful World of Gene McDaniels	1963	$30
❑ LST-7311 [S]	The Wonderful World of Gene McDaniels	1963	$30
❑ LRP-3215 [M]	Tower of Strength	1962	$30
❑ LST-7215 [S]	Tower of Strength	1962	$40

ODE

❑ SP-77028	Natural Juices	1975	$15

SUNSET

❑ SUM-1122 [M]	Facts of Life	1967	$15
❑ SUS-5122 [S]	Facts of Life	1967	$18

UNITED ARTISTS

❑ UA-LA447-E	The Very Best of Gene McDaniels	1975	$12

MCDERMOT, TOM

STOMP OFF

❑ SOS-1024	New Rags	198?	$25

MCDONALD, COUNTRY JOE
See COUNTRY JOE AND THE FISH.

MCDONALD, KATHI

CAPITOL

❑ ST-11224	Insane Asylum	1974	$30

MCDONALD, MARIE

RCA VICTOR

❑ LPM-1585 [M]	The Body Sings!, The	1957	$50

MCDONALD, MICHAEL
Also see THE DOOBIE BROTHERS; THE REGENTS

ARISTA

❑ ABM-2006	That Was Then -- The Early Recordings of Michael McDonald	1982	$50

MOBILE FIDELITY

❑ 1-149	If That's What It Takes	1985	$50
— Audiophile vinyl			

REPRISE

❑ 25979	Take It to Heart	1990	$18

WARNER BROS.

❑ 23703	If That's What It Takes	1982	$12
❑ 25291	No Lookin' Back	1985	$12

MCDONALD, SKEETS

CAPITOL

❑ T1040 [M]	Goin' Steady with the Blues	1958	$100

COLUMBIA

❑ CL2170 [M]	Call Me Skeets	1964	$30
❑ CS8970 [S]	Call Me Skeets	1964	$30

FORTUNE

❑ 3001	The Tattooed Lady and Other Songs	1969	$50

SEARS

❑ SPS-116 [R]	Skeets	196?	$30

MCDONOUGH, DICK, AND CARL KRESS

JAZZ ARCHIVES

❑ JA-32	The Guitar Genius of Dick McDonough and Carl Kress	198?	$25

MCDOWELL, MISSISSIPPI FRED

ARHOOLIE

❑ F-1021 [M]	Delta Blues	1964	$50
❑ F-1027 [M]	Delta Blues, Volume 2	1966	$50
❑ F-1068	Keep Your Lamp Trimmed and Burning	1973	$25
❑ F-1046	Mississippi Fred McDowell and His Blues Boys	1970	$30

CAPITOL

❑ ST-403	I Do Not Play No Rock and Roll	1970	$30

JUST SUNSHINE

❑ JSS-4	Mississippi Fred McDowell 1904-1972	1973	$18

MILESTONE

❑ MLP-3003 [M]	Long Way from Home	1966	$30

Number	Title	Yr	NM
❏ MLS-93003 [S]	Long Way from Home	1966	$40

SIRE

Number	Title	Yr	NM
❏ SES-97018	Mississippi Fred McDowell in London	1970	$30

MCDOWELL, RONNIE

CURB

Number	Title	Yr	NM
❏ 10602	I'm Still Missing You	1988	$10

EPIC

Number	Title	Yr	NM
❏ FE38981	Country Boy's Heart	1983	$12
❏ PE38981	Country Boy's Heart	1985	$10
— Budget-line reissue with new prefix			
❏ JE36821	Going, Going ... Gone	1980	$12
❏ PE36821	Going, Going ... Gone	198?	$10
— Budget-line reissue with new prefix			
❏ FE37399	Good Time Lovin' Man	1981	$12
❏ PE37399	Good Time Lovin' Man	198?	$10
— Budget-line reissue with new prefix			
❏ FE38314	Greatest Hits	1983	$12
❏ FE39954	In a New York Minute	1985	$12
❏ JE36336	Love So Many Ways	1980	$12
❏ FE38017	Love to Burn	1982	$12
❏ PE38017	Love to Burn	198?	$10
— Budget-line reissue with new prefix			
❏ PE40643	Older Women and Other Greatest Hits	1987	$12
❏ FE38514	Personally	1983	$12
❏ PE38514	Personally	1985	$10
— Budget-line reissue with new prefix			
❏ JE36142	Rockin' You Easy, Lovin' You Slow	1979	$12
❏ PE36142	Rockin' You Easy, Lovin' You Slow	198?	$10
— Budget-line reissue with new prefix			
❏ FE39329	Willing	1984	$12

MCA CURB

Number	Title	Yr	NM
❏ 5725	All Tied Up in Love	1986	$10

SCORPION

Number	Title	Yr	NM
❏ 8028	I Love You, I Love You, I Love You	1978	$18
❏ 0010	Live at the Fox	1978	$18
❏ 8021	The King Is Gone	1977	$25

MCDUFF, JACK

ATLANTIC

Number	Title	Yr	NM
❏ 1463 [M]	A Change Is Gonna Come	1966	$35
❏ SD1463 [S]	A Change Is Gonna Come	1966	$50
❏ SD1498	Double Barreled Soul	1968	$35
❏ 1472 [M]	Tobacco Road	1967	$30
❏ SD1472 [S]	Tobacco Road	1967	$35

BLUE NOTE

Number	Title	Yr	NM
❏ BST-84322	Down Home Style	1969	$35
❏ BST-84334	Moon Rappin'	1970	$35
❏ BST-84348	To Seek a New Home	1970	$35
❏ BST-84358	Who Knows	1971	$35

CADET

Number	Title	Yr	NM
❏ CH-50024	Check This Out	1973	$30
❏ CH-50051	Fourth Dimension	1974	$30
❏ LPS-817	Getting Our Thing Together	1969	$35
❏ LPS-831	Gin and Orange	1970	$35
❏ CH-60031	Magnetic Feel	1975	$30
❏ LPS-812	Natural Thing	1968	$35
❏ CH-60017	The Healin' System	1972	$30

CHESS

Number	Title	Yr	NM
❏ 19004	Sophisticated Funk	1976	$30

FANTASY

Number	Title	Yr	NM
❏ OJC-326	Brother Jack Meets the Boss	1988	$25
— Reissue of Prestige 7228			
❏ OJC-222	The Honeydripper	198?	$25
— Reissue of Prestige 7199			
❏ OJC-324	Tough 'Duff	1988	$25
— Reissue of Prestige 7185			

MUSE

Number	Title	Yr	NM
❏ MR-5361	The Re-Entry	1989	$30

PRESTIGE

Number	Title	Yr	NM
❏ PRST-7771	Best of the Big Soul Band	1970	$35
❏ PRLP-7174 [M]	Brother Jack	1960	$250
❏ PRST-7785	Brother Jack	1970	$35
❏ PRLP-7481 [M]	Brother Jack McDuff's Greatest Hits	1967	$75
❏ PRST-7481 [S]	Brother Jack McDuff's Greatest Hits	1967	$50
❏ PRLP-7220 [M]	Goodnight, It's Time to Go	1961	$250
❏ PRST-7220 [S]	Goodnight, It's Time to Go	1961	$250
❏ PRLP-7492 [M]	Hallelujah Time!	1967	$75
❏ PRST-7492 [S]	Hallelujah Time!	1967	$50
❏ PRLP-7422 [M]	Hot Barbeque	1966	$25
❏ PRST-7422 [S]	Hot Barbeque	1966	$75
❏ PRST-7642	I Got a Woman	1969	$50
❏ PRST-7596	Jack McDuff Plays for Beautiful People	1969	$50
❏ PRLP-7274 [M]	Live!	1963	$40
❏ PRST-7274 [S]	Live!	1963	$40
❏ PRLP-7286 [M]	Live! At the Jazz Workshop	1964	$40
❏ PRST-7286 [S]	Live! At the Jazz Workshop	1964	$40
❏ PRST-7703	Live! The Best of Brother Jack McDuff	1969	$50
❏ PRLP-7228 [M]	Mellow Gravy -- Brother Jack Meets the Boss	1962	$175

Number	Title	Yr	NM
❏ PRST-7228 [S]	Mellow Gravy -- Brother Jack Meets the Boss	1962	$175
❏ PRST-7851	On With It	1973	$30
❏ PRLP-7333 [M]	Prelude	1964	$75
❏ PRST-7333 [S]	Prelude	1964	$75
❏ 24013	Rock Candy	1972	$35
❏ PRLP-7259 [M]	Screamin'	1963	$40
❏ PRST-7259 [S]	Screamin'	1963	$40
❏ PRLP-7404 [M]	Silk and Soul	1965	$75
❏ PRST-7404 [S]	Silk and Soul	1965	$75
❏ PRLP-7265 [M]	Somethin' Slick!	1963	$40
❏ PRST-7265 [S]	Somethin' Slick!	1963	$40
❏ PRST-7567	Soul Circle	1968	$50
❏ PRST-7666	Steppin' Out	1969	$50
❏ PRLP-7362 [M]	The Concert McDuff Recorded Live!	1965	$75
❏ PRST-7362 [S]	The Concert McDuff Recorded Live!	1965	$75
❏ PRLP-7323 [M]	The Dynamic Jack McDuff	1964	$40
❏ PRST-7323 [S]	The Dynamic Jack McDuff	1964	$40
❏ PRLP-7199 [M]	The Honeydripper	1961	$250
❏ PRST-7529	The Midnight Sun	1968	$50
❏ PRST-7814	Tough 'Duff	1971	$35
❏ PRLP-7185 [M]	Tough 'Duff	1960	$250
❏ PRLP-7476 [M]	Walk On By	1967	$75
❏ PRST-7476 [S]	Walk On By	1967	$50

MCENTIRE, REBA

MCA

Number	Title	Yr	NM
❏ 1P-8162	For My Broken Heart	1991	$30
— Only released on vinyl through Columbia House			
❏ 5585	Have I Got a Deal for You	1985	$10
❏ 5475	Just a Little Love	1984	$10
❏ 42031	Merry Christmas to You	1987	$12
❏ R164184	Merry Christmas to You	1987	$15
— BMG Direct Marketing edition			
❏ 5516	My Kind of Country	1984	$10
❏ 42134	Reba	1988	$10
❏ R244602	Reba Live	1989	$30
— BMG Direct Marketing version; no regular retail version			
❏ 2P-7933	Reba Live	1989	$30
— Columbia House edition; no regular retail version			
❏ 5979	Reba McEntire's Greatest Hits	1987	$10
❏ 10016	Rumor Has It	1990	$25
❏ 6294	Sweet Sixteen	1989	$12
❏ 42030	The Last One to Know	1987	$10
❏ 5807	What Am I Gonna Do About You	1986	$10
❏ 5691	Whoever's in New England	1986	$10

MERCURY

Number	Title	Yr	NM
❏ 812781-1	Behind the Scene	1983	$25
❏ SRM-1-5029	Feel the Fire	1980	$30
❏ 822887-1	Feel the Fire	1986	$12
— Reissue			
❏ SRM-1-6003	Heart to Heart	1981	$30
❏ SRM-1-5017	Out of a Dream	1979	$40
❏ SRM-1-1177	Reba McEntire	1977	$150
❏ SRM-1-5002	Reba McEntire	1977	$40
— Reissue of 1177			
❏ 822455-1	Reba Nell McEntire	1986	$12
❏ 824342-1	The Best of Reba McEntire	1985	$12
❏ SRM-1-4047	Unlimited	1982	$30
❏ 822882-1	Unlimited	1986	$12
— Reissue			

MCEUEN, JOHN

WARNER BROS.

Number	Title	Yr	NM
❏ 25266	John McEuen	1985	$10

MCFADDEN, BOB

BRUNSWICK

Number	Title	Yr	NM
❏ BL54056 [M]	Songs Our Mummy Taught Us	1959	$250
❏ BL754056 [S]	Songs Our Mummy Taught Us	1959	$300

MCFADDEN AND WHITEHEAD

PHILADELPHIA INT'L.

Number	Title	Yr	NM
❏ JZ35800	McFadden and Whitehead	1979	$15

TSOP

Number	Title	Yr	NM
❏ JZ36773	I Heard It in a Love Song	1980	$15

MCFARLAND, GARY

ABC IMPULSE!

Number	Title	Yr	NM
❏ AS-46 [S]	Points of Departure	1968	$35
❏ AS-9112 [S]	Profiles	1968	$35
❏ AS-9122 [S]	Simpatico	1968	$35
❏ AS-9104 [S]	Tijuana Jazz	1968	$35

BUDDAH

Number	Title	Yr	NM
❏ BDS95001	Butterscotch Rum	1967	$50

COBBLESTONE

Number	Title	Yr	NM
❏ CST9019	Requiem for Gary McFarland	1972	$50

IMPULSE!

Number	Title	Yr	NM
❏ A-46 [M]	Point of Departure	1963	$250
❏ AS-46 [S]	Points of Departure	1963	$160
❏ A-9112 [M]	Profiles	1966	$250
❏ AS-9112 [S]	Profiles	1966	$160
❏ A-9122 [M]	Simpatico	1966	$250

Number	Title	Yr	NM
❏ AS-9122 [S]	Simpatico	1966	$160
❏ A-9104 [M]	Tijuana Jazz	1966	$250
❏ AS-9104 [S]	Tijuana Jazz	1966	$250

SKYE

Number	Title	Yr	NM
❏ SK-8	America the Beautiful	1969	$50
❏ SK-2	Does the Sun Really Shine on the Moon?	1968	$50
❏ SK-11	Slaves	1970	$75
❏ SK-14	Today	1970	$75

VERVE

Number	Title	Yr	NM
❏ V/V6-8674	Gary McFarland	1965	$0
— Canceled			
❏ V-8443 [M]	How to Succeed in Business Without Really Trying	1962	$50
❏ V6-8443 [S]	How to Succeed in Business Without Really Trying	1962	$75
❏ V-8738 [M]	Scorpio and Other Signs	1967	$150
❏ V6-8738 [S]	Scorpio and Other Signs	1967	$40
❏ V-8603 [M]	Soft Samba	1964	$75
❏ V6-8603 [S]	Soft Samba	1964	$75
❏ V-8682 [M]	Soft Samba Strings	1966	$75
❏ V6-8682 [S]	Soft Samba Strings	1966	$75
❏ V6-8786	Sympathetic Vibrations	1969	$75
❏ V-8518 [M]	The Gary McFarland Orchestra with Special Guest Soloist Bill Evans	1963	$75
❏ V6-8518 [S]	The Gary McFarland Orchestra with Special Guest Soloist Bill Evans	1963	$75
❏ V-8632 [M]	The "In" Sound	1965	$40
❏ V6-8632 [S]	The "In" Sound	1965	$150

MCFERRIN, BOBBY

BLUE NOTE

Number	Title	Yr	NM
❏ BT-85110	Spontaneous Inventions	1986	$15

ELEKTRA/MUSICIAN

Number	Title	Yr	NM
❏ E1-60023	Bobby McFerrin	1982	$12
❏ 60366	The Voice	1985	$12

EMI MANHATTAN

Number	Title	Yr	NM
❏ E1-48059	Simple Pleasures	1988	$10
❏ E1-548059	Simple Pleasures	1988	$12
— Columbia House edition			

MCGARITY, LOU

ARGO

Number	Title	Yr	NM
❏ LP-654 [M]	Blue Lou	1960	$30
❏ LPS-654 [S]	Blue Lou	1960	$40

JUBILEE

Number	Title	Yr	NM
❏ JGM-1108 [M]	Some Like It Hot	1959	$50

MCGEE, SAM AND KIRK, AND THE CROOK BROTHERS

STARDAY

Number	Title	Yr	NM
❏ SLP-182 [M]	Opry Old Timers	1962	$40

MCGHEE, BROWNIE

BLUESVILLE

Number	Title	Yr	NM
❏ BVLP-1042 [M]	Brownie's Blues	1962	$100
— Blue label, silver print			
❏ BVLP-1042 [M]	Brownie's Blues	1964	$30
— Blue label, trident logo at right			

FANTASY

Number	Title	Yr	NM
❏ OBC-505	Brownie's Blues	198?	$15

FOLKWAYS

Number	Title	Yr	NM
❏ FP-30 [10]	Brownie McGhee Blues	1951	$175
❏ FA-2030 [10]	Brownie McGhee Blues	1951	$175
❏ 3557	Brownie McGhee Sings the Blues	197?	$15
❏ 2421/2	Traditional Blues Vol. 1 and 2	197?	$18

SAVOY JAZZ

Number	Title	Yr	NM
❏ SJL-1204	Jumpin' the Blues	1989	$15

MCGHEE, HOWARD

ARGO

Number	Title	Yr	NM
❏ LP-4020 [M]	House Warmin'	1963	$30
❏ LPS-4020 [S]	House Warmin'	1963	$30

BETHLEHEM

Number	Title	Yr	NM
❏ BCP-6055 [M]	Dusty Blue	1961	$300
❏ BCPS-6055 [S]	Dusty Blue	1961	$300
❏ BCP-61 [M]	Life Is Just a Bowl of Cherries	1957	$300
❏ BCP-6039	That Bop Thing	197?	$30
— Reissue of 42, distributed by RCA Victor			
❏ BCP-42 [M]	The Return of Howard McGhee	1956	$650

BLACK LION

Number	Title	Yr	NM
❏ 305	Shades of Blue	197?	$30

BLUE NOTE

Number	Title	Yr	NM
❏ BLP-5024 [10]	Howard McGhee, Volume 2	1953	$300
❏ BLP-5012 [10]	Howard McGhee's All Stars/ Howard McGhee-Fats Navarro Sextet	1952	$300

CADET

Number	Title	Yr	NM
❏ LP-4020 [M]	House Warmin'	1966	$30
❏ LPS-4020 [S]	House Warmin'	1966	$35

Number	Title	Yr	NM
CONTEMPORARY			
❑ M-3596 [M]	Maggie's Back in Town	1961	$250
❑ S-7596 [S]	Maggie's Back in Town	1961	$250
DIAL			
❑ LP-217 [10]	Night Music	1951	$300
HI-LO			
❑ HL-6001 [10]	Jazz Goes to the Battlefront, Vol. 1	1952	$300
❑ HL-6002 [10]	Jazz Goes to the Battlefront, Vol. 2	1952	$300
SAVOY			
❑ MG-12026 [M]	Howard McGhee and Milt Jackson	1955	$100
SAVOY JAZZ			
❑ SJL-2219	Maggie	197?	$35
STEEPLECHASE			
❑ SCS-1024	Just Be There	198?	$30
STORYVILLE			
❑ 4077	Jazzbrothers	198?	$30
❑ 4080	Young at Heart	198?	$30
UNITED ARTISTS			
❑ UAJ-14028 [M]	Nobody Knows You When You're Down and Out	1963	$30
❑ UAJS-15028 [S]	Nobody Knows You When You're Down and Out	1963	$40
ZIM			
❑ 2004	Cookin' Time	197?	$30
❑ 2006	Live at Emerson's	197?	$30

MCGHEE, STICK, AND JOHN LEE HOOKER

Number	Title	Yr	NM
AUDIO LAB			
❑ AL-1520 [M]	Highway of Blues	1959	$350

MCGILLIS, KELLY, AND MICHAEL HEDGES

Number	Title	Yr	NM
WINDHAM HILL			
❑ WH-0700	Santabear's First Christmas	1986	$15
— McGillis narrates Side 1; Hedges plays music on both sides			

MCGLOHON, LOONIS

Number	Title	Yr	NM
AUDIOPHILE			
❑ AP-166	Loonis in London	1982	$25

MCGOVERN, MAUREEN

Number	Title	Yr	NM
20TH CENTURY			
❑ T-474	Academy Award Performances	1975	$15
❑ T-439	Nice to Be Around	1974	$15
❑ T-419	The Morning After	1973	$15
CBS			
❑ BFM42314	Another Woman in Love	1987	$12
❑ BFM44500	State of the Heart	1988	$12
WARNER BROS.			
❑ BSK3329	Maureen McGovern	1979	$12

MCGOVERN, PATTY, AND THOMAS TALBERT

Number	Title	Yr	NM
ATLANTIC			
❑ 1245 [M]	Wednesday's Child	1956	$300
— Black label			
❑ 1245 [M]	Wednesday's Child	1961	$175
— Multicolor label, white "fan" logo at right			

MCGRATH, BAT, AND DON POTTER

Number	Title	Yr	NM
EPIC			
❑ BN26499	Introducing	1969	$18

MCGRAW, TIM

Number	Title	Yr	NM
CURB			
❑ 77886-2P [DJ]	Everywhere	1997	$30
— Promo-only picture disc			

MCGREGOR, CHRIS, BROTHERHOOD OF BREATH

Number	Title	Yr	NM
VENTURE			
❑ 90988	Country Cooking	1988	$25

MCGRIFF, JIMMY, AND JUNIOR PARKER

Number	Title	Yr	NM
CAPITOL			
❑ ST-569	Dudes Doin' Business	1971	$35
UNITED ARTISTS			
❑ UAS-6814 [B]	100 Proof Black Magic	1971	$25
❑ UAS-5597 [B]	Jimmy McGriff and Junior Parker	1972	$30

MCGRIFF, JIMMY

Number	Title	Yr	NM
BLUE NOTE			
❑ BST-84374	Black Pearl	1971	$35
❑ BST-84350	Electric Funk	1970	$35
❑ BST-84364	Something to Listen To	1971	$35
CAPITOL			
❑ ST-616	Soul Sugar	1970	$50
COLLECTABLES			
❑ COL-5147	Blues for Mr. Jimmy	198?	$25

Number	Title	Yr	NM
GROOVE MERCHANT			
❑ 2203	Black and Blues	1971	$35
❑ 520	Come Together	1973	$30
❑ 509	Fly Dude	1973	$35
❑ 4403 [B]	Flyin' Time	197?	$25
❑ 3300	Giants of the Organ In Concert	1974	$35
❑ 2205	Good Things Don't Happen Every Day	1971	$35
❑ 503	Groove Grease	1972	$35
❑ 529	If You're Ready Come Go with Me	1974	$30
❑ 506	Let's Stay Together	1972	$35
❑ 534	Main Squeeze	1975	$30
❑ 3311	Mean Machine	1976	$30
❑ 3309	Stump Juice	1976	$30
JAM			
❑ 02	City Lights	1982	$30
❑ 05	Movin' Upside the Blues	1983	$30
LRC			
❑ 9320	Outside Looking In	1978	$35
❑ 9316	Tailgunner	1977	$35
MILESTONE			
❑ M-9163	Blue to the 'Bone	1988	$25
❑ M-9116	Countdown	1984	$25
❑ M-9126	Skywalk	1985	$25
❑ M-9135	State of the Art	1986	$25
❑ M-9148	The Starting Five	1987	$25
QUINTESSENCE			
❑ 25061	Soul	1978	$30
SOLID STATE			
❑ SS-18017	A Bag Full of Blues	1968	$50
❑ SM-17002 [M]	A Bag Full of Soul	1966	$35
❑ SS-18002 [S]	A Bag Full of Soul	1966	$50
❑ SS-18060	A Thing to Come By	1969	$50
❑ SM-17006 [M]	Cherry	1967	$50
❑ SS-18006 [S]	Cherry	1967	$50
❑ SS-18036	Honey	1968	$50
❑ SS-18030	I've Got a New Woman	1968	$50
❑ SS-18053	Step I	1969	$50
❑ SM-17001 [M]	The Big Band of Jimmy McGriff	1966	$35
❑ SS-18001 [S]	The Big Band of Jimmy McGriff	1966	$50
❑ SS-18063	The Way You Look Tonight	1970	$50
❑ SS-18045	The Worm	1968	$50
SUE			
❑ LP-1039 [M]	Blues for Mister Jimmy	1965	$75
❑ STLP-1039 [S]	Blues for Mister Jimmy	1965	$40
❑ LP-1018 [M]	Christmas with McGriff	1963	$75
❑ STLP-1018 [S]	Christmas with McGriff	1963	$40
❑ LP-1012 [M]	I've Got a Woman	1962	$75
❑ STLP-1012 [S]	I've Got a Woman	1962	$40
❑ LP-1017 [M]	Jimmy McGriff at the Apollo	1963	$75
❑ STLP-1017 [S]	Jimmy McGriff at the Apollo	1963	$40
❑ LP-1020 [M]	Jimmy McGriff at the Organ	1963	$75
❑ STLP-1020 [S]	Jimmy McGriff at the Organ	1963	$40
❑ LP-1013 [M]	One of Mine	1963	$75
❑ STLP-1013 [S]	One of Mine	1963	$40
❑ LP-1043 [M]	Toast to Greatest Hits	1966	$50
❑ STLP-1043 [S]	Toast to Greatest Hits	1966	$75
❑ LP-1033 [M]	Topkapi	1964	$75
❑ STLP-1033 [S]	Topkapi	1964	$40
SUNSET			
❑ SUS-5264	The Great Jimmy McGriff	1969	$25
VEEP			
❑ VP-13522 [M]	Greatest Organ Hits	1967	$75
❑ VPS-16522 [S]	Greatest Organ Hits	1967	$50
❑ VP-13515 [M]	Live Where the Action Is	1966	$50

Number	Title	Yr	NM
❑ VPS-16515 [S]	Live Where the Action Is	1966	$30

MCGUFFEY LANE

Number	Title	Yr	NM
ATCO			
❑ SD 38-144	Aqua Dream	1982	$12
❑ 90020	Let the Hard Times Roll	1983	$10
❑ SD 38-133	McGuffey Lane	1980	$12
ATLANTIC AMERICA			
❑ 90155	Day By Day	1984	$10

MCGUINN, CLARK, & HILLMAN

Number	Title	Yr	NM
CAPITOL			
❑ ST-12043	City	1980	$15
❑ SW-11910	McGuinn, Clark & Hillman	1979	$15

MCGUINN, ROGER
Also see THE BYRDS; McGUINN AND HILLMAN; McGUINN, CLARK AND HILLMAN.

Number	Title	Yr	NM
ARISTA			
❑ AL8648	Back from Rio	1991	$18
COLUMBIA			
❑ PC34154	Cardiff Rose	1976	$15
❑ KC32956	Peace On You	1974	$15
❑ PC33541	Roger McGuinn & Band	1975	$15
❑ KC31946	Roger McGuinn	1973	$15
❑ AS353 [DJ]	The Roger McGuinn Airplay Anthology	1977	$30
— Promo only; also includes Byrds tracks			
❑ PC34656	Thunderbyrd	1977	$15

MCGUINN AND HILLMAN

Number	Title	Yr	NM
CAPITOL			
❑ SOO-12108	McGuinn and Hillman	1980	$12

MCGUINNESS FLINT

Number	Title	Yr	NM
CAPITOL			
❑ ST-794	Happy Birthday, Ruthy Baby	1971	$15
❑ SMAS-625	McGuinness Flint	1971	$15

MCGUIRE, BARRY, AND BARRY KANE

Number	Title	Yr	NM
HORIZON			
❑ WP-1608 [M]	Barry and Barry: Here and Now!	1962	$30
❑ SWP-1608 [S]	Barry and Barry: Here and Now!	1962	$30

MCGUIRE, BARRY
Also see THE NEW CHRISTY MINSTRELS.

Number	Title	Yr	NM
ABC DUNHILL			
❑ DS-50033	The World's Last Private Citizen	1968	$30
DUNHILL			
❑ D-50003 [M]	Eve of Destruction	1965	$50
❑ DS-50003 [S]	Eve of Destruction	1965	$75
❑ D-50005 [M]	This Precious Time	1966	$30
❑ DS-50005 [S]	This Precious Time	1966	$30
HORIZON			
❑ WP-1636 [M]	The Barry McGuire Album	1963	$30
❑ ST-1636 [S]	The Barry McGuire Album	1963	$40
MIRA			
❑ LP-3000 [M]	The Barry McGuire Album	1965	$25
— Reissue of Horizon LP			
❑ LPS-3000 [S]	The Barry McGuire Album	1965	$30
— Reissue of Horizon LP			
MYRRH			
❑ MSA-6531	Lighten Up	1975	$15
❑ MSA-6519	Seeds	1974	$15
ODE			
❑ SP-77004	Barry McGuire with the Doctor	1970	$18

MCGUIRE, PHYLLIS
Also see THE McGUIRE SISTERS.

Number	Title	Yr	NM
ABC-PARAMOUNT			
❑ 552 [M]	Phyllis McGuire Sings	1966	$18
❑ S-552 [S]	Phyllis McGuire Sings	1966	$25

MCGUIRE SISTERS, THE
Also see PHYLLIS McGUIRE.

Number	Title	Yr	NM
ABC-PARAMOUNT			
❑ 530 [M]	The McGuire Sisters Today	1966	$18
❑ S-530 [S]	The McGuire Sisters Today	1966	$25
CORAL			
❑ CRL56123 [10]	By Request	1955	$50
❑ CRL57097 [M]	Children's Holiday	1956	$40
❑ CRL57026 [M]	Do You Remember When	1956	$40
❑ CRL57225 [M]	Greetings from the McGuire Sisters	1958	$30
❑ CRL57033 [M]	He	1956	$40
❑ CRL57337 [M]	His and Hers	1960	$25
❑ CRL757337 [S]	His and Hers	1960	$30
❑ CRL57303 [M]	In Harmony with Him	1959	$30
❑ CRL757303 [S]	In Harmony with Him	1959	$40
❑ CRL57385 [M]	Just for Old Times' Sake	1961	$25
❑ CRL757385 [S]	Just for Old Times' Sake	1961	$30
❑ CRL57296 [M]	May You Always	1959	$25
❑ CRL757296 [S]	May You Always	1959	$30
❑ CRL57180 [M]	Musical Magic	1957	$30
❑ CRL57349 [M]	Our Golden Favorites	1961	$25
❑ CRL757349 [R]	Our Golden Favorites	196?	$15
❑ CRL57443 [M]	Showcase	196?	$25
❑ CRL757443 [R]	Showcase	196?	$15

Number	Title	Yr	NM
❏ CRL57052 [M]	Sincerely	1956	$40
❏ CRL57415 [M]	Songs Everybody Knows	1962	$18
❏ CRL757415 [S]	Songs Everybody Knows	1962	$25
❏ CRL57398 [M]	Subways Are for Sleeping	1961	$18
❏ CRL757398 [S]	Subways Are for Sleeping	1961	$25
❏ CRL57217 [M]	Sugartime	1958	$30
❏ CRL57028 [M]	'S Wonderful	1956	$40
❏ CRL57134 [M]	Teenage Party	1957	$30
❏ CXB6 [M]	The Best of the McGuire Sisters	1965	$30
❏ 7CXB6 [P]	The Best of the McGuire Sisters	1965	$30
❏ CRL57145 [M]	While the Lights Are Low	1957	$30

MCA

Number	Title	Yr	NM
❏ 4119	The Best of the McGuire Sisters	1978	$15

— Reissue of Coral 6

VOCALION

Number	Title	Yr	NM
❏ VL3685 [M]	Children's Holiday	1960	$25
❏ VL3798 [M]	The McGuire Sisters	1967	$18
❏ VL73798 [R]	The McGuire Sisters	1967	$15

MCHARGUE, ROSY

JUMP

Number	Title	Yr	NM
❏ JL-8 [10]	Dixie Combo	1955	$75

MCINTOSH, LADD

SEA BREEZE

Number	Title	Yr	NM
❏ 2007	Energy	198?	$25

MCINTYRE, HAL

COLUMBIA

Number	Title	Yr	NM
❏ CL6124 [10]	Dance Date	1950	$50

FORUM

Number	Title	Yr	NM
❏ F-9018 [M]	It Seems Like Only Yesterday	196?	$30
❏ SF-9018 [S]	It Seems Like Only Yesterday	196?	$35

HINDSIGHT

Number	Title	Yr	NM
❏ HSR-172	Hal McIntyre and His Orchestra 1943-45	198?	$25

ROULETTE

Number	Title	Yr	NM
❏ R-25079 [M]	It Seems Like Only Yesterday	1959	$25
❏ SR-25079 [S]	It Seems Like Only Yesterday	1959	$30

MCINTYRE, KALAPARUSHA MAURICE

BLACK SAINT

Number	Title	Yr	NM
❏ BSR-0037	Peace and Blessings	198?	$30

DELMARK

Number	Title	Yr	NM
❏ DS-425	Forces and Feelings	197?	$25
❏ DS-419	Humility	1969	$25

MCINTYRE, KEN

FANTASY

Number	Title	Yr	NM
❏ OJC-252	Looking Ahead	1987	$30

INNER CITY

Number	Title	Yr	NM
❏ IC-2014	Hindsight	1976	$40
❏ IC-2039	Home	197?	$75
❏ IC-2065	Introducing the Vibrations	1977	$75
❏ IC-2049	Open Horizon	1976	$50

NEW JAZZ

Number	Title	Yr	NM
❏ NJLP-8247 [M]	Looking Ahead	1960	$175

— Purple label

| ❏ NJLP-8247 [M] | Looking Ahead | 1965 | $175 |

— Blue label, trident logo at right

| ❏ NJLP-8259 [M] | Stone Blues | 1961 | $175 |

— Purple label

| ❏ NJLP-8259 [M] | Stone Blues | 1965 | $175 |

— Blue label, trident logo at right

STEEPLECHASE

Number	Title	Yr	NM
❏ SCS-1114	Chasing the Sun	198?	$35
❏ SCS-1014	Hindsight	198?	$50
❏ SCS-1039	Home	198?	$35
❏ SCS-1065	Introducing the Vibrations	198?	$35
❏ SCS-1049	Open Horizon	198?	$35

UNITED ARTISTS

Number	Title	Yr	NM
❏ UAL-3336 [M]	Way Way Out	1964	$100
❏ UAS-6336 [S]	Way Way Out	1964	$150
❏ UAJ-14015 [M]	Year of the Iron Sheep	1962	$150
❏ UAJS-15015 [S]	Year of the Iron Sheep	1962	$120

MCKAY, SCOTTY

ACE

Number	Title	Yr	NM
❏ LP-1017 [M]	Tonight In Person	1961	$100

MCKAY, STUART

RCA VICTOR

Number	Title	Yr	NM
❏ LJM-1021 [M]	Stuart McKay and His Woods	1955	$50

MCKEE, MARIA

GEFFEN

Number	Title	Yr	NM
❏ GHS24229	Maria McKee	1989	$12

MCKENDREE SPRING

DECCA

Number	Title	Yr	NM
❏ DL75104	McKendree Spring	1969	$18
❏ DL75332	McKendree Spring 3	1972	$18
❏ DL75230	Second Thoughts	1970	$18
❏ DL75385	Tracks	1972	$18

MCA

Number	Title	Yr	NM
❏ 277	McKendree Spring	1973	$12

— Reissue of Decca 75104

| ❏ 44 | McKendree Spring 3 | 1973 | $12 |

— Reissue of Decca 75332

| ❏ 370 | Spring Suite | 1973 | $15 |
| ❏ 50 | Tracks | 1973 | $12 |

— Reissue of Decca 75385

PYE

Number	Title	Yr	NM
❏ 12108	Get Me to the Country	1975	$15
❏ 12124	Too Young to Feel This Old	1976	$15

MCKENNA, DAVE, AND HALL OVERTON

BETHLEHEM

Number	Title	Yr	NM
❏ BCP-6049 [M]	Dual Piano Jazz	1960	$300
❏ BCPS-6049 [S]	Dual Piano Jazz	1960	$300

MCKENNA, DAVE; SCOTT HAMILTON; JAKE HANNA

CONCORD JAZZ

Number	Title	Yr	NM
❏ CJ-97	No Bass Hit	1979	$30

MCKENNA, DAVE

ABC-PARAMOUNT

Number	Title	Yr	NM
❏ ABC-104 [M]	Solo Piano	1956	$40

CHIAROSCURO

Number	Title	Yr	NM
❏ 175	Dave "Fingers" McKenna	197?	$30
❏ 136	Dave McKenna Quartet Featuring Zoot Sims	197?	$35
❏ 202	McKenna	1978	$30
❏ 119	Piano Solos	197?	$35

CONCORD JAZZ

Number	Title	Yr	NM
❏ CJ-227	Celebration of Hoagy Carmichael	1984	$25
❏ CJ-292	Dancing in the Dark	1986	$25
❏ CJ-174	Dave McKenna Plays Music of Harry Warren	198?	$25
❏ CJ-99	Giant Strides	1979	$30
❏ CJ-123	Left Handed Complement	1980	$30
❏ CJ-313	My Friend the Piano	1987	$25
❏ CJ-365	No More Ouzo for Puzo	1989	$30
❏ CJ-261	The Key Man	1985	$25

EPIC

Number	Title	Yr	NM
❏ LN3558 [M]	Dave McKenna	1959	$75
❏ BN527 [S]	Dave McKenna	1959	$75

FAMOUS DOOR

Number	Title	Yr	NM
❏ 122	No Holds Barred	1978	$30

HALCYON

Number	Title	Yr	NM
❏ 108	Cookin' at Michael's Pub	197?	$35

SHIAH

Number	Title	Yr	NM
❏ MK-1	By Myself	198?	$30

MCKENZIE, BOB AND DOUG

MERCURY

Number	Title	Yr	NM
❏ SRM-1-4034	Great White North	1981	$15

MCKENZIE, RED, AND EDDIE CONDON

JAZZOLOGY

Number	Title	Yr	NM
❏ J-110	Chicagoans (1944)	198?	$25

MCKENZIE, SCOTT

ODE

Number	Title	Yr	NM
❏ SP-77007	Stained Glass Morning	1970	$18
❏ Z1244002 [S]	The Voice of Scott McKenzie	1967	$25
❏ Z1244001 [M]	The Voice of Scott McKenzie	1967	$75

MCKINLEY, RAY, AND EDDIE SAUTER

SAVOY

Number	Title	Yr	NM
❏ MG-12024 [M]	Borderline	1955	$75

MCKINLEY, RAY

Also see GLENN MILLER ORCHESTRA.
Drummer, male singer and bandleader. Also see PEANUTS HUCKO; GLENN MILLER ORCHESTRA.

ALLEGRO ELITE

Number	Title	Yr	NM
❏ 4129 [10]	Ray McKinley and His Famous Orchestra	195?	$150
❏ 4015 [10]	Ray McKinley Plays Sauter and Others	195?	$50

SAVOY JAZZ

Number	Title	Yr	NM
❏ SJK-2261	The Most Versatile Band in the World	198?	$30

MCKINLEY, RAY/JOE MARSALA

DECCA

Number	Title	Yr	NM
❏ DL5262 [10]	Dixieland Jazz Battle, Vol. 2	1950	$175

MCKINLEY, TOM, AND ED SCHULLER

GM

Number	Title	Yr	NM
❏ 3001	Life Cycle	1982	$25

MCKINNEY, HAROLD

TRIBE

Number	Title	Yr	NM
❏ 2233	Voices and Rhythms	197?	$40

MCKINNEY'S COTTON PICKERS

RCA VICTOR

Number	Title	Yr	NM
❏ LPT-24 [10]	McKinney's Cotton Pickers	1952	$75

X

Number	Title	Yr	NM
❏ LVA-3031 [10]	McKinney's Cotton Pickers	1954	$50

MCKUEN, ROD; TAK SHINDO; JULIE MEREDITH

IMPERIAL

Number	Title	Yr	NM
❏ LP-9092 [M]	The Yellow Unicorn	1960	$40
❏ LP-12036 [S]	The Yellow Unicorn	1960	$50

MCKUEN, ROD

BUDDAH

Number	Title	Yr	NM
❏ BDS-5138	Cycles	197?	$15

CAPITOL

Number	Title	Yr	NM
❏ ST2838 [S]	Love Movement	1968	$18
❏ T2838 [M]	Love Movement	1968	$30
❏ T2079 [M]	Rod McKuen Sings Rod McKuen	1964	$18
❏ ST2079 [S]	Rod McKuen Sings Rod McKuen	1964	$25

DECCA

Number	Title	Yr	NM
❏ DL8946 [M]	Alone After Dark	1959	$25
❏ DL78946 [S]	Alone After Dark	1959	$30
❏ DL8882 [M]	Anywhere I Wander	1958	$25
❏ DL78882 [S]	Anywhere I Wander	1958	$30
❏ DL4969 [M]	Very Warm	1968	$25
❏ DL74969 [S]	Very Warm	1968	$18

EPIC

Number	Title	Yr	NM
❏ BN26370 [S]	In Search of Eros	1968	$18
❏ BN26370 [M]	In Search of Eros	1968	$30

— White label promo only; in stereo cover with "Epic Mono" sticker

EVEREST

Number	Title	Yr	NM
❏ 3208	Desire Has No Special Time	1968	$18
❏ 3267	Life Is	197?	$18

HIFI

Number	Title	Yr	NM
❏ R419 [M]	Beatsville	1960	$25
❏ SR419 [S]	Beatsville	1960	$30
❏ R407 [M]	Time of Desire	1958	$25
❏ SR407 [S]	Time of Desire	1958	$30

HORIZON

Number	Title	Yr	NM
❏ WP-1612 [M]	New Sounds in Folk Music	1963	$25
❏ ST-1612 [S]	New Sounds in Folk Music	1963	$30
❏ WPLP-1632 [M]	There's a Hoot Tonight	1963	$25
❏ WPLP-1632 [S]	There's a Hoot Tonight	1963	$30

IN

Number	Title	Yr	NM
❏ 1003 [M]	Seasons in the Sun	1964	$25
❏ S-1003 [S]	Seasons in the Sun	1964	$30

JUBILEE

Number	Title	Yr	NM
❏ J-5013 [M]	Mr. Oliver Twist	1962	$25
❏ SJ-5013 [S]	Mr. Oliver Twist	1962	$30

KAPP

Number	Title	Yr	NM
❏ KL-1538 [M]	In a Lonely Place	1967	$25
❏ KS-3538 [S]	In a Lonely Place	1967	$18

LIBERTY

Number	Title	Yr	NM
❏ LRP-3011 [M]	Lazy Afternoon	1956	$40

RCA VICTOR

Number	Title	Yr	NM
❏ LSP-4010	A Single Man	1968	$18

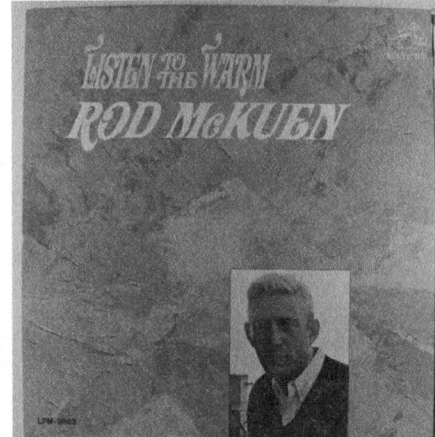

Number	Title	Yr	NM
❏ LPM-3863 [M]	Listen to the Warm	1967	$25
❏ LSP-3863 [S]	Listen to the Warm	1967	$18
❏ LPM-3635 [M]	Other Kinds of Songs	1966	$18

Number	Title	Yr	NM
❏ LSP-3635 [S]	Other Kinds of Songs	1966	$25
❏ LPM-3424 [M]	Rod McKuen Sings His Own	1965	$18
❏ LSP-3424 [S]	Rod McKuen Sings His Own	1965	$25
❏ LSP-4127	The Best of Rod McKuen	1969	$18
❏ LPM-3508 [M]	The Loner	1966	$18
❏ LSP-3508 [S]	The Loner	1966	$25
❏ LPM-3786 [M]	Through European Windows	1967	$25
❏ LSP-3786 [S]	Through European Windows	1967	$18

STANYAN

Number	Title	Yr	NM
❏ 5010	A Boy Named Charlie Brown	1970	$18
❏ 5051	Amsterdam Concert	1972	$18
❏ 5072	A Portrait of Rod McKuen	1972	$15
❏ 4010	A Single Man	197?	$12
❏ 5005	Blessings in Shades of Green	1970	$15
❏ 10009	Concerto No. 1; Four Statements	197?	$15
❏ 9001	Concerto No. 1 for Four Harpsichords and Orchestra	197?	$15
❏ 9006	Concerto No. 2 for Guitar and Orchestra; Five Pieces	197?	$15
❏ 9012	Concerto No. 3 for Piano and Orchestra	1972	$15
❏ 5040	Evening in Vienna	1972	$15
❏ 5006	Folk Album	1970	$15
❏ 5032	Have a Nice Day	1973	$15
❏ STS-001	In Concert	197?	$18
—Originals are numbered, limited editions			
❏ 5048	Listen to the Warm	197?	$18
❏ 5075	Live at the Sydney Opera House	197?	$15
❏ 5016	Live in London!	1971	$18
❏ 5009	Love's Been Good to Me	1970	$15
❏ 9010	McKuen Conducts McKuen	1972	$15
❏ 1894	Pastorale	197?	$15
❏ 5047	Pastures Green	197?	$15
❏ 9008	Piano Variations	197?	$15
❏ 5025	Rod	197?	$15
❏ 5042	Rod McKuen Grand Tour, Vol. 3	1972	$15
❏ 5031	Rod McKuen's Greatest Hits, Vol. 3	197?	$15
❏ 2688	Rod McKuen's Greatest Hits, Vol. 4	197?	$12
❏ 2560	Rod McKuen's Greatest Hits 2	197?	$12
❏ 5022	Rod McKuen Sings Jacques Brel	197?	$15
❏ 9015	Seascapes; Plains of My Country	197?	$15
❏ STS-003	Seasons in the Sun	197?	$18
❏ 5004	Seasons in the Sun Vol. 2	197?	$15
❏ 5046	Seasons in the Sun Vols. 1 and 2	197?	$18
❏ 9005	Symphony No. 1: "All Men Love Something	197?	$15
❏ 5020	Try Rod McKuen in Your Own Home	197?	$15

SUNSET

Number	Title	Yr	NM
❏ SUS-5273	In the Beginning	1970	$12

TRADITION

Number	Title	Yr	NM
❏ 2063 [M]	A San Francisco Hippie Trip	1967	$30

WARNER BROS.

Number	Title	Yr	NM
❏ BS2817	Alone	1974	$15
❏ 2WS2731	Back to Carnegie Hall	1973	$18
❏ WS1722	Beautiful Strangers	1968	$18
❏ WS1772	Greatest Hits of Rod McKuen	1969	$18
❏ ST-92042	Greatest Hits of Rod McKuen	1969	$25
—Capitol Record Club edition			
❏ WS1758	Lonesome Cities	1968	$18
❏ BS2931	McKuen Country	1976	$12
❏ WS1837	New Ballads	1970	$15
❏ BS2638	Odyssey	1973	$15
❏ 2WS1894	Pastorale	1971	$18
❏ 2WS1794	Rod McKuen at Carnegie Hall	1969	$25
❏ 2WS1947	Rod McKuen Grand Tour	1971	$18
❏ BS2688	Rod McKuen's Greatest Hits, Vol. 4	1973	$15
❏ BS2560	Rod McKuen's Greatest Hits 2	1970	$15
❏ BS2785	Seasons in the Sun	1974	$15

MCKUSICK, HAL

BETHLEHEM

Number	Title	Yr	NM
❏ BCP-16 [M]	East Coast Jazz/8	1955	$300

CORAL

Number	Title	Yr	NM
❏ CRL57131 [M]	Hal McKusick Quintet	1957	$120
❏ CRL57116 [M]	Jazz at the Academy	1957	$100

DECCA

Number	Title	Yr	NM
❏ DL9209 [M]	Cross Section -- Saxes	1958	$150
❏ DL79209 [S]	Cross Section -- Saxes	1958	$150

MCA

Number	Title	Yr	NM
❏ 1379	Hal McKusick Quintet Featuring Art Farmer 1957	198?	$15

PRESTIGE

Number	Title	Yr	NM
❏ PRLP-7135 [M]	Triple Exposure	1957	$650

RCA VICTOR

Number	Title	Yr	NM
❏ LPM-1164 [M]	Hal McKusick in the 20th Century Drawing Room	1956	$100
❏ LPM-1366 [M]	The Jazz Workshop	1957	$120

MCLACHLAN, SARAH

ARISTA

Number	Title	Yr	NM
❏ RTH-2013	Afterglow	2004	$30
—Audiophile vinyl issue by Classic Records			
❏ RTH-2000	Fumbling Toward Ecstasy and The Freedom Sessions	1997	$40
—Audiophile vinyl issue of both CDs on 2-LP set by Classic Records, with one bonus track			
❏ RTH-2005	Solace	2002	$30
—Audiophile vinyl reissue by Classic Records			
❏ RTH-18970	Surfacing	1999	$30
—Audiophile vinyl issue by Classic Records			
❏ AL8594	Touch	1989	$25
❏ RTH-2004	Touch	2002	$30
—Audiophile vinyl reissue by Classic Records			

MCLAIN, DENNY

CAPITOL

Number	Title	Yr	NM
❏ ST2881	Denny McLain at the Organ	1968	$30
❏ ST-204	Denny McLain In Las Vegas	1969	$30

MCLAIN, TOMMY

CRAZY CAJUN

Number	Title	Yr	NM
❏ 1050	Good Mornin' Lousiana	1978	$30

JIN

Number	Title	Yr	NM
❏ 9009	Tommy McLain	1975	$30

STARFLITE

Number	Title	Yr	NM
❏ 36028	Backwoods Bayou Adventure	1979	$18

MCLAUGHLIN, JOHN

CBS

Number	Title	Yr	NM
❏ FM45578	Mediterranean Concerto	1989	$35

CELLULOID

Number	Title	Yr	NM
❏ CEL-5010	Devotion	198?	$25
—Reissue of Douglas 31568			

COLUMBIA

Number	Title	Yr	NM
❏ PC34372	A Handful of Beauty	1977	$30
—No bar code on cover			
❏ JC35785	Electric Dreams	1979	$25
❏ JC35326	Electric Guitarist	1978	$30
—No bar code on cover			
❏ FC37152	Friday Night in San Francisco	1981	$25
—With Al DiMeola and Paco De Lucia			
❏ JC34980	Natural Elements	1977	$30
—No bar code on cover			
❏ FC38645	Passion, Grace & Fire	1983	$25
—With Al DiMeola and Paco De Lucia			
❏ PC34162	Shakti with John McLaughlin	1976	$30
—No bar code on cover			
❏ JC36355	The Best of John McLaughlin	1980	$30
❏ PC36355	The Best of John McLaughlin	198?	$20
—Reissue with new prefix			

DOUGLAS

Number	Title	Yr	NM
❏ KZ31568	Devotion	1972	$35
—Reissue of 4			
❏ 4	Devotion	1970	$50
❏ KZ30766	My Goals Beyond	1971	$35
—Original issue			

DOUGLAS CASABLANCA

Number	Title	Yr	NM
❏ ADLP-6003	My Goals Beyond	1976	$30
—Reissue of Douglas 30766; second issue of this album			

ELEKTRA/MUSICIAN

Number	Title	Yr	NM
❏ E1-60031	My Goals Beyond	1982	$30
—Third issue of this album			

POLYDOR

Number	Title	Yr	NM
❏ PD-5510	Extrapolation	1972	$50
❏ PD-1-6074	Extrapolation	1972	$30
—Reissue of 5510			

PYE

Number	Title	Yr	NM
❏ 12103	Where Fortune Smiles	1975	$50
—Recorded in 1970; this was the first U.S. issue of this material			

RELATIVITY

Number	Title	Yr	NM
❏ 88561-8061-1	Adventures in Radioland	1986	$30

RYKO ANALOGUE

Number	Title	Yr	NM
❏ RALP-0051	My Goals Beyond	1987	$50
—Clear vinyl; fourth issue of this album			

WARNER BROS.

Number	Title	Yr	NM
❏ BSK3619	Belo Horizonte	1981	$35
❏ 25190	Mahavishnu	1985	$25
❏ 23723	Music Spoken Here	1982	$25

MCLAWLER, SARAH

VEE JAY

Number	Title	Yr	NM
❏ LP-1030 [M]	At the Break of Day	1961	$75
—With Richard Otto			

MCLEAN, DON

ARISTA

Number	Title	Yr	NM
❏ AL4149	Prime Time	1978	$12

CAPITOL

Number	Title	Yr	NM
❏ B002431201 [B]	American Pie	2016	$25
❏ C1-48080	Love Tracks	1988	$12

CASABLANCA

Number	Title	Yr	NM
❏ NBLP7173	Chain Lightning	1979	$0
—Canceled			

EMI AMERICA

Number	Title	Yr	NM
❏ ST-17255	Don McLean's Greatest Hits, Then and Now	1987	$12

LIBERTY

Number	Title	Yr	NM
❏ LN-10037	American Pie	1980	$10
—Reissue of United Artists 5535			
❏ LN-10211	Homeless Brother	198?	$10
—Reissue of United Artists 315			
❏ LN-10157	Tapestry	1982	$10
—Reissue of United Artists 5522			

MEDIARTS

Number	Title	Yr	NM
❏ 41-4	Tapestry	1970	$25

MILLENNIUM

Number	Title	Yr	NM
❏ BXL1-7762	Believers	1981	$12
❏ BXL1-7756	Chain Lightning	1981	$12

UNITED ARTISTS

Number	Title	Yr	NM
❏ UAS-5535	American Pie	1971	$15
❏ UAS-5651	Don McLean	1972	$15
❏ UA-LA315-G	Homeless Brother	1974	$15
❏ UA-LA161-F	Playin' Favorites	1973	$15
❏ UA-LA652-H2	Solo	1976	$18
❏ UAS-5522	Tapestry	1971	$15
—Reissue of Mediarts LP			

MCLEAN, JACKIE, AND MICHAEL CARVIN

INNER CITY

Number	Title	Yr	NM
❏ IC-2028	Antiquity	197?	$35

STEEPLECHASE

Number	Title	Yr	NM
❏ SCS-1028	Antiquity	198?	$30

MCLEAN, JACKIE

ADLIB

Number	Title	Yr	NM
❏ ADL-6601 [M]	The Jackie McLean Quintet	1955	$4000

BLUE NOTE

Number	Title	Yr	NM
❏ BLP-4218 [M]	Action Action Action	1965	$120
—With "New York, USA" address on label			
❏ BST-84218 [S]	Action Action Action	1965	$150
—With "New York, USA" address on label			
❏ BST-84218 [S]	Action Action Action	1967	$30
—With "A Division of Liberty Records" on label			
❏ BLP-4089 [M]	A Fickle Sonance	1961	$800
—With W. 63rd St. address on label			
❏ BLP-4089 [M]	A Fickle Sonance	1963	$300
—With "New York, USA" address on label			
❏ BST-84089 [S]	A Fickle Sonance	1961	$350
—With W. 63rd St. address on label			
❏ BST-84089 [S]	A Fickle Sonance	1963	$300
—With "New York, USA" address on label			
❏ BST-84089 [S]	A Fickle Sonance	1967	$175
—With "A Division of Liberty Records" on label			
❏ BLP-4067 [M]	Bluesnik	1961	$400
—With W. 63rd St. address on label			
❏ BLP-4067 [M]	Bluesnik	1963	$100
—With "New York, USA" address on label			
❏ BST-84067 [S]	Bluesnik	1961	$250
—With W. 63rd St. address on label			
❏ BST-84067 [S]	Bluesnik	1963	$75
—With "New York, USA" address on label			
❏ BST-84067 [S]	Bluesnik	1967	$75
—With "A Division of Liberty Records" on label			
❏ B1-84067 [S]	Bluesnik	1989	$30
—The Finest in Jazz Since 1939" reissue			
❏ BST-84284	'Bout Soul	1968	$100
—With "A Division of Liberty Records" on label			
❏ BLP-4038 [M]	Capuchin Swing	1960	$600
—Deep groove; with W. 63rd St. address on label			
❏ BLP-4038 [M]	Capuchin Swing	1960	$175
—W. 63rd St. address on label, either with no "deep groove" or with the groove on only one side			
❏ BLP-4038 [M]	Capuchin Swing	1963	$100
—With "New York, USA" address on label			
❏ BST-84038 [S]	Capuchin Swing	1960	$300
—With W. 63rd St. address on label			
❏ BST-84038 [S]	Capuchin Swing	1963	$75
—With "New York, USA" address on label			
❏ BST-84038 [S]	Capuchin Swing	1967	$75
—With "A Division of Liberty Records" on label			
❏ LT-994	Consequences	1979	$25
❏ BST-84345	Demon's Dance	1969	$100
—With "A Division of Liberty Records" on label			
❏ BST-84345	Demon's Dance	198?	$25
—The Finest in Jazz Since 1939" reissue			
❏ BLP-4165 [M]	Destination... Out!	1964	$120

Number	Title	Yr	NM
— With "New York, USA" address on label			
❏ BST-84165 [S]	Destination... Out!	197?	$20
— Dark blue label with white stylized "B"			
❏ BST-84165 [S]	Destination... Out!	1964	$150
— With "New York, USA" address on label			
❏ BST-84165 [S]	Destination... Out!	1967	$40
— With "A Division of Liberty Records" on label			
❏ BN-LA483-4047	Hipnosis	1975	$75
❏ BLP-4179 [M]	It's Time!	1964	$150
— With "New York, USA" address on label			
❏ BST-84179 [S]	It's Time!	1964	$150
— With "New York, USA" address on label			
❏ BST-84179 [S]	It's Time!	1967	$30
— With "A Division of Liberty Records" on label			
❏ BLP-4116 [M]	Jackie McLean Quintet	1962	$0
— Canceled			
❏ BST-84116 [S]	Jackie McLean Quintet	1962	$0
— Canceled			
❏ BLP-4051 [M]	Jackie's Bag	1960	$700
— Deep groove; with W. 63rd St. address on label			

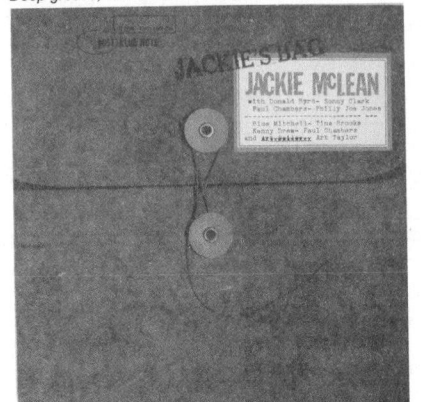

Number	Title	Yr	NM
❏ BLP-4051 [M]	Jackie's Bag	1963	$150
— With "New York, USA" address on label			
❏ BST-84051 [S]	Jackie's Bag	1960	$300
— With W. 63rd St. address on label			
❏ BST-84051 [S]	Jackie's Bag	1963	$75
— With "New York, USA" address on label			
❏ BST-84051 [S]	Jackie's Bag	1967	$75
— With "A Division of Liberty Records" on label			
❏ BST-84051 [S]	Jackie's Bag	1985	$30
— The Finest in Jazz Since 1939" reissue			
❏ BLP-4223 [M]	Jackknife	1965	$0
— Canceled			
❏ BST-84223 [S]	Jackknife	1965	$0
— Canceled			
❏ BN-LA457-H2	Jackknife	1975	$75
— First issue of unreleased material from 1960s			
❏ BLP-4106 [M]	Let Freedom Ring	1962	$300
— With "New York, USA" address on label			
❏ BST-84106 [S]	Let Freedom Ring	1962	$250
— With "New York, USA" address on label			
❏ BST-84106 [S]	Let Freedom Ring	1967	$40
— With "A Division of Liberty Records" on label			
❏ BST-84106 [S]	Let Freedom Ring	198?	$30
— The Finest in Jazz Since 1939" reissue			
❏ BLP-4262 [M]	New and Old Gospel	1967	$300
— With "A Division of Liberty Records" on label			
❏ BST-84262 [S]	New and Old Gospel	1967	$120
— With "A Division of Liberty Records" on label			
❏ BLP-4236 [M]	New Frequency	1966	$0
— Canceled			
❏ BST-84236 [S]	New Frequency	1966	$0
— Canceled			
❏ BLP-4013 [M]	New Soil	1959	$500
— Deep groove" version; W. 63rd St. address on label			
❏ BLP-4013 [M]	New Soil	1959	$300
— Regular version, W. 63rd St. address on label			
❏ BLP-4013 [M]	New Soil	1963	$150
— With "New York, USA" address on label			
❏ BST-4013 [S]	New Soil	1959	$300
— Deep groove" version; W. 63rd St. address on label			
❏ BST-4013 [S]	New Soil	1959	$250
— Regular version, W. 63rd St. address on label			
❏ BST-4013 [S]	New Soil	1963	$40
— With "New York, USA" address on label			
❏ BST-84013 [S]	New Soil	1967	$75
— With "A Division of Liberty Records" on label			
❏ B1-84013 [S]	New Soil	1989	$30
— The Finest in Jazz Since 1939" reissue			
❏ BLP-4137 [M]	One Step Beyond	1963	$120
— With "New York, USA" address on label			
❏ BST-84137 [S]	One Step Beyond	1963	$150
— With "New York, USA" address on label			
❏ BST-84137 [S]	One Step Beyond	1967	$40

Number	Title	Yr	NM
— With "A Division of Liberty Records" on label			
❏ BST-84137 [S]	One Step Beyond	198?	$30
— The Finest in Jazz Since 1939" reissue			
❏ BST-84137 [S]	One Step Beyond	197?	$20
— Dark blue label with black stylized "B"			
❏ BLP-4215 [M]	Right Now!	1965	$175
— With "New York, USA" address on label			
❏ BST-84215 [S]	Right Now!	1965	$150
— With "New York, USA" address on label			
❏ BST-84215 [S]	Right Now!	1967	$30
— With "A Division of Liberty Records" on label			
❏ BLP-4024 [M]	Swing, Swang, Swingin'	1959	$1200
— Deep groove" version; W. 63rd St. address on label			
❏ BLP-4024 [M]	Swing, Swang, Swingin'	1959	$500
— Regular version, W. 63rd St. address on label			
❏ BLP-4024 [M]	Swing, Swang, Swingin'	1963	$150
— With "New York, USA" address on label			
❏ BST-84024 [S]	Swing, Swang, Swingin'	1959	$400
— With W. 63rd St. address on label			
❏ BST-84024 [S]	Swing, Swang, Swingin'	1963	$100
— With "New York, USA" address on label			
❏ BST-84024 [S]	Swing, Swang, Swingin'	1967	$75
— With "A Division of Liberty Records" on label			
❏ BST-84427	Tippin' the Scales	198?	$35
❏ LT-1085	Vertigo	1980	$25
BOPLICITY			
❏ BOP-2	Swing, Swang, Swingin'	198?	$25
FANTASY			
❏ OJC-056	4, 5 and 6	198?	$30
❏ OJC-253	A Long Drink of the Blues	1987	$30
❏ OJC-074	Jackie McLean & Co.	198?	$30
❏ OJC-1717	Jackie's Pal -- Introducing Bill Hardman	198?	$30
❏ OJC-426	Lights Out!	1990	$35
❏ OJC-197	Makin' the Changes	1985	$30
❏ OJC-098	McLean's Scene	198?	$30
❏ OJC-354	Strange Blues	198?	$30
INNER CITY			
❏ IC-2013	Ghetto Lullaby	197?	$35
❏ IC-2001	Live at Montmartre	197?	$35
❏ IC-6029	New Wine	1978	$35
❏ IC-2023	New York Calling	197?	$35
❏ IC-2009	Ode to Super	197?	$35
JOSIE			
❏ JJM-3503 [M]	Jackie McLean Sextet	1963	$75
❏ JJM-3507 [M]	Jackie McLean Sextet	1963	$75
❏ JLPS-3503 [S]	Jackie McLean Sextet	1963	$40
❏ JLPS-3507 [S]	Jackie McLean Sextet	1963	$40
JUBILEE			
❏ JLP-1093 [M]	Jackie McLean Plays Fat Jazz	1959	$250
❏ JLP-1064 [M]	The Jackie McLean Quintet	1958	$175
MOSAIC			
❏ MQ6-150	The Complete Blue Note 1964-66 Jackie McLean Sessions	1993	$250
— Limited edition of 5,000			
NEW JAZZ			
❏ NJLP-8279 [M]	4, 5 and 6	1962	$250
— Purple label			
❏ NJLP-8279 [M]	4, 5 and 6	1965	$175
— Blue label, trident logo at right			
❏ NJLP-8253 [M]	A Long Drink of the Blues	1961	$500
— Purple label			
❏ NJLP-8253 [M]	A Long Drink of the Blues	1965	$175
— Blue label, trident logo at right			
❏ NJLP-8312 [M]	Alto Madness	1963	$0
— Canceled; reassigned to Status			
❏ NJLP-8323 [M]	Jackie McLean & Co.	1963	$0
— Canceled; reassigned to Status			
❏ NJLP-8263 [M]	Lights Out!	1961	$250
— Purple label			
❏ NJLP-8263 [M]	Lights Out!	1965	$175
— Blue label, trident logo at right			
❏ NJLP-8231 [M]	Makin' the Changes	1960	$600
— Purple label			
❏ NJLP-8231 [M]	Makin' the Changes	1965	$175
— Blue label, trident logo at right			
❏ NJLP-8212 [M]	McLean's Scene	1958	$400
— Purple label			
❏ NJLP-8212 [M]	McLean's Scene	1965	$175
— Blue label, trident logo at right			
❏ NJLP-8290 [M]	Steeplechase	1962	$250
— Purple label			
❏ NJLP-8290 [M]	Steeplechase	1965	$175
— Blue label, trident logo at right			
PRESTIGE			
❏ PRLP-7048 [M]	4, 5 and 6	1956	$1500
— 446 W. 50th St., N.Y.C." address on yellow label			
❏ PRLP-7114 [M]	Alto Madness	1957	$1000
— Yellow label			
❏ MPP-2512	Alto Madness	198?	$30
❏ P-24076	Contour	1977	$50
❏ PRLP-7087 [M]	Jackie McLean & Co.	1957	$600
— 446 W. 50th St., N.Y.C." address on label			

Number	Title	Yr	NM
❏ PRLP-7068 [M]	Jackie's Pal -- Introducing Bill Hardman	1956	$2000
— 446 W. 50th St., N.Y.C." address on yellow label			
❏ PRLP-7035 [M]	Lights Out!	1956	$1000
— 446 W. 50th St., N.Y.C." address on yellow label			
❏ PRST-7757	Lights Out!	1970	$75
❏ PRLP-7500 [M]	Strange Blues	1967	$40
❏ PRST-7500 [R]	Strange Blues	1967	$75
RCA VICTOR			
❏ AFL1-3230 [S]	Monuments	1979	$30
ROULETTE			
❏ RE-129	Echoes of an Era (Tune-Up)	1976	$35
STATUS			
❏ ST-8312 [M]	Alto Madness	1965	$75
❏ ST-8323 [M]	Jackie McLean & Co.	1965	$75
STEEPLECHASE			
❏ SCS-1013	A Ghetto Lullaby	198?	$30
❏ SCC-6005	Dr. Jackie	198?	$30
❏ SCS-1001	Live at Montmartre	198?	$30
❏ SCS-1023	New York Calling	198?	$30
❏ SCS-1009	Ode to Super	198?	$30
❏ SCS-1006	The Meeting	198?	$30
❏ SCS-1020	The Source	198?	$30
TRIP			
❏ TLX-5027	Two Sides of Jackie McLean	197?	$50

MCLEAN, RENE

Number	Title	Yr	NM
INNER CITY			
❏ IC-2037	Watch Out	197?	$35
STEEPLECHASE			
❏ SCS-1037	Watch Out!	198?	$30

MCLOLLIE, OSCAR

Number	Title	Yr	NM
CROWN			
❏ CLP-5016 [M]	Oscar McLollie and His Honey Jumpers	1956	$400

— Opinions differ as to whether this LP actually exists. Value is probably conservative.

MCLUHAN, MARSHALL

Number	Title	Yr	NM
COLUMBIA			
❏ CL2701 [M]	The Medium Is the Message	1967	$30
❏ CS9501 [S]	The Medium Is the Message	1967	$30

MCLUHAN

Number	Title	Yr	NM
BRUNSWICK			
❏ BL754177	Anomaly	1972	$25

MCMAHON, ED

Number	Title	Yr	NM
CAMEO			
❏ C-2009 [M]	And Me...I'm Ed McMahon	1967	$30
❏ SC-2009 [S]	And Me...I'm Ed McMahon	1967	$30
RCA CAMDEN			
❏ CAL-1083 [M]	What Do You Want to Be When You Grow Up?	1965	$25
❏ CAS-1083 [S]	What Do You Want to Be When You Grow Up?	1965	$30

MCMANUS, JILL

Number	Title	Yr	NM
CONCORD JAZZ			
❏ CJ-242	Symbols of Hopi	1984	$25

MCNABB, TED

Number	Title	Yr	NM
EPIC			
❏ LN3663 [M]	Ted McNabb and Company	1959	$150
❏ BN558 [S]	Ted McNabb and Company	1959	$100

MCNAIR, BARBARA

Number	Title	Yr	NM
AUDIO FIDELITY			
❏ AFSD-6222	More Today Than Yesterday	1969	$25
❏ ST-92074	More Today Than Yesterday	1969	$30
— Capitol Record Club edition			
MOTOWN			

Number	Title	Yr	NM
☐ 644 [M]	Here I Am	1966	$50
☐ S-644 [S]	Here I Am	1966	$75
☐ S-680	The Real Barbara McNair	1969	$30
SIGNATURE			
☐ SM1042 [M]	Love Talk	1960	$40
☐ SS1042 [S]	Love Talk	1960	$50
WARNER BROS.			
☐ W1541 [M]	I Enjoy Being a Girl	1964	$30
☐ WS1541 [S]	I Enjoy Being a Girl	1964	$30
☐ W1570 [M]	The Livin' End	1964	$30
☐ WS1570 [S]	The Livin' End	1964	$30

MCNALLY, BOB
HANDCRAFTED

Number	Title	Yr	NM
☐ HCR100	Handmade Christmas Music 1983		$12

MCNEELY, BIG JAY
COLLECTABLES

Number	Title	Yr	NM
☐ COL-5133	Golden Classics	198?	$12
FEDERAL			
☐ 295-96 [10]	Big Jay McNeely	1955	$3000
☐ 395-530 [M]	Big Jay McNeely in 3-D	1956	$800
KING			
☐ 650 [M]	Big "J" in 3-D	1959	$500
SAVOY			
☐ MG-15045 [10]	A Rhythm and Blues Concert	1955	$2000
—VG value 1000; VG+ value 1500			
WARNER BROS.			
☐ W1533 [M]	Big Jay McNeely	1963	$100
☐ WS1533 [S]	Big Jay McNeely	1963	$150

MCNEELY, JIM
GATEMOUTH

Number	Title	Yr	NM
☐ 1001	The Plot Thickens	1980	$30
MUSE			
☐ MR-5378	The Plot Thickens	198?	$25
STEEPLECHASE			
☐ SCS-4001	Rain's Dance	198?	$30

MCNEIL, JOHN
STEEPLECHASE

Number	Title	Yr	NM
☐ SCS-1154	Clean Sweep	198?	$30
☐ SCS-1099	Embarkation	1978	$30
☐ SCS-1117	Faun	198?	$30
☐ SCS-1183	I've Got the World on a String	198?	$30
☐ SCS-1128	Look to the Sky	198?	$30
☐ SCS-1133	The Glass Room	1979	$30

MCNEILL, DON
CORAL

Number	Title	Yr	NM
☐ CRL57288 [M]	Book, Candle, Prayer	1958	$30
☐ CRL57291 [M]	March Around the Breakfast Table	1958	$30

MCNEILL, LLOYD
ASHA

Number	Title	Yr	NM
☐ 3	Washington Suite	1976	$35

MCNICHOL, KRISTY AND JIMMY
RCA VICTOR

Number	Title	Yr	NM
☐ AFL1-2875	Kristy and Jimmy McNichol	1978	$25

MCPARTLAND, JIMMY
BRUNSWICK

Number	Title	Yr	NM
☐ BL54018 [M]	Dixieland Band	1955	$75
☐ BL58049 [10]	Shades of Bix	1953	$100
EPIC			
☐ LN3371 [M]	Jimmy McPartland's Dixieland	1956	$100
☐ LN3463 [M]	The Music Man" Goes Dixieland, The	1958	$100
☐ BN506 [S]	The Music Man" Goes Dixieland, The	1958	$75
HARMONY			
☐ HS11264	Dixieland	1968	$30
JAZZOLOGY			
☐ J-16 [M]	Jimmy McPartland On Stage	196?	$35
☐ J-137	One Night Stand	1986	$25
JAZZTONE			
☐ J-1227 [M]	The Middle Road	1956	$40
MCA			
☐ 4110	Shades of Bix	197?	$30
MERCURY			
☐ MG-20460 [M]	Meet Me in Chicago	1959	$150
☐ SR-60143 [S]	Meet Me in Chicago	1959	$150
PALACE			
☐ M-708 [M]	Dixieland Vol. 1	196?	$35
RCA CAMDEN			
☐ CAL-549 [M]	That Happy Dixieland Jazz	1960	$30

RCA VICTOR

Number	Title	Yr	NM
☐ LPV-549 [M]	That Happy Dixieland Jazz	1966	$25

MCPARTLAND, JIMMY/PAUL BARBARIN
JAZZTONE

Number	Title	Yr	NM
☐ J-1241 [M]	Dixieland Now and Then	195?	$30

MCPARTLAND, MARIAN, AND GEORGE SHEARING
SAVOY

Number	Title	Yr	NM
☐ MG-12016 [M]	Great Britain's Marion McPartland and George Shearing	1955	$50

MCPARTLAND, MARIAN
ARGO

Number	Title	Yr	NM
☐ LP-640 [M]	Marion McPartland at the London House	1959	$40
☐ LPS-640 [S]	Marion McPartland at the London House	1959	$30
BAINBRIDGE			
☐ 1045	Marian McPartland with Ben Tucker	198?	$25
CAPITOL			
☐ T699 [M]	After Dark	1956	$75
☐ T574 [M]	Marion McPartland at the Hickory House	1955	$85
☐ T785 [M]	Marion McPartland Trio	1957	$85
CONCORD JAZZ			
☐ CJ-86	From This Moment On	1979	$25
☐ CJ-118	Marian McPartland at the Festival	1981	$25
☐ CJ-326	Marian McPartland Plays the Music of Billy Strayhorn	1987	$25
☐ CJ-202	Personal Choice	1982	$25
☐ CJ-101	Portrait of Marian McPartland	1980	$25
☐ CJ-272	Willow Creek and Other Ballads	1985	$25
DOT			
☐ DLP-25907	My Old Flame	1969	$85
HALCYON			
☐ 103	Ambience	1971	$35
☐ 105	Delicate Balance	1972	$35
☐ 100	Interplay	1970	$35
☐ 117	Live at the Carlyle	1979	$30
☐ 109	Marian McPartland Plays Alec Wilder	197?	$35
☐ 115	Now's the Time	1978	$30
☐ 111	Solo Concert at Haverford	197?	$30
IMPROV			
☐ 7115	A Fine Romance	1976	$30
SAVOY			
☐ MG-15019 [10]	Jazz at Storyville, Volume 3	1952	$100
☐ MG-15032 [10]	Jazz at the Hickory House	1953	$100
☐ MG-12005 [M]	Lullaby of Birdland	1955	$75
☐ MG-15027 [10]	Marion McPartland	1953	$100
☐ MG-12004 [M]	Marion McPartland in Concert	1955	$75
☐ MG-15021 [10]	Piano Moods	1952	$100
SAVOY JAZZ			
☐ SJL-2248	Marian McPartland at the Hickory House	198?	$35
TIME			
☐ 52073 [M]	Bossa Nova Plus Soul	1963	$30
☐ S-2073 [S]	Bossa Nova Plus Soul	1963	$30
☐ 52189 [M]	West Side Story	196?	$30
☐ S-2189 [S]	West Side Story	196?	$30

MCPARTLAND, MARIAN AND JIMMY
HALCYON

Number	Title	Yr	NM
☐ 116	Goin' Back a Ways	198?	$30
☐ 107	Live at the Monticello	197?	$35
☐ 114	Swingin'	197?	$30
IMPROV			
☐ 7122	Wanted!	1977	$30

MCPEAK, CURTIS
ABC-PARAMOUNT

Number	Title	Yr	NM
☐ ABC-446 [M]	Bluegrass Hillbillies	1963	$25
☐ ABCS-446 [S]	Bluegrass Hillbillies	1963	$30

MCPHATTER, CLYDE
Also see THE DRIFTERS.
ALLEGIANCE

Number	Title	Yr	NM
☐ AV-5029	The Pretty One	198?	$12
ATLANTIC			
☐ 8031 [M]	Clyde	1959	$500
—Black label			
☐ 8031 [M]	Clyde	1960	$400
—White "bullseye" label			

Number	Title	Yr	NM
☐ 8031 [M]	Clyde	1960	$250
—Brown and purple label			
☐ 8024 [M]	Love Ballads	1958	$500
—Black label			
☐ 8024 [M]	Love Ballads	1960	$250
—Brown and purple label			
☐ 8024 [M]	Love Ballads	1960	$400
—White "bullseye" label			
☐ 8077 [M]	The Best of Clyde McPhatter	1963	$250
DECCA			
☐ DL75231	Welcome Home	1970	$30
MERCURY			
☐ MG-20783 [M]	Clyde McPhatter's Greatest Hits	1963	$30
☐ SR-60783 [S]	Clyde McPhatter's Greatest Hits	1963	$40
☐ MG-20655 [M]	Golden Blues Hits	1961	$50
☐ SR-60655 [S]	Golden Blues Hits	1961	$80
☐ MG-20915 [M]	Live at the Apollo	1964	$30
☐ SR-60915 [S]	Live at the Apollo	1964	$40
☐ MG-20711 [M]	Lover Please	1962	$50
☐ SR-60711 [S]	Lover Please	1962	$80
☐ MG-20750 [M]	Rhythm and Soul	1962	$50
☐ SR-60750 [S]	Rhythm and Soul	1962	$80
☐ MG-20902 [M]	Songs of the Big City	1964	$30
☐ SR-60902 [S]	Songs of the Big City	1964	$40
☐ MG-20597 [M]	Ta Ta	1960	$50
☐ SR-60262 [S]	Ta Ta	1960	$80
MGM			
☐ E-3866 [M]	Clyde McPhatter's Greatest Hits	1960	$80
☐ SE-3866 [S]	Clyde McPhatter's Greatest Hits	1960	$100
☐ E-3775 [M]	Let's Start Over Again	1959	$175
☐ SE-3775 [S]	Let's Start Over Again	1959	$250
WING			
☐ MGW-12224 [M]	May I Sing for You?	1962	$30
☐ SRW-16224 [S]	May I Sing for You?	1962	$30

MCPHEE, JOE
CJR

Number	Title	Yr	NM
☐ 2	Nation Time	197?	$30
☐ 4	Pieces of Light	197?	$30
☐ 3	Trinity	197?	$30
HAT ART			
☐ 2033	Po Music: A Future Retrospective	1987	$35
HAT HUT			
☐ 0A	Black Magic Man	1974	$30
☐ 0P	Glasses	1978	$25
☐ 0I/J	Graphics	1977	$30
☐ 01	Old Eyes	1979	$25
☐ 0D	Rotation	1977	$25
☐ 0C	Tenor	1976	$25
☐ 1987/8	Topology	1981	$30
☐ 0O	Variations on a Blue Line/Round Midnight	1978	$25

MCPHERSON, CHARLES
MAINSTREAM

Number	Title	Yr	NM
☐ MRL-329	Charles McPherson	1972	$35
☐ MRL-365	Siku Ya Bibi	1973	$35
☐ MRL-395	Today's Man	1974	$35
PRESTIGE			
☐ PRLP-7359 [M]	Bebop Revisited	1965	$30
☐ PRST-7359 [S]	Bebop Revisited	1965	$40
☐ PRLP-7427 [M]	Con Alma!	1966	$30
☐ PRST-7427 [S]	Con Alma!	1966	$40
☐ PRST-7559	From This Moment On	1968	$30
☐ PRST-7603	Horizons	1969	$30
☐ PRST-7743	McPherson's Mood	1970	$25
☐ PRLP-7480 [M]	The Charles McPherson Quintet Live!	1967	$40
☐ PRST-7480 [S]	The Charles McPherson Quintet Live!	1967	$30

Number	Title	Yr	NM
XANADU			
❏ 115	Beautiful	1976	$30
❏ 170	Free Bop	1979	$30
❏ 131	Live in Tokyo	1977	$30
❏ 149	New Horizons	1978	$30

MCQUAIG, SCOTT

UNIVERSAL

❏ UVL-76000	Scott McQuaig	1989	$12

MCRAE, CARMEN

ACCORD

❏ SN-7152	Love Songs	1981	$25

ATLANTIC

❏ 8143 [M]	For Once in My Life	1967	$50
❏ SD8143 [S]	For Once in My Life	1967	$35
❏ SD1568	Just a Little Lovin'	1971	$30
❏ 8165 [M]	Portrait of Carmen	1968	$75
❏ SD8165 [S]	Portrait of Carmen	1968	$35
❏ SD 2-904	The Great American Songbook	1971	$50
❏ SD8200 [S]	The Sound of Silence	1968	$35
❏ 8200 [M]	The Sound of Silence	1968	$75

— *Mono is white label promo only; "d/j copy monaural" sticker on front cover*

BAINBRIDGE

❏ 6221	The Sound of Silence	198?	$25

BETHLEHEM

❏ BCP-1023 [10]	Carmen McRae	1955	$300

BLUE NOTE

❏ BN-LA635-G	Can't Hide Love	1976	$30
❏ BN-LA462-G	I Am Music	1975	$30
❏ BN-LA709-H2	The Great Music Hall	1977	$35
❏ LWB-709	The Great Music Hall	1981	$30

— *Reissue of BN-LA709-H2*

BUDDAH

❏ B2D-6501	I'm Coming Home Again	1980	$35

CATALYST

❏ 7904	As Time Goes By	197?	$30

COLUMBIA

❏ CL1730 [M]	Lover Man	1962	$50
❏ CS8530 [S]	Lover Man	1962	$75
❏ CL1943 [M]	Something Wonderful	1962	$50
❏ CS8743 [S]	Something Wonderful	1962	$75

CONCORD JAZZ

❏ CJ-342	Fine and Mellow	1988	$25
❏ CJ-128	Two for the Road	1980	$25
❏ CJ-235	You're Looking at Me: A Collection of Nat King Cole Songs	1984	$25

DECCA

❏ DL8583 [M]	After Glow	1957	$175

— *Black label, silver print*

❏ DL8583 [M]	After Glow	1960	$50

— *Black label with color bars*

❏ DL8815 [M]	Birds of a Feather	1959	$150

— *Black label, silver print*

❏ DL8815 [M]	Birds of a Feather	1960	$50

— *Black label with color bars*

❏ DL8347 [M]	Blue Moon	1957	$150

— *Black label, silver print*

❏ DL8347 [M]	Blue Moon	1960	$50

— *Black label with color bars*

❏ DL8173 [M]	By Special Request	1955	$175

— *Black label, silver print*

❏ DL8173 [M]	By Special Request	1960	$50

— *Black label with color bars*

❏ DL8738 [M]	Carmen for Cool Ones	1958	$120

— *Black label, silver print*

❏ DL8738 [M]	Carmen for Cool Ones	1960	$50

— *Black label with color bars*

❏ DL8662 [M]	Mad About the Man	1958	$150

— *Black label, silver print*

❏ DL8662 [M]	Mad About the Man	1960	$50

— *Black label with color bars*

❏ DL8267 [M]	Torchy!	1956	$175

— *Black label, silver print*

❏ DL8267 [M]	Torchy!	1960	$50

— *Black label with color bars*

FOCUS

❏ FL-334 [M]	Bittersweet	1964	$35
❏ FS-334 [S]	Bittersweet	1964	$50

GROOVE MERCHANT

❏ 522	A Whole Lot of Human Feeling	1973	$30
❏ 531	Ms. Jazz	1974	$30
❏ 4401	Velvet Soul	197?	$35

HARMONY

❏ KH32177	Carmen McRae Sings Billie Holiday	1972	$25
❏ HL7452 [M]	Yesterdays	1968	$50
❏ HS11252 [S]	Yesterdays	1968	$30

Number	Title	Yr	NM
JAZZ MAN			
❏ 5004	Carmen McRae and the Kenny Clarke/Francy Boland Big Band	198?	$25

KAPP

❏ KL-1117 [M]	Book of Ballads	1958	$75
❏ KS-3000 [S]	Book of Ballads	1958	$75
❏ KL-1169 [M]	Something to Swing About	1960	$75
❏ KS-3053 [S]	Something to Swing About	1960	$75
❏ KL-1541 [M]	This Is Carmen McRae	1967	$50
❏ KS-3541 [S]	This Is Carmen McRae	1967	$35
❏ KL-1135 [M]	When You're Away	1959	$75
❏ KS-3018 [S]	When You're Away	1959	$75

MAINSTREAM

❏ 56084 [M]	Alfie	1966	$35
❏ S-6084 [S]	Alfie	1966	$50
❏ 800	Alive!	1974	$35
❏ 309	Carmen McRae	1971	$30
❏ 352	Carmen McRae In Person	1972	$30
❏ 338	Carmen's Gold	1972	$30
❏ 56044 [M]	Haven't We Met?	1965	$35
❏ S-6044 [S]	Haven't We Met?	1965	$50
❏ 56091 [M]	In Person/San Francisco	1967	$30
❏ S-6091 [S]	In Person/San Francisco	1967	$35
❏ 387	I Want You	1972	$30
❏ S-6110	Live & Wailin'	1968	$35
❏ 403	Live and Doin' It	1974	$30
❏ 56028 [M]	Second to None	1965	$35
❏ S-6028 [S]	Second to None	1965	$50
❏ 56065 [M]	Woman Talk	1966	$35
❏ S-6065 [S]	Woman Talk	1966	$50

MCA

❏ 4111	The Greatest of Carmen McRae	197?	$30

NOVUS

❏ 3086-1-N	Carmen Sings Monk	1990	$30

PAUSA

❏ 9003	Can't Hide Love	198?	$25

QUINTESSENCE

❏ 25021	Ms. Jazz	1978	$25

— *Reissue of Groove Merchant 531*

STANYAN

❏ 10115	Mad About the Man	197?	$30

TEMPONIC

❏ 29562	Carmen	1972	$30

TIME

❏ 52104 [M]	Live at Sugar Hill	1960	$50
❏ S-2104 [S]	Live at Sugar Hill	1960	$75

VOCALION

❏ VL3697 [M]	Carmen McRae	1963	$35
❏ VL73828	My Foolish Heart	1969	$30

MCRITCHIE, GREG

CADET

❏ LP-4058 [M]	Fighting Back	1967	$30
❏ LPS-4058 [S]	Fighting Back	1967	$35

ZEPHYR

❏ 12005 [M]	Easy Jazz on a Fish Beat Bass	1959	$300

MCSHANN, JAY

ATLANTIC

❏ SD8804	The Big Apple Bash	1979	$30
❏ 90047	The Big Apple Bash	198?	$25

— *Reissue of 8804*

❏ SD8800	The Last of Jay McShann	197?	$30

CAPITOL

❏ T2645 [M]	McShann's Piano	1967	$40
❏ ST2645 [S]	McShann's Piano	1967	$40

CLASSIC JAZZ

❏ 128	Confessin' the Blues	197?	$30

DECCA

❏ DL5503 [10]	Kansas City Memories	1954	$500

— *CHARLIE PARKER appears on this LP*

❏ DL9236 [M]	Kansas City Memories	1958	$300
❏ DL79236 [R]	Kansas City Memories	196?	$35

MASTER JAZZ

❏ 8113	Going to Kansas City	197?	$35

MCA

❏ 1338	The Early Bird	198?	$25

SACKVILLE

❏ 3040	Airmail Special	198?	$25
❏ 3019	A Tribute to Fats Waller	198?	$25
❏ 3011	Crazy Legs and Friday Strut	1977	$25
❏ 3035	Just a Little So and So	198?	$25
❏ 3021	Kansas City Hustle	198?	$25
❏ 3006	The Man from Muskogee	198?	$25
❏ 3025	Tuxedo Junction	1980	$25

MCTELL, BLIND WILLIE

BLUESVILLE

❏ BVLP-1040 [M]	Last Session	1962	$120

— *Blue label, silver print*

❏ BVLP-1040 [M]	Last Session	1964	$30

Number	Title	Yr	NM
— *Blue label, trident logo at right*			
MELODEON			
❏ 7323 [M]	1940	1956	$175

MCTELL, RALPH

CAPITOL

❏ ST-240	Eight Frames a Second	1969	$15

REPRISE

❏ MS2121	Not Till Tomorrow	1973	$12

MCVICKER, DANA

CAPITOL

❏ C1-46967	Dana McVicker	1988	$12

MCVIE, CHRISTINE

Also see CHICKEN SHACK; FLEETWOOD MAC.

SIRE

❏ SASD-7522	The Legendary Christine Perfect Album	1976	$18

— *Original with ABC distribution*

❏ SR6022	The Legendary Christine Perfect Album	1978	$12

— *Reissue with Warner Bros. distribution*

WARNER BROS.

❏ 25059	Christine McVie	1984	$10
❏ 25059 [DJ]	Christine McVie	1984	$30

— *Promo on Quiex II vinyl*

MCWILLIAMS, DAVID

KAPP

❏ KS-3547 [B]	Days of Pearly Spencer	1968	$30

MEADE, DONNA

MERCURY

❏ 834624-1	Love's Last Stand	1988	$12

MEADER, VAUGHN

CADENCE

❏ CSBLL-1	The Experiment/After Dinner Conversations/Relatively Speaking/Motorcade//But Vote!/Economy Lunch/Press Conference	1962	$10

— *Jukebox issue; small hole, plays at 33 1/3 rpm*

❏ CSBLL-1 [PS]	The First Family	1962	$12
❏ CLP3060 [M]	The First Family	1962	$12
❏ CLP3065 [M]	The First Family, Volume Two	1963	$25
❏ CLP25065 [S]	The First Family, Volume Two	1963	$30

KAMA SUTRA

❏ KSBS-2038	The Second Coming	1971	$18

LAURIE

❏ LLP-2035 [M]	Take That!	1966	$18

VERVE

❏ V-15042 [M]	Have Some Nuts	1964	$18
❏ V6-15042 [S]	Have Some Nuts	1964	$25
❏ V-15050 [M]	If the Shoe Fits	1965	$18

MEADOW

Supposedly, Laura Branigan was in this group.

PARAMOUNT

❏ PAS-6066	The Friend Ship	1973	$25

MEADOWS, DOROTHY, AND JOHN EASTMAN

INTERNATIONAL AWARD SERIES

❏ AK-X-8 [M]	Christmas Songs for the Family	196?	$15

MEAT LOAF

Also see THE POPCORN BLIZZARD; STONEY AND MEATLOAF.

ATLANTIC

❏ 81698	Blind Before I Stop	1986	$10

CLEVELAND INT'L.

❏ FE36007	Dead Ringer	1981	$10
❏ PE36007	Dead Ringer	198?	$10

— *Budget-line reissue*

EPIC

❏ PE34974	Bat Out of Hell	1977	$12

— *Orange label; originals do not have bar code on back cover*

❏ JE34974	Bat Out of Hell	1979	$10

— *Dark blue label*

❏ E9934974 [PD]	Bat Out of Hell	1978	$25
❏ HE44974	Bat Out of Hell	1981	$40

— *Half-speed mastered edition*

❏ PE34974	Bat Out of Hell	1985	$10

— *Dark blue label; bar code on cover*

❏ FE38444	Midnight at the Lost and Found	1983	$10

RCA VICTOR

❏ AFL1-5451	Bad Attitude	1985	$10

Number	Title	Yr	NM
VIRGIN			
❏ 09463-63147-1	Bat Out of Hell III: The Monster Is Loose	2006	$25

MEAT PUPPETS

LONDON

Number	Title	Yr	NM
❏ 1109 [10]	Raw Meat	1994	$25
—Promo-only five-song 10-inch EP			
❏ 828484-1	Too High to Die	1994	$25
—Includes bonus 10-inch EP (double value for DJ stamp on cover)			

MERCURY

❏ 828665-1	No Joke!	1995	$18

SST

❏ 150 [B]	Huevos	1987	$30
❏ 009 [B]	Meat Puppets	1982	$30
❏ 019 [B]	Meat Puppets II	1984	$30
❏ 100 [B]	Mirage	1986	$25
❏ 253	Monsters	1989	$18
❏ 265	No Strings Attached	1990	$25
❏ 049 [10]	Out My Way	1986	$25
—10-inch EP			
❏ 039 [B]	Up on the Sun	1985	$30

MEATMEN, THE

HOMESTEAD

❏ 009	War of the Superbikes	198?	$18

TOUCH & GO

❏ TGLP 001	We're the Meatmen...And You Suck	198?	$18

MECCA, LOU

BLUE NOTE

❏ BLP-5067 [10]	Lou Mecca Quartet	1955	$300

MECKI MARK MEN, THE

LIMELIGHT

❏ LS-86068	Running in the Summer Night	1969	$30
❏ LS-86054	The Mecki Mark Men	1968	$30

MECO

ARISTA

❏ AL8-8098	Ewok Celebration	1983	$15
❏ AL5-8235	Ewok Celebration	198?	$12
—Reissue of 8098			
❏ AL9598	Pop Goes the Movies	1982	$15
❏ AL9605	Swingtime's Greatest Hits	1982	$12

CASABLANCA

❏ NBLP7260	Meco's Impressions of An American Werewolf in London	1981	$15
❏ NBLP7155	Moondancer	1979	$15
❏ NBLP7196	Music from Star Trek and Music from The Black Hole	1980	$15
❏ NBLP7136	Superman and Other Galactic Heroes	1979	$15

MILLENNIUM

❏ MNLP8004	Encounters of Every Kind	1977	$15
❏ MNLP8001	Star Wars and Other Galactic Funk	1977	$15
❏ MNLP8009	The Wizard of Oz	1978	$15
—Black vinyl			
❏ MNLP8009	The Wizard of Oz	1978	$30
—Gold vinyl			

RSO

❏ RO-1-3086 [10]	Meco Plays Music from The Empire Strikes Back	1980	$18
—Four-song EP			

MEDALLION ORCHESTRA & CHORUS, THE

MEDALLION

❏ ML7512 [M]	Deck the Halls: The Sound of Christmas	196?	$15

MEDEIROS, GLENN

AMHERST

❏ AMH-3313	Glenn Medeiros	1987	$12
❏ 4400	Not Me	1988	$12

MCA

❏ 6399	Glenn Medeiros	1990	$15
—Different album than Amherst 3313			
❏ 6286	Not Me	1988	$10
—Reissue of Amherst 4400			

MEDIUM

GAMMA

❏ GS-503	Medium	196?	$150

MEDLEY, BILL

A&M

❏ SP-3505	A Song for You	1971	$15
❏ SP-3517	Smile	1972	$15

Number	Title	Yr	NM
LIBERTY			
❏ LT-1097	Sweet Thunder	1981	$10
—Reissue of United Artists 1097			

MGM

❏ E-4583 [M]	Bill Medley 100%	1968	$50
—Mono is yellow label promo only			
❏ SE-4583 [S]	Bill Medley 100%	1968	$25
❏ SE-4741	Gone	1970	$18
❏ SE-4702	Nobody Knows	1970	$18
❏ SE-4603	Soft and Soulful	1969	$25
❏ SE-4640	Someone Is Standing Outside	1969	$25

RCA VICTOR

❏ MHL1-8519 [EP]	I Still Do	1985	$10
❏ BXL1-4434	Right Here and Now	1982	$12
❏ CPL1-5352	Still Hung Up on You	1984	$12

UNITED ARTISTS

❏ UA-LA929-H	Lay a Little Lovin' on Me	1978	$12
❏ LT-1097	Sweet Thunder	1980	$12

MEEUWSEN, TERRY ANN

SANDY

❏ SRS-9003	Meet Terry	1976	$30

MEHEGAN, JOHN, AND EDDIE COSTA

SAVOY

❏ MG-12049 [M]	A Pair of Pianos	1956	$40

MEHEGAN, JOHN

EPIC

❏ LA16007 [M]	Act of Jazz	1960	$40
❏ BA17007 [S]	Act of Jazz	1960	$75

PERSPECTIVE

❏ PR-1 [M]	From Barrelhouse to Bop	195?	$50

SAVOY

❏ MG-12028 [M]	Reflections	1956	$40
❏ MG-15054 [10]	The Last Mehegan	1955	$85

TJ

❏ LP-1 [M]	Casual Affair	1959	$40

MEISNER, RANDY

Also see EAGLES.

ASYLUM

❏ 6E-140	Randy Meisner	1978	$12

EPIC

❏ NJE36748 [B]	One More Song	1980	$12
❏ FE38121	Randy Meisner	1982	$12

MEL AND TIM

BAMBOO

❏ BMS-8001	Good Guys Only Win in the Movies	1970	$30

STAX

❏ STS-5501	Mel and Tim	1974	$25
❏ STS-3007	Starting All Over Again	1972	$25

MELACHRINO, GEORGE

RCA VICTOR

❏ LPM-1045 [M]	Christmas in High Fidelity	1954	$30
❏ LPM-1329 [M]	I'll Walk Beside You	1956	$25
❏ LPM-1110 [M]	Immortal Ladies	1955	$25
❏ LPM-1762 [M]	Lisbon at Twilight	1958	$18
❏ LSP-1762 [S]	Lisbon at Twilight	1958	$25
❏ LPM-1184 [M]	Masquerade	1955	$25
❏ LPM-1307 [M]	Melachrino on Broadway	1956	$25
❏ LPM-1005 [M]	Music for Courage and Confidence	195?	$30
❏ LPM-1028 [M]	Music for Daydreaming	195?	$30
❏ LPM-1000 [M]	Music for Dining	195?	$30
❏ LPM-1002 [M]	Music for Reading	195?	$30
❏ LPM-1001 [M]	Music for Relaxation	195?	$30
❏ LPM-1027 [M]	Music for Two People Alone	195?	$30
❏ LPM-1006 [M]	Music to Help You Sleep	195?	$30
❏ LPM-1029 [M]	Music to Work or Study By	195?	$30
❏ LPM-1008 [M]	Show Tunes	195?	$30
❏ LPM-1261 [M]	Sounds of Paris	1956	$25
❏ LPM-1757 [M]	Strauss Waltzes	1958	$18
❏ LSP-1757 [S]	Strauss Waltzes	1958	$25
❏ LPM-1330 [M]	Those Beautiful Strings	1956	$25

MELANIE

ABC

❏ ABND-879	From the Beginning/Twelve Great Performances	1975	$12

ACCORD

❏ SN-7191	Beautiful People	1982	$12
❏ SN-7109	What Have They Done to My Song Ma	1981	$12

AMHERST

❏ AMH-3302	Am I Real or What	1985	$12

ATLANTIC

❏ SD18190	Photograph	1976	$12

BLANCHE

❏ BL6177	Arabesque	1982	$12

Number	Title	Yr	NM
BUDDAH			
❏ BDS-5024	Born to Be	1969	$18
❏ BDS-5060	Candles in the Rain	1970	$18
❏ BDS-95005	Four Sides of Melanie	1972	$18
❏ BDS-5095	Garden in the City	1971	$15
❏ BDS-5066	Leftover Wine	1970	$18
❏ BDS-5041	Melanie	1969	$18
❏ BDS-5074	My First Album	1971	$15
❏ BDS-5132	Please Love Me	1973	$15
❏ B2D-5664	The Best...Melanie	197?	$18
❏ BDS-95000	The Good Book	1971	$18

MIDSONG

❏ MCA-3033	Phonogenic: Not Just Another Pretty Face	1978	$12

NEIGHBORHOOD

❏ 3000	As I See It Now	1974	$15
❏ 47001	Gather Me	1971	$15
❏ 48001	Madrugada	1974	$15
❏ 49001	Melanie at Carnegie Hall	1973	$18
❏ 47005	Stoneground Words	1972	$15
❏ 3001	Sunsets and Other Beginnings	1975	$15

PICKWICK

❏ SPC-3317	Try the Real Thing	197?	$12

TOMATO

❏ TOM-2-9003	Ballroom Streets	1979	$15

MELCHER, TERRY

REPRISE

❏ MS2185	Terry Melcher	1974	$18

MELDONIAN, DICK

PROGRESSIVE

❏ 7062	Plays Gene Roland Music	198?	$25
❏ 7033	Some of These Days	1979	$30
❏ 7058	The Jersey Swing Concerts	198?	$25

STATINAS

❏ SLP-8076	It's a Wonderful World	1985	$25

MELILLO, MIKE

RED RECORD

❏ VPA-188	'Live and Well	1986	$30
❏ VPA-170	Piano Solo	198?	$30

MELIS, JOSE

DIPLOMAT

❏ DS-2260 [S]	Jose Melis and the Metropolitan Strings	196?	$12
❏ D-2260 [M]	Jose Melis and the Metropolitan Strings	196?	$12

HARMONY

❏ HL7150 [M]	Exciting TV Star Jose Melis	195?	$15

MERCURY

❏ MG20008 [M]	Classics the South American Way	195?	$18
❏ MG20738 [M]	Everybody's Favorites	1962	$15
❏ SR60738 [S]	Everybody's Favorites	1962	$18
❏ MG25035 [10]	Jose Melis	195?	$30
❏ MG20709 [M]	Jose Melis at the Opera	1962	$15
❏ SR60709 [S]	Jose Melis at the Opera	1962	$18
❏ MG20684 [M]	Jose Melis at the Pops Concert	1962	$15
❏ SR60684 [S]	Jose Melis at the Pops Concert	1962	$18
❏ SR60648 [S]	Jose Melis in Movieland	1961	$18
❏ MG20648 [M]	Jose Melis in Movieland	1961	$15
❏ MG20610 [M]	Jose Melis on Broadway	1961	$15
❏ SR60610 [S]	Jose Melis on Broadway	1961	$18
❏ MG25119 [10]	Latin-American Piano	195?	$30
❏ MG20127 [M]	Latin American Stylings	195?	$18
❏ MG20275 [M]	Tonight It's Music	195?	$18

MGM

❏ E-3527 [M]	Jose Melis of the Jack Paar Show	1957	$18
❏ E-262 [10]	The Jose Melis Trio	1955	$30

MUSICOR

❏ MS-3071 [S]	Piano Classics the South American Way	1967	$15
❏ MM-2071 [M]	Piano Classics the South American Way	1967	$15

PALACE

❏ P-84 [M]	Dance Party with Jose Melis	195?	$15

SEECO

❏ CELP423 [M]	Christmas with Melis	1959	$18
❏ CELP-414 [M]	Jose Melis at Midnight	1959	$18
❏ CELP-4140 [S]	Jose Melis at Midnight	1959	$25
❏ CELP-4620 [S]	Jose Melis Plays Jack Paar's Favorites	1960	$18
❏ CELP-462 [M]	Jose Melis Plays Jack Paar's Favorites	1960	$15
❏ CELP-445 [M]	Jose Melis Plays the Latin Way	1960	$15
❏ CELP-4450 [S]	Jose Melis Plays the Latin Way	1960	$18
❏ CELP-471 [M]	Our Love	1961	$15
❏ CELP-4710 [S]	Our Love	1961	$18
❏ CELP-4360 [S]	The Many Moods of Jose Melis	1960	$18
❏ CELP-436 [M]	The Many Moods of Jose Melis	1960	$15

Number	Title	Yr	NM
❏ CELP-411 [M]	Tonight with Jose Melis	1958	$18

MELIS, MARCELLO
BLACK SAINT

Number	Title	Yr	NM
❏ BSR-0073	Angedras	1983	$30
❏ BSR-0023	Free to Dance	198?	$30
❏ BSR-0012	New Village on the Left	198?	$30

MELLE, GIL
BLUE NOTE

Number	Title	Yr	NM
❏ BLP-5033 [10]	Gil Melle Quintet, Volume 2	1953	$800
❏ BLP-5054 [10]	Gil Melle Quintet, Volume 3	1954	$800
❏ BLP-5063 [10]	Gil Melle Quintet, Volume 4 -- Five Impressions of Color	1954	$800
❏ BLP-5020 [10]	Gil Melle Quintet/Sextet	1953	$800
❏ B1-92168	Mindscape	1989	$35
❏ BLP-1517 [M]	Patterns in Jazz	1956	$800
—"Deep groove" version; Lexington Ave. address on label			

Number	Title	Yr	NM
❏ BLP-1517 [M]	Patterns in Jazz	1956	$800
—Regular version, Lexington Ave. address on label			

FANTASY

Number	Title	Yr	NM
❏ OJC-1753	Gil's Guests	198?	$35
❏ OJC-1712	Melle Plays Primitive Modern	198?	$35

PRESTIGE

Number	Title	Yr	NM
❏ PRLP-7063 [M]	Gil's Guests	1956	$300
—Yellow label with W. 50th St. address			
❏ PRLP-7040 [M]	Melle Plays Primitive Modern	1956	$300
—Yellow label with W. 50th St. address			
❏ PRLP-7097 [M]	Quadrama	1957	$300
—Yellow label			

VERVE

Number	Title	Yr	NM
❏ V6-8744	Tome VI	1968	$40

MELLENCAMP, JOHN
Includes records as "Johnny Cougar," "John Cougar," and "John Cougar Mellencamp."
COLUMBIA

Number	Title	Yr	NM
❏ C69602	John Mellencamp	1998	$18

HEAR MUSIC

Number	Title	Yr	NM
❏ HRM30895	Life, Death, Love and Freedom	2008	$25

MCA

Number	Title	Yr	NM
❏ 2225 [B]	Chestnut Street Incident	1977	$30
—As "Johnny Cougar			

MERCURY

Number	Title	Yr	NM
❏ 838220-1	Big Daddy	1989	$12
❏ 832465-1	The Lonesome Jubilee	1987	$10

MOBILE FIDELITY

Number	Title	Yr	NM
❏ 1-222	The Lonesome Jubilee	1995	$40
—Audiophile vinyl			

RIVA

Number	Title	Yr	NM
❏ RVL7501 [B]	American Fool	1982	$12
—As "John Cougar			
❏ RVL7401 [B]	John Cougar	1979	$18
—As "John Cougar			
❏ RVL7403	Nothin' Matters and What If It Did	1980	$12
—As "John Cougar			
❏ 824865-1	Scarecrow	1985	$10
—As "John Cougar Mellencamp			
❏ RVL7504	Uh-Huh	1983	$10
—As "John Cougar Mellencamp			

MELLO-KINGS, THE
COLLECTABLES

Number	Title	Yr	NM
❏ COL-5020 [B]	Greatest Hits	198?	$15

HERALD

Number	Title	Yr	NM
❏ H-1013 [M]	Tonight-Tonight	1960	$500
—Yellow label			
❏ H-1013 [M]	Tonight-Tonight	196?	$300
—Multi-color label			

RELIC

Number	Title	Yr	NM
❏ LP-5035	Greatest Hits	198?	$15

MELLO-LARKS, THE
RCA CAMDEN

Number	Title	Yr	NM
❏ CAL-530 [M]	Just for a Lark	1959	$40

MELROSE, FRANK
ABC-PARAMOUNT

Number	Title	Yr	NM
❏ 0(# unknown) [M]	Kansas City Frank Melrose	1956	$50

MELTON, LEVY, AND THE DEY BROTHERS
COLUMBIA

Number	Title	Yr	NM
❏ KC31279	Levy Melton and the Dey Brothers	1972	$25

MELTZER, DAVID AND TINA
VANGUARD

Number	Title	Yr	NM
❏ VSD-6619	Poet Song	1969	$50

MELVIN, HAROLD, AND THE BLUE NOTES
PHILADELPHIA INT'L.

Number	Title	Yr	NM
❏ ZS731648	Be for Real//Ebony Woman/ Let It Be You	1971	$25
—Stereo jukebox issue; small hole, plays at 33 1/3 rpm			
❏ ZS731648 [PS]	Harold Melvin and the Blue Notes	1971	$25

ABC

Number	Title	Yr	NM
❏ AB-1041	Now Is the Time	1978	$30
❏ AB-969	Reaching for the World	1977	$30

MCA

Number	Title	Yr	NM
❏ 5261	All Things Happen in Time	1981	$15

PHILADELPHIA INT'L.

Number	Title	Yr	NM
❏ KZ32407	Black & Blue	1973	$15
❏ ZQ32407 [Q]	Black & Blue	1973	$30
❏ PZ34232	Collector's Item -- All Their Greatest Hits!	1976	$30
❏ KZ31648	Harold Melvin and the Blue Notes	1972	$30
❏ PZ33148	To Be True	1975	$20
❏ PZ33808	Wake Up Everybody	1975	$25
❏ PZQ33808 [Q]	Wake Up Everybody	1975	$30

PHILLY WORLD

Number	Title	Yr	NM
❏ 90187	Talk It Up (Tell Everybody)	1985	$25

SOURCE

Number	Title	Yr	NM
❏ 3197	The Blue Album	1980	$15

MEMBERS ONLY
MUSE

Number	Title	Yr	NM
❏ MR-5332	Members Only	1987	$25
❏ MR-5348	Members Only…Too: The Way You Make Me Feel	1989	$30

MEMPHIS MINNIE
MCA

Number	Title	Yr	NM
❏ 1370	Moanin' the Blues	198?	$18

PORTRAIT

Number	Title	Yr	NM
❏ RJ44072	I Ain't No Bad Gal	1988	$18

MEMPHIS NIGHTHAWKS, THE
DELMARK

Number	Title	Yr	NM
❏ DS-216	The Memphis Nighthawks	197?	$35

GOLDEN CREST

Number	Title	Yr	NM
❏ GC-4162	Stabilizer	1977	$30

MEMPHIS SLIM
BATTLE

Number	Title	Yr	NM
❏ BM-6118 [M]	Alone with My Friends	1963	$50
❏ BM-6122 [M]	Baby Please Come Home	1963	$50

BLUESVILLE

Number	Title	Yr	NM
❏ BVLP-1053 [M]	All Kinds of Blues	1962	$150
—Blue label, silver print			
❏ BVLP-1053 [M]	All Kinds of Blues	1964	$30
—Blue label, trident logo at right			
❏ BVLP-1018 [M]	Just Blues	1961	$120
—Blue label, silver print			
❏ BVLP-1018 [M]	Just Blues	1964	$30
—Blue label, trident logo at right			
❏ BVLP-1031 [M]	No Strain	1961	$120
—Blue label, silver print			
❏ BVLP-1031 [M]	No Strain	1964	$30
—Blue label, trident logo at right			
❏ BVLP-1075 [M]	Steady Rollin' Blues	1963	$150
—Blue label, silver print			
❏ BVLP-1075 [M]	Steady Rollin' Blues	1964	$30
—Blue label, trident logo at right			

BUDDAH

Number	Title	Yr	NM
❏ BDS-7505	Mother Earth	1969	$25

CANDID

Number	Title	Yr	NM
❏ CM-8024 [M]	Memphis Slim U.S.A.	1962	$75
❏ CS-9024 [S]	Memphis Slim U.S.A.	1962	$100
❏ CM-8023 [M]	Slim's Tribute to Big Bill Broonzy	1961	$75
❏ CS-9023 [S]	Slim's Tribute to Big Bill Broonzy	1961	$100

CHESS

Number	Title	Yr	NM
❏ LP-1455 [M]	Memphis Slim	1961	$175
—Black label			
❏ LP-1510 [M]	The Real Folk Blues	1966	$100

DISC

Number	Title	Yr	NM
❏ D-105 [M]	If the Rabbit Had a Gun	1964	$40

FOLKWAYS

Number	Title	Yr	NM
❏ FG-3536 [M]	Chicago Blues	1961	$12
❏ FG-3535 [M]	Memphis Slim…And the Real Honky Tonk	1960	$120
❏ FG-3524 [M]	The Real Boogie Woogie	1959	$120

JUBILEE

Number	Title	Yr	NM
❏ JGM-8003 [M]	Legend of the Blues	1967	$30
❏ JGS-8003 [S]	Legend of the Blues	1967	$30

KING

Number	Title	Yr	NM
❏ 885 [M]	Memphis Slim Sings Folk Blues	1964	$50

SCEPTER

Number	Title	Yr	NM
❏ SM-535 [M]	Self Portrait	1966	$25
❏ SMS-535 [S]	Self Portrait	1966	$30

SPIN-O-RAMA

Number	Title	Yr	NM
❏ 149 [M]	Lonesome Blues	196?	$25

STRAND

Number	Title	Yr	NM
❏ SL-1046 [M]	The World's Foremost Blues Singer	1962	$40
❏ SLS-1046 [S]	The World's Foremost Blues Singer	1962	$50

UNITED ARTISTS

Number	Title	Yr	NM
❏ UAL-3137 [M]	Broken Soul Blues	1961	$75
❏ UAS-6137 [S]	Broken Soul Blues	1961	$100

VEE JAY

Number	Title	Yr	NM
❏ LP-1012 [M]	Memphis Slim at the Gate of the Horn	1959	$250
—Maroon label			
❏ LP-1012 [M]	Memphis Slim at the Gate of the Horn	1961	$120
—Black rainbow label, oval logo			

MEMPHIS WILLIE B
BLUESVILLE

Number	Title	Yr	NM
❏ BVLP-1048 [M]	Hard Working Man Blues	1962	$150
—Blue label, silver print			
❏ BVLP-1048 [M]	Hard Working Man Blues	1964	$30
—Blue label, trident logo at right			
❏ BVLP-1034 [M]	Introducing Memphis Willie B	1961	$150
—Blue label, silver print			
❏ BVLP-1034 [M]	Introducing Memphis Willie B	1964	$30
—Blue label, trident logo at right			

MEN, THE
SNAT-5

Number	Title	Yr	NM
❏ 2001 [B]	Hermeneutics	1981	$30

MEN AT WORK
COLUMBIA

Number	Title	Yr	NM
❏ ARC37978	Business as Usual	1982	$10
❏ FC37978	Business as Usual	1982	$10
—New prefix to reflect list-price increase			
❏ HC47978	Business as Usual	1983	$30
—Half-speed mastered edition			
❏ QC38660	Cargo	1983	$10
❏ HC48660	Cargo	1983	$30

Number	Title	Yr	NM
—Half-speed mastered edition			
❏ PC38660	Cargo	198?	$10
—Reissue with new prefix			
❏ A2S1650 [DJ]	Cargo (World Premiere Weekend)	1983	$25
—Promo-only two-record package of interviews and music			
❏ FC40078	Two Hearts	1985	$10
MOBILE FIDELITY			
❏ MFSLP1025 [B]	Cargo	2014	$50

MEN WITHOUT HATS
BACKSTREET

❏ 39002	Rhythm of Youth	1983	$15
❏ 5436	Rhythm of Youth	1983	$12
—Reissue			

MCA

❏ 5487	Folk of the 80's, Part 3	1984	$12

MERCURY

❏ 842000-1	In the 21st Century	1989	$12

STIFF

❏ TEES-12-01 [EP]	Folk of the 80's	1981	$30
—Reissue of Trend 10-inch EP			

TREND

❏ HATS-001 [10]	Folk of the 80's	1981	$30
—10-inch four-song EP; possibly released only in Canada			

MENDELSON, STAN
LAND O' JAZZ

❏ 2674	Storyville Piano	1978	$25

MENDES, SERGIO
A&M

❏ SP-5250	Arara	1989	$30
❏ SP-4984	Confetti	1984	$25
❏ SP-4197	Crystal Illusions	1969	$35
❏ LP-122 [M]	Equinox	1967	$35
❏ SP-4122 [S]	Equinox	1967	$35
❏ SP-4160	Fool on the Hill	1968	$35
❏ SP-3108	Fool on the Hill	198?	$20
—Budget-line reissue			
❏ SP-4252	Greatest Hits	1970	$35
❏ SP-3258	Greatest Hits	198?	$20
—Budget-line reissue			
❏ SP-4137	Look Around	1968	$35
❏ SP-4315	Pais Tropical	1971	$30
❏ SP-4353	Primal Roots	1972	$30
❏ SP-4937	Sergio Mendes	1983	$25
❏ LP-116 [M]	Sergio Mendes and Brasil '66	1966	$30
❏ SP-4116 [S]	Sergio Mendes and Brasil '66	1966	$35
❏ SP-5135	Sergio Mendes and Brasil '86	1986	$25
❏ SP-4284	Stillness	1970	$35
❏ SP-3522	The Sergio Mendes Foursider	1973	$35
❏ SP-6012	The Sergio Mendes Foursider	198?	$25
—Budget-line reissue			
❏ SP-4236	Ye-Me-Le	1969	$35

ATLANTIC

❏ 1466 [M]	Great Arrival	1966	$35
❏ SD1466 [S]	Great Arrival	1966	$50
❏ 8177 [M]	Sergio Mendes' Favorite Things	1968	$40
—White label promo only			
❏ SD8177 [S]	Sergio Mendes' Favorite Things	1968	$50
❏ 8112 [M]	Sergio Mendes In Person at the El Matador	1967	$50
❏ SD8112 [S]	Sergio Mendes In Person at the El Matador	1967	$35
❏ 1480 [M]	The Beat of Brazil	1967	$50
❏ SD1480 [S]	The Beat of Brazil	1967	$35
❏ 1434 [M]	The Swinger from Rio	1965	$35
❏ SD1434 [S]	The Swinger from Rio	1965	$50

BELL

❏ 1119	Love Music	1973	$25
❏ 1305	Vintage 74	1974	$25

CAPITOL

❏ T2294 [M]	In a Brazilian Bag	1965	$175
❏ ST2294 [S]	In a Brazilian Bag	1965	$250

ELEKTRA

❏ 7E-1055	Homecooking	1976	$25
❏ 6E-214	Magic Lady	1980	$25
❏ 7E-1027	Sergio Mendes	1975	$25
❏ EQ-1027 [Q]	Sergio Mendes	1975	$40
❏ 6E-134	Sergio Mendes and Brasil '88	1978	$25
❏ 7E-1102	Sergio Mendes and the New Brasil '77	1977	$25

MOBILE FIDELITY

❏ 1-118	Sergio Mendes and Brasil '66	1984	$150
—Audiophile vinyl			

PHILIPS

❏ PHM200263 [M]	Quiet Nights	1968	$50
❏ PHS600263 [S]	Quiet Nights	1968	$35

PICKWICK

❏ SPC-3149	So Nice	1972	$25

TOWER

❏ T5052 [M]	In a Brazilian Bag	1966	$85

Number	Title	Yr	NM
—Reissue of Capitol 2294			
❏ ST5052 [S]	In a Brazilian Bag	1966	$175
—Reissue of Capitol 2294			

MENGELBERG, MISHA
SOUL NOTE

❏ SN-1104	Change of Season	1985	$30

MENTAL AS ANYTHING
A&M

❏ SP-4946	Creatures of Leisure	1983	$15
❏ SP-4921	If You Leave Me, Can I Come Too?	1982	$15

COLUMBIA

❏ C45367	Cyclone Raymond	1989	$12
❏ BFC40299	Fundamental	1985	$12
❏ FC44144	Mouth to Mouth	1988	$12

MENUHIN, YEHUDI
MERCURY LIVING PRESENCE

❏ SR90003 [S]	Bartok: Violin Concerto No. 2	1959	$80
—With Antal Dorati/Minneapolis Symphony Orch.; maroon label, no "Vendor: Mercury Record Corporation			
❏ SR90003 [S]	Bartok: Violin Concerto No. 2	196?	$30
—With Antal Dorati/Minneapolis Symphony Orch.; maroon label, with "Vendor: Mercury Record Corporation			

MENZA, DON
CATALYST

❏ 7617	First Flight	1976	$35

PALO ALTO

❏ PA-8010	Flip Pocket	1981	$30

PAUSA

❏ 7170	Horn of Plenty	1985	$25

REAL TIME

❏ RT-301	Burnin'	198?	$35

VOSS

❏ VLP1-42931	Horn of Plenty	1988	$25

MENZLES, HAMISH
MUSIC IS MEDICINE

❏ 9028	Jazz Tracks	1979	$30

MEPHISTOPHELES
REPRISE

❏ RS6355 [B]	In Frustration I Hear Singing	1969	$75

MERCER, JOHNNY
CAPITOL

❏ T907 [M]	Ac-Cent-Tchu-Ate the Positive	1957	$175
❏ H214 [10]	Johnny Mercer Sings	1950	$300
❏ H210 [10]	Music of Jerome Kern	1950	$300

JUPITER

❏ JLP-1001 [M]	Johnny Mercer Sings Just for Fun	1956	$150

PAUSA

❏ PR9062	Jonny Mercer Sings Jonny Mercer	1986	$25
—Name is indeed misspelled on the label as "Jonny"			

MERCER, MABEL, AND BOBBY SHORT
ATLANTIC

❏ SD 2-604	Mabel Mercer and Bobby Short at Town Hall	1968	$25

MERCER, MABEL
ATLANTIC

❏ 1213 [M]	Mabel Mercer Sings Cole Porter	1955	$300
—Black label			
❏ 1213 [M]	Mabel Mercer Sings Cole Porter	1961	$175
—Multicolor label, white "fan" logo at right			
❏ 1213 [M]	Mabel Mercer Sings Cole Porter	1963	$35
—Multicolor label, black "fan" logo at right			
❏ 81264	Mabel Mercer Sings Cole Porter	1985	$25
❏ 1322 [M]	Merely Marvelous Mabel Mercer	1960	$300
—Black label			
❏ SD1322 [S]	Merely Marvelous Mabel Mercer	1960	$300
—Green label			
❏ 1322 [M]	Merely Marvelous Mabel Mercer	1961	$175
—Multicolor label, white "fan" logo at right			
❏ 1322 [M]	Merely Marvelous Mabel Mercer	1963	$35
—Multicolor label, black "fan" logo at right			
❏ SD1322 [S]	Merely Marvelous Mabel Mercer	1961	$175

Number	Title	Yr	NM
—Multicolor labels, white "fan" logo at right			
❏ SD1322 [S]	Merely Marvelous Mabel Mercer	1963	$25
—Multicolor labels, black "fan" logo at right			
❏ 1244 [M]	Midnight at Mabel Mercer's	1956	$300
—Black label			
❏ 1244 [M]	Midnight at Mabel Mercer's	1961	$175
—Multicolor label, white "fan" logo at right			
❏ 1244 [M]	Midnight at Mabel Mercer's	1963	$35
—Multicolor label, black "fan" logo at right			
❏ 1301 [M]	Once in a Blue Moon	1959	$300
—Black label			
❏ SD1301 [S]	Once in a Blue Moon	1959	$300
—Green label			
❏ 1301 [M]	Once in a Blue Moon	1961	$175
—Multicolor label, white "fan" logo at right			
❏ 1301 [M]	Once in a Blue Moon	1963	$35
—Multicolor label, black "fan" logo at right			
❏ SD1301 [S]	Once in a Blue Moon	1961	$175
—Multicolor labels, white "fan" logo at right			
❏ SD1301 [S]	Once in a Blue Moon	1963	$25
—Multicolor labels, black "fan" logo at right			
❏ ALS-402 [10]	Songs by Mabel Mercer, Volume 1	1954	$300
❏ ALS-403 [10]	Songs by Mabel Mercer, Volume 2	1954	$300
❏ 2-602 [M]	The Art of Mabel Mercer	1959	$300
—Black labels			
❏ 2-602 [M]	The Art of Mabel Mercer	1961	$300
—Multicolor labels, white "fan" logo at right			
❏ 2-602 [M]	The Art of Mabel Mercer	1963	$50
—Multicolor labels, black "fan" logo at right			
❏ SD 2-605	The Second Town Hall Concert	1969	$25
—Red and green label with "1841 Broadway" address			
❏ SD 2-605	The Second Town Hall Concert	1975	$15
—Red and green label with "75 Rockefeller Plaza" address			

AUDIOPHILE

❏ AP-161/2	Echoes of My Life	197?	$35

DECCA

❏ DL4472 [M]	Mabel Mercer Sings	1964	$35
❏ DL74472 [S]	Mabel Mercer Sings	1964	$25

STANYAN

❏ SR10108 [M]	For Always	1974	$30

MERCHANTS OF DREAM, THE
A&M

❏ SP-4149	Strange Night Voyage	1969	$30

MERCURY, FREDDIE
Also see QUEEN.
COLUMBIA

❏ FC40071 [B]	Mr. Bad Guy	1985	$18

MERCURY REV
COLUMBIA

❏ C53030	Yerself Is Steam	1992	$15

MERCY
SUNDI

❏ SRLP-803 [B]	The Mercy & Love (Can Make You Happy)	1969	$30
—Has the original version of the title song plus filler instrumentals			

WARNER BROS.

❏ WS1799	Love (Can Make You Happy)	1969	$18
—Love (Can Make You Happy)" was re-recorded for this LP			

MERCY DEE
ARHOOLIE

❏ F-1007 [M]	Mercy Dee	1961	$75

BLUESVILLE

❏ BVLP-1039 [M]	A Pity and a Shame	1962	$100
—Blue label, silver print			
❏ BVLP-1039 [M]	A Pity and a Shame	1964	$30
—Blue label, trident logo at right			

MEREDITH, BUDDY
STARDAY

❏ SLP-225 [M]	Sing Me a Heart Song	1963	$30

MEREDITH, BURGESS
COLPIX

❏ CP-452 [M]	Burgess Meredith Sings Songs from "How the West Was Won"	1964	$25
❏ SCP-452 [S]	Burgess Meredith Sings Songs from "How the West Was Won"	1964	$30

EPIC

❏ LN3656 [M]	Songs and Stories of the Gold Rush	1961	$30

Number	Title	Yr	NM
❏ BN590 [S]	Songs and Stories of the Gold Rush	1961	$30

MERIAN, LEON
SEECO

Number	Title	Yr	NM
❏ CELP-459 [M]	Fiorello!	1960	$175
❏ CELP-4590 [S]	Fiorello!	1960	$175
❏ CELP-447 [M]	This Time the Swing's On Me	1960	$150
❏ CELP-4470 [S]	This Time the Swing's On Me	1960	$150

MERIWETHER, ROY
CAPITOL

Number	Title	Yr	NM
❏ ST-102	Soul Knight	1969	$75

COLUMBIA

Number	Title	Yr	NM
❏ CL2498 [M]	Popcorn and Soul Groovin' at the Movies	1966	$35
❏ CS9298 [S]	Popcorn and Soul Groovin' at the Movies	1966	$25
❏ CL2744 [M]	Soul Invader	1968	$30
❏ CS9544 [S]	Soul Invader	1968	$35
❏ CL2433 [M]	Soup and Onions (Soul Cookin')	1966	$35
❏ CS9233 [S]	Soup and Onions (Soul Cookin')	1966	$25
❏ CL2584 [M]	Stone Truth	1967	$25
❏ CS9384 [S]	Stone Truth	1967	$35

MERKIN
WINDI

Number	Title	Yr	NM
❏ 1004/5	Music from Merkin	1972	$400

MERMAIDS, THE
See THE MURMAIDS.

MERMAN, ETHEL
DECCA

Number	Title	Yr	NM
❏ DXA153 [M]	A Musical Autobiography	195?	$40
—Black label, silver print			
❏ DL8178 [M]	A Musical Autobiography, Volume 1	195?	$30
—Black label, silver print			
❏ DL8179 [M]	A Musical Autobiography, Volume 2	195?	$30
—Black label, silver print			
❏ DL9028 [M]	Memories	1955	$40
❏ DL5053 [10]	Songs She Made Famous	1950	$75

MERRILL, HELEN, AND JOHN LEWIS
MERCURY

Number	Title	Yr	NM
❏ SRM-1-1150	Helen Merrill and John Lewis	197?	$30

MERRILL, HELEN
ATCO

Number	Title	Yr	NM
❏ 33-112 [M]	American Country Songs	1959	$175

CATALYST

Number	Title	Yr	NM
❏ 7912	Autumn Love	197?	$75
❏ 7903	Helen Sings, Teddy Swings	197?	$75

DRG

Number	Title	Yr	NM
❏ SL-5204	The Rodgers & Hammerstein Album	1987	$30

EMARCY

Number	Title	Yr	NM
❏ MG-36078 [M]	Dream of You	1956	$175
—Blue label with drummer logo			
❏ MG-36078 [M]	Dream of You	1958	$150
—Blue label, double oval at top, "Emarcy Jazz" between the two ovals under "Mercury"			
❏ MG-36006 [M]	Helen Merrill	1955	$1750
—Blue label with drummer logo			
❏ MG-36057 [M]	Helen Merrill with Strings	1955	$150
—Blue label with drummer logo			
❏ MG-36107 [M]	Merrill at Midnight	1957	$175
—Blue label with drummer logo			
❏ MG-36107 [M]	Merrill at Midnight	1958	$300
—Blue label, double oval at top, "Emarcy Jazz" between the two ovals under "Mercury"			
❏ MG-36134 [M]	The Nearness of You	1958	$350

INNER CITY

Number	Title	Yr	NM
❏ IC-1125	Casa Forte	198?	$35
❏ IC-1080	Chasin' the Bird	198?	$35
❏ IC-1060	Something Special	1978	$35

LANDMARK

Number	Title	Yr	NM
❏ LLP-1308	A Shade of Difference	1986	$30

MAINSTREAM

Number	Title	Yr	NM
❏ 56014 [M]	The Artistry of Helen Merrill	1965	$30
❏ S-6014 [S]	The Artistry of Helen Merrill	1965	$30

MERCURY

Number	Title	Yr	NM
❏ 826340-1	The Complete Helen Merrill on Mercury	1985	$100

METROJAZZ

Number	Title	Yr	NM
❏ E-1010 [M]	You've Got a Date with the Blues	1958	$120
❏ SE-1010 [S]	You've Got a Date with the Blues	1958	$175

MILESTONE

Number	Title	Yr	NM
❏ M-9019	Shade of Difference	1969	$25
❏ MLP-1003 [M]	The Feeling Is Mutual	1967	$40
❏ MLS-9003 [S]	The Feeling Is Mutual	1967	$30

OWL

Number	Title	Yr	NM
❏ 044	Music Makers	1986	$75

TRIP

Number	Title	Yr	NM
❏ TLP-5526	Helen Merrill Sings	197?	$35
❏ TLP-5552	Helen Merrill with Strings	197?	$35

MERRILL, TONI
RAMA

Number	Title	Yr	NM
❏ RLP-5004 [M]	Songs from the Heart	1957	$100

MERRY-GO-ROUND, THE
A&M

Number	Title	Yr	NM
❏ LP-132 [M]	The Merry-Go-Round	1967	$75
❏ SP-4132 [S]	The Merry-Go-Round	1967	$30

RHINO

Number	Title	Yr	NM
❏ RNLP126	The Best of the Merry-Go-Round	1985	$12

MERRYWEATHER, NEIL
CAPITOL

Number	Title	Yr	NM
❏ SKAO-220	Merryweather	1969	$18
❏ STBB-278	Word of Mouth	1969	$25

KENT

Number	Title	Yr	NM
❏ KST-546	Neil Merryweather and the Boers	197?	$18

MERCURY

Number	Title	Yr	NM
❏ SRM-1-1024	Kryptonite	1975	$15
❏ SRM-1-1007 [B]	Space Rangers	1974	$15

MERRYWEATHER AND CAREY
RCA VICTOR

Number	Title	Yr	NM
❏ LSP-4442	Ivar Avenue Reunion	1970	$18
❏ LSP-4485	Vacuum Cleaner	1971	$18

MERSEYBEATS, THE
ARC INTERNATIONAL

Number	Title	Yr	NM
❏ 834 [M]	England's Best Sellers	1964	$40

MERSEYBOYS, THE
VEE JAY

Number	Title	Yr	NM
❏ VJ-1101 [M]	The 15 Greatest Songs of the Beatles	1964	$150
—With typographical error on label "Saluting Their Return to Amercia"; this album is not known to exist in stereo			
❏ VJ-1101 [M]	The 15 Greatest Songs of the Beatles	1964	$150
—Without typographical error on label "Saluting Their Return To America"; this album is not known to exist in stereo			
❏ VJ-1101 [DJ]	The 15 Greatest Songs of the Beatles	1964	$175
—White label, blue and black print; with typographical error on label: "Saluting Their Return to Amercia"			
❏ VJ-1101 [DJ]	The 15 Greatest Songs of the Beatles	1964	$175
—White label, all-blue print; without typographical error on label: "Saluting Their Return To America"			

MERTENS, TEDDY
4 CORNERS OF THE WORLD

Number	Title	Yr	NM
❏ FCL-4229 [M]	Trumpet in the Night	1966	$18
❏ FCS-4229 [S]	Trumpet in the Night	1966	$25

MESHEL, BILLY
PROBE

Number	Title	Yr	NM
❏ CPLP-4502	The Love Songs of A. Wilbur Meshel	1969	$25

MESMERIZING EYE, THE
SMASH

Number	Title	Yr	NM
❏ MGS-27090 [M]	Psychedelia -- A Musical Light Show	1967	$150
❏ SRS-67090 [S]	Psychedelia -- A Musical Light Show	1967	$80

MESSENGERS, THE (1)
RARE EARTH

Number	Title	Yr	NM
❏ RS-509	The Messengers	1969	$25

MESSINA, JIM
Also see BUFFALO SPRINGFIELD; LOGGINS AND MESSINA; POCO.
AUDIO FIDELITY

Number	Title	Yr	NM
❏ DFM-3037 [M]	The Dragsters	1964	$100
❏ DFS-7037 [S]	The Dragsters	1964	$150

COLUMBIA

Number	Title	Yr	NM
❏ JC36141	Oasis	1979	$12

THIMBLE

Number	Title	Yr	NM
❏ TLP-3	Jim Messina	197?	$18

WARNER BROS.

Number	Title	Yr	NM
❏ BSK3559	Messina	1981	$12
❏ BSK3559 [DJ]	Messina	1981	$25
—Promo-only version on Quiex II vinyl			
❏ 23825	One More Mile	1983	$12

MESSNER, JOHNNY
HINDSIGHT

Number	Title	Yr	NM
❏ HSR-186	Johnny Messner and His Hotel McAlpin Orchestra 1939-40	198?	$25

METALLICA
ELEKTRA

Number	Title	Yr	NM
❏ 60812	...And Justice for All	1988	$30
❏ 60757 [EP]	Garage Days Re-Revisited	1987	$50
❏ 62299	Garage Inc.	1998	$30
❏ 60766	Kill 'Em All	1987	$18
—Reissue of Megaforce 069 with two extra tracks			
❏ 61923	Load	1996	$25
❏ 60439	Master of Puppets	1986	$25
❏ 61113	Metallica	1991	$75
❏ 62126	Re-Load	1997	$30
❏ 60396	Ride the Lightning	1984	$25
❏ 62504	S&M	1999	$25
❏ 62853	St. Anger	2003	$30

MEGAFORCE

Number	Title	Yr	NM
❏ MRI 069	Kill 'Em All	1983	$40
❏ MRI 069 [PD]	Kill 'Em All	1983	$50
—Un-numbered version			
❏ MRI 069 [PD]	Kill 'Em All	1983	$150
—Numbered limited edition version			
❏ MRI769	Ride the Lightning	1984	$40

RHINO

Number	Title	Yr	NM
❏ R1-76156	Vinyl Box Set	2004	$250
—Limited edition of 5,000 numbered copies; includes their first four albums pressed on two records each, the "Garage Days Re-Revisited" EP and the picture disc "Creeping Death"			

WARNER BROS.

Number	Title	Yr	NM
❏ 470780	...And Justice for All	2008	$50
❏ 470716	...And Justice for All	2008	$25
❏ 508732	Death Magnetic	2008	$25
❏ 512119	Death Magnetic	2008	$150
—Deluxe box			
❏ 343676	Kill 'Em All	2008	$30
❏ 470908	Master of Puppets	2008	$30
❏ 511830	Metallica	2008	$25
❏ 424572	Ride the Lightning	2008	$16

METERS, THE
JOSIE

Number	Title	Yr	NM
❏ JOS-4011	Look-Ka Py Py	1970	$100

Number	Title	Yr	NM
❏ JOS-4012 [B]	Struttin'	1970	$100
❏ JOS-4010	The Meters	1969	$100

REPRISE

Number	Title	Yr	NM
❏ MS2076	Cabbage Alley	1972	$50
❏ MS2228	Fire on the Bayou	1975	$40
❏ MS2200	Rejuvenation	1974	$40
❏ MS2252	Trick Bag	1976	$40

ROUNDER

Number	Title	Yr	NM
❏ 2104	Good Old Funky Music	1990	$25
❏ 2103	Look-Ka Py Py	1990	$25
—Reissue of Josie 4011			

SUNDAZED

Number	Title	Yr	NM
❏ LP5081	Kickback	2001	$15

VIRGO

Number	Title	Yr	NM
❏ 12002	The Best of the Meters	1972	$50

WARNER BROS.

Number	Title	Yr	NM
❏ BS3042	New Directions	1977	$30

Number	Title	Yr	NM

METHENY, MIKE
HEADFIRST
| ❏ 9712 | Blue Jay Sessions | 198? | $25 |

MCA/IMPULSE!
| ❏ 5755 | Day In, Night Out | 1986 | $25 |

METHENY, PAT, AND LYLE MAYS
ECM
| ❏ ECM1-1190 | As Falls Wichita, So Falls Wichita Falls | 1981 | $25 |

—*Distributed by Warner Bros.*

METHENY, PAT, AND ORNETTE COLEMAN
GEFFEN
| ❏ GHS24096 | Song X | 1986 | $25 |

METHENY, PAT
ECM
| ❏ ECM2-1180 | 80/81 | 1980 | $35 |

—*Distributed by Warner Bros.*
| ❏ ECM1-1155 | American Garage | 1979 | $25 |

—*Distributed by Warner Bros.*
| ❏ PRO-A-810 [DJ] | An Hour with Pat Metheny | 1979 | $120 |

—*Promo-only music and interviews*
| ❏ ECM-1-1073 | Bright Size Life | 1976 | $30 |

—*Distributed by Polydor*
| ❏ ECM-1-1073 | Bright Size Life | 1979 | $25 |

—*Reissue, distributed by Warner Bros.*
| ❏ 25008 | First Circle | 1984 | $25 |
| ❏ 1278 | First Circle | 1984 | $30 |

—*Made in Germany*
| ❏ PRO 030 [DJ] | Live in Concert | 1977 | $120 |

—*Promo-only release*
| ❏ ECM1-1131 | New Chautauqua | 1979 | $25 |

—*Distributed by Warner Bros.*
| ❏ ECM1-1216 | Offramp | 1982 | $25 |

—*Distributed by Warner Bros.*
| ❏ ECM1-1114 | Pat Metheny Group | 1978 | $25 |

—*Distributed by Warner Bros.*
| ❏ 25006 | Rejoicing | 1984 | $25 |
| ❏ 1271 | Rejoicing | 1984 | $30 |

—*Made in Germany*
| ❏ 23791 | Travels | 1983 | $35 |
| ❏ 1252/3 | Travels | 1983 | $50 |

—*Made in Germany*
| ❏ ECM1-1097 | Watercolors | 1977 | $30 |

—*Distributed by Warner Bros.*
| ❏ 823270-1 | Works | 1984 | $30 |

—*Made in West Germany (not issued in U.S.)*

GEFFEN
❏ GHS24245	Letter from Home	1989	$35
❏ GHS24293	Question and Answer	1990	$50
❏ GHS24145	Still Life (Talking)	1987	$25

WARNER BROS.
| ❏ WBMS-106 [DJ] | Live on Tour | 1979 | $75 |

—*Part of "The Warner Bros. Music Show" series; promo only*

METHOD ACTOR
The lead singer was Washington, D.C. cult favorite Eva Cassidy.
(LABEL UNKNOWN)
| ❏ 0(# unknown) | Method Actor | 1988 | $500 |

METRONOMES, THE (U)
STRAND
| ❏ SL-1057 [M] | The Fabulous Metronomes Sing the Standard Hits | 1962 | $30 |
| ❏ SLS-1057 [S] | The Fabulous Metronomes Sing the Standard Hits | 1962 | $40 |

WYNNE
| ❏ 106 [M] | And Now... The Metronomes | 1960 | $120 |

METROPOLITAN JAZZ OCTET
ARGO
| ❏ LP-659 [M] | The Legend of Bix | 1960 | $30 |

METROS, THE (1)
RCA VICTOR
| ❏ LPM-3776 [M] | Sweetest One | 1967 | $100 |
| ❏ LSP-3776 [S] | Sweetest One | 1967 | $150 |

METROS, THE (3)
MTM
| ❏ ST-71054 | The Metros | 1986 | $15 |

METROTONES, THE
COLUMBIA
| ❏ CL6341 [10] | Tops in Rock and Roll | 1955 | $300 |

MEXICALI BRASS, THE
CUSTOM
| ❏ CS10 [S] | Jingle Bells | 196? | $15 |

MEYERS, AUGIE
ATLANTIC AMERICA
| ❏ 90856 | My Main Squeeze | 1988 | $12 |

PARAMOUNT
| ❏ PAS-6065 | You Ain't Rollin' Your Roll Rite | 1973 | $25 |

POLYDOR
| ❏ 24-4069 | Western Head Music Co. | 1971 | $25 |

TEXAS RE-CORD
| ❏ 1002 | Live at the Longneck | 197? | $30 |

MEZZROW, MEZZ
BLUE NOTE
| ❏ BLP-7023 [10] | Mezz Mezzrow and His Band | 1952 | $300 |

LONDON
| ❏ TKL-93092 [10] | A La Schola Cantorum | 195? | $75 |

RCA VICTOR
| ❏ LJM-1006 [M] | Mezzin' Around | 1954 | $50 |

SWING
| ❏ SW-8409 | Paris 1955, Volume 1 | 1986 | $25 |

X
| ❏ LVA-3027 [10] | Mezz Mezzrow | 1954 | $150 |
| ❏ LVA-3015 [10] | Mezz Mezzrow's Swing Session | 1954 | $150 |

MFG
HAT HUT
| ❏ 0S/T | MFG in Minnesota | 1978 | $30 |

MFSB
PHILADELPHIA INT'L.
❏ KZ32707	Love Is the Message	1974	$12
❏ ZQ32707 [Q]	Love Is the Message	1974	$30
❏ KZ32046	MFSB	1973	$12
❏ PZ33845	Philadelphia Freedom	1975	$12
❏ PZQ33845 [Q]	Philadelphia Freedom	1975	$30
❏ PZ34238	Summertime	1976	$12
❏ PZ34658	The End of Phase One	1977	$12
❏ JZ35516	The Gamble-Huff Orchestra	1978	$12
❏ PZ33158	Universal Love	1975	$12

TSOP
| ❏ JZ36405 | Mysteries of the World | 1980 | $12 |

MIAMI SOUND MACHINE
AUDIOFON
| ❏ AUS5426 | Live Again -- Renacer | 1977 | $300 |

—*First 600 have a cover where the backdrop is clearly visible*
| ❏ AUS5426 | Live Again -- Renacer | 1977 | $250 |

—*The rest have a cover with a blue and yellow "tropical" background*
| ❏ AUS5427 | Miami Sound Machine | 1978 | $250 |

—*Spanish-language version*

CBS INTERNATIONAL
| ❏ DSL10335 | 7Up Presenta Los Hits de Miami Sound Machine | 1983 | $175 |

—*Only available in the Miami area from 7Up dealers*
| ❏ DIL10349 | A Toda Maquina | 1984 | $40 |

—*Spanish-language version of "Eyes of Innocence," their first all-English LP*
| ❏ DML10306 | Imported | 1980 | $50 |

—*Reissue of 10455*
| ❏ DKL10455 | Imported | 1979 | $150 |

—*Reissue of MSM album*
| ❏ DHL10311 | Miami Sound Machine | 1980 | $150 |

—*Different album than Electric Cat 226 and its later issues*
| ❏ DIL10320 | Otra Vez | 1981 | $50 |
| ❏ DIL10375 | Primitive Love | 1985 | $30 |

—*Edition mostly distributed in Puerto Rico, with three Spanish-language tracks replacing three English tracks*
| ❏ DIL10330 | Rio | 1982 | $50 |

ELECTRIC CAT
| ❏ ECS226 [B] | Miami Sound Machine | 1978 | $300 |

—*Mostly English-language version*

EPIC
| ❏ BFE39622 | Eyes of Innocence | 1984 | $18 |

—*Original issue*
| ❏ PE39622 | Eyes of Innocence | 1986 | $10 |

—*Reissue with new prefix*
| ❏ BFE40131 | Primitive Love | 1985 | $15 |

—*The band's breakthrough LP to non-Hispanic audiences, and the last one not to have Gloria Estefan prominently credited; original issue*
| ❏ FE40131 | Primitive Love | 1986 | $10 |

—*Reissue with new prefix*

MSM
| ❏ ERK 0714 | Imported | 1979 | $250 |

TOP HITS
| ❏ TH-AM2185 | Live Again -- Renacer | 1982 | $100 |

—*Reissue of Audiofon LP of the same name*
| ❏ TH-AM2228 | Lo Mejor De Miami Sound Machine -- A Portrait of the Originals | 1983 | $50 |

—*Compilation from first two Spanish-language LPs*
| ❏ TH-AM2187 | Miami Sound Machine | 1982 | $150 |

—*Reissue of Electric Cat LP of the same name*

MICHAEL, GEORGE
COLUMBIA
| ❏ OC40867 | Faith | 1987 | $12 |
| ❏ C46898 | Listen Without Prejudice (Volume 1) | 1990 | $15 |

MICHAELS, HILLY
WARNER BROS.
| ❏ BSK3431 [B] | Calling All Girls | 1980 | $18 |

WARNER BROS.
| ❏ BSK3566 [B] | Lumia | 1981 | $15 |

MICHAELS, LEE
A&M
❏ SP-4302	5th	1971	$18
❏ SP-4249	Barrel	1970	$18
❏ SP-4140	Carnival of Life	1968	$40
❏ SP-4199	Lee Michaels	1969	$18
❏ SP-3158	Lee Michaels	198?	$10

—*Budget-line reissue*
❏ SP-3518	Live	1973	$18
❏ SP-4152	Recital	1968	$25
❏ SP-4336	Space and First Takes	1972	$18

COLUMBIA
❏ KC32275	Nice Day for Something	1973	$15
❏ CQ32275 [Q]	Nice Day for Something	1973	$50
❏ KC32846	Tailface	1974	$15

MICKELSON, PAUL
CONSOLE
| ❏ CS-3005 [S] | Christmas Concert at the Console | 1961 | $18 |

RCA VICTOR
| ❏ LPM-1115 [M] | Christmas Bells | 1955 | $25 |
| ❏ LPM-1517 [M] | The Best of Christmas | 1957 | $25 |

MICKEY AND SYLVIA
Also see MICKEY BAKER; SYLVIA
RCA CAMDEN
| ❏ CAL-863 [M] | Love Is Strange | 1965 | $50 |
| ❏ CAS-863(e) [R] | Love Is Strange | 1965 | $30 |

RCA VICTOR
| ❏ APM1-0327 | Do It Again | 1973 | $15 |

VIK
| ❏ LX-1102 [M] | New Sounds | 1957 | $400 |

MICROSCOPIC SEPTET, THE
OSMOSIS
| ❏ 0(# unknown) | Off Beat Glory | 198? | $30 |

STASH
| ❏ ST-276 | Beauty Based on Science | 1988 | $25 |

MIDDLE OF THE ROAD
RCA VICTOR
| ❏ LSP-4674 | Acceleration | 1972 | $15 |

MIDDLEBROOKS, HARRY
AVI
| ❏ AV-6033 | Give It Time | 197? | $15 |

CAPITOL
| ❏ T2850 [M] | Funny How Time Slips Away | 1968 | $30 |
| ❏ ST-2850 [S] | Funny How Time Slips Away | 1968 | $15 |

MIDDLETON, EDDIE
EPIC
| ❏ PE34882 | Eddie Middleton | 1977 | $12 |

MIDLER, BETTE
ATLANTIC
| ❏ 81933 | Beaches | 1988 | $12 |
| ❏ SD7270 | Bette Midler | 1973 | $15 |

—*1841 Broadway address on label; with poster*
| ❏ SW-95507 | Bette Midler | 1973 | $25 |

—*Longines Record Club edition*
❏ SD19151	Broken Blossom	1977	$12
❏ SD16022	Divine Madness	1980	$12
❏ SD 2-9000	Live! At Last	1977	$15
❏ PR275 [DJ]	Live! At Last Specially Edited for Air Play	1977	$18

—*Promo-only 14-track sampler*
| ❏ 81291 | Mud Will Be Flung Tonight! | 1985 | $12 |
| ❏ R163898 | Mud Will Be Flung Tonight! | 1985 | $15 |

—*RCA Music Service edition*
❏ 80070	No Frills	1983	$12
❏ 82129	Some People's Lives	1990	$15
❏ SD18155	Songs for the New Depression	1976	$12

Number	Title	Yr	NM
❑ 7238 [M]	The Divine Miss M	1972	$50

—Mono is promo only; white label, "dj copy monaural" sticker on stereo cover

| ❑ QD7238 [Q] | The Divine Miss M | 1973 | $30 |
| ❑ SD7238 [S] | The Divine Miss M | 1972 | $12 |

—1841 Broadway" address on label

| ❑ SD16010 | The Rose | 1979 | $12 |
| ❑ SD16004 | Thighs and Whispers | 1979 | $12 |

MOBILE FIDELITY

| ❑ MOFI1-022 [B] | The Rose - The Original Soundtrack Recording | 2012 | $75 |

RHINO

| ❑ R1553201 [B] | A Gift of Love | 2016 | $40 |

—pink vinyl

MIDNIGHT OIL

COLUMBIA

| ❑ BFC38996 | 10,9,8,7,6,5,4,3,2,1 | 1983 | $15 |
| ❑ C45398 | Blue Sky Mining | 1990 | $15 |

—All copies on blue vinyl

| ❑ BFC40967 | Diesel and Dust | 1987 | $15 |
| ❑ FC40967 | Diesel and Dust | 1988 | $12 |

—Reissue; "02" added to rear-cover bar code

| ❑ BFC39987 | Red Sails in the Sunset | 1984 | $15 |

MIDNIGHT STAR

SOLAR

❑ 60454	Headlines	1986	$12
❑ D1-72564	Midnight Star	1988	$12
❑ 60241	No Parking on the Dance Floor	1983	$12
❑ 60384	Planetary Invasion	1984	$12
❑ S-19	Standing Together	1981	$15
❑ BXL1-3491	The Beginning	1980	$25
❑ 60145	Victory	1982	$15

MIDNIGHTERS, THE

FEDERAL

| ❑ 295-90 [10] | Their Greatest Hits | 1954 | $8000 |

—VG value 4000; VG+ value 6000

| ❑ 541 | Their Greatest Hits | 1955 | $1500 |

—Red cover

| ❑ 541 [M] | Their Greatest Hits | 1955 | $1000 |

—Yellow cover

| ❑ 581 [M] | The Midnighters, Volume 2 | 1955 | $1200 |

KING

| ❑ 541 [M] | Their Greatest Jukebox Hits | 1958 | $400 |

—Crownless black label, "King" is two inches wide on label

| ❑ 541 [M] | Their Greatest Jukebox Hits | 196? | $300 |

—Crownless black label, "King" is three inches wide on label. Above two have a girl on the cover.

| ❑ 541 [M] | Their Greatest Jukebox Hits | 196? | $250 |

—Reissue with Hank Ballard on cover

| ❑ 581 [M] | The Midnighters, Volume 2 | 1958 | $300 |

—Crownless black label, "King" is two inches wide on label

| ❑ 581 [M] | The Midnighters, Volume 2 | 196? | $250 |

—Crownless black label, "King" is three inches wide on label

MIGHTY BABY

HEAD

| ❑ LPS-025 | Mighty Baby | 1969 | $150 |

MIGHTY CLOUDS OF JOY

ABC

❑ D-899	Kickin'	1975	$12
❑ D-1038	Live and Direct	1977	$12
❑ D-986	The Truth Is the Power	1976	$12

ABC DUNHILL

| ❑ DSX-50177 | It's Time | 1974 | $12 |

HOB

| ❑ 288 | Live" Zion Songs | 196? | $18 |

KING

| ❑ SG3-1107 | Out Talking to Yourself | 1970 | $18 |

MCA

| ❑ 28008 | Family Circle | 198? | $10 |

—Reissue of Peacock 114

| ❑ 28030 | God Bless America | 198? | $10 |

—Reissue of Peacock 170

| ❑ 28032 | Live at the Apollo | 198? | $10 |

—Reissue of Peacock 173

| ❑ 28017 | Mighty Clouds of Joy At the Music Hall | 198? | $10 |

—Reissue of Peacock 134

| ❑ 28028 | Songs of Rev. Julius Cheeks and the Nightingales | 198? | $10 |

—Reissue of Peacock 163

| ❑ 28019 | The Best of Mighty Clouds of Joy | 198? | $10 |

—Reissue of Peacock 136

| ❑ 28040 | The Best of Mighty Clouds of Joy -- Volume 2 | 198? | $10 |
| ❑ 28012 | The Bright Side | 198? | $10 |

—Reissue of Peacock 121

| ❑ 28025 | The Untouchables | 198? | $10 |

—Reissue of Peacock 151

| ❑ 1091 | The Very Best of Mighty Clouds of Joy | 198? | $12 |

MYRRH

❑ MSB-6663	Cloudburst	1980	$12
❑ WR-8121	Mighty Clouds Alive	1984	$12
❑ MSB-6694	Miracle Man	1982	$12
❑ MSB-6712	Request Line	1983	$12
❑ WR-8122	Sing and Shout	1984	$12
❑ MSB-6681	The Truth Is the Power	1981	$12

PEACOCK

THE MIGHTY CLOUDS OF JOY

❑ 114 [B]	Family Circle	196?	$25
❑ 170	God Bless America	1971	$18
❑ 173	Live at the Apollo	1972	$18
❑ 134	Mighty Clouds of Joy At the Music Hall	196?	$25
❑ 161	Out Talking to Yourself	196?	$25
❑ 163	Songs of Rev. Julius Cheeks and the Nightingales	196?	$25
❑ 136	The Best of Mighty Clouds of Joy	196?	$25
❑ 121	The Bright Side	196?	$25
❑ 151	The Untouchables	196?	$25

PRIORITY

| ❑ RV37707 | Changing Times | 1982 | $12 |

MIGHTY FAITH INCREASERS, THE

KING

| ❑ 814 [M] | A Festival of Spiritual Songs | 1962 | $175 |
| ❑ 806 [M] | The Mighty Faith Increasers with Willa Dorsey | 1962 | $175 |

MIGHTY LEMON DROPS, THE

REPRISE

| ❑ 26017 | Laughter | 1989 | $12 |

SIRE

❑ 25788	Happy Head	1988	$12
❑ 25595	Out of Hand	1987	$12
❑ 25532	The Mighty Lemon Drops	1986	$12

MIGHTY MIGHTY BOSSTONES

BIG RIG

| ❑ BR101 | Don't Know How to Party | 1993 | $50 |

—Includes one 12-inch plaid picture disc and a 10-inch record called "Skacore"

| ❑ BR102 [10] | Question the Answers | 1994 | $50 |

—Two 10-inch records; includes one song not on the CD version

BIG RIG/ISLAND

| ❑ 314 542451-1 | Pay Attention | 2000 | $30 |

SIDE ONE DUMMY

| ❑ SDLP-1234 | A Jackknife to a Swan | 2002 | $30 |

TAANG!

| ❑ 44 | Devils Night Out | 1991 | $30 |
| ❑ 49 | More Noise & Other Disturbances | 1991 | $30 |

MIGHTY RYEDERS

SUN GLO

| ❑ SG456 [B] | Help Us Spread The Message | 1978 | $4500 |

MIGLIORI, JAY

DISCOVERY

| ❑ DS-859 | The Courage | 198? | $25 |

PBR

| ❑ 5 | Count the Nights and Times | 197? | $35 |

TRANSITION

| ❑ TRLP-18 [M] | Jay Migliori Quintet | 1956 | $0 |

—Canceled

MIKE & ELSE

SKANDISC

| ❑ SK-1519 | Juleglede (Christmas Joy) | 1977 | $12 |

MIKE + THE MECHANICS

ATLANTIC

| ❑ 81923 | Living Years | 1989 | $12 |
| ❑ PR820 [DJ] | Mike on Mike | 1985 | $25 |

—Promo-only music and interviews

| ❑ PR2543 [DJ] | Mike on Mike II | 1989 | $18 |

—Promo-only music and interviews

| ❑ 81287 | Mike + The Mechanics | 1985 | $12 |

MIL-COMBO, THE

CAPITOL

| ❑ T579 [M] | The Mil-Combo | 1955 | $100 |

MILANOV, ZINKA

RCA VICTOR RED SEAL

| ❑ LSC-2303 [S] | Operatic Arias by Puccini | 1959 | $40 |

—Originals on "shaded dog" label

MILBURN, AMOS

ALADDIN

| ❑ LP-704 [10] | Rockin' the Boogie | 1952 | $8000 |

—Red vinyl, blue cover

| ❑ LP-704 [10] | Rockin' the Boogie | 1952 | $4000 |

—Black vinyl

| ❑ LP-810 [M] | Rockin' the Boogie | 1957 | $0 |

—Canceled

IMPERIAL

| ❑ LP-9176 [M] | Million Sellers | 1962 | $500 |

MOSAIC

| ❑ MQ10-155 | The Complete Aladdin Recordings of Amos Milburn | 199? | $180 |

—Limited editon of 3,500

MOTOWN

| ❑ 608 [M] | The Return of Amos Milburn, "The" Blues Boss | 1963 | $900 |

SCORE

| ❑ LP-4035 [M] | Amos Milburn Sings the Blues | 1958 | $0 |

—Canceled

| ❑ LP-4012 [M] | Let's Have a Party | 1957 | $800 |

MILBURN, AMOS/WYNONIE HARRIS/ETC.

ALADDIN

| ❑ LP-703 [10] | Party After Hours | 1952 | $8000 |

—Red vinyl, blue cover

| ❑ LP-703 [10] | Party After Hours | 1952 | $4000 |

—Black vinyl

MILES, BARRY

CENTURY

| ❑ 1070 | Fusion Is… | 1979 | $25 |

—Audiophile edition

CHARLIE PARKER

| ❑ PLP-804 [M] | Miles of Genius | 1962 | $30 |
| ❑ PLP-804S [S] | Miles of Genius | 1962 | $30 |

GRYPHON

| ❑ 783 | Fusion Is… | 1978 | $30 |

LONDON

| ❑ XPS661 | Magic Theatre | 1975 | $30 |
| ❑ XPS651 | Silverlight | 1975 | $30 |

MAINSTREAM

| ❑ MRL-382 | Scatbird | 1974 | $35 |
| ❑ MRL-353 | White Heat | 1973 | $35 |

POPPY

| ❑ PY-40009 | Barry Miles | 1970 | $25 |

RCA VICTOR

| ❑ BGL1-2200 | Sky Train | 1977 | $30 |

MILES, BOB

OPTIMISM

| ❑ OP-2003 | Windstorm | 198? | $25 |

MILES, BUDDY

ATLANTIC

| ❑ SD 2-4000 | Sneak Attack | 1982 | $15 |

CASABLANCA

| ❑ NBLP7024 | Bicentennial Gathering of the Tribes | 1976 | $12 |
| ❑ NBLP7019 | More Miles Per Gallon | 1975 | $12 |

COLUMBIA

❑ KC33089	All the Faces	1974	$15
❑ KC32694	Booger Bear	1973	$15
❑ CQ32694 [Q]	Booger Bear	1973	$30
❑ KC32048	Chapter VII	1973	$15
❑ CQ32048 [Q]	Chapter VII	1973	$30

Number	Title	Yr	NM

MERCURY
❏ SRM-1-608	A Message to the People	1971	$18
❏ SRM-2-7500	Buddy Miles Live	1971	$18
❏ SR-61222	Electric Church	1969	$25
❏ SR-61196	Expressway to Your Skull	1968	$25
❏ SR-61280	Them Changes	1970	$18
❏ SR-61313	We Got to Live Together	1970	$18

MILES, BUTCH
DREAMSTREET
❏ 102	Lady Be Good	1980	$30

FAMOUS DOOR
❏ 132	Butch Miles Salutes Chick Webb	1979	$30
❏ 142	Butch Miles Salutes Gene Krupa	1982	$25
❏ 135	Butch Miles Swings Some Standards	1981	$25
❏ 124	Encore	1978	$30
❏ 145	Hail to the Chief	1982	$25
❏ 117	Miles of Swing	1977	$30
❏ 150	More Miles… More Standards	1985	$25

MILES, DICK
CAPITOL
❏ ST2925	The Last Goodbye	1968	$18

MILES, LIZZIE
COOK
❏ 1183 [M]	Hot Songs My Mother Taught Me	195?	$75
❏ 1182 [M]	Moans and Blues	195?	$75
❏ 1181 [10]	Queen Mother of the Rue Royale	1955	$100
❏ 1184 [M]	Torchy Lullabies My Mother Taught Me	195?	$75

— Black vinyl
❏ 1184 [M]	Torchy Lullabies My Mother Taught Me	195?	$250

— Rose-colored vinyl

MILES, LUKE "LONG GONE"
WORLD PACIFIC
❏ WP-1820 [M]	Country Born	1964	$30
❏ ST-1820 [S]	Country Born	1964	$30

MILESTONE JAZZSTARS, THE
MILESTONE
❏ 55006	Milestone Jazzstars In Concert	1978	$35

MILKWOOD (1)
A&M
❏ SP-4226	Under Milkwood	1969	$300

MILKWOOD (2)
PARAMOUNT
❏ PAS-6046 [B]	How's the Weather?	1973	$50

MILKWOOD TAPESTRY
METROMEDIA
❏ MD-1007	Milkwood Tapestry	1969	$85

MILL CITY SEVEN, THE
JAZZOLOGY
❏ J-19	The Mill City Seven	1974	$25

MILLARD & DYCE
KAYMAR
❏ KS-7-265	Open	1973	$75

MILLENNIUM
COLUMBIA
❏ CS9663	Begin	1968	$30

MILLER, ASHLEY
COMMAND
❏ COM-K-1SD [S]	Christmas Carols with Organ and Chimes	1963	$18

— Sold only at Korvettes department stores
❏ COM-K-1 [M]	Christmas Carols with Organ and Chimes	1963	$15

— Sold only at Korvettes department stores

MILLER, CHUCK
MERCURY
❏ MG-20195 [M]	After Hours	1956	$100

MILLER, CLARENCE "BIG
COLUMBIA
❏ CL1808 [M]	Big Miller Sings, Twists, Shouts and Preaches	1962	$30
❏ CS8608 [S]	Big Miller Sings, Twists, Shouts and Preaches	1962	$30
❏ CL1611 [M]	Revelation and the Blues	1961	$30

Number	Title	Yr	NM
❏ CS8411 [S]	Revelation and the Blues	1961	$30

UNITED ARTISTS
❏ UAL-3047 [M]	Did You Ever Hear the Blues?	1959	$40
❏ UAS-6047 [S]	Did You Ever Hear the Blues?	1959	$75

MILLER, DON
KING
❏ 712 [M]	The Don Miller Quartet	1960	$75

MILLER, EDDIE, AND ARMAND HUG
LAND O' JAZZ
❏ 5876	Just Friends	1979	$30

MILLER, EDDIE
CAPITOL
❏ T614 [M]	Classics in Jazz	1955	$100

FAMOUS DOOR
❏ 131	It's Miller Time	1979	$30

MILLER, EDDIE/GEORGE VAN EPS
JUMP
❏ JL-5 [10]	Eddie Miller/George Van Eps	1953	$50

MILLER, FRANKIE
AUDIO LAB
❏ AL-1562 [M]	The Fine Country Singing of Frankie Miller	1963	$175

STARDAY
❏ SLP-339 [M]	Blackland Farmer	1965	$75
❏ SLP-134 [M]	Country Music's Great New Star	1961	$150
❏ SLP-199 [M]	The True Country Style of Frankie Miller	1962	$150

MILLER, GARY
CIRCLE
❏ 2	Gary Miller and the Celebration Road Show Live On Stage	197?	$25

MILLER, GLENN, ORCHESTRA
GRP
❏ GRP-A-1002	In the Digital Mood	1983	$25

MILLER, GLENN, ORCHESTRA (BUDDY DEFRANCO, DIRECTOR)
EPIC
❏ LN24206 [M]	Something New	1966	$75
❏ BN26206 [S]	Something New	1966	$85

PARAMOUNT
❏ PAS-5034	The Glenn Miller Orchestra	1970	$30

RCA VICTOR
❏ LPM-3819 [M]	In the Mod	1967	$35
❏ LSP-3819 [S]	In the Mod	1967	$30
❏ LPM-3971 [M]	The Glenn Miller Orchestra Makes the Goin' Great	1968	$40
❏ LSP-3971 [S]	The Glenn Miller Orchestra Makes the Goin' Great	1968	$30
❏ LPM-3880 [M]	The Glenn Miller Orchestra Returns to the Glen Island Casino	1968	$25
❏ LSP-3880 [S]	The Glenn Miller Orchestra Returns to the Glen Island Casino	1968	$30

MILLER, GLENN, ORCHESTRA (RAY MCKINLEY, DIRECTOR)
EPIC
❏ LN24133 [M]	Glenn Miller Time -- 1965	1965	$85
❏ BN26133 [S]	Glenn Miller Time -- 1965	1965	$40
❏ LN24157 [M]	Great Songs of the 60's	1965	$85
❏ BN26157 [S]	Great Songs of the 60's	1965	$50

RCA VICTOR
❏ LPM-2193 [M]	Dance, Anyone?	1960	$30
❏ LSP-2193 [S]	Dance, Anyone?	1960	$30
❏ LPM-2519 [M]	Echoes of Glenn Miller	1962	$30
❏ LSP-2519 [S]	Echoes of Glenn Miller	1962	$30
❏ LPM-2436 [M]	Glenn Miller Time	1961	$30
❏ LSP-2436 [S]	Glenn Miller Time	1961	$30
❏ LPM-1948 [M]	On Tour with the New Glenn Miller Orchestra	1959	$30
❏ LSP-1948 [S]	On Tour with the New Glenn Miller Orchestra	1959	$40
❏ LPM-1678 [M]	Something Old, New, Borrowed and Blue	1958	$30
❏ LSP-1678 [S]	Something Old, New, Borrowed and Blue	1958	$40
❏ LPM-2270 [M]	The Authentic Sound of the New Glenn Miller Orchestra -- Today	1961	$30
❏ LSP-2270 [S]	The Authentic Sound of the New Glenn Miller Orchestra -- Today	1961	$30
❏ LPM-2080 [M]	The Great Dance Bands of the 30's and 40's	1960	$30
❏ LSP-2080 [S]	The Great Dance Bands of the 30's and 40's	1960	$30

Number	Title	Yr	NM
❏ ANL1-2975(e) [S]	The Great Dance Bands of the 30's and 40's	1978	$10

— Reissue of LSP-2080
❏ LPM-1852 [M]	The Miller Sound	1959	$30
❏ LSP-1852 [S]	The Miller Sound	1959	$40
❏ LPM-1522 [M]	The New Glenn Miller Orchestra in Hi-Fi	1957	$30
❏ LSP-1522 [S]	The New Glenn Miller Orchestra in Hi-Fi	1958	$40

MILLER, GLENN
20TH CENTURY
❏ T2-904	Remember Glenn	197?	$35

20TH CENTURY FOX
❏ TFM-3159 [M]	This Is Glenn Miller and His Greatest Orchestra, Volume 1	1964	$35
❏ TFS-4159 [R]	This Is Glenn Miller and His Greatest Orchestra, Volume 1	1964	$25
❏ TFM-3160 [M]	This Is Glenn Miller and His Greatest Orchestra, Volume 2	1964	$35
❏ TFS-4160 [R]	This Is Glenn Miller and His Greatest Orchestra, Volume 2	1964	$25

20TH FOX
❏ TCF-100-2 [M]	Glenn Miller and His Orchestra Original Film Sound Tracks	1958	$30
❏ TCF-100-2S [R]	Glenn Miller and His Orchestra Original Film Sound Tracks	1961	$25
❏ FOX3020 [M]	Glenn Miller's Original Film Soundtracks, Volume 1	1958	$50

— Half of 101
❏ FOX3021 [M]	Glenn Miller's Original Film Soundtracks, Volume 2	1958	$50

— Half of 101

BANDSTAND
❏ BS-7136	A Million Dreams Ago	198?	$25

BLUEBIRD
❏ 6360-1-RB	Maj. Glenn Miller and the Army Air Force Band	1987	$25
❏ AXM2-5512	The Complete Glenn Miller Volume 1, 1938-39	1975	$30
❏ AXM2-5514	The Complete Glenn Miller Volume 2, 1939	1976	$30
❏ AXM2-5534	The Complete Glenn Miller Volume 3, 1939-40	1976	$30
❏ AXM2-5558	The Complete Glenn Miller Volume 4, 1940	1978	$30
❏ AXM2-5565	The Complete Glenn Miller Volume 5, 1940	1979	$30
❏ AXM2-5569	The Complete Glenn Miller Volume 6, 1940-41	1980	$30
❏ AXM2-5570	The Complete Glenn Miller Volume 7, 1941	1980	$30
❏ AXM2-5571	The Complete Glenn Miller Volume 8, 1941-42	1980	$30
❏ AXM2-5574	The Complete Glenn Miller Volume 9, 1939-42	1980	$30
❏ 9785-1-RB	The Popular Recordings 1938-1942	1989	$30

EPIC
❏ LA16002 [M]	Glenn Miller	1960	$40

EVEREST
❏ 4005/5	His Complete Recordings on Columbia (1928-1938) As Player and Conductor	1982	$30

— Box set with 8-page booklet

HARMONY
❏ HS11393 [R]	Collector's Choice	1970	$30

INTERMEDIA
❏ QS-5045	A String of Pearls	198?	$20

KOALA
❏ AW14186	Chattanooga Choo Choo	1979	$30

MERCURY
❏ 826635-1	Glenn Miller In Hollywood	1986	$30

— Reissue of material formerly on 20th Century

MOVIETONE
❏ MTM-1003 [M]	Glenn Miller's Shindig	1965	$35
❏ MTS-72003 [R]	Glenn Miller's Shindig	1965	$25
❏ MTS-72018 [R]	The Glenn Miller Years	1967	$30

PAIR
❏ PDL2-1003	Original Recordings, Volume 1	1986	$30
❏ PDL2-1036	Original Recordings, Volume 2	1986	$30

PICKWICK
❏ DL2-0168	A String of Pearls	197?	$25

— Reissue of RCA Camden ACL2-0168
❏ ACL-7009	Parade of Hits	1976	$20

RCA
❏ 7648-1-R	Pure Gold	1988	$10
❏ 7652-1-R	The Best of Glenn Miller	1988	$10

RCA CAMDEN
❏ ACL2-0168	A String of Pearls	1973	$30
❏ CXS-9004	Sunrise Serenade	197?	$30
❏ CAL-751 [M]	The Great Glenn Miller	1963	$35

Number	Title	Yr	NM
❏ CAS-751(e) [R]	The Great Glenn Miller	1963	$30
❏ CAL-2128 [M]	The Nearness of You and Others	1967	$35
❏ CAS-2128 [R]	The Nearness of You and Others	1967	$30
❏ CAS-2267	The One and Only Glenn Miller	1968	$25
❏ CAL-829 [M]	The Original Recordings	1964	$35
❏ CAS-829(e) [R]	The Original Recordings	1964	$30
❏ ACL-0503	This Time the Dream's On Me	1974	$20

RCA SPECIAL PRODUCTS
Number	Title	Yr	NM
❏ DMM4-0322	Glenn Miller	1978	$25

—Box set; mail-order offer

RCA VICTOR
Number	Title	Yr	NM
❏ CPM2-0693	A Legendary Performer	1974	$30
❏ CPL1-2080	A Legendary Performer, Volume 2	1976	$25
❏ CPL1-2495	A Legendary Performer, Volume 3	1977	$25
❏ LPM-3657 [M]	Blue Moonlight	1966	$35
❏ LSP-3657 [R]	Blue Moonlight	1966	$35
❏ LPM-6100 [M]	For the Very First Time…	195?	$50

—Black "Long Play" labels in leatherette spiral-bound binder

Number	Title	Yr	NM
❏ LPT-31 [10]	Glenn Miller	1951	$75
❏ VPM-6019	Glenn Miller: A Memorial 1944-1969	1969	$35
❏ LPT-6700 [M]	Glenn Miller and His Orchestra Limited Edition	1953	$175

—Silver labels with red print in leatherette spiral-bound binder

Number	Title	Yr	NM
❏ LPT-6700 [M]	Glenn Miller and His Orchestra Limited Edition -- Second Pressing	195?	$75

—Black "Long Play" labels in leatherette spiral-bound binder

Number	Title	Yr	NM
❏ LPT-6701 [M]	Glenn Miller and His Orchestra Limited Edition Volume Two	1954	$120

—Black "Long Play" labels in leatherette spiral-bound binder

Number	Title	Yr	NM
❏ LPT-6701 [M]	Glenn Miller and His Orchestra Limited Edition Volume Two -- Second Pressing	195?	$75

—Black "Long Play" labels in leatherette spiral-bound binder; identified as "Second Pressing" throughout

Number	Title	Yr	NM
❏ LPT-6702 [M]	Glenn Miller Army Air Force Band	1955	$120

—Black "Long Play" labels in leatherette spiral-bound binder

Number	Title	Yr	NM
❏ LPT-6702 [M]	Glenn Miller Army Air Force Band	195?	$75

—Same as above, but in box rather than in binder

Number	Title	Yr	NM
❏ LPM-1193 [M]	Glenn Miller Concert	1956	$40
❏ LPT-16 [10]	Glenn Miller Concert -- Volume 1	1951	$75
❏ LPT-30 [10]	Glenn Miller Concert -- Volume 2	1951	$75
❏ LPT-3001 [10]	Glenn Miller Concert -- Volume 3	195?	$75
❏ LPM-6101 [M]	Glenn Miller On the Air	1963	$40
❏ LSP-6101 [R]	Glenn Miller On the Air	1963	$30
❏ LPM-2767 [M]	Glenn Miller On the Air Volume 1	1963	$35
❏ LSP-2767 [R]	Glenn Miller On the Air Volume 1	1963	$25
❏ LPM-2768 [M]	Glenn Miller On the Air Volume 2	1963	$35
❏ LSP-2768 [R]	Glenn Miller On the Air Volume 2	1963	$25
❏ LPM-2769 [M]	Glenn Miller On the Air Volume 3	1963	$35
❏ LSP-2769 [R]	Glenn Miller On the Air Volume 3	1963	$25
❏ PR-114 [M]	Glenn Miller Originals	1962	$25

—Promotional item for Salada Foods Inc.

Number	Title	Yr	NM
❏ LPT-1016 [M]	Juke Box Saturday Night	1955	$50
❏ LPM-1494 [M]	Marvelous Miller Moods	1957	$40
❏ PRM-181 [M]	Moonlight Serenade	1965	$35
❏ ANL1-0974	Pure Gold	1975	$20
❏ AYL1-3666	Pure Gold	1980	$10
❏ LPT-3057 [10]	Selections from the Film "The Glenn Miller Story"	1954	$75
❏ LPM-1192 [M]	Selections from "The Glenn Miller Story" and Other Hits	1956	$40
❏ LSP-1192(e) [R]	Selections from "The Glenn Miller Story" and Other Hits	196?	$35

—Black label, dog on top

Number	Title	Yr	NM
❏ AFL1-1192	Selections from "The Glenn Miller Story" and Other Hits	1977	$20
❏ AYL1-3759	Selections from "The Glenn Miller Story" and Other Hits	1981	$10
❏ LPT-3067 [10]	Sunrise Serenade	1954	$75
❏ LPM-3377 [M]	The Best of Glenn Miller	1965	$35
❏ LSP-3377(e) [R]	The Best of Glenn Miller	1965	$25

—Black label

Number	Title	Yr	NM
❏ AYL1-3871	The Best of Glenn Miller	1981	$10
❏ LSP-3377(e) [R]	The Best of Glenn Miller	1969	$20

—Orange label

Number	Title	Yr	NM
❏ LPM-3564 [M]	The Best of Glenn Miller Volume 2	1966	$35
❏ LSP-3564 [R]	The Best of Glenn Miller Volume 2	1966	$25
❏ AYL1-3809	The Best of Glenn Miller Volume 2	1981	$10
❏ LSP-4125 [R]	The Best of Glenn Miller Volume 3	1969	$30
❏ AFL1-2825	The Best of Glenn Miller Volume 3	1978	$20
❏ AYL1-3810	The Best of Glenn Miller Volume 3	1981	$10

Number	Title	Yr	NM
❏ LPM-3873 [M]	The Chesterfield Broadcasts, Volume 1	1967	$35
❏ LSP-3873 [R]	The Chesterfield Broadcasts, Volume 1	1967	$25
❏ ANL1-1139	The Chesterfield Broadcasts, Volume 1	1975	$20
❏ LSP-3981 [R]	The Chesterfield Broadcasts, Volume 2	1968	$30
❏ LPM-1506 [M]	The Glenn Miller Carnegie Hall Concert	1957	$40
❏ LOP-1005 [M]	The Marvelous Miller Medleys	1958	$40
❏ LPM-1973 [M]	The Marvelous Miller Medleys	1959	$30
❏ LSP-1973 [R]	The Marvelous Miller Medleys	196?	$35
❏ LPT-1031 [M]	The Nearness of You	1955	$50
❏ LPM-1189 [M]	The Sound of Glenn Miller	1956	$40
❏ LPT-3002 [M]	This Is Glenn Miller	195?	$75
❏ LPM-1190 [M]	This Is Glenn Miller	1956	$40
❏ VPM-6080	This Is Glenn Miller's Army Air Force Band	1972	$35
❏ LPT-3036 [10]	This Is Glenn Miller -- Volume 2	195?	$75

READER'S DIGEST
Number	Title	Yr	NM
❏ RD4-64 [R]	The Unforgettable Glenn Miller	1968	$25

SANDY HOOK
Number	Title	Yr	NM
❏ SH2055	Uncle Sam Presents the Band of the Army Air Forces Training Command	1981	$25

SPRINGBOARD
Number	Title	Yr	NM
❏ SPX-6013	Remember Glenn	1973	$30

SUNBEAM
Number	Title	Yr	NM
❏ SB-232	Glenn Miller and His Chesterfield Orchestra	1984	$25

TIME-LIFE
Number	Title	Yr	NM
❏ STBB-01	Big Bands: Glenn Miller	1983	$35
❏ STBB-29	Big Bands: Glenn Miller: Take Two	1986	$35
❏ STBB-17	Big Bands: Major Glenn Miller	1985	$35

MILLER, JODY

CAPITOL
Number	Title	Yr	NM
❏ T2412 [M]	Home of the Brave	1965	$18
❏ ST2412 [S]	Home of the Brave	1965	$25
❏ T2446 [M]	Jody Miller Sings the Great Hits of Buck Owens	1966	$18
❏ ST2446 [S]	Jody Miller Sings the Great Hits of Buck Owens	1966	$25
❏ T2349 [M]	Queen of the House	1965	$18
❏ ST2349 [S]	Queen of the House	1965	$25
❏ ST-11169	The Best of Jody Miller	1973	$15
❏ ST2996	The Nashville Sound of Jody Miller	1968	$18
❏ T1913 [M]	Wednesday's Child Is Full of Woe	1963	$30
❏ ST1913 [S]	Wednesday's Child Is Full of Woe	1963	$40

EPIC
Number	Title	Yr	NM
❏ KE33349	Country Girl	1975	$15
❏ KE32386	Good News!	1973	$15
❏ PE34446	Here's Jody	1977	$15
❏ E30659	He's So Fine	1971	$15
❏ KE32569	House of the Rising Sun	1974	$15
❏ E30282	Look at Mine	1971	$15
❏ KE31706	There's a Party Goin' On	1972	$15
❏ KE33934	Will You Love Me Tomorrow?	1976	$15

MILLER, MARCUS

WARNER BROS.
Number	Title	Yr	NM
❏ 25074	Marcus Miller	1984	$30
❏ 23806	Suddenly	1983	$35

MILLER, MARY K.

INERGI
Number	Title	Yr	NM
❏ ILP-1000	Mary K. Miller	197?	$15

MILLER, MICKEY

FOLKWAYS
Number	Title	Yr	NM
❏ FA-2393 [M]	American Folk Songs	1959	$35

MILLER, MITCH

ATLANTIC
Number	Title	Yr	NM
❏ SD8277	Peace Sing Along with Mitch	1970	$15

COLUMBIA
Number	Title	Yr	NM
❏ G30250	34 All Time Great Sing Along Selections	1970	$15
❏ CL1205	Christmas Sing Along with Mitch	1958	$18

—Originals have gatefold cover with eight detachable lyric sheets inside

Number	Title	Yr	NM
❏ CS8027 [S]	Christmas Sing Along with Mitch	1959	$25

—Originals have gatefold cover with eight detachable lyric sheets inside

Number	Title	Yr	NM
❏ PC39298	Christmas Sing Along with Mitch	1984	$10
❏ CL1773 [M]	Family Sing Along with Mitch	1962	$15
❏ CS8573 [S]	Family Sing Along with Mitch	1962	$18

Number	Title	Yr	NM
❏ CL1389 [M]	Fireside Sing Along with Mitch	1959	$18
❏ CS8184 [S]	Fireside Sing Along with Mitch	1959	$25
❏ CL1316 [M]	Folk Songs Sing Along with Mitch	1959	$18
❏ CS8118 [S]	Folk Songs Sing Along with Mitch	1959	$25
❏ CL1568 [M]	Happy Times! Sing Along with Mitch	1961	$15
❏ CS8368 [S]	Happy Times! Sing Along with Mitch	1961	$18
❏ CL1701 [M]	Holiday Sing Along with Mitch	1961	$15
❏ CS8501 [S]	Holiday Sing Along with Mitch	1961	$18
❏ 3C39297	Holiday Sing Along with Mitch	1984	$10
❏ CL2063 [M]	Hymn Sing Along with Mitch	1963	$15
❏ CS8863 [S]	Hymn Sing Along with Mitch	1963	$18
❏ CL779 [M]	It's So Peaceful in the Country	1956	$25

—Red and black label with 6 "eye" logos

Number	Title	Yr	NM
❏ CL1475 [M]	March Along with Mitch	1960	$15
❏ CL1542 [M]	Memories Sing Along with Mitch	1960	$15
❏ CS8342 [S]	Memories Sing Along with Mitch	1960	$18
❏ CL6222 [10]	Mitch Miller with Horns and Chorus	195?	$30
❏ CL1544 [M]	Mitch's Greatest Hits	1961	$15
❏ CS8638 [R]	Mitch's Greatest Hits	1963	$12
❏ CL1102 [M]	Mitch's Marches	1957	$18
❏ CL601 [M]	Mmmmitch!	1954	$25

—Maroon label, gold print

Number	Title	Yr	NM
❏ CL1243 [M]	More Sing Along with Mitch	1958	$18
❏ CS8043 [S]	More Sing Along with Mitch	1959	$25
❏ CL1864 [M]	Night Time Sing Along with Mitch	1963	$15
❏ CS8664 [S]	Night Time Sing Along with Mitch	1963	$18
❏ CL1331 [M]	Party Sing Along with Mitch	1959	$18
❏ CS8138 [S]	Party Sing Along with Mitch	1959	$25
❏ CL1727 [M]	Rhythm Sing Along with Mitch	1962	$15
❏ CS8527 [S]	Rhythm Sing Along with Mitch	1962	$18
❏ CL1414 [M]	Saturday Night Sing Along with Mitch	1960	$15
❏ CS8211 [S]	Saturday Night Sing Along with Mitch	1960	$18
❏ CL1457 [M]	Sentimental Sing Along with Mitch	1960	$15
❏ CS8251 [S]	Sentimental Sing Along with Mitch	1960	$18
❏ CL1160 [M]	Sing Along with Mitch	1958	$18
❏ CS8004 [S]	Sing Along with Mitch	1959	$25

—Red and black label with 6 "eye" logos

Number	Title	Yr	NM
❏ CS8004	Sing Along with Mitch	1963	$15

—Red label

Number	Title	Yr	NM
❏ CS8004	Sing Along with Mitch	1970	$10

—Orange label

Number	Title	Yr	NM
❏ PC8004	Sing Along with Mitch	198?	$10

—Reissue with new prefix

Number	Title	Yr	NM
❏ CL1283 [M]	Still More! Sing Along with Mitch	1959	$18
❏ CS8099 [S]	Still More! Sing Along with Mitch	1959	$25
❏ CL1628 [M]	TV Sing Along with Mitch	1961	$15
❏ CS8428 [S]	TV Sing Along with Mitch	1961	$18
❏ CL1671 [M]	Your Request Sing Along with Mitch	1961	$15
❏ CS8471 [S]	Your Request Sing Along with Mitch	1961	$18

DECCA
Number	Title	Yr	NM
❏ DL4777 [M]	Dance and Sing Along with Mitch	1966	$12
❏ DL74777 [S]	Dance and Sing Along with Mitch	1966	$15

HARMONY
Number	Title	Yr	NM
❏ HS11273	Everybody Sing Along with Mitch	1968	$12
❏ HS11241	Fireside Sing Along with Mitch	1968	$12
❏ HL7404 [M]	March Along with Mitch	1967	$15
❏ HS11204 [S]	March Along with Mitch	1967	$15
❏ HS11242	Memories Sing Along with Mitch	1968	$12
❏ HS11354	Night Time Sing Along with Mitch	1970	$12

MILLER, MRS.

AMARET
Number	Title	Yr	NM
❏ 5000	Mrs. Miller Does Her Thing	1969	$25

CAPITOL
Number	Title	Yr	NM
❏ T2494 [M]	Mrs. Miller's Greatest Hits	1966	$30
❏ ST2494 [S]	Mrs. Miller's Greatest Hits	1966	$30
❏ T2734 [M]	The Country Soul of Mrs. Miller	1967	$30
❏ ST2734 [S]	The Country Soul of Mrs. Miller	1967	$30
❏ T2579 [M]	Will Success Spoil Mrs. Miller?	1966	$30
❏ ST2579 [S]	Will Success Spoil Mrs. Miller?	1966	$30

MILLER, MULGREW

LANDMARK
Number	Title	Yr	NM
❏ LLP-1525	From Day to Day	1990	$30

Number	Title	Yr	NM
❏ LLP-1507	Keys to the City	198?	$25
❏ LLP-1519	The Countdown	1989	$30
❏ LLP-1515	Wingspan	1988	$25
❏ LLP-1511	Work!	1986	$25

MILLER, NED
CAPITOL

Number	Title	Yr	NM
❏ ST2914	In the Name of Love	1968	$18
❏ T2330 [M]	Ned Miller Sings the Songs of Ned Miller	1965	$25
❏ ST2330 [S]	Ned Miller Sings the Songs of Ned Miller	1965	$30
❏ T2586 [M]	Teardrop Lane	1967	$25
❏ ST2586 [S]	Teardrop Lane	1967	$25
❏ T2414 [M]	The Best of Ned Miller	1966	$18
❏ ST2414 [S]	The Best of Ned Miller	1966	$25

FABOR
❏ FLP-1001 [M]	From a Jack to a King	1963	$40
— Black vinyl			
❏ FLP-1001 [M]	From a Jack to a King	1963	$150
— Colored vinyl			

MILLER, PUNCH
HERWIN
| ❏ 108 | Jazz Rarities 1929-30 | 197? | $25 |
IMPERIAL
| ❏ LP-9160 [M] | Hongo Fongo | 1962 | $175 |
JAZZ CRUSADE
| ❏ 2016 | Oh Lady Be Good | 196? | $35 |
JAZZOLOGY
| ❏ JCE-12 | Kid Punch | 1967 | $35 |
| ❏ J-17 | River's in Mourning | 197? | $25 |

MILLER, ROGER
20TH CENTURY
| ❏ T-592 | Making a Name for Myself | 1979 | $15 |
COLUMBIA
| ❏ KC32449 | Dear Folks Sorry I Haven't Written Lately | 1973 | $18 |
| ❏ KC33472 | Supersongs | 1975 | $18 |
HILLTOP
| ❏ 6109 | King of the Road | 197? | $12 |
| ❏ 6131 | Little Green Apples | 197? | $12 |
MCA
| ❏ 5722 | Roger Miller | 1986 | $12 |
MERCURY
❏ SR-61297	A Trip in the Country	1970	$18
❏ 826261-1	Golden Hits	198?	$10
— Reissue of Smash 67073			
❏ SR-61361	The Best of Roger Miller	1971	$18
NASHVILLE
| ❏ 2046 | The Amazing Roger Miller | 196? | $15 |
PICKWICK
| ❏ SPC-3226 | Engine #9 | 197? | $12 |
| ❏ PTP-2057 | King High | 1973 | $15 |
RCA CAMDEN
❏ CAL-851 [M]	Roger Miller	1964	$15
❏ CAS-851 [S]	Roger Miller	1964	$18
❏ CAL-903 [M]	The One and Only Roger Miller	1965	$15
❏ CAS-903 [S]	The One and Only Roger Miller	1965	$18
SMASH
❏ SRS-67103	A Tender Look at Love	1968	$25
❏ MGS-27049 [M]	Dang Me	196?	$15
— Yet another retitled version of "Roger and Out"			
❏ SRS-67049 [S]	Dang Me	196?	$18
— Yet another retitled version of "Roger and Out"			
❏ SRS-67049 [S]	Dang Me/Chug-a-Lug	196?	$18
— Retitled version of "Roger and Out"			
❏ MGS-27049 [M]	Dang Me/Chug-a-Lug	196?	$15
— Retitled version of "Roger and Out"			
❏ MGS-27073 [M]	Golden Hits	1965	$18
❏ SRS-67073 [S]	Golden Hits	1965	$25
❏ MGS-27049 [M]	Roger and Out	1964	$18
❏ SRS-67049 [S]	Roger and Out	1964	$25
❏ SRS-67123	Roger Miller	1969	$25
❏ SRS-67129	Roger Miller 1970	1970	$25
❏ MGS-27068 [M]	The 3rd Time Around	1965	$18
❏ SRS-67068 [S]	The 3rd Time Around	1965	$25
❏ MGS-27061 [M]	The Return of Roger Miller	1965	$18
❏ SRS-67061 [S]	The Return of Roger Miller	1965	$25
❏ MGS-27092 [M]	Walkin' in the Sunshine	1967	$25
❏ SRS-67092 [S]	Walkin' in the Sunshine	1967	$25
❏ MGS-27096 [M]	Waterhole #3	1967	$30
❏ SRS-67096 [S]	Waterhole #3	1967	$25
❏ MGS-27075 [M]	Words and Music	1966	$18
❏ SRS-67075 [S]	Words and Music	1966	$25
STARDAY
❏ 3011	Painted Poetry	1978	$12
❏ SLP-318 [M]	The Country Side of Roger Miller	196?	$30
— Retitled version of "Wild Child"			
❏ SLP-318 [M]	Wild Child Roger Miller	1965	$30
❏ T-90241 [M]	Wild Child Roger Miller	1965	$40
— Capitol Record Club edition			

Number	Title	Yr	NM
❏ DT-90241 [R]	Wild Child Roger Miller	1965	$40
— Capitol Record Club edition			

WINDSONG
| ❏ BHL1-2337 | Off the Wall | 1977 | $15 |

MILLER, STEVE, BAND
CAPITOL
❏ ST-12216	Abracadabra	1982	$12
❏ SVBB-11114	Anthology	1972	$18
❏ R223186	Anthology	197?	$18
— RCA Music Service edition			
❏ SO-11630	Book of Dreams	1977	$12
❏ SEAX-11903 [PD]	Book of Dreams	1978	$18
❏ SN-16323	Book of Dreams	1984	$10
❏ C1-48303	Born 2 B Blue	1988	$12
❏ SKAO-184 [B]	Brave New World	1969	$30
— Black label with colorband			
❏ SKAO-184	Brave New World	1970	$18
— Green label			
❏ SN-16078	Brave New World	1980	$10
❏ SKAO-8-0184	Brave New World	1969	$30
— Capitol Record Club edition; black label with colorband			
❏ SKAO2920	Children of the Future	1968	$30
— Black label with colorband			
❏ SKAO2920	Children of the Future	1970	$18
— Green label			
❏ SN-16262	Children of the Future	1982	$10
❏ STBB-717	Children of the Future/Living in the U.S.A.	1971	$18
— Repackage of 2920 and 2984 (with new title for the latter)			
❏ ST-12121	Circle of Love	1981	$12
❏ SN-16357	Circle of Love	1985	$10
❏ ST-11497	Fly Like an Eagle	1976	$12
❏ SN-16339	Fly Like an Eagle	1984	$10
❏ 21185	Fly Like an Eagle	1999	$25
— Limited-edition reissue on 180-gram vinyl			
❏ SOO-11872 [DJ]	Greatest Hits 1974-1978	1978	$30
— Promo only on blue vinyl			
❏ SOO-11872	Greatest Hits 1974-1978	1978	$12
❏ SN-16321	Greatest Hits 1974-1978	1984	$10
❏ SJ-12339	Italian X-Rays	1985	$12
❏ PJ-12445	Living in the 20th Century	1987	$12
❏ SKAO-436	Number 5	1970	$18
❏ SKAO-80436	Number 5	1970	$25
— Capitol Record Club edition			
❏ SMAS-11022	Recall the Beginning…A Journey from Eden	1972	$18
❏ SW-748	Rock Love	1971	$18
❏ ST2984	Sailor	1968	$30
— Black label with colorband			
❏ ST2984	Sailor	1970	$18
— Green label			
❏ SN-16263	Sailor	1982	$10
❏ ST-12263	Steve Miller Live	1983	$12
❏ SMAS-11235	The Joker	1973	$12
❏ ST-331 [B]	Your Saving Grace	1969	$30
❏ SN-16079	Your Saving Grace	1980	$10
DCC COMPACT CLASSICS
| ❏ LPZ-2028 | Greatest Hits 1974-1978 | 1996 | $50 |
| — Audiophile vinyl | | | |
MOBILE FIDELITY
| ❏ Jan-0021 | Fly Like an Eagle | 1979 | $50 |
| — Audiophile vinyl | | | |

MILLER, STEVE, BAND/QUICKSILVER MESSENGER SERVICE/THE BAND
Also see each artist's individual listings.
CAPITOL
| ❏ STCR-288 [B] | Sailor/Quicksilver Messenger Service/Music from Big Pink | 1969 | $50 |
| — Special 3-LP box set combining these three LPs, also listed separately in each group's listing, in one package | | | |

MILLER, STEVEN
HIPPOCKET
| ❏ HP-102 | Singing Whale Songs in a Low Voice | 1983 | $15 |
WINDHAM HILL
| ❏ WH-0102 | Singing Whale Songs in a Low Voice | 1987 | $12 |
| — Reissue of HipPocket 102 | | | |

MILLI VANILLI
ARISTA
| ❏ AL8592 | Girl You Know It's True | 1989 | $12 |
| ❏ AL8622 | The Remix Album | 1990 | $15 |

MILLINDER, LUCKY
ALAMAC
| ❏ QSR-2425 | Lucky Millinder and His Orchestra 1941-43 | 198? | $25 |
HINDSIGHT
| ❏ HSR-233 | The Uncollected Lucky Millinder and His Orchestra 1942 | 198? | $25 |

Number	Title	Yr	NM
	MCA		
❏ 1357	Let It Roll	198?	$30

MILLMAN, JACK
DECCA
| ❏ DL8156 [M] | Jazz Studio 4 | 1955 | $175 |
ERA
❏ EL-20005 [M]	Blowing Up a Storm	1956	$75
— Red vinyl			
❏ EL-20005 [M]	Blowing Up a Storm	1956	$40
— Black vinyl			
LIBERTY
| ❏ LJH-6007 [M] | Shades of Things to Come | 1956 | $50 |

MILLS, ALAN
FOLKWAYS
❏ FC-7677 [M]	Animals, Vol. 1	1956	$50
❏ FW-3000 [M]	Canada's Story in Song	1960	$40
❏ FC-7750 [M]	Christmas Songs from Many Lands	1956	$35
❏ FP-29 [10]	Folk Songs of French Canada	1952	$75
❏ FW-6929 [M]	Folk Songs of French Canada	195?	$40
❏ FP-831 [10]	Folk Songs of Newfoundland	1953	$50
❏ FW-6831 [M]	Folk Songs of Newfoundland	195?	$35
❏ FC-7208 [M]	French Folk Songs for Children	1957	$35
❏ FC-7018 [M]	French Folk Songs for Children in English	1957	$35
❏ FC-7642 [M]	More Animals, Vol. 2	1956	$30
❏ FW-3001 [M]	O Canada: A History in Song	1956	$30
❏ FA-2313 [M]	Songs of the Sea	1957	$35
❏ FW-8771 [M]	We'll Rant and We'll Roar: Songs of Newfoundland	1958	$30
SCHOLASTIC
| ❏ FC-7750 [M] | Christmas Songs from Many Lands | 196? | $20 |
| — Reissue of Folkways album with same contents | | | |

MILLS, FRANK
CAPITOL
❏ SN-16290	A Special Christmas	198?	$10
❏ ST-12388	Music Box Dancer	1985	$10
❏ ST-12421	Traveler	1985	$10
POLYDOR
❏ PD-1-6192	Music Box Dancer	1979	$12
❏ PD-1-6225	Sunday Morning	1980	$12
❏ PD-1-6305	The Frank Mills Album	1982	$12

MILLS, HAYLEY
BUENA VISTA
| ❏ BV-3311 [M] | Let's Get Together | 1962 | $40 |
| ❏ STER-3311 [S] | Let's Get Together | 1962 | $40 |

MILLS, MRS.
LIBERTY
| ❏ LRP-3359 [M] | My Mother -- The Ragtime Piano Player | 1964 | $15 |
| ❏ LST-7359 [S] | My Mother -- The Ragtime Piano Player | 1964 | $18 |

MILLS, STEPHANIE
20TH CENTURY
❏ T-700	Stephanie	1981	$12
❏ T-603	Sweet Sensation	1980	$12
❏ T-583	Whatcha Gonna Do ... With My Lovin'?	1979	$12
ABC
| ❏ ABCD-869 | Movin' in the Right Direction | 1975 | $18 |
CASABLANCA
❏ 832519-1	In My Life: Greatest Hits	1987	$12
❏ 822421-1	I've Got the Cure	1984	$12
❏ 811364-1	Merciless	1983	$12
❏ NBLP7265	Tantalizingly Hot	1982	$12
MCA
❏ 6312	Home	1989	$12
❏ 5996	If I Were Your Woman	1987	$10
❏ 10260	Something Real	1992	$18
❏ 5669	Stephanie Mills	1985	$10
MOTOWN
❏ M6-859S1	For the First Time	1975	$15
❏ M5-227-V1	For the First Time	1982	$10
— Reissue of 859			
❏ 6033ML	Love Has Lifted Me	1983	$50

MILLS BROTHERS, THE
ABC
| ❏ 4004 | 16 Great Performances | 1975 | $12 |
| ❏ 1027 | The Best of the Mills Brothers, Volume 2 | 1978 | $15 |
ABC SONGBIRD
| ❏ SBDP-255 | Inspiration | 1974 | $12 |
DECCA
| ❏ DL5050 [10] | Barber Shop Ballads | 1950 | $175 |
| ❏ DL5051 [10] | Barber Shop Ballads | 1950 | $175 |

Number	Title	Yr	NM
❑ DL8890 [M]	Barber Shop Harmony	1959	$150
❑ DL5516 [10]	Four Boys and a Guitar	1954	$175
❑ DL8827 [M]	Glow with the Mills Brothers	1958	$120
❑ DL75174 [R]	Golden Favorites, Volume 2	1970	$12
❑ DL8892 [M]	Harmonizin' with the Mills Brothers	1959	$100
❑ DL5506 [10]	Meet the Mills Brothers	1954	$175
❑ DL8219 [M]	Memory Lane	1956	$120
❑ DL8491 [M]	One Dozen Roses	1957	$120
❑ DL4084 [M]	Our Golden Favorites	1960	$25
❑ DL74084 [R]	Our Golden Favorites	196?	$15
❑ DL8209 [M]	Singin' and Swingin'	1956	$175
❑ DL5102 [10]	Souvenir Album	1950	$175
❑ DL8148 [M]	Souvenir Album	1955	$175
❑ DXB193 [M]	The Best of the Mills Brothers	1965	$25
❑ DXSB7193 [R]	The Best of the Mills Brothers	1965	$25
❑ DL8664 [M]	The Mills Brothers in Hi-Fi	1958	$150
❑ DL5337 [10]	Wonderful Words	1951	$250

DOT

❑ DLP-3465 [M]	Beer Barrel Polka and Other Hits	1962	$75
❑ DLP-25465 [S]	Beer Barrel Polka and Other Hits	1962	$75
❑ DLP-25927	Dream	1969	$75
❑ DLP-25809	Fortuosity	1968	$75
❑ DLP-3565 [M]	Gems by the Mills Brothers	1964	$75
❑ DLP-25565 [S]	Gems by the Mills Brothers	1964	$75
❑ DLP-3208 [M]	Great Barbershop Hits	1959	$85
❑ DLP-25208 [S]	Great Barbershop Hits	1959	$85
❑ DLP-3368 [M]	Great Hawaiian Hits	1961	$75
❑ DLP-25368 [S]	Great Hawaiian Hits	1961	$85
❑ DLP-3568 [M]	Hymns We Love	1964	$75
❑ DLP-25568 [S]	Hymns We Love	1964	$75
❑ DLP-25232 [S]	Merry Christmas	1959	$85

—Same as above, but in stereo; with cursive "Dot" logo

| ❑ DLP-3232 [M] | Merry Christmas | 1959 | $85 |
| ❑ DLP-25232 [S] | Merry Christmas | 1968 | $75 |

—With "Dot"/"Paramount" logo

❑ DLP-3103 [M]	Mmmm, The Mills Brothers	1958	$25
❑ DLP-25103 [S]	Mmmm, The Mills Brothers	1958	$85
❑ DLP-25872	My Shy Violet	1968	$75
❑ DLP-3363 [M]	San Antonio Rose	1961	$75
❑ DLP-25363 [S]	San Antonio Rose	1961	$85
❑ DLP-3592 [M]	Say Si Si and Other Great Latin Hits	1964	$75
❑ DLP-25592 [S]	Say Si Si and Other Great Latin Hits	1964	$75
❑ DLP-3652 [M]	Ten Years of Hits 1954-1964	1965	$75
❑ DLP-25652 [S]	Ten Years of Hits 1954-1964	1965	$75
❑ DLP-3744 [M]	That Country Feeling	1966	$75
❑ DLP-25744 [S]	That Country Feeling	1966	$75
❑ DLP-3508 [M]	The End of the World	1963	$75
❑ DLP-25508 [S]	The End of the World	1963	$75
❑ DLP-3157 [M]	The Mills Brothers' Great Hits	1958	$85
❑ DLP-25157 [S]	The Mills Brothers' Great Hits	1958	$85

—Black vinyl

| ❑ DLP-25157 [S] | The Mills Brothers' Great Hits | 195? | $250 |

—Blue vinyl

❑ DLP-3308 [M]	The Mills Brothers' Great Hits, Volume 2	1960	$75
❑ DLP-25308 [S]	The Mills Brothers' Great Hits, Volume 2	1960	$85
❑ DLP-25960	The Mills Brothers In Motion	1970	$75
❑ DLP-3783 [M]	The Mills Brothers Live	1967	$75
❑ DLP-25783 [S]	The Mills Brothers Live	1967	$75
❑ DLP-3237 [M]	The Mills Brothers Sing	1960	$85
❑ DLP-25237 [S]	The Mills Brothers Sing	1960	$85
❑ DL-3766 [M]	The Mills Brothers Today	1966	$75
❑ DLP-25766 [S]	The Mills Brothers Today	1966	$75
❑ DLP-3699 [M]	These Are the Mills Brothers	1966	$75
❑ DLP-25699 [S]	These Are the Mills Brothers	1966	$75
❑ DLP-3338 [M]	Yellow Bird	1960	$85
❑ DLP-25338 [S]	Yellow Bird	1960	$150

EVEREST ARCHIVE OF FOLK & JAZZ

| ❑ 300 | The Mills Brothers | 197? | $12 |
| ❑ 328 | The Mills Brothers, Volume 2 | 197? | $12 |

GNP CRESCENDO

| ❑ GNP-9106 | Four Boys and a Guitar | 197? | $12 |

HAMILTON

| ❑ HL-116 [M] | The Mills Brothers Sing for You | 1964 | $15 |
| ❑ HS-12116 [S] | The Mills Brothers Sing for You | 1964 | $15 |

MARK 56

| ❑ 709 | Original Radio Broadcasts | 197? | $12 |

MCA

❑ 717	16 Great Performances	1980	$10
❑ 132	Golden Favorites, Volume 2	1973	$12
❑ 15029	Merry Christmas	198?	$12
❑ 188	Old Golden Favorites	1973	$12
❑ 4039	The Best of the Mills Brothers	197?	$12
❑ 1556	The Mills Brothers	198?	$12
❑ 27083	The Mills Brothers Great Hits	1980	$10
❑ 28116	Were You There	198?	$10

MCA SPECIAL MARKETS

| ❑ MSM2-35067 | Classic Mills Brothers | 198? | $12 |

PARAMOUNT

| ❑ PAS-6038 | A Donut and a Dream | 1973 | $15 |

❑ PAS-5025	No Turnin' Back	1971	$15
❑ PAS-1010	The Best of the Mills Brothers	1973	$15
❑ PAS-1027	The Best of the Mills Brothers, Volume 2	1974	$20
❑ PAS-6024	What a Wonderful World	1972	$15

PICKWICK

❑ SPC-3076	14 Karat Gold	196?	$12
❑ SPC-3107	Anytime	197?	$12
❑ SPC-3220	Cab Driver	197?	$12
❑ SPC-3137	Dream a Little Dream	197?	$12
❑ SPC-1025	Merry Christmas	1979	$12

—Reissue of Dot album with one fewer track

❑ 2008	Songs You Remember	197?	$12
❑ 2030	The Mills Brothers	1973	$12
❑ SPC-3556	The Mills Brothers	1976	$10
❑ SPC-3158	Till We Meet Again	197?	$12

RANWOOD

❑ 7035	22 Great Hits	1985	$12
❑ 8152	50th Anniversary	197?	$12
❑ 8123	Cab Driver	197?	$12
❑ 8198	Command Performance	198?	$10
❑ 8139	Country's Greatest Hits	197?	$12
❑ 8133	The Mills Brothers Story	197?	$12

SUNNYVALE

| ❑ 1023 | Timeless | 1978 | $12 |

VOCALION

❑ VL3607 [M]	In a Mellow Tone	196?	$15
❑ VL73607 [R]	In a Mellow Tone	196?	$12
❑ VL73859 [R]	Such Sweet Singing	1969	$12

MILSAP, RONNIE

PAIR

| ❑ PDL2-1105 | Back on My Mind Again | 1986 | $15 |
| ❑ PDL2-1031 | Believe It! | 1986 | $15 |

PICKWICK

| ❑ JS-6179 | Plain and Simple | 197? | $12 |

RCA

| ❑ R183710 | Back to the Grindstone | 1991 | $25 |

—Only released on vinyl through BMG Direct Marketing

| ❑ 9588-1-R | Stranger Things Have Happened | 1989 | $12 |

RCA VICTOR

❑ APL1-1666	20-20 Vision	1976	$15
❑ APL1-0846	A Legend in My Time	1975	$18
❑ APD1-0846 [Q]	A Legend in My Time	1975	$30
❑ 5624-1-R	Christmas with Ronnie Milsap	1986	$12
❑ CPL1-7166	Collector's Series	1986	$10
❑ AHL1-3772	Greatest Hits	1980	$12
❑ AHL1-5425	Greatest Hits, Vol. 2	1985	$12
❑ 6425-1-R	Heart and Soul	1987	$12
❑ 7618-1-R	Heart and Soul	1988	$10

—Reissue of 6245

| ❑ AHL1-3346 | Images | 1979 | $15 |
| ❑ AYL1-4171 | Images | 1981 | $10 |

—Best Buy Series" reissue

| ❑ AHL1-4311 | Inside Ronnie Milsap | 1982 | $12 |
| ❑ AYL1-5142 | Inside Ronnie Milsap | 1984 | $10 |

—Best Buy Series" reissue

| ❑ AFL1-2439 | It Was Almost Like a Song | 1977 | $15 |
| ❑ AYL1-5139 | It Was Almost Like a Song | 1984 | $10 |

—Best Buy Series" reissue

| ❑ AHL1-4670 | Keyed Up | 1983 | $12 |
| ❑ AYL1-5435 | Keyed Up | 1985 | $10 |

—Best Buy Series" reissue

❑ AHL1-7194	Lost in the Fifties Tonight	1986	$12
❑ AHL1-3563	Milsap Magic	1980	$12
❑ APL1-1223	Night Things	1975	$18
❑ AHL1-5016	One More Try for Love	1984	$12
❑ AFL1-2780	Only One Love in My Life	1978	$15
❑ AAL1-3932	Out Where the Bright Lights Are Glowing	1981	$12
❑ APL1-0500	Pure Love	1974	$18
❑ APD1-0500 [Q]	Pure Love	1974	$30
❑ AYL1-3899	Pure Love	1981	$10

—Best Buy Series" reissue

| ❑ APL1-2043 | Ronnie Milsap Live | 1976 | $15 |
| ❑ AYL1-4255 | Ronnie Milsap Live | 1982 | $10 |

—Best Buy Series" reissue

| ❑ AHL1-4060 | There's No Gettin' Over Me | 1981 | $12 |
| ❑ AYL1-5140 | There's No Gettin' Over Me | 1984 | $10 |

—Best Buy Series" reissue

| ❑ APL1-0338 | Where My Heart Is | 1973 | $25 |
| ❑ AYL1-3760 | Where My Heart Is | 1980 | $10 |

—Best Buy Series" reissue

TIME-LIFE

| ❑ STW-110 | Country Music | 1981 | $12 |

WARNER BROS.

| ❑ BS2870 | A Rose By Any Other Name | 1975 | $18 |
| ❑ WS1934 | Ronnie Milsap | 1971 | $25 |

MILTON, ROY

KENT

| ❑ KLP-5054 [M] | The Great Roy Milton | 1963 | $50 |
| ❑ KST-554 [R] | The Great Roy Milton | 196? | $30 |

MIMMS, GARNET, AND THE ENCHANTERS

ARISTA

| ❑ AL4153 | Garnet Mimms Has It All | 1978 | $15 |

UNITED ARTISTS

❑ UAL3396 [M]	As Long As I Have You	1964	$50
❑ UAS6396 [S]	As Long As I Have You	1964	$80
❑ UAL3305 [M]	Cry Baby and 11 Other Hits	1963	$100
❑ UAS6305 [S]	Cry Baby and 11 Other Hits	1963	$150
❑ UAL3498 [M]	I'll Take Good Care of You	1966	$50
❑ UAS6498 [S]	I'll Take Good Care of You	1966	$80

MINASI, DOM

BLUE NOTE

| ❑ BN-LA426 | I Have the Feeling I've Been Here | 1975 | $35 |
| ❑ BN-LA258 | When Joanna Loved Me | 1974 | $35 |

MINCE, JOHNNY

JAZZOLOGY

| ❑ J-163 | Summer of '79 | 1989 | $25 |
| ❑ J-126 | The Master Comes Home | 1985 | $25 |

MONMOUTH-EVERGREEN

| ❑ 7090 | Summer of '79 | 1979 | $30 |

MIND EXPANDERS, THE

DOT

| ❑ DLP-3773 [M] | What's Happening | 1967 | $120 |
| ❑ DLP-25773 [S] | What's Happening | 1967 | $100 |

MIND GARAGE, THE

RCA VICTOR

| ❑ LSP-4218 | The Mind Garage | 1969 | $30 |
| ❑ LSP-4319 | The Mind Garage Again! | 1970 | $30 |

MINDBENDERS, THE

FONTANA

| ❑ MGF-27554 [M] | A Groovy Kind of Love | 1966 | $40 |

—With "Don't Cry No More

| ❑ MGF-27554 [M] | A Groovy Kind of Love | 1966 | $30 |

—With "Ashes to Ashes

| ❑ SRF-67554 [R] | A Groovy Kind of Love | 1966 | $30 |

—With "Don't Cry No More

| ❑ SRF-67554 [R] | A Groovy Kind of Love | 1966 | $25 |

—With "Ashes to Ashes

MINEO, SAL

EPIC

| ❑ LN3405 [M] | Sal | 1958 | $175 |

MINERVA JAZZ BAND

STOMP OFF

| ❑ SOS-1117 | A Pile of Logs and Stone Called Home | 1986 | $25 |

MINGUS, CHARLES

ABC IMPULSE!

| ❑ AS-35 [S] | Black Saint and Sinner Lady | 1968 | $250 |

—Black label with red ring

| ❑ AS-60 [S] | Charlie Mingus Plays Piano | 1968 | $250 |

—Black label with red ring

| ❑ AS-54 [S] | Mingus, Mingus, Mingus, Mingus, Mingus | 1968 | $250 |

—Black label with red ring

| ❑ AS-9234 | Reevaluation -- The Impulse Years | 1973 | $35 |

ATLANTIC

| ❑ SD1700 | 3 or 4 Shades | 1977 | $30 |
| ❑ 1305 [M] | Blues & Roots | 1959 | $300 |

—White "bullseye" label

| ❑ 1305 [M] | Blues & Roots | 1961 | $300 |

—Multicolor label, white "fan" logo at right

| ❑ 1305 [M] | Blues & Roots | 1964 | $30 |

—Multicolor label, black "fan" logo at right

| ❑ SD1305 [S] | Blues & Roots | 1959 | $300 |

—White "bullseye" label

| ❑ SD1305 [S] | Blues & Roots | 1961 | $300 |

—Multicolor label, white "fan" logo at right

| ❑ SD1305 [S] | Blues & Roots | 1964 | $25 |

—Multicolor label, black "fan" logo at right

❑ SD1677	Changes 1	1975	$30
❑ SD1678	Changes 2	1975	$30
❑ SD3001	Charles Mingus at Antibes	1979	$35
❑ SD8801	Cumbia & Jazz Fusion	197?	$30
❑ SD8803	Me, Myself An Eye	1979	$30
❑ SD1667	Mingus at Carnegie Hall	1974	$30
❑ SD1653	Mingus Moves	1974	$30
❑ 1377 [M]	Oh, Yeah	1961	$175

—Multicolor label, white "fan" logo at right

| ❑ 1377 [M] | Oh, Yeah | 1964 | $25 |

—Multicolor label, black "fan" logo at right

| ❑ SD1377 [S] | Oh, Yeah | 1961 | $175 |

—Multicolor label, white "fan" logo at right

| ❑ SD1377 [S] | Oh, Yeah | 1964 | NM |

—Multicolor label, black "fan" logo at right

Number	Title	Yr	NM
SD 3-600	Passions of a Man: The Charles Mingus Anthology	1980	$25
1237 [M]	Pithecanthropus Erectus	1956	$300
—Black label			
1237 [M]	Pithecanthropus Erectus	1961	$175
—Multicolor label, white "fan" logo at right			
1237 [M]	Pithecanthropus Erectus	1964	$25
—Multicolor label, black "fan" logo at right			
SD8809	Pithecanthropus Erectus	1981	$30
SD8805	Something Like a Bird	1979	$30
SD 2-302	The Art of Charles Mingus	1973	$35
SD1555	The Best of Charles Mingus	1970	$35
1260 [M]	The Clown	1957	$300
—Black label			
1260 [M]	The Clown	1961	$175
—Multicolor label, white "fan" logo at right			
1260 [M]	The Clown	1964	$25
—Multicolor label, black "fan" logo at right			
90142	The Clown	198?	$25
1417 [M]	Tonight at Noon	1964	$30
SD1417 [S]	Tonight at Noon	1964	$30

BARNABY

BR-5012	Charles Mingus Presents	1978	$30
Z30561	Charles Mingus Presents the Quartet	1971	$35
BR-6015	Stormy Weather	1976	$30
KZ31034	The Candid Recordings	1972	$35

BETHLEHEM

BCP-6026 [M]	A Modern Jazz Symposium of Jazz and Poetry	1958	$300
BCP-6019 [M]	East Coasting	1957	$300
BCP-6019	East Coasting	197?	$35
—Reissue, distributed by RCA Victor			
BCP-65 [M]	The Jazz Experiment of Charlie Mingus	1956	$300

BLUEBIRD

5644-1-RB	New Tijuana Moods	1986	$35

CANDID

CD-8005 [M]	Charles Mingus Presents Charles Mingus	1960	$40

CS-9005 [S]	Charles Mingus Presents Charles Mingus	1960	$50
CD-8021 [M]	Mingus	1960	$40
CS-9021 [S]	Mingus	1960	$50

CHARLES MINGUS

JWS-001/2	Mingus at Monterey	1966	$700
—Single-pocket jacket with sepia-tone photo on front			
JWS-001/2	Mingus at Monterey	1966	$300
—Gatefold jacket with color photo on front; "This album can be purchased only by mail" on back cover			
JWS-001/2	Mingus at Monterey	1968	$75
—Gatefold jacket with color photo on front; distributed by Fantasy			
JWS-005	My Favorite Quintet	1966	$300
—"This album can be purchased only by mail" on back cover			
JWS-013/14	Special Music Written For (But Not Heard At) Monterey	1966	$1000
—Single-pocket jacket; "This album can be purchased only by mail" on back cover			
JWS-009	Town Hall Concert 1964, Vol. 1	1966	$300
—"This album can be purchased only by mail" on back cover			

COLUMBIA

G30628	Better Git It in Your Soul	1971	$25
CG30628	Better Git It in Your Soul	197?	$30
—Reissue with new prefix			
KG31814	Charles Mingus and Friends	1973	$25
KC31039	Let My Children Hear Music	1972	$35
PC31039	Let My Children Hear Music	198?	$20
—Reissue with new prefix			
CL1370 [M]	Mingus Ah Um	1959	$100
—Red and black label with six "eye" logos			
CL1370 [M]	Mingus Ah Um	1963	$40

Number	Title	Yr	NM
—Red label with "Guaranteed High Fidelity" at bottom			
CL1370 [M]	Mingus Ah Um	1966	$30
—Red label with "360 Sound Mono" at bottom			
CS8171 [S]	Mingus Ah Um	1959	$120
—Red and black label with six "eye" logos			
CS8171 [S]	Mingus Ah Um	1963	$50
—Red label with "360 Sound Stereo" in black at bottom			
CS8171 [S]	Mingus Ah Um	1966	$40
—Red label with "360 Sound Stereo" in white at bottom			
CS8171 [S]	Mingus Ah Um	1971	$35
—Orange label, "Columbia" repeated along edge			
PC8171	Mingus Ah Um	198?	$20
—Budget-line reissue with new prefix			
CS8171 [S]	Mingus Ah Um	199?	$30
—Classic Records reissue on audiophile vinyl			
CL1440 [M]	Mingus Dynasty	1960	$30
—Red and black label with six "eye" logos			
CL1440 [M]	Mingus Dynasty	1963	$25
—Red label with "Guaranteed High Fidelity" at bottom			
CL1440 [M]	Mingus Dynasty	1966	$35
—Red label with "360 Sound Mono" at bottom			
CS8236 [S]	Mingus Dynasty	1960	$40
—Red and black label with six "eye" logos			
CS8236 [S]	Mingus Dynasty	1963	$30
—Red label with "360 Sound Stereo" in black at bottom			
CS8236 [S]	Mingus Dynasty	1966	$25
—Red label with "360 Sound Stereo" in white at bottom			
CS8236 [S]	Mingus Dynasty	1971	$30
—Orange label, "Columbia" repeated along edge			
JG35717	Nostalgia in Times Square	1979	$35

COLUMBIA JAZZ MASTERPIECES

CJ40648	Mingus Ah Um	1987	$25
CJ44050	Shoes of the Fisherman's Wife	1988	$25

DEBUT

DEB-123 [M]	Mingus at the Bohemia	1956	$500
DLP-1 [M]	Strings and Keys	1953	$500
DEB-139 [M]	The Charlie Mingus Quintet + Max Roach	1956	$0
—Canceled			

ENJA

3077	Mingus in Europe	198?	$30

EVEREST ARCHIVE OF FOLK & JAZZ

235	Charlie Mingus	1969	$30

FANTASY

6002 [M]	Chazz!	1962	$50
—Red vinyl			
6002 [M]	Chazz!	1962	$30
—Black vinyl			
86002 [R]	Chazz!	196?	$30
—Blue vinyl			
86002 [R]	Chazz!	196?	$35
—Black vinyl			
JWS-001/2	Mingus at Monterey	1969	$25
—Reissue of Charles Mingus 001/2			
OJC-045	Mingus at the Bohemia	198?	$25
JWS-005	My Favorite Quintet	1969	$35
—Reissue of Charles Mingus 005			
6017 [M]	Right Now -- Live at the Jazz Workshop	1966	$30
86017 [S]	Right Now -- Live at the Jazz Workshop	1966	$30
OJC-237	Right Now -- Live at the Jazz Workshop	198?	$25
6009 [M]	The Charlie Mingus Quartet + Max Roach	1963	$30
86009 [R]	The Charlie Mingus Quartet + Max Roach	196?	$35
OJC-440	The Charlie Mingus Quartet + Max Roach	1990	$30
OJC-042	Town Hall Concert 1964	198?	$25
JWS-009	Town Hall Concert 1964, Vol. 1	1969	$35
—Reissue of Charles Mingus 009			

GATEWAY

7026	His Final Work	1979	$30

GRP/IMPULSE!

217	Charlie Mingus Plays Piano	1997	$250
—Reissue on audiophile vinyl			

IMPULSE!

A-35 [M]	Black Saint and Sinner Lady	1963	$120
AS-35 [S]	Black Saint and Sinner Lady	1963	$160
A-60 [M]	Charlie Mingus Plays Piano	1964	$120
AS-60 [S]	Charlie Mingus Plays Piano	1964	$160
A-54 [M]	Mingus, Mingus, Mingus, Mingus, Mingus	1963	$120
AS-54 [S]	Mingus, Mingus, Mingus, Mingus, Mingus	1963	$160

JAZZ MAN

5002	Mingus	198?	$30
5048	Mingus Presents	198?	$30

JAZZTONE

J-1226 [M]	Jazz Experiment	1956	$75
J-1271 [M]	The Jazz Experiments of Charlie Mingus	1957	$50

Number	Title	Yr	NM

JOSIE

JOZ-3508 [M]	Mingus Three	1963	$30
JLPS-3508 [R]	Mingus Three	1963	$25

JUBILEE

JLP-1054 [M]	Mingus Trio	1958	$100

LIMELIGHT

LM-82015 [M]	Mingus Revisited	1965	$30
LS-86105 [S]	Mingus Revisited	1965	$30

MCA IMPULSE!

MCA-39119	Mingus, Mingus, Mingus, Mingus, Mingus	198?	$25
MCA-5649	The Black Saint and the Sinner Lady	1986	$25

MERCURY

MG-20627 [M]	Pre-Bird	1961	$150
SR-60627 [S]	Pre-Bird	1961	$150

MOSAIC

MQ4-143	The Complete 1959 CBS Charles Mingus Sessions	199?	$175
MR4-111	The Complete Candid Recordings of Charles Mingus	199?	$250
—Limited editon of 7,500			

PERIOD

SPL-1107 [10]	Jazzical Moods, Volume 1	1955	$250
SLP-1111 [10]	Jazzical Moods, Volume 2	1955	$250

PRESTIGE

24010	Charles Mingus	197?	$35
24100	Mingus at Monterey	198?	$35
24092	Portrait	1980	$35
24028	Reincarnation of a Lovebird	197?	$35
34001	The Great Concert	197?	$25

QUINTESSENCE

25171	Soul Fusion	197?	$30

RCA VICTOR

LPM-2533 [M]	Tijuana Moods	1962	$40
LSP-2533 [S]	Tijuana Moods	1962	$50
APL1-0939	Tijuana Moods	1974	$30
—Reissue of 2533			
LSP-2533 [S]	Tijuana Moods	199?	$30
—Classic Records reissue on audiophile vinyl			

SAVOY

MG-15050 [10]	Charlie Mingus	1955	$250
MG-12059 [M]	Jazz Composers Workshop	1956	$150

SAVOY JAZZ

SJL-1113	Jazz Workshop	197?	$25

SOLID STATE

SS-18024	Town Hall Concert	1968	$25
SS-18019	Wonderland	1968	$50

TRIP

5040	Charles Mingus Trio and Sextet	197?	$25
5017	Mingus Moods	197?	$25
5513	Mingus Revisited	197?	$25

UNITED ARTISTS

UAL-4036 [M]	Jazz Portraits	1959	$40
UAS-5036 [S]	Jazz Portraits	1959	$50
UAJ-14024 [M]	Town Hall Concert	1963	$40
UAJS-15024 [S]	Town Hall Concert	1963	$50
UAJ-14005 [M]	Wonderland	1962	$40
UAJS-15005 [S]	Wonderland	1962	$150
UAS-5637	Wonderland	1972	$30

WHO'S WHO IN JAZZ

21005	Lionel Hampton Presents Charles Mingus	1978	$35

MINGUS DYNASTY

ELEKTRA

6E-248	Chair in the Sky	1980	$25

SOUL NOTE

SN-1142	Mingus' Sound of Love	1988	$30
SN-1042	Reincarnation	1982	$30

MINIMAL KIDDS

INTUITION

C1-46879	No Age	1989	$30

MINION, FRANK

BETHLEHEM

BCP-6033 [M]	Forward Sound	1959	$250
BCP-6052 [M]	The Soft Land of Make Believe	1961	$250
BCPS-6052 [S]	The Soft Land of Make Believe	1961	$250

MINISTRY

ARISTA

AL6608	With Sympathy	1983	$14
AL68016	With Sympathy	198?	$12
—Reissue			

SIRE

25799	The Land of Rape and Honey	1988	$15

Number	Title	Yr	NM
❏ 26004	The Mind Is a Terrible Thing to Taste	1989	$15
❏ 25309	Twitch	1986	$15

WARNER BROS.

Number	Title	Yr	NM
❏ 45838	Filth Pig	1996	$25

WAX TRAX!

Number	Title	Yr	NM
❏ 035	Twelve Inch Singles 1981-84	1985	$18

MINK DEVILLE

ATLANTIC

Number	Title	Yr	NM
❏ SD19311	Coup De Grace	1981	$15
❏ 81623	Sportin' Life	1985	$10
❏ 80115	Where Angels Fear to Tread	1983	$12

CAPITOL

Number	Title	Yr	NM
❏ ST-11955	Le Chat Bleu	1980	$15
❏ ST-11631	Mink DeVille	1977	$15
❏ SW-11780	Return to Magenta	1978	$15
❏ SN-16282	Return to Magenta	1982	$10

—*Budget-line reissue*

| ❏ SN-16281 | Savoir Faire | 1982 | $10 |

—*Budget-line reissue of self-titled album*

MINNEAPOLIS MADRIGAL SINGERS, THE

LUTHERAN

Number	Title	Yr	NM
❏ TRF6910 [M]	Twelve Days of Christmas	1961	$18

MINNEAPOLIS SYMPHONY ORCHESTRA (ANTAL DORATI, CONDUCTOR)

MERCURY LIVING PRESENCE

Number	Title	Yr	NM
❏ SR90007 [S]	Albeniz-Artos: Iberia; Falla: Interlude and Dance	1959	$80

—*Maroon label, no "Vendor: Mercury Record Corporation*

| ❏ SR90098 [S] | Bartok: Suite No. 2 | 1959 | $40 |

—*Maroon label, no "Vendor: Mercury Record Corporation*

| ❏ SR90011 [S] | Beethoven: Symphony No. 3 | 1959 | $40 |

—*Maroon label, no "Vendor: Mercury Record Corporation*

| ❏ SR90288 [S] | Bloch: Sinfonia Brave; Peterson, Wayne: Free Variations for Orchestra | 196? | $100 |

—*Maroon label, no "Vendor: Mercury Record Corporation*

| ❏ SR90171 [S] | Brahms: Symphony No. 2 | 196? | $30 |

—*Maroon label, no "Vendor: Mercury Record Corporation*

| ❏ SR90172 [S] | Copland: Rodeo; El Salon Mexico; Danzon Cubano | 196? | $150 |

—*Maroon label, no "Vendor: Mercury Record Corporation*

| ❏ SR90172 [S] | Copland: Rodeo; El Salon Mexico; Danzon Cubano | 196? | $50 |

—*Maroon label, with "Vendor: Mercury Record Corporation*

| ❏ SR90248 [S] | Dorati: Symphony; Nocturne; Capriccio | 196? | $160 |

—*Maroon label, with "Vendor: Mercury Record Corporation*

| ❏ SR90499 [S] | Dorati: Symphony; Nocturne and Capriccio | 196? | $25 |

—*Maroon label, with "Vendor: Mercury Record Corporation*

| ❏ SR90132 [S] | Kodaly: Hary Janos Suite; Bartok: Hungarian Sketches; Rumanian Dances | 1960 | $120 |

—*Maroon label, no "Vendor: Mercury Record Corporation*

| ❏ SR90132 [S] | Kodaly: Hary Janos Suite; Bartok: Hungarian Sketches; Rumanian Dances | 196? | $30 |

—*Maroon label, with "Vendor: Mercury Record Corporation*

| ❏ SR90217 [S] | Mussorgsky: Pictures at an Exhibition | 196? | $220 |

—*Maroon label, no "Vendor: Mercury Record Corporation*

| ❏ SR90217 [S] | Mussorgsky: Pictures at an Exhibition | 196? | $40 |

—*Maroon label, with "Vendor: Mercury Record Corporation*

| ❏ SR90431 [S] | Offenbach: Gaite Parisienne; Gershwin: An American in Paris | 1965 | $25 |

—*Maroon label, no "Vendor: Mercury Record Corporation*

| ❏ SR90016 [S] | Offenbach: Gaite Parisienne; Strauss, Johann: Graduation Ball | 1959 | $25 |

—*Maroon label, no "Vendor: Mercury Record Corporation*

| ❏ SR90298 [S] | Respighi: Pines and Fountains of Rome | 196? | $50 |

—*Maroon label, no "Vendor: Mercury Record Corporation*

| ❏ SR90298 [S] | Respighi: Pines and Fountains of Rome | 196? | $30 |

—*Maroon label, with "Vendor: Mercury Record Corporation*

| ❏ SR90195 [S] | Rimsky-Korsakov: Scheherazade | 196? | $40 |

—*Maroon label, no "Vendor: Mercury Record Corporation*

| ❏ SR90139 [S] | Rossini: Overtures | 196? | $30 |

—*Maroon label, no "Vendor: Mercury Record Corporation*

| ❏ SR90139 [S] | Rossini: Overtures | 196? | $40 |

—*Maroon label, with "Vendor: Mercury Record Corporation"* (a rare case where the second edition is more sought after than the first)

| ❏ SR90282 [S] | Schuller: Seven Studies on Themes of Paul Klee; Fetler: Contrasts for Orchestra | 196? | $150 |

—*Maroon label, no "Vendor: Mercury Record Corporation*

| ❏ SR90282 [S] | Schuller: Seven Studies on Themes of Paul Klee; Fetler: Contrasts for Orchestra | 196? | $50 |

—*Maroon label, with "Vendor: Mercury Record Corporation*

Number	Title	Yr	NM
❏ SR90202 [S]	Strauss, Richard: Don Juan; Death and Transfiguration	196?	$100

—*Maroon label, no "Vendor: Mercury Record Corporation*

| ❏ SR90253 [S] | Stravinsky: Le Sacre du Printemps (The Rite of Spring) | 196? | $75 |

—*Maroon label, no "Vendor: Mercury Record Corporation*

| ❏ SR90253 [S] | Stravinsky: Le Sacre du Printemps (The Rite of Spring) | 196? | $25 |

—*Maroon label, with "Vendor: Mercury Record Corporation*

| ❏ SR90216 [S] | Stravinsky: Petrouchka | 196? | $100 |

—*Maroon label, no "Vendor: Mercury Record Corporation*

| ❏ SR90216 [S] | Stravinsky: Petrouchka | 196? | $30 |

—*Maroon label, with "Vendor: Mercury Record Corporation*

| ❏ SR90201 [S] | Tchaikovsky: March Slave; Polonaise and Waltz; Francesca da Rimini | 196? | $40 |

—*Maroon label, no "Vendor: Mercury Record Corporation*

| ❏ SR90201 [S] | Tchaikovsky: March Slave; Polonaise and Waltz; Francesca da Rimini | 196? | $30 |

—*Maroon label, no "Vendor: Mercury Record Corporation*

| ❏ SR90178 [S] | The Strauss Family Album | 196? | $25 |

—*Maroon label, no "Vendor: Mercury Record Corporation*

MINNEAPOLIS SYMPHONY ORCHESTRA (STANISLAW SKROWACZEWSKI, CONDUCTOR)

MERCURY LIVING PRESENCE

Number	Title	Yr	NM
❏ SR90060 [S]	Khachatourian: Gayne Ballet; Shostakovich: Symphony No. 5	1960	$300

—*Maroon label, no "Vendor: Mercury Record Corporation*

| ❏ SR90356 [S] | Mendelssohn: Symphony No. 4; Schubert: Symphony No. 5 | 196? | $30 |

—*Maroon label, no "Vendor: Mercury Record Corporation*

| ❏ SR90315 [S] | Prokofiev: Romeo and Juliet Ballet Suites 1 and 2 | 196? | $50 |

—*Maroon label, no "Vendor: Mercury Record Corporation*

| ❏ SR90315 [S] | Prokofiev: Romeo and Juliet Ballet Suites 1 and 2 | 196? | $25 |

—*Maroon label, with "Vendor: Mercury Record Corporation*

| ❏ SR90218 [S] | Schubert: Symphony in B "Unfinished" | 196? | $75 |

—*Maroon label, no "Vendor: Mercury Record Corporation*

| ❏ SR90218 [S] | Schubert: Symphony in B "Unfinished" | 196? | $25 |

—*Maroon label, with "Vendor: Mercury Record Corporation*

| ❏ SR90272 [S] | Schubert: Symphony No. 7 (9) in C | 196? | $50 |

—*Maroon label, no "Vendor: Mercury Record Corporation*

MINNELLI, LIZA

A&M

Number	Title	Yr	NM
❏ SP-4164	Come Saturday Morning	1969	$18
❏ SP-4345	Live at the Olympia	1971	$18
❏ SP-4141 [M]	Liza Minnelli	1968	$30

—*Mono copies have stereo numbers, but the labels are mono white label promos*

❏ SP-4141 [S]	Liza Minnelli	1968	$18
❏ SP-3524	Liza Minnelli Foursider	1973	$18
❏ SP-6013	Liza Minnelli Foursider	198?	$12

—*Reissue of 3524*

| ❏ SP-4272 | New Feelin' | 1970 | $18 |

CAPITOL

Number	Title	Yr	NM
❏ T2271 [M]	It Amazes Me	1965	$25
❏ ST2271 [S]	It Amazes Me	1965	$30
❏ SM-2271	It Amazes Me	1976	$12

—*Reissue with new prefix*

❏ T2174 [M]	Liza! Liza!	1964	$25
❏ ST2174 [S]	Liza! Liza!	1964	$30
❏ ST-11080	Maybe This Time	1972	$15
❏ SM-11080	Maybe This Time	197?	$12

—*Reissue with new prefix*

❏ T2448 [M]	There Is a Time	1966	$25
❏ ST2448 [S]	There Is a Time	1966	$30
❏ SM-11803	There Is a Time	1978	$12

—*Reissue of ST 2448*

COLUMBIA

Number	Title	Yr	NM
❏ PC32854	Live at the Winter Garden	1974	$18
❏ KC32149	Liza Minnelli The Singer	1973	$18
❏ PC32149	Liza Minnelli The Singer	198?	$10

—*Budget-line reissue*

❏ CQ32149 [Q]	Liza Minnelli The Singer	1973	$30
❏ KC31762	Liza with a "Z	1972	$18
❏ PC31762	Liza with a "Z	198?	$10

—*Budget-line reissue*

| ❏ PC34887 | Tropical Nights | 1977 | $15 |

EPIC

Number	Title	Yr	NM
❏ OE45098	Results	1989	$18

TELARC

Number	Title	Yr	NM
❏ 15502	Liza Minnelli at Carnegie Hall	1987	$18

MINNIE PEARL

STARDAY

Number	Title	Yr	NM
❏ SLP-380 [M]	America's Beloved Minnie Pearl	1965	$40
❏ SLP-224 [M]	Howdee!	1963	$40
❏ SLP-397 [M]	The Country Music Story	1966	$30

MINOR THREAT

DISCHORD

Number	Title	Yr	NM
❏ 10 [B]	Out of Step	1983	$50

—*Second stock pressing, gray back cover with photos*

| ❏ 10 [DJ] | Out of Step | 1983 | $500 |

—*Test pressing of 50; black silkscreen cover with sheep logo; paste-on back cover; blank labels; plain innersleeve with rubber stamp*

| ❏ 10 [B] | Out of Step | 1983 | $80 |

—*First stock pressing, black back cover with lyrics*

| ❏ 12 [EP] | The First Two 7" On a 12 | 1984 | $35 |

MINT CONDITION

PERSPECTIVE

Number	Title	Yr	NM
❏ 2896810011	Meant to Be Mint	1991	$18

MINT TATTOO

DOT

Number	Title	Yr	NM
❏ DLP-25918 [B]	Mint Tattoo	1969	$40

MINUTEMEN

Also see FIREHOSE. Featuring Mike Watt.

NEW ALLIANCE

Number	Title	Yr	NM
❏ 017 [B]	The Politics of Time	1984	$40

SST

Number	Title	Yr	NM
❏ 058 [B]	3-Way Tie (For Last)	1985	$30
❏ 068 [B]	Ballot Result	1987	$30
❏ 016 [EP]	Buzz or Howl Under the Influence of Heat	1983	$30
❏ 028 [B]	Double Nickels on the Dime	1984	$30
❏ PSST E-28 [DJ]	Excerpts from Double Nickels on the Dime	1984	$50

—*One-sided promo LP with etched B-side and sticker on blank cover*

| ❏ 034 [EP] | Project Mersh | 1985 | $30 |
| ❏ 277 [B] | The Politics of Time | 198? | $25 |

—*Reissue of New Alliance 017*

| ❏ 004 [B] | The Punch Line | 1981 | $40 |
| ❏ 004 [B] | The Punch Line | 1981 | $50 |

—*Original copies have white labels*

| ❏ 014 [B] | What Makes a Man Start Fires? | 1983 | $30 |
| ❏ 014 [B] | What Makes a Man Start Fires? | 1983 | $40 |

—*Original version has yellow labels and no UPC code*

MIRABAI

ATLANTIC

Number	Title	Yr	NM
❏ SD18144	Mirabai	1975	$12

MIRACLES, THE

COLUMBIA

Number	Title	Yr	NM
❏ PC34460	Love Crazy	1977	$15
❏ PCQ34460 [Q]	Love Crazy	1977	$75
❏ JC34910	The Miracles	1978	$15

MOTOWN

Number	Title	Yr	NM
❏ M5-136V1	Away We a Go-Go	1981	$10

—*Reissue of Tamla 271*

| ❏ 5254ML | Christmas with the Miracles | 1982 | $10 |

—*Reissue of Tamla 236*

| ❏ M5-217V1 | Doin' Mickey's Monkey | 1981 | $10 |

—*Reissue of Tamla 245*

| ❏ M5-133V1 | Do It Baby | 1981 | $10 |

—*Reissue of Tamla 334*

| ❏ M5-210V1 | Greatest Hits, Vol. 2 | 1981 | $10 |

—*Reissue of Tamla 280*

| ❏ M8-238M2 | Greatest Hits from the Beginning | 1982 | $15 |

—*Reissue of Tamla 254*

| ❏ M5-160V1 | Hi, We're the Miracles | 1981 | $10 |

—*Reissue of Tamla 220*

| ❏ M5-220V1 | Recorded Live on Stage | 1981 | $10 |

—*Reissue of Tamla 241*

| ❏ M793R3 | Smokey Robinson and the Miracles Anthology | 1974 | $25 |
| ❏ 5253ML | The Season for Miracles | 1982 | $10 |

—*Reissue of Tamla 307*

| ❏ M5-156V1 | The Tears of a Clown | 1981 | $10 |

—*Reissue of Tamla 276*

TAMLA

Number	Title	Yr	NM
❏ TS320	1957-1972	1972	$25
❏ TS306	A Pocket Full of Miracles	1970	$18
❏ T271 [M]	Away We a Go-Go	1966	$30
❏ TS271 [S]	Away We a Go-Go	1966	$30
❏ T236 [M]	Christmas with the Miracles	1963	$300

—*Originals have two globes on the top of the label*

| ❏ T6-339 | City of Angels | 1975 | $15 |
| ❏ T223 [M] | Cookin' with the Miracles | 1962 | $800 |

—*White label*

Number	Title	Yr	NM
❏ T245 [M]	Doin' Mickey's Monkey	1963	$250
❏ TS245 [S]	Doin' Mickey's Monkey	1963	$300
❏ T6-334	Do It Baby	1974	$15
❏ T6-336	Don't Cha Love It	1975	$15
❏ TS318	Flying High Together	1972	$18
❏ TS297	Four in Blue	1969	$25
❏ T267 [M]	Going to a Go-Go	1966	$30
❏ TS267 [S]	Going to a Go-Go	1966	$40
❏ T7-357	Greatest Hits	1977	$15
❏ TS280	Greatest Hits, Vol. 2	1968	$30
❏ T254 [M]	Greatest Hits from the Beginning	1965	$75
❏ TS254 [P]	Greatest Hits from the Beginning	1965	$40
❏ T220 [M]	Hi We're the Miracles	1961	$600
—White label			
❏ T230 [M]	I'll Try Something New	1962	$600
— White label			
❏ TS289	Live!	1969	$25

Number	Title	Yr	NM
❏ T276 [M]	Make It Happen	1967	$40
❏ TS276 [S]	Make It Happen	1967	$30
❏ TS312	One Dozen Roses	1971	$18
❏ T325F	Renaissance	1973	$15
❏ T290 [M]	Special Occasion	1968	$80
❏ TS290 [S]	Special Occasion	1968	$25
❏ T238 [M]	The Fabulous Miracles	1963	$300
❏ T241 [M]	The Miracles On Stage	1963	$250
❏ T6-344	The Power of Music	1976	$15
❏ TS307	The Season for Miracles	1970	$18
❏ TS276 [S]	The Tears of a Clown	1970	$18
—Retitled version of "Make It Happen"			
❏ TS295	Time Out for Smokey Robinson & the Miracles	1969	$25
❏ TS301	What Love Has…Joined Together	1970	$18
❏ T238 [M]	You've Really Got a Hold on Me	1963	$250
—Retitled version of "The Fabulous Miracles"			

MIRETTES, THE
REVUE
Number	Title	Yr	NM
❏ RS-7205	In the Midnight Hour	1968	$18

UNI
| ❏ 73062 | Whirlpool | 1969 | $18 |

MIRROR IMAGE
PICKWICK
| ❏ SPC-1026 | Disco Noel | 1979 | $12 |
| ❏ SPC-1027 | Yuletide Disco | 1979 | $12 |

MISFITS, THE
The famous punk band. Also see GLENN DANZIG; SAMHAIN.
CAROLINE
❏ 7515	Collection II	1995	$150
—Clear vinyl (500 made); sealed copies have bar code at upper right or not at all			
❏ 7515	Collection II	1995	$40
—Red vinyl (6,000 made); sealed copies have bar code roughly 1 inch from bottom of back cover			
❏ 7515	Collection II	1995	$30
—Green vinyl (3,500 made); sealed copies have bar code roughly 1/4 to 1/2 inch from bottom of back cover			
❏ 7511	Static Age	1995	$0
—Canceled; finally released on 7520			
❏ 7520	Static Age	1997	$150
—Purple vinyl (500 made)			
❏ 7520	Static Age	1997	$40
—Red vinyl (2,000 made)			
❏ 7520	Static Age	1997	$30
—Yellow vinyl (1,000 made)			

GEFFEN
| ❏ GEF25126 [B] | American Psycho | 1997 | $50 |

PLAN 9
❏ PL9-03 [EP]	Die, Die My Darling	1984	$300
—500 on purple vinyl			
❏ PL9-03 [EP]	Die, Die My Darling	1984	$300

Number	Title	Yr	NM
—500 on white vinyl (distributed by Caroline)			
❏ PL9-03 [EP]	Die, Die My Darling	1984	$15
—Common issue on black vinyl (distribued by Caroline)			
❏ PL9-02	Earth A.D.	1983	$800
—200 on dark purple vinyl			
❏ PL9-02	Earth A.D.	1983	$500
—500 on yellow vinyl			
❏ PL9-02	Earth A.D.	1983	$600
—200 on clear vinyl with red and blue swirls			
❏ PL9-02	Earth A.D.	1983	$1500
—100 on green vinyl			
❏ PL9-02	Earth A.D.	1983	$15
—At least 10,000 on black vinyl (distributed by Caroline)			
❏ PL9-08 [EP]	Evilive	1987	$150
—2,000 on green vinyl (distributed by Caroline)			
❏ PL9-08 [EP]	Evilive	1987	$25
—Black vinyl (distributed by Caroline)			
❏ PL9-06	Legacy of Brutality	1986	$500
—500 on red vinyl			
❏ PL9-06	Legacy of Brutality	1986	$300
—500 on white vinyl			
❏ PL9-06	Legacy of Brutality	1986	$5000
—16 (!!) on pink vinyl; VG value 2000; VG+ value 3500			
❏ PL9-06	Legacy of Brutality	1986	$25
—Black vinyl (distributed by Caroline)			
❏ PL9-09	Misfits	1988	$15

ROADRUNNER
| ❏ RR8658-1 | Famous Monsters | 1999 | $25 |
| —Picture disc | | | |

RUBY/SLASH
❏ JRR804	Walk Among Us	1982	$150
—Original red cover; has custom innersleeve and insert			
❏ JRR804	Walk Among Us	1982	$50
—Purple cover with innersleeve and insert			

SLASH
| ❏ 25756 | Walk Among Us | 1988 | $25 |
| —Reissue of JRR 804; some copies came with a Halloween bag, which can double or even triple the value! | | | |

MISSING PERSONS
CAPITOL
Number	Title	Yr	NM
❏ ST-12465	Color in Your Life	1986	$12
❏ MLP-15001 [EP]	Missing Persons	1982	$15
❏ ST-12315	Rhyme & Reason	1984	$12
❏ SN-16359	Rhyme & Reason	1985	$10
—Budget-line reissue			
❏ ST-12228	Spring Session M	1982	$15
❏ SN-16460	Spring Session M	1987	$10
—Budget-line reissue			

MISSOURI
PANAMA
| ❏ 1022 | Missouri | 1977 | $30 |

MISSOURIANS, THE
X
| ❏ LVA-3020 [10] | Harlem in the Twenties, Volume 1 | 1954 | $50 |

MISTER SPATS
PAUSA
| ❏ 7194 | Love Speaks | 1986 | $25 |

MISTLETOE DISCO BAND
HOLIDAY
| ❏ HDY-1019 | More Christmas Disco | 1980 | $12 |

MISTLETOE PLAYERS, THE
MISTLETOE
| ❏ MLP-1236 | A Golden Hour of Christmas Stories | 1978 | $12 |

MISTLETOE SINGERS, THE
MISTLETOE
| ❏ MLX-1211 | Happy Holidays | 197? | $18 |

MIT
HAT HUT
| ❏ 18 | MIT | 198? | $35 |

MITCHELL, BILLY
CATALYST
| ❏ 7611 | Now's the Time | 1976 | $30 |

OPTIMISM
| ❏ OP-2501 | Faces | 1987 | $25 |
| ❏ OP-2502 | In Focus | 1988 | $25 |

PAUSA
| ❏ 7158 | Blue City Jam | 198? | $25 |
| ❏ 7192 | Night Theme | 1986 | $25 |

SMASH
| ❏ MGS-27042 [M] | A Little Juicy | 1962 | $30 |

Number	Title	Yr	NM
❏ SRS-67042 [S]	A Little Juicy	1962	$30
❏ MGS-27027 [M]	This Is Billy Mitchell	1962	$30
❏ SRS-67027 [S]	This Is Billy Mitchell	1962	$30

TRIP
| ❏ 5534 | Billy Mitchell with Bobby Hutcherson | 197? | $25 |

XANADU
| ❏ 158 | Colossus of Detroit | 1978 | $30 |
| ❏ 182 | De Lawd's Blues | 198? | $25 |

MITCHELL, BLUE
ABC IMPULSE!
| ❏ AS-9328 | African Violet | 1977 | $35 |
| ❏ IA-9347 | Summer Soft | 1978 | $35 |

BLUE NOTE
❏ BST-84324	Bantu Village	1969	$40
—With "A Division of Liberty Records" on label			
❏ BLP-4257 [M]	Boss Horn	1967	$150
—With "A Division of Liberty Records" on label			
❏ BST-84257 [S]	Boss Horn	1967	$30
—With "A Division of Liberty Records" on label			
❏ BLP-4228 [M]	Bring It Home to Me	1966	$150
—New York, USA" on label			
❏ BST-84228 [S]	Bring It Home to Me	1966	$50
—With "New York, USA" address on label			
❏ BST-84228 [S]	Bring It Home to Me	1967	$75
—With "A Division of Liberty Records" on label			
❏ BST-84300	Collision in Black	1968	$30
—With "A Division of Liberty Records" on label			
❏ BLP-4214 [M]	Down With It	1965	$150
—New York, USA" on label			
❏ BST-84214 [M]	Down With It	1965	$50
—With "New York, USA" address on label			
❏ BST-84214 [S]	Down With It	1967	$75
—With "A Division of Liberty Records" on label			
❏ BST-84272	Heads Up!	1968	$30
—With "A Division of Liberty Records" on label			
❏ BLP-4142 [M]	Step Lightly	1963	$0
—Canceled			
❏ BST-84142 [S]	Step Lightly	1963	$0
—Canceled			
❏ LT-1082	Step Lightly	1980	$50
❏ BLP-4178 [M]	The Thing to Do	1964	$175
—New York, USA" on label			
❏ BST-84178 [S]	The Thing to Do	1964	$100
—With "New York, USA" address on label			
❏ BST-84178 [S]	The Thing to Do	1967	$75
—With "A Division of Liberty Records" on label			
❏ BST-84178 [S]	The Thing to Do	1985	$30
—The Finest in Jazz Since 1939" reissue			

FANTASY
| ❏ OJC-6009 | Blues on My Mind | 198? | $30 |
| ❏ OJC-615 | The Big Six | 1991 | $35 |

FORTISSIMO
| ❏ XK8006 | Brasses and Strings | 1961 | $175 |
| —Red vinyl; record plays from the inside out | | | |

JAM
| ❏ 5002 | Last Dance | 1977 | $50 |

MAINSTREAM
❏ MRL-315	Blue Mitchell	1971	$150
❏ MRL-374	Blue's Blues	1973	$40
❏ MRL-413	Booty	1974	$75
❏ MRL-400	Graffiti Blues	1974	$40
❏ MRL-392	Last Tango = Blues	1973	$175
—Reproductions exist			
❏ MRL-402	Many Shades of Blue Mitchell	1974	$40
❏ MRL-343	Vital	1972	$150

MCA
| ❏ 29050 | African Violet | 1980 | $25 |
| ❏ 29051 | Summer Soft | 1980 | $25 |

MILESTONE
| ❏ M-47055 | A Blue Time | 1979 | $75 |

MOSAIC
| ❏ MQ6-178 | The Complete Blue Note Sessions | 199? | $150 |

RCA VICTOR
| ❏ APL1-1493 | Funktion Junction | 1976 | $50 |
| ❏ APL1-1109 | Stratosonic Nuances | 1975 | $75 |

RIVERSIDE
❏ RLP-414 [M]	A Sure Thing	1962	$175
❏ RS-9414 [S]	A Sure Thing	1962	$175
❏ RLP-336 [M]	Blue's Moods	1960	$250
❏ RS-9336 [S]	Blue's Moods	1960	$250
❏ 6045	Blue's Moods	197?	$35
❏ RLP 12-309 [M]	Blue Soul	1959	$300
❏ RLP-1155 [S]	Blue Soul	1959	$300
❏ RLP 12-293 [M]	Out of the Blue	1958	$300
❏ RLP-1131 [S]	Out of the Blue	1959	$300
❏ RLP-367 [M]	Smooth as the Wind	1961	$250
❏ RS-9367 [S]	Smooth as the Wind	1961	$250
❏ RLP 12-273 [M]	The Big Six	1958	$300
❏ RLP-439 [M]	The Cup Bearers	1963	$175
❏ RS-9439 [S]	The Cup Bearers	1963	$175

Number	Title	Yr	NM
MITCHELL, CHAD, TRIO			
COLPIX			
❑ CP-463 [M]	Everybody's Listening	1964	$25
❑ SCP-463 [S]	Everybody's Listening	1964	$30
❑ CP-411 [M]	The Chad Mitchell Trio	1961	$25
❑ SCP-411 [S]	The Chad Mitchell Trio	1961	$30
KAPP			
❑ KL-1313 [M]	Chad Mitchell Trio In Action	1963	$25
❑ KS-3313 [S]	Chad Mitchell Trio In Action	1963	$30
❑ KL-1262 [M]	Mighty Day on Campus	1962	$25
❑ KS-3262 [S]	Mighty Day on Campus	1962	$30
❑ KGP-102BI [M]	My Gift to You	196?	$50
— Three-record boxed set containing KL-1262, KL-1281 and KL-1313 on mid-1960s reissue labels (black with white circle and "Kapp" vertical logo at top)			
❑ KL-1334 [M]	The Best of Chad Mitchell Trio	1963	$25
❑ KS-3334 [S]	The Best of Chad Mitchell Trio	1963	$30
❑ KL-1281 [M]	The Chad Mitchell Trio at the Bitter End	1962	$25
❑ KS-3281 [S]	The Chad Mitchell Trio at the Bitter End	1962	$30
MERCURY			
❑ MG-20891 [M]	Reflecting	1964	$18
❑ SR-60891 [S]	Reflecting	1964	$25
❑ MG-20838 [M]	Singin' Our Mind	1963	$18
❑ SR-60838 [S]	Singin' Our Mind	1963	$25
MITCHELL, CHAD			
BELL			
❑ 6028	Chad	1969	$18
WARNER BROS.			
❑ W1706 [M]	A Feeling of Love	1967	$25
❑ WS1706 [S]	A Feeling of Love	1967	$18
❑ W1667 [M]	Chad Mitchell Himself	1966	$18
❑ WS1667 [S]	Chad Mitchell Himself	1966	$25
MITCHELL, FREDDIE			
ALLEGRO ROYALE			
❑ 1600 [M]	That Boogie Beat	195?	$75
MITCHELL, GROVER			
STASH			
❑ ST-277	Truckin' with Grover Mitchell and His Orchestra	1988	$25
MITCHELL, GUY			
COLUMBIA			
❑ CL1211 [M]	Guy in Love	1958	$40
❑ CS8011 [S]	Guy in Love	1959	$50
❑ CL1226 [M]	Guy's Greatest Hits	1959	$50
— Red and black label with six "eye" logos			
❑ CL1226 [M]	Guy's Greatest Hits	1962	$30
— Guaranteed High Fidelity" on red label			
❑ CL1226 [M]	Guy's Greatest Hits	1965	$25
— 360 Sound Mono" on red label			
❑ CL6231 [10]	Open Spaces	1953	$80
❑ CL1552 [M]	Sunshine Guitar	1960	$30
❑ CS8352 [S]	Sunshine Guitar	1960	$40
KING			
❑ 644 [M]	Sincerely Yours	1959	$300
NASHVILLE			
❑ 2074	Heartaches	1970	$15
STARDAY			
❑ 432	Singin' Up a Storm	1969	$25
❑ 412	Traveling Shoes	1968	$25
MITCHELL, JONI			
ASYLUM			
❑ 7E-1001	Court and Spark	1974	$12
❑ EQ-1001 [Q]	Court and Spark	1974	$100
❑ BB-701	Don Juan's Reckless Daughter	1977	$15
❑ SD5057	For the Roses	1972	$12
❑ 7E-1087	Hejira	1976	$12

Number	Title	Yr	NM
❑ AB-202 [B]	Miles of Aisles	1974	$12
❑ 5E-505	Mingus	1979	$25
❑ BB-704	Shadows and Light	1980	$30
❑ 7E-1051	The Hissing of Summer Lawns	1975	$12
❑ EQ-1051 [Q]	The Hissing of Summer Lawns	1975	$100
DCC COMPACT CLASSICS			
❑ LPZ-2069	Blue	2000	$0
— Audiophile vinyl; canceled			
❑ LPZ-2044	Court and Spark	1997	$120
— Audiophile vinyl			
GEFFEN			
❑ GHS24172	Chalk Mark in a Rain Storm	1988	$10
❑ GHS24074	Dog Eat Dog	1985	$10
❑ GEF24302	Night Ride Home	1991	$18
❑ GHS2019	Wild Things Run Fast	1982	$10
❑ PRO-A-1081 [DJ]	Wild Things Run Fast Sampler	1982	$15
— Promo-only 4-song EP			
NAUTILUS			
❑ NR-11	Court and Spark	1980	$75
— Audiophile vinyl			
REPRISE			
❑ MS2038	Blue	1970	$18
❑ RS6341	Clouds	1969	$25
— With "W7" and "r:" logos on two-tone orange label			
❑ RS6341	Clouds	1970	$15
— With only "r:" logo on all-orange (tan) label			
❑ RS6293 [S]	Joni Mitchell	1968	$25
— With "W7" and "r:" logos on two-tone orange label			
❑ RS6293 [S]	Joni Mitchell	1970	$15
— With only "r:" logo on all-orange (tan) label			
❑ R6293 [M]	Joni Mitchell	1968	$150
— White label promo; evidently, no stock copies were issued in mono			
❑ RS6376	Ladies of the Canyon	1970	$25
— With "W7" and "r:" logos on two-tone orange label			
❑ RS6376	Ladies of the Canyon	1970	$15
— With only "r:" logo on all-orange (tan) label			
RHINO VINYL			
❑ 74842	Blue	2007	$30
— Reissue on 180-gram vinyl; has replica Reprise label			
MITCHELL, MARTY			
MC			
❑ MC6-511S1	You Are the Sunshine of My Life	1977	$15
MITCHELL, OLLIE			
PAUSA			
❑ 7128	Blast Off	198?	$25
MITCHELL, PAUL			
VERVE			
❑ V-8713 [M]	Live at the Atlanta Playboy Club	1967	$25
❑ V6-8713 [S]	Live at the Atlanta Playboy Club	1967	$30
MITCHELL, PRICE			
BRYLEN			
❑ BN-4402	Can't Live Without You	1982	$12
GRT			
❑ 8008	Mr. Country Soul	197?	$18
SUNBIRD			
❑ SN-50108	The Best of Price Mitchell	1979	$15
MITCHELL, RED, AND HAROLD LAND			
ATLANTIC			
❑ 1376 [M]	Hear Ye!	1961	$175
— Multicolor label, white "fan" logo at right			
❑ 1376 [M]	Hear Ye!	1964	$25
— Multicolor label, black "fan" logo at right			
❑ SD1376 [S]	Hear Ye!	1961	$175
— Multicolor label, white "fan" logo at right			
❑ SD1376 [S]	Hear Ye!	1964	$30
— Multicolor label, black "fan" logo at right			
MITCHELL, RED			
BETHLEHEM			
❑ BCP-1033 [10]	Happy Minors	1955	$400
❑ BCP-38 [M]	Jam for Your Bread	1956	$300
CONTEMPORARY			
❑ C-3538 [M]	Presenting Red Mitchell	1957	$300
FANTASY			
❑ OJC-158	Presenting Red Mitchell	198?	$30
PACIFIC JAZZ			
❑ PJ-22 [M]	Rejoice	1961	$30
❑ ST-22 [S]	Rejoice	1961	$40

Number	Title	Yr	NM
PAUSA			
❑ 7018	Red Mitchell Meets Manusardi	198?	$25
STEEPLECHASE			
❑ SCS-1161	Chocolate Cadillac	198?	$30
MITCHELL, ROSCOE			
Also see ART ENSEMBLE OF CHICAGO. Reeds player.			
BLACK SAINT			
❑ BSR-0050	3 X 4 Eye	198?	$30
❑ BSR-0070	Roscoe Mitchell and Sound and Space Ensembles	198?	$30
DELMARK			
❑ D-408 [M]	Roscoe Mitchell Sextet	1966	$30
❑ DS-408 [S]	Roscoe Mitchell Sextet	1966	$25
NESSA			
❑ N-2	Congliptious	1968	$30
❑ N-14/15	L-R-G/The Maze/S II Examples	1980	$25
❑ N-9/10	Nonaah	1977	$30
❑ N-5	Old/Quartet	197?	$35
❑ N-20	Snurdy McGurdy and Her Dancin' Shoes	1981	$35
MITCHELL, WHITEY			
ABC-PARAMOUNT			
❑ ABC-126 [M]	Whitey Mitchell Sextette	1956	$150
MITCHELL, WILLIE			
BEARSVILLE			
❑ BRK3520	... Listen ... Dance	1980	$12
HI			
❑ HL-32029 [M]	Driving Beat	1966	$30
❑ SHL-32029 [S]	Driving Beat	1966	$30
❑ HL-32021 [M]	Hold It	1964	$30
❑ SHL-32021 [S]	Hold It	1964	$30
❑ HL-32026 [M]	It's Dance Time	1965	$30
❑ SHL-32036 [S]	It's Dance Time	1965	$30
❑ SHL-32048	On Top	1969	$30
❑ HL-32039 [M]	Ooh Baby, You Turn Me On	1967	$30
❑ SHL-32039 [S]	Ooh Baby, You Turn Me On	1967	$30
❑ SHL-32058	Robin's Nest	1970	$30
❑ SHL-32045	Solid Soul	1968	$30
❑ SHL-32050	Soul Bag	1969	$30
❑ HL-32010 [M]	Sunrise Serenade	1963	$40
❑ SHL-32010 [S]	Sunrise Serenade	1963	$30
❑ SHL-32068/9	The Best of Willie Mitchell	1971	$30
❑ HL-32034 [M]	The Hit Sound of Willie Mitchell	1967	$30
❑ SHL-32034 [S]	The Hit Sound of Willie Mitchell	1967	$30
❑ SHL-32056	The Many Moods of Willie Mitchell	1970	$30
❑ SHL-32042	Willie Mitchell Live	1968	$30
❑ 8002	Willie Mitchell Live	1977	$12
MITCHELL-RUFF DUO, THE			
ATLANTIC			
❑ 1458 [M]	After This Message	1966	$25
❑ SD1458 [S]	After This Message	1966	$30
❑ 1374 [M]	The Catbird Seat	1961	$175
— Multicolor label, white "fan" logo at right			
❑ 1374 [M]	The Catbird Seat	1964	$35
— Multicolor label, black "fan" logo at right			
❑ SD1374 [S]	The Catbird Seat	1961	$175
— Multicolor label, white "fan" logo at right			
❑ SD1374 [S]	The Catbird Seat	1964	$50
— Multicolor label, black "fan" logo at right			
EPIC			
❑ LN3318 [M]	Campus Concert	1956	$100
❑ LN3221 [M]	The Mitchell-Ruff Duo	1956	$100
FORUM			
❑ F-9031 [M]	Jazz Mission to Moscow	196?	$30
— Reissue of Roulette R-52034			
❑ SF-9031 [S]	Jazz Mission to Moscow	196?	$35
— Reissue of Roulette SR-52034			
MAINSTREAM			
❑ MRL-335	Strayhorn	1972	$35
ROULETTE			
❑ R-52002 [M]	Appearing Nightly	1958	$40
❑ SR-52002 [S]	Appearing Nightly	1959	$30
❑ R-52025 [M]	Jazz for Juniors	1959	$30
❑ SR-52025 [S]	Jazz for Juniors	1959	$30
❑ R-52034 [M]	Jazz Mission to Moscow	1959	$30
❑ SR-52034 [S]	Jazz Mission to Moscow	1959	$30
❑ R-52013 [M]	The Mitchell-Ruff Duo Plus Strings and Brass	1958	$40
❑ SR-52013 [S]	The Mitchell-Ruff Duo Plus Strings and Brass	1959	$30
❑ R-52037 [M]	The Sound of Music	1960	$30
❑ SR-52037 [S]	The Sound of Music	1960	$30
MITCHELL TRIO, THE			
MERCURY			
❑ MG-21049 [M]	That's the Way It's Gonna Be	1965	$18
❑ SR-61049 [S]	That's the Way It's Gonna Be	1965	$25

Number	Title	Yr	NM
❏ MG-20944 [M]	The Slightly Irreverent Mitchell Trio	1964	$18
❏ SR-60944 [S]	The Slightly Irreverent Mitchell Trio	1964	$25
❏ MG-20992 [M]	Typical American Boys	1965	$18
❏ SR-60992 [S]	Typical American Boys	1965	$25
❏ MG-21067 [M]	Violets of Dawn	1966	$18
❏ SR-61067 [S]	Violets of Dawn	1966	$25

REPRISE

Number	Title	Yr	NM
❏ R-6258 [M]	Alive	1967	$25
❏ RS-6258 [S]	Alive	1967	$18

MITCHELLS, THE
METROJAZZ

Number	Title	Yr	NM
❏ E-1012 [M]	Get Those Elephants Out'a Here	1958	$200
❏ SE-1012 [S]	Get Those Elephants Out'a Here	1958	$175

MITCHUM, ROBERT
CAPITOL

Number	Title	Yr	NM
❏ T853 [M]	Calypso -- Is Like So...	1957	$150

MONUMENT

Number	Title	Yr	NM
❏ MLP-8066 [M]	That Man, Robert Mitchum, Sings	1967	$30
❏ SLP-18066 [S]	That Man, Robert Mitchum, Sings	1967	$30

MIXTURES, THE (1)
LINDA

Number	Title	Yr	NM
❏ 3301 [M]	Stompin' at the Rainbow	1962	$150

MIZE, BILLY
IMPERIAL

Number	Title	Yr	NM
❏ LP-12441	This Time and Place	1969	$25

UNITED ARTISTS

Number	Title	Yr	NM
❏ UAS-6781	You're Alright with Me	1971	$18

ZODIAC

Number	Title	Yr	NM
❏ 5007	Love 'n' Stuff	1976	$15

MJT + 3
ARGO

Number	Title	Yr	NM
❏ LP-621 [M]	Daddy-O Presents MJT + 3	1957	$40

TRIP

Number	Title	Yr	NM
❏ 5025	Branching Out	197?	$30

VEE JAY

Number	Title	Yr	NM
❏ LP-3008 [M]	Make Everybody Happy	1960	$30
❏ SR-3008 [S]	Make Everybody Happy	1960	$30
❏ LP-3014 [M]	MJT + 3	1961	$30
❏ SR-3014 [S]	MJT + 3	1961	$30
❏ LP-1013 [M]	Walter Perkins' MJT + 3	1959	$30
❏ SR-1013 [S]	Walter Perkins' MJT + 3	1959	$40

MOB, THE
COLOSSUS

Number	Title	Yr	NM
❏ CS-1006	The Mob	1971	$25

MGM

Number	Title	Yr	NM
❏ SE-4839	The Mob	1972	$18

PRIVATE STOCK

Number	Title	Yr	NM
❏ PS-2005	The Mob	1975	$15

MOBLEY, HANK
BLUE NOTE

Number	Title	Yr	NM
❏ BLP-4230 [M]	A Caddy for Daddy	1966	$1000
— With "New York, USA" address on label			
❏ BST-84230 [S]	A Caddy for Daddy	1966	$400
— With "New York, USA" address on label			
❏ BST-84230 [S]	A Caddy for Daddy	1967	$40
— With "A Division of Liberty Records" on label			
❏ BST-84431	Another Workout	1986	$50
❏ B1-33582	A Slice Off the Top	1995	$35
— The Finest in Jazz Since 1939" reissue			
❏ BLP-4209 [M]	Dippin'	1965	$175
— With "New York, USA" address on label			
❏ BST-84209 [S]	Dippin'	1965	$150
— With "New York, USA" address on label			
❏ BST-84209 [S]	Dippin'	1967	$40
— With "A Division of Liberty Records" on label			
❏ BST-84425	Far Away Lands	1985	$50
❏ BLP-1560 [M]	Hank	1957	$1000
— Deep groove" version (deep indentation under label on both sides)			
❏ BLP-1560 [M]	Hank	1957	$1500
— Regular version, W. 63rd St. address on label			
❏ BLP-1560 [M]	Hank	1963	$140
— With "New York, USA" address on label			
❏ BST-81560 [R]	Hank	1967	$25
— With "A Division of Liberty Records" on label			
❏ BLP-1550 [M]	Hank Mobley	1957	$1200
— Deep groove" version; W.63rd St. address on label			
❏ BLP-1550 [M]	Hank Mobley	1957	$300
— Regular version, W. 63rd St. address on label			
❏ BLP-1550 [M]	Hank Mobley	1963	$175
— With "New York, USA" address on label			

Number	Title	Yr	NM
❏ BST-81550 [R]	Hank Mobley	1967	$25
— With "A Division of Liberty Records" on label			
❏ BLP-1568 [M]	Hank Mobley	1957	$10000
— Deep groove" version; W. 63rd St. address on label			
❏ BLP-1568 [M]	Hank Mobley	1957	$800
— Regular version, W. 63rd St. address on label			
❏ BLP-1568 [M]	Hank Mobley	1963	$100
— With "New York, USA" address on label			
❏ BST-1568 [S]	Hank Mobley	1959	$400
— Deep groove" version; W. 63rd St. address on label			
❏ BST-1568 [S]	Hank Mobley	1959	$250
— Regular version, W. 63rd St. address on label			
❏ BST-1568 [S]	Hank Mobley	1963	$40
— With "New York, USA" address on label			
❏ BST-81568 [S]	Hank Mobley	1967	$25
— With "A Division of Liberty Records" on label			
❏ BLP-4241 [M]	Hank Mobley	1966	$0
— Canceled			
❏ BST-84241 [S]	Hank Mobley	1966	$0
— Canceled			
❏ BLP-1568 [M]	Hank Mobley	200?	$75
— 200-gram reissue, distributed by Classic Records			
❏ BLP-1544 [M]	Hank Mobley and His All Stars	1957	$800
— Deep groove" version; W. 63rd St. address on label			
❏ BLP-1544 [M]	Hank Mobley and His All Stars	1957	$300
— Regular version, W. 63rd St. address on label			
❏ BLP-1544 [M]	Hank Mobley and His All Stars	1963	$250
— With "New York, USA" address on label			
❏ BST-81544 [R]	Hank Mobley and His All Stars	1967	$25
— With "A Division of Liberty Records" on label			
❏ BLP-5066 [10]	Hank Mobley Quartet	1955	$1500
❏ BLP-1540 [M]	Hank Mobley with Donald Byrd and Lee Morgan	1957	$700
— Deep groove" version; W. 63rd St. address on label			
❏ BLP-1540 [M]	Hank Mobley with Donald Byrd and Lee Morgan	1957	$1000
— Deep groove" version, Lexington Ave. address on label			
❏ BLP-1540 [M]	Hank Mobley with Donald Byrd and Lee Morgan	1963	$850
— With "New York, USA" address on label			
❏ BST-81540 [R]	Hank Mobley with Donald Byrd and Lee Morgan	1967	$25
— With "A Division of Liberty Records" on label			
❏ BST-84273	High Voltage	1986	$30
— The Finest in Jazz Since 1939" reissue			
❏ BLP-4273 [M]	Hi Voltage	1968	$500
— With "A Division of Liberty Records" address on label			
❏ BST-84273 [S]	Hi Voltage	1968	$150
— With "A Division of Liberty Records" on label			
❏ BLP-4149 [M]	No Room for Squares	1963	$250
— With "New York, USA" address on label			
❏ BST-84149 [S]	No Room for Squares	1963	$150
— With "New York, USA" address on label			
❏ BST-84149 [S]	No Room for Squares	1967	$40
— With "A Division of Liberty Records" on label			
❏ B1-84149	No Room for Squares	1989	$35
— The Finest in Jazz Since 1939" reissue			
❏ BLP-1574 [M]	Peckin' Time	1958	$1500
— Deep groove" version; W. 63rd St. address on label			
❏ BLP-1574 [M]	Peckin' Time	1958	$300
— Regular version, W. 63rd St. address on label			
❏ BLP-1574 [M]	Peckin' Time	1963	$250
— With "New York, USA" address on label			
❏ BST-81574 [R]	Peckin' Time	1967	$25
— With "A Division of Liberty Records" on label			
❏ B1-81574	Peckin' Time	1988	$30
— The Finest in Jazz Since 1939" reissue			
❏ BST-84288	Reach Out!	1968	$100
— With "A Division of Liberty Records" on label			
❏ BLP-4058 [M]	Roll Call	1961	$800
— With W. 63rd St. address on label			
❏ BLP-4058 [M]	Roll Call	1963	$150
— With "New York, USA" address on label			
❏ BST-84058 [S]	Roll Call	1961	$250
— With W. 63rd St. address on label			
❏ BST-84058 [S]	Roll Call	1963	$40
— With "New York, USA" address on label			
❏ BST-84058 [S]	Roll Call	1967	$75
— With "A Division of Liberty Records" on label			
❏ BST-84058	Roll Call	199?	$30
— 180-gram reissue; distributed by Classic Records			
❏ LT-995	Slice Off the Top	1979	$50
❏ BLP-4031 [M]	Soul Station	1960	$1000
— Deep groove" version; W. 63rd St. address on label			
❏ BLP-4031 [M]	Soul Station	1960	$250
— Regular version, W. 63rd St. address on label			
❏ BLP-4031 [M]	Soul Station	1963	$100
— With "New York, USA" address on label			
❏ BST-84031 [S]	Soul Station	1960	$250
— With W. 63rd St. address on label			
❏ BST-84031 [S]	Soul Station	1963	$40
— With "New York, USA" address on label			

Number	Title	Yr	NM
❏ BST-84031 [S]	Soul Station	1967	$75
— With "A Division of Liberty Records" on label			
❏ BST-84031	Soul Station	1987	$35
— The Finest in Jazz Since 1939" reissue			
❏ BST-84435	Straight No Filter	1986	$75
❏ BST-84329	The Flip	1969	$100
— With "A Division of Liberty Records" on label			
❏ BLP-4186 [M]	The Turnaround!	1964	$250
— With "New York, USA" address on label			
❏ BST-84186 [S]	The Turnaround!	1964	$150
— With "New York, USA" address on label			
❏ BST-84186 [S]	The Turnaround!	1967	$40
— With "A Division of Liberty Records" on label			
❏ B1-84186	The Turnaround!	1989	$35
— The Finest in Jazz Since 1939" reissue			
❏ LT-1045	Thinking of Home	1980	$75
❏ LT-1081	Third Season	1981	$75
❏ BLP-4080 [M]	Workout	1961	$1000
— With W. 63rd St. address on label			

Number	Title	Yr	NM
❏ BLP-4080 [M]	Workout	1963	$600
— With "New York, USA" address on label			
❏ BST-84080 [S]	Workout	1961	$250
— With W. 63rd St. address on label			
❏ BST-84080 [S]	Workout	1963	$300
— With "New York, USA" address on label			
❏ BST-84080 [S]	Workout	1967	$75
— With "A Division of Liberty Records" on label			
❏ B1-84080	Workout	1988	$30
— The Finest in Jazz Since 1939" reissue			

NEW JAZZ

Number	Title	Yr	NM
❏ NJLP-8311 [M]	52nd Street Theme	1963	$0
— Canceled; reassigned to Status			

PRESTIGE

Number	Title	Yr	NM
❏ PRST-7661	Hank Mobley's Message	1969	$75
❏ P-24063	Messages	1976	$75
❏ PRLP-7061 [M]	Mobley's Message	1956	$800
— Yellow label with W. 50th St. address			
❏ PRLP-7082 [M]	Mobley's Second Message	1957	$650
— Yellow label with W. 50th St. address			
❏ PRST-7667	Mobley's Second Message	1969	$75

SAVOY

Number	Title	Yr	NM
❏ MG-12092 [M]	Jazz Message #2	1956	$400

STATUS

Number	Title	Yr	NM
❏ ST-8311 [M]	52nd Street Theme	1965	$100

MOBY GRAPE
Also see ALEXANDER "SKIP" SPENCE.

COLUMBIA

Number	Title	Yr	NM
❏ MGS1	Grape Jam	1968	$25
❏ C31098	Great Grape	1972	$18
❏ CL2698 [M]	Moby Grape	1967	$175
— Cover has Don Stephenson "giving the finger" on his washboard			
❏ CS9498 [S]	Moby Grape	1967	$150
— Cover has Don Stephenson "giving the finger" on his washboard			
❏ CL2698 [M]	Moby Grape	1967	$50
— Cover has offending finger airbrushed out			
❏ CS9498 [S]	Moby Grape	1967	$25
— Cover has offending finger airbrushed out			
❏ CS9498	Moby Grape	1971	$15
— Orange label; with poster			
❏ CS9696	Moby Grape '69	1969	$25
❏ 2698/9498	Moby Grape Poster	1967	$18
— Poster has Don Stephenson "giving the finger" on his washboard			
❏ 2698/9498	Moby Grape Poster	1967	$10
— Poster has offending finger airbrushed out			
❏ CS9912	Truly Fine Citizen	1969	$25
❏ CS9613 [M]	Wow	1968	$40
— Special Mono Radio Station Copy" with white label			

Number	Title	Yr	NM
❏ CS9613	Wow	1968	$25
❏ CXS3	Wow/Grape Jam	1968	$30
—Joint release of the two albums under one cover			
❏ CXS3	Wow/Grape Jam	1971	$18
—Orange labels			

ESCAPE

| ❏ ESA1 | Live Grape | 1978 | $18 |

HARMONY

| ❏ KH30392 | Omaha | 1971 | $18 |

REPRISE

| ❏ RS6460 | 20 Granite Creek | 1971 | $25 |

SUNDAZED

❏ LP-5227	Grape Jam	2007	$25
—Reissue of Columbia MGS 1			
❏ LP-5225 [M]	Moby Grape	2007	$30
—Reissue of Columbia 2698 with poster			
❏ LP-5228	Moby Grape '69	2007	$18
—Reissue of Columbia 9696			
❏ LP-5226	Wow	2007	$25
—Reissue of Columbia 9613			

MOCEDADES

TARA

| ❏ 53000 | Eres Tu "Touch the Wind" | 1974 | $15 |

MOD AND THE ROCKERS

JUSTICE

| ❏ JLP-153 | Mod and the Rockers Now! | 1967 | $400 |

MODELS, THE

GEFFEN

| ❏ GHS24100 | Out of Mind Out of Sight | 1986 | $12 |

WINDSONG

| ❏ BXL1-3642 | Yes with My Body | 1980 | $15 |

MODERN ENGLISH

SIRE

❏ 23821	After the Snow	1982	$12
❏ 25066	Ricochet Days	1984	$12
❏ 25343	Stop Start	1986	$12

TVT

| ❏ 2810 | Pillow Lips | 1990 | $12 |

MODERN FOLK QUARTET, THE

WARNER BROS.

❏ W1546 [M]	Changes	1964	$30
❏ WS1546 [S]	Changes	1964	$30
❏ W1511 [M]	The Modern Folk Quartet	1963	$30
❏ WS1511 [S]	The Modern Folk Quartet	1963	$30

MODERN JAZZ DISCIPLES, THE

NEW JAZZ

❏ NJLP-8222 [M]	Modern Jazz Disciples	1959	$300
—Purple label			
❏ NJLP-8222 [M]	Modern Jazz Disciples	1965	$175
—Blue label, trident logo at right			
❏ NJLP-8240 [M]	Right Down Front	1960	$175
—Purple label			
❏ NJLP-8240 [M]	Right Down Front	1965	$175
—Blue label, trident logo at right			

MODERN JAZZ QUARTET, THE

APPLE

❏ STAO-3360	Space	1970	$30
❏ STAO-5-3360	Space	1970	$100
—Capitol Record Club edition			
❏ ST-3353	Under the Jasmine Tree	1969	$30
❏ ST-5-3353	Under the Jasmine Tree	1969	$100
—Capitol Record Club edition			

ATLANTIC

❏ 1420 [M]	A Quartet Is a Quartet Is a Quartet	1964	$35
❏ SD1420 [S]	A Quartet Is a Quartet Is a Quartet	1964	$25
—Multicolor label, black "fan" logo at right			
❏ SD1420 [S]	A Quartet Is a Quartet Is a Quartet	1969	$25
—Red and green label			
❏ 1468 [M]	Blues at Carnegie Hall	1967	$35
❏ SD1468 [S]	Blues at Carnegie Hall	1967	$35
—Blue and green label, black "fan" logo at right			
❏ SD1468 [S]	Blues at Carnegie Hall	1969	$30
—Red and green label			
❏ SD1652	Blues on Bach	1974	$30
❏ SQ1652 [Q]	Blues on Bach	1974	$30
❏ 1429 [M]	Collaboration -- The Modern Jazz Quartet with Laurindo Almeida	1964	$30
❏ SD1429 [S]	Collaboration -- The Modern Jazz Quartet with Laurindo Almeida	1969	$25
—Red and green label			

Number	Title	Yr	NM
❏ SD1429 [S]	Collaboration -- The Modern Jazz Quartet with Laurindo Almeida	1964	$35
—Multicolor label, black "fan" logo at right			
❏ 1231 [M]	Fontessa	1956	$300
—Black label			
❏ 1231 [M]	Fontessa	1960	$300
—Multicolor label, white "fan" logo at right			
❏ 1231 [M]	Fontessa	1963	$50
—Multicolor label, black "fan" logo at right			
❏ SD1231 [S]	Fontessa	1958	$300
—Green label			
❏ SD1231 [S]	Fontessa	1960	$300
—Multicolor label, white "fan" logo at right			
❏ SD1231 [S]	Fontessa	1963	$50
—Multicolor label, black "fan" logo at right			
❏ SD1231 [S]	Fontessa	1969	$25
—Red and green label			
❏ 1449 [M]	Jazz Dialogue	1966	$30
❏ SD1449 [S]	Jazz Dialogue	1966	$35
—Multicolor label, black "fan" logo at right			
❏ SD1449 [S]	Jazz Dialogue	1969	$25
—Red and green label			
❏ SD1623	Legendary Profile	1973	$30
❏ 1486 [M]	Live at the Lighthouse	1967	$25
❏ SD1486 [S]	Live at the Lighthouse	1967	$30
—Multicolor label, black "fan" logo at right			
❏ SD1486 [S]	Live at the Lighthouse	1969	$25
—Red and green label			
❏ 1381 [M]	Lonely Woman	1962	$175
❏ SD1381 [S]	Lonely Woman	1962	$175
—Multicolor label, black "fan" logo at right			
❏ SD1381 [S]	Lonely Woman	1969	$25
—Red and green label			
❏ SD8806	More from the Last Concert	198?	$25
❏ 1284 [M]	No Sun in Venice	1958	$300
—Black label			
❏ 1284 [M]	No Sun in Venice	1960	$300
—Multicolor label, white "fan" logo at right			
❏ 1284 [M]	No Sun in Venice	1963	$35
—Multicolor label, black "fan" logo at right			
❏ SD1284 [S]	No Sun in Venice	1958	$300
—Green label			
❏ SD1284 [S]	No Sun in Venice	1960	$300
—Multicolor label, white "fan" logo at right			
❏ SD1284 [S]	No Sun in Venice	1963	$30
—Multicolor label, black "fan" logo at right			
❏ SD1284 [S]	No Sun in Venice	1969	$25
—Red and green label			
❏ SD1589	Plastic Dreams	1972	$30
❏ 1325 [M]	Pyramid	1960	$300
—Black label			
❏ 1325 [M]	Pyramid	1961	$175
—Multicolor label, white "fan" logo at right			
❏ 1325 [M]	Pyramid	1963	$35
—Multicolor label, black "fan" logo at right			
❏ SD1325 [S]	Pyramid	1960	$300
—Green label			
❏ SD1325 [S]	Pyramid	1961	$175
—Multicolor label, white "fan" logo at right			
❏ SD1325 [S]	Pyramid	1963	$30
—Multicolor label, black "fan" logo at right			
❏ SD1325 [S]	Pyramid	1969	$25
—Red and green label			
❏ SD 2-301	The Art of the Modern Jazz Quartet	1973	$35
❏ SD1546	The Best of the Modern Jazz Quartet	1970	$30
❏ 1390 [M]	The Comedy	1963	$50
❏ SD1390 [S]	The Comedy	1963	$50
—Multicolor label, black "fan" logo at right			
❏ SD1390 [S]	The Comedy	1969	$25
—Red and green label			
❏ 2-603 [M]	The European Concert	1961	$175
—Multicolor labels, white "fan" logo at right			
❏ 2-603 [M]	The European Concert	1963	$50
—Multicolor labels, black "fan" logo at right			
❏ SD 2-603 [S]	The European Concert	1961	$175
—Multicolor labels, white "fan" logo at right			
❏ SD 2-603 [S]	The European Concert	1963	$50
—Multicolor labels, black "fan" logo at right			
❏ SD 2-603 [S]	The European Concert	1969	$35
—Red and green labels			
❏ 1385 [M]	The European Concert, Volume 1	1962	$175
❏ SD1385 [S]	The European Concert, Volume 1	1962	$175
—Multicolor label, black "fan" logo at right			
❏ SD1385 [S]	The European Concert, Volume 1	1969	$25
—Red and green label			
❏ 1386 [M]	The European Concert, Volume 2	1962	$175
❏ SD1386 [S]	The European Concert, Volume 2	1962	$175
—Multicolor label, black "fan" logo at right			
❏ SD1386 [S]	The European Concert, Volume 2	1969	$25

Number	Title	Yr	NM
—Red and green label			
❏ SD 2-909	The Last Concert	1975	$35
❏ SQ 2-909 [Q]	The Last Concert	1975	$40
❏ 1265 [M]	The Modern Jazz Quartet	1957	$300
—Black label			
❏ 1265 [M]	The Modern Jazz Quartet	1960	$175
—Multicolor label, white "fan" logo at right			
❏ 1265 [M]	The Modern Jazz Quartet	1963	$175
—Multicolor label, black "fan" logo at right			
❏ 1359 [M]	The Modern Jazz Quartet and Orchestra	1961	$300
—Multicolor label, white "fan" logo at right			
❏ 1359 [M]	The Modern Jazz Quartet and Orchestra	1963	$175
—Multicolor label, black "fan" logo at right			
❏ SD1359 [S]	The Modern Jazz Quartet and Orchestra	1961	$250
—Multicolor label, white "fan" logo at right			
❏ SD1359 [S]	The Modern Jazz Quartet and Orchestra	1963	$175
—Multicolor label, black "fan" logo at right			
❏ SD1359 [S]	The Modern Jazz Quartet and Orchestra	1969	$25
—Red and green label			
❏ 1247 [M]	The Modern Jazz Quartet at the Music Inn	1956	$300
—Black label			
❏ 1247 [M]	The Modern Jazz Quartet at the Music Inn	1960	$175
—Multicolor label, white "fan" logo at right			
❏ 1247 [M]	The Modern Jazz Quartet at the Music Inn	1963	$175
—Multicolor label, black "fan" logo at right			
❏ 90049	The Modern Jazz Quartet at the Music Inn	1983	$25
❏ 1299 [M]	The Modern Jazz Quartet at the Music Inn, Volume 2	1958	$300
—Black label			
❏ 1299 [M]	The Modern Jazz Quartet at the Music Inn, Volume 2	1960	$175
—Multicolor label, white "fan" logo at right			
❏ 1299 [M]	The Modern Jazz Quartet at the Music Inn, Volume 2	1963	$175
—Multicolor label, black "fan" logo at right			
❏ SD1299 [S]	The Modern Jazz Quartet at the Music Inn, Volume 2	1958	$300
—Green label			
❏ SD1299 [S]	The Modern Jazz Quartet at the Music Inn, Volume 2	1960	$175
—Multicolor label, white "fan" logo at right			
❏ SD1299 [S]	The Modern Jazz Quartet at the Music Inn, Volume 2	1963	$175
—Multicolor label, black "fan" logo at right			
❏ SD1299 [S]	The Modern Jazz Quartet at the Music Inn, Volume 2	1969	$25
—Red and green label			
❏ 1440 [M]	The Modern Jazz Quartet Plays Gershwin's "Porgy and Bess"	1965	$30
❏ SD1440 [S]	The Modern Jazz Quartet Plays Gershwin's "Porgy and Bess"	1965	$35
—Multicolor label, black "fan" logo at right			
❏ SD1440 [S]	The Modern Jazz Quartet Plays Gershwin's "Porgy and Bess"	1969	$25
—Red and green label			
❏ 1414 [M]	The Sheriff	1964	$35
❏ SD1414 [S]	The Sheriff	1964	$25
—Multicolor label, black "fan" logo at right			
❏ SD1414 [S]	The Sheriff	1969	$25
—Red and green label			
❏ 1345 [M]	Third Stream Music	1960	$300
—Multicolor label, white "fan" logo at right			
❏ 1345 [M]	Third Stream Music	1963	$30
—Multicolor label, black "fan" logo at right			
❏ SD1345 [S]	Third Stream Music	1960	$300
—Multicolor label, white "fan" logo at right			
❏ SD1345 [S]	Third Stream Music	1963	$35
—Multicolor label, black "fan" logo at right			
❏ SD1345 [S]	Third Stream Music	1969	$25
—Red and green label			
❏ 81761	Three Windows	1987	$25

EASTWEST

| ❏ 90826 | For Ellington | 1988 | $25 |

FANTASY

❏ OJC-002	Concorde	1982	$25
❏ OJC-057	Django	198?	$25
❏ OJC-125	Modern Jazz Quartet/Milt Jackson Quintet	198?	$25

LITTLE DAVID

| ❏ LD3001 | In Memoriam | 1975 | $30 |
| ❏ 90130 | In Memoriam | 198? | $25 |

MOBILE FIDELITY

❏ 1-206	Blues at Carnegie Hall	1994	$40
—Audiophile vinyl			
❏ Jan-0090	Live at the Lighthouse	1982	$50
—Audiophile vinyl			
❏ 1-205	The Modern Jazz Quartet	1994	$40
—Audiophile vinyl			

Number	Title	Yr	NM
❑ 1-228	The Modern Jazz Quartet at the Music Inn, Volume 2	1995	$75

—Audiophile vinyl

PABLO

❑ 2405423	The Best of the Modern Jazz Quartet	198?	$25
❑ 2310917	Topsy: This One's for Basie	198?	$25

PABLO LIVE

❑ 2308243	Reunion at Budokan	198?	$25
❑ 2308244	Together Again... At Montreux Jazz Festival	198?	$25

PABLO TODAY

❑ 2312142	Together Again	1984	$25

PRESTIGE

❑ PRLP-7005 [M]	Concorde	1955	$300

— Yellow label originals

❑ 16-1 [M]	Concorde	1955	$500

— This album plays at 16 2/3 rpm and is marked as such; white label; one side has the Modern Jazz Quartet, the other side has Milt Jackson

❑ PRLP-7057 [M]	Django	1956	$325

— Yellow label originals

❑ PRST-7749	First Recordings	1970	$30
❑ PRLP-7059 [M]	Modern Jazz Quartet/Milt Jackson Quintet	1956	$300

— Yellow label originals

❑ 24005	The Modern Jazz Quartet	197?	$35
❑ PRLP-170 [10]	The Modern Jazz Quartet, Volume 2	1953	$350
❑ PRLP-7421 [M]	The Modern Jazz Quartet Play for Lovers	1966	$25
❑ PRST-7421 [R]	The Modern Jazz Quartet Play for Lovers	1966	$30
❑ PRLP-7425 [M]	The Modern Jazz Quartet Plays Jazz Classics	1966	$25
❑ PRST-7425 [R]	The Modern Jazz Quartet Plays Jazz Classics	1966	$30
❑ PRLP-160 [10]	The Modern Jazz Quartet with Milt Jackson	1953	$350

SAVOY

❑ MG-12046 [M]	Modern Jazz Quartet	1955	$300

SOLID STATE

❑ SS-18035	The Modern Jazz Quartet on Tour	1968	$30

UNITED ARTISTS

❑ UAL-4072 [M]	Patterns	1960	$30
❑ UAS-5072 [S]	Patterns	1960	$30

MODERN JAZZ QUINTET, THE

SURREY

❑ S-1030 [M]	Q.T. Hush	1966	$30
❑ SS-1030 [S]	Q.T. Hush	1966	$30

MODERN JAZZ SEXTET, THE

AMERICAN RECORDING SOCIETY

❑ G-429 [M]	The Modern Jazz Sextet	1957	$300

NORGRAN

❑ MGN-1076 [M]	The Modern Jazz Sextet	1956	$250

VERVE

❑ VE-1-2533	Dizzy Meets Sonny	197?	$30
❑ MGV-8166 [M]	The Modern Jazz Sextet	1957	$300
❑ V-8166 [M]	The Modern Jazz Sextet	1961	$175

MODERN JAZZ SOCIETY, THE

AMERICAN RECORDING SOCIETY

❑ G-432 [M]	A Concert of Contemporary Music	1957	$300

NORGRAN

❑ MGN-1040 [M]	A Concert of Contemporary Music	1955	$300

VERVE

❑ MGV-8131 [M]	A Concert of Contemporary Music	1957	$300
❑ V-8131 [M]	A Concert of Contemporary Music	1961	$250
❑ VSP-18 [M]	Little David's Fugue	1966	$25

— As "The Modern Jazz Ensemble"

❑ VSPS-18 [R]	Little David's Fugue	1966	$30

— As "The Modern Jazz Ensemble"

MODERN JAZZ STARS, THE

CROWN

❑ CLP-5009 [M]	Jazz Masquerade	1957	$30

— Original edition has black label with silver print

❑ CLP-5008 [M]	Jazz Surprise	1957	$30

MODERN JAZZ TRIO

See MJT + 3.
See MJT + 3. (JZ)

MODERN LOVERS, THE

See JONATHAN RICHMAN AND THE MODERN LOVERS.

4 MEN WITH BEARDS

❑ 4M523LP [B]	The Modern Lovers		$25

BMG

❑ 15056V [B]	The Modern Lovers	2015	$50

— Limited edition of 1000, blue/black vinyl

MODERN MANDOLIN QUARTET, THE

LOST LAKE ARTS

❑ LL-0095	Modern Mandolin Quartet	1988	$30

MODERNAIRES, THE

COLUMBIA

❑ CL2584 [10]	Juke Box Saturday Night	1955	$40
❑ CL2490 [M]	The Modernaires Salute Herb Alpert and the Tijuana Brass	1966	$15
❑ CS9290 [S]	The Modernaires Salute Herb Alpert and the Tijuana Brass	1966	$18
❑ CL6043 [10]	Tributes in Tempo	1950	$40

HARMONY

❑ HL7023 [M]	Juke Box Saturday Night	195?	$25

LIBERTY

❑ LN-10215	The Modernaires Sing the Great Glenn Miller Instrumentals	198?	$12

MERCURY

❑ MG-20546 [M]	Like Swung	1960	$18
❑ SR-60220 [S]	Like Swung	1960	$25

UNITED ARTISTS

❑ WWS8510 [S]	The Modernaires Sing the Great Glenn Miller Instrumentals	196?	$25
❑ WW3510 [S]	The Modernaires Sing the Great Glenn Miller Instrumentals	196?	$18
❑ WW7524 [M]	We Remember Tommy Dorsey, Too!	196?	$18
❑ WWS8524 [S]	We Remember Tommy Dorsey, Too!	196?	$25

WING

❑ SRW-16231 [S]	Like Swung	196?	$18
❑ MGW-12231 [M]	Like Swung	196?	$15

MODUGNO, DOMENICO

DECCA

❑ DL8853 [M]	Encore	1959	$40
❑ DL8808 [M]	Nel Blu Dipinto Di Blu (Volare) and Other Italian Favorites	1958	$50
❑ DL4133 [M]	Viva Italia	1961	$30

MODULATIONS, THE

BUDDAH

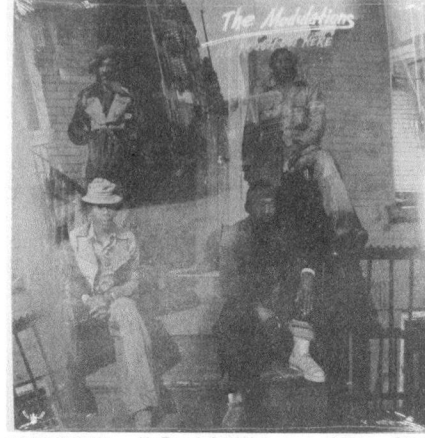

❑ BDS-5638 [B]	It's Rough Out Here	1975	$100

—Reproductions exist

MOER, PAUL

DEL-FI

❑ DFLP-1212 [M]	Contemporary Jazz Classics	1961	$250
❑ DFST-1212 [S]	Contemporary Jazz Classics	1961	$250

MOFFATT, HUGH

PHILO

❑ PH-1111	Loving You	1987	$12
❑ PH-1127	Troubadour	1989	$15

MOFFATT, KATY

COLUMBIA

❑ PC34172	Katy Moffatt	1976	$18
❑ JC34774	Kissin' in the California Sun	1977	$18

PHILO

❑ PH-1133	Child Bride	1990	$15
❑ PH-1128	Walkin' on the Moon	1989	$15

MOFFETT, CHARLES

SAVOY

❑ MG-12194	The Gift	1969	$25

MOFFETT, CHARNETT

BLUE NOTE

❑ B1-91650	Beauty Within	1989	$35
❑ BT-46993	Nett Man	1987	$25

MOJO JAZZIN' FIVE

STOMP OFF

❑ SOS-1086	South Side Chicago Style	1985	$25

MOJO MEN, THE

GRT

❑ 10003	Mojo Magic	1969	$30

MOLE, MIFF

JAZZOLOGY

❑ J-105	Milt Mole and His World Jam Session Band, 1944	198?	$25
❑ JCE-5 [M]	The Immortal Miff Mole	1964	$35

MOLE, MIFF/EDMUND HALL

BRUNSWICK

❑ BL58042 [10]	Battle of Jazz, Volume 4	1953	$75

MOLENAT, CLAUDE

VANGUARD

❑ VSD-319	Trumpet/Organ/Rhythm	197?	$30

MOLLY HATCHET

CAPITOL

❑ C1-92114	Lightning Strikes Twice	1989	$15

EPIC

❑ AS99844 [DJ]	Beatin' the Odds	1980	$40

—Promo-only picture disc

❑ FE36572	Beatin' the Odds	1980	$12
❑ E240137	Double Trouble Live	1985	$18
❑ AS99694 [DJ]	Flirtin' with Disaster	1979	$40

—Promo-only picture disc

❑ JE36110	Flirtin' with Disaster	1979	$12
❑ JE35347	Molly Hatchet	1978	$15

—Orange label

❑ JE35347	Molly Hatchet	1979	$12

—Dark blue label

❑ PE35347	Molly Hatchet	198?	$10

—Budget-line reissue with new prefix

❑ FE38429	No Guts... No Glory	1983	$12
❑ PE38429	No Guts... No Glory	198?	$10

—Budget-line reissue with new prefix

❑ AS991320 [DJ]	Take No Prisoners	1981	$30

—Promo-only picture disc

❑ FE37480	Take No Prisoners	1981	$12
❑ PE37480	Take No Prisoners	198?	$10

—Budget-line reissue with new prefix

❑ FE39621	The Deed Is Done	1984	$12

MOLOCH

ENTERPRISE

❑ ENS-1002	Moloch	1969	$30

MOM & DADS, THE

GNP CRESCENDO

❑ GNP-2173	20 Favorite Waltzes	1986	$10
❑ GNP-2068	Again!	1973	$12
❑ GNP-2130	Blue Hawaii	1980	$12
❑ GNP-2078	Dance with the Mom & Dads	1974	$12
❑ GNP-2106	Down the River of Golden Dreams	1977	$12
❑ GNP-2092	Dream	1975	$12
❑ 2GNP-2123	Golden Country	1979	$15
❑ GNP-2150	Good Night Sweetheart	1985	$10
❑ GNP-2117	Gratefully Yours	1978	$12
❑ GNP-2063	In the Blue Canadian Rockies	1972	$12
❑ GNP-2084	Love Is a Beautiful Song	1974	$12
❑ GNP-2125	Love Letters in the Sand	1979	$12
❑ GNP-2096	Memories	1976	$12
❑ GNP-2110	One Dozen Roses	1977	$12
❑ GNP-2189	Red Sails in the Sunset	1987	$10
❑ GNP-2072	Reminiscing	1973	$12
❑ GNP-2065	Souvenirs	1972	$12
❑ GNP-2102	Summertime	1976	$12
❑ GNP-2087	The Best of the Mom & Dads	1975	$12
❑ GNP-2082	The Mom & Dads Play Your Favorite Hymns	1974	$12
❑ GNP-2061	The Rangers Waltz	1971	$12
❑ 2GNP-2129	The Very Best of the Mom & Dads	1980	$15
❑ GNP-2136	To Mom & Dad With Love from the Mom & Dads	1980	$12
❑ GNP-2139	Waltz Across Texas	1981	$12
❑ GNP-2108	Whispering Hope	1977	$12

MOMENTS, THE

R&B trio. For legal reasons, their records on EMI America, EMI Manhattan, Panoramic and Polydor were issued under the name "Ray, Goodman and Brown."

CHESS

❑ CH2-92517	Greatest Hits	198?	$15

Number	Title	Yr	NM
POLYDOR			
❏ PD-1-6240	Ray, Goodman & Brown	1979	$12
❏ PD-1-6299	Ray, Goodman & Brown II	1980	$12
❏ PD-1-6341	Stay	1981	$12
STANG			
❏ ST-1003	A Moment with the Moments	1970	$30
❏ 2ST-1033	Greatest Hits	1977	$25
❏ ST-1015	Live at the Miss Black America Pageant	1972	$25
❏ ST-1026	Look at Me	1975	$18
❏ ST-1004	Moments Greatest Hits	1971	$25
❏ ST-1030	Moments With You	1976	$18
❏ ST-1022	My Thing	1973	$18
❏ ST-1000	Not On the Outside, But On the Inside Strong	1969	$30
❏ ST-1034	Sharp	1978	$18
❏ ST-1019	The Best of the Moments	1975	$18
❏ ST-1006	The Moments Live at the New York State Womans Prison	1971	$30
❏ ST-1002	The Moments On Top	1970	$30
❏ ST-1009	The Other Side of the Moments	1972	$30
❏ ST-1023	The Sexy Moments	1974	$18

MOM'S APPLE PIE

Number	Title	Yr	NM
BROWN BAG			
❏ BB-LA073-F	Mom's Apple Pie #2	1973	$18
❏ 14200 [B]	Mom's Apple Pie	1972	$40
—With vulva showing in the apple pie			
❏ 14200 [B]	Mom's Apple Pie	1972	$30
—With barbed wire wall covering the former opening. This is much rarer than the first version, though less sought-after			

MONCUR, GRACHAN, III

Number	Title	Yr	NM
BLUE NOTE			
❏ BLP-4153 [M]	Evolution	1963	$75
❏ BST-84153 [S]	Evolution	1963	$30
—With "New York, USA" address on label			
❏ BST-84153 [S]	Evolution	1967	$35
—With "A Division of Liberty Records" on label			
❏ BST-84153 [S]	Evolution	1986	$25
—The Finest in Jazz Since 1939" reissue			
❏ BLP-4177 [M]	Some Other Stuff	1964	$75
❏ BST-84177 [S]	Some Other Stuff	1964	$30
—With "New York, USA" address on label			
❏ BST-84177 [S]	Some Other Stuff	1967	$35
—With "A Division of Liberty Records" on label			
JCOA			
❏ 1009	Echoes of Prayer	197?	$35
PICCADILLY			
❏ 3520	African Concepts	198?	$25

MONDAY BLUES

Number	Title	Yr	NM
VAULT			
❏ 133	The Phil Spector Song Book	1970	$25

MONEY, EDDIE

Number	Title	Yr	NM
COLUMBIA			
❏ FC40096	Can't Hold Back	1986	$12
❏ PC34909	Eddie Money	1977	$15
—No bar code on back cover			
❏ JC34909	Eddie Money	198?	$10
—Reissue with bar code on back cover			
❏ PC34909	Eddie Money	1977	$15
—No bar code on back cover			
❏ 1P-7982	Greatest Hits Sound of Money	1989	$18
—Columbia House edition; only U.S. vinyl version			
❏ JC35598	Life for the Taking	1979	$12
❏ PC35598	Life for the Taking	198?	$10
—Budget-line reissue with new prefix			
❏ FC37960	No Control	1982	$12
❏ OC44302	Nothing to Lose	1988	$12
❏ FC36514	Playing for Keeps	1980	$12
❏ C46756	Right Here	1991	$18
❏ FC38862	Where's the Party?	1983	$12

MONEY, ZOOT

Number	Title	Yr	NM
EPIC			
❏ LN24241 [M]	All Happening Zoot Money's Big Roll Band at Klooks Kleek	1966	$35

MONICA, CORBETT

Number	Title	Yr	NM
DOT			
❏ DLP-3303 [M]	For Laughs1	1960	$30

MONITORS, THE (1)

Number	Title	Yr	NM
SOUL			
❏ SS-714	Greetings, We're the Monitors	1969	$75

MONK, MEREDITH

Number	Title	Yr	NM
ECM			
❏ 1197	Dolmen Music	198?	$25
❏ 23792	Turtle Dreams	1983	$25

Number	Title	Yr	NM
LOVELY			
❏ 1051	Key	198?	$25

MONK, THELONIOUS, AND JOHN COLTRANE

Number	Title	Yr	NM
FANTASY			
❏ OJC-039	Thelonious Monk with John Coltrane	198?	$30
JAZZLAND			
❏ JLP-46 [M]	Thelonious Monk with John Coltrane	1961	$200
❏ JLP-946 [S]	Thelonious Monk with John Coltrane	1961	$175
MILESTONE			
❏ M-47011	Monk/Trane	1973	$50
RIVERSIDE			
❏ RLP-490 [M]	Thelonious Monk with John Coltrane	1965	$150
—Reissue of Jazzland 46			
❏ RS-9490 [S]	Thelonious Monk with John Coltrane	1965	$40
—Reissue of Jazzland 946			

MONK, THELONIOUS

Number	Title	Yr	NM
ANALOGUE PRODUCTIONS			
❏ AP-37	The Riverside Tenor Sessions	1999	$300
BANDSTAND			
❏ BDLP-1516	April in Paris	1992	$30
❏ BDLP-1505	Blue Monk	1992	$30
BLACK LION			
❏ 152	Something in Blue	1972	$50
❏ 197	The Man I Love	1973	$50
BLUE NOTE			
❏ BLP-5002 [10]	Genius of Modern Music, Vol. 1	1952	$800
❏ BLP-1510 [M]	Genius of Modern Music, Vol. 1	1956	$400
—Deep groove" version; Lexington Ave. address on label			
❏ BLP-1510 [M]	Genius of Modern Music, Vol. 1	1958	$250
—Deep groove" edition, W. 63rd St. address on label			
❏ BLP-1510 [M]	Genius of Modern Music, Vol. 1	1963	$100
—New York, USA" address on label			
❏ BLP-81510 [R]	Genius of Modern Music, Vol. 1	1968	$150
—A Division of Liberty Records" on label			
❏ BST-81510	Genius of Modern Music, Vol. 1	1985	$30
—The Finest in Jazz Since 1939" reissue			
❏ BLP-5009 [10]	Genius of Modern Music, Vol. 2	1952	$800
❏ BLP-1511 [M]	Genius of Modern Music, Vol. 2	1956	$800
—Deep groove" version; Lexington Ave. address on label			
❏ BLP-1511 [M]	Genius of Modern Music, Vol. 2	1958	$400
—Deep groove" edition, W. 63rd St. address on label			
❏ BLP-1511 [M]	Genius of Modern Music, Vol. 2	1963	$175
—New York, USA" address on label			
❏ BLP-81511 [R]	Genius of Modern Music, Vol. 2	1968	$150
—A Division of Liberty Records" on label			
❏ BST-81511	Genius of Modern Music, Vol. 2	1985	$30
—The Finest in Jazz Since 1939" reissue			
❏ BN-LA579-H2	The Complete Genius	1976	$50
❏ LWB-579	The Complete Genius	1981	$35
—Reissue of BN-LA579-H2			
COLUMBIA			
❏ JG35720	Always Know	1979	$50
❏ CL2038 [M]	Criss-Cross	1963	$75
—Guaranteed High Fidelity" on label			
❏ CS8838 [S]	Criss-Cross	1963	$120
—360 Sound Stereo" in black on label			
❏ CL2038 [M]	Criss-Cross	1966	$50
—360 Sound Mono" on label			
❏ CL2038 [M]	Criss-Cross	199?	$30
—180-gram reissue			
❏ CS8838 [S]	Criss-Cross	1966	$75
—360 Sound Stereo" in white on label			
❏ CS9775	Greatest Hits	1969	$50
—Red "360 Sound" label			
❏ CS9775	Greatest Hits	1971	$30
—Orange label			
❏ PC9775	Greatest Hits	198?	$20
—Reissue with new prefix			
❏ CL2184 [M]	It's Monk's Time	1964	$75
—Guaranteed High Fidelity" on label			
❏ CS8984 [S]	It's Monk's Time	1964	$140
—360 Sound Stereo" in black on label			
❏ CL2184 [M]	It's Monk's Time	1966	$50
—360 Sound Mono" on label			
❏ CS8984 [S]	It's Monk's Time	1966	$75
—360 Sound Stereo" in white on label			
❏ CS8984 [S]	It's Monk's Time	199?	$30

Number	Title	Yr	NM
—180-gram reissue			
❏ C238030	Live at the It Club	1983	$75
—Original edition			
❏ C238030	Live at the It Club	199?	$35
—180-gram reissue			
❏ C238269	Live at the Jazz Workshop	1983	$75
❏ CL2416 [M]	Misterioso	1966	$75
—360 Sound Mono" on label			
❏ CS9216 [S]	Misterioso	1966	$75
—360 Sound Stereo" on red label			
❏ CL2416 [M]	Misterioso	199?	$30
—180-gram reissue			
❏ CL2291 [M]	Monk	1965	$75
—Guaranteed High Fideilty" on label			
❏ CS9091 [S]	Monk	1965	$150
—360 Sound Stereo" in black on label			
❏ CS9091 [S]	Monk	1966	$75
—360 Sound Stereo" in white on label			
❏ CS9091 [S]	Monk	199?	$30
—180-gram reissue			
❏ CL2291 [M]	Monk	1966	$50
—360 Sound Mono" on label			
❏ CL2164 [M]	Monk Big Band and Quartet In Concert	1964	$75
—Guaranteed High Fidelity" on label			
❏ CS8964 [S]	Monk Big Band and Quartet In Concert	1964	$175
—360 Sound Stereo" in black on label			
❏ CL2164 [M]	Monk Big Band and Quartet In Concert	1966	$50
—360 Sound Mono" on label			
❏ CS8964 [S]	Monk Big Band and Quartet In Concert	1966	$75
—360 Sound Stereo" in white on label			
❏ CS8964 [S]	Monk Big Band and Quartet In Concert	199?	$30
—180-gram reissue			
❏ CS9806	Monk's Blues	1969	$175
—Red "360 Sound" label			
❏ CS9806	Monk's Blues	1971	$35
—Orange label			
❏ PC9806	Monk's Blues	198?	$20
—Reissue with new prefix; most have bar codes on back cover			
❏ PC9806	Monk's Blues	199?	$30
—180-gram reissue			
❏ CL1965 [M]	Monk's Dream	1963	$75
—Guaranteed High Fideilty" on label			
❏ CS8765 [S]	Monk's Dream	1963	$140
—360 Sound Stereo" in black on label			
❏ CL1965 [M]	Monk's Dream	1966	$50
—360 Sound Mono" on label			
❏ CS8765 [S]	Monk's Dream	1966	$75
—360 Sound Stereo" in white on label			
❏ CS8765 [S]	Monk's Dream	199?	$30
—180-gram reissue			
❏ CL2349 [M]	Solo Monk	1965	$75
—360 Sound Mono" on label			
❏ CS9149 [S]	Solo Monk	1965	$40
—Red "360 Sound" label			
❏ CS9149	Solo Monk	1971	$30
—Orange label			
❏ PC9149	Solo Monk	198?	$20
—Reissue with new prefix; most have bar codes			
❏ PC9149	Solo Monk	199?	$30
—180-gram reissue			
❏ CL2651 [M]	Straight No Chaser	1967	$150
—Red label with "Mono			
❏ CS9451 [S]	Straight No Chaser	1967	$40
—Red "360 Sound" label			
❏ CS9451	Straight No Chaser	1971	$30
—Orange label			
❏ PC9451	Straight No Chaser	198?	$20
—Reissue with new prefix			
❏ PC9451	Straight No Chaser	199?	$30
—180-gram reissue			
❏ C238510	The Tokyo Concerts	1984	$50
—Original edition			
❏ C238510	The Tokyo Concerts	199?	$35
—180-gram reissue			
❏ CS9632 [S]	Underground	1968	$75
—Red "360 Sound" label			
❏ CS9632	Underground	1971	$30
—Orange label			
❏ PC9632	Underground	198?	$20
—Reissue with new prefix			
❏ CS9632 [M]	Underground	1968	$150
—White label promo only with stereo number; "Special Mono Radio Station Copy" sticker on stereo cover			
❏ PC9632	Underground	199?	$30
—180-gram reissue			
❏ KG32892	Who's Afraid of the Big Band Monk	1974	$75
❏ KG32892	Who's Afraid of the Big Band Monk	199?	$35
—180-gram reissue			

Number	Title	Yr	NM
COLUMBIA JAZZ MASTERPIECES			
❑ CJ40786	Monk's Dream	1987	$25
❑ CJ44297	The Composer	1988	$30
❑ CJ40785	Underground	1987	$25
COLUMBIA LIMITED EDITION			
❑ LE10122	Criss-Cross	197?	$30
COLUMBIA MUSICAL TREASURY			
❑ DS338	Monk's Miracles	1967	$75
— Columbia Record Club exclusive			
EVEREST ARCHIVE OF FOLK & JAZZ			
❑ FS-336	Piano Solos	1978	$30
FANTASY			
❑ OJC-362	5 By Monk By 5	1989	$30
❑ OJC-231	Alone in San Francisco	1987	$30
❑ OJC-026	Brilliant Corners	198?	$30
❑ OJC-206	Misterioso	1985	$30
❑ OJC-016	Monk	198?	$30
❑ OJC-488	Monk in Italy	1991	$30
❑ OJC-084	Monk's Music	198?	$30
❑ OJC-301	Mulligan Meets Monk	1988	$30
❑ OJC-254	Thelonious Himself	1987	$30
❑ OJC-103	Thelonious in Action	198?	$30
❑ OJC-305	Thelonious Monk at the Blackhawk	1988	$30
❑ OJC-135	Thelonious Monk at Town Hall	1984	$30
❑ OJC-024	Thelonious Monk Plays Duke Ellington	198?	$30
❑ OJC-059	Thelonious Monk/Sonny Rollins	198?	$30
❑ OJC-010	Thelonious Monk Trio	198?	$30
❑ OJC-064	The Unique Thelonious Monk	198?	$30
GATEWAY			
❑ GSLP-7023	Monk's Music	197?	$35
GNP CRESCENDO			
❑ 9008	Thelonious Monk	197?	$35
JAZZ MAN			
❑ 5017	Something in Blue	1980	$30
MILESTONE			
❑ M-47060	April in Paris/Live	198?	$50
❑ M-9124	Blues Five Spot	1984	$35
❑ M-47023	Brilliance	1975	$75
❑ M-9115	Evidence	1983	$30
❑ M-47064	Memorial Album	1982	$50
❑ M-47004	Pure Monk	1972	$50
❑ M-47067	'Round Midnight	198?	$50
❑ M-47043	Thelonious Monk at the Five Spot	1978	$50
❑ M-47033	Thelonious Monk In Person	1976	$75
❑ M-47052	The Riverside Trios	1980	$50
MOSAIC			
❑ MR4-112	The Complete Black Lion and Vogue Recordings	199?	$300
— Limited edition of 7,500			
❑ MR4-101	The Complete Blue Note Recordings of Thelonious Monk	198?	$250
— Limited edition of 7,500			
ORIGINAL JAZZ CLASSICS			
❑ CJC084 [B]	Monk's Music	2015	$25
PICCADILLY			
❑ 3521	Monkisms	198?	$30
PRESTIGE			
❑ PRST-7848	Blue Monk, Volume 2	197?	$35
❑ PRLP-7053 [M]	Monk	1956	$2500
— Reissue of 150; yellow label with W. 50th St. address. Andy Warhol cover.			
❑ PRST-7159 [M]	Monk's Moods	1959	$250
— Reissue of 7027; yellow label with Bergenfield, N.J. address			
❑ PRST-7751	Reflections, Volume 1	1970	$50
❑ PRST-7656	The Genius of Thelonious Monk	1969	$50
❑ PRLP-7363 [M]	The Golden Monk	1965	$75
— Reissue of 7245			
❑ PRST-7363 [R]	The Golden Monk	1965	$50
❑ PRLP-7508 [M]	The High Priest	1967	$150
— Reissue of 7159			
❑ PRST-7508 [R]	The High Priest	1967	$50
❑ PRLP-7027 [M]	Thelonious Monk	1956	$700
— Reissue of 142 and 189 on one 12-inch record; yellow label with W. 50th St. address; label calls this "Thelonious Monk Trio"			
❑ PR-24006	Thelonious Monk	1971	$50
❑ PRLP-180 [10]	Thelonious Monk Quintet	1954	$800
❑ PRLP-166 [10]	Thelonious Monk Quintet with Sonny Rollins and Julius Watkins	1953	$800
❑ PRLP-7075 [M]	Thelonious Monk/Sonny Rollins	1957	$500
— Reissue of 166; yellow label with W. 50th St. address			
❑ PRLP-142 [10]	Thelonious Monk Trio	1953	$800
❑ PRLP-189 [10]	Thelonious Monk Trio	1954	$800
❑ PRLP-7245 [M]	We See	1962	$300
— Reissue of 7053			
❑ PRLP-7169 [M]	Work	1959	$250
— Reissue of 7075			
RIVERSIDE			
❑ RLP 12-305 [M]	5 By Monk By 5	1959	$300

Number	Title	Yr	NM
—Blue label with reel and microphone logo			
❑ RLP1150 [S]	5 By Monk By 5	1959	$350
— Black label with reel and microphone logo			
❑ 6086	5 By Monk By 5	197?	$30
❑ 6163	Alone in San Francisco	198?	$30
❑ RS-3037	Best of Thelonious Monk	1969	$150
❑ RLP 12-226 [M]	Brilliant Corners	1957	$1000
— White label with blue print			
❑ RLP 12-226 [M]	Brilliant Corners	1958	$300
— Blue label with reel and microphone logo			
❑ RS-3009 [R]	CT Meets Monk	1968	$150
❑ 6107	Meet Thelonious Monk and Gerry Mulligan	197?	$30
❑ RM-3000 [M]	Mighty Monk	1967	$150
❑ RS-3000 [S]	Mighty Monk	1967	$150
❑ RLP 12-279 [M]	Misterioso	1958	$300
— Blue label with reel-and-microphone logo			
❑ RLP1133 [S]	Misterioso	1958	$300
— Black label with reel and microphone logo			
❑ 6119	Misterioso	197?	$30
❑ RLP-491 [M]	Monk in France	1965	$175
❑ RS-9491 [S]	Monk in France	1965	$175
❑ RS-3015 [R]	Monk Plays Duke	1968	$150
❑ RLP 12-242 [M]	Monk's Music	1957	$700
— White label with blue print			
❑ RLP 12-242 [M]	Monk's Music	1958	$300
— Blue label with reel and microphone logo			
❑ RLP1101 [S]	Monk's Music	1959	$300
— Black label with reel and microphone logo			
❑ RM-3004 [M]	Monk's Music	1967	$150
❑ RS-3004 [S]	Monk's Music	1967	$150
❑ 6207	Monk's Music	1983	$50
❑ RLP 12-247 [M]	Mulligan Meets Monk	1957	$400
— White label with blue print			
❑ RLP 12-247 [M]	Mulligan Meets Monk	1958	$300
— Blue label with reel and microphone logo			
❑ RLP1106 [S]	Mulligan Meets Monk	1959	$300
— Black label with reel and microphone logo			
❑ RS-3047	Panorama!	1970	$150
❑ R-022	The Complete Riverside Recordings	1987	$500
❑ RLP 12-312 [M]	Thelonious Alone in San Francisco	1959	$250
— Blue label with reel and microphone logo			
❑ RLP1158 [S]	Thelonious Alone in San Francisco	1959	$250
— Black label with reel and microphone logo			
❑ RLP 12-235 [M]	Thelonious Himself	1957	$400
— White label with blue print			
❑ RLP 12-235 [M]	Thelonious Himself	1958	$300
— Blue label with reel and microphone logo			
❑ 6053 [M]	Thelonious Himself	197?	$30
❑ RLP235 [B]	Thelonious Himself	2016	$25
❑ 6102	Thelonious in Action	197?	$30
❑ RLP 12-262 [M]	Thelonious in Action Recorded at the Five Spot Café, New York, With Johnny Griffin	1958	$300
— Blue label with reel and microphone logo			
❑ RLP1190 [S]	Thelonious in Action Recorded at the Five Spot Café, New York, With Johnny Griffin	1960	$250
— Black label with reel and microphone logo			
❑ 6198	Thelonious Monk at the Blackhawk	198?	$30
❑ 6183	Thelonious Monk at Town Hall	198?	$30
❑ RLP-443 [M]	Thelonious Monk in Italy	1963	$175
❑ RS-9443 [S]	Thelonious Monk in Italy	1963	$175
❑ RLP 12-201 [M]	Thelonious Monk Plays Duke Ellington	1955	$900
— White label with blue print			

Number	Title	Yr	NM
❑ RLP 12-201 [M]	Thelonious Monk Plays Duke Ellington	1958	$150
— Blue label with reel and microphone logo			
❑ 6039 [M]	Thelonious Monk Plays Duke Ellington	197?	$30

Number	Title	Yr	NM
❑ RLP 12-323 [M]	Thelonious Monk Quartet Plus Two at the Blackhawk	1960	$250
— Blue label with reel and microphone logo			
❑ RLP1171 [S]	Thelonious Monk Quartet Plus Two at the Blackhawk	1960	$250
— Black label with reel and microphone logo			
❑ RLP-421 [M]	Thelonious Monk's Greatest Hits	1962	$175
❑ RS-9421 [S]	Thelonious Monk's Greatest Hits	1962	$175
❑ RLP 12-300 [M]	The Thelonious Monk Orchestra at Town Hall	1959	$250
— Blue label with reel and microphone logo			
❑ RLP1138 [S]	The Thelonious Monk Orchestra at Town Hall	1959	$250
— Black label with reel and microphone logo			
❑ RS-9483/4 [S]	The Thelonious Monk Story	1965	$120
❑ RLP-483/4 [M]	The Thelonious Monk Story	1965	$140
❑ RLP-483	The Thelonious Monk Story, Volume 1	1965	$175
❑ RS-9483	The Thelonious Monk Story, Volume 1	1965	$175
❑ RLP-484	The Thelonious Monk Story, Volume 2	1965	$175
❑ RS-9484	The Thelonious Monk Story, Volume 2	1965	$175
❑ RLP 12-209 [M]	The Unique Thelonious Monk	1956	$500
— White label with blue print			
❑ RLP 12-209 [M]	The Unique Thelonious Monk	1958	$300
— Blue label with reel and microphone logo			
❑ 6068 [M]	The Unique Thelonious Monk	197?	$30
❑ RLP-460/1 [M]	Two Hours with Thelonious Monk	1963	$175
❑ RS-9460/1 [S]	Two Hours with Thelonious Monk	1963	$175
❑ RS-3020X [R]	Two Hours with Thelonious Monk	1969	$150
TRIP			
❑ 5022	Pure Monk	1974	$30
XANADU			
❑ 202	Live at the Village Gate	1985	$35

MONKEES, THE

Also see DOLENZ, JONES & TORK; DOLENZ, JONES, BOYCE & HART; MICKEY DOLENZ; DAVY JONES; MICHAEL NESMITH.

Number	Title	Yr	NM
COLGEMS			
❑ CGLP-102	I'm a Believer/Mary, Mary/When Love Comes Knockin' (At Your Door)//(I'm Not Your) Steppin' Stone/The Kind of Girl I Could Love/She	1966	$200
— Jukebox issue; small hole, plays at 33 1/3 rpm			
❑ CGLP-102 [PS]	More of the Monkees	1966	$300
ARISTA			
❑ AL-8525	More of the Monkees	1988	$15
❑ AL-8524	The Monkees	1988	$15
❑ AL4089	The Monkees' Greatest Hits	1976	$15
— Reissue of Bell LP			
❑ AL8-8313	The Monkees' Greatest Hits	198?	$10
— Reissue of Arista 4089			
❑ AL9-8432	Then & Now...The Best of the Monkees	1986	$15
BELL			
❑ 6081	Re-Focus	1972	$30
COLGEMS			
❑ SCOS-1001	A Barrel Full of Monkees	1971	$85
❑ COS-119	Changes	1970	$100
❑ COSO-5008	Head	1968	$50
❑ COS-113	Instant Replay	1969	$40
❑ COM-102 [M]	More of the Monkees	1966	$40
❑ COS-102 [S]	More of the Monkees	1966	$35
❑ COS-104 [S]	Pisces, Aquarius, Capricorn & Jones Ltd.	1967	$40
❑ COM-104 [M]	Pisces, Aquarius, Capricorn & Jones Ltd.	1967	$175
❑ COM-109 [M]	The Birds, the Bees & the Monkees	1968	$300
❑ COS-109 [S]	The Birds, the Bees & the Monkees	1968	$25
❑ COM-101 [M]	The Monkees	1966	$40
— First pressing: Side 1, Song 5 listed as "Papa Jean's Blues			
❑ COM-101 [M]	The Monkees	1966	$30
— Second pressing: Side 1, Song 5 listed as "Papa Gene's Blues" (RE after number on upper right back cover)			
❑ COS-101 [S]	The Monkees	1966	$40
— First pressing: Side 1, Song 5 listed as "Papa Jean's Blues			
❑ COS-101 [S]	The Monkees	1966	$30
— Second pressing: Side 1, Song 5 listed as "Papa Gene's Blues" (RE after number on upper right back cover)			
❑ PRS-329	The Monkees' Golden Hits	1971	$150
— RCA Special Products edition			
❑ COS-115	The Monkees Greatest Hits	1969	$40
❑ COM-103 [M]	The Monkees' Headquarters	1967	$100
— First pressing: Back cover, center bottom photo is of two of the LP's producers			
❑ COS-103 [S]	The Monkees' Headquarters	1967	$35
— First pressing: Back cover, center bottom photo is of two of the LP's producers			

Number	Title	Yr	NM
❏ COM-103 [M]	The Monkees' Headquarters	1967	$30

—Second pressing: Back cover, center bottom photo is of producers plus the Monkees with beards; "RE" on upper right back cover

Number	Title	Yr	NM
❏ COS-103 [S]	The Monkees' Headquarters	1967	$30

—Second pressing: Back cover, center bottom photo is of producers plus the Monkees with beards; "RE" on upper right back cover

Number	Title	Yr	NM
❏ COS-117	The Monkees Present	1969	$50

FSH

Number	Title	Yr	NM
❏ 71110	Live, 20th Anniversary Tour	1987	$25

—Live album sold at tour stops

LAURIE HOUSE

Number	Title	Yr	NM
❏ LH-8009	The Monkees	1974	$25

— TV mail-order offer

PAIR

Number	Title	Yr	NM
❏ ARPDL2-1109	Hit Factory	1986	$25

RCA SPECIAL PRODUCTS

Number	Title	Yr	NM
❏ DPL2-0188	The Monkees	1976	$30

— TV mail-order offer

RHINO

Number	Title	Yr	NM
❏ RNLP-70148	Changes	1986	$20
❏ RNLP-145	Head	1985	$15
❏ RNLP-146	Instant Replay	1985	$15
❏ RNLP-70139	Live 1967	1987	$25
❏ RNLP-70150	Missing Links	1987	$15
❏ RNLP-701 [PD]	Monkee Business	1982	$18
❏ RNLP-113	Monkee Flips	1984	$15
❏ RNLP-70142	More of the Monkees	1986	$15
❏ RNLP-70141	Pisces, Aquarius, Capricorn & Jones Ltd.	1986	$15
❏ RNIN-70706	Pool It!	1987	$20
❏ RNLP-144	The Birds, the Bees and the Monkees	1985	$15
❏ RNLP-70140	The Monkees	1986	$15
❏ RNLP-70143	The Monkees' Headquarters	1986	$15
❏ RNLP-147	The Monkees Present	1985	$15

SILHOUETTE

Number	Title	Yr	NM
❏ SM-10012 [PD]	Tails of the Monkees	1983	$18

SILVER EAGLE

Number	Title	Yr	NM
❏ SE-1048	The Best of the Monkees	1986	$18

— TV mail-order offer

SUNDAZED

Number	Title	Yr	NM
❏ LP5046	More of the Monkees	1996	$12
❏ LP5048	Pisces, Aquarius, Capricorn & Jones Ltd.	1996	$12
❏ LP5049	The Birds, the Bees, and the Monkees	1996	$12

—All of the above are on colored vinyl with bonus tracks and posters

Number	Title	Yr	NM
❏ LP5045	The Monkees	1996	$12
❏ LP5047	The Monkees Headquarters	1996	$12

MONNIER, ALAIN

HAT HUT

Number	Title	Yr	NM
❏ 3505	Tribulat	198?	$35

MONOCHROME SET

4 MEN WITH BEARDS

Number	Title	Yr	NM
❏ 4M531LP [B]	Love Zombies		$25
❏ 4M530LP [B]	Strange Boutique		$25

MONRO, MATT

CAPITOL

Number	Title	Yr	NM
❏ SKAO-152	Best of Matt Monro	1969	$12
❏ T2608 [M]	Here's to My Lady	1966	$15
❏ ST2608 [S]	Here's to My Lady	1966	$18
❏ T2683 [M]	Invitation to Broadway	1967	$15
❏ ST2683 [S]	Invitation to Broadway	1967	$18
❏ T2730 [M]	Invitation to the Movies/Born Free	1967	$18
❏ ST2730 [S]	Invitation to the Movies/Born Free	1967	$15
❏ T2801 [M]	These Years	1968	$18
❏ ST2801 [S]	These Years	1968	$15
❏ T2540 [M]	This Is the Life	1966	$15
❏ ST2540 [S]	This Is the Life	1966	$18

LIBERTY

Number	Title	Yr	NM
❏ LRP-3423 [M]	All My Loving	1965	$15
❏ LST-7423 [S]	All My Loving	1965	$18
❏ LRP-3256 [M]	From Hollywood With Love	1962	$18
❏ LST-7256 [S]	From Hollywood With Love	1962	$25
❏ LRP-3240 [M]	Matt Monro	1962	$18
❏ LST-7240 [S]	Matt Monro	1962	$25
❏ LRP-3459 [M]	Matt Monro's Best	1966	$15
❏ LST-7459 [S]	Matt Monro's Best	1966	$18
❏ LRP-3402 [M]	Walk Away	1965	$15
❏ LST-7402 [S]	Walk Away	1965	$18
❏ LRP-3437 [M]	Yesterday	1966	$15
❏ LST-7437 [S]	Yesterday	1966	$18

LONDON

Number	Title	Yr	NM
❏ LL1611 [M]	Blue and Sentimental	1957	$30

PICKWICK

Number	Title	Yr	NM
❏ SPC-3147	This Is All I Ask	197?	$12

WARWICK

Number	Title	Yr	NM
❏ W2045 [M]	My Kind of Girl	1961	$30

Number	Title	Yr	NM
❏ WST2045 [S]	My Kind of Girl	1961	$50

MONROE, BILL

COLUMBIA

Number	Title	Yr	NM
❏ FC38904	Columbia Historic Editions	1983	$15

DECCA

Number	Title	Yr	NM
❏ DL75135	A Voice from On High	1969	$25
❏ DL75010	Bill Monroe's Greatest Hits	1968	$25
❏ DL4601 [M]	Bluegrass Instrumentals	1965	$25
❏ DL74601 [S]	Bluegrass Instrumentals	1965	$30
❏ DL4266 [M]	Bluegrass Ramble	1962	$30
❏ DL74266 [S]	Bluegrass Ramble	1962	$40
❏ DL4382 [M]	Bluegrass Special	1963	$30
❏ DL74382 [S]	Bluegrass Special	1963	$30
❏ DL4896 [M]	Bluegrass Time	1967	$30
❏ DL74896 [S]	Bluegrass Time	1967	$25
❏ DL75281	Country Music Hall of Fame	1972	$25
❏ DL4537 [M]	I'll Meet You in Chuch Sunday Morning	1964	$30
❏ DL74537 [S]	I'll Meet You in Church Sunday Morning	1964	$30
❏ DL8769 [M]	I Saw the Light	1959	$50
❏ DL78769 [S]	I Saw the Light	1959	$80
❏ DL75213	Kentucky Bluegrass	1970	$25
❏ DL8731 [M]	Knee Deep in Bluegrass	1958	$50
❏ DL78731 [S]	Knee Deep in Bluegrass	1958	$80
❏ DL4080 [M]	Mr. Bluegrass	1960	$30
❏ DL74080 [S]	Mr. Bluegrass	1960	$40
❏ DL4327 [M]	My All Time Country Favorites	1962	$30
❏ DL74327 [S]	My All Time Country Favorites	1962	$30
❏ DL4780 [M]	The High Lonesome Sound of Bill Monroe	1966	$25
❏ DL74780 [S]	The High Lonesome Sound of Bill Monroe	1966	$30

HARMONY

Number	Title	Yr	NM
❏ HL7315 [M]	Bill Monroe's Best	1964	$25
❏ HL7290 [M]	The Great Bill Monroe and His Bluegrass Boys	1961	$30
❏ HS11335 [R]	The Great Bill Monroe and His Bluegrass Boys	1969	$18
❏ HL7338 [M]	The Original Bluegrass Sound	1965	$25

MCA

Number	Title	Yr	NM
❏ 131	A Voice from On High	1973	$15

— Reissue of Decca 75135

Number	Title	Yr	NM
❏ 8002	Bean Blossom	1973	$25
❏ 3209	Bean Blossom '79	1979	$18
❏ 765	Bean Blossom '79	198?	$12

— Reissue of 3209

Number	Title	Yr	NM
❏ 5435	Bill Monroe and Friends	1984	$15
❏ 5625	Bill Monroe and the Stars of the Bluegrass Hall of Fame	1985	$15
❏ 17	Bill Monroe's Greatest Hits	1973	$15

— Reissue of Decca 75010

Number	Title	Yr	NM
❏ 2251	Bill Monroe Sings Bluegrass, Body and Soul	1977	$18
❏ 708	Bill Monroe Sings Bluegrass, Body and Soul	198?	$12

— Reissue of 2251

Number	Title	Yr	NM
❏ 104	Bluegrass Instrumentals	1973	$15

— Reissue of Decca 74601

Number	Title	Yr	NM
❏ 2315	Bluegrass Memories	1978	$18
❏ 88	Bluegrass Ramble	1973	$15

— Reissue of Decca 74266

Number	Title	Yr	NM
❏ 97	Bluegrass Special	1973	$15

— Reissue of Decca 74382

Number	Title	Yr	NM
❏ 116	Bluegrass Time	1973	$15

— Reissue of Decca 74896

Number	Title	Yr	NM
❏ 140	Country Music Hall of Fame	1973	$15

— Reissue of Decca 75281

Number	Title	Yr	NM
❏ 226	I'll Meet You in Church Sunday Morning	1973	$15

— Reissue of Decca 74537

Number	Title	Yr	NM
❏ 527	I Saw the Light	197?	$15

— Reissue of Decca 78769

Number	Title	Yr	NM
❏ 136	Kentucky Bluegrass	1973	$15

— Reissue of Decca 75213

Number	Title	Yr	NM
❏ 82	Mr. Bluegrass	1973	$15

— Reissue of Decca 74080

Number	Title	Yr	NM
❏ 426	Road of Life	1974	$18
❏ 4090	The Best of Bill Monroe	197?	$18
❏ 110	The High Lonesome Sound of Bill Monroe	1973	$15

— Reissue of Decca 74780

Number	Title	Yr	NM
❏ 500	Uncle Pen	197?	$15
❏ 2173	Weary Traveler	1976	$18
❏ 707	Weary Traveler	198?	$12

— Reissue of 2173

RCA CAMDEN

Number	Title	Yr	NM
❏ CAL-719 [M]	Father of Bluegrass Music	1962	$30

MONROE, CHARLIE

STARDAY

Number	Title	Yr	NM
❏ SLP-372 [M]	Charlie Monroe Sings Again	1966	$30
❏ SLP-361 [M]	Lord, Build Me a Cabin	1965	$30

MONROE, MARILYN

20TH CENTURY

Number	Title	Yr	NM
❏ T-901 [B]	Remember Marilyn	1973	$30

20TH FOX

Number	Title	Yr	NM
❏ FXG-5000 [M]	Marilyn	1962	$175
❏ SXG-5000 [R]	Marilyn	1962	$150
❏ F/SXG-5000	Marilyn Bonus Photo	1962	$50

ASCOT

Number	Title	Yr	NM
❏ AM-13008 [M]	Marilyn Monroe	1963	$75
❏ AS-16008 [S]	Marilyn Monroe	1963	$50

CLEOPATRA

Number	Title	Yr	NM
❏ 3258 [B]	Diamonds Are A Girl's Best Friend		$18
❏ 8202 [B]	Diamonds Are A Girl's Best Friend - 50th Anniversary Edition		$30

—picture disc

Number	Title	Yr	NM
❏ 8992 [B]	Golden Collection		$30
❏ 5364 [B]	Greatest Moments		$25
❏ 3042 [B]	The Essential Masters		$25

MOVIETONE

Number	Title	Yr	NM
❏ 1016 [M]	The Unforgettable Marilyn Monroe	1967	$30
❏ 72016 [R]	The Unforgettable Marilyn Monroe	1967	$25

SANDY HOOK

Number	Title	Yr	NM
❏ SH-2013 [PD]	Rare Recordings 1948-1962	1980	$30

STET

Number	Title	Yr	NM
❏ DS-15005	Never Before and Never Again	1980	$18

MONROE, VAUGHN

DOT

Number	Title	Yr	NM
❏ DLP-3548 [M]	Great Gospels -- Great Hymns	1963	$75
❏ DLP-25548 [S]	Great Gospels -- Great Hymns	1963	$75
❏ DLP-3470 [M]	Great Themes of Famous Bands and Famous Singers	1962	$75
❏ DLP-25470 [S]	Great Themes of Famous Bands and Famous Singers	1962	$75
❏ DLP-3431 [M]	His Greatest Hits	1962	$75
❏ DLP-25431 [S]	His Greatest Hits	1962	$75
❏ DLP-3584 [M]	His Greatest Hits, Volume 2	1964	$75
❏ DLP-25584 [S]	His Greatest Hits, Volume 2	1964	$75
❏ DLP-3419 [M]	Surfer's Stomp	1962	$85
❏ DLP-25419 [S]	Surfer's Stomp	1962	$100

HAMILTON

Number	Title	Yr	NM
❏ HLP-137 [M]	Racing with the Moon	1965	$12
❏ HLP-12137 [S]	Racing with the Moon	1965	$15

RCA CAMDEN

Number	Title	Yr	NM
❏ CAL-329 [M]	Dance with Me	1956	$30
❏ CAL-354 [M]	Dreamland Special	1956	$30

RCA VICTOR

Number	Title	Yr	NM
❏ LPM-1493 [M]	House Party	1957	$30
❏ LPM-3817 [M]	The Best of Vaughn Monroe	1967	$25
❏ LSP-3817 [R]	The Best of Vaughn Monroe	1967	$15
❏ ANL1-1140	The Best of Vaughn Monroe	1976	$10
❏ LPM-1799 [M]	There I Sing, Swing It Again	1958	$30
❏ LSP-1799 [S]	There I Sing, Swing It Again	1958	$30
❏ VPM-6073	This Is Vaughn Monroe	1972	$20
❏ LPM-3048 [10]	Vaughn Monroe Caravan	1952	$40
❏ LPM-13 [10]	Vaughn Monroe Plays Victor Herbert for Dancing	1952	$40

MONROE BROTHERS, THE

BLUEBIRD

Number	Title	Yr	NM
❏ AXM2-5510	Feast Here Tonight	197?	$18

MONROES, THE

ALFA

Number	Title	Yr	NM
❏ AAE-15015 [EP]	The Monroes	1982	$25

MONTAGE

LAURIE

Number	Title	Yr	NM
❏ SLP-2049	Montage	1969	$25

MONTANA, PATSY

SIMS

Number	Title	Yr	NM
❏ 122 [M]	The New Sound of Patsy Montana	1964	$50

STARDAY

Number	Title	Yr	NM
❏ SLP-376 [M]	Cowboy's Sweetheart	1966	$30

MONTANA

LABOR

Number	Title	Yr	NM
❏ 5	Montana	198?	$30

MONTANA SLIM

DECCA

Number	Title	Yr	NM
❏ DL8917 [M]	I'm Ragged But I'm Right	1959	$75
❏ DL4092 [M]	The Dynamite Trail	1960	$50
❏ DL74092 [S]	The Dynamite Trail	1960	$75

RCA CAMDEN

Number	Title	Yr	NM
❏ CAL-846 [M]	32 Wonderful Years	1965	$25
❏ CAS-846 [R]	32 Wonderful Years	1965	$15
❏ CAL-668 [M]	Reminiscin' with Montana Slim	1962	$30
❏ CAL-527 [M]	Wilf Carter/Montana Slim	1958	$40

Number	Title	Yr	NM
STARDAY			
❏ SLP-389 [M]	Wilf Carter	1966	$30
❏ SLP-300 [M]	Wilf Carter As Montana Slim	1964	$30

MONTARROYOS, MARCIO

Number	Title	Yr	NM
BLACK SUN			
❏ 15001	Samba Solstice	1987	$30
COLUMBIA			
❏ FC38952	Carioca	1983	$25
LORIMAR			
❏ FC37929	Magic Moment	1982	$25
PM			
❏ 014	Marcio Montarroyos and Stone Alliance	1977	$35

MONTE, LOU

Number	Title	Yr	NM
RCA CAMDEN			
❏ CAL-455 [M]	Here's Lou Monte	195?	$15
RCA VICTOR			
❏ LPM-3705 [M]	Good Time Songs	1967	$18
❏ LSP-3705 [S]	Good Time Songs	1967	$15
❏ LPM-1976 [M]	Italian House Party	1959	$25
❏ LSP-1976 [S]	Italian House Party	1959	$30
❏ LPM-1651 [M]	Lou Monte Sings for You	1957	$30
❏ LPM-1877 [M]	Songs for Pizza Lovers	1958	$30
❏ LPM-3672 [M]	The Best of Lou Monte	1966	$18
❏ LSP-3672 [S]	The Best of Lou Monte	1966	$15
REPRISE			
❏ R-6005 [M]	Great Italian-American Hits	1961	$25
❏ R9-6005 [S]	Great Italian-American Hits	1961	$30
❏ R-6014 [M]	Live in Person	1961	$25
❏ R9-6014 [S]	Live in Person	1961	$30
❏ R-6099 [M]	More Italian Fun Songs	1963	$25
❏ R9-6099 [S]	More Italian Fun Songs	1963	$30
❏ R-6058 [M]	Pepino The Italian Mouse & Other Italian Fun Songs	1962	$25
❏ R9-6058 [S]	Pepino The Italian Mouse & Other Italian Fun Songs	1962	$30
❏ R-6118 [M]	The Golden Hits of Lou Monte	1964	$18
❏ RS-6118 [S]	The Golden Hits of Lou Monte	1964	$25
ROULETTE			
❏ R-25126 [M]	Italiano U.S.A.	1960	$25
❏ SR-25126 [S]	Italiano U.S.A.	1960	$30
❏ R-25257 [M]	The Magic World of Italy	1963	$18
❏ SR-25257 [S]	The Magic World of Italy	1963	$25

MONTEGO JOE

Number	Title	Yr	NM
ESP-DISK'			
❏ S-1067	Montego Joe's HARYOU Percussion Ensemble	1968	$250
PRESTIGE			
❏ PRLP-7336 [M]	Arriba Con Montego Joe	1964	$30
❏ PRST-7336 [S]	Arriba Con Montego Joe	1964	$30
❏ PRLP-7413 [M]	Wild and Warm	1966	$75
❏ PRST-7413 [S]	Wild and Warm	1966	$75

MONTENEGRO, HUGO

Includes some of his soundtracks; others are in the "Soundtracks" and "Television Albums" sections.

Number	Title	Yr	NM
20TH CENTURY FOX			
❏ S-4204	Lady in Cement	1968	$25
20TH FOX			
❏ 3018 [M]	The 20th Century Strings, Volume 1	1959	$25
BAINBRIDGE			
❏ 1002	American Musical Theatre, Volume 1 (1924-1935)	198?	$10
❏ 1003	American Musical Theatre, Volume 2 (1935-1945)	198?	$10
❏ 1004	American Musical Theatre, Volume 3 (1946-1952)	198?	$10
❏ 1005	American Musical Theatre, Volume 4 (1953-1960)	198?	$10
❏ 1009	Big Band Boogie	198?	$10
❏ 1021	Camelot	198?	$10
❏ 1028	Hugo Montenegro Plays the Movies	198?	$10
GWP			
❏ 2003	The Dawn of Dylan	1971	$18
MAINSTREAM			
❏ 56101 [M]	Camelot	1967	$18
❏ S-6101 [S]	Camelot	1967	$15
RCA CAMDEN			
❏ CAS-2309	Hawaiian Wedding Song	1969	$12
❏ CAL-729 [M]	In a Sentimental Mood	196?	$15
❏ CAS-729 [S]	In a Sentimental Mood	196?	$15
RCA VICTOR			
❏ LSP-4273	Colours of Love	1970	$15
❏ LPM-3540 [M]	Come Spy with Me	1966	$15
❏ LSP-3540 [S]	Come Spy with Me	1966	$18
❏ LSP-4104	Good Vibrations	1969	$18
❏ LPM-4022 [M]	Hang 'Em High	1968	$40
❏ LSP-4022 [S]	Hang 'Em High	1968	$18
❏ APL1-0413	Hugo in Wonderland	1974	$15
❏ ARD1-0413 [Q]	Hugo in Wonderland	1974	$20
❏ ARD1-0001 [Q]	Love Theme from "The Godfather"	1972	$18

Number	Title	Yr	NM
❏ LSP-4631	Mammy Blue	1971	$15
❏ LSP-4170	Moog Power	1969	$25
❏ LPM-3927 [M]	Music from A Fistful of Dollars & For a Few Dollars More & The Good, The Bad and The Ugly	1968	$25
❏ LSP-3927 [S]	Music from A Fistful of Dollars & For a Few Dollars More & The Good, The Bad and The Ugly	1968	$18
❏ ANL1-1094	Music from A Fistful of Dollars & For a Few Dollars More & The Good, The Bad and The Ugly	1975	$12
❏ ARD1-0132 [Q]	Neil's Diamonds	1973	$20
❏ ARD1-0784 [Q]	Others by Brothers	1974	$20
❏ LSP-4537	People…One to One	1971	$15
❏ APL1-1024	Rocket Man	1975	$15
❏ APD1-1024 [Q]	Rocket Man	1975	$30
❏ APD1-0025 [Q]	Scenes and Themes	1973	$30
❏ LSP-4361	The Best of Hugo Montenegro	1970	$15
❏ AFL1-4361	The Best of Hugo Montenegro	1977	$12
❏ ANL1-2348	The Neil Diamond Songbook	1977	$12
❏ LSP-2958 [S]	The Young Beat of Rome	1964	$18
❏ LPM-2958 [M]	The Young Beat of Rome	1964	$15
❏ VPS-6036	This Is Hugo Montenegro	1971	$18
TIME			
❏ 52035 [M]	American Musical Theatre, Volume 1 (1924-1935)	196?	$15
❏ S-2035 [S]	American Musical Theatre, Volume 1 (1924-1935)	196?	$18
❏ 52036 [M]	American Musical Theatre, Volume 2 (1935-1945)	196?	$15
❏ S-2036 [S]	American Musical Theatre, Volume 2 (1935-1945)	196?	$18
❏ 52037 [M]	American Musical Theatre, Volume 3 (1946-1952)	1961	$15
❏ S-2037 [S]	American Musical Theatre, Volume 3 (1946-1952)	1961	$18
❏ 52038 [M]	American Musical Theatre, Volume 4 (1953-1960)	1961	$15
❏ S-2038 [S]	American Musical Theatre, Volume 4 (1953-1960)	1961	$18
❏ 52030 [M]	Arriba	196?	$18
❏ S-2030 [S]	Arriba	196?	$25
❏ 52020 [M]	Boogie Woogie and Bongos	196?	$18
❏ S-2020 [S]	Boogie Woogie and Bongos	196?	$25
❏ 52018 [M]	Cha Chas for Dancing	196?	$18
❏ S-2018 [S]	Cha Chas for Dancing	196?	$25
❏ 52044 [M]	Great Songs from Motion Pictures Vol. 1 (1927-1937)	1961	$15
❏ S-2044 [S]	Great Songs from Motion Pictures Vol. 1 (1927-1937)	1961	$18
❏ 52045 [M]	Great Songs from Motion Pictures Vol. 2 (1938-1944)	1961	$15
❏ S-2045 [S]	Great Songs from Motion Pictures Vol. 2 (1938-1944)	1961	$18
❏ 52046 [M]	Great Songs from Motion Pictures Vol. 3 (1945-1960)	1961	$15
❏ S-2046 [S]	Great Songs from Motion Pictures Vol. 3 (1945-1960)	1961	$18
❏ TDM3003 [M]	Italy - Ciao	196?	$18
❏ TDS3003 [S]	Italy - Ciao	196?	$25
❏ 52051 [M]	Montenegro in Italy	196?	$15
❏ S-2051 [S]	Montenegro in Italy	196?	$18
VIK			
❏ LX-1106 [M]	Ellington Fantasy	1957	$30
❏ LX-1089 [M]	Loves of My Life	1957	$30

MONTEROSE, J.R.

Number	Title	Yr	NM
BLUE NOTE			
❏ BLP-1536 [M]	J.R. Monterose	1956	$1500
—Deep groove" version; Lexington Ave. address on label			
❏ BLP-1536 [M]	J.R. Monterose	1956	$800
—Deep groove" version, W. 63rd St. address on label			
❏ BLP-1536 [M]	J.R. Monterose	1963	$175
—With "New York, USA" address on label			
❏ BST-81536 [R]	J.R. Monterose	1967	$35
—With "A Division of Liberty Records" on label			
❏ BLP-1536 [M]	J.R. Monterose	2003	$150
—200-gram reissue; distributed by Classic Records			
CADENCE JAZZ			
❏ CJ-1013	Bebop Loose and Live	198?	$50
JARO			
❏ JAM-5004 [M]	The Message	1959	$1000
❏ JAS-8004 [S]	The Message	1959	$1000
PROGRESSIVE			
❏ PRO7049	Lush Life	1979	$75
STUDIO 4			
❏ 100 [M]	J.R. Monterose in Action	195?	$2000
UPTOWN			
❏ 272	J.R. Monterose in Albany	1980	$35
❏ 276	J.R. Monterose in Duo with Tommy Flanagan….And a Little Pleasure	198?	$35
XANADU			
❏ 126	Straight Ahead	197?	$50

MONTEZ, CHRIS

Number	Title	Yr	NM
A&M			
❏ LP-128 [M]	Foolin' Around	1967	$30

Number	Title	Yr	NM
❏ SP-4128 [S]	Foolin' Around	1967	$25
❏ LP-115 [M]	The More I See You/Call Me	1966	$25
❏ ST-4115 [S]	The More I See You/Call Me	1966	$30
❏ LP-120 [M]	Time After Time	1966	$18
❏ SP-4120 [S]	Time After Time	1966	$25
❏ LP-157 [M]	Watch What Happens	1967	$18
❏ SP-4157 [S]	Watch What Happens	1967	$25
MONOGRAM			
❏ M-100 [M]	Let's Dance and Have Some Kinda' Fun!!!	1963	$400

MONTGOMERY, BUDDY

Number	Title	Yr	NM
ABC IMPULSE!			
❏ AS-9192	This Rather Than That	1970	$250
BEAN			
❏ 102	Ties	197?	$35
LANDMARK			
❏ LLP-1518	So Why Not?	1989	$30
❏ LLP-1512	Ties of Love	1987	$25
MILESTONE			
❏ M-9015	Two-Sided Album	1969	$25

MONTGOMERY, DAVID, AND CECIL LYTLE

Number	Title	Yr	NM
KLAVIER			
❏ 533	Rags and Blues	197?	$30
SONIC ARTS			
❏ 6	Ragtime Piano for Four Hands	197?	$25
—Direct-to-disc recording			

MONTGOMERY, LITTLE BROTHER

Number	Title	Yr	NM
BLUESVILLE			
❏ BVLP-1012 [M]	Tasty Blues	1961	$100
—Blue label, silver print			
❏ BVLP-1012 [M]	Tasty Blues	1964	$30
—Blue label with trident logo at right			
RIVERSIDE			
❏ RS-9410 [S]	Little Brother Montgomery, Chicago Living Legend	1962	$40
❏ RLP-410 [M]	Little Brother Montgomery, Chicago Living Legend	1962	$30

MONTGOMERY, MARIAN

Number	Title	Yr	NM
CAPITOL			
❏ T1962 [M]	Let There Be Love, Let There Be Swing, Let There Be Marian Montgomery	1963	$75
❏ ST1962 [S]	Let There Be Love, Let There Be Swing, Let There Be Marian Montgomery	1963	$75
❏ T2185 [M]	Lovin' Is Livin'	1964	$75
❏ ST2185 [S]	Lovin' Is Livin'	1964	$75
❏ T1884 [M]	Marian Montgomery Swings for Winners and Losers	1963	$75
❏ ST1884 [S]	Marian Montgomery Swings for Winners and Losers	1963	$75
DECCA			
❏ DL4773 [M]	What's New?	1965	$25
❏ DL74773 [S]	What's New?	1965	$30

MONTGOMERY, MELBA

Also see GEORGE JONES; CHARLIE LOUVIN; GENE PITNEY.

Number	Title	Yr	NM
CAPITOL			
❏ ST-468	Don't Keep Me Lonely Too Long	1970	$18
❏ ST-328	The Big, Wonderful Country World of Melba Montgomery	1969	$18
—This is the title on the cover; the label calls this "The Big, Beautiful Country World of Melba Montgomery			
ELEKTRA			
❏ CM-2	Don't Let the Good Times Fool You	1975	$12
❏ EKS-75069	Melba Montgomery	1973	$15
❏ EKS-75079	No Charge	1974	$12
❏ CM-6	The Greatest Gift of All	1975	$12
HILLTOP			
❏ JS-6031	Miss Country Music	196?	$15
MUSICOR			
❏ MM-2074 [M]	Country Girl	1966	$18
❏ MS-3074 [S]	Country Girl	1966	$25
❏ MM-2114 [M]	Don't Keep Me Lonely Too Long	1967	$25
❏ MS-3114 [S]	Don't Keep Me Lonely Too Long	1967	$25
❏ MM-2113 [M]	Melba Toast	1967	$25
❏ MS-3113 [S]	Melba Toast	1967	$25
❏ MM-2097 [M]	The Hallelujah Road	1966	$18
❏ MS-3097 [S]	The Hallelujah Road	1966	$25
STARDAY			
❏ SLP-352 [M]	Queen of Country Music	1965	$30
UNITED ARTISTS			
❏ UAL-3341 [M]	America's Number One Country and Western Girl Singer	1964	$25
❏ UAS-6341 [S]	America's Number One Country and Western Girl Singer	1964	$30

Number	Title	Yr	NM
❑ UAL-3369 [M]	Down Home	1964	$25
❑ UAS-6369 [S]	Down Home	1964	$30
❑ UAL-3391 [M]	I Can't Get Used to Being Lonely	1965	$25
❑ UAS-6391 [S]	I Can't Get Used to Being Lonely	1965	$30

MONTGOMERY, MONK
CHISA
| ❑ CS-806 | Bass Odyssey | 1971 | $25 |
| ❑ CS-801 | It's Never Too Late | 1970 | $25 |

PHILADELPHIA INT'L.
| ❑ KZ33153 [B] | Reality | 1974 | $75 |

MONTGOMERY, WES
A&M
❑ LP-2001 [M]	A Day in the Life	1967	$50
❑ SP-3001 [S]	A Day in the Life	1967	$30
❑ SP9-3001	A Day in the Life	1983	$35

—Audio Master Plus" reissue
| ❑ SP-3006 | Down Here on the Ground | 1968 | $35 |
| ❑ SP9-3006 | Down Here on the Ground | 1983 | $35 |

—Audio Master Plus" reissue
❑ SP-4247	Greatest Hits	1970	$35
❑ SP-3012	Road Song	1968	$35
❑ SP9-3012	Road Song	1984	$35

—Audio Master Plus" reissue

ACCORD
| ❑ SN-7170 | The Classic Sound of Wes Montgomery | 1981 | $25 |

BLUE NOTE
| ❑ BN-LA531-H2 | Beginnings | 1976 | $75 |
| ❑ LWB-531 | Beginnings | 1981 | $75 |

—Reissue of BN-LA531-H2

DCC COMPACT CLASSICS
| ❑ LPZ-2014 | Goin' Out of My Head | 1996 | $40 |

—Audiophile vinyl

FANTASY
❑ OJC-034	A Dynamic New Sound	198?	$30
❑ OJC-261	Boss Guitar	1987	$30
❑ OJC-106	Full House	198?	$30
❑ OJC-368	Fusion! Wes Montgomery with Strings	198?	$30
❑ OJC-489	Guitar on the Go	1991	$35
❑ OJC-089	Movin' Along	198?	$30
❑ OJC-144	Portrait of Wes	198?	$30
❑ OJC-233	So Much Guitar!	198?	$30
❑ OJC-036	The Incredible Jazz Guitar of Wes Montgomery	198?	$30

MGM
| ❑ GAS-120 | Wes Montgomery (Golden Archive Series) | 1970 | $35 |

MILESTONE
❑ 9110	Encores	1983	$25
❑ 47051	Groove Brothers	1979	$30
❑ 47040	Movin'	197?	$30
❑ 47030	Pretty Blue	197?	$30
❑ 47065	The Alternative Wes Montgomery	1982	$30
❑ 47013	Wes Montgomery and Friends	1973	$35
❑ 47003	While We're Young	1972	$35
❑ 47057	Yesterdays	198?	$30

MOBILE FIDELITY
| ❑ MFSL-508 | Bumpin' | 198? | $150 |

—Original Master Recording" at top of cover

PACIFIC JAZZ
❑ PJ-10104 [M]	Easy Groove	1966	$35
❑ ST-20104 [S]	Easy Groove	1966	$50
❑ PJ-10130 [M]	Kismet	1967	$50
❑ ST-20130 [S]	Kismet	1967	$35
❑ PJ-5 [M]	Montgomeryland	1960	$75
❑ ST-5 [S]	Montgomeryland	1960	$40
❑ ST-20137	Portrait of Wes Montgomery	1968	$35

PICCADILLY
| ❑ 3584 | Jazz Guitar | 198? | $25 |

RIVERSIDE
❑ RLP 12-310 [M]	A Dynamic New Sound	1959	$300
❑ RLP-459 [M]	Boss Guitar	1963	$175
❑ RS-9459 [S]	Boss Guitar	1963	$175
❑ 6111	Boss Guitar	197?	$25
❑ RLP-434 [M]	Full House	1962	$700
❑ RS-9434 [S]	Full House	1962	$175
❑ 6069	Full House	197?	$25
❑ RLP-472 [M]	Fusion! Wes Montgomery with Strings	1964	$175
❑ RS-9472 [S]	Fusion! Wes Montgomery with Strings	1964	$175
❑ 6210	Fusion! Wes Montgomery with Strings	198?	$25
❑ RLP-494 [M]	Guitar on the Go	1965	$175
❑ RS-9494 [S]	Guitar on the Go	1965	$175
❑ 6168	Guitar on the Go	198?	$25
❑ RM-3002 [M]	In the Wee Small Hours	1967	$150

—Reissue of 472
| ❑ RS-3002 [S] | In the Wee Small Hours | 1967 | $150 |

—Reissue of 9472
| ❑ RS-3036 | March 6, 1925-June 15, 1968 | 1968 | $150 |

Number	Title	Yr	NM
❑ RLP-342 [M]	Movin' Along	1960	$250
❑ RS-9342 [S]	Movin' Along	1960	$250
❑ 6199	Movin' Along	198?	$25
❑ RLP1156 [S]	New Concepts in Jazz Guitar	1959	$300
❑ RS-3046	Panorama	1969	$150
❑ RLP-492 [M]	Portrait of Wes	1965	$175
❑ RS-9492 [S]	Portrait of Wes	1965	$175
❑ 6202	Portrait of Wes	198?	$25
❑ RS-3014	'Round Midnight	1968	$150

—Reissue of 1156
❑ RLP-382 [M]	So Much Guitar!	1961	$250
❑ RS-9382 [S]	So Much Guitar!	1961	$250
❑ 6100	So Much Guitar!	197?	$25
❑ RS-3039	The Best of Wes Montgomery	1968	$150
❑ 6080	The Dynamic New Jazz Sound of Wes Montgomery	197?	$25
❑ RLP 12-320 [M]	The Incredible Jazz Guitar of Wes Montgomery	1960	$600
❑ RLP1169 [S]	The Incredible Jazz Guitar of Wes Montgomery	1960	$250
❑ 6046	The Incredible Jazz Guitar of Wes Montgomery	197?	$25
❑ RS-3012	This Is Wes Montgomery	1968	$150

—Reissue of 9459

VERVE
❑ V-8625 [M]	Bumpin'	1965	$35
❑ V6-8625 [S]	Bumpin'	1965	$50
❑ V-8672 [M]	California Dreaming	1967	$50
❑ V6-8672 [S]	California Dreaming	1967	$35
❑ V6-8796	Eulogy	1970	$35
❑ V-8642 [M]	Goin' Out of My Head	1966	$35
❑ V6-8642 [S]	Goin' Out of My Head	1966	$50
❑ V6-8804	Just Walkin'	1971	$35
❑ V-8610 [M]	Movin' Wes	1965	$35
❑ V6-8610 [S]	Movin' Wes	1965	$50
❑ V3HB-8839	Return Engagement	1974	$35
❑ VE-2-2513	Small Group Recording	197?	$35
❑ V-8653 [M]	Tequila	1966	$35
❑ V6-8653 [S]	Tequila	1966	$25
❑ V-8714 [M]	The Best of Wes Montgomery	1967	$50
❑ V6-8714 [S]	The Best of Wes Montgomery	1967	$35
❑ V6-8757	The Best of Wes Montgomery, Vol. 2	1968	$35
❑ V6-8813	The History of Wes Montgomery	1972	$35
❑ V6-8765	Willow Weep for Me	1969	$35

MONTGOMERY BROTHERS, THE
FANTASY
| ❑ OJC-138 | Groove Yard | 198? | $25 |
| ❑ 3308 [M] | The Montgomery Brothers | 1960 | $50 |

—Red vinyl
| ❑ 3308 [M] | The Montgomery Brothers | 1960 | $30 |

—Black vinyl
| ❑ 8052 [S] | The Montgomery Brothers | 1960 | $40 |

—Blue vinyl
| ❑ 8052 [S] | The Montgomery Brothers | 1960 | $30 |

—Black vinyl
| ❑ 3323 [M] | The Montgomery Brothers in Canada | 1961 | $50 |

—Red vinyl
| ❑ 3323 [M] | The Montgomery Brothers in Canada | 1961 | $30 |

—Black vinyl
| ❑ 8066 [S] | The Montgomery Brothers in Canada | 1961 | $40 |

—Blue vinyl
| ❑ 8066 [S] | The Montgomery Brothers in Canada | 1961 | $30 |

—Black vinyl
❑ OJC-283	The Montgomery Brothers in Canada	1987	$25
❑ 3376 [M]	Wes' Best	1967	$25
❑ 8376 [S]	Wes' Best	1967	$35

PACIFIC JAZZ
| ❑ PJ-17 [M] | Wes, Buddy and Monk Montgomery | 1961 | $30 |

RIVERSIDE
❑ RLP-362 [M]	Groove Yard	1961	$250
❑ RS-9362 [S]	Groove Yard	1961	$250
❑ 6141	Groove Yard	198?	$30

WORLD PACIFIC
| ❑ PJ-1240 [M] | The Montgomery Brothers and Five Others | 1957 | $175 |
| ❑ WP-1240 [M] | The Montgomery Brothers and Five Others | 1958 | $175 |

—Reissue with new prefix

MONTOLIU, TETE
CONTEMPORARY
| ❑ C-14004 | Lunch in L.A. | 1980 | $30 |

ENJA
| ❑ 2040 | Songs for Love | 197? | $35 |

INNER CITY
❑ IC-2017	Catalonian Fire	197?	$35
❑ IC-2021	Music for Perla	197?	$35
❑ IC-2029	Tete!	197?	$35

Number	Title	Yr	NM
PAUSA			
❑ 7057	Piano for Nuria	1979	$25
STEEPLECHASE			
❑ SCS-1152/3	Boston Concert	1981	$50
❑ SCS-1148	Catalonian Nights Vol. 1	1980	$30
❑ SCS-1185	Face to Face	198?	$30
❑ SCS-1137	I Wanna Talk About You	1980	$30
❑ SCS-1054	Tete-a-Tete	197?	$30
❑ SCS-1199	That's All	198?	$30
❑ SCS-1108	Tootie's Tempo	198?	$30
TIMELESS			
❑ 304	Catalonian Folksongs	1979	$30

MONTROSE, JACK
ATLANTIC
| ❑ 1223 [M] | Arranged, Played, Composed by Jack Montrose with Bob Gordon | 1956 | $300 |

—Black label
| ❑ 1223 [M] | Arranged, Played, Composed by Jack Montrose with Bob Gordon | 1961 | $300 |

—Multicolor label, white "fan" logo at right
| ❑ 1223 [M] | Arranged, Played, Composed by Jack Montrose with Bob Gordon | 1964 | $35 |

—Multicolor label, black "fan" logo at right

PACIFIC JAZZ
| ❑ PJ-1208 [M] | Jack Montrose Sextet | 1955 | $175 |

—Red vinyl
| ❑ PJ-1208 [M] | Jack Montrose Sextet | 1955 | $100 |

—Black vinyl

RCA VICTOR
| ❑ LPM-1451 [M] | Blues and Vanilla | 1957 | $50 |
| ❑ LPM-1572 [M] | The Horns Full | 1957 | $50 |

WORLD PACIFIC
| ❑ WP-1208 [M] | Jack Montrose Sextet | 1958 | $175 |

MONTROSE
Also see SAMMY HAGAR; GAMMA; VAN HALEN; CHICKENFOOT.
ENIGMA
| ❑ ST-73264 | Mean | 1987 | $12 |
| ❑ D1-73323 | Speed of Sound | 1988 | $12 |

WARNER BROS.
❑ BS2963	Jump On It	1976	$12
❑ BS2740	Montrose	1974	$15
❑ BSK3106	Montrose	1978	$10

—Reissue of 2740
| ❑ BS2823 | Paper Money | 1974 | $12 |
| ❑ BS2892 | Warner Bros. Presents Montrose! | 1975 | $12 |

MONTY PYTHON
ARISTA
| ❑ AL4039 [B] | Matching Tie & Handkerchief | 1975 | $30 |

—Side 2 is "trick tracked," with two different routines depending on where you place the needle at the start
| ❑ AL8357 | Matching Tie and Handkerchief | 198? | $10 |

—Reissue; we don't know whether Side 2 maintains the trick groove on this issue
| ❑ AL4073 | Monty Python Live! At City Center | 1976 | $25 |
| ❑ AL8353 | Monty Python Live! At City Center | 198? | $10 |

—Reissue
| ❑ AB9536 | Monty Python's Contractual Obligation Album | 1980 | $25 |
| ❑ AL8343 | Monty Python's Contractual Obligation Album | 198? | $10 |

—Reissue
| ❑ SP-101 [DJ] | Monty Python's Contractual Obligation Sampler | 1980 | $30 |

—One side is censored, the other is uncensored
| ❑ AL4050 | The Album of the Soundtrack of the Trailer of the Film of "Monty Python and the Holy Grail | 1975 | $25 |
| ❑ AL8355 | The Album of the Soundtrack of the Trailer of the Film of "Monty Python and the Holy Grail | 198? | $10 |

—Reissue
| ❑ AB9580 | The Monty Python Instant Record Collection | 1981 | $18 |
| ❑ AL8296 | The Monty Python Instant Record Collection | 198? | $10 |

—Reissue

BBC
| ❑ 22073 | Monty Python's Flying Circus | 1980 | $25 |

—Excerpts from TV shows; pressed by Columbia, possibly for exclusive use by the record club

BUDDAH
| ❑ BDS5656 | The Worst of Monty Python | 1976 | $25 |

—Repackage of the two Charisma LPs

Number	Title	Yr	NM

CHARISMA
❏ CAS1049 [B]	Another Monty Python Record	1972	$30
❏ CAS1063 [B]	Monty Python's Previous Record	1972	$30

MCA
❏ 6121	Monty Python and the Meaning of Life	1983	$15

PYE
❏ 12116	Monty Python's Flying Circus	1975	$25

VIRGIN
❏ 90865	The Final Rip Off	1988	$25

WARNER BROS.
❏ BSK3396	Life of Brian	1979	$18

MOODY, CLYDE

KING
❏ 891 [M]	The Best of Clyde Moody	1964	$100

OLD HOMESTEAD
❏ 90013	Moody's Blues -- Bluesy Bluegrass	197?	$18

MOODY, JAMES

ARGO
❏ LP-695 [M]	Another Bag	1962	$30
❏ LPS-695 [S]	Another Bag	1962	$40
❏ LP-740 [M]	Comin' On Strong	1964	$30
❏ LPS-740 [S]	Comin' On Strong	1964	$30
❏ LP-603 [M]	Flute 'n the Blues	1956	$40
—Reissue of Creative 603			
❏ LP-725 [M]	Great Day	1963	$30
❏ LPS-725 [S]	Great Day	1963	$30
❏ LP-666 [M]	Hey! It's James Moody	1960	$30
❏ LPS-666 [S]	Hey! It's James Moody	1960	$40
❏ LP-648 [M]	James Moody	1959	$40
❏ LPS-648 [S]	James Moody	1959	$30
❏ LP-637 [M]	Last Train from Overbrook	1959	$40
❏ LPS-637 [S]	Last Train from Overbrook	1959	$30
❏ LP-613 [M]	Moody's Mood for Love	1957	$40
❏ LP-679 [M]	Moody with Strings	1961	$30
❏ LPS-679 [S]	Moody with Strings	1961	$40

BLUE NOTE
❏ BLP-5006 [10]	James Moody and His Modernists	1952	$300
❏ BLP-5005 [10]	James Moody with Strings	1952	$300

CADET
❏ LP-695 [M]	Another Bag	1966	$30
❏ LPS-695 [S]	Another Bag	1966	$35
❏ LP-740 [M]	Comin' On Strong	1966	$30
❏ LPS-740 [S]	Comin' On Strong	1966	$35
❏ LP-756 [M]	Cookin' the Blues	1965	$25
❏ LPS-756 [S]	Cookin' the Blues	1965	$30
❏ 2CA-60010	Everything About Sax and Flute	1972	$25
❏ LP-603 [M]	Flute 'n the Blues	1966	$35
❏ LP-725 [M]	Great Day	1966	$30
❏ LPS-725 [S]	Great Day	1966	$35
❏ LP-666 [M]	Hey! It's James Moody	1966	$30
❏ LPS-666 [S]	Hey! It's James Moody	1966	$35
❏ LP-648 [M]	James Moody	1966	$30
❏ LPS-648 [S]	James Moody	1966	$35
❏ LP-637 [M]	Last Train from Overbrook	1966	$30
❏ LPS-637 [S]	Last Train from Overbrook	1966	$35
❏ LP-613 [M]	Moody's Mood for Love	1966	$35
❏ LP-679 [M]	Moody with Strings	1966	$30
❏ LPS-679 [S]	Moody with Strings	1966	$35

CHESS
❏ CH-91548	Flute 'n' the Blues	198?	$25
❏ 2ACMJ-403	Moody's Mood	1976	$35
❏ CH-91522	The Great Day	198?	$25

CREATIVE
❏ LP-603 [M]	Flute 'n Blues	1956	$175

DIAL
❏ LP-209 [10]	James Moody, His Saxophone and His Band	1950	$400

EMARCY
❏ MG-26040 [10]	Moodsville	1954	$300
❏ MG-26004 [10]	The Moody Story	1954	$300
❏ MG-36031 [M]	The Moody Story	1955	$250

FANTASY
❏ OJC-188	James Moody's Moods	1985	$25

MILESTONE
❏ M-9023	Blues and Other Colors	1970	$25
❏ M-9005	Brass Figures	1968	$25

MUSE
❏ MR-5020	Feelin' It Together	1974	$30
❏ MR-5001	Never Again!	1973	$30

NOVUS
❏ 3026-1-N	Moving Forward	1988	$25
❏ 3004-1-N	Something Special	1986	$25
❏ 3063-1-N	Sweet and Lovely	1989	$30

PAULA
❏ LPS-4003	Sax and Flute Man	197?	$30

PAUSA
❏ 7029	Too Heavy for Words	1979	$25

PRESTIGE
❏ PRST-7625	Don't Look Away Now!	1969	$35
❏ PRLP-7011 [M]	Hi-Fi Party	1955	$300
❏ PRST-7740	Hi-Fi Party, Volume 2	1970	$35
❏ 24015	James Moody	197?	$35
❏ PRLP-198 [10]	James Moody and His Band	1954	$300
❏ PRLP-110 [10]	James Moody Favorites, No. 1	1951	$300
❏ PRLP-125 [10]	James Moody Favorites, No. 2	1952	$300
❏ PRLP-146 [10]	James Moody Favorites, No. 3	1953	$300
❏ PRLP-7431 [M]	James Moody's Greatest Hits	1967	$30
❏ PRST-7431 [R]	James Moody's Greatest Hits	1967	$35
❏ PRLP-7441 [M]	James Moody's Greatest Hits, Volume 2	1967	$30
❏ PRST-7441 [R]	James Moody's Greatest Hits, Volume 2	1967	$35
❏ PRLP-7056 [M]	James Moody's Moods	1956	$300
❏ PRLP-7072 [M]	Moody	1956	$300
❏ PRLP-157 [10]	Moody in France	1953	$350
❏ PRLP-192 [10]	Moody's Mood	1954	$300
❏ PRST-7554	Moody's Moods	1968	$35
❏ PRLP-7179 [M]	Moody's Workshop	1960	$250
❏ PRST-7663	Moody's Workshop	1969	$35
❏ PRLP-7036 [M]	Wail, Moody, Wail	1956	$300
❏ PRST-7853	Wail Moody Wail, Volume 3	1971	$35

ROOST
❏ RST-405 [10]	James Moody in France	1951	$300

SCEPTER
❏ SRM-525 [M]	Running the Gamut	1965	$25
❏ SPS-525 [S]	Running the Gamut	1965	$30

TRIP
❏ 5521	The Moody Story (1951-52)	197?	$25

VANGUARD
❏ VSD-79404	Beyond	1978	$30
❏ VSD-79381	Sun Journey	1976	$30
❏ VSD-79366	Timeless	1975	$30

MOODY, JAMES/GEORGE WALLINGTON

BLUE NOTE
❏ B-6503 [M]	The Beginning and End of Bop	1969	$30

MOODY, PHIL

SOMERSET
❏ P-10400 [M]	Intimate Jazz	1959	$30

MOODY BLUES, THE
Also see GRAEME EDGE; JUSTIN HAYWARD; DENNY LAINE; RAY THOMAS.

COMPLEAT
❏ 672008	Early Blues	1985	$18
—Reissue of London 1964-66 material			

DERAM
❏ DE16012 [M]	Days of Future Passed	1968	$500
❏ DES18012 [S]	Days of Future Passed	1968	$25
—With large "DERAM" on top half of label			
❏ 820006-1 [S]	Days of Future Passed	1985	$10
❏ DES18012 [S]	Days of Future Passed	1968	$30
—With "LONDON" under "DERAM" on top half of label			
❏ DES18017	In Search of the Lost Chord	1968	$25
—Originals have gatefold covers			
❏ 820168-1	In Search of the Lost Chord	1985	$10
❏ DES18051 [R]	In the Beginning	1971	$25
❏ DES18025	On the Threshold of a Dream	1969	$25
—Originals have gatefold covers and lyric booklet			
❏ 820170-1	On the Threshold of a Dream	1985	$10

LONDON
❏ PS690/1	Caught Live + 5	1977	$15
❏ 820161-1	Caught Live + 5	1985	$10
❏ LL3428 [M]	Go Now -- The Moody Blues #1	1965	$50
❏ PS428 [R]	Go Now -- The Moody Blues #1	1965	$40
❏ PS708 [DJ]	Octave	1978	$30
—Promo only on blue vinyl			
❏ PS708	Octave	1978	$12
❏ 820329-1	Octave	1986	$10

MOBILE FIDELITY
❏ Jan-0042	Days of Future Passed	1980	$150
—Audiophile vinyl			
❏ 1-232	Every Good Boy Deserves Favour	1995	$75
—Audiophile vinyl			
❏ 1-215	On the Threshold of a Dream	1994	$50
—Audiophile vinyl			
❏ 1-151	Seventh Sojourn	1984	$80
—Audiophile vinyl			
❏ 1-253	To Our Children's Children's Children	1996	$75
—Audiophile vinyl			

NAUTILUS
❏ NR-21	On the Threshold of a Dream	1981	$75
—Audiophile vinyl			

❏ NR-21 [B]	On the Threshold of a Dream	1981	$50
—Audiophile vinyl; DBX-encoded version			

POLYDOR
❏ 840 659-1	Greatest Hits (1967-1988)	1989	$18
❏ 835 756-1	Sur La Mer	1988	$15
❏ 829 179-1	The Other Side of Life	1986	$12

THRESHOLD
❏ THS3	A Question of Balance	1970	$18
—White label with purple logo; gatefold cover			
❏ THS3	A Question of Balance	197?	$12
—Blue label; no gatefold			
❏ 820211-1	A Question of Balance	1985	$10
❏ SMAS-93329	A Question of Balance	1971	$25
—Capitol Record Club edition			
❏ THS5	Every Good Boy Deserves Favour	1971	$18
—White label with purple logo; gatefold cover			
❏ THS5	Every Good Boy Deserves Favour	197?	$15
—Blue label; gatefold cover			
❏ 820160-1	Every Good Boy Deserves Favour	1985	$10
❏ THS5	Every Good Boy Deserves Favour	197?	$12
—Blue label; no gatefold			
❏ TR-1-2901	Long Distance Voyager	1981	$12
❏ 820105-1	Long Distance Voyager	1985	$10
❏ THS7	Seventh Sojourn	1972	$18
—White label with purple logo; gatefold cover			
❏ THS7	Seventh Sojourn	197?	$15
—Blue label; gatefold cover			
❏ 820159-1	Seventh Sojourn	1985	$10
❏ THS7	Seventh Sojourn	197?	$12
—Blue label; no gatefold			
❏ THX-100 [DJ]	Special Interview Kit	1971	$175
—Includes script			
❏ TR-1-2902	The Present	1982	$12
❏ 810119-1	The Present	1983	$10
❏ THS12/13	This Is the Moody Blues	1974	$18
❏ 820007-1	This Is the Moody Blues	1985	$10
❏ THS1	To Our Children's Children's Children	1969	$18
—White label with purple logo; gatefold cover			
❏ THS1	To Our Children's Children's Children	197?	$12
—Blue label; no gatefold			
❏ 820155-1	Voices in the Sky/The Best of the Moody Blues	1985	$12

VARESE VINTAGE
❏ 302 067 415 1 [B]	Go Now - Moody Blues #1	2016	$20

MOOG MACHINE, THE

COLUMBIA
❏ CS9959	Christmas Becomes Electric	1969	$25
❏ CS9921	Switched-On Rock	1969	$25

MOON, KEITH
Also see THE WHO.

TRACK/MCA
❏ 2136	Two Sides of the Moon	1975	$25

MOON, THE

IMPERIAL
❏ LP-12444	The Moon	1969	$40
❏ LP-12381	Without Earth	1968	$40

MOONDOC, JEMEEL

CADENCE JAZZ
❏ CJ-1006	New York Live	198?	$25

SOUL NOTE
❏ SN-1051	Judy's Bounce	1981	$30

Number	Title	Yr	NM
❏ SN-1041	Konstanze's Delight	1981	$30

MOONDOG
COLUMBIA

| ❏ KC30897 | Moondog 2 | 1971 | $50 |

— With booklet (deduct 20 percent if missing)
COLUMBIA MASTERWORKS

| ❏ MS7335 | Moondog | 1969 | $30 |

— Gray label with "360 Sound Stereo" at bottom

| ❏ MS7335 | Moondog | 2001 | $15 |

— 180-gram reissue
EPIC

| ❏ LG1002 [10] | Moondog and His Friends | 1954 | $300 |

FANTASY

| ❏ OJC-1741 | Moondog | 1990 | $20 |

MOONDOG

| ❏ 1 | Snaketime Series by Moondog | 1956 | $800 |

— With paper insert; deduct 25 percent if it is missing
MUSICAL HERITAGE SOCIETY

| ❏ MHS3803 | Moondog | 1978 | $40 |

PRESTIGE

| ❏ PRLP-7042 [M] | Moondog | 1956 | $300 |

— Yellow label with W. 50th St. address

| ❏ PRLP-7069 [M] | More Moondog | 1957 | $300 |

— Yellow label with W. 50th St. address

| ❏ PRLP-7099 [M] | The Story of Moondog | 1957 | $500 |

— Yellow label with W. 50th St. address. Andy Warhol cover.

MOONEY, ART
CORONET

❏ CXS-138 [S]	Cha Cha Cha with Art Mooney	196?	$15
❏ CX-138 [M]	Cha Cha Cha with Art Mooney	196?	$12
❏ CX-220 [M]	Dance and Dream	196?	$15
❏ CXS-220 [S]	Dance and Dream	196?	$15

DECCA

| ❏ DL4207 [M] | Songs Everybody Knows | 1962 | $15 |
| ❏ DL74207 [S] | Songs Everybody Knows | 1962 | $18 |

DIPLOMAT

| ❏ DS-2218 [S] | Cha Cha Cha with Art Mooney | 196? | $15 |
| ❏ DS-2246 [S] | Sing Along | 196? | $15 |

HURRAH

| ❏ H-1002 [M] | Big Band Dance Time | 1962 | $12 |
| ❏ HS-1002 [S] | Big Band Dance Time | 1962 | $15 |

KAPP

❏ KL-1405 [M]	Jump for Joy!	1964	$15
❏ KS-3405 [S]	Jump for Joy!	1964	$18
❏ KL-1421 [M]	Sentimental Love Songs of World War II	1965	$15
❏ KS-3421 [S]	Sentimental Love Songs of World War II	1965	$18

LION

| ❏ L-70062 [M] | Those Happy Banjos | 1958 | $18 |

MGM

| ❏ E-3649 [M] | Art Mooney and His Orchestra in Hi-Fi Play for Dancing | 1958 | $25 |

— Reissue of 3628 with new cover and title

❏ E-3616 [M]	Art Mooney in Hi-Fi Dixieland	1957	$25
❏ E-3431 [M]	Art Mooney Presents the Happy Minstrels	1956	$30
❏ E-206 [10]	Banjo Bonanza	1953	$30
❏ E-3899 [M]	Spectacular Voices with Banjos	1961	$15
❏ SE-3899 [S]	Spectacular Voices with Banjos	1961	$18
❏ E-3628 [M]	Sunrise to Sunrise	1958	$40

— Quickly deleted and reissued as 3649 with a new title

| ❏ E-121 [10] | Sunset to Sunrise | 1952 | $30 |

PIROUETTE

| ❏ FM-45 [M] | Cha Cha Cha with Art Mooney | 196? | $12 |

PROMENADE

| ❏ 2218 [M] | Cha Cha Cha with Art Mooney | 196? | $12 |
| ❏ 2246 [M] | Sing Along | 196? | $12 |

RCA VICTOR

| ❏ LPM-3739 [M] | The Best of Art Mooney | 1967 | $25 |
| ❏ LSP-3739 [S] | The Best of Art Mooney | 1967 | $15 |

SPIN-O-RAMA

❏ MK-3079 [M]	Cha Cha Cha with Art Mooney	196?	$12
❏ S-45 [S]	Cha Cha Cha with Art Mooney	196?	$15
❏ M-93 [M]	Dancetime	196?	$12
❏ S-93 [S]	Dancetime	196?	$15

TIARA

| ❏ TM-7545 [M] | Cha Cha Cha with Art Mooney | 196? | $12 |

MOONEY, JOE
ATLANTIC

| ❏ 1255 [M] | Lush Life | 1958 | $300 |

— Black label

| ❏ 1255 [M] | Lush Life | 1961 | $175 |

— Multicolor label, white "fan" logo at right
COLUMBIA

❏ CL2186 [M]	The Greatness of Joe Mooney	1964	$35
❏ CS8986 [S]	The Greatness of Joe Mooney	1964	$25
❏ CL2345 [M]	The Happiness of Joe Mooney	1965	$30
❏ CS9145 [S]	The Happiness of Joe Mooney	1965	$35

DECCA

| ❏ DL8468 [M] | On the Rocks | 1957 | $120 |
| ❏ DL5555 [10] | You Go to My Head | 1955 | $350 |

MOONGLOWS, THE
CHESS

| ❏ LP1430 [M] | Look! It's the Moonglows | 1959 | $500 |
| ❏ CH-9193 | Look! It's the Moonglows | 1987 | $15 |

— Reissue of 1430

| ❏ LP1471 [M] | The Best of Bobby Lester & the Moonglows | 1962 | $300 |

— Black label

| ❏ LP1471 [M] | The Best of Bobby Lester & the Moonglows | 1966 | $50 |

— Blue, fading to white label

| ❏ CH-9111 | Their Greatest Sides | 1986 | $15 |

CONSTELLATION

| ❏ C-2 [M] | Collectors Showcase -- The Moonglows | 1964 | $150 |

— Light blue lettering

| ❏ C-2 [M] | Collectors Showcase -- The Moonglows | 1964 | $50 |

— Dark blue lettering
LOST-NITE

| ❏ LP-23 [10] | The Moonglows | 1981 | $15 |

RCA VICTOR

| ❏ LSP-4722 | The Return of the Moonglows | 1972 | $18 |

MOONLIGHT BROADCASTERS, THE
STOMP OFF

| ❏ SOS-1193 | Radio Nights | 1991 | $25 |

MOONLIGHTERS, THE
CENTURY

| ❏ 29132 | An Evening with the Moonlighters | 197? | $25 |

MOONRAKERS, THE
SHAMLEY

| ❏ 704 | Together | 1968 | $40 |

MOONSHINERS, THE
VILLAGE GATE

| ❏ 2002 [M] | Breakout! | 1964 | $25 |

MOOR, DET
Actually producer and composer Robert Mersey.
GALLANT

| ❏ GT4001 [M] | Great Jazz from Great TV | 1962 | $40 |

MOORE, ADA
DEBUT

| ❏ DLP-15 [10] | Jazz Workshop | 1955 | $300 |

FANTASY

| ❏ OJC-1701 | Ada Moore | 1985 | $25 |

MOORE, BOB
HICKORY

| ❏ LP-131 [M] | Viva Bob Moore | 1965 | $18 |
| ❏ LPS-131 [S] | Viva Bob Moore | 1965 | $25 |

MONUMENT

❏ MLP-8008 [M]	Mexico	1967	$15
❏ SLP-18008 [S]	Mexico	1967	$18
❏ MLP-4005 [M]	Mexico and Other Great Hits!	1961	$25
❏ SLP-4005 [S]	Mexico and Other Great Hits!	1961	$30

MOORE, BOBBY, AND THE RHYTHM ACES
CHECKER

| ❏ LP-3000 [M] | Searching for My Love | 1966 | $30 |
| ❏ LPS-3000 [R] | Searching for My Love | 1966 | $25 |

MOORE, BREW
FANTASY

| ❏ 3264 [M] | Brew Moore | 1958 | $50 |

— Red vinyl

| ❏ 3264 [M] | Brew Moore | 1958 | $30 |

— Black vinyl

| ❏ OJC-049 | Brew Moore | 198? | $25 |
| ❏ 6013 [M] | Brew Moore in Europe | 1962 | $150 |

— Red vinyl

| ❏ 6013 [M] | Brew Moore in Europe | 1962 | $35 |

— Black vinyl

| ❏ 86013 [S] | Brew Moore in Europe | 1962 | $100 |

— Blue vinyl

| ❏ 86013 [S] | Brew Moore in Europe | 1962 | $25 |

— Black vinyl

| ❏ 3222 [M] | The Brew Moore Quintet | 1956 | $100 |

— Red vinyl

| ❏ 3222 [M] | The Brew Moore Quintet | 1956 | $40 |

— Black vinyl

| ❏ OJC-100 | The Brew Moore Quintet | 198? | $25 |

SAVOY

| ❏ MG-9028 [10] | Tenor Sax | 1953 | $175 |

STEEPLECHASE

| ❏ SCS-6016 | If I Had You | 198? | $30 |
| ❏ SCS-6019 | I Should Care | 198? | $30 |

STORYVILLE

| ❏ 4019 | No More Brew | 198? | $25 |

MOORE, CHARLIE, AND BILL NAPIER
KING

❏ 1021 [M]	Brand New Country & Western Songs	1967	$30
❏ KS-1021 [S]	Brand New Country & Western Songs	1967	$25
❏ 992 [M]	City Folks Back on the Farm	1966	$30
❏ KS-992 [S]	City Folks Back on the Farm	1966	$40
❏ 917 [M]	Country Hymnal	1964	$40
❏ 982 [M]	Country Music Goes to Viet Nam	1966	$30
❏ KS-982 [S]	Country Music Goes to Viet Nam	1966	$40
❏ 828 [M]	Folk 'n' Hill	1963	$50
❏ 1017 [M]	Gospel and Sacred Songs	1967	$30
❏ KS-1017 [S]	Gospel and Sacred Songs	1967	$25
❏ 936 [M]	Songs of the Lonesome Truck Drivers	1965	$30
❏ KS-936 [S]	Songs of the Lonesome Truck Drivers	1965	$40
❏ 1014 [M]	Spectacular Instrumentals	1967	$30
❏ KS-1014 [S]	Spectacular Instrumentals	1967	$25
❏ 880 [M]	The Best of Charlie Moore and Bill Napier	1964	$50

MOORE, DANNY
EVEREST

| ❏ LPBR-5211 [M] | Folk Songs from Here and There | 1963 | $25 |
| ❏ SDBR-1211 [S] | Folk Songs from Here and There | 1963 | $30 |

MOORE, DEBBY
TOP RANK

| ❏ RM-12-301 [M] | My Kind of Blues | 1959 | $40 |

MOORE, DOROTHY
MALACO

❏ 6359	Definitely Dorothy	1979	$15
❏ 6353	Dorothy Moore	1977	$18
❏ 7455	Feel the Love	1990	$15
❏ 6351	Misty Blue	1976	$15
❏ 6356	Once More with Feeling	1978	$15
❏ 7363	Talk to Me	1980	$18

REJOICE/A&M

| ❏ WR8326 | Givin' It Straight to You | 1986 | $18 |

VOLT

| ❏ 3401 | Time Out for Me | 1988 | $15 |
| ❏ 3405 | Winner | 1989 | $15 |

MOORE, DUDLEY
ATLANTIC

| ❏ 1403 [M] | Beyond the Fringe and All That Jazz | 1963 | $35 |
| ❏ SD1403 [S] | Beyond the Fringe and All That Jazz | 1963 | $75 |

LONDON

| ❏ PS558 | Dudley Moore Trio | 1969 | $75 |

MOORE, GATEMOUTH
AUDIO FIDELITY

| ❏ AFLP-1921 [M] | Revival! | 196? | $75 |
| ❏ AFSD-5921 [S] | Revival! | 196? | $100 |

BLUESWAY

| ❏ BLS6074 | After 21 Years | 1973 | $25 |

KING

| ❏ 684 [M] | Gatemouth Moore Sings Blues | 1960 | $5000 |

MOORE, GLEN, AND DAVID FRIESEN
VANGUARD

| ❏ VSD-79383 | Glen Moore and David Friesen In Concert | 1976 | $30 |

Number	Title	Yr	NM
MOORE, JACKIE			
ATLANTIC			
❑ SD7285	Sweet Charlie Babe	1973	$18
COLUMBIA			
❑ JC35991	On My Way	1979	$12
❑ JC36455	With Your Love	1980	$12
KAYVETTE			
❑ 801	Make Me Feel Like a Woman	1975	$18
MOORE, JERRY			
ESP-DISK'			
❑ 1061	Life Is a Constant Journey Home	1968	$250
MOORE, LATTIE			
AUDIO LAB			
❑ AL-1573 [M]	Country Side	1962	$175
❑ AL-1555 [M]	The Best of Lattie Moore	1960	$250
DERBYTOWN			
❑ 102 [M]	Lattie Moore	196?	$40
MOORE, MARILYN			
BETHLEHEM			
❑ BCP-73 [M]	Moody	1957	$300
MOORE, MELBA			
ACCORD			
❑ SN-7129	Sweet Melba	1981	$12
BUDDAH			
❑ BDS-5720	Dancin' with Melba	1979	$12
❑ BDS-5677	Melba	1976	$12
❑ BDS-5629	Peach Melba	1975	$12
❑ BDS-5695	Portrait of Melba Moore	1977	$12
❑ BDS-5657	This Is It	1976	$12
CAPITOL			
❑ ST-12471	A Lot of Love	1986	$12
❑ ST-12305	Never Say Never	1983	$12
❑ ST-12382	Read My Lips	1985	$12
❑ C1-92355	Soul Exposed	1990	$15
❑ ST-12243	The Other Side of the Rainbow	1982	$12
EMI AMERICA			
❑ ST-17060	What a Woman Needs	1981	$12
EPIC			
❑ JE36128	Burn	1979	$12
❑ JE36412	Closer	1980	$12
❑ JE35507	Melba	1978	$12
MERCURY			
❑ SR-61287	I Got Love	1970	$18
❑ SRM-1-622	Live!	1972	$15
❑ SR-61255	Living to Give	1970	$18
❑ SR-61321	Look What You're Doing to the Man	1971	$18
MOORE, OSCAR			
CHARLIE PARKER			
❑ PLP-830 [M]	The Fabulous Oscar Moore Guitar	1962	$30
❑ PLP-830S [S]	The Fabulous Oscar Moore Guitar	1962	$30
SKYLARK			
❑ SKLP-19 [M]	Oscar Moore Trio	1954	$150
TAMPA			
❑ TP-22 [M]	Galivantin' Guitar	1957	$175
— Colored vinyl			
❑ TP-22 [M]	Galivantin' Guitar	1958	$175
— Black vinyl			
❑ TP-16 [M]	Oscar Moore Trio	1957	$175
— Colored vinyl			
❑ TP-16 [M]	Oscar Moore Trio	1958	$175
— Black vinyl			
MOORE, PHIL, JR.			
Pianist.			
ATLANTIC			
❑ SD1530	Right On	1969	$35
MOORE, PHIL			
CLEF			
❑ MGC-635 [M]	Music for Moderns	1954	$300
STRAND			
❑ SL-1004 [M]	Polynesian Paradise	1959	$40
❑ SLS-1004 [S]	Polynesian Paradise	1959	$50
MOORE, RALPH			
LANDMARK			
❑ LLP-1526	Furthermore	1990	$30
❑ LLP-1520	Images	1988	$25
MOORE, REGGIE			
MAINSTREAM			
❑ MRL-380	Furioso	1972	$25
❑ MRL-341	Wishbone	1971	$50

Number	Title	Yr	NM
MOORE, SCOTTY			
EPIC			
❑ LN24103 [M]	The Guitar That Changed the World	1964	$75
❑ BN26103 [S]	The Guitar That Changed the World	1964	$85
GUINNESS			
❑ GNS-36038 [B]	What's Left	1977	$25
MOORE, SHELLEY			
ARGO			
❑ LP-4016 [M]	For the First Time	1962	$30
❑ LPS-4016 [S]	For the First Time	1962	$40
MOORE, THURSTON			
DGC			
❑ 24810	Psychic Hearts	1995	$16
MOORE, TIM			
ABC DUNHILL			
❑ DSX-50132	Of Woodstock and Other Places	1973	$15
A SMALL RECORD COMPANY			
❑ SRS-10001	Tim Moore	1974	$30
ASYLUM			
❑ 7E-1042	Behind the Eyes	1975	$12
❑ 6E-179	High Contrast	1979	$12
❑ 7E-1019	Tim Moore	1974	$12
❑ 7E-1088	White Shadows	1977	$12
ELEKTRA			
❑ 60463	Flash Forward	1985	$12
MOORE, WILD BILL			
JAZZLAND			
❑ JLP-54 [M]	Bottom Groove	1961	$30
❑ JLP-954 [S]	Bottom Groove	1961	$40
❑ JLP-38 [M]	Wild Bill's Beat	1961	$75
❑ JLP-938 [S]	Wild Bill's Beat	1961	$40
MOORMAN, DENNIS			
INDIA NAVIGATION			
❑ IN-1055	Circles of Destiny	198?	$30
MORAN, GAYLE			
WARNER BROS.			
❑ BSK3339	I Loved You Then, I Love You Now	1980	$12
MORAN, PAT			
AUDIO FIDELITY			
❑ AFLP-1875 [M]	This Is Pat Moran	1958	$40
❑ AFSD-5875 [S]	This Is Pat Moran	1958	$50
BETHLEHEM			
❑ BCP-6007 [M]	Pat Moran Quartet	1956	$300
❑ BCP-6018 [M]	While at Birdland	1957	$300
MORATH, MAX			
EPIC			
❑ LN24066 [M]	Celebrated Maestro	1963	$85
❑ BN26066 [S]	Celebrated Maestro	1963	$40
JAZZOLOGY			
❑ JCE-52 [M]	All Play Together	1969	$30
RCA VICTOR			
❑ LSO-1159	Max Morath at the Turn of the Century	1969	$30
SAVOY			
❑ MG-12091 [M]	Introducing Max Morath	196?	$25
VANGUARD			
❑ VSD-79378	Jonah Man and Others of the Bert Williams Era	1976	$25
❑ VSD-79391	Living a Ragtime Life: A One-Man Show	1977	$30
❑ VSD-79418	Max Morath in Jazz Country	1979	$25
❑ VSD-83/84	Max Morath Plays Ragtime	197?	$35
❑ VSD-79402	Ragtime Women	1977	$25
❑ VRS-39/40	The Best of Scott Joplin and Other Rag Classics	1972	$35
❑ VSD-73106	The Best of Scott Joplin and Other Rag Classics	198?	$30
❑ VSD-79429	The Great American Piano Bench	1980	$25
❑ VSD-310	The World of Scott Joplin	197?	$30
❑ VSD-351	The World of Scott Joplin, Vol. 2	197?	$30
MOREL, TERRY			
BETHLEHEM			
❑ BCP-47 [M]	Songs of a Woman in Love	1956	$300
MORELLO, JOE, AND GARY BURTON			
OVATION			
❑ OV-1714	Percussive Jazz	197?	$30

Number	Title	Yr	NM
MORELLO, JOE			
INTRO			
❑ 608 [M]	Joe Morello Sextet	1957	$175
OVATION			
❑ OV-1197	Joe Morello	197?	$35
RCA VICTOR			
❑ LPM-2486 [M]	It's About Time	1961	$30
❑ LSP-2486 [S]	It's About Time	1961	$30
MORENO, RITA			
STRAND			
❑ L-1039 [M]	Rita Moreno Sings	1962	$30
❑ SL-1039 [S]	Rita Moreno Sings	1962	$40
WYNNE			
❑ WLP-103 [M]	Warm, Wild, Wonderful	1964	$25
❑ WLP-703 [S]	Warm, Wild, Wonderful	1964	$30
MOREY STORE BAND, THE			
SOUND MACHINE			
❑ 49007	Cry for the Dreamer	197?	$150
MORGAN, DICK			
RIVERSIDE			
❑ RLP 12-329 [M]	Dick Morgan at the Showboat	1960	$250
❑ RLP-1183 [S]	Dick Morgan at the Showboat	1960	$250
❑ RLP-347 [M]	See What I Mean?	1960	$250
❑ RS-9347 [S]	See What I Mean?	1960	$250
❑ RLP-383 [M]	Settin' In	1961	$250
❑ RS-9383 [S]	Settin' In	1961	$250
MORGAN, FRANK			
ANTILLES			
❑ 91320	Mood Indigo	1989	$30
CONTEMPORARY			
❑ C-14026	Bebop Lives!	1987	$25
❑ C-14045	Double Image	1988	$25
❑ C-14013	Easy Living	198?	$25
❑ C-14021	Lament	1986	$25
❑ C-14039	Major Changes	1988	$25
❑ C-14052	Reflections	1989	$30
❑ C-14045	Yardbird Suite	1988	$25
GENE NORMAN			
❑ GNP-12 [M]	Frank Morgan	1955	$120
— Red vinyl			
GNP CRESCENDO			
❑ GNPS-9014	Frank Morgan with Conte Candoli	197?	$25
SAVOY JAZZ			
❑ SJL-1201	Bird Calls	198?	$25
WHIPPET			
❑ WLP-704 [M]	Frank Morgan	1956	$150
MORGAN, GEORGE			
4 STAR			
❑ 002	From This Moment On	1975	$15
COLUMBIA			
❑ CL1631 [M]	Golden Memories	1961	$30
❑ CS8431 [S]	Golden Memories	1961	$30
❑ CL1044 [M]	Morgan, By George	1957	$50
❑ CL2333 [M]	Red Roses for a Blue Lady	1965	$25
❑ CS9133 [S]	Red Roses for a Blue Lady	1965	$30
❑ PC33894	Remembering George Morgan	1975	$15
❑ CL2111 [M]	Tender Lovin' Care	1964	$25
❑ CS8911 [S]	Tender Lovin' Care	1964	$30
MCA			
❑ 461	Candy Mountain Melody	1974	$15
❑ 422	Red Rose from the Blue Side of Town/Somewhere Around Midnight	1974	$15
STARDAY			
❑ SLP-417	Barbara	1969	$25
❑ SLP-400	Candy Kisses	1967	$30
❑ SLP-410	Country Hits by Candlelight	1967	$30
❑ SLP-413	Steal Away	1968	$25
STOP			
❑ 10009	George Morgan Sings Like a Bird	1969	$18
MORGAN, JANE			
ABC			
❑ S-638	A Jane Morgan Happening	1968	$15
COLPIX			
❑ CP497 [M]	The Jane Morgan Album	1966	$18
❑ SCP497 [S]	The Jane Morgan Album	1966	$25
❑ CP469 [M]	The Last Time I Saw Paris	1964	$25
❑ SCP469 [S]	The Last Time I Saw Paris	1964	$30
EPIC			
❑ LN24211 [M]	Fresh Flavor	1966	$15
❑ BN26211 [S]	Fresh Flavor	1966	$18
❑ LN24166 [M]	In My Style	1965	$15
❑ BN26166 [S]	In My Style	1965	$18
❑ LN24247 [M]	Kiss Tomorrow Goodbye	1967	$25

Number	Title	Yr	NM
❏ BN26247 [S]	Kiss Tomorrow Goodbye	1967	$15
❏ LN24190 [M]	Today's Hits…Tomorrow's Golden Favorites	1966	$15
❏ BN26190 [S]	Today's Hits…Tomorrow's Golden Favorites	1966	$18

HARMONY

❏ HS11398	Sounds of Silence	1970	$12

KAPP

❏ KL-1080 [M]	All the Way	1958	$30
❏ KL-1191 [M]	Ballads of Lady Jane	1960	$18
❏ KS-3191 [S]	Ballads of Lady Jane	1960	$25
❏ KL-1247 [M]	Big Hits from Broadway	1961	$18
❏ KS-3247 [S]	Big Hits from Broadway	1961	$25
❏ KS-3001 [S]	Broadway in Stereo	1959	$30
❏ KL-1066 [M]	Fascination	1957	$30
❏ KS-3017 [S]	Fascination	1959	$30
❏ KS-3066 [S]	Fascination	1962	$25
❏ UXL-5006 [M]	Great Songs from the Great Shows of the Century	195?	$40
❏ KL-1129 [M]	Jane in Spain	1959	$30
❏ KS-3014 [S]	Jane in Spain	1959	$30
❏ KL-1023 [M]	Jane Morgan	1956	$30
❏ KL-1093 [M]	Jane Morgan	1958	$30
❏ KL-1268 [M]	Jane Morgan at the Cocoanut Grove	1962	$18
❏ KS-3268 [S]	Jane Morgan at the Cocoanut Grove	1962	$25
❏ KL-1329 [M]	Jane Morgan's Greatest Hits	1963	$15
❏ KS-3329 [S]	Jane Morgan's Greatest Hits	1963	$18
❏ KL-1170 [M]	Jane Morgan Time	1959	$25
❏ KS-3054 [S]	Jane Morgan Time	1959	$30
❏ KL-1250 [M]	Love Makes the World Go 'Round	1961	$18
❏ KS-3250 [S]	Love Makes the World Go 'Round	1961	$25
❏ KL-1275 [M]	More Golden Hits	1962	$18
❏ KS-3275 [S]	More Golden Hits	1962	$25
❏ KJM-1 [DJ]	Radio Station Sampler	196?	$30
—Promo only, gatefold cover			
❏ KL-1239 [M]	Second Time Around	1961	$18
❏ KS-3239 [S]	Second Time Around	1961	$25
❏ KL-1089 [M]	Something Old, New, Borrowed, Blue	1958	$30
❏ KL-1089S [S]	Something Old, New, Borrowed, Blue	1958	$40
❏ KL-1105 [M]	The Day the Rains Came	1958	$30
❏ KL-1105S [S]	The Day the Rains Came	1958	$40
❏ KL-1246 [M]	The Great Golden Hits	1961	$18
❏ KS-3246 [S]	The Great Golden Hits	1961	$25
❏ KL-1296 [M]	What Now My Love	1962	$18
❏ KS-3296 [S]	What Now My Love	1962	$25

MCA

❏ 537	Jane Morgan's Greatest Hits	197?	$12

RCA VICTOR

❏ LSP-4322	Jane Morgan in Nashville	1970	$15
❏ LSP-4171	Traces of Love	1969	$15

MORGAN, JAYE P.

ALLEGRO ELITE

❏ 4111 [M]	Jaye P. Morgan Sings	195?	$15

BEVERLY HILLS

❏ 24	What Are You Doing the Rest of Your Life	1970	$30

MAYFAIR

❏ 9739 [M]	Life Is Just a Bowl of Cherries	195?	$18

MGM

❏ E-3867 [M]	Down South	1960	$30
❏ SE-3867 [S]	Down South	1960	$30
❏ E-3774 [M]	Slow and Easy	1959	$30
❏ SE-3774 [S]	Slow and Easy	1959	$30
❏ E-3940 [M]	That Country Sound	1961	$30
❏ SE-3940 [S]	That Country Sound	1961	$30
❏ E-3830 [M]	Up North	1960	$30
❏ SE-3830 [S]	Up North	1960	$30

RCA VICTOR

❏ LPM-1155 [M]	Jaye P. Morgan	1955	$50
❏ LPM-1682 [M]	Just You, Just Me	1958	$40

RONDO-LETTE

❏ A-13 [M]	Jaye P. Morgan Sings	1958	$30

ROYALE

❏ 18147 [10]	Jaye P. Morgan and Orchestra	195?	$25

TOPS

❏ L-1739 [M]	Life Is Just a Bowl of Cherries	195?	$18

MORGAN, LEE

BLUE NOTE

❏ BLP-1590 [M]	Candy	1958	$3500
—Deep groove" version; W. 63rd St. address on label			
❏ BLP-1590 [M]	Candy	1958	$350
—Regular edition, W. 63rd St. address on label			
❏ BST-1590 [S]	Candy	1959	$1000
—Deep groove" version; W. 63rd St. address on label			
❏ BST-1590 [S]	Candy	1959	$300
—Regular edition, W. 63rd St. address on label			
❏ BLP-1590 [M]	Candy	1963	$250
—New York, USA" address on label			
❏ BST-1590 [S]	Candy	1963	$140
—New York, USA" address on label			
❏ BST-84289	Caramba!	1969	$175
—A Division of Liberty Records" on label			
❏ BST-84312	Charisma	1969	$150
—A Division of Liberty Records" on label			
❏ BLP-1575 [M]	City Lights	1958	$3500
—Deep groove" version; W. 63rd St. address on label			
❏ BLP-1575 [M]	City Lights	1958	$250
—Regular edition, W. 63rd St. address on label			
❏ BST-1575 [S]	City Lights	1959	$800
—Deep groove" version; W. 63rd St. address on label			
❏ BST-1575 [S]	City Lights	1959	$300
—Regular edition, W. 63rd St. address on label			
❏ BLP-1575 [M]	City Lights	1963	$250
—New York, USA" address on label			
❏ BST-1575 [S]	City Lights	1963	$175
—New York, USA" address on label			
❏ BLP-4222 [M]	Cornbread	1967	$175
—New York, USA" on label			
❏ BST-84222 [S]	Cornbread	1967	$175
—New York, USA" address on label			
❏ BST-84222 [S]	Cornbread	1968	$75
—A Division of Liberty Records" on label			
❏ BLP-4243 [M]	Delightfulee Morgan	1967	$400
❏ BST-84243 [S]	Delightfulee Morgan	1967	$120
—New York, USA" address on label			
❏ BST-84243 [S]	Delightfulee Morgan	1968	$75
—A Division of Liberty Records" on label			
❏ BST-84243	Delightfulee Morgan	198?	$30
—The Finest in Jazz Since 1939" reissue			
❏ LT-1091	Infinity	1981	$40
❏ BST-84901	Lee Morgan	1972	$75
—A Division of United Artists" on blue and white labels			
❏ BLP-1541 [M]	Lee Morgan, Volume 2	1957	$2000
—Deep groove" version; Lexington Ave. address on label			
❏ BLP-1541 [M]	Lee Morgan, Volume 2	1957	$700
—Deep groove" edition, W. 63rd St. address on label			
❏ BLP-1541 [M]	Lee Morgan, Volume 2	1963	$400
—New York, USA" on label			
❏ BLP-1557 [M]	Lee Morgan, Volume 3	1957	$1200
—Deep groove" version; W. 63rd St. address on label			
❏ BLP-1557 [M]	Lee Morgan, Volume 3	1957	$500
—Regular edition, W. 63rd St. address on label			
❏ BLP-1557 [M]	Lee Morgan, Volume 3	1963	$250
—New York, USA" address on label			
❏ BST-89906	Lee Morgan at the Lighthouse	1970	$150
❏ BLP-1538 [M]	Lee Morgan Indeed!	1957	$2500
—Deep groove" version; Lexington Ave. address on label			
❏ BLP-1538 [M]	Lee Morgan Indeed!	1957	$1000
—Deep groove" edition, W. 63rd St. address on label			
❏ BLP-1538 [M]	Lee Morgan Indeed!	1963	$2000
—New York, USA" address on label			
❏ BLP-1538 [M]	Lee Morgan Indeed!	200?	$150
—200-gram edition; distributed by Classic Records			
❏ BLP-4034 [M]	Lee-Way	1960	$800
—Deep groove" version; W. 63rd St. address on label			
❏ BLP-4034 [M]	Lee-Way	1960	$300
—Regular edition, W. 63rd St. address on label			
❏ BST-84034 [S]	Lee-Way	1960	$175
—Regular edition, W. 63rd St. address on label			
❏ BLP-4034 [M]	Lee-Way	1963	$250
—New York, USA" address on label			
❏ BST-84034 [S]	Lee-Way	1963	$40
—New York, USA" address on label			
❏ BST-84034 [S]	Lee-Way	1968	$75
—A Division of Liberty Records" on label			
❏ B1-32089	Lee-Way	1995	$50
❏ BN-LA224-G	Memorial Album	1974	$50
❏ BN-LA582-4047	Procrastinator	1977	$75
❏ BLP-4169 [M]	Search for the New Land	1965	$250
—New York, USA" on label			
❏ BST-84169 [S]	Search for the New Land	1965	$175

—New York, USA" address on label			
❏ BST-84169 [S]	Search for the New Land	1968	$75
—A Division of Liberty Records" on label			
❏ LT-987	Sonic Boom	1979	$75
❏ LT-1031	Taru	1980	$40
❏ B1-91138	The Best of Lee Morgan	1988	$35
❏ BLP-1578 [M]	The Cooker	1958	$1300
—Deep groove" version; W. 63rd St. address on label			
❏ BLP-1578 [M]	The Cooker	1958	$250
—Regular edition, W. 63rd St. address on label			
❏ BST-1578 [S]	The Cooker	1959	$2000
—Deep groove" version; W. 63rd St. address on label			
❏ BST-1578 [S]	The Cooker	1959	$250
—Regular edition, W. 63rd St. address on label			
❏ BLP-1578 [M]	The Cooker	1963	$250
—New York, USA" address on label			
❏ BST-1578 [S]	The Cooker	1963	$150
—New York, USA" address on label			
❏ BST-81578 [S]	The Cooker	1968	$75
—A Division of Liberty Records" on label			
❏ BLP-4212 [M]	The Gigolo	1966	$200
—New York, USA" on label			
❏ BST-84212 [S]	The Gigolo	1966	$175
—New York, USA" address on label			
❏ BST-84212 [S]	The Gigolo	1968	$75
—A Division of Liberty Records" on label			
❏ BST-84212	The Gigolo	1986	$30
—The Finest in Jazz Since 1939" reissue			
❏ B1-33579	The Procrastinator	1995	$50
❏ BST-84426	The Rajah	1984	$150
❏ BLP-4199 [M]	The Rumproller	1966	$200
—New York, USA" on label			
❏ BST-84199 [S]	The Rumproller	1966	$175
—New York, USA" address on label			
❏ BST-84199 [S]	The Rumproller	1968	$75
—A Division of Liberty Records" on label			
❏ BLP-4157 [M]	The Sidewinder	1964	$200
—New York, USA" on label			
❏ BST-84157 [S]	The Sidewinder	1964	$175
—New York, USA" address on label			
❏ BST-84157 [S]	The Sidewinder	1968	$75
—A Division of Liberty Records" on label			
❏ LN-10075	The Sidewinder	1981	$35
—Budget-line reissue			
❏ BST-84157	The Sidewinder	1985	$30
—The Finest in Jazz Since 1939" reissue			
❏ B1-46137	The Sidewinder	1997	$50
❏ BST-84335	The Sixth Sense	1969	$120
—A Division of Liberty Records" on label			
❏ LT-1058	Tom Cat	1980	$40

FANTASY

❏ OJC-310	Take Twelve	198?	$30

GNP CRESCENDO

❏ GNP-2079	Lee Morgan	1973	$50

JAZZLAND

❏ JLP-80 [M]	Take Twelve	1962	$150
❏ JLP-980 [S]	Take Twelve	1962	$120

MOSAIC

❏ MQ6-162 [B]	The Complete Blue Note Lee Morgan Fifties Sessions	1995	$1000

PRESTIGE

❏ MPP-2510	Take Twelve	198?	$30

SAVOY

❏ MG-12091 [M]	Introducing Lee Morgan	1956	$500

SUNSET

❏ SUS-5269	All the Way	1969	$35

TRADITION

❏ 2079	The Genius of Lee Morgan	1969	$50

TRIP

❏ 5037	A Date with Lee	1974	$35
❏ 5041	Live Sessions	1975	$75
❏ 5029	One of a Kind	1974	$35
❏ 5020	Speedball	1974	$35
❏ 5003	Two Sides of Lee Morgan	1974	$75

VEE JAY

❏ LP-3015 [M]	Expoobident	1960	$175
❏ SR-3015 [S]	Expoobident	1960	$250
❏ LP-3007 [M]	Here's Lee Morgan	1960	$175
❏ SR-3007 [S]	Here's Lee Morgan	1960	$175
❏ VJS-3007	Here's Lee Morgan	1986	$35
—Reissue on reactivated label			
❏ E-4000	Lee Morgan 1938-1972	198?	$50
❏ VJ-2508 [M]	Lee Morgan Quintet	1965	$120
❏ VJS-2508 [S]	Lee Morgan Quintet	1965	$175

MORGAN, LENNY

PALO ALTO

❏ PA-8007	It's About Time	1981	$30

MORGAN, LORRIE

RCA

❏ 9594-1-R	Leave the Light On	1989	$15
❏ R183848	Something in Red	1991	$25

Number	Title	Yr	NM

— Only available on vinyl through BMG Direct Marketing

MORGAN, RUSS
CAPITOL

Number	Title	Yr	NM
❑ T1703 [M]	Medleys in the Morgan Manner	1962	$75
❑ ST1703 [S]	Medleys in the Morgan Manner	1962	$85
❑ T2158 [M]	Music in the Country Manner	1964	$75
❑ ST2158 [S]	Music in the Country Manner	1964	$50

CIRCLE

❑ CLP-87	Music in the Morgan Manner (1938)	198?	$25
❑ C-9	Russ Morgan and His Orchestra 1936	198?	$25

DECCA

❑ DL8423 [M]	A Lovely Way to Spend an Evening (Songs of Jimmy McHugh)	1957	$120

— Black label, silver print

❑ DL8423 [M]	A Lovely Way to Spend an Evening (Songs of Jimmy McHugh)	196?	$30

— Black label with color bars

❑ DL8581 [M]	Cheerful Little Earful (Songs of Harry Warren)	195?	$25

— Black label, silver print

❑ DL8581 [M]	Cheerful Little Earful (Songs of Harry Warren)	196?	$30

— Black label with color bars

❑ DL5278 [10]	College Marching Songs	195?	$30
❑ DL8332 [M]	Does Your Heart Beat for Me	1956	$175

— Black label, silver print

❑ DL8332 [M]	Does Your Heart Beat for Me	196?	$30

— Black label with color bars

❑ DL4503 [M]	Does Your Heart Beat for Me	1964	$30
❑ DL74503 [S]	Does Your Heart Beat for Me	1964	$35
❑ DL8337 [M]	Everybody Dance	1956	$175

— Black label, silver print

❑ DL8337 [M]	Everybody Dance	196?	$30

— Black label with color bars

❑ DL5324 [10]	Everybody Dance to the Music of Russ Morgan	195?	$30
❑ DL8746 [M]	Kitten on the Keys	195?	$25

— Black label, silver print

❑ DL8746 [M]	Kitten on the Keys	196?	$30

— Black label with color bars

❑ DL5324 [10]	Morgan-Airs	1951	$250
❑ DL5098 [10]	Music in the Morgan Manner	1950	$120
❑ DL8828 [M]	Songs Everybody Knows	1958	$150

— Black label, silver print

❑ DL8828 [M]	Songs Everybody Knows	196?	$30

— Black label with color bars

❑ DL78828 [S]	Songs Everybody Knows	1958	$150

— Black label, silver print

❑ DL78828 [S]	Songs Everybody Knows	196?	$35

— Black label with color bars

❑ DL8336 [M]	Tap Dancing for Pleasure	1956	$175

— Black label, silver print

❑ DL8336 [M]	Tap Dancing for Pleasure	196?	$30

— Black label with color bars

❑ DXB196 [M]	The Best of Russ Morgan	1965	$25
❑ DXSB7196 [R]	The Best of Russ Morgan	1965	$35
❑ DL8642 [M]	Velvet Violins	1957	$120

— Black label, silver print

❑ DL8642 [M]	Velvet Violins	196?	$30

— Black label with color bars

EVEREST

❑ LPBR-5083 [M]	Dance Along	1960	$30
❑ SDBR-1083 [S]	Dance Along	1960	$35
❑ LPBR-5055 [M]	Let's All Sing with Russ Morgan and Eddie Wilser	1959	$30
❑ SDBR-1055 [S]	Let's All Sing with Russ Morgan and Eddie Wilser	1959	$35
❑ LPBR-5129 [M]	Morgan Time	1961	$30
❑ SDBR-1129 [S]	Morgan Time	1961	$35
❑ LPBR-5054 [M]	Music in the Morgan Manner	1959	$30
❑ SDBR-1054 [S]	Music in the Morgan Manner	1959	$35
❑ LPBR-5095 [M]	Russ Morgan and His Wolverine Band	1960	$30
❑ SDBR-1095 [S]	Russ Morgan and His Wolverine Band	1960	$35
❑ LPBR-5130 [M]	Russ Morgan at Catalina	1961	$30
❑ SDBR-1130 [S]	Russ Morgan at Catalina	1961	$35

GNP CRESCENDO

❑ GNPS-9015	The Best of Russ Morgan	197?	$25

HINDSIGHT

❑ HSR-145	Russ Morgan and His Orchestra 1937-38	198?	$25
❑ HSR-404	Russ Morgan and His Orchestra Play 22 Original Big Band Recordings	198?	$30

MCA

❑ 92	Golden Favorites	1973	$25
❑ 4036	The Best of Russ Morgan	197?	$30

PICKWICK

❑ PC-3030 [M]	Dance Along	196?	$25
❑ SPC-3030 [S]	Dance Along	196?	$30
❑ PC-3016 [M]	There Goes That Song	196?	$25
❑ SPC-3016 [S]	There Goes That Song	196?	$30

Number	Title	Yr	NM

RUSS MORGAN PRESENTS

❑ RMP-1000	Russ Morgan Presents "Music in the Morgan Manner"	1967	$35

SEARS

❑ SPS-413 [R]	Does Your Heart Beat for Me?	196?	$25

SUNSET

❑ SUM-1142 [M]	Does Your Heart Beat for Me	1967	$30
❑ SUS-5142 [S]	Does Your Heart Beat for Me	1967	$25

VEE JAY

❑ VJ-1125 [M]	His Greatest Hits	1964	$35
❑ VJS-1125 [S]	His Greatest Hits	1964	$25
❑ VJ-1139 [M]	Red Roses for a Blue Lady	1965	$35
❑ VJS-1139 [S]	Red Roses for a Blue Lady	1965	$25
❑ E-4009 [M]	Russ Morgan 1904-1969	1975	$35

VOCALION

❑ VL3695 [M]	Hoop-De-Doo Polkas and Waltzes	196?	$30
❑ VL3601 [M]	Let's Dance	195?	$30
❑ VL3792 [M]	Music in the Morgan Manner	196?	$30
❑ VL73792 [R]	Music in the Morgan Manner	196?	$25

MORGEN
PROBE

❑ CPLP-4507	Morgen	1969	$175

MORISSETTE, ALANIS
MAVERICK

❑ 47094	Supposed Former Infatuation Junkie	1998	$18
❑ R1553461 [B]	The Demos 1994-1998	2016	$20

MORLY GREY
STARSHINE

❑ 69000	The Only Truth	1969	$250

MORMON TABERNACLE CHOIR
BOOK-OF-THE-MONTH

❑ 71-6406	Christmas Celebration	1980	$30

— Contains 20-page lyric booklet

CBS MASTERWORKS

❑ XM38299	Christmas Carols Around the World	1982	$10
❑ IM39034	Faith of Our Fathers	1984	$12
❑ FM37297	Gloria!	1982	$12
❑ M37828	Serenade	1985	$12
❑ IM37206	Silent Night -- The Greatest Hits of Christmas	1981	$15
❑ M2X39102	The Great Choruses of Bach and Handel	1984	$15
❑ MG37853	The Greatest Hits of Christmas	1982	$18
❑ IM36661	The Power and the Glory	1981	$12
❑ FM37286	The Twenties	1982	$12
❑ FM37200	When You Wish Upon a Star	1981	$12

COLUMBIA HOUSE

❑ 1P6075	Christmas with the Mormon Tabernacle Choir	1973	$12
❑ 6P6007	The Mormon Tabernacle Choir	1973	$30
❑ 2P7437	The Mormon Tabernacle Choir Christmas Treasury	1982	$18
❑ 3P6240	The Mormon Tabernacle Choir's Greatest Hits (Includes Christmas with the Mormon Tabernacle Choir)	1974	$25
❑ 1P6008	What Child Is This	1973	$15

COLUMBIA LIMITED EDITION

❑ LE10091 [B]	Christmas Carols Around the World	1976	$12
❑ LE10461	Hymns and Songs of Brotherhood	197?	$10

COLUMBIA MASTERWORKS

❑ M34134	A Jubilant Song	1976	$12
❑ ML5497 [M]	A Mighty Fortress	1960	$15

— Gray and black label with six "eye" logos

❑ MS6162 [S]	A Mighty Fortress	1960	$18

— Gray and black label with six "eye" logos

❑ ML6461 [M]	Anvil Chorus: Favorite Opera Choruses	1967	$15
❑ MS7061 [S]	Anvil Chorus: Favorite Opera Choruses	1967	$15
❑ MS7149	Beautiful Dreamer	1968	$15

— Gray "360 Sound" label

❑ ML6079 [M]	Beloved Choruses Volume Two	1964	$15
❑ MS6679 [S]	Beloved Choruses Volume Two	1964	$18
❑ M35868	Beyond the Blue Horizon	1980	$12
❑ ML6235 [M]	Bless This House	1966	$12
❑ MS6835 [S]	Bless This House	1966	$15
❑ M2L286 [M]	Brahms: A German Requiem Sung in English	1963	$18
❑ M2S686 [S]	Brahms: A German Requiem Sung in English	1963	$25

— Gray label, "360 Sound Stereo" in black

❑ ML5684 [M]	Christmas Carols Around the World	1961	$15
❑ MS6284 [S]	Christmas Carols Around the World	1961	$18

— Same as ML 5684, but in stereo

Number	Title	Yr	NM
❑ M32227	Cielito Lindo -- The Mormon Tabernacle Choir En Espanol	1973	$15
❑ M30647	Climb Every Mountain	1971	$12
❑ ML5048 [M]	Concert of Sacred Music	1955	$25
❑ ML6121 [M]	God Bless America	1965	$15
❑ MS6721 [S]	God Bless America	1965	$18
❑ M30054	God of Our Fathers	1970	$15
❑ M35120	Hail to the Victors!	1978	$12
❑ MS7292	Hallelujah Chorus: The Great Handel Choruses	1969	$15

— Gray "360 Sound" label

❑ M2L263 [M]	Handel: Messiah	1959	$25

— Gray and black labels with six "eye" logos

❑ M2S607 [S]	Handel: Messiah	1959	$30

— Gray and black labels with six "eye" logos

❑ ML5714 [M]	Hymns and Songs of Brotherhood	1962	$15
❑ MS6314 [S]	Hymns and Songs of Brotherhood	1962	$18
❑ MS7405	Jesu, Joy of Man's Desiring: The Great Bach Choruses	1970	$15

— Gray "360 Sound" label

❑ M30077	Joy to the World	1970	$15
❑ XM30077	Joy to the World	197?	$12

— Reissue of M 30077

❑ M35825	Memories: Songs America Loves Best	1980	$12
❑ M33440	Music and the Spoken Word	1975	$12
❑ M35148	Robertson: Oratorio from the Book of Mormon	1978	$12
❑ MG33710	Rock of Ages	1975	$15
❑ ML6308 [M]	Sing Unto God	1966	$12
❑ MS6908 [S]	Sing Unto God	1966	$15
❑ ML5203 [M]	Songs of Faith and Devotion	1957	$25
❑ M34538	Songs of Thanks	1977	$12
❑ ML5659 [M]	Songs of the North & South 1861-1865	1961	$15

— Gray and black label with six "eye" logos

❑ MS6259 [S]	Songs of the North & South 1861-1865	1961	$18

— Gray and black label with six "eye" logos

❑ M32298	Stars & Stripes Forever	1973	$12
❑ ML5364 [M]	The Beloved Choruses	1958	$18

— Gray and black label with six "eye" logos

❑ MS6058 [S]	The Beloved Choruses	1958	$25

— Gray and black label with six "eye" logos

❑ M32935	The Great "Messiah" Choruses	1974	$12
❑ ML5592 [M]	The Holly and the Ivy	1960	$15
❑ MS6192 [S]	The Holly and the Ivy	1960	$18

— Same as ML 5592, but in stereo

❑ MS6499 [S]	The Joy of Christmas	1963	$18

— Same as ML 5899, but in stereo

❑ ML5899 [M]	The Joy of Christmas	1963	$15

— With the New York Philharmonic conducted by Leonard Bernstein

❑ ML5302 [M]	The Lord Is My Shepherd	1958	$18

— Gray and black label with six "eye" logos

❑ MS6019 [S]	The Lord Is My Shepherd	1958	$25

— Gray and black label with six "eye" logos

❑ ML5386 [M]	The Lord's Prayer	1959	$18

— Gray and black label with six "eye" logos

❑ MS6068 [S]	The Lord's Prayer	1959	$25

— Gray and black label with six "eye" logos

❑ ML5767 [M]	The Lord's Prayer Volume II	1962	$15
❑ MS6367 [S]	The Lord's Prayer Volume II	1962	$18
❑ MG31081	The Mormon Tabernacle Choir Album	1972	$18
❑ ML6019 [M]	The Mormon Tabernacle Choir at the World's Fair	1964	$25
❑ MS6619 [S]	The Mormon Tabernacle Choir at the World's Fair	1964	$30
❑ ML2077 [10]	The Mormon Tabernacle Choir of Salt Lake City	1949	$40

— Their first album

❑ ML4789 [M]	The Mormon Tabernacle Choir of Salt Lake City	195?	$30

— Reissue of two 10-inch LPs onto one 12-inch LP

❑ ML2098 [10]	The Mormon Tabernacle Choir of Salt Lake City Volume II	1950	$30
❑ ML6351 [M]	The Mormon Tabernacle Choir's Greatest Hits	1966	$12
❑ MS6951 [S]	The Mormon Tabernacle Choir's Greatest Hits	1966	$15

— Same as ML 6351, but in stereo

❑ ML6486 [M]	The Mormon Tabernacle Choir's Greatest Hits, Volume 2	1967	$15
❑ MS7086 [S]	The Mormon Tabernacle Choir's Greatest Hits, Volume 2	1967	$15
❑ MS7399	The Mormon Tabernacle Choir's Greatest Hits, Volume 3	1970	$15
❑ ML5222 [M]	The Mormon Tabernacle Choir Sings Christmas Carols	1957	$25
❑ ML6177 [M]	The Mormon Tabernacle Choir Sings Christmas Carols	1965	$15

— A new recording of ML 5222

❑ MS6777 [S]	The Mormon Tabernacle Choir Sings Christmas Carols	1965	$18

Number	Title	Yr	NM
— Same as ML 6177, but in stereo			
ML6412 [M]	The Old Beloved Songs	1967	$15
MS7012 [S]	The Old Beloved Songs	1967	$15
ML5423 [M]	The Spirit of Christmas	1959	$15
MS6100 [S]	The Spirit of Christmas	1959	$18
— Same as ML 5500, but in stereo			
ML5819 [M]	This Is My Country	1962	$15
MS6419 [S]	This Is My Country	1962	$18
M2L303 [M]	This Is My Country	1963	$18
M2S703 [S]	This Is My Country	1963	$25
— Gray label, "360 Sound Stereo" in black; not to be confused with the single-record LP of the same name			
ML6147 [M]	This Land Is Your Land	1965	$15
MS6747 [S]	This Land Is Your Land	1965	$18
M34546	White Christmas	1977	$15
— In box with insert of Christmas recipes			

COLUMBIA SPECIAL PRODUCTS

P14245	For All the Saints	1977	$15
— Mfg by CBS for Covenant Recordings			
P14247	I Know That My Redeemer Lives	1977	$15
— Mfg by CBS for Covenant Recordings			
P14303	It's Christmas!	1977	$15
— Mfg by CBS for Covenant Recordings			
P14244	Lift Thine Eyes	1977	$15
— Mfg by CBS for Covenant Recordings			
P14243	Nearer My God to Thee	1977	$15
— Mfg by CBS for Covenant Recordings			
P14246	Now the Day Is Over	1977	$15
— Mfg by CBS for Covenant Recordings			
P15935	Songs of Faith	1983	$12
CSS1667	The Mormon Tabernacle Choir in South Carolina -- Tricentennial Concert	1970	$25

FRANKLIN MINT

0(no cat #)	The Greatest Songs of Christmas	1980	$30
— Maroon vinyl; the choir's first digital recording			

HARMONY

HS11370	Faith of Our Fathers	1970	$15
HS11272	Onward Christian Soldiers	1968	$12
KH30673	The Mormon Tabernacle Choir Sings Songs of Christmas	1971	$12

READER'S DIGEST

P215176/7	50th Anniversary Album	1980	$25
RBA-128/A	Climb Ev'ry Mountain: The Mormon Tabernacle Choir Sings Great Songs of Inspiration	1988	$30
RD4A-221-1	Merry Christmas from the Mormon Tabernacle Choir	1981	$12
RD4-093	The Mormon Tabernacle Choir Sings	1973	$30

REALM

3V8039	The Mormon Tabernacle Choir's Greatest Hits (Includes Christmas with the Mormon Tabernacle Choir)	197?	$18
— Reissue of Columbia House 6240			

TIME-LIFE

SMT104	Christmas Celebration	1987	$25
— Same contents as Book-of-the-Month LP. Side 1, 2 and 6 are identical; Side 3 is BOTM's Side 5, Side 4 is BOTM's Side 3, and Side 5 is BOTM's Side 4.			

MORMON TABERNACLE ORGAN AND CHIMES

COLUMBIA MASTERWORKS

ML6037 [M]	Christmas with the Mormon Tabernacle Organ and Chimes	1964	$15
MS6637 [S]	Christmas with the Mormon Tabernacle Organ and Chimes	1964	$18

MORNING DEW, THE

ROULETTE

SR-42049	The Morning Dew	1970	$300

MORNING GLORY

FONTANA

SRF-67573 [B]	Two Suns Worth	1968	$35

MORNINGLORY

TOYA

STLP-003	Growing	1972	$40

MORRIS, AUDREY

BETHLEHEM

BCP-6010 [M]	The Voice of Audrey Morris	1956	$300

MORRIS, GARY

UNIVERSAL

UVL-76010	Every Christmas	1989	$15
— Same as Warner Bros. 25760 with one track deleted and one added			
UVL-76005	Stones	1989	$12

WARNER BROS.

25279	Anything Goes...	1985	$10
25760	Every Christmas	1988	$12
25069	Faded Blue	1984	$10
BSK3658	Gary Morris	1982	$10
25581	Hits	1987	$10
25438	Plain Brown Wrapper	1986	$10
23738	Why Lady Why	1983	$10

MORRIS, GREG

DOT

DLP-25881	For You	1968	$25

MORRIS, MARLOWE

COLUMBIA

CL1819 [M]	Play the Thing	1962	$25
CS8619 [S]	Play the Thing	1962	$30

MORRISON, HAROLD

DECCA

DL4680 [M]	Hoss, He's the Boss	1965	$18
DL74680 [S]	Hoss, He's the Boss	1965	$25

MORRISON, SAM

CHIAROSCURO

184	Natural Layers	197?	$30

INNER CITY

IC-6017	Dune	197?	$35

MORRISON, VAN

BANG

BLP-218 [M]	Blowin' Your Mind	1967	$150
— With the true "Brown Eyed Girl" lyric, "Makin' love in the green grass behind the stadium with you.			

BLPS-218 [S]	Blowin' Your Mind	1967	$100
— With the true "Brown Eyed Girl" lyric, "Makin' love in the green grass behind the stadium with you.			
BLBS-218 [S]	Blowin' Your Mind	1968	$25
— With the censored "Brown Eyed Girl" lyric, "Laughin' and a-runnin', hey hey, behind the stadium with you," part of which was spliced in from another part of the song!			
BLB-218 [M]	Blowin' Your Mind	1968	$150
— With the censored "Brown Eyed Girl" lyric, "Laughin' and a-runnin', hey hey, behind the stadium with you," part of which was spliced in from another part of the song. This has been confirmed to exist in mono.			
BLPS-400	T.B. Sheets	1973	$25
BLPS-222	The Best of Van Morrison	1970	$18

DIRECT DISK

SD-16604	Moondance	1981	$150
— Audiophile vinyl			

LOST HIGHWAY

B0005968-01	Pay the Devil	2006	$15

MERCURY

822895-1	A Sense of Wonder	1985	$10
839262-1	Avalon Sunset	1989	$12
847100-1	Enlightenment	1990	$18
834496-1	Irish Heartbeat	1988	$10
— With the Chieftains			
818336-1	Live at the Grand Opera House, Belfast	1985	$12
830077-1	No Guru, No Method, No Teacher	1986	$10
832585-1	Poetic Champions Compose	1987	$10
841970-1	The Best of Van Morrison	1990	$18

POLYDOR

8391661	It's Too Late to Stop Now	2008	$30
1775313	Tupelo Honey	2008	$25

WARNER BROS.

BS2987	A Period of Transition	1977	$15
— "Burbank" palm-tree labels			
BS2987	A Period of Transition	1979	$10
— Later white or tan label			
WS1768	Astral Weeks	1968	$30
— With "W7" logo on green label			
WS1768	Astral Weeks	1970	$15
— With "WB" logo on green label			
WS1768	Astral Weeks	1973	$12
— "Burbank" palm-tree label			
WS1768	Astral Weeks	1979	$10
— Later white or tan label			
BSK3652	Beautiful Vision	1981	$15
R13652 [B]	Beautiful Vision	2016	$25
BSK3462	Common One	1980	$15
BS2712	Hard Nose the Highway	1973	$15
— "Burbank" palm-tree label			
BS2712	Hard Nose the Highway	1979	$10
— Later white or tan label			
WS1884	His Band and the Street Choir	1970	$18
— With "WB" logo on green label			
WS1884	His Band and the Street Choir	1973	$12
— "Burbank" palm-tree label			
WS1884	His Band and the Street Choir	1979	$10
— Later white or tan label			
23802	Inarticulate Speech of the Heart	1983	$15
HS3390	Into the Music	1979	$15
2BS2760	It's Too Late to Stop Now	1974	$18
— "Burbank" palm-tree labels			
2BS2760	It's Too Late to Stop Now	1979	$10
— Later white or tan label			
WBMS-102 [DJ]	Live at the Roxy	1978	$40
WS1835	Moondance	1969	$25
— With "W7" logo on green label			
WS1835	Moondance	1970	$15
— With "WB" logo on green label			
WS1835	Moondance	1973	$12
— "Burbank" palm-tree label			
BSK3103	Moondance	1977	$12
— Reissue with new number; "Burbank" palm-tree label			
BSK3103	Moondance	1979	$10
— Later white or tan label			
WS2633	Saint Dominic's Preview	1972	$18
— With "WB" logo on green label			
WS2633	Saint Dominic's Preview	1973	$12
— "Burbank" palm-tree label			
WS2633	Saint Dominic's Preview	1979	$10
— Later white or tan label			
WS1950	Tupelo Honey	1971	$18
— With "WB" logo on green label, plus poster			
WS1950	Tupelo Honey	1973	$12
— "Burbank" palm-tree label			
WS1950	Tupelo Honey	1979	$10
— Later white or tan label			
BS2805	Veedon Fleece	1974	$15
— "Burbank" palm-tree labels			
BS2805	Veedon Fleece	1979	$10
— Later white or tan label			
BSK3212	Wavelength	1978	$15

MORRISSEY, PAT

MERCURY

MG-20197 [M]	I'm Pat Morrissey, I Sing	1957	$175

MORRISSEY
Also see THE SMITHS.

ATTACK

86001	You Are the Quarry	2004	$30

DECCA

SKL6003	Greatest Hits	2008	$30

LOST HIGHWAY

1257801	Years of Refusal	2009	$25

PARLOPHONE

825646299485 [B]	Vauxhall and I	2014	$35
825646348831 [B]	Your Arsenal	2014	$30

SIRE

R153729 [B]	Viva Hate	1988	$30
— BMG Direct Marketing edition			
25699 [B]	Viva Hate	1988	$18

MORROW, BUDDY

EPIC

LN24095 [M]	Big Band Beatlemania	1964	$75
BN26095 [S]	Big Band Beatlemania	1964	$75
LN24171 [M]	Campus After Dark	1965	$75
BN26171 [S]	Campus After Dark	1965	$85

HINDSIGHT

HSR-154	Buddy Morrow 1963-64	198?	$25

MERCURY

MG-20764 [M]	A Collection of 33 All-Time Dance Favorites	1963	$150
SR-60764 [S]	A Collection of 33 All-Time Dance Favorites	1963	$150
MG-20204 [M]	A Salute to the Fabulous Dorseys	1957	$150

Number	Title	Yr	NM
❏ MG-20221 [M]	Golden Trombone	1956	$150
❏ MG-20372 [M]	Just We Two	195?	$150
❏ SR-60018 [S]	Just We Two	1958	$150
❏ MG-20396 [M]	Night Train	195?	$150
❏ SR-60009 [S]	Night Train	1958	$150
❏ MG-20702 [M]	Night Train Goes to Hollywood	1962	$150
❏ SR-60702 [S]	Night Train Goes to Hollywood	1962	$150
❏ MG-20062 [M]	Shall We Dance?	195?	$150
❏ MG-20290 [M]	Tribute to Tommy Dorsey	1957	$150

RCA VICTOR
❏ LPM-2018 [M]	Big Band Guitar	1959	$30
❏ LSP-2018 [S]	Big Band Guitar	1959	$40
❏ LPM-1925 [M]	Dancing Tonight To Morrow	1958	$30
❏ LSP-1925 [S]	Dancing Tonight To Morrow	1958	$40
❏ LPM-2180 [M]	Double Impact	1960	$30
❏ LSP-2180 [S]	Double Impact	1960	$40
❏ LPM-2042 [M]	Impact	1959	$30
❏ LSP-2042 [S]	Impact	1959	$40
❏ LPM-1427 [M]	Night Train	1956	$40
❏ LPM-2208 [M]	Poe for Moderns	1960	$30
❏ LSP-2208 [S]	Poe for Moderns	1960	$40

WING
❏ MGW-12102 [M]	Dance Date	196?	$30
❏ SRW-16102 [R]	Dance Date	196?	$30
❏ MGW-12105 [M]	Tribute to a Sentimental Gentleman	196?	$30

MORSE, ELLA MAE
CAPITOL
❏ H513 [10]	Barrelhouse Boogie and the Blues	1954	$400
❏ T513 [M]	Barrelhouse Boogie and the Blues	1955	$300
❏ T1802 [M]	Hits of Ella Mae Morse and Freddie Slack	1962	$175
❏ ST1802 [S]	Hits of Ella Mae Morse and Freddie Slack	1962	$250
❏ M-11971 [M]	Hits of Ella Mae Morse and Freddie Slack	197?	$20

— Reissue
| ❏ T898 [M] | Morse Code | 1957 | $300 |
— Turquoise label

MORSE, ROBERT, AND CHARLES NELSON REILLY
CAPITOL
| ❏ T1862 [M] | A Jolly Theatrical Christmas | 1963 | $25 |
| ❏ ST1862 [S] | A Jolly Theatrical Christmas | 1963 | $30 |

MORTIMER, AZIE
BETHLEHEM
| ❏ BLP-10006 | The Feeling of Jazz | 197? | $35 |

MORTIMER
PHILIPS
| ❏ PHS600267 | Mortimer | 1969 | $30 |

MORTON, ANN J.
PRAIRIE DUST
| ❏ 1661 | My Friends Call Me Annie | 197? | $18 |

MORTON, BENNY / JIMMY HAMILTON
MOSAIC
| ❏ MR1-115 | The Benny Morton and Jimmy Hamilton Blue Note Swingtets | 199? | $75 |
— Limited edition of 7,500

MORTON, JELLY ROLL
BIOGRAPH
| ❏ 1004 | Rare Piano Rolls 1924-1926 | 197? | $25 |
BLUEBIRD
| ❏ 6588-1-RB | Jelly Roll Morton & His Red Hot Peppers | 1988 | $30 |
CIRCLE
❏ L-14001 [M]	The Saga of Mr. Jelly Lord Volume 1: Jazz Started in New Orleans	1951	$120
❏ L-14002 [M]	The Saga of Mr. Jelly Lord Volume 2: Way Down Yonder	1951	$120
❏ L-14003 [M]	The Saga of Mr. Jelly Lord Volume 3: Jazz Is Strictly Music	1951	$120
❏ L-14004 [M]	The Saga of Mr. Jelly Lord Volume 4: The Spanish Tinge	1951	$120
❏ L-14005 [M]	The Saga of Mr. Jelly Lord Volume 5: Bad Man Ballads	1951	$120
❏ L-14006 [M]	The Saga of Mr. Jelly Lord Volume 6: Jazz Piano Soloist #1	1951	$120
❏ L-14007 [M]	The Saga of Mr. Jelly Lord Volume 7: Everyone Had His Style	1951	$120
❏ L-14008 [M]	The Saga of Mr. Jelly Lord Volume 8: Jelly and the Blues	1951	$120
❏ L-14009 [M]	The Saga of Mr. Jelly Lord Volume 9: Alabama Bound	1951	$120

Number	Title	Yr	NM
❏ L-14010 [M]	The Saga of Mr. Jelly Lord Volume 10: Jazz Piano Soloist #2	1951	$120
❏ L-14011 [M]	The Saga of Mr. Jelly Lord Volume 11: In New Orleans	1951	$120
❏ L-14012 [M]	The Saga of Mr. Jelly Lord Volume 12: I'm the Winin' Boy	1951	$120

COMMODORE
| ❏ DL-30000 [M] | New Orleans Memories | 1950 | $150 |
| ❏ XFL-14942 | New Orleans Memories | 198? | $30 |
EVEREST ARCHIVE OF FOLK & JAZZ
| ❏ 267 | Jelly Roll Morton | 197? | $25 |
JAZZ PANORAMA
| ❏ 1804 [10] | Peppers | 1951 | $150 |
| ❏ 1810 [10] | Peppers | 1951 | $150 |
MAINSTREAM
| ❏ 56020 [M] | Jelly Roll Morton | 1965 | $30 |
| ❏ S-6020 [R] | Jelly Roll Morton | 1965 | $30 |
MILESTONE
| ❏ M-2003 [M] | Immortal Jelly Roll Morton | 1970 | $30 |
| ❏ 47018 | Jelly Roll Morton 1923-24 | 197? | $35 |
RCA VICTOR
❏ LPT-32 [10]	A Treasury of Immortal Performances	1952	$150
❏ LPV-524 [M]	Hot Jazz, Pop Jazz, Hokum and Hilarity	1965	$25
❏ LPV-559 [M]	I Thought I Heard Buddy Bolden Say	1966	$25
❏ LPV-546 [M]	Mr. Jelly Lord	1966	$25
❏ LPV-508 [M]	Stomps and Joys	1965	$25
❏ LPM-1649 [M]	The King of New Orleans Jazz	1957	$50
RIVERSIDE
❏ RLP-1038 [10]	Classic Jazz Piano, Volume 1	1954	$300
❏ RLP-1041 [10]	Classic Jazz Piano, Volume 2	1954	$300
❏ RLP 12-111 [M]	Classic Piano Solos	1955	$300
❏ RLP 12-133 [M]	Jelly Roll Morton Plays and Sings	1956	$300
❏ RLP-1027 [10]	Jelly Roll Morton's Kings of Jazz: His Rarest Recordings	1954	$300
❏ RLP-9001 [M]	Library of Congress Recordings Volume 1	1955	$300
❏ RLP-9002 [M]	Library of Congress Recordings Volume 2	1955	$300
❏ RLP-9003 [M]	Library of Congress Recordings Volume 3	1955	$300
❏ RLP-9004 [M]	Library of Congress Recordings Volume 4	1955	$300
❏ RLP-9005 [M]	Library of Congress Recordings Volume 5	1955	$300
❏ RLP-9006 [M]	Library of Congress Recordings Volume 6	1955	$300
❏ RLP-9007 [M]	Library of Congress Recordings Volume 7	1955	$300
❏ RLP-9008 [M]	Library of Congress Recordings Volume 8	1955	$300
❏ RLP-9009 [M]	Library of Congress Recordings Volume 9	1955	$300
❏ RLP-9010 [M]	Library of Congress Recordings Volume 10	1955	$300
❏ RLP-9011 [M]	Library of Congress Recordings Volume 11	1955	$300
❏ RLP-9012 [M]	Library of Congress Recordings Volume 12	1955	$300
❏ RLP 12-132 [M]	Mr. Jelly Lord	1956	$300
❏ RLP 12-140 [M]	Rags and Blues	1956	$300
❏ RLP-1018 [10]	Rediscovered Solos	1953	$300
❏ RLP 12-128 [M]	The Incomparable Jelly Roll Morton	1956	$300
❏ RLP 12-102 [M]	The New Orleans Rhythm Kings with Jelly Roll Morton	1955	$300
TIME-LIFE
| ❏ STL-J-07 | Giants of Jazz | 1979 | $50 |
TRIP
| ❏ J-1 | Piano Roll Solos | 197? | $25 |
X
| ❏ LX-3008 [10] | Red Hot Peppers, Volume 1 | 1954 | $150 |
| ❏ LVA-3028 [10] | Red Hot Peppers, Volume 2 | 1954 | $150 |

MOSBY, JOHNNY AND JONIE
CAPITOL
❏ ST-286	Hold Me	1969	$18
❏ ST-414	I'll Never Be Free	1970	$18
❏ ST-170	Just Hold My Hand	1969	$18
❏ ST2903	Make a Left and Then a Right	1968	$18
❏ ST-556	My Happiness	1970	$18
❏ ST-737	Oh, Love of Mine	1971	$18
COLUMBIA
| ❏ CL2297 [M] | Mr. & Mrs. Country Music | 1965 | $18 |
| ❏ CS9097 [S] | Mr. & Mrs. Country Music | 1965 | $25 |
HARMONY
| ❏ HS11389 | Mr. & Mrs. Country Music | 1970 | $12 |
STARDAY
| ❏ SLP-328 [M] | The New Sweethearts of Country Music | 1965 | $30 |

MOSCA, SAL
CHOICE
| ❏ 1022 | For You | 1979 | $30 |

Number	Title	Yr	NM
INTERPLAY			
❏ 7712	Sal Mosca Music	197?	$30

MOSCHNER, PINGUIN
SOUND ASPECTS
| ❏ 05 | Tuba Love Story | 1986 | $30 |

MOSES, BOB
GRAMAVISION
| ❏ 8307 | Visit with the Great Spirit | 1983 | $25 |
| ❏ 8203 | When Elephants Dream of Music | 198? | $25 |

MOSES, KATHRYN
PM
| ❏ 017 | Music in My Heart | 1979 | $30 |

MOSHER, JIMMY
DISCOVERY
| ❏ 860 | A Chick from Chelsea | 1981 | $25 |

MOSLEY, BOB
REPRISE
| ❏ MS2068 [B] | Bob Mosley | 1972 | $30 |

MOSS, ANNE MARIE
STASH
| ❏ ST-211 | Don't You Know Me | 198? | $25 |

MOSS, BUDDY
BIOGRAPH
| ❏ 12019 | Rediscovery | 197? | $18 |

MOSS, GENE
RCA VICTOR
| ❏ LPM-2977 [M] | Dracula's Greatest Hits | 1964 | $30 |
| ❏ LSP-2977 [S] | Dracula's Greatest Hits | 1964 | $40 |

MOSSE, SANDY
ARGO
❏ LP-609 [M]	Chicago Scene	1957	$50
❏ LP-639 [M]	Relaxin' with Sandy Mosse	1959	$30
❏ LPS-639 [S]	Relaxin' with Sandy Mosse	1959	$40

MOST, ABE
LIBERTY
| ❏ LJH-6004 [M] | Mister Clarinet | 1955 | $75 |

MOST, SAM
BETHLEHEM
❏ BCP-18 [M]	I'm Nuts About the Most: East Coast Jazz, Volume 7	1955	$300
❏ BCP-6008 [M]	Musically Yours	1956	$300
❏ BCP-75 [M]	Sam Most Plays Bird, Bud, Monk and Miles	1957	$300
❏ BCP-78 [M]	The Amazing Sam Most with Strings	1958	$300
CATALYST
| ❏ 7609 | But Beautiful | 1976 | $30 |
DEBUT
| ❏ DLP-11 [10] | Sam Most Sextet | 1954 | $350 |
VANGUARD
| ❏ VRS-8014 [10] | Sam Most Sextet | 1954 | $100 |
XANADU
❏ 141	Flute Flight	1977	$30
❏ 173	Flute Talk	1980	$30
❏ X-3001	Flute Talk	1980	$30
— Audiophile edition
| ❏ 160 | From the Attic of My Mind | 198? | $25 |
| ❏ 133 | Mostly Flute | 1976 | $30 |

MOTELS, THE
Also see MARTHA DAVIS.
CAPITOL
| ❏ ST-12177 | All Four One | 1982 | $12 |
| ❏ SN-16420 | All Four One | 198? | $10 |
— Budget-line reissue
| ❏ ST-12177 [DJ] | All Four One | 1982 | $25 |
— Promo-only high-grade vinyl pressing (different front cover)
| ❏ ST-12070 | Careful | 1980 | $12 |
| ❏ SN-16347 | Careful | 1985 | $10 |
— Budget-line reissue
| ❏ ST-12288 | Little Robbers | 1983 | $12 |
| ❏ SN-16355 | Little Robbers | 1985 | $10 |
— Budget-line reissue
❏ SJ-12378	Shock	1985	$12
❏ ST-11996	The Motels	1979	$12
❏ SN-16343	The Motels	1985	$10
— Budget-line reissue

Number	Title	Yr	NM

MOTEN, BENNIE

BLUEBIRD
❏ 9768-1-RB	Bennie Moten's Kansas City Orchestra	1989	$30

HISTORICAL
❏ 9	Bennie Moten's Kansas City Orchestra	1966	$25

RCA VICTOR
❏ LPV-514 [M]	Bennie Moten's Great Band of 1930-32	1965	$25

X
❏ LX-3004 [10]	Kansas City Jazz, Volume 1	1954	$75
❏ LVA-3025 [10]	Kansas City Jazz, Volume 2	1954	$75
❏ LVA-3038 [10]	Kansas City Jazz, Volume 3	1954	$75

MOTHER EARTH

MERCURY
❏ SR-61194	Living with the Animals	1968	$30
❏ SR-61226	Make a Joyful Noise	1969	$25
❏ SR-61270	Satisfied	1970	$25
❏ SR-61230	Tracy Nelson Country	1969	$25

REPRISE
❏ RS6431	Bring Me Home	1971	$18
❏ MS2054	Tracy Nelson/Mother Earth	1972	$18

MOTHER LOVE BONE
PEARL JAM related.

POLYDOR
❏ 843191-1	Apple	1990	$40

STARDOG
❏ 839011-1 [EP]	Shine	1989	$40
—Four songs on side one, the same four songs on side two

MOTHERLODE

BUDDAH
❏ BDS-5108	Tapped Out	1970	$18
❏ BDS-5046	When I Die	1969	$18

MOTHER'S BOYS

AUDIOPHILE
❏ AP-100	Stompin' Hot! Singin' Sweet!	1970	$30

MOTHERS OF INVENTION, THE
See FRANK ZAPPA.

MOTIAN, PAUL

ECM
❏ 1028	Conception Vessel	197?	$35
❏ 1108	Dance	1977	$25
❏ 1283	It Should Have Happened a Long Time Ago	1985	$30
❏ 1138	Le Voyage	1979	$25
❏ 1222	Psalm	198?	$25
❏ 1048	Tribute	197?	$30

SOUL NOTE
❏ SN-1124	Jack of Clubs	1986	$30
❏ 121224	One Time Out	1990	$35
❏ SN-1074	The Story of Maryam	1983	$30

MOTIONS, THE (3)

PHILIPS
❏ PHS600317	Electric Baby	1969	$25

MOTLEY CRUE

ELEKTRA
❏ 60829	Dr. Feelgood	1989	$15
❏ 60725	Girls, Girls, Girls	1987	$12
❏ 60395 [EP]	Helter Skelter	1984	$40
—Picture disc with four songs; includes poster and insert (deduct 50 percent if missing)
❏ 60289	Shout at the Devil	1982	$12
❏ 60418	Theatre of Pain	1985	$12
❏ 60174	Too Fast for Love	1982	$15
—Reissue of Leathur LP with slight revisions

LEATHUR
❏ LR-1281	Too Fast for Love	1981	$250
—First pressing with white lettering on cover
❏ LR-1281	Too Fast for Love	1981	$175
—Second pressing with red lettering on cover. Both Leathur pressings contain "Stick to Your Guns," which was not on the Elektra reissue

MOTLEY/HIP-O SELECT
❏ B0004791-01	Too Fast for Love	2005	$25
—Reissue of Leathur LP with bonus 7-inch single, Stick to Your Guns/Toast of the Town

MOTORHEAD
Formed by Lemmy of HAWKWIND fame.

BRONZE
❏ BMG15015V [B]	No Sleep Til Hammersmith	2015	$25
❏ BMG15013V [B]	Overkill	2015	$25
—180g

CLEOPATRA
❏ 9335 [B]	Roundhouse - February 18, 1978		$35

DRASTIC PLASTIC
❏ DPRLP53 [B]	Motorhead	2015	$25
—150g clear vinyl with black swirl

EMI AMERICA
❏ LN-10340	On Parole	1986	$25
—First U.S. issue of early U.K. LP

ENIGMA
❏ D1-75405	No Sleep at All	1988	$35
❏ D1-73536	The Birthday Party	1990	$30

ISLAND
❏ 90233	No Remorse	1984	$40
—Regular cover
❏ 90236	No Remorse	1984	$40
—Leather cover

MERCURY
❏ SRM-1-4011	Ace of Spades	1980	$40
❏ 811265-1	Another Perfect Day	1983	$40
❏ SRM-1-4042	Iron Fist	1982	$40

PROFILE
❏ PRO-3243	Ace of Spades	1986	$20
—Reissue of Mercury 4011
❏ PRO-3242	Bomber	1986	$40
—First U.S. issue of early U.K. LP
❏ PRO-3244	No Sleep 'Til Hammersmith	1986	$25
—Reissue of Mercury 4023
❏ PAL-1223	Orgasmatron	1986	$40
❏ PRO-3241	Overkill	1986	$40
—First U.S. issue of early U.K. LP
❏ PAL-1240	Rock 'N' Roll	1987	$40

SANCTUARY
❏ BMG15057V [B]	Ace of Spades	2015	$25
—180g
❏ 5312076	No Sleep 'Til Hammersmith	2008	$25

WTG
❏ N46858 [B]	1916	1991	$40

MOTORS, THE
DUCKS DELUXE and BRAM TCHAIKOVSKY related.

VIRGIN
❏ JZ35348	Approved by the Motors	1978	$12
❏ VA13139	Tenement Steps	1980	$12
❏ PZ34924	The Motors	1977	$15

MOTT THE HOOPLE
Includes two albums as MOTT, after IAN HUNTER left the band. Also see IAN HUNTER.

ATLANTIC
❏ SD8304 [B]	Brain Capers	1972	$50
❏ SD8272 [B]	Mad Shadows	1970	$50
❏ SD8258 [B]	Mott the Hoople	1970	$75
—With "1841 Broadway" address and no mention of Warner Communications on label
❏ SD8258	Mott the Hoople	198?	$10
—With Warner Communications "W" logo on label
❏ SD7297	Rock and Roll Queen	1974	$30
❏ SD8284 [B]	Wildlife	1971	$50

COLUMBIA
❏ KC31750	All the Young Dudes	1972	$20
❏ PC31750	All the Young Dudes	198?	$10
—Budget-line reissue
❏ PC33705 [B]	Drive On	1975	$20
—released under the abbreviated name Mott
❏ KC32425	Mott	1973	$25
❏ PC32425	Mott	198?	$10
—Budget-line reissue
❏ PC33282	Mott the Hoople Live	1974	$20
—No bar code on cover
❏ PC33282	Mott the Hoople Live	198?	$10
—Reissue with bar code on cover
❏ PC34368	Mott the Hoople's Greatest Hits	1976	$15
—No bar code on cover
❏ PC34368	Mott the Hoople's Greatest Hits	198?	$10
—Reissue with bar code on cover
❏ PC34236 [B]	Shouting and Pointing	1976	$15
—released under the abbreviated name Mott
❏ PC32871	The Hoople	1974	$18
❏ PCQ32871 [Q]	The Hoople	1974	$100

MOTTOLA, TONY

ABC
❏ S-738	16 Great Performances	1972	$12
❏ X-770	Mister Guitar	1973	$12

COMMAND
❏ 33-900 [M]	Amor -- Mexico/S.A.	1966	$15
❏ SD900 [S]	Amor -- Mexico/S.A.	1966	$18
❏ 33-885 [M]	Command Performance	1965	$15
❏ SD885 [S]	Command Performance	1965	$18
❏ 33-823 [M]	Country and Western Folk Songs	1962	$15
❏ SD823 [S]	Country and Western Folk Songs	1962	$18
❏ 33-877 [M]	Guitar -- Paris	1964	$15

❏ SD877 [S]	Guitar -- Paris	1964	$18
❏ QD-40001 [Q]	Guitar -- Paris	1972	$30
❏ 33-908 [M]	Guitar -- U.S.A.	1967	$15
❏ SD908 [S]	Guitar -- U.S.A.	1967	$15
❏ 33-889 [M]	Love Songs -- Mexico/S.A.	1965	$15
❏ SD889 [S]	Love Songs -- Mexico/S.A.	1965	$18
❏ 33-807 [M]	Mr. Big	1961	$15
❏ SD807 [S]	Mr. Big	1961	$18
❏ 33-816 [M]	Roman Guitar	1962	$15
❏ SD816 [S]	Roman Guitar	1962	$18
❏ 33-836 [M]	Roman Guitar, Volume Two	1962	$15
❏ SD836 [S]	Roman Guitar, Volume Two	1962	$18
❏ 33-847 [M]	Romantic Guitar	1963	$15
❏ SD847 [S]	Romantic Guitar	1963	$18
❏ 33-864 [M]	Sentimental Guitar	1964	$15
❏ SD864 [S]	Sentimental Guitar	1964	$18
❏ 33-841 [M]	Spanish Guitar	1963	$15
❏ SD841 [S]	Spanish Guitar	1963	$18
❏ 33-828 [M]	String Band Strum-Along	1962	$15
❏ SD828 [S]	String Band Strum-Along	1962	$18

PICKWICK
❏ SPC-3610	Spanish Guitar	1978	$10

PROJECT 3
❏ PR-5010	A Latin Love-In	1967	$15
❏ PR4C-5010 [Q]	A Latin Love-In	1973	$30
❏ PR-5050	Close to You	1971	$15
❏ PR-6007/8	Favorite Things: The Best of Tony Mottola	1975	$18
❏ PR-6025/6	Feelings	198?	$15
❏ PR-5101	Goin' Out of My Head	197?	$12
❏ PR-5003	Heart and Soul	1967	$15
❏ PR-5094	I Only Have Eyes for You	197?	$12
❏ PR-5020	Lush, Latin & Lovely	1968	$15
❏ PR4C-5020 [Q]	Lush, Latin & Lovely	1973	$30
❏ PR-5032	Roma Oggi/Rome Today	1969	$15
❏ PR4C-5032 [Q]	Roma Oggi/Rome Today	1973	$30
❏ PR-5062	Superstar Guitar	1972	$15
❏ PR4C-5062 [Q]	Superstar Guitar	1973	$20
❏ PR-6031/2	The Best of Tony Mottola	198?	$15
❏ PR-5041	The Tony Touch	1970	$15
❏ PR4C-5041 [Q]	The Tony Touch	1973	$30
❏ PR-5069	Tony and Strings	1973	$15
❏ PR4C-5069 [Q]	Tony and Strings	1973	$30
❏ PR-5035	Tony Mottola Joins the Guitar Underground	1969	$15
❏ PR-5044	Tony Mottola's Guitar Factory	1970	$15
❏ PR-5082	Tony Mottola with the Brass Menagerie	1974	$15
❏ PR4C-5078 [Q]	Tony Mottola with the Quad Guitars	1974	$20
❏ PR-5074	Two Guitars	1974	$12
❏ PR-5025	Warm, Wild & Wonderful	1968	$15
❏ PR4C-5025 [Q]	Warm, Wild & Wonderful	1973	$30
❏ PR-5058	Warm Feelings	1971	$15

MOULD, BOB
Also see HUSKER DU; SUGAR.

VIRGIN
❏ 91395	Black Sheets of Rain	1990	$15
❏ PR3512 [EP]	Rust Bucket Coliseum	1990	$18
—Promo-only five-track release
❏ 91240	Workbook	1989	$15

MOULE, KEN

LONDON
❏ LL1673 [M]	Ken Moule Arranges for...	1957	$50
—Label calls this "Cool Moule"

MOUNT ALVERNIA SEMINARY CHOIR

ABC-PARAMOUNT
❏ 211 [M]	Christmas in a Monastery: The Sons of St. Francis Sing	1957	$25

MOUNT RUSHMORE

DOT
❏ DLP-25898	High on Mount Rushmore	1968	$25
❏ DLP-25934	Mount Rushmore '69	1969	$25

MOUNTAIN
Also see WEST, BRUCE AND LAING.

COLUMBIA
❏ KC33008	Avalanche	1974	$15
❏ CQ33008 [Q]	Avalanche	1974	$40
❏ PC33008	Avalanche	197?	$10
—Budget-line reissue
❏ KC32079	The Best of Mountain	1973	$15
❏ CQ32079 [Q]	The Best of Mountain	1973	$40
❏ PC32079	The Best of Mountain	198?	$10
—Budget-line reissue
❏ CG32818	Twin Peaks	1974	$18
❏ PG32818	Twin Peaks	198?	$12
—Budget-line reissue

SCOTTI BROTHERS
❏ FZ40006	Go for Your Life	1985	$12

WINDFALL
❏ 5501	Flowers of Evil	1971	$18
❏ 4501	Mountain Climbing!	1970	$18
❏ 5502	Mountain Live (The Road Goes Ever On)	1972	$18

Number	Title	Yr	NM
❏ 5500	Nantucket Sleighride	1971	$18
—Deduct 20% if inserts are missing			

MOUNTAIN BUS
GOOD
Number	Title	Yr	NM
❏ 101	Sundance	1971	$250

MOUNTAIN RAMBLERS, THE
ATLANTIC
Number	Title	Yr	NM
❏ 1347 [M]	Blue Ridge Mountain Music	1962	$30
❏ SD1347 [S]	Blue Ridge Mountain Music	1962	$30

MOURNING REIGN, THE
BEAT ROCKET
Number	Title	Yr	NM
❏ BR102	The Mourning Reign	1999	$15

MOUTH AND MACNEIL
PHILIPS
Number	Title	Yr	NM
❏ PHS700000	How Do You Do?	1972	$15
❏ PHS700003	Mouth & MacNeil II	1973	$15

MOUZON, ALPHONSE
BLUE NOTE
Number	Title	Yr	NM
❏ BN-LA058-H2	Essence of Mystery	1973	$35
❏ BN-LA222-H2	Funky Snakefoot	1974	$25
❏ BN-LA584-H2	Man Incognito	1976	$35
❏ BN-LA398-H2	Mind Transplant	1975	$35

OPTIMISM
Number	Title	Yr	NM
❏ OP-6003	Back to Jazz	198?	$25
❏ OP-6002	Early Spring	198?	$25
❏ OP-6001	Love, Fantasy	198?	$25
❏ OP-6004	Morning Sun	198?	$25

PAUSA
Number	Title	Yr	NM
❏ 7196	Back to Jazz	1986	$25
❏ 7087	By All Means	198?	$25
❏ 7107	Morning Sun	198?	$25
❏ 7182	The 11th House	1985	$25
❏ 7173	The Sky Is the Limit	1985	$25
❏ 7054	Virtue	197?	$25

MOVE, THE
Also see ELECTRIC LIGHT ORCHESTRA; ROY WOOD.
A&M
Number	Title	Yr	NM
❏ SP-4259 [B]	Shazam	1969	$30
❏ SP-3181	Shazam	1982	$12
—Budget-line reissue of 4259			
❏ SP-3625 [B]	The Best of the Move	1974	$30

CAPITOL
Number	Title	Yr	NM
❏ ST-658 [B]	Looking On	1971	$30
❏ ST-811 [B]	Message from the Country	1971	$30

UNITED ARTISTS
Number	Title	Yr	NM
❏ UAS-5666	Split Ends	1972	$18

MOVER, BOB
CHOICE
Number	Title	Yr	NM
❏ 1015	On the Move	1977	$30

VANGUARD
Number	Title	Yr	NM
❏ VSD-79408	Bob Mover	1978	$25

XANADU
Number	Title	Yr	NM
❏ 187	In the True Tradition	198?	$25
❏ 194	Things Unseen	198?	$25

MOVIEES, THE
SUNDAZED
Number	Title	Yr	NM
❏ LP5073	Become One of Them	2000	$15

MOVING SIDEWALKS, THE
TANTARA
Number	Title	Yr	NM
❏ 6919 [B]	Flash	1968	$350

MOYE, DON
AECO
Number	Title	Yr	NM
❏ 01	Sun Percussion, Vol. 1	1980	$35

MOYET, ALISON
COLUMBIA
Number	Title	Yr	NM
❏ BFC39956	Alf	1985	$12
❏ BFC40653	Raindancing	1987	$12

MOZIAN, ROGER KING
CLEF
Number	Title	Yr	NM
❏ MGC-166 [10]	The Colorful Music of Roger King Mozian	1954	$300

MOZZ, THE
MESA
Number	Title	Yr	NM
❏ R1-79018	Mystique and Identity	1989	$35

MR. BIG (1)
ARISTA
Number	Title	Yr	NM
❏ AL4083 [B]	Photographic Smile	1976	$18

MR. BIG (2)
U.S.-based hard rock band featuring TALAS and DAVID LEE ROTH bassist Billy Sheehan.
ATLANTIC
Number	Title	Yr	NM
❏ A1-82209	Lean Into It	1991	$25
—U.S. version issued on vinyl only through Columbia House			
❏ 81990	Mr. Big	1989	$12

MR. BUNGLE
Features Mike Patton from FAITH NO MORE.
WARNER BROS.
Number	Title	Yr	NM
❏ 45963	Disco Volante	1995	$25
—Originals have bonus 7-inch single (listed separately)			

MR. GASSER AND THE WEIRDOS
CAPITOL
Number	Title	Yr	NM
❏ T2010 [M]	Hot Rod Hootenanny	1963	$150
❏ ST2010 [S]	Hot Rod Hootenanny	1963	$120
❏ T2057 [M]	Rods n' Ratfinks	1963	$150
—Add 25% if ratfink decal is enclosed			
❏ ST2057 [S]	Rods n' Ratfinks	1963	$120
—Add 25% if ratfink decal is enclosed			
❏ T2114 [M]	Surfink!	1964	$175
—With bonus single in pocket on cover: "Santa Barbara"/"Midnight Run" by the Super Stocks			
❏ T2114 [M]	Surfink!	1964	$150
—Without bonus single			
❏ ST2114 [S]	Surfink!	1964	$250
—With bonus single in pocket on cover: "Santa Barbara"/"Midnight Run" by the Super Stocks			
❏ ST2114 [S]	Surfink!	1964	$175
—Without bonus single			

MR. MISTER
RCA
Number	Title	Yr	NM
❏ 6276-1-R	Go On	1987	$10
❏ AFL1-4864	I Wear the Face	1984	$12
❏ AFL1-7180	Welcome to the Real World	1985	$10
—Reissue			
❏ NFL1-8045	Welcome to the Real World	1985	$15
—Original issue			

MR. SHORT STUFF
SPIVEY
Number	Title	Yr	NM
❏ 1005	Mr. Short Stuff	196?	$25

MRUBATA, MCCOY
JIVE
Number	Title	Yr	NM
❏ 1254-1-J	Firebird	1989	$30

MTUME UMOJA ENSEMBLE
STRATA-EAST
Number	Title	Yr	NM
❏ SES-1972-4	Alkebu-Lan, Land of the Blacks	1972	$50

MU
CAS
Number	Title	Yr	NM
❏ 300	Mu	1971	$300

MUDHONEY
Also see GREEN RIVER.
REPRISE
Number	Title	Yr	NM
❏ 45477	Five Dollar Bob's Mock Cooter Stew	1993	$18
❏ 45840	My Brother the Cow	1994	$18

SUB POP
Number	Title	Yr	NM
❏ 105PD [PD]	Every Good Boy Deserves Fudge	1991	$30
—Picture disc -- limited edition of 2,500			

Number	Title	Yr	NM
❏ SP500 [B]	March to Fuzz	2000	$35
❏ 44	Mudhoney	1989	$30
—First 3,000 have gatefold sleeve and poster			
❏ 44	Mudhoney	1989	$25

Number	Title	Yr	NM
—Without gatefold and poster			
❏ 70765 [B]	Mudhoney	2008	$18
❏ SP-555 [B]	Since We've Become Translucent	2002	$25
❏ 21 [EP]	Superfuzz Bigmuff	1988	$30
—With poster			
❏ 21 [EP]	Superfuzz Bigmuff	1988	$25
—Without poster			

SUPER ELECTRO
Number	Title	Yr	NM
❏ SE10	Tomorrow Hit Today	1998	$15

MUGWUMPS, THE
WARNER BROS.
Number	Title	Yr	NM
❏ W1697 [M]	The Mugwumps	1967	$75
❏ WS1697 [S]	The Mugwumps	1967	$30

MUHAMMAD, IDRIS
FANTASY
Number	Title	Yr	NM
❏ F-9581	Foxhuntin'	1979	$35
❏ F-9598	Make It Count	1980	$35
❏ F-9566	You Ain't No Friend of Mine	1978	$35

KUDU
Number	Title	Yr	NM
❏ 38	Boogie to the Top	1978	$25
❏ 27	House of the Rising Sun	1976	$30
❏ 17	Power of Soul	1974	$30
❏ 34	Turn This Mutha Out	1977	$25

PRESTIGE
Number	Title	Yr	NM
❏ 10005	Black Rhythm Revolution	1971	$40
❏ 10036	Peace and Rhythm	1971	$30

THERESA
Number	Title	Yr	NM
❏ 110	Kabsha	198?	$35

MULCAY, JIMMY AND MILDRED
JUBILEE
Number	Title	Yr	NM
❏ JGM-5017 [M]	Magic Millions	1962	$30

MULDAUR, GEOFF & MARIA
CARTHAGE
Number	Title	Yr	NM
❏ CGLP-4428	Pottery Pie	198?	$12

REPRISE
Number	Title	Yr	NM
❏ MS2073	Sweet Potatoes	1972	$15

MULDAUR, GEOFF
FOLKLORE
Number	Title	Yr	NM
❏ FRLP-14004 [M]	Sleepy Man Blues	1964	$30
❏ FRST-14004 [S]	Sleepy Man Blues	1964	$40

PRESTIGE
Number	Title	Yr	NM
❏ PRST-7727	Sleepy Man Blues	1969	$25
—Reissue of Folklore LP			

MULDAUR, MARIA
MYRRH
Number	Title	Yr	NM
❏ MSB-6685	There Is a Love	1984	$12

REPRISE
Number	Title	Yr	NM
❏ MS2148	Maria Muldaur	1973	$15
❏ MS2235	Sweet Harmony	1976	$15
❏ MS2194	Waitress in a Donut Shop	1974	$15
❏ MS4-2194 [Q]	Waitress in a Donut Shop	1974	$30

TAKOMA
Number	Title	Yr	NM
❏ 7084	Gospel Nights	1980	$15

TUDOR
Number	Title	Yr	NM
❏ 109902	Sweet & Sour	1983	$12

WARNER BROS.
Number	Title	Yr	NM
❏ BSK3305	Open Your Eyes	1979	$12
❏ BSK3162	Southern Winds	1978	$12

MULL, MARTIN
ABC
Number	Title	Yr	NM
❏ AB-997	I'm Everyone I've Ever Loved	1977	$12
❏ AA-1064	Sex and Violins	1978	$12

CAPRICORN
Number	Title	Yr	NM
❏ CP 0155	Days of Wine and Neurosis	1975	$15
❏ CP 0106	Martin Mull	1972	$15
❏ CP 0117	Martin Mull and His Fabulous Furniture	1973	$15
❏ CP 0195	No Hits Four Errors	1977	$12
❏ CP 0126	Normal	1974	$15

ELEKTRA
Number	Title	Yr	NM
❏ 6E-200	Near Perfect	1979	$12

MCA
Number	Title	Yr	NM
❏ 795	I'm Everyone I've Ever Loved	1980	$10
—Reissue of ABC 997			

MULLER, WERNER
DECCA
Number	Title	Yr	NM
❏ DL8388 [M]	O, Tannenbaum (Christmas on the Rhine)	1956	$25
—Black label, silver print			
❏ DL8388 [M]	O, Tannenbaum (Christmas on the Rhine)	1960	$15
—Black label with color bars; album credited to "Mixed Chorus and Orchestra" (Muller's name is on the jacket spine only);			

Number	Title	Yr	NM
revised contents thus:			
❑ DL78388 [S]	O, Tannenbaum (Christmas on the Rhine)	1960	$18
MCA			
❑ 15023	O, Tannenbaum (Christmas on the Rhine)	197?	$10
—Reissue still credited to "Mixed Chorus and Orchestra			

MULLICAN, MOON

Number	Title	Yr	NM
AUDIO LAB			
❑ AL-1568 [M]	Instrumentals	1962	$175
CORAL			
❑ CRL57235 [M]	Moon Over Mullican	1958	$500
HILLTOP			
❑ JS-6033	Good Times Gonna Roll Again	1966	$30
KAPP			
❑ KS-3600	Showcase	1968	$30
KING			
❑ 628 [M]	Moon Mullican Plays and Sings 16 of His Favorite Tunes	1959	$175
❑ 937 [M]	Moon Mullican Sings 24 of His Favorite Tunes	1965	$50
❑ 555 [M]	Moon Mullican Sings His All-Time Greatest Hits	1958	$250
❑ 681 [M]	The Many Moods of Moon Mullican	1960	$175
NASHVILLE			
❑ 2080	I'll Sail My Ship Alone	1970	$25
SPAR			
❑ SP-3005 [M]	Mister Honky Tonk Man	1965	$150
STARDAY			
❑ SLP-267 [M]	Mister Piano Man	1964	$50
❑ SLP-135 [M]	Playin' and Singin'	1963	$150
❑ SLP-398 [M]	The Unforgettable Moon Mullican	1967	$40
STERLING			
❑ ST-601 [M]	I'll Sail My Ship Alone	1958	$250

MULLIGAN, GERRY, AND CHET BAKER

Number	Title	Yr	NM
CTI			
❑ 6054	The Carnegie Hall Concert, Volume 1	1976	$30
❑ 6055	The Carnegie Hall Concert, Volume 2	1976	$30
JAZZTONE			
❑ J-1253 [M]	Mulligan and Baker!	1957	$40

MULLIGAN, GERRY, AND SHORTY ROGERS

Number	Title	Yr	NM
CAPITOL			
❑ T691 [M]	Modern Sounds	1956	$250
❑ T2025 [M]	Modern Sounds	1963	$175
❑ DT2025 [R]	Modern Sounds	1963	$175

MULLIGAN, GERRY

Number	Title	Yr	NM
A&M			
❑ SP-3036	The Age of Steam	1971	$35
CAPITOL			
❑ H439 [10]	Gerry Mulligan and His Ten-Tette	1953	$300
CHIAROSCURO			
❑ 155	Idol Gossip	1977	$30
COLUMBIA			
❑ CL1932 [M]	Jeru	1963	$30
—Red label, "Guaranteed High Fidelity" at bottom			
❑ CS8732 [S]	Jeru	1963	$30
—Red label, "360 Sound Stereo" in black at bottom			
❑ CL1932 [M]	Jeru	1965	$15
—Red label, "360 Sound Mono" at bottom			
❑ CS8732 [S]	Jeru	1965	$35
—Red label, "360 Sound Stereo" in white at bottom			
❑ CL1932 [M]	Jeru	1963	$150
—Red and black label with six "eye" logos			
❑ JC34803	The Arranger (1946-57)	1977	$30
❑ CL1307 [M]	What Is There to Say?	1959	$40
—Red and black label with six "eye" logos			
❑ CS8116 [S]	What Is There to Say?	1959	$40
—Red and black label with six "eye" logos			
❑ CL1307 [M]	What Is There to Say?	1963	$30
—Red label, "Guaranteed High Fidelity" or "360 Sound Mono" at bottom			
❑ CS8116 [S]	What Is There to Say?	1963	$35
—Red label, "360 Sound Stereo" at bottom			
CONCORD JAZZ			
❑ CJ-300	Soft Lights and Sweet Music	1986	$25
CROWN			
❑ CLP-5363 [M]	The Great Gerry Mulligan	196?	$35
❑ CST-363 [R]	The Great Gerry Mulligan	196?	$30
DRG			
❑ MRS-506	Gerry Mulligan and Dave Grusin	198?	$25
❑ SL-5194	Walk on the Water	1980	$25

Number	Title	Yr	NM
EMARCY			
❑ MG-36101 [M]	Mainstream of Jazz	1956	$250
❑ MG-36056 [M]	Presenting the Gerry Mulligan Sextet	1955	$250
FANTASY			
❑ 3-6 [10]	Gerry Mulligan Quartet	1953	$250
—Green vinyl			
❑ 3-6 [10]	Gerry Mulligan Quartet	1953	$250
—Red vinyl			
❑ 3-6 [10]	Gerry Mulligan Quartet	1953	$175
—Black vinyl			
❑ OJC-003	Mulligan Plays Mulligan	1982	$25
GENE NORMAN			
❑ GNP-3 [10]	Gerry Mulligan Quartet	1952	$300
GRP			
❑ GR-1003	Little Big Horn	198?	$25
LIMELIGHT			
❑ LM-82004 [M]	Butterfly with Hiccups	1964	$30
❑ LS-86004 [S]	Butterfly with Hiccups	1964	$30
❑ LM-82030 [M]	Feelin' Good	1965	$30
❑ LS-86030 [S]	Feelin' Good	1965	$30
❑ LM-82021 [M]	If You Can't Beat 'Em, Join 'Em	1965	$30
❑ LS-86021 [S]	If You Can't Beat 'Em, Join 'Em	1965	$30
❑ LM-82040 [M]	Something Borrowed, Something Blue	1966	$25
❑ LS-86040 [S]	Something Borrowed, Something Blue	1966	$30
MERCURY			
❑ MG-20453 [M]	A Profile of Gerry Mulligan	1959	$150
MOBILE FIDELITY			
❑ 1-179	At the Village Vanguard	1985	$50
—Audiophile vinyl			
❑ 1-241	Blues in Time	1996	$50
—Audiophile vinyl			
❑ 1-234	Gerry Mulligan Meets Ben Webster	1995	$50
—Audiophile vinyl			
MOSAIC			
❑ MR5-102	The Complete Pacific Jazz and Capitol Recordings of the Original Gerry Mulligan Quartet and Tentette	198?	$175
ODYSSEY			
❑ 32160290	Jeru	1968	$30
❑ 32160258	What Is There to Say?	1968	$30
PACIFIC JAZZ			
❑ PJ-50 [M]	California Concerts	1962	$30
❑ PJ-1228 [M]	Gerry Mulligan at Storyville	1957	$175
❑ PJLP-1 [10]	Gerry Mulligan Quartet	1953	$300
❑ PJLP-5 [10]	Gerry Mulligan Quartet	1953	$300
❑ PJ-1201 [M]	Gerry Mulligan Sextet	1955	$175
❑ PJ-38 [M]	Konitz Meets Mulligan	1962	$30
❑ PJLP-10 [10]	Lee Konitz and the Gerry Mulligan Quartet	1954	$300
❑ PJLP-2 [10]	Lee Konitz Plays with the Gerry Mulligan Quartet	1953	$300
❑ PJM-406 [M]	Lee Konitz with the Gerry Mulligan Quartet	1956	$175
❑ PJ-1210 [M]	Paris Concert	1956	$175
❑ PJ-10102 [M]	Paris Concert	1966	$25
❑ ST-20102 [S]	Paris Concert	1966	$25
❑ PJ-47 [M]	Reunion with Chet Baker	1962	$30
❑ ST-47 [S]	Reunion with Chet Baker	1962	$30
❑ T90061 [M]	Reunion with Chet Baker	196?	$75
—Capitol Record Club edition			
❑ PJ-8 [M]	The Genius of Gerry Mulligan	1960	$40
❑ ST-20140 [R]	The Genius of Gerry Mulligan	1968	$35
❑ PJ-1207 [M]	The Original Mulligan Quartet	1955	$175
❑ PJ-75 [M]	Timeless	1963	$30
PAR			
❑ PAD-703	Symphonic Dreams	1987	$25
PAUSA			
❑ 9010	The Genius of Gerry Mulligan	198?	$25
PHILIPS			
❑ PHM200108 [M]	Night Lights	1963	$300
❑ PHS600108 [S]	Night Lights	1963	$300
❑ PHM200077 [M]	Spring Is Sprung	1963	$25
❑ PHS600077 [S]	Spring Is Sprung	1963	$30
PRESTIGE			
❑ PRLP-120 [10]	Gerry Mulligan Blows	1952	$300
❑ PRLP-7251 [M]	Historically Speaking	1963	$40
—Yellow label			
❑ 24016	Mulligan/Baker	1972	$35
❑ PRLP-7006 [M]	Mulligan Plays Mulligan	1956	$150
—Yellow label			
❑ PRLP-141 [10]	Mulligan Too Blows	1953	$300
SUNSET			
❑ SUM-1117 [M]	Concert Days	1966	$35
❑ SUS-5117 [S]	Concert Days	1966	$30
TRIP			
❑ 5561	Gerry Mulligan Sextet	197?	$25
❑ 5531	Profile (1955-56)	197?	$25

Number	Title	Yr	NM
UNITED ARTISTS			
❑ UAL-4085 [M]	Nightwatch	1960	$40
❑ UAS-5085 [S]	Nightwatch	1960	$50
VERVE			
❑ V-8478 [M]	Blues in Time	1962	$25
❑ V6-8478 [S]	Blues in Time	1962	$30
❑ V-8515 [M]	Gerry Mulligan '63 -- The Concert Jazz Band	1963	$25
❑ V6-8515 [S]	Gerry Mulligan '63 -- The Concert Jazz Band	1963	$30
❑ MGV-8388 [M]	Gerry Mulligan and the Concert Jazz Band	1960	$175
❑ V6-8388 [S]	Gerry Mulligan and the Concert Jazz Band	1961	$30
❑ V-8388 [M]	Gerry Mulligan and the Concert Jazz Band	1961	$25
❑ MGV-8396 [M]	Gerry Mulligan and the Concert Jazz Band at the Village Vanguard	1960	$175
❑ V6-8396 [S]	Gerry Mulligan and the Concert Jazz Band at the Village Vanguard	1961	$50
❑ V-8396 [M]	Gerry Mulligan and the Concert Jazz Band at the Village Vanguard	1961	$40
❑ UMV-2057	Gerry Mulligan and the Concert Jazz Band at the Village Vanguard	198?	$30
❑ V-8415 [M]	Gerry Mulligan and the Concert Jazz Band Presents a Concert in Jazz	1961	$30
❑ V6-8415 [S]	Gerry Mulligan and the Concert Jazz Band Presents a Concert in Jazz	1961	$30
❑ MGV-8343 [M]	Gerry Mulligan Meets Ben Webster	1959	$150
❑ MGVS-6104 [S]	Gerry Mulligan Meets Ben Webster	1960	$175
❑ V-8343 [M]	Gerry Mulligan Meets Ben Webster	1961	$25
❑ V-8534 [M]	Gerry Mulligan Meets Ben Webster	1963	$35
❑ V6-8534 [S]	Gerry Mulligan Meets Ben Webster	1963	$25
❑ UMJ-3093	Gerry Mulligan Meets Ben Webster	198?	$30
❑ MGV-8367 [M]	Gerry Mulligan Meets Johnny Hodges	1960	$175
❑ V6-8367 [S]	Gerry Mulligan Meets Johnny Hodges	1961	$30
❑ MGVS-6137 [S]	Gerry Mulligan Meets Johnny Hodges	1960	$0
—Canceled			
❑ V-8367 [M]	Gerry Mulligan Meets Johnny Hodges	1961	$25
❑ V-8536 [M]	Gerry Mulligan Meets Johnny Hodges	1963	$35
❑ V6-8536 [S]	Gerry Mulligan Meets Johnny Hodges	1963	$25
❑ V-8535 [M]	Gerry Mulligan Meets Stan Getz	1963	$35
❑ V6-8535 [S]	Gerry Mulligan Meets Stan Getz	1963	$25
❑ UMV-2652	Gerry Mulligan Presents a Concert in Jazz	198?	$30
❑ VSP-6 [M]	Gerry's Time	1966	$35
❑ VSPS-6 [R]	Gerry's Time	1966	$30
❑ MGV-8249 [M]	Getz Meets Mulligan in Hi-Fi	1958	$150
❑ MGVS-6003 [S]	Getz Meets Mulligan in Hi-Fi	1960	$150
❑ V-8249 [M]	Getz Meets Mulligan in Hi-Fi	1961	$25
❑ V6-8249 [S]	Getz Meets Mulligan in Hi-Fi	1961	$30
❑ VE-2-2537	Mulligan & Getz & Desmond	1980	$35
❑ V-8567 [M]	The Essential Gerry Mulligan	1964	$30
❑ V6-8567 [S]	The Essential Gerry Mulligan	1964	$35
❑ V-8438 [M]	The Gerry Mulligan Concert Jazz Band On Tour with Guest Soloist Zoot Sims	1962	$30
❑ V6-8438 [S]	The Gerry Mulligan Concert Jazz Band On Tour with Guest Soloist Zoot Sims	1962	$30
❑ MGV-8246 [M]	The Gerry Mulligan-Paul Desmond Quartet	1958	$150
❑ V-8246 [M]	The Gerry Mulligan-Paul Desmond Quartet	1961	$25
❑ V-8466 [M]	The Gerry Mulligan Quartet	1962	$30
❑ V6-8466 [S]	The Gerry Mulligan Quartet	1962	$30
WHO'S WHO IN JAZZ			
❑ 21007	Lionel Hampton Presents Gerry Mulligan	1978	$30
WING			
❑ MGW-12335 [M]	Night Lights	1964	$30
❑ SRW-16335 [S]	Night Lights	1964	$35
WORLD PACIFIC			
❑ WP-1201 [M]	California Concerts	1958	$175
❑ WP-1228 [M]	Gerry Mulligan at Storyville	1958	$175
❑ ST-1006 [S]	Gerry Mulligan at Storyville	1958	$250
❑ WP-1273 [M]	Lee Konitz Plays with the Gerry Mulligan Quartet	1959	$175
—Reissue of 406			
❑ PJM-406 [M]	Lee Konitz with the Gerry Mulligan Quartet	1958	$175
❑ WP-1210 [M]	Paris Concert	1958	$175
❑ PJ-1241 [M]	Reunion with Chet Baker	1957	$300
❑ WP-1241 [M]	Reunion with Chet Baker	1958	$175
❑ ST-1007 [S]	Reunion with Chet Baker	1958	$175
❑ PJ-1237 [M]	The Gerry Mulligan Songbook, Volume 1	1957	$300
❑ WP-1237 [M]	The Gerry Mulligan Songbook, Volume 1	1958	$175

Number	Title	Yr	NM
❑ ST-1001 [S]	The Gerry Mulligan Songbook, Volume 1	1958	$250
❑ WP-1207 [M]	The Original Mulligan Quartet	1958	$175

MULLIGAN, GERRY/BUDDY DEFRANCO
GENE NORMAN
❑ GNP-26 [M]	The Gerry Mulligan Quartet with Chet Baker/Buddy DeFranco Quartet	1957	$100

—Combined reissue of two 10-inch LPs

❑ GNP-56 [M]	The Gerry Mulligan Quartet with Chet Baker/Buddy DeFranco Quartet	196?	$40

—Reissue of 26

GNP CRESCENDO
❑ GNPS-56 [R]	The Gerry Mulligan Quartet with Chet Baker/Buddy DeFranco Quartet	196?	$25

MULLIGAN, GERRY/KAI WINDING/RED RODNEY
NEW JAZZ
❑ NJLP-8306 [M]	Broadway	1963	$0

—Canceled; reassigned to Status

STATUS
❑ ST-8306 [M]	Broadway	1965	$40

MULLIGAN, GERRY/PAUL DESMOND
FANTASY
❑ 3220 [M]	Gerry Mulligan Quartet/Paul Desmond Quintet	1956	$100

—Red vinyl; combined reissue of two 10-inch LPs

❑ 3220 [M]	Gerry Mulligan Quartet/Paul Desmond Quintet	1956	$40

—Black vinyl

MULLINS, DEE
PLANTATION
❑ PLP-4	The Continuing Story	1969	$18

MULLINS, ROB
FLYING PIANO
❑ FPR102	Red Shoes	1982	$35
NOVA
| ❑ 8810 | 5th Gear | 1988 | $25 |

MULLOY, BOB
CLASSIC CHRISTMAS
❑ CCR-1932	The Musical Magic of Christmas Organ and Chimes	1977	$12

MULTIPLICATION ROCK (SOUNDTRACK)
CAPITOL
❑ SJA-11174	Multiplication Rock	1973	$40

MUMY, BILL
BB
❑ 103	Bill Mumy	1980	$30

MUNGO JERRY
JANUS
❑ JLS-3027	Memoirs of a Stockbroker	1972	$18
❑ JLS3027 [B]	Memoirs of a Stockbroker	1971	$18
❑ JXS-7000	Mungo Jerry	1970	$18
❑ JXS7000 [B]	Mungo Jerry	12.00	$

MUNOZ
INDIA NAVIGATION
❑ IN-1034	Rendezvous with Now	1978	$35

MUNSON, ESTELLA
MEL-SO'NANCE
❑ SLP-33-100	Christmas Is In the Air	1968	$15

MUNSTERS, THE
DECCA
❑ DL4588 [M]	The Munsters	1964	$150
❑ DL74588 [S]	The Munsters	1964	$175

MURE, BILLY
EVEREST
❑ LPBR-5067 [M]	A String of Trumpets	1960	$25
❑ SDBR-1067 [S]	A String of Trumpets	1960	$30
❑ LPBR-5072 [M]	Songs of Hank Williams	1960	$25
❑ SDBR-1072 [S]	Songs of Hank Williams	1960	$30
❑ LPBR-5120 [M]	Strictly Cha-Cha-Cha	1961	$25
❑ SDBR-1120 [S]	Strictly Cha-Cha-Cha	1961	$30
KAPP
| ❑ KL-1253 [M] | Tough Strings | 1961 | $25 |
| ❑ KS-3253 [S] | Tough Strings | 1961 | $30 |
MGM
| ❑ E-4406 [M] | Happy Guitars | 1966 | $25 |
| ❑ SE-4406 [S] | Happy Guitars | 1966 | $30 |

Number	Title	Yr	NM
❑ E-4189 [M]	Maria Elena and Other Great Songs	1964	$25
❑ SE-4189 [S]	Maria Elena and Other Great Songs	1964	$30
❑ E-3780 [M]	Supersonic Guitars	1959	$30
❑ SE-3780 [S]	Supersonic Guitars	1959	$50
❑ E-3807 [M]	Supersonic Guitars, Vol. 2	1959	$30
❑ SE-3807 [S]	Supersonic Guitars, Vol. 2	1959	$50
❑ E-4131 [M]	Teen Bossa Nova	1963	$25
❑ SE-4131 [S]	Teen Bossa Nova	1963	$30
PREMIER
| ❑ PM-9014 [M] | Blue Hawaii | 196? | $12 |

—Side 1 by Billy Mure; Side 2 by Harry Kaapuni and His Royal Hawaiians

RCA VICTOR
❑ LPM-1694 [M]	Fireworks	1958	$30
❑ LSP-1694 [S]	Fireworks	1958	$40
❑ LPM-1536 [M]	Supersonic Guitars in Hi-Fi	1957	$40
❑ LPM-1869 [M]	Supersonic in Flight	1959	$30
❑ LSP-1869 [S]	Supersonic in Flight	1959	$50
SPIN-O-RAMA
| ❑ S147 [M] | Blue Hawaii | 196? | $12 |

—Side 1 by Billy Mure; Side 2 by Harry Kaapuni and His Royal Hawaiians

❑ S157 [M]	Hawaiian Moods	196?	$12

—One side by Billy Mure; one side by Luke Leilani

STRAND
❑ SL-1010 [M]	Hawaiian Percussion	1961	$30
❑ SLS-1010 [S]	Hawaiian Percussion	1961	$40
❑ SL-1070 [M]	Pink Hawaii	1962	$25
❑ SLS-1070 [S]	Pink Hawaii	1962	$30
❑ SL-1021 [M]	'Round the World in Percussion	1961	$30
❑ SLS-1021 [S]	'Round the World in Percussion	1961	$40
SUNSET
| ❑ SUS-5173 | Songs of Hank Williams | 196? | $15 |

—Reissue of Everest SDBR-1072 with fewer tracks

UNITED ARTISTS
❑ UAL-3031 [M]	Bandstand Record Hop	1959	$40
❑ UAS-6031 [S]	Bandstand Record Hop	1959	$75

MURIBUS, GEORGE
CATALYST
❑ 7602	Brazilian Tapestry	1976	$30
❑ 7619	Trio '77	1977	$30

MURMAIDS, THE
CHATTAHOOCHEE
❑ CHLP-628 [M]	The Mermaids Resurface!	1981	$30

MURPHEY, MICHAEL
A&M
❑ SP-4388	Cosmic Cowboy Souvenir	1973	$15
❑ SP-3137	Cosmic Cowboy Souvenir	198?	$10

—Budget-line reissue

❑ SP-4358	Geronimo's Cadillac	1972	$15
❑ SP-3134	Geronimo's Cadillac	198?	$10

—Budget-line reissue

EMI AMERICA
❑ ST-17143	The Best of Michael Martin Murphey	1984	$12
❑ LN-10310	The Heart Never Lies	1986	$10

—Budget-line reissue

EPIC
❑ KE33290	Blue Sky -- Night Thunder	1975	$12
❑ PE33290	Blue Sky -- Night Thunder	197?	$10

—Reissue with new prefix & dark blue label

❑ PE34220	Flowing Free Forever	1976	$12
❑ JE35013	Lonewolf	1978	$12
❑ KE32835	Michael Murphey	1974	$15
❑ JE35742	Peaks, Valleys, Honky-Tonks & Alleys	1979	$12
❑ PE33851	Swans Against the Sun	1975	$12
❑ PEQ33851 [Q]	Swans Against the Sun	1975	$16
LIBERTY
| ❑ LT-51120 | Michael Martin Murphey | 1982 | $12 |
| ❑ LT-51150 | The Heart Never Lies | 1983 | $12 |
WARNER BROS.
❑ 25500	Americana	1987	$12
❑ 25894	Land of Enchantment	1989	$15
❑ 25644	River of Time	1988	$12
❑ 25369	Tonight We Ride	1986	$12

MURPHY, EDDIE
COLUMBIA
❑ FC39005	Comedian	1983	$12
❑ AS991763 [DJ]	Comedian	1983	$25

—Promo-only picture disc

❑ 9C939151	Comedian	1983	$18

—Stock version of picture disc

❑ FC39952	How Could It Be	1985	$12
❑ OC40970	So Happy	1989	$15
THE ENTERTAINMENT COMPANY
| ❑ FC38180 | Eddie Murphy | 1982 | $12 |
| ❑ AS1607 [EP] | Special Censored Versions | 1982 | $15 |

Number	Title	Yr	NM

—Promo-only collection of "safe for airplay" routines from FC 38180

MURPHY, ELLIOTT
POLYDOR
❑ PD-5061	Aquashow	1973	$25

—First edition with "Like a Great Gatsby" listed as a song title

RCA VICTOR
❑ APL1-0916	Lost Generation	1975	$25

—Orange or tan labels

❑ APL1-1318	Night Lights	1976	$25

—Orange or tan labels

MURPHY, JAC
MUSIC IS MEDICINE
❑ 9003	Child's Gift	1978	$30
❑ 9016	Erin Eileen	198?	$30

MURPHY, JIMMY
SUGAR HILL
❑ SH-3702	Electricity	1978	$15

MURPHY, LYLE
CONTEMPORARY
❑ C-3506 [M]	Gone with the Woodwinds	1955	$250
GENE NORMAN
❑ GNP-9 [10]	Four Saxophones in Twelve Tones	1954	$120
❑ GNP-152 [M]	Four Saxophones in Twelve Tones	195?	$50
❑ GNP-33 [M]	New Orbits in Sound	1957	$50
INNER CITY
| ❑ IC-1133 | Ultimate Odyssey | 198? | $35 |

MURPHY, MARK
AUDIOPHILE
❑ AP-132	Mark Murphy Sings Dorothy Fields and Cy Coleman	197?	$25
CAPITOL
❑ T1299 [M]	Hip Parade	1960	$75
❑ ST1299 [S]	Hip Parade	1960	$75
❑ T1458 [M]	Playing the Field	1960	$75
❑ ST1458 [S]	Playing the Field	1960	$75
❑ T1177 [M]	This Could Be the Start of Something	1959	$75
❑ ST1177 [S]	This Could Be the Start of Something	1959	$75
DECCA
| ❑ DL8632 [M] | Let Yourself Go | 1958 | $150 |
| ❑ DL8390 [M] | Meet Mark Murphy | 1957 | $120 |
FANTASY
| ❑ OJC-141 | Rah | 198? | $25 |
| ❑ OJC-367 | That's How I Love the Blues | 198? | $25 |
FONTANA
| ❑ MGF-27537 [M] | A Swingin' Singin' Affair | 1965 | $25 |
| ❑ SRF-67537 [S] | A Swingin' Singin' Affair | 1965 | $30 |
MILESTONE
| ❑ M-9145 | Night Mood | 1987 | $25 |
| ❑ M-9154 | September Ballads | 1988 | $25 |
MUSE
❑ MR-5355	Beauty and the Beast	198?	$25
❑ MR-5253	Bop for Kerouac	1981	$30
❑ MR-5297	Brazil Song (Cancoes do Brasil)	1983	$25
❑ MR-5009	Bridging a Gap	197?	$30
❑ MR-5359	Kerouac, Then and Now	198?	$30
❑ MR-5345	Living Room	1986	$25
❑ MR-5041	Mark II	197?	$30
❑ MR-5078	Mark Murphy Sings	1975	$30
❑ MR-5308	Mark Murphy Sings Nat's Choice	1985	$25
❑ MR-5320	Mark Murphy Sings Nat's Choice, Vol. 2	1986	$25
❑ MR-5213	Satisfaction Guaranteed	1980	$25
❑ MR-5102	Stolen Moments	1978	$30
❑ MR-5286	The Artistry of Mark Murphy	1982	$25
PAUSA
| ❑ 7023 | Midnight Mood | 1979 | $25 |
| ❑ 9042 | This Could Be the Start of Something | 1985 | $25 |
RIVERSIDE
❑ RLP-395 [M]	Rah	1961	$250
❑ RS-9395 [S]	Rah	1961	$250
❑ 6064	Rah	197?	$30
❑ 6091	That's How I Love the Blues	197?	$30
❑ RLP-441 [M]	That's How I Love the Blues!	1962	$175
❑ RS-9441 [S]	That's How I Love the Blues!	1962	$175

MURPHY, ROSE
AUDIOPHILE
❑ AP-70	Rose Murphy	198?	$30
MCA
| ❑ 1558 | Rose Murphy Sings Again | 1983 | $35 |
ROYALE
| ❑ VLP-6079 [10] | Chi-Chi Girl | 195? | $100 |

Number	Title	Yr	NM
❏ 1835 [10]	Rose Murphy and Quartette	195?	$100
UNITED ARTISTS			
❏ UAJ-14025 [M]	Jazz, Joy and Happiness	1962	$50
❏ UAJS-15025 [S]	Jazz, Joy and Happiness	1962	$75
VERVE			
❏ MGV-2070 [M]	Not Cha-Cha But Chi-Chi	1957	$175
❏ V-2070 [M]	Not Cha-Cha But Chi-Chi	1961	$30

MURPHY, TURK
ATLANTIC
❏ SD1613	The Many Faces of Ragtime	1972	$30

COLUMBIA
❏ CL6257 [10]	Barrelhouse Jazz	1953	$50
❏ CL595 [M]	Barrelhouse Jazz	1954	$40
—Maroon label, gold print			
❏ CL595 [M]	Barrelhouse Jazz	1955	$40
—Red and black label with six "eye" logos			
❏ CL650 [M]	Dancing Jazz	1955	$50
—Maroon label, gold print			
❏ CL650 [M]	Dancing Jazz	1955	$40
—Red and black label with six "eye" logos			
❏ CL559 [M]	The Music of Jelly Roll Morton	1954	$40
—Maroon label, gold print			
❏ CL559 [M]	The Music of Jelly Roll Morton	1955	$40
—Red and black label with six "eye" logos			
❏ CL546 [M]	When the Saints Go Marching In	1953	$40
—Maroon label, gold print			
❏ CL546 [M]	When the Saints Go Marching In	1955	$85
—Red and black label with six "eye" logos			

FORUM
❏ F-9017 [M]	Turk Murphy and His Jazz Band at the Roundtable	196?	$30
—Reissue of Roulette R-25076			
❏ SF-9017 [S]	Turk Murphy and His Jazz Band at the Roundtable	196?	$35
—Reissue of Roulette SR-25076			

GHB
❏ 91	Turk Murphy, Volume 1	198?	$25
❏ 92	Turk Murphy, Volume 2	198?	$25
❏ 93	Turk Murphy, Volume 3	198?	$25

GOOD TIME JAZZ
❏ L-12026 [M]	San Francisco Jazz, Volume 1	1955	$50
❏ L-12027 [M]	San Francisco Jazz, Volume 2	1955	$50
❏ L-7 [10]	Turk Murphy with Claire Austin	1952	$50

MERRY MAKERS
❏ S-105	Turk Murphy San Francisco Jazz Band	197?	$35
❏ S-106	Turk Murphy's Jazz Band	197?	$35

MOTHERLODE
❏ 0103	Turk Murphy's Jazz Band, Vol. 1	1973	$30
❏ 0104	Turk Murphy's Jazz Band, Vol. 2	1973	$30

MPS
❏ MC-22097	Live!	197?	$35

RCA VICTOR
❏ LPM-2501 [M]	Let the Good Times Roll	1962	$25
❏ LSP-2501 [S]	Let the Good Times Roll	1962	$30

ROULETTE
❏ R-25088 [M]	Music for Wise Guys	1960	$25
❏ SR-25088 [S]	Music for Wise Guys	1960	$30
❏ R-25076 [M]	Turk Murphy and His Jazz Band at the Roundtable	1959	$25
❏ SR-25076 [S]	Turk Murphy and His Jazz Band at the Roundtable	1959	$30

SONIC ARTS
❏ 14	Natural High	1979	$35

STOMP OFF
❏ SOS-1161	Southern Stomps	1989	$25
❏ SOS-1155	Turk at Carnegie	1988	$25

VERVE
❏ MGV-1013 [M]	Music for Losers	1957	$175
❏ V-1013 [M]	Music for Losers	1961	$25
❏ MGV-1015 [M]	Turk Murphy on Easy Street	1957	$150
❏ V-1015 [M]	Turk Murphy on Easy Street	1961	$25

MURPHY, WALTER
MCA
❏ 6114	Themes from E.T. and More	1982	$12

PRIVATE STOCK
❏ PS2015	A Fifth of Beethoven	1976	$12
❏ PS7010	Phantom of the Opera	1978	$12
❏ PS2028	Rhapsody in Blue	1977	$12

MURRAY, ANNE, AND GLEN CAMPBELL
CAPITOL
❏ SW-869	Anne Murray/Glen Campbell	1971	$15
❏ SN-16144	Anne Murray/Glen Campbell	1980	$10

Number	Title	Yr	NM
—Budget-line reissue			

MURRAY, ANNE
CAPITOL
❏ ST-12039	A Country Collection	1980	$12
❏ SN-16338	A Country Collection	198?	$10
—Budget-line reissue			
❏ ST-12301	A Little Good News	1983	$12
❏ ST-667	Anne Murray	1971	$15
❏ SOO-12110	Anne Murray's Greatest Hits	1980	$12
❏ ST-11024	Annie	1972	$12
❏ C1-48764	As I Am	1988	$12
❏ C1-90886	Christmas	1987	$10
❏ SN-16232	Christmas Wishes	1981	$12
—Original issue was on the budget-line series			
❏ ST-11324	Country	1974	$12
❏ SN-16213	Country	1981	$10
—Budget-line reissue			
❏ ST-11172	Danny's Song	1973	$12
❏ SN-16211	Danny's Song	1981	$10
—Budget-line reissue			
❏ C1-92072	Greatest Hits Volume II	1989	$15
❏ PJ-12562	Harmony	1987	$12
❏ SJ-12363	Heart Over Mind	1984	$12
❏ ST-11354	Highly Prized Possession	1974	$12
❏ SN-16081	Highly Prized Possession	1980	$10
—Budget-line reissue			
❏ SOO-12012	I'll Always Love You	1979	$12
❏ ST-11559	Keeping in Touch	1976	$12
❏ SN-16082	Keeping in Touch	1980	$10
—Budget-line reissue			
❏ ST-11743	Let's Keep It That Way	1978	$12
❏ SN-16341	Let's Keep It That Way	198?	$10
—Budget-line reissue			
❏ ST-11266	Love Song	1974	$12
❏ SN-16212	Love Song	1981	$10
—Budget-line reissue			
❏ SW-11849	New Kind of Feeling	1979	$12
❏ SN-16283	New Kind of Feeling	1982	$10
—Budget-line reissue			
❏ ST-579	Snowbird	1970	$15
❏ SOO-12064	Somebody's Waiting	1980	$12
❏ SJ-12466	Something to Talk About	1986	$12
❏ ST-821	Talk It Over in the Morning	1971	$15
❏ SN-16080	Talk It Over in the Morning	1980	$10
—Budget-line reissue			
❏ ST-12225	The Hottest Night of the Year	1982	$12
❏ SN-16233	There's a Hippo in My Tub	1981	$12
—Original issue was on the budget-line series			
❏ ST-11433	Together	1975	$12
❏ SN-16282	Together	1982	$10
—Budget-line reissue			
❏ SOO-12144	Where Do You Go When You Dream	1981	$12

CAPITOL NASHVILLE
❏ R173232	You Will	1990	$25
—Only released on vinyl through BMG Direct Marketing			

PICKWICK
❏ SPC-3350	What About Me	197?	$10

MURRAY, DAVID
ADELPHI
❏ 5002	Low Class Conspiracy	1976	$35

BLACK SAINT
❏ BSR-0089	Children	1986	$30
❏ BSR-0055	Home	198?	$30
❏ BSR-0018	Interboogieology	198?	$35
❏ 120105	I Want to Talk About You	1990	$35
❏ BSR-0085	Live at Sweet Basil, Vol. 1	1985	$30
❏ 120095	Live at Sweet Basil, Vol. 2	1986	$30
❏ BSR-0045	Ming	198?	$30
❏ BSR-0075	Morning Song	1984	$30
❏ BSR-0065	Murray's Steps	1983	$30
❏ BSR-0039	Sweet Lovely	198?	$30
❏ 120110	The Hill	1990	$35

HAT ART
❏ 2016	3D Family	1986	$35

HAT HUT
❏ 0U/V	The Third Family	1979	$25

INDIA NAVIGATION
❏ IN-1026	Flowers for Albert	197?	$35
❏ IN-1044	Live, Volume 2	1979	$35
❏ IN-1032	Live at the Ocean Club	1978	$35

PORTRAIT
❏ OR44432	Ming's Samba	1989	$30

RED RECORD
❏ VPA-129	Last of the Hipman	198?	$30

MURRAY, SUNNY
ESP-DISK'
❏ 1032 [M]	Sunny Murray	1966	$250
❏ S-1032 [S]	Sunny Murray	1966	$250

JIHAD
❏ 663 [M]	Sunny's Time Now	1967	$250

Number	Title	Yr	NM

MURRAY THE "K
See VARIOUS ARTISTS COLLECTIONS.

MUSCLE SHOALS HORNS, THE
BANG

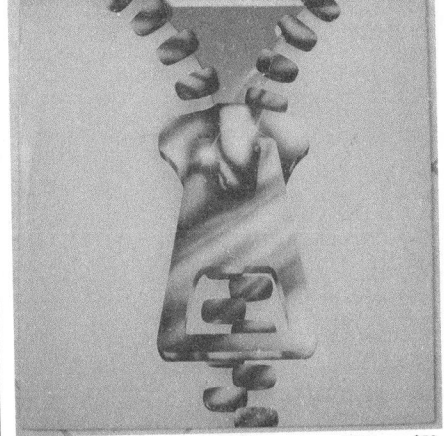

❏ BLP-403 [B]	Born to Get Down	1975	$50

MUSIC ASYLUM, THE
UNITED ARTISTS
❏ UAS-6778	Commit Thyself	1970	$25

MUSIC CITY SINGERS, THE
HALO
❏ 1003	Christmas Favorites	196?	$18
—Includes Bobby Russell, Bill Pursell, Boots Randolph, Willie Ackerman, The Jordanaires and the Anita Kerr Singers, among others			

MUSIC CITY SOUNDS, THE
MGM
❏ SE-4672	The Music City Sounds Featuring Lloyd Green and Pete Wade	1970	$18

MUSIC COMPANY, THE
CRESTVIEW
❏ CRS-3057	Hard and Heavy	196?	$75

MIRWOOD
❏ M-7002 [M]	Rubber Soul Jazz	1966	$50
❏ MS-7002 [S]	Rubber Soul Jazz	1966	$75

MUSIC EMPORIUM, THE
SENTINEL
❏ 69001 [B]	The Music Emporium	1969	$4000

SUNDAZED
❏ LP5078	The Music Emporium	2001	$18
—First legitimate reissue of the original			

MUSIC EXPLOSION, THE
LAURIE
❏ LLP-2040 [M]	Little Bit O'Soul	1967	$25
❏ SLLP-2040 [S]	Little Bit O'Soul	1967	$30

MUSIC IMPROVISATION COMPANY, THE
ECM
❏ 1005	The Music Improvisation Company	197?	$35

MUSIC MACHINE, THE
ORIGINAL SOUND
❏ 5015 [M]	(Turn On) The Music Machine	1966	$40
❏ 8875 [S]	(Turn On) The Music Machine	1966	$50

SUNDAZED
❏ LP5038	Ignition	2000	$15

WARNER BROS.
❏ W1732 [M]	Bonniwell's Music Machine	1967	$75
❏ WS1732 [S]	Bonniwell's Music Machine	1967	$40

MUSICAL YOUTH
MCA
❏ 5454 [B]	Different Style	1983	$15
❏ 5389 [B]	The Youth of Today	1983	$15

MUSRA, PHIL
INTEX SOUND
❏ 84 [B]	Creatorspaces	1974	$500

Number	Title	Yr	NM

MUSSELWHITE, CHARLIE
VANGUARD

Number	Title	Yr	NM
❏ VSD-79287	Charlie Musselwhite	1968	$25
❏ VRS-9232 [M]	Stand Back! Here Comes Charlie Musselwhite's South Side Band	1966	$25
❏ VSD-79232 [S]	Stand Back! Here Comes Charlie Musselwhite's South Side Band	1966	$30
❏ VSD-6258	Tennessee Woman	1969	$25

MUSSO, VIDO
CROWN

| ❏ CLP-5029 [M] | Teenage Dance Party | 1957 | $50 |
| ❏ CLP-5007 [M] | The Swingin'st | 1957 | $50 |

— Reissue of Modern LP

MODERN

| ❏ MLP-1207 [M] | The Swingin'st | 1956 | $150 |

MUSSULLI, BOOTS
CAPITOL

| ❏ H6506 [10] | Boots Mussulli | 1955 | $250 |
| ❏ T6506 [M] | Boots Mussulli | 1955 | $100 |

MUSTANGS, THE
PROVIDENCE

| ❏ PLP-001 [M] | Dartell Stomp | 1964 | $50 |

MUTZIE
SUSSEX

| ❏ SUX-7001 | Light of Your Shadow | 1970 | $30 |

MY BLOODY VALENTINE
CREATION/RELATIVITY

| ❏ 1006 [B] | Isn't Anything | 1989 | $35 |

MYA
INTERSCOPE

| ❏ 490640-1 | Fear of Flying | 2000 | $18 |
| ❏ 90166 | Mya | 1998 | $15 |

MYERS, AMINA CLAUDINE
BLACK SAINT

| ❏ BSR-0078 | Circle of Time | 1984 | $30 |

MINOR MUSIC

| ❏ MM-012 | Country Girl | 1987 | $25 |
| ❏ MM-002 | Jumping in the Sugar Bowl | 198? | $30 |

NOVUS

| ❏ 3030-1-N | Amina | 1988 | $25 |
| ❏ 3064-1-N | In Touch | 1989 | $30 |

MYERS, DAVE
CAROLE

| ❏ 8002 [M] | Greatest Racing Themes | 1967 | $50 |

DEL-FI

❏ DFLP-1239 [M]	Hangin' Twenty	1963	$100
❏ DFST-1239 [S]	Hangin' Twenty	1963	$180
❏ DLF-1239	Hangin' Twenty	1998	$15

MYERSON, BESS
MGM

| ❏ E-3785 [M] | Fashions in Music | 1959 | $30 |
| ❏ SE-3785 [S] | Fashions in Music | 1959 | $40 |

MYLES, ALANNAH
ATLANTIC

| ❏ 81956 | Alannah Myles | 1989 | $15 |

MYRICK, BERL
STRATA-EAST

Number	Title	Yr	NM
❏ SES-102-74	Live 'n Well	1974	$30

MYRICK, GARY, AND THE FIGURES
EPIC

| ❏ NJE36524 | Gary Myrick and the Figures | 1980 | $15 |
| ❏ JE36524 | Gary Myrick and the Figures | 1981 | $12 |

— Reissue with amended prefix

| ❏ B5E38637 [EP] | Language | 1983 | $12 |
| ❏ AS1389 [DJ] | Live Sampler | 1982 | $16 |

— Four live tracks, including one unreleased song

| ❏ ARE37429 | Living in a Movie | 1981 | $12 |
| ❏ AS912 [DJ] | Talks in Stereo | 1981 | $40 |

— Side one has studio tracks, side two has live versions of songs on side one

GEFFEN

| ❏ GHS24076 | Stand for Love | 1985 | $12 |

MYSTERIOUS FLYING ORCHESTRA, THE
RCA VICTOR

| ❏ APL1-2137 | The Mysterious Flying Orchestra | 1977 | $50 |

MYSTIC ASTROLOGICAL CRYSTAL BAND, THE
CAROLE

❏ S-8003	Clip Out, Put On Book	1968	$30
❏ 8001 [M]	Mystic Astrological Crystal Band	1967	$30
❏ S-8001 [S]	Mystic Astrological Crystal Band	1967	$30

MYSTIC MOODS ORCHESTRA, THE
BAINBRIDGE

| ❏ 6216 | Another Stormy Night | 1983 | $10 |
| ❏ 6211 | Country Lovin' Folk | 1982 | $10 |

— Reissue of Sound Bird 8512

| ❏ 6206 | Emotions | 1982 | $10 |

— Reissue of Sound Bird 7505

| ❏ 6210 | English Muffins | 1982 | $10 |
| ❏ 6215 | Erogenous | 1982 | $10 |

— Reissue of Sound Bird 7509

❏ 6212	Extensions	1982	$10
❏ 6209	Highway One	1982	$10
❏ 6207	Love Token	1982	$10
❏ 6203	Mexico!	1982	$10
❏ 6202	Moods for a Stormy Night	1982	$10

— Reissue of Sound Bird 7504

| ❏ 6201 | More Than Music | 1982 | $10 |
| ❏ 6204 | Nightide | 1982 | $10 |

— Reissue of Sound Bird 7502

| ❏ 6205 | One Stormy Night | 1982 | $10 |

— Reissue of Sound Bird 7501

| ❏ 6208 | Stormy Weekend | 1982 | $10 |

— Reissue of Sound Bird 7506

| ❏ 6219 | Summer Moods | 1985 | $10 |

MOBILE FIDELITY

| ❏ Jan-002 | Cosmic Forces | 1979 | $40 |

— Audiophile vinyl

| ❏ Jan-001 | Emotions | 1979 | $50 |

— Audiophile vinyl

| ❏ Jan-003 | Stormy Weekend | 1979 | $30 |

— Audiophile vinyl

PHILIPS

❏ PHS600351	Country Lovin' Folk	1971	$15
❏ PHS600277	Emotions	1968	$15
❏ PHS600349	English Muffins	1970	$15
❏ PHS600301	Extensions	1969	$15
❏ PHS600321	Love Token	1969	$15
❏ PHM200250 [M]	Mexican Trip	1967	$18
❏ PHS600250 [S]	Mexican Trip	1967	$15
❏ PHM200231 [M]	More Than Music	1967	$18
❏ PHS600231 [S]	More Than Music	1967	$15
❏ PHM200213 [M]	Nightide	1966	$15
❏ PHS600213 [S]	Nightide	1966	$18
❏ PHM200205 [M]	One Stormy Night	1966	$15
❏ PHS600205 [S]	One Stormy Night	1966	$18
❏ PHS600342	Stormy Weekend	1970	$15
❏ PHM200260 [M]	The Mystic Moods of Love	1968	$18
❏ PHS600260 [S]	The Mystic Moods of Love	1968	$15

SOUND BIRD

❏ 8508	Alone Together	1978	$10
❏ 7510	Being with You	1976	$12
❏ SQ7510 [Q]	Being with You	1976	$16
❏ 8510	Being with You	1978	$10

— Reissue of Sound Bird 7510

❏ 8511	Cosmic Forces	1978	$10
❏ 8512	Country Lovin' Folk	1978	$10
❏ 7505	Emotions	1975	$10
❏ 7509	Erogenous	1975	$10

— Reissue of Warner Bros. 2786

| ❏ SQ7509 [Q] | Erogenous | 1975 | $18 |

— Reissue of Warner Bros. BS4 2786

| ❏ 7508 | Love the One You're With | 1975 | $10 |

— Reissue of Warner Bros. 2577

| ❏ SQ7508 [Q] | Love the One You're With | 1975 | $18 |

— Reissue of Warner Bros. BS4 2577

Number	Title	Yr	NM
❏ 7503	Man and...	1975	$10
❏ 8505	Midnight	1978	$10
❏ 8503	Misty	1978	$10
❏ 7504	Moods for a Stormy Night	1975	$10
❏ 7502	Nightide	1975	$10

— Reissue of Warner Bros. 2593

| ❏ 7501 | One Stormy Night | 1975 | $10 |

— Reissue of Warner Bros. 2594

| ❏ 8514 | Simple | 1978 | $10 |
| ❏ 7506 | Stormy Weekend | 1975 | $10 |

— Reissue of Warner Bros. 2596

| ❏ 7507 | Touch | 1975 | $10 |
| ❏ SQ7507 [Q] | Touch | 1975 | $18 |

WARNER BROS.

❏ BS2690	Awakening	1973	$15
❏ BS42690 [Q]	Awakening	1974	$16
❏ BS2745	Clear Light	1974	$15
❏ BS42745 [Q]	Clear Light	1974	$16
❏ BS2597	Emotions	1972	$12

— Reissue of Philips 600-277

❏ BS2786	Erogenous	1974	$12
❏ BS42786 [Q]	Erogenous	1974	$16
❏ BS2648	Highway One	1973	$15
❏ BS42648 [Q]	Highway One	1974	$16
❏ BS2577	Love the One You're With	1972	$15
❏ BS42577 [Q]	Love the One You're With	1974	$16
❏ BS2595	Love Token	1972	$12

— Reissue of Philips 600-321

| ❏ BS2593 | Nightide | 1972 | $12 |

— Reissue of Philips 600-213

| ❏ BS2594 | One Stormy Night | 1972 | $12 |

— Reissue of Philips 600-205

| ❏ BS2596 | Stormy Weekend | 1972 | $12 |

— Reissue of Philips 600-342

| ❏ BS2598 | The Mystic Moods of Love | 1972 | $12 |

— Reissue of Philips 600-260

MYSTIC NUMBER NATIONAL BANK, THE
PROBE

| ❏ CPLP-4501 | The Mystic Number National Bank | 1969 | $25 |

MYSTIC SIVA
VO

| ❏ 19713 | Mystic Siva | 1971 | $1000 |

MYSTICS, THE
AMBIENT SOUND

| ❏ FZ37716 | Crazy for You | 1982 | $12 |

COLLECTABLES

| ❏ COL-5043 | 16 Golden Classics | 198? | $12 |

N

N.E.R.D.
VIRGIN

| ❏ 91457 [B] | Fly or Die | 2004 | $18 |

| ❏ 12622 [B] | In Search of... | 2002 | $30 |

N.W.A.
PRIORITY

| ❏ SPRO30080 [DJ] | Greatest Hits/In-Store Play | 1996 | $25 |

— Promo-only "clean" versions for retailer use

RUTHLESS

❏ 7224 [EP]	100 Miles and Runnin'	1990	$18
❏ 57126	Efil4zaggin (Niggaz4life)	1991	$25
❏ 50561	Greatest Hits	1996	$18

Number	Title	Yr	NM
❑ 57119	N.W.A. and the Posse	1990	$18
— Reissue of MRC 1057			
❑ MRC1057	N.W.A. and the Posse	1987	$30

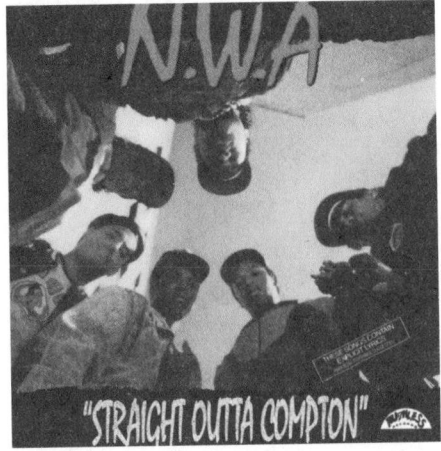

Number	Title	Yr	NM
❑ 57102 [B]	Straight Outta Compton	1989	$25

NABORS, JIM
CAPITOL SPECIAL MARKETS

❑ SL-8136	20 All-Time Favorites	1977	$12

COLUMBIA

❑ KC33401	A Very Special Love Song	1974	$15
❑ PC33401	A Very Special Love Song	1979	$10
— Budget-line reissue			
❑ C30129	Everything Is Beautiful	1970	$15
❑ C30449	For the Good Times/The Jim Nabors Hour	1971	$15
❑ CS9817	Galveston	1969	$15
❑ KG31591	Great Love Songs	1972	$18
❑ PG31591	Great Love Songs	198?	$12
— Budget-line reissue			
❑ C30810	Help Me Make It Through the Night	1971	$15
❑ CQ30810 [Q]	Help Me Make It Through the Night	1971	$30
❑ C30671	How Great Thou Art	1971	$15
❑ 3C30671	How Great Thou Art	198?	$10
— Budget-line reissue			
❑ KC32950	It's My Life	1973	$15
❑ CL2665 [M]	Jim Nabors By Request	1967	$15
❑ CS9465 [S]	Jim Nabors By Request	1967	$18
❑ CL2731 [M]	Jim Nabors' Christmas Album	1967	$15
❑ CS9531 [S]	Jim Nabors' Christmas Album	1967	$15
— Originals with "360 Sound" label			
❑ CS9531	Jim Nabors' Christmas Album	1970	$12
— Later editions with orange label			
❑ CL2558 [M]	Jim Nabors Sings Love Me with All Your Heart	1966	$15
❑ CS9358 [S]	Jim Nabors Sings Love Me with All Your Heart	1966	$18
❑ CS9620	Kiss Me Goodbye	1968	$15
❑ C31630	Merry Christmas	1972	$12
❑ KC32909	Peace in the Valley	1973	$15
❑ PC32909	Peace in the Valley	1979	$10
— Budget-line reissue			
❑ CL2368 [M]	Shazam! (Gomer Pyle, U.S.M.C.)	1965	$25
❑ CS9168 [S]	Shazam! (Gomer Pyle, U.S.M.C.)	1965	$30
❑ CS1020	The Jim Nabors Hour	1970	$15
❑ PC9716	The Lord's Prayer	1979	$10
— Budget-line reissue			
❑ CS9716	The Lord's Prayer and Other Sacred Songs	1968	$15
❑ CG33618	The Lord's Prayer/How Great Thou Art	1975	$18
❑ CL2703 [M]	The Things I Love	1967	$15
❑ CS9503 [S]	The Things I Love	1967	$18
❑ KC32377	The Twelfth of Never	1972	$15
❑ KC31336	The Way of Love	1972	$15
❑ KG31973	The World of Jim Nabors	1972	$18
❑ PG31973	The World of Jim Nabors	1979	$12
— Budget-line reissue			

COLUMBIA SPECIAL PRODUCTS

❑ P13507	Somewhere My Love	1977	$12

HARMONY

❑ KH30398	More	1971	$12

PAIR

❑ PDL2-1097	On the Country Side	1986	$15
❑ PDL2-1077	The Very Special Warmth of Jim Nabors	1986	$15

Number	Title	Yr	NM
RANWOOD			
❑ R-7017	22 Great Hymn and Country Favorites	1984	$15
❑ R-8178	I See God	1977	$12
❑ R-8157	Old Time Religion	1976	$12
❑ R-8176	Sincerely	1977	$12
❑ R-8164	Town & Country	1976	$12
REALM			
❑ 1V-8170	Christmas with Jim Nabors	1982	$10

NAGLE, RON
WARNER BROS.

❑ WS1902 [B]	Bad Rice	1970	$25

NAJEE
EMI

❑ E1-92248	Tokyo Blue	1990	$12

EMI AMERICA

❑ ST-17241	Najee's Theme	1986	$12

EMI MANHATTAN

❑ E1-90096	Day By Day	1988	$12

NAKAMURA, TERUO
POLYDOR

❑ PD-1-6119	Manhattan Special	1977	$25
❑ PD-1-6097	Rising Sun	1977	$25

NAKED EYES
EMI AMERICA

❑ ST-17116	Fuel for the Fire	1984	$12
❑ ST-17089	Naked Eyes	1983	$15

NAKED RAYGUN
CAROLINE

❑ 1348	Jettison	1988	$25
❑ 1642	Raygun...Naked Raygun	1990	$25
❑ 1371	Understand?	1989	$25
HAUNTED TOWN			
❑ HTR11	Free Shit	2001	$12
HOMESTEAD			
❑ HMS 045	All Rise	1985	$30
❑ HMS 008	Throb Throb	1984	$30
— First edition has lyric sheet			
❑ HMS 008	Throb Throb	1984	$25
— Second edition has lyric innersleeve			
RUTHLESS			
❑ 03 [EP]	Basement Screams	1983	$100

NAMYSLOVSKI, ZBIGNIEW
INNER CITY

❑ IC-1130	Air Condition	198?	$30
❑ IC-1048	Namyslovski	197?	$35

NANCE, RAY
SOLID STATE

❑ SS-18062 [B]	Body and Soul	1969	$25

NANTON, MORRIS
PRESTIGE

❑ PRLP-7345 [M]	Preface	1964	$25
❑ PRST-7345 [S]	Preface	1964	$30
❑ PRLP-7409 [M]	Something We've Got	1965	$25
❑ PRST-7409 [S]	Something We've Got	1965	$30
❑ PRLP-7467 [M]	Soul Fingers	1966	$25
❑ PRST-7467 [S]	Soul Fingers	1966	$30
WARNER BROS.			
❑ W-1256 [M]	Flower Drum Song	1958	$30
❑ WS-1256 [S]	Flower Drum Song	1958	$30
❑ W-1279 [M]	The Original Jazz Performance of "Roberta	1959	$30
❑ WS-1279 [S]	The Original Jazz Performance of "Roberta	1959	$30

NAPOLEON, PHIL
CAPITOL

❑ ST1428 [S]	In the Land of Dixie	1961	$30
❑ T1428 [M]	In the Land of Dixie	1961	$50
❑ T1344 [M]	Phil Napoleon and the Memphis Five	1960	$30
❑ ST1344 [S]	Phil Napoleon and the Memphis Five	1960	$50
❑ ST1535 [S]	Tenderloin Dixieland	1961	$30
❑ T1535 [M]	Tenderloin Dixieland	1961	$50
COLUMBIA			
❑ CL2505 [10]	Two-Beat	1955	$100
EMARCY			
❑ MG-26008 [10]	Dixieland Classics Vol. 1	1954	$250
❑ MG-36033 [M]	Dixieland Classics Vol. 1	1955	$100
❑ MG-26009 [10]	Dixieland Classics Vol. 2	1954	$250
JOLLY ROGER			
❑ 5006 [10]	Dixieland By Phil Napoleon	1954	$50

Number	Title	Yr	NM
MERCURY			
❑ MG-25078 [10]	Dixieland Classics Vol. 1	1953	$175
❑ MG-25079 [10]	Dixieland Classics Vol. 2	1953	$175

NAPOLEON XIV
RHINO

❑ RNLP816	They're Coming to Take Me Away, Ha-Haaa!	1985	$15

WARNER BROS.

❑ W1661 [M]	They're Coming to Take Me Away, Ha-Haaa!	1966	$100
❑ WS1661 [S]	They're Coming to Take Me Away, Ha-Haaa!	1966	$150

NARAHARA, STEVE
PAUSA

❑ 7177	Odyssey	1985	$25
❑ 7153	Sierra	1982	$25

NARELL, ANDY
HIPPOCKET

❑ HP-103	Light in Your Eyes	1983	$30
— Original issue			
❑ HP-105	Slow Motion	1985	$30
— Original issue			
❑ HP-101	Stickman	1981	$30
— Original issue			
INNER CITY			
❑ IC-1053	Hidden Treasure	1979	$35
WINDHAM HILL			
❑ WH-0103	Light in Your Eyes	1987	$25
— Reissue of HipPocket 103			
❑ WH-0120	Little Secrets	1989	$30
❑ WH-0105	Slow Motion	1987	$25
— Reissue of HipPocket 105			
❑ WH-0101	Stickman	1987	$25
— Reissue of HipPocket 101			
❑ WH-0107	The Hammer	1987	$25

NARK, VAUGHN
STATIRAS

❑ SLP-8070	El Tigre	1985	$25

NARZ, JACK
DOT

❑ DLP-3244 [M]	Sing the Folk Hits with Jack Narz	1960	$30
❑ DLP-25244 [S]	Sing the Folk Hits with Jack Narz	1960	$30

NAS
COLUMBIA

❑ C286930	God's Son	2002	$18
❑ C2S41881 [DJ]	I Am	1999	$25
— Promo-only version in generic black sleeve			
❑ C268773	I Am	1999	$18
❑ C57694	Illmatic	1994	$30
❑ C292072	Illmatic	2004	$18
— 10th anniversary reissue with bonus material			
❑ C67015	It Was Written	1996	$15
❑ C263930	Nastradamus	1999	$18
❑ C285736	Stillmatic	2001	$18
❑ C492065	Street's Disciple	2004	$30
❑ C285275	The Lost Tapes	2002	$18

NASCIMENTO, MILTON
A&M

❑ SP-3019	Courage	1969	$25
❑ SP9-3019	Courage	198?	$35
— Audiophile reissue (clearly marked as such)			
❑ SP-4719	Journey to Dawn	1979	$35
❑ SP-4611	Milton	1976	$25
❑ LP-0(# unknown) [M]	Milton Nascimento	1967	$30
❑ SP-0(# unknown) [S]	Milton Nascimento	1967	$25
COLUMBIA			
❑ FC45239	Miltons	1989	$30
❑ FC44277	Yauarate	1987	$25
INTUITION			
❑ B1-90790	Milagre Dos Peixes	1988	$30
— Originally issued in Brazil in 1973			
POLYDOR			
❑ 827638-1	Encontros E Despedidas	1986	$30
VERVE			
❑ 831349-1	A Barca Dos Amantes	1986	$30

NASH, GRAHAM, AND DAVID CROSBY
ABC

❑ AA-1042	Crosby/Nash -- Live	1977	$12
❑ AA-1102	The Best of Crosby/Nash	1978	$12

Number	Title	Yr	NM

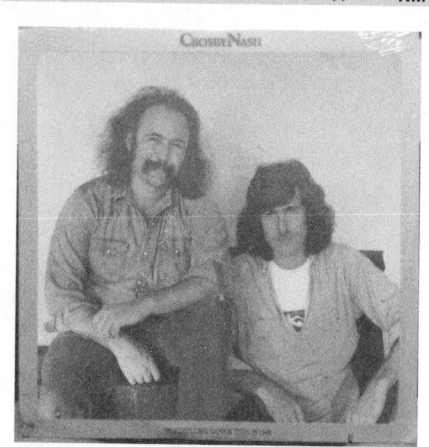

❑ ABCD-956 [B]	Whistling Down the Wire	1976	$12
❑ ABCD-902 [B]	Wind on the Water	1975	$12
ATLANTIC			
❑ SD7220	Graham Nash/David Crosby	1972	$15
MCA			
❑ 37008	The Best of Crosby/Nash	198?	$10
— Reissue of ABC 1102			
❑ 37007	Wind on the Water	198?	$10
— Reissue of ABC 902			

NASH, GRAHAM
Also see CROSBY, STILLS AND NASH; CROSBY, STILLS, NASH & YOUNG; THE HOLLIES.

ATLANTIC			
❑ 81633	Innocent Eyes	1986	$10
❑ SD7204	Songs for Beginners	1971	$15
❑ SD7288	Wild Tales	1974	$12
CAPITOL			
❑ SWAK-12014	Earth & Sky	1980	$12

NASH, JOHNNY

ABC-PARAMOUNT			
❑ 299 [M]	I Got Rhythm	1959	$30
❑ S-299 [S]	I Got Rhythm	1959	$40
❑ 244 [M]	Johnny Nash	1958	$30
❑ S-244 [S]	Johnny Nash	1959	$40
❑ 344 [M]	Let's Get Lost	1960	$30
❑ S-344 [S]	Let's Get Lost	1960	$40
❑ 276 [M]	Quiet Hour	1959	$30
❑ S-276 [S]	Quiet Hour	1959	$40
❑ 383 [M]	Studio Time	1961	$30
❑ S-383 [S]	Studio Time	1961	$40
ARGO			
❑ LP-4038 [M]	Composer's Choice	1964	$25
❑ LPS-4038 [S]	Composer's Choice	1964	$30
EPIC			
❑ PE32828	Celebrate Life	1974	$18
❑ KE31607	I Can See Clearly Now	1972	$18
— Yellow label			
❑ KE31607	I Can See Clearly Now	1973	$15
— Orange label			
❑ KE32158	My Merry-Go-Round	1973	$18
JAD			

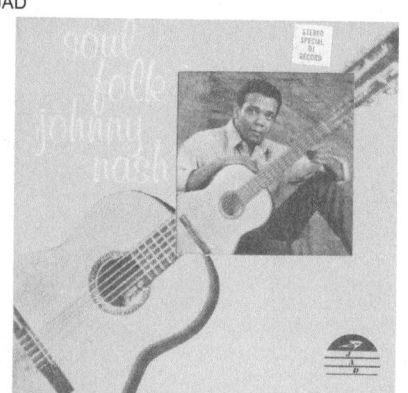

❑ JS-1006 [B]	Folk Soul	1970	$30
❑ JS-1207	Hold Me Tight	1968	$30
❑ JS-1001 [B]	Prince of Peace	1969	$30

NASH, PAUL

REVELATION			
❑ 32	A Jazz Composer's Ensemble	1980	$35
SOUL NOTE			
❑ SN-1107	Second Impression	1986	$30

NASH, TED & DICK

LIBERTY			
❑ LJH-6011 [M]	The Brothers Nash	1956	$50

NASH, TED

COLUMBIA			
❑ CL989 [M]	Star Eyes	1957	$40
CONCORD JAZZ			
❑ CJ-106	Conception	1980	$25
STARLITE			
❑ LP-6001 [10]	Ted Nash	1954	$50

NASHVILLE ALL STARS, THE

RCA VICTOR			
❑ LPM-2302 [M]	After the Riot at Newport	1960	$40
❑ LSP-2302 [S]	After the Riot at Newport	1960	$50
RCA VICTOR RECORD CLUB			
❑ CPM-0114 [M]	All-Time Country and Western Hits	1966	$15
❑ CSP-0114 [S]	All-Time Country and Western Hits	1966	$18
❑ CPM-0126 [M]	That Happy Nashville Sound	1967	$18
❑ CSP-0126 [S]	That Happy Nashville Sound	1967	$15

NASHVILLE DEPOE

GUINNESS			
❑ GNS36061 [B]	Nashville Depoe	1977	$175

NASHVILLE GUITARS, THE

MONUMENT			
❑ MLP-8058 [M]	The Nashville Guitars	1966	$18
❑ SLP-18058 [S]	The Nashville Guitars	1966	$25
❑ MLP-18093	The Nashville Guitars at Home	1968	$18

NASHVILLE JAZZ MACHINE, THE

AM-PM			
❑ 14	Where's Eli?	1986	$25

NASHVILLE PUSSY

AMPHETAMINE REPTILE			
❑ AMREP-69	Let Them Eat Pussy	1999	$30
RESERVATION			
❑ REZP-1 [PD]	Say Something Nasty	2003	$18
— Picture disc; 1,000 pressed			
TVT			
❑ 3340-1	High as Hell	2000	$30

NASHVILLE TEENS, THE

LONDON			
❑ LL3407 [M]	Tobacco Road	1964	$120
❑ PS407 [R]	Tobacco Road	1964	$100

NASTOS, NICK

STRAND			
❑ SL-1097 [M]	Guitars on Fire	1962	$25
❑ SLS-1097 [S]	Guitars on Fire	1962	$30

NATAL, NANETTE

BENYO			
❑ BY-3335	Hi-Fi Baby	198?	$30
❑ BY-3334	Wild in Reverie	198?	$30

NATIONAL GALLERY, THE

PHILIPS			
❑ PHS600266	The National Gallery (Performing Musical Interpretations of the Paintings of Paul Klee)	1968	$25

NATIONAL JAZZ ENSEMBLE

CHIAROSCURO			
❑ 140	National Jazz Ensemble	197?	$30
❑ 151	National Jazz Ensemble, Volume 2	197?	$25

NATIONAL LAMPOON

BANANA			
❑ BTS6006 [B]	Lemmings	1973	$25
❑ BTS6008	Missing White House Tapes	1974	$18
❑ BTS38 [B]	Radio Dinner	1972	$25
EPIC			
❑ PE33410	Gold Turkey	1974	$15
— Orange label			
❑ PE33410 [B]	Gold Turkey	1979	$10
— Dark blue label			
❑ PE33956	Goodbye Pop	1975	$15
— Orange label			
❑ PE33956	Goodbye Pop	1979	$10
— Dark blue label			
LABEL 21			
❑ IMP-2001	That's Not Funny, That's Sick!	1978	$12

❑ PIC-2001 [PD]	That's Not Funny, That's Sick!	1978	$25
❑ IMP-2002	The White Album	1979	$12
MCA			
❑ 27023	Lemmings	198?	$10
❑ 27024	Radio Dinner	198?	$10
PASSPORT			
❑ PB6018	Sex, Drugs, Rock and Roll and the End of the World	1982	$12
VISA			
❑ 7008 [B]	Greatest Hits of the National Lampoon	1978	$15
❑ 2001	That's Not Funny, That's Sick!	198?	$10
❑ 2002	The White Album	198?	$10

NATIONAL SYMPHONY ORCHESTRA (HOWARD MITCHELL, CONDUCTOR)

RCA VICTOR RED SEAL			
❑ LSC-2261 [S]	Shostakovich: Symphony No. 5	1959	$50
— Original with "shaded dog" label			

NATIONAL YOUTH JAZZ ORCHESTRA

RCA VICTOR			
❑ LPL1-5116	11 Plus	197?	$35

NATURAL ESSENCE

FANTASY			
❑ F-9440	In Search of Happiness	1974	$30

NATURAL FOUR, THE

CURTOM			
❑ CU5004	Heaven Right Here on Earth	1975	$25
❑ CRT-8600	The Natural Four	1974	$25

NATURAL LIFE

ASI			
❑ 5006	All Music	1977	$30
❑ 5001	Natural Life	1977	$30
❑ 5005	Unnamed Land	1977	$30
CELEBRATION			
❑ 5001	Natural Life	197?	$35
❑ 5005	Unnamed Land	1975	$35

NATURAL PROGRESSIONS

PALO ALTO/TBA			
❑ TBA-248	Rumor Has It	1989	$30

NAUGHTON, BOBBY

OTIC			
❑ 1009	Nauxtagram	1979	$30
❑ 1005	The Haunt	1976	$35
❑ 1003	Understanding	197?	$35

NAUGHTY BY NATURE

ARISTA			
❑ 19047	Nineteen Naughty Nine -- Nature's Fury	1999	$25
TOMMY BOY			
❑ TBLP-1069	19 Naughty III	1993	$25
❑ TBLP-1310	Nature's Finest: Naughty by Nature's Greatest Hits	1999	$18
❑ TBLP-1051	Naughty By Nature	1991	$18
❑ TBLP-1111	Poverty's Paradise	1995	$15

NAUSEEF, MARK

CMP			
❑ CMP-16-ST	Personal Note	198?	$25
❑ CMP-21-ST	Sura	198?	$25
❑ CMP-25-ST	Wun Wun	1987	$25

NAVARRO, FATS

BLUE NOTE			
❑ BLP-5004 [10]	Fats Navarro Memorial Album	1952	$1000
❑ BN-LA507-H2	Prime Source	1976	$35
❑ BLP-1531 [M]	The Fabulous Fats Navarro, Vol. 1	1956	$500
— Deep groove" version; Lexington Ave. address on label			
❑ BLP-1531 [M]	The Fabulous Fats Navarro, Vol. 1	1956	$250
— Deep groove" version, W. 63rd St. address on label			
❑ BLP-1531 [M]	The Fabulous Fats Navarro, Vol. 1	1963	$100
— With "New York, USA" address on label			
❑ BST-81531 [R]	The Fabulous Fats Navarro, Vol. 1	196?	$30
— With "A Divison of Liberty Records" on label			
❑ BST-81531	The Fabulous Fats Navarro, Vol. 1	1985	$30
— The Finest in Jazz Since 1939" reissue			
❑ BLP-1532 [M]	The Fabulous Fats Navarro, Vol. 2	1956	$500
— Deep groove" version; Lexington Ave. address on label			
❑ BLP-1532 [M]	The Fabulous Fats Navarro, Vol. 2	1956	$250

Number	Title	Yr	NM

— Deep groove" version, W. 63rd St. address on label

THE FABULOUS FATS NAVARRO

blue note 1532 volume 2

❏ BLP-1532 [M]	The Fabulous Fats Navarro, Vol. 2	1963	$100

— With "New York, USA" address on label

| ❏ BST-81532 [R] | The Fabulous Fats Navarro, Vol. 2 | 196? | $30 |

— With "A Divison of Liberty Records" on label

| ❏ BST-81532 | The Fabulous Fats Navarro, Vol. 2 | 1985 | $30 |

— The Finest in Jazz Since 1939" reissue

RIVERSIDE
| ❏ RS-3019 | Good Bait | 1968 | $150 |

SAVOY
❏ MG-12011 [M]	Fats Navarro Memorial	1955	$175
❏ MG-9005 [10]	New Sounds in Modern Music	1952	$400
❏ MG-9019 [10]	New Trends Of Jazz	1952	$400
❏ MG-12133 [M]	Nostalgia	1958	$150

SAVOY JAZZ
| ❏ SJL-2216 | Fat Girl | 197? | $30 |
| ❏ SJC-416 | Memorial Album | 1985 | $25 |

NAVARRO, FATS/KAI WINDING/BREW MOORE

SAVOY
| ❏ MG-12119 [M] | In the Beginning…Bebop | 1957 | $75 |

NAVARRO, JOEY

ANTILLES
| ❏ 90985 | On the Rocks | 1988 | $25 |

NAVARRO, TOMMY, AND THE SUNDIALERS

URANIA
| ❏ UR-900 [M] | Twist Around the Town | 1961 | $175 |
| ❏ US-5900 [S] | Twist Around the Town | 1961 | $250 |

NAZARETH

A&M
❏ SP-4901	2XS	1982	$12
❏ SP-4562	Close Enough for Rock 'N' Roll	1976	$12
❏ SP-3109	Close Enough for Rock 'N' Roll	1981	$10

— Budget-line reissue
| ❏ SP-3168 | Exercises | 1982 | $10 |

— Reissue of Warner Bros. 2639
| ❏ SP-4666 | Expect No Mercy | 1977 | $12 |
| ❏ SP-4511 | Hair of the Dog | 1975 | $12 |

| ❏ SP-3225 [B] | Hair of the Dog | 1984 | $10 |
— Budget-line reissue

| ❏ SP-4643 | Hot Tracks | 1977 | $12 |
| ❏ SP-3226 | Hot Tracks | 1984 | $10 |
— Budget-line reissue
❏ SP-3609	Loud 'N' Proud	1974	$12
❏ SP-4799	Malice in Wonderland	1980	$12
❏ SP-3169	Nazareth	1982	$10
— Reissue of Warner Bros. 2615
❏ SP-4741	No Mean City	1979	$12
❏ SP-4610	Play 'N' the Game	1976	$12
❏ SP-3641	Rampant	1974	$12
❏ SP-4396	Razamanaz	1973	$18
— First edition with brown label
❏ SP-4396	Razamanaz	1974	$12
❏ SP-6703	'Snaz	1981	$15
❏ SP-4844	The Fool Circle	1981	$12

MCA
| ❏ 5458 | Sound Elixir | 1983 | $12 |

WARNER BROS.
| ❏ BS2639 [B] | Exercises | 1972 | $30 |
| ❏ BS2615 [B] | Nazareth | 1972 | $30 |

NAZZ (1)
Also see TODD RUNDGREN.

RHINO
❏ RNLP109	Nazz	1984	$18
❏ RNLP111	Nazz III	1984	$18
❏ RNLP110	Nazz Nazz	1984	$18
❏ RNLP116	The Best of Nazz	1984	$18
❏ R170116	The Best of Nazz	1987	$15

SGC
❏ SD5001	Nazz	1968	$40
❏ SD5004	Nazz III	1970	$40
❏ 5002 [M]	Nazz Nazz	1969	$175
— Promo-only mono pressing on red vinyl
| ❏ SD5002 [S] | Nazz Nazz | 1969 | $40 |
— Red vinyl
| ❏ SD5002 [S] | Nazz Nazz | 1969 | $100 |
— Black vinyl

NBC SYMPHONY ORCHESTRA (LEOPOLD STOKOWSKI, COND.)

RCA VICTOR RED SEAL
| ❏ LSC-2555 [S] | The Sound of Stokowski and Wagner | 1961 | $75 |
— Originals with "shaded dog" label
| ❏ LSC-2555 [S] | The Sound of Stokowski and Wagner | 1964 | $30 |
— Second editions with "white dog" label

NDEGEOCELLO, ME'SHELL

MAVERICK
| ❏ PRO-A-6622 [DJ] | Plantation Lullabies | 1993 | $25 |
— Promo-only U.S. vinyl release

NECKBONES, THE

FAT POSSUM
| ❏ 80304-1 [B] | Souls On Fire | 1997 | $18 |

NECROS

RESTLESS
| ❏ 72203 | Tangled Up | 1986 | $15 |

TOUCH & GO
| ❏ 2 | Conquest for Death | 1983 | $80 |

NEELY, DON

MERRY MAKERS
| ❏ 108 | Don Neely's Royal Society Jazz Orchestra | 197? | $25 |

STOMP OFF
| ❏ SOS-1208 | Ain't That a Grand and Glorious Feeling? | 1991 | $30 |

NEELY, JIMMY

TRU-SOUND
| ❏ TRU-15002 [M] | Misirlou | 1962 | $40 |

NEELY, SAM

A&M
| ❏ SP-3626 | Sam Neely | 1974 | $15 |

CAPITOL
| ❏ ST-873 | Long Road to Texas | 1972 | $18 |
| ❏ ST-11097 | Loving You Just Crossed My Mind | 1972 | $15 |
— Reissued version of ST-873
| ❏ SMAS-11143 | Sam Neely -- 2 | 1973 | $15 |

NEFF, HILDEGARDE

LONDON
| ❏ PS596 | From Here On It Gets Rough | 1971 | $25 |

NEGATIVLAND

SEELAND
| ❏ 003 | A Big 10-8 Place | 1985 | $15 |
| ❏ 001 [B] | Negativland | 1981 | $35 |
— Every copy has a different cover
| ❏ 002 | Points | 1982 | $15 |
— Black vinyl
| ❏ 002 | Points | 1982 | $18 |
— Blue vinyl

SST
| ❏ 133 | Escape from Noise | 1987 | $25 |
— With booklet
❏ 292 [EP]	Guns	1992	$10
❏ 252	Helter Stupid	1989	$15
❏ 272 [EP]	U2	1990	$300
— Withdrawn thanks to pressure from the record company of U2 (the band)

NEIDLINGER, BUELL

ANTILLES
| ❏ AN-1014 | Swingrass '83 | 1983 | $25 |

NEIGHBORHOOD, THE

BIG TREE
| ❏ 2001 | Debut | 1970 | $18 |

NEIGHB'RHOOD CHILDREN

ACTA
| ❏ 8005 [M] | The Neighb'rhood Children | 1968 | $100 |
| ❏ 38005 [S] | The Neighb'rhood Children | 1968 | $150 |

SUNDAZED
| ❏ LP5023 | Long Years in Space | 199? | $18 |

NEIL, FRED

CAPITOL
❏ ST-294	Everybody's Talkin'	1969	$30
❏ T2665 [M]	Fred Neil	1966	$30
❏ ST2665 [S]	Fred Neil	1966	$40
— With color photo on back
| ❏ ST2665 [S] | Fred Neil | 1967 | $30 |
— With black & white photo on back
| ❏ T2862 [M] | Fred Neil Sessions | 1968 | $40 |
| ❏ ST2862 [S] | Fred Neil Sessions | 1968 | $30 |

ELEKTRA
❏ EKL-293 [M]	Bleecker and MacDougal	1965	$30
❏ EKS-7293 [S]	Bleecker and MacDougal	1965	$40
❏ EKS-74073	Little Bit of Rain	1970	$25
— Reissue of 7293

SUNDAZED
| ❏ LP5107 | Bleecker and MacDougal | 2002 | $15 |

NEKTAR

CLEOPATRA
❏ 9223 [B]	A Spoonful Of Time		$35
❏ CLP514 [B]	A Tab In The Ocean	2013	$35
❏ 9958 [B]	Journey To The Centre Of The Eye		$35
❏ CLP9958 [B]	Journey To The Centre Of The Eye	2013	$35
❏ 7.41157E+11 [B]	Magic is a Child	2014	$30
❏ 9296 [B]	Recycled - Deluxe Edition		$30
❏ CLP297 [B]	Remember the Future	2013	$35
❏ CLP676 [B]	...Sounds Like This	2013	$35
❏ CLP495 [B]	Time Machine	2013	$35

PASSPORT
❏ PPSD-98017 [B]	A Tab in the Ocean	1976	$40
❏ PPSD-98005 [B]	Down to Earth	1975	$40
❏ PPSD-98011 [B]	Recycled	1976	$50

| ❏ PPS-98002 [B] | Remember the Future | 1974 | $50 |

POLYDOR
| ❏ PD-1-6115 | Magic Is a Child | 1977 | $30 |

Number	Title	Yr	NM

VISA
| ❏ IMP9001 | Thru the Ears | 1979 | $15 |

NELL, BOB
CADENCE JAZZ
| ❏ CJR-1022 | Chasin' a Classic | 198? | $25 |

NELOMS, BOB
INDIA NAVIGATION
| ❏ IN-1050 | Pretty Music | 198? | $30 |

NELSON, LOUIS
GHB
❏ 158	Everybody's Talkin' 'Bout the Piron Band	198?	$25
❏ GHB-25	The Big Four, Vol. 1	196?	$35
❏ GHB-26	The Big Four, Vol. 2	196?	$35

NELSON, OLIVER, AND LOU DONALDSON
CHESS
| ❏ 2ACMJ-404 | Back Talk | 1976 | $35 |
| ❏ CH2-92515 | Back Talk | 198? | $30 |

NELSON, OLIVER; KING CURTIS; JIMMY FORREST
PRESTIGE
❏ PRLP-7223 [M]	Soul Battle	1962	$175
— Yellow label			
❏ PRST-7223 [S]	Soul Battle	1962	$175

NELSON, OLIVER
ABC IMPULSE!
❏ AS-9132 [S]	Happenings	1968	$250
— With Hank Jones; black label with red ring			
❏ AS-9153 [S]	Live From Los Angeles	1968	$250
— Black label with red ring			
❏ AS-9113 [S]	Michelle	1968	$250
— Black label with red ring			
❏ AS-75 [S]	More Blues and the Abstract Truth	1968	$250
— Black label with red ring			
❏ AS-75 [S]	More Blues and the Abstract Truth	1975	$30
— Green, blue, purple "target" label			
❏ AS-9168 [S]	Soulful Brass	1968	$120
— Black label with red ring			
❏ AS-9129 [S]	Sound Pieces	1968	$250
— Black label with red ring			
❏ AS-5 [S]	The Blues and the Abstract Truth	1968	$250
— Black label with red ring			
❏ AS-9144 [S]	The Kennedy Dream	1968	$250
— Black label with red ring			
❏ AS-9147 [S]	The Spirit of '67	1968	$250
— With Pee Wee Russell; black label with red ring			
❏ IA-9335-2	Three Dimensions	1978	$250

ARGO
| ❏ LP-737 [M] | Fantabulous | 1964 | $50 |
| ❏ LPS-737 [S] | Fantabulous | 1964 | $50 |

BLUEBIRD
| ❏ 6993-1-RB | Black, Brown and Beautiful | 1989 | $35 |
| — Reissue of Flying Dutchman 10116 | | | |

CADET
❏ LPS-737 [S]	Fantabulous	1966	$35
— Fading blue label			
❏ LP-737 [M]	Fantabulous	1966	$75
— Fading blue label			

FANTASY
❏ OJC-227	Meet Oliver Nelson	198?	$30
❏ OJC-089	Screamin' the Blues	198?	$30
❏ OJC-325	Soul Battle	1988	$30
❏ OJC-099	Straight Ahead	198?	$30

FLYING DUTCHMAN
❏ FD-10134	Berlin Dialogue	1972	$75
❏ FD-10116	Black, Brown and Beautiful	1971	$40
— Reissue of 116			
❏ FD-116	Black, Brown and Beautiful	1970	$75
❏ CYL2-1449	Dream Deferred	1976	$75
❏ BDL1-0592	Oliver Nelson in London	1974	$75
❏ BDL1-0825	Skull Session	1975	$175
— Reproductions exist			
❏ FD-10149	Swiss Suite	1973	$75

GRP IMPULSE!
❏ IMP-212	More Blues and the Abstract Truth	1997	$250
— Reissue on audiophile vinyl			
❏ IMP-154	The Blues and the Abstract Truth	1995	$35
— Reissue on audiophile vinyl			

IMPULSE!
❏ A-9132 [M]	Happenings	1967	$160
— With Hank Jones			
❏ AS-9132 [S]	Happenings	1967	$120
— With Hank Jones			

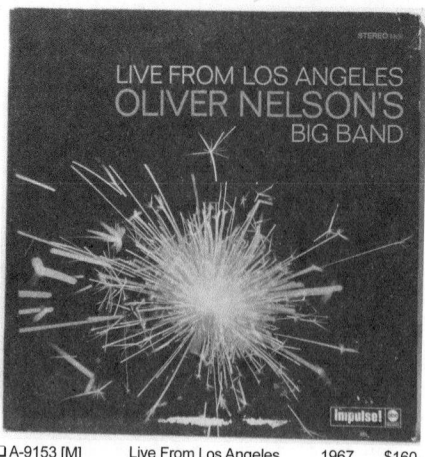

❏ A-9153 [M]	Live From Los Angeles	1967	$160
❏ AS-9153 [S]	Live From Los Angeles	1967	$120
❏ A-9113 [M]	Michelle	1966	$120
❏ AS-9113 [S]	Michelle	1966	$160
❏ A-75 [M]	More Blues and the Abstract Truth	1964	$250

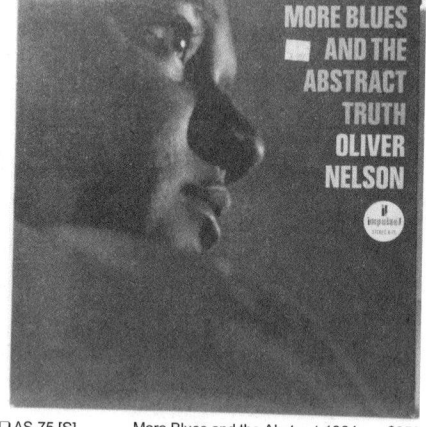

❏ AS-75 [S]	More Blues and the Abstract Truth	1964	$250
❏ A-9129 [M]	Sound Pieces	1966	$160
❏ AS-9129 [S]	Sound Pieces	1966	$160
❏ A-5 [M]	The Blues and the Abstract Truth	1961	$250
— Original cover has an abstract painting and lists Bill Evans' name first			
❏ AS-5 [S]	The Blues and the Abstract Truth	1961	$120
— Original cover has an abstract painting and lists Bill Evans' name first			
❏ A-5 [M]	The Blues and the Abstract Truth	196?	$160
— Later cover has Oliver Nelson clearly indicated as leader and features a photo of him at the right			
❏ AS-5 [S]	The Blues and the Abstract Truth	196?	$250
— Later cover has Oliver Nelson clearly indicated as leader and features a photo of him at the right			
❏ A-9144 [M]	The Kennedy Dream	1967	$160
❏ AS-9144 [S]	The Kennedy Dream	1967	$120
❏ A-9147 [M]	The Spirit of '67	1967	$250
— With Pee Wee Russell			
❏ AS-9147 [S]	The Spirit of '67	1967	$120
— With Pee Wee Russell			

INNER CITY
| ❏ IC-6008 | Stolen Moments | 1977 | $35 |

MCA
❏ 29052	More Blues and the Abstract Truth	1980	$25
❏ 5888	More Blues and the Abstract Truth	1987	$25
— Another reissue			
❏ 29063	The Blues and the Abstract Truth	1980	$25
❏ 4148	Three Dimensions	1980	$30

MCA IMPULSE!
| ❏ MCA-5888 | More Blues and the Abstract Truth | 1987 | $25 |
| ❏ MCA-5659 | The Blues and the Abstract Truth | 1985 | $30 |

MOODSVILLE
❏ MVLP-13 [M]	Nocturne	1960	$150
— Green label			
❏ MVLP-13 [M]	Nocturne	1965	$50
— Blue label, trident logo at right			

NEW JAZZ
❏ NJLP-8224 [M]	Meet Oliver Nelson	1959	$250
— Purple label			
❏ NJLP-8224 [M]	Meet Oliver Nelson	1965	$175
— Blue label, trident logo at right			
❏ NJLP-8243 [M]	Screamin' the Blues	1960	$250
— Purple label			
❏ NJLP-8324 [M]	Screamin' the Blues	1963	$0
— Canceled			
❏ NJLP-8243 [M]	Screamin' the Blues	1965	$175
— Blue label, trident logo at right			
❏ NJLP-8255 [M]	Straight Ahead	1961	$250
— Purple label			
❏ NJLP-8255 [M]	Straight Ahead	1965	$175
— Blue label, trident logo at right			
❏ NJLP-8233 [M]	Takin' Care of Business	1960	$250
— Purple label			
❏ NJLP-8233 [M]	Takin' Care of Business	1965	$175
— Blue label, trident logo at right			

PRESTIGE
❏ PRLP-7225 [M]	Afro/American Sketches	1962	$175
❏ PRST-7225 [S]	Afro/American Sketches	1962	$175
❏ P-24060	Images	1976	$50
❏ PRLP-7236 [M]	Main Stem	1962	$175
❏ PRST-7236 [S]	Main Stem	1962	$175

STATUS
| ❏ ST-8324 [M] | Screamin' the Blues | 1965 | $50 |

UNITED ARTISTS
| ❏ UAJ-14019 [M] | Impressions of Phaedra | 1962 | $50 |
| ❏ UAJS-15019 [S] | Impressions of Phaedra | 1962 | $100 |

VERVE
❏ V-8508 [M]	Full Nelson	1963	$40
❏ V6-8508 [S]	Full Nelson	1963	$50
❏ V6-8743 [S]	Leonard Feather Presents the Sound of Feeling and the Sound of Oliver Nelson	1968	$150

NELSON, OZZIE
AIRCHECK
| ❏ 19 | Ozzie Nelson and His Orchestra On the Air | 198? | $25 |

HINDSIGHT
❏ HSR-189	Ozzie Nelson and His Orchestra 1937	198?	$25
❏ HSR-208	Ozzie Nelson and His Orchestra 1938	198?	$25
❏ HSR-107	Ozzie Nelson and His Orchestra 1940-42	198?	$25

NELSON, RICK "COUGAR
JAZZOLOGY
| ❏ J-123 | Steppin' Out | 198? | $25 |

NELSON, RICKY
CAPITOL
| ❏ SOO-12109 | Playing to Win | 1981 | $12 |

DECCA
❏ DL4944 [M]	Another Side of Rick	1967	$30
❏ DL74944 [S]	Another Side of Rick	1967	$30
❏ DL4660 [M]	Best Always	1965	$30
❏ DL74660 [S]	Best Always	1965	$40
❏ DL4779 [M]	Bright Lights and Country Music	1966	$30
❏ DL74779 [S]	Bright Lights and Country Music	1966	$30
❏ DL4827 [M]	Country Fever	1967	$30
❏ DL74827 [S]	Country Fever	1967	$30
❏ DL4419 [M]	For Your Sweet Love	1963	$30
❏ DL74419 [S]	For Your Sweet Love	1963	$40
❏ DL4678 [M]	Love and Kisses	1965	$30
❏ DL74678 [S]	Love and Kisses	1965	$40
❏ DL5014 [M]	Perspective	1968	$80
— Mono copies are promo only			
❏ DL75014 [S]	Perspective	1968	$30
❏ DL75162	Rick Nelson In Concert	1970	$30

Number	Title	Yr	NM
DL74479 [S]	Rick Nelson Sings "For You"	1963	$50
DL4479 [M]	Rick Nelson Sings "For You"	1963	$35
DL75236	Rick Sings Nelson	1970	$30
—Deduct 20 percent if poster is missing			
DL75297	Rudy the Fifth	1971	$30
DL4608 [M]	Spotlight on Rick	1964	$30
DL74608 [S]	Spotlight on Rick	1964	$40
DL4559 [M]	The Very Thought of You	1964	$30
DL74559 [S]	The Very Thought of You	1964	$40

EMI AMERICA

Number	Title	Yr	NM
SQ-17192	The Very Best of Rick Nelson	1986	$12
—Reissue of United Artists UA-LA330			

EPIC

Number	Title	Yr	NM
JE34420	Intakes	1977	$15
FE40388	The Memphis Sessions	1986	$12

EPIC/NU-DISK

Number	Title	Yr	NM
3E36868 [10]	Four You	1981	$15

IMPERIAL

Number	Title	Yr	NM
LP9167 [M]	Album Seven by Rick	1962	$40
—Black label with stars			
LP9167 [M]	Album Seven by Rick	1964	$30
—Black label with pink and white at left			
LP9167 [M]	Album Seven by Rick	1966	$25
—Black label with green and white at left			
LP12082 [S]	Album Seven by Rick	1962	$150
—Black label with silver print			
LP12082 [S]	Album Seven by Rick	1964	$40
—Black label with pink and white at left			
LP12082 [S]	Album Seven by Rick	1966	$30
—Black label with green and white at left			
LP9244 [M]	A Long Vacation	1963	$40
—Black label with stars			
LP9244 [M]	A Long Vacation	1964	$30
—Black label with pink and white at left			
LP9244 [M]	A Long Vacation	1966	$25
—Black label with green and white at left			
LP12244 [R]	A Long Vacation	1964	$25
—Black label with pink and white at left			
LP12244 [R]	A Long Vacation	1966	$18
—Black label with green and white at left			
LP12218 [R]	Best Sellers	1964	$25
—Black label with pink and white at left			
LP12218 [R]	Best Sellers	1966	$18
—Black label with green and white at left			
LP9218 [M]	Best Sellers by Rick Nelson	1963	$40
—Black label with stars			
LP9218 [M]	Best Sellers by Rick Nelson	1964	$30
—Black label with pink and white at left			
LP9218 [M]	Best Sellers by Rick Nelson	1966	$25
—Black label with green and white at left			
LP9223 [M]	It's Up to You	1963	$40
—Black label with stars			
LP9223 [M]	It's Up to You	1964	$30
—Black label with pink and white at left			
LP9223 [M]	It's Up to You	1966	$25
—Black label with green and white at left			
LP9232 [M]	Million Sellers	1963	$40
—Black label with stars			
LP9232 [M]	Million Sellers	1964	$30
—Black label with pink and white at left			
LP9232 [M]	Million Sellers	1966	$25
—Black label with green and white at left			
LP12232 [R]	Million Sellers	1964	$25
—Black label with pink and white at left			
LP12232 [R]	Million Sellers	1966	$18
—Black label with green and white at left			
LP9122 [M]	More Songs by Ricky	1960	$85
—Black label with stars			
LP9122 [M]	More Songs by Ricky	1964	$30
—Black label with pink and white at left			
LP9122 [M]	More Songs by Ricky	1966	$25
—Black label with green and white at left			
LP12059 [DJ]	More Songs by Ricky	1960	$1000
—Promo copy on blue vinyl. Add 20 percent for enclosed poster.			
LP12059 [S]	More Songs by Ricky	1960	$150
—Black label with silver print			
LP12059 [S]	More Songs by Ricky	1964	$40
—Black label with pink and white at left			
LP12059 [S]	More Songs by Ricky	1966	$30
—Black label with green and white at left			
LP9152 [M]	Rick Is 21	1961	$40
—Black label with stars			
LP9152 [M]	Rick Is 21	1964	$30
—Black label with pink and white at left			
LP9152 [M]	Rick Is 21	1966	$25
—Black label with green and white at left			
LP12071 [S]	Rick Is 21	1961	$150
—Black label with silver print			
LP12071 [S]	Rick Is 21	1964	$40
—Black label with pink and white at left			
LP12071 [S]	Rick Is 21	1966	$30
—Black label with green and white at left			
LP9251 [M]	Rick Nelson Sings for You	1964	$40
—Black label with stars			
LP9251 [M]	Rick Nelson Sings for You	1964	$30
—Black label with pink and white at left			
LP9251 [M]	Rick Nelson Sings for You	1966	$25
—Black label with green and white at left			
LP12251 [R]	Rick Nelson Sings for You	1964	$30
—Black label with silver print			
LP12251 [R]	Rick Nelson Sings for You	1964	$25
—Black label with pink and white at left			
LP12251 [R]	Rick Nelson Sings for You	1966	$18
—Black label with green and white at left			
LP9048 [M]	Ricky	1957	$150
—Black label with stars			
LP9048 [M]	Ricky	1964	$30
—Black label with pink and white at left			
LP9048 [M]	Ricky	1966	$25
—Black label with green and white at left			
LP12392 [R]	Ricky	1968	$18
—Rechanneled reissue of 9048			
LP9050 [M]	Ricky Nelson	1958	$150
—Black label with stars			
LP9050 [M]	Ricky Nelson	1964	$30
—Black label with pink and white at left			
LP9050 [M]	Ricky Nelson	1966	$25
—Black label with green and white at left			
LP12393 [R]	Ricky Nelson	1968	$18
—Rechanneled reissue of 9050			
LP9061 [M]	Ricky Sings Again	1959	$150
—Black label with stars			
LP9061 [M]	Ricky Sings Again	1964	$30
—Black label with pink and white at left			
LP9061 [M]	Ricky Sings Again	1966	$25
—Black label with green and white at left			
LP12090 [S]	Ricky Sings Again	1962	$175
—Black label with silver print			
LP12090 [S]	Ricky Sings Again	1964	$40
—Black label with pink and white at left			
LP12090 [S]	Ricky Sings Again	1966	$30
—Black label with green and white at left			
LP9082 [M]	Songs by Ricky	1959	$85
—Black label with stars			
LP9082 [M]	Songs by Ricky	1964	$30
—Black label with pink and white at left			
LP9082 [M]	Songs by Ricky	1966	$25
—Black label with green and white at left			
LP12030 [S]	Songs by Ricky	1959	$250
—Black label with silver print			
LP12030 [S]	Songs by Ricky	1964	$40
—Black label with pink and white at left			
LP12030 [S]	Songs by Ricky	1966	$30
—Black label with green and white at left			

LIBERTY

Number	Title	Yr	NM
LN-10304	I Need You	1986	$10
—Reissue of Sunset 5205			
LXB-9960	Legendary Masters	198?	$15
—Reissue of United Artists 9960			
LM-1004	Ricky	1981	$10
—Reissue of United Artists 1004			
LM-51004	Ricky	1983	$10
—Reissue of Liberty 1004			
LN-10305	Ricky Nelson	1986	$10
—Another reissue			
LN-10134	Ricky Sings Again	1982	$12
—Reissue of Imperial 12090			
LN-10205	Souvenirs	1983	$10
LN-10253	Teen Age Idol	1984	$10

MCA

Number	Title	Yr	NM
6163	All My Best	1986	$12
62	Garden Party	1973	$15
—Reissue of Decca 75391			
2-4004	Rick Nelson Country	1973	$18
3	Rick Nelson In Concert	1973	$15
—Reissue of Decca 75162			
25983	Rick Nelson In Concert The Troubadour, 1969	1987	$12
—Reissue of MCA 3 with revised title			
20	Rick Sings Nelson	1973	$15
—Reissue of Decca 75236			
37	Rudy the Fifth	1973	$15
—Reissue of Decca 75297			
1517	The Decca Years	1982	$10
383	Windfall	1974	$18

RHINO

Number	Title	Yr	NM
RNLP215	Greatest Hits	1985	$15
R1-70215	Greatest Hits	1987	$12
RNDF259 [PD]	Greatest Hits	1985	$18
R1-71114	Live 1983-1985	1989	$15

SUNSET

Number	Title	Yr	NM
SUS-5205	I Need You	1968	$18
SUM-1118 [M]	Ricky Nelson	1966	$18
SUS-5118 [P]	Ricky Nelson	1966	$25

TIME-LIFE

Number	Title	Yr	NM
SRNR31	Rick Nelson: 1957-1972	1989	$18

UNITED ARTISTS

Number	Title	Yr	NM
UAS-9960	Legendary Masters	1971	$30
LM-1004	Ricky	1980	$12
—Reissue of Imperial 9048			
UA-LA330-E	The Very Best of Rick Nelson	1974	$15

VERVE

Number	Title	Yr	NM
V2083 [M]	Teen Time	1957	$500
—Has three Ricky Nelson songs plus tracks by four others; usually treated as Rick's LP because of his prominence on the cover			

NELSON, SANDY

IMPERIAL

Number	Title	Yr	NM
LP9329 [M]	Beat That #!!@* Drum	1966	$15
LP12329 [S]	Beat That #!!@* Drum	1966	$18
LP9237 [M]	Beat That Drum	1963	$18
LP12237 [S]	Beat That Drum	1963	$25
LP9258 [M]	Be True to Your School	1964	$18
LP12258 [S]	Be True to Your School	1964	$25
LP12367	Boogaloo Beat	1968	$15
LP9298 [M]	Boss Beat	1965	$18
LP12298 [S]	Boss Beat	1965	$25
LP9340 [M]	Cheetah Beat	1967	$15
LP12340 [S]	Cheetah Beat	1967	$18
LP9204 [M]	Compelling Percussion	1962	$25
LP12204 [S]	Compelling Percussion	1962	$30
LP9203 [M]	Country Style	1962	$25
LP12203 [S]	Country Style	1962	$30
LP9283 [M]	Drum Discotheque	1965	$18
LP12283 [S]	Drum Discotheque	1965	$25
LP9189 [M]	Drummin' Up a Storm	1962	$25
LP12189 [S]	Drummin' Up a Storm	1962	$30
LP9287 [M]	Drums A Go-Go	1965	$18
LP12287 [S]	Drums A Go-Go	1965	$25
LP9168 [M]	Drums Are My Beat!	1962	$25
—Black label with stars			
LP12083 [S]	Drums Are My Beat!	1962	$30
LP9168 [M]	Drums Are My Beat!	1964	$18
—Pink, white and black label			
LP9202 [M]	Golden Hits	1962	$25
LP12202 [P]	Golden Hits	1962	$30
LP12451	Groovy	1970	$15
LP9136 [M]	He's a Drummer Boy	1961	$30
LP12089 [R]	He's a Drummer Boy	1962	$30
LP9305 [M]	In" Beat	1966	$18
LP12305 [S]	In" Beat	1966	$25
LP9159 [M]	Let There Be Drums	1962	$30
LP12080 [R]	Let There Be Drums	1962	$30
LP9272 [M]	Live! In Las Vegas	1964	$25
LP12272 [R]	Live! In Las Vegas	1964	$18
LP12439	Manhattan Spiritual	1969	$15
LP9203 [M]	On the Wild Side	1966	$18
—Same LP as above, but new title on cover			
LP12203 [S]	On the Wild Side	1966	$25
—Same LP as above, but new title on cover			
LP12424	Rebirth of the Beat	1969	$15
LP12400	Rock and Roll Revival	1968	$15
LP9249 [M]	Sandy Nelson Plays	1963	$18
LP12249 [S]	Sandy Nelson Plays	1963	$25
LP9105 [M]	Sandy Nelson Plays Teen Beat	1960	$30
LP12044 [S]	Sandy Nelson Plays Teen Beat	1960	$40
LP9362 [M]	Soul Drums	1967	$18
LP12362 [S]	Soul Drums	1967	$15
LP9314 [M]	Super Drums	1966	$18
LP12314 [S]	Super Drums	1966	$25
LP9215 [M]	Teenage House Party	1963	$25
LP12215 [S]	Teenage House Party	1963	$30
LP9278 [M]	Teen Beat '65	1965	$18
LP12278 [S]	Teen Beat '65	1965	$25
LP9345 [M]	The Beat Goes On	1967	$15
LP12345 [S]	The Beat Goes On	1967	$18
LP9224 [M]	The Best of the Beats	1963	$18
LP12224 [S]	The Best of the Beats	1963	$25
—Black label			
LP12224 [S]	The Best of the Beats	1963	$18
—Black, pink and white label			

LIBERTY

Number	Title	Yr	NM
LN-10209	Collectors' Gems, Vol. 2	1983	$10
LN-10172	The Very Best of Sandy Nelson	1982	$10

PICKWICK

Number	Title	Yr	NM
SPC-3605	And Then There Were Drums	1978	$12

SUNSET

Number	Title	Yr	NM
SUS-5224	And There Were Drums (Drums and More Drums)	1968	$12
SUS-5261	Heavy Drums	1969	$12
SUS-5291	Sandy Nelson Plays Fats Domino Hits	1970	$12
SUM-1166 [M]	Teen Drums	1967	$12
SUS-5166 [S]	Teen Drums	1967	$15
SUM-1114 [M]	Walking Beat	1966	$12
SUS-5114 [S]	Walking Beat	1966	$15

UNITED ARTISTS

Number	Title	Yr	NM
UA-LA440-E	The Very Best of Sandy Nelson	1975	$15

Number	Title	Yr	NM

NELSON, TRACY

ADELPHI
| ❏ 4119 | Doin' It My Way | 1981 | $12 |

ATLANTIC
| ❏ SD7310 [B] | Tracy Nelson | 1974 | $15 |

COLUMBIA
| ❏ KC31759 | Poor Man's Paradise | 1973 | $15 |

FLYING FISH
| ❏ FF-209 | Come See About Me | 1980 | $12 |
| ❏ FF-052 | Homemade Songs | 1978 | $12 |

MCA
| ❏ 494 | Sweet Soul Music | 1975 | $15 |
| ❏ 2203 | Time Is On My Side | 1976 | $15 |

PRESTIGE
❏ PRLP7393 [M]	Deep Are the Roots	1965	$30
❏ PRST7393 [S]	Deep Are the Roots	1965	$30
❏ PRST7726	Deep Are the Roots	1969	$18

NELSON, WILLIE, AND DAVID ALLAN COE

PLANTATION
| ❏ PLP41 | Willie and David | 1980 | $12 |

— One side is solo songs by Willie Nelson, the other side solo songs by David Allan Coe

NELSON, WILLIE, AND FARON YOUNG

COLUMBIA
| ❏ FC39484 | Funny How Time Slips Away | 1984 | $12 |
| ❏ PC39484 | Funny How Time Slips Away | 1985 | $10 |

— Budget-line reissue

NELSON, WILLIE, AND HANK SNOW

COLUMBIA
| ❏ FC39977 | Brand on My Heart | 1984 | $12 |
| ❏ PC39977 | Brand on My Heart | 1985 | $10 |

— Budget-line reissue

NELSON, WILLIE, AND KRIS KRISTOFFERSON

COLUMBIA
| ❏ FC39531 | Music from Songwriter | 1984 | $12 |

NELSON, WILLIE, AND LEON RUSSELL

COLUMBIA
| ❏ KC236064 | One for the Road | 1979 | $18 |

NELSON, WILLIE, AND RAY PRICE

COLUMBIA
| ❏ JC36476 | San Antonio Rose | 1980 | $12 |
| ❏ PC36476 | San Antonio Rose | 198? | $10 |

— Budget-line reissue

NELSON, WILLIE, AND ROGER MILLER

COLUMBIA
| ❏ FC38013 | Old Friends | 1982 | $12 |
| ❏ PC38013 | Old Friends | 198? | $10 |

— Budget-line reissue

NELSON, WILLIE, AND WEBB PIERCE

COLUMBIA
| ❏ FC38095 | In the Jailhouse Now | 1982 | $12 |
| ❏ PC38095 | In the Jailhouse Now | 198? | $10 |

— Budget-line reissue

NELSON, WILLIE

ALLEGIANCE
| ❏ AV-5010 | Wild & Willie | 1983 | $12 |
| ❏ AV-5005 | Willie or Won't He | 1983 | $12 |

ATLANTIC
| ❏ SD7291 | Phases and Stages | 1974 | $25 |
| ❏ SD7262 | Shotgun Willie | 1973 | $25 |

COLUMBIA
❏ FC45046	A Horse Called Music	1989	$12
❏ FC37951	Always on My Mind	1982	$12
❏ HC47951	Always on My Mind	1982	$50

— Half-speed mastered edition
| ❏ 9C939943 [PD] | Always on My Mind | 1985 | $25 |
| ❏ PC37951 | Always on My Mind | 1984 | $10 |

— Budget-line reissue
| ❏ FC39363 | Angel Eyes | 1984 | $12 |
| ❏ PC39363 | Angel Eyes | 1985 | $10 |

— Budget-line reissue
| ❏ FC39145 | City of New Orleans | 1984 | $12 |
| ❏ PC39145 | City of New Orleans | 1985 | $10 |

— Budget-line reissue
| ❏ FC39990 | Half Nelson | 1985 | $12 |

— Duets with 10 different artists
| ❏ PC39990 | Half Nelson | 1986 | $10 |

— Budget-line reissue
| ❏ FC40056 | Highwayman | 1985 | $12 |

— Waylon Jennings/Willie Nelson/Johnny Cash/Kris Kristofferson

| ❏ C45240 | Highwayman 2 | 1990 | $18 |

— Waylon Jennings/Willie Nelson/Johnny Cash/Kris Kristofferson
| ❏ S236752 | Honeysuckle Rose | 1980 | $15 |

— Over half of the LP is by Willie
❏ FC40487	Island in the Sea	1987	$12
❏ FC40008	Me and Paul	1985	$12
❏ PC40008	Me and Paul	1986	$10

— Budget-line reissue
| ❏ FC39894 | Partners | 1986 | $12 |
| ❏ PC39894 | Partners | 1987 | $10 |

— Budget-line reissue
| ❏ JC36189 | Pretty Paper | 1979 | $12 |
| ❏ KC33482 | Red Headed Stranger | 1975 | $18 |

— No bar code on back cover
| ❏ HC43482 | Red Headed Stranger | 1982 | $40 |

— Half-speed mastered edition
| ❏ PC33482 [B] | Red Headed Stranger | 1979 | $10 |

— With bar code on back cover; budget-line reissue
❏ FC36883	Somewhere Over the Rainbow	1981	$12
❏ JC35305 [B]	Stardust	1978	$12
❏ HC45305	Stardust	1981	$80

— Half-speed mastered edition
| ❏ JC35305 | Stardust | 2000 | $30 |

— Classic Records reissue on audiophile vinyl
| ❏ JS36327 | The Electric Horseman | 1979 | $12 |

— Side 2 by Dave Grusin
| ❏ FC40327 | The Promiseland | 1986 | $12 |
| ❏ PC34092 | The Sound in Your Mind | 1976 | $15 |

— No bar code on back cover
| ❏ PC34092 | The Sound in Your Mind | 1979 | $10 |

— With bar code on back cover; budget-line reissue
| ❏ KC34112 | The Troublemaker | 1976 | $15 |

— No bar code on back cover
| ❏ PC34112 | The Troublemaker | 1979 | $10 |

— With bar code on back cover; budget-line reissue
| ❏ JC34695 | To Lefty From Willie | 1977 | $15 |
| ❏ PC34695 | To Lefty From Willie | 1979 | $10 |

— Budget-line reissue
| ❏ QC38248 | Tougher Than Leather | 1983 | $12 |
| ❏ HC48248 | Tougher Than Leather | 1983 | $50 |

— Half-speed mastered edition
| ❏ PC38248 | Tougher Than Leather | 1984 | $10 |

— Budget-line reissue
❏ FC44431	What a Wonderful World	1988	$12
❏ KC235642	Willie and Family Live	1978	$18
❏ CX38250	Willie Nelson	1983	$120
❏ KC237542	Willie Nelson's Greatest Hits (& Some That Will Be)	1981	$15
❏ JC36188	Willie Nelson Sings Kristofferson	1979	$12
❏ PC36188	Willie Nelson Sings Kristofferson	1980	$10

— Budget-line reissue
| ❏ FC39110 | Without a Song | 1983 | $12 |
| ❏ PC39110 | Without a Song | 1984 | $10 |

— Budget-line reissue

DELTA
| ❏ DLP-1157 | Diamonds in the Rough | 1982 | $12 |

FRIDAY MUSIC
| ❏ FRM37951 [B] | Always On My Mind | 2015 | $25 |

HEARTLAND
| ❏ HL1038/9 | The Best of Willie Nelson | 1987 | $18 |

LIBERTY
❏ LRP-3239 [M]	...And Then I Wrote	1962	$40
❏ LST-7239 [S]	...And Then I Wrote	1962	$50
❏ LN-10013	Country Willie	1980	$10

— Budget-line reissue
❏ LRP-3308 [M]	Here's Willie Nelson	1963	$40
❏ LST-7308 [S]	Here's Willie Nelson	1963	$50
❏ LN-10118	The Best of Willie Nelson	1982	$10

— Budget-line reissue

LOST HIGHWAY
❏ B0004706-01	Countryman	2005	$15
❏ B0006939-01	Songbird	2006	$18
❏ B0006079-01	You Don't Know Me: The Songs of Cindy Walker	2006	$15

PAIR
❏ PDL2-1007	Country Winners	1986	$15
❏ PDL2-1114	Good Hearted Woman	1986	$15
❏ PDL2-1032	Once More with Feeling	1986	$15

PICKWICK
❏ ACL1-7018	Columbus Stockade Blues	1976	$10
❏ ACL1-0326	Country Winners	1976	$10
❏ SPC-3584	Hello Walls	1978	$12
❏ ACL1-0705	Spotlight on Willie Nelson	1976	$10

PLANTATION

| ❏ PLP-24 [B] | The Longhorn Jamboree Presents: Willie Nelson & His Friends | 1976 | $12 |

— Also includes tracks by David Allan Coe, Jerry Lee Lewis and Carl Perkins

RCA CAMDEN
❏ CAS-2444	Columbus Stockade Blues	1970	$18
❏ ACL1-7018	Columbus Stockade Blues	1975	$12
❏ ACL1-0326	Country Winners	1973	$15
❏ ACL1-0705	Spotlight on Willie Nelson	1974	$15

RCA VICTOR
| ❏ APL1-2210 | Before His Time | 1977 | $12 |
| ❏ AYL1-3671 | Before His Time | 1980 | $10 |

— Best Buy Series" reissue
❏ LSP-4294	Both Sides Now	1970	$25
❏ AHL1-5470	Collector's Series	1985	$12
❏ LPM-3528 [M]	Country Favorites, Willie Nelson Style	1966	$25
❏ LSP-3528 [S]	Country Favorites, Willie Nelson Style	1966	$30
❏ LPM-3659 [M]	Country Music Concert	1966	$25
❏ LSP-3659 [S]	Country Music Concert	1966	$30
❏ LPM-3418 [M]	Country Willie -- His Own Songs	1965	$25
❏ LSP-3418 [S]	Country Willie -- His Own Songs	1965	$30
❏ AHL1-3549	Danny Davis & Willie Nelson with the Nashville Brass	1980	$12
❏ CPL1-5174	Don't You Ever Get Tired of Hurting Me	1984	$12
❏ LSP-4057	Good Times	1968	$25
❏ LSP-4404	Laying My Burdens Down	1970	$25
❏ LPM-3748 [M]	Make Way for Willie Nelson	1967	$25
❏ LSP-3748 [S]	Make Way for Willie Nelson	1967	$30
❏ LSP-4111	My Own Peculiar Way	1969	$25
❏ AHL1-4819	My Own Way	1983	$12
❏ AYL1-5438	My Own Way	1985	$10

— Best Buy Series" reissue
| ❏ AHL1-3243 | Sweet Memories | 1979 | $12 |
| ❏ AYL1-4300 | Sweet Memories | 1982 | $10 |

— Best Buy Series" reissue
❏ LPM-3937 [M]	Texas in My Soul	1968	$150
❏ LSP-3937 [S]	Texas in My Soul	1968	$25
❏ AHL1-4420	The Best of Willie Nelson	1982	$12
❏ AYL1-5143	The Best of Willie Nelson	1984	$10

— Best Buy Series" reissue
❏ AHL1-4045	The Minstrel Man	1981	$12
❏ LPM-3858 [M]	The Party's Over and Other Great Willie Nelson Songs	1967	$30
❏ LSP-3858 [S]	The Party's Over and Other Great Willie Nelson Songs	1967	$25
❏ LSP-4653	The Picture	1972	$25
❏ LSP-4760	The Willie Way	1972	$25
❏ APL1-1234	What Can You Do to Me Now	1975	$15
❏ AYL1-3958	What Can You Do to Me Now	1981	$10

— Best Buy Series" reissue
❏ CPL1-7158	Willie	1986	$12
❏ LSP-4568	Willie Nelson & Family	1971	$25
❏ APL1-1487	Willie Nelson Live	1976	$15
❏ AYL1-4165	Willie Nelson Live	1981	$10

— Best Buy Series" reissue
| ❏ LSP-4568 | Yesterday's Wine | 1971 | $25 |
| ❏ AYL1-3800 | Yesterday's Wine | 1980 | $10 |

— Best Buy Series" reissue
| ❏ ANL1-1102 | Yesterday's Wine | 1975 | $12 |

SONGBIRD
| ❏ 3258 | Family Bible | 1980 | $12 |

SUNSET
| ❏ SUM-1138 [M] | Hello Walls | 1966 | $18 |
| ❏ SUS-5138 [S] | Hello Walls | 1966 | $25 |

TAKOMA
| ❏ TAK-7104 | The Legend Begins | 1983 | $12 |

TIME-LIFE
| ❏ P16946 | Country and Western Classics | 1983 | $25 |

UNITED ARTISTS
| ❏ UA-LA410-G | Country Willie | 1975 | $18 |

Number	Title	Yr	NM
□ UA-LA574-H2	Texas Country	1975	$25
□ UA-LA086-E	The Best of Willie Nelson	1973	$18
—Reissue of Liberty tracks			
□ UA-LA930-G	There'll Be No Teardrops Tonight	1978	$18

NELSON
DGC
| □ DGC-24290 | After the Rain | 1990 | $18 |

NENA
EPIC
□ BFE39294	99 Luftballons	1984	$15
□ PE39294	99 Luftballons	198?	$10
—Budget-line reissue with new prefix			
□ FE40144	It's All in the Game	1985	$12

NEON PHILHARMONIC, THE
Also see TUPPER SAUSSY.
WARNER BROS.
| □ WS1769 | The Moth Confesses | 1968 | $30 |
| □ WS1804 [B] | The Neon Philharmonic | 1969 | $18 |

NEP-TUNES, THE
FAMILY
| □ FLP-152 [M] | Surfer's Holiday | 1963 | $250 |
| □ SFLP-152 [S] | Surfer's Holiday | 1963 | $300 |

NEPTUNE, JOHN KAIZAN
FORTUNA
| □ 17030 | Dance for the One in Six | 198? | $25 |
INNER CITY
| □ IC-6077 | Bamboo | 198? | $30 |
| □ IC-6078 | Shogun | 198? | $30 |
MILESTONE
| □ M-9113 | West of Somewhere | 1981 | $30 |

NERO, PAUL
SUNSET
| □ LP-303 [M] | Play the Music of Paul Nero and His Hi-Fiddles | 1956 | $75 |

NERO, PETER
ARISTA
| □ AL4034 | Disco, Dance and Love Themes | 1976 | $12 |
BAINBRIDGE
| □ BT-6268 | The Sounds of Love | 1987 | $12 |
COLUMBIA
□ PC33136	Greatest Hits	1974	$12
□ CS1009	I'll Never Fall in Love Again	1970	$12
□ CS9800	I've Gotta Be Me	1969	$15
□ C30586	Love Story	1971	$12
□ KC32689	Say, Has Anybody Seen My Sweet Gypsy Rose	1973	$12
□ KC31105	Summer of '42	1971	$12
□ CQ31105 [Q]	Summer of '42	1971	$20
□ KC31335	The First Time Ever (I Saw Your Face)	1972	$12
□ C231982	The World of Peter Nero	1972	$15
CONCORD JAZZ
| □ CJ-48 | Now | 1978 | $25 |
CRYSTAL CLEAR
| □ 6001 | The Wiz | 198? | $25 |
| *—Direct-to-disc recording* | | | |
MODE
| □ LP-117 [M] | Bernie Nerow Trio | 1957 | $250 |
| *—As "Bernie Nerow* | | | |
PREMIER
| □ PM-2011 [M] | Just for You | 1963 | $50 |
| □ PS-2011 [R] | Just for You | 1963 | $30 |
RCA CAMDEN
□ CAL-2228 [M]	If Ever I Would Leave You	1968	$18
□ CAS-2228 [S]	If Ever I Would Leave You	1968	$15
□ CAL-2139 [M]	Peter Nero Plays Born Free and Others	1967	$18
□ CAS-2139 [S]	Peter Nero Plays Born Free and Others	1967	$15
RCA VICTOR
□ LPM-3313 [M]	Career Girls	1965	$18
□ LSP-3313 [S]	Career Girls	1965	$25
□ LPM-2536 [M]	For the Nero-Minded	1962	$18
□ LSP-2536 [S]	For the Nero-Minded	1962	$25
□ LPM-2638 [M]	Hail the Conquering Nero	1963	$18
□ LSP-2638 [S]	Hail the Conquering Nero	1963	$25
□ LSP-4072	Impressions (Great Songs of Burt Bacharach and Hal David)	1968	$15
□ LSP-4205	Love Trip	1969	$15
□ ADL1-0284	Music Festival of Hits	1973	$15
□ LPM-3871 [M]	Nero-ing In on the Hits	1968	$18
□ LSP-3871 [S]	Nero-ing In on the Hits	1968	$15
□ LPM-2383 [M]	New Piano in Town	1961	$18
□ LSP-2383 [S]	New Piano in Town	1961	$25
□ LPM-2710 [M]	Peter Nero in Person	1963	$18

Number	Title	Yr	NM
□ LSP-2710 [S]	Peter Nero in Person	1963	$25
□ LPM-3610 [M]	Peter Nero On Tour	1966	$15
□ LSP-3610 [S]	Peter Nero On Tour	1966	$18
□ LSP-3936 [S]	Peter Nero Plays Love Is Blue and Ten Other Great Songs	1968	$15
□ LPM-3936 [M]	Peter Nero Plays Love Is Blue and Ten Other Great Songs	1968	$18
□ LPM-3550 [M]	Peter Nero -- Up Close	1966	$15
□ LSP-3550 [S]	Peter Nero -- Up Close	1966	$18
□ LPM-2334 [M]	Piano Forte	1961	$18
□ LSP-2334 [S]	Piano Forte	1961	$25
□ LPM-3720 [M]	Plays a Salute to Herb Alpert and the Tijuana Brass	1967	$18
□ LSP-3720 [S]	Plays a Salute to Herb Alpert and the Tijuana Brass	1967	$15
□ LPM-2853 [M]	Reflections	1964	$18
□ LSP-2853 [S]	Reflections	1964	$25
□ LPM-2935 [M]	Songs You Won't Forget	1964	$18
□ LSP-2935 [S]	Songs You Won't Forget	1964	$25
□ LPM-2827 [M]	Sunday in New York	1964	$18
□ LSP-2827 [S]	Sunday in New York	1964	$25
□ PRM-241 [M]	Tender Is the Night	1967	$18
□ PRS-241 [S]	Tender Is the Night	1967	$25
—Special-products release			
□ LPM-2978 [M]	The Best of Peter Nero	1965	$18
□ LSP-2978 [S]	The Best of Peter Nero	1965	$25
□ LPM-2618 [M]	The Colorful Peter Nero	1963	$18
□ LSP-2618 [S]	The Colorful Peter Nero	1963	$25
□ LPM-3496 [M]	The Screen Scene	1966	$15
□ LSP-3496 [S]	The Screen Scene	1966	$18
□ LPM-3814 [M]	Xochimilco	1967	$18
□ LSP-3814 [S]	Xochimilco	1967	$15
□ LPM-2484 [M]	Young and Warm and Wonderful	1962	$18
□ LSP-2484 [S]	Young and Warm and Wonderful	1962	$25

NERVOUS EATERS
ACE OF HEARTS
| □ 1007 | Hot Steel and Acid | 1986 | $12 |
ELEKTRA
| □ 6E-282 | Nervous Eaters | 1980 | $18 |

NESBITT, JIM
CHART
□ CHS-1031 [B]	Runnin' Bare	1970	$25
□ CHM-1005 [M]	Truck Drivin' Cat with Nine Wives	1968	$30
□ CHS-1005 [S]	Truck Drivin' Cat with Nine Wives	1968	$25

NESMITH, MICHAEL
Also see MIKE, JOHN AND BILL; THE MONKEES.
PACIFIC ARTS
□ 7-116	And the Hits Just Keep On Comin'	1978	$18
—Reissue of RCA 4695			
□ 7-106	Compilation	1976	$25
□ 7-107 [B]	From a Radio Engine to the Photon Wing	1977	$35
□ ILPA-9486	From a Radio Engine to the Photon Wing	1977	$18
—Original issue			

□ 7-130 [B]	Infinite Rider on the Big Dogma	1979	$18
□ 7-118	Live at the Palais	1978	$18
□ 7-117	Pretty Much Your Standard Ranch Stash	1978	$18
—Reissue of RCA APL1-0164			
□ (no #) [DJ]	The Michael Nesmith Radio Special	1979	$40
□ 11-101A	The Prison	197?	$50
—Boxed set with booklet			
□ 7-101	The Prison	197?	$25
—Standard cover			
RCA VICTOR
| □ LSP-4695 [B] | And the Hits Just Keep On Comin' | 1972 | $50 |

Number	Title	Yr	NM
□ LSP-4415	Loose Salute	1970	$30
□ LSP-4371	Magnetic South	1970	$30
□ LSP-4497	Nevada Fighter	1971	$30
□ APL1-0164	Pretty Much Your Standard Ranch Stash	1973	$30
□ LSP-4563	Tantamount to Treason	1971	$30
RHINO
| □ R1-70168 | The Newer Stuff | 1989 | $15 |

NESTICO, SAMMY
MARK
| □ 32244 | Swingaphonic | 1969 | $25 |
SEA BREEZE
| □ SBD-103 | Night Flight | 1986 | $25 |

NETHERWORLD
R.E.M.
| □ 4441 [B] | Netherworld | 196? | $85 |

NEUMANN, ROGER
SEA BREEZE
| □ SBD-102 | Introducing Roger Neumann's Rather Large Band | 1983 | $25 |

NEUSTADT, LISA, AND THE ANGEL BAND WITH JEAN REDPATH
PHILO
| □ 1068 | Shout for Joy: An Unusual Collection of Traditional Carols | 1980 | $15 |

NEVIL, ROBBIE
EMI MANHATTAN
| □ E1-48359 | A Place Like This | 1988 | $12 |
MANHATTAN
| □ ST-53006 | Robbie Nevil | 1986 | $12 |

NEVILLE, AARON
MINIT

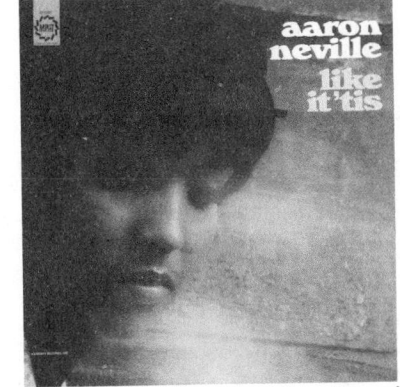

| □ LP40007 [M] | Like It 'Tis | 1967 | $85 |
| □ LP24007 [R] | Like It 'Tis | 1967 | $30 |
PAR-LO
| □ 1 [M] | Tell It Like It Is | 1967 | $175 |
| □ 1 [S] | Tell It Like It Is | 1967 | $250 |

NEVILLE BROTHERS, THE
Also see AARON NEVILLE. (SC2)
Also see AARON NEVILLE.
CAPITOL
| □ ST-11865 | The Neville Brothers | 1978 | $30 |

NEW AMERICAN GUITAR ENSEMBLE
REVERE
| □ RR182 | A Collection of Favorite Christmas Carols | 1983 | $12 |
| □ RR842 | Songs, Hymns and Carols | 1984 | $12 |

NEW APOCALYPSE, THE
M.T.A.
| □ S-5017 | Stainless Soul | 1970 | $25 |

NEW BIRTH, THE
ARIOLA AMERICA
| □ SW-9017 | Platinum City | 1979 | $12 |
BUDDAH
| □ BDS-5636 | Blind Baby | 1975 | $12 |
COLLECTABLES
| □ COL-5100 | Golden Classics | 1988 | $12 |
RCA VICTOR
□ LSP-4526	Ain't No Big Thing, But It's Growing	1971	$18
□ LSP-4797	Birth Day	1973	$15
□ ANL1-2145	Birth Day	1977	$12
—Reissue of 4797			

Number	Title	Yr	NM
❑ APL1-0494	Comin' From All Ends	1974	$12
❑ LSP-4697	Coming Together	1972	$18
❑ AFL1-4411	I'm Back	1982	$12
❑ APL1-0285 [B]	It's Been a Long Time	1974	$12
❑ APD1-0285 [Q]	It's Been a Long Time	1974	$30
❑ APL1-1021	The Best of the New Birth	1975	$12
❑ LSP-4450	The New Birth	1970	$18

WARNER BROS.

❑ BSK3071	Behold the Mighty Army	1977	$12
❑ BS2953	Love Potion	1976	$12

NEW BLACK EAGLE JAZZ BAND

DIRTY SHAME

❑ 2002	On the River	197?	$25

GHB

❑ GHB-59	New Black Eagle Jazz Band	1973	$30

PHILO

❑ 1086	New Black Eagle Jazz Band at Symphony Hall: 10th Anniversary	198?	$30

STOMP OFF

❑ SOS-1147	Don't Monkey With It	1988	$25
❑ SOS-1065	Dreaming the Hours Away	1984	$25
❑ SOS-1048	Live at the World Music Concourse	198?	$25
❑ SOS-1054	Live at the World Music Concourse, Volume 2	198?	$25
❑ SOS-1091	Mt. Gretna Week-End, Vol. 1	1985	$25
❑ SOS-1092	Mt. Gretna Week-End, Vol. 2	1985	$25

NEW CHRISTY MINSTRELS, THE
Also see BARRY McGUIRE; KENNY ROGERS.

COLUMBIA

❑ CL2369 [M]	Chim Chim Cher-ee	1965	$25
❑ CS9169 [S]	Chim Chim Cher-ee	1965	$30
❑ CS9709	Chitty Chitty Bang Bang	1969	$25
❑ CS9356 [S]	Christmas with the Christies	1966	$30
❑ CL2556 [M]	Christmas with the Christies	1966	$25
❑ CL2303 [M]	Cowboys and Indians	1965	$25
❑ CS9103 [S]	Cowboys and Indians	1965	$30
❑ CL2479 [M]	Greatest Hits	1966	$25
❑ CS9279 [S]	Greatest Hits	1966	$30
❑ CS9331 [S]	In Italy…In Italian	1966	$30
❑ CL2531 [M]	In Italy…In Italian	1966	$25
❑ CL2187 [M]	Land of Giants	1964	$25
❑ CS8987 [S]	Land of Giants	1964	$30
❑ CL2096 [M]	Merry Christmas	1963	$25
❑ CS8896 [S]	Merry Christmas	1963	$30
❑ CL2542 [M]	New Kick	1967	$25
❑ CS9342 [S]	New Kick	1967	$30
❑ CS9616 [M]	On Tour Through Motortown	1968	$50

— White label promo only; "Special Mono Radio Station Copy" sticker on front

❑ CS9616 [S]	On Tour Through Motortown	1968	$25
❑ CL2055 [M]	Ramblin' Feturing Green, Green	1963	$25
❑ CS8855 [S]	Ramblin' Feturing Green, Green	1963	$30
❑ CL2017 [M]	Tall Tales! Legends & Nonsense	1963	$25
❑ CS8817 [S]	Tall Tales! Legends & Nonsense	1963	$30
❑ CL1872 [M]	The New Christy Minstrels	1962	$25
❑ CS8672 [S]	The New Christy Minstrels	1962	$30
❑ CL1941 [M]	The New Christy Minstrels In Person	1963	$25
❑ CS8741 [S]	The New Christy Minstrels In Person	1963	$30
❑ CL2280 [M]	The Quiet Sides of the New Christy Minstrels	1965	$25
❑ CS9080 [S]	The Quiet Sides of the New Christy Minstrels	1965	$30
❑ CL2384 [M]	The Wandering Minstrels	1965	$25
❑ CS9184 [S]	The Wandering Minstrels	1965	$30
❑ CL2159 [M]	Today	1964	$25
❑ CS8959 [S]	Today	1964	$30

GREGAR

❑ 102 [B]	You Need Someone to Love	1970	$18

NEW COLONY SIX, THE
MERCURY

www.jovemguarda1965-elvandir.blogspot.com

Number	Title	Yr	NM
❑ SR-61228 [B]	Attacking a Straw Man	1969	$30
❑ SR-61165 [B]	Revelations	1968	$30

SENTAR

❑ LP-101 [M]	Breakthrough	1966	$500
❑ ST-3001 [M]	Colonization	1967	$50
❑ SST-3001 [S]	Colonization	1967	$75

SUNDAZED

❑ LP5007	At the River's Edge	1995	$12

NEW DAWN, THE
HOOT

❑ GR 704569	There's a New Dawn	1970	$1000

NEW DIMENSIONS, THE
SUNDAZED

❑ LP-5025	The Best of the New Dimensions	199?	$12

SUTTON

❑ SU-331 [M]	Deuces and Eights	1963	$100
❑ SSU-331 [S]	Deuces and Eights	1963	$150
❑ SU-336 [M]	Soul Surf	1964	$40
❑ SSU-336 [S]	Soul Surf	1964	$50
❑ SU-332 [M]	Surf 'N' Bongos	1963	$40
❑ SSU-332 [S]	Surf 'N' Bongos	1963	$50

NEW EDITION
MCA

❑ 5679	All for Love	1985	$10
❑ 39040 [EP]	Christmas All Over the World	1985	$10
❑ 42207	Heart Break	1988	$10
❑ 11480	Home Again	1996	$18
❑ 5515	New Edition	1984	$10
❑ 5912	Under the Blue Moon	1986	$10

STREETWISE

❑ 3301	Candy Girl	1983	$15

NEW ESTABLISHMENT, THE
COLGEMS

❑ COS-118	The New Establishment	1970	$0

— Scheduled but never released

NEW GLENN MILLER ORCHESTRA
See GLENN MILLER ORCHESTRA (in the M's).

NEW GRASS REVIVAL
CAPITOL

❑ C1-90739	Friday Night in America	1989	$15

EMI AMERICA

❑ ST-17216	New Grass Revival	1986	$12

FLYING FISH

❑ FF-083	Barren County	1979	$18
❑ FF-254	Commonwealth	198?	$15
❑ FF-016	Fly Through the Country	1975	$18
❑ FF-050	Too Late to Turn Back	1977	$18
❑ FF-032	When the Storm Is Over	1976	$18

STARDAY

❑ SLP-482	New Grass Revival	1973	$18

SUGAR HILL

❑ SH-3771	Live!	1989	$15
❑ SH-3745	On the Boulevard	198?	$12

NEW HERITAGE KEYBOARD QUARTET
BLUE NOTE

❑ BN-LA099-H2	New Heritage Keyboard Quartet	1973	$30

NEW KIDS ON THE BLOCK
COLUMBIA

❑ BFC40985	Hangin' Tough	1988	$15

— Original with three-letter prefix on spine and short bar code on back cover; all versions have only a "C" prefix on the label

❑ FC40985	Hangin' Tough	1988	$10

— Reissue with only "FC" on spine and longer bar code on back cover; all versions have only a "C" prefix on the label

❑ OC40985	Hangin' Tough	1988	$10

— Yet another version with a different prefix on spine and a long bar code on back cover; all versions have only a "C" prefix on the label

❑ FC45280	Merry Merry Christmas	1989	$15
❑ BFC40475	New Kids on the Block	1987	$15

— Original with short bar code on back cover

❑ FC40475	New Kids on the Block	1988	$10

— Reissue with longer bar code on back cover; both versions have only the "C" prefix on the label

❑ C45129	Step by Step	1990	$15

NEW LEGION ROCK SPECTACULAR, THE
SPECTACULAR

❑ 7777	Wild Ones!	1975	$75

NEW LONDON CHORALE, THE
MYRRH

❑ 6658	The Young Messiah	1981	$15

Number	Title	Yr	NM

NEW MCKINNEY'S COTTON PICKERS, THE
BOUNTIFUL

❑ 38000	The New McKinney's Cotton Pickers	1972	$35
❑ 38001	You're Driving Me Crazy	1974	$35

NEW MIX, THE
UNITED ARTISTS

❑ UAS-6678	The New Mix	1968	$25

NEW MUSIC ENSEMBLE
NME

❑ 101 [B]	New Music Ensemble	1964	$250

NEW ORDER
Also see JOY DIVISION.

FACTORY

❑ FACTUS8 [EP]	1981-1982	1983	$25
❑ FACTUS50	Movement	1981	$25

— Originals have no bar code

❑ FACTUS50	Movement	1981	$50

— Purple vinyl (looks more black, but will appear purple when held to a light)

❑ FACTUS50	Movement	198?	$15

— With bar code on cover

❑ FACTUS12 [B]	Power, Corruption and Lies	1983	$25

QWEST

❑ 25511 [B]	Brotherhood	1986	$15
❑ PRO-A-5970 [DJ]	In Order	1993	$50

— Promo only six-song, 44-minute compilation; orange vinyl

❑ 25289	Low Life	1985	$12
❑ 25308	Power, Corruption and Lies	1985	$12

— Reissue of Factory FACTUS 12

❑ 25621 [B]	Substance	1987	$30
❑ R100938	Technique	1989	$15

— BMG Direct Marketing edition

❑ 25845	Technique	1989	$15

NEW ORLEANS ALL STARS, THE
DIXIELAND JUBILEE

❑ DJ-502	In Concert	196?	$35

NEW ORLEANS CREOLE ORCHESTRA
SOUTHLAND

❑ 234 [M]	New Orleans Creole Jazz Band	1962	$35

NEW ORLEANS HERITAGE HALL JAZZ BAND
DIXIELAND JUBILEE

❑ DJ-512	New Orleans Heritage Hall Jazz Band	197?	$30

NEW ORLEANS NIGHTHAWKS, THE
GHB

❑ 98	The New Orleans Nighthawks	1979	$25

NEW ORLEANS RAGTIME ORCHESTRA
ARHOOLIE

❑ 1058	New Orleans Ragtime Orchestra	197?	$30

DELMARK

❑ DS-214	Grace and Beauty	197?	$30

VANGUARD

❑ VSD-69/70	New Orleans Ragtime Orchestra	197?	$35

NEW ORLEANS RASCALS, THE
STOMP OFF

❑ SOS-1074	Love Song of the Nile	1984	$25
❑ SOS-1113	The New Orleans Rascals at Preservation Hall	1986	$25

NEW ORLEANS RHYTHM KINGS

BRUNSWICK

Number	Title	Yr	NM
❏ BL58011 [10]	Dixieland Jazz	1950	$120

KINGS OF JAZZ

Number	Title	Yr	NM
❏ NLJ-18009/10	New Orleans Rhythm Kings Heritage	198?	$35

MILESTONE

Number	Title	Yr	NM
❏ 47020	New Orleans Rhythm Kings	197?	$35

NEW ORLEANS SHUFFLERS, THE

KINGSWAY

Number	Title	Yr	NM
❏ KL-700 [M]	The New Orleans Shufflers	1955	$50

NEW RENAISSANCE SOCIETY, THE

HANNA-BARBERA

Number	Title	Yr	NM
❏ HLP-9504 [M]	Baroque n' Stones	1966	$25
❏ HST-9504 [S]	Baroque n' Stones	1966	$30

NEW RIDERS OF THE PURPLE SAGE

JERRY GARCIA was briefly in this group.

A&M

Number	Title	Yr	NM
❏ SP-4818	Feelin' All Right	1981	$12

COLUMBIA

Number	Title	Yr	NM
❏ PC33145	Brujo	1974	$18

— Originals have no bar code

Number	Title	Yr	NM
❏ KC31930	Gypsy Cowboy	1972	$18
❏ PC31930	Gypsy Cowboy	1979	$10

— Budget-line reissue

Number	Title	Yr	NM
❏ PC32870	Home, Home on the Road	1974	$18

— Originals have no bar code

Number	Title	Yr	NM
❏ KC30888	New Riders of the Purple Sage	1971	$18
❏ PC30888 [B]	New Riders of the Purple Sage	1979	$10

— Budget-line reissue

Number	Title	Yr	NM
❏ PC33688	Oh, What a Mighty Time	1975	$18

— Originals have no bar code

Number	Title	Yr	NM
❏ KC31284	Powerglide	1972	$18
❏ PC31284	Powerglide	1979	$10

— Budget-line reissue

Number	Title	Yr	NM
❏ KC32450 [B]	The Adventures of Panama Red	1973	$18
❏ CQ32450 [Q]	The Adventures of Panama Red	1974	$30
❏ PC32450	The Adventures of Panama Red	1979	$10

— Budget-line reissue

Number	Title	Yr	NM
❏ PC34367	The Best of New Riders of the Purple Sage	1976	$15

— Originals have no bar code

Number	Title	Yr	NM
❏ PC34367	The Best of New Riders of the Purple Sage	1979	$10

— Budget-line reissue with bar code

MCA

Number	Title	Yr	NM
❏ 2307	Marin County Line	1977	$15
❏ 632	Marin County Line	1980	$10

— Reissue of 2307

Number	Title	Yr	NM
❏ 2196	New Riders	1976	$15
❏ 2248	Who Are These Guys	1977	$15

RELIX

Number	Title	Yr	NM
❏ RRLP-2024	Before Time Began	1986	$10
❏ RRLP-2025	Vintage NRPS	1987	$10

NEW SEEKERS, THE

ELEKTRA

Number	Title	Yr	NM
❏ EKS-74088	Beautiful People	1971	$15
❏ EKS-75034	Circles	1972	$15
❏ EKS-74108 [B]	New Colours	1971	$15
❏ EKS-75051	The Best of the New Seekers	1973	$15
❏ EQ-5051 [Q]	The Best of the New Seekers	1973	$30
❏ EKS-74115	We'd Like to Teach the World to Sing	1971	$15

MGM VERVE

Number	Title	Yr	NM
❏ V5090	Come Softly to Me	1972	$12
❏ V5098	Pinball Wizards	1973	$12
❏ V5095	The History of the New Seekers	1973	$12

NEW SOCIETY, THE

RCA VICTOR

Number	Title	Yr	NM
❏ LPM-3676 [M]	The Barock Sound of the New Society	1966	$30
❏ LSP-3676 [S]	The Barock Sound of the New Society	1966	$30

NEW STRANGERS, THE

FOLKLORE

Number	Title	Yr	NM
❏ FRLP-14027 [M]	Meet the New Strangers	1964	$25
❏ FRST-14027 [S]	Meet the New Strangers	1964	$30

NEW SUNSHINE JAZZ BAND

BIOGRAPH

Number	Title	Yr	NM
❏ 12058	Too Much Mustard	197?	$30

FLYING DUTCHMAN

Number	Title	Yr	NM
❏ BDL1-0549	Old Rags	1974	$30

NEW SYMPHONY ORCHESTRA OF LONDON (ALEXANDER GIBSON, CONDUCTOR)

RCA VICTOR RED SEAL

Number	Title	Yr	NM
❏ LSC-2225 [S]	Witches' Brew	1959	$400

— Original with "shaded dog" label

Number	Title	Yr	NM
❏ LSC-2225 [S]	Witches' Brew	199?	$30

— Classic Records reissue

NEW SYMPHONY ORCHESTRA OF LONDON (RAYMOND AGOULT, CONDUCTOR)

RCA VICTOR RED SEAL

Number	Title	Yr	NM
❏ LSC-2134 [S]	Overture! Overture!	1959	$50

— Original with "shaded dog" label; issued with two different covers

Number	Title	Yr	NM
❏ LSC-2134 [S]	Overture! Overture!	199?	$30

— Classic Records reissue

NEW SYMPHONY ORCHESTRA OF LONDON (RONALD BINGE, CONDUCTOR)

RCA VICTOR RED SEAL

Number	Title	Yr	NM
❏ LSC-2399 [S]	Mendelssohniana	1960	$300

— Originals with "shaded dog" label

NEW TROUBADOURS, THE

LORIAN

Number	Title	Yr	NM
❏ 39340	Festival of Light: A Collection of Original Christmas Songs	1980	$15

NEW TWEEDY BROTHERS, THE

RIDON

Number	Title	Yr	NM
❏ 234	The New Tweedy Brothers	1968	$2000

— With oversized hexagonal cover designed to look like a sugar cube

Number	Title	Yr	NM
❏ 234	The New Tweedy Brothers	1968	$400

— With plain white cover

Number	Title	Yr	NM
❏ SLP234 [B]	The New Tweedy Brothers!	1968	$3500

NEW VAUDEVILLE BAND, THE

FONTANA

Number	Title	Yr	NM
❏ MGF-27688 [M]	The New Vaudeville Band on Tour	1967	$15
❏ SRF-67688 [P]	The New Vaudeville Band on Tour	1967	$15
❏ MGF-27560 [M]	Winchester Cathedral	1966	$18

— With "Whatever Happened to Phyllis Puke" and "Diana Goodbye"

Number	Title	Yr	NM
❏ MGF-27560 [M]	Winchester Cathedral	1966	$18

— With "Oh, Donna Clara"; record has mono number and actually plays in mono; the number "27560" is in the trail-off

Number	Title	Yr	NM
❏ SRF-67560 [P]	Winchester Cathedral	1966	$18

— With "Whatever Happened to Phyllis Puke" and "Diana Goodbye"

Number	Title	Yr	NM
❏ SRF-67560 [P]	Winchester Cathedral	1966	$15

— With "Oh, Donna Clara"

Number	Title	Yr	NM
❏ MGF-27560 [P]	Winchester Cathedral	1966	$15

— With "Oh, Donna Clara"; record has mono number, but plays stereo; the number "2/67560" is in trail-off area

NEW WAVE, THE

CANTERBURY

Number	Title	Yr	NM
❏ CLPS-1501	The New Wave	1967	$30

NEW YANKEE RHYTHM KINGS, THE

STOMP OFF

Number	Title	Yr	NM
❏ SOS-1015	Jazz Band	198?	$25
❏ SOS-1050	Live at the Strata-Capitol	1982	$25
❏ SOS-1067	Together at Last	1984	$25

NEW YORK ART QUARTET, THE

ESP-DISK'

Number	Title	Yr	NM
❏ 1004 [M]	The New York Art Quartet	1965	$250
❏ S-1004 [S]	The New York Art Quartet	1965	$250

NEW YORK BASS VIOLIN CHOIR

STRATA-EAST

Number	Title	Yr	NM
❏ SES-8003	New York Bass Violin Choir	1980	$35

NEW YORK CITY

CHELSEA

Number	Title	Yr	NM
❏ BCL1-0198	I'm Doin' Fine Now	1973	$18
❏ CHL500	Soulful Road	1974	$18
❏ CHL514	The Best of New York City	1977	$15

NEW YORK CITY GAY MEN'S CHORUS

PRO ARTE

Number	Title	Yr	NM
❏ 159	A Festival of Song	198?	$15

NEW YORK DOLLS

Also see DAVID JOHANSEN; SYLVAIN SYLVAIN.

CLEOPATRA

Number	Title	Yr	NM
❏ 8124 [B]	Trashed In Paris '73		$30

— picture disc

MERCURY

Number	Title	Yr	NM
❏ SRM-1-1001	In Too Much Too Soon	1974	$40
❏ SRM-1-675	New York Dolls	1973	$40
❏ 1786413	New York Dolls	2008	$25

Number	Title	Yr	NM
❏ 826094-1 [B]	Night of the Living Dolls	1985	$15

NEW YORK JAZZ GUITAR ENSEMBLE, THE

CHOICE

Number	Title	Yr	NM
❏ CRS-6831	4 On 6 x 5	1986	$30

NEW YORK JAZZ QUARTET, THE (1)

CORAL

Number	Title	Yr	NM
❏ CRL57136 [M]	Music For Suburban Living	1958	$250
❏ CRL757136 [S]	Music For Suburban Living	1958	$175

ELEKTRA

Number	Title	Yr	NM
❏ EKL-118 [M]	Gone Native	1957	$50
❏ EKL-115 [M]	The New York Jazz Quartet	1957	$50

SAVOY

Number	Title	Yr	NM
❏ MG-12172 [M]	Adam's Theme	1960	$30
❏ MG-12175 [M]	Gone Native	1961	$30

NEW YORK JAZZ QUARTET, THE (2)

ENJA

Number	Title	Yr	NM
❏ 3083	Oasis	1981	$30

INNER CITY

Number	Title	Yr	NM
❏ IC-3024	Blues for Sarka	1978	$35
❏ IC-3011	Surge	197?	$35

SALVATION

Number	Title	Yr	NM
❏ 703	Concert in Japan	197?	$30

NEW YORK JAZZ REPERTORY COMPANY, THE

ATLANTIC

Number	Title	Yr	NM
❏ SD1671	The Music of Louis Armstrong	1975	$25

NEW YORK JAZZ SEXTET, THE

SCEPTER

Number	Title	Yr	NM
❏ S-526 [M]	New York Jazz Sextet	1964	$25
❏ SS-526 [S]	New York Jazz Sextet	1964	$30

NEW YORK MARY

ARISTA/FREEDOM

Number	Title	Yr	NM
❏ AF1019	New York Mary	1975	$35
❏ AF1035	Piece of the Apple	1976	$35

NEW YORK ORIGINATORS, THE

PARAMOUNT

Number	Title	Yr	NM
❏ RS-201 [10]	The New York Style	1952	$75

NEW YORK PHILHARMONIC ORCHESTRA (BRUNO WALTER, CONDUCTOR)

COLUMBIA MASTERWORKS

Number	Title	Yr	NM
❏ ML4001 [M]	Mendelssohn: Violin Concerto	1948	$40

— Violinist: Nathan Milstein; the very first modern microgroove LP!

Number	Title	Yr	NM
❏ ML4001 [M]	Mendelssohn: Violin Concerto	1999	$30

— Violinist: Nathan Milstein; Classic Records commemorative reissue

NEW YORK PRO MUSICA ANTIQUA

COUNTERPOINT/ESOTERIC

Number	Title	Yr	NM
❏ CPT521 [M]	English Medieval Christmas Carols	196?	$25
❏ CPTS5521 [S]	English Medieval Christmas Carols	196?	$18

Number	Title	Yr	NM

NEW YORK ROCK ENSEMBLE, THE
ATCO
Number	Title	Yr	NM
❏ SD 33-294	Faithful Friends	1969	$18
❏ SD 33-312	Reflections	1970	$18
❏ SD 33-240	The New York Rock 'n' Roll Ensemble	1968	$18

COLUMBIA
| ❏ KC31317 | Freedomburger | 1972 | $18 |
| ❏ C30033 | Roll Over | 1970 | $18 |

NEW YORK SAXOPHONE QUARTET, THE
20TH CENTURY FOX
| ❏ TFM-3150 [M] | The New York Saxophone Quartet | 1964 | $25 |
| ❏ TFS-3150 [S] | The New York Saxophone Quartet | 1964 | $30 |

MARK
| ❏ 32322 | The New York Saxophone Quartet | 1969 | $25 |

STASH
| ❏ ST-220 | An American Experience | 198? | $25 |
| ❏ ST-210 | New York Saxophone Quartet | 198? | $25 |

NEW YORK VOICES
GRP
| ❏ GR-9589 | New York Voices | 1989 | $30 |

NEWBAN
GUINNESS
| ❏ GNS36004 [B] | Newban | 1977 | $150 |
| ❏ GNS36017 [B] | Newban 2 | | $50 |

NEWBEATS, THE
HICKORY
❏ LPM122 [M]	Big Beat Sounds by the Newbeats	1965	$50
❏ LPS122 [S]	Big Beat Sounds by the Newbeats	1965	$150
❏ LPM120 [M]	Bread and Butter	1964	$50
❏ LPS120 [S]	Bread and Butter	1964	$175
❏ T90701 [M]	Bread and Butter	1965	$175
— Capitol Record Club edition			
❏ DT90701 [R]	Bread and Butter	1965	$175
— Capitol Record Club edition			
❏ ST90701 [S]	Bread and Butter	1965	$250
— Capitol Record Club edition			
❏ LPM128 [M]	Run Baby Run	1965	$50

| ❏ LPS128 [S] | Run Baby Run | 1965 | $150 |

NEWBERGER, ELI, AND JIMMY MAZZY
STOMP OFF
| ❏ SOS-1109 | Shake It Down | 1986 | $25 |

NEWBORN, PHINEAS
ATLANTIC
❏ 1235 [M]	Here Is Phineas	1956	$300
— Black label			
❏ SD1235 [S]	Here Is Phineas	1958	$300
— Green label			
❏ 1235 [M]	Here Is Phineas	1961	$175
— Multicolor label, white "fan" logo at right			
❏ SD1235 [S]	Here Is Phineas	1961	$175
— Multicolor label, white "fan" logo at right			
❏ 1235 [M]	Here Is Phineas	1964	$35
— Multicolor label, black "fan" logo at right			
❏ SD1235 [S]	Here Is Phineas	1964	$30
— Multicolor label, black "fan" logo at right			
❏ SD1672	Solo Piano	1975	$30
❏ 90534	The Piano Artistry of Phineas Newborn	1986	$25

CONTEMPORARY
❏ C-7648	Back Home	198?	$15
❏ M-3611 [M]	Great Jazz Piano	1962	$250
❏ S-7611 [S]	Great Jazz Piano	1962	$250

Number	Title	Yr	NM
❏ S-7622 [S]	Please Send Me Someone to Love	1969	$85
❏ M-3615 [M]	The Newborn Touch	1964	$250
❏ S-7615 [S]	The Newborn Touch	1964	$250
❏ M-3600 [M]	The World of Piano!	1961	$250
❏ S-7600 [S]	The World of Piano!	1961	$250

FANTASY
❏ OJC-175	A World of Piano	198?	$25
❏ OJC-388	Great Jazz Piano	1989	$30
❏ OJC-270	The Newborn Touch	1988	$25
❏ OJC-175	The World of Piano!	198?	$25

PABLO
| ❏ 2310801 | Look Out, Phineas Is Back | 197? | $30 |

RCA VICTOR
❏ LPM-1873 [M]	Fabulous Phineas	1958	$50
❏ LSP-1873 [S]	Fabulous Phineas	1958	$40
❏ LPM-1589 [M]	Phineas Newborn Plays Jamaica	1957	$50
❏ LPM-1421 [M]	Phineas' Rainbow	1957	$50
❏ LPM-1474 [M]	While the Lady Sleeps	1957	$150

ROULETTE
❏ R-52043 [M]	I Love a Piano	1960	$30
❏ SR-52043 [S]	I Love a Piano	1960	$30
❏ R-52031 [M]	Piano Portraits	1959	$30
❏ SR-52031 [S]	Piano Portraits	1959	$30

NEWBURY, MICKEY
ABC HICKORY
❏ HA-44011	Eye on the Sparrow	1978	$12
❏ HA-44002	Rusty Tracks	1977	$12
❏ HB-44017	The Sailor	1979	$12

ELEKTRA
❏ EKS-74107 [B]	'Frisco Mabel Joy	1971	$12
❏ EQ-4107 [Q]	'Frisco Mabel Joy	1974	$30
❏ EKS-75055	Heaven Help the Child	1973	$12
❏ 7E-1007	I Came to Hear the Music	1974	$12
❏ 7E-1030	Lovers	1975	$12
❏ EK-PROMO20 [DJ]	Recorded Live at Montezuma Hall, San Diego State University, March 6, 1973	1973	$40

MCA
❏ 803	Eye on the Sparrow	198?	$10
— Reissue			
❏ 802	Rusty Tracks	198?	$10
— Reissue			
❏ 945	Sweet Memories	1985	$12
❏ 804	The Sailor	198?	$10
— Reissue			

MERCURY
| ❏ SR61236 | Looks Like Rain | 1969 | $18 |

RCA VICTOR
| ❏ LSP-4043 | Harlequin Melodies | 1968 | $18 |

NEWHART, BOB
HARMONY
| ❏ HS11344 | The Very Funny Bob Newhart | 196? | $15 |

MURRAY HILL
| ❏ OP2529 | The Best of the Button-Down Mind | 197? | $25 |

WARNER BROS.
❏ W1417 [M]	Behind the Button-Down Mind of Bob Newhart	1961	$30
❏ WS1417 [S]	Behind the Button-Down Mind of Bob Newhart	1961	$25
❏ W1517 [M]	Bob Newhart Faces Bob Newhart (Faces Bob Newhart)	1964	$30
❏ W1672 [M]	The Best of Bob Newhart	1966	$30
❏ WS1672 [S]	The Best of Bob Newhart	1966	$30
— Gold label			
❏ WS1672 [S]	The Best of Bob Newhart	1968	$25
— Green "W7" label			
❏ WS1672 [S]	The Best of Bob Newhart	1970	$18
— Green "WB" label			
❏ WS1672 [S]	The Best of Bob Newhart	1973	$15
— Burbank" palm-trees label			
❏ WS1672 [S]	The Best of Bob Newhart	1979	$10
— White or tan label			
❏ 2N1399 [M]	The Bob Newhart Deluxe Edition	1961	$50
❏ 2NS1399 [S]	The Bob Newhart Deluxe Edition	1961	$40
❏ W1379 [M]	The Button-Down Mind of Bob Newhart	1960	$30
❏ WS1379 [S]	The Button-Down Mind of Bob Newhart	1960	$30
❏ W1467 [M]	The Button-Down Mind on TV	1962	$30
❏ WS1467 [S]	The Button-Down Mind on TV	1962	$25
❏ W1393 [M]	The Button-Down Mind Strikes Back!	1960	$30
❏ WS1393 [S]	The Button-Down Mind Strikes Back!	1960	$30
❏ W1588 [M]	The Windmills Are Weakening	1965	$30
❏ W1717 [M]	This Is It	1967	$30

Number	Title	Yr	NM

NEWLEY, ANTHONY
LONDON
❏ LL3461 [M]	Genius	1966	$15
❏ PS461 [S]	Genius	1966	$18
❏ LL3156 [M]	Love Is a Now and Then Thing	1960	$25
❏ LL3262 [M]	This Is Tony Newley	1962	$18
❏ LL3252 [M]	Tony	1962	$18
❏ PS244 [S]	Tony	1962	$30

RCA VICTOR
❏ LPM-3839 [M]	Doctor Dolittle	1967	$15
❏ LSP-3839 [S]	Doctor Dolittle	1967	$18
❏ LPM-2925 [M]	In My Solitude	1964	$18
❏ LSP-2925 [S]	In My Solitude	1964	$25
❏ LPM-3614 [M]	Newly Recorded	1966	$15
❏ LSP-3614 [S]	Newly Recorded	1966	$18
❏ LSP-4163	The Best of Anthony Newley	1969	$15
❏ LPM-3347 [M]	Who Can I Turn To	1965	$15
❏ LSP-3347 [S]	Who Can I Turn To	1965	$18

NEWMAN, BOB
AUDIO LAB
| ❏ AL-1536 [M] | The Kentucky Colonel | 1959 | $250 |

NEWMAN, DAVID "FATHEAD
ATLANTIC
❏ SD1505	Bigger and Better	1968	$25
❏ 1399 [M]	Fathead Comes On	1962	$175
❏ SD1399 [S]	Fathead Comes On	1962	$40
❏ 81965	Fire! Live at the Village Vanguard	1989	$30
❏ 81725	Heads Up	1987	$25
❏ SD1489	House of David	1968	$25
❏ SD1600	Lonely Avenue	1972	$35
❏ SD1524	Many Facets	1969	$35
❏ SD1662	Newmanism	1974	$30
❏ 1304 [M]	Ray Charles Presents David "Fathead" Newman	1959	$300
— Black label			
❏ 1304 [M]	Ray Charles Presents David "Fathead" Newman	1961	$175
— Multicolor label with white "fan" logo			
❏ 1304 [M]	Ray Charles Presents David "Fathead" Newman	1964	$30
— Multicolor label with black "fan" logo			
❏ SD1304 [S]	Ray Charles Presents David "Fathead" Newman	1959	$300
— Green label			
❏ SD1304 [S]	Ray Charles Presents David "Fathead" Newman	1961	$175
— Multicolor label with white "fan" logo			
❏ SD1304 [S]	Ray Charles Presents David "Fathead" Newman	1964	$35
— Multicolor label with black "fan" logo			
❏ 1366 [M]	Straight Ahead	1961	$175
— Multicolor label with white "fan" logo			
❏ 1366 [M]	Straight Ahead	1964	$30
— Multicolor label with black "fan" logo			
❏ SD1366 [S]	Straight Ahead	1961	$175
— Multicolor label with white "fan" logo			
❏ SD1366 [S]	Straight Ahead	1964	$35
— Multicolor label with black "fan" logo			
❏ SD1590	The Best of David "Fathead" Newman	1972	$35
❏ SD1638	The Weapon	1973	$35

COTILLION
| ❏ SD18002 | Captain Buckles | 1970 | $25 |

MUSE
| ❏ MR-5234 | Resurgence | 1981 | $25 |
| ❏ MR-5283 | Still Hard Times | 1982 | $25 |

PRESTIGE
❏ 10104	Concrete Jungle	1978	$35
❏ 10106	Keep the Dream Alive	1978	$35
❏ 10108	Scratch My Back	1979	$35

WARNER BROS.
| ❏ BS2984 | Front Money | 1977 | $25 |
| ❏ BS2917 | Mr. Fathead | 1976 | $25 |

NEWMAN, JIMMY
DECCA
❏ DL4748 [M]	Artificial Rose	1966	$25
❏ DL74748 [S]	Artificial Rose	1966	$30
❏ DL75065	Born to Love You	1968	$25
❏ DL4398 [M]	Folk Songs of the Bayou Country	1963	$40
❏ DL74398 [S]	Folk Songs of the Bayou Country	1963	$50
❏ DL4221 [M]	Jimmy Newman	1962	$30
❏ DL74221 [S]	Jimmy Newman	1962	$30
❏ DL4781 [M]	Jimmy Newman Sings Country Songs	1966	$25
❏ DL74781 [S]	Jimmy Newman Sings Country Songs	1966	$30
❏ DL4960 [M]	The Jimmy Newman Way	1967	$30
❏ DL74960 [S]	The Jimmy Newman Way	1967	$25
❏ DL4885 [M]	The World of Country Music	1967	$30
❏ DL74885 [S]	The World of Country Music	1967	$25

DOT
| ❏ DLP-3690 [M] | A Fallen Star | 1965 | $30 |
| ❏ DLP-3736 [M] | Country Crossroads | 1966 | $30 |

Number	Title	Yr	NM
❏ DLP-25736 [R]	Country Crossroads	1966	$25
MGM			
❏ E-4045 [M]	Songs by Jimmy Newman	1962	$30
❏ SE-4045 [S]	Songs by Jimmy Newman	1962	$30
❏ E-3777 [M]	This Is Jimmy Newman	1959	$30
❏ SE-3777 [S]	This Is Jimmy Newman	1959	$30

NEWMAN, JOE, AND JOE WILDER

CONCORD JAZZ

Number	Title	Yr	NM
❏ CJ-262	Joe Newman and Joe Wilder	1985	$30

NEWMAN, JOE

AMERICAN RECORDING SOCIETY

Number	Title	Yr	NM
❏ G-447 [M]	Basically Swing	1958	$40
❏ G-451 [M]	New Sounds In Swing	1958	$40
CORAL			
❏ CRL57208 [M]	Soft Swingin' Jazz	1958	$50
❏ CRL57121 [M]	The Happy Cats	1957	$50
FANTASY			
❏ OJC-185	Good 'N Groovy	1985	$25
❏ OJC-419	Jive At Five	1990	$30
JAZZTONE			
❏ J-1217 [M]	New Sounds In Swing	1956	$40
❏ J-1265 [M]	Swing Lightly	1957	$40
❏ J-1220 [M]	The Count's Men	1956	$40
MERCURY			
❏ MG-20696 [M]	Joe Newman At Count Basie's	1962	$150
❏ SR-60696 [S]	Joe Newman At Count Basie's	1962	$150
PRESTIGE			
❏ 2509	Jive At Five	198?	$30
RAMA			
❏ LP-1003 [M]	Locking Horns	1957	$400
RCA VICTOR			
❏ LPM-1118 [M]	All I Want To Do Is Swing	1955	$150

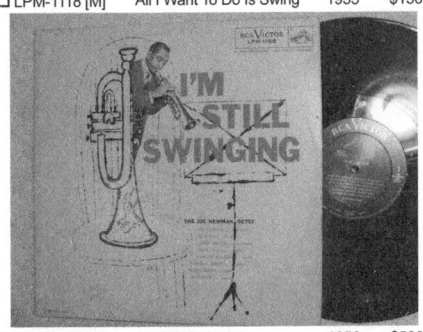

Number	Title	Yr	NM
❏ LPM-1198 [M]	I'm Still Swinging	1956	$500
—Andy Warhol cover.			
❏ LPM-1324 [M]	Salute To Satch	1956	$100
ROULETTE			
❏ R-52014 [M]	Joe Newman With Woodwinds	1958	$40
❏ SR-52014 [S]	Joe Newman With Woodwinds	1958	$30
❏ R-52009 [M]	Locking Horns	1958	$40
❏ SR-52009 [S]	Locking Horns	1958	$30
STASH			
❏ ST-219	In a Mellow Mood	198?	$25
STORYVILLE			
❏ STLP-905 [M]	I Feel Like a Newman	1956	$150
❏ STLP-318 [10]	Joe Newman and the Boys In the Band	1955	$175
SWINGVILLE			
❏ SVLP-2019 [M]	Good 'N Groovy	1961	$50
—Purple label			
❏ SVLP-2019 [M]	Good 'N Groovy	1965	$30
—Blue label, trident logo at right			
❏ SVLP-2011 [M]	Jive At Five	1961	$50
—Purple label			
❏ SVLP-2011 [M]	Jive At Five	1965	$30
—Blue label, trident logo at right			
❏ SVLP-2027 [M]	Joe's Hap'nin's	1961	$75
—Purple label			
❏ SVST-2027 [S]	Joe's Hap'nin's	1961	$75
—Red label			
❏ SVLP-2027 [M]	Joe's Hap'nin's	1965	$30
—Blue label, trident logo at right			
❏ SVST-2027 [S]	Joe's Hap'nin's	1965	$30
—Blue label, trident logo at right			
TRIP			
❏ 5548	Live at Basie's	197?	$12
VANGUARD			
❏ VRS-8007 [10]	Joe Newman and His Band	1954	$250
VIK			
❏ LX-1060 [M]	The Midgets	1957	$100

WORLD PACIFIC

Number	Title	Yr	NM
❏ WP-1288 [M]	Countin'	1960	$175
❏ ST-1288 [S]	Countin'	1960	$175

NEWMAN, JOE/RUBY BRAFF

HALL OF FAME

Number	Title	Yr	NM
❏ 601	Swing Lightly	197?	$25

NEWMAN, PHYLLIS

SIRE

Number	Title	Yr	NM
❏ SES-97002	Those Were the Days	1969	$25

NEWMAN, RANDY

REPRISE

Number	Title	Yr	NM
❏ RS6373	12 Songs	1970	$18
—With "W7" and "r:" logos on two-tone orange label			
❏ RS6373	12 Songs	1970	$12
—With only "r:" logo on all-orange (tan) label			
❏ MS2193	Good Old Boys	1974	$12
❏ MS42193 [Q]	Good Old Boys	1974	$20
❏ 25773	Land of Dreams	1988	$12
❏ RS6286	Randy Newman	1968	$25
—Cover with Randy standing in the clouds			
❏ RS6286	Randy Newman	1968	$18
—Cover with close-up of Randy's face; "W7" and "r:" logos on two-tone orange label			
❏ RS6286	Randy Newman	1970	$15
—With only "r:" logo on all-orange (tan) label			
❏ RS6459	Randy Newman/Live	1971	$12
❏ MS2064	Sail Away	1972	$18
—With no song titles listed on back			
❏ MS2064	Sail Away	1972	$12
—With song titles listed on back			
RHINO			
❏ R16286 [B]	Randy Newman	2014	$25
WARNER BROS.			

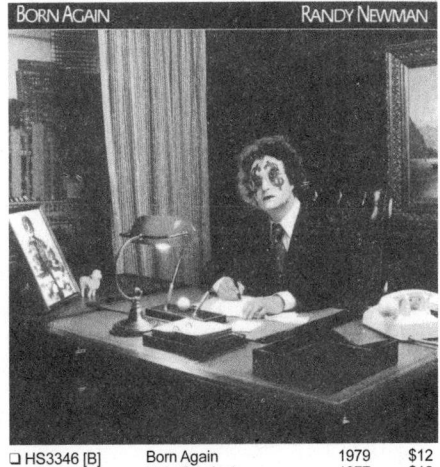

Number	Title	Yr	NM
❏ HS3346 [B]	Born Again	1979	$12
❏ BSK3079	Little Criminals	1977	$12
❏ 23755	Trouble in Paradise	1983	$12

NEWPORT ALL STARS, THE

BASF

Number	Title	Yr	NM
❏ 20717	A Tribute to Duke	1972	$35
BLACK LION			
❏ 303	Newport All Stars	197?	$30
CONCORD JAZZ			
❏ CJ-343	European Tour	1988	$25
—As "The Newport Jazz Festival All-Stars			

NEWTON, CAM

INNER CITY

Number	Title	Yr	NM
❏ IC-1059	The Motive Behind the Smile	1979	$35
❏ IC-1079	Welcome Aliens	1980	$35

NEWTON, JAMES

BLUE NOTE

Number	Title	Yr	NM
❏ BT-85109	The African Flower	1986	$30
CELESTIAL HARMONIES			
❏ CEL-012	Echo Canyon	1984	$30
❏ 13012	Echo Canyon	198?	$25
—Reissue with new number			
❏ 14030	James Newton in Venice	1988	$30
ECM			
❏ 1214	Axum	1981	$25
GRAMAVISION			
❏ 8205	James Newton	1982	$25
❏ GR-8304	Luella	1983	$25
INDIA NAVIGATION			
❏ IN-1046	Mystery School	1980	$30

Number	Title	Yr	NM
❏ IN-1037	Paseo Del Mar	197?	$35
❏ IN-1051	Portraits	198?	$30

NEWTON, JUICE

CAPITOL

Number	Title	Yr	NM
❏ ST-11682	Come to Me	1977	$18
❏ SN-16242	Come to Me	1982	$10
—Budget-line reissue			
❏ ST-12294	Dirty Looks	1983	$12
❏ SN-16356	Dirty Looks	1985	$10
—Budget-line reissue			
❏ SJ-12353	Greatest Hits	1984	$12
❏ SN-16471	Greatest Hits	1987	$10
—Budget-line reissue			
❏ ST-12136	Juice	1981	$12
❏ SN-16313	Juice	1984	$10
—Budget-line reissue			
❏ ST-12210	Quiet Lies	1982	$12
❏ SN-16314	Quiet Lies	1984	$10
—Budget-line reissue			
❏ ST-12000	Take Heart	1980	$18
❏ SN-16244	Take Heart	1982	$10
—Budget-line reissue			
❏ ST-11811	Well-Kept Secret	1978	$18
❏ SN-16243	Well-Kept Secret	1982	$10
—Budget-line reissue			
RCA			
❏ 8376-1-R	Ain't Gonna Cry	1989	$12
❏ 6371-1-R	Emotion	1987	$12
❏ 5646-1-R	Old Flame	1986	$12
—Reissue of 5493 with slightly different lineup			
RCA VICTOR			
❏ APL1-1722	After Dust Settled	1977	$18
❏ AYL1-4038	After Dust Settled	1982	$10
—Best Buy Series" reissue			
❏ AFL1-4995	Can't Wait All Night	1984	$12
❏ APL1-1004	Juice Newton and Silver Spur	1975	$25
❏ AYL1-4037	Juice Newton and Silver Spur	1982	$10
—Best Buy Series" reissue			
❏ AFL1-5493	Old Flame	1985	$15

NEWTON, LAUREN

HAT HUT

Number	Title	Yr	NM
❏ 3511	Timbre	1982	$35

NEWTON, WAYNE

20TH CENTURY

Number	Title	Yr	NM
❏ T-576	Change of Heart	1979	$12
ARIES II			
❏ WY201	Wayne Newton Christmas	1979	$12
CAPITOL			
❏ T1973 [M]	Danke Schoen	1963	$18
❏ ST1973 [S]	Danke Schoen	1963	$25
❏ SM-11972	Danke Schoen	1979	$12
—Reissue			
❏ T2832 [M]	God Is Alive	1968	$25
❏ ST2832 [S]	God Is Alive	1968	$18
❏ ST-617	How I Got This Way	1971	$18
❏ T2635 [M]	It's Only the Good Times	1967	$18
❏ ST2635 [S]	It's Only the Good Times	1967	$25
❏ STBB-487	Merry Christmas to You	1970	$18
❏ T2335 [M]	Red Roses for a Blue Lady	1965	$18
❏ ST2335 [S]	Red Roses for a Blue Lady	1965	$25
❏ SM-2335	Red Roses for a Blue Lady	197?	$12
—Reissue			
❏ T2714 [M]	Song of the Year...Wayne Newton Style	1967	$25
❏ ST2714 [S]	Song of the Year...Wayne Newton Style	1967	$18
❏ T2588 [M]	Songs for a Merry Christmas	1966	$15
❏ ST2588 [S]	Songs for a Merry Christmas	1966	$18
❏ T2389 [M]	Summer Wind	1965	$18
❏ ST2389 [S]	Summer Wind	1965	$25
❏ T2797 [M]	The Best of Wayne Newton	1967	$25
❏ ST2797 [S]	The Best of Wayne Newton	1967	$18
❏ SN-16083	The Best of Wayne Newton	1980	$10
—Budget-line reissue			
❏ SKAO-137	The Best of Wayne Newton, Volume 2	1968	$18
❏ T2563 [M]	The Old Rugged Cross	1966	$18
❏ ST2563 [S]	The Old Rugged Cross	1966	$25
❏ SM-2563	The Old Rugged Cross	197?	$12
—Reissue			
❏ T2029 [M]	Wayne Newton In Person	1964	$18
❏ ST2029 [S]	Wayne Newton In Person	1964	$25
❏ T2445 [M]	Wayne Newton -- Now!	1966	$18
❏ ST2445 [S]	Wayne Newton -- Now!	1966	$25
❏ T2130 [M]	Wayne Newton Sings Hit Songs	1964	$18
❏ ST2130 [S]	Wayne Newton Sings Hit Songs	1964	$25
❏ T2847 [M]	Wayne Newton -- The Greatest	1968	$25
❏ ST2847 [S]	Wayne Newton -- The Greatest	1968	$18
CAPITOL PICKWICK SERIES			
❏ PC-3459 [M]	Everybody Loves Somebody	196?	$12
❏ SPC-3459 [S]	Everybody Loves Somebody	196?	$12

Number	Title	Yr	NM
❏ PC-3461 [M]	Michelle	196?	$12
❏ SPC-3461 [S]	Michelle	196?	$12
❏ PC-3455 [M]	Somewhere My Love	196?	$12
❏ SPC-3455 [S]	Somewhere My Love	196?	$12
❏ PC-3464 [M]	Wow! Wayne Newton Live	196?	$12
❏ SPC-3464 [S]	Wow! Wayne Newton Live	196?	$12

CHELSEA

❏ CHE1003	Can't You Hear the Song?	1972	$15
❏ CHE1001	Daddy Don't You Walk So Fast	1972	$15
❏ CHL-513	Daddy Don't You Walk So Fast	1976	$12
— Reissue of 1001			
❏ CHL-507	Midnight Idol	1975	$12
❏ BCL1-0367	Pour Me a Little More Wine	1973	$15
❏ CHL-504	The Best of Wayne Newton Live	1974	$12
❏ CHL-512	Tomorrow	1976	$12
❏ CHE1006	While We're Still Young	1973	$15

CURB

❏ 10607	Coming Home	1989	$15

MGM

❏ SE-4593	Christmas Isn't Christmas Without You	1968	$15
❏ SE-4594	Dreams of the Everyday Housewife/Town and Country	1969	$15
❏ E-4549 [M]	One More Time	1968	$25
❏ SE-4549 [S]	One More Time	1968	$15
❏ E-4523 [M]	Walking on New Grass	1968	$25
❏ SE-4523 [S]	Walking on New Grass	1968	$15

WORD

❏ WST-8586	Only Believe	1972	$15

NEWTON, WOOD

ELEKTRA

❏ 6E-176	Wood Newton	1979	$12

NEWTON-JOHN, OLIVIA

GEFFEN

❏ GHS24257	Warm and Tender	1989	$15

MCA

❏ 2148	Clearly Love	1975	$12
❏ 3015	Clearly Love	1977	$10
— Reissue			
❏ 37061	Clearly Love	1980	$10
— Reissue			
❏ 2186	Come On Over	1976	$12
❏ 3016	Come On Over	1977	$10
— Reissue			
❏ 37062	Come On Over	1980	$10
— Reissue			
❏ 2223	Don't Stop Believin'	1976	$12
❏ 3017	Don't Stop Believin'	1977	$10
— Reissue			
❏ 37063	Don't Stop Believin'	1980	$10
— Reissue			
❏ 2133	Have You Never Been Mellow	1975	$12
❏ 3014	Have You Never Been Mellow	1977	$10
— Reissue			
❏ 411	If You Love Me Let Me Know	1974	$18
— Originals have incorrect song title: "I Love You, I Honestly Love You"			
❏ 411	If You Love Me Let Me Know	1974	$12
— With corrected song title: "I Honestly Love You"			
❏ 3013	If You Love Me Let Me Know	1977	$10
— Reissue			
❏ 389	Let Me Be There	1973	$18
❏ 3012	Let Me Be There	1977	$10
— Reissue			
❏ 2280	Making a Good Thing Better	1977	$12
❏ 3018	Making a Good Thing Better	1977	$10
— Reissue			
❏ 3028	Olivia Newton-John's Greatest Hits	1977	$12
❏ 5347	Olivia's Greatest Hits, Vol. 2	1982	$10
❏ 5229	Physical	1981	$10
❏ 16011	Physical	1982	$30
— Audiophile edition			
❏ 6151	Soul Kiss	1985	$10
❏ 6245	The Rumour	1988	$10
❏ 3067	Totally Hot	1978	$12
❏ 37123	Totally Hot	1981	$10
— Reissue			

MOBILE FIDELITY

❏ Jan-0040 [B]	Totally Hot	1980	$25
— Audiophile vinyl			

UNI

❏ 73117	If Not for You	1971	$100

NEXT MORNING, THE

CALLA

❏ SC-2002	The Next Morning	1972	$150

NGCUKANA, EZRA

JIVE

❏ 1250-1-J	You Think You Know Me	1989	$30

NICE, THE

Keith Emerson, later of EMERSON, LAKE AND PALMER, was in this group.

COLUMBIA SPECIAL PRODUCTS

❏ P11634	Ars Longa Vita Brevis	1973	$15
❏ P11635	The Nice	1973	$15
❏ P11633	Thoughts of Emerlist Davjack	1973	$15

IMMEDIATE

❏ Z12-52020 [B]	Ars Longa Vita Brevis	1969	$30
❏ Z12-52022 [B]	The Nice	1969	$30
❏ Z1252004 [B]	Thoughts of Emerlist Davjack	1968	$30

MERCURY

❏ SR61324	Elegy	1971	$15
❏ SR61295	Five Bridges	1970	$15
❏ SRM-2-6500	Keith Emerson with The Nice	1972	$18

SIRE

❏ SASH-3710	The Vintage Years	1975	$18

NICHOLAS, ALBERT

DELMARK

❏ DS-209	Albert Nicholas with Art Hodes' All-Star Stompers	1964	$25

GHB

❏ 64	The Albert Nicholas/John Defferary Jazztet	197?	$30

NICHOLAS, ALBERT/SIDNEY BECHET

RIVERSIDE

❏ RLP-12-216 [M]	Creole Reeds	1956	$300
— White label, blue print			
❏ RLP-12-216 [M]	Creole Reeds	1959	$300
— Blue label, microphone logo at top			

NICHOLAS, GEORGE "BIG NICK"

INDIA NAVIGATION

❏ IN-1061	Big and Warm	1985	$30
❏ IN-1066	Big Nick	1986	$30

NICHOLAS, JOSEPH "WOODEN JOE"

AMERICA MUSIC

❏ 640 [10]	A Nite at Artesian Hall With Wooden Joe	1951	$75

NICHOLAS, PAUL

RSO

❏ RS-1-3028	Paul Nicholas	1977	$15

NICHOLAS BROTHERS, THE

MERCURY

❏ MG-20355 [M]	We Do Sing, Too	1958	$30

NICHOLS, HERBIE

BETHLEHEM

❏ BCP-81 [M]	Love Gloom Cash and Love	1957	$300
❏ BCP-6028	The Bethlehem Years	197?	$35
— Distributed by RCA Victor			

BLUE NOTE

❏ BLP-1519 [M]	Herbie Nichols Trio	1956	$600
— Deep groove" version, Lexington Ave. address on label			
❏ BLP-1519 [M]	Herbie Nichols Trio	1956	$500
— Deep groove" edition, W. 63rd St. address on label			
❏ BLP-1519 [M]	Herbie Nichols Trio	1963	$500
— With "New York, USA" address on label			
❏ BST-81519 [R]	Herbie Nichols Trio	1967	$50
— With "A Division of Liberty Records" on label			
❏ BLP-1519 [M]	Herbie Nichols Trio	1971	$250
— A Division of United Artists" on label			
❏ BLP-5068 [10]	The Prophetic Herbie Nichols, Volume 1	1955	$1200
❏ BLP-5069 [10]	The Prophetic Herbie Nichols, Volume 2	1955	$1200
❏ BN-LA485-H2	Third World	1975	$40

MOSAIC

❏ MR5-118	The Complete Blue Note Recordings of Herbie Nichols	1987	$250
— Limited edition of 7,500			

NICHOLS, KEITH

STOMP OFF

❏ SOS-1159	Chitterlin' Strut	1988	$25
❏ SOS-1135	Doctors Jazz	1987	$25

NICHOLS, MIKE, AND ELAINE MAY

MERCURY

❏ OCM2200 [M]	An Evening with Mike Nichols and Elaine May	1961	$30
❏ OCS6200 [S]	An Evening with Mike Nichols and Elaine May	1961	$40
❏ MG20376 [M]	Improvisations to Music	1959	$30
❏ SR60040 [S]	Improvisations to Music	1959	$40
❏ MG20680 [M]	Nichols and May Examine Doctors	1962	$30
❏ SR60680 [S]	Nichols and May Examine Doctors	1962	$30
❏ SRM-2-628	Retrospect	1972	$25
❏ SR60997 [S]	The Best of Nichols and May	1965	$30
❏ MG20997 [M]	The Best of Nichols and May	1965	$25

NICHOLS, NICHELLE

EPIC

❏ BN26351 [S]	Down to Earth	1968	$40
❏ LN24351 [M]	Down to Earth	1968	$100
— White label promo only; in stereo cover with "Mono" sticker			

NICHOLS, RED, AND THE FIVE PENNIES

AUDIOPHILE

❏ AP-1 [M]	Red Nichols and Band	195?	$50
❏ AP-7 [M]	Syncopated Chamber Music, Volume 1	195?	$50
❏ AP-8 [M]	Syncopated Chamber Music, Volume 2	195?	$50

BRUNSWICK

❏ BL58008 [10]	Classics, Volume 1	1950	$100
❏ BL58009 [10]	Classics, Volume 2	1950	$100
❏ BL54008 [M]	For Collectors Only	1954	$50
❏ BL54047 [M]	The Red Nichols Story	1959	$50
❏ BL58027 [10]	Volume 3	1951	$100

CAPITOL

❏ T2065 [M]	Blues and Old-Time Rags	1963	$85
❏ ST2065 [S]	Blues and Old-Time Rags	1963	$40
❏ T1297 [M]	Dixieland Dinner Dance	1960	$85
❏ ST1297 [S]	Dixieland Dinner Dance	1960	$40
❏ T775 [M]	Hot Pennies	1956	$100
❏ H215 [10]	Jazz Time	1950	$175
❏ T1051 [M]	Parade of the Pennies	1958	$50
❏ ST1051 [S]	Parade of the Pennies	1958	$75
❏ T1803 [M]	The All-Time Hits of Red Nichols	1962	$85
❏ ST1803 [S]	The All-Time Hits of Red Nichols	1962	$50

CIRCLE

❏ CLP-110	Red Nichols and His Orchestra 1936	1987	$25

CONCERT DISC

❏ CS-53	Red Nichols and His Five Pennies	1961	$25

HALL OF FAME

❏ 619	Red Nichols and His Five Pennies	197?	$25

JAZZOLOGY

❏ J-90	Red Nichols and His Five Pennies	198?	$25

MARK 56

❏ 612	Red Nichols and His Five Pennies	197?	$30

MCA

❏ 1518	The Rarest Brunswick Masters	198?	$25

MOBILE FIDELITY

❏ Jan-0093 [B]	Red Nichols and the Five Pennies at Marineland	1982	$25
— Audiophile vinyl			

PAUSA

❏ 9022	All Time Hits	198?	$25

PICCADILLY

❏ 3570	Big Band Series/Original Recordings	198?	$25

STARDUST

❏ SD-122 [M]	Red Nichols and His "Five Pennies	196?	$30
❏ SDS-122 [S]	Red Nichols and His "Five Pennies	196?	$30

SUNBEAM

❏ 12	Popular Concert 1928-32	197?	$30
❏ 137	Red Nichols and His Five Pennies 1929-31	1973	$25

NICHOLS-JACOBY DREAMLAND SYNCOPATORS

STOMP OFF

❏ SOS-1150	Territory Jazz	1988	$25

NICKEL BAG, THE

KAMA SUTRA

❏ KLPS-8066 [S]	Doing Their Love Thing	1968	$30
❏ KLP-8066 [M]	Doing Their Love Thing	1968	$75
— Both stock and promo copies exist			

NICKS, STEVIE

Also see FLEETWOOD MAC; TOM PETTY AND THE HEARTBREAKERS.

Number	Title	Yr	NM
ATLANTIC			
❏ 1P-8160	TimeSpace -- The Best of Stevie Nicks	1991	$25
— Columbia House edition; only US vinyl version			
MOBILE FIDELITY			
❏ 1-121	Bella Donna	1984	$100
— Audiophile vinyl			
MODERN			
❏ MR 38-139	Bella Donna	1981	$12
❏ PR-2881 [DJ]	Reflections from the Other Side of the Mirror	1989	$25
— Promo-only interview album with script			
❏ 90479	Rock a Little	1985	$12
❏ 91245	The Other Side of the Mirror	1989	$12
❏ 90084	The Wild Heart	1983	$12

NICO
Also see THE VELVET UNDERGROUND.

Number	Title	Yr	NM
4 MEN WITH BEARDS			
❏ 4M138LP [B]	Chelsea Girl		$25
❏ 4M113LP [B]	Desertshore		$25
❏ 4M113 [B]	Desertshore	2013	$25
CLEOPATRA			
❏ 8916 [B]	All Tomorrow's Parties		$30
— picture disc			
❏ 9925 [B]	Reims Cathedral - December 13, 1974	2012	$25
ELEKTRA			
❏ EKS-74029 [B]	The Marble Index	1968	$150
❏ EKS74029 [B]	The Marble Index	1968	$150
ISLAND			
❏ ILPS-9311 [B]	The End	1975	$100
❏ ILPS9311 [B]	The End	1974	$100
PVC			
❏ 8938 [B]	Camera Obscura	1985	$30
REPRISE			
❏ RS6424 [B]	Desertshore	1970	$150

Number	Title	Yr	NM
❏ RS6424 [B]	Desert Shore	1970	$150
VERVE			
❏ V-5032 [M]	Chelsea Girl	1967	$300
❏ V6-5032 [S]	Chelsea Girl	1967	$150
❏ V5032 [M]	Chelsea Girl	1967	$300
❏ V65032 [S]	Chelsea Girl	1967	$150

NIEBLA, EDUARDO, AND ANTONIO FORCIONE

Number	Title	Yr	NM
VENTURE			
❏ 90655	Celebration	1988	$25

NIEHAUS, LENNIE

Number	Title	Yr	NM
CAMBRIA			
❏ C-1016	Shades of Dring	1981	$50
CONTEMPORARY			
❏ C-2513 [10]	Lennie Niehaus, Vol. 1: The Quintet	1954	$300
❏ C-2517 [10]	Lennie Niehaus, Vol. 2: The Octet	1954	$300
❏ C-3503 [M]	Lennie Niehaus, Vol. 3: The Octet No. 2	1955	$300
❏ C-3510 [M]	Lennie Niehaus, Vol. 4: The Quintets & Strings	1956	$300
❏ C-3524 [M]	Lennie Niehaus, Vol. 5: The Sextet	1956	$300
❏ C-3518 [M]	The Lennie Niehaus Quintet	1956	$300

Number	Title	Yr	NM
❏ C-3540 [M]	Zounds! Lennie Niehaus, Vol. 2: The Octet	1957	$300
EMARCY			
❏ MG-36118 [M]	I Swing for You	1957	$150
FANTASY			
❏ OJC-319	The Lennie Niehaus Quintet	198?	$30
MERCURY			
❏ MG-20555 [M]	I Swing for You	1960	$150
❏ SR-60123 [S]	I Swing for You	1960	$150

NIELSEN, GERTRUDE

Number	Title	Yr	NM
DECCA			
❏ DL5138 [10]	Gertrude Nielsen	1951	$50

NIEMACK, JUDY, AND SIMON WETTENHALL

Number	Title	Yr	NM
INNER CITY			
❏ IC-1115	Night Sprite	198?	$30
SEA BREEZE			
❏ 2001	By Heart	1980	$30

NIEWOOD, GERRY

Number	Title	Yr	NM
A&M			
❏ SP-3409	Slow, Hot Wind	1977	$25
HORIZON			
❏ SP-719	Gerry Niewood and Timepiece	1976	$30

NIGHT OWLS, THE

Number	Title	Yr	NM
VALMOR			
❏ 79 [M]	Twisting the Oldies	1962	$150

NIGHT RANGER
DAMN YANKEES related. Guitarist Brad Gillis was briefly in OZZY OSBOURNE's band.

Number	Title	Yr	NM
BOARDWALK			
❏ NB1-33259	Dawn Patrol	1982	$15
MCA			
❏ 5460	Dawn Patrol	1984	$10
— Reissue of Boardwalk LP			
❏ 5456	Midnight Madness	1984	$10
MCA CAMEL			
❏ 5593 [B]	7 Wishes	1985	$10
❏ 5839	Big Life	1987	$10

NIGHT SHADOWS, THE

Number	Title	Yr	NM
HOTTRAX			
❏ 1450	Invasion of the Acid Eaters	1982	$30
❏ 1430	Live at the Spot	1981	$30

Number	Title	Yr	NM
❏ 1414 [B]	The Square Root of Two	1979	$50
— Reissue of Spectrum LP			
SPECTRUM			
❏ 2001	The Square Root of Two	1968	$1000
— With neither bonus 45 nor psychedelic poster			
❏ 2001	The Square Root of Two	1968	$1100
— With bonus 45, but no poster			
❏ 2001	The Square Root of Two	1968	$1200
— With poster, but no 45			
❏ 2001	The Square Root of Two	1968	$1500
— With both 45 and poster			

NIGHTCAPS, THE

Number	Title	Yr	NM
VANDAN			
❏ VRLP-8124	Wine, Wine, Wine	196?	$175

NIGHTCRAWLERS, THE

Number	Title	Yr	NM
KAPP			
❏ KL-1520 [M]	The Little Black Egg	1967	$75
❏ KS-3520 [S]	The Little Black Egg	1967	$40

NIGHTHAWKS, THE

Number	Title	Yr	NM
ALADDIN			
❏ LP-101	Rock and Roll	197?	$250

NIGHTINGALE, MAXINE

Number	Title	Yr	NM
HIGHRISE			
❏ HR101	It's a Beautiful Thing	198?	$15
RCA VICTOR			
❏ AFL1-3528	Bittersweet	1980	$12
UNITED ARTISTS			
❏ UA-LA731-G	Night Life	1977	$15
❏ UA-LA626-G	Right Back Where We Started From	1976	$15
WINDSONG			
❏ BXL1-3404	Lead Me On	1979	$12

NIGHTWIND

Number	Title	Yr	NM
PAUSA			
❏ 7127	Casual Romance	198?	$25

NILES, JOHN JACOB

Number	Title	Yr	NM
BOONE-TOLLIVER			
❏ BTR-22 [10]	American Folk Songs to Dulcimer Accompaniment	195?	$50
❏ BTR-23 [10]	Ballads	195?	$50
RCA CAMDEN			
❏ CAL-330 [M]	50th Anniversary Album	195?	$30
❏ CAL-219 [M]	American Folk and Gambling Songs	195?	$30
❏ CAL-245 [M]	American Folk Songs	195?	$30
TRADITION			
❏ TLP-1036 [M]	An Evening with John Jacob Niles	195?	$30
❏ TLP-1023 [M]	I Wonder As I Wander	1957	$30

NILSSON

Number	Title	Yr	NM
MUSICOR			
❏ MUS-2505 [S]	Early Tymes	1977	$18
PICKWICK			
❏ SPC-3321 [B]	Rock 'N' Roll	1977	$12
RAPPLE			
❏ ABL1-0220	Son of Dracula	1974	$15
RCA VICTOR			
❏ LPM-3956 [M]	Aerial Ballet	1968	$50
❏ LSP-3956 [S]	Aerial Ballet	1968	$25
— "Stereo" on black label			
❏ LSP-3956 [S]	Aerial Ballet	1969	$18
— Orange label, non-flexible vinyl			
❏ LSP-4543	Aerial Pandemonium Ballet	1971	$15
— Collection of tracks from 3874 and 3956, remixed with, in some cases, new vocals			
❏ APL1-0097	A Little Touch of Schmilsson in the Night	1973	$15
❏ AYL1-3761	A Little Touch of Schmilsson in the Night	1980	$10
— Best Buy Series" reissue			
❏ APL1-0817	Duit On Mon Dei	1975	$15
❏ APD1-0817 [Q]	Duit On Mon Dei	1975	$30
❏ AFL1-2798	Greatest Hits	1978	$15
❏ LSP-4197	Harry	1969	$18
— Orange label, non-flexible vinyl			
❏ AFL1-2276	Knnillssonn	1977	$15
❏ LSP-4515 [B]	Nilsson Schmilsson	1971	$15
❏ APD1-0319 [Q]	Nilsson Schmilsson	1974	$30
❏ ANL1-3464	Nilsson Schmilsson	1979	$10
❏ APL1-0203	Nilsson Sings Newman	1974	$12
— Reissue of LSP-4289			
❏ LSP-4289	Nilsson Sings Newman	1970	$15
— Orange label, non-flexible vinyl			
❏ LPM-3874 [M]	Pandemonium Shadow Show	1967	$40
❏ LSP-3874 [S]	Pandemonium Shadow Show	1967	$25

Number	Title	Yr	NM
—Stereo" on black label			
❏ LSP-3874 [S]	Pandemonium Shadow Show	1969	$18
—Orange label			
❏ CPL1-0570	Pussy Cats	1974	$25
❏ APD1-0570 [Q]	Pussy Cats	1974	$40
❏ APL1-1031	Sandman	1976	$15
❏ APD1-1031 [Q]	Sandman	1976	$30
❏ SPS-33-567 [DJ]	Scatalogue	197?	$150
❏ LSP-4717	Son of Schmilsson	1972	$15
—With custom black "Victor" label			
❏ AYL1-3812	Son of Schmilsson	1980	$10
—Best Buy Series" reissue			
❏ APL1-1119	That's the Way It Is	1976	$15
❏ LSPX-1003	The Point!	1971	$15
❏ AYL1-3811	The Point!	1980	$10
—Best Buy Series" reissue			
❏ LSP-4417	The Point!	1971	$12
—Reissue of LSPX-1003			
❏ (no #) [M]	The True One	1967	$250
—Boxed set with mono copy of RCA Victor 3874, two photos, button, poster, sticker, bios			

SUNDAZED
❏ LP5468 [B]	Aerial Ballet	2014	$30
❏ LP5467 [B]	Pandemonium Shadow Show	2014	$30

TOWER
❏ T5095 [M]	Spotlight on Nilsson	1967	$25
❏ ST5095 [S]	Spotlight on Nilsson	1967	$25
❏ DT5165 [R]	Spotlight on Nilsson	1969	$18

NIMMONS, PHIL

CLEF
❏ MGC-753 [M]	The Canadian Scene Via Phil Nimmons	1955	$0
—Canceled; issued on Verve 8025			

VERVE
❏ MGV-8376 [M]	Nimmons 'n' Nine	1960	$150
❏ MGVS-6153 [S]	Nimmons 'n' Nine	1960	$0
—Canceled			
❏ V-8376 [M]	Nimmons 'n' Nine	1961	$25
❏ MGV-8025 [M]	The Canadian Scene Via Phil Nimmons	1957	$175
❏ V-8025 [M]	The Canadian Scene Via Phil Nimmons	1961	$25

NIMOY, LEONARD

CAEDMON
❏ TC-1526	Green Hills of Earth	1977	$30
❏ TC-1479	The Illustrated Man	1976	$30
❏ TC-1466	The Martian Chronicles	1976	$30
❏ TC-1520	War of the Worlds	1977	$30

DOT
❏ DLP3794 [M]	Mr. Spock's Music from Outer Space	1967	$50

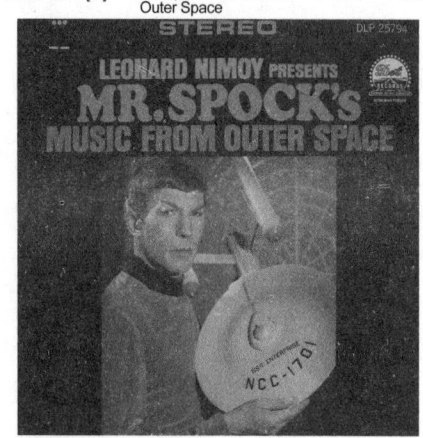

❏ DLP25794 [S]	Mr. Spock's Music from Outer Space	1967	$100
❏ DLP25966	The New World of Leonard Nimoy	1969	$75
❏ DLP25910	The Touch of Leonard Nimoy	1969	$75
❏ DLP3883 [M]	The Way I Feel	1968	$100
—Stereo cover with "Monaural" sticker; label is black stock copy			
❏ DLP25883 [S]	The Way I Feel	1968	$75
❏ DLP3835 [M]	Two Sides of Leonard Nimoy	1968	$50
❏ DLP25835 [S]	Two Sides of Leonard Nimoy	1968	$100

JRT
❏ 0(# unknown)	The Mysterious Golem	1982	$40

PARAMOUNT
❏ PAS-1030	Outer Space/Inner Mind	1970	$50

PICKWICK
❏ SPC-3199	Space Odyssey	197?	$50

SEARS
❏ SPS-491	Leonard Nimoy	196?	$100

NINE INCH NAILS
Industrial rock vehicle for Trent Reznor.

NOTHING
Number	Title	Yr	NM
❏ 1169701 [S]	The Downward Spiral	2008	$30

NOTHING/INTERSCOPE
❏ 490473	The Fragile	1999	$150
—Also called "Halo Fourteen			
❏ 490744	Things Falling Apart	2000	$25
—Also called "Halo Sixteen			
❏ B0004553-01	With Teeth	2005	$30

NOTHING/TVT
❏ 2610	Pretty Hate Machine	1990	$25
—Also called "Halo Two			

NOTHING/TVT/INTERSCOPE
❏ DMD1903 [EP]	Broken	1992	$40
—Also called "Halo Five"; promo-only vinyl release; six songs on one side of a 12-inch record and two bonus tracks, "Physical (You're So)" and "Suck," on a bonus 7-inch record			
❏ 96093 [EP]	Fixed	1992	$40
—Also called "Halo Six			
❏ PR5509 [DJ]	The Downward Spiral	1994	$75
—Also called "Halo Eight"; vinyl is promo only			

RYKODISC
❏ RLP10386-1	Pretty Hate Machine	2006	$25
—Reissue of TVT album of the same title			

999

POLYDOR
❏ PD1-6256	Biggest Prize in Sport	1980	$14
❏ PD1-6307	Biggest Tour in Sport	1980	$14
❏ PD1-6322	Concrete	1981	$15

PVC
❏ 7999 [B]	High Energy Plan	1979	$15

1910 FRUITGUM COMPANY

BUDDAH
❏ BDS-5022	1,2,3 Red Light	1968	$30
❏ BDS-5027	Goody, Goody Gumdrops	1969	$30
❏ BDS-5043	Hard Ride	1969	$30
❏ BDS-5036	Indian Giver	1969	$30
❏ BDS-5057 [B]	Juiciest Fruitgum	1970	$30
❏ BDM-5010 [M]	Simon Says	1968	$100
—Appears to be promo only; "Mono" sticker on stereo cover			
❏ BDS-5010 [S]	Simon Says	1968	$30

NINETEENTH WHOLE, THE

EASTBOUND
❏ EB-9003	Smilin'	1970	$250

---

94 EAST
Early recordings by PRINCE.

HOT PINK
❏ HLP3223	Minneapolis Genius -- 94 East	1977	$40
—Deduct 25% for cut-outs			

---

98 DEGREES

MOTOWN
❏ 3145307961	98 Degrees	1997	$18

NIRVANA
The 1990s grunge group. Dave Grohl now leads FOO FIGHTERS and is also in THEM CROOKED VULTURES.

DGC
❏ DGC225105 [B]	From The Muddy Banks Of The Wishkah	2016	$35
❏ 25105	From the Muddy Banks of the Wishkah	1996	$25
❏ 24504	Incesticide	1992	$30
—All copies on blue swirl vinyl			

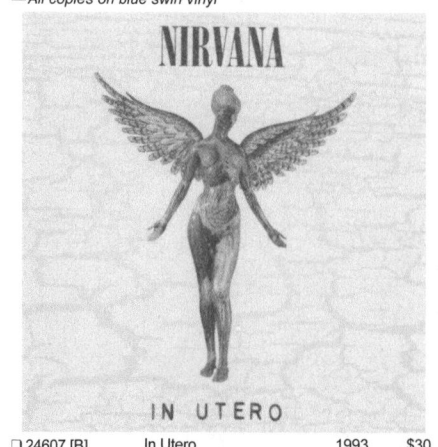

❏ 24607 [B]	In Utero	1993	$30

Number	Title	Yr	NM
—All copies on clear vinyl			
❏ 24727	MTV Unplugged in New York	1994	$25
—White vinyl version			
❏ 24727 [B]	MTV Unplugged in New York	1994	$40
—Black vinyl, issued simultaneously with white vinyl version; color of vinyl cannot be determined without opening the shrink wrap			
❏ 24425 [B]	Nevermind	1991	$30
—All copies on black vinyl			

MOBILE FIDELITY
❏ 1-258	Nevermind	1996	$300
—Audiophile vinyl			

SUB POP
❏ SP34	Bleach	1989	$250
—First 1,000 were pressed on white vinyl			
❏ SP34	Bleach	1989	$250
—Second 1,000 were pressed on black vinyl and include a poster			
❏ SP34 [B]	Bleach	1989	$75
—Red vinyl			
❏ SP34 [B]	Bleach	1989	$80
—Pink vinyl			
❏ SP34	Bleach	1989	$175
—Red and white swirl vinyl			
❏ SP34 [B]	Bleach	1989	$80
—Purple vinyl			
❏ 70034 [B]	Bleach	2000	$30
—Reissue			

NIRVANA (1)
The 1960s psychedelic group.

BELL
❏ 6024 [B]	All of Us	1969	$75
❏ 6015 [B]	The Story of Simon Simopath	1968	$75

NIRVANA (2)

METROMEDIA
❏ MD-1018	Nirvana	1970	$30

NISTICO, SAL

BEE HIVE
❏ BH-7006	Neo/Nistico	1980	$30

JAZZLAND
❏ JLP-66 [M]	Heavyweights	1962	$30
❏ JLP-966 [S]	Heavyweights	1962	$40

RIVERSIDE
❏ RLP-457 [M]	Comin' On Up	1963	$175
❏ RS-9457 [S]	Comin' On Up	1963	$175

NITE-LITERS, THE

RCA VICTOR
❏ LSP-4580	Instrumental Directions	1972	$18
❏ LSP-4493	Morning, Noon & The Nite-Liters	1971	$18

NITTY GRITTY DIRT BAND

LIBERTY
❏ LST-7611	Alive	1969	$30
❏ LMAS-5553	All the Good Times	1981	$10
❏ LO-974	An American Dream	1981	$10
❏ LKCL-670	Dirt, Silver and Gold	1981	$15
❏ LT-51146	Let's Go	1982	$12
❏ LT-1042	Make a Little Magic	1981	$10
❏ LST-7540	Rare Junk	1968	$30
❏ LRP-3516 [M]	Ricochet	1967	$30
❏ LST-7516 [S]	Ricochet	1967	$30
❏ LWB-184	Stars and Stripes Forever	1981	$12
❏ LRP-3501 [M]	The Nitty Gritty Dirt Band	1967	$30
❏ LST-7501 [S]	The Nitty Gritty Dirt Band	1967	$30
❏ LST-7642 [DJ]	Uncle Charlie and His Dog Teddy	1970	$120
—Leatherette promo pack with LP, two other discs, photos, booklet			
❏ LST-7642 [B]	Uncle Charlie and His Dog Teddy	1970	$30
—Standard issue of LP			
❏ LTAO-7642	Uncle Charlie and His Dog Teddy	1981	$10
❏ LWCL-51158	Will the Circle Be Unbroken	1986	$18

MCA
❏ 6407	The Rest of the Dream	1990	$15

UNITED ARTISTS
❏ UAS-5553	All the Good Times	1972	$18
❏ UA-LA974-H	An American Dream	1979	$12
❏ UA-LA670-L3	Dirt, Silver and Gold	1976	$25
❏ UA-LA469-G	Dream	1975	$15
❏ LW-1106	Jealousy	1981	$12
❏ LT-1042	Make a Little Magic	1980	$12
❏ UA-LA184-J2	Stars and Stripes Forever	1974	$18
❏ UA-LA830-H	The Chicken Chronicles	1978	$12
❏ UA-LA854-H	The Dirt Band	1978	$12
❏ UAS-9801	Will the Circle Be Unbroken	1972	$30

Number	Title	Yr	NM
UNIVERSAL			
❑ UVL2-12500	Will the Circle Be Unbroken, Volume Two	1989	$25
WARNER BROS.			
❑ 25573	Hold On	1987	$10
❑ 25830	More Great Dirt: The Best of the Nitty Gritty Dirt Band, Vol. 2	1989	$12
❑ 25304	Partners, Brothers and Friends	1985	$10
❑ 25113	Plain Dirt Fashion	1984	$10
❑ 25382	Twenty Years of Dirt: The Best of the Nitty Gritty Dirt Band	1986	$10
❑ 25722	Workin' Band	1988	$10

NITZINGER
BLOODROCK related.

Number	Title	Yr	NM
20TH CENTURY			
❑ T-518 [B]	Live Better Electrically	1976	$15
CAPITOL			
❑ SMAS-11091	Nitzinger	1972	$25
❑ SMAS-11122	One Foot in History	1973	$25

NITZSCHE, JACK

Number	Title	Yr	NM
REPRISE			
❑ R6200 [M]	Chopin '66	1966	$30
❑ RS6200 [S]	Chopin '66	1966	$30
❑ R6115 [M]	Dance to the Hits of the Beatles	1964	$50
❑ RS6115 [S]	Dance to the Hits of the Beatles	1964	$75
❑ MS2092	St. Giles Cripplegate	1972	$25
❑ R6101 [M]	The Lonely Surfer	1963	$85
❑ R9-6101 [S]	The Lonely Surfer	1963	$175
— Pink, gold and green label			
❑ RS6101 [S]	The Lonely Surfer	197?	$25
— With only "r:" logo on all-orange (tan) label			

NIX, DON

Number	Title	Yr	NM
CREAM			
❑ 1001	Gone Too Long	1979	$12
ELEKTRA			
❑ EKS-74101	Living by the Days	1971	$15
ENTERPRISE			
❑ ENS-1032	Hobos, Heroes and Street Corner Clowns	1974	$15

NIXON, MOJO, AND SKID ROPER

Number	Title	Yr	NM
ENIGMA			
❑ ST-73272	Bo-Day-Shus!!!	1987	$15
RESTLESS			
❑ 72127	Frenzy	1986	$15
❑ 72185 [EP]	Get Out of My Way	1986	$12
— Clear vinyl			
❑ 72056	Mojo Nixon and Skid Roper	1985	$15

NIXON, NICK

Number	Title	Yr	NM
MERCURY			
❑ SRM-1-1175	Nick Nixon	1977	$12

NKRUMAH, KWAME

Number	Title	Yr	NM
COLUMBIA			
❑ CS9863	Ninth Son	1969	$30

NO DOUBT
Featuring Gwen Stefani.

Number	Title	Yr	NM
TRAUMA/INTERSCOPE			
❑ 069-490441-1	Return of Saturn	2000	$18
❑ 069-493195-1	Rock Steady	2001	$40
❑ 92580-1 [B]	Tragic Kingdom	1995	$150

NOACK, EDDIE

Number	Title	Yr	NM
WIDE WORLD			
❑ 2001	Remembering Jimmie Rodgers	1970	$30

NOBLE, NICK

Number	Title	Yr	NM
COLUMBIA			
❑ CS9810	I'm Gonna Make You Love Me	1969	$18
LIBERTY			
❑ LRP-3302 [M]	Relax	1963	$25
❑ LST-7302 [M]	Relax	1963	$30
MERCURY			
❑ MG-20182 [M]	You Don't Know What Love Is	1956	$30
WING			
❑ MGW-12184 [M]	Music for Lovers	196?	$18

NOBLES, CLIFF

Number	Title	Yr	NM
MOON SHOT			
❑ 601	Pony the Horse	1969	$40
PHIL-L.A. OF SOUL			
❑ 4001	The Horse	1968	$75

NOCK, MIKE

Number	Title	Yr	NM
ECM			
❑ 1220	Ondas	1981	$25
IAI			
❑ 373851	Almanac	197?	$35
TIMELESS			
❑ 313	In Out and Around	1978	$30
TOMATO			
❑ TOM-8009	Climbing	1979	$35

NOCTURNES, THE

Number	Title	Yr	NM
MGM			
❑ E-154 [10]	Melodies from Far Away Places	195?	$75

NOEL (1)

Number	Title	Yr	NM
4TH & B'WAY			
❑ 4009	Noel	1988	$12

NO/GAP JAZZ BAND, THE

Number	Title	Yr	NM
NO/GAP			
❑ 7444001	Live	197?	$35
❑ 7444002	No/Gap Jazz Band	197?	$35

NOGUEZ, JACKY

Number	Title	Yr	NM
JAMIE			
❑ JLP-3007 [M]	Chow Chow Bambina	1959	$25
❑ JLPS-3007 [S]	Chow Chow Bambina	1959	$30
❑ JLP-3013 [M]	Dance Along with Jacky Noguez	1960	$25
❑ JLPS-3013 [S]	Dance Along with Jacky Noguez	1960	$30
❑ JLP-3012 [M]	Jacky Noguez	1960	$25
❑ JLPS-3012 [S]	Jacky Noguez	1960	$30

NOLAND, TERRY

Number	Title	Yr	NM
BRUNSWICK			
❑ BL54041 [M]	Terry Noland	1958	$600
— Buddy Holly plays guitar			

NOONE, JIMMIE

Number	Title	Yr	NM
BRUNSWICK			
❑ BL58006 [10]	The Apex Club Orchestra	1950	$50
MCA			
❑ 1313	Jimmie Noone and Earl Hines at the Apex Club	198?	$25

NOONE, JIMMY, JR.

Number	Title	Yr	NM
STOMP OFF			
❑ SOS-1121	Jimmy Remembers Jimmie	1986	$25

NOONE, PETER

Number	Title	Yr	NM
JOHNSTON			
❑ ARZ37369	One of the Glory Boys	1982	$12

NORDINE, KEN

Number	Title	Yr	NM
BLUE THUMB			
❑ BTS-33	How Are Things in Your Town?	1971	$75
❑ BTS-35	Ken Nordine	1972	$50
DECCA			
❑ DL8550 [M]	Concert in the Sky	1957	$175
DOT			
❑ DLP-3115 [M]	Love Words	1958	$250
❑ DLP-25115 [S]	Love Words	1959	$300
❑ DLP-3142 [M]	My Baby	1959	$150
❑ DLP-25142 [S]	My Baby	1959	$200
❑ DLP-3196 [M]	Next!	1959	$150

Number	Title	Yr	NM
❑ DLP-25196 [S]	Next!	1959	$200
❑ DLP-3096 [M]	Son of Word Jazz	1958	$150
❑ DLP-25096 [S]	Son of Word Jazz	1959	$300
❑ DLP-25880	The Best of Word Jazz	1968	$100

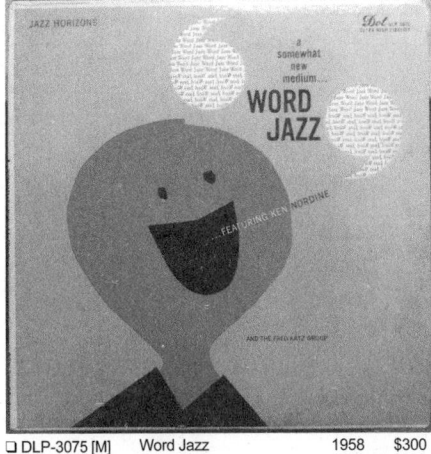

Number	Title	Yr	NM
❑ DLP-3075 [M]	Word Jazz	1958	$300
❑ DLP-25075 [S]	Word Jazz	1959	$300
❑ DLP-3301 [M]	Word Jazz, Vol. 2	1960	$300
❑ DLP-25301 [S]	Word Jazz, Vol. 2	1960	$300
FM			
❑ 304 [M]	Passion In the Desert	1963	$30
❑ S-304 [S]	Passion In the Desert	1963	$40
HAMILTON			
❑ HL-102 [M]	The Voice of Love	1964	$30
❑ HL-12102 [S]	The Voice of Love	1964	$40
PHILIPS			
❑ PHM200224 [M]	Colors	1966	$100
❑ PHS600224 [S]	Colors	1966	$150
❑ PHM200258 [M]	Ken Nordine Does Robert Shure's "Twink	1967	$30
❑ PHS600258 [S]	Ken Nordine Does Robert Shure's "Twink	1967	$40
SNAIL			
❑ SR-1003	Grandson of Word Jazz	1987	$30
❑ SR-1001	Stare with Your Ears	1979	$30
VERSION			
❑ VLP101 [10]	Passion In the Desert	1957	$250

NORMA JEAN

Number	Title	Yr	NM
HARMONY			
❑ HL7363 [M]	Country's Favorite	1966	$25
❑ HS11163 [R]	Country's Favorite	1966	$18
RCA CAMDEN			
❑ CAL-2218 [M]	Heaven Help the Working Girl	1968	$40
❑ CAS-2218 [S]	Heaven Help the Working Girl	1968	$18
❑ CAS-2511	It Wasn't God Who Made Honky Tonk Angels	1972	$18
RCA VICTOR			
❑ LSP-4341	Another Man Loved Me Last Night	1970	$25
❑ LSP-3977	Body and Mind	1968	$30
❑ LSP-4146	Country Giants	1969	$30
❑ LPM-3910 [M]	Heaven's Just a Prayer Away	1967	$50
❑ LSP-3910 [S]	Heaven's Just a Prayer Away	1967	$30
❑ LSP-4745	I Guess That Comes From Being Poor	1972	$25
❑ LSP-4446	It's Time for Norma Jean	1970	$30
❑ LPM-3836 [M]	Jackson Ain't a Very Big Town	1967	$30
❑ LSP-3836 [S]	Jackson Ain't a Very Big Town	1967	$30
❑ LPM-2961 [M]	Let's Go All the Way	1964	$30
❑ LSP-2961 [S]	Let's Go All the Way	1964	$30
❑ LSP-4060	Love's a Woman's Job	1968	$30
❑ LSP-4510	Norma Jean	1971	$25
❑ LSP-4587	Norma Jean Sings	1971	$25
❑ LPM-3664 [M]	Norma Jean Sings a Tribute to Kitty Wells	1966	$30
❑ LSP-3664 [S]	Norma Jean Sings a Tribute to Kitty Wells	1966	$30
❑ LPM-3700 [M]	Norma Jean Sings Porter Wagoner	1967	$30
❑ LSP-3700 [S]	Norma Jean Sings Porter Wagoner	1967	$30
❑ LPM-3541 [M]	Please Don't Hurt Me	1966	$30
❑ LSP-3541 [S]	Please Don't Hurt Me	1966	$30
❑ LPM-3449 [M]	Pretty Miss Norma Jean	1965	$30
❑ LSP-3449 [S]	Pretty Miss Norma Jean	1965	$30
❑ LSP-4691	Thank You for Loving Me	1972	$25
❑ LSP-4227	The Best of Norma Jean	1969	$30
❑ APL1-0170	The Only Way to Hold Your Man	1973	$18

Number	Title	Yr	NM

NORMAN, GENE, GROUP
GNP CRESCENDO
| ❏ GNP-2015 [M] | Dylan Jazz | 1965 | $25 |
| ❏ GNPS-2015 [S] | Dylan Jazz | 1965 | $30 |

NORMAN, JESSYE
PHILIPS
| ❏ 420180-1 | Christmastide | 1987 | $12 |
| —Pressed in Europe for export | | | |

NORMAN, LARRY
A founding father of Christian rock. Also see PEOPLE.
AB
| ❏ 777 | Streams of White Light Into Darkened Corners | 1977 | $30 |
CAPITOL
| ❏ ST-446 | Upon This Rock | 1970 | $30 |
IMPACT

| ❏ 3121 [B] | Upon This Rock | 197? | $25 |
MGM
| ❏ SE-4942 | So Long Ago the Garden | 1974 | $40 |
ONE WAY
❏ 4847	Bootleg	1972	$40
—Gatefold cover			
❏ 900	Bootleg	1972	$30
—Regular cover			
❏ 7397	Street Level	1971	$30
PHYDEAUX
| ❏ BONE-777-6 | Almost So Long Ago the Garden | 1981 | $18 |
| ❏ ARF-777-6 | Almost So Long Ago the Garden | 1984 | $15 |
SOLID ROCK
| ❏ 2001 [B] | In Another Land | 1976 | $18 |
| ❏ 2007 | Something New Under the Son | 1981 | $18 |
STREET LEVEL
❏ ROCK-888-5	Only Visiting This Planet	1978	$18
—Gatefold cover			
❏ ROCK-888-5	Only Visiting This Planet	1978	$15
—Regular cover			
VERVE
❏ V6-5092	Only Visiting This Planet	1973	$30
—Tri-fold cover			
❏ V6-5092	Only Visiting This Planet	1973	$40
—Gatefold cover			

NORRIS, WALTER, AND ALADAR PAGE
INNER CITY
| ❏ IC-3028 | Synchronicity | 1979 | $35 |

NORRIS, WALTER, AND GEORGE MRAZ
ENJA
| ❏ 2044 | Drifting | 197? | $35 |

NORRIS, WALTER
ENJA
| ❏ 2044 | Drifting | 198? | $30 |
PROGRESSIVE
| ❏ PRO-7039 | Stepping on Cracks | 198? | $30 |

NORTH, FREDDIE
MANKIND
| ❏ 205 [B] | Cuss the Wind | 1973 | $40 |
| ❏ 204 | Friend | 1971 | $30 |

NORTH, JAY
KEM
| ❏ 27 | Look Who's Singing! | 1960 | $150 |

NORTHCOTT, TOM
UNI
| ❏ 73108 | Upside Downside | 1971 | $25 |

NORTHERN
GUINNESS
| ❏ GNS36060 [B] | Lady Luck | 1977 | $25 |

NORTHERN FRONT
KADER
| ❏ 0(# unknown) | Furniture Store | 1975 | $150 |

NORVO, RED, AND ROSS TOMPKINS
CONCORD JAZZ
| ❏ CJ-90 | Red Norvo and Ross Tompkins | 1979 | $25 |

NORVO, RED
ALLEGRO
| ❏ 1739 [M] | Red Norvo Jazz Trio | 195? | $40 |
BLUEBIRD
| ❏ 6278-1-RB | Just a Mood | 1987 | $25 |
CAPITOL
| ❏ T616 [M] | Classics in Jazz | 1955 | $175 |
CHARLIE PARKER
| ❏ PLP-833 [M] | Pretty Is the Only Way To Fly | 1962 | $30 |
| ❏ PLP-833S [S] | Pretty Is the Only Way To Fly | 1962 | $30 |
CIRCLE
| ❏ 3 | Red Norvo and His Orchestra 1938 | 198? | $25 |
COMMODORE
| ❏ FL-20023 [10] | Town Hall Concert, Volume 1 | 1952 | $175 |
| ❏ FL-20027 [10] | Town Hall Concert, Volume 2 | 1952 | $175 |
CONTEMPORARY
| ❏ C-3534 [M] | Music To Listen To Red Norvo By | 1957 | $300 |
| ❏ S-7009 [S] | Music To Listen To Red Norvo By | 1959 | $300 |
CONTINENTAL
| ❏ C-16005 [M] | Mainstream Jazz | 1962 | $35 |
| ❏ CS-16005 [S] | Mainstream Jazz | 1962 | $25 |
DECCA
| ❏ DL5501 [10] | Dancing on the Ceiling | 1953 | $175 |
DIAL
| ❏ LP-903 [M] | Fabulous Jazz Session | 1951 | $600 |
DISCOVERY
❏ DL-3012 [10]	Red Norvo Trio	1950	$300
❏ DL-3018 [10]	Red Norvo Trio	1952	$300
❏ DL-4005 [M]	Red Norvo Trio, Volume 1	1951	$300
DOT
| ❏ DLP-3126 [M] | Windjammer City Style | 1958 | $200 |
| ❏ DLP-25126 [S] | Windjammer City Style | 1958 | $100 |
EMARCY
| ❏ MG-26002 [10] | Improvisation | 1954 | $250 |
ENCORE
| ❏ EE-22009 | Original 1933-38 Recordings | 1968 | $35 |
EPIC
| ❏ LN3128 [M] | Red Norvo and His All Stars | 1955 | $150 |
FAMOUS DOOR
❏ 116	Red Norvo in New York	197?	$30
❏ 108	Second Time Around	197?	$30
❏ 105	Vibes A La Red	197?	$30
FANTASY
❏ OJC-155	Music To Listen To Red Norvo By	198?	$25
❏ 3-12 [10]	Red Norvo Trio	1953	$175
—Colored vinyl			
❏ 3-12 [10]	Red Norvo Trio	1953	$150
—Black vinyl			
❏ 3-19 [M]	Red Norvo Trio	1955	$100
—Red vinyl			
❏ 3-19 [M]	Red Norvo Trio	195?	$40
—Black vinyl			
❏ OJC-641	Red Norvo Trio	1991	$30
❏ 3218 [M]	Red Norvo With Strings	1956	$175
—Red vinyl			
❏ 3218 [M]	Red Norvo With Strings	195?	$40
—Black vinyl			
❏ 3244 [M]	The Red Norvo Trios	1957	$100
—Red vinyl			
❏ 3244 [M]	The Red Norvo Trios	195?	$40
—Black vinyl			
LIBERTY
| ❏ LRP-3035 [M] | Ad Lib | 1957 | $40 |
| ❏ LJH-6012 [M] | Vibe-rations In Hi-Fi | 1956 | $50 |

MERCURY
| ❏ 830966-1 | Improvisations | 1987 | $25 |
PAUSA
| ❏ 9015 | All Star Sessions | 198? | $25 |
PRESTIGE
| ❏ 24108 | The Trios | 198? | $35 |
RAVE
| ❏ 101 [M] | Red Norvo Quintet | 1956 | $100 |
RCA VICTOR
❏ LPM-1420 [M]	Hi Five	1957	$40
❏ LSP-1711 [S]	Red Norvo In Stereo	1958	$50
❏ LPM-1729 [M]	Red Plays the Blues	1958	$40
❏ LSP-1729 [S]	Red Plays the Blues	1958	$50
❏ LPM-1449 [M]	Some of My Favorites	1957	$40
REFERENCE RECORDINGS
| ❏ RR-8 | The Forward Look | 1983 | $25 |
| ❏ RR-8-UHGR | The Forward Look | 1983 | $40 |
RONDO-LETTE
| ❏ A-28 [M] | Red Norvo Trio | 1958 | $30 |
SAVOY
| ❏ MG-12093 [M] | Midnight On Cloud 69 | 1956 | $100 |
| ❏ MG-12088 [M] | Move! | 1956 | $100 |
SAVOY JAZZ
| ❏ SJL-2212 | Red Norvo Trio | 197? | $30 |
SPOTLITE
| ❏ 107 | Fabulous Jam | 197? | $25 |
STASH
| ❏ ST-230 | Just Friends | 1984 | $25 |
STEREO RECORDS
| ❏ S-7009 [S] | Music To Listen To Red Norvo By | 1958 | $50 |
TAMPA
❏ TP-35 [M]	Norvo Naturally	1957	$250
—Colored vinyl			
❏ TP-35 [M]	Norvo Naturally	1958	$175
—Black vinyl			
TIME-LIFE
| ❏ STL-J-14 | Giants of Jazz | 1980 | $50 |
X
| ❏ LXA-3034 [M] | Red's Blue Room | 1955 | $175 |
XANADU
| ❏ 199 | Time in His Hands | 198? | $25 |

NORVO, RED/CAL TJADER
JAZZTONE
| ❏ J-1277 [M] | Delightfully Light | 195? | $40 |

NORVO, RED/GEORGIE AULD
GOLDEN ERA
| ❏ 15016 [M] | The Great Dance Bands, Vol. 2 | 195? | $40 |

NORWOOD, DOROTHY
I AM
| ❏ 4002-1-M | A Wonderful Day | 1990 | $18 |
JEWEL
| ❏ 0134 | He's a Friend | 1978 | $18 |
SAVOY
❏ SL-14598	Answer Me Dear Jesus	198?	$18
❏ MG14190 [M]	Bereaved Child	196?	$30
❏ MG14244	Brother Came Too Late	196?	$30
❏ MG14309	Come By Here	1973	$30
❏ MG14140 [M]	Denied Mother	196?	$30
❏ MG14266	Despondent Wife	196?	$30
❏ SL-14515	Faithful Daughter	198?	$18
❏ SL-14557	God Can	198?	$18
❏ MG14127 [M]	He Will Never Let Go My Hand	196?	$30
❏ MG14259	Jesus Picked Up the Pieces	196?	$30
❏ MG14083 [M]	Johnny and Jesus	196?	$30
❏ MG14217	Just in Time	196?	$30
❏ MG14295	Just the Two of Us	1972	$30
—With Lois Snead			
❏ SL-14630	Look What They've Done to My Child	198?	$18
❏ MG14157 [M]	Soldier from Vietnam	196?	$30
❏ SL-14651	Somebody Here	198?	$18
—With the Allen Darling Ensemble			
❏ MG14107 [M]	The Bell Didn't Toll	196?	$30
❏ MG14169 [M]	The Dorothy Norwood Singers	196?	$30
❏ SL-7042	The Mountain Climbers	1979	$25
❏ MG14093 [M]	The Old Lady's House	196?	$30
❏ MG14175 [M]	The Singing Slave	196?	$30
❏ MG14212	The Stories Behind the Songs	196?	$30
❏ MG14282	Three Little Pigs	197?	$30
—With Lois Snead			
❏ SL-14716	Up Where We Belong	1983	$18
WORD
| ❏ WR-8420 | Mother's Son | 1988 | $12 |

Number	Title	Yr	NM

NOSY PARKER
(NO LABEL)

| 0(no cat #) | Nosy Parker | 1975 | $300 |

NOTES FROM THE UNDERGROUND
VANGUARD

| VSD-6502 | Notes from the Underground | 1970 | $100 |

NOTHING, CHARLIE
TAKOMA

| C-1015 | The Psychedelic Saxophone of Charlie Nothing | 1967 | $75 |

NOTO, SAM
XANADU

127	Act One	1976	$30
103	Entrance!	1975	$15
144	Notes to You	1977	$30
168	Noto-Riety	198?	$25

NOVA LOCAL, THE
DECCA

| DL74977 | Nova 1 | 1968 | $80 |
| DL4997 [M] | Nova 1 | 1968 | $175 |

NOVAC, JERRY
EMBRYO

| 527 | The 5th Word | 1970 | $30 |

NOVELLS, THE
MOTHER'S

| MLPS-73 | A Happening | 1968 | $50 |

NOW CREATIVE ARTS JAZZ ENSEMBLE, THE
ARHOOLIE

| 8002 | Now | 1969 | $25 |

NOZERO, LARRY
STRATA

| 109-75 | Time | 1975 | $25 |

NRBQ
ANNUIT COEPTIS

| 1001/2 | Scraps/Workshop | 1976 | $25 |

— *Reissue of Kama Sutra LPs*

BEARSVILLE

| 23817 | Grooves in Orbit | 1983 | $12 |

COLUMBIA

| CS9858 | NRBQ | 1969 | $30 |

— *360 Sound Stereo" label*

| CS9858 | NRBQ | 1970 | $15 |

— *Orange label*

| PC9858 | NRBQ | 198? | $10 |

— *Budget-line reissue*

KAMA SUTRA

| KSBS-2045 [B] | Scraps | 1972 | $30 |
| KSBS-2065 [B] | Workshop | 1973 | $40 |

MERCURY

| SRM-1-3712 | NRBQ at Yankee Stadium | 1978 | $18 |
| 824462-1 | NRBQ at Yankee Stadium | 1984 | $12 |

— *Reissue*

RED ROOSTER

| 101 | All Hopped Up | 1977 | $18 |

ROUNDER

3029	All Hopped Up	1979	$15
EP-2501 [EP]	Christmas Wish	1985	$15
3108	God Bless Us All	1988	$12
3030	Kick Me Hard	1979	$15
3109	Live! Diggin' Uncle Q	1988	$12
3098	Lou and the Q	1986	$12

— *With pro wrestler Captain Lou Albano*

3090	RC Cola & a Moon Pie	1987	$12
3055	Scraps	1982	$12
3066	Tapdancin' Bats	1983	$12
3048	Tiddlywinks	1980	$15

SUNDAZED

| LP-5162 | Atsa My Band | 2003 | $18 |
| LP-5184 | Scraps | 2007 | $18 |

— *Reissue of Kama Sutra 2045*

| LP-5185 | Workshop | 2007 | $18 |

— *Reissue of Kama Sutra 2065*

VIRGIN

| 91291 | Wild Weekend | 1989 | $12 |

NU SHOOZ
ATLANTIC

| 81647 | Poolside | 1986 | $12 |
| 81804 | Told U So | 1988 | $12 |

NUBIN, KATI BELL
VERVE

| MGV-8372 [M] | Soul, Soul Searchin' | 1960 | $0 |

— *Canceled*

| MGV-3004 [M] | Soul, Soul Searchin' | 1960 | $100 |
| MGVS-6147 [S] | Soul, Soul Searchin' | 1960 | $0 |

— *Canceled*

| V-3004 [M] | Soul, Soul Searchin' | 1961 | $40 |
| V6-3004 [S] | Soul, Soul Searchin' | 1961 | $50 |

NUCLEUS
MAINSTREAM

| S-6120 | Nucleus | 1969 | $50 |

NUDIE
NUDIE

| 3203 | Nudie and His Mandolin | 196? | $40 |

NUGENT, TED
Also see THE AMBOY DUKES; ST. PARADISE. One-time vocalist Charlie Huhn is now in FOGHAT.

ATLANTIC

81812	If You Can't Lick 'Em... Lick 'Em	1988	$12
81632	Little Miss Dangerous	1986	$12
SD19365	Nugent	1982	$12
80125	Penetrator	1984	$12

EPIC

| JE34700 | Cat Scratch Fever | 1977 | $15 |

— *Orange label*

| PE34700 [B] | Cat Scratch Fever | 198? | $10 |

— *Reissue with dark blue label and bar code*

| KE235069 | Double Live Gonzo! | 1978 | $18 |

— *Orange labels*

| PE34121 [B] | Free-for-All | 1976 | $15 |

— *Orange label*

| PEQ34121 [Q] | Free-for-All | 1976 | $30 |
| PE34121 | Free-for-All | 1979 | $10 |

— *Reissue with dark blue label and bar code*

| FE37667 | Great Gonzos! The Best of Ted Nugent | 1981 | $12 |
| PE37667 | Great Gonzos! The Best of Ted Nugent | 198? | $10 |

— *Budget-line reissue*

| FE37084 | Intensities in 10 Cities | 1981 | $12 |
| PE37084 | Intensities in 10 Cities | 198? | $10 |

— *Budget-line reissue*

FE36404	Scream Dream	1980	$12
FE36000	State of Shock	1979	$12
AS99-607 [PD]	State of Shock	1979	$30

— *Promo-only picture disc*

| PE36000 [B] | State of Shock | 198? | $10 |

— *Budget-line reissue*

| PE33692 | Ted Nugent | 1975 | $15 |

— *Orange label*

| PE33692 | Ted Nugent | 1979 | $10 |

— *Reissue with dark blue label and bar code*

| FE35551 | Weekend Warriors | 1978 | $15 |

— *Orange label*

| PE35551 [B] | Weekend Warriors | 198? | $10 |

— *Reissue with dark blue label and bar code*

NUMAN, GARY
ATCO

SD 38-143	Dance	1981	$12
90014 [B]	I, Assassin	1982	$15
SD 38-117	Replicas	1979	$12

— *With Tubeway Army*

| SD 32-103 | Telekon | 1980 | $12 |

| SD 38-120 [B] | The Pleasure Principle | 1979 | $15 |
| SD 32-106 | Tubeway Army: The First Album | 1980 | $12 |

— *First American issue of U.K. debut*

I.R.S.

| 82003 | New Anger | 1988 | $12 |

NUMA

| 1005 | Strange Charm | 1985 | $12 |

NUNEZ, FLIP
CATALYST

| 7603 | My Own Time and Space | 1976 | $30 |

NUNS, THE
BOMP!

| 4010 [B] | The Nuns | 1980 | $30 |

POSH BOY

| 105 [B] | The Nuns | 1980 | $30 |

— *Same album as the Bomp! release*

NUROCK, KIRK
LABOR

| 13 | Natural Sound | 1981 | $30 |

NUTTER, MAYF
CAPITOL

| ST-11194 | The First Batch | 1973 | $15 |

GNP CRESCENDO

| GNPS-2104 | Goin' Skinny Dippin' | 1976 | $15 |

NUTTY SQUIRRELS, THE
COLUMBIA

| CL1589 [M] | Bird Watching | 1961 | $75 |

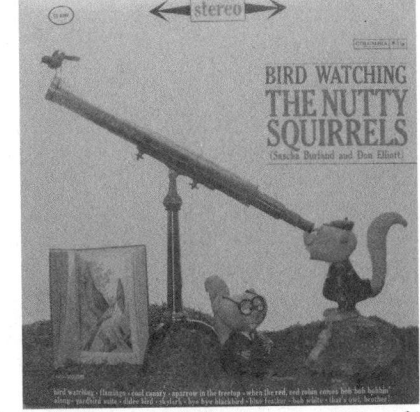

| CS8389 [S] | Bird Watching | 1961 | $40 |

HANOVER

| HML-8014 [M] | The Nutty Squirrels | 1960 | $150 |

MGM

| E-4272 [M] | A Hard Day's Night | 1964 | $75 |
| SE-4272 [S] | A Hard Day's Night | 1964 | $75 |

NYE, LOUIS
RIVERSIDE

| RLP-842 [M] | Heigh-Ho, Madison Avenue | 1960 | $30 |

NYRO, LAURA
COLUMBIA

| KC30259 | Christmas and the Beads of Sweat | 1970 | $18 |

— *360 Sound Stereo" label*

Number	Title	Yr	NM
❏ KC30259	Christmas and the Beads of Sweat	1970	$12
—Orange label			
❏ PC30259	Christmas and the Beads of Sweat	198?	$10
—Budget-line reissue			
❏ CL2826 [M]	Eli and the Thirteenth Confession	1968	$40
❏ CS9626 [S]	Eli and the Thirteenth Confession	1968	$18
—360 Sound Stereo" label			
❏ CS9626	Eli and the Thirteenth Confession	1970	$12
—Orange label			
❏ PC9626 [B]	Eli and the Thirteenth Confession	198?	$10
—Budget-line reissue			
❏ KC30987	Gonna Take a Miracle	1971	$18
❏ PC30987 [B]	Gonna Take a Miracle	197?	$10
—Budget-line reissue			
❏ FC39215	Mother's Spiritual	1984	$12
❏ JC35449	Nested	1978	$15
❏ PC35449	Nested	198?	$10
—Budget-line reissue			
❏ CS9737 [B]	New York Tendaberry	1969	$18
—360 Sound Stereo" label			
❏ CS9737	New York Tendaberry	1970	$12
—Orange label			
❏ PC9737	New York Tendaberry	198?	$10
—Budget-line reissue			
❏ PC234331 [DJ]	Season of Lights…Laura Nyro in Concert	1977	$50
—Promo only in plain cardboard jacket; this LP was edited to one LP for release			
❏ JC34786	Season of Lights…Laura Nyro in Concert	1977	$15
—Edited version of above			
❏ PC33912	Smile	1976	$15
—No bar code on cover			
❏ KC31410	The First Songs	1973	$18
—Reissue of Verve Forecast 3020			
❏ PC31410	The First Songs	197?	$10
—Budget-line reissue			

VERVE FOLKWAYS
Number	Title	Yr	NM
❏ FT-3020 [M]	Laura Nyro -- More Than a New Discovery	1967	$35
❏ FTS-3020 [S]	Laura Nyro -- More Than a New Discovery	1967	$35

VERVE FORECAST
Number	Title	Yr	NM
❏ FTS-3029	Laura Nyro	1968	$0
—Canceled			
❏ ST93036	Laura Nyro -- More Than a New Discovery	1968	$30
—Capitol Record Club edition			
❏ FTS-3020 [S]	Laura Nyro (The First Songs)	1967	$30

—The First Songs" is found on the label and back cover, but not on the front cover or the spine; this has the same material as the Verve Folkways LP but in a different order

O

O.C.
PAYDAY
Number	Title	Yr	NM
❏ 524399-1	Jewelz	1997	$15

WILD PITCH
Number	Title	Yr	NM
❏ E1-30928	Word…Life	1994	$25

OAK
MERCURY
Number	Title	Yr	NM
❏ SRM-1-3802	Oak	1979	$12
❏ SRM-1-4009	Set the Night on Fire	1980	$12

OAK RIDGE BOYS, THE
ABC
Number	Title	Yr	NM
❏ AA-1135	Have Arrived	1979	$15
❏ AA-1065	Room Service	1978	$12

ABC/DOT
Number	Title	Yr	NM
❏ DA-2093	Y'all Come Back Saloon	1977	$12

ACCORD
Number	Title	Yr	NM
❏ SN-7138	Spiritual Jubilee	198?	$12
❏ SN-7159	Spiritual Jubilee -- Volume 2	198?	$12
❏ SN-7199	Spiritual Jubilee -- Volume 3	198?	$12

CADENCE
Number	Title	Yr	NM
❏ CLP-3019 [M]	The Oak Ridge Quartet	1958	$75

CANAAN
Number	Title	Yr	NM
❏ 9625	Together	1966	$25
—With the Harvesters			

COLUMBIA
Number	Title	Yr	NM
❏ FC37737	All Our Favorite Songs	1981	$12

Number	Title	Yr	NM
❏ KC33935	Old Fashioned, Down Home, Hand Clappin', Foot Stompin', Southern Style, Gospel Quartet Music	1976	$15
❏ PC37711	Old Fashoned Gospel Quartet Music	1984	$10
❏ KC33057	Sky High	1975	$15
❏ PC33057	Sky High	197?	$10
—Reissue			
❏ PC38467	Smoky Mountain Gospel	1984	$10
❏ PC35202	The Best of the Oak Ridge Boys	1978	$12
❏ KC32742	The Oak Ridge Boys	1974	$15
❏ PC32742	The Oak Ridge Boys	197?	$10
—Reissue			

HEARTWARMING
Number	Title	Yr	NM
❏ HWS3091	International	1971	$18
❏ HWS3036	Thanks	1971	$18
❏ HWS3159	The Light	1972	$18

INTERMEDIA
Number	Title	Yr	NM
❏ QS-5012	Glory Train	198?	$12

LIBERTY
Number	Title	Yr	NM
❏ LN-10046	The Oak Ridge Boys at Their Best	1981	$10

MCA
Number	Title	Yr	NM
❏ 42311	American Dreams	1989	$12
❏ 5390	American Made	1983	$12
❏ 1447	American Made	1985	$10
—Budget-line reissue			
❏ 5294	Bobbie Sue	1982	$12
❏ 5365	Christmas	1982	$12
❏ 5799	Christmas Again	1986	$12
❏ 5455	Deliver	1983	$12
❏ 1446	Deliver	1985	$10
—Budget-line reissue			

Number	Title	Yr	NM
❏ 5209 [B]	Fancy Free	1981	$12
❏ 5150	Greatest Hits	1980	$12
❏ 5496	Greatest Hits 2	1984	$12
❏ AA-1135	Have Arrived	1979	$12
❏ 37221	Have Arrived	1984	$10
—Budget-line reissue			
❏ 42036	Heartbeat	1987	$12
❏ 42205	Monongahela	1988	$12
❏ 37153	Room Service	198?	$10
—Budget-line reissue			
❏ 5714	Seasons	1986	$12
❏ 5555	Step On Out	1985	$12
❏ L33-2-1276 [DJ]	Step On Out" World Premiere	1985	$30
—Promo-only interview and music LP with no script or cover			
❏ 3220	Together	1980	$12
❏ 37223	Together	1984	$10
—Budget-line reissue			
❏ 5945	Where the Fast Lane Ends	1987	$12
❏ 37222	Y'all Come Back Saloon	1984	$10
—Budget-line reissue			

NASHVILLE
Number	Title	Yr	NM
❏ 2086	Higher Power	1970	$18

POWER PAK
Number	Title	Yr	NM
❏ 716	The Oak Ridge Boys	197?	$12

PRIORITY
Number	Title	Yr	NM
❏ PU37711	Old Fashoned Gospel Quartet Music	1981	$12
❏ PU38467	Smoky Mountain Gospel	1983	$12

RCA
Number	Title	Yr	NM
❏ R164223	Unstoppable	1991	$18
—Only released on vinyl through BMG Direct Marketing			

SKYLITE
Number	Title	Yr	NM
❏ RLP-6030 [M]	I Wouldn't Take Nothing for My Journey Now	1965	$25
❏ SRLP-6030 [S]	I Wouldn't Take Nothing for My Journey Now	1965	$30
❏ RLP-6045 [M]	River of Love	1967	$25
❏ SRLP-6045 [S]	River of Love	1967	$30

Number	Title	Yr	NM
❏ RLP-6020 [M]	The Oak Ridge Boys Sing for You	1964	$25
❏ SRLP-6020 [S]	The Oak Ridge Boys Sing for You	1964	$30
❏ RLP-6040 [M]	The Solid Gospel Sound of the Oak Ridge Boys	1966	$25
❏ SRLP-6040 [S]	The Solid Gospel Sound of the Oak Ridge Boys	1966	$30

STARDAY
Number	Title	Yr	NM
❏ SLP-356 [M]	The Sensational Oak Ridge Boys	1965	$30

UNITED ARTISTS
Number	Title	Yr	NM
❏ UAL3554 [M]	The Oak Ridge Boys at Their Best	1966	$25
❏ UAS6554 [S]	The Oak Ridge Boys at Their Best	1966	$30
❏ LN-10046	The Oak Ridge Boys at Their Best	1979	$12

WARNER BROS.
Number	Title	Yr	NM
❏ W1521 [M]	Folk-Minded Spirituals for Spiritual-Minded Folks	1963	$25
❏ WS1521 [S]	Folk-Minded Spirituals for Spiritual-Minded Folks	1963	$30
❏ W1497 [M]	With Sounds of Nashville	1963	$25
❏ WS1497 [S]	With Sounds of Nashville	1963	$30

OAKEY, PHILIP AND GIORGIO MORODER
A&M
Number	Title	Yr	NM
❏ SP-5080	Philip Oakey and Giorgio Moroder	1985	$10

OAKLEY, LEON
GHB
Number	Title	Yr	NM
❏ GHB-153	Leon Oakley and the Flying Duces	198?	$25

STOMP OFF
Number	Title	Yr	NM
❏ SOS-1013	New Orleans Joys	198?	$25

OAKTOWN'S 3.5.7.
BUST IT
Number	Title	Yr	NM
❏ C1-92996	Fully Loaded	1991	$18

CAPITOL
Number	Title	Yr	NM
❏ C1-90926	Wild and Loose	1989	$12

OASIS
EPIC
Number	Title	Yr	NM
❏ 34-78216	Wonderwall/Round Are Way	1996	$4
❏ E94493	Don't Believe the Truth	2005	$25

HELTER SKELTER
Number	Title	Yr	NM
❏ 88697-00754-1	Stop the Clocks	2006	$50
—Pressed in Europe but imported by Sony BMG for U.S. distribution			

O'BANION, JOHN
ELEKTRA
Number	Title	Yr	NM
❏ 6E-342	John O'Banion	1981	$12

OBEIDO, RAY
WINDHAM HILL
Number	Title	Yr	NM
❏ WH-0115	Perfect Crime	1989	$30

OBERNKIRCHEN CHILDREN'S CHOIR
ANGEL
Number	Title	Yr	NM
❏ 35914 [M]	Christmas Songs	196?	$15
—Conducted by Edith Moeller			
❏ S-35914 [S]	Christmas Songs	196?	$18
—Same as above, but in stereo			
❏ ANG.65021 [M]	Christmas Songs	1955	$25

OBOLER, ARCH
CAPITOL
Number	Title	Yr	NM
❏ T1763 [M]	Drop Dead! An Exercise in Horror	1962	$30
❏ ST1763 [S]	Drop Dead! An Exercise in Horror	1962	$30

O'BRIAN, HUGH
ABC-PARAMOUNT
Number	Title	Yr	NM
❏ ABC-203 [M]	TV's Wyatt Earp Sings	1957	$75

O'BRIEN, HOD
UPTOWN
Number	Title	Yr	NM
❏ 278	Bits and Pieces	198?	$25

O'BRYAN
CAPITOL
Number	Title	Yr	NM
❏ ST-12332	Be My Lover	1984	$12
❏ ST-12192	Doin' Alright	1982	$12
❏ ST-12520	Surrender	1986	$12
❏ ST-12256	You and I	1983	$12

O'BRYANT, JIMMY
BIOGRAPH
Number	Title	Yr	NM
❏ 12002 [M]	Jimmy O'Bryant's Washboard Wonders 1924-26	1968	$30

Number	Title	Yr	NM
O'BRYANT, JOAN			
FOLKWAYS			
❑ FA-2338 [M]	American Ballads and Folksongs	1958	$50
❑ FA-2134 [M]	Folksongs and Ballads of Kansas	1957	$35
OCASEK, RIC			
GEFFEN			
❑ GHS2022	Beatitude	1983	$10
❑ R144634	This Side of Paradise	1986	$12
—RCA Music Service edition			
❑ 24098	This Side of Paradise	1986	$10
OCEAN, BILLY			
EPIC			
❑ FE38129	Inner Feelings	1982	$18
❑ PE38129	Inner Feelings	1985	$10
—Budget-line reissue with new prefix			
❑ FE37406	Nights (Feel Like Gettin' Down)	1981	$18
❑ PE37406	Nights (Feel Like Gettin' Down)	1985	$10
—Budget-line reissue with new prefix			
JIVE			
❑ 1271-1-J	Greatest Hits	1989	$12
JIVE/ARISTA			
❑ JL8-8409	Love Zone	1986	$10
❑ JL8-8213	Suddenly	1984	$18
—Original cover: Photo of Billy Ocean on blue background			
❑ JL8-8213	Suddenly	1984	$10
—Second cover: Drawing of Billy Ocean on white background			
❑ JL8-8495	Tear Down These Walls	1988	$10
OCEAN			
KAMA SUTRA			
❑ KSBS-2064	Give Tomorrow's Children One More Chance	1972	$15
❑ KSBS-2033	Put Your Hand in the Hand	1971	$15
OCEAN BLUE, THE			
SIRE			
❑ 25906	The Ocean Blue	1989	$15
OCHS, PHIL			
A&M			
❑ SP-6511	Chords of Fame	1976	$18
—Reissue of 4599			
❑ SP-4599	Chords of Fame	1974	$30
—Original edition			
❑ SP-4253	Phil Ochs Greatest Hits	1970	$25
❑ SP-3125 [B]	Phil Ochs Greatest Hits	198?	$10
—Budget-line reissue			
❑ LP-133 [M]	Pleasures of the Harbor	1967	$30
❑ SP-4133 [S]	Pleasures of the Harbor	1967	$25
❑ SP-4181	Rehearsals for Retirement	1969	$25
❑ SP-4148 [S]	Tape from California	1968	$25
❑ LP-148 [M]	Tape from California	1968	$50
—Mono is white label promo only; "Monaural" sticker at upper right corner of stereo cover			
CARTHAGE			
❑ CGLP-4427	All the News That's Fit to Sing	198?	$12
❑ CGLP-4422	I Ain't Marching Anymore	198?	$12
ELEKTRA			
❑ EKL-269 [M]	All the News That's Fit to Sing	1964	$30
—Gold label with "guitar player" logo			
❑ EKL-269 [M]	All the News That's Fit to Sing	1966	$25
—Gold label with stylized "E" logo			
❑ EKS-7269 [S]	All the News That's Fit to Sing	1964	$40
—Gold label with "guitar player" logo			
❑ EKS-7269 [S]	All the News That's Fit to Sing	1966	$30
—Gold label with stylized "E" logo			
❑ EKL-287 [M]	I Ain't Marching Anymore	1965	$30
—Gold label with "guitar player" logo			
❑ EKL-287 [M]	I Ain't Marching Anymore	1966	$25
—Gold label with stylized "E" logo			
❑ EKS-7287 [S]	I Ain't Marching Anymore	1965	$40
—Gold label with "guitar player" logo			
❑ EKS-7287 [S]	I Ain't Marching Anymore	1966	$30
—Gold label with stylized "E" logo			
❑ EKS-7287 [S]	I Ain't Marching Anymore	1975	$15
—Butterfly label with small Warner Communications logo			
❑ EKL-310 [M]	Phil Ochs in Concert	1966	$25
❑ EKS-7310 [S]	Phil Ochs in Concert	1966	$30
FOLKWAYS			
❑ FD-5362	Broadside Tapes 1 (#14)	1979	$20
❑ FB-5321	Phil Ochs Interviews	197?	$15
❑ FB-5320	Phil Ochs Sings Songs for Broadside (#10)	1976	$15

Number	Title	Yr	NM
PICKWICK			
❑ SPC-3707	Rehearsals for Retirement	197?	$12
RHINO			
❑ RNLP-70080	A Toast to Those Who Are Gone	1986	$12
SMITHSONIAN/FOLKWAYS			
❑ SF-40008	Broadside Tapes 1 (#14)	1989	$20
O'CONNELL, BILL			
INNER CITY			
❑ IC-1035	Searching	197?	$35
O'CONNELL, HELEN			
MARK 56			
❑ 711	Christmas with Helen O'Connell	19??	$15
VIK			
❑ LX-1093 [M]	Green Eyes	1957	$40
O'CONNOR, CARROLL			
A&M			
❑ SP-4340	Remembering You	1972	$30
AUDIO FIDELITY			
❑ AFSD-6727	Carroll O'Connor Sings for Old P.F.A.R.T.S.	1976	$30
O'CONNOR, SINEAD			
CHRYSALIS			
❑ R133512	I Do Not Want What I Haven't Got	1990	$18
—BMG Direct Marketing edition			
❑ F1-21759	I Do Not Want What I Haven't Got	1990	$15
❑ R163660	The Lion and the Cobra	1988	$12
—BMG Direct Marketing edition			
❑ BFV41612	The Lion and the Cobra	1987	$10
❑ F1-21612	The Lion and the Cobra	1989	$15
—Reissue			
OCTOBER COUNTRY			
EPIC			
❑ BN26381 [B]	October Country	1968	$25
ODA			
LOUD			
❑ A 0011	Oda	1973	$250
O'DAY, ALAN			
PACIFIC			
❑ PC4300	Appetizers	1977	$12
❑ PC4301	Oh Johnny!	1979	$12
VIVA			
❑ VV2679	Caress Me Pretty Music	1973	$20
O'DAY, ANITA			
ADVANCE			
❑ LSP-8 [10]	Anita O'Day Specials	1951	$300
AMERICAN RECORDING SOCIETY			
❑ G-426 [M]	For Oscar	1957	$40
BASF			
❑ MB20750	Recorded Live at the Berlin Jazz Festival	1973	$25
BOB THIELE MUSIC			
❑ BBM1-0595 [M]	Hi Ho Trailus Boot Whip	1974	$35
CLEF			
❑ MGC-130 [10]	Anita O'Day Collates	1953	$300
CORAL			
❑ CRL-56073 [10]	Singin' and Swingin'	1953	$175
DOCTOR JAZZ			
❑ FW39418	Hi Ho Trailus Boot Whip	198?	$25
EMILY			
❑ 13081	Angel Eyes	1981	$30
❑ 83084	A Song for You	1984	$30
❑ 92685	Big Band Concert 1985	1985	$30
❑ 11579	Live at Mingos	1979	$35
❑ 102479	Live at the City	1979	$35
❑ 42181	Live at the City: The Second Set	1981	$30
❑ 9579	Live at Tokyo	1979	$35
❑ 11279	My Ship	1979	$35
❑ 32383	The Night Has a Thousand Eyes	1983	$30
GLENDALE			
❑ 6001	Anita O'Day	197?	$30
❑ 6000	Once Upon a Summertime	197?	$30
GNP CRESCENDO			
❑ GNPS-2126	Mello' Day	197?	$25
NORGRAN			
❑ MGN-1057 [M]	An Evening With Anita O'Day	1956	$250
❑ MGN-1049 [M]	Anita O'Day	1955	$300
❑ MGN-30 [10]	Songs By Anita O'Day	1954	$175

Number	Title	Yr	NM
PAUSA			
❑ 7092	Anita O'Day in Berlin	198?	$25
VERVE			
❑ V-8442 [M]	All the Sad Young Men	1962	$30
❑ V6-8442 [S]	All the Sad Young Men	1962	$40
❑ MGV-8147 [M]	An Evening With Anita O'Day	1957	$0
—Canceled			
❑ MGV-2050 [M]	An Evening With Anita O'Day	1957	$150
❑ V-2050 [M]	An Evening With Anita O'Day	1961	$25
❑ MGV-2000 [M]	Anita	1956	$175
❑ V-2000 [M]	Anita	1961	$75
❑ 829261-1	Anita	1986	$25

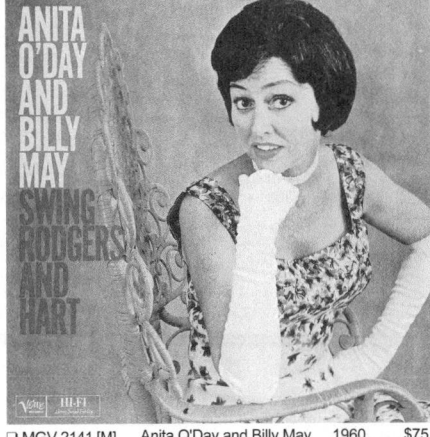

Number	Title	Yr	NM
❑ MGV-2141 [M]	Anita O'Day and Billy May Swing Rodgers and Hart	1960	$75
❑ V-2141 [M]	Anita O'Day and Billy May Swing Rodgers and Hart	1961	$75
❑ V6-2141 [S]	Anita O'Day and Billy May Swing Rodgers and Hart	1961	$75
❑ V-8514 [M]	Anita O'Day and the Three Sounds	1963	$30
❑ V6-8514 [S]	Anita O'Day and the Three Sounds	1963	$30
❑ MGV-2113 [M]	Anita O'Day At Mr. Kelly's	1958	$175
❑ MGVS-6043 [S]	Anita O'Day At Mr. Kelly's	1960	$175
❑ V-2113 [M]	Anita O'Day At Mr. Kelly's	1961	$75
❑ V6-2113 [S]	Anita O'Day At Mr. Kelly's	1961	$75
❑ UMV-2550	Anita O'Day At Mr. Kelly's	198?	$30
❑ MGV-8283 [M]	Anita O'Day Sings the Winners	1958	$175
❑ MGVS-6002 [S]	Anita O'Day Sings the Winners	1960	$175
❑ V-8283 [M]	Anita O'Day Sings the Winners	1961	$75
❑ V6-8283 [S]	Anita O'Day Sings the Winners	1961	$75
❑ V-8485 [M]	Anita O'Day Sings the Winners	1962	$25
❑ V6-8485 [S]	Anita O'Day Sings the Winners	1962	$30
❑ UMV-2536	Anita O'Day Sings the Winners	198?	$30
❑ MGV-2118 [M]	Anita O'Day Swings Cole Porter	1959	$175
❑ MGVS-6059 [S]	Anita O'Day Swings Cole Porter	1960	$175
❑ V-2118 [M]	Anita O'Day Swings Cole Porter	1961	$75
❑ V6-2118 [S]	Anita O'Day Swings Cole Porter	1961	$75
❑ MGV-8259 [M]	Anita Sings the Most	1958	$175
❑ V-8259 [M]	Anita Sings the Most	1961	$75
❑ MGV-8312 [M]	Cool Heat -- Anita O'Day Sings Jimmy Giuffre Arrangements	1959	$150
❑ MGVS-6046 [S]	Cool Heat -- Anita O'Day Sings Jimmy Giuffre Arrangements	1960	$150
❑ V-8312 [M]	Cool Heat -- Anita O'Day Sings Jimmy Giuffre Arrangements	1961	$25
❑ V6-8312 [S]	Cool Heat -- Anita O'Day Sings Jimmy Giuffre Arrangements	1961	$30
❑ UMV-2679	Cool Heat -- Anita O'Day Sings Jimmy Giuffre Arrangements	198?	$30
❑ V-8572 [M]	Incomparable! Anita O'Day	1964	$30
❑ V6-8572 [S]	Incomparable! Anita O'Day	1964	$30
❑ MGV-2154 [M]	I Remember Billie Holiday	1960	$0
—Canceled			
❑ MGV-2043 [M]	Pick Yourself Up With Anita O'Day	1957	$175
❑ V-2043 [M]	Pick Yourself Up With Anita O'Day	1961	$25
❑ MGV-2086 [M]	'S Wonderful	1957	$0
—Canceled			
❑ VE-2-2534	The Big Band Sessions	1979	$35
❑ MGV-8140 [M]	The Lady Is a Tramp	1957	$0
—Canceled			
❑ MGV-2049 [M]	The Lady Is a Tramp	1957	$175
❑ V-2049 [M]	The Lady Is a Tramp	1961	$25

Number	Title	Yr	NM
❏ V-8483 [M]	This Is Anita	1962	$30
❏ V6-8483 [R]	This Is Anita	1962	$35
❏ V-8472 [M]	Time For Two	1962	$30
❏ V6-8472 [S]	Time For Two	1962	$40
❏ UMJ-3287	Time For Two	198?	$30
❏ MGV-2157 [M]	Trav'lin' Light	1960	$75
❏ V-2157 [M]	Trav'lin' Light	1961	$25
❏ V6-2157 [S]	Trav'lin' Light	1961	$30
❏ MGV-2145 [M]	Waiter, Make Mine Blues	1960	$75
❏ V-2145 [M]	Waiter, Make Mine Blues	1961	$25
❏ V6-2145 [S]	Waiter, Make Mine Blues	1961	$30

O'DAY, MOLLY
AUDIO LAB
❏ AL-1544 [M]	Music for the Country Folks	1960	$30

HARMONY
❏ HL7299 [M]	The Unforgettable Molly O'Day	1963	$25

STARDAY
❏ SLP-367 [B]	The Living Legend of Country Music	1966	$30

O'DAY, TOMMY
NU TRAYL
❏ NLP-6005	Tommy O'Day	1977	$18
❏ NLP-6006	Tommy O'Day Sings Today's Woman	1978	$18

ODD SQUAD
RAP-A-LOT
❏ SPRO50781 [EP]	Hot Club Wax	1994	$15
— Promo-only six-song sampler			

O'DELL, DOYE
ERA
❏ EL-20004 [M]	Doye	1956	$50
— Red vinyl			
❏ EL-20004 [M]	Doye	1956	$30
— Black vinyl			

SAGE
❏ C-36 [M]	Crossroads	195?	$30

O'DELL, KENNY
CAPRICORN
❏ CP 0140	Kenny O'Dell	1974	$15
❏ CPN 0211	Let's Shake Hands and Come Out Lovin'	1978	$15

VEGAS
❏ 401	Beautiful People	1968	$30

ODETTA
ALCAZAR
❏ ALC-104	Christmas Spirituals	198?	$12

EVEREST ARCHIVE OF FOLK & JAZZ
❏ 273	Odetta	1973	$15

FANTASY
❏ 3-15 [10]	Odetta and Larry	1955	$50
❏ F-3252 [M]	Odetta and Larry	1957	$50
— Dark red vinyl			
❏ F-3252 [M]	Odetta and Larry	1958	$30
❏ F-8345	Odetta and Larry	1963	$15
— Reissue of 3252			
❏ OBC-509	Odetta and the Blues	198?	$25
— Reissue of Riverside LP			

RCA VICTOR
❏ LPM-2792 [M]	It's a Mighty World	1964	$18
❏ LSP-2792 [S]	It's a Mighty World	1964	$25
❏ LPM-3457 [M]	Odetta in Japan	1965	$18
❏ LSP-3457 [S]	Odetta in Japan	1965	$25
❏ LPM-3324 [M]	Odetta Sings Dylan	1965	$18
❏ LSP-3324 [S]	Odetta Sings Dylan	1965	$25
❏ LPM-2643 [M]	Odetta Sings Folk Songs	1963	$25
❏ LSP-2643 [S]	Odetta Sings Folk Songs	1963	$30
❏ LPM-2923 [M]	Odetta Sings of Many Things	1964	$18
❏ LSP-2923 [S]	Odetta Sings of Many Things	1964	$25
❏ LPM-2573 [M]	Sometimes I Feel Like Crying	1962	$25
❏ LSP-2573 [S]	Sometimes I Feel Like Crying	1962	$30

RIVERSIDE
❏ RLP-417 [M]	Odetta and the Blues	1962	$175
❏ RS-9417 [S]	Odetta and the Blues	1962	$175

ROSE QUARTZ
❏ RQ-101	Movin' It On	1987	$12

TRADITION
❏ TRP-1025 [M]	Odetta at the Gate of Horn	1958	$30
❏ TRP-1010 [M]	Odetta Sings Ballads and Blues	1957	$30
❏ TRP-1052 [M]	The Best of Odetta	1967	$25
❏ TRS-2052 [R]	The Best of Odetta	1967	$18

VANGUARD
❏ VRS-9066 [M]	Ballads for Americans	1960	$50
❏ VSD-2057 [S]	Ballads for Americans	1960	$75
❏ VRS-9079 [M]	Christmas Spirituals	1961	$40
❏ VSD-2079 [S]	Christmas Spirituals	1961	$50
❏ VSD-43/44	Essential Odetta	1973	$18
❏ VRS-9059 [M]	My Eyes Have Seen	1960	$3
❏ VSD-2046 [S]	My Eyes Have Seen	1960	$40
❏ VRS-9076 [M]	Odetta at Carnegie Hall	1961	$40
❏ VSD-2072 [S]	Odetta at Carnegie Hall	1961	$75
❏ VRS-3003 [M]	Odetta at Carnegie Hall	1967	$30
❏ VSD-73003 [S]	Odetta at Carnegie Hall	1967	$30
❏ VRS-9103 [M]	Odetta at Town Hall	1962	$30
❏ VSD-2109 [S]	Odetta at Town Hall	1962	$40
❏ VRS-9137 [M]	One Grain of Sand	1963	$25
❏ VSD-2153 [S]	One Grain of Sand	1963	$30

ODRICH, RON
CLASSIC JAZZ
❏ 35	Blackstick	1978	$30

ODYSSEY
RCA VICTOR
❏ AFL1-3526	Hang Together	1980	$12
❏ AFL1-4240	Happy Together	1982	$12
❏ AFL1-3031	Hollywood Party Tonight	1978	$12
❏ AFL1-3910	I Got the Melody	1981	$12
❏ APL1-2204	Odyssey	1977	$12

ODYSSEY
TIGER LILY
❏ 698 [B]	Electric One	1976	$500

O'FARRILL, CHICO
ABC IMPULSE!
❏ AS-9135 [S]	Nine Flags	1968	$35

CLEF
❏ MGC-131 [10]	Afro-Cuban	1953	$350
❏ MGC-132 [10]	Chico O'Farrill Jazz	1953	$350
❏ MGC-699 [M]	Chico O'Farrill Jazz	1956	$250

IMPULSE!
❏ AS-9135 [S]	Nine Flags	1967	$250
❏ A-9135 [M]	Nine Flags	1967	$120

NORGRAN
❏ MGN-31 [10]	Chico O'Farrill	1954	$175
❏ MGN-28 [10]	Latino Dance Sessions	1954	$250
❏ MGN-27 [10]	Mambo Dance Sessions	1954	$175
❏ MGN-9 [10]	The Second Afro-Cuban Jazz Suite	1954	$175

VERVE
❏ MGV-8083 [M]	Jazz North of the Border and South of the Border	1957	$175
❏ V-8083 [M]	Jazz North of the Border and South of the Border	1961	$30
❏ MGV-2003 [M]	Mambo/Latino Dances	1956	$250
❏ V-2003 [M]	Mambo/Latino Dances	1961	$30
❏ MGV-2024 [M]	Music From South America	1956	$250
❏ V-2024 [M]	Music From South America	1961	$30

OFF BROADWAY USA
ATLANTIC
❏ SD19263	On	1980	$25
❏ SD19287	Quick Turns	1981	$18

OFFSPRING, THE
COLUMBIA
❏ C69661 [B]	Americana	1998	$30
❏ C61419	Conspiracy of One	2000	$18
❏ C67810	Ixnay on the Hombre	1997	$18
❏ C89026	Splinter	2003	$18

EPITAPH
❏ 86424 [B]	Ignition	1992	$30
❏ 86432	Smash	1994	$18

NEMESIS
❏ 6	The Offspring	1989	$150
— Original issue, 5,000 copies pressed			

NITRO
❏ 86460	The Offspring	1995	$15
— Reissue of Nemesis LP			

OGERMAN, CLAUS, AND MICHAEL BRECKER
ECM
❏ 23698	Cityscape	1982	$25

OGERMAN, CLAUS
JAZZ MAN
❏ 5015	Aranjuez	198?	$30

RCA VICTOR
❏ LPM-3640 [M]	Saxes Mexicano	1966	$25
❏ LSP-3640 [S]	Saxes Mexicano	1966	$30
❏ LPM-3366 [M]	Soul Searchin'	1965	$25
❏ LSP-3366 [S]	Soul Searchin'	1965	$30
❏ LPM-3455 [M]	Watusi Trumpets	1965	$25
❏ LSP-3455 [S]	Watusi Trumpets	1965	$30

UNITED ARTISTS
❏ UAL-3206 [M]	Sing Along in German	1962	$25
❏ UAS-6206 [S]	Sing Along in German	1962	$30

WARNER BROS.
❏ BS3006	Gate of Dreams	1977	$25

O'GWYNN, JAMES
MERCURY
❏ MG-20727 [M]	The Best of James O'Gwynn	1962	$30
❏ SR-60727 [S]	The Best of James O'Gwynn	1962	$40

PLANTATION
❏ 21	Greatest Hits	197?	$15

WING
❏ MGW-12290 [M]	Heartaches and Memories	1964	$25
❏ SRW-16290 [S]	Heartaches and Memories	1964	$30

O'HARA, MAUREEN
COLUMBIA
❏ CL1750 [M]	Maureen O'Hara Sings Her Favorite Irish Songs	1962	$40
❏ CS8550 [S]	Maureen O'Hara Sings Her Favorite Irish Songs	1962	$50

RCA VICTOR
❏ LPM-1953 [M]	Love Letters	1959	$50
❏ LSP-1953 [S]	Love Letters	1959	$75

OHIO EXPRESS, THE
BUDDAH
❏ BDS5026	Chewy, Chewy	1969	$25
❏ BDS5037 [B]	Mercy	1969	$25
❏ BDM1018 [M]	The Ohio Express	1968	$40
— Stereo cover with "mono" sticker attached; white label promo			
❏ BDS5018 [S]	The Ohio Express	1968	$25
❏ BDS5058	The Very Best of the Ohio Express	1970	$25

CAMEO
❏ C20000 [M]	Beg, Borrow and Steal	1967	$30
❏ CS20000 [S]	Beg, Borrow and Steal	1967	$40

OHIO PLAYERS, THE
ACCORD
❏ SN-7102	Young and Ready	1981	$10

ARISTA
❏ AB4226	Everybody Up	1979	$10

BOARDWALK
❏ FW37090	Tenderness	1981	$10

CAPITOL
❏ ST-192	Observations in Time	1969	$50
❏ ST-11291	The Ohio Players	1974	$15
— Reissue of 192			

MERCURY
❏ SRM-1-3701	Angel	1977	$12
❏ SRM-1-1088	Contradiction	1976	$12
❏ SRM-1-1013	Fire	1974	$12
❏ SRM-1-1038	Honey	1975	$12
❏ SRM-1-3730	Jass-Ay-Lay-Dee	1978	$12
❏ SRM-1-3707	Mr. Mean	1977	$12
❏ SRM-1-1122	Ohio Players Gold	1976	$12
❏ 824461-1	Ohio Players Gold	198?	$10
— Reissue of 1122			
❏ SRM-1-705	Skin Tight	1974	$15
— Red label			
❏ SRM-1-705 [B]	Skin Tight	1974	$12
— Chicago skyline label			

TRACK
❏ TRK58810	Back	1988	$12

TRIP
❏ 8029	First Impression	1972	$15

UNITED ARTISTS
❏ UA-LA502-E	The Very Best of The Ohio Players	1975	$15

WESTBOUND
❏ 1003	Climax	1974	$18
❏ 2021	Ecstasy	1973	$25
❏ 222	Ecstasy	1976	$15
— Reissue of 2021			
❏ 1005	Ohio Players Greatest Hits	1975	$18
❏ 2015	Pain	1972	$25
❏ 219	Pain	1976	$15
— Reissue of 2015			
❏ 2017	Pleasure	1973	$25
❏ 220	Pleasure	1976	$15
— Reissue of 2017			
❏ 211	Rattlesnake	1975	$15
❏ 304	The Best of the Early Years	1977	$18

OHLSON, CURTIS
INTIMA
❏ D1-73358	Better Than Ever	1989	$30
❏ SJE-73274	So Fast	1987	$25

OHNO, SHUNZO
INNER CITY
❏ IC-1108	Quarter Moon	198?	$30

OINGO BOINGO
A&M
❏ SP-4959	Good for Your Soul	1983	$12
❏ SP-3252	Good for Your Soul	1984	$10

Number	Title	Yr	NM
—Reissue of 4959			
❏ SP-4903	Nothing to Fear	1982	$12
❏ SP-3251	Nothing to Fear	1984	$10
—Reissue of 4930			
❏ SP-4863	Only a Lad	1981	$12

Number	Title	Yr	NM
❏ SP-3250 [B]	Only a Lad	1984	$10
—Reissue of 4863			
❏ SP-5217	Skeletons in the Closet	1988	$12

I.R.S.
❏ SP-70400 [10]	Oingo Boingo	1980	$15
—Four-song 10-inch EP			
❏ SP-70400	Oingo Boingo	1980	$15
—Limited edition 12" version			

MCA
❏ 5811	BOI-NGO	1987	$12
❏ 8030	Boingo Alive	1988	$15
❏ 6365	Dark at the End of the Tunnel	1990	$12
❏ L33-18137 [DJ]	Dark at the End of the Tunnel	1990	$40
—Promo-only picture disc			
❏ 5665	Dead Man's Party	1985	$12

O'JAYS, THE

BELL
❏ 6014	Back on Top	1968	$25
❏ 6082	The O'Jays	1973	$15

EMI
❏ E1-93390	Emotionally Yours	1991	$18
❏ E1-96420	Home for Christmas	1991	$18
❏ E1-90921	Serious	1989	$12

IMPERIAL
❏ LP9290 [M]	Comin' Through	1965	$40
❏ LP12290 [S]	Comin' Through	1965	$50

KORY
❏ 1006	The O'Jays	1977	$12

LIBERTY
❏ LN-10119	Greatest Hits	1980	$10
—Budget-line reissue of Imperial material			

MINIT
❏ LP-40008 [M]	Soul Sounds	1967	$40
❏ LP-24008 [S]	Soul Sounds	1967	$50

NEPTUNE
❏ 202	The O'Jays in Philadelphia	1969	$30

PHILADELPHIA INT'L.
❏ KZ31712 [B]	Back Stabbers	1972	$15
❏ ASZ140 [DJ]	Everything You Always Wanted to Hear by the O'Jays But Were Afraid to Ask For	1975	$18
❏ PZ33807	Family Reunion	1975	$12
—No bar code on back cover			
❏ PZQ33807 [Q]	Family Reunion	1975	$20
❏ PZ33807	Family Reunion	198?	$10
—Budget-line reissue with bar code			
❏ FZ39251	Greatest Hits	1984	$12
❏ FZ36027	Identify Yourself	1979	$12
❏ 53036	Let Me Touch You	1987	$12
❏ 53015	Love Fever	1985	$12
❏ PZ34245	Message in the Music	1976	$12
❏ FZ37999	My Favorite Person	1982	$12
❏ KZ32408	Ship Ahoy	1973	$12
❏ PZQ32408 [Q]	Ship Ahoy	1974	$20
❏ PZ32408	Ship Ahoy	198?	$10
—Budget-line reissue			
❏ JZ35355	So Full of Love	1978	$12
❏ PZ35355	So Full of Love	198?	$10
—Budget-line reissue			
❏ PZ33150	Survival	1975	$12
❏ PZG35024	The O'Jays' Collector's Items	1978	$15
❏ Z235024	The O'Jays' Collector's Items	198?	$12

Number	Title	Yr	NM
—Reissue			
❏ KZ32120	The O'Jays in Philadelphia	1973	$15
—Reissue of Neptune LP			
❏ KZ32953	The O'Jays Live in London	1974	$12
❏ PZQ32953 [Q]	The O'Jays Live in London	1974	$20
❏ PZ34684	Travelin' at the Speed of Thought	1977	$12
❏ FZ38518	When Will I See You Again	1983	$12
❏ PZ38518	When Will I See You Again	1985	$10
—Budget-line reissue			

SUNSET
❏ SUS-5222	Full of Soul	1968	$18
—Reissue of Imperial LP			

TSOP
❏ FZ36416	The Year 2000	1980	$12

UNITED ARTISTS
❏ UAS-5655	The O'Jays Greatest Hits	1972	$15

VOLCANO
❏ 31149	Love You to Tears	1997	$18

O'KANES, THE

COLUMBIA
❏ BFC40459	The O'Kanes	1986	$10
❏ FC44066	Tired of the Runnin'	1988	$10

O'KAYSIONS, THE

ABC
❏ S-664	Girl Watcher	1968	$40

O'KEEFE, DANNY

ATLANTIC
❏ SD7264	Breezy Stories	1973	$15
❏ SD18125	So Long, Harry Truman	1975	$15

COTILLION
❏ SD9036	Danny O'Keefe	1971	$18

FIRST AMERICAN
❏ 7700	The Seattle Tapes	1977	$15
❏ 7721	The Seattle Tapes, Volume 2	1979	$15

PANORAMA
❏ 105	Introducing Danny O'Keefe	1966	$40

SIGNPOST
❏ SD8404	O'Keefe	1972	$15

WARNER BROS.
❏ BS3050	American Roulette	1977	$12
❏ BSK3314	Global Blues	1978	$12
❏ PRO760 [DJ]	The O'Keefe File	1977	$18

OL' DIRTY BASTARD

ELEKTRA
❏ ED6187 [DJ]	N***a Please	1999	$25
—Promo-only version			
❏ 62414	Nigga Please	1999	$18
❏ 61659	Return to the 36 Chambers: The Dirty Version	1995	$18
❏ ED5796 [DJ]	Return to the 36 Chambers: The Dirty Version	1995	$18
—Promo-only version			

OL' SKOOL

UNIVERSAL
❏ 53104	Ol' Skool	1998	$15

OLA AND THE JANGLERS

GNP CRESCENDO
❏ GNPS-2050	Let's Dance/What a Way to Die	1969	$25

OLAY, RUTH

ABC
❏ ABC-573 [M]	Soul In the Night	1966	$25
❏ ABCS-573 [S]	Soul In the Night	1966	$30

EMARCY
❏ MG-36125 [M]	Olay! The New Sound Of Ruth Olay	1958	$250

EVEREST
❏ LPBR-5218 [M]	Olay! OK	1963	$30
❏ SDBR-1218 [S]	Olay! OK	1963	$30

LAUREL
❏ 501	Ruth Olay Sings Jazz Today	198?	$30

MERCURY
❏ MG-20390 [M]	Easy Living	1959	$150
❏ SR-60069 [S]	Easy Living	1959	$150

UNITED ARTISTS
❏ UAL-3115 [M]	Ruth Olay In Person	1960	$30
❏ UAS-4115 [S]	Ruth Olay In Person	1960	$40

OLD & IN THE WAY
JERRY GARCIA heads a bluegrass band!

ROUND
❏ RX-103	Old & In the Way	1975	$30

SUGAR HILL
❏ SH-3746	Old & In the Way	1987	$12
—Reissue of Round LP			

OLD AND NEW DREAMS

BLACK SAINT
❏ 120113	A Tribute to Blackwell	1990	$35
❏ BSR-0013	Old and New Dreams	198?	$35

ECM
❏ ECM1-1154	Old and New Dreams	1979	$35
—Distributed by Warner Bros.			
❏ ECM1-1205	Playing	1981	$35
—Distributed by Warner Bros.			

OLDFIELD, MIKE

VIRGIN
❏ VR13143 [B]	Airborn	1980	$30
—U.S.-only compilation, which may make it much more valuable overseas			
❏ 91270	Earth Moving	1990	$15
❏ VR 13-109	Hergest Ridge	1974	$25
—First issue of this album			
❏ VR 13-109 [DJ]	Hergest Ridge	1974	$35
—Promo only; banded for airplay			
❏ 90590	Hergest Ridge	1987	$10
—Reissue of Virgin International 2013			
❏ 90645	Islands	1988	$12
❏ PZ33913	Ommadawn	1975	$30
—Original U.S. issue of this album			
❏ PZ33913 [DJ]	Ommadawn	1975	$40
—Promo only; banded for airplay			
❏ PZQ33913 [Q]	Ommadawn	1975	$150
❏ 90591	The Killing Fields	1987	$12
❏ 90894	The Orchestral Tubular Bells	1989	$12
—Reissue of 13-115			
❏ VR 13-115	The Orchestral Tubular Bells	1975	$20
❏ VR 13-105	Tubular Bells	1973	$18
—First stereo issue of this album			
❏ QD 13-105 [Q]	Tubular Bells	1974	$150
❏ VR13135	Tubular Bells	1979	$12
—Third stereo issue of this album			
❏ PZ34116	Tubular Bells	1976	$15
—Second stereo issue of this album (note the "PZ" prefix)			
❏ 90589	Tubular Bells	1987	$10
—Fifth stereo issue of this album			

VIRGIN/EPIC
❏ ARE37983	Five Miles Out	1982	$12
❏ FE37358	QE2	1981	$12
❏ PE34116	Tubular Bells	1982	$10
—Fourth stereo issue of this album (note the "PE" prefix)			
❏ HE44116	Tubular Bells	1982	$30
—Half-speed mastered edition			

VIRGIN INTERNATIONAL
❏ VI-2013	Hergest Ridge	1979	$12
—Reissue of 13-109; not to be confused with UK pressings that have only a "V" prefix			
❏ VI-2043	Ommadawn	1979	$12
—Reissue of 33913; not to be confused with UK pressings that have only a "V" prefix			

OLDHAM, ANDREW

LONDON
❏ LL3457 [M]	The Rolling Stones Songbook	1965	$150
❏ PS457 [S]	The Rolling Stones Songbook	1965	$175

PARROT
❏ PA61003 [M]	East Meets West	1965	$250
❏ PAS71003 [S]	East Meets West	1965	$300

OLDHAM, DOUG

IMPACT
❏ R3193	Christmas with Doug Oldham	1972	$15

OLENN, JOHNNY

LIBERTY
❏ LRP-3029 [M]	Just Rollin' with Johnny Olenn	1956	$300

O'LENO, LARRY

PAINTED SMILES
❏ 1348	Larry O'Leno Sings Billy Strayhorn	198?	$30

OLIPHANT, GRASELLA

ATLANTIC
❏ 1438 [M]	The Grass Roots	1965	$35
❏ SD-1438 [S]	The Grass Roots	1965	$25

OLIVA, TONY

KUBANY
❏ SD-600	My Favorite Music	1966	$30

OLIVER, DAVID

Number	Title	Yr	NM
MERCURY			
❏ SRM-1-1183	David Oliver	1978	$12
❏ SRM-1-3831	Here's to You	1980	$12
❏ SRM-1-3747	Mind Magic	1979	$12
❏ SRM-1-3784	Rain Fire	1979	$12

OLIVER, JIMMY

Number	Title	Yr	NM
SUE			
❏ LP-1041 [M]	Hits A-Go-Go	1966	$25
❏ STLP-1041 [S]	Hits A-Go-Go	1966	$30

OLIVER, KING

Number	Title	Yr	NM
BRUNSWICK			
❏ BL58020 [10]	King Oliver	1950	$120
DECCA			
❏ DL79246	Papa Joe	1969	$35
EPIC			
❏ LA16003 [M]	King Oliver and His Orchestra	1960	$75
❏ BA17003 [R]	King Oliver and His Orchestra	1960	$50
❏ LN3208 [M]	King Oliver Featuring Louis Armstrong	1956	$150
HERWIN			
❏ 106	Zulus Ball/Working Man Blues	197?	$30
LONDON			
❏ AL3510 [10]	King Oliver Plays the Blues	195?	$100
MCA			
❏ 1309	Papa Joe	198?	$25
MILESTONE			
❏ M-2006	The Immortal King Oliver	197?	$35
RCA VICTOR			
❏ LPV-529 [M]	King Oliver In New York	1965	$30
RIVERSIDE			

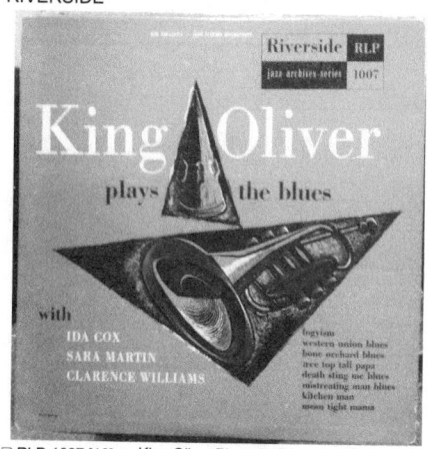

Number	Title	Yr	NM
❏ RLP-1007 [10]	King Oliver Plays the Blues	1953	$100
X			
❏ LVA-3018 [10]	King Oliver's Uptown Jazz	1954	$150

OLIVER, SY

Number	Title	Yr	NM
MOBILE FIDELITY			
❏ 1-242	Oliver's Twist/Easy Walkin'	1996	$50
—Audiophile vinyl			

OLIVER

Number	Title	Yr	NM
CREWE			
❏ CR-1333	Good Morning Starshine	1969	$18
❏ CR-1344	Oliver Again	1970	$18
UNITED ARTISTS			
❏ UAS-5511	Prisms	1971	$18

OLIVER AND THE TWISTERS

Number	Title	Yr	NM
COLPIX			
❏ CP-423 [M]	Look Who's Twistin' Everybody	1961	$40

OLIVIER, SIR LAWRENCE

Number	Title	Yr	NM
GOLDEN			
❏ XMK4014 [M]	Christmas Carol" by Charles Dickens, A	196?	$0

OLIVOR, JANE

Number	Title	Yr	NM
COLUMBIA			
❏ PC34917	Chasing Rainbows	1977	$12
—Original issue with no bar code			
❏ PC34917	Chasing Rainbows	198?	$10
—Budget-line reissue with bar code			
❏ PC34274	First Night	1977	$12
—Original issue with no bar code			
❏ PC34274	First Night	198?	$10
—Budget-line reissue with bar code			
❏ FC37938	In Concert	1982	$10
❏ PC37938	In Concert	198?	$10
—Budget-line reissue with new prefix			
❏ JC35437	Stay the Night	1978	$10
❏ PC35437	Stay the Night	198?	$10
—Budget-line reissue with new prefix			
❏ JC36335	The Best Side of Goodbye	1980	$10
❏ PC36335	The Best Side of Goodbye	198?	$10
—Budget-line reissue with new prefix			

OLLIE AND THE NIGHTINGALES

Number	Title	Yr	NM
STAX			
❏ STS-2021	Ollie and the Nightingales	1969	$50

OLSEN, DOROTHY

Number	Title	Yr	NM
RCA VICTOR			
❏ LPM-1606 [M]	I Know Where I'm Going	1957	$30

OLSEN, GEORGE

Number	Title	Yr	NM
RCA VICTOR			
❏ LPV-549 [M]	George Olsen and His Music	1968	$25

OLSHER, LESLEY

Number	Title	Yr	NM
VITAL			
❏ VTL-011	Lesley	1993	$25

OLSSON, NIGEL

Number	Title	Yr	NM
BANG			
❏ JZ36491	Changing Tides	1980	$12
❏ JZ35792	Nigel	1979	$12
ROCKET			
❏ L33-1962 [DJ]	Drummers Can Sing Too!	1975	$25
—Promo-only interview album			
❏ PIG-2158	Nigel Olsson	1975	$15
UNI			
❏ 73113	Nigel Olsson's Drum Orchestra	1971	$18

OLYMPIA BRASS BAND OF NEW ORLEANS

Number	Title	Yr	NM
AUDIOPHILE			
❏ AP-108	Olympia Brass Band of New Orleans	197?	$30
BASF			
❏ 20678	New Orleans Street Parade	197?	$30
BIOGRAPH			
❏ VPS-4	Here Come Da Great Olympia Jazz Band	197?	$30

OLYMPIC RUNNERS

Number	Title	Yr	NM
LONDON			
❏ PS668	Don't Let Up	1975	$18
❏ PS678	Hot to Trot	1977	$18
❏ PS658	Out in Front	1975	$18
❏ PS653	Put the Music Where Your Mouth Is	1974	$18
POLYDOR			
❏ PD-1-6196	Dancealot	1979	$15

OLYMPICS, THE

Number	Title	Yr	NM
ARVEE			
❏ A-424 [M]	Dance by the Light of the Moon	1961	$120
❏ A-423 [M]	Doin' the Hully Gully	1960	$160
❏ A-429 [M]	Party Time	1961	$120
EVEREST			
❏ 4109	The Olympics	1981	$12
MIRWOOD			
❏ MW-7003 [M]	Something Old, Something New	1966	$40
❏ MS-7003 [S]	Something Old, Something New	1966	$50
POST			
❏ 8000	The Olympics Sing	196?	$30
RHINO			
❏ RNDF-207	The Official Record Album of the Olympics	1983	$15
TRI-DISC			
❏ 1001 [M]	Do the Bounce	1963	$100

O'MALLEY, LENORE

Number	Title	Yr	NM
POLYDOR			
❏ PD-1-6253	First Be a Woman	1980	$18
❏ PD-1-6321	Lenore	1981	$18

OMAR AND THE HOWLERS

Number	Title	Yr	NM
AMAZING			
❏ AM1003	Big Leg Beat	1980	$30
AUSTIN			
❏ 8401	I Told You So	1984	$15

Number	Title	Yr	NM
COLUMBIA			
❏ BFC40815	Hard Times in the Land of Plenty	1987	$12
❏ FC44102	Wall of Pride	1988	$12

OMNIBUS

Number	Title	Yr	NM
UNITED ARTISTS			
❏ UAS-6743	Omnibus	1970	$40

ONE

Number	Title	Yr	NM
VILLAGE			
❏ 0(# unknown)	Creation Earth	1977	$50
—Includes posters			

ONE 2 MANY

Number	Title	Yr	NM
A&M			
❏ SP-5237	Mirror	1988	$10

ONE CAUSE ONE EFFECT

Number	Title	Yr	NM
CAPITOL			
❏ C1-94847	Drop the Axxe	1991	$18

101 STRINGS

Number	Title	Yr	NM
ALSHIRE			
❏ S-7100	The Glory of Christmas	1966	$15
❏ XM-4	The Glory of Christmas	197?	$10
—Reissue of 7100			

100 PROOF AGED IN SOUL

Number	Title	Yr	NM
HOT WAX			
❏ 712	100 Proof Aged in Soul	1971	$18
❏ 704	Somebody's Been Sleeping in My Bed	1970	$18

100 VOICES OF CHRISTMAS, THE

Number	Title	Yr	NM
DESIGN			
❏ SDLP-X-15 [S]	Silent Night	196?	$18
—Same as above, but in stereo			
❏ DLP-X-15 [M]	Silent Night	196?	$15

101 NORTH

Number	Title	Yr	NM
CAPITOL			
❏ C1-90911	101 North	1988	$12
—Reissue of Valley Vue 72945			
❏ C1-92510	Forever Yours	1991	$18
VALLEY VUE			
❏ D1-72945	101 North	1988	$18

ONE TO ONE

Number	Title	Yr	NM
WARNER BROS.			
❏ 25390	Forward Your Emotions	1986	$15

112

Number	Title	Yr	NM
BAD BOY			
❏ 73039 [B]	Part III	2000	$15

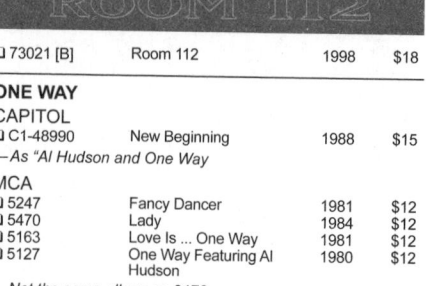

Number	Title	Yr	NM
❏ 73021 [B]	Room 112	1998	$18

ONE WAY

Number	Title	Yr	NM
CAPITOL			
❏ C1-48990	New Beginning	1988	$15
—As "Al Hudson and One Way"			
MCA			
❏ 5247	Fancy Dancer	1981	$12
❏ 5470	Lady	1984	$12
❏ 5163	Love Is ... One Way	1981	$12
❏ 5127	One Way Featuring Al Hudson	1980	$12
—Not the same album as 3178			

Number	Title	Yr	NM
❏ 3178	One Way Featuring Al Hudson	1979	$12
❏ 5823	One Way IX	1986	$12
❏ 5428	Shine on Me	1983	$12
❏ 5279	Who's Foolin' Who	1982	$12
❏ 5369	Wild Night	1982	$12
❏ 5552	Wrap Your Body	1985	$12

O'NEAL, ALEXANDER
TABU
❏ FZ39331	Alexander O'Neal	1985	$10
❏ OZ44492	All Mixed Up	1989	$12
❏ Z45349	All True Man	1991	$18
❏ FZ40320	Hearsay	1987	$10
❏ OZ45016	My Gift to You	1988	$12

O'NEAL, JOHNNY
CONCORD JAZZ
| ❏ CJ-228 | Coming Out | 198? | $25 |

O'NEAL, SHAQUILLE
JIVE
| ❏ 41529 | Shaq Diesel | 1993 | $18 |

— Issued in generic cover
| ❏ 41550 | Shaq-Fu: Da Return | 1994 | $15 |

T.W.ISM.
| ❏ INT2-90087 | You Can't Stop the Reign | 1996 | $18 |
| ❏ 6064 [EP] | You Can't Stop the Reign | 1996 | $10 |

— Promo only four-track sampler

ONENESS OF JUJU
BLACK FIRE

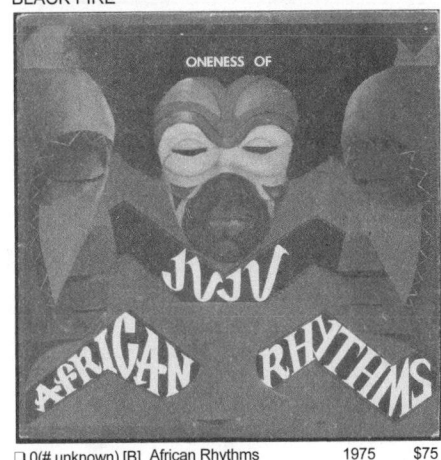

| ❏ 0(# unknown) [B] | African Rhythms | 1975 | $75 |
| ❏ 0(# unknown) | Space Jungle Luv | 1976 | $75 |

STRATA-EAST
| ❏ SES-19735 | A Message from Mozambique | 1973 | $150 |

— As "Juju"
| ❏ SES-7420 | Chapter 2: Nia | 1974 | $150 |

— As "Juju"

ONLY ONES, THE
DRASTIC PLASTIC
| ❏ DPRLP44 [B] | The Only Ones | 2015 | $30 |

— numbered, green and clear vinyl editions

ONO, YOKO
Also see JOHN LENNON.

APPLE
❏ SVBB-3399 [B]	Approximately Infinite Universe	1973	$150
❏ SW-3412 [B]	Feeling the Space	1973	$100
❏ SVBB-3380 [B]	Fly	1971	$150
❏ SW-3373 [B]	Yoko Ono Plastic Ono Band	1970	$50

CAPITOL
| ❏ SPRO-11219 [DJ] | Rising Mixes | 1996 | $30 |

— Promo-only vinyl EP of six remixes from the CD "Rising"

GEFFEN
| ❏ GHS2004 | Season of Glass | 1981 | $15 |

POLYDOR
| ❏ PD-1-6364 | It's Alright (I See Rainbows) | 1982 | $12 |
| ❏ 823289-1 | It's Alright (I See Rainbows) | 1984 | $10 |

— Reissue
| ❏ 827530-1 [B] | Starpeace | 1985 | $15 |

ONYX
DEF JAM
| ❏ 536988-1 | Shut 'Em Down | 1998 | $18 |
| ❏ 230 [DJ] | Shut 'Em Down | 1998 | $25 |

— Promo-only version in generic cover

Number	Title	Yr	NM
JMJ/RAL			
❏ 529265-1	All We Got Iz Us	1995	$15

OPA
MILESTONE
| ❏ M-9069 | Goldenwings | 1976 | $30 |
| ❏ M-9078 | Magic Time | 1977 | $30 |

OPEN SKY
PM
| ❏ PMR-001 | Open Sky | 1974 | $35 |
| ❏ PMR-003 | Spirit in the Sky | 1975 | $35 |

OPHELIA RAGTIME ORCHESTRA
STOMP OFF
| ❏ SOS-1108 | Echoes from the Snowball Club | 1986 | $25 |

OPUS
POLYDOR
| ❏ 827953-1 | Up and Down | 1985 | $12 |

OPUS SEVEN
SOURCE
| ❏ 27000 | Thoughts | 1979 | $18 |

ORANG UTAN
BELL
| ❏ 6054 | Orang Utan | 1971 | $40 |

ORANGE COLORED SKY
UNI
| ❏ 73031 | Orange Colored Sky | 1968 | $50 |

ORANGE THEN BLUE
GM RECORDINGS
| ❏ GM-3006 | Music for Jazz Orchestra | 1987 | $25 |

ORANGE WEDGE
(NO LABEL)
| ❏ 0(no cat #) | No One Left But Me | 1975 | $300 |
| ❏ 0(no cat #) | Wedge | 1975 | $300 |

ORBACH, JERRY
MGM
| ❏ E-4056 [M] | Jerry Orbach Off Broadway | 1963 | $25 |
| ❏ SE-4056 [S] | Jerry Orbach Off Broadway | 1963 | $30 |

ORBISON, ROY
ACCORD
| ❏ SN-7150 | Ooby Dooby | 1981 | $10 |

ASYLUM
| ❏ 6E-198 | Laminar Flow | 1979 | $15 |

BUCKBOARD
| ❏ BBS-1015 | Roy Orbison's Golden Hits | 197? | $12 |

CANDELITE
| ❏ P212946 | The Living Legend of Roy Orbison | 1976 | $18 |

DCC COMPACT CLASSICS
| ❏ LPZ-2042 | The All-Time Greatest Hits of Roy Orbison | 1997 | $120 |

— Audiophile vinyl

DESIGN
| ❏ DLP-164 [M] | Orbiting with Roy Orbison | 196? | $18 |
| ❏ DLPS-164 [R] | Orbiting with Roy Orbison | 196? | $12 |

HALLMARK
| ❏ SHM-824 | The Exciting Roy Orbison | 197? | $10 |

HITS UNLIMITED
| ❏ 233-0 | My Spell on You | 1982 | $10 |

MERCURY
| ❏ SRM-1-1045 | I'm Still in Love with You | 1975 | $15 |

MGM
❏ E-4514 [M]	Cry Softly, Lonely One	1967	$30
❏ SE-4514 [S]	Cry Softly, Lonely One	1967	$35
❏ SE-4683	Hank Williams the Roy Orbison Way	1970	$30
❏ SE-4867	Memphis	1972	$18
❏ SE-4934	Milestones	1973	$18
❏ SE-4835	Roy Orbison Sings	1972	$18
❏ E-4424 [M]	Roy Orbison Sings Don Gibson	1967	$30
❏ SE-4424 [S]	Roy Orbison Sings Don Gibson	1967	$35
❏ T-91173 [M]	Roy Orbison Sings Don Gibson	1967	$35

— Capitol Record Club edition
| ❏ ST-91173 [S] | Roy Orbison Sings Don Gibson | 1967 | $35 |

— Capitol Record Club edition
❏ E-4379 [M]	The Classic Roy Orbison	1966	$30
❏ SE-4379 [S]	The Classic Roy Orbison	1966	$35
❏ T-90928 [M]	The Classic Roy Orbison	1966	$35

— Capitol Record Club edition

Number	Title	Yr	NM
❏ ST-90928 [S]	The Classic Roy Orbison	1966	$35

— Capitol Record Club edition
❏ SE-4659	The Great Songs of Roy Orbison	1970	$30
❏ SE-4636	The Many Moods of Roy Orbison	1969	$30
❏ E-4322 [M]	The Orbison Way	1965	$30
❏ SE-4322 [S]	The Orbison Way	1965	$35
❏ T-90631 [M]	The Orbison Way	1965	$35

— Capitol Record Club edition
| ❏ ST-90631 [S] | The Orbison Way | 1965 | $35 |

— Capitol Record Club edition
❏ E-4308 [M]	There Is Only One Roy Orbison	1965	$30
❏ SE-4308 [S]	There Is Only One Roy Orbison	1965	$35
❏ T90454 [M]	There Is Only One Roy Orbison	1965	$40

— Capitol Record Club edition
| ❏ ST90454 [S] | There Is Only One Roy Orbison | 1965 | $40 |

— Capitol Record Club edition

MONUMENT

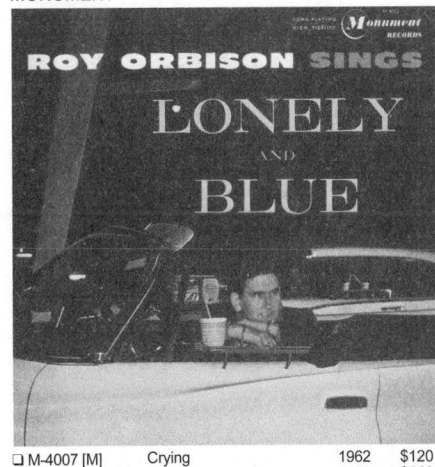

❏ M-4007 [M]	Crying	1962	$120
❏ SM-14007 [S]	Crying	1962	$600
❏ MLP-8023 [M]	Early Orbison	1964	$30
❏ SLP-18023 [S]	Early Orbison	1964	$50
❏ MLP-8003 [M]	In Dreams	1963	$50

— White and rainbow label
| ❏ MLP-8003 [M] | In Dreams | 1964 | $30 |

— Green and gold label
| ❏ SLP-18003 [S] | In Dreams | 1963 | $150 |

— White and rainbow label
| ❏ SLP-18003 [S] | In Dreams | 1964 | $50 |

— Green and gold label
❏ MC-6620	In Dreams	1977	$15
❏ M-4002 [M]	Lonely and Blue	1961	$175
❏ SM-14002 [S]	Lonely and Blue	1961	$600
❏ MLP-8024 [M]	More of Roy Orbison's Greatest Hits	1964	$30
❏ SLP-18024 [S]	More of Roy Orbison's Greatest Hits	1964	$40
❏ MC-6621	More of Roy Orbison's Greatest Hits	1977	$15
❏ MLP-8035 [M]	Orbisongs	1965	$30
❏ SLP-18035 [S]	Orbisongs	1965	$35
❏ MG-7600	Regeneration	1976	$18
❏ M-4009 [M]	Roy Orbison's Greatest Hits	1962	$50
❏ MLP-8000 [M]	Roy Orbison's Greatest Hits	1963	$30
❏ SM-14009 [S]	Roy Orbison's Greatest Hits	1962	$100
❏ SLP-18000 [S]	Roy Orbison's Greatest Hits	1963	$40
❏ MC-6619	Roy Orbison's Greatest Hits	1977	$15
❏ KZG31484	The All-Time Greatest Hits of Roy Orbison	1972	$30
❏ MP-8600	The All-Time Greatest Hits of Roy Orbison	1977	$16
❏ KWG38384	The All-Time Greatest Hits of Roy Orbison	1982	$12
❏ MLP-8045 [M]	The Very Best of Roy Orbison	1966	$30
❏ SLP-18045 [P]	The Very Best of Roy Orbison	1966	$35

— "It's Over" is rechanneled
| ❏ MC-6622 | The Very Best of Roy Orbison | 1977 | $15 |

RHINO
❏ R171493	For the Lonely: A Roy Orbison Anthology	1988	$15
❏ R170711	The Classic Roy Orbison	1989	$15
❏ R170916	The Sun Years	1989	$18

S&P
| ❏ 507 | The All-Time Greatest Hits of Roy Orbison | 2004 | $40 |

— Reissue on 180-gram vinyl

SUN
| ❏ LP-1260 [M] | Roy Orbison at the Rock House | 1961 | $600 |
| ❏ 113 | The Original Sound | 1969 | $15 |

Number	Title	Yr	NM
TIME-LIFE			
❑ SRNR34	Roy Orbison 1960-1965	1990	$25
—Box set in "The Rock 'n' Roll Era" series			
TRIP			
❑ TLX-8505	The Best of Roy Orbison	197?	$10
VIRGIN			
❑ 91295	A Black and White Night	1990	$18
❑ 90604	In Dreams: The Greatest Hits	1987	$15
—Re-recordings of his original hits			
❑ 91058	Mystery Girl	1989	$12

ORCHESTRA OF THE EIGHTH DAY

Number	Title	Yr	NM
FLYING FISH			
❑ FF-292	Music for the End	1982	$35

ORCHESTRA U.S.A.

Number	Title	Yr	NM
COLPIX			
❑ CP-448 [M]	Orchestra U.S.A. Debut	1964	$175
❑ SCP-448 [S]	Orchestra U.S.A. Debut	1964	$175
COLUMBIA			
❑ CL2247 [M]	Jazz Journey	1963	$30
❑ CS9047 [S]	Jazz Journey	1963	$30
RCA VICTOR			
❑ LPM-3498 [M]	The Sextet Of Orchestra U.S.A.	1965	$25
❑ LSP-3498 [S]	The Sextet Of Orchestra U.S.A.	1965	$30

ORCHESTRAL MANOEUVRES IN THE DARK

Number	Title	Yr	NM
A&M			
❑ SP-5077	Crush	1985	$10
❑ SP6-5027	Junk Culture	1984	$10
❑ R184156	The Best of O.M.D.	1988	$15
—BMG Direct Marketing edition			
❑ SP-5186	The Best of O.M.D.	1988	$12
❑ R114546	The Pacific Age	1986	$15
—RCA Music Service edition			
❑ SP-5144	The Pacific Age	1986	$12
VIRGIN			
❑ 91006	Dazzle Ships	1988	$12
—Reissue			
❑ 90611	Orchestral Manoeuvres in the Dark	1987	$12
—Reissue			
❑ 90612	Organisation	1987	$12
—First U.S. issue of early LP			
VIRGIN/EPIC			
❑ ARE37721	Architecture and Morality	1981	$18
❑ FE37411	Orchestral Manoeuvres in the Dark	1981	$18
VIRIGN/EPIC			
❑ BFE38543	Dazzle Ships	1983	$15

ORCHIDS, THE (U)

Number	Title	Yr	NM
ROULETTE			
❑ R-25169 [M]	Twistin' at the Roundtable	1962	$40
❑ SR-25169 [S]	Twistin' at the Roundtable	1962	$35

OREGON

Number	Title	Yr	NM
ECM			
❑ 25025	Crossing	1985	$25
❑ 23796	Oregon	1983	$25
ELEKTRA			
❑ AB-304	In Performance	1979	$35
❑ 6E-154	Out of the Woods	1978	$25
❑ 6E-224	Roots in the Sky	1979	$25
MOBILE FIDELITY			
❑ 1-514	Distant Hills	198?	$150
—Audiophile vinyl			
PORTRAIT			
❑ OR44465	45th Parallel	1989	$30
TERRA			
❑ T-1	Music of Another Present Era	1985	$25
VANGUARD			
❑ VSD-79341	Distant Hills	1973	$30
❑ VSQ-40031 [Q]	Distant Hills	1974	$40
❑ VSD-79370	Friends	1976	$30
❑ VSD-79358	In Concert	1975	$30
❑ VSD-79419	Moon and Mind	1979	$30
❑ VSD-79326	Music of Another Present Era	197?	$30
❑ VSD-79432	Our First Record	1980	$30
❑ VSD-109/10	The Essential Oregon	198?	$35
❑ VSD-79397	Violin	1978	$30
❑ VSD-79350	Winter Light	1974	$30

OREGON AND ELVIN JONES

Number	Title	Yr	NM
VANGUARD			
❑ VSD-79377	Together	1977	$30

ORGAN GRINDERS, THE

Number	Title	Yr	NM
MERCURY			
❑ SR-61282	Out of the Egg	1970	$30

ORGANIZED KONFUSION

Number	Title	Yr	NM
HOLLYWOOD			
❑ HB-61406	Stress: The Extinction Agenda	1994	$30
—Vinyl may be promo only			
PRIORITY			
❑ 50560	The Equinox	1997	$15

ORIENT EXPRESS, THE

Number	Title	Yr	NM
MAINSTREAN			
❑ S-6117	The Orient Express	1969	$100

ORIGINAL CAMELLIA JAZZ BAND

Number	Title	Yr	NM
NEW ORLEANS			
❑ 7207	Original Camellia Jazz Band	198?	$25

ORIGINAL CASTE, THE

Number	Title	Yr	NM
T-A			
❑ 5003	One Tin Soldier	1970	$18

ORIGINAL DIXIELAND JAZZ BAND, THE

Number	Title	Yr	NM
GHB			
❑ GHB-100	Original Dixieland Jazz Band 1943	198?	$12
RCA VICTOR			
❑ LPV-547 [M]	The Original Dixieland Jazz Band	1968	$25
X			
❑ LX-3007 [M]	The Original Dixieland Jazz Band	1954	$50

ORIGINAL LAST POETS, THE

See THE LAST POETS.

ORIGINAL MEMPHIS FIVE, THE

Number	Title	Yr	NM
FOLKWAYS			
❑ RBF-26	The Original Memphis Five	197?	$35

ORIGINAL SALTY DOGS, THE

Number	Title	Yr	NM
BLACKBIRD			
❑ 12003	Traditional Classics	1967	$35
GHB			
❑ 58	Free Wheeling	1968	$35
❑ 44	The Original Salty Dogs	1967	$35
❑ 62	The Right Track	197?	$30
STOMP OFF			
❑ SOS-1115	Honky Tonk Town	1987	$25

ORIGINAL SURFARIS, THE
See THE SURFARIS (2).

ORIGINAL TWISTERS, THE

Number	Title	Yr	NM
WING			
❑ MGW-12217 [M]	Come On and Twist	1962	$25
❑ SRW-16217 [S]	Come On and Twist	1962	$30

ORIGINAL WASHBOARD BAND, THE

Number	Title	Yr	NM
RCA VICTOR			
❑ LSP-1958 [S]	Scrubbin' and Pickin'	1959	$30
❑ LPM-1958 [M]	Scrubbin' and Pickin'	1959	$25

ORIGINALS, THE (1)

Number	Title	Yr	NM
FANTASY			
❑ F-9546	Another Time, Another Place	1978	$12
❑ F-9577	Come Away with Me	1979	$12
MOTOWN			
❑ M7-826	California Sunset	1975	$18
❑ M5-110V	Motown Superstar Series, Vol. 10	1982	$12
PHASE II			
❑ JW37075	Yesterday and Today	1981	$15
SOUL			
❑ SS-716	Baby I'm for Real	1969	$40
❑ SS-743	California Sunset	1974	$0
—Unreleased			
❑ S7-746	Communique	1976	$18
❑ SS-734	Definitions	1971	$25
❑ S7-749	Down to Love Town	1977	$18
❑ SS-729	Naturally Together	1971	$30
❑ SS-724	Portrait of the Originals	1970	$30
❑ SS-740	The Game Called…	1973	$18

ORIGINOO GUNN CLAPPAZ

Number	Title	Yr	NM
PRIORITY			
❑ 50577	Da Storm	1996	$18

ORIOLES, THE

Number	Title	Yr	NM
BIG A			
❑ LP-2001	The Orioles' Greatest All-Time Hits	1969	$30
CHARLIE PARKER			
❑ PLP-816 [M]	Modern Sounds of the Orioles	1962	$100
❑ PLP-816S [S]	Modern Sounds of the Orioles	1962	$150
COLLECTABLES			
❑ COL-5014	Sonny Til and the Orioles' Greatest Hits	198?	$15
MURRAY HILL			
❑ M61234	For Collectors Only	1983	$40

ORION, P.J., AND THE MAGNATES

Number	Title	Yr	NM
MAGNATE			
❑ 122459	P.J. Orion and the Magnates	196?	$175

ORION

Number	Title	Yr	NM
SUN			
❑ 1028 [B]	Fresh	1983	$12
❑ 1025	Glory	1982	$12
❑ 1019	Orion Country	1980	$12
❑ 1012	Orion Reborn	1978	$30
—White cover, also known as the "coffin cover			
❑ 1012	Orion Reborn	1978	$12
—Blue cover			
❑ 1021	Rockabilly	1981	$12
❑ 1017	Sunrise	1979	$12

ORION THE HUNTER
With Barry Goudreau, formerly of BOSTON.

Number	Title	Yr	NM
PORTRAIT			
❑ BFR39239	Orion the Hunter	1984	$18

ORLANDO, JAY

Number	Title	Yr	NM
DOBRE			
❑ 1040	Jay Orlando Loves Earl Bostic	197?	$30

ORLANDO, TONY

Number	Title	Yr	NM
CASABLANCA			
❑ NBLP7153	I Got Rhythm	1979	$12
❑ NBLP7209	Living for the Music	1980	$12
EPIC			
❑ BG33785	Before Dawn	1975	$18
❑ BN611 [S]	Bless You and 11 Other Great Hits	1961	$40
❑ LN3808 [M]	Bless You and 11 Other Great Hits	1961	$30

ORLEANS

Number	Title	Yr	NM
ABC			
❑ AA-1058-2	Before the Dance	1977	$15
❑ ABCX-795	Orleans	1973	$18
❑ AC-30011	The ABC Collection	1976	$12
ASYLUM			
❑ 7E-1029	Let There Be Music	1975	$12
❑ 7E-1070	Waking and Dreaming	1976	$12
INFINITY			
❑ INF-9006	Forever	1979	$12
MCA			
❑ 5767	Grown Up Children	1986	$10
❑ 5110	Orleans	1980	$12
RADIO			
❑ 90012	One of a Kind	1982	$12

ORLONS, THE

Number	Title	Yr	NM
CAMEO			
❑ C1033 [M]	All the Hits by the Orlons	1962	$75
❑ C1073 [M]	Down Memory Lane with the Orlons	1964	$50
❑ C1054 [M]	Not Me	1963	$50
❑ C1041 [M]	South Street	1963	$75
❑ C1061 [M]	The Orlons' Biggest Hits	1964	$50
❑ C1020 [M]	The Wah-Watusi	1962	$75

ORLONS, THE / THE DOVELLS
Also see each artist's individual listings.

Number	Title	Yr	NM
CAMEO			
❑ C1067 [M]	Golden Hits of the Orlons and the Dovells	1964	$50

ORNBERG, THOMAS

Number	Title	Yr	NM
STOMP OFF			
❑ SOS-1043	Come Back, Sweet Papa	198?	$25

ORPHAN EGG

Number	Title	Yr	NM
CAROLE			
❑ CARS-8004	Orphan Egg	1968	$40

Number	Title	Yr	NM

ORPHANN
O.M.I.
| ❏ 70021 | Up for Adoption | 1977 | $150 |

ORPHEON CELESTA
STOMP OFF
| ❏ SOS-1083 | Gare de Lyon | 1985 | $25 |
| ❏ SOS-1095 | Shim-Me-Sha-Wabble | 1985 | $25 |

ORPHEUS
MGM
| ❏ SE-4569 [S] | Ascending | 1968 | $25 |
| ❏ E-4569 [M] | Ascending | 1968 | $75 |

—Known copies are yellow label promos with "DJ Monaural" sticker on stereo cover

❏ SE-4599	Joyful	1969	$25
❏ E-4524 [M]	Orpheus	1968	$75
❏ SE-4524 [S]	Orpheus	1968	$18

ORR, BENJAMIN
ELEKTRA
| ❏ R152406 | The Lace | 1986 | $15 |

—RCA Music Service edition

| ❏ 60460 | The Lace | 1986 | $12 |

ORRALL, ROBERT ELLIS
RCA VICTOR
❏ AFL1-4853	Contain Yourself	1984	$10
❏ AFL1-4081	Fixation	1981	$10
❏ MFL1-8502 [EP]	Special Pain	1983	$10

ORSTED PEDERSEN, NIELS-HENNING, AND KENNETH KNUDSEN
STEEPLECHASE
| ❏ SCS-1068 | Pictures | 198? | $30 |

ORSTED PEDERSEN, NIELS-HENNING, AND SAM JONES
INNER CITY
| ❏ IC-2055 | Double Bass | 197? | $35 |
STEEPLECHASE
| ❏ SCS-1055 | Double Bass | 198? | $30 |

ORSTED PEDERSEN, NIELS-HENNING
INNER CITY
| ❏ IC-2041 | Jaywalkin' | 197? | $35 |
STEEPLECHASE
❏ SCS-1125	Dancing on the Tables	1979	$30
❏ SCS-1041	Jaywalkin'	198?	$30
❏ SCS-1083	Trio 1	198?	$30
❏ SCS-1093	Trio 2	198?	$30

ORTEGA, ANTHONY
BETHLEHEM
| ❏ BCP-79 [M] | Jazz For Young Moderns | 1957 | $300 |
DISCOVERY
| ❏ 788 | Rain Dance | 1978 | $30 |
HERALD
| ❏ HLP-0101 [M] | A Man and His Horn | 1956 | $75 |
REVELATION
| ❏ REV-M3 [M] | New Dance | 1968 | $40 |
| ❏ REV-3 [S] | New Dance | 1968 | $25 |
VANTAGE
| ❏ VLP-2 [10] | Anthony Ortega | 1954 | $120 |

ORTEGA, FRANKIE
DOBRE
| ❏ 1043 | Smokin' | 197? | $30 |
IMPERIAL
| ❏ LP-9025 [M] | Piano Stylings | 1956 | $175 |
| ❏ LP-12011 [S] | Piano Stylings | 1959 | $175 |
JUBILEE
❏ JLP-1106 [M]	77 Sunset Strip	1959	$30
❏ JGS-1106 [S]	77 Sunset Strip	1959	$40
❏ JGM-1112 [M]	Frankie Ortega at the Embers	1960	$25
❏ JGS-1112 [S]	Frankie Ortega at the Embers	1960	$30
❏ JLP-1080 [M]	Swingin' Abroad	1958	$30
❏ SDJLP-1080 [S]	Swingin' Abroad	1958	$30
❏ JLP-1051 [M]	Twinkling Pinkies	1958	$30

ORTEGA/DOMANICO/WEST/GOODWIN
REVELATION
| ❏ REV-7 [S] | Permutations | 1969 | $30 |

ORY, KID
COLUMBIA
| ❏ CL6145 [10] | Kid Ory & His Creole Dixieland Band | 1950 | $150 |
| ❏ CL835 [M] | Kid Ory | 1955 | $75 |

DIXIELAND JUBILEE
| ❏ DJ-519 | Kid Ory at the Dixieland Jubilee | 198? | $25 |
FOLKLYRIC
| ❏ 9008 | Kid Ory's Creole Jazz Band | 197? | $25 |
GOOD TIME JAZZ
❏ L-12022 [M]	Kid Ory's Creole Jazz Band, 1944-45	1955	$50
❏ L-21 [10]	Kid Ory's Creole Jazz Band, 1953	1954	$50
❏ L-12004 [M]	Kid Ory's Creole Jazz Band, 1954	1954	$40
❏ L-12008 [M]	Kid Ory's Creole Jazz Band, 1955	1955	$50
❏ L-12016 [M]	Kid Ory's Creole Jazz Band, 1956	1955	$50
❏ L-12041/2	Kid Ory's Favorites!	1961	$50

| ❏ S-10041/2 [S] | Kid Ory's Favorites! | 1961 | $75 |
| ❏ M-12045 [M] | This Kid's the Greatest! | 1962 | $30 |
STORYVILLE
| ❏ 4064 | Kid Ory Plays the Blues | 198? | $25 |
VAULT
| ❏ 9006 | Kid Ory Live! | 196? | $35 |
VERVE
❏ MGV-1022 [M]	Dance with Kid Ory or Just Listen	1957	$175
❏ MGVS-6125 [S]	Dance with Kid Ory or Just Listen	1960	$150
❏ V-1022 [M]	Dance with Kid Ory or Just Listen	1961	$25
❏ V6-1022 [S]	Dance with Kid Ory or Just Listen	1961	$35
❏ MGV-1026 [M]	Dixieland Marching Songs	1957	$175
❏ V-1026 [M]	Dixieland Marching Songs	1961	$25
❏ V6-1026 [S]	Dixieland Marching Songs	1961	$35
❏ MGV-8254 [M]	Kid Ory In Europe	1958	$175
❏ V-8254 [M]	Kid Ory In Europe	1961	$25
❏ MGV-1017 [M]	Kid Ory Plays W.C. Handy	1957	$175
❏ MGVS-6061 [S]	Kid Ory Plays W.C. Handy	1960	$150
❏ V-1017 [M]	Kid Ory Plays W.C. Handy	1961	$25
❏ V6-1017 [S]	Kid Ory Plays W.C. Handy	1961	$35
❏ MGV-1030 [M]	Kid Ory Sings French Traditional Songs	1957	$175

—Canceled

❏ MGV-1014 [M]	Song of the Wanderer	1957	$175
❏ MGVS-6011 [S]	Song of the Wanderer	1960	$150
❏ V-1014 [M]	Song of the Wanderer	1961	$25
❏ V6-1014 [S]	Song of the Wanderer	1961	$35
❏ V-8456 [M]	Storyville Nights	1962	$30
❏ V6-8456 [S]	Storyville Nights	1962	$25
❏ MGV-1016 [M]	The Kid From New Orleans	1957	$175
❏ V-1016 [M]	The Kid From New Orleans	1961	$25
❏ MGV-1023 [M]	The Original Jazz	1957	$175
❏ MGVS-6126 [S]	The Original Jazz	1960	$0

—Canceled

| ❏ V-1023 [M] | The Original Jazz | 1961 | $25 |
| ❏ V6-1023 [S] | The Original Jazz | 1961 | $35 |

ORY, KID/JOHNNY WITTWER
JAZZ MAN
| ❏ LP-2 [10] | Kid Ory's Creole Band/ Johnny Wittwer Trio | 1954 | $50 |

OSBORNE, JEFFREY
A&M
❏ SP-5017	Don't Stop	1984	$10
❏ SP-5103	Emotional	1986	$10
❏ SP-3272	Jeffrey Osborne	198?	$10

—Budget-line reissue of 4896

❏ SP-4896	Jeffrey Osborne	1982	$10
❏ SP-5205	One Love -- One Dream	1988	$10
❏ SP-4940	Stay with Me Tonight	1983	$10
ARISTA
| ❏ AL8620 | Only Human | 1990 | $18 |

OSBORNE, JIMMIE
AUDIO LAB
| ❏ AL-1527 [M] | Singing Songs He Wrote | 1959 | $150 |
KING
❏ 782 [M]	Golden Harvest	1963	$50
❏ 941 [M]	Jimmie Osborne's Golden Harvest	1965	$40
❏ 730 [M]	The Legendary Jimmy Osborne	1961	$50
❏ 892 [M]	The Very Best of Jimmie Osborne	1964	$40

OSBORNE, MARY
STASH
| ❏ ST-215 | Now and Then | 198? | $25 |
WARWICK
| ❏ W-2004 [M] | A Girl and Her Guitar | 1960 | $150 |
| ❏ W-2004ST [S] | A Girl and Her Guitar | 1960 | $120 |

OSBORNE, WILL
AIRCHECK
| ❏ 37 | Will Osborne and His Orchestra On the Air | 198? | $25 |
HINDSIGHT
| ❏ HSR-197 | Will Osborne and His Orchestra 1936 | 198? | $25 |

OSBORNE BROTHERS, THE
CMH
❏ 6206 [B]	#1	197?	$12
❏ 9011	Bluegrass Collection	1978	$18
❏ 6231	Bluegrass Concerto	197?	$15
❏ 6256	Bobby and His Mandolin	1981	$15
❏ 9008	From Rocky Top to Muddy Bottom	1977	$18
❏ 4501	Greatest Bluegrass Hits, Vol. 1	198?	$15
❏ 6244	Kentucky Calling Me	1980	$15
❏ 9016	The Essential Bluegrass Album	1979	$18

— With MacWiseman

DECCA
❏ DL75356	Bobby & Sonny	1972	$18
❏ DL75321	Country Roads	1971	$18
❏ DL75079	Favorite Hymns by the Osborne Brothers	1969	$25
❏ DL4903 [M]	Modern Sounds of Bluegrass Music	1967	$18
❏ DL74903 [S]	Modern Sounds of Bluegrass Music	1967	$25
❏ DL75204	Ru-Beeeee	1970	$25
❏ DL75271	The Osborne Brothers	1971	$18
❏ DL4767 [M]	Up This Hill and Down	1966	$18
❏ DL74767 [S]	Up This Hill and Down	1966	$25
❏ DL75128	Up to Date and Down to Earth	1969	$25
❏ DL4602 [M]	Voices in the Bluegrass	1965	$18
❏ DL74602 [S]	Voices in the Bluegrass	1965	$25
❏ DL4993 [M]	Yesterday, Today and The Osborne Brothers	1968	$30
❏ DL74993 [S]	Yesterday, Today and The Osborne Brothers	1968	$25
MCA
| ❏ 125 | Favorite Hymns by the Osborne Brothers | 1973 | $15 |

—Reissue of Decca 75079

| ❏ 135 | Ru-Beeeee | 1973 | $15 |

—Reissue of Decca 75204

| ❏ 4086 | The Best of the Osborne Brothers | 1974 | $18 |
| ❏ 105 | Voices in the Bluegrass | 1973 | $15 |

—Reissue of Decca 74602

| ❏ 119 | Yesterday, Today and The Osborne Brothers | 1973 | $15 |

—Reissue of Decca 74993

MGM
❏ E-4090 [M]	Bluegrass Instrumentals	1962	$30
❏ SE-4090 [S]	Bluegrass Instrumentals	1962	$30
❏ E-4018 [M]	Bluegrass Music	1962	$30
❏ SE-4018 [S]	Bluegrass Music	1962	$30
❏ E-3734 [M]	Country Pickin' and Hillside Singin'	1959	$50
❏ E-4149 [M]	Cuttin' Grass	1963	$30
❏ SE-4149 [S]	Cuttin' Grass	1963	$30
❏ GAS140	The Osborne Brothers (Golden Archives Series)	1970	$25
RCA VICTOR
| ❏ AHL1-4324 | Bluegrass Spectacular | 1982 | $12 |
| ❏ AYL1-5436 | Bluegrass Spectacular | 1985 | $10 |

—Best Buy Series" reissue

ROUNDER
| ❏ SS-04 | The Osborne Brothers | 198? | $15 |
| ❏ SS-03 | The Osborne Brothers with Red Allen | 1981 | $15 |
SUGAR HILL
❏ SH-3754	Once More, Vol. 1	1986	$12
❏ SH-3758	Once More, Vol. 2	1987	$12
❏ SH-3764	Singing, Shouting Praises	1988	$12
❏ SH-3740	Some Things I Want to Sing About	1984	$12

OSBOURNE, OZZY
Also see BLACK SABBATH; QUIET RIOT; URIAH HEEP; RAINBOW; BADLANDS; NIGHT RANGER.

CBS ASSOCIATED

Number	Title	Yr	NM
❏ FZ38987	Bark at the Moon	1983	$12
❏ PZ38987	Bark at the Moon	1985	$10

—Budget-line reissue with new prefix

Number	Title	Yr	NM
❏ AS1828 [DJ]	Interview with Ozzy	1984	$30
❏ Z46795	No More Tears	1991	$25
❏ FZ44245	No Rest for the Wicked	1988	$12
❏ ZX240714	Ozzy Osbourne/Randy Rhoads Tribute	1987	$15
❏ 9Z940543 [EP]	The Ultimate Live Ozzy	1986	$40

—Picture disc with live material

Number	Title	Yr	NM
❏ FZ40026	The Ultimate Sin	1986	$12

JET

Number	Title	Yr	NM
❏ JZ36812	Blizzard of Ozz	1981	$12
❏ AS991372 [PD]	Diary of a Madman	1981	$40

—Promo-only picture disc

Number	Title	Yr	NM
❏ FZ37492	Diary of a Madman	1981	$12
❏ 8Z837640 [EP]	Mr. Crowley	1982	$30

—Three-song picture disc with live material

Number	Title	Yr	NM
❏ ZX238350	Speak of the Devil	1982	$18

O'SHEA, MILO

COLUMBIA

Number	Title	Yr	NM
❏ CS9647	An Evening in Dublin	1969	$25

OSIBISA

ANTILLES

Number	Title	Yr	NM
❏ 7058	Ojah Awake	1978	$12
❏ 7051	Welcome Home	1978	$12

BUDDAH

Number	Title	Yr	NM
❏ BDS-5136	Super Fly T.N.T.	1973	$30

DECCA

Number	Title	Yr	NM
❏ DL75368	Heads	1972	$18
❏ DL75285	Osibisa	1971	$18
❏ DL75327	Woyaya	1972	$18

ISLAND

Number	Title	Yr	NM
❏ ILPS9411	Ojah Awake	1977	$12
❏ ILPS9355	Welcome Home	1976	$12

MCA

Number	Title	Yr	NM
❏ 32	Osibisa	1973	$12

—Reissue of Decca 75285

Number	Title	Yr	NM
❏ 43	Woyaya	1973	$12

—Reissue of Decca 75327

WARNER BROS.

Number	Title	Yr	NM
❏ BS2732	Happy Children	1973	$12
❏ BS2802	Osibirock	1974	$12

OSIPOV STATE RUSSIAN FOLK ORCHESTRA (VITALY GNUTOV, CONDUCTOR)

MERCURY LIVING PRESENCE

Number	Title	Yr	NM
❏ SR90310 [S]	Balalaika Favorites	196?	$100

—Maroon label, no "Vendor: Mercury Record Corporation"

Number	Title	Yr	NM
❏ SR90310 [S]	Balalaika Favorites	196?	$50

—Maroon label, with "Vendor: Mercury Record Corporation"

Number	Title	Yr	NM
❏ SR90310 [S]	Balalaika Favorites	196?	$30

—Third edition: Dark red (not maroon) label

Number	Title	Yr	NM
❏ SR90310 [S]	Balalaika Favorites	1998	$30

—Classic Records reissue

OSIRIS

MARLIN

Number	Title	Yr	NM
❏ 2234	O-Zone	1979	$25

WARNER BROS.

Number	Title	Yr	NM
❏ BSK3311	Since Before Our Time	1978	$25

OSKAR, LEE

ELEKTRA

Number	Title	Yr	NM
❏ 6E-150	Before the Rain	1978	$12
❏ 5E-526	My Road, Our Road	1981	$12

UNITED ARTISTS

Number	Title	Yr	NM
❏ UA-LA594-G	Lee Oskar	1976	$12

OSLIN, K.T.

RCA

Number	Title	Yr	NM
❏ 5924-1-R	80's Ladies	1987	$12
❏ 8369-1-R	This Woman	1988	$12

OSMOND, DONNY

CAPITOL

Number	Title	Yr	NM
❏ C1-92354	Donny Osmond	1989	$15
❏ C1-94051	Eyes Don't Lie	1990	$18

MGM

Number	Title	Yr	NM
❏ SE-4886	Alone Together	1973	$30

—With tear-off 10x10 photo intact; deduct 60 percent if missing

Number	Title	Yr	NM
❏ M3G-4930	A Time for Us	1973	$12
❏ M3G-4978	Donny	1974	$12
❏ SE-4872	My Best to You	1972	$12
❏ SE-4820	Portrait of Donny	1972	$12
❏ SE-4782	The Donny Osmond Album	1971	$15

Number	Title	Yr	NM
❏ SE-4854	Too Young	1972	$12
❏ SE-4797	To You with Love, Donny	1971	$12

POLYDOR

Number	Title	Yr	NM
❏ PD-1-6067	Disco Train	1976	$10
❏ PD-1-6109	Donald Clark Osmond	1977	$10

OSMOND, DONNY AND MARIE

MGM

Number	Title	Yr	NM
❏ M3G-4968	I'm Leaving It All Up to You	1974	$12
❏ M3G-4996	Make the World Go Away	1975	$12

POLYDOR

Number	Title	Yr	NM
❏ PD-1-6068	Donny & Marie -- Featuring Songs from Their Television Show	1976	$10
❏ PD-1-6083	Donny & Marie -- New Season	1976	$10
❏ PD-1-6169	Goin' Coconuts	1978	$10
❏ PD-1-6127	Winning Combination	1978	$10

OSMOND, JIMMY

MGM

Number	Title	Yr	NM
❏ SE-4855	Killer Joe	1972	$12
❏ M3G-4916	Little Arrows	1975	$15

OSMOND, MARIE

CAPITOL

Number	Title	Yr	NM
❏ C1-48968	All in Love	1988	$10
❏ ST-12516	I Only Wanted You	1986	$10
❏ C1-91781	Steppin' Stone	1989	$12
❏ ST-12414	There's No Stopping Your Heart	1985	$10

MGM

Number	Title	Yr	NM
❏ M3G-4944	In My Little Corner of the World	1974	$15
❏ SE-4910	Paper Roses	1973	$15
❏ M3G-4979	Who's Sorry Now	1975	$15

POLYDOR

Number	Title	Yr	NM
❏ PD-1-6099	This Is the Way That I Feel	1977	$10

OSMONDS, THE
Includes records as "The Osmond Brothers." (Most of these were pre-1970, before Donny was a member of the group.) Also see DONNY OSMOND.

ELEKTRA

Number	Title	Yr	NM
❏ 60180	The Osmond Brothers	1982	$12

MERCURY

Number	Title	Yr	NM
❏ SRM-1-3766	Steppin' Out	1979	$12

METRO

Number	Title	Yr	NM
❏ M543 [M]	We Sing You a Merry Christmas	1965	$18

—Reissue of 4187 with one track missing and remaining contents rearranged

Number	Title	Yr	NM
❏ MS543 [S]	We Sing You a Merry Christmas	1965	$25

MGM

Number	Title	Yr	NM
❏ MG-2-5012	Around the World -- Live in Concert	1975	$15
❏ SE-4851	Crazy Horses	1972	$15
❏ SE-4770	Homemade	1971	$30

—With tear-off poster intact; deduct 60 percent if poster is not attached

Number	Title	Yr	NM
❏ M3G-4939	Love Me for a Reason	1974	$12
❏ SE-4724	Osmonds	1971	$15
❏ SE-4796	Phase-III	1972	$15
❏ E-4146 [M]	Songs We Sang on the Andy Williams Show	1963	$30
❏ SE-4146 [S]	Songs We Sang on the Andy Williams Show	1963	$30

—As "The Osmond Brothers"

Number	Title	Yr	NM
❏ E-4291 [M]	The New Sound of the Osmond Brothers	1965	$25
❏ SE-4291 [S]	The New Sound of the Osmond Brothers	1965	$30
❏ T90403 [M]	The New Sound of the Osmond Brothers	1965	$40

—Capitol Record Club edition

Number	Title	Yr	NM
❏ ST90403 [S]	The New Sound of the Osmond Brothers	1965	$40

—Capitol Record Club edition

Number	Title	Yr	NM
❏ E-4235 [M]	The Osmond Brothers Sing the All-Time Hymn Favorites	1964	$25
❏ SE-4235 [S]	The Osmond Brothers Sing the All-Time Hymn Favorites	1964	$30
❏ SE-4826	The Osmonds "Live	1972	$18
❏ SE-4902	The Plan	1973	$12
❏ M3G-4993	The Proud One	1975	$12
❏ PM-7 [M]	The Travels of Jaimie McPheeters	1963	$50

—Side 1: Dialogue from TV show; Side 2: Osmond Brothers tracks. AC Spark Plugs promo.

Number	Title	Yr	NM
❏ E-4187 [M]	We Sing You a Merry Christmas	1963	$30

—As "The Osmond Brothers"

Number	Title	Yr	NM
❏ SE-4187 [S]	We Sing You a Merry Christmas	1963	$30
❏ PM-9 [M]	We Sing You a Merry Christmas	1963	$40

—Special-products issue for AC Spark Plug dealers

POLYDOR

Number	Title	Yr	NM
❏ PD-1-6077	Brainstorm	1976	$12

Number	Title	Yr	NM
❏ PD-2-8001	The Osmond Christmas Album	1976	$18

—Includes group, solo and duet recordings

Number	Title	Yr	NM
❏ PD-2-9005	The Osmonds Greatest Hits	1977	$15

WARNER BROS.

Number	Title	Yr	NM
❏ 25070	One Way Rider	1984	$10

OSTERWALD, HAZY

BALLY

Number	Title	Yr	NM
❏ BAL-12004 [M]	Swiss Jazz	1956	$40

O'SULLIVAN, GILBERT

EPIC

Number	Title	Yr	NM
❏ JE37013	Off Centre	1981	$12

MAM

Number	Title	Yr	NM
❏ 5	Back to Front	1972	$18
❏ 4	Gilbert O'Sullivan -- Himself	1972	$18
❏ 7	I'm a Writer, Not a Fighter	1973	$18
❏ 10	Stranger in My Own Backyard	1974	$18

OSWALD, LEE HARVEY
The below are documentary records, all based on the same radio interview.

EYEWITNESS

Number	Title	Yr	NM
❏ 1002	Lee Harvey Oswald Speaks	1967	$100

INCA

Number	Title	Yr	NM
❏ 1001	Oswald: Self Portrait in Red	1965	$150

KEY

Number	Title	Yr	NM
❏ 880	The President's Assassin Speaks	1964	$150

OTB

BLUE NOTE

Number	Title	Yr	NM
❏ BT-85128	Inside Track	1986	$30
❏ B1-85141	Live at Mt. Fuji	1987	$30
❏ BT-85118	Out of the Blue	1985	$30
❏ B1-93006	Spiral Staircase	1989	$35

OTHER HALF, THE (1)

ACTA

Number	Title	Yr	NM
❏ 38004	The Other Half	1968	$150

OTHER HALF, THE (2)

7/2

Number	Title	Yr	NM
❏ 0 (no cat #)	The Other Half	1966	$1500

—Album has been counterfeited, but those records are translucent when held to a light, originals are not

OTHER ONES, THE

VIRGIN

Number	Title	Yr	NM
❏ 90576	The Other Ones	1987	$10

OTIS, JOHNNY

ALLIGATOR

Number	Title	Yr	NM
❏ AL-4726	The New Johnny Otis Show	1982	$12

CAPITOL

Number	Title	Yr	NM
❏ C1-92858	The Capitol Years	1989	$18
❏ T940 [M]	The Johnny Otis Show	1958	$300

DIG

Number	Title	Yr	NM
❏ 104 [M]	Rock and Roll Hit Parade, Volume 1	1957	$900

—Gold cover with thick cardboard and thick vinyl records. Counterfeits have noticeably thinner vinyl.

Number	Title	Yr	NM
❏ 104 [M]	Rock and Roll Hit Parade, Volume 1	1958	$600

—Yellow cover with thick cardboard and thick vinyl records. Counterfeits have noticeably thinner vinyl.

EPIC

Number	Title	Yr	NM
❏ BN26524 [B]	Cuttin' Up	1970	$30
❏ EG30473	The Johnny Otis Show Live at Monterey	1971	$30

KENT

Number	Title	Yr	NM
❏ KST-534	Cold Shot	1968	$30

SAVOY

Number	Title	Yr	NM
❏ SJL-2230	The Original Johnny Otis Show	1978	$18
❏ SJL-2252	The Original Johnny Otis Show, Vol. 2	1980	$18

OTIS, SHUGGIE

EPIC

Number	Title	Yr	NM
❏ KE30752	Freedom Flight	1971	$18
❏ BN26511	Here Comes Shuggie Otis	1970	$18
❏ PE33059	Inspiration Information	1975	$18

OTIS AND CARLA
Also see OTIS REDDING; CARLA THOMAS.

Number	Title	Yr	NM

STAX

☐ ST-716 [M]	King and Queen	1967	$35
☐ STS-716 [S]	King and Queen	1967	$50

SUNDAZED

☐ LP5069 [S]	King and Queen	2001	$15

— *Reissue on 180-gram vinyl*

OTTE, HANS

KUCKUCK

☐ KU-069/70	Das Buch der Klänge	1984	$35

OTTO'S CHEMICAL LOUNGE

HOMESTEAD

☐ HMS 023	Spillover	1985	$15

OTWAY, JOHN

STIFF

☐ NEW3 [B]	I Did It Otway	1981	$25

STIFF/EPIC

☐ USE5 [B]	Deep Thought	1980	$25

OUSLEY, HAROLD

BETHLEHEM

☐ BCP-6059 [M]	Tenor Sax	1961	$250
☐ SBCP-6059 [S]	Tenor Sax	1961	$250

COBBLESTONE

☐ 9017	The Kid!	1971	$30

MUSE

☐ MR-5141	Sweet Double Hipness	1979	$30
☐ MR-5107	The People's Groove	197?	$35

OUTCASTS, THE (2)

CICADELIC

☐ CIC-988	Live! Standing Room Only	1985	$18
☐ CIC-987	Meet the Outcasts	1985	$18

OUTFIELD, THE

COLUMBIA

☐ OC40619	Bangin'	1987	$10
☐ BFC40027	Play Deep	1985	$10
☐ OC44449	Voices of Babylon	1989	$12

MCA

☐ 10111	Diamond Days	1990	$15

OUTKAST

LAFACE

☐ 26053	Aquemini	1998	$18
☐ 6153 [DJ]	Aquemini	1998	$25

— *Promo-only censored version*

☐ 26029	Atliens	1996	$18
☐ 26072	Stankonia	2000	$18

OUTLAW BLUES BAND, THE

BLUESWAY

☐ BLS-6020	Breakin' In	1969	$30
☐ BLS-6021	The Outlaw Blues Band	1968	$30

OUTLAWS

Southern rock" band; few, if any, of their releases used the word "The" before their name. Also see LYNYRD SKYNYRD.

ARISTA

☐ A2L8300	Bring It Back Alive	1978	$15
☐ A2L8608	Bring It Back Alive	198?	$12

— *Reissue*

☐ A2L8114	Bring It Back Alive	198?	$12

— *Second reissue*

☐ AL9542	Ghost Riders	1980	$12
☐ AL9614	Greatest Hits of the Outlaws/ High Tides Forever	1982	$12
☐ AL8319	Greatest Hits of the Outlaws/ High Tides Forever	198?	$10

Number	Title	Yr	NM

— *Reissue*

☐ AL4135	Hurry Sundown	1977	$12
☐ AL8369	Hurry Sundown	198?	$10

— *Reissue*

☐ AL9507	In the Eye of the Storm	1979	$12
☐ AL4070 [B]	Lady in Waiting	1976	$12
☐ AQ4070 [Q]	Lady in Waiting	1976	$20
☐ AL9584	Los Hombres Malo	1982	$12
☐ AL4042	Outlaws	1975	$12
☐ AL8301	Outlaws	198?	$10

— *Reissue*

☐ AB4205	Playin' to Win	1978	$12
☐ SP-132 [EP]	Radio Remixes	1982	$15

— *Promo-only four-song sampler*

DIRECT DISC

☐ SD16617	Outlaws	198?	$50

— *Audiophile vinyl*

PAIR

☐ PDL2-1050	The Outlaws	1986	$15

PASHA

☐ BFZ40512	Soldiers of Fortune	1986	$10

OUTSIDERS, THE

CAPITOL

☐ T2745 [M]	Happening "Live!	1967	$30
☐ ST2745 [S]	Happening "Live!	1967	$30
☐ T2636 [M]	In	1967	$30
☐ ST2636 [S]	In	1967	$30
☐ T2568 [M]	The Outsiders Album #2	1966	$30
☐ ST2558 [S]	The Outsiders Album #2	1966	$30
☐ T2501 [M]	Time Won't Let Me	1966	$30

☐ ST2501 [S]	Time Won't Let Me	1966	$30

RHINO

☐ RNLP-70132	The Best of the Outsiders (1965-1968)	1986	$12

OVATIONS, THE (1)

MGM

☐ SE-4945	Having a Party	1973	$18

SOUNDS OF MEMPHIS

☐ 7001	Hooked on a Feeling	1972	$25

OVERKILL

MEGAFORCE

☐ MRI1469	Feel the Fire	1985	$15

MEGAFORCE/ATLANTIC

☐ 81792 [EP]	Fuck You!	1987	$12
☐ 81735	Taking Over	1987	$12
☐ 82045	The Years of Decay	1989	$15
☐ 81865	Under the Influence	1988	$12

OVERSTREET, PAUL

RCA

☐ R150526	Heroes	1991	$18

— *Only available on vinyl through BMG Direct Marketing*

☐ 9717-1-R	Sowin' Love	1989	$15

RCA VICTOR

☐ NFL1-8007	Paul Overstreet	1983	$15

OVERSTREET, TOMMY

ABC

☐ AB-1066	Better Me	1978	$15

ABC DOT

☐ DOSD-2027	Greatest Hits Vol. One	1975	$18
☐ DO-2086	Hangin' 'Round	1977	$15
☐ DOSD-2016 [B]	I'm a Believer	1975	$18
☐ DOSD-2038	The Tommy Overstreet Show Live from the Silver Slipper	1975	$18
☐ DOSD-2056	Turn On to Tommy Overstreet	1976	$18

Number	Title	Yr	NM

☐ DO-2071	Vintage '77	1977	$15

DOT

☐ DLP-25992	Gwen (Congratulations)	1971	$25
☐ DLP-26003	Heaven Is My Woman's Love	1972	$25
☐ DOS-26010	My Friends Call Me T.O.	1973	$25
☐ DLP-25994	This Is Tommy Overstreet	1972	$25
☐ DOS-26021	Woman, Your Name Is My Song	1974	$25

ELEKTRA

☐ 6E-178	I'll Never Let You Down	1979	$12
☐ 6E-292	The Best of Tommy Overstreet	1980	$12
☐ 6E-226	The Real Tommy Overstreet	1979	$12

MCA

☐ 797	Better Me	198?	$10

— *Reissue*

☐ 646	Hangin' 'Round	198?	$10

— *Reissue*

☐ 645	Vintage '77	198?	$10

— *Reissue*

OWEN, JIM

EPIC

☐ PEG34852	A Song for Us All: A Salute to Hank Williams	1977	$25

OWEN, REG

DECCA

☐ DL8859 [M]	Under Paris Skies	1959	$25
☐ DL78859 [S]	Under Paris Skies	1959	$30

PALETTE

☐ PZ-1018 [M]	Fiorello!	1960	$25
☐ SPZ-31018 [S]	Fiorello!	1960	$30
☐ PZ-1004 [M]	Get Happy	1960	$25
☐ SPZ-31004 [S]	Get Happy	1960	$30
☐ 1001 [M]	Manhattan Spiritual	1959	$30
☐ S-1001 [S]	Manhattan Spiritual	1959	$40

RCA VICTOR

☐ LPM-1582 [M]	Coffee Break	1958	$25
☐ LSP-1582 [S]	Coffee Break	1958	$30
☐ LPM-1914 [M]	Cuddle Up a Little Closer	1959	$25
☐ LSP-1914 [S]	Cuddle Up a Little Closer	1959	$30
☐ LPM-1907 [M]	Deep in a Dream	1959	$30
☐ LPM-1580 [M]	Dreaming	1958	$30
☐ LPM-1908 [M]	Girls Were Made to Take Care of Boys	1959	$25
☐ LSP-1908 [S]	Girls Were Made to Take Care of Boys	1959	$30
☐ LPM-1597 [M]	Holiday Abroad in Dublin	1958	$25
☐ LSP-1597 [S]	Holiday Abroad in Dublin	1958	$30
☐ LPM-1599 [M]	Holiday Abroad in London	1958	$25
☐ LSP-1599 [S]	Holiday Abroad in London	1958	$30
☐ LPM-1906 [M]	I'll Sing You 1,000 Love Songs	1959	$25
☐ LSP-1906 [S]	I'll Sing You 1,000 Love Songs	1959	$30
☐ LPM-1542 [M]	The Best of Irving Berlin	1957	$30
☐ LPM-1675 [M]	The British Isles	1958	$25
☐ LSP-1675 [S]	The British Isles	1958	$30
☐ LPM-1915 [M]	You Don't Know Paree	1959	$30

OWEN-B

MUS-I-COL

☐ 101209	Owen-B	1970	$75

OWENS, BONNIE

CAPITOL

☐ T2600 [M]	All of Me Belongs to You	1967	$30
☐ ST2600 [S]	All of Me Belongs to You	1967	$30
☐ T2403 [M]	Don't Take Advantage of Me	1965	$25
☐ ST2403 [S]	Don't Take Advantage of Me	1965	$30
☐ ST-341	Hi-Fi to Cry By	1969	$30
☐ ST-195	Lead Me On	1969	$30
☐ ST-557	Mother's Favorite Hymns	1970	$30
☐ ST2861	Somewhere Between	1968	$30

OWENS, BUCK, AND SUSAN RAYE

CAPITOL

☐ ST-558	Great White Horse	1970	$18
☐ ST-837	Merry Christmas from Buck Owens and Susan Raye	1971	$18
☐ ST-11084	The Best of Buck Owens and Susan Raye	1972	$18
☐ ST-11204	The Good Old Days (Are Here Again)	1973	$18
☐ ST-448	We're Gonna Get Together	1970	$25

OWENS, BUCK

CAPITOL

☐ C1-92893	Act Naturally	1989	$18
☐ SMAS-11180	Ain't It Amazing, Gracie	1973	$18
☐ STBB-486	A Merry "Hee Haw" Christmas	1970	$30
☐ ST2902	A Night on the Town	1968	$30
☐ ST-194	Anywhere U.S.A.	1969	$25
☐ ST-11222	Arms Full of Empty	1972	$18
☐ T2353 [M]	Before You Go/No One But You	1965	$30
☐ ST2353 [S]	Before You Go/No One But You	1965	$30

Number	Title	Yr	NM
❏ ST-685	Bridge Over Troubled Water	1971	$18
❏ T1489 [M]	Buck Owens	1961	$40
—Black colorband label, Capitol logo at left			
❏ STCL-574	Buck Owens	1970	$40
❏ T1489 [M]	Buck Owens	1962	$30
—Black colorband label, Capitol logo at top			
❏ ST2994	Buck Owens, The Guitar Player	1968	$30
❏ T2715 [M]	Buck Owens and His Buckaroos in Japan	1967	$25
❏ ST2715 [S]	Buck Owens and His Buckaroos in Japan	1967	$30
❏ ST-232	Buck Owens in London	1969	$25
❏ ST 8-0232	Buck Owens in London	1969	$30
— Capitol Record Club edition			
❏ T1482 [M]	Buck Owens Sings Harlan Howard	1961	$40
❏ ST1482 [S]	Buck Owens Sings Harlan Howard	1961	$50
❏ T1989 [M]	Buck Owens Sings Tommy Collins	1963	$40
❏ ST1989 [S]	Buck Owens Sings Tommy Collins	1963	$50
❏ T2556 [M]	Carnegie Hall Concert	1966	$25
❏ ST2556 [S]	Carnegie Hall Concert	1966	$30
❏ ST2977	Christmas Shopping	1968	$30
❏ T2396 [M]	Christmas with Buck Owens and His Buckaroos	1965	$25
❏ ST2396 [S]	Christmas with Buck Owens and His Buckaroos	1965	$30
❏ SWBB-257	Close-Up	1969	$25
— Reissue of "Together Again" and "No One But You"			
❏ T2497 [M]	Dust on Mother's Bible	1966	$25
❏ ST2497 [S]	Dust on Mother's Bible	1966	$30
❏ C1-91132	Hot Dog!	1988	$15
❏ T2186 [M]	I Don't Care	1964	$30
❏ ST2186 [S]	I Don't Care	1964	$30
❏ ST-11136	In the Palm of Your Hand	1973	$18
❏ ST2841 [S]	It Takes People Like You to Make People Like Me	1968	$30
❏ T2841 [M]	It Takes People Like You to Make People Like Me	1968	$40
❏ T2283 [M]	I've Got a Tiger by the Tail	1965	$30
❏ ST2283 [S]	I've Got a Tiger by the Tail	1965	$30
❏ ST-131	I've Got You on My Mind Again	1969	$25
❏ ST-628	I Wouldn't Live in New York City	1970	$25
❏ ST-11105	Live at the White House	1972	$18
❏ SPRO2980/1 [DJ]	Minute Masters	1966	$50
— Promo-only excerpts of 24 songs			
❏ ST-11332	Monster's Holiday	1974	$18
❏ T1879 [M]	On the Bandstand	1963	$40
❏ ST1879 [S]	On the Bandstand	1963	$50
❏ T2650 [M]	Open Up Your Heart	1967	$25
❏ ST2650 [S]	Open Up Your Heart	1967	$30
❏ T2443 [M]	Roll Out the Red Carpet for Buck Owens & The Buckaroos	1966	$25
❏ ST2443 [S]	Roll Out the Red Carpet for Buck Owens & The Buckaroos	1966	$30
❏ ST2962	Sweet Rosie Jones	1968	$30
❏ ST-212	Tall Dark Stranger	1969	$25
❏ T2105 [M]	The Best of Buck Owens	1964	$30
❏ ST2105 [S]	The Best of Buck Owens	1964	$30
❏ ST2897	The Best of Buck Owens, Vol. 2	1968	$30
❏ ST-830	The Best of Buck Owens, Vol. 4	1971	$18
❏ SKAO-145	The Best of Buck Owens, Volume 3	1969	$25
❏ ST-11471	The Best of Buck Owens, Volume 6	1976	$18
❏ ST-11273	The Best of Buck Owens Volume 5	1973	$18
❏ T2367 [M]	The Instrumental Hits of Buck Owens & the Buckaroos	1965	$30
❏ ST2367 [S]	The Instrumental Hits of Buck Owens & the Buckaroos	1965	$30
❏ ST-476	The Kansas City Song	1970	$25
❏ T2135 [M]	Together Again/My Heart Skips a Beat	1964	$30
❏ ST2135 [S]	Together Again/My Heart Skips a Beat	1964	$30
❏ DT1489 [R]	Under Your Spell Again	1968	$30
— Duophonic" reissue of mono original with new title			
❏ ST-11390	Weekend Daddy	1974	$18
❏ T1777 [M]	You're for Me	1962	$40
❏ ST1777 [S]	You're for Me	1962	$50
❏ ST-439	Your Mother's Prayer	1970	$25
❏ T2760 [M]	Your Tender Loving Care	1967	$30
❏ ST2760 [S]	Your Tender Loving Care	1967	$30
COUNTRY MUSIC FOUNDATION			
❏ CMF-012	Live at Carnegie Hall	198?	$15
LABREA			
❏ 1017 [M]	Buck Owens	1961	$150
❏ 8017 [S]	Buck Owens	1961	$175

STARDAY

Number	Title	Yr	NM
❏ SLP-324 [B]	Coutnry Hit Maker #1	1964	$30
❏ SLP-172	The Fabulous Country Music Sound of Buck Owens	1962	$50
TIME-LIFE			
❏ STW-114	Country Music	1981	$12
WARNER BROS.			
❏ BS2952	Buck 'Em	1976	$15
❏ BS3087	Our Old Mansion	1977	$15

OWENS, CHARLES

Number	Title	Yr	NM
DISCOVERY			
❏ 811	Music of Harry Warren, Volume 1	1980	$30
❏ 787	Two Quartets	1978	$30
VAULT			
❏ LP-0(# unknown)	I Stand Alone	196?	$50

OXFORD, VERNON

Number	Title	Yr	NM
RCA VICTOR			
❏ LPM-3704 [M]	Woman, Let Me Sing You a Song	1967	$40
❏ LSP-3704 [S]	Woman, Let Me Sing You a Song	1967	$30
ROUNDER			
❏ 0123	His and Hers	198?	$18
❏ 0091	If I Had My Wife to Love Over	198?	$18
❏ 0156	Keepin' It Country	1982	$18

OZ KNOZZ

Number	Title	Yr	NM
OZONE			
❏ O2-1000	Ruff Mix	1975	$500

OZARK MOUNTAIN DAREDEVILS

Number	Title	Yr	NM
A&M			
❏ SP-4662	Don't Look Down	1977	$15
❏ SP-3654	It'll Shine When It Shines	1974	$15
❏ SP-3192	It'll Shine When It Shines	198?	$10
— Budget-line reissue			
❏ SP-6006	It's Alive	1978	$18
❏ SP-4601	Men from Earth	1976	$15
❏ SP-3202	The Best of Ozark Mountain Daredevils	1982	$12
❏ SP-4549	The Car Over the Lake Album	1975	$15
❏ SP-4411	The Ozark Mountain Daredevils	1973	$15
❏ SP-3110	The Ozark Mountain Daredevils	198?	$10
— Budget-line reissue			
COLUMBIA			
❏ JC36375	Ozark Mountain Daredevils	1980	$12
SOUNDS GREAT			
❏ SG-5004	The Lost Cabin Sessions	1985	$12

OZONE, MAKOTO

Number	Title	Yr	NM
COLUMBIA			
❏ FC40240	After	1986	$25
❏ BFC39624	Makoto Ozone	1985	$25
❏ FC40676	Now You Know	1987	$25

OZONE

Number	Title	Yr	NM
MOTOWN			
❏ 6037ML	Glasses	1983	$25
❏ 6011ML	Li'l Suzy	1982	$25
❏ M8-962M1	Send It	1981	$25

P

P. FUNK ALL STARS

Number	Title	Yr	NM
CBS ASSOCIATED			
❏ FZ39168	Urban Dancefloor Guerrilas	1983	$18

P.F.M.

Number	Title	Yr	NM
ASYLUM			
❏ 7E-1071 [B]	Chocolate Kings	1976	$15
❏ 7E-1101 [B]	Jet Lag	1977	$15
MANTICORE			
❏ MA6-502 [B]	P.F.M. 'Cook'	1974	$25
❏ MC66668 [B]	Photos of Ghosts	1973	$25
❏ MC66673 [B]	The World Became the World	1974	$20

P.H. PHACTOR

Number	Title	Yr	NM
PICCADILLY			
❏ PIC-3343	Merryjuana	1980	$150

— Cover spells the group's name "Factor" but the label has it "Phactor

P.M. DAWN

Number	Title	Yr	NM
GEE STREET			
❏ 6768 [DJ]	The Bliss Album	1993	$25

— Promo-only vinyl edition

P.M. DAWN

Number	Title	Yr	NM
GEE STREET			
❏ 524147-1	Jesus Wept	1995	$25
❏ PRLP-6768-1 [DJ]	The Bliss Album...?	1993	$25

— Promo-only vinyl edition

PABLO CRUISE

Number	Title	Yr	NM
A&M			
❏ SP-4625	A Place in the Sun	1977	$12
❏ SP-3236	A Place in the Sun	198?	$10
— Budget-line reissue of 4625			
❏ SP-4575	Lifeline	1976	$12
❏ SP-4909	Out of Our Hands	1983	$12
❏ SP-4528	Pablo Cruise	1975	$12
❏ SP-3111	Pablo Cruise	198?	$10
— Budget-line reissue of 4528			
❏ SP-3712	Part of the Game	1979	$12
❏ SP-3726	Reflector	1981	$12
❏ SP-4697	Worlds Away	1978	$12
❏ SP-3198	Worlds Away	198?	$10
— Budget-line reissue of 4697			
MOBILE FIDELITY			

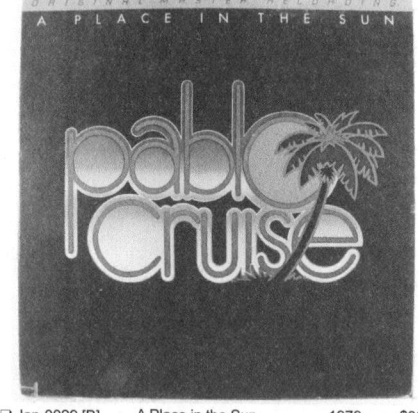

Number	Title	Yr	NM
❏ Jan-0029 [B]	A Place in the Sun	1979	$30
— Audiophile vinyl			
NAUTILUS			
❏ NR-6	Lifeline	1980	$25
— Audiophile vinyl			
❏ NR-28	Worlds Away	1981	$25
— Audiophile vinyl			

PAC-MAN

Number	Title	Yr	NM
KID STUFF			
❏ KSS-5029	Christmas Album	1982	$18

— Written and produced by Patrick McBride and Dana Walden

PACE, JOHNNY

Number	Title	Yr	NM
RIVERSIDE			
❏ RLP 12-292 [M]	Chet Baker Introduces Johnny Pace	1958	$300
❏ RLP-1130 [S]	Chet Baker Introduces Johnny Pace	1959	$300

Number	Title	Yr	NM

PACERS, THE
RAZORBACK
| ❏ 121 [M] | You Asked For It | 1965 | $150 |

PACHECO, MIKE
INTERLUDE
| ❏ MO-513 [M] | Hot Skins | 1959 | $40 |
| ❏ ST-1013 [S] | Hot Skins | 1959 | $30 |
TAMPA
| ❏ TP-30 [M] | Bongo Date | 1957 | $250 |
— Colored vinyl
| ❏ TP-30 [M] | Bongo Date | 1958 | $175 |
— Black vinyl
| ❏ TP-21 [M] | Bongo Session | 1957 | $250 |
— Colored vinyl
| ❏ TP-21 [M] | Bongo Session | 1958 | $175 |
— Black vinyl
| ❏ TP-10 [M] | Bongo Skins | 1957 | $250 |
— Colored vinyl
| ❏ TP-10 [M] | Bongo Skins | 1958 | $175 |
— Black vinyl

PACIFIC COAST RAGTIMERS, THE
CIRCLE
| ❏ CLP-1376 | The Pacific Coast Ragtimers | 199? | $30 |

PACIFIC DRIFT
DERAM
| ❏ DES18040 | Feelin' Free | 1970 | $25 |

PACIFIC GAS & ELECTRIC
ABC DUNHILL
| ❏ DSX-50157 | Pacific Gas and Electric Starring Charlie Allen | 1974 | $15 |
BRIGHT ORANGE
| ❏ 701 | Get It On | 1968 | $40 |
COLUMBIA
| ❏ CS1017 | Are You Ready | 1970 | $18 |
— 360 Sound" label
| ❏ CS1017 | Are You Ready | 1970 | $15 |
— Orange label
| ❏ CS9900 | Pacific Gas and Electric | 1969 | $18 |
— 360 Sound" label
| ❏ CS9900 | Pacific Gas and Electric | 1970 | $15 |
— Orange label
| ❏ C30362 | PG&E | 1971 | $15 |
| ❏ C32019 | The Best of Pacific Gas & Electric | 1972 | $15 |
POWER
| ❏ 701 | Get It On | 1969 | $30 |

PACIFIC OCEAN
V.M.C.
| ❏ 135 | Pacific Ocean | 1969 | $25 |

PACK, MARSHALL
STARDAY
| ❏ SLP-120 [M] | Marshall Pack | 1960 | $40 |

PACKERS, THE
PURE SOUL MUSIC
| ❏ 1001 [S] | Hole in the Wall | 1966 | $25 |

PACKHAM, GREG
STASH
| ❏ ST-242 | Action Reaction | 198? | $25 |

PADDOCK JAZZ BAND
BIOGRAPH
| ❏ CEN-10 | Paddock Jazz Band | 197? | $25 |

PAGE, GENE
ARISTA
| ❏ AL4174 | Close Encounters | 1978 | $12 |
| ❏ AL4262 | Love Starts After Dark | 1980 | $12 |
ATLANTIC
| ❏ SD18111 | Hot City | 1974 | $15 |
| ❏ SD18161 | Lovelock! | 1975 | $15 |

PAGE, HOT LIPS
CONTINENTAL
| ❏ 16007 [M] | Hot and Cozy | 1962 | $75 |
ONYX
| ❏ 207 | After Hours | 197? | $30 |
XANADU
| ❏ 107 | Trumpet at Minton's | 197? | $30 |

PAGE, JIMMY, AND ROBERT PLANT
Also see each artist's individual listings.

ATLANTIC
| ❏ 82706 [B] | No Quarter | 1994 | $30 |

| ❏ 83092 | Walking Into Clarksdale | 1998 | $25 |
— With all four sides of music correct
| ❏ 83092 | Walking Into Clarksdale | 1998 | $25 |
— Pressing error with Side 2's music repeated on Side 3

PAGE, JIMMY
Also see LED ZEPPELIN; JIMMY PAGE AND ROBERT PLANT; THE YARDBIRDS; THE FIRM; HONEYDRIPPERS.
CLEOPATRA
| ❏ 2914 [B] | Burn Up | | $25 |
| ❏ 8207 [B] | Burn Up | | $30 |
— picture disc
| ❏ 1236 [B] | No Introduction Necessary - Deluxe Edition | | $25 |
GEFFEN
| ❏ GHS24188 | Outrider | 1988 | $12 |
SPRINGBOARD
| ❏ SPB-4038 | Special Early Works | 1972 | $30 |

PAGE, LARRY, ORCHESTRA
RHINO
| ❏ RNDF-257 [PD] | Kinky Music | 1984 | $15 |
| ❏ RNLP-058 | Kinky Music | 1984 | $12 |

PAGE, MILTON
DIPLOMAT
| ❏ X-1016 | Pipe Organ | 196? | $12 |
— Reissue of Promenade album with same contents in same order
PROMENADE
| ❏ CH-1006 | Pipe Organ | 196? | $18 |

PAGE, PATTI
ACCORD
| ❏ SN-7206 | Special Thoughts | 1982 | $12 |
COLUMBIA
❏ CL2505 [M]	America's Favorite Hymns	1966	$15
❏ CS9305 [S]	America's Favorite Hymns	1966	$18
❏ CL2414 [M]	Christmas with Patti Page	1965	$15
❏ CS9214 [S]	Christmas with Patti Page	1965	$18
❏ CS9666	Gentle on My Mind	1968	$18
❏ CS9999	Honey Come Back	1970	$15
❏ CL2353 [M]	Hush, Hush, Sweet Charlotte	1965	$18
❏ CS9153 [S]	Hush, Hush, Sweet Charlotte	1965	$25
❏ CL2132 [M]	Love After Midnight	1964	$18
❏ CS8932 [S]	Love After Midnight	1964	$25
❏ CL2526 [M]	Patti Page's Greatest Hits	1966	$15
❏ CS9326 [S]	Patti Page's Greatest Hits	1966	$18
— 360 Sound" label
| ❏ CS9326 | Patti Page's Greatest Hits | 1970 | $12 |
— Orange label
| ❏ PC9326 | Patti Page's Greatest Hits | 198? | $10 |
— Budget-line reissue
❏ CL2049 [M]	Say Wonderful Things	1963	$18
❏ CS8849 [S]	Say Wonderful Things	1963	$25
❏ CL2761 [M]	Today My Way	1967	$25
❏ CS9561 [S]	Today My Way	1967	$18
EMARCY
❏ MG-36074 [M]	In the Land of Hi-Fi	1956	$250
❏ SR-80000 [S]	In the Land of Hi-Fi	1959	$250
❏ MG-36116 [M]	The East Side	1957	$250
❏ MG-36136 [M]	The West Side	1957	$250
HARMONY
| ❏ KH30407 | Green, Green Grass of Home | 1971 | $12 |
| ❏ HS11381 | Stand By Your Man | 1970 | $12 |
MERCURY
❏ MG-25209 [10]	And I Thought About You	1954	$40
❏ MG-20909 [M]	Blue Dream Street	1964	$25
❏ SR-60909 [S]	Blue Dream Street	1964	$30
❏ MG-25109 [10]	Christmas	1951	$40
❏ MG20093 [M]	Christmas with Patti Page	1956	$30
❏ 822740-1	Christmas with Patti Page	1987	$12
— Reissue
❏ MG-20615 [M]	Country & Western Golden Hits	1961	$25
❏ SR-60615 [S]	Country & Western Golden Hits	1961	$30
❏ MG-25101 [10]	Folksong Favorites	1951	$40
❏ MG-20712 [M]	Golden Hits of the Boys	1962	$25
❏ SR-60712 [S]	Golden Hits of the Boys	1962	$30
❏ MG-20689 [M]	Go On Home	1962	$25
❏ SR-60689 [S]	Go On Home	1962	$30
❏ SR-61344	I'd Rather Be Sorry	1971	$15
❏ MG-20406 [M]	I'll Remember April	1959	$30
❏ SR-60081 [S]	I'll Remember April	1959	$40
❏ MG-20405 [M]	Indiscretion	1959	$30
❏ SR-60059 [S]	Indiscretion	1959	$40
❏ MG-20388 [M]	I've Heard That Song Before	1957	$30
❏ SR-60011 [S]	I've Heard That Song Before	1959	$40
❏ MG-20573 [M]	Just a Closer Walk with Thee	1960	$30
❏ SR-60233 [S]	Just a Closer Walk with Thee	1960	$40
❏ MG-25196 [10]	Just Patti	1954	$40
❏ MG-20387 [M]	Let's Get Away from It All	1957	$30
❏ SR-60010 [S]	Let's Get Away from It All	1959	$40

❏ MG-20226 [M]	Manhattan Tower	1956	$30
❏ MG-20099 [M]	Music for Two in Love	1955	$30
❏ MG-20095 [M]	Page I	1955	$30
❏ MG-20096 [M]	Page II	1955	$30
❏ MG-20097 [M]	Page III	1955	$30
❏ MG-20101 [M]	Page IV	1955	$30
❏ MG-20398 [M]	Patti Page On Camera	1958	$30
❏ SR-60025 [S]	Patti Page On Camera	1959	$40
❏ MG-20758 [M]	Patti Page On Stage	1963	$25
❏ SR-60758 [S]	Patti Page On Stage	1963	$30
❏ MG-20495 [M]	Patti Page's Golden Hits	1960	$30
❏ SR-60495 [S]	Patti Page's Golden Hits	196?	$30
❏ MG-20794 [M]	Patti Page's Golden Hits, Volume 2	1963	$25
❏ SR-60794 [S]	Patti Page's Golden Hits, Volume 2	1963	$30
❏ MG-20599 [M]	Patti Page Sings and Stars In "Elmer Gantry	1960	$30
❏ SR-60260 [S]	Patti Page Sings and Stars In "Elmer Gantry	1960	$30
❏ MG-25185 [10]	Patti Sings for Romance	1954	$40
❏ MG-25197 [10]	Patti's Songs	1954	$40
❏ MG-20076 [M]	Romance on the Range	1955	$30
❏ MG-25210 [10]	So Many Memories	1954	$40
❏ MG-25059 [10]	Songs	1950	$40
❏ MG-25187 [10]	Song Souvenirs	1954	$40
❏ MG-25154 [10]	Tennessee Waltz	1952	$40
❏ SR-60114 [S]	The East Side	1959	$150
❏ PKW-118	The Most	1969	$18
❏ MG-20952 [M]	The Nearness of You	1965	$18
❏ SR-60952 [S]	The Nearness of You	1965	$25
❏ MG-20819 [M]	The Singing Rage	1963	$25
❏ SR-60819 [S]	The Singing Rage	1963	$30
❏ MG-20100 [M]	The Voice of Patti Page	1955	$30
❏ MG-20318 [M]	The Waltz Queen	1957	$40
— With one image of Patti Page on cover; "Custom High Fidelity" and Mercury logo at upper right of front cover
| ❏ SR-60049 [S] | The Waltz Queen | 1959 | $40 |
| ❏ MG-20318 [M] | The Waltz Queen | 1959 | $35 |
— With two images of Patti Page on cover; Mercury logo at upper left of front cover, "High Custom Fidelity" in white strip along bottom front cover
❏ SR-60113 [S]	The West Side	1959	$150
❏ MG-20102 [M]	This Is My Song	1955	$30
❏ MG-20417 [M]	Three Little Words	1960	$30
❏ SR-60037 [S]	Three Little Words	1960	$40
❏ MG-20098 [M]	You Go to My Head	1955	$30
PLANTATION
| ❏ 548 | Aces | 1981 | $12 |
WING
| ❏ MGW12174 [M] | Christmas with Patti Page | 196? | $25 |
— Same contents and order as Mercury 20093
❏ MGW12250 [M]	Let's Get Away from It All	196?	$15
❏ SRW16250 [S]	Let's Get Away from It All	196?	$18
❏ MGW12121 [M]	The Waltz Queen	196?	$15
❏ SRW16121 [S]	The Waltz Queen	196?	$18

PAGE, SID, AND DAVID SHELANDER
BAINBRIDGE
| ❏ 6257 | Odyssey | 198? | $25 |

PAGE, TOMMY
SIRE
| ❏ 26148 | Paintings in My Mind | 1990 | $15 |
| ❏ 25740 | Tommy Page | 1988 | $12 |

PAICH, MARTY
BETHLEHEM
| ❏ BCP-44 [M] | Jazz City Workshop | 1956 | $300 |
CADENCE
| ❏ CLP-3010 [M] | Marty Paich Big Band | 1958 | $50 |
DISCOVERY
❏ 829	I Get A Boot Out of You	198?	$25
❏ 844	New York Scene	198?	$25
❏ DS-857	What's New	198?	$25
GENE NORMAN
| ❏ GNP-10 [10] | Marty Paich Octet | 1955 | $120 |
— Red vinyl
| ❏ GNP-21 [M] | Marty Paich Octet | 1956 | $100 |
INTERLUDE
❏ MO-514 [M]	Like Wow -- Jazz 1960	1960	$30
❏ ST-1014 [S]	Like Wow -- Jazz 1960	1960	$30
❏ MO-509 [M]	Revel Without a Pause	1959	$30
❏ ST-1009 [S]	Revel Without a Pause	1959	$30
MODE
| ❏ LP-110 [M] | Jazz Band Ball | 1957 | $100 |
| ❏ LP-105 [M] | Marty Paich Trio | 1957 | $100 |
RCA VICTOR
❏ LPM-2164 [M]	Piano Quartet	1960	$25
❏ LSP-2164 [S]	Piano Quartet	1960	$30
❏ LPM-2259 [M]	Piano Quartet	1960	$25
❏ LSP-2259 [S]	Piano Quartet	1960	$30
REPRISE
| ❏ RS-6206 [S] | The Rock-Jazz Incident | 1966 | $35 |
| ❏ R-6206 [M] | The Rock-Jazz Incident | 1966 | $30 |
TAMPA
| ❏ TP-23 [M] | Hot Piano | 1957 | $300 |
— Probably the original title

Number	Title	Yr	NM
❑ TP-23 [M]	Jazz for Relaxation	1957	$300
— Colored vinyl			
❑ TP-23 [M]	Jazz for Relaxation	1958	$250
— Black vinyl			
❑ TP-28 [M]	Marty Paich Quintet Featuring Art Pepper	1957	$1000
— Red vinyl			
❑ TP-28 [M]	Marty Paich Quintet Featuring Art Pepper	1958	$400
— Black vinyl			

WARNER BROS.

❑ W1349 [M]	I Get A Boot Out of You	1959	$400
❑ WS1349 [S]	I Get A Boot Out of You	1959	$180
❑ W1296 [M]	The Broadway Bit	1959	$1200
❑ WS1296 [S]	The Broadway Bit	1959	$600

PAIGE, JANIS

BALLY

❑ BAL-12008 [M]	Let's Fall in Love	1957	$40

PAIR, THE

LIBERTY

❑ LRP-3461 [M]	In"-Citement	1966	$18
❑ LST-7461 [S]	In"-Citement	1966	$25
❑ LRP-3504 [M]	It's a Wonderful World	1967	$18
❑ LST-7504 [S]	It's a Wonderful World	1967	$25
❑ LRP-3440 [M]	The Pair Extraordinaire	1966	$18
❑ LST-7440 [S]	The Pair Extraordinaire	1966	$25
❑ LRP-3410 [M]	The Pair Live! At the Ice House	1965	$25
❑ LST-7410 [S]	The Pair Live! At the Ice House	1965	$30

PAISLEYS, THE

AUDIO CITY

❑ 70	Cosmic Mind at Play	1970	$250

PALANCE, JACK

WARNER BROS.

❑ WS1865	Palance	1970	$30

PALEY, TOM

ELEKTRA

❑ EKL-12 [M]	Folk Songs from the Southern Appalachians	195?	$40

PALM BEACH BAND BOYS, THE

RCA VICTOR

❑ LPM-3808 [M]	The Palm Beach Band Boys Strike Again	1967	$18
❑ LSP-3808 [S]	The Palm Beach Band Boys Strike Again	1967	$12
❑ LPM-3734 [M]	Winchester Cathedral	1966	$15
❑ LSP-3734 [S]	Winchester Cathedral	1966	$12

PALMER, BRUCE

VERVE FORECAST

❑ FTS-3086 [B]	The Cycle Is Complete	1970	$30

PALMER, EARL

LIBERTY

❑ LRP-3201 [M]	Drumsville	1961	$30
❑ LST-7201 [S]	Drumsville	1961	$40
❑ LRP-3227 [M]	Percolator Twist	1962	$30
❑ LST-7227 [S]	Percolator Twist	1962	$40

PALMER, JEFF

AUDIOQUEST

❑ AQ-LP-1014	Ease On	1993	$35

STATIRAS

❑ SLP-8081	Laser Wizzard	1987	$30

PALMER, ROBERT

EMI MANHATTAN

❑ E1-48057	Heavy Nova	1988	$12

ISLAND

❑ 842301-1	Addictions Volume I	1990	$12
❑ 91318	Addictions Volume I	1989	$15
— Original pressing available only for a short time			
❑ ILPS9595	Clues	1980	$12
❑ 90493	Clues	1986	$10
❑ ILPS9476	Double Fun	1978	$15
— Original copies of the above four albums were NOT distributed by Warner Bros.			
❑ 90494	Double Fun	1986	$10
❑ ILPS9665	Maybe It's Live	1982	$12
❑ ILPS9372	Pressure Drop	1976	$15
❑ 90087	Pressure Drop	1984	$10
❑ 90065	Pride	1983	$12
❑ 90471	Riptide	1985	$12
❑ PRO-819 [DJ]	Secrets	1979	$25
— Promo-only picture disc			
❑ PRO-819 [DJ]	Secrets	1979	$35
— Promo-only picture disc			
❑ ILPS9544	Secrets	1979	$12
❑ 90089	Secrets	1984	$10

Number	Title	Yr	NM
❑ ILPS9294 [B]	Sneakin' Sally Through the Alley	1975	$18
❑ 90086	Sneakin' Sally Through the Alley	1984	$10
❑ ILPS9420	Some People Can Do What They Like	1977	$15

WARNER BROS.

❑ WBMS-111 [DJ]	Live in Boston	1979	$30
— Part of "The Warner Bros. Music Show"			
❑ WBMS-111 [DJ]	Live in Boston	1979	$25
— Part of "The Warner Bros. Music Show"			

PALMER, ROY

RIVERSIDE

❑ RLP-1020 [10]	Roy Palmer's State Street Ramblers	1953	$300

PALMER, SINGLETON

DIXIELAND JUBILEE

❑ DJ-513	At the Opera House	197?	$25
❑ DJ-511	Dixie by Gaslight	197?	$25

NORMAN

❑ NS-206 [M]	At the Opera House	1963	$35
❑ NL-106 [M]	At the Opera House	1963	$30
❑ NS-201 [S]	Dixie by Gaslight	1962	$35
❑ NL-101 [M]	Dixie by Gaslight	1962	$30
❑ NL-110 [M]	The Best Dixieland Band	1965	$30
❑ NS-210 [S]	The Best Dixieland Band	1965	$35

PALMIER, REMO

CONCORD JAZZ

❑ CJ-76	Remo Palmier	1979	$25

PALMIERI, EDDIE

EPIC

❑ JE35523	Lucumi Macumba Voodoo	1978	$25

INTUITION

❑ C1-91353	Sueno	1989	$30

PAMEIJER, PAM

STOMP OFF

❑ SOS-1134	Jelly Roll Morton: 100 Years	1987	$25
❑ SOS-1194	Little Bits	1989	$25
❑ SOS-1172	London Blues	1988	$25

PANDIT, KORLA

FANTASY

❑ 3350 [M]	Christmas with Korla Pandit	1962	$40
— Red vinyl			
❑ 3350 [M]	Christmas with Korla Pandit	1962	$30
— Black vinyl			
❑ 8350 [S]	Christmas with Korla Pandit	1962	$50
— Blue vinyl			
❑ 8350 [S]	Christmas with Korla Pandit	1962	$30
— Black vinyl			
❑ 3329 [M]	Hypnotique	1961	$40
— Red vinyl			
❑ 3329 [M]	Hypnotique	1961	$30
— Black vinyl			
❑ 8075 [S]	Hypnotique	1961	$50
— Blue vinyl			
❑ 8075 [S]	Hypnotique	1961	$30
— Black vinyl			
❑ 3286 [M]	Korla Pandit at the Pipe Organ	1959	$40
— Red vinyl			
❑ 3286 [M]	Korla Pandit at the Pipe Organ	1959	$30
— Black vinyl			
❑ 8018 [S]	Korla Pandit at the Pipe Organ	1960	$50
— Blue vinyl			
❑ 8018 [S]	Korla Pandit at the Pipe Organ	1960	$30
— Black vinyl			
❑ 3304 [M]	Korla Pandit in Concert	1960	$40
— Red vinyl			
❑ 3304 [M]	Korla Pandit in Concert	1960	$30
— Black vinyl			
❑ 8049 [S]	Korla Pandit in Concert	1960	$50
— Blue vinyl			
❑ 8049 [S]	Korla Pandit in Concert	1960	$30
— Black vinyl			
❑ 3347 [M]	Korla Pandit in Paris	1962	$30
❑ 3347 [M]	Korla Pandit in Paris	1962	$30
❑ 3284 [M]	Latin Holiday	1959	$40
— Red vinyl			
❑ 3284 [M]	Latin Holiday	1959	$30
— Black vinyl			
❑ 8027 [S]	Latin Holiday	1960	$50
— Blue vinyl			
❑ 8027 [S]	Latin Holiday	1960	$30
— Black vinyl			
❑ 3327 [M]	Love Letters	1961	$40
— Red vinyl			

Number	Title	Yr	NM
❑ 3327 [M]	Love Letters	1961	$30
— Black vinyl			
❑ 8070 [S]	Love Letters	1961	$50
— Blue vinyl			
❑ 8070 [S]	Love Letters	1961	$30
— Black vinyl			
❑ 3342 [M]	Music for Meditation	1962	$40
— Red vinyl			
❑ 3342 [M]	Music for Meditation	1962	$30
— Black vinyl			
❑ 8342 [S]	Music for Meditation	1962	$50
— Blue vinyl			
❑ 8342 [S]	Music for Meditation	1962	$30
— Black vinyl			
❑ 3334 [M]	Music of Hollywood	1962	$40
— Red vinyl			
❑ 3334 [M]	Music of Hollywood	1962	$30
— Black vinyl			
❑ 8086 [S]	Music of Hollywood	1962	$50
— Blue vinyl			
❑ 8086 [S]	Music of Hollywood	1962	$30
— Black vinyl			
❑ 3320 [M]	Music of Mystery and Romance	1961	$40
— Red vinyl			
❑ 3320 [M]	Music of Mystery and Romance	1961	$30
— Black vinyl			
❑ 8061 [S]	Music of Mystery and Romance	1961	$50
— Blue vinyl			
❑ 8061 [S]	Music of Mystery and Romance	1961	$30
— Black vinyl			
❑ 3272 [M]	Music of the Exotic East	1958	$40
— Red vinyl			
❑ 3272 [M]	Music of the Exotic East	1958	$30
— Black vinyl			
❑ 8013 [S]	Music of the Exotic East	1960	$50
— Blue vinyl			
❑ 8013 [S]	Music of the Exotic East	1960	$30
— Black vinyl			
❑ 3293 [M]	Speak to Me of Love	1959	$40
— Red vinyl			
❑ 3293 [M]	Speak to Me of Love	1959	$30
— Black vinyl			
❑ 8039 [S]	Speak to Me of Love	1960	$50
— Blue vinyl			
❑ 8039 [S]	Speak to Me of Love	1960	$30
— Black vinyl			
❑ 3288 [M]	Tropical Magic	1959	$40
— Red vinyl			
❑ 3288 [M]	Tropical Magic	1959	$30
— Black vinyl			
❑ 8034 [S]	Tropical Magic	1960	$50
— Blue vinyl			
❑ 8034 [S]	Tropical Magic	1960	$30
— Black vinyl			

NATIONAL CUSTOM

❑ NCR 12-574	Fantastique!	196?	$30

SYMPATHY FOR THE RECORD INDUSTRY

❑ SFTRI387	Exotica 2000	1996	$15

VITA

❑ VLP-14 [10]	Rememb'ring with Korla Pandit	195?	$100

PANICS, THE

CHANCELLOR

❑ CHL-5026 [M]	Panicsville	1962	$30
❑ CHLS-5026 [S]	Panicsville	1962	$40

PHILIPS

❑ PHM200159 [M]	Discotheque Dance Party	1964	$18
❑ PHS600159 [S]	Discotheque Dance Party	1964	$25

PANTERA

Offshoots include DOWN, SUPERJOINT RITUAL, DAMAGEPLAN, REBEL MEETS REBEL and HELLYEAH!.

EASTWEST

❑ 92302	Far Beyond Driven	1994	$250
❑ 62068	Official Live: 101 Proof	1997	$150
❑ 61908	The Great Southern Trendkill	1996	$30

ELEKTRA

❑ 62451	Reinventing the Steel	2000	$35

METAL MAGIC

❑ MMR1985	I Am the Night	1985	$150
❑ MMR1283	Metal Magic	1983	$175
❑ MMR1988	Power Metal	1988	$120
❑ MMR1984	Projects in the Jungle	1984	$150

PAPA DOO RUN RUN

TELARC

❑ 70501	California Project	1985	$12

Number	Title	Yr	NM

PAPER GARDEN, THE
MUSICOR

| ❏ MS-3175 [B] | The Paper Garden | 1968 | $75 |

PAPER LACE
MERCURY

| ❏ SRM-1-1008 | Paper Lace | 1974 | $15 |

PAPPALARDI, FELIX
A&M

| ❏ SP-4586 | Creation | 1976 | $12 |
| ❏ SP-4729 | Don't Worry Me | 1979 | $12 |

PARADISE ISLANDERS, THE
DECCA

| ❏ DL4122 [M] | Christmas in Hawaii | 1961 | $15 |
| ❏ DL74122 [S] | Christmas in Hawaii | 1961 | $18 |

PARAGONS, THE & THE HARPTONES
MUSICTONE

| ❏ M-8001 [M] | The Paragons vs. the Harptones | 1964 | $50 |

PARAGONS, THE & THE JESTERS
JOSIE

| ❏ 4008 [M] | The Paragons Meet the Jesters | 1962 | $250 |

JUBILEE

| ❏ JLP-1098 [M] | The Paragons Meet the Jesters | 1959 | $300 |

— Blue label, black vinyl

| ❏ JLP-1098 [M] | The Paragons Meet the Jesters | 1959 | $1500 |

— Multi-color splash vinyl; VG value 750; VG+ value 1125

| ❏ JLP-1098 [M] | The Paragons Meet the Jesters | 196? | $175 |

— Flat black label

| ❏ JLP-1098 [M] | The Paragons Meet the Jesters | 196? | $75 |

— Black label with multi-color logo

WINLEY

| ❏ LP-6003 [M] | War! The Jesters vs. the Paragons | 195? | $500 |

PARAGONS, THE
COLLECTABLES

| ❏ COL-5035 | The Best of the Paragons | 198? | $12 |

LOST-NITE

| ❏ LLP-4 [10] | The Best of the Paragons | 1981 | $12 |

— Red vinyl; in die-cut cover with sticker

PARAMOR, NORRIE
CAPITOL

❏ T10238 [M]	Amor Amor	196?	$15
❏ ST10238 [S]	Amor Amor	196?	$18
❏ T10212 [M]	Autumn	196?	$15
❏ ST10212 [S]	Autumn	196?	$18
❏ T10025 [M]	In London…In Love	196?	$25
❏ ST10025 [S]	In London…In Love	196?	$30
❏ T2071 [M]	In London…In Love Again	1964	$25
❏ ST2071 [S]	In London…In Love Again	1964	$30
❏ T2526 [M]	In Tokyo -- In Love	1966	$15
❏ ST2526 [S]	In Tokyo -- In Love	1966	$18
❏ T10052 [M]	London After Dark	196?	$15
❏ T10130 [M]	Norrie Paramor's Moods	196?	$15
❏ T2357 [M]	Warm and Willing	1965	$15
❏ ST2357 [S]	Warm and Willing	1965	$18

POLYDOR

| ❏ 24-6006 | Love at First Sight | 1970 | $12 |

PARAMOUNT JAZZ BAND OF BOSTON
STOMP OFF

| ❏ SOS-1205 | Ain't Cha Glad | 1991 | $25 |

PARAMOUNT THEATRE ORCHESTRA, THE
STOMP OFF

| ❏ SOS-1089 | Lolly Pops | 1985 | $25 |

PARANOISE
ANTILLES

| ❏ 90986 | Constant Fear | 1988 | $35 |

PARENTI, TONY
JAZZOLOGY

❏ J-11 [M]	Downtown Boys	1965	$35
❏ J-41	Jazz Goes Underground	197?	$25
❏ J-26	Jean Kittrell with Tony Parenti and His Blues Blowers	196?	$35
❏ J-31 [M]	Night at Jimmy Ryan's	196?	$35
❏ J-15	Ragtime	196?	$35
❏ J-21 [M]	Ragtime Jubilee	1967	$35
❏ J-71	The Final Bar	197?	$25
❏ J-1 [M]	Tony Parenti	1962	$35
❏ JCE-1 [10]	Tony Parenti and His New Orleanians	1962	$25

RIVERSIDE

| ❏ RLP 12-205 [M] | Ragtime | 1956 | $300 |

— White label, blue print

| ❏ RLP 12-205 [M] | Ragtime | 195? | $30 |

— Blue label, microphone logo at top

PARENTI, TONY/THE DIXIELAND RHYTHM KINGS
JAZZTONE

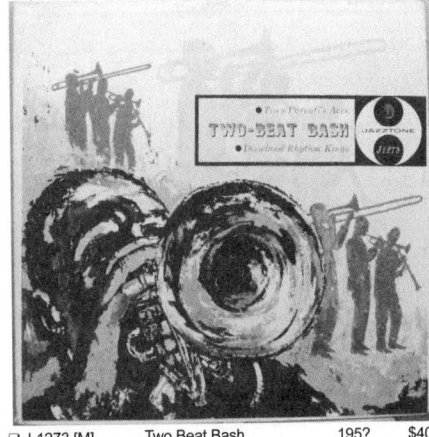

| ❏ J-1273 [M] | Two Beat Bash | 195? | $40 |

PARHAM, TINY
FOLKLYRIC

| ❏ 9028 | Hot Chicago Jazz | 198? | $25 |

X

| ❏ LVA-3039 [10] | Tiny Parham's South Side Jazz | 1955 | $85 |

PARIS, BOBBY
TETRAGRAMMATON

| ❏ T-105 [S] | Let Me Show You the Way | 1968 | $40 |
| ❏ M-2105 [M] | Let Me Show You the Way | 1968 | $150 |

PARIS, FREDDIE
RCA VICTOR

| ❏ LSP-4064 | Lovin' Mood | 1968 | $25 |

PARIS, JACK
2-J

| ❏ 101 | My Music, My Friends | 197? | $18 |
| ❏ 102 | Strawberries and Butterflies | 197? | $18 |

50 STATES

| ❏ 1005 | Nashville Heart and Soul | 197? | $18 |
| ❏ 1002 | Southern Session | 197? | $18 |

PARIS, JACKIE, AND ANNE MARIE MOSS
DIFFERENT DRUMMER

| ❏ 1004 | Maisonette | 197? | $35 |

PARIS, JACKIE
ABC IMPULSE!

| ❏ AS-17 [S] | The Song Is Paris | 1968 | $250 |

AUDIOPHILE

| ❏ 158 | Jackie Paris | 198? | $25 |

BRUNSWICK

| ❏ BL-54019 [M] | Skylark | 1957 | $150 |

CORAL

| ❏ CRL-56118 [10] | That Paris Mood | 195? | $100 |

EASTWEST

| ❏ 4002 [M] | The Jackie Paris Sound | 1958 | $300 |

EMARCY

| ❏ MG-36095 [M] | Songs by Jackie Paris | 1956 | $250 |

IMPULSE!

| ❏ A-17 [M] | The Song Is Paris | 1962 | $120 |
| ❏ AS-17 [S] | The Song Is Paris | 1962 | $160 |

TIME

| ❏ T-70009 [M] | Jackie Paris Sings the Lyrics of Ira Gershwin | 1959 | $40 |
| ❏ ST-70009 [S] | Jackie Paris Sings the Lyrics of Ira Gershwin | 1959 | $50 |

WING

| ❏ MGW-60004 [M] | Songs by Jackie Paris | 1956 | $100 |

PARIS, PRISCILLA
Also see THE PARIS SISTERS.
HAPPY TIGER

| ❏ HT-1002 | Priscilla Loves Billy | 1968 | $40 |

YORK

| ❏ 4005 [M] | Priscilla Sings Herself | 1967 | $30 |
| ❏ 4005-S [S] | Priscilla Sings Herself | 1967 | $40 |

PARIS
CAPITOL

| ❏ ST-11560 | Big Towne, 2061 | 1976 | $15 |
| ❏ ST-11464 | Paris | 1975 | $15 |

PARIS CONSERVATOIRE ORCHESTRE (ALBERT WOLFF, CONDUCTOR)
RCA VICTOR RED SEAL

| ❏ LSC-2301 [S] | Adam: Giselle | 1959 | $50 |

— Original with "shaded dog" label

PARIS CONSERVATOIRE ORCHESTRE (ANATOLE FISTOULARI, CONDUCTOR)
RCA VICTOR RED SEAL

| ❏ LSC-2400 [S] | Ballet Music from the Opera | 1960 | $400 |

— Original with "shaded dog" label

| ❏ LSC-2400 [S] | Ballet Music from the Opera | 199? | $30 |

— Classic Records reissue

PARIS CONSERVATOIRE ORCHESTRE (HUGH RIGNOLD, CONDUCTOR)
RCA VICTOR RED SEAL

| ❏ LSC-2485 [S] | Delibes: Sylvia and Coppelia Ballet Suites | 1961 | $100 |

— Original with "shaded dog" label

PARIS CONSERVATOIRE ORCHESTRE (JEAN-PAUL MOREL, CONDUCTOR)
RCA VICTOR RED SEAL

| ❏ LSC-6094 [S] | Albaniz: Iberia; Ravel: Rapsodie Espagnole | 196? | $400 |

— Original with "shaded dog" label

PARIS CONSERVATOIRE ORCHESTRE (JEAN MARTINON, CONDUCTOR)
RCA VICTOR RED SEAL

| ❏ LSC-2272 [S] | Prokofiev: Symphony No. 5 | 1959 | $100 |

— Original with "shaded dog" label

| ❏ LSC-2288 [S] | Prokofiev: Symphony No. 7 | 1959 | $100 |

— Original with "shaded dog" label

| ❏ LSC-2288 [S] | Prokofiev: Symphony No. 7 | 199? | $30 |

— Classic Records reissue

PARIS CONSERVATOIRE ORCHESTRE (PIERRE MONTEUX, CONDUCTOR)
RCA VICTOR RED SEAL

| ❏ LSC-2085 [S] | Stravinsky: The Rite of Spring | 1958 | $50 |

— Original with "shaded dog" label

| ❏ LSC-2085 [S] | Stravinsky: The Rite of Spring | 1964 | $40 |

— Second issue with "white dog" label

PARIS PILOT
HIP

| ❏ 7004 | Paris Pilot | 1970 | $30 |

PARIS SISTERS, THE
Also see PRISCILLA PARIS.
REPRISE

| ❏ R-6259 [M] | Everything Under the Sun | 1967 | $40 |
| ❏ RS-6359 [S] | Everything Under the Sun | 1967 | $75 |

SIDEWALK

| ❏ T5906 [M] | Golden Hits of the Paris Sisters | 1967 | $50 |
| ❏ DT5906 [R] | Golden Hits of the Paris Sisters | 1967 | $30 |

UNIFILMS

| ❏ 505 [M] | The Paris Sisters Sing Songs from Glass House | 1966 | $40 |
| ❏ S-505 [S] | The Paris Sisters Sing Songs from Glass House | 1966 | $50 |

PARIS WASHBOARD
STOMP OFF

| ❏ SOS-1182 | When We're Smiling | 1988 | $25 |

PARISH HALL
FANTASY

| ❏ 8398 | Parish Hall | 1969 | $25 |

PARKER, BILLIE JEAN
RCA VICTOR

| ❏ LPM-3967 [M] | The Truth About Bonnie and Clyde | 1968 | $40 |
| ❏ LSP-3967 [S] | The Truth About Bonnie and Clyde | 1968 | $18 |

PARKER, BILLY (2)
STRATA-EAST

| ❏ SES-19754 | Freedom of Speech | 1975 | $30 |

Number	Title	Yr	NM

PARKER, CHARLIE; DIZZY GILLESPIE; RED NORVO

DIAL

Number	Title	Yr	NM
❏ LP-903 [M]	Fabulous Jam Session	1951	$600

PARKER, CHARLIE

ALAMAC

| ❏ QSR2430 | Charlie Parker's All Stars 1950 | 198? | $30 |

AMERICAN RECORDING SOCIETY

| ❏ G-441 [M] | Now's the Time | 1957 | $150 |

BARONET

❏ B-105 [M]	A Handful of Modern Jazz	1962	$50
❏ BS-105 [R]	A Handful of Modern Jazz	1962	$30
❏ B-107 [M]	The Early Bird	1962	$50
❏ BS-107 [R]	The Early Bird	1962	$30

BIRDLAND

| ❏ 425 [10] | A Night at Carnegie Hall | 1956 | $300 |

BLUE NOTE

| ❏ BT-85108 | Charlie Parker at Storyville | 198? | $30 |

BLUE RIBBON

| ❏ 8011 [M] | The Early Bird | 1962 | $50 |
| ❏ S-8011 [R] | The Early Bird | 1962 | $30 |

CHARLIE PARKER

❏ PLP-401 [M]	Bird Is Free	1961	$40
❏ PLP-407 [M]	Bird Symbols	1961	$40
❏ PLP-406 [M]	Charlie Parker	1961	$40
❏ CP-513 [M]	Charlie Parker Plus Strings	196?	$40
❏ PLP-701	Historical Masterpieces	196?	$120
❏ CP-2-502 [M]	Live at Rockland Palace, September 26, 1952	1961	$150
❏ PLP-408 [M]	Once There Was Bird	1961	$40
❏ PLP-404 [M]	The Happy Bird	1961	$40

CLEF

❏ MGC-512 [10]	Bird and Diz	1954	$400
—Reissue of Mercury 512			
❏ MGC-157 [10]	Charlie Parker	1954	$400
❏ MGC-609 [M]	Charlie Parker Big Band	1954	$400
❏ MGC-501 [10]	Charlie Parker with Strings	1954	$400
—Reissue of Mercury 501			
❏ MGC-675 [M]	Charlie Parker with Strings	1955	$400
❏ MGC-101 [10]	Charlie Parker with Strings	1958	$0
—Canceled			
❏ MGC-509 [10]	Charlie Parker with Strings, No. 2	1954	$400
—Reissue of Mercury 509			
❏ MGC-725 [M]	Night and Day	1956	$350
❏ MGC-513 [10]	South of the Border	1954	$400
—Reissue of Mercury 513			
❏ MGC-646 [M]	The Magnificent Charlie Parker	1955	$700

COLUMBIA

❏ JC34832	Bird with Strings Live	1977	$30
❏ JG34808	One Night in Birdland	1977	$35
❏ C234808	One Night in Birdland	198?	$30
—Reissue with new prefix			
❏ JC34831	Summit Meeting	1977	$30

CONCERT HALL JAZZ

| ❏ 1017 [10] | The Art of Charlie Parker, Vol. 2 | 1955 | $120 |
| ❏ 1004 [10] | The Fabulous Bird | 1955 | $120 |

CONTINENTAL

| ❏ 16004 [M] | Bird Lives | 1962 | $40 |

DEBUT

| ❏ DEB-611 [M] | Bird on 52nd Street | 196? | $175 |

DIAL

❏ LP-904 [M]	Alternate Masters	1951	$600
❏ LP-905 [M]	Alternate Masters	1951	$1400
❏ LP-203 [10]	Charlie Parker	1949	$2500
❏ LP-201 [10]	Charlie Parker Quintet	1949	$1000
❏ LP-202 [10]	Charlie Parker Quintet	1949	$800
❏ LP-207 [10]	Charlie Parker Sextet	1949	$800
❏ LP-901 [M]	The Bird Blows the Blues	1949	$4000
—Limited edition of 300 copies on opaque red vinyl; designed as a mail-order offer; issued with a generic gray cover; also has a pale yellow Dial label similiar to the label's 78 rpm design			
❏ LP-901 [M]	The Bird Blows the Blues	1950	$600
—Commercial version of mail-order album			

ELEKTRA/MUSICIAN

| ❏ 60019 | One Night in Washington | 1982 | $25 |

ESP-DISK'

| ❏ ESP-BIRD-2 | Broadcast Performances 1948-1949, Vol. 2 | 1973 | $175 |

EVEREST ARCHIVE OF FOLK & JAZZ

❏ 214	Charlie Parker	1969	$30
❏ 254	Charlie Parker, Vol. 3	197?	$25
❏ 295	Charlie Parker, Vol. 4	197?	$25
❏ 315	Charlie Parker, Vol. 5	197?	$25
❏ 232	Charlie Parker, Volume 2	1970	$25

FANTASY

❏ 6012 [M]	Bird at St. Nick's	1964	$75
❏ OJC-041	Bird at St. Nick's	1983	$25
❏ 86012 [R]	Bird at St. Nick's	1964	$35
❏ 6011 [M]	Bird on 52nd St.	1964	$75

Number	Title	Yr	NM
❏ 86011 [R]	Bird on 52nd St.	1964	$35
❏ OJC-114	Bird on 52nd St.	198?	$25
❏ OJC-044	Jazz at Massey Hall	198?	$25

HALL OF FAME

| ❏ 617 | Giants of Jazz | 197? | $25 |
| ❏ 620 | Takin' Off | 197? | $25 |

JAZZTONE

❏ J-1204 [M]	Giants of Modern Jazz	1955	$150
❏ J-0(# unknown) [M]	The Art of Charlie Parker, Vol. 2	1955	$150
❏ J-1214 [M]	The Fabulous Bird	1955	$150
❏ J-1240 [M]	The Saxes of Stan Getz and Charlie Parker	1957	$150

JAZZ WORKSHOP

| ❏ JWS-500 [M] | Bird at St. Nick's | 1958 | $250 |
| ❏ JWS-501 [M] | Bird on 52nd Street | 1958 | $250 |

LES JAZZ COOL

❏ 101 [M]	Les Jazz Cool, Volume 1	1960	$150
❏ 102 [M]	Les Jazz Cool, Volume 2	1960	$150
❏ 103 [M]	Les Jazz Cool, Volume 3	1960	$150

MERCURY

❏ MGC-512 [10]	Bird and Diz	1952	$500
❏ MG-35010 [10]	Charlie Parker with Strings	1950	$600
❏ MGC-101 [10]	Charlie Parker with Strings	1950	$500
—Reissue of 35010			
❏ MGC-501 [10]	Charlie Parker with Strings	1951	$500
—Reissue of 101 with new number			
❏ MGC-109 [10]	Charlie Parker with Strings, Volume 2	1950	$500
❏ MGC-509 [10]	Charlie Parker with Strings, Volume 2	1952	$500
—Reissue of 109 with new number			
❏ MGC-513 [10]	South of the Border	1952	$500

MGM

| ❏ M3G-4949 | Archetypes | 1974 | $30 |

MOSAIC

| ❏ MR10-129 | The Complete Dean Benedetti Recordings of Charlie Parker | 199? | $200 |

ONYX

| ❏ 221 | First Recordings with Jay McShann | 197? | $30 |

PHOENIX

❏ 10	New Bird	197?	$25
❏ 12	New Bird, Vol. 2	197?	$25
❏ 17	Yardbird in Lotusland	197?	$25

PICKWICK

| ❏ SPC-3054 [R] | Yardbird | 196? | $25 |
| ❏ PC-3054 [M] | Yardbird | 196? | $25 |

PRESTIGE

| ❏ 24009 | Charlie Parker | 197? | $35 |
| ❏ 24024 | Parker/Powell/Mingus/Roach | 197? | $35 |

ROOST

| ❏ LP-2210 [M] | All Star Sextet | 1958 | $250 |
| ❏ LP-2257 [M] | The World of Charlie Parker | 1963 | $40 |

SAVOY

❏ MG-12152 [M]	An Evening at Home with the Bird	196?	$40
❏ MG-12138 [M]	Bird's Night -- The Music of Charlie Parker	1958	$150
❏ MG-9000 [10]	Charlie Parker	1950	$1400
❏ MG-9001 [10]	Charlie Parker, Volume 2	1951	$500
❏ MG-9010 [10]	Charlie Parker, Volume 3	1952	$500
❏ MG-9011 [10]	Charlie Parker, Volume 4	1952	$500
❏ MG-12000 [M]	Charlie Parker Memorial	1955	$200
❏ MG-12009 [M]	Charlie Parker Memorial, Volume 2	1955	$200
❏ MG-12186 [M]	Newly Discovered Sides by the Immortal Charlie Parker	1966	$75
❏ MG-12179 [M]	The "Bird" Returns	196?	$75
❏ MG-12079 [M]	The Charlie Parker Story	1956	$200
❏ MG-12014 [M]	The Genius of Charlie Parker	1955	$200
❏ MG-12001 [M]	The Immortal Charlie Parker	1955	$200

SAVOY JAZZ

❏ SJL-2201	Bird: The Savoy Recordings	1976	$35
❏ SJL-1108	Bird at the Roost	197?	$30
❏ SJL-1173	Bird at the Roost, Vol. 3	1987	$25
❏ SJL-2259	Bird at the Roost: The Complete Royal Roost Performances, Vol. 1	198?	$35
❏ SJL-2260	Bird at the Roost: The Complete Royal Roost Performances, Vol. 2	1986	$35
❏ SJL-1107	Encores	197?	$30
❏ SJL-1129	Encores, Vol. 2	198?	$25
❏ SJL-1132	One Night in Chicago	198?	$25
❏ SJL-1208	Original Bird: The Best on Savoy	198?	$25
❏ SJL-5500	The Complete Savoy Studio Sessions	197?	$75

SPOTLITE

❏ 101	Charlie Parker on Dial, Vol. 1	197?	$25
❏ 102	Charlie Parker on Dial, Vol. 2	197?	$25
❏ 103	Charlie Parker on Dial, Vol. 3	197?	$25
❏ 104	Charlie Parker on Dial, Vol. 4	197?	$25
❏ 105	Charlie Parker on Dial, Vol. 5	197?	$25
❏ 106	Charlie Parker on Dial, Vol. 6	197?	$25

Number	Title	Yr	NM

STASH

| ❏ ST-260 | Birth of the Bebop | 1986 | $25 |
| ❏ ST-280 | The Bird You Never Heard | 1988 | $25 |

TRIP

| ❏ 5039 | Birdology | 197? | $35 |
| ❏ 5035 | The Master | 197? | $30 |

UPFRONT

| ❏ UPF-172 | Live Sessions | 197? | $25 |

VERVE

❏ MGV-8004 [M]	April in Paris (The Genius of Charlie Parker #2)	1957	$175
❏ V-8004 [M]	April in Paris (The Genius of Charlie Parker #2)	1961	$75
❏ V6-8004 [R]	April in Paris (The Genius of Charlie Parker #2)	196?	$30
❏ 50-5263 [M]	April in Paris (The Genius of Charlie Parker #2)	197?	$35
—Book-of-the-Month Club edition of 8004			
❏ 837176-1	Bird: The Original Recordings of Charlie Parker	1987	$25
❏ MGV-8006 [M]	Bird and Diz (The Genius of Charlie Parker #4)	1957	$175
❏ V-8006 [M]	Bird and Diz (The Genius of Charlie Parker #4)	1961	$75
❏ V6-8006 [R]	Bird and Diz (The Genius of Charlie Parker #4)	196?	$30
❏ 817442-1	Bird on Verve, Vol. 1: Charlie Parker with Strings	1985	$25
❏ 817443-1	Bird on Verve, Vol. 2: Bird and Diz	1985	$25
❏ 817444-1	Bird on Verve, Vol. 3: More Charlie Parker with Strings	1985	$25
❏ 817445-1	Bird on Verve, Vol. 4: Afro-Cuban Jazz	1985	$25
❏ 817446-1	Bird on Verve, Vol. 5: Charlie Parker	1985	$25
❏ 817447-1	Bird on Verve, Vol. 6: South of the Border	1985	$25
❏ 817448-1	Bird on Verve, Vol. 7: Big Band	1985	$25
❏ 817449-1	Bird on Verve, Vol. 8: Charlie Parker in Hi-Fi	1985	$25
❏ V6-8787 [R]	Bird Set	1969	$35
❏ VSP-23 [M]	Bird Wings	1966	$50
❏ VSPS-23 [R]	Bird Wings	1966	$30
❏ MGV-8007 [M]	Charlie Parker Plays Cole Porter (The Genius of Charlie Parker #5)	1957	$175
❏ V-8007 [M]	Charlie Parker Plays Cole Porter (The Genius of Charlie Parker #5)	1961	$75
❏ V6-8007 [R]	Charlie Parker Plays Cole Porter (The Genius of Charlie Parker #5)	196?	$30
❏ VE-2-2508	Charlie Parker Sides	197?	$35
❏ 833564-1	Charlie Parker Sides	198?	$25
❏ UMV-2562	Charlie Parker with Strings	198?	$25
❏ MGV-8008 [M]	Fiesta (The Genius of Charlie Parker #6)	1957	$175
❏ V-8008 [M]	Fiesta (The Genius of Charlie Parker #6)	1961	$75
❏ V6-8008 [R]	Fiesta (The Genius of Charlie Parker #6)	196?	$30
❏ UMV-2617	Jazz Perennial	198?	$25
❏ MGV-8009 [M]	Jazz Perennial (The Genius of Charlie Parker #7)	1957	$175
❏ V-8009 [M]	Jazz Perennial (The Genius of Charlie Parker #7)	1961	$75
❏ V6-8009 [R]	Jazz Perennial (The Genius of Charlie Parker #7)	196?	$30
❏ MGV-8003 [M]	Night and Day (The Genius of Charlie Parker #1)	1957	$175
❏ V-8003 [M]	Night and Day (The Genius of Charlie Parker #1)	1961	$75
❏ V6-8003 [R]	Night and Day (The Genius of Charlie Parker #1)	196?	$30
❏ UMV-2029	Now's the Time	198?	$25
❏ V6-8005 [R]	Now's the Time (The Genius of Charlie Parker #3)	196?	$30
❏ V-8005 [M]	Now's the Time (The Genius of Charlie Parker #3)	1961	$75
❏ MGV-8005 [M]	Now's the Time (The Genius of Charlie Parker #3)	1957	$175
❏ V3HB-8840	Return Engagement	197?	$35
❏ UMV-2030	Swedish Schnapps	198?	$25
❏ MGV-8010 [M]	Swedish Schnapps (The Genius of Charlie Parker #8)	1957	$175
❏ V-8010 [M]	Swedish Schnapps (The Genius of Charlie Parker #8)	1961	$75
❏ V6-8010 [R]	Swedish Schnapps (The Genius of Charlie Parker #8)	196?	$30
❏ MGV-8100-3 [M]	The Charlie Parker Story	1957	$300
—Combines 8000, 8001 and 8002 in a box set			
❏ V-8100-3 [M]	The Charlie Parker Story	1961	$120
—Combines 8000, 8001 and 8002 in a box set			
❏ MGV-8000 [M]	The Charlie Parker Story, Volume 1	1957	$175
❏ V-8000 [M]	The Charlie Parker Story, Volume 1	1961	$75
❏ V6-8000 [R]	The Charlie Parker Story, Volume 1	196?	$30
❏ MGV-8001 [M]	The Charlie Parker Story, Volume 2	1957	$175
❏ V-8001 [M]	The Charlie Parker Story, Volume 2	1961	$75
❏ V6-8001 [R]	The Charlie Parker Story, Volume 2	196?	$30
❏ MGV-8002 [M]	The Charlie Parker Story, Volume 3	1957	$175
❏ V-8002 [M]	The Charlie Parker Story, Volume 3	1961	$75

Number	Title	Yr	NM
❏ V6-8002 [R]	The Charlie Parker Story, Volume 3	196?	$30
❏ 823250-1	The Cole Porter Songbook	1986	$25
❏ V-8409 [M]	The Essential Charlie Parker	1961	$75
❏ V6-8409 [R]	The Essential Charlie Parker	196?	$30
❏ VE-2-2501	The Verve Years 1948-50	197?	$35
❏ VE-2-2512	The Verve Years 1950-51	197?	$35
❏ VE-2-2523	The Verve Years 1952-54	197?	$35

VOGUE

❏ LAE-12002 [M]	Memorial Album	1955	$175

WARNER BROS.

❏ 6BS3159	The Complete Dial Recordings	1977	$175
—Limited edition of 4,000 box sets			
❏ 2WB3198	The Very Best of Bird	1977	$50

ZIM

❏ 1006	Apartment Jam	197?	$30
❏ 1003	At the Pershing Ballroom, Chicago, 1950	197?	$30
❏ 1001	Lullaby in Rhythm	197?	$30

PARKER, CHARLIE/COLEMAN HAWKINS/ GEORGIE AULD

JAM

❏ 5006	Unearthed Masters, Vol. 1	198?	$25

PARKER, CHARLIE/DIZZY GILLESPIE

EMUS

❏ ES-12027 [R]	Charlie Parker / Dizzy Gillespie	197?	$30

PARKER, CHARLIE/DIZZY GILLESPIE/BUD POWELL/MAX ROACH

SAVOY

❏ MG-9034 [10]	Bird, Diz, Bud, Max	1953	$600

PARKER, CHARLIE/STAN GETZ/WARDELL GRAY

DESIGN

❏ DLP-183 [M]	Charlie Parker/Stan Getz/ Wardell Gray	196?	$35

PARKER, FESS

COLUMBIA

❏ CL666 [M]	Walt Disney's Davy Crockett, King of the Wild Frontier	1955	$150

DISNEYLAND

❏ DQ-1336	Cowboy and Indian Songs	1969	$30
❏ DQ-1269 [M]	Pecos Bill and Other Stories in Song	1965	$30
❏ WDA-3602 [M]	Three Adventures of Davy Crockett	1958	$50
—Reissue of Columbia 666			
❏ DQ-1315 [M]	Three Adventures of Davy Crockett	1968	$30
—Another reissue, this time of 1926			
❏ ST-1926 [M]	Three Adventures of Davy Crockett	1963	$30
—Reissue of 3602			
❏ WDL-3041 [M]	Westward Ho the Wagons	1959	$30
—Reissue of 4008			
❏ WDL-4006 [M]	Westward Ho the Wagons	1956	$100
❏ WDL-3006 [M]	Yarns and Songs	1957	$40
❏ WDL-1007 [M]	Yarns and Songs of the West	1959	$30
—Reissue of 3006			

RCA VICTOR

❏ LPM-2973 [M]	Fess Parker Sings About Daniel Boone, Davy Crockett and Abe Lincoln	1964	$30
❏ LSP-2973 [S]	Fess Parker Sings About Daniel Boone, Davy Crockett and Abe Lincoln	1964	$30

PARKER, GRAHAM
Includes records with THE RUMOUR.

ARISTA

❏ AL9589	Another Grey Area	1982	$12
❏ AL6-8374	Another Grey Area	1985	$10
—Budget-line reissue			
❏ SP-63 [DJ]	Live Sparks	1979	$35
❏ SP-63 [DJ]	Live Sparks	1979	$35
❏ AL6-8391	Look Back in Anger	1985	$12
❏ AL4223	Squeezing Out Sparks	1979	$15
❏ AL6-8363	Squeezing Out Sparks	1985	$10
—Budget-line reissue			
❏ AL8-8023	The Real Macaw	1983	$12
❏ AL6-8352	The Real Macaw	1985	$10
—Budget-line reissue			
❏ AL9517	The Up Escalator	1980	$12
❏ AL6-8356	The Up Escalator	1985	$10
—Budget-line reissue			

ELEKTRA

❏ 60388	Steady Nerves	1985	$12

MERCURY

❏ SRM-1-1117	Heat Treatment	1976	$18
❏ SRM-1-1095	Howlin' Wind	1976	$18

Number	Title	Yr	NM
❏ 826097-1 [B]	Pourin' It All Out: The Mercury Years	1985	$18
❏ SRM-1-3706	Stick to Me	1977	$18
❏ 824808-1	Stick to Me	1985	$15
—Reissue with new number			
❏ SRM-2-100 [B]	The Parkerilla	1978	$25
—Originals have gatefold sleeves			

RCA

❏ 9876-1-R	Human Soul	1989	$12
❏ 8316-1-R	The Mona Lisa's Sister	1988	$12

ROCK THE HOUSE

❏ RTH-2817-1 [B]	12 Haunted Episodes	1995	$40

PARKER, JACY

VERVE

❏ V-8424 [M]	Spotlight On Jacy Parker	1962	$40
❏ V6-8424 [S]	Spotlight On Jacy Parker	1962	$50

PARKER, JOHN

GOLDEN CREST

❏ GC-3051	Dixieland	196?	$35

PARKER, JUNIOR, AND BOBBY BLAND

ABC DUKE

❏ DLP-72	Blues Consolidated	1974	$18

DUKE

❏ DLP-72 [M]	Blues Consolidated	1961	$175

PARKER, JUNIOR

ABC

❏ AC-30010	The ABC Collection	1976	$18

ABC DUKE

❏ DLP-76	Driving Wheel	1974	$18
❏ DLP-83	The Best of Junior Parker	1974	$18

BLUE ROCK

❏ SRB-64004	Honey-Drippin' Blues	1969	$18

BLUESWAY

❏ BLS-6066	Sometime Tomorrow	1973	$18

CAPITOL

❏ ST-564	Outside Man	1970	$18

DUKE

❏ DLP-76 [M]	Driving Wheel	1962	$175
—With Cadillac on front cover			
❏ DLP-76 [M]	Driving Wheel	196?	$150
—With Wagon Wheel on front cover			
❏ DLP-83	The Best of Junior Parker	1967	$50
❏ DLPS-83 [P]	The Best of Junior Parker	1967	$40

GROOVE MERCHANT

❏ 513	Love Ain't Nothin'	1974	$18

MCA

❏ 27046	The Best of Junior Parker	1980	$12

MERCURY

❏ MG-21101 [M]	Like It Is	1967	$30
❏ SR-61101 [S]	Like It Is	1967	$30

MINIT

❏ 24024	Blues Man	1969	$30

UNITED ARTISTS

❏ UAS-6823	I Tell Stories Sad and True	1971	$18

PARKER, KIM

SOUL NOTE

❏ SN-1063	Good Girl	1982	$30
❏ SN-1033	Havin' Myself a Time	1981	$30
❏ SN-1133	Sometimes I'm Blue	1986	$30

PARKER, KNOCKY, AND SMOKEY MONTGOMERY

CIRCLE

❏ CLP-10001	Texas Swing, Vol. 1: The Barrelhouse	1987	$25
❏ CLP-10002	Texas Swing, Vol. 2: The Boogie-Woogie	1987	$25
❏ CLP-10003	Texas Swing, Vol. 3: … And the Blues	1987	$25
❏ CLP-10004	Texas Swing, Vol. 4: Smokey and the Bearkats	1987	$25

PARKER, KNOCKY

AUDIOPHILE

❏ AP-28 [M]	Boogie Woogie Maxine	1956	$40
❏ AP-102/5	The Complete Piano Works of Jelly Roll Morton	196?	$50
—In box with booklet; it's unknown whether the volumes also were issued individually			

EUPHONIC

❏ 1216	Classic Rags and Nostalgia	198?	$25
❏ 1215	Eight on Eighty-Eight	198?	$25

GHB

❏ GHB-19	Knocky Parker	1967	$35
❏ 150	Knocky Parker and the Cake-Walkin' Jazz Band	1981	$25

JAZZOLOGY

❏ J-81	Cakewalk to Ragtime	197?	$25

PROGRESSIVE

Number	Title	Yr	NM
❏ PLP-1 [10]	New Orleans Stomps	1954	$50

PARKER, LEO

BLUE NOTE

❏ BLP-4087 [M]	Let Me Tell You 'Bout It	1961	$150
—With 61st St. address on label			
❏ BST-84087 [S]	Let Me Tell You 'Bout It	1961	$100
—With 61st St. address on label			
❏ BLP-4087 [M]	Let Me Tell You 'Bout It	1963	$75
—With "New York, USA" address on label			
❏ BST-84087 [S]	Let Me Tell You 'Bout It	1963	$30
—With "New York, USA" address on label			
❏ BST-84087 [S]	Let Me Tell You 'Bout It	1967	$35
—With "A Division of Liberty Records" on label			
❏ LT-1076	Rollin' with Leo	1980	$25
❏ BLP-4095 [M]	Rollin' with Leo	1961	$0
—Canceled			
❏ BST-84095 [S]	Rollin' with Leo	1986	$30
—Originally scheduled for 1961 release, this was the first issue on its originally assigned number			

CHESS

❏ LPV-413	The Late, Great King of Baritone Sax	1971	$35

COLLECTABLES

❏ COL-5329	Back to the Baritones	198?	$25

SAVOY

❏ MG-9009 [10]	Leo Parker	1952	$300
❏ MG-9018 [10]	New Trends in Modern Music	1952	$300

PARKER, MAYNARD

PRESTIGE

❏ 10054	Midnight Rider	1973	$25

PARKER, RAY, JR.

ARISTA

❏ AL9543	A Woman Needs Love	1981	$12
—As "Ray Parker Jr. and Raydio"			
❏ AL8-8266	Chartbusters	1984	$12
❏ AL9612	Greatest Hits	1982	$12
❏ AB4163	Raydio	1978	$18
—As "Raydio"			
❏ AB4212	Rock On	1979	$18
—As "Raydio"			
❏ AL8-8280	Sex and the Single Man	1985	$12
❏ AL9590	The Other Woman	1982	$12
❏ AL9515	Two Places at the Same Time	1980	$12
—As "Ray Parker Jr. and Raydio"			
❏ AL8-8087	Woman Out of Control	1983	$12

GEFFEN

❏ GHS24124	After Dark	1987	$12

MCA

❏ 10327	I Love You Like You Are	1991	$15

PARKER, ROBERT

NOLA

❏ LP-1001 [M]	Barefootin'	1966	$40

PARKER FAMILY, THE

AUDIO LAB

❏ AL-1548 [M]	Songs for Salvation	196?	$175
❏ AL-1574 [M]	Songs for Salvation, Vol. 2	196?	$175

KING

❏ 932 [M]	Just a Real Nice Family	1965	$40

PARKINS, LEROY

BETHLEHEM

❏ BCP-6047 [M]	LeRoy Parkins and His Yazoo River Band	1960	$300
❏ SBCP-6047 [S]	LeRoy Parkins and His Yazoo River Band	1960	$300

PARKS, ANDY

CAPITOL

❏ T2799 [M]	Sex, School…And Like Other Pressures	1967	$25
❏ ST2799 [S]	Sex, School…And Like Other Pressures	1967	$25

PARKS, MICHAEL

FIRST AMERICAN

❏ 7781	You Don't Know Me	1983	$12

MGM

❏ SE-4717	Blue	1970	$18
❏ SE-4646	Closing the Gap	1969	$18
❏ SE-4662	Long Lonesome Highway	1970	$18
❏ SE-4784	The Best of Michael Parks	1971	$18

VERVE

❏ V6-5079	Lost and Found	1971	$18

Number	Title	Yr	NM

PARKS, VAN DYKE
SUNDAZED
| ❏ LP-5141 | Discover America | 2002 | $18 |

—Reissue on 180-gram vinyl

| ❏ LP-5140 | Song Cycle | 2002 | $18 |

—Reissue on 180-gram vinyl

WARNER BROS.
❏ BS2878	Clang of the Yankee Reaper	1975	$15
❏ BS2589	Discover America	1972	$15
❏ 23829	Jump!	1984	$15
❏ WS1727	Song Cycle	1968	$30

—Gold label

| ❏ WS1727 [B] | Song Cycle | 1968 | $30 |

—Green label with "W7" box logo

| ❏ WS1727 | Song Cycle | 1970 | $15 |

—Green label with "WB" shield logo

| ❏ 25968 | Tokyo Rose | 1989 | $15 |

PARLAN, HORACE
BLUE NOTE
| ❏ BST-84134 | Happy Frame of Mind | 1986 | $30 |

—"The Finest in Jazz Since 1939" issue

| ❏ BLP-4062 [M] | Headin' South | 1961 | $300 |

—With W. 63rd St. address on label

| ❏ BST-84062 [S] | Headin' South | 1961 | $300 |

—With W. 63rd St. address on label

| ❏ BLP-4062 [M] | Headin' South | 1963 | $75 |

—With "New York, USA" address on label

| ❏ BST-84062 [S] | Headin' South | 1963 | $30 |

—With "New York, USA" address on label

| ❏ BST-84062 [S] | Headin' South | 1967 | $35 |

—With "A Division of Liberty Records" on label

| ❏ BLP-4028 [M] | Movin' and Groovin' | 1960 | $300 |

—Deep groove" version (deep indentation under label on both sides)

| ❏ BLP-4028 [M] | Movin' and Groovin' | 1960 | $175 |

—Regular version, W. 63rd St. address on label

| ❏ BST-84028 [S] | Movin' and Groovin' | 1960 | $300 |

—With W. 63rd St. address on label

| ❏ BLP-4028 [M] | Movin' and Groovin' | 1963 | $75 |

—With "New York, USA" address on label

| ❏ BST-84028 [S] | Movin' and Groovin' | 1963 | $30 |

—With "New York, USA" address on label

| ❏ BST-84028 [S] | Movin' and Groovin' | 1967 | $35 |

—With "A Division of Liberty Records" on label

| ❏ BLP-4074 [M] | On the Spur of the Moment | 1961 | $175 |

—With W. 63rd St. address on label

| ❏ BST-84074 [S] | On the Spur of the Moment | 1961 | $150 |

—With 61st St. address on label

| ❏ BLP-4074 [M] | On the Spur of the Moment | 1961 | $150 |

—With 61st St. address on label

| ❏ BST-84074 [S] | On the Spur of the Moment | 1961 | $250 |

—With W. 63rd St. address on label

| ❏ BLP-4074 [M] | On the Spur of the Moment | 1963 | $75 |

—With "New York, USA" address on label

| ❏ BST-84074 [S] | On the Spur of the Moment | 1963 | $30 |

—With "New York, USA" address on label

| ❏ BST-84074 [S] | On the Spur of the Moment | 1967 | $35 |

—With "A Division of Liberty Records" on label

| ❏ BST-4074 | On the Spur of the Moment | 199? | $30 |

—Classic Records reissue on audiophile vinyl

| ❏ BLP-4043 [M] | Speakin' My Piece | 1960 | $500 |

—Deep groove" version (deep indentation under label on both sides)

| ❏ BLP-4043 [M] | Speakin' My Piece | 1960 | $175 |

—Regular version, W. 63rd St. address on label

| ❏ BST-84043 [S] | Speakin' My Piece | 1963 | $30 |

—With "New York, USA" address on label

| ❏ BLP-4043 [M] | Speakin' My Piece | 1963 | $75 |

—With "New York, USA" address on label

| ❏ BST-84043 [S] | Speakin' My Piece | 1960 | $100 |

—With W. 63rd St. address on label

| ❏ BST-84043 [S] | Speakin' My Piece | 1967 | $35 |

—With "A Division of Liberty Records" on label

| ❏ BLP-4082 [M] | Up and Down | 1961 | $150 |

—With 61st St. address on label

| ❏ BST-84082 [S] | Up and Down | 1961 | $150 |

—With 61st St. address on label

| ❏ BLP-4082 [M] | Up and Down | 1963 | $75 |

—With "New York, USA" address on label

| ❏ BST-84082 [S] | Up and Down | 1963 | $30 |

—With "New York, USA" address on label

| ❏ BST-84082 [S] | Up and Down | 1967 | $35 |

—With "A Division of Liberty Records" on label

| ❏ BLP-4037 [M] | Us Three | 1960 | $1000 |

—Deep groove" version (deep indentation under label on both sides)

| ❏ BLP-4037 [M] | Us Three | 1960 | $175 |

—Regular version, W. 63rd St. address on label

| ❏ BST-84037 [S] | Us Three | 1960 | $100 |

—With W. 63rd St. address on label

| ❏ BLP-4037 [M] | Us Three | 1963 | $75 |

—With "New York, USA" address on label

| ❏ BST-84037 [S] | Us Three | 1967 | $35 |

—With "A Division of Liberty Records" on label

| ❏ BST-84037 [S] | Us Three | 1963 | $30 |

—With "New York, USA" address on label

INNER CITY
| ❏ IC-2012 | Arrival | 197? | $35 |
| ❏ IC-2056 | No Blues | 197? | $35 |

MOSAIC
| ❏ MQ8-197 | The Complete Horace Parlan Blue Note Sessions | 2000 | $175 |

STEEPLECHASE
❏ SCS-1012	Arrival	198?	$30
❏ SCS-1124	Blue Parlan	198?	$30
❏ SCS-1076	Frank-ly Speaking	198?	$30
❏ SCS-1194	Glad I Met You	198?	$30
❏ SCS-1178	Like Someone in Love	1983	$30
❏ SCS-1141	Musically Yours	198?	$30
❏ SCS-1056	No Blues	198?	$30
❏ SCS-1167	The Maestro	198?	$30

PARLET
CASABLANCA
| ❏ NBLP7146 | Invasion of the Booty Snatchers | 1979 | $25 |
| ❏ NBLP7094 | Pleasure Principle | 1978 | $25 |

PARLIAMENT
Also see GEORGE CLINTON; FUNKADELIC; THE PARLIAMENTS.
CASABLANCA
❏ NBLP7014	Chocolate City	1975	$85
❏ NBLP7084	Funkentelechy vs. the Placebo Syndrome	1977	$75
❏ 824501-1	Funkentelechy vs. the Placebo Syndrome	1985	$25

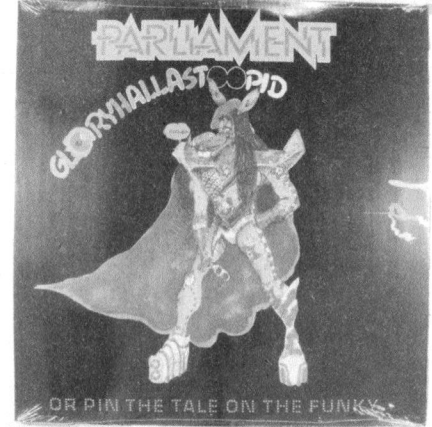

❏ NBLP7195 [B]	Gloryhallastoopid (Or Pin the Tale on the Funky)	1979	$75
❏ 822637-1	Greatest Hits	1984	$25
❏ NBLP7022	Mothership Connection	1976	$75
❏ 824502-1	Mothership Connection	1985	$25
❏ NBLP7125	Motor-Booty Affair	1978	$75
❏ NBPIX7125 [PD]	Motor-Booty Affair	1978	$85
❏ NBLP7053	Parliament Live/P. Funk Earth Tour	1977	$85
❏ NBLP7034	The Clones of Dr. Funkenstein	1976	$75
❏ NBLP7249	Trombipulation	1980	$75
❏ NBLP9003	Up for the Down Stroke	1974	$75

—Original pressing, distributed by Warner Bros.

| ❏ NBLP7002 | Up for the Down Stroke | 1974 | $85 |

INVICTUS
| ❏ ST-7302 | Osmium | 1970 | $175 |

PARR, JOHN
ATLANTIC
| ❏ 80180 | John Parr | 1984 | $10 |
| ❏ 81689 | Running the Endless Mile | 1986 | $10 |

PARSONS, ALAN, PROJECT
20TH CENTURY
| ❏ T-508 [B] | Tales of Mystery and Imagination - Edgar Allan Poe | 1976 | $18 |

ARISTA
| ❏ AL8204 | Ammonia Avenue | 1984 | $12 |
| ❏ AL8289 | Ammonia Avenue | 1985 | $10 |

—Reissue

| ❏ SP-68 [DJ] | Audio Guide to the Alan Parsons Project | 1979 | $50 |

—Contains first four APP LPs plus a two-record set of other Parsons work

| ❏ SP-68 [DJ] | Audio Guide to the Alan Parsons Project | 1979 | $50 |

—Contains first four APP LPs plus a two-record set of other Parsons work

| ❏ SP-140 [DJ] | Complete Audio Guide to the 1982 Alan Parsons Project | | $100 |

—Contains first six APP LPs plus a two-record set of other Parsons work

| ❏ SP-140 [DJ] | Complete Audio Guide to the 1982 Alan Parsons Project | | $100 |

—Contains first six APP LPs plus a two-record set of other Parsons work

| ❏ AB9504 | Eve | 1979 | $12 |
| ❏ AL8318 | Eve | 1985 | $10 |

—Reissue

| ❏ AL9599 | Eye in the Sky | 1982 | $12 |
| ❏ AL8290 | Eye in the Sky | 1985 | $10 |

—Reissue

❏ AL8448	Gaudi	1987	$10
❏ AL7002	I Robot	1977	$12
❏ AL8040	I Robot	1983	$10

—Reissue

| ❏ AB4180 | Pyramid | 1978 | $12 |
| ❏ AL8320 | Pyramid | 1985 | $10 |

—Reissue

| ❏ AL8384 | Stereotomy | 1986 | $18 |

—First editions came in an oversize vinyl jacket

| ❏ AL8384 | Stereotomy | 1986 | $10 |

—With regular LP jacket

❏ AL8193	The Best of the Alan Parsons Project	1983	$10
❏ AL8486	The Best of the Alan Parsons Project, Vol. 2	1987	$10
❏ AL8487	The Instrumental Works of the Alan Parsons Project	1988	$12
❏ AL9518	The Turn of a Friendly Card	1980	$12
❏ AL8315	The Turn of a Friendly Card	1985	$10

—Reissue

| ❏ ALPD8263 [DJ] | Vulture Culture | 1985 | $30 |

—Promo-only picture disc

| ❏ ALPD8263 [DJ] | Vulture Culture | 1985 | $30 |

—Promo-only picture disc

| ❏ AL8263 | Vulture Culture | 1985 | $12 |

CASABLANCA
| ❏ 822784-1 | Tales of Mystery and Imagination - Edgar Allan Poe | 1984 | $12 |

—Reissue of 20th Century LP

MOBILE FIDELITY
| ❏ Jan-0084 | I Robot | 1982 | $75 |

—Audiophile vinyl

| ❏ MFQR 1-084 | I Robot | 1982 | $150 |

—Audiophile vinyl; Ultra High Quality pressing in box

| ❏ 1-204 | Tales of Mystery and Imagination - Edgar Allan Poe | 1994 | $75 |

—Audiophile vinyl

PARSONS, GRAM
An important figure in the melding of country with rock. EMMYLOU HARRIS appears on some of his solo recordings. Also see THE BYRDS; THE FLYING BURRITO BROTHERS; THE INTERNATIONAL SUBMARINE BAND.

REPRISE
| ❏ MS2123 [B] | G.P. | 1973 | $25 |
| ❏ MS2171 [B] | Grievous Angel | 1974 | $25 |

RHINO
❏ R1541107 [B]	Alternate Takes From GP And Grievous Angel	2014	$40
❏ R-12123 [B]	GP	2014	$30
❏ R-12171 [B]	Grievous Angel	2014	$30

SIERRA
| ❏ 8702 | Early Years, Volume 1 (1963-65) | 1979 | $12 |
| ❏ SP-1963 | Early Years, Volume 1 (1963-65) | 198? | $10 |

—Reissue of 8702

| ❏ GP-1973 | Gram Parsons and the Fallen Angels Live '73 | 1982 | $12 |

SUNDAZED
| ❏ LP5076 | Another Side of This Life | 2000 | $15 |

PARTON, DOLLY
COLUMBIA
| ❏ C46882 | Eagle When She Flies | 1991 | $25 |

—Available on vinyl only through Columbia House

| ❏ FC40968 | Rainbow | 1987 | $12 |
| ❏ FC44384 | White Limozeen | 1989 | $15 |

MONUMENT
❏ SLP-18136	As Long As I Love	1970	$25
❏ MLP-8085 [M]	Hello, I'm Dolly	1967	$30
❏ SLP-18085 [S]	Hello, I'm Dolly	1967	$40
❏ KZG33876	Hello, I'm Dolly	1975	$25
❏ 7623	In the Beginning	197?	$15
❏ KZG31913	The World of Dolly	1972	$25

PAIR
| ❏ PDL2-1009 | Just the Way I Am | 1986 | $15 |
| ❏ PDL2-1116 | Portrait | 1986 | $15 |

RCA
| ❏ 5706-1-R | The Best of Dolly Parton, Vol. 3 | 1987 | $12 |

Number	Title	Yr	NM
❏ 6497-1-R	The Best There Is	1987	$12

RCA CAMDEN

Number	Title	Yr	NM
❏ CAS-2583	Just the Way I Am	1972	$12
❏ ACL1-0307	Mine	1973	$12

RCA VICTOR

Number	Title	Yr	NM
❏ AYL1-4830	9 to 5 and Odd Jobs	1984	$10

—Best Buy Series" reissue

❏ AHL1-3852	9 to 5 and Odd Jobs	1980	$15
❏ APL1-1665	All I Can Do	1976	$15
❏ LSP-4387	A Real Live Dolly	1970	$30

—Four songs feature Porter Wagoner

❏ APD1-0286 [Q]	Bubbling Over	1974	$30
❏ APL1-0286	Bubbling Over	1973	$15
❏ AHL1-4691	Burlap & Satin	1983	$12
❏ AYL1-5437	Burlap & Satin	1985	$10

—Best Buy Series" reissue

❏ LSP-4603	Coat of Many Colors	1971	$25
❏ AHL1-5471	Collector's Series	1985	$12
❏ APL1-1221	Dolly	1975	$15
❏ AHL1-3546	Dolly Dolly Dolly	1980	$15
❏ LSP-4762	Dolly Parton Sings	1972	$18
❏ LSP-4398	Golden Streets of Glory	1971	$25
❏ AHL1-3361	Great Balls of Fire	1979	$15
❏ AHL1-4422	Greatest Hits	1982	$15
❏ AFL1-2797	Heartbreaker	1978	$15
❏ AYL1-3665	Heartbreaker	1980	$10

—Best Buy Series" reissue

❏ AHL1-4289	Heartbreak Express	1982	$15
❏ AYL1-4829	Here You Come Again	1984	$10

—Best Buy Series" reissue

❏ AFL1-2544	Here You Come Again	1977	$15
❏ LSP-4099	In the Good Old Days	1969	$25
❏ AYL1-3898	Jolene	1981	$10

—Best Buy Series" reissue

❏ APL1-0473	Jolene	1974	$15
❏ LSP-4507	Joshua	1971	$25
❏ LPM-3949 [M]	Just Because I'm a Woman	1968	$150
❏ LSP-3949 [S]	Just Because I'm a Woman	1968	$30

—Stereo" on black label

❏ LSP-3949 [S]	Just Because I'm a Woman	1968	$25

—Orange label

❏ APL1-0712	Love Is Like a Butterfly	1974	$15
❏ LSP-4188	My Blue Ridge Mountain Boy	1969	$25
❏ LSP-4752	My Favorite Song Writer: Porter Wagoner	1972	$25
❏ APL1-0033	My Tennessee Mountain Home	1973	$15
❏ AYL1-3764	My Tennessee Mountain Home	1980	$10

—Best Buy Series" reissue

❏ AYL1-3980	New Harvest	1981	$10

—Best Buy Series" reissue

❏ APL1-2188	New Harvest...First Gathering	1977	$15
❏ DJL1-2314 [DJ]	Personal Music Dialogue with Dolly Parton	1976	$30
❏ AHL1-5414	Real Love	1985	$12
❏ APL1-0950	The Bargain Store	1975	$15
❏ LSP-4449	The Best of Dolly Parton	1970	$25
❏ AYL1-5146	The Best of Dolly Parton	1984	$10

—Best Buy Series" reissue

❏ APL1-1117	The Best of Dolly Parton	1975	$15
❏ LSP-4288	The Fairest of Them All	1970	$25
❏ AHL1-4940	The Great Pretender	1984	$12
❏ AHL1-9508	Think About Love	1986	$12
❏ LSP-4686	Touch Your Woman	1972	$25

TIME-LIFE

❏ STW-107	Country Music	1981	$12

PARTON, DOLLY/FAYE TUCKER

SOMERSET

Number	Title	Yr	NM
❏ SF-29400	Dolly Parton Sings Country Oldies	1968	$18
❏ S-9700 [M]	Hits Made Famous by Country Queens	1963	$30
❏ SF-19700 [S]	Hits Made Famous by Country Queens	1963	$30

—Dolly Parton sings songs made famous by Kitty Wells

TIME

❏ 2108	Country & Western Soul	1963	$40

PARTON, DOLLY/GEORGE JONES

STARDAY

❏ LP429 [P]	Dolly Parton and George Jones	1968	$40

—One side of Dolly in stereo, one side of "Possum" in rechanneled stereo

PARTON, DOLLY/LINDA RONSTADT/EMMYLOU HARRIS

WARNER BROS.

❏ 25491	Trio	1987	$12

PARTON, STELLA

ELEKTRA

❏ 7E-1111	Country Sweet	1977	$15
❏ 6E-191	Love Ya	1979	$15
❏ 6E-126	Stella Parton	1978	$15
❏ 6E-229	The Best of Stella Parton	1979	$15

SOUL, COUNTRY & BLUES

Number	Title	Yr	NM
❏ 6006	I Want to Hold You in My Dreams Tonight	1975	$25

TOWN HOUSE

❏ ST-7005	So Far So Good	1982	$15

PARTRIDGE FAMILY, THE

BELL

❏ 6066	A Partridge Family Christmas Card	1971	$40

—With attached Christmas card

❏ 6066	A Partridge Family Christmas Card	1971	$20

—Without Christmas card

❏ 6066 [B]	A Partridge Family Christmas Card	1971	$25

—With Christmas card printed on the cover (later pressing)

❏ 1137	Bulletin Board	1973	$75
❏ 1122	Crossword Puzzle	1973	$50
❏ 6050	The Partridge Family Album	1970	$25
❏ 6050	The Partridge Family Album Bonus Photo	1970	$20

❏ 1107 [B]	The Partridge Family At Home with Their Greatest Hits	1972	$30
❏ 1111	The Partridge Family Notebook	1972	$30
❏ 6072 [B]	The Partridge Family Shopping Bag	1972	$35

—includes free plastic shopping bag

❏ 6072	The Partridge Family Shopping Bag	1972	$25
❏ 6064	The Partridge Family Sound Magazine	1971	$30
❏ 1319	The World of the Partridge Family	1974	$50
❏ 6059	Up to Date	1971	$25
❏ 6059	Up to Date Book Cover	1971	$20

LAURIE HOUSE

❏ H-8014	The Partridge Family	197?	$50

PASS, JOE, AND ARNOLD ROSS

PACIFIC JAZZ

❏ PJ-48 [M]	Sounds of Synanon	1962	$30
❏ ST-48 [S]	Sounds of Synanon	1962	$30

PASS, JOE, AND JIMMY ROWLES

PABLO

❏ 2310865	Checkmate	1982	$30

PASS, JOE, AND NIELS-HENNING ORSTED PEDERSEN

PABLO

❏ 2310830	Chops	1979	$30

PABLO LIVE

❏ 2308811	North Sea Nights	1979	$30

PASS, JOE, AND PAULINHO DA COSTA

PABLO

❏ 2310824	Tudo Bem!	1978	$30

PASS, JOE, AND ROBERT CONTI

DISCOVERY

❏ 906	The Living Legends	1985	$30

PASS, JOE; TOOTS THIELMANS; NIELS-HENNING ORSTED PEDERSEN

PABLO LIVE

❏ 2308233	Live in the Netherlands	1981	$30

PASS, JOE

BASF

❏ 20738	Intercontinental	197?	$35

BLUE NOTE

Number	Title	Yr	NM
❏ LT-1103	Joy Spring	1981	$25
❏ LT-1053	The Complete "Catch Me" Sessions	1980	$30

DISCOVERY

❏ DS-776	Guitar Interludes	197?	$30
❏ DS-906	The Living Legends	1986	$25

FANTASY

❏ OJC-602	I Remember Charlie Parker	1991	$30
❏ OJC-382	Montreux '77	1989	$25

PABLO

❏ 2310931	Blues for Fred	198?	$25
❏ 2310877	Eximious	198?	$30
❏ 2310752	Montreux '75	1976	$30
❏ 2310936	One for My Baby	1989	$30
❏ 2310716	Portrait of Duke Ellington	1975	$30
❏ 2310939	Summer Nights	1990	$35
❏ 2310593	The Best of Joe Pass	198?	$30
❏ 2405419	The Best of Joe Pass	198?	$25
❏ 2310788	Virtuoso #2	1976	$30
❏ 2310805	Virtuoso #3	1978	$30
❏ 2640102	Virtuoso #4	198?	$35
❏ 2310708	Virtuoso	1974	$35
❏ 2310912	Whitestone	198?	$25

PABLO LIVE

❏ 2308249	Joe Pass at Akron University	1987	$25
❏ 2620114	Joe Pass Trio Live at Donte's	198?	$35
❏ 2308239	Live at Long Beach City College	1987	$25
❏ 2308212	Montreux '77	1978	$30

PABLO TODAY

❏ 2312109	I Remember Charlie Parker	1979	$30
❏ 2312133	Joe Pass Loves Gershwin	198?	$30

PACIFIC JAZZ

❏ PJ-73 [M]	Catch Me!	1963	$30
❏ ST-73 [S]	Catch Me!	1963	$30
❏ PJ-85 [M]	For Django	1964	$30
❏ ST-85 [S]	For Django	1964	$30
❏ LN-10132	For Django	198?	$20

—Budget-line reissue

❏ LN-10086	Simplicity	198?	$20

—Budget-line reissue

PAUSA

❏ 7043	Intercontinental	198?	$25

WORLD PACIFIC

❏ WP-1844 [M]	A Sign of the Times	1966	$150
❏ ST-21844 [S]	A Sign of the Times	1966	$150
❏ WP-1865 [M]	Simplicity	1967	$150
❏ ST-21865 [S]	Simplicity	1967	$150
❏ WP-1854 [M]	The Stones Jazz	1967	$150
❏ ST-21854 [S]	The Stones Jazz	1967	$150

PASSPORT

ATCO

❏ SD 36-107	Cross-Collateral	1975	$30
❏ SD 36-149	Iguacu	1977	$25
❏ SD 36-132	Infinity Machine	1976	$30
❏ SD7042	Looking Thru	1974	$30

ATLANTIC

❏ SD19304	Blue Tattoo	1981	$25
❏ SD18162	Doldinger Jubilee '75	1976	$30
❏ 80034	Earthborn	1982	$25
❏ SD19233	Garden of Eden	1979	$25
❏ 81727	Heavy Nights	1986	$25
❏ 80144	Man in the Mirror	1983	$25
❏ SD19265	Oceanliner	1980	$25
❏ 81251	Running in Real Time	1985	$25
❏ SD19177	Sky Blue	1978	$25
❏ 81937	Talk Back	1989	$25

REPRISE

❏ MS2143	Doldinger	1973	$35

PASTEL SIX, THE

ZEN

❏ 1001 [M]	The Cinnamon Cinder	1963	$150

PASTICHE

NOVA

❏ 8707	That's R & B-Bop	198?	$30

PASTOR, GUY

DISCOVERY

❏ DS-918	This Is It	1986	$25

PASTOR, TONY

CIRCLE

❏ CLP-121	Tony Pastor and His Orchestra 1942-47	198?	$25
❏ 31	Tony Pastor and His Orchestra 1944-47	198?	$25

EVEREST

❏ LPBR-5031 [M]	P.S. – Plays and Sings Shaw	1959	$35
❏ SDBR-1031 [S]	P.S. – Plays and Sings Shaw	1959	$25

Number	Title	Yr	NM
FORUM			
❑ F-9009 [M]	Let's Dance with Tony Pastor	196?	$30
❑ SF-9009 [S]	Let's Dance with Tony Pastor	196?	$30
ROULETTE			
❑ R-25027 [M]	Guy Pastor and His Dad	1958	$75
❑ R-25024 [M]	Let's Dance	1958	$75
X			
❑ LXA-3025 [10]	Tony Pastor's Best	1954	$150

PASTORIUS, JACO

Number	Title	Yr	NM
EPIC			
❑ PE33949 [B]	Jaco Pastorius	1976	$40
IAI			
❑ 373846 [B]	Jaco	1975	$40
WARNER BROS.			
❑ 23876 [B]	Invitation	1983	$30
❑ BSK3535 [B]	Word of Mouth	1981	$75

PATCHEN, KENNETH, WITH THE CHAMBER JAZZ SEXTET

Number	Title	Yr	NM
CADENCE			
❑ CLP-3004 [M]	Kenneth Patchen Reads His Poetry	1957	$300

PATE, JOHNNY

Number	Title	Yr	NM
GIG			
❑ GLP-100 [M]	Subtle Sounds	1956	$400
KING			
❑ 611 [M]	A Date with Johnny Pate	1959	$100
❑ 561 [M]	Jazz Goes Ivy League	1958	$100
❑ 584 [M]	Swingin' Flute	1958	$100
STEPHENY			
❑ 4002 [M]	Johnny Pate at the Blue Note	1957	$150
TALISMAN			
❑ TLP-1 [10]	Johnny Pate Trio	1956	$120

PATITUCCI, JOHN

Number	Title	Yr	NM
GRP			
❑ GR-1049	John Patitucci	1988	$25
❑ GR-9583	On the Corner	1989	$30

PATRON SAINTS, THE

Number	Title	Yr	NM
(NO LABEL)			
❑ JT-1001	Fohhob Bohob	1969	$3000

—100 copies were pressed; VG value 1000; VG+ value 2000

Number	Title	Yr	NM
PATRON SAINT			
❑ JT-1001	Fohhob Bohob	1997	$30

—Authorized reissue with bonus 7-inch single; numbered edition of 500

PATTERSON, DON

Number	Title	Yr	NM
CADET			
❑ LPS-787 [S]	Goin' Down Home	1967	$25
❑ LP-787 [M]	Goin' Down Home	1967	$30
MUSE			
❑ MR-5121	Movin' Up	1977	$30
❑ MR-5005	The Return of Don Patterson	1974	$35
❑ MR-5032	These Are Soulful Days	1975	$35
❑ MR-5148	Why Not	1979	$30
PRESTIGE			
❑ PRST-7772	Best of Jazz Giants	1971	$35
❑ PRST-7563	Boppin' and Burnin'	1968	$25
❑ PRST-7738	Brothers-4	1970	$35
❑ PRST-7816	Donnybrook	1971	$35
❑ PRST-7533 [S]	Four Dimensions	1967	$25
❑ PRLP-7533 [M]	Four Dimensions	1967	$30
❑ PRST-7613	Funk You	1969	$25
❑ PRST-7349 [S]	Hip Cake Walk	1965	$30
❑ PRLP-7349 [M]	Hip Cake Walk	1965	$30
❑ PRST-7415 [S]	Holiday Soul	1965	$30
❑ PRLP-7415 [M]	Holiday Soul	1966	$30
❑ PRST-7510 [S]	Mellow Soul	1967	$25
❑ PRLP-7510 [M]	Mellow Soul	1967	$30
❑ PRST-7640	Oh, Happy Days!	1969	$25
❑ PRST-7577	Opus De Don	1968	$25
❑ PRST-7381 [S]	Patterson's People	1965	$30
❑ PRLP-7381 [M]	Patterson's People	1965	$30
❑ PRST-7430 [S]	Satisfaction	1966	$30
❑ PRLP-7430 [M]	Satisfaction	1966	$30
❑ PRST-7484 [S]	Soul Happening!	1967	$25
❑ PRLP-7484 [M]	Soul Happening!	1967	$30
❑ PRST-7704	The Best of Don Patterson	1969	$35
❑ PRST-7466 [S]	The Boss Men	1967	$30
❑ PRLP-7466 [M]	The Boss Men	1967	$30
❑ PRST-7331 [S]	The Exciting New Organ of Don Patterson	1964	$30
❑ PRLP-7331 [M]	The Exiting New Organ of Don Patterson	1964	$30
❑ PRST-7852	Tune Up	1971	$35

PATTERSON, KELLEE

Number	Title	Yr	NM
BLACK JAZZ			
❑ QD-12	Maiden Voyage	1974	$25

PATTERSON SINGERS, THE

Number	Title	Yr	NM
ATCO			
❑ SD 33-380	The Patterson Singers	1972	$25
KING			
❑ 763 [M]	Gospel Songs by the Patterson Singers	1962	$50
❑ KS-1129	Jesus Knows	1971	$25
MINIT			
❑ LP-40021	The Soul of Gospel	1969	$25
VEE JAY			
❑ LP-5017 [M]	My Prayer	1962	$30
❑ LP-5046 [M]	Songs of Faith	1963	$25
❑ SR-5046 [S]	Songs of Faith	1963	$30
❑ LP-5032 [M]	The Lord's Prayer	1963	$30
❑ LP-5060 [M]	The Soul of the Patterson Singers	1964	$25

PATTO

Number	Title	Yr	NM
ISLAND			
❑ SW-9322	Roll 'Em, Smoke 'Em, Put Another Line Out	1972	$30
VERTIGO			

Number	Title	Yr	NM
❑ VEL-1008 [B]	Hold Your Fire	1972	$120
❑ VEL-1001	Patto	1971	$100

PATTON, "BIG" JOHN

Number	Title	Yr	NM
BLUE NOTE			
❑ BST-84340 [S]	Accent on the Blues	1970	$30

—With "A Division of Liberty Records" on label

❑ BLP-4130 [M]	Along Came John	1963	$75
❑ BST-84130 [S]	Along Came John	1963	$40

—With "New York, USA" address on label

❑ BST-84130 [S]	Along Came John	1967	$35

—With "A Division of Liberty Records" on label

❑ BLP-4143 [M]	Blue John	1963	$0

—Canceled

❑ BST-84143 [S]	Blue John	1986	$30

—The Finest in Jazz Since 1939" issue; originally scheduled for 1963 release, but canceled

❑ BLP-4229 [M]	Got a Good Thing Goin'	1966	$75
❑ BST-84229 [S]	Got a Good Thing Goin'	1966	$30

—With "New York, USA" address on label

❑ BST-84229 [S]	Got a Good Thing Goin'	1967	$35

—With "A Division of Liberty Records" on label

❑ BLP-4239 [M]	Let 'Em Roll	1966	$75
❑ BST-84239 [S]	Let 'Em Roll	1966	$30

—With "New York, USA" address on label

❑ BST-84239 [S]	Let 'Em Roll	1967	$35

—With "A Division of Liberty Records" on label

❑ BLP-4192 [M]	Oh Baby!	1964	$75
❑ BST-84192 [S]	Oh Baby!	1964	$30

—With "New York, USA" address on label

❑ BST-84192 [S]	Oh Baby!	1967	$35

—With "A Division of Liberty Records" on label

❑ BST-84281 [S]	That Certain Feeling	1968	$30

—With "A Division of Liberty Records" on label

❑ BLP-4174 [M]	The Way I Feel	1964	$75
❑ BST-84174 [S]	The Way I Feel	1964	$30

—With "New York, USA" address on label

❑ BST-84174 [S]	The Way I Feel	1967	$35

—With "A Division of Liberty Records" on label

❑ BST-84306 [S]	Understanding	1969	$30

—With "A Division of Liberty Records" on label

PATTON, CHARLEY

Number	Title	Yr	NM
ORIGIN JAZZ LIBRARY			
❑ OJL-1 [M]	The Immortal Charley Patton No. 1	1962	$30
❑ OJL-7 [M]	The Immortal Charley Patton No. 2	1962	$30
YAZOO			
❑ 2010	Founder of the Delta Blues	197?	$30

Number	Title	Yr	NM
❑ 2001	King of the Delta Blues	197?	$30

PATTON, JIMMY

Number	Title	Yr	NM
MOON			
❑ 101 [M]	Make Room for the Blues	1966	$40
SIMS			
❑ 127 [M]	Blue Darlin'	1965	$40
SOURDOUGH			
❑ 127 [M]	Blue Darlin'	1965	$50
STEREOPHONIC			
❑ LP-1002 [S]	Take 30 Minutes with Jimmy Patton	196?	$120

PAUL, BILLY

Number	Title	Yr	NM
PHILADELPHIA INT'L.			
❑ ZS731793 [PS]	360 Degrees of Billy Paul	1972	$15
❑ ZS731793	I'm Just a Prisoner//Am I Black Enough for You/I'm Gonna Make It This Time	1972	$15

—Jukebox issue; small hole, plays at 33 1/3 rpm

Number	Title	Yr	NM
GAMBLE			
❑ SG-5002	Feeling Good at the Cadillac Club	1968	$30
ICHIBAN			
❑ ICH-1025	Wide Open	198?	$12
NEPTUNE			
❑ 201	Ebony Woman	1970	$25
PHILADELPHIA INT'L.			
❑ KZ31793	360 Degrees of Billy Paul	1972	$15
❑ ZQ31793 [Q]	360 Degrees of Billy Paul	1972	$40
❑ KZ32118	Ebony Woman	1973	$15

—Reissue of Neptune LP

❑ KZ32119	Feeling Good at the Cadillac Club	1973	$15

—Reissue of Gamble LP

❑ JZ35756	First Class	1979	$12
❑ Z30580	Going East	1971	$15
❑ PZ33157	Got My Head On Straight	1975	$12
❑ PZ34389	Let 'Em In	1976	$12
❑ KZ32952	Live in Europe	1974	$12
❑ ZQ32952 [Q]	Live in Europe	1974	$30
❑ PZ34923	Only the Strong Survive	1977	$12
❑ Z236314	The Best of Billy Paul	1980	$18
❑ KZ32409	War of the Gods	1973	$12
❑ ZQ32409 [Q]	War of the Gods	1973	$50
❑ PZ33843	When Love Is New	1975	$12
TOTAL EXPERIENCE			
❑ TEL8-5711	Lately	1985	$12

PAUL, JOYCE

Number	Title	Yr	NM
UNITED ARTISTS			
❑ UAS-6684	Heartaches, Laughter and Tears	1968	$18

PAUL, LES, AND MARY FORD

The well-known pop duo had one of their hits make the country charts. Also see CHET ATKINS AND LES PAUL.

Number	Title	Yr	NM
CAPITOL			
❑ H356 [10]	Bye Bye Blues	1952	$100

Number	Title	Yr	NM
❑ T356 [M]	Bye Bye Blues	1955	$50
❑ H577 [10]	Les and Mary	1955	$100
❑ W577 [M]	Les and Mary	1955	$50
❑ H416 [10]	The Hit Makers	1953	$100
❑ T416 [M]	The Hit Makers	1955	$50
❑ T1476 [M]	The Hits of Les and Mary	1960	$30
❑ DT1476 [R]	The Hits of Les and Mary	1960	$25
❑ H226 [10]	The New Sound, Volume 1	1950	$100
❑ T226 [M]	The New Sound, Volume 1	1955	$50
❑ H286 [10]	The New Sound, Volume 2	1951	$100
❑ T286 [M]	The New Sound, Volume 2	1955	$50
❑ SM-286	The New Sound, Volume 2	197?	$12
❑ ST-11308	The World Is Still Waiting for the Sunrise	1974	$15

Number	Title	Yr	NM
❏ SM-11308	The World Is Still Waiting for the Sunrise	197?	$12

— *Reissue with new prefix*

| ❏ T802 [M] | Time to Dream | 1956 | $50 |

CAPITOL SPECIAL MARKETS

| ❏ SLCR-8130 | The All-Time Greatest Hits of Les Paul and Mary Ford | 1980 | $25 |

— *Produced for Murray Hill Records (979462)*

COLUMBIA

Number	Title	Yr	NM
❏ CL1821 [M]	Bouquet of Roses	1962	$25
❏ CS8621 [S]	Bouquet of Roses	1962	$30
❏ CL1276 [M]	Lovers' Luau	1959	$25
❏ CS8086 [S]	Lovers' Luau	1959	$30
❏ CL1928 [M]	Swingin' South	1963	$18
❏ CS8728 [S]	Swingin' South	1963	$25
❏ CL1688 [M]	Warm and Wonderful	1962	$25
❏ CS8488 [S]	Warm and Wonderful	1962	$30

HARMONY

| ❏ HL7333 [M] | The Fabulous Les Paul and Mary Ford | 1965 | $15 |
| ❏ HS11133 [S] | The Fabulous Les Paul and Mary Ford | 1965 | $15 |

PICKWICK

| ❏ SPC-3122 | Brazil | 197? | $12 |

PAUL, LES

CAPITOL

| ❏ N-16286 | Early Les Paul | 1982 | $10 |

DECCA

❏ DL-5376 [10]	Galloping Guitars	1952	$150
❏ DL-5018 [10]	Hawaiian Paradise	1949	$150
❏ DL8589 [M]	More of Les	1957	$40

GLENDALE

| ❏ 6014 [B] | The Les Paul Trio | 198? | $15 |

LONDON

| ❏ 50016 | Multi-Trackin' | 1979 | $15 |

LONDON PHASE 4

| ❏ SP-44101 | Les Paul Now! | 1968 | $18 |

VOCALION

| ❏ VL3849 [M] | The Guitar Artistry of Les Paul | 196? | $18 |
| ❏ VL73849 [R] | The Guitar Artistry of Les Paul | 196? | $15 |

PAUL, LOUIS

ENTERPRISE

| ❏ ENS-1034 | Reflections of the Way It Really Is | 1971 | $18 |

PAUL AND PAULA

PHILIPS

❏ PHM200101 [M]	Holiday for Teens	1963	$35
❏ PHS600101 [S]	Holiday for Teens	1963	$40
❏ PHM200078 [M]	Paul and Paula Sing for Young Lovers	1963	$30
❏ PHS600078 [S]	Paul and Paula Sing for Young Lovers	1963	$40
❏ PHM200089 [M]	We Go Together	1963	$30
❏ PHS600089 [S]	We Go Together	1963	$40

PAUL MESSIS

STATE RECORDS

| ❏ THSLP005 [S] | Case Closed | 2013 | $25 |

— *Limited edition; 500 copies pressed on 180-gram vinyl. With a front-laminated flip-back sleeve. Released in the U.K. on April 23, 2013. Pricing based on range seen on amazon.com as of 26 June 2013.*

PAULIN, DOC

FOLKWAYS

| ❏ FA2856 | Doc Paulin's Marching Band | 198? | $30 |

PAULO, MICHAEL

MCA

| ❏ 42295 | One Passion | 1989 | $30 |

PAULSON, PAT

RUBICON/MERCURY

| ❏ SR61251 | Live at the Ice House | 1970 | $18 |
| ❏ SR61179 | Pat Paulson for President | 1968 | $25 |

PAUPERS, THE

VERVE FORECAST

❏ FTS-3051	Ellis Island	1968	$18
❏ FT-3026 [M]	Magic People	1967	$25
❏ FTS-3026 [S]	Magic People	1967	$25

PAVAROTTI, LUCIANO

LONDON

| ❏ OS26473 | O Holy Night | 1976 | $18 |

— *Original U.S.-distributed version has "London" without "ffrr" on upper right front cover and a white back cover.*

| ❏ OS26473 | O Holy Night | 198? | $15 |

— *Later pressings have "London/ffrr" on upper right front cover and have a yellow back cover*

PAVLOV'S DOG

ABC

Number	Title	Yr	NM
❏ D-866	Pampered Menial	1975	$30

COLUMBIA

| ❏ PC33964 | At the Sound of the Bell | 1976 | $15 |
| ❏ PC33552 | Pampered Menial | 1976 | $15 |

— *Reissue of ABC album*

PAVONE, RITA

RCA VICTOR

❏ LPM-2900 [M]	Rita Pavone	1964	$18
❏ LSP-2900 [S]	Rita Pavone	1964	$25
❏ LPM-2996 [M]	Small Wonder	1965	$18
❏ LSP-2996 [S]	Small Wonder	1965	$25

PAXTON, GARY

NEW PAX

❏ NP-33033	More from the Astonishing, Outrageous, Amazing, Incredible, Unbelievable World of Gary S. Paxton	1977	$15
❏ NP-33080	(Some of) The Best of Gary S. Paxton (So Far)	1980	$15
❏ NP-33005	The Astonishing, Outrageous, Amazing, Incredible, Unbelievable Different World of Gary S. Paxton	1976	$15
❏ NP-33048	The Gospel According to Gary S.	1979	$15

PAX

| ❏ R-2411 | Gary Sanford Paxton | 1979 | $15 |
| ❏ R-2406 | Terminally Weird but Godly Right/Anchored in the Rock of Ages | 1978 | $15 |

PAXTON, GEORGE

HINDSIGHT

| ❏ HSR-184 | George Paxton and His Orchestra 1944-45 | 198? | $25 |

PAXTON, TOM

ELEKTRA

❏ EKL-298 [M]	Ain't That News	1965	$25
❏ EKS-7298 [S]	Ain't That News	1965	$30
❏ EKS-74019	Morning Again	1968	$25
❏ EKL-317 [M]	Outward Bound	1966	$25
❏ EKS-7317 [S]	Outward Bound	1966	$30
❏ EKL-277 [M]	Ramblin' Boy	1964	$25
❏ EKS-7277 [S]	Ramblin' Boy	1964	$30
❏ 7E-2003	The Compleat Tom Paxton	1971	$25
❏ EKS-74043	The Things I Notice Now	1969	$18
❏ EKS-74066	Tom Paxton 6	1970	$18

FLYING FISH

❏ FF-414	And Loving You	1987	$12
❏ FF-280	Even a Gray Day	1983	$12
❏ FF-356	One Million Lawyers...And Other Disasters	1986	$12
❏ FF-486	Politics	199?	$15
❏ FF-408	The Marvellous Toy and Other Gallimaufry	1987	$12
❏ FF-519	The Very Best of Tom Paxton	199?	$15

GASLIGHT

| ❏ GV-116 [M] | I'm the Man Who Built the Bridges | 1962 | $100 |

HOGEYE

| ❏ 004 | Bulletin...We Interrupt This Record | 198? | $12 |

MOUNTAIN RAILROAD

| ❏ 52796 | The Paxton Report | 198? | $15 |
| ❏ 52792 | Up and Up | 1980 | $15 |

PRIVATE STOCK

| ❏ PS-2002 | Something in My Life | 1975 | $15 |

REPRISE

❏ RS6443	How Come the Sun	1971	$18
❏ MS2144	New Songs for Old Friends	1973	$18
❏ MS2096	Peace Will Come	1972	$18

VANGUARD

| ❏ VSD-79411 | Heroes | 1978 | $15 |
| ❏ VSD-79395 | New Songs from the Briarpatch | 1977 | $15 |

PAYCHECK, JOHNNY

ACCORD

| ❏ SN-7173 | Extra Special | 1981 | $12 |

ALLEGIANCE

| ❏ AV-435 | I Don't Need to Know That Right Now | 198? | $10 |

CERTRON

| ❏ 7002 | Johnny Paycheck Again | 1970 | $18 |

EPIC

❏ KE33943	11 Months and 29 Days	1975	$12
❏ KE35444	Armed and Crazy	1978	$12
❏ FE37345	Encore	1981	$12
❏ PE37345	Encore	198?	$10

— *Budget-line reissue*

| ❏ JE36200 | Everybody's Got a Family -- Meet Mine | 1979 | $12 |

Number	Title	Yr	NM
❏ KE33091	Greatest Hits	1974	$12
❏ PE33091	Greatest Hits	198?	$10

— *Budget-line reissue*

| ❏ KE35623 | Greatest Hits, Volume 2 | 1978 | $12 |
| ❏ PE35623 | Greatest Hits, Volume 2 | 198? | $10 |

— *Budget-line reissue*

❏ PE39943	John Austin Paycheck	1984	$10
❏ FE38322	Johnny Paycheck's Biggest Hits	1983	$12
❏ FE37933	Lovers and Losers	1982	$12
❏ KE33354	Loving You Beats All I've Ever Seen	1975	$12
❏ FE36761	Mr. Hag Told My Story	1981	$12
❏ PE36761	Mr. Hag Told My Story	1981	$10

— *Budget-line reissue*

❏ JE36496	New York Town	1980	$12
❏ E31141	She's All I Got	1971	$15
❏ PE34693	Slide Off of Your Satin Sheets	1976	$12
❏ KE31702	Somebody Loves Me	1972	$15
❏ KE31449	Someone to Give My Love To	1972	$15
❏ KE32387	Something About You I Love	1973	$15
❏ KE32570	Song and Dance Man	1973	$15
❏ KE35045	Take This Job and Shove It	1977	$12
❏ PE35045	Take This Job and Shove It	198?	$10

— *Budget-line reissue*

INTERMEDIA

| ❏ QS-5018 | Back On the Job | 198? | $10 |

LITTLE DARLIN'

❏ SLD-8010	Country Soul	1968	$30
❏ LD-4004 [M]	Gospeltime in My Fashion	1967	$25
❏ SLD-8004 [S]	Gospeltime in My Fashion	1967	$30
❏ LD-4001 [M]	Johnny Paycheck at Carnegie Hall	1966	$25
❏ SLD-8001 [S]	Johnny Paycheck at Carnegie Hall	1966	$30
❏ SLD-8012	Johnny Paycheck's Greatest Hits	1968	$30
❏ LD-4006 [M]	Johnny Paycheck Sings Jukebox Charlie	1967	$30
❏ SLD-8006 [S]	Johnny Paycheck Sings Jukebox Charlie	1967	$30
❏ LD-4003 [M]	The Lovin' Machine	1966	$25
❏ SLD-8003 [S]	The Lovin' Machine	1966	$30
❏ SLD-8023	Wherever You Are	1969	$30

MERCURY

| ❏ 830404-1 | Modern Times | 1987 | $12 |

POWER PAK

| ❏ PO-284 | Johnny Paycheck At His Best | 197? | $10 |

PAYNE, BENNIE

KAPP

| ❏ KL-1004 [M] | Bennie Payne Plays and Sings | 1955 | $100 |

PAYNE, CECIL, AND DUKE JORDAN

MUSE

| ❏ MR-5015 | Brooklyn Brothers | 1974 | $35 |

PAYNE, CECIL

CHARLIE PARKER

❏ PLP-801 [M]	Cecil Payne Performing Charlie Parker's Music	1962	$40
❏ PLP-801S [S]	Cecil Payne Performing Charlie Parker's Music	1962	$50
❏ PLP-506 [M]	Shaw Nuff	1962	$30
❏ PLP-506S [S]	Shaw Nuff	1962	$30

MUSE

| ❏ MR-5061 | Bird Gets the Worm | 1976 | $30 |

SAVOY

| ❏ MG-12147 [M] | Patterns of Jazz | 1959 | $100 |

SAVOY JAZZ

| ❏ SJL-1167 | Patterns | 1986 | $25 |

SIGNAL

| ❏ S-1203 [M] | Cecil Payne Quintet and Quartet | 1955 | $600 |

STRATA-EAST

| ❏ SES-19734 | The Zodiac | 1973 | $30 |

PAYNE, DENNIS, AND THE RENEGADES

RED MAN

| ❏ 1492 | We're Indian | 1969 | $175 |

PAYNE, FREDA

ABC

| ❏ D-901 | Out of Payne Comes Love | 1976 | $15 |

ABC DUNHILL

| ❏ DSX-50176 | Payne and Pleasure | 1974 | $18 |

ABC IMPULSE!

| ❏ AS-53 [S] | After the Lights Go Down Low...And Much More | 1968 | $35 |

CAPITOL

❏ ST-12003	Hot	1979	$15
❏ ST-11700	Stares and Whispers	1977	$15
❏ ST-11864	Supernatural	1978	$15

Number	Title	Yr	NM

IMPULSE!

Number	Title	Yr	NM
❏ A-53 [M]	After the Lights Go Down Low…And Much More	1964	$250
❏ AS-53 [S]	After the Lights Go Down Low…And Much More	1964	$160
❏ A53 [B]	After The Lights Go Down Low And Much More!!!	1963	$12

INVICTUS

❏ ST-7301 [B]	Band of Gold	1970	$25
❏ ST7301 [B]	Band of Gold	1970	$10
❏ SMAS-7307	Contact	1971	$18
❏ SMAS7307 [B]	Contact	1971	$10
❏ Z32493	Reaching Out	1973	$18
❏ KZ32493 [B]	Reaching Out	1973	$12
❏ ST-9804	The Best of Freda Payne	1972	$18

MGM

❏ GAS-128	Freda Payne (Golden Archive Series)	1970	$18
❏ E-4370 [M]	How Do You Say I Don't Love You Anymore	1966	$30
❏ SE-4370 [S]	How Do You Say I Don't Love You Anymore	1966	$30
❏ E4370 [B]	How Do You Say I Don't Love You Anymore	1966	$12

PAYNE, JIMMY

EPIC

| ❏ BN26372 | Woman, Woman! What Does It Take? | 1968 | $25 |

PAYNE, JOHN, AND LOUIS LEVIN

ARISTA/FREEDOM

| ❏ AF1025 | Bedtime | 1976 | $30 |
| ❏ AF1036 | The Razor's Edge | 1976 | $30 |

MERCURY

| ❏ SRM-1-1166 | John Payne/Louis Levin Band | 1977 | $25 |

PAYNE, LEON

STARDAY

| ❏ SLP-236 [M] | Americana | 1963 | $50 |
| ❏ SLP-231 [M] | Leon Payne: A Living Legend of Country Music | 1963 | $100 |

PEACE, JOE

RITE

| ❏ 29917 | Finding Peace | 1972 | $250 |

PEACHES AND HERB

COLUMBIA

| ❏ FC38746 | Remember | 1983 | $12 |

DATE

❏ TEM3005 [M]	For Your Love	1967	$30
❏ TES4005 [S]	For Your Love	1967	$25
❏ TEM3007 [M]	Golden Duets	1968	$30
❏ TES4007 [S]	Golden Duets	1968	$25
❏ TEM3004 [M]	Let's Fall in Love	1967	$25
❏ TES4004 [S]	Let's Fall in Love	1967	$30
❏ TES4012	Peaches and Herb's Greatest Hits	1968	$25

EPIC

| ❏ E36089 | Love Is Strange | 1979 | $12 |
| —Reissue of Date material |
| ❏ JE36099 | Peaches and Herb's Greatest Hits | 1979 | $12 |
| —Reissue of Date 4012 |

MCA

| ❏ 2261 | Peaches and Herb | 1977 | $15 |

POLYDOR

❏ PD-1-6172	2 Hot!	1978	$12
❏ PD-1-6332	Sayin' Something!	1981	$12
❏ PD-1-6239	Twice the Fire	1979	$12
❏ PD-1-6298	Worth the Wait	1980	$12

PEACOCK, GARY

ECM

❏ 1119	December Poems	1979	$30
❏ 1165	Shift in the Wind	1981	$25
❏ 1101	Tale of Another	1977	$30
❏ 1210	Voice from the Past	1982	$25

PEAGLER, CURTIS

PABLO

| ❏ 2310930 | I'll Be Around | 1988 | $25 |

PEANUT BUTTER CONSPIRACY, THE

CHALLENGE

| ❏ 2000 | For Children of All Ages | 1969 | $30 |

COLUMBIA

❏ CL2790 [M]	The Great Conspiracy	1968	$40
❏ CS9590 [S]	The Great Conspiracy	1968	$30
❏ CL2654 [M]	The Peanut Butter Conspiracy Is Spreading	1967	$80
❏ CS9454 [S]	The Peanut Butter Conspiracy Is Spreading	1967	$30

PEARL HARBOUR AND THE EXPLOSIONS

WARNER BROS.

Number	Title	Yr	NM
❏ BSK3515	Don't Follow Me, I'm Lost Too	1981	$12
—Pearl Harbor solo, with members of The Clash
❏ BSK3404	Pearl Harbor and the Explosions	1980	$15

PEARL JAM

Also see GREEN RIVER; MOTHER LOVE BONE; SOUNDGARDEN.

EPIC

❏ E263365	Binaural	2000	$50
❏ E269752	Live on Two Legs	1998	$50
❏ E385738	Lost Dogs	2004	$30
—CD version was issued in 2003
❏ E67500	No Code	1996	$30
—Includes one of four sets of six 12x12 trading cards
❏ E493535	Rearviewmirror: Greatest Hits	2004	$50
❏ E286825	Riot Act	2002	$50
❏ E66900	Vitalogy	1994	$25
❏ E53136	Vs.	1993	$25
❏ E68164	Yield	1998	$50

EPIC ASSOCIATED

| ❏ Z47857 | Ten | 1991 | $12 |
| —Album not released on U.S. vinyl until 1994 |

J

| ❏ 82876-71467-1 | Pearl Jam | 2006 | $25 |
| — With 36-page lyric booklet; number is nowhere on the packaging or labels, but is only in the trail-off wax of the records |

PEARLS BEFORE SWINE

4 MEN WITH BEARDS

| ❏ 4M234 [B] | The Use of Ashes | 2013 | $25 |

ADELPHI

| ❏ 4111 | The Best of Pearls Before Swine | 198? | $18 |

ESP-DISK

❏ 1075	Balaklava	1968	$100
❏ 1054 [M]	One Nation Under Ground	1967	$140
❏ 1054 [S]	One Nation Under Ground	1967	$150
—Sepia-tone cover with white border
❏ 1054 [S]	One Nation Under Ground	1967	$150
—Sepia-tone cover with no border
❏ 1054 [S]	One Nation Under Ground	1967	$150
—Black and white cover
❏ 1054 [S]	One Nation Under Ground	1968	$75
—Full-color cover
❏ 1054	One Nation Under Ground Bonus Poster	1967	$75

REPRISE

❏ RS6467	Beautiful Lies You Could Live In	1971	$40
❏ RS6442	City of Gold	1971	$40
❏ RS6364	These Things Too	1969	$30
❏ RS6405	The Use of Ashes	1970	$30

PEARSON, ALBIE

VIBRANT

| ❏ 1501 | Albie Pearson | 1973 | $30 |

PEARSON, DUKE

ATLANTIC

❏ 3002 [M]	Honeybuns	196?	$35
❏ SD3002 [S]	Honeybuns	196?	$35
❏ SD3005	Prairie Dog	196?	$35

BLUE NOTE

❏ BST-84344	How Insensitive	1970	$50
❏ B1-35220	I Don't Care Who Knows It	1996	$30
❏ BST-84276	Introducing Duke Pearson's Big Band	1968	$75
❏ BN-LA317-G	It Could Only Happen with You	1974	$35
❏ BST-84323	Merry Ole Soul	1970	$50
❏ BST-84308	Now Hear This	1969	$75
❏ BLP-4022 [M]	Profile -- Duke Pearson	1959	$400
—Deep groove" version (deep indentation under label on both sides)
❏ BLP-4022 [M]	Profile -- Duke Pearson	1959	$175
—Regular version with W. 63rd St. address on label
❏ BLP-4022 [M]	Profile -- Duke Pearson	1963	$150
—With New York, USA address on label
❏ BST-84022 [S]	Profile -- Duke Pearson	1959	$120
—With W. 63rd St. address on label
❏ BST-84022 [S]	Profile -- Duke Pearson	1963	$50
—With New York, USA address on label
❏ BST-84022 [S]	Profile -- Duke Pearson	1967	$30
—With "A Division of Liberty Records" on label
❏ BLP-4252 [M]	Sweet Honey Bee	1966	$150
❏ BST-84252 [S]	Sweet Honey Bee	1966	$75
—With New York, USA address on label
❏ BST-84252 [S]	Sweet Honey Bee	1967	$30
—With "A Division of Liberty Records" on label
❏ B1-89792	Sweet Honey Bee	1993	$30
—Reissue of 84252

Number	Title	Yr	NM
❏ BLP-4035 [M]	Tender Feelin's	1960	$500
—Deep groove" version (deep indentation under label on both sides)
❏ BLP-4035 [M]	Tender Feelin's	1960	$175
—Regular version with W. 63rd St. address on label
❏ BLP-4035 [M]	Tender Feelin's	1963	$150
—With New York, USA address on label
❏ BST-84035 [S]	Tender Feelin's	1960	$120
—With W. 63rd St. address on label
❏ BST-84035 [S]	Tender Feelin's	1963	$50
—With New York, USA address on label
❏ BST-84035 [S]	Tender Feelin's	1967	$30
—With "A Division of Liberty Records" on label
❏ BST-84293	The Phantom	1969	$75
❏ BST-84267	The Right Touch	1968	$75
❏ B1-28269	The Right Touch	1994	$30
—Reissue of 84267
❏ BLP-4191 [M]	Wahoo!	1965	$150
❏ BST-84191 [S]	Wahoo!	1965	$75
—With New York, USA address on label
❏ BST-84191 [S]	Wahoo!	1967	$30
—With "A Division of Liberty Records" on label
❏ B1-84191	Wahoo!	1986	$30
—The Finest in Jazz Since 1939" reissue

JAZZ LINE

| ❏ 3302 [B] | Hush! | 1962 | $350 |

JAZZTIME

| ❏ 33-02 [M] | Hush! | 1962 | $700 |

PRESTIGE

| ❏ PRST-7729 | Dedication | 1970 | $35 |

PEBBLES

MCA

| ❏ 10025 | Always | 1990 | $18 |
| ❏ 42094 | Pebbles | 1987 | $12 |

PEBBLES AND BAMM BAMM

HANNA-BARBERA

| ❏ HLP-2040 [M] | On the Good Ship Lollipop | 1966 | $150 |

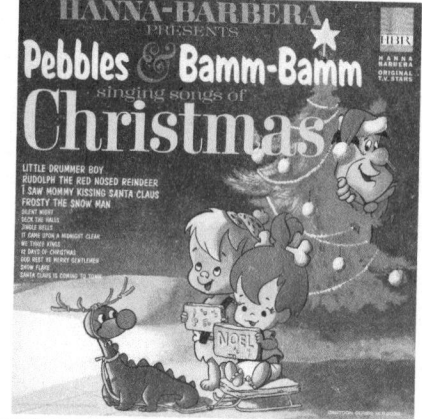

| ❏ HLP-2033 [M] | Pebbles and Bamm-Bamm Sing Songs of Christmas | 1965 | $120 |

PECK, BERT, AND THE KINGS OF DIXIELAND

PAULA

| ❏ 2225 | New Orleans Beat | 197? | $12 |

PECK, GREGORY

DECCA

| ❏ DLP8009 [M] | Lullaby of Christmas | 1949 | $0 |
| ❏ DL78009 [R] | Lullaby of Christmas | 1966 | $0 |

PECORA, SANTO

CLEF

| ❏ MGC-123 [10] | Santo Pecora Collates | 1953 | $300 |
| —With either Mercury or Clef cover; all labels are Clef |

MERCURY

| ❏ MGC-123 [10] | Dixieland Jazz Band | 1953 | $0 |
| —Canceled; released on Clef 123 |

SOUTHLAND

| ❏ SLP-213 [M] | Santo Pecora | 1955 | $75 |

VIK

| ❏ XLA-1081 [M] | Dixieland Mardi Gras | 1957 | $50 |

PEDERSEN, HERB

EPIC

| ❏ PE34933 | Sandman | 1977 | $18 |
| ❏ PE34225 | South by Southwest | 1976 | $18 |

SUGAR HILL

| ❏ SH-3738 | Lonesome Feeling | 1984 | $15 |

Number	Title	Yr	NM

PEDICIN, MICHAEL, JR.
OPTIMISM
❏ OP-3211	Angles	1989	$30
❏ OP-3106	City Song	198?	$25

PEDICIN, MIKE
APOLLO
❏ LP-484 [M]	Musical Medicine	1957	$175

PEEBLES, ANN
HI
❏ XSHL-32079	I Can't Stand the Rain	1974	$25
❏ HLP-6002	If This Is Heaven	1977	$15
❏ SHL-32059	Part Time Love	1971	$25
❏ HLP-8005	Part Time Love	197?	$15
—Reissue of 32059			
❏ SHL-32065	Straight from the Heart	1972	$25
❏ HLP-8009	Straight from the Heart	197?	$15
—Reissue of 32065			
❏ SHL-32091	Tellin' It	1975	$25
❏ HLP-6007	The Handwriting Is On the Wall	1978	$15

PEEL, DAVE
CHART
❏ CHS-1039	Move Two Mountains	1971	$18

PEEL, DAVID
APPLE
❏ SW-3391 [B]	The Pope Smokes Dope	1972	$50
ELEKTRA
❏ EKS-74032 [B]	Have a Marijuana	1968	$40
❏ EKS-74069 [B]	The American Revolution	1970	$40

PEELS, THE
KARATE
❏ 5402 [M]	Juanita Banana	1966	$100

PEGGY SUE
DECCA
❏ DL75215	All American Husband	1970	$30
❏ DL75153	Dynamite!	1969	$30

PEGGY SUE AND SONNY WRIGHT (2)
COUNTRY INT'L.
❏ 732	One Side of Peggy Sue and Sonny Wright	198?	$25

PEIFFER, BERNARD
DECCA
❏ DL9203 [M]	Piano Ala Mood	1958	$150
❏ DL79203 [S]	Piano Ala Mood	1958	$150
❏ DL8626 [M]	The Astounding Bernard Peiffer	1958	$120
❏ DL9218 [M]	The Pied Peiffer of the Piano	1959	$100
❏ DL79218 [S]	The Pied Peiffer of the Piano	1959	$100
EMARCY
❏ MG-36080 [M]	Bernie's Tunes	1956	$250
❏ MG-26036 [10]	Le Most	1954	$250
LAURIE
❏ LLP-1008 [M]	Cole Porter's "Can Can	1960	$30
❏ SLP-1008 [S]	Cole Porter's "Can Can	1960	$30
❏ LLP-1006 [M]	Modern Jazz for People Who Like Original Music	1960	$300
❏ SLP-1006 [S]	Modern Jazz for People Who Like Original Music	1960	$300
NORGRAN
❏ MGN-11 [10]	Bernard Peiffer Et Son Trio	1954	$175

PELL, DAVE, AND JOE WILLIAMS
GNP CRESCENDO
❏ GNPS-2124	Prez & Joe: In Celebration of Lester Young	1979	$25

PELL, DAVE
ATLANTIC
❏ 1216 [M]	Jazz and Romantic Places	1955	$300
—Black label			
❏ 1216 [M]	Jazz and Romantic Places	1961	$175
—Multicolor label, white "fan" logo at right			
❏ 1249 [M]	Love Story	1956	$300
—Black label			
❏ 1249 [M]	Love Story	1961	$175
—Multicolor label, white "fan" logo at right			
CAPITOL
❏ T925 [M]	I Had the Craziest Dream	1958	$75
—Turquoise label			
❏ T1687 [M]	I Remember John Kirby	1962	$50
❏ ST1687 [S]	I Remember John Kirby	1962	$75
❏ T1512 [M]	Old South Wails	1961	$25
❏ ST1512 [S]	Old South Wails	1961	$75
❏ T1309 [M]	The Big Small Bands	1960	$40
❏ ST1309 [S]	The Big Small Bands	1960	$75

CORAL
❏ CRL57248 [M]	Swingin' School Songs	1958	$30
❏ CRL757248 [S]	Swingin' School Songs	1958	$30
GNP CRESCENDO
❏ GNPS-2122	Prez Conference	1978	$25
HEADFIRST
❏ 715	Live at Alfonse's	198?	$30
KAPP
❏ KL-1034 [M]	Dave Pell Plays Burke and Van Heusen	1956	$40
❏ KL-1036 [M]	Dave Pell Plays Irving Berlin	1957	$40
❏ KL-1025 [M]	Dave Pell Plays Rodgers and Hart	1956	$30
LIBERTY
❏ LRP-3321 [M]	Jazz Voices in Video	1963	$35
❏ LST-7321 [S]	Jazz Voices in Video	1963	$25
❏ LST-7631 [S]	Man-Ha-Man-Ha	1969	$35
❏ LST-7298 [S]	Today;s Hits in Jazz	1961	$25
❏ LRP-3298 [M]	Today's Hits in Jazz	1961	$35
PRI
❏ 3003 [M]	Dave Pell Plays Artie Shaw's Big Band Sounds	196?	$25
❏ 3004 [M]	Dave Pell Plays Benny Goodman's Big Band Sounds	196?	$25
❏ 3007 [M]	Dave Pell Plays Duke Ellington's Big Band Sounds	196?	$25
❏ 3002 [M]	Dave Pell Plays Harry James' Big Band Sounds	196?	$25
❏ 3005 [M]	Dave Pell Plays Lawrence Welk's Big Band Sounds	196?	$25
❏ 3009 [M]	Dave Pell Plays Mantovani's Big Band Sounds	196?	$25
❏ 3006 [M]	Dave Pell Plays Perez Prado's Big Band Sounds	196?	$25
❏ 3011 [M]	Dave Pell Plays the Big Band Sounds	196?	$25
❏ 3010 [M]	Dave Pell Plays the Dorsey Brothers' Big Band Sounds	196?	$25
RCA VICTOR
❏ LPM-1662 [M]	Campus Hop	1957	$50
❏ LPM-1320 [M]	Jazz Goes Dancing	1956	$50
❏ LPM-1524 [M]	Pell of a Time	1957	$50
❏ LPM-1394 [M]	Swingin' in the Ol' Corral	1957	$50
TREND
❏ TL-1003 [10]	Dave Pell Plays Irving Berlin	1953	$120
❏ TL-1501 [M]	Dave Pell Plays Rodgers and Hart	1954	$150

PEMBROKE, MIKE
JAZZOLOGY
❏ J-24	Mike Pembroke's Hot Seven	197?	$25

PENAZZI, ANDRE
DAUNTLESS
❏ 7020 [S]	Organ Jazz Samba Percussion	1963	$25
❏ 2020 [M]	Organ Jazz Samba Percussion	1963	$35

PENDERGRASS, TEDDY
Also see HAROLD MELVIN AND THE BLUE NOTES.
ASYLUM
❏ 60317	Love Language	1984	$10
❏ 60447	Workin' It Back	1985	$10
ELEKTRA
❏ 60775	Joy	1988	$10
PHILADELPHIA INT'L.
❏ FZ39252	Greatest Hits	1984	$12
❏ FZ38646	Heaven Only Knows	1983	$12
❏ PZ38646	Heaven Only Knows	1985	$10
—Budget-line reissue with new prefix			
❏ HZ47491	It's Time for Love	198?	$40
—Half-speed mastered edition			
❏ FZ37491	It's Time for Love	1981	$12
❏ PZ37491	It's Time for Love	198?	$10
—Budget-line reissue with new prefix			
❏ PZ35095	Life Is a Song Worth Singing	1978	$12
—No bar code on back cover			
❏ PZ35095	Life Is a Song Worth Singing	198?	$10
—With bar code on back cover			
❏ FZ36003	Teddy	1979	$12
❏ PZ36003	Teddy	198?	$10
—Budget-line reissue with new prefix			
❏ KZ236294	Teddy Live! Coast to Coast	1979	$15
❏ PZ34390	Teddy Pendergrass	1977	$12
—No bar code on back cover			
❏ PZ34390	Teddy Pendergrass	198?	$10
—With bar code on back cover			
❏ FZ38118	This One's for You	1982	$12
❏ PZ38118	This One's for You	198?	$10
—Budget-line reissue with new prefix			
❏ FZ36745	TP	1980	$12
❏ PZ36745	TP	198?	$10
—Budget-line reissue with new prefix			

PENGUINS, THE
COLLECTABLES
❏ COL-5045	Golden Classics	198?	$12
DOOTO
❏ DTL-204 [M]	The Best Vocal Groups… Rhythm and Blues	1959	$250
—Reissue of Dootone 204; blue and yellow label			
❏ DTL-204 [M]	The Best Vocal Groups… Rhythm and Blues	196?	$150
—Black label with gold/orange/blue ring. This is NOT a counterfeit.			
❏ DTL-242 [M]	The Cool, Cool Penguins	1959	$700
—Red and yellow label			
❏ DTL-242 [M]	The Cool, Cool Penguins	1959	$700
—Blue and yellow label			
❏ DTL-242 [M]	The Cool, Cool Penguins	196?	$250
—Black label with gold/orange/blue ring. This is NOT a counterfeit.			
DOOTONE
❏ DTL-204 [M]	The Best Vocal Groups… Rhythm and Blues	1957	$1500
—Also includes tracks by the Medallions, Don Julian and the Meadowlarks, and the Dootones. Flat maroon label.			
❏ DTL-204 [M]	The Best Vocal Groups… Rhythm and Blues	195?	$500
—As above; glossy maroon label			

PENN, MICHAEL
RCA
❏ 9692-1-R	March	1989	$12

PENNINGTON, RAY
DIMENSION
❏ DLP-5007	Memories	1983	$15
MONUMENT
❏ SLP-18145	Ray Pennington Sings for the Other Woman	1970	$18

PENNY, HANK
AUDIO LAB
❏ AL-1508 [M]	Hank Penny Sings	1959	$250

PENNY AND JEAN
RCA VICTOR
❏ LPM-2244 [M]	Two for the Road	1961	$25
❏ LSP-2244 [S]	Two for the Road	1961	$30

PENSYL, KIM
OPTIMISM
❏ OP-3210	Pensyl Sketches #1	1988	$25

PENTAGON
EAST WIND
❏ 10002	Pentagon	1979	$50

PENTANGLE, THE
GREEN LINNET
❏ SIF-3048	So Early in the Spring	1990	$15
REPRISE
❏ RS6372 [B]	Basket of Light	1969	$30
—With "W7" and "r." logos on two-tone orange label			
❏ RS6372 [B]	Basket of Light	1970	$25
—With only "r." logo on all-orange (tan) label			
❏ RS6430	Cruel Sister	1971	$18
❏ RS6463	Reflection	1971	$18
❏ MS2100	Solomon's Seal	1972	$18
❏ 2RS6334	Sweet Child	1969	$30
—With "W7" and "r." logos on two-tone orange label			
❏ 2RS6334	Sweet Child	1970	$25
—With only "r." logo on all-orange (tan) label			
❏ RS6315	The Pentangle	1968	$25
—With "W7" and "r." logos on two-tone orange label			
❏ RS6315 [B]	The Pentangle	1970	$18
—With only "r." logo on all-orange (tan) label			
SHANACHIE
❏ 79066	A Maid That's Deep in Love	198?	$12
VARRICK
❏ VR-026	In the Round	1986	$12
❏ VR-017	Open the Door	1985	$12

PEOPLE
CAPITOL
❏ ST-151	Both Sides of People	1969	$25
❏ ST2924	I Love You	1968	$25
PARAMOUNT
❏ PAS-5013	There Are People	1970	$25

PEOPLE'S CHOICE
PHILADELPHIA INT'L.
❏ JZ35363	Turn Me Loose	1978	$12
TSOP
❏ KZ33154	Boogie Down U.S.A.	1975	$12

Number	Title	Yr	NM
❏ PZ34124	We Got the Rhythm	1976	$12

PEPLOWSKI, KEN
CONCORD JAZZ

Number	Title	Yr	NM
❏ CJ-344	Double Exposure	1988	$25
❏ CJ-376	Sonny Side	1989	$30

PEPPER, ART
ANALOGUE PRODUCTIONS

Number	Title	Yr	NM
❏ AP 017	Art Pepper + Eleven: Modern Jazz Classics	199?	$30

— Reissue on audiophile vinyl

❏ AP 010	Art Pepper Meets the Rhythm Section	199?	$30

— Reissue on audiophile vinyl

❏ AP 012	Smack Up!	199?	$30

— Reissue on audiophile vinyl

❏ APR3013	So in Love	199?	$35
❏ APR3014	The Intimate Art Pepper	199?	$35
❏ APR3012	The New York Album	199?	$35

ARTISTS HOUSE

❏ AH9412	So in Love	1979	$35

BLUE NOTE

❏ BN-LA591-H2	Early Art	1976	$75
❏ LT-1064	Omega Alpha	1980	$50

CONTEMPORARY

❏ C-7650	Art Pepper at the Village Vanguard, Vol. 4: More for Les	1986	$35
❏ M-3568 [M]	Art Pepper + Eleven: Modern Jazz Classics	1959	$300
❏ S-7568 [S]	Art Pepper + Eleven: Modern Jazz Classics	1959	$300
❏ C-3532 [M]	Art Pepper Meets the Rhythm Section	1957	$700
❏ S-7532 [S]	Art Pepper Meets the Rhythm Section	1959	$300
❏ S-7643	Friday Night at the Village Vanguard	1980	$35
❏ M-3573 [M]	Gettin' Together!	1960	$300
❏ S-7573 [S]	Gettin' Together!	1960	$300
❏ M-3607 [M]	Intensity	1963	$250
❏ S-7607 [S]	Intensity	1963	$250
❏ S-7633	Living Legend	1975	$50
❏ S-7639	No Limit	1978	$50
❏ C-7644	Saturday Night at the Village Vanguard	198?	$35
❏ M-3602 [M]	Smack Up!	1961	$250
❏ S-7602 [S]	Smack Up!	1961	$250
❏ S-7638	The Trip	1977	$50
❏ S-7630	The Way It Was!	1972	$50

— Originals have orange labels

❏ S-7642	Thursday Night at the Village Vanguard	1979	$50

DISCOVERY

❏ DS-837	Among Friends	1981	$50
❏ 3019 [10]	Art Pepper Quartet	1952	$600
❏ 3023 [10]	Art Pepper Quintet	1954	$600

FANTASY

❏ OJC-338	Art Pepper Meets the Rhythm Section	198?	$30
❏ OJC-474	Art Pepper Today	1990	$35
❏ OJC-695	Friday Night at the Village Vanguard	199?	$30
❏ OJC-169	Gettin' Together	198?	$30
❏ OJC-387	Intensity	1989	$30
❏ OJC-408	Living Legend	1990	$35
❏ OJC-341	Modern Jazz Classics	198?	$30
❏ OJC-411	No Limit	1990	$35
❏ OJC-696	Saturday Night at the Village Vanguard	199?	$30
❏ OJC-176	Smack Up!	198?	$30
❏ OJC-475	Straight Life	1990	$35
❏ OJC-410	The Trip	1990	$35
❏ OJC-389	The Way It Was	1989	$30

GALAXY

❏ GXY-5145	Art Lives	1983	$35
❏ GXY-5151	Art Pepper Quartet: The Maiden Voyage Sessions, Part 3	198?	$50
❏ GXY-5119	Art Pepper Today	1979	$35
❏ GXY-5148	Art Works	1984	$35
❏ GXY-5143	Goin' Home	1982	$35
❏ GXY-5128	Landscape	1980	$50
❏ GXY-5141	One September Afternoon	1981	$50
❏ GXY-5142	Roadgame	1982	$30
❏ GXY-5127	Straight Life	1979	$35
❏ GXY-5123	Tete-a-Tete	198?	$35
❏ GXY-5154	The New York Album	1985	$50
❏ GXY-5140	Winter Moon	1980	$35

INTERLUDE

❏ MO-512 [M]	Art Pepper Quartet	1959	$50
❏ ST-1012 [S]	Art Pepper Quartet	1959	$40

INTERPLAY

❏ 7718	Among Friends	1979	$50

INTRO

❏ 606 [M]	Modern Art	1957	$2500

JAZZ WEST

❏ JLP-10 [M]	The Return of Art Pepper	1956	$600

MOSAIC

Number	Title	Yr	NM
❏ MR3-105	The Complete Pacific Jazz Small Group Recordings of Art Pepper	198?	$100

ONYX

❏ 219	Omega Man / Omega Man	197?	$25

PACIFIC JAZZ

❏ PJ-60 [M]	The Artistry of Pepper	1962	$40

SAVOY

❏ MG-12089 [M]	Surf Ride	1956	$150

SAVOY JAZZ

❏ SJL-2217	Discoveries	197?	$35

SCORE

❏ SLP-4030 [M]	Modern Art	1958	$300
❏ SLP-4031 [M]	The Art Pepper-Red Norvo Sextet	1958	$150
❏ SLP-4032 [M]	The Return of Art Pepper	1958	$150

STEREO RECORDS

❏ S-7018 [S]	Art Pepper Meets the Rhythm Section	1958	$100

TAMPA

❏ TP-20 [M]	Art Pepper Quartet	1957	$500

— Red vinyl

❏ TP-20 [M]	Art Pepper Quartet	1958	$300

— Black vinyl

❏ TS-1001 [S]	Art Pepper Quartet	1959	$1250

XANADU

❏ 108	The Early Show	197?	$25
❏ 117	The Late Show	198?	$25

PEPPER, ART/SHELLY MANNE
CHARLIE PARKER

❏ PLP-836 [M]	Pepper/Manne	1963	$30
❏ PLP-836S [S]	Pepper/Manne	1963	$30

PEPPER, ART/SONNY REDD
REGENT

❏ MG-6069 [M]	Two Altos	1959	$50

SAVOY

❏ MG-12215 [M]	Art Pepper-Sonny Redd	1969	$25

PEPPER, JIM
EMBRYO

❏ SD-731	Pepper's Powwow	196?	$40

PEPPERMINT, DANNY
CARLTON

❏ LP-20001 [M]	Twist with Danny Peppermint	1962	$40
❏ STLP-20001 [S]	Twist with Danny Peppermint	1962	$50

PEPPERMINT RAINBOW, THE
DECCA

❏ DL75129	Will You Be Staying After Sunday	1969	$25

PEPPERMINT TROLLEY COMPANY, THE
ACTA

❏ A-8007 [M]	The Peppermint Trolley Company	1968	$150

— In stereo cover with "Monaural" sticker

❏ A-38007 [S]	The Peppermint Trolley Company	1968	$35

PEPPERS, THE
EVENT

❏ EV6901	Pepper Box	1974	$18

PERAZA, ARMANDO
SKYE

❏ S-5D	Wild Thing	1970	$35

PERE UBU
Pioneering Cleveland industrialists, featuring Dave Thomas.

BLANK

❏ 01 [B]	The Modern Dance	1978	$75

CHRYSALIS

❏ CHR1207	Dub Housing	1979	$30

ENIGMA

❏ D1-73343	The Tenement Year	1988	$18

FONTANA

❏ 838237-1	Cloudland	1989	$15

ROUGH TRADE

❏ ROUGH US10	390 Degrees of Simulated Stereo	1981	$25
❏ ROUGH US21	Song of the Bailing Man	1982	$25
❏ ROUGH US4	The Art of Walking	1980	$40

— First 1,800 were incorrectly mastered

❏ ROUGH US4	The Art of Walking	1980	$25

— Revised version: Vocal added on "Arabia"; "Miles" is

---

shortened

Number	Title	Yr	NM
❏ ROUGH US7	The Modern Dance	1981	$25

— Reissue of Blank 001

PERHACS, LINDA
KAPP

❏ KS-3636	Parallelograms	1970	$250

PERIGEO
RCA VICTOR

❏ TPL1-1228	Fata Morgana	197?	$35
❏ TPL1-1080	Genealogia	197?	$35
❏ TPL1-1175	The Valley of the Temples	197?	$35
❏ APL1-1175	The Valley of the Temples	197?	$30

— Reissue with new prefix

PERKINS, BILL, AND RICHIE KAMUCA
LIBERTY

❏ LRP-3051 [M]	Tenors Head On	1957	$100

PERKINS, BILL, AND THE SAN FRANCISCANS
FAMOUS DOOR

❏ 128	The Other Bill	197?	$25

PERKINS, BILL; ART PEPPER; RICHIE KAMUCA
PACIFIC JAZZ

❏ PJM-401 [M]	Just Friends	1956	$250

WORLD PACIFIC

❏ PJM-401 [M]	Just Friends	1958	$300

PERKINS, BILL
CONTEMPORARY

❏ C-14011	Journey to the East	1985	$30

INTERPLAY

❏ 7721	Confluence	1979	$75
❏ 8606	Remembrance of Dino's	1990	$30

LIBERTY

❏ LRP-3293 [M]	Bossa Nova with Strings Attached	1963	$40
❏ LST-7293 [S]	Bossa Nova with Strings Attached	1963	$50

PACIFIC JAZZ

❏ PJ-1221 [M]	The Bill Perkins Octet On Stage	1956	$120

RIVERSIDE

❏ RS-3052	Quietly There	1969	$150

SEA BREEZE

❏ SB-2006	Many Ways to Go	1980	$25

WORLD PACIFIC

❏ WP-1221 [M]	The Bill Perkins Octet On Stage	1958	$175

PERKINS, CARL
ACCORD

❏ SN-7169	Presenting Carl Perkins	1982	$12

ALBUM GLOBE

❏ 8118	Country Soul	1980	$12
❏ 9037	Goin' Back to Memphis	1980	$12

ALLEGIANCE

❏ AV-5001	The Heart and Soul of Carl Perkins	198?	$12

BULLDOG

❏ BDL-2034	Twenty Golden Pieces	198?	$12

COLUMBIA

❏ CS9981	Boppin' the Blues	1970	$30

— Red "360 Sound Stereo" label

❏ PC9981	Boppin' the Blues	198?	$10

— Budget-line reissue

❏ CS9981	Boppin' the Blues	1970	$15

— Orange label

❏ CS9833	Carl Perkins' Greatest Hits	1969	$30

— Red "360 Sound Stereo" label

❏ CS9931	Carl Perkins On Top	1969	$30

— Red "360 Sound Stereo" label

❏ FC37961	The Survivors	1982	$12

— With Johnny Cash and Jerry Lee Lewis

❏ PC37961	The Survivors	198?	$10

— Budget-line reissue

❏ CL1234 [M]	Whole Lotta Shakin'	1958	$400
❏ CL1234 [DJ]	Whole Lotta Shakin'	1958	$800

— White label promo

COLUMBIA LIMITED EDITION

❏ LE10117	Carl Perkins' Greatest Hits	1974	$15

— Limited Edition" brown label

DESIGN

❏ DLP-611 [M]	Tennessee	1963	$30
❏ SDLP-611 [R]	Tennessee	1963	$25

DOLLIE

❏ 4001	Country Boy's Dream	1967	$30
❏ ST-91428	Country Boy's Dream	1967	$40

— Capitol Record Club edition

Number	Title	Yr	NM
HARMONY			
❏ KH31179	Brown Eyed Handsome Man	1971	$15
❏ HS11385	Carl Perkins	1970	$18
❏ KH31792	Greatest Hits	1972	$15
HILLTOP			
❏ 6103	Matchbox	197?	$15
JET			
❏ JZ35604	Ol' Blue Suede's Back	1978	$12
❏ JT-LA856-H	Ol' Blue Suede's Back	1978	$18
KOALA			
❏ AW14164	Country Soul	198?	$12
MCA DOT			
❏ 39035	Carl Perkins	1985	$12
MERCURY			
❏ SRM-1-691	My Kind of Country	1973	$15
RHINO			
❏ RNLP-70221	Original Sun Greatest Hits (1955-1957)	1986	$15
ROUNDER			
❏ SS-27	Honky Tonk Gal: Rare and Unissued Sun Masters	1989	$15
SMASH			
❏ 830002-1	Class of '55	1986	$15
—With Jerry Lee Lewis, Roy Orbison and Johnny Cash			
SUEDE			
❏ 002	Live at Austin City Limits	1981	$12
SUN			
❏ LP-112	Blue Suede Shoes	1969	$15
❏ LP-111	Original Golden Hits	1969	$15
❏ SLP-1225 [M]	Teen Beat -- The Best of Carl Perkins	1961	$500
—Reissue with new title			
❏ SLP-1225 [M]	The Dance Album of Carl Perkins	1957	$1200
SUNNYVALE			
❏ 9330803	The Sun Story, Vol. 3	1977	$15
TRIP			
❏ TLP-8503	The Best of Carl Perkins	1974	$15
UNIVERSAL			
❏ UVL-76001	Born to Rock	1989	$18

PERKINS, CARL (2)
Jazz pianist.
Pianist. Not to be confused with the rock 'n' roll singer of the same name.

Number	Title	Yr	NM
DOOTO			
❏ DL-211 [M]	Introducing Carl Perkins	196?	$35
DOOTONE			
❏ DL-211 [M]	Introducing Carl Perkins	1956	$120
—Black vinyl			
❏ DL-211 [M]	Introducing Carl Perkins	1956	$250
—Red vinyl			

PERKINS, TONY

Number	Title	Yr	NM
EPIC			
❏ LN3394 [M]	Tony Perkins	1957	$50
RCA VICTOR			
❏ LPM-1679 [M]	From My Heart	1958	$40
❏ LSP-1679 [S]	From My Heart	1958	$75
❏ LPM-1853 [M]	On a Rainy Afternoon	1958	$40
❏ LSP-1853 [S]	On a Rainy Afternoon	1958	$75

PERREY, JEAN-JACQUES

Number	Title	Yr	NM
PICKWICK			
❏ PC-3160 [M]	The Happy Moog	196?	$25
❏ SPC-3160 [S]	The Happy Moog	196?	$30
—Silver label			
VANGUARD			
❏ VSD-6549	Moog Indigo	1969	$40
❏ VSD-79286	The Amazing New Electronic Pop Sound of Jean-Jackques Perrey	1968	$75

PERREY-KINGSLEY

Number	Title	Yr	NM
VANGUARD			
❏ VSD-6525	Kaleidoscopic Vibrations	1969	$75
❏ VSD-71/72	The Essential Perrey & Kingsley	197?	$30
❏ VRS-9222 [M]	The In Sound from Way Out!	1966	$75
❏ VSD-79222 [S]	The In Sound from Way Out!	1966	$75

PERRI

Number	Title	Yr	NM
ZEBRA			
❏ ZEB-5684	Celebrate!	1986	$25
❏ ZR-5007	Perri	198?	$30
❏ ZEB-42017	The Flight	1987	$25

PERRINE, PEP

Number	Title	Yr	NM
HIDEOUT			
❏ 1003 [M]	Pep Perrine Live and In Person	196?	$120

PERRY, STEVE

Number	Title	Yr	NM
COLUMBIA			
❏ FC39334	Street Talk	1984	$12

PERRY, VILO

Number	Title	Yr	NM
GUINNESS			
❏ GNS36055 [B]	Standing Room Only	1977	$175

PERSIP, CHARLIE

Number	Title	Yr	NM
BETHLEHEM			
❏ BCP-6046 [M]	Charlie Persip and the Jazz Statesmen	1960	$250
❏ SBCP-6046 [S]	Charlie Persip and the Jazz Statesmen	1960	$250
❏ BCP-6046	Right Down Front	197?	$30
—Reissue, distributed by RCA Victor			
SOUL NOTE			
❏ SN-1079	In Case You Missed It	1985	$30
❏ 121179	No Dummies Allowed	1990	$35
STASH			
❏ ST-209	The Charlie Persip & Gerry LaFum Superband	198?	$25

PERSON, HOUSTON

Number	Title	Yr	NM
20TH CENTURY			
❏ W-205	Houston Person	196?	$30
FANTASY			
❏ OJC-332	Goodness!	1988	$25
MERCURY			
❏ SRM-1-1151	Harmony	1977	$30
❏ SRM-1-1104	Pure Pleasure	1976	$30
MUSE			
❏ MR-5289	Always on My Mind	1986	$25
❏ MR-5344	Basics	1989	$30
❏ MR-5260	Heavy Juice	1982	$25
❏ MR-5376	Something in Common	1989	$30
❏ MR-5110	Stolen Sweets	1977	$30
❏ MR-5199	Suspicions	1980	$30
❏ MR-5136	The Big Horn	197?	$30
❏ MR-5178	The Nearness of You	197?	$30
❏ MR-5331	The Talk of the Town	1987	$25
❏ MR-5231	Very Personal	1981	$25
❏ MR-5433	Why Not!	1991	$35
❏ MR-5161	Wild Flower	1977	$30
PRESTIGE			

Number	Title	Yr	NM
❏ PRST-7566 [B]	Blue Odyssey	1968	$25
❏ 10044	Broken Windows, Empty Hallways	1972	$25
❏ PRST-7517	Chocomotive	1968	$25
❏ PRST-7678	Goodness!	1969	$25
❏ 10017	Houston Express	1971	$25
❏ 10003	Person to Person	1971	$30
❏ PRST-7621	Soul Dance!	1969	$25
❏ 10055	Sweet Buns and Barbeque	1973	$35
❏ PRST-7779	The Best of Houston Person	1970	$25
❏ PRST-7767	The Truth!	1970	$25
❏ PRST-7548	Trust in Me	1968	$25
❏ PRLP-7491 [M]	Underground Soul	1967	$30
❏ PRST-7491 [S]	Underground Soul	1967	$25
SAVOY			
❏ 14471	Gospel Soul	197?	$30
WESTBOUND			
❏ 213	Get Outa My Way	1975	$35
❏ 205	Houston Person '75	1975	$35

PERSSON, AAKE

Number	Title	Yr	NM
EMARCY			
❏ MG-26039 [10]	Swedish Modern	1954	$250

PERSSON, AAKE/ARNE DOMNERUS

Number	Title	Yr	NM
PRESTIGE			
❏ PRLP-173 [10]	Aake Persson Swedish All Stars	1953	$350

PERSSON, BENT

Number	Title	Yr	NM
STOMP OFF			
❏ SOS-1167	Livin' High in London	198?	$25

PERSUADERS, THE
More than one group?

Number	Title	Yr	NM
ATCO			
❏ SD7046	Best Thing That Ever Happened to Me	1974	$25
❏ SD7021	The Persuaders	1973	$25
CALLA			
❏ PZ34802	It's All About Love	1977	$18
COLLECTABLES			
❏ COL-5139	Thin Line Between Love and Hate (Golden Classics)	198?	$12
WIN OR LOSE			
❏ SD 33-387	Thin Line Between Love and Hate	1972	$30

PERSUADERS, THE (2)
Surf group.

Number	Title	Yr	NM
SATURN			
❏ SAT-5000 [M]	Surfer's Nightmare	1963	$300
❏ SATS-5000 [S]	Surfer's Nightmare	1963	$400

PERSUASIONS, THE

Number	Title	Yr	NM
A&M			
❏ SP-3656	I Just Want to Sing with My Friends	1974	$15
❏ SP-3635	More Than Before	1974	$15
CAPITOL			
❏ ST-11101	Spread the Word	1972	$30
❏ ST-872	Street Corner Symphony	1972	$30
❏ ST-791	We Came to Play	1971	$30
❏ SM-791	We Came to Play	197?	$12
—Reissue with new prefix			
CATAMOUNT			
❏ 905	Stardust	197?	$40
ELEKTRA			
❏ 7E-1099	Chirpin'	1977	$15
FLYING FISH			
❏ FF-093	Comin' At Ya	1979	$15
MCA			
❏ 326	We Still Ain't Got No Band	1973	$18
REPRISE			
❏ RS6394	Acapella	1970	$30
ROUNDER			
❏ 3053	Good News	1981	$12
❏ 3083	No Frills	1984	$12

PERUNA JAZZMEN, THE

Number	Title	Yr	NM
STOMP OFF			
❏ SOS-1003	Come On and Stomp, Stomp, Stomp	1981	$25
❏ SOS-1020	Mean Blues	198?	$25
❏ SOS-1105	Smoke House Blues	1986	$25

PET SHOP BOYS

Number	Title	Yr	NM
EMI			
❏ E1-34023	Alternative	1995	$100
—Box set pressed in UK for import into the US (regular UK pressings have gatefold sleeves)			
❏ E1-28105	Disco 2	1994	$15
EMI AMERICA			
❏ SQ-17246	Disco	1986	$12
❏ R164390	Please	1986	$15
—BMG Direct Marketing edition			
❏ PW-17193	Please	1986	$12
EMI MANHATTAN			
❏ R153678	Actually	1987	$15
—BMG Direct Marketing edition			
❏ ELJ-46972	Actually	1987	$12
❏ E1-90263	Actually	1988	$25
—Limited set with bonus 12" record of "Always on My Mind" (SPRO-04055/6) included			
❏ R100681	Introspective	1988	$15
—BMG Direct Marketing edition			
❏ E1-90868	Introspective	1988	$12
❏ 4233 [DJ]	Special Limited Edition: Introspective Club Mixes	1988	$75
—Promo-only set of three 12" records of remixes			
❏ E1-90868 [DJ]	Special Limited Edition Club Mixes	1988	$175
—Promo-only set of three 12-inch singles of remixes, which can also be found separately (SPRO-04231/2; SPRO-04233/41; SPRO-04242/3); this is for the complete package with outer sticker			

PETER, PAUL AND MARY

Number	Title	Yr	NM
GOLD CASTLE			
❏ D1-71316	A Holiday Celebration	1988	$12
❏ R164086	A Holiday Celebration	1988	$15
—Same as above, except BMG Direct Marketing edition			

Number	Title	Yr	NM
❏ 171001	No Easy Walk to Freedom	1987	$15
❏ D1-71301	No Easy Walk to Freedom	1988	$12
—Reissue of 171001			

PETER, PAUL AND MARY
❏ 830331	Such Is Love	1983	$25

WARNER BROS.
❏ W1700 [M]	Album 1700	1967	$30
❏ WS1700 [S]	Album 1700	1967	$30
—Gold label			
❏ WS1700 [S]	Album 1700	1968	$15
—Green "W7" label			
❏ WS1700 [S]	Album 1700	1970	$12
—Any later Warner Bros. label			
❏ W1589 [M]	A Song Will Rise	1965	$25
❏ WS1589 [S]	A Song Will Rise	1965	$30
—Gold label			
❏ WS1589 [S]	A Song Will Rise	1968	$12
—Any later Warner Bros. label			
❏ W1507 [M]	In the Wind	1963	$25
❏ WS1507 [S]	In the Wind	1963	$30
—Gold label			
❏ WS1507 [S]	In the Wind	1968	$12
—Any later Warner Bros. label			
❏ WS1751	Late Again	1968	$18
—Green "W7" label			
❏ WS1751	Late Again	1970	$12
—Any later Warner Bros. label			
❏ W1473 [M]	(Moving)	1963	$25
❏ WS1473 [S]	(Moving)	1963	$30
—Gold label			
❏ WS1473 [S]	(Moving)	1968	$12
—Any later Warner Bros. label (green "W7", green "WB", palm trees, white label)			
❏ W1449 [M]	Peter, Paul and Mary	1962	$25

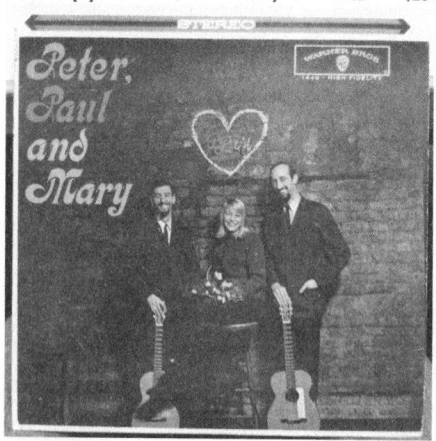

❏ WS1449 [S]	Peter, Paul and Mary	1962	$30
—Gold label			
❏ WS1449 [S]	Peter, Paul and Mary	1968	$15
—Green "W7" label			
❏ WS1449 [S]	Peter, Paul and Mary	1970	$12
—Any later Warner Bros. label (green "WB", palm trees, white label)			
❏ W1648 [M]	Peter, Paul and Mary Album	1966	$25
❏ WS1648 [S]	Peter, Paul and Mary Album	1966	$30
—Gold label			
❏ WS1648 [S]	Peter, Paul and Mary Album	1968	$12
—Any later Warner Bros. label			
❏ 2W1555 [M]	Peter, Paul and Mary In Concert	1964	$30
❏ 2WS1555 [S]	Peter, Paul and Mary In Concert	1964	$30
—Gold labels			
❏ 2WS1555 [S]	Peter, Paul and Mary In Concert	1968	$15
—Any later Warner Bros. label			
❏ WS1785	Peter, Paul and Mommy	1969	$18
—Green "W7" label			
❏ WS1785	Peter, Paul and Mommy	1970	$12
—Any later Warner Bros. label			
❏ BSK3231	Reunion	1978	$12
❏ W1615 [M]	See What Tomorrow Brings	1965	$25
❏ WS1615 [S]	See What Tomorrow Brings	1965	$30
—Gold label			
❏ WS1615 [S]	See What Tomorrow Brings	1968	$12
—Any later Warner Bros. label			
❏ BS2552	(Ten) Years Together -- The Best of Peter, Paul and Mary	1970	$18
—Green "WB" label			
❏ BS2552	(Ten) Years Together -- The Best of Peter, Paul and Mary	1973	$15
—Burbank" palm-trees label			
❏ BSK3105	(Ten) Years Together -- The Best of Peter, Paul and Mary	1977	$12
—Burbank" palm-trees label			

Number	Title	Yr	NM
❏ BSK3105	(Ten) Years Together -- The Best of Peter, Paul and Mary	1979	$10
—White or tan label			

PETER AND GORDON
CAPITOL
❏ T2115 [M]	A World Without Love	1964	$30
❏ ST2115 [S]	A World Without Love	1964	$30
❏ ST2882 [S]	Hot, Cold and Custard	1968	$30
❏ T2220 [M]	I Don't Want to See You Again	1964	$25
❏ ST2220 [S]	I Don't Want to See You Again	1964	$30
❏ T2324 [M]	I Go to Pieces	1965	$25
❏ ST2324 [S]	I Go to Pieces	1965	$30
❏ T2747 [M]	In London for Tea	1967	$18
❏ ST2747 [S]	In London for Tea	1967	$25
❏ T2729 [M]	Knight in Rusty Armour	1967	$25
❏ ST2729 [S]	Knight in Rusty Armour	1967	$25
❏ T2664 [M]	Lady Godiva	1967	$25
❏ ST2664 [S]	Lady Godiva	1967	$25
❏ T2430 [M]	Peter and Gordon Sing the Hits of Nashville	1966	$25
❏ ST2430 [S]	Peter and Gordon Sing the Hits of Nashville	1966	$30
❏ T2549 [M]	The Best of Peter and Gordon	1966	$18
—Black label with colorband			
❏ ST2549 [P]	The Best of Peter and Gordon	1966	$25
—Black label with colorband; "Woman" is rechanneled			
❏ T2549 [M]	The Best of Peter and Gordon	1967	$15
—Starline" label			
❏ ST2549 [P]	The Best of Peter and Gordon	1967	$18
—Starline" label			
❏ SN-16084 [S]	The Best of Peter and Gordon	1979	$10
❏ T2368 [M]	True Love Ways	1965	$25
❏ ST2368 [S]	True Love Ways	1965	$30
❏ T2477 [M]	Woman	1966	$25
❏ ST2477 [P]	Woman	1966	$30
—Woman" is rechanneled			

PETERS, BROCK
UNITED ARTISTS
❏ UAL-3127 [M]	Brock Peters	1963	$25
❏ UAS-6127 [S]	Brock Peters	1963	$30
❏ UAL-3062 [M]	Brock Peters at the Village Gate	1961	$30
❏ UAS-6062 [S]	Brock Peters at the Village Gate	1961	$30
❏ UAL-3041 [M]	Sing'a Man	1960	$30
❏ UAS-6041 [S]	Sing'a Man	1960	$40

PETERS, RAY
JCW
❏ 1333	From the Heart	1968	$30

PETERS, ROBERTA
RCA VICTOR RED SEAL
❏ LSC-2379 [S]	Roberta Peters in Recital	1960	$25
—Original with "shaded dog" label			

PETERSEN, EDWARD
DELMARK
❏ DS-445	Upward Spiral	1990	$30

PETERSEN, PAUL
COLPIX
❏ CP-429 [M]	Lollipops and Roses	1962	$50
❏ SCP-429 [S]	Lollipops and Roses	1962	$75
❏ CP-442 [M]	My Dad	1963	$50
❏ SCP-442 [S]	My Dad	1963	$75

PETERSON, COLLEEN
CAPITOL
❏ ST-11567	Beginning to Feel Like Home	1976	$15
❏ ST-11714	Colleen	1978	$15
❏ ST-11835	Takin' My Boots Off	1978	$15

PETERSON, HANNIBAL MARVIN
ENJA
❏ 3085	Angels of Atlanta	1981	$30

INNER CITY
❏ IC-3020	Antibes	197?	$35

PETERSON, JEANNE ARLAND
CELEBRATION
❏ 5004	Jeanne Arland Peterson	197?	$35

PETERSON, OSCAR, AND HERB ELLIS
BASF
❏ 20723	Hello Herbie	1969	$35

PAUSA
❏ PR7085	Hello Herbie	1981	$25
—Reissue			

Number	Title	Yr	NM

PETERSON, OSCAR, AND MILT JACKSON
PABLO
❏ 2310881	Two of the Few	1983	$30

PETERSON, OSCAR, AND STEPHANE GRAPPELLI
JAZZ MAN
❏ 5054	Time After Time	1983	$30

PABLO
❏ 2310907	Violins No End	198?	$30
—With Stuff Smith			

PRESTIGE
❏ 24041	Oscar Peterson Featuring Stephane Grappelli	1974	$35

PETERSON, OSCAR
AMERICAN RECORDING SOCIETY
❏ G-415 [M]	An Oscar for Peterson	1957	$40
❏ G-438 [M]	Oscar Peterson Trio at Newport	1957	$40

BASF
❏ 20869	Another Day	1975	$35
❏ MC20668	A Rare Mood	1976	$35
❏ 25101	Exclusively for My Friends	1972	$35
❏ MC21281	Great Connection	1974	$35
❏ 25156	In a Mellow Mood	1973	$35
❏ 20905	In Tune	1973	$30
❏ 20713	Motions and Emotions	1972	$30
❏ 20908	Reunion Blues	1973	$35
❏ MC20879	Tracks	1974	$35
❏ 20734	Tristeza on Piano	1972	$30
❏ 20868	Walking the Line	1973	$175

BOOK-OF-THE-MONTH
❏ 61-7546	Easy Does It	1984	$75

CLEF
❏ MGC-698 [M]	An Evening with the Oscar Peterson Duo/Quartet	1956	$300
❏ MGC-697 [M]	Keyboard Music by Oscar Peterson	1956	$300
❏ MGC-695 [M]	Nostalgic Memories by Oscar Peterson	1956	$300
❏ MGC-107 [10]	Oscar Peterson at Carnegie Hall	1951	$350
❏ MGC-110 [10]	Oscar Peterson Collates	1952	$350
❏ MGC-127 [10]	Oscar Peterson Collates No. 2	1953	$300
❏ MGC-106 [10]	Oscar Peterson Piano Solos	1951	$300
—Reissue of Mercury 25024			
❏ MGC-603 [M]	Oscar Peterson Plays Cole Porter	1953	$300
❏ MGC-708 [M]	Oscar Peterson Plays Count Basie	1956	$300
❏ MGC-606 [M]	Oscar Peterson Plays Duke Ellington	1953	$300
❏ MGC-605 [M]	Oscar Peterson Plays George Gershwin	1953	$300
❏ MGC-649 [M]	Oscar Peterson Plays Harold Arlen	1955	$300
❏ MGC-648 [M]	Oscar Peterson Plays Harry Warren	1955	$300
❏ MGC-604 [M]	Oscar Peterson Plays Irving Berlin	1953	$300
❏ MGC-623 [M]	Oscar Peterson Plays Jerome Kern	1954	$300
❏ MGC-650 [M]	Oscar Peterson Plays Jimmy McHugh	1955	$300
❏ MGC-119 [10]	Oscar Peterson Plays Pretty	1952	$350
❏ MGC-155 [10]	Oscar Peterson Plays Pretty No. 2	1954	$300
❏ MGC-624 [M]	Oscar Peterson Plays Richard Rodgers	1954	$300
❏ MGC-625 [M]	Oscar Peterson Plays Vincent Youmans	1954	$300
❏ MGC-145 [10]	Oscar Peterson Sings	1954	$300
❏ MGC-694 [M]	Recital by Oscar Peterson	1956	$300
❏ MGC-696 [M]	Tenderly -- Music by Oscar Peterson	1956	$300
❏ MGC-116 [10]	The Oscar Peterson Quartet	1952	$350
❏ MGC-688 [M]	The Oscar Peterson Quartet	1956	$300
—Reissue of 116			
❏ MGC-168 [10]	The Oscar Peterson Quartet No. 2	1954	$300
❏ MGC-751 [M]	The Oscar Peterson Trio at the Stratford Shakesperean Festival, Volume 1	1955	$0
—Canceled			
❏ MGC-752 [M]	The Oscar Peterson Trio at the Stratford Shakesperean Festival, Volume 2	1955	$0
—Canceled			

DCC COMPACT CLASSICS
❏ LPZ-2021	West Side Story	1996	$200
—Audiophile vinyl			

EMARCY
❏ 405	Oscar Peterson Trio Transition	1976	$35

FANTASY
❏ OJC-383	Oscar Peterson and the Bassists -- Montreux '77	1989	$25
❏ OJC-378	Oscar Peterson Jam -- Montreux '77	1989	$25
❏ OJC-498	Skol	1991	$25
❏ OJC-627	The Good Life	1991	$25

Number	Title	Yr	NM
OJC-603	Trumpet Summit Meets the Oscar Peterson Big Four	1991	$25

LIMELIGHT

Number	Title	Yr	NM
LM-82039 [M]	Blues Etude	1966	$35
LS-86039 [S]	Blues Etude	1966	$35
LM-82010 [M]	Canadiana Suite	1965	$35
LS-86010 [S]	Canadiana Suite	1965	$25
LM-82023 [M]	Eloquence	1965	$35
LS-86023 [S]	Eloquence	1965	$50
LM-82044 [M]	Soul Espanol	1967	$50
LS-86044 [S]	Soul Espanol	1967	$35
LM-82029 [M]	With Respect to Nat	1966	$35
LS-86029 [S]	With Respect to Nat	1966	$50

MERCURY

Number	Title	Yr	NM
MGC-107 [10]	Oscar Peterson at Carnegie Hall	1951	$300
MGC-110 [10]	Oscar Peterson Collates	1952	$300
MG-25024 [10]	Oscar Peterson Piano Solos	1950	$300
MGC-106 [10]	Oscar Peterson Piano Solos	1951	$300
MGC-603 [M]	Oscar Peterson Plays Cole Porter	1953	$300
MGC-606 [M]	Oscar Peterson Plays Duke Ellington	1953	$300
MGC-605 [M]	Oscar Peterson Plays George Gershwin	1953	$300
MGC-604 [M]	Oscar Peterson Plays Irving Berlin	1953	$300
MGC-119 [10]	Oscar Peterson Plays Pretty	1952	$300
MG-20975 [M]	Oscar Peterson Trio + One	1964	$150
SR-60975 [S]	Oscar Peterson Trio + One	1964	$150
MGC-116 [10]	The Oscar Peterson Quartet	1952	$300

MGM

Number	Title	Yr	NM
GAS-133	Oscar Peterson (Golden Archive Series)	1970	$30

MOBILE FIDELITY

Number	Title	Yr	NM
1-243	Very Tall	1995	$150

—Audiophile vinyl

PABLO

Number	Title	Yr	NM
2625705	A Salle Pleyel	1975	$35
2640101	Freedom Songbook	1983	$35
2310796	Giants	1977	$30
2625702	History of An Artist	1975	$35
2310895	History of An Artist, Volume 2	1983	$30
2310918	If You Could See Me Now	1987	$25
2310817	Jousts	1979	$30
2310940	Live	1990	$30
2310747	Montreux '75	1976	$30
2310742	Oscar Peterson and Clark Terry	1976	$30
2310740	Oscar Peterson and Dizzy Gillespie	1976	$30
2310741	Oscar Peterson and Harry Edison	1976	$30
2310743	Oscar Peterson and Jon Faddis	1976	$30
2310739	Oscar Peterson and Roy Eldridge	1976	$30
2310927	Oscar Peterson + Harry Edison + Eddie "Cleanhead" Vinson	1988	$25
2625711	Oscar Peterson in Russia	1976	$30
2310779	Porgy and Bess	1976	$30
2310701	The Trio	1975	$30

PABLO LIVE

Number	Title	Yr	NM
2308224	Digital at Montreux	1980	$30
2620115	Live at the Northsea Jazz Festival, 1980	1981	$35
2308231	Nigerian Marketplace	1982	$30
2308213	Oscar Peterson and the Bassists -- Montreux '77	1978	$30
2308208	Oscar Peterson Jam -- Montreux '77	1977	$30
2308232	Skol	1982	$30
2308241	The Good Life	1983	$30
2620111	The London Concert	1979	$35
2620112	The Paris Concert	1979	$35

PABLO TODAY

Number	Title	Yr	NM
2312129	A Royal Wedding Suite	198?	$30
2312108	Night Child	1979	$30
2313103	Silent Partner	1980	$30
2312135	The Personal Touch	1982	$30

PAUSA

Number	Title	Yr	NM
PR7059	Action	1980	$25
PR7135	Another Day	1983	$25

—Reissue of BASF 20869

Number	Title	Yr	NM
PR7064	Girl Talk	1980	$25
PR7113	Great Connection	1983	$25

—Reissue of BASF 21281

Number	Title	Yr	NM
PR7073	In Tune	1980	$25

—Reissue of BASF 20905

Number	Title	Yr	NM
PR7044	Mellow Mood	1979	$25
PR7102	Motions and Emotions	1982	$25

—Reissue of BASF 20713

Number	Title	Yr	NM
PR7069	My Favorite Instrument	1980	$25
PR7099	Reunion Blues	1981	$25

—Reissue of BASF 20908

Number	Title	Yr	NM
PR7080	The Way I Really Play	1981	$25
PR7124	Tristeza on Piano	1983	$25

—Reissue of BASF 20734

PRESTIGE

Number	Title	Yr	NM
PRST-7690	Easy Walker	1969	$35
PRST-7649	Oscar Peterson Plays for Lovers	1969	$35
PRST-7595	Soul-O!	1968	$35
PRST-7620	The Great Oscar Peterson on Prestige!	1969	$35

RCA VICTOR

Number	Title	Yr	NM
LPT-3006 [10]	This Is Oscar Peterson	1952	$250

TRIP

Number	Title	Yr	NM
5560	Eloquence	197?	$25

VERVE

Number	Title	Yr	NM
V-8516 [M]	Affinity	1963	$75
V6-8516 [S]	Affinity	1963	$75
MGV-2048 [M]	An Evening with Oscar Peterson	1957	$300

—Reissue of Clef 698

Number	Title	Yr	NM
V-2048 [M]	An Evening with Oscar Peterson	1961	$50
MGV-8082 [M]	An Evening with Oscar Peterson	1957	$0

—Canceled

Number	Title	Yr	NM
MGV-8287 [M]	A Night on the Town	1958	$120
MGVS-6036 [S]	A Night on the Town	1960	$0

—Canceled

Number	Title	Yr	NM
V-8287 [M]	A Night on the Town	1961	$50
V-8476 [M]	Bursting Out with the All Star Big Band!	1962	$30
V6-8476 [S]	Bursting Out with the All Star Big Band!	1962	$75
MGV-8399 [M]	Carnival	1960	$0

—Canceled

Number	Title	Yr	NM
MGV-2002 [M]	In a Romantic Mood -- Oscar Peterson with Strings	1956	$250
V-2002 [M]	In a Romantic Mood -- Oscar Peterson with Strings	1961	$50
MGV-2047 [M]	Keyboard Music by Oscar Peterson	1957	$300

—Reissue of Clef 697

Number	Title	Yr	NM
V-2047 [M]	Keyboard Music by Oscar Peterson	1961	$50
MGV-8081 [M]	Keyboard Music by Oscar Peterson	1957	$175

—Canceled

Number	Title	Yr	NM
821988-1	Motions and Emotions	1984	$25

—Reissue

Number	Title	Yr	NM
V-8538 [M]	Night Train	1963	$75
V6-8538 [S]	Night Train	1963	$75
BOMC 70-5601 [S]	Night Train	197?	$75

—Book-of-the-Month Club edition

Number	Title	Yr	NM
V-8740 [M]	Night Train, Volume 2	1967	$50
V6-8740 [S]	Night Train, Volume 2	1967	$35
MGV-2045 [M]	Nostalgic Memories by Oscar Peterson	1957	$300

—Reissue of Clef 695

Number	Title	Yr	NM
V-2045 [M]	Nostalgic Memories by Oscar Peterson	1961	$50
MGV-8079 [M]	Nostalgic Memories by Oscar Peterson	1957	$175

—Canceled

Number	Title	Yr	NM
UMV-2626	Oscar Peterson at the Concertgebouw	198?	$25
UMV-2502	Oscar Peterson at the Stratford Shakespearean Festival	198?	$25
MGV-8092 [M]	Oscar Peterson Plays Count Basie	1957	$300

—Reissue of Clef 708

Number	Title	Yr	NM
V-8092 [M]	Oscar Peterson Plays Count Basie	1961	$50
MGV-2119 [M]	Oscar Peterson Plays "My Fair Lady"	1958	$150
MGVS-6060 [S]	Oscar Peterson Plays "My Fair Lady"	1960	$150
V-2119 [M]	Oscar Peterson Plays "My Fair Lady"	1961	$50
V6-2119 [S]	Oscar Peterson Plays "My Fair Lady"	1961	$35

—Reissue of 6060

Number	Title	Yr	NM
V-8581 [M]	Oscar Peterson Plays "My Fair Lady"	1964	$35
V6-8581 [S]	Oscar Peterson Plays "My Fair Lady"	1964	$50
MGV-2052 [M]	Oscar Peterson Plays the Cole Porter Songbook	1957	$300

—Reissue of Clef 603

Number	Title	Yr	NM
MGVS-6083 [S]	Oscar Peterson Plays the Cole Porter Songbook	1960	$150
V6-2052 [S]	Oscar Peterson Plays the Cole Porter Songbook	1961	$35

—Reissue of 6083

Number	Title	Yr	NM
V-2052 [M]	Oscar Peterson Plays the Cole Porter Songbook	1961	$50
821987-1	Oscar Peterson Plays the Cole Porter Songbook	1986	$25

—Reissue of 2053

Number	Title	Yr	NM
MGV-2055 [M]	Oscar Peterson Plays the Duke Ellington Songbook	1957	$300

—Reissue of Clef 606

Number	Title	Yr	NM
MGVS-6086 [S]	Oscar Peterson Plays the Duke Ellington Songbook	1960	$150
V-2055 [M]	Oscar Peterson Plays the Duke Ellington Songbook	1961	$50
V6-2055 [S]	Oscar Peterson Plays the Duke Ellington Songbook	1961	$35

—Reissue of 6086

Number	Title	Yr	NM
MGV-2054 [M]	Oscar Peterson Plays the George Gershwin Songbook	1957	$300

—Reissue of Clef 605

Number	Title	Yr	NM
MGVS-6085 [S]	Oscar Peterson Plays the George Gershwin Songbook	1960	$150
V-2054 [M]	Oscar Peterson Plays the George Gershwin Songbook	1961	$50
V6-2054 [S]	Oscar Peterson Plays the George Gershwin Songbook	1961	$35

—Reissue of 6085

Number	Title	Yr	NM
823249-1	Oscar Peterson Plays the George Gershwin Songbook	1985	$25

—Reissue of 2054

Number	Title	Yr	NM
MGV-2060 [M]	Oscar Peterson Plays the Harold Arlen Songbook	1957	$300

—Reissue of Clef 649

Number	Title	Yr	NM
MGVS-6091 [S]	Oscar Peterson Plays the Harold Arlen Songbook	1960	$150
V-2060 [M]	Oscar Peterson Plays the Harold Arlen Songbook	1961	$50
V6-2060 [S]	Oscar Peterson Plays the Harold Arlen Songbook	1961	$35

—Reissue of 6091

Number	Title	Yr	NM
MGV-2059 [M]	Oscar Peterson Plays the Harry Warren Songbook	1957	$300

—Reissue of Clef 648

Number	Title	Yr	NM
MGVS-6090 [S]	Oscar Peterson Plays the Harry Warren Songbook	1960	$150
V-2059 [M]	Oscar Peterson Plays the Harry Warren Songbook	1961	$50
V6-2059 [S]	Oscar Peterson Plays the Harry Warren Songbook	1961	$35

—Reissue of 6090

Number	Title	Yr	NM
MGV-2053 [M]	Oscar Peterson Plays the Irving Berlin Songbook	1957	$300

—Reissue of Clef 604

Number	Title	Yr	NM
MGVS-6084 [S]	Oscar Peterson Plays the Irving Berlin Songbook	1960	$150
V-2053 [M]	Oscar Peterson Plays the Irving Berlin Songbook	1961	$50
V6-2053 [S]	Oscar Peterson Plays the Irving Berlin Songbook	1961	$35

—Reissue of 6084

Number	Title	Yr	NM
MGV-2056 [M]	Oscar Peterson Plays the Jerome Kern Songbook	1957	$300

—Reissue of Clef 623

Number	Title	Yr	NM
MGVS-6087 [S]	Oscar Peterson Plays the Jerome Kern Songbook	1960	$150
V-2056 [M]	Oscar Peterson Plays the Jerome Kern Songbook	1961	$50
V6-2056 [S]	Oscar Peterson Plays the Jerome Kern Songbook	1961	$35

—Reissue of 6087

Number	Title	Yr	NM
825865-1	Oscar Peterson Plays the Jerome Kern Songbook	1985	$25

—Reissue of 2056

Number	Title	Yr	NM
MGV-2061 [M]	Oscar Peterson Plays the Jimmy McHugh Songbook	1957	$300

—Reissue of Clef 650

Number	Title	Yr	NM
MGVS-6092 [S]	Oscar Peterson Plays the Jimmy McHugh Songbook	1960	$150
V-2061 [M]	Oscar Peterson Plays the Jimmy McHugh Songbook	1961	$50
V6-2061 [S]	Oscar Peterson Plays the Jimmy McHugh Songbook	1961	$35

—Reissue of 6092

Number	Title	Yr	NM
MGV-2057 [M]	Oscar Peterson Plays the Richard Rodgers Songbook	1957	$300

—Reissue of Clef 624

Number	Title	Yr	NM
MGVS-6088 [S]	Oscar Peterson Plays the Richard Rodgers Songbook	1960	$150
V-2057 [M]	Oscar Peterson Plays the Richard Rodgers Songbook	1961	$50
V6-2057 [S]	Oscar Peterson Plays the Richard Rodgers Songbook	1961	$35

—Reissue of 6088

Number	Title	Yr	NM
MGV-2058 [M]	Oscar Peterson Plays the Vincent Youmans Songbook	1957	$0

—Reissue planned but canceled

Number	Title	Yr	NM
MGVS-6089 [S]	Oscar Peterson Plays the Vincent Youmans Songbook	1960	$0

—Canceled

Number	Title	Yr	NM
V6-8775	Oscars -- Oscar Peterson Plays the Academy Awards	1969	$35
MGV-2004 [M]	Pastel Moods by Oscar Peterson	1956	$250
V-2004 [M]	Pastel Moods by Oscar Peterson	1961	$50
MGV-8340 [M]	Porgy and Bess	1959	$150
MGVS-6098 [S]	Porgy and Bess	1960	$0

—Canceled

Number	Title	Yr	NM
V-8340 [M]	Porgy and Bess	1961	$50
V6-8340 [S]	Porgy and Bess	1961	$35
V-8660 [M]	Put On a Happy Face	1966	$35
V6-8660 [S]	Put On a Happy Face	1966	$50
MGV-2044 [M]	Recital by Oscar Peterson	1957	$250

—Reissue of Clef 694

Number	Title	Yr	NM
V-2044 [M]	Recital by Oscar Peterson	1961	$50
MGV-8078 [M]	Recital by Oscar Peterson	1957	$0

—Canceled

Number	Title	Yr	NM
V3HB-8842	Return Engagement	1975	$35
833552	Return Engagement	198?	$30

—Reissue of 8842 (though the labels may still use the old number)

Number	Title	Yr	NM
MGV-2012 [M]	Romance -- The Vocal Styling of Oscar Peterson	1956	$350

Number	Title	Yr	NM

—Reissue of Clef 145

Number	Title	Yr	NM
❏ V-2012 [M]	Romance -- The Vocal Styling of Oscar Peterson	1961	$50
❏ MGV-2079 [M]	Soft Sands	1957	$150
❏ V-2079 [M]	Soft Sands	1961	$50
❏ V-8681 [M]	Something Warm	1966	$35
❏ V6-8681 [S]	Something Warm	1966	$50
❏ MGV-8334 [M]	Songs for a Swingin' Affair -- A Jazz Portrait of Sinatra	1959	$150
❏ MGVS-6071 [S]	Songs for a Swingin' Affair -- A Jazz Portrait of Sinatra	1960	$150
❏ V-8334 [M]	Songs for a Swingin' Affair -- A Jazz Portrait of Sinatra	1961	$50
❏ V6-8334 [S]	Songs for a Swingin' Affair -- A Jazz Portrait of Sinatra	1961	$35

—Reissue of 6071

❏ 825769-1	Songs for a Swingin' Affair -- A Jazz Portrait of Sinatra	1985	$25

—Reissue of 8334

❏ VSP-11 [M]	Stage Right	1966	$30
❏ VSPS-11 [S]	Stage Right	1966	$35
❏ MGV-8364 [M]	Swinging Brass with the Oscar Peterson Trio	1959	$150
❏ MGVS-6119 [S]	Swinging Brass with the Oscar Peterson Trio	1960	$100
❏ V-8364 [M]	Swinging Brass with the Oscar Peterson Trio	1961	$50
❏ V6-8364 [S]	Swinging Brass with the Oscar Peterson Trio	1961	$35

—Reissue of 6119

❏ MGV-2046 [M]	Tenderly -- Music by Oscar Peterson	1957	$250

—Reissue of Clef 696

❏ V-2046 [M]	Tenderly -- Music by Oscar Peterson	1961	$50
❏ MGV-8080 [M]	Tenderly -- Music by Oscar Peterson	1957	$0

—Canceled

❏ MGV-8351 [M]	The Jazz Soul of Oscar Peterson	1959	$150
❏ MGVS-6116 [S]	The Jazz Soul of Oscar Peterson	1960	$0

—Canceled

❏ V-8351 [M]	The Jazz Soul of Oscar Peterson	1961	$50
❏ V-8482 [M]	The Modern Jazz Quartet and the Oscar Petereson Trio at the Opera House	1962	$175

—Reissue of 8269

❏ V6-8482 [S]	The Modern Jazz Quartet and the Oscar Petereson Trio at the Opera House	1962	$175

—Reissue of 8269

❏ MGV-8366 [M]	The Music from "Fiorello!	1960	$100
❏ MGVS-6134 [S]	The Music from "Fiorello!	1960	$0

—Canceled

❏ V-8366 [M]	The Music from "Fiorello!	1961	$50
❏ V3G-8828	The Newport Years	1974	$30
❏ V6-8810	The Oscar Peterson Collection	1972	$35
❏ 30-5606 [M]	The Oscar Peterson Quartet #1	197?	$30

—Book-of-the-Month Club edition

❏ MGV-8072 [M]	The Oscar Peterson Quartet No. 1	1957	$175
❏ V-8072 [M]	The Oscar Peterson Quartet No. 1	1961	$50
❏ MGV-8368 [M]	The Oscar Peterson Trio at J.A.T.P.	1960	$150
❏ V-8368 [M]	The Oscar Peterson Trio at J.A.T.P.	1961	$50
❏ MGV-8268 [M]	The Oscar Peterson Trio at the Concertgebouw	1958	$150
❏ V-8268 [M]	The Oscar Peterson Trio at the Concertgebouw	1961	$50
❏ MGV-8024 [M]	The Oscar Peterson Trio at the Stratford Shakespearean Festival	1957	$175
❏ V-8024 [M]	The Oscar Peterson Trio at the Stratford Shakespearean Festival	1961	$50
❏ V-8591 [M]	The Oscar Peterson Trio Plays	1964	$35
❏ V6-8591 [S]	The Oscar Peterson Trio Plays	1964	$50
❏ 825099-1	The Oscar Peterson Trio Set	1985	$25
❏ MGV-2156 [M]	The Oscar Peterson Trio with David Rose	1958	$0

—Canceled

❏ V-8562 [M]	The Oscar Peterson Trio with Nelson Riddle	1963	$75
❏ V6-8562 [S]	The Oscar Peterson Trio with Nelson Riddle	1963	$75
❏ MGV-8239 [M]	The Oscar Peterson Trio with Sonny Stitt, Roy Eldredge and Jo Jones at Newport	1958	$150
❏ V-8239 [M]	The Oscar Peterson Trio with Sonny Stitt, Roy Eldredge and Jo Jones at Newport	1961	$50
❏ MGV-8269 [M]	The Oscar Peterson Trio with the Modern Jazz Quartet at the Opera House	1958	$150
❏ MGVS-6069 [S]	The Oscar Peterson Trio with the Modern Jazz Quartet at the Opera House	1960	$150
❏ V-8269 [M]	The Oscar Peterson Trio with the Modern Jazz Quartet at the Opera House	1961	$50

❏ V6-8269 [S]	The Oscar Peterson Trio with the Modern Jazz Quartet at the Opera House	1961	$35

—Reissue of 6069

❏ V-8480 [M]	The Sound of the Trio	1962	$75
❏ V6-8480 [S]	The Sound of the Trio	1962	$75
❏ V-8420 [M]	The Trio -- Live from Chicago	1961	$75
❏ V6-8420 [S]	The Trio -- Live from Chicago	1961	$75
❏ V-8700 [M]	Thoroughly Modern '20s	1967	$35
❏ V6-8700 [S]	Thoroughly Modern '20s	1967	$35
❏ 821849-1	Tracks	1985	$25
❏ 821663-1	Travelin' On	1985	$25
❏ V-8429 [M]	Very Tall	1962	$75
❏ V6-8429 [S]	Very Tall	1962	$75
❏ V-8606 [M]	We Get Requests	1965	$35
❏ V6-8606 [S]	We Get Requests	1965	$50
❏ 810047-1	We Get Requests	1986	$25
❏ V-8454 [M]	West Side Story	1962	$75
❏ V6-8454 [S]	West Side Story	1962	$75

WING

❏ SRW16351	Canadiana Suite	1969	$30

PETERSON, OSCAR/GERRY MULLIGAN

VERVE

❏ V-8559 [M]	The Oscar Peterson Trio and the Gerry Mulligan Four at Newport	1963	$75
❏ V6-8559 [S]	The Oscar Peterson Trio and the Gerry Mulligan Four at Newport	1963	$75

PETERSON, PAT

ENJA

❏ 4020	Introducing Pat Peterson	1982	$30

PETERSON, PETE

PAUSA

❏ 7163	Jazz Journey	1984	$25
❏ 7191	Playin' in the Park	1986	$25
❏ 7143	Texas State of Mind	1982	$25

PETERSON, RALPH

BLUE NOTE

❏ B1-92750	Tri-Angular	1989	$30
❏ B1-91730	V	1989	$30

PETERSON, RAY

DECCA

❏ DL75307	Ray Peterson Country	1971	$25

MGM

❏ E-4277 [M]	The Other Side of Ray Peterson	1965	$30
❏ SE-4277 [S]	The Other Side of Ray Peterson	1965	$30
❏ E-4250 [M]	The Very Best of Ray Peterson	1964	$30
❏ SE-4250 [S]	The Very Best of Ray Peterson	1964	$30

RCA CAMDEN

❏ CAL-2119 [M]	Goodnight My Love	1966	$15
❏ CAS-2119 [S]	Goodnight My Love	1966	$15

RCA VICTOR

❏ LPM-2297 [M]	Tell Laura I Love Her	1960	$150
❏ LSP-2297 [S]	Tell Laura I Love Her	1960	$175

UNI

❏ 73078	Missing You/Featuring His Greatest Hits!	1969	$25

PETERSTEIN, SHORTY

WORLD PACIFIC

❏ WP-1274 [M]	The Wide Weird World of Shorty Petterstein	1959	$175

PETRUCCIANI, MICHEL

BLUE NOTE

❏ B1-48679	Michel Plays Petrucciani	1988	$25
❏ B1-92563	Music	1989	$30
❏ BT-85124	Pianism	1987	$25
❏ BT-85133	Power of Three	1987	$25

GEORGE WEIN COLLECTION

❏ GW-3001	100 Hearts	1984	$30
❏ GW-3006	Live at the Village Vanguard	1985	$30

PETTIFORD, OSCAR

ABC-PARAMOUNT

❏ ABC-227 [M]	O.P.'s Jazz Men: Oscar Pettiford Orchestra in Hi-Fi, Vol. 2	1958	$120
❏ ABCS-227 [S]	O.P.'s Jazz Men: Oscar Pettiford Orchestra in Hi-Fi, Vol. 2	1958	$150
❏ ABC-135 [M]	Oscar Pettiford Orchestra in Hi-Fi	1956	$150

BETHLEHEM

❏ BCP-1019 [10]	Basically Duke	1955	$300
❏ BCP-1003 [10]	Oscar Pettiford	1954	$300
❏ BCP-33 [M]	Oscar Pettiford Sextet	1955	$300

❏ BCP-6007	The Finest of Oscar Pettiford	197?	$35

—Reissue, distributed by RCA Victor

DEBUT

❏ DLP-8 [10]	Oscar Pettiford Sextet	1954	$500

FANTASY

❏ 6010 [M]	My Little Cello	1964	$40
❏ 86010 [R]	My Little Cello	1964	$50
❏ 6015 [M]	The Essen Jazz Festival	1964	$40
❏ 86015 [R]	The Essen Jazz Festival	1964	$50
❏ OJC-112	The New Sextet	198?	$30

JAZZLAND

❏ JLP-64 [M]	Last Recordings by the Late, Great Bassist	1962	$75
❏ JLP-964 [R]	Last Recordings by the Late, Great Bassist	1962	$40

JAZZ MAN

❏ 5036	Blue Brothers	1981	$30

PRESTIGE

❏ PRST-7813	Memorial Album	1971	$50

SAVOY JAZZ

❏ SJL-1172	Discoveries	1986	$30

PETTIFORD, OSCAR/RED MITCHELL

BETHLEHEM

❏ BCP-2 [M]	Jazz Mainstream	1957	$300

PETTIFORD, OSCAR/VINNIE BURKE

BETHLEHEM

❏ BCP-6 [M]	Bass by Pettiford/Burke	1957	$300

PETTY, NORMAN, TRIO

COLUMBIA

❏ CL1092 [M]	Moondreams	1958	$175

TOP RANK

❏ R-639 [M]	Petty for Your Thoughts	1960	$30
❏ RS-639 [S]	Petty for Your Thoughts	1960	$40

VIK

❏ LX-1073 [M]	Corsage	1957	$80

PETTY, TOM, AND THE HEARTBREAKERS

Includes Tom Petty solo. Also see STEVIE NICKS; TRAVELING WILBURYS.

AMERICAN

❏ 44285-1	Highway Companion	2007	$30

—180-gram issue; CD released in 2006

BACKSTREET

❏ BSR-5105	Damn the Torpedoes	1979	$12
❏ BSR-5160	Hard Promises	1981	$12
❏ BSR-5360	Long After Dark	1982	$12

MCA

❏ 1486	Damn the Torpedoes	1987	$10
❏ 6253	Full Moon Fever	1989	$12
❏ 37239	Hard Promises	1984	$10

❏ 10317 [B]	Into the Great Wide Open	1991	$25
❏ 5836	Let Me Up (I've Had Enough)	1987	$12
❏ 2-8021	Pack Up the Plantation -- Live!	1985	$15
❏ 5486	Southern Accents	1985	$12
❏ 37143	Tom Petty and the Heartbreakers	1982	$10
❏ 37116	You're Gonna Get It!	1982	$10

REPRISE

❏ 544259-1 [B]	Hypnotic Eye	2014	$25
❏ 553679-1 [B]	Kiss My Amps Live Volume 2	2016	$25

—Limited edition, 180g

SHELTER

❏ TP-12677 [DJ]	Official Live 'Leg	1977	$75

—Promo-only live album with letter to radio (has been counterfeited)

❏ TP-12677 [DJ]	Official Live 'Leg	1977	$75

—Promo-only live album with letter to radio (has been

Number	Title	Yr	NM
counterfeited)			
❏ SRL-52006 [B]	Tom Petty and the Heartbreakers	1976	$25
— Original copies were distributed by ABC			
❏ SRL-52006	Tom Petty and the Heartbreakers	1979	$15
— Later copies were distributed by MCA			
❏ DA-52029 [DJ]	You're Gonna Get It!	1978	$30
— Promo only on red vinyl			
❏ DA-52029 [DJ]	You're Gonna Get It!	1978	$30
— Promo only on red vinyl			
❏ DA-52029	You're Gonna Get It!	1978	$18
— Original copies were distributed by ABC			
❏ DA-52029	You're Gonna Get It!	1979	$15
— Later copies were distributed by MCA			

WARNER BROS.
Number	Title	Yr	NM
❏ 47294	Echo	1999	$25
❏ 46285	Songs and Music from the Motion Picture "She's the One	1996	$12
❏ 47955	The Last DJ	2002	$25
❏ 45759	Wildflowers	1994	$30

PFEIFER, DIANE
CAPITOL
Number	Title	Yr	NM
❏ ST-12046	Diane Pfeifer	1980	$12

PHAFNER
DRAGON
Number	Title	Yr	NM
❏ LP-101	Overdrive	1971	$3000
— VG value 1000; VG+ value 2000			

PHAIR, LIZ
MATADOR
Number	Title	Yr	NM
❏ OLE 051-1	Exile in Guyville	1992	$25
❏ OLE107-1	Whip-Smart	1994	$15
❏ OLE191-1	Whitechocolatespaceegg	1998	$18

PHANTOM'S DIVINE COMEDY
CAPITOL
Number	Title	Yr	NM
❏ ST-11313	The Phantom's Divine Comedy, Part One	1974	$85

PHILADELPHIA BRASS ENSEMBLE, THE
COLUMBIA MASTERWORKS
Number	Title	Yr	NM
❏ ML6433 [M]	A Festival of Carols in Brass	1967	$18
❏ MS7033 [S]	A Festival of Carols in Brass	1967	$18
— 360 Sound" label			
❏ MS7033 [S]	A Festival of Carols in Brass	1970	$15
— Gray label ringed with six orange "Columbia"s			
❏ XMS7033 [S]	A Festival of Carols in Brass	197?	$12
— Reissue with new prefix			

PHILADELPHIA EXPERIMENT, THE
ATLANTIC
Number	Title	Yr	NM
❏ 93042	The Philadelphia Experiment	2001	$20

PHILADELPHIA ORCHESTRA (ORMANDY)
COLUMBIA MASTERWORKS
Number	Title	Yr	NM
❏ ML6039 [M]	A Christmas Festival	1964	$15
❏ MS6639 [S]	A Christmas Festival	1964	$18
— With the Temple University Concert Choir and the St. Francis de Sales Boychoir			
❏ MS7161	Greatest Christmas Hits	1968	$15
— 360 Sound" label			
❏ MS7161	Greatest Christmas Hits	1970	$12
— Gray label ringed with six orange "Columbia"s			
❏ ML5769 [M]	The Glorious Sound of Christmas	1962	$15
❏ MS6369 [S]	The Glorious Sound of Christmas	1962	$18

RCA GOLD SEAL
Number	Title	Yr	NM
❏ AGL1-4088	Christmas with Eugene Ormandy and the Philadelphia Orchestra	1981	$10
— Reissue of RCA Red Seal LSC-3326			

RCA RED SEAL
Number	Title	Yr	NM
❏ LSC-3326	The Greatest Hits of Christmas	1972	$12
❏ ARL1-0257	The Greatest Hits of Christmas, Volume 2	1973	$12

PHILARMONICS, THE
CAPRICORN
Number	Title	Yr	NM
❏ CPN 0179	The Masters in Philadelphia	1977	$30

PHILBIN, REGIS
MERCURY
Number	Title	Yr	NM
❏ SR-61169	It's Time for Regis!	1968	$30

PHILHARMONIA HUNGARICA (ANTAL DORATI, CONDUCTOR)
MERCURY LIVING PRESENCE
Number	Title	Yr	NM
❏ SR90183 [S]	Bartok: Dance Suite; Deux Portraits; Mikrokosmos	196?	$120

Number	Title	Yr	NM
— Maroon label, no "Vendor: Mercury Record Corporation			
❏ SR90208 [S]	Haydn: Symphonies 94 and 103	196?	$40
— Maroon label, no "Vendor: Mercury Record Corporation			
❏ SR90179 [S]	Kodaly: Dances of Galanta; Marosszek Dancves; Bartok-Weiner: Two Romanian Dances	196?	$40
— Maroon label, no "Vendor: Mercury Record Corporation			
❏ SR90199 [S]	Respighi: Ancient Airs and Dances, Suites 1-3	196?	$75
— Maroon label, no "Vendor: Mercury Record Corporation			
❏ SR90199 [S]	Respighi: Ancient Airs and Dances, Suites 1-3	196?	$40
— Maroon label, with "Vendor: Mercury Record Corporation			
❏ SR90199 [S]	Respighi: Ancient Airs and Dances, Suites 1-3	196?	$25
— Third edition: Dark red (not maroon) label			
❏ SR90200 [S]	Tchaikovsky: Serenade in C; Arensky: Tchaikovsky Variations	196?	$100
— Maroon label, no "Vendor: Mercury Record Corporation			
❏ SR90190 [S]	Wienerwalzer Paprika	196?	$25
— Maroon label, no "Vendor: Mercury Record Corporation			

PHILLIPS, BARRE
ECM
Number	Title	Yr	NM
❏ 1149	Barre Phillips II	198?	$30
❏ 1257	Call Me When You Get There	198?	$30
❏ 1076	Mountainscapes	1976	$30
❏ 1011	Music for Two Basses	197?	$35

OPUS ONE
Number	Title	Yr	NM
❏ 2	Journal Violone	197?	$35

PHILLIPS, BILL
DECCA
Number	Title	Yr	NM
❏ DL4897 [M]	Bill Phillips' Style	1967	$30
❏ DL74897 [S]	Bill Phillips' Style	1967	$30
❏ DL75022	Country Action	1968	$25
❏ DL75182	Little Boy Sad	1970	$25
❏ DL4792 [M]	Put It Off Until Tomorrow	1966	$30
❏ DL74792 [S]	Put It Off Until Tomorrow	1966	$40

GUINNESS
Number	Title	Yr	NM
❏ GNS36069 [B]	The Bill Phillips Project	1977	$20

HARMONY
Number	Title	Yr	NM
❏ HL7309 [M]	Bill Phillips' Best	1964	$25

PHILLIPS, ESTHER
ATLANTIC
Number	Title	Yr	NM
❏ 8102 [M]	And I Love Him	1965	$50
— Cover has a pink Cupid on it			
❏ 8102 [M]	And I Love Him	1966	$30
— Cover has a black photo on it			
❏ SD8102 [S]	And I Love Him	1965	$100
— Cover has a pink Cupid on it			
❏ SD8102 [S]	And I Love Him	1966	$40
— Cover has a black photo on it			
❏ SD1565	Burnin'	1970	$75
❏ SD1680	Confessin' the Blues	1975	$35
❏ 90670	Confessin' the Blues	1987	$25
— Reissue of 1680			
❏ 8122 [M]	Esther	1966	$30
❏ SD8122 [S]	Esther	1966	$40
❏ 8130 [M]	The Country Side of Esther Phillips	1966	$30
— Reissue of Lenox 227			
❏ SD8130 [S]	The Country Side of Esther Phillips	1966	$40
— Reissue of Lenox S-227			

CBS ASSOCIATED
Number	Title	Yr	NM
❏ PZ40935	From a Whisper to a Scream	1988	$10
— Reissue of Kudu 05			
❏ PZ40710	What a Diff'rence a Day Makes	1987	$10
— Reissue of Kudu 23			

KING
Number	Title	Yr	NM
❏ 622 [M]	Memory Lane	1959	$4000

KUDU
Number	Title	Yr	NM
❏ 09	Alone Again, Naturally	1972	$15
❏ 14	Black-Eyed Blues	1973	$15
❏ 31	Capricorn Princess	1976	$15
❏ 28	For All We Know	1976	$15
❏ 05	From a Whisper to a Scream	1972	$15
❏ 18	Performance	1974	$15
❏ 23	What a Diff'rence a Day Makes	1975	$15

LENOX
Number	Title	Yr	NM
❏ 227 [M]	Release Me	1962	$150
❏ S-227 [S]	Release Me	1962	$250

MERCURY
Number	Title	Yr	NM
❏ SRM-1-4005	A Good Black Is Hard to Crack	1981	$12
❏ SRM-1-3733	All About Esther Phillips	1978	$12
❏ SRM-1-3769	Here's Esther -- Are You Ready?	1979	$12
❏ SRM-1-1187	You've Come a Long Way, Baby	1977	$12

MUSE
Number	Title	Yr	NM
❏ MR-5302	A Way to Say Goodbye	1986	$30

SAVOY JAZZ
Number	Title	Yr	NM
❏ SJL-2258	The Complete Savoy Recordings	1984	$25

PHILLIPS, FLIP, AND WOODY HERMAN
CENTURY
Number	Title	Yr	NM
❏ 1090	Together	1978	$35

PHILLIPS, FLIP
BRUNSWICK
Number	Title	Yr	NM
❏ BL58032 [10]	Tenor Sax Stylings	1953	$175

CHOICE
Number	Title	Yr	NM
❏ 1013	Phillips' Head	197?	$30

CLEF
Number	Title	Yr	NM
❏ MGC-693 [M]	Flip	1956	$300
❏ MGC-105 [10]	Flip Phillips	1953	$350
❏ MGC-109 [10]	Flip Phillips Collates	1953	$350
❏ MGC-133 [10]	Flip Phillips Collates No. 2	1953	$350
❏ MGC-691 [M]	Flip Wails	1956	$300
❏ MGC-158 [10]	Jumping Moods with Flip Phillips	1954	$350
❏ MGC-740 [M]	Rock with Flip	1956	$300
❏ MGC-692 [M]	Swinging with Flip Phillips and His Orchestra	1956	$300
❏ MGC-634 [M]	The Flip Phillips-Buddy Rich Trio	1954	$300
❏ MGC-637 [M]	The Flip Phillips Quintet	1954	$300

CONCORD JAZZ
Number	Title	Yr	NM
❏ CJ-358	A Real Swinger	1988	$25
❏ CJ-334	A Sound Investment	1988	$25

DOCTOR JAZZ
Number	Title	Yr	NM
❏ FW39419	A Melody from the Sky	198?	$25

MERCURY
Number	Title	Yr	NM
❏ MGC-105 [10]	Flip Phillips	1951	$300
❏ MGC-109 [10]	Flip Phillips Collates	1952	$300
❏ MGC-133 [10]	Flip Phillips Collates No. 2	1953	$0
— Canceled; issued on Clef			
❏ MG-25023 [10]	Flip Phillips Quartet	1950	$300

ONYX
Number	Title	Yr	NM
❏ 214	Flip Phillips in Florida	197?	$30

PROGRESSIVE
Number	Title	Yr	NM
❏ PRO-7063	Flipenstein	198?	$25

SUE
Number	Title	Yr	NM
❏ STLP-1035 [S]	Flip Phillips Revisited	1965	$40
❏ LP-1035 [M]	Flip Phillips Revisited	1965	$30

VERVE
Number	Title	Yr	NM
❏ MGV-8077 [M]	Flip	1957	$175
❏ V-8077 [M]	Flip	1961	$30
❏ MGV-8075 [M]	Flip Wails	1957	$175
❏ V-8075 [M]	Flip Wails	1961	$30
❏ MGV-8116 [M]	Rock with Flip	1957	$100
❏ V-8116 [M]	Rock with Flip	1961	$30
❏ MGV-8076 [M]	Swingin' with Flip	1957	$175
❏ V-8076 [M]	Swingin' with Flip	1961	$30

PHILLIPS, GENE
CROWN
Number	Title	Yr	NM
❏ CLP-5375 [M]	Gene Phillips and the Rockers	1963	$40

PHILLIPS, JOHN
ABC DUNHILL
Number	Title	Yr	NM
❏ DS-50077	John Phillips (John the Wolfking of L.A.)	1970	$18

PHILLIPS, MICHELLE
A&M
Number	Title	Yr	NM
❏ SP-4651	Victim of Romance	1977	$18

PHILLIPS, SHAWN
A&M
Number	Title	Yr	NM
❏ SP-4402	Bright White	1973	$15
❏ SP-4324	Collaboration	1972	$18
❏ SP-4324	Contribution	1970	$18
❏ SP-4539	Do You Wonder	1975	$15
❏ SP-4363	Faces	1972	$15
❏ SP-3135	Faces	198?	$10
— Budget-line reissue			
❏ SP-3662	Furthermore	1974	$15
❏ SP-4582	Rumpelstiltskin's Resolve	1976	$15
❏ SP-4282	Second Contribution	1971	$18
❏ SP-3128	Second Contribution	198?	$10
— Budget-line reissue			
❏ SP-4650	Spaced	1977	$15

CHAMELEON
Number	Title	Yr	NM
❏ D1-74764	Beyond Here Be Dragons	1988	$12

RCA VICTOR
Number	Title	Yr	NM
❏ AFL1-3028	Transcendence	1978	$12
❏ AYL1-3873	Transcendence	1981	$10
— Best Buy Series" reissue			

Number	Title	Yr	NM

PHILLIPS, SONNY
MUSE
❏ MR-5157	I Concentrate on You	1979	$30
❏ MR-5118	My Black Flower	1977	$15

PRESTIGE
❏ PRST-7799	Black Magic	1970	$25
❏ 10007	Black On Black	1971	$25
❏ PRST-7737	Sure 'Nuff	1970	$25

PHILLIPS, STU
CAPITOL
❏ T2356 [M]	Feels Like Lovin'	1965	$30
❏ ST2356 [S]	Feels Like Lovin'	1965	$30

RCA VICTOR
❏ LPM-3717 [M]	Grassroots Country	1967	$30
❏ LSP-3717 [S]	Grassroots Country	1967	$30
❏ LPM-4012 [M]	Our Last Rendezvous	1968	$50
❏ LSP-4012 [S]	Our Last Rendezvous	1968	$30
❏ LPM-3619 [M]	Singin' Stu Phillips	1966	$25
❏ LSP-3619 [S]	Singin' Stu Phillips	1966	$30

PHILLIPS, WARREN, AND THE ROCKETS
PARROT
❏ PAS71044	Rocked Out	1970	$30

PHILLIPS, WOOLF
CORAL
❏ CRL56036 [10]	Woolf Phillips Plays Duke Ellington Songs	1951	$150

PHILOSOPHERS, THE
PHILO
❏ 1001	After Sundown	1969	$175

PHIPPS FAMILY, THE
STARDAY
❏ SLP-248 [M]	Echoes of the Carter Family	1963	$30
❏ SLP-195 [M]	Old Time Pickin' and Singin'	1962	$30
❏ SLP-139 [M]	The Phipps Family Sings the Most Requested Sacred Songs of the Carter Family	1961	$40

PHLUPH
VERVE
❏ V6-5054 [B]	Phluph	1968	$35

PHOENIX SYMPHONY RAGTIME ENSEMBLE
WORLD JAZZ
❏ 12	Phoenix Symphony Ragtime Ensemble	197?	$25

PIAF, EDITH
CAPITOL
❏ T10210 [M]	Piaf	1959	$30
❏ T10348 [M]	Piaf and Sarapo at the Bobido	1963	$18
❏ ST10348 [S]	Piaf and Sarapo at the Bobido	1963	$25
❏ T10368 [M]	Piaf at the Olympia	1964	$18
❏ ST10368 [S]	Piaf at the Olympia	1964	$25
❏ T10283 [M]	Piaf of Paris	1961	$18
❏ ST10283 [S]	Piaf of Paris	1961	$25
❏ T10295 [M]	Potpourri Par Piaf	1962	$18
❏ ST10295 [S]	Potpourri Par Piaf	1962	$25
❏ DTCL2953	The Edith Piaf Deluxe Set	1968	$30

COLUMBIA
❏ CL6223 [10]	Encore Parisiennes	1952	$50
❏ CL898 [M]	La Vie En Rose	1956	$40

DECCA
❏ DL6004 [10]	Chansons de Cafes du Paris	1951	$75

PHILIPS
❏ PCC208 [M]	Adieu, Edith Piaf, Little Sparrow	1964	$25

POLYDOR VOX
❏ PL3050 [10]	Edith Piaf Sings	195?	$100

PIANO CHOIR, THE
STRATA-EAST
❏ SES-19730 [B]	Handscapes	1973	$30
❏ SES-19750	Handscapes 2	1975	$25

PIANO RED
ARHOOLIE
❏ 1064	William Perryman (Alone with Piano)	197?	$30

EUPHONIC
❏ 1212	Percussive Piano	198?	$25

GROOVE
❏ LG-1001 [M]	Jump Man, Jump	1956	$0
—The existence of this LP has not been confirmed			
❏ LG-1002 [M]	Piano Red in Concert	1956	$600

KING
❏ KS-1117	Happiness Is Piano Red	1970	$50

RCA CAMDEN
❏ ACL1-0547	Rockin' with Red	1974	$30

SOUTHLAND
❏ 8	Willie Perryman-Piano Red- Dr. Feelgood	1983	$35

PIANO ROLLS AND VOICES, THE
RCA VICTOR
❏ LSP-4000	All Time Christmas Hits	1968	$18

PIATIGORSKI, GREGOR
RCA VICTOR RED SEAL
❏ LSC-2490 [S]	Dvorak: Cello Concerto	1961	$40
—With Charles Munch/Boston Symphony Orch.; original with "shaded dog" label			
❏ LSC-2490 [S]	Dvorak: Cello Concerto	199?	$30
—With Charles Munch/Boston Symphony Orch.; Classic Records reissue			

PIAZZA, MARGUERITE
HALO
❏ 1009	Joys of Christmas	1977	$12

PICHON, WALTER "FATS
DECCA
❏ DL8390 [M]	Appearing Nightly	1956	$40

PICKARD, SORRELLS
DECCA
❏ DL75338	Sorrells Pickard	1972	$18

PICKETT, BOBBY "BORIS
GARPAX
❏ GPX57001 [M]	The Original Monster Mash	1962	$175
❏ SGP67001 [S]	The Original Monster Mash	1962	$300

PARROT
❏ XPAS71063 [R]	The Original Monster Mash	1973	$30
—Reissue of Garpax LP with four tracks deleted and one added			

PICKETT, WILSON
ATLANTIC
❏ SD8300	Don't Knock My Love	1971	$18
❏ SD8215 [B]	Hey Jude	1969	$30
❏ SD8175 [B]	I'm in Love	1968	$30
❏ 8114 [M]	In the Midnight Hour	1965	$50
❏ SD8114 [R]	In the Midnight Hour	1965	$40
❏ SD8250	Right On	1970	$25
❏ 8151 [M]	The Best of Wilson Pickett	1967	$40
❏ SD8151 [R]	The Best of Wilson Pickett	1967	$30
❏ 81283	The Best of Wilson Pickett	1985	$12
❏ 8290 [M]	The Best of Wilson Pickett, Vol. II	1971	$35
—Mono copies are promo only			
❏ SD8290 [S]	The Best of Wilson Pickett, Vol. II	1971	$18
❏ 8129 [M]	The Exciting Wilson Pickett	1966	$50
❏ SD8129 [R]	The Exciting Wilson Pickett	1966	$40
❏ SD8183 [B]	The Midnight Mover	1968	$30
❏ 8145 [M]	The Sound of Wilson Pickett	1967	$50

THE SOUND OF WILSON PICKETT

❏ SD8145 [P]	The Sound of Wilson Pickett	1967	$50
❏ 8136 [M]	The Wicked Pickett	1967	$50
❏ SD8136 [R]	The Wicked Pickett	1967	$40
❏ SD8270	Wilson Pickett in Philadelphia	1970	$25
❏ SD 2-501	Wilson Pickett's Greatest Hits	1973	$25

BIG TREE
❏ SD76011	Funky Situation	1978	$15

DOUBLE-L
❏ DL-2300 [M]	It's Too Late	1963	$50
❏ SDL-8300 [S]	It's Too Late	1963	$80

EMI AMERICA
❏ SW-17019	I Want You	1979	$15
❏ SW-17043	Right Track	1981	$15

MOTOWN
❏ 6244ML	American Soul Man	1987	$12

RCA VICTOR
❏ ANL1-2149	Join Me and Let's Be Free	1977	$12
—Reissue			
❏ APL1-0856	Join Me and Let's Be Free	1975	$18
❏ APL1-0312	Miz Lena's Boy	1973	$18
❏ LSP-4858	Mr. Magic Man	1973	$18
❏ APL1-0495	Pickett in the Pocket	1974	$18

TRIP
❏ 8010	Wickedness	1972	$12

UPFRONT
❏ UPF-127 [S]	It's Too Late	197?	$12

WAND
❏ WD-672 [M]	Great Wilson Pickett Hits	1966	$30
❏ WDS-672 [R]	Great Wilson Pickett Hits	1966	$25

WICKED
❏ 9001	Chocolate Mountain	1976	$30

PIECES OF A DREAM
ELEKTRA
❏ 60270	Imagine This	1984	$25
❏ 6E-350	Pieces of a Dream	1981	$25
❏ 60142	We Are One	1982	$25

MANHATTAN
❏ ST-53023	Joyride	1986	$25

PIERANUNZI, ENRICO, AND ART FARMER
SOUL NOTE
❏ SN-1021	Isis	198?	$30

PIERANUNZI, ENRICO
SOUL NOTE
❏ 121221	No Man's Land	1990	$35

PIERCE, BILLIE AND DEDE
ARHOOLIE
❏ 2016	New Orleans Music	197?	$25

BIOGRAPH
❏ CEN-15	Billie and Dede Pierce at Luthjen's	197?	$25

JAZZOLOGY
❏ JCE-25	New Orleans Legends Live, Vol. 15	196?	$35

RIVERSIDE
❏ RLP-394 [M]	Blues and Tonks From the Delta	1961	$250
❏ RS-9394 [R]	Blues and Tonks From the Delta	1961	$250
❏ RLP-370 [M]	Blues in the Classic Tradition	1961	$250
❏ RS-9370 [R]	Blues in the Classic Tradition	1961	$250

PIERCE, BILLY
SUNNYSIDE
❏ SSC-1026	Give and Take	1988	$25
❏ SSC-1013	William the Conqueror	1986	$25

PIERCE, BOBBY
COBBLESTONE
❏ 9016	Introducing Bobby Pierce	197?	$35

MUSE
❏ MR-5030	New York	1974	$30
❏ MR-5304	Piercing	198?	$25

PIERCE, DEDE
BIOGRAPH
❏ CEN-5	Dede Pierce and the New Orleans Stompers	197?	$25

PIERCE, NAT; DICK COLLINS; CHARLIE MARIANO
FANTASY
❏ OJC-118	Nat Pierce-Dick Collins Nonet/Charlie Mariano Sextet	198?	$25
❏ 3224 [M]	Nat Pierce-Dick Collins Nonet/Charlie Mariano Sextet	1956	$120
—Red vinyl			
❏ 3224 [M]	Nat Pierce-Dick Collins Nonet/Charlie Mariano Sextet	195?	$75
—Black vinyl			

PIERCE, NAT; MILT HINTON; BARRY GALBRAITH; OSIE JOHNSON
MUSIC MINUS ONE
❏ Vol.1 [M]	Nat Pierce and Milt Hinton and Barry Galbraith and Osie Johnson	1956	$30
—With sheet music attached			

Number	Title	Yr	NM

PIERCE, NAT
CORAL
| ❏ CRL57128 [M] | Chamber Music for Moderns | 1957 | $50 |
| ❏ CRL57091 [M] | Kansas City Memories | 1957 | $50 |
FANTASY
| ❏ 3-14 [10] | Nat Pierce and the Herdsmen Featuring Dick Collins | 1954 | $100 |
—Red vinyl
| ❏ 3-14 [10] | Nat Pierce and the Herdsmen Featuring Dick Collins | 1954 | $100 |
—Blue vinyl
KEYNOTE
| ❏ LP-1101 [M] | Nat Pierce Octet and Tentette | 1955 | $100 |
RCA VICTOR
| ❏ LPM-2543 [M] | Big Band at the Savoy Ballroom | 1962 | $30 |
| ❏ LSP-2543 [S] | Big Band at the Savoy Ballroom | 1962 | $30 |
VANGUARD
| ❏ VRS-8017 [10] | Nat Pierce Bandstand | 1955 | $120 |
ZIM
| ❏ 2003 | Ballad of Jazz Street | 198? | $25 |
| ❏ 1005 | Nat Pierce and His Orchestra | 197? | $30 |

PIERCE, WEBB; MARVIN RAINWATER; STUART HAMBLEN
AUDIO LAB
| ❏ AL-1563 [M] | Sing for You | 1960 | $250 |

PIERCE, WEBB
DECCA
| ❏ DL8889 [M] | Bound for the Kingdom | 1959 | $40 |
—Black label, silver print
| ❏ DL8889 [M] | Bound for the Kingdom | 196? | $30 |
—Black label with color bar
| ❏ DL78889 [S] | Bound for the Kingdom | 1959 | $50 |
—Black label, silver print
| ❏ DL78889 [S] | Bound for the Kingdom | 196? | $30 |
—Black label with color bar
❏ DL4384 [M]	Bow Thy Head	1963	$30
❏ DL74384 [S]	Bow Thy Head	1963	$30
❏ DL4659 [M]	Country Music Time	1965	$30
❏ DL74659 [S]	Country Music Time	1965	$30
❏ DL4294 [M]	Cross Country	1962	$30
❏ DL74294 [S]	Cross Country	1962	$40
❏ DL4144 [M]	Fallen Angel	1961	$30
❏ DL74144 [S]	Fallen Angel	1961	$40
❏ DL4964 [M]	Fool, Fool, Fool	1968	$50
❏ DL74964 [S]	Fool, Fool, Fool	1968	$30
❏ DL4110 [M]	Golden Favorites	1961	$30
❏ DL74110 [S]	Golden Favorites	1961	$40
❏ DL4218 [M]	Hideaway Heart	1962	$30
❏ DL74218 [S]	Hideaway Heart	1962	$40
❏ DL75393	I'm Gonna Be a Swinger	1972	$25
❏ DL4358 [M]	I've Got a New Heartache	1963	$30
❏ DL74358 [S]	I've Got a New Heartache	1963	$30
❏ DL8728 [M]	Just Imagination	1957	$50
—Black label, silver print
| ❏ DL8728 [M] | Just Imagination | 196? | $30 |
—Black label with color bar
❏ DL75168	Love Ain't Never Gonna Be No Better	1970	$30
❏ DL4604 [M]	Memory #1	1965	$30
❏ DL74604 [S]	Memory #1	1965	$30
❏ DL75210	Merry-Go-Round World	1970	$25
❏ DL4486 [M]	Sands of Gold	1964	$30
❏ DL74486 [S]	Sands of Gold	1964	$30
❏ DL75071	Saturday Night	1969	$30
❏ DL4739 [M]	Sweet Memories	1966	$30

| ❏ DL74739 [S] | Sweet Memories | 1966 | $30 |
| ❏ DL5536 [10] | That Wondering Boy | 1954 | $120 |

Number	Title	Yr	NM

| ❏ DL8295 [M] | That Wondering Boy | 1956 | $75 |
—Black label, silver print
| ❏ DL8295 [M] | That Wondering Boy | 196? | $30 |
—Black label with color bar
| ❏ DL75280 | The Webb Pierce Road Show | 1971 | $25 |
| ❏ DXB181 [M] | The Webb Pierce Story | 1964 | $30 |
—Deduct 25% if booklet is missing
| ❏ DXSB7181 [S] | The Webb Pierce Story | 1964 | $40 |
—Deduct 25% if booklet is missing
❏ DL4079 [M]	Walking the Streets	1960	$30
❏ DL74079 [S]	Walking the Streets	1960	$40
❏ DL8899 [M]	Webb!	1959	$40
—Black label, silver print
| ❏ DL78899 [S] | Webb! | 1959 | $50 |
—Black label, silver print
| ❏ DL8899 [M] | Webb! | 196? | $30 |
—Black label with color bar
| ❏ DL78899 [M] | Webb! | 196? | $30 |
—Black label with color bar
| ❏ DL8129 [M] | Webb Pierce | 1955 | $75 |
—Black label, silver print
| ❏ DL8129 [M] | Webb Pierce | 196? | $30 |
—Black label with color bar
❏ DL74999	Webb Pierce's Greatest Hits	1968	$30
❏ DL75132	Webb Pierce Sings This Thing	1969	$30
❏ DL4782 [M]	Webb's Choice	1966	$30
❏ DL74782 [S]	Webb's Choice	1966	$30
❏ DL4015 [M]	Webb with a Beat	1960	$30
❏ DL74015 [S]	Webb with a Beat	1960	$40
❏ DL4844 [M]	Where'd Ya Stay Last Night	1967	$30
❏ DL74844 [S]	Where'd Ya Stay Last Night	1967	$30
KING
| ❏ 648 [M] | The One and Only Webb Pierce | 1959 | $80 |
MCA
| ❏ 130 | Greatest Hits | 1973 | $15 |
| ❏ 513 | I'm Gonna Be a Swinger | 197? | $15 |
—Reissue of Decca 75393
| ❏ 4087 | The Best of Webb Pierce | 1974 | $18 |
VOCALION
| ❏ VL73911 | Country Favorites | 1970 | $18 |
| ❏ VL73830 | Country Songs | 1968 | $15 |

PIKE, DAVE
ATLANTIC
| ❏ 1457 [M] | Jazz for the Jet Set | 1966 | $75 |
| ❏ SD1457 [S] | Jazz for the Jet Set | 1966 | $25 |
BASF
❏ 20739	Infra-Red	1972	$35
❏ 25112	Riff for Rent	1973	$25
❏ 21541	Salamao	1974	$35
COLUMBIA JAZZ ODYSSEY
| ❏ PC37011 | Pike's Peak | 1981 | $25 |
—Reissue of Epic 17025
DECCA
| ❏ DL4568 [M] | Manhattan Latin | 1965 | $35 |
| ❏ DL74568 [S] | Manhattan Latin | 1965 | $25 |
EPIC
| ❏ LA-16025 [M] | Pike's Peak | 1962 | $75 |
| ❏ BA-17025 [S] | Pike's Peak | 1962 | $75 |
MOODSVILLE
| ❏ MVLP-36 [M] | Dave Pike Plays the Jazz Version of "Oliver | 1963 | $50 |
—Green label
| ❏ MVLP-36 [M] | Dave Pike Plays the Jazz Version of "Oliver | 1965 | $30 |
—Blue label, trident logo at right
MUSE
❏ MR-5203	Let the Minstrels Play On	1980	$25
❏ MR-5261	Moon Bird	198?	$25
❏ MR-5092	Times Out of Mind	197?	$30
NEW JAZZ
| ❏ NJLP-8281 [M] | Bossa Nova Carnival | 1962 | $175 |
—Purple label
| ❏ NJLP-8281 [M] | Bossa Nova Carnival | 1965 | $175 |
—Blue label, trident logo at right
| ❏ NJLP-8284 [M] | Limbo Carnival | 1962 | $175 |
—Purple label
| ❏ NJLP-8284 [M] | Limbo Carnival | 1965 | $175 |
—Blue label, trident logo at right
RIVERSIDE
| ❏ RLP-360 [M] | It's Time for David Pike | 1961 | $250 |
| ❏ RS-9360 [S] | It's Time for David Pike | 1961 | $250 |
TIMELESS
| ❏ LPSJP-302 | Bluebird | 1990 | $30 |
VORTEX
| ❏ 2007 | The Doors of Perception | 1970 | $25 |

PIKE, PETE
AUDIO LAB
| ❏ AL-1559 [M] | Pete Pike | 1960 | $150 |

Number	Title	Yr	NM

PILHOFER, HERB
ARGO
| ❏ LP-657 [M] | Jazz | 1960 | $30 |
| ❏ LPS-657 [S] | Jazz | 1960 | $30 |
SOUND 80
| ❏ DLR103 | Spaces | 198? | $30 |
ZEPHYR
| ❏ ZP-12103-G [M] | Dick and Don Maw Present the Herb Pilhofer Octet -- Jazz from the North Coast, Volume 2 | 1959 | $75 |

PILLOW, RAY
ABC
| ❏ ABCS-665 | Ray Pillow Sings | 1968 | $18 |
ABC DOT
| ❏ DOSD-2013 | Countryfied | 1975 | $15 |
CAPITOL
❏ T2738 [M]	Even When It's Bad, It's Good!	1967	$25
❏ ST2738 [S]	Even When It's Bad, It's Good!	1967	$18
❏ T2417 [M]	Presenting Ray Pillow	1965	$18
❏ ST2417 [S]	Presenting Ray Pillow	1965	$25
HILLTOP
| ❏ JS-6164 | Wonderful Day | 197? | $15 |
MEGA
| ❏ 1017 | Slippin' Around with Ray Pillow | 1972 | $18 |
PLANTATION
| ❏ PLP-6 | People Music | 1970 | $18 |

PILOT (1)
EMI
| ❏ ST-11488 | January | 1976 | $12 |
| ❏ ST-11368 | Pilot | 1975 | $12 |

PILOT (2)
RCA VICTOR
| ❏ LSP-4730 | Pilot | 1972 | $15 |
| ❏ LSP-4825 | Point of View | 1973 | $25 |

PILTZECKER, TED
SEA BREEZE
| ❏ SB-2027 | Destinations | 1986 | $25 |

PINDER, MICHAEL
THRESHOLD
| ❏ THS18 | The Promise | 1976 | $15 |

PINE, COURTNEY
ANTILLES
❏ 510769-1	Closer to Home	1992	$50
❏ 90697	Destiny's Song + The Image of Pursuance	1987	$30
❏ 8700	Journey to the Urge Within	1986	$35
❏ 91334	The Vision's Tale	1989	$30

PINERA, MIKE
CAPRICORN
| ❏ CPN 0202 [B] | Isla | 1978 | $18 |
SPECTOR
| ❏ 00001 [B] | Forever, Mike Pinera | 1979 | $18 |

PINETOPPERS, THE
CORAL
| ❏ CRL56200 [10] | Square Dances | 195? | $40 |
| ❏ CRL57048 [M] | The Pinetoppers | 195? | $30 |
DECCA
| ❏ DL8348 [M] | Saturday Night Barn Dance | 1956 | $30 |

PINK FLOYD
Also see SYD BARRETT; ROGER WATERS; RICHARD WRIGHT.
CAPITOL
| ❏ SN-16337 | Atom Heart Mother | 1985 | $12 |
—Budget-line reissue
| ❏ SN-16230 [B] | More | 1982 | $15 |
—Budget-line reissue
| ❏ SN-16330 | Obscured by Clouds | 1985 | $12 |
—Budget-line reissue
| ❏ SPRO-8116/7 [DJ] | Pink Floyd Tour '75 | 1975 | $120 |
| ❏ SN-16234 [B] | Relics | 1982 | $18 |
—Budget-line reissue
| ❏ SEAX-11902 [PD] | The Dark Side of the Moon | 1978 | $80 |
| ❏ ST-12276 [M] | Works | 1983 | $25 |
COLUMBIA
| ❏ TC37680 [B] | A Collection of Great Dance Songs | 1981 | $25 |
| ❏ HC47680 | A Collection of Great Dance Songs | 1982 | $50 |
—Half-speed mastered edition

Number	Title	Yr	NM
❏ PC37680	A Collection of Great Dance Songs	198?	$10

—Budget-line reissue

Number	Title	Yr	NM
❏ OC40599	A Momentary Lapse of Reason	1987	$12
❏ AP-1 [DJ]	Animals	1977	$175

—White cover, with the song "Pigs" edited for airplay

Number	Title	Yr	NM
❏ JC34474 [DJ]	Animals	1977	$150

—Demonstration Not for Sale" on label; also has insert

Number	Title	Yr	NM
❏ JC34474 [B]	Animals	1977	$45
❏ PFRLP02 [B]	A Saucerful of Secrets	2016	$25
❏ PC244484 [B]	Delicate Sound of Thunder	1988	$30
❏ PFRLP3 [B]	Music From The Film More	2016	$25
❏ AS736 [DJ]	Off the Wall	1979	$175

—Sampler from 2-LP set

Number	Title	Yr	NM
❏ C64200	The Division Bell	1994	$150

—U.S. pressings on blue vinyl

Number	Title	Yr	NM
❏ QC38243	The Final Cut	1983	$12
❏ AS1636 [DJ]	The Final Cut	1983	$30

—White label, record banded for airplay

Number	Title	Yr	NM
❏ 88875184181 [B]	The Piper At The Gates Of Dawn	2016	$25

—180g

Number	Title	Yr	NM
❏ PC236183 [B]	The Wall	1979	$30
❏ HC246183	The Wall	1983	$300

—Half-speed mastered edition

Number	Title	Yr	NM
❏ PFRLP4 [B]	Ummagumma	2016	$40

—180g

Number	Title	Yr	NM
❏ PC33453 [B]	Wish You Were Here	1975	$25

—Standard copy (no blue wraparound) without bar code

Number	Title	Yr	NM
❏ PC33453 [DJ]	Wish You Were Here	1975	$300

—Blue cover with photo and title on jacket; unbanded record

Number	Title	Yr	NM
❏ PC33453 [B]	Wish You Were Here	1975	$35

—Original copies had a blue wraparound with title/artist sticker. Most buyers threw this out upon opening the LP!

Number	Title	Yr	NM
❏ PCQ33453 [Q]	Wish You Were Here	1975	$300
❏ HC33453 [B]	Wish You Were Here	1981	$100

—Half-speed mastered edition (original)

Number	Title	Yr	NM
❏ HC43453 [B]	Wish You Were Here	1982	$50

—Half-speed mastered edition (reissue)

Number	Title	Yr	NM
❏ PC33453 [DJ]	Wish You Were Here	1975	$300

—White cover, "Special DJ Copy"; banded for airplay

EMI

Number	Title	Yr	NM
❏ 32700	Pulse	1995	$150

—Pressed in U.K. for U.S. release; box set with 12x12 hardback book; identical to British pressings except for American bar code (67065) on shrink wrap

HARVEST

Number	Title	Yr	NM
❏ SABB-11257 [B]	A Nice Pair	1973	$40

—sleeve censors breasts and replaces Phang dental surgery with a gargling monk

Number	Title	Yr	NM
❏ SABB-11257 [B]	A Nice Pair	1973	$35

—original sleeve shows uncensored breasts and WR Phang dental surgery

Number	Title	Yr	NM
❏ SKAO-382 [B]	Atom Heart Mother	1970	$45

—Without title on front cover

Number	Title	Yr	NM
❏ SKAO-382	Atom Heart Mother	197?	$18

—With title on front cover

Number	Title	Yr	NM
❏ SMAS-832	Meddle	1971	$18
❏ ST-11198	More	1973	$15

—Reissue of Tower 5169

Number	Title	Yr	NM
❏ ST-11078 [B]	Obscured by Clouds	1972	$30
❏ SW-759 [B]	Relics	1971	$40
❏ SMAS-11163 [B]	The Dark Side of the Moon	1973	$35

—With poster and two stickers

Number	Title	Yr	NM
❏ SMAS-11163 [B]	The Dark Side of the Moon	1973	$25

—With no inserts

Number	Title	Yr	NM
❏ SKBB-388 [B]	Ummagumma	1969	$75

—With the soundtrack LP from "Gigi" leaning against wall on front cover

Number	Title	Yr	NM
❏ SKBB-388	Ummagumma	1970	$25

—With white LP cover leaning against wall on front cover

MOBILE FIDELITY

Number	Title	Yr	NM
❏ 1-202 [B]	Atom Heart Mother	1994	$85

—Audiophile vinyl

Number	Title	Yr	NM
❏ 1-190 [B]	Meddle	1987	$300

—Audiophile vinyl

Number	Title	Yr	NM
❏ Jan-0017 [B]	The Dark Side of the Moon	1980	$175

—Audiophile vinyl

Number	Title	Yr	NM
❏ MFQR-017	The Dark Side of the Moon	1982	$500

—Audiophile vinyl; "Ultra High Quality Recording" in box

TOWER

Number	Title	Yr	NM
❏ ST5131	A Saucerful of Secrets	1968	$100

—Orange label

Number	Title	Yr	NM
❏ ST5131	A Saucerful of Secrets	1968	$40

—Multi-color striped label

Number	Title	Yr	NM
❏ ST5169	More	1968	$50
❏ T5093 [M]	Pink Floyd (The Piper at the Gates of Dawn)	1967	$450
❏ ST5093 [S]	Pink Floyd (The Piper at the Gates of Dawn)	1967	$100

—Orange label

Number	Title	Yr	NM
❏ ST5093 [S]	Pink Floyd (The Piper at the Gates of Dawn)	1968	$60

—Multi-color striped label

PINKARD AND BOWDEN

WARNER BROS.

Number	Title	Yr	NM
❏ 25299	PG-13	1985	$10
❏ 25057	Writers in Disguise	1984	$10

PIPER, WARDELL

MIDSONG INT'L.

Number	Title	Yr	NM
❏ MSI-009	Wardell Piper	1979	$15

PIPKINS, THE

CAPITOL

Number	Title	Yr	NM
❏ ST-483	Gimme Dat Ding	1970	$30

PIRANHAS, THE

CUSTOM FIDELITY

Number	Title	Yr	NM
❏ 1452	Somethin' Fishy	1969	$175

PIRCHNER, WERNER; HARRY PEPI; JACK DEJOHNETTE

ECM

Number	Title	Yr	NM
❏ 1237	Trio Recordings	1985	$30

PIROUETTE ORCHESTRA AND CHORUS, THE

PIROUETTE

Number	Title	Yr	NM
❏ XFM-58	Christmas Sing Along	195?	$18

PISANO, JOHNNY, AND BILLY BEAN

DECCA

Number	Title	Yr	NM
❏ DL9206 [M]	Makin' It	1958	$150
❏ DL79206 [S]	Makin' It	1958	$150
❏ DL9219 [S]	Take Your Pick	1958	$150
❏ DL79219 [S]	Take Your Pick	1958	$150

PISTORIOUS, STEVE

JAZZOLOGY

Number	Title	Yr	NM
❏ J-78	Classic Piano Rags	197?	$25

PITNEY, GENE, AND GEORGE JONES

MUSICOR

Number	Title	Yr	NM
❏ MM-2044 [M]	For the First Time! Two Great Singers Together: George Jones and Gene Pitney	1965	$30
❏ MS-3044 [S]	For the First Time! Two Great Singers Together: George Jones and Gene Pitney	1965	$30
❏ MM-2065 [M]	It's Country Time Again	1965	$30
❏ MS-3065 [S]	It's Country Time Again	1965	$30

PITNEY, GENE, AND MELBA MONTGOMERY

MUSICOR

Number	Title	Yr	NM
❏ MM-2077 [M]	Being Together	1966	$30
❏ MS-3077 [S]	Being Together	1966	$30

PITNEY, GENE

MUSIC DISC

Number	Title	Yr	NM
❏ MDS1006	America's Greatest Country Songs	1969	$15
❏ MDS1014	Baby, I Need Your Lovin'	1969	$15
❏ MDS1003	The Man Who Shot Liberty Valance	1969	$15
❏ MDS1005	Town Without Pity	1969	$15
❏ MDS1008	Twenty Four Hours from Tulsa	1969	$15

MUSICOR

Number	Title	Yr	NM
❏ MM-2095 [M]	Backstage I'm Lonely	1966	$25
❏ MS-3095 [S]	Backstage I'm Lonely	1966	$30
❏ MM-2085 [M]	Big Sixteen, Vol. 3	1966	$25
❏ MS-3085 [S]	Big Sixteen, Vol. 3	1966	$30
❏ MM-2006 [M]	Blue Gene	1963	$30
❏ MS-3006 [S]	Blue Gene	1963	$40
❏ MM-2015 [M]	Gene Italiano	1964	$30

Number	Title	Yr	NM
❏ MS-3015 [S]	Gene Italiano	1964	$30
❏ MM-2072 [M]	Gene Pitney En Espanol	1965	$30
❏ MS-3072 [S]	Gene Pitney En Espanol	1965	$30
❏ MM-2007 [M]	Gene Pitney Meets the Fair Young Ladies of Folkland	1964	$30
❏ MS-3007 [S]	Gene Pitney Meets the Fair Young Ladies of Folkland	1964	$40
❏ MM-2008 [M]	Gene Pitney's Big Sixteen	1964	$30
❏ MS-3008 [S]	Gene Pitney's Big Sixteen	1964	$40
❏ MS-3161	Gene Pitney Sings Burt Bacharach	1968	$25
❏ MM-2004 [M]	Gene Pitney Sings Just for You	1963	$30
❏ MS-3004 [S]	Gene Pitney Sings Just for You	1963	$40
❏ MS-3183	Gene Pitney Sings the Platters' Golden Platters	1970	$18
❏ MM-2043 [M]	Gene Pitney's More Big Sixteen	1965	$30
❏ MS-3043 [P]	Gene Pitney's More Big Sixteen	1965	$30
❏ MS-3193	Gene Pitney Super Star	1971	$18
❏ MM-2134 [M]	Golden Greats	1967	$30
❏ MS-3134 [S]	Golden Greats	1967	$25
❏ MS-3233	Golden Hour	1972	$18
❏ MM-2102 [M]	Greatest Hits of All Times	1966	$25
❏ MS-3102 [P]	Greatest Hits of All Times	1966	$30
❏ MM-2056 [M]	I Must Be Seeing Things	1965	$30
❏ MS-3056 [S]	I Must Be Seeing Things	1965	$30
❏ MM-2019 [M]	It Hurts to Be in Love	1964	$30
❏ MS-3019 [P]	It Hurts to Be in Love	1964	$30
❏ MM-2117 [M]	Just One Smile	1967	$25
❏ MS-3117 [S]	Just One Smile	1967	$30
❏ MM-2069 [M]	Looking Through the Eyes of Love	1965	$30
❏ MS-3069 [S]	Looking Through the Eyes of Love	1965	$30
❏ MM-2100 [M]	Messumo Mi Puo Giudicare	1966	$25
❏ MS-3100 [S]	Messumo Mi Puo Giudicare	1966	$30
❏ MM-2003 [M]	Only Love Can Break a Heart	1962	$40

—Brown label

Number	Title	Yr	NM
❏ MM-2003 [M]	Only Love Can Break a Heart	1963	$30

—Black label

Number	Title	Yr	NM
❏ MS-3003 [S]	Only Love Can Break a Heart	1962	$50

—Brown label

Number	Title	Yr	NM
❏ MS-3003 [S]	Only Love Can Break a Heart	1963	$30

—Black label

Number	Title	Yr	NM
❏ MS-3164	She's a Heartbreaker	1968	$25
❏ MS-3206	Ten Years After	1971	$18
❏ MUX-4600	The Best of Gene Pitney (Double Gold Series)	1977	$18
❏ MM-2104 [M]	The Country Side of Gene Pitney	1967	$25
❏ MS-3104 [S]	The Country Side of Gene Pitney	1967	$30
❏ MM-2101 [M]	The Gene Pitney Show	1966	$25
❏ MS-3101 [S]	The Gene Pitney Show	1966	$30
❏ M2S-3148 [S]	The Gene Pitney Story	1968	$30

—Add 40% if bonus photo is enclosed

Number	Title	Yr	NM
❏ M2-3148 [M]	The Gene Pitney Story	1968	$40

—Mono is promo only

Number	Title	Yr	NM
❏ MS-3174	The Greatest Hits of Gene Pitney	1969	$25
❏ MM-2001 [M]	The Many Sides of Gene Pitney	1962	$50

—Brown label

Number	Title	Yr	NM
❏ MM-2001 [M]	The Many Sides of Gene Pitney	1963	$30

—Black label

Number	Title	Yr	NM
❏ MS-3001 [R]	The Many Sides of Gene Pitney	1962	$30

—Brown label

Number	Title	Yr	NM
❏ MS-3001 [R]	The Many Sides of Gene Pitney	1963	$25

—Black label

Number	Title	Yr	NM
❏ MM-2005 [M]	World-Wide Winners	1963	$30
❏ MS-3005 [P]	World-Wide Winners	1963	$40
❏ MM-2108 [M]	Young and Warm and Wonderful	1967	$25
❏ MS-3108 [S]	Young and Warm and Wonderful	1967	$30

RHINO

Number	Title	Yr	NM
❏ RNDA-1102	Anthology (1961-1968)	1984	$15

SPRINGBOARD

Number	Title	Yr	NM
❏ SPB-4057	Gene Pitney	1975	$12

PIXIES

Features Frank Black, now a prolific solo artist.

4AD

Number	Title	Yr	NM
❏ 70010 [B]	Bossanova	2008	$18
❏ CAD3425 [B]	Doolittle 25	2015	$40
❏ 71014	Trompe La Monde	2008	$18

ELEKTRA

Number	Title	Yr	NM
❏ 60963	Bossanova	1990	$18
❏ 60856	Doolittle	1989	$25
❏ 60856 [DJ]	Doolittle	1989	$15

—Promo-only on audiophile vinyl

Number	Title	Yr	NM
❏ PR-8127 [DJ]	Live	1989	$75

—Promo-only seven-song live collection of mostly songs from their pre-Elektra days

Number	Title	Yr	NM
ROUGH TRADE			
❏ ROUGH US38	Surfer Rosa	1988	$25
PIXIES THREE, THE			
MERCURY			
❏ MG-20912 [M]	Party with the Pixies Three	1964	$175
❏ SR-60912 [S]	Party with the Pixies Three	1964	$250
PIZZARELLI, BUCKY, AND BUD FREEMAN			
FLYING DUTCHMAN			
❏ BDL1-1378	Buck & Bud	1976	$30
PIZZARELLI, BUCKY, AND VINNIE BURKE			
SAVOY			
❏ MG-12158 [M]	Music Minus Many Men	1960	$30
PIZZARELLI, BUCKY			
FLYING DUTCHMAN			
❏ BDL1-1120	Nightwings	1975	$30
MONMOUTH-EVERGREEN			
❏ 7066	Bucky Pizzarelli Plays Beiderbecke, Challis, Kress	197?	$35
❏ 7093	Bucky Pizzarelli with the Care Pierre Trio	197?	$30
❏ 7082	Bucky's Bunch	197?	$30
❏ 7047	Green Guitar Blues	197?	$35
STASH			
❏ ST-213	Love Songs	198?	$25
❏ ST-263	Solo Flight	1987	$25
PIZZARELLI, BUCKY AND JOHN JR.			
STASH			
❏ ST-207	2 x 7 = Pizzarelli	1980	$30
❏ ST-239	Swinging Sevens	198?	$25
PIZZARELLI, JOHN JR.			
STASH			
❏ ST-256	Hit That Jive, Jack!	1985	$25
❏ ST-226	I'm Hip	1983	$25
❏ ST-267	Sing! Sing! Sing!	1987	$25
PIZZI, RAY			
DISCOVERY			
❏ 853	Espressivo	1982	$25
❏ 801	The Love Letter	1980	$25
PABLO			
❏ 2310795	Conception	197?	$30
PLACE, MARY KAY			
COLUMBIA			
❏ PC34908	Aimin' to Please	1977	$12
❏ KC34353	Tonite! At the Capri Lounge Loretta Haggers	1976	$12
PLAIN JANE			
HOBBIT			
❏ 5000	Plain Jane	1969	$30
PLANET, JANET			
SEA BREEZE			
❏ SB-2026	Sweet Thunder	1986	$30
PLANET P			
Features Tony Carey of RAINBOW and solo fame.			
GEFFEN			
❏ GHS4000	Planet P	1983	$15
MCA			
❏ 8019	Pink World	1984	$25
— As "Planet P Project			
❏ L33-1227 [EP]	Pink World	1984	$15
— Promo-only pink vinyl EP			
PLANET PATROL			
TOMMY BOY			
❏ TBLP-1002	Planet Patrol	1983	$40
— Originals on purple vinyl			
❏ TBLP-1002	Planet Patrol	1983	$18
— Black vinyl			
PLANT, ROBERT			
Also see THE HONEYDRIPPERS; LED ZEPPELIN. (SC2)			
ES PARANZA			
❏ 90485 [EP]	Little by Little Collector's Edition	1985	$10
❏ 91336	Manic Nirvana	1990	$18
❏ PR2244 [DJ]	Non-Stop Go	1988	$30
— Promo-only interview album			
❏ 90863	Now and Zen	1988	$10
❏ 90265	Shaken 'n' Stirred	1985	$10
❏ 90101	The Principle of Moments	1983	$10
SWAN SONG			
❏ SS8512	Pictures at Eleven	1982	$12

Number	Title	Yr	NM
PLANT & SEE			
WHITE WHALE			
❏ WWS-7120	Plant & See	1969	$30
PLASMATICS			
CAPITOL			
❏ ST-12237	Coup d'Etat	1982	$18
PVC			
❏ 8929	Beyond the Valley of 1984	1983	$18
— Reissue of Stiff USE-11			
❏ 6908	Metal Priestess	1983	$18
— Reissue of Stiff WOW-666			
STIFF			
❏ USE-11	Beyond the Valley of 1984	1981	$40
❏ WOW-666 [EP]	Metal Priestess	1981	$35
❏ USE-9	New Hope for the Wretched	1980	$30
VICE SQUAD			
❏ VS105/106 [EP]	Meet the Plasmatics	1979	$100
PLASTER CASTERS, THE			
BLUESTIME			
❏ BTS-9001 [B]	The Plaster Casters Blues Band	1969	$75
PLASTIC BERTRAND			
SIRE			
❏ SRK6061	Plastic Bertrand	1978	$25
PLASTIC COW, THE			
DOT			
❏ DLP25961 [B]	The Plastic Cow Goes Moooooog	1969	$30
PLASTIC ONO BAND			
See JOHN LENNON; YOKO ONO.			
PLATINUM BLONDE			
EPIC			
❏ BFE40147	Alien Shores	1985	$12
❏ BFE40949	Contact	1987	$12
PLATTERS, THE			
More than one group has used this name over the years, but all are related. Also see TONY WILLIAMS.			
CANDELITE MUSIC			
❏ CMI1000	The 50 Golden Hits of the Platters	197?	$40
COLUMBIA SPECIAL PRODUCTS			
❏ P11834 [S]	Christmas with the Platters	1973	$18
— Reissue of Mercury SR-60841 with fewer tracks			
FEDERAL			
❏ 549 [M]	The Platters	1957	$1600
— Records on Federal 651 are bootlegs from the 1970s			
KING			
❏ 5002	19 Hits of the Platters	197?	$15
❏ 651 [M]	The Platters	1959	$800
— Records on Federal 651 are bootlegs from the 1970s			
❏ KLP-651 [M]	The Platters	1987	$12
— Reissue with "Highland Records" on label			
MERCURY			
❏ MG-20933 [M]	10th Anniversary Album	1964	$25
❏ SR-60933 [S]	10th Anniversary Album	1964	$30
❏ MG-20841 [M]	Christmas with the Platters	1963	$30
❏ SR-60841 [S]	Christmas with the Platters	1963	$40
— Same as above, but in stereo			
❏ MG-20613 [M]	Encore of Broadway Golden Hits	1961	$25
❏ SR-60613 [S]	Encore of Broadway Golden Hits	1961	$30
❏ MG-20472 [M]	Encore of Golden Hits	1960	$30
❏ SR-60243 [P]	Encore of Golden Hits	1960	$40
— Original: Black label, silver print; 12 songs on LP			
❏ 828254-1	Encore of Golden Hits	198?	$10
— Reissue			
❏ SR-60243 [P]	Encore of Golden Hits	1965	$30
— Second edition: Red label, "MERCURY" in white across top; may or may not have "Gold Record Award" insignia on back cover; 12 songs on LP			
❏ SR-60243 [P]	Encore of Golden Hits	1975	$15
— Chicago skyline label; album has 10 songs			
❏ MG-20893 [M]	Encore of Golden Hits of the Groups	1964	$25
❏ SR-60893 [S]	Encore of Golden Hits of the Groups	1964	$30
❏ MG-20589 [M]	Life Is Just a Bowl of Cherries	1960	$30
❏ SR-60245 [S]	Life Is Just a Bowl of Cherries	1960	$30
❏ MG-20759 [M]	Moonlight Memories	1963	$25
❏ SR-60759 [S]	Moonlight Memories	1963	$30
❏ MG-20591 [M]	More Encore of Golden Hits	1960	$30
❏ SR-60252 [S]	More Encore of Golden Hits	1960	$30
❏ 828246-1	More Encore of Golden Hits	198?	$10
— Reissue			
❏ SRM-1-4050	Platterama	1982	$12

Number	Title	Yr	NM
❏ MG-20481 [M]	Reflections	1960	$30
❏ SR-60160 [S]	Reflections	1960	$30
❏ MG-20410 [M]	Remember When?	1959	$30
❏ SR-60087 [S]	Remember When?	1959	$50
❏ MG-20669 [M]	Song for the Lonely	1962	$25
❏ SR-60669 [S]	Song for the Lonely	1962	$30
❏ MG-20298 [M]	The Flying Platters	1957	$150
❏ MG-20366 [M]	The Flying Platters Around the World	1958	$30
❏ SR-60043 [S]	The Flying Platters Around the World	1959	$50
❏ MG-20983 [M]	The New Soul of the Platters	1965	$18
❏ SR-60983 [S]	The New Soul of the Platters	1965	$25
❏ MG-20146 [M]	The Platters	1956	$150
❏ MG-20216 [M]	The Platters, Volume Two	1956	$150
❏ MG-20782 [M]	The Platters Present All-Time Movie Hits	1963	$25
❏ SR-60782 [S]	The Platters Present All-Time Movie Hits	1963	$30
❏ MG-20808 [M]	The Platters Sing Latino	1963	$25
❏ SR-60808 [S]	The Platters Sing Latino	1963	$30
MUSIC DISC			
❏ MDS-1002	Only You	1969	$15
MUSICOR			
❏ MM-2125 [M]	Going Back to Detroit	1967	$18
❏ MS-3125 [S]	Going Back to Detroit	1967	$18
❏ MS-3231	Golden Hour	1973	$15
❏ MS-3171	I Get the Sweetest Feeling	1968	$18
❏ MM-2091 [M]	I Love You 1,000 Times	1966	$18
❏ MS-3091 [S]	I Love You 1,000 Times	1966	$25
❏ MM-2141 [M]	New Golden Hits of the Platters	1967	$25
❏ MS-3141 [S]	New Golden Hits of the Platters	1967	$18
❏ MS-3185	Singing the Great Hits Our Way	1969	$18
❏ MS-3156	Sweet, Sweet Lovin'	1968	$18
❏ MS-3254	The Golden Hits of the Platters	1973	$15
❏ MM-2111 [M]	The Platters Have the Magic Touch	1966	$18
❏ MS-3111 [S]	The Platters Have the Magic Touch	1966	$25
PICKWICK			
❏ PTP-2083	Only You	1973	$15
❏ SPC-3236	Super Hits	197?	$12
RHINO			
❏ RNFP-71495	Anthology (1955-1967)	1986	$15
SPRINGBOARD			
❏ SPB-4059	The Platters	197?	$12
WING			
❏ MGW-12346 [M]	10th Anniversary Album	196?	$15
❏ SRW-16346 [S]	10th Anniversary Album	196?	$15
❏ MGW-12112 [M]	Encores!	1959	$30
— With liner notes on back cover			
❏ MGW-12112 [M]	Encores!	196?	$18
— With photos of other Wing LPs on back cover			
❏ SRW-16112 [R]	Encores!	196?	$15
❏ MGW-12226 [M]	Flying Platters	1963	$15
❏ SRW-16226 [S]	Flying Platters	1963	$15
❏ MGW-12272 [M]	Reflections	1964	$15
❏ SRW-16272 [S]	Reflections	1964	$15
PLAXICO, LONNIE			
MUSE			
❏ MR-5389	Plaxico	1989	$30
PLAYER			
CASABLANCA			
❏ NBLP7217	Room with a View	1980	$12
RCA VICTOR			
❏ AFL1-4186	Spies of Life	1982	$12
RSO			
❏ RS-1-3036	Danger Zone	1978	$12
❏ RS-1-3026	Player	1977	$12
PLAYERS, THE			
MINIT			
❏ LP-40006 [M]	He'll Be Back	1966	$30
❏ LP-24006 [S]	He'll Be Back	1966	$30
PLAYMATES, THE			
FORUM			
❏ F-9012 [M]	At Play with the Playmates	196?	$15
❏ SF-9012 [S]	At Play with the Playmates	196?	$18
❏ F-9021 [M]	Broadway Show Stoppers	196?	$15
❏ SF-9021 [S]	Broadway Show Stoppers	196?	$18
❏ F-16001 [M]	The Playmates Visit West of the Indies	1960	$18
❏ SF-16001 [S]	The Playmates Visit West of the Indies	1960	$25
ROULETTE			
❏ R-25043 [M]	At Play with the Playmates	1958	$30
❏ SR-25043 [S]	At Play with the Playmates	1958	$30
❏ R-25084 [M]	Broadway Show Stoppers	1961	$25
❏ SR-25084 [S]	Broadway Show Stoppers	1961	$30
❏ R-25001 [M]	Calypso	1957	$30
❏ R-25068 [M]	Cuttin' Capers	1960	$25
❏ SR-25068 [S]	Cuttin' Capers	1960	$30
❏ R-25059 [M]	Rock and Roll Record Hop	1959	$25
❏ SR-25059 [S]	Rock and Roll Record Hop	1959	$30

Number	Title	Yr	NM

PLEASANT, BU
MUSE
| ❏ MR-5033 | Ms. Bu | 1975 | $30 |

PLEASURE FAIR, THE
With Robb Royer, later of BREAD.
UNI
| ❏ 3008 [M] | The Pleasure Fair | 1967 | $25 |
| ❏ 73008 [S] | The Pleasure Fair | 1967 | $25 |

PLIMSOULS, THE
BEAT
| ❏ BE-1001 [EP] | Zero Hour | 1980 | $30 |
GEFFEN
| ❏ GHS4002 | Everywhere at Once | 1983 | $15 |
PLANET
| ❏ 13 [B] | The Plimsouls | 1981 | $30 |

PLONSKY, JOHN
GOLDEN CREST
| ❏ GC-3014 [M] | Cool Man, Cool | 1958 | $30 |

PLUGZ
FATIMA
| ❏ 80 | Better Luck | 1981 | $30 |
PLUG/REAL LIFE
| ❏ 01 | Electrify Me | 1979 | $75 |

PLUM NELLY
CAPITOL
| ❏ ST-692 [B] | Deceptive Lines | 1971 | $30 |

PLUMMER, BILL
ABC IMPULSE!
| ❏ A-9164 [M] | Bill Plummer and the Cosmic Brotherhood | 1968 | $160 |
| ❏ AS-9164 [S] | Bill Plummer and the Cosmic Brotherhood | 1968 | $250 |

PLYMOUTH FESTIVAL CHORUS AND ORCHESTRA
PLYMOUTH MUSIC SERIES
| ❏ 45379 | The Season to Shine | 1986 | $15 |
— *Available only at Donaldsons stores in the Minneapolis-St. Paul area*
PRO ARTE
| ❏ PAD152 | Ralph Vaughan Williams: Carols (et al.) | 1983 | $15 |
| ❏ PAD257 | Stephen Paulus: So Hallow'd Is the Time | 1984 | $15 |

PO' BOYS, THE
DECCA
❏ DL4725 [M]	Bill Anderson Presents the Po' Boys	1966	$25
❏ DL74725 [S]	Bill Anderson Presents the Po' Boys	1966	$30
❏ DL4884 [M]	The Po' Boys Pick Again	1967	$30
❏ DL74884 [S]	The Po' Boys Pick Again	1967	$25
MCA
| ❏ 337 | The Rich Sounds of Bill Anderson's Po' Boys | 1973 | $18 |

POCO
ABC
❏ D-890	Head Over Heels	1975	$12
❏ D-989	Indian Summer	1977	$12
❏ AA-1099	Legend	1978	$15
❏ D-946	Rose of Cimarron	1976	$12
ATLANTIC
| ❏ 80008 | Ghost Town | 1982 | $12 |
| ❏ 80148 | Inamorata | 1984 | $12 |
EPIC

❏ KE31601	A Good Feelin' to Know	1972	$18
— *Yellow label*			
❏ KE31601	A Good Feelin' to Know	1973	$12
— *Orange label*			
❏ PE31601	A Good Feelin' to Know	198?	$10
— *Budget-line reissue*			
❏ PE33192	Cantamos	1974	$15
— *Orange label*			
❏ PCQ33192 [Q]	Cantamos	1974	$30
❏ KE32354	Crazy Eyes	1973	$15
— *Orange label*			
❏ EQ32354 [Q]	Crazy Eyes	1973	$30
❏ PE32354	Crazy Eyes	1979	$10
— *Blue label*			
❏ KE30209	Deliverin'	1971	$18
— *Yellow label*			
❏ KE30209	Deliverin'	1973	$12
— *Orange label*			
❏ EQ30209 [Q]	Deliverin'	1972	$30
❏ KE30753	From the Inside	1971	$18
— *Yellow label*			
❏ KE30753	From the Inside	1973	$12
— *Orange label*			
❏ E30753	From the Inside	1973	$12
— *Reissue with new prefix*			
❏ PE33336	Live	1976	$15
— *Orange label*			
❏ BN26460	Pickin' Up the Pieces	1969	$18
— *Yellow label*			
❏ BN26460	Pickin' Up the Pieces	1973	$12
— *Orange label*			
❏ BN26522	Poco	1970	$18
— *Yellow label*			
❏ BN26522 [B]	Poco	1973	$12
— *Orange label*			
❏ KE32895	Seven	1974	$15
— *Orange label*			
❏ EQ32895 [Q]	Seven	1974	$30
❏ JE36210	The Songs of Paul Cotton	1980	$12
❏ JE36211	The Songs of Richie Furay	1980	$12
❏ PEG33537	The Very Best of Poco	1975	$18
— *Orange labels*			
MCA
❏ 5363	Backtracks	1983	$12
❏ 5227	Blue and Gray	1981	$12
❏ 5288	Cowboys & Englishmen	1982	$12
❏ 37009	Head Over Heels	1980	$10
— *Budget-line reissue*			
❏ 37011	Indian Summer	1980	$10
— *Budget-line reissue*			
❏ AA-1099	Legend	1979	$12
— *Reissue of ABC 1099*			
❏ 37117	Legend	1981	$10
— *Budget-line reissue*			
❏ 37010	Rose of Cimarron	1980	$10
— *Budget-line reissue*			
❏ 5132	Under the Gun	1980	$12
❏ 37160	Under the Gun	198?	$10
— *Budget-line reissue*			
MOBILE FIDELITY
| ❏ Jan-0020 | Legend | 1979 | $50 |
| — *Audiophile vinyl* | | | |
RCA
| ❏ 9694-1-R | Legacy | 1989 | $12 |

PODEWELL, POLLY
AUDIOPHILE
| ❏ AP-136 | All of Me | 1980 | $25 |

POGUES, THE
ENIGMA
| ❏ ST-73225 | Red Roses for Me | 1986 | $30 |
ISLAND
| ❏ 90872 | If I Should Fall from Grace With God | 1988 | $15 |
RHINO
| ❏ R1542004 [B] | Live in London (with Joe Strummer) | 2014 | $50 |
| — *credited to the Pogues with Joe Strummer* | | | |
STIFF/MCA
| ❏ 36015 [EP] | Poguetry in Motion | 1986 | $35 |
| ❏ 5744 | Rum, Sodomy and the Lash | 1985 | $35 |

POI DOG PONDERING
COLUMBIA
❏ CAS1856 [DJ]	Interchords	1989	$25
— *Promo-only interview and music*			
❏ CAS2219 [EP]	Untitled (Fruitless)	1990	$18
— *Promo-only six-song sampler*			
❏ C45403	Wishing Like a Mountain and Thinking Like the Sea	1990	$15
TEXAS HOTEL
| ❏ 16 [EP] | Circle Around the Sun | 198? | $10 |
| ❏ 11 [EP] | Poi Dog Pondering | 1988 | $10 |

POINDEXTER, BUSTER
RCA
| ❏ 9665-1-R | Buster Goes Berserk | 1989 | $15 |
| ❏ 6633-1-R | Buster Poindexter | 1987 | $15 |

POINDEXTER, PONY
EPIC
| ❏ LA-16035 [M] | Pony's Express | 1962 | $150 |
| ❏ BA-17035 [S] | Pony's Express | 1962 | $175 |
INNER CITY
| ❏ IC-1062 | Poindexter | 198? | $30 |
NEW JAZZ
❏ NJLP-8297 [M]	Gumbo	1963	$0
— *Canceled*			
❏ NJLP-8285 [M]	Pony Poindexter Plays the Big Ones	1962	$175
— *Purple label*			
❏ NJLP-8285 [M]	Pony Poindexter Plays the Big Ones	1965	$175
— *Blue label, trident logo at right*			
PRESTIGE
| ❏ PRLP-16001 [M] | Gumbo | 1964 | $40 |

POINTER, ANITA
RCA
| ❏ 6419-1-R | Love for What It Is | 1987 | $10 |

POINTER, BONNIE
MOTOWN
❏ M7-911R1	Bonnie Pointer	1978	$15
❏ M7-929M1	Bonnie Pointer	1979	$12
— *The above two are different albums*			
PRVATE I
| ❏ FZ39406 | If the Price Is Right | 1984 | $10 |

POINTER, JUNE
COLUMBIA
| ❏ FC44315 | June Pointer | 1989 | $15 |
PLANET
| ❏ BXL1-4508 | Baby Sister | 1983 | $12 |

POINTER, NOEL
BLUE NOTE
| ❏ BN-LA736-H | Phantazia | 1977 | $30 |
LIBERTY
❏ LT-1094	All My Reasons	1981	$25
❏ LN-10256	All My Reasons	198?	$20
— *Budget-line reissue*			
❏ LT-1050	Calling	1981	$20
— *Reissue of United Artists 1050*			
❏ LT-51123	Direct Hit	1982	$25
❏ LO-848	Hold On	1981	$20
— *Reissue of United Artists 848*			
❏ LN-10235	Hold On	198?	$20
— *Budget-line reissue*			
❏ LN-10236	Phantazia	198?	$20
— *Budget-line reissue*			
UNITED ARTISTS
| ❏ LT-1050 | Calling | 1980 | $25 |
| ❏ UA-LA848-H | Hold On | 1978 | $25 |

POINTER SISTERS, THE
ABC BLUE THUMB
❏ BT-6023	Having a Party	1977	$15
❏ BT-6021	Steppin	1975	$15
❏ BTSY-6026	The Best of the Pointer Sisters	1976	$18
BLUE THUMB
❏ BTS-8002	Live at the Opera House	1974	$18
❏ BTS-6009	That's a Plenty	1974	$15
❏ BTS-48	The Pointer Sisters	1973	$15
MCA
| ❏ 3275 | Retrospect | 1981 | $12 |
| — *Reissue of Blue Thumb material* | | | |
MOTOWN
| ❏ 6287ML | Right Rhythm | 1990 | $15 |
PLANET
❏ P-18	Black and White	1981	$12
❏ BXL1-4705	Break Out	1983	$12
— *Original does not have "I'm So Excited"*			
❏ BEL1-4705A	Break Out	1984	$10
— *Reissue has "I'm So Excited" plus a remix of "Jump (For My Love)"*			
❏ P-1	Energy	1978	$12
❏ 60203	Pointer Sisters' Greatest Hits	1982	$12
❏ P-9003	Priority	1979	$12
❏ BXL1-4355	So Excited!	1982	$12
❏ P-9	Special Things	1980	$12
RCA
| ❏ 5609-1-R | Hot Together | 1986 | $12 |
| ❏ 6562-1-R | Serious Slammin' | 1988 | $12 |

Number	Title	Yr	NM

RCA VICTOR
❑ AYL1-5092 — Black and White — 1985 — $10
— *Budget-line reissue*
❑ AJL1-5487 — Contact — 1985 — $12
❑ AYL1-5091 — Energy — 1985 — $10
— *Budget-line reissue*
❑ AYL1-5089 — Priority — 1985 — $10
— *Budget-line reissue*
❑ AYL1-5088 — Special Things — 1985 — $10
— *Budget-line reissue*

POISON
First name in "hair metal."

CAPITOL
❑ C1-598046 — Swallow This Live — 1991 — $40
— *Vinyl version available only from Columbia House*

CAPITOL/ENIGMA
❑ C1-91813 — Flesh & Blood — 1990 — $15
— *With blood dripping from letters "Flesh & Blood"*
❑ C1-91813 — Flesh & Blood — 1990 — $15
— *With blood airbrushed out of front cover photo*
❑ C1-591813 — Flesh & Blood — 1990 — $15
— *Columbia House club edition*
❑ ST-12523 — Look What the Cat Dragged In — 1986 — $10
❑ ST-512523 — Look What the Cat Dragged In — 1986 — $12
— *Columbia House club edition*
❑ R144402 — Look What the Cat Dragged In — 1986 — $12
— *BMG Direct Marketing club edition*
❑ C1-48493 — Open Up and Say...Ahh! — 1988 — $15
— *With uncropped front cover photo (woman's tongue is fully visible)*
❑ C1-48493 — Open Up and Say...Ahh! — 1988 — $10
— *With cropped front cover photo (woman's tongue is cut off; large black bars at top and bottom of cover)*
❑ SPRO79319/22 — Open Up and Say...Ahh! World Premiere Weekend — 1988 — $30
— *Special radio-only version to promote the LP's release*

POITIER, SIDNEY
WARNER BROS.
❑ W1561 [M] — Poitier Meets Plato — 1965 — $30
❑ WS1561 [S] — Poitier Meets Plato — 1965 — $30

POLAD, MIKE
JAZZOLOGY
❑ J-77 — The Cascades — 197? — $25

POLCER, ED
JAZZOLOGY
❑ J-150 — In the Condon Tradition — 1987 — $25

POLICE, THE
Also see STEWART COPELAND; KLARK KENT; STING; ANDY SUMMERS.

A&M
❑ R173924 — Every Breath You Take -- The Singles — 1986 — $15
— *BMG Direct Marketing edition*
❑ SP-3902 — Every Breath You Take -- The Singles — 1986 — $12
❑ R123571 — Ghost in the Machine — 1981 — $15
— *RCA Music Service edition*
❑ SP-3730 — Ghost in the Machine — 1981 — $12
❑ SP-3730 [DJ] — Ghost in the Machine — 1981 — $1000
— *Special prototype picture disc that lights up when placed on a turntable*
❑ R124159 — Outlandos d'Amour — 1979 — $15
— *RCA Music Service edition*
❑ SP-4753 — Outlandos d'Amour — 1979 — $15
❑ SP-3311 — Outlandos d'Amour — 198? — $10
— *Reissue*
❑ R153349 — Reggatta de Blanc — 1979 — $15
— *RCA Music Service edition*
❑ SP-3713 [10] — Reggatta de Blanc — 1979 — $40
— *Two 10" records with poster*
❑ SP-4792 — Reggatta de Blanc — 1979 — $15
❑ SP-3312 — Reggatta de Blanc — 198? — $10
— *Reissue*
❑ SP-6018 [10] — Reggatta de Blanc — 1980 — $30
— *Reissue of SP-3713*
❑ R134070 — Synchronicity — 1983 — $15
— *RCA Music Service edition*
❑ SP-3735 — Synchronicity — 1983 — $40
— *With gold, silver and bronze color bands on cover; used on audiophile pressings*
❑ SP-3735 — Synchronicity — 1983 — $12
— *With blue, yellow and red color bands; 93 versions of this cover exist, none more valuable than any other*
❑ 3937351 — Synchronicity — 2008 — $25
— *Black & white cover*
❑ R130108 — Zenyatta Mondatta — 1980 — $15
— *RCA Music Service edition*
❑ SP-3720 — Zenyatta Mondatta — 1980 — $12
❑ 1775311 — Zenyatta Mondatta — 2008 — $25

Number	Title	Yr	NM

NAUTILUS

❑ NR-40 [B] — Ghost in the Machine — 1982 — $40
— *Audiophile vinyl*
❑ NR-19 [B] — Zenyatta Mondatta — 1981 — $50
— *Audiophile vinyl*

POLK, LUCY ANN
INTERLUDE
❑ MO-504 [M] — Easy Livin' — 1959 — $150
❑ ST-1004 [S] — Easy Livin' — 1959 — $100
MODE
❑ LP-115 [M] — Lucky Lucy Ann — 1957 — $175
TREND
❑ TL-1008 [10] — Lucy Ann Polk with Dave Pell — 1954 — $175

POLL WINNERS, THE
CONTEMPORARY
❑ M-3581 [M] — Exploring the Scene — 1960 — $300
❑ S-7581 [S] — Exploring the Scene — 1960 — $300
❑ M-3576 [M] — Poll Winners Three — 1960 — $250
❑ S-7576 [S] — Poll Winners Three — 1960 — $250
❑ C-3535 [M] — The Poll Winners — 1957 — $300
❑ S-7535 [S] — The Poll Winners — 1959 — $300
❑ C-3556 [M] — The Poll Winners Ride Again — 1958 — $300
❑ S-7556 [S] — The Poll Winners Ride Again — 1959 — $300
STEREO RECORDS
❑ S-7010 [S] — The Poll Winners — 1958 — $50
❑ S-7029 [S] — The Poll Winners Ride Again — 1958 — $50

POLLACK, BEN
BRUNSWICK
❑ BL58025 [10] — Ben Pollack — 1951 — $75
SAVOY
❑ MG-12207 [M] — Dixieland Strut — 196? — $25
❑ MG-12090 [M] — Pick a Rib Boys — 1956 — $50
X
❑ LX-3003 [10] — Ben Pollack and His Orchestra Featuring Benny Goodman — 1954 — $75

POLLARD, TERRY
BETHLEHEM
❑ BCP-1015 [10] — Terry Pollard — 1954 — $300

POLLARD, TERRY/BOBBY SCOTT
BETHLEHEM
❑ BCP-1 [M] — Young Moderns — 1957 — $300

POLLUTION
CAPITOL
❑ ST-205 — Heir: Pollution — 1969 — $25
PROPHECY
❑ SD6051 — Pollution — 1971 — $25
❑ SD6067 — Pollution II — 1972 — $25

POLNAREFF, MICHEL
4 CORNERS OF THE WORLD
❑ FCL-4240 [M] — French Rock-Blues — 1967 — $18
❑ FCS-4240 [S] — French Rock-Blues — 1967 — $25
ATLANTIC
❑ SD18153 — Michel Polnareff — 1976 — $12

POLYPHONIC SPREE
CHERRY RED
❑ BRED588 [S] — Yes, It's True — 2013 — $20
— *Released Aug. 6, 2013.*

Number	Title	Yr	NM

POMEROY, HERB
ROULETTE
❑ R-52001 [M] — Life Is A Many Splendored Gig — 1958 — $120
❑ SR-52001 [S] — Life Is A Many Splendored Gig — 1958 — $150
SHIAH
❑ HP-1 — Pramlatta's Hips — 1980 — $50
TRANSITION
❑ TRLP-1 [M] — Jazz in a Stable — 1956 — $400
— *Deduct 25 percent if booklet is missing*
UNITED ARTISTS
❑ UAL-4015 [M] — Band in Boston — 1959 — $175
❑ UAS-5015 [S] — Band in Boston — 1959 — $120

PONCE, PONCIE
WARNER BROS.
❑ W1453 [M] — Poncie Ponce Sings — 1962 — $25
❑ WS1453 [S] — Poncie Ponce Sings — 1962 — $30

PONDER, JIMMY
ABC IMPULSE!
❑ IA-9313 — Illusions — 197? — $30
❑ IA-9327 — White Room — 197? — $30
CADET
❑ CA-50048 — While My Guitar Gently Weeps — 1974 — $30
MILESTONE
❑ M-9121 — Down Here on the Ground — 1984 — $25
❑ M-9132 — So Many Stars — 1985 — $25
MUSE
❑ MR-5347 — Jump — 1988 — $25
❑ MR-5324 — Mean Streets, No Bridges — 1987 — $25

PONTY, JEAN-LUC
ATLANTIC
❑ SD19253 — A Taste for Passion — 1979 — $25
❑ SD18163 — Aurora — 1976 — $25
❑ SD19158 — Aurora — 1978 — $20
— *Reissue of 18163*
❑ SD16020 — Civilized Evil — 1980 — $25
❑ SD19189 — Cosmic Messenger — 1978 — $25
❑ SD19110 — Enigmatic Ocean — 1977 — $25
❑ 81276 — Fables — 1985 — $20
❑ SD18195 — Imaginary Voyage — 1976 — $25
❑ SD19136 — Imaginary Voyage — 1978 — $20
— *Reissue of 18195*
❑ A1-80098 — Individual Choice — 1983 — $20
❑ SD19229 — Jean-Luc Ponty: Live — 1979 — $25
❑ SD19333 — Mystical Adventures — 1982 — $25
❑ 80185 — Open Mind — 1984 — $20
❑ SD18138 — Upon the Wings of Music — 1975 — $25
BASF
❑ 21288 — Open Strings — 1973 — $50
❑ 20645 — Sunday Walk — 1972 — $50
BLUE NOTE
❑ BN-LA632-H2 — Cantaloupe Island — 1976 — $50
❑ LWB-632 — Cantaloupe Island — 1981 — $30
— *Reissue of BN-LA632-H2*
❑ LT-1102 — Live at Donte's — 1981 — $25
COLUMBIA
❑ FC45252 — Storytelling — 1989 — $35
❑ FC40983 — The Gift of Time — 1987 — $20
DIRECT DISC
❑ SD-16603 — Cosmic Messenger — 1980 — $75
— *Audiophile vinyl*
INNER CITY
❑ IC-1005 — Jean-Luc Ponty and Stephane Grappelli — 197? — $25
❑ IC-1003 — Live at Montreux: Sonata Erotica — 1976 — $35
PAUSA
❑ PR-7014 — Jean-Luc Ponty Meets Giorgio Gaslini — 1979 — $25
❑ PR-7065 — Open Strings — 1980 — $25
— *Reissue of BASF 21288*
❑ PR-7033 — Sunday Walk — 1980 — $25
— *Reissue of BASF 20645*
❑ PA9001 — The Jean-Luc Ponty Experience — 1982 — $50
PRESTIGE
❑ PRST-7676 — Critic's Choice — 1969 — $50
WORLD PACIFIC
❑ ST-20156 — Electric Connection — 1969 — $175
❑ ST-20134 — More Than Meets the Ear — 1969 — $175
WORLD PACIFIC JAZZ
❑ ST-20172 — King Kong -- Jean-Luc Ponty Plays the Music of Frank Zappa — 1970 — $175
❑ ST-20168 — The Jean-Luc Ponty Experience — 1969 — $175

Number	Title	Yr	NM

POOBAH
A.E.I.
| ❏ A-LP-1 | U.S. Rock | 1976 | $300 |

PEPPERMINT
| ❏ PP-1180 | Steamroller | 1979 | $175 |

RITE
| ❏ 0(no cat #) | Let Me In | 1972 | $600 |

POOLE, BILLIE
RIVERSIDE
❏ RLP-458 [M]	Confessin' the Blues	1963	$175
❏ RS-9458 [S]	Confessin' the Blues	1963	$175
❏ RLP-425 [M]	Sermonette	1962	$175
❏ RS-9425 [S]	Sermonette	1962	$175

POOLE, BRIAN, AND THE TREMELOES
AUDIO FIDELITY
❏ AFLP2151 [M]	Brian Poole Is Here	1966	$40
❏ AFSD2151 [R]	Brian Poole Is Here	1966	$30
❏ AFLP2177 [M]	The Tremeloes Are Here	1967	$75
— Reissue of above album with new title
| ❏ AFSD2177 [R] | The Tremeloes Are Here | 1967 | $30 |
— Reissue of above album with new title

POP WILL EAT ITSELF
NOTHING
| ❏ 95887 | Amalgamation | 1994 | $12 |

RCA
| ❏ 9742-1-R | This Is the Day...This Is the Hour...This Is This! | 1989 | $18 |

ROUGH TRADE
| ❏ ROUGH033 | Box Frenzy! | 1988 | $18 |
| ❏ ROUGH022 | Now for a Feast | 198? | $18 |

POPCORN BLIZZARD, THE (1)
DE-LITE
| ❏ DE-2004 [B] | Explode! | 1969 | $50 |

POPE JOHN PAUL II
INFINITY
| ❏ INF9899 | Pope John Paul II Sings at the Festival of Sacrosong | 1979 | $15 |

VOX CHRISTIANA
| ❏ VC3004/5 | Christmas Midnight Mass | 1979 | $18 |
— Recording of the December 24, 1978 Mass at St. Peter's Basilica at the Vatican

POPE JOHN XXIII
MERCURY
| ❏ 200 [M] | Pope John XXIII | 1963 | $18 |
— Tribute album released after his death

POPKIN, LENNY
CHOICE
| ❏ 1027 | Falling Free | 198? | $25 |

POPPIES, THE
EPIC
| ❏ LN24200 [M] | Lullaby of Love | 1966 | $40 |
| ❏ BN26200 [S] | Lullaby of Love | 1966 | $50 |

POPPY FAMILY, THE
LONDON
| ❏ PS599 | Seeds | 1971 | $18 |
| ❏ PS574 | Which Way You Goin' Billy? | 1970 | $18 |

PORCELAIN BEARMEAT
DILL PICKLE
| ❏ 3468 | Free Love, Free Sex, Free Music | 1971 | $25 |

PORNO FOR PYROS
Direct descendant of JANE'S ADDICTION.
WARNER BROS.
| ❏ 45228 | Porno for Pyros | 1993 | $18 |

PORT OF HARLEM JAZZMEN, THE
MOSAIC
| ❏ MR1-108 | The Complete Recordings of the Port of Harlem Jazzmen | 198? | $25 |

PORTAL, MICHEL
HARMONIA MUNDI
| ❏ HM-5186 | Turbulence | 1987 | $30 |

PORTER, DAVID
ENTERPRISE
❏ ENS-1012	David Porter...Into a Real Thing	1971	$25
❏ ENS-1009	Gritty, Groovy, & Gettin' It	1970	$25
❏ ENS-1026	Sweat and Love	1973	$25
❏ ENS-1019	Victim of the Joke?	1972	$25

PORTER, JERRY
MIRROR
| ❏ SWB-123 [M] | Don't Bother Me! | 1966 | $150 |

PORTER, NOLAN
ABC
| ❏ ABCX-766 | Nolan | 1973 | $120 |

LIZARD
| ❏ A-20102 | No Apologies | 1971 | $30 |
—As "Nolan

PORTER, PEPPER
FIRST AMERICAN
| ❏ FA-7756 | Invasion | 1980 | $30 |

PORTER TWIN DISC MUSIC BOX, THE
PORTER
| ❏ 103 | Music Box Nutcracker Suite and More Christmas Favorites | 1984 | $15 |

PORTISHEAD
LONDON/GO BEAT
| ❏ 539189-1 | (Music by) Portishead | 1997 | $15 |

PORTSMOUTH SINFONIA
ANTILLES
| ❏ AN-7002 [B] | Hallelujah - At The Royal Albert Hall | 1974 | $40 |

POSEY, SANDY
COLUMBIA
| ❏ KC31594 | Why Don't We Go Somewhere and Love | 1972 | $15 |

MGM
❏ E-4418 [M]	Born a Woman	1966	$18
❏ SE-4418 [S]	Born a Woman	1966	$25
❏ E-4480 [M]	I Take It Back	1967	$30
❏ SE-4480 [S]	I Take It Back	1967	$25
❏ E-4525 [M]	Looking at You	1968	$50
❏ SE-4525 [S]	Looking at You	1968	$18
❏ GAS-125	Sandy Posey (Golden Archive Series)	1970	$18
❏ E-4455 [M]	Single Girl	1967	$25
❏ SE-4455 [S]	Single Girl	1967	$25
❏ ST-91110	Single Girl	1967	$30
— Capitol Record Club issue
| ❏ E-4509 [M] | The Best of Sandy Posey | 1967 | $30 |
| ❏ SE-4509 [S] | The Best of Sandy Posey | 1967 | $25 |

POSEY, SANDY/ SKEETER DAVIS
GUSTO
| ❏ 0005 | The Best of Sandy Posey/ Skeeter Davis | 198? | $10 |

POSSUM
CAPITOL
| ❏ ST-648 [B] | Possum | 1970 | $18 |

POSSUM HUNTERS, THE
TAKOMA
| ❏ C-1010 [B] | Death on Lee Highway | 1970 | $40 |

POST, MIKE
ELEKTRA
| ❏ 60028 [EP] | Television Theme Songs | 1982 | $10 |

MGM
| ❏ M3G-5005 | Railhead Overture | 1975 | $12 |

POLYDOR
| ❏ 833985-1 | Theme from L.A. Law and Otherwise | 1987 | $10 |

RCA VICTOR
| ❏ AFL1-5415 | Mike Post | 1985 | $12 |

POTENZA, FRANK
PALO ALTO/TBA
| ❏ TB-206 | Sand Dance | 198? | $25 |
| ❏ TB-222 | Soft and Warm | 1987 | $25 |

POTLIQUOR
CAPITOL
| ❏ ST-11998 | Potliquor | 1979 | $15 |

JANUS
❏ JLS-3033	Levee Blues	1972	$25
❏ JLS-3036	Louisiana Rock and Roll	1973	$25
❏ JLS-3002	Potliquor	1970	$25

POTTER, CURTIS
DOT
| ❏ DLP-25988 | Here Comes Curtis Potter | 1971 | $25 |

STEP ONE
| ❏ 0020 | All I Need Is Time | 1987 | $25 |
| ❏ 0004 | Down in Texas Today | 1984 | $25 |

POTTER, TOMMY
EASTWEST
| ❏ 4001 [M] | Tommy Potter's Hard Funk | 1958 | $350 |

POTTS, BILL
COLPIX
| ❏ CP-451 [M] | Bye Bye Birdie | 1963 | $30 |
| ❏ SCP-451 [S] | Bye Bye Birdie | 1963 | $40 |

UNITED ARTISTS
| ❏ UAL-4032 [M] | The Jazz Soul of Porgy and Bess | 1959 | $30 |
| ❏ UAS-5032 [S] | The Jazz Soul of Porgy and Bess | 1959 | $40 |

POWELL, ADAM CLAYTON
JUBILEE
| ❏ JGM2062 [M] | Keep the Faith, Baby! | 1967 | $18 |

POWELL, ANDREW, AND THE PHILHARMONIA ORCHESTRA
MOBILE FIDELITY
| ❏ 1-175 | The Best of the Alan Parsons Project | 1986 | $30 |
—Audiophile vinyl

POWELL, BADEN
BASF
❏ 25155	Canto on Guitar	197?	$25
❏ 29194	Estudios	197?	$35
❏ 29057	Images on Guitar	197?	$35
❏ 29623	Tristeza on Guitar	197?	$35

COLUMBIA
| ❏ KC32441 | Solitude on Guitar | 1974 | $30 |

PAUSA
| ❏ 7078 | Tristeza on Guitar | 198? | $25 |

POWELL, BUD
BLACK LION
| ❏ 153 | Invisible Cage | 1974 | $50 |

BLUE NOTE
| ❏ BST-84430 | Alternate Takes | 1985 | $50 |
| ❏ BLP-1571 [M] | Bud! | 1957 | $400 |
—Deep groove" version; W. 63rd St. address on label
| ❏ BLP-1571 [M] | Bud! | 1957 | $300 |
—Regular version, W. 63rd St. address on label
| ❏ BST-1571 [S] | Bud! | 1959 | $600 |
—Deep groove" version; W. 63rd St. address on label
| ❏ BST-1571 [S] | Bud! | 1959 | $300 |
—Regular version, W. 63rd St. address on label
| ❏ BLP-1571 [M] | Bud! | 1963 | $250 |
—With "New York, USA" address on label
| ❏ BST-1571 [S] | Bud! | 1963 | $150 |
—With "New York, USA" address on label
| ❏ BST-81571 [S] | Bud! | 1967 | $75 |
—With "A Division of Liberty Records" on label
| ❏ BST-81571 [S] | Bud! | 1986 | $30 |
—The Finest in Jazz Since 1939" reissue
| ❏ BLP-5003 [10] | The Amazing Bud Powell, Vol. 1 | 1951 | $1000 |
| ❏ BLP-1503 [M] | The Amazing Bud Powell, Vol. 1 | 1955 | $400 |
—Deep groove" version; Lexington Ave. address on label
| ❏ BLP-1503 [M] | The Amazing Bud Powell, Vol. 1 | 1958 | $500 |
—Deep groove" version, W. 63rd St. address on label
| ❏ BLP-1503 [M] | The Amazing Bud Powell, Vol. 1 | 1963 | $100 |
—With "New York, USA" address on label
| ❏ BST-81503 [R] | The Amazing Bud Powell, Vol. 1 | 1967 | $60 |
—With "A Division of Liberty Records" on label
| ❏ B1-81503 [M] | The Amazing Bud Powell, Vol. 1 | 1989 | $35 |
—The Finest in Jazz Since 1939" reissue
| ❏ BLP-5041 [10] | The Amazing Bud Powell, Vol. 2 | 1954 | $1000 |
| ❏ BLP-1504 [M] | The Amazing Bud Powell, Vol. 2 | 1955 | $500 |
—Deep groove" version; Lexington Ave. address on label
| ❏ BLP-1504 [M] | The Amazing Bud Powell, Vol. 2 | 1963 | $100 |
—With "New York, USA" address on label
| ❏ BLP-1504 [M] | The Amazing Bud Powell, Vol. 2 | 1958 | $300 |
—Deep groove" version, W. 63rd St. address on label
| ❏ BST-81504 [R] | The Amazing Bud Powell, Vol. 2 | 1967 | $50 |
—With "A Division of Liberty Records" on label
| ❏ B1-81504 [M] | The Amazing Bud Powell, Vol. 2 | 1989 | $35 |
—The Finest in Jazz Since 1939" reissue
| ❏ B1-93204 | The Best of Bud Powell | 1989 | $35 |
| ❏ BLP-4009 [M] | The Scene Changes | 1959 | $800 |
—Deep groove" version; W. 63rd St. address on label
| ❏ BLP-4009 [M] | The Scene Changes | 1959 | $250 |
—Regular version, W. 63rd St. address on label
| ❏ BST-4009 [S] | The Scene Changes | 1959 | $1250 |
—Deep groove" version; W. 63rd St. address on label

Number	Title	Yr	NM
❏ BST-4009 [S]	The Scene Changes	1959	$175
—Regular version, W. 63rd St. address on label			
❏ BLP-4009 [M]	The Scene Changes	1963	$100
—With "New York, USA" address on label			
❏ BST-4009 [S]	The Scene Changes	1963	$40
—With "New York, USA" address on label			
❏ BST-84009 [S]	The Scene Changes	1967	$50
—With "A Division of Liberty Records" on label			
❏ BLP-1598 [M]	The Time Waits	1959	$400
—Deep groove" version; W. 63rd St. address on label			
❏ BLP-1598 [M]	The Time Waits	1959	$300
—Regular version, W. 63rd St. address on label			
❏ BST-1598 [S]	The Time Waits	1959	$300
—Deep groove" version; W. 63rd St. address on label			
❏ BST-1598 [S]	The Time Waits	1959	$175
—Regular version, W. 63rd St. address on label			
❏ BLP-1598 [M]	The Time Waits	1963	$100
—With "New York, USA" address on label			
❏ BST-1598 [S]	The Time Waits	1963	$40
—With "New York, USA" address on label			
❏ BST-81598 [S]	The Time Waits	1967	$50
—With "A Division of Liberty Records" on label			
CLEF			
❏ MGC-102 [10]	Bud Powell Piano Solos	1953	$0
—Canceled			
❏ MGC-502 [10]	Bud Powell Piano Solos	1954	$400
❏ MGC-507 [10]	Bud Powell Piano Solos, No. 2	1954	$400
❏ MGC-610 [M]	Bud Powell's Moods	1954	$350
❏ MGC-739 [M]	The Genius of Bud Powell	1956	$350
COLUMBIA			
❏ CL2292 [M]	A Portrait of Thelonious	1965	$40
❏ CS9092 [S]	A Portrait of Thelonious	1965	$50
—Red label with "360 Sound Stereo			
COLUMBIA JAZZ ODYSSEY			
❏ PC36805	A Portrait of Thelonious	1980	$25
COMMODORE			
❏ XFL-14943	The World Is Waiting	198?	$35
DEBUT			
❏ DLP-3 [10]	Jazz at Massey Hall, Volume 2	1953	$800
DELMARK			
❏ DL-406 [M]	Bouncing with Bud	1966	$40
❏ DS-9406 [S]	Bouncing with Bud	1966	$50
❏ DS-406	Bouncing with Bud	1987	$30
DISCOVERY			
❏ 830	Bud Powell in Paris	198?	$30
ELEKTRA/MUSICIAN			
❏ E1-60030	Inner Fires	1982	$30
ESP-DISK'			
❏ BUD-1	Broadcast Performances 1953	197?	$150
❏ 1066 [S]	Bud Powell at the Blue Note Café, Paris	1968	$175
FANTASY			
❏ 6006 [M]	Bud Powell Trio	1962	$100
—Red vinyl			
❏ 6006 [M]	Bud Powell Trio	1962	$40
—Black vinyl			
❏ 86006 [R]	Bud Powell Trio	1962	$40
—Blue vinyl			
❏ 86006 [R]	Bud Powell Trio	1962	$25
—Black vinyl			
❏ OJC-111	Jazz at Massey Hall, Volume 2	198?	$30
MAINSTREAM			
❏ MRL-385	Ups 'n' Downs	1973	$75
MERCURY			
❏ MG-35012 [10]	Bud Powell Piano	1950	$600
❏ MGC-102 [10]	Bud Powell Piano	1950	$500
❏ MGC-502 [10]	Bud Powell Piano Solos	1951	$500
❏ MGC-507 [10]	Bud Powell Piano Solos, No. 2	1951	$500
❏ MGC-610 [M]	Bud Powell's Moods	1953	$400
MOSAIC			
❏ MR5-116	The Complete Bud Powell Blue Note Recordings (1949-1958)	199?	$300
MYTHIC SOUND			
❏ MS-6002	Burning in the USA, 1953-55	199?	$30
❏ MS-6003	Cookin' at Saint-Germain, 1957-59	199?	$30
❏ MS-6001	Early Years of a Genius, 1944-48	199?	$30
❏ MS-6005	Groovin' at the Blue Note, 1959-61	199?	$30
❏ MS-6008	Holiday in Edenville, 1964	199?	$30
❏ MS-6004	Relaxin' at Home, 1961-64	199?	$30
❏ MS-6009	Return to Birdland, 1964	199?	$30
❏ MS-6007	Tribute to Thelonious, 1964	199?	$30
❏ MS-6006	Writin' for Duke, 1963	199?	$30
NORGRAN			
❏ MGN-1098 [M]	Bud Powell '57	1957	$350
❏ MGN-1064 [M]	Bud Powell's Moods	1956	$300
❏ MGN-23 [10]	Bud Powell Trio	1954	$500

Number	Title	Yr	NM
❏ MGN-1063 [M]	Jazz Giant	1956	$300
❏ MGN-1017 [M]	Jazz Original	1955	$300
❏ MGN-1077 [M]	Piano Interpretations by Bud Powell	1956	$300
QUINTESSENCE			
❏ 25381	Bud Powell	1980	$30
RCA VICTOR			
❏ LPM-1423 [M]	Strictly Powell	1957	$175
—Reproductions exist			
❏ LPM-1507 [M]	Swingin' with Bud	1957	$120
—Reproductions exist			
REPRISE			
❏ R-6098 [M]	Bud Powell in Paris	1964	$40
❏ R9-6098 [S]	Bud Powell in Paris	1964	$75
ROOST			
❏ LP-401 [10]	Bud Powell Trio	1950	$650
❏ LP-412 [10]	Bud Powell Trio	1953	$500
❏ LP-2224 [M]	Bud Powell Trio	1957	$175
ROULETTE			
❏ R-52115 [M]	The Return of Bud Powell -- His First New Recordings Since 1958	1965	$30
❏ SR-52115 [S]	The Return of Bud Powell -- His First New Recordings Since 1958	1965	$40
STEEPLECHASE			
❏ SCC-6001	Bud Powell at the Golden Circle, Vol. 1	198?	$35
❏ SCC-6002	Bud Powell at the Golden Circle, Vol. 2	198?	$35
❏ SCC-6009	Bud Powell at the Golden Circle, Vol. 3	198?	$35
❏ SCC-6014	Bud Powell at the Golden Circle, Vol. 4	198?	$35
❏ SCC-6017	Bud Powell at the Golden Circle, Vol. 5	198?	$35
VERVE			
❏ MGV-8218 [M]	Blues in the Closet	1958	$175
❏ V-8218 [M]	Blues in the Closet	1961	$30
❏ MGV-8185 [M]	Bud Powell '57	1957	$175
❏ V-8185 [M]	Bud Powell '57	1961	$30
❏ UMV-2571	Bud Powell '57	198?	$25
❏ MGV-8154 [M]	Bud Powell's Moods	1957	$175
❏ V-8154 [M]	Bud Powell's Moods	1961	$30
❏ MGV-8153 [M]	Jazz Giant	1957	$175
❏ V-8153 [M]	Jazz Giant	1961	$30
❏ MGV-8167 [M]	Piano Interpretations by Bud Powell	1957	$175
❏ V-8167 [M]	Piano Interpretations by Bud Powell	1961	$30
❏ UMV-2573	Piano Interpretations by Bud Powell	198?	$25
❏ MGV-8115 [M]	The Genius of Bud Powell	1957	$175
❏ V-8115 [M]	The Genius of Bud Powell	1961	$30
❏ VE-2-2506	The Genius of Bud Powell, Vol. 1	197?	$35
❏ VE-2-2526	The Genius of Bud Powell, Vol. 2	197?	$35
❏ VSP-34 [M]	The Jazz Legacy of Bud Powell	1966	$25
❏ VSPS-34 [R]	The Jazz Legacy of Bud Powell	1966	$30
❏ MGV-8301 [M]	The Lonely One…	1959	$150
❏ V-8301 [M]	The Lonely One…	1961	$30
❏ VSP-37 [M]	This Was Bud Powell	1966	$25
❏ VSPS-37 [R]	This Was Bud Powell	1966	$30
XANADU			
❏ 102	Bud in Paris	1975	$35

POWELL, DICK

DECCA

❏ DL8837 [M]	Song Book	1959	$40

RPC

❏ 105 [M]	The Wonderful Teens	1962	$30

POWELL, JANE

COLUMBIA MASTERWORKS

❏ ML2045 [10]	A Date with Jane Powell	1949	$100
❏ ML2034 [10]	Romance	1949	$100

LION

❏ L-70111 [M]	Jane Powell Sings	1960	$25

MGM

❏ E-3451 [M]	Something Wonderful	1957	$40

VERVE

❏ MGV-2023 [M]	Can't We Be Friends?	1957	$40

POWELL, JIMMY (1)

DECCA

❏ DL75216	Jimmy Powell	1970	$15

POWELL, JIMMY (2)

JUBILEE

❏ JGM8001 [M]	In a Sentimental Mood	1966	$35

POWELL, LOVEY

TRANSITION

❏ TRLP-1 [M]	Lovelady	1956	$150
—Deduct 25 percent if booklet is missing			

Number	Title	Yr	NM
POWELL, MEL			
CAPITOL			
❏ T615 [M]	Classics in Jazz	1955	$85
COMMODORE			
❏ XFL-14943	The World Is Waiting	1979	$25
PAUSA			
❏ 9023	The Unavailable Mel Powell	198?	$25
VANGUARD			
❏ VRS-8015 [10]	Bandstand	1954	$100
❏ VRS-8501 [M]	Borderline	1954	$50
❏ VRS-8519 [M]	Easy Swing	1955	$150
❏ VRS-8004 [10]	Mel Powell Septet	1953	$100
❏ VRS-8506 [M]	Out on a Limb	1955	$150
❏ VRS-8502 [M]	Thigamagig	1954	$50
POWELL, ROGER			
ATLANTIC			
❏ SD7251	Cosmic Furnace	1973	$35
POWELL, SELDON			
ROOST			
❏ LP-2205 [M]	Seldon Powell Plays	1956	$250
❏ LP-2220 [M]	Seldon Powell Sextet	1956	$300
POWELL, SPECS			
ROULETTE			
❏ R-52004 [M]	Movin' In	1958	$30
❏ SR-52004 [S]	Movin' In	1958	$30
STRAND			
❏ SL-1027 [M]	Specs Powell Presents Big Band Jazz	1961	$25
❏ SLS-1027 [S]	Specs Powell Presents Big Band Jazz	1961	$30
POWER STATION, THE			
CAPITOL			
❏ R123577	The Power Station	1985	$15
—RCA Music Service edition			
❏ SJ-12380	The Power Station	1985	$12
POWER TOOLS			
ANTILLES			
❏ 90627	Strange Meeting	1987	$25
POWERS, CHRIS			
CIRCLE			
❏ CLP-89	Chris Powers and His Orchestra 1985	1986	$25
POWERS, JOEY			
AMY			
❏ 8001 [M]	Midnight Mary	1964	$30
POWERS OF BLUE, THE			
MTA			
❏ 1002 [M]	Flipout	1967	$30
❏ 5002 [S]	Flipout	1967	$30
POWERSOURCE			
POWERVISION			
❏ 0(# unknown)	Shelter from the Storm	1986	$15
POWRIE, GLENNA			
MUSE			
❏ MR-5392	Ashja	1990	$30
POZAR, ROBERT			
SAVOY			
❏ MG-12189 [M]	Good Golly, Miss Nancy	1967	$25
POZO-SECO SINGERS, THE			
DON WILLIAMS was in this group.			
CERTRON			
❏ CS-7007	Spend Some Time with Me	1970	$18
COLUMBIA			
❏ CL2600 [M]	I Can Make It with You	1967	$25
❏ CS9400 [S]	I Can Make It with You	1967	$18
❏ CS9656	Shades of Time	1968	$18
❏ CL2515 [M]	Time/I'll Be Gone	1966	$18
❏ CS9315 [S]	Time/I'll Be Gone	1966	$25
POWER PAK			
❏ 285	The Pozo-Seco Singers with Don Williams	198?	$12
PRADO, PEREZ			
RCA CAMDEN			
❏ CAL-547 [M]	Latino!	1960	$50
❏ CAL-409 [M]	Mambo Happy!	1957	$50
RCA VICTOR			
❏ LPM-2133 [M]	A Touch of Tabasco	1960	$50
❏ LSP-2133 [S]	A Touch of Tabasco	1960	$75
❏ LPM-2104 [M]	Big Hits by Prado	1959	$75
❏ LSP-2104 [S]	Big Hits by Prado	1959	$40

Number	Title	Yr	NM
❏ LPM-3330 [M]	Dance Latino	1965	$35
❏ LSP-3330 [S]	Dance Latino	1965	$50
❏ LPM-1883 [M]	Dilo (Ugh!)	1958	$75
❏ LSP-1883 [S]	Dilo (Ugh!)	1959	$40
❏ LPM-2571 [M]	Exotic Suite	1962	$50
❏ LSP-2571 [S]	Exotic Suite	1962	$75
❏ LPM-1257 [M]	Havana 3 A.M.	1956	$40
❏ LPM-1459 [M]	Latin Satin	1957	$40
❏ LPM-3108 [10]	Mambo by the King	1953	$120
❏ LPM-1196 [M]	Mambo by the King	1956	$40
❏ LPM-1075 [M]	Mambo Mania	1955	$50
❏ LPM-2610 [M]	Our Man in Latin America	1963	$50
❏ LSP-2610 [S]	Our Man in Latin America	1963	$75
❏ LPM-21 [10]	Perez Prado Plays Mucho Mambo for Dancing	1951	$120
❏ LPM-2028 [M]	Pops and Prado	1959	$75
❏ LSP-2028 [S]	Pops and Prado	1959	$40
❏ LPM-1556 [M]	Prez	1958	$75
❏ LSP-1556 [S]	Prez	1959	$40
❏ ANL1-1941	Pure Gold	1975	$25
❏ LPM-2308 [M]	Rockambo	1961	$50
❏ LSP-2308 [S]	Rockambo	1961	$75
❏ LPM-3732 [M]	The Best of Perez Prado	1967	$50
❏ LSP-3732 [S]	The Best of Perez Prado	1967	$35
❏ LPM-2379 [M]	The New Dance La Chunga	1961	$50
❏ LSP-2379 [S]	The New Dance La Chunga	1961	$75
❏ LPM-2524 [M]	The Twist Goes Latin	1962	$50
❏ LSP-2524 [S]	The Twist Goes Latin	1962	$75
❏ VPS-6066	This Is Perez Prado	1972	$35
❏ LPM-1101 [M]	Voodoo Suite (and Six All-Time Greats)	1955	$50

UNITED ARTISTS

Number	Title	Yr	NM
❏ LS-61032	Estas Si Viven (The Living End)	196?	$35

PRATT, ANDY
COLUMBIA

Number	Title	Yr	NM
❏ KC31722	Andy Pratt	1973	$12

NEMPEROR

❏ SD438	Resolution	1976	$12
❏ SD443	Shiver in the Night	1977	$12

POLYDOR

❏ 24-4015	Records Are Like Life	1970	$15

PRATT & MCCLAIN
ABC DUNHILL

❏ DSX-50164	Pratt-McClain	1974	$15

REPRISE

❏ MS2250	Pratt & McClain Featuring "Happy Days	1976	$12

PREACHER ROLLO
KING

❏ 295-101 [10]	Dixieland	195?	$120

MGM

❏ E-3259 [M]	Dixieland Favorites	1955	$75
❏ E-95 [10]	Preacher Rollo and the Five Saints	1951	$100
❏ E-217 [10]	Preacher Rollo at the Jazz Band Ball	1953	$100
❏ E-3403 [M]	Swanee River Jazz	1956	$50

PREFAB SPROUT
EPIC

❏ BFE44208	From Langley Park to Memphis	1988	$12
❏ E46132	Jordan: The Comeback	1990	$15
❏ BFE40100	Two Wheels Good	1985	$12

PORTRAIT

❏ BFR39872	Swoon	1984	$12

PRELUDE
ISLAND

❏ ILPS9282	After the Gold Rush	1974	$15

PYE

❏ 12139	Back Into the Light	1976	$15
❏ 12120	Owlcreek Incident	1975	$15

PREMIERS, THE (1)
WARNER BROS.

❏ W1565 [M]	Farmer John	1964	$40
❏ WS1565 [S]	Farmer John	1964	$50

PRESERVATION HALL JAZZ BAND
CBS MASTERWORKS

❏ FM44856	New Orleans, Vol. 4	1989	$30
❏ FM37780	New Orleans, Volume 2	1982	$25
❏ FM38650	New Orleans, Volume 3	1983	$25
❏ FM44996	The Best of Preservation Hall Jazz Band	1989	$30

COLUMBIA MASTERWORKS

❏ M34549	Preservation Hall Jazz Band	1977	$30

PRESIDENT, THE
ELEKTRA/MUSICIAN

❏ 60799	Bring Yr Camera	1989	$30

PRESIDENTS, THE (1)
SUSSEX

Number	Title	Yr	NM
❏ SXBX-7005	5-10-15-20 (25-30 Years of Love)	1970	$30

PRESLEY, ELVIS
BMG/SUN

❏ 82876-61205-1	Elvis at Sun	2004	$18

BOXCAR

❏ (no #) [B]	Having Fun with Elvis on Stage	1974	$250

—All-talking record sold at Elvis concerts in 1974

COLLECTABLES

❏ COL-0165 [B]	Elvis Top Album Collection, Volume 1	2003	$175

—Contains reproductions, on red vinyl, of five RCA albums (LPM-1254, LPM-1382, LSP-2370, LSP-2426 and APL2-2587) using facsimiles of original labels, covers, inner sleeves and inserts; with poster and all in wooden box

❏ COL-0166	Elvis Top Album Collection, Volume 2	2003	$150

—Contains reproductions, on red vinyl, of five RCA albums (LPM-1515, LOC-1035, LSP-2256, LSP-2999 and CPL2-2642) using facsimiles of original labels, covers, inner sleeves and inserts; with poster and all in wooden box

DCC COMPACT CLASSICS

❏ LPZ-2040	24 Karat Hits!	1997	$120

—Audiophile vinyl

❏ LPZ-2037 [S]	Elvis Is Back!	1997	$120

—Audiophile vinyl

FOTOPLAY

❏ FSP-1001 [PD]	To Elvis: Love Still Burning	1978	$30

—Tribute-song picture disc of Elvis; in plastic bag with 11x11 insert

❏ FSP-1001 [PD]	To Elvis: Love Still Burning	1978	$30

—In white cardboard cover with black printing

❏ FSP-1001 [PD]	To Elvis: Love Still Burning	1978	$18

—In black cardboard cover with white printing

FRIDAY MUSIC

❏ FRM2075 [B]	50,000,000 Elvis Fans Can't Be Wrong (Elvis' Gold Records Vol. 2)	2014	$35

GOLDEN EDITIONS

❏ GEL-101	The First Year (Elvis, Scotty and Bill)	1979	$25
❏ KING-1	The First Year (Elvis, Scotty and Bill)	1979	$18

GREAT NORTHWEST

❏ GNW-4005	The Elvis Tapes	1977	$15
❏ GV-2004	The King Speaks (February 1961, Memphis, Tennessee)	1977	$12

—Label says this is on "Green Valley" while sleeve says "Great Northwest

❏ GNW-4006 [B]	The King Speaks (February 1961, Memphis, Tennessee)	1977	$15

—Both label and sleeve say this is on "Great Northwest

GREEN VALLEY

❏ GV-2001	Elvis Exclusive Live Press Conference (Memphis, Tennessee, February 1961)	1977	$40

—Issued with two slightly different covers

❏ GV-2001/3	Elvis (Speaks to You)	1978	$30

—Elvis interviews plus tracks by the Jordanaires

GUSTO

❏ SD-995	Interviews with Elvis (Canada 1957)	1978	$40

—Reissue of Great Northwest album

HALW

❏ HALW-0001	The First Years	1978	$30

—With stamped, limited edition number

❏ HALW-0001	The First Years	1978	$25

—Without limited edition number

K-TEL

❏ NU9900	Love Songs	1981	$25

LOUISIANA HAYRIDE

❏ LH-3061	Beginning Years	1984	$35

—With booklet and facsimile contract

MARVENCO

❏ 101	Beginning (1954-1955)	1988	$18

—Pink vinyl with booklet and facsimile contract

MOBILE FIDELITY

❏ Jan-0059	From Elvis in Memphis	1982	$50

—Audiophile vinyl

MUSIC WORKS

❏ PB-3601	The First Live Recordings	1984	$18
❏ PB-3602	The Hillbilly Cat	1984	$18

OAK

❏ 1003	Vintage 1955 Elvis	1990	$75

PAIR

❏ PDL2-1010	Double Dynamite	1982	$25
❏ PDL2-1185	Elvis Aron Presley Forever	1988	$25

Number	Title	Yr	NM
❏ PDL2-1037	Remembering	1983	$30

PICKWICK

❏ CAS-2440	Almost in Love	1975	$15
❏ CAS-2595	Burning Love And Hits from His Movies, Vol. 2	1975	$25

—First cover contains a notice about the upcoming "Aloha from Hawaii" show

❏ CAS-2595	Burning Love And Hits from His Movies, Vol. 2	1976	$20

—Reissue deletes the "Aloha from Hawaii" notice

❏ CAL-2518	C'mon Everybody	1975	$15
❏ DL2-5001	Double Dynamite	1975	$35
❏ CAS-2428 [M]	Elvis' Christmas Album	1975	$15

—Same contents as RCA Camden LP; no Christmas trim on border; despite the "CAS" catalog number, this album is mono

❏ CAS-2428 [M]	Elvis' Christmas Album	1976	$12

—Same as above, but with Christmas trim on cover border; despite the "CAS" catalog number, this album is mono

❏ CAS-2304	Elvis Sings Flaming Star	1976	$12
❏ CAS-2567	Elvis Sings Hits from His Movies, Volume 1	1975	$12
❏ ACL-7007	Frankie and Johnny	1976	$12
❏ CAS-2533	I Got Lucky	1975	$12
❏ CAS-2408	Let's Be Friends	1975	$12
❏ ACL-7064	Mahalo from Elvis	1978	$25
❏ CAS-2611	Separate Ways	1975	$12
❏ 0(no cat #)	The Pickwick Pack (unofficial title)	1978	$75

—Seven Pickwick albums in special package and cardboard wrapper; one of the LPs is Elvis' Christmas Album

❏ 0(no cat #)	The Pickwick Pack (unofficial title)	1979	$75

—Seven Pickwick albums in special package and cardboard wrapper; one of the LPs is Frankie and Johnny

❏ CAL-2472	You'll Never Walk Alone	1975	$15

PREMORE

❏ PL-589	Early Elvis (1954-1956 Live at the Louisiana Hayride)	1989	$30

RCA

❏ 82876-51108-1	2nd to None	2003	$30
❏ 07863-68079-1	30 #1 Hits	2002	$25
❏ 3114-1-R	Collectors Gold	1991	$250
❏ 07863-67642-1	Elvis' Golden Records	1997	$30

—Reissue for the Tower Records chain with 6 bonus tracks

❏ 07863-67643-1	Elvis' Golden Records Volume 2 -- 50,000,000 Elvis Fans Can't Be Wrong	1997	$30

—Reissue for the Tower Records chain with 10 bonus tracks

❏ 9586-1-R	Elvis Gospel 1957-1971 (Known Only to Him)	1989	$40
❏ 8468-1-R	Elvis in Nashville (1956-1971)	1988	$40
❏ 6313-1-R	Elvis Talks!	1987	$30
❏ 9589-1-R	Essential Elvis, Vol. 2 (Stereo '57)	1989	$30
❏ 6738-1-R	Essential Elvis: The First Movies	1988	$30
❏ 5600-1-R	Return of the Rocker	1986	$25
❏ 6985-1-R	The Alternate Aloha	1988	$25
❏ 6414-1-R	The Complete Sun Sessions	1987	$35
❏ 2227-1-R	The Great Performances	1990	$40
❏ 6221-1-R	The Memphis Record	1987	$30
❏ 2023-1-R	The Million Dollar Quartet	1990	$15

—With Jerry Lee Lewis, Carl Perkins, and perhaps Johnny Cash

❏ 6382-1-R	The Number One Hits	1987	$30
❏ 6383-1-R	The Top Ten Hits	1987	$30

RCA CAMDEN

❏ CAS-2440 [B]	Almost in Love	1970	$60

—Last song on Side 2 is "Stay Away, Joe

❏ CAS-2440	Almost in Love	1973	$35

—Last song on Side 2 is "Stay Away

❏ CAS-2595	Burning Love And Hits from His Movies, Vol. 2	1972	$35

—With star on front cover advertising a bonus photo, the presence of which doubles the value of this LP

❏ CAS-2595 [B]	Burning Love And Hits from His Movies, Vol. 2	1972	$25

—No star on cover, no bonus photo

❏ CAL-2518	C'mon Everybody	1971	$30
❏ CAL-2428 [M]	Elvis' Christmas Album	1970	$100

—Blue label, non-flexible vinyl

❏ CAL-2428 [M]	Elvis' Christmas Album	1971	$15

—Blue label, flexible vinyl

❏ CAS-2304	Elvis Sings Flaming Star	1969	$30
❏ CAS-2567	Elvis Sings Hits from His Movies, Volume 1	1972	$25
❏ CAL-2533	I Got Lucky	1971	$30
❏ CAS-2408	Let's Be Friends	1970	$30
❏ CAS-2611	Separate Ways	1973	$30
❏ CALX-2472	You'll Never Walk Alone	1971	$18
❏ CAL-2472	You'll Never Walk Alone	1974	$30

RCA SPECIAL PRODUCTS

❏ SVL3-0710	50 Years -- 50 Hits	1985	$30
❏ DPL2-0056(e)	Elvis	1973	$50

—Mustard labels

❏ DPL2-0056(e)	Elvis	1973	$30

—Blue labels

❏ CAL-2428 [M]	Elvis' Christmas Album	1986	$30

—Reissue for The Special Music Company

Number	Title	Yr	NM
❏ DPL2-0056(e)	Elvis Commemorative Album	1978	$100

—*Reissue of "Elvis" (same number) with new title and gold vinyl*

Number	Title	Yr	NM
❏ DPL1-0647	Elvis Country	1984	$30
❏ DPL2-0168	Elvis in Hollywood	1976	$75

—*Blue labels; with 20-page booklet*

Number	Title	Yr	NM
❏ DVM1-0704	Elvis (One Night with You)	1984	$75

—*With poster (deduct 25% if missing)*

Number	Title	Yr	NM
❏ SVL2-0824	Good Rockin' Tonight	1988	$25
❏ DVL2-0728	His Songs of Faith and Inspiration	1986	$50
❏ DML1-0264	His Songs of Inspiration	1977	$18
❏ DPL5-0347	Memories of Elvis (A Lasting Tribute to the King of Rock 'N' Roll)	1978	$100
❏ DML1-0437	Rock 'N Roll Forever	1981	$18
❏ DML3-0632	The Elvis Presley Collection	1984	$100

—*Available through Candelite Music via mail order*

Number	Title	Yr	NM
❏ DML5-0263	The Elvis Story	1977	$75

—*Available through Candelite Music via mail order*

Number	Title	Yr	NM
❏ DML1-0413	The Greatest Moments in Music	1980	$18
❏ DML1-0348	The Greatest Show on Earth	1978	$18
❏ DVL1-0461	The Legendary Magic of Elvis Presley	1980	$18
❏ DML6-0412 [B]	The Legendary Recordings of Elvis Presley	1979	$120

RCA VICTOR

Number	Title	Yr	NM
❏ KKL1-7065	A Canadian Tribute	1978	$30

—*Gold vinyl, embossed cover*

Number	Title	Yr	NM
❏ LPM-2011 [M]	A Date with Elvis	1965	$60

—*"Monaural" on label*

Number	Title	Yr	NM
❏ LSP-2011(e) [R]	A Date with Elvis	1965	$60

—*Black label, "Stereo Electronically Reprocessed" on label*

Number	Title	Yr	NM
❏ LPM-2011 [M]	A Date with Elvis	1959	$650

—*"Long Play" on label; gatefold cover, no sticker on cover*

Number	Title	Yr	NM
❏ LPM-2011 [M]	A Date with Elvis	1959	$800

—*"Long Play" on label; gatefold cover, with sticker on cover*

Number	Title	Yr	NM
❏ LPM-2011 [M]	A Date with Elvis	1963	$275

—*"Mono" on label; no gatefold cover*

Number	Title	Yr	NM
❏ LSP-2011(e) [R]	A Date with Elvis	1968	$35

—*Orange label, non-flexible vinyl*

Number	Title	Yr	NM
❏ LSP-2011(e) [R]	A Date with Elvis	1971	$30

—*Orange label, flexible vinyl*

Number	Title	Yr	NM
❏ LSP-2011(e) [R]	A Date with Elvis	1975	$30

—*Tan label*

Number	Title	Yr	NM
❏ LSP-2011(e) [R]	A Date with Elvis	1977	$20

—*Black label, dog near top*

Number	Title	Yr	NM
❏ AFL1-2011(e) [R]	A Date with Elvis	1977	$20

—*Black label, dog near top; includes copies with sticker wrapped around spine with new number*

Number	Title	Yr	NM
❏ CPM6-5172	A Golden Celebration	1984	$150
❏ CPL1-0341	A Legendary Performer, Volume 1	1974	$30

—*Includes booklet (deduct 40% if missing); with die-cut hole in front cover*

Number	Title	Yr	NM
❏ CPL1-0341	A Legendary Performer, Volume 1	1986	$18

—*No die-cut hole in cover and no booklet*

Number	Title	Yr	NM
❏ CPL1-1349	A Legendary Performer, Volume 2	1976	$30

—*Includes booklet (deduct 40% if missing); with die-cut hole in front cover*

Number	Title	Yr	NM
❏ CPL1-1349	A Legendary Performer, Volume 2	1976	$75

—*Without false starts and outtakes of "Such a Night" and "Cane and a High Starched Collar," which are supposed to be there. End of matrix number may be "31.*

Number	Title	Yr	NM
❏ CPL1-1349	A Legendary Performer, Volume 2	1986	$18

—*No die-cut hole in cover and no booklet*

Number	Title	Yr	NM
❏ CPL1-3078 [PD]	A Legendary Performer, Volume 3	1978	$30

—*Picture disc applied to blue vinyl LP; with booklet (deduct 40% if missing)*

Number	Title	Yr	NM
❏ CPL1-3082 [B]	A Legendary Performer, Volume 3	1978	$30

—*Includes booklet (deduct 40% if missing); with die-cut hole in front cover*

Number	Title	Yr	NM
❏ CPL1-3082	A Legendary Performer, Volume 3	1986	$10

—*No die-cut hole in cover and no booklet*

Number	Title	Yr	NM
❏ CPL1-4848	A Legendary Performer, Volume 4	1983	$30

—*Includes booklet (deduct 40% if missing); with die-cut hole in front cover*

Number	Title	Yr	NM
❏ CPL1-4848	A Legendary Performer, Volume 4	1986	$25

—*No die-cut hole in cover*

Number	Title	Yr	NM
❏ CPL2-2642 [S]	Aloha from Hawaii Via Satellite	2003	$35

—*Red vinyl, "DRL 13359" in trail-off wax, "DRL-23359" on back cover, "BMG Special Products" logo on back cover, from box "Elvis Top Album Collection Volume 2"*

Number	Title	Yr	NM
❏ VPSX-6089 [Q]	Aloha from Hawaii Via Satellite	1973	$300

—*Dark orange labels, "QuadraDisc" on top, "RCA" on bottom*

Number	Title	Yr	NM
❏ VPSX-6089 [Q]	Aloha from Hawaii Via Satellite	1973	$5000

—*Stokely-Van Camp employee version with Saturn-shaped*

sticker on front cover with "Chicken of the Sea" and mermaid (beware: this has been counterfeited); VG value 2500; VG+ value 3750

Number	Title	Yr	NM
❏ VPSX-6089 [Q]	Aloha from Hawaii Via Satellite	1973	$60

—*Lighter orange labels, "RCA" on side*

Number	Title	Yr	NM
❏ CPL2-2642 [Q]	Aloha from Hawaii Via Satellite	1984	$18

—*New prefix; single-pocket instead of gatefold jacket*

Number	Title	Yr	NM
❏ R213736 [S]	Aloha from Hawaii Via Satellite	1973	$80

—*RCA Record Club edition in stereo instead of quadraphonic; orange labels*

Number	Title	Yr	NM
❏ R213736 [S]	Aloha from Hawaii Via Satellite	1975	$80

—*RCA Record Club edition in stereo instead of quadraphonic; tan labels*

Number	Title	Yr	NM
❏ R213736 [S]	Aloha from Hawaii Via Satellite	1977	$35

—*RCA Record Club edition in stereo instead of quadraphonic; black labels, dog near top*

Number	Title	Yr	NM
❏ CPD2-2642 [Q]	Aloha from Hawaii Via Satellite	1975	$50

—*Orange labels*

Number	Title	Yr	NM
❏ CPD2-2642 [Q]	Aloha from Hawaii Via Satellite	1977	$150

—*Black labels, dog near top*

Number	Title	Yr	NM
❏ VPSX-6089 [DJ]	Aloha from Hawaii Via Satellite	1973	$2000

—*Orange or dark orange label; with white timing sticker on front cover*

Number	Title	Yr	NM
❏ AFL1-5430	Always on My Mind	1985	$25

—*All copies on purple vinyl*

Number	Title	Yr	NM
❏ AFL1-5353	A Valentine Gift for You	1985	$25

—*Red vinyl*

Number	Title	Yr	NM
❏ AFL1-5353	A Valentine Gift for You	1985	$12

—*Black vinyl*

Number	Title	Yr	NM
❏ LSP-4429	Back in Memphis	1970	$45

—*Orange label, non-flexible vinyl*

Number	Title	Yr	NM
❏ LSP-4429	Back in Memphis	1971	$35

—*Orange label, flexible vinyl*

Number	Title	Yr	NM
❏ LSP-4429	Back in Memphis	1975	$35

—*Tan label*

Number	Title	Yr	NM
❏ LSP-4429	Back in Memphis	1977	$20

—*Black label, dog near top*

Number	Title	Yr	NM
❏ AFL1-4429	Back in Memphis	1977	$20

—*Black label, dog near top; with sticker wrapped around spine with new number*

Number	Title	Yr	NM
❏ LSP-2426 [S]	Blue Hawaii	2003	$35

—*Red vinyl; "DRL 13358" in trail-off wax; "BMG Special Products" logo on back cover; from box "Elvis Top Album Collection Volume 1"*

Number	Title	Yr	NM
❏ LSP-2426 [S]	Blue Hawaii	197?	$1200

—*One-of-a-kind blue vinyl pressing with black label, dog near top*

Number	Title	Yr	NM
❏ LPM-2426 [M]	Blue Hawaii	1961	$200

—*"Long Play" on label; with sticker on cover advertising the presence of "Can't Help Falling in Love" and "Rock-a-Hula Baby"*

Number	Title	Yr	NM
❏ LPM-2426 [M]	Blue Hawaii	1963	$60

—*"Mono" on label*

Number	Title	Yr	NM
❏ LPM-2426 [M]	Blue Hawaii	1964	$45

—*"Monaural" on label*

Number	Title	Yr	NM
❏ LPM-2426 [M]	Blue Hawaii	1962	$80

—*"Long Play" on label; no sticker on front cover*

Number	Title	Yr	NM
❏ LSP-2426 [S]	Blue Hawaii	1961	$250

—*"Living Stereo" on label and upper right front cover; with sticker on cover advertising the presence of "Can't Help Falling in Love" and "Rock-a-Hula Baby"*

Number	Title	Yr	NM
❏ LSP-2426 [S]	Blue Hawaii	1962	$125

—*"Living Stereo" on label and upper right front cover; no sticker on front cover*

Number	Title	Yr	NM
❏ LSP-2426 [S]	Blue Hawaii	1964	$60

—*"Stereo" on label; "Victor Stereo" on upper right front cover*

Number	Title	Yr	NM
❏ LSP-2426 [S]	Blue Hawaii	1968	$50

—*Orange label, non-flexible vinyl*

Number	Title	Yr	NM
❏ LSP-2426 [S]	Blue Hawaii	1971	$35

—*Orange label, flexible vinyl*

Number	Title	Yr	NM
❏ LSP-2426 [S]	Blue Hawaii	1975	$35

—*Tan label*

Number	Title	Yr	NM
❏ LSP-2426 [S]	Blue Hawaii	1977	$20

—*Black label, dog near top*

Number	Title	Yr	NM
❏ AFL1-2426 [S]	Blue Hawaii	1977	$1815

—*Black label, dog near top; with sticker wrapped around spine with new number*

Number	Title	Yr	NM
❏ AYL1-3683 [S]	Blue Hawaii	1980	$12

—*"Best Buy Series" reissue*

Number	Title	Yr	NM
❏ LPM-3893 [M]	Clambake	1967	$350
❏ LSP-3893 [S]	Clambake	1967	$80
❏ APL1-2565	Clambake	1977	$25
❏ LPM/LSP-3893	Clambake Bonus Photo	1967	$50
❏ R233299(e)	Country Classics	1980	$40

—*RCA Music Service exclusive*

Number	Title	Yr	NM
❏ R244069	Country Memories	1978	$40

—*RCA Music Service exclusive*

Number	Title	Yr	NM
❏ LPM-3787 [M]	Double Trouble	1967	$85

—*With bonus photo announcement on cover*

Number	Title	Yr	NM
❏ LPM-3787 [M]	Double Trouble	1967	$125

—*With no bonus photo announcement on cover*

Number	Title	Yr	NM
❏ LSP-3787 [S]	Double Trouble	1967	$80

—*With bonus photo announcement on cover*

Number	Title	Yr	NM
❏ LSP-3787 [S]	Double Trouble	1967	$85

—*With no bonus photo announcement on cover; black label "Stereo*

Number	Title	Yr	NM
❏ LSP-3787 [S]	Double Trouble	1968	$50

—*Orange label, non-flexible vinyl*

Number	Title	Yr	NM
❏ LSP-3787 [S]	Double Trouble	1975	$35

—*Tan label*

Number	Title	Yr	NM
❏ LSP-3787 [S]	Double Trouble	1977	$20

—*Black label, dog near top*

Number	Title	Yr	NM
❏ APL1-2564 [S]	Double Trouble	1977	$20

—*Black label, dog near top; includes copies with sticker wrapped around spine with new number*

Number	Title	Yr	NM
❏ LPM/LSP-3787	Double Trouble Bonus Photo	1967	$60
❏ LPM-1382 [M]	Elvis	2003	$25

—*Red vinyl; "DRC 13271" in trail-off wax; "BMG Special Products" logo on back cover; from box "Elvis Top Album Collection Volume 1"*

Number	Title	Yr	NM
❏ LPM-1382 [M]	Elvis	1956	$400

—*Back cover has ads for other albums. At least 11 different variations of this are known, all of equal value.*

Number	Title	Yr	NM
❏ LPM-1382 [M]	Elvis	1956	$400

—*Back cover has no ads for other albums. "Long Play" on label.*

Number	Title	Yr	NM
❏ LPM-1382 [M]	Elvis	1956	$1000

—*With alternate take of "Old Shep" on side 2. Matrix number on the "Old Shep" side ends in "15S," "17S" or "19S," but should be played for positive ID. On alternate take, Elvis sings "he grew old AND his eyes were growing dim" (no AND on standard press)*

Number	Title	Yr	NM
❏ LPM-1382 [M]	Elvis	1956	$400

—*With tracks listed on labels as "Band 1" through "Band 6"*

Number	Title	Yr	NM
❏ LPM-1382 [M]	Elvis	1963	$125

—*Mono" on label*

Number	Title	Yr	NM
❏ LPM-1382 [M]	Elvis	1965	$80

—*Monaural" on label*

Number	Title	Yr	NM
❏ LSP-1382(e) [R]	Elvis	1962	$300

—*Stereo Electronically Reprocessed" and silver "RCA Victor" on label*

Number	Title	Yr	NM
❏ LSP-1382(e) [R]	Elvis	1964	$0

—*Stereo Electronically Reprocessed" and white "RCA Victor" on label*

Number	Title	Yr	NM
❏ LSP-1382(e) [R]	Elvis	1968	$40

—*Orange label, non-flexible vinyl*

Number	Title	Yr	NM
❏ LSP-1382(e) [R]	Elvis	1971	$25

—*Orange label, flexible vinyl*

Number	Title	Yr	NM
❏ LSP-1382(e) [R]	Elvis	1975	$18

—*Tan label*

Number	Title	Yr	NM
❏ LSP-1382(e) [R]	Elvis	1976	$15

—*Black label, dog near top*

Number	Title	Yr	NM
❏ AFL1-1382(e) [R]	Elvis	1977	$15

—*Black label, dog near top; includes copies with sticker wrapped around spine with new number*

Number	Title	Yr	NM
❏ AFM1-5199 [M]	Elvis	1984	$25

—*50th Anniversary reissue in mono with banner*

Number	Title	Yr	NM
❏ APL1-0283	Elvis	1973	$50
❏ CPL8-3699 [B]	Elvis Aron Presley	1980	$250

—*Box set; regular issue with booklet*

Number	Title	Yr	NM
❏ CPL8-3699 [B]	Elvis Aron Presley	1980	$300

Number	Title	Yr	NM

—Box set; "Reviewer Series" edition (will be identified as such on the cover)
❏ DJL1-3729 [DJ] — Elvis Aron Presley (Excerpts) — 1980 — $175
—Promo-only excerpts of songs from box set
❏ DJL1-3781 [DJ] — Elvis Aron Presley (Selections) — 1980 — $175
—Promo-only complete versions of songs from box set
❏ LSP-4776 — Elvis As Recorded at Madison Square Garden — 1972 — $30
—Orange label
❏ SPS-33-571 [DJ] — Elvis As Recorded at Madison Square Garden — 1972 — $350
—Radio Station Banded Special Version"; came in plain white cover with stickers
❏ LSP-4776 — Elvis As Recorded at Madison Square Garden — 1975 — $25
—Tan label
❏ LSP-4776 — Elvis As Recorded at Madison Square Garden — 1976 — $18
—Black label, dog near top
❏ AFL1-4776 — Elvis As Recorded at Madison Square Garden — 1977 — $15
—Black label, dog near top; includes copies with sticker wrapped around spine with new number
❏ AQL1-4776 — Elvis As Recorded at Madison Square Garden — 1980 — $10
—Another reissue with new prefix
❏ LSP-4776 [DJ] — Elvis As Recorded at Madison Square Garden — 1972 — $175
—Orange label; with white timing sticker on front cover
❏ LOC-1035 — Elvis' Christmas Album — 2003 — $25
—Red vinyl; not to be mistaken for the unique 1957 version, as this has "DRL 13265" number in trail-off wax and BMG Special Products logo and "This is a replica of the original packaging" on back cover; from box "Elvis Top Album Collection Volume 2
❏ LOC-1035 [M] — Elvis' Christmas Album — 1957 — $600
—Gatefold cover; title printed in gold on LP spine; includes bound-in booklet but not sticker
❏ LOC-1035 [M] — Elvis' Christmas Album — 1957 — $800
—Gatefold cover; title printed in silver on LP spine; includes bound-in booklet but not sticker
❏ LOC-1035 [M] — Elvis' Christmas Album — 1957 — $20000
—Red vinyl; unique; VG value 7500; VG+ value 11250
❏ AFM1-5486 [M] — Elvis' Christmas Album — 1985 — $25
—Same as LOC-1035; green vinyl with booklet
❏ AFM1-5486 [M] — Elvis' Christmas Album — 1985 — $18
—Same as LOC-1035; black vinyl with booklet
❏ LPM-1951 [M] — Elvis' Christmas Album — 1958 — $300
—Same contents as LOC-1035, but with non-gatefold blue cover; "Long Play" at bottom of label
❏ LPM-1951 [M] — Elvis' Christmas Album — 1963 — $175
—Mono" at bottom of label: "RE" on lower left front cover (photos on back were altered)
❏ LPM-1951 [M] — Elvis' Christmas Album — 1964 — $40
—Monaural" at bottom of label; "RE" on lower left front cover
❏ LSP-1951(e) [R] — Elvis' Christmas Album — 1968 — $75
—Orange label, non-flexible vinyl
❏ LSP-1951(e) [R] — Elvis' Christmas Album — 1964 — $50
—Black label, dog on top; "Stereo Electronically Reprocessed" at bottom of label
❏ LOC-1035 [M] — Elvis' Christmas Album Sticker — 1957 — $250
—Gold sticker with "To_____" and "From_____" blanks
❏ LSP-4460 — Elvis Country ("I'm 10,000 Years Old") — 1971 — $40
—Orange label, non-flexible vinyl
❏ LSP-4460 — Elvis Country ("I'm 10,000 Years Old") — 1971 — $30
—Orange label, flexible vinyl
❏ LSP-4460 — Elvis Country ("I'm 10,000 Years Old") — 1975 — $30
—Tan label
❏ LSP-4460 — Elvis Country ("I'm 10,000 Years Old") — 1976 — $18
—Black label, dog near top
❏ AFL1-4460 — Elvis Country ("I'm 10,000 Years Old") — 1977 — $15
—Black label, dog near top; includes copies with sticker wrapped around spine with new number
❏ AYL1-3956 — Elvis Country ("I'm 10,000 Years Old") — 1981 — $10
—Best Buy Series" reissue
❏ LSP-4460 — Elvis Country ("I'm 10,000 Years Old") — 197? — $2000
—Green vinyl; black label, dog near top
❏ LSP-4460 — Elvis Country ("I'm 10,000 Years Old") Bonus Photo — 1971 — $18
—Available in either orange-label pressing
❏ LPM-3450 [M] — Elvis for Everyone — 1965 — $75
❏ LSP-3450 [P] — Elvis for Everyone — 1965 — $75
—Black label, "Stereo" on label
❏ LSP-3450 [P] — Elvis for Everyone — 1968 — $40
—Orange label, non-flexible vinyl
❏ LSP-3450 [P] — Elvis for Everyone — 1971 — $25
—Orange label, flexible vinyl
❏ LSP-3450 [P] — Elvis for Everyone — 1975 — $25
—Tan label

❏ LSP-3450 [P] — Elvis for Everyone — 1976 — $15
—Black label, dog near top
❏ AFL1-3450 — Elvis for Everyone — 1977 — $15
—Black label, dog near top; includes copies with sticker wrapped around spine with new number
❏ AYL1-4232 [P] — Elvis for Everyone — 1982 — $10
—Best Buy Series" reissue
❏ LPM-1707 [M] — Elvis' Golden Records — 1964 — $40
—Monaural" on label; "RE2" on back cover
❏ LPM-1707 [M] — Elvis' Golden Records — 1958 — $300
—Title on cover in light blue letters; no song titles listed on front cover
❏ LPM-1707 [M] — Elvis' Golden Records — 1958 — $250
—Title on cover in light blue letters; no song titles listed on front cover; "RE" on back cover
❏ LPM-1707 [M] — Elvis' Golden Records — 1963 — $75
—Mono" on label; title on cover in white letters; song titles added to front cover
❏ LSP-1707(e) [R] — Elvis' Golden Records — 1962 — $250
—Stereo Electronically Reprocessed" and silver "RCA Victor" on label
❏ LSP-1707(e) [R] — Elvis' Golden Records — 1964 — $50
—Stereo Electronically Reprocessed" and white "RCA Victor" on label
❏ LSP-1707(e) [R] — Elvis' Golden Records — 1968 — $30
—Orange label, non-flexible vinyl
❏ LSP-1707(e) [R] — Elvis' Golden Records — 1971 — $25
—Orange label, flexible vinyl
❏ LSP-1707(e) [R] — Elvis' Golden Records — 1975 — $25
—Tan label
❏ LSP-1707(e) [R] — Elvis' Golden Records — 1976 — $15
—Black label, dog near top
❏ AFL1-1707(e) [R] — Elvis' Golden Records — 1977 — $15
—Black label, dog near top; includes copies with sticker wrapped around spine with new number
❏ AQL1-1707(e) [R] — Elvis' Golden Records — 1979 — $12
—Another reissue with new prefix
❏ AFM1-5196 [M] — Elvis' Golden Records — 1984 — $25
—50th Anniversary reissue in mono with banner
❏ LPM-2765 [M] — Elvis' Golden Records, Volume 3 — 1963 — $175
—Mono" on label
❏ LPM-2765 [M] — Elvis' Golden Records, Volume 3 — 1964 — $75
—Monaural" on label
❏ LSP-2765 [S] — Elvis' Golden Records, Volume 3 — 1963 — $175
—Stereo" and silver "RCA Victor" on black label
❏ LSP-2765 [S] — Elvis' Golden Records, Volume 3 — 1964 — $50
—Stereo" and white "RCA Victor" on black label
❏ LSP-2765 [S] — Elvis' Golden Records, Volume 3 — 1968 — $40
—Orange label, non-flexible vinyl
❏ LSP-2765 [S] — Elvis' Golden Records, Volume 3 — 1975 — $25
—Tan label
❏ LSP-2765 [S] — Elvis' Golden Records, Volume 3 — 1976 — $15
—Black label, dog near top
❏ AFL1-2765 [S] — Elvis' Golden Records, Volume 3 — 1977 — $15
—Black label, dog near top; includes copies with sticker wrapped around spine with new number
❏ LPM-3921 [M] — Elvis' Gold Records, Volume 4 — 1968 — $2000
—Monaural" on label
❏ LSP-3921 [P] — Elvis' Gold Records, Volume 4 — 1968 — $50
—Stereo" and white "RCA Victor" on black label
❏ LSP-3921 [P] — Elvis' Gold Records, Volume 4 — 1968 — $40
—Orange label, non-flexible vinyl
❏ LSP-3921 [P] — Elvis' Gold Records, Volume 4 — 1975 — $30
—Tan label
❏ LSP-3921 [P] — Elvis' Gold Records, Volume 4 — 1976 — $15
—Black label, dog near top
❏ AFL1-3921 [P] — Elvis' Gold Records, Volume 4 — 1976 — $18
—Tan label with new prefix
❏ AFL1-3921 [P] — Elvis' Gold Records, Volume 4 — 1977 — $15
—Black label, dog near top; includes copies with sticker wrapped around spine with new number
❏ LSP-3921 [P] — Elvis' Gold Records, Volume 4 — 197? — $25
—Orange label, flexible vinyl
❏ AFL1-4941 — Elvis' Gold Records, Volume 5 — 1984 — $12
❏ LPM-2075 [M] — Elvis' Gold Records Volume 2 -- 50,000,000 Elvis Fans Can't Be Wrong — 1960 — $300
—Long Play" on label; "Magic Millions" on upper right front cover with RCA Victor logo
❏ LPM-2075 [M] — Elvis' Gold Records Volume 2 -- 50,000,000 Elvis Fans Can't Be Wrong — 1963 — $100
—Mono" on label; "RE" on lower right front cover

❏ LPM-2075 [M] — Elvis' Gold Records Volume 2 -- 50,000,000 Elvis Fans Can't Be Wrong — 1964 — $50
—Monaural" on label; label has words "50,000,000 Elvis Presley Fans Can't Be Wrong
❏ LSP-2075(e) [R] — Elvis' Gold Records Volume 2 -- 50,000,000 Elvis Fans Can't Be Wrong — 1964 — $50
—Stereo Electronically Reprocessed" and white "RCA Victor" on label
❏ LPM-2075 [M] — Elvis' Gold Records Volume 2 -- 50,000,000 Elvis Fans Can't Be Wrong — 1964 — $50
—Monaural" on label; label only has "Elvis' Gold Records - Vol. 2
❏ LSP-2075(e) [R] — Elvis' Gold Records Volume 2 -- 50,000,000 Elvis Fans Can't Be Wrong — 1962 — $250
—Stereo Electronically Reprocessed" on label; label has words "50,000,000 Elvis Presley Fans Can't Be Wrong
❏ LSP-2075(e) [R] — Elvis' Gold Records Volume 2 -- 50,000,000 Elvis Fans Can't Be Wrong — 1975 — $30
—Tan label
❏ LSP-2075(e) [R] — Elvis' Gold Records Volume 2 -- 50,000,000 Elvis Fans Can't Be Wrong — 1968 — $30
—Orange label, non-flexible vinyl
❏ LSP-2075(e) [R] — Elvis' Gold Records Volume 2 -- 50,000,000 Elvis Fans Can't Be Wrong — 1971 — $30
—Orange label, flexible vinyl
❏ LSP-2075(e) [R] — Elvis' Gold Records Volume 2 -- 50,000,000 Elvis Fans Can't Be Wrong — 1976 — $15
—Black label, dog near top
❏ AFL1-2075(e) [R] — Elvis' Gold Records Volume 2 -- 50,000,000 Elvis Fans Can't Be Wrong — 1977 — $15
—Black label, dog near top; includes copies with sticker wrapped around spine with new number
❏ AFM1-5197 [M] — Elvis' Gold Records Volume 2 -- 50,000,000 Elvis Fans Can't Be Wrong — 1984 — $25
—50th Anniversary reissue in mono with banner
❏ APL2-2587 — Elvis in Concert — 2003 — $25
—Red vinyl; "DRL 13360" in trail-off wax; "This is a replica of the original packaging" on back cover and all inserts; "DRL-23360" on back cover; from box "Elvis Top Album Collection Volume 1
❏ APL2-2587 — Elvis in Concert — 1977 — $30
❏ CPL2-2587 — Elvis in Concert — 1982 — $40
❏ AFL2-2587 — Elvis in Concert — 197? — $1000
—Both records on translucent blue vinyl; possibly an in-house demo at the RCA Indianapolis pressing plant
❏ LSP-4428 [B] — Elvis in Person at the International Hotel, Las Vegas, Nevada — 1970 — $75
—Orange label, non-flexible vinyl
❏ LSP-4428 — Elvis in Person at the International Hotel, Las Vegas, Nevada — 1971 — $40
—Orange label, flexible vinyl
❏ LSP-4428 — Elvis in Person at the International Hotel, Las Vegas, Nevada — 1975 — $30
—Tan label
❏ LSP-4428 — Elvis in Person at the International Hotel, Las Vegas, Nevada — 1976 — $18
—Black label, dog near top
❏ AFL1-4428 — Elvis in Person at the International Hotel, Las Vegas, Nevada — 1977 — $15
—Black label, dog near top; includes copies with sticker wrapped around spine with new number
❏ AYL1-3892 — Elvis in Person at the International Hotel, Las Vegas, Nevada — 1981 — $10
—Best Buy Series" reissue
❏ LPM-2231 [M] — Elvis Is Back! — 1960 — $175
—With sticker attached to front cover. Side 2, Song 4 is listed as "The Girl Next Door.
❏ LPM-2231 [M] — Elvis Is Back! — 1960 — $175
—With sticker attached to front cover. Side 2, Song 4 is listed as "The Girl Next Door Went a-Walking.
❏ LPM-2231 [M] — Elvis Is Back! — 1960 — $250
—With no sticker attached to front cover. Side 2, Song 4 is listed as "The Girl Next Door.
❏ LPM-2231 [M] — Elvis Is Back! — 1960 — $250
—With no sticker attached to front cover. Side 2, Song 4 is listed as "The Girl Next Door Went a-Walking.
❏ LPM-2231 [M] — Elvis Is Back! — 1963 — $75
—Mono" on label; song titles printed on front cover
❏ LPM-2231 [M] — Elvis Is Back! — 1964 — $75
—Monaural" on label
❏ LSP-2231 [S] — Elvis Is Back! — 1960 — $300
—Living Stereo" on label; with sticker attached to front cover. Side 2, Song 4 is listed as "The Girl Next Door.
❏ LSP-2231 [S] — Elvis Is Back! — 1960 — $300
—Living Stereo" on label; with sticker attached to front cover. Side 2, Song 4 is listed as "The Girl Next Door Went

Number	Title	Yr	NM

a-Walking.
❏ LSP-2231 [S] Elvis Is Back! 1960 $300
— Living Stereo" on label; with no sticker attached to front cover. Side 2, Song 4 is listed as "The Girl Next Door.
❏ LSP-2231 [S] Elvis Is Back! 1960 $300
— Living Stereo" on label; with no sticker attached to front cover. Side 2, Song 4 is listed as "The Girl Next Door Went a-Walking.
❏ LSP-2231 [S] Elvis Is Back! 1964 $75
— Stereo" on label; song titles printed on front cover
❏ LSP-2231 [S] Elvis Is Back! 1968 $40
— Orange label, non-flexible vinyl
❏ LSP-2231 [S] Elvis Is Back! 1975 $25
— Tan label
❏ LSP-2231 [S] Elvis Is Back! 1976 $18
— Black label, dog on top
❏ AFL1-2231 Elvis Is Back! 1977 $15
— Black label, dog near top; includes copies with sticker wrapped around spine with new number
❏ LPM-4088 Elvis (NBC-TV Special) 1968 $40
— Orange label, non-flexible vinyl
❏ LPM-4088 Elvis (NBC-TV Special) 1971 $30
— Orange label, flexible vinyl
❏ LPM-4088 Elvis (NBC-TV Special) 1975 $25
— Tan label
❏ LPM-4088 Elvis (NBC-TV Special) 1976 $18
— Black label, dog near top
❏ AFM1-4088 Elvis (NBC-TV Special) 1977 $15
— Black label, dog near top; includes copies with sticker wrapped around spine with new number
❏ AYM1-3894 Elvis (NBC-TV Special) 1981 $10
— Best Buy Series" reissue
❏ LSP-4671 Elvis Now 1972 $30
— Orange label
❏ LSP-4671 Elvis Now 1975 $30
— Tan label
❏ LSP-4671 Elvis Now 1976 $18
— Black label, dog near top
❏ AFL1-4671 Elvis Now 1977 $15
— Black label, dog near top; includes copies with sticker wrapped around spine with new number
❏ LSP-4671 [DJ] Elvis Now 1972 $150
— Orange label; with white timing sticker on front cover
❏ LPM-1254 [M] Elvis Presley 2003 $25
— Red vinyl; "DRL 13272" in trail-off wax; "BMG Special Products" logo on back cover; from box "Elvis Top Album Collection Volume 1
❏ LSP-1254(e) [R] Elvis Presley 1968 $30
— Orange label, non-flexible vinyl
❏ LPM-1254 [M] Elvis Presley 1956 $800
— Version 1: "Long Play" on label; "Elvis" in pale pink, "Presley" in pale green on cover; pale green logo box in upper right front cover

❏ LPM-1254 [M] Elvis Presley 1956 $600
— Version 2: "Long Play" on label; "Elvis" in pale pink, "Presley" in neon green on cover; neon green logo box in upper right front cover
❏ LPM-1254 [M] Elvis Presley 1956 $300
— Version 3: "Long Play" on label; "Elvis" in pale pink, "Presley" in neon green on cover; black logo box in upper right front cover
❏ LPM-1254 [M] Elvis Presley 1958 $300
— Version 4: "Long Play" on label; "Elvis" in neon pink, almost red, "Presley" in neon green on cover; black logo box in upper right front cover
❏ LPM-1254 [M] Elvis Presley 1963 $175
— Mono" on label; cover photo is slightly left of center, otherwise same as Version 4 above
❏ LPM-1254 [M] Elvis Presley 1964 $75
— Monaural" on label
❏ LSP-1254(e) [R] Elvis Presley 1965 $40
— Stereo Electronically Reprocessed" and white "RCA Victor"

on label
❏ LSP-1254(e) [R] Elvis Presley 1962 $250
— Stereo Electronically Reprocessed" and silver "RCA Victor" on label
❏ LSP-1254(e) [R] Elvis Presley 1975 $18
— Tan label
❏ LSP-1254(e) [R] Elvis Presley 1976 $15
— Black label, dog near top
❏ AFL1-1254(e) [R] Elvis Presley 1977 $15
— Black label, dog near top; includes copies with sticker wrapped around spine with new number
❏ AFM1-5198 [M] Elvis Presley 1984 $25
— 50th Anniversary reissue in mono with banner
❏ DJM1-0835 [DJ] Elvis Presley Interview Record: An Audio Self-Portrait 1984 $100
— Promotional item for "50th Anniversary" series; later issued as RCA 6313-1-R
❏ CPL1-0606 Elvis Recorded Live on Stage in Memphis 1974 $30
— Orange label
❏ DJL1-0606 [DJ] Elvis Recorded Live on Stage in Memphis 1974 $350
— Special banded version for radio airplay
❏ APD1-0606 [Q] Elvis Recorded Live on Stage in Memphis 1974 $300
— RCA QuadraDisc" labels
❏ CPL1-0606 Elvis Recorded Live on Stage in Memphis 1975 $30
— Tan label
❏ AFL1-0606 Elvis Recorded Live on Stage in Memphis 1977 $15
— Black label, dog near top; includes copies with sticker wrapped around spine with new number
❏ CPL1-2901 Elvis Sings for Children and Grownups Too! 1978 $25
— With two slits for removable greeting card on back cover (card should be with package)
❏ CPL1-2901 Elvis Sings for Children and Grownups Too! 1978 $12
— With greeting card graphic printed on back cover, and no slits on back cover
❏ LSP-4579 [B] Elvis Sings the Wonderful World of Christmas 1971 $40
— Orange label. Bonus postcard is priced separately
❏ ANL1-1936 Elvis Sings the Wonderful World of Christmas 1975 $18
— New number; same contents as LSP-4579. Orange label.
❏ ANL1-1936 Elvis Sings the Wonderful World of Christmas 1976 $15
— Tan label
❏ ANL1-1936 Elvis Sings the Wonderful World of Christmas 1977 $12
— Black label, dog near top
❏ LSP-4579 [B] Elvis Sings the Wonderful World of Christmas Postcard 1971 $30
❏ APL1-1039 Elvis Today 1975 $75
— Orange label
❏ APD1-1039 [Q] Elvis Today 1975 $300
— RCA QuadraDisc" labels
❏ APL1-1039 Elvis Today 1975 $30
— Tan label
❏ APD1-1039 [Q] Elvis Today 1977 $250
— Black label, dog near top; quadraphonic reissue
❏ AFL1-1039 Elvis Today 1977 $15
— Black label, dog near top; includes copies with sticker wrapped around spine with new number
❏ LPM-1990 [M] For LP Fans Only 1959 $300
— Long Play" on label
❏ LPM-1990 [M] For LP Fans Only 1963 $100
— Mono" on label
❏ LPM-1990 [M] For LP Fans Only 1964 $50
— Monaural" on label
❏ LSP-1990(e) [R] For LP Fans Only 1965 $300
— Stereo Electronically Reprocessed" on label; error cover with same photo on both front and back
❏ LSP-1990(e) [R] For LP Fans Only 1965 $50
— Stereo Electronically Reprocessed" on label; normal cover with different front and back cover photos
❏ LSP-1990(e) [R] For LP Fans Only 1968 $30
— Orange label, non-flexible vinyl
❏ LSP-1990(e) [R] For LP Fans Only 1975 $25
— Tan label
❏ LSP-1990(e) [R] For LP Fans Only 1976 $15
— Black label, dog near top
❏ AFL1-1990(e) [R] For LP Fans Only 1977 $15
— Black label, dog near top; includes copies with sticker wrapped around spine with new number
❏ LPM-3553 [M] Frankie and Johnny 1966 $75
❏ LSP-3553 [S] Frankie and Johnny 1966 $75
— Stereo" on black label
❏ LPM/LSP-3553 Frankie and Johnny Bonus Print 1966 $75
❏ LSP-4155 From Elvis in Memphis 1975 $30
— Tan label
❏ LSP-4155 From Elvis in Memphis 1976 $18
— Black label, dog near top
❏ LSP-4155 From Elvis in Memphis 1969 $40
— Orange label, non-flexible vinyl

❏ LSP-4155 From Elvis in Memphis 1971 $30
— Orange label, flexible vinyl
❏ AFL1-4155 From Elvis in Memphis 1977 $15
— Black label, dog near top; includes copies with sticker wrapped around spine with new number
❏ LSP-4155 From Elvis in Memphis Bonus Photo 1969 $40
❏ APL1-1506 From Elvis Presley Boulevard, Memphis, Tennessee 1976 $30
— Tan label
❏ AFL1-1506 From Elvis Presley Boulevard, Memphis, Tennessee 1977 $15
— Black label, dog near top; with sticker wrapped around spine with new number (old number still on label)
❏ AFL1-1506 From Elvis Presley Boulevard, Memphis, Tennessee 1977 $12
— Black label, dog near top; new number is on cover and label
❏ R234340 From Elvis with Love 1978 $40
— RCA Music Service exclusive
❏ LSP-6020 [B] From Memphis to Vegas/ From Vegas to Memphis 1969 $175
— Orange labels, non-flexible vinyl; with composers of "Words" correctly listed as Barry, Robin and Maurice Gibb
❏ LSP-6020 From Memphis to Vegas/ From Vegas to Memphis 1969 $175
— Orange labels, non-flexible vinyl; with composers of "Words" incorrectly listed as Tommy Boyce and Bobby Hart
❏ LSP-6020 From Memphis to Vegas/ From Vegas to Memphis 1971 $40
— Orange labels, flexible vinyl
❏ LSP-6020 From Memphis to Vegas/ From Vegas to Memphis Bonus Photos 1969 $50
— Four different photos came with LP, but no more than two per set. Value is for any two different of the four photos.
❏ LSP-6020 From Memphis to Vegas/ From Vegas to Memphis Bonus Photos 1975 $30
— Tan labels
❏ LSP-6020 From Memphis to Vegas/ From Vegas to Memphis Bonus Photos 1976 $25
— Black label, dog near top
❏ LPM-2756 [M] Fun in Acapulco 1963 $100
— Mono" on label
❏ LPM-2756 [M] Fun in Acapulco 1964 $50
— Monaural" on label
❏ LSP-2756 [S] Fun in Acapulco 1963 $150
— Stereo" and silver "RCA Victor" on black label
❏ LSP-2756 [S] Fun in Acapulco 1964 $75
— Stereo" and white "RCA Victor" on black label
❏ LSP-2756 [S] Fun in Acapulco 1968 $40
— Orange label, non-flexible vinyl
❏ LSP-2756 [S] Fun in Acapulco 1975 $30
— Tan label
❏ LSP-2756 [S] Fun in Acapulco 1976 $15
— Black label, dog near top
❏ AFL1-2756 [S] Fun in Acapulco 1977 $15
— Black label, dog near top; includes copies with sticker wrapped around spine with new number
❏ LSP-2256 [S] G.I. Blues 2003 $25
— Red vinyl; "DRL 13273" in trail-off wax; "BMG Special Products" logo on back cover; from box "Elvis Top Album Collection Volume 2
❏ LPM-2256 [M] G.I. Blues 1960 $500
— Long Play" on label; with sticker on front cover advertising the presence of "Wooden Heart"
❏ LPM-2256 [M] G.I. Blues 1960 $120
— Long Play" on label; with no sticker on front cover
❏ LPM-2256 [M] G.I. Blues 1963 $150
— Mono" on label
❏ LPM-2256 [M] G.I. Blues 1964 $50
— Monaural" on label
❏ LSP-2256 [S] G.I. Blues 1960 $600
— Living Stereo" on label; with sticker on front cover advertising the presence of "Wooden Heart"
❏ LSP-2256 [S] G.I. Blues 1960 $150
— Living Stereo" on label; with no sticker on front cover
❏ LSP-2256 [S] G.I. Blues 1964 $50
— Stereo" on black label
❏ LSP-2256 [S] G.I. Blues 1968 $40
— Orange label, non-flexible vinyl
❏ LSP-2256 [S] G.I. Blues 1971 $25
— Orange label, flexible vinyl
❏ LSP-2256 [S] G.I. Blues 1975 $30
— Tan label
❏ LSP-2256 [S] G.I. Blues 1976 $15
— Black label, dog near top
❏ AYL1-3735 [S] G.I. Blues 1980 $10
— Best Buy Series" reissue
❏ AFL1-2256 [S] G.I. Blues 1977 $15
— Black label, dog near top; includes copies with sticker wrapped around spine with new number
❏ LSP-3338 [S] Girl Happy 1971 $25
— Orange label, flexible vinyl

Number	Title	Yr	NM
❏ LPM-3338 [M]	Girl Happy	1965	$75
❏ LSP-3338 [S]	Girl Happy	1965	$75
— *Stereo" on black label*			
❏ LSP-3338 [S]	Girl Happy	1968	$40
— *Orange label, non-flexible vinyl*			
❏ LSP-3338 [S]	Girl Happy	1975	$30
— *Tan label*			
❏ LSP-3338 [S]	Girl Happy	1976	$15
— *Black label, dog near top*			
❏ AFL1-3338 [S]	Girl Happy	1977	$15
— *Black label, dog near top; includes copies with sticker wrapped around spine with new number*			
❏ LPM-2621 [M]	Girls! Girls! Girls!	1962	$100
— *Long Play" on label*			
❏ LPM-2621 [M]	Girls! Girls! Girls!	1963	$75
— *Mono" on label*			
❏ LPM-2621 [M]	Girls! Girls! Girls!	1964	$40
— *Monaural" on label*			
❏ LSP-2621 [S]	Girls! Girls! Girls!	1962	$250
— *Living Stereo" on label*			
❏ LSP-2621 [S]	Girls! Girls! Girls!	1964	$75
— *Stereo" on black label*			
❏ LSP-2621 [S]	Girls! Girls! Girls!	1968	$40
— *Orange label, non-flexible vinyl*			
❏ LSP-2621 [S]	Girls! Girls! Girls!	1971	$25
— *Orange label, flexible vinyl*			
❏ LSP-2621 [S]	Girls! Girls! Girls!	1975	$30
— *Tan label*			
❏ LSP-2621 [S]	Girls! Girls! Girls!	1976	$15
— *Black label, dog near top*			
❏ AFL1-2621 [S]	Girls! Girls! Girls!	1977	$15
— *Black label, dog near top; includes copies with sticker wrapped around spine with new number*			
❏ LPM/LSP-2621 [B]	Girls! Girls! Girls! Bonus 1963 Calendar	1962	$250
— *With listing of other Elvis records on back*			
❏ CPL1-0475	Good Times	1974	$50
— *Orange label*			
❏ CPL1-0475	Good Times	1976	$15
— *Black label, dog near top*			
❏ AFL1-0475	Good Times	1977	$15
— *Black label, dog near top; includes copies with sticker wrapped around spine with new number*			
❏ AHL1-2347	Greatest Hits, Volume One	1981	$30
— *With embossed cover*			
❏ AHL1-2347	Greatest Hits, Volume One	1983	$18
— *Without embossed cover*			
❏ AAL1-3917	Guitar Man	1981	$30

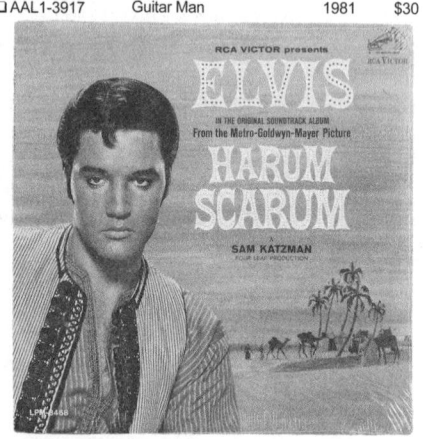

Number	Title	Yr	NM
❏ LPM-3468 [M]	Harum Scarum	1965	$75
❏ LSP-3468 [S]	Harum Scarum	1965	$75
— *Stereo" on black label*			
❏ APL1-2558 [S]	Harum Scarum	1977	$15
— *Black label, dog near top*			
❏ AYL1-3734 [S]	Harum Scarum	1980	$10
— *Best Buy Series" reissue*			
❏ LPM/LSP-3468	Harum Scarum Bonus Photo	1965	$75
❏ CPM1-0818	Having Fun with Elvis on Stage	1974	$30
— *Commercial issue of Boxcar LP; orange label*			
❏ CPM1-0818	Having Fun with Elvis on Stage	1975	$25
— *Tan label*			
❏ AFM1-0818	Having Fun with Elvis on Stage	1977	$30
— *Black label, dog near top*			
❏ LSP-4690	He Touched Me	1972	$40
— *Orange label*			
❏ LSP-4690	He Touched Me	1975	$25
— *Tan label*			
❏ LSP-4690	He Touched Me	1976	$18
— *Black label, dog near top*			
❏ AFL1-4690	He Touched Me	1977	$15
— *Black label, dog near top; includes copies with sticker wrapped around spine with new number*			

Number	Title	Yr	NM
❏ LSP-4690 [DJ]	He Touched Me	1972	$150
— *Orange label; with white timing sticker on front cover*			
❏ AFL1-2772	He Walks Beside Me	1978	$30
— *Includes 20-page photo booklet*			
❏ LPM-2328 [M]	His Hand in Mine	1960	$175
— *Long Play" on label*			
❏ LPM-2328 [M]	His Hand in Mine	1963	$75
— *Mono" on label*			
❏ LPM-2328 [M]	His Hand in Mine	1964	$50
— *Monaural" on label*			
❏ LSP-2328 [S]	His Hand in Mine	1960	$250
— *Living Stereo" on label*			
❏ LSP-2328 [S]	His Hand in Mine	1964	$700
— *Stereo" and silver "RCA Victor" on black label*			
❏ LSP-2328 [S]	His Hand in Mine	1964	$175
— *Stereo" and white "RCA Victor" on black label*			
❏ LSP-2328 [S]	His Hand in Mine	1968	$50
— *Orange label, non-flexible vinyl*			
❏ LSP-2328 [S]	His Hand in Mine	1975	$25
— *Tan label*			
❏ ANL1-1319 [S]	His Hand in Mine	1976	$18
— *Reissue with more tightly cropped photo of Elvis on front cover*			
❏ AYL1-3935 [S]	His Hand in Mine	1981	$10
— *Best Buy Series" reissue; includes copies with sticker wrapped around spine with new number*			
❏ LSP-2328 [S]	His Hand in Mine	197?	$25
— *Orange label, flexible vinyl*			
❏ LPM-3758 [M]	How Great Thou Art	1967	$75
— *Mono Dynagroove" on label*			
❏ LSP-3758 [S]	How Great Thou Art	1967	$75
— *Stereo Dynagroove" on black label*			
❏ LSP-3758 [S]	How Great Thou Art	1968	$40
— *Orange label, non-flexible vinyl*			
❏ LSP-3758 [S]	How Great Thou Art	1971	$30
— *Orange label, flexible vinyl*			
❏ LSP-3758 [S]	How Great Thou Art	1975	$25
— *Tan label*			
❏ LSP-3758 [S]	How Great Thou Art	1976	$15
— *Black label, dog near top*			
❏ AFL1-3758 [S]	How Great Thou Art	1977	$15
— *Black label, dog near top; includes copies with sticker wrapped around spine with new number*			
❏ AQL1-3758 [S]	How Great Thou Art	1979	$12
— *Reissue with new prefix*			
❏ (no #) [B]	International Hotel, Las Vegas Nevada, Presents Elvis, 1969	1969	$3000
— *Gift box to guests at Elvis' July 31-Aug, 1, 1969 shows. Includes LPM-4088 and LSP-4155; press release; 1969 catalog; three photos; and thank-you note from Elvis and the Colonel. Most of the value is for the box; VG value 1250; VG+ value 1875*			
❏ (no #) [B]	International Hotel, Las Vegas Nevada, Presents Elvis, 1970	1970	$3000
— *Gift box to guests at Elvis' Jan. 28, 1970 show. Includes LSP-6020 and 47-9791; press release; 1970 catalog; photo; booklet; and dinner menu. Most of the value is for the box; VG value 1250; VG+ value 1875*			
❏ LPM-2697 [M]	It Happened at the World's Fair	1963	$175
❏ LSP-2697 [S]	It Happened at the World's Fair	1963	$250
— *Living Stereo" and silver "RCA Victor" on black label*			
❏ LSP-2697 [S]	It Happened at the World's Fair	1964	$100
— *Stereo" and white "RCA Victor" on black label*			
❏ APL1-2568 [S]	It Happened at the World's Fair	1977	$15
❏ LPM/LSP-2697	It Happened at the World's Fair Photo	1963	$300
❏ AHL1-4678	I Was the One	1983	$12
❏ LPM-1884 [M]	King Creole	1958	$250
— *Long Play" on label; contrary to some other sources, this was NOT issued with a bonus photo*			
❏ LPM-1884 [M]	King Creole	1963	$100
— *Mono" on label*			
❏ LPM-1884 [M]	King Creole	1964	$75
— *Monaural" on label*			
❏ LSP-1884(e) [R]	King Creole	1962	$175
— *Stereo Electronically Reprocessed" and silver "RCA Victor" on label*			
❏ LSP-1884(e) [R]	King Creole	1964	$75
— *Stereo Electronically Reprocessed" and white "RCA Victor" on label*			
❏ LSP-1884(e) [R]	King Creole	1968	$40
— *Orange label, non-flexible vinyl*			
❏ LSP-1884(e) [R]	King Creole	1971	$25
— *Orange label, flexible vinyl*			
❏ LSP-1884(e) [R]	King Creole	1975	$25
— *Tan label*			
❏ LSP-1884(e) [R]	King Creole	1976	$15
— *Black label, dog near top*			
❏ AFL1-1884(e) [R]	King Creole	1977	$15
— *Black label, dog near top; includes copies with sticker wrapped around spine with new number*			

Number	Title	Yr	NM
❏ AYL1-3733 [R]	King Creole	1980	$10
— *Best Buy Series" reissue; includes copies with sticker wrapped around spine with new number*			
❏ LSP-2894 [S]	Kissin' Cousins	1968	$40
— *Orange label, non-flexible vinyl*			
❏ LPM-2894 [M]	Kissin' Cousins	1964	$100
— *Mono" on label; front cover has a small black and white photo of six cast members in lower right*			
❏ LPM-2894 [M]	Kissin' Cousins	1964	$250
— *Mono" on label; front cover does NOT have black and white photo in lower right*			
❏ LPM-2894 [M]	Kissin' Cousins	1964	$150
— *Monaural" on label; front cover has a small black and white photo of six cast members in lower right*			
❏ LPM-2894 [M]	Kissin' Cousins	1964	$250
— *Monaural" on label; front cover does NOT have black and white photo in lower right*			
❏ LSP-2894 [S]	Kissin' Cousins	1964	$120
— *Stereo" and silver "RCA Victor" on black label; front cover has a small black and white photo of six cast members in lower right*			
❏ LSP-2894 [S]	Kissin' Cousins	1964	$250
— *Stereo" and silver "RCA Victor" on black label; front cover does NOT have black and white photo in lower right*			
❏ LSP-2894 [S]	Kissin' Cousins	1964	$75
— *Stereo" and white "RCA Victor" on black label; all front covers have the cast photo in lower right*			
❏ LSP-2894 [S]	Kissin' Cousins	1971	$25
— *Orange label, flexible vinyl*			
❏ LSP-2894 [S]	Kissin' Cousins	1975	$30
— *Tan label*			
❏ LSP-2894 [S]	Kissin' Cousins	1976	$15
— *Black label, dog near top*			
❏ AFL1-2894 [S]	Kissin' Cousins	1977	$15
— *Black label, dog near top; includes copies with sticker wrapped around spine with new number*			
❏ AYL1-4115 [S]	Kissin' Cousins	1981	$10
— *Best Buy Series" reissue; includes copies with sticker wrapped around spine with new number*			
❏ LSP-2894 [S]	Kissin' Cousins	1976	$1500
— *Black label, dog near top; blue vinyl*			
❏ LSP-4530	Love Letters from Elvis	1971	$40
— *Orange label; "Love Letters from" on one line of cover, "Elvis" on a second line*			
❏ LSP-4530	Love Letters from Elvis	1971	$30
— *Orange label; "Love Letters" on one line of cover; "from" on a second line, "Elvis" on a third line*			
❏ LSP-4530	Love Letters from Elvis	1975	$30
— *Tan label; "Love Letters from" on one line of cover, "Elvis" on a second line*			
❏ LSP-4530	Love Letters from Elvis	1975	$30
— *Tan label; "Love Letters" on one line of cover; "from" on a second line, "Elvis" on a third line*			
❏ LSP-4530	Love Letters from Elvis	1976	$25
— *Black label, dog near top*			
❏ AFL1-4530	Love Letters from Elvis	1977	$15
— *Black label, dog near top; includes copies with sticker wrapped around spine with new number*			
❏ LPM-1515 [M]	Loving You	2003	$25
— *Red vinyl; "DRL 13268" in trail-off wax; "BMG Special Products" logo on back cover; from box "Elvis Top Album Collection Volume 2*			
❏ LSP-1515(e) [R]	Loving You	1975	$25
— *Tan label*			
❏ LSP-1515(e) [R]	Loving You	1976	$15
— *Black label, dog near top*			
❏ LPM-1515 [M]	Loving You	1957	$400
— *Long Play" on label*			
❏ LPM-1515 [M]	Loving You	1963	$250
— *Mono" on label*			
❏ LPM-1515 [M]	Loving You	1964	$50
— *Monaural" on label*			
❏ LSP-1515(e) [R]	Loving You	1962	$175
— *Stereo Electronically Reprocessed" and silver "RCA Victor" on label*			
❏ LSP-1515(e) [R]	Loving You	1964	$50
— *Stereo Electronically Reprocessed" and white "RCA Victor" on label*			
❏ LSP-1515(e) [R]	Loving You	1968	$40
— *Orange label, non-flexible vinyl*			
❏ LSP-1515(e) [R]	Loving You	1971	$25
— *Orange label, flexible vinyl*			
❏ AFL1-1515(e) [R]	Loving You	1977	$15
— *Black label, dog near top; includes copies with sticker wrapped around spine with new number*			
❏ CPL1-4395	Memories of Christmas	1982	$18
— *With greeting card (deduct 1/3 if missing)*			
❏ AFK1-2428	Moody Blue	1977	$5000
— *Alternate cover slick (never put on an actual cover), with the words "Moody Blue" inside the large word "Elvis." See any late-1970s Elvis inner sleeve for a black and white photo of the scrapped cover; VG value 1500; VG+ value 2250*			
❏ AFL1-2428 [DJ]	Moody Blue	1977	$2500
— *Experimental colored vinyl pressings (with no cover), any color or combination except blue or black*			

Number	Title	Yr	NM
❏ AFL1-2428	Moody Blue	1977	$12
—Blue vinyl			
❏ AFL1-2428 [B]	Moody Blue	1977	$300
—Black vinyl			
❏ AQL1-2428	Moody Blue	1979	$30
—Reissue with new prefix			
❏ LSP-4362	On Stage February, 1970	1970	$40
—Orange label, non-flexible vinyl			
❏ LSP-4362	On Stage February, 1970	1971	$30
—Orange label, flexible vinyl			
❏ LSP-4362	On Stage February, 1970	1975	$30
—Tan label			
❏ LSP-4362	On Stage February, 1970	1976	$30
—Black label, dog near top			
❏ AFL1-4362	On Stage February, 1970	1977	$15
—Black label, dog near top; includes copies with sticker wrapped around spine with new number			
❏ AQL1-4362	On Stage February, 1970	1983	$10
—Reissue with some cover changes			
❏ AQL1-3279 [B]	Our Memories of Elvis	1979	$30
❏ AQL1-3448	Our Memories of Elvis, Volume 2	1979	$25
❏ LPM-3643 [M]	Paradise, Hawaiian Style	1966	$75
❏ LSP-3643 [S]	Paradise, Hawaiian Style	1966	$75
—Stereo" on black label			
❏ LSP-3643 [S]	Paradise, Hawaiian Style	1968	$40
—Orange label, non-flexible vinyl			
❏ LSP-3643 [S]	Paradise, Hawaiian Style	1971	$25
—Orange label, flexible vinyl			
❏ LSP-3643 [S]	Paradise, Hawaiian Style	1975	$18
—Tan label			
❏ LSP-3643 [S]	Paradise, Hawaiian Style	1976	$15
—Black label, dog near top			
❏ AFL1-3643 [S]	Paradise, Hawaiian Style	1977	$15
—Black label, dog near top; includes copies with sticker wrapped around spine with new number			
❏ LPM-2523 [M]	Pot Luck with Elvis	1962	$175
—Long Play" on label			
❏ LPM-2523 [M]	Pot Luck with Elvis	1964	$175
—Monaural" on label			
❏ LSP-2523 [S]	Pot Luck with Elvis	1962	$175
—Living Stereo" on label			
❏ LSP-2523 [S]	Pot Luck with Elvis	1964	$75
—Stereo" on black label			
❏ LSP-2523 [S]	Pot Luck with Elvis	1968	$40
—Orange label, non-flexible vinyl			
❏ LSP-2523 [S]	Pot Luck with Elvis	1975	$25
—Tan label			
❏ LSP-2523 [S]	Pot Luck with Elvis	1976	$15
—Black label, dog near top			
❏ AFL1-2523 [S]	Pot Luck with Elvis	1977	$15
—Black label, dog near top; includes copies with sticker wrapped around spine with new number			
❏ APL1-0873	Promised Land	1975	$75
—Orange label			
❏ APD1-0873 [Q]	Promised Land	1975	$300
—RCA QuadraDisc" label			
❏ APL1-0873	Promised Land	1975	$25
—Tan label			
❏ AFL1-0873	Promised Land	1977	$18
—Black label, dog near top			
❏ APD1-0873 [Q]	Promised Land	1977	$250
—Black label, dog near top; quadraphonic reissue			
❏ DJL1-3455 [DJ]	Pure Elvis	1979	$800
—Promo-only item for Our Memories of Elvis, Volume 2; contains original version of five songs on one side, "unsweetened" versions of same songs on the other			
❏ ANL1-0971(e)	Pure Gold	1975	$18
—Orange label			
❏ ANL1-0971(e)	Pure Gold	1976	$15
—Yellow label			
❏ AYL1-3732	Pure Gold	1980	$10
—Best Buy Series" reissue			
❏ APL1-0388	Raised on Rock/For Ol' Times Sake	1973	$30
—Orange label			
❏ APL1-0388	Raised on Rock/For Ol' Times Sake	1975	$30
—Tan label			
❏ APL1-0388	Raised on Rock/For Ol' Times Sake	1977	$15
—Black label, dog near top			
❏ AFL1-5418	Reconsider Baby	1985	$25
—All copies on blue vinyl			
❏ AFM1-5182	Rocker	1984	$25
❏ LSP-2999 [S]	Roustabout	2003	$25
—Red vinyl, "DRL 13269" in trail-off wax; "BMG Special Products" logo on back cover; from box "Elvis Top Album Collection Volume 2			
❏ LPM-2999 [M]	Roustabout	1964	$175
—Mono" on label			
❏ LPM-2999 [M]	Roustabout	1965	$75
—Monaural" on label			
❏ LSP-2999 [S]	Roustabout	1964	$700
—Stereo" and silver "RCA Victor" on black label			
❏ LSP-2999 [S]	Roustabout	1964	$75

Number	Title	Yr	NM
—Stereo" and white "RCA Victor" on black label			
❏ LSP-2999 [S]	Roustabout	1968	$40
—Orange label, non-flexible vinyl			
❏ LSP-2999 [S]	Roustabout	1971	$25
—Orange label, flexible vinyl			
❏ LSP-2999 [S]	Roustabout	1975	$25
—Tan label			
❏ LSP-2999 [S]	Roustabout	1976	$15
—Black label, dog near top			
❏ AFL1-2999 [S]	Roustabout	1977	$15
—Black label, dog near top; includes copies with sticker wrapped around spine with new number			
❏ PRS-279 [B]	Singer Presents Elvis Singing Flaming Star and Others	1968	$175
—Sold only at Singer sewing machine dealers; reissued on RCA Camden 2304			
❏ LSP-2370 [S]	Something for Everybody	2003	$25
—Red vinyl; "DRL 13270" in trail-off wax; "BMG Special Products" logo on back cover; from box "Elvis Top Album Collection Volume 1			
❏ LPM-2370 [M]	Something for Everybody	1961	$175
—Long Play" on label; back cover advertises RCA Compact 33 singles and doubles			
❏ LPM-2370 [M]	Something for Everybody	1963	$100
—Mono" on label; back cover advertises "Viva Las Vegas" EP			
❏ LPM-2370 [M]	Something for Everybody	1964	$50
—Monaural" on label; back cover advertises "Viva Las Vegas" EP			
❏ LSP-2370 [S]	Something for Everybody	1961	$300
—Living Stereo" on label; back cover advertises RCA Compact 33 singles and doubles			
❏ LSP-2370 [S]	Something for Everybody	1963	$175
—Stereo" and silver "RCA Victor" on black label; back cover advertises Elvis' Christmas Album and His Hand in Mine LPs and "Viva Las Vegas" EP			
❏ LSP-2370 [S]	Something for Everybody	1964	$50
—Stereo" and white "RCA Victor" on black label; back cover advertises "Viva Las Vegas" EP			
❏ LSP-2370 [S]	Something for Everybody	1968	$40
—Orange label, non-flexible vinyl; final back cover change advertises Elvis (NBC-TV Special), Elvis' Christmas Album and His Hand in Mine LPs			
❏ LSP-2370 [S]	Something for Everybody	1971	$25
—Orange label, flexible vinyl			
❏ LSP-2370 [S]	Something for Everybody	1975	$25
—Tan label			
❏ LSP-2370 [S]	Something for Everybody	1976	$15
—Black label, dog near top			
❏ AFL1-2370 [S]	Something for Everybody	1977	$15
—Black label, dog near top; includes copies with sticker wrapped around spine with new number			
❏ AYL1-4116 [S]	Something for Everybody	1981	$10
—Best Buy Series" reissue; includes copies with sticker wrapped around spine with new number			
❏ UNRM-5697/8 [DJ]	Special Christmas Programming	1967	$1200
—White label promo. Add 25% for script.			
❏ SP-33-461 [DJ]	Special Palm Sunday Programming	1967	$1000
—White label promo. Add 25% for cue sheet.			
❏ LSP-3989 [S]	Speedway	1971	$25
—Orange label, flexible vinyl			
❏ LSP-3989 [S]	Speedway	1975	$25
—Tan label			

LPM-3989

Number	Title	Yr	NM
❏ LPM-3989 [M]	Speedway	1968	$3500
❏ LSP-3989 [S]	Speedway	1968	$75
—Stereo" on black label			
❏ LSP-3989 [S]	Speedway	1968	$40
—Orange label, non-flexible vinyl			
❏ LSP-3989 [S]	Speedway	1976	$15
—Black label, dog near top			
❏ AFL1-3989 [S]	Speedway	1977	$15
—Black label, dog near top; includes copies with sticker wrapped around spine with new number			

Number	Title	Yr	NM
❏ LPM/LSP-3989	Speedway Bonus Photo	1968	$50
❏ LPM-3702 [M]	Spinout	1966	$75
❏ LSP-3702 [S]	Spinout	1966	$75
—Stereo" on black label			
❏ APL1-2560 [S]	Spinout	1977	$15
—Black label, dog near top			
❏ AYL1-3684 [S]	Spinout	1980	$10
—Best Buy Series" reissue			
❏ LPM/LSP-3702	Spinout Bonus Photo	1966	$75
❏ LSP-4445	That's the Way It Is	1970	$100
—Orange label, non-flexible vinyl			
❏ LSP-4445	That's the Way It Is	1971	$30
—Orange label, flexible vinyl			
❏ LSP-4445	That's the Way It Is	1975	$25
—Tan label			
❏ LSP-4445	That's the Way It Is	1976	$18
—Black label, dog near top			
❏ AFL1-4445	That's the Way It Is	1977	$15
—Black label, dog near top; includes copies with sticker wrapped around spine with new number			
❏ AYL1-4114	That's the Way It Is	1981	$10
—Best Buy Series" reissue; includes copies with sticker wrapped around spine with new number			
❏ AHL1-4530	The Elvis Medley	1982	$15
❏ R244047	The Legendary Concert Performances	1978	$40
—RCA Music Service exclusive			
❏ LPM-6402	The Other Sides: Worldwide 50 Gold Award Hits, Vol. 2	1971	$80
—Orange labels, flexible vinyl; with blurb for inserts on cover			
❏ LPM-6402	The Other Sides: Worldwide 50 Gold Award Hits, Vol. 2	1975	$30
—Tan labels			
❏ LPM-6402	The Other Sides: Worldwide 50 Gold Award Hits, Vol. 2	1977	$25
—Black labels, dog near top			
❏ LPM-6402	The Other Sides: Worldwide 50 Gold Award Hits, Vol. 2 Poster	1971	$30
❏ LPM-6402	The Other Sides: Worldwide 50 Gold Award Hits, Vol. 2 Swatch and Envelope	1971	$30
❏ APM1-1675	The Sun Sessions	1976	$25
—Tan label			
❏ APM1-1675	The Sun Sessions	1976	$15
—Black label, dog near top			
❏ AFM1-1675	The Sun Sessions	1977	$18
—Black label, dog near top; includes copies with sticker wrapped around spine with new number			
❏ AYM1-3893	The Sun Sessions	1981	$10
—Best Buy Series" reissue; includes copies with sticker wrapped around spine with new number			
❏ CPL2-4031	This Is Elvis	1980	$18
❏ APL1-2274	Welcome to My World	1977	$25
—Black label, dog near top			
❏ AFL1-2274	Welcome to My World	1977	$15
—Black label, dog near top; includes copies with sticker wrapped around spine with new number			
❏ AQL1-2274	Welcome to My World	1979	$12
—Black label, dog near top; includes copies with sticker wrapped around spine with new number			
❏ LPM-6401	Worldwide 50 Gold Award Hits, Vol. 1	1970	$100
—Orange labels, non-flexible vinyl; with blurb for photo book on cover			
❏ LPM-6401	Worldwide 50 Gold Award Hits, Vol. 1	1970	$100
—Orange labels, flexible vinyl; with blurb for photo book on cover			
❏ LPM-6401	Worldwide 50 Gold Award Hits, Vol. 1	1975	$40
—Tan labels			
❏ LPM-6401	Worldwide 50 Gold Award Hits, Vol. 1	1977	$30
—Black labels, dog near top			
❏ LPM-6401	Worldwide 50 Gold Award Hits, Vol. 1 Photo Book	1970	$40
—Two different books have been found in this LP box; price is for either			
❏ R213690	Worldwide Gold Award Hits, Parts 1 & 2	1974	$120
—RCA Record Club version; one label is orange, the other is tan (orange label on both records is unknown)			
❏ R213690	Worldwide Gold Award Hits, Parts 1 & 2	1974	$40
—RCA Record Club version; tan labels			
❏ R213690	Worldwide Gold Award Hits, Parts 1 & 2	1977	$30
—RCA Record Club version; black labels, dog near top			
❏ R214657	Worldwide Gold Award Hits, Parts 3 & 4	1978	$25
—RCA Record Club version; black labels, dog near top			

READER'S DIGEST

Number	Title	Yr	NM
❏ RDA-242/D	Elvis Sings Country Favorites	1984	$75
❏ RD4A-181/D	Elvis Sings Inspirational Favorites	1983	$25
❏ RBA-072/D	Great Hits of 1956-57	1987	$25
❏ RD-10/A [B]	His Greatest Hits	1979	$400
—White box			

Number	Title	Yr	NM
❏ 010/A	His Greatest Hits	1990	$40
— White box			
❏ 010/A	His Greatest Hits	1983	$75
— Yellow box			
❏ RB4-191/A	The Legend Lives On	1986	$75
SHOW-LAND			
❏ LP-2001	The First of Elvis	1979	$150
SILHOUETTE			
❏ 10001/2	Personally Elvis	1979	$30
— Interview records; no music			
SUN			
❏ 1001 [B]	The Sun Years -- Interviews and Memories	1977	$30
— With "Memphis, Tennessee" on label			
❏ 1001 [B]	The Sun Years -- Interviews and Memories	1977	$15
— With "Nashville, U.S.A." on label; white cover with brown print			
❏ 1001 [B]	The Sun Years -- Interviews and Memories	1977	$25
— With "Nashville, U.S.A." on label; dark yellow cover with brown print			
TIME-LIFE			
❏ STW-106	Country Music	1981	$25
❏ STL-106	Elvis Presley: 1954-1961	1986	$30
❏ STL-126	Elvis: the King: 1954-1965	1989	$100

PRESNELL, HARVE
MGM

Number	Title	Yr	NM
❏ E-4266 [M]	New Echoes of the Old West	1965	$25
❏ SE-4266 [S]	New Echoes of the Old West	1965	$30
❏ E-4194 [M]	The World's Greatest Love Songs	1964	$25
❏ SE-4194 [S]	The World's Greatest Love Songs	1964	$30

PRESTER, ROB
ANTILLES

Number	Title	Yr	NM
❏ 90967	Trillum	1988	$25

PRESTI, IDA, AND ALEXANDRE LAGOYA
MERCURY LIVING PRESENCE

Number	Title	Yr	NM
❏ SR90457 [S]	Baroque Music for Two Guitars	196?	$40
— Maroon label, with "Vendor: Mercury Record Corporation"			
❏ SR90380 [S]	Four Concertos for Two Guitars by Vivaldi	196?	$30
— Maroon label, no "Vendor: Mercury Record Corporation"			
❏ SR90427 [S]	Spanish Music for Two Guitars	196?	$30
— Maroon label, no "Vendor: Mercury Record Corporation"			

PRESTIGE BLUES SWINGERS, THE
PRESTIGE

Number	Title	Yr	NM
❏ PRST-7787	Outskirts of Town	1970	$35
❏ PRLP-7145 [M]	Outskirts of Town	1958	$300
SWINGVILLE			
❏ SVLP-2013 [M]	Stasch	1960	$250
— Blue label, trident logo at right			
❏ SVLP-2013 [M]	Stasch	1965	$50
— Purple label			

PRESTIGE JAZZ QUARTET, THE
PRESTIGE

Number	Title	Yr	NM
❏ PRLP-7108 [M]	The Prestige Jazz Quartet	1957	$300

PRESTON, BILLY
A&M

Number	Title	Yr	NM
❏ SP-4587	Billy Preston	1976	$15
❏ SP-3526	Everybody Likes Some Kind of Music	1973	$15
❏ SP-4657	It's a Whole New Thing	1977	$15
❏ SP-4532	It's My Pleasure	1975	$15
❏ SP-3507	I Wrote a Simple Song	1971	$15
❏ SP-3637	Live European Tour	1974	$15
❏ SP-3516	Music Is My Life	1972	$15
❏ SP-3205	The Best of Billy Preston	1982	$12
❏ SP-3645	The Kids & Me	1974	$15
APPLE			
❏ ST-3370	Encouraging Words	1970	$25
❏ ST-3359	That's the Way God Planned It	1969	$50
— Cover has close-up of Billy Preston			
❏ ST-3359	That's the Way God Planned It	1972	$25
— Cover has multiple images of Billy Preston			
BUDDAH			
❏ BDS-7502	Billy Preston	1969	$18
CAPITOL			
❏ T2607 [M]	Club Meetin'	1967	$0
— The above versions of Club Meetin' may not exist			
❏ DT2607 [R]	Club Meetin'	1967	$0
❏ T2532 [M]	Wildest Organ in Town!	1966	$50
❏ ST2532 [S]	Wildest Organ in Town!	1966	$40

DERBY

Number	Title	Yr	NM
❏ LPM-701 [M]	16 Year Old Soul	1963	$300
EXODUS			
❏ 304 [M]	Early Hits of 1965	1965	$30
GNP CRESCENDO			
❏ GNPS-2071	Soul'd Out	1973	$18
MCA			
❏ 28037	Gospel Soul	198?	$10
— Reissue of Peacock LP			
MOTOWN			
❏ M7-958	Billy Preston & Syreeta	1981	$12
❏ M7-925	Late at Night	1980	$12
❏ 6020ML	Pressin' On	1982	$12
❏ M8-941	The Way I Am	1981	$12
MYRRH			
❏ MSB-6605	Behold	1978	$15
❏ MSB-6607	Universal Love	1979	$15
PEACOCK			
❏ 179	Gospel Soul	197?	$15
PICKWICK			
❏ SPC-3315	Organ Transplant	197?	$12
VEE JAY			
❏ LP-1142 [M]	Greatest Hits	1966	$40
❏ LPS-1142 [S]	Greatest Hits	1966	$75
❏ LP-1123 [M]	The Most Exciting Organ Ever	1965	$40
❏ LPS-1123 [S]	The Most Exciting Organ Ever	1965	$75

PRESTON, JOHNNY
MERCURY

Number	Title	Yr	NM
❏ MG-20609 [M]	Come Rock with Me	1960	$150
❏ SR-60609 [S]	Come Rock with Me	1960	$175
❏ MG-20592 [M]	Running Bear	1960	$150
❏ SR-60250 [S]	Running Bear	1960	$175
— Black label			
❏ SR-60250 [S]	Running Bear	1981	$15
— Reissue on Chicago skyline label			
WING			
❏ MGW-12246 [M]	Running Bear	1963	$25
❏ SRW-16246 [S]	Running Bear	1963	$30

PRETENDERS
NAUTILUS

Number	Title	Yr	NM
❏ NR-38	Pretenders	1982	$50
— Audiophile vinyl			
SIRE			
❏ MINI3563 [EP]	Extended Play	1981	$12
❏ R144453	Get Close	1986	$15
— RCA Music Service edition			
❏ 25488	Get Close	1986	$12
❏ 23980	Learning to Crawl	1983	$12
❏ 23980 [DJ]	Learning to Crawl	1983	$30
— Promo-only Quiex II pressing; otherwise, same as above			
❏ 26219	Packed!	1990	$15
❏ SRK6083	Pretenders	1980	$12
❏ SRK3572	Pretenders II	1981	$12
❏ R133248	The Singles	1987	$15
— BMG Direct Marketing edition; otherwise, same as 25664			
❏ 25664	The Singles	1987	$12
WARNER BROS.			
❏ WBMS-142 [DJ]	Get Close Interview	1987	$25
— Part of "The Warner Bros. Music Show" series			
❏ WBMS-114 [DJ]	Pretenders Live	1980	$30
— Part of "The Warner Bros. Music Show" series; comes in red die-cut cover			
❏ WBMS-121 [DJ]	Pretenders Live (Star Fleet)	1982	$25
— Part of "The Warner Bros. Music Show" series; comes in black cover with white sticker			

PRETTY POISON
SVENGALI

Number	Title	Yr	NM
❏ SRPP-1 [EP]	Laced	1984	$25
VIRGIN			
❏ R144099	Catch Me I'm Falling	1988	$15
— BMG Direct Marketing edition			
❏ 90885	Catch Me I'm Falling	1987	$12

PRETTY THINGS, THE
BIG BEAT

Number	Title	Yr	NM
❏ WIK-24 [B]	Live at Heartbreak Hotel	1985	$15
FONTANA			
❏ MGF-27544 [M]	The Pretty Things	1965	$100
❏ SRF-67544 [P]	The Pretty Things	1965	$100
NORTON			
❏ TED-1001 [10]	Defecting Grey	2000	$30
❏ 283	Get the Picture?	2000	$15
❏ 284	Midnight to Six	2000	$15
❏ 282	The Pretty Things	2000	$15
RARE EARTH			
❏ RS515	Parachute	1970	$25
❏ R549R2	Real Pretty	1976	$18
— The two prior Rare Earth albums in one package			

Number	Title	Yr	NM
❏ RS506 [B]	S.F. Sorrow	1969	$75
— Original covers are rounded at top			
❏ RS506	S.F. Sorrow	1969	$30
— Later copies are standard in shape			
SIRE			
❏ SASH-3713 [B]	The Vintage Years	1976	$30
SWAN SONG			
❏ SS8414 [B]	Savage Eye	1976	$18
❏ SS8411 [B]	Silk Torpedo	1975	$18
WARNER BROS.			
❏ BSK3466 [B]	Cross Talk	1980	$18
❏ BS2680 [B]	Freeway Madness	1973	$15

PREVIN, ANDRE, AND RUSS FREEMAN
CONTEMPORARY

Number	Title	Yr	NM
❏ C-3537 [M]	Double Play!	1957	$300
❏ S-7011 [S]	Double Play!	1959	$300
STEREO RECORDS			
❏ S-7011 [S]	Double Play!	1958	$150

PREVIN, ANDRE; HERB ELLIS; SHELLY MANNE; RAY BROWN
COLUMBIA

Number	Title	Yr	NM
❏ CL2018 [M]	Four to Go	1963	$50
❏ CS8818 [S]	Four to Go	1963	$75

PREVIN, ANDRE
ANGEL

Number	Title	Yr	NM
❏ DS-37780	A Different Kind of Blues	1981	$25
❏ S-1-37799	It's a Breeze	1981	$25
COLUMBIA			
❏ CL2034 [M]	Andre Previn in Hollywood	1963	$35
— Red label with "Guaranteed High Fidelity" at bottom			
❏ CS8834 [S]	Andre Previn in Hollywood	1963	$50
— Red label with "360 Sound Stereo" in black at bottom			
❏ CL2034 [M]	Andre Previn in Hollywood	1966	$30
— Red label with "360 Sound Mono" at bottom			
❏ CS8834 [S]	Andre Previn in Hollywood	1966	$35
— Red label with "360 Sound Stereo" in white at bottom			
❏ CL1649 [M]	A Touch of Elegance	1961	$50
— Red and black label with six "eye" logos			
❏ CS8449 [S]	A Touch of Elegance	1961	$75
— Red and black label with six "eye" logos			
❏ CL1569 [M]	Camelot	1961	$50
— Red and black label with six "eye" logos			
❏ CS8369 [S]	Camelot	1961	$75
— Red and black label with six "eye" logos			
❏ CL1569 [M]	Camelot	1963	$30
— Red label with "Guaranteed High Fidelity" or "360 Sound Mono" at bottom			
❏ CS8369 [S]	Camelot	1963	$35
— Red label with "360 Sound Stereo" at bottom			
❏ CL1786 [M]	Faraway Part of Town	1962	$50
— Red and black label with six "eye" logos			
❏ CS8586 [S]	Faraway Part of Town	1962	$75
— Red and black label with six "eye" logos			
❏ CL1786 [M]	Faraway Part of Town	1963	$30
— Red label with "Guaranteed High Fidelity" or "360 Sound Mono" at bottom			
❏ CS8586 [S]	Faraway Part of Town	1963	$35
— Red label with "360 Sound Stereo" at bottom			
❏ CL1530 [M]	Give My Regards to Broadway	1960	$50
— Red and black label with six "eye" logos			
❏ CS8330 [S]	Give My Regards to Broadway	1960	$75
— Red and black label with six "eye" logos			
❏ CL1530 [M]	Give My Regards to Broadway	1963	$30
— Red label with "Guaranteed High Fidelity" or "360 Sound Mono" at bottom			
❏ CS8330 [S]	Give My Regards to Broadway	1960	$35
— Red label with "360 Sound Stereo" at bottom			
❏ CL1437 [M]	Like Love	1960	$35
— Red and black label with six "eye" logos			
❏ CS8233 [S]	Like Love	1960	$50
— Red and black label with six "eye" logos			
❏ CL1437 [M]	Like Love	1963	$30
— Red label with "Guaranteed High Fidelity" or "360 Sound Mono" at bottom			
❏ CS8233 [S]	Like Love	1963	$35
— Red label with "360 Sound Stereo" at bottom			
❏ CL1741 [M]	Mack the Knife and Other Kurt Weill Music	1962	$50
— Red and black label with six "eye" logos			
❏ CS8541 [S]	Mack the Knife and Other Kurt Weill Music	1962	$75
— Red and black label with six "eye" logos			
❏ CL1741 [M]	Mack the Knife and Other Kurt Weill Music	1963	$30
— Red label with "Guaranteed High Fidelity" or "360 Sound Mono" at bottom			
❏ CS8541 [S]	Mack the Knife and Other Kurt Weill Music	1962	$35

Number	Title	Yr	NM

—Red label with "360 Sound Stereo" at bottom
| ❏ CL2195 [M] | My Fair Lady | 1964 | $35 |

—Red label with "Guaranteed High Fidelity" at bottom
| ❏ CS8995 [S] | My Fair Lady | 1964 | $50 |

—Red label with "360 Sound Stereo" in black at bottom
| ❏ CL2195 [M] | My Fair Lady | 1966 | $30 |

—Red label with "360 Sound Mono" at bottom
| ❏ CS8995 [S] | My Fair Lady | 1966 | $35 |

—Red label with "360 Sound Stereo" in white at bottom
| ❏ CL2294 [M] | Popular Previn | 1965 | $35 |

—Red label with "Guaranteed High Fidelity" at bottom
| ❏ CS9094 [S] | Popular Previn | 1965 | $50 |

—Red label with "360 Sound Stereo" in black at bottom
| ❏ CS9094 [S] | Popular Previn | 1966 | $35 |

—Red label with "360 Sound Stereo" in white at bottom
| ❏ CL2294 [M] | Popular Previn | 1966 | $30 |

—Red label with "360 Sound Mono" at bottom
| ❏ CL1495 [M] | Rhapsody in Blue | 1960 | $35 |

—Red and black label with six "eye" logos
| ❏ CS8286 [S] | Rhapsody in Blue | 1960 | $50 |

—Red and black label with six "eye" logos
| ❏ CS8286 [S] | Rhapsody in Blue | 1963 | $35 |

—Red label with "360 Sound Stereo" at bottom
| ❏ CL1495 [M] | Rhapsody in Blue | 1963 | $30 |

—Red label with "Guaranteed High Fidelity" or "360 Sound Mono" at bottom
| ❏ CS8733 [S] | Sittin' on a Rainbow: The Music of Harold Arlen | 1963 | $50 |

—Red label, "360 Sound Stereo" in black at bottom
| ❏ CL1933 [M] | Sittin' on a Rainbow: The Music of Harold Arlen | 1963 | $35 |

—Guaranteed High Fidelity" on label
| ❏ CL1888 [M] | The Light Fantastic | 1962 | $50 |

—Red and black label with six "eye" logos
| ❏ CS8688 [S] | The Light Fantastic | 1962 | $75 |

—Red and black label with six "eye" logos
| ❏ CL1888 [M] | The Light Fantastic | 1963 | $30 |

—Red label with "Guaranteed High Fidelity" or "360 Sound Mono" at bottom
| ❏ CS8688 [S] | The Light Fantastic | 1963 | $35 |

—Red label with "360 Sound Stereo" at bottom
| ❏ CL2114 [M] | The Soft and Swinging Music of Jimmy McHugh | 1964 | $35 |

—Red label with "Guaranteed High Fidelity" at bottom
| ❏ CS8914 [S] | The Soft and Swinging Music of Jimmy McHugh | 1964 | $50 |

—Red label with "360 Sound Stereo" in black at bottom
| ❏ CS8914 [S] | The Soft and Swinging Music of Jimmy McHugh | 1966 | $35 |

—Red label with "360 Sound Stereo" in white at bottom
| ❏ CL2114 [M] | The Soft and Swinging Music of Jimmy McHugh | 1966 | $30 |

—Red label with "360 Sound Mono" at bottom
| ❏ CL1595 [M] | Thinking of You | 1961 | $50 |

—Red and black label with six "eye" logos
| ❏ CS8395 [S] | Thinking of You | 1961 | $75 |

—Red and black label with six "eye" logos
| ❏ CL1595 [M] | Thinking of You | 1963 | $30 |

—Red label with "Guaranteed High Fidelity" or "360 Sound Mono" at bottom
| ❏ CS8395 [S] | Thinking of You | 1963 | $35 |

—Red label with "360 Sound Stereo" at bottom

CONTEMPORARY
❏ M-3586 [M]	Andre Previn Plays Harold Arlen	1960	$300
❏ S-7586 [S]	Andre Previn Plays Harold Arlen	1960	$300
❏ M-3567 [M]	Andre Previn Plays Jerome Kern	1959	$300
❏ S-7567 [S]	Andre Previn Plays Jerome Kern	1959	$300
❏ M-3558 [M]	Andre Previn Plays Vernon Duke	1959	$300
❏ S-7558 [S]	Andre Previn Plays Vernon Duke	1959	$300
❏ C-3548 [M]	Gigi	1958	$50
❏ S-7548 [S]	Gigi	1959	$300
❏ M-3570 [M]	Jazz Trio, King Size	1959	$300
❏ S-7570 [S]	Jazz Trio, King Size	1959	$300
❏ M-3575 [M]	Like Previn	1960	$250
❏ S-7575 [S]	Like Previn	1960	$250
❏ C-3543 [M]	Pal Joey	1957	$300
❏ S-7543 [S]	Pal Joey	1959	$300
❏ M-3572 [M]	West Side Story	1960	$250
❏ S-7572 [S]	West Side Story	1960	$250

CORONET
| ❏ 170 | Featuring Andre Previn | 196? | $30 |
| ❏ 181 | The Magic Sounds of Andre Previn | 196? | $30 |

DECCA
❏ DL4115 [M]	Andre Previn Plays Pretty	1961	$30
❏ DL74115 [S]	Andre Previn Plays Pretty	1961	$35
❏ DL4350 [M]	But Beautiful	1963	$30
❏ DL74350 [S]	But Beautiful	1963	$35
❏ DL8341 [M]	Hollywood at Midnight	1957	$120
❏ DL8131 [M]	Let's Get Away from It All	1955	$175

EVEREST ARCHIVE OF FOLK & JAZZ
| ❏ 247 | Early Years | 1970 | $25 |

FANTASY
| ❏ OJC-157 | Double Play! | 198? | $25 |
—Reissue of Contemporary 7011
| ❏ OJC-170 | Like Previn | 198? | $25 |
—Reissue of Contemporary 7575
| ❏ OJC-637 | Pal Joey | 1991 | $30 |
| ❏ OJC-422 | West Side Story | 1990 | $25 |

GUEST STAR
| ❏ 1436 | Piano Greats | 196? | $30 |

HARMONY
❏ HL7429 [M]	Camelot	1967	$30
❏ HS11229 [S]	Camelot	1967	$30
❏ HL7348 [M]	Misty	1965	$30
❏ HS11148 [S]	Misty	1965	$30
❏ HL7407 [M]	Starlight Piano	196?	$30
❏ HS11207 [S]	Starlight Piano	196?	$30

JAZZ ODYSSEY
| ❏ 32160260 | Mack the Knife and Other Kurt Weill Music | 196? | $30 |
—Reissue of Columbia 8541

MGM
❏ E-4186 [M]	Andre Previn -- Composer, Conductor, Arranger, Pianist	1964	$35
❏ SE-4186 [M]	Andre Previn -- Composer, Conductor, Arranger, Pianist	1964	$50
❏ E-3811 [M]	Like Blue	1960	$50
❏ SE-3811 [M]	Like Blue	1960	$75
❏ E-3716 [M]	Secret Songs for Young Lovers	1959	$50
❏ SE-3716 [M]	Secret Songs for Young Lovers	1959	$75

MOBILE FIDELITY
| ❏ Jan-0095 | West Side Story | 1982 | $75 |
—Audiophile vinyl

MONARCH
| ❏ 203 [10] | All Star Jazz | 1952 | $175 |
| ❏ 204 [10] | Andre Previn Plays Duke | 1952 | $175 |

PRI
| ❏ 3026 [S] | The World's Most Honored Pianist | 1962 | $75 |
—Issued on yellow vinyl

RCA CAMDEN
| ❏ CAL-792 [M] | Love Walked In | 1964 | $30 |
| ❏ CAS-792 [R] | Love Walked In | 1964 | $25 |

RCA VICTOR
❏ LPM-3806 [M]	All Alone	1967	$35
❏ LSP-3806 [S]	All Alone	1967	$30
❏ LPM-36 [10]	Andre Previn By Request	1951	$175
❏ LPT-3002 [10]	Andre Previn Plays Harry Warren	1952	$175
❏ LPM-3491 [M]	Andre Previn Plays Music of the Young Hollywood Composers	1966	$30
❏ LSP-3491 [S]	Andre Previn Plays Music of the Young Hollywood Composers	1966	$35
❏ LPM-3551 [M]	Andre Previn with Voices	1966	$30
❏ LSP-3551 [S]	Andre Previn with Voices	1966	$35
❏ LPM-1011 [M]	Gershwin	1955	$50
❏ ANL1-2805	Pure Gold	1978	$25
❏ LPM-1356 [M]	Three Little Words	1957	$40

SPRINGBOARD
| ❏ SPB-4053 | After Dark | 197? | $25 |

STEREO RECORDS
| ❏ S-7020 [S] | Gigi | 1958 | $150 |
| ❏ S-7004 [S] | Pal Joey | 1958 | $150 |

STRAND
| ❏ SL1074 [M] | Andre Previn Plays | 1962 | $30 |
| ❏ SLS1074 [S] | Andre Previn Plays | 1962 | $35 |

VERVE
| ❏ V-8565 [M] | The Essential Andre Previn | 1963 | $30 |
| ❏ V6-8565 [S] | The Essential Andre Previn | 1963 | $35 |

PREVITE, ROBERT

SOUND ASPECTS
| ❏ SAS 008 | Bump the Renaissance | 1986 | $30 |

PRICE, ALAN
Also see THE ANIMALS.

ACCORD
| ❏ SJA-7904 | It's Priceless | 1982 | $12 |

JET
| ❏ JT-LA809-H | Alan Price | 1977 | $12 |
—The "H" suffix is on the label, but the front and back cover, inner sleeve and spine have a "G" prefix; it's not known if any labels have a "G" prefix
| ❏ JZ35710 | Lucky Day | 1979 | $12 |
| ❏ NJZ36510 | Rising Sun | 1980 | $12 |

PARROT
| ❏ PAS71018 [P] | The Price Is Right | 1968 | $30 |

TOWNHOUSE
| ❏ SN-7126 | House of the Rising Sun | 1981 | $12 |

WARNER BROS.
| ❏ BS2783 [B] | Between Today and Yesterday | 1974 | $18 |

| ❏ BS2710 [B] | O Lucky Man | 1973 | $18 |

PRICE, KENNY

BOONE
| ❏ 1211 | One Hit Follows Another | 1967 | $30 |
| ❏ 1214 | Southern Bound | 1968 | $30 |

DIMENSION
| ❏ DLP-5000 | The Best of Both | 1980 | $15 |

RCA VICTOR
❏ APL1-0208	30 California Women	1973	$18
❏ LSP-4605	Charlotte Fever	1971	$25
❏ LSP-4224	Happy Tracks	1969	$25
❏ LSP-4373	Northeast Arkansas Mississippi County Bootlegger	1970	$25
❏ LSP-4839	Sea of Heartbreak	1973	$25
❏ LSP-4681	Supersideman	1972	$25
❏ LSP-4292	The Heavyweight	1970	$25
❏ LSP-4469	The Red Foley Songbook	1971	$25
❏ LSP-4527	The Sheriff of Boone County	1971	$25
❏ LSP-4225	Walking on New Grass	1969	$25
❏ LSP-4763	You Almost Slipped My Mind	1972	$25

PRICE, LEONTYNE

LONDON
❏ OS25280 [S]	A Christmas Offering	1961	$30
❏ 5644 [M]	A Christmas Offering	1961	$25
❏ 410198-1	Noel! Noel!	1983	$12

LONDON JUBILEE
| ❏ 411614-1 | A Christmas Offering | 1984 | $12 |
—Reissue of London 25280

RCA VICTOR RED SEAL
| ❏ LSC-2279 [S] | A Program of Song | 1959 | $25 |
—Original with "shaded dog" label
| ❏ LSC-2600 [S] | Swing Low, Sweet Chariot | 1962 | $30 |
—Original with "shaded dog" label

PRICE, LLOYD

ABC
| ❏ X-763 | 16 Greatest Hits | 1972 | $18 |
| ❏ DW-94842 | 16 Greatest Hits | 1972 | $25 |
—Capitol Record Club edition
| ❏ S-297 | Mr. Personality | 1967 | $18 |
—Reissue on revised label
| ❏ S-324 [R] | Mr. Personality's Big 15 | 1968 | $18 |
—Reissue on revised label
| ❏ AC-30006 | The ABC Collection | 1976 | $18 |

ABC-PARAMOUNT
❏ ABC-382 [M]	Cookin' with Lloyd Price	1961	$40
❏ ABCS-382 [S]	Cookin' with Lloyd Price	1961	$50
❏ ABC-366 [M]	Lloyd Price Sings the Million Sellers	1961	$40
❏ ABCS-366 [S]	Lloyd Price Sings the Million Sellers	1961	$50
❏ ABC-297 [M]	Mr. Personality	1959	$40
❏ ABCS-297 [S]	Mr. Personality	1959	$100
❏ ABC-324 [M]	Mr. Personality's 15 Hits	1960	$40
—Label calls this "Mr. Personality's Big Hits"
❏ ABC-315 [M]	Mr. Personality Sings the Blues	1960	$40
❏ ABCS-315 [S]	Mr. Personality Sings the Blues	1960	$100
❏ ABC-277 [M]	The Exciting Lloyd Price	1959	$40
❏ ABCS-277 [S]	The Exciting Lloyd Price	1959	$150
❏ ABC-346 [M]	The Fantastic Lloyd Price	1960	$40
❏ ABCS-346 [R]	The Fantastic Lloyd Price	196?	$30

DOUBLE-L
❏ DL-2303 [M]	Misty	1963	$30
❏ SDL-8303 [S]	Misty	1963	$40
❏ DL-2301 [M]	The Lloyd Price Orchestra	1963	$30
❏ SDL-8301 [S]	The Lloyd Price Orchestra	1963	$40

GRAND PRIX
| ❏ 422 [M] | Mr. Rhythm and Blues | 196? | $15 |
| ❏ S-422 [R] | Mr. Rhythm and Blues | 196? | $12 |

GUEST STAR
| ❏ G-1910 [M] | Come to Me | 196? | $15 |
| ❏ GS-1910 [R] | Come to Me | 196? | $12 |

JAD
| ❏ 1002 | Lloyd Price Now | 1969 | $30 |

LPG
| ❏ 001 | Music…Music | 1976 | $12 |

MCA
| ❏ 1503 | Greatest Hits | 1982 | $10 |

MONUMENT
| ❏ MLP-8032 [M] | Lloyd Swings for Sammy | 1965 | $30 |
| ❏ SLP-18032 [S] | Lloyd Swings for Sammy | 1965 | $40 |

PICKWICK
| ❏ SPC-3518 | Big Hits | 197? | $10 |

SCEPTER CITATION
| ❏ CTN-18006 | The Best of Lloyd Price | 1972 | $12 |

SPECIALTY
| ❏ SP-2105 [M] | Lloyd Price | 1959 | $180 |
| ❏ SP-2105 | Lloyd Price | 198? | $15 |
—1980s reissue

Column 1 — PRICE, LLOYD / PRICE, RAY

Number	Title	Yr	NM
TRIP			
❏ TOP 16-5	16 Greatest Hits	1976	$12
TURNTABLE			
❏ TTS-5001	Lloyd Price Now	197?	$18
UPFRONT			
❏ UPF-126	Misty	197?	$15

PRICE, RAY

Number	Title	Yr	NM
ABC DOT			
❏ DOSD-2062	Hank 'n Me	1976	$15
❏ DO-2053	Rainbows and Tears	1976	$15
❏ DO-2073	Reunited	1977	$15
❏ DO-2037	Say I Do	1975	$15
COLUMBIA			
❏ CL2528 [M]	Another Bridge to Burn	1966	$18
❏ CS9328 [S]	Another Bridge to Burn	1966	$25
❏ JC37061	A Tribute to Willie and Kris	1982	$12
❏ CL2289 [M]	Burning Memories	1965	$18
❏ CS9089 [S]	Burning Memories	1965	$25
❏ CL2677 [M]	Danny Boy	1967	$25
❏ CS9477 [S]	Danny Boy	1967	$18
❏ CL1494 [M]	Faith	1960	$30
❏ CS8285 [S]	Faith	1960	$40
❏ C30106	For the Good Times	1970	$15
❏ CQ30106 [Q]	For the Good Times	1972	$30
❏ CG33633	For the Good Times/I Won't Mention It Again	1975	$18
—*Reissue of two LPs in one package*			
❏ PC34710	Help Me	1977	$15
❏ PC33560	If You Change Your Mind	1975	$15
❏ C30510	I Won't Mention It Again	1971	$15
❏ CL2189 [M]	Love Life	1964	$18
❏ CS8989 [S]	Love Life	1964	$25
❏ CL1971 [M]	Night Life	1963	$18
❏ CS8771 [S]	Night Life	1963	$25
❏ KG31364	Ray Price's All-Time Greatest Hits	1972	$18
❏ CS9861	Ray Price's Christmas Album	1969	$18
❏ CL1566 [M]	Ray Price's Greatest Hits	1961	$30
❏ CS8866 [R]	Ray Price's Greatest Hits	1964	$15
❏ PC8866	Ray Price's Greatest Hits	198?	$10
—*Reissue with new prefix*			
❏ CL2670 [M]	Ray Price's Greatest Hits, Volume 2	1967	$25
❏ CS9470 [S]	Ray Price's Greatest Hits, Volume 2	1967	$18
❏ CL1015 [M]	Ray Price Sings Heart Songs	1957	$50
❏ CL1756 [M]	San Antonio Rose	1962	$25
❏ CS8556 [S]	San Antonio Rose	1962	$30
❏ KC32033	She's Got to Be a Saint	1973	$15
❏ PC32033	She's Got to Be a Saint	197?	$10
—*Reissue with new prefix*			
❏ CS9733	She Wears My Ring	1968	$18
❏ CS9822	Sweetheart of the Year	1969	$18
❏ CL2806 [M]	Take Me As I Am	1968	$30
❏ CS9606 [S]	Take Me As I Am	1968	$18
❏ CL1148 [M]	Talk to Your Heart	1958	$40
❏ PC34160	The Best of Ray Price	1976	$15
❏ KC31546	The Lonesomest Lonesome	1972	$15
❏ CL2382 [M]	The Other Woman	1965	$18
❏ CS9182 [S]	The Other Woman	1965	$25
❏ GP28	The World of Ray Price	1970	$18
❏ CL2606 [M]	Touch My Heart	1967	$25
❏ CS9406 [S]	Touch My Heart	1967	$18
❏ CG30878	Welcome to My World	1971	$18
❏ CL2339 [M]	Western Strings	1965	$25
❏ CS9139 [S]	Western Strings	1965	$30
❏ KC32777	You're the Best Thing That Ever Happened to Me	1973	$15
❏ PC32777	You're the Best Thing That Ever Happened to Me	197?	$10
—*Reissue with new prefix*			
❏ CS9918	You Wouldn't Know Love	1970	$18
COLUMBIA LIMITED EDITION			
❏ LE10142	Love Life	197?	$12
—*Reissue of Columbia CS 8989*			
HARMONY			
❏ HL7440 [M]	Born to Lose	1967	$15
❏ HS11240 [S]	Born to Lose	1967	$15
❏ HL7372 [M]	Collectors' Choice	196?	$15
❏ HS11172 [R]	Collectors' Choice	196?	$15
❏ HS11373	I Fall to Pieces	1969	$12
❏ KH30272	Make the World Go Away	1970	$12
MONUMENT			
❏ 7633	Always Me	1979	$12
MYRRH			
❏ 6532	This Time, Lord	1975	$15
PAIR			
❏ PDL2-1044	Happens to Be the Best	1986	$15
❏ PDL2-1096	Priceless	1986	$15
❏ PDL2-1044	Ray Price Happens to Be the Best!	1986	$15
ROUNDER			
❏ SS-22	The Honky Tonk Years	1986	$12
WORD			
❏ 8780	How Great Thou Art	1978	$15
❏ 8723	Precious Memories	197?	$15

Column 2 — PRICE, RUTH / SAMMY / VINCENT / VITO / PRIDE, CHARLEY

PRICE, RUTH

Number	Title	Yr	NM
AVA			
❏ A-54 [M]	Live and Beautiful	1963	$40
❏ AS-54 [S]	Live and Beautiful	1963	$50
CONTEMPORARY			
❏ M-3590 [M]	Ruth Price with Shelly Manne at the Manne-Hole	1961	$250
❏ S-7590 [S]	Ruth Price with Shelly Manne at the Manne-Hole	1961	$250
KAPP			
❏ KL-1006 [M]	My Name Is Ruth Price. I Sing.	1955	$150
❏ KL-1054 [M]	The Party's Over	1957	$150
ROOST			
❏ LP-2217 [M]	Ruth Price Sings!	1956	$150

PRICE, SAMMY

Number	Title	Yr	NM
CIRCLE			
❏ 73	Sammy Price and His Musicians, 1944	1985	$25
CLASSIC JAZZ			
❏ 106	Fire	198?	$25
CONCERT HALL JAZZ			
❏ 1008 [10]	Barrelhouse and Blues	1955	$75
JAZZTONE			
❏ J-1207 [M]	Barrelhouse and Blues	1956	$40
❏ J-1236 [M]	Les Jeunesses Musicales	1956	$40
❏ J-1260 [M]	The Price Is Right	1957	$40
SAVOY			
❏ MG-14004	Rock	196?	$35
WORLD WIDE			
❏ 20016	Blues and Boogie	196?	$35

PRICE, VINCENT

Number	Title	Yr	NM
CAEDMON			
❏ TC1429	A Graveyard of Ghost Tales	1974	$18
❏ TC-1059 [M]	Vincent Price Reads Poems of Shelley	196?	$30
CAPITOL			
❏ SWBB-342	Witchcraft/Magic	1969	$30
CAPITOL CUSTOM			
❏ SGP-6258/9 [S]	The World of the 21st Century	1965	$40
—*Blue vinyl*			
❏ SGP-6256/7 [S]	The World Tomorrow	1965	$40
—*Blue vinyl*			
COLUMBIA MASTERWORKS			
❏ ML5668 [M]	America the Beautiful	1961	$30
DOT			
❏ DLP-3195 [M]	Gallery	1962	$30
❏ DLP-25195 [S]	Gallery	1962	$30
NELSON INDUSTRIES			
❏ 0(# unknown)	International Cooking Course	1977	$40

PRICE, VITO

ARGO

Number	Title	Yr	NM
❏ LP-631 [M]	Swingin' the Loop	1958	$300
❏ LPS-631 [S]	Swingin' the Loop	1958	$300

PRIDE, CHARLEY

Number	Title	Yr	NM
16TH AVENUE			
❏ ST-70550	After All This Time	1987	$15
❏ D1-70551	I'm Gonna Love Her on the Radio	1988	$15
❏ D1-70554	Moody Woman	1989	$15
PAIR			
❏ PDL2-1023	Country in My Soul	1986	$15
RCA CAMDEN			
❏ CAS-2584	The Incomparable Charley Pride	1972	$18

Column 3 — RCA VICTOR

Number	Title	Yr	NM
RCA VICTOR			
❏ APL1-0397	Amazing Love	1974	$18
❏ APD1-0397 [Q]	Amazing Love	1974	$40
❏ AYL1-4074	Amazing Love	1981	$10
—*Best Buy Series" reissue*			
❏ LSP-4742	A Sunshiny Day with Charley Pride	1972	$25
❏ AHL1-5851	Back to the Country	1986	$12
❏ AHL1-2963	Burgers and Fries	1978	$15
❏ AYL1-4252	Burgers and Fries	1982	$10
—*Best Buy Series" reissue*			
❏ APL1-1038	Charley	1975	$18
❏ APD1-1038 [Q]	Charley	1975	$40
❏ LSP-4094	Charley Pride -- In Person	1969	$25
❏ ANL1-0996	Charley Pride -- In Person	1975	$12
—*Reissue of LSP-4094*			
❏ AHL1-4524	Charley Pride Live	1983	$12
❏ APL1-0315	Charley Pride Presents the Pridesmen	1973	$18
❏ LSP-4367	Charley Pride's 10th Album	1970	$25
❏ AHL1-4287	Charley Pride Sings Everybody's Choice	1982	$12
❏ LSP-4617	Charley Pride Sings Heart Songs	1971	$25
❏ LSP-4406	Christmas in My Home Town	1970	$25
❏ ANL1-1934	Christmas in My Home Town	1976	$10
—*Reissue of LSP-4406*			
❏ CPL1-7049	Collector's Series	1985	$12
❏ LPM-3645 [M]	Country Charley Pride	1966	$30
❏ LSP-3645 [S]	Country Charley Pride	1966	$30
❏ AHL1-4662	Country Classics	1983	$12
❏ APL1-0534	Country Feelin'	1974	$18
❏ LSP-4513	Did You Think to Pray	1971	$25
❏ LSP-4468	From Me to You	1971	$25
❏ AHL1-4151	Greatest Hits	1981	$12
❏ AYL1-5147	Greatest Hits	1984	$10
—*Best Buy Series" reissue*			
❏ AHL1-5426	Greatest Hits, Volume 2	1985	$12
❏ LSP-4560	I'm Just Me	1971	$25
❏ ANL1-1214	I'm Just Me	1975	$12
—*Reissue of LSP-4560*			
❏ AYL1-3874	I'm Just Me	1981	$10
—*Best Buy Series" reissue*			
❏ LSP-4290	Just Plain Charley	1970	$25
❏ LPM-3952 [M]	Make Mine Country	1968	$75
❏ LSP-3952 [S]	Make Mine Country	1968	$25
❏ AHL1-4822	Night Games	1983	$12
❏ APL1-0757	Pride of America	1974	$18
❏ APD1-0757 [Q]	Pride of America	1974	$40
❏ AHL1-3905	Roll On Mississippi	1981	$12
❏ APL1-2261	She's Just an Old Love Turned Memory	1977	$15
❏ AYL1-4166	She's Just an Old Love Turned Memory	1981	$10
—*Best Buy Series" reissue*			
❏ AHL1-2478	Someone Loves You Honey	1978	$15
❏ AYL1-3676	Someone Loves You Honey	1980	$10
—*Best Buy Series" reissue*			
❏ LSP-4837	Songs of Love by Charley Pride	1973	$18
❏ LSP-4041	Songs of Pride -- Charley, That Is	1968	$25
❏ APL1-1359	Sunday Morning with Charley Pride	1976	$18
❏ APD1-1359 [Q]	Sunday Morning with Charley Pride	1976	$40
❏ AYL1-3740	Sunday Morning with Charley Pride	1980	$10
—*Best Buy Series" reissue*			
❏ APL1-0217	Sweet Country	1973	$18
❏ APD1-0217 [Q]	Sweet Country	1973	$40
❏ LSP-4223	The Best of Charley Pride	1969	$25
❏ AHL1-4223	The Best of Charley Pride	198?	$12
—*Reissue of LSP-4223*			
❏ AYL1-5148	The Best of Charley Pride	1984	$10
—*Best Buy Series" reissue*			
❏ APL1-2023	The Best of Charley Pride, Vol. III	1976	$15
❏ LSP-4682	The Best of Charley Pride, Volume 2	1972	$25
❏ AHL1-4682	The Best of Charley Pride, Volume 2	198?	$12
—*Reissue of LSP-4682*			
❏ AHL1-7174	The Best There Is	1986	$12
❏ LPM-3895 [M]	The Country Way	1967	$30
❏ LSP-3895 [S]	The Country Way	1967	$25
❏ APL1-1241	The Happiness of Having You	1975	$18
❏ APD1-1241 [Q]	The Happiness of Having You	1975	$40
❏ AYL1-3943	The Happiness of Having You	1981	$10
—*Best Buy Series" reissue*			
❏ AHL1-5031	The Power of Love	1984	$12
❏ LPM-3775 [M]	The Pride of Country Music	1967	$30
❏ LSP-3775 [S]	The Pride of Country Music	1967	$25
❏ AHL1-3548	There's a Little Bit of Hank in Me	1980	$15
❏ AYL1-4831	There's a Little Bit of Hank in Me	1983	$10
—*Best Buy Series" reissue*			
❏ LSP-4153	The Sensational Charley Pride	1969	$25
❏ AHL1-3441	You're My Jamaica	1979	$15
READER'S DIGEST			
❏ RDA-217	Charley Pride's Country	1979	$40

Number	Title	Yr	NM

TEE VEE/RCA SPECIAL PRODUCTS
| DVL2-0208 | Favorites | 1976 | $18 |

— Label calls this "Charley's Favorites"

TIME-LIFE
| STW-101 | Country Music | 1981 | $12 |

PRIDE
WARNER BROS.
| WS1848 | Pride | 1970 | $30 |

PRIEST, MAXI
VIRGIN
| 90957 | Maxi Priest | 1988 | $15 |

PRIESTER, JULIAN
ECM
| 1044 | Love, Love | 197? | $75 |

— Only issued in Germany?

| 1098 | Polarization | 1977 | $75 |

— Only issued in Germany?

JAZZLAND
| JLP-25 [M] | Spiritsville | 1960 | $50 |
| JLP-925 [S] | Spiritsville | 1960 | $150 |

RIVERSIDE
6081	Keep Swingin'	197?	$35
RLP 12-316 [M]	Keep Swingin'	1960	$250
RLP1163 [S]	Keep Swingin'	1960	$250

PRIMA, LOUIS, AND KEELY SMITH
CAPITOL
T1160 [M]	Hey Boy! Hey Girl!	1959	$100
T1531 [M]	The Hits of Louis and Keely	1961	$75
ST1531 [S]	The Hits of Louis and Keely	1961	$75
SM-1531	The Hits of Louis and Keely	197?	$12

— Reissue with new prefix

CORONET
| CX121 [M] | Louis Prima Digs Keely Smith | 196? | $25 |

DOT
DLP-3210 [M]	Louis and Keely!	1959	$85
DLP-25210 [S]	Louis and Keely!	1959	$100
DLP-3266 [M]	Louis and Keely on Stage	1960	$85
DLP-25266 [S]	Louis and Keely on Stage	1960	$85
DLP-3263 [M]	Together	1960	$85
DLP-25263 [S]	Together	1960	$85

FLEET
| 101 [M] | Louis Prima Digs Keely Smith | 196? | $25 |

RHINO
| RNLP-70225 | Zooma Zooma: The Best of Louis Prima Featuring Keely Smith | 1986 | $25 |

SPIN-O-RAMA
| 74 [M] | Box of Oldies | 196? | $20 |

PRIMA, LOUIS
BRUNSWICK
| BL754183 | The Prima Generation '72 | 1972 | $100 |

CAPITOL
T1797 [M]	Lake Tahoe Prima Style	1962	$75
ST1797 [S]	Lake Tahoe Prima Style	1962	$75
T1010 [M]	Las Vegas Prima Style	1958	$100
T1132 [M]	Strictly Prima	1959	$75
T836 [M]	The Call of the Wildest	1957	$100
T755 [M]	The Wildest	1956	$100
T1723 [M]	The Wildest Comes Home	1962	$75
ST1723 [S]	The Wildest Comes Home	1962	$75
T908 [M]	The Wildest Show at Tahoe	1957	$100

COLUMBIA
| CL1206 [M] | Breakin' It Up! | 1959 | $40 |

DOT
DLP-3385 [M]	Blue Moon	1961	$85
DLP-25385 [S]	Blue Moon	1961	$85
DLP-3410 [M]	Doin' the Twist	1961	$85
DLP-25410 [S]	Doin' the Twist	1961	$85
DLP-3262 [M]	His Greatest Hits	1960	$85
DLP-25262 [S]	His Greatest Hits	1960	$85
DLP-3264 [M]	Pretty Music Prima Style	1960	$85
DLP-25264 [S]	Pretty Music Prima Style	1960	$85
DLP-3392 [M]	Return of the Wildest!	1961	$85
DLP-25392 [S]	Return of the Wildest!	1961	$85
DLP-3272 [M]	The Wildest Clan	1960	$85
DLP-25272 [S]	The Wildest Clan	1960	$85
DLP-3352 [M]	Wonderland by Night	1960	$200
DLP-25352 [S]	Wonderland by Night	1960	$200

GOLDEN TONE
| 326 [M] | Italian Favorites | 196? | $12 |

— Label calls this "Italian Songs"; one side is by Louis Prima, the other side by Phil Brito

HANNA-BARBERA
| HLP-8502 [M] | The Golden Hits of Louis Prima | 1966 | $30 |

MERCURY
| MG-25142 [10] | Louis Prima Plays | 1953 | $175 |

PRIMA
ST 0074	Angelina	1973	$30
PS3003 [S]	King of Clubs	1964	$150
PM3003 [M]	King of Clubs	1964	$150
PM3001 [M]	Prima Show in the Casbar	1963	$40
PS3001 [S]	Prima Show in the Casbar	1963	$75
ST 0072	The Prima Generation	1972	$50

RONDO-LETTE
| A-25 [M] | Louis Prima Entertains | 1959 | $30 |
| A-9 [M] | Louis Prima in All His Moods | 1959 | $30 |

SAVOY JAZZ
| SJL-2264 | Play Pretty for the People | 198? | $15 |

TOPS
| 9759 [M] | Italian Favorites | 195? | $20 |

PRIMUS
CAROLINE
| CAROL1619 | Frizzle Fry | 1990 | $100 |

— Red vinyl

| CAROL1620 | Suck on This | 1990 | $75 |

— Clear vinyl

INTERSCOPE
069-490414-01	Antipop	1999	$30
INT2-90126	Brown Album	1997	$50
92553	Tales from the Punchbowl	1995	$100

MOBILE FIDELITY
| LMF45-001 [EP] | Animals Should Not Try to Act Like Humans | 2004 | $75 |

— Original Master Recording" at top of cover; plays at 45 rpm

PRAWN SONG/INTERSCOPE
| 7-72738-1 [B] | Pork Soda | 1993 | $80 |

PRINCE, BOB
RCA VICTOR
| LPM-2435 [M] | Opus Jazz | 1961 | $50 |
| LSP-2435 [S] | Opus Jazz | 1961 | $75 |

WARNER BROS.
W1276 [M]	Charleston 1970	1959	$50
WS1276 [S]	Charleston 1970	1959	$75
W1240 [M]	N.Y. Export: Op. Jazz from Ballets U.S.A.; Ballet Music from Leonard Bernstein's West Side Story	1958	$50
WS1240 [S]	N.Y. Export: Op. Jazz from Ballets U.S.A.; Ballet Music from Leonard Bernstein's West Side Story	1958	$75

PRINCE, ROLAND
VANGUARD
| VSD-79371 | Color Visions | 197? | $25 |
| VSD-79388 | Free Spirit | 197? | $25 |

PRINCE

Includes records as "Prince and the Revolution," "Prince and the N.P.G." (or New Power Generation); plus later releases as an unpronounceable glyph. Also see 94 EAST.

ARISTA
| 14624 [B] | Rave Un2 the Joy Fantastic | 1999 | $150 |

NPG
| 5533641 [B] | For You | 2016 | $25 |

NPG/BELLMARK
| 71003 [EP] | The Beautiful Experience | 1994 | $75 |

NPG/REDLINE
| 70004 [B] | The Rainbow Children | 2001 | $250 |

PAISLEY PARK
| R124370 [B] | Around the World in a Day | 1985 | $35 |

— RCA Music Service edition

| 25286 [B] | Around the World in a Day | 1985 | $40 |

— Original copies have a fold-over flap (deduct 25% or more if missing)

| R234107 [B] | Graffiti Bridge | 1990 | $60 |

— Also includes The Time, Tevin Campbell; BMG Direct Marketing edition

| 27493 [B] | Graffiti Bridge | 1990 | $40 |

— Also includes The Time, Tevin Campbell

| R154087 [B] | Lovesexy | 1988 | $40 |

— BMG Direct Marketing edition

| 25720 [B] | Lovesexy | 1988 | $60 |
| 25720-DJ [DJ] | Lovesexy | 1988 | $100 |

— Gold stamped and stickered cover (no UPC) with promo labels; tracks are banded

| R140234 [B] | Parade | 1986 | $40 |

— RCA Music Service edition

25395 [B]	Parade	1986	$50
25577 [B]	Sign "O" The Times	1987	$60
W1-25577 [B]	Sign "O" The Times	1987	$50

— Columbia House edition

| R261991 [B] | Sign "O" The Times | 1987 | $50 |

— BMG Direct Marketing edition

| 25677 | The Black Album | 1987 | $1500 |

— Withdrawn prior to release, though a few copies escaped. Numerous counterfeits exist on other labels and colored vinyl.

| 25677-DJ | The Black Album | 1987 | $3000 |

— Entire album on two 12-inch records that play at 45 RPM

WARNER BROS.
| R252483 [B] | 1999 | 1982 | $50 |

— RCA Music Service edition

| 23720 [B] | 1999 | 1982 | $70 |
| R160344 [B] | Batman (Soundtrack) | 1989 | $25 |

— BMG Direct Marketing edition

| 25936 [B] | Batman (Soundtrack) | 1989 | $25 |
| PRO-A-7270 [DJ] | Come | 1994 | $200 |

— Promo-only vinyl

BSK3601 [B]	Controversy	1981	$80
BSK3478 [B]	Dirty Mind	1980	$85
BSK3150 [B]	For You	1978	$100

— First edition on Burbank "palm trees" label

| BSK3150 [B] | For You | 1978 | $60 |

— White WB label

BSK3366 [B]	Prince	1979	$85
5533651 [B]	Prince	2016	$25
R160175 [B]	Purple Rain	1984	$50

— RCA Music Service edition; includes poster

| 25110 [B] | Purple Rain | 1984 | $100 |

— Purple vinyl; comes with poster

| 25110 [B] | Purple Rain | 1984 | $60 |

— With poster

| PRO-A-7330 [DJ] | The Black Album | 1994 | $100 |

— Promo-only vinyl

| 45793 [DJ] | The Black Album | 1994 | $250 |

— White vinyl; 300 copies, numbered in gold on the label (from 051 to 350)

| 45793 [DJ] | The Black Album | 1994 | $150 |

— Peach vinyl; 1,000 copies

| 45793 [DJ] | The Black Album | 1994 | $500 |

— Gray marbled vinyl; 50 copies

| PRO-A-7835 [DJ] | The Gold Experience | 1995 | $300 |

— Promo-only gold vinyl with numbered gold foil jacket

PRINCE BUSTER
RCA VICTOR
| LPM-3792 [M] | Ten Commandments | 1967 | $75 |
| LSP-3792 [S] | Ten Commandments | 1967 | $35 |

PRINCE IGOR AND THE CZAR
DIFFERENT DRUMMER
| 1002 | From Russia | 197? | $35 |

PRINCETON TRIANGLE JAZZ BAND
BIOGRAPH
| 12014 | College Jazz in the '20s | 1969 | $35 |

PRINE, JOHN
ASYLUM
6E-139	Bruised Orange	1978	$15
6E-222	Pink Cadillac	1979	$15
6E-286	Storm Windows	1980	$15

ATLANTIC
SD18127	Common Sense	1975	$15
SD7240	Diamonds in the Rough	1972	$15
SD8296	John Prine	1971	$15
SD19156	John Prine	1978	$12

— Reissue of 8296

| SD18202 | Prime Prine -- The Best of John Prine | 1976 | $15 |
| SD7274 | Sweet Revenge | 1973 | $15 |

OH BOY
| 002 | Aimless Love | 198? | $12 |
| OBR-034 | Fair & Square | 2007 | $30 |

— Contains four bonus tracks not on the CD version

| 003 | German Afternoons | 198? | $12 |
| 005 | John Prine Live | 1986 | $18 |

PRINZ, ROSEMARY
PHAROS
| MN-10001 [M] | TV's Penny Sings | 1966 | $25 |
| SN-30001 [S] | TV's Penny Sings | 1966 | $30 |

PRITCHARD, DAVID
INNER CITY
| IC-1070 | City Dreams | 1979 | $30 |
| IC-1047 | Light-Year | 1978 | $30 |

PRITCHETT, GEORGE
KINNICKINNICK
| 101 | By Request | 197? | $25 |

PROBERT, GEORGE
GHB
| GHB-70 | The Incredible George Probert | 197? | $25 |

PROBY, P.J.
LIBERTY
| LRP-3497 [M] | Enigma | 1967 | $35 |
| LST-7497 [S] | Enigma | 1967 | $30 |

Number	Title	Yr	NM
❑ LRP-3515 [M]	Phenomenon	1967	$40
❑ LST-7515 [S]	Phenomenon	1967	$30
❑ LRP-3421 [M]	P.J. Proby	1965	$25
❑ LST-7421 [S]	P.J. Proby	1965	$30
❑ LRP-3406 [M]	Somewhere/Go Go P.J. Proby	1965	$25
❑ LST-7406 [S]	Somewhere/Go Go P.J. Proby	1965	$30
❑ LST-7561 [B]	What's Wrong with My World?	1968	$30

PROCESSION
SMASH

❑ SRS-67122	Procession	1969	$25

PROCLAIMERS, THE
CHRYSALIS

❑ R152320	Sunshine on Leith	1989	$14
—BMG Music Service edition			
❑ F1-21668	Sunshine on Leith	1989	$15
❑ FV41602	This Is the Story	1988	$15

PROCOL HARUM
Also see THE PARAMOUNTS (4); ROBIN TROWER.
A&M

❑ SP-4179	A Salty Dog	1969	$18
❑ SP-3123	A Salty Dog	1979	$10
—Reissue of 4179			
❑ SP-4373	A Whiter Shade of Pale	1972	$15
—Reissue of Deram 18008 with one more track			
❑ SP-4294	Broken Barricades	1971	$15
❑ SP-4261	Home	1970	$15
❑ SP-4335	Procol Harum Live in Concert with the Edmonton Symphony Orchestra	1972	$15
❑ SP-8503 [DJ]	Procol Harum Lives	197?	$300
—Promo-only box set with press kit, photos, keychain and interview LP			
❑ SP-8503 [DJ]	Procol Harum Lives	197?	$30
—Interview LP alone			
❑ SP-4151	Shine On Brightly	1968	$30
❑ SP-4401	The Best of Procol Harum	1973	$15
❑ SP-3259	The Best of Procol Harum	198?	$10
—Reissue of 4401			

CHRYSALIS

❑ CHR1058	Exotic Birds and Fruit	1974	$15
—Green label with "3300 Warner Blvd." address			
❑ PV41058	Exotic Birds and Fruit	1985	$10
❑ CHR1058	Exotic Birds and Fruit	1977	$12
—Blue label with New York address			
❑ CHR1037	Grand Hotel	1973	$15
—Green label with "3300 Warner Blvd." address			
❑ PV41037	Grand Hotel	1985	$10
❑ CHR1037	Grand Hotel	1977	$12
—Blue label with New York address			
❑ CHR1080	Procol's Ninth	1975	$15
—Green label with "3300 Warner Blvd." address			
❑ PV41080	Procol's Ninth	1985	$10
❑ CHR1080	Procol's Ninth	1977	$12
—Blue label with New York address			
❑ CHR1130	Something Magic	1977	$12

DERAM

❑ DE16008 [M]	Procol Harum	1967	$120
❑ DES18008 [R]	Procol Harum	1967	$40
❑ DE/ S16008/18008	Procol Harum Poster	1967	$30

PROCOPE, RUSSELL
DOT

❑ DLP3010 [M]	The Persuasive Sax of Russell Procope	1956	$100

PRODIGY
MAVERICK

❑ PRO-A-8929 [DJ]	The Fat of the Land	1997	$30
—Promo-only U.S. vinyl in generic white sleeve			

PRODUCERS, THE
MARATHON

❑ MR111	Run For Your Life	198?	$25

PORTRAIT

❑ NJR37097	The Producers	1981	$15
❑ ARR38060	You Make the Heat	1982	$15

PROFESSOR LONGHAIR
ATLANTIC

❑ SD7225	New Orleans Piano	1972	$30

PROVINE, DOROTHY
WARNER BROS.

❑ W1394 [M]	The Roaring 20's	1961	$25
❑ WS1394 [S]	The Roaring 20's	1961	$30
❑ W1419 [M]	The Vamp of the Roaring 20's	1961	$25
❑ WS1419 [S]	The Vamp of the Roaring 20's	1961	$30

Number	Title	Yr	NM
PRUETT, JEANNE			
ALLEGIANCE			
❑ AV-5028	Stand By Your Man	1984	$12
DECCA			
❑ DL75360	Love Me	1972	$18
DOT/MCA			
❑ 39031	Jeanne Pruett	1985	$12
MCA			
❑ 479	Honey on His Hands	1975	$15
❑ 388	Jeanne Pruett	1974	$15
❑ 503	Love Me	1975	$15
—Reissue of Decca LP			
❑ 338	Satin Sheets	1973	$15

PRYOR, RICHARD
AUDIOFIDELITY

❑ 349 [PD]	Richard Pryor Live	198?	$18

DOVE

❑ RS6325	Richard Pryor	1968	$25

LAFF

❑ A196	Are You Serious???	1977	$15
❑ A200	Black Ben	1978	$12
❑ 226	Blackjack	198?	$10
—Reissue of 146			
❑ A146	Craps: After Hours	1971	$15
❑ A184	Down 'N' Dirty	197?	$15
❑ A212	Holy Smoke	1980	$12
❑ A209	Insane	1980	$12
❑ A206	Outrageous	1979	$12
❑ A170	Pryor Goes Foxx Hunting	197?	$15
❑ A216	Rev. Du Rite	1981	$12
❑ 279	Richard Pryor Live	198?	$10
❑ A188	Richard Pryor Meets Richard and Willie and the S.L.A.	1976	$15
❑ 227	Show Biz	198?	$10
—Reissue of 200			
❑ 0(# unknown)	Supernigger	198?	$10
❑ A221	The Very Best of Richard Pryor	1982	$12
❑ A198	Who Me? I'm Not Him	1977	$15
❑ A202	Wizard of Comedy	1978	$12

PARTEE

❑ PBS-2404	That Nigger's Crazy	1974	$18

REPRISE

❑ MS2227	Is It Something I Said?	1975	$15
❑ MSK2285	Is It Something I Said?	1977	$12
—Reissue of 2227			
❑ RS6325	Richard Pryor	197?	$15
—Reissue of Dove LP			
❑ MS2241	That Nigger's Crazy	197?	$15
—Reissue of Partee LP			
❑ MSK2287	That Nigger's Crazy	1977	$12
—Reissue of Reprise 2241			

TIGER LILY

❑ TL14023 [B]	L.A. Jail	1977	$50

WARNER BROS.

❑ BS2960	Bicentennial Nigger	1976	$15
❑ BSK3114	Bicentennial Nigger	1977	$12
—Reissue of 2960			
❑ 23981	Richard Pryor: Here and Now	1983	$12
❑ BSK3660	Richard Pryor Live on the Sunset Strip	1982	$12
❑ BSK3057	Richard Pryor's Greatest Hits	1977	$12
❑ 2BSK3364	Wanted	1978	$15

PRYSOCK, ARTHUR
DECCA

❑ DL4628 [M]	Showcase	1965	$35
❑ DL74628 [S]	Showcase	1965	$50
❑ DL4581 [M]	Strictly Sentimental	1965	$35
❑ DL74581 [S]	Strictly Sentimental	1965	$50

KING

❑ KS-1088	Fly My Love	1970	$30
❑ KS-1064	The Country Side of Arthur Prysock	1969	$30
❑ KS-1067	The Lord Is My Shepherd	1970	$30
❑ KS-1134	Unforgettable	1971	$30
❑ KS-1066	Where the Soul Trees Go	1970	$30

MCA

❑ 3061	Here's To Good Friends	1978	$25

MGM

❑ SE-4694	Arthur Prysock	1970	$30
❑ GAS-134	Arthur Prysock (Golden Archive Series)	1970	$30

MILESTONE

❑ M-9139	A Rockin' Good Way	1986	$25
❑ M-9146	This Guy's in Love with You	1987	$25
❑ M-9157	Today's Love Songs, Tomorrow's Blues	1988	$25

OLD TOWN

❑ LP-2009 [M]	A Double Header with Arthur Prysock	1965	$40
❑ Dec-004	All My Life	1976	$30

Number	Title	Yr	NM
❑ LP-2006 [M]	A Portrait of Arthur Prysock	1963	$40
❑ T-90604 [M]	A Portrait of Arthur Prysock	1965	$85
—Capitol Record Club edition			
❑ ST-90604 [S]	A Portrait of Arthur Prysock	1965	$85
—Capitol Record Club edition			
❑ Dec-001	Arthur Prysock '74	1973	$30
❑ OT12005	Arthur Prysock Does It Again	1977	$30
❑ LP-2004 [M]	Arthur Prysock Sings Only for You	1962	$150
❑ LP-2005 [M]	Coast to Coast	1963	$40
❑ LP-2007 [M]	Everlasting Songs for Everlasting Lovers	1964	$40
❑ LP-2010 [M]	In a Mood	1965	$40
❑ LP-2008 [M]	Intimately Yours	1964	$40
❑ LP-102 [M]	I Worry About You	1962	$150
❑ Dec-002	Love Makes It Right	1974	$30

POLYDOR

❑ PD-2-8901	Silk and Satin	1977	$35

VERVE

❑ V6-650	24 Karat Hits	1969	$35
❑ V-5012 [M]	A Portrait of Arthur Prysock	1967	$35
❑ V6-5012 [S]	A Portrait of Arthur Prysock	1967	$35
❑ V-5009 [M]	Art and Soul	1966	$30
❑ V6-5009 [S]	Art and Soul	1966	$35
❑ V6-5059	I Must Be Doing Something Right	1968	$30
❑ V-5029 [M]	Love Me	1968	$35
❑ V6-5029 [S]	Love Me	1968	$30
❑ V-5014 [M]	Mister Prysock	1967	$35
❑ V6-5014 [S]	Mister Prysock	1967	$35
❑ V-5011 [M]	The Best of Arthur Prysock	1967	$30
❑ V6-5011 [S]	The Best of Arthur Prysock	1967	$35
❑ V-5038 [M]	The Best of Arthur Prysock, Number 2	1968	$50
—All mono copies appear to be yellow label promos			
❑ V6-5038 [S]	The Best of Arthur Prysock, Number 2	1968	$30
❑ V6-5070	This Is My Beloved	1969	$30
❑ V-5048 [M]	To Love or Not to Love	1968	$75
—May be promo only			
❑ V6-5048 [S]	To Love or Not to Love	1968	$30

PRYSOCK, ARTHUR/COUNT BASIE
VERVE

❑ V-8646 [M]	Arthur Prysock/Count Basie	1966	$35
❑ V6-8646 [S]	Arthur Prysock/Count Basie	1966	$50
❑ 827011-1	Arthur Prysock/Count Basie	1985	$20
—Reissue			

PRYSOCK, RED
MERCURY

❑ MG-20211 [M]	Fruit Boots	1957	$120
❑ MG-20088 [M]	Rock 'n Roll	1955	$250
❑ MG-20512 [M]	Swing Softly Red	1958	$50
❑ SR-60188 [S]	Swing Softly Red	1959	$100
❑ MG-20307 [M]	The Beat	1957	$100

WING

❑ MGW-12007 [M]	Fruit Boots	1959	$40
—Originals have liner notes on back cover			
❑ MGW-12007 [M]	Fruit Boots	196?	$25
—Reissues have other LPs listed on back cover			
❑ SRW-16007 [S]	Fruit Boots	196?	$15

PSEUDO ECHO
EMI AMERICA

❑ ST-17130	Pseudo Echo	1985	$12

RCA

❑ 5730-1-R	Love An Adventure	1987	$15
—Without "Funkytown"			
❑ 5730-1-RX	Love An Adventure	1987	$10
—With "Funkytown"			
❑ 8503-1-R	Race	1989	$12

PSYCHEDELIC FURS
COLUMBIA

❑ FC44377	All of This and Nothing	1988	$12
❑ FC45412	Book of Days	1989	$12

Number	Title	Yr	NM
❑ ARC38261 [B]	Forever Now	1982	$12
❑ PC38261	Forever Now	198?	$10
— Budget-line reissue			
❑ AS1296 [DJ]	Interchords	1981	$30
❑ AS1296 [DJ]	Interchords	1981	$30
❑ CAS1310 [DJ]	Interchords with Richard Butler	1988	$25
❑ CAS 01310 [DJ]	Interchords with Richard Butler	1988	$18
❑ FC40466	Midnight to Midnight	1987	$12
❑ BFC39278	Mirror Moves	1984	$12
❑ PC39278	Mirror Moves	198?	$10
— Budget-line reissue			
❑ NFC36791	Psychedelic Furs	1980	$15
❑ CAS2719 [DJ]	Richard Butler Interview	1987	$18
❑ CAS2719 [DJ]	Richard Butler Interview	1987	$18
❑ NFC37339	Talk Talk Talk	1981	$12
❑ PC37339	Talk Talk Talk	1983	$10
— Budget-line reissue			
❑ PC36791	The Psychedelic Furs	198?	$10
— Budget-line reissue			

PSYCHOTIC PINEAPPLE, THE

RICHMOND
❑ 6026 [B]	Where's the Party	1980	$30

PUBLIC ENEMY

ATOMIC POP
❑ 0001	There's a Poison Goin' On	1999	$30
— Red vinyl			

DEF JAM
❑ C247374	Apocalypse 91... The Enemy Strikes Black	1991	$18
❑ C45413	Fear of a Black Planet	1990	$15
❑ C253014	Greatest Misses	1993	$18
❑ 558130-1	He Got Game	1998	$18
❑ BFW44303	It Takes a Nation of Millions to Hold Us Back	1988	$15
❑ 523362-1	Muse Sick-N-Hour Mess Age	1994	$12
❑ BFC40658	Yo! Bum Rush the Show	1987	$15

PUBLIC IMAGE LTD.
Includes Johnny Rotten - now as Lydon - from the SEX PISTOLS.

4 MEN WITH BEARDS
❑ 4M517LP [B]	Second Edition		$30
❑ 4M518LP [B]	The Flowers of Romance		$25

ELEKTRA
❑ 60491	Live in Tokyo	1985	$12
❑ 60438	Public Image Ltd. Album	1986	$12
❑ 60365	This Is What You Want... This Is What You'll Get	1984	$12

ISLAND
❑ 2WX3288	Second Edition	1980	$25

LIGHT IN THE ATTIC
❑ LITA100 [B]	First Edition	2013	$30

VIRGIN
❑ 91062	9	1989	$12
❑ 90642	Happy	1987	$12

WARNER BROS.
❑ BSK3536	Flowers of Romance	1981	$15
❑ 2WX3288 [B]	Second Edition	198?	$30
— Reissue			

PUCHO AND THE LATIN SOUL BROTHERS

PRESTIGE
❑ PRST-7555	Big Stick	1968	$30
❑ PRST-7616	Dateline	1969	$30
❑ PRST-7572	Heat!	1968	$30
❑ PRLP-7471 [M]	Pucho and the Latin Soul Brothers	1967	$40
❑ PRST-7471 [S]	Pucho and the Latin Soul Brothers	1967	$30
❑ PRLP-7502 [M]	Saffron and Soul	1967	$40
❑ PRST-7502 [S]	Saffron and Soul	1967	$30
❑ PRLP-7528 [M]	Shuckin' and Jivin'	1967	$50
❑ PRST-7528 [S]	Shuckin' and Jivin'	1967	$30
❑ PRST-7679	The Best of Pucho and the Latin Soul Brothers	1969	$30

PUCKETT, GARY, AND THE UNION GAP

COLUMBIA
❑ CS1042	Gary Puckett and the Union Gap's Greatest Hits	1970	$25
❑ CS9715 [S]	Incredible	1968	$25
❑ CL2915 [M]	Incredible	1968	$75
— Red label stock copy with "Mono" on label; this has been confirmed to exist			
❑ C30862	The Gary Puckett Album	1971	$18
❑ CS9935	The New Gary Puckett and the Union Gap Album	1969	$25
❑ CS9612 [S]	Woman, Woman	1968	$25
— As "The Union Gap Featuring Gary Puckett"			
❑ CL2812 [M]	Woman, Woman	1968	$40
— As "The Union Gap Featuring Gary Puckett"			
❑ CS9664 [S]	Young Girl	1968	$25
❑ CL2864 [M]	Young Girl	1968	$50
— Red label stock copy with "Mono" on label; this has been confirmed to exist			
❑ CS9664 [M]	Young Girl	1968	$75
— White label promo with stereo number and "Mono" on label; "Special Mono Radio Station Copy" sticker and timing strip on front cover			

HARMONY
❑ KH31184	Lady Willpower	1972	$12

PUENTE, TITO

CONCORD PICANTE
❑ CJP-250	El Rey	1984	$25
❑ CJP-283	Mambo Diablo	1985	$25
❑ CP-207	On Broadway	1983	$25
❑ CJP-354	Salsa Meets Jazz	1988	$25
❑ CJP-301	Sensacion	1987	$25
❑ CJP-329	Un Poco Loco	1987	$25

DECCA
❑ DL74910 [S]	Brasilia Nueve	1967	$25
❑ DL4910 [M]	Brasilia Nueve	1967	$30

GNP CRESCENDO
❑ GNPS-2048 [S]	Puente Now!	197?	$25
— Reissue of 70			
❑ GNP-70 [M]	The Exciting Tito Puente Band in Hollywood	196?	$30

RCA VICTOR
❑ LPM-2187 [M]	Cha Cha at Grossinger's	1959	$30
❑ LSP-2187 [S]	Cha Cha at Grossinger's	1959	$40
❑ LPM-1251 [M]	Cuban Carnival	1955	$75
❑ LPM-1692 [M]	Dance Mania	1958	$30
❑ LSP-1692 [S]	Dance Mania	1958	$40
❑ LPM-1874 [M]	Dancing Under Latin Skies	1958	$30
❑ LSP-1874 [S]	Dancing Under Latin Skies	1958	$40
❑ LPM-1392 [M]	Let's Cha-Cha with Puente	1957	$40
❑ LPM-1354 [M]	Mambo on Broadway	1957	$40
❑ LPM-2113 [M]	Mucho Cha Cha Cha	1959	$30
❑ LSP-2113 [S]	Mucho Cha Cha Cha	1959	$40
❑ LPM-1479 [M]	Mucho Puente	1957	$40
❑ LPM-1447 [M]	Night Beat	1957	$40
❑ LPM-1312 [M]	Puente Goes Jazz	1956	$75
❑ LPM-2299 [M]	Revolving Bandstand	1960	$30
❑ LSP-2299 [S]	Revolving Bandstand	1960	$40
❑ LPM-2257 [M]	Tambo	1960	$30
❑ LSP-2257 [S]	Tambo	1960	$40
❑ LPM-2974 [M]	The Best of Tito Puente	1964	$30
❑ LSP-2974(e) [P]	The Best of Tito Puente	1964	$35
❑ LSP-1617 [S]	Top Percussion	1958	$40
❑ LPM-1617 [M]	Top Percussion	1958	$30

ROULETTE
❑ R-25193 [M]	Bossa Nova	1962	$25
❑ SR-25193 [S]	Bossa Nova	1962	$30
❑ R-25276 [M]	My Fair Lady" Goes Latin	1964	$25
❑ SR-25276 [S]	My Fair Lady" Goes Latin	1964	$30

TICO
❑ LP-1151 [M]	20th Anniversary	1967	$30
❑ SLP-1151 [S]	20th Anniversary	1967	$25
❑ LP-1032 [M]	Basic Cha Cha Cha	1957	$50
❑ LP-1127 [M]	Carnival in Harlem	196?	$25
❑ SLP-1127 [S]	Carnival in Harlem	196?	$30
❑ JMTS-1440	Ce' Magnifique	198?	$35
❑ LP-128 [10]	Cha Cha Cha, Volume 1	195?	$100
❑ LP-130 [10]	Cha Cha Cha, Volume 2	195?	$100
❑ LP-134 [10]	Cha Cha Cha, Volume 3	195?	$100
❑ LP-1025 [M]	Cha Cha Cha at the El Morocco	1956	$75
❑ LP-1136 [M]	Cuba Y Puerto Ricon Son	196?	$25
❑ SLP-1136 [S]	Cuba Y Puerto Ricon Son	196?	$30
❑ JMTS-1439	Dance Mania 80's	198?	$35
❑ LP-1010 [M]	Dance the Cha Cha Cha	195?	$75
❑ LP-1116 [M]	De Mi Para Ti	196?	$30
❑ SLP-1116 [S]	De Mi Para Ti	196?	$30
❑ LP-1109 [M]	El Mundo Latino de Tito Puente	196?	$30
❑ SLP-1109 [S]	El Mundo Latino de Tito Puente	196?	$30
❑ SLP-1172	El Rey (The King)	1968	$25
❑ LP-1086 [M]	El Rey Tito: Bravo Puente	1962	$30
❑ SLP-1086 [S]	El Rey Tito: Bravo Puente	1962	$40
— This album contains the original version of "Oye Como Va," later a hit for Santana			
❑ SLP-1154 [S]	El Rey Y Yo (The King and I)	1967	$25
❑ LP-1154 [M]	El Rey Y Yo (The King and I)	1967	$30
❑ LP-1106 [M]	Excitente Ritmo	196?	$30
❑ SLP-1106 [S]	Excitente Ritmo	196?	$30
❑ JMTS-1425	Homenaje a Beny More	1978	$35
❑ LP-1131 [M]	Homenaje a Rafael Hernandez	196?	$25
❑ SLP-1131 [S]	Homenaje a Rafael Hernandez	196?	$30
❑ LP-133 [10]	Instrumental Mambos	195?	$100
❑ JMTS-1430	La Pareja	1978	$35
❑ LP-1003 [M]	Mambo and Me	1955	$85
❑ LP-1001 [M]	Mamborama	1955	$85
❑ LP-101 [10]	Mambos, Volume 1	1951	$150
❑ LP-103 [10]	Mambos, Volume 2	1952	$100
❑ LP-107 [10]	Mambos, Volume 3	195?	$100
❑ LP-114 [10]	Mambos, Volume 4	195?	$100
❑ LP-116 [10]	Mambos, Volume 5	195?	$100
❑ LP-131 [10]	Mambos, Volume 8	195?	$100
❑ LP-1006 [M]	Mambos for Lovers	1955	$85
❑ LP-1115 [M]	Mucho Puente	196?	$30
❑ SLP-1115 [S]	Mucho Puente	196?	$30
❑ SLP-1083 [S]	Pachanga Con Puente	1961	$40
❑ LP-1083 [M]	Pachanga Con Puente	1961	$30
❑ SLP-1214	P'alante!	1970	$25

Number	Title	Yr	NM
❑ CLP-1301	Para Los Rumberos	1972	$35
❑ LP-1058 [M]	Puente in Love	1959	$40
❑ LP-1011 [M]	Puente in Percussion	1956	$75
❑ SLP-1203	The Best of Tito Puente	1969	$25
❑ LP-120 [10]	The King of the Mambo and His Orchestra	195?	$100
❑ JMTS-1413	The Legend	1976	$35
❑ CLP-1308	Tito Puente and His Concert Orchestra	1972	$35
❑ LP-124 [10]	Tito Puente at the Vibes and His Rhythm Quartet	195?	$100
❑ LP-1093 [M]	Tito Puente Bailables	1963	$30
❑ SLP-1093 [S]	Tito Puente Bailables	1963	$30
❑ SLP-1191	Tito Puente En El Puente (On the Bridge)	1969	$25
❑ LP-1088 [M]	Tito Puente in Puerto Rico	1963	$30
❑ SLP-1088 [S]	Tito Puente in Puerto Rico	1963	$30
❑ SLP-1121 [S]	Tito Puente Swings/The Exciting Lupe Sings	196?	$30
❑ LP-1121 [M]	Tito Puente Swings/The Exciting Lupe Sings	196?	$25
❑ LP-1049 [M]	Tito Puente Swings/ Vicentico Valdes Sings	1958	$50
❑ SLP-1125 [S]	Tu Y Yo (You 'n' Me)	196?	$30
❑ LP-1125 [M]	Tu Y Yo (You 'n' Me)	196?	$25
❑ CLP-1322	Unlimited Tito	1974	$35
❑ LP-1085 [M]	Vaya Puente	1962	$30
❑ SLP-1085 [S]	Vaya Puente	1962	$40

PUFF DADDY

BAD BOY
❑ 73012	No Way Out	1997	$15

PUGSLEY MUNION

J&S
❑ SLP-001	Just Like You	1969	$150

PUKWANA, DUDU

ARISTA/FREEDOM
❑ AF1041	Diamond	1977	$30

PULLEN, DON, AND MILFORD GRAVES

PULLEN-GRAVES MUSIC
❑ 0(# unknown)	Graves-Pullen Duo	1967	$50

S.R.P.
❑ LP-290	Nommo	1968	$40

PULLEN, DON

ATLANTIC
❑ SD8802	Montreux '77	1978	$30
❑ SD1699	Tomorrow's Promises	1977	$30

BLACK SAINT
❑ BSR-0004	Capricorn Rising	198?	$30
❑ BSR-0080	Evidence of Things Unseen	198?	$30
❑ BSR-0010	Healing Force	198?	$30
❑ BSR-0028	Milano Strut	198?	$30
❑ BSR-0038	The Magic Triangle	198?	$30
❑ BSR-0088	The Sixth Sense	1986	$30
❑ BSR-0019	Warriors	198?	$30

BLUE NOTE
❑ B1-91785	New Beginnings	1989	$30

SACKVILLE
❑ 3008	Solo Piano Record	198?	$25

PULLEN, WHITEY

CROWN
❑ CLP-5332 [M]	Whitey Pullen	1963	$40
❑ CST-332 [R]	Whitey Pullen	1963	$15

PULLINS, LEROY

KAPP
❑ KS-3557	Funny Bones and Hearts	1968	$30
❑ KL-1488 [M]	I'm a Nut	1966	$30
❑ KS-3488 [S]	I'm a Nut	1966	$30

PULSE

POISON RING
❑ 2237	Pulse	1969	$30

PUMA, JOE

BETHLEHEM
❑ BCP-1012 [10]	East Coast Jazz 3	1954	$300

COLUMBIA
❑ CL1618 [M]	Like Tweet	1961	$30
❑ CS8418 [S]	Like Tweet	1961	$40

DAWN
❑ DLP-1118 [M]	Wild Kitten	1957	$200

JUBILEE
❑ JLP-1070 [M]	Joe Puma Jazz	1958	$100

PUNCH & HANDY'S CALIFORNIA CRUSADERS

GHB
❑ 191	Punch & Handy's California Crusaders, Vol. 1	1985	$25
❑ 192	Punch & Handy's California Crusaders, Vol. 2	1985	$25

Number	Title	Yr	NM
❏ 193	Punch & Handy's California Crusaders, Vol. 3	1985	$25

PURCELL, JOHN
MINOR MUSIC

Number	Title	Yr	NM
❏ MM-006	Third Kind of Blue	1986	$30

PURDIE, BERNARD
DATE

Number	Title	Yr	NM
❏ TEM3006 [M]	Soul Drums	1967	$25
❏ TES4006 [S]	Soul Drums	1967	$25

PRESTIGE

| ❏ 10013 | Purdie Good | 1971 | $20 |
| ❏ 10038 | Shaft | 1972 | $25 |

PURE ENERGY
PRISM

| ❏ PLP-1007 | Pure Energy | 1980 | $25 |

PURE LOVE AND PLEASURE
ABC DUNHILL

| ❏ DS-50076 | A Record of Pure Love and Pleasure | 1970 | $18 |

PURE PRAIRIE LEAGUE
CASABLANCA

| ❏ NBLP-7212 | Firin' Up | 1980 | $12 |
| ❏ NBLP-7255 | Something in the Night | 1981 | $12 |

PAIR

| ❏ PDL2-1034 | Home on the Range | 1986 | $15 |

RCA VICTOR

| ❏ LSP-4769 [B] | Bustin' Out | 1972 | $18 |

❏ AFL1-4769 [B]	Bustin' Out	1977	$12
—Reissue of LSP-4769			
❏ AYL1-4656	Bustin' Out	1984	$10
—Best Buy Series" reissue			
❏ AFL1-3335	Can't Hold Back	1979	$15
❏ APL1-1924	Dance	1976	$15
❏ AYL1-3723	Dance	1981	$10
—Best Buy Series" reissue			
❏ APL1-1247	If the Shoe Fits	1976	$15
❏ APD1-1247 [Q]	If the Shoe Fits	1976	$30
❏ AYL1-3717	If the Shoe Fits	1981	$10
—Best Buy Series" reissue			
❏ AFL1-2590	Just Fly	1978	$15
❏ AYL1-3718	Just Fly	1981	$10
—Best Buy Series" reissue			
❏ CPL2-2404	Live!! Takin' the Stage	1977	$18
❏ LSP-4650	Pure Prairie League	1972	$15
❏ AFL1-4650	Pure Prairie League	1977	$12
—Reissue of LSP-4650			
❏ AYL1-3719	Pure Prairie League	1981	$10
—Best Buy Series" reissue			
❏ APL1-0933	Two Lane Highway	1975	$15
❏ APD1-0933 [Q]	Two Lane Highway	1975	$30
❏ AYL1-3669	Two Lane Highway	1980	$10
—Best Buy Series" reissue			

PURIFY, JAMES AND BOBBY
BELL

❏ 6003 [M]	James and Bobby Purify	1966	$30
❏ S-6003 [S]	James and Bobby Purify	1966	$30
❏ 6010 [M]	The Pure Sound of the Purifys	1967	$30
❏ S-6010 [S]	The Pure Sound of the Purifys	1967	$30

MERCURY

| ❏ SRM-1-1134 | The Purify Brothers | 1977 | $15 |

PURIM, FLORA, AND AIRTO
CROSSOVER

Number	Title	Yr	NM
❏ CR-5001	The Magicians	1988	$25
❏ CR-5003	The Sun Is Out	1989	$35

GEORGE WEIN COLLECTION

| ❏ GW-3007 | Humble People | 1986 | $25 |

PURIM, FLORA
FANTASY

❏ OJC-315	Butterfly Dreams	1988	$20
—Reissue of Milestone 9052			
❏ OJC-619	Stories to Tell	1991	$30
—Reissue of Milestone 9058			

MILESTONE

❏ M-9070	500 Miles High	1976	$30
❏ M-9052	Butterfly Dreams	1973	$35
❏ M-9077	Encounter	1977	$35
❏ M-9095	Love Reborn	1980	$30
❏ M-9075	Nothing Will Be As It Was... Tomorrow	1977	$50
❏ M-9065	Open Your Eyes You Can Fly	1976	$35
❏ M-9058	Stories to Tell	1974	$35
❏ FPM-4005 [Q]	Stories to Tell	1975	$40
❏ M-9081	That's What She Said	1978	$30

VIRGIN

| ❏ 90995 | The Midnight Sun | 1988 | $30 |

WARNER BROS.

❏ BSK3344	Carry On	1979	$35
❏ BSK3168	Everyday, Everynight	1978	$30
❏ BS2985	Nothing Will Be As It Was... Tomorrow	1977	$30

PURPLE GANG, THE
SIRE

| ❏ SES97006 [B] | The Purple Gang Strikes | 1969 | $75 |

PURPLE IMAGE
MAP CITY

| ❏ 3015 | Purple Image | 1971 | $50 |

PURSELL, BILL
COLUMBIA

❏ CL2077 [M]	Chasing a Dream	1964	$18
❏ CS8877 [S]	Chasing a Dream	1964	$25
❏ CL1992 [M]	Our Winter Love	1963	$18
❏ CS8792 [S]	Our Winter Love	1963	$25
❏ CL2421 [M]	Remembered Love	1965	$18
❏ CS9221 [S]	Remembered Love	1965	$25

PURVIS, PAM, AND BOB ACKERMAN
BLACKHAWK

| ❏ BKH-51201 | Heart Song | 1986 | $25 |

PUSSY GALORE
BUY OUR RECORDS

| ❏ 10 [EP] | Pussy Gold 5000 | 1986 | $50 |

CAROLINE

| ❏ CAROL1369 | Dial "M" for Motherfucker | 1989 | $30 |
| ❏ CAROL1337 | Right Now! | 1987 | $30 |

SHOVE

| ❏ 2 | Groovy Hate Fuck | 1986 | $50 |

PUTMAN, CURLY
ABC

❏ ABC-618 [M]	Lonesome	1967	$30
❏ ABCS-618 [S]	Lonesome	1967	$18
❏ ABCS-686	World of Country Music	1969	$18

PUYANA, RAFAEL
MERCURY LIVING PRESENCE

❏ SR90369 [S]	Bach for Harpsichord	196?	$30
—Maroon label, no "Vendor: Mercury Record Corporation			
❏ SR90369 [S]	Bach for Harpsichord	196?	$30
—Maroon label, with "Vendor: Mercury Record Corporation			
❏ SR90322 [S]	Bachs: Harpsichord Music	196?	$25
—Maroon label, no "Vendor: Mercury Record Corporation			
❏ SR90411 [S]	Baroque Masterpieces for the Harpsichord	196?	$30
—Maroon label, no "Vendor: Mercury Record Corporation			
❏ SR90259 [S]	Picchi: Belli d'Arpsichordo; Frescobaldi: Music for Harpsichord	196?	$25
—Maroon label, no "Vendor: Mercury Record Corporation			
❏ SR90459 [S]	Soler: Harpsichord Music	196?	$30
—Maroon label, with "Vendor: Mercury Record Corporation			
❏ SR90304 [S]	The Golden Age of Harpsichord Music	196?	$25
—Maroon label, no "Vendor: Mercury Record Corporation			

PUZZLE
ABC

| ❏ ABCS-671 | Puzzle | 1969 | $25 |

PYLE, ARTIMUS
Also see LYNYRD SKYNYRD.
MCA

Number	Title	Yr	NM
❏ 5313 [B]	A.P.B.	1982	$30
❏ 39003	Nightcaller	1983	$30

PYLE, JACK
CAMEO

| ❏ C-1017 [M] | Listen Son...And Other Readings by Jack Pyle | 1963 | $25 |

PYRAMIDS, THE (1)
BEST

❏ LPM-1001 [M]	The Original Penetration! And Other Favorites	1964	$300
—Original issue with "Walkin' the Dog			
❏ BR16501 [M]	The Original Penetration! And Other Favorites	1964	$250
—Reissue with "Road Runnah			
❏ BS36501 [R]	The Original Penetration! And Other Favorites	1964	$120

SUNDAZED

| ❏ LP-5012 | Penetration! The Best of the Pyramids | 1995 | $12 |

PYTHON LEE JACKSON
GNP CRESCENDO

| ❏ GNPS-2066 | In a Broken Dream | 1972 | $18 |

Q

Q-FEEL
JIVE/ARISTA

| ❏ VA66005 | Q-Feel | 1983 | $15 |

Q-TIP
ARISTA

| ❏ 14619 | Amplified | 1999 | $18 |

Q
EPIC

| ❏ PE34691 | Dancin' Man | 1977 | $15 |

QUADRANT
PABLO

| ❏ 2310837 | Quadrant | 1978 | $30 |

PABLO TODAY

| ❏ 2312117 | Quadrant Toasts Duke Ellington/All Too Soon | 1980 | $30 |

QUARTERFLASH
GEFFEN

❏ GHS24078 [B]	Back Into Blue	1985	$12
❏ GHS2003 [B]	Quarterflash	1981	$12
❏ GHS4011 [B]	Take Another Picture	1983	$12

QUARTETTE TRES BIEN
ATLANTIC

| ❏ 1461 [M] | Bully! | 1966 | $30 |
| ❏ SD1461 [S] | Bully! | 1966 | $20 |

DECCA

❏ DL4547 [M]	Boss Tres Bien	1964	$30
❏ DL74547 [S]	Boss Tres Bien	1964	$25
❏ DL4958 [M]	Four of a Kind	1967	$20
❏ DL74958 [S]	Four of a Kind	1967	$30
❏ DL4893 [M]	Here It Is	1967	$18
❏ DL74893 [S]	Here It Is	1967	$30
❏ DL4791 [M]	In" Motion	1966	$30
❏ DL74791 [S]	In" Motion	1966	$20
❏ DL4548 [M]	Kilimanjaro	1964	$30
❏ DL74548 [S]	Kilimanjaro	1964	$25
❏ DL75044	Our Thing	1969	$30
❏ DL4715 [M]	Sky High	1966	$30
❏ DL74715 [S]	Sky High	1966	$20
❏ DL4617 [M]	Spring Into Spring	1965	$30
❏ DL74617 [S]	Spring Into Spring	1965	$20
❏ DL4675 [M]	Stepping Out	1965	$30
❏ DL74675 [S]	Stepping Out	1965	$18
❏ DL4822 [M]	Where It's At	1966	$30
❏ DL74822 [S]	Where It's At	1966	$35

GNP

❏ GNP-107 [M]	Kilimanjaro	1963	$25
❏ GNPS-107 [S]	Kilimanjaro	1963	$30
❏ GNP-102 [M]	Quartette Tres Bien	1962	$25
❏ GNPS-102 [S]	Quartette Tres Bien	1962	$30

QUARTZ
MARLIN

| ❏ 2216 | Quartz | 1978 | $15 |

POLYDOR

| ❏ PD-1-6203 | Camel in the City | 1979 | $18 |

Number	Title	Yr	NM

QUATEMAN, BILL
COLUMBIA
| ❏ KC31761 | Bill Quateman | 1973 | $15 |

RCA VICTOR
❏ AFL1-2879	Just Like You	1979	$12
❏ APL1-2027	Night After Night	1977	$12
❏ APL1-2434	Shot in the Dark	1977	$12

QUATERMASS
HARVEST
| ❏ SKAO-314 [B] | Quatermass | 1970 | $50 |

QUATRO, MICHAEL
EVOLUTION
| ❏ 3021 | Look Deeply Into the Mirror | 1973 | $30 |
— As "Mike Quatro Jam Band"
| ❏ 3011 | Paintings | 1972 | $30 |
— As "Mike Quatro Jam Band"

KOALA
| ❏ KOA14631 | Into the Mirror | 1979 | $18 |
— New version of similar 1973 album on Evolution

PRODIGAL
| ❏ P6-10010S1 [B] | Dancers, Romancers, Dreamers and Schemers | 1976 | $18 |
| ❏ P6-10016S1 | Gettin' Ready | 1977 | $18 |

SPECTOR
| ❏ SW-70003 | Bottom Line | 1981 | $18 |

UNITED ARTISTS
| ❏ UA-LA420-G | In Collaboration with the Gods | 1975 | $25 |

QUATRO, SUZI
ARISTA
| ❏ AL4035 [B] | Your Mama Won't Like Me | 1975 | $15 |

BELL
| ❏ 1313 [B] | Quatro | 1974 | $18 |
| ❏ 1302 | Suzi Quatro | 1974 | $18 |

DREAMLAND
| ❏ DL-1-5006 | Rock Hard | 1980 | $12 |

RSO
| ❏ RS-1-3044 | If You Knew Suzi... | 1979 | $12 |
| ❏ RS-1-3064 | Suzi...And Other Four Letter Words | 1980 | $12 |

QUATTLEBAUM, DOUG
BLUESVILLE
| ❏ BVLP-1065 [M] | Softee Man Blues | 1963 | $75 |
— Blue label, silver print
| ❏ BVLP-1065 [M] | Softee Man Blues | 1964 | $25 |
— Blue label, trident logo at right

QUAZAR
ARISTA
| ❏ AB4187 [B] | Quazar | 1978 | $15 |

QUEBEC, IKE
BLUE NOTE
| ❏ BLP-4098 [M] | Blue and Sentimental | 1962 | $125 |
— With "New York, USA" address on label
| ❏ BST-84098 [S] | Blue and Sentimental | 1962 | $25 |
— With "New York, USA" address on label
| ❏ BLP-4098 [M] | Blue and Sentimental | 1962 | $175 |
— With 61st St. address on label
| ❏ BST-84098 [S] | Blue and Sentimental | 1962 | $75 |
— With 61st St. address on label
| ❏ BST-84098 [S] | Blue and Sentimental | 1967 | $30 |
— With "A Division of Liberty Records" on label
| ❏ BST-84098 [S] | Blue and Sentimental | 1986 | $25 |
— The Finest in Jazz Since 1939" reissue
| ❏ BLP-4114 [M] | Bossa Nova Soul Samba | 1962 | $75 |
| ❏ BST-84114 [S] | Bossa Nova Soul Samba | 1962 | $40 |
— With "New York, USA" address on label
| ❏ BST-84114 [S] | Bossa Nova Soul Samba | 1967 | $35 |
— With "A Division of Liberty Records" on label
| ❏ BLP-4103 [M] | Easy Living | 1962 | $0 |
— Canceled
| ❏ BST-84103 [S] | Easy Living | 1987 | $30 |
— The Finest in Jazz Since 1939" issue; originally scheduled for 1962 release
| ❏ BLP-4093 [M] | Heavy Soul | 1962 | $75 |
— With "New York, USA" address on label
| ❏ BST-84093 [S] | Heavy Soul | 1961 | $25 |
— With "New York, USA" address on label
| ❏ BLP-4093 [M] | Heavy Soul | 1961 | $175 |
— With 61st St. address on label
| ❏ BST-84093 [S] | Heavy Soul | 1961 | $75 |
— With 61st St. address on label
| ❏ BST-84093 [S] | Heavy Soul | 1967 | $30 |
— With "A Division of Liberty Records" on label
| ❏ B1-32090 | Heavy Soul | 1995 | $35 |
— The Finest in Jazz Since 1939" reissue
| ❏ BLP-4105 [M] | It Might As Well Be Spring | 1962 | $75 |
| ❏ BST-84105 [S] | It Might As Well Be Spring | 1962 | $40 |
— With "New York, USA" address on label
| ❏ BST-84105 [S] | It Might As Well Be Spring | 1967 | $35 |
— With "A Division of Liberty Records" on label
| ❏ BST-84114 | Soul Samba | 199? | $30 |
— Classic Records reissue on audiophile vinyl
| ❏ LT-1052 | With a Song in My Heart | 1980 | $25 |

MOSAIC
| ❏ MR3-121 | The Complete Blue Note 45 Sessions of Ike Quebec | 199? | $75 |
| ❏ MR4-107 | The Complete Blue Note Forties Recordings of Ike Quebec and John Hardee | 199? | $150 |

QUEEN & PAUL RODGERS
Also see FREE; BAD COMPANY; THE FIRM.
HOLLYWOOD
| ❏ D261601 [B] | The Cosmos Rocks | 2008 | $30 |

QUEEN
Also see FREDDIE MERCURY.
CAPITOL
❏ SMAS-12476	A Kind of Magic	1986	$12
❏ C1-92357	The Miracle	1989	$18
❏ ST-12322	The Works	1984	$12

DCC COMPACT CLASSICS
| ❏ LPZ-2072 [B] | A Night at the Opera | 2000 | $175 |
— Audiophile vinyl

ELEKTRA
| ❏ 6E-101 [B] | A Day at the Races | 1977 | $12 |
— Butterfly, red, or red/black labels
| ❏ 7E-1053 | A Night at the Opera | 1975 | $12 |
— Butterfly, red, or red/black labels
| ❏ 60128 | Hot Space | 1982 | $12 |
| ❏ 6E-166 [B] | Jazz | 1978 | $18 |
— With poster of the nude bicycle race
| ❏ 6E-166 | Jazz | 1978 | $10 |
— Without poster of the nude bicycle race. Some copies had a sticker on the shrink wrap with an address at which the poster was available free.
| ❏ BB-702 | Live Killers | 1979 | $15 |
| ❏ 6E-112 [DJ] | News of the World | 1977 | $175 |
— White label promo with oversize cover and press kit
| ❏ 6E-112 | News of the World | 1977 | $12 |
| ❏ EKS-75064 [DJ] | Queen | 1973 | $50 |
— White label promo
| ❏ EKS-75064 | Queen | 1973 | $30 |
— With "Queen" gold-embossed on the cover
| ❏ EKS-75064 | Queen | 1973 | $12 |
— With "Queen" printed on the cover; butterfly, red, or red/black labels
| ❏ EQ-5064 [Q] | Queen | 1973 | $50 |
| ❏ EKS-75082 [DJ] | Queen II | 1974 | $50 |
— White label promo
| ❏ EKS-75082 | Queen II | 1974 | $12 |
— Butterfly, red, or red/black labels
| ❏ 5E-564 | Queen's Greatest Hits | 1981 | $15 |
| ❏ 7E-1026 [DJ] | Sheer Heart Attack | 1974 | $50 |
— White label promo
| ❏ 7E-1026 | Sheer Heart Attack | 1974 | $12 |
— Butterfly, red, or red/black labels
| ❏ 5E-513 | The Game | 1980 | $18 |
— With shiny, mirrorlike cover; all copies have custom white labels
| ❏ 5E-513 | The Game | 1980 | $12 |
— With dull gray cover; all copies have custom white labels

HOLLYWOOD
❏ D262101	A Day at the Races	2008	$25
❏ D436601	A Kind of Magic	2009	$25
❏ D262001	A Night at the Opera	2008	$25
❏ D436501	Flash Gordon	2009	$25
❏ D436701	Innuendo	2009	$25
❏ D002083101 [B]	Live at the Rainbow '74	2014	$300
❏ 62017	Made in Heaven	1996	$25
— White vinyl; imported from Europe; the only distinguishing mark to make this a U.S. version is the Hollywood bar code, which was stuck to the shrink wrap
| ❏ D436401 | News of the World | 2009 | $25 |
| ❏ D436301 | Queen | 2009 | $25 |

| ❏ ED-62005 [PD] | Queen at the BBC | 1995 | $150 |
— Promo-only picture disc (no U.S. stock vinyl)
| ❏ D261801 | Queen II | 2008 | $25 |
| ❏ D261901 [B] | Sheer Heart Attack | 2008 | $25 |

MOBILE FIDELITY
| ❏ 1-256 [B] | A Day at the Races | 1996 | $120 |
— Audiophile vinyl
| ❏ Jan-0067 [B] | A Night at the Opera | 1980 | $150 |
— Audiophile vinyl
| ❏ 1-211 | The Game | 1995 | $150 |
— Audiophile vinyl

VIRGIN
| ❏ 00602547202703 [B] | A Day at the Races | 2015 | $30 |
| ❏ 00602547202680 [B] | Sheer Heart Attack | 2015 | $40 |

QUEEN CITY RAGTIME ENSEMBLE
STOMP OFF
| ❏ SOS-1138 | Everybody's Rag | 1987 | $25 |

QUEEN LATIFAH
MOTOWN
| ❏ 530895-1 | Order in the Court | 1998 | $18 |
| ❏ 37463 08951 [DJ] | Order in the Court | 1998 | $18 |
— Promo-only eight-song sampler from LP

TOMMY BOY
| ❏ TB1022 | All Hail the Queen | 1989 | $18 |
| ❏ TB1035 | Nature of a Sista' | 1991 | $18 |

QUEEN PEN
INTERSCOPE
| ❏ INT2-90151 | My Melody | 1997 | $18 |

MOTOWN
| ❏ 013785-1 | Conversations with Queen | 2001 | $15 |

QUEEN'S NECTORINE MACHINE, THE
ABC
| ❏ S-666 | The Mystical Powers of Roving Tarot Gamble | 1969 | $40 |

QUEENS OF THE STONE AGE
Offshoot of KYUSS; also see EAGLES OF DEATH METAL.
IPECAC
| ❏ IPC-41 [B] | Songs for the Deaf | 2002 | $25 |

MAN'S RUIN
| ❏ MR151 | Queens of the Stone Age | 1998 | $120 |
— 2,500 copies on black vinyl; beware of counterfeits; counterfeits lack "MR 151" in the trail-off wax
| ❏ MR151 | Queens of the Stone Age | 1998 | $300 |
— Approximately 200 copies on green vinyl
| ❏ MR151 | Queens of the Stone Age | 1998 | $300 |
— Approximately 200 copies on blue vinyl
| ❏ MR151 | Queens of the Stone Age | 1998 | $300 |
— Approximately 300 copies on orange-yellow vinyl

QUEENSRYCHE
206 RECORDS
| ❏ R-101 [EP] | Queensryche | 1983 | $85 |

EMI
| ❏ E1-92806 [B] | Empire | 1990 | $18 |
| ❏ E1-30711 [B] | Promised Land | 1994 | $30 |

EMI AMERICA
| ❏ MLP-19006 [EP] | Queensryche | 1983 | $15 |
| ❏ SPRO-MLP-19006 [DJ] | Queensryche | 1983 | $40 |
— White label version in film can
| ❏ ST-17197 | Rage for Order | 1986 | $12 |
— Black circle on front cover
| ❏ ST-17197 | Rage for Order | 1986 | $18 |
— Blue circle on front cover
| ❏ ST-17134 [DJ] | The Warning | 1984 | $40 |

Number	Title	Yr	NM
—Promo-only "High Quality Vinyl" pressing			
❑ ST-17134	The Warning	1984	$12
EMI MANHATTAN			
❑ E1-48640	Operation: Mindcrime	1988	$15
❑ SPRO-04136/7 [PD]	Operation: Mindcrime	1988	$100
—Promo-only picture disc			
❑ SPRO-04194 [DJ]	Speak the Word	1988	$25
—Promo-only interview album			
RHINO			
❑ R1-73306	Operation: Mindcrime II	2006	$25

QUEERS, THE

Number	Title	Yr	NM
CLEARVIEW			
❑ 0(no cat #) [B]	Suck This	1995	$30
—Picture disc			
HOPELESS			
❑ HR643	Beyond the Valley of the Assfuckers	2000	$12
❑ HR636 [B]	Punk Rock Confidential	1998	$25
LOOKOUT!			
❑ LK 081	Beat Off	199?	$12
❑ LK140	Don't Back Down	1996	$12
❑ LK 090	Grow Up	1995	$12
—Reissue of rare Shakin' Street original			
❑ LK 066	Love Songs for the Retarded	199?	$12
❑ LK114 [B]	Move Back Home	1995	$18
SELFLESS			
❑ SFLS-28	Rocket to Russia	1994	$25
—Tour edition; 300 on pink vinyl			
SHAKIN' STREET			
❑ 010	Grow Up	1990	$250
—Only 100-150 copies exist of a planned pressing of 500 (others were destroyed at the plant)			

QUEST

Number	Title	Yr	NM
PATHFINDER			
❑ PTF-8839	Natural Selection	1988	$12

? (QUESTION MARK) AND THE MYSTERIANS

Number	Title	Yr	NM
CAMEO			
❑ C-2004 [M]	96 Tears	1966	$150

Number	Title	Yr	NM
❑ CS-2004 [P]	96 Tears	1966	$100
—96 Tears," "I Need Somebody," "Up Side" and "8-Teen" are rechanneled			
❑ C-2006 [M]	Action	1967	$300
❑ CS-2006 [P]	Action	1967	$150
—Don't Hold It Against Me," "Like a Rose" and "Girl (You Captivate Me)" are rechanneled			
COLLECTABLES			
❑ COL2004 [B]	Featuring 96 Tears	1997	$15
—Re-recorded tracks; orange vinyl			
NORTON			
❑ 262 [B]	Do You Feel It Baby?	1998	$18
—Live album recorded in 1997			

QUICK, THE

Number	Title	Yr	NM
A&M			
❑ SP-5140	Wah Wah	1986	$12
EPIC			
❑ FE37989	One Light in a Blackout	1982	$10

QUICKSAND

Number	Title	Yr	NM
POLYDOR			
❑ 517685-1DJ [DJ]	Slip	1993	$40
—U.S. vinyl is promo only; contains a bonus track, "How Soon Is Now," that is not on the CD of the same number			
REVELATION			
❑ 43	Manic Compression	1995	$12

QUICKSILVER MESSENGER SERVICE

Number	Title	Yr	NM
CAPITOL			
❑ SVBB-11165	Anthology	1973	$25
❑ SMAS-11002	Comin' Thru	1972	$18
❑ ST-120	Happy Trails	1969	$30
—Black label with colorband			
❑ ST-120 [B]	Happy Trails	1973	$15
—Orange label			
❑ SN-16090	Happy Trails	1980	$10
—Budget-line reissue			
❑ SMAS-498	Just for Love	1970	$30
—Lime green label			
❑ SMAS-498	Just for Love	1973	$15
—Orange label			
❑ SN-16093	Just for Love	1980	$10
—Budget-line reissue			
❑ ST-12496	Peace By Piece	1986	$12
❑ SW-819	Quicksilver	1971	$30
—Red label with stylized "C" at top			
❑ SW-819	Quicksilver	1973	$15
—Orange label			
❑ SN-16091	Quicksilver	1980	$10
—Budget-line reissue			
❑ ST2904	Quicksilver Messenger Service	1968	$40
—Black label with colorband; glossy black cover with red and silver foil-like printing			
❑ ST-2904	Quicksilver Messenger Service	1969	$25
—Lime green or red label			
❑ ST-2904 [B]	Quicksilver Messenger Service	1973	$15
—Orange label			
❑ SN-16089	Quicksilver Messenger Service	1980	$10
—Budget-line reissue			
❑ SKAO-391	Shady Grove	1969	$30
—Lime green label			
❑ SKAO-391	Shady Grove	1973	$15
—Orange label			
❑ SN-16094	Shady Grove	1980	$10
—Budget-line reissue			
❑ SM-391	Shady Grove	1976	$12
—Reissue on yellow label and new prefix			
❑ ST-11462	Solid Silver	1975	$18
❑ SM-11820	Solid Silver	1978	$12
—Reissue of 11462			
❑ SMAS-630	What About Me	1970	$30
—Lime green label			
❑ SMAS-630	What About Me	1973	$15
—Orange label			
❑ SN-16092	What About Me	1980	$10
—Budget-line reissue			
CLEOPATRA			
❑ CLP1559 [B]	Fillmore Auditorium, Nov. 5th, 1966	2014	$40
❑ CLP0432 [B]	Live At The Fillmore June 7,1968	2013	$35
❑ CLP0795 [B]	Live At The Winterland Ballroom, December 1, 1973	2013	$35

QUIET RIOT

OZZY OSBOURNE guitarist Randy Rhoads was on this band's first two albums, issued only in Japan.

Number	Title	Yr	NM
PASHA			
❑ QZ39516 [B]	Condition Critical	1984	$10
❑ 8Z839203	Metal Health	1983	$25
—Picture disc in plastic sleeve with sticker			
❑ BFZ38443	Metal Health	1983	$10
—Original edition with full prefix			
❑ FZ38443 [B]	Metal Health	1983	$10
—Later edition with shorter prefix			
❑ PZ38443	Metal Health	198?	$10
—Later edition yet with new prefix and longer bar code on back			
❑ OZ40321	QR III	1986	$10
❑ OZ40981	Quiet Riot	1988	$10

QUIET SUN

Number	Title	Yr	NM
ANTILLES			
❑ AN-7008 [B]	Mainstream	1975	$30

QUIGLEY, JACK

Number	Title	Yr	NM
SAND			
❑ C-30 [M]	Class In Session	196?	$30
—Red vinyl; may or may not exist on black vinyl			
❑ CS-30 [S]	Class In Session	196?	$25
❑ C-38 [M]	D'Jever	196?	$25
❑ CS-38 [S]	D'Jever	196?	$30
❑ C-28 [M]	Jack Quigley in Hollywood	196?	$30
—Red vinyl; may or may not exist on black vinyl			
❑ CS-28 [S]	Jack Quigley in Hollywood	196?	$25
❑ C-32 [M]	Listen! Quigley	196?	$30
—Red vinyl; may or may not exist on black vinyl			
❑ CS-32 [S]	Listen! Quigley	196?	$25

QUILL, GENE

Number	Title	Yr	NM
ROOST			
❑ LP-2229 [M]	Three Bones and a Quill	1958	$50

QUILL

Number	Title	Yr	NM
COTILLION			
❑ SD9017 [B]	Quill	1970	$30

QUINICHETTE, PAUL, AND FRANK FOSTER

Number	Title	Yr	NM
DECCA			
❑ DL8058 [M]	Jazz Studio 1	1954	$175

QUINICHETTE, PAUL

Number	Title	Yr	NM
BIOGRAPH			
❑ BLP-12066	The Kid from Denver	199?	$75
DAWN			
❑ DLP-1109 [M]	The Kid from Denver	1956	$150
EMARCY			
❑ MG-36003 [M]	Moods	1955	$250
❑ MG-26035 [10]	Sequel	1954	$300
❑ MG-26022 [10]	The Vice 'Pres'	1954	$300

Number	Title	Yr	NM
❑ MG-36027 [M]	The Vice 'Pres'	1955	$120
FANTASY			
❑ OJC-076	On the Sunny Side	198?	$30
PRESTIGE			
❑ PRLP-7147 [M]	Basie Reunion	1958	$300
❑ P-24109	Basie Reunions	198?	$35
❑ PRLP-7127 [M]	For Basie	1957	$300
—Yellow label with W. 50th St. address			
❑ PRLP-7103 [M]	On the Sunny Side	1957	$350
—Yellow label with W. 50th St. address			
STATUS			
❑ ST-2036 [M]	For Basie	1966	$25
—Reissue of Swingville 2036			
SWINGVILLE			
❑ SVLP-2037 [M]	Basie Reunion	1962	$50
—Purple label			
❑ SVLP-2037 [M]	Basie Reunion	1965	$30
—Blue label, trident logo at right			
❑ SVLP-2036 [M]	For Basie	1965	$30
—Blue label, trident logo at right			
❑ SVLP-2036 [M]	For Basie	1962	$50
—Purple label			
TRIP			
❑ TLP-5542	The Vice 'Pres'	197?	$75
UNITED ARTISTS			
❑ UAL-4024 [M]	Like Basie	1959	$50
❑ UAS-5024 [S]	Like Basie	1959	$40
❑ UAL-4054 [M]	Like Who?	1959	$40
❑ UAS-5054 [S]	Like Who?	1959	$30
❑ UAL-4077 [M]	Paul Quinichette	1960	$40
❑ UAS-5077 [S]	Paul Quinichette	1960	$50

QUINICHETTE, PAUL/GENE ROLAND

Number	Title	Yr	NM
DAWN			
❑ DLP-1112 [M]	Jazzville	1957	$150

QUINN, ANTHONY

Number	Title	Yr	NM
CAPITOL			
❑ ST-116 [B]	In My Own Way... I Love You	1969	$30

QUINN, CARMEL

Number	Title	Yr	NM
COLUMBIA			
❑ CL629 [M]	Arthur Godfrey Presents Carmel Quinn	1955	$30

QUINTESSENCE

Number	Title	Yr	NM
ISLAND			
❑ SW-9305	Dive Deep	1971	$30
❑ SMAS-9301	Quintessence	1971	$30

Number	Title	Yr	NM

QUINTET, THE
DEBUT

Number	Title	Yr	NM
❏ DLP-2 [10]	Jazz at Massey Hall	1953	$400
❏ DEB-124 [M]	Jazz at Massey Hall	1956	$300
❏ DLP-4 [10]	Jazz at Massey Hall, Volume 3	1953	$400

FANTASY

❏ 6006 [M]	Jazz at Massey Hall	1962	$50
—Red vinyl			
❏ 6006 [R]	Jazz at Massey Hall	1962	$30
—Black vinyl			
❏ 86006 [M]	Jazz at Massey Hall	1962	$30
—Blue vinyl			
❏ 86006 [R]	Jazz at Massey Hall	1962	$25
—Black vinyl			
❏ OJC-044	Jazz at Massey Hall	198?	$15

UNITED ARTISTS

❏ UAS-5514	Future Tense	1971	$18
❏ UAS-5599	The Quintet	1972	$18

QUINTET OF THE HOT CLUB OF FRANCE, THE
CAPITOL

❏ T2045 [M]	Hot Club of France	1964	$75
❏ DT2045 [R]	Hot Club of France	1964	$40

DIAL

❏ LP-214 [10]	Django Reinhardt and the Hot Club Quintet	1951	$300
❏ LP-218 [10]	Django Reinhardt and the Quintet	1951	$300

LONDON

❏ LB-810 [10]	Hot Club Quintet	1954	$120
❏ LL1344 [M]	Swing from Paris	1956	$100

PRESTIGE

❏ PRST-7614 [R]	First Recordings	1969	$35

QUIRE
RCA VICTOR

❏ BGL1-1700	Quire	1976	$30

QUIST, JACK
GRUDGE

❏ 451	Where Does Love Go	1989	$18

QUIVER
WARNER BROS.

❏ BS2630	Gone in the Morning	1972	$18
❏ WS1939	Quiver	1971	$18

R

R.E.M.
A&M

❏ B1301501	Murmur	2009	$25
❏ B1302901	Reckoning	2009	$25

I.R.S.

❏ SP-70502 [EP]	Chronic Town	1982	$15
—Original pressings have a custom gargoyle label			
❏ SP-70502 [EP]	Chronic Town	1982	$10
—Later pressings have a standard I.R.S. label			
❏ SP-70054	Dead Letter Office	1987	$15
❏ R163503	Document	1987	$15
—BMG Direct Marketing edition			

❏ 42059 [B]	Document	1987	$12
❏ R100701	Eponymous	1988	$15
—BMG Direct Marketing edition			
❏ 6262	Eponymous	1988	$12
❏ 5592	Fables of the Reconstruction	1985	$15

Number	Title	Yr	NM
❏ R173669	Lifes Rich Pageant	1986	$14
—RCA Music Service edition			
❏ 5783	Lifes Rich Pageant	1986	$15
❏ SP-70014	Murmur	1983	$15
—Reissue?			
❏ SP-70604	Murmur	1983	$18
—Original number?			
❏ SP-70044	Reckoning	1984	$15

MOBILE FIDELITY

❏ 1-231	Murmur	1995	$50
—Audiophile vinyl			
❏ 1-261	Reckoning	1996	$100
—Audiophile vinyl			

RHINO

❏ R1541570 [B]	Unplugged 1991 & 2001 - The Complete Sessions	2014	$40

WARNER BROS.

❏ 418620	Accelerate	2008	$30
❏ R1-78422	Around the Sun	2004	$25
❏ 45055 [B]	Automatic for the People	1992	$18
❏ R100715	Green	1988	$15
—BMG Direct Marketing edition			
❏ 25795	Green	1988	$15
❏ W1-25795	Green	1988	$18
—Columbia House edition			
❏ 45740 [B]	Monster	1994	$25
❏ 46320 [B]	New Adventures in Hi-Fi	1996	$30
❏ R124762 [B]	Out of Time	1991	$30
—BMG Direct Marketing edition; one of the last BMG vinyl releases			
❏ 26496 [B]	Out of Time	1991	$25
❏ 303740	R.E.M. Live	2008	$40
❏ 47946	Reveal	2001	$25
❏ PRO-A-3377 [DJ]	Should We Talk About the Weather?	1988	$40
—Promo-only interviews and music			
❏ 47112	Up	1998	$18

R.P.S.
MARS

❏ 0(# unknown)	R.P.S.	197?	$100

RA, SUN
ROARATORIO

❏ ROAR40 [B]	The Intergalactic Thing	2016	$30

RABBITT, EDDIE
ELEKTRA

❏ CM-3	Eddie Rabbitt	1975	$18
❏ 6E-276	Horizon	1980	$12
❏ 6E-181	Loveline	1979	$12
❏ 7E-1105	Rabbitt	1977	$18
—Butterfly label			
❏ 7E-1105	Rabbitt	198?	$10
—Red label			
❏ 60160	Radio Romance	1982	$12
❏ 7E-1065	Rocky Mountain Music	1976	$18
—Butterfly label			
❏ 7E-1065	Rocky Mountain Music	198?	$10
—Red label			
❏ 5E-532	Step by Step	1981	$12
❏ 6E-235	The Best of Eddie Rabbitt	1979	$12
❏ 6E-127	Variations	1978	$15

RCA

❏ 6373-1-R	I Wanna Dance with You	1988	$10

RCA VICTOR

❏ AHL1-7041	Rabbitt Trax	1986	$10

WARNER BROS.

❏ 25278	#1's	1985	$12
❏ 23925	Greatest Hits, Volume II	1983	$12
❏ 6E-276	Horizon	1983	$10
—Reissue of Elektra LP			
❏ 6E-181	Loveline	1983	$10
—Reissue of Elektra LP			
❏ 60160	Radio Romance	1983	$10
—Reissue of Elektra LP			
❏ 7E-1065	Rocky Mountain Music	1983	$10
—Reissue of Elektra LP			
❏ 5E-532	Step by Step	1983	$10
—Reissue of Elektra LP			
❏ 6E-235	The Best of Eddie Rabbitt	1983	$10
—Reissue of Elektra LP			
❏ 25251	The Best Year of My Life	1984	$12
❏ 6E-127	Variations	1983	$10
—Reissue of Elektra LP			

RABBITT, JIMMY
CAPITOL

❏ ST-11491	Jimmy Rabbitt and Renegade	1976	$15

RABBLE, THE
ROULETTE

❏ SR-42010	The Rabble	1968	$175

Number	Title	Yr	NM

RACHABANE, BARNEY
JIVE

❏ 1253-1-J	Barney's Way	1989	$30

RACKET SQUAD, THE
JUBILEE

❏ JGS-8026	Corners of Your Mind	1969	$40
❏ JGS-8015	The Racket Squad	1968	$40

RACONTEURS, THE
ELEKTRA

❏ 60815 [DJ]	Blind Man's Zoo	1989	$18
—Promo-only audiophile pressing (promo labels)			
❏ 60738 [DJ]	In My Tribe	1987	$15
—Promo-only audiophile pressing			
❏ 5270 [DJ]	Interview	1987	$30
—Lenny Kaye interviews Natalie Merchant; promo only			

RADER, DON
DISCOVERY

❏ 796	Wallflower	1979	$30

PBR

❏ 10	Now	197?	$30

RADICE, MARK
PARAMOUNT

❏ PAS-6033	Mark Radice	1972	$40

ROADSHOW

❏ RS-LA788-G	Intense	1977	$18

UNITED ARTISTS

❏ UA-LA629-G	Ain't Nothin' But a Party	1976	$18

RADIO BIRDMAN
4 MEN WITH BEARDS

❏ 4M527LP [B]	Radios Appear		$25

SIRE

❏ SRK6050	Radio Appears	1978	$40

RADIO CITY MUSIC HALL ORCHESTRA
CONTINENTAL

❏ CR-1009	Merry Christmas America from the Radio City Music Hall	1972	$15
—Same contents as Continental CR-1004			
❏ CR-1004	Merry Christmas New York from the Radio City Music Hall	1972	$15

RCA VICTOR

❏ LOP-1010 [M]	Christmas Holidays at Radio City Music Hall	1958	$25
—With gatefold and 10-page bound-in booklet with fold-open poster of the Rockettes			
❏ LSO-1010 [S]	Christmas Holidays at Radio City Music Hall	1958	$40
—"Living Stereo" banner on cover			

RADIOHEAD
PARLOPHONE

❏ 7243 8 55229 1 8 [B]	OK Computer	2016	$25

XL

❏ XLLP790 [B]	A Moon Shaped Pool	2016	$25

RADKE, FRED, AND MIKE VAX
MUSIC IS MEDICINE

❏ 9052	The First Reunion	198?	$30

RAE, CHARLOTTE
VANGUARD

❏ VRS-9004 [M]	Songs I Taught My Mother	1956	$100

RAE, JOHN
SAVOY

❏ MG-12156 [M]	Opus De Jazz, Volume 2	1960	$40

RAEBURN, BOYD
AIRCHECK

❏ 20	Rhythms by Boyd Raeburn	197?	$25

CIRCLE

❏ 22	Boyd Raeburn and His Orchestra 1944-45	198?	$25
❏ CLP-113	More Boyd Raeburn and His Orchestra 1944-45	1987	$25

COLUMBIA

❏ CL889 [M]	Dance Spectacular	1956	$40
❏ CL957 [M]	Fraternity Rush	1957	$40
❏ CL1073 [M]	Teen Rock	1958	$50

MUSICRAFT

❏ 505	Experiments in Big Band Jazz 1945	198?	$25

SAVOY

❏ MG-12040 [M]	Boyd Meets Stravinsky	1955	$100

Number	Title	Yr	NM
❏ MG-15010 [10]	Innovations by Boyd Raeburn, Volume 1	1951	$175
❏ MG-15011 [10]	Innovations by Boyd Raeburn, Volume 2	1951	$175
❏ MG-15012 [10]	Innovations by Boyd Raeburn, Volume 3	1951	$175
❏ MG-12025 [M]	Man With the Horns	1955	$100

SAVOY JAZZ

❏ SJL-2250	Jewels Plus	1980	$75
❏ SJC-406	Man With the Horns	1985	$35

RAELETTS, THE

TANGERINE

❏ TRCS-1515	Yesterday, Today, Tomorrow	1972	$18

RAFF, RENEE

AUDIO FIDELITY

❏ AFLP-2142 [M]	Among the Stars	1965	$35
❏ AFSD-6142 [S]	Among the Stars	1965	$25

RAFFERTY, GERRY

ABC/BLUE THUMB

❏ 6031	Can I Have My Money Back?	1978	$15

BLUE THUMB

❏ BTS-58	Can I Have My Money Back?	1973	$25

LIBERTY

❏ LO-840	City to City	1981	$10
—Reissue of United Artists 840			
❏ LOO-958	Night and Day	1981	$10
—Reissue of United Artists 958			
❏ LT-51132	Sleepwalking	1982	$12
❏ LOO-1039	Snakes and Ladders	1981	$10
—Reissue of United Artists 1039			

MOBILE FIDELITY

❏ Jan-0058 [B]	City to City	1980	$100
—Audiophile vinyl			

PARLOPHONE

❏ 825646321933 [B]	City to City	2014	$30

POLYDOR

❏ 835449-1	North and South	1988	$12

UNITED ARTISTS

❏ UA-LA840-H	City to City	1978	$12
❏ UA-LA958-I	Night Owl	1979	$12
❏ LOO-1039	Snakes and Ladders	1980	$12

VISA

❏ 7006 [B]	Gerry Rafferty	1978	$15
—Reissue of Blue Thumb material			

RAFFI

MCA

❏ 10043	Raffi's Christmas Album	1990	$18
—Reissue of Shoreline LP			

SHORELINE

❏ SL-0226	Raffi's Christmas Album	1983	$12
❏ R154088	Raffi's Christmas Album	198?	$18
—Same as above, but BMG Direct Marketing edition			

RAGE AGAINST THE MACHINE
AUDIOSLAVE related.

EPIC

❏ E57523	Evil Empire	1996	$25
❏ E52959	Rage Against The Machine	1996	$25
—CD and cassette released in 1992			
❏ E69630	The Battle of Los Angeles	1999	$25

RAGTIME BANJO COMMISSION, THE

GHB

❏ GHB-154	The Ragtime Banjo Commission	1981	$25

RAHIM, EMANUEL K., AND THE KAHLIQA

COBBLESTONE

❏ 9014	Total Submission	1972	$30

RAHMLEE

HEADFIRST

❏ 9703	Rise of the Phoenix	198?	$30

RAI, VASANT

VANGUARD

❏ VSD-79414	Autumn Song	1978	$30
❏ VSD-79379	Spring Flowers	197?	$30

RAIDERS, THE (3)

LIBERTY

❏ LRP-3225 [M]	Twistin' the Country Classics	1962	$30
❏ LST-7225 [S]	Twistin' the Country Classics	1962	$30

Number	Title	Yr	NM

RAIN

PROJECT 3

❏ PR5072SD	New Rock Group	1972	$30

WHAZOO

❏ USR-3049	Live Christmas Night	1969	$175
—Issued with no cover			

RAINBOW
Also see DEEP PURPLE; ELF; DIO; RONNIE DIO; FANDANGO; YNGWIE MALMSTEEN; MSG.

CLEOPATRA

❏ CLO0047 [B]	Boston 1981	2016	$40
—red vinyl			

MERCURY

❏ 815305-1	Bent Out of Shape	1983	$12
❏ 827987-1	Finyl Vinyl	1986	$14
❏ SRM-1-4041	Straight Between the Eyes	1982	$12

OYSTER

❏ OY-2-1801	On Stage	1977	$18
❏ OY-1-1601	Rainbow Rising	1976	$15
❏ OY-6049	Ritchie Blackmore's Rainbow	1975	$18

POLYDOR

❏ PD-1-6316	Difficult to Cure	1981	$12
❏ 825383-1	Difficult to Cure	1985	$10
—Reissue			
❏ PD-1-6221	Down to Earth	1979	$12
❏ 823705-1	Down to Earth	1985	$10
—Reissue			
❏ PX-1-502 [EP]	Jealous Lover	1981	$10
❏ 881516-1 [EP]	Jealous Lover	1985	$10
—Reissue			
❏ PD-1-6143	Long Live Rock 'n' Roll	1978	$12
❏ 825090-1	Long Live Rock 'n' Roll	1985	$10
—Reissue			
❏ 823656-1	On Stage	1985	$15
—Reissue			
❏ 823655-1	Rainbow Rising	1985	$10
—Reissue			
❏ 825089-1	Ritchie Blackmore's Rainbow	1985	$9
—Reissue			

RAINBOW (2)

GNP CRESCENDO

❏ GNPS-2049	After the Storm	1969	$30

RAINBOW (3)

INNER CITY

❏ IC-6001	Crystal Green	197?	$35

RAINBOW PRESS, THE

MR. G

❏ 9004	Sunday Funnies	1969	$30
❏ 9003	There's a War On	1968	$30

RAINBOW PROMISE, THE

NEW WINE

❏ LPS-251-01	The Rainbow Promise	1970	$300

RAINCOATS, THE

ROUGH TRADE

❏ ROUGH US13 [B]	Odyshape	1981	$40

SOUNDS LIKE

❏ 12 [EP]	The Raincoats	1994	$25

RAINDROPS, THE (1)

JUBILEE

❏ JGM-5023 [M]	The Raindrops	1963	$175
❏ JGS-5023 [S]	The Raindrops	1963	$300

Number	Title	Yr	NM

RAINER, TOM

MUSIC IS MEDICINE

❏ 9042	Night Music	198?	$30

RAINES, LEON

ATLANTIC AMERICA

❏ 90237	Leon Raines	1984	$12

RAINEY, CHUCK

COBBLESTONE

❏ 9008	Chuck Rainey Coalition	1972	$25

RAINEY, MA

BIOGRAPH

❏ LP-12001	Blues the World Forgot	1968	$20
❏ LP-12011	Oh My Babe Blues	197?	$15
❏ LP-12032	Queen of the Blues	197?	$15

MILESTONE

❏ 2008	Blame It on the Blues	196?	$20
❏ 2017	Down in the Basement	197?	$15
❏ 2001	Immortal Ma Rainey	1967	$20
❏ 47042	Ma Rainey	197?	$20

RIVERSIDE

❏ RLP 12-137 [M]	Broken Hearted Blues	1956	$300
❏ RLP 12-108 [M]	Ma Rainey	1955	$300
❏ RLP-1003 [10]	Ma Rainey, Vol. 1	1953	$300
❏ RLP-1016 [10]	Ma Rainey, Vol. 2	1953	$300
❏ RLP-1045 [10]	Ma Rainey, Vol. 3	1954	$300

RAINFORD, TINA

EPIC

❏ KE35034	Silver Angel	1977	$15

RAINWATER, MARVIN

CROWN

❏ CLP-5307 [M]	Marvin Rainwater	196?	$15
❏ CST-307 [R]	Marvin Rainwater	196?	$15

GUEST STAR

❏ GS-1435 [M]	Country and Western Star	196?	$15

MGM

❏ E-4046 [M]	Gonna Find Me a Bluebird	1962	$100
❏ SE-4046 [R]	Gonna Find Me a Bluebird	1962	$50
❏ E-3721 [M]	Marvin Rainwater Sings with a Beat	1958	$120
❏ E-3534 [M]	Songs by Marvin Rainwater	1957	$175

SPIN-O-RAMA

❏ SPM-109 [M]	Golden Country Hits	196?	$15

RAINY DAZE, THE

UNI

❏ 3002 [M]	That Acapulco Gold	1967	$25
❏ 73002 [S]	That Acapulco Gold	1967	$30

RAITT, BONNIE

CAPITOL

❏ C1-96111	Luck of the Draw	1991	$18
❏ C1-91268	Nick of Time	1989	$15

DCC COMPACT CLASSICS

❏ LPZ-2031	Luck of the Draw	1997	$100
—Audiophile vinyl			
❏ LPZ-2025	Nick of Time	1996	$100
—Audiophile vinyl			

WARNER BROS.

❏ WS1953	Bonnie Raitt	1971	$18
—Green "WB" label			
❏ WS1953	Bonnie Raitt	1973	$15
—Burbank" palm trees label			
❏ WS1953	Bonnie Raitt	1979	$10
—White or tan label			
❏ BS2643	Give It Up	1972	$18
—Green "WB" label			
❏ BS2643	Give It Up	1973	$15
—Burbank" palm trees label			
❏ BS2643	Give It Up	1979	$10
—White or tan label			
❏ BSK3630	Green Light	1982	$15
❏ BS2864	Home Plate	1975	$15
—Burbank" palm trees label			
❏ BS2864	Home Plate	1979	$10
—White or tan label			
❏ 25486	Nine Lives	1986	$12
❏ BS2818	Streetlights	1974	$15
—Burbank" palm trees label			
❏ BS2818	Streetlights	1979	$10
—White or tan label			
❏ BS2990	Sweet Forgiveness	1977	$15
—Burbank" palm trees label			
❏ BS2990	Sweet Forgiveness	1979	$10
—White or tan label			
❏ BS2729	Takin' My Time	1973	$15
—Burbank" palm trees label			
❏ BS2729	Takin' My Time	1979	$10
—White or tan label			

Number	Title	Yr	NM
❏ HS3369	The Glow	1979	$15

RAITT, JOHN
CAPITOL

Number	Title	Yr	NM
❏ T583 [M]	Highlights of Broadway	1955	$30
❏ T714 [M]	Mediterranean Magic	1956	$30
❏ T1058 [M]	Under Open Skies	1958	$30
❏ ST1058 [S]	Under Open Skies	1958	$40

RAKES, PAL
ATLANTIC AMERICA

Number	Title	Yr	NM
❏ 90964	Midnight Rain	1988	$12

RAKIM
UNIVERSAL

Number	Title	Yr	NM
❏ U2-53113	The 18th Letter	1997	$18

— Generic black cover with large sticker

RALKE, DON
CROWN

Number	Title	Yr	NM
❏ CLP-5019 [M]	Bongo Madness	1957	$30

WARNER BROS.

Number	Title	Yr	NM
❏ W1321 [M]	Bourbon Street Beat	1959	$30
❏ WS1321 [S]	Bourbon Street Beat	1959	$30
❏ W1360 [M]	But You've Never Heard Gershwin with Bongos	1960	$25
❏ WS1360 [S]	But You've Never Heard Gershwin with Bongos	1960	$30
❏ W1398 [M]	The Savage and Sensuous Bongos	1960	$30
❏ WS1398 [S]	The Savage and Sensuous Bongos	1960	$30

RALSTON, BOB
RCA CAMDEN

Number	Title	Yr	NM
❏ CAL-994 [M]	Christmas Hymns and Carols	196?	$15
❏ CAS-994 [S]	Christmas Hymns and Carols	196?	$18

RAM, BUCK
MERCURY

Number	Title	Yr	NM
❏ MG-20392 [M]	The Magic Touch	1960	$30
❏ SR-60067 [S]	The Magic Touch	1960	$40

RAM
POLYDOR

Number	Title	Yr	NM
❏ 24-5013	Where (In Conclusion)	1972	$30

RAM JAM
EPIC

Number	Title	Yr	NM
❏ JE35287	Portrait of the Artist as a Young Man	1978	$14
❏ PE34885	Ram Jam	1977	$15

RAMATAM
ATLANTIC

Number	Title	Yr	NM
❏ SD7261	In April Came the Dawning of the Red Suns	1973	$18
❏ SD7236	Ramatam	1972	$18

RAMBEAU, EDDIE
DYNO VOICE

Number	Title	Yr	NM
❏ 9001 [M]	Concrete and Clay	1965	$25
❏ DS-9001 [S]	Concrete and Clay	1965	$30

RAMIREZ, RAM
MASTER JAZZ

Number	Title	Yr	NM
❏ 8122	Rampant Ram	1973	$30

RAMONE, DEE DEE
SIRE

Number	Title	Yr	NM
❏ 25884	Standing in the Spotlight	1988	$20

RAMONES, THE
Marky Ramone was in DUST; also see DEE DEE RAMONE.
RADIOACTIVE

Number	Title	Yr	NM
❏ 11273 [B]	Adios Amigos!	1995	$30
❏ 10615	Mondo Bizarro	1992	$40

SIRE

Number	Title	Yr	NM
❏ 25433	Animal Boy	1986	$25
❏ 25905	Brain Drain	1989	$25
❏ SRK6077	End of the Century	1980	$20
❏ 25641	Halfway to Sanity	1987	$20
❏ SRK3571	Pleasant Dreams	1981	$20
❏ PRO-A-996 [DJ]	Pleasant Dreams Radio Sampler	1980	$30
❏ SASD-7520	Ramones	1976	$100

— First issue, distributed by ABC

❏ SR6020 [B]	Ramones	1978	$75

— Reissue, distributed by Warner Bros.; originals have no bar code

❏ SA-7528 [B]	Ramones Leave Home	1977	$150

— First issue, distributed by ABC, with "Carbona Not Glue"

❏ SA-7528	Ramones Leave Home	1977	$30

— Second issue, distributed by ABC, with "Sheena Is a Punk

— Rocker" replacing "Carbona Not Glue

❏ SR6031	Ramones Leave Home	1978	$30

— Third issue, distributed by Warner Bros., tracks as on second issue; originals have no bar code

Number	Title	Yr	NM
❏ 25709	RamonesMania	1988	$25
❏ SRK6063	Road to Ruin	1979	$20
❏ PRO-A-756 [DJ]	Road to Ruin Radio Sampler	1978	$35
❏ SRK6042	Rocket to Russia	1978	$20
❏ PRO-A-605 [DJ]	Rock 'n' Roll High School Radio Sampler	1979	$30
❏ 23800	Subterranean Jungle	1983	$20
❏ 25187	Too Tough to Die	1984	$18

RAMPART STREET PARADERS, THE
COLUMBIA

Number	Title	Yr	NM
❏ CL785 [M]	Dixieland My Dixieland	1956	$75
❏ CL648 [M]	Rampart and Vine	1955	$50

— Maroon label, gold print

❏ CL648 [M]	Rampart and Vine	1956	$75

— Red and black label with six "eye" logos

❏ CL1061 [M]	Texas! U.S.A.	1957	$75

HARMONY

Number	Title	Yr	NM
❏ HL7214 [M]	Real Dixieland	196?	$35

RAMSAY, OBRAY
PRESTIGE

Number	Title	Yr	NM
❏ PRLP-13020 [M]	Folk Songs from the Three Laurels	1961	$30
❏ PRLP-13009 [M]	Obray Ramsay Sings Jimmie Rodgers Favorites	1960	$30

RIVERSIDE

Number	Title	Yr	NM
❏ RLP-12-649 [M]	Banjo Songs of the Blue Ridge and Great Smokies	196?	$30

RAND, CHARLES
PREMIER

Number	Title	Yr	NM
❏ XMS-10 [S]	Christmas Organ in the Ken Griffin Style	196?	$18

— Same as above, but in stereo

❏ XM-10 [M]	Christmas Organ in the Ken Griffin Style	196?	$15

RANDALL, TONY, AND JACK KLUGMAN
LONDON

Number	Title	Yr	NM
❏ XPS903	The Odd Couple Sings	1973	$50

RANDALL, TONY
IMPERIAL

Number	Title	Yr	NM
❏ LP-9090 [M]	Tony Randall	1958	$30

MERCURY

Number	Title	Yr	NM
❏ MG-21108 [M]	Vo, Vo, De Oh, Doe	1967	$25
❏ SR-61108 [S]	Vo, Vo, De Oh, Doe	1967	$30
❏ MG-21128 [M]	Warm and Wavery	1967	$25
❏ SR-61128 [S]	Warm and Wavery	1967	$30

RANDAZZO, TEDDY
ABC-PARAMOUNT

Number	Title	Yr	NM
❏ 352 [M]	Journey to Love	1961	$30
❏ S-352 [S]	Journey to Love	1961	$40
❏ 421 [M]	Teddy Randazzo Twists	1962	$30
❏ S-421 [S]	Teddy Randazzo Twists	1962	$40

COLPIX

Number	Title	Yr	NM
❏ CP-445 [M]	Big Wide World	1963	$30
❏ SCP-445 [S]	Big Wide World	1963	$40

VIK

Number	Title	Yr	NM
❏ LX-1121 [M]	I'm Confessin'	1958	$250

RANDI, DON
CAPITOL

Number	Title	Yr	NM
❏ ST-287	Love Theme from Romeo and Juliet	1969	$25

PALOMAR

Number	Title	Yr	NM
❏ 24002 [M]	Don Randi!	1965	$35
❏ 34002 [S]	Don Randi!	1965	$25

POPPY

Number	Title	Yr	NM
❏ PY-5701	Don Randi Trio at the Baked Potato	1972	$35

REPRISE

Number	Title	Yr	NM
❏ R-6229 [M]	Revolver Jazz	1966	$25
❏ RS-6229 [S]	Revolver Jazz	1966	$30

VERVE

Number	Title	Yr	NM
❏ V-8524 [M]	Last Night With the Don Randi Trio	1963	$30
❏ V6-8524 [S]	Last Night With the Don Randi Trio	1963	$35
❏ V-8469 [M]	Where Do We Go From Here?	1962	$30
❏ V6-8469 [S]	Where Do We Go From Here?	1962	$35

WORLD PACIFIC

Number	Title	Yr	NM
❏ WP-1297 [M]	Feelin' Like Blues	1960	$150
❏ ST-1297 [S]	Feelin' Like Blues	1960	$150

RANDOLPH, BOOTS
MONUMENT

Number	Title	Yr	NM
❏ MLP-8029 [M]	12 Monstrous Sax Hits	1965	$18
❏ SLP-18029 [S]	12 Monstrous Sax Hits	1965	$25
❏ SLP18127	Boots and Stockings	1969	$18
❏ 6610	Boots and Stockings	197?	$12

— Reissue of 18127

❏ MLP-8037 [M]	Boots Randolph Plays More Yakety Sax	1965	$18
❏ SLP-18037 [S]	Boots Randolph Plays More Yakety Sax	1965	$25
❏ 6602	Boots Randolph Plays More Yakety Sax	197?	$12

— Reissue of 18037

❏ KZ31908	Boots Randolph Plays the Great Hits of Today	1972	$15
❏ 6615	Boots Randolph Plays the Great Hits of Today	197?	$12

— Reissue of 31908

❏ MLP-8002 [M]	Boots Randolph's Yakety Sax	1963	$25
❏ SLP-18002 [S]	Boots Randolph's Yakety Sax	1963	$30
❏ 6600	Boots Randolph's Yakety Sax	197?	$12

— Reissue of 18002

❏ KZ33298	Boots Randolph's Yakety Sax	1974	$15
❏ MLP-8082 [M]	Boots Randolph with the Knightsbridge Strings & Voices	1967	$25
❏ SLP-18082 [S]	Boots Randolph with the Knightsbridge Strings & Voices	1967	$18
❏ 6606	Boots Randolph with the Knightsbridge Strings & Voices	197?	$12

— Reissue of 18082

❏ SLP-18147	Boots with Brass	1970	$18
❏ 6613	Boots with Brass	197?	$12

— Reissue of 18147

❏ MLP-8066 [M]	Boots with Strings	1966	$18
❏ SLP-18066 [S]	Boots with Strings	1966	$25
❏ 6604	Boots with Strings	197?	$12

— Reissue of 18066

❏ BZ33852	Boots with Strings	1975	$18
❏ 6618	Cool Boots	197?	$12

— Reissue of 33803

❏ KZ33803	Cool Boots	1975	$15
❏ 6617	Country Boots	197?	$12

— Reissue of 32912

❏ KZ32912	Country Boots	1974	$15
❏ JW38396	Dedication	1983	$12
❏ 7602	Greatest Hits	1977	$12
❏ PW38388	Greatest Hits	1983	$12
❏ MLP-8015 [M]	Hip Boots	1964	$18
❏ SLP-18015 [S]	Hip Boots	1964	$25
❏ 6601	Hip Boots	197?	$12

— Reissue of 18015

❏ SLP-18144	Hit Boots 1970	1970	$18
❏ 6612	Hit Boots 1970	197?	$12

— Reissue of 18144

❏ Z30678	Homer Louis Randolph, III	1971	$15
❏ 6614	Homer Louis Randolph, III	197?	$12

— Reissue of 30678

❏ DS632	King of Yakety	197?	$18

— Manufactured by CBS Direct Marketing Services

❏ 8604	Party Boots	197?	$15

— Reissue of 34082

❏ Z234082	Party Boots	1976	$18
❏ 7627	Put a Little Sax	1978	$12
❏ 7611	Sax Appeal	1977	$12
❏ MC6605	Sax-Sational	1976	$12

— Reissue of 18079

❏ MLP-8079 [M]	Sax-Sational	1967	$25
❏ SLP-18079 [S]	Sax-Sational	1967	$18
❏ KZ32292	Sentimental Journey	1973	$15
❏ 6616	Sentimental Journey	197?	$12

— Reissue of 32292

❏ SLP-18092	Sunday Sax	1968	$25
❏ 6607	Sunday Sax	197?	$12

— Reissue of 18092

❏ MLP-8042 [M]	The Fantastic Boots Randolph	1966	$18
❏ SLP-18042 [S]	The Fantastic Boots Randolph	1966	$25
❏ 6603	The Fantastic Boots Randolph	197?	$12

— Reissue of 18042

❏ SLP-18099	The Sound of Boots	1968	$25
❏ 6608	The Sound of Boots	197?	$12

— Reissue of 18099

❏ ZG30963	The World of Boots Randolph	1971	$18
❏ SLP-18111	...With Love/The Seductive Sax of Boots Randolph	1969	$18
❏ 6609	...With Love/The Seductive Sax of Boots Randolph	197?	$12

— Reissue of 18111

❏ SLP-18128	Yakety Revisited	1969	$18
❏ 6611	Yakety Revisited	197?	$12

— Reissue of 18128

RCA CAMDEN

Number	Title	Yr	NM
❏ CAL-865 [M]	Sweet Talk	1965	$18
❏ CAS-865 [R]	Sweet Talk	1965	$15
❏ ACL-9003	Yakety Sax	1972	$15
❏ CAL-825 [M]	Yakin' Sax Man	1964	$18

Number	Title	Yr	NM

❑ CAS-825 [S] | Yakin' Sax Man | 1964 | $18

RCA VICTOR
❑ LPM-2165 [M] | Yakety Sax | 1960 | $40
❑ LSP-2165 [S] | Yakety Sax | 1960 | $50

RANDY AND THE RAINBOWS
AMBIENT SOUND
❑ FZ37715 | C'mon, Let's Go | 1982 | $15
❑ ASR-601 | Remember | 1985 | $15

RANELIN, PHIL
TRIBE
❑ PRSD-2226 | Message from the Tribe | 197? | $150
❑ TRCD4006 | The Time Is Now! | 1974 | $100

RANEY, DOUG
STEEPLECHASE
❑ SCS-1191 | Black and White | 198? | $30
❑ SCS-1105 | Cuttin' Loose | 198? | $30
❑ SCS-1212 | Guitar, Guitar, Guitar | 198? | $30
❑ SCS-1166 | I'll Close My Eyes | 1982 | $30
❑ SCS-1082 | Introducing Doug Raney | 1978 | $30
❑ SCS-1200 | Lazy Bird | 198? | $30
❑ SCS-1144 | Listen | 1981 | $30

RANEY, JIMMY
ABC-PARAMOUNT
❑ ABC-129 [M] | Jimmy Raney Featuring Bob Brookmeyer | 1956 | $250
❑ ABC-167 [M] | Jimmy Raney in Three Attitudes | 1957 | $175

BIOGRAPH
❑ LP-12060 | Too Marvelous for Words | 198? | $30

DAWN
❑ DLP-1120 [M] | Jimmy Raney Visits Paris | 1958 | $150

FANTASY
❑ OJC-1706 | Jimmy Raney/A | 1985 | $30

MUSE
❑ MR-5004 | Strings and Swings | 1973 | $40

NEW JAZZ
❑ NJLP-1103 [10] | Jimmy Raney Ensemble Introducing Phil Woods | 1953 | $500
❑ NJLP-1101 [10] | Jimmy Raney Quartet Featuring Hall Overton | 1953 | $500

PAUSA
❑ 7021 | Momentum | 197? | $30

PRESTIGE
❑ PRLP-7089 [M] | Jimmy Raney/A | 1957 | $300
— Yellow label with W. 50th St. address
❑ PRLP-203 [10] | Jimmy Raney Ensemble | 1955 | $400
❑ PRLP-179 [10] | Jimmy Raney in Sweden | 1954 | $400
❑ PRLP-156 [10] | Jimmy Raney Plays | 1953 | $400
❑ PRLP-201 [10] | Jimmy Raney Quartet | 1955 | $400
❑ PRLP-199 [10] | Jimmy Raney Quintet | 1954 | $400

XANADU
❑ 116 | Influence | 197? | $75
❑ 132 | Live in Tokyo | 197? | $75
❑ 140 | Solo | 1977 | $75

RANEY, JIMMY AND DOUG
STEEPLECHASE
❑ SCS-1134 | Duets | 1980 | $35
❑ SCS-1184 | Nardis | 198? | $35
❑ SCS-1118 | Stolen Moments | 198? | $35

RANEY, JIMMY/GEORGE WALLINGTON
EMARCY
❑ MG-36121 [M] | Swingin' in Sweden | 1958 | $250

RANEY, SUE, AND BOB FLORENCE
DISCOVERY
❑ DS-931 | Flight of Fancy: A Journey of Alan and Marilyn Bergman | 1987 | $25
❑ DS-939 | Quietly There | 1988 | $25

RANEY, SUE
CAPITOL
❑ T2032 [M] | All By Myself | 1964 | $85
❑ ST2032 [S] | All By Myself | 1964 | $50
❑ T1335 [M] | Songs for a Raney Day | 1960 | $50
❑ ST1335 [S] | Songs for a Raney Day | 1960 | $75

DISCOVERY
❑ DS-913 | Ridin' High | 1984 | $25
❑ DS-875 | Sue Raney Sings the Music of Johnny Mandel | 1982 | $25

IMPERIAL
❑ LP-9323 [M] | Alive and In Love | 1966 | $175
❑ LP-12323 [S] | Alive and In Love | 1966 | $175
❑ LP-9355 [M] | New and Now | 1967 | $175
❑ LP-12355 [S] | New and Now | 1967 | $175
❑ LP-9376 [M] | With a Little Help from My Friends | 1968 | $200
❑ LP-12376 [S] | With a Little Help from My Friends | 1968 | $175

RANEY, WAYNE
KING
❑ 588 [M] | Songs from the Hills | 1958 | $150

NASHVILLE
❑ NLP-2002 | Radio Gospel and Sacred Favorites | 196? | $18

STARDAY
❑ SLP-279 [M] | Don't Try to Be What You Ain't | 1964 | $40
❑ SLP-124 [M] | Wayne Raney and the Raney Family | 1960 | $40

RANGELL, NELSON
GRP
❑ GR-9593 | Playing for Keeps | 1989 | $30

RANGER, ANDY
DOT
❑ DLP-3028 [M] | The Song That Never Ends | 1956 | $75

RANK AND FILE
RHINO
❑ RNLP70830 | Rank and File | 1987 | $12

SLASH
❑ 25087 | Long Gone Dead | 1984 | $15
❑ 23833 | Sundown | 1983 | $12
❑ SR114 | Sundown | 1982 | $15

RANKIN, KENNY
ATLANTIC
❑ SD19271 | After the Roses | 1980 | $12

LITTLE DAVID
❑ LD1009 | Inside | 1975 | $12
❑ LD1003 | Like a Seed | 1972 | $12
❑ SD3000 | Silver Morning | 1974 | $12
❑ 90131 | Silver Morning | 1984 | $10
— Reissue of 3000
❑ LD1013 | The Kenny Rankin Album | 1977 | $12

MERCURY
❑ SR-61240 | Family | 1969 | $15
❑ MG-21141 [M] | Mind Dusters | 1967 | $18
❑ SR-61141 [S] | Mind Dusters | 1967 | $15

RAPEMAN
TOUCH & GO
❑ 19 [B] | Budd | 1988 | $30
❑ 36 [B] | Two Nuns and a Pack Mule | 1989 | $30

RAPPIN' DUKE
JWP
❑ 6969 | Que Pasa? | 1985 | $12

RARE BIRD
ABC
❑ X-715 | As Your Mind Flies | 1972 | $18

POLYDOR
❑ PD6506 | Born Again | 1974 | $18
❑ PD5530 | Epic Forest | 1973 | $18
❑ PD6502 | Somebody's Watching | 1974 | $18

PROBE
❑ 4514 | Rare Bird | 1970 | $30

RARE EARTH
MOTOWN
❑ M5-202V1 | Ecology | 1981 | $10
❑ 5229ML | Get Ready | 1982 | $10
❑ M5-116V1 | Motown Superstar Series, Vol. 16 | 1981 | $12

PRODIGAL
❑ P7-10025 | Band Together | 1978 | $12
❑ P7-10027 | Grand Slam | 1979 | $12
❑ P6-10019 | Rare Earth | 1977 | $12

RARE EARTH
❑ R6-548 | Back to Earth | 1975 | $15
❑ RS514 | Ecology | 1970 | $18
❑ RS510 | Generation | 1970 | $500
— At least one copy of this album has been confirmed to exist
❑ RS507 | Get Ready | 1969 | $30
— Original cover has a rounded top
❑ RS507 | Get Ready | 1970 | $15
— Regular square cover
❑ R6-546 | Ma | 1973 | $15
❑ R7-550 | Midnight Lady | 1976 | $15
❑ RS520 | One World | 1971 | $18
❑ R534 | Rare Earth in Concert | 1971 | $18
❑ R543 | Willie Remembers | 1972 | $15

VERVE
❑ V6-5066 | Dreams/Answers | 1968 | $50

RASCALS, THE
ATLANTIC
❑ 8134 [M] | Collections | 1967 | $30
❑ SD8134 [S] | Collections | 1967 | $30
— Green and blue label

Number	Title	Yr	NM

❑ SD8134 [S] | Collections | 1969 | $15
— Red and green label
❑ SD 2-901 [B] | Freedom Suite | 1969 | $40
❑ ST-137 [DJ] | Freedom Suite Sampler | 1969 | $50
❑ 8148 [M] | Groovin' | 1967 | $30
❑ SD8148 [S] | Groovin' | 1967 | $30
— Green and blue label
❑ SD8148 [S] | Groovin' | 1969 | $15
— Red and green label
❑ 8169 [M] | Once Upon a Dream | 1968 | $80
❑ SD8169 [S] | Once Upon a Dream | 1968 | $30
— Green and blue label
❑ SD8169 [S] | Once Upon a Dream | 1969 | $15
— Red and green label
❑ 8276 [M] | Search and Nearness | 1970 | $50
— Mono is promo only; cover has "dj copy monaural" sticker on front
❑ SD8276 [S] | Search and Nearness | 1970 | $18
❑ 8246 [M] | See | 1969 | $50
— Mono is promo only; cover has "dj copy monaural" sticker on front
❑ SD8246 [S] | See | 1969 | $18
❑ 8123 [M] | The Young Rascals | 1966 | $75
❑ SD8123 [S] | The Young Rascals | 1966 | $40
— Green and blue label
❑ SD8123 [S] | The Young Rascals | 1966 | $50
— Purple and green label
❑ SD8123 [S] | The Young Rascals | 1969 | $15
— Red and green label
❑ 8190 [M] | Time Peace/The Rascals' Greatest Hits | 1968 | $50
— Mono is promo only
❑ SD8190 [S] | Time Peace/The Rascals' Greatest Hits | 1968 | $30
— Green and blue label
❑ SD8190 [S] | Time Peace/The Rascals' Greatest Hits | 1968 | $18
— Purple and gold label
❑ SD8190 [S] | Time Peace/The Rascals' Greatest Hits | 1969 | $15
— Red and green label

COLUMBIA
❑ G30462 | Peaceful World | 1971 | $18
❑ KC31103 | The Island of Real | 1972 | $15

PAIR
❑ PDL2-1106 | Rock and Roll Treasures | 1986 | $18

RHINO
❑ RNLP70238 | Collections | 1988 | $12
❑ R1-70241 | Freedom Suite | 1988 | $12
❑ RNLP70239 | Groovin' | 1988 | $12
❑ R1-70240 | Once Upon a Dream | 1988 | $12
❑ R1-70242 | Searching for Ecstasy: The Rest of the Rascals 1969-1972 | 1988 | $12
❑ RNLP70237 | The Young Rascals | 1988 | $12

SUNDAZED
❑ LP5117 | Collections | 2002 | $15
❑ LP5118 | Groovin' | 2002 | $15
❑ LP5119 | Once Upon a Dream | 2002 | $15
❑ LP5116 | The Young Rascals | 2002 | $15

WARNER SPECIAL PRODUCTS
❑ SP-2502 | 24 Greatest Hits | 1971 | $25

WES FARRELL
❑ PFT-1002 [DJ] | Songs from the Rascals | 197? | $30
— Promo-only publisher's demo

RASPBERRIES
Also see ERIC CARMEN; THE CHOIR.
CAPITOL
❑ ST-11123 | Fresh | 1972 | $25
❑ SK-11036 [B] | Raspberries | 1972 | $75
— Originals have red labels and a "scratch 'n' sniff" cover, the smell of which fades over time
❑ ST-11036 | Raspberries | 1973 | $25
— Orange label, "Capitol" at bottom
❑ ST-11524 | Raspberries' Best Featuring Eric Carmen | 1976 | $18
❑ SN-16095 | Raspberries' Best Featuring Eric Carmen | 1979 | $12
❑ SMAS-11220 | Side 3 | 1973 | $25
— With cover cut in the shape of a basket of raspberries
❑ ST-11329 | Starting Over | 1974 | $25

MOBILE FIDELITY
❑ MOFI1-032 [B] | Raspberries' Best - Featuring Eric Carmen | 2013 | $40

RATCHELL
DECCA
❑ DL75330 | Ratchell | 1972 | $18
❑ DL75365 | Ratchell 2 | 1972 | $18

RATHBONE, BASIL
CAEDMON
❑ TC1028 [M] | Basil Rathbone Reads Edgar Allan Poe | 195? | $30
❑ TC1115 [M] | Basil Rathbone Reads Edgar Allan Poe, Vol. 2 | 195? | $30

Number	Title	Yr	NM
❏ TC1195 [M]	Basil Rathbone Reads Edgar Allan Poe, Vol. 3	196?	$30
❏ TC1120 [M]	Stories of Hawthorne	195?	$30
❏ TC1197 [M]	Stories of Hawthorne, Vol. 2	196?	$30
❏ TC1172 [M]	Stories of Sherlock Holmes, Vol. 1	1963	$30
❏ TC1208 [M]	Stories of Sherlock Holmes, Vol. 2	1966	$30
❏ TC1220 [M]	Stories of Sherlock Holmes, Vol. 3	1967	$30
❏ TC1240 [M]	Stories of Sherlock Holmes, Vol. 4	1967	$30
❏ TC1044 [M]	The Happy Prince and Other Oscar Wilde Fairy Tales	195?	$30

COLUMBIA MASTERWORKS

Number	Title	Yr	NM
❏ ML4081 [10]	A Christmas Carol	1950	$50
❏ ML4038 [10]	Peter and the Wolf; Treasure Island	1949	$50

CO-STAR

Number	Title	Yr	NM
❏ C-107 [M]	The Brothers Karamazov	196?	$25
❏ CS-107 [S]	The Brothers Karamazov	196?	$30

DECCA

Number	Title	Yr	NM
❏ DL9109 [M]	Selections from The Jungle Book	1962	$30

RATIONALS, THE

CREWE

Number	Title	Yr	NM
❏ CR-1334	The Rationals	1969	$40

RATTLES, THE

MERCURY

Number	Title	Yr	NM
❏ MG21127 [M]	The Rattles' Greatest Hits	1967	$100
❏ SR61127 [R]	The Rattles' Greatest Hits	1967	$50

RATTLESNAKE ANNIE

COLUMBIA

Number	Title	Yr	NM
❏ B6C40678	Rattlesnake Annie	1987	$12

RATZER, KARL

CMP

Number	Title	Yr	NM
❏ CMP-13-ST	Dancing on a String	198?	$25

VANGUARD

Number	Title	Yr	NM
❏ VSD-79407	In Search of the Ghost	1978	$30
❏ VSD-79423	Street Talk	1979	$30

RAULSTON, FRED

INNER CITY

Number	Title	Yr	NM
❏ IC-1054	Open Stream	197?	$30
❏ IC-1085	Uncharted Waters	198?	$30

SEA BREEZE

Number	Title	Yr	NM
❏ SBD-104	Fred's Rescue	1987	$25

RAVA, ENRICO

BLACK SAINT

Number	Title	Yr	NM
❏ BSR-0011	Il Giro Del Giorno	198?	$30

ECM

Number	Title	Yr	NM
❏ 1122	Enrico Rava Quartet	1978	$30
❏ 1224	Opening Night	1981	$25
❏ 1063	Pilgrim	197?	$30
❏ 1078	Plot	1976	$30

SOUL NOTE

Number	Title	Yr	NM
❏ SN-1064	Andanada	198?	$30
❏ SN-1114	String Band	1985	$30

RAVAZZA, CARL

HINDSIGHT

Number	Title	Yr	NM
❏ HSR-117	Carl Ravazza and His Orchestra 1940-44	198?	$25

RAVEN, EDDY

ABC DOT

Number	Title	Yr	NM
❏ DOSD-2031	This Is Eddy Raven	1975	$18

DIMENSION

Number	Title	Yr	NM
❏ DLP-5001	Eyes	1980	$18

ELEKTRA

Number	Title	Yr	NM
❏ 5E-545	Desperate Dreams	1981	$15

LA LOUISIANNE

Number	Title	Yr	NM
❏ 127	That Cajun Country Sound	197?	$25

MCA

Number	Title	Yr	NM
❏ 910	Thank God for Kids	198?	$10

RCA

Number	Title	Yr	NM
❏ 5728-1-R	Right Hand Man	1987	$10
❏ 6815-1-R	The Best of Eddy Raven	1988	$10

RCA VICTOR

Number	Title	Yr	NM
❏ AHL1-5040	I Could Use Another You	1984	$10
❏ AHL1-5456	Love and Other Hard Times	1985	$10

UNIVERSAL

Number	Title	Yr	NM
❏ UVL-76003	Temporary Sanity	1989	$12

WARNER BROS.

Number	Title	Yr	NM
❏ 5E-545	Desperate Dreams	1983	$10

— *Reissue of Elektra 5E-545*

RAVEN

COLUMBIA

Number	Title	Yr	NM
❏ CS9903	Raven	1969	$25

DISCOVERY

Number	Title	Yr	NM
❏ 36133	Live at the Inferno	1967	$100

RAVENS, THE

HARLEM HIT PARADE

Number	Title	Yr	NM
❏ 1007	The Ravens	1975	$12

REGENT

Number	Title	Yr	NM
❏ MG-6062 [M]	Write Me a Letter	1957	$300

— *Green label*

Number	Title	Yr	NM
❏ MG-6062 [M]	Write Me a Letter	195?	$175

— *Red label*

SAVOY JAZZ

Number	Title	Yr	NM
❏ SJL-2227	The Greatest Group of Them All	1978	$15

RAVENSCROFT, THURL

DOT

Number	Title	Yr	NM
❏ DLP-3430 [M]	Great Hits	1962	$30
❏ DLP-25430 [S]	Great Hits	1962	$40

RAW

CORAL

Number	Title	Yr	NM
❏ CRL757515 [B]	Raw Holly	1971	$40

RAW SPITT

UNITED ARTISTS

Number	Title	Yr	NM
❏ UAS-6795	Maybe You Ain't Black	1971	$30

RAWLINS, STEVE

SEA BREEZE

Number	Title	Yr	NM
❏ SB-3003	Step Right Up	1985	$25

RAWLS, LOU

CAPITOL CREATIVE PRODUCTS

Number	Title	Yr	NM
❏ SU-479	Another Saturday Night/Chain Gang/Cool Train//Take Me for What I Am/Win Your Love/What Makes the Ending So Sad	1970	$15

— *Stereo jukebox issue; small hole, plays at 33 1/3 rpm*

Number	Title	Yr	NM
❏ SU-479 [PS]	Bring It on Home	1970	$15

ALLEGIANCE

Number	Title	Yr	NM
❏ AV-5016	Trying As Hard As I Can	198?	$12

BELL

Number	Title	Yr	NM
❏ 1318	She's Gone	1974	$15

BLUE NOTE

Number	Title	Yr	NM
❏ B1-91937	At Last	1989	$15
❏ B1-93841	It's Supposed to Be Fun	1990	$18
❏ B1-91441	Stormy Monday	1990	$15

— *Reissue of Capitol 1714*

CAPITOL

Number	Title	Yr	NM
❏ T1824 [M]	Black and Blue	1963	$25
❏ ST1824 [S]	Black and Blue	1963	$30
❏ ST-479	Bring It on Home	1970	$18
❏ SWBB-261	Close-Up	1969	$25

— *Reissue of 1824 and 2042 in one package*

Number	Title	Yr	NM
❏ STBB-720	Down Here on the Ground/I'd Rather Drink Muddy Water	1971	$25
❏ T2864 [M]	Feelin' Good	1968	$30
❏ ST2864 [S]	Feelin' Good	1968	$18
❏ T2401 [M]	Lou Rawls and Strings	1965	$25
❏ ST2401 [S]	Lou Rawls and Strings	1965	$30
❏ T2632 [M]	Lou Rawls Carryin' On!	1966	$18
❏ ST2632 [S]	Lou Rawls Carryin' On!	1966	$25
❏ T2459 [M]	Lou Rawls Live!	1966	$18
❏ ST2459 [S]	Lou Rawls Live!	1966	$25
❏ SM-2459	Lou Rawls Live!	197?	$12

— *Reissue with new prefix*

Number	Title	Yr	NM
❏ SN-16097	Lou Rawls Live!	1980	$10

— *Budget-line reissue*

Number	Title	Yr	NM
❏ T2566 [M]	Lou Rawls Soulin'	1966	$18
❏ ST2566 [S]	Lou Rawls Soulin'	1966	$25
❏ SM-2566	Lou Rawls Soulin'	197?	$12

— *Reissue with new prefix*

Number	Title	Yr	NM
❏ ST2790 [S]	Merry Christmas, Ho, Ho, Ho	1967	$15
❏ T2790 [M]	Merry Christmas, Ho, Ho, Ho	1967	$18
❏ T2273 [M]	Nobody But Lou	1965	$25
❏ ST2273 [S]	Nobody But Lou	1965	$30
❏ T1714 [M]	Stormy Monday	1962	$25
❏ ST1714 [S]	Stormy Monday	1962	$30
❏ SM-1714	Stormy Monday	197?	$12

— *Reissue with new prefix*

Number	Title	Yr	NM
❏ T2756 [M]	That's Lou	1967	$25
❏ ST2756 [S]	That's Lou	1967	$18
❏ SKBB-11585	The Best from Lou Rawls	1976	$15
❏ SKAO2948	The Best of Lou Rawls	1968	$18
❏ SM-2948	The Best of Lou Rawls	197?	$12

— *Reissue with new prefix*

Number	Title	Yr	NM
❏ SN-16096	The Best of Lou Rawls	1980	$10

— *Budget-line reissue*

Number	Title	Yr	NM
❏ ST-122	The Way It Was	1969	$18
❏ ST-215	The Way It Was -- The Way It Is	1969	$18
❏ ST 8-0215	The Way It Was -- The Way It Is	1969	$25

— *Capitol Record Club edition*

Number	Title	Yr	NM
❏ T2042 [M]	Tobacco Road	1964	$25
❏ ST2042 [S]	Tobacco Road	1964	$30
❏ T2713 [M]	Too Much!	1967	$25

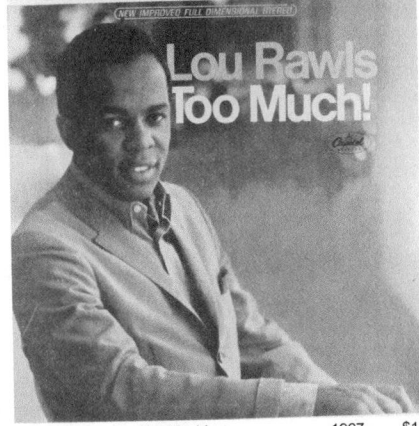

Number	Title	Yr	NM
❏ ST2713 [S]	Too Much!	1967	$18
❏ ST2927	You're Good for Me	1968	$18
❏ ST-325	Your Good Thing	1969	$18
❏ ST-427	You've Made Me So Very Happy	1970	$18

EPIC

Number	Title	Yr	NM
❏ FE39403	Close Company	1984	$12
❏ FE40210	Love All Your Blues Away	1986	$12
❏ FE37448	Now Is the Time	1982	$12
❏ FE38553	When the Night Comes	1983	$12

MGM

Number	Title	Yr	NM
❏ SE-4861	A Man of Value	1973	$15
❏ SE-4965	Live at the Century Plaza	1974	$15
❏ SE-4771	Natural Man	1971	$15
❏ SE-4809	Silk & Soul	1972	$15

PHILADELPHIA INT'L.

Number	Title	Yr	NM
❏ PZ33957	All Things in Time	1976	$12

— *No bar code on cover*

Number	Title	Yr	NM
❏ PZ33957	All Things in Time	198?	$10

— *With bar code on cover*

Number	Title	Yr	NM
❏ FZ39285	Classics	1984	$12
❏ JZ36006	Let Me Be Good to You	1979	$12
❏ PZ36006	Let Me Be Good to You	198?	$10

— *Budget-line reissue*

Number	Title	Yr	NM
❏ PZ235517	Lou Rawls Live	1978	$15
❏ JZ36774	Shades of Blue	1980	$12
❏ JZ36304	Sit Down and Talk to Me	1979	$12
❏ PZ36304	Sit Down and Talk to Me	198?	$10

— *Budget-line reissue*

Number	Title	Yr	NM
❏ PZ34488	Unmistakably Lou	1977	$12
❏ PZ34488	Unmistakably Lou	1986	$10

— *Budget-line reissue*

Number	Title	Yr	NM
❏ JZ35036	When You Hear Lou, You've Heard It All	1977	$12

PICKWICK

Number	Title	Yr	NM
❏ SPC-3156	Come On In, Mr. Blues	1971	$12
❏ SPC-3228	Gee Baby	1972	$12

POLYDOR

Number	Title	Yr	NM
❏ PD-1-6086	Naturally	1976	$12

RAY, DAVE

ELEKTRA

Number	Title	Yr	NM
❏ EKL-319 [M]	Fine Soft Land	1966	$25
❏ EKS-7319 [S]	Fine Soft Land	1966	$30
❏ EKL-284 [M]	Snaker's Here	1965	$25
❏ EKS-7284 [S]	Snaker's Here	1965	$30

RAY, DIANE

MERCURY

Number	Title	Yr	NM
❏ MG-20903 [M]	The Exciting Years	1964	$100
❏ SR-60903 [S]	The Exciting Years	1964	$150

RAY, JAMES

CAPRICE

Number	Title	Yr	NM
❏ LP-1002 [M]	James Ray	1962	$100
❏ SLP-1002 [S]	James Ray	1962	$120

RAY, JOHNNIE

COLUMBIA

Number	Title	Yr	NM
❏ CL1093 [M]	At the Desert Inn in Las Vegas	1957	$50
❏ CL2510 [10]	I Cry for You	1955	$80

— *House Party Series" issue*

Number	Title	Yr	NM
❏ CL6199 [10]	Johnnie Ray	1951	$100
❏ CL1227 [M]	Johnnie Ray's Greatest Hits	1958	$40

— *Red and black label with 6 "eye" logos*

Number	Title	Yr	NM
❑ CL1227 [M]	Johnnie Ray's Greatest Hits	1962	$30
—*Guaranteed High Fidelity" on label*			
❑ CL1227 [M]	Johnnie Ray's Greatest Hits	1965	$18
—*360 Sound" label*			
❑ CL1385 [M]	On the Trail	1959	$40
❑ CS8180 [S]	On the Trail	1959	$50
❑ CL961 [M]	The Big Beat	1957	$50
❑ CL1225 [M]	'Til Morning	1958	$40
—*Red and black label with six "eye" logos*			
❑ CL1225 [M]	'Til Morning	1963	$25
—*Red label with either "Guranteed High Fidelity" or "360 Sound Mono" at bottom*			

COLUMBIA SPECIAL PRODUCTS
Number	Title	Yr	NM
❑ P13086	Greatest Hits	197?	$12

EPIC
| ❑ LN1120 [10] | Johnnie Ray | 1955 | $100 |

HARMONY
| ❑ H30609 | The Best of Johnnie Ray | 1971 | $15 |

LIBERTY
| ❑ LRP-3221 [M] | Johnnie Ray | 1962 | $25 |
| ❑ LST-7221 [S] | Johnnie Ray | 1962 | $30 |

SUNSET
| ❑ SUM-1125 [M] | Mr. Cry | 196? | $15 |
| ❑ SUS-5125 [S] | Mr. Cry | 196? | $15 |

RAY, WADE
ABC-PARAMOUNT
Number	Title	Yr	NM
❑ ABC-539 [M]	A Ray of Country Sun	1966	$18
❑ ABCS-539 [S]	A Ray of Country Sun	1966	$25

RCA CAMDEN
| ❑ CAS-2107 | Walk Softly | 1969 | $18 |

RAYBURN, MARGIE
LIBERTY
| ❑ LRP-3126 [M] | Margie | 1959 | $30 |
| ❑ LST-7126 [S] | Margie | 1959 | $40 |

RAYE, JERRY
DEVILLE
| ❑ LP-101 [M] | The Many Sides of Jerry Raye and Fenwyck | 1967 | $600 |

RAYE, MARTHA
EPIC
| ❑ LG3061 [M] | Here's Martha Raye | 1954 | $40 |

RAYE, SUSAN
CAPITOL
Number	Title	Yr	NM
❑ ST-11179	Cheating Game	1973	$15
❑ ST-11255	Hymns by Susan Raye	1974	$15
❑ ST-875	(I've Got a) Happy Heart	1972	$18
❑ ST-11135	Love Sure Feels Good in My Heart	1973	$15
❑ ST-11055	My Heart Has a Mind of Its Own	1972	$15
❑ ST-543	One Night Stand	1970	$18
❑ ST-807	Pitty, Pitty, Patter	1971	$18
❑ ST-11223	Plastic Trains, Paper Planes	1973	$15
❑ ST-11333	Singing	1974	$15
❑ ST-11282	The Best of Susan Raye	1974	$15
❑ ST-11393	Whatch Gonna Do with a Dog Like That	1975	$15
❑ ST-11106	Wheel of Fortune	1972	$15
❑ ST-736	Willy Jones	1971	$18

UNITED ARTISTS
| ❑ UA-LA764-G | Susan Raye | 1977 | $15 |

RAYMOND, LEW
TOPS
❑ L-1583 [M]	For Men Only	1958	$40
—*Jayne Mansfield is the cover model*			
❑ L-1647 [M]	Million Sellers	1960	$30
—*Mary Tyler Moore is the cover model*			

RCA VICTOR SYMPHONY ORCHESTRA (KIRIL KONDRASHIN, CONDUCTOR)
RCA VICTOR RED SEAL
Number	Title	Yr	NM
❑ LSC-2398 [S]	Khachaturian: Masquerade Suite; Kabalevsky: The Comedians	1960	$120
—*Original with "shaded dog" label*			
❑ LSC-2398 [S]	Khachaturian: Masquerade Suite; Kabalevsky: The Comedians	1964	$150
—*Second edition with "white dog" label*			
❑ LSC-2398 [S]	Khachaturian: Masquerade Suite; Kabalevsky: The Comedians	1969	$30
—*Third edition with no dog on label*			
❑ LSC-2398 [S]	Khachaturian: Masquerade Suite; Kabalevsky: The Comedians	199?	$30
—*Classic Records reissue*			
❑ LSC-2323 [S]	Tchaikovsky: Capriccio Italien; Rimsky-Korsakov: Capriccio Espagnole	1959	$40
—*Original with "shaded dog" label*			

| ❑ LSC-2323 [S] | Tchaikovsky: Capriccio Italien; Rimsky-Korsakov: Capriccio Espagnole | 199? | $30 |
| —*Classic Records reissue* | | | |

RCA VICTOR SYMPHONY ORCHESTRA (LEOPOLD STOKOWSKI, CONDUCTOR)
RCA VICTOR RED SEAL
Number	Title	Yr	NM
❑ LSC-2612 [S]	Handel: Royal Fireworks Music; Water Music	1962	$30
—*Original with "shaded dog" label*			
❑ LSC-2612 [S]	Handel: Royal Fireworks Music; Water Music	1964	$25
—*Second edition with "white dog" label*			
❑ LSC-2471 [S]	Rhapsodies	196?	$40
—*Original with "shaded dog" label or second edition with "white dog" label*			
❑ LSC-2471 [S]	Rhapsodies	199?	$30
—*Classic Records reissue*			

RCA VICTOR SYMPHONY ORCHESTRA (ROBERT RUSSELL BENNETT, CONDUCTOR)
RCA VICTOR RED SEAL
| ❑ LSC-2238 [S] | It's Classic But It's Good | 1959 | $25 |
| —*Original with "shaded dog" label* | | | |

RE-FLEX
CAPITOL
Number	Title	Yr	NM
❑ ST-12314 [DJ]	The Politics of Dancing	1983	$18
—*High-grade vinyl edition (sticker on cover)*			
❑ ST-12314	The Politics of Dancing	1983	$12

REA, CHRIS
COLUMBIA
Number	Title	Yr	NM
❑ FC37664	Chris Rea	1981	$12
❑ JC36435	Tennis	1980	$12

GEFFEN
| ❑ GHS24232 | New Light Through Old Windows | 1989 | $15 |

MOTOWN
| ❑ 6245ML | Dancing with Strangers | 1987 | $12 |

UNITED ARTISTS
| ❑ UA-LA959-H | Deltics | 1979 | $12 |
| ❑ UA-LA879-H | Whatever Happened to Benny Santini? | 1978 | $15 |

READY FOR THE WORLD
MCA
Number	Title	Yr	NM
❑ 5829	Long Time Coming	1986	$10
❑ 5594	Ready for the World	1985	$10
❑ 42198	Ruff 'N' Ready	1988	$10
❑ 10224	Straight Down to Business	1991	$18

REAGAN, RONALD
DECCA
Number	Title	Yr	NM
❑ DL4943 [M]	Freedom's Finest Hour	1967	$30
❑ DL74943 [S]	Freedom's Finest Hour	1967	$30

KEY
| ❑ 690 [M] | Rendezvous with Destiny | 1964 | $30 |

X
| ❑ LVA-3051 [M] | Tales from the Great Book | 1956 | $40 |

REAL LIFE
CURB
Number	Title	Yr	NM
❑ CRB-10624	Let's Fall in Love	1989	$12
❑ D1-77271	Lifetime	1990	$15
❑ CRB-10614	Send Me an Angel '89	1989	$12

MCA CURB
❑ 5834	Down Comes the Hammer	1986	$12
❑ 5639	Flame	1985	$12
❑ 5459	Heartland	1983	$12
❑ 1443	Heartland	1985	$10
—*Budget-line reissue*			

REALLY RED
C.I.A.
| ❑ 06 | Teaching You the Fear | 1981 | $100 |

REAVES, GILES, AND JOHN GOIN
MCA
| ❑ 6283 | Letting Go | 1989 | $15 |

REBECCA AND THE SUNNY BROOK FARMERS
MUSICOR
| ❑ MS-3176 [B] | Rebecca and the Sunny Brook Farmers | 1969 | $50 |

REBILLOT, PAT
ATLANTIC
| ❑ SD1663 | Free Fall | 1974 | $30 |

REBIRTH
AVANT GARDE
| ❑ AVS-135 | Rebirth | 1971 | $50 |

REBIRTH BRASS BAND
ARHOOLIE
Number	Title	Yr	NM
❑ 1092	Here to Stay	1986	$25
—*As "Rebirth Jazz Band of New Orleans*			

ROUNDER
| ❑ 2093 | Feel Like Funkin' It Up | 1989 | $30 |

REBROFF, IVAN
CBS MASTERWORKS
| ❑ IM38658 | Christmas with Ivan Rebroff | 1983 | $12 |

REBS, THE
FREDLO
| ❑ 6830 | 1968 A.D. Break Through | 1968 | $400 |

RECOIL
PAUSA
| ❑ 7117 | Pardon My Fantasy | 198? | $25 |
| ❑ 7168 | The Fantasy Continues | 1985 | $25 |

RECORD, EUGENE
WARNER BROS.
Number	Title	Yr	NM
❑ BS3018	Eugene Record	1977	$18
❑ BSK3097	Trying to Get to You	1978	$18
❑ BSK3284	Welcome to My Fantasy	1979	$18

RECORDS, THE
VIRGIN
Number	Title	Yr	NM
❑ VA13140	Crashes	1980	$15
❑ VA13130 [B]	The Records	1979	$25
—*With bonus 4-song EP "Abracadabra" (deduct 33% if missing)*			

VIRGIN INTERNATIONAL
| ❑ VI2206 | Music on Both Sides | 1982 | $12 |

RED, SONNY
BLUE NOTE
Number	Title	Yr	NM
❑ BLP-4032 [M]	Out of the Blue	1960	$400
—*Deep groove" version (deep indentation under label on both sides)*			
❑ BLP-4032 [M]	Out of the Blue	1960	$175
—*Regular version, W. 63rd St. address on label*			
❑ ST-84032 [S]	Out of the Blue	1960	$75
—*With W. 63rd St. address on label*			
❑ BLP-4032 [M]	Out of the Blue	1963	$75
—*With "New York, USA" address on label*			
❑ ST-84032 [S]	Out of the Blue	1963	$25
—*With "New York, USA" address on label*			
❑ ST-84032 [S]	Out of the Blue	1967	$35
—*With "A Division of Liberty Records" on label*			

FANTASY
| ❑ OJC-148 | Images | 198? | $25 |

JAZZLAND
❑ JLP-32 [M]	Breezin'	1960	$30
❑ JLP-932 [M]	Breezin'	1960	$40
❑ JLP-74 [M]	Images	1962	$30
❑ JLP-974 [S]	Images	1962	$40
❑ JLP-59 [M]	The Mode	1961	$250
❑ JLP-959 [S]	The Mode	1961	$250

MAINSTREAM
| ❑ MRL-324 | Sonny Red | 1971 | $35 |

RED, WHITE AND BLUE (GRASS)
GRC
Number	Title	Yr	NM
❑ 5002	Red, White and Blue (Grass)	1973	$18
❑ 10003	Red, White and Blue (Grass) Pickin' Up!	1974	$18

MERCURY
| ❑ SRM-1-1165 | Red, White and Blue (Grass) and Company | 1977 | $15 |

RED CRAYOLA, THE
INTERNATIONAL ARTISTS
Number	Title	Yr	NM
❑ 7	God Bless the Red Crayola	1968	$75
❑ 7	God Bless the Red Crayola	1979	$18
—*Reissue with "Masterfonics" in trail-off wax*			
❑ 2 [M]	Parable of the Arable Land	1968	$120
❑ 2 [S]	Parable of the Arable Land	1968	$100
❑ 2	Parable of the Arable Land	1979	$18
—*Reissue with "Masterfonics" in trail-off wax*			

RED HOT CHILI PEPPERS
Drummer Chad Smith is also in CHICKENFOOT.
EMI
Number	Title	Yr	NM
❑ E1-92152	Mother's Milk	1989	$25
❑ E1-29665 [B]	Out in L.A.	1994	$25

EMI AMERICA
❑ ST-17168	Freaky Styley	1985	$18
❑ ST-17128	Red Hot Chili Peppers	1984	$18
❑ E1-48036	The Uplift Mofo Party Plan	1987	$18

EMI MANHATTAN
| ❑ E1-90869 [EP] | The Abbey Road E.P. | 1988 | $20 |

Number	Title	Yr	NM
WARNER BROS.			
❏ PRO-A-5170 [DJ]	Blood Sugar Sex Magik	1991	$50

—Radio-ready" version of LP, this is the only U.S. vinyl release of this album

Number	Title	Yr	NM
❏ 48140	By the Way	2002	$30
❏ 47386	Californication	1999	$75
❏ 5533401 [B]	Greatest Hits	2016	$25
❏ 43391-1	Stadium Arcadium	2006	$40

—150-gram version; records are contained in two gatefold sleeves inside a slipcase

Number	Title	Yr	NM
❏ 49996-1	Stadium Arcadium	2006	$100

—180-gram version; box set contains records in individual sleeves plus two 12x12 booklets

Number	Title	Yr	NM
❏ 5552391 [B]	The Getaway	2016	$40
RED ONION JAZZ BAND, THE			
BIOGRAPH			
❏ LP-12012	There'll Be a Hot Time in the Old Town Tonight	1969	$35
RIVERSIDE			
❏ RLP 12-260 [M]	Dance Off Both Your Shoes In Hi-Fi	1958	$300
RED ONIONS AND OTTILIE			
STOMP OFF			
❏ SOS-1090	Mad Dog	1985	$25
RED RIVER DAVE			
CONTINENTAL			
❏ 1507 [M]	Red River Dave Sings	1962	$30
VARSITY			
❏ 6962 [10]	Red River Dave	1951	$80
RED ROSE RAGTIME BAND			
STOMP OFF			
❏ SOS-1128	A Rose Is a Rose Is a Rose	1987	$25
RED ROSELAND CORNPICKERS, THE			
STOMP OFF			
❏ SOS-1101	Double Talk	1985	$25
❏ SOS-1133	Handful of Keith	1987	$25
❏ SOS-1153	Red Hot Band	1988	$25
❏ SOS-1102	That's No Bargain	1985	$25
RED SKY			
GUINNESS			
❏ GNS36067 [B]	Red Sky	1977	$300
RED WING BLACKBIRDS RAGTIME BAND			
STOMP OFF			
❏ SOS-1018	Two-Step Ball	198?	$25
REDBONE, LEON			
AUGUST			
❏ AS8890	Christmas Island	1988	$18
WARNER BROS.			
❏ BS3165	Champagne Charlie	1978	$30
❏ BS2971	Double Time	1977	$25
❏ BS2888	On the Track	1975	$25
REDBONE			
EPIC			
❏ KE31598	Already Here	1972	$18
❏ KE33053	Bearded Dreams Through Turquoise Eyes	1974	$18
❏ EQ33053 [Q]	Bearded Dreams Through Turquoise Eyes	1974	$30
❏ KEG33456	Come & Get Your Redbone	1975	$25
❏ KE30815	Message from a Drum	1972	$18
❏ EQ30815 [Q]	Message from a Drum	1973	$30

Number	Title	Yr	NM
❏ E30109 [B]	Potlatch	1970	$18
❏ EGP501 [B]	Redbone	1970	$30

Number	Title	Yr	NM
❏ KE32462	Wovoka	1974	$18
RCA VICTOR			
❏ AFL1-2352	Cycles	1977	$15
REDD, FREDDIE, AND HAMPTON HAWES			
FANTASY			
❏ OJC-1705	Piano: East/West	1985	$25
NEW JAZZ			
❏ NJLP-8307 [M]	Movin'	1963	$0

—Canceled; reassigned to Status

Number	Title	Yr	NM
PRESTIGE			
❏ PRLP-7067 [M]	Piano: East/West	1956	$300
STATUS			
❏ ST-8307 [M]	Movin'	1965	$40
REDD, FREDDIE			
BLUE NOTE			
❏ BLP-4027 [M]	Music From "The Connection	1960	$300

—Deep groove" version (deep indentation under label on both sides)

Number	Title	Yr	NM
❏ BLP-4027 [M]	Music From "The Connection	1963	$75

—With "New York, USA" address on label

Number	Title	Yr	NM
❏ BST-84027 [S]	Music From "The Connection	1967	$20

—With "A Division of Liberty Records" on label

Number	Title	Yr	NM
❏ BLP-4027 [M]	Music From "The Connection	1960	$250

—Regular version, W. 63rd St. on label

Number	Title	Yr	NM
❏ BST-84027 [S]	Music From "The Connection	1960	$150

—With W. 63rd St. address on label

Number	Title	Yr	NM
❏ BST-84027 [S]	Music From "The Connection	1963	$50

—With "New York, USA" address on label

Number	Title	Yr	NM
❏ BLP-4045 [M]	Shades of Redd	1960	$1000

—Deep groove" version (deep indentation under label on both sides)

Number	Title	Yr	NM
❏ BLP-4045 [M]	Shades of Redd	1963	$300

—With "New York, USA" address on label

Number	Title	Yr	NM
❏ BST-84045 [S]	Shades of Redd	1960	$0

—Canceled

Number	Title	Yr	NM
❏ BLP-4045 [M]	Shades of Redd	1960	$300

—Regular version, W. 63rd St. address on label

Number	Title	Yr	NM
FANTASY			
❏ OJC-1748	San Francisco Suite For Jazz Trio	1990	$30
INTERPLAY			
❏ 7715	Straight Ahead	1979	$30
MOSAIC			
❏ MR3-124	The Complete Blue Note Recordings of Freddie Redd	199?	$30
PRESTIGE			
❏ PRLP-197 [10]	Introducing the Freddie Redd Trio	1954	$300
RIVERSIDE			
❏ RLP 12-250 [M]	San Francisco Suite For Jazz Trio	1957	$350
❏ 6184	San Francisco Suite For Jazz Trio	198?	$30
REDD, VI			
ATCO			
❏ 33-157 [M]	Lady Soul	1963	$30
❏ SD 33-157 [S]	Lady Soul	1963	$40
UNITED ARTISTS			
❏ UAJ-14016 [M]	Bird Call	1962	$40
❏ UAJS-15016 [S]	Bird Call	1962	$50
REDD KROSS			
ATLANTIC			
❏ 82148	Third Eye	1990	$12
BIG TIME			
❏ 6034-1	Neurotica	1987	$15
FRONTIER			
❏ 4609-1-L [B]	Born Innocent	1991	$25

—Reissue

Number	Title	Yr	NM
❏ FLP1018	Born Innocent	1986	$15

—Reissue

Number	Title	Yr	NM
GASATANKA			
❏ E1170 [B]	Teen Babies from Monsanto	1984	$25
POSH BOY			
❏ 1010 [EP]	Annette's Got the Hits	1987	$25

—Reissue

Number	Title	Yr	NM
❏ 1010 [EP]	Red Cross	1980	$25
SMOKE			
❏ SMK7-103	Born Innocent	1982	$18
SYMPATHY FOR THE RECORD INDUSTRY			
❏ 260 [10]	2,500 Redd Kross Fans Can't Be Wrong	1993	$25

Number	Title	Yr	NM
REDDING, GENE			
HAVEN			
❏ ST-9200	Blood Brother	1974	$25
REDDING, OTIS			
ATCO			
❏ SD 37-265	I Can't Turn You Loose/Pain in My Heart//Mr. Pitiful/Any Ole Way/Respect	1968	$30

—Stereo jukebox issue; small hole, plays at 33 1/3 rpm

Number	Title	Yr	NM
❏ SD 37-265 [PS]	Otis Redding In Person at the Whiskey A-Go-Go	1968	$30
ATLANTIC			
❏ SD70419	(Sittin' on) The Dock of the Bay/Let Me Come On Home/Open the Door//The Glory of Love/Tramp/Ole Man Trouble	1968	$30

—Stereo jukebox issue; small hole, plays at 33 1/3 rpm

Number	Title	Yr	NM
❏ SD70419 [PS]	The Dock of the Bay	1968	$30

—Cover says "Volt" but the label of the record is Atlantic

Number	Title	Yr	NM
4 MEN WITH BEARDS			
❏ 4M105	The Great Otis Redding Sings Soul Ballads	2002	$18

—Reissue on 180-gram vinyl

Number	Title	Yr	NM
ATCO			
❏ SD 33-287	Complete & Unbelievable... The Otis Redding Dictionary of Soul	1969	$18

—Reissue of Volt 415

Number	Title	Yr	NM
❏ SD 33-261	History of Otis Redding	1968	$18

—Reissue of Volt 418

Number	Title	Yr	NM
❏ SD 33-289	Love Man	1969	$18
❏ SD 33-284	Otis Blue/Otis Redding Sings Soul	1969	$18

—Reissue of Volt 412

Number	Title	Yr	NM
❏ SD 33-265	Otis Redding In Person at the Whiskey A-Go-Go	1968	$18
❏ SD 33-286	Otis Redding Live in Europe	1969	$18

—Reissue of Volt 416

Number	Title	Yr	NM
❏ R180253 [B]	Pain In My Heart	2014	$75
❏ 33-161 [M]	Pain in My Heart	1964	$300
❏ SD 33-161 [R]	Pain in My Heart	1968	$300
❏ SD 33-333	Tell the Truth	1970	$18
❏ SD 2-801	The Best of Otis Redding	1972	$25
❏ SD 33-288 [B]	The Dock of the Bay	1969	$25

—Reissue of Volt 419

Number	Title	Yr	NM
❏ SD 33-252 [S]	The Immortal Otis Redding	1968	$18
❏ 33-252 [M]	The Immortal Otis Redding	1968	$50

—Mono is white label promo only

Number	Title	Yr	NM
❏ SD 33-285	The Soul Album	1969	$18

—Reissue of Volt 413

Number	Title	Yr	NM
ATLANTIC			
❏ SD19346	Recorded Live	198?	$12
❏ 81282	The Best of Otis Redding	1985	$12
❏ 81762	The Otis Redding Story	1987	$30
PAIR			
❏ PDL2-1062	The Legend of Otis Redding	1984	$18
SUNDAZED			
❏ LP5063 [M]	Complete & Unbelievable ... The Otis Redding Dictionary of Soul	2001	$15

—Reissue on 180-gram vinyl

Number	Title	Yr	NM
❏ LP5064 [M]	Otis Blue/Otis Redding Sings Soul	2001	$15

—Reissue on 180-gram vinyl

Number	Title	Yr	NM
❏ LP5133 [S]	Otis Redding In Person at the Whiskey A-Go-Go	2003	$15

—Reissue on 180-gram vinyl

Number	Title	Yr	NM
❏ LP5134 [S]	Otis Redding Live in Europe	2003	$15

—Reissue on 180-gram vinyl

Number	Title	Yr	NM
❏ LP5172 [S]	The Dock of the Bay	2003	$15

—Reissue on 180-gram vinyl

Number	Title	Yr	NM
❏ LP5132 [S]	The Soul Album	2003	$15

—Reissue on 180-gram vinyl

Number	Title	Yr	NM
VOLT			
❏ 415 [M]	Complete & Unbelievable... The Otis Redding Dictionary of Soul	1966	$100
❏ S-415 [S]	Complete & Unbelievable... The Otis Redding Dictionary of Soul	1966	$75
❏ 418 [M]	History of Otis Redding	1967	$40
❏ S-418 [S]	History of Otis Redding	1967	$30
❏ 412 [M]	Otis Blue/Otis Redding Sings Soul	1965	$100
❏ S-412 [S]	Otis Blue/Otis Redding Sings Soul	1965	$75
❏ 416 [M]	Otis Redding Live in Europe	1967	$30
❏ S-416 [S]	Otis Redding Live in Europe	1967	$40
❏ S-419	The Dock of the Bay	1968	$30
❏ 411 [M]	The Great Otis Redding Sings Soul Ballads	1965	$120
❏ S-411 [R]	The Great Otis Redding Sings Soul Ballads	1968	$120
❏ 413 [M]	The Soul Album	1966	$100
❏ S-413 [S]	The Soul Album	1966	$75

Number	Title	Yr	NM

REDDINGS, THE
BELIEVE IN A DREAM
❏ JZ36875	Awakening	1980	$12
❏ FZ38690	Back to Basics	1983	$12
❏ FZ37175	Class	1981	$12
❏ FZ37974	Steamin' Hot	1982	$12
POLYDOR
❏ 823324-1	If Looks Could Kill	1985	$10
❏ 835292-1	The Reddings	1988	$12

REDDY, HELEN
CAPITOL
❏ SO-11640	Ear Candy	1977	$12
❏ ST-11348	Free and Easy	1974	$12
❏ SN-16249	Free and Easy	198?	$10
—Budget-line reissue			
❏ ST-857	Helen Reddy	1971	$18
❏ SN-16098	Helen Reddy	1980	$10
—Budget-line reissue			
❏ ST-11467	Helen Reddy's Greatest Hits	1975	$12
—Orange label			
❏ SW-11467	Helen Reddy's Greatest Hits	1978	$10
—Purple label			
❏ SN-16333	Helen Reddy's Greatest Hits	1984	$10
—Budget-line reissue			
❏ ST-11068	I Am Woman	1972	$12
❏ SN-16099	I Am Woman	1980	$10
—Budget-line reissue			
❏ ST-762	I Don't Know How to Love Him	1971	$18
❏ SN-16100	I Don't Know How to Love Him	1980	$10
—Budget-line reissue			
❏ SKBO-11873	Live	1979	$15
❏ SN-16250	Live	198?	$10
—Budget-line reissue			
❏ SMAS-11213	Long Hard Climb	1973	$12
❏ SN-16101	Long Hard Climb	1980	$10
—Budget-line reissue			
❏ SO-11284	Love Song for Jeffrey	1974	$12
❏ SN-16195	Love Song for Jeffrey	198?	$10
—Budget-line reissue			
❏ ST-11547	Music, Music	1976	$12
❏ ST-11418	No Way to Treat a Lady	1975	$12
❏ SN-16196	No Way to Treat a Lady	1980	$10
—Budget-line reissue			
❏ SO-11949	Reddy	1979	$12
❏ SN-16200	Reddy	1980	$10
—Budget-line reissue			
❏ SOO-12068	Take What You Find	1980	$12
❏ SN-16248	Take What You Find	198?	$10
—Budget-line reissue			
❏ SW-11759	We'll Sing in the Sunshine	1978	$12
❏ SN-16199	We'll Sing in the Sunshine	1980	$10
—Budget-line reissue			
MCA
❏ 5376	Imagination	198?	$10
PAIR
❏ PDL2-1066	Lust for Life	1986	$15

REDEYE
PENTAGRAM
❏ PR-10006 [B]	One Man's Poison	1971	$25
❏ PE-10003 [B]	Redeye	1970	$25

REDMAN, DEWEY, AND ED BLACKWELL
BLACK SAINT
❏ BSR-0093	Red and Black in Willisau	1985	$30

REDMAN, DEWEY
ABC IMPULSE!
❏ AS-9300	Coincide	1974	$35
❏ AS-9250	The Ear of the Behearer	1973	$35
ARISTA/FREEDOM
❏ AF1011	Look for the Black Star	1976	$30
BLACK SAINT
❏ 120123	Living on the Edge	1990	$35
ECM
❏ 1225	The Struggle Continues	1981	$25
GALAXY
❏ 5118	Musics	1980	$30
❏ 5130	Soundsigns	198?	$30

REDMAN, DON
GOLDEN CREST
❏ GC-3017 [M]	Park Avenue Patter	1958	$40
RCA VICTOR
❏ LPV-520 [M]	Master of the Big Band	1965	$25
ROULETTE
❏ R-25070 [M]	Dixieland in High Society	1960	$25
❏ SR-25070 [S]	Dixieland in High Society	1960	$30
STEEPLECHASE
❏ SCC-6020	For Europeans Only	198?	$30

REDMAN, GEORGE
SKYLARK
❏ SKLP-20 [10]	The George Redman Group	1954	$175

REDMOND, EDGAR
DISQUE-PHENOMENON
❏ 2696 [10]	Edgar Redmond & the Modern String Ensemble	1965	$30

REDNOW, EIVETS
See STEVIE WONDER.

REDOLFI, MICHEL
HAT ART
❏ 2002	Sonic Waters	1986	$35

REDPATH, JEAN
ELEKTRA
❏ EKL-274 [M]	Laddie Lie Near Me	1964	$16
❏ EKS-7274 [S]	Laddie Lie Near Me	1964	$25
❏ EKL-214 [M]	Scottish Ballad Book	1962	$25
❏ EKL-224 [M]	Songs of Love, Lilt and Laughter	1963	$25
PRESTIGE
❏ PR-13041 [M]	Skipping Barefoot Through the Heather	1962	$30

REECE, DIZZY, AND TUBBY HAYES
SAVOY
❏ MG-12111 [M]	Changing the Jazz at Buckingham Palace	1957	$150

REECE, DIZZY
BEE HIVE
❏ BH-7001	Manhattan Project	1978	$75
BLUE NOTE
❏ BLP-4006 [M]	Blues in Trinity	1958	$400
—Deep groove" version; W. 63rd St. address on label			
❏ BLP-4006 [M]	Blues in Trinity	1958	$175
—Regular version, W. 63rd St. address on label			
❏ BST-4006 [S]	Blues in Trinity	1959	$600
—Deep groove" version; W. 63rd St. address on label			
❏ BST-4006 [S]	Blues in Trinity	1959	$120
—Regular version, W. 63rd St. address on label			
❏ BLP-4006 [M]	Blues in Trinity	1963	$100
—With "New York, USA" address on label			
❏ BST-4006 [S]	Blues in Trinity	1963	$30
—With "New York, USA" address on label			
❏ BST-84006 [S]	Blues in Trinity	1967	$75
—With "A Division of Liberty Records" on label			
❏ B1-32093	Blues in Trinity	1995	$35
❏ BLP-4033 [M]	Soundin' Off	1960	$800
—Deep groove" version; W. 63rd St. address on label			
❏ BLP-4033 [M]	Soundin' Off	1960	$250
—Regular version, W. 63rd St. address on label			
❏ BST-84033 [S]	Soundin' Off	1960	$175
—With W. 63rd St. address on label			
❏ BLP-4033 [M]	Soundin' Off	1963	$150
—With "New York, USA" address on label			
❏ BST-84033 [S]	Soundin' Off	1963	$40
—With "New York, USA" address on label			
❏ BST-84033 [S]	Soundin' Off	1967	$75
—With "A Division of Liberty Records" on label			
❏ BLP-4023 [M]	Star Bright	1959	$300
—Deep groove" version; W. 63rd St. address on label			
❏ BLP-4023 [M]	Star Bright	1959	$175
—Regular version, W. 63rd St. address on label			
❏ BST-84023 [S]	Star Bright	1959	$120
—With W. 63rd St. address on label			
❏ BLP-4023 [M]	Star Bright	1963	$100
—With "New York, USA" address on label			
❏ BST-84023 [S]	Star Bright	1963	$40
—With "New York, USA" address on label			
❏ BST-84023 [S]	Star Bright	1967	$75
—With "A Division of Liberty Records" on label			
❏ BLP-4023 [M]	Star Bright	200?	$75
—200-gram reissue; distributed by Classic Records			
DISCOVERY
❏ DS-839	Moose the Mooche	1982	$50
IMPERIAL
❏ LP-9043 [M]	London Jazz	1957	$200
NEW JAZZ
❏ NJLP-8274 [M]	Asia Minor	1962	$175
—Purple label			
❏ NJLP-8274 [M]	Asia Minor	1965	$175
—Blue label, trident logo at right			

REED, A.C.
ALLIGATOR
❏ AL-4757	I'm in the Wrong Business!	1988	$15

Number	Title	Yr	NM
ICE CUBE
❏ 1057	Take These Blues and Shove 'Em!	1982	$18
ROOSTER BLUES
❏ R7606	Take These Blues and Shove 'Em!	1982	$12

REED, JERRY
CAPITOL
❏ ST-12492	Lookin' at You	1986	$10
HARMONY
❏ H30547	I'm Movin' On	1971	$12
RCA CAMDEN
❏ CAS-2585	Oh What a Woman!	1972	$12
❏ ACL1-0331	Tupelo Mississippi Flash	1973	$12
RCA VICTOR
❏ APL1-0544	A Good Woman's Love	1974	$15
❏ LSP-4069	Alabama Wild Man	1968	$25
❏ LSP-4147	Better Things in Life	1969	$25
❏ APL1-1861	Both Barrels	1976	$15
❏ AHL1-5472	Collector's Series	1985	$12
❏ LSP-4293	Cookin'	1970	$25
❏ AHL1-4021	Dixie Dreams	1981	$15
❏ AHL1-2516	East Bound and Down	1977	$15
❏ AYL1-3677	East Bound and Down	1980	$10
—Best Buy Series" reissue			
❏ LSP-4391 [B]	Georgia Sunshine	1970	$30
❏ AHL1-5176	Greatest Hits	1984	$12
❏ AHL1-3359	Half Singin' & Half Pickin'	1979	$15
❏ LSP-4838	Hot A' Mighty!	1973	$18
❏ LSP-4750	Jerry Reed	1972	$18
❏ LSP-4204	Jerry Reed Explores Guitar Country	1969	$25
❏ AHL1-3453	Jerry Reed Live!	1979	$15
❏ AYL1-4167	Jerry Reed Live!	1982	$10
—Best Buy Series" reissue			
❏ AHL1-2346	Jerry Reed Rides Again	1977	$15
❏ AHL1-3604	Jerry Reed Sings Jim Croce	1980	$15
❏ LSP-4596	Ko-Ko Joe	1971	$18
❏ APL1-0238	Lord, Mr. Ford	1973	$15
❏ APD1-0238 [Q]	Lord, Mr. Ford	1973	$40
❏ LSP-4707	Me and Chet	1972	$18
—With Chet Atkins			
❏ ANL1-2167	Me and Chet	1976	$12
—Reissue of 4707			
❏ APL1-0787	Mind Your Love	1974	$15
❏ LPM-3978 [M]	Nashville Underground	1968	$100
❏ LSP-3978 [S]	Nashville Underground	1968	$25
❏ AHL1-4692	Ready	1983	$12
❏ APL1-1226	Red Hot Picker	1975	$15
❏ LSP-4660	Smell the Flowers	1972	$18
❏ AHL1-2764	Sweet Love Feelings	1978	$15
❏ AHL1-3771	Texas Bound and Flyin'	1980	$15
❏ AYL1-4394	Texas Bound and Flyin'	1982	$10
—Best Buy Series" reissue			
❏ LSP-4729	The Best of Jerry Reed	1972	$18
❏ AHL1-4529	The Bird	1982	$12
❏ AYL1-5151	The Bird	1984	$10
—Best Buy Series" reissue			
❏ AHL1-4315	The Man with the Golden Thumb	1982	$12
❏ LPM-3756 [M]	The Unbelievable Guitar and Voice of Jerry Reed	1967	$30
❏ LSP-3756 [S]	The Unbelievable Guitar and Voice of Jerry Reed	1967	$25
❏ APL1-0356	The Uptown Poker Club	1973	$15
❏ LSP-4506	When You're Hot, You're Hot	1971	$18
❏ ANL1-1345	When You're Hot, You're Hot	1975	$12
—Reissue of 4506			

REED, JIMMY
ANTILLES
❏ 7007	Cold Chills	197?	$18
BLUESVILLE
❏ BLS-6054	I Ain't From Chicago	1973	$18
❏ BLS-6073	Jimmy Reed at Carnegie Hall	1973	$25
❏ BLS-6067	The Ultimate Jimmy Reed	1973	$18
BLUESWAY
❏ BLS-6015	Big Boss Man	1968	$25
❏ BLS-6024	Down in Virginia	1969	$25
❏ BL-6009 [M]	Soulin'	1967	$25
❏ BLS-6009 [S]	Soulin'	1967	$25
❏ BL-6004 [M]	The New Jimmy Reed Album	1967	$25
❏ BLS-6004 [S]	The New Jimmy Reed Album	1967	$25
BUDDAH
❏ BDS-4003	The Very Best of Jimmy Reed	1969	$18
—Reissue of Vee Jay 1039			
CHAMELEON
❏ D1-74762	Bright Lights, Big City	1988	$12
EVEREST ARCHIVE OF FOLK & JAZZ
❏ 234	Jimmy Reed	197?	$15
GNP CRESCENDO
❏ GNPS-10006	The Best of Jimmy Reed	1974	$18
SUNSET
❏ SUS-5218	Somethin' Else	1968	$15

Number	Title	Yr	NM
TRADITION			
❏ 2069	Wailin' the Blues	1969	$15
TRIP			
❏ 8012	History of Jimmy Reed	1971	$18
VEE JAY			
❏ VJS-7303	Blues Is My Business	198?	$12
❏ LP-1022 [M]	Found Love	1959	$250
—Maroon label			
❏ LP-1022 [M]	Found Love	1961	$100
—Black label with colorband			
❏ LP-1004 [M]	I'm Jimmy Reed	1958	$220
—Maroon label			
❏ LP-1004 [M]	I'm Jimmy Reed	1961	$100
—Black label with colorband			
❏ VJLP-1004	I'm Jimmy Reed	198?	$12
—Reissue with glossy labels			
❏ 2LP-1035 [M]	Jimmy Reed at Carnegie Hall	1961	$50
❏ 2SR-1035 [S]	Jimmy Reed at Carnegie Hall	1961	$80
❏ VJLP2-1035	Jimmy Reed at Carnegie Hall	198?	$15
—Reissue with glossy labels			
❏ LP-1095 [M]	Jimmy Reed at Soul City	1964	$40
❏ VJLP-1095	Jimmy Reed at Soul City	198?	$12
—Reissue with glossy labels			
❏ LP-1050 [M]	Just Jimmy Reed	1962	$40
❏ SR-1050 [S]	Just Jimmy Reed	1962	$75
❏ LP-1080 [M]	More of the Best of Jimmy Reed	1964	$40
❏ SR-1080 [S]	More of the Best of Jimmy Reed	1964	$175
❏ LP-1025 [M]	Now Appearing	1960	$100
❏ VJLP-1025	Now Appearing	198?	$12
—Reissue with glossy labels			
❏ LP-1008 [M]	Rockin' with Reed	1959	$250
—Maroon label			
❏ LP-1008 [M]	Rockin' with Reed	1961	$100
—Black label with colorband			
❏ VJLP-1008	Rockin' with Reed	198?	$12
—Reissue with glossy labels			
❏ LP-1067 [M]	T'Ain't No Big Thing…But He Is Jimmy Reed	1963	$40
❏ SR-1067 [S]	T'Ain't No Big Thing…But He Is Jimmy Reed	1963	$75
❏ LP-1073 [M]	The 12 String Guitar Blues	1963	$40
❏ SR-1073 [S]	The 12 String Guitar Blues	1963	$175
❏ LP-1039 [M]	The Best of Jimmy Reed	1962	$40
❏ SR-1039 [S]	The Best of Jimmy Reed	1962	$75
❏ VJLP-1039	The Best of Jimmy Reed	198?	$12
—Reissue with glossy labels			
❏ LP-1072 [M]	The Best of the Blues	1963	$40
❏ LP-8501 [M]	The Legend, The Man	1965	$40
❏ VJS-8501 [S]	The Legend, The Man	1965	$175
❏ VJLP-8501	The Legend, The Man	198?	$12
—Reissue with glossy labels			

REED, LOU, AND JOHN CALE

SIRE

Number	Title	Yr	NM
❏ 26140 [B]	Songs for Drella	1990	$25

REED, LOU

Also see THE PRMITIVES; THE VELVET UNDERGROUND.

ARISTA

Number	Title	Yr	NM
❏ ALB6-8390	City Lights -- Classic Performances by Lou Reed	1985	$12
❏ AL9522 [B]	Growing Up in Public	1980	$25
❏ AL8502 [B]	Live! Take No Prisoners	1978	$40
❏ R252506	Rock and Roll Diary 1967-1980	1980	$25
—RCA Music Service edition			
❏ A2L8603	Rock and Roll Diary 1967-1980	1980	$25
❏ AL118434	Rock and Roll Diary 1967-1980	198?	$16
—Reissue			
❏ AL4100	Rock and Roll Heart	1976	$18
—Originals on light blue labels			
❏ AL4169 [B]	Street Hassle	1978	$25
❏ AL4229 [B]	The Bells	1979	$25
DIRECT DISK			
❏ 0(no cat #) [DJ]	The Blue Mask	1982	$175
—Only exists on test pressings; no stock copies made			
RCA			
❏ 88691958021 [B]	Rock N Roll Animal	2012	$30
❏ 88875071411 [B]	Transformer	2015	$25
RCA VICTOR			
❏ APL1-0207 [B]	Berlin	1973	$40
❏ AYL1-4388	Berlin	1983	$10
—Best Buy Series reissue			
❏ APL1-0915 [B]	Coney Island Baby	1976	$30
❏ ANL1-2480	Coney Island Baby	1977	$10
—Reissue			
❏ AYL1-3807	Coney Island Baby	1980	$10
—Best Buy Series reissue			
❏ AFL1-4568 [B]	Legendary Hearts	1983	$25
❏ LSP-4701 [B]	Lou Reed	1972	$30
❏ APL1-0959 [B]	Lou Reed Live	1975	$25
❏ AFL1-0959	Lou Reed Live	1977	$10

Number	Title	Yr	NM
—Reissue			
❏ AYL1-3752	Lou Reed Live	1980	$10
—Best Buy Series reissue			
❏ CPL2-1101 [B]	Metal Machine Music	1975	$100
—Orange or brown label			
❏ CPD2-1101 [Q]	Metal Machine Music	1975	$400
❏ AFL1-7190 [B]	Mistrial	1986	$25
❏ AFL1-4998 [B]	New Sensations	1984	$25
❏ APL1-0472 [B]	Rock & Roll Animal	1974	$35
❏ AFL1-0472	Rock & Roll Animal	1977	$10
—Reissue			
❏ AYL1-3664	Rock & Roll Animal	1980	$10
—Best Buy Series reissue			
❏ CPL1-0611	Sally Can't Dance	1974	$25
❏ AFL1-0611	Sally Can't Dance	1977	$10
—Reissue			
❏ AYL1-4555	Sally Can't Dance	1983	$10
—Best Buy Series reissue			
❏ DJL1-4266 [DJ]	Special Radio Series, Vol. XVII	1980	$30
—Promo-only with insert			
❏ AFL1-4221 [B]	The Blue Mask	1982	$25
❏ AYL1-4780	The Blue Mask	1984	$10
—Best Buy Series reissue			
❏ DJL1-4267 [DJ]	The Blue Mask Interview Album	1982	$30
❏ DJL1-4345 [DJ]	The Blue Mask Sampler	1982	$15
—Three-song EP released to radio			
❏ LSP-4807	Transformer	1972	$25
❏ AFL1-4807	Transformer	1977	$10
—Reissue			
❏ AYL1-3806	Transformer	1980	$10
—Best Buy Series reissue			
❏ APL1-2001	Walk on the Wild Side	1977	$15
❏ AFL1-2001	Walk on the Wild Side	1978	$10
—Reissue			
❏ AYL1-3753	Walk on the Wild Side	1980	$10
—Best Buy Series reissue			
SIRE			
❏ R101058	New York	1989	$15
—BMG Music Service edition			
❏ 25829 [B]	New York	1989	$25

REED, LUCY

FANTASY

Number	Title	Yr	NM
❏ 3212 [M]	The Singing Reed	1956	$175
—Red vinyl			
❏ 3212 [M]	The Singing Reed	195?	$100
—Black vinyl			
❏ 3243 [M]	This Is Lucy Reed	1957	$175
—Red vinyl			
❏ 3243 [M]	This Is Lucy Reed	195?	$100
—Black vinyl			

REED, LULA

KING

Number	Title	Yr	NM
❏ 604 [M]	Blue and Moody	1958	$2000

REED, VIVIAN

EPIC

Number	Title	Yr	NM
❏ BN26412	Vivian Reed	1968	$40
H&L			
❏ 69017	Brown Sugar	1976	$25
UNITED ARTISTS			
❏ UA-LA911-H	Another Side	1978	$18
❏ UA-LA970-H	Ready and Waiting	1979	$18

REED, WAYMON

ARTISTS HOUSE

Number	Title	Yr	NM
❏ 10	46th and 8th	1980	$30

REESE, DELLA

ABC

Number	Title	Yr	NM
❏ 612 [M]	Della on Strings of Blue	1967	$25
❏ S-612 [S]	Della on Strings of Blue	1967	$20
❏ 569 [M]	Della Reese Live	1966	$20
❏ S-569 [S]	Della Reese Live	1966	$25
❏ S-636	I Gotta Be Me…This Trip Out	1968	$20
❏ 589 [M]	One More Time	1967	$20
❏ S-589 [S]	One More Time	1967	$20
❏ AC-30002	The ABC Collection	1976	$20
ABC-PARAMOUNT			
❏ ABC-524 [M]	C'mon and Hear Della Reese	1965	$25
❏ ABCS-524 [S]	C'mon and Hear Della Reese	1965	$25
❏ ABC-540 [M]	I Like It Like Dat!	1966	$20
❏ ABCS-540 [S]	I Like It Like Dat!	1966	$25
AVCO EMBASSY			
❏ 33004	Black Is Beautiful	1969	$20
❏ 33017	Right Now	1970	$20
JAZZ A LA CARTE			
❏ 3	One of a Kind	1978	$20

Number	Title	Yr	NM
JUBILEE			
❏ JLP-1071 [M]	A Date with Della Reese at Mr. Kelly's in Chicago	1959	$30
—Originals have blue labels			
❏ SDJLP-1071 [S]	A Date with Della Reese at Mr. Kelly's in Chicago	1959	$30
—Originals have blue labels			
❏ JGM-1071 [M]	A Date with Della Reese at Mr. Kelly's in Chicago	196?	$25
—Black label with all-silver print			
❏ JGM-1071 [M]	A Date with Della Reese at Mr. Kelly's in Chicago	1963	$25
—Black label, multi-colored spokes around "jubilee			
❏ SDJLP-1071 [S]	A Date with Della Reese at Mr. Kelly's in Chicago	1959	$30
—Black label with all-silver print			
❏ SDJLP-1071 [S]	A Date with Della Reese at Mr. Kelly's in Chicago	1962	$25
—Black label, multi-colored spokes around "jubilee," yellow spoke goes almost to center hole			
❏ JGS-1071 [S]	A Date with Della Reese at Mr. Kelly's in Chicago	1965	$25
—Black label, multi-colored spokes around "jubilee," yellow spoke goes nowhere near center hole; new prefix			
❏ JLP-1083 [M]	Amen	1959	$30
❏ SDJLP-1083 [S]	Amen	1959	$30
❏ JLP-1116 [M]	And That Reminds Me	1960	$30
❏ JLP-1026 [M]	Melancholy Baby	1957	$30
❏ JGM-5002 [M]	The Best of Della Reese	196?	$20
❏ JGS-5002 [S]	The Best of Della Reese	196?	$25
❏ JLP-1095 [M]	The Story of the Blues	1960	$30
—Original labels are black with all-silver print			
❏ SDJLP-1095 [S]	The Story of the Blues	1960	$30
—Original labels are black with all-silver print			
❏ JLP-1095 [M]	The Story of the Blues	1960	$25
—Black label, multi-colored spokes around "jubilee," yellow spoke goes almost to center hole			
❏ JGM-1095 [M]	The Story of the Blues	1962	$25
—Black label, multi-colored spokes around "jubilee," yellow spoke goes almost to center hole; new prefix			
❏ JGS-1095 [S]	The Story of the Blues	1964	$25
—Black label, multi-colored spokes around "jubilee," yellow spoke goes nowhere near center hole			
❏ SDJLP-1095 [S]	The Story of the Blues	1962	$30
—Black label, multi-colored spokes around "jubilee," yellow spoke goes almost to center hole			
❏ JLP-1109 [M]	What Do You Know About Love	1960	$30
PICKWICK			
❏ SPC-3058	And That Reminds Me	196?	$15
RCA VICTOR			
❏ LPM-2157 [M]	Della	1960	$25

Number	Title	Yr	NM
❏ LSP-2157 [S]	Della	1960	$30
❏ LPM-2204 [M]	Della by Starlight	1960	$25
❏ LSP-2204 [S]	Della by Starlight	1960	$30
❏ LPM-2280 [M]	Della Della Cha-Cha-Cha	1961	$25
❏ LSP-2280 [S]	Della Della Cha-Cha-Cha	1961	$30
❏ LPM-2568 [M]	Della on Stage	1962	$25
❏ LSP-2568 [S]	Della on Stage	1962	$30
❏ LPM-2872 [M]	Della Reese at Basin Street East	1964	$25
❏ LSP-2872 [S]	Della Reese at Basin Street East	1964	$30
❏ LPM-2814 [M]	Moody	1963	$25
❏ LSP-2814 [S]	Moody	1963	$30
❏ LPM-2391 [M]	Special Delivery	1961	$25
❏ LSP-2391 [S]	Special Delivery	1961	$30
❏ LSP-4651	The Best of Della Reese	1972	$15
❏ LPM-2419 [M]	The Classic Della	1962	$25
❏ LSP-2419 [S]	The Classic Della	1962	$30
❏ LPM-2711 [M]	Waltz with Me, Della	1963	$25
❏ LSP-2711 [S]	Waltz with Me, Della	1963	$30

REEVES, DEL, AND BILLIE JO SPEARS

UNITED ARTISTS

Number	Title	Yr	NM
❏ UA-LA649-G	By Request: Del and Billie Jo	1976	$18

Number	Title	Yr	NM

REEVES, DEL, AND BOBBY GOLDSBORO
UNITED ARTISTS
❏ UAL3615 [M]	Our Way of Life	1967	$50
❏ UAS6615 [S]	Our Way of Life	1967	$25

REEVES, DEL
KOALA
| ❏ KO14188 | Del Reeves | 1980 | $15 |
PLAYBACK
| ❏ 12002 | Here's Del Reeves | 1988 | $18 |
STARDAY
| ❏ 998 | Greatest Hits | 197? | $12 |
SUNSET
❏ SUS-5279	Country Concert Live!	1969	$15
❏ SUS-5321	Out in the Country	1970	$15
❏ SUS-5230	Wonderful World of Country Music	1968	$15
UNITED ARTISTS
❏ UA-LA687-G	10th Anniversary	1977	$15
❏ UAS-6830	Before Goodbye	1972	$25
❏ UAS-6733	Big Daddy Del	1970	$25
❏ UAL-3441 [M]	Del Reeves Sings Girl on the Billboard	1965	$30
❏ UAS-6441 [S]	Del Reeves Sings Girl on the Billboard	1965	$30
❏ UAL-3468 [M]	Del Reeves Sings Jim Reeves	1966	$25
❏ UAS-6468 [S]	Del Reeves Sings Jim Reeves	1966	$30
❏ UA-LA364-G	Del Reeves with Strings and Things	1975	$18
❏ UAL-3458 [M]	Doodle-Oo-Doo-Doo	1965	$25
❏ UAS-6458 [S]	Doodle-Oo-Doo-Doo	1965	$30
❏ UAS-6705	Down at Good Time Charlie's	1969	$25
❏ UAS-6789	Friends and Neighbors	1971	$25
❏ UAL-3530 [M]	Gettin' Any Feed for Your Chickens?	1966	$25
❏ UAS-6530 [S]	Gettin' Any Feed for Your Chickens?	1966	$30
❏ UA-LA204-G	Live at the Palomino Club	1974	$18
❏ UAS-6674	Looking at the World Through a Windshield	1968	$25
❏ UAS-6643	Running Wild	1968	$25
❏ UAL-3528 [M]	Santa's Boy	1966	$25
❏ UAS-6528 [S]	Santa's Boy	1966	$30
❏ UAL-3595 [M]	Six of One, Half a Dozen of the Other	1967	$30
❏ UAS-6595 [S]	Six of One, Half a Dozen of the Other	1967	$25
❏ UAL-3488 [M]	Special Delivery	1966	$25
❏ UAS-6488 [S]	Special Delivery	1966	$30
❏ UAL-3571 [M]	Struttin' My Stuff	1967	$30
❏ UAS-6571 [S]	Struttin' My Stuff	1967	$25
❏ UAS-6635	The Best of Del Reeves	1968	$25
❏ UAS-6758	The Best of Del Reeves, Vol. 2	1970	$25
❏ UAS-6820	The Del Reeves Album	1971	$25
❏ UAS-6612 [S]	The Little Church in the Dell	1967	$30
❏ UAL-3612 [M]	The Little Church in the Dell	1967	$30
❏ UA-LA235	The Very Best of Del Reeves	1974	$18
❏ UA-LA044-F	Trucker's Paradise	1973	$18

REEVES, DIANNE
BLUE NOTE
| ❏ BT-46906 | Dianne Reeves | 1987 | $25 |
EMI
| ❏ E1-92401 | Never Too Far | 1990 | $30 |
PALO ALTO
| ❏ PA-8026 | Welcome to My Love | 1983 | $35 |
PALO ALTO/TBA
| ❏ TB-203 | For Every Heart | 1984 | $30 |

REEVES, JIM, AND PATSY CLINE
MCA
| ❏ 5319 | Remembering Jim Reeves and Patsy Cline | 1982 | $18 |
RCA VICTOR
| ❏ AHL1-4127 | Greatest Hits | 1981 | $18 |
| ❏ AYL1-5152 | Greatest Hits | 1984 | $12 |
—Best Buy Series" reissue

REEVES, JIM
ABBOTT
| ❏ LP-5001 [M] | Jim Reeves Sings | 1956 | $2000 |
—VG value 1000; VG+ value 1500
COUNTRY MUSIC FOUNDATION
| ❏ CMF-008 | Live at the Opry | 198? | $12 |
PAIR
| ❏ PDL2-1002 | The Country Side of Jim Reeves | 1986 | $15 |
RCA CAMDEN
❏ CAL-583 [M]	According to My Heart	1960	$25
❏ CAS-583 [R]	According to My Heart	1960	$25
❏ CAL-784 [M]	Good 'N' Country	1963	$25
❏ CAS-784 [S]	Good 'N' Country	1963	$25
❏ CAL-842 [M]	Have I Told You Lately That I Love You?	1964	$25

Number	Title	Yr	NM
❏ CAS-842 [S]	Have I Told You Lately That I Love You?	1964	$25
❏ CAX-9001	Jim Reeves	1972	$25
❏ ACL1-0123	Kimberley Jim	1973	$18
❏ CAL-686 [M]	The Country Side of Jim Reeves	1962	$25
❏ CAS-686 [S]	The Country Side of Jim Reeves	1962	$25
❏ CAS-2532	Young and Country	1971	$18

RCA VICTOR
❏ CPL1-1891	A Legendary Performer	1976	$25
❏ APL1-0039	Am I That Easy to Forget	1973	$25
❏ AHL1-4865	A Special Collection	1983	$15
❏ LPM-3987 [M]	A Touch of Sadness	1968	$75
❏ LSP-3987 [S]	A Touch of Sadness	1968	$25
❏ LPM-2487 [M]	A Touch of Velvet	1962	$30
❏ LSP-2487 [S]	A Touch of Velvet	1962	$30
❏ LPM-1410 [M]	Bimbo	1957	$250
—Reissue of Abbott LP
❏ LPM-3793 [M]	Blue Side of Lonesome	1967	$30
❏ LSP-3793 [S]	Blue Side of Lonesome	1967	$25
❏ AHL1-5424	Collector's Series	1985	$15
❏ LPM-3542 [M]	Distant Drums	1966	$25
❏ LSP-3542 [P]	Distant Drums	1966	$30
—Overnight" and "The Gods Were Angry with Me" are rechanneled
| ❏ AHL1-3454 | Don't Let Me Cross Over | 1979 | $18 |
| ❏ AYL1-4833 | Don't Let Me Cross Over | 1983 | $12 |
—Best Buy Series" reissue
| ❏ LPM-2223 [M] | Featuring He'll Have to Go and Other Favorites | 1960 | $30 |
—Black and white cover (original)
| ❏ LSP-2223 [S] | Featuring He'll Have to Go and Other Favorites | 1960 | $40 |
—Black and white cover (original)
| ❏ LPM-2223 [M] | Featuring He'll Have to Go and Other Favorites | 1962 | $25 |
—Color cover (reissue)
| ❏ LSP-2223 [S] | Featuring He'll Have to Go and Other Favorites | 1962 | $30 |
—Color cover (reissue)
❏ LPM-2605 [M]	Gentleman Jim	1963	$30
❏ LSP-2605 [S]	Gentleman Jim	1963	$30
❏ LPM-1685 [M]	Girls I Have Known	1958	$75
❏ LPM-1950 [M]	God Be With You	1958	$40
❏ LSP-1950 [S]	God Be With You	1958	$50
❏ APL1-0330	Great Moments with Jim Reeves	1973	$25
❏ APL1-0537	I'd Fight the World	1974	$25
❏ APL1-1224	I Love You Because	1976	$25
❏ AYL1-4835	I Love You Because	1983	$12
—Best Buy Series" reissue
❏ APL1-2309	It's Nothin' to Me	1977	$18
❏ LPM-1576 [M]	Jim Reeves	1957	$100
❏ AHL1-2720	Jim Reeves	1978	$18
❏ LSP-4112	Jim Reeves and Some Friends	1969	$25
❏ LSP-4062	Jim Reeves On Stage	1968	$25
❏ LSP-4475	Jim Reeves Writes You a Record	1971	$25
❏ CPL2-5044	Just for You	1984	$18
❏ LPM-2780 [M]	Kimberley Jim	1964	$30
❏ LSP-2780 [S]	Kimberley Jim	1964	$30
❏ LSP-4749	Missing You	1972	$25
❏ LPM-2854 [M]	Moonlight and Roses	1964	$30
❏ LSP-2854 [S]	Moonlight and Roses	1964	$30
❏ LPM-3903 [M]	My Cathedral	1967	$30
❏ LSP-3903 [S]	My Cathedral	1967	$30
❏ LSP-4646	My Friend	1972	$25
❏ ANL1-3014	Pure Gold, Volume 1	1978	$15
❏ AYL1-3936	Pure Gold, Volume 1	1980	$12
—Best Buy Series" reissue
❏ LPM-1256 [M]	Singing Down the Lane	1956	$250
❏ LSP-4528	Something Special	1971	$25
❏ APL1-1037	Songs of Love	1975	$25
❏ AYL1-4836	Songs of Love	1983	$12
—Best Buy Series" reissue
❏ LPM-2001 [M]	Songs to Warm the Heart	1959	$40
❏ LSP-2001 [S]	Songs to Warm the Heart	1959	$50
❏ LPM-2339 [M]	Talkin' to Your Heart	1961	$30
❏ LSP-2339 [S]	Talkin' to Your Heart	1961	$30
❏ LPM-2284 [M]	Tall Tales and Short Tempers	1961	$30
❏ LSP-2284 [S]	Tall Tales and Short Tempers	1961	$30
❏ LPM-2890 [M]	The Best of Jim Reeves	1964	$25
❏ LSP-2890 [S]	The Best of Jim Reeves	1964	$30
❏ AYL1-3678	The Best of Jim Reeves	1980	$15
—Best Buy Series" reissue
| ❏ LPM-3482 [M] | The Best of Jim Reeves, Vol. II | 1966 | $25 |
| ❏ LSP-3482(e) [P] | The Best of Jim Reeves, Vol. II | 1966 | $30 |
—This album is at least partially, and possibly entirely, in rechanneled stereo
| ❏ AYL1-4168 | The Best of Jim Reeves, Vol. II | 1981 | $12 |
—Best Buy Series" reissue
| ❏ AHL1-3271 | The Best of Jim Reeves, Volume IV | 1979 | $18 |
| ❏ AYL1-4075 | The Best of Jim Reeves, Volume IV | 1981 | $12 |
—Best Buy Series" reissue
| ❏ APL1-0793 | The Best of Jim Reeves Sacred Songs | 1974 | $25 |
| ❏ AYL1-3765 | The Best of Jim Reeves Sacred Songs | 1980 | $12 |
—Best Buy Series" reissue

Number	Title	Yr	NM
❏ AYL1-4838	The Best of Jim Reeves Vol. III	1983	$12
—Best Buy Series" reissue
❏ LSP-4187	The Best of Jim Reeves Volume III	1969	$25
❏ LPM-2704 [M]	The International Jim Reeves	1963	$30
❏ LSP-2704 [S]	The International Jim Reeves	1963	$30
❏ LPM-2216 [M]	The Intimate Jim Reeves	1960	$30
❏ LSP-2216 [S]	The Intimate Jim Reeves	1960	$40
❏ AHL1-4531	The Jim Reeves Medley	1983	$12
❏ LPM-2968 [M]	The Jim Reeves Way	1965	$25
❏ LSP-2968 [S]	The Jim Reeves Way	1965	$30
❏ AHL1-3827	There's Always Me	1980	$15
❏ AYL1-4839	There's Always Me	1983	$12
—Best Buy Series" reissue
❏ LPM-2758 [M]	Twelve Songs of Christmas	1963	$30
❏ LSP-2758 [S]	Twelve Songs of Christmas	1963	$30
❏ ANL1-1927	Twelve Songs of Christmas	1976	$10
—Reissue of LSP-2758
❏ LPM-3427 [M]	Up Through the Years	1965	$25
❏ LSP-3427 [S]	Up Through the Years	1965	$30
❏ LPM-2552 [M]	We Thank Thee	1962	$30
❏ LSP-2552 [S]	We Thank Thee	1962	$30
❏ AYL1-4840	We Thank Thee	1983	$12
—Best Buy Series" reissue
| ❏ LPM-3709 [M] | Yours Sincerely, Jim Reeves | 1966 | $25 |
| ❏ LSP-3709(e) [P] | Yours Sincerely, Jim Reeves | 1966 | $30 |
—This album is at least partially, and possibly entirely, in rechanneled stereo
TIME-LIFE
| ❏ STW-113 | Country Music | 1981 | $12 |

REEVES, MARTHA
ARISTA
| ❏ AL4105 | The Rest of My Life | 1976 | $15 |
FANTASY
| ❏ F-9591 | Gotta Keep Moving | 1980 | $15 |
| ❏ F-9549 | We'll Meet Again | 1978 | $15 |
MCA
| ❏ 414 | Martha Reeves | 1974 | $15 |

REFLECTIONS, THE (1)
GOLDEN WORLD
| ❏ 300 [M] | (Just Like) Romeo and Juliet | 1964 | $175 |

REGENT CONCERT ORCHESTRA, THE
REGENT
| ❏ 6091 [M] | Amor | 1958 | $50 |
—Cover model is Jayne Mansfield

REGENTS, THE (1)
GEE
❏ GLP-706 [M]	Barbara Ann	1961	$175
❏ SGLP-706 [S]	Barbara Ann	1961	$300
❏ SGLP-706	Barbara Ann	197?	$30
—Reissue by Publishers Central Bureau (clearly marked as such on cover)

REGENTS, THE (U)
CAPITOL
| ❏ KAO2153 [M] | Live at the AM-PM Discotheque | 1964 | $50 |
| ❏ SKAO2153 [S] | Live at the AM-PM Discotheque | 1964 | $75 |

REHAK, FRANK/ALEX SMITH
DAWN
| ❏ DLP-1107 [M] | Jazzville, Vol. 2 | 1956 | $150 |

REICH, STEVE
COLUMBIA MASTERWORKS
| ❏ MS7265 [B] | Live / Electric Music | 1968 | $60 |
ECM
❏ 11129 [B]	Music For 18 Musicians	1978	$80
❏ 11168 [B]	Octet • Music For A Large Ensemble • Violin Phase	1980	$25
❏ 11215 [B]	Tehillim	1982	$40
ELEKTRA/NONESUCH
| ❏ 9791701 [B] | Drumming | 1987 | $30 |
| ❏ 9791691 [B] | Early Works | 1987 | $50 |
NONESUCH
| ❏ 9791381-F [B] | Sextet / Six Marimbas | 1986 | $35 |
| ❏ 79101 [B] | The Desert Music | 1985 | $50 |
SUPERIOR VIADUCT
| ❏ SV096 [B] | Four Organs / Phase Patterns | 2016 | $30 |

REICHMAN, JOE
CIRCLE
| ❏ CLP-84 | The Pagliacci of the Piano | 1986 | $25 |
HINDSIGHT
| ❏ HSR-166 | Joe Reichman and His Orchestra 1944-49 | 198? | $25 |

Number	Title	Yr	NM
RCA CAMDEN			
❏ CAL-230 [M]	Show Tunes of Broadway	1954	$40
❏ CAL-133 [M]	Tea for Two	195?	$35
REID, CLARENCE			
ATCO			
❏ SD 33-307	Dancin' with Nobody But You Babe	1969	$30
REID, IRENE			
MGM			
❏ E-4159 [M]	It's Only the Beginning for Irene Reid	1963	$25
❏ SE-4159 [S]	It's Only the Beginning for Irene Reid	1963	$30
POLYDOR			
❏ 24-4040	The World Needs What I Need	1971	$35
VERVE			
❏ V-8621 [M]	Room for One More	1965	$35
❏ V6-8621 [S]	Room for One More	1965	$25
REID, RUFUS			
SUNNYSIDE			
❏ SSC-1010	Seven Minds	1985	$25
THERESA			
❏ 111	Perpetual Stroll	1980	$30
REID, TERRY			
4 MEN WITH BEARDS			
❏ 4M108LP [B]	River		$25
ABC			
❏ X-935	Seed of Memory	1976	$15
ATLANTIC			
❏ SD7259	River	1973	$15
CAPITOL			
❏ SW-11857	Rogue Waves	1978	$15
EPIC			
❏ BN26427	Bang, Bang You're Terry Reid	1968	$18
❏ BN26477	Terry Reid	1969	$18
REILLY, JACK			
CAROUSEL			
❏ 1001	Blue-Sean-Green	197?	$35
❏ 1002	Tributes	197?	$35
REVELATION			
❏ 36	Brinksman	198?	$25
❏ 35	Together (Again)… For the First Time	198?	$25
REINER, CARL, AND MEL BROOKS			
CAPITOL			
❏ W1618 [M]	2000 and One Years	1961	$18
❏ SW1618 [S]	2000 and One Years	1961	$25
❏ W1529 [M]	2000 Years	1961	$18
❏ SW1529 [S]	2000 Years	1961	$25
❏ W1815 [M]	At the Cannes Film Festival	1962	$18
❏ SW1815 [S]	At the Cannes Film Festival	1962	$25
❏ ST2981	The Best of the 2000 Year Old Man	1968	$18
WARNER BROS.			
❏ BS2741	2000 and Thirteen	1973	$18
❏ 3XX2744	The Incomplete Works of Reiner and Brooks	1973	$30
WORLD PACIFIC			
❏ WP-1401 [M]	2000 Years	1960	$30
REINHARDT, DJANGO			
ANGEL			
❏ ANG-36985	Django Reinhardt and the Quintet of the Hot Club of France	197?	$25
❏ ANG.60011 [10]	Django's Guitar	1955	$175
❏ ANG.60003 [10]	Le Jazz Hot	1954	$175
BLUEBIRD			
❏ 9988-1-RB	Djangology 49	1990	$30
CAPITOL			
❏ TBO10226 [M]	The Best of Django Reinhardt	1960	$100
—Black colorband labels, Capitol logo at left			
CLEF			
❏ MGC-516 [10]	The Great Artistry of Django Reinhardt	1954	$300
COLUMBIA			
❏ C31479	Swing It Lightly	1972	$30
❏ PC31479	Swing It Lightly	198?	$20
—Budget-line reissue			
EMARCY			
❏ 66004	Jazz Hot	1967	$150
EPITAPH			
❏ E-4002	Django Reinhardt 1910-1953	1975	$35

Number	Title	Yr	NM
EVEREST ARCHIVE OF FOLK & JAZZ			
❏ FS-212 [R]	Django Reinhardt	1968	$25
❏ FS-255	Django Reinhardt, Vol. 3	197?	$25
❏ FS-306	Django Reinhardt, Vol. 4	197?	$25
❏ FS-230 [R]	Django Reinhardt, Volume II	1969	$25
GNP CRESCENDO			
❏ GNP-9031	Django Reinhardt 1934	197?	$25
❏ GNP-9023	Django Reinhardt 1935	197?	$25
❏ GNP-9019	Django Reinhardt 1935-39	197?	$25
❏ GNP-9001	Django Reinhardt and the Quintet of the Hot Club of France	196?	$25
❏ GNP-9039	Legendary Django Reinhardt	198?	$25
❏ GNP-9002	Parisian Swing	197?	$25
❏ GNP-9038	The Immortal Django Reinhardt	198?	$25
INNER CITY			
❏ IC-1106	Compositions	198?	$30
❏ IC-1104	Django Reinhardt and the Quintet of the Hot Club of France	198?	$30
❏ IC-1105	Solos/Duos/Trios, Vol. 2	198?	$30
❏ IC-7004	The Versatile Giant	198?	$30
JAY			
❏ 3008 [10]	Django Reinhardt	1954	$180
MERCURY			
❏ MGC-516 [10]	The Great Artistry of Django Reinhardt	1953	$300
PERIOD			
❏ SPL-1100 [10]	Django Reinhardt Memorial, Volume 1	1954	$120
❏ SPL-1101 [10]	Django Reinhardt Memorial, Volume 2	1954	$120
❏ SPL-1102 [10]	Django Reinhardt Memorial, Volume 3	1954	$120
❏ SPL-1201 [M]	Django Reinhardt Memorial Album, Volume 1	1956	$50
❏ SPL-1201 [M]	Django Reinhardt Memorial Album, Volume 2	1956	$50
❏ SPL-1203 [M]	Django Reinhardt Memorial Album, Volume 3	1956	$50
❏ SPL-1204 [M]	The Best of Django Reinhardt	1956	$50
❏ SPL-2204 [R]	The Best of Django Reinhardt	196?	$30
PRESTIGE			
❏ PRST-7633 [R]	Django Reinhardt and American Jazz Giants	1969	$35
RCA VICTOR			
❏ LPM-2319 [M]	Djangology	1961	$40
❏ LSP-2319 [R]	Djangology	196?	$30
❏ LPM-1100 [M]	Django Reinhardt	1955	$150
REPRISE			
❏ R-6075 [M]	The Immortal Django Reinhardt	1963	$30
❏ R9-6075 [R]	The Immortal Django Reinhardt	1963	$35
SUTTON			
❏ SU-274 [M]	Django Reinhardt and His Guitar	1966	$25
❏ SSU-274 [R]	Django Reinhardt and His Guitar	1966	$30
SWING			
❏ SW-8420/7	Djangologie USA Volumes 1-7	1988	$75
REMAINS, THE			
EPIC			
❏ LN24214 [M]	The Remains	1966	$250
❏ BN26214 [S]	The Remains	1966	$300
SPOONFED			
❏ SFD-3205	The Remains	1978	$18
—Red vinyl			
SUNDAZED			
❏ LP5015	A Session with the Remains	199?	$12
❏ LP5055	The Remains	1999	$15
❏ SEP 10-162 [10]	The Remains	2000	$10
REMINGTON, DAVE			
JUBILEE			
❏ JLP-1017 [M]	Chicago Jazz Reborn	1956	$40
TEMPUS			
❏ TL-101 [M]	Danceable Dixieland Jazz	1958	$40
VEE JAY			
❏ LP-3030 [M]	Dixie Chicago Style	1962	$25
❏ SR-3030 [S]	Dixie Chicago Style	1962	$30
❏ LP-3009 [M]	Dixie on the Rocks	1960	$30
❏ SR-3009 [S]	Dixie on the Rocks	1960	$30
REMINGTON, HERB			
D			
❏ 1376	Herby Remington Plays the Steel	197?	$15
HILLTOP			
❏ JM-6020 [M]	Herby Remington Rides Again	196?	$18
❏ JS-6020 [S]	Herby Remington Rides Again	196?	$15

Number	Title	Yr	NM
STONEWAY			
❏ 138	Pure Remington Steel	197?	$15
UNITED ARTISTS			
❏ UAL-3167 [M]	Steel Guitar Holiday	1961	$30
❏ UAS-6167 [S]	Steel Guitar Holiday	1961	$30
REMINGTON, RITA			
HILLTOP			
❏ JS-6050	The Loretta Lynn Songbook	197?	$15
PLANTATION			
❏ 511	Country Girl Gold	197?	$15
REMLER, EMILY			
CONCORD JAZZ			
❏ CJ-265	Catwalk	1985	$25
❏ CJ-356	East to Wes	1988	$25
❏ CJ-162	Firefly	1981	$25
❏ CJ-195	Take Two	1982	$25
❏ CJ-236	Transitions	1984	$25
RENA, KID			
CIRCLE			
❏ L-409 [10]	Kid Rena Delta Jazz Band	1951	$100
RENAISSANCE			
CAPITOL/SOVEREIGN			
❏ ST-11216	Ashes Are Burning	1973	$18
❏ SWBC-11871	In the Beginning	1978	$18
—Combines 11116 and 11216 in one package			
❏ SMAS-11116	Prologue	1972	$18
ELEKTRA			
❏ EKS-74068 [B]	Renaissance	1969	$35
I.R.S.			
❏ SP-70019	Camera Camera	1981	$12
❏ SP-70033	Time Line	1983	$12
MOBILE FIDELITY			
❏ Jan-0099	Scheherazade and Other Stories	1982	$75
—Audiophile vinyl			
SIRE			
❏ SRK6049	A Song for All Seasons	1978	$15
❏ SRK6068	Azure d'Or	1979	$15
❏ SASD-3902	Live at Carnegie Hall	1976	$18
❏ 2XS6029	Live at Carnegie Hall	1977	$15
—Reissue of 3902			
❏ SASD-7526	Novella	1977	$15
❏ SR6024	Novella	1977	$12
—Reissue of 7526			
❏ SASD-7510	Scheherazade and Other Stories	1975	$15
❏ SR6017	Scheherazade and Other Stories	1977	$12
—Reissue of 7510			
❏ SAS-7502	Turn of the Cards	1974	$15
❏ SR6015	Turn of the Cards	1977	$12
—Reissue of 7502			
RENAUD, HENRI			
CONTEMPORARY			
❏ C-2502 [10]	The Henri Renaud All-Stars	1953	$300
PERIOD			
❏ SPL-1211 [M]	The Birdlanders	1954	$100
❏ SPL-1212 [M]	The Birdlanders	1954	$100
RENAY, DIANE			
20TH CENTURY FOX			
❏ TF-3133 [M]	Navy Blue	1964	$100
❏ TFS-4133 [S]	Navy Blue	1964	$175
RENDELL, DON			
JAZZLAND			
❏ JLP-51 [M]	Roarin'	1961	$30
❏ JLP-951 [S]	Roarin'	1961	$40
RENE, GOOGIE			
CLASS			
❏ LP-5001 [M]	Beautiful Weekend	1957	$30
❏ LP-200 [M]	Flapjacks	1963	$25
❏ LP-5003 [M]	Googie Rene Presents Romesville	1959	$30
RENDEZVOUS			
❏ M-1311 [M]	Beautiful Weekend	196?	$18
❏ M-1313 [S]	Romseville	196?	$18
RENE, HENRI			
IMPERIAL			
❏ LP-9096 [M]	Swingin' 59	1960	$175
❏ LP-12040 [S]	Swingin' 59	1960	$175
❏ LP-9074 [M]	White Heat	1959	$200
❏ LP-12021 [S]	White Heat	1959	$200
RCA CAMDEN			
❏ CAL-312 [M]	In Love Again	195?	$35
❏ CAL-353 [M]	Melodic Magic	195?	$35
❏ CAL-130 [M]	Portfolio for Easy Listening	195?	$35

Number	Title	Yr	NM

RCA VICTOR

Number	Title	Yr	NM
❑ LPM-1947 [M]	Compulsion to Swing	1958	$30
❑ LSP-1947 [S]	Compulsion to Swing	1958	$30
❑ LSA-2396 [S]	Dynamic Dimensions	1961	$30
❑ LPM-3076 [10]	Listen to Rene	1953	$40
❑ LPM-1046 [M]	Music for Bachelors	1955	$120

—Cover model is Jayne Mansfield

Number	Title	Yr	NM
❑ LPM-1583 [M]	Music for the Weaker Sex	1957	$30
❑ LPM-1033 [M]	Passion in Paint	1955	$100
❑ LPM-2002 [M]	Riot in Rhythm	1959	$25
❑ LSP-2002 [S]	Riot in Rhythm	1959	$30
❑ LPM-3049 [10]	Serenade to Love	1953	$40

RENE AND RENE

WHITE WHALE

Number	Title	Yr	NM
❑ WWS-7119	Lo Mucho Que Te Quiero	1968	$18

RENO, DON, AND BILL HARRELL

JALYN

Number	Title	Yr	NM
❑ JLP-108 [M]	Bluegrass Favorites	1964	$30
❑ JLP-119 [M]	The Most Requested Songs	1966	$30

KING

Number	Title	Yr	NM
❑ KSD-1033	All the Way to Reno	1968	$25
❑ KSD-1029	A Variety of New Sacred Gospel Songs	1968	$25
❑ KSD-1068	I'm Using My Bible for a Roadmap	1969	$25

RENO, JACK

ATCO

Number	Title	Yr	NM
❑ SD 33-251	Meet Jack Reno	1968	$30

DERBYTOWN

Number	Title	Yr	NM
❑ 101	Yellow Pages	197?	$25

DOT

Number	Title	Yr	NM
❑ DLP25946	I'm a Good Man in a Bad Frame of Mind	1969	$30
❑ DLP25921	I Want One	1968	$30

TARGET

Number	Title	Yr	NM
❑ 1313	Hitchin' a Ride	1972	$25

RENO, RONNIE

MCA

Number	Title	Yr	NM
❑ 472	For the First Time	1974	$15

RENO AND SMILEY

DOT

Number	Title	Yr	NM
❑ DLP-3490 [M]	Bluegrass Hits	1963	$30
❑ DLP-25490 [S]	Bluegrass Hits	1963	$30

KING

Number	Title	Yr	NM
❑ 914 [M]	A Bluegrass Tribute to Cowboy Copas	1964	$100
❑ 816 [M]	Another Day with Reno and Smiley	1962	$100
❑ 646 [M]	A Variety of Country Songs	1959	$150
❑ 787 [M]	Banjo Special	1962	$100
❑ 776 [M]	Country Singing and Instrumentals	1962	$100
❑ 701 [M]	Country Songs	1959	$150
❑ 579 [M]	Folk Ballads and Instrumentals	1958	$150
❑ 756 [M]	Folk Songs of the Civil War	1961	$150
❑ 621 [M]	Good Old Country Ballads	1959	$150
❑ 693 [M]	Hymns Sacred and Gospel	1959	$150
❑ KSD-1044	I Know You're Married	1969	$30
❑ 911 [M]	On the Road with Reno and Smiley	1964	$100
❑ 552 [M]	Reno and Smiley Instrumentals	1958	$150
❑ 550 [M]	Sacred Songs	1958	$120
❑ 617 [M]	Someone Will Love Me in Heaven	1959	$150
❑ 853 [M]	The 15 Greatest Hymns of All Time	1963	$100
❑ KSD-1091	The Best of Reno and Smiley	1970	$30
❑ 874 [M]	The True Meaning of Christmas	1963	$150
❑ 874 [M]	The True Meaning of Christmas	1963	$100
❑ 861 [M]	The World's Best Five String Banjo	1963	$100
❑ 718 [M]	Wanted	1961	$150

RENTIE, DAMON

PALO ALTO/TBA

Number	Title	Yr	NM
❑ TB-212	Designated Hitter	198?	$25
❑ TB-219	Don't Look Back	1986	$25
❑ TB-230	Skyline	1987	$25

RENZI, MIKE

STASH

Number	Title	Yr	NM
❑ ST-273	A Beautiful Friendship	1988	$25

REO SPEEDWAGON

EPIC

Number	Title	Yr	NM
❑ KE236444	A Decade of Rock and Roll 1970 to 1980	1980	$15
❑ FE38100	Good Trouble	1982	$12
❑ PE38100	Good Trouble	198?	$10

—Budget-line reissue

Number	Title	Yr	NM
❑ HE48100	Good Trouble	1982	$30

—Half-speed mastered edition

Number	Title	Yr	NM
❑ FE36844	Hi Infidelity	1980	$10
❑ HE46844	Hi Infidelity	1982	$30

—Half-speed mastered edition

Number	Title	Yr	NM
❑ FE40444	Life As We Know It	1987	$10
❑ PE32948	Lost in a Dream	1974	$15

—Orange label

Number	Title	Yr	NM
❑ PE32948	Lost in a Dream	1979	$10

—Dark blue label

Number	Title	Yr	NM
❑ PEQ32948 [Q]	Lost in a Dream	1974	$30
❑ FE35988	Nine Lives	1979	$12
❑ PE35988	Nine Lives	198?	$10

—Budget-line reissue

Number	Title	Yr	NM
❑ PE34143	R.E.O.	1976	$15

—Orange label

Number	Title	Yr	NM
❑ PE34143	R.E.O.	1979	$10

—Dark blue label

Number	Title	Yr	NM
❑ E31089	REO Speedwagon	1972	$18

—Yellow label original

Number	Title	Yr	NM
❑ KE31089	REO Speedwagon	1973	$15

—Orange label

Number	Title	Yr	NM
❑ PE31089	REO Speedwagon	1979	$10

—Dark blue label

Number	Title	Yr	NM
❑ PEG34494	REO Speedwagon Live/You Get What You Play For	1977	$18

—Orange labels

Number	Title	Yr	NM
❑ PEG34494	REO Speedwagon Live/You Get What You Play For	1979	$15

—Dark blue labels

Number	Title	Yr	NM
❑ KE31745	R.E.O./T.W.O.	1972	$18

—Yellow label original

Number	Title	Yr	NM
❑ KE31745	R.E.O./T.W.O.	1973	$15

—Orange label

Number	Title	Yr	NM
❑ PE31745	R.E.O./T.W.O.	1979	$10

—Dark blue label

Number	Title	Yr	NM
❑ KE32378	Ridin' the Storm Out	1973	$15

—Orange label

Number	Title	Yr	NM
❑ PE32378	Ridin' the Storm Out	1979	$10

—Dark blue label

Number	Title	Yr	NM
❑ E45246	The Earth, a Small Man, His Dog and a Chicken	1990	$15
❑ OE44202	The Hits	1988	$12
❑ PE33338	This Time We Mean It	1975	$15

—Orange label

Number	Title	Yr	NM
❑ PE33338	This Time We Mean It	1979	$10

—Dark blue label

Number	Title	Yr	NM
❑ PEQ33338 [Q]	This Time We Mean It	1975	$30
❑ QE39593	Wheels Are Turnin'	1984	$10
❑ JE35082	You Can Tune a Piano, But You Can't Tuna Fish	1978	$15

—Orange label; no bar code on back cover

Number	Title	Yr	NM
❑ JE35082	You Can Tune a Piano, But You Can't Tuna Fish	1978	$12

—Orange label; with bar code on back cover

Number	Title	Yr	NM
❑ JE35082	You Can Tune a Piano, But You Can't Tuna Fish	1979	$10

—Dark blue label

Number	Title	Yr	NM
❑ PE35082	You Can Tune a Piano, But You Can't Tuna Fish	198?	$10
❑ HE45082	You Can Tune a Piano, But You Can't Tuna Fish	198?	$40

—Half-speed mastered edition

REPARATA AND THE DELRONS

AVCO EMBASSY

Number	Title	Yr	NM
❑ AVE-33008	Rock and Roll Revolution	1970	$30

WORLD ARTISTS

Number	Title	Yr	NM
❑ WAM-2006 [M]	Whenever a Teenager Cries	1965	$50
❑ WAS-3006 [S]	Whenever a Teenager Cries	1965	$75

REPERCUSSION UNIT

CMP

Number	Title	Yr	NM
❑ CMP-31-ST	In Need Again	1987	$25

REPLACEMENTS, THE

Featuring PAUL WESTERBERG.

RHINO

Number	Title	Yr	NM
❑ 25557	Pleased to Meet Me	2008	$25
❑ R1548945 [B]	The Sire Years	2016	$80
❑ 25330	Tim	2008	$25

SIRE

Number	Title	Yr	NM
❑ PRO-A-4632 [DJ]	Don't Sell Or Buy...It's Crap	1991	$30

—Promo-only 5-track sampler

Number	Title	Yr	NM
❑ R101024	Don't Tell a Soul	1989	$18

—BMG Music Service edition

Number	Title	Yr	NM
❑ 25831	Don't Tell a Soul	1989	$15
❑ PRO-A-3633 [DJ]	Live Inconcerated	1989	$50

—Five live tracks and one studio track, each of which is repeated on the other side

Number	Title	Yr	NM
❑ 25557	Pleased to Meet Me	1987	$15
❑ 25330	Tim	1985	$15

TWIN/TONE

Number	Title	Yr	NM
❑ TTR8332 [B]	Hootenanny	1983	$30
❑ R1773760 [B]	Hootenanny	2016	$30
❑ TTR8441 [B]	Let It Be	1984	$30
❑ R1773761 [B]	Let It Be	2016	$25
❑ TTR8123 [B]	Sorry, Ma, Forgot to Take Out the Trash	1981	$30

Number	Title	Yr	NM
❑ R1773762 [B]	Sorry Ma, Forgot To Take Out The Trash	2016	$25
❑ R1773763 [B]	Stink ("Kids Don't Follow" Plus Seven)	2016	$25
❑ TTR8228 [EP]	The Replacements Stink	1982	$30

WARNER BROS.

Number	Title	Yr	NM
❑ WBMS-148 [DJ]	An Interview with Paul Westerberg	1987	$50

—Part of "The Warner Bros. Music Show" promotional series

REPRISE REPERTORY THEATRE, THE

Artists who were signed to Reprise Records at the time, including ROSEMARY CLOONEY, BING CROSBY, SAMMY DAVIS, JR., DEAN MARTIN, FRANK SINATRA and JO STAFFORD, perform new versions of famous musicals under this collective name.

REPRISE

Number	Title	Yr	NM
❑ F-2015 [M]	Finian's Rainbow	1964	$30

—Gatefold cover

Number	Title	Yr	NM
❑ F-2015 [M]	Finian's Rainbow	196?	$25

—Standard cover

Number	Title	Yr	NM
❑ FS-2015 [S]	Finian's Rainbow	1964	$40

—Gatefold cover

Number	Title	Yr	NM
❑ FS-2015 [S]	Finian's Rainbow	196?	$30

—Standard cover

Number	Title	Yr	NM
❑ F-2016 [M]	Guys and Dolls	1964	$30

—Gatefold cover

Number	Title	Yr	NM
❑ F-2016 [M]	Guys and Dolls	196?	$25

—Standard cover

Number	Title	Yr	NM
❑ FS-2016 [S]	Guys and Dolls	1964	$40

—Gatefold cover

Number	Title	Yr	NM
❑ FS-2016 [S]	Guys and Dolls	196?	$30

—Standard cover

Number	Title	Yr	NM
❑ F-2017 [M]	Kiss Me, Kate	1964	$30

—Gatefold cover

Number	Title	Yr	NM
❑ F-2017 [M]	Kiss Me, Kate	196?	$25

—Standard cover

Number	Title	Yr	NM
❑ FS-2017 [S]	Kiss Me, Kate	1964	$40

—Gatefold cover

Number	Title	Yr	NM
❑ FS-2017 [S]	Kiss Me, Kate	196?	$30

—Standard cover

Number	Title	Yr	NM
❑ F-2018 [M]	South Pacific	1964	$30

—Gatefold cover

Number	Title	Yr	NM
❑ F-2018 [M]	South Pacific	196?	$25

—Standard cover

Number	Title	Yr	NM
❑ FS-2018 [S]	South Pacific	1964	$40

—Gatefold cover

Number	Title	Yr	NM
❑ FS-2018 [S]	South Pacific	196?	$30

—Standard cover

Number	Title	Yr	NM
❑ F-2019 [M]	The Reprise Repertory Theatre	1964	$250

—Box set of all four of the above LPs in gatefold covers

Number	Title	Yr	NM
❑ FS-2019 [S]	The Reprise Repertory Theatre	1964	$300

—Box set of all four of the above LPs in gatefold covers

RESIDENTS, THE

CRYPTIC

Number	Title	Yr	NM
❑ S-18335SP-2	For Elsie	1987	$150

—Green vinyl one-sided LP

ENIGMA

Number	Title	Yr	NM
❑ 73547	The King & Eye	1989	$18

EPISODE

Number	Title	Yr	NM
❑ ED21	The Census Taker (Soundtrack)	1985	$100

—Red vinyl

Number	Title	Yr	NM
❑ ED21	The Census Taker (Soundtrack)	1985	$25

RALPH

Number	Title	Yr	NM
❑ RR 0278 [B]	Duck Stab	1978	$50

—First version: Green titles box on back

Number	Title	Yr	NM
❑ RR 0278 [B]	Duck Stab	1978	$40

—Second version: Yellow titles box on back

Number	Title	Yr	NM
❑ RR87521 [B]	Duck Stab	1988	$18

—New number, red vinyl

Number	Title	Yr	NM
❑ RR87521	Duck Stab	1988	$12

—New number, black vinyl

Number	Title	Yr	NM
❑ ESK7906 [B]	Eskimo	1979	$75

—First version: White vinyl, gatefold cover

Number	Title	Yr	NM
❑ ESK7906 [B]	Eskimo	1979	$50

—Second version: Black vinyl, gatefold

Number	Title	Yr	NM
❑ ESK7906 [B]	Eskimo	1979	$40

—Third version: Black vinyl, standard cover

Number	Title	Yr	NM
❑ RZ7906 [PD]	Eskimo	1979	$30

—Picture disc

Number	Title	Yr	NM
❑ RR1276	Fingerprince	1977	$100

—First version: Dark brown cover, "First Pressing" written on back cover

Number	Title	Yr	NM
❑ RR1276	Fingerprince	1977	$25

—Second version: Lighter brown cover

Number	Title	Yr	NM
❑ RR1276	Fingerprince	1977	$12

—Third version: Color cover

Number	Title	Yr	NM
❑ RR82761	Fingerprince	1988	$15

—New number, purple vinyl

Number	Title	Yr	NM
❑ RR82761	Fingerprince	1988	$12

—New number, black vinyl

Number	Title	Yr	NM
❑ OP-011 [PD]	Freak Show	1991	$80

—Picture disc

❑ OP-011 [DJ]	Freak Show	1991	$175

—Promo-only black vinyl pressing; 400 made

❑ RZ8402	George & James	1984	$30

—First edition: Rejected mix with "Re-1" in trail-off

❑ RZ8402	George & James	1984	$12

—Second edition: Approved mix with "Re-5" in trail-off

❑ RZ8402	George & James	1984	$50

—Re-5" in trail-off, clear vinyl

❑ RZ8252	Intermission	1982	$14

—Red vinyl

❑ RZ8252	Intermission	1982	$15
❑ RZ8152	Mark of the Mole	1981	$50

—Signed brown vinyl edition with lyrics

❑ RZ8152	Mark of the Mole	1981	$12
❑ RR 0274	Meet the Residents	1974	$250

—First version: "Meet the Beatles" LP parody cover and "First Edition" on back cover

❑ RR 0677 [B]	Meet the Residents	1977	$175

—Second version: "She Loves You" picture sleeve parody cover, split "a" Ralph logo

❑ RR 0677 [B]	Meet the Residents	1977	$150

—Third version: same cover as second version, black "a" Ralph logo

❑ RR 0677 [B]	Meet the Residents	1977	$100

—Fourth version: same cover as second version, modified and orange back cover

❑ RR88521	Meet the Residents	1988	$18

—Original "Meet the Beatles" parody cover restored, white vinyl

❑ RR88521	Meet the Residents	1988	$15

—Original "Meet the Beatles" parody cover restored, black vinyl

❑ RZ7707 [PD]	Meet the Residents	1986	$30

—Picture disc, with original cover on one side, replacement cover on other

❑ RR1174	Not Available	1978	$30

—Purple label, mis-mastered, "Re-1" in trail-off vinyl

❑ RR1174	Not Available	1978	$18

—Orange label, remastered, "Re-3" in trail-off vinyl

❑ RR1174	Not Available	1978	$15

—Green label, address is "444 Grove

❑ RR1174	Not Available	1978	$12

—Green label, address is "109 Minna

❑ DJ7901 [DJ]	Please Do Not Steal It!	1979	$40

—Promo-only sampler

❑ RZ8302	Residue	1983	$15
❑ RZ8652	Stars & Hank Forever	1986	$40

—Blue vinyl

❑ RZ8652	Stars & Hank Forever	1986	$12
❑ RZ8552	The Big Bubble	1985	$100

—Pink vinyl

❑ RZ8552	The Big Bubble	1985	$15
❑ RZ8602	The Eyeball Show (The 13th Anniversary Show) Live in Japan	1986	$100

—White vinyl

❑ RZ8602	The Eyeball Show (The 13th Anniversary Show) Live in Japan	1986	$12
❑ Mole Show 001	The Mole Show (The Roxy)	1983	$30
❑ C-002A	The Mole Show (The Roxy)	1983	$40

—Picture disc

❑ RZ8052	The Residents Commercial Album	1980	$25

—First version: Purple Ralph logo, songs listed in wrong order

❑ RZ8052	The Residents Commercial Album	1980	$18

—Second version: Corrected song order, green logo

❑ RZ8052	The Residents Commercial Album	1980	$15

—Third version: Green vinyl

❑ RR1075 [B]	The Third Reich 'N' Roll	1976	$250

—First version of 1,000: Liner notes inside, orange carrot

❑ RR1075 [B]	The Third Reich 'N' Roll	1976	$175

—Second version: Gray carrot, split "a" Ralph logo

❑ RR1075	The Third Reich 'N' Roll	1976	$15

—Third version: Orange carrot, black "a" Ralph logo

❑ RR1075	The Third Reich 'N' Roll	1976	$12

—Fourth version: Gray carrot, black "a" Ralph logo

❑ RR1075	The Third Reich 'N' Roll	1976	$1500

—Numbered box set on marbled vinyl, silkscreened cover and lithographs inside

❑ RR1075 [B]	The Third Reich 'N' Roll	1976	$150

—Censored cover with swastikas obscured, pressed in U.S. for export to Germany

❑ RZ8202	The Tunes of Two Cities	1982	$15

—First edition: "444 Grove Street" address

❑ RZ8202	The Tunes of Two Cities	1982	$12

—Second edition: "109 Minna Street" address

❑ RR8315	Title in Limbo	1983	$15

—With Renaldo and The Loaf

❑ RZ8452	Whatever Happened to Vileness Fats?	1984	$100

—Red vinyl

Number	Title	Yr	NM
❑ RZ8452	Whatever Happened to Vileness Fats?	1984	$15

RYKO ANALOGUE

❑ RALP-0044-2 [B]	God in Three Persons	1988	$40

—Clear vinyl

❑ RALP-0045-2	God in Three Persons Instrumental	1988	$18

—Clear vinyl

UWEB

❑ 0011	Stranger Than Supper	1990	$30

—Fan club issue

RESNICK, ART
CAPRI

❑ 74015	A Gift	198?	$25

SYMPOSIUM

❑ 2005	Jungleopolis	197?	$35

RESTIVO, JOHNNY
RCA VICTOR

❑ LPM-2149 [M]	Oh, Johnny!	1959	$75
❑ LSP-2149 [S]	Oh, Johnny!	1959	$150

RESTLESS HEART
RCA

❑ 8317-1-R	Big Dreams in a Small Town	1988	$10
❑ 9961-1-R	Fast Movin' Train	1990	$15
❑ 5648-1-R	Wheels	1986	$10

RCA VICTOR

❑ CPL1-5369	Restless Heart	1985	$10

RESTUM, WILLIE
GONE

❑ LP-5011 [M]	Willie Restum at the Dream Lounge	1960	$300

ROULETTE

❑ R-25152 [M]	Dream Bar	1961	$75

RETURN TO FOREVER
COLUMBIA

❑ PC34682	Musicmagic	1977	$30

—No bar code on cover

❑ PC34682	Musicmagic	1985	$20

—Reissue with bar code

❑ PCQ34682 [Q]	Musicmagic	1977	$75
❑ JC35281	Return to Forever Live	1979	$25
❑ PC34076	Romantic Warrior	1976	$30

—No bar code on cover

❑ PC34076	Romantic Warrior	198?	$20

—Reissue with bar code

❑ JC36359	The Best of Return to Forever	1980	$30
❑ PC36359	The Best of Return to Forever	198?	$25

—Budget-line reissue with new prefix

ECM

❑ 1022ST	Return to Forever	197?	$35

—Original issue; made in Germany

❑ ECM-1-1022	Return to Forever	197?	$30

—Distributed by Polydor

POLYDOR

❑ PD-5536	Hymn of the Seventh Galaxy	1973	$30
❑ 825336-1	Hymn of the Seventh Galaxy	198?	$20

—Reissue

❑ PD-5525	Light as a Feather	1973	$30
❑ PD-6512	No Mystery	1975	$30
❑ PD-6509	Where Have I Known You Before	1974	$30

REVELERS, THE
RONDO-LETTE

❑ A-50 [M]	Jazz at the Downstairs Club	1962	$25
❑ SA-50 [S]	Jazz at the Downstairs Club	1962	$30

REVELLS, THE
REPRISE

❑ R-6160 [M]	The Go Sound of the Slots	1965	$175
❑ RS-6160 [S]	The Go Sound of the Slots	1965	$250

REVELS, THE (2)
IMPACT

❑ LPM-1 [M]	Revels on a Rampage	1964	$500

SUNDAZED

❑ LP5010	Intoxica! The Best of the Revels	1994	$12

REVENGERS, THE
METRO

❑ M-565 [M]	Batman and Other Supermen	1966	$30
❑ MS-565 [S]	Batman and Other Supermen	1966	$40

Number	Title	Yr	NM

REVERBERI
PAUSA

❑ 7003	Reverberi and ...	198?	$25
❑ 7016	Timer	198?	$25

UNITED ARTISTS

❑ UA-LA813-H	Stairway to Heaven	1977	$30

REVERE, PAUL, AND THE RAIDERS
COLUMBIA

❑ CL2755 [M]	A Christmas Present… And Past	1967	$75
❑ CS9555 [S]	A Christmas Present… And Past	1967	$30
❑ CS9905	Alias Pink Puzz	1969	$25
❑ KG31464	All-Time Greatest Hits	1972	$25
❑ CS9964	Collage	1970	$25
❑ KC31106	Country Wine	1972	$18
❑ CL2805 [M]	Goin' to Memphis	1968	$100
❑ CS9605 [S]	Goin' to Memphis	1968	$25
❑ KCL2662 [M]	Greatest Hits	1967	$30

—Add 20% if booklet is included; at least some copies actually are stereo with the "XSS" prefix on the label's master numbers rather than "XLP," though we don't know if all of them are

❑ KCS9462 [P]	Greatest Hits	1967	$30

—Add 20% if booklet is included

❑ PC35593	Greatest Hits	1978	$12
❑ C30386	Greatest Hits, Volume 2	1971	$25
❑ CS9753	Hard 'N' Heavy (With Marshmallow)	1969	$25

—Black and white cover

❑ CS9753	Hard 'N' Heavy (With Marshmallow)	1969	$30

—Color cover

❑ CL2307 [M]	Here They Come!	1965	$30

—Guaranteed High Fidelity" on label

❑ CL2307 [M]	Here They Come!	1965	$25

—360 Sound Mono" on label

❑ CS9107 [S]	Here They Come!	1965	$40

—360 Sound Stereo" in black on label

❑ CS9107 [S]	Here They Come!	1965	$30

—360 Sound Stereo" in white on label

❑ C30768	Indian Reservation	1971	$18
❑ CL2451 [M]	Just Like Us!	1966	$30
❑ CS9251 [S]	Just Like Us!	1966	$30
❑ CL2508 [M]	Midnight Ride	1966	$30
❑ CS9308 [S]	Midnight Ride	1966	$30
❑ CL2721 [M]	Revolution!	1967	$30
❑ CS9521 [S]	Revolution!	1967	$30
❑ CS9665	Something Happening	1968	$25
❑ CL2595 [M]	The Spirit of '67	1966	$30

❑ CS9395 [S]	The Spirit of '67	1966	$30
❑ GP12	Two All Time Great Selling LPs	1969	$30

—Combines 9395 and 9521 in one package; red labels

❑ GP12	Two All Time Great Selling LPs	1971	$25

—Combines 9395 and 9521 in one package; orange labels

COLUMBIA LIMITED EDITION

❑ LE10170 [S]	Midnight Ride	197?	$18

—Reissue of 9308

COLUMBIA SPECIAL PRODUCTS

❑ P13512	Goin' to Memphis	197?	$18

ERA

❑ NU5880	The Great Raider Reunion	1983	$15

—Re-recordings

GARDENA

❑ LP-G-1000 [M]	Like, Long Hair	1961	$600

HARMONY

❑ KH30975	Good Thing	1971	$15
❑ KH31183	Movin' On	1972	$15
❑ H30089	Paul Revere and the Raiders Featuring Mark Lindsay	1970	$15

Number	Title	Yr	NM
JERDEN			
❑ JRL-7004 [M]	Paul Revere and the Raiders In the Beginning	1966	$100
❑ JRS-7004 [R]	Paul Revere and the Raiders In the Beginning	1966	$30
❑ T-90709 [M]	Paul Revere and the Raiders In the Beginning	1966	$80
— Capitol Record Club edition			
❑ DT-90709 [R]	Paul Revere and the Raiders In the Beginning	1966	$50
— Capitol Record Club edition			
PICKWICK			
❑ SPC-3176 [R]	Paul Revere and the Raiders	1969	$12
SANDE			
❑ S-1001 [M]	Paul Revere and the Raiders	1963	$1200
— Original version with "Sande" and no mention of "Etiquette" in trail-off area			
❑ S-1001 [M]	Paul Revere and the Raiders	1979	$30
— Legitimate reissue with "Sande" and "Etiquette" in trail-off area			
SEARS			
❑ SPS-493	Paul Revere and the Raiders	1969	$30
REVEREND HORTON HEAT			
SUB POP			
❑ 250	Liquor in the Front	1994	$15
❑ 96 [10]	Smoke 'Em If You Got 'Em	1991	$15
❑ 202	The Full Custom Gospel Sounds of Reverend Horton Heat	1993	$15
REVOLTING COCKS			
WAX TRAX!			
❑ 7063 [B]	Beers Steers and Queers	1990	$18
❑ 017 [B]	Big Sexy Land	1986	$18
❑ 037 [B]	You Goddamned Son of a Bitch	1988	$18
REVOLUTIONARY ENSEMBLE, THE			
ESP-DISK'			
❑ S-3007	The Revolutionary Ensemble at Peace Church	196?	$120
HORIZON			
❑ SP-708	People's Republic	1975	$30
INDIA NAVIGATION			
❑ IN-1023	Manhattan Cycles	197?	$35
INNER CITY			
❑ IC-3016	The Revolutionary Ensemble	197?	$30
REX			
Hard rock band with two records; later solo albums are as REX SMITH.			
COLUMBIA			
❑ PC34399	Rex	1976	$18
❑ PC34865	Where Do We Go from Here	1977	$18
REXROTH, KENNETH, AND LAWRENCE FERLINGHETTI			
FANTASY			
❑ 7002 [M]	Poetry Readings from the Cellar	1957	$250
— Red vinyl			
❑ 7002 [M]	Poetry Readings from the Cellar	1957	$150
— Black vinyl			
REXROTH, KENNETH			
FANTASY			
❑ 7008 [M]	Poetry and Jazz at the Blackhawk	1958	$250
— Red vinyl			
❑ 7008 [M]	Poetry and Jazz at the Blackhawk	1958	$150
— Black vinyl			
REY, ALVINO			
CAPITOL			
❑ T808 [M]	Aloha	1957	$75
❑ T1262 [M]	Ping Pong!	1959	$50
❑ ST1262 [S]	Ping Pong!	1959	$75
❑ T1085 [M]	Swinging Fling	1958	$75
❑ ST1085 [S]	Swinging Fling	1958	$75
❑ T1395 [M]	That Lonely Feeling	1960	$50
❑ ST1395 [S]	That Lonely Feeling	1960	$75
HINDSIGHT			
❑ HSR-196	Alvino Rey and His Orchestra 1940-41	198?	$25
❑ HSR-121	Alvino Rey and His Orchestra 1946	198?	$25
❑ HSR-167	Alvino Rey and His Orchestra 1946, Vol. 2	198?	$25

Number	Title	Yr	NM
REYNOLDS, ART, SINGERS			
CAPITOL			
❑ ST-191	It's a Wonderful World	1969	$25
❑ T2811 [M]	Long Dusty Road	1967	$30
❑ ST2811 [S]	Long Dusty Road	1967	$25
❑ ST2900	Soul-Gospel Sounds	1968	$25
❑ T2534 [M]	Tellin' It Like It Is	1966	$25
❑ ST2534 [S]	Tellin' It Like It Is	1966	$30
REYNOLDS, BURT			
MERCURY			
❑ MK-4 [DJ]	A Burt Reynolds Radio Special	1973	$30
❑ SRM-1-693	Ask Me What I Am	1973	$18
REYNOLDS, DEBBIE			
DOT			
❑ DLP-3295 [M]	Am I That Easy to Forget?	1960	$30
❑ DLP-25295 [S]	Am I That Easy to Forget?	1960	$40
— Black vinyl			
❑ DLP-25295 [S]	Am I That Easy to Forget?	1960	$100
— Blue vinyl			
❑ DLP-3191 [M]	Debbie	1959	$30
❑ DLP-25191 [S]	Debbie	1959	$40
❑ DLP-3298 [M]	Fine and Dandy	1960	$25
❑ DLP-25298 [S]	Fine and Dandy	1960	$30
❑ DLP-3492 [M]	Tammy	1963	$25
❑ DLP-25492 [S]	Tammy	1963	$30
K-TEL			
❑ NU9190	Do It Debbie's Way	1983	$12
— Exercise record			
METRO			
❑ M-535 [M]	Raise a Ruckus	196?	$25
❑ MS-535 [S]	Raise a Ruckus	196?	$25
MGM			
❑ E-3806 [M]	From Debbie with Love	1959	$40
REYNOLDS, JODY			
TRU-GEMS			
❑ 1002	Endless Sleep	1978	$15
REYNOLDS, LAWRENCE			
WARNER BROS.			
❑ WS1825	Jesus Is a Soul Man	1969	$25
REYNOLDS, TEDDY, AND THE TWISTERS			
CROWN			
❑ CLP-5247 [M]	The Twist	1962	$30
❑ CST-247 [S]	The Twist	1962	$40
REYNOLDS, TOMMY			
AUDIO LAB			
❑ AL-1509 [M]	Dixieland All-Stars	1958	$150
KING			
❑ 395-510 [M]	Jazz for Happy Feet	1956	$100
ROYALE			
❑ 18117 [10]	Tommy Reynolds Orchestra with Bon Bon	195?	$100
REYS, RITA			
COLUMBIA			
❑ CL903 [M]	The Cool Voice of Rita Reys with Art Blakey and the Jazz Messengers	1956	$175
EPIC			
❑ LN3522 [M]	Her Name Is Rita Reys	1957	$175
INNER CITY			
❑ IC-1157	Songs of Antonio Carlos Jobim	198?	$35
REZILLOS, THE			
SIRE			
❑ SR6057 [B]	Can't Stand the Rezillos	1978	$18
RHEIMS, ROBERT			
CATHEDRAL			
❑ R-101	Christmas Organ and Chimes by Robert Rheims	198?	$12
— Reissue of UA sets			
RHEIMS			
❑ LP-6010 [M]	For the Whole Family at Christmas	1961	$15
❑ ST-7710 [S]	For the Whole Family at Christmas	1961	$18
❑ LP-6006 [M]	Merry Christmas Carols	1958	$18
— Black vinyl			
❑ LP-6006 [M]	Merry Christmas Carols	1958	$25
— Red vinyl with lyric innersleeve			
❑ ST-7706 [S]	Merry Christmas Carols	1958	$30
— Green vinyl with lyric innersleeve			
❑ ST-7706 [S]	Merry Christmas in Carols	1958	$18
❑ LP-6008 [M]	We Wish You a Merry Christmas	1959	$18

Number	Title	Yr	NM
❑ ST-7708 [S]	We Wish You a Merry Christmas	1959	$18
UNITED ARTISTS			
❑ UXS-96	Christmas Organ and Chimes by Robert Rheims	1972	$18
— Reissue of earlier material in "Superpak			
❑ UA-LA351-E2	Christmas Organ and Chimes by Robert Rheims	1974	$15
— Reissue of United Artists 96			
RHINOCEROS			
ELEKTRA			
❑ EKS-74075	Better Times Are Coming	1970	$25
❑ EKS-74030 [B]	Rhinoceros	1968	$30
❑ EKS-74056	Satin Chickens	1969	$25
RHODES, EMITT			
A&M			
❑ SP-4254	The American Dream	1971	$18
— Reissue contains "Saturday Night" and a framed photo of Rhodes on cover			
❑ SP-4254	The American Dream	1970	$30
— Original album contains "You're a Very Lovely Woman" and has Rhodes in front of a paint-covered backdrop on cover			
ABC DUNHILL			
❑ DS-50089	Emitt Rhodes	1970	$15
❑ DS-50122	Farewell to Paradise	1972	$15
❑ DS-50111	Mirror	1971	$15
RHODES, GEORGE			
GROOVE			
❑ LG-1005 [M]	Real George!	1956	$75
RHODES, TODD			
KING			
❑ 658 [M]	Dance Music	1960	$800
❑ 295-88 [10]	Todd Rhodes Playing His Greatest Hits	1954	$1500
RHYNE, MEL			
JAZZLAND			
❑ JLP-16 [M]	Organizing	1960	$30
❑ JLP-916 [S]	Organizing	1960	$40
RHYTHM AND BLU			
GRAMAVISION			
❑ 18-8608	Rhythm and Blu	1986	$30
RHYTHM COMBINATION, THE			
BASF			
❑ 25124	Power Play	197?	$35
❑ 21751	Waitaminute	197?	$35
RHYTHM DEVILS, THE			
PASSPORT			
❑ PB-9844	The Rhythm Devils Play River Music	1980	$25
RHYTHM HERITAGE			
ABC			
❑ D-934	Disco-Fied	1976	$12
❑ D-987	Last Night on Earth	1977	$12
❑ AA-1037	The Sky's the Limit	1978	$12
RHYTHM MASTERS, THE (1)			
ACE			
❑ LP-1010 [M]	Hymns and Spirituals	1961	$150
RHYTHM ROCKERS (1)			
CHALLENGE			
❑ CHL-617 [M]	Soul Surfin'	1963	$125
RHYTHMIC UNION, THE			
INNER CITY			
❑ IC-1100	Gentle Awakening	198?	$30
RHYZE			
20TH CENTURY			
❑ T-639	Rhyze to the Top	1981	$30
RICE, BOBBY G.			
AUDIOGRAPH			
❑ 6000	Bobby G. Rice	1982	$12
❑ 7772	Bobby's Back	1982	$12
DOOR KNOB			
❑ 1008	New Beginning	198?	$15
GRT			
❑ 8011	Instant Rice -- The Best of Bobby G.	1976	$15
❑ 8001	She Sure Laid the Lonelies on Me	1974	$15
❑ 8016	With Love from Bobby G. Rice	1977	$15
❑ 8003	Write Me a Letter	1975	$15

Number	Title	Yr	NM
METROMEDIA COUNTRY			
❏ BML1-0186	You Lay So Easy on My Mind	1973	$25
ROYAL AMERICAN			
❏ 1003	Hit After Hit	1972	$25
SUNBIRD			
❏ SN-50106	Greatest Hits	1980	$15
RICE, DARYLE			
AUDIOPHILE			
❏ AP-141	I Walk with Music	1980	$25
RICH, BUDDY, AND MAX ROACH			
MERCURY			
❏ MG-20448 [M]	Rich Versus Roach	1959	$250
❏ SR-60133 [S]	Rich Versus Roach	1959	$300
RICH, BUDDY, AND SWEETS EDISON			
NORGRAN			
❏ MGN-1038 [M]	Buddy Rich and Sweets Edison	1955	$150
VERVE			
❏ MGV-8129 [M]	Buddy and Sweets	1957	$250
—Reissue of Norgran 1038			
❏ V-8129 [M]	Buddy and Sweets	1961	$50
RICH, BUDDY			
ARGO			
❏ LP-676 [M]	Playtime	1961	$75
❏ LPS-676 [S]	Playtime	1961	$40
EMARCY			
❏ EMS-2-402	Both Sides	1976	$35
❏ 66006	Driver	1967	$150
EVEREST ARCHIVE OF FOLK & JAZZ			
❏ 260	Buddy Rich	197?	$35
GREAT AMERICAN			
❏ 1030	Class of '78	1978	$50
—Direct-to-disc version of Gryphon 781			
GROOVE MERCHANT			
❏ 3307	The Big Band Machine	1976	$30
❏ 3303	The Last Blues Album, Vol. 1	1975	$30
❏ 528	The Roar of '74	1974	$30
❏ 4407	Tuff Dude!	197?	$35
❏ 3301	Very Live at Buddy's Place	1974	$30
GRYPHON			
❏ 781	Class of '78	1978	$30
LIBERTY			
❏ 11006	Keep the Customer Satisfied	1970	$35
MCA			
❏ 5186	The Buddy Rich Band	1981	$25
MERCURY			
❏ MG-20451 [M]	Richcraft	1959	$250
❏ SR-60136 [S]	Richcraft	1959	$300
❏ MG-20461 [M]	The Voice Is Rich	1959	$175
❏ SR-60144 [S]	The Voice Is Rich	1959	$250
NORGRAN			
❏ MGN-26 [10]	Buddy Rich Swingin'	1954	$250
❏ MGN-1031 [M]	Sing and Swing with Buddy Rich	1955	$175
❏ MGN-1052 [M]	The Swingin' Buddy Rich	1955	$120
—Reissue of 26			

Number	Title	Yr	NM
❏ MGN-1078 [M]	The Wailing Buddy Rich	1956	$75
❏ MGN-1088 [M]	This One's for Basie	1956	$300
PACIFIC JAZZ			
❏ ST-20126	A New One	1968	$50
❏ PJ-10117 [M]	Big Swing Face	1967	$75
❏ ST-20117 [S]	Big Swing Face	1967	$50
❏ LN-10090	Big Swing Face	1981	$20
—Budget-line reissue			
❏ PJ-10113 [M]	Swingin' New Big Band	1966	$75

Number	Title	Yr	NM
❏ ST-20113 [S]	Swingin' New Big Band	1966	$50
❏ LN-10089	Swingin' New Big Band	1981	$20
—Budget-line reissue			
PAUSA			
❏ 9004	Buddy & Soul	1983	$25
QUINTESSENCE			
❏ 25051	Mr. Drums	1978	$30
RCA VICTOR			
❏ LSP-4593	A Different Drummer	1971	$30
❏ ANL1-1090	A Different Drummer	1975	$25
—Reissue of 4593			
❏ CPL2-2273	Buddy Rich Plays & Plays & Plays	1977	$35
❏ LSP-4666	Rich in London	1972	$30
❏ AFL1-4666	Rich in London	1977	$25
—Reissue with new prefix			
❏ APL1-1503	Speak No Evil	1976	$30
❏ LSP-4802	Stick It	1972	$30
❏ AFL1-4802	Stick It	1977	$25
—Reissue with new prefix			
UNITED ARTISTS			
❏ UXS-86	Buddy Rich Superpak	1972	$35
VERVE			
❏ V-8712 [M]	Big Band Shout	1967	$50
❏ V6-8712 [S]	Big Band Shout	1967	$35
❏ V-8425 [M]	Blues Caravan	1962	$75
❏ V6-8425 [S]	Blues Caravan	1962	$75
❏ VSP-40 [M]	Buddy Rich at J.A.T.P.	1966	$35
❏ VSPS-40 [R]	Buddy Rich at J.A.T.P.	1966	$30
❏ MGV-8285 [M]	Buddy Rich in Miami	1958	$175
❏ V-8285 [M]	Buddy Rich in Miami	1961	$50
❏ MGV-2075 [M]	Buddy Rich Just Sings	1957	$175
❏ V-2075 [M]	Buddy Rich Just Sings	1961	$50
❏ MGV-2009 [M]	Buddy Rich Sings Johnny Mercer	1956	$175
❏ V-2009 [M]	Buddy Rich Sings Johnny Mercer	1961	$50
❏ V-8471 [M]	Burnin' Beat	1962	$75
❏ V6-8471 [S]	Burnin' Beat	1962	$75
❏ V-8484 [M]	Drum Battle: Gene Krupa vs. Buddy Rich	1962	$75
❏ V6-8484 [S]	Drum Battle: Gene Krupa vs. Buddy Rich	1962	$75
❏ V6-8824	Monster	1973	$35
❏ V6-8778	Super Rich	1969	$35
❏ MGV-8142 [M]	The Swingin' Buddy Rich	1957	$175
—Reissue of Norgran 1052			
❏ V-8142 [M]	The Swingin' Buddy Rich	1961	$50
❏ MGV-8168 [M]	The Wailing Buddy Rich	1957	$250
—Reissue of Norgran 1078			
❏ V-8168 [M]	The Wailing Buddy Rich	1961	$50
❏ MGV-8176 [M]	This One's for Basie	1957	$300
—Reissue of Norgran 1086			
❏ V-8176 [M]	This One's for Basie	1961	$50
WHO'S WHO IN JAZZ			
❏ 21006	Lionel Hampton Presents Buddy Rich	1978	$30
WORLD PACIFIC			
❏ WPS-20158	Buddy & Soul	1969	$150
❏ WPS-20133	Mercy, Mercy	1968	$150
❏ WPS-20169	The Best of Buddy Rich	1970	$150
❏ WPS-20113	The Buddy Rich Big Band	1968	$150
RICH, CHARLIE			
BUCKBOARD			
❏ 1019	The Entertainer	197?	$12
COLUMBIA SPECIAL PRODUCTS			
❏ P213663	Super Hits	197?	$18
ELEKTRA			
❏ 6E-301	Once a Drifter	1981	$12
EPIC			
❏ KE32247	Behind Closed Doors	1973	$15
❏ PE32247	Behind Closed Doors	197?	$10
—Reissue			
❏ CQ32247 [Q]	Behind Closed Doors	1973	$30
❏ E30214	Boss Man	1970	$25
❏ AS50 [DJ]	Charlie Rich	1973	$30
—Promo-only compilation			
❏ JE35394	Classic Rich, Vol. 1	1978	$12
❏ JE35624	Classic Rich, Vol. 2	1978	$12
❏ AS139 [DJ]	Everything You Always Wanted to Hear by Charlie Rich But Were Afraid to Ask For	1976	$30
—Promo-only sampler			
❏ PE33455	Every Time You Touch Me (I Get High)	1975	$15
❏ PEQ33455 [Q]	Every Time You Touch Me (I Get High)	1975	$30
❏ PE34240	Greatest Hits	1976	$12
—Without bar code on cover			
❏ PE34240	Greatest Hits	1979	$10
—With bar code on cover			
❏ PE34891	Rollin' with the Flow	1977	$12
❏ BN26376	Set Me Free	1968	$25
❏ PE33545	Silver Linings	1976	$12
❏ PE34444	Take Me	1977	$12
❏ PE34444	Take Me	1977	$12
❏ KE31933	The Best of Charlie Rich	1972	$18

Number	Title	Yr	NM
—Yellow label; add 80 percent if bonus record AE7 1065 and its special sleeve are still there			
❏ KE31933	The Best of Charlie Rich	1973	$15
—Orange label			
❏ CQ31933 [Q]	The Best of Charlie Rich	1972	$30
❏ BN26516	The Fabulous Charlie Rich	1970	$25
❏ PE33250	The Silver Fox	1974	$15
❏ PEQ33250 [Q]	The Silver Fox	1974	$30
❏ PE32531	Very Special Love Songs	1974	$15
❏ PEQ32531 [Q]	Very Special Love Songs	1974	$30
GROOVE			
❏ GM-1000 [M]	Charlie Rich	1964	$175
❏ GS-1000 [S]	Charlie Rich	1964	$300
HARMONY			
❏ KH32166	I Do My Swingin' at Home	1973	$15
HI			
❏ HL12037 [M]	Charlie Rich Sings Country and Western	1967	$30
❏ SHL32037 [S]	Charlie Rich Sings Country and Western	1967	$25
❏ SHL32084	Charlie Rich Sings the Songs of Hank Williams & Others	1974	$15
—Reissue of 32037			
❏ 8006	I'm So Lonesome I Could Cry	198?	$10
—Reissue of Hi 32084			
HILLTOP			
❏ 6160	Entertainer of the Year	197?	$12
❏ 6139	Lonely Weekends	197?	$12
❏ 6149	Songs for Beautiful Girls	1974	$12
MERCURY			
❏ SRM-2-7505	Fully Realized	1974	$18
PHILLIPS INTERNATIONAL			
❏ PLP-1970 [M]	Lonely Weekends	1960	$600
PICKWICK			
❏ ACL-7001	Too Many Teardrops	1975	$12
POWER PAK			
❏ PO-245	Arkansas Traveler	197?	$12
❏ PO-241	There Won't Be Anymore	197?	$12
❏ PO-252	The Silver Fox	197?	$12
QUICKSILVER			
❏ QS-1005	Midnight Blue	198?	$15
RCA CAMDEN			
❏ CAS-2417	The Versatile and Talented Charlie Rich	1970	$12
RCA VICTOR			
❏ LPM-3537 [M]	Big Boss Man	1966	$40
❏ LSP-3557 [S]	Big Boss Man	1966	$50
❏ APL1-2260	Big Boss Man/My Mountain Dew	1977	$15
❏ AHL1-5496	Collector's Series	1985	$10
❏ APL1-0857	Greatest Hits	1975	$15
❏ APL1-1242	Now Everybody Knows	1975	$15
❏ APL1-0686	She Called Me Baby	1974	$15
❏ ANL1-2424	She Called Me Baby	1977	$12
—Reissue of APL1-0686			
❏ LPM-3352 [M]	That's Rich	1965	$40
❏ LSP-3352 [S]	That's Rich	1965	$50
❏ APL1-0433	There Won't Be Anymore	1974	$15
❏ APL1-0258	Tomorrow Night	1973	$15
❏ ANL1-1542	Tomorrow Night	1976	$12
—Reissue			
SMASH			
❏ MGS-27078 [M]	The Best Years	1966	$30
❏ SRS-67070 [S]	The Best Years	1966	$40
❏ MGS-27070 [M]	The Many New Sides of Charlie Rich	1965	$30
❏ SRS-67070 [S]	The Many New Sides of Charlie Rich	1965	$40
SUN			
❏ 1003 [B]	20 Golden Hits	1979	$18
—Gold vinyl			
❏ LP123 [B]	A Time for Tears	1971	$18
❏ KH134 [B]	Golden Treasures	1974	$18
❏ LP110 [B]	Lonely Weekend	1970	$18
❏ LP135 [B]	Sun's Best of Charlie Rich	1974	$18
❏ LP132 [B]	The Early Years	1974	$18
❏ LP133 [B]	The Memphis Sound of Charlie Rich	1974	$18
❏ 1007	The Original Charlie Rich	1979	$12
SUNNYVALE			
❏ 9330	The Sun Story Vol. 2	1977	$12
TIME-LIFE			
❏ STW-115	Country Music	1981	$12
TRIP			
❏ TLP-8502	The Best of Charlie Rich	1974	$15
UNITED ARTISTS			
❏ UA-LA876-H	I Still Believe in Love	1978	$15
❏ UA-LA925-H	The Fool Strikes Again	1978	$12
WING			
❏ SRW-16375	A Lonely Weekend	1969	$15
RICH, DAVE			
STOP			
❏ 10007	Soul Brother	196?	$30

Number	Title	Yr	NM

RICH, DON

Also see THE BUCKAROOS.

CAPITOL
❏ ST-643	That Fiddlin' Man	1970	$30

RICH, LISA
DISCOVERY
❏ 908	Listen Here	1986	$25

TREND
❏ 541	Touch of the Rare	1986	$25

RICHARD, CLIFF
ABC-PARAMOUNT
❏ 321 [M]	Cliff Sings	1960	$150
❏ S-321 [S]	Cliff Sings	1960	$120
❏ 391 [M]	Listen to Cliff	1961	$150
❏ S-391 [S]	Listen to Cliff	1961	$120

EMI AMERICA
❏ SN-16253	Every Face Tells a Story	1981	$10
❏ ST-17105	Give a Little Bit More	1983	$12
❏ SN-16220	Green Light	1981	$10
❏ SN-16221	I'm Nearly Famous	1981	$10
❏ SW-17039	I'm No Hero	1980	$12
❏ ST-17081	Now You See Me, Now You Don't	1982	$12
❏ SW-17018	We Don't Talk Anymore	1979	$12
❏ SW-17059	Wired for Sound	1981	$12

EPIC
❏ LN24115 [M]	Cliff Richard in Spain	1965	$50
❏ BN26115 [S]	Cliff Richard in Spain	1965	$75
❏ LN24089 [M]	It's All in the Game	1964	$50
❏ BN26089 [S]	It's All in the Game	1964	$75
❏ LN24063 [M]	Summer Holiday	1963	$50
❏ BN26063 [S]	Summer Holiday	1963	$75
❏ LN24145 [M]	Swingers' Paradise	1963	$40
❏ BN24145 [S]	Swingers' Paradise		$75

ROCKET
❏ PIG-2268	Every Face Tells a Story	1977	$15
❏ BXL1-2958	Green Light	1978	$15
❏ PIG-2210 [B]	I'm Nearly Famous	1976	$18

WORD
❏ WR-8306	Walking in the Light	1985	$15

RICHARD AND JIM
CAPITOL
❏ T2058 [M]	Folk Songs and Country Sounds	1964	$25
❏ ST2058 [S]	Folk Songs and Country Sounds	1964	$30
❏ T2287 [M]	Two Boys from Alabama	1965	$25
❏ ST2287 [S]	Two Boys from Alabama	1965	$30

RICHARDS, ANN
ATCO
❏ 33-136 [M]	Ann, Man!	1961	$40
❏ SD 33-136 [S]	Ann, Man!	1961	$75

CAPITOL
❏ T1087 [M]	I'm Shooting High	1959	$100
❏ ST1087 [S]	I'm Shooting High	1959	$150
❏ T1406 [M]	The Many Moods of Ann Richards	1960	$150
❏ ST1406 [S]	The Many Moods of Ann Richards	1960	$175
❏ T1495 [M]	Two Much!	1961	$150
❏ ST1495 [S]	Two Much!	1961	$175

VEE JAY
❏ LP-1070 [M]	Live...At the Losers	1963	$40
❏ SR-1070 [S]	Live...At the Losers	1963	$50

RICHARDS, EMIL
ABC IMPULSE!
❏ AS-9188 [S]	Journey to Bliss	1969	$250
❏ AS-9182 [S]	Spirit of '76	1968	$250

UNI
❏ 3008 [M]	New Sound	1967	$30
❏ 73008 [S]	New Sound	1967	$25
❏ 3003 [M]	New Time Element	1967	$30
❏ 73003 [S]	New Time Element	1967	$25

RICHARDS, JOHNNY
BETHLEHEM
❏ BCP-6011 [M]	Something Else by Johnny Richards	1956	$300
❏ BCP-6032	Something Else by Johnny Richards	197?	$50

— Reissue, distributed by RCA Victor

CAPITOL
❏ T981 [M]	Experiments In Sound	1958	$75

— Turquoise label
❏ T885 [M]	Wide Range	1957	$250

— Turquoise label

CORAL
❏ CRL57304 [M]	Walk Softly/Run Wild	1959	$120
❏ CRL757304 [S]	Walk Softly/Run Wild	1959	$100

Number	Title	Yr	NM

CREATIVE WORLD
❏ ST-1052	Wide Range	198?	$35

DISCOVERY
❏ DS-915	Je Vous Adore	1986	$75

ROULETTE
❏ SR-25351 [S]	Aqui Se Habla Espanol	1967	$30
❏ R-25351 [M]	Aqui Se Habla Espanol	1967	$30
❏ R-52114 [M]	My Fair Lady, My Way	1964	$75
❏ SR-52114 [S]	My Fair Lady, My Way	1964	$40
❏ R-52008 [M]	The Rites of Diablo	1958	$100
❏ SR-52008 [S]	The Rites of Diablo	1958	$75

RICHARDS, KEITH
VIRGIN
❏ 90973	Talk Is Cheap	1988	$15

RICHARDS, RED
SACKVILLE
❏ 2017	I'm Shooting High	198?	$30

WEST 54
❏ 8005	Mellow Tone	1980	$30
❏ 8000	Soft Buns	1979	$30

RICHARDS, SUE
ABC DOT
❏ DOSD-2012	A Girl Named Sue	1974	$15
❏ DOSD-2052	Sweet Sensuous Feelings	1976	$15

RICHARDS, TREVOR
STOMP OFF
❏ SOS-1222	The Trevor Richards New Orleans Trio	1991	$30

RICHARDS, TRUDY
CAPITOL
❏ T838 [M]	Crazy in Love	1957	$30

RICHARDSON, JEROME
NEW JAZZ
❏ NJLP-8205 [M]	Jerome Richardson Sextet	1958	$175

— Purple label
❏ NJLP-8205 [M]	Jerome Richardson Sextet	1965	$175

— Blue label, trident logo at right
❏ NJLP-8226 [M]	Roamin' with Richardson	1959	$400

— Purple label
❏ NJLP-8226 [M]	Roamin' with Richardson	1965	$175

— Blue label, trident logo at right

UNITED ARTISTS
❏ UAJ-14006 [M]	Going to the Movies	1962	$30
❏ UAJS-15006 [S]	Going to the Movies	1962	$40

VERVE
❏ V-8729 [M]	Groove Merchant	1967	$25
❏ V6-8729 [S]	Groove Merchant	1967	$35

RICHARDSON, JIMMY
STARDAY
❏ SLP-126 [M]	Sweet with a Beat	1960	$30

RICHARDSON, RALPH; PAUL SCHOFIELD; AND CAST
CAEDMON
❏ TC91135 [S]	A Christmas Carol	1960	$18

— Green, blue and white label; front cover says "Sir Ralph Richardson"; number on jacket is "TC 1135S"
❏ TC1135 [M]	A Christmas Carol	197?	$15

— Blue and white label; front cover says "Ralph Richardson"; 1960 copyright date added to label and jacket

RICHARDSON, WALLY
PRESTIGE
❏ PRST-7569	Soul Guru	1969	$25

RICHARDSON, WARREN S., JR.
COTILLION
❏ SD9013	Warren S. Richardson, Jr.	1970	$30

RICHIE, LIONEL
MOTOWN
❏ MOT-6338	Back to Front	1992	$30

— U.S. vinyl available only through Columbia House
❏ 6059ML	Can't Slow Down	1983	$10
❏ R110767	Can't Slow Down	1983	$12

— RCA Music Service edition
❏ 6158ML	Dancing on the Ceiling	1986	$10
❏ 6007ML	Lionel Richie	1982	$10
❏ 5386ML	The Composer	1986	$10

— Includes songs he wrote and performed with the Commodores, plus "Endless Love" with Diana Ross

RICHIE, LITTLE JOE
See LITTLE JOE.

Number	Title	Yr	NM

RICHMAN, JONATHAN, AND THE MODERN LOVERS
BESERKLEY
❏ JBZ 0060	Back in Your Life	1979	$12

— Distributed by Playboy/CBS
❏ 10060	Back in Your Life	1980	$15

— Reissue -- change in distributing label to Elektra
❏ BZ-0048	Jonathan Richman and the Modern Lovers	1976	$30

— Distributed by GRT
❏ JBZ 0048	Jonathan Richman and the Modern Lovers	1976	$30

— Distributed by Playboy/CBS
❏ JBZ 0055	Modern Lovers "Live	1978	$14

— Distributed by Playboy/CBS
❏ PZ34800	Rock 'N' Roll with the Modern Lovers	1977	$14

— Distributed by Playboy/CBS
❏ BZ-0053	Rock 'N' Roll with the Modern Lovers	1977	$25

— Distributed by Janus/GRT
❏ JBZ 0050	The Modern Lovers	1978	$30

— Distributed by Playboy/CBS
❏ BZ-0050	The Modern Lovers	1976	$30

— Distributed by GRT

BOMP!
❏ 4021	The Original Modern Lovers	1981	$25

— Same album as Mohawk releasse

HOME OF THE HITS
❏ HH-1910	The Modern Lovers	1975	$50

MOHAWK
❏ SCALP 0002	The Original Modern Lovers	1981	$30

RHINO
❏ RNLP70095	Back in Your Life	1986	$15

— Reissue
❏ RNLP70092	Jonathan Richman and the Modern Lovers	1986	$15

— Reissue
❏ RNLP70094	Modern Lovers "Live	1986	$15

— Reissue
❏ RNLP70093	Rock 'N' Roll with the Modern Lovers	1986	$15

— Reissue
❏ RNLP70091	The Modern Lovers	1986	$15

— Reissue

ROUNDER
❏ 9024	Jonathan Goes Country	1990	$15
❏ 9021	Jonathan Richman	1989	$15
❏ 9014	Modern Lovers '88	1988	$15

SIRE
❏ 23939	Jonathan Sings!	1983	$15

VAPOR
❏ 48216	Her Mystery Not of High Heels and Eye Shadow	2001	$18
❏ 47086	I'm So Confused	1998	$18

RICHMOND, DANNIE
ABC IMPULSE!
❏ AS-98 [S]	Dannie Richmond	1968	$35

GATEMOUTH
❏ 1004	Dannie Richmond Quintet	1980	$30

IMPULSE!
❏ AS-98 [S]	Dannie Richmond	1966	$120
❏ A-98 [M]	Dannie Richmond	1966	$250

RED RECORD
❏ VPA-161	Dionysius	198?	$30

SOUL NOTE
❏ SN-1005	Ode to Mingus	198?	$30

RICHMOND, MIKE, AND ANDY LA VERNE
STEEPLECHASE
❏ SCS-1101	For Us	198?	$30

RICHMOND, MIKE
INNER CITY
❏ IC-1065	Dream Waves	1978	$30

RICKLES, DON
WARNER BROS.
❏ WS1779	Don Rickles Speaks!	1969	$18
❏ WS1745	Hello Dummy!	1968	$18

RICKS, JIMMY
Also see THE RAVENS.

JUBILEE
❏ JGS-8021	Tell Her You Love Her	1969	$50

MAINSTREAM
❏ 56050 [M]	Vibrations	1965	$50
❏ S-6050 [S]	Vibrations	1965	$75

SIGNATURE
❏ SM-1032 [M]	Jimmy Ricks	1961	$300
❏ SM-1032 [M]	Jimmy Ricks	1961	$250

— White label promo

Number	Title	Yr	NM

RIDDLE, NELSON

ALSHIRE
| 5203 | Bridge Over Troubled Water | 197? | $12 |

AVON
| 10170 | Avon Wishes You a Happy Holiday and a Joyous New Year | 1970 | $18 |

— *Given to Avon salespeople*

CAPITOL
T1365 [M]	Can-Can	1961	$25
ST1365 [S]	Can-Can	1961	$30
T893 [M]	C'mon, Get Happy	1957	$30
T813 [M]	Hey, Let Yourself Go	1957	$30
T1817 [M]	Love Is a Game of Poker	1962	$25
ST1817 [S]	Love Is a Game of Poker	1962	$30
T1571 [M]	Love Tide	1961	$25
ST1571 [S]	Love Tide	1961	$30
T1670 [M]	Magic Moments from "The Gay Life	1962	$25
ST1670 [S]	Magic Moments from "The Gay Life	1962	$30
T1869 [M]	More Hit TV Themes	1963	$25
ST1869 [S]	More Hit TV Themes	1963	$30
T1771 [M]	Route 66 Theme and Other Great TV Themes	1962	$30
ST1771 [S]	Route 66 Theme and Other Great TV Themes	1962	$30
T915 [M]	Sea of Dreams	1958	$30
TAO1259 [M]	Sing a Song with Riddle	1960	$25
STAO1259 [S]	Sing a Song with Riddle	1960	$30
T1990 [M]	The Best of Nelson Riddle	1963	$18
DT1990 [P]	The Best of Nelson Riddle	1963	$18
SM-11764	The Best of Nelson Riddle	1976	$12
T1148 [M]	The Joy of Living	1959	$25
ST1148 [S]	The Joy of Living	1959	$30
T753 [M]	The Tender Touch	1956	$30

DAYBREAK
| DS2015 | Viva Legrand! | 197? | $25 |

HARMONY
| HS11320 | Nelson Riddle and His Orchestra Play the Wonderful Nat King Cole Songs | 1969 | $15 |

LIBERTY
LRP-3508 [M]	The Bright and the Beautiful	1967	$18
LST-7508 [S]	The Bright and the Beautiful	1967	$18
LST-3532 [M]	The Riddle of Today	1967	$25
LST-7532 [S]	The Riddle of Today	1967	$18

PICKWICK
| PC3007 [M] | Witchcraft | 1965 | $18 |
| SPC3007 [R] | Witchcraft | 1965 | $15 |

REPRISE
R-6071 [M]	Come Blow Your Horn	1963	$18
R9-6071 [S]	Come Blow Your Horn	1963	$25
R-6138 [M]	Great Music, Great Films, Great Sounds	1964	$18
RS-6138 [S]	Great Music, Great Films, Great Sounds	1964	$25
R-6162 [M]	Nat	1965	$18
RS-6162 [S]	Nat	1965	$25
R-6120 [M]	White on White," "Shangri-La," "Charade" and Other Hits of 1964	1964	$18
RS-6120 [S]	White on White," "Shangri-La," "Charade" and Other Hits of 1964	1964	$25

SEARS
| SP-406 [M] | Witchcraft | 196? | $18 |
| SPS-406 [R] | Witchcraft | 196? | $15 |

SOLID STATE
| SS-18013 | Music for Wives and Lovers | 1967 | $25 |
| ST-91083 | Music for Wives and Lovers | 1967 | $30 |

— *Capitol Record Club edition*

SUNSET
| SUS-5233 | The Riddle Touch | 1968 | $15 |

UNITED ARTISTS
| UAS6670 | The Contemporary Sound of Nelson Riddle | 1968 | $25 |
| ST-91566 | The Contemporary Sound of Nelson Riddle | 1968 | $30 |

— *Capitol Record Club edition*

RIDERS IN THE SKY

MCA
42180	Riders Radio Theater	1988	$10
42040	The Cowboy Way	1987	$10
42305	The Riders Go Commercial	1989	$12

ROUNDER
0147	Cowboy Jubilee	1981	$12
0186	Live	1984	$12
0220	New Trails	1986	$12
0170	Prairie Serenade	1982	$12
8011	Saddle Pals	1985	$12
0102	Three on the Trail	1980	$12
1038	Weeds and Water	1983	$12

RIDERS OF THE PURPLE SAGE, THE
See FOY WILLING.

RIDLEY, LARRY

STRATA-EAST
| SES-19759 | Sum of the Parts | 1975 | $30 |

RIEDEL, GEORGE

PHILIPS
| PHM200140 [M] | Jazz Ballet | 1964 | $35 |
| PHS600140 [S] | Jazz Ballet | 1964 | $25 |

RIEMANN, KURT

INNOVATIVE COMMUNICATION
| KS 80.047 | Electronic Nightworks | 1987 | $30 |

RIFKIN, JOSHUA

NONESUCH
| H-71248 | Piano Rags by Scott Joplin | 1970 | $30 |
| H-71264 | Piano Rags by Scott Joplin, Vol. 2 | 1971 | $30 |

RIG

CAPITOL
| ST-473 [B] | Rig | 1970 | $30 |

RIGHTEOUS BROTHERS, THE

HAVEN
| ST-9201 | Give It to the People | 1974 | $18 |
| ST-9203 | Sons of Mrs. Righteous | 1975 | $18 |

MGM
| SE-4885 | The History of the Righteous Brothers | 1973 | $18 |
| GAS-102 | The Righteous Brothers (Golden Archive Series) | 1970 | $18 |

MOONGLOW
| MLP-1001 [M] | Right Now! | 1963 | $40 |
| MSP-1001 [S] | Right Now! | 1963 | $75 |

MLP-1002 [M]	Some Blue-Eyed Soul	1964	$40
MSP-1002 [S]	Some Blue-Eyed Soul	1964	$75
MLP-1004 [M]	The Best of the Righteous Brothers	1966	$30
MSP-1004 [S]	The Best of the Righteous Brothers	1966	$30
MLP-1003 [M]	This Is New!	1965	$40
MSP-1003 [S]	This Is New!	1965	$75

PHILLES
PHLP-4009 [M]	Back to Back	1965	$30
PHLPS-4009 [S]	Back to Back	1965	$40
T-90677 [M]	Back to Back	1965	$30
— *Capitol Record Club edition*
| ST-90677 [S] | Back to Back | 1965 | $40 |
— *Capitol Record Club edition*
PHLP-4008 [M]	Just Once in My Life	1965	$30
PHLPS-4008 [S]	Just Once in My Life	1965	$40
PHLP-4007 [M]	You've Lost That Lovin' Feelin'	1964	$40
PHLPS-4007 [S]	You've Lost That Lovin' Feelin'	1964	$50
T-90692 [M]	You've Lost That Lovin' Feelin'	1965	$50
— *Capitol Record Club edition*
| ST-90692 [S] | You've Lost That Lovin' Feelin' | 1965 | $50 |
— *Capitol Record Club edition*

RHINO
| R1-71488 | Anthology | 1989 | $18 |

VERVE
V-5004 [M]	Go Ahead and Cry	1966	$25
V6-5004 [S]	Go Ahead and Cry	1966	$30
ST-90921 [S]	Go Ahead and Cry	1966	$30
— *Capitol Record Club edition*
V-5020 [M]	Greatest Hits	1967	$30
V6-5020 [S]	Greatest Hits	1967	$25
823662-1	Greatest Hits	198?	$12
V6-5071	Greatest Hits, Vol. 2	1969	$25
V6-5058	One for the Road	1968	$30
— *With The Blossoms credited on the back cover*
| V6-5058 | One for the Road | 1968 | $25 |
— *Without The Blossoms credited on the back cover*
V6-5076	Re-Birth	1970	$25
V-5010 [M]	Sayin' Somethin'	1967	$25
V6-5010 [S]	Sayin' Somethin'	1967	$30
T-91057 [M]	Sayin' Somethin'	1967	$30
— *Capitol Record Club edition*
| ST-91057 [S] | Sayin' Somethin' | 1967 | $30 |
— *Capitol Record Club edition*
V-5001 [M]	Soul and Inspiration	1966	$25
V6-5001 [S]	Soul and Inspiration	1966	$30
ST-90669 [S]	Soul and Inspiration	1966	$30
— *Capitol Record Club edition*
V-5031 [M]	Souled Out	1967	$40
V6-5031 [S]	Souled Out	1967	$25
V6-5051	Standards	1968	$25

RILEY, BILLY LEE

GNP CRESCENDO
| GNP-2020 [M] | Billy Lee Riley | 1966 | $18 |
| GNPS-2020 [S] | Billy Lee Riley | 1966 | $25 |

MERCURY
MG-20974 [M]	Beatlemania Harmonica	1965	$25
SR-60974 [S]	Beatlemania Harmonica	1965	$30
MG-20965 [M]	Big Harmonica Special	1964	$25
SR-60965 [S]	Big Harmonica Special	1964	$30
MG-20958 [M]	The Whiskey A-Go-Go Presents Billy Lee Riley	1964	$25
SR-60958 [S]	The Whiskey A-Go-Go Presents Billy Lee Riley	1964	$30

RILEY, DOUG

PM
| 07 | Dreams | 1977 | $30 |

RILEY, JEANNIE C.

ALLEGIANCE
| AV-5026 | Tears, Joys and Memories | 198? | $12 |

CAPITOL
| ST-177 | The Songs of Jeannie C. Riley | 1969 | $18 |

LITTLE DARLIN'
| SLD8011 | Sock Soul | 1968 | $25 |

MGM
SE-4849	Down to Earth	1973	$15
SE-4805	Give Myself a Party	1972	$15
SE-4909	Just Jeannie C. Riley	1973	$15
SE-4891	When Love Has Gone Away	1973	$15

PICKWICK
| 6098 | The Girl Most Likely | 197? | $12 |
| 6119 | The World of Country | 197? | $12 |

PLANTATION
PLP8	Country Girl	1970	$18
508	Country Queens	197?	$15
PLP1 [S]	Harper Valley P.T.A.	1968	$25
PLM1 [M]	Harper Valley P.T.A.	1968	$75
PLP16	Jeannie	1971	$18
PLP13	Jeannie C. Riley's Greatest Hits	1971	$18
PLP11	The Generation Gap	1970	$18
PLP3	Things Go Better with Love	1969	$18
PLP2	Yearbooks and Yesterdays	1969	$18

POWER PAK
| 250 | Country Gold | 197? | $12 |

RILEY, TERRY

CBS
| M35164 [B] | Shri Camel | 1980 | $50 |

CELESTIAL HARMONIES
| CEL018/019 [B] | The Harp Of New Albion | 1986 | $80 |

COLUMBIA MASTERWORKS
| MS7315 [B] | A Rainbow In Curved Air | 1969 | $40 |
| MS7178 [B] | In C | 1968 | $50 |

GRAMAVISION
| 1870141 (2) [B] | Cadenza On The Night Plain And Other String Quartets | 1985 | $60 |

MASS ART
| M131 [B] | Reed Streams | 1967 | $500 |

RIMINGTON, SAMMY

GHB
GHB-181	Sammy Rimington and the Mouldy Five, Vol. 1	1985	$25
GHB-182	Sammy Rimington and the Mouldy Five, Vol. 2	1985	$25
GHB-94	Sammy Rimington Plays George Lewis Classics	198?	$25

JAZZ CRUSADE
| 1005 | Sammy Rimington Plays George Lewis Classics | 196? | $35 |

PROGRESSIVE
| PRO-7077 | The Exciting Sax of Sammy Rimington | 1987 | $25 |

Number	Title	Yr	NM
RINCON SURFSIDE BAND, THE			
DUNHILL			
❏ D50001 [M]	Surfing Songbook	1965	$250
❏ DS50001 [S]	Surfing Songbook	1965	$300
RIOPELLE, JERRY			
CAPITOL			
❏ ST-732	Jerry Riopelle	1971	$18
❏ ST-863	Second Album	1971	$18
RIOS, MIGUEL			
A&M			
❏ SPX-4267	A Song of Joy	1970	$18
RIOS, WALDO DE LOS			
UNITED ARTISTS			
❏ UAS-5554	Mozartmania	1972	$15
❏ UAS-6802	Sinfonias	1971	$15
VAULT			
❏ VS-126 [B]	International Hits	1969	$30
WARNER BROS.			
❏ BS2801	Operas	1974	$15
RIOT			
ARIOLA			
❏ ARL5007	Rock City	1977	$18
CAPITOL			
❏ ST12081	Narita	1979	$15
❏ SN16271	Narita	1982	$12
CBS			
❏ Z45132	The Privilege of Power	1990	$14
❏ BFZ44232	Thundersteel	1988	$15
ELEKTRA			
❏ 55546	Fire Down Under	1981	$15
❏ 60134	Restless Breed	1982	$12
❏ 67969	Riot Live	1982	$25
FIRE-SIGN			
❏ 87001	Rock City	1977	$30
GRAND SLAMM			
❏ SLAM6	Born In America	1989	$14
QUALITY			
❏ QUS1008	Born In America	1983	$15
RIP CHORDS, THE			
COLUMBIA			
❏ CL2151 [M]	Hey Little Cobra and Other Hot Rod Hits	1964	$40
—Guaranteed High Fidelity" on label			
❏ CS8951 [S]	Hey Little Cobra and Other Hot Rod Hits	1964	$50
❏ CL2151 [M]	Hey Little Cobra and Other Hot Rod Hits	1966	$30
—360 Sound Mono" on label			
❏ CL2216 [M]	Three Window Coupe	1964	$75
❏ CS9016 [S]	Three Window Coupe	1964	$80
RIPERTON, MINNIE			
ACCORD			
❏ SN-7205	Wistful Memories	1981	$12
CAPITOL			
❏ SN-12005	Adventures in Paradise	1979	$12
—Reissue of Epic 33454			
❏ SN-16146	Adventures in Paradise	1980	$10
—Budget-line reissue			
❏ SOO-12097	Love Lives Forever	1980	$12
❏ SO-11936	Minnie	1979	$12
❏ SN-12004	Perfect Angel	1979	$12
—Reissue of Epic 32561			
❏ SN-16145	Perfect Angel	1980	$10
—Budget-line reissue			
❏ SN-12006	Stay in Love	1979	$12
—Reissue of Epic 34191			
❏ SN-16147	Stay in Love	1980	$10
—Budget-line reissue			
❏ ST-12189	The Best of Minnie Riperton	1981	$12
EPIC			
❏ PE33454	Adventures in Paradise	1975	$15
❏ PEQ33454 [Q]	Adventures in Paradise	1975	$40
❏ KE32561	Perfect Angel	1974	$15
❏ EQ32561 [Q]	Perfect Angel	1974	$40
❏ PE34191	Stay in Love	1977	$15
GRT			
❏ 30001	Come To My Garden	1970	$18
JANUS			
❏ 7011	Come To My Garden	1974	$15
—Reissue of GRT LP			
RIPPINGTONS, THE			
GRP			
❏ GR-9588	Tourist in Paradise	1989	$30
❏ GR-9618	Welcome to the St. James Club	1990	$35

Number	Title	Yr	NM
PASSPORT JAZZ			
❏ PJ88042	Kilimanjaro	1988	$30
❏ PJ88019	Moonlighting	1987	$30
RIPPY, RODNEY ALLEN			
BELL			
❏ 1311	Take Life a Little Easier	1974	$25
RISERS, THE			
IMPERIAL			
❏ LP-9269 [M]	She's a Bad Motorcycle	1964	$150
❏ LP-12269 [S]	She's a Bad Motorcycle	1964	$175
RISING SONS, THE			
SUNDAZED			
❏ LP5054	The Rising Sons	200?	$15
RISING STORM, THE			
ARF! ARF!			
❏ 007	Alive in Anover Again	1983	$120
REMNANT			
❏ BBA-3571	Calm Before the Rising Storm	1968	$1200
—VG value 600; VG+ value 900			
STANTON PARK			
❏ 001	Calm Before the Rising Storm	1991	$25
—Reissue of Remnant album			
RITCHIE, JEAN			
TRADITION			
❏ TLP1031	Carols of All Seasons	1959	$0
RITCHIE FAMILY, THE			
20TH CENTURY			
❏ T-498	Brazil	1975	$12
CASABLANCA			
❏ NBLP-7166	Bad Reputation	1979	$12
❏ NBLP-7223	Give Me a Break	1980	$12
MARLIN			
❏ 2206	African Queens	1977	$12
❏ 2215	American Generation	1978	$12
❏ 2201	Arabian Nights	1976	$12
❏ 2203	Life Is Music	1977	$12
RCA VICTOR			
❏ AFL1-4601	All Night, All Night	1983	$12
❏ AFL1-4324	I'll Do My Best	1982	$12
RITENOUR, LEE			
ELEKTRA			
❏ 60358	Banded Together	1984	$25
❏ 6E-192	Feel the Night	1979	$25
❏ 6E-331	Rit	1981	$25
❏ 60186	Rit/2	1982	$25
❏ 6E-136	The Captain's Journey	1978	$25
ELEKTRA/MUSICIAN			
❏ 60310	On the Line	1983	$25
❏ 60024	Rio	1982	$25
EPIC			
❏ PE34426	Captain Fingers	1977	$25
—Orange label			
❏ PE34426	Captain Fingers	1979	$20
—Dark blue label			
❏ PE33947	First Course	1976	$25
—Orange label			
❏ PE33947	First Course	1979	$20
—Dark blue label			
❏ JE36527	The Best of Lee Ritenour	1980	$25
❏ PE36527	The Best of Lee Ritenour	198?	$20
—Budget-line reissue			
GRP			
❏ GR-9594	Color Rit	1989	$30
❏ GR-1021	Earth Run	1986	$25
❏ GR-9570	Festival	1988	$25
❏ GR-1042	Portrait	1987	$25
❏ GR-1017	Rio	1986	$20
❏ GR-9615	Stolen Moments	1990	$35
MOBILE FIDELITY			
❏ 1-147	Captain Fingers	1985	$50
—Audiophile vinyl			
NAUTILUS			
❏ NR-41	Rit	198?	$40
—Audiophile vinyl			
RITTER, TEX			
BUCKBOARD			
❏ BBS1030	Tex Ritter	198?	$12
CAPITOL			
❏ SKC-11241	An American Legend	1973	$30
❏ T1292 [M]	Blood on the Saddle	1960	$30
—Black colorband label, logo at left			
❏ T1292 [M]	Blood on the Saddle	1962	$25

Number	Title	Yr	NM
—Black colorband label, logo at top			
❏ ST1292 [S]	Blood on the Saddle	1960	$40
—Black colorband label, logo at left			
❏ ST1292 [S]	Blood on the Saddle	1962	$30
—Black colorband label, logo at left			
❏ T1910 [M]	Border Affair	1963	$25
❏ ST1910 [S]	Border Affair	1963	$30
❏ T2890 [M]	Bum Tiddl Dee Bum Bum!	1968	$50
❏ ST2890 [S]	Bum Tiddl Dee Bum Bum!	1968	$30
❏ ST-213	Chuck Wagon Days	1969	$25
❏ ST-11503	Comin' After Jinny	1976	$18
❏ H4004 [10]	Cowboy Favorites	195?	$180
❏ ST-11351	Fall Away	1974	$18
❏ ST-467	Green Green Valley	1970	$25
❏ T1623 [M]	Hillbilly Heaven	1961	$30
—Black colorband label, logo at left			
❏ T1623 [M]	Hillbilly Heaven	1962	$25
—Black colorband label, logo at left			
❏ ST1623 [S]	Hillbilly Heaven	1961	$40
—Black colorband label, logo at left			
❏ ST1623 [S]	Hillbilly Heaven	1962	$30
—Reissue with new prefix			
❏ SM-1623	Hillbilly Heaven	1976	$12
—Reissue with new prefix			
❏ T2786 [M]	Just Beyond the Moon	1967	$30
❏ ST2786 [S]	Just Beyond the Moon	1967	$30
❏ T1100 [M]	Psalms	1959	$50
—Black colorband label, logo at left			
❏ T1100 [M]	Psalms	1962	$30
—Black colorband label, logo at top			
❏ T971 [M]	Songs from the Western Screen	1958	$100
—Turquoise or gray label			
❏ T971 [M]	Songs from the Western Screen	1959	$40
—Black colorband label, logo at left			
❏ T971 [M]	Songs from the Western Screen	1962	$30
—Black colorband label, logo at top			
❏ ST-11037	Supercountrylegendary	1972	$18
❏ T2743 [M]	Sweet Land of Liberty	1967	$30
❏ ST2743 [S]	Sweet Land of Liberty	1967	$30
❏ ST2974	Tex Ritter's Wild West	1968	$30
❏ T2595 [M]	The Best of Tex Ritter	1966	$30
❏ DT2595 [R]	The Best of Tex Ritter	1966	$18
❏ T2402 [M]	The Friendly Voice of Tex Ritter	1965	$25
❏ ST2402 [S]	The Friendly Voice of Tex Ritter	1965	$30
❏ W1562 [M]	The Lincoln Hymns	1961	$30
❏ SW1562 [S]	The Lincoln Hymns	1961	$40
HILLTOP			
❏ JS-6138	High Noon	196?	$15
❏ JS-6075	Love You As Big As Texas	196?	$15
❏ PTP-2020	My Kinda Songs	197?	$18
❏ JS-6155	Tex	197?	$15
❏ JS-6043	Tex Ritter Sings His Hits	196?	$15
LABREA			
❏ L-8036 [M]	Jamboree, Nashville Style	196?	$25
❏ LS-8036 [S]	Jamboree, Nashville Style	196?	$30
PREMIER			
❏ 9023	Tex Ritter and the Rio Grande River Boys	196?	$15
RITZ, LYLE			
VERVE			
❏ MGV-8333 [M]	50th State Jazz	1959	$150
❏ MGVS-6070 [S]	50th State Jazz	1960	$120
❏ V-8333 [M]	50th State Jazz	1961	$30
❏ V6-8333 [S]	50th State Jazz	1961	$25
❏ MGV-2087 [M]	How About Uke?	1957	$175
RITZ, THE			
PAUSA			
❏ 7190	Born to Bop	1986	$25
RIVERA, HECTOR			
WING			
❏ MGW-12197 [M]	Let's Cha Cha Cha	1960	$25
RIVERA, LUIS, AND DOC BAGBY			
KING			
❏ 631 [M]	Battle of the Organs	1959	$150
RIVERA, LUIS			
IMPERIAL			
❏ LP-9139 [M]	Filet of Soul	1961	$30
RIVERS, BOB, COMEDY CORP			
CRITIQUE			
❏ 90671	Twisted Christmas	1987	$15
RIVERS, JAMES			
SPINDLETOP			
❏ STP-101	The Dallas Sessions	1986	$30

Number	Title	Yr	NM

RIVERS, JERRY
STARDAY
| ❏ SLP-281 [M] | Fantastic Fiddlin' and Tall Tales | 1964 | $30 |

RIVERS, JOHNNY
IMPERIAL
| ❏ LP-4-2293 [PS] | Johnny Rivers Rocks the Folk | 196? | $30 |
| ❏ LP-4-2293 | Where Have All the Flowers Gone/Michael (Row the Boat Ashore)/Tall Oak Tree// Mr. Tambourine Man/Green, Green/Blowin' in the Wind | 196? | $30 |
— Stereo jukebox issue; small hole, plays at 33 1/3 rpm

ATLANTIC
| ❏ SD7301 | The Road | 1974 | $15 |

BIG TREE
| ❏ BT76004 | Outside Help | 1977 | $15 |

CAPITOL
| ❏ T2161 [M] | The Sensational Johnny Rivers | 1964 | $25 |
| ❏ ST2161 [S] | The Sensational Johnny Rivers | 1964 | $30 |

COLUMBIA
| ❏ FE38429 | Not a Through Street | 1983 | $12 |
| ❏ PE38429 | Not a Through Street | 1985 | $10 |
— Budget-line reissue

EPIC
| ❏ PE33681 | New Lovers and Old Friends | 1975 | $15 |

IMPERIAL
| ❏ LP-9307 [M] | ...And I Know You Wanna Dance | 1966 | $25 |
— Black label with pink and white at left
| ❏ LP-12307 [S] | ...And I Know You Wanna Dance | 1966 | $30 |
— Black label with pink and white at left
| ❏ LP-9307 [M] | ...And I Know You Wanna Dance | 1966 | $15 |
— Black label with green and white at left
| ❏ LP-12307 [S] | ...And I Know You Wanna Dance | 1966 | $18 |
— Black label with green and white at left
❏ LP-12427	A Touch of Gold	1969	$25
❏ LP-9334 [M]	Changes	1966	$18
❏ LP-12334 [S]	Changes	1966	$25
❏ LP-9274 [M]	Here We A-Go-Go Again!	1964	$25
— Black label with pink and white at left
| ❏ LP-12274 [S] | Here We A-Go-Go Again! | 1964 | $30 |
— Black label with pink and white at left
| ❏ LP-9274 [M] | Here We A-Go-Go Again! | 1966 | $15 |
— Black label with green and white at left
| ❏ LP-12274 [S] | Here We A-Go-Go Again! | 1966 | $18 |
— Black label with green and white at left
| ❏ LP-9264 [M] | Johnny Rivers at the Whiskey A-Go-Go | 1964 | $25 |
— Black label with pink and white at left
| ❏ LP-12264 [S] | Johnny Rivers at the Whiskey A-Go-Go | 1964 | $30 |
— Black label with pink and white at left
| ❏ LP-9264 [M] | Johnny Rivers at the Whiskey A-Go-Go | 1966 | $15 |
— Black label with green and white at left
| ❏ LP-12264 [S] | Johnny Rivers at the Whiskey A-Go-Go | 1966 | $18 |
— Black label with green and white at left
❏ LP-9324 [M]	Johnny Rivers' Golden Hits	1966	$18
❏ LP-12324 [S]	Johnny Rivers' Golden Hits	1966	$25
❏ LP-9280 [M]	Johnny Rivers In Action!	1965	$25
— Black label with pink and white at left
| ❏ LP-12280 [S] | Johnny Rivers In Action! | 1965 | $30 |
— Black label with pink and white at left
| ❏ LP-9280 [M] | Johnny Rivers In Action! | 1966 | $15 |
— Black label with green and white at left
| ❏ LP-12280 [S] | Johnny Rivers In Action! | 1966 | $18 |
— Black label with green and white at left
| ❏ LP-9293 [M] | Johnny Rivers Rocks the Folk | 1965 | $25 |
— Black label with pink and white at left
| ❏ LP-12293 [S] | Johnny Rivers Rocks the Folk | 1965 | $30 |
— Black label with pink and white at left
| ❏ LP-9293 [M] | Johnny Rivers Rocks the Folk | 1966 | $15 |
— Black label with green and white at left
| ❏ LP-12293 [S] | Johnny Rivers Rocks the Folk | 1966 | $18 |
— Black label with green and white at left
| ❏ LP-9284 [M] | Meanwhile Back at the Whiskey a-Go-Go | 1965 | $25 |
— Black label with pink and white at left
| ❏ LP-12284 [S] | Meanwhile Back at the Whiskey a-Go-Go | 1965 | $30 |
— Black label with pink and white at left
| ❏ LP-9284 [M] | Meanwhile Back at the Whiskey a-Go-Go | 1966 | $15 |
— Black label with green and white at left
| ❏ LP-12284 [S] | Meanwhile Back at the Whiskey a-Go-Go | 1966 | $18 |

Number	Title	Yr	NM

— Black label with green and white at left
❏ LP-12372 [S]	Realization	1968	$25
❏ LP-9372 [M]	Realization	1968	$40
❏ LP-9341 [M]	Rewind	1967	$25
❏ LP-12341 [S]	Rewind	1967	$25
❏ LP-16001	Slim Slo Slider	1970	$25

LIBERTY
| ❏ LW-12427 | A Touch of Gold | 198? | $10 |
— Budget-line reissue
| ❏ LN-10154 | Blue Suede Shoes | 1981 | $10 |
— Budget-line reissue
| ❏ LN-10121 | Changes | 1981 | $10 |
— Budget-line reissue
| ❏ LO-12324 | Johnny Rivers' Golden Hits | 198? | $10 |
— Budget-line reissue
| ❏ LN-10120 | The Best of Johnny Rivers | 1981 | $10 |

MCA
| ❏ 917 | Greatest Hits | 1985 | $12 |

PICKWICK
❏ SPC-3191	If You Want It, I Got It	196?	$15
❏ PC-3022 [M]	Johnny Rivers	196?	$18
❏ SPC-3022 [R]	Johnny Rivers	196?	$15
— First pressing covers have no "electronically enhanced for STEREO" at upper right
| ❏ SPC-3022 [R] | Johnny Rivers | 196? | $12 |
— Later covers have "electronically enhanced for STEREO" at upper right

RSO
| ❏ RS-1-3082 | Borrowed Time | 1980 | $12 |

SEARS
| ❏ SPS-487 | Groovin' | 1968 | $30 |
| ❏ SPS-417 | Mr. Teenage | 196? | $30 |

SOUL CITY
| ❏ SC1007-1 | Greatest Hits | 1998 | $25 |
— 500 copies, each autographed by Johnny Rivers

SUNSET
❏ SUS-5251	The Early Years	1969	$12
❏ SUS-5157 [S]	Whiskey A-Go-Go Revisited	1967	$12
❏ SUM-1157 [M]	Whiskey A-Go-Go Revisited	1967	$15

UNART
| ❏ M-20007 [M] | The Great Johnny Rivers | 1967 | $15 |
| ❏ S-21007 [S] | The Great Johnny Rivers | 1967 | $15 |

UNITED ARTISTS
❏ UA-LA075-F	Blue Suede Shoes	1973	$15
❏ UAL-3386 [M]	Go, Johnny, Go	1964	$25
❏ UAS-6386 [S]	Go, Johnny, Go	1964	$30
❏ T-90813 [M]	Go, Johnny, Go	1965	$30
— Capitol Record Club edition
| ❏ ST-90813 [S] | Go, Johnny, Go | 1965 | $30 |
— Capitol Record Club edition
❏ UAS-5532	Home Grown	1971	$18
❏ USX-93	Johnny Rivers Superpak	1971	$25
❏ UAS-5650	L.A. Reggae	1972	$18
❏ UA-LA253-G	The Very Best of Johnny Rivers	1974	$15
❏ UA-LA387-E	The Very Best of Johnny Rivers	1975	$15
❏ UA-LA486-G	Wild Night	1976	$15

WARNER BROS.
| ❏ R133498 [S] | Johnny Rivers' Golden Hits | 197? | $30 |
— RCA Music Service edition of Imperial LP-12324 on "Burbank" palm trees label; why this was pressed on Warner Bros. is anyone's guess, but it doesn't appear to be an error

RIVERS, MAVIS
CAPITOL
| ❏ T1210 [M] | Take a Number | 1959 | $75 |
| ❏ ST1210 [S] | Take a Number | 1959 | $85 |

DELOS
| ❏ DMS-4002 | It's a Good Day | 1983 | $30 |

REPRISE
❏ R-2002 [M]	Mavis	1961	$30
❏ R9-2002 [S]	Mavis	1961	$40
❏ R-6074 [M]	Mavis Rivers Meets Shorty Rogers	1963	$30
❏ RS-6074 [S]	Mavis Rivers Meets Shorty Rogers	1963	$30

VEE JAY
| ❏ VJ-1132 [M] | We Remember Mildred Bailey | 1964 | $30 |
| ❏ VJS-1132 [S] | We Remember Mildred Bailey | 1964 | $40 |

RIVERS, RAY
INSIGHT
| ❏ 202 | Let Me Hear Some Jazz | 198? | $25 |

PROJECT 3
| ❏ PR5110SD | Cool Cat on a Jazz Guitar | 1983 | $25 |

RIVERS, SAM, AND DAVE HOLLAND
IAI
| ❏ 373843 | Sam Rivers and Dave Holland | 197? | $35 |
| ❏ 373848 | Sam Rivers and Dave Holland, Vol. 2 | 1976 | $35 |

Number	Title	Yr	NM

RIVERS, SAM
ABC IMPULSE!
❏ AS-9286	Crystals	1974	$35
❏ AS-9302	Hues	1974	$35
❏ IA-9352	Sam Rivers Live	1978	$35
❏ AS-9316	Sizzle	1975	$35
❏ AS-9251	Streams	1973	$35

BLACK SAINT
| ❏ BSR-0064 | Colours | 1982 | $30 |

BLUE NOTE
| ❏ BLP-4249 [M] | A New Conception | 1966 | $150 |
| ❏ BST-84249 [S] | A New Conception | 1966 | $75 |
— With "New York, USA" address on label
| ❏ BST-84249 [S] | A New Conception | 1967 | $50 |
— With "A Division of Liberty Records" on label
| ❏ BLP-4206 [M] | Contours | 1965 | $75 |
| ❏ BST-84206 [S] | Contours | 1965 | $30 |
— With "New York, USA" address on label
| ❏ BST-84206 [S] | Contours | 1967 | $25 |
— With "A Division of Liberty Records" on label
| ❏ BLP-4261 [M] | Dimensions and Extensions | 1966 | $0 |
— Canceled
| ❏ BST-84261 [S] | Dimensions and Extensions | 1986 | $30 |
— The Finest in Jazz Since 1939" label; originally scheduled for 1966 release
| ❏ BLP-4184 [M] | Fuchsia Swing Song | 1964 | $75 |
| ❏ BST-84184 [S] | Fuchsia Swing Song | 1964 | $30 |
— With "New York, USA" address on label
| ❏ BST-84184 [S] | Fuchsia Swing Song | 1967 | $25 |
— With "A Division of Liberty Records" on label
| ❏ BN-LA453-H2 | Involution | 1975 | $35 |

ECM
| ❏ 1162 | Contrasts | 1980 | $30 |

MCA
| ❏ 4149 | Live Trio Session | 198? | $30 |

PAUSA
| ❏ 7015 | The Quest | 198? | $25 |

RED RECORD
| ❏ VPA-106 | The Quest | 198? | $30 |

TOMATO
| ❏ TOM-8002 | Waves | 1979 | $30 |

RIVERSIDE JAZZ STARS, THE
RIVERSIDE
| ❏ RLP-397 [M] | A Jazz Version of "Kean | 1961 | $250 |
| ❏ RS-9397 [S] | A Jazz Version of "Kean | 1961 | $250 |

RIVIERAS, THE (1)
POST
| ❏ 2000 | The Rivieras Sing | 196? | $40 |

RIVIERAS, THE (2)
RIVIERA
| ❏ 701 [M] | Campus Party | 1964 | $300 |
U.S.A.
| ❏ 102 [M] | Let's Have a Party | 1964 | $175 |

RIVINGTONS, THE
LIBERTY

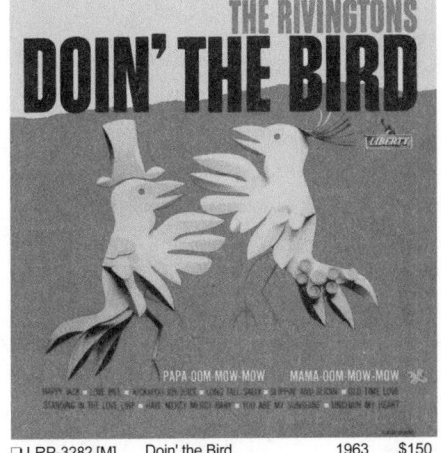

| ❏ LRP-3282 [M] | Doin' the Bird | 1963 | $150 |
| ❏ LST-7282 [S] | Doin' the Bird | 1963 | $250 |

RIZZI, TONY
MILAGRO
| ❏ 1000 | Tony Rizzi Plays Charlie Christian | 197? | $30 |

STARLITE
| ❏ 6002 [10] | Tony Rizzi Guitar | 1954 | $50 |

Number	Title	Yr	NM

ROACH, FREDDIE

BLUE NOTE

Number	Title	Yr	NM
❏ BLP-4190 [M]	All That's Good	1965	$75
❏ BST-84190 [S]	All That's Good	1965	$30
— With "New York, USA" address on label			
❏ BST-84190 [S]	All That's Good	1967	$35
— With "A Division of Liberty Records" on label			
❏ BLP-4168 [M]	Brown Sugar	1964	$75
❏ BST-84168 [S]	Brown Sugar	1964	$30
— With "New York, USA" address on label			
❏ BST-84168 [S]	Brown Sugar	1967	$35
— With "A Division of Liberty Records" on label			
❏ BLP-4113 [M]	Down to Earth	1962	$75
❏ BST-84113 [S]	Down to Earth	1962	$30
— With "New York, USA" address on label			
❏ BST-84113 [S]	Down to Earth	1967	$35
— With "A Division of Liberty Records" on label			
❏ BLP-4158 [M]	Good Move	1964	$75
❏ BST-84158 [S]	Good Move	1964	$30
— With "New York, USA" address on label			
❏ BST-84158 [S]	Good Move	1967	$35
— With "A Division of Liberty Records" on label			
❏ BLP-4128 [M]	Mo' Greens, Please	1963	$75
❏ BST-84128 [S]	Mo' Greens, Please	1963	$30
— With "New York, USA" address on label			
❏ BST-84128 [S]	Mo' Greens, Please	1967	$35
— With "A Division of Liberty Records" on label			

PRESTIGE

Number	Title	Yr	NM
❏ PRLP-7507 [M]	Mocha Motion	1967	$30
❏ PRST-7507 [S]	Mocha Motion	1967	$25
❏ PRLP-7521 [M]	My People -- Soul People	1967	$30
❏ PRST-7521 [S]	My People -- Soul People	1967	$25
❏ PRLP-7490 [M]	The Soul Book	1967	$30
❏ PRST-7490 [S]	The Soul Book	1967	$25

ROACH, MAX, AND ANTHONY BRAXTON

BLACK SAINT

Number	Title	Yr	NM
❏ BSR-0024 [B]	Birth and Rebirth	198?	$18

HAT HUT

| ❏ 06 | One in Two -- Two in One | 1980 | $50 |

ROACH, MAX, AND ARCHIE SHEPP

HAT HUT

| ❏ 13 | The Long March | 1980 | $50 |

ROACH, MAX, AND CECIL TAYLOR

SOUL NOTE

| ❏ SN-1100/1 | Historic Concerts | 1985 | $35 |

ROACH, MAX, AND CLIFFORD BROWN

See CLIFFORD BROWN.

ROACH, MAX, AND CONNIE CROTHERS

NEW ARTISTS

| ❏ NA-1001 | Swish | 198? | $30 |

ROACH, MAX, AND STAN LEVEY

LIBERTY

| ❏ LRP-3064 [M] | Drummin' the Blues | 1957 | $175 |

ROACH, MAX; SONNY CLARK; GEORGE DUVIVIER

TIME

| ❏ 52101 [M] | Max Roach, Sonny Clark, George Duvivier | 1962 | $75 |
| ❏ S-2101 [S] | Max Roach, Sonny Clark, George Duvivier | 1962 | $40 |

ROACH, MAX

ABC IMPULSE!

| ❏ AS-16 [S] | It's Time | 1968 | $160 |
| ❏ AS-8 [S] | Percussion Bitter Sweet | 1968 | $250 |

ARGO

| ❏ LP-623 [M] | Max | 1958 | $150 |
| ❏ LPS-623 [S] | Max | 1958 | $40 |

ATLANTIC

❏ 1467 [M]	Drums Unlimited	1966	$50
❏ SD1467 [S]	Drums Unlimited	1966	$75
❏ SD1587	Lift Every Voice and Sing	1972	$30
❏ 1435 [M]	Max Roach Trio Featuring the Legendary Hasaan	1965	$50
❏ SD1435 [S]	Max Roach Trio Featuring the Legendary Hasaan	1965	$75
❏ SD1510 [S]	Members Don't Get Weary	1968	$50

BAINBRIDGE

| ❏ 1042 | Max Roach | 198? | $25 |
| ❏ 1044 | Max Roach/George Duvivier/Sonny Clark | 198? | $25 |

CANDID

| ❏ CD-8002 [M] | We Insist -- Freedom Now Suite | 1960 | $120 |
| ❏ CS-9002 [S] | We Insist -- Freedom Now Suite | 1960 | $120 |

DEBUT

Number	Title	Yr	NM
❏ DLP-13 [10]	Max Roach Quartet Featuring Hank Mobley	1954	$400

EMARCY

❏ MG-36108 [M]	Jazz in 3/4 Time	1957	$250
❏ SR-80002 [S]	Jazz in 3/4 Time	1959	$250
❏ 826456-1	Jazz in 3/4 Time	1986	$25
❏ MG-36132 [M]	Max Roach + 4 on the Chicago Scene	1958	$120
❏ MG-36098 [M]	Max Roach + 4	1957	$250
❏ SR-80001 [S]	Max Roach + 4	1959	$250
❏ MG-36140 [M]	Max Roach Plus Four At Newport	1958	$120
❏ SR-80010 [S]	Max Roach Plus Four At Newport	1959	$250
❏ MG-36144 [M]	Max Roach with the Boston Percussion Ensemble	1958	$120
❏ SR-80015 [S]	Max Roach with the Boston Percussion Ensemble	1959	$250
❏ 814190-1	Standard Time	198?	$30
❏ MG-36127 [M]	The Max Roach 4 Plays Charlie Parker	1958	$175
❏ SR-80019 [S]	The Max Roach 4 Plays Charlie Parker	1959	$250

FANTASY

❏ OJC-304	Deeds, Not Words	1988	$25
❏ OJC-202	Max Roach Quartet Featuring Hank Mobley	1985	$25
❏ 6007 [M]	Speak Brother, Speak	1963	$75
❏ 86007 [S]	Speak Brother, Speak	1963	$75

HAT ART

| ❏ 4026 | The Long March | 1986 | $75 |

IMPULSE!

❏ A-16 [M]	It's Time	1962	$250
❏ AS-16 [S]	It's Time	1962	$250
❏ A-8 [M]	Percussion Bitter Sweet	1961	$250
❏ AS-8 [S]	Percussion Bitter Sweet	1961	$160

JAZZLAND

| ❏ JLP-79 [M] | Conversation | 1962 | $75 |
| ❏ JLP-979 [S] | Conversation | 1962 | $75 |

MCA

| ❏ 29053 | It's Time | 1980 | $25 |

MERCURY

❏ MG-20539 [M]	Moon Faced and Starry-Eyed	1960	$150
❏ SR-60215 [S]	Moon Faced and Starry-Eyed	1960	$175
❏ MG-20760 [M]	Parisian Sketches	1962	$150
❏ SR-60760 [S]	Parisian Sketches	1962	$150
❏ MG-20491 [M]	Quiet As It's Kept	1959	$150
❏ SR-60170 [S]	Quiet As It's Kept	1959	$175
❏ MG-20911 [M]	The Many Sides of Max	1964	$150
❏ SR-60911 [S]	The Many Sides of Max	1964	$150

MILESTONE

| ❏ 47061 | Conversations | 198? | $35 |

RIVERSIDE

❏ RLP 12-280 [M]	Deeds, Not Words	1958	$300
❏ RLP-1122 [S]	Deeds, Not Words	1959	$300
❏ RS-3018 [S]	Deeds, Not Words	1968	$150

SOUL NOTE

❏ SN-1109	Easy Winners	1985	$30
❏ SN-1053	In the Light	1982	$30
❏ SN-1003	Pictures in a Frame	198?	$30
❏ SN-1103	Scott Free	1985	$30
❏ SN-1093	Survivors	1985	$30

TIME

❏ T-70003 [M]	Award Winning Drummer	1959	$175
❏ ST-70003 [S]	Award Winning Drummer	1959	$120
❏ 52087 [M]	Max Roach	1962	$40
❏ S-2087 [S]	Max Roach	1962	$40

TRIP

| ❏ TLP-5559 | Jazz in 3/4 Time | 197? | $30 |
| ❏ TLP-5522 | Max Roach + 4 | 197? | $30 |

ROACH, MAX/ART BLAKEY

BLUE NOTE

| ❏ BLP-5010 [10] | Max Roach Quintet / Art Blakey and His Band | 1952 | $1000 |

ROAD, THE

KAMA SUTRA

❏ KSBS-2032 [B]	Cognition	1970	$30
❏ KLPS-8075	The Road	1969	$25
❏ KSBS-2012	The Road	1970	$18
— Reissue of 8075			

ROAD RUNNERS, THE

BEAT ROCKET

| ❏ BR104 | The Road Runners | 1999 | $15 |

LONDON

| ❏ LL3381 [M] | The New Mustang (And Other Hot Rod Hits) | 1964 | $250 |
| ❏ PS381 [S] | The New Mustang (And Other Hot Rod Hits) | 1964 | $300 |

ROANE, STEPHEN

LABOR

| ❏ 2 | Siblings | 1980 | $30 |

ROARING SEVEN JAZZBAND, THE

STOMP OFF

Number	Title	Yr	NM
❏ SOS-1019	Hot Dance	198?	$25

ROBBINS, ADELAIDE/MARIAN MCPARTLAND/ BARBARA CARROLL

SAVOY

| ❏ MG-12097 [M] | Lookin' for a Boy | 1957 | $50 |

ROBBINS, DENNIS

MCA

| ❏ 5720 | The First of Me | 1986 | $10 |

ROBBINS, HARGUS "PIG

CHART

| ❏ CHS-1011 | One More Time | 196? | $18 |

ELEKTRA

❏ 7E-1110	Country Instrumentalist of the Year	1977	$15
❏ 6E-129	Pig in a Poke	1978	$15
❏ 6E-185	Unbreakable Hearts	1979	$15

TIME

| ❏ 52107 [M] | A Bit of Country Piano | 1963 | $25 |
| ❏ S-2107 [S] | A Bit of Country Piano | 1963 | $30 |

ROBBINS, MARTY

ARTCO

| ❏ 110 | The Best of Marty Robbins | 1973 | $40 |

CBS SPECIAL PRODUCTS

| ❏ P17730 | The Great Love Songs | 1984 | $12 |

COLUMBIA

❏ PC34448	Adios Amigo	1977	$15
— No bar code on cover			
❏ PC34448	Adios Amigo	198?	$10
— With bar code on cover			
❏ C238870	A Lifetime of Song 1951-1982	1983	$18
❏ JC36085	All Around Cowboy	1979	$15
❏ PC36085	All Around Cowboy	198?	$10
— Budget-line reissue			
❏ CG31361	All Time Greatest Hits	1972	$25
❏ FC38309	Biggest Hits	1982	$15
❏ KC31341	Bound for Old Mexico (Great Hits from South of the Border)	1973	$18
❏ CL2817 [M]	By the Time I Get to Phoenix	1968	$75
❏ CS9617 [S]	By the Time I Get to Phoenix	1968	$25
❏ CS9617 [M]	By the Time I Get to Phoenix	1968	$50
— Special Mono Radio Station Copy" with stereo number and "Mono" on white label			
❏ CL2735 [M]	Christmas with Marty Robbins	1967	$50

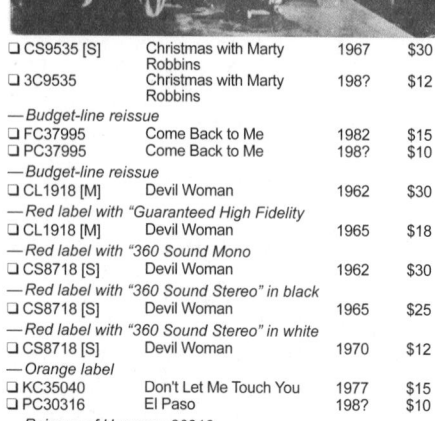

❏ CS9535 [S]	Christmas with Marty Robbins	1967	$30
❏ 3C9535	Christmas with Marty Robbins	198?	$12
— Budget-line reissue			
❏ FC37995	Come Back to Me	1982	$15
❏ PC37995	Come Back to Me	198?	$10
— Budget-line reissue			
❏ CL1918 [M]	Devil Woman	1962	$30
— Red label with "Guaranteed High Fidelity			
❏ CL1918 [M]	Devil Woman	1965	$18
— Red label with "360 Sound Mono			
❏ CS8718 [S]	Devil Woman	1962	$30
— Red label with "360 Sound Stereo" in black			
❏ CS8718 [S]	Devil Woman	1965	$25
— Red label with "360 Sound Stereo" in white			
❏ CS8718 [S]	Devil Woman	1970	$12
— Orange label			
❏ KC35040	Don't Let Me Touch You	1977	$15
❏ PC30316	El Paso	198?	$10
— Reissue of Harmony 30316			

Number	Title	Yr	NM
❏ PC34303	El Paso City	198?	$10
— With bar code on cover			
❏ PC34303	El Paso City	1976	$15
— No bar code on cover			
❏ FC37353	Encore	1981	$15
❏ PC37353	Encore	198?	$10
— Budget-line reissue			
❏ JC36860	Everything I've Always Wanted	1981	$15
❏ KC35629	Greatest Hits Vol. IV	1978	$15
❏ CL1349 [M]	Gunfighter Ballads and Trail Songs	1959	$30
— Red and black label with six "eye" logos			
❏ CL1349 [M]	Gunfighter Ballads and Trail Songs	1963	$18
— Red label with "Guaranteed High Fidelity" or "360 Sound Mono			
❏ CS8158 [S]	Gunfighter Ballads and Trail Songs	1959	$40
— Red and black label with six "eye" logos			
❏ CS8158 [S]	Gunfighter Ballads and Trail Songs	1963	$25
— Red label with "360 Sound Stereo			
❏ CS8158 [S]	Gunfighter Ballads and Trail Songs	1971	$12
— Orange label			
❏ PC8158	Gunfighter Ballads and Trail Songs	198?	$10
— Reissue with new prefix			
❏ CG33630	Gunfighter Ballads and Trail Songs/My Woman, My Woman, My Wife	1976	$18
❏ KC32586	Have I Told You Lately That I Love You	1974	$18
❏ CL2040 [M]	Hawaii's Calling Me	1963	$30
— Red label with "Guaranteed High Fidelity			
❏ CL2040 [M]	Hawaii's Calling Me	1965	$18
— Red label with "360 Sound Mono			
❏ CS8840 [S]	Hawaii's Calling Me	1963	$30
— Red label with "360 Sound Stereo" in black			
❏ CS8840 [S]	Hawaii's Calling Me	1965	$25
— Red label with "360 Sound Stereo" in white			
❏ CL2176 [M]	Island Woman	1964	$30
— Red label with "Guaranteed High Fidelity			
❏ CS8976 [S]	Island Woman	1964	$40
— Red label with "360 Sound Stereo" in black			
❏ CL2176 [M]	Island Woman	1965	$25
— Red label with "360 Sound Mono			
❏ CS8976 [S]	Island Woman	1965	$30
— Red label with "360 Sound Stereo" in white			
❏ CS9811	It's a Sin	1969	$25
— Red "360 Sound" label			
❏ CS9811	It's a Sin	1970	$12
— Orange label			
❏ KC31628	I've Got a Woman's Love	1972	$18
❏ CS9725	I Walk Alone	1968	$25
— Red "360 Sound" label			
❏ CS9725	I Walk Alone	1970	$12
— Orange label			
❏ CL1666 [M]	Just a Little Sentimental	1961	$30
— Red and black label with six "eye" logos			
❏ CL1666 [M]	Just a Little Sentimental	1963	$18
— Red label with "Guaranteed High Fidelity" or "360 Sound Mono			
❏ CS8466 [S]	Just a Little Sentimental	1961	$30
— Red and black label with six "eye" logos			
❏ CS8466 [S]	Just a Little Sentimental	1963	$25
— Red label with "360 Sound Stereo			
❏ KC239575	Long, Long Ago	1984	$18
❏ CL1801 [M]	Marty After Midnight	1962	$50
— Red and black label with six "eye" logos			
❏ CL1801 [M]	Marty After Midnight	1962	$25
— Red label with "Guaranteed High Fidelity			
❏ CL1801 [M]	Marty After Midnight	1965	$18
— Red label with "360 Sound Mono			
❏ CS8601 [S]	Marty After Midnight	1962	$100
— Red and black label with six "eye" logos			
❏ CS8601 [S]	Marty After Midnight	1962	$30
— Red label with "360 Sound Stereo" in black			
❏ CS8601 [S]	Marty After Midnight	1965	$25
— Red label with "360 Sound Stereo" in white			
❏ CL1189 [M]	Marty Robbins	1958	$100
— Red and black label with six "eye" logos			
❏ CL1189 [M]	Marty Robbins	1963	$25
— Red label with "Guaranteed High Fidelity" or "360 Sound Mono			
❏ KG31361	Marty Robbins' All-Time Greatest Hits	1972	$25
❏ C30571	Marty Robbins' Greatest Hits Vol. III	1971	$18
❏ PC30571	Marty Robbins' Greatest Hits Vol. III	198?	$10
— Budget-line reissue			
❏ GP15	Marty's Country	1969	$30
❏ CL1325 [M]	Marty's Greatest Hits	1959	$100
— Red and black label with six "eye" logos			
❏ CL1325 [M]	Marty's Greatest Hits	1963	$25
— Red label with "Guaranteed High Fidelity" or "360 Sound Mono			

Number	Title	Yr	NM
❏ CS8639 [P]	Marty's Greatest Hits	1962	$30
— Red label with "360 Sound Stereo" in black			
❏ CS8639 [P]	Marty's Greatest Hits	1965	$25
— Red label with "360 Sound Stereo" in white			
❏ CS8639 [P]	Marty's Greatest Hits	1970	$12
— Orange label			
❏ PC8639	Marty's Greatest Hits	198?	$10
— Reissue with new prefix			
❏ CL1635 [M]	More Greatest Hits	1961	$30
— Red and black label with six "eye" logos			
❏ CL1635 [M]	More Greatest Hits	1963	$18
— Red label with "Guaranteed High Fidelity" or "360 Sound Mono			
❏ CS8435 [S]	More Greatest Hits	1961	$30
— Red and black label with six "eye" logos			
❏ CS8435 [S]	More Greatest Hits	1963	$25
— Red label with "360 Sound Stereo			
❏ CS8435 [S]	More Greatest Hits	1971	$12
— Orange label			
❏ PC8435	More Greatest Hits	198?	$10
— Reissue with new prefix			
❏ CL1481 [M]	More Gunfighter Ballads and Trail Songs	1960	$40
— Red and black label with six "eye" logos			
❏ CL1481 [M]	More Gunfighter Ballads and Trail Songs	1963	$18
— Red label with "Guaranteed High Fidelity" or "360 Sound Mono			
❏ CS8272 [S]	More Gunfighter Ballads and Trail Songs	1960	$40
— Red and black label with six "eye" logos			
❏ CS8272 [S]	More Gunfighter Ballads and Trail Songs	1963	$25
— Red label with "360 Sound Stereo			
❏ CS8272 [S]	More Gunfighter Ballads and Trail Songs	1971	$12
— Orange label			
❏ PC8272	More Gunfighter Ballads and More	198?	$10
— Reissue with new prefix			
❏ CL2645 [M]	My Kind of Country	1967	$30
❏ CS9445 [S]	My Kind of Country	1967	$25
❏ CS9978	My Woman, My Woman, My Wife	1970	$25
— Red "360 Sound" label			
❏ CS9978	My Woman, My Woman, My Wife	1970	$18
— Orange label			
❏ KC33476	No Sign of Loneliness Here	1976	$15
❏ CL1855 [M]	Portrait of Marty	1962	$40
❏ CS8655 [S]	Portrait of Marty	1962	$50
❏ CL1855/CS 8655	Portrait of Marty Bonus Photo	1962	$30
❏ CL2072 [M]	Return of the Gunfighter	1963	$25
— Red label with "Guaranteed High Fidelity			
❏ CL2072 [M]	Return of the Gunfighter	1965	$18
— Red label with "360 Sound Mono			
❏ CS8872 [S]	Return of the Gunfighter	1963	$30
— Red label with "360 Sound Stereo" in black			
❏ CS8872 [S]	Return of the Gunfighter	1965	$25
— Red label with "360 Sound Stereo" in white			
❏ CS8872 [S]	Return of the Gunfighter	1970	$12
— Orange label			
❏ CL2220 [M]	R.F.D.	1964	$25
— Red label with "Guaranteed High Fidelity			
❏ CL2220 [M]	R.F.D.	1965	$18
— Red label with "360 Sound Mono			
❏ CS9020 [S]	R.F.D.	1964	$30
— Red label with "360 Sound Stereo" in black			
❏ CS9020 [S]	R.F.D.	1965	$25
— Red label with "360 Sound Stereo" in white			
❏ CL2601 [10]	Rock 'N Roll 'N Robbins	1956	$1000
❏ FC38603	Some Memories Just Won't Die	1983	$15
❏ CL1087 [M]	Song of the Islands	1957	$120
— Red and black label with six "eye" logos			
❏ CL1087 [M]	Song of the Islands	1963	$25
— Red label with "Guaranteed High Fidelity" or "360 Sound Mono			
❏ CS9425 [R]	Song of the Islands	1967	$18
❏ CL2527 [M]	The Drifter	1966	$18
❏ CS9327 [S]	The Drifter	1966	$25
— Red "360 Sound" label			
❏ CS9327 [S]	The Drifter	1970	$12
— Orange label			
❏ FC37541	The Legend	1982	$15
❏ PC37541	The Legend	1985	$10
— Budget-line reissue			
❏ JC35446	The Performer	1979	$15
❏ CL976 [M]	The Song of Robbins	1957	$150
— Red and black label with six "eye" logos			
❏ CL976 [M]	The Song of Robbins	1963	$25
— Red label with "Guaranteed High Fidelity" or "360 Sound Mono			
❏ CS9421 [R]	The Song of Robbins	1967	$18
— Red "360 Sound" label			
❏ CS9421 [R]	The Song of Robbins	1970	$12

Number	Title	Yr	NM
— Orange label			
❏ G30881	The World of Marty Robbins	1971	$25
❏ C30816	Today	1971	$18
❏ CL2725 [M]	Tonight Carmen	1967	$30
❏ CS9525 [S]	Tonight Carmen	1967	$25
— Red "360 Sound" label			
❏ CS9525 [S]	Tonight Carmen	1970	$12
— Orange label			
❏ CL2304 [M]	Turn the Lights Down Low	1965	$30
— Red label with "Guaranteed High Fidelity			
❏ CL2304 [M]	Turn the Lights Down Low	1965	$18
— Red label with "360 Sound Mono			
❏ CS9104 [S]	Turn the Lights Down Low	1965	$30
— Red label with "360 Sound Stereo" in black			
❏ CS9104 [S]	Turn the Lights Down Low	1965	$25
— Red label with "360 Sound Stereo" in white			
❏ CL2448 [M]	What God Has Done	1966	$18
❏ CS9248 [S]	What God Has Done	1966	$25
— Red "360 Sound" label			
❏ CS9248 [S]	What God Has Done	1970	$12
— Orange label			
❏ JC36507	With Love	1980	$15

COLUMBIA LIMITED EDITION

Number	Title	Yr	NM
❏ LE10045	By the Time I Get to Phoenix	197?	$12
❏ LE10579	Devil Woman	197?	$12
❏ LE10575	From the Heart	197?	$12
❏ LE10030	It's a Sin	197?	$12
❏ LE10033	My Kind of Country	197?	$12
❏ LE10022	Portrait of Marty	197?	$12
❏ LE10144	R.F.D.	197?	$12
❏ LE10576	Streets of Laredo	197?	$12
❏ LE10578	The Song of Robbins	197?	$12
❏ LE10577	The Story of My Life	197?	$12
❏ LE10046	Today	197?	$12
❏ LE10189	Tonight Carmen	197?	$12
❏ LE10145	Turn the Lights Down Low	197?	$12

COLUMBIA MUSICAL TREASURY

Number	Title	Yr	NM
❏ P5S5812	Marty	1972	$40

COLUMBIA RECORD CLUB

Number	Title	Yr	NM
❏ DS445	Bend in the River	1968	$40

COLUMBIA SPECIAL PRODUCTS

Number	Title	Yr	NM
❏ P17138	Banquet of Songs	1983	$12
❏ C11311	By the Time I Get to Phoenix	1972	$18
❏ C11513	By the Time I Get to Phoenix	1973	$18
❏ C10980 [S]	Christmas with Marty Robbins	1972	$18
— Stereo reissue; "Distributed by Apex Rendezvous, Inc." on back cover			
❏ P13358	Christmas with Marty Robbins	1976	$15
❏ 3P16578	Classics	1983	$25
❏ P16914	Country Classics	1983	$12
❏ P17209	Country Cowboy	1983	$12
❏ P17136	Forever Yours	1983	$12
❏ P14035	Legendary Music Man	1977	$15
❏ P15812	Marty Robbins' Best	1982	$12
❏ P12416	Marty Robbins' Own Favorites	1974	$18
❏ C11122	Marty's Greatest Hits	1972	$15
❏ P16561	Reflections	1982	$12
❏ P17120	Sincerely	1983	$12
❏ P17367	Song of the Islands	1983	$12
❏ P17137	That Country Feeling	1983	$12
❏ P14613	The Best of Marty Robbins	1978	$12
❏ P17159	The Great Marty Robbins	1983	$12
❏ P17206	The Legendary Marty Robbins	1983	$12
❏ P15594	The Number One Cowboy	1981	$12

DECCA

Number	Title	Yr	NM
❏ DL75389	This Much a Man	1972	$18

HARMONY

Number	Title	Yr	NM
❏ KH30316	El Paso	1971	$15
❏ KH31257	Marty Robbins Favorites	1972	$15
❏ HS11338	Singing the Blues	1969	$18
❏ H31258	Songs of the Islands	1972	$25
❏ KH32286	Streets of Laredo	1973	$15
❏ HS11409	The Story of My Life	1970	$18

MCA

Number	Title	Yr	NM
❏ 27060	20th Century Drifter	1983	$18
— Reissue of older material			
❏ 421	Good'n Country	1974	$18
❏ 342	Marty Robbins	1973	$18
❏ 61	This Much a Man	1973	$15
— Reissue of Decca LP			

READER'S DIGEST

Number	Title	Yr	NM
❏ RDA-054/A	His Greatest Hits and Finest Performances	1983	$30

TIME-LIFE

Number	Title	Yr	NM
❏ STW-109	Country Music	1981	$15

ROBBINS, RONNY

COLUMBIA

Number	Title	Yr	NM
❏ CS9944	Columbia Records Presents Marty Robbins Jr.	1970	$30
— As "Marty Robbins, Jr.			

Number	Title	Yr	NM

ROBBS, THE
MERCURY
| ❏ SR-61130 [S] | The Robbs | 1967 | $30 |
| ❏ MG-21130 [M] | The Robbs | 1967 | $40 |

ROBERT, GEORGE
CONTEMPORARY
| ❏ C-14037 | Sun Dance | 1988 | $25 |

ROBERTINO
KAPP
❏ KS-3338 [S]	Italia Mia	1963	$25
❏ KL-1338 [M]	Italia Mia	1963	$18
❏ KS-3252 [S]	O Sole Mio	1962	$25
❏ KL-1252 [M]	O Sole Mio	1962	$18
❏ KS-3471 [S]	The Best of Robertino	1966	$18
❏ KL-1471 [M]	The Best of Robertino	1966	$15
❏ KS-3293 [S]	The Young Italian Singing Sensation	1962	$25
❏ KL-1293 [M]	The Young Italian Singing Sensation	1962	$18

ROBERTS, AUSTIN
CHELSEA
| ❏ CES-1004 | Austin Roberts | 1972 | $15 |
| ❏ BCL1-0199 | The Last Thing on My Mind | 1973 | $15 |
NEW PAX
| ❏ NP-33016 | 8 Days (A Personal Journey) | 1977 | $15 |
PRIVATE STOCK
| ❏ PS-5000 | Rocky | 1975 | $15 |

ROBERTS, DAVID THOMAS
STOMP OFF
❏ SOS-1021	An Album of Early Folk Rags	198?	$25
❏ SOS-1132	The Amazon Rag	1986	$25
❏ SOS-1075	Through the Bottomlands	1985	$25

ROBERTS, GEORGE
COLUMBIA
| ❏ CL1384 [M] | Meet Mr. Roberts -- George Roberts and His Big Bass Trombone | 195? | $100 |

ROBERTS, HANK
JMT
| ❏ 834416-1 | Black Pastels | 1988 | $25 |

ROBERTS, HOWARD
ABC IMPULSE!
| ❏ AS-9207 | Antelope Freeway | 1972 | $35 |
| ❏ AS-9299 | Equinox Express Elevator | 1974 | $35 |
CAPITOL
❏ T2609 [M]	All-Time Great Instrumental Hits	1966	$85
❏ ST2609 [S]	All-Time Great Instrumental Hits	1966	$50
❏ T1887 [M]	Color Him Funky	1963	$85
❏ ST1887 [S]	Color Him Funky	1963	$75
❏ T2400 [M]	Goodies	1965	$85
❏ ST2400 [S]	Goodies	1965	$50
❏ T2824 [M]	Guilty	1967	$50
❏ ST2824 [S]	Guilty	1967	$85
❏ SM-1961 [S]	H.R. Is A Dirty Guitar Player	1976	$25
—Reissue with new prefix			
❏ T1961 [M]	H.R. Is A Dirty Guitar Player	1963	$85
❏ ST1961 [S]	H.R. Is A Dirty Guitar Player	1963	$50
❏ T2716 [M]	Jaunty -- Jolly	1967	$75
❏ ST2716 [S]	Jaunty -- Jolly	1967	$85
❏ ST2901 [S]	Out Of Sight -- But In Mind	1968	$50
❏ T2214 [M]	Something's Cookin'	1965	$50
❏ ST2214 [S]	Something's Cookin'	1965	$50
❏ ST-11247	Sounds	1974	$30
❏ ST-336	Spinning Wheel	1970	$50
❏ T2478 [M]	Whatever's Fair	1966	$75
❏ ST2478 [S]	Whatever's Fair	1966	$50
CONCORD JAZZ
❏ CJ-53	The Real Howard Roberts	1978	$25
DISCOVERY
❏ 812	Turning to Spring	1980	$30
NORGRAN
❏ MGN-1106 [M]	Mr. Roberts Plays Guitar	1955	$0
—Canceled			
VERVE
❏ MGV-8305 [M]	Good Pickin's	1959	$150
❏ V-8305 [M]	Good Pickin's	1961	$30
❏ MGV-8192 [M]	Mr. Roberts Plays Guitar	1957	$175
❏ V-8192 [M]	Mr. Roberts Plays Guitar	1961	$30
❏ UMV-2673	Mr. Roberts Plays Guitar	198?	$30
❏ VSP-29 [M]	The Movin' Man	1966	$25
❏ VSPS-29 [R]	The Movin' Man	1966	$30
❏ V-8662 [M]	Velvet Groove	1966	$25
❏ V6-8662 [S]	Velvet Groove	1966	$35

ROBERTS, JUDY
INNER CITY
| ❏ IC-1078 | Judy Roberts Band | 198? | $30 |
| ❏ IC-1138 | Nights in Brazil | 198? | $30 |

Number	Title	Yr	NM
❏ IC-1088	The Other World	198?	$30
PAUSA
❏ 7147	Judy Roberts Trio	198?	$25
❏ 7176	You Are There	1985	$25

ROBERTS, KENNY
STARDAY
❏ SLP-434	Country Music Singing Sensation	1969	$25
❏ SLP-336 [M]	Indian Love Call	1965	$40
❏ SLP-406 [M]	The Incredible Kenny Roberts	1967	$30
VOCALION
❏ VL73770	Kenny Roberts Sings Country Songs	196?	$15

ROBERTS, LUCKEY, AND WILLIE "THE LION" SMITH
GOOD TIME JAZZ
| ❏ L-12035 [M] | Harlem Piano Solos | 1958 | $40 |
| ❏ S-10035 [S] | Harlem Piano Solos | 1958 | $30 |

ROBERTS, LUCKEY
PERIOD
| ❏ RL-1929 [M] | Happy Go Luckey | 1956 | $40 |

ROBERTS, MARCUS
NOVUS
| ❏ 3078-1-N | Deep in the Shed | 1990 | $35 |
| ❏ 3051-1-N | The Truth Is Spoken Here | 1989 | $30 |

ROBERTS, PAT
DOT
| ❏ DLP-26011 | This Is Pat Roberts | 1973 | $18 |

ROBERTS, PERNELL
RCA VICTOR
| ❏ LPM-2662 [M] | Come All Ye Fair and Tender Ladies | 1963 | $30 |
| ❏ LSP-2662 [S] | Come All Ye Fair and Tender Ladies | 1963 | $40 |

ROBERTS, ROCKY, AND THE AIREDALES
BRUNSWICK
❏ BL754133 [S]	Rocky Roberts and the Airedales	1968	$25
❏ BL54133 [M]	Rocky Roberts and the Airedales	1968	$100
—Mono is yellow label promo only			

ROBERTS, WILLIAM NEIL
KLAVIER
| ❏ 510 | Great Scott! | 197? | $30 |
| ❏ 516 | Scott Joplin Ragtime, Vol. 2 | 1974 | $30 |

ROBERTSON, DALE
RCA VICTOR
| ❏ LPM-2158 [M] | Dale Robertson Presents His Album of Western Classics | 1959 | $100 |
| ❏ LSP-2158 [S] | Dale Robertson Presents His Album of Western Classics | 1959 | $150 |

ROBERTSON, DON
RCA VICTOR
| ❏ LPM-3348 [M] | Heart on My Sleeve | 1965 | $25 |
| ❏ LSP-3348 [S] | Heart on My Sleeve | 1965 | $30 |

ROBERTSON, HERB
JMT
| ❏ 834420-1 | Shades of Bud Powell | 1988 | $25 |

ROBERTSON, PAUL
PALO ALTO
| ❏ PA-8013 | Old Friends, New Friends | 1982 | $25 |
| ❏ PA-8002 | The Song Is You | 1981 | $25 |

ROBERTSON, PERRY
CHIAROSCURO
| ❏ 190 | The Traveler | 1977 | $18 |

ROBERTSON, ROBBIE
GEFFEN
| ❏ GEF-24160 | Robbie Robertson | 1987 | $12 |
| ❏ GEF24303 | Storyville | 1991 | $30 |

ROBERTSON, TEXAS JIM
DESIGN
| ❏ DLP-115 [M] | Golden Hits of Country and Western Music | 196? | $15 |
| ❏ DLP-132 [M] | Sacred Country & Western Songs | 196? | $15 |

Number	Title	Yr	NM
GRAND PRIX
❏ 185 [M]	Texas Jim Robertson Sings the Great Hits of Country & Western	196?	$18
MASTERSEAL
❏ 0(# unknown) [10]	Eight Top Western Hits	195?	$75
STRAND
❏ 1016 [M]	Texas Jim Robertson	1961	$40

ROBESON, PAUL
COLUMBIA MASTERWORKS
| ❏ ML4105 [10] | Spirituals | 1949 | $100 |
| ❏ ML2038 [10] | Swing Low Sweet Chariot | 1949 | $100 |
VANGUARD
❏ VSD-79193 [S]	Ballad for Americans: Carnegie Hall Concert, Vol. 2	1965	$25
❏ VRS-9193 [M]	Ballad for Americans: Carnegie Hall Concert, Vol. 2	1965	$25
❏ VSD-57/58	Essential Paul Robeson	197?	$25
❏ VRS-9051 [M]	Paul Robeson at Carnegie Hall	1960	$30
❏ VRS-9037 [M]	Spirituals and Folksongs	1959	$75

ROBICHAUX, JOE
FOLKLYRIC
| ❏ 9032 | Joe Robichaux and the Hot New Orleans Rhythm Boys | 198? | $25 |

ROBINS, CAROL JOY
OPTIMISM
| ❏ OP-3202 | Joy Sings the Blues | 1988 | $25 |

ROBINS, THE (1)
GNP CRESCENDO
| ❏ GNPS-9034 [B] | The Best of the Robins | 1975 | $25 |
WHIPPET
| ❏ WLP-703 [M] | Rock 'n' Roll with the Robins | 1958 | $800 |

ROBINSON, FLOYD
RCA VICTOR
| ❏ LPM-2162 [M] | Floyd Robinson | 1960 | $100 |
| ❏ LSP-2162 [S] | Floyd Robinson | 1960 | $120 |

ROBINSON, FREDDY
ENTERPRISE
| ❏ ENS-1025 | Freddy Robinson at the Drive-In | 1972 | $30 |
PACIFIC JAZZ
| ❏ ST-20176 | Hot Fun in the Summertime | 1971 | $35 |
| ❏ ST-20162 | The Coming Atlantis | 1970 | $35 |

ROBINSON, JIM, AND BILLIE AND DEDE PIERCE
ATLANTIC
| ❏ 1409 [M] | Jim Robinson and Billie & DeDe Pierce | 1963 | $50 |
| ❏ SD1409 [S] | Jim Robinson and Billie & DeDe Pierce | 1963 | $50 |

ROBINSON, JIM
BIOGRAPH
| ❏ CEN-8 | Jim Robinson and His New Orleans Band | 197? | $25 |
| ❏ CEN-16 | Jim Robinson and His New Orleans Joymakers | 197? | $25 |
CENTER
| ❏ PLP-1 [M] | Jim Robinson and His New Orleans Band | 196? | $35 |
GHB
❏ GHB-196	1944 Revisited	1986	$25
❏ GHB-185	Big Jim's Little Six	1986	$25
❏ GHB-28	Jim Robinson at the Jacinto Ballroom	197?	$30
JAZZ CRUSADE
❏ 2015	1944 Revisited	196?	$35
❏ 2005	Jim Robinson	1965	$35
❏ 2010	Jim Robinson's Little Six	196?	$35
PEARL
❏ PS-5	Economy Hall Breakdown	197?	$30
RIVERSIDE
❏ RLP-393 [M]	Jim Robinson Plays Spirituals and Blues	1961	$250
❏ RS-9393 [R]	Jim Robinson Plays Spirituals and Blues	1961	$250
❏ RLP-369 [M]	Jim Robinson's New Orleans Band	1961	$250
❏ RS-9369 [R]	Jim Robinson's New Orleans Band	1961	$250

ROBINSON, JOHNNY
EPIC
| ❏ BN26528 | Memphis High | 1970 | $25 |

Number	Title	Yr	NM

ROBINSON, PERRY
IAI
☐ 373856 | Kundalini | 1978 | $35
SAVOY
☐ MG-12202 [M] | East of Suez | 196? | $35
☐ MG-12177 [M] | Funk Dumpling | 1962 | $30
SAVOY JAZZ
☐ SJL-1180 | Funk Dumpling | 198? | $25

ROBINSON, PETE
TESTAMENT
☐ 4401 | Dialogues for Piano and Reeds | 197? | $30

ROBINSON, PETER MANNING
CMG
☐ CML-8018 | Phoenix Rising | 1989 | $30

ROBINSON, SMOKEY, AND THE MIRACLES
See THE MIRACLES.

ROBINSON, SMOKEY
MOTOWN
☐ M5-197V1 | A Quiet Storm | 1981 | $10
— Reissue of Tamla 337
☐ 5349ML | Being with You | 1983 | $10
— Reissue of Tamla 375
☐ M5-154V1 | Deep in My Soul | 1981 | $10
— Reissue of Tamla 350
☐ MOT-6268 | Love, Smokey | 1990 | $15
☐ M5-118V1 | Motown Superstar Series, Vol. 18 | 1981 | $12
☐ MOT-6226 | One Heartbeat | 1987 | $12
☐ M5-168V1 | Pure Smokey | 1981 | $10
— Reissue of Tamla 331
☐ M5-134V1 | Smokey | 1981 | $10
— Reissue of Tamla 328
☐ 5267ML | Where There;s Smoke | 1982 | $10
— Reissue of Tamla 366
TAMLA
☐ T6-337 | A Quiet Storm | 1975 | $15
☐ T8-375 | Being with You | 1981 | $12
☐ 6064TL | Blame It on Love & All the Great Hits | 1983 | $12
☐ T6-350 | Deep in My Soul | 1977 | $15
☐ 6098TL | Essar | 1984 | $12
☐ T7-359 | Love Breeze | 1978 | $15
☐ T6-331 | Pure Smokey | 1974 | $15
☐ 6156TL | Smoke Signals | 1986 | $12
☐ T328 | Smokey | 1973 | $15
☐ T6-341 | Smokey's Family Robinson | 1976 | $15
☐ T9-363 | Smokin' | 1979 | $18
☐ 6030TL | Touch the Sky | 1983 | $12
☐ T8-367 | Warm Thoughts | 1980 | $12
☐ T7-366 | Where There's Smoke | 1979 | $12
☐ 6001TL | Yes It's You Lady | 1982 | $12
UNIVERSAL MOTOWN
☐ 5316009 | A Quiet Storm | 2009 | $25

ROBINSON, SPIKE, AND AL COHN
CAPRI
☐ 71787 | Henry B. Meets Alvin G. | 1987 | $25

ROBINSON, SPIKE
CAPRI
☐ 72185 | It's a Wonderful World | 1985 | $25
☐ 8984 | London Reprise | 1984 | $25
☐ 71785 | Spring Can Really Hang You Up the Most | 1985 | $25
DISCOVERY
☐ 870 | This Is Always: The Music of Harry Warren, Vol. 2 | 198? | $25

ROBINSON, SUGAR CHILE
CAPITOL
☐ T589 [M] | Boogie Woogie | 1955 | $250

ROBINSON, SUGAR RAY
CONTINENTAL
☐ CLP-16009 | I'm Still Swinging | 195? | $25

ROBINSON, TOM, BAND
GEFFEN
☐ GHS24053 | Hope and Glory | 1984 | $12
HARVEST
☐ STBB-11778 [B] | Power in the Darkness | 1978 | $25
☐ ST-11930 | TRB 2 | 1979 | $15
I.R.S.
☐ SP-70013 | Tom Robinson's Sector 27 | 1980 | $15

ROBINSON, VICKI SUE
RCA VICTOR
☐ AFL1-2294 | Half and Half | 1978 | $15
☐ APL1-1256 | Never Gonna Let You Go | 1976 | $15
☐ AYL1-3949 | Turn the Beat Around | 1981 | $10
☐ APL1-1829 | Vicki Sue Robinson | 1977 | $15

ROBINSON, WANDA
PERCEPTION
☐ 18 [B] | Black Ivory | 1971 | $18

ROBINSON/LANGWORTHY/AXT JAZZ TRIO, THE
ASHLAND
☐ 4963 | The Robinson/Langworthy/ Axt Jazz Trio | 198? | $30

ROBISON, CARSON
COLUMBIA
☐ CL2551 [10] | Square Dance | 1955 | $100
☐ CL6029 [10] | Square Dance | 1949 | $100
MGM
☐ E-13 [M] | Call Your Own Square Dances | 195? | $75
☐ E-3594 [M] | Life Gets Tee-Jus, Don't It | 1958 | $50
☐ E-3258 [M] | Square Dances | 1955 | $30
☐ E-557 [10] | Square Dances with Calls | 1952 | $75
RCA VICTOR
☐ LPM-3030 [10] | Square Dances | 1952 | $75
☐ LPM-1238 [M] | Square Dances | 1956 | $30

ROCCA, ANTONIO
MGM
☐ E-4183 [M] | In This Corner...The Musical World of Antonio Rocca | 1963 | $25
☐ SE-4183 [S] | In This Corner...The Musical World of Antonio Rocca | 1963 | $30

ROCHE, BETTY
BETHLEHEM
☐ BCP-64 [M] | Take the "A" Train | 1956 | $300
☐ BCP-6026 | Take the "A" Train | 197? | $50
— Reissue, distributed by RCA Victor
FANTASY
☐ OJC-1718 | Singin' and Swingin' | 198? | $30
PRESTIGE
☐ PRLP-7198 [M] | Lightly and Politely | 1961 | $175
☐ PRLP-7187 [M] | Singin' and Swingin' | 1961 | $250

ROCHES, THE
MCA
☐ 10020 | We Three Kings | 1990 | $25
RHINO
☐ RNEP-70616 [EP] | No Trespassing | 1987 | $18
WARNER BROS.
☐ 25321 [B] | Another World | 1985 | $15
☐ 23735 [B] | Keep On Doing | 1982 | $18
☐ BSK3475 [B] | Nurds | 1980 | $18
☐ BSK3298 [B] | The Roches | 1979 | $18

ROCHESTER-VEASLEY BAND, THE
GRAMAVISION
☐ 18-8505 | One Minute of Love | 1986 | $25

ROCK, MATTY
LEMANS
☐ LPC-15 | Polskie Koledy (Polish-American Christmas Carols) | 1972 | $15

ROCK-A-TEENS, THE
ROULETTE
☐ R-25109 [M] | Woo-Hoo | 1960 | $175
☐ SR-25109 [S] | Woo-Hoo | 1960 | $300

ROCK ISLAND
PROJECT 3
☐ PR-4005SD | Rock Island | 1970 | $30

ROCKATS
ISLAND
☐ ILPS9626 | Live at the Ritz | 1981 | $30

ROCKETS, THE (4)
WHITE WHALE
☐ WWS-7116 | The Rockets | 1968 | $30

ROCKETS
ELEKTRA
☐ 6E-351 | Back Talk | 1981 | $12
☐ 60143 | Rocket Roll | 1982 | $12
RSO
☐ RS1-3071 | No Ballads | 1980 | $15
☐ RS1-3047 | The Rockets | 1979 | $15
TORTOISE INT'L.
☐ BYL1-2572 [B] | Love Transfusion | 1977 | $18

ROCKIN' FOO
HOBBIT
☐ HB-5001 [B] | Rockin' Foo | 1969 | $30

ROCKIN' REBELS, THE
SWAN
☐ SLP-509 [M] | Wild Weekend | 1963 | $250

ROCKIN' SIDNEY
EPIC
☐ B5E40153 [EP] | My Toot Toot | 1985 | $10
ZBC
☐ LP-100 | A Holiday Celebration with Rockin' Sidney | 1983 | $18

ROCKPILE
Also see DAVE EDMUNDS; NICK LOWE.
COLUMBIA
☐ JC36886 | Seconds of Pleasure | 1980 | $18
— Includes bonus EP, "Nick Lowe and Dave Edmunds Sing the Everly Brothers.

ROCKWELL, ROBERT
ASI
☐ 5002 | Androids | 1977 | $30
CELEBRATION
☐ 5002 | Androids | 197? | $35

ROCKWELL
MOTOWN
☐ 6122ML | Captured | 1985 | $12
☐ 6052ML | Somebody's Watching Me | 1984 | $12
☐ 6178ML | The Genie | 1986 | $12

ROCKY FELLERS, THE
SCEPTER
☐ SP-512 [M] | Killer Joe | 1964 | $30
☐ SPS-512 [S] | Killer Joe | 1964 | $40

RODGER, MART
GHB
☐ GHB-224 | Jazz Tale of Two Cities | 198? | $25

RODGERS, GENE
EMARCY
☐ MG-36145 [M] | Jazz Comes to the Astor | 1958 | $175

RODGERS, IKE
RIVERSIDE
☐ RLP-1013 [10] | The Trombone of Ike Rodgers | 1953 | $300

RODGERS, JIMMIE (1)
RCA VICTOR
☐ CPL1-2504 | A Legendary Performer | 1977 | $12
☐ LPM-2531 [M] | Country Music Hall of Fame | 1962 | $100
☐ LPM-2213 [M] | Jimmie the Kid | 1961 | $100
☐ LPM-2112 [M] | My Rough and Rowdy Ways | 1960 | $100
☐ ANL1-1209 | My Rough and Rowdy Ways | 1976 | $12
☐ LPM-2865 [M] | My Time Ain't Long | 1964 | $50
☐ LPM-1232 [M] | Never No Mo' Blues -- A Memorial Album | 1955 | $175
☐ LPM-3315 [M] | The Best of the Legendary Jimmie Rodgers | 1965 | $40
☐ LSP-3315 [R] | The Best of the Legendary Jimmie Rodgers | 1965 | $25
☐ AHL1-3315 | The Best of the Legendary Jimmie Rodgers | 197? | $10
— Reissue with new prefix
☐ DPL2-0075 | The Legendary Jimmie Rodgers, Vol. 1 | 1974 | $40
— Special-products issue for Country Music Magazine
☐ LPM-2634 [M] | The Short But Brilliant Life of Jimmie Rodgers | 1963 | $100
☐ VPS-6091(e) | This Is Jimmie Rodgers | 1971 | $25
☐ LPM-1640 [M] | Train Whistle Blues | 1957 | $175
☐ LPM-3073 [10] | Travelin' Blues | 1952 | $500
☐ LPT-3037 [10] | Yodelingly Yours Jimmie Rodgers, Volume 1 | 1953 | $500
☐ LPT-3038 [10] | Yodelingly Yours Jimmie Rodgers, Volume 2 | 1953 | $500
☐ LPT-3039 [10] | Yodelingly Yours Jimmie Rodgers, Volume 3 | 1953 | $500
ROUNDER
☐ 1056 | First Sessions 1927-1928 | 1990 | $15
☐ 1057 | The Early Years 1928-1929 | 1990 | $15

RODGERS, JIMMIE (2)
A&M
☐ SP-130 [M] | Child of Clay | 1967 | $30
☐ SP-4130 [S] | Child of Clay | 1967 | $18
☐ SP-4242 | Troubled Times | 1970 | $18
☐ SP-4187 | Windmills of Your Mind | 1969 | $18
ACCORD
☐ SN-7198 | Honeycomb & Other Hits | 198? | $12

Number	Title	Yr	NM

DOT
❑ DLP-3579 [M]	12 Great Hits	1964	$18
❑ DLP-25579 [S]	12 Great Hits	1964	$25
❑ DLP3657 [M]	Christmas with Jimmie	1965	$15
❑ DLP25657 [S]	Christmas with Jimmie	1965	$18
❑ DLP-3710 [M]	Country Music 1966	1966	$18
❑ DLP-25710 [S]	Country Music 1966	1966	$25
❑ DLP-3614 [M]	Deep Purple	1965	$18
❑ DLP-25614 [S]	Deep Purple	1965	$25
❑ DLP-3815 [M]	Golden Hits/15 Hits of Jimmie Rodgers	1967	$25
❑ DLP-25815 [S]	Golden Hits/15 Hits of Jimmie Rodgers	1967	$18
❑ DLP-3525 [M]	Honeycomb & Kisses Sweeter Than Wine	1963	$18
❑ DLP-25525 [S]	Honeycomb & Kisses Sweeter Than Wine	1963	$25
❑ DLP-3717 [M]	It's Over	1966	$18
❑ DLP-25717 [S]	It's Over	1966	$25
❑ DLP-3496 [M]	Jimmie Rodgers Folk Concert	1963	$18
❑ DLP-25496 [S]	Jimmie Rodgers Folk Concert	1963	$25
❑ DLP-3780 [M]	Love Me, Please Love Me	1967	$18
❑ DLP-25780 [S]	Love Me, Please Love Me	1967	$25
❑ DLP-3502 [M]	My Favorite Hymns	1963	$18
❑ DLP-25502 [S]	My Favorite Hymns	1963	$25
❑ DLP-25453 [S]	No One Will Ever Know	1962	$25
❑ DLP-3453 [M]	No One Will Ever Know	1962	$18
❑ DLP-3687 [M]	The Nashville Sound	1966	$18
❑ DLP-25687 [S]	The Nashville Sound	1966	$25
❑ DLP-3556 [M]	The World I Used to Know	1964	$18
—Retitled version of above			
❑ DLP-25556 [S]	The World I Used to Know	1964	$25
—Retitled version of above			
❑ DLP-3556 [M]	Town and Country	1964	$25
❑ DLP-25556 [S]	Town and Country	1964	$30

FORUM
❑ F-9025 [M]	At Home with Jimmie Rodgers: An Evening of Folk Songs	196?	$15
❑ SF-9025 [S]	At Home with Jimmie Rodgers: An Evening of Folk Songs	196?	$15
❑ SF-9059 [S]	Jimmie Rodgers Sings Folk Songs	196?	$15
❑ F-9059 [M]	Jimmie Rodgers Sings Folk Songs	196?	$15
❑ F-9049 [M]	Just for You	196?	$15
❑ SF-9049 [S]	Just for You	196?	$15

HAMILTON
❑ HL-114 [M]	6 Favorite Hymns and 6 Favorite Folk Ballads	1964	$15
❑ HS-12114 [S]	6 Favorite Hymns and 6 Favorite Folk Ballads	1964	$15
❑ HL-148 [M]	12 Immortal Songs	196?	$15
❑ HS-12148 [S]	12 Immortal Songs	196?	$15

PARAMOUNT
❑ PAS-2-1042	Honeycomb	1974	$18

PICKWICK
❑ SPC-3106	Am I That Easy to Forget	196?	$15
❑ SPC-3599	Big Hits	197?	$12
❑ PC-3040 [M]	Jimmie Rodgers	196?	$15
❑ SPC-3040 [S]	Jimmie Rodgers	196?	$15

ROULETTE
❑ R-25179 [M]	15 Million Sellers	1962	$30
❑ SR-25179 [P]	15 Million Sellers	1962	$30
—White label with colored spokes			
❑ SR-25179 [P]	15 Million Sellers	1962	$25
—Orange and yellow label			
❑ R-25128 [M]	At Home with Jimmie Rodgers: An Evening of Folk Songs	1960	$30
❑ SR-25128 [S]	At Home with Jimmie Rodgers: An Evening of Folk Songs	1960	$40
❑ R-25199 [M]	Folk Songs	1963	$25
❑ SR-25199 [S]	Folk Songs	1963	$30
❑ R-25057 [M]	His Golden Year	1959	$30
❑ R25095 [M]	It's Christmas Once Again	1959	$30
❑ SR25095 [S]	It's Christmas Once Again	1959	$50
❑ R-25020 [M]	Jimmie Rodgers	1959	$30
—White label with colored spokes			
❑ R-25020 [M]	Jimmie Rodgers	1957	$50
—Black label			
❑ R-25042 [M]	Jimmie Rodgers Sings Folk Songs	1958	$50
—Black label			
❑ R-25042 [M]	Jimmie Rodgers Sings Folk Songs	1959	$30
—White label with colored spokes			
❑ R-25033 [M]	Number One Ballads	1958	$50
—Black label			
❑ R-25033 [M]	Number One Ballads	1959	$30
—White label with colored spokes			
❑ R-25160 [M]	The Best of Jimmie Rodgers' Folk Tunes	1961	$30
❑ SR-25160 [S]	The Best of Jimmie Rodgers' Folk Tunes	1961	$40
—Black vinyl			
❑ SR-25160 [S]	The Best of Jimmie Rodgers' Folk Tunes	1961	$300
—Red vinyl			
❑ R-25150 [M]	The Folk Song World of Jimmie Rodgers	1961	$30
❑ SR-25150 [S]	The Folk Song World of Jimmie Rodgers	1961	$40
❑ R-25071 [M]	TV Favorites	1959	$30
❑ SR-25071 [S]	TV Favorites	1959	$50
❑ R-25081 [M]	Twilight on the Trail	1959	$30
❑ SR-25081 [S]	Twilight on the Trail	1959	$50
❑ R-25103 [M]	When the Spirit Moves You	1960	$30
❑ SR-25103 [S]	When the Spirit Moves You	1960	$40
❑ SR-42006	Yours Truly	1968	$18

RODGERS, PAUL

ATLANTIC
❑ 80121	Cut Loose	1983	$10

RODITI, CLAUDIO

MILESTONE
❑ M-9158	Gemini Man	198?	$25
❑ M-9175	Slow Fire	198?	$25

RODMAN, JUDY

MTM
❑ ST-71060	A Place Called Love	1987	$12
❑ D1-71069	Goin' to Work	1988	$12
❑ ST-71050	Judy	1986	$12

RODNEY, RED, AND IRA SULLIVAN

ELEKTRA/MUSICIAN
❑ 60261	Sprint	198?	$25
❑ 60020	The Spirit Within	1982	$25

RODNEY, RED

ARGO
❑ LP-643 [M]	Red Rodney Returns	1959	$50
❑ LSP-643 [S]	Red Rodney Returns	1959	$40

FANTASY
❑ 3208 [M]	Modern Music from Chicago	1956	$250
—Red vinyl			
❑ 3208 [M]	Modern Music from Chicago	195?	$100
—Black vinyl			
❑ OJC-048	Modern Music from Chicago	198?	$25

MUSE
❑ MR-5307	Alive in New York	1986	$25
❑ MR-5034	Bird Lives!	1975	$30
❑ MR-5371	Bird Lives!	1989	$25
❑ MR-5135	Home Free	197?	$30
❑ MR-5209	Live at the Village Vanguard	1980	$30
❑ MR-5274	Night and Day	1981	$25
❑ MR-5088	Red Tornado	1975	$30
❑ MR-5111	Red White and Blues	1977	$30
❑ MR-5046	Superbop	197?	$30
❑ MR-5290	The 3 R's	198?	$25

ONYX
❑ 204	Red Arrow	197?	$30

PRESTIGE
❑ PRLP-122 [10]	Red Rodney	1952	$350

SAVOY
❑ MG-12148 [M]	Fiery Red Rodney	1959	$150

SIGNAL
❑ S-1206 [M]	Red Rodney 1957	1957	$600
❑ S-1206 [S]	Red Rodney 1957	199?	$30
—Classic Records reissue on audiophile vinyl (in stereo)			

RODRIGUEZ, JOHNNY

CAPITOL
❑ C1-90040	Gracias	1988	$12

EPIC
❑ FE37103	After the Rain	1981	$12
❑ FE38321	Biggest Hits	1982	$12
❑ FE39172	Foolin' with Fire	1984	$12
❑ FE38806	For Every Rose	1983	$12
❑ FE39583	Full Circle	1985	$12
❑ JE36587	Gypsy	1980	$12
❑ JE36014	Rodriguez	1979	$12
❑ JE36274	Through My Eyes	1980	$12

MERCURY
❑ SRM-1-686	All I Ever Meant to Do Was Sing	1973	$18
❑ SR-61378	Introducing Johnny Rodriguez	1973	$18
❑ SRM-1-5015	Johnny Rodriguez Was Here	1979	$15
❑ SRM-1-5003	Just for You	1977	$15
❑ SRM-1-1032	Just Get Up and Close the Door	1975	$18
❑ SRM-1-5011	Love Me with All You Heart	1978	$15
❑ SRM-1-1057	Love Put a Song in My Heart	1975	$18
❑ SRM-1-699	My Third Album	1974	$18
❑ SRM-1-1144	Practice Makes Perfect	1977	$15
❑ SRM-1-1110	Reflecting	1976	$15
❑ SRM-1-5022	Sketches	1980	$15
❑ SRM-1-1012	Songs About Ladies and Love	1974	$18
❑ SRM-1-1078	The Greatest Hits of Johnny Rodriguez	1976	$18
❑ 826271-1	The Greatest Hits of Johnny Rodriguez	1985	$10
—Reissue			

RODRIGUEZ, WILLIE

RIVERSIDE
❑ RLP-469 [M]	Flatjacks	1963	$175
❑ RS-9469 [S]	Flatjacks	1963	$175

RODRIQUEZ, BOBBY

SEA BREEZE
❑ SB-2030	Tell An Amigo	1986	$25

ROE, TOMMY

ABC
❑ S-700	12 in a Roe/A Collection of Tommy Roe's Greatest Hits	1969	$25
❑ X-762	16 Greatest Hits	1972	$18
❑ S-732	Beginnings	1971	$18
❑ S-683	Dizzy	1969	$25
❑ 594 [M]	It's Now Winters Day	1967	$25
❑ S-594 [S]	It's Now Winters Day	1967	$30
❑ 610 [M]	Phantasy	1967	$40
❑ S-610 [S]	Phantasy	1967	$40
❑ S-467 [R]	Something for Everybody	1968	$50
—Issued in rechanneled stereo four years after its original release			
❑ T-90883 [M]	Sweet Pea	1966	$40
—Capitol Record Club issue			
❑ ST-90883 [S]	Sweet Pea	1966	$40
—Capitol Record Club issue			
❑ S-714	We Can Make Music	1970	$18

ABC-PARAMOUNT
❑ 432 [M]	Sheila	1962	$40
❑ S-432 [S]	Sheila	1962	$50
❑ 467 [M]	Something for Everybody	1964	$30
❑ 575 [M]	Sweet Pea	1966	$30
❑ S-575 [S]	Sweet Pea	1966	$40

ACCORD
❑ SN-7155	Sheila	1981	$12

MCA
❑ 1519	Collectibles -- Greatest Hits	1982	$10

MONUMENT
❑ PZ34182	Energy	1976	$15
❑ 7604	Energy	1977	$12
—Reissue of 34182			
❑ 7614	Full Bloom	1977	$12

PICKWICK
❑ SPC-3361	Dizzy	197?	$12

ROESSLER, GEORGE

EAGLE
❑ SM-4195	Still Life and Old Dreams	1985	$25

ROGERS, BOB

INDIGO
❑ 1501 [M]	All That and This, Too	1961	$40

ROGERS, DANN

IA
❑ 5000	Hearts Under Fire	1979	$15

MCA
❑ 42025	Still Runnin'	1987	$10

ROGERS, DAVID

ATLANTIC
❑ SD7283	Farewell to the Ryman	1973	$25
❑ SD7306	Hey There Girl	1974	$18
❑ SD7266	Just Thank Me	1973	$18

COLUMBIA
❑ CS1023	A World Called You	1970	$18
❑ KC31506	Need You	1972	$18
❑ C30972	She Don't Make Me Cry	1971	$18

REPUBLIC
❑ 5907	I'm Gonna Love You Right Out of This World	1976	$15
❑ 5003	Lovingly	197?	$15

UNITED ARTISTS
❑ UA-LA422-G	A Whole Lotta Livin' in a House	1975	$15

ROGERS, ERIC, CHORALE AND ORCHESTRA

LONDON PHASE 4
❑ SP44027	The Glory of Christmas	196?	$15

ROGERS, JULIE

MERCURY
❑ MG-20981 [M]	Julie Rogers	1965	$18
❑ SR-60981 [S]	Julie Rogers	1965	$25

ROGERS, KENNY, AND DOLLY PARTON

RCA VICTOR
❑ ASL1-5307	Once Upon a Christmas	1984	$12

ROGERS, KENNY, AND DOTTIE WEST

UNITED ARTISTS
❑ UA-LA946-H	Classics	1979	$12

Number	Title	Yr	NM
❏ UA-LA864-G	Every Time Two Fools Collide	1978	$12

ROGERS, KENNY, AND THE FIRST EDITION
See THE FIRST EDITION.

ROGERS, KENNY
Also see THE BOBBY DOYLE THREE; THE FIRST EDITION; THE NEW CHRISTY MINSTRELS; THE SCHOLARS (1).

LIBERTY
❏ LOO-51115	Christmas	1981	$12
❏ LN-10240	Christmas	198?	$10
— Reissue of LOO 51115			
❏ LO-754	Daytime Friends	1981	$10
— Reissue of United Artists 754			
❏ LN-10249	Daytime Friends	1984	$10
— Budget-line reissue			
❏ LO-51154	Duets	1984	$10
❏ LOO-1035	Gideon	1981	$10
— Reissue of United Artists 1035			
❏ LN-10243	Gideon	1984	$10
— Budget-line reissue			
❏ LOO-979	Kenny	1981	$10
— Reissue of United Artists 979			
❏ LN-10248	Kenny	1984	$10
— Budget-line reissue			
❏ LO-689	Kenny Rogers	1981	$10
— Reissue of United Artists 689			
❏ LN-10208	Kenny Rogers	1983	$10
— Budget-line reissue			
❏ LOO-1072	Kenny Rogers' Greatest Hits	1980	$10
❏ LO-51157	Love Is What We Make It	1985	$10
❏ LO-607	Love Lifted Me	1981	$10
— Reissue of United Artists 607			
❏ LN-10207	Love Lifted Me	1984	$10
— Budget-line reissue			
❏ LO-903	Love Or Something Like It	1981	$10
— Reissue of United Artists 903			
❏ LN-10250	Love Or Something Like It	1984	$10
— Budget-line reissue			
❏ LO-51124	Love Will Turn You Around	1982	$10
❏ LN-10246	Love Will Turn You Around	1984	$10
— Budget-line reissue			
❏ LOO-1108	Share Your Love	1981	$10
❏ LO-835	Ten Years of Gold	1981	$10
— Reissue of United Artists 835			
❏ LN-10254	Ten Years of Gold	1984	$10
— Budget-line reissue			
❏ LO-934	The Gambler	1981	$10
— Reissue of United Artists 934			
❏ LN-10247	The Gambler	1984	$10
— Budget-line reissue			
❏ LV-51152	Twenty Greatest Hits	1983	$10
❏ LO-51143	We've Got Tonight	1983	$10
❏ LN-10245	We've Got Tonight	1984	$10
— Budget-line reissue			

MOBILE FIDELITY
❏ Jan-0049	Kenny Rogers' Greatest Hits	1981	$25
— Audiophile vinyl			
❏ Jan-0044	The Gambler	1981	$25
— Audiophile vinyl			

RCA
❏ 8371-1-R	Greatest Hits	1988	$10
❏ 6484-1-R	I Prefer the Moonlight	1987	$10
❏ 5833-1-R	They Don't Make Them Like They Used To	1986	$10

RCA VICTOR
❏ AFL1-4697	Eyes That See in the Dark	1983	$10
❏ AFL1-4697	Eyes That See in the Dark	1983	$250
— Picture disc on one side, regular RCA label on other; possibly an in-house demo at the RCA Indianapolis pressing plant			
❏ AJL1-7023	The Heart of the Matter	1985	$10
❏ AJL1-5335	What About Me	1984	$10

REPRISE
❏ 25973	Christmas in America	1989	$15
❏ R144593	Love Is Strange	1990	$25
— Only available on vinyl from BMG Direct Marketing			
❏ 25792	Something Inside So Strong	1989	$12

UNITED ARTISTS
❏ UA-LA754-G	Daytime Friends	1977	$12
❏ LOO-1035	Gideon	1980	$12
❏ LWAK-979	Kenny	1979	$12
❏ UA-LA689-G	Kenny Rogers	1976	$12
❏ UA-LA607-G	Love Lifted Me	1976	$18
❏ UA-LA903-H	Love Or Something Like It	1978	$12
❏ UA-LA835-H	Ten Years of Gold	1978	$12
❏ UA-LA934-H [B]	The Gambler	1978	$12

ROGERS, ROD, TERI SUMMERS, AND THE LIBRETTOS

CARNAGE PRESS
❏ 0(# unknown)	MSR Madness: Beat of the Traps	199?	$0

ROGERS, RONNIE

MTM
❏ ST-71065	Tough Times Don't Last	1988	$12

ROGERS, ROY, AND DALE EVANS

CAPITOL
❏ T2818 [M]	Christmas Is Always	1967	$30
❏ ST2818 [S]	Christmas Is Always	1967	$30
❏ T1745 [M]	The Bible Tells Me So	1962	$40
❏ ST1745 [S]	The Bible Tells Me So	1962	$50

GOLDEN
❏ A198-7 [M]	16 Great Songs of the Old West	1958	$100
— Originals have black labels and "198" prefix			
❏ LP7 [M]	A Child's Introduction to the West (16 Great Songs of the Old West)	196?	$40
— Yellow label, "LP" prefix			
❏ A298-81 [M]	Peter Cottontail	1962	$75
— Originals have black labels and "298" prefix			
❏ A198-6 [M]	Roy Rogers' and Dale Evans' Song Wagon	1958	$100
— Originals have black labels and "198" prefix			

RCA VICTOR
❏ LPM-1439 [M]	Sweet Hour of Prayer	1957	$100

ROGERS, ROY

20TH CENTURY
❏ T-487	Happy Trails to You	1975	$18

CAPITOL
❏ ST-785	A Man from Duck Run	1971	$25
❏ ST-594	The Country Side of Roy Rogers	1970	$25

RCA
❏ 3024-1-RRE [PD]	Roy Rogers Tribute	1991	$40
— Picture disc; only vinyl edition of this release			

RCA CAMDEN
❏ CAL-1074 [M]	Lore of the West	1966	$30
❏ CAS-1074(e) [R]	Lore of the West	1966	$18
❏ CAL-1054 [M]	Pecos Bill	1964	$30
❏ CAS-1054(e) [R]	Pecos Bill	1964	$18
❏ CAS-1097 [R]	Peter Cottontail and His Friends	1968	$18
❏ CAL-1097 [M]	Peter Cottontail and His Friends	1968	$30

RCA VICTOR
❏ LPM-3168 [M]	Hymns of Faith	1954	$250
❏ LBY-1022 [M]	Jesus Loves Me	1959	$50
— On the "Children's Bluebird Series			
❏ LPM-3041 [M]	Roy Rogers Souvenir Album	1952	$300

ROGERS, SHORTY, AND ANDRE PREVIN

RCA VICTOR
❏ LPM-1018 [M]	Collaboration	1954	$75

ROGERS, SHORTY, AND BUDD SHANK

CONCORD JAZZ
❏ CJ-223	Yesterday, Today and Forever	1983	$25

ROGERS, SHORTY

ATLANTIC
❏ 1232 [M]	Martians, Come Back	1956	$300
— Black label			
❏ SD1232 [S]	Martians, Come Back	1958	$300
— Green label			
❏ 1232 [M]	Martians, Come Back	1961	$175
— Multicolor label, white "fan" logo at right			
❏ SD1232 [S]	Martians, Come Back	1961	$175
— Multicolor label, white "fan" logo at right			
❏ 1232 [M]	Martians, Come Back	1963	$25
— Multicolor label, black "fan" logo at right			
❏ SD1232 [S]	Martians, Come Back	1963	$35
— Multicolor label, black "fan" logo at right			
❏ 90042	The Swinging Mr. Rogers	1983	$25
❏ 1212 [M]	The Swinging Mr. Rogers	1955	$300
— Black label			
❏ 1212 [M]	The Swinging Mr. Rogers	1961	$175
— Multicolor label, white "fan" logo at right			
❏ 1212 [M]	The Swinging Mr. Rogers	1963	$25
— Multicolor label, black "fan" logo at right			
❏ 1270 [M]	Way Up There	1957	$300
— Black label			
❏ 1270 [M]	Way Up There	1961	$175
— Multicolor label, white "fan" logo at right			
❏ 1270 [M]	Way Up There	1963	$25
— Multicolor label, black "fan" logo at right			

BLUEBIRD
❏ 5917-1-RB	Short Stops	1987	$35

CAPITOL
❏ T1960 [M]	Gospel Mission	1963	$75
❏ ST1960 [S]	Gospel Mission	1963	$50
❏ H294 [10]	Modern Sounds	1952	$300

DISCOVERY
❏ 843	Jazz Waltz	1982	$25

MGM
❏ E-3798 [M]	Shorty Rogers Meets Tarzan	1960	$30
❏ SE-3798 [S]	Shorty Rogers Meets Tarzan	1960	$40

MOSAIC
❏ MR6-125	The Complete Atlantic and EMI Jazz Recordings of Shorty Rogers	199?	$175
— Limited edition of 7,500			

PAUSA
❏ 9016	14 Historic Arrangements and Performances	198?	$25

RCA VICTOR
❏ LPM-1763 [M]	Afro-Cuban Influence	1958	$40
❏ LSP-1763 [S]	Afro-Cuban Influence	1958	$50
❏ LPM-1975 [M]	Chances Are It Swings	1959	$40
❏ LSP-1975 [S]	Chances Are It Swings	1959	$50
❏ LPM-1334 [M]	Collaboration	1956	$75
❏ LPM-3138 [10]	Cool and Crazy	1953	$250
❏ LPM-1696 [M]	Gigi Goes Jazz	1958	$50
❏ LSP-1696 [S]	Gigi Goes Jazz	1958	$75
❏ LPM-1564 [M]	Portrait of Shorty	1957	$75
❏ LPM-1195 [M]	Shorty Rogers and His Giants	1956	$150
❏ LJM-1004 [M]	Shorty Rogers Courts the Count	1954	$100
❏ LPM-3137 [10]	Shorty Rogers' Giants	1953	$250
❏ LPM-1428 [M]	Shorty Rogers Plays Richard Rogers	1957	$75
❏ LPM-1350 [M]	The Big Shorty Rogers Express	1957	$75
❏ LPM-2110 [M]	The Swingin' Nutcracker	1960	$40
❏ LSP-2110 [S]	The Swingin' Nutcracker	1960	$50
❏ LPM-1997 [M]	The Wizard of Oz	1959	$40
❏ LSP-1997 [S]	The Wizard of Oz	1959	$50
❏ LPM-1326 [M]	Wherever the Five Winds Blow	1956	$140

REPRISE
❏ R-6050 [M]	Bossa Nova	1962	$25
❏ R9-6050 [S]	Bossa Nova	1962	$30
❏ R-6060 [M]	Jazz Waltz	1962	$25
❏ R9-6060 [S]	Jazz Waltz	1962	$30

WARNER BROS.
❏ W1443 [M]	4th Dimension Jazz	1961	$75
❏ WS1443 [S]	4th Dimension Jazz	1961	$75

XANADU
❏ 148	Popi	198?	$25

ROGERS, STAN

FOGARTY'S COVE
❏ FCM 002	Between the Breaks... Live	1979	$0
— Canadian only; contains First Christmas			

ROGERS, TIMMIE

PHILIPS
❏ PHM200088 [M]	If I Were President	1963	$30
❏ PHS600088 [S]	If I Were President	1963	$40

ROHRS, DONNIE

AD-KORP
❏ 0112	Daddy and Daughter Time	197?	$15

ROKES, THE

RCA VICTOR INTERNATIONAL
❏ FPM-185 [M]	Che Mondo Strano	1967	$100

ROLAND, GENE

BRUNSWICK
❏ BL54114 [M]	Swingin' Friends	1963	$40
❏ BL754114 [S]	Swingin' Friends	1963	$50

DAWN
❏ DLP-1122 [M]	Jazzville, Volume 4	1958	$100

ROLAND, JOE

BETHLEHEM
❏ BCP-17 [M]	Joe Roland Quintet	1955	$300

SAVOY
❏ MG-15034 [10]	Joe Roland Quartet	1954	$120
❏ MG-15047 [10]	Joe Roland Quartet	1954	$120
❏ MG-12039 [10]	Joltin' Joe Roland	1955	$75

ROLDINGER, ADELHARD

ECM
❏ 1221	Schattseite	1981	$30

ROLLAND, BRIAN

WUMAT
❏ WM-1001	Guitar Bazaar	198?	$30

ROLLING STONES, THE
Also see BRIAN JONES; RONNIE WOOD; MICK TAYLOR; MICK JAGGER; KEITH RICHARDS.

ABKCO
❏ 018771940210 [B]	12 x 5	2014	$25
❏ 18771-9477-1	Aftermath UK	2003	$25

Number	Title	Yr	NM

—180-gram vinyl reissue pressed in U.S. by RTI, though cover says "Made in E.U."; with loose outer bag; cover has number "882 323-1

| ❏ 18771-9539-1 | Beggars Banquet | 2003 | $25 |

—180-gram vinyl reissue pressed in U.S. by RTI, though cover says "Made in E.U."; with loose outer bag; cover has number "882 330-1

| ❏ 18771-9500-1 | Between the Buttons UK | 2003 | $25 |

—180-gram vinyl reissue pressed in U.S. by RTI, though cover says "Made in E.U."; with loose outer bag; cover has number "882 326-1

| ❏ 18771-9001-1 | Big Hits (High Tide and Green Grass) | 2003 | $25 |

—180-gram vinyl reissue pressed in U.S. by RTI, though cover says "Made in E.U."; with loose outer bag; number on cover is "882 322-1

| ❏ 18771-9375-1 | England's Newest Hit Makers -- The Rolling Stones | 2003 | $25 |

—180-gram vinyl reissue pressed in U.S. by RTI, though cover says "Made in E.U."; with loose outer bag; cover has number "882 316-1

| ❏ 18771-9005-1 | Get Yer Ya-Ya's Out! | 2003 | $25 |

—180-gram vinyl reissue pressed in U.S. by RTI, though cover says "Made in E.U."; with loose outer bag; cover has number "882 333-1

| ❏ 018771900511 [B] | Get Yer Ya-Yas Out | 2014 | $25 |
| ❏ 18771-9667-1 | Hot Rocks 1964-1971 | 2003 | $40 |

—180-gram vinyl reissue pressed in U.S. by RTI, though cover says "Made in E.U."; with loose outer bag; cover has number "882 334-1

| ❏ 18771-9004-1 | Let It Bleed | 2003 | $25 |

—180-gram vinyl reissue pressed in U.S. by RTI, though cover says "Made in E.U."; with loose outer bag; cover has number "882 332-1

| ❏ ANA1 [P] | Metamorphosis | 1975 | $25 |
| ❏ 18771-9006-1 | Metamorphosis | 2003 | $25 |

—180-gram vinyl reissue pressed in U.S. by RTI, though cover says "Made in E.U."; with loose outer bag; cover has number "882 344-1

| ❏ AB-4224 [B] | Necrophilia | 1973 | $10000 |

—Canceled; covers exist. Value is for complete tri-fold cover.

| ❏ 18771-9430-1 | Out of Our Heads UK | 2003 | $25 |

—180-gram vinyl reissue pressed in U.S. by RTI, though cover says "Made in E.U."; with loose outer bag; cover has number "882 319-1

| ❏ 1218-1 | Singles Collection: The London Years | 1989 | $50 |
| ❏ MPD-1 [DJ] | Songs of the Rolling Stones | 1975 | $700 |

—Band in field" cover

| ❏ MPD-1 [DJ] | Songs of the Rolling Stones | 1975 | $3000 |

—Rock and Roll Circus" cover; VG value 1000; VG+ value 2000

| ❏ 18771-9002-1 | Their Satanic Majesties Request | 2003 | $25 |

—180-gram vinyl reissue pressed in U.S. by RTI, though cover says "Made in E.U."; with loose outer bag; cover has number "882 329-1

| ❏ DVL2-0268 [P] | The Rolling Stones' Greatest Hits | 1977 | $25 |

—RCA Special Products mail-order offer

EAGLE

| ❏ ERDVLP070 [B] | Some Girls (Live In Texas '78) | 2012 | $40 |

—gatefold sleeve includes DVD

EAGLE ROCK

❏ EV306949 [B]	Hampton Coliseum 1981	2014	$40
❏ EV306959 [B]	LA Forum (Live in 1975)	2014	$40
❏ ERDVLP092 [B]	Live at the Tokyo Dome	2015	$50
❏ ERDVLP095 [B]	Live in Leeds 1982	2016	$50
❏ EV307549 [B]	Totally Stripped	2016	$40

LONDON

| ❏ LL3402 [M] | 12 x 5 | 1964 | $250 |

—Maroon label with "London/ffrr" in a box at top

| ❏ LL3402 [M] | 12 x 5 | 1964 | $75 |

—Maroon label with "London" unboxed at top

| ❏ LL3402 [M] | 12 x 5 | 1964 | $10000 |

—Maroon label with "London" unboxed at top; possibly unique blue vinyl pressing; VG value 5000; VG+ value 7500

| ❏ LL3402 [M] | 12 x 5 | 1965 | $40 |

—Red or maroon label with "London" boxed at top

| ❏ PS402 [R] | 12 x 5 | 1964 | $30 |

—Dark blue label with "London" unboxed at top

| ❏ PS402 [R] | 12 x 5 | 1965 | $25 |

—Dark blue label with "London" boxed at top

❏ LL3476 [M]	Aftermath	1966	$75
❏ PS476 [S]	Aftermath	1966	$65
❏ PS509	Back Behind and In Front	1967	$5000

—Prototype cover slick for an unreleased LP; the same number was used for "Flowers

| ❏ PS539 [S] | Beggars Banquet | 1968 | $30 |

—With all songs credited to "Jagger-Richard

| ❏ PS539 [S] | Beggars Banquet | 1968 | $25 |

—With "Rev. Wilkins: credited as composer of "Prodigal Son

| ❏ PS539 | Beggars Banquet | 1968 | $10000 |

—Original "toilet graffiti" cover slick (not on a cover)

| ❏ LL3499 [M] | Between the Buttons | 1967 | $175 |

Number	Title	Yr	NM
❏ PS499 [S]	Between the Buttons	1967	$25
❏ NP1 [M]	Big Hits (High Tide and Green Grass)	1966	$8000

—With two lines of type on the front cover, all in small letters

| ❏ NP1 [M] | Big Hits (High Tide and Green Grass) | 1966 | $50 |

—With five lines of type on the front cover, all in capital letters

| ❏ NPS1 [R] | Big Hits (High Tide and Green Grass) | 1966 | $25 |
| ❏ LL3451 [M] | December's Children (and Everybody's) | 1965 | $40 |

—Maroon label with "London" unboxed at top

| ❏ LL3451 [M] | December's Children (and Everybody's) | 1966 | $30 |

—Maroon label with "London" boxed at top

| ❏ PS451 [P] | December's Children (and Everybody's) | 1965 | $30 |

—Dark blue label with "London" unboxed at top

| ❏ PS451 [P] | December's Children (and Everybody's) | 1966 | $25 |

—Dark blue label with "London" boxed at top. "Look What You've Done" is in true stereo; all other tracks are rechanneled.

| ❏ LL3375 [DJ] | England's Newest Hit Makers -- The Rolling Stones | 1964 | $3000 |

—White label promo

| ❏ LL3375 [M] | England's Newest Hit Makers -- The Rolling Stones | 1964 | $300 |

—Maroon label with "Full Frequency Range Recording" inside horizontal lines that go through the center hole; lower left-hand corner of cover advertises a bonus photo

| ❏ PS375 [R] | England's Newest Hit Makers -- The Rolling Stones | 1964 | $300 |

—Dark blue label; lower left-hand corner of cover advertises a bonus photo

| ❏ LL3375 [M] | England's Newest Hit Makers -- The Rolling Stones | 1965 | $75 |

—Maroon label with "London" unboxed at top

| ❏ LL3375 [M] | England's Newest Hit Makers -- The Rolling Stones | 1966 | $40 |

—Red or maroon label with "London" boxed at top

| ❏ PS375 [R] | England's Newest Hit Makers -- The Rolling Stones | 1965 | $30 |

—Dark blue label with "London" unboxed at top

| ❏ PS375 [R] | England's Newest Hit Makers -- The Rolling Stones | 1966 | $25 |

—Dark blue label with "London" boxed at top

❏ LL3375	England's Newest Hit Makers -- The Rolling Stones Bonus Photo	1964	$250
❏ LL3509 [M]	Flowers	1967	$175
❏ PS509 [P]	Flowers	1967	$25

—Have You Seen Your Mother, Baby, Standing in the Shadow?" and "Mother's Little Helper" are rechanneled; all others are true stereo

| ❏ PS509 [M] | Flowers | 197? | $10 |

—Some later "stereo" copies of this LP are actually entirely in mono

❏ NPS5 [S]	Get Yer Ya-Ya's Out!	1970	$25
❏ LL3493 [M]	Got Live If You Want It!	1966	$75
❏ PS493 [P]	Got Live If You Want It!	1966	$25

—Fortune Teller" is rechanneled (it's actually an early studio recording with overdubbed crowd noise)

| ❏ 2PS606/7 [P] | Hot Rocks 1964-1971 | 1971 | $1000 |

—With alternate versions of "Brown Sugar" and "Wild Horses" unavailable elsewhere. The date "11-5-71" or "11-18-71" is in the Side 4 trail-off area.

| ❏ 2PS606/7 [P] | Hot Rocks 1964-1971 | 1971 | $25 |

—With regular versions of all tracks. All of Side 1 and "Mothers Little Helper" and "19th Nervous Breakdown" on Side 2 are rechanneled. All of Side 3 and 4 are stereo.

Number	Title	Yr	NM
❏ NPS4 [S]	Let It Bleed	1969	$30

—With poster

| ❏ NPS4 [S] | Let It Bleed | 1969 | $25 |

—Without poster

| ❏ NPS-4 | Let It Bleed | 1970 | $10000 |

—One-of-a-kind red/yellow/blue/green vinyl (all on the same record!); VG value 5000; VG+ value 7500

| ❏ 2PS626/7 [P] | More Hot Rocks (Big Hits and Fazed Cookies) | 1972 | $25 |

—All of Sides 1 and 4 are rechanneled; Side 2 and 3, except "Have You Seen Your Mother, Baby, Standing in the Shadow?" are in true stereo

| ❏ LL3429 [M] | Out of Our Heads | 1965 | $250 |

—Maroon label with "London/ffrr" in a box at top

| ❏ LL3429 [M] | Out of Our Heads | 1965 | $40 |

—Maroon label with "London" unboxed at top

| ❏ LL3429 [M] | Out of Our Heads | 1966 | $30 |

—Red or maroon label with "London" boxed at top

| ❏ PS429 [R] | Out of Our Heads | 1965 | $150 |

—Dark blue label with "London/ffrr" in a box at top and "Made in England by the Decca Record Co. Ltd." at top edge

| ❏ PS429 [R] | Out of Our Heads | 1965 | $30 |

—Dark blue label with "London" unboxed at top

| ❏ PS429 [R] | Out of Our Heads | 1965 | $25 |

—Dark blue label with "London" boxed at top

| ❏ NP2 [M] | Their Satanic Majesties Request | 1967 | $300 |
| ❏ NPS2 [S] | Their Satanic Majesties Request | 1967 | $50 |

—With 3-D cover

| ❏ NPS2 [S] | Their Satanic Majesties Request | 197? | $10 |

—Without 3-D cover

| ❏ LL3420 [M] | The Rolling Stones, Now! | 1965 | $250 |

—Maroon label with "London/ffrr" in a box at top. Add 20% for complete liner notes (or sticker) on back cover (both columns of type about equal in length).

| ❏ LL3420 [M] | The Rolling Stones, Now! | 1965 | $75 |

—Maroon label with "London" unboxed at top and no lines on label. Add 20% for complete liner notes (or sticker) on back cover (both columns of type about equal in length).

| ❏ LL3420 [M] | The Rolling Stones, Now! | 1966 | $40 |

—Red or maroon label with "London" boxed at top and censored liner notes (second column an inch shorter than the first column)

| ❏ PS420 [R] | The Rolling Stones, Now! | 1965 | $75 |

—Dark blue label with "London" unboxed at top. Add 20% for complete liner notes (or sticker) on back cover (both columns of type about equal in length).

| ❏ PS420 [R] | The Rolling Stones, Now! | 1966 | $50 |

—Dark blue label with "London" boxed at top. Add 20% for censored liner notes (or sticker) on back cover (second column an inch shorter than the first column; "offensive" notes were quietly restored in the 1970s).

| ❏ LL3420 [M] | The Rolling Stones, Now! | 1965 | $400 |

—Maroon label with "London" unboxed, but with "ffrr" ear above "London" and "Full Frequency Range Recording" inside horizontal lines that go through the center hole

| ❏ LL3420 [M] | The Rolling Stones, Now! | 1965 | $400 |

—Maroon label with "London" unboxed, with horizontal lines that go through the center hole, but with NO "ffrr" ear at the top and NO "Full Frequency Range Recording" between the horizontal lines

| ❏ RSD-1 [DJ] | The Rolling Stones -- The Promotional Album | 1969 | $3000 |

—Not to be confused with imports of this rare promo; VG value 1000; VG+ value 2000

| ❏ NPS3 [P] | Through the Past, Darkly (Big Hits Vol. 2) | 1969 | $25 |

—With hexagonal cover

| ❏ NPS3 [P] | Through the Past, Darkly (Big Hits Vol. 2) | 197? | $25 |

—Reissue with regular square cover

| ❏ NPS3 [PD] | Through the Past, Darkly (Big Hits Vol. 2) | 1969 | $6000 |

—Prototype picture discs that used the cover art from "Big Hits (High Tide and Green Grass)" either on one or both sides; VG value 3000; VG+ value 4500

LONDON/ABKCO

| ❏ 74021 [M] | 12 x 5 | 1986 | $10 |

—Digitally Remastered from Original Master Recording" on cover; red label

| ❏ 74761 [S] | Aftermath | 1986 | $10 |

—Digitally Remastered from Original Master Recording" on cover; red label

| ❏ 75391 [S] | Beggars Banquet | 1986 | $25 |

—Digitally Remastered from Original Master Recording" on cover; red label; original banned "toilet cover" released for the first time on this reissue

| ❏ 74991 [S] | Between the Buttons | 1986 | $10 |

—Digitally Remastered from Original Master Recording" on cover; red label

| ❏ 80011 [M] | Big Hits (High Tide and Green Grass) | 1986 | $10 |

—Digitally Remastered from Original Master Recording" on cover; red label

Number	Title	Yr	NM
❑ 74511 [M]	December's Children (and Everybody's)	1986	$10

—Digitally Remastered from Original Master Recording" on cover; red label

❑ 73751 [M]	England's Newest Hit Makers -- The Rolling Stones	1986	$10

—Digitally Remastered from Original Master Recording" on cover; red label

❑ 75091 [S]	Flowers	1986	$10

—Digitally Remastered from Original Master Recording" on cover; red label

❑ 80051	Get Yer Ya-Ya's Out!	1986	$10

—Digitally Remastered from Original Master Recording" on cover; red label

❑ 74931 [S]	Got Live If You Want It!	1986	$10

—Digitally Remastered from Original Master Recording" on cover; red label

❑ 62671 [P]	Hot Rocks 1964-1971	1986	$30

—Digitally Remastered from Original Master Recording" on cover; red label; same stereo content as original

❑ 80041	Let It Bleed	1986	$10

—Digitally Remastered from Original Master Recording" on cover; red label

❑ 62671 [P]	More Hot Rocks (Big Hits and Fazed Cookies)	1986	$30

—Digitally Remastered from Original Master Recording" on cover; red label

❑ 74291 [P]	Out of Our Heads	1986	$10

—Digitally Remastered from Original Master Recording" on cover; red label

❑ 80021 [S]	Their Satanic Majesties Request	1986	$10

—Digitally Remastered from Original Master Recording" on cover; red label

❑ 74201 [P]	The Rolling Stones, Now!	1986	$10

—Digitally Remastered from Original Master Recording" on cover; red label; four tracks are in true stereo

❑ 80031 [S]	Through the Past, Darkly (Big Hits Vol. 2)	1986	$10

—Digitally Remastered from Original Master Recording" on cover; red label

MOBILE FIDELITY

❑ Jan-0087	Some Girls	1982	$150

—Audiophile vinyl

❑ Jan-0060 [B]	Sticky Fingers	1980	$85

—Audiophile vinyl

❑ RC-1	The Rolling Stones	1984	$500

—London LPs pressed on audiophile vinyl in box

RADIO PULSEBEAT NEWS

❑ 4 [B]	It's Here Luv!!	1965	$250

—Ed Rudy interview album; this has been counterfeited, but originals can be identified thus: Charlie Watts' jacket should be completely black with no white marks; the label is very clear; the vinyl is all black

ROLLING STONES

❑ COC79104	Black and Blue	1976	$25
❑ FC40495	Black and Blue	1986	$10

—Reissue on CBS

❑ OC40250	Dirty Work	1986	$10

—Originals came with red shrink wrap; add 50% if it is still with the package

❑ COC16015 [B]	Emotional Rescue	1980	$25

—Originally released with a large poster wrapped around the outside of the record jacket

❑ COC16015	Emotional Rescue	1980	$25

—Without poster

❑ FC40500	Emotional Rescue	1986	$10

—Reissue on CBS

❑ COC 2-2900	Exile on Main St.	1973	$25

—Reissue covers have two pockets, one for each record

❑ CG240489	Exile on Main St.	1986	$25

—Reissue on CBS

❑ COC 2-2900 [B]	Exile on Main St.	1972	$30

—Original covers have Unipak design -- cover has to be opened to remove the records. Add 33% for sheet of postcards.

❑ C47456 [B]	Flashpoint	1991	$30
❑ COC59101	Goats Head Soup	1973	$30

—With bonus photo

❑ COC59101	Goats Head Soup	1973	$25

—Without bonus photo

❑ COC39106	Goats Head Soup	1977	$10

—Reissue on Atlantic

❑ FC40492	Goats Head Soup	1986	$10

—Reissue on CBS

❑ PR164 [DJ]	Interview with Mick Jagger by Tom Donahue	1971	$250

—Yellow label

❑ COC79101	It's Only Rock 'n' Roll	1974	$25
❑ FC40493	It's Only Rock 'n' Roll	1986	$10

—Reissue on CBS

❑ COC39100	Jamming with Edward	1972	$30

—Not an official Stones album, this includes Jagger, Watts and Wyman with Ry Cooder and Nicky Hopkins

❑ COC39100 [DJ]	Jamming with Edward	1972	$200

—White label stereo promo

❑ COC39100 [M]	Jamming with Edward	1972	$350

—White label mono promo

❑ COC 2-9001	Love You Live	1977	$25
❑ CG240496	Love You Live	1986	$25

—Reissue on CBS

❑ COC79102	Made in the Shade	1975	$25
❑ COC39107	Made in the Shade	1977	$10

—Reissue on Atlantic

❑ FC40494	Made in the Shade	1986	$10

—Reissue on CBS

❑ 90176	Rewind (1971-1984)	1984	$30
❑ FC40505	Rewind (1971-1984)	1986	$10

—Reissue on CBS

❑ COC39108	Some Girls	1978	$30

—With all women's faces visible. Nine different color schemes exist for the front cover.

❑ COC39108	Some Girls	1978	$25

—With "cover under reconstruction." Nine different color schemes exist for the front cover.

❑ FC40499	Some Girls	1986	$10

—Reissue on CBS

❑ OC45333	Steel Wheels	1989	$25
❑ COC59100 [M]	Sticky Fingers	1971	$2500

—White label mono promo

❑ COC59100 [DJ]	Sticky Fingers	1971	$300

—White label stereo promo

❑ COC59100	Sticky Fingers	1971	$25

—With working zipper

❑ FC40488	Sticky Fingers	1986	$10

—Reissue on CBS with photo of zipper only

❑ COC39105	Sticky Fingers	1977	$25

—Reissue on Atlantic with working zipper

❑ COC39105	Sticky Fingers	1977	$10

—Reissue on Atlantic with photo of zipper only

❑ 376 4821 [B]	Sticky Fingers	2015	$25
❑ COC39113	Still Life (American Concert 1981)	1982	$25
❑ COC39114 [PD]	Still Life (American Concert 1981)	1982	$40
❑ FC40503	Still Life (American Concert 1981)	1986	$10

—Reissue on CBS

❑ COC16028	Sucking in the Seventies	1981	$25
❑ FC40501	Sucking in the Seventies	1986	$10

—Reissue on CBS

❑ COC16052	Tattoo You	1981	$25
❑ FC40502	Tattoo You	1986	$10

—Reissue on CBS

❑ 90120	Undercover	1983	$25

—With stickers intact

❑ 90120	Undercover	1983	$10

—With stickers peeled off

❑ FC40504	Undercover	1986	$10

—Reissue on CBS has no stickers on cover

VIRGIN

❑ V3012	A Bigger Bang	2005	$30

—Alternate number is "00946 3300671 3"; pressed in the EU for U.S. distribution

❑ 8447121	Bridges to Babylon	1997	$100

—U.S. versions pressed in U.K., but have "Virgin Records America Inc." on back cover

❑ 47864	Exile on Main St.	1999	$50

—Limited-edition reissue with 180-gram vinyl and all original inserts

❑ 8467401 [B]	No Security	1998	$30

—U.S. versions pressed in U.K., but have "Virgin Records America Inc." on back cover

❑ 47867	Some Girls	1999	$30

—Limited-edition reissue with 180-gram vinyl and original inserts (except it has the "cover under reconstruction" inner sleeve)

❑ 47863	Sticky Fingers	1999	$30

—Limited-edition reissue with 180-gram vinyl and original working zipper cover

❑ V2801(8 41040 1) [B]	Stripped	1995	$25

—U.S. versions pressed in U.K., but have UPC code paste-over with "Marketed and Distributed by Caroline Records

❑ V2750(8 39782 1)	Voodoo Lounge	1994	$30

—U.S. versions pressed in U.K., but have UPC code paste-over and blue sticker "Marketed by Caroline

ROLLINI, ADRIAN

MERCURY

❑ MG-20011 [M]	Chopsticks	1953	$150

SUNBEAM

❑ 134	Adrian Rollini and His Orchestra 1933-34	197?	$25

ROLLINS, SONNY; CLIFFORD BROWN; MAX ROACH

PRESTIGE

❑ PRST-7821	Three Giants	1971	$30
❑ PRLP-7291 [M]	Three Giants	1964	$40
❑ PRST-7291 [R]	Three Giants	1964	$75

ROLLINS, SONNY

ABC IMPULSE!

❑ AS-9121 [S]	East Broadway Run Down	1968	$35

—Black label with red ring

❑ AS-9236	Reevaluation: The Impulse Years	1973	$250

❑ AS-91 [S]	Sonny Rollins On Impulse!	1968	$120

—Black label with red ring

❑ IA-9349	There Will Never Be Another You	1978	$35

ANALOGUE PRODUCTIONS

❑ AP 008	Way Out West	199?	$75

—180-gram audiophile vinyl

BLUEBIRD

❑ 5634-1-RB	The Quartets Featuring Jim Hall	1986	$50

BLUE NOTE

❑ BLP-1581 [M]	A Night at the Village Vanguard	1958	$2000

—Deep groove" version; W. 63rd St. address on label

❑ BLP-1581 [M]	A Night at the Village Vanguard	1958	$1500

—Regular version, W. 63rd St. address on label

❑ BLP-1581 [M]	A Night at the Village Vanguard	1963	$350

—With "New York, USA" address on label

❑ BST-81581 [R]	A Night at the Village Vanguard	1967	$40

—With "A Division of Liberty Records" on label

❑ BST-81581 [M]	A Night at the Village Vanguard, Vol. 1	1987	$30

—The Finest in Jazz Since 1939" reissue

❑ BN-LA475-H2	More from the Vanguard	1975	$35
❑ BLP-4001 [M]	Newk's Time	1958	$600

—Deep groove" version; W. 63rd St. address on label

❑ BLP-4001 [M]	Newk's Time	1958	$175

—Regular version, W. 63rd St. address on label

❑ BST-4001 [S]	Newk's Time	1959	$300

—Deep groove" version; W. 63rd St. address on label

❑ BST-4001 [S]	Newk's Time	1959	$250

—Regular version, W. 63rd St. address on label

❑ BLP-4001 [M]	Newk's Time	1963	$120

—With "New York, USA" address on label

❑ BST-4001 [S]	Newk's Time	1963	$40

—With "New York, USA" address on label

❑ BST-84001 [S]	Newk's Time	1967	$50

—With "A Division of Liberty Records" on label

❑ BST-84001 [S]	Newk's Time	198?	$30

Number	Title	Yr	NM
— The Finest in Jazz Since 1939" reissue			
❏ BLP-1542 [M]	Sonny Rollins	1957	$1200
— Deep groove" version; Lexington Ave. address on label			
❏ BLP-1542 [M]	Sonny Rollins	1958	$500
— Deep groove" version, W. 63rd St. address on label			
❏ BLP-1542 [M]	Sonny Rollins	1963	$175
— With "New York, USA" address on label			
❏ BST-81542 [R]	Sonny Rollins	1967	$35
— With "A Division of Liberty Records" on label			
❏ BN-LA401-H2	Sonny Rollins	1975	$75
❏ BST-81542	Sonny Rollins	1985	$30
— The Finest in Jazz Since 1939" reissue			
❏ BLP-1558 [M]	Sonny Rollins, Volume 2	1957	$1000
— Deep groove" version; W. 63rd St. address on label			
❏ BLP-1558 [M]	Sonny Rollins, Volume 2	1957	$400
— Regular version, W. 63rd St. address on label			
❏ BLP-1558 [M]	Sonny Rollins, Volume 2	1963	$175
— With "New York, USA" address on label			
❏ BST-81558 [R]	Sonny Rollins, Volume 2	1967	$35
— With "A Division of Liberty Records" on label			
❏ BST-81558	Sonny Rollins, Volume 2	1985	$30
— The Finest in Jazz Since 1939" reissue			
❏ B1-93203	The Best of Sonny Rollins	1989	$35
CONTEMPORARY			
❏ C-7651	Alternate Takes	1986	$35
❏ M-3564 [M]	Sonny Rollins and the Contemporary Leaders	1959	$300
❏ S-7564 [S]	Sonny Rollins and the Contemporary Leaders	1959	$300
❏ C-3530 [M]	Way Out West	1957	$300
❏ S-7530 [S]	Way Out West	1959	$300
DCC COMPACT CLASSICS			
❏ LPZ-2008	Saxophone Colossus	1995	$200
— 180-gram audiophile vinyl			
❏ LPZ-2022	Tenor Madness	1996	$175
— 180-gram audiophile vinyl			
EVEREST ARCHIVE OF FOLK & JAZZ			
❏ FS-220 [R]	Sonny Rollins with Guest Artist Thad Jones	1968	$30
FANTASY			
❏ OJC-067	Freedom Suite	198?	$30
❏ OJC-314	Horn Culture	198?	$30
❏ OJC-058	Moving Out	198?	$30
❏ OJC-620	Nucleus	1991	$35
❏ OJC-291	Saxophone Colossus	198?	$30
❏ OJC-348	Sonny Boy	198?	$30
❏ OJC-340	Sonny Rollins and the Contemporary Leaders	198?	$35
❏ OJC-214	Sonny Rollins Plays for Bird	198?	$30
❏ OJC-243	Sonny Rollins Plus 4	1987	$30
❏ OJC-011	Sonny Rollins with the Modern Jazz Quartet	1982	$30
❏ OJC-124	Tenor Madness	198?	$30
❏ OJC-468	The Cutting Edge: Montreux 1974	198?	$30
❏ OJC-312	The Next Album	1988	$30
❏ OJC=029	The Sound of Sonny	198?	$30
❏ OJC-337	Way Out West	198?	$30
❏ OJC-007	Work Time	1982	$30
GATEWAY			
❏ GS-7204	The Sound of Sonny	1977	$25
GRP IMPULSE!			
❏ IMP-161 [M]	East Broadway Run Down	199?	$150
— 180-gram audiophile reissue			
❏ IMP-223	Sonny Rollins On Impulse!	1997	$150
— 180-gram reissue			
IMPULSE!			
❏ A-9121 [M]	East Broadway Run Down	1967	$160
❏ AS-9121 [S]	East Broadway Run Down	1967	$250
❏ A-91 [M]	Sonny Rollins On Impulse!	1966	$250
❏ AS-91 [S]	Sonny Rollins On Impulse!	1966	$160
JAZZLAND			
❏ JLP-86 [M]	Shadow Waltz	1962	$175
❏ JLP-986 [S]	Shadow Waltz	1962	$140
❏ JLP-72 [M]	Sonny's Time	1962	$175
❏ JLP-972 [S]	Sonny's Time	1962	$140
MCA			
❏ 4127	Great Moments with Sonny Rollins	198?	$30
❏ 29054	Sonny Rollins On Impulse!	1980	$25
❏ 29055	There Will Never Be Another You	1980	$25
MCA IMPULSE!			
❏ MCA-5655	Sonny Rollins On Impulse!	1986	$25
METROJAZZ			
❏ E-1002 [M]	Sonny Rollins and the Big Brass	1958	$350
❏ SE-1002 [S]	Sonny Rollins and the Big Brass	1958	$300
❏ E-1011 [M]	Sonny Rollins at Music Inn	1958	$350
❏ SE-1011 [S]	Sonny Rollins at Music Inn	1958	$350
MILESTONE			
❏ M-9155	Dancing in the Dark	1988	$30
❏ M-9090	Don't Ask	1979	$30
❏ M-55005	Don't Stop the Carnival	1978	$50
❏ M-9080	Easy Living	1977	$30
❏ M-9179	Falling in Love with Jazz	1990	$35
❏ M-47007	Freedom Suite Plus	1973	$50

Number	Title	Yr	NM
❏ M-9150	G-Man	1987	$30
❏ M-9051	Horn Culture	1974	$30
❏ M-9098	Love at First Sight	1980	$30
❏ M-9104	No Problem	1981	$25
❏ M-9064	Nucleus	1975	$30
❏ M-9108	Reel Life	1982	$25
❏ M-9122	Sunny Days, Starry Nights	1984	$25
❏ M-9059	The Cutting Edge: Montreux 1974	1975	$30
❏ M-9042	The Next Album	197?	$30
❏ M-9074	The Way I Feel	1976	$30
PRESTIGE			
❏ PRLP-7058 [M]	Moving Out	1956	$750
— Yellow label with W. 50th St. address			
❏ PRLP-7058 [M]	Moving Out	1958	$300
— Yellow label with Bergenfield, N.J. address			
❏ PRLP-7095 [M]	Rollins Plays for Bird	1957	$500
— Yellow label with W. 50th St. address			
❏ PRLP-7079 [M]	Saxophone Colossus	1957	$2500
— Yellow label with W. 50th St. address			
❏ PRLP-7326 [M]	Saxophone Colossus	1964	$120
❏ PRST-7326 [R]	Saxophone Colossus	1964	$75
❏ P-24050	Saxophone Colossus and More	1974	$50
❏ PRLP-7269 [M]	Sonny and the Stars	1963	$175
❏ PRST-7269 [R]	Sonny and the Stars	1963	$40
❏ PRLP-7207 [M]	Sonny Boy	1961	$250
❏ PR-24004	Sonny Rollins	1972	$75
❏ PRLP-190 [10]	Sonny Rollins	1954	$600
❏ PRST-7553 [R]	Sonny Rollins Plays for Bird	1968	$75
❏ PRLP-7433 [M]	Sonny Rollins Plays Jazz Classics	1967	$200
❏ PRST-7433 [R]	Sonny Rollins Plays Jazz Classics	1967	$75
❏ PRLP-7038 [M]	Sonny Rollins Plus 4	1956	$400
— Yellow label with W. 50th St. address			
❏ PRLP-137 [10]	Sonny Rollins Quartet	1952	$800
❏ PRLP-186 [10]	Sonny Rollins Quartet	1954	$700
❏ PRLP-7029 [M]	Sonny Rollins with the Modern Jazz Quartet	1956	$750
— Orange cover; original edition has the wrong catalog number at upper left (PR 7020), but the record has the correct number			
❏ PRLP-7029 [M]	Sonny Rollins with the Modern Jazz Quartet	1956	$300
— Orange cover; second edition has the correct catalog number, "Prestige LP 7029," in upper left inside an orange box			
❏ PRLP-7029 [M]	Sonny Rollins with the Modern Jazz Quartet	1956	$300
— Brown and yellow cover; catalog number at upper left is "Prestige Hi-Fil LP 7029"; record has yellow label with W. 50th St. address			
❏ P-24082	Taking Care of Business	1978	$50
❏ PRLP-7047 [M]	Tenor Madness	1956	$300
— Yellow label with W. 50th St. address			
❏ PRST-7657 [R]	Tenor Madness	1969	$75
❏ PRLP-7047 [M]	Tenor Madness	1958	$250
— Yellow label with Bergenfield, N.J. address			
❏ PRST-7856	The First Recordings	1972	$30
❏ PRLP-7126 [M]	Tour de Force	1957	$300
— Yellow label with W. 50th St. address			
❏ P-24096	Vintage Sessions	1981	$50
❏ PRST-7750	Worktime	1970	$30
❏ PRLP-7020 [M]	Work Time	1956	$500
— Yellow label with W. 50th St. address			
❏ PRLP-7246 [M]	Work Time	1962	$175
❏ PRST-7246 [R]	Work Time	1962	$40
QUINTESSENCE			
❏ QJ-25181	Green Dolphin Street	1978	$30
RCA			
❏ ORGM1078 [B]	The Bridge	2016	$40
— blue vinyl, 180 gram. Vinyl Me, Please club issue			
RCA VICTOR			
❏ LPM-2927 [M]	Now's the Time	1964	$75
❏ LSP-2927 [S]	Now's the Time!	1964	$75
❏ LSP-2927 [S]	Now's the Time!	199?	$75
— Classic Records reissue on audiophile vinyl			
❏ LPM-2612 [M]	Our Man In Jazz	1962	$75
❏ LSP-2612 [S]	Our Man In Jazz	1962	$120
❏ LSP-2612 [S]	Our Man In Jazz	199?	$75
— Classic Records reissue on audiophile vinyl			
❏ ANL1-2809	Pure Gold	1978	$25
❏ LPM-2712 [M]	Sonny Meets Hawk!	1963	$75
❏ LSP-2712 [S]	Sonny Meets Hawk!	1963	$120
❏ LSP-2712 [S]	Sonny Meets Hawk!	199?	$75
— Classic Records reissue on audiophile vinyl			
❏ LPM-2527 [M]	The Bridge	1962	$40
— Black label, dog on top, "Long 33 1/3 Play" at bottom			
❏ LSP-2527 [S]	The Bridge	1962	$140
— Black label, dog on top, "Living Stereo" at bottom			
❏ APL1-0859	The Bridge	1975	$50
— Reissue of LSP-2527; orange or tan label			
❏ AFL1-0859	The Bridge	1977	$30
— Reissue with new prefix; black label, dog at 1 o'clock			
❏ LSP-2527 [S]	The Bridge	199?	$75
— Classic Records reissue on audiophile vinyl			
❏ LSP-2527-45	The Bridge	1999	$120
— Classic Records reissue; 4 single-sided LPs that play at 45 rpm			

Number	Title	Yr	NM
❏ LPM-3355 [M]	The Standard Sonny Rollins	1965	$75
❏ LSP-3355 [S]	The Standard Sonny Rollins	1965	$75
❏ LPM-2572 [M]	What's New?	1962	$75
❏ LSP-2572 [S]	What's New?	1962	$120
RIVERSIDE			
❏ RLP-258 [M]	Freedom Suite	1958	$300
❏ RS-3010 [S]	Freedom Suite	1968	$150
❏ SMJ-6044	Freedom Suite	1974	$50
❏ RLP 12-241 [M]	The Sound of Sonny	1957	$750
— White label, blue print			
❏ RLP 12-241 [M]	The Sound of Sonny	1959	$250
— Blue label, microphone logo at top			
❏ RLP-1124 [S]	The Sound of Sonny	1959	$250
STEREO RECORDS			
❏ S-7017 [S]	Way Out West	1958	$250
VERVE			
❏ V-8430 [M]	Sonny Rollins/Brass, Sonny Rollins/Trio	1962	$40
❏ V6-8430 [S]	Sonny Rollins/Brass, Sonny Rollins/Trio	1962	$75
❏ UMV-2555	Sonny Rollins/Brass, Sonny Rollins/Trio	198?	$25
❏ VSP-32 [M]	Tenor Titan	1966	$35
❏ VSPS-32 [S]	Tenor Titan	1966	$30

ROLLINS, SONNY/JIMMY CLEVELAND

Number	Title	Yr	NM
PERIOD			
❏ SPL-1204 [M]	Sonny Rollins Plays/Jimmy Cleveland Plays	1956	$2000

ROLLINS BAND, THE
As in Henry Rollins of BLACK FLAG.

Number	Title	Yr	NM
1/4 STICK			
❏ 0002	Turned On	1990	$18
IMAGO			
❏ 21034	Weight	1994	$18

ROMAN NEW ORLEANS JAZZ BAND, THE

Number	Title	Yr	NM
RCA VICTOR			
❏ LPT-3033 [10]	Around the World in Jazz -- Italy	1953	$40

ROMANTICS, THE

Number	Title	Yr	NM
NEMPEROR			
❏ BFZ38880	In Heat	1983	$12
❏ JZ36881	National Breakout	1980	$12
❏ FZ40106	Rhythm Romance	1985	$12
❏ ARZ37435	Strictly Personal	1981	$12

❏ JZ36273 [B]	The Romantics	1980	$12

ROMAO, DOM UM

Number	Title	Yr	NM
MUSE			
❏ MR-5013	Dom Um Romao	1974	$35
❏ MR-5049	Spirit of the Times	197?	$30
PABLO			
❏ 2310777	Hotmosphere	197?	$30

ROMEO VOID

Number	Title	Yr	NM
415 RECORDS			
❏ A-0004	It's a Condition	1981	$18
❏ A-0007 [EP]	Never Say Never	1981	$30
COLUMBIA			
❏ ARC38182	Benefactor	1982	$12
❏ PC38182	Benefactor	198?	$10
— Reissue			
❏ BFC39155	Instincts	1984	$12
❏ PC39155	Instincts	1985	$10
— Reissue			
❏ PC38178 [EP]	Never Say Never	1982	$15
— Reissue			

Number	Title	Yr	NM

ROMEOS, THE (1)
MARK II

Number	Title	Yr	NM
❏ 1001	Precious Memories	1967	$30

ROMERO, CELEDONIO; CELIN; PEPE; AND ANGEL
MERCURY LIVING PRESENCE

Number	Title	Yr	NM
❏ SR90434 [S]	An Evening of Flamenco Music	1965	$30
— Maroon label, with "Vendor: Mercury Record Corporation			
❏ SR90417 [S]	Spain's Royal Family of the Guitar	196?	$30
— Maroon label, no "Vendor: Mercury Record Corporation			
❏ SR90295 [S]	The Royal Family of the Spanish Guitar	196?	$30
— Maroon label, no "Vendor: Mercury Record Corporation			
❏ SR90295 [S]	The Royal Family of the Spanish Guitar	196?	$30
— Maroon label, with "Vendor: Mercury Record Corporation			

ROMERO, CELEDONIO
MERCURY LIVING PRESENCE

Number	Title	Yr	NM
❏ SR90296 [S]	Guitar Music from the Courts of Spain	196?	$30
— Maroon label, no "Vendor: Mercury Record Corporation			

ROMERO, CESAR
TOPS

Number	Title	Yr	NM
❏ L-1631 [M]	Songs by a Latin Lover	1958	$30

ROMERO, PEPE
MERCURY LIVING PRESENCE

Number	Title	Yr	NM
❏ SR90297 [S]	Flamenco	196?	$40
— Maroon label, no "Vendor: Mercury Record Corporation			

ROMERO, RAOUL
SEA BREEZE

Number	Title	Yr	NM
❏ SB-2031	The Music of Raoul Romero	1987	$25

ROMNEY, HUGH
Later known as "Wavy Gravy."
WORLD PACIFIC

Number	Title	Yr	NM
❏ WP-1805 [M]	Third Stream Humor	1962	$30
❏ ST-1805 [S]	Third Stream Humor	1962	$40

RONDO, DON
JUBILEE

Number	Title	Yr	NM
❏ JLP-1081 [M]	Have You Met Don Rondo	195?	$25
❏ JLP-1052 [M]	Rondo	195?	$25

VOCALION

Number	Title	Yr	NM
❏ VL73897	Two Different Worlds	1970	$15

RONETTES, THE
COLPIX

Number	Title	Yr	NM
❏ CP-486 [M]	The Ronettes Featuring Veronica	1965	$250
— Gold label			
❏ CP-486 [M]	The Ronettes Featuring Veronica	1965	$150
— Blue label			
❏ SCP-486 [S]	The Ronettes Featuring Veronica	1965	$300
— Gold label			
❏ SCP-486 [S]	The Ronettes Featuring Veronica	1965	$175
— Blue label			

PHILLES

Number	Title	Yr	NM
❏ PHLP-4006 [M]	Presenting the Fabulous Ronettes Featuring Veronica	1964	$800
— Blue and black label			
❏ PHLP-4006 [M]	Presenting the Fabulous Ronettes Featuring Veronica	1964	$400
— Yellow and red label			
❏ PHLP-ST-4006 [S]	Presenting the Fabulous Ronettes Featuring Veronica	1965	$600
❏ T-90721 [M]	Presenting the Fabulous Ronettes Featuring Veronica	1965	$300
— Capitol Record Club edition			
❏ ST-90721 [S]	Presenting the Fabulous Ronettes Featuring Veronica	1965	$400
— Capitol Record Club edition			

RONEY, WALLACE
MUSE

Number	Title	Yr	NM
❏ MR-5346	Intuition	1989	$30
❏ MR-5372	The Standard Bearer	1990	$30
❏ MR-5335	Verses	1987	$25

RONNIE AND THE DEADBEATS
CHECK

Number	Title	Yr	NM
❏ 103 [M]	Groovin' with Ronnie and the Deadbeats	197?	$25

RONNIE AND THE POMONA CASUALS
DONNA

Number	Title	Yr	NM
❏ 2113 [M]	Everybody Jerk	1965	$30

RONNY AND THE DAYTONAS
BEAT ROCKET

Number	Title	Yr	NM
❏ BR119	G.T.O.	199?	$15
— Reissue of Mala 4001 with four bonus tracks			
❏ BR120	Sandy	199?	$15
— Reissue of Mala 4002 with three bonus tracks			

MALA

Number	Title	Yr	NM
❏ 4001 [M]	G.T.O.	1964	$120
❏ 4002 [M]	Sandy	1966	$100
❏ 4002S [S]	Sandy	1966	$150

SUNDAZED

Number	Title	Yr	NM
❏ LP5050	G.T.O. -- Best of the Mala Recordings	1997	$12

RONSON, MICK
Also see DAVID BOWIE; MOTT THE HOOPLE.
RCA VICTOR

Number	Title	Yr	NM
❏ APL1-0681 [B]	Play Don't Worry	1975	$25
❏ APL1-0353 [B]	Slaughter on 10th Avenue	1974	$25

RONSTADT, LINDA
Also see DOLLY PARTON/LINDA RONSTADT/EMMYLOU HARRIS. Also see STONE PONEYS.
ASYLUM

Number	Title	Yr	NM
❏ 60765	Canciones De Mi Padre	1988	$15
❏ SD5064	Don't Cry Now	1973	$12
❏ 60474	For Sentimental Reasons	1987	$12
❏ 60185	Get Closer	1982	$12
❏ 7E-1092	Greatest Hits	1976	$15
❏ 6E-106	Greatest Hits	1977	$12
❏ 5E-516	Greatest Hits, Volume 2	1980	$12
❏ 7E-1072	Hasten Down the Wind	1976	$12
— Clouds" label			
❏ 7E-1072	Hasten Down the Wind	1976	$18
— Solid blue label with white stylized "a" at top			
❏ 5E-540	Keeping Out of Mischief	1981	$0
— Canceled			
❏ 6E-155	Living in the U.S.A.	1978	$12
❏ DP-401 [PD]	Living in the U.S.A.	1978	$30
❏ 60387	Lush Life	1984	$12
❏ 5E-510	Mad Love	1980	$12
❏ 7E-1045	Prisoner in Disguise	1975	$12
❏ 60489	'Round Midnight: The Nelson Riddle Sessions	1987	$30
❏ 6E-104	Simple Dreams	1977	$12
❏ 60260	What's New	1983	$12

CAPITOL

Number	Title	Yr	NM
❏ SKBB-11629	A Retrospective	1977	$18
— Also includes Stone Poneys tracks			
❏ SN-16133	Beginnings	1980	$10
❏ ST-11269	Different Drum	1974	$15
— Also includes Stone Poneys tracks			
❏ SN-16299	Different Drum	198?	$10
— Budget-line reissue			
❏ ST-208	Hand Sown…Home Grown	1969	$25
— Black label with colorband			
❏ ST-208	Hand Sown…Home Grown	1970	$18
— Green label			
❏ ST-208	Hand Sown…Home Grown	1971	$15
— Red label			
❏ SN-16130	Hand Sown…Home Grown	1980	$10
❏ ST-11358	Heart Like a Wheel	1974	$15
❏ SW-11358	Heart Like a Wheel	1975	$12
❏ SMAS-635	Linda Ronstadt	1972	$15
❏ SN-16132	Linda Ronstadt	1980	$10
❏ ST-407	Silk Purse	1970	$18
— Green label			
❏ ST-407	Silk Purse	1971	$15
— Red label			
❏ SN-16131	Silk Purse	1980	$10
❏ ST-8-0407	Silk Purse	1970	$25
— Capitol Record Club edition			

DCC COMPACT CLASSICS

Number	Title	Yr	NM
❏ LPZ-2048	Greatest Hits	1997	$100
— Audiophile vinyl			
❏ LPZ-2065	Greatest Hits, Volume Two	1998	$40
— Audiophile vinyl			

ELEKTRA

Number	Title	Yr	NM
❏ 60872	Cry Like a Rainstorm, Howl Like the Wind	1989	$15

MOBILE FIDELITY

Number	Title	Yr	NM
❏ 1-158	What's New	1984	$50
— Audiophile vinyl			

NAUTILUS

Number	Title	Yr	NM
❏ NR-26	Simple Dreams	1982	$50
— Audiophile vinyl			

PAIR

Number	Title	Yr	NM
❏ PDL2-1070	Prime of Life	1986	$15
❏ PDL2-1125	Rockfile	1986	$15

Number	Title	Yr	NM
TPM/RHINO EXCLUSIVE			
❏ 306	Prisoner in Disguise	2008	$25

ROOFTOP SINGERS, THE
VANGUARD

Number	Title	Yr	NM
❏ VRS-9134 [M]	Good Time	1964	$20
❏ VSD-79134 [S]	Good Time	1964	$25
❏ VRS-9190 [M]	Rainy River	1965	$18
❏ VSD-79190 [S]	Rainy River	1965	$25
❏ VRS-9123 [M]	Walk Right In	1963	$20
❏ VSD-2136 [S]	Walk Right In	1963	$25

ROOMFUL OF BLUES
ANTILLES

Number	Title	Yr	NM
❏ 7071	Let's Have a Party!	1980	$25

BLUE FLAME

Number	Title	Yr	NM
❏ 1001	Hot Little Mama	197?	$30

ISLAND

Number	Title	Yr	NM
❏ ILPS9474	Roomful of Blues	1977	$30

ROONEY, MICKEY
RCA VICTOR

Number	Title	Yr	NM
❏ LPM-1520 [M]	Mickey Rooney Sings George M. Cohan	1957	$100

ROS, EDMUNDO
LONDON

Number	Title	Yr	NM
❏ PS114 [S]	Rhythms of the South	195?	$18

ROSE, BIFF
BUDDAH

Number	Title	Yr	NM
❏ BDS-5076	Children of Light	1971	$15
— Reissue of Tetragrammaton 116			
❏ BDS-5078	Half Live at the Bitter End	1971	$15
❏ BDS-5069	Ride On!	1970	$15
❏ BDS-5075	The Thorn in Mrs. Rose's Side	1971	$15
— Reissue of Tetragrammaton 103			

TETRAGRAMMATON

Number	Title	Yr	NM
❏ T-116	Children of Light	1969	$18
❏ T-103	The Thorn in Mrs. Rose's Side	1968	$18

UNITED ARTISTS

Number	Title	Yr	NM
❏ UAS-5594	Uncle Jesus Auntie Christ	1972	$15

ROSE, DAVID
CAPITOL

Number	Title	Yr	NM
❏ ST2853	Christmas Album	1968	$18
❏ T2717 [M]	Holiday for Strings	1967	$18
❏ ST2717 [S]	Holiday for Strings	1967	$15
❏ ST-124	Something Fresh	1969	$18
❏ T2627 [M]	The Bible	1966	$15
❏ ST2627 [S]	The Bible	1966	$18
❏ ST-290	The Little Drummer Boy	1969	$15
— Reissue of 2853			

DINO

Number	Title	Yr	NM
❏ DP-3001	Miracle	1972	$15

KAPP

Number	Title	Yr	NM
❏ KL-1100 [M]	Great Waltzes of the Fabulous Century	1958	$25
❏ K-1100-S [S]	Great Waltzes of the Fabulous Century	1958	$30
❏ KXL-5004 [M]	Songs of the Fabulous Thirties	1958	$30
❏ KX-5004-S [S]	Songs of the Fabulous Thirties	1958	$30
❏ KL-1205 [M]	Songs of the Fabulous Thirties, Vol. 1	1960	$18
❏ KS-3205 [S]	Songs of the Fabulous Thirties, Vol. 1	1960	$25
❏ KL-1206 [M]	Songs of the Fabulous Thirties, Vol. 2	1960	$18
❏ KS-3206 [S]	Songs of the Fabulous Thirties, Vol. 2	1960	$25
❏ KS-3010 [S]	Waltzes in Stereo	1959	$30

LION

Number	Title	Yr	NM
❏ L-70109 [M]	Magic Melodies	1959	$25

METRO

Number	Title	Yr	NM
❏ M585 [M]	Among the Stars	1966	$15
❏ MS585 [S]	Among the Stars	1966	$15
❏ M502 [M]	Deep Purple	1965	$15
❏ MS502 [R]	Deep Purple	1965	$15

MGM

Number	Title	Yr	NM
❏ E-4004 [M]	21 Channel Sound	1962	$18
❏ SE-4004 [S]	21 Channel Sound	1962	$25
❏ E-3469 [M]	A Merry Christmas to You	1956	$30
— Yellow label			
❏ E-3469 [M]	A Merry Christmas to You	1960	$18
— Black label			
❏ E-532 [10]	A Sentimental Journey with David Rose	1950	$75
❏ E-3592 [M]	Autumn Leaves	1957	$30
— Yellow label			
❏ SE-3592 [S]	Autumn Leaves	1959	$30
— Yellow label			
❏ E-3067 [M]	Beautiful Music to Love By	1953	$30
— Yellow label			

Number	Title	Yr	NM
❑ E-3894 [M]	Box-Office Blockbusters	1961	$18
❑ SE-3894 [S]	Box-Office Blockbusters	1961	$25
❑ E-3952 [M]	Butterfield-8	1961	$18
❑ SE-3952 [S]	Butterfield-8	1961	$25
❑ E-3953 [M]	Cimarron	1961	$18
❑ SE-3953 [S]	Cimarron	1961	$25
❑ E-3852 [M]	Concert with a Beat!	1960	$18
❑ SE-3852 [S]	Concert with a Beat!	1960	$25
❑ E-3960 [M]	David Rose and His Concert Orchestra Play His Dramatic Music from the NBC-TV Series "Bonanza"	1961	$30
❑ SE-3960 [S]	David Rose and His Concert Orchestra Play His Dramatic Music from the NBC-TV Series "Bonanza"	1961	$40
❑ GAS-129	David Rose and His Orchestra (Golden Archive Series)	1970	$12
❑ E-85 [10]	David Rose and His Orchestra Play Music of George Gershwin	1951	$40
❑ E-3748 [M]	David Rose Plays David Rose	1959	$25
— Yellow label			
❑ SE-3748 [S]	David Rose Plays David Rose	1959	$25
— Yellow label			
❑ E-3640 [M]	David Rose Plays Music from "Gigi	1958	$30
— Yellow label			
❑ SE-3640 [S]	David Rose Plays Music from "Gigi	1958	$30
— Yellow label			
❑ E-3746 [M]	David Rose Plays the Music from "Whoop Up!	1959	$25
— Yellow label			
❑ SE-3746 [S]	David Rose Plays the Music from "Whoop Up!	1959	$30
— Yellow label			
❑ E-3950 [M]	Exodus	1961	$18
❑ SE-3950 [S]	Exodus	1961	$25
❑ E-3108 [M]	Fiddlin' for Fun	1954	$30
— Yellow label			
❑ E-3481 [M]	Hi Fiddles	1957	$30
— Yellow label			
❑ E-3215 [M]	Holiday for Strings	1955	$30
— Yellow label			
❑ E-506 [10]	Holiday for Strings	1950	$75
❑ E-3101 [M]	Let's Fall in Love	1954	$30
— Yellow label			
❑ E-3289 [M]	Lover's Serenade	1955	$30
— Yellow label			
❑ E-4144 [M]	Love Theme from "Cleopatra" and Music from Other Great Motion Pictures	1963	$18
❑ SE-4144 [S]	Love Theme from "Cleopatra" and Music from Other Great Motion Pictures	1963	$25
❑ E-3123 [M]	Love Walked In -- The Music of George Gershwin	1954	$30
— Yellow label			
❑ E-4099 [M]	More, More, More, Music of the Stripper	1963	$18
❑ SE-4099 [S]	More, More, More, Music of the Stripper	1963	$25
❑ E-3612 [M]	Music from Jamaica	1957	$30
— Yellow label			
❑ E-3397 [M]	Music from Motion Pictures	1956	$30
— Yellow label			
❑ E-3134 [M]	Nostalgia	1954	$30
— Yellow label			
❑ E-4285 [M]	Quick, Before It Melts and Other Selections	1965	$18
❑ SE-4285 [S]	Quick, Before It Melts and Other Selections	1965	$25
❑ E-3603 [M]	Reflections in the Water	1957	$30
— Yellow label			
❑ E-3716 [M]	Secret Songs for Young Lovers	1959	$25
— With Andre Previn; yellow label			
❑ SE-3716 [S]	Secret Songs for Young Lovers	1959	$30
— With Andre Previn; yellow label			
❑ E-3255 [M]	Sentimental Journey	1955	$30
— Yellow label			
❑ E-515 [10]	Serenades	1950	$75
❑ E-3895 [M]	Spectacular Strings	1961	$18
❑ SE-3895 [S]	Spectacular Strings	1961	$25
❑ E-4271 [M]	The Americanization of Emily and Other Great Movie Themes	1964	$18
❑ SE-4271 [S]	The Americanization of Emily and Other Great Movie Themes	1964	$25
❑ E-196 [10]	The Magic Music Box	1953	$40
❑ E-3555 [M]	The Song Is You -- Melodies of Jerome Kern	1957	$30
— Yellow label			
❑ T-90534 [M]	The Stripper and Other Fun Songs for the Family	1965	$25
— Capitol Record Club edition			
❑ ST-90534 [S]	The Stripper and Other Fun Songs for the Family	1965	$25
— Capitol Record Club edition			

Number	Title	Yr	NM
❑ E-4062 [M]	The Stripper and Other Fun Songs for the Family	1962	$18
— Black label			
❑ SE-4062 [S]	The Stripper and Other Fun Songs for the Family	1962	$25
— Black label			
❑ SE-4062 [S]	The Stripper and Other Fun Songs for the Family	1968	$15
— Blue and gold label			
❑ E-4307 [M]	The Velvet Beat	1965	$15
❑ SE-4307 [S]	The Velvet Beat	1965	$18
❑ ST-90754 [S]	The Velvet Beat	1965	$25
— Capitol Record Club edition			
❑ E-4155 [M]	The Very Best of David Rose	1963	$15
❑ SE-4155 [S]	The Very Best of David Rose	1963	$18
❑ E-4077 [M]	The Wonderful World of the Brothers Grimm	1962	$18
❑ SE-4077 [S]	The Wonderful World of the Brothers Grimm	1962	$25

ROSE, DAVID (2)
INNER CITY

❑ IC-1058	The Distance Between Dreams	197?	$30

ROSE, TIM
CAPITOL

❑ ST-673	Love, A Kind of Hate Story	1970	$15

COLUMBIA

❑ CS9772 [B]	Thru Rose Colored Glasses	1969	$18
❑ CS9577 [B]	Tim Rose	1968	$18

PLAYBOY

❑ P-101	Tim Rose	1972	$15

TIGER LILY

❑ TL14055 [B]	Unfinished Song	1976	$250

ROSE, WALLY
BLACKBIRD

❑ 12007	Wally Rose on Piano	196?	$30
❑ 12010	Whippin' the Keys	197?	$30

COLUMBIA

❑ CL782 [M]	Cake Walk to Lindy Hop	1956	$40
❑ CL2535 [10]	Honky-Tonkin'	1955	$40
— House Party Series" reissue			
❑ CL6260 [10]	Wally Rose	1953	$50

GOOD TIME JAZZ

❑ S-10034 [S]	Ragtime Classics	1960	$25
❑ L-12034 [M]	Ragtime Classics	1960	$35

STOMP OFF

❑ SOS-1057	Wally Rose Revisited	1982	$25

ROSE
MILLENNIUM

❑ BXL1-7749	Worlds Apart	1979	$35

ROSE GARDEN, THE
ATCO

❑ 33-225 [M]	The Rose Garden	1968	$75
❑ SD 33-225 [S]	The Rose Garden	1968	$30

ROSE MARIE
KAPP

❑ KFL-4500 [M]	Songs for Single Girls	1964	$30

ROSE ROYCE
ATLANTIC

❑ 81944	Perfect Lover	1989	$15

EPIC

❑ FE37939	Stronger Than Ever	1982	$18

MONTAGE

❑ MA110	Music Magic	1984	$18

OMNI

❑ 90557	Fresh Cut	1987	$15
❑ 90641	The Best of Rose Royce	1988	$25

WHITFIELD

❑ WHK3512	Golden Touch	1980	$18
❑ WHK3457	Greatest Hits	1980	$15
❑ WHK3620	Jump Street	1981	$18
❑ WH3074	Rose Royce II/In Full Bloom	1977	$15
❑ WHK3227	Rose Royce III/Strikes Again!	1978	$15
❑ WHS3387	Rose Royce IV/Rainbow Connection	1979	$15

ROSELLI, JIMMY
UNITED ARTISTS

❑ UAS-6665	3 A.M.	1968	$15
❑ UAS-6635	Core Napulitano	1968	$18
❑ UAS-6698	Core Spezzato	1969	$18
❑ UAS-6775	I'te Voglio Bene Assale	1970	$15
❑ UAS-6747	It's Been Swell	1970	$15
❑ UXS-83	Jimmy Roselli Superpak	1972	$18
❑ UAS-6724	Let Me Sing	1969	$15

Number	Title	Yr	NM
❑ UAL-3429 [M]	Life & Love Italian Style	1965	$15
❑ UAS-6429 [S]	Life & Love Italian Style	1965	$18
❑ UAL-3430 [M]	Mala Femmina	1965	$15
❑ UAS-6430 [S]	Mala Femmina	1965	$18
❑ UAL-3467 [M]	New York: My Port of Call	1966	$15
❑ UAS-6467 [S]	New York: My Port of Call	1966	$18
❑ UAL-3451 [M]	Saloon Songs	1966	$15
❑ UAS-6451 [S]	Saloon Songs	1966	$18
❑ UAL-3585 [M]	Saloon Songs, Vol. 2	1967	$15
❑ UAS-6585 [S]	Saloon Songs, Vol. 2	1967	$18
❑ UAS-5641	Simmo 'e Napule	1972	$15
❑ UAL-3564 [M]	Sold Out	1967	$15
❑ UAS-6564 [S]	Sold Out	1967	$18
❑ UAS-6645	The Best of Jimmy Roselli	1968	$18
❑ UAL3539 [M]	The Christmas Album	1966	$18
❑ UAS6539 [S]	The Christmas Album	1966	$18
❑ UAL-3438 [M]	The Great Ones!	1965	$15
❑ UAS-6438 [S]	The Great Ones!	1965	$18
❑ UAL-3544 [M]	The Italian Album	1966	$15
❑ UAS-6544 [S]	The Italian Album	1966	$18
❑ UAL-3611 [M]	There Must Be a Way	1967	$18
❑ UAS-6611 [S]	There Must Be a Way	1967	$18

ROSENGREN, BERNT
STOMP OFF

❑ SOS-1177	Surprise Party	198?	$25

ROSEWOMAN, MICHELE
ENJA

❑ R1-79607	Contrast High	1990	$35

SOUL NOTE

❑ SN-1072	The Source	1984	$30

ROSIE AND THE ORIGINALS
BRUNSWICK

❑ BL54102 [M]	Lonely Blue Nights with Rosie	1961	$175
❑ BL754102 [S]	Lonely Blue Nights with Rosie	1961	$250

ROSIE O'GRADY'S GOOD TIME BAND
DIRECT DISK

❑ DD-103	Dixieland	1979	$25
— Audiophile recording			

ROSNES, RENEE
BLUE NOTE

❑ B1-93561	Renee Rosnes	1990	$35

ROSOLINO, FRANK
BETHLEHEM

❑ BCP-26 [M]	I Play Trombone	1955	$300

CAPITOL

❑ T6509 [M]	Frankly Speaking	1955	$175
❑ H6507 [10]	Frank Rosolino	1954	$300
❑ T6507 [M]	Frank Rosolino	1955	$175

INTERLUDE

❑ MO-500 [M]	The Legend of Frank Rosolino	1959	$100
❑ ST-1000 [S]	The Legend of Frank Rosolino	1959	$75

MODE

❑ LP-107 [M]	Frank Rosolino Quintet	1957	$175

REPRISE

❑ R-6016 [M]	Turn Me Loose	1961	$75
❑ R9-6016 [S]	Turn Me Loose	1961	$100

SACKVILLE

❑ 2014	Thinking About You	198?	$50

SPECIALTY

❑ SPS-2161	Free for All	1974	$40

ROSS, ANNIE; DOROTHY DUNN; SHELBY DAVIS
SAVOY

❑ MG-12060 [M]	Singin' 'N Swingin'	1956	$75

ROSS, ANNIE
Also see LAMBERT, HENDRICKS AND ROSS.

DECCA

❑ DL4922 [M]	Fill My Heart with Song	1967	$40
❑ DL74922 [S]	Fill My Heart with Song	1967	$30

KIMBERLY

❑ 2018 [M]	Annie Ross Sings A Song With Mulligan!	1963	$40
❑ 11018 [S]	Annie Ross Sings A Song With Mulligan!	1963	$40

WORLD PACIFIC

❑ WP-1285 [M]	A Gasser!	1960	$175
❑ ST-1285 [S]	A Gasser!	1960	$175
❑ WP-1253 [M]	Annie Ross Sings A Song With Mulligan!	1959	$300
❑ ST-1020 [S]	Annie Ross Sings A Song With Mulligan!	1959	$175
❑ WP-1808 [M]	Gypsy	1959	$175
❑ ST-1028 [S]	Gypsy	1959	$175

Number	Title	Yr	NM

ROSS, ARNOLD
CLEF
| ❏ MGC-134 [10] | Arnold Ross | 1953 | $0 |

— Evidently canceled

DISCOVERY
| ❏ DL-2006 [M] | Arnold Ross | 1954 | $300 |

MERCURY
| ❏ MGC-134 [10] | Arnold Ross | 1952 | $300 |

ROSS, CHARLIE
ACCORD
| ❏ SN-7007 | High Cost of Loving | 1982 | $12 |

ROSS, DIANA, AND MARVIN GAYE
MOTOWN
| ❏ M7-803 [B] | Diana & Marvin | 1973 | $25 |
| ❏ M5-124V1 | Diana & Marvin | 1981 | $10 |

— Reissue

ROSS, DIANA, AND THE SUPREMES
See THE SUPREMES.

ROSS, DIANA
MOTOWN
❏ M13-960C2	All the Great Hits	1981	$15
❏ M7-877R2	An Evening with Diana Ross	1977	$18
❏ M7-890R1	Baby It's Me	1977	$15
❏ M8-936	Diana	1980	$12
❏ MS-719	Diana!	1971	$18
❏ M5-155V1	Diana!	1981	$10

— Reissue of 719

❏ MS-711	Diana Ross	1970	$18
❏ M6-861S1	Diana Ross	1976	$15
❏ M5-135V1	Diana Ross	1981	$10

— Reissue of 711

| ❏ 5294ML | Diana Ross | 1983 | $10 |

— Reissue of 861

❏ 6049ML2	Diana Ross Anthology	1983	$18
❏ M6-869S1	Diana Ross' Greatest Hits	1976	$15
❏ M6-801S1	Diana Ross Live at Caesars Palace	1974	$15
❏ M5-169V1	Diana Ross Live at Caesars Palace	1981	$10

— Reissue of 801

❏ M5-214V1	Duets with Diana	1981	$12
❏ MS-724	Everything Is Everything	1970	$18
❏ M-758D	Lady Sings the Blues	1972	$18

— With booklet; all but four tracks are by Diana Ross

❏ M7-812V1	Last Time I Saw Him	1974	$15
❏ M7-907R1	Ross	1978	$15
❏ MS-723	Surrender	1971	$18
❏ M8-923M1	The Boss	1979	$12
❏ M5-198V1	The Boss	1981	$10

— Reissue of 923

❏ 37463-6377-1	The Remixes	1994	$15
❏ M8-951M1	To Love Again	1981	$12
❏ M-772L	Touch Me in the Morning	1973	$18
❏ M5-163V1	Touch Me in the Morning	1981	$10

— Reissue of 772

| ❏ MOT-6274 | Workin' Overtime | 1989 | $12 |

NAUTILUS
| ❏ NR-37 [B] | Diana | 1981 | $40 |

— Audiophile vinyl

RCA VICTOR
❏ AFL1-5422	Eaten Alive	1985	$10
❏ 6388-1-R	Red Hot Rhythm and Blues	1987	$10
❏ AFL1-4677	Ross	1983	$10
❏ AFL1-4384	Silk Electric	1982	$12
❏ AFL1-5009	Swept Away	1984	$10
❏ AFL1-4153	Why Do Fools Fall in Love	1981	$12
❏ AYL1-5162	Why Do Fools Fall in Love	1985	$10

— Best Buy Series" reissue

ROSS, JACK
DOT
| ❏ DLP-3429 [M] | Cinderella | 1962 | $25 |
| ❏ DLP-25429 [S] | Cinderella | 1962 | $30 |

ROSS, JACKIE
CHESS
| ❏ LP-1489 [M] | In Full Bloom | 1966 | $30 |
| ❏ LPS-1489 [S] | In Full Bloom | 1966 | $40 |

ROSS, JERIS
ABC DOT
| ❏ DOSD-2046 | Jeris Ross | 1976 | $15 |

ROSS, JOE E.
ROULETTE
| ❏ R-25281 [M] | Love Songs from a Cop | 1965 | $30 |
| ❏ SR-25281 [S] | Love Songs from a Cop | 1965 | $30 |

ROSS, RONNIE
ATLANTIC
| ❏ 1333 [M] | The Jazz Makers | 1960 | $300 |
| ❏ SD1333 [S] | The Jazz Makers | 1960 | $300 |

ROSS, SPENCER
COLUMBIA
| ❏ CL1525 [M] | Spencer Ross and His Orchestra | 1960 | $25 |
| ❏ CS0(# unknown) [S] | Spencer Ross and His Orchestra | 1960 | $30 |

ROSS, STAN
DEL-FI
| ❏ DFLP-1233 [M] | My Son the Copy Cat | 1963 | $30 |
| ❏ DFST-1233 [S] | My Son the Copy Cat | 1963 | $40 |

ROSS-LEVINE BAND, THE
HEADFIRST
| ❏ 9701 | That Summer Something | 198? | $30 |

ROTARY CONNECTION
CADET
| ❏ CS-50006 [B] | Hey Love | 1971 | $30 |

CADET CONCEPT
❏ LPS-317	Aladdin	1968	$30
❏ LSP-328 [B]	Dinner Music	1970	$30
❏ LPS318 [B]	Peace	1969	$30
❏ LP-312 [M]	Rotary Connection	1968	$100

— Mono appears to be promo only

| ❏ LPS-312 [S] | Rotary Connection | 1968 | $30 |
| ❏ LPS-322 [B] | Songs | 1969 | $30 |

ROTH, DAVID LEE
Also see VAN HALEN.
WARNER BROS.
❏ 26477	A Little Ain't Enough	1991	$18
❏ 25222 [EP]	Crazy from the Heat	1985	$10
❏ 25470	Eat 'Em and Smile	1986	$10
❏ 25671	Skyscraper	1988	$10

ROTH, LILLIAN
EPIC
| ❏ LN3206 [M] | I'll Cry Tomorrow | 1957 | $30 |

TOPS
| ❏ L-1567 [M] | Lillian Roth Sings | 1958 | $30 |

ROUND, JONATHAN
WESTBOUND
| ❏ 2009 | Jonathan Round | 1971 | $30 |

— Round cover

| ❏ 2009 [B] | Jonathan Round | 1972 | $25 |

— Square cover

ROUND ROBIN
CHALLENGE
| ❏ LP-620 [M] | The Land of 1,000 Dances | 1965 | $30 |

DOMAIN
| ❏ 101 [M] | Greatest Dance Hits Slauson Style | 1964 | $40 |

ROUSE, CHARLIE, AND PAUL QUINICHETTE
BETHLEHEM
| ❏ BCP-6021 [M] | The Chase Is On | 1958 | $250 |

ROUSE, CHARLIE
BLUE NOTE
| ❏ BLP-4119 [M] | Bossa Nova Bacchanal | 1962 | $75 |
| ❏ BST-84119 [S] | Bossa Nova Bacchanal | 1962 | $40 |

— With "New York, USA" address on label

| ❏ BST-84119 [S] | Bossa Nova Bacchanal | 196? | $25 |

— With "A Division of Liberty Records" on label

DOUGLAS
| ❏ 7044 | Cinnamon Flower | 197? | $35 |

EPIC
❏ LA16018 [M]	We Paid Our Dues	1961	$100
❏ BA17018 [S]	We Paid Our Dues	1961	$150
❏ LA16012 [M]	Yeah!	1960	$700
❏ BA17012 [S]	Yeah!	1960	$250
❏ BA17012 [S]	Yeah!	199?	$75

— Classic Records reissue on audiophile vinyl

FANTASY
| ❏ OJC-491 | Takin' Care of Business | 1991 | $30 |

JAZZLAND
| ❏ JLP-19 [M] | Takin' Care of Business | 1960 | $40 |
| ❏ JLP-919 [S] | Takin' Care of Business | 1960 | $50 |

LANDMARK
| ❏ LLP-1521 | Epistrophy | 1989 | $30 |

STORYVILLE
| ❏ 4079 | Moment's Notice | 198? | $25 |

STRATA-EAST
| ❏ SES-19746 | Two Is One | 1974 | $30 |

ROUTERS, THE
WARNER BROS.
❏ W1524 [M]	1963's Great Instrumental Hits	1964	$30
❏ WS1524 [S]	1963's Great Instrumental Hits	1964	$40
❏ W1559 [M]	Charge!	1964	$30
❏ WS1559 [S]	Charge!	1964	$30
❏ W1595 [M]	Go Go Go with the Chuck Berry Songbook	1965	$25
❏ WS1595 [S]	Go Go Go with the Chuck Berry Songbook	1965	$30
❏ W1490 [M]	Let's Go! with the Routers	1963	$40
❏ WS1490 [S]	Let's Go! with the Routers	1963	$50

ROVA
BLACK SAINT
| ❏ 120126 | Beat Kennel | 1987 | $30 |
| ❏ BSR-0076 | Rova Plays Lacy -- Favorite Street | 1984 | $30 |

HAT ART
| ❏ 2013 | Saxophone Diplomacy | 1986 | $35 |
| ❏ 2032 | The Crowd | 198? | $35 |

METALANGUAGE
❏ 118	As Was	1981	$35
❏ 101	Cinema Rovate	1978	$50
❏ 0(# unknown)	Daredevils	1979	$50
❏ 106	The Removal of Secrecy	1979	$50

ROVERS, THE
CLEVELAND INT'L.
| ❏ FE37706 | Pain in My Past | 1982 | $12 |
| ❏ JE37107 | Wasn't That a Party | 1981 | $12 |

ROWLAND, DAVE
ELEKTRA
| ❏ 5E-525 | Pleasure | 1981 | $10 |

— As "Dave Rowland and Sugar

| ❏ 60011 | Sugar Free | 1982 | $10 |

ROWLES, JIMMY, AND GEORGE MRAZ
PROGRESSIVE
| ❏ PRO-7009 | Music's the Only Thing on My Mind | 1981 | $35 |

ROWLES, JIMMY
ANDEX
| ❏ A-3007 [M] | Weather in a Jazz Vane | 1958 | $50 |
| ❏ AS-3007 [S] | Weather in a Jazz Vane | 1958 | $40 |

CAPITOL
| ❏ T1831 [M] | Kinda Groovy! | 1963 | $150 |
| ❏ ST1831 [S] | Kinda Groovy! | 1963 | $85 |

CHOICE
| ❏ CRS1014 | Grandpaws | 1976 | $50 |
| ❏ CRS1023 | Paws That Refresh | 1979 | $35 |

COLUMBIA
| ❏ FC37639 | Jimmy Rowles Plays Duke Ellington and Billy Strayhorn | 1981 | $35 |
| ❏ JC34873 | Peacocks | 1979 | $35 |

CONTEMPORARY
| ❏ C-14032 | I'm Glad There Is You | 1988 | $30 |
| ❏ C-14016 | Jimmy Rowles/Red Mitchell Trio | 1986 | $30 |

HALCYON
| ❏ HAL110 | Special Magic | 197? | $25 |

INTERLUDE
| ❏ MO-515 [M] | Upper Classmen | 1959 | $75 |
| ❏ ST-1015 [S] | Upper Classmen | 1959 | $40 |

JAZZZ
| ❏ 103 | Jazz Is a Fleeting Moment | 1976 | $75 |

LIBERTY
| ❏ LRP-3003 [M] | Rare -- But Well Done | 1955 | $175 |

SIGNATURE
| ❏ SM-6011 [M] | Fiorello Uptown, Mary Sunshine Downtown | 1960 | $120 |
| ❏ SS-6011 [S] | Fiorello Uptown, Mary Sunshine Downtown | 1960 | $175 |

STASH
| ❏ ST-227 | Peacocks | 198? | $25 |

TAMPA
| ❏ TP-8 [M] | Let's Get Acquainted with Jazz… For People Who Hate Jazz | 1957 | $300 |

— Colored vinyl

| ❏ TP-8 [M] | Let's Get Acquainted with Jazz… For People Who Hate Jazz | 1958 | $300 |
| ❏ TPS-8 [S] | Let's Get Acquainted with Jazz… For People Who Hate Jazz | 1958 | $175 |

XANADU
| ❏ 157 | Make Such Beautiful Music Together | 1980 | $35 |

ROWLES, JOHN
KAPP
| ❏ KS-3637 | Cheryl Moana Marie | 1971 | $18 |
| ❏ KS-3597 | Exciting | 1969 | $18 |

Number	Title	Yr	NM

MCA
| ❑ 549 | John Rowles | 197? | $12 |

ROWLES, STACY AND JIMMY
CONCORD JAZZ
| ❑ CJ-249 | Tell It Like It Is | 1984 | $25 |

ROXETTE
CAPITOL
| ❑ MLP-15018 [EP] | Heartland | 1984 | $40 |
EMI
| ❑ E1-91098 | Look Sharp! | 1989 | $18 |

ROXY MUSIC
Also see BRYAN FERRY.
ATCO
| ❑ SD 36-106 [B] | Country Life | 1975 | $30 |
— Original cover shows two semi-naked women on a grassy background
| ❑ SD 36-106A | Country Life | 1975 | $12 |
— Revised cover deletes women, leaves only the grassy background
| ❑ SD 32-102 | Flesh + Blood | 1980 | $12 |
| ❑ SD 36-134 | For Your Pleasure | 1975 | $15 |
— Reissue of Warner Bros. BS 2696; originals have yellow labels
❑ SD 38-103	Greatest Hits	1977	$12
❑ SD 38-114	Manifesto	1979	$12
❑ SD 38-114 [PD]	Manifesto	1979	$30
— Picture disc
| ❑ SD 36-127 | Siren | 1975 | $12 |
— Originals have yellow labels
| ❑ SD7045 | Stranded | 1974 | $15 |
| ❑ 90122 | The Atlantic Years (1973-80) | 1983 | $12 |

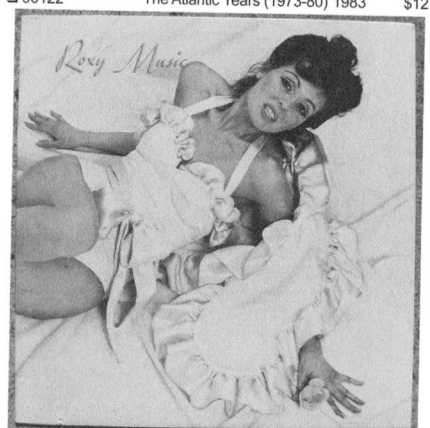

| ❑ SD 36-133 [B] | The First Roxy Music Album | 1975 | $15 |
— Reissue of Reprise MS 2114; originals have yellow labels
| ❑ SD 36-139 | Viva! Roxy Music (Live) | 1976 | $12 |
— Originals have yellow labels
REPRISE
| ❑ MS2114 [B] | Roxy Music | 1972 | $35 |
| ❑ 25857 | Street Life: 20 Greatest Hits | 1989 | $18 |
— By "Bryan Ferry & Roxy Music"
WARNER BROS.
❑ 23686	Avalon	1982	$12
❑ BS2696	For Your Pleasure	1973	$30
❑ 23808 [EP]	Musique -- The High Road	1983	$10

ROY, BOBBIE
CAPITOL
| ❑ ST-11086 | I'm Your Woman | 1972 | $15 |

ROY, WILLIAM
AUDIOPHILE
| ❑ AP-213 | When I Sing Alone | 1986 | $25 |

ROY C
MERCURY
❑ SRM-1-1192	More	1978	$18
❑ SRM-1-1056	Nice	1976	$18
❑ SRM-1-678 [B]	Sex and Soul	1974	$25

ROYAL, BILLY JOE
ATLANTIC AMERICA
❑ 90508	Looking Ahead	1986	$12
❑ 91064	Tell It Like It Is	1989	$12
❑ 90658	The Royal Treatment	1987	$12
COLUMBIA
❑ CL2781 [M]	Billy Joe Royal	1967	$30
❑ CS9581 [S]	Billy Joe Royal	1967	$30
❑ CS9974	Cherry Hill Park	1969	$30
❑ CL2403 [M]	Down in the Boondocks	1965	$25
❑ CS9203 [S]	Down in the Boondocks	1965	$30

Number	Title	Yr	NM

KAT FAMILY
| ❑ JW37342 | Billy Joe Royal | 1982 | $12 |
MERCURY
| ❑ SRM-1-3837 | Billy Joe Royal | 1980 | $12 |

ROYAL, ERNIE
URANIA
| ❑ UJLP-1203 [M] | Accent on Trumpet | 1955 | $175 |

ROYAL, MARSHALL
CONCORD JAZZ
| ❑ CJ-88 | First Chair | 1979 | $25 |
| ❑ CJ-125 | Royal Blue | 1980 | $25 |
EVEREST
| ❑ LPBR-5087 [M] | Gordon Jenkins Presents Marshall Royal | 1960 | $30 |
| ❑ SDBR-1087 [S] | Gordon Jenkins Presents Marshall Royal | 1960 | $30 |

ROYAL GUARDSMEN, THE
HOLIDAY
| ❑ HDY1913 | Merry Snoopy's Christmas | 1980 | $12 |
— Reissue of Laurie 2042
LAURIE
| ❑ LLP2042 [M] | Snoopy and His Friends | 1967 | $50 |
— With "Merry Snoopy's Christmas" poster still attached to back cover
| ❑ LLP2042 [M] | Snoopy and His Friends | 1967 | $40 |
— With "Merry Snoopy's Christmas" poster missing
| ❑ SLP2042 [S] | Snoopy and His Friends | 1967 | $30 |
— With "Merry Snoopy's Christmas" poster still attached to back cover
| ❑ SLP2042 [S] | Snoopy and His Friends | 1967 | $25 |
— With "Merry Snoopy's Christmas" poster missing
❑ SLP-2046	Snoopy for President	1968	$30
❑ LLP-2038 [M]	Snoopy vs. the Red Baron	1967	$40
❑ SLP-2038 [S]	Snoopy vs. the Red Baron	1967	$30
❑ LLP-2039 [M]	The Return of the Red Baron	1967	$50
❑ SLP-2039 [S]	The Return of the Red Baron	1967	$30

ROYAL OPERA HOUSE ORCHESTRA (ALEXANDER GIBSON, CONDUCTOR)
RCA VICTOR RED SEAL
| ❑ LSC-2449 [S] | Gounod: Ballet Music of Faust; Bizet: Carmen | 1960 | $1000 |
— Original with "shaded dog" label
| ❑ LSC-2449 [S] | Gounod: Ballet Music of Faust; Bizet: Carmen | 199? | $30 |
— Classic Records reissue

ROYAL OPERA HOUSE ORCHESTRA (ANATOLE FISTOULARI, CONDUCTOR)
RCA VICTOR RED SEAL
| ❑ LSC-2285 [S] | Walton: Facade Suite | 1959 | $250 |
— Original with "shaded dog" label
| ❑ LSC-2285 [S] | Walton: Facade Suite | 199? | $30 |
— Classic Records reissue

ROYAL OPERA HOUSE ORCHESTRA (ERNEST ANSERMET, CONDUCTOR)
RCA VICTOR RED SEAL
| ❑ LDS-6065 [S] | The Royal Ballet Gala Performances | 195? | $1200 |
— Original with "shaded dog" labels
| ❑ LDS-6065 [S] | The Royal Ballet Gala Performances | 199? | $40 |
— Classic Records reissue at 33 1/3 rpm
| ❑ LDS-6065 [S] | The Royal Ballet Gala Performances | 199? | $120 |
— Classic Records reissue at 45 rpm

ROYAL OPERA HOUSE ORCHESTRA (HUGO RIGNOLD, CONDUCTOR)
RCA VICTOR RED SEAL
| ❑ LSC-2135 [S] | Prokofiev: Cinderella | 1958 | $0 |
— No mention of Classic Records on cover; unknown
| ❑ LSC-2135 [S] | Prokofiev: Cinderella | 199? | $30 |
— Classic Records issue; this album is not known to have been issued in stereo before this.
| ❑ LSC-2450 [S] | Schumann: Carnaval; Meyerbeer: Les Patineurs | 1960 | $75 |
— Original with "shaded dog" label
| ❑ LSC-2450 [S] | Schumann: Carnaval; Meyerbeer: Les Patineurs | 199? | $30 |
— Classic Records reissue

ROYAL OPERA HOUSE ORCHESTRA (JEAN MOREL, CONDUCTOR)
RCA VICTOR RED SEAL
| ❑ LSC-6094 [S] | Albeniz: Iberia (Complete); Ravel: Rapsodie Espagnole | 196? | $400 |
— Original with "shaded dog" labels

Number	Title	Yr	NM

| ❑ LSC-6094 [S] | Albeniz: Iberia (Complete); Ravel: Rapsodie Espagnole | 199? | $40 |
— Classic Records reissue
| ❑ LSC-2327 [S] | Bizet: L'Arlesienne Suites | 1960 | $180 |
— Original with "shaded dog" label
| ❑ LSC-2327 [S] | Bizet: L'Arlesienne Suites | 199? | $30 |
— Classic Records reissue

ROYAL OPERA HOUSE ORCHESTRA (SIR GEORGE SOLTI, CONDUCTOR)
RCA VICTOR RED SEAL
| ❑ LSC-2313 [S] | Venice | 1959 | $150 |
— Original with "shaded dog" label
| ❑ LSC-2313 [S] | Venice | 199? | $30 |
— Classic Records reissue

ROYAL PHILHARMONIC ORCHESTRA, THE
RCA VICTOR CLUB RECORD
| ❑ CM-305 [M] | Joyful and Triumphant | 1963 | $15 |
— For the Reader's Digest Music Guide
| ❑ CSC-305 [S] | Joyful and Triumphant | 1963 | $18 |
— For the Reader's Digest Music Guide

ROYAL PHILHARMONIC ORCHESTRA (RENE LEIBOWITZ, CONDUCTOR)
RCA VICTOR RED SEAL
| ❑ VCS-2659 [S] | The Power of the Orchestra | 1962 | $300 |
— Original with "shaded dog" label

ROYAL PLAYBOYS, THE
WALDORF
| ❑ 33-136 [10] | Rock and Roll/New Orleans Blues | 195? | $500 |

ROYAL TEENS, THE
COLLECTABLES
| ❑ COL-5094 | Short Shorts: Golden Classics | 198? | $12 |
MUSICOR
| ❑ MS-3186 | Newies But Oldies | 1970 | $25 |
TRU-GEMS
| ❑ 1001 | Short Shorts & Others | 1975 | $25 |

ROYALETTES, THE
MGM
❑ E-4332 [M]	It's Gonna Take a Miracle	1965	$25
❑ SE-4332 [S]	It's Gonna Take a Miracle	1965	$30
❑ E-4366 [M]	The Elegant Sound of the Royalettes	1966	$25
❑ SE-4366 [S]	The Elegant Sound of the Royalettes	1966	$30

ROYALS, THE (1)
FEDERAL
| ❑ 567 | The Best of the Royals | 197? | $18 |
— This is a bootleg album

RUBBER BAND, THE (2)
GRT
❑ 10015	Beatles Songbook	1969	$30
❑ 10000	Cream Songbook	1969	$30
❑ 10007	Hendrix Songbook	1969	$30

RUBBER CITY REBELS
CAPITOL
| ❑ ST-12100 [B] | Rubber City Rebels | 1980 | $50 |

RUBBER MEMORY
R.P.C.
| ❑ 69401 | Welcome | 196? | $1000 |

RUBEN AND THE JETS
MERCURY
| ❑ SRM-1-694 [B] | Con Safos | 1974 | $30 |
| ❑ SRM-1-659 [B] | For Real | 1973 | $35 |

RUBENSTEIN, ARTUR
RCA VICTOR RED SEAL
| ❑ LSC-2120 [S] | Beethoven: Piano Concerto No. 1 | 1959 | $30 |
— With Josef Krips/NBC "Symphony of the Air" Orchestra; original with "shaded dog" label
| ❑ LSC-2121 [S] | Beethoven: Piano Concerto No. 2 | 1959 | $25 |
— With Josef Krips/NBC "Symphony of the Air" Orchestra; original with "shaded dog" label
| ❑ LSC-2122 [S] | Beethoven: Piano Concerto No. 3 | 1959 | $25 |
— With Josef Krips/NBC "Symphony of the Air" Orchestra; original with "shaded dog" label
| ❑ LSC-2123 [S] | Beethoven: Piano Concerto No. 4 | 1959 | $25 |
— With Josef Krips/NBC "Symphony of the Air" Orchestra; original with "shaded dog" label

Number	Title	Yr	NM
❏ LSC-2124 [S]	Beethoven: Piano Concerto No. 5	1959	$25

— With Josef Krips/NBC "Symphony of the Air" Orchestra; original with "shaded dog" label

❏ LSC-1831 [S]	Brahms: Piano Concerto No. 1	1958	$0

— With the Chicago Symphony (Fritz Reiner cond.); no mention of Classic Records on cover; unknown

❏ LSC-1831 [S]	Brahms: Piano Concerto No. 1	199?	$30

— With the Chicago Symphony (Fritz Reiner cond.); Classic Records issue; this album is not known to have been issued in stereo before this

❏ LSC-2296 [S]	Brahms: Piano Concerto No. 2	1959	$25

— With Josef Krips/RCA Victor Symphony Orchestra; original with "shaded dog" label

❏ LSC-2459 [S]	Brahms: Piano Sonata in F; Intermezzo; Romance	1961	$40

— Original with "shaded dog" label

❏ LSC-2370 [S]	Chopin: Ballades 1-4	1960	$25

— Original with "shaded dog" label

❏ LDS-2554 [S]	Chopin: Piano Sonatas No. 2 and 3	1961	$30

— Original with "shaded dog" label

❏ LSC-2368 [S]	Chopin: Scherzos 1-4	1960	$25

— Original with "shaded dog" label

❏ LSC-2566 [S]	Grieg: Piano Concerto	1962	$25

— Original with "shaded dog" label

❏ LSC-2429 [S]	Grieg: Piano Concerto in A; Lizst: Piano Concerto No. 1	1960	$30

— Original with "shaded dog" label

❏ LSC-2636 [S]	Mozart: Piano Concerto No. 17; Schubert: Impromptus	1962	$40

— Original with "shaded dog" label

❏ LSC-2068 [S]	Rachmaninoff: Piano Concerto No. 2; Lizst: Piano Conceto No. 1	1958	$30

— Original with "shaded dog" label

❏ LSC-2430 [S]	Rachmaninoff: Rhapsody on a Theme of Paganini	1960	$25

— With Fritz Reiner/Chicago Symphony Orchestra; original with "shaded dog" label

❏ LSC-2430 [S]	Rachmaninoff: Rhapsody on a Theme of Paganini	199?	$30

— With Fritz Reiner/Chicago Symphony Orchestra; Classic Records reissue

❏ LSC-2605 [S]	Rubenstein at Carnegie Hall	1962	$25

— Original with "shaded dog" label

❏ LSC-2234 [S]	Saint-Saens: Piano Concerto No. 2	1959	$25

— With the Symphony of the Air Orchestra (Alfred Wallenstein, conductor); original with "shaded dog" label

❏ LSC-2234 [S]	Saint-Saens: Piano Concerto No. 2	199?	$30

— With the Symphony of the Air Orchestra (Alfred Wallenstein, conductor); Classic Records reissue

❏ LSC-2256 [S]	Schubert: Piano Concerto in A	1959	$25

— With Josef Krips/RCA Victor Symphony Orchestra; original with "shaded dog" label

❏ LSC-2265 [S]	The Rubenstein Story	1959	$30

— With Alfred Wallerstein/NBC Symphony Orchestra; original with "shaded dog" label and gatefold cover

RUBETTES
STATE

Number	Title	Yr	NM
❏ MCA-2193 [B]	Rubettes	1976	$18

RUBIN, STAN
CORAL

❏ CRL57185 [M]	Dixieland Goes Broadway	1959	$30
❏ CRL757185 [S]	Dixieland Goes Broadway	1959	$30

JUBLIEE

❏ JLP-1003 [M]	College Jazz Comes to Carnegie Hall	1955	$50
❏ JLP-1024 [M]	Stan Rubin in Morocco	1956	$40
❏ JLP-1001 [M]	The College All Stars at Carnegie Hall	1955	$50
❏ JLP-4 [10]	The Tigertown Five, Vol. 1	1954	$50
❏ JLP-5 [10]	The Tigertown Five, Vol. 2	1954	$50
❏ JLP-6 [10]	The Tigertown Five, Vol. 3	1954	$50
❏ JLP-1016 [M]	Tigertown Five	1956	$40

PRINCETON

❏ LP-102 [10]	The Stan Rubin Tigertown Five	1954	$75

RCA VICTOR

❏ LPM-1200 [M]	Dixieland Bash	1956	$40
❏ LPM-3277 [10]	Stan Rubin's Dixieland Comes to Carnegie Hall	1955	$75

RUBY AND THE ROMANTICS
ABC

❏ S-638	More Than Yesterday	1968	$25

KAPP

❏ KL-1323 [M]	Our Day Will Come	1963	$30
❏ KS-3323 [S]	Our Day Will Come	1963	$40
❏ KL-1526 [M]	Ruby and the Romantics	1967	$30
❏ KS-3526 [S]	Ruby and the Romantics	1967	$30

Number	Title	Yr	NM
❏ KL-1458 [M]	The Greatest Hits Album	1966	$25
❏ KS-3458 [S]	The Greatest Hits Album	1966	$30
❏ KL-1341 [M]	Till Then	1963	$30
❏ KS-3341 [S]	Till Then	1963	$30

MCA

❏ 541	The Greatest Hits Album	197?	$12

PICKWICK

❏ SPC-3519	Makin' Out	197?	$12

RUCKER, ELLYN
CAPRI

❏ 10187	Ellyn	1987	$30

RUDD, ROSWELL, AND STEVE LACY
SOUL NOTE

❏ SN-1054	Regeneration	1982	$30

RUDD, ROSWELL
ABC IMPULSE!

❏ AS-9126 [S]	Everywhere	1968	$35

ARISTA/FREEDOM

❏ AF1006	Flexible Flyer	1975	$30
❏ AF1029	Inside Job	1976	$30

IMPULSE!

❏ A-9126 [M]	Everywhere	1967	$80
❏ AS-9126 [S]	Everywhere	1967	$120

JCOA

❏ 1007	The Numatik String Band	197?	$35

RUEDEBUSCH, DICK
ASCOT

❏ AM-13017 [M]	Dick Ruedebusch	1964	$30
❏ AS-16017 [S]	Dick Ruedebusch	1964	$35

JUBILEE

❏ JGS-5015 [S]	Dick Ruedebusch Remembers the Greats	1962	$25
❏ JGM-5015 [M]	Dick Ruedebusch Remembers the Greats	1962	$35
❏ JGS-5008 [S]	Meet Mr. Trumpet	1962	$25
❏ JGM-5008 [M]	Meet Mr. Trumpet	1962	$35
❏ JGS-5021 [S]	Mr. Trumpet, Volume 2	1963	$25
❏ JGM-5021 [M]	Mr. Trumpet, Volume 2	1963	$35

RUFF, WILLIE
COLUMBIA

❏ CS9603	The Smooth Side of Willie Ruff	1968	$25

— Red "360 Sound" label

RUFFIN, DAVID
Also see DARYL HALL AND JOHN OATES; JIMMY AND DAVID RUFFIN; THE TEMPTATIONS; THE VOICE MASTERS.

MOTOWN

❏ M7-895	At His Best	1978	$15
❏ M5-211V1	At His Best	1981	$10

— Reissue

❏ M733	David Ruffin	1971	$0

— Canceled

❏ M-762	David Ruffin	1973	$15
❏ M6-866	Everything's Coming Up Love	1976	$15
❏ MS-696	Feelin' Good	1969	$18
❏ M6-885	In My Stride	1977	$15
❏ M6-818	Me 'N' Rock 'N' Roll Are Here to Stay	1974	$15
❏ MS-685	My Whole World Ended	1969	$25
❏ M5-146V1	My Whole World Ended	1981	$10

— Reissue

❏ M6-849	Who I Am	1975	$15

WARNER BROS.

❏ BSK3416	Gentleman Ruffin	1980	$12
❏ BSK3306	So Soon We Change	1979	$12

RUFFIN, JIMMY
RSO

❏ RS-1-3078	Sunrise	1980	$12

SOUL

❏ S-708	Ruff'n Ready	1969	$30
❏ SS-727	The Groove Governor	1970	$25
❏ 704 [M]	Top Ten	1967	$50

— One-color cover

❏ 704 [M]	Top Ten	1967	$30

— Full-color cover

❏ S-704 [S]	Top Ten	1967	$30

RUFFIN, JIMMY AND DAVID
MOTOWN

❏ M5-108V1	Motown Superstar Series, Vol. 8	1981	$12

SOUL

❏ SS-728	I Am My Brother's Keeper	1970	$25

RUFUS
ABC

Number	Title	Yr	NM
❏ D-975	Ask Rufus	1977	$12
❏ AA-1098	Numbers	1979	$12
❏ AA-1098 [PD]	Numbers	1979	$25

— Promo-only picture disc

❏ X-809	Rags to Rufus	1974	$12
❏ X-783	Rufus	1973	$12
❏ D-909	Rufus Featuring Chaka Khan	1975	$12
❏ D-837	Rufusized	1974	$12
❏ AA-1049	Street Player	1978	$12
❏ AA-1049 [PD]	Street Player	1978	$30

— Promo-only picture disc

COMMAND

❏ CQD-40024 [Q]	Rags to Rufus	1974	$30
❏ CQD-40023 [Q]	Rufusized	1974	$30

MCA

❏ 37037	Ask Rufus	1980	$10

— Reissue of ABC 975

❏ 5270	Camouflage	1982	$12
❏ 5103	Masterjam	1979	$12
❏ 37157	Masterjam	198?	$10

— Reissue of 5103

❏ 37039	Numbers	1980	$10

— Reissue of ABC 1098

❏ 5159	Party 'Til You're Broke	1981	$12
❏ 37034	Rags to Rufus	1980	$10

— Reissue of ABC 809

❏ 642	Rufus	1980	$10

— Reissue of ABC 783

❏ 37036	Rufus Featuring Chaka Khan	1980	$10

— Reissue of ABC 909

❏ 37035	Rufusized	1980	$10

— Reissue of ABC 837

❏ 37038	Street Player	1980	$10

— Reissue of ABC 1049

❏ 5339	The Very Best of Rufus	1983	$12

WARNER BROS.

❏ 23679	Live: Stompin' at the Savoy	1983	$15
❏ 23753	Seal in Red	1984	$12

RUFUS AND CARLA
STAX

❏ STX-4124	Chronicle	1979	$18

RUGBYS, THE
AMAZON

❏ 1000	Hot Cargo	1970	$25

RUGOLO, PETE
COLUMBIA

❏ CL604 [M]	Adventures in Rhythm	1955	$75

— Maroon label, gold print

❏ CL604 [M]	Adventures in Rhythm	1956	$40

— Red and black label with six "eye" logos

❏ CL6289 [10]	Introducing Pete Rugolo	1954	$75
❏ CL635 [M]	Introducing Pete Rugolo	1955	$75

— Maroon label, gold print

❏ CL635 [M]	Introducing Pete Rugolo	1956	$40

— Red and black label with six "eye" logos

❏ CL689 [M]	Rugolomania	1956	$40

— Red and black label with six "eye" logos

EMARCY

❏ MG-36082 [M]	Music for Hi-Fi Bugs	1956	$250
❏ MG-36115 [M]	Out on a Limb	1957	$250
❏ MG-36122 [M]	Percussion at Work	1958	$250
❏ MG-36143 [M]	Rugolo Plays Kenton	1958	$250

HARMONY

❏ HL7003 [M]	New Sounds	195?	$35

MERCURY

❏ PPS-2023 [M]	10 Saxophones and 2 Basses	196?	$150
❏ PPS-6023 [S]	10 Saxophones and 2 Basses	196?	$150
❏ PPS-6016 [S]	10 Trombones and 2 Guitars	196?	$150
❏ PPS-2016 [S]	10 Trombones and 2 Guitars	196?	$150
❏ PPS-6001 [S]	10 Trombones Like 2 Pianos	196?	$150
❏ PPS-2001 [S]	10 Trombones Like 2 Pianos	196?	$150
❏ MG-0(# unknown) [M]	An Adventure in Sound: Reeds	1958	$175
❏ SR-60039 [S]	An Adventure in Sound: Reeds	1959	$175
❏ MG-20261 [M]	Brass in Hi-Fi	1958	$175
❏ SR-60044 [S]	Brass in Hi-Fi	1959	$150
❏ MG-20118 [M]	Music from Outer Space	1957	$150
❏ MG-20260 [M]	Reeds in Hi-Fi	1958	$175
❏ SR-60043 [S]	Reeds in Hi-Fi	1959	$150

RUIZ, HILTON
INNER CITY

❏ IC-2036	Piano Man	197?	$35

NOVUS

❏ 3024-1-N	El Camino (The Road)	1988	$25
❏ 3011-1-N	Something Grand	1987	$25
❏ 3053-1-N	Strut	1989	$30

Number	Title	Yr	NM

STASH
| ❏ ST-248 | Cross Currents | 1985 | $25 |

STEEPLECHASE
❏ SCS-1078	Excitation	198?	$30
❏ SCS-1094	New York Hilton	198?	$30
❏ SCS-1036	Piano Man	198?	$30
❏ SCS-1158	Steppin' Into Beauty	198?	$30

RUIZ, JORGE LOPEZ
CATALYST
| ❏ 7908 | Amor Buenos Aires | 197? | $30 |

RUMBLERS, THE
DOT
| ❏ DLP-3509 [M] | Boss! | 1963 | $50 |
| ❏ DLP-25509 [S] | Boss! | 1963 | $75 |

DOWNEY
| ❏ DLP-1001 [M] | Boss! | 1963 | $180 |

| ❏ DLPS-1001 [S] | Boss! | 1963 | $300 |

RUMMEL, JACK
STOMP OFF
| ❏ SOS-1118 | Back to Ragtime | 1986 | $25 |

RUMOUR, THE
GRAHAM PARKER's band.
ARISTA
| ❏ AL4235 | Frogs, Sprouts, Clogs & Krauts | 1979 | $15 |

HANNIBAL
| ❏ 1305 | Purity of Essence | 1981 | $18 |

MERCURY
| ❏ SRM-1-1174 | Max | 1977 | $18 |

RUMPLESTILTSKIN
BELL
| ❏ 6047 | Rumpelstiltskin | 1970 | $30 |

RUMSEY, HOWARD
CONTEMPORARY
❏ C-2506 [10]	Howard Rumsey's Lighthouse All-Stars	1953	$300
❏ C-3508 [M]	Howard Rumsey's Lighthouse All-Stars, Vol. 3	1955	$250
❏ C-3520 [M]	Howard Rumsey's Lighthouse All-Stars, Vol. 4: Oboe/Flute	1956	$250
❏ C-3504 [M]	Howard Rumsey's Lighthouse All-Stars, Vol. 6	1955	$250
❏ C-2513 [10]	Howard Rumsey's Lighthouse All-Stars, Volume 1: The Quintet	1954	$300
❏ C-2515 [10]	Howard Rumsey's Lighthouse All-Stars, Volume 2: The Octet	1954	$300
❏ C-2510 [10]	Howard Rumsey's Lighthouse All-Stars, Volume 4	1954	$300
❏ C-3517 [M]	In the Solo Spotlight	1956	$250
❏ C-14051	Jazz Invention	1989	$30
❏ C-3509 [M]	Lighthouse at Laguna	1955	$250
❏ C-3528 [M]	Music for Lighthousekeeping	1957	$300
❏ S-7008 [S]	Music for Lighthousekeeping	1959	$300
❏ C-2501 [10]	Sunday Jazz a la Lighthouse	1953	$300
❏ C-3501 [M]	Sunday Jazz a la Lighthouse	1955	$250

FANTASY
❏ OJC-266	Howard Rumsey's Lighthouse All-Stars, Vol. 3	198?	$25
❏ OJC-154	Howard Rumsey's Lighthouse All-Stars, Vol. 4: Oboe/Flute	198?	$25
❏ OJC-386	Howard Rumsey's Lighthouse All-Stars, Vol. 6	1989	$25
❏ OJC-451	In the Solo Spotlight	1990	$30
❏ OJC-406	Lighthouse at Laguna	1989	$25
❏ OJC-151	Sunday Jazz a la Lighthouse	198?	$25

Number	Title	Yr	NM

LIBERTY
| ❏ LRP-3045 [M] | Double or Nothin' | 1957 | $50 |
| ❏ LST-7014 [S] | Double or Nothin' | 1959 | $40 |

LIGHTHOUSE
| ❏ LP-300 [M] | Jazz Rolls-Royce | 1958 | $40 |
| ❏ LP-301 [M] | Sunday Jazz a la Lighthouse | 1958 | $40 |
—*Red vinyl*

OMEGA
| ❏ OML-5 [M] | Jazz Rolls-Royce | 1960 | $30 |
| ❏ OSL-5 [S] | Jazz Rolls-Royce | 1960 | $30 |

PHILIPS
| ❏ PHM200012 [M] | Jazz Structures | 1961 | $25 |
| ❏ PHS600012 [S] | Jazz Structures | 1961 | $30 |

STEREO RECORDS
| ❏ S-7008 [S] | Music for Lighthousekeeping | 1958 | $150 |

RUN-D.M.C.
ARISTA
| ❏ 16400 | Crown Royal | 2001 | $18 |

PROFILE
❏ PRO-1401 [B]	Back from Hell	1990	$18
❏ PRO-1205	King of Rock	1985	$15
❏ PRO-1217	Raising Hell	1986	$15
❏ PRO-1202	Run-D.M.C.	1984	$15
❏ PRO-1419	Together Forever: Greatest Hits 1983-1991	1991	$18
❏ PRO-1265	Tougher Than Leather	1988	$15

RUNAWAYS, THE
Also see LITA FORD; JOAN JETT AND THE BLACKHEARTS.

MARILYN
| ❏ USM1004 [B] | Born to Be Bad | 1991 | $30 |

MERCURY
❏ SRM-1-3740 [B]	Live in Japan	1978	$75
❏ SRM-1-1126	Queens of Noise	1977	$30
❏ SRM-1-1090	The Runaways	1976	$30
❏ SRM-1-3705	Waiting for the Night	1977	$30

RHINO
| ❏ RNDF-250 [PD] | Little Lost Girls | 1982 | $30 |
| ❏ RNLP-70861 | Little Lost Girls | 1987 | $15 |
—*Reissue of Rhino 250 on regular vinyl*
| ❏ RNEP-602 [EP] | Mama Weer All Crazee Now | 1983 | $18 |

RUNDGREN, TODD
Also see NAZZ (1); UTOPIA.

AMPEX
| ❏ A-10105 | Runt | 1970 | $175 |
—*LP jacket and label list 10 tracks, but the album has 12*
| ❏ A-10105 [B] | Runt | 1970 | $120 |
—*LP jacket and label list 10 tracks, but the album has 11*

| ❏ A-10105 [B] | Runt | 1970 | $75 |
—*LP jacket and label list 10 tracks and album actually has 10*

BEARSVILLE
❏ BR2133	A Wizard/A True Star	1973	$15
❏ 2BRX6986	Back to the Bars	1978	$15
❏ BR6963	Faithful	1976	$12
❏ BHS3522	Healing	1981	$12
—*Add $5 if bonus 7-inch 33 1/3 single (Time Heals/Tiny Demons) is included*
❏ BRK6981	Hermit of Mink Hollow	1978	$12
❏ PRO597 [DJ]	Ikon/Todd Rundgren Interview	1974	$150
❏ BR6957	Initiation	1975	$12
❏ A-10105	Runt	1971	$30
—*Reissue with new label*
| ❏ BR2046 | Runt | 1972 | $18 |
—*Another reissue, after switch from Ampex to Warner Bros. distribution*
| ❏ 2BX2066 | Something/Anything? | 1972 | $30 |
—*Regular copy with black vinyl*

Number	Title	Yr	NM

| ❏ 2BX2066 | Something/Anything? | 1972 | $250 |
—*White label with one record on red vinyl and the other on blue vinyl*
| ❏ A-10116 [B] | The Ballad of Todd Rundgren | 1971 | $150 |
| ❏ BR2047 | The Ballad of Todd Rundgren | 1972 | $18 |
—*Reissue of 10116*
❏ 23732	The Ever Popular Tortured Artist Effect	1983	$12
❏ PRO524 [DJ]	The Todd Rundgren Radio Show	1972	$175
❏ 2BR6952	Todd	1974	$18
❏ PRO-A-788 [DJ]	Todd Rundgren Radio Sampler	1978	$50
—*Highlights of "Back to the Bars" plus interview of Todd by Patti Smith*

MOBILE FIDELITY
| ❏ 2-225 | Something/Anything? | 1995 | $75 |
—*Audiophile vinyl*

RHINO
❏ R1-71491	Anthology (1968-1985)	1989	$25
❏ RNLP70864	A Wizard/A True Star	1987	$12
❏ RNDA71109	Back to the Bars	1987	$15
❏ RNLP70868	Faithful	1987	$12
❏ RNLP70874	Healing	1987	$12
❏ RNLP70871	Hermit of Mink Hollow	1988	$12
❏ RNLP70866	Initiation	1987	$12
❏ RNLP70862	Runt	1987	$12
❏ RNDA71107	Something/Anything?	1987	$15
❏ RNLP70863	The Ballad of Todd Rundgren	1987	$12
❏ RNLP70876	The Ever Popular Tortured Artist Effect	1988	$12
❏ RNDA71108	Todd	1987	$15

WARNER BROS.
| ❏ 25128 | A Cappella | 1985 | $12 |
| ❏ 25881 | Nearly Human | 1989 | $18 |

RUSH, MERRILEE
BELL
| ❏ 6020 [S] | Angel of the Morning | 1968 | $25 |
| ❏ 6020 [M] | Angel of the Morning | 1968 | $40 |
—*Mono is white label promo only with "Monaural" on label; sticker with "This is a monaural record for radio station play only" on cover*

LIBERTY
| ❏ LN-10166 | Merilee Rush | 1981 | $10 |
—*Budget-line reissue*

UNITED ARTISTS
| ❏ UA-LA735-G | Merilee Rush | 1977 | $12 |

RUSH, OTIS
BLUE HORIZON
| ❏ BH-4602 | Blues Masters, Volume 2 | 1968 | $30 |
| ❏ BH-4805 | Chicago Blues | 1970 | $30 |

COTILLION
| ❏ SD9006 | Mourning in the Morning | 1969 | $30 |

RUSH, TOM
COLUMBIA
❏ KC33054	Ladies Love Outlaws	1974	$15
❏ KC31306	Merrimack County	1972	$15
❏ PC33907	The Best of Tom Rush	1976	$15
❏ CS9972	Tom Rush	1970	$18
—*Red "360 Sound" label*
| ❏ CS9972 | Tom Rush | 1970 | $15 |
—*Orange label*
| ❏ C30402 | Wrong End of the Rainbow | 1970 | $15 |

ELEKTRA
❏ EKS-74062	Classic Rush	1971	$18
❏ EKL-308 [M]	Take a Little Walk with Me	1966	$18
❏ EKS-7308 [S]	Take a Little Walk with Me	1966	$18
❏ EKS-74018 [B]	The Circle Game	1968	$18
❏ EKL-288 [M]	Tom Rush	1965	$18
❏ EKS-7288 [S]	Tom Rush	1965	$18

FANTASY
| ❏ 24709 | Tom Rush | 1973 | $18 |
—*Reissue of Prestige/Folklore recordings*

FOLKLORE
| ❏ FRLP-14003 [M] | Got a Mind to Ramble | 1964 | $25 |
| ❏ FRST-14003 [S] | Got a Mind to Ramble | 1964 | $30 |

LY CORNU
| ❏ SA-70-2 | Tom Rush at the Unicorn | 1962 | $150 |

PRESTIGE
❏ PR-7374 [M]	Blues -- Songs -- Ballads	1965	$25
❏ PRST-7374 [S]	Blues -- Songs -- Ballads	1965	$30
❏ PRST-7536	Got a Mind to Ramble	1968	$18
—*Reissue of Folklore LP*

RUSH
ATLANTIC
❏ 83728	Feedback	2004	$16
❏ R183728 [B]	Feedback	2016	$20
❏ 82040	Presto	1989	$18

Number	Title	Yr	NM
❏ 83531	Vapor Trails	2002	$30
MERCURY			
❏ SRM-1-1079	2112	1976	$12
— Chicago skyline" label			
❏ 822545-1	2112	1985	$10
— Reissue with new number			
❏ SRM-1-1079	2112	1983	$10
— Black label			
❏ SRM-1-1184	A Farewell to Kings	1977	$12
— Chicago skyline" label			
❏ 822546-1	A Farewell to Kings	1985	$10
— Reissue with new number			
❏ SRM-1-1184	A Farewell to Kings	1983	$10
— Black label			
❏ SRM-2-7508	All the World's a Stage	1976	$15
— Chicago skyline" labels			
❏ 822552-1	All the World's a Stage	1985	$12
— Reissue with new number			
❏ SRM-2-7508	All the World's a Stage	1983	$12
— Black labels			
❏ SRM-3-9200	Archives	1978	$25
— Chicago skyline" labels			
❏ 822553-1	Archives	1985	$18
— Reissue with new number			
❏ SRM-3-9200	Archives	1983	$25
— Black labels			
❏ 836346-1	A Show of Hands	1988	$15
❏ SRM-1-1046	Caress of Steel	1975	$12
— Chicago skyline" label			
❏ 822543-1	Caress of Steel	1985	$10
— Reissue with new number			
❏ SRM-1-1046	Caress of Steel	1983	$10
— Black label			
❏ MK-32 [DJ]	Everything Your Listener Ever Wanted to Hear by Rush ... But You Were Afraid to Play	1977	$175
❏ SRM-2-7001	Exit... Stage Left	1981	$15
❏ 822551-1	Exit...Stage Left	1985	$12
— Reissue with new number			
❏ SRM-1-1023	Fly by Night	1975	$12
— Chicago skyline" label			
❏ 822542-1	Fly by Night	1985	$10
— Reissue with new number			
❏ SRM-1-1023	Fly by Night	1983	$10
— Black label			
❏ 818476-1	Grace Under Pressure	1984	$12
❏ SRM-1-3743	Hemispheres	1978	$12
— Chicago skyline" label; with poster			
❏ SRP-1-1300 [PD]	Hemispheres	1979	$40
❏ 822547-1	Hemispheres	1985	$10
— Reissue with new number			
❏ SRM-1-3743	Hemispheres	1983	$10
— Black label			
❏ 832464-1	Hold Your Fire	1987	$12
❏ SRM-1-4013	Moving Pictures	1981	$12
— Custom label			
❏ 822549-1	Moving Pictures	1985	$10
— Reissue with new number			
❏ SRM-1-4001	Permanent Waves	1980	$12
— Custom label			
❏ 822548-1	Permanent Waves	1985	$10
— Reissue with new number			
❏ 826098-1	Power Windows	1985	$12
❏ B002238501 [B]	Power Windows	2016	$25
❏ SRM-1-1011	Rush	1974	$12
— Based on the LP's release date, original copies theoretically have red labels, rather than the common "Chicago skyline" labels; those would be worth at least twice this price			
❏ 822541-1	Rush	1985	$10
— Reissue with new number			
❏ SRM-1-1011	Rush	1983	$10
— Black label			
❏ MK-185 [DJ]	Rush 'N' Roulette	1981	$120
— Promo-only six-track EP that has six grooves cut in it; the song it plays is based on where you place the stylus			
❏ SRM-1-4063	Signals	1982	$12
❏ 822550-1	Signals	1985	$10
— Reissue with new number			

RUSHEN, PATRICE

Number	Title	Yr	NM
ARISTA			
❏ AL-8401	Watch Out!	1987	$12
ELEKTRA			
❏ 60465	Anthology of Patrice Rushen	1986	$12
❏ 6E-160	Patrice	1978	$12
❏ 60360	Patrice Rushen Now	1984	$12
❏ 6E-243	Pizzazz	1979	$12
❏ 6E-302	Posh	1980	$12
❏ 60015	Straight from the Heart	1982	$12
PRESTIGE			
❏ 10098	Before the Dawn	1976	$25
❏ 10110	Let There Be Funk	1980	$20
❏ 10089	Prelusion	1974	$25
❏ 10101	Shout It Out	1977	$20

RUSHING, JIMMY; ADA MOORE; BUCK CLAYTON

Number	Title	Yr	NM
COLUMBIA			
❏ CL778 [M]	Cat Meets Chick	1956	$75

RUSHING, JIMMY

Also see CHAMPION JACK DUPREE AND JIMMY RUSHING.

Number	Title	Yr	NM
AUDIO LAB			
❏ AL-1512 [M]	Two Shades of Blue	1959	$120
BLUESWAY			
❏ BL-6005 [M]	Everyday I Have the Blues	1967	$25
❏ BLS-6005 [S]	Everyday I Have the Blues	1967	$25
❏ BLS-6017	Livin' the Blues	1968	$25
❏ BLS-6057	Sent for You Yesterday	1973	$20
COLPIX			
❏ CP-446 [M]	Five Feet of Soul	1963	$40
❏ SCP-446 [S]	Five Feet of Soul	1963	$75
— The existence of this record has been confirmed			
COLUMBIA			
❏ CL1605 [M]	Jimmy Rushing and the Smith Girls	1961	$30
❏ CS8405 [S]	Jimmy Rushing and the Smith Girls	1961	$40
❏ CL1152 [M]	Little Jimmy Rushing and the Big Brass	1958	$40
❏ CS8060 [S]	Little Jimmy Rushing and the Big Brass	1958	$50
❏ C236419	Mister Five by Five	1979	$15
❏ CL1401 [M]	Rushing Lullabies	1959	$40
❏ CS8196 [S]	Rushing Lullabies	1959	$50
❏ CL963 [M]	The Jazz Odyssey of James Rushing, Esq.	1957	$40
JAZZTONE			
❏ J-1244 [M]	Listen to the Blues	195?	$40
MASTER JAZZ			
❏ 8104	Gee, Baby	197?	$20
❏ 8120	Who Was It Sang That Song?	1971	$35
RCA VICTOR			
❏ LSP-4566	You and Me The Used to Be	1972	$35
VANGUARD			
❏ VRS-65/66	Essential Jimmy Rushing	197?	$20
❏ VRS-8518 [M]	Going to Chicago	1957	$100
❏ VRS-8513 [M]	If This Ain't the Blues	1957	$100
❏ VSD-2008 [S]	If This Ain't the Blues	1958	$150
❏ VRS-8011 [10]	Jimmy Rushing Sings the Blues	1955	$250
❏ VRS-8505 [M]	Listen to the Blues	1955	$150
❏ VSD-73007	Listen to the Blues	1967	$20

RUSKIN-SPEAR, ROGER

Number	Title	Yr	NM
UNITED ARTISTS			
❏ UA-LA097-F	Electric Shocks	1973	$30

RUSSELL, ANNA

Number	Title	Yr	NM
COLUMBIA MASTERWORKS			
❏ ML4928 [M]	Anna Russell's Guide to Concert Audiences	1955	$30
❏ ML4594 [M]	Anna Russell Sings?	1953	$30
❏ ML4733 [M]	Anna Russell Sings! Again?	1954	$30
❏ ML5295 [M]	A Practical Banana Promotion	1959	$50
❏ ML5036 [M]	A Square Talk on Popular Music	1956	$30
❏ ML5195 [M]	In Darkest Africa	1957	$30
❏ MG31199	The Anna Russell Album?	1972	$25

RUSSELL, BOBBY

Number	Title	Yr	NM
ELF			
❏ 9501	Unlimited	1970	$18
❏ 9500 [S]	Words, Music, Laughter & Tears	1969	$25
❏ 9500 [M]	Words, Music, Laughter & Tears	1969	$50
— Mono copies are white label promo only and say "Monaural" on the label			
UNITED ARTISTS			
❏ UAS-5548	Saturday Morning Confusion	1971	$15

RUSSELL, GENE

Number	Title	Yr	NM
BLACK JAZZ			
❏ 1	New Direction	1972	$30
❏ QD-10	Talk to My Lady	1973	$30
OVATION			
❏ OV-1803	Listen Here	197?	$30
SEA BREEZE			
❏ SB-3001	Autumn Leaves	198?	$25

RUSSELL, GEORGE

Number	Title	Yr	NM
BASF			
❏ 25125	Live at Beethoven Hall	1973	$35
BLUE NOTE			
❏ BT-85132	So What	1987	$35
❏ BT-85103	The African Game	198?	$30
CONCEPT			
❏ 02	Listen to the Silence	197?	$30

Number	Title	Yr	NM
DECCA			
❏ DL9220 [M]	George Russell at the Five Spot	1958	$120
❏ DL79220 [S]	George Russell at the Five Spot	1958	$120
❏ DL4183 [M]	George Russell in Kansas City	1961	$30
❏ DL74183 [S]	George Russell in Kansas City	1961	$40
❏ DL9219 [M]	Jazz in the Space Age	1958	$120
❏ DL79219 [S]	Jazz in the Space Age	1958	$120
❏ DL9216 [M]	New York, N.Y.	1958	$150
❏ DL79216 [S]	New York, N.Y.	1958	$150
FANTASY			
❏ OJC-070	Ezz-thetics	198?	$25
❏ OJC-232	Stratusphunk	198?	$25
❏ OJC-616	The Outer View	1991	$30
❏ OJC-365	The Stratus Seekers	198?	$25
FLYING DUTCHMAN			
❏ FD-10124	Electronic Sonata for Souls Loved by Nature	1971	$35
❏ FD-124	Electronic Sonata for Souls Loved by Nature	1970	$25
❏ FD-10122	Othello Ballet Suite/ Electronic Organ Sonata No. 1	1971	$35
❏ FD-122	Othello Ballet Suite/ Electronic Organ Sonata No. 1	1970	$25
MCA			
❏ 4017	New York, N.Y./Jazz in the Space Age	1974	$35
MGM			
❏ E-3321 [M]	George Russell Octets	1955	$100
MILESTONE			
❏ 47027	Outer Thoughts	197?	$35
PETE			
❏ 1107	Easy Listening	1969	$35
RCA VICTOR			
❏ LPM-1372 [M]	Jazz Workshop	1957	$100
❏ LPM-2534 [M]	Jazz Workshop	1962	$30
❏ LSP-2534 [R]	Jazz Workshop	1962	$35
RIVERSIDE			
❏ RLP-375 [M]	Ezz-thetics	1961	$250
❏ RS-9375 [S]	Ezz-thetics	1961	$250
❏ 6112	Ezz-thetics	197?	$30
❏ RS-3043	George Russell Sextet	1970	$150
❏ RLP-341 [M]	Stratusphunk	1960	$250
❏ RS-9341 [S]	Stratusphunk	1960	$250
❏ RLP-440 [M]	The Outer View	1963	$175
❏ RS-9440 [S]	The Outer View	1963	$175
❏ RS-3016	The Outer View	1968	$150
❏ RLP-412 [M]	The Stratus Seekers	1962	$175
❏ RS-9412 [S]	The Stratus Seekers	1962	$175
SOUL NOTE			
❏ SN-1034	Electronic Sonata for Souls Loved by Nature 1969	198?	$30
❏ SN-1009	Electronic Sonata for Souls Loved by Nature 1980	1980	$30
❏ SN-1024	Listen to the Silence (A Mass for Our Time)	198?	$30
❏ SN-1049	Live in an American Time Spiral	1983	$30
❏ SN-1039	New York Big Band	198?	$30
❏ SN-1014	Othello Ballet Suite	198?	$30
❏ SN-1044/5	The Essence of George Russell	198?	$35
❏ SN-1029	Trip to Pillar-Guri	198?	$30
❏ SN-1019	Vertical Form VI	198?	$30
STRATA-EAST			
❏ SES-19761	Electronic Sonata for Souls Loved by Nature	1976	$25

RUSSELL, HAL

Number	Title	Yr	NM
NESSA			
❏ N-25	Generation	1982	$50
❏ N-21	NRG Ensemble	1981	$50

RUSSELL, JANE

Number	Title	Yr	NM
MGM			
❏ E-3715 [M]	Jane Russell	1959	$50
❏ SE-3715 [S]	Jane Russell	1959	$150

RUSSELL, JIMMY

Number	Title	Yr	NM
CUCA			
❏ 4100 [M]	Jimmy Russell Trio	1965	$30
DORIAN			
❏ 1020	The Swingin'est	1968	$35

RUSSELL, JOHNNY

Number	Title	Yr	NM
MERCURY			
❏ SRM-1-5019	Perspectives	1979	$15
RCA VICTOR			
❏ LSP-4851	Catfish John/Chained	1973	$18
❏ APL-1211	Here Comes Johnny Russell	1975	$18
❏ LSP-4588	Mr. and Mrs. Untrue	1971	$18
❏ APL1-0345	Rednecks, White Socks and Blue Ribbon Beer	1973	$18
❏ ANL1-2165	Rednecks, White Socks and Blue Ribbon Beer	1977	$12

Number	Title	Yr	NM
—Reissue			
❏ APL1-0542	She's in Love with a Rodeo Man	1974	$18

RUSSELL, KURT
CAPITOL

Number	Title	Yr	NM
❏ SKAO-492	Kurt Russell	1970	$30

RUSSELL, LEON, AND MARC BENNO
See ASYLUM CHOIR.

RUSSELL, LEON
MCA

Number	Title	Yr	NM
❏ 37114	Best of Leon	1980	$10
— Reissue of Shelter 52004			
❏ 685	Carney	1979	$10
— Reissue of Shelter 52011			
❏ 682	Leon Russell	1979	$10
— Reissue of Shelter 52007			
❏ 683	Leon Russell and the Shelter People	1979	$10
— Reissue of Shelter 52008			
❏ 686	Will O' the Wisp	1979	$10
— Reissue of Shelter 52020			

PARADISE

Number	Title	Yr	NM
❏ BSK3172	Americana	1978	$15
❏ 0002	Hank Wilson Vol. II	1984	$15
❏ BSK3341	Life and Love	1979	$15
❏ BSK3066	Make Love to the Music	1977	$15
— As "Leon and Mary Russell"			
❏ BSK3532	The Live Album	1981	$12
❏ PR2943	Wedding Album	1976	$15
— As "Leon and Mary Russell"			

SHELTER

Number	Title	Yr	NM
❏ 52004	Best of Leon	1976	$12
❏ SW-8911	Carney	1972	$18
❏ SR2121	Carney	1974	$15
— Reissue of 8911			
❏ 52011	Carney	1977	$12
— Reissue of 2121			
❏ SW-8923	Hank Wilson's Back, Vol. 1	1973	$18
— As "Hank Wilson"			
❏ 52014	Hank Wilson's Back, Vol. 1	1977	$12
— Reissue of 8923			
❏ STCO-8917	Leon Live	1973	$25
❏ SHE-1001	Leon Russell	1968	$25
❏ SW-8901	Leon Russell	1970	$18
— Early reissue of 1001			
❏ SR2118	Leon Russell	1974	$15
— Reissue of 8901			
❏ 52007	Leon Russell	1977	$12
— Reissue of 2118			
❏ SW-8903	Leon Russell and the Shelter People	1971	$18
❏ SR2119	Leon Russell and the Shelter People	1974	$15
— Reissue of 8903			
❏ 52008	Leon Russell and the Shelter People	1977	$12
— Reissue of 2119			
❏ SR2108	Stop All That Jazz	1974	$18
❏ 52016	Stop All That Jazz	1977	$12
— Reissue of 2108			
❏ SR2138	Will O' the Wisp	1975	$18
❏ 52020	Will O' the Wisp	1977	$12
— Reissue of 2138			

RUSSELL, LINDA, AND COMPANIE
FLYING FISH

Number	Title	Yr	NM
❏ FF402	Sing We All Merrily (A Colonial Christmas)	1986	$12

RUSSELL, LUIS
COLUMBIA

Number	Title	Yr	NM
❏ CG32338	Luis Russell and the Louisiana Swing Orchestra	1973	$35
❏ PG32338	Luis Russell and the Louisiana Swing Orchestra	197?	$30
— Reissue with new prefix			

RUSSELL, PEE WEE, AND RUBY BRAFF
SAVOY

Number	Title	Yr	NM
❏ MG-12034 [M]	Jazz At Storyville, Volume 1	1955	$75
❏ MG-12041 [M]	Jazz at Storyville, Volume 2	1955	$75

RUSSELL, PEE WEE
ABC IMPULSE!

Number	Title	Yr	NM
❏ AS-96 [S]	Ask Me Now	1968	$35
❏ AS-9137 [S]	College Concert of Pee Wee Russell with Henry "Red" Allen	1968	$35
❏ IA-9359	Salute to Newport	1979	$35

ATLANTIC

Number	Title	Yr	NM
❏ ALS-126 [10]	Pee Wee Russell All Stars	1952	$350

BARNABY

Number	Title	Yr	NM
❏ BR-5018	Jazz Reunion	197?	$30

BELL

Number	Title	Yr	NM
❏ LP-42 [M]	Pee Wee Russell Plays Pee Wee	1961	$30
❏ LPS-42 [S]	Pee Wee Russell Plays Pee Wee	1961	$30

COLUMBIA

Number	Title	Yr	NM
❏ CL1985 [M]	New Groove	1963	$35
❏ CS8785 [S]	New Groove	1963	$25

COMMODORE

Number	Title	Yr	NM
❏ XFL-16440	Three Deuces and Hot Four: The Pied Piper of Jazz	198?	$25

COUNTERPOINT

Number	Title	Yr	NM
❏ 0(# unknown) [M]	Portrait of Pee Wee	1957	$75

DCC COMPACT CLASSICS

Number	Title	Yr	NM
❏ LPZ-2024	Portrait of Pee Wee	1996	$30
— Audiophile vinyl			

DISC

Number	Title	Yr	NM
❏ DLP-0(# unknown) [10]	Jazz Ensemble	195?	$120

DOT

Number	Title	Yr	NM
❏ DLP-3253 [M]	Pee Wee Russell Plays	1960	$85
❏ DLP-25253 [S]	Pee Wee Russell Plays	1960	$85

ESOTERIC

Number	Title	Yr	NM
❏ 565 [M]	Pee Wee Russell All Stars	1959	$40
❏ 5565 [S]	Pee Wee Russell All Stars	1959	$30

EVEREST ARCHIVE OF FOLK & JAZZ

Number	Title	Yr	NM
❏ 233 [R]	Pee Wee Russell	1969	$25

FANTASY

Number	Title	Yr	NM
❏ OJC-1708	Rhythmakers and Teagarden	1985	$25

IMPULSE!

Number	Title	Yr	NM
❏ A-96 [M]	Ask Me Now	1966	$120
❏ AS-96 [S]	Ask Me Now	1966	$120
❏ A-9137 [M]	College Concert of Pee Wee Russell with Henry "Red" Allen	1967	$120
❏ AS-9137 [S]	College Concert of Pee Wee Russell with Henry "Red" Allen	1967	$250

MAINSTREAM

Number	Title	Yr	NM
❏ 56026 [M]	A Legend	1965	$35
❏ S-6026 [S]	A Legend	1965	$25

MCA

Number	Title	Yr	NM
❏ 4150	Salute to Newport	198?	$30

PRESTIGE

Number	Title	Yr	NM
❏ 24051	Jam Session in Swingville	198?	$35
❏ PRST-7672 [R]	The Pee Wee Russell Memorial Album	1969	$35

RIVERSIDE

Number	Title	Yr	NM
❏ RLP 12-141 [M]	Rhythmakers and Teagarden	1955	$300

SAVOY JAZZ

Number	Title	Yr	NM
❏ SJL-2228	The Individualism of Pee Wee Russell	197?	$35

STEREO-CRAFT

Number	Title	Yr	NM
❏ RTN-105 [M]	Pee Wee Plays Pee Wee	196?	$25
❏ RTS-105 [S]	Pee Wee Plays Pee Wee	196?	$30

STORYVILLE

Number	Title	Yr	NM
❏ STLP-308 [10]	Pee Wee Russell	1954	$100
❏ STLP-909 [M]	We're In the Money	1956	$50

SWINGVILLE

Number	Title	Yr	NM
❏ SVLP-2008 [M]	Swingin' with Pee Wee	1960	$50
— Purple label			
❏ SVLP-2008 [M]	Swingin' with Pee Wee	1965	$30
— Blue label, trident logo at right			

TIME-LIFE

Number	Title	Yr	NM
❏ STL-J-17	Giants of Jazz	1981	$50

XANADU

Number	Title	Yr	NM
❏ 192	Over the Rainbow	198?	$25

RUSSELL, PEE WEE/BILLY BANKS
JAZZ PANORAMA

Number	Title	Yr	NM
❏ 1808 [10]	Pee Wee Russell / Billy Banks	1951	$100

RUSSIAN JAZZ QUARTET, THE
ABC IMPULSE!

Number	Title	Yr	NM
❏ AS-80 [S]	Happiness	1968	$35

IMPULSE!

Number	Title	Yr	NM
❏ A-80 [M]	Happiness	1965	$250
❏ AS-80 [S]	Happiness	1965	$120

RUSSIN, BABE
DOT

Number	Title	Yr	NM
❏ DLP-3060 [M]	To Soothe the Savage	1956	$150

RUSSO, BILL
ATLANTIC

Number	Title	Yr	NM
❏ 1241 [M]	The World of Alcina	1956	$300
— Black label			
❏ 1241 [M]	The World of Alcina	1961	$175
— Multicolor label, white "fan" logo at right			

DEE GEE

Number	Title	Yr	NM
❏ 1001 [10]	A Recital in New American Music	1952	$250

FM

Number	Title	Yr	NM
❏ 302 [M]	Stereophony	1963	$30
❏ S-302 [S]	Stereophony	1963	$30

ROULETTE

Number	Title	Yr	NM
❏ R-52045 [M]	School of Rebellion	1960	$30
❏ SR-52045 [S]	School of Rebellion	1960	$30
❏ R-52063 [M]	Seven Deadly Sins	1960	$30
❏ SR-52063 [S]	Seven Deadly Sins	1960	$30

RUSTIX
RARE EARTH

Number	Title	Yr	NM
❏ RS-508	Bedlam	1969	$18
— Regular cover			
❏ RS-508	Bedlam	1969	$30
— Rounded-top cover			
❏ RS-513	Come On, People	1970	$15

RUSTY AND DOUG
See RUSTY AND DOUG KERSHAW.

RUTHERFORD, PAUL
EMANEM

Number	Title	Yr	NM
❏ 3305	Gentle Harm of the Bourgeoisie	197?	$30

RUTLES, THE
WARNER BROS.

Number	Title	Yr	NM
❏ HS3151 [B]	The Rutles	1978	$30
— With bound-in booklet			
❏ PRO-A-723 [DJ]	The Rutles	1978	$30
— Yellow vinyl with five songs and "banana" label			

RYAN, BUCK, AND SMITTY IRWIN
MONUMENT

Number	Title	Yr	NM
❏ MLP-8031 [M]	Ballads and Bluegrass	1965	$25
❏ SLP-18031 [S]	Ballads and Bluegrass	1965	$30

RYAN, CHARLIE
HILLTOP

Number	Title	Yr	NM
❏ JM-6006 [M]	Hot Rod Lincoln Drags Again	1964	$50
❏ JS-6006 [R]	Hot Rod Lincoln Drags Again	1964	$30

KING

Number	Title	Yr	NM
❏ 751 [M]	Hot Rod Lincoln	1961	$400

RYDELL, BOBBY
CAMEO

Number	Title	Yr	NM
❏ C-2001 [M]	16 Golden Hits	1965	$25
❏ SC-2001 [R]	16 Golden Hits	1965	$25

Number	Title	Yr	NM
❏ C-1019 [M]	All the Hits	1962	$30
— Black vinyl			
❏ C-1019 [M]	All the Hits	1962	$175
— Red vinyl			
❏ C-1040 [M]	All the Hits, Volume 2	1963	$30
❏ SC-1040 [P]	All the Hits, Volume 2	1963	$40
❏ C-1010 [M]	Bobby Rydell Salutes "The Great Ones"	1961	$30
❏ SC-1010 [S]	Bobby Rydell Salutes "The Great Ones"	1961	$40
❏ C-1028 [M]	Bobby Rydell's Biggest Hits, Volume 2	1962	$30
❏ C-1009 [M]	Bobby's Biggest Hits	1961	$100
— Original with die-cut cover and textured inner sleeve			
❏ C-1009 [M]	Bobby's Biggest Hits	1961	$30
— Standard cover			
❏ C-1007 [M]	Bobby Sings	1960	$50
❏ C-1043 [M]	Bye Bye Birdie	1963	$30
❏ C-1080 [M]	Forget Him	1964	$25

Number	Title	Yr	NM
❏ SC-1080 [R]	Forget Him	1964	$25
❏ C-1011 [M]	Rydell at the Copa	1961	$30
❏ SC-1011 [S]	Rydell at the Copa	1961	$40
❏ C-1070 [M]	The Top Hits of 1963	1963	$25

—Came with bonus single, also numbered 1070

❏ SC-1070 [S]	The Top Hits of 1963	1963	$30

—Came with bonus single, also numbered 1070

❏ C-1006 [M]	We Got Love	1959	$75
❏ C-1055 [M]	Wild (Wood) Days	1963	$25
❏ SC-1055 [S]	Wild (Wood) Days	1963	$30

CAPITOL

❏ T2281 [M]	Somebody Loves You	1965	$18
❏ ST2281 [S]	Somebody Loves You	1965	$25

P.I.P.

❏ 6818	Born with a Smile	1976	$12

SPIN-O-RAMA

❏ 143 [M]	Starring Bobby Rydell	196?	$15
❏ S-143 [S]	Starring Bobby Rydell	196?	$15

STRAND

❏ SL-1120 [M]	Bobby Rydell Sings	196?	$30
❏ SLS-1120 [R]	Bobby Rydell Sings	196?	$25

VENISE

❏ 10035 [M]	Twistin'	1962	$30

—Also includes tracks by Barry Norman and Stephen Garrick

RYDELL, BOBBY/CHUBBY CHECKER
Also see each artist's individual listings.

CAMEO

❏ C1013 [M]	Bobby Rydell/Chubby Checker	1961	$30
❏ C-1063 [M]	Chubby Checker and Bobby Rydell	1963	$25

RYDER, MITCH, AND THE DETROIT WHEELS

CREWE

❏ CR-1335	All Mitch Ryder Hits!	1969	$18

—Reissue of New Voice 2004

NEW VOICE

❏ 2004 [M]	All Mitch Ryder Hits!	1967	$40
❏ NVS-2004 [S]	All Mitch Ryder Hits!	1967	$25
❏ 2002 [M]	Breakout…!!!	1966	$30

—Without "Devil with a Blue Dress On/Good Golly Miss Molly

❏ 2002 [M]	Breakout…!!!	1966	$25

—With "Devil with a Blue Dress On/Good Golly Miss Molly

❏ S-2002 [S]	Breakout…!!!	1966	$30

—Without "Devil with a Blue Dress On/Good Golly Miss Molly

❏ S-2002 [S]	Breakout…!!!	1966	$30

—With "Devil with a Blue Dress On/Good Golly Miss Molly

❏ S-2005	Mitch Ryder Sings the Hits	1968	$25
❏ 2003 [M]	Sock It To Me!	1967	$75
❏ S-2003 [S]	Sock It To Me!	1967	$30
❏ 2000 [M]	Take a Ride	1966	$30
❏ S-2000 [S]	Take a Ride	1966	$30

RHINO

❏ R1-70941	Rev Up: The Best of Mitch Ryder and the Detroit Wheels	1989	$15

SUNDAZED

❏ LP5083	Breakout ... !!!	2001	$15

—Reissue on 180-gram vinyl

VIRGO

❏ 12001	The Best of Mitch Ryder and the Detroit Wheels	1972	$15

RYDER, MITCH

DYNO VOICE

❏ 1901 [M]	What Now My Love	1967	$75
❏ 31901 [S]	What Now My Love	1967	$25

RIVA

❏ RV7503	Never Kick a Sleeping Dog	1983	$12

SEEDS & STEMS

❏ 7801	How I Spent My Summer Vacation	1978	$15
❏ 7804	Naked But Not Dead	1980	$15

RYG, JORGEN

EMARCY

❏ MG-36099 [M]	Jorgen Ryg Jazz Quartet	1956	$250

RYLES, JOHN WESLEY

ABC

❏ AB-1112	Love's Sweet Pain	1979	$15
❏ AB-1056	Shine on Me	1978	$15

ABC DOT

❏ DO-2089	John Wesley Ryles	1977	$15

COLUMBIA

❏ CS9768	Kay	1969	$25

MCA

❏ 644	John Wesley Ryles	198?	$10

—Budget-line reissue of ABC Dot 2089

❏ 3183	Let the Night Begin	1979	$15
❏ 750	Let the Night Begin	198?	$10

—Budget-line reissue

Number	Title	Yr	NM
❏ 798	Love's Sweet Pain	198?	$10

—Budget-line reissue of ABC 1112

❏ 643	Shine on Me	198?	$10

—Budget-line reissue of ABC 1056

PLANTATION

❏ 517	Reconsider Me	197?	$15

RYPDAL, TERJE

ECM

❏ 1083	After the Rain	1977	$30
❏ 1303	Chaser	1986	$25
❏ 1144	Descendre	1979	$30
❏ 1067/8	Odyssey	1976	$35
❏ 1125	Terje Rypdal/Miroslav Vitous/Jack DeJohnette To Be Continued	1979	$30
❏ 1192	To Be Continued	198?	$25
❏ 1110	Waves	1978	$35
❏ 1031	What Comes After	1974	$35
❏ 1045	Whenever I Seem to Be Far Away	1975	$30

S

SAAD, SUE, AND THE NEXT

PLANET

❏ 4	Sue Saad and the Next	1979	$15

SABIEN, RANDY

FLYING FISH

❏ FF-297	In a Fog	198?	$25

SABRES, THE

RCA VICTOR

❏ LPM-1376 [M]	Ridin' High with the Sabres	1956	$75

SABU, PAUL

MCA

❏ 3236	Sabu	1980	$15

—As "Sabu

OCEAN/ARIOLA AMERICA

❏ SW-49902	Sabu	1979	$30

—As "Sabu

SABU

ALEGRE

❏ 802 [M]	Jazz Espagnole	195?	$300

BLUE NOTE

❏ BLP-1561 [M]	Palo Congo	1957	$800

—Deep groove" version (deep indentation under label on both sides)

❏ BLP-1561 [M]	Palo Congo	1957	$350

—Regular version, W. 63rd St. address on label

❏ BLP-1561 [M]	Palo Congo	1963	$175

—With "New York, USA" address on label

❏ BST-81561 [R]	Palo Congo	1967	$35

—With "A Division of Liberty Records" on label

SACBE

DISCOVERY

❏ 864	Street Corner	198?	$25

TREND

❏ TR-521	Aztlan	1979	$30
❏ TR-544	The Sleeping Lady	1986	$25

SACHS, AARON

BETHLEHEM

❏ BCP-1008 [10]	Aaron Sachs Quintet	1954	$300

DAWN

❏ DLP-1114 [M]	Jazzville, Volume 3	1957	$100

RAMA

❏ LP-1004 [M]	Clarinet and Co.	1957	$100

SACHS, AARON/HANK D'AMICO

BETHLEHEM

❏ BCP-7 [M]	We Brought Our "Axes	1955	$300

SACKVILLE ALL-STARS, THE

SACKVILLE

❏ 3028	Saturday Night Function	198?	$25

SACRED MUSHROOM, THE
Members of this group were later in POCO and PURE PRAIRIE LEAGUE.

PARALLAX

❏ P-4001	The Sacred Mushroom	1969	$175

Number	Title	Yr	NM
SADE			
EPIC			
❏ OE44210	Stronger Than Pride	1988	$12
❏ E266686	The Best of Sade	1994	$18

PORTRAIT

❏ BFR39581	Diamond Life	1984	$15
❏ BFR40263	Promise	1985	$12

SADI, FATS

BLUE NOTE

❏ BLP-5061 [10]	The Swinging Fats Sadi Combo	1955	$300

SADLER, SSGT. BARRY

RCA VICTOR

❏ LPM-3605 [M]	A" Team, The	1966	$35
❏ LSP-3605 [S]	A" Team, The	1966	$25
❏ LPM-3691 [M]	Back Home	1967	$35
❏ LSP-3691 [S]	Back Home	1967	$18
❏ LPM-3547 [M]	Ballads of the Green Berets	1966	$35
❏ LSP-3547 [S]	Ballads of the Green Berets	1966	$25

SAGA

ATLANTIC

❏ 81794	Wildest Dreams	1987	$12

POLYDOR

❏ PD-1-6209	Saga	1979	$18

PORTRAIT

❏ BFR40145	Behaviour	1985	$10
❏ FR38999	Heads or Tales	1983	$10
❏ ARR38246	Worlds Apart	1982	$12
❏ FR38246	Worlds Apart	1982	$10

—Reissue with new prefix

SAGITTARIUS

COLUMBIA

❏ CS9644 [B]	Present Tense	1968	$35

TOGETHER

❏ STT-1002 [B]	The Blue Marble	1969	$75

—With two bonus photos; deduct 25 percent if missing

SAHL, MORT

FANTASY

❏ 7005 [M]	Mort Sahl at Sunset	196?	$40

—Red vinyl

❏ 7005 [M]	Mort Sahl at Sunset	196?	$30

—Black vinyl

GNP CRESCENDO

❏ GNPS-2070	Sing a Song of Watergate	1973	$18

MERCURY

❏ MG-21112 [M]	Anyway…Onward	1967	$25
❏ SR-61112 [S]	Anyway…Onward	1967	$25

REPRISE

❏ R-5003 [M]	Mort Sahl On Relationships	1961	$40
❏ R9-5003 [S]	Mort Sahl On Relationships	1961	$50

—Joan Collins appears on the cover

❏ R-5002 [M]	The New Frontier	1961	$25
❏ R9-5002 [S]	The New Frontier	1961	$30

VERVE

❏ MGV-15004 [M]	1960: Look Forward in Anger	1959	$25
❏ MGV-15006 [M]	A Way of Life	1960	$25
❏ V-15049 [M]	Great Moments of Comedy	1965	$18
❏ MGV-15012 [M]	Mort Sahl at the Hungry I	1960	$25
❏ MGVS-15012 [S]	Mort Sahl at the Hungry I	1960	$30
❏ MGV-15002 [M]	The Future Lies Ahead	1959	$25
❏ V-15021 [M]	The Next President	1961	$25
❏ V6-15021 [S]	The Next President	1961	$30

SAHM, DOUG
Also see SIR DOUGLAS QUINTET.

ABC DOT

❏ DO-2057	Texas Rock for Country Rollers	1976	$18

ANTONE'S

❏ ANT-0008	Juke Box Music	1989	$15

ATLANTIC

❏ SD7254	Doug Sahm and Band	1973	$18

MERCURY

❏ SRM-1-655 [B]	Rough Edges	1972	$35

TAKOMA

❏ TAK-7075	Hell of a Spell	1980	$15

TEARDROP

❏ TD-5000	The West Side Sound Rolls Again	1982	$15

WARNER BROS.

❏ BS2810	Groovers Paradise	1974	$25

SAILCAT

ELEKTRA

❏ EKS-75029	Sailcat	1972	$18

Number	Title	Yr	NM

SAIN, OLIVER
ABAT
| 406 | Bus Stop | 1974 | $25 |
| 404 | Main Man | 1973 | $25 |

SAINT ETIENNE
PLAIN
PLAIN178 [B]	Foxbase Alpha	2013	$30
PLAIN179 [B]	So Tough	2013	$30
PLAIN180 [B]	Tiger Bay	2014	$35

SAINT STEVEN
PROBE
| CPLP-4506 | Over the Hills | 1969 | $85 |

SAINTE-MARIE, BUFFY
ABC
| D-929 | Sweet America | 1976 | $15 |
MCA
| 405 | Buffy | 1974 | $15 |
| 451 | Changing Woman | 1975 | $15 |
VANGUARD
VRS9250 [M]	Fire & Fleet & Candlelight	1967	$35
VSD79250 [S]	Fire & Fleet & Candlelight	1967	$25
VSD79300 [B]	Illuminations	1969	$25
VSD79280 [B]	I'm Gonna Be a Country Girl Again	1968	$25
VRS9142 [M]	It's My Way	1964	$30
VSD79142 [S]	It's My Way	1964	$30
VRS9211 [M]	Little Wheel Spin and Spin	1966	$25
VSD79211 [S]	Little Wheel Spin and Spin	1966	$25
VRS9171 [M]	Many a Mile	1965	$25
VSD79171 [S]	Many a Mile	1965	$25
VSD79312 [B]	Moon Shot	1972	$25
VSQ40003 [Q]	Moon Shot	1972	$40
VSD79340	Native Child: Odyssey	1974	$15
VSD79330	Quiet Places	1973	$15
VSQ40020 [Q]	Quiet Places	1973	$40
VSD79311 [B]	She Used to Wanna Be a Ballerina	1971	$25
VSD3/4	The Best of Buffy Sainte-Marie	1970	$25
VMS73113	The Best of Buffy Sainte-Marie	1985	$12
VSD33/34	The Best of Buffy Sainte-Marie, Vol. 2	1974	$18

SAINTS, THE
4 MEN WITH BEARDS
| 4M529LP [B] | Eternally Yours | | $25 |
| 4M502LP [B] | (I'm) Stranded | | $25 |
HARVEST
| RP1156436 [B] | Eternally Yours | 2015 | $20 |
—limited edition, translucent green vinyl
SIRE

| SRK6055 [B] | Eternally Yours | 1978 | $30 |
| SR6039 | (I'm) Stranded | 1977 | $30 |
TVT
| 2111 | All Fools Day | 1987 | $12 |
| 2121 | Prodigal Son | 1988 | $12 |

SAKAMOTO, KYU
CAPITOL
| T10349 [M] | Sukiyaki and Other Japanese Hits | 1963 | $30 |
| DT10349 [R] | Sukiyaki and Other Japanese Hits | 1963 | $18 |

SALEM MASS
SALEM MASS
| SM-101 | Witch Burning | 1972 | $300 |

SALES, SOUPY
ABC-PARAMOUNT
517 [M]	Soupy Sales Sez Do the Mouse and Other Teen Hits	1965	$30
S-517 [S]	Soupy Sales Sez Do the Mouse and Other Teen Hits	1965	$30
503 [M]	Spy with a Pie	1965	$30
S-503 [S]	Spy with a Pie	1965	$30
MCA
| 5274 | Still Soupy After All These Years | 1981 | $15 |
MOTOWN
| MS686 | A Bag of Soup | 1969 | $30 |
REPRISE
R6010 [M]	The Soupy Sales Show	1961	$30
R96010 [S]	The Soupy Sales Show	1961	$40
R6052 [M]	Up in the Air	1962	$30
R96052 [S]	Up in the Air	1962	$40

SALIM, A.K.
PRESTIGE
| PRLP-7379 [M] | Afro-Soul Drum Orgy | 1966 | $30 |
| PRST-7379 [S] | Afro-Soul Drum Orgy | 1966 | $30 |
SAVOY
MG-12132 [M]	Blues Suite	1958	$50
SST-13001 [S]	Blues Suite	1959	$40
MG-12118 [M]	Pretty for the People	1957	$100
MG-12102 [M]	The Flute Suite	1957	$100

SALIS, ANTONELLO
HAT HUT
| 10 | Orange Juice/Nice Food | 1980 | $35 |

SALLYANGIE
WARNER BROS.
| WS1783 [B] | Children of the Sun | 1969 | $35 |

SALSOUL ORCHESTRA, THE
SALSOUL
| SZS5507 | Christmas Jollies | 1976 | $15 |
| CA-1001 | Christmas Jollies | 198? | $10 |
—Reissue
| SA8547 | Christmas Jollies II | 1981 | $15 |
| CA-1004 | Christmas Jollies II | 198? | $10 |
—Reissue
SA-8508	Greatest Disco Hits/Music for Non-Stop Dancing	1978	$12
SA-8552	Heat It Up	1982	$12
SA-8528	How High	1980	$12
SZS5515	Magic Journey	1977	$12
SZS5502	Nice 'n' Naasty	1976	$12
SA-8516	Street Sense	1979	$12
SZS5501	The Salsoul Orchestra	1975	$12
SA-8500	Up the Yellow Brick Road	1978	$12

SALT-N-PEPA
LONDON
| 828392-1 | Very Necessary | 1993 | $15 |
LONDON/RED ANT
| 828959-1 | Brand New | 1997 | $15 |
NEXT PLATEAU
| PL1011 | A Salt with a Deadly Pepa | 1988 | $15 |
| PL1019 | Blacks' Magic | 1989 | $15 |

SALT CITY FIVE, THE
JUBILEE
JLP-13 [10]	Salt City Five	1955	$75
JLP-1012 [M]	Salt City Five	1956	$40
JLP-24 [10]	Salt City Five, Volume 2	1955	$75

SALT WATER TAFFY
BUDDAH
| BDS-5021 | Finders Keepers | 1968 | $25 |

SALUZZI, DINO
ECM
| 1251 | Kultrum | 198? | $30 |
| 25042 | Once Upon a Time… Far Away in the South | 1986 | $25 |

SALVADOR, DOM
MUSE
| MR-5085 | My Family | 1976 | $30 |

SALVADOR, SAL
BEE HIVE
| BH-7009 | Juicy Lucy | 1979 | $30 |
| BH-7002 | Starfingers | 1978 | $30 |
BETHLEHEM
BCP-59 [M]	Frivolous Sal	1956	$300
BCP-39 [M]	Shades of Sal Salvador	1956	$300
BCP-74 [M]	Tribute to the Greats	1957	$300
BLUE NOTE
| BLP-5035 [10] | Sal Salvador Quintet | 1954 | $300 |
CAPITOL
| H6505 [10] | Sal Salvador | 1954 | $250 |
| T6505 [M] | Sal Salvador | 1955 | $175 |
DAUNTLESS
| DM-4307 [M] | You Ain't Heard Nothin' Yet | 1963 | $75 |
| DS-6307 [S] | You Ain't Heard Nothin' Yet | 1963 | $40 |
DECCA
DL4026 [M]	Beat for This Generation	1959	$150
DL74026 [S]	Beat for This Generation	1959	$150
DL9210 [M]	Colors in Sound	1958	$120
DL79210 [S]	Colors in Sound	1958	$120
GOLDEN CREST
| GC-1001 [M] | Sal Salvador Quartet | 1961 | $30 |
| GCS-1001 [S] | Sal Salvador Quartet | 1961 | $30 |
GP
| 5010 | Live at the University of Bridgeport | 197? | $30 |
ROULETTE
| R-25262 [M] | Music To Stop Smoking By | 1964 | $25 |
| RS-25262 [S] | Music To Stop Smoking By | 1964 | $30 |
STASH
ST-224	In Our Own Sweet Way	198?	$25
ST-251	Sal Salvador Plays Gerry Mulligan	1985	$25
ST-234	Sal Salvador Plays the World's Greatest Standards	198?	$25

SALVATION
ABC
| S-653 | Gypsy Carnival Caravan | 1968 | $25 |
| S-623 [B] | Salvation | 1968 | $30 |

SAM AND DAVE
ATLANTIC
| SD8205 | I Thank You | 1968 | $30 |
| 81718 | Soul Men | 1987 | $12 |
—Reissue of Stax 725
| SD8218 | The Best of Sam and Dave | 1969 | $25 |
| 81279 | The Best of Sam and Dave | 1985 | $12 |
GUSTO
| 0045 | Sweet and Funky Gold | 197? | $12 |
ROULETTE
| R-25323 [M] | Sam and Dave | 1966 | $50 |
| SR-25323 [S] | Sam and Dave | 1966 | $40 |
STAX
ST-712 [M]	Double Dynamite	1966	$75
STS-712 [S]	Double Dynamite	1966	$40
ST-708 [M]	Hold On, I'm Comin'	1966	$75
STS-708 [S]	Hold On, I'm Comin'	1966	$50
ST-725 [M]	Soul Men	1967	$75
STS-725 [S]	Soul Men	1967	$40
UNITED ARTISTS
| UA-LA524-G | Back At 'Cha! | 1975 | $15 |

SAM THE SHAM AND THE PHARAOHS
ATLANTIC
| SD8271 | Hard and Heavy | 1971 | $18 |
—As "Sam Samudio
MGM
E-4407 [M]	Lil' Red Riding Hood	1966	$30
SE-4407 [S]	Lil' Red Riding Hood	1966	$30
E-4477 [M]	Nefertiti	1967	$30
SE-4477 [S]	Nefertiti	1967	$30
E-4347 [M]	On Tour	1966	$30
SE-4347 [S]	On Tour	1966	$30
SE-4526	Ten of Pentacles	1968	$25
E-4422 [M]	The Best of Sam the Sham and the Pharoahs	1967	$25
SE-4422 [S]	The Best of Sam the Sham and the Pharoahs	1967	$30
E-4317 [M]	Their Second Album	1965	$30
SE-4317 [S]	Their Second Album	1965	$30
SE-4477	The Sam The Sham Revue	1968	$25
—Retitled reissue
| T90422 [M] | Wooly Bully | 1965 | $75 |
—Capitol Record Club edition
| ST90422 [S] | Wooly Bully | 1965 | $50 |
—Capitol Record Club edition
| E-4297 [M] | Wooly Bully | 1965 | $30 |
| SE-4297 [S] | Wooly Bully | 1965 | $40 |
POLYDOR
| 827917-1 | The Best of Sam the Sham and the Pharoahs | 1985 | $12 |
RHINO
| RNLP-122 | Pharoahization: The Best of Sam the Sham and the Pharoahs (1965-1967) | 1986 | $12 |

SAMHAIN
Also see THE MISFITS; DANZIG.
PLAN 9
| PL9-04 [M] | Initium | 1984 | $150 |
—500 on red vinyl
| PL9-04 | Initium | 1984 | $300 |
—No more than 100 on marbled black and white vinyl
| PL9-04 | Initium | 1984 | $50 |

Number	Title	Yr	NM

—Black vinyl; "8-84" scrawled in trail-off wax
☐ PL9-04 | Initium | 1984 | $300
—100 on white vinyl
☐ PL9-04 | Initium | 1984 | $400
—Pink vinyl "error" pressing
☐ PL9-07 | November Coming Fire | 1986 | $175
—200 on orange vinyl
☐ PL9-07 | November Coming Fire | 1986 | $30
—Regular issue on black vinyl
☐ PL9-05 [EP] | Unholy Passion | 1985 | $100
—Black vinyl, tan cover (original)
☐ PL9-05 [EP] | Unholy Passion | 1985 | $150
—Red vinyl, maroon cover
☐ PL9-05 [EP] | Unholy Passion | 1985 | $150
—White vinyl, tan cover
☐ PL9-05 [EP] | Unholy Passion | 1985 | $15
—Black vinyl, maroon cover

SAMI, ABDULLAH
ABDULLAH SAMI
☐ 802326 [B] | Piece Of Time | 1978 | $1200

SAMI JO
MGM
☐ M3G-4998 | Sami Jo | 1975 | $15
MGM SOUTH
☐ S3G703 | It Could Have Been Me | 1974 | $15

SAMMES, MIKE, SINGERS
COMPOSE
☐ S98032 | White Christmas | 1970 | $18

SAMPLE, JOE, AND DAVID T. WALKER
CRUSADERS
☐ 16004 | Swing Street Café | 198? | $50
—Audiophile vinyl
MCA
☐ 5785 | Swing Street Café | 198? | $25

SAMPLE, JOE; RAY BROWN; SHELLY MANNE
EAST WIND
☐ 10001 | The Three | 1976 | $50
INNER CITY
☐ IC-6007 | The Three | 197? | $35

SAMPLE, JOE
ABC
☐ AA-1126 | Carmel | 1979 | $30
☐ AA-1050 | Rainbow Seeker | 1978 | $25
CRUSADERS
☐ 16001 | Carmel | 198? | $50
—Audiophile vinyl
MCA
☐ 37210 | Carmel | 198? | $20
—Budget-line reissue
☐ AA-1126 | Carmel | 1979 | $25
—Reissue of ABC 1126
☐ 5481 | Oasis | 1985 | $25
☐ AA-1050 | Rainbow Seeker | 1979 | $20
—Reissue of ABC 1050
☐ 5978 | Roles | 1987 | $25
☐ 5397 | The Hunter | 1983 | $25
☐ 5172 | Voices in the Rain | 1981 | $25
☐ 27077 | Voices in the Rain | 198? | $20
—Budget-line reissue
MOBILE FIDELITY
☐ Jan-0016 | Rainbow Seeker | 1979 | $75
—Audiophile vinyl
STORYVILLE
☐ 4000 | Fancy Dance | 1980 | $30
WARNER BROS.
☐ 26318 | Ashes to Ashes | 1990 | $35
☐ 25781 | Spellbound | 1989 | $30

SAMPLES, JUNIOR
CHART
☐ CHS-1045 | Best of Junior Samples | 1970 | $18
☐ CHS-1007 | Bull Session at Bulls Gap | 1968 | $18
☐ CHS-1021 | That's a Hee Haw | 1969 | $18
☐ CHM-1002 [M] | The World of Junior Samples | 1967 | $25
☐ CHS-1002 [S] | The World of Junior Samples | 1967 | $25
HILLTOP
☐ JS-6113 | Moonshining | 197? | $12

SAMPSON, EDGAR
CORAL
☐ CRL57049 [M] | Swing Softly Sweet Sampson | 1957 | $40

MCA
☐ 1354 | Sampson Swings Again | 198? | $25

SAMS, GEORGE
HAT HUT
☐ 3506 | Nomadic Winds | 198? | $30

SAMUELS, DAVID
MCA
☐ 6328 | Ten Degrees North | 1988 | $25

SAN REMO GOLDEN STRINGS
GORDY
☐ G-923 [M] | Hungry for Love | 1967 | $30
☐ GS-923 [S] | Hungry for Love | 1967 | $30
☐ GS-928 [S] | Swing | 1968 | $25
☐ GLP-928 [M] | Swing | 1968 | $75
—Mono is white label promo only; stereo cover has "Monaural Record DJ Copy" sticker on front
RIC-TIC
☐ 901 [M] | Hungry for Love | 1966 | $50
☐ S-901 [S] | Hungry for Love | 1966 | $75

SAN SEBASTIAN STRINGS, THE
STANYAN
☐ 10043 | La Mer | 1972 | $12
WARNER BROS.
☐ BS2768 | Bouquet -- The Best of the San Sebastian Strings | 1974 | $12
☐ WS1795 | For Lovers | 1969 | $15
☐ WS1764 | Home to the Sea | 1968 | $15
☐ ST-91618 | Home to the Sea | 1968 | $18
—Capitol Record Club edition
☐ 4WS2754 | Seasons | 1973 | $25
☐ BS2707 | Summer | 1973 | $12
☐ BS4-2707 [Q] | Summer | 1973 | $20
☐ 3WS1827 | The Complete Sea | 1969 | $25
☐ W1705 [M] | The Earth | 1967 | $18
☐ WS1705 [S] | The Earth | 1967 | $15
☐ W1670 [M] | The Sea | 1967 | $18
☐ WS1670 [S] | The Sea | 1967 | $15
☐ 3WS1730 | The Sea, The Earth, The Sky | 1968 | $25
☐ WS1720 | The Sky | 1968 | $15
☐ WS1839 | The Soft Sea | 1970 | $15
☐ BS2622 | Winter | 1972 | $12
☐ BS2837 | With Love | 1975 | $12

SANBORN, DAVID
REPRISE
☐ 25715 | Close-Up | 1988 | $25
WARNER BROS.
☐ 25479 | A Change of Heart | 1987 | $25
☐ 23650 | As We Speak | 1982 | $25
☐ 23906 | Backstreet | 1983 | $25
☐ BSK3189 | Heart to Heart | 1978 | $25
☐ BSK3379 | Hideaway | 1980 | $25
☐ BS3051 | Promise Me the Moon | 1977 | $25
☐ BS2957 | Sanborn | 1976 | $25
☐ 25150 | Straight from the Heart | 1985 | $25
☐ BS2873 | Taking Off | 1975 | $25
☐ BSK3546 | Voyeur | 1981 | $25

SANCHEZ, PONCHO
CONCORD PICANTE
☐ CJP-239 | Bien Sabroso | 198? | $25
☐ CJP-286 | El Conguero | 1985 | $25
☐ CJP-340 | Fuente | 1988 | $25
☐ CJP-369 | La Familia | 1989 | $25
☐ CJP-310 | Papa Gato | 1987 | $25
☐ CJP-201 | Sonando | 198? | $25
DISCOVERY
☐ 799 | Poncho | 1979 | $30
☐ 813 | Straight Ahead | 1980 | $30

SANCIOUS, DAVID
ELEKTRA/MUSICIAN
☐ 60130 | The Bridge | 1982 | $25

SANCTON, TOMMY
GHB
☐ GHB-52 | Tommy Sancton's Galvanized Washboard Band | 1969 | $30

SANCTUARY
Morphed into NEVERMORE.
COLUMBIA
☐ 45085 | Into The Mirror Black | 1990 | $16
☐ BFE40920 | Refuge Denied | 1987 | $12

SANDALS, THE
WORLD PACIFIC
☐ WP-1818 [M] | Scrambler | 1964 | $100
—As "The Sandells"
☐ ST-1818 [S] | Scrambler | 1964 | $150
—As "The Sandells"; black vinyl

☐ ST-1818 [S] | Scrambler | 1964 | $300
—As "The Sandells"; red vinyl
☐ WP-1832 [M] | The Endless Summer | 1966 | $30

WORLD-PACIFIC STEREO

THE ORIGINAL SOUND-TRACK MUSIC FROM BRUCE BROWN'S

The Endless Summer

THE SANDALS

☐ ST-1832 [S] | The Endless Summer | 1966 | $30
☐ ST-21884 | The Last of the Ski Bums | 1969 | $30
—With skiers' silhouettes on cover
☐ ST-21884 | The Last of the Ski Bums | 1969 | $30
—With Volkswagon bus on cover

SANDBERG, CARL
COLUMBIA MASTERWORKS
☐ ML5539 [M] | Flat Rock Ballads | 1959 | $25
DECCA
☐ DL9105 [M] | Cowboy Songs and Negro Spirituals | 1964 | $25
☐ DL5135 [10] | The People, Yes | 1950 | $50
LYRICHORD
☐ LL-4 [10] | American Songbag | 1951 | $50
☐ LL-66 [M] | The Great Carl Sandburg | 1957 | $30

SANDBERG, PAUL
MANNA
☐ MS-2068 | The Wonder and Warmth of Christmas | 1980 | $12

SANDERS, ANNETTE
SOVEREIGN
☐ SOV-502 | The Time Is Right | 198? | $30

SANDERS, ED
REPRISE
☐ MS2105 [B] | Beer Cans on the Moon | 1972 | $30
☐ RS-6374 [B] | Sanders' Truckstop | 1969 | $50

SANDERS, FELICIA
COLUMBIA
☐ CL654 [M] | Felicia Sanders at the Blue Angel | 1955 | $30
☐ CL713 [M] | Girl Meets Boy | 1955 | $30
DECCA
☐ DL8762 [M] | That Certain Feeling | 1958 | $30
☐ DL78762 [S] | That Certain Feeling | 1959 | $40

SANDERS, GEORGE
ABC-PARAMOUNT
☐ ABC-231 [M] | The George Sanders Touch | 1958 | $30

SANDERS, PHAROAH
ABC IMPULSE!
☐ AS-9219 | Black Unity | 1972 | $35
☐ AQ-9219 [Q] | Black Unity | 1974 | $250
☐ AS-9261 | Elevation | 1974 | $30
☐ AQ-9261 [Q] | Elevation | 1974 | $250
☐ AS-9190 | Jewels of Thought | 1970 | $250
☐ AS-9181 | Karma | 1969 | $250
☐ AS-9227 | Live at the East | 1973 | $35
☐ AQ-9227 [Q] | Live at the East | 1974 | $250
☐ ASD-9280 | Love in Us All | 1975 | $30
☐ AQ-9280 [Q] | Love in Us All | 1975 | $250
☐ AS-9199 | Summun Bukmun Umyum | 1970 | $250
☐ A-9138 [M] | Tauhid | 1967 | $250
☐ AS-9138 [S] | Tauhid | 1967 | $250
☐ AS-9229 | The Best of Pharoah Sanders | 1973 | $250
☐ AS-9206 | Thembi | 1971 | $35
☐ AS-9254 | Village of the Pharoahs | 1974 | $30
☐ AQ-9254 [Q] | Village of the Pharoahs | 1974 | $250
☐ AS-9233 | Wisdom Through Music | 1973 | $35
ARISTA
☐ AL4161 | Love Will Find a Way | 1978 | $30
ESP-DISK'
☐ 1003 [M] | Pharoah's First | 1965 | $120
☐ S-1003 [S] | Pharoah's First | 1965 | $120

Number	Title	Yr	NM
GRP/IMPULSE!			
❏ IMP-219	Black Unity	199?	$35
—*Reissue on audiophile vinyl*			
INDIA NAVIGATION			
❏ IN-1027	Pharoah	1977	$30
MCA			
❏ 29058	Jewels of Thought	1981	$20
—*Reissue of Impulse 9190*			
❏ 29057	Karma	1981	$20
—*Reissue of Impulse 9181*			
❏ 29056	Tauhid	1981	$20
—*Reissue of Impulse 9138*			
❏ 4151	The Best of Pharoah Sanders	1981	$30
—*Reissue of Impulse 9229*			
❏ 29059	Thembi	1981	$20
—*Reissue of Impulse 9206*			
SIGNATURE			
❏ FA40952	Oh Lord, Let Me Do No Wrong	1989	$30
STRATA-EAST			
❏ 19733	Izipho Sam (My Gifts)	1973	$35
THERESA			
❏ 118	Heart Is a Melody	1986	$25
❏ 108/9	Journey to the One	1980	$35
❏ 116	Pharoah Sanders Live	1985	$25
❏ 112/13	Rejoice	1981	$35
❏ 121	Shukuru	1986	$25
TIMELESS			
❏ SJP-253	Africa	1990	$30
UPFRONT			
❏ 150	Spotlight	1973	$30

SANDERS, RAY

Number	Title	Yr	NM
IMPERIAL			
❏ LP-12447	Feelin' Good Is Easy	1969	$18
REPUBLIC			
❏ 5004	I Don't Want to Be Alone Tonight	1977	$15
UNITED ARTISTS			
❏ UAS-6822	Ray Sanders	1972	$15

SANDERS, THE

Number	Title	Yr	NM
AIRBORNE			
❏ 61003	Into Every Life	1988	$15

SANDKE, JORDAN

Number	Title	Yr	NM
STASH			
❏ ST-259	Rhythm Is Our Business	1986	$25

SANDKE, RANDY

Number	Title	Yr	NM
STASH			
❏ ST-264	New York Stories	1987	$25

SANDLER AND YOUNG

Number	Title	Yr	NM
CAPITOL			
❏ ST-449	Honey Come Back	1970	$15
❏ T2802 [M]	More and More	1967	$18
❏ ST2802 [S]	More and More	1967	$15
❏ T2686 [M]	On the Move	1967	$15
❏ ST2686 [S]	On the Move	1967	$18
❏ ST-241	Pretty Things Come in Twos	1969	$15
❏ T2598 [M]	Side by Side	1966	$15
—*also known as "Tony Sandler and Ralph Young*			
❏ ST2598 [S]	Side by Side	1966	$18
❏ ST2967	The Christmas World of Sandler and Young	1968	$15
❏ ST-159	Together	1968	$15
HOLIDAY			
❏ HDY1942	Happy Holidays!	1981	$10
—*Reissue of True Value 2 (almost identical front cover, different back cover)*			
RALTON			
❏ SY200	Re-Discover Christmas	19??	$18
—*Has same contents as "Happy Holidays, Volume 11"; is this the original?*			
TRUE VALUE			
❏ 1	Happy Holidays, Album Eleven	1975	$12
—*Sold only at True Value Hardware stores*			
❏ 2	Happy Holidays! Album Twelve	1976	$12
—*Sold only at True Value Hardware stores*			

SANDOLE, DENNIS

Number	Title	Yr	NM
FANTASY			
❏ 3251 [M]	Compositions and Arrangements for Guitar	1958	$30

SANDOLE BROTHERS, THE

Number	Title	Yr	NM
FANTASY			
❏ 3209 [M]	Modern Music from Philadelphia	1956	$250
—*Red vinyl*			

Number	Title	Yr	NM
❏ 3209 [M]	Modern Music from Philadelphia	1957	$300
—*Black vinyl*			

SANDOVAL, ARTURO

Number	Title	Yr	NM
GRP			
❏ GR-9634	Flight to Freedom	1991	$35

SANDPIPERS, THE

Number	Title	Yr	NM
A&M			
❏ SP-4328	A Gift of Song	1972	$15
❏ SP-4262	Come Saturday Morning	1970	$15
❏ SP-3525	Foursider	1973	$15
❏ SP-6014	Foursider	198?	$12
—*Reissue of 3525*			
❏ SP-4246	Greatest Hits	1970	$15
❏ LP-117 [M]	Guantanamera	1966	$15
❏ SP-4117 [S]	Guantanamera	1966	$18
❏ SP-4135	Misty Roses	1967	$15
❏ SP-4147	Softly	1968	$15
❏ LP-125 [M]	The Sandpipers	1967	$18
❏ SP-4125 [S]	The Sandpipers	1967	$15
❏ SP-4159	The Spanish Album	1969	$15
❏ SP-4180	The Wonder of You	1969	$15

SANDS, EVIE

Number	Title	Yr	NM
A&M			
❏ SP-4239 [B]	Any Way That You Want Me	1969	$35
HAVEN			
❏ ST-9202	Estate of Mind	1975	$25
RCA VICTOR			
❏ AFL1-2943	Suspended Animation	1979	$18

SANDS, TOMMY

Number	Title	Yr	NM
CAPITOL			
❏ T1426 [M]	Dream with Me	1961	$30
❏ ST1426 [S]	Dream with Me	1961	$40
❏ T1364 [M]	Sands at the Sands	1960	$30
❏ ST1364 [S]	Sands at the Sands	1960	$40
❏ T1081 [M]	Sands Storm	1959	$50
❏ T929 [M]	Sing Boy Sing	1958	$75
❏ T848 [M]	Steady Date with Tommy Sands	1957	$75
❏ T1123 [M]	This Thing Called Love	1959	$30
❏ ST1123 [S]	This Thing Called Love	1959	$40
❏ T1239 [M]	When I'm Thinking of You	1960	$30
❏ ST1239 [S]	When I'm Thinking of You	1960	$40
GREEN LINNET			
❏ SIF-3044	Singing of the Times	1989	$15

SANG, SAMANTHA

Number	Title	Yr	NM
LIBERTY			
❏ LN-10017	From Dance to Love	1980	$10
—*Budget-line reissue*			
PRIVATE STOCK			
❏ PS-7009	Emotion	1978	$12
UNITED ARTISTS			
❏ UA-LA965-H	From Dance to Love	1979	$12

SANGUMA

Number	Title	Yr	NM
ODE NEW ZEALAND			
❏ SODE-194	Sanguma	1986	$30

SANTA CLAUS

Number	Title	Yr	NM
CAPITOL			
❏ T2836	Santa's Own Christmas	1967	$18

SANTA ESMERALDA

Number	Title	Yr	NM
CASABLANCA			
❏ NBLP7175	Another Cha-Cha	1979	$15
❏ NBLP7109	Beauty	1978	$15
❏ NBLP7216	Don't Be Shy Tonight	1980	$15
❏ NBLP7080	Don't Let Me Be Misunderstood	1977	$15
❏ NBLP7088	House of the Rising Sun	1978	$15

SANTA FE

Number	Title	Yr	NM
RTV			
❏ 301	Good Earth	197?	$30

SANTAMARIA, MONGO

Number	Title	Yr	NM
ATLANTIC			
❏ SD8252	Feelin' Alright	1970	$30
❏ SD1567	Mongo '70	1970	$30
❏ SD1593	Mongo at Montreux	1972	$30
❏ SD1581	Mongo's Way	1971	$30
❏ SD1621 [S]	Up from the Roots	1972	$30
❏ 1621 [M]	Up from the Roots	1972	$75
—*Mono is white label promo only; "d/j copy monaural" sticker on stereo cover*			
BATTLE			
❏ B-6129 [M]	Mongo at the Village Gate	1964	$50
❏ BS-96129 [S]	Mongo at the Village Gate	1964	$75
❏ B-6120 [M]	Watermelon Man!	1963	$50
❏ BS-96120 [S]	Watermelon Man!	1963	$75

Number	Title	Yr	NM
COLUMBIA			
❏ CS9988	All Strung Out	1970	$35
❏ CL2411 [M]	El Bravo	1966	$30
❏ CS9211 [S]	El Bravo	1966	$35
❏ CL2298 [M]	El Pussy Cat	1965	$50
—*With "Guaranteed High Fidelity" in black at bottom of red label*			
❏ CS9098 [S]	El Pussy Cat	1965	$75
—*With "360 Sound Stereo" in black at bottom of red label*			
❏ CL2298 [M]	El Pussy Cat	1965	$30
—*With "360 Sound Mono" in white at bottom of red label*			
❏ CS9098 [S]	El Pussy Cat	1965	$35
—*With "360 Sound Stereo" in white at bottom of red label*			
❏ CL2473 [M]	Hey! Let's Party	1966	$30
❏ CS9273 [S]	Hey! Let's Party	1966	$35
❏ CL2375 [M]	La Bamba	1965	$35
❏ CS9175 [S]	La Bamba	1965	$50
❏ CL2612 [M]	Mongomania	1967	$35
❏ CS9412 [S]	Mongomania	1967	$30
❏ CL2770 [M]	Mongo Santamaria Explodes at the Village Gate	1967	$35
❏ CS9570 [S]	Mongo Santamaria Explodes at the Village Gate	1967	$30
❏ CS1060	Mongo's Greatest Hits	1970	$30
❏ PC1060	Mongo's Greatest Hits	198?	$20
—*Reissue with new prefix*			
❏ CL2375 [M]	Mr. Watermelon Man	196?	$30
—*Retitled reissue*			
❏ CS9175 [S]	Mr. Watermelon Man	196?	$35
—*Retitled reissue*			
❏ CS9653	Soul Bag	1968	$35
❏ CS9780	Stone Soul	1969	$35
❏ CS9937	Workin' on a Groovy Thing	1969	$35
CONCORD JAZZ			
❏ CJ-387	Ole Ola	1989	$30
CONCORD PICANTE			
❏ CJP-362	Soca Me Nice	1988	$25
❏ CJP-327	Soy Yo	1987	$25
FANTASY			
❏ 3324 [M]	Arriba!	1961	$40
—*Red vinyl*			
❏ 3324 [M]	Arriba!	1961	$75
—*Black vinyl*			
❏ 8067 [S]	Arriba!	1962	$75
—*Blue vinyl*			
❏ 8067 [S]	Arriba!	1962	$50
—*Black vinyl*			
❏ 3328 [M]	Mas Sabroso	1962	$40
—*Red vinyl*			
❏ 3328 [M]	Mas Sabroso	1962	$75
—*Black vinyl*			
❏ 8071 [S]	Mas Sabroso	1962	$75
—*Blue vinyl*			
❏ 8071 [S]	Mas Sabroso	1962	$50
—*Black vinyl*			
❏ 8351 [S]	Mighty Mongo	1963	$50
❏ 3351 [M]	Mighty Mongo	1963	$35
❏ 3291 [M]	Mongo	1959	$40
—*Red vinyl*			
❏ 3291 [M]	Mongo	1959	$75
—*Black vinyl*			
❏ 8032 [S]	Mongo	1962	$75
—*Blue vinyl*			
❏ 8032 [S]	Mongo	1962	$50
—*Black vinyl*			
❏ OJC-490	Mongo at the Village Gate	1991	$30
—*Reissue of Riverside 93529*			
❏ 3311 [M]	Mongo in Havana	1960	$40
—*Red vinyl*			
❏ 3311 [M]	Mongo in Havana	1960	$75
—*Black vinyl*			
❏ 8055 [S]	Mongo in Havana	1962	$75
—*Blue vinyl*			
❏ 8055 [S]	Mongo in Havana	1962	$50
—*Black vinyl*			
❏ 8373	Mongo Santamaria's Greatest Hits	1967	$30
❏ MPF-4529	Mongo Santamaria's Greatest Hits	198?	$20
—*Budget-line reissue*			
❏ 9431	Mongo Y La Lupe	1974	$30
❏ 3302 [M]	Our Man in Havana	1960	$40
—*Red vinyl*			
❏ 3302 [M]	Our Man in Havana	1960	$75
—*Black vinyl*			
❏ 8045 [S]	Our Man in Havana	1962	$75
—*Blue vinyl*			
❏ 8045 [S]	Our Man in Havana	1962	$50
—*Black vinyl*			
❏ 3314 [M]	Sabroso	1960	$40
—*Red vinyl*			
❏ 3314 [M]	Sabroso	1960	$75
—*Black vinyl*			
❏ 8058 [S]	Sabroso	1962	$75
—*Blue vinyl*			
❏ 8058 [S]	Sabroso	1962	$50
—*Black vinyl*			

Number	Title	Yr	NM
❏ OJC-281	Sabroso	1987	$25
— Reissue of 8058			
❏ OJC-626	Summertime	1991	$30
— Reissue of Pablo 2308 229			
❏ 3335 [M]	Viva Mongo!	1962	$40
— Red vinyl			
❏ 3335 [M]	Viva Mongo!	1962	$75
— Black vinyl			
❏ 8087 [S]	Viva Mongo!	1962	$75
— Blue vinyl			
❏ 8087 [S]	Viva Mongo!	1962	$50
— Black vinyl			
❏ 3267 [M]	Yambu	1959	$40
— Red vinyl			
❏ 3267 [M]	Yambu	1959	$75
— Black vinyl			
❏ 8012 [S]	Yambu	1962	$75
— Blue vinyl			
❏ 8012 [S]	Yambu	1962	$50
— Black vinyl			
❏ OJC-276	Yambu	1987	$25
— Reissue of 8012			

HARMONY
Number	Title	Yr	NM
❏ H30291	The Dock of the Bay	1971	$25

MILESTONE
❏ 47038	Skins	1976	$35
❏ 47012	Watermelon Man	1974	$35

PABLO
❏ 2308229	Summertime	1980	$30

PRESTIGE
❏ 24018	Afro Roots	1973	$35

RIVERSIDE
❏ R-3008 [M]	Explosion	1967	$150
❏ RS-3008 [S]	Explosion	1968	$150
❏ RM-3008 [M]	Explosion	1968	$150
❏ RLP-423 [M]	Go, Mongo!	1962	$175
❏ RS-9423 [S]	Go, Mongo!	1962	$175
❏ RM-3529 [M]	Mongo at the Village Gate	1963	$175
❏ RS-93529 [S]	Mongo at the Village Gate	1963	$175
❏ RM-3523 [M]	Mongo Introduces La Lupe	1963	$175
❏ RS-93523 [S]	Mongo Introduces La Lupe	1963	$175
❏ RM-3530 [M]	Mongo Santamaria Explodes!	1964	$175
❏ RS-93530 [S]	Mongo Santamaria Explodes!	1964	$175
❏ RS-3045	Mongo Soul	1969	$150

TICO
❏ LP-137 [10]	Chango	1955	$175
❏ LP-1037 [M]	Chango: Mongo Santamaria's Drums and Chants	1957	$120
❏ LP-1149 [M]	Mongo Santamaria's Drums and Chants	1967	$50

SANTANA, CARLOS, AND BUDDY MILES

COLUMBIA
❏ KC31308	Carlos Santana and Buddy Miles! Live!	1972	$15
❏ PC31308	Carlos Santana and Buddy Miles! Live!	197?	$10
— Reissue with new prefix			

SANTANA, CARLOS, AND MAHAVISHNU JOHN MCLAUGHLIN

COLUMBIA
❏ KC32034	Love Devotion Surrender	1973	$25
❏ PC32034	Love Devotion Surrender	197?	$20
— Reissue with new prefix			

SANTANA, CARLOS

COLUMBIA
❏ FC40875	Blues for Salvador	1987	$12
❏ FC38642	Havana Moon	1983	$12
❏ JC35686	Oneness/Silver Dreams-Golden Reality	1979	$12
❏ AS573 [DJ]	The Solo Guitar of Devadip Carlos Santana	1979	$18
❏ C236590	The Swing of Delight	1980	$15

SANTANA
Also see JOURNEY; CARLOS SANTANA; GREGG ROLIE.

ARISTA
❏ 19080	Supernatural	2000	$40
— Classic Records audiophile vinyl issue in gatefold cover with booklet			

CICADELIC
❏ 1004	Santana '68	1988	$15

CLEOPATRA
❏ CLP1816 [B]	1968 San Francisco	2014	$30
❏ 8203 [B]	The Early San Francisco Years		$30
— picture disc			

COLUMBIA
❏ KC30130	Abraxas	1970	$18
— Original copies have a poster			

Number	Title	Yr	NM
❏ KC30130	Abraxas	197?	$12
— With no poster			
❏ PC30130	Abraxas	1985	$10
❏ CQ30130 [Q]	Abraxas	1972	$40
❏ HC40130 [B]	Abraxas	1981	$150
— Half-speed mastered edition			
❏ JC30130	Abraxas	1977	$10
❏ PC33576	Amigos	1976	$15
— No bar code on cover			
❏ PCQ33576 [Q]	Amigos	1976	$30
❏ PC33576	Amigos	1979	$10
— With bar code on cover			
❏ FC39527	Beyond Appearances	1985	$12
❏ PC39527	Beyond Appearances	198?	$10
— Budget-line reissue			
❏ PC33135	Borboletta	1974	$15
— No bar code on cover			
❏ PC33135	Borboletta	1979	$10
— With bar code on cover			
❏ PCQ33135 [Q]	Borboletta	1974	$30
❏ KC31610	Caravanserai	1972	$15
❏ PC31610	Caravanserai	197?	$10
❏ PCQ31610 [Q]	Caravanserai	1974	$40
❏ JC34423	Festival	1977	$15
❏ JCQ34423 [Q]	Festival	1977	$30
❏ PC34423	Festival	198?	$10
❏ FC40272	Freedom	1987	$12
❏ FC35600	Inner Secrets	1978	$15
❏ PC35600	Inner Secrets	198?	$10
— Budget-line reissue			
❏ FC36154	Marathon	1979	$15
❏ PC36154	Marathon	198?	$10
— Budget-line reissue			
❏ C234914	Moonflower	1977	$18
❏ CS9781	Santana	1969	$18
— 360 Sound" on label			
❏ CS9781	Santana	1970	$12
— Orange label			
❏ PC9781	Santana	198?	$10
❏ KC30595	Santana	1971	$15
— Not the same album as CS 9781; this is often called "Santana III"			
❏ CQ30595 [Q]	Santana	1972	$40
❏ PC30595	Santana	197?	$10
❏ PCQ32964 [Q]	Santana	1974	$40
— Quadraphonic issue of their debut album (9781)			
❏ PC33050	Santana's Greatest Hits	1974	$15
— No bar code on cover			
❏ JC33050	Santana's Greatest Hits	1977	$10
❏ PCQ33050 [Q]	Santana's Greatest Hits	1974	$40
❏ FC38122	Shango	1982	$15
❏ PC38122	Shango	198?	$10
— Budget-line reissue			
❏ C236590	Swing of Delight	1980	$18
❏ C3X44344	Viva Santana	1988	$25
❏ PC32455	Welcome	1973	$15
— No bar code on cover			
❏ PC32455	Welcome	1979	$10
— With bar code on cover			
❏ PCQ32455 [Q]	Welcome	1974	$40
❏ FC37158	Zebop!	1981	$15
❏ HC47158	Zebop!	1981	$40
— Half-speed mastered edition			
❏ PC37158	Zebop!	198?	$10
— Budget-line reissue			

MOBILE FIDELITY
❏ MOFI1-039 [B]	Santana III	2014	$75

SANTA'S HELPERS

DESIGN
❏ SDLPX-30 [S]	All I Want for Christmas Are My Two Front Teeth	196?	$15

SANTIAGO, MIKE

CHIAROSCURO
❏ 193	White Trees	1978	$30

SANTO AND JOHNNY

CANADIAN AMERICAN
❏ CALP-1008 [M]	Around the World with Santo and Johnny	1962	$30
❏ SCALP-1008 [S]	Around the World with Santo and Johnny	1962	$40
❏ CALP-1006 [M]	Come On In	1962	$30
❏ SCALP-1006 [S]	Come On In	1962	$40
❏ CALP-1002 [M]	Encore	1960	$40
❏ SCALP-1002 [S]	Encore	1960	$50
❏ CALP-1004 [M]	Hawaii	1961	$40
❏ SCALP-1004 [S]	Hawaii	1961	$40
❏ CALP-1014 [M]	In the Still of the Night	1963	$30
❏ SCALP-1014 [S]	In the Still of the Night	1963	$40
❏ CALP-1018 [M]	Mucho	1965	$30
❏ SCALP-1018 [S]	Mucho	1965	$40
❏ CALP-1011 [M]	Off Shore	1963	$30
❏ SCALP-1011 [S]	Off Shore	1963	$40
❏ CALP-1001 [M]	Santo & Johnny	1959	$75
❏ SCALP-1001 [S]	Santo & Johnny	1959	$100
❏ CALP-1017 [M]	The Beatles' Greatest Hits	1965	$40
❏ SCALP-1017 [S]	The Beatles' Greatest Hits	1965	$50
❏ CALP-1016 [M]	Wish You Love	1964	$30

Number	Title	Yr	NM
❏ SCALP-1016 [S]	Wish You Love	1964	$40

IMPERIAL
❏ LP-9363 [M]	Brilliant Guitar Sounds	1967	$18
❏ LP-12363 [S]	Brilliant Guitar Sounds	1967	$25
❏ LP-12366	Golden Guitars	1968	$18
❏ LP-12418	On the Road Again	1968	$18

SANTOS, LARRY

CASABLANCA
❏ NBLP7061	Don't Let the Music Stop	1977	$15
❏ NBLP7030	You Are Everything I Need	1976	$15

EVOLUTION
❏ 2002	Just a Man	1969	$25
❏ 2015	Morning Sun	1971	$18

SANTOS, MOACIR

BLUE NOTE
❏ BN-LA483-G	Carnival of the Spirits	1975	$35
❏ BN-LA007-F	Maestro	1972	$25
❏ BN-LA260-G	Saudade	1974	$35

DISCOVERY
❏ 795	Opus 3, No. 1	1979	$30

SANTOS BROTHERS, THE

METROJAZZ
❏ E-1015 [M]	Jazz For Two Trumpets	1958	$120
❏ SE-1015 [S]	Jazz For Two Trumpets	1958	$120

SAPODILLA PUNCH

PHILIPS
❏ PHS600312	Sapodilla Punch	1969	$25

SAPPHIRE THINKERS, THE

HOBBIT
❏ HB-5003	From Within	1969	$30

SAPPHIRES, THE (1)

COLLECTABLES
❏ COL-5007	Who Do You Love	198?	$12

SWAN
❏ LP-513 [M]	Who Do You Love	1964	$300

SARACHO

ABC IMPULSE!
❏ AS-9247	En Medio	1974	$35

SARBIB, SAHEB

CADENCE JAZZ
❏ CJR-1010	Aisha	198?	$25
❏ CJR-1001	Live at the Public Theatre	198?	$25
❏ CJR-1008	U.F.O. -- Live on Tour	198?	$25

SOUL NOTE
❏ SN-1098	It Couldn't Happen Without You	198?	$30
❏ SN-1048	Sessions	198?	$30

SARSTEDT, PETER

UNITED ARTISTS
❏ UAS-5558	Every Word You Say Is Written Down	1971	$12

WORLD PACIFIC
❏ WPS-21899	As Though It Were a Movie	1969	$18
❏ WPS-21895 [B]	Where Do You Go To, My Lovely	1969	$25

SASH, LEON

DELMARK
❏ DS-9416	I Remember Newport	1968	$35

STORYVILLE
❏ STLP-917 [M]	Leon Sash Quartet	1956	$50

SASKIA AND SERGE

ABC HICKORY
❏ HB-44008	Saskia and Serge	1978	$12

SATAN AND THE DISCIPLES

GOLDBAND
❏ 7750 [B]	Underground	1969	$100

SATANS, THE

(NO LABEL)
❏ 0(no cat #) [M]	Raisin' Hell	1962	$300

SATAN'S FOUR

B.T. PUPPY
❏ BTS-1010	Mixed Soul	1970	$175
— With the Cinnamon Angels			

SATCHMO LEGACY BAND, THE

SOUL NOTE
❏ 121116	Salute to Pops, Vol. 1	1990	$35

Number	Title	Yr	NM

SATIN STRINGS
SUTTON
| ❑ SU101X [M] | Satin Strings Play for Christmas | 196? | $15 |
| ❑ SSU101X [S] | Satin Strings Play for Christmas | 196? | $18 |

SATOH, MASAHIKO
ENJA
| ❑ 2008 | Trinity | 197? | $35 |
PORTRAIT
| ❑ OR44194 | Amorphism | 1989 | $30 |

SATTERFIELD, ESTHER
A&M
| ❑ SP-3408 | Once I Loved | 1974 | $25 |
| ❑ SP-3411 | The Need to Be | 1975 | $25 |

SAUNDERS, HERM
VOGUE
| ❑ 101 [10] | Music at the Bantam Cock | 1953 | $250 |
WARNER BROS.
| ❑ W1269 [M] | That Celestial Feeling | 1959 | $25 |
| ❑ W1234 [M] | The Tinkling Piano in the Next Apartment | 1958 | $30 |

SAUNDERS, MERL
CRYSTAL CLEAR
| ❑ 5006 | Do I Move You | 1980 | $50 |
— *Direct-to-disc recording*
FANTASY
| ❑ 9421 | Fire Up | 1973 | $50 |
— *With Jerry Garcia and Tom Fogerty*
❑ 8421	Heavy Turbulence	1972	$35
❑ MPF-4533	Keystone Encores, Vol. 1	1988	$30
❑ MPF-4534	Keystone Encores, Vol. 2	1988	$30
❑ 9503	Leave Your Hat On	1976	$30
❑ 79002	Live at the Keystone	197?	$50
❑ MPF-4535	Live at the Keystone, Vol. 1	1988	$30
❑ MPF-4536	Live at the Keystone, Vol. 2	1988	$30
❑ 9460	Saunders	1974	$35
GALAXY
| ❑ 8209 | Soul Grooving | 197? | $35 |

SAUNDERS, TEDDY
DISCOVERY
| ❑ 809 | Sue Blue | 1980 | $30 |

SAUNDERS, TOM
BOUNTIFUL
| ❑ 38002 | Tom Saunders' Surf Side Six | 197? | $35 |

SAUSSY, TUPPER
Also see THE NEON PHILARMONIC.
Pianist. In the pop-rock world, he was composer for The Neon Philharmonic, who had one hit, "Morning Girl," in 1969.
MONUMENT
❑ MLP-8034 [M]	A Swinger's Guide to "Mary Poppins	1965	$25
❑ SLP-18034 [S]	A Swinger's Guide to "Mary Poppins	1965	$30
❑ MLP-8004 [M]	Discover Tupper Saussy	1964	$25
❑ SLP-18004 [S]	Discover Tupper Saussy	1964	$30
❑ MLP-8027 [M]	Said I to Shostakovitch	1965	$25
❑ SLP-18027 [S]	Said I to Shostakovitch	1965	$30

SAUTER-FINEGAN; CHICAGO SYMPHONY ORCHESTRA (FRITZ REINER, CONDUCTOR)
RCA VICTOR RED SEAL
| ❑ LM-1888 [M] | Concerto for Jazz Band and Orchestra | 1954 | $75 |

SAUTER-FINEGAN
GOLDEN ERA
| ❑ 15071 | Sauter-Finegan Orchestra Revisited | 198? | $25 |
RCA VICTOR
❑ LPM-1240 [M]	Adventure In Time	1956	$120
❑ LPM-1051 [M]	Concert Jazz	1955	$120
❑ LJM-1003 [M]	Inside Sauter-Finegan	1954	$175
❑ LPM-2473 [M]	Inside Sauter-Finegan Revisited	1961	$75
❑ LSP-2473 [S]	Inside Sauter-Finegan Revisited	1961	$40
❑ LPM-1634 [M]	Memories of Goodman and Miller	1958	$150
❑ LPM-3115 [10]	New Directions in Music	1953	$250
❑ LPM-1227 [M]	New Directions in Music	1956	$120
❑ LPM-1104 [M]	Sons of Sauter-Finegan	1955	$120
❑ LPM-1497 [M]	Straight Down the Middle	1957	$150
❑ LPM-1009 [M]	The Sound of Sauter-Finegan	1954	$175
❑ LPM-1341 [M]	Under Analysis	1957	$150
UNITED ARTISTS
| ❑ WWR3511 [M] | The Return of the Doodletown Fifers | 1959 | $40 |
| ❑ WWS7511 [S] | The Return of the Doodletown Fifers | 1959 | $150 |

SAVAGE GRACE
REPRISE
| ❑ RS6399 | Savage Grace | 1970 | $30 |
| ❑ RS6484 [B] | Savage Grace 2 | 1971 | $30 |

SAVAGE RESURRECTION
MERCURY
| ❑ MG-21156 [M] | Savage Resurrection | 1968 | $250 |
| ❑ SR-61156 [S] | Savage Resurrection | 1968 | $150 |

SAVAGE ROSE
POLYDOR
| ❑ 24-6001 | In the Plain | 1969 | $25 |
— *Gatefold cover*

SAVALAS, TELLY
AUDIO FIDELITY
| ❑ AFSD-6271 | Telly Savalas | 1975 | $18 |
MCA
| ❑ 436 | Telly | 1974 | $18 |
| ❑ 2160 | Who Loves Ya Baby | 1976 | $18 |

SAVATAGE
TRANS-SIBERIAN ORCHESTRA related.
ATLANTIC
❑ 81634	Fight for the Rock	1986	$12
❑ 82008	Gutter Ballet	1990	$18
❑ 81775	Hall of the Mountain King	1987	$12
❑ 81247	Power of the Night	1985	$15
COMBAT
| ❑ 8018 | Sirens | 1986 | $15 |
— *Reissue of Par LP with new cover*
| ❑ MX6016 [EP] | The Dungeons Are Calling | 1985 | $18 |
PAR
| ❑ PAR-1050 | Sirens | 1983 | $400 |
— *Blue vinyl*
| ❑ PAR-1050 | Sirens | 1983 | $250 |
— *Black vinyl*

SAVITT, BUDDY
PARKWAY
| ❑ P-7012 [M] | The Most Heard Sax in the World | 1962 | $30 |
| ❑ SP-7012 [S] | The Most Heard Sax in the World | 1962 | $150 |

SAVITT, JAN
HINDSIGHT
| ❑ HSR-213 | Jan Savitt and His Top Hatters 1939 | 198? | $25 |

SAVOY BROWN
Also see FOGHAT.
GNP CRESCENDO
| ❑ GNPS-2196 | Kings of Boogie | 1989 | $12 |
| ❑ GNPS-2193 | Make Me Sweat | 1988 | $12 |
LONDON
❑ APS638	Boogie Brothers	1974	$12
❑ PS718	Savage Return	1978	$12
❑ PS670	Skin 'n' Bone	1976	$12
❑ LC-50000	The Best of Savoy Brown	1977	$12
❑ PS659	Wire Fire	1975	$12
PARROT
❑ PAS71029	A Step Further	1969	$18
❑ PAS71027	Blue Matter	1969	$30
❑ PAS71024	Getting to the Point	1968	$30
❑ XPAS71052	Hellbound Train	1972	$18
❑ XPAS71059	Jack the Toad	1973	$18
❑ XPAS71057	Lion's Share	1972	$18
❑ PAS71042	Looking In	1970	$18
❑ PAS71036	Raw Sienna	1970	$18
❑ PAS71047	Street Corner Talking	1971	$18
TOWN HOUSE
| ❑ SKBK-7003 | Greatest Hits Live in Concert | 1982 | $18 |
| ❑ ST-7002 | Rock 'n' Roll Warriors | 1981 | $15 |

SAWBUCK
FILLMORE
| ❑ Z31248 | Sawbuck | 1972 | $25 |

SAWYER, RAY
CAPITOL
| ❑ ST-11591 | Ray Sawyer | 1976 | $12 |

SAWYER BROWN
CAPITOL
❑ ST-12517	Out Goin' Cattin'	1986	$10
❑ ST-12391	Sawyer Brown	1985	$10
❑ ST-12438	Shakin'	1985	$10
❑ CLT-46923	Somewhere in the Night	1987	$10
❑ C1-92358	The Boys Are Back	1989	$12
❑ C1-90417	Wide Open	1988	$10

SAXON, SKY
Later recorded with THE SEEDS. Also see RITCHIE MARSH.
GNP CRESCENDO
| ❑ GNP-2040 [M] | A Full Spoon of Seedy Blues | 1967 | $75 |
| ❑ GNPS-2040 [S] | A Full Spoon of Seedy Blues | 1967 | $40 |

SAXONS, THE
MIRASONIC
| ❑ A-1017 [M] | The Saxons | 1966 | $40 |
| ❑ AS-1017 [S] | The Saxons | 1966 | $100 |

SAYE, JOE
EMARCY
❑ MG-36147 [M]	A Double Shot of Saye	1958	$250
❑ SR-80022 [S]	A Double Shot of Saye	1958	$250
❑ MG-36112 [M]	A Wee Bit of Jazz	1957	$250
❑ MG-36072 [M]	Scotch on the Rocks	1956	$250
MERCURY
| ❑ SR-60052 [S] | A Wee Bit of Jazz | 1959 | $175 |

SAYER, LEO
CHRYSALIS
| ❑ PV41087 | Another Year | 1985 | $10 |
— *Reissue of Warner Bros. 2885*
| ❑ PV41125 | Endless Flight | 1985 | $10 |
— *Reissue of Warner Bros. 3101*
| ❑ PV41240 | Here | 1985 | $10 |
— *Reissue of Warner Bros. 3374*
| ❑ PV41198 | Leo Sayer | 1985 | $10 |
— *Reissue of Warner Bros. 3200*
| ❑ PV41154 | Thunder in My Heart | 1985 | $10 |
— *Reissue of Warner Bros. 3089*
WARNER BROS.
❑ BS2885	Another Year	1975	$12
❑ BS2962	Endless Flight	1976	$12
❑ BSK3101	Endless Flight	1977	$10
— *Reissue of 2962*
❑ 25073	Have You Ever Been in Love	1984	$12
❑ BSK3374	Here	1979	$12
❑ BS2836	Just a Boy	1974	$12
❑ BSK3200	Leo Sayer	1978	$12
❑ BSK3483	Living in a Fantasy	1980	$12
❑ BS2738	Silverbird	1973	$15
❑ BSK3089	Thunder in My Heart	1977	$12
❑ 23560	World Radio	1982	$12

SAYLES SILVER LEAF RAGTIME
GHB
| ❑ GHB-8 | Sayles Sugar Leaf Ragtime | 196? | $35 |

SCAFFOLD, THE
BELL
| ❑ 6018 [S] | Thank U Very Much | 1968 | $75 |
| ❑ 6018 [M] | Thank U Very Much | 1968 | $100 |
— *Mono copies are promo only*

SCAGGS, BOZ
ATLANTIC
| ❑ SD8239 | Boz Scaggs | 1969 | $15 |
| ❑ SD19166 | Boz Scaggs | 1977 | $10 |
COLUMBIA
❑ KC30976	Boz Scaggs & Band	1971	$12
❑ PC30976	Boz Scaggs & Band	197?	$10
❑ JC37429	Down Two Then Left	1977	$12
❑ PC37249	Down Two Then Left	198?	$10
— *Budget-line reissue*
| ❑ FC36841 | Hits! | 1980 | $12 |
| ❑ PC36841 | Hits! | 198? | $10 |
— *Budget-line reissue*
| ❑ A2S71 [DJ] | KSAN Live Concert | 1974 | $50 |
— *Promo-only set released in plain cardboard jacket*
| ❑ FC36106 | Middle Man | 1980 | $12 |
| ❑ PC36106 | Middle Man | 198? | $10 |
— *Budget-line reissue*
❑ KC30454	Moments	1971	$12
❑ PC30454	Moments	197?	$10
❑ KC31384	My Time	1972	$12
❑ PC31384	My Time	197?	$10
❑ FC40463	Other Roads	1988	$12
❑ JC33920	Silk Degrees	1977	$12
— *Early reissue with new prefix*
| ❑ PC33920 | Silk Degrees | 1985 | $10 |
— *Budget-line reissue; bar code on back cover*
| ❑ HC43920 | Silk Degrees | 1981 | $30 |
— *Half-speed mastered edition*
| ❑ PC33920 | Silk Degrees | 1976 | $15 |
— *Original edition with "PC" prefix and no bar code on back cover*
| ❑ KC32760 | Slow Dancer | 1974 | $15 |
— *Original cover has Boz Scaggs on a beach in only a bathing suit*
| ❑ KC32760 | Slow Dancer | 1974 | $12 |
— *Second cover has a male dancer who is not Boz Scaggs*
| ❑ PC32760 | Slow Dancer | 197? | $10 |
| ❑ AS203 [DJ] | The Boz Scaggs Sampler | 1976 | $25 |

Number	Title	Yr	NM

SCALETTA, DON
CAPITOL
❏ T2328 [M]	All in Good Time	1965	$85
❏ ST2328 [S]	All in Good Time	1965	$50
❏ T2204 [M]	Any Time, Any Groove	1965	$85
❏ ST2204 [S]	Any Time, Any Groove	1965	$50
VERVE
| ❏ V-5027 [M] | Sunday Afternoon at the Trident | 1967 | $25 |
| ❏ V6-5027 [S] | Sunday Afternoon at the Trident | 1967 | $35 |

SCAMPS, THE
PROJECT
| ❏ 8002 [M] | Teen Dance and Sing Along Party | 1962 | $40 |

SCANDAL
COLUMBIA
❏ 5C38194 [EP]	Scandal	1983	$12
❏ PC38194 [EP]	Scandal	198?	$10
— Reissue with new prefix			
❏ 8C839905 [EP]	Scandal featuring Patty Smyth	1985	$25
— Picture disc EP with four of the group's biggest hits			
❏ FC39173	Warrior	1984	$12

SCANIAZZ
STOMP OFF
❏ SOS-1056	It's Right Here for You	198?	$25
❏ SOS-1004	Messin' Around	198?	$25
❏ SOS-1038	Sunset Café Stomp	198?	$25

SCARBURY, JOEY
ELEKTRA
| ❏ 5E-537 | America's Greatest Hero | 1981 | $12 |

SCARS ON BROADWAY
INTERSCOPE
| ❏ 1159201 | Scars on Broadway | 2008 | $25 |

SCHAEFER, HAL
DISCOVERY
| ❏ DS781 | Extraordinary Jazz Pianist | 1979 | $30 |
RCA VICTOR
| ❏ LPM-1106 [M] | Just Too Much | 1955 | $120 |
| ❏ LPM-1199 [M] | The RCA Victor Jazz Workshop | 1956 | $120 |
RENAISSANCE
| ❏ 1000 | Extraordinary Jazz Pianist | 197? | $35 |
UNITED ARTISTS
| ❏ UAL-3021 [M] | Ten Shades of Blue | 1959 | $75 |
| ❏ UAS-6021 [S] | Ten Shades of Blue | 1959 | $50 |

SCHAERLI, PETER
HAT ART
| ❏ 2037 | Schnipp Schnapp | 1987 | $35 |

SCHAFER, KERMIT
JUBILEE
❏ BL-1 [M]	Blooperama	196?	$25
❏ JGM-2001 [M]	Comedy of Errors	196?	$25
❏ JGM-2008 [M]	Foot 'n Mouth Club	196?	$25
❏ JGM-2007 [M]	Funny Boners	196?	$25
❏ JGM-2005 [M]	Off the Record	196?	$25
❏ LP-2 [10]	Pardon My Blooper!	1954	$40
❏ PMB-1 [M]	Pardon My Blooper! Volume 1	1958	$25
❏ LP-3 [10]	Pardon My Blooper! Volume 2	1954	$40
❏ PMB-2 [M]	Pardon My Blooper! Volume 2	1958	$25
❏ LP-19 [10]	Pardon My Blooper! Volume 3	1955	$40
❏ PMB-3 [M]	Pardon My Blooper! Volume 3	1958	$25
❏ PMB-4 [M]	Pardon My Blooper! Volume 4	1958	$25
❏ PMB-5 [M]	Pardon My Blooper! Volume 5	1959	$25
❏ PMB-6 [M]	Pardon My Blooper! Volume 6	1959	$25
❏ PMB-7 [M]	Pardon My Blooper! Volume 7	1959	$25
❏ PMB-8 [M]	Pardon My Blooper! Volume 8	1959	$25
❏ QPMB-10 [M]	Pardon My Quiz Blooper!	196?	$25
❏ SPMB-9 [M]	Pardon My Sports Blooper!	196?	$25
❏ WPMB-11 [M]	Pardon My Washington Blooper!	196?	$25
❏ JGM-2003 [M]	Prize Bloopers	196?	$25
❏ JGM-2002 [M]	Slipped Disks	196?	$25
❏ JLP-1000 [M]	Special Edition: Pardon My Blooper	195?	$30
❏ JGM-2006 [M]	Station Breaks	196?	$25
❏ JGM-2004 [M]	Super Bloopers	196?	$25
❏ KS-1 [M]	The Best of Bloopers	1959	$30

SCHECKTER, JANE
DRG
| ❏ MRS-711 | I've Got My Standards | 1989 | $30 |

SCHEER MUSIC
PALO ALTO
| ❏ TB-204 | High Rise | 198? | $30 |
| ❏ PA-8025 | Rappin' It Up | 198? | $30 |

SCHIFRIN, LALO
AMERICAN INT'L.
| ❏ AILP3003 | The Amityville Horror | 1979 | $25 |
AUDIO FIDELITY
❏ AFLP-1981 [M]	Bossa Nova -- New Brazilian Jazz	1962	$50
❏ AFSD-5981 [S]	Bossa Nova -- New Brazilian Jazz	1962	$75
❏ AFLP-2117 [M]	Eso Es Latino Jazz	1963	$50
❏ AFSD-6117 [S]	Eso Es Latino Jazz	1963	$75
❏ AFSD-6195	The Other Side of Lalo Schifrin	1968	$35
COLGEMS
| ❏ COMO-5003 [M] | Murderer's Row | 1967 | $150 |
| ❏ COSO-5003 [S] | Murderer's Row | 1967 | $200 |
CTI
| ❏ 5000 | Black Widow | 1976 | $30 |
| ❏ 5003 | Towering Toccata | 1977 | $30 |
DOT
❏ DLP-3833 [M]	Cool Hand Luke	1968	$250
❏ DLP-25833 [M]	Cool Hand Luke	1968	$250
❏ DLP-3831 [M]	Music from Mission: Impossible	1967	$200
❏ DLP-25831 [M]	Music from Mission: Impossible	1967	$100
❏ DLP-25852	There's a Whole Lot of Schifrin Goin' On	1968	$150
DRG
| ❏ SBL-12591 | The Fourth Protocol | 1987 | $35 |
ENTR'ACTE
| ❏ ERS-6510 | The Eagle Has Landed/The Four Musketeers | 1980 | $30 |
| ❏ ERS-6508 | Voyage of the Damned | 1977 | $75 |
MCA
❏ 25137	Liquidator	1966	$20
❏ 2374	Nunzio	1978	$30
❏ 2284	Rollercoaster	1977	$35
❏ 25012	The Cincinnati Kid	1986	$20
❏ 5185	The Competition	1980	$25
MGM
❏ E-4156 [M]	Between Broadway and Hollywood	1963	$35
❏ SE-4156 [S]	Between Broadway and Hollywood	1963	$50
❏ E-4413ST [M]	Liquidator	1966	$50
❏ SE-4413ST [S]	Liquidator	1966	$75
❏ SE-4742	Medical Center and Other Great Themes	1971	$50
❏ E-4110 [M]	Piano, Strings and Bossa Nova	1963	$35
❏ SE-4110 [S]	Piano, Strings and Bossa Nova	1963	$50
❏ E-4313 [M]	The Cincinnati Kid	1965	$50
❏ SE-4313 [S]	The Cincinnati Kid	1965	$75
NAUTILUS
| ❏ NR-51 | Ins and Outs | 198? | $40 |
| — Audiophile vinyl | | | |
PALO ALTO
| ❏ 8055 | Ins and Outs | 1983 | $30 |
PARAMOUNT
| ❏ PAS-5004 | Mannix | 1969 | $75 |
| ❏ PAS-5002 | More Music from Mission: Impossible | 1969 | $40 |
ROULETTE
❏ R52088 [M]	Lalo Brilliance	1962	$50
❏ SR52088 [S]	Lalo Brilliance	1962	$75
❏ SR-42013	Lalole" -- The Latin Sound	1968	$35
TABU
| ❏ JZ35436 | Gypsies | 1978 | $30 |
| ❏ JZ36091 | No One Home | 1979 | $30 |
TETRAGRAMMATON
| ❏ T-5006 | Che! | 1969 | $75 |
TICO
| ❏ LP-1070 [M] | Piano Espanol | 1960 | $75 |
| ❏ LPS-1070 [S] | Piano Espanol | 1960 | $75 |
VARESE SARABANDE
| ❏ STV-81198 | The Osterman Weekend | 1983 | $25 |
VERVE
❏ V6-8785	Insensatez	1968	$35
❏ V-8601 [M]	New Fantasy	1964	$35
❏ V6-8601 [S]	New Fantasy	1964	$50
❏ V-8624 [M]	Once a Thief and Other Themes	1965	$35
❏ V6-8624 [S]	Once a Thief and Other Themes	1965	$50
❏ V6-8801	Rock Requiem	1971	$30
❏ V-8543 [M]	Samba Paros Dos	1963	$35
— With Bob Brookmeyer			
❏ V6-8543 [S]	Samba Paros Dos	1963	$50
— With Bob Brookmeyer			
❏ V-8654 [M]	The Dissection and Reconstruction of Music from the Past	1966	$35
❏ V6-8654 [S]	The Dissection and Reconstruction of Music from the Past	1966	$50
WARNER BROS.
❏ BSK3328	Boulevard Nights	1979	$25
❏ WS1777	Bullitt	1968	$120
❏ BS2727	Enter the Dragon	1973	$120

SCHILLER, LAWRENCE
CAPITOL
❏ KAO2652 [M]	Homosexuality in the American Male	1967	$40
❏ TAO2574 [M]	LSD	1966	$150
❏ KAO2630 [M]	Why Did Lenny Bruce Die?	1967	$40

SCHILLING, PETER
ELEKTRA
❏ 60265	Error in the System	1983	$12
❏ 60863	The Different Story	1989	$12
❏ 60404	Things to Come	1985	$12

SCHLAMME, MARTHA
VANGUARD
❏ VRS497 [M]	Chansons de Noel	1956	$75
❏ VRS-9019 [M]	Folk Songs of Many Lands	195?	$30
❏ VRS-9011 [M]	Raisins and Almonds and Other Jewish Folk Songs	195?	$30

SCHMIT, TIMOTHY B.
ASYLUM
| ❏ 60359 | Playin' It Cool | 1984 | $12 |
MCA
| ❏ 6420 | Tell Me the Truth | 1990 | $18 |
| ❏ 42049 | Timothy B. | 1987 | $12 |

SCHNEIDER, ERIC, AND EARL HINES
GATEMOUTH
| ❏ 1003 | Eric and Earl | 1980 | $30 |

SCHNEIDER, ERIC
GATEMOUTH
| ❏ 1005 | Eric's Alley | 1981 | $30 |

SCHNEIDER, FRED
WARNER BROS.
| ❏ 25158 | Fred Schneider and the Shake Society | 1984 | $15 |

SCHNEIDER, JOHN
MCA
❏ 5668	A Memory Like You	1986	$10
❏ 42033	Greatest Hits	1987	$10
❏ 5789	Take the Long Way Home	1986	$10
❏ 5495	Too Good to Stop Now	1984	$10
❏ 5583	Tryin' to Outrun the Wind	1985	$10
❏ 5973	You Ain't Seen the Last of Me	1987	$10
SCOTTI BROTHERS
❏ FZ38712	If You Believe	1983	$12
❏ FZ37400	Now or Never	1981	$12
❏ FZ37956	Quiet Man	1982	$12
❏ FZ37617	White Christmas	1981	$12
❏ 3Z37617	White Christmas	198?	$10
— Budget-line reissue with new prefix			

SCHNEIDER, KENT
DELMARK
| ❏ DS-418 | Celebration for Modern Man | 197? | $30 |

SCHNITTER, DAVID
MUSE
❏ MR-5222	Glowing	1980	$30
❏ MR-5153	Goliath	1977	$30
❏ MR-5108	Invitation	197?	$30
❏ MR-5197	Thundering	1979	$30

SCHOEN, VIC
DECCA
| ❏ DL8132 [M] | Letter to Laura | 195? | $75 |
| ❏ DL8081 [M] | Music for a Rainy Night | 195? | $75 |
KAPP
| ❏ KL-1097 [M] | Great Songs from All Over the World | 1959 | $50 |
| ❏ K-1097-S [S] | Great Songs from All Over the World | 1959 | $75 |
MAINSTREAM
❏ 56036 [M]	Corcovado Trumpets	196?	$50
❏ S-6036 [S]	Corcovado Trumpets	196?	$50
❏ MMS705	Girls with Brass	197?	$30
RCA VICTOR
| ❏ LPM-2344 [M] | Brass Laced with Strings | 196? | $35 |
| ❏ LSA-2344 [S] | Brass Laced with Strings | 196? | $75 |

Number	Title	Yr	NM

SCHOOF, MANFRED
ECM
❑ 19004	Scales	1980	$30

SCHORY, DICK
CONCERT DISC
❑ SC-21 [M]	Re-Percussion	1957	$75

RCA VICTOR
❑ LPM-2806 [M]	Dick Schory on Tour	1964	$25
❑ LSP-2806 [S]	Dick Schory on Tour	1964	$30
❑ LSA-2485 [S]	Holiday for Percussion	1962	$40
❑ LPM-2485 [M]	Holiday for Percussion	1962	$30
❑ LPM-1866 [M]	Music for Bang, Barroom and Harp	1958	$75
❑ LSP-1866 [S]	Music for Bang, Barroom and Harp	1958	$250
❑ LPM-2125 [M]	Music to Break Any Mood	1960	$30
❑ LSP-2125 [S]	Music to Break Any Mood	1960	$150
❑ LPM-2738 [M]	Politely Percussive	1963	$30
❑ LSP-2738 [S]	Politely Percussive	1963	$40
❑ LSA-2306 [S]	Runnin' Wild	1960	$40
❑ LSA-2382 [S]	Stereo Action Goes Broadway	1961	$40
❑ LSP-2613 [S]	Supercussion	1963	$40
❑ LPM-2926 [M]	The Happy Hits	1964	$25
❑ LSP-2926 [S]	The Happy Hits	1964	$30
❑ LPM-2289 [M]	Wild Percussion and Horns A-Plenty	1960	$30
❑ LSP-2289 [S]	Wild Percussion and Horns A-Plenty	1960	$75

SCHULLER, GUNTHER
ANGEL
❑ S-36060	Joplin	197?	$30

ATLANTIC
❑ SD1368 [S]	Jazz Abstractions	1963	$50
—Multicolor label, black "fan" logo at right			
❑ 1368 [M]	Jazz Abstractions	1961	$175
—Multicolor label, white "fan" logo at right			
❑ SD1368 [S]	Jazz Abstractions	1961	$175
—Multicolor label, white "fan" logo at right			
❑ 1368 [M]	Jazz Abstractions	1963	$50
—Multicolor label, black "fan" logo at right			

GM RECORDINGS
❑ GM-3010	Jumpin' in the Future	1989	$30

GOLDEN CREST
❑ 31043	Happy Feet: A Tribute to Paul Whiteman	197?	$30
❑ 31042	The Road from Rags to Jazz	197?	$35

SCHUMANN, WALTER
CAPITOL
❑ L9016 [10]	Christmas in the Air!	1952?	$35
—Reissue with red label and new prefix			
❑ H9016 [10]	Christmas in the Air!	1951	$40
—Original issue with purple label			
❑ H285 [10]	Songs of the Ivy League	195?	$40
—Purple label original			
❑ L285 [10]	Songs of the Ivy League	195?	$30
—Reissue with red label; has the same cover as the original, except the "H" has been blacked out and an "L" stamped next to it			
❑ H297 [10]	The Voices of Walter Schumann	195?	$40
❑ T297 [M]	The Voices of Walter Schumann	1955	$30

PICKWICK
❑ PCX-1003 [M]	The Christmas Voices of Walter Schumann	196?	$18
—Reissue of Capitol material; record is not banded			
❑ SPCX-1003 [R]	The Christmas Voices of Walter Schumann	196?	$12
—Same as above, except in rechanneled stereo			

RCA VICTOR
❑ LPM-1025 [M]	Exploring the Unknown	1955	$50
❑ LPM-1465 [M]	Scrapbook: The Voices of Walter Schumann	1957	$25
❑ LPM-1141 [M]	The Voices of Christmas	1955	$25
—Original cover has all-yellow lettering on front cover and eight LP/EP covers on back			
❑ LPM-1141 [M]	The Voices of Christmas	1956	$25
—Second cover has red and yellow lettering on front cover and no LP/EP covers on back			
❑ LPM-1558 [M]	Walter Schumann Presents the Voices	1958	$18
❑ LSP-1558 [S]	Walter Schumann Presents the Voices	1958	$25
❑ LPM-1477 [M]	When We Were Young	1957	$25

SCHUUR, DIANE
GRP
❑ GR-1010	Deedles	1984	$25
❑ GR-1039	Diane Schuur and the Count Basie Orchestra	1987	$25
❑ GR-9628	Pure Schuur	1991	$35
❑ GR-1022	Schuur Thing	1985	$25
❑ GR-9567	Talkin' 'Bout You	1988	$25
❑ GR-9591	The Diane Schuur Collection	1989	$30
❑ GR-1030	Timeless	1986	$25

MUSIC IS MEDICINE
❑ 9057	Pilot of My Destiny	1982	$25

SCHUYLER, KNOBLOCH & BICKHARDT
MTM
❑ ST-71064	No Easy Horses	1987	$12

SCHUYLER, KNOBLOCH & OVERSTREET
MTM
❑ ST-71058	S-K-O	1986	$12

SCHUYLER, THOM
CAPITOL
❑ SQ-12298	Brave Heart	1983	$12

SCHWARTZ, CHARLES
INNER CITY
❑ IC-1015	Professor Jive	197?	$35
❑ IC-1164	Solo Brothers	198?	$30

PABLO TODAY
❑ 2312115	Mother--! Mother--!	1980	$35

SCHWARTZ, JONATHAN
MUSE
❑ MR-5325	Anyone Would Love You	1986	$25

SCHWARTZ, THORNEL
ARGO
❑ LP-704 [M]	Soul Cookin'	1962	$30
❑ LPS-704 [S]	Soul Cookin'	1962	$30

SCHWEIZER, IRENE, AND RUDIGER CARL
HAT HUT
❑ 0X	The Very Centre of Middle Europe	1979	$35

SCIANNI, JOSEPH
SAVOY
❑ MG-12185 [M]	New Concepts	1965	$30

SCOBEY, BOB
AMERICAN RECORDING SOCIETY
❑ G-408 [M]	Bob Scobey's Frisco Band	1956	$40

DOWN HOME
❑ MGD-1 [M]	Bob Scobey's Frisco Band with Clancy Hayes	1954	$50

GOOD TIME JAZZ
❑ L-22 [10]	Bob Scobey's Frisco Band	1954	$50
❑ L-12032 [M]	Bob Scobey's Frisco Band, Volume 1	1957	$40
❑ L-12033 [M]	Bob Scobey's Frisco Band, Volume 2	1957	$40
❑ L-14 [10]	Bob Scobey's Frisco Band Vol. 2	1954	$50
❑ L-12006 [M]	Bob Scobey's Frisco Band with Clancy Hayes	1955	$50

DIRECT FROM SAN FRANCISCO!

❑ L-12023 [M]	Direct from San Francisco	1955	$40
❑ L-12009 [M]	Scobey and Clancy	1955	$50

JANSCO
❑ 6250	The Great Bob Scobey, Volume 1	1967	$35
❑ 6252	The Great Bob Scobey, Volume 2	1967	$35
❑ 5231	The Great Bob Scobey, Volume 3	1967	$35

RCA VICTOR
❑ LPM-1344 [M]	Beauty and the Beat	1957	$40
❑ LPM-1567 [M]	Between 18th and 19th on Any Street	1957	$40
❑ LPM-1700 [M]	College Classics	1958	$40
❑ LPM-2086 [M]	Rompin' and Stompin'	1959	$30
❑ LSP-2086 [S]	Rompin' and Stompin'	1959	$40

❑ LPM-1889 [M]	Something's Always Happening on the River	1958	$40
❑ LSP-1889 [S]	Something's Always Happening on the River	1958	$75
❑ LPM-1448 [M]	Swingin' on the Golden Gate	1957	$40

VERVE
❑ MGV-1001 [M]	Bob Scobey's Band	1956	$250
❑ V-1001 [M]	Bob Scobey's Band	1961	$25
❑ MGV-1009 [M]	Music from Bourbon Street	1956	$250
❑ V-1009 [M]	Music from Bourbon Street	1961	$25
❑ MGV-1011 [M]	The San Francisco Jazz of Bob Scobey	1957	$100
❑ V-1011 [M]	The San Francisco Jazz of Bob Scobey	1961	$25

SCOFIELD, JOHN
ARISTA/NOVUS
❑ AN3018	Who's Who?	1980	$30

BLUE NOTE
❑ B1-92894	Time on My Hands	1990	$35

ENJA
❑ 4038	Out Like a Light	1982	$30
❑ 4004	Shinola	1981	$30

GRAMAVISION
❑ 18-8702-1	Blue Matter	1987	$25
❑ GR-8405	Electric Outlet	1984	$25
❑ R1-79400	Flat Out	1989	$30
❑ 18-8508-1	Still Warm	1985	$25

INNER CITY
❑ IC-3022	John Scofield Live	197?	$35
❑ IC-3030	Rough House	1979	$30

SCOGGINS, JOHN
TIGER LILY
❑ TL14059 [B]	Pressed for Time	1976	$300

SCOOBY DOO
ZEPHYR
❑ ZMP-12002 [M]	Jerry Leiber Presents Scooby Doo	1959	$150

SCOOBY DOO AND FRIENDS
PETER PAN
❑ 8214	Exciting Christmas Stories	1978	$18
—With voices from the TV series: Don Messick, Casey Kasem, Frank Welker, Heather North, Pat Stevens.			

SCORPION
TOWER
❑ ST5171	Scorpion	1969	$50

SCORPIONS
Rudolph Schenker's brother Michael was briefly a member - twice.
BILLINGSGATE
❑ 1004 [B]	Lonesome Crow	1974	$40

MERCURY
❑ SRM-1-3825	Animal Magnetism	1980	$12
❑ 822556-1	Animal Magnetism	198?	$10
—Reissue of 3825			
❑ 842002-1	Best of Rockers 'N' Ballads	1989	$12
❑ SRM-1-4039	Blackout	1982	$12
❑ 818885-1	Blackout	198?	$10
—Reissue of 4039			
❑ 846908-1	Crazy World	1990	$18
❑ 814981-1	Love at First Sting	1984	$12
—With man and woman on cover			
❑ 822038-1	Love at First Sting	1984	$15
—Reissue with band on cover			
❑ SRM-1-3795	Lovedrive	1979	$12
❑ 822555-1	Lovedrive	198?	$10
—Reissue of 3795			
❑ 832963-1	Savage Amusement	1988	$12
❑ 824344-1	World Wide Live	1985	$15

RCA VICTOR
❑ AFL1-3516	Best of Scorpions	1979	$12
❑ AFL1-5085	Best of Scorpions, Vol. 2	1984	$12
❑ PPL1-4025	Fly to the Rainbow	1975	$15
❑ AFL1-4025	Fly to the Rainbow	1977	$12
—Reissue with new prefix			
❑ AYL1-5057	Fly to the Rainbow	1984	$10
—Best Buy Series" reissue			
❑ PPL1-4128	In Trance	1976	$15
❑ AFL1-4128	In Trance	1977	$12
—Reissue with new prefix			
❑ AYL1-4657	In Trance	1983	$10
—Best Buy Series" reissue			
❑ AFL1-2628	Taken by Force	1978	$15
❑ CPL2-3039	Toyko Tapes	1978	$18
❑ PPL1-4225	Virgin Killer	1977	$15
❑ AYL1-3659	Virgin Killer	1980	$10
—Best Buy Series" reissue			

SCOT, PATRICIA
ABC-PARAMOUNT
❑ 301 [M]	Once Around the Clock	1959	$25
❑ S-301 [S]	Once Around the Clock	1959	$30

Number	Title	Yr	NM
SCOTT, BOBBY			
ABC-PARAMOUNT			
ABC-148 [M]	Bobby Scott and Two Horns	1957	$50
ABC-102 [M]	Scott Free	1956	$50
ATLANTIC			
1355 [M]	A Taste of Honey	1960	$300
— Multicolor label, white "fan" logo at right			
SD1355 [S]	A Taste of Honey	1960	$300
— Multicolor label, white "fan" logo at right			
1341 [M]	The Compleat Musician	1960	$300
— Multicolor label, white "fan" logo at right			
SD1341 [S]	The Compleat Musician	1960	$300
— Multicolor label, white "fan" logo at right			
BETHLEHEM			
BCP-1004 [10]	Great Scott	1954	$300
BCP-8 [M]	The Compositions of Bobby Scott	1957	$300
BCP-1009 [10]	The Compositions of Bobby Scott, Volume 1	1954	$300
BCP-1029 [10]	The Compositions of Bobby Scott, Volume 2	1955	$300
MERCURY			
MG-20854 [M]	108 Pounds of Heartache	1963	$150
SR-60854 [S]	108 Pounds of Heartache	1963	$150
MG-20995 [M]	I Had a Ball	1964	$150
SR-60995 [S]	I Had a Ball	1964	$150
MG-20701 [M]	Joyful Noises	1962	$150
SR-60701 [S]	Joyful Noises	1962	$150
MG-20767 [M]	When the Feeling Hits You	1963	$150
SR-60767 [S]	When the Feeling Hits You	1963	$150
VERVE			
MGV-8326 [M]	Bobby Scott Plays the Music of Leonard Bernstein	1959	$175
MGVS-6065 [S]	Bobby Scott Plays the Music of Leonard Bernstein	1960	$120
V-8326 [M]	Bobby Scott Plays the Music of Leonard Bernstein	1961	$30
V6-8326 [S]	Bobby Scott Plays the Music of Leonard Bernstein	1961	$25
MGV-2106 [M]	Bobby Scott Sings the Best of Lerner and Loewe	1958	$175
MGVS-6030 [S]	Bobby Scott Sings the Best of Lerner and Loewe	1960	$120
V-2106 [M]	Bobby Scott Sings the Best of Lerner and Loewe	1961	$30
V6-2106 [S]	Bobby Scott Sings the Best of Lerner and Loewe	1961	$25
MGV-8297 [M]	Serenate -- Bobby Scott, Pianist	1959	$150
MGVS-6031 [S]	Serenate -- Bobby Scott, Pianist	1960	$150
V-8297 [M]	Serenate -- Bobby Scott, Pianist	1961	$30
V6-8297 [S]	Serenate -- Bobby Scott, Pianist	1961	$25
SCOTT, CALVIN			
STAX			
STS-2046	I'm Not Blind... I Just Can't See	1972	$100
SCOTT, CHRISTOPHER			
DECCA			
DL75243	More Switched-On Bacharach	1970	$18
DL75141	Switched-On Bacharach	1969	$18
MCA			
282	Switched-On Bacharach	1973	$15
— Reissue of Decca 75141			
SCOTT, CLIFFORD, AND LES MCCANN			
PACIFIC JAZZ			
PJ-66 [M]	Out Front	1963	$40
— Colored vinyl			
PJ-66 [M]	Out Front	1963	$25
— Black vinyl			
ST-66 [S]	Out Front	1963	$50
— Colored vinyl			
ST-66 [S]	Out Front	1963	$30
— Black vinyl			
SCOTT, CLIFFORD			
WORLD PACIFIC			
WP-1825 [M]	Lavender Sax	1964	$150
ST-1825 [S]	Lavender Sax	1964	$175
WP-1811 [M]	The Big Ones	1964	$150
— Black vinyl			
ST-1811 [S]	The Big Ones	1964	$150
— Black vinyl			
WP-1811 [M]	The Big Ones	1964	$175
— Green vinyl			
ST-1811 [S]	The Big Ones	1964	$175
— Green vinyl			
SCOTT, FREDDIE			
COLPIX			
CP-461 [M]	Freddie Scott Sings and Sings and Sings	1964	$75
— Gold label			
CP-461 [M]	Freddie Scott Sings and Sings and Sings	1965	$40
— Blue label			
SCP-461 [S]	Freddie Scott Sings and Sings and Sings	1964	$120
— Gold label			
SCP-461 [R]	Freddie Scott Sings and Sings and Sings	1965	$30
— Blue label			
COLUMBIA			
CL2258 [M]	Everything I Have Is Yours	1964	$25
CS9058 [S]	Everything I Have Is Yours	1964	$30
CL2660 [M]	Lonely Man	1967	$25
CS9460 [S]	Lonely Man	1967	$30
PROBE			
CPLP-4517	I Shall Be Released	1970	$30
SHOUT			
SLP-501 [M]	Are You Lonely for Me	1967	$25
SLPS-501 [S]	Are You Lonely for Me	1967	$30
SCOTT, HAZEL			
CAPITOL			
H364 [10]	Late Show	1953	$175
COLUMBIA			
CL6090 [10]	Great Scott	1950	$100
CORAL			
CRL56057 [10]	Hazel Scott	1952	$100
DEBUT			
DLP-16 [10]	Relaxed Piano Moods	1955	$300
DECCA			
DL8474 [M]	'Round Midnight	1957	$120
DL5130 [10]	Swinging the Classics	1950	$175
FANTASY			
OJC-1702	Relaxed Piano Moods	1985	$25
TIOCH			
TD-1013	Afterhours	198?	$25
SCOTT, JACK			
CAPITOL			
T2035 [M]	Burning Bridges	1964	$100
ST2035 [S]	Burning Bridges	1964	$175
ST-8-2035	Burning Bridges	196?	$250
— Capitol Record Club edition			
CARLTON			
LP-12-107 [M]	Jack Scott	1959	$175
STLP-12-107 [S]	Jack Scott	1959	$400
— With "Stereo" in felt letters vertically along the left of cover			
STLP-12-107 [S]	Jack Scott	1959	$300
— With "Stereo" in felt letters horizontally along the top of cover			
STLP-12-107 [S]	Jack Scott	1959	$250
— With "Stereo" printed across the top			
LP-12-122 [M]	What Am I Living For	1959	$120
STLP-12-122 [S]	What Am I Living For	1959	$320
JADE			
J33-113	Jack Is Back	198?	$18
J33-114	The Way I Rock	198?	$18
PONIE			
563	Jack Scott	1974	$18
7055	Jack Scott	1977	$18
TOP RANK			
RM-319 [M]	I Remember Hank Williams	1960	$250
SM-619 [S]	I Remember Hank Williams	1960	$300
RM-348 [M]	The Spirit Moves Me	1961	$250
SM-648 [S]	The Spirit Moves Me	1961	$300
RM-326 [M]	What in the World's Come Over You	1960	$250
SM-626 [S]	What in the World's Come Over You	1960	$300
SCOTT, JIMMY			
SAVOY			
MG-12181 [M]	If You Only Knew	1963	$40
MG-12150 [M]	The Fabulous Little Jimmy Scott	1959	$40
MG-12301 [M]	The Fabulous Songs of Jimmy Scott	1969	$35
MG-12302 [M]	The Fabulous Voice of Jimmy Scott	1969	$35
MG-12027 [M]	Very Truly Yours	1955	$85
MG-12300 [M]	Very Truly Yours	1969	$35
TANGERINE			
TRC-1501 [M]	Falling in Love Is Wonderful	1963	$250
TRCS-1501 [S]	Falling in Love Is Wonderful	1963	$300
SCOTT, LINDA			
CANADIAN AMERICAN			
CALP-1007 [M]	Great Scott!! Her Greatest Hits	1962	$150
SCALP-1007 [S]	Great Scott!! Her Greatest Hits	1962	$175
CALP-1005 [M]	Starlight, Starbright	1961	$150
SCALP-1005 [S]	Starlight, Starbright	1961	$175
CONGRESS			
CGL-3001 [M]	Linda	1962	$40
CGS-3001 [S]	Linda	1962	$50
KAPP			
KL-1424 [M]	Hey, Look at Me Now	1965	$40
KS-3424 [S]	Hey, Look at Me Now	1965	$50
SCOTT, LIZABETH			
VIK			
LX-1130 [M]	Lizabeth	1958	$150
SCOTT, PEGGY, AND JO JO BENSON			
SSS INTERNATIONAL			
2	Lover's Heaven	1969	$30
1	Soulshake	1968	$30
SCOTT, ROBERT WILLIAM			
WARNER BROS.			
WS1886	Robert William Scott	1970	$35
SCOTT, SHIRLEY, AND CLARK TERRY			
ABC IMPULSE!			
AS-9133 [S]	Soul Duo	1968	$35
IMPULSE!			
A-9133 [M]	Soul Duo	1967	$120
AS-9133 [S]	Soul Duo	1967	$250
SCOTT, SHIRLEY			
ABC IMPULSE!			
AS-73 [S]	Everybody Loves a Lover	1968	$35
AS-51 [S]	For Members Only	1968	$35
AS-9141	Girl Talk	1967	$35
AS-67 [S]	Great Scott!	1968	$35
AS-93 [S]	Latin Shadows	1968	$35
AS-9109	On a Clear Day	1968	$35
AS-81 [S]	Queen of the Organ	1968	$35
AS-9119	Shirley Scott Plays the Big Bands	1968	$35
IA-9341	The Great Live Sessions	1978	$35
ATLANTIC			
SD1561	Something	1970	$35
SD1532	Soul Saxes	1969	$35
SD1515	Soul Song	1968	$35
CADET			
CA-50025	Lean On Me	1972	$30
CA-50009	Mystical Lady	1972	$30
CA-50036	Superstition	1973	$30
FANTASY			
OJC-328	Blue Flames	1988	$25
IMPULSE!			
A-73 [M]	Everybody Loves a Lover	1964	$250
AS-73 [S]	Everybody Loves a Lover	1964	$120
A-51 [M]	For Members Only	1963	$250
AS-51 [S]	For Members Only	1963	$120
A-9141 [M]	Girl Talk	1967	$120
AS-9141 [S]	Girl Talk	1967	$250
A-67 [M]	Great Scott!	1964	$250
AS-67 [S]	Great Scott!	1964	$120
A-93 [M]	Latin Shadows	1965	$250
AS-93 [S]	Latin Shadows	1965	$120
A-9109 [M]	On a Clear Day	1967	$250
AS-9109 [S]	On a Clear Day	1967	$120
A-81 [M]	Queen of the Organ	1965	$250
AS-81 [S]	Queen of the Organ	1965	$120
A-9119 [M]	Shirley Scott Plays the Big Bands	1966	$250
AS-9119 [S]	Shirley Scott Plays the Big Bands	1966	$120
MCA			
4152	The Great Live Sessions	1980	$30
MOODSVILLE			
MVLP-19 [M]	Like Cozy	1961	$50
— Green label			
MVST-19 [S]	Like Cozy	1961	$50
— Green label			
MVLP-19 [M]	Like Cozy	1965	$30
— Blue label, trident logo at right			
MVST-19 [S]	Like Cozy	1965	$30
— Blue label, trident logo at right			
MVLP-5 [M]	Shirley Scott Trio	1960	$50
— Green label			
MVLP-5 [M]	Shirley Scott Trio	1965	$30
— Blue label, trident logo at right			
MUSE			
MR-5388	Oasis	1990	$30
PRESTIGE			
PRLP-7338 [M]	Blue Flames	1965	$30
PRST-7338 [S]	Blue Flames	1965	$30
PRLP-7376 [M]	Blue Seven	1965	$30
PRST-7376 [S]	Blue Seven	1965	$30
PRLP-7305 [M]	Drag 'Em Out	1964	$40
PRST-7305 [S]	Drag 'Em Out	1964	$50
PRLP-7143 [M]	Great Scott!	1958	$300
PRLP-7262 [M]	Happy Talk	1963	$40
PRST-7262 [S]	Happy Talk	1963	$50
PRLP-7205 [M]	Hip Soul	1961	$250
— Yellow label, Bergenfield, NJ address			
PRLP-7205 [M]	Hip Soul	1965	$25

Number	Title	Yr	NM
—Blue label, trident logo at right			
❏ PRLP-7226 [M]	Hip Twist	1962	$175
— Yellow label, Bergenfield, NJ address			
❏ PRST-7226 [S]	Hip Twist	1962	$175
— Silver label, Bergenfield, NJ address			
❏ PRLP-7226 [M]	Hip Twist	1965	$25
—Blue label, trident logo at right			
❏ PRST-7226 [S]	Hip Twist	1965	$30
—Blue label, trident logo at right			
❏ PRLP-7182 [M]	Mucho, Mucho	1960	$250
❏ PRLP-7440 [M]	Now's the Time	1967	$30
❏ PRST-7440 [S]	Now's the Time	1967	$30
❏ PRLP-7283 [M]	Satin Doll	1963	$40
❏ PRST-7283 [S]	Satin Doll	1963	$50
❏ PRLP-7155 [M]	Scottie	1959	$250
❏ PRLP-7163 [M]	Scottie Plays Duke	1959	$250
❏ PRLP-7240 [M]	Shirley Scott Plays Horace Silver	1962	$175
❏ PRST-7240 [S]	Shirley Scott Plays Horace Silver	1962	$175
❏ PRLP-7195 [M]	Shirley's Sounds	1961	$250
❏ PRST-7195 [S]	Shirley's Sounds	1961	$250
❏ PRLP-7173 [M]	Soul Searching	1960	$250
❏ PRLP-7312 [M]	Soul Shoutin'	1964	$40
— Yellow label, Bergenfield, NJ address			
❏ PRST-7312 [S]	Soul Shoutin'	1964	$50
— Silver label, Bergenfield, NJ address			
❏ PRLP-7312 [M]	Soul Shoutin'	1965	$25
—Blue label, trident logo at right			
❏ PRST-7312 [S]	Soul Shoutin'	1965	$30
—Blue label, trident logo at right			
❏ PRLP-7392 [M]	Soul Sisters	1965	$30
❏ PRST-7392 [S]	Soul Sisters	1965	$30
❏ PRST-7456 [S]	Stompin'	1968	$30
❏ PRLP-7360 [M]	Sweet Soul	1965	$30
❏ PRST-7360 [S]	Sweet Soul	1965	$30
❏ PRST-7773	The Best for Beautiful People	1970	$25
❏ PRST-7707 [S]	The Best of Shirley Scott and Stanley Turrentine	1969	$25
❏ PRLP-7267 [M]	The Soul Is Willing	1963	$40
— Yellow label, Bergenfield, NJ address			
❏ PRST-7267 [S]	The Soul Is Willing	1963	$50
— Silver label, Bergenfield, NJ address			
❏ PRLP-7267 [M]	The Soul Is Willing	1965	$25
—Blue label, trident logo at right			
❏ PRST-7267 [S]	The Soul Is Willing	1965	$30
—Blue label, trident logo at right			
❏ PRST-7845	The Soul Is Willing	1971	$35
❏ PRLP-7328 [M]	Travelin' Light	1964	$30
❏ PRST-7328 [S]	Travelin' Light	1964	$30
❏ PRLP-7424 [M]	Workin'	1966	$75
❏ PRST-7424 [S]	Workin'	1966	$75

STRATA-EAST

❏ SES-7430	One for Me	197?	$25

SCOTT, TOM

A&M

❏ SP-4330	Great Scott!	1972	$35

ABC IMPULSE!

❏ A-9163 [M]	Honeysuckle Breeze	1967	$250
❏ AS-9163 [S]	Honeysuckle Breeze	1967	$160
❏ AS-9171	Rural Still Life	1968	$250

ATLANTIC

❏ 80106	Target	1983	$25

COLUMBIA

❏ FC37419	Apple Juice	1981	$25
❏ JC35557	Intimate Strangers	1978	$25
❏ PC35557	Intimate Strangers	198?	$20
—Budget-line reissue			
❏ JC36137	Street Beat	1979	$25
❏ JC36352	The Best of Tom Scott	1980	$25

ELEKTRA/MUSICIAN

❏ 60162	Desire	1982	$25

Number	Title	Yr	NM
FLYING DUTCHMAN			
❏ 106	Hair	1969	$50
❏ 114	Paint Your Wagon	1970	$50
❏ BDL1-0833	Tom Scott in L.A.	1975	$30
❏ AYL1-3875	Tom Scott in L.A.	1980	$20
— Best Buy Series" reissue			
❏ BXL1-0833	Tom Scott in L.A.	197?	$25
— Second edition; new prefix, "RE" on cover			
GRP			
❏ GR-9571	Flashpoint	1988	$25
❏ GR-1044	Streamlines	1987	$25
MCA			
❏ 29060	Rural Still Life	198?	$20
— Reissue of Impulse 9171			
ODE			
❏ PE34966	Blow It Out	1977	$25
❏ SP-77033	New York Connection	1976	$25
❏ PE34959	New York Connection	1977	$20
— Reissue of 77033			
❏ SP-77029	Tom Cat	1975	$25
❏ PE34956	Tom Cat	1977	$20
— Reissue of 77029			
❏ SP-77021	Tom Scott and the L.A. Express	1974	$25
❏ PE34952	Tom Scott and the L.A. Express	1977	$20
— Reissue of 77021			
SOUNDWINGS			
❏ SW-202	Tom Scott	1986	$25

SCOTT, TONY, AND JIMMY KNEPPER

CARLTON

❏ LP-12-113 [M]	Free Blown Jazz	1959	$50
❏ ST-12-113 [S]	Free Blown Jazz	1959	$50

SCOTT, TONY, AND MAT MATTHEWS

BRUNSWICK

❏ BL58057 [10]	Jazz for GI's	1954	$120

SCOTT, TONY, AND TERRY GIBBS

BRUNSWICK

❏ BL58058 [10]	Hi-Fi Jazz	1955	$120

SCOTT, TONY

ABC-PARAMOUNT

❏ ABC-235 [M]	South Pacific	1958	$30
❏ ABCS-235 [S]	South Pacific	1958	$30

BRUNSWICK

❏ BL58040 [10]	Music After Midnight	1953	$120
❏ BL54021 [M]	Tony Scott In Hi-Fi	1957	$100
❏ BL58056 [10]	Tony Scott Quartet	1954	$120
❏ BL54056 [M]	Tony Scott Quartet	1957	$120

CORAL

❏ CRL57239 [M]	52nd Street Scene	1958	$50
❏ CRL757239 [S]	52nd Street Scene	1958	$40

MUSE

❏ MR-5230	Golden Moments	198?	$25
❏ MR-5266	I'll Remember	198?	$25

PERFECT

❏ PL-12010 [M]	My Kind of Jazz	1960	$40
❏ PL-14010 [S]	My Kind of Jazz	1960	$50

RCA VICTOR

❏ LPM-1353 [M]	A Touch of Tony Scott	1956	$100
❏ LPM-1268 [M]	Both Sides of Tony Scott	1956	$100
❏ LJM-1022 [M]	Scott's Fling	1955	$100
❏ LPM-1452 [M]	The Complete Tony Scott	1957	$100

SEECO

❏ SLP-428 [M]	Hi-Fi Land of Jazz	1959	$175
❏ SLP-4280 [S]	Hi-Fi Land of Jazz	1959	$175
❏ SLP-425 [M]	The Modern Art of Jazz	1959	$300
❏ SLP-4250 [S]	The Modern Art of Jazz	1959	$300

SIGNATURE

❏ SM-6001 [M]	Gypsy	1959	$50
❏ SS-6001 [S]	Gypsy	1959	$40

SOUL NOTE

❏ SN-1083	African Bird: Come Back! Mother Africa	1984	$30

SUNNYSIDE

❏ SSC-1015	Sung Heroes	1987	$25

VERVE

❏ V6-8788 [S]	Homage to Lord Krishna	1969	$35
❏ V-8742 [M]	Music for Yoga Meditation and Other Joys	1967	$25
❏ V6-8742 [S]	Music for Yoga Meditation and Other Joys	1967	$35
❏ V-8634 [M]	Music for Zen Meditation	1965	$35
❏ V6-8634 [S]	Music for Zen Meditation	1965	$25

SCOTT, WALTER

MUSICLAND U.S.A.

❏ LP-3502 [M]	Great Scott	1967	$25
❏ SLP-3502 [S]	Great Scott	1967	$30

WHITE WHALE

❏ WWS-7131	Walter Scott	1970	$25

Number	Title	Yr	NM
SCOTT-HERON, GIL			
Includes records with Brian Jackson.			
ARISTA			
❏ AL9514	1980	1980	$25
❏ AL4147	Bridges	1977	$25
❏ AL4044	From South Africa to South Carolina	1975	$25
❏ A2L5001	It's Your World	1976	$30
❏ AL9606	Moving Target	1982	$25
❏ AL9540	Real Eyes	1980	$25
❏ AL9566	Reflections	1981	$25
❏ AB4189	Secrets	1978	$25
❏ ALB6-8306	The Best of Gil Scott-Heron	1985	$20
—Reissue of 8248			
❏ AL8248	The Best of Gil Scott-Heron	1984	$25
❏ AL4030	The First Minute of a New Day	1975	$25
❏ AL8301	The Mind of Gil Scott-Heron	1980	$35
BLUEBIRD			
❏ 6994-1-RB	The Revolution Will Not Be Televised	1988	$30
FLYING DUTCHMAN			
❏ FD-10153	Free Will	1972	$50
❏ FD-10143	Pieces of a Man	1971	$50
❏ BXL1-2834	Pieces of a Man	1978	$30
— Reissue of 10143			
❏ AYL1-3819	Pieces of a Man	1980	$20
— Best Buy Series" reissue			
❏ BLD1-0613 [B]	The Revolution Will Not Be Televised	1974	$30
❏ BXL1-0613	The Revolution Will Not Be Televised	1978	$30
— Reissue with new prefix			
❏ AYL1-3818	The Revolution Will Not Be Televised	1980	$20
— Best Buy Series" reissue			
STRATA-EAST			
❏ SES-19742	Winter in America	1974	$75

SCOTTO, RENATA

RCA RED SEAL

❏ ARL1-4136	Christmas with Renata Scotto at St. Patrick's Cathedral	1981	$12

SCOTTSVILLE SQUIRREL BARKERS, THE
Chris Hillman, later of THE BYRDS, makes his first appearance on record here.

CROWN

❏ CLP-5346 [M]	Bluegrass Favorites	1963	$50
❏ CST-346 [S]	Bluegrass Favorites	1963	$75

SCRAMBLERS, THE

CROWN

❏ CLP-5384 [M]	Cycle Psychos	1964	$25
❏ CST-384 [S]	Cycle Psychos	1964	$30

DIPLOMAT

❏ D-2316 [M]	Motorcycle Scramble	1964	$25
❏ DS-2316 [S]	Motorcycle Scramble	1964	$30

WYNCOTE

❏ W-9048 [M]	Little Honda	1964	$25
❏ SW-9048 [S]	Little Honda	1964	$30

SCREAMING BLUE MESSIAHS

ELEKTRA

❏ 60755 [DJ]	Bikini Red	1987	$15
—Promo-only pressing on audiophile vinyl			
❏ 60755	Bikini Red	1987	$12
❏ 60755 [DJ]	Bikini Red	1987	$15
— Promo-only pressing on audiophile vinyl			
❏ 60488	Gun-Shy	1985	$18
❏ 60859 [DJ]	Totally Religious	1989	$15
—Promo-only pressing on audiophile vinyl			
❏ 60859	Totally Religious	1989	$12
❏ 60859 [DJ]	Totally Religious	1989	$15
— Promo-only pressing on audiophile vinyl			

SCREAMING GYPSY BANDITS

BAR-B-Q

❏ 22185	In the Eye	1973	$100
❏ 04	The Dancer Inside You	1974	$100

SCREAMING TREES
Also see MARK LANEGAN.

EPIC

❏ E48996 [B]	Sweet Oblivion	1992	$18
❏ E46800 [B]	Uncle Anesthesia	1991	$18

SST

❏ 260 [B]	Anthology	1991	$30
❏ 248 [B]	Buzz Factory	1989	$25
❏ 132 [B]	Even If and Especially When	1987	$25
❏ 188 [B]	Invisible Lantern	1988	$25
❏ 105 [EP]	Other Worlds	1986	$25
— Reissue of Velvetone cassette-only release			

VELVETONE

❏ 86002	Clairvoyance	1986	$40

Number	Title	Yr	NM

SCRITTI POLITTI

WARNER BROS.

❑ R144294	Cupid & Psyche '85	1985	$12

—*RCA Music Service edition*

| ❑ 25302 | Cupid & Psyche '85 | 1985 | $10 |
| ❑ R100460 | Provision | 1988 | $15 |

—*BMG Direct Marketing edition*

| ❑ 25686 | Provision | 1988 | $12 |

SCROOGE BROTHERS, THE

RHINO

| ❑ RNEP70514 [EP] | Commercial Christmasland | 1987 | $10 |

—*Reissue of Enigma EP*

SCRUGGS, EARL

COLUMBIA

❑ FC39586	American Made, World Played	1984	$12
❑ PC33416	Anniversary Special, Volume One	1975	$12
❑ JC35319	Bold & New	1978	$12
❑ JC36509	Country Comfort	1980	$12
❑ C32268	Dueling Banjos	1973	$15
❑ PC32268	Dueling Banjos	198?	$10

—*Budget-line reissue with bar code*

❑ PC34346	Family Portrait	1976	$12
❑ KC31354	I Saw the Light	1972	$18
❑ C31758	Live at Kansas State	1972	$15
❑ PC31758	Live at Kansas State	198?	$10

—*Budget-line reissue with bar code*

| ❑ PC34464 | Live from Austin City Limits | 1977 | $12 |

—*No bar code on back cover*

| ❑ PC34464 | Live from Austin City Limits | 198? | $10 |

—*Budget-line reissue with bar code*

❑ CS1007	Nashville's Rock	1970	$18
❑ KC32943	Rockin' 'Cross the Country	1974	$15
❑ PC34878	Strike Anywhere	1977	$12
❑ FC39370	Super Jammin'	1984	$12
❑ KC32426	The Earl Scruggs Revue	1973	$15
❑ PC34090	The Earl Scruggs Revue, Volume II	1976	$12
❑ JC36084	Today and Forever	1979	$12
❑ PC36084	Today and Forever	198?	$10

—*Budget-line reissue with bar code*

| ❑ FC38295 | Top of the World | 1983 | $12 |
| ❑ PC38295 | Top of the World | 1985 | $10 |

—*Budget-line reissue with new prefix*

SEA, JOHNNY

HILLTOP

| ❑ JM-6018 | Everybody's Favorite | 196? | $15 |

PHILIPS

❑ PHM200194 [M]	Live at the Bitter End	1965	$25
❑ PHS600194 [S]	Live at the Bitter End	1965	$30
❑ PHM200139 [M]	World of a Country Boy	1964	$25
❑ PHS600139 [S]	World of a Country Boy	1964	$30

WARNER BROS.

| ❑ W1659 [M] | Day for Decision | 1966 | $18 |
| ❑ WS1659 [S] | Day for Decision | 1966 | $25 |

SEA HAGS

CHRYSALIS

| ❑ FV41665 | Sea Hags | 1989 | $12 |

SEA LEVEL

ARISTA

| ❑ AL9531 | Ball Room | 1980 | $12 |

CAPRICORN

❑ CPN 0198	Cats on the Coast	1978	$12
❑ CPN 0227	Long Walk on a Short Pier	1979	$12
❑ CPN 0212	On the Edge	1978	$12
❑ CP 0178	Sea Level	1977	$12

SEALS, DAN

CAPITOL

| ❑ 1P7999 | On Arrival | 1990 | $25 |

—*Only available on vinyl from Columbia House*

| ❑ C1-46976 | Rage On | 1988 | $10 |
| ❑ CLT-48308 | The Best | 1988 | $10 |

EMI AMERICA

❑ PW-17231	On the Front Line	1986	$10
❑ ST-17131	San Antone	1984	$10
❑ ST-17166	Won't Be Blue Anymore	1985	$10

LIBERTY

| ❑ LT-51149 | Rebel Heart | 1983 | $12 |

SEALS, TROY

ATLANTIC

| ❑ SD7281 | Now Prresenting Troy Seals | 1973 | $15 |

COLUMBIA

| ❑ KC34271 | Troy Seals | 1976 | $15 |

SEALS AND CROFTS

K-TEL

| ❑ NU9610 | Collection: 16 of Their Greatest Hits | 1979 | $15 |

NAUTILUS

| ❑ NR-10 [B] | Summer Breeze | 1980 | $35 |

—*Audiophile vinyl*

T-A

| ❑ 5004 | Down Home | 1970 | $30 |
| ❑ 5001 | Seals and Crofts | 1969 | $30 |

WARNER BROS.

| ❑ BS2699 | Diamond Girl | 1973 | $15 |

—*Burbank" palm-tree label*

| ❑ BS2699 | Diamond Girl | 1979 | $10 |

—*White or tan label*

❑ BS42699 [Q]	Diamond Girl	1974	$40
❑ BS2907	Get Closer	1976	$12
❑ BS2886	Greatest Hits	1975	$12
❑ BSK3109	Greatest Hits	1977	$10

—*Reissue; any label variation*

❑ BS2848	I'll Play for You	1975	$12
❑ BS42848 [Q]	I'll Play for You	1975	$30
❑ 2WS2809 [B]	Seals & Crofts I and II	1974	$25

—*Reissue of the two T-A LPs in one package*

| ❑ BS2976 | Sudan Village | 1976 | $12 |
| ❑ BS2629 | Summer Breeze | 1972 | $15 |

—*Green "WB" label*

| ❑ BS2629 | Summer Breeze | 1973 | $12 |

—*Burbank" palm-tree label*

| ❑ BS2629 | Summer Breeze | 1979 | $10 |

—*White or tan label*

❑ BS42629 [Q]	Summer Breeze	1974	$40
❑ BSK3165	Takin' It Easy	1978	$12
❑ BSK3365	The Longest Road	1980	$12
❑ BS2761	Unborn Child	1974	$15
❑ BS42761 [Q]	Unborn Child	1974	$40
❑ BS2568	Year of Sunday	1971	$15

—*Green "WB" label*

| ❑ BS2568 | Year of Sunday | 1973 | $12 |

—*Burbank" palm-tree label*

SEALY, JOE

SACKVILLE

| ❑ 4007 | Clear Vision | 198? | $25 |

SEARCH PARTY, THE

CENTURY CUSTOM

| ❑ 32013 | Montgomery Chapel | 1969 | $2000 |

SEARCHERS, THE

KAPP

| ❑ KL-1363 [M] | Meet the Searchers | 1964 | $40 |

—*With black and blue label*

| ❑ KS-3363 [S] | Meet the Searchers | 1964 | $50 |

—*With black and blue label*

| ❑ KL-1363 [M] | Meet the Searchers | 1964 | $30 |

—*With black label*

| ❑ KS-3363 [S] | Meet the Searchers | 1964 | $30 |

—*With black label*

❑ KL-1477 [M]	Take Me for What I'm Worth	1966	$30
❑ KS-3477 [S]	Take Me for What I'm Worth	1966	$30
❑ KL-1412 [M]	The New Searchers LP	1965	$30
❑ KS-3412 [S]	The New Searchers LP	1965	$30
❑ KL-1449 [M]	The Searchers No. 4	1965	$30
❑ KS-3419 [S]	The Searchers No. 4	1965	$30
❑ KL-1409 [M]	This Is Us	1964	$30

—*Version 1: No sticker on front cover*

| ❑ KS-3409 [S] | This Is Us | 1964 | $30 |

—*Version 1: No sticker on front cover*

| ❑ KL-1409 [M] | This Is Us | 1964 | $30 |

—*Version 2: With sticker on front cover referring to "Love Potion No. 9*

| ❑ KS-3409 [S] | This Is Us | 1964 | $30 |

—*Version 2: With sticker on front cover referring to "Love Potion No. 9*

MERCURY

| ❑ MG-20914 [M] | Hear! Hear! | 1964 | $50 |

—*White label promo*

| ❑ MG-20914 [M] | Hear! Hear! | 1964 | $50 |

—*Version 1: With only the title on the front cover*

| ❑ SR-60914 [S] | Hear! Hear! | 1964 | $40 |

—*Version 1: With only the title on the front cover*

| ❑ MG-20914 [M] | Hear! Hear! | 1964 | $40 |

—*Version 2: With sticker "Live from the Star Club" on cover*

| ❑ SR-60914 [S] | Hear! Hear! | 1964 | $30 |

—*Version 2: With sticker "Live from the Star Club" on cover*

| ❑ MG-20914 [M] | Hear! Hear! | 1964 | $30 |

—*Version 3: With "Live from the Star Club" imprinted on cover*

| ❑ SR-60914 [S] | Hear! Hear! | 1964 | $30 |

—*Version 3: With "Live from the Star Club" imprinted on cover*

| ❑ MG-20994 [M] | The Searchers Meet the Rattles | 1965 | $150 |
| ❑ SR-60994 [S] | The Searchers Meet the Rattles | 1965 | $75 |

PYE

| ❑ 501 | The Searchers | 197? | $18 |

—*Reissue of Kapp hits*

| ❑ 508 | The Searchers, Vol. 2 | 1976 | $18 |

RHINO

| ❑ RNLP162 | Greatest Hits | 1985 | $12 |
| ❑ R1-70162 | Greatest Hits | 1988 | $10 |

—*Reissue of RNLP 162*

SIRE

| ❑ SRK3523 | Love's Melodies | 1981 | $12 |
| ❑ SRK6082 | The Searchers | 1980 | $12 |

SEARS, AL

AUDIO LAB

| ❑ AL-1540 [M] | Dance Music with a Swing Beat | 1959 | $120 |

SWINGVILLE

| ❑ SVLP-2018 [M] | Swing's the Thing | 1961 | $50 |

—*Purple label*

| ❑ SVLP-2018 [M] | Swing's the Thing | 1965 | $30 |

—*Blue label, trident logo at right*

SEARS GOLDEN STRINGS, THE

SEARS

| ❑ SPX-503 [M] | White Christmas | 196? | $15 |
| ❑ SPSX-503 [S] | White Christmas | 196? | $18 |

SEATRAIN

A&M

| ❑ SP-4171 | Sea Train | 1969 | $18 |

CAPITOL

| ❑ SMAS-829 | Marblehead Messenger | 1971 | $18 |
| ❑ SN-16103 | Marblehead Messenger | 1980 | $10 |

—*Budget-line reissue*

| ❑ SMAS-650 | Seatrain | 1970 | $18 |
| ❑ SN-16102 | Seatrain | 1980 | $10 |

—*Budget-line reissue*

WARNER BROS.

| ❑ BS2692 | Watch | 1973 | $15 |

SEBASTIAN, JOHN

Also see THE LOVIN' SPOONFUL.

MGM

| ❑ SE-4654 | John B. Sebastian | 1969 | $18 |
| ❑ SE-4720 | John Sebastian Live | 1970 | $18 |

REPRISE

| ❑ MS2036 [B] | Cheapo-Cheapo Productions Presents Real Live John Sebastian | 1971 | $15 |
| ❑ RS6379 | John B. Sebastian | 1969 | $25 |

—*Same album as MGM 4654, but a different mix*

❑ MS2187	Tarzana Kid	1974	$15
❑ MS2041	The Four of Us	1971	$15
❑ MS2249	Welcome Back	1976	$15

RHINO

| ❑ R1-70170 | The Best of John Sebastian (1969-1976) | 1989 | $15 |

SEBESKY, DON

CTI

| ❑ CTX-6031/2 | Giant Box | 1974 | $35 |
| ❑ 6061 | The Rape of El Morro | 197? | $30 |

DOCTOR JAZZ

| ❑ FW40155 | Moving Lines | 1986 | $25 |

GNP CRESCENDO

| ❑ GNPS-2164 | Full Circle | 198? | $25 |

GRYPHON

| ❑ 791 | Three Works for Jazz Soloists and Symphony Orchestra | 1980 | $35 |

MOBILE FIDELITY

| ❑ 1-503 | Three Works for Jazz Soloists and Symphony Orchestra | 198? | $75 |

—*Audiophile vinyl*

VERVE

| ❑ V6-8756 | Don Sebesky and the Jazz-Rock Syndrome | 1968 | $25 |

SECOND TIME, THE

TOWER

| ❑ ST5146 [B] | Listen to the Music | 1968 | $30 |

SECRET OYSTER

PETERS INT'L.

| ❑ 9003 | Furtive Pearl | 1973 | $30 |
| ❑ 9009 | Sea Son | 1974 | $30 |

SEDAKA, NEIL, AND THE TOKENS WITH THE COINS

CROWN

| ❑ CLP-5366 [M] | Neil Sedaka and the Tokens and the Coins | 1963 | $40 |
| ❑ CST-366 [R] | Neil Sedaka and the Tokens and the Coins | 1963 | $40 |

Number	Title	Yr	NM

SEDAKA, NEIL
51 WEST

Number	Title	Yr	NM
❏ Q16003	I'm a Song	1979	$15

ACCORD

| ❏ SN-7152 | Singer, Songwriter, Melody Maker | 1981 | $12 |

ELEKTRA

❏ 6E-161	All You Need Is Music	1978	$12
❏ 6E-102	A Song	1977	$12
❏ 6E-259	In the Pocket	1980	$12
❏ 6E-348	Neil Sedaka Now	1981	$12

INTERMEDIA

| ❏ QS5015 | Superbird | 1982 | $12 |

KIRSHNER

| ❏ KES-111 | Emergence | 1971 | $18 |
| ❏ KES-117 | Solitaire | 1972 | $18 |

MCA

| ❏ 5466 | Come See About Me | 1984 | $12 |
| ❏ 2357 | Sedaka's Back | 1978 | $12 |

— *Reissue of Rocket 463*

ORBIT

| ❏ RB-17196 | Bravo! | 1983 | $12 |

PICKWICK

| ❏ ACL1-7006 | Breaking Up Is Hard to Do | 197? | $10 |

POLYDOR

| ❏ 831235-1 | My Friend | 1986 | $12 |

RCA CAMDEN

| ❏ ACL1-7006 | Breaking Up Is Hard to Do | 197? | $12 |

RCA SPECIAL PRODUCTS

| ❏ DPL2-0149 | Original Hits | 1975 | $25 |

RCA VICTOR

❏ LPM-2317 [M]	Circulate	1960	$100
❏ LSP-2317 [S]	Circulate	1960	$150
❏ APL1-1789	Emergence	1976	$15

— *Reissue of Kirshner 111*

| ❏ R133511 | Let's Go Steady Again | 1976 | $18 |

— *RCA Record Club edition*

❏ LPM-2421 [M]	Little Devil" and His Other Hits	1961	$100
❏ LSP-2421 [S]	Little Devil" and His Other Hits	1961	$150
❏ VPL1-1540	Live in Australia	1976	$15
❏ LPM-2035 [M]	Neil Sedaka	1959	$150
❏ LSP-2035 [S]	Neil Sedaka	1959	$130
❏ LPM-2627 [M]	Neil Sedaka Sings His Greatest Hits	1962	$75
❏ LSP-2627 [S]	Neil Sedaka Sings His Greatest Hits	1962	$100

— *Black label, dog on top, "Living Stereo" at bottom*

| ❏ APL1-0928 | Neil Sedaka Sings His Greatest Hits | 1975 | $15 |

— *Reissue of LSP-2627*

| ❏ AFL1-0928 | Neil Sedaka Sings His Greatest Hits | 1977 | $12 |

— *Reissue with new prefix*

| ❏ ANL1-3465 | Neil Sedaka Sings His Greatest Hits | 1979 | $10 |

— *Reissue of AFL1-0928*

| ❏ LSP-2627 [S] | Neil Sedaka Sings His Greatest Hits | 1969 | $25 |

— *Reissue; orange label*

❏ ANL1-0879	Oh! Carol	1975	$12
❏ ANL1-1314	Pure Gold	1976	$12
❏ AFL1-2254	Sedaka -- The '50s and '60s	1977	$12
❏ APL1-1790	Solitaire	1976	$15

— *Reissue of Kirshner 117*

| ❏ AFL1-2524 | The Many Sides of Neil Sedaka | 1978 | $12 |

ROCKET

❏ PIG-2297	Neil Sedaka's Greatest Hits	1977	$15
❏ MCA-463	Sedaka's Back	1974	$15
❏ PIG-2195	Steppin' Out	1976	$15
❏ PIG-2157	The Hungry Years	1975	$15

ROLLER SKATE

| ❏ TLA-50172 | Is Anybody Gonna Miss You | 1982 | $18 |

SEDUCTION
VENDETTA

| ❏ SP-5280 | Nothing Matters Without Love | 1989 | $15 |

SEEDS, THE
Also see SKY SAXON.

GNP CRESCENDO

❏ GNP-2040 [M]	A Full Spoon of Seedy Blues	1968	$175
❏ GNPS-2040 [S]	A Full Spoon of Seedy Blues	1968	$30
❏ GNP-2033 [M]	A Web of Sound	1967	$500
❏ GNPS-2033 [S]	A Web of Sound	1967	$40
❏ ST-91224	A Web of Sound	1968	$30

— *Capitol Record Club edition*

| ❏ GNPS-2107 | Fallin' Off the Edge | 1977 | $12 |
| ❏ GNP-2038 [M] | Future | 1967 | $175 |

— *Deduct 25% if two inserts are missing*

| ❏ GNPS-2038 [S] | Future | 1967 | $30 |

— *Deduct 25% if two inserts are missing*

| ❏ GNPS-2043 | Raw and Alive | 1968 | $30 |

Number	Title	Yr	NM
❏ GNP-2023 [M]	The Seeds	1966	$80
❏ GNPS-2023 [S]	The Seeds	1966	$40

SEEGER, BERT
ANTILLES

| ❏ AN-7088 | Because They Can | 198? | $25 |
| ❏ AN-7086 | Time to Burn | 198? | $25 |

SEEGER, PEGGY, BARBARA AND PENNY
FOLKWAYS

| ❏ FC-7553 [10] | American Folk Songs for Christmas | 195? | $100 |

SCHOLASTIC

| ❏ SC7553 [M] | American Folk Songs for Christmas | 1966 | $25 |

— *Reissue of Folkways material*

SEEGER, PEGGY
FOLKLORE

| ❏ FRLP-14016 [M] | The Best of Peggy Seeger | 196? | $30 |

FOLK-LYRIC

| ❏ FL114 [M] | American Folksongs for Banjo | 196? | $30 |
| ❏ FL120 [M] | Popular Ballads | 196? | $30 |

FOLKWAYS

❏ FC-7551 [10]	Animal Folksongs for Children	1957	$120
❏ FP-49 [10]	Folk Songs of Courting and Complaint	1955	$120
❏ FP-2049 [10]	Folk Songs of Courting and Complaint	195?	$150
❏ FW-8563 [M]	From Where I Stand	1982	$15

PRESTIGE

| ❏ PRLP-13058 [M] | A Song for You and Me | 1962 | $30 |
| ❏ PRLP-13005 [M] | The Best of Peggy Seeger | 1961 | $30 |

RIVERSIDE

| ❏ RLP-12-655 [M] | Folksongs and Ballads | 1958 | $40 |

TOPIC

| ❏ 10T-9 [10] | Peggy Seeger | 1956 | $150 |

SEEGER, PETE, PENNY AND MICHAEL
PRESTIGE

| ❏ PRLP-7375 [M] | Pete, Penny and Michael Seeger | 1965 | $25 |
| ❏ PRST-7375 [S] | Pete, Penny and Michael Seeger | 1965 | $30 |

SEEGER, PETE
ARAVEL

| ❏ AB1006 [M] | Live Hootenanny | 1963 | $18 |

BROADSIDE

| ❏ 502 | Pete Seeger Sings and Answers Questions | 1970 | $18 |

BULLDOG

| ❏ BDL-2011 | 20 Golden Pieces of Pete Seeger | 198? | $12 |

CAPITOL

❏ W2172 [M]	Folk Songs	1964	$25
❏ DW2172 [R]	Folk Songs	1964	$15
❏ T2718 [M]	Freight Train	1967	$25
❏ DT2718 [R]	Freight Train	1967	$15

COLUMBIA

❏ CL1947 [M]	Children's Concert at Town Hall	1963	$30
❏ CS8747 [S]	Children's Concert at Town Hall	1963	$30
❏ CL2503 [M]	Dangerous Songs?	1966	$18

❏ CS9303 [S]	Dangerous Songs?	1966	$25
❏ CL2432 [M]	God Bless the Grass	1966	$18
❏ CS9232 [S]	God Bless the Grass	1966	$25
❏ CL2257 [M]	I Can See a New Day	1965	$18
❏ CS9057 [S]	I Can See a New Day	1965	$25
❏ CS9717	Pete Seeger Now	1968	$18
❏ CL2616 [M]	Pete Seeger's Greatest Hits	1967	$25

Number	Title	Yr	NM
❏ CS9416 [S]	Pete Seeger's Greatest Hits	1967	$18
❏ PC9416	Pete Seeger's Greatest Hits	198?	$10

— *Reissue with new prefix*

❏ CL1668 [M]	Pete Seeger Story Songs	1961	$30
❏ CS8468 [S]	Pete Seeger Story Songs	1961	$30
❏ C30739	Rainbow Race	1971	$15
❏ CL2334 [M]	Strangers and Cousins	1964	$18
❏ CS9134 [S]	Strangers and Cousins	1964	$25
❏ CL1916 [M]	The Bitter and the Sweet	1962	$30
❏ CS8716 [S]	The Bitter and the Sweet	1962	$30
❏ KG31949	The World of Pete Seeger	1972	$18
❏ CL2705 [M]	Waist Deep in the Big Muddy	1967	$25
❏ CS9505 [S]	Waist Deep in the Big Muddy	1967	$18
❏ CL2101 [M]	We Shall Overcome	1963	$18
❏ CS8901 [S]	We Shall Overcome	1963	$25
❏ CS9873	Young vs. Old	1969	$18

DISC

| ❏ D-101 [M] | Sing with Seeger | 1964 | $25 |

EVEREST ARCHIVE OF FOLK & JAZZ

| ❏ 201 | Pete Seeger | 1966 | $15 |

FOLKWAYS

❏ FI-8371 [M]	12-String Guitar As Played by Leadbelly	1962	$25
❏ FA-2319 [M]	American Ballads	1957	$50
❏ FTS-31017 [R]	American Ballads	1968	$20
❏ FA-2320 [M]	American Favorite Ballads, Vol. 1	1957	$50
❏ FA-2321 [M]	American Favorite Ballads, Vol. 2	1958	$50
❏ FA-2322 [M]	American Favorite Ballads, Vol. 3	1958	$50
❏ FA-2323 [M]	American Favorite Ballads, Vol. 4	1961	$50
❏ FA-2445 [M]	American Favorite Ballads, Vol. 5: Tunes and Songs As Sung by Pete Seeger	1962	$50
❏ FP-701 [10]	American Folk Songs for Children	195?	$175
❏ FC-7601 [10]	American Folk Songs for Children	1953	$150
❏ FC-7674 [M]	American Game and Activity Songs for Children	1962	$25
❏ FH-5251 [M]	American Industrial Ballads	1956	$35
❏ FP-43 [10]	A Pete Seeger Sampler	195?	$175
❏ FA-2043 [10]	A Pete Seeger Sampler	1954	$150
❏ FH-5485 [M]	Ballads of Sacco and Vanzetti	1963	$35
❏ FTS-31040 [R]	Banks of Marble and Other Songs	1974	$25
❏ FW-6912 [10]	Bantu Choral Folk Songs	1955	$150
❏ FC-7611 [M]	Birds, Beasts, Bugs and Bigger Fishes	1954	$75
❏ FP-710 [10]	Birds, Beasts, Bugs and Little Fishes	1954	$120
❏ FC-7610 [10]	Birds, Beasts, Bugs and Little Fishes	1954	$150
❏ FH-5302 [M]	Broadside Ballads, Vol. 2	1963	$35
❏ FA-2456 [M]	Broadsides	1964	$30
❏ FH-5210 [M]	Champlain Valley Songs	1960	$40
❏ FP-3 [10]	Darling Corey	1950	$120
❏ FA-2003 [10]	Darling Corey	1950	$150
❏ FH-5257	Fifty Sail On Newburgh Bay	1976	$20
❏ FI-8354 [M]	Folksinger's Guitar Guide Vol. 1: An Instruction Record	1955	$35
❏ FP-911 [10]	Folk Songs of Four Continents	195?	$120
❏ FW-6911 [10]	Folk Songs of Four Continents	1955	$150
❏ 5003	Frontier Ballads	1954	$150
❏ FA-2175 [10]	Frontier Ballads, Volume 1	1954	$150
❏ FA-2176 [10]	Frontier Ballads, Volume 2	1954	$150
❏ FA-2501 [M]	Gazette, Vol. 1	1958	$50
❏ FA-2502 [M]	Gazette, Vol. 2	1962	$30
❏ FW-6843 [10]	German Folk Songs	1954	$150
❏ 37232	God Bless the Grass	1982	$15
❏ FP-45 [10]	Goofing Off Suite	195?	$120
❏ FA-2045 [10]	Goofing Off Suite	1954	$150
❏ FA-2450 [M]	Highlights of Pete Seeger at the Village Gate with Memphis Slim and Willie Dixon	1960	$50
❏ FN-2511 [M]	Hootenanny Tonight!	195?	$35
❏ FI-8303 [M]	How to Play the Five String Banjo	195?	$35
❏ FS-3851 [M]	Indian Summer	1960	$35

— *With Michael Seeger*

❏ FP-10 [10]	Lonesome Valley	195?	$120
❏ FA-2010 [10]	Lonesome Valley	195?	$150
❏ FA-2453 [M]	Love Songs for Friends and Foes	1956	$40
❏ FA-2439 [M]	Nonesuch	196?	$35
❏ FA-2412 [M]	Pete Seeger and Sonny Terry	1958	$35
❏ FA-2451 [M]	Pete Seeger at the Village Gate -- Vol. 2	1960	$35
❏ FH-5702	Pete Seeger Sings and Answers Questions	1968	$30
❏ FTS-31022 [R]	Pete Seeger Sings Leadbelly	1968	$15
❏ FTS-31002 [R]	Pete Seeger Sings Woody Guthrie	1968	$15
❏ FA-2454 [M]	Rainbow Quest	1960	$30
❏ FXM-36055	Sing Along	1980	$18
❏ FN-2513 [M]	Sing Out! Hootenanny	1963	$25
❏ FA-2455 [M]	Sing Out with Pete!	1961	$25
❏ FC-7526 [M]	Song and Play Time	195?	$50
❏ FH-5233 [M]	Songs of Struggle and Protest 1930-50	1959	$35

Number	Title	Yr	NM
❏ FH-5436 [M]	Songs of the Spanish Civil War, Vol. 1	1961	$35
❏ FC-7020 [10]	Songs to Grow On -- Vol. 2	1951	$150
❏ FC-7027 [10]	Songs to Grow On -- Vol. 3	1951	$150
❏ FQ-8354 [M]	The Folksinger's Guitar Gude	1955	$40
❏ FT-35001	The Nativity: By Sholem Asch	1963	$20
❏ FA-2311 [M]	Traditional Christmas Carols	1956	$30
❏ FTS-32311 [R]	Traditional Christmas Carols	1967	$20
❏ FTS-31018 [R]	Wimoweh and Other Songs of Freedom and Protest	1968	$15
❏ FA-2452 [M]	With Voices Together We Sing	1956	$30
❏ FH-5595 [M]	WNEW's Story of Selma	1965	$25
❏ 7527	Zhitkov's How I Hunted the Little Fellows	1980	$15

HARMONY

❏ HS11337	John Henry and Other Folk Favorites	1969	$15

ODYSSEY

❏ 32160266	3 Saints, 4 Sinners and 6 Other People	1968	$18

OLYMPIC

❏ 7102	America's Balladeer	1973	$15

PAIR

❏ PDL2-1076	Clearwater Classics	1986	$15

PHILIPS

❏ PHM 2-300 [M]	The Story of the Nativity	1963	$25
❏ PHS 2-300 [S]	The Story of the Nativity	1963	$30
❏ PHM 2-300 [M]	The Story of the Nativity	1963	$25
❏ PHS 2-300 [S]	The Story of the Nativity	1963	$30

SMITHSONIAN FOLKWAYS

❏ SF-40024	Traditional Christmas Carols	1989	$15

STINSON

❏ SLP-57 [10]	A Pete Seeger Concert	1953	$150
❏ SLP-52 [10]	Lincoln Brigade	1953	$150
❏ SLP-90 [10]	Pete	1963	$30

TRADITION

❏ 2107	Folk Music of the World	1973	$15

VANGUARD

❏ VSD-97/98	The Essential Pete Seeger	1978	$18
❏ VSD-73111	The Essential Pete Seeger, Vol. 1	198?	$10
❏ VSD-73112	The Essential Pete Seeger, Vol. 2	198?	$10

VERVE FOLKWAYS

❏ FV-9013 [M]	Folk Music Live at the Village Gate	1965	$30
❏ FVS-9013 [S]	Folk Music Live at the Village Gate	1965	$30
❏ FV-9020 [M]	Little Boxes and Other Broadsides	1965	$35
❏ FVS-9020 [S]	Little Boxes and Other Broadsides	1965	$35
❏ FV-9008 [M]	Pete Seeger and Big Bill Broonzy in Concert	1965	$25
❏ FVS-9008 [S]	Pete Seeger and Big Bill Broonzy in Concert	1965	$35
❏ FV-9009 [M]	Pete Seeger On Campus	1965	$30
❏ FVS-9009 [S]	Pete Seeger On Campus	1965	$30

WARNER BROS.

❏ BSK3329	Circles and Seasons	1979	$15

SEEKERS, THE

CAPITOL

❏ T2369 [M]	A World of Our Own	1965	$15
❏ DT2369 [R]	A World of Our Own	1965	$15
❏ T2431 [M]	Georgy Girl	1966	$25
❏ ST2431 [S]	Georgy Girl	1966	$18
❏ SM-2746 [P]	The Best of the Seekers	197?	$12
❏ SN-16104 [S]	The Best of the Seekers	1980	$10
❏ T2746 [M]	The Best of the Seekers	1967	$15
❏ ST2746 [S]	The Best of the Seekers	1967	$15

— *Red and white "target" Starline label; though the cover has an "ST" prefix, the record and trail-off wax have a "DT" prefix; "Morningtown Ride," "Turn, Turn, Turn," and "We're Moving On" are in stereo*

❏ ST2746 [P]	The Best of the Seekers	196?	$12

— *Red and white "star" Starline label*

❏ T2319 [M]	The New Seekers	1965	$15
❏ ST2319 [S]	The New Seekers	1965	$18
❏ ST-135 [S]	The Seekers Live	1969	$15
❏ SKAO2821 [S]	The Seekers Seen in Green	1968	$18
❏ KAO2821 [M]	The Seekers Seen in Green	1968	$75

MARVEL

❏ 2060 [M]	The Seekers	1965	$15
❏ 3060 [R]	The Seekers	1965	$12

SEELY, JEANNIE

DECCA

❏ DL75093	Jeannie Seely	1969	$18
❏ DL75228	Please Be My New Love	1970	$18

HARMONY

❏ KH31029	Make the World Go Away	1972	$15

MCA

❏ 385	Can I Sleep in Your Arms/ Lucky Ladies	1973	$15

Number	Title	Yr	NM
MONUMENT			
❏ KZ31911	Greatest Hits	1973	$18
❏ 6640	Greatest Hits	1977	$15

— *Reissue of 31911*

❏ SLP-18091	I'll Love You More	1968	$25
❏ SLP-18104	Little Things	1968	$25
❏ MLP-8073 [M]	Thanks, Hank!	1967	$30
❏ SLP-18073 [S]	Thanks, Hank!	1967	$25
❏ MLP-8057 [M]	The Seely Style	1966	$18

— *Title on label is "The Jeannie Seely Style*

❏ SLP-18057 [S]	The Seely Style	1966	$25

— *Title on label is "The Jeannie Seely Style*

SEGAL, GEORGE

PHILIPS

❏ PHM200242 [M]	The Yama-Yama Man	1967	$50
❏ PHS600242 [S]	The Yama-Yama Man	1967	$50

SIGNATURE

❏ BSL1-0654	A Touch of Ragtime	1976	$35

SEGALL, RICKY

BELL

❏ 1138	Ricky Segall and the Segalls	1973	$25

SEGER, BOB

CAPITOL

❏ SOO-12041	Against the Wind	1980	$12
❏ ST-11378	Beautiful Loser	1975	$12

— *Originals have orange labels*

❏ ST-11378	Beautiful Loser	1978	$10

— *Purple label with large Capitol logo*

❏ SN-16315	Beautiful Loser	1984	$10
❏ ST-731	Brand New Morning	1971	$150
❏ SPRO-8433 [DJ]	Consensus Cuts Edited for Airplay from "Live Bullet	1976	$30
❏ SPRO-8433 [DJ]	Consensus Cuts Edited for Airplay from "Live Bullet	1976	$30
❏ C1-30334	Greatest Hits	1994	$18
❏ C1-99774	It's a Mystery	1995	$0

— *Canceled*

❏ PT-12398	Like a Rock	1986	$12
❏ SKBB-11523	Live Bullet	1976	$18

— *Originals have orange labels*

❏ SKBB-11523	Live Bullet	1978	$15

— *Purple label with large Capitol logo*

❏ SKBB-11523	Live Bullet	1983	$15

— *Black label, print in colorband*

❏ STBK-11523	Live Bullet	1988	$15

— *Purple label with smaller Capitol logo*

❏ SKAO-499	Mongrel	1970	$30
❏ SM-499	Mongrel	1977	$10
❏ SN-16106	Mongrel	1980	$10
❏ ST-11557	Night Moves	1976	$12
❏ 0(no cat #) [PD]	Night Moves	1977	$40

— *Promo-only picture disc*

❏ STBK-12182	Nine Tonight	1981	$18
❏ ST-236	Noah	1969	$100
❏ ST-172 [B]	Ramblin' Gamblin' Man	1969	$50

— *Black label with colorband*

❏ SM-172	Ramblin' Gamblin' Man	1977	$10
❏ SN-16105	Ramblin' Gamblin' Man	1980	$10
❏ R124284	Ramblin' Gamblin' Man	197?	$25

— *Orange label, "Capitol"at bottom; RCA Music Service edition with B-side label error listing the title as "Ramblin' Bamblin' Man*

❏ ST-11748	Seven	1978	$12
❏ SN-16108	Seven	1980	$10
❏ ST-11746	Smokin' O.P.'s	1978	$12
❏ SN-16107	Smokin' O.P.'s	1980	$10
❏ SW-11698	Stranger in Town	1978	$12
❏ SEAX-11904 [PD]	Stranger in Town	1978	$30
❏ ST-12254	The Distance	1983	$12
❏ C1-91134	The Fire Inside	1991	$15

Number	Title	Yr	NM
MOBILE FIDELITY			
❏ 1-127	Against the Wind	1983	$50

— *Audiophile vinyl*

❏ Jan-0034 [B]	Night Moves	1980	$80

— *Audiophile vinyl*

PALLADIUM

❏ P-1006	Smokin' O.P.'s	1972	$30

REPRISE

❏ MS2126	Back in '72	1973	$75
❏ MS2184	Seven	1974	$25
❏ MS2109	Smokin' O.P.'s	1972	$18

SEGO BROTHERS AND NAOMI, THE

GOSPEL TIME

❏ 5007	From the Soul	196?	$30
❏ 5018	Gospel Concert Special	196?	$25

HARVEST

❏ 1001	Keeping It Gospel	196?	$30

HEART WARMING

❏ 3154	Featuring Naomi	1972	$30
❏ 3056	Happy Day	196?	$30
❏ 3433	It Will Be Different the Next Time	1976	$30
❏ 3144	Meetin' Time	1972	$30
❏ 3186	Sorry I Never Knew You	1972	$30
❏ 3206	The Dearest Friend I Ever Had	1973	$30
❏ 1955	This World Has Turned Me Down	196?	$30
❏ 3279	What a Happy Time	1974	$30
❏ 1952	With the Help of God	196?	$30

RUNA

❏ 1942	Completely Gospel	196?	$30
❏ 1941	Gospel Singing	196?	$30

SCRIPTURE

❏ 122	Far Above the Starry Skies	196?	$30
❏ 121	The Best of the Sego Brothers and Naomi	196?	$30

SILVER STAFF

❏ 15003	I Pray My Way Out of Trouble	196?	$30

SIMS

❏ 134	With the Help of God	196?	$40

SING

❏ 9092S [S]	One Day Late	196?	$40
❏ 9092M [M]	One Day Late	196?	$30
❏ 9091M [M]	Sego Brothers and Naomi	196?	$30
❏ 9091S [S]	Sego Brothers and Naomi	196?	$40

SONGS OF FAITH

❏ 150	Daddy Sang Bass	1969	$30
❏ 117	From the Soul	196?	$30
❏ 158	Golden Hits of the Sego Brothers and Naomi	1970	$30
❏ 141	Gospel Music On Stage with the Sego Brothers and Naomi	196?	$30
❏ 133	He'll Walk By Your Side	196?	$30
❏ 126	Hem of His Garment	196?	$30
❏ 143	I'm Longing for Home	196?	$30
❏ 103	Satisfied with Me	196?	$30
❏ 147	Somebody Touched Me	196?	$30
❏ 121	The Award Winning Sego Brothers and Naomi	196?	$30
❏ 168	The Sego Brothers and Naomi at Grandfather Mountain	197?	$30
❏ 156	The Sego Brothers and Naomi Featuring W.R. Sego	1969	$30
❏ 110	The Sego Brothers and Naomi Sing the Gospel	1963	$30
❏ 145	The Sego Brothers and Naomi Sing Weapon of Prayer	196?	$25
❏ 137	Will the Circle Be Unbroken	196?	$30

SUPREME

❏ 33003	I Pray My Way Out of Trouble	196?	$30

VISTA

❏ 1224	Old Time Singing	196?	$30

SEIFERT, ZBIGNIEW

CAPITOL

❏ ST-11618	Zbigniew Seifert	197?	$30

PAUSA

❏ 7077	Man of the Light	1979	$25

SELAH JUBILEE QUARTET, THE

REMINGTON

❏ 1023 [10]	Spirituals	1951	$250

SELECTER, THE

CHRYSALIS

❏ CHR1306	Celebrate the Bullet	1981	$12
❏ PV41306	Celebrate the Bullet	198?	$10

— *Reissue*

❏ CHR1274	Too Much Pressure	1980	$12
❏ PV41274	Too Much Pressure	1983	$10

— *Reissue*

Number	Title	Yr	NM

SELENA
CAPITOL/EMI LATIN

❏ H1-42299 [B]	16 Super Exitos Originales	1990	$100
❏ H1-42144 [B]	Selena Y Los Dinos	1989	$100
❏ H1-42359 [B]	Ven Conmingo	1990	$100

CBS DISCOS

❏ RRL80323 [B]	Personal Best	1990	$100

GP

❏ LP-1002	Alpha	1986	$500
❏ LP-1009	And the Winner Is…	1987	$250
❏ LP-1005	Menequito De Trapo	1986	$300

RP

❏ LP-8803	Dulce Amor	1988	$175
❏ LP-8801	Preciosa	1988	$175

SELLARS, MARILYN
KOALA

❏ 14154	Raised on Country Sunshine	198?	$12

MEGA

❏ MLPS-609	Gather Me	1974	$15
❏ MLPS-602	One Day at a Time	1974	$15

ZODIAC

❏ ZLP-5005	Marilyn	1977	$15
❏ ZLP-5001	One Day at a Time	1976	$15

SELLERS, BROTHER JOHN
VANGUARD

❏ VRS-9036 [M]	Blues and Folk Songs	1957	$120
❏ VRS-8005 [10]	Brother John Sellers: Folk Songs and Blues	1954	$150

SELLERS, PETER, AND SOPHIA LOREN
ANGEL

❏ 35910 [M]	Peter Sellers and Sophia Loren	1961	$40
❏ S35910 [S]	Peter Sellers and Sophia Loren	1961	$50

SELLERS, PETER
ACAPELLA

❏ 1 [B]	Fool Brittania	1963	$35

—With Joan Collins and Anthony Newley

ANGEL

❏ 35884 [M]	The Best of Sellers	1960	$30
❏ S35884 [S]	The Best of Sellers	1960	$40

EMI AMERICA

❏ SN-16396	Songs for Swingin' Sellers	1986	$25

—First American issue of 1959 U.K. LP

SEMBELLO, MICHAEL
A&M

❏ SP-5044	Without Walls	1986	$25

WARNER BROS.

❏ 23920	Bossa Nova Hotel	1983	$12

SENATOR BOBBY
PARKWAY

❏ P7057 [M]	Boston Soul with the Hardly-Worthit Players	1967	$25
❏ SP7057 [S]	Boston Soul with the Hardly-Worthit Players	1967	$25

SENENSKY, BERNIE
PM

❏ 021	Free Spirit	1986	$25
❏ 06	New Life	197?	$30

SENOFSKY, BERL
RCA VICTOR RED SEAL

❏ LSC-2488 [S]	Debussy: Violin Sonata; Faure: Violin Sonata No. 1 in A	1961	$40

—With Gary Graffman, piano; original with "shaded dog" label

SENSATIONS, THE
ARGO

❏ LP-4022 [M]	Let Me In/Music, Music, Music	1963	$500

SENTINALS, THE
DEL-FI

❏ DFLP-1232 [M]	Big Surf!	1963	$150
❏ DFST-1232 [S]	Big Surf!	1963	$175
❏ DLF1232	Big Surf!	1997	$15
❏ DFLP-1241 [M]	Surfer Girl	1963	$80
❏ DFST-1241 [S]	Surfer Girl	1963	$150
❏ DLF1241	Surfer Girl	1997	$15

SUTTON

❏ SU-338 [M]	Vegas Go-Go	1964	$40
❏ SSU-338 [S]	Vegas Go-Go	1964	$50

SERENDIPITY SINGERS, THE
PHILIPS

❏ PHM200190 [M]	Love, Lies and Flying Festoons	1965	$18
❏ PHS600190 [S]	Love, Lies and Flying Festoons	1965	$25
❏ PHM200151 [M]	Take Your Shoes Off with the Serendipity Singers	1964	$18
❏ PHS600151 [S]	Take Your Shoes Off with the Serendipity Singers	1964	$25
❏ PHM200134 [M]	The Many Sides of the Serendipity Singers	1964	$18
❏ PHS600134 [S]	The Many Sides of the Serendipity Singers	1964	$25
❏ PHM200115 [M]	The Serendipity Singers	1964	$18
❏ PHS600115 [S]	The Serendipity Singers	1964	$25
❏ PHM200180 [M]	We Belong Together	1965	$18
❏ PHS600180 [S]	We Belong Together	1965	$25

SERPENT POWER
VANGUARD

❏ VRS-9252 [M]	Serpent Power	1967	$300
❏ VSD-79252 [S]	Serpent Power	1967	$180

SERRANO, PAUL
RIVERSIDE

❏ RLP-359 [M]	Blues Holiday	1961	$250
❏ RS-9359 [S]	Blues Holiday	1961	$250

SERRY, JOHN
CHRYSALIS

❏ CHS1279	Jazziz	1979	$25

SERTL, DOUG
DISCOVERY

❏ 920	Groovin'	1986	$25

SESSIONS, RONNIE
MCA

❏ 2285	Ronnie Sessions	1977	$12

SETE, BOLA
ANALOGUE PRODUCTIONS

❏ APR3003	Tour de Force	199?	$35

COLUMBIA

❏ KC32375	Goin' to Rio	1973	$30

DANCING CAT

❏ DC-3005	Jungle Suite	1985	$30

FANTASY

❏ OJC-290	Autentico!	1987	$25
❏ 3375 [M]	Autentico!	1966	$35
❏ 8375 [S]	Autentico!	1966	$25
❏ OJC-286	Bossa Nova	1987	$25
❏ 3349 [M]	Bossa Nova	1963	$35
❏ 8349 [S]	Bossa Nova	1963	$25
❏ 8417	Shebaba	1971	$15
❏ OJC-288	The Incomparable Bola Sete	1987	$25
❏ 3364 [M]	The Incomparable Bola Sete	1965	$35
❏ 8364 [S]	The Incomparable Bola Sete	1965	$25
❏ 3369 [M]	The Solo Guitar of Bola Sete	1966	$35
❏ 8369 [S]	The Solo Guitar of Bola Sete	1966	$25
❏ 7358 [S]	Tour de Force	1965	$50
❏ 3358 [M]	Tour de Force	1965	$35

LOST LAKE ARTS

❏ LL-82	Ocean	1981	$25

—Reissue of Takoma LP

PARAMOUNT

❏ PAS-5011	Workin' on a Groovy Thing	1970	$35

TAKOMA

❏ C-1049	Ocean	1975	$30

VERVE

❏ V-8689 [M]	Bola Sete At the Monterey Jazz Festival	1967	$25
❏ V6-8689 [S]	Bola Sete At the Monterey Jazz Festival	1967	$35

SETTLE, MIKE
REPRISE

❏ R-6149 [M]	The Mike Settle Shindig	1965	$25
❏ RS-6149 [S]	The Mike Settle Shindig	1965	$30

SETZER, BRIAN
Also see STRAY CATS.
EMI AMERICA

❏ ST-17178	The Knife Feels Like Justice	1986	$12
❏ ST-517178	The Knife Feels Like Justice	1986	$15

—Columbia House edition

EMI MANHATTAN

❏ E1-46963	Live Nude Guitars	1988	$15

INTERSCOPE

❏ 90183	The Dirty Boogie	1998	$35

—As "The Brian Setzer Orchestra

SURFDOG

❏ 67124	Ignition!	2001	$35

—As "Brian Setzer '68 Comeback Special"; red vinyl

SEVEN BLENDS, THE
ROULETTE

❏ R-25172 [M]	Twistin' at the Miami Beach Peppermint Lounge	1962	$25
❏ SR-25172 [S]	Twistin' at the Miami Beach Peppermint Lounge	1962	$30

SEVENTH AVENUE
I.T.I.

❏ JL-022	Heads Up	1986	$30

SEVENTH AVENUE STOMPERS
SAVOY JAZZ

❏ SJL-1139	Fidgety Feet	198?	$25

SEVENTH SONS, THE
ESP-DISK'

❏ 1078	The Seventh Sons	1967	$75

SEVENTH WAVE, THE
JANUS

❏ 7021	Psi-Fi	1975	$25
❏ 7008	Things to Come	1974	$25

SEVERINSON, DOC
ABC

❏ S-737 [B]	16 Great Performances	1971	$15
❏ X-771	Trumpets, Crumpets	1973	$25

AMHERST

❏ AMH-3319	Facets	1988	$25
❏ AMH-3311	The Tonight Show Band with Doc Severinson	1986	$25
❏ AMH-3312	The Tonight Show Band with Doc Severinson, Vol. II	1987	$25

COMMAND

❏ RS 33-904 [M]	Command Performances	1966	$30
❏ RS904SD [S]	Command Performances	1966	$35
❏ RS937SD	Doc Severinson with Strings	1969	$30
❏ RS 33-893 [M]	Fever!	1966	$30
❏ RS893SD [S]	Fever!	1966	$35
❏ QD-40003 [Q]	Fever!	1972	$40
❏ RS 33-883 [M]	High, Wide and Wonderful	1965	$35
❏ RS883SD [S]	High, Wide and Wonderful	1965	$50
❏ RS 33-901 [M]	Live!	1966	$30
❏ RS901SD [S]	Live!	1966	$35
❏ RS 33-909 [M]	Swinging and Singing	1967	$35
❏ RS909SD [S]	Swinging and Singing	1967	$30
❏ RS 33-819 [M]	Tempestuous Trumpet	1961	$25
❏ RS819SD [S]	Tempestuous Trumpet	1961	$50
❏ RS952SD	The Best of Doc Severinson	1970	$30
❏ RS 33-837 [M]	The Big Band's Back in Town	1962	$35
❏ RS837SD [S]	The Big Band's Back in Town	1962	$50
❏ RS950SD	The Closet	1970	$30
❏ RS927SD	The Great Arrival	1968	$30
❏ RS 33-917 [M]	The New Sound	1967	$35
❏ RS917SD [S]	The New Sound	1967	$30
❏ RS 33-859 [M]	Torch Songs for Trumpet	1963	$35
❏ RS859SD [S]	Torch Songs for Trumpet	1963	$25

EPIC

❏ PE34925	A Brand New Thing	1977	$25
❏ PE34078	Night Journey	1976	$25

EVEREST ARCHIVE OF FOLK & JAZZ

❏ 334	Doc Severinson and Friends	1978	$25

FIRSTLINE

❏ FDLP5001	London Sessions	1980	$30

JUNO

❏ 1001	I Feel Good	1970	$30

MCA

❏ 4168	The Best of Doc Severinson	198?	$25

PICKWICK

❏ SPC3627	Tempestuous Trumpet	1978	$20
❏ SPC-3608	Torch Songs for Trumpet	1978	$20

RCA VICTOR

❏ LSP-4522	Brass Roots	1971	$30
❏ LSP-4669	Doc	1972	$30
❏ AFL1-4669	Doc	1977	$25

—Reissue with new prefix

❏ APL1-0273	Rhapsody for Now!	1973	$30

SEVERSON, PAUL
ACADEMY

❏ MWJ-1 [M]	Midwest Jazz	1956	$50

SEVILLA, JORGE
VERVE

❏ MGV-8342 [M]	The Incredible Guitar of Jorge Sevilla	1959	$175
❏ MGVS-6103 [S]	The Incredible Guitar of Jorge Sevilla	1960	$150
❏ V-8342 [M]	The Incredible Guitar of Jorge Sevilla	1961	$30
❏ V6-8342 [S]	The Incredible Guitar of Jorge Sevilla	1961	$25

SEVILLE, DAVID
LIBERTY

❏ LRP-3073 [M]	The Music of David Seville	1957	$150
❏ LRP-3092 [M]	The Witch Doctor	1958	$120

Number	Title	Yr	NM

SEWARD, ALEC
BLUESVILLE
| ❏ BVLP-1076 [M] | Creepin' Blues | 1963 | $100 |

— Blue label, silver print
| ❏ BVLP-1076 [M] | Creepin' Blues | 1964 | $30 |

— Blue label, trident logo at right

SEX CLARK FIVE
BLOOD MONEY
| ❏ ERATO59 | Battle of Sex Clark Five | 1989 | $25 |
RECORDS TO RUSSIA
| ❏ LP408 | Strum & Drum! | 1986 | $120 |

— Test pressing with 24 tracks
| ❏ LP408 | Strum & Drum! | 1987 | $25 |

— First pressing: 20 tracks, photos are halftones
| ❏ LP408 | Strum & Drum! | 1987 | $18 |

— Second pressing: 20 tracks, no halftones, different back photo
SKYCLAD
| ❏ (NOT) BM131 [B] | Antedium | 1992 | $25 |

SEX PISTOLS
Johnny Rotten would later join Public Image Ltd.
RESTLESS
❏ 72255 [B]	Better Live Than Dead	1988	$25
❏ 72511 [B]	Live at Chelmsford Top Security Prison	1990	$25
❏ 72257	The Ex-Pistols: The Swindle Continues	1988	$15
❏ 72256 [EP]	The Mini-Album	1988	$15
RHINO/WARNER BROS.
| ❏ 3147 [B] | Never Mind the Bollocks Here's the Sex Pistols | 2008 | $25 |
SKYCLAD
| ❏ SEX6 [B] | We've Cum For Your Children | 1988 | $25 |
WARNER BROS.
| ❏ BSK3147 [B] | Never Mind the Bollocks Here's the Sex Pistols | 1978 | $50 |

— With sticker "Contains Sub-Mission"
| ❏ BSK3147 [B] | Never Mind the Bollocks Here's the Sex Pistols | 1978 | $30 |

— Any other version with custom label
| ❏ BSK3147 [B] | Never Mind the Bollocks Here's the Sex Pistols | 1978 | $25 |

— With white WB label

SEYMOUR, PHIL
BOARDWALK
| ❏ FW36996 | Phil Seymour | 1980 | $15 |
| ❏ NB1-33252 | Phil Seymour 2 | 1982 | $18 |

SHA NA NA
ACCORD
| ❏ SN-7115 | Remember Then | 1981 | $12 |
| ❏ SN-7146 | Sh-Boom | 1981 | $12 |
BUDDAH
| ❏ BDM-5692 | Rock & Roll Is Here to Stay! | 1978 | $12 |
| ❏ BDM-5703 | The Best of Sha Na Na | 1978 | $12 |
EMUS
| ❏ ES-12037 | On Stage | 1978 | $12 |
KAMA SUTRA
❏ KSBS-2075	From the Streets of New York	1973	$18
❏ KSBS-2600	Hot Sox	1974	$18
❏ KSBS-2010	Rock & Roll Is Here to Stay!	1969	$18
❏ KSBS-2077	Rock & Roll Is Here to Stay!	1974	$18
❏ KSBS-2034	Sha Na Na	1971	$18
❏ KSBS-2605	Sha Na Now	1975	$18
❏ KSBS-2609	The Best…Sha Na Na	1976	$18
❏ KSBS-2073	The Golden Age of Rock 'n' Roll	1973	$25
❏ KSBS-2050	The Night Is Still Young	1972	$18
NASHVILLE
| ❏ NR-12348-122 | Rockin' in the 80's | 1980 | $15 |
REALM
| ❏ 2V8058 | All-Time Greatest Rock 'n' Roll Hits | 1977 | $18 |
| ❏ 1V8059 | Rock 'n' Roll Dance Party | 1977 | $15 |

SHACKLEFORDS, THE
CAPITOL
| ❏ T2450 [M] | The Shacklefords | 1966 | $25 |
| ❏ ST2450 [S] | The Shacklefords | 1966 | $30 |
MERCURY
| ❏ MG-20806 [M] | Until You've Heard the Shacklefords | 1963 | $25 |
| ❏ SR-60806 [S] | Until You've Heard the Shacklefords | 1963 | $30 |

SHADES OF BLUE
IMPACT
| ❏ IM-101 [M] | Happiness Is the Shades of Blue | 1966 | $100 |
| ❏ IM-1001 [S] | Happiness Is the Shades of Blue | 1966 | $75 |

SHADES OF JOY
FONTANA
| ❏ SRF-67592 | Shades of Joy | 1969 | $25 |

SHADOW PROJECT
LIVELY ART
| ❏ ARTY37 [B] | Shadow Project | 1991 | $40 |

SHADOWS, THE (1)
ATLANTIC
| ❏ 8084 [M] | Out of the Shadows | 1962 | $250 |

— Canada-only release?
❏ 8089 [M]	Surfing with the Shadows	1963	$175
❏ SD8089 [S]	Surfing with the Shadows	1963	$300
❏ 8097 [M]	The Shadows Know	1964	$150
❏ SD8097 [S]	The Shadows Know	1964	$250

SHADOWS OF KNIGHT, THE
DUNWICH
❏ 667 [M]	Back Door Men	1966	$75
❏ S-667 [S]	Back Door Men	1966	$100
❏ 666 [M]	Gloria	1966	$100
❏ S-666 [S]	Gloria	1966	$150
SUNDAZED
| ❏ LP5035 | Back Door Men | 1999 | $15 |

— Reissue on 180-gram vinyl
| ❏ LP5034 | Gloria | 1999 | $15 |

— Reissue on 180-gram vinyl
| ❏ LP5006 | Raw and Live at the Cellar 1966 | 1992 | $12 |
SUPER K
| ❏ SKS-6002 | The Shadows of Knight | 1969 | $50 |

SHADRACK
IGL
| ❏ 132 | Chameleon | 1971 | $300 |

SHAFRAN, DANIEL
RCA VICTOR RED SEAL
| ❏ LSC-2553 [S] | Shostakovich: Cello Sonata; Schubert: Arpeggione Sonata | 1961 | $120 |

— Original with "shaded dog" label

SHAGGS, THE (2)
MCM
| ❏ 1295 [B] | Wink | 1967 | $300 |

— No number on label -- this number is found in the trail-off wax on each side

SHAGGS, THE (3)
ROUNDER
| ❏ 3032 | Philosophy of the World | 1980 | $30 |
| ❏ 3056 | Shaggs' Own Thing | 1982 | $30 |
THIRD WORLD
| ❏ 3001 | Philosophy of the World | 1969 | $2000 |

SHAGGY
MCA
| ❏ 112096 | Hotshot | 2000 | $18 |
| ❏ 112827 | Hotshot Ultramix | 2002 | $18 |
VIRGIN
| ❏ 44487 | Midnite Lover | 1997 | $15 |

SHAKATAK
POLYDOR
| ❏ 823017-1 | Drivin' Hard | 1987 | $25 |
| ❏ 839578-1 | Manic and Cool | 1989 | $30 |

SHAKERS, THE
AUDIO FIDELITY
| ❏ AFLP-2155 [M] | The Shakers Break It All | 1966 | $40 |
| ❏ AFSD-6155 [S] | The Shakers Break It All | 1966 | $50 |

SHAKEY JAKE
BLUESVILLE
| ❏ BVLP-1008 [M] | Good Times | 1960 | $120 |

— Blue label, silver print
| ❏ BVLP-1008 [M] | Good Times | 1964 | $30 |

— Blue label, trident logo at right
| ❏ BVLP-1027 [M] | Mouth Harp Blues | 1961 | $120 |

— Blue label, silver print
| ❏ BVLP-1027 [M] | Mouth Harp Blues | 1964 | $30 |

— Blue label, trident logo at right
WORLD PACIFIC
| ❏ WPS-21886 | Blues Makers | 196? | $30 |

SHAKEY VICK
JANUS
| ❏ JLS-3000 [B] | Little Woman, You're So Sweet | 1970 | $30 |

SHALAMAR
SOLAR
❏ BXL1-3479	Big Fun	1979	$15
❏ ST-72556	Circumstantial Evidence	1987	$12
❏ BXL1-2895	Disco Gardens	1978	$18
❏ S-28	Friends	1982	$12
❏ BXL1-3984	Go For It	1981	$15
❏ BXL1-4262	Greatest Hits	1982	$15
❏ 60385	Heart Break	1984	$12
❏ 60239	The Look	1983	$12
❏ BZL1-3577	Three for Love	1980	$12
❏ Z75315	Wake Up	1990	$15
SOUL TRAIN
| ❏ BVL1-2289 | Uptown Festival | 1977 | $18 |

SHAM 69
SIRE
| ❏ SRK-6060 | Tell Us the Truth | 1978 | $18 |

SHANGRI-LAS, THE
COLLECTABLES
| ❏ COL-5011 | Remember…Their Greatest Hits | 198? | $12 |
MERCURY
| ❏ MG-21099 [M] | The Shangri-Las' Golden Hits | 1966 | $75 |
| ❏ SR-61099 [S] | The Shangri-Las' Golden Hits | 1966 | $100 |
POLYDOR
| ❏ 824807-1 | Golden Hits of the Shangri-Las | 1985 | $12 |
POST
| ❏ 4000 | The Shangri-Las Sing | 196? | $25 |
RED BIRD
| ❏ 20104 [M] | I Can Never Go Home Anymore | 1966 | $175 |

— Retitled version with title song added and "Sophisticated Boom Boom" dropped
| ❏ 20101 [M] | Leader of the Pack | 1965 | $250 |
| ❏ 20104 [M] | Shangri-Las '65 | 1965 | $250 |

SHANK, BUD
BAINBRIDGE
| ❏ CRS-6830 | Live at the Haig | 1985 | $25 |
CONCORD CONCERTO
| ❏ CC-2002 | Explorations 1980: Suite for Flute and Piano | 1981 | $25 |
CONCORD JAZZ
❏ CJ-126	Crystal Comments	1980	$25
❏ CJ-58	Heritage	1979	$30
❏ CJ-20	Sunshine Express	1976	$30
CONTEMPORARY
❏ C-14027	Bud Shank at Jazz Alley	1987	$25
❏ C-14012	California Concert	1985	$25
❏ C-14031	Serious Swingers	1988	$25

— With the Bill Perkins Quartet
| ❏ C-14019 | That Old Feeling | 1986 | $25 |
| ❏ C-14048 | Tomorrow's Rainbow | 1989 | $25 |
CROWN
| ❏ CLP-5311 [M] | Bud Shank | 1963 | $35 |
| ❏ CST-311 [R] | Bud Shank | 1963 | $30 |
KIMBERLY
| ❏ 2025 [M] | The Talents of Bud Shank | 1963 | $25 |
| ❏ 11025 [S] | The Talents of Bud Shank | 1963 | $30 |
MUSE
| ❏ 5309 | This Bud's for You | 198? | $25 |
NOCTURNE
| ❏ NLP-2 [10] | Compositions of Shorty Rogers | 1953 | $250 |
PACIFIC JAZZ
❏ PJ-58 [M]	Bossa Nova Jazz Samba	1962	$30
❏ ST-58 [S]	Bossa Nova Jazz Samba	1962	$30
❏ PJ-64 [M]	Brassamba Bossa Nova	1963	$25
❏ ST-64 [S]	Brassamba Bossa Nova	1963	$30
❏ PJLP-20 [10]	Bud Shank and Bob Brookmeyer	1954	$120
❏ PJ-89 [M]	Bud Shank and His Brazilian Friends	1965	$25
❏ ST-89 [S]	Bud Shank and His Brazilian Friends	1965	$30
❏ PJ-10110 [M]	Bud Shank and the Sax Section	1966	$35
❏ ST-20110 [S]	Bud Shank and the Sax Section	1966	$25
❏ LN-10091	Bud Shank and the Sax Section	198?	$25
❏ PJ-4 [M]	Bud Shank Plays Tenor	1960	$30
❏ ST-4 [S]	Bud Shank Plays Tenor	1960	$30
❏ PJ-1205 [M]	Bud Shank/Shorty Rogers	1955	$100
❏ PJLP-14 [10]	Bud Shank with Three Trombones	1954	$120
❏ PJ-1226 [M]	Flute 'n Oboe	1957	$75
❏ PJ-1219 [M]	Jazz at Cal-Tech	1956	$75

Number	Title	Yr	NM
❏ PJ-21 [M]	New Groove	1961	$30
❏ ST-21 [S]	New Groove	1961	$30
❏ PJ-1213 [M]	Strings and Trombones	1956	$100
❏ PJ-1215 [M]	The Bud Shank Quartet	1956	$100
❏ PJ-1230 [M]	The Bud Shank Quartet	1957	$75
❏ PJM-411 [M]	The Swing's to TV	1957	$75
❏ ST-20157	Windmills of Your Mind	1969	$35

SUNSET
❏ SUM-1132 [M]	I Hear Music	1967	$50
❏ SUS-5132 [S]	I Hear Music	1967	$30

WORLD PACIFIC
❏ ST-21868	A Spoonful of Jazz	1968	$150
❏ WP-1855 [M]	Brazil! Brazil! Brazil!	1967	$150
❏ ST-21855 [S]	Brazil! Brazil! Brazil!	1967	$150
❏ WP-1864 [M]	Bud Shank Plays Music from Today's Movies	1967	$150
❏ ST-21864 [S]	Bud Shank Plays Music from Today's Movies	1967	$150
❏ WP-1205 [M]	Bud Shank/Shorty Rogers	1958	$175
❏ WP-1845 [M]	California Dreaming	1966	$150
❏ ST-21845 [S]	California Dreaming	1966	$150
❏ WP-1827 [M]	Flute, Oboe and Strings	1965	$150
❏ ST-21827 [S]	Flute, Oboe and Strings	1965	$150
❏ WP-1286 [M]	Flute 'n Alto	1960	$150
❏ ST-1286 [S]	Flute 'n Alto	1960	$175
❏ WP-1226 [M]	Flute 'n Oboe	1958	$175
❏ WP-1819 [M]	Folk 'n Flute	1965	$150
❏ ST-21819 [S]	Folk 'n Flute	1965	$150
❏ WP-1853 [M]	Girl in Love	1967	$150
❏ ST-21853 [S]	Girl in Love	1967	$150
❏ WP-1259 [M]	Holiday in Brazil	1959	$175
❏ ST-1018 [S]	Holiday in Brazil	1959	$150
❏ WP-1251 [M]	I'll Take Romance	1958	$175
❏ WP-1416 [M]	Improvisations	1961	$150
❏ WP-1219 [M]	Jazz at Cal-Tech	1958	$175
❏ WP-1299 [M]	Koto 'n Flute	1960	$150
❏ ST-1299 [S]	Koto 'n Flute	1960	$175
❏ WP-1424 [M]	Koto 'n Flute	1962	$150
❏ WP-1281 [M]	Latin Contrasts	1959	$175
❏ ST-1281 [S]	Latin Contrasts	1959	$150
❏ ST-20170	Let It Be	1970	$150
❏ ST-21873	Magical Mystery Tour	1968	$150
❏ WP-1840 [M]	Michelle	1966	$150
❏ ST-21840 [S]	Michelle	1966	$150
❏ WP-1215 [M]	The Bud Shank Quartet	1958	$175
❏ WP-1230 [M]	The Bud Shank Quartet	1958	$175
❏ WPM-411 [M]	The Swing's to TV	1958	$175
❏ ST-1002 [S]	The Swing's to TV	1959	$150
❏ PJM-411 [M]	The Swing's to TV	1958	$175

SHANK, BUD/CHET BAKER

KIMBERLY
❏ 2016 [M]	Swinging Soundtrack	1963	$25
❏ 11016 [S]	Swinging Soundtrack	1963	$30

SHANKAR, ANANDA

REPRISE
❏ RS-6398	Ananda Shankar	1970	$25

SHANKAR, L.

ZAPPA
❏ SRZ-1-1602	Touch Me There	1979	$25

SHANKAR, RAVI

ANGEL
❏ S36806	Concerto for Sitar and Orchestra	1972	$15
❏ 35468 [M]	Music of India	196?	$30
❏ DS-37935	Raga-Mala (Sitar Concert No. 2)	1983	$12
❏ DS-37920	Raga Mishra Piloo	1982	$12
❏ 36418 [M]	West Meets East	1967	$30
— With Yahudi Menuhin			
❏ S36418 [S]	West Meets East	1967	$25
— With Yahudi Menuhin			
❏ S36026 [S]	West Meets East, Vol. 2	1968	$18

APPLE
❏ SWAO-3384	Raga	1971	$30
❏ SVBB-3396	Ravi Shankar In Concert	1973	$40

BLUESVILLE
❏ BVLP-1078 [M]	The Master Musician of India	1964	$30

CAPITOL
❏ T10497 [M]	Exotic Sitar and Sarod	196?	$25
❏ ST10497 [S]	Exotic Sitar and Sarod	196?	$30
❏ SP-10561	Raga Parameshwari	1972	$15
❏ ST10504	Ravi	196?	$18
❏ T2720 [M]	Three Ragas	1967	$25
❏ DT2720 [R]	Three Ragas	1967	$18
❏ T10482 [M]	Two Raga Moods	196?	$25
❏ ST10482 [S]	Two Raga Moods	196?	$30

COLUMBIA
❏ OS3230	Chappaqua	1968	$18
❏ CL2496 [M]	Sounds of India	1966	$18
❏ CS9296 [S]	Sounds of India	1966	$25
❏ CL2760 [M]	The Genius of Ravi Shankar	1967	$35
❏ CS9560 [S]	The Genius of Ravi Shankar	1967	$18
❏ WL119 [M]	The Sounds of India	196?	$30

DARK HORSE
❏ SP22007	Music Festival from India	1975	$15
❏ SP22002	Shankar Family and Friends	1974	$15

DEUTCHE GRAMMOPHON
❏ 2531356	Homage to Mahatma Gandhi; Homage to Baba Allauddin	198?	$12
❏ 2531381	Pad Hasapa, for Koto; etc.	198?	$12
❏ 2531280	Raga Jogeshwari	198?	$12
❏ 2531216	Ragas Hameer & Gara	198?	$12

FANTASY
❏ 24714	Ragas	1973	$18

ORIENTAL
❏ BGRP-108	Raga Sanjh Kalyan	198?	$12

PRIVATE MUSIC
❏ 2044-1-P	Inside the Kremlin	1989	$12
❏ 2016-1-P	The Shankar Project: Tana Mana	1988	$12

SPARK
❏ 06	Transmigration Macabre	1973	$15

WORLD PACIFIC
❏ ST-21454	Charly	1969	$18
❏ WPS-26201	His Festival from India	1968	$25
❏ WP-1422 [M]	India's Master Musician	1965	$18
❏ ST-21422 [S]	India's Master Musician	1965	$25
❏ ST-21464	Morning Raga/Evening Raga	1970	$18
❏ WP-1432 [M]	Portrait of Genius	1966	$18
❏ ST-21432 [S]	Portrait of Genius	1966	$25
❏ WP-1431 [M]	Ragas and Talas	1966	$18
❏ ST-21431 [S]	Ragas and Talas	1966	$25
❏ WP-1442 [M]	Ravi Shankar at the Monterey International Pop Festival	1967	$25
❏ ST-21442 [S]	Ravi Shankar at the Monterey International Pop Festival	1967	$25
❏ ST-21467	Ravi Shankar at Woodstock	1970	$18
❏ WP-1421 [M]	Ravi Shankar In Concert	1965	$18
❏ ST-21421 [S]	Ravi Shankar In Concert	1965	$25
❏ WP-1430 [M]	Ravi Shankar In London	1966	$18
❏ ST-21430 [S]	Ravi Shankar In London	1966	$25
❏ WP-1441 [M]	Ravi Shankar in New York	1967	$18
❏ ST-21441 [S]	Ravi Shankar in New York	1967	$25
❏ ST-21449	Ravi Shankar in San Francisco	1968	$25
❏ WP-1434 [M]	Sound of the Sitar	1967	$18
❏ ST-21434 [S]	Sound of the Sitar	1967	$25
❏ WP-1438 [M]	Three Ragas	1967	$18
❏ ST-21438 [S]	Three Ragas	1967	$25

SHANKAR

ECM
❏ 25016	Song for Everyone	1985	$25
❏ 25039	The Epidemics	1986	$25
❏ 25004	Vision	1985	$25
❏ 1195	Who's to Know	198?	$30

SHANNON, DEL

AMY
❏ 8006 [M]	1,661 Seconds with Del Shannon	1965	$50
❏ S-8006 [S]	1,661 Seconds with Del Shannon	1965	$100
❏ 8004 [M]	Del Shannon Sings Hank Williams	1965	$50
❏ S-8004 [S]	Del Shannon Sings Hank Williams	1965	$100
❏ 8003 [M]	Handy Man	1964	$50
❏ S-8003 [S]	Handy Man	1964	$100

BIG TOP
❏ 12-1308 [M]	Little Town Flirt	1963	$175
❏ 12-1308 [B]	Little Town Flirt	1963	$1000
—One side is mono, one side is stereo; should be played to identify			
❏ 12-1308 [S]	Little Town Flirt	1963	$1500
—Stereo copies are not identified as such on either cover or label; some, but not all, copies have an "S" in the dead wax. Playing is the best way to identify.			
❏ 12-1303 [M]	Runaway	1961	$300
❏ 12-1303 [S]	Runaway	1961	$1600

DOT
❏ DLP3824 [M]	The Best of Del Shannon	1967	$50
❏ DLP25824 [R]	The Best of Del Shannon	1967	$40

ELEKTRA
❏ 5E-568	Drop Down and Get Me	1981	$12

LIBERTY
❏ LRP-3539 [M]	The Further Adventures of Charles Westover	1967	$50
❏ LST-7539 [S]	The Further Adventures of Charles Westover	1967	$100
❏ LRP-3453 [M]	This Is My Bag	1966	$30
❏ LST-7453 [S]	This Is My Bag	1966	$40
❏ LRP-3479 [M]	Total Commitment	1966	$30
❏ LST-7479 [S]	Total Commitment	1966	$40

PICKWICK
❏ SPC-3595 [R]	The Best of Del Shannon	197?	$12

POST
❏ 9000 [R]	Del Shannon Sings	196?	$40

RHINO
❏ RNLP-71056 [M]	Runaway Hits	1986	$12

SIRE
❏ SASH-3708 [P]	The Vintage Years	1975	$30

TWIRL
❏ 5001 [M]	Del Shannon's Greatest Hits	196?	$250
—LP was never issued; price is for front cover slick, which is known to exist			

UNITED ARTISTS
❏ UA-LA151-E	Del Shannon Live in England	1973	$30

SHANNON, HUGH

ATLANTIC
❏ ALS-406 [10]	Hugh Shannon Sings	195?	$150

SHANTY BOYS, THE

ELEKTRA
❏ EKL-142 [M]	Off-Beat Folk Songs	1958	$30

SHAPIRO, HELEN

EPIC
❏ LN24075 [M]	A Teenager in Love	1962	$40
❏ BN26075 [S]	A Teenager in Love	1962	$40

SHARKEY, FEARGAL

A&M
❏ SP6-5108	Feargal Sharkey	1985	$12

VIRGIN
❏ 90895	Wish	1988	$12

SHARKS

MCA
❏ 351	First Water	1973	$18
❏ 415	Jab It in Your Eye	1974	$18

SHARON, RALPH

ARGO
❏ LP-635 [M]	2:38 A.M.	1958	$40

BETHLEHEM
❏ BCP-13 [M]	Mr. & Mrs. Jazz	1955	$300
❏ BCP-41 [M]	Ralph Sharon Trio	1956	$300

COLUMBIA
❏ CL2321 [M]	Do I Hear a Waltz?	1965	$30
❏ CS9121 [S]	Do I Hear a Waltz?	1965	$30

GORDY
❏ G-903 [M]	Modern Innovations on Country & Western Themes	1963	$250

LONDON
❏ LB-842 [10]	Autumn Leaves	1954	$50
❏ LL1488 [M]	Easy Jazz	1956	$40
❏ LB-733 [10]	Spring Fever	1953	$50
❏ LL1339 [M]	Spring Fever/Autumn Leaves	1955	$50

RAMA
❏ RLP-1001 [M]	Jazz Around the World	1957	$50

SHARP, DEE DEE, AND CHUBBY CHECKER

CAMEO
❏ C-1029 [M]	Down to Earth	1962	$40
❏ SC-1029 [S]	Down to Earth	1962	$50

SHARP, DEE DEE

CAMEO
❏ C-2002 [M]	18 Golden Hits	1964	$40
❏ SC-2002 [S]	18 Golden Hits	1964	$50
❏ C-1027 [M]	All the Hits	1962	$40
❏ SC-1027 [S]	All the Hits	1962	$50
❏ C-1032 [M]	All the Hits, Vol. 2	1963	$40
❏ SC-1032 [S]	All the Hits, Vol. 2	1963	$50
❏ C-1062 [M]	Biggest Hits	1963	$40
❏ C-1050 [M]	Do the Bird	1963	$40
❏ SC-1050 [S]	Do the Bird	1963	$50
❏ C-1074 [M]	Down Memory Lane	1963	$40
❏ C-1018 [M]	It's Mashed Potato Time	1962	$75
❏ C-1022 [M]	Songs of Faith	1962	$40
❏ SC-1022 [S]	Songs of Faith	1962	$50

PHILADELPHIA INT'L.
❏ JZ36370	Dee Dee	1980	$12
❏ PZ33839	Happy 'Bout the Whole Thing	1976	$12
❏ PZ34437	What Color Is Love	1977	$12

SHARP, RANDY

NAUTILUS
❏ NR-1	First in Line	1980	$40
— Standard cover			
❏ NR-1	First in Line	1980	$50
— Styrofoam cover			

SHARPE, RAY

AWARD
❏ LMP-711 [M]	Welcome Back, Linda Lu	1964	$120

SHARPE, SUNDAY

UNITED ARTISTS
❏ UA-LA362-G	I'm Having Your Baby	1975	$15

Number	Title	Yr	NM
SHARROCK, SONNY			
4 MEN WITH BEARDS			
❏ 4M103LP [B]	Black Woman		$25
VORTEX			
❏ 2014	Black Woman	1970	$25
SHATNER, WILLIAM			
CLEOPATRA			
❏ 7062 [B]	Seeking Major Tom		$75
DECCA			
❏ DL5043 [M]	The Transformed Man	1969	$175
— Mono is white label promo only; in stereo cover with "Monaural" sticker			
❏ DL75043 [S]	The Transformed Man	1969	$100
K-TEL			
❏ NC494 [B]	Captain of the Starship	1978	$75
— Reissue of Lemli album			
LEMLI			
❏ 9400 [B]	William Shatner -- Live!	1977	$50
SHAVER, BILLY JOE			
CAPRICORN			
❏ CPN 0192	Gypsy Boy	1977	$15
❏ CPN 0171	Wings	1976	$15
COLUMBIA			
❏ FC37959	Billy Joe Shaver	1982	$12
❏ FC37078	I'm Just an Old Chunk of Coal	1981	$12
MONUMENT			
❏ KZ32293	Old Five and Dimers Like Me	1973	$18
❏ 7621	Old Five and Dimers Like Me	1978	$12
— Reissue of 32293			
ZOO			
❏ 1104	Unshaven: Live at Smith's Olde Bar	1995	$18
SHAVERS, CHARLIE			
AAMCO			
❏ 310 [M]	The Most Intimate Charlie Shavers	1959	$40
BETHLEHEM			
❏ BCP-27 [M]	Gershwin, Shavers and Strings	1955	$300
❏ BCP-1007 [10]	Horn o' Plenty	1954	$300
❏ BCP-67 [M]	The Complete Charlie Shavers with Maxine Sullivan	1957	$300
❏ BCP-6005 [M]	The Finest of Charlie Shavers: The Most Intimate	1976	$30
— Reissue, distributed by Caytronics			
❏ BCP-1021 [10]	The Most Intimate Charlie Shavers	1955	$300
❏ BCP-5002 [M]	The Most Intimate Charlie Shavers	1958	$250
CAPITOL			
❏ T1883 [M]	Excitement Unlimited	1963	$40
❏ ST1883 [S]	Excitement Unlimited	1963	$75
EVEREST			
❏ LPBR-5070 [M]	Girl of My Dreams	1960	$25
❏ SDBR-1070 [S]	Girl of My Dreams	1960	$30
❏ LPBR-5108 [M]	Here Comes Charlie	1960	$25
❏ SDBR-1108 [S]	Here Comes Charlie	1960	$30
❏ LPBR-5127 [M]	Like Charlie	1961	$25
❏ SDBR-1127 [S]	Like Charlie	1961	$30
JAZZTONE			
❏ J-1229 [M]	Flow Gently, Sweet Rhythm	1956	$40
MGM			
❏ E-3809 [M]	Charlie Digs Dixie	1960	$30
❏ SE-3809 [S]	Charlie Digs Dixie	1960	$30
❏ E-3765 [M]	Charlie Digs Paree	1959	$30
❏ SE-3765 [S]	Charlie Digs Paree	1959	$30
PERIOD			
❏ SPL-1113 [10]	Flow Gently, Sweet Rhythm	1955	$120
PHOENIX			
❏ 21	Trumpet Man	197?	$25
SHAW, ARTIE			
AIRCHECK			
❏ 11	Artie Shaw and His Orchestra 1939-40	197?	$25
ALLEGRO			
❏ 1405 [M]	An Hour with Artie Shaw	1955	$50
❏ 1466 [M]	Artie Shaw Hour	1955	$50
ALLEGRO EILTE			
❏ 4023 [10]	Artie Shaw Plays	195?	$40
❏ 4107 [10]	Artie Shaw Plays Cole Porter	195?	$40
BLUEBIRD			
❏ AXM2-5580	The Complete Artie Shaw, Volume 7: Retrospective	198?	$35
❏ AXM2-5517	The Complete Artie Shaw, Volume 1 (1938-39)	197?	$35

Number	Title	Yr	NM
❏ AXM2-5533	The Complete Artie Shaw, Volume 2 (1939)	197?	$35
❏ AXM2-5556	The Complete Artie Shaw, Volume 3 (1939-40)	1979	$35
❏ AXM2-5572	The Complete Artie Shaw, Volume 4 (1940-41)	1980	$35
❏ AXM2-5576	The Complete Artie Shaw, Volume 5 (1941-42)	198?	$35
❏ AXM2-5579	The Complete Artie Shaw, Volume 6 (1942-45)	198?	$35
❏ 7637-1-RB	The Complete Gramercy Five Sessions	1989	$30
CAPITOL			
❏ ST2992	Artie Shaw Re-Creates His Great '38 Band	1968	$85
CLEF			
❏ MGC-159 [10]	Artie Shaw and His Gramercy Five, Volume 1	1954	$250
❏ MGC-160 [10]	Artie Shaw and His Gramercy Five, Volume 2	1954	$250
❏ MGC-630 [M]	Artie Shaw and His Gramercy Five, Volume 3	1954	$250
❏ MGC-645 [M]	Artie Shaw and His Gramercy Five, Volume 4	1955	$250
COLUMBIA MASTERWORKS			
❏ ML4260 [M]	Modern Music for Clarinet	1950	$300
DECCA			
❏ DL5286 [10]	Artie Shaw Dance Program	195?	$50
❏ DL8309 [M]	Did Someone Say Party?	1956	$175
— Black label, silver print			
❏ DL5524 [10]	Speak to Me of Love	195?	$50
ENCORE			
❏ EE22023	Free for All	196?	$35
EPIC			
❏ LG1102 [10]	Artie Shaw	1955	$150
❏ LN3150 [M]	Artie Shaw and His Orchestra	1955	$100
❏ LG1006 [10]	Artie Shaw with Strings	1954	$150
❏ LN3112 [M]	Artie Shaw with Strings	1955	$100
❏ LG1017 [10]	Non-Stop Flight	1954	$150
EVEREST ARCHIVE OF FOLK & JAZZ			
❏ 248	Artie Shaw	1970	$25
HINDSIGHT			
❏ HSR-139	Artie Shaw and His Orchestra, 1938	198?	$25
❏ HSR-140	Artie Shaw and His Orchestra, 1938, Volume 2	198?	$25
❏ HSR-176	Artie Shaw and His Orchestra, 1938-39	198?	$25
❏ HSR-148	Artie Shaw and His Orchestra, 1939	198?	$25
❏ HSR-149	Artie Shaw and His Orchestra, 1939, Volume 2	198?	$25
❏ HSR-401	Artie Shaw and His Orchestra Play 22 Original Big Band Recordings	198?	$30
INSIGHT			
❏ 204	Artie Shaw and His Orchestra (1938-39)	198?	$25
LION			
❏ L-70058 [M]	Artie Shaw Plays Irving Berlin and Cole Porter	1958	$30
MCA			
❏ 4081	The Best of Artie Shaw	197?	$30
MGM			
❏ E-517 [10]	Artie Shaw Plays Cole Porter	1950	$50
MUSICRAFT			
❏ 503	Artie Shaw and His Orchestra, Volume 1	198?	$25
❏ 507	Artie Shaw and His Orchestra, Volume 2	198?	$25
PAIR			
❏ PDL2-1012	Original Recordings	1986	$30
RCA CAMDEN			
❏ ACL1-0509	Greatest Hits	1974	$25
❏ CAL-584 [M]	One Night Stand	1959	$25
❏ CAL-908 [M]	September Song and Other Favorites	196?	$25
❏ CAL-465 [M]	The Great Artie Shaw	195?	$25
RCA VICTOR			
❏ LPM-1648 [M]	A Man and His Dream	1957	$40
❏ LPM-1570 [M]	Any Old Time	1957	$300
— although signed AW, this Andy Warhol cover was not fully acknowledged until 2007			
❏ LPM-1241 [M]	Artie Shaw and His Gramercy Five	1956	$40
❏ LPT-28 [10]	Artie Shaw Favorites	195?	$50
❏ LPM-1217 [M]	Back Bay Shuffle	1956	$40
❏ ANL1-2151	Backbay Shuffle	1977	$25
❏ LPM-1201 [M]	Both Feet in the Groove	1956	$400
— Andy Warhol cover.			
❏ LPM-30 [10]	Four Star Favorites	1955	$75
❏ LPT-6000 [M]	In the Blue Room/In the Café Rouge	195?	$50
— Originals are in a box; silver labels, red print			
❏ LPM-1244 [M]	Moonglow	1956	$40
❏ LPT-1020 [M]	My Concerto	195?	$40
❏ ANL1-1089	The Best of Artie Shaw	1975	$25
❏ LPM-3675 [M]	The Best of Artie Shaw	1967	$25
❏ LSP-3675 [R]	The Best of Artie Shaw	1967	$30

Number	Title	Yr	NM
❏ LPT-3013 [10]	This Is Artie Shaw	1952	$50
❏ VPM-6039	This Is Artie Shaw	197?	$35
❏ VPM-6062	This Is Artie Shaw, Volume 2	1972	$35
❏ VPM-6062	This Is Artie Shaw, Volume 2	1976	$30
— Black labels, dog near top			
ROYALE			
❏ 18135 [10]	The Best in Dance Music	195?	$30
SUNBEAM			
❏ 207	New Music 1936-37	197?	$25
TIME-LIFE			
❏ STBB-06	Big Bands: Artie Shaw	1983	$35
❏ STBB-26	Big Bands: Encore: Artie Shaw	1986	$35
VERVE			
❏ MGV-2014 [M]	I Can't Get Started	1956	$250
❏ V-2014 [M]	I Can't Get Started	1961	$25
❏ MGV-2015 [M]	Sequence in Music	1956	$250
❏ V-2015 [M]	Sequence in Music	1961	$25
SHAW, BOBO			
BLACK SAINT			
❏ BSR-0021	Junk Trap	198?	$30
MUSE			
❏ MR-5268	Bugle Boy Bop	198?	$30
❏ MR-5232	P'NKJ'ZZ	198?	$35
SHAW, GENE			
ARGO			
❏ LP-707 [M]	Breakthrough	1962	$30
❏ LPS-707 [S]	Breakthrough	1962	$30
❏ LP-743 [M]	Carnival Sketches	1964	$30
❏ LPS-743 [S]	Carnival Sketches	1964	$30
❏ LP-726 [M]	Debut In Blues	1963	$175
❏ LPS-726 [S]	Debut In Blues	1963	$175
CHESS			
❏ CH-91564	Debut In Blues	198?	$25
SHAW, GEORGE			
PALO ALTO/TBA			
❏ TBA-218	Encounters	1986	$25
❏ TBA-223	Let Yourself Go	1987	$25
SHAW, LEE			
CADENCE JAZZ			
❏ CJR-1021	OK!	198?	$25
SHAW, MARLENA			
BLUE NOTE			
❏ BN-LA143-F	From the Depths of My Soul	1974	$35
❏ BN-LA606-G	Just a Matter	1976	$35
❏ BST-84422	Marlena	1972	$35
❏ BN-LA397-G	Who Is This Bitch, Anyway?	1975	$35
CADET			
❏ LPS-803	Different Bags	1968	$50
❏ LPS-833	Spice of Life	1969	$50
COLUMBIA			
❏ JC35073	Acting Up	1978	$30
❏ PC34458	Sweet Beginnings	1977	$30
❏ JC35632	Take a Bite	1979	$30
❏ JC36367	The Best of Marlena Shaw	1980	$25
VERVE			
❏ 831438-1	It Is Love	1987	$25
❏ 837312-1	Love Is In Flight	1988	$25
SHAW, ROBERT, CHORALE			
RCA CAMDEN			
❏ CAL-448 [M]	Joy to the World	1958	$15
— Reissue of RCA Red Seal LM-1112			
RCA VICTOR RED SEAL			
❏ LSC-2598 [S]	23 Glee Club Favorites	1962	$40
— Original with "shaded dog" label			
❏ LSC-2402 [S]	A Chorus of Love	1960	$25
— Original with "shaded dog" label or second edition with "white dog" label			
❏ LSC-2199 [S]	A Mighty Fortress	1959	$25
— Original with "shaded dog" label			
❏ LSC-2273 [S]	Bach, J.S.: Cantata 4	1959	$25
— Original with "shaded dog" label			
❏ LM-1112 [M]	Christmas Hymns and Carols	1952	$30
— Original has 2" brown border around all four sides of front cover			
❏ LM-2139 [M]	Christmas Hymns and Carols, Volume 1	1957	$25
— Original cover has "LM-2139" with "RCA Victor" in box on upper right			
❏ LM-2139 [M]	Christmas Hymns and Carols, Volume 1	1958	$16
— Second cover has "LM-2139" in lower left corner; small "RE" is on front cover			
❏ LSC-2139 [S]	Christmas Hymns and Carols, Volume 1	1958	$25
— Original with "shaded dog" label			

Number	Title	Yr	NM
❏ LM-1112 [M]	Christmas Hymns and Carols, Volume I	1954	$25
— Mostly pink front cover with "Enhanced Sound" at top and under dog on label			
❏ LM-1711 [M]	Christmas Hymns and Carols Vol. 2	195?	$25
— Pink "ornaments" cover; maroon label, large dog on top			
❏ LM-1711 [M]	Christmas Hymns and Carols Volume II	1954	$30
— Original carolers cover; red label with outline of dog			
❏ LSC-2247 [S]	Deep River and Other Spirituals	1959	$25
— Original with "shaded dog" label			
❏ LSC-2580 [S]	I'm Goin' to Sing	1962	$40
— Original with "shaded dog" label			
❏ LSC-2231 [S]	On Stage	1959	$25
— Original with "shaded dog" label			
❏ LSC-2416 [S]	Operatic Choruses	1960	$25
— Original with "shaded dog" label			
❏ LSC-2551 [S]	Sea Shanties	1961	$30
— Original with "shaded dog" label			
❏ LM-2684 [M]	The Many Moods of Christmas	1963	$15
❏ LSC-2684 [S]	The Many Moods of Christmas	1963	$18
❏ LSC-2295 [S]	The Stephen Foster Song Book	1959	$25
— Original with "shaded dog" label			
❏ LSC-2403 [S]	What Wondrous Love	1960	$25
— Original with "shaded dog" label			

SHAW, RON
PACIFIC CHALLENGER
Number	Title	Yr	NM
❏ 152	Goin' Home	1978	$15

SHAW, SANDIE
REPRISE
Number	Title	Yr	NM
❏ R-6191 [M]	Me	1966	$100
❏ RS-6191 [S]	Me	1966	$50
❏ R-6166 [M]	Sandie Shaw	1965	$75
❏ RS-6166 [R]	Sandie Shaw	1965	$75

SHAW, SERENA
RAMA
Number	Title	Yr	NM
❏ RLP-5001 [M]	Cry My Love	1956	$400

SHAW, TOMMY
A&M
Number	Title	Yr	NM
❏ SP-5020	Girls with Guns	1984	$12
❏ SP-5097	What If	1985	$12
ATLANTIC
| ❏ 81798 | Ambition | 1987 | $12 |

SHAW, WOODY
COLUMBIA
Number	Title	Yr	NM
❏ FC36383	For Sure	1980	$30
❏ JC35309	Rosewood	1977	$30
❏ JC35560	Stepping	1978	$30
❏ FC36519	The Best of Woody Shaw	1980	$25
❏ JC35977	Woody III	1979	$30
CONTEMPORARY
| ❏ C-7627/8 | Blackstone Legacy | 1971 | $85 |
| ❏ C-7632 | Song of Songs | 197? | $35 |
ELEKTRA/MUSICIAN
| ❏ 60131 | Master of the Art | 1983 | $25 |
| ❏ 60299 | Night Music | 1984 | $25 |
ENJA
| ❏ 4018 | Lotus Flower | 1982 | $30 |
FANTASY
| ❏ OJC-180 | Song of Songs | 198? | $25 |
MOSAIC
| ❏ MR4-142 | The Complete CBS Studio Recordings of Woody Shaw | 199? | $100 |
MUSE
❏ MR-5139	Concert Ensemble '76	1977	$30
❏ MR-5338	Imagination	1988	$25
❏ MR-5298	In the Beginning	198?	$25
❏ MR-5074	Love Dance	1976	$30
❏ MR-5058	Moontrane	1975	$30
❏ MR-5103	Red's Fantasy	197?	$30
❏ MR-5318	Setting Standards	198?	$25
❏ MR-5329	Solid	1987	$25
❏ MR-5160	The Iron Men	198?	$30
RED RECORD
| ❏ VPA-168 | The Time Is Right | 198? | $30 |

SHAWN, DICK
20TH CENTURY FOX
Number	Title	Yr	NM
❏ TFM-3124 [M]	Dick Shawn Sings with His Little People	1964	$25
❏ TFS-4124 [S]	Dick Shawn Sings with His Little People	1964	$30

SHAY, DOROTHY
CAPITOL
Number	Title	Yr	NM
❏ H517 [10]	Broadway Ditties	195?	$50
❏ H444 [10]	Park Avenue Hillbilly	195?	$50
COLUMBIA
❏ CL6089 [10]	Coming 'Round the Mountain	1950	$50
❏ CL6003 [10]	Dorothy Shay Sings	1948	$50
— With envelope-like cover			
HARMONY
| ❏ HL7017 [M] | Coming 'Round the Mountain | 195? | $30 |

SHAY, SHERYL
LAUREL
Number	Title	Yr	NM
❏ LR-506	Sophisticated Lady	1985	$30

SHEA, GEORGE BEVERLY
RCA CAMDEN
Number	Title	Yr	NM
❏ CAL-850 [M]	Christmas with George Beverly Shea	196?	$15
❏ CAS-850 [S]	Christmas with George Beverly Shea	196?	$15
RCA VICTOR
❏ LPM-1406 [M]	A Billy Graham Crusade in Song	1956	$25
❏ LPM-1967 [M]	Blessed Assurance	1959	$18
❏ LSP-1967 [S]	Blessed Assurance	1959	$25
❏ LPM-2064 [M]	Christmas Hymns	1959	$18
❏ LSP-2064 [S]	Christmas Hymns	1959	$25
❏ LPM-1349 [M]	Evening Prayer	1956	$25
❏ LPM-1062 [M]	Evening Vespers	1955	$25
❏ LPM-1564 [M]	George Beverly Shea	1957	$25
❏ LPM-1187 [M]	Inspirational Songs	1955	$25
❏ LPM-1235 [M]	Sacred Songs	1956	$25
❏ LPM-3904 [M]	The Best of George Beverly Shea, Vol. II	1968	$30
❏ LSP-3904 [S]	The Best of George Beverly Shea, Vol. II	1968	$15
❏ LPM-1949 [M]	The Love of God	1958	$18
❏ LSP-1949 [S]	The Love of God	1958	$25
❏ LPM-1642 [M]	Through the Years	1957	$25

SHEA, TOM
STOMP OFF
Number	Title	Yr	NM
❏ SOS-1022	Little Wabash Special	198?	$25

SHEARING, GEORGE, AND MEL TORME
CONCORD JAZZ
Number	Title	Yr	NM
❏ CJ-294	An Elegant Evening	1985	$25
❏ CJ-248	An Evening at Charlie's	1984	$25
❏ CJ-190	An Evening with George Shearing and Mel Torme	1982	$25
❏ CJ-341	A Vintage Year	1988	$25
❏ CJ-219	Top Drawer	1983	$25

SHEARING, GEORGE, AND THE MONTGOMERY BROTHERS
FANTASY
Number	Title	Yr	NM
❏ OJC-040	George Shearing and the Montgomery Brothers	198?	$25
JAZZLAND
❏ JLP-55 [M]	Love Walked In	1961	$75
— Cover has Shearing and the brothers			
❏ JLP-55 [M]	Love Walked In	1962	$75
— Cover has a woman			
❏ JLP-955 [S]	Love Walked In	1961	$40
— Cover has Shearing and the brothers			
❏ JLP-955 [S]	Love Walked In	1962	$75
— Cover has a woman			
RIVERSIDE
| ❏ 6087 | George Shearing and the Montgomery Brothers | 197? | $25 |
| *— Reissue of Jazzland LP* | | | |

SHEARING, GEORGE
CAPITOL
Number	Title	Yr	NM
❏ XE 3-1715 [S]	Be-Bop Irishman/I'll Be Around	1962	$75
— Small hole, plays at 33 1/3 rpm			
❏ XE 4-1715 [S]	Jumpin' with Symphony Sid/ Cocktails for Two	1962	$75
— Small hole, plays at 33 1/3 rpm			
❏ XE 5-1715 [S]	Lullaby of Birdland (Part 1)/ (Part 2)	1962	$75
— Small hole, plays at 33 1/3 rpm			
❏ XE 2-1715 [S]	Monophraseology/My New Mambo	1962	$75
— Small hole, plays at 33 1/3 rpm			
❏ XE 1-1715 [S]	The Outlaw/When April Comes Again	1962	$75
— Small hole, plays at 33 1/3 rpm			
BASF
❏ MC-25612	Continental Experience	1975	$30
❏ 25340	Light, Airy and Swinging	1973	$30
❏ 25351	The Way We Are	1974	$30
CAPITOL
❏ T858 [M]	Black Satin	1957	$150
— Turquoise label			
❏ T858 [M]	Black Satin	1959	$100
— Black label with colorband, logo on left			
❏ T858 [M]	Black Satin	1962	$85
— Black label with colorband, logo on top			
❏ ST858 [S]	Black Satin	1959	$100
— Black label with colorband, logo on left			
❏ ST858 [S]	Black Satin	1962	$85
— Black label with colorband, logo on top			
❏ SM-11800	Black Satin	1978	$25
❏ T1124 [M]	Blue Chiffon	1959	$100
— Black label with colorband, logo on left			
❏ T1124 [M]	Blue Chiffon	1962	$85
— Black label with colorband, logo on top			
❏ ST1124 [S]	Blue Chiffon	1959	$150
— Black label with colorband, logo on left			
❏ ST1124 [S]	Blue Chiffon	1962	$100
— Black label with colorband, logo on top			
❏ T1873 [M]	Bossa Nova	1963	$85
❏ ST1873 [S]	Bossa Nova	1963	$100
❏ T1038 [M]	Burnished Brass	1958	$100
— Black label with colorband, logo on left			
❏ T1038 [M]	Burnished Brass	1962	$85
— Black label with colorband, logo on top			
❏ ST1038 [S]	Burnished Brass	1959	$150
— Black label with colorband, logo on left			
❏ ST1038 [S]	Burnished Brass	1962	$100
— Black label with colorband, logo on top			
❏ T1755 [M]	Concerto for My Love	1962	$85
❏ ST1755 [S]	Concerto for My Love	1962	$100
❏ T2143 [M]	Deep Velvet	1964	$75
❏ ST2143 [S]	Deep Velvet	1964	$85
❏ ST-181	Fool on the Hill	1969	$75
❏ T1187 [M]	George Shearing On Stage	1959	$100
— Black label with colorband, logo on left			
❏ T1187 [M]	George Shearing On Stage	1962	$85
— Black label with colorband, logo on top			
❏ ST1187 [S]	George Shearing On Stage	1959	$150
— Black label with colorband, logo on left			
❏ ST1187 [S]	George Shearing On Stage	1962	$100
— Black label with colorband, logo on top			
❏ T2699 [M]	George Shearing Today	1967	$85
❏ ST2699 [M]	George Shearing Today	1967	$75
❏ T2372 [M]	Here and Now	1965	$75
❏ ST2372 [S]	Here and Now	1965	$85
❏ T1992 [M]	Jazz Concert	1963	$85
❏ ST1992 [S]	Jazz Concert	1963	$100
❏ T1827 [M]	Jazz Moments	1963	$85
❏ ST1827 [S]	Jazz Moments	1963	$100
❏ T1275 [M]	Latin Affair	1960	$100
— Black label with colorband, logo on left			
❏ T1275 [M]	Latin Affair	1962	$85
— Black label with colorband, logo on left			
❏ ST1275 [S]	Latin Affair	1960	$150
— Black label with colorband, logo on left			
❏ ST1275 [S]	Latin Affair	1962	$100
— Black label with colorband, logo on top			
❏ T737 [M]	Latin Escapade	1957	$150
— Turquoise label			
❏ T737 [M]	Latin Escapade	1959	$100
— Black label with colorband, logo on left			
❏ T737 [M]	Latin Escapade	1962	$85
— Black label with colorband, logo on top			
❏ DT737 [R]	Latin Escapade	196?	$75
❏ SM-11454	Latin Escapade	197?	$25
❏ T1082 [M]	Latin Lace	1958	$100
— Black label with colorband, logo on left			
❏ T1082 [M]	Latin Lace	1962	$85
— Black label with colorband, logo on top			
❏ ST1082 [S]	Latin Lace	1958	$150
— Black label with colorband, logo on left			
❏ ST1082 [S]	Latin Lace	1962	$100
— Black label with colorband, logo on top			
❏ T2326 [M]	Latin Rendezvous	1965	$75
❏ ST2326 [S]	Latin Rendezvous	1965	$85
❏ T1567 [M]	Mood Latino	1961	$100
— Black label with colorband, logo on left			
❏ T1567 [M]	Mood Latino	1962	$85
— Black label with colorband, logo on left			
❏ ST1567 [S]	Mood Latino	1961	$150
— Black label with colorband, logo on left			
❏ ST1567 [S]	Mood Latino	1962	$100
— Black label with colorband, logo on top			
❏ T943 [M]	Night Mist	1957	$150
— Turquoise label			
❏ T2048 [M]	Old Gold and Ivory	1964	$75
❏ ST2048 [S]	Old Gold and Ivory	1964	$50
❏ T1416 [M]	On the Sunny Side of the Strip	1960	$100
— Black label with colorband, logo on left			
❏ T1416 [M]	On the Sunny Side of the Strip	1962	$50
— Black label with colorband, logo on top			
❏ ST1416 [S]	On the Sunny Side of the Strip	1960	$150
— Black label with colorband, logo on left			
❏ ST1416 [S]	On the Sunny Side of the Strip	1962	$100
— Black label with colorband, logo on top			
❏ T2272 [M]	Out of the Woods	1965	$75

Number	Title	Yr	NM
❏ ST2272 [S]	Out of the Woods	1965	$50
❏ T2447 [M]	Rare Form	1965	$75
❏ ST2447 [S]	Rare Form	1965	$50
❏ T1715 [M]	San Francisco Scene	1962	$50
❏ ST1715 [S]	San Francisco Scene	1962	$100
❏ T1628 [M]	Satin Affair	1961	$100
—Black label with colorband, logo on left			
❏ T1628 [M]	Satin Affair	1962	$50
—Black label with colorband, logo on top			
❏ ST1628 [S]	Satin Affair	1961	$150
—Black label with colorband, logo on left			
❏ ST1628 [S]	Satin Affair	1962	$100
—Black label with colorband, logo on top			
❏ T909 [M]	Shearing Piano	1957	$150
—Turquoise label			
❏ T909 [M]	Shearing Piano	1959	$100
—Black label with colorband, logo on left			
❏ T2567 [M]	That Fresh Feeling	1966	$75
❏ ST2567 [S]	That Fresh Feeling	1966	$50
❏ T2104 [M]	The Best of George Shearing	1964	$75
❏ ST2104 [S]	The Best of George Shearing	1964	$85
❏ SM-2104	The Best of George Shearing	1977	$25
—Reissue with new prefix			
❏ SKAO-139	The Best of George Shearing, Vol. 2	1969	$75
❏ T648 [M]	The Shearing Spell	1956	$150
—Turquoise label			
❏ T648 [M]	The Shearing Spell	1959	$100
—Black label with colorband, logo on left			
❏ T1472 [M]	The Shearing Touch	1961	$100
—Black label with colorband, logo on left			
❏ T1472 [M]	The Shearing Touch	1962	$50
—Black label with colorband, logo on top			
❏ ST1472 [S]	The Shearing Touch	1961	$150
—Black label with colorband, logo on left			
❏ ST1472 [S]	The Shearing Touch	1962	$100
—Black label with colorband, logo on top			
❏ SM-1472	The Shearing Touch	1977	$25
—Reissue with new prefix			
❏ T1874 [M]	Touch Me Softly	1963	$50
❏ ST1874 [S]	Touch Me Softly	1963	$100
❏ T720 [M]	Velvet Carpet	1956	$150
—Turquoise label			
❏ T720 [M]	Velvet Carpet	1959	$100
—Black label with colorband, logo on left			
❏ T720 [M]	Velvet Carpet	1962	$50
—Black label with colorband, logo on top			
❏ DT720 [R]	Velvet Carpet	196?	$50
❏ T1334 [M]	White Satin	1960	$100
—Black label with colorband, logo on left			
❏ T1334 [M]	White Satin	1962	$75
—Black label with colorband, logo on top			
❏ ST1334 [S]	White Satin	1960	$150
—Black label with colorband, logo on left			
❏ ST1334 [S]	White Satin	1962	$100
—Black label with colorband, logo on top			
CONCORD CONCERTO			
❏ CC-2010	George Shearing and Barry Tuckwell Play the Music of Cole Porter	1986	$25
CONCORD JAZZ			
❏ CJ-171	Alone Together	1981	$25
❏ CJ-357	A Perfect Match	1988	$25
—With Ernestine Anderson			
❏ CJ-110	Blues Alley Jazz	1980	$25
❏ CJ-335	Breakin' Out	1988	$25
❏ CJ-346	Dexterity	1988	$25
❏ CJ-177	First Edition	1982	$25
❏ CJ-388	George Shearing in Dixieland	1989	$30
❏ CJ-281	Grand Piano	1985	$25
❏ CJ-246	Live at the Café Carlyle	1984	$25
❏ CJ-318	More Grand Piano	1987	$25
❏ CJ-132	On a Clear Day	1981	$25
—With Brian Torff			
❏ CJ-400	Piano	1989	$30
❏ CJ-371	The Spirit of 176	1989	$30
—With Hank Jones			
DISCOVERY			
❏ DL-3002 [10]	George Shearing Quintet	1950	$300
EVEREST ARCHIVE OF FOLK & JAZZ			
❏ 236	The Early Years, Vol. 2	1969	$25
❏ 223	Young George Shearing	1968	$25
LONDON			
❏ LL1343 [M]	By Request	1956	$75
❏ LL295 [10]	Souvenirs	1951	$120
MGM			
❏ E-252 [10]	An Evening with George Shearing	1954	$150

Number	Title	Yr	NM
❏ E-3122 [M]	An Evening with The George Shearing Quintet	1955	$30
❏ E-90 [10]	A Touch of Genius	1951	$150
❏ E-155 [10]	I Hear Music	1952	$150
❏ E-3266 [M]	I Hear Music	1955	$85
❏ E-4041 [M]	Satin Latin	1962	$35
❏ SE-4041 [R]	Satin Latin	1962	$30
❏ E-3175 [M]	Shearing Caravan	1955	$85
❏ E-3293 [M]	Shearing in Hi-Fi	1955	$85
❏ E-4043 [M]	Smooth and Swinging	1962	$35
❏ SE-4043 [R]	Smooth and Swinging	1962	$30
❏ E-4042 [M]	Soft and Silky	1962	$35
❏ SE-4042 [R]	Soft and Silky	1962	$30
❏ E-4169 [M]	The Very Best of George Shearing	1963	$35
❏ SE-4169 [R]	The Very Best of George Shearing	1963	$30
❏ E-3265 [M]	Touch of Genius	1955	$85
❏ E-226 [10]	When Lights Are Low	1953	$150
❏ E-3264 [M]	When Lights Are Low	1955	$85
❏ GAS-143	You're Hearing George Shearing	1970	$30
❏ E-3216 [M]	You're Hearing George Shearing	1955	$85
❏ E-3796 [M]	You're Hearing the Best of George Shearing	1960	$35
❏ E-518 [10]	You're Hearing the George Shearing Quartet	1950	$120
MOSAIC			
❏ MQ7-157	The Complete Capitol Live Recordings of George Shearing	199?	$300
PAUSA			
❏ 7072	500 Miles High	1979	$25
❏ 7088	Getting in the Swing of Things	1981	$25
❏ 9036	Jazz Moments	1985	$25
❏ 9065	Latin Affair	1986	$25
❏ 7035	Light, Airy and Swinging	1977	$25
❏ 7116	On Target	198?	$25
❏ PR7049	The Reunion	1977	$25
—With Stephane Grappelli			
❏ 9030	The Shearing Touch	198?	$25
PICKWICK			
❏ SPC-3039	Lullaby of Birdland	197?	$25
❏ SPC-3100	You Stepped Out of a Dream	197?	$25
SAVOY			
❏ MG-15003 [10]	Piano Solo	1951	$120
SAVOY JAZZ			
❏ SJL-1117	So Rare	198?	$25
SHEBA			
❏ 105	As Requested	197?	$30
❏ 107	GAS	197?	$30
❏ 104	George Shearing Quartet	197?	$30
❏ 103	George Shearing Trio	197?	$30
❏ 106	Music to Hear	197?	$30
❏ 101	Out of This World	197?	$30
VERVE			
❏ VSP-9 [M]	Classic Shearing	1966	$35
❏ VSPS-9 [R]	Classic Shearing	1966	$30
❏ 827977-1	Lullaby of Birdland	1986	$30
❏ 821664-1	My Ship	198?	$25

SHEEN, MICKEY

HERALD

Number	Title	Yr	NM
❏ HLP-0105 [M]	Have Swing, Will Travel	1956	$75

SHELDON, JACK

CAPITOL

Number	Title	Yr	NM
❏ T1851 [M]	Out!	1963	$50
❏ ST1851 [S]	Out!	1963	$50
❏ T2029 [M]	Play Buddy, Play!	1966	$50
❏ ST2029 [S]	Play Buddy, Play!	1966	$50

CONCORD JAZZ

Number	Title	Yr	NM
❏ CJ-339	Hollywood Heroes	1988	$25
❏ CJ-229	Stand By for Jack Sheldon	1983	$25

GENE NORMAN

Number	Title	Yr	NM
❏ GNP-60 [M]	Jack's Groove	1961	$40

GNP CRESCENDO

Number	Title	Yr	NM
❏ GNPS-60	Jack's Groove	196?	$30
❏ GNPS-9036	Jack Sheldon and His All-Star Band	197?	$25
❏ GNPS-2029 [S]	Play, Buddy, Play!	1966	$30
❏ GNP-2029 [M]	Play, Buddy, Play!	1966	$35

JAZZ WEST

Number	Title	Yr	NM
❏ JWLP-1 [10]	Get Out of Town	1955	$400
❏ JWLP-2 [10]	Jack Sheldon Quintet	1955	$400
❏ JWLP-6 [M]	The Quartet and the Quintet	1956	$800

REAL TIME

Number	Title	Yr	NM
❏ 303	Playin' It Straight	1981	$35

REPRISE

Number	Title	Yr	NM
❏ R-2004 [M]	A Jazz Profile of Ray Charles	1961	$30
❏ R9-2004 [S]	A Jazz Profile of Ray Charles	1961	$30

SHELDON, NINA

PLUG

Number	Title	Yr	NM
❏ PLUG-2	Secret Places	1986	$30

SHELLS, THE

CANDELITE

Number	Title	Yr	NM
❏ 1000	Accapella	197?	$18

COLLECTABLES

Number	Title	Yr	NM
❏ COL-5077 [B]	Golden Classics	198?	$15

SHELTON, RICKY VAN

COLUMBIA

Number	Title	Yr	NM
❏ C46855	Backroads	1990	$25
—Vinyl available only through Columbia House			
❏ FC44221	Loving Proof	1988	$10
❏ FC45269	Ricky Van Shelton Sings Christmas	1989	$15
❏ C45250	RVS III	1990	$18
❏ B6C40602	Wild-Eyed Dream	1987	$10

SHELTON, ROSCOE

EXCELLO

Number	Title	Yr	NM
❏ LP-8002 [M]	Roscoe Shelton Sings	1961	$600

SOUND STAGE 7

Number	Title	Yr	NM
❏ SSS-5002 [M]	Soul in His Music, Music in His Soul	1966	$40
❏ SSS-15002 [S]	Soul in His Music, Music in His Soul	1966	$50

SHENANDOAH

COLUMBIA

Number	Title	Yr	NM
❏ C48885	Greatest Hits	1992	$25
—Vinyl available only through Columbia House			
❏ BFC40788	Shenandoah	1987	$12
❏ FC44468	The Road Not Taken	1989	$15

SHEP AND THE LIMELITES

HULL

Number	Title	Yr	NM
❏ 1001 [M]	Our Anniversary	1962	$1200

ROULETTE

Number	Title	Yr	NM
❏ R-25350 [M]	Our Anniversary	1967	$100
❏ SR-25350 [R]	Our Anniversary	1967	$50

SHEPARD, JEAN, AND RAY PILLOW

CAPITOL

Number	Title	Yr	NM
❏ T2537 [M]	I'll Take the Dog	1966	$18
❏ ST2537 [S]	I'll Take the Dog	1966	$25

SHEPARD, JEAN

CAPITOL

Number	Title	Yr	NM
❏ ST2966	A Real Good Woman	1968	$18
❏ ST-559	A Woman's Hand	1970	$18
❏ ST-441	Best By Request	1970	$18
❏ SM-11409	For the Good Times	1975	$12
❏ T1525 [M]	Got You on My Mind	1961	$30
❏ ST1525 [S]	Got You on My Mind	1961	$30
❏ T2690 [M]	Heart, We Did All That We Could	1967	$18
❏ ST2690 [S]	Heart, We Did All That We Could	1967	$18
❏ T1663 [M]	Heartaches and Tears	1962	$30
❏ ST1663 [S]	Heartaches and Tears	1962	$30
❏ T2871 [M]	Heart to Heart	1968	$40
❏ ST2871 [S]	Heart to Heart	1968	$18
❏ ST-738	Here and Now	1971	$18
❏ ST-171	I'll Fly Away	1969	$18
❏ T2416 [M]	It's a Man Every Time	1965	$15
❏ ST2416 [S]	It's a Man Every Time	1965	$18
❏ ST-815	Just As Soon As I Get Over Loving You	1971	$18
❏ ST-11049	Just Like Walkin' in the Sunshine	1972	$15
❏ T2187 [M]	Lighthearted and Blue	1964	$18
❏ ST2187 [S]	Lighthearted and Blue	1964	$25
❏ T1126 [M]	Lonesome Love	1959	$40
❏ T2547 [M]	Many Happy Hangovers	1966	$15
❏ ST2547 [S]	Many Happy Hangovers	1966	$18
❏ ST-321	Seven Lonely Days	1969	$18

Number	Title	Yr	NM
❏ T728 [M]	Songs of a Love Affair	1956	$75
❏ T1922 [M]	The Best of Jean Shepherd	1963	$30
❏ DT1922 [R]	The Best of Jean Shepherd	1963	$18
❏ T1253 [M]	This Is Jean Shepard	1959	$40
❏ T2765 [M]	Your Forevers Don't Last Very Long	1967	$25
❏ ST2765 [S]	Your Forevers Don't Last Very Long	1967	$18

HILLTOP

Number	Title	Yr	NM
❏ JS-6068	Under Your Spell Again	197?	$12

UNITED ARTISTS

Number	Title	Yr	NM
❏ UA-LA307-R	I'll Do Anything It Takes	1974	$15
❏ UA-LA525-G	I'm a Believer	1975	$15
❏ UA-LA685-G	Jean Shepard's Greatest Hits	1976	$12
❏ UA-LA609	Mercy, Ain't Love Good	1976	$15
❏ UA-LA363-G	Poor Sweet Baby and Ten More Bill Anderson Songs	1975	$15
❏ UA-LA144-F	Slippin' Away	1973	$15

SHEPARD, TOMMY

CORAL

Number	Title	Yr	NM
❏ CRL57110 [M]	Shepard's Flock	1957	$100

SHEPHERD, CYBILL

PARAMOUNT

Number	Title	Yr	NM
❏ PAS-1018	Cybill Does It...to Cole Porter	1974	$50

— With poster

SHEPHERD, JEAN

ELEKTRA

Number	Title	Yr	NM
❏ EKL-172 [M]	Jean Shepherd and Other Foibles	1959	$50

SHEPP, ARCHIE, AND BILL DIXON

SAVOY

Number	Title	Yr	NM
❏ MG-12184 [M]	Archie Shepp and the New Contemporary 5/The Bill Dixon 7-Tette	1964	$250

— White bordered cover

Number	Title	Yr	NM
❏ MG-12184 [M]	Archie Shepp and the New Contemporary 5/The Bill Dixon 7-Tette	1965	$175

— Purple bordered cover

Number	Title	Yr	NM
❏ MG-12178 [M]	The Archie Shepp-Bill Dixon Quartet	1962	$30

SHEPP, ARCHIE, AND DOLLAR BRAND

DENON

Number	Title	Yr	NM
❏ 7532	Duet	197?	$35

SHEPP, ARCHIE, AND HORACE PARLAN

STEEPLECHASE

Number	Title	Yr	NM
❏ SCS-1079	Goin' Home	197?	$30
❏ SCS-1139	Trouble in Mind	1980	$30

SHEPP, ARCHIE

ABC IMPULSE!

Number	Title	Yr	NM
❏ AS-9222	Africa Blues	197?	$35
❏ AS-9231	Cry of My People	1973	$35
❏ AS-86 [S]	Fire Music	1968	$35
❏ AS-9188	For Losers	1970	$250
❏ AS-71 [S]	Four for Trane	1968	$35
❏ AS-9262	Kwanza	1974	$35
❏ AS-9118 [S]	Live In San Francisco	1968	$35
❏ AS-9134 [S]	Mama Too Tight	1968	$35
❏ AS-97 [S]	On This Night	1968	$35
❏ AS-9154 [S]	The Magic of Ju Ju	1968	$250
❏ AS-9170 [S]	The Way Ahead	1969	$250
❏ AS-9212	Things Have Got to Change	197?	$35
❏ AS-9162 [S]	Three for a Quarter, One for a Dime	1968	$250

ARISTA/FREEDOM

Number	Title	Yr	NM
❏ AF1027	Montreux 1	197?	$30
❏ AF1034	Montreux 2	197?	$30
❏ AF1016	There's a Trumpet in My Soul	1975	$30

BASF

Number	Title	Yr	NM
❏ 20651	Donaueschingen Festival	197?	$35

BLACK SAINT

Number	Title	Yr	NM
❏ BSR-0002	A Sea of Faces	198?	$30

DELMARK

Number	Title	Yr	NM
❏ DL-409 [M]	Archie Shepp in Europe	1968	$30
❏ DS-9409 [S]	Archie Shepp in Europe	1968	$25

DENON

Number	Title	Yr	NM
❏ 7543	Lady Bird	197?	$35
❏ 7538	Live in Tokyo	197?	$35

GRP/IMPULSE!

Number	Title	Yr	NM
❏ IMP-218	Four for Trane	199?	$35

— Reissue on audiophile vinyl

IMPULSE!

Number	Title	Yr	NM
❏ A-86 [M]	Fire Music	1965	$120
❏ AS-86 [S]	Fire Music	1965	$120
❏ A-71 [M]	Four for Trane	1964	$120
❏ AS-71 [S]	Four for Trane	1964	$120
❏ A-9118 [M]	Live In San Francisco	1967	$120
❏ AS-9118 [S]	Live In San Francisco	1967	$120
❏ A-9134 [M]	Mama Too Tight	1967	$120
❏ AS-9134 [S]	Mama Too Tight	1967	$120
❏ A-97 [M]	On This Night	1966	$120
❏ AS-97 [S]	On This Night	1966	$120

INNER CITY

Number	Title	Yr	NM
❏ IC-1001	Doodlin'	197?	$35
❏ IC-3002	Steam	1976	$30

PRESTIGE

Number	Title	Yr	NM
❏ 10034	Black Gypsy	197?	$35
❏ 10066	Coral Rock	197?	$35

SACKVILLE

Number	Title	Yr	NM
❏ 3026	I Know About the Life	198?	$25

SOUL NOTE

Number	Title	Yr	NM
❏ SN-1102	Down Home in New York	1985	$30

STEEPLECHASE

Number	Title	Yr	NM
❏ SCS-1149	Looking at Bird	198?	$30
❏ SCS-1169	Mama Rose	1982	$30
❏ SCS-6013	The House I Live In	198?	$30

TIMELESS

Number	Title	Yr	NM
❏ SJP-287	Lover Man	1990	$30

VARRICK

Number	Title	Yr	NM
❏ VR-005	The Good Life	198?	$25

SHEPPARD, ANDY

ANTILLES

Number	Title	Yr	NM
❏ 90692	Andy Sheppard	1988	$25

SHEPPARD, T.G.

COLUMBIA

Number	Title	Yr	NM
❏ FC40796	1ne 4 the $	1987	$10
❏ FC44307	Biggest Hits (1985-1987)	1988	$10
❏ FC44421	Crossroads	1989	$12
❏ FC40310	It Still Rains in Memphis	1986	$10
❏ FC40007	Livin' on the Edge	1985	$10

HITSVILLE

Number	Title	Yr	NM
❏ H6-404S1	Solitary Man	1976	$15

MELODYLAND

Number	Title	Yr	NM
❏ ME6-403S1	Motels and Memories	1976	$15
❏ ME6-401S1	T.G. Sheppard	1975	$15

WARNER BROS.

Number	Title	Yr	NM
❏ BSK3353	3/4 Lonely	1979	$10
❏ BSK3259	Daylight	1978	$10
❏ BSK3600	Finally!	1982	$10
❏ 25329	Greatest Hits, Volume 2	1985	$10
❏ BSK3528	I Love 'Em All	1981	$10
❏ 25149	One Owner Heart	1984	$10
❏ 23726	Perfect Stranger	1982	$10
❏ 23911	Slow Burn	1983	$10
❏ BSK3423	Smooth Sailin'	1980	$10
❏ BSK3133	T.G.	1978	$12

— Burbank" palm trees label

Number	Title	Yr	NM
❏ BSK3133	T.G.	1979	$10

— White label

Number	Title	Yr	NM
❏ 25282	T.G.	1985	$10
❏ 23841	T.G. Sheppard's Greatest Hits	1983	$10

SHEPPARDS, THE

COLLECTABLES

Number	Title	Yr	NM
❏ COL-5078	Golden Classics	198?	$12

CONSTELLATION

Number	Title	Yr	NM
❏ C-4 [M]	Collectors Showcase: The Sheppards	1964	$100
❏ CS-4 [R]	Collectors Showcase: The Sheppards	1964	$40

SOLID SMOKE

Number	Title	Yr	NM
❏ SS-8028	18 Dusty Diamonds	1984	$12
❏ SS-8004	The Sheppards	1980	$12

SHERIFF

CAPITOL

Number	Title	Yr	NM
❏ ST-12227	Sheriff	1983	$12
❏ C1-91216	Sheriff	1988	$12

— Reissue of 12227

SHERLEY, GLEN

MEGA

Number	Title	Yr	NM
❏ 1006	Glen Sherley	1971	$15

SHERMAN, ALLAN

JUBLIEE

Number	Title	Yr	NM
❏ JGM5019 [M]	More Folk Songs by Allan Sherman	1963	$25

— Two early Allan Sherman sides plus comedy bits by others

RCA RED SEAL

Number	Title	Yr	NM
❏ LM-2773 [M]	Peter and the Commissar	1964	$25
❏ LSC-2773 [S]	Peter and the Commissar	1964	$30

— With Arthur Fiedler and the Boston Pops Orchestra

RHINO

Number	Title	Yr	NM
❏ RNLP70818	A Gift of Laughter	1986	$12
❏ RNLP-005	The Best of Allan Sherman	198?	$12

WARNER BROS.

Number	Title	Yr	NM
❏ W1539 [M]	Allan in Wonderland	1964	$15
❏ WS1539 [S]	Allan in Wonderland	1964	$18

— Gold label

Number	Title	Yr	NM
❏ W1649 [M]	Allan Sherman -- Live	1966	$15
❏ WS1649 [S]	Allan Sherman -- Live	1966	$18

— Gold label

Number	Title	Yr	NM
❏ W1569 [M]	For Swingin' Livers Only!	1964	$15
❏ WS1569 [S]	For Swingin' Livers Only!	1964	$18
❏ W1604 [M]	My Name Is Allan	1965	$15
❏ WS1604 [S]	My Name Is Allan	1965	$18

— Gold label

Number	Title	Yr	NM
❏ W1487 [M]	My Son, the Celebrity	1963	$18
❏ WS1487 [S]	My Son, the Celebrity	1963	$25

— Gold label

Number	Title	Yr	NM
❏ W1475 [M]	My Son, the Folk Singer	1962	$18
❏ WS1475 [S]	My Son, the Folk Singer	1962	$25

— Gold label

Number	Title	Yr	NM
❏ W1501 [M]	My Son, the Nut	1963	$18
❏ WS1501 [S]	My Son, the Nut	1963	$25

— Gold label

Number	Title	Yr	NM
❏ W1684 [M]	Togetherness	1967	$18
❏ WS1684 [S]	Togetherness	1967	$25

— Gold label

SHERMAN, BOBBY

METROMEDIA

Number	Title	Yr	NM
❏ MD1014	Bobby Sherman	1969	$18
❏ MD1038	Bobby Sherman Christmas Album	1970	$18
❏ KMD1048	Bobby Sherman's Greatest Hits	1972	$15
❏ MD1045	Getting Together	1971	$18
❏ MD1028	Here Comes Bobby	1970	$18
❏ MD1060	Just for You	1973	$18
❏ MD1040	Portrait of Bobby	1971	$18
❏ MD1032	With Love, Bobby	1970	$18

SHERMAN, MARK

COLUMBIA

Number	Title	Yr	NM
❏ BFC40360	A New Balance	1986	$25

SHERRILL, JOYA

20TH CENTURY FOX

Number	Title	Yr	NM
❏ TFL-3170 [M]	Joya Sherrill Sings Duke Ellington	196?	$30
❏ TFS-4170 [S]	Joya Sherrill Sings Duke Ellington	196?	$30

COLUMBIA

Number	Title	Yr	NM
❏ CL1378 [M]	Sugar and Spice	1959	$30
❏ CS8178 [S]	Sugar and Spice	1960	$30

DESIGN

Number	Title	Yr	NM
❏ DLP-22 [M]	Joya Sherrill Jumps with Sammy Davis, Jr.	196?	$30

SHERRYS, THE

GUYDEN

Number	Title	Yr	NM
❏ GLP503 [M]	At the Hop with the Sherrys	1963	$300

SHERWOOD, BOBBY

CAPITOL

Number	Title	Yr	NM
❏ H463 [10]	Bobby Sherwood	1954	$100
❏ H320 [10]	Classics in Jazz	1952	$150
❏ T320 [M]	Classics in Jazz	1955	$85

IAJRC

Number	Title	Yr	NM
❏ LP35	Out of Sherwood's Forest	198?	$25

JUBILEE

Number	Title	Yr	NM
❏ JLP-1040 [M]	I'm an Old Cowhand	1957	$30
❏ JLP-1061 [M]	Pal Joey	1958	$30
❏ SDJLP-1061 [S]	Pal Joey	1959	$30

SHEW, BOBBY, AND BILL MAYS

JAZZ HOUNDS

Number	Title	Yr	NM
❏ 03	Telepathy	198?	$25

SHEW, BOBBY, AND CHUCK FINDLEY

DELOS

Number	Title	Yr	NM
❏ DMS-4003	Trumpets No End	1984	$25

SHEW, BOBBY

INNER CITY

Number	Title	Yr	NM
❏ IC-1077	Outstanding in His Field	197?	$30

JAZZ HOUNDS

Number	Title	Yr	NM
❏ 02	Play Song	1980	$25

PAUSA

Number	Title	Yr	NM
❏ 7171	Breakfast Wine	1985	$25
❏ 7198	Shewhorn	1986	$25

SHIELDS, BILL

OPTIMISM

Number	Title	Yr	NM
❏ OP-9001	Shieldstone	198?	$25

SHIELDS, ROGER

TURNABOUT

Number	Title	Yr	NM
❏ 34579	The Age of Ragtime	197?	$25

Number	Title	Yr	NM

SHIGETA, JAMES
CHOREO
Number	Title	Yr	NM
❏ A-7 [M]	We Speak the Same Language	1962	$30
❏ AS-7 [S]	We Speak the Same Language	1962	$30

SHIHAB, SAHIB
ARGO
| ❏ LP-742 [M] | Summer Dawn | 1964 | $400 |
| ❏ LPS-742 [S] | Summer Dawn | 1964 | $30 |
CHESS
| ❏ CH-91563 | Summer Dawn | 198? | $25 |
SAVOY
| ❏ MG-12124 [M] | Jazz Sahib | 1957 | $50 |
SAVOY JAZZ
| ❏ SJL-2245 | All-Star Sextets | 197? | $30 |
| ❏ SJC-409 | Jazz Sahib | 1985 | $25 |

SHIHAB, SAHIB/HERBIE MANN
SAVOY
| ❏ MG-12112 [M] | The Jazz We Heard Last Summer | 1957 | $50 |

SHILOH
AMOS
| ❏ AAS-7015 | Shiloh | 1971 | $100 |

SHINER, MERVIN
LITTLE DARLIN'
| ❏ 8018 | In the Ghetto | 1970 | $18 |

SHIP, THE
ELEKTRA
| ❏ EKS-75036 [B] | The Ship | 1972 | $35 |

SHIRELLES, THE
RCA VICTOR
| ❏ LSP-4581 | Happy and In Love | 1971 | $18 |
| ❏ LSP-4698 | The Shirelles | 1972 | $18 |
RHINO
| ❏ RNDA-1101 | Anthology (1959-1967) | 1984 | $15 |
SCEPTER
| ❏ SPM-505 [M] | A Twist Party | 1962 | $100 |
| ❏ SPS-505 [S] | A Twist Party | 1965 | $150 |

❏ SPM-504 [M]	Baby It's You	1962	$150
❏ SPS-504 [S]	Baby It's You	1965	$150
❏ SPS-569	Eternally Soul	1968	$30
❏ SPM-511 [M]	Foolish Little Girl	1963	$50
❏ SPS-511 [S]	Foolish Little Girl	1965	$100
❏ SPM-514 [M]	It's a Mad, Mad, Mad, Mad World	1963	$40
❏ SPS-514 [S]	It's a Mad, Mad, Mad, Mad World	1963	$50
❏ SPS-2-599	Remember When	1972	$25
❏ SPM-562 [M]	Spontaneous Combustion	1967	$40
❏ SPS-562 [S]	Spontaneous Combustion	1967	$50
❏ SPM-507 [M]	The Shirelles' Greatest Hits	1962	$40
❏ SPS-507 [S]	The Shirelles' Greatest Hits	1965	$50
❏ SPM-560 [M]	The Shirelles' Greatest Hits, Volume 2	1967	$25
❏ SPS-560 [S]	The Shirelles' Greatest Hits, Volume 2	1967	$30
❏ SPM-516 [M]	The Shirelles Sing the Golden Oldies	1964	$40
❏ SPS-516 [S]	The Shirelles Sing the Golden Oldies	1964	$50
❏ S-502 [M]	The Shirelles Sing to Trumpets and Strings	1961	$250

— Scepter" in scroll at top of label

| ❏ SPM-502 [M] | The Shirelles Sing to Trumpets and Strings | 1962 | $75 |

— Scepter Records" at left of label

| ❏ SPS-502 [S] | The Shirelles Sing to Trumpets and Strings | 1965 | $150 |
| ❏ S-501 [M] | Tonight's the Night | 1961 | $250 |

— Scepter" in scroll at top of label

| ❏ SPM-501 [M] | Tonight's the Night | 1962 | $75 |

— Scepter Records" at left of label

| ❏ SPS-501 [M] | Tonight's the Night | 1965 | $150 |

SPRINGBOARD
| ❏ 4006 | The Shirelles Sing Their Very Best | 1973 | $10 |

UNITED ARTISTS
| ❏ UA-LA340-E | The Very Best of the Shirelles | 1974 | $12 |

SHIRLEY, DON
AUDIO FIDELITY
| ❏ AFLP-1897 [M] | Don Shirley | 1959 | $25 |
| ❏ AFSD-5897 [S] | Don Shirley | 1959 | $30 |
CADENCE
❏ CLP-1015 [M]	Don Shirley Duo	1956	$40
❏ CLP-3035 [M]	Don Shirley Plays Birdland Lullabies	1960	$30
❏ CLP-3032 [M]	Don Shirley Plays Gershwin	1960	$30
❏ CLP-3034 [M]	Don Shirley Plays Love Songs	1960	$30
❏ CLP-3036 [M]	Don Shirley Plays Showtunes	1960	$30
❏ CLP-3033 [M]	Don Shirley Plays Standards	1960	$30
❏ CLP-3007 [M]	Don Shirley Solos	1958	$30
❏ CLP-3008 [M]	Don Shirley with Two Basses	1958	$30
❏ CLP-3057 [M]	Drown in My Own Tears	1962	$25
❏ CLP-25057 [S]	Drown in My Own Tears	1962	$30
❏ CLP-1009 [M]	Orpheus in the Underworld	1956	$40
❏ CLP-3037 [M]	Orpheus in the Underworld	1960	$30

— Reissue of 1009

❏ CLP-3048 [M]	Pianist Extraordinary	1962	$25
❏ CLP-25048 [S]	Pianist Extraordinary	1962	$30
❏ CLP-3049 [M]	Piano Arrangements of Spirituals	1962	$25
❏ CLP-25049 [S]	Piano Arrangements of Spirituals	1962	$30
❏ CLP-1004 [M]	Piano Perspectives	1955	$40
❏ CLP-1001 [M]	Tonal Expressions	1955	$40
❏ CLP-3046 [M]	Trio	1961	$25
❏ CLP-25046 [S]	Trio	1961	$30
COLUMBIA
| ❏ CL2396 [M] | Water Boy | 1965 | $18 |
| ❏ CS9196 [S] | Water Boy | 1965 | $25 |

SHIRLEY (AND COMPANY)
VIBRATION
| ❏ 128 | Shame Shame Shame | 1975 | $12 |

SHIRLEY AND LEE
ALADDIN
| ❏ 807 [M] | Let the Good Times Roll | 1956 | $1500 |
IMPERIAL
| ❏ LP-9179 [M] | Let the Good Times Roll | 1962 | $300 |

— Reissue of Aladdin LP

SCORE
| ❏ SLP-4023 [M] | Let the Good Times Roll | 1957 | $800 |

— Reissue of Aladdin LP

WARWICK
| ❏ W-2028 [M] | Let the Good Times Roll | 1961 | $175 |
| ❏ W-2028ST [S] | Let the Good Times Roll | 1961 | $300 |

SHIRTS, THE
CAPITOL
❏ SW-12085	Inner Sleeve	1980	$15
❏ ST-11944	Street Light Shine	1979	$14
❏ SW-11791	The Shirts	1978	$14

SHIVA'S HEADBAND
APE
| ❏ 1001 | Psychedelic Yesterday | 1981 | $25 |
ARMADILLO
| ❏ 0(no cat #) | Coming to a Head | 1969 | $300 |
CAPITOL
| ❏ ST-538 | Take Me to the Mountains | 1970 | $75 |

SHOCKED, MICHELLE
MERCURY
| ❏ 838878-1 | Captain Swing | 1989 | $12 |
| ❏ PRO797 [DJ] | Live | 1990 | $25 |

— Five-song mini-LP for radio stations with custom jacket

| ❏ PRO797 [DJ] | Live | 1990 | $25 |

— Five-song mini-LP for radio stations with custom jacket

| ❏ 834924-1 | Short Sharp Shocked | 1988 | $12 |
| ❏ 834581-1 | The Texas Campfire Tapes | 1988 | $15 |

SHOCKING BLUE, THE
COLOSSUS
| ❏ CS-1000 | The Shocking Blue | 1970 | $30 |

SHOEMAKE, CHARLIE, AND BILL HOLMAN
PAUSA
| ❏ 7180 | Collaboration | 1985 | $25 |

SHOEMAKE, CHARLIE, AND HAROLD LAND
CMG
| ❏ CML-8016 | Stand-Up Guys | 1989 | $30 |

SHOEMAKE, CHARLIE
DISCOVERY
❏ 856	Away from the Crowd	198?	$25
❏ 894	Charlie Shoemake Plays the Music of David Raksin	1986	$25
❏ 924	I Think We're Almost There	1987	$25
MUSE
| ❏ MR-5221 | Blue Shoe | 1979 | $30 |
| ❏ MR-5193 | Sunstroke | 1978 | $30 |

SHOES
BLACK VINYL
| ❏ 51477 | Black Vinyl Shoes | 1977 | $100 |
ELEKTRA
❏ 60146	Boomerang	1982	$12
❏ 6E-244	Present Tense	1979	$12
❏ AS11570 [DJ]	Shoes on Ice -- Live	1982	$40

— Promo-only 7-song live record; issued in generic jacket

| ❏ AS11570 [DJ] | Shoes on Ice -- Live | 1982 | $50 |

— Promo-only 7-song live record; issued in generic jacket

| ❏ 6E-303 | Tongue Twister | 1980 | $12 |
(NO LABEL)
| ❏ 0(no cat #) | One in Versailles | 1976 | $120 |
PVC
| ❏ 7904 | Black Vinyl Shoes | 1979 | $25 |

SHONDELL, TROY
EVEREST
| ❏ 5206 [M] | The Many Sides of Troy Shondell | 1963 | $50 |
| ❏ 1206 [S] | The Many Sides of Troy Shondell | 1963 | $100 |
SUNSET
| ❏ SUM-1174 [M] | This Time | 1967 | $18 |
| ❏ SUS-5174 [S] | This Time | 1967 | $18 |

SHOOTERS, THE
EPIC
| ❏ FE44326 | Solid as a Rock | 1989 | $12 |
| ❏ FE40885 | The Shooters | 1987 | $10 |

SHOOTING STAR
EPIC
❏ FE38020	3 Wishes	1982	$12
❏ BFE38683	Burning	1983	$12
❏ NFE37407	Hang On for Your Life	1981	$12
❏ PE37720	Shooting Star	1982	$10

— Reissue of Virgin VA 13133

GEFFEN
| ❏ GHS24056 | Silent Scream | 1985 | $12 |
VIRGIN
| ❏ VA13133 | Shooting Star | 1979 | $12 |

SHOPPE, THE
MTM
| ❏ ST-71051 | The Shoppe | 1986 | $12 |

SHORE, DINAH
BAINBRIDGE
| ❏ 6232 | Once Upon a Summertime | 198? | $12 |
CAPITOL
❏ T1247 [M]	Dinah, Yes Indeed	1959	$25
❏ ST1247 [S]	Dinah, Yes Indeed	1959	$30
❏ T1655 [M]	Dinah Down Home	1962	$25
❏ ST1655 [S]	Dinah Down Home	1962	$30
❏ T1422 [M]	Dinah Sings/Previn Plays	1960	$25
❏ ST1422 [S]	Dinah Sings/Previn Plays	1960	$30
❏ T1354 [M]	Dinah Sings Some Blues with Red	1960	$75
❏ ST1354 [S]	Dinah Sings Some Blues with Red	1960	$75
❏ T1296 [M]	Somebody Loves Me	1959	$25
❏ ST1296 [S]	Somebody Loves Me	1959	$30
❏ T1704 [M]	The Fabulous Hits of Dinah Shore	1962	$25

— Black label with colorband, logo at left

| ❏ T1704 [M] | The Fabulous Hits of Dinah Shore | 1962 | $15 |

— Black label with colorband, logo at top

| ❏ ST1704 [S] | The Fabulous Hits of Dinah Shore | 1962 | $30 |

— Black label with colorband, logo at left

| ❏ ST1704 [S] | The Fabulous Hits of Dinah Shore | 1962 | $18 |

— Black label with colorband, logo at top

COLUMBIA
| ❏ CL6004 [10] | Dinah Shore Sings | 1949 | $50 |

Number	Title	Yr	NM
❑ CL6069 [10]	Reminiscing	1949	$50
❑ C34395	The Best of Dinah Shore	1977	$12
HARMONY			
❑ HL7188 [M]	Buttons and Bows	195?	$18
❑ HL7010 [M]	Dinah Shore Sings Cole Porter and Richard Rodgers	195?	$25
❑ HL7239 [M]	Lavender Blue	1959	$18
PICKWICK			
❑ SPC-3524	It's So Nice to Have a Man Around the House	197?	$10
PROJECT 3			
❑ PR-5018SD	Songs for Sometime Losers	1968	$18
RCA CAMDEN			
❑ CAL-477 [M]	I'm Your Girl	1959	$18
❑ CAL-572 [M]	Vivacious Dinah Shore	1960	$18
RCA VICTOR			
❑ LPM-1214 [M]	Bouquet of Blues	1956	$30
❑ LPM-3103 [10]	Dinah Shore Sings the Blues	1953	$40
❑ LPM-1154 [M]	Holding Hands at Midnight	1955	$30
❑ LPM-1719 [M]	Moments Like These	1958	$30
❑ ANL1-1158	The Best of Dinah Shore	1976	$12
❑ LPM-3214 [10]	The Dinah Shore TV Show	1954	$40
REPRISE			
❑ R-6150 [M]	The Lower East Side Revisited	1965	$15
❑ RS-6150 [S]	The Lower East Side Revisited	1965	$18
SEAGULL			
❑ LG-8203	Oh Lonesome Me	198?	$12
STANYAN			
❑ 10071	Dinah Sings the Blues	197?	$12
❑ 10139	For Always	1977	$12
❑ 10125	Once Upon a Summertime	197?	$12

SHORT, BOBBY

Number	Title	Yr	NM
ATLANTIC			
❑ 81715	50 from Bobby Short	1987	$75
❑ 1230 [M]	Bobby Short	1956	$300
—*Black label*			
❑ 1230 [M]	Bobby Short	1961	$300
—*White "fan" logo at right of label*			
❑ 1230 [M]	Bobby Short	1963	$50
—*Black "fan" logo at right of label*			
❑ SD 2-610	Bobby Short Celebrates Rodgers and Hart	197?	$35
❑ SD 2-608	Bobby Short Is K-RA-Z-Y for Gershwin	1973	$35
❑ SD 2-606	Bobby Short Loves Cole Porter	1972	$50
❑ 81778	Guess Who's in Town: The Lyrics of Andy Razaf	1988	$25
❑ SD1535	Jump for Joy	1969	$30
❑ SD 2-609	Live at the Café Carlyle	1974	$35
❑ SD 2-607	Mad About Noel Coward	1972	$50
❑ SD1574	Nobody Else But Me	1971	$30
❑ 1321 [M]	On the East Side	1960	$300
—*Black label*			
❑ 1321 [M]	On the East Side	1961	$175
—*White "fan" logo at right of label*			
❑ 1321 [M]	On the East Side	1963	$35
—*Black "fan" logo at right of label*			
❑ SD1321 [S]	On the East Side	1960	$300
—*Green label*			
❑ SD1321 [S]	On the East Side	1961	$175
—*White "fan" logo at right of label*			
❑ SD1321 [S]	On the East Side	1963	$50
—*Black "fan" logo at right of label*			
❑ SD1689	Personal	1977	$30
❑ 1285 [M]	Sing Me a Swing Song	1958	$300
—*Black label*			
❑ 1285 [M]	Sing Me a Swing Song	1961	$175
—*White "fan" logo at right of label*			
❑ 1285 [M]	Sing Me a Swing Song	1963	$35
—*Black "fan" logo at right of label*			
❑ 1214 [M]	Songs by Bobby Short	1955	$300
—*Black label*			
❑ 1214 [M]	Songs by Bobby Short	1961	$175
—*White "fan" logo at right of label*			
❑ 1214 [M]	Songs by Bobby Short	1963	$35
—*Black "fan" logo at right of label*			
❑ 1262 [M]	Speaking of Love	1958	$300
—*Black label*			
❑ 1262 [M]	Speaking of Love	1961	$175
—*White "fan" logo at right of label*			
❑ SD1262 [S]	Speaking of Love	1959	$300
—*Green label*			
❑ SD1262 [S]	Speaking of Love	1961	$175
—*White "fan" logo at right of label*			
❑ 1302 [M]	The Mad Twenties	1959	$300
—*Black label*			
❑ 1302 [M]	The Mad Twenties	1961	$175
—*White "fan" logo at right of label*			
❑ 1302 [M]	The Mad Twenties	1963	$35
—*Black "fan" logo at right of label*			
❑ SD1302 [S]	The Mad Twenties	1959	$300
—*Green label*			

Number	Title	Yr	NM
❑ SD1302 [S]	The Mad Twenties	1961	$175
—*White "fan" logo at right of label*			
❑ SD1302 [S]	The Mad Twenties	1963	$50
—*Black "fan" logo at right of label*			
❑ SD1664	The Mad Twenties	1974	$30
❑ SD1620	The Very Best of Bobby Short	1973	$30
ELEKTRA			
❑ E1-60002	Moments Like This	1982	$25

SHORT CROSS

Number	Title	Yr	NM
GRIZZLY			
❑ S-16013 [B]	Arising	1970	$300

SHORTER, ALAN

Number	Title	Yr	NM
VERVE			
❑ V6-8769	Orgasm	1969	$25

SHORTER, WAYNE

Number	Title	Yr	NM
BLUE NOTE			
❑ BST-84232	Adam's Apple	1967	$50
❑ BST-84232	Adam's Apple	1985	$25
—*The Finest in Jazz Since 1939" reissue*			
❑ LT-1056	Etcetera	1980	$30
❑ B1-33581	Etcetera	1995	$35
❑ BLP-4182 [M]	Juju	1965	$150
❑ BST-84182 [S]	Juju	1965	$75
—*With New York, USA address on label*			
❑ BST-84182 [S]	Juju	1967	$35
—*With "A Division of Liberty Records" on label*			
❑ BST-84182	Juju	198?	$25
—*The Finest in Jazz Since 1939" reissue*			
❑ BN-LA014-G	Moto Grosso Feio	1973	$35
❑ BLP-4173 [M]	Night Drreamer	1964	$150
❑ BST-84173 [S]	Night Drreamer	1964	$75
—*With New York, USA address on label*			
❑ BST-84173 [S]	Night Drreamer	1967	$35
—*With "A Division of Liberty Records" on label*			
❑ BST-84297	Schizophrenia	1969	$50
❑ B1-32096	Schizophrenia	1995	$35
❑ BLP-4194 [M]	Speak No Evil	1966	$150
❑ BST-84194 [S]	Speak No Evil	1966	$75
—*With New York, USA address on label*			
❑ BST-84194 [S]	Speak No Evil	1967	$35
—*With "A Division of Liberty Records" on label*			
❑ B1-46509	Speak No Evil	1997	$35
—*Reissue on 180-gram vinyl*			
❑ BST-84332	Super Nova	1970	$50
❑ BLP-4219 [M]	The All Seeing Eye	1966	$150
❑ BST-84219 [S]	The All Seeing Eye	1966	$75
—*With New York, USA address on label*			
❑ BST-84219 [S]	The All Seeing Eye	1967	$35
—*With "A Division of Liberty Records" on label*			
❑ B1-29100	The All Seeing Eye	1994	$35
❑ B1-91141	The Best of Wayne Shorter	1988	$25
❑ BST-84363	The Odyssey of Iska	1971	$35
❑ LT-988	The Soothsayer	1979	$30
COLUMBIA			
❑ FC40055	Atlantis	1985	$25
❑ FC44110	Joy Ryder	1988	$25
❑ PC33418	Native Dancer	1975	$30
—*Originals have no bar code*			
❑ PC33418	Native Dancer	198?	$20
—*Reissue with bar code*			
❑ FC40373	Phantom Navigator	1987	$25
GNP CRESCENDO			
❑ GNPS-2075	Wayne Shorter	1973	$35
TRIP			
❑ 5009	Shorter Moments	1974	$30
VEE JAY			
❑ LP-3006 [M]	Introducing Wayne Shorter	1960	$40
❑ SR-3006 [S]	Introducing Wayne Shorter	1960	$150
❑ VJS-3006	Introducing Wayne Shorter	1986	$30
—*1980s reissue on thinner vinyl*			
❑ LP-3057 [M]	Second Genesis	1963	$75
❑ SR-3057 [S]	Second Genesis	1963	$40
❑ VJS-3057	Second Genesis	198?	$30
—*1980s reissue on thinner vinyl*			
❑ LP-3029 [M]	Wayning Moments	1962	$75
❑ SR-3029 [S]	Wayning Moments	1962	$40
❑ VJS-3029	Wayning Moments	198?	$30
—*1980s reissue on thinner vinyl*			

SHOTGUN LTD.

Number	Title	Yr	NM
PROPHESY			
❑ 6050	Shotgun Ltd.	1971	$25

SHOWMEN, THE

Number	Title	Yr	NM
COLLECTABLES			
❑ COL-5162	Golden Classics	198?	$12

SHQ

Number	Title	Yr	NM
ESP-DISK'			
❑ 1080 [S]	The Uhu Sleeps Only During the Day	1969	$120

SHRINER, HERB

Number	Title	Yr	NM
COLUMBIA			
❑ CL774 [M]	Herb Shriner On Stage	1957	$30
DOT			
❑ DLP-3149 [M]	Polka Dot Party	1959	$30
❑ DLP-25149 [S]	Polka Dot Party	1959	$40

SHU, EDDIE

Number	Title	Yr	NM
BETHLEHEM			
❑ BCP-1013 [10]	I Only Have Eyes For Shu	1954	$300

SHU, EDDIE/BOB HARDAWAY

Number	Title	Yr	NM
BETHLEHEM			
❑ BCP-3 [M]	Jazz Practitioners	1957	$180

SHU, EDDIE/JOE ROLAND/"WILD" BILL DAVIS

Number	Title	Yr	NM
MERCER			
❑ LP-1002 [10]	New Stars, New Sounds, Volume 1	1951	$175

SHULMAN, JOEL

Number	Title	Yr	NM
JAMAL			
❑ 5162	Peninah	197?	$50

SHUMATE, TED, AND IRA SULLIVAN

Number	Title	Yr	NM
PAUSA			
❑ 7188	Gulfstream	1986	$25

SHYLO

Number	Title	Yr	NM
COLUMBIA			
❑ PC34161	Flower of the South	1976	$15

SICKNICKS, THE

Number	Title	Yr	NM
AMY			
❑ 2 [M]	Sick #2	1961	$50

SIDE OF THE ROAD GANG, THE

Number	Title	Yr	NM
CAPITOL			
❑ ST-11526	The Side of the Road Gang	1976	$15

SIDEKICKS, THE

Number	Title	Yr	NM
RCA VICTOR			
❑ LPM-3712 [M]	Fifi the Flea	1966	$40
❑ LSP-3712 [S]	Fifi the Flea	1966	$30

SIDEWINDERS, THE

Number	Title	Yr	NM
RCA VICTOR			
❑ LSP-4694	The Sidewinders	1972	$25

SIDMAN, DAVID

Number	Title	Yr	NM
CADENCE JAZZ			
❑ CJR-1033	Shades of Meaning	1988	$25

SIDRAN, BEN

Number	Title	Yr	NM
ANTILLES			
❑ AN-1012	Bop City	1984	$30
❑ AN-1004	Old Songs for the New Depression	1981	$35
ARISTA			
❑ AB4178	A Little Kiss in the Night	1978	$35
❑ AL4081	Free in America	1976	$30
❑ AB4218	Live at Montreux	1979	$30
❑ AL4131	The Doctor Is In	1977	$30
BLUEBIRD			
❑ 6575-1-RB	That's Life I Guess	1990	$35
BLUE THUMB			
❑ BTS-6012	Don't Let Go	1974	$50
❑ BTS-40	I Lead a Life	1972	$40
❑ BTS-55	Puttin' In Time on Planet Earth	1973	$50
CAPITOL			
❑ ST-825	Feel Your Groove	1971	$100
HORIZON			
❑ SP-741	The Cat and the Hat	1980	$30
MAGENTA			
❑ MA-0204	On the Cool Side	1985	$25
❑ MA-0206	On the Live Side	1986	$25
WINDHAM HILL			
❑ WH-0108	Too Hot to Touch	1988	$30

SIEGEL, DAN

Number	Title	Yr	NM
CBS ASSOCIATED			
❑ OZ44490	Late One Night	1989	$30
❑ BZ44026	Northern Nights	1987	$25
INNER CITY			
❑ IC-1046	Nite Ride	197?	$30
❑ IC-1134	Oasis	198?	$30
❑ IC-1111	The Hot Shot	198?	$30
PAUSA			
❑ 7164	Another Time	1984	$25
❑ 7179	On the Edge	1985	$25
❑ 7142	Reflections	198?	$25

Number	Title	Yr	NM

SIEGEL-SCHWALL BAND, THE
VANGUARD
❏ VRS-9249 [M]	Say Siegel-Schwall	1967	$30
❏ VSD-79249 [S]	Say Siegel-Schwall	1967	$30
❏ VSD-79289	Shake!	1968	$25
❏ VSD-6562	Siegel-Schwall '70	1970	$25
❏ VRS-9235 [M]	The Siegel-Schwall Band	1966	$40
❏ VSD-79235 [S]	The Siegel-Schwall Band	1966	$40

WOODEN NICKEL
❏ BWL1-0121	953 West	1973	$25
❏ BWL1-0288	Last Summer -- Live	1974	$25
❏ BWL1-0554	R.I.P.	1974	$25
❏ WNS-1010	Sleepy Hollow	1972	$30
❏ WNS-1002	The Siegel-Schwall Band	1971	$30

SIGLER, BUNNY
GOLD MIND
| ❏ 9503 | I've Always Wanted to Sing... Not Just Write Songs | 1979 | $15 |
| ❏ 7502 | Let Me Party with You | 1978 | $15 |

PARKWAY
| ❏ P-50000 [M] | Let the Good Times Roll | 1967 | $40 |
| ❏ PS-50000 [S] | Let the Good Times Roll | 1967 | $40 |

PHILADELPHIA INT'L.
❏ KZ33249 [B]	Keep Smilin'	1974	$18
❏ PZ34267 [B]	My Music	1976	$30
❏ KZ32589	That's How Long I'll Be Loving You	1974	$18

SALSOUL
| ❏ SA-8531 | Let It Snow | 1980 | $15 |

SIGNATURES, THE
WARNER BROS.
❏ W1353 [M]	Prepare to Flip!	1959	$75
❏ WS1353 [S]	Prepare to Flip!	1959	$40
❏ W1250 [M]	The Signatures Sing In	1958	$75
❏ WS1250 [S]	The Signatures Sing In	1958	$40

WHIPPET
| ❏ WLP-702 [M] | The Signatures -- Their Voices and Instruments | 1957 | $120 |

SIGNORELLI, FRANK
DAVIS
| ❏ JD-103 [M] | Piano Moods | 1951 | $150 |

SIGUE SIGUE SPUTNIK
EMI
| ❏ E1-48700 [B] | Dress for Excess | 1989 | $15 |

MANHATTAN
| ❏ ST-53033 [B] | Flaunt It | 1986 | $35 |

SILHOUETTES, THE
GOODWAY
| ❏ GLP-100 [B] | The Silhouettes 1958-1968/ Get a Job | 1968 | $500 |

SILK
ABC
| ❏ S-694 | Smooth As Raw Silk | 1969 | $30 |

SILKIE, THE
FONTANA
❏ MGF27548 [M]	You've Got to Hide Your Love Away	1965	$100
—With full-color cover			
❏ MGF27548 [M]	You've Got to Hide Your Love Away	1965	$75
—With purplish, black and white cover			
❏ SRF67548 [R]	You've Got to Hide Your Love Away	1965	$50
—With full-color cover			
❏ SRF67548 [R]	You've Got to Hide Your Love Away	1965	$40
—With purplish, black and white cover			

SILL, JUDEE
4 MEN WITH BEARDS
| ❏ 4M121LP [B] | Heart Food | | $25 |
| ❏ 4M120LP [B] | Judee Sill | | $25 |

SILLY SURFERS, THE
MERCURY
| ❏ MG-20977 [M] | The Sounds of the Silly Surfers | 1965 | $100 |
| ❏ SR-60977 [S] | The Sounds of the Silly Surfers | 1965 | $150 |

SILLY SURFERS, THE / THE WEIRD-OHS
HAIRY
| ❏ 101 [M] | The Sounds of the Silly Surfers/The Sounds of the Weird-Ohs | 1964 | $175 |

SILVA, ALAN
CHIAROSCURO
| ❏ 2015 | The Shout: Portrait for a Small Woman | 197? | $30 |

ESP-DISK'
| ❏ 1091 [S] | Alan Silva | 1969 | $120 |

SILVA, MARCOS
CROSSOVER
| ❏ CR-5004 | Here We Go | 1987 | $25 |
| ❏ CR-5006 | White and Black | 1989 | $30 |

SILVEIRA, RICARDO
VERVE FORECAST
| ❏ 835054-1 | Long Distance | 1988 | $25 |
| ❏ 837696-1 | Sky Light | 1989 | $30 |

SILVER, HORACE
BLUE NOTE
❏ BLP-4017 [M]	Blowin' the Blues Away	1959	$300
—Deep groove" version; W. 63rd St. address on label			
❏ BLP-4017 [M]	Blowin' the Blues Away	1959	$250
—Regular edition, W. 63rd St. address on label			
❏ BLP-4017 [M]	Blowin' the Blues Away	1963	$100
—New York, USA" address on label			
❏ BST-84017 [S]	Blowin' the Blues Away	1959	$250
—W. 63rd St. address on label			
❏ BST-84017 [S]	Blowin' the Blues Away	1963	$40
—New York, USA" address on label			
❏ BST-84017 [S]	Blowin' the Blues Away	1967	$75
—A Division of Liberty Records" on label			
❏ BST-84017	Blowin' the Blues Away	1985	$30
—The Finest in Jazz Since 1939" reissue			
❏ BLP-4076 [M]	Doin' the Thing at the Village Gate	1961	$175
—W. 63rd St. address on label			
❏ BLP-4076 [M]	Doin' the Thing at the Village Gate	1963	$175
—New York, USA" address on label			
❏ BST-84076 [S]	Doin' the Thing at the Village Gate	1961	$250
—W. 63rd St. address on label			
❏ BST-84076 [S]	Doin' the Thing at the Village Gate	1963	$175
—New York, USA" address on label			
❏ BST-84076 [S]	Doin' the Thing at the Village Gate	1967	$75
—A Division of Liberty Records" on label			
❏ B1-84076	Doin' the Thing at the Village Gate	1989	$30
—The Finest in Jazz Since 1939" reissue			
❏ BLP-4008 [M]	Finger Poppin'	1959	$400
—Deep groove" version; W. 63rd St. address on label			
❏ BLP-4008 [M]	Finger Poppin'	1959	$250
—Regular edition, W. 63rd St. address on label			
❏ BLP-4008 [M]	Finger Poppin'	1963	$100
—New York, USA" address on label			
❏ BST-4008 [S]	Finger Poppin'	1959	$500
—Deep groove" version; W. 63rd St. address on label			
❏ BST-4008 [S]	Finger Poppin'	1959	$200
—Regular edition, W. 63rd St. address on label			
❏ BST-4008 [S]	Finger Poppin'	1963	$40
—New York, USA" address on label			
❏ BST-84008 [S]	Finger Poppin'	1967	$50
—With "A Division of Liberty Records" on label			
❏ B1-84008	Finger Poppin'	198?	$30
—The Finest in Jazz Since 1939" reissue			
❏ BLP-1589 [M]	Further Explorations	1958	$300
—Deep groove" version; W. 63rd St. address on label			
❏ BLP-1589 [M]	Further Explorations	1958	$400
—Regular edition, W. 63rd St. address on label			
❏ BLP-1589 [M]	Further Explorations	1963	$175
—New York, USA" address on label			
❏ BST-1589 [S]	Further Explorations	1959	$1000
—Deep groove" version; W. 63rd St. address on label			
❏ BST-1589 [S]	Further Explorations	1959	$350
—Regular edition, W. 63rd St. address on label			
❏ BST-1589 [S]	Further Explorations	1963	$175
—New York, USA" address on label			
❏ BST-81589 [S]	Further Explorations	1967	$50
—With "A Division of Liberty Records" on label			
❏ BLP-4042 [M]	Horace-Scope	1960	$400
—Deep groove" version; W. 63rd St. address on label			
❏ BLP-4042 [M]	Horace-Scope	1960	$250
—Regular edition, W. 63rd St. address on label			
❏ BLP-4042 [M]	Horace-Scope	1963	$100
—New York, USA" address on label			
❏ BST-84042 [S]	Horace-Scope	1960	$250
—W. 63rd St. address on label			
❏ BST-84042 [S]	Horace-Scope	1963	$40
—New York, USA" address on label			
❏ BST-84042 [S]	Horace-Scope	1967	$75
—A Division of Liberty Records" on label			
❏ BN-LA402-H2	Horace Silver	1975	$75
❏ BLP-1518 [M]	Horace Silver and the Jazz Messengers	1956	$700
—Deep groove" version; Lexington Ave. address on label			
❏ BLP-1518 [M]	Horace Silver and the Jazz Messengers	1956	$300
—Deep groove" edition, W. 63rd St. address on label			

❏ BLP-1518 [M]	Horace Silver and the Jazz Messengers	1963	$250
—New York, USA" on label			
❏ BST-81518 [R]	Horace Silver and the Jazz Messengers	1967	$75
—A Division of Liberty Records" on label			
❏ BST-81518	Horace Silver and the Jazz Messengers	1985	$35
—The Finest in Jazz Since 1939" reissue			
❏ BLP-5058 [10]	Horace Silver Quintet	1955	$700
❏ BLP-5062 [10]	Horace Silver Quintet	1955	$700
❏ BLP-5034 [10]	Horace Silver Trio, Vol. 2	1954	$800
❏ BLP-5018 [10]	New Faces	1953	$800
❏ BST-84420	Phase Three "All	1972	$150
—A Division of United Artists Records" on blue and white label			
❏ BST-84277	Serenade to a Soul Sister	1968	$175
—A Division of Liberty Records" on label			
❏ LWB-1033	Silver and Strings Play Music of the Spheres	1980	$75
❏ BN-LA406-G	Silver 'n' Brass	1975	$50
❏ BN-LA853-H	Silver 'n' Percussion	1978	$35
❏ BN-LA708-G	Silver 'n' Voices	1977	$50
❏ BN-LA581-G	Silver 'n' Wood	1976	$75
❏ BLP-4131 [M]	Silver's Serenade	1963	$200
—New York, USA" on label			
❏ BST-84131 [S]	Silver's Serenade	1963	$175
—New York, USA" address on label			
❏ BST-84131 [S]	Silver's Serenade	1967	$75
—A Division of Liberty Records" on label			
❏ BLP-1539 [M]	Six Pieces of Silver	1957	$1000
—Deep groove" version; Lexington Ave. address on label			
❏ BLP-1539 [M]	Six Pieces of Silver	1957	$600
—Deep groove" edition, W. 63rd St. address on label			
❏ BLP-1539 [M]	Six Pieces of Silver	1963	$250
—New York, USA" address on label			
❏ BST-81539 [R]	Six Pieces of Silver	1967	$50
—With "A Division of Liberty Records" on label			
❏ B1-81539	Six Pieces of Silver	1988	$30
—The Finest in Jazz Since 1939" reissue			
❏ B1-46548	Song for My Father	1997	$35
—Reissue on 180-gram vinyl			
❏ BLP-4185 [M]	Song for My Father (Cantiga Para Meu Pai)	1965	$200
—New York, USA" on label			
❏ BST-84185 [S]	Song for My Father (Cantiga Para Meu Pai)	1965	$140
—New York, USA" address on label			
❏ BST-84185 [S]	Song for My Father (Cantiga Para Meu Pai)	1967	$75
—A Division of Liberty Records" on label			
❏ BST-84185	Song for My Father (Cantiga Para Meu Pai)	1985	$30
—The Finest in Jazz Since 1939" reissue			
❏ BLP-1520 [M]	Spotlight on Drums	1956	$600
—Deep groove" version; Lexington Ave. address on label			
❏ BLP-1520 [M]	Spotlight on Drums	1956	$300
—Deep groove" edition, W. 63rd St. address on label			
❏ BLP-1520 [M]	Spotlight on Drums	1963	$250
—New York, USA" address on label			
❏ BST-81520 [R]	Spotlight on Drums	1967	$50
—With "A Division of Liberty Records" on label			
❏ BN-LA945-H	Sterling Silver	1979	$35
❏ BST-84352	That Healin' Feelin' (Phase 1)	1970	$175
—A Division of Liberty Records" on label			
❏ BST-84325	The Best of Horace Silver	1970	$75
—A Division of Liberty Records" on label			
❏ B1-91143	The Best of Horace Silver	1988	$30
❏ B1-93206	The Best of Horace Silver, Vol. 2	1989	$30
❏ BLP-4220 [M]	The Cape Verdean Blues	1965	$200
❏ BST-84220 [S]	The Cape Verdean Blues	1965	$140
—New York, USA" address on label			
❏ BST-84220 [S]	The Cape Verdean Blues	1967	$75
—A Division of Liberty Records" on label			
❏ B1-81520	The Horace Silver Trio	1989	$30
—The Finest in Jazz Since 1939" reissue			
❏ BLP-4250 [M]	The Jody Grind	1966	$175
—A Division of Liberty Records" on label			
❏ BST-84250	The Jody Grind	1966	$120
—New York, USA" address on label			
❏ BST-84250 [S]	The Jody Grind	1967	$75
—A Division of Liberty Records" on label			
❏ BN-LA054-F	The Pursuit of the 27th Man	1973	$35
—Dark blue label with black stylized "b" at upper right			
❏ BLP-1562 [M]	The Stylings of Silver	1957	$1250
—Deep groove" version; W. 63rd St. address on label			
❏ BLP-1562 [M]	The Stylings of Silver	1957	$250
—Regular edition, W. 63rd St. address on label			
❏ BLP-1562 [M]	The Stylings of Silver	1963	$250
—New York, USA" address on label			
❏ BST-1562 [S]	The Stylings of Silver	1959	$1200
—Deep groove" version; W. 63rd St. address on label			
❏ BST-1562 [S]	The Stylings of Silver	1959	$200
—Regular edition, W. 63rd St. address on label			
❏ BST-1562 [S]	The Stylings of Silver	1963	$100
—New York, USA" address on label			
❏ BST-81562 [S]	The Stylings of Silver	1967	$50
—With "A Division of Liberty Records" on label			

Number	Title	Yr	NM
❏ BLP-4110 [M]	The Tokyo Blues	1962	$200
—New York, USA" on label			
❏ BST-84110 [S]	The Tokyo Blues	1962	$175
—New York, USA" address on label			
❏ BST-84110 [S]	The Tokyo Blues	1967	$75
—A Division of Liberty Records" on label			
❏ BST-84368	Total Response (Phase 2)	1971	$200
❏ BST-84309	You Gotta Take a Little Love	1969	$150
—A Division of Liberty Records" on label			
EPIC			
❏ LN3326 [M]	Silver's Blue	1956	$300
❏ LA16006 [M]	Silver's Blue	1959	$300
—Reissue with new cover			
❏ BA17006 [R]	Silver's Blue	196?	$150

SILVER
ARISTA

Number	Title	Yr	NM
❏ AL4076	Silver	1976	$15

SILVER APPLES
KAPP

Number	Title	Yr	NM
❏ KS-3584 [B]	Contact	1969	$40
❏ KS-3562 [B]	Silver Apples	1968	$40
—Add 1/3 if poster is enclosed			

SILVER CONVENTION
MIDLAND INT'L.

Number	Title	Yr	NM
❏ BKL1-1824	Madhouse	1976	$12
❏ BKL1-1129	Save Me	1975	$12
❏ BKL1-1369	Silver Convention	1976	$12
MIDSONG INT'L.			
❏ BKL1-2296	Golden Girls	1977	$12
❏ BXL1-2296	Golden Girls	1978	$10
—Reissue with new prefix			
❏ BXL1-1824	Madhouse	1978	$10
—Reissue with new prefix			
❏ BXL1-1129	Save Me	1978	$10
—Reissue with new prefix			
❏ BXL1-1369	Silver Convention	1978	$10
—Reissue with new prefix			

SILVERHEAD
MCA

Number	Title	Yr	NM
❏ MCA306 [B]	Silverhead	1972	$25
❏ MCA391 [B]	Sixteen and Savaged	1973	$25

SILVERS, PHIL
COLUMBIA

Number	Title	Yr	NM
❏ CL1011 [M]	Phil Silvers and the Swinging Brass	1957	$50
HARMONY			
❏ HL7170 [M]	Bugle Calls for Big Band	196?	$30

SILVERSTEIN, SHEL
ATLANTIC

Number	Title	Yr	NM
❏ 8072 [M]	Inside Folk Songs	1962	$30
❏ SD8072 [S]	Inside Folk Songs	1962	$40
CADET			
❏ LP4054 [M]	Drain My Brain	1966	$30
❏ LPS4054 [S]	Drain My Brain	1966	$30
❏ LP4052 [M]	I'm So Good I Don't Have to Brag!	1965	$30
❏ LPS4052 [S]	I'm So Good I Don't Have to Brag!	1965	$30
COLUMBIA			
❏ FC40219	A Light in the Attic	1985	$12
❏ KC31119	Freakin' at the Freakers' Ball	1972	$18
❏ PC31119	Freakin' at the Freakers' Ball	1979	$10
—Budget-line reissue			
❏ FC39412	Where the Sidewalk Ends	1984	$12
❏ 9C939611 [PD]	Where the Sidewalk Ends	1984	$30
—Picture disc			
CRESTVIEW			
❏ CRV804 [M]	Stag Party	1963	$30
❏ CRS7804 [S]	Stag Party	1963	$30
ELEKTRA			
❏ EKL-176 [M]	Hairy Jazz	1961	$150
❏ EKS-7176 [S]	Hairy Jazz	1961	$175
FLYING FISH			
❏ FF-211	Conch Train Robbery	1980	$15
JANUS			
❏ 2JLS3052	Crouching on the Outside	1973	$18
PARACHUTE			
❏ 20512 [DJ]	Selected Cuts from Songs and Stories	1978	$25
—Promo-only EP			
❏ RRLP-9007	Songs and Stories	1978	$15
RCA VICTOR			
❏ LSP-4192	A Boy Named Sue (And His Other Country Songs)	1969	$25

SIMEON, OMER
CONCERT HALL JAZZ

Number	Title	Yr	NM
❏ 1014 [10]	Clarinet A La Creole	195?	$50
DISC			
❏ DLP-748 [10]	Omer Simeon Trio With James P. Johnson	195?	$250

SIMEONE, HARRY, CHORALE
20TH CENTURY FOX

Number	Title	Yr	NM
❏ TFM-3100 [M]	The Little Drummer Boy	1963	$15
—Reissue of FOX-3002 with same contents			
❏ TFS-3100 [S]	The Little Drummer Boy	1963	$18
—Same as above, but in stereo ("The Little Drummer Boy" is mono)			
❏ T-580	The Little Drummer Boy	1978	$12
—Another reissue of S 3100			
❏ 3100 [M]	The Little Drummer Boy	1966	$12
—Reissue of TFM-3100 (distributed by ABC)			
❏ S-3100 [S]	The Little Drummer Boy	1966	$15
—Reissue of TFS-3100 (distributed by ABC)			
20TH FOX			
❏ FOX-3002 [M]	Sing We Now of Christmas	1959	$30
—With no mention of "The Little Drummer Boy" at bottom of front cover			
❏ FOX-3002 [M]	Sing We Now of Christmas	1959	$25
—With "The Little Drummer Boy" mentioned at bottom of front cover			
❏ SFX-3002 [S]	Sing We Now of Christmas	1959	$25
—Sky blue label			
DIPLOMAT			
❏ XS1018	The Little Drummer Boy	196?	$15
—Abridged reissue of 20th Fox material			
KAPP			
❏ KL1450 [M]	The Little Drummer Boy	1965	$15
—With re-recording of the title song			
❏ KS3450 [S]	The Little Drummer Boy	1965	$18
MERCURY			
❏ MG20820 [M]	The Wonderful Songs of Christmas	1963	$18
❏ SR60820 [S]	The Wonderful Songs of Christmas	1963	$25
MISTLETOE			
❏ MLP-1201 [S]	The Little Drummer Boy	1973	$10
—Reissue of TFS 3100 with same contents			

SIMMONS, "JUMPIN'" GENE
HI

Number	Title	Yr	NM
❏ HL2018 [M]	Jumpin' Gene Simmons	1964	$50
❏ SHL32018 [S]	Jumpin' Gene Simmons	1964	$80

SIMMONS, GENE
Also see KISS.
CASABLANCA

Number	Title	Yr	NM
❏ NBLP7120	Gene Simmons	1978	$25
❏ NBPIX7120 [PD]	Gene Simmons	1978	$80

SIMMONS, JEFF
REPRISE

Number	Title	Yr	NM
❏ RS-6391	Lucille Has Messed Up My Mind	1969	$30
STRAIGHT			
❏ STS-1057	Lucille Has Messed Up My Mind	1969	$100

SIMMONS, NORMAN
ARGO

Number	Title	Yr	NM
❏ LP-607 [M]	Norman Simmons Trio	1956	$40
CREATIVE			
❏ LP-607 [M]	Interpolations	1956	$100
MILLJAC			
❏ MLP-1002	I'm the Blues	1981	$35
❏ MLP-1001	Midnight Creeper	1979	$35

SIMMONS, PATRICK
ELEKTRA

Number	Title	Yr	NM
❏ 60225	Arcade	1983	$12

SIMMONS, SONNY
ARHOOLIE

Number	Title	Yr	NM
❏ 8003 [S]	Manhattan Egos	1969	$35
CONTEMPORARY			
❏ S-7625/6	Burning Spirits	1970	$85
❏ M-3623 [M]	Rumasuma	1966	$175
❏ S-7623 [S]	Rumasuma	1966	$175
ESP-DISK'			
❏ 1043 [M]	Music from the Spheres	1967	$120
❏ S-1043 [S]	Music from the Spheres	1967	$120
❏ 1030 [M]	Sonny Simmons	1966	$120
❏ S-1030 [S]	Sonny Simmons	1966	$120

SIMON, ALAN
CADENCE JAZZ

Number	Title	Yr	NM
❏ CJR-1027	Rainsplash	198?	$25

SIMON, CARLY
Also see THE SIMON SISTERS.
ARISTA

Number	Title	Yr	NM
❏ AL-8443	Coming Around Again	1987	$10
❏ AL-8526	Greatest Hits Live	1988	$10
❏ AL-8650	Have You Seen Me Lately?	1990	$15
❏ AL-8582	My Romance	1990	$15
DIRECT DISK			
❏ SD-16608	Boys in the Trees	1980	$50
—Audiophile vinyl			
ELEKTRA			
❏ 7E-1064	Another Passenger	1976	$12
❏ EQ-1064 [Q]	Another Passenger	1976	$0
—Not released			
❏ EKS-75016	Anticipation	1971	$15
❏ 6E-128	Boys in the Trees	1978	$12
❏ EKS-74082	Carly Simon	1971	$15
❏ EQ-4082 [Q]	Carly Simon	1974	$30
❏ 7E-1002	Hotcakes	1974	$12
❏ EQ-1002 [Q]	Hotcakes	1974	$30
❏ EKS-75049	No Secrets	1972	$15
—With lyrics on innersleeve			
❏ EKS-75049	No Secrets	1973	$12
—Without lyrics on innersleeve			
❏ EQ-5049 [Q]	No Secrets	1974	$30
❏ 7E-1033	Playing Possum	1975	$12
❏ EQ-1033 [Q]	Playing Possum	1975	$30
❏ 5E-506	Spy	1979	$12
❏ 7E-1048	The Best of Carly Simon	1975	$12
❏ EQ-1048 [Q]	The Best of Carly Simon	1975	$30
❏ 6E-109	The Best of Carly Simon	1977	$10
—Reissue of 7E-1048			
EPIC			
❏ FE39970	Spoiled Girl	1985	$12
WARNER BROS.			
❏ BSK3443	Come Upstairs	1980	$12
❏ 23886	Hello Big Man	1983	$12
❏ BSK3592	Torch	1981	$12

SIMON, FRANK
AUDIO LAB

Number	Title	Yr	NM
❏ AL-1552 [M]	Four Star Hits	1960	$175

SIMON, FRED
WNDHAM HILL

Number	Title	Yr	NM
❏ WH-1071	Usually/Always	1988	$25

SIMON, JOE
BUDDAH

Number	Title	Yr	NM
❏ BDS-7512	Joe Simon	1969	$30
COMPLEAT			
❏ 671015-1	Mr. Right	1985	$15
POSSE			
❏ 10003	By Popular Demand	1982	$15
❏ 10002	Glad You Came My Way	1981	$15
SOUND STAGE 7			
❏ KZ31916	Greatest Hits	1972	$15
❏ SSS-15008	Joe Simon…Better Than Ever	1969	$30
❏ SSS-15004	No Sad Songs	1968	$40
❏ SSM-5003	Pure Soul	1967	$30
❏ SSS-15003 [S]	Pure Soul	1967	$40
❏ SSS-15005	Simon Sings	1968	$40
❏ SSS-15009	The Best of Joe Simon	1972	$18
❏ SSS-15006	The Chokin' Kind	1969	$30
❏ ZG33879	The Chokin' Kind/Joe Simon…Better Than Ever	1975	$18
❏ 5000	The World of Joe Simon	197?	$15
—Reissue of 32536			
❏ ZG32536	The World of Joe Simon	1974	$18
SPRING			
❏ SPR-6716	Bad Case of Love	1977	$18
❏ SPR-5702	Drowning in the Sea of Love	1972	$30
❏ SPR-6713	Easy to Love	1976	$18
❏ SPR-6706	Get Down	1975	$18
❏ SPR-6720	Love Vibrations	1979	$18
❏ SPR-6702	Mood, Heart and Soul	1974	$18
❏ SPR-5705	Simon Country	1973	$18
❏ SPR-5704	The Power of Joe Simon	1973	$30
❏ SPR-4701	The Sounds of Simon	1971	$30
❏ SPR-6710	Today	1975	$18

SIMON, PAUL
Includes records under various pseudonyms, such as "Paul Kane," "Jerry Landis" and "True Taylor." Also see SIMON AND GARFUNKEL; TICO AND THE TRIUMPHS; TOM AND JERRY (1).
COLUMBIA

Number	Title	Yr	NM
❏ C5X37581 [B]	Collected Works	1981	$100
—Contains his first four post-S&G solo albums plus the elusive "Paul Simon Songbook," otherwise unavailable in U.S.			
❏ JC35032	Greatest Hits, Etc.	1977	$12
❏ HC45032 [B]	Greatest Hits, Etc.	1981	$75

Number	Title	Yr	NM
—Half-speed mastered edition			
❏ KC30750	Paul Simon	1972	$12
❏ CQ30750 [Q]	Paul Simon	1974	$50
❏ PC32855	Paul Simon in Concert -- Live Rhymin'	1974	$12
❏ PC33540	Still Crazy After All These Years	1975	$12
—Original release has no bar code on cover			
❏ PCQ33540 [Q]	Still Crazy After All These Years	1975	$30
❏ HC43540 [B]	Still Crazy After All These Years	1981	$75
—Half-speed mastered edition			
❏ PC33540	Still Crazy After All These Years	1980	$10
—With bar code on cover			
❏ 61579	The Paul Simon Songbook	1965	$0
—British import; never released in U.S. on its own (U.S. counterfeits and bootlegs exist)			
❏ KC32280	There Goes Rhymin' Simon	1973	$12
❏ CQ32280 [Q]	There Goes Rhymin' Simon	1974	$50
❏ PC32280	There Goes Rhymin' Simon	1980	$10
CONCORD			
❏ CRE3978101 [B]	Stranger to Stranger	2016	$25
DCC COMPACT CLASSICS			
❏ LPZ-2060	Paul Simon	1998	$30
—Audiophile vinyl			
❏ LPZ-2062	There Goes Rhymin' Simon	1998	$30
—Audiophile vinyl			
WARNER BROS.			
❏ 25447	Graceland	1986	$12
❏ 23942 [DJ]	Hearts and Bones	1983	$25
—Promo only on Quiex II vinyl			
❏ 23942 [DJ]	Hearts and Bones	1983	$25
—Promo only on Quiex II vinyl			
❏ 23942	Hearts and Bones	1983	$12
❏ 25789	Negotiations and Love Songs	1988	$18
❏ HS3472	One-Trick Pony	1980	$12
❏ 25588	Paul Simon	1988	$15
❏ 25590	Paul Simon in Concert -- Live Rhymin'	1988	$15
❏ 46814	Songs from The Capeman	1997	$100
❏ 25591	Still Crazy After All These Years	1988	$15
❏ 49982-1	Surprise	2006	$18
❏ WBMS-140 [DJ]	The Paul Simon Interview Show	1986	$50
—Promo-only "Graceland"-era program in the "Warner Bros. Music Show" series			
❏ 25589	There Goes Rhymin' Simon	1988	$15
❏ 26098	The Rhythm of the Saints	1990	$18

SIMON, RALPH
GRAMAVISION

Number	Title	Yr	NM
❏ 8002	Time Being	1981	$25

SIMON AND BARD
FLYING FISH

Number	Title	Yr	NM
❏ FF-243	Musaic	1980	$25
❏ FF-262	Tear It Up	1982	$25
❏ FF-321	The Enormous Radio	198?	$25

SIMON AND GARFUNKEL
Also see ART GARFUNKEL; PAUL SIMON; TOM AND JERRY (1).
CBS

Number	Title	Yr	NM
❏ KCS9914	Bridge Over Troubled Water	1970	$18
—360 Sound Stereo" on label; pressed in U.S. for export			
COLUMBIA			
❏ KCS9529 [M]	Bookends	1968	$50
—White label "Special Mono Radio Station Copy			
❏ KCS9529 [S]	Bookends	1968	$15
—360 Sound Stereo" on label; add 25% for poster			
❏ KCS9529 [S]	Bookends	1970	$12
—Orange label			
❏ PC9529 [S]	Bookends	197?	$10
—Budget-line reissue			
❏ KCL2729 [M]	Bookends	1968	$250
—Red label, "Mono" at bottom			
❏ KCS9914	Bridge Over Troubled Water	1970	$15
—360 Sound Stereo" on label			
❏ KCS9914	Bridge Over Troubled Water	1970	$12
—Orange label			
❏ PC9914	Bridge Over Troubled Water	198?	$10
—Budget-line reissue			
❏ HC49914	Bridge Over Troubled Water	1982	$30
—Half-speed mastered edition			
❏ CQ30995 [Q]	Bridge Over Troubled Water	1971	$40
❏ JC9914	Bridge Over Troubled Water	197?	$10
—Reissue with new prefix			
❏ KCS9914	Bridge Over Troubled Water	2000	$30
—Classic Records reissue on audiophile vinyl			
❏ PCQ30995 [Q]	Bridge Over Troubled Water	1974	$40
—Reissue with new prefix; possibly the only difference between this and the original is a sticker on the cover with the new number			

Number	Title	Yr	NM
❏ C5X37587	Collected Works	1981	$40
❏ CL2563 [M]	Parsley, Sage, Rosemary and Thyme	1966	$25
❏ CS9363 [S]	Parsley, Sage, Rosemary and Thyme	1966	$18
—360 Sound Stereo" on label			
❏ CS9363 [S]	Parsley, Sage, Rosemary and Thyme	1970	$12
—Orange label			
❏ PC9363 [S]	Parsley, Sage, Rosemary and Thyme	197?	$10
—Budget-line reissue			
❏ KC31350	Simon and Garfunkel's Greatest Hits	1972	$15
—Original covers are slightly oversized			
❏ JC31350	Simon and Garfunkel's Greatest Hits	197?	$10
—Reissue with new prefix			
❏ HC41350	Simon and Garfunkel's Greatest Hits	1982	$30
—Half-speed mastered edition			
❏ CS9269 [S]	Sounds of Silence	1970	$12
—Orange label			
❏ CL2469 [M]	Sounds of Silence	1966	$30
—With "Simon and Garfunkel" and "Sounds of Silence" in all capital letters on front cover with no list of songs			
❏ CL2469 [M]	Sounds of Silence	1966	$25
—With "Simon and Garfunkel" and "Sounds of Silence" in large upper and lowercase letters on front cover with all song titles listed; "Tiger Beat" magazine is pictured twice on back cover			
❏ CS9269 [S]	Sounds of Silence	1966	$30
—With "Simon and Garfunkel" and "Sounds of Silence" in all capital letters on front cover with no list of songs			
❏ CS9269 [S]	Sounds of Silence	1966	$25
—With "Simon and Garfunkel" and "Sounds of Silence" in large upper and lowercase letters on front cover with all song titles listed; "Tiger Beat" magazine is pictured twice on back cover			
❏ PC9269 [S]	Sounds of Silence	198?	$10
—Budget-line reissue			
❏ JC9269	Sounds of Silence	197?	$10
—Reissue with new prefix			
❏ CL2469 [M]	Sounds of Silence	1966	$25
—With "Simon and Garfunkel" and "Sounds of Silence" in large upper and lowercase letters on front cover with all song titles listed; "Tiger Beat" magazines on back cover are airbrushed out			
❏ CS9269 [S]	Sounds of Silence	1966	$15
—With "Simon and Garfunkel" and "Sounds of Silence" in large upper and lowercase letters on front cover with all song titles listed; "Tiger Beat" magazines on back cover are airbrushed out			
❏ CL2249 [M]	Wednesday Morning, 3 A.M.	1964	$30
—Guaranteed High Fidelity" on label			
❏ CL2249 [M]	Wednesday Morning, 3 A.M.	1965	$25
—Mono" on label			
❏ CS9049 [S]	Wednesday Morning, 3 A.M.	1964	$30
—360 Sound Stereo" in black on label			
❏ CS9049 [S]	Wednesday Morning, 3 A.M.	1965	$18
—360 Sound Stereo" in white on label			
❏ CS9049 [S]	Wednesday Morning, 3 A.M.	1970	$12
—Orange label			
❏ PC9049 [S]	Wednesday Morning, 3 A.M.	197?	$10
—Budget-line reissue			
MOBILE FIDELITY			
❏ 1-173	Bridge Over Troubled Water	198?	$75
—Audiophile vinyl			
PICKWICK			
❏ PC-3059 [M]	The Hit Sounds of Simon and Garfunkel	1966	$75
❏ SPC-3059 [R]	The Hit Sounds of Simon and Garfunkel	1966	$30
SEARS			
❏ SPS-435	Simon and Garfunkel	196?	$30
TEE VEE			
❏ TV-2002 [B]	The Complete Collection	1980	$100
—Alternate number is Columbia Special Products P5-15333; also contains solo material by both Paul Simon and Art Garfunkel, plus a rare true stereo mix of "You Don't Know Where Your Interest Lies"			
WARNER BROS.			
❏ 2BSK3654	The Concert in Central Park	1982	$15

SIMON SISTERS, THE
CARLY SIMON and her sister Lucy.
COLUMBIA

Number	Title	Yr	NM
❏ CC24506	The Lobster Quadrille	1969	$25
—Special edition with booklet			
❏ CR21525 [B]	The Lobster Quadrille	1969	$25
❏ CR21539	The Simon Sisters Sing for Children	1972	$18
KAPP			
❏ KL-1397 [M]	Cuddlebug	1964	$40
❏ KS-3397 [S]	Cuddlebug	1964	$50
❏ KL-1359 [M]	Winkin', Blinkin' and Nod	1964	$30

Number	Title	Yr	NM
❏ KS-3359 [S]	Winkin', Blinkin' and Nod	1964	$40

SIMONE, NINA
ACCORD

Number	Title	Yr	NM
❏ SN-7108	In Concert	1981	$25
BETHLEHEM			
❏ BCP-6028 [M]	Jazz As Played in an Exclusive Side Street Club	1959	$250
❏ SBCP-6028 [S]	Jazz As Played in an Exclusive Side Street Club	1959	$250
❏ BCP-6041 [M]	Nina Simone and Her Friends	1960	$300
❏ SBCP-6041 [S]	Nina Simone and Her Friends	1960	$300
—With Carmen McRae and Chris Connor			
❏ BCP-6003	Nina Simone's Finest	197?	$30
❏ BCP-6028 [M]	The Original Nina Simone	1961	$1500
—Retitled reissue			
❏ SBCP-6028 [S]	The Original Nina Simone	1961	$1500
—Retitled reissue			
CANYON			
❏ 7705	Gifted and Black	1971	$35
COLPIX			
❏ CP-465 [M]	Folksy Nina	1964	$75
❏ SCP-465 [S]	Folksy Nina	1964	$75
❏ CP-419 [M]	Forbidden Fruit	1961	$75
❏ SCP-419 [S]	Forbidden Fruit	1961	$75
❏ CP-412 [M]	Nina at Newport	1960	$75
❏ SCP-412 [S]	Nina at Newport	1960	$75
❏ CP-409 [M]	Nina at Town Hall	1960	$75
❏ SCP-409 [S]	Nina at Town Hall	1960	$75
❏ CP-443 [M]	Nina's Choice	1963	$75
❏ SCP-443 [S]	Nina's Choice	1963	$75
❏ CP-455 [M]	Nina Simone at Carnegie Hall	1963	$75
❏ SCP-455 [S]	Nina Simone at Carnegie Hall	1963	$75
❏ CP-421 [M]	Nina Simone at the Village Gate	1961	$75
❏ SCP-421 [S]	Nina Simone at the Village Gate	1961	$75
❏ CP-425 [M]	Nina Sings Ellington	1962	$75
❏ SCP-425 [S]	Nina Sings Ellington	1962	$75
❏ CP-496 [M]	Nina with Strings	1966	$75
❏ SCP-496 [S]	Nina with Strings	1966	$75
❏ CP-407 [M]	The Amazing Nina Simone	1959	$75
❏ SCP-407 [S]	The Amazing Nina Simone	1959	$75
CTI			
❏ 7084	Baltimore	1978	$30
PHILIPS			
❏ PHM200148 [M]	Broadway...Blues...Ballads	1964	$35
❏ PHS600148 [S]	Broadway...Blues...Ballads	1964	$50
❏ PHM200172 [M]	I Put a Spell on You	1965	$35
❏ PHS600172 [S]	I Put a Spell on You	1965	$400
❏ PHM200202 [M]	Let It All Out	1966	$35
❏ PHS600202 [S]	Let It All Out	1966	$50
❏ PHM200135 [M]	Nina Simone In Concert	1964	$35
❏ PHS600135 [S]	Nina Simone In Concert	1964	$50
❏ PHM200187 [M]	Pastel Blues	1965	$35
❏ PHS600187 [S]	Pastel Blues	1965	$50
❏ PHS600298	The Best of Nina Simone	1969	$50
❏ 822846-1	The Best of Nina Simone	198?	$25
❏ PHM200219 [M]	The High Priestess of Soul	1967	$35
❏ PHS600219 [S]	The High Priestess of Soul	1967	$50
❏ PHM200207 [M]	Wild Is the Wind	1966	$35
❏ PHS600207 [S]	Wild Is the Wind	1966	$50
PM			
❏ 018	A Very Rare Evening	1979	$30
QUINTESSENCE			
❏ 25421	Silk and Soul	1979	$25
RCA VICTOR			
❏ LSP-4248	Black Gold	1970	$35
❏ LSP-4757	Emergency Ward!	1972	$35
❏ LSP-4536	Here Comes the Sun	1971	$35
❏ AFL1-4536	Here Comes the Sun	1977	$25
—Reissue with new prefix			
❏ APL1-0241	It Is Finished -- Nina 1974	1974	$30
❏ AFL1-0241	It Is Finished -- Nina 1974	1977	$25
—Reissue with new prefix			
❏ LSP-4102	Nina Simone and Piano	1968	$35
❏ LPM-3789 [M]	Nina Simone Sings the Blues	1967	$75
❏ LSP-3789 [S]	Nina Simone Sings the Blues	1967	$35
❏ LSP-4065	'Nuff Said	1968	$35
❏ APL1-1788	Poets	1976	$30
❏ AFL1-1788	Poets	1977	$25
—Reissue with new prefix			
❏ LPM-3837 [M]	Silk and Soul	1967	$75
❏ LSP-3837 [S]	Silk and Soul	1967	$35
❏ LSP-4374	The Best of Nina Simone	1970	$35
❏ AFL1-4374	The Best of Nina Simone	1977	$25
—Reissue with new prefix			
❏ LSP-4152	To Love Somebody	1969	$35
SALSOUL			
❏ SA-8546	Little Girl Blue	1982	$25
TRIP			
❏ 8021	Black Is the Color	1973	$30
❏ 8020	Live in Europe	1973	$30
❏ 9521	Portrait	197?	$25

Number	Title	Yr	NM

VERVE
| ❏ 831437-1 | Let It Be Me | 1987 | $25 |

SIMONE
COLUMBIA
| ❏ FC44275 | Vicio | 1988 | $30 |

SIMPKINS, ANDY, AND DAVE MACKAY
STUDIO 7
| ❏ 403 | Happying | 197? | $30 |

SIMPLE MINDS
A&M
| ❏ R209526 | Live in the City of Light | 1987 | $25 |
—BMG Direct Marketing edition
| ❏ SP-6850 | Live in the City of Light | 1987 | $18 |
| ❏ SP-6-4928 | New Gold Dream (81-82-83-84) | 1982 | $15 |
—Originals have gold and purple marbled vinyl
| ❏ R142320 | Once Upon a Time | 1985 | $15 |
—RCA Music Service edition; has front and back covers reversed
❏ SP-5092	Once Upon a Time	1985	$10
❏ SP-6-4981	Sparkle in the Rain	1984	$12
❏ R101142	Street Fighting Years	1989	$15
—BMG Direct Marketing edition
| ❏ SP-3927 | Street Fighting Years | 1989 | $12 |

PVC
| ❏ 7910 | Life in a Day | 1979 | $25 |

STIFF
| ❏ TEES-102 | Themes for Great Cities | 1982 | $20 |

VIRGIN
| ❏ 90858 | Life in a Day | 1988 | $12 |
—Reissue of PVC 7910
| ❏ 90859 | Real to Real Cacophony | 1988 | $12 |
—First U.S. edition of early LP
| ❏ 90610 | Sister Feelings Call | 1987 | $12 |
—First U.S. issue of LP originally released in 1981

SIMPLY RED
ELEKTRA
| ❏ R101012 | A New Flame | 1989 | $15 |
—BMG Direct Marketing edition
| ❏ 60828 | A New Flame | 1989 | $12 |
| ❏ R152858 | Men and Women | 1987 | $12 |
—RCA Music Service edition
| ❏ 60727 | Men and Women | 1987 | $10 |
| ❏ R153936 | Picture Book | 1985 | $12 |
—RCA Music Service edition
| ❏ 60452 | Picture Book | 1985 | $10 |
| ❏ ED5236 [DJ] | Simply Red Billboard Interview | 1989 | $40 |
—Nelson George interviews Mick Hucknall and Lamont Dozier; promo-only
| ❏ ED5236 [DJ] | Simply Red Interview | 1989 | $30 |
—Nelson George interviews Mick Hucknall and Lamont Dozier; promo-only

SIMPSON, CAROLE
CAPITOL
| ❏ T878 [M] | All About Carole | 1957 | $175 |
TOPS
| ❏ L-1732 [M] | Singin' and Swingin' | 1960 | $30 |

SIMPSON, CASS
ABC-PARAMOUNT
| ❏ ABC-103 [M] | Cass Simpson | 1956 | $40 |

SIMPSON, RED
CAPITOL
❏ T2829 [M]	A Bakersfield Dozen	1967	$30
❏ ST2829 [S]	A Bakersfield Dozen	1967	$25
❏ ST-11231	A Trucker's Christmas	1973	$18
❏ ST-881	I'm a Truck	1972	$18
❏ T2468 [M]	Roll, Truck, Roll	1966	$18
❏ ST2468 [S]	Roll, Truck, Roll	1966	$25
❏ T2569 [M]	The Man Behind the Badge	1966	$18
❏ ST2569 [S]	The Man Behind the Badge	1966	$25
❏ ST-11093	The Very Real Red Simpson	1973	$18
❏ T2691 [M]	Truck Drivin' Fool	1967	$25
❏ ST2691 [S]	Truck Drivin' Fool	1967	$25
PORTLAND
| ❏ 1005 [M] | Hello, I'm a Truck | 1965 | $100 |
SEA SHELL
| ❏ 16253 | Ramblin' Road | 198? | $15 |

SIMPSON, VALERIE
TAMLA
❏ T6-351	Keep It Comin'	1977	$15
❏ T317	Valerie Simpson	1972	$18
❏ T311	Valerie Simpson Exposed	1971	$18

Number	Title	Yr	NM

SIMPSONS, THE
GEFFEN
| ❏ GHS24308 | The Simpsons Sing the Blues | 1990 | $30 |

SIMS, FRANKIE LEE
SPECIALTY
| ❏ SPS-2124 | Lucy Mae Blues | 1970 | $40 |

SIMS, ZOOT, AND BUDDY RICH
QUINTESSENCE
| ❏ 25041 | Air Mail Special | 197? | $30 |

SIMS, ZOOT, AND HARRY "SWEETS" EDISON
FANTASY
| ❏ OJC-499 | Just Friends | 1991 | $30 |
PABLO
| ❏ 2310841 | Just Friends | 198? | $25 |

SIMS, ZOOT, AND JIMMY ROWLES
PABLO
| ❏ 2310803 | Lucky | 1977 | $30 |

SIMS, ZOOT; JIMMY RANEY; JIM HALL
MAINSTREAM
❏ MRL-358	Otra Vez	1972	$30
❏ 56013 [M]	Two Jims and Zoot	1965	$25
❏ S-6013 [S]	Two Jims and Zoot	1965	$30

SIMS, ZOOT; TONY SCOTT; AL COHN
JAZZLAND
| ❏ JLP-11 [M] | East Coast Sounds | 1960 | $40 |
| ❏ JLP-911 [S] | East Coast Sounds | 1960 | $40 |

SIMS, ZOOT
ABC IMPULSE!
| ❏ AS-9131 [S] | The Waiting Game | 1968 | $120 |
—Black label with red ring
ABC-PARAMOUNT
| ❏ ABC-155 [M] | Zoot Sims Plays Alto, Tenor and Baritone | 1957 | $175 |
| ❏ ABC-198 [M] | Zoot Sims Plays Four Altos | 1957 | $175 |
ARGO
| ❏ LP-608 [M] | Zoot | 1956 | $700 |
—Color cover
| ❏ LP-608 [M] | Zoot | 1957 | $175 |
—Black and white cover
BETHLEHEM
| ❏ BCP-6027 | Down Home | 197? | $50 |
—Reissue, distributed by RCA Victor
| ❏ BCP-6051 [M] | Down Home | 1960 | $500 |
| ❏ SBCP-6051 [S] | Down Home | 1960 | $300 |
BIOGRAPH
| ❏ 12062 | One to Blow On | 198? | $25 |
CADET
| ❏ LP-608 [M] | Zoot | 1966 | $50 |
—Fading blue label
CHOICE
| ❏ 1006 | Party | 197? | $35 |
CLASSIC JAZZ
| ❏ 21 | Zoot Sims and Bucky Pizzarelli | 197? | $30 |
COLPIX
❏ CP-435 [M]	New Beat Bossa Nova	1962	$40
❏ SCP-435 [S]	New Beat Bossa Nova	1962	$50
❏ CP-437 [M]	New Beat Bossa Nova, Volume 2	1962	$40
❏ SCP-437 [S]	New Beat Bossa Nova, Volume 2	1962	$50
DAWN
| ❏ DLP-1102 [M] | The Modern Art of Jazz | 1956 | $300 |
| ❏ DLP-1115 [M] | Zoot Sims Goes to Jazzville | 1957 | $250 |
DISCOVERY
| ❏ DL-3015 [10] | The Zoot Sims Quartet In Paris | 1951 | $300 |
FAMOUS DOOR
| ❏ HL-2000 | At Ease | 197? | $35 |
FANTASY
❏ OJC-444	The Gershwin Brothers	1990	$35
❏ OJC-228	Zoot!	198?	$30
❏ OJC-242	Zoot Sims Quartets	1987	$30
GROOVE MERCHANT
| ❏ 533 | Nirvana | 197? | $35 |
IMPULSE!
| ❏ A-9131 [M] | The Waiting Game | 1967 | $250 |
| ❏ AS-9131 [S] | The Waiting Game | 1967 | $250 |
JAZZLAND
| ❏ JLP-2 [M] | Zoot Sims Quintet | 1960 | $40 |
| ❏ JLP-92 [S] | Zoot Sims Quintet | 1960 | $75 |

Number	Title	Yr	NM

MCA
| ❏ 29069 | Zoot Sims Plays Four Altos | 1980 | $25 |
NEW JAZZ
| ❏ NJLP-8280 [M] | Good Old Zoot | 1962 | $175 |
| ❏ NJLP-8309 [M] | Koo Koo | 1963 | $0 |
—Canceled; reassigned to Status
| ❏ NJLP-8302 [M] | Trotting | 1963 | $0 |
—Canceled; reassigned to Status
| ❏ NJLP-1102 [10] | Zoot Sims in Hollywood | 1954 | $350 |
PABLO
❏ 2310783	Hawthorne Nights	197?	$30
❏ 2310868	I Wish I Were Twins	198?	$25
❏ 2310903	Quietly There	198?	$25
❏ 2310770	Soprano Sax	197?	$30
❏ 2310898	Suddenly It's Spring	198?	$25
❏ 2310861	Swinger	198?	$25
❏ 2405406	The Best of Zoot Sims	198?	$25
❏ 2310744	The Gershwin Brothers	197?	$30
❏ 2310872	The Innocent Years	198?	$25
❏ 2310831	Warm Tenor	1979	$30
PABLO TODAY
| ❏ 2312120 | Zoot Sims Plays Duke Ellington/Passion Flower | 1980 | $30 |
PACIFIC JAZZ
| ❏ PJ-20 [M] | Choice | 1961 | $40 |
PRESTIGE
❏ PRST-7817	First Recordings!	1970	$35
❏ PRLP-117 [10]	Swingin' with Zoot Sims	1951	$300
❏ PRLP-118 [10]	Tenor Sax Favorites	1951	$300
❏ PRLP-16009 [M]	Trotting	1963	$75
❏ P-24061	Zootcase	197?	$50
❏ PRLP-138 [10]	Zoot Sims All Stars	1953	$300
❏ PRLP-7026 [M]	Zoot Sims Quartets	1956	$300
—Yellow label with W. 50th St. address
| ❏ PRLP-202 [10] | Zoot Sims Quintet | 1955 | $300 |
RIVERSIDE
| ❏ 6103 | Zoot | 197? | $30 |
| ❏ RLP 12-228 [M] | Zoot! | 1957 | $300 |
SEECO
| ❏ CELP-452 [M] | The Modern Art of Jazz | 1960 | $300 |
| ❏ CELP-4520 [S] | The Modern Art of Jazz | 1960 | $300 |
STATUS
| ❏ ST-8280 [M] | Good Old Zoot | 1965 | $40 |
| ❏ ST-8309 [M] | Koo Koo | 1965 | $40 |
SWING
| ❏ SW-8417 | Zoot Sims in Paris | 1987 | $25 |
TRIP
| ❏ 5548 | You 'n Me | 197? | $25 |
UNITED ARTISTS
❏ UAL-4040 [M]	A Night at the Half Note	1959	$40
❏ UAS-5040 [S]	A Night at the Half Note	1959	$50
❏ UAJ-14013 [M]	Zoot Sims in Paris	1962	$40
❏ UAJS-15013 [S]	Zoot Sims in Paris	1962	$150
ZIM
| ❏ 1008 | Nash-ville | 198? | $25 |

SIN SAY SHUNS, THE
VENETT
| ❏ V-940 [M] | I'll Be There | 1966 | $40 |
| ❏ VS-940 [S] | I'll Be There | 1966 | $50 |

SINATRA, FRANK; DEAN MARTIN; SAMMY DAVIS, JR.
ARTANIS
| ❏ ARZ102 | The Summit | 1999 | $0 |
—Canceled

SINATRA, FRANK
ARTANIS
| ❏ ARZ101 | Sinatra '57 In Concert | 1999 | $0 |
—Canceled
BOOK-OF-THE-MONTH
| ❏ (# unknown) | Tommy Dorsey/Frank Sinatra: The Complete Sessions | 1983 | $200 |
CAPITOL
| ❏ W894 [M] | A Jolly Christmas from Frank Sinatra | 1957 | $85 |
—Original mono with gray label
| ❏ W894 [M] | A Jolly Christmas from Frank Sinatra | 1958 | $150 |
—Black colorband label, logo at left
❏ W1538 [M]	All the Way	1961	$100
❏ SW1538 [S]	All the Way	1961	$150
❏ SN-16205	All the Way	198?	$20
—Budget-line reissue
| ❏ W803 [M] | A Swingin' Affair! | 1957 | $150 |
—Gray label
| ❏ W803 [M] | A Swingin' Affair! | 1957 | $100 |
—Black label with colorband
❏ DW803 [R]	A Swingin' Affair!	196?	$75
❏ SM-11502	A Swingin' Affair!	1976	$25
❏ W789 [M]	Close to You	1957	$150
—Gray label

Number	Title	Yr	NM
❏ W789 [M]	Close to You	1959	$100
— Black label with colorband			
❏ DW789 [R]	Close to You	196?	$75
❏ DWBB-254 [R]	Close-Up	1969	$100
— Reissue in one package of "This Is Sinatra" and "This Is Sinatra, Volume Two"			
❏ W1069 [M]	Come Dance with Me!	1959	$100
❏ SW1069 [S]	Come Dance with Me!	1959	$150
❏ SN-16203	Come Dance with Me!	198?	$20
— Budget-line reissue			
❏ W920 [M]	Come Fly with Me	1958	$75
— Gray label			
❏ W920 [M]	Come Fly with Me	1959	$100
— Black label with colorband			
❏ SW920 [S]	Come Fly with Me	1959	$150
❏ SM-920	Come Fly with Me	197?	$20
❏ SY-4528 [S]	Come Fly with Me	197?	$25
— Reissue of SW 920 with orange label and "Capitol" at bottom			
❏ SM-11801	Come Swing with Me	1978	$25
❏ W1594 [M]	Come Swing with Me!	1961	$100
❏ SW1594 [S]	Come Swing with Me!	1961	$150
❏ C1-89611	Duets	1993	$100
❏ T2602 [M]	Forever Frank	1966	$100
❏ DT2602 [R]	Forever Frank	1966	$75
❏ T735 [M]	Frank Sinatra Conducts Tone Poems of Color	1956	$250
— Turquoise label			
❏ T735 [M]	Frank Sinatra Conducts Tone Poems of Color	1959	$75
— Black label with colorband			
❏ PRO-2974/5 [DJ]	Frank Sinatra Minute Masters	1965	$75
— Edited version of 20 songs			
❏ DKAO-374 [R]	Frank Sinatra's Greatest Hits	1969	$75
❏ W1053 [M]	Frank Sinatra Sings for Only the Lonely	1958	$75
— Gray label			
❏ W1053 [M]	Frank Sinatra Sings for Only the Lonely	1959	$100
— Black label with colorband			
❏ SW1053 [S]	Frank Sinatra Sings for Only the Lonely	1959	$150
— Originals do not include "It's a Lonesome Old Town" and "Spring Is Here"			
❏ SW1053 [S]	Frank Sinatra Sings for Only the Lonely	196?	$150
— Later releases restore "It's a Lonesome Old Town" and "Spring Is Here"			
❏ SN-16202	Frank Sinatra Sings for Only the Lonely	198?	$20
— Budget-line reissue			
❏ SY-4533 [S]	Frank Sinatra Sings for Only the Lonely	197?	$25
— Reissue of SW-1053 on orange label with "Capitol" at bottom			
❏ W581 [M]	In the Wee Small Hours	1955	$85
— Gray label original			
❏ W581 [M]	In the Wee Small Hours	1959	$150
— Black label with colorband			
❏ DW581 [R]	In the Wee Small Hours	196?	$75
❏ SM-581	In the Wee Small Hours	197?	$20
❏ H1-581 [10]	In the Wee Small Hours, Part 1	1955	$300
❏ H2-581 [10]	In the Wee Small Hours, Part 2	1955	$300
❏ W1164 [M]	Look to Your Heart	1959	$150
❏ DW1164 [R]	Look to Your Heart	196?	$75
❏ N-16148	Look to Your Heart	198?	$20
— Budget-line reissue			
❏ N-16112	My One and Only Love	198?	$20
— Budget-line reissue			
❏ STBB-724	My One and Only Love/ Sentimental Journey	1971	$50
❏ STBB-500724	My One and Only Love/ Sentimental Journey	197?	$50
— Columbia Record Club edition of STBB-724			
❏ W1417 [M]	Nice 'N' Easy	1960	$100
❏ SW1417 [S]	Nice 'N' Easy	1960	$30
❏ SN-16204	Nice 'N' Easy	198?	$20
— Budget-line reissue			
❏ W1221 [M]	No One Cares	1959	$100
❏ SW1221 [S]	No One Cares	1959	$150
❏ SM-1221	No One Cares	197?	$20
❏ ST-11309	One More for the Road	1973	$25
❏ W1676 [M]	Point of No Return	1962	$100
❏ SW1676 [S]	Point of No Return	1962	$150
❏ SM-1676	Point of No Return	197?	$20
❏ SABB-11367 [P]	Round #1	1974	$50
❏ PRO-2163/4/5/6 [DJ]	Selections from Sinatra, The Great Years	1962	$85
❏ W90986 [M]	Sentimental Journey	1966	$150
— Capitol Record Club issue			
❏ DW90986 [R]	Sentimental Journey	1966	$50
— Capitol Record Club issue			
❏ SN-16113	Sentimental Journey	198?	$20
— Budget-line reissue			
❏ WCO1762 [M]	Sinatra, The Great Years	1962	$150
❏ SWCO1762 [P]	Sinatra, The Great Years	1962	$85
❏ W1729 [M]	Sinatra Sings…Of Love and Things	1962	$100
❏ SW1729 [P]	Sinatra Sings…Of Love and Things	1962	$100

Number	Title	Yr	NM
❏ SN-16149	Sinatra Sings…Of Love and Things	198?	$20
— Budget-line reissue			
❏ W1825 [M]	Sinatra Sings Rodgers and Hart	1963	$100
❏ DW1825 [R]	Sinatra Sings Rodgers and Hart	1963	$75
❏ STBB-95191	Sinatra Sings the Great Ones	1973	$100
— Longines Symphonette (formerly Capitol) Record Club issue			
❏ W2301 [M]	Sinatra Sings the Select Cole Porter	1965	$100
❏ DW2301 [R]	Sinatra Sings the Select Cole Porter	1965	$75
❏ T2123 [M]	Sinatra Sings the Select Harold Arlen	1964	$175
— Only released in Canada, Australia and the UK			
❏ W1994 [M]	Sinatra Sings the Select Johnny Mercer	1963	$100
❏ DW1994 [R]	Sinatra Sings the Select Johnny Mercer	1963	$75
❏ W1491 [M]	Sinatra's Swingin' Session!!!	1961	$100
❏ SW1491 [S]	Sinatra's Swingin' Session!!!	1961	$150
❏ SM-1491	Sinatra's Swingin' Session!!!	197?	$20
❏ W653 [M]	Songs for Swingin' Lovers!	1956	$175
— Gray label; cover has Sinatra facing away from the embracing couple			
❏ W653 [M]	Songs for Swingin' Lovers!	1956	$85
— Gray label; cover has Sinatra facing toward the embracing couple			
❏ W653 [M]	Songs for Swingin' Lovers!	1959	$150
— Black label with colorband			
❏ DW653 [R]	Songs for Swingin' Lovers!	196?	$75
❏ SM-653	Songs for Swingin' Lovers!	197?	$20
❏ DQBO91261 [R]	Songs for the Young at Heart	196?	$150
— Capitol Record Club issue			
❏ H488 [10]	Songs for Young Lovers	1954	$250
❏ W1432 [M]	Songs for Young Lovers	1960	$100
❏ DW1432 [R]	Songs for Young Lovers	1960	$75
❏ H528 [10]	Swing Easy	1954	$250
❏ W1429 [M]	Swing Easy	1960	$100
❏ DW1429 [R]	Swing Easy	1960	$75
❏ W587 [M]	Swing Easy/Songs for Young Lovers	1955	$85
— Gray label original; 12-inch version of two 10-inch LPs			
❏ W587 [M]	Swing Easy/Songs for Young Lovers	1959	$150
— Black label with colorband			
❏ T1919 [M]	Tell Her You Love Her	1963	$100
❏ DT1919 [R]	Tell Her You Love Her	1963	$75
❏ DKAO2900 [R]	The Best of Frank Sinatra	1968	$35
❏ SN-16109	The Best of Frank Sinatra	198?	$20
— Budget-line reissue			
❏ C1-94777	The Capitol Years	1990	$300
— With book and wraparound banner. Only 5,000 were pressed			
❏ TFL-2814 [M]	The Frank Sinatra Deluxe Set	1968	$300
❏ STFL2814 [P]	The Frank Sinatra Deluxe Set	1968	$250
❏ T2036 [M]	The Greatest Hits of Frank Sinatra	1964	$100
❏ DT2036 [R]	The Greatest Hits of Frank Sinatra	1964	$75
❏ T2700 [M]	The Movie Songs	1967	$100
❏ DT2700 [R]	The Movie Songs	1967	$75
❏ SN-16111	The Night We Called It a Day	198?	$20
— Budget-line reissue			
❏ T894 [M]	The Sinatra Christmas Album	196?	$100
— Reissue of A Jolly Christmas with Frank Sinatra with same contents; some copies have this cover and "A Jolly Christmas" labels			
❏ SM-894 [R]	The Sinatra Christmas Album	197?	$20
— Reissue in rechanneled stereo; any color label			
❏ DT894 [R]	The Sinatra Christmas Album	196?	$25
— Rechanneled reissue of A Jolly Christmas with Frank Sinatra with same contents; some copies have this cover and "A Jolly Christmas" labels			
❏ DNFR7630 [P]	The Sinatra Touch	19??	$250
❏ T768 [M]	This Is Sinatra!	1956	$150
— Turquoise label			
❏ T768 [M]	This Is Sinatra!	196?	$100
— Black "Starline" label			
❏ T768 [M]	This Is Sinatra!	196?	$50
— Gold "Starline" label			
❏ DT768 [R]	This Is Sinatra!	196?	$75
❏ M-11883	This Is Sinatra!	1979	$25
❏ W982 [M]	This Is Sinatra, Volume Two	1958	$85
— Gray label			
❏ W982 [M]	This Is Sinatra, Volume Two	1959	$100
— Black label with colorband, logo at left			
❏ DW982 [R]	This Is Sinatra, Volume Two	196?	$75
❏ DN-16268	This Is Sinatra, Volume Two	198?	$20
— Budget-line reissue			
❏ W982 [M]	This Is Sinatra, Volume Two	1963	$50
— Black label with colorband, logo at top			
❏ DN-16110	What Is This Thing Called Love	198?	$20
— Budget-line reissue			

Number	Title	Yr	NM
❏ STBB-529	What Is This Thing Called Love?/The Night We Called It a Day	1970	$75
❏ SN-16267	Where Are You	198?	$20
— Budget-line reissue			
❏ W855 [M]	Where Are You?	1957	$150
— Gray label			
❏ W855 [M]	Where Are You?	1959	$100
— Black label with colorband			
❏ SW855 [S]	Where Are You?	1959	$85
— Originals do not include "I Cover the Waterfront"			
❏ SW855 [S]	Where Are You?	196?	$150
— Later releases restore "I Cover the Waterfront"			
CAPITOL PICKWICK SERIES			
❏ PC-3457 [M]	Just One of Those Things	196?	$75
❏ SPC-3457 [R]	Just One of Those Things	196?	$25
❏ PC-3463 [M]	My Cole Porter	196?	$75
❏ SPC-3463 [R]	My Cole Porter	196?	$40
❏ PC-3456 [M]	Nevertheless	196?	$75
❏ SPC-3456 [R]	Nevertheless	196?	$25
❏ PC-3450 [M]	The Nearness of You	196?	$75
❏ SPC-3450 [R]	The Nearness of You	196?	$25
❏ PC-3458 [M]	This Love of Mine	196?	$75
❏ SPC-3458 [R]	This Love of Mine	196?	$25
❏ PC-3452 [M]	Try a Little Tenderness	196?	$75
❏ SPC-3452 [R]	Try a Little Tenderness	196?	$25
COLUMBIA			
❏ CL953 [M]	Adventures of the Heart	1957	$75
❏ PC40707	Christmas Dreaming	1987	$75
— Reissue of CL 1032 with an extra track			
❏ CL1032 [M]	Christmas Dreaming	1957	$175
❏ CL6019 [10]	Christmas Songs by Sinatra	1948	$200
— With "gingerbread man" cover			
❏ CL6019 [10]	Christmas Songs by Sinatra	1949	$175
— With green vinylite cover			
❏ CL2542 [M]	Christmas with Sinatra	1955	$120
— House Party Series" release			
❏ CL1359 [M]	Come Back to Sorrento	1959	$75
❏ CL6096 [10]	Dedicated to You	1952	$200
— Three of the tracks on this LP are alternate takes unavailable on vinyl anywhere else			
❏ CL606 [M]	Frankie	1955	$85
— Cover has drawing of Frank Sinatra wearing a hat			
❏ CL606 [M]	Frankie	1955	$85
— Cover has Frank with Debbie Reynolds			
❏ CL6059 [10]	Frankly Sentimental	1951	$120
❏ CL884 [M]	Frank Sinatra Conducts Music of Alec Wilder	1956	$40
— Reissue of Columbia Masterworks ML 4271			
❏ CL2913 [M]	Frank Sinatra in Hollywood	1968	$175
❏ CS9713 [R]	Frank Sinatra in Hollywood	1968	$30
❏ CL2521 [10]	Get Happy	1955	$120
— House Party Series" release			
❏ CL2474 [M]	Greatest Hits, The Early Years, Vol. 1	1966	$35
❏ CS9274 [R]	Greatest Hits, The Early Years, Vol. 1	1966	$25
❏ PC9274	Greatest Hits, The Early Years, Vol. 1	197?	$20
❏ CL2572 [M]	Greatest Hits, The Early Years, Vol. 2	1966	$35
❏ CS9372 [R]	Greatest Hits, The Early Years, Vol. 2	1966	$25
❏ PC9372	Greatest Hits, The Early Years, Vol. 2	197?	$20
❏ C2X40897	Hello Young Lovers	1988	$75
❏ KG31358	In the Beginning	1971	$40
— Original edition; titles of songs at left on front cover			
❏ PG31358	In the Beginning	197?	$30
— Revised version; titles of songs at right on front cover			
❏ CL6290 [10]	I've Got a Crush on You	1954	$120
❏ CL2539 [10]	I've Got a Crush on You	1955	$120
— House Party Series" release; different contents from CL 6290			
❏ CL1241 [M]	Love Is a Kick	1958	$75
❏ CL1136 [M]	Put Your Dreams Away	1958	$75
❏ CL1448 [M]	Reflections	1959	$120
❏ PC44238 [M]	Sinatra Rarities	1989	$40
❏ CL6143 [10]	Sing and Dance with Frank Sinatra	1953	$120
❏ CL6087 [10]	Songs by Sinatra, Volume 1	1952	$120
❏ CL902 [M]	That Old Feeling	1956	$75
❏ CL1297 [M]	The Broadway Kick	1958	$75
❏ S3L42 [M]	The Essential Frank Sinatra	1966	$200
❏ S3S42 [R]	The Essential Frank Sinatra	1966	$150
❏ CL2739 [M]	The Essential Frank Sinatra, Volume 1	1967	$75
❏ CS9539 [R]	The Essential Frank Sinatra, Volume 1	1967	$30
❏ CL2740 [M]	The Essential Frank Sinatra, Volume 2	1967	$75
❏ CS9540 [R]	The Essential Frank Sinatra, Volume 2	1967	$30
❏ CL2741 [M]	The Essential Frank Sinatra, Volume 3	1967	$75
❏ CS9541 [R]	The Essential Frank Sinatra, Volume 3	1967	$30
❏ C2L6 [M]	The Frank Sinatra Story	1958	$75
❏ CL743 [M]	The Voice	1956	$75
❏ CL743 [M]	The Voice	1999	$75
— Classic Records reissue on audiophile vinyl			
❏ C6X40343	The Voice: The Columbia Years 1943-1952	1986	$175

Number	Title	Yr	NM
❏ CAS2475 [DJ]	The Voice: The Columbia Years Sampler	1986	$40
❏ CAS2475 [DJ]	The Voice: The Columbia Years Sampler	1986	$40
❏ CL6001 [10]	The Voice of Frank Sinatra	1949	$140
—Original in pink paper cover			
❏ CL6001 [10]	The Voice of Frank Sinatra	1950	$120
—Blue cardboard cover			

COLUMBIA MASTERWORKS

❏ ML4271 [M]	Frank Sinatra Conducts Music of Alec Wilder	1955	$200

HARMONY

❏ HS11390 [R]	Frank Sinatra	1969	$35
❏ KH30318 [R]	Greatest Hits, Early Years	1971	$35
❏ HL7400 [M]	Have Yourself a Merry Little Christmas	1967	$75
❏ HS11200 [R]	Have Yourself a Merry Little Christmas	1967	$50
—At least two different cover designs exist			
❏ HL7405 [M]	Romantic Scenes from the Early Years	1967	$75
❏ HS11205 [R]	Romantic Scenes from the Early Years	1967	$30
❏ HS11277 [R]	Someone to Watch Over Me	1968	$35

LONGINES SYMPHONETTE

❏ LS-308A	Sinatra: The Works	1972	$175
❏ LS-309A	Sinatra: The Works	1973	$40
—Abridged version of LS-308A			
❏ SYS-5637	Sinatra Like Never Before	1972	$75
—Bonus LP with purchase of LS-308A			

MOBILE FIDELITY

❏ 1-135 [M]	A Jolly Christmas from Frank Sinatra	1984	$150
—Audiophile vinyl using the original title			
❏ Jan-0086	Nice 'N' Easy	1981	$40
—Audiophile vinyl			
❏ MFSL1-409 [B]	Point of No Return	2014	$50
❏ SC-1	Sinatra	1983	$800
—Audiophile vinyl; only two of the 16 records in this box were released individually			

PAIR

❏ PDL2-1027	All-Time Classics	1986	$30
❏ PDL2-1122	Classic Performances	1986	$30
❏ PDL2-1028	Timeless	1986	$30

QWEST

❏ 25145	L.A. Is My Lady	1984	$30

RCA VICTOR

❏ LPT-3063 [10]	Fabulous Frankie	1953	$120
❏ LPM-1569 [M]	Frankie and Tommy	1957	$120
—First issue of this LP			
❏ AFL1-4741 [R]	Radio Years (Sinatra/Dorsey/Stordahl)	1983	$35
❏ CPL2-4334	The Sinatra/Dorsey Sessions, Vol. 1	1982	$75
❏ CPL2-4335	The Sinatra/Dorsey Sessions, Vol. 2	1982	$75
❏ CPL2-4336	The Sinatra/Dorsey Sessions, Vol. 3	1982	$75
❏ LPV-583 [M]	This Love of Mine	1971	$40
❏ LPM-1569 [M]	Tommy Plays, Frankie Sings	1957	$40
—Second issue with new title			
❏ LPM-1632 [M]	We Three	1958	$120
—First issue			
❏ LPM-1632 [M]	We Three	1958	$40
—Second issue, "RE" on cover			
❏ APL1-0497 [R]	What'll I Do	1974	$30
❏ ANL1-1050 [R]	What'll I Do	1976	$25

REPRISE

❏ F1007 [M]	All Alone	1962	$35
❏ R91007 [S]	All Alone	1962	$50
❏ FS1030	A Man Alone & Other Songs of Rod McKuen	1969	$35
❏ FS1030	A Man Alone & Other Songs of Rod McKuen	1969	$400
—Signed copies with gatefold cover and hardbound book; 400 made			
❏ SMAS-92081	A Man Alone & Other Songs of Rod McKuen	1969	$100
—Capitol Record Club edition			
❏ 2F1016 [M]	A Man and His Music	1965	$50
❏ 2FS1016 [S]	A Man and His Music	1965	$75
❏ 5004 [DJ]	A Man and His Music, Part II	1966	$250
—Promotional album for use by Budweiser			
❏ 5004 [DJ]	A Man and His Music, Part II	1966	$300
—Promotional album for use by Budweiser			
❏ 2F/2FS1016	A Man and His Music Special Box	1965	$250
—Blue slipcase with embossed silver front, raised letters, plus 4-page booklet and a signed card (deduct 50% if card missing). Add this to LP value.			
❏ FS1027	Cycles	1969	$35
❏ F1011 [M]	Days of Wine and Roses, Moon River, and Other Academy Award Winners	1964	$35
❏ FS1011 [S]	Days of Wine and Roses, Moon River, and Other Academy Award Winners	1964	$50
❏ FS1024	Francis A. and Edward K.	1968	$50
❏ F1021 [M]	Francis Albert Sinatra & Antonio Carlos Jobim	1967	$30

Number	Title	Yr	NM
❏ FS1021 [S]	Francis Albert Sinatra & Antonio Carlos Jobim	1967	$35
❏ R173798 [S]	Francis Albert Sinatra & Antonio Carlos Jobim	2004	$35
—180-gram reissue			
❏ FS1025	Frank Sinatra's Greatest Hits	1968	$35
❏ FS1032	Frank Sinatra's Greatest Hits, Vol. 2	1970	$0
—Canceled?			
❏ FS1034	Frank Sinatra's Greatest Hits, Vol. 2	1972	$35
❏ FS4-1034 [Q]	Frank Sinatra's Greatest Hits, Vol. 2	1974	$40
❏ F1022 [M]	Frank Sinatra (The World We Knew)	1967	$35
❏ FS1022 [S]	Frank Sinatra (The World We Knew)	1967	$35
❏ F1006 [M]	Great Songs from Great Britain	1962	$100
—Only released in the UK			
❏ R91006 [S]	Great Songs from Great Britain	1962	$150
—Only released in the UK			
❏ F1003 [M]	I Remember Tommy	1961	$50
❏ R91003 [S]	I Remember Tommy	1961	$75
❏ 5409 [DJ]	I Sing the Songs	1976	$50
❏ 5409 [DJ]	I Sing the Songs	1976	$150
❏ F1012 [M]	It Might As Well Be Swing	1964	$35
❏ FS1012 [S]	It Might As Well Be Swing	1964	$50
❏ F1018 [M]	Moonlight Sinatra	1966	$35
❏ SYS1018 [S]	Moonlight Sinatra	1966	$50
❏ F1015 [M]	My Kind of Broadway	1965	$35
❏ FS1015 [S]	My Kind of Broadway	1965	$50
❏ FS1029	My Way	1969	$35
❏ FS41029 [Q]	My Way	1974	$40
❏ FS2155	Ol' Blue Eyes Is Back	1973	$30
❏ FS42155 [Q]	Ol' Blue Eyes Is Back	1974	$40
❏ F1001 [M]	Ring-a-Ding-Ding!	1961	$50

❏ R91001 [S]	Ring-a-Ding-Ding!	1961	$30
❏ F1014 [M]	September of My Years	1965	$35
❏ FS1014 [S]	September of My Years	1965	$50
❏ R173799 [S]	September of My Years	2004	$35
—180-gram reissue			
❏ FS2305	She Shot Me Down	1981	$30
❏ F1004 [M]	Sinatra & Strings	1962	$35
❏ R91004 [S]	Sinatra & Strings	1962	$50
❏ R6167 [M]	Sinatra '65	1965	$35
❏ RS6167 [S]	Sinatra '65	1965	$50
❏ FS1033	Sinatra and Company	1971	$35
❏ F1005 [M]	Sinatra and Swingin' Brass	1962	$35
❏ R91005 [S]	Sinatra and Swingin' Brass	1962	$50
❏ 2F1019 [M]	Sinatra at the Sands	1966	$50
❏ 2FS1019 [S]	Sinatra at the Sands	1966	$75
❏ F1008 [M]	Sinatra-Basie	1963	$35
❏ R91008 [S]	Sinatra-Basie	1963	$50
❏ F6045 [M]	Sinatra Conducts Music from Pictures and Plays	1962	$75
❏ R96045 [S]	Sinatra Conducts Music from Pictures and Plays	1962	$40
❏ FS1028	SinatraJobim	1969	$4000
—Unreleased; test pressings exist (value is for one of these). 8-track tapes also exist and are 10% of this value; VG value 1000; VG+ value 1000			
❏ R-1010 [M]	Sinatra's Sinatra	1963	$35
—Gatefold jacket; some copies have a large photo of Sinatra holding a pack of Lucky Strikes at the right side of the inside gatefold; we don't yet know the relative rarity of these variations, or which came first, or whether they also exist on stereo copies			
❏ R-1010 [M]	Sinatra's Sinatra	1963	$35
—Gatefold jacket; some copies have eight photos of previous Frank Sinatra Reprise LPs at the right side of the inside gatefold; we don't yet know the relative rarity of these variations, or which came first, or whether they also exist on stereo copies			
❏ R91010 [S]	Sinatra's Sinatra	1963	$50
❏ R91002 [M]	Sinatra Swings	1961	$100
—Retitled version of "Swing Along with Me"; Capitol threatened legal action because of its "Come Swing With Me!"			

Number	Title	Yr	NM
collection			
❏ R91002 [S]	Sinatra Swings	1961	$150
—Retitled version of "Swing Along with Me"; Capitol threatened legal action because of its "Come Swing With Me!" collection			
❏ FS2207	Sinatra -- The Main Event Live	1974	$30
❏ F1013 [M]	Softly, As I Leave You	1964	$35
❏ FS1013 [S]	Softly, As I Leave You	1964	$50
❏ FS2195	Some Nice Things I've Missed	1974	$30
❏ FS42194 [Q]	Some Nice Things I've Missed	1974	$40
❏ 5230 [DJ]	Songbook, Vol. 1	1971	$50
❏ 5230 [DJ]	Songbook, Vol. 1	1971	$150
❏ 5267 [DJ]	Songbook, Vol. 2	1972	$150
❏ 5267 [DJ]	Songbook, Vol. 2	1972	$200
❏ F1017 [M]	Strangers in the Night	1966	$30
❏ FS1017 [S]	Strangers in the Night	1966	$35
❏ F1002 [M]	Swing Along with Me	1961	$40
—Original title			
❏ R91002 [S]	Swing Along with Me	1961	$150
—Original title			
❏ F1020 [M]	That's Life	1966	$30
❏ FS1020 [S]	That's Life	1966	$35
❏ F1009 [M]	The Concert Sinatra	1963	$35
❏ R91009 [S]	The Concert Sinatra	1963	$75
—Original pressings declare this was recorded in "35mm Stereo			
❏ R91009 [S]	The Concert Sinatra	196?	$50
—Without cover reference to "35mm Stereo			
❏ FS1023	The Sinatra Christmas Album	1967	$200
—Album never released; value is for cover slick			
❏ 3FS2300	Trilogy: Past, Present, Future	1980	$50
❏ FS1031	Watertown	1970	$75
—With gatefold and poster			
❏ SMAS-93119	Watertown	1970	$150
—Capitol Record Club edition; does not contain poster			

TIME-LIFE

❏ SLGD-02	Legendary Singers: Frank Sinatra	1985	$75

SINATRA, NANCY
RCA VICTOR

❏ LSP-4645	Nancy and Lee Again	1972	$30
—With Lee Hazlewood			
❏ VPS-6078	This Is Nancy Sinatra	1972	$50
❏ LSP-4774	Woman	1973	$30

REPRISE

❏ R-6202 [M]	Boots	1966	$30
❏ RS-6202 [S]	Boots	1966	$35
❏ ST-91341 [S]	Boots	1967	$50
—Capitol Record Club edition			
❏ R-6251 [M]	Country, My Way	1967	$50
❏ RS-6251 [S]	Country, My Way	1967	$35
❏ R-6207 [M]	How Does That Grab You?	1966	$30
❏ RS-6207 [S]	How Does That Grab You?	1966	$35
❏ R-6277 [M]	Movin' with Nancy	1967	$50
❏ RS-6277 [S]	Movin' with Nancy	1967	$35
❏ ST-91349 [S]	Movin' with Nancy	1967	$40
—Capitol Record Club edition			
❏ RS-6333 [B]	Nancy	1969	$40
❏ RS-6273 [B]	Nancy and Lee	1968	$35
—With Lee Hazlewood			
❏ R-6221 [M]	Nancy in London	1966	$40
❏ RS-6221 [S]	Nancy in London	1966	$35
❏ RS-6409 [B]	Nancy's Greatest Hits	1970	$30
❏ R-6239 [M]	Sugar	1967	$50
❏ RS-6239 [S]	Sugar	1967	$35

RHINO

❏ RNLP-70227 [B]	Boots: Nancy Sinatra's All-Time Hits (1966-1970)	1987	$15
❏ R1-70166 [B]	Fairy Tales and Fantasies: The Best of Nancy and Lee	1989	$15
—With Lee Hazlewood			

SINCEROS, THE
COLUMBIA

❏ NFC37349	Pet Rock	1980	$12
❏ JC36134	The Sound of Sunbathing	1979	$15

SINFIELD, PETE
Also see KING CRIMSON.

MANTICORE

❏ MC66667 [B]	Still	1973	$30

SING A SONG WITH THE BEATLES
TOWER

❏ KAO5000 [M]	Sing a Song with the Beatles	1965	$300
—No artist listed on label			
❏ DKAO5000 [R]	Sing a Song with the Beatles	1965	$300

SINGER, HAL, AND CHARLIE SHAVERS
PRESTIGE

❏ PRLP-7153 [M]	Blue Stompin'	1959	$250

Number	Title	Yr	NM

SWINGVILLE
| ❏ SVLP-2023 [M] | Blue Stompin' | 1961 | $50 |

— *Purple label*
| ❏ SVLP-2023 [M] | Blue Stompin' | 1965 | $30 |

— *Blue label, trident logo at right*

SINGER ORCHESTRA, THE
SINGER
| ❏ HE-M-1 [M] | Favorite Christmas Songs from Singer | 1964 | $18 |

— *Cover photo of the cast of "The Donna Reed Show"*
| ❏ HE-S-1 [S] | Favorite Christmas Songs from Singer | 1964 | $25 |

— *Cover photo of the cast of "The Donna Reed Show"*

SINGERS UNLIMITED, THE
BASF
| ❏ 21852 | The Four of Us | 197? | $30 |
| ❏ 20903 | Try to Remember | 197? | $30 |

PAUSA
❏ 7100	A Cappella I	198?	$25
❏ 7101	A Cappella II	198?	$25
❏ 7076	A Cappella III	1979	$25
❏ 7062	A Special Blend	197?	$25
❏ 7136	Composer's Corner: The Singers Unlimited Sing Music of Lennon, McCartney and Ellington	198?	$30
❏ 7109	Easy to Love	198?	$25
❏ 7118	Eventide	198?	$25
❏ 7068	Feeling Free	197?	$25
❏ 7121	Four of Us	198?	$25
❏ 7039	Friends	197?	$25
❏ 7048	Just in Time	197?	$25
❏ 7056	The Singers Unlimited with Rob McConnell and the Boss Brass	197?	$25

VERVE
❏ 815671-1	A Cappella	1985	$25
❏ 821859-1	Christmas	198?	$30
❏ 817486-1	The Singers Unlimited with Rob McConnell and the Boss Brass	198?	$25

SINGING NUN, THE
PHILIPS
❏ PCC209 [M]	Her Joy, Her Songs	1964	$18
❏ PCC609 [S]	Her Joy, Her Songs	1964	$18
❏ PCC203 [M]	Soeur Sourire: The Singing Nun	1963	$25
❏ PCC603 [S]	Soeur Sourire: The Singing Nun	1963	$18

SINGING NUNS, THE
SN
| ❏ 001 [S] | O Bambino | 197? | $15 |

— *No relation to the "Dominique" lady.*

SINGLE BULLET THEORY
NEMPEROR
| ❏ ARZ38368 | Single Bullet Theory | 1983 | $12 |

SINGLETON, CHARLIE
RCA CAMDEN
| ❏ CAL-713 [M] | Big Twist Hits | 1962 | $25 |
| ❏ CAS-713 [S] | Big Twist Hits | 1962 | $30 |

SINGLETON, MARGIE
ASHLEY
| ❏ 3003 | Margie Singleton Sings Country Music with Soul | 1968 | $18 |

PICKWICK
| ❏ SPC-3133 | Harper Valley P.T.A. | 197? | $12 |

UNITED ARTISTS
| ❏ UAL-3459 [M] | Crying Time | 1965 | $18 |
| ❏ UAS-6459 [S] | Crying Time | 1965 | $25 |

SINGLETON, ZUTTY/ART TATUM
BRUNSWICK
| ❏ BL58038 [10] | Battle of Jazz, Vol. 2 | 1953 | $50 |

SIOUXSIE AND THE BANSHEES
GEFFEN
❏ GHS24049	A Kiss in the Dream House	1984	$12
❏ GHS24030	Hyaena	1984	$12
❏ GHS24047	Join Hands	1984	$12
❏ GHS24050	Juju	1984	$12

— *Reissue of PVC 8903*
| ❏ GHS24048 | Kaleidoscope | 1984 | $12 |

— *Reissue of PVC 7921*
| ❏ GHS24052 | Nocturne | 1984 | $12 |
| ❏ GHS24051 | Once Upon a Time: The Singles | 1984 | $12 |

— *Reissue of PVC 8906*
❏ GHS24205	Peepshow	1988	$12
❏ GEF24387 [B]	Superstition	1991	$25
❏ GEF24630	The Rapture	1995	$18

| ❏ GHS24046 | The Scream | 1984 | $12 |

— *Reissue of Polydor PD1-6207*
| ❏ GHS24134 | Through the Looking Glass | 1987 | $12 |
| ❏ GHS24092 | Tinderbox | 1986 | $12 |

POLYDOR
| ❏ PD1-6207 | The Scream | 1978 | $30 |

PVC
| ❏ 8903 | Ju Ju | 1981 | $30 |

— *Original copies include bonus single "Israel"/"Red Over White*
| ❏ 7921 | Kaleidoscope | 1980 | $30 |
| ❏ 8906 | Once Upon a Time: The Singles | 1981 | $25 |

— *With poster and inner sleeve*

WARNER BROS.
| ❏ WBMS-138 [DJ] | The Tinderbox Interview | 1986 | $30 |

— *Part of "The Warner Bros. Music Show"*

SIR DOUGLAS QUINTET
Also see THE DEVONS; DOUG SAHM.
ABC DOT
| ❏ DO-2057 | Texas Rock for Country Rollers | 1976 | $18 |

— *As "Sir Doug and the Texas Tornadoes"*

ATLANTIC
| ❏ SD7287 | Texas Tornado | 1974 | $18 |

— *As "Sir Douglas Band"*

BEAT ROCKET
| ❏ BR123 | The Best of the Sir Douglas Quintet | 2000 | $15 |

— *Reissue of Tribe LP on 180-gram vinyl*
| ❏ BR124 | The Sir Douglas Quintet Is Back! | 2000 | $15 |

— *New compilation of Tribe material on 180-gram vinyl*

PHILIPS
| ❏ PHS600344 | 1 + 1 + 1 = 4 | 1970 | $30 |
| ❏ PHS600353 | The Return of Doug Saldana | 1971 | $30 |

R&M
| ❏ UDL-2343 | The Tracker | 1981 | $25 |

SMASH
❏ SRS-67115	Mendocino	1969	$30
❏ SRS-67108	Sir Douglas Quintet + 2 = Honkey Blues	1968	$30
❏ SRS-67130	Together After Five	1970	$30

TAKOMA
❏ TAK-7088	Border Wave	1981	$20
❏ TAK-7095	Sir Douglas Quintet Live	1985	$15
❏ TAK-7086	The Best of the Sir Douglas Quintet	1980	$15

TRIBE
| ❏ TR37001 [M] | The Best of the Sir Douglas Quintet | 1966 | $80 |
| ❏ TRS47001 [R] | The Best of the Sir Douglas Quintet | 1966 | $50 |

VARRICK
| ❏ 004 | Quintessence | 1983 | $15 |

SIR LANCELOT
MERCURY
| ❏ MG-25159 [10] | Calypso | 1952 | $50 |

SIR LORD BALTIMORE
MERCURY
| ❏ SR-61328 | Kingdom Come | 1970 | $30 |
| ❏ SRM-1-613 | Sir Lord Baltimore | 1971 | $30 |

SIRAVO, GEORGE
AD-LIB
| ❏ 226 [M] | Out on a Limb | 196? | $35 |
| ❏ S-226 [S] | Out on a Limb | 196? | $25 |

COLUMBIA
| ❏ CL6146 [10] | Your Dance Date with George Siravo | 1951 | $40 |

DECCA
| ❏ DL8464 [M] | Portraits in Hi-Fi | 1957 | $120 |

EPIC
| ❏ LN3803 [M] | Everything Goes | 1961 | $85 |
| ❏ BN607 [S] | Everything Goes | 1961 | $40 |

KAPP
| ❏ KL-1016 [M] | Polite Jazz | 1956 | $30 |

MERCURY
| ❏ MG-20327 [M] | Darling, Please Forgive Me | 1958 | $175 |

RCA CAMDEN
| ❏ CAL-505 [M] | Siravo Swing Session | 1959 | $35 |
| ❏ CAS-505 [S] | Siravo Swing Session | 1959 | $25 |

RCA VICTOR
| ❏ LPM-1970 [M] | Swingin' in Hi-Fi in Studio A | 1959 | $30 |
| ❏ LSP-1970 [S] | Swingin' in Hi-Fi in Studio A | 1959 | $30 |

TIME
| ❏ 52115 [M] | And Then I Wrote Richard Rodgers | 196? | $35 |

❏ S-2115 [S]	And Then I Wrote Richard Rodgers	196?	$25
❏ S-2019 [S]	Seductive Strings	196?	$25
❏ 52019 [M]	Seductive Strings	196?	$35

VIK
| ❏ LX-1091 [M] | Old But New | 1957 | $30 |
| ❏ LX-1125 [M] | Swing Hi, Swing Fi | 1958 | $30 |

SIREN
ELEKTRA
| ❏ EKS-74087 | Strange Locomotion | 1971 | $25 |

SISTER DOUBLE HAPPINESS
REPRISE
| ❏ PRO05010 [DJ] | Heart and Mind | 1991 | $50 |

— *Available as stock copy on cassette and CD only*
| ❏ PRO-A-5010 [DJ] | Heart and Mind | 1991 | $50 |

— *Vinyl is promo only*

SST
| ❏ 162 | Sister Double Happiness | 1988 | $12 |

SISTER SLEDGE
ATCO
| ❏ SD 36-105 | Circle of Love | 1975 | $25 |

ATLANTIC
| ❏ 81255 | When the Boys Meet the Girls | 1985 | $12 |

COTILLION
❏ SD16027	All American Girls	1981	$12
❏ 90069	Bet Cha Say That to All the Girls	1983	$12
❏ SD16012	Love Somebody Today	1980	$12
❏ SD5231	The Sisters	1982	$12
❏ SD9919	Together	1976	$25
❏ SD5209	We Are Family	1979	$12

SISTERS OF MERCY
ELEKTRA
| ❏ 60405 [B] | First and Last and Always | 1985 | $25 |
| ❏ 60762 [B] | Floodland | 1987 | $25 |

MOBILE FIDELITY
| ❏ MOFI1-021 [B] | Floodland | 2013 | $35 |

SIVUCA
VANGUARD
| ❏ VSD-79352 | Live at the Village Gate | 197? | $30 |
| ❏ VSD-79337 | Sivuca | 197? | $35 |

SIX, THE
BETHLEHEM
| ❏ BCP-28 [M] | The Six | 1955 | $300 |
| ❏ BCP-57 [M] | The View From Jazzbo's Head | 1956 | $300 |

SIX AND SEVEN-EIGHTHS STRING BAND, THE
FOLKWAYS
| ❏ FP-2671 [M] | The Six and Seven-Eighths String Band | 195? | $40 |
| ❏ FP-671 [M] | The Six and Seven-Eighths String Band | 1951 | $50 |

SIZEMORE, ARTHUR
DECCA
| ❏ DL4785 [M] | Mountain Ballads and Old Hymns | 1966 | $30 |
| ❏ DL74785 [S] | Mountain Ballads and Old Hymns | 1966 | $40 |

SKAGGS, RICKY, AND KEITH WHITLEY
REBEL
| ❏ 1504 | Second Generation Bluegrass | 1972 | $25 |
| ❏ 1550 | That's It | 1975 | $25 |

SKAGGS, RICKY
ATLANTIC
| ❏ 82834 | Solid Ground | 1995 | $18 |

EPIC
❏ FE40623	Comin' Home to Stay	1988	$10
❏ FE39410	Country Boy	1984	$12
❏ FE39409	Favorite Country Songs	1985	$12
❏ FE37996	Highways and Heartaches	1982	$12
❏ FE45027	Kentucky Thunder	1989	$12
❏ FE40103	Live in London	1985	$12
❏ FE40309	Love's Gonna Get Ya!	1986	$10
❏ EAS2022 [DJ]	The Ricky Skaggs Story	1990	$30

— *Promo-only interview record*
| ❏ FE37193 | Waitin' for the Sun to Shine | 1981 | $12 |

ROUNDER
| ❏ 0151 | Family and Friends | 1982 | $15 |

SUGAR HILL
| ❏ SH-3711 | Skaggs and Rice | 1980 | $15 |
| ❏ SH-3706 | Sweet Temptation | 1979 | $15 |

Number	Title	Yr	NM

SUGAR HILL/EPIC
| ❏ FE38954 | Don't Cheat in Our Hometown | 1983 | $12 |

SKELTON, RED
LIBERTY
❏ LRP-3477 [M]	Music from the Heart	1966	$25
❏ LST-7477 [S]	Music from the Heart	1966	$30
❏ LRP-3425 [M]	Red Skelton Conducts	1966	$25
❏ LST-7425 [S]	Red Skelton Conducts	1966	$30

SKID ROW (1)
Cream-like band featuring GARY MOORE.
EPIC
| ❏ E30913 | 34 Hours | 1971 | $30 |
| ❏ E30404 | Skid Row | 1971 | $30 |

SKID ROW (2)
New Jersey hard rockers featuring SEBASTIAN BACH.
ATLANTIC
| ❏ 81936 [B] | Skid Row | 1989 | $15 |
| ❏ 1P-8136 | Slave to the Grind | 1991 | $30 |
— U.S. vinyl version available only from Columbia House; all copies are the censored version with "Beggars Day

SKIN ALLEY
STAX
| ❏ STS-3013 | Two Quid Deal | 1973 | $25 |
— With poster

SKINNER, CORNELIA AND OTIS
RCA CAMDEN
| ❏ CAL-190 [M] | Cornelia Skinner with Otis Skinner | 1955 | $30 |

SKINNER, JIMMIE
DECCA
| ❏ DL4132 [M] | Country Singer | 1961 | $40 |
MERCURY
❏ MG-20700 [M]	Jimmie Skinner Sings Jimmie Rodgers	1962	$30
❏ SR-60700 [S]	Jimmie Skinner Sings Jimmie Rodgers	1962	$30
❏ MG-20352 [M]	Songs That Make the Jukebox Play	1957	$100
STARDAY
| ❏ SLP-240 [M] | Jimmie Skinner | 1963 | $40 |
VETCO
| ❏ 3001 [B] | Jimmie Skinner Sings Bluegrass | 1976 | $25 |
WING
| ❏ MGW-12277 [M] | Country Blues | 1964 | $30 |
| ❏ SRW-16277 [R] | Country Blues | 1964 | $18 |

SKIP AND THE CREATIONS
JUSTICE
| ❏ 0(# unknown) | Mobam | 196? | $400 |

SKJELBRED, RAY
EUPHONIC
| ❏ 1223 | Chicago High Life | 198? | $25 |
STOMP OFF
| ❏ SOS-1097 | Gin Mill Blues | 1985 | $25 |
| ❏ SOS-1124 | Stompin' 'Em Down | 1987 | $25 |

SKUNKS, THE
TEEN TOWN
| ❏ TTLP-101 | Getting Started | 1968 | $50 |

SKY
RCA VICTOR
| ❏ LSP-4514 | Sailor's Delight | 1971 | $18 |
| ❏ LSP-4457 | Sky | 1970 | $18 |

SKYLARK
CAPITOL
| ❏ ST-11048 | Skylark | 1972 | $18 |
| ❏ ST-11256 | Skylark 2 | 1973 | $15 |

SKYLINERS, THE
CALICO
| ❏ LP-3000 [M] | The Skyliners | 1959 | $600 |
— Yellow and blue label
| ❏ LP-3000 [M] | The Skyliners | 196? | $250 |
— Blue label
KAMA SUTRA
| ❏ KSBS-2026 | Once Upon a Time | 1971 | $30 |
ORIGINAL SOUND
❏ OS-5010 [M]	Since I Don't Have You	1963	$50
❏ OSS-8873 [S]	Since I Don't Have You	1963	$80
❏ OSS-8873 [S]	Since I Don't Have You	197?	$18
— Reissue on thinner vinyl

SKYWALK
ZEBRA
| ❏ ZEB-42204 | Paradiso | 1988 | $25 |
| ❏ ZEB-5680 | Silent Witness | 1986 | $25 |
— Reissue of 5004
| ❏ ZR5004 | Silent Witness | 1984 | $30 |
| ❏ ZEB-5715 | The Bohemians | 1986 | $25 |

SLACK, FREDDIE
EMARCY
| ❏ MG-36094 [M] | Boogie-Woogie on the 88 | 1956 | $250 |
PAUSA
| ❏ 9027 | Behind the Eight-Beat | 198? | $25 |

SLADE
CBS ASSOCIATED
| ❏ FZ39336 | Keep Your Hands Off My Power Supply | 1984 | $12 |
| ❏ PZ39336 | Keep Your Hands Off My Power Supply | 1985 | $10 |
— Budget-line reissue
| ❏ FZ39976 | Rogues Gallery | 1985 | $15 |
| ❏ BFZ40908 | You Boyz Make Big Noize | 1986 | $15 |
COTILLION
| ❏ SD9035 [B] | Play It Loud | 1970 | $150 |
FONTANA
| ❏ SRF-67598 [B] | Ballzy | 1969 | $250 |

| ❏ SRF-67598 [DJ] | Ballzy | 1969 | $175 |
— White label promo
POLYDOR
| ❏ PD-5508 | Slade Alive! | 1972 | $18 |
| ❏ PD-5524 | Slayed? | 1973 | $18 |
REPRISE
| ❏ MS2173 | Sladest | 1973 | $18 |
WARNER BROS.
❏ BS2936	Nobody's Fools	1976	$25
❏ BS2865	Slade in Flame	1975	$18
❏ BS2770	Stomp Your Hands, Clap Your Feet	1974	$18

SLAGLE, STEVE
ATLANTIC
| ❏ 81657 | Rio Highlife | 1986 | $25 |

SLATER, DAVID
CAPITOL
| ❏ C1-91181 | Be with Me | 1989 | $12 |
| ❏ C1-48307 | Exchange of Hearts | 1988 | $10 |

SLATKIN, FELIX
LIBERTY
❏ LRP-3150 [M]	Fantastic Percussion	1960	$18
❏ LST-7150 [S]	Fantastic Percussion	1960	$25
❏ LMM-13021 [M]	Fantastic Strings Play Fantastic Themes	1962	$18
❏ LSS-14021 [S]	Fantastic Strings Play Fantastic Themes	1962	$25
❏ LMM-13024 [M]	Hoedown	1963	$18
❏ LSS-14024 [S]	Hoedown	1963	$25
❏ LMM-13019 [M]	Inspired Themes from the Inspired Films	1962	$18
❏ LSS-14019 [S]	Inspired Themes from the Inspired Films	1962	$25
❏ LMM-13011 [M]	Many Splendored Themes	1962	$18
❏ LSS-14011 [S]	Many Splendored Themes	1962	$25
❏ LRP-3287 [M]	Our Winter Love	1963	$15
❏ LST-7287 [S]	Our Winter Love	1963	$18
❏ LMM-13001 [M]	Paradise Found	1960	$18
❏ LSS-14001 [S]	Paradise Found	1960	$25
❏ LMM-13008 [M]	Street Scene	1961	$18
❏ LSS-14008 [S]	Street Scene	1961	$25
❏ LMM-13027 [M]	The Ballad of New Orleans	1963	$18
❏ LSS-14027 [S]	The Ballad of New Orleans	1963	$25

SUNSET
❏ SUM-1106 [M]	Love Strings	196?	$15
❏ SUS-5106 [S]	Love Strings	196?	$15
❏ SUM-1141 [M]	Seasons Greetings	196?	$15
❏ SUS-5141 [S]	Seasons Greetings	196?	$15
❏ SUM-1170 [M]	Tender Strings	196?	$15
❏ SUS-5170 [S]	Tender Strings	196?	$15
UNITED ARTISTS
| ❏ UAS-6818 | Classic Country | 1971 | $12 |

SLAUGHTER
CHRYSALIS
| ❏ R120666 [EP] | Stick It Live | 1990 | $25 |
— Vinyl version available only through BMG Direct Marketing
| ❏ F1-21702 [DJ] | Stick It To Ya | 1990 | $30 |
— Black generic sleeve with hole; numbered edition of 500 with sticker that says "Limited Edition Special Vinyl Pressing Metal Radio Only
| ❏ F1-21911 | The Wild Life | 1992 | $25 |
— Vinyl version available only through Columbia House

SLAWSON, BRIAN
CBS/FM
| ❏ 5M42069 [EP] | A Yule Log | 1985 | $10 |

SLAYER
AMERICAN
| ❏ C269192 | Diabolus in Musica | 1998 | $30 |
COMBAT
| ❏ MX8020 | Hell Awaits | 1985 | $25 |
DEF AMERICAN
| ❏ DFS24307 | Seasons in the Abyss | 1990 | $25 |
DEF JAM
| ❏ GHS24131 | Reign in Blood | 1986 | $25 |
| ❏ GHS24203 | South of Heaven | 1988 | $14 |
METAL BLADE
| ❏ 72297 | Hell Awaits | 1988 | $16 |
— Reissue of Combat LP
| ❏ MBR1037 [PD] | Live Undead | 1984 | $30 |
— Limited edition picture disc
| ❏ 72217 | Live Undead | 1987 | $25 |
| ❏ 71034 | Show No Mercy | 198? | $15 |
— Early reissue of 1034
| ❏ E1034 | Show No Mercy | 1983 | $25 |
| ❏ 72214 [PD] | Show No Mercy | 1987 | $30 |
— Picture disc in plastic sleeve

SLEAZE
SING SING
| ❏ SING0-49 [B] | Sleaze | 2012 | $30 |

SLEDD, PATSY
MEGA
| ❏ 1020 | Yours Sincerely | 1973 | $15 |

SLEDGE, PERCY
ATLANTIC
❏ SD8180	Take Time to Know Her	1968	$50
❏ SD8210	The Best of Percy Sledge	1969	$30
❏ 8146 [M]	The Percy Sledge Way	1967	$50
❏ SD8146 [S]	The Percy Sledge Way	1967	$50
❏ 80212	The Ultimate Collection: When a Man Loves a Woman	1983	$15
❏ 8132 [M]	Warm and Tender Soul	1966	$50
❏ SD8132 [R]	Warm and Tender Soul	1966	$30
❏ 8125 [M]	When a Man Loves a Woman	1966	$50
❏ SD8125 [R]	When a Man Loves a Woman	1966	$30
CAPRICORN
| ❏ CP 0147 | I'll Be Your Everything | 1974 | $18 |
MONUMENT
| ❏ FW38532 | Percy! | 1983 | $15 |

SLEEP
TUPELO
| ❏ TUPLP34 | Volume One | 1992 | $25 |

SLEEPERS
ADOLESCENT
| ❏ ARTT 007 | Painless Nights | 1981 | $15 |

SLEET, DON
JAZZLAND
| ❏ JLP-45 [M] | All Members | 1961 | $30 |
| ❏ JLP-945 [S] | All Members | 1961 | $30 |

SLICK, GRACE
Also see THE GREAT SOCIETY; JEFFERSON AIRPLANE; JEFFERSON STARSHIP; PAUL KANTNER AND GRACE SLICK.

Number	Title	Yr	NM
GRUNT			
❏ BFL1-0347 [B]	Manhole	1974	$18
❏ AYL1-3736	Manhole	1981	$10
—Best Buy Series" reissue			
RCA VICTOR			
❏ AFL1-3544	Dreams	1980	$12
❏ DJL1-3923 [DJ]	RCA Special Radio Series	1981	$25
❏ AQL1-3851	Welcome to the Wrecking Ball	1981	$12
❏ DJL1-3922 [DJ]	Welcome to the Wrecking Ball Interview	1981	$25
SLICKAPHONICS			
ENJA			
❏ 4024	Wow Bag	1982	$30
SLICKEE BOYS			
DACOIT			
❏ 1001	Separated Vegetables	1977	$100
—Limited edition of 100 copies			
GIANT			
❏ GR16037-1	Live at Last	1989	$12
LIMP			
❏ 1003	Separated Vegetables	1980	$30
—Limited edition of 300 copies; reissue with new cover			
TWIN/TONE			
❏ TTR8337	Cybernetic Dreams of Pi	1983	$18
❏ TTR8544	Uh Oh, No Breaks	1985	$15
SLIDER-GLENN			
I.T.I.			
❏ JL-031	A Whispered Warning	1986	$25
REEL DREAMS			
❏ 1007	A Whispered Warning	1983	$35
SLIM JIM			
SOMA			
❏ MG1225 [M]	Slim Jim Sings	1958	$40
SLINGER, CEES			
TIMELESS			
❏ LPSJP-225	Sling Shot	1990	$30
SLITS, THE			
4 MEN WITH BEARDS			
❏ 4M506LP [B]	Cut		$25
ANTILLES			
❏ AN-7077	Cut	1979	$40
SLOAN, P.F.			
ATCO			
❏ SD 33-268	Measure of Pleasure	1968	$30
DUNHILL			
❏ D-50004 [M]	Songs of Our Times	1965	$30
❏ DS-50004 [S]	Songs of Our Times	1965	$30
❏ D-50007 [M]	Twelve More Times	1966	$30
❏ DS-50007 [S]	Twelve More Times	1966	$30
MUMS			
❏ KZ31260	Raised on Records	1972	$25
RHINO			
❏ RNLP-70133	Precious Times: The Best of P.F. Sloan	1986	$12
SLOANE, CAROL			
AUDIOPHILE			
❏ AP-195	Sophisticated Lady	1985	$25
CHOICE			
❏ 1025	Cottontail	1979	$35
COLUMBIA			
❏ CL1923 [M]	Carol Sloane Live at 30th Street	1963	$75
❏ CS8723 [S]	Carol Sloane Live at 30th Street	1963	$100
❏ CL1766 [M]	Out of the Blue	1962	$75
❏ CS8566 [S]	Out of the Blue	1962	$100
CONTEMPORARY			
❏ C-14049	Love You Madly	1989	$35
❏ C-14060	The Real Thing	1990	$35
PROGRESSIVE			
❏ PRO-7047	Carol Sings	1978	$30
SLY AND THE FAMILY STONE			
EPIC			
❏ E237071	Anthology	1981	$18
❏ LN24324 [M]	A Whole New Thing	1967	$100
❏ BN26324 [S]	A Whole New Thing	1967	$25
❏ E30335 [B]	A Whole New Thing	1971	$15
—Reissue of 26324			
❏ BN26371 [S]	Dance to the Music	1968	$18
❏ E30334	Dance to the Music	1971	$15
—Reissue of 26371			
❏ LN24371 [M]	Dance to the Music	1968	$100

Number	Title	Yr	NM
❏ AS264 [DJ]	Everything You Always Wanted to Hear by Sly and the Family Stone But Were Afraid to Ask For	1976	$30
—Promo-only compilation			
❏ AS264 [DJ]	Everything You Always Wanted to Hear by Sly and the Family Stone But Were Afraid to Ask For	1976	$30
—Promo-only compilation			
❏ KE32134	Fresh	1973	$12
—Orange label			
❏ PE34348	Heard Ya Missed Me, Well I'm Back	1976	$12
—Orange label			
❏ PE33835	High on You	1975	$12
—Orange label			
❏ PEQ33835 [Q]	High on You	1975	$40
❏ BN26397	Life	1968	$18
❏ E30333	Life	1971	$15
—Reissue of 26397			
❏ KE30325	Sly and the Family Stone's Greatest Hits	1970	$15
—Yellow label, gatefold cover			
❏ EQ30325 [Q]	Sly and the Family Stone's Greatest Hits	1971	$175
—Has alternate mixes of "Hot Fun in the Summertime," "Thank You" and "Everybody Is a Star," which are not rechanneled stereo as they are on other LPs			
❏ PE30325	Sly and the Family Stone's Greatest Hits	1979	$10
—Budget-line reissue			
❏ PE32930	Small Talk	1974	$12
—Orange label			
❏ PEQ32930 [Q]	Small Talk	1974	$40
❏ BN26456	Stand!	1969	$18
❏ PE26456	Stand!	1986	$10
—Budget-line reissue			
❏ JE35974	Ten Years Too Soon	1979	$12
❏ KE30986	There's a Riot Goin' On	1971	$15
—Yellow label, gatefold cover			
EPIC LEGACY			
❏ 88875063701 [B]	Live at the Fillmore East	2015	$30
—Limited editions in red, green, black vinyl			
WARNER BROS.			
❏ 23700	Ain't But the Right Way	1983	$12
❏ BSK3303	Back on the Right Track	1979	$12
SLY FOX			
CAPITOL			
❏ ST-12367	Let's Go All the Way	1985	$10
❏ ST-512367	Let's Go All the Way	1985	$12
—Columbia House edition			
SMACK, THE			
AUDIO HOUSE			
❏ 0(# unknown)	The Smack	1968	$2000
SMALL, DANNY			
UNITED ARTISTS			
❏ UAJ-14004 [M]	Woman She Was Born for Sorrow	1962	$25
❏ UAJS-15004 [S]	Woman She Was Born for Sorrow	1962	$30
SMALL, MILLIE			
SMASH			
❏ MGS-27055 [M]	My Boy Lollipop	1964	$75
❏ SRS-67055 [R]	My Boy Lollipop	1964	$50
SMALL FACES			
Also see FACES.			
4 MEN WITH BEARDS			
❏ 4M182LP [B]	From The Beginning		$25
❏ 4M181LP [B]	Small Faces		$25
ACCORD			
❏ AN-7157	By Appointment	1982	$12
ATLANTIC			
❏ SD19171	78 in the Shade	1978	$12
❏ SD19113	Playmates	1977	$12
COMPLEAT			
❏ 67-2004	Big Music	1985	$15
❏ 67-5003	Ogden's Nut Gone Flake	1985	$12
—Reissue			
IMMEDIATE			
❏ Z1252008 [S]	Ogden's Nut Gone Flake	1968	$75
—Originals have a round cover			
❏ 4225	Ogden's Nut Gone Flake	1973	$18
—Reissue has a standard square cover			
❏ Z1252002 [S]	There Are But Four Small Faces	1967	$50
—Color cover (counterfeits have either black and white or black and green covers)			
MGM			
❏ M3F-4955	Archetypes	1974	$15

Number	Title	Yr	NM
PRIDE			
❏ PRD 0001 [R]	Early Faces	1972	$18
❏ PRD 0014 [P]	The History of the Small Faces	1973	$15
SIRE			
❏ SASH-3709	The Vintage Years	1976	$18
VARESE SARABANDE			
❏ 302 067 183 1 [B]	There Are But Four Small Faces	2013	$25
SMALLEY, JUNE			
CIRCLE			
❏ C-6	June Smalley Swings America	1979	$25
SMALLS, CLIFF			
MASTER JAZZ			
❏ 8131	Swing and Things	197?	$30
SMART SET, THE			
WARNER BROS.			
❏ W-1203 [M]	A New Experience in Vocal Styles	1958	$30
❏ WS-1203 [S]	A New Experience in Vocal Styles	1958	$40
SMASHING PUMPKINS			
Featuring Billy Corgan.			
CAROLINE			
❏ 45879 [B]	Adore	1998	$40
—Different cover than CD version, and the entire LP was remixed into mono			
❏ 1705	Gish	1991	$75
—Originals do not have the word "Remastered" under the bar code			
❏ 1705	Gish	199?	$25
—With "Remastered" under the bar code			
❏ 48936	Machina/The Machines of God	2000	$30
—With bound-in booklet			
❏ 1767	Pisces Iscariot	1994	$300
—First 2,000 copies, hand-numbered on back cover, came with a bonus 7-inch single			
❏ 1767 [B]	Pisces Iscariot	1994	$175
—Regular pressing on colored vinyl, not numbered, no bonus 7-inch single			
❏ 1740 [B]	Siamese Dream	1993	$150
—Originals have dark red vinyl			
❏ 1740	Siamese Dream	199?	$50
—Pink marbled vinyl			
CONSTANTINOPLE			
❏ CR 01-04	Machina II/The Friends and Enemies of Modern Music	2000	$3000
—Exactly 25 copies were pressed as two 12-inch and three 10-inch records, with the presumption that at least some of them would be bootlegged onto CDs and into downloadable files via the Internet. (This has indeed happened, so many fans have heard the music.) It's not known whether any of the 25 copies have left the hands of their original recipients, so the price above is highly speculative and probably conservative; VG value 1000; VG+ value 2000			
SMECK, ROY			
ABC-PARAMOUNT			
❏ ABC-329 [M]	Adventures in Paradise	1960	$30
❏ ABCS-329 [S]	Adventures in Paradise	1960	$40
❏ ABC-358 [M]	Adventures in Paradise, Volume 2	1961	$30
❏ ABCS-358 [S]	Adventures in Paradise, Volume 2	1961	$30
❏ ABC-414 [M]	Adventures in Paradise, Volume 3	1962	$30
❏ ABCS-414 [S]	Adventures in Paradise, Volume 3	1962	$30
❏ ABC-462 [M]	Adventures in Paradise, Volume 4	1963	$30
❏ ABCS-462 [S]	Adventures in Paradise, Volume 4	1963	$30
❏ ABC-234 [M]	Hi-Fi Paradise	1958	$40
❏ ABC-484 [M]	I Love to Hear a Banjo	1964	$30
❏ ABCS-484 [S]	I Love to Hear a Banjo	1964	$30
❏ ABC-174 [M]	Melodies with Memories	1957	$40
❏ ABC-379 [M]	Roy Smeck, His Singing Guitar and Paradise Serenaders	1961	$30
❏ ABCS-379 [S]	Roy Smeck, His Singing Guitar and Paradise Serenaders	1961	$30
❏ ABC-119 [M]	South Seas Serenade	1956	$40
❏ ABC-412 [M]	Stringing Along	1962	$30
❏ ABCS-412 [S]	Stringing Along	1962	$30
❏ ABC-309 [M]	The Happy Banjo	1959	$30
❏ ABCS-309 [S]	The Happy Banjo	1959	$40
❏ ABC-330 [M]	The Haunting Hawaiian Guitar	1960	$30
❏ ABCS-330 [S]	The Haunting Hawaiian Guitar	1960	$30
❏ ABC-279 [M]	The Magic Ukulele	1959	$30
❏ ABCS-279 [S]	The Magic Ukulele	1959	$40
❏ ABC-452 [M]	The Many Guitar Moods of Roy Smeck	1963	$30

Number	Title	Yr	NM
❑ ABCS-452 [S]	The Many Guitar Moods of Roy Smeck	1963	$30

CORAL
Number	Title	Yr	NM
❑ CRL56013 [10]	Drifting and Dreaming	195?	$120

DECCA
Number	Title	Yr	NM
❑ DL8674 [M]	Memories of You	1958	$40
—Black label, silver print			
❑ DL5458 [10]	Memory Lane	1953	$150
❑ DL5473 [10]	Songs of the Range	1953	$150

X
Number	Title	Yr	NM
❑ LPA-3016 [10]	Christmas in Hawaii	195?	$120
❑ LPX-3012 [10]	South of the Border	1954	$120

SMIAROWSKI, MIKE
SMEAR
Number	Title	Yr	NM
❑ SMR-891	Island Fantasy	1990	$35

SMILE (1)
PICKWICK
Number	Title	Yr	NM
❑ SPC-3288	Smile	1973	$30

SMITH, "FIDDLIN' " ARTHUR
STARDAY
Number	Title	Yr	NM
❑ SLP-202 [M]	Rare Old Time Fiddle Tunes	1962	$30

SMITH, AL
BLUESVILLE
Number	Title	Yr	NM
❑ BVLP-1069 [M]	Blues Shout	196?	$25
❑ BVLP-1001 [M]	Hear My Blues	1960	$100
— Blue label, silver print			
❑ BVLP-1001 [M]	Hear My Blues	1964	$30
— Blue label, trident logo at right			
❑ BVLP-1014 [M]	Midnight Special	1961	$100
— Blue label, silver print			
❑ BVLP-1014 [M]	Midnight Special	1964	$30
— Blue label, trident logo at right			

SMITH, ARTHUR "GUITAR BOOGIE
ABC-PARAMOUNT
Number	Title	Yr	NM
❑ ABC-441 [M]	Arthur "Guitar" Smith and Voices	1963	$25
❑ ABCS-441 [S]	Arthur "Guitar" Smith and Voices	1963	$30

DOT
Number	Title	Yr	NM
❑ DLP-3769 [M]	A Tribute to Jim Reeves	1966	$18
❑ DLP-25769 [S]	A Tribute to Jim Reeves	1966	$25
❑ DLP-3636 [M]	Great Country and Western Hits	1965	$18
❑ DLP-25636 [S]	Great Country and Western Hits	1965	$25
❑ DLP-3600 [M]	Original Guitar Boogie	1964	$25
❑ DLP-25600 [S]	Original Guitar Boogie	1964	$30
❑ DLP-3642 [M]	Singing on the Mountain with the Crossroads Quartet	1965	$25
❑ DLP-25642 [S]	Singing on the Mountain with the Crossroads Quartet	1965	$30

MGM
Number	Title	Yr	NM
❑ E-533 [10]	Fingers on Fire	1955	$150
❑ E-3525 [M]	Fingers on Fire	1957	$100
❑ E-236 [10]	Foolish Questions	1954	$120
❑ E-3301 [M]	Specials	1955	$100

MONUMENT
Number	Title	Yr	NM
❑ Z32259	Battling Banjos	1973	$15

STARDAY
Number	Title	Yr	NM
❑ SLP-216 [M]	Arthur "Guitar Boogie" Smith Goes to Town	1963	$30
❑ SLP-186 [M]	Arthur Smith and the Crossroads Quartet	1962	$40
❑ SLP-266 [M]	Down Home	1964	$30
❑ SLP-241 [M]	In Person	1963	$30
❑ SLP-173 [M]	Mister Guitar	1962	$30

SMITH, BARTON
FOLKWAYS
Number	Title	Yr	NM
❑ FSP-33856	Realizations	198?	$30

SMITH, BESSIE
COLUMBIA
Number	Title	Yr	NM
❑ CG30126	Any Woman's Blues	1971	$35
❑ CG30818	Empress	1972	$35
❑ CG30450	Empty Bed Blues	1971	$35
❑ CG31093	Nobody's Blues But Mine	1972	$35
❑ GL503 [M]	The Bessie Smith Story, Volume 1	1951	$50
—Maroon label, gold print			
❑ CL855 [M]	The Bessie Smith Story, Volume 1	1956	$30
—Red and black label with six "eye" logos			
❑ CL855 [M]	The Bessie Smith Story, Volume 1	1963	$35
—Red label with "Guaranteed High Fidelity" or "360 Sound Mono			
❑ GL504 [M]	The Bessie Smith Story, Volume 2	1951	$50
—Maroon label, gold print			
❑ CL856 [M]	The Bessie Smith Story, Volume 2	1956	$30

Number	Title	Yr	NM
—Red and black label with six "eye" logos			
❑ CL856 [M]	The Bessie Smith Story, Volume 2	1963	$35
—Red label with "Guaranteed High Fidelity" or "360 Sound Mono			
❑ GL505 [M]	The Bessie Smith Story, Volume 3	1951	$50
—Maroon label, gold print			
❑ CL857 [M]	The Bessie Smith Story, Volume 3	1956	$30
—Red and black label with six "eye" logos			
❑ CL857 [M]	The Bessie Smith Story, Volume 3	1963	$35
—Red label with "Guaranteed High Fidelity" or "360 Sound Mono			
❑ GL506 [M]	The Bessie Smith Story, Volume 4	1951	$50
—Maroon label, gold print			
❑ CL858 [M]	The Bessie Smith Story, Volume 4	1956	$30
—Red and black label with six "eye" logos			
❑ CL858 [M]	The Bessie Smith Story, Volume 4	1963	$35
—Red label with "Guaranteed High Fidelity" or "360 Sound Mono			
❑ C247091	The Complete Recordings Volume 1: Empress of the Blues	1991	$25
—Box set; none of the subsequent volumes came out on vinyl			
❑ GP33	The World's Greatest Blues Singer	1970	$25

COLUMBIA MASTERWORKS
Number	Title	Yr	NM
❑ ML4801 [M]	The Bessie Smith Story, Volume 1	1954	$40
❑ ML4802 [M]	The Bessie Smith Story, Volume 2	1954	$40
❑ ML4809 [M]	The Bessie Smith Story, Volume 3	1954	$40
❑ ML4810 [M]	The Bessie Smith Story, Volume 4	1954	$40

TIME-LIFE
Number	Title	Yr	NM
❑ STL-J-28	Giants of Jazz	1982	$50

SMITH, BILL
CONTEMPORARY
Number	Title	Yr	NM
❑ M-3591 [M]	Folk Jazz	1961	$250
❑ S-7591 [S]	Folk Jazz	1961	$250

ONARI
Number	Title	Yr	NM
❑ 04	Pick a Number	198?	$30

SMITH, BOB
KENT
Number	Title	Yr	NM
❑ KST-551	The Visit	1970	$150
—Deduct 25 percent if poster is missing			

SMITH, BOBBY
CMH
Number	Title	Yr	NM
❑ 6225	Smokin' Bluegrass	198?	$12

SMITH, BUSTER
ATLANTIC
Number	Title	Yr	NM
❑ 1323 [M]	The Legendary Buster Smith	1960	$300
—Black label			
❑ 1323 [M]	The Legendary Buster Smith	1961	$175
—Multi-color label, white "fan" logo			
❑ SD1323 [S]	The Legendary Buster Smith	1960	$300
—Green label			
❑ SD1323 [S]	The Legendary Buster Smith	1961	$175
—Multi-color label, white "fan" logo			

SMITH, CAL
DECCA
Number	Title	Yr	NM
❑ DL75369	I've Found Someone of My Own	1972	$18

KAPP
Number	Title	Yr	NM
❑ KL-1504 [M]	All the World Is Lonely Now	1966	$30
❑ KS-3504 [S]	All the World Is Lonely Now	1966	$25
❑ KS-3608	Cal Smith Sings It Takes Me All Night Long	1969	$25
❑ KS-3585	Drinking Champagne	1968	$25
❑ KL-1537 [M]	Goin' to Cal's Place	1967	$30
❑ KS-3537 [S]	Goin' to Cal's Place	1967	$25
❑ KS-3642	The Best of Cal Smith	1969	$18
❑ KL-1544 [M]	Travelin' Man	1968	$40
—White label promo only; in stereo cover with "Mono" sticker			
❑ KS-3544 [S]	Travelin' Man	1968	$25

MCA
Number	Title	Yr	NM
❑ 344	Cal Smith	1973	$12
—Reissue of Decca LP			
❑ 424	Country Bumpkin	1974	$12
❑ 2266	I Just Came Home to Count the Memories	1977	$12
❑ 467	It's Time to Pay the Fiddler	1975	$12
❑ 2172	Jason's Farm	1976	$12
❑ 485	My Kind of Country	1975	$12
❑ 70	The Best of Cal Smith	1973	$12
—Reissue of Kapp 3642			

SMITH, CARL; LEFTY FRIZZELL; MARTY ROBBINS
COLUMBIA
Number	Title	Yr	NM
❑ CL2544 [10]	Carl, Lefty and Marty	1955	$500

SMITH, CARL
ABC HICKORY
Number	Title	Yr	NM
❑ HB-44015	The Silver-Tongued Cowboy	1978	$15
❑ HB-44005	This Lady Loves Me	1977	$15

COLUMBIA
Number	Title	Yr	NM
❑ C30548	Bluegrass	1971	$25
❑ CL2579 [10]	Carl Smith	1955	$150
❑ FC38906	Carl Smith	198?	$12
❑ CL1937 [M]	Carl Smith's Greatest Hits	1962	$30
❑ CS8737 [S]	Carl Smith's Greatest Hits	1962	$30
❑ CS9807	Carl Smith's Greatest Hits, Vol. 2	1969	$25
❑ CS9870	Carl Smith Sings a Tribute to Roy Acuff	1969	$25
❑ C30215	Carl Smith with the Tunesmiths	1970	$25
❑ CS9688 [S]	Country on My Mind	1968	$25
❑ CL2888 [M]	Country on My Mind	1968	$50
❑ CL2822 [M]	Deep Water	1968	$30
❑ CS9622 [S]	Deep Water	1968	$25
❑ C31277	Don't Say You're Mine	1972	$25
❑ CL1740 [M]	Easy to Please	1961	$30
❑ CS8540 [S]	Easy to Please	1961	$30
❑ CS9786	Faded Love and Winter Roses	1969	$25
❑ KC31606	If This Is Goodbye	1972	$25
❑ CS9898	I Love You Because	1970	$25
❑ CL2293 [M]	I Want to Live and Love	1965	$25
❑ CS9093 [S]	I Want to Live and Love	1965	$30
❑ CL2358 [M]	Kisses Don't Lie	1965	$25
❑ CS9158 [S]	Kisses Don't Lie	1965	$30
❑ CL1172 [M]	Let's Live a Little	1958	$75
❑ CL2501 [M]	Man with a Plan	1966	$25
❑ CS9301 [S]	Man with a Plan	1966	$30
❑ CL9023 [10]	Sentimental Songs	195?	$150
❑ CL1022 [M]	Smith's the Name	1957	$75
❑ CL9026 [10]	Softly and Tenderly	195?	$100
❑ CL959 [M]	Sunday Down South	1957	$75
❑ GP31	The Carl Smith Anniversary Album/20 Years of Hits	1970	$30
❑ CL1532 [M]	The Carl Smith Touch	1960	$30
❑ CS8352 [S]	The Carl Smith Touch	1960	$30
❑ CL2610 [M]	The Country Gentleman	1967	$25
❑ CS9410 [S]	The Country Gentleman	1967	$30
❑ CL2687 [M]	The Country Gentleman Sings His Favorites	1967	$30
❑ CS9487 [S]	The Country Gentleman Sings His Favorites	1967	$25
❑ CL2173 [M]	There Stands the Glass	1964	$25
❑ CS8973 [S]	There Stands the Glass	1964	$30
❑ CL2091 [M]	The Tall, Tall Gentleman	1963	$25
❑ CS8891 [S]	The Tall, Tall Gentleman	1963	$30

HICKORY/MGM
Number	Title	Yr	NM
❑ H3G4522	The Girl I Love	1975	$15
❑ H3G4518	The Way I Lose My Mind	1975	$15

ROUNDER
Number	Title	Yr	NM
❑ SS-25	Old Lonesome Times	1988	$12

SMITH, CARRIE
AUDIOPHILE
Number	Title	Yr	NM
❑ AP-164	Fine and Mellow	198?	$25

CLASSIC JAZZ
Number	Title	Yr	NM
❑ 139	Do Your Duty	197?	$35

WEST 54
Number	Title	Yr	NM
❑ 8002	Carrie Smith	197?	$35

SMITH, CONNIE, AND NAT STUCKEY
RCA VICTOR
Number	Title	Yr	NM
❑ LSP-4300	Sunday Morning	1970	$18
❑ LSP-4190	Young Love	1969	$25

SMITH, CONNIE
COLUMBIA
Number	Title	Yr	NM
❑ KC32185	A Lady Named Smith	1973	$15
❑ KC33414	Connie Smith Sings Hank Williams Gospel	1975	$15
❑ KC32492	God Is Abundant	1973	$15
❑ KC34270	I Don't Want to Talk It Over Anymore	1976	$15
❑ KC33375	I Got a Lot of Hurtin' Done Today/I've Got My Baby on My Mind	1975	$15
❑ KC33055	I Never Knew (What That Song Meant Before)	1974	$15
❑ KC32581	That's the Way Love Goes	1974	$15
❑ KC34877	The Best of Connie Smith	1977	$15
❑ KC33918	The Song We Fell in Love To	1976	$15

MONUMENT
Number	Title	Yr	NM
❑ 7624	New Horizons	1978	$15
❑ 7609	Pure Connie Smith	1977	$15

RCA CAMDEN
Number	Title	Yr	NM
❑ CAS-2550	City Lights -- Country Favorites	1972	$12
❑ CAL-2120 [M]	Connie in the Country	1967	$18
❑ CAS-2120 [S]	Connie in the Country	1967	$15
❑ ACL1-0250	Even the Bad Times Are Good	1973	$12
— With Nat Stuckey			

Number	Title	Yr	NM
❏ CAS-2495	My Heart Has a Mind of Its Own	1971	$12

RCA VICTOR

Number	Title	Yr	NM
❏ LSP-4694	Ain't We Having a Good Time	1972	$18
❏ LSP-4229	Back in Baby's Arms	1969	$25
❏ LPM-3628 [M]	Born to Sing	1966	$25
❏ LSP-3628 [S]	Born to Sing	1966	$30
❏ LSP-4598	Come Along and Walk with Me	1971	$25
❏ LSP-4132	Connie's Country	1969	$25
❏ LPM-3341 [M]	Connie Smith	1965	$25
❏ LSP-3341 [S]	Connie Smith	1965	$30
❏ APL1-0275	Connie Smith's Greatest Hits, Volume 1	1973	$15
❏ LPM-3768 [M]	Connie Smith Sings Bill Anderson	1967	$30
❏ LSP-3768 [S]	Connie Smith Sings Bill Anderson	1967	$25
❏ LPM-3589 [M]	Connie Smith Sings Great Sacred Songs	1966	$25
❏ LSP-3589 [S]	Connie Smith Sings Great Sacred Songs	1966	$30
❏ LPM-3444 [M]	Cute 'n' Country	1965	$25
❏ LSP-3444 [S]	Cute 'n' Country	1965	$30
❏ LPM-3725 [M]	Downtown Country	1967	$30
❏ LSP-3725 [S]	Downtown Country	1967	$25
❏ APL1-0188	Dream Painter	1973	$15
❏ LSP-4748	If It Ain't Love" And Other Great Dallas Frazier Songs	1972	$18
❏ LSP-4002 [S]	I Love Charley Brown	1968	$25
❏ LPM-4002 [M]	I Love Charley Brown	1968	$100
❏ LSP-4394	I Never Once Stopped Loving You	1970	$25
❏ LSP-4537	Just One Time	1971	$18
❏ LSP-4840	Love Is the Look You're Looking For	1973	$18
❏ LPM-3520 [M]	Miss Smith Goes to Nashville	1966	$25
❏ LSP-3520 [S]	Miss Smith Goes to Nashville	1966	$30
❏ APL1-0607	Now	1974	$15
❏ LPM-3889 [M]	Soul of Country Music	1968	$50
❏ LSP-3889 [S]	Soul of Country Music	1968	$25
❏ LSP-4077	Sunshine and Rain	1968	$25
❏ LPM-3848 [M]	The Best of Connie Smith	1967	$30
❏ LSP-3848 [S]	The Best of Connie Smith	1967	$25

—Black label, dog on top, "Stereo Dynagroove" at bottom

Number	Title	Yr	NM
❏ LSP-3848 [S]	The Best of Connie Smith	1969	$15

—Orange label

Number	Title	Yr	NM
❏ LSP-4324	The Best of Connie Smith Volume II	1970	$25
❏ LSP-4474	Where's My Castle	1971	$18

SMITH, DAN

BIOGRAPH

Number	Title	Yr	NM
❏ LP-12036	God Is Not Dead	197?	$25

SMITH, DARDEN

COLUMBIA

Number	Title	Yr	NM
❏ CAS3034 [DJ]	Interchords	1988	$18

—Promo-only interview record

EPIC

Number	Title	Yr	NM
❏ E40938	Darden Smith	1988	$12
❏ EAS1282 [EP]	Live Tracks: Darden Smith	1988	$18

—Promo-only three-song live EP

REDI MIX

Number	Title	Yr	NM
❏ RM 001	Native Soil	1986	$25

SMITH, DEREK

PROGRESSIVE

Number	Title	Yr	NM
❏ PRO-7055	Derek Smith Plays Jerome Kern	198?	$25
❏ PRO-7002	Love for Sale	197?	$30
❏ PRO-7035	The Man I Love	197?	$30

SMITH, DWAYNE, AND ART JOHNSON

CAFÉ

Number	Title	Yr	NM
❏ L-729	Heartbound	1985	$25

SMITH, EFFIE

JUBILEE

Number	Title	Yr	NM
❏ JGM-2057 [M]	Dial That Telephone	1966	$30

SMITH, ELLIOTT

BONG LOAD

Number	Title	Yr	NM
❏ BL-48	Figure 8	2000	$30
❏ BL-35	XO	1998	$25

KILL ROCK STARS

Number	Title	Yr	NM
❏ KRS-269	Either/Or	1997	$15
❏ KRS-246	Elliott Smith	1995	$15

SMITH, ETHEL

DECCA

Number	Title	Yr	NM
❏ DL8187 [M]	Christmas Music	1955	$25

—Black label, silver print

SMITH, GREG AND BEV

INTIMA

Number	Title	Yr	NM
❏ SJE-73291	Mr. and Mrs. Smith: No Baggage	1987	$30

SMITH, GREGG, SINGERS

TURNABOUT

Number	Title	Yr	NM
❏ QTV34710 [Q]	The World Rejoices	1977	$20

SMITH, HAL

JAZZOLOGY

Number	Title	Yr	NM
❏ J-136	Hal Smith and His Rhythmakers with Butch Thompson	1985	$25

STOMP OFF

Number	Title	Yr	NM
❏ SOS-1078	Do What Ory Say!	1985	$25

SMITH, HUEY "PIANO

ACE

Number	Title	Yr	NM
❏ LP-1015 [M]	For Dancing	1961	$300
❏ 2038	Good Old Rock & Roll	198?	$18
❏ LP-1004 [M]	Having a Good Time	1959	$400
❏ LP-2021	Rock 'N' Roll Revival	197?	$30
❏ LP-1027 [M]	'Twas the Night Before Christmas	1962	$300
❏ LP-1027 [M]	'Twas the Night Before Christmas	198?	$18

—Reissue with "Dr. John Band" credited on front cover and label

GRAND PRIX

Number	Title	Yr	NM
❏ K-418 [M]	Huey "Piano" Smith	196?	$25
❏ KS-418 [R]	Huey "Piano" Smith	196?	$15

RHINO

Number	Title	Yr	NM
❏ RNLP-70222	Serious Clownin': The History of Huey "Piano" Smith and the Clowns	1986	$15

SMITH, HURRICANE

CAPITOL

Number	Title	Yr	NM
❏ ST-11139 [B]	Hurricane Smith	1972	$15

SMITH, JABBO

MCA

Number	Title	Yr	NM
❏ 1347	Ace of Rhythm	198?	$25

MELODEON

Number	Title	Yr	NM
❏ 7326	Trumpet Ace of the 20s, Vol. 1	197?	$30
❏ 7327	Trumpet Ace of the 20s, Vol. 2	197?	$30

SMITH, JACK

BEL CANTO

Number	Title	Yr	NM
❏ BCM-37 [M]	You Asked for It: Jack Smith Sings	1959	$30
❏ SR-1015 [S]	You Asked for It: Jack Smith Sings	1959	$30

SMITH, JENNIE

CANADIAN AMERICAN

Number	Title	Yr	NM
❏ CALP-1010 [M]	Nightly Yours on the Steve Allen Show	1963	$30

COLUMBIA

Number	Title	Yr	NM
❏ CL1242 [M]	Love Among the Young	1959	$30
❏ CS8028 [S]	Love Among the Young	1959	$40

DOT

Number	Title	Yr	NM
❏ DLP-3586 [M]	Jennie	1964	$18
❏ DLP-25586 [S]	Jennie	1964	$25

RCA VICTOR

Number	Title	Yr	NM
❏ LPM-1523 [M]	Jennie	1957	$40

SMITH, JERRY

ABC

Number	Title	Yr	NM
❏ ABCS-692	Truck Stop	1969	$18

DECCA

Number	Title	Yr	NM
❏ DL75241	Drivin' Home, Steppin' Out	1970	$18
❏ DL75311	The Touch of Love	1972	$18

RANWOOD

Number	Title	Yr	NM
❏ R-8126	Ragtime	197?	$12
❏ R-8111	The New Sound of Jerry Smith and His Pianos	197?	$12

SMITH, JIMMY, AND WES MONTGOMERY

VERVE

Number	Title	Yr	NM
❏ V-8678 [M]	Jimmy and Wes, The Dynamic Duo	1967	$50
❏ V6-8678 [M]	Jimmy and Wes, The Dynamic Duo	1967	$35
❏ UMV-2069	Jimmy and Wes, The Dynamic Duo	198?	$25

—Reissue of 8678

Number	Title	Yr	NM
❏ V6-8766	The Further Adventures of Jimmy Smith and Wes Montgomery	1969	$35

SMITH, JIMMY

BLUE NOTE

Number	Title	Yr	NM
❏ BLP-1547 [M]	A Date with Jimmy Smith, Vol. 1	1957	$250

—Deep groove" version (deep indentation under label on both sides)

Number	Title	Yr	NM
❏ BLP-1547 [M]	A Date with Jimmy Smith, Vol. 1	1957	$1000

—Regular edition, W. 63rd St. address on label

Number	Title	Yr	NM
❏ BLP-1547 [M]	A Date with Jimmy Smith, Vol. 1	1963	$250

—With New York, USA address on label

Number	Title	Yr	NM
❏ BST-81547 [R]	A Date with Jimmy Smith, Vol. 1	1967	$30
❏ BLP-1548 [M]	A Date with Jimmy Smith, Vol. 2	1957	$250

—Deep groove" version (deep indentation under label on both sides)

Number	Title	Yr	NM
❏ BLP-1548 [M]	A Date with Jimmy Smith, Vol. 2	1957	$800

—Regular edition, W. 63rd St. address on label

Number	Title	Yr	NM
❏ BLP-1548 [M]	A Date with Jimmy Smith, Vol. 2	1963	$300

—With New York, USA address on label

Number	Title	Yr	NM
❏ BST-81548 [R]	A Date with Jimmy Smith, Vol. 2	1967	$30
❏ BLP-4117 [M]	Back at the Chicken Shack	1963	$150
❏ BST-84117 [S]	Back at the Chicken Shack	1963	$75

—With New York, USA address on label

Number	Title	Yr	NM
❏ BST-84117 [S]	Back at the Chicken Shack	1967	$35

—With "A Division of Liberty Records" on label

Number	Title	Yr	NM
❏ BST-84117	Back at the Chicken Shack	1985	$25

—The Finest in Jazz Since 1939" reissue

Number	Title	Yr	NM
❏ BLP-4235 [M]	Bucket!	1966	$150
❏ BST-84235 [M]	Bucket!	1966	$75

—With New York, USA address on label

Number	Title	Yr	NM
❏ BST-84235 [S]	Bucket!	1967	$35

—With "A Division of Liberty Records" on label

Number	Title	Yr	NM
❏ LT-992	Confirmation	1979	$25
❏ LT-1054	Cool Blues	1980	$25
❏ BLP-4030 [M]	Crazy Baby	1960	$250

—Deep groove" version (deep indentation under label on both sides)

Number	Title	Yr	NM
❏ BLP-4030 [M]	Crazy Baby	1960	$175

—Regular edition, W. 63rd St. address on label

Number	Title	Yr	NM
❏ BLP-4030 [M]	Crazy Baby	1963	$150

—With New York, USA address on label

Number	Title	Yr	NM
❏ BST-84030 [S]	Crazy Baby	1960	$150

—With W. 63rd St. address on label

Number	Title	Yr	NM
❏ BST-84030 [S]	Crazy Baby	1963	$50

—With New York, USA address on label

Number	Title	Yr	NM
❏ BST-84030 [S]	Crazy Baby	1967	$35

—With "A Division of Liberty Records" on label

Number	Title	Yr	NM
❏ B1-84030	Crazy Baby	1988	$25

—The Finest in Jazz Since 1939" reissue

Number	Title	Yr	NM
❏ B1-85125	Go For Whatcha Know	198?	$25
❏ BLP-1585 [M]	Groovin' at Small's Paradise, Vol. 1	1958	$300

—Deep groove" version (deep indentation under label on both sides)

Number	Title	Yr	NM
❏ BLP-1585 [M]	Groovin' at Small's Paradise, Vol. 1	1958	$300

—Regular edition, W. 63rd St. address on label

Number	Title	Yr	NM
❏ BLP-1585 [M]	Groovin' at Small's Paradise, Vol. 1	1963	$250

—With New York, USA address on label

Number	Title	Yr	NM
❏ BST-1585 [S]	Groovin' at Small's Paradise, Vol. 1	1959	$300

—Deep groove" version (deep indentation under label on both sides)

Number	Title	Yr	NM
❏ BST-1585 [S]	Groovin' at Small's Paradise, Vol. 1	1959	$250

—Regular edition, W. 63rd St. address on label

Number	Title	Yr	NM
❏ BST-1585 [S]	Groovin' at Small's Paradise, Vol. 1	1963	$175

—With New York, USA address on label

Number	Title	Yr	NM
❏ BST-81585 [S]	Groovin' at Small's Paradise, Vol. 1	1967	$35
❏ BST-81586 [S]	Groovin' at Small's Paradise, Vol. 1	1967	$35
❏ BLP-1586 [M]	Groovin' at Small's Paradise, Vol. 2	1958	$300

—Deep groove" version (deep indentation under label on both sides)

Number	Title	Yr	NM
❏ BLP-1586 [M]	Groovin' at Small's Paradise, Vol. 2	1958	$300

—Regular edition, W. 63rd St. address on label

Number	Title	Yr	NM
❏ BLP-1586 [M]	Groovin' at Small's Paradise, Vol. 2	1963	$250

—With New York, USA address on label

Number	Title	Yr	NM
❏ BST-1586 [S]	Groovin' at Small's Paradise, Vol. 2	1959	$400

—Deep groove" version (deep indentation under label on both sides)

Number	Title	Yr	NM
❏ BST-1586 [S]	Groovin' at Small's Paradise, Vol. 2	1959	$250

—Regular edition, W. 63rd St. address on label

Number	Title	Yr	NM
❏ BST-1586 [S]	Groovin' at Small's Paradise, Vol. 2	1963	$175

—With New York, USA address on label

Number	Title	Yr	NM
❏ BLP-4050 [M]	Home Cookin'	1961	$250

—With W. 63rd St. address on label

Number	Title	Yr	NM

HOME COOKIN'
THE INCREDIBLE JIMMY SMITH
WITH PERCY FRANCE/KENNY BURRELL/DONALD BAILEY

Number	Title	Yr	NM
❏ BLP-4050 [M]	Home Cookin'	1963	$75

—With New York, USA address on label

❏ BST-84050 [S]	Home Cookin'	1961	$150

—With W. 63rd St. address on label

❏ BST-84050 [S]	Home Cookin'	1963	$50

—With New York, USA address on label

❏ BST-84050 [S]	Home Cookin'	1967	$35

—With "A Division of Liberty Records" on label

❏ BLP-4002 [M]	House Party	1959	$500

—Deep groove" version (deep indentation under label on both sides)

❏ BLP-4002 [M]	House Party	1959	$175

—Regular edition, W. 63rd St. address on label

❏ BLP-4002 [M]	House Party	1963	$150

—With New York, USA address on label

❏ BST-4002 [S]	House Party	1959	$175

—Deep groove" version (deep indentation under label on both sides)

❏ BST-4002 [S]	House Party	1959	$150

—Regular edition, W. 63rd St. address on label

❏ BST-4002 [S]	House Party	1963	$50

—With New York, USA address on label

❏ BST-84002 [S]	House Party	1967	$35
❏ BST-84002	House Party	1985	$25

—The Finest in Jazz Since 1939" reissue

❏ BLP-4255 [M]	I'm Movin' On	1967	$150
❏ BST-84255 [S]	I'm Movin' On	1967	$50
❏ BN-LA400-H2	Jimmy Smith	1975	$35
❏ BLP-1512 [M]	Jimmy Smith at the Organ, Vol. 1	1956	$350

—Deep groove" version (deep indentation under label on both sides)

❏ BLP-1512 [M]	Jimmy Smith at the Organ, Vol. 1	1956	$850

—Regular edition, Lexington Ave. address on label

❏ BLP-1512 [M]	Jimmy Smith at the Organ, Vol. 1	1963	$150

—With New York, USA address on label

❏ BLP-1551 [M]	Jimmy Smith at the Organ, Vol. 1	1957	$250

—Deep groove" version (deep indentation under label on both sides)

❏ BLP-1551 [M]	Jimmy Smith at the Organ, Vol. 1	1957	$300

—Regular edition, W. 63rd St. address on label

❏ BLP-1551 [M]	Jimmy Smith at the Organ, Vol. 1	1963	$250

—With New York, USA address on label

❏ BST-81512 [R]	Jimmy Smith at the Organ, Vol. 1	1967	$30
❏ BST-81551 [R]	Jimmy Smith at the Organ, Vol. 1	1967	$30
❏ BLP-1514 [M]	Jimmy Smith at the Organ, Vol. 2	1956	$350

—Deep groove" version (deep indentation under label on both sides)

❏ BLP-1514 [M]	Jimmy Smith at the Organ, Vol. 2	1956	$1000

—Regular edition, Lexington Ave. address on label

❏ BLP-1514 [M]	Jimmy Smith at the Organ, Vol. 2	1963	$175

—With New York, USA address on label

❏ BLP-1552 [M]	Jimmy Smith at the Organ, Vol. 2	1957	$250

—Deep groove" version (deep indentation under label on both sides)

❏ BLP-1552 [M]	Jimmy Smith at the Organ, Vol. 2	1957	$300

—Regular edition, W. 63rd St. address on label

❏ BLP-1552 [M]	Jimmy Smith at the Organ, Vol. 2	1963	$250

—With New York, USA address on label

❏ BST-81514 [R]	Jimmy Smith at the Organ, Vol. 2	1967	$30
❏ BST-81552 [R]	Jimmy Smith at the Organ, Vol. 2	1967	$30

Number	Title	Yr	NM
❏ BLP-4100 [M]	Jimmy Smith Plays Fats Waller	1962	$250

—With 61st St. address on label

❏ BLP-4100 [M]	Jimmy Smith Plays Fats Waller	1963	$150

—With New York, USA address on label

❏ BST-84100 [S]	Jimmy Smith Plays Fats Waller	1962	$150

—With 61st St. address on label

❏ BST-84100 [S]	Jimmy Smith Plays Fats Waller	1963	$50

—With New York, USA address on label

❏ BST-84100 [S]	Jimmy Smith Plays Fats Waller	1967	$35

—With "A Division of Liberty Records" on label

❏ BLP-1563 [M]	Jimmy Smith Plays Pretty Just for You	1957	$175

—Regular edition, W. 63rd St. address on label

❏ BLP-1563 [M]	Jimmy Smith Plays Pretty Just for You	1957	$250

—Deep groove" version (deep indentation under label on both sides)

❏ BLP-1563 [M]	Jimmy Smith Plays Pretty Just for You	1963	$0

—With New York, USA address on label

❏ BST-1563 [S]	Jimmy Smith Plays Pretty Just for You	1959	$175

—Deep groove" version (deep indentation under label on both sides)

❏ BST-1563 [S]	Jimmy Smith Plays Pretty Just for You	1959	$150

—Regular edition, W. 63rd St. address on label

❏ BST-1563 [S]	Jimmy Smith Plays Pretty Just for You	1963	$175

—With New York, USA address on label

❏ BST-81563 [S]	Jimmy Smith Plays Pretty Just for You	1967	$35
❏ BST-89901	Jimmy Smith's Greatest Hits!	1969	$75
❏ LWB-89901	Jimmy Smith's Greatest Hits!	198?	$35
❏ BLP-4078 [M]	Midnight Special	1961	$250

—With 61st St. address on label

❏ BLP-4078 [M]	Midnight Special	1963	$150

—With New York, USA address on label

❏ BST-84078 [S]	Midnight Special	1961	$150

—With 61st St. address on label

❏ BST-84078 [S]	Midnight Special	1963	$50

—With New York, USA address on label

❏ BST-84078 [S]	Midnight Special	1967	$35

—With "A Division of Liberty Records" on label

❏ B1-84078	Midnight Special	1989	$25

—The Finest in Jazz Since 1939" reissue

❏ LT-1092	On the Sunny Side	1981	$25
❏ BST-84269	Open House	1968	$50
❏ BST-84296	Plain Talk	1969	$50
❏ BLP-4164 [M]	Prayer Meetin'	1964	$150
❏ BST-84164 [S]	Prayer Meetin'	1964	$75

—With New York, USA address on label

❏ BST-84164 [S]	Prayer Meetin'	1967	$35

—With "A Division of Liberty Records" on label

❏ B1-84164	Prayer Meetin'	1988	$25

—The Finest in Jazz Since 1939" reissue

❏ BLP-4141 [M]	Rockin' the Boat	1963	$150
❏ BST-84141 [S]	Rockin' the Boat	1963	$75

—With New York, USA address on label

❏ BST-84141 [S]	Rockin' the Boat	1967	$35

—With "A Division of Liberty Records" on label

❏ BLP-4200 [M]	Softly as a Summer Breeze	1965	$150
❏ BST-84200 [S]	Softly as a Summer Breeze	1965	$75

—With New York, USA address on label

❏ BST-84200 [S]	Softly as a Summer Breeze	1967	$35

—With "A Division of Liberty Records" on label

❏ B1-91140	The Best of Jimmy Smith	1988	$25
❏ BLP-1528 [M]	The Incredible Jimmy Smith at Club Baby Grand, Wilmington, Delaware, Vol. 1	1956	$1000

—Deep groove" version (deep indentation under label on both sides)

❏ BLP-1528 [M]	The Incredible Jimmy Smith at Club Baby Grand, Wilmington, Delaware, Vol. 1	1956	$800

—Regular edition, Lexington Ave. address on label

❏ BLP-1528 [M]	The Incredible Jimmy Smith at Club Baby Grand, Wilmington, Delaware, Vol. 1	1963	$150

—With New York, USA address on label

❏ BST-81528 [R]	The Incredible Jimmy Smith at Club Baby Grand, Wilmington, Delaware, Vol. 1	1967	$30
❏ BLP-1529 [M]	The Incredible Jimmy Smith at Club Baby Grand, Wilmington, Delaware, Vol. 2	1956	$1000

—Deep groove" version (deep indentation under label on both sides)

❏ BLP-1529 [M]	The Incredible Jimmy Smith at Club Baby Grand, Wilmington, Delaware, Vol. 2	1956	$755

—Regular edition, Lexington Ave. address on label

❏ BLP-1529 [M]	The Incredible Jimmy Smith at Club Baby Grand, Wilmington, Delaware, Vol. 2	1963	$175

—With New York, USA address on label

Number	Title	Yr	NM
❏ BST-81529 [R]	The Incredible Jimmy Smith at Club Baby Grand, Wilmington, Delaware, Vol. 2	1967	$30
❏ BLP-1525 [M]	The Incredible Jimmy Smith at the Organ, Vol. 3	1956	$175

—Deep groove" version (deep indentation under label on both sides)

❏ BLP-1525 [M]	The Incredible Jimmy Smith at the Organ, Vol. 3	1956	$200

—Regular edition, Lexington Ave. address on label

❏ BLP-1525 [M]	The Incredible Jimmy Smith at the Organ, Vol. 3	1963	$150

—With New York, USA address on label

❏ BST-81525 [R]	The Incredible Jimmy Smith at the Organ, Vol. 3	1967	$30
❏ BLP-4011 [M]	The Sermon	1959	$250

—Deep groove" version (deep indentation under label on both sides)

❏ BLP-4011 [M]	The Sermon	1959	$175

—Regular edition, W. 63rd St. address on label

❏ BLP-4011 [M]	The Sermon	1963	$150

—With New York, USA address on label

❏ BST-4011 [S]	The Sermon	1959	$175

—Deep groove" version (deep indentation under label on both sides)

❏ BST-4011 [S]	The Sermon	1959	$150

—Regular edition, W. 63rd St. address on label

❏ BST-4011 [S]	The Sermon	1963	$50

—With New York, USA address on label

❏ BST-84011 [S]	The Sermon	1967	$35
❏ BLP-1556 [M]	The Sounds of Jimmy Smith	1957	$2000

—Deep groove" version (deep indentation under label on both sides)

❏ BLP-1556 [M]	The Sounds of Jimmy Smith	1957	$300

—Regular edition, W. 63rd St. address on label

❏ BLP-1556 [M]	The Sounds of Jimmy Smith	1963	$250

—With New York, USA address on label

❏ BST-81556 [R]	The Sounds of Jimmy Smith	1967	$30

ELEKTRA/MUSICIAN

❏ 60301	Keep On Comin'	1984	$25
❏ 60175	Off the Top	1983	$25

GUEST STAR

❏ G1914 [M]	Jimmy Smith	196?	$30
❏ 1344 [M]	Jimmy Smith	196?	$30

INNER CITY

❏ 1121	The Cat Strikes Again	1981	$25

MERCURY

❏ SRM-1-1189	It's Necessary	1977	$25
❏ SRM-1-1127	Sit On It!	1976	$25
❏ SRM-1-3716	Unfinished Business	1978	$25

METRO

❏ M-521 [M]	Jimmy Smith at the Village Gate	1965	$175
❏ MS-521 [S]	Jimmy Smith at the Village Gate	1965	$175
❏ M-568 [M]	Live In Concert/The Incredible Jimmy Smith	196?	$175
❏ M-568 [S]	Live In Concert/The Incredible Jimmy Smith	196?	$175

MGM

❏ SE-4751	I'm Gon' Git Myself Together	1971	$30
❏ GAS-107	Jimmy Smith (Golden Archive Series)	1970	$35
❏ SE-4709	The Other Side	1970	$30

MILESTONE

❏ M-9176	Prime Time	198?	$25

MOSAIC

❏ MQ5-154 [B]	The Complete February 1957 Jimmy Smith Blue Note Sessions	199?	$1000

PICKWICK

❏ SPC-3023	Stranger in Paradise	196?	$25

PRIDE

❏ 6011	Black Smith	1974	$30

SUNSET

❏ SUM-1175 [M]	Jimmy Smith Plays the Standards	1967	$35
❏ SUS-5175 [S]	Jimmy Smith Plays the Standards	1967	$30
❏ SUS-5316	Just Friends	1971	$30

VERVE

❏ V6-652-2	24 Karat Hits	196?	$35
❏ V-8552 [M]	Any Number Can Win	1963	$30
❏ V6-8552 [S]	Any Number Can Win	1963	$75
❏ V-8474 [M]	Bashin'	1962	$30
❏ V6-8474 [S]	Bashin'	1962	$40
❏ 823308-1	Bashin'	1986	$25

—Reissue of 8474

❏ V6-8809	Bluesmith	1973	$30
❏ V-8604 [M]	Christmas '64	1964	$50
❏ V6-8604 [S]	Christmas '64	1964	$75
❏ V-8666 [M]	Christmas Cookin'	1966	$50
❏ V6-8666 [S]	Christmas Cookin'	1966	$75
❏ V-8641 [M]	Got My Mojo Workin'	1966	$35
❏ V6-8641 [S]	Got My Mojo Workin'	1966	$50
❏ MAS-90751 [M]	Got My Mojo Workin'	1966	$100

—Capitol Record Club edition

❏ SMAS-90751 [S]	Got My Mojo Workin'	1966	$75

Number	Title	Yr	NM
❑ V6-8794	Groove Drops	1970	$35
❑ V6-8814	History of Jimmy Smith	1973	$35
❑ V-8544 [M]	Hobo Flats	1963	$30
❑ V6-8544 [S]	Hobo Flats	1963	$30
❑ V-8667 [M]	Hoochie Coochie Man	1966	$35
❑ V6-8667 [S]	Hoochie Coochie Man	1966	$50
❑ V6-8750	Livin' It Up!	1968	$35
❑ V-8628 [M]	Organ Grinder Swing	1965	$35
❑ V6-8628 [S]	Organ Grinder Swing	1965	$50
❑ UMV-2073	Organ Grinder Swing	198?	$25
—Reissue of 8628			
❑ V-8652 [M]	Peter and the Wolf	1966	$50
❑ V6-8652 [S]	Peter and the Wolf	1966	$75
❑ V6-8800	Plain Brown Wrapper	1971	$30
❑ V6-8832	Portuguese Soul	1974	$30
❑ V-8705 [M]	Respect	1967	$50
❑ V6-8705 [S]	Respect	1967	$35
❑ V6-8806	Root Down	1972	$30
❑ V6-8745 [S]	Stay Loose	1968	$35
❑ V-8721 [M]	The Best of Jimmy Smith	1967	$50
❑ V6-8721 [S]	The Best of Jimmy Smith	1967	$35
❑ V6-8770	The Boss	1969	$35
❑ V-8587 [M]	The Cat	1964	$30
❑ V6-8587 [S]	The Cat	1964	$75
❑ V-8618 [M]	The Monster	1965	$35
❑ V6-8618 [S]	The Monster	1965	$50
❑ SMAS-90643 [S]	The Monster	1965	$150
—Capitol Record Club edition			
❑ V-8583 [M]	Who's Afraid of Virginia Woolf?	1964	$50
❑ V6-8583 [S]	Who's Afraid of Virginia Woolf?	1964	$75

SMITH, JOHNNY "HAMMOND
See JOHNNY HAMMOND.

SMITH, JOHNNY
LEGENDE
Number	Title	Yr	NM
❑ 1401 [10]	Annotations of the Muses	1955	$150

ROOST
❑ R-410 [10]	A Three-Dimension Sound Recording of Jazz at NBC with the Johnny Smith Quintet	1953	$175
❑ LP-2239 [M]	Dear Little Sweetheart	1960	$30
❑ SLP-2239 [S]	Dear Little Sweetheart	1960	$40
❑ LP-2238 [M]	Designed for You	1960	$30
❑ SLP-2238 [S]	Designed for You	1960	$40
❑ LP-2233 [M]	Easy Listening	1959	$40
❑ SLP-2233 [S]	Easy Listening	1959	$30
❑ LP-2237 [M]	Favorites	1959	$40
❑ SLP-2237 [S]	Favorites	1959	$30
❑ LP-2231 [M]	Flower Drum Song	1958	$40
❑ SLP-2231 [S]	Flower Drum Song	1958	$30
❑ LP-2242 [M]	Guitar and Strings	1960	$30
❑ SLP-2242 [S]	Guitar and Strings	1960	$40
❑ LP-2254 [M]	Guitar World	1963	$30
❑ SLP-2254 [S]	Guitar World	1963	$30
❑ R-421 [10]	In a Mellow Mood	1954	$150
❑ R-424 [10]	In a Sentimental Mood	1954	$150
❑ LP-2223 [M]	Johnny Smith Foursome, Volume 1	1956	$50
❑ LP-2228 [M]	Johnny Smith Foursome, Volume 2	1957	$50
❑ LP-2201 [M]	Johnny Smith Plays Jimmy Van Heusen	1955	$100
❑ LP-2250 [M]	Johnny Smith Plays Jimmy Van Heusen	1963	$30
❑ SLP-2250 [S]	Johnny Smith Plays Jimmy Van Heusen	1963	$30
❑ LP-2243 [M]	Johnny Smith Plus the Trio	1960	$30
❑ SLP-2243 [S]	Johnny Smith Plus the Trio	1960	$40
❑ LP-2203 [M]	Johnny Smith Quartet	1955	$100
❑ R-413 [10]	Johnny Smith Quintet	1953	$120
❑ LP-2248 [M]	Man with the Blue Guitar	1962	$30
❑ SLP-2248 [S]	Man with the Blue Guitar	1962	$40
❑ LP-2215 [M]	Moods	1956	$75
❑ LP-2211 [M]	Moonlight in Vermont	1956	$100
❑ LP-2216 [M]	New Quartet	1956	$75
❑ LP-2259 [M]	Reminiscing	1965	$30
❑ SLP-2259 [S]	Reminiscing	1965	$30
❑ LP-2246 [M]	The Sound of the Johnny Smith Guitar	1961	$30
❑ SLP-2246 [S]	The Sound of the Johnny Smith Guitar	1961	$40

VERVE
❑ V-8692 [M]	Johnny Smith	1967	$30
❑ V6-8692 [S]	Johnny Smith	1967	$25
❑ V-8737 [M]	Johnny Smith's Kaleidoscope	1968	$30
❑ V6-8737 [S]	Johnny Smith's Kaleidoscope	1968	$25
❑ V6-8767 [S]	Phase II	1969	$25

SMITH, KATE
RCA VICTOR
Number	Title	Yr	NM
❑ LPM-3607 [M]	The Kate Smith Christmas Album	1966	$15
❑ LSP-3607 [S]	The Kate Smith Christmas Album	1966	$18
—Same as above, but in stereo			

TOPS
| ❑ L1677 [M] | Christmas with Kate | 195? | $18 |

SMITH, KEELY
Also see LOUIS PRIMA AND KEELY SMITH.

CAPITOL
Number	Title	Yr	NM
❑ W914 [M]	I Wish You Love	1957	$100
—Turquoise label			
❑ W914 [M]	I Wish You Love	1959	$75
—Black label with colorband, Capitol logo at left			
❑ W914 [M]	I Wish You Love	1962	$40
—Black label with colorband, Capitol logo at top			
❑ SW914 [S]	I Wish You Love	1959	$75
—Black label with colorband, Capitol logo at left			
❑ SW914 [S]	I Wish You Love	1962	$40
—Black label with colorband, Capitol logo at top			
❑ T1073 [M]	Politely!	1958	$85
—Black label with colorband, Capitol logo at left			
❑ T1073 [M]	Politely!	1962	$40
—Black label with colorband, Capitol logo at top			
❑ ST1073 [S]	Politely!	1959	$100
—Black label with colorband, Capitol logo at left			
❑ ST1073 [S]	Politely!	1962	$50
—Black label with colorband, Capitol logo at top			
❑ T1145 [M]	Swingin' Pretty	1959	$85
—Black label with colorband, Capitol logo at left			
❑ T1145 [M]	Swingin' Pretty	1962	$40
—Black label with colorband, Capitol logo at top			
❑ ST1145 [S]	Swingin' Pretty	1959	$100
—Black label with colorband, Capitol logo at left			
❑ ST1145 [S]	Swingin' Pretty	1962	$50
—Black label with colorband, Capitol logo at top			

DOT
❑ DLP-3345 [M]	A Keely Christmas	1961	$85
❑ DLP-25345 [S]	A Keely Christmas	1961	$85
❑ DLP-3415 [M]	Because You're Mine	1962	$85
❑ DLP-25415 [S]	Because You're Mine	1962	$85
❑ DLP-3241 [M]	Be My Love	1959	$85
❑ DLP-25241 [S]	Be My Love	1959	$85
❑ DLP-3460 [M]	Cherokeely Swings	1962	$85
❑ DLP-25460 [S]	Cherokeely Swings	1962	$85
❑ DLP-3287 [M]	Dearly Beloved	1961	$85
❑ DLP-25287 [S]	Dearly Beloved	1961	$85
❑ DLP-3265 [M]	Swing, You Lovers	1960	$85
❑ DLP-25265 [S]	Swing, You Lovers	1960	$85
❑ DLP-3423 [M]	Twist with Keely Smith	1962	$85
❑ DLP-25423 [S]	Twist with Keely Smith	1962	$85
❑ DLP-3461 [M]	What Kind of Fool Am I	1962	$85
❑ DLP-25461 [S]	What Kind of Fool Am I	1962	$85

HARMONY
| ❑ HS11333 | That Old Black Magic | 1968 | $15 |

REPRISE
❑ R-6142 [M]	Keely Smith Sings the John Lennon/Paul McCartney Songbook	1964	$30
❑ RS-6142 [S]	Keely Smith Sings the John Lennon/Paul McCartney Songbook	1964	$30
❑ R-6086 [M]	Little Girl Blue, Little Girl New	1963	$25
❑ R9-6086 [S]	Little Girl Blue, Little Girl New	1963	$30
❑ R-6175 [M]	That Old Black Magic	1965	$25
❑ RS-6175 [S]	That Old Black Magic	1965	$30
❑ R-6132 [M]	The Intimate Keely Smith	1964	$25
❑ RS-6132 [S]	The Intimate Keely Smith	1964	$30

SMITH, KEITH
GHB
Number	Title	Yr	NM
❑ GHB-27	Keith Smith's Climax Jazz Band	196?	$30

SMITH, LAVERGNE
COOK
| ❑ LP-1081 [10] | Angel in the Absinthe House | 1955 | $175 |

SAVOY
| ❑ MG-12031 [M] | New Orleans Nightingale | 1955 | $75 |

VIK
| ❑ LX-1056 [M] | La Vergne Smith | 1956 | $50 |

SMITH, LEO
BLACK SAINT
| ❑ BSR-0053 | Go in Numbers | 198? | $30 |

ECM
| ❑ 1143 | Divine Love | 1979 | $30 |

KABELL
| ❑ CM-1 | Creative Music-1 | 197? | $35 |

NESSA
| ❑ N-19 | Spirit Catcher | 1980 | $35 |

SACKVILLE
| ❑ 3030 | Rastafari | 198? | $25 |

SMITH, LONNIE
BLUE NOTE
❑ BST-84351	Drives	1971	$35
❑ B1-28266	Drives	1994	$35
❑ B1-31880	Live at Club Mozambique	1995	$35
❑ BST-84326	Move Your Hand	1970	$35
❑ B1-31249	Move Your Hand	1996	$35
❑ BST-84290	Think!	1968	$50
❑ BST-84313	Turning Point	1969	$50

CHIAROSCURO
Number	Title	Yr	NM
❑ 2019	When the Night Is Right	1979	$30

COLUMBIA
| ❑ CL2696 [M] | Finger-Lickin' Good Soul Organ | 1967 | $75 |
| ❑ CS9496 [S] | Finger-Lickin' Good Soul Organ | 1967 | $50 |

GROOVE MERCHANT
| ❑ 3308 | Afro-Desia | 1975 | $30 |
| ❑ 3312 | Keep On Lovin' | 1976 | $30 |

KUDU
| ❑ 02 | Mama Wailer | 1972 | $30 |

SMITH, LONNIE LISTON
BLUEBIRD
Number	Title	Yr	NM
❑ 6996-1-RB	Golden Dreams	1988	$25

COLUMBIA
❑ JC35654	Exotic Mysteries	1979	$25
❑ JC36373	Love Is the Answer	1980	$25
❑ JC35332	Loveland	1978	$25
❑ JC36141	Song for the Children	1979	$25
❑ JC36366	The Best of Lonnie Liston Smith	1980	$25

DOCTOR JAZZ
❑ FW38447	Dreams of Tomorrow	1983	$25
❑ FW40063	Rejuvenation	1985	$25
❑ FW39420	Silhouettes	1984	$25

FLYING DUTCHMAN
❑ 10163	Astral Travelling	1973	$30
❑ BDL1-0591	Cosmic Funk	1974	$30
❑ BXL1-0591	Cosmic Funk	1978	$20
—Reissue with new prefix			
❑ BDL1-0934	Expressions	1975	$30
❑ BXL1-0934	Expressions	1978	$20
—Reissue with new prefix			
❑ BDL1-1460	Reflections of a Golden Dream	1976	$30
❑ BXL1-1460	Reflections of a Golden Dream	1978	$20
—Reissue with new prefix			
❑ BDL1-1196	Visions of a New World	1975	$30
❑ BXL1-1196	Visions of a New World	1978	$20
—Reissue with new prefix			

RCA VICTOR
❑ APL1-2433	Live!	1977	$25
❑ AFL1-2433	Live!	1978	$20
—Reissue with new prefix			
❑ APL1-1822	Renaissance	1976	$25
❑ AFL1-1822	Renaissance	1978	$20
—Reissue with new prefix			
❑ AFL1-2897	The Best of Lonnie Liston Smith	1978	$25

STARTRAK
| ❑ STA-4021 | Love Goddess | 198? | $25 |

SMITH, LOUIS
BLUE NOTE
❑ BLP-1584 [M]	Here Comes Louis Smith	1958	$1000
—Deep groove" version (deep indentation under label on both sides)			
❑ BLP-1584 [M]	Here Comes Louis Smith	1958	$800
—Regular version, W. 63rd St. address on label			
❑ BST-1584 [S]	Here Comes Louis Smith	1959	$800
—Deep groove" version (deep indentation under label on both sides)			
❑ BST-1584 [S]	Here Comes Louis Smith	1959	$800
—Regular version, W. 63rd St. address on label			
❑ BST-81584 [S]	Here Comes Louis Smith	1967	$35
—With "A Division of Liberty Records" on label			
❑ BLP-1594 [M]	Smithville	1958	$1500
—Deep groove" version (deep indentation under label on both sides)			
❑ BLP-1594 [M]	Smithville	1958	$1500
—Regular version, W. 63rd St. address on label			
❑ BST-1594 [S]	Smithville	1959	$800
—Deep groove" version (deep indentation under label on both sides)			
❑ BST-1594 [S]	Smithville	1959	$600
—Regular version, W. 63rd St. address on label			
❑ BST-81594 [S]	Smithville	1967	$35
—With "A Division of Liberty Records" on label			

STEEPLECHASE
| ❑ SCS-1096 | Just Friends | 198? | $30 |
| ❑ SCS-1121 | Prancin' | 1979 | $30 |

SMITH, MARGO
20TH CENTURY
| ❑ T-490 | Margo Smith | 1975 | $15 |

WARNER BROS.
❑ BSK3286	A Woman	1979	$12
❑ BSK3464	Diamonds and Chills	1980	$12
❑ BSK3173	Don't Break the Heart That Loves You	1978	$12
❑ BS3049	Happiness	1977	$12
❑ BSK3388	Just Margo	1979	$12

Number	Title	Yr	NM
❏ BS2955	Song Bird	1976	$12

SMITH, MARVIN "SMITTY

CONCORD JAZZ

Number	Title	Yr	NM
❏ CJ-325	Keeper of the Drums	1987	$25
❏ CJ-379	The Road Less Traveled	1989	$30

SMITH, MICHAEL

STORYVILLE

Number	Title	Yr	NM
❏ 4014	Reflection on Progress	1980	$30

SMITH, MIKE

DELMARK

Number	Title	Yr	NM
❏ DS-444	Unit 7: A Tribute to Cannonball Adderley	1990	$30

SMITH, O.C.

CARIBOU

Number	Title	Yr	NM
❏ PZ34471	Together	1977	$30

COLUMBIA

Number	Title	Yr	NM
❏ CS9756	For Once in My Life	1969	$15
❏ C30664	Help Me Make It Through the Night	1971	$25
❏ CS9680 [M]	Hickory Holler Revisited	1968	$75
— White label promo "Special Mono Radio Station Copy" with stereo number			
❏ CS9680 [S]	Hickory Holler Revisited	1968	$25
❏ KC33247	La La Peace Song	1974	$25
❏ CS9908	O.C. Smith at Home	1969	$15
❏ C30227	O.C. Smith's Greatest Hits	1970	$15
❏ CL2714 [M]	The Dynamic O.C. Smith	1967	$75
❏ CS9514 [S]	The Dynamic O.C. Smith	1967	$40

FAMILY

Number	Title	Yr	NM
❏ 1000	Dreams Come True	1980	$18

HARMONY

Number	Title	Yr	NM
❏ KH30317	O.C. Smith	1971	$12

MOTOWN

Number	Title	Yr	NM
❏ 6019ML	Love Changes	1982	$30

RENDEZVOUS

Number	Title	Yr	NM
❏ 50006	What'cha Gonna Do	1986	$18

SHADY BROOK

Number	Title	Yr	NM
❏ SB-012	Love Is Forever	1978	$15

SOUTH BAY

Number	Title	Yr	NM
❏ SB1001	Love Changes	1982	$30

SMITH, OSBORNE

ARGO

Number	Title	Yr	NM
❏ LP-4000 [M]	Eyes of Love	1960	$30
❏ LPS-4000 [S]	Eyes of Love	1960	$40

SMITH, PATTI, GROUP

ARISTA

Number	Title	Yr	NM
❏ R100469	Dreams of Life	1988	$15
— BMG Music Service edition			
❏ AL8453	Dreams of Life	1988	$12
❏ AB4171	Easter	1978	$15
❏ ALB6-8349	Easter	198?	$10
— Reissue			
❏ AL4066 [B]	Horses	1975	$18
— With the word "Horses" in white letters on the front cover			
❏ ALB6-8362	Horses	198?	$10
— Reissue			
❏ AL4066 [B]	Horses	1975	$25
— With the word "Horses" in black letters on the front cover			
❏ AL4097	Radio Ethiopia	1977	$15
❏ ALB6-8379	Radio Ethiopia	198?	$10
— Reissue			
❏ AB4221	Wave	1979	$12
❏ AL8546	Wave	1990	$10
— Reissue			

COLUMBIA

Number	Title	Yr	NM
❏ C290330	Trampin'	2004	$18

SMITH, PAUL; RAY BROWN; LOUIS BELLSON

DISCWASHER

Number	Title	Yr	NM
❏ 001	Intensive Care	1979	$25

SMITH, PAUL

CAPITOL

Number	Title	Yr	NM
❏ T665 [M]	Cascades	1955	$85
❏ T757 [M]	Cool and Sparkling	1956	$75
❏ T1017 [M]	Delicate Jazz	1958	$75
❏ ST1017 [S]	Delicate Jazz	1958	$75
❏ H493 [10]	Liquid Sounds	1954	$175
❏ T829	Softly, Baby	1957	$85

DISCOVERY

Number	Title	Yr	NM
❏ DL-3009 [10]	Paul Smith	1950	$300
❏ DL-3017 [10]	Paul Smith Trio	1952	$300

MGM

Number	Title	Yr	NM
❏ E-4057 [M]	Memories of Paris	1962	$25
❏ SE-4057 [S]	Memories of Paris	1962	$30

OUTSTANDING

Number	Title	Yr	NM
❏ 09	Heavy Jazz	197?	$30
❏ 011	Heavy Jazz, Vol. 2	1978	$30
❏ 024	Jazz Spotlight on Ellington and Rodgers	1980	$35
❏ 023	Jazz Spotlight on Porter and Gershwin	1980	$35
❏ 04	The Art Tatum Touch	197?	$30
❏ 07	The Art Tatum Touch, Vol. 2	197?	$30
❏ 05	The Ballad Touch	197?	$30
❏ 02	The Master Touch	197?	$30
❏ 012	This One Cooks!	197?	$30

PAUSA

Number	Title	Yr	NM
❏ 7172	Paul Smith Plays Steve Allen	1985	$25

SAVOY

Number	Title	Yr	NM
❏ MG-12094 [M]	By the Fireside	1956	$50

SKYLARK

Number	Title	Yr	NM
❏ SKLP-13 [10]	Paul Smith Quartet	1954	$120

TAMPA

Number	Title	Yr	NM
❏ TP-9 [M]	Fine, Sweet and Tasty	1957	$250
— Colored vinyl			
❏ TP-9 [M]	Fine, Sweet and Tasty	1958	$175
— Black vinyl			

VERVE

Number	Title	Yr	NM
❏ MGV-4051 [M]	Carnival! In Percussion	1961	$30
❏ V-4051 [M]	Carnival! In Percussion	1961	$25
❏ V6-4051 [S]	Carnival! In Percussion	1961	$30
❏ MGV-2148 [M]	Latin Keyboards and Percussion	1960	$150
❏ V-2148 [M]	Latin Keyboards and Percussion	1961	$25
❏ V6-2148 [S]	Latin Keyboards and Percussion	1961	$35
❏ MGV-2130 [M]	The Big Men	1960	$175
❏ MGVS-6135 [S]	The Big Men	1960	$175
❏ V-2130 [M]	The Big Men	1961	$25
❏ V6-2130 [S]	The Big Men	1961	$35
❏ MGV-2128 [M]	The Sound of Music	1960	$100
❏ MGVS-6128 [S]	The Sound of Music	1960	$100
❏ V-2128 [M]	The Sound of Music	1961	$25
❏ V6-2128 [S]	The Sound of Music	1961	$35

VOSS

Number	Title	Yr	NM
❏ VLP1-42937	The Good Life	1988	$25

SMITH, PINE TOP

BRUNSWICK

Number	Title	Yr	NM
❏ BL58003 [10]	Pine Top Smith	1950	$120

SMITH, PLATO

LAND O' JAZZ

Number	Title	Yr	NM
❏ 1972	Dixieland Dance Date	1972	$25

SMITH, RAY

COLUMBIA

Number	Title	Yr	NM
❏ CL1937 [M]	Ray Smith's Greatest Hits	1963	$30
❏ CS8737 [S]	Ray Smith's Greatest Hits	1963	$30

JUDD

Number	Title	Yr	NM
❏ JLPA-701 [M]	Travelin' with Ray	1960	$700

STOMP OFF

Number	Title	Yr	NM
❏ SOS-1012	Jungle Blues	198?	$30

T

Number	Title	Yr	NM
❏ 56062 [M]	The Best of Ray Smith	196?	$150

WIX

Number	Title	Yr	NM
❏ 1000	I'm Gonna Rock Some More	197?	$18

SMITH, RICHARD

CMG

Number	Title	Yr	NM
❏ CML-8011	Puma Creek	1988	$25

SMITH, ROBERT CURTIS

BLUESVILLE

Number	Title	Yr	NM
❏ BVLP-1064 [M]	Clarksdale Blues	1963	$100
— Blue label, silver print			
❏ BVLP-1064 [M]	Clarksdale Blues	1964	$30
— Blue label, trident logo at right			

SMITH, ROGER

WARNER BROS.

Number	Title	Yr	NM
❏ W1305 [M]	Beach Romance	1960	$40
❏ WS1305 [S]	Beach Romance	1960	$50

SMITH, RUSSELL

CAPITOL

Number	Title	Yr	NM
❏ ST-12197	Russell Smith	1982	$10

EPIC

Number	Title	Yr	NM
❏ FE40918	This Little Town	1988	$10

SMITH, SAMMI

ELEKTRA

Number	Title	Yr	NM
❏ 7E-1058	As Long As There's a Sunday	1976	$12
❏ 7E-1108	Mixed Emotions	1977	$12

HARMONY

Number	Title	Yr	NM
❏ H30616	The World of Sammi Smith	1971	$12

MEGA

Number	Title	Yr	NM
❏ 31-1000	Help Me Make It Through the Night	1971	$15
❏ 31-1007	Lonesome	1971	$15
❏ MLPS-601	Rainbow in Daddy's Eyes	1974	$15
❏ MLPS-604	Sammi's Greatest Hits	1974	$15
❏ 31-1011	Something Old, Something New, Something Blue	1972	$15
❏ 31-1019	The Best of Sammi Smith	1973	$15
❏ 31-1021	The Toast of '45	1973	$15
❏ MLPS-612	Today I Started Loving You Again	1975	$15

PICKWICK

Number	Title	Yr	NM
❏ 6167	Help Me Make It Through the Night	197?	$12

ZODIAC

Number	Title	Yr	NM
❏ 5004	Her Way	1976	$12

SMITH, SOMETHIN', AND THE REDHEADS

EPIC

Number	Title	Yr	NM
❏ LN3373 [M]	Put the Blame on Mame	196?	$30
❏ LN3138 [M]	Somethin' Smith and the Redheads	1959	$35

MGM

Number	Title	Yr	NM
❏ E-3941 [M]	Ain't We Got Fun Kinda Songs	1961	$30
❏ SE-3941 [S]	Ain't We Got Fun Kinda Songs	1961	$35

SMITH, STEVE

COLUMBIA

Number	Title	Yr	NM
❏ FC44334	Fiafiaga	1988	$25
❏ FC38955	Vital Information	1983	$25

SMITH, STUFF

20TH FOX

Number	Title	Yr	NM
❏ FTM-3008 [M]	Sweet Singin' Stuff	1959	$30
❏ FTS-3008 [S]	Sweet Singin' Stuff	1959	$30

BASF

Number	Title	Yr	NM
❏ 20650	Black Violin	197?	$35

EVEREST ARCHIVE OF FOLK & JAZZ

Number	Title	Yr	NM
❏ 238	Stuff Smith/Guest Artist: Stphane Grappelly	1970	$25

PRESTIGE

Number	Title	Yr	NM
❏ PRST-7691 [R]	The Stuff Smith Memorial Album	1969	$35

STORYVILLE

Number	Title	Yr	NM
❏ 4087	Swingin' Stuff	198?	$25

VERVE

Number	Title	Yr	NM
❏ MGV-8339 [M]	Cat on a Hot Fiddle	1959	$175
❏ MGVS-6097 [S]	Cat on a Hot Fiddle	1960	$150
❏ V-8339 [M]	Cat on a Hot Fiddle	1961	$25
❏ V6-8339 [S]	Cat on a Hot Fiddle	1961	$35
❏ MGV-8282 [M]	Have Violin, Will Swing	1958	$150
❏ V-8282 [M]	Have Violin, Will Swing	1961	$25
❏ MGV-8206 [M]	Soft Winds	1958	$150
❏ V-8206 [M]	Soft Winds	1961	$25
❏ MGV-8270 [M]	Stephane Grappelli With Stuff Smith	1958	$0
— Canceled			
❏ MGV-2041 [M]	Stuff Smith	1957	$0
— Canceled			

SMITH, TAB

CHECKER

Number	Title	Yr	NM
❏ LP-2971 [M]	Tab Smith	1960	$600
— White label promo with multi-color vinyl			
❏ LP-2971 [M]	Tab Smith	1960	$150
— Regular issue			

UNITED

Number	Title	Yr	NM
❏ LP-001 [10]	Music Styled by Tab Smith	1955	$250
❏ LP-003 [10]	Red, Hot and Cool Blues	1955	$250

SMITH, TOMMY

BLUE NOTE

Number	Title	Yr	NM
❏ B1-91930	Step by Step	1989	$30

STOMP OFF

Number	Title	Yr	NM
❏ SOS-1162	South Side Strut: A Tribute to Don Ewell	1989	$25

SMITH, VERDELLE

CAPITOL

Number	Title	Yr	NM
❏ T2476 [M]	In My Room	1966	$250
❏ ST2476 [S]	In My Room	1966	$300

SMITH, WARREN

LIBERTY

Number	Title	Yr	NM
❏ LRP-3199 [M]	The First Country Collection of Warren Smith	1961	$50
❏ LST-7199 [S]	The First Country Collection of Warren Smith	1961	$80

Number	Title	Yr	NM

SMITH, WHISTLING JACK
DERAM
| ❑ DE16006 [M] | I Was Kaiser Bill's Batman | 1967 | $30 |
| ❑ DES18006 [S] | I Was Kaiser Bill's Batman | 1967 | $25 |

SMITH, WILL
COLUMBIA
❑ C268683	Big Willie Style	1997	$18
❑ C286189	Born to Reign	2002	$18
❑ C269985	Willennium	1999	$18

SMITH, WILLIE "THE LION", AND DON EWELL
SACKVILLE
| ❑ 2004 | Grand Piano | 198? | $25 |

SMITH, WILLIE "THE LION
BLACK LION
| ❑ 156 | Pork and Beans | 197? | $35 |
BLUE CIRCLE
| ❑ 1500-33 [10] | Willie "The Lion" Smith | 1952 | $175 |
CHIAROSCURO
| ❑ 104 | Live at Blues Alley | 197? | $35 |
COMMODORE
| ❑ DL-30004 [M] | The Lion of the Piano | 1951 | $150 |
| ❑ XFL-15775 | Willie "The Lion" Smith | 198? | $25 |
DIAL
| ❑ LP-305 [10] | Harlem Memories | 1953 | $300 |
DOT
| ❑ DLP-3094 [M] | The Lion Roars | 1958 | $150 |
GNP CRESCENDO
| ❑ GNP-9011 | Willie "The Lion" Smith | 197? | $25 |
GRAND AWARD
| ❑ GA-33-368 [M] | The Legend of Willie Smith | 1956 | $50 |
MAINSTREAM
| ❑ 56027 [M] | A Legend | 1965 | $30 |
| ❑ S-6027 [R] | A Legend | 1965 | $35 |
RCA VICTOR
| ❑ LSP-6016 | Memoirs | 1968 | $25 |
URANIA
| ❑ UJLP-1207 [M] | Accent On Piano | 1955 | $300 |

SMITH, WILLIE
EMARCY
| ❑ MG-26000 [10] | Relaxin' After Hours | 1954 | $150 |
GNP CRESCENDO
| ❑ GNPS-2055 | The Best -- Alto Saxophone Supreme | 196? | $25 |
MERCURY
| ❑ MG-25075 [10] | Alto Sax Artistry | 1950 | $250 |

SMITH-GLAMANN QUINTET
BETHLEHEM
| ❑ BCP-22 [M] | Smith-Glamann Quintet | 1955 | $300 |

SMITH
ABC DUNHILL
| ❑ DS-50056 | A Group Called Smith | 1969 | $18 |
| ❑ DS-50081 | Minus-Plus | 1970 | $18 |

SMITHEREENS, THE
CAPITOL
| ❑ C1-91194 | 11 | 1989 | $15 |
CAPITOL/ENIGMA
| ❑ R130120 | Green Thoughts | 1988 | $15 |
| — BMG Direct Marketing edition |
| ❑ C1-48375 | Green Thoughts | 1988 | $12 |
ENIGMA
| ❑ 73220 [EP] | Beauty and Sadness | 1988 | $10 |
| — Remixed version of Little Ricky 103 with one track deleted |
| ❑ R164050 | Especially for You | 1987 | $15 |
| — BMG Direct Marketing edition |
| ❑ SEAX-73258 [PD] | Especially for You | 1986 | $25 |
| — Picture disc in plastic sleeve, sticker on sleeve |
❑ ST-73208	Especially for You	1986	$12
❑ 0(no cat #) [DJ]	Live at the Roxy -- Special Forces Radio Concert	1986	$40
❑ 0(no cat #) [DJ]	Live at the Roxy -- Special Forces Radio Concert	1986	$40
LITTLE RICKY
| ❑ 103 [EP] | Beauty and Sadness | 1983 | $40 |

SMITHS, THE
Also see MORRISSEY.
SIRE
❑ 25669	Louder Than Bombs	1987	$18
❑ 25269	Meat Is Murder	1985	$18
❑ 25786	Rank	1988	$15
❑ 25649	Strangeways, Here We Come	1987	$14
❑ 25426	The Queen Is Dead	1986	$18
❑ 25065	The Smiths	1984	$18

WARNER BROS.
| ❑ WBMS-130 [DJ] | Music and Interviews | 1985 | $75 |
| — Part of "The Warner Bros. Music Show" series; one side is The Smiths; the other side is The Blasters |
| ❑ WBMS-130 [DJ] | The Warner Bros. Music Show | 1985 | $14 |
| — One side: The Smiths; the other side: The Blasters |

SMITHSONIAN JAZZ REPERTORY ENSEMBLE, THE
SMITHSONIAN
| ❑ N-021 | The Music of Fats Waller and James P. Johnson | 1988 | $35 |

SMOKE, THE (1)
California group. Jimmy Greenspoon, later a member of THREE DOG NIGHT, appears on the LP cover, but not on the record itself.
SIDEWALK
| ❑ ST5912 | The Smoke | 1968 | $40 |

SMOKE, THE (2)
Houston-based group.
UNI
| ❑ 73052 | The Smoke | 1969 | $30 |
| ❑ 73065 | The Smoke at George's Coffee Shop | 1970 | $30 |

SMOKE RISE, THE
PARAMOUNT
| ❑ PAS-9000 [B] | The Survival of St. Joan | 1971 | $30 |
| — With booklet |

SMOKER, PAUL
SOUND ASPECTS
| ❑ SAS-006 | Mississippi River Rat | 1985 | $30 |

SMOKESTACK LIGHTNIN'
BELL
| ❑ 6026 | Off the Wall | 1969 | $25 |

SMOKIE
MCA
| ❑ 2152 | Smokey | 1975 | $15 |
| — As "Smokey |
RSO
| ❑ RS-1-3029 | Bright Lights and Back Alleys | 1978 | $12 |
| ❑ RS-1-3005 | Midnight Café | 1976 | $12 |

SMOKY BABE
BLUESVILLE
| ❑ BVLP-1063 [M] | Hottest Brand Going | 1963 | $100 |
| — Blue label, silver print |
| ❑ BVLP-1063 [M] | Hottest Brand Going | 1964 | $30 |
| — Blue label, trident logo at right |
FOLK-LYRIC
| ❑ FL-108 [M] | Smokey Babe | 196? | $150 |

SMOTHERS, SMOKEY
KING
| ❑ 779 [M] | The Backporch Blues | 1962 | $1000 |

SMOTHERS BROTHERS, THE
MERCURY
❑ MG-20989 [M]	Aesop's Fables the Smothers Brothers Way	1965	$18
❑ SR-60989 [S]	Aesop's Fables the Smothers Brothers Way	1965	$25
❑ MGDJ-20 [DJ]	Best of the Smothers Brothers	1964	$40
❑ MGDJ-20 [DJ]	Best of the Smothers Brothers	1964	$40
❑ MG-20862 [M]	Curb Your Tongue, Knave!	1963	$18
❑ SR-60862 [S]	Curb Your Tongue, Knave!	1963	$25
❑ MG-21089 [M]	Golden Hits of the Smothers Brothers, Vol. 2	1966	$18
❑ SR-61089 [S]	Golden Hits of the Smothers Brothers, Vol. 2	1966	$25
❑ MG-20904 [M]	It Must Have Been Something I Said!	1964	$18
❑ SR-60904 [S]	It Must Have Been Something I Said!	1964	$25
❑ MGDJ-25 [DJ]	It's Brothers Smothers Month	1964	$40
❑ MGDJ-25 [DJ]	It's Brothers Smothers Month	1964	$40
❑ MG-21051 [M]	Mom Always Liked You Best!	1965	$18
❑ SR-61051 [S]	Mom Always Liked You Best!	1965	$25
❑ SR-61193	Smothers Comedy Brothers Hour	1968	$25
❑ MG-21064 [M]	The Smothers Brothers Play It Straight	1966	$18

Number	Title	Yr	NM

❑ SR-61064 [S]	The Smothers Brothers Play It Straight	1966	$25
❑ MG-20611 [M]	The Songs and Comedy of the Smothers Brothers!	1962	$18
❑ SR-60611 [S]	The Songs and Comedy of the Smothers Brothers!	1962	$25
❑ MG-20675 [M]	The Two Sides of the Smothers Brothers	1962	$18
❑ SR-60675 [S]	The Two Sides of the Smothers Brothers	1962	$25
❑ MG-20777 [M]	(Think Ethnic!)	1963	$18
❑ SR-60777 [S]	(Think Ethnic!)	1963	$25
❑ MG-20948 [M]	Tour De Farce American History and Other Unrelated Subjects	1964	$18
❑ SR-60948 [S]	Tour De Farce American History and Other Unrelated Subjects	1964	$25
RHINO
| ❑ R1-70188 | Sibling Revelry: The Best of the Smothers Brothers | 1988 | $12 |

SNAKEFINGER
RALPH
❑ SN8353	Against the Grain	1983	$15
❑ SNK7909	Chewing Hides the Sound	1979	$15
❑ SN8053	Greener Postures	1980	$15
❑ SN8203	Manual of Errors	1982	$15

SNAP
ARISTA
| ❑ AL8536 | World Power | 1990 | $15 |

SNEAKY PETE
SHILO
| ❑ 4086 | Sneaky Pete | 1979 | $30 |

SNELL, TONY
ESP-DISK'
| ❑ 3004 | Medieval and Latter Day Lays | 197? | $25 |

SNIFF 'N' THE TEARS
ATLANTIC
| ❑ SD19242 | Fickle Heart | 1979 | $14 |
| — With full version of "Driver's Seat" |
| ❑ SD19242 | Fickle Heart | 1979 | $12 |
| — Some pressings erroneously contain an edit of "Driver's Seat" with the entire first verse missing |
| ❑ SD19272 | The Game's Up | 1980 | $12 |
MCA
| ❑ 5242 | Love Action | 1981 | $12 |
| ❑ 821 | Love Action | 1983 | $10 |
| — Budget-line reissue |

SNOOP DOGG
Also includes records credited to "Snoop Doggy Dogg."
DEATH ROW/INTERSCOPE
| ❑ 92279 | Doggystyle | 1993 | $50 |
| — As "Snoop Doggy Dogg |
| ❑ INT2-90038 | Tha Doggfather | 1996 | $50 |
| — As "Snoop Doggy Dogg |
GEFFEN
| ❑ B0003763-01 | R&G (Rhythm & Gangsta): The Masterpiece | 2004 | $18 |
NO LIMIT
| ❑ 50006 | Da Game Is to Be Sold, Not to Be Told | 1998 | $30 |
| ❑ 50062 | No Limit Top Dogg | 1999 | $30 |
PRIORITY
| ❑ 39157 | Paid Tha Cost to Be Tha Bo$$ | 2002 | $30 |
| ❑ P123225 | Tha Last Meal | 2000 | $30 |

Number	Title	Yr	NM

SNOW, HANK, AND ANITA CARTER
RCA VICTOR
❏ LPM-2580 [M]	Together Again	1962	$30
❏ LSP-2580 [S]	Together Again	1962	$40

SNOW, HANK, AND CHET ATKINS
RCA VICTOR
❏ LSP-4254	By Special Request - C.B. Atkins and C.E. Snow	1970	$25
❏ LPM-2952 [M]	Reminiscing	1964	$30
❏ LSP-2952 [S]	Reminiscing	1964	$30

SNOW, HANK, AND KELLY FOXTON
RCA VICTOR
❏ AHL1-3496	Lovingly Yours	1980	$12
❏ AYL1-3987	Win Some, Lose Some, Lonesome	1981	$12

SNOW, HANK; PORTER WAGONER; HANK LOCKLIN
RCA VICTOR
❏ LPM-2723 [M]	Three Country Gentlemen	1963	$30
❏ LSP-2723 [S]	Three Country Gentlemen	1963	$40

SNOW, HANK
PAIR
❏ PDL2-1004	I'm Movin' On	1986	$15

RCA CAMDEN
❏ ACL1-0540	I'm Movin' On	1974	$12
❏ CAS-2348	I Went to Your Wedding	1969	$15
❏ CAS-2513	Lonesome Whistle	1972	$15
❏ CAS-2443	Memories Are Made of This	1970	$15
❏ CAL-2160 [M]	My Early Favorites	1967	$18
❏ CAS-2160 [S]	My Early Favorites	1967	$15
❏ CAS-2257 [B]	My Nova Scotia Home	1968	$15
❏ CAL-836 [M]	Old and Great Songs	1964	$18
❏ CAS-836 [S]	Old and Great Songs	1964	$15
❏ ACL1-0124	Snowbird	1973	$12
❏ CAS-2235	Somewhere Along Life's Highway	1968	$15
❏ CAL-910 [M]	The Highest Bidder	1965	$15
❏ CAS-910 [S]	The Highest Bidder	1965	$18
❏ CAL-782 [M]	The Last Ride	1963	$30
❏ CAS-782 [R]	The Last Ride	1963	$18
❏ CAS-2560	The Legend of Old Doc Brown	1972	$15
❏ CAL-722 [M]	The One and Only Hank Snow	1962	$30
❏ CAS-722 [R]	The One and Only Hank Snow	1962	$18
❏ CAL-514 [M]	The Singing Ranger	1959	$25
❏ CAS-514 [R]	The Singing Ranger	196?	$15
❏ CAL-680 [M]	The Southern Cannonball	1961	$30
❏ CAS-680 [R]	The Southern Cannonball	196?	$18
❏ CXS-9009	The Wreck of the 97	197?	$18
❏ CAL-964 [M]	Travelin' Blues	1966	$15
❏ CAS-964 [S]	Travelin' Blues	1966	$18
❏ ACL2-0337	When My Blue Moon Turns to Gold Again	197?	$18

RCA VICTOR
❏ APL1-2400	#104 -- Still Movin' On	1977	$15
❏ LSP-4601	Award Winners	1971	$25
❏ LPM-2458 [M]	Big Country Hits	1961	$30
❏ LSP-2458 [S]	Big Country Hits	1961	$40
❏ LPM-3826 [M]	Christmas with Hank Snow	1967	$30
❏ LSP-3826 [S]	Christmas with Hank Snow	1967	$30
❏ AHL1-5497	Collector's Series	1986	$12
❏ LPM-1419 [M]	Country and Western Jamboree	1957	$100
❏ LPM-3026 [10]	Country Classics	1952	$250
❏ LPM-1233 [M]	Country Classics	1956	$100
❏ LSP-4379	Cure for the Blues	1970	$25
❏ LPM-3378 [M]	Gloryland March	1965	$30
❏ LSP-3378 [S]	Gloryland March	1965	$30
❏ LPM-3595 [M]	Gospel Train	1966	$30
❏ LSP-3595 [S]	Gospel Train	1966	$40
❏ APL1-0162	Grand Ole Opry Favorites	1973	$18
❏ ANL1-1207	Grand Ole Opry Favorites	1975	$12
— Reissue of APL1-0162			
❏ LPM-3548 [M]	Guitar Stylings of Hank Snow	1966	$40
❏ LSP-3548 [S]	Guitar Stylings of Hank Snow	1966	$35
❏ LPM-3131 [10]	Hank Snow Salutes Jimmie Rodgers	1953	$180
❏ LPM-3267 [10]	Hank Snow's Country Guitar	1954	$180
❏ LPM-1435 [M]	Hank Snow's Country Guitar	1957	$100
❏ LPM-3070 [10]	Hank Snow Sings	1952	$180
❏ LSP-4306	Hank Snow Sings in Memory of Jimmie Rodgers	1970	$25
❏ LPM-2043 [M]	Hank Snow Sings Jimmie Rodgers Songs	1959	$50
❏ LSP-2043 [S]	Hank Snow Sings Jimmie Rodgers Songs	1959	$150
❏ LPM-1638 [M]	Hank Snow Sings Sacred Songs	1958	$75
❏ LPM-2285 [M]	Hank Snow Souvenirs	1961	$30
❏ LSP-2285 [S]	Hank Snow Souvenirs	1961	$40
❏ LPM-3471 [M]	Heartbreak Trail - A Tribute to the Sons of the Pioneers	1966	$30
❏ LSP-3471 [S]	Heartbreak Trail - A Tribute to the Sons of the Pioneers	1966	$30
❏ APL1-0441	Hello Love	1974	$18
❏ LPM-3965 [M]	Hits, Hits and More Hits	1968	$175
❏ LSP-3965 [S]	Hits, Hits and More Hits	1968	$30
❏ AHL1-3511	Instrumentally Yours	1980	$15

❏ LPM-2675 [M]	I've Been Everywhere	1963	$30
❏ LSP-2675 [S]	I've Been Everywhere	1963	$40
❏ LPM-1113 [M]	Just Keep a-Movin'	1955	$150
❏ APL1-1361	Live from Evangel Temple	1976	$15
— With Jimmy Snow			
❏ LPM-2812 [M]	More Hank Snow Souvenirs	1964	$30
❏ LSP-2812 [S]	More Hank Snow Souvenirs	1964	$30
❏ AHL1-3208	Mysterious Lady	1979	$15
❏ LPM-1156 [M]	Old Doc Brown and Other Narrations	1955	$150
❏ LPM-2705 [M]	Railroad Man	1963	$30
❏ LSP-2705 [S]	Railroad Man	1963	$40
❏ LSP-4122	Snow in All Seasons	1969	$30
❏ LPM-3737 [M]	Snow in Hawaii	1967	$30
❏ LSP-3737 [S]	Snow in Hawaii	1967	$30
❏ LPM-2901 [M]	Songs of Tragedy	1964	$30
❏ LSP-2901 [S]	Songs of Tragedy	1964	$30
❏ LPM-3857 [M]	Spanish Fire Ball and Other Great Hank Snow Stylings	1967	$30
❏ LSP-3857 [S]	Spanish Fire Ball and Other Great Hank Snow Stylings	1967	$30
❏ LSP-4032	Tales of the Yukon	1968	$30
❏ APL1-0608	That's You and Me	1974	$18
❏ LPM-3478 [M]	The Best of Hank Snow	1966	$25
❏ LSP-3478 [S]	The Best of Hank Snow	1966	$30
❏ ANL1-3470	The Best of Hank Snow	1980	$10
❏ LSP-4798	The Best of Hank Snow, Vol. 2	1972	$18
❏ LSP-4708	The Jimmie Rodgers Story	1972	$18
❏ ANL1-2194	The Jimmie Rodgers Story	1977	$12
— Reissue of 4708			
❏ DPL2-0134	The Living Legend	197?	$150
— RCA Special Products release			
❏ LPM-6014 [M]	This Is My Story	1966	$40
❏ LSP-6014 [S]	This Is My Story	1966	$50
❏ LSP-4501	Tracks and Trains	1971	$25
❏ APL1-0908	You're Easy to Love	1975	$18
❏ LPM-3317 [M]	Your Favorite Country Hits	1965	$30
❏ LSP-3317 [S]	Your Favorite Country Hits	1965	$30

READER'S DIGEST
❏ RDA-216	I'm Movin' On	197?	$120

SCHOOL OF MUSIC
❏ 1149 [M]	The Guitar	1958	$300
— Deduct 20 percent if instruction book is missing			

SNOW, PHOEBE
COLUMBIA
❏ JC35456	Against the Grain	1978	$12
❏ PC34387	It Looks Like Snow	1976	$12
— Original with no bar code			
❏ PC34387	It Looks Like Snow	198?	$10
— Budget-line reissue with bar code			
❏ JC34875	Never Letting Go	1977	$12
❏ PC33952	Second Childhood	1976	$12
— Original with no bar code			
❏ PCQ33952 [Q]	Second Childhood	1976	$20
❏ PC33952	Second Childhood	198?	$10
— Budget-line reissue with bar code			
❏ JC37091	The Best of Phoebe Snow	1981	$12
❏ PC37091	The Best of Phoebe Snow	1981	$10
— Budget-line reissue			

DCC COMPACT CLASSICS
❏ LPZ-2027	Phoebe Snow	1996	$30
— Audiophile vinyl			

ELEKTRA
❏ 60852	Something Real	1989	$12

MCA
❏ 37119	Phoebe Snow	198?	$10
— Budget-line reissue of Shelter LP			

MIRAGE
❏ SD19297	Rock Away	1981	$12

SHELTER
❏ 2109	Phoebe Snow	1974	$12
❏ 52017	Phoebe Snow	1977	$10
— Reissue with ABC distribution			

SNOW, VALAIDA
SWING
❏ SW-8455/6	Swing Is the Thing	198?	$30

SNOW
EPIC
❏ BN26435 [B]	Snow	1969	$30

SNOWBALL
GUINNESS
❏ GNS36065 [B]	Snowball	1977	$250

SNOWDEN, ELMER
FANTASY
❏ OJC-1756	Harlem Banjo	198?	$25

IAJRC
❏ LP12	Elmer Snowden 1924-63	198?	$25

RIVERSIDE
❏ RLP-348 [M]	Harlem Banjo	1960	$250
❏ RS-9348 [S]	Harlem Banjo	1960	$250

SNUFF
ELEKTRA
❏ 60149	Snuff	1982	$12

SNYDER, TERRY, AND THE ALL-STARS
See ENOCH LIGHT.

SOBULE, JILL
MCA
❏ 6375	Things Here Are Different	1990	$16

SOCIAL DISTORTION
13TH FLOOR
❏ SD1301 [B]	Mommy's Little Monster	1983	$75
— Standard cover with lyric sheet			
❏ SD1301 [B]	Mommy's Little Monster	1983	$100
— Gatefold cover			

EPIC
❏ E46055	Social Distortion	1990	$25
❏ E47948 [B]	Somewhere Between Heaven and Hell	1992	$30

EPIC/550 MUSIC
❏ E64380	White Light, White Heat, White Trash	1996	$15

RESTLESS
❏ 72251 [B]	Prison Bound	1988	$30

TIME BOMB
❏ 43516 [B]	Live at the Roxy	1998	$2000
❏ 43502 [B]	Mainliner (Wreckage from the Past)	1995	$25
❏ 43500 [B]	Mommy's Little Monster	1995	$30
❏ 43501	Prison Bound	1995	$18

TRIPLE X
❏ 51019	Mommy's Little Monster	1989	$25
— Clear vinyl			

SOCIAL UNREST
LIBERTINE
❏ LSU1 [EP]	Rat in a Maze	1982	$30
❏ LSU2461 [B]	SU-2000	1985	$30

SOCIETY OF SEVEN
SILVER SWORD
❏ 7012	How Has Your Love Life Been?	1970	$25

SOCOLOW, FRANK
BETHLEHEM
❏ BCP-70 [M]	Sounds By Socolow	1957	$300

SOFT CELL
SIRE
❏ 23694 [EP]	Non-Stop Ecstatic Dancing	1982	$15
❏ BSK3647	Non-Stop Erotic Cabaret	1981	$15
❏ 23989 [EP]	Soul Inside	1983	$15
❏ 23769 [B]	The Art of Falling Apart	1983	$25
— With limited 12-inch EP			
❏ 25096 [B]	This Last Night	1984	$15

SOFT MACHINE, THE
ACCORD
❏ SN-7178	Memories	1981	$12

COLUMBIA
❏ KC31604 [B]	5	1972	$18
❏ C30754 [B]	Fourth	1971	$18
❏ KC32716	Seven	1974	$15
❏ KG32260	Six	1973	$18
❏ G30339 [B]	Third	1970	$25

COMMAND
❏ 964SD	Soft Machine	1973	$18
— Reissue of Probe LPs in one package			

PROBE
❏ CPLP-4500 [B]	The Soft Machine	1968	$75
— Cover with moving parts			
❏ CPLP-4500	The Soft Machine	1969	$25
— Regular cover			
❏ CPLP-4505 [B]	The Soft Machine, Vol. 2	1969	$40

SOFTWARE
HEADFIRST
❏ 9707	Marbles	198?	$30

INNOVATIVE COMMUNICATION
❏ KS 80.050	Chip-Meditation	1987	$35
❏ D1-74766	Digital Dance	1988	$30
❏ KS 80.055	Electronic Universe	1987	$50
❏ IC 80.064	Syn-Code/Live in Concert	1988	$35

SOHO
ATCO
❏ 91585	Goddess	1990	$15

Number	Title	Yr	NM

SOLAL, MARTIAL

CAPITOL
☐ T10261 [M]	Martial Solal	1960	$75
☐ ST10261 [S]	Martial Solal	1960	$75
☐ T10354 [M]	Vive La France! Viva La Jazz! Vive Solal!	1961	$50
☐ ST10354 [S]	Vive La France! Viva La Jazz! Vive Solal!	1961	$75

CONTEMPORARY
| ☐ C-2512 [10] | French Modern Sounds | 1954 | $300 |

LIBERTY
| ☐ LRP-3335 [M] | Martial Solal in Concert | 1963 | $35 |
| ☐ LST-7335 [S] | Martial Solal in Concert | 1963 | $25 |

MILESTONE
☐ MSP-9014	On Home Ground	1969	$35
☐ MLP-1001 [M]	Solal!	1967	$30
☐ MSP-9001 [S]	Solal!	1967	$35

PAUSA
| ☐ 7061 | Four Keys | 197? | $25 |
| ☐ 7103 | Movability | 198? | $25 |

RCA VICTOR
| ☐ LPM-2777 [M] | Martial Solal at Newport '63 | 1963 | $35 |
| ☐ LSP-2777 [S] | Martial Solal at Newport '63 | 1963 | $25 |

SOUL NOTE
| ☐ SN-1060 | Bluesine | 1983 | $30 |

SOLAR PLEXUS

INNER CITY
| ☐ IC-1087 | Earth Songs | 1980 | $30 |
| ☐ IC-1067 | Solar Plexus | 1979 | $30 |

SOLOFF, LEW

PROJAZZ
| ☐ PAD-601 | Hanalei Bay | 1986 | $25 |

SOLUTION, THE

FIRST AMERICAN
| ☐ 7776 | It's Only Just Begun | 198? | $25 |

SOMERSET STRINGS, THE

EPIC
| ☐ LN3159 [M] | Music for Christmas at Home | 1955 | $25 |

SOMMER, ELKE

MGM
| ☐ E-4321 [M] | Love in Any Language | 1965 | $30 |
| ☐ SE-4321 [S] | Love in Any Language | 1965 | $30 |

SOMMERS, JOANIE

COLUMBIA
| ☐ CL2495 [M] | Come Alive | 1966 | $25 |
| ☐ CS9295 [S] | Come Alive | 1966 | $30 |

DISCOVERY
| ☐ DS-883 | Dream | 1983 | $15 |
—*With Bob Florence*

WARNER BROS.
| ☐ B1348 [M] | Behind Closed Doors at a Recording Session | 1960 | $175 |
—*Record comes in a box with a booklet included*
☐ W1436 [M]	For Those Who Think Young	1962	$30
☐ WS1436 [S]	For Those Who Think Young	1962	$40
☐ W1412 [M]	Joanie Sommers	1961	$30
☐ WS1412 [S]	Joanie Sommers	1961	$40
☐ W1470 [M]	Johnny Get Angry	1962	$40
☐ WS1470 [S]	Johnny Get Angry	1962	$50
☐ W1474 [M]	Let's Talk About Love	1962	$30
☐ WS1474 [S]	Let's Talk About Love	1962	$40
☐ W1346 [M]	Positively the Most	1960	$400
☐ WS1346 [S]	Positively the Most	1960	$300
☐ W1575 [M]	Softly, The Brazilian Sound	1964	$30
☐ WS1575 [S]	Softly, The Brazilian Sound	1964	$30
☐ W1504 [M]	Sommers' Seasons	1963	$30
☐ WS1504 [S]	Sommers' Seasons	1963	$30

SOMOA

PROJAZZ
| ☐ PAD-645 | No Band Is an Island | 1987 | $25 |

SON VOLT

WARNER BROS.
| ☐ 46518 | Straightaways | 1997 | $15 |
| ☐ 47059 | Wide Swing Tremolo | 1998 | $15 |

SONDHEIM, ALAN

ESP-DISK'
| ☐ 1048 [S] | Ritual-All-7-70 | 1969 | $150 |
| ☐ 1082 [S] | T'Other Little Tune | 1969 | $150 |

SONIC YOUTH

DGC
☐ 24485 [B]	Dirty	1992	$35
☐ 24632	Experimental Jet Set, Trash and No Star	1994	$40
☐ 24297	Goo	1990	$30
☐ 24825	Washing Machine	1995	$40

ENIGMA
| ☐ 75403 | Daydream Nation | 1988 | $30 |

GEFFEN
| ☐ 490650-1 | NYC Ghosts and Flowers | 2000 | $18 |
| ☐ B002374001 [B] | Rather Ripped | 2016 | $20 |

GOOFIN'
☐ GOO 05	Dirty (Deluxe Edition)	2003	$30
☐ GOO 07	Goo (Deluxe Edition)	2005	$30
☐ GOO 04	Murray Street	2002	$15
☐ GOO11	Rather Ripped	2006	$15
☐ GOO 06	Sonic Nurse	2004	$18
☐ GOO 08	Sonic Youth	2006	$25
—*Reissue of 1982 debut album with a second record of bonus tracks*
| ☐ GOO021 [B] | Spinhead Sessions • 1986 | 2016 | $20 |

HOMESTEAD
| ☐ HMS 016 [B] | Bad Moon Rising | 1985 | $40 |
| ☐ HMS 021 [EP] | Death Valley '69 | 1985 | $40 |
—*With Lydia Lunch*

KONKURRENT
| ☐ FISH-9 | In the Fishtank | 2002 | $18 |
—*With I.C.P. and The Ex; U.S. editions are distributed by Touch and Go Records*

MOBILE FIDELITY
| ☐ 1-257 | Goo | 1996 | $150 |
—*Audiophile vinyl*

MY SO-CALLED RECORDS
| ☐ 3 | A Thousand Leaves | 1998 | $18 |

NEUTRAL
☐ 9 [B]	Confusion Is Sex	1983	$100
☐ N-1 [EP]	Sonic Youth	1982	$150
☐ 01 [EP]	Sonic Youth	1982	$150

RHINO
| ☐ R171591 [B] | Made in U.S.A. (Soundtrack) | 1995 | $30 |
—*Clear vinyl record and sleeve; music recorded in 1986*

SST
| ☐ 096 [B] | Confusion Is Sex | 1987 | $50 |
—*Reissue of Neutral 9*
☐ 059 [B]	Evol	1986	$75
☐ 155 [EP]	Master Dik	1988	$40
☐ 134 [B]	Sister	1987	$30
☐ 097 [EP]	Sonic Youth	1987	$30
☐ 080 [EP]	Starpower	1986	$50

SYR
| ☐ 1 [B] | Anagrama | 1997 | $12 |
—*Red vinyl*
| ☐ 4 | Goodbye 20th Century | 1999 | $18 |
| ☐ 3 | Invito Al Cielo | 1998 | $12 |
—*With Jim O'Rourke; clear vinyl*
| ☐ 5 | Kim Gordon - DJ Olive - Ikue Mori | 2000 | $15 |
| ☐ 2 [B] | Slaapkamers Met Slagroom | 1997 | $30 |
—*Teal vinyl*

SONICS, THE (2); THE WAILERS; THE GALAXIES

ETIQUETTE
| ☐ ETALB-025 [M] | Merry Christmas | 1965 | $500 |
| ☐ ETALB-025 | Merry Christmas | 1984 | $12 |
—*Flimsier vinyl, with date on back cover*

SONICS, THE (2)

BEAT ROCKET
| ☐ BR114 | Introducing the Sonics | 199? | $15 |

BOMP!
| ☐ 4011 | Sinderella | 1980 | $18 |

BUCKSHOT
| ☐ 01 | Explosives | 1973 | $250 |

ETIQUETTE
| ☐ ETALB-024 [M] | Here Are the Sonics!!! | 1965 | $350 |
—*Red label*
| ☐ ETALB-024 [M] | Here Are the Sonics!!! | 1965 | $300 |
—*Purple label*
| ☐ ETLPS-024 [S] | Here Are the Sonics!!! | 1965 | $400 |
—*Red label*
| ☐ ETLPS-024 [S] | Here Are the Sonics!!! | 1965 | $300 |
—*Purple label*
| ☐ ETLPS-024 | Here Are the Sonics!!! | 1984 | $16 |
—*Purple label, flimsier vinyl, with date on back cover*
☐ ETALB-027 [M]	The Sonics Boom	1966	$500
☐ ETLPS-027 [R]	The Sonics Boom	1966	$250
☐ ETLPS-027	The Sonics Boom	1984	$12
—*Flimsier vinyl, with date on back cover*

FIRST AMERICAN
☐ FA-7779	Fire and Ice	1983	$25
☐ FA-7715	Original Northwest Punk	1978	$25
☐ FA-7719	Unreleased	1980	$25

JERDEN
| ☐ JRL-7007 [M] | Introducing the Sonics | 1967 | $300 |
| ☐ JRS-7007 [R] | Introducing the Sonics | 1967 | $175 |

ReVox
| ☐ RVUSA002 [B] | Live at Easy Street | 2016 | $100 |
—*Limited edition*

SONN, LARRY

CORAL
| ☐ CRL57057 [M] | The Sound of Sonn | 1956 | $40 |

DOT
| ☐ DLP-9005 [M] | Jazz Band Having a Ball | 1958 | $85 |
| ☐ DLP-29005 [S] | Jazz Band Having a Ball | 1958 | $85 |

SONNIER, JO-EL

RCA
☐ 6374-1-R	Come On Joe	1988	$10
☐ 9718-1-R	Have a Little Faith	1990	$15
☐ 8396-RDJ [DJ]	Jo-El	1989	$18
—*Promo-only sampler*

ROUNDER
| ☐ 3049 | Cajun Life | 1988 | $12 |

SONNY

ATCO
| ☐ 33-229 [M] | Inner Views | 1967 | $25 |
| ☐ SD 33-229 [S] | Inner Views | 1967 | $25 |

SONNY AND CHER

ATCO
☐ 33-214 [M]	Good Times	1967	$18
☐ SD 33-214 [S]	Good Times	1967	$25
☐ 33-203 [M]	In Case You're in Love	1967	$18
☐ SD 33-203 [S]	In Case You're in Love	1967	$25
☐ 33-177 [M]	Look At Us	1965	$40
—*Without white box that says "Includes Their Big Hit 'I Got You Babe'" (original)*
| ☐ SD 33-177 [S] | Look At Us | 1965 | $30 |
—*Without white box that says "Includes Their Big Hit 'I Got You Babe'" (original)*
| ☐ 33-177 [M] | Look At Us | 1965 | $18 |
—*With white box that says "Includes Their Big Hit 'I Got You Babe'" (second edition)*
| ☐ SD 33-177 [S] | Look At Us | 1965 | $18 |
—*With white box that says "Includes Their Big Hit 'I Got You Babe'" (second edition)*
| ☐ A2M5177 [M] | Sonny & Cher's Greatest Hits | 1967 | $35 |
—*Columbia Record Club exclusive*
| ☐ A2S5178 [S] | Sonny & Cher's Greatest Hits | 1967 | $30 |
—*Columbia Record Club exclusive*
☐ SD11000	The Beat Goes On	1975	$18
☐ 33-219 [M]	The Best of Sonny and Cher	1967	$25
☐ SD 33-219 [S]	The Best of Sonny and Cher	1967	$25
—*"What Now My Love," "A Beautiful Story," "But You're Mine" and "Laugh at Me" are rechanneled*
| ☐ SD 2-804 | The Two of Us | 1972 | $25 |
—*Combines "Look at Us" and "In Case You're in Love"*
| ☐ 33-183 [M] | The Wondrous World of Sonny and Cher | 1966 | $18 |
| ☐ SD 33-183 [S] | The Wondrous World of Sonny and Cher | 1966 | $25 |

KAPP
| ☐ KS-3660 | All I Ever Need Is You | 1972 | $18 |
—*Orange and red swirl label*
| ☐ ST-94312 | All I Ever Need Is You | 1972 | $25 |
—*Capitol Record Club edition*
| ☐ KS-3660 | All I Ever Need Is You | 1972 | $25 |
—*Black label with red "Kapp" cap at top*
| ☐ KS-3660 | All I Ever Need Is You | 1972 | $30 |
—*Red label with red "Kapp" cap at top*
| ☐ KRS-5560 | All I Ever Need Is You | 1972 | $15 |
—*Reissue; orange and red swirl label; some of these have a sticker on the front cover with the new number with no difference in value*
| ☐ KS-3654 | Sonny & Cher Live | 1971 | $18 |

MCA
| ☐ 2021 | All I Ever Need Is You | 1973 | $15 |
—*Reissue of Kapp 3660*
☐ 2117	Greatest Hits	1974	$15
☐ 2101	Mama Was a Rock & Roll Singer Papa Used to Write All Her Songs	1973	$15
☐ 2009	Sonny & Cher Live	1973	$15
—*Reissue of Kapp 3654*
| ☐ 2-8004 | Sonny & Cher Live in Las Vegas, Vol. 2 | 1973 | $18 |

PAIR
| ☐ PDL2-1140 | Sonny & Cher At Their Best | 1986 | $15 |

REPRISE
| ☐ R6177 [M] | Baby Don't Go | 1965 | $30 |
| ☐ RS6177 [P] | Baby Don't Go | 1965 | $30 |
—*By "Sonny & Cher & Friends" (also includes The Lettermen, Bill Medley and The Blendells)*

TVP
| ☐ TVP-1021 | The Hits of Sonny & Cher | 1977 | $15 |

Number	Title	Yr	NM

SONNY AND THE DEMONS

UNITED ARTISTS
❏ UAL-3316 [M]	Drag Kings	1964	$75
❏ UAS-6316 [S]	Drag Kings	1964	$80

SONS OF BIX, THE

JAZZOLOGY
❏ J-99	Copenhagen	1983	$25
❏ J-59	Ostrich Walk	1979	$25

SONS OF CHAMPLIN, THE

ARIOLA AMERICA
❏ ST-50007	A Circle Filled with Love	1976	$12
❏ SW-50017	Loving Is Why	1977	$12
❏ SW-50002	The Sons of Champlin	1975	$12

CAPITOL
❏ ST-675	Follow Your Heart	1971	$25
❏ SWBB-200 [B]	Loosen Up Naturally	1969	$75
—With the F-word clearly visible as part of the cover artwork			
❏ SWBB-200	Loosen Up Naturally	1969	$30
—With the F-word scratched off the cover artwork			
❏ SWBB-200 [B]	Loosen Up Naturally	1969	$35
—With the F-word airbrushed off the cover artwork			
❏ SKAO-322	The Sons	1969	$30

COLUMBIA
❏ KC32341	Welcome to the Dance	1973	$18

GOLDMINE
❏ GM94930	The Sons of Champlin	1975	$25

SONS OF CHAMPLIN
❏ 0(no cat #)	Minus Seeds and Stems	1969	$500

SONS OF HEROES

MCA
❏ 39010	Sons of Heroes	1983	$25

SONS OF THE PIONEERS

COLUMBIA
❏ FC37439	The Sons of the Pioneers: Columbia Historical Edition	1981	$12

MCA
❏ 730	Tumbleweed Trails	198?	$12

RCA CAMDEN
❏ CAL-587 [M]	Room Full of Roses	1960	$25
❏ CAL-413 [M]	Wagons West	1958	$25
❏ CAS-413 [R]	Wagons West	1963	$15

RCA VICTOR
❏ ANL1-2332	A Country-Western Songbook	1977	$18
❏ LPM-3714 [M]	Campfire Favorites	1967	$30
❏ LSP-3714 [S]	Campfire Favorites	1967	$25
❏ LPM-2118 [M]	Cool Water	1960	$30
❏ LSP-2118 [S]	Cool Water	1960	$30
❏ AYL1-3679	Cool Water	1980	$12
❏ LPM-2855 [M]	Country Fare	1964	$25
❏ LSP-2855 [S]	Country Fare	1964	$30
❏ LPM-3032 [10]	Cowboy Classics	1952	$150
❏ LPM-3095 [10]	Cowboy Hymns and Spirituals	1952	$150
❏ LPM-2957 [M]	Down Memory Trail	1964	$25
❏ LSP-2957 [S]	Down Memory Trail	1964	$30
❏ LPM-1130 [M]	Favorite Cowboy Songs	1955	$75
❏ LPM-1431 [M]	How Great Thou Art	1957	$75
❏ LPM-2652 [M]	Hymns of the Cowboy	1963	$25
❏ LSP-2652 [S]	Hymns of the Cowboy	1963	$30
❏ LPM-3351 [M]	Legends of the West	1965	$18
❏ LSP-3351 [S]	Legends of the West	1965	$25
❏ AYM1-4092	Let's Go West Again	1981	$12
❏ LPM-2356 [M]	Lure of the West	1961	$30
❏ LSP-2356 [S]	Lure of the West	1961	$30
❏ LPM-1483 [M]	One Man's Songs	1957	$75
❏ LPM-2603 [M]	Our Men Out West	1963	$25
❏ LSP-2603 [S]	Our Men Out West	1963	$30
❏ LPM-3964 [M]	South of the Border	1968	$100
❏ LSP-3964 [S]	South of the Border	1968	$25
❏ LPM-3476 [M]	The Best of Sons of the Pioneers	1966	$18
❏ LSP-3476 [S]	The Best of Sons of the Pioneers	1966	$25
❏ ANL1-3468	The Best of the Sons of the Pioneers	1980	$12
❏ LPM-3554 [M]	The Songs of Bob Nolan	1966	$18
❏ LSP-3554 [S]	The Songs of Bob Nolan	1966	$25
❏ LPM-2737 [M]	Trail Dust	1963	$25
❏ LSP-2737 [S]	Trail Dust	1963	$30
❏ LPM-2456 [M]	Tumbleweed Trails	1962	$30
❏ LSP-2456 [S]	Tumbleweed Trails	1962	$30
❏ LPM-3162 [10]	Western Classics	1953	$150
❏ PRM-104 [M]	Westward Ho!	1961	$30
—Special-products issue			

READER'S DIGEST
❏ RBA-135-A	Down Memory Trail with the Sons of the Pioneers	1981	$75

SILVER SPUR
❏ S581	Celebration: Commemorating 50 Years of the Sons of the Pioneers	1982	$18

SONS OF THE PURPLE SAGE

TOPS
❏ L-1588 [M]	Western Favorites	1959	$25

WALDORF
❏ 143 [10]	Songs of the Golden West	1955	$50

SOPHOMORES, THE (1)

SEECO
❏ CELP-451 [M]	The Sophomores	1958	$250

SOPRANO SUMMIT

CHIAROSCURO
❏ 149	Chalumeau Blue	197?	$30
❏ 178	Crazy Rhythm	1977	$30

CONCORD JAZZ
❏ CJ-52	Live at Concord '77	1977	$30
❏ CJ-29	Soprano Summit in Concert	1976	$30

JAZZOLOGY
❏ J-56	Live at Big Horn Jazzfest	197?	$25

SOPWITH "CAMEL," THE

KAMA SUTRA
❏ KSBS-2063	Hello Hello	1973	$25
❏ KLP-8060 [M]	The Sopwith Camel	1967	$30
❏ KLPS-8060 [S]	The Sopwith Camel	1967	$30

REPRISE
❏ MS2108	The Miraculous Hump Returns	1973	$30

SOSKIN, MARK

PRESTIGE
❏ 10109	Rhythm Vision	1979	$35

SOSSON, MARSHALL

TOWN HALL
❏ M-26	Virtuoso Jazz Violin Classics	197?	$30

SOTHERN, ANN

CRAFTSMAN
❏ C-8061 [M]	It's Ann Sothern Time	1961	$25

TOPS
❏ L-1611 [M]	Sothern Exposure	1959	$30

SOUCHON, DR. EDMOND

GHB
❏ GHB-6	Dr. Edmond Souchon	1963	$35
❏ GHB-131	Dr. Edmond Souchon and the Milneburg Boys	1969	$30

GOLDEN CREST
❏ GC-3021	Dixieland of New Orleans	196?	$35
❏ GC-3065	Minstrel Days	196?	$35

SOUTHLAND
❏ 231	Dr. Edmond Souchon and the Milneburg Boys	1962	$35

SOUL, DAVID

PRIVATE STOCK
❏ PS-2019	David Soul	1977	$12
❏ PS-7001	Playing to an Audience of One	1977	$12

SOUL, JIMMY

SPQR
❏ E16001	If You Wanna Be Happy	1963	$175

SOUL ASYLUM

A&M
❏ 7503153181 [B]	...And the Horse They Rode In On	1990	$25
—Blue vinyl			
❏ SP-5197	Hang Time	1988	$18

COLUMBIA
❏ C67618	Candy From a Stranger	1998	$15
❏ C48898 [B]	Grave Dancers Union	1993	$25
❏ C57616	Let Your Dim Light Shine	1995	$15

TWIN/TONE
❏ TTR88144 [EP]	Clam Dip & Other Delights	1988	$25
❏ TTR8666 [B]	Made to Be Broken	1986	$25
❏ TTR8439	Say You Will, Clarence...Karl Sold the Truck	1984	$25
❏ TTR8691 [B]	While You Were Out	1986	$25

SOUL CHILDREN, THE

EPIC
❏ PE33902	Finders Keepers	1976	$18
❏ PE34455	Where Is Your Woman Tonight	1977	$18

STAX
❏ STX-4120	Chronicle	1979	$15
❏ STS-5507	Friction	1974	$30
❏ STS-3003	Genesis	1972	$30
❏ STX-4105	Open Door Policy	1978	$18
❏ STS-2018	Soul Children	1969	$30
❏ STS-2043	The Best of Two Worlds	1971	$30

SOUL FINDERS, THE

RCA CAMDEN
❏ CAL-2239 [M]	An Explosive Album of Soul	1968	$40
❏ CAS-2239 [S]	An Explosive Album of Soul	1968	$40
❏ CAL-2170 [M]	Sweet Soul Music	1967	$40
❏ CAS-2170 [S]	Sweet Soul Music	1967	$40

SOUL FLUTES

A&M
❏ SP-3009	Trust in Me	1968	$25

SOUL GENERATION, THE

EBONY SOUNDS
❏ 2000 [B]	Beyond Body and Soul	1972	$30

SOUL SEARCHERS
See CHUCK BROWN AND THE SOUL SEARCHERS.

SOUL SET, THE

JOHNSON
❏ 1001	The Soul Set	196?	$30

SOUL SISTERS, THE

SUE
❏ LP-1022 [M]	I Can't Stand It	1964	$250
❏ STLP-1022 [S]	I Can't Stand It	1964	$400

SOUL SOCIETY, THE

DOT
❏ DLP-25842	Satisfaction	1969	$30

SOUL STIRRERS, THE

SPECIALTY
❏ SP-2106 [M]	The Soul Stirrers Featuring Sam Cooke	1959	$50

SOUL SURVIVORS

ATCO
❏ SD 33-277	Take Another Look	1969	$30

CRIMSON
❏ CR-502 [M]	When the Whistle Blows Anything Goes	1967	$50
❏ CR-502S [S]	When the Whistle Blows Anything Goes	1967	$30

TSOP
❏ KZ33186	The Soul Survivors	1975	$15

SOULFUL STRINGS, THE

CADET
❏ LPS-805	Another Exposure	1968	$30
❏ 50022	Best of the Soulful Strings	1973	$30
❏ LPS-846	Gamble-Huff	1971	$25
❏ LPS-796	Groovin' with the Soulful Strings	1967	$30
❏ LPS-820	In Concert/Back by Demand	1969	$30
❏ LP-776 [M]	Paint It Black	1967	$35
❏ LPS-776 [S]	Paint It Black	1967	$30
❏ LPS-834	String Fever	1969	$30
❏ LPS-814	The Magic of Christmas	1968	$30

SOUND FOUNDATION

SMOBRO
❏ 9001	Sound Foundation	1971	$30

SOUND OF FEELING

LIMELIGHT
❏ LS-86063	Spleen	1969	$25

SOUND SYMPOSIUM, THE

DOT
❏ DLP-25952	Bob Dylan Interpreted	1969	$25
❏ DLP-3871 [M]	Paul Simon Interpreted	1968	$30
—Stereo cover with white "Monaural" sticker; label is regular stock copy			
❏ DLP-25871 [S]	Paul Simon Interpreted	1968	$25

SOUNDGARDEN
Also see SOUNDGARDEN.

A&M
❏ 7502153741 [B]	Badmotorfinger	1991	$75
—Limited edition on yellow vinyl			
❏ 31454 0526-1	Down on the Upside	1996	$25
❏ SP-17951 [DJ]	Louder Than Live	1990	$50
—Promo-only live album on blue vinyl			
❏ SP-17951 [DJ]	Louder Than Live	1990	$100
—Promo-only live album on blue vinyl			
❏ SP-5252	Louder Than Live	1989	$25
—Black vinyl			
❏ SP-5252	Louder Than Live	1989	$75
—Green vinyl			
❏ SP-5252	Louder Than Live	1989	$40

Number	Title	Yr	NM
—Red vinyl			
❏ 31454 01981	Superunknown	1994	$30
—Gold vinyl			
❏ 31454 01981	Superunknown	1994	$30
—Blue vinyl			
❏ 31454 01981	Superunknown	1994	$30
—Clear vinyl			

SST
❏ 911 [10]	Flower	1988	$30
❏ 231 [EP]	Flower	1988	$35
❏ 201 [B]	Ultramega OK	1988	$40

SUB POP
❏ 17 [EP]	Fopp	1988	$75
❏ 12 [EP]	Screaming Life	1987	$300
—First 500 copies on orange vinyl			
❏ 12 [EP]	Screaming Life	1987	$50
—Black vinyl			
❏ 12 [EP]	Screaming Life	1987	$35
—Reissues on any color vinyl except black or orange			

SOUNDS OF OUR TIMES, THE
CAPITOL
❏ ST-182	Galveston	1969	$15
❏ ST-117	Hey Jude	1969	$15
❏ ST-8-0117	Hey Jude	1969	$18
—Capitol Record Club edition			
❏ T2817 [M]	Music of the Flower Children	1968	$25
❏ ST2817 [S]	Music of the Flower Children	1968	$15
❏ T2892 [M]	The Sounds of Our Time Play "Love Is Blue"	1968	$30
❏ ST2892 [S]	The Sounds of Our Time Play "Love Is Blue"	1968	$15

SOUNDS OF SUNSHINE
P.I.P.
❏ 6823	Nadia's Theme	1976	$12

RANWOOD
❏ 8089	Love Means You Never Have to Say You're Sorry	1971	$12
❏ 8095	Today Is the First Day (Of the Rest of Your Life)	1972	$12

SOUNDS OF THE CITY EXPERIENCE
TIGER LILY
❏ TL14065 [B]	Sounds of the City Experience	1000.00	$

SOUNDS ORCHESTRAL
JANUS
❏ JLS-3014 [B]	One More Time	197?	$25

PARKWAY
❏ P7046 [M]	Cast Your Fate to the Wind	1965	$25
❏ SP7046 [S]	Cast Your Fate to the Wind	1965	$50
❏ P7050 [M]	Impressions of James Bond	1966	$35
❏ SP7050 [S]	Impressions of James Bond	1966	$75
❏ P7047 [M]	The Soul of Sounds Orchestral	1965	$25
❏ SP7047 [S]	The Soul of Sounds Orchestral	1965	$50

SOUNDSTAGE ALL-STARS, THE
DOT
❏ DLP-3204 [M]	More "Peter Gunn	1959	$85
❏ DLP-25204 [S]	More "Peter Gunn	1959	$85

SOUP
ARF ARM
❏ 1	Soup	1970	$120

BIG TREE
❏ BTS2007	The Album Soup	1971	$35

SOUP DRAGONS
BIG LIFE/MERCURY
❏ 842985-1	Lovegod	1990	$15

MERCURY
❏ 522732-1	Hydrophonic	1994	$15
—Clear vinyl			

SIRE
❏ 25666	Hang Ten!	1987	$10
❏ 25702	This Is Our Art	1988	$10

SOUTH, EDDIE
CHESS
❏ ACMJ-415	South Side Jazz	197?	$30

MERCURY
❏ MG-20401 [M]	The Distinguished Violin of Eddie South	1959	$150
❏ SR-60070 [S]	The Distinguished Violin of Eddie South	1959	$150

SWING
❏ SW-8405	Eddie South	1985	$25

TRIP
❏ 5803	Dark Angel of the Fiddle	197?	$25

SOUTH, JOE
ACCORD
❏ SN-7119	Party People	1981	$12

CAPITOL
❏ ST-11074	A Look Inside	1972	$15
❏ ST-392	Don't It Make You Want to Go Home	1969	$18
❏ ST-235	Games People Play	1969	$18
❏ ST-108	Introspect	1968	$25
❏ ST-845	Joe South	1972	$15
❏ ST-450	Joe South's Greatest Hits	1970	$18
❏ SM-450	Joe South's Greatest Hits	1977	$10
—Reissue with new prefix			
❏ ST-637	So the Seeds Are Growing	1971	$15

ISLAND
❏ ILPS-9328	Midnight Rainbows	1975	$12

MINE
❏ MSG-1100	The Joe South Story	1971	$18
❏ MSG-1100	Walkin' Shoes	1971	$15
—Reissue with new title			

NASHVILLE
❏ 2092	You're the Reason	1970	$15

PICKWICK
❏ SPC-3314	Games People Play	197?	$12

SOUTH 40
METROBEAT
❏ MBS-1000	Live at the Someplace Else	1968	$30

SOUTH CENTRAL AVENUE MUNICIPAL BLUES BAND
BLUESWAY
❏ BL-6018	The Soul of Bonnie and Clyde	1968	$30

SOUTH FRISCO JAZZ BAND, THE
SFJB
❏ 2-1978	Diggin' Clams	1978	$35

STOMP OFF
❏ SOS-1180	Broken Promises	1988	$25
❏ SOS-1103	Jones Law Blues	1985	$25
❏ SOS-1027	Live at Earthquake McGoon's	198?	$25
❏ SOS-1143	Sage Hen Strut	1987	$25
❏ SOS-1035	These Cats Are Diggin' Us	198?	$25

VAULT
❏ S-9008	Hot Tamale Man	196?	$35

SOUTH TAMPA HORN BAND
GUINNESS
❏ GNS36009 [B]	South Tampa Horn Band	1977	$300

SOUTHER, HILLMAN, FURAY BAND, THE
ASYLUM
❏ 7E-1006	The Souther, Hillman, Furay Band	1974	$12
❏ 7E-1036	Trouble in Paradise	1975	$12
❏ EQ-1036 [Q]	Trouble in Paradise	1975	$30

SOUTHER, J.D.
ASYLUM
❏ 7E-1059	Black Rose	1976	$12
❏ SD5055 [B]	John David Souther	1972	$18

COLUMBIA
❏ JC36093	You're Only Lonely	1979	$12
❏ PC36093	You're Only Lonely	198?	$10
—Budget-line reissue			

WARNER BROS.
❏ 25081	Home By Dawn	1985	$12

SOUTHERN, HAL
SAGE & SAND
❏ 46	You Got a Man on Your Hands	1967	$30

SOUTHERN, JERI
CAPITOL
❏ T1278 [M]	Jeri Southern at the Crescendo	1960	$75
—Black colorband label, Capitol logo at left			
❏ ST1278 [S]	Jeri Southern at the Crescendo	1960	$85
—Black colorband label, Capitol logo at left			
❏ T1278 [M]	Jeri Southern at the Crescendo	1963	$85
—Black colorband label, Capitol logo at top			
❏ ST1278 [S]	Jeri Southern at the Crescendo	1963	$50
—Black colorband label, Capitol logo at top			
❏ T1173 [M]	Jeri Southern Meets Cole Porter	1959	$75
—Black colorband label, Capitol logo at left			
❏ ST1173 [S]	Jeri Southern Meets Cole Porter	1959	$85
—Black colorband label, Capitol logo at left			
❏ T1173 [M]	Jeri Southern Meets Cole Porter	1963	$85
—Black colorband label, Capitol logo at top			
❏ ST1173 [S]	Jeri Southern Meets Cole Porter	1963	$50
—Black colorband label, Capitol logo at top			

DECCA
❏ DL5531 [10]	Intimate Songs	1954	$175
❏ DL8472 [M]	Jeri Southern Gently Jumps	1957	$120
❏ DL8745 [M]	Prelude to a Kiss	1958	$150
❏ DL8761 [M]	Southern Hospitality	1958	$150
❏ DL8055 [M]	Southern Style	1955	$175
❏ DL8394 [M]	When Your Heart's on Fire	1956	$175
❏ DL8214 [M]	You Better Go Now	1956	$175

FORUM
❏ F-9030 [M]	Jeri Southern Meets Johnny Smith	196?	$30
❏ SF-9030 [S]	Jeri Southern Meets Johnny Smith	196?	$35

PAUSA
❏ PR9054	Jeri Southern Meets Cole Porter	1986	$25
—Reissue of Capitol ST 1173			

ROULETTE
❏ R-25039 [M]	Coffee, Cigarettes and Memories	1958	$40
❏ R-52016 [M]	Jeri Southern Meets Johnny Smith	1958	$40
❏ RS-52016 [S]	Jeri Southern Meets Johnny Smith	1958	$50
❏ R-52010 [M]	Southern Breeze	1958	$40
❏ RS-52010 [S]	Southern Breeze	1958	$50

STANYAN
❏ SR10106	You Better Go Now	1974	$35
—Reissue of Decca DL 8214			

SOUTHERN CALIFORNIA MORMON CHOIR, THE
CAPITOL
❏ T2590 [M]	The Southern California Mormon Chior Sings the Songs of Christmas	1966	$15
❏ ST2590 [S]	The Southern California Mormon Chior Sings the Songs of Christmas	1966	$18

SOUTHERN CULTURE ON THE SKIDS
LLOYD STREET
❏ SO17737	Southern Culture on the Skids	1985	$100

SAFEHOUSE
❏ SH-2114-1 [PD]	Ditch Diggin'	1994	$30
—Picture disc			

TELSTAR
❏ 20	Dirt Track Date	1995	$40
❏ TR-40 [B]	Liquored Up and Lacquered Down	2000	$18
❏ TR30	Plastic Seat Sweat	1997	$15

YEP ROC
❏ LP-YEP-2120	Double Wide and Live	2006	$25
❏ 2063	Mojo Box	2004	$18

SOUTHERN PACIFIC
WARNER BROS.
❏ 25409	Killbilly Hill	1986	$10
❏ 25206	Southern Pacific	1985	$10
❏ 25609	Zuma	1988	$10

SOUTHERN STOMPERS, THE
STOMP OFF
❏ SOS-1215	Echoes of King Oliver's Jazz Band	1991	$25

SOUTHERN UNIVERSITY JAZZ BAND ENSEMBLE
JAZZSTRONAUTS
❏ LP1 [B]	Live at the 1971 American College Jazz Festival	1971	$1000

SOUTHSIDE JOHNNY AND THE ASBURY JUKES
ATLANTIC
❏ 81654	At Least We Got Shoes	1986	$10

CYPRESS
❏ YL-0115	Slow Dance	1988	$12

EPIC
❏ JE36246	Havin' a Party with Southside Johnny	1979	$12
❏ PE36246	Havin' a Party with Southside Johnny	198?	$10
—Budget-line reissue with new prefix			
❏ JE35488	Hearts of Stone	1978	$12
—Orange label, no bar code			
❏ PE35488	Hearts of Stone	198?	$10
—Dark blue label, bar code on back cover			
❏ PE34180	I Don't Want to Go Home	1976	$12
—Orange label, no bar code			
❏ PE34180	I Don't Want to Go Home	1979	$10
—Dark blue label, most have bar codes on back cover			

Number	Title	Yr	NM
❏ AS275 [DJ]	Jukes Live at the Bottom Line	1976	$30
❏ PE34668	This Time It's for Real	1977	$12
— Orange label, no bar code			
❏ PE34668	This Time It's for Real	198?	$10
— Dark blue label, bar code on back cover			
MERCURY			
❏ SRM-2-8602	Live -- Reach Out and Touch the Sky	1981	$15
❏ 826285-1	Live -- Reach Out and Touch the Sky	198?	$12
— Reissue of 8602			
❏ SRM-1-3836	Love Is a Sacrifice	1980	$12
❏ SRM-1-3793	The Jukes	1979	$12
MIRAGE			
❏ 90186	In the Heat	1984	$12
❏ 90113	Trash It Up!	1983	$12

SOUTHWEST F.O.B.
HIP

Number	Title	Yr	NM
❏ 7001 [B]	Smell of Incense	1969	$40

SOVINE, RED
CHART

Number	Title	Yr	NM
❏ 2056	It'll Come Back	1974	$18
❏ 1052	The Greatest Grand Ol' Opry	1972	$18
DECCA			
❏ DL4736 [M]	Country Music Time	1966	$30
❏ DL74736 [R]	Country Music Time	1966	$25
❏ DL4445 [M]	Red Sovine	1963	$30
❏ DL74445 [R]	Red Sovine	1963	$25
GUSTO			
❏ 3010	16 All-Time Favorites	1978	$15
MGM			
❏ E-3465 [M]	Red Sovine	1957	$75
NASHVILLE			
❏ 2044	A Dear John Letter	196?	$15
❏ 2056	Anytime	196?	$15
❏ 2083	Don't Take Your Love to Town	1969	$15
❏ 2033	Giddy-Up Go	196?	$15
POWER PAK			
❏ 270	Phantom 309	197?	$12
STARDAY			
❏ SLP-436	Classic Narrations	1968	$25
❏ SLP-441	Closing Time 'Til Dawn	1969	$25
❏ SLP-363 [M]	Giddy-Up Go	1966	$25
❏ T-90712 [M]	Giddy-Up Go	1966	$30
— Capitol Record Club edition			
❏ ST-90712 [S]	Giddy-Up Go	1966	$30
— Capitol Record Club edition			
❏ SLP-197 [M]	Golden Country Ballads of the 1960s	1962	$40
❏ SLP-405 [M]	I Didn't Jump the Fence	1967	$25
❏ SLP-459	I Know You're Married But I Love You Still	1970	$25
❏ SLP-341 [M]	Little Rosa	1965	$30
❏ SLP-414 [M]	Phantom 309	1967	$25
❏ 991	Red Sovine's 16 Greatest Hits	1977	$18
❏ SLP-427	Sunday with Sovine	1968	$25
❏ 968	Teddy Bear	1976	$18
❏ SLP-420	Tell Maude I Slipped	1968	$25
❏ SLP-357	That's Truckdrivin'	196?	$25
❏ 952	The Best of Red Sovine	197?	$18
❏ SLP-396 [M]	The Nashville Sound of Red Sovine	1967	$25
❏ SLP-132 [M]	The One and Only Red Sovine	1961	$40
❏ SLP-383 [M]	Town and Country Action	1966	$25
❏ SLP-445	Who Am I	1969	$25
❏ 970	Woodrow Wilson Sovine	1977	$18
VOCALION			
❏ VL3829 [M]	The Country Way	196?	$18
❏ VL73829 [R]	The Country Way	196?	$15

SPACE
1750 ARCH

Number	Title	Yr	NM
❏ 1806	An Interesting Breakfast Conversation	198?	$30
HAND			
❏ 5167	Space	1969	$30

SPACEK, SISSY
ATLANTIC AMERICA

Number	Title	Yr	NM
❏ 90100	Hangin' Up My Heart	1983	$12

SPACEMEN, THE
ROULETTE

Number	Title	Yr	NM
❏ R-25322 [M]	Music for Batman and Robin	1966	$40
❏ SR-25322 [S]	Music for Batman and Robin	1966	$50
❏ R-25275 [M]	Rockin' in the 25th Century	1964	$30
❏ SR-25275 [S]	Rockin' in the 25th Century	1964	$40

SPANDAU BALLET
CHRYSALIS

Number	Title	Yr	NM
❏ CHR1353	Diamond	1982	$12

Number	Title	Yr	NM
❏ FV41353	Diamond	1983	$10
— Reissue of CHR 1353			
❏ PV41353	Diamond	1986	$10
— Reissue of FV 41353 with new prefix			
❏ CHR1331	Journeys to Glory	1981	$15
❏ FV41331	Journeys to Glory	1983	$10
— Reissue			
❏ FV41473	Parade	1984	$12
❏ FV41498	The Singles Collection	1985	$12
❏ FV41403	TRUE	1983	$10
— Reissue with new prefix			
❏ B6V41403	TRUE	1983	$15
— Original prefix			
EPIC			
❏ FE40642	Through the Barricades	1987	$15
MOBILE FIDELITY			
❏ 1-152	TRUE	1984	$40
— Audiophile vinyl			

SPANIELS, THE
LOST-NITE

Number	Title	Yr	NM
❏ LLP-19 [10]	The Spaniels	1981	$15
— Red vinyl			
VEE JAY			
❏ LP-1002 [M]	Goodnite, It's Time to Go	1958	$600
— Maroon label; group pictured on cover			
❏ LP-1002 [M]	Goodnite, It's Time to Go	1961	$250
— Black label; dogs on cover			
❏ VJLP-1002 [M]	Goodnite, It's Time to Go	198?	$15
— Legitimate reissue on flimsier vinyl than originals			
❏ LP-1024 [M]	The Spaniels	1960	$300

SPANIER, MUGGSY
AVA

Number	Title	Yr	NM
❏ A-12 [M]	Columbia, the Gem of the Ocean	1963	$30
❏ AS-12 [S]	Columbia, the Gem of the Ocean	1963	$35
COMMODORE			
❏ FL-30016 [M]	Chicago Jazz	1957	$50
❏ XFL-15777	Muggsy Spanier at Nick's New York, April 1944	198?	$25
❏ FL-20009 [10]	Spanier's Ragtimers	1950	$150
DECCA			
❏ DL5552 [10]	Hot Horn	1955	$175
EMARCY			
❏ MG-26011 [10]	Muggsy Spanier and His Dixieland Band	1954	$150
EVEREST ARCHIVE OF FOLK & JAZZ			
❏ 226	Muggsy Spanier	1968	$25
❏ 326	Muggsy Spanier, Vol. 2	197?	$25
GLENDALE			
❏ GLS6024	One of a Kind	198?	$25
JAZZ ARCHIVES			
❏ JA-44	Jazz from California	198?	$25
❏ JA-30	Little David Play Your Harp	198?	$25
JAZZOLOGY			
❏ J-33	Muggsy Spanier	197?	$25
❏ J-115	Relaxin' at Touro -- 1952	198?	$25
LONDON			
❏ AL-3503 [S]	Muggsy, Tesch and the Chicagoans	195?	$30
❏ LL3528 [M]	Muggsy Spanier and the Bucktown Five	1959	$40
MERCURY			
❏ MG-25095 [10]	Muggsy Spanier and His Dixieland Band	1953	$250
❏ MG-20171 [M]	Muggsy Spanier and His Dixieland Band	1956	$150
RCA VICTOR			
❏ LPM-3043 [10]	Ragtime Favorites	195?	$120
❏ LPM-1295 [M]	The Great 16	1956	$50
RIVERSIDE			
❏ RLP 12-107 [M]	Classic Early Recordings	1955	$300
❏ RLP-1004 [10]	Muggsy Spanier and Frank Teschemacher	1953	$300
❏ RLP-1035 [10]	Muggsy Spanier and His Bucktown Five	1954	$300
RKO			
❏ ULP130 [M]	Chicago Jazz	195?	$25
STINSON			
❏ SLP30 [M]	Muggsy Spanier's Ragtimers, Vol. 1	1962	$50
— Red vinyl			
❏ SLP30 [M]	Muggsy Spanier's Ragtimers, Vol. 1	1962	$30
— Black vinyl			
❏ SLP31 [M]	Muggsy Spanier's Ragtimers, Vol. 2	1962	$50
— Red vinyl			
❏ SLP31 [M]	Muggsy Spanier's Ragtimers, Vol. 2	1962	$30
— Black vinyl			

Number	Title	Yr	NM
STORYVILLE			
❏ 4053	Hot Horn	198?	$25
❏ 4020	Muggsy Spanier	198?	$25
❏ 4056	Muggsy Spanier at Club Hangover	198?	$25
TRIP			
❏ 5532	Dixieland Session	197?	$25
WEATHERS INDUSTRIES			
❏ W-5401 [M]	Dynamic Dixie	1954	$75
ZEE GEE			
❏ 101 [10]	Muggsy Spanier's Ragtimers, Vol. 1	195?	$120
❏ 102 [10]	Muggsy Spanier's Ragtimers, Vol. 2	195?	$120

SPANKY AND OUR GANG
EPIC

Number	Title	Yr	NM
❏ PE33580	Change	1975	$15
MERCURY			
❏ SR-61183	Anything You Choose/ Without Rhyme or Reason	1969	$25
❏ SR-61161	Like to Get to Know You	1968	$25
❏ SR-61326	Live	1971	$18
❏ MG-21124 [M]	Spanky and Our Gang	1967	$30
❏ SR-61124 [S]	Spanky and Our Gang	1967	$25
❏ SR-61227	Spanky's Greatest Hit(s)	1969	$25
RHINO			
❏ RNLP-70131	The Best of Spanky and Our Gang (1967-1969)	1986	$15

SPANN, LES
JAZZLAND

Number	Title	Yr	NM
❏ JLP-35 [M]	Gemini	1961	$30
❏ JLP-935 [S]	Gemini	1961	$30

SPANN, LUCILLE
BLUESWAY

Number	Title	Yr	NM
❏ BLS-6070	Cry Before I Go	1974	$30

SPANN, OTIS
BARNABY

Number	Title	Yr	NM
❏ Z30246	Otis Spann Is the Blues	1970	$25
❏ KZ31290	Walking the Blues	1972	$25
BLUE HORIZON			
❏ BH4802	The Biggest Thing Since Colossus	1970	$30
BLUES TIME			
❏ 9006	Sweet Giant of the Blues	1970	$25
BLUESWAY			
❏ BLS-6063	Heart Loaded with Trouble	1973	$25
❏ BL-6003 [M]	The Blues Is Where It's At	1967	$30
❏ BLS-6003 [S]	The Blues Is Where It's At	1967	$30
❏ BLS-6013	The Bottom of the Blues	1968	$30
CANDID			
❏ CM-8001 [M]	Otis Spann Is the Blues	1966	$175
❏ CS-9001 [S]	Otis Spann Is the Blues	1966	$250
LONDON			
❏ PS551	Cracked Spanner Head	1969	$30
❏ PS543	Raw Blues	1968	$30
PRESTIGE			
❏ PRST-7719	The Blues Will Never Die	1969	$25
TESTAMENT			
❏ T-2211	Otis Spann's Chicago Blues	1966	$40
VANGUARD			
❏ VSD-6514	Cryin' Time	1970	$25

SPARKS, MELVIN
MUSE

Number	Title	Yr	NM
❏ MR-5248	Sparkling	1981	$35
PRESTIGE			
❏ 10039	Akilah!	1973	$25
❏ 10016	Spark Plug	1972	$25
❏ 10001	Sparks!	1971	$25
WESTBOUND			
❏ 204	Melvin Sparks '75	1975	$25

SPARKS, RANDY
VERVE

Number	Title	Yr	NM
❏ MGV-2103 [M]	Randy Sparks	1959	$30
❏ MGV-2143 [M]	Randy Sparks Three	1960	$30
❏ MGV-2126 [M]	Walkin' the Low Road	1960	$30

SPARKS
ANTILLES

Number	Title	Yr	NM
❏ ANT-7044	Kimono My House	198?	$12
— Reissue of Island 9272			
ATLANTIC			
❏ SD19347	Angst in My Pants	1982	$12
❏ 80160	Pulling Rabbits Out of a Hat	1984	$12
❏ 80055	Sparks in Outer Space	1983	$12

Number	Title	Yr	NM

BEARSVILLE

Number	Title	Yr	NM
❏ BR2110 [B]	A Woofer in Tweeter's Clothing	1973	$30
❏ BV2048 [B]	Halfnelson	1971	$50

— Original issue of "Sparks" as "Halfnelson

| ❏ BV2048 [B] | Sparks | 1972 | $25 |

— Reissue under the group's new name

COLUMBIA

| ❏ PC34359 [B] | Big Beat | 1976 | $15 |

— Originals have no bar code

| ❏ PC34901 | Introducing Sparks | 1977 | $12 |

— Originals have no bar code

ELEKTRA

| ❏ 6E-186 | No. 1 in Heaven | 1979 | $12 |

IN THE RED

| ❏ ITR131 | Hello Young Lovers | 2006 | $15 |

ISLAND

| ❏ ILPS-9345 [B] | Indiscreet | 1975 | $18 |

— Originals have black label and no Warner Bros. distribution

| ❏ ILPS-9272 [B] | Kimono My House | 1974 | $18 |

— Originals have multicolor island-scene label

| ❏ 5318093 | Kimono My House | 2009 | $25 |
| ❏ ILPS-9312 | Propaganda | 1975 | $15 |

— Originals have multicolor island-scene label

MCA CURB

| ❏ 5780 | Music That You Can Dance To | 1986 | $12 |

RCA VICTOR

| ❏ AFL1-4091 | Whomp That Sucker | 1981 | $12 |

RHINO

| ❏ R1-70841 | Interior Design | 1988 | $12 |

SPARROW, THE

COLUMBIA

| ❏ CS9758 | John Kay and Sparrow | 1969 | $40 |

— Red "360 Sound" label

SPARROWS, THE

ELKAY

| ❏ 3009 [M] | That Mersey Sound | 1964 | $40 |

SPATS, THE

ABC-PARAMOUNT

| ❏ 502 [M] | Cookin' with the Spats | 1965 | $25 |
| ❏ S-502 [S] | Cookin' with the Spats | 1965 | $30 |

SPAULDING, JAMES

MUSE

| ❏ MR-5369 | Brilliant Corners | 1989 | $25 |
| ❏ MR-5413 | Gotstabe a Better Way! | 1990 | $30 |

STORYVILLE

| ❏ 4034 | Jame Spaulding Plays the Legacy of Duke | 1980 | $30 |

SPEARS, BILLIE JO

CAPITOL

❏ ST-560	Country Girl	1970	$18
❏ ST-688	Just Singin'	1971	$18
❏ ST-397	Miss Sincerity	1969	$18
❏ ST-224	Mr. Walker, It's All Over!	1969	$18
❏ SM-11887	The Best of Billie Jo Spears	1979	$12
❏ ST-114	The Voice of Billie Jo Spears	1969	$25
❏ ST-454	With Love	1970	$18

LIBERTY

❏ LN-10018	Blanket on the Ground	1980	$10
❏ LN-10021	If You Want Me	1980	$10
❏ LN-10020	I Will Survive	1980	$10
❏ LN-10019	Love Ain't Gonna Wait for Us	1980	$10
❏ LT-1074	Only the Hits	1981	$10

UNITED ARTISTS

❏ UA-LA508-G	Billie Jo	1975	$12
❏ UA-LA390-G	Blanket on the Ground	1975	$12
❏ UA-LA748-G	If You Want Me	1977	$12
❏ UA-LA684-G	I'm Not Easy	1976	$12
❏ UA-LA859-G	Lonely Hearts Club	1977	$12
❏ UA-LA921-H	Love Ain't Gonna Wait for Us	1978	$12
❏ LT-1018	Standing Tall	1980	$12
❏ LT-983	The Singles Album	1979	$12
❏ UA-LA608-G	What I've Got in Mind	1976	$12

SPECIAL EFX

GRP

❏ GR-9581	Confidential	1989	$30
❏ GR-1048	Double Feature	1988	$25
❏ GR-1014	Modern Manners	1986	$25
❏ GR-1033	Mystique	1987	$25
❏ GR-1025	Slice of Life	1987	$25
❏ GR-1007	Special EFX	1986	$25

SPECIALS, THE

CHRYSALIS

| ❏ CHR1303 | More Specials | 1980 | $15 |
| ❏ PV41303 | More Specials | 1983 | $10 |

— Reissue

| ❏ CHR1265 | The Specials | 1979 | $18 |
| ❏ PV41265 | The Specials | 1986 | $12 |

— Reissue

SPECTOR, RONNIE

COLUMBIA

| ❏ C40620 | Unfinished Business | 1987 | $12 |

POLISH

| ❏ PRG-808 | Siren | 1980 | $15 |

SPELLBINDERS, THE

COLUMBIA

| ❏ CL2514 [M] | The Magic of the Spellbinders | 1966 | $25 |
| ❏ CS9314 [S] | The Magic of the Spellbinders | 1966 | $30 |

SPENCE, ALEXANDER "SKIP

Also see MOBY GRAPE.

COLUMBIA

| ❏ CS9831 | Oar | 1969 | $75 |

SUNDAZED

| ❏ LP5030 | Oar | 2000 | $25 |

— Reissue on 180-gram vinyl

SPENCE, JOSEPH

ROUNDER

| ❏ 2021 | Living on the Hallelujah Side | 198? | $0 |

— Contains one Christmas song: Santa Claus Is Coming to Town

SPENCER, JEREMY

ATLANTIC

| ❏ SD19236 | Flee | 1979 | $12 |

COLUMBIA

| ❏ KC31990 | Jeremy Spencer and the Children of God | 1972 | $18 |

SPENCER, JON, BLUES EXPLOSION

CAROLINE

| ❏ 1719 [B] | Jon Spencer Blues Explosion | 1992 | $18 |

CRYPT

| ❏ 29 [B] | Crypt Style | 1991 | $30 |

MATADOR

| ❏ OLE322-1 | Acme | 1998 | $12 |
| ❏ 0(# unknown) [DJ] | Controversial Negro | 1997 | $30 |

— Promo-only vinyl issue of a Japanese live CD

❏ OLE52-1 [B]	Extra Width	1993	$18
❏ OLE193-1	Now I Got Worry	1996	$12
❏ OLE105-1 [B]	Orange	1994	$18
❏ OLE376-1	Xtra-Acme USA	1999	$18

SPENCER, LEON, JR.

PRESTIGE

❏ 10042	Bad Walking Woman	1973	$25
❏ 10033	Louisiana Slim	1972	$25
❏ 10011	Sneak Preview!	1971	$25
❏ 10063	Where I'm Coming From	197?	$35

SPENCER, TRACIE

CAPITOL

| ❏ C1-92153 | Make the Difference | 1990 | $15 |
| ❏ C1-48186 | Tracie Spencer | 1988 | $10 |

SPHEERIS, JIMMY

COLUMBIA

| ❏ C30988 | The Isle of View | 1972 | $18 |
| ❏ KC32157 | The Original Tap Dancing Kid | 1973 | $18 |

EPIC

| ❏ PE34276 | Ports of the Heart | 1976 | $15 |
| ❏ PE33565 | The Dragon Is Dancing | 1975 | $15 |

SPHERE (1)

STRATA

| ❏ 103-74 | Inside Ourselves | 1974 | $35 |

SPHERE (2)

ELEKTRA/MUSICIAN

| ❏ 60313 | Flight Path | 1984 | $25 |
| ❏ 60166 | Four in One | 1982 | $25 |

RED RECORD

| ❏ VPA-191 | Sphere On Tour | 1986 | $30 |

VERVE

| ❏ 837032-1 | Bird Songs | 198? | $25 |
| ❏ 831674-1 | Four for All | 1987 | $25 |

SPHEROE

INNER CITY

| ❏ IC-1034 | Spheroe | 197? | $35 |

SPIDER-MAN

LIFESONG

| ❏ LS6001 [B] | Rock Reflections of a Superhero | 1976 | $40 |

SPIDERS, THE (1)

IMPERIAL

| ❏ LP-9142 [M] | I Didn't Wanna Do It | 1961 | $600 |

SPIEGEL, VICTOR

EAGLE

| ❏ SM-4197 | Wind on the Water | 1985 | $30 |

SPIN DOCTORS

EPIC

| ❏ E52907 | Turn It Upside Down | 1994 | $12 |

SPINAL TAP

MCA

| ❏ 10514 [PD] | Break Like the Wind | 1992 | $18 |

— Picture disc (only U.S. vinyl version of this LP)

SPINNERS, THE

TIME

| ❏ 52092 [M] | Party -- My Pad After Surfin' | 1963 | $30 |
| ❏ S-2092 [S] | Party -- My Pad After Surfin' | 1963 | $30 |

SPINNERS

ATLANTIC

❏ SD19318	Can't Shake This Feelin'	1981	$12
❏ SD19256	Dancin' and Lovin'	1980	$12
❏ SD19219	From Here to Eternally	1979	$15
❏ 80020	Grand Slam	1982	$12
❏ SD18181	Happiness is Being with the Spinners	1976	$15
❏ SD16032	Labor of Love	1981	$12
❏ SD19270	Love Trippin'	1980	$12
❏ SD7296	Mighty Love	1974	$15
❏ SD18118	New and Improved	1974	$15
❏ QD18118 [Q]	New and Improved	1974	$30
❏ SD18141	Pick of the Litter	1975	$15
❏ QD18141 [Q]	Pick of the Litter	1975	$30
❏ SD7256	Spinners	1973	$15
❏ QD7256 [Q]	Spinners	1974	$30
❏ SD19146	Spinners/8	1977	$15
❏ SD 2-910	Spinners Live!	1975	$18
❏ SD19179	The Best of the Spinners	1978	$15
❏ SD19100	Yesterday, Today & Tomorrow	1977	$15

MIRAGE

| ❏ 90456 | Lovin' Feelings | 1985 | $12 |

MOTOWN

❏ M5-109V1	Motown Superstar Series, Vol. 9	1982	$10
❏ M769	The Best of the Spinners	1973	$18
❏ M5-199V1	The Best of the Spinners	1981	$15

— Reissue of Motown 769

❏ M639 [M]	The Original Spinners	1967	$30
❏ MS639 [P]	The Original Spinners	1967	$30
❏ M5-132V1	The Original Spinners	1981	$15

— Reissue of Motown 639

V.I.P.

| ❏ 405 | 2nd Time Around | 1970 | $40 |

VOLT

| ❏ V-3403 | Down to Business | 1989 | $15 |

SPINORAMA ORCHESTRA AND CHORUS, THE

SPIN-O-RAMA

| ❏ XMK-4012 [M] | Christmas Sing Along | 195? | $18 |

SPINOZZA, DAVID

A&M

| ❏ SP-4677 | Spinozza | 1978 | $25 |

Number	Title	Yr	NM

SPIRAL STARECASE
COLUMBIA
❏ CS9852	More Today Than Yesterday	1969	$30

—360 Sound" label

SPIRIT
EPIC
❏ KE31175	Feedback	1972	$25

—Yellow label
❏ KE31175	Feedback	1973	$12

—Orange label
❏ KEG31457	Spirit	1972	$18

—Reissue of Ode 44004 and 44016 in one package; yellow labels
❏ PEG31457	Spirit	197?	$15

—Reissue with new prefix and orange labels
❏ KE32271	The Best of Spirit	1973	$15
❏ PE32271	The Best of Spirit	1979	$10

—Dark blue label; bar code on cover
❏ KE31461	The Family That Plays Together	1972	$15

—Reissue of Ode 44014 with slightly different cover; yellow label
❏ KE31461	The Family That Plays Together	1973	$12

—Orange label
❏ BG33761 [B]	The Family That Plays Together/Feedback	1976	$18
❏ E30267 [B]	Twelve Dreams of Dr. Sardonicus	1970	$30

—Yellow label
❏ KE30267	Twelve Dreams of Dr. Sardonicus	1973	$12

—Orange label
❏ PE30267	Twelve Dreams of Dr. Sardonicus	197?	$10

—Orange or dark blue label, with or without bar code
I.R.S.
❏ 82007	Rapture in the Chambers	1989	$15

MERCURY
❏ SRM-1-1094	Farther Along	1976	$15
❏ SRM-1-1122	Future Games	1977	$15
❏ SRM-1-1053	Son of Spirit	1975	$15
❏ SRM-2-804 [B]	Spirit of '76	1975	$25
❏ 818514-1	Spirit of '84	1984	$12

ODE
❏ Z1244016	Clear Spirit	1969	$30
❏ Z1244004 [S]	Spirit	1968	$30
❏ Z1244003 [M]	Spirit	1968	$300
❏ Z1244014	The Family That Plays Together	1968	$30

POTATO
❏ 2001	Live	1978	$12

RHINO
❏ RNSP-303	Potatoland	1981	$12

SUNDAZED
❏ LP5082	Clear	2001	$16
❏ LP5068	Eventide	2000	$16
❏ LP5067	Now or Anywhere	2000	$16
❏ LP5085	The Family That Plays Together	2001	$16

SPIRIT OF NEW ORLEANS JAZZ BAND, THE
GHB
❏ GHB-247	The Spirit of New Orleans Jazz Band	198?	$25

SPIRITS AND WORM
A&M
❏ SP-4229	Spirits and Worm	1969	$800

SPIRITUAL CONCEPT
PHILADELPHIA INT'L.
❏ KZ32404 [B]	Spiritual Concept	1973	$35

SPITFIRE BAND, THE
COLUMBIA
❏ FC39891	Flight III	1985	$25

SPIVAK, CHARLIE
CIRCLE
❏ 17	Charlie Spivak and His Orchestra: Now!	1981	$25
❏ 16	Charlie Spivak and His Orchestra 1942	198?	$25
❏ CLP-80	Charlie Spivak and His Orchestra 1946	1985	$25

HINDSIGHT
❏ HSR-188	Charlie Spivak and His Orchestra 1941	198?	$25
❏ HSR-105	Charlie Spivak and His Orchestra 1943-46	198?	$25

INSIGHT
❏ 215	Charlie Spivak and His Orchestra 1943-46	198?	$25

SPIVAK, DUBBY
AUDIOPHILE
❏ AP-189	Dubby Swings Lightly	1986	$25

SPIVEY, VICTORIA
SPIVEY
❏ LP-1001 [M]	Basket of Blues	1962	$30
❏ LP-1009 [M]	Encore for the Chicago Blues	1964	$30
❏ LP-2001 [M]	Recorded Legacy of the Blues	196?	$30
❏ LP-1015 [M]	Spivey's Blues Cavalcade	196?	$30
❏ LP-1012 [M]	Spivey's Blues Parade	196?	$30
❏ LP-1017 [M]	Spivey's Blues Showcase	196?	$30
❏ LP-1008 [M]	The Bluesmen of the Muddy Waters Band	1964	$30
❏ LP-1010 [M]	The Bluesmen of the Muddy Waters Band, Volume Two	1964	$30
❏ LP-1006 [M]	The Queen and Her Knights	1964	$30
❏ LP-1005 [M]	Three Kings and a Queen	1964	$50

—Bob Dylan plays on this LP; no blurb on cover
❏ LP-1004 [M]	Three Kings and a Queen	196?	$30

—"Historic Tracks, Bob Dylan Appears with Big Joe Williams" blurb on cover
❏ LP-1014 [M]	Three Kings and a Queen, Volume Two	196?	$30
❏ LP-1002 [M]	Victoria and Her Blues	1963	$30

SPLINTER
DARK HORSE
❏ SP-22006	Harder to Live	1975	$25
❏ SP-22001	The Place I Love	1974	$25
❏ DH3073	Two Man Band	1977	$30

SPLIT ENZ
Featuring the Finn brothers.
A&M
❏ SP-4963	Conflicting Emotions	1984	$12
❏ SP-3153	Frenzy	1981	$15

—First U.S. issue of 1979 recordings
❏ SP-3289	History Never Repeats: The Best of Split Enz	1987	$15
❏ SP-4894	Time & Tide	1982	$15
❏ SP-3256	Time & Tide	1984	$10

—Reissue
❏ SP-4822	True Colours	1980	$12

—All copies are laser etched on one side; mostly purple cover with yellow triangles
❏ SP-3235	True Colours	1984	$25

—Reissue; record is NOT laser etched
❏ SP-4822	True Colours	1980	$12

—All copies are laser etched on one side; mostly red cover with green triangles
❏ SP-4822	True Colours	1980	$12

—All copies are laser etched on one side; mostly yellow cover with blue triangles
❏ SP-4822	True Colours	1980	$12

—All copies are laser etched on one side; mostly blue cover with orange triangles
❏ SP-4848	Waiata	1981	$12
❏ SP-3255	Waiata	1984	$10

—Reissue
CHRYSALIS
❏ CHR1145	Disrythmia	1977	$15
❏ PV41145	Disrythmia	198?	$10

—Budget-line reissue of CHR 1145
❏ CHR1131	Mental Notes	1976	$15
❏ PV41131	Mental Notes	198?	$10

—Budget-line reissue of CHR 1131

SPOELSTRA, MARK
ELEKTRA
❏ EKL-283 [M]	Five and Twenty Questions	1965	$25
❏ EKS-7283 [S]	Five and Twenty Questions	1965	$30
❏ EKL-307 [M]	State of Mind	1966	$25
❏ EKS-7307 [S]	State of Mind	1966	$30

VERVE FOLKWAYS
❏ FV-9018 [M]	The Times I've Had	196?	$25
❏ FVS-9018 [S]	The Times I've Had	196?	$30

SPOKESMEN, THE
DECCA
❏ DL4712 [M]	The Dawn of Correction	1965	$30
❏ DL74712 [S]	The Dawn of Correction	1965	$30

SPONTANEOUS COMBUSTION
CAPITOL
❏ ST-11021	Spontaneous Combustion	1972	$30

FLYING DUTCHMAN
❏ 102	Spontaneous Combustion	1969	$30

HARVEST
❏ SW-11095	Triad	1972	$30

SPONTANEOUS MUSIC ENSEMBLE, THE
EMANEM
❏ 303	Face to Face	1974	$25

SPOOKY TOOTH
Also see PATTO; GARY WRIGHT; FOREIGNER.

A&M
❏ SP-4225	Ceremony	1970	$25
❏ SP-4194	Spooky Two	1969	$25
❏ SP-3124	Spooky Two	198?	$10

—Budget-line reissue
❏ SP-4266	The Last Puff	1970	$25
❏ SP-4300	Tobacco Road	1971	$18

—Reissue of Bell LP
❏ SP-4385	You Broke My Heart So I Busted Your Jaw	1973	$18

ACCORD
❏ SN-7168	Hell or High Water	1982	$12

BELL
❏ 6019 [M]	Spooky Tooth	1968	$175

—Mono is white label promo only; record is stereo cover
❏ 6019 [S]	Spooky Tooth	1968	$30

ISLAND
❏ SW-9292	The Mirror	1974	$15
❏ ILPS-9337	Witness	1974	$12
❏ SW-9255	Witness	1973	$15

SPOTTS, ROGER HAMILTON
SEA BREEZE
❏ SB-5004	Roger Hamilton Spotts and His Big Band	1986	$25

SPRAGUE, PETER
CONCORD JAZZ
❏ CJ-237	Musica Del Mar	1984	$25
❏ CJ-277	Na Pali Coast	1985	$25

XANADU
❏ 184	Bird Raga	198?	$25
❏ 176	Dance of the Universe	1980	$30
❏ 193	Message Sent on the Wind	1982	$25
❏ 183	The Path	1981	$25

SPRING
UNITED ARTISTS
❏ UAS-5571 [DJ]	Spring	1972	$150

—Special promo package in 12x12 folder; includes LP, press kit and a packet of seeds
❏ UAS-5571	Spring	1972	$30
❏ UAS-5571 [DJ]	Spring	1972	$150

—Special promo package in 12x12 folder; includes LP, press kit and a packet of seeds

SPRING STREET STOMPERS, THE
JUBILEE
❏ JLP-1004 [M]	I Go, Hook, Line and Sinker	1955	$250
❏ JLP-1002 [M]	The Spring Street Stompers at Carnegie Hall	1955	$50

SPRINGFIELD, BOBBY LEE
EPIC
❏ B6E40816	All Fired Up!	1987	$10

SPRINGFIELD, DUSTY
REAL GONE MUSIC
❏ RGM0444 [B]	Faithful	2016	$25

—orange vinyl
4 MEN WITH BEARDS
❏ 4M112	Dusty in Memphis	2002	$18

—Reissue on 180-gram vinyl
ABC DUNHILL
❏ DSX-50128	Cameo	1973	$18
❏ DSX-50186	Longings	1974	$0

—Unreleased
ATLANTIC
❏ SD8249	A Brand New Me	1970	$18

❏ 8249 [DJ]	A Brand New Me	1970	$40

—Mono white label promo

Number	Title	Yr	NM
❏ SD8214 [B]	Dusty in Memphis	1969	$35

— *Originals have purple and brown labels*

❏ SD8214	Dusty in Memphis	1969	$18

— *Second pressings have green and red labels*

CASABLANCA

❏ NBLP-7271	White Heat	1982	$15

LIBERTY

❏ LN-10024	It Begins Again	1980	$10

— *Budget-line reissue of United Artists LP of same name*

❏ LN-10026	Living Without Your Love	1980	$10

— *Budget-line reissue of United Artists LP of same name*

PHILIPS

❏ PHM-200156 [M]	Dusty	1964	$35
❏ PHS-600156 [P]	Dusty	1964	$40
❏ PHM-200220 [M]	Dusty Springfield's Golden Hits	1966	$30

— *With "Goin' Back"*

❏ PHM-200220 [M]	Dusty Springfield's Golden Hits	1967	$35

— *Without "Goin' Back"*

❏ PHS-600220 [P]	Dusty Springfield's Golden Hits	1966	$35

— *With "Goin' Back"*

❏ PHS-600220 [P]	Dusty Springfield's Golden Hits	1967	$30

— *Without "Goin' Back"*

❏ PHM-200303 [M]	Everything's Coming Up Dusty	1967	$35
❏ PHS-600303 [S]	Everything's Coming Up Dusty	1967	$30
❏ PHM-200174 [M]	Oooooo Weeeee!	1965	$40
❏ PHS-600174 [S]	Oooooo Weeeee!	1965	$50
❏ PHM-200133 [M]	Stay Awhile	1964	$35
❏ PHS-600133 [P]	Stay Awhile	1964	$40
❏ PHM-200256 [M]	The Look of Love	1967	$35
❏ PHS-600256 [S]	The Look of Love	1967	$30
❏ PHM-200210 [M]	You Don't Have to Say You Love Me	1966	$35
❏ PHS-600210 [S]	You Don't Have to Say You Love Me	1966	$40

POLYDOR

❏ 824467-1	Dusty Springfield's Golden Hits	1985	$12

UNITED ARTISTS

❏ UA-LA791	It Begins Again	1978	$18
❏ UA-LA936	Living Without Your Love	1979	$18

WING

❏ SRW-16380	Just Dusty	196?	$15
❏ PKW-2-120	Something Special	196?	$25

SPRINGFIELD, RICK

CAPITOL

❏ SMAS-11047	Beginnings	1972	$25
❏ SN-16251	Beginnings	1981	$10

— *Budget-line reissue*

❏ SMAS-11206	Comic Book Heroes	1973	$40

— *Withdrawn and reissued on Columbia*

CHELSEA

❏ 515	Wait for Night	1976	$18

COLUMBIA

❏ KC32704	Comic Book Heroes	1973	$18
❏ PC32704	Comic Book Heroes	1981	$10

— *Budget-line reissue*

MERCURY

❏ 824107-1	Beautiful Feelings	1984	$12

RCA

❏ 9817-1-R	Rick Springfield's Greatest Hits	1989	$15
❏ 6620-1-R	Rock of Life	1988	$10

RCA VICTOR

❏ ABL1-4935	Hard to Hold	1984	$12
❏ AFL1-4660	Living in Oz	1983	$12
❏ AFL1-4125	Success Hasn't Spoiled Me Yet	1982	$12
❏ AYL1-4767	Success Hasn't Spoiled Me Yet	1983	$10

— *Best Buy Series" reissue*

❏ AJL1-5370	Tao	1985	$12
❏ AFL1-4235	Wait for Night	1982	$12

— *Reissue of Chelsea LP*

❏ ARL1-3697	Working Class Dog	1981	$12
❏ AYL1-4766	Working Class Dog	1983	$10

— *Best Buy Series" reissue*

SPRINGFIELD RIFLE, THE

BURDETTE

❏ ST-5159	The Springfield Rifle	1969	$30

SPRINGFIELDS, THE

PHILIPS

❏ PHM200076 [M]	Folksongs from the Hills	1963	$30
❏ PHS600076 [S]	Folksongs from the Hills	1963	$40
❏ PHM200052 [M]	Silver Threads and Golden Needles	1962	$30
❏ PHS600052 [S]	Silver Threads and Golden Needles	1962	$40

SPRINGSTEEN, BRUCE

COLUMBIA

Number	Title	Yr	NM
❏ C269746 [B]	18 Tracks	1999	$30
❏ AS978 [DJ]	As Requested Around the World	1981	$80
❏ AS978 [DJ]	As Requested Around the World	1981	$80
❏ QC38653	Born in the U.S.A.	1984	$12
❏ PC33795 [DJ]	Born to Run	1975	$1200

— *Test pressing with "Bruce Springsteen -- Born to Run" in script print. Also includes mailing envelope, letter from CBS and orange patch*

❏ PC33795 [DJ]	Born to Run	1975	$150

— *White label promo*

❏ PC33795 [DJ]	Born to Run	1975	$1200

— *Test pressing with "Bruce Springsteen -- Born to Run" in script print. Also includes mailing envelope, letter from CBS and orange patch; VG value 400; VG+ value 800*

❏ PC33795 [DJ]	Born to Run	1975	$150

— *White label promo*

❏ PC33795	Born to Run	1975	$30

— *Jon Landau's name is misspelled "John" on the back cover*

❏ PC33795	Born to Run	1975	$18

— *Sticker with the correct spelling of Jon Landau is on the back cover*

❏ PC33795	Born to Run	1975	$12

— *Jon Landau's name is correct on the back cover*

❏ JC33795	Born to Run	1977	$10
❏ HC33795 [B]	Born to Run	1981	$100

— *Half-speed mastered edition (original)*

❏ HC43795 [B]	Born to Run	1982	$75

— *Half-speed mastered edition (reissue)*

❏ PC33795	Born to Run	1999	$40

— *Classic Records reissue, identified as such on back cover; "error" first pressing with no gatefold*

❏ PC33795	Born to Run	1999	$30

— *Classic Records reissue, identified as such on back cover; corrected pressing with gatefold*

❏ PC33795 [B]	Born to Run	2015	$25
❏ AS1957 [DJ]	Bruce Springsteen	1985	$40

— *Five-song mini-LP with five B-sides of singles from Born in the U.S.A.*

❏ AS1957 [DJ]	Bruce Springsteen	1987	$30

— *Five-song mini-LP with five B-sides of singles from Born in the U.S.A.; second pressings say so on the label*

❏ AS1957 [DJ]	Bruce Springsteen	1985	$40

— *Five-song mini-LP with five B-sides of singles from Born in the U.S.A.*

❏ AS1957 [DJ]	Bruce Springsteen	1987	$30

— *Five-song mini-LP with five B-sides of singles from Born in the U.S.A.; second pressings say so on the label*

❏ AS2543 [DJ]	Bruce Springsteen and the E Street Band: Live 1975-1985	1986	$30

— *Sampler from 5-LP live set*

❏ C5X40558	Bruce Springsteen and the E Street Band: Live 1975-1985	1986	$40
❏ CAS2543 [DJ]	Bruce Springsteen and the E Street Band: Live 1975-1985	1986	$75

— *Sampler from 5-LP live set*

❏ 3C44445 [EP]	Chimes of Freedom	1988	$12
❏ JC35318 [DJ]	Darkness on the Edge of Town	1978	$150

— *White label promo*

❏ JC35318 [B]	Darkness on the Edge of Town	1978	$18

— *Original pressings have thick paper innersleeves and small titles on back cover*

❏ JC35318	Darkness on the Edge of Town	198?	$10

— *Later pressings have thin paper innersleeves and larger titles on back cover*

❏ 0(# unknown) [PD]	Darkness on the Edge of Town	1978	$250

— *Promo-only picture disc*

❏ JC35318 [DJ]	Darkness on the Edge of Town	1978	$150

— *White label promo*

❏ HC45318 [B]	Darkness on the Edge of Town	1981	$75

— *Half-speed mastered edition*

❏ C293900	Devils and Dust	2005	$25
❏ C267404 [B]	Greatest Hits	1995	$25
❏ KC31903 [DJ]	Greetings from Asbury Park, N.J.	1973	$250

— *Promotional copy with timing strip and "Bruce Springsteen Fact Sheet" attached to back cover. Authentic fact sheets are on glossy stock*

❏ KC31903 [DJ]	Greetings from Asbury Park, N.J.	1973	$250

— *Promotional copy with timing strip and "Bruce Springsteen Fact Sheet" attached to back cover. Authentic fact sheets are on glossy stock*

❏ KC31903	Greetings from Asbury Park, N.J.	1973	$25
❏ PC31903	Greetings from Asbury Park, N.J.	1975	$12

— *Without bar code on cover*

❏ PC31903	Greetings from Asbury Park, N.J.	1979	$10

— *With bar code on cover*

Number	Title	Yr	NM
❏ JC31903	Greetings from Asbury Park, N.J.	1977	$10

— *Reissue of the first PC-prefix version*

❏ C53000 [B]	Human Touch	1992	$18
❏ C385490	Live in New York City	2001	$25

— *As of press date, all known copies contain "Born to Run," but the song is not listed on either the record jacket or label*

❏ C53001 [B]	Lucky Town	1992	$18
❏ 88697-17060-1	Magic	2007	$18
❏ TC38358	Nebraska	1982	$12
❏ QC38358 [B]	Nebraska	2015	$25
❏ C67484	The Ghost of Tom Joad	1995	$25
❏ C286600	The Rising	2002	$25
❏ PC236854 [DJ]	The River	1980	$100

— *White label promo, with photocopied letter from CBS*

❏ PC236854 [DJ]	The River	1980	$50

— *White label promo, without letter*

❏ PC236854 [DJ]	The River	1980	$100

— *White label promo, with photocopied letter from CBS*

❏ PC236854 [DJ]	The River	1980	$50

— *White label promo, without letter*

❏ PC236854 [B]	The River	1980	$25
❏ PC236854 [B]	The River	2015	$35
❏ KC32432 [B]	The Wild, The Innocent & the E Street Shuffle	2015	$20

— *Record Store Day release*

❏ KC32432	The Wild, the Innocent & the E Street Shuffle	1973	$25
❏ PC32432	The Wild, the Innocent & the E Street Shuffle	1975	$12

— *Without bar code on cover*

❏ PC32432	The Wild, the Innocent & the E Street Shuffle	1979	$10

— *With bar code on cover*

❏ JC32432	The Wild, the Innocent & the E Street Shuffle	1977	$10

— *Reissue of the first PC-prefix version*

❏ OC40999	Tunnel of Love	1987	$12

SPUR

CINEMA

❏ CSLP-1500	Spur of the Moment	196?	$100

SPYRO GYRA

AMHERST

❏ AMH-1014	Spyro Gyra	1978	$35

GRP

❏ GR-9608	Fast Forward	1990	$35

INFINITY

❏ INF-9004	Morning Dance	1979	$30

MCA

❏ 6893	Access All Areas	1984	$30
❏ 5606	Alternating Currents	1985	$25
❏ 5753	Breakout	1986	$25
❏ 37176	Carnaval	198?	$20

— *Budget-line reissue*

❏ 5149	Carnaval	1981	$25
❏ 16010	Catching the Sun	1982	$40

— *Audiophile vinyl*

❏ 5108	Catching the Sun	1980	$25
❏ 1445	City Kids	1986	$20

— *Budget-line reissue*

❏ 5431	City Kids	1983	$25
❏ 5238	Freetime	1981	$25
❏ 5368	Incognito	1982	$25
❏ 37148	Morning Dance	198?	$20

— *Reissue of Infinity LP*

❏ 6309	Point of View	1989	$30
❏ 6235	Rites of Summer	1988	$25
❏ 37149	Spyro Gyra	198?	$20

— *Reissue of Amherst LP*

❏ 42046	Stories Without Words	1987	$25

NAUTILUS

❏ NR-9	Morning Dance	1979	$40

— *Audiophile vinyl*

SQUEEZE

A&M

❏ SP-4802	Argybargy	1980	$15
❏ SP-3232	Argybargy	198?	$10

— *Reissue*

❏ SP-5161	Babylon and On	1987	$12
❏ SP-4759	Cool for Cats	1979	$15
❏ SP-3231	Cool for Cats	198?	$10

— *Reissue*

❏ SP-5085	Cosi Fan Tutti Frutti	1985	$12
❏ SP-4854	East Side Story	1981	$12
❏ SP-3253	East Side Story	198?	$10

— *Reissue*

❏ R124200	Frank	1989	$15

— *BMG Music Service edition*

❏ SP-5278	Frank	1989	$12
❏ SP-4922	Singles 45's and Under	1983	$12
❏ SP-3413 [EP]	Six Squeeze Songs Crammed Into One 10-Inch Record	1979	$18

— *10-inch EP in 12-inch "squeezed" jacket*

❏ SP-4899	Sweets from a Stranger	1982	$12

Number	Title	Yr	NM
—With flap removed or never there			
❏ SP-4899	Sweets from a Stranger	1982	$15
—Original pressings have a 2-inch flap on the right side of the			
front cover with critics' raves			
❏ SP-3254	Sweets from a Stranger	198?	$10
—Reissue; none of these have 2-inch flap			
❏ SP-4687 [B]	U.K. Squeeze	1978	$30
—First pressing on red vinyl			
❏ SP-4687	U.K. Squeeze	1978	$15
—Later pressings on black vinyl			
❏ SP-3185	U.K. Squeeze	198?	$10
—Reissue			

SQUIRES, ROSEMARY
MGM
| ❏ E3597 [M-DJ] | My Love is a Wanderer | 1000.00 | $ |

SQUIRREL NUT ZIPPERS
MAMMOTH
❏ MR 0137	Hot	1996	$10
❏ MR 0169	Perennial Favorites	1998	$10
❏ MR 0105	The Inevitable	1995	$10

SRC
As in Scott Richard Case.
CAPITOL
❏ ST-134 [B]	Milestones	1969	$50
❏ ST2991 [B]	SRC	1968	$100
❏ SKAO-273 [B]	Travellers Tale	1970	$50

ST. ANTHONY'S FIRE
ZONK
| ❏ 0(# unknown) | St. Anthony's Fire | 1968 | $400 |

ST. CLAIRE, BETTY
JUBILEE
❏ JLP-23 [10]	Cool and Clearer	1955	$150
❏ JLP-15 [10]	Hal McKusick Plays -- Betty St. Clair Sings	1955	$175
❏ JLP-1011 [M]	What Is There to Say?	1956	$50
SEECO
❏ SLP-456 [M]	Betty St. Claire at Basin Street	1960	$150
❏ SLP-4560 [S]	Betty St. Claire at Basin Street	1960	$150

ST. CLOUD, ENDLE
INTERNATIONAL ARTISTS
| ❏ IA-12 | Thank You All Very Much | 1970 | $75 |

ST. CYR, JOHNNY
SOUTHLAND
| ❏ 212 | Johnny St. Cyr and His Hot Five | 196? | $50 |

ST. GERMAIN
BLUE NOTE
| ❏ 25114 | Tourist | 2000 | $30 |

ST. LOUIS JIMMY
BLUESVILLE
❏ BVLP-1028 [M]	Goin' Down Blues	1961	$175
—Blue label, silver print			
❏ BVLP-1028 [M]	Goin' Down Blues	1964	$75
—Blue label, trident logo at right			

ST. LOUIS RAGTIMERS, THE
AUDIOPHILE
| ❏ AP-122 | Songs of the Showboat Era | 197? | $25 |
| ❏ AP-116 | The St. Louis Ragtimers | 1977 | $25 |

ST. OLAF CHOIRS, THE
ST. OLAF
| ❏ E-661/2 | Born a Child & Yet a King: Christmas at St. Olaf College/Volume II | 19?? | $18 |

ST. PARADISE
Also see TED NUGENT; MONTROSE.
WARNER BROS.
| ❏ BSK3281 | St. Paradise | 1979 | $15 |

ST. PATRICK'S CATHEDRAL CHOIR
ROULETTE
| ❏ R25142 [M] | Sings Christmas Songs (Volume 2) | 1960 | $18 |

ST. PETERS, CRISPIAN
JAMIE
| ❏ JLPM-3027 [M] | The Pied Piper | 1966 | $30 |
| ❏ JLPS-3027 [R] | The Pied Piper | 1966 | $25 |

ST. PETER'S CHOIR
CORAL
| ❏ CRL56015 [10] | Hark! The Herald Angels Sing | 1950 | $40 |

ST. SHAW, MIKE
REPRISE
| ❏ R-6128 [M] | The Mike St. Shaw Trio | 1964 | $25 |
| ❏ RS-6128 [S] | The Mike St. Shaw Trio | 1964 | $30 |

ST JOHN, BRIDGET
4 MEN WITH BEARDS
❏ 4M188LP [B]	Ask Me No Questions		$25
❏ 4M189LP [B]	Songs For The Gentle Man		$25
❏ 4M190LP [B]	Thank You For...		$25

STACEY Q
ATLANTIC
❏ 81676	Better Than Heaven	1986	$12
❏ 81802	Hard Machine	1988	$12
❏ 81962	Nights Like This	1989	$12

STACKRIDGE
DECCA
| ❏ DL75317 | Stackridge | 1971 | $30 |
MCA
| ❏ 308 [B] | Friendliness | 1973 | $15 |
SIRE
| ❏ SASD-7509 [B] | Extravaganza | 1975 | $15 |
| ❏ SASD-7503 [B] | Pinafore Days | 1974 | $15 |

STACY, JESS
AIRCHECK
| ❏ 26 | Jess Stacy On the Air | 198? | $25 |
ATLANTIC
❏ 1225 [M]	A Tribute to Benny Goodman	1956	$300
—Black label			
❏ 90664	A Tribute to Benny Goodman	1988	$25
BRUNSWICK
❏ BL58029 [10]	Piano Solos	1951	$100
❏ BL54017 [M]	Piano Solos	1956	$50
CHIAROSCURO
❏ 177	Stacy's Still Swinging	1978	$30
❏ 133	Stacy Still Swings	197?	$30
COLUMBIA
❏ CL6147 [10]	Piano Moods	1950	$150
COMMODORE
❏ XFL-15358	Jess Stacy and Friends	198?	$25
HANOVER
❏ HL-8010 [M]	The Return of Jess Stacy	1964	$35
❏ HS-8010 [S]	The Return of Jess Stacy	1964	$25
JAZZOLOGY
❏ JCE-90	Blue Notion	198?	$25

STADLER, HEINER
LABOR
❏ 7001	Brains on Fire	197?	$35
❏ 7002	Brains on Fire, Vol. 2	1974	$35
❏ 7003	Ecstasy	197?	$35
❏ 7006	Jazz Alchemy	197?	$35

STAETER, TED
ATLANTIC
❏ 1218 [M]	Ted Staeter's New York	1955	$300
—Multicolor label, white "fan" logo at right			
❏ 1218 [M]	Ted Staeter's New York	1961	$175
—Black label			

STAFFORD, JIM
MGM
| ❏ M3G-4947 | Jim Stafford | 1974 | $12 |
| ❏ M3G-4984 | Not Just Another Pretty Foot | 1975 | $12 |
POLYDOR
| ❏ PD-1-6072 | Jim Stafford | 1976 | $10 |
| *—Reissue of MGM 4947* | | | |

STAFFORD, JO, AND GORDON MACRAE
CAPITOL
❏ T423 [M]	Memory Songs	1955	$100
❏ H247 [10]	Sunday Evening Songs	1952	$150
❏ T1916 [M]	There's Peace in the Valley	1963	$50
❏ ST1916 [S]	There's Peace in the Valley	1963	$75
❏ SM-11890 [B]	There's Peace in the Valley	1978	$12
—Reissue			
❏ T1696 [M]	Whispering Hope	1962	$100
❏ ST1696 [S]	Whispering Hope	1962	$150

STAFFORD, JO
BAINBRIDGE
| ❏ 6234 | Look at Me Now | 1982 | $12 |
CAPITOL
❏ H75 [10]	American Folk Songs	1950	$150
❏ T1653 [M]	American Folk Songs	1962	$50
❏ ST1653 [S]	American Folk Songs	1962	$75
❏ H197 [10]	Autumn in New York	195?	$150
❏ T197 [M]	Autumn in New York	1955	$100
—Turquoise or gray label			
❏ T197 [M]	Autumn in New York	1959	$75
—Black colorband label, Capitol logo at left			
❏ T423 [M]	Memory Songs	1955	$100
—Turquoise or gray label			
❏ T423 [M]	Memory Songs	1959	$75
—Black colorband label, Capitol logo at left			
❏ H247 [10]	Songs for Sunday Evening	195?	$150
❏ H9014 [10]	Songs of Faith	1950	$150
❏ H435 [10]	Starring Jo Stafford	1953	$150
❏ T435 [M]	Starring Jo Stafford	1955	$100
—Turquoise or gray label			
❏ T435 [M]	Starring Jo Stafford	1959	$75
—Black colorband label, Capitol logo at left			
❏ T2069 [M]	Sweet Hour of Prayer	1964	$50
❏ ST2069 [S]	Sweet Hour of Prayer	1964	$75
❏ T1921 [M]	The Hits of Jo Stafford	1963	$50
❏ ST1921 [S]	The Hits of Jo Stafford	1963	$75
❏ SM-11889	The Hits of Jo Stafford	1979	$12
❏ T2166 [M]	The Joyful Season	1964	$40
❏ ST2166 [S]	The Joyful Season	1964	$75
❏ SM-1696	Whispering Hope	1977	$25
—Reissue with new prefix			
COLUMBIA
❏ CL2591 [10]	A Gal Named Jo	1955	$50
❏ CL6210 [10]	As You Desire Me	1952	$50
❏ CL1339 [M]	Ballad of the Blues	1959	$30
❏ CS8139 [S]	Ballad of the Blues	1959	$40
❏ CL6286 [10]	Garden of Prayer	1954	$50
❏ CL691 [M]	Happy Holiday	1955	$85
❏ CL1262 [M]	I'll Be Seeing You	1959	$30
❏ CS8080 [S]	I'll Be Seeing You	1959	$40
❏ CL1561 [M]	Jo + Jazz	1960	$40
❏ CS8361 [S]	Jo + Jazz	1960	$75
❏ CL1228 [M]	Jo Stafford's Greatest Hits	1958	$40
—Red and black label with six "eye" logos			
❏ CL1228 [M]	Jo Stafford's Greatest Hits	1963	$25
—Red label with "Guaranteed High Fidelity" in black			
❏ CL1228 [M]	Jo Stafford's Greatest Hits	1965	$25
—Red label with "360 Sound Mono" in white			
❏ CL6238 [10]	Jo Stafford Sings Broadway's Best	1953	$50
❏ CL584 [M]	Jo Stafford Sings Broadway's Best	1954	$40
—Maroon label, gold print			
❏ CL584 [M]	Jo Stafford Sings Broadway's Best	1955	$40
—Red and black label with six "eye" logos			
❏ CL1043 [M]	Jo Stafford Sings Songs of Scotland	1957	$40
❏ CL6274 [10]	My Heart's in the Highland	1954	$50
❏ CL578 [M]	New Orleans	1954	$40
—Maroon label, gold print			
❏ CL6268 [10]	New Orleans	1954	$50
❏ CL578 [M]	New Orleans	1955	$40
—Red and black label with six "eye" logos			
❏ CL968 [M]	Once Over Lightly	1957	$40
❏ CL910 [M]	Ski Trails	1956	$40
❏ CL2501 [10]	Soft and Sentimental	1955	$50
❏ CL1124 [M]	Swingin' Down Broadway	1958	$40
CORINTHIAN
❏ COR-118	Broadway Revisited	198?	$12
❏ COR-119	By Request	198?	$12
❏ COR-105	G.I. Jo	1977	$12
❏ COR-106	Greatest Hits	1977	$12
❏ COR-115	International Hits	197?	$12
❏ COR-114	Jo + Blues	197?	$12
❏ COR-112	Jo + Broadway	197?	$12
❏ COR-108	Jo + Jazz	197?	$12
❏ COR-110	Jo Stafford Sings American Folk Songs	197?	$12
❏ COR-123	Music of My Life	1986	$12
❏ COR-113	Ski Trails	197?	$12
❏ COR-111	Songs of Faith, Hope and Love	197?	$12
DECCA
❏ DL74973	Jo Stafford's Greatest Hits	1968	$20
DOT
❏ DLP-3673 [M]	Do I Hear a Waltz?	1966	$75
❏ DLP-25673 [S]	Do I Hear a Waltz?	1966	$85
❏ DLP-3745 [M]	This Is Jo Stafford	1967	$75
❏ DLP-25745 [S]	This Is Jo Stafford	1967	$85
REPRISE
❏ R-6090 [M]	Getting Sentimental Over Tommy Dorsey	1963	$25
❏ R9-6090 [S]	Getting Sentimental Over Tommy Dorsey	1963	$30
STANYAN
❏ 10073	Look at Me Now	197?	$15
TIME-LIFE
❏ SLGD-14	Legendary Singers: Jo Stafford	1986	$20
VOCALION
❏ VL73856 [R]	Happy Holidays	1968	$15
❏ VL73892	In the Mood for Love	1970	$15
❏ VL73866 [R]	Sweet Singer of Songs	1969	$15

Number	Title	Yr	NM

STAFFORD, MARILYN, AND THE ERNIE CARSON BAND
CIRCLE
| ❏ C-66 | Jazz Goes Country | 198? | $25 |

STAFFORD, TERRY
ATLANTIC
| ❏ SD7282 | Say, Has Anybody Seen My Sweet Gypsy Rose | 1974 | $15 |

CRUSADER
| ❏ CLP-1001 [M] | Suspicion! | 1964 | $40 |
| ❏ CLP-1001S [S] | Suspicion! | 1964 | $75 |

STAINED GLASS
CAPITOL
| ❏ ST-242 | Aurora | 1969 | $30 |
| ❏ ST-154 | Crazy Horse Roads | 1969 | $30 |

STALEY, KAREN
MCA
| ❏ 42112 | Wildest Dreams | 1988 | $12 |

STALLINGS, MARY, AND CAL TJADER
FANTASY
❏ 3325 [M]	Cal Tjader Plays, Mary Stallings Sings	1962	$50
—Red vinyl			
❏ 3325 [M]	Cal Tjader Plays, Mary Stallings Sings	1962	$30
—Black vinyl			
❏ 8068 [S]	Cal Tjader Plays, Mary Stallings Sings	1962	$40
—Blue vinyl			
❏ 8068 [S]	Cal Tjader Plays, Mary Stallings Sings	1962	$25
—Black vinyl			

STAMEY, CHRIS
COYOTE
| ❏ TTC8564 | Christmas Time | 1985 | $12 |

STAMM, MARVIN
PALO ALTO
| ❏ PA-8022 | Stampede | 198? | $25 |
VERVE
| ❏ V6-8759 | Machinations | 1968 | $25 |

STAMPEDERS
BELL
| ❏ 6068 | Sweet City Woman | 1971 | $18 |
CAPITOL
| ❏ ST-11288 | From the Fire | 1973 | $15 |
| ❏ ST-11328 | New Day | 1974 | $15 |
QUALITY
| ❏ 1001 | Hit the Road | 1976 | $15 |

STAMPLEY, JOE
ABC
| ❏ AC-30031 | The ABC Collection | 1976 | $15 |
ABC DOT
❏ DOSD-2059	All These Things	1976	$15
❏ DOSD-2023	Joe Stampley's Greatest Hits Volume 1	1975	$15
❏ DOSD-2006	Take Me Home to Somewhere	1974	$15
ACCORD
❏ SN-7156	Early Years	1982	$12
DOT
❏ DLP-26002	If You Touch Me (You've Got to Love Me)	1972	$18
❏ DLP-26020	I'm Still Loving You	1974	$18
❏ DLP-26007	Soul Song	1973	$18
EPIC
❏ JE36484	After Hours	1980	$12
❏ FE38364	Backslidin'	1982	$12
❏ FE38319	Biggest Hits	1982	$12
❏ PE33546	Billy, Get Me a Woman	1975	$15
❏ FE37343	Encore	1981	$12
❏ KE35622	Greatest Hits	1978	$12
❏ PE35622	Greatest Hits	198?	$10
—Budget-line reissue with new prefix			
❏ KE36016	I Don't Lie	1979	$12
❏ FE37927	I'm Goin' Hurtin'	1982	$12
❏ FE37055	I'm Gonna Love You Back to Loving You Again	1981	$12
❏ KE33356	Joe Stampley	1975	$15
❏ FE38964	Memory Lane	1983	$12
❏ KE35543	Red Wine and Blue Memories	1978	$15
❏ PE34732	Saturday Nite Dance	1977	$15
❏ FE39960	Still Be Lovin' You	1985	$10
❏ PE34356	Ten Songs About Her	1976	$15
❏ KE34036	The Sheik of Chicago	1976	$15

MCA
| ❏ 27022 | The Very Best of Joe Stampley | 198? | $10 |

STANDBACK
SEA BREEZE
| ❏ SB-3004 | Norwegian Wood | 198? | $25 |

STANDELLS, THE
LIBERTY
| ❏ LRP-3384 [M] | The Standells In Person at P.J.'s | 1964 | $100 |
| ❏ LST-7384 [S] | The Standells In Person at P.J.'s | 1964 | $150 |
RHINO
❏ RNLP-115	Rarities	1983	$12
❏ RNLP-107	The Best of the Standells	1983	$12
❏ RNLP-70176	The Best of the Standells (Golden Archive Series)	1987	$12
SUNSET
❏ SUM-1136 [M]	Live and Out of Sight	1966	$30
❏ SUS-5136 [S]	Live and Out of Sight	1966	$30
TOWER
❏ T5027 [M]	Dirty Water	1966	$75
❏ ST5027 [R]	Dirty Water	1966	$50
❏ T5049 [M]	The Hot Ones	1966	$100
❏ ST5049 [S]	The Hot Ones	1966	$75
❏ T5098 [M]	Try It	1967	$100
❏ ST5098 [S]	Try It	1967	$75
❏ T5044 [M]	Why Pick on Me	1966	$50
❏ ST5044 [S]	Why Pick on Me	1966	$75

STANKO, TOMASZ
ECM
| ❏ 1071 | Balladyna | 1976 | $30 |

STANLEY, MICHAEL, BAND
ARISTA
| ❏ AL4182 | Cabin Fever | 1978 | $12 |
| ❏ AL4236 | Greatest Hints | 1979 | $12 |
EMI AMERICA
❏ SW-17040	Heartland	1980	$12
❏ SN-16352	Heartland	1985	$10
—Budget-line reissue			
❏ ST-17071	MSB	1982	$12
❏ SN-16392	MSB	1986	$10
—Budget-line reissue			
❏ SW-17056	North Coast	1981	$12
❏ ST-17100	You Can't Fight Fashion	1983	$12
❏ SN-16353	You Can't Fight Fashion	1985	$10
—Budget-line reissue			
EPIC
❏ PE33917	Ladies' Choice	1976	$15
—Original with orange label and no bar code			
❏ PE33917	Ladies' Choice	198?	$10
—Reissue with dark blue label and bar code			
❏ PEG34661	Stagepass	1977	$18
❏ PE33492	You Break It…You Bought It!	1975	$15
—Original with orange label and no bar code			
❏ PE33492	You Break It…You Bought It!	198?	$10
—Reissue with dark blue label and bar code			
MCA
❏ 372	Friends and Legends	1973	$15
TUMBLEWEED
❏ TWS106	Michael Stanley	1972	$25
—Blue textured cover			

STANLEY, PAUL
Also see KISS.
CASABLANCA
| ❏ NBLP-7123 | Paul Stanley | 1978 | $30 |
| ❏ NBPIX-7123 [PD] | Paul Stanley | 1978 | $75 |

STANLEY, RALPH
JALYN
❏ JLP-118 [M]	Old Time Music	1966	$30
❏ JLP-129 [M]	Ralph Stanley and the Clinch Mountain Boys	196?	$30
❏ JLP-120 [M]	The Bluegrass Sound of Ralph Stanley	1966	$30
KING
❏ KSD-1028	Brand New Country Songs by Ralph Stanley	1968	$25
❏ KSD-1046	How Far to Little Rock?	1969	$25
❏ KSD-1032	Over the Sunset Hill	1968	$25
❏ KSD-1069	The Hills of Home	1969	$25

STANLEY BROTHERS, THE
CABIN CREEK
| ❏ LP-203 [M] | Bluegrass Gospel Favorites | 1966 | $75 |
HARMONY
| ❏ HL7291 [M] | The Stanley Brothers | 1961 | $30 |
KING
❏ 963 [M]	A Collection of Gospel and Sacred Songs	1966	$30
❏ 791 [M]	Award Winners	1962	$100
❏ KS-791 [S]	Award Winners	1962	$150
❏ 864 [M]	Country Folk Music Spotlight	1964	$50
❏ 690 [M]	Everybody's Country Favorites	1961	$100
❏ KS-690 [S]	Everybody's Country Favorites	1961	$150
❏ 872 [M]	Five String Banjo Hootenanny	1964	$50
❏ 698 [M]	For the Good People	1961	$100
❏ 805 [M]	Good Old Camp Meeting Songs	1963	$100
❏ KS-805 [S]	Good Old Camp Meeting Songs	1963	$150
❏ 645 [M]	Hymns and Sacred Songs	1960	$100
❏ 918 [M]	Hymns of the Cross	1964	$50
❏ 834 [M]	Just Because	1964	$50
❏ 750 [M]	Old Time Camp Meeting	1962	$100
❏ 953 [M]	The Best of the Stanley Brothers	1966	$30
❏ 924 [M]	The Remarkable Stanley Brothers Play and Sing Bluegrass Songs for You	1965	$50
❏ 615 [M]	The Stanley Brothers	1959	$150
❏ 772 [M]	The Stanley Brothers and the Clinch Mountain Boys Sing the Songs They Like Best	1962	$100
❏ 1013 [M]	The Stanley Brothers Sing the Best-Loved Sacred Songs of the Carter Family	1967	$30
❏ KS-1013 [S]	The Stanley Brothers Sing the Best-Loved Sacred Songs of the Carter Family	1967	$30
❏ 719 [M]	The Stanleys In Person	1961	$100
❏ KS-719 [S]	The Stanleys In Person	1961	$150
MERCURY
❏ MG-20349 [M]	Country Pickin' and Singin'	1958	$100
❏ MG-20884 [M]	Hard Times	1963	$30
❏ SR-60884 [S]	Hard Times	1963	$30
STARDAY
❏ SLP-384 [M]	Jacob's Vision	1966	$30
❏ SLP-106 [M]	Mountain Song Favorites	1959	$50
❏ SLP-122 [M]	Sacred Songs from the Hills	1960	$50
❏ SLP-201 [M]	The Mountain Music Sound of the Stanley Brothers	1962	$40
VINTAGE
❏ ZK-002 [M]	The Stanley Brothers Live at Antioch College	1961	$80

STANSFIELD, LISA
ARISTA
❏ R134198	Affection	1990	$15
—BMG Music Service edition			
❏ AL-8554	Affection	1990	$12
❏ 19012	The #1 Remixes	1998	$18

STAPLE SINGERS, THE
20TH CENTURY
| ❏ T-636 | Hold On to Your Dream | 1981 | $12 |
ARCHIVE OF GOSPEL MUSIC
| ❏ 62 | The Staple Singers | 1968 | $15 |
| ❏ 72 | The Staple Singers, Vol. 2 | 1969 | $15 |
BUDDAH
| ❏ BDS-2009 | The Best of the Staple Singers | 1969 | $25 |
| ❏ BDS-7508 | Will the Circle Be Unbroken | 1969 | $25 |
CURTOM
| ❏ CU5005 | Let's Do It Again | 1975 | $15 |
EPIC
❏ LN24132 [M]	Amen	1965	$25
❏ BN26132 [S]	Amen	1965	$30
❏ LN24332 [M]	For What It's Worth	1967	$30
❏ BN26332 [S]	For What It's Worth	1967	$25
❏ LN24163 [M]	Freedom Highway	1965	$25
❏ BN26163 [S]	Freedom Highway	1965	$30
❏ LN24237 [M]	Pray On	1967	$30
❏ BN26237 [S]	Pray On	1967	$25
❏ EG30635	The Staple Singers Make You Happy	1971	$25
❏ BN26373	What the World Needs Now Is Love	1968	$25
❏ LN24196 [M]	Why	1966	$25
❏ BN26196 [S]	Why	1966	$30
FANTASY
❏ 9442	The 25th Day of December	1973	$18
❏ 9423	Use What You Got	1973	$18
HARMONY
❏ KH31775	Tell It Like It Is	1972	$15
MILESTONE
❏ 47028	A Great Day	197?	$18
PICKWICK
❏ 7001	The Staple Singers	197?	$12
PRIVATE I
❏ BFZ40109	The Staple Singers	1985	$12
❏ FZ39460	The Turning Point	1984	$12
STAX
❏ STS-3002	Be Altitude: Respect Yourself	1972	$18
❏ STX-4116	Be Altitude: Respect Yourself	198?	$12
—Reissue of 3002			

Number	Title	Yr	NM
❏ STS-3015	Be What You Are	1973	$18
❏ MPS-8553	Be What You Are	1990	$15
—Reissue of 3015			
❏ STX-4119	Chronicle	198?	$12
❏ STS-5515	City in the Sky	1974	$18
❏ STS-2004	Soul Folk in Action	1968	$30
❏ STS-5523	The Best of the Staple Singers	1975	$18
❏ STS-2034	The Staple Swingers	1971	$25
❏ MPS-8511	This Time Around	198?	$12
❏ STS-2016	We'll Get Over	1969	$25
❏ MPS-8532	We'll Get Over	198?	$12
—Reissue of 2016			
TRIP			
❏ 7014	Swing Low	197?	$12
❏ 7019	The Best of the Staple Singers	197?	$12
❏ 8014	The Other Side of the Staple Singers	1972	$12
❏ 7000	Uncloudy Day	197?	$12
VEE JAY			
❏ LP-5019 [M]	Best of the Staple Singers	1962	$30
❏ LP-5014 [M]	Swing Low	1961	$30
❏ LP-5030 [M]	Swing Low Sweet Chariot	1963	$30
❏ LP-5000 [M]	Uncloudy Day	1959	$30
❏ LP-5008 [M]	Will the Circle Be Unbroken	1960	$30
VEE JAY/CHAMELEON			
❏ D1-74782	The Best of the Staple Singers	1988	$18
WARNER BROS.			
❏ BS3084	Family Tree	1977	$15
—As "The Staples			
❏ BS2945	Pass It On	1976	$15
—As "The Staples			
❏ BSK3192	Unlock Your Mind	1978	$15
—As "The Staples			

STAPLES, MAVIS

Number	Title	Yr	NM
CURTOM			
❏ CU5019	A Piece of the Action	1977	$15
PAISLEY PARK			
❏ 25798	Time Waits for No One	1989	$15
STAX			
❏ STX-4118	Mavis Staples	198?	$12
—Reissue of Volt 6007			
❏ MPS-8539	Only for the Lonely	1987	$12
—Reissue of Volt 6010			
VOLT			
❏ VOS-6007	Mavis Staples	1969	$25
❏ VOS-6010	Only for the Lonely	1970	$25
WARNER BROS.			
❏ BSK3319	Oh What a Feeling	1979	$15

STAPLETON, CYRIL

Number	Title	Yr	NM
RICHMOND			
❏ S30057 [S]	Children's Christmas Album	196?	$18

STARCASTLE

Number	Title	Yr	NM
EPIC			
❏ 34935 [PD]	Citadel	1978	$50
—Picture disc, possibly promo only			
❏ PE34935	Citadel	1977	$15
—Orange label			
❏ PE34375	Fountains of Light	1977	$15
—Orange label			
❏ AS296 [DJ]	Fountains of Light Banded for Airplay	1977	$40
—White label, promo-only version with separations between tracks			
❏ JE35441	Real to Reel	1978	$15
—Orange label			
❏ PE33914 [B]	Starcastle	1976	$15
—Orange label			

STARCHER, BUDDY

Number	Title	Yr	NM
DECCA			
❏ DL4796 [M]	History Repeats Itself	1966	$25
❏ DL74796 [S]	History Repeats Itself	1966	$30
STARDAY			
❏ SLP-211 [M]	Buddy Starcher and His Mountain Guitar	1962	$30
❏ SLP-382 [M]	History Repeats Itself	1966	$30

STARFIRES, THE (4)

Number	Title	Yr	NM
OHIO RECORDING SERVICE			
❏ 34 [M]	The Starfires Play	1964	$50

STARFIRES, THE (5)

Number	Title	Yr	NM
LABREA			
❏ LS-8018 [M]	Teenbeat A-Go-Go	1965	$50

STARK NAKED

Number	Title	Yr	NM
RCA VICTOR			
❏ LSP-4592	Stark Naked	1971	$30

STARKER, JANOS

Number	Title	Yr	NM
MERCURY LIVING PRESENCE			
❏ SR90480 [S]	Bach, J.S.: Three Sonatas	196?	$250
—Maroon label, with "Vendor: Mercury Record Corporation			
❏ SR90370 [S]	Bach: Suites 2 and 5 for Solo Violin	196?	$100
—Maroon label, no "Vendor: Mercury Record Corporation			
❏ SR90370 [S]	Bach: Suites 2 and 5 for Solo Violin	196?	$40
—Third edition: Dark red (not maroon) label			
❏ SR90370 [S]	Bach: Suites 2 and 5 for Solo Violin	196?	$75
—Maroon label, with "Vendor: Mercury Record Corporation			
❏ SR90405 [S]	Bartok: First Rhapsody; Mendelssohn: Various Concertantes; Martinu: Rossini Variations; et al.	196?	$120
—Maroon label, no "Vendor: Mercury Record Corporation			
❏ SR90405 [S]	Bartok: First Rhapsody; Mendelssohn: Various Concertantes; Martinu: Rossini Variations; et al.	196?	$75
—Maroon label, with "Vendor: Mercury Record Corporation			
❏ SR90405 [S]	Bartok: First Rhapsody; Mendelssohn: Various Concertantes; Martinu: Rossini Variations; et al.	196?	$40
—Third edition: Dark red (not maroon) label			
❏ SR90392 [S]	Brahms: Cello Sonatas No. 1 and 2	196?	$175
—Maroon label, no "Vendor: Mercury Record Corporation			
❏ SR90392 [S]	Brahms: Cello Sonatas No. 1 and 2	196?	$50
—Maroon label, with "Vendor: Mercury Record Corporation			
❏ SR90303 [S]	Dvorak: Cello Concerto; Bruch: Kol Nidre	196?	$120
—With Antal Dorati/London Symphony Orchestra; maroon label, no "Vendor: Mercury Record Corporation			
❏ SR90303 [S]	Dvorak: Cello Concerto; Bruch: Kol Nidre	196?	$80
—With Antal Dorati/London Symphony Orchestra; maroon label, with "Vendor: Mercury Record Corporation			
❏ SR90303 [S]	Dvorak: Cello Concerto; Bruch: Kol Nidre	196?	$40
—With Antal Dorati/London Symphony Orchestra; third edition (dark red, not maroon, label)			
❏ SR90320 [S]	Mendelssohn: Cello Sonata; Chopin: Cello Sonata in G	196?	$150
—Maroon label, no "Vendor: Mercury Record Corporation			
❏ SR90320 [S]	Mendelssohn: Cello Sonata; Chopin: Cello Sonata in G	196?	$75
—Maroon label, with "Vendor: Mercury Record Corporation			
❏ SR90347 [S]	Schumann: Cello Concerto; Lalo: Cello Concerto	196?	$120
—With Stanislaw Skrowaczewski/London Symphony Orchestra; maroon label, no "Vendor: Mercury Record Corporation			
❏ SR90347 [S]	Schumann: Cello Concerto; Lalo: Cello Concerto	196?	$40
—With Stanislaw Skrowaczewski/London Symphony Orchestra; maroon label, with "Vendor: Mercury Record Corporation			

STARLAND VOCAL BAND

Number	Title	Yr	NM
WINDSONG			
❏ BXL1-3536	4 x 4	1980	$15
❏ BXL1-2598	Late Nite Radio	1978	$15
❏ BHL1-2239	Rear View Mirror	1977	$15
❏ BHL1-1351	Starland Vocal Band	1976	$15

STARR, EDWIN

Number	Title	Yr	NM
20TH CENTURY			
❏ T-559	Clean	1978	$12
❏ T-538	Edwin Starr	1977	$12
❏ T-591	Happy Radio	1979	$12
❏ T-615	Stronger Than You	1980	$12
❏ T-634	The Best of Edwin Starr	1981	$12
GORDY			
❏ GS-940	25 Miles	1969	$30
❏ GS-956	Involved	1971	$25
❏ GS-945	Just We Two	1969	$25
—With Blinky			
❏ GS-931	Soul Master	1968	$30
❏ GS-948	War & Peace	1970	$25
GRANITE			
❏ 1005	Free to Be Myself	1975	$15
MOTOWN			
❏ M5-103V1	Superstar Series, Vol. 3	1981	$12
❏ M5-170V1	War & Peace	1981	$12
PICKWICK			
❏ SPC-3387	25 Miles	197?	$12

STARR, KAY

Number	Title	Yr	NM
ABC			
❏ S-631	When the Lights Go On Again	1968	$30
CAPITOL			
❏ T1468 [M]	All Starr Hits	1961	$75
❏ ST1468 [S]	All Starr Hits	1961	$75
❏ T1681 [M]	I Cry by Night	1962	$50
❏ ST1681 [S]	I Cry by Night	1962	$75
❏ T580 [M]	In a Blue Mood	1955	$100
❏ T1795 [M]	Just Plain Country	1962	$40
❏ ST1795 [S]	Just Plain Country	1962	$75
❏ ST-8-1795 [S]	Just Plain Country	196?	$75
—Capitol Record Club edition			
❏ T1438 [M]	Kay Starr, Jazz Singer	1960	$75
❏ ST1438 [S]	Kay Starr, Jazz Singer	1960	$85
❏ ST-11323	Kay Starrs Again	1974	$12
❏ SM-11323	Kay Starrs Again	1977	$10
—Reissue with new prefix			
❏ T1303 [M]	Losers Weepers	1960	$75
❏ ST1303 [S]	Losers Weepers	1960	$75
❏ T1254 [M]	Movin'	1959	$75
❏ ST1254 [S]	Movin'	1959	$75
❏ SM-11880	Movin'	1979	$12
❏ T1374 [M]	Movin' on Broadway	1960	$75
❏ ST1374 [S]	Movin' on Broadway	1960	$75
❏ T1358 [M]	One More Time	1960	$75
❏ ST1358 [S]	One More Time	1960	$75
❏ H211 [10]	Songs by Starr	1950	$250
❏ T211 [M]	Songs by Starr	1955	$100
❏ T2550 [M]	Tears and Heartaches/Old Records	1966	$40
❏ ST2550 [S]	Tears and Heartaches/Old Records	1966	$40
❏ T2106 [M]	The Fabulous Favorites	1964	$100
❏ ST2106 [S]	The Fabulous Favorites	1964	$25
❏ H415 [10]	The Hits of Kay Starr	1953	$250
❏ T415 [M]	The Hits of Kay Starr	1955	$100
—Turquoise or gray label			
❏ T415 [M]	The Hits of Kay Starr	1958	$75
—Black label with colorband, Capitol logo at left			
❏ T415 [M]	The Hits of Kay Starr	1962	$25
—Black label with colorband, Capitol logo at top			
❏ DT415 [R]	The Hits of Kay Starr	196?	$50
❏ H363 [10]	The Kay Starr Style	1953	$250
❏ T363 [M]	The Kay Starr Style	1955	$100
CORONET			
❏ CX-106 [M]	Kay Starr Sings	196?	$15
❏ CXS-106 [S]	Kay Starr Sings	196?	$15
GNP CRESCENDO			
❏ GNPS-2090	Back to the Roots	1975	$12
❏ GNPS-2083	Country	1974	$12
HINDSIGHT			
❏ HSR-214	Kay Starr 1947	1985	$12
LIBERTY			
❏ LRP-9001 [M]	Swingin' with the Starr	1956	$50
❏ LRP-3280 [M]	Swingin' with the Starr	1963	$30
—Reissue of 9001			
PARAMOUNT			
❏ PAS-5001	How About This	1969	$15
RCA CAMDEN			
❏ CAL-567 [M]	Kay Starr	196?	$15
RCA VICTOR			
❏ LPM-1549 [M]	Blue Starr	1957	$30
❏ LPM-2055 [M]	I Hear the Word	1959	$30
❏ LSP-2055 [S]	I Hear the Word	1959	$30
❏ ANL1-1311	Pure Gold	1976	$10
❏ LPM-1720 [M]	Rockin' with Kay	1958	$50
❏ LPM-1149 [M]	The One and Only Kay Starr	1955	$40
RONDO-LETTE			
❏ A-3 [M]	Them There Eyes	1958	$30
SUNSET			
❏ SUM-1126 [M]	Portrait of a Starr	196?	$25
❏ SUS-5126 [R]	Portrait of a Starr	196?	$12

STARR, KAY/ERROLL GARNER

Number	Title	Yr	NM
CROWN			
❏ CLP-5003 [M]	Singin' Kay Starr, Swingin' Erroll Garner	1957	$30
MODERN			
❏ MLP-1203 [M]	Singin' Kay Starr, Swingin' Erroll Garner	1956	$100

STARR, KENNY

Number	Title	Yr	NM
MCA			
❏ 2177	The Blind Man in the Bleachers	1975	$12

STARR, LUCILLE

Number	Title	Yr	NM
A&M			
❏ LP-107 [M]	French Song	1966	$30
EPIC			
❏ BN26436	Lonely Street	1969	$30

STARR, RINGO

Also see THE BEATLES; GEORGE HARRISON AND FRIENDS.

Number	Title	Yr	NM
APPLE			
❏ SMAS-3368 [B]	Beaucoups of Blues	1970	$30
❏ SW-3422	Blast from Your Past	1975	$18
❏ SW-3417	Goodnight Vienna	1974	$15

Number	Title	Yr	NM
❏ SWAL-3413	Ringo	1973	$25

—*Standard issue with booklet; Side 1, Song 2 identified on cover as "Hold On"*

| ❏ SWAL-3413 | Ringo | 1974 | $30 |

—*Later issue with booklet; Side 1, Song 2 identified on cover as "Have You Seen My Baby"*

| ❏ SWAL-3413 | Ringo | 1973 | $400 |

—*With a 5:26 version of "Six O'Clock." On later copies, the song is shortened to 4:05 though the label still says 5:26. All known copies have a promo punch-hole in top corner of jacket; on Side 2 record, "Six O'Clock" will be the widest track.*

| ❏ SW-3365 [B] | Sentimental Journey | 1970 | $30 |

ATLANTIC

| ❏ SD18193 | Ringo's Rotogravure | 1976 | $18 |

—*Deduct 2/3 for cut-outs*

| ❏ SD18193 [DJ] | Ringo's Rotogravure | 1976 | $30 |

—*With "DJ Only" scrawled into trail-off area*

| ❏ SD19108 | Ringo the 4th | 1977 | $18 |

—*Deduct 1/2 for cut-outs*

| ❏ SD19108 [DJ] | Ringo the 4th | 1977 | $30 |

—*With "DJ Only" scrawled into trail-off area*

BOARDWALK

| ❏ NB1-33246 | Stop and Smell the Roses | 1981 | $12 |

—*Deduct 1/2 for cut-outs*

CAPITOL

| ❏ SN-16235 | Beaucoups of Blues | 198? | $25 |

—*Green label budget-line reissue*

| ❏ SN-16236 | Blast from Your Past | 198? | $18 |

—*Green label budget-line reissue*

| ❏ SN-16219 | Goodnight Vienna | 198? | $30 |

—*Green label budget-line reissue*

| ❏ SN-16114 | Ringo | 198? | $18 |

—*Green label budget-line reissue with all errors corrected*

| ❏ SW-3365 | Sentimental Journey | 197? | $40 |

—*Purple label, large Capitol logo*

| ❏ SN-16218 | Sentimental Journey | 198? | $30 |

—*Green label budget-line reissue*

PORTRAIT

| ❏ JR35378 | Bad Boy | 1978 | $18 |

—*Deduct 1/3 for cut-outs*

| ❏ JR35378 [DJ] | Bad Boy | 1978 | $150 |

—*White label promo with "Advance Promotion" on label; in plain white cover*

| ❏ JR35378 [DJ] | Bad Boy | 1978 | $30 |

—*Regular white-label promo in standard jacket*

RHINO

| ❏ R170199 | Starr Struck: Ringo's Best 1976-1983 | 1989 | $30 |

RYKODISC

| ❏ RALP 0190 | Ringo Starr and His All-Starr Band | 1990 | $30 |

—*With limited, numbered obi (deduct $5 if missing)*

STARR, SALLY

ARCADE

| ❏ 1001 [M] | Our Gal Sal | 1960 | $100 |

CLYMAX

| ❏ 1001 [M] | Our Gal Sal | 1959 | $250 |

STARS ON

21 RECORDS

| ❏ 90291 | Soul Revue | 1985 | $18 |

RADIO

❏ RR16044	Stars On Long Play	1981	$12
❏ RR19314	Stars On Long Play II	1981	$12
❏ RR19349	Stars On Long Play III	1982	$12

STARSHIP

GRUNT

| ❏ BXL1-5488 | Knee Deep in the Hoopla | 1985 | $10 |
| ❏ 6413-1-G | No Protection | 1987 | $10 |

RCA

| ❏ 9693-1-R | Love Among the Cannibals | 1989 | $12 |

STARSHIP ORCHESTRA

COLUMBIA

| ❏ NJC36456 | Celestial Sky | 1980 | $25 |

STARZ

CAPITOL

❏ ST-11730	Attention Shoppers!	1978	$12
❏ ST-11861	Coliseum Rock	1978	$12
❏ SPRO-8657/8 [DJ]	Live at Municipal Auditorium, Louisville, March 30, 1978	1978	$30

—*Promo-only "Superstars Radio Network Presents" album*

| ❏ ST-11539 | Starz | 1976 | $12 |
| ❏ SW-11617 | Violation | 1977 | $25 |

—*Gold vinyl*

| ❏ SW-11617 | Violation | 1977 | $12 |

—*Black vinyl*

Number	Title	Yr	NM

METAL BLADE

| ❏ 73430 | Live in Action | 1989 | $15 |

VIOLATION

| ❏ 0001 | Live in America | 1983 | $18 |

STATE STREET ACES, THE

STOMP OFF

❏ SOS-1106	Old Folks Shuffle	198?	$25
❏ SOS-1041	Pass Out Lightly	198?	$25
❏ SOS-1011	Stuff	198?	$25

STATE STREET RAMBLERS, THE

HERWIN

| ❏ 104 | The State Street Ramblers, Vol. 1 | 197? | $30 |
| ❏ 105 | The State Street Ramblers, Vol. 2 | 197? | $30 |

STATLER BROTHERS, THE

COLUMBIA

❏ CL2449 [M]	Flowers on the Wall	1966	$30
❏ CS9249 [S]	Flowers on the Wall	1966	$30
❏ PC9249	Flowers on the Wall	198?	$10

—*Reissue with new prefix*

| ❏ C31560 | How Great Thou Art | 197? | $12 |

—*Reissue of Harmony 31560*

| ❏ CS9878 [B] | Oh Happy Day | 1969 | $30 |
| ❏ PC9878 | Oh Happy Day | 198? | $10 |

—*Reissue with new prefix*

❏ CL2719 [M]	The Big Hits	1967	$30
❏ CS9519 [S]	The Big Hits	1967	$30
❏ PC9519	The Big Hits	198?	$10

—*Reissue with new prefix*

| ❏ KG31557 | The World of the Statler Brothers | 1972 | $25 |
| ❏ CG31557 | The World of the Statler Brothers | 198? | $15 |

—*Reissue with new prefix*

HARMONY

❏ H30610	Big Country Hits	1971	$15
❏ KH32256	Do You Love Me Tonight	1973	$15
❏ KH31560	How Great Thou Art	1972	$15

MERCURY

❏ SRM-1-5027	10th Anniversary	1980	$15
❏ 812282-1	10th Anniversary	1983	$10
❏ 818652-1	Atlanta Blue	1984	$12
❏ SR-61317	Bed of Rose's	1970	$18
❏ 826247-1	Bed of Rose's	1986	$10
❏ SRM-1-676	Carry Me Back	1973	$18
❏ 812284-1	Carry Me Back	1983	$10
❏ SRM-1-5012 [B]	Christmas Card	1978	$12
❏ 822743-1	Christmas Card	1985	$10
❏ 824785-1	Christmas Present	1985	$12
❏ SR-61367	Country Music "Then and Now	1972	$18
❏ 826260-1	Country Music "Then and Now	1986	$10
❏ SRM-1-5007	Entertainers...On and Off the Record	1978	$15
❏ 812283-1	Entertainers...On and Off the Record	1983	$10
❏ 826782-1	Four for the Show	1986	$12
❏ SRM-1-1077	Harold, Lew, Phil & Don	1976	$18
❏ 826269-1	Harold, Lew, Phil & Don	1986	$10
❏ SRM-1-1052	Holy Bible: New Testament	1975	$18
❏ 826268-1	Holy Bible: New Testament	1986	$10
❏ SRM-1-1051	Holy Bible: Old Testament	1975	$18
❏ 826267-1	Holy Bible: Old Testament	1986	$10
❏ SRM-2-101	Holy Bible/The Old and New Testaments	1978	$25

—*Reissue of 1051 and 1052 in one package*

❏ 826264-1	Holy Bible/The Old and New Testaments	1986	$12
❏ SR-61358	Innerview	1972	$18
❏ 826259-1	Innerview	1986	$10
❏ 832404-1	Maple Street Memories	1987	$12
❏ 824420-1	Pardners in Rhyme	1985	$12
❏ SR-61349	Pictures of Moments to Remember	1971	$18
❏ 826710-1	Radio Gospel Favorites	1986	$12
❏ SRM-1-5001	Short Stories	1977	$15
❏ 826280-1	Short Stories	1986	$10
❏ SRM-1-1019	Sons of the Motherland	1975	$18
❏ 838231-1	Statler Brothers Live -- Sold Out	1989	$18
❏ SRM-1-707	Thank You World	1974	$18
❏ SRM-1-1037	The Best of the Statler Brothers	1975	$15
❏ 822524-1	The Best of the Statler Brothers	1984	$10
❏ SRM-1-5024	The Best of the Statler Brothers Rides Again, Volume II	1980	$15
❏ 822525-1	The Best of the Statler Brothers Rides Again, Volume II	1984	$10
❏ SRM-1-1125	The Country America Loves	1977	$18
❏ 826275-1	The Country America Loves	1986	$10
❏ SRM-1-4048	The Legend Goes On	1982	$15
❏ 826278-1	The Legend Goes On	1986	$10
❏ SRM-1-5016	The Originals	1979	$15
❏ 826281-1	The Originals	1986	$10
❏ SR-61374	The Statler Brothers Sing Country Symphonies in E Major	1973	$18

Number	Title	Yr	NM
❏ 834626-1	The Statlers Greatest Hits	1988	$12
❏ 812184-1	Today	1983	$12
❏ SRM-1-6002	Years Ago	1981	$15

PRIORITY

| ❏ PU37709 | Country Gospel | 1982 | $12 |

REALM

| ❏ 2V8077 | The Very Best of the Statler Brothers | 1977 | $18 |

TIME-LIFE

| ❏ STW-105 | Country Music | 1981 | $12 |

STATON, CANDI

FAME

❏ 1800	Candi Staton	1972	$25
❏ ST-4201	I'm a Prisoner	1970	$25
❏ ST-4202	Stand By Your Man	1971	$25

WARNER BROS.

❏ BS2830	Candi	1974	$15
❏ BSK3428	Candi Staton	1980	$15
❏ BSK3333	Chance	1979	$15
❏ BSK3207	House of Love	1978	$15
❏ BS3040	Music Speaks Louder Than Words	1977	$15
❏ BS2948	Young Hearts Run Free	1976	$15

STATON, DAKOTA

CAPITOL

| ❏ T1387 [M] | Ballads and the Blues | 1960 | $150 |

—*Black label with colorband, Capitol logo at left*

| ❏ ST1387 [S] | Ballads and the Blues | 1960 | $75 |

—*Black label with colorband, Capitol logo at left*

| ❏ T1387 [M] | Ballads and the Blues | 1962 | $85 |

—*Black label with colorband, Capitol logo at top*

| ❏ ST1387 [S] | Ballads and the Blues | 1962 | $100 |

—*Black label with colorband, Capitol logo at top*

| ❏ T1170 [M] | Crazy He Calls Me | 1959 | $150 |

—*Black label with colorband, Capitol logo at left*

| ❏ T1170 [M] | Crazy He Calls Me | 1962 | $85 |

—*Black label with colorband, Capitol logo at top*

| ❏ ST1170 [S] | Crazy He Calls Me | 1959 | $75 |

—*Black label with colorband, Capitol logo at left*

| ❏ ST1170 [S] | Crazy He Calls Me | 1962 | $100 |

—*Black label with colorband, Capitol logo at top*

| ❏ T1490 [M] | Dakota | 1961 | $150 |

—*Black label with colorband, Capitol logo at left*

| ❏ T1490 [M] | Dakota | 1962 | $85 |

—*Black label with colorband, Capitol logo at top*

| ❏ ST1490 [S] | Dakota | 1961 | $75 |

—*Black label with colorband, Capitol logo at left*

| ❏ ST1490 [S] | Dakota | 1962 | $100 |

—*Black label with colorband, Capitol logo at top*

❏ T1649 [M]	Dakota at Storyville	1962	$100
❏ ST1649 [S]	Dakota at Storyville	1962	$150
❏ T1054 [M]	Dynamic!	1958	$150

—*Black label with colorband, Capitol logo at left*

| ❏ T1054 [M] | Dynamic! | 1962 | $85 |

—*Black label with colorband, Capitol logo at top*

| ❏ ST1054 [S] | Dynamic! | 1959 | $75 |

—*Black label with colorband, Capitol logo at left*

| ❏ ST1054 [S] | Dynamic! | 1962 | $100 |

—*Black label with colorband, Capitol logo at top*

| ❏ T1003 [M] | In the Night | 1958 | $175 |

—*Turquoise or gray label*

| ❏ T1003 [M] | In the Night | 1959 | $150 |

—*Black label with colorband, Capitol logo at left*

| ❏ M-1003 | In the Night | 1976 | $25 |

—*Reissue with new prefix*

| ❏ T1325 [M] | More Than the Most | 1960 | $150 |

—*Black label with colorband, Capitol logo at left*

| ❏ T1325 [M] | More Than the Most | 1962 | $85 |

—*Black label with colorband, Capitol logo at top*

| ❏ ST1325 [S] | More Than the Most | 1960 | $85 |

—*Black label with colorband, Capitol logo at left*

| ❏ ST1325 [S] | More Than the Most | 1962 | $100 |

—*Black label with colorband, Capitol logo at top*

| ❏ T1597 [M] | 'Round Midnight | 1961 | $150 |

—*Black label with colorband, Capitol logo at left*

| ❏ T1597 [M] | 'Round Midnight | 1962 | $50 |

—*Black label with colorband, Capitol logo at top*

| ❏ ST1597 [S] | 'Round Midnight | 1961 | $85 |

—*Black label with colorband, Capitol logo at left*

| ❏ ST1597 [S] | 'Round Midnight | 1962 | $100 |

—*Black label with colorband, Capitol logo at top*

| ❏ T1427 [M] | Softly | 1961 | $150 |

—*Black label with colorband, Capitol logo at left*

| ❏ T1427 [M] | Softly | 1962 | $50 |

—*Black label with colorband, Capitol logo at top*

| ❏ ST1427 [S] | Softly | 1961 | $85 |

—*Black label with colorband, Capitol logo at left*

| ❏ ST1427 [S] | Softly | 1962 | $100 |

—*Black label with colorband, Capitol logo at top*

| ❏ T876 [M] | The Late, Late Show | 1957 | $175 |

—*Turquoise or gray label*

| ❏ T876 [M] | The Late, Late Show | 1959 | $150 |

Number	Title	Yr	NM

—Black label with colorband, Capitol logo at left
❏ T876 [M] — The Late, Late Show — 1962 — $85
—Black label with colorband, Capitol logo at top
❏ DT876 [R] — The Late, Late Show — 196? — $75
❏ SM-876 — The Late, Late Show — 1977 — $25
—Reissue with new prefix
❏ T1241 [M] — Time to Swing — 1959 — $150
—Black label with colorband, Capitol logo at left
❏ T1241 [M] — Time to Swing — 1962 — $50
—Black label with colorband, Capitol logo at top
❏ ST1241 [S] — Time to Swing — 1959 — $85
—Black label with colorband, Capitol logo at left
❏ ST1241 [S] — Time to Swing — 1962 — $100
—Black label with colorband, Capitol logo at top

GROOVE MERCHANT
❏ 4410 — Confessin' — 197? — $35
❏ 521 — I Want a Country Man — 1973 — $30
❏ 510 — Madame Foo-Foo — 1972 — $30
❏ 532 — Ms. Soul — 1974 — $30

LONDON
❏ LL3495 [M] — Dakota '67 — 1967 — $50
❏ PS495 [S] — Dakota '67 — 1967 — $35

MUSE
❏ MR-5401 — Dakota Staton — 1991 — $35

UNITED ARTISTS
❏ UAL-3355 [M] — Dakota Staton with Strings — 1964 — $50
❏ UAS-6355 [S] — Dakota Staton with Strings — 1964 — $75
❏ UAL-3292 [M] — From Dakota with Love — 1963 — $50
❏ UAS-6292 [S] — From Dakota with Love — 1963 — $75
❏ UAL-3312 [M] — Live and Swinging — 1963 — $50
❏ UAS-6316 [S] — Live and Swinging — 1963 — $75

VERVE
❏ V6-8799 — I've Been There — 1971 — $35

STATUS CYMBAL, THE
RCA VICTOR
❏ LPM-3993 [M] — In the Morning — 1968 — $50
❏ LSP-3993 [S] — In the Morning — 1968 — $25

STATUS QUO
A&M
❏ SP-3615 [B] — Hello! — 1974 — $18
❏ SP-4381 [B] — Piledriver — 1973 — $18
❏ SP-3649 [B] — Quo — 1974 — $18

CADET CONCEPT

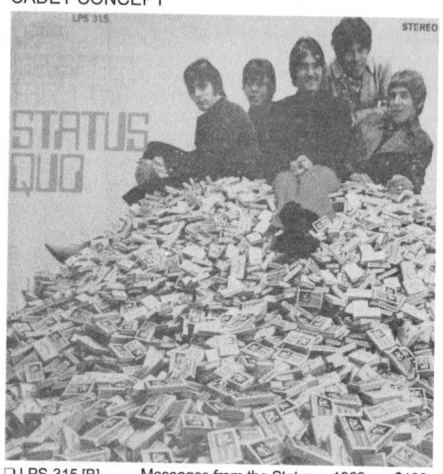

❏ LPS-315 [B] — Messages from the Status Quo — 1968 — $100

CAPITOL
❏ ST-11381 — On the Level — 1975 — $12
❏ ST-11749 — Rockin' All Over the World — 1978 — $12
❏ ST-11509 — Status Quo — 1976 — $12
❏ SKBB-11623 — Status Quo Live — 1977 — $15

JANUS
❏ JLS-3018 [B] — Ma Kelly's Greasy Spoon — 1970 — $30

MERCURY
❏ 836651-1 — Status Quo — 1989 — $15

PYE
❏ 3301 [B] — Dog of Two Head — 1971 — $30

RIVA
❏ 7402 — Now Here This — 1980 — $15

STEAGALL, RED
ABC
❏ AB-1051 — Hang On Feelin' — 1978 — $15

ABC DOT
❏ DO-2078 — For All Our Cowboy Friends — 1977 — $15
❏ DOSD-2055 — Lone Star Beer and Bob Wills Music — 1976 — $18
❏ DOSD-2068 — Texas Red — 1976 — $15

CAPITOL
❏ ST-11321 — Finer Things in Life — 1974 — $15
❏ ST-11228 — If You've Got the Time, I've Got the Song — 1973 — $15
❏ ST-11056 — Party Dolls and Wine — 1972 — $25
❏ ST-11162 — Somewhere My Love — 1973 — $15

MCA
❏ 680 — For All Our Cowboy Friends — 198? — $10
—Reissue of ABC Dot 2078
❏ 681 — Hang On Feelin' — 198? — $10
—Reissue of ABC 1051
❏ 985 — Lone Star Beer and Bob Wills Music — 1986 — $12
—Reissue of ABC Dot 2055

STEALERS WHEEL
A&M
❏ SP-4419 — Ferguslie Park — 1974 — $15
❏ SP-4517 — Right or Wrong — 1974 — $15
❏ SP-4377 [B] — Stealers Wheel — 1973 — $18
❏ SP-4708 — Stuck in the Middle with You -- The Best of Stealers Wheel — 1978 — $12

STEAM
MERCURY
❏ SR61254 [B] — Steam — 1969 — $30

STEAMHAMMER
EPIC
❏ BN26490 — Reflection — 1969 — $30
❏ BN26552 — Steamhammer — 1970 — $30

STEARNS, JUNE
COLUMBIA
❏ CS9783 — River of Regret — 1969 — $25

STEEL
EPIC
❏ E30875 — Steel — 1971 — $25

STEELE, JAN & CAGE, JOHN
ANTILLES
❏ AN-7031 [B] — Voices and Instruments — 1976 — $50

STEELE, JOAN, AND JOHN MAGALDI
AUDIOPHILE
❏ AP-156 — Lonesome No More — 198? — $25

STEELE, JOAN
AUDIOPHILE
❏ AP-94 — 'Round Midnight — 1975 — $30

STEELE, TOMMY
LIBERTY
❏ LRP-3426 [M] — Everything's Coming Up Broadway — 1965 — $25
❏ LST-7426 [S] — Everything's Coming Up Broadway — 1965 — $30
❏ LRP-3566 [M] — Sixpenny Millionaire — 1968 — $30
—Stereo cover with "Audition Mono LP Not for Sale" sticker attached; label is stock
❏ LST-7566 [S] — Sixpenny Millionaire — 1968 — $18

LONDON
❏ LL1770 [M] — Rock Around the World — 195? — $50

STEELEYE SPAN
BIG TREE
❏ BTS2004 [B] — Please to See the King — 1971 — $35

CHRYSALIS
❏ CHR1091 — All Around My Hat — 1975 — $18
—Green label, "3300 Warner Blvd." address
❏ CHR1091 — All Around My Hat — 1977 — $15
—Blue label, New York address
❏ CHR1008 — Below the Salt — 1972 — $18
—Green label, "3300 Warner Blvd." address
❏ CHR1008 — Below the Salt — 1977 — $15
—Blue label, New York address
❏ CHR1071 — Commoners Crown — 1975 — $18
—Green label, "3300 Warner Blvd." address
❏ CHR1071 — Commoners Crown — 1977 — $15
—Blue label, New York address
❏ CHR1120 — Hark the Village Wait — 1976 — $18
—First US issue of debut LP; green label; "3300 Warner Blvd." address
❏ CHR1120 — Hark the Village Wait — 1977 — $15
—Blue label, New York address
❏ CHR1199 — Live at Last — 1978 — $15
❏ CHR1053 — Now We Are Six — 1974 — $18
—Green label, "3300 Warner Blvd." address
❏ CHR1053 — Now We Are Six — 1977 — $15
—Blue label, New York address
❏ CHR1046 — Parcel of Rogues — 1973 — $18
—Green label, "3300 Warner Blvd." address

❏ CHR1046 — Parcel of Rogues — 1977 — $15
—Blue label, New York address
❏ CHR1119 — Please to See the King — 1976 — $18
—Reissue of Big Tree LP; green label, "3300 Warner Blvd." address
❏ CHR1119 — Please to See the King — 1977 — $15
—Blue label, New York address
❏ CHR1123 — Rocket Cottage — 1976 — $18
—Green label, "3300 Warner Blvd." address
❏ CHR1123 — Rocket Cottage — 1977 — $15
—Blue label, New York address
❏ CHR1151 — Storm Force Ten — 1978 — $15
❏ CHR1121 — Ten Man Mop — 1976 — $18
—First US issue of third UK LP; green label, "3300 Warner Blvd." address
❏ CHR1121 — Ten Man Mop — 1977 — $15
—Blue label, New York address
❏ CHR21136 — The Steeleye Span Story: Original Masters — 1977 — $18
❏ V2X41136 — The Steeleye Span Story: Original Masters — 1984 — $15
—Reissue of 1136

MOBILE FIDELITY
❏ Jan-0027 [B] — All Around My Hat — 1980 — $100
—Audiophile vinyl

PAIR
❏ CRPDL-2-1021 — Dogs and Ferrets — 1983 — $18

SHANACHIE
❏ 79059 — All Around My Hat — 1989 — $15
❏ 79063 — Back in Line — 1989 — $15
❏ 79039 — Below the Salt — 1989 — $15
❏ 79052 — Hark the Village Wait — 1989 — $15
❏ 79060 — Now We Are Six — 1989 — $15
❏ 79045 — Parcel of Rogues — 1989 — $15
❏ 79071/2 [B] — Portfolio — 1990 — $30
❏ 64020 — Tempted and Tried — 1989 — $15
❏ 79049 — Ten Man Mop — 1989 — $15

TAKOMA
❏ TAK-7097 — Sails of Silver — 1981 — $15

STEELY DAN
Also see DONALD FAGEN.
ABC
❏ AA-1006 — Aja — 1977 — $15
❏ 758 — Can't Buy a Thrill — 1972 — $15
—Black label
❏ 758 — Can't Buy a Thrill — 1974 — $12
—Multicolor label
❏ 779 — Countdown to Ecstasy — 1973 — $15
—Black label
❏ 779 — Countdown to Ecstasy — 1974 — $12
—Multicolor label
❏ AK-1107 — Greatest Hits — 1978 — $18
❏ 2022-1107 — Greatest Hits — 1978 — $25
—Canadian import on gold vinyl, widely available in U.S.
❏ 846 — Katy Lied — 1975 — $15

❏ 806 [B] — Pretzel Logic — 1974 — $15
—Black label
❏ 806 — Pretzel Logic — 1974 — $12
—Multicolor label
❏ 931 — The Royal Scam — 1976 — $15

ABC DUNHILL
❏ SMAS-94976 — Can't Buy a Thrill — 1973 — $30
—Capitol Record Club edition pressed on the wrong label

COMMAND
❏ QD-40009 [Q] — Can't Buy a Thrill — 1974 — $50
—Second issue with no border around the cover
❏ QD-40009 [Q] — Can't Buy a Thrill — 1974 — $75
—First issue with wide border around outside of cover
❏ QD-40010 [Q] — Countdown to Ecstasy — 1974 — $50
❏ QD-40015 [Q] — Pretzel Logic — 1974 — $50

Number	Title	Yr	NM

GEFFEN
❏ MCA1693	Gaucho	2008	$25

MCA
❏ AA-1006	Aja	1980	$12
❏ 1688	Aja	1987	$10
❏ 37040	Can't Buy a Thrill	1980	$10
❏ 1591	Can't Buy a Thrill	1987	$10
❏ 37041	Countdown to Ecstasy	1980	$10
❏ 1592	Countdown to Ecstasy	1987	$10
❏ 6102	Gaucho	1980	$12
❏ 16009	Gaucho	1981	$50

—Audiophile pressing
❏ 1693	Gaucho	1987	$10

—Many in the 1500 and 1600 series have a gold stamp with the new number on the cover
❏ 5324	Gold	1982	$12
❏ 16016	Gold	1982	$50

—Audiophile pressing
❏ 37243	Gold	1984	$10
❏ 2-6008	Greatest Hits	1980	$15
❏ 37043	Katy Lied	1980	$10
❏ 1594	Katy Lied	1987	$10
❏ 37042	Pretzel Logic	1980	$10
❏ 1593	Pretzel Logic	1987	$10
❏ 37044	The Royal Scam	1980	$10
❏ 1595	The Royal Scam	1987	$10

MOBILE FIDELITY
❏ Jan-0033 [B]	Aja	1980	$100

—Audiophile vinyl
❏ Jan-007 [B]	Katy Lied	1979	$150

—Audiophile vinyl

STEGALL, KEITH

EPIC
❏ B6E39892	Keith Stegall	1985	$10

STEIG, JEREMY, AND EDDIE GOMEZ

CMP
❏ CMP-3-ST	Lend Me Your Ears	198?	$25
❏ CMP-6-ST	Music for Flute and Double Bass	198?	$25
❏ CMP-12-ST	Rain Forest	198?	$25

ENJA
❏ 2098	Outlaws	198?	$30

INNER CITY
❏ IC-3015	Outlaws	197?	$30

STEIG, JEREMY

BLUE NOTE
❏ BST-84354	Wayfaring Stranger	1970	$25

CAPITOL
❏ SM-662	Energy	1976	$25

—Reissue with new prefix
❏ ST-662	Energy	1971	$35

COLUMBIA
❏ CL2136 [M]	Flute Fever	1964	$30
❏ CS8936 [S]	Flute Fever	1964	$35
❏ KC32579	Monium	1974	$30
❏ KC33297	Temple of Birth	1975	$30

CTI
❏ 7075	Firefly	1977	$30

GROOVE MERCHANT
❏ 2204	Fusion	197?	$35

SOLID STATE
❏ SS-18068	Legwork	1970	$35
❏ SS-18059	This Is Jeremy Steig	1969	$35

STEIN, ANDY

STOMP OFF
❏ SOS-1146	Goin' Places	1987	$25

STEIN, HAL, AND WARREN FITZGERALD

PROGRESSIVE
❏ PLP-1002 [M]	Hal Stein-Warren Fitzgerald Quintet	1955	$500

STEIN, LOU

AUDIOPHILE
❏ AP-198	Solo Piano	1984	$25

BRUNSWICK
❏ BL58053 [10]	Lou Stein	1953	$150

CHIAROSCURO
❏ CR-2027	Temple of the Gods	1979	$35
❏ 140	Tribute to Tatum	197?	$30

CORAL
❏ CRL57201 [M]	Sing Around the Piano	1958	$50
❏ CRL57003 [M]	Sweet and Lovely	195?	$30

DREAMSTREET
❏ DR-106	Lou Stein Trio Live at the Dome	1986	$25

EPIC
❏ LN3186 [M]	From Broadway to Paris	1955	$100
❏ LG3101 [M]	House Top	1955	$100

Number	Title	Yr	NM
❏ LN3148 [M]	Three, Four and Five	1955	$100

JUBILEE
❏ JLP-1019 [M]	Eight for Kicks, Four for Laughs	1956	$40
❏ JLP-8 [10]	Six for Kicks	1954	$150

MASTERSEAL
❏ MS33-1812 [M]	Mood Music for Beer and Pretzels	1957	$35

MERCURY
❏ SR-60054 [S]	Honky Tonk Piano	1959	$150
❏ MG-20364 [M]	Honky Tonk Piano	195?	$20
❏ MG-20159 [M]	Honky Tonk Piano	195?	$25
❏ MG-20469 [M]	Honky Tonk Piano and a Hot Banjo	1960	$150
❏ SR-60151 [S]	Honky Tonk Piano and a Hot Banjo	1960	$150
❏ MG-20271 [M]	Saloon Favorites	195?	$20

MUSICOR
❏ MM-2057 [M]	Hey Louie! Play Melancholy Baby!	1967	$35
❏ MS-3057 [S]	Hey Louie! Play Melancholy Baby!	1967	$30

WING
❏ SRW-16219 [S]	The Lou Stein-Way of Piano Pleasure	196?	$35
❏ MGW-12219 [M]	The Lou Stein-Way of Piano Pleasure	196?	$30

WORLD JAZZ
❏ WJLPS-17	Lou Stein and Friends	1980	$30

STEINBERG, DAVID

COLUMBIA
❏ KC32563	Booga Booga	1974	$12
❏ PC33390	Goodbye to the Seventies	1975	$12

ELEKTRA
❏ EKS-74063	Disguised as a Normal Person	1970	$15

UNI
❏ 73013	The Incredible Shrinking God	1968	$18

STEINMAN, JIM

CLEVELAND INT'L.
❏ FE36531	Bad for Good	1981	$18

—With bonus 7-inch 33 1/3 small hole single AE7 1232, "The Storm"/"Rock and Roll Dreams Come Through," and its picture sleeve (deduct 50 percent if missing)

STEPHENS, LEIGH
BLUE CHEER guitarist.

PHILIPS
❏ PHS600294	Red Weather	1969	$100

STEPPENWOLF
Also see SPARROW.

ABC
❏ AC-30008	The ABC Collection	1976	$18

ABC DUNHILL
❏ DSX-50135	16 Greatest Hits	1973	$25
❏ DSX-50053	At Your Birthday Party	1969	$25
❏ DS-50060	Early Steppenwolf	1969	$25

—Actually a 1967 concert by Sparrow (pre-Steppenwolf)
❏ DSX-50110	For Ladies Only	1971	$25
❏ DS-50066	Monster	1969	$25
❏ DSX-50124	Rest in Peace	1972	$25
❏ DS-50029 [S]	Steppenwolf	1968	$25
❏ DSX-50090	Steppenwolf 7	1970	$25
❏ DSX-50099	Steppenwolf Gold/Their Great Hits	1971	$25
❏ DSD-50075	Steppenwolf 'Live'	1970	$30
❏ DS-50037	The Second	1968	$30

—With chrome border on cover
❏ DS-50037	The Second	1968	$30

—With white border on cover

DUNHILL
❏ SKAO-93083	Monster	1969	$30

—Capitol Record Club edition on old-style Dunhill label
❏ D-50029 [M]	Steppenwolf	1968	$250
❏ DS-50029 [S]	Steppenwolf	1968	$40
❏ ST-91487	Steppenwolf	1968	$30

—Capitol Record Club edition

EPIC
❏ PE33583	Hour of the Wolf	1975	$15
❏ JE34382	Reborn to Be Wild	1977	$15
❏ PE34120	Skullduggery	1976	$15

MCA
❏ 37049	16 Greatest Hits	1979	$10
❏ 1599	16 Greatest Hits	198?	$10

—Reissue of 37049
❏ 37045	Steppenwolf	1979	$10
❏ 37047	Steppenwolf 7	1979	$10
❏ DSX-50099	Steppenwolf Gold/Their Great Hits	1980	$15

—Columbia House edition on blue rainbow label, but retaining the original ABC Dunhill catalog number
❏ 2-6013	Steppenwolf 'Live'	198?	$12
❏ 37046	The Second	1979	$10

MUMS
❏ PZ33093	Slow Flux	1974	$18

NAUTILUS
❏ NR-53	Wolftracks	198?	$50

—As "John Kay and Steppenwolf"; audiophile vinyl

PICKWICK
❏ SPC-3603	Best of Steppenwolf	1978	$12

STEPS AHEAD

ELEKTRA/MUSICIAN
❏ 60441	Magnetic	1986	$25
❏ 60351	Modern Times	1985	$25
❏ 60168	Steps	1983	$25

STERLING, ARNOLD

JAM
❏ 010	Here's Brother Sterling	198?	$30

STERN, LENI

ENJA
❏ R1-79602	Secrets	1989	$30

STERN, MIKE

ATLANTIC
❏ 82027	Jigsaw	1990	$30
❏ 81840	Time in Place	1988	$25
❏ 81656	Upside Downside	1986	$25

STEVENS, APRIL

AUDIO LAB
❏ AL-1534 [M]	Torrid Tunes	1959	$250

IMPERIAL
❏ LP-9118 [M]	Teach Me Tiger	1960	$75
❏ LP-12055 [S]	Teach Me Tiger	1960	$150

STEVENS, CAT

A&M
❏ SP-4735	Back to Earth	1978	$15
❏ SP-3623	Buddha and the Chocolate Box	1974	$15
❏ QU-53623 [Q]	Buddha and the Chocolate Box	1974	$30
❏ SP-4365	Catch Bull at Four	1972	$15
❏ QU-54365 [Q]	Catch Bull at Four	1974	$0

—Not released
❏ SP-3736	Footsteps in the Dark -- Greatest Hits, Volume Two	1984	$12
❏ SP-3285	Footsteps in the Dark -- Greatest Hits, Volume Two	1986	$10

—Reissue of 3736
❏ SP-4391	Foreigner	1973	$15
❏ QU-54391 [Q]	Foreigner	1974	$30
❏ SP-4519	Greatest Hits	1975	$15
❏ QU-54519 [Q]	Greatest Hits	1975	$30
❏ SP-4702	Izitso	1977	$15
❏ SP-4260	Mona Bone Jakon	1970	$15

—Brown label
❏ SP-4260	Mona Bone Jakon	1974	$12

—Mostly silver label with gradually fading "A&M
❏ SP-3160	Mona Bone Jakon	198?	$10

—Reissue of 4260
❏ SP-4555	Numbers	1975	$15
❏ SP-4280	Tea for the Tillerman	1971	$15

—Brown label
❏ SP-4280	Tea for the Tillerman	1974	$12

—Mostly silver label with gradually fading "A&M
❏ QU-54280 [Q]	Tea for the Tillerman	1974	$0

—Not released
❏ SP-4313	Teaser and the Firecat	1971	$15

—Brown label
❏ SP-4313	Teaser and the Firecat	1974	$12

—Mostly silver label with gradually fading "A&M
❏ QU-54313 [Q]	Teaser and the Firecat	1974	$0

—Not released

ANALOGUE PRODUCTIONS
❏ APP9135-45 [B]	Tea for the Tillerman	2015	$50

—45rpm

DERAM
❏ DE16005 [M]	Matthew and Son	1967	$175
❏ DES18005 [P]	Matthew and Son	1967	$25
❏ DES18005/10 [P]	Matthew and Son/New Masters	1971	$18
❏ DES18010 [S]	New Masters	1968	$30
❏ DES18061 [P]	Very Young and Early Songs	1972	$15

LONDON
❏ LC-5010	Cat's Cradle	1977	$15
❏ 820321-1	Cat's Cradle	1985	$10

MOBILE FIDELITY
❏ 1-254	Izitso	1996	$40

—Audiophile vinyl
❏ Jan-0035 [B]	Tea for the Tillerman	1979	$75

—Audiophile vinyl
❏ MFQR-035 [B]	Tea for the Tillerman	1984	$175

—Ultra High Quality Recording in a box

Number	Title	Yr	NM
❏ 1-244 [B]	Teaser and the Firecat	1996	$75
—Audiophile vinyl			

STEVENS, CLIVE
CAPITOL
Number	Title	Yr	NM
❏ ST-11263	Atmospheres	1973	$35
❏ SM-11675	Atmospheres	1976	$25
❏ ST-11320	Voyage to Uranus	1974	$35
❏ SM-11676	Voyage to Uranus	1976	$25

STEVENS, CONNIE
HARMONY
Number	Title	Yr	NM
❏ HS11312	The Hank Williams Songbook	1969	$18

WARNER BROS.
Number	Title	Yr	NM
❏ W1208 [M]	Conchetta	1958	$50
❏ WS1208 [S]	Conchetta	1958	$75
❏ W1432 [M]	Connie	1962	$30
❏ WS1432 [S]	Connie	1962	$40

THE NEW SINGING SENSATION OF TELEVISION
CONNIE STEVENS
AS "CRICKET" IN THE
WARNER BROS. SERIES "HAWAIIAN EYE"

Number	Title	Yr	NM
❏ WS1382 [S]	Connie Stevens from "Hawaiian Eye"	1960	$40
❏ W1382 [M]	Connie Stevens from "Hawaiian Eye"	1960	$30
❏ W1431 [M]	From Me to You	1962	$30
❏ WS1431 [S]	From Me to You	1962	$40
❏ W1460 [M]	The Hank Williams Songbook	1962	$30
❏ WS1460 [S]	The Hank Williams Songbook	1962	$40

STEVENS, DODIE
DOT
Number	Title	Yr	NM
❏ DLP-3212 [M]	Dodie Stevens	1960	$30
❏ DLP-25212 [S]	Dodie Stevens	1960	$40
❏ DLP-3323 [M]	Over the Rainbow	1960	$30
❏ DLP-25323 [S]	Over the Rainbow	1960	$40
❏ DLP-3371 [M]	Pink Shoelaces	1961	$30
❏ DLP-25371 [S]	Pink Shoelaces	1961	$40

STEVENS, EVEN
DAKAR
Number	Title	Yr	NM
❏ DK-76905	Even Stevens	1973	$30

ELEKTRA
Number	Title	Yr	NM
❏ 7E-1113	Thorn on a Rose	1977	$15

STEVENS, JEFF, AND THE BULLETS
ATLANTIC AMERICA
Number	Title	Yr	NM
❏ 90556	Bolt Out of the Blue	1987	$12

STEVENS, LEITH
CORAL
Number	Title	Yr	NM
❏ CRL57283 [M]	Jazz Themes for Cops and Robbers	1958	$50

DECCA
Number	Title	Yr	NM
❏ DL5515 [10]	Jazz Themes in "The Wild One	1954	$175

STEVENS, MIKE
NOVUS
Number	Title	Yr	NM
❏ 3042-1-N	Light Up the Night	1988	$25
❏ 3080-1-N	Set the Spirit Free	1990	$30

STEVENS, PK
GUINNESS
Number	Title	Yr	NM
❏ GNS36019 [B]	Your Love Is A Very Special Thing To Me	1977	$30

STEVENS, RAY
BARNABY
Number	Title	Yr	NM
❏ 6003	Boogity Boogity	1974	$15
❏ Z1235005	Everything Is Beautiful	1970	$18
❏ KZ32139	Losin' Streak	1972	$15
❏ 6012	Misty	1975	$15

Number	Title	Yr	NM
❏ BR15007	Nashville	1973	$15
❏ 5005	Nashville	1974	$12
—Reissue of 15007			
❏ Z30770	Ray Stevens' Greatest Hits	1971	$15
❏ 5004	Ray Stevens' Greatest Hits	1974	$12
—Reissue of 30770			
❏ ZQ30770 [Q]	Ray Stevens' Greatest Hits	1971	$30
❏ Z30092	Ray Stevens…Unreal!!!	1970	$15
❏ 6018	The Very Best of Ray Stevens	1975	$15
❏ Z30809	Turn Your Radio On	1972	$15
❏ ZQ30809 [Q]	Turn Your Radio On	1972	$30

MCA
Number	Title	Yr	NM
❏ 42303	Beside Myself	1989	$12
❏ 42020	Crackin' Up!	1987	$12
❏ 5918	Greatest Hits	1987	$12
❏ 42062	Greatest Hits, Volume 2	1987	$12
❏ 5517	He Thinks He's Ray Stevens	1984	$12
❏ 5635	I Have Returned	1985	$12
❏ 42172	I Never Made a Record I Didn't Like	1988	$12
❏ 5795	Surely You Joust	1986	$12

MERCURY
Number	Title	Yr	NM
❏ MG-20732 [M]	1,837 Seconds of Humor	1962	$40
❏ SR-60732 [S]	1,837 Seconds of Humor	1962	$50
❏ 812780-1	Me	1984	$12
❏ SR-61272	The Best of Ray Stevens	1968	$18
❏ MG-20828 [M]	This Is Ray Stevens	1963	$30
❏ SR-60828 [S]	This Is Ray Stevens	1963	$30

MONUMENT
Number	Title	Yr	NM
❏ SLP-18102	Even Stevens	1968	$18
❏ SLP-18115	Gitarzan	1969	$18
❏ SLP-18134	Have a Little Talk with Myself	1970	$18

PICKWICK
Number	Title	Yr	NM
❏ SPC-3266	Rock and Roll Show	1971	$12

PRIORITY
Number	Title	Yr	NM
❏ PU38075	Turn Your Radio On	1982	$12
—Reissue of Barnaby 30809			

RCA VICTOR
Number	Title	Yr	NM
❏ CPL1-7161	Collector's Series	1986	$12
❏ AHL1-4288	Don't Laugh Now	1982	$12
❏ AHL1-4727	Greatest Hits	1983	$12
❏ AYL1-5153	Greatest Hits	1985	$10
—Best Buy Series" reissue			
❏ AHL1-3841	One More Last Chance	1981	$12
❏ AHL1-3574	Shriner's Convention	1980	$12
❏ AYL1-4253	Shriner's Convention	1982	$10
—Best Buy Series" reissue			

WARNER BROS.
Number	Title	Yr	NM
❏ BS3195	Be Your Own Best Friend	1978	$12
❏ BS2997	Feel the Music	1977	$12
❏ BS2914	Just for the Record	1976	$12
❏ BSK3332	The Feeling's Not Right Again	1979	$12
❏ BS3098	There Is Something...	1977	$12

STEVENS, SHAKIN'
EPIC
Number	Title	Yr	NM
❏ FE37415	Get Shakin'	1981	$14
❏ BFE38449	Give Me Your Heart Tonight	1983	$12
❏ 3E36924 [10]	Shakin' Stevens	1981	$10
❏ BFE39286	The Bop Won't Stop	1983	$12
❏ ARE38022	You Drive Me Crazy	1982	$12

STEVENS, TERRI
EVEREST
Number	Title	Yr	NM
❏ LPBR-5088 [M]	It's Been a Long, Long Time	1960	$25
❏ SDBR-1088 [S]	It's Been a Long, Long Time	1960	$30

STEVENSON, B.W.
MCA
Number	Title	Yr	NM
❏ 3215	Lifeline	1980	$12

RCA VICTOR
Number	Title	Yr	NM
❏ LSP-4685	B.W. Stevenson	1972	$18
❏ APL1-0410	Calabasas	1974	$15
❏ APD1-0410 [Q]	Calabasas	1974	$30
❏ LSP-4794	Lead Free	1972	$18
❏ APL1-0088	My Maria	1973	$15
❏ APL1-2394	The Best of B.W. Stevenson	1977	$12

WARNER BROS.
Number	Title	Yr	NM
❏ BS3012	Lost	1977	$12
❏ BS2901	We Be Sailin'	1976	$12

STEVIE B
LMR
Number	Title	Yr	NM
❏ LP-5531	In My Eyes	1989	$18
❏ 2307-1-R	Love & Emotion	1990	$18
❏ LP-5500	Party Your Body	1988	$15

STEWARD, ALEC
BLUESVILLE
Number	Title	Yr	NM
❏ BVLP-1076 [M]	Creepin' Blues	1963	$100
—Blue label, silver print			
❏ BVLP-1076 [M]	Creepin' Blues	1964	$30
—Blue label, trident logo at right			

STEWARD, HERB
AVA
Number	Title	Yr	NM
❏ A-9 [M]	So Pretty	1962	$30
❏ AS-9 [S]	So Pretty	1962	$30

FAMOUS DOOR
Number	Title	Yr	NM
❏ 139	Three Horns of Herb Steward	1981	$30

STEWART, AL
ARISTA
Number	Title	Yr	NM
❏ AL9520 [B]	24 Carrots	1980	$18
❏ A2L8607 [B]	Live/Indian Summer	1981	$25
❏ AL9525	Modern Times	1980	$12
—Reissue of Janus 7012			
❏ AL9524	Past, Present and Future	1980	$12
—Reissue of Janus 3063			
❏ AL6-8359	Past, Present and Future	198?	$10
—Reissue of Arista 9524			
❏ AL4190 [B]	Time Passages	1978	$18
❏ AL6-8342	Time Passages	198?	$10
—Reissue of 4190			
❏ AL9503	Year of the Cat	1979	$12
—Reissue of Janus 7022			
❏ AL6-8326	Year of the Cat	198?	$10
—Reissue of Arista 9503			

ENIGMA
Number	Title	Yr	NM
❏ D1-73316 [B]	Last Days of the Century	1988	$25

EPIC
Number	Title	Yr	NM
❏ BN26564 [B]	Love Chronicles	1970	$40

JANUS
Number	Title	Yr	NM
❏ 7012 [B]	Modern Times	1975	$35
❏ 3063 [B]	Past, Present and Future	1974	$30
❏ 7026 [DJ]	The Early Years	1977	$30
—Promo-only condensation of 2-LP set with rubber-stamp cover			
❏ 7026 [B]	The Early Years	1977	$25
❏ 7026 [DJ]	The Early Years	1977	$35
—Promo-only condensation of 2-LP set with rubber-stamp cover			
❏ 7022	Year of the Cat	1976	$15

MOBILE FIDELITY
Number	Title	Yr	NM
❏ Jan-0082	Time Passages	1981	$75
—Audiophile vinyl			
❏ Jan-009 [B]	Year of the Cat	1979	$150
—Audiophile vinyl			

NAUTILUS
Number	Title	Yr	NM
❏ NR-34	24 Carrots	198?	$30
—Audiophile vinyl			

PASSPORT
Number	Title	Yr	NM
❏ PB-6042 [B]	Russians and Americans	1986	$18

STEWART, AMII
ARIOLA AMERICA
Number	Title	Yr	NM
❏ SW50054	Knock on Wood	1979	$15
❏ SW50072	Paradise Bird	1979	$12

STEWART, ANDY
CAPITOL
Number	Title	Yr	NM
❏ T10320 [M]	Andy Stewart's Scotland	196?	$18
❏ ST10320 [S]	Andy Stewart's Scotland	196?	$25

EPIC
Number	Title	Yr	NM
❏ LF18027 [M]	A Scottish Soldier	196?	$15
❏ BF19027 [S]	A Scottish Soldier	196?	$18
❏ LF18048 [M]	I'm Off to Bonnie Scotland	196?	$15
❏ BF19048 [S]	I'm Off to Bonnie Scotland	196?	$18
❏ LF18031 [M]	Tunes of Glory	196?	$15
❏ BF19031 [S]	Tunes of Glory	196?	$18

WARWICK
Number	Title	Yr	NM
❏ W3043 [M]	A Scottish Soldier	1961	$25
❏ WST3043 [S]	A Scottish Soldier	1961	$30

STEWART, BILLY
CHESS
Number	Title	Yr	NM
❏ LPS-1547	Billy Stewart Remembered	1970	$30
❏ LP-1513 [M]	Billy Stewart Teaches Old Standards New Tricks	1967	$30
❏ LPS-1513 [S]	Billy Stewart Teaches Old Standards New Tricks	1967	$40
❏ CH-50059	Cross My Heart	1974	$18
❏ LP-1496 [M]	I Do Love You	1965	$100
—Red cover, black "wheel			
❏ LP-1496 [M]	I Do Love You	196?	$30
—Green "woman" cover			
❏ LPS-1496 [S]	I Do Love You	1965	$150
—Red cover, black "wheel			
❏ LPS-1496 [S]	I Do Love You	196?	$40
—Green "woman" cover			
❏ CH-9104	The Greatest Sides	198?	$12
❏ LP-1499 [M]	Unbelievable	1966	$30
❏ LPS-1499 [S]	Unbelievable	1966	$40

Number	Title	Yr	NM

STEWART, BOB

DAWN
❑ DLP-1103 [M]	Let's Talk About Love	1956	$50

JMT
❑ 834414-1	First Line	1988	$25

STASH
❑ ST-266	In a Sentimental Mood	1987	$25

STEWART, DAVE

ARISTA
❑ AL9-8626	Dave Stewart and the Spiritual Cowboys	1990	$12

STEWART, GARY, AND DEAN DILLON

RCA VICTOR
❑ AHL1-4310	Brotherly Love	1982	$12
❑ MHL1-8602 [EP]	Those Were the Days	1983	$10

STEWART, GARY

HIGHTONE
❑ HT-8014	Brand New	1988	$15

MCA
❑ 488	You're Not the Woman You Used to Be	1975	$15

RCA VICTOR
❑ AHL1-3627	Cactus and a Rose	1980	$12
❑ AHL1-5498	Collector's Series	1985	$10
❑ AHL1-3288	Gary	1979	$12
❑ AYL1-4254	Greatest Hits	1982	$10
❑ AHL1-2779	Little Junior	1978	$12
❑ APL1-0900	Out of Hand	1975	$12
❑ AYL1-3944	Out of Hand	1981	$10
—*Best Buy Series" reissue*			
❑ APL1-1225	Steppin' Out	1976	$12
❑ AYL1-3769	Steppin' Out	1981	$10
—*Best Buy Series" reissue*			
❑ APL1-2199	Your Place or Mine	1977	$12

STEWART, HELYNE

CONTEMPORARY
❑ M-3601 [M]	Love Moods	1962	$250
❑ S-7601 [S]	Love Moods	1962	$250

STEWART, JIMMY

BLACKHAWK
❑ BKH-50301	The Touch	1986	$25

CADENCE JAZZ
❑ CJR-1018	An Engineer of Sounds	198?	$25

CATALYST
❑ 7621	Fire Flower	1977	$30

STEWART, JOHN
Also see THE KINGSTON TRIO.

AFFORDABLE DREAMS
❑ AD-01	Trancas	1984	$12

ALLEGIANCE
❑ AV-431	Blondes	1982	$12

CAPITOL
❑ ST-203	California Bloodlines	1969	$18
❑ SN-16150	California Bloodlines	198?	$10
—*Budget-line reissue*			
❑ ST2975	Signals Through the Glass	1968	$25
❑ SM-2975	Signals Through the Glass	1977	$12
—*Reissue with new prefix*			
❑ ST-540	Willard	1970	$18
❑ SN-16151	Willard	198?	$10
—*Budget-line reissue*			

CYPRESS
❑ 661117-1	Punch the Big Guy	1987	$12

HOMECOMING
❑ HC-0200	Centennial	1984	$12
❑ HC-0300	The Last Campaign	1985	$12
❑ HC-0500	The Trio Years	1986	$12

RCA VICTOR
❑ LSP-4827	Cannons in the Rain	1973	$15
❑ AYL1-3731	Cannons in the Rain	1981	$10
—*Best Buy Series" reissue*			
❑ AFL1-3513	John Stewart in Concert	1980	$12
❑ CPL2-0265	The Phoenix Concerts – Live	1974	$18
❑ APL1-0816	Wingless Angels	1975	$15

RSO
❑ RS-1-3051	Bombs Away Dream Babies	1979	$12
❑ RS-1-3074	Dream Babies Go Hollywood	1980	$12
❑ RS-1-3027	Fire in the Wind	1977	$12

WARNER BROS.
❑ BS2611	Sunstorm	1972	$15
❑ WS1948	The Lonesome Picker Rides Again	1971	$15

STEWART, REDD

AUDIO LAB
❑ AL-1528 [M]	Redd Stewart Sings Favorite Old Time Tunes	1959	$250

HICKORY/MGM
❑ H3G-4512	I Remember	1974	$18

STEWART, REX, AND DICKIE WELLS

RCA VICTOR
❑ LPM-2024 [M]	Chatter Jazz	1959	$30
❑ LSP-2024 [S]	Chatter Jazz	1959	$30

STEWART, REX

AMERICAN RECORDING SOCIETY
❑ G-448 [M]	The Big Challenge	1958	$40

ATLANTIC
❑ 1209 [M]	Big Jazz	1956	$300

CONCERT HALL JAZZ
❑ 1202 [M]	Dixieland On Location	1954	$100

DIAL
❑ LP-215 [10]	Ellingtonia	1951	$300

FELSTED
❑ 7001 [M]	Rendezvous with Rex	1958	$40
❑ 2001 [S]	Rendezvous with Rex	1958	$30

GRAND AWARD
❑ GA 33-414 [M]	Just for Kicks	195?	$40

HALL OF FAME
❑ 624	Reunion	197?	$25

JAZZOLOGY
❑ J-36	The Irrepressible Rex Stewart	197?	$30

JAZZTONE
❑ J-1202 [M]	Dixieland Free-for-All	1956	$40
❑ J-1268 [M]	The Big Challenge	1957	$75
❑ J-1285 [M]	The Big Reunion	1957	$75

MASTER JAZZ
❑ 8123	Rendezvous with Rex	197?	$30

PRESTIGE
❑ PRST-7728	Memorial Album	1970	$35
❑ PRST-7812	Trumpet Jive!	1971	$35
—*With Wingy Manone*			

SWING
❑ SW-8414	Porgy and Bess Revisited	1986	$25

SWINGVILLE
❑ SVLP-2006 [M]	The Happy Jazz of Rex Stewart	1960	$50
—*Purple label*			
❑ SVLP-2006 [M]	The Happy Jazz of Rex Stewart	1965	$30
—*Blue label, trident logo at right*			

UNITED ARTISTS
❑ UAL-4009 [M]	Henderson Homecoming	1959	$40
❑ UAS-5009 [S]	Henderson Homecoming	1959	$30

URANIA
❑ UJLP-2012 [M]	Cool Fever	1955	$175

WARNER BROS.
❑ W1260 [M]	Porgy and Bess Revisited	1958	$40
❑ WS1260 [S]	Porgy and Bess Revisited	1958	$30

X
❑ LX-3001 [10]	Rex Stewart and His Orchestra	1954	$150

STEWART, REX/ILLINOIS JACQUET

GRAND AWARD
❑ GA 33-315 [M]	Rex Stewart Plays Duke/ Uptown Jazz	1955	$50

STEWART, REX/PEANUTS HUCKO

JAZZTONE
❑ J-1250 [M]	Dedicated Jazz	1957	$40

STEWART, ROD
Also see JEFF BECK; FACES; PYTHON LEE JACKSON; SHOTGUN EXPRESS.

ACCORD
❑ SN-7142	Rod the Mod	1981	$15

DCC COMPACT CLASSICS
❑ LPZ-2010	Never a Dull Moment	1995	$30
—*Audiophile vinyl*			

J
❑ 55710	As Time Goes By... The Great American Songbook Vol. 2	2003	$18
❑ 62182	Stardust... The Great American Songbook Volume III	2004	$18

MERCURY
❑ SRM-1-609	Every Picture Tells a Story	1971	$18
—*Original cover has an attached, perforated poster*			
❑ SRM-1-609	Every Picture Tells a Story	1971	$12

—*With poster missing; red label*			
❑ 822385-1	Every Picture Tells a Story	1984	$10
❑ SR-61264	Gasoline Alley	1970	$25
—*Cover is textured, most noticeably on the pebbles*			
❑ SR-61264	Gasoline Alley	1971	$18
—*Cover is not textured; red label*			
❑ 824881-1	Gasoline Alley	1985	$10
❑ SRM-1-646	Never a Dull Moment	1972	$15
—*Red label*			
❑ SRM-1-697	Rod Stewart/Faces Live: Coast to Coast Overtures and Beginners	1973	$18
—*By "Rod Stewart/Faces*			
❑ SRM-1-680	Sing It Again Rod	1973	$15
—*Red label*			
❑ 824882-1	Sing It Again Rod	1985	$10
❑ SRM-1-1017	Smiler	1974	$15
—*Chicago skyline cover*			
❑ SRM-2-7507	The Best of Rod Stewart	1976	$18
❑ 826287-1	The Best of Rod Stewart	1985	$15
❑ SRM-2-7509	The Best of Rod Stewart, Volume 2	1977	$18
❑ 822791-1	The Best of Rod Stewart, Volume 2	1985	$15
❑ SR-61237	The Rod Stewart Album	1969	$30
—*Cover is yellow with no black border*			
❑ SR-61237	The Rod Stewart Album	1971	$18
—*Cover is yellow with black border; red label*			

MOBILE FIDELITY
❑ Jan-0054	Blondes Have More Fun	1980	$40
—*Audiophile vinyl*			

PRIVATE STOCK
❑ PS-2021	A Shot of Rhythm and Blues	1976	$18

SPRINGBOARD
❑ SPB-4063	Rod Stewart and Steampacket	197?	$15
❑ SPB-4030	Rod Stewart and The Faces	197?	$15

TRIP
❑ TOP-16-31	Looking Back/16 Early Hits	1974	$15

UNITED DISTRIBUTORS
❑ UDL-2391	The Day Will Come	1981	$25

WARNER BROS.
❑ 23743 [DJ]	Absolutely Live	1982	$35
—*Promo only on Quiex II vinyl*			
❑ 23743	Absolutely Live	1982	$15
❑ 23743 [DJ]	Absolutely Live	1982	$30
—*Promo only on Quiex II vinyl*			
❑ BS2938	A Night on the Town	1976	$12
❑ BSK3116	A Night on the Town	1977	$10
—*Reissue of 2938*			
❑ BS2875	Atlantic Crossing	1975	$12
❑ BSK3108	Atlantic Crossing	1977	$10
—*Reissue of 2875*			
❑ BSK3261	Blondes Have More Fun	1978	$12
❑ BSP3276 [PD]	Blondes Have More Fun	1978	$25
❑ 23877	Body Wishes	1983	$10
❑ 23877 [DJ]	Body Wishes	1983	$30
—*Promo only on Quiex II vinyl*			
❑ 25095	Camouflage	1984	$10
—*Issued with 16 different back covers, all of equal value, that, when assembled, form a giant poster*			
❑ 26158	Downtown Train: Selections from the Storyteller Anthology	1990	$15
❑ HS3485	Foolish Behaviour	1980	$12
❑ BSK3092	Foot Loose and Fancy Free	1977	$12
❑ 25884	Out of Order	1988	$10
❑ 25446	Rod Stewart	1986	$10
❑ HS3373	Rod Stewart Greatest Hits	1979	$12
❑ BSK3602	Tonight I'm Yours	1981	$12

STEWART, SANDY

AUDIOPHILE
❑ AP-205	Sandy Stewart Sings Songs of Jerome Kern	1985	$25
—*Accompanied by Dick Hyman on piano*			

COLPIX
❑ CP-441 [M]	My Coloring Book	1963	$75
❑ SCP-441 [S]	My Coloring Book	1963	$75

STEWART, SLAM, AND BUCKY PIZZARELLI

STASH
❑ ST-201	Dialogue	1978	$30

STEWART, SLAM

JAZZ MAN
❑ 5010	Slam Stewart with Milt Buckner and Jo Jones	198?	$25

SAVOY
❑ MG-12067 [M]	Bowin' Singin' Slam	1956	$40

STEWART, SLY

SCULPTURE
❑ SCP-2001	San Francisco Recordings 1964-1967	197?	$25
—*As "Sly Stone*			

Number	Title	Yr	NM

STEWART, TOM
ABC-PARAMOUNT
| ❏ ABC-117 [M] | Tom Stewart Sextette/ Quintet | 1956 | $50 |

STEWART, TOMMY
PROGRESSIVE
| ❏ PRO-7009 | Tommy Stewart and His Orchestra | 198? | $25 |

STEWART, WYNN, AND JAN HOWARD
CHALLENGE
| ❏ CHL-611 [M] | Sweethearts of Country Music | 1961 | $50 |
STARDAY
| ❏ SLP-421 | Wynn Stewart and Jan Howard Sing Their Hits | 1968 | $30 |

STEWART, WYNN, AND WEBB PIERCE
DESIGN
| ❏ DLP-604 [M] | Country and Western Stars | 196? | $15 |
STEREO-SPECTRUM
| ❏ SLP-604 [R] | Country and Western Stars | 196? | $15 |

STEWART, WYNN
CAPITOL
❏ ST-113	In Love	1969	$25
❏ T2737 [M]	It's Such a Pretty World Today	1967	$25
❏ ST2737 [S]	It's Such a Pretty World Today	1967	$30
❏ ST-214	Let the Whole World Sing It with Me	1969	$25
❏ T2849 [M]	Love's Gonna Happen to Me	1968	$30
❏ ST2849 [S]	Love's Gonna Happen to Me	1968	$25
❏ ST2921	Something Pretty	1968	$25
❏ T2332 [M]	The Songs of Wynn Stewart	1965	$25
❏ ST2332 [S]	The Songs of Wynn Stewart	1965	$30
❏ ST-324	Yours Forever	1969	$25
HILLTOP
| ❏ JM-6050 [M] | Above and Beyond the Call of Love | 1967 | $18 |
| ❏ JS-6050 [S] | Above and Beyond the Call of Love | 1967 | $15 |
PLAYBOY
| ❏ PB416 | After the Storm | 1976 | $12 |
WRANGLER
| ❏ W-1006 [M] | Wynn Stewart | 1962 | $30 |
| ❏ W-31006 [S] | Wynn Stewart | 1962 | $40 |

STEWART FAMILY, THE
KING
| ❏ 687 [M] | Country Sacred Songs | 1960 | $30 |
| ❏ 695 [M] | Golden Country Favorites | 1960 | $30 |

STIDHAM, ARBEE
BLUESVILLE
| ❏ BVLP-1021 [M] | Tired of Wandering | 1961 | $150 |
—Blue label, silver print
| ❏ BVLP-1021 [M] | Tired of Wandering | 1964 | $30 |
—Blue label, trident logo at right
FOLKWAYS
| ❏ F-31033 | There's Always Tomorrow | 1973 | $25 |

STIFF LITTLE FINGERS
4 MEN WITH BEARDS
| ❏ 4M526LP [B] | Inflammable Material | | $25 |
CAROLINE
| ❏ 1377 | See You Up There | 1990 | $15 |
CHRYSALIS
❏ CHR1339	Go For It	1981	$25
❏ CHR1300	Hanx	1980	$25
❏ CHR1270	Nobody's Heroes	1980	$25
ROUGH TRADE
| ❏ ROUGH US5 | Inflammable Material | 1980 | $30 |
—Released in U.K. in 1979

STILES, DANNY, AND BILL WATROUS
FAMOUS DOOR
❏ HL-103	In Tandem	1974	$50
❏ 126	In Tandem -- Into the 80s	1980	$35
❏ HL-112	One More Time	1977	$50

STILLROVEN, THE
SUNDAZED
| ❏ LP-5020 | Cast Thy Burden Upon the Stillroven | 199? | $12 |

STILLS, STEPHEN
ATLANTIC
❏ SD7250	Down the Road	1973	$15
❏ SD 2-903	Manassas	1972	$18
❏ 80177	Right By You	1984	$10
❏ SD7202	Stephen Stills	1970	$15
❏ SD7206	Stephen Stills 2	1971	$15
❏ SD18156	Stephen Stills Live	1975	$15
❏ SD18201	Still Stills -- The Best of Stephen Stills	1976	$12
COLUMBIA
| ❏ PC34348 | Illegal Stills | 1976 | $12 |
| ❏ PC33575 | Stills | 1975 | $12 |
—No bar code on cover
| ❏ PCQ33575 [Q] | Stills | 1975 | $30 |
| ❏ PC33575 | Stills | 198? | $10 |
—Bar code on cover
| ❏ JC35380 | Thoroughfare Gap | 1978 | $12 |

STILLS-YOUNG BAND, THE
REPRISE
| ❏ MS2253 | Long May You Run | 1976 | $12 |

STING
Also see THE POLICE.
A&M
| ❏ SP-3295 [EP] | ...Nada Como El Sol | 1988 | $25 |
—Spanish versions of songs from "...Nothing Like the Sun"
| ❏ R273965 | ...Nothing Like the Sun | 1987 | $14 |
—BMG Direct Marketing edition
| ❏ SP-6402 | ...Nothing Like the Sun | 1987 | $15 |
| ❏ R150266 | The Dream of the Blue Turtles | 1985 | $15 |
—RCA Music Service edition
| ❏ SP-3750 | The Dream of the Blue Turtles | 1985 | $12 |
| ❏ 750216405-1 | The Soul Cages | 1991 | $15 |
MOBILE FIDELITY
| ❏ 1-185 | The Dream of the Blue Turtles | 1985 | $25 |
—Audiophile vinyl

STINGERS, THE
CROWN
| ❏ CLP-5476 [M] | Guitars A Go Go | 196? | $30 |
| ❏ CST-476 [S] | Guitars A Go Go | 196? | $40 |

STINSON BROTHERS, THE
CANADIAN AMERICAN
| ❏ CALP-1012 [M] | The Stinson Brothers in Las Vegas | 196? | $25 |
| ❏ SCALP-1012 [S] | The Stinson Brothers in Las Vegas | 196? | $30 |

STITES, GARY
CARLTON
| ❏ LP-120 [M] | Lonely for You | 1960 | $100 |
| ❏ STLP-120 [S] | Lonely for You | 1960 | $120 |

STITT, SONNY, AND GENE AMMONS
See GENE AMMONS AND SONNY STITT.

STITT, SONNY
ABC IMPULSE!
| ❏ AS-52 [S] | Salt and Pepper | 1968 | $250 |
—With Paul Gonsalves; black label with red ring
| ❏ AS-43 [S] | Sonny Stitt Now! | 1968 | $250 |
—Black label with red ring
| ❏ AS-43 [S] | Sonny Stitt Now! | 1975 | $30 |
—Green, purple, blue "target" label
ARGO
❏ LP-661 [M]	Burnin'	1960	$40
❏ LPS-661 [S]	Burnin'	1960	$150
❏ LP-730 [M]	Move On Over	1964	$40
❏ LPS-730 [S]	Move On Over	1964	$150
❏ LP-744 [M]	My Main Man	1965	$40
❏ LPS-744 [S]	My Main Man	1965	$150
❏ LP-709 [M]	Rearin' Back	1962	$40
❏ LPS-709 [S]	Rearin' Back	1962	$150
❏ LP-629 [M]	Sonny Stitt	1958	$150
❏ LP-683 [M]	Sonny Stitt at the D.J. Lounge	1961	$40
❏ LPS-683 [S]	Sonny Stitt at the D.J. Lounge	1961	$150
ATLANTIC
❏ SD3008	Deuces Wild	1970	$50
❏ 1395 [M]	Sonny Stitt and the Top Brass	1962	$175
❏ SD1395 [S]	Sonny Stitt and the Top Brass	1962	$175
❏ 90139	Sonny Stitt and the Top Brass	198?	$30
❏ 1418 [M]	Stitt Plays Bird	1964	$75
❏ SD1418 [S]	Stitt Plays Bird	1964	$40
BLACKHAWK
| ❏ 528 | Good Life | 1982 | $30 |
BLACK LION
| ❏ 307 | Night Work | 197? | $30 |
CADET
| ❏ LP-661 [M] | Burnin' | 1966 | $50 |
—Fading blue label
| ❏ LPS-661 [S] | Burnin' | 1966 | $75 |
—Fading blue label
| ❏ CA-661 | Burnin' | 197? | $30 |
—Yellow and pink label
| ❏ 2CA-50039 | I Cover the Waterfront | 1974 | $75 |
| ❏ LP-760 [M] | Inter-Action | 1966 | $75 |
—Fading blue label
| ❏ LPS-760 [S] | Inter-Action | 1966 | $40 |
—Fading blue label
| ❏ LP-730 [M] | Move On Over | 1966 | $50 |
—Fading blue label
| ❏ LPS-730 [S] | Move On Over | 1966 | $75 |
—Fading blue label
| ❏ CA-730 [S] | Move On Over | 197? | $30 |
—Yellow and pink label
| ❏ CA-50026 | Mr. Bojangles | 1973 | $40 |
| ❏ LP-744 [M] | My Main Man | 1966 | $50 |
—Fading blue label
| ❏ LPS-744 [S] | My Main Man | 1966 | $75 |
—Fading blue label
| ❏ CA-60040 | Never Can Say Goodbye | 1975 | $50 |
| ❏ LP-709 [M] | Rearin' Back | 1966 | $50 |
—Fading blue label
| ❏ LPS-709 [S] | Rearin' Back | 1966 | $75 |
—Fading blue label
| ❏ CA-709 | Rearin' Back | 197? | $30 |
—Yellow and pink label
| ❏ CA-50060 | Satan | 1974 | $50 |
| ❏ LP-629 [M] | Sonny Stitt | 1966 | $50 |
—Fading blue label
| ❏ CA-629 [R] | Sonny Stitt | 197? | $25 |
—Yellow and pink label
| ❏ LP-683 [M] | Sonny Stitt at the D.J. Lounge | 1966 | $50 |
—Fading blue label
| ❏ LPS-683 [S] | Sonny Stitt at the D.J. Lounge | 1966 | $75 |
—Fading blue label
| ❏ CA-683 | Sonny Stitt at the D.J. Lounge | 197? | $30 |
—Yellow and pink label
| ❏ LP-770 [M] | Soul In the Night | 1966 | $75 |
—Fading blue label
| ❏ LPS-770 [S] | Soul In the Night | 1966 | $40 |
—Fading blue label
CATALYST
| ❏ 7608 | Forecast | 1976 | $50 |
—With Red Holloway
| ❏ 7616 | I Remember Bird | 1977 | $50 |
| ❏ 7620 | Tribute to Duke Ellington | 1977 | $35 |
CHESS
| ❏ 2ACMJ-405 | Interaction | 197? | $50 |
—With Zoot Sims
| ❏ CH-9317 | Sonny Stitt | 1990 | $30 |
| ❏ CH-91523 | Sonny Stitt at the D.J. Lounge | 198? | $30 |
COBBLESTONE
| ❏ CST-9021 | Constellation | 1973 | $50 |
| ❏ CST-9013 | Tune-Up | 1972 | $75 |
COLPIX
| ❏ CP-499 [M] | Broadway Soul | 1964 | $75 |
| ❏ SCP-499 [S] | Broadway Soul | 1964 | $40 |
DELMARK
| ❏ DS-426 | Made for Each Other | 1972 | $50 |
FANTASY
| ❏ OJC-060 | Kaleidoscope | 198? | $30 |
| ❏ OJC-009 | Sonny Stitt/Bud Powell/J.J. Johnson | 198? | $30 |
FLYING DUTCHMAN
| ❏ BDL1-1197 | Dumpy Mama | 1975 | $75 |
| ❏ BDL1-1538 | Stomp Off Let's Go | 1976 | $50 |
GALAXY
| ❏ 8204 | In the Beginning | 197? | $50 |
GRP/IMPULSE!
| ❏ IMP-210 | Salt and Pepper | 1997 | $35 |
—Reissue on audiophile vinyl
IMPULSE!
| ❏ A-52 [M] | Salt and Pepper | 1964 | $160 |
| ❏ AS-52 [S] | Salt and Pepper | 1964 | $250 |
—With Paul Gonsalves
| ❏ A-43 [M] | Sonny Stitt Now! | 1963 | $250 |
| ❏ AS-43 [S] | Sonny Stitt Now! | 1963 | $250 |
JAZZLAND
| ❏ JLP-71 [M] | Low Flame | 1962 | $40 |
| ❏ JLP-971 [S] | Low Flame | 1962 | $150 |
JAZZ MAN
| ❏ 5040 | Night Work | 198? | $30 |
—Reissue of Black Lion LP
JAZZTONE
| ❏ J-1231 [M] | Early Modern | 1956 | $175 |
| ❏ J-1263 [M] | Early Modern | 1957 | $120 |
MUSE
❏ MR-5006	12!	1973	$35
❏ MR-5129	Blues for Duke	1978	$30
❏ MR-5323	Constellation	1986	$35

Number	Title	Yr	NM
— Reissue of Cobblestone 9021			
❏ MR-5228	In Style	1982	$30
❏ MR-5067	Mellow	1975	$50
❏ MR-5091	My Buddy: Sonny Stitt Plays for Gene Ammons	1976	$35
❏ MR-5204	Sonny's Back	1981	$35
❏ MR-5023	The Champ	1974	$35
❏ MR-5269	The Last Stitt Sessions, Vol. 1	1983	$35
❏ MR-5280	The Last Stitt Sessions, Vol. 2	1984	$35
❏ MR-5334	Tune-Up	1987	$35
— Reissue of Cobblestone 9013			

NEW JAZZ

Number	Title	Yr	NM
❏ NJLP-103 [10]	Sonny Stitt and Bud Powell	1950	$500

PACIFIC JAZZ

Number	Title	Yr	NM
❏ PJ-71 [M]	My Mother's Eyes	1963	$175
❏ ST-71 [S]	My Mother's Eyes	1963	$175

PAULA

Number	Title	Yr	NM
❏ 4004	Soul Girl	1974	$30

PHOENIX

Number	Title	Yr	NM
❏ 19	Battles	197?	$25
❏ 15	Superstitt	197?	$25

PRESTIGE

Number	Title	Yr	NM
❏ PRLP-7248 [M]	All God's Chillun Got Rhythm	1962	$175
— Yellow label with Bergenfield, N.J. address			
❏ PRLP-7248 [M]	All God's Chillun Got Rhythm	1964	$40
— Blue label with trident logo			
❏ PRST-7248 [R]	All God's Chillun Got Rhythm	1962	$175
❏ PRST-7769	Best for Lovers	1970	$75
❏ P-10032	Black Vibrations	1972	$75
❏ PRST-7839	Bud's Blues	1974	$50
❏ PRLP-126 [10]	Favorites, Volume 1	1952	$400
❏ PRLP-148 [10]	Favorites, Volume 2	1953	$400
❏ P-24044	Genesis	1974	$50
❏ 10048	Goin' Down Slow	1973	$75
❏ PRLP-7077 [M]	Kaleidoscope	1957	$300
— Yellow label with W. 50th St address			
❏ PRLP-111 [10]	Mr. Saxophone	1951	$400
❏ PRLP-7436 [M]	Night Crawler	1966	$40
— Blue label, trident logo at right			
❏ PRST-7436 [S]	Night Crawler	1966	$150
— Blue label, trident logo at right			
❏ PRST-7759	Night Letter	1970	$50
❏ PRLP-7452 [M]	'Nuther Fu'ther	1966	$40
— Blue label, trident logo at right			
❏ PRST-7452 [S]	'Nuther Fu'ther	1966	$150
— Blue label, trident logo at right			
❏ PRST-7452 [S]	'Nuther Fu'ther	197?	$75
— Green label			
❏ PRLP-7459 [M]	Pow!	1967	$150
— Blue label, trident logo at right			
❏ PRST-7459 [S]	Pow!	1967	$40
— Blue label, trident logo at right			
❏ PRLP-7302 [M]	Primitive Soul!	1964	$175
— Yellow label with Bergenfield, N.J. address			
❏ PRLP-7302 [M]	Primitive Soul!	1965	$40
— Blue label with trident logo			
❏ PRST-7302 [S]	Primitive Soul!	1964	$140
— Silver label			
❏ PRST-7302 [S]	Primitive Soul!	1965	$40
— Blue label with trident logo			
❏ PRLP-7332 [M]	Shangri-La	1964	$40
— Blue label, trident logo at right			
❏ PRST-7332 [S]	Shangri-La	1964	$150
— Blue label, trident logo at right			
❏ P-10074	So Doggone Good	1974	$35
❏ PRLP-103 [10]	Sonny Stitt Plays	1951	$400
❏ PRLP-7024 [M]	Sonny Stitt with Bud Powell and J.J. Johnson	1956	$450
❏ PRST-7372	Soul Electricity	1969	$75
❏ PRLP-7372 [M]	Soul People	1965	$40
— Blue label, trident logo at right			
❏ PRST-7372 [S]	Soul People	1965	$150
— Blue label, trident logo at right			
❏ PRST-7372 [S]	Soul People	197?	$75
— Green label			
❏ PRLP-7297 [M]	Soul Shack	1964	$175
— Yellow label with Bergenfield, N.J. address			
❏ PRLP-7297 [M]	Soul Shack	1965	$40
— Blue label with trident logo			
❏ PRST-7297 [S]	Soul Shack	1964	$140
— Silver label with Bergenfield, N.J. address			
❏ PRST-7297 [S]	Soul Shack	1965	$40
— Blue label with trident logo			
❏ PRLP-7244 [M]	Stitt Meets Brother Jack	1962	$175
— Yellow label with Bergenfield, N.J. address			
❏ PRLP-7244 [M]	Stitt Meets Brother Jack	1964	$40
— Blue label, trident logo			
❏ PRST-7244 [S]	Stitt Meets Brother Jack	1962	$175
❏ PRLP-7133 [M]	Stitt's Bits	1958	$250
❏ PRST-7585	Stitt's Bits, Volume 1	1968	$75
❏ PRST-7612	Stitt's Bits, Volume 2	1969	$75
❏ PRST-7701	The Best of Sonny Stitt with Brother Jack McDuff	1969	$75

Number	Title	Yr	NM
❏ P-10012	Turn It On	1971	$75

PROGRESSIVE

Number	Title	Yr	NM
❏ PRO-7034	Sonny Stitt Meets Sadik Hakim	1978	$75

ROOST

Number	Title	Yr	NM
❏ LP-2219 [M]	37 Minutes and 48 Seconds with Sonny Stitt	1957	$175
❏ LP-2235 [M]	A Little Bit of Stitt	1959	$140
❏ SLP-2235 [S]	A Little Bit of Stitt	1959	$120
❏ LP-1203 [M]	Battle of Birdland	1955	$250
❏ LP-2247 [M]	Feelin's	1962	$120
❏ SLP-2247 [S]	Feelin's	1962	$120
❏ LP-418 [10]	Jazz at the Hi-Hat	1954	$400
❏ LP-2245 [M]	Sonny Side Up	1960	$175
❏ SLP-2245 [S]	Sonny Side Up	1960	$175
❏ LP-1208 [M]	Sonny Stitt	1956	$250
❏ LP-2208 [M]	Sonny Stitt	1957	$250
❏ LP-2253 [M]	Sonny Stitt Goes Latin	1963	$150
❏ SLP-2253 [S]	Sonny Stitt Goes Latin	1963	$150
❏ LP-2252 [M]	Sonny Stitt in Orbit	1963	$150
❏ SLP-2252 [S]	Sonny Stitt in Orbit	1963	$150
❏ LP-415 [10]	Sonny Stitt Plays Arrangements from the Pen of Johnny Richards	1952	$400
❏ LP-2204 [M]	Sonny Stitt Plays Arrangements of Quincy Jones	1957	$175
❏ LP-2226 [M]	Sonny Stitt with the New Yorkers	1958	$175
❏ LP-2244 [M]	Stittsville	1960	$140
❏ SLP-2244 [S]	Stittsville	1960	$175
❏ LP-2230 [M]	The Saxophone of Sonny Stitt	1959	$140
❏ SLP-2230 [S]	The Saxophone of Sonny Stitt	1959	$120
❏ LP-2240 [M]	The Sonny Side of Stitt	1960	$140
❏ SLP-2240 [S]	The Sonny Side of Stitt	1960	$120

ROULETTE

Number	Title	Yr	NM
❏ R-25348 [M]	I Keep Comin' Back	1967	$40
❏ SR-25348 [S]	I Keep Comin' Back	1967	$75
❏ SR-42035	Make Someone Happy	1969	$50
❏ SR-25354 [S]	Parallel-O-Stitt	1968	$75
❏ R-25354 [M]	Parallel-O-Stitt	1968	$150
❏ SR-42048	Stardust	1970	$50
❏ SR-5002	Stardust	197?	$35
— Reissue of 42048			
❏ R-25339 [M]	The Matadors Meet the Bull	1965	$40
❏ SR-25339 [S]	The Matadors Meet the Bull	1965	$150
❏ R-25343 [M]	What's New?	1966	$75
❏ SR-25343 [S]	What's New?	1966	$40

SAVOY

Number	Title	Yr	NM
❏ MG-9006 [10]	All Star Series: Sonny Stitt	1953	$300
❏ MG-9012 [10]	New Sounds in Modern Music	1953	$300
❏ MG-9014 [10]	New Trends Of Jazz	1953	$300

SAVOY JAZZ

Number	Title	Yr	NM
❏ SJL-1165	Symphony Hall Swing	1986	$35

SOLID STATE

Number	Title	Yr	NM
❏ SS-18057	Come Hither	1969	$50
❏ SS-18047	Little Green Apples	1968	$50

TRIP

Number	Title	Yr	NM
❏ TLX-5008	Two Sides of Sonny Stitt	1974	$35

UPFRONT

Number	Title	Yr	NM
❏ UPF-196	Sonny's Blues	197?	$30

VERVE

Number	Title	Yr	NM
❏ MGV-8219 [M]	New York Jazz	1957	$175
❏ V-8219 [M]	New York Jazz	1961	$75
❏ UMV-2558	New York Jazz	198?	$30
❏ MGV-8250 [M]	Only the Blues	1958	$150
❏ V-8250 [M]	Only the Blues	1961	$75
❏ UMV-2634	Only the Blues	198?	$30
❏ MGV-8324 [M]	Personal Appearance	1959	$150
❏ V-8324 [M]	Personal Appearance	1961	$75
❏ V6-8837	Previously Unreleased Recordings	1974	$30
❏ MGV-8377 [M]	Saxophone Supremacy	1960	$150
❏ MGVS-6154 [S]	Saxophone Supremacy	1960	$0
— Canceled			
❏ V-8377 [M]	Saxophone Supremacy	1961	$75
❏ V-8380 [M]	Sommy Stitt Swings the Most	1961	$75
❏ MGV-8262 [M]	Sonny Side Up	1958	$120
❏ V-8262 [M]	Sonny Side Up	1961	$75
❏ MGV-8403 [M]	Sonny Stitt	1960	$0
— Canceled			
❏ MGV-8374 [M]	Sonny Stitt Blows the Blues	1960	$150
❏ MGVS-6149 [S]	Sonny Stitt Blows the Blues	1960	$150
❏ V-8374 [M]	Sonny Stitt Blows the Blues	1961	$75
❏ V6-8374 [S]	Sonny Stitt Blows the Blues	1961	$50
❏ MGVS-6149	Sonny Stitt Blows the Blues	1996	$40
— Audiophile reissue by Classic Records			
❏ MGVS-6149-45	Sonny Stitt Blows the Blues	1999	$40
— Audiophile reissue by Classic Records; plays at 45 rpm			
❏ MGV-8309 [M]	Sonny Stitt Plays Jimmy Giuffre Arrangements	1959	$150
❏ MGVS-6041 [S]	Sonny Stitt Plays Jimmy Giuffre Arrangements	1960	$150
❏ V-8309 [M]	Sonny Stitt Plays Jimmy Giuffre Arrangements	1961	$75
❏ V6-8309 [S]	Sonny Stitt Plays Jimmy Giuffre Arrangements	1961	$50
❏ MGV-8344 [M]	Sonny Stitt Sits In with the Oscar Peterson Trio	1959	$150

Number	Title	Yr	NM
❏ MGVS-6108 [S]	Sonny Stitt Sits In with the Oscar Peterson Trio	1960	$150
❏ V-8344 [M]	Sonny Stitt Sits In with the Oscar Peterson Trio	1961	$75
❏ V6-8344 [S]	Sonny Stitt Sits In with the Oscar Peterson Trio	1961	$50
❏ MGV-8380 [M]	Sonny Stitt Swings the Most	1960	$150
❏ MGVS-6162 [S]	Sonny Stitt Swings the Most	1960	$0
— Canceled			
❏ MGV-8306 [M]	The Hard Swing	1959	$150
❏ MGVS-6038 [S]	The Hard Swing	1960	$150
❏ V-8306 [M]	The Hard Swing	1961	$75
❏ V6-8306 [S]	The Hard Swing	1961	$50
❏ V-8451 [M]	The Sensual Sound of Sonny Stitt	1962	$50
❏ V6-8451 [S]	The Sensual Sound of Sonny Stitt	1962	$75

WHO'S WHO IN JAZZ

Number	Title	Yr	NM
❏ 21022	Sonny, Sweets and Jaws	1981	$35
❏ 21025	The Bubba's Sessions	1982	$35

STOCKHAUSEN, KARLHEINZ

CANDIDE

Number	Title	Yr	NM
❏ CE31001 [B]	Prozession	1968	$50
❏ CE31002 [B]	Refrain; Kontakte	1968	$30

CBS

Number	Title	Yr	NM
❏ 32 21 000 [B]	Complete Piano Music	1967	$50
❏ 32 11 0044 [B]	Mikrophonie I - Mikrophonie II	1967	$35

COLUMBIA MASTERWORKS

Number	Title	Yr	NM
❏ ML5275 [B]	Le Marteau Sans Maître / Nr. 5 Zeitmasse For Five Woodwinds	1958	$50
— one side only by Stockhausen; side one by Pierre Boulez			

MAINSTREAM

Number	Title	Yr	NM
❏ MS5003 [B]	Zyklus • Refrain / Transición II	1970	$80

NONESUCH

Number	Title	Yr	NM
❏ H71157 [B]	Momente (1965 Version)	1967	$25

ODYSSEY

Number	Title	Yr	NM
❏ 32 16 0153 [B]	Le Marteau Sans Maître / Nr. 5 Zeitmasse For Five Woodwinds	1967	$40

TIME

Number	Title	Yr	NM
❏ 58001 [M]	Zyklus • Refrain / Transición II	1961	$80
❏ S8001 [S]	Zyklus • Refrain / Transición II	1961	$60

VARESE INTERNATIONAL

Number	Title	Yr	NM
❏ VC81008 [B]	Prozession (1967 Version)	1977	$20

STOECKLEIN, VAL

DOT

Number	Title	Yr	NM
❏ DLP-3904 [M]	Grey Life	1968	$150
— Label is black, as if stock copy, but record is found inside stereo (25904) cover with "Monaural Promotion Not for Sale" sticker on front			
❏ DLP-25904 [S]	Grey Life	1968	$40

STOKES, CARL B.

FLYING DUTCHMAN

Number	Title	Yr	NM
❏ FD-130	The Mayor and the People	1970	$150

STOKOWSKI, LEOPOLD

RCA VICTOR RED SEAL

Number	Title	Yr	NM
❏ LSC-2593 [S]	Inspiration	1962	$25
— Original with "shaded dog" label			

THE BACH GUILD

Number	Title	Yr	NM
❏ BGS-70696	In Dulci Jubilo: A Baroque Concert	1967	$15

STOLOFF, MORRIS

DECCA

Number	Title	Yr	NM
❏ DL8574 [M]	This Is Kim	1957	$75
— Black label, silver print; Kim Novak is the cover model			

STOLTZMAN, RICHARD

RCA

Number	Title	Yr	NM
❏ 5944-1-RC	New York Counterpoint	1987	$25

RCA VICTOR

Number	Title	Yr	NM
❏ AML1-7124	Begin Sweet World	1986	$25

STONE, ANGIE

J

Number	Title	Yr	NM
❏ 80813-20013-1	Mahogany Soul	2001	$30
❏ 82876-56215-1	Stone Love	2004	$18

STONE, CLIFFIE

CAPITOL

Number	Title	Yr	NM
❏ T1230 [M]	Cool Cowboy	1959	$30
❏ ST1230 [S]	Cool Cowboy	1959	$40
❏ T1685 [M]	It's Fun to Square Dance	1962	$25
❏ ST1685 [S]	It's Fun to Square Dance	1962	$30
❏ KAO1555 [M]	Original Cowboy Sing-A-Long	1961	$30
❏ SKAO1555 [S]	Original Cowboy Sing-A-Long	1961	$40
❏ T1286 [M]	Square Dance Promenade	1960	$30
❏ ST1286 [S]	Square Dance Promenade	1960	$40

Number	Title	Yr	NM
❑ H4009 [10]	Square Dances	195?	$75
❑ T1080 [M]	The Party's on Me	1958	$40

TOWER

❑ T5073 [M]	Together Again	1967	$30
❑ ST5073 [S]	Together Again	1967	$30

STONE, KIRBY, FOUR

CADENCE

❑ CLP1023 [M]	Man I Flipped	1958	$30

COLUMBIA

❑ CL1211 [M]	Baubles, Bangles and Beads	1959	$25
❑ CS8014 [S]	Baubles, Bangles and Beads	1959	$30
❑ CL1714 [M]	Guys and Dolls	1961	$25
❑ CS8514 [S]	Guys and Dolls	1961	$30
❑ CL1290 [M]	The "Go" Sound of the Kirby Stone Four	1959	$25
❑ CS8130 [S]	The "Go" Sound of the Kirby Stone Four	1959	$30
❑ CL1646 [M]	The Kirby Stone Four at the Playboy Club	1960	$25
❑ CS8446 [S]	The Kirby Stone Four at the Playboy Club	1960	$30
❑ CL1356 [M]	The Kirby Stone Touch	1959	$25
❑ CS8164 [S]	The Kirby Stone Touch	1959	$30

TOPS

❑ L-1582 [M]	The Kirby Stone Four	1957	$30

STONE, ROLAND

ACE

❑ LP-1018 [M]	Just a Moment	1961	$175

STONE, SLY

CLEOPATRA

❑ 6612 [B]	I'm Back! Family & Friends		$25

STONE ALLIANCE

PM

❑ 015	Con Amigos	197?	$30
❑ 020	Heads Up	197?	$30
❑ 013	Stone Alliance	197?	$30

STONE CIRCUS, THE

MAINSTREAM

❑ S-6119	The Stone Circus	1969	$100

STONE COUNTRY

RCA VICTOR

❑ LSP-3958	Stone Country	1968	$25

STONE HARBOUR

STONE HARBOUR

❑ 398	Stone Harbour Emerges	197?	$500

STONE PONEYS

Also see LINDA RONSTADT.

CAPITOL

❑ T2763 [M]	Evergreen, Vol. 2	1967	$150
❑ ST2763 [S]	Evergreen, Vol. 2	1967	$30
❑ ST2863	Linda Ronstadt/Stone Poneys and Friends Vol. III	1968	$50
❑ T2666 [M]	The Stone Poneys	1967	$100
❑ ST2666 [S]	The Stone Poneys	1967	$30
❑ ST-11383	The Stone Poneys Featuring Linda Ronstadt	1974	$12

PICKWICK

❑ SPC-3298	Stoney End	1976	$15

STONE ROSES, THE

SILVERTONE

❑ 1184-1-J	The Stone Roses	1989	$15

STONE TEMPLE PILOTS

Also see VELVET REVOLVER.

ATLANTIC

❑ 82607 [B]	Purple	1994	$25
❑ 82871	Tiny Music -- Music from the Vatican Gift Shop	1996	$25

STONE THE CROWS

POLYDOR

❑ PD-5037	Continuous Performance	1972	$25
❑ 24-4019	Stone the Crows	1970	$25
❑ PD-5020	Teenage Licks	1972	$25

STONEGROUND

WARNER BROS.

❑ 2WS1956	Family Album	1971	$25
❑ WS1895	Stoneground	1971	$18
❑ BS2645	Stoneground 3	1972	$14

STONEHILL, RANDY

ONE WAY

❑ JC-31252	Born Twice	1972	$75

STONEMANS, THE

MGM

❑ E-4511 [M]	All in the Family	1968	$30
❑ SE-4511 [S]	All in the Family	1968	$25
❑ SE-4613	A Stoneman Christmas	1968	$25
❑ E-4453 [M]	Stoneman's Country	1967	$25
❑ SE-4453 [S]	Stoneman's Country	1967	$30
❑ SE-4578	The Great Stonemans	1968	$25
❑ GAS-124	The Stonemans (Golden Archive Series)	1970	$18
❑ E-4363 [M]	Those Singin' Swingin' Stompin' Sensational Stonemans	1966	$25
❑ SE-4363 [S]	Those Singin' Swingin' Stompin' Sensational Stonemans	1966	$30

RCA VICTOR

❑ LSP-4431	California Blues	1970	$18
❑ LSP-4264	Dawn of the Stonemans' Age	1970	$18
❑ LSP-4343	In All Honesty	1970	$18

STARDAY

❑ SLP-393 [M]	White Lightning	1965	$40

WORLD PACIFIC

❑ WP-1828 [M]	Big Ball in Monterey	1964	$30
❑ ST-1828 [S]	Big Ball in Monterey	1964	$40

STONEWALL

TIGER LILY

❑ TL14013DJ [B]	Stonewall	1976	$15000

STONEY AND MEATLOAF

Also see MEAT LOAF.

PRODIGAL

❑ 10	Stoney and Meatloaf	1978	$15

RARE EARTH

❑ R528 [B]	Stoney and Meatloaf	1971	$40

STOOGES, THE

See IGGY AND THE STOOGES.

ELEKTRA

❑ EKS74101 [B]	Fun House	1970	$175

—By "The Stooges"; red label with large stylized "E" (butterfly label, deduct 60%)

❑ EKS74051 [B]	The Stooges	1969	$1500

—By "The Stooges"; red label with large stylized "E" (butterfly label, deduct 60%)

❑ 74051 [B]	The Stooges	1969	$3000

—Promo with unique folder cover, media reviews and biog, hype letter, three publicity photos and promo poster.

RHINO

❑ R1525148 [B]	Have Some Fun: Live at Ungano's	2015	$25

SUNDAZED

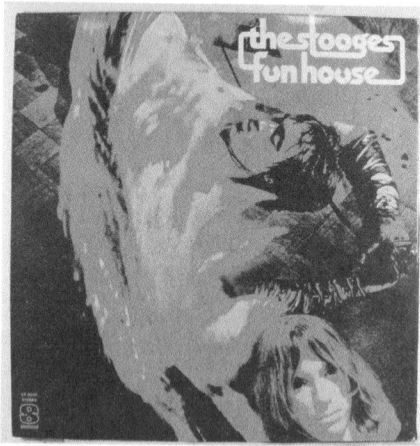

❑ LP5150 [B]	Fun House	2002	$20

—By "The Stooges"; reissue on 180-gram vinyl

STOOKEY, PAUL

WARNER BROS.

❑ BS2674	One Night Stand	1973	$12

—As "Noel Paul Stookey

❑ WS1912	Paul and...	1971	$12

STOPAK, BERNIE

STASH

❑ ST-274	Remember Me	1988	$25

STORDAHL, AXEL

DECCA

❑ DL8933 [M]	Christmas in Scandinavia	1960	$18
❑ DL78933 [S]	Christmas in Scandinavia	1960	$25

STORIES

KAMA SUTRA

❑ KSBS-2068	About Us	1973	$30

—Gatefold; does NOT contain "Brother Louie

❑ KSBS-2068	About Us	1973	$18

—Gatefold cover; "Brother Louie" added as the last song on side 2

❑ KSBS-2068	About Us	1973	$15

—Regular cover; "Brother Louie" added as the last song on side 2

❑ KSBS-2051	Stories	1972	$15
❑ KSBS-2078	Traveling Underground	1974	$15

STORM, BILLY

BUENA VISTA

❑ BV-3315 [M]	Billy Storm	1963	$150
❑ STER-3315 [S]	Billy Storm	1963	$120

FAMOUS

❑ F-504	This Is the Night	1969	$150

STORM, GALE

DOT

❑ DLP-3011 [M]	Gale Storm	1956	$50
❑ DLP-3098 [M]	Gale Storm Hits	1958	$40
❑ DLP-3209 [M]	Gale Storm Sings	1959	$30
❑ DLP-25209 [S]	Gale Storm Sings	1959	$40
❑ DLP-3017 [M]	Sentimental Me	1956	$50
❑ DLP-3197 [M]	Softly and Tenderly	1959	$30
❑ DLP-25197 [S]	Softly and Tenderly	1959	$40

HAMILTON

❑ HLP-171 [M]	I Don't Want to Walk	1966	$15
❑ HLP-12171 [S]	I Don't Want to Walk	1966	$18

MCA

❑ 1504	Gale Storm	198?	$12

STORY, CARL

MERCURY

❑ MG-20323 [M]	Gospel Quartet Favorites	1958	$40
❑ MG-20584 [M]	More Gospel Quartet Favorites	1961	$30
❑ SR-60584 [S]	More Gospel Quartet Favorites	1961	$40

STARDAY

❑ SLP-278 [M]	All Day Sacred Singing	1964	$40
❑ SLP-137 [M]	All Day Singing with Dinner on the Ground	1961	$40
❑ SLP-107 [M]	America's Favorite Country Gospel Artist	1959	$50
❑ SLP-152 [M]	Get Religion	1962	$40
❑ SLP-127 [M]	Gospel Revival	1961	$40
❑ SLP-219 [M]	Mighty Close to Heaven	1963	$40
❑ SLP-411 [M]	My Lord Keeps a Record	1968	$30
❑ SLP-315 [M]	Sacred Songs of Life and the Hereafter	1965	$40
❑ SLP-348 [M]	There's Nothing on Earth (That Heaven Can't Cure)	1965	$40

STORYVILLE STOMPERS, THE

TROPICANA

❑ 1204 [M]	New Orleans Jazz	195?	$40

STOVER, SMOKEY

ARGO

❑ LP-652 [DJ]	Smokey Stover's Original Firemen	1960	$75

—White label, multi-color vinyl

❑ LP-652	Smokey Stover's Original Firemen	1960	$30
❑ LPS-652 [S]	Smokey Stover's Original Firemen	1960	$30

JAZZOLOGY

❑ J-53	Smokey Stover and the Original Firemen	197?	$25

STOWAWAYS, THE

JUSTICE

❑ JLP-148	The Stowaways	1968	$500

STOWELL, JOHN

INNER CITY

❑ IC-1030	Golden Delicious	197?	$30

STRADIVARI STRINGS, THE

SPIN-O-RAMA

❑ 590 [M]	String Along with Me	196?	$30
❑ S-590 [S]	String Along with Me	196?	$40

—Cover model on the above LP is Jayne Mansfield

STRAIT, GEORGE

HEARTLAND

❑ HL1172/3	The Very Best of George Strait	1991	$18

MCA

❑ 5750	#7	1986	$12
❑ 42266	Beyond the Blue Neon	1989	$10
❑ R153641	Chill of an Early Fall	1991	$25

Number	Title	Yr	NM

—Only released on vinyl through BMG Direct Marketing

❏ 5518	Does Fort Worth Ever Cross Your Mind	1984	$12
❏ 5567	Greatest Hits	1985	$12
❏ 42035	Greatest Hits, Volume Two	1987	$10
❏ 10532	Holding My Own	1992	$25

—Only available on vinyl through Columbia House

❏ 42114	If You Ain't Lovin' You Ain't Livin'	1988	$10
❏ 6415	Livin' It Up	1990	$15
❏ 5800	Merry Christmas Strait to You	1986	$12
❏ R134172	Merry Christmas Strait to You	1986	$15

—BMG Direct Marketing version

❏ 5913	Ocean Front Property	1987	$12
❏ 5450	Right or Wrong	1983	$12
❏ 5605	Something Special	1985	$12
❏ 5248	Strait Country	1981	$12
❏ 27092	Strait Country	1984	$10

—Reissue of 5248

| ❏ 5320 | Strait from the Heart | 1982 | $12 |
| ❏ 10450 | Ten Strait Hits | 1992 | $25 |

—Only available on vinyl through Columbia House

STRAND, LES

FANTASY

| ❏ 3242 [M] | Jazz Classics on the Baldwin Organ | 1956 | $50 |

—Red vinyl

| ❏ 3242 [M] | Jazz Classics on the Baldwin Organ | 195? | $25 |

—Black vinyl

| ❏ 3231 [M] | Les Strand on the Baldwin Organ | 1956 | $50 |

—Red vinyl

| ❏ 3231 [M] | Les Strand on the Baldwin Organ | 195? | $25 |

—Black vinyl

STRANGE, BILLY

CHESS

| ❏ CH2-6027 | One More Time | 1988 | $15 |

COLISEUM

| ❏ CM-1001 [M] | Limbo Rock | 1962 | $40 |

GNP CRESCENDO

❏ GNPS-2039	A James Bond Double Feature	1967	$15
❏ GNP-2024 [M]	Billy Strange Plays Roger Miller Hits	1966	$15
❏ GNPS-2024 [S]	Billy Strange Plays Roger Miller Hits	1966	$18
❏ GNP-2012 [M]	Billy Strange Plays the Hits	1965	$15
❏ GNPS-2012 [S]	Billy Strange Plays the Hits	1965	$18
❏ GNP-2030 [M]	Billy Strange with the Challengers	1966	$18
❏ GNPS-2030 [S]	Billy Strange with the Challengers	1966	$25
❏ GNPS-2094	Dyn-o-mite Guitar	197?	$12
❏ GNP-2009 [M]	English Hits of '65	1965	$15
❏ GNPS-2009 [S]	English Hits of '65	1965	$18
❏ GNP-98 [M]	Five String Banjo	1964	$15
❏ GNPS-98 [S]	Five String Banjo	1964	$18
❏ GNP-2016 [M]	Folk Rock Hits	1965	$15
❏ GNPS-2016 [S]	Folk Rock Hits	1965	$18
❏ GNP-2006 [M]	Goldfinger	1965	$15
❏ GNPS-2006 [S]	Goldfinger	1965	$18
❏ GNPS-2046	Great Western Themes	1969	$15
❏ GNP-2022 [M]	In the Mexican Bag	1966	$15
❏ GNPS-2022 [S]	In the Mexican Bag	1966	$18
❏ GNP-97 [M]	Mr. Guitar	1963	$15
❏ GNPS-97 [S]	Mr. Guitar	1963	$18
❏ GNPS-2041	Railroad Man	1968	$15
❏ GNP-2019 [M]	Secret Agent File	1966	$15
❏ GNPS-2019 [S]	Secret Agent File	1966	$18
❏ GNP-2037 [M]	The Best of Billy Strange	1967	$15
❏ GNPS-2037 [S]	The Best of Billy Strange	1967	$15
❏ GNP-2004 [M]	The James Bond Theme	1964	$15
❏ GNPS-2004 [S]	The James Bond Theme	1964	$18
❏ GNP-94 [M]	Twelve String Guitar	1963	$15
❏ GNPS-94 [S]	Twelve String Guitar	1963	$18

SUNSET

| ❏ SUS-5209 | Mr. Guitar | 1968 | $12 |

SURREY

| ❏ SS-1002 | The Best of Billy Strange | 1965 | $18 |

TRADITION

| ❏ 2080 | Strange Country | 1969 | $12 |

STRANGE, RICHARD

PVC

| ❏ 7917 [B] | The Live Rise of Richard Strange | 1980 | $30 |

STRANGE

OUTER GALAXIE

| ❏ 1001 | Raw Power | 1976 | $150 |
| ❏ 1000 | Translucent World | 1973 | $150 |

STRANGEBREW

ABC

| ❏ ABCS-672 [B] | Very Strangebrew | 1969 | $30 |

STRANGELOVES, THE

BANG

| ❏ BLP-211 [M] | I Want Candy | 1965 | $175 |
| ❏ BLPS-211 [S] | I Want Candy | 1965 | $150 |

STRANGERS, THE

CAPITOL

❏ ST-590	Getting to Know Merle Haggard's Strangers	1970	$25
❏ ST-796	Honky Tonkin'	1971	$25
❏ ST-169	Instrumental Sounds of Merle Haggard's Strangers	1969	$25
❏ ST-445	Introducing My Friends the Strangers	1970	$25
❏ ST-11141	Totally Instrumental with One Exception...	1973	$18

STRANGLERS, THE

A&M

| ❏ SP-4706 [B] | Black and White | 1978 | $30 |

—Grey marbled wax; first 75,000 released with white-vinyl EP (FREE-9)

| ❏ SP-4706 | Black and White | 1978 | $15 |

—Black vinyl without bonus single

| ❏ SP-4659 [B] | No More Heroes | 1977 | $25 |
| ❏ SP-4648 [B] | Rattus Norvegicus | 1977 | $25 |

—With bonus single "Peasant in the Big Shitty"/"Choosie Suzie" (FREE-3)

EMI AMERICA

| ❏ SQ-17207 | La Folie | 1986 | $18 |

—U.S. issue of 1981 U.K. release

| ❏ ST-17189 | The Men in Black | 1986 | $18 |

—Reissue

EPIC

❏ FE44209	All Live and All of the Night	1988	$12
❏ BFE39959	Aural Sculpture	1985	$15
❏ BFE40607	Dreamtime	1986	$12
❏ BFE38542	Feline	1983	$15
❏ E46120	Stranglers 10	1990	$12
❏ E47081	The Stranglers Greatest Hits 1977-1990	1990	$15

I.R.S.

| ❏ SP70011 [B] | Stranglers IV | 1980 | $25 |

—combines tracks from the 1979 "The Raven" LP (unreleased in US) and singles

STIFF AMERICA

| ❏ USE-10 [B] | The Men in Black | 1981 | $30 |

STRATAVARIOUS

ROULETTE

| ❏ RS3019 | Stratavarious | 1976 | $30 |

STRATTON, DON

ABC-PARAMOUNT

| ❏ ABC-118 [M] | Modern Jazz with Dixieland Roots | 1956 | $250 |

STRAWBERRY ALARM CLOCK

SUNDAZED

❏ LP5441 [B]	Best Of The Strawberry Alarm Clock	2013	$25
❏ LP5440 [B]	The World In A Sea Shell	2013	$25
❏ LP5439 [B]	Wake Up...It's Tomorrow	2013	$25

UNI

❏ 73054	Good Morning Starshine	1969	$40
❏ 3014 [M]	Incense and Peppermints	1967	$150
❏ 73014 [S]	Incense and Peppermints	1967	$40
❏ 73074	The Best of the Strawberry Alarm Clock	1970	$40
❏ 73035	The World in a Sea Shell	1968	$40
❏ 73025	Wake Up It's Tomorrow	1968	$40

VOCALION

| ❏ VL73915 | Changes | 1971 | $50 |

STRAWBS, THE

A&M

❏ SP-6005	Best of the Strawbs	1978	$15
❏ SP-4383	Bursting at the Seams	1973	$18
❏ SP-4304	From the Witchwood	1971	$18
❏ SP-4506	Ghosts	1975	$18
❏ SP-4344	Grave New World	1972	$18
❏ SP-3607	Hero and Heroine	1974	$18
❏ SP-4288	Just a Collection of Antiques and Curios	1971	$18
❏ SP-4544	Nomadness	1975	$18

ARISTA

| ❏ AB4172 | Deadlines | 1978 | $12 |

OYSTER

| ❏ OY-1604 | Burning for You | 1977 | $15 |
| ❏ OY-1603 | Deep Cuts | 1976 | $15 |

STRAY CATS

Also see BRIAN SETZER.

CLEOPATRA

| ❏ CLP1747 [B] | Live at the Roxy 1981 | 2014 | $25 |

EMI

| ❏ R101178 | Blast Off | 1989 | $18 |

—BMG Music Service edition

EMI AMERICA

| ❏ ST-17070 | Built for Speed | 1982 | $12 |
| ❏ ST-517070 | Built for Speed | 1982 | $12 |

—Columbia House edition

| ❏ SO-17102 [B] | Rant 'n' Rave with the Stray Cats | 1983 | $12 |
| ❏ SN-16354 | Rant 'n' Rave with the Stray Cats | 1985 | $10 |

—Budget-line reissue

| ❏ ST-17226 | Rock Therapy | 1986 | $18 |

MOBILE FIDELITY

| ❏ 1-125 | Built for Speed | 1983 | $0 |

—Released only on cassette

STRAYHORN, BILLY

FELSTED

| ❏ 7008 [M] | Billy Strayhorn Septet | 1958 | $100 |
| ❏ 2008 [S] | Billy Strayhorn Septet | 1958 | $75 |

MASTER JAZZ

| ❏ 8116 | Cue for Sax | 197? | $35 |

MERCER

| ❏ LP-1005 [10] | Billy Strayhorn and All-Stars | 1951 | $250 |
| ❏ LP-1001 [10] | Billy Strayhorn Trio | 1951 | $250 |

ROULETTE

| ❏ R-52119 [M] | Live! | 1965 | $25 |
| ❏ SR-52119 [S] | Live! | 1965 | $30 |

SOLID STATE

| ❏ SS-18031 | The Peaceful Side of Billy Strayhorn | 1968 | $35 |

UNITED ARTISTS

| ❏ UAJ-14010 [M] | The Peaceful Side of Billy Strayhorn | 1962 | $40 |
| ❏ UAJS-15010 [S] | The Peaceful Side of Billy Strayhorn | 1962 | $50 |

STRAZZERI, FRANK

CATALYST

| ❏ 7607 | After the Rain | 1976 | $30 |
| ❏ 7623 | Straz | 1977 | $30 |

CREATIVE WORLD

| ❏ ST-3003 | View From Within | 197? | $30 |

DISCOVERY

| ❏ DS-933 | Kat Dancin' | 1987 | $25 |

GLENDALE

| ❏ 6002 | Frames | 197? | $30 |

REVELATION

| ❏ REV-10 | That's Him and This Is New | 1969 | $30 |

SEA BREEZE

| ❏ SB-1007 | Relaxin' | 198? | $30 |

STREET, MEL

GRT

❏ 8010	Mel Street's Greatest Hits	1976	$15
❏ 8004	Smokey Mountain Memories	1975	$15
❏ 8002	Two Way Street	1974	$15

METROMEDIA COUNTRY

| ❏ 5001 | Borrowed Angel | 1972 | $18 |
| ❏ BML1-0281 | The Town Where You Live/ Walk Softly on the Bridges | 1973 | $15 |

POLYDOR

| ❏ PD-1-6144 | Country Soul | 1978 | $12 |
| ❏ PD-1-6114 | Mel Street | 1977 | $12 |

SUNBIRD

❏ 1000	Many Moods of Mel	1980	$15
❏ ST-50102	Some Special Moments	1980	$15
❏ ST-50101	The Very Best of Mel Street	1980	$12

Number	Title	Yr	NM

STREET NOISE
EVOLUTION
❏ 2010	Street Noise	1970	$25

STREET PEOPLE
MUSICOR
❏ MS-3189	Jennifer Tomkins	1970	$25

STREET PLAYERS
ARIOLA AMERICA
❏ SW-50071	Dancin' Fever	1979	$25

STREETDANCER
DHARMA
❏ 807	Rising	197?	$35
FUTURE
❏ 2001	Streetdancer	197?	$35

STREISAND, BARBRA
COLUMBIA
❏ 7-30378 [PS]	Stoney End	1971	$15
❏ 7-30378	Stoney End/Just a Little Lovin' (Early in the Mornin')/Maybe/I Don't Know Where I Stand/If You Could Read My Mind	1971	$15

—Jukebox issue; small hole, plays at 33 1/3 rpm
❏ CL2757 [M]	A Christmas Album	1967	$30
❏ CS9557 [S]	A Christmas Album	1967	$25

—Red "360 Sound Stereo" label
❏ CS9557 [S]	A Christmas Album	1970	$10

—Orange label
❏ PC9557	A Christmas Album	198?	$10

—Reissue with new prefix and bar code
❏ OC45369	A Collection: Greatest Hits.. And More	1989	$18
❏ CS9710	A Happening in Central Park	1968	$18

—Red "360 Sound Stereo" label
❏ CS9710	A Happening in Central Park	1970	$12

—Orange label
❏ PC9710	A Happening in Central Park	197?	$10

—Reissue with new prefix
❏ JS34403	A Star Is Born	1976	$15

—With Kris Kristofferson
❏ KC30792	Barbra Joan Streisand	1971	$18
❏ CQ30792 [Q]	Barbra Joan Streisand	1972	$40
❏ PC30792	Barbra Joan Streisand	197?	$10

—Reissue with new prefix
❏ KC32655	Barbra Streisand…And Other Musical Instruments	1973	$15
❏ PC32655	Barbra Streisand…And Other Musical Instruments	197?	$10

—Reissue with new prefix
❏ PC32801	Barbra Streisand Featuring The Way We Were and All In Love Is Fair	1974	$25

—Original version with this title on spine and label, and no title on front cover
❏ KCS9968	Barbra Streisand's Greatest Hits	1970	$18

—Red "360 Sound Stereo" label
❏ KCS9968	Barbra Streisand's Greatest Hits	1970	$12

—Orange label
❏ PC9968	Barbra Streisand's Greatest Hits	197?	$10

—Reissue with new prefix
❏ JC9968	Barbra Streisand's Greatest Hits	197?	$10

—Another reissue with a new prefix (postdates PC)
❏ FC35679	Barbra Streisand's Greatest Hits, Volume 2	1978	$15
❏ HC45679	Barbra Streisand's Greatest Hits, Volume 2	1980	$30

—Half-speed mastered edition
❏ PC33095	Butterfly	1974	$15

—Original with no bar code
❏ PC33095	Butterfly	198?	$10

—Reissue with bar code
❏ PCQ33095 [Q]	Butterfly	1974	$30
❏ CL2478 [M-DJ]	Color Me Barbra	1966	$250

—Promo only on red vinyl (white label)
❏ CS9278 [S-DJ]	Color Me Barbra	1966	$250

—Promo only on red vinyl (white label)
❏ CL2478 [M]	Color Me Barbra	1966	$18
❏ CL2478 [M]	Color Me Barbra	1966	$250

—Promo only on red vinyl (white label)
❏ CS9278 [S]	Color Me Barbra	1966	$25

—Red "360 Sound Stereo" label
❏ CS9278 [S]	Color Me Barbra	1966	$250

—Promo only on red vinyl (white label)
❏ CS9278 [S]	Color Me Barbra	1970	$12

—Orange label
❏ PC9278	Color Me Barbra	197?	$10

—Reissue with new prefix
❏ QC39480	Emotion	1984	$12
❏ FC36750	Guilty	1980	$12
❏ HC46750	Guilty	1982	$30

—Half-speed mastered edition
❏ CL2547 [M]	Je M'Appelle Barbra	1966	$18
❏ CS9347 [S]	Je M'Appelle Barbra	1966	$25

—Red "360 Sound Stereo" label
❏ CS9347 [S]	Je M'Appelle Barbra	1970	$12

—Orange label
❏ PC9347	Je M'Appelle Barbra	197?	$10

—Reissue with new prefix
❏ PC33815	Lazy Afternoon	1975	$15

—Original with no bar code
❏ PCQ33815 [Q]	Lazy Afternoon	1975	$40
❏ PC33815	Lazy Afternoon	198?	$10

—Reissue with bar code
❏ KC31760	Live Concert at the Forum	1972	$18
❏ CQ31760 [Q]	Live Concert at the Forum	1972	$40
❏ PC31760	Live Concert at the Forum	197?	$10

—Reissue with new prefix
❏ TC37678	Memories	1981	$12
❏ HC47678	Memories	1982	$30

—Half-speed mastered edition
❏ CL2336 [M]	My Name Is Barbra	1965	$25

—Guaranteed High Fidelity" on label
❏ CL2336 [M]	My Name Is Barbra	1966	$15

—360 Sound Mono" on label
❏ CS9136 [S]	My Name Is Barbra	1965	$30

—360 Sound Stereo" in black on label
❏ CS9136 [S]	My Name Is Barbra	1966	$18

—360 Sound Stereo" in white on label
❏ CS9136 [S]	My Name Is Barbra	1970	$12

—Orange label
❏ PC9136	My Name Is Barbra	197?	$10

—Reissue with new prefix

❏ CL2409 [M]	My Name Is Barbra, Two	1965	$18
❏ CS9209 [S]	My Name Is Barbra, Two	1965	$25

—Red "360 Sound Stereo" label
❏ CS9209 [S]	My Name Is Barbra, Two	1970	$12

—Orange label
❏ PC9209	My Name Is Barbra, Two	197?	$10

—Reissue with new prefix
❏ OC40788	One Voice	1987	$12
❏ CL2215 [M]	People	1964	$25

—Guaranteed High Fidelity" on label
❏ CL2215 [M]	People	1966	$15

—360 Sound Mono" on label
❏ CS9015 [S]	People	1964	$30

—360 Sound Stereo" in black on label
❏ CS9015 [S]	People	1966	$18

—360 Sound Stereo" in white on label
❏ CS9015 [S]	People	1970	$12

—Orange label
❏ PC9015	People	197?	$10

—Reissue with new prefix
❏ CL2682 [M]	Simply Streisand	1967	$30
❏ CS9482 [S]	Simply Streisand	1967	$25

—Red "360 Sound Stereo" label
❏ CS9482 [S]	Simply Streisand	1970	$12

—Orange label
❏ PC9482	Simply Streisand	197?	$10

—Reissue with new prefix
❏ JC35375	Songbird	1978	$15
❏ PC35275	Songbird	198?	$10

—Budget-line reissue
❏ KC30378	Stoney End	1971	$18
❏ CQ30378 [Q]	Stoney End	1972	$40
❏ PC30378	Stoney End	197?	$10

—Reissue with new prefix
❏ JC34830	Streisand Superman	1977	$15
❏ PC34830	Streisand Superman	198?	$10

—Budget-line reissue
❏ CL2007 [M]	The Barbra Streisand Album	1963	$25

—Guaranteed High Fidelity" on label
❏ CL2007 [M]	The Barbra Streisand Album	1966	$15

—360 Sound Mono" on label
❏ CS8807 [S]	The Barbra Streisand Album	1963	$30

—360 Sound Stereo" in black on label
❏ CS8807 [S]	The Barbra Streisand Album	1966	$18

—360 Sound Stereo" in white on label
❏ CS8807 [S]	The Barbra Streisand Album	1970	$12

—Orange label
❏ PC8807	The Barbra Streisand Album	197?	$10

—Reissue with new prefix
❏ OC40092	The Broadway Album	1985	$12
❏ AS1779 [DJ]	The Legend of Barbra Streisand	1983	$30

—Promo-only interview LP for "Yentl
❏ A2S1779 [DJ]	The Legend of Barbra Streisand	1983	$150

—Promo-only interview LP for "Yentl
❏ CL2054 [M-DJ]	The Second Barbra Streisand Album	1963	$250

—Promo only on blue vinyl (white label)
❏ CS8854 [S-DJ]	The Second Barbra Streisand Album	1963	$250

—Promo only on blue vinyl (white label)
❏ CL2054 [M]	The Second Barbra Streisand Album	1963	$250

—Promo only on blue vinyl (white label)
❏ CL2054 [M]	The Second Barbra Streisand Album	1963	$25

—Guaranteed High Fidelity" on label
❏ CL2054 [M]	The Second Barbra Streisand Album	1966	$15

—360 Sound Mono" on label
❏ CS8854 [S]	The Second Barbra Streisand Album	1963	$250

—Promo only on blue vinyl (white label)
❏ CS8854 [S]	The Second Barbra Streisand Album	1963	$30

—360 Sound Stereo" in black on label
❏ CS8854 [S]	The Second Barbra Streisand Album	1966	$18

—360 Sound Stereo" in white on label
❏ CS8854 [S]	The Second Barbra Streisand Album	1970	$12

—Orange label
❏ PC8854	The Second Barbra Streisand Album	197?	$10

—Reissue with new prefix
❏ CL2154 [M]	The Third Album	1964	$25

—Guaranteed High Fidelity" on label
❏ CL2154 [M]	The Third Album	1966	$15

—360 Sound Mono" on label
❏ CS8954 [S]	The Third Album	1964	$30

—360 Sound Stereo" in black on label
❏ CS8954 [S]	The Third Album	1966	$18

—360 Sound Stereo" in white on label
❏ CS8954 [S]	The Third Album	1970	$12

—Orange label
❏ PC8954	The Third Album	197?	$10

—Reissue with new prefix
❏ PC32801	The Way We Were	1974	$15

—Revised version; has this title on spine, label and front cover
❏ PCQ32801 [Q]	The Way We Were	1974	$40
❏ HC42801	The Way We Were	1982	$30

—Half-speed mastered edition
❏ JC32801	The Way We Were	197?	$10

—Reissue with new prefix
❏ OC40880	Till I Loved You	1988	$12
❏ FC36258	Wet	1979	$12
❏ CS9816	What About Today?	1969	$18

—Red "360 Sound Stereo" label
❏ CS9816	What About Today?	1970	$12

—Orange label
❏ PC9816	What About Today?	197?	$10

—Reissue with new prefix
❏ JS39152	Yentl	1983	$12

COLUMBIA MASTERWORKS
❏ M33452	Classical Barbra	1976	$15

STRENGTH, "TEXAS" BILL
RE-CAR
❏ 2022	Greatest Hits	1967	$30

STRIDER
WARNER BROS.
❏ BS2722 [B]	Exposed	1973	$30

STRING-A-LONGS, THE
ATCO
❏ SD 33-241 [S]	Wide World Hits	1969	$30
❏ 33-241 [M]	Wide World Hits	1969	$50

—Mono is white label promo only
DOT
❏ DLP-3723 [M]	Great Instrumental Hits	1966	$25
❏ DLP-25723 [S]	Great Instrumental Hits	1966	$30
❏ DLP-3463 [M]	Matilda	1962	$30
❏ DLP-25463 [S]	Matilda	1962	$30

WARWICK
❏ W-2036 [M]	Pick-A-Hit Featuring "Wheels	1961	$50

Number	Title	Yr	NM
❏ W-2036ST [S]	Pick-A-Hit Featuring "Wheels"	1961	$100

STRING CHEESE
WOODEN NICKEL
Number	Title	Yr	NM
❏ WNS-1001 [B]	String Cheese	1971	$30

STRING TRIO OF NEW YORK
BLACK SAINT
Number	Title	Yr	NM
❏ BSR-0048	Area Code 212	198?	$30
❏ BSR-0058	Common Goal	198?	$30
❏ BSR-0031	First String	198?	$30
❏ BSR-0068	Rebirth of a Feeling	1984	$30

STRINGBEAN
STARDAY
Number	Title	Yr	NM
❏ SLP-215 [M]	A Salute to Uncle Dave Macon	1963	$50
❏ SLP-142 [M]	Old Time Pickin' and Singin' with Stringbean	1961	$75
❏ SLP-179 [M]	Stringbean	1962	$50
❏ SLP-260 [M]	Way Back in the Hills of Old Kentucky	1964	$50

STROLLERS, THE
SCORE
Number	Title	Yr	NM
❏ SLP-4026 [M]	Swinging Flute in Hi-Fi	1958	$150

STRONG, BARRETT
CAPITOL
Number	Title	Yr	NM
❏ ST-11376 [B]	Stronghold	1975	$18

STRONG, NOLAN, AND THE DIABLOS
FORTUNE
Number	Title	Yr	NM
❏ LP-8010 [M]	Fortune of Hits	1961	$220
— Purple label, thick vinyl			
❏ LP-8010 [M]	Fortune of Hits	196?	$50
— Yellow label			
❏ LP-8010 [M]	Fortune of Hits	197?	$18
— Purple label, thinner, more flexible vinyl			
❏ LP-8012 [M]	Fortune of Hits, Vol. 2	1962	$220
— Purple label, thick vinyl			
❏ LP-8012 [M]	Fortune of Hits, Vol. 2	196?	$50
— Yellow label			
❏ LP-8012 [M]	Fortune of Hits, Vol. 2	197?	$18
— Purple label, thinner, more flexible vinyl			
❏ LP-8015 [M]	Mind Over Matter	1963	$300
— Purple label, thick vinyl			
❏ LP-8015 [M]	Mind Over Matter	196?	$75
— Yellow label			
❏ LP-8015 [M]	Mind Over Matter	197?	$25
— Purple label, thinner, more flexible vinyl			

STROZIER, FRANK
INNER CITY
Number	Title	Yr	NM
❏ IC-2066	Remember Me	197?	$35
JAZZLAND
Number	Title	Yr	NM
❏ JLP-56 [M]	Long Night	1961	$30
❏ JLP-956 [S]	Long Night	1961	$30
❏ JLP-70 [M]	March of the Siamese Children	1962	$30
❏ JLP-970 [S]	March of the Siamese Children	1962	$30
STEEPLECHASE
Number	Title	Yr	NM
❏ SCS-1066	Remember Me	198?	$30
VEE JAY
Number	Title	Yr	NM
❏ LP-3005 [M]	Fantastic Frank Strozier	1960	$30
❏ SR-3005 [S]	Fantastic Frank Strozier	1960	$40

STRUMMER, JOE
Also see THE CLASH.
EPIC
Number	Title	Yr	NM
❏ E45372	Earthquake Weather	1989	$15

STRUNK, JUD
COLUMBIA
Number	Title	Yr	NM
❏ CS9990	Downeast Viewpoint	1970	$18
HARMONY
Number	Title	Yr	NM
❏ KH32344	Mr. Bojangles and Other Favorites	1973	$12
MCA
Number	Title	Yr	NM
❏ 2309	A Semi-Reformed Tequila Crazed Gypsy	1977	$12
MGM
Number	Title	Yr	NM
❏ SE-4898	Daisy a Day	1973	$15
❏ SE-4790	Jones General Store	1972	$15

STRUNZ & FARAH
MILESTONE
Number	Title	Yr	NM
❏ M-9123	Frontera	1984	$25
❏ M-9136	Guitarras	1985	$25

STRYPER
Christian metal pioneers.

ENIGMA
Number	Title	Yr	NM
❏ D1-73317	In God We Trust	1988	$12
❏ 72077	Soldiers Under Command	1985	$25
— White vinyl			
❏ 72077	Soldiers Under Command	1985	$15
— Black vinyl			
❏ ST-73211	Soldiers Under Command	1985	$12
— Reissue with new number			
❏ ST-73207	The Yellow and Black Attack	1985	$25
— Reissue with eight tracks; blue vinyl, round sleeve			
❏ E-1064	The Yellow and Black Attack	1984	$40
— Original with six tracks; yellow vinyl			
❏ 71064	The Yellow and Black Attack	1984	$25
— Original with six tracks; black vinyl			
❏ ST-73207	The Yellow and Black Attack	1985	$12
— Reissue with eight tracks; black vinyl, square sleeve			
❏ PJAS-73237	To Hell with the Devil	1986	$25
— Cover has band as winged angels in battle			
❏ SEAX-73277	To Hell with the Devil	1986	$30
— Picture disc in plastic sleeve			
❏ PJAS-73237	To Hell with the Devil	1986	$12
— Cover is black			

STUART, MARTY
COLUMBIA
Number	Title	Yr	NM
❏ B6C40302	Marty Stuart	1986	$30
MCA
Number	Title	Yr	NM
❏ 42312	Hillbilly Rock	1989	$18
❏ R170076	Tempted	1990	$30
— Vinyl version available only through BMG Direct Marketing			
RIDGE RUNNER
Number	Title	Yr	NM
❏ RRR 0013	Marty	1978	$30
SUGAR HILL
Number	Title	Yr	NM
❏ 3726	Busy Bee Café	1981	$30

STUART, MARY
BELL
Number	Title	Yr	NM
❏ 1133	Mary Stuart	1973	$25
COLUMBIA
Number	Title	Yr	NM
❏ CL6333 [10]	Joanne Sings	1954	$40

STUART, RORY
CADENCE JAZZ
Number	Title	Yr	NM
❏ CJR-1016	Nightwork	1983	$25
SUNNYSIDE
Number	Title	Yr	NM
❏ SSC-1021	Hurricane	1988	$25

STUARTI, ENZO
MISTLETOE
Number	Title	Yr	NM
❏ MLP-1237	Comin' Home for Christmas	1978	$12

STUBBLEFIELD, JOHN
SOUL NOTE
Number	Title	Yr	NM
❏ SN-1095	Confessin'	1985	$30
STORYVILLE
Number	Title	Yr	NM
❏ 4011	Prelude	197?	$30

STUBO, THORGEIR
CADENCE JAZZ
Number	Title	Yr	NM
❏ CJR-1036	End of a Tune	1988	$25
❏ CJR-1030	Rhythm-A-Ning	1987	$25

STUCKEY, NAT
MCA
Number	Title	Yr	NM
❏ 2184	Independence	1976	$15
PAULA
Number	Title	Yr	NM
❏ LP-2196 [M]	All My Tomorrows	1967	$25
❏ LPS-2196 [S]	All My Tomorrows	1967	$30
❏ LPS-2203	Country Favorites	1968	$30
❏ LP-2192 [M]	Nat Stuckey Sings	1966	$25
❏ LPS-2192 [S]	Nat Stuckey Sings	1966	$30
RCA CAMDEN
Number	Title	Yr	NM
❏ ACL1-0780	In the Ghetto	1974	$12
RCA VICTOR
Number	Title	Yr	NM
❏ LSP-4389	Country Fever	1970	$18
❏ LSP-4635	Forgive Me for Calling You Darling	1972	$18
❏ LSP-4743 [B]	Is It Any Wonder That I Love You	1972	$18
❏ LSP-4123	Keep 'Em Country	1969	$25
❏ LSP-4090	Nat Stuckey Sings	1968	$25
❏ LSP-4226	New Country Roads	1969	$25
❏ LSP-4330	Old Man Willie	1970	$18
❏ LSP-4559	Only a Woman Like You	1971	$18
❏ LSP-4477	She Wakes Me with a Kiss Every Morning	1971	$18
❏ APD1-0080 [Q]	Take Time to Love Her/I Used It All on You	1973	$40
— QuadraDisc; may not exist in regular stereo			
❏ APL1-0541	The Best of Nat Stuckey	1974	$18

STUDDARD, RUBEN
J
Number	Title	Yr	NM
❏ 54639	Soulful	2003	$18

STUERMER, DARYL
GRP
Number	Title	Yr	NM
❏ GR-9573	Steppin' Out	1988	$25

STUFFY AND HIS FROZEN PARACHUTE BAND
PARAMOUNT
Number	Title	Yr	NM
❏ PAS-6070 [B]	Stuffy and His Frozen Parachute Band	1974	$30
— Reissue of Water Street 1002			
WATER STREET
Number	Title	Yr	NM
❏ WST1002 [B]	Stuffy and His Frozen Parachute Band	1974	$75

STURR, JIMMY
STARR
Number	Title	Yr	NM
❏ R-BS-116	Polka Christmas in My Home Town	1979	$18

STUTTGART BAROQUE ENSEMBLE (MARCEL COURAND, CONDUCTOR)
MERCURY LIVING PRESENCE
Number	Title	Yr	NM
❏ SR90402 [S]	Couperin: Les Nations (selections); Rameau: Concerts en Sextuor Nos. 1, 4, 5 and 6	196?	$50
— Maroon label, no "Vendor: Mercury Record Corporation			

STYLE COUNCIL, THE
GEFFEN
Number	Title	Yr	NM
❏ GHS24103	Home and Abroad	1986	$12
❏ GHS24061	Internationalists	1985	$12
❏ GHS4029	My Ever Changing Moods	1984	$12
POLYDOR
Number	Title	Yr	NM
❏ 835785-1	Confessions of a Pop Group	1988	$15
❏ 815277-1 [EP]	Introducing the Style Council	1983	$10
❏ 831443-1	The Cost of Loving	1987	$15

STYLISTICS, THE
AMHERST
Number	Title	Yr	NM
❏ AMH-744	All-Time Classics	1986	$12
❏ AMH-746	Greatest Love Hits	1986	$12
❏ AMH-743	The Best of the Stylistics	1986	$12
❏ AMH-745	The Best of the Stylistics, Vol. 2	1986	$12
AVCO
Number	Title	Yr	NM
❏ AV-69004	Heavy	1974	$18
❏ AV-69001	Let's Put It All Together	1974	$18
❏ 11010	Rockin' Roll Baby	1973	$25
❏ 11006	Round 2: The Stylistics	1972	$25
❏ 69008	Thank You Baby	1975	$18
❏ AV-69005	The Best of the Stylistics	1975	$18
❏ AV-33023	The Stylistics	1971	$25
❏ 69010	You Are Beautiful	1975	$18
H&L
Number	Title	Yr	NM
❏ 69013	Fabulous	1976	$15
❏ 69032	Wonder Woman	1978	$15
MERCURY
Number	Title	Yr	NM
❏ SRM-1-3727	In Fashion	1978	$15
❏ SRM-1-3753	Love Spell	1979	$15
PHILADELPHIA INT'L.
Number	Title	Yr	NM
❏ FZ37955	1982	1982	$12
TSOP
Number	Title	Yr	NM
❏ FZ37458	Closer Than Close	1981	$12
❏ JZ36470	Hurry Up This Way Again	1980	$12

STYX
A&M
Number	Title	Yr	NM
❏ SP-6514	Caught in the Act	1984	$15
❏ SP-3711	Cornerstone	1979	$30
— Silver vinyl pressing, reportedly for fan club members			
❏ SP-3711	Cornerstone	1979	$12
❏ SP-3239	Cornerstone	1984	$10
❏ SP-4604	Crystal Ball	1976	$12
❏ SP-3218	Crystal Ball	1984	$10
❏ 7502153271	Edge of the Century	1990	$25
❏ SP-4559	Equinox	1975	$12
❏ SP-3217	Equinox	1984	$10
❏ SP-3734	Kilroy Was Here	1983	$12
❏ SP-3719	Paradise Theater	1981	$12
❏ SP-3240	Paradise Theater	1984	$10
— 3200 series LPs are reissues			
❏ SP-4724	Pieces of Eight	1978	$12
❏ SP-3224	Pieces of Eight	1984	$10
❏ PR-4724 [PD]	Pieces of Eight	1978	$30
❏ SP-17222 [DJ]	Radio Sampler and Interview Album	1983	$30
— Promo only; with "Kilroy Was Here" album graphic on cover			
❏ SP-17053 [DJ]	Styx Radio Special	1978	$40
— Promo-only box set			
❏ SP-17053 [DJ]	Styx Radio Special	1978	$40
— Promo-only box set			
❏ SP-4637	The Grand Illusion	1977	$12
❏ SP-3223	The Grand Illusion	1984	$10

Number	Title	Yr	NM
❏ SP-8431 [DJ]	The Styx Radio Special	1977	$30
—Promo only; green cover			
MOBILE FIDELITY			
❏ Jan-0026	The Grand Illusion	1979	$30
—Audiophile vinyl			
NAUTILUS			
❏ NR-27	Cornerstone	1982	$25
—Audiophile vinyl			
❏ NR-45	Paradise Theater	198?	$30
—Audiophile vinyl			
❏ NR-15	Pieces of Eight	1981	$30
—Audiophile vinyl			
RCA VICTOR			
❏ AFL1-3597	Best of Styx	1979	$12
❏ AYL1-4756	Best of Styx	1982	$10
❏ AFL1-3594	Lady	1979	$12
—Retitled version of "Styx II"			
❏ AYL1-4233	Lady	1981	$10
—Retitled version of "Styx II"			
❏ AFL1-3596	Miracles	1979	$12
—Retitled version of "Man of Miracles"			
❏ AFL1-3595	Serpent	1979	$12
—Retitled version of "The Serpent Is Rising"			
❏ AFL1-3593	Styx	1979	$12
❏ AYL1-3888	Styx	1980	$10
WOODEN NICKEL			
❏ BWL1-2250	Best of Styx	1977	$15
❏ BWL1-0638	Man of Miracles	1974	$30
—Original version contains "Lies"			
❏ BWL1-0638	Man of Miracles	1974	$25
—Second version contains "Best Thing"			
❏ WNS-1008	Styx	1972	$25
❏ BWL1-1008	Styx	1975	$18
❏ WNS-1012	Styx II	1973	$25
—With die-cut cover			
❏ BWL1-1012	Styx II	1975	$18
❏ BWL1-0287	The Serpent Is Rising	1974	$25

SUB-ZERO BAND, THE

SUB-ZERO

Number	Title	Yr	NM
❏ 1172	The Sub-Zero Band	197?	$250

SUBRAMANIAM, DR. L.

CRUSADERS

Number	Title	Yr	NM
❏ 16003	Blossom	198?	$25
—Audiophile vinyl			
DISCOVERY			
❏ DS-202	Indian Classical Music	198?	$30
MCA			
❏ 5784	Blossom	1986	$25
MILESTONE			
❏ M-9130	Conversations	1985	$25
❏ M-9138	Mani & Co.	1986	$25
❏ M-9114	Spanish Wave	198?	$30
STORYVILLE			
❏ 4075	Garland	198?	$25
TREND			
❏ 524	Fantasy Without Limits	1980	$30

SUDHALTER, DICK

AUDIOPHILE

Number	Title	Yr	NM
❏ AP-159	Friends with Pleasure	1981	$25
STOMP OFF			
❏ SOS-1207	Get Out and Get Under the Moon	1991	$30

SUDLER, MONETTE

INNER CITY

Number	Title	Yr	NM
❏ IC-2062	Time for a Change	197?	$35
STEEPLECHASE			
❏ SCS-1087	Brighter Days for You	198?	$30
❏ SCS-1102	Live in Europe	198?	$30
❏ SCS-1062	Time for a Change	198?	$30

SUEDE

WARNER BROS.

Number	Title	Yr	NM
❏ SUELPX001 [B]	Bloodsports	2013	$30

SUGAR
Featuring BOB MOULD, formerly of HUSKER DU.

RYKO ANALOGUE

Number	Title	Yr	NM
❏ RALP10300	File Under: Easy Listening	1994	$15

SUGAR BEARS, THE
KIM CARNES was in this group.

BIG TREE

Number	Title	Yr	NM
❏ BTS-2009	Introducing the Sugar Bears	1972	$25

SUGAR CREEK

METROMEDIA

Number	Title	Yr	NM
❏ MD1020	Please Tell a Friend	1969	$75

Number	Title	Yr	NM

SUGAR HILL GANG

SUGAR HILL

Number	Title	Yr	NM
❏ SH249 [B]	8th Wonder	1981	$25
❏ SH9206 [B]	Livin' in the Fast Lane	1984	$18
❏ SH245 [B]	Sugar Hill Gang	1980	$30

SUGARCUBES, THE

ELEKTRA

Number	Title	Yr	NM
❏ 60860	Here Today, Tomorrow, Next Week!	1989	$15
❏ 60860 [DJ]	Here Today, Tomorrow, Next Week!	1989	$18
—White label promo on audiophile vinyl			
❏ 60801	Life's Too Good	1988	$15
❏ 60801 [DJ]	Life's Too Good	1988	$18
—White label promo on audiophile vinyl			

SUGARLOAF

BRUT

Number	Title	Yr	NM
❏ 6006	I Got a Song	1973	$18
CLARIDGE			
❏ 1000	Don't Call Us, We'll Call You	1975	$15
LIBERTY			
❏ LST-11010 [B]	Spaceship Earth	1971	$25
❏ LST-7640	Sugarloaf	1970	$25

SUGARPLUM FAIRY AND CAST, THE

RCA CAMDEN

Number	Title	Yr	NM
❏ CAL-1101 [M]	'Twas the Night Before Christmas	1968	$18
❏ CAS-1101 [S]	'Twas the Night Before Christmas	1968	$15

SUICIDAL TENDENCIES

CAROLINE

Number	Title	Yr	NM
❏ CAROL1336	Join the Army	1987	$18
EPIC			
❏ 6E45244	Controlled by Hatred/Feel Like Shit...Deja Vu	1989	$15
❏ FE44288	How Will I Laugh Tomorrow When I Can't Even Smile Today	1988	$15
❏ E45389	Lights...Camera...Revolution	1990	$15
FRONTIER			
❏ 4604-1-L	Suicidal Tendencies	198?	$18
❏ 1011	Suicidal Tendencies	1983	$18

SUICIDE

ANTILLES

Number	Title	Yr	NM
❏ AN-7080 [B]	Alan Vega-Martin Rev	1980	$18
RED STAR			
❏ RS-1 [B]	Suicide	1977	$30
❏ RED-800	Suicide	1980	$14
—Reissue of RS-1			
SUPERIOR VIADUCT			
❏ SV109 [B]	Suicide	2016	$30
❏ SV110 [B]	Suicide - Alan Vega, Martin Rev	2016	$30
WAX TRAX!			
❏ 7072 [B]	A Way of Life	1989	$25

SUICIDE COMMANDOS

BLANK

Number	Title	Yr	NM
❏ 002	The Suicide Commandos Make a Record	1977	$30
TWIN/TONE			
❏ TTR7906	The Commandos Commit Suicide Dance Concert	1979	$85
—Limited edition of 1,000 copies			

SUKMAN, HARRY

LIBERTY

Number	Title	Yr	NM
❏ LRP-3135 [M]	Command Performance	1959	$25
❏ LST-7135 [S]	Command Performance	1959	$30
❏ LRP-3005 [M]	Nightfall	1955	$25
❏ LRP-3151 [M]	The Franz Liszt Story	1960	$25
❏ LST-7151 [S]	The Franz Liszt Story	1960	$30

SULIEMAN, IDREES

NEW JAZZ

Number	Title	Yr	NM
❏ NJLP-8202 [M]	Roots	1958	$175
—Purple label			
❏ NJLP-8202 [M]	Roots	1958	$250
—Yellow label			
❏ NJLP-8202 [M]	Roots	1965	$175
—Blue label, trident logo at right			
STEEPLECHASE			
❏ SCS-1202	Bird's Grass	198?	$30
❏ SCS-1052	Now Is the Time	198?	$30

SULLIVAN, CHARLES

INNER CITY

Number	Title	Yr	NM
❏ IC-1012	Genesis	1975	$35

Number	Title	Yr	NM

SULLIVAN, FRANK

REVELATION

Number	Title	Yr	NM
❏ 34	First Impressions	1981	$25

SULLIVAN, IRA

ATLANTIC

Number	Title	Yr	NM
❏ 1476 [M]	Horizons	1967	$30
❏ SD-1476 [S]	Horizons	1967	$35
DELMARK			
❏ DL-402 [M]	Blue Stroll	1961	$30
❏ DS-402 [S]	Blue Stroll	1961	$40
❏ DS-422	Nicky's Tune	1970	$50
DISCOVERY			
❏ 873	Horizons	1983	$30
—Reissue of Atlantic SD 1476			
FLYING FISH			
❏ FF-27075	Ira Sullivan	198?	$25
—Reissue			
❏ FF-075	Ira Sullivan	1978	$30
GALAXY			
❏ 5137	Multimedia	198?	$30
❏ 5114	Peace	1979	$30
HORIZON			
❏ SP-706	Ira Sullivan	1976	$30
MUSE			
❏ MR-5242	Ira Sullivan Does It All!	1981	$35
PAUSA			
❏ 7169	Strings Attached	1985	$30
STASH			
❏ ST-208	The Incredible Ira Sullivan	1980	$50
VEE JAY			
❏ VJS-3003 [S]	Bird Lives!	198?	$30
—Reissue with new prefix on thinner vinyl			
❏ LP-3003 [M]	Bird Lives!	1960	$50
❏ SR-3003 [S]	Bird Lives!	1960	$75

SULLIVAN, JIM

MERCURY

Number	Title	Yr	NM
❏ MG-21137 [M]	Sitar Beat	1967	$25
❏ SR-61137 [S]	Sitar Beat	1967	$25

SULLIVAN, JOE

CAPITOL

Number	Title	Yr	NM
❏ T636 [M]	Classics in Jazz	1955	$85
DOWN HOME			
❏ MGD-2 [M]	Mr. Piano Man: The Music of Joe Sullivan	1956	$50
EPIC			
❏ LG1003 [10]	Joe Sullivan Plays Fats Waller Compositions	1954	$175
FOLKWAYS			
❏ FJ-2851	Joe Sullivan Piano	197?	$30
RIVERSIDE			
❏ RLP 12-202 [M]	New Solos by an Old Master	1955	$300
TIME-LIFE			
❏ STL-J-27	Giants of Jazz	1982	$50
VERVE			
❏ MGV-1002 [M]	Mr. Piano Man: The Music of Joe Sullivan	1957	$175
❏ V-1002 [M]	Mr. Piano Man: The Music of Joe Sullivan	1961	$25

SULLIVAN, MAXINE, AND BOB WILBER

MONMOUTH-EVERGREEN

Number	Title	Yr	NM
❏ 6917	Bob & Maxine	1969	$35
❏ 6919	Maxine Sullivan and Bob Wilber	1969	$30

SULLIVAN, MAXINE

ATLANTIC

Number	Title	Yr	NM
❏ 81783	Together	1987	$25
AUDIOPHILE			
❏ AP-193	Good Morning, Life!	1986	$25
❏ AP-185	It Was Great Fun	1984	$25
❏ AP-167	Maxine	1985	$25
❏ AP-154	Maxine Sullivan and the Ike Isaacs Trio	198?	$25
❏ AP-128	We Just Couldn't Say Goodbye	1979	$25
CIRCLE			
❏ 47	Maxine Sullivan and John Kirby 1940	198?	$25
CONCORD JAZZ			
❏ CJ-288	Uptown	1986	$25
EVEREST ARCHIVE OF FOLK & JAZZ			
❏ 307	Maxine Sullivan with Jack Teagarden	197?	$25
MONMOUTH-EVERGREEN			
❏ 7038	Sullivan, Shakespeare and Hyman	197?	$35

Number	Title	Yr	NM
PERIOD			
❏ SPL-1207 [M]	Maxine Sullivan, Volume 2	1956	$50
❏ RL-1909 [M]	Maxine Sullivan 1956	1956	$50
STASH			
❏ ST-257	Maxine Sullivan Sings the Music of Burton Lane	1986	$25
❏ ST-244	The Great Songs from the Cotton Club by Harold Arlen and Ted Koehler	1985	$25

SULLIVAN, PAT, JAZZ ORCHESTRA

Number	Title	Yr	NM
PJS			
❏ WRC1-2536	Stairway Down to the Stars	1985	$25

SUMAC, YMA

Number	Title	Yr	NM
CAPITOL			
❏ ST1169 [S]	Fuego del Andes	1959	$50
❏ T1169 [M]	Fuego del Andes	1959	$40
❏ L423 [10]	Inca Taqui	1953	$150
❏ T770 [M]	Legend of the Jivaro	1956	$50
— Turquoise label			
❏ T770 [M]	Legend of the Jivaro	1963	$25
— Black colorband label, "Capitol" at top			
❏ SM-299 [M]	Legend of the Sun Virgin	197?	$15
❏ L299 [10]	Legend of the Sun Virgin	1952	$120
❏ T299 [M]	Legend of the Sun Virgin	1955	$50
❏ M-11892	Mambo!	1979	$15
❏ H564 [10]	Mambo!	1954	$150
❏ T564 [M]	Mambo!	1955	$50
❏ H244 [10]	Voice of the Xtabay	1952	$150
❏ DW684 [R]	Voice of the Xtabay and Inca Taqui	1963	$18
❏ SM-684	Voice of the Xtabay and Inca Taqui	197?	$15
— On this reissue, Side 1 is in mono			
❏ W684 [M]	Voice of the Xtabay and Inca Taqui	1955	$50
— Gray label			
❏ W684 [M]	Voice of the Xtabay and Inca Taqui	1963	$25
— Black colorband label, "Capitol" at top			
CORAL			
❏ CRL56058 [10]	Presenting Yma Sumac	1952	$120
LONDON			
❏ XPS608	Miracles	1972	$25

SUMMER, DONNA

Number	Title	Yr	NM
ATLANTIC			
❏ 81987	Another Place and Time	1989	$15
CASABLANCA			
❏ NBLP7150	Bad Girls	1979	$15
❏ 822557-1	Bad Girls	1984	$12
❏ NBLP7038	Four Seasons of Love	1976	$12
❏ NBLP7201	Greatest Hits, Vol. 1	1979	$10
❏ NBLP7202	Greatest Hits, Vol. 2	1979	$10
❏ 822559-1	Greatest Hits, Vol. 2	1984	$10
❏ NBLP7056	I Remember Yesterday	1977	$12
❏ NBLP7119	Live and More	1978	$15
❏ 811123-1	Live and More	1985	$12
❏ NBLP7078	Once Upon a Time...	1977	$15
❏ NBLP7191	On the Radio -- Greatest Hits Vols. 1 and 2	1979	$15
❏ 822558-1	On the Radio -- Greatest Hits Vols. 1 and 2	1984	$12
❏ NBPIX7119 [PD]	The Best of Live and More	1979	$25
❏ 822560-1	Walk Away	1984	$10
❏ NBLP7244	Walk Away -- Collector's Edition (The Best of 1977-1980)	1980	$12
EPIC			
❏ E269910	Live and More Encore	1999	$18
GEFFEN			
❏ GHS24102	All Systems Go	1987	$12
❏ GHS24040 [DJ]	Cats Without Claws	1984	$18
— Promo only on Quiex II vinyl			
❏ GHS24040	Cats Without Claws	1984	$12
❏ GHS2005	Donna Summer	1982	$12
❏ GHS2000	The Wanderer	1980	$12
MERCURY			
❏ 812265-1	She Works Hard for the Money	1983	$12
❏ 826144-1	The Summer Collection	1985	$12
OASIS			
❏ OCLP5004	A Love Trilogy	1976	$15
❏ OCLP5003	Love to Love You Baby	1975	$15
— Add 50% if poster is included			
❏ 822792-1	Love to Love You Baby	1985	$10

SUMMER SOUNDS, THE

Number	Title	Yr	NM
LAUREL			
❏ 90973	Up Down	196?	$1000

SUMMERHILL

Number	Title	Yr	NM
TETRAGRAMMATON			
❏ T-114	Summerhill	1969	$30

SUMMERLIN, ED

Number	Title	Yr	NM
ECCLESIA			
❏ ER-101 [M]	Liturgical Jazz	1959	$75

SUMMERS, ANDREW ROWAN

Number	Title	Yr	NM
FOLKWAYS			
❏ FA-2348 [M]	Andrew Rowan Summers	1957	$35
❏ FA-2002 [10]	Christmas Carols	195?	$75
❏ FC7502 [M]	Christmas Carols	196?	$20
❏ FA-2361 [M]	Hymns and Carols	195?	$35
❏ FA-2021 [10]	Seeds of Love	1951	$50
❏ FP-21 [10]	Seeds of Love	1951	$50
❏ FA-2044 [10]	The Faulse Lady	1954	$75
❏ FP-44 [10]	The Faulse Lady	1954	$75
❏ FA-2041 [10]	The Lady Gay	1954	$75
❏ FP-41 [10]	The Lady Gay	1954	$75
❏ FA-2364 [M]	The Unquiet Grave and Other American Tragic Ballads	195?	$30

SUMMERS, ANDY, AND ROBERT FRIPP

Number	Title	Yr	NM
A&M			
❏ SP9-5011	Bewitched	1984	$12
❏ SP-4913	I Advance Masked	1982	$12
❏ SP-17299 [DJ]	Speak Out Interview	1982	$30
— Issued in generic cover with sticker			
❏ SP-17299 [DJ]	Speak Out Interview	1982	$30
— Issued in generic cover with sticker			

SUMMERS, ANDY

Number	Title	Yr	NM
MCA			
❏ 42007	XYZ	1987	$12
PRIVATE MUSIC			
❏ 2039-1-P	Mysterious Barricades	1988	$12

SUMMERS, BILL

Number	Title	Yr	NM
PRESTIGE			
❏ 10103	Cayenne	1977	$35
❏ 10102	Feel the Heat	1977	$35
❏ 10105	Straight to the Bank	1978	$35

SUN, JOE

Number	Title	Yr	NM
ELEKTRA			
❏ 60010	I Ain't Honky Tonkin' No More	1982	$10
OVATION			
❏ 1755	Livin' on Honky Tonk Time	1980	$12
❏ 1734	Old Flames	1978	$12
❏ 1743	Out of Your Mind	1979	$12

SUN RA

Number	Title	Yr	NM
A&M			
❏ SP-5260 [B]	Blue Delight	1989	$175
ABC IMPULSE!			
❏ AS-9245 [B]	Angels and Demons at Play	1974	$300
❏ AS-9294	Art Forms from Dimensions Tomorrow	1974	$0
— Canceled?			
❏ AS-9255 [B]	Astro Black	1973	$300
❏ AS-9239 [B]	Atlantis	1973	$300
❏ AS-9291	Cosmic Tones for Mental Therapy	1974	$0
— Canceled?			
❏ AS-9297	Crystal Spears	1974	$0
— Canceled?			
❏ AS-9296	Cymbals	1974	$0
— Canceled?			
❏ AS-9270	Fate in a Pleasant Mood	1974	$250
❏ ASD-9265 [B]	Jazz in Silhouette	1974	$1200
❏ AS-9295	Monorails and Satellites	1974	$0
— Canceled?			
❏ AS-9289	My Brother the Wind	1974	$0
— Canceled?			
❏ AS-9287	Night of the Purple Moon	1974	$0
— Canceled?			
❏ AS-9293	Other Planes of There	1974	$0
— Canceled?			
❏ ASD-9298	Pathways to Unknown Worlds	1975	$300
❏ AS-9288	Planet Earth	1974	$0
— Canceled?			
❏ AS-9290	Sound Sound Pleasure	1974	$0
— Canceled?			
❏ AS-9271	Super Sonic Sounds	1974	$250
❏ ASD-9276 [B]	The Bad and the Beautiful	1974	$300
❏ AS-9243	The Magic City	1973	$250
❏ AS-9242 [B]	The Nubians of Plutonia	1974	$1200
❏ 1974 [B]	Welcome to Saturn	1974	$300
❏ ASD-9292	We Travel the Spaceways	1974	$300
— May only exist as a promo or test pressing			
AFFINITY			
❏ AFF10	The Solar-Myth Approach Volume I	1978	$300
❏ AFF76	The Solar-Myth Approach Volume II	1978	$300
BASF			
❏ 20748	It's After the End of the World	1971	$300
BLACK LION			
❏ 106	Pictures of Infinity	197?	$300

Number	Title	Yr	NM
BLACK SAINT			
❏ 120111	Hours After	1990	$175
❏ 120101	Reflections in Blue	1987	$250
BLUE THUMB			
❏ BTS-41 [Q]	Space Is the Place	1973	$175
— All copies are quad			
DELMARK			
❏ DS-414 [R]	Sound of Joy	1968	$300
❏ DL-411 [M]	Sun Song	1967	$300
❏ DS-411 [R]	Sun Song	1967	$300
— Reissue of Transition 10			
DIW			
❏ DIWP-2 [PD]	Cosmo Omnibus Imaginable Illusion: Live at Pit-Inn	1988	$300
— Picture disc; limited to under 1,000 copies			
❏ 8024 [B]	Cosmo Omnibus Imaginable Illusion: Live at Pit-Inn	1988	$250
ESP-DISK'			
❏ S-1045 [S]	Nothing Is	1969	$300
❏ 1014 [M]	The Heliocentric Worlds of Sun Ra, Volume 1	1966	$300
❏ S-1014 [S]	The Heliocentric Worlds of Sun Ra, Volume 1	1966	$300
— Reproductions exist of this LP			
❏ 1017 [M]	The Heliocentric Worlds of Sun Ra, Volume 2	1966	$300
— With voices overdubbed on "The Sun Myth			
❏ S-1017 [S]	The Heliocentric Worlds of Sun Ra, Volume 2	1966	$300
— With voices overdubbed on "The Sun Myth			
❏ 1017 [M]	The Heliocentric Worlds of Sun Ra, Volume 2	1966	$300
— Without voices overdubbed on "The Sun Myth			
❏ S-1017 [S]	The Heliocentric Worlds of Sun Ra, Volume 2	1966	$300
— Without voices overdubbed on "The Sun Myth			
HAT ART			
❏ 2017	Sunrise in Different Directions	1986	$250
HAT HUT			
❏ 17	Sunrise in Different Directions	1980	$250
HORO			
❏ HDP-25/26	New Steps	1978	$250
❏ HDP-23/24	Other Voices, Other Blues	1978	$300
❏ HDP-19/20	Unity	1978	$300
IAI			
❏ 373850	Solo Piano Volume 1	197?	$300
❏ 373858	St. Louis Blues	1978	$300
INNER CITY			
❏ IC-1020	Cosmos	1978	$300
— Original edition; reproductions exist			
❏ IC-1039	Live at Montreux	1978	$300
JIHAD			
❏ 1968 [S]	A Black Mass	1968	$500
— Black and white cover			
❏ 1968 [S]	A Black Mass	1968	$800
— Color cover			
LEO			
❏ LR-154	Love in Outer Space: Live in Utrecht	1988	$250
MELTDOWN			
❏ MPA-1	John Cage Meets Sun Ra	1987	$250
PHILLY JAZZ			
❏ PJ-666	Lanquidity	1978	$300
— Reproductions exist			
❏ PJ-1007	Of Mythic Worlds	1980	$300
PRAXIS			
❏ CM110	Live at Praxis 84 Volume 3	1985	$250
❏ CM108	Live at Praxis Volume 1	1984	$300

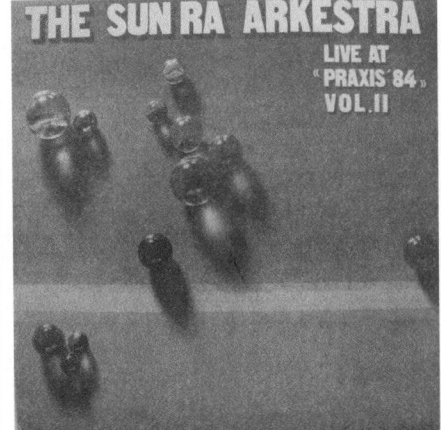

Number	Title	Yr	NM
❏ CM109 [B]	Live at Praxis Volume 2	1985	$100

Number	Title	Yr	NM
❏ CM106	Sun Ra Arkestra Meets Salah Ragab in Egypt	1983	$300

RECOMMENDED

Number	Title	Yr	NM
❏ RR-11	Nuits de la Fondation Maeght Volume I	1981	$300
—Reissue of Shandar 10.001; plays at 45 rpm			

ROUNDER

Number	Title	Yr	NM
❏ 3035	Strange Celestial Road	1982	$300
—Reproductions exist			

SATURN

Number	Title	Yr	NM
❏ A/B-1984SG-9 [B]	A Fireside Chat with Lucifer	1984	$1200
❏ 19841 [B]	A Fireside Chat with Lucifer	1984	$500
❏ SR-9956-2/O/P [M]	Angels and Demons at Play	1965	$800
—Red label; metallic gold cover			
❏ LP-407 [M]	Angels and Demons at Play	196?	$400
—Chicago address on label; reproductions exist			
❏ SR-9956 [M]	Art Forms of Dimensions Tomorrow	1965	$1200
—Red label; reproductions exist			
❏ LP-404 [M]	Art Forms of Dimensions Tomorrow	1969	$500
—Chicago address on label; reproductions exist			
❏ ESR-507 [S]	Atlantis	1969	$800
—El Saturn" label			
❏ 527-529-530 [B]	A Tonal View of Times Tomorrow		$2000
❏ 10480 [B]	Aurora Borealis	1980	$500
❏ 123180 [B]	Beyond the Purple Star Zone	1981	$500
❏ C/D-1984SG-9 [B]	Celestial Love	1984	$1300
❏ 19842 [B]	Celestial Love	1984	$500
❏ ESR-520 [B]	Continuation	1969	$800
❏ LP-520 [B]	Continuation	1970	$500
❏ LP-408 [S]	Cosmic Tones for Mental Therapy	1967	$1200
—Red label; Sun Ra art on cover; reproductions exist			
❏ KH-2772 [S]	Cosmic Tones for Mental Therapy	196?	$800
—Blue cover; Chicago address on label			
❏ 1981 [B]	Dance of Innocent Passion	1981	$1200
❏ 72579 [B]	Days of Happiness		$1500
—hand pasted sleeve			
❏ LP-485 [B]	Deep Purple	1973	$1000
❏ LP-538 [B]	Discipline 27-II	1973	$750
❏ CMIJ78 [B]	Disco 3000	1978	$750
❏ SR-9956-2/A/B [M]	Fate in a Pleasant Mood	1965	$800
—Red label; reproductions exist			
❏ LP-202 [M]	Fate in a Pleasant Mood	196?	$400
—Chicago address on label			
❏ 72579 [B]	God Is More Than Love Can Ever Be	1979	$500
❏ 13188III/12988II [B]	Hidden Fire 1	1988	$400
❏ 13088A/12988B [B]	Hidden Fire 2	1988	$400
❏ 101185 [B]	Hiroshima	1985	$500
❏ ESR-508 [S]	Holiday for Soul-Dance	1969	$600
—El Saturn" label; reproductions exist			
❏ LP-849 [B]	Horizon	1974	$500
❏ 1217718 [B]	Horizon	1974	$500
❏ 6680 [B]	I, Pharaoh	1980	$750
—El Saturn" label			
❏ LP-203 [M]	Interstellar Low Ways	1969	$750
—Chicago address on label; reproductions exist			
❏ 144000 [B]	Invisible Shield	197?	$1200
❏ LP-5786 [M]	Jazz in Silhouette	1958	$1500
—Yellow label			
❏ LP-205 [M]	Jazz in Silhouette	1967	$500
—Red label			
❏ LP-205 [M]	Jazz in Silhouette	1967	$300
—Green label			
❏ 1984A/B [B]	Just Friends	1984	$300
❏ MS87976 [B]	Live at Montreux	1976	$750
❏ 1272 [B]	Live in Egypt 1	1973	$800
❏ 19783 [B]	Media Dream	1978	$1000
❏ 1978 [B]	Media Dream	1978	$500
❏ LP-509 [M]	Monorails and Satellites	1968	$800
—El Saturn" label; reproductions exist			
❏ LP-519 [S]	Monorails and Satellites, Vol. II	1969	$800
—El Saturn" label			
❏ ESR-1970 [B]	My Brother the Wind	1970	$750
❏ ESR-521 [B]	My Brother the Wind	1970	$750
—Reproductions exist			
❏ LP-521 [B]	My Brother the Wind	197?	$500
❏ SRA-2000 [B]	My Brother the Wind, Volume II	1971	$750
❏ ESR-523 [B]	My Brother the Wind, Volume II	1971	$750
—Reproductions exist			
❏ 77771	Nidhamu	197?	$300
❏ 7771	Nidhamu	197?	$300
❏ 1982 [B]	Nuclear War	1982	$300
❏ IX SR72881 [B]	Oblique Parallax	1981	$250
❏ 91379 [B]	Omniverse	1979	$1200
❏ 101679 [B]	On Jupiter	1979	$800
—El Saturn" label			
❏ KH-98766 [M]	Other Planes of There	1966	$1000
—Red label; reproductions exist			
❏ LP-206 [M]	Other Planes of There	1967	$800

Number	Title	Yr	NM
—Chicago address on label			
❏ 61674 [B]	Out Beyond the Kingdom Of	1974	$750
❏ 9121385	Outer Reach Intensity-Energy	1985	$250
❏ LP-530	Outer Spaceways Incorporated	1974	$250
—Chicago address on label			
❏ LP-530	Outer Spaceways Incorporated	1974	$350
—Philadelphia address on label			
❏ LP-564	Pathways to Unknown Worlds	1974	$0
—Canceled?			
❏ IX/1983-220 [B]	Ra to the Rescue	1983	$350
❏ SR-9956-2-M/N [M]	Rocket #9 Take Off For the Planet Venus	1966	$500
—Cover has "burning candle" logo			
❏ GH-9954-E/F[M]	Secrets of the Sun	1965	$1500
—Red label			
❏ LP-208 [M]	Secrets of the Sun	196?	$1000
—Chicago address on label			
❏ 11179 [B]	Sleeping Beauty	1979	$800
❏ LP-747 [B]	Some Blues But Not the Kind That's Blue	1977	$250
❏ 1014077 [B]	Some Blues But Not the Kind That's Blue	1977	$750
❏ 101477 [B]	Some Blues But Not the Kind That's Blue	1977	$750
❏ 7877	Somewhere Over the Rainbow	1977	$250
❏ LP-487 [B]	Song of the Stargazers	1979	$300
❏ 6161 [B]	Song of the Stargazers	1979	$2000
❏ 19782 [B]	Sound Mirror	1978	$750
❏ LP-512 [B]	Sound Sun Pleasure!!	1970	$600
—Reproductions exist			
❏ LP-527 [B]	Space Probe	197?	$750
❏ 14200-A/B [B]	Space Probe	197?	$600
❏ LP-502 [S]	Strange Strings	1967	$800
—Red label; reproductions exist			
❏ 92074 [B]	Sub Underground	1974	$600
❏ IHNY-165 [B]	Sun Ra and His Arkestra Featuring Pharoah Sanders and Black Harold	1976	$750
❏ SR-9956-11A/B [M]	Sun Ra Visits Planet Earth	1966	$800
—Red label; reproductions exist			
❏ LP-207 [M]	Sun Ra Visits Planet Earth	1968	$500
—Minneapolis address on label			
❏ LP-207 [M]	Sun Ra Visits Planet Earth	196?	$600
—El Saturn" label			
❏ SRLP-0216 [M]	Super-Sonic Jazz	1957	$2000
—Blank cover			
❏ SRLP-0216 [M]	Super-Sonic Jazz	1957	$3000
—Silk-screened cover			
❏ SRLP-0216 [M]	Super-Sonic Jazz	1958	$1250
—Purple "keyboard" cover			
❏ SRLP-0216 [M]	Super-Sonic Jazz	1965	$800
—Blue or green cover			
❏ LP-204 [M]	Super-Sonic Sounds	1968	$750
—Blue or green cover; Chicago address on label			
❏ LP-772 [B]	Taking a Chance on Chances	1977	$500
❏ 92074 [B]	Temple U		$750
—hand drawn sleeve			
❏ 81774 [B]	The Antique Blacks	1974	$700
❏ ESR-532 [B]	The Bad and the Beautiful	196?	$1000
—Chicago address on label; reproductions exist			
❏ LP-529 [B]	The Invisible Shield	1974	$750
—Philadelphia address on label			
❏ LP-529	The Invisible Shield	1974	$250
—Chicago address on label			
❏ SR-9956-11E/F[M]	The Lady with the Golden Stockings	1966	$600
—Cover is generic and says "Tonal Views of Times Tomorrow			
❏ LPB-711 [M]	The Magic City	1966	$800
—Red label; reproductions exist			
❏ LP-403 [M]	The Magic City	196?	$600
—Chicago address on label			
❏ LP-522 [B]	The Night of the Purple Moon	197?	$400
—Reproductions exist			
❏ LP-406 [M]	The Nubians of Plutonia	1969	$400
—Chicago address on label; reproductions exist			
❏ LP-771	The Soul Vibrations of Man	1977	$250
❏ ESR-5000 [B]	Universe in Blue	1972	$750
❏ LP-200 [B]	Universe in Blue	197?	$500
❏ 91780 [B]	Voice of the Eternal Tomorrow	1980	$350
❏ HK-5445 [M]	We Travel the Spaceways	1966	$800
—Red label			
❏ LP-409 [M]	We Travel the Spaceways	196?	$600
—El Saturn" label; reproductions exist			
❏ LP-539 [B]	What's New?	197?	$1500
❏ 752 [B]	What's New?	197?	$800
❏ 52375 [B]	What's New?	1975	$500
❏ LP-405	When Angels Speak of Love	196?	$300
❏ LP-1966 [B]	When Angels Speak of Love	1966	$1200
—Red cover with a "sideways" image of Sun Ra			
❏ 101485	When Spaceships Appear	1985	$300
❏ LP-402 [M]	When Sun Comes Out	196?	$400
❏ LP-2066 [M]	When Sun Comes Out	1963	$400

Number	Title	Yr	NM
—Blank cover			
❏ LP-2066 [M]	When Sun Comes Out	1963	$500
—Green cover with yellow sun			
❏ LP-2066 [M]	When Sun Comes Out	1963	$500
—Black ameboid figure on cover			
❏ LP-2066 [M]	When Sun Comes Out	1967	$300
—Spaceman at piano cover; reproductions exist			

SATURN/RECOMMENDED

Number	Title	Yr	NM
❏ SRRD-1 [B]	Cosmo Sun Connection	1985	$800

SAVOY

Number	Title	Yr	NM
❏ MG-12169 [M]	The Futuristic Sounds of Sun Ra	1961	$300

SAVOY JAZZ

Number	Title	Yr	NM
❏ SJL-1141	We Are in the Future	1984	$300

SHANDAR

Number	Title	Yr	NM
❏ SR 10.001	Nuits de la Fondation Maeght Volume I	1971	$300
❏ SR 10.003	Nuits de la Fondation Maeght Volume II	1971	$300

SWEET EARTH

Number	Title	Yr	NM
❏ SER1003	The Other Side of the Sun	1979	$300
—Reproductions exist			

THOTH INTERGALACTIC

Number	Title	Yr	NM
❏ KH-2772 [S]	Cosmic Tones for Mental Therapy	1969	$300
❏ KH-1272	Live in Egypt 1	1973	$6300
❏ 7771	Nidhamu	197?	$300
❏ KH-98766 [M]	Other Planes of There	1969	$300
❏ KH-5472 [M]	Strange Strings	196?	$300
❏ LPB-711 [M]	The Magic City	1969	$300
❏ IR-1972	The Night of the Purple Moon	1970	$300

TOTAL ENERGY

Number	Title	Yr	NM
❏ NER3029	It Is Forbidden	2001	$175
—Green vinyl			
❏ NER3026	Life Is Beautiful	1999	$175
❏ NER3021	Outer Space Employment Agency	1999	$175

TRANSITION

Number	Title	Yr	NM
❏ TLP-10 [M]	Jazz by Sun Ra	1957	$2500
—With booklet (deduct 1/5 if missing)			

SUNDAY FUNNIES, THE

RARE EARTH

Number	Title	Yr	NM
❏ RS-538	Benediction	1972	$15
❏ RS-526 [B]	The Sunday Funnies	1971	$18

SUNDAYS, THE

DGC

Number	Title	Yr	NM
❏ 24277 [B]	Reading, Writing and Arithmetic	1990	$80

SUNDBOM, LARS "SUMPEN

GHB

Number	Title	Yr	NM
❏ GHB-148	Hemma Hos Sumpen	1979	$25

SUNDOWNERS, THE

LIBERTY

Number	Title	Yr	NM
❏ LRP-3269 [M]	Folk Songs for the Rich	1962	$25
❏ LST-7269 [S]	Folk Songs for the Rich	1962	$30

SUNGLOWS, THE
See SUNNY AND THE SUNLINERS.

SUNKEL, PHIL

ABC-PARAMOUNT

Number	Title	Yr	NM
❏ ABC-225 [M]	Gerry Mulligan and Bob Brookmeyer Play Phil Sunkel's Jazz Concerto Grosso	1958	$75
❏ ABCS-225 [S]	Gerry Mulligan and Bob Brookmeyer Play Phil Sunkel's Jazz Concerto Grosso	1958	$50
❏ ABC-136 [M]	Jazz Band	1956	$100

SUNNA

ASTRALWERKS

Number	Title	Yr	NM
❏ ASW49708-1	One Minute Science	2000	$30

SUNNY AND THE SUNLINERS

KEY-LOC

Number	Title	Yr	NM
❏ 3008 [M]	Adelante	196?	$30
❏ 3005 [M]	A Little Brown-Eyed Soul	196?	$30
❏ 3004 [M]	Canta Sunny	196?	$30
❏ 3002 [M]	No Te Chifles	196?	$30
❏ 3009 [M]	Sky High	196?	$30
❏ 3001 [M]	Smile Now, Cry Later	196?	$30
❏ 3003 [M]	Sunny and the Sunliners Live in Hollywood	196?	$30
❏ 3010 [M]	The Missing Link	196?	$30
❏ 3006 [M]	This Is My Band	196?	$30
❏ 3007 [M]	Versatile	196?	$30

Number	Title	Yr	NM
SUNGLOW			
❏ SLP-101 [M]	Sunny Ozuna and the Sunglows	1963	$150
—As "The Sunglows			
❏ SLP-102 [M]	The Fabulous Sunglows	1964	$150
—As "The Sunglows			
❏ SLP-103 [M]	The Original Peanuts	1965	$100
—As "The Sunglows			
❏ SLP-103S [S]	The Original Peanuts	1965	$150
—As "The Sunglows			
TEAR DROP			
❏ LPM-2001 [M]	Las Vegas Welcomes Sunny and the Sunliners	1964	$40
❏ LPM-2000 [M]	Talk to Me	1963	$150
❏ LPM-2008 [M]	Teardrop Presents Sunny and the Sunliners	196?	$40
SUNNY DAY REAL ESTATE			
SUB POP			
❏ SP-246	Diary	1994	$40
—Aqua vinyl			
❏ SP-246	Diary	1994	$25
—Black vinyl			
❏ SP-409	How It Feels to Be Something On	1997	$30
❏ SP-316	Sunny Day Real Estate	1995	$25
❏ SP-485	Sunny Day Real Estate Live	1999	$30
TIME BOMB			
❏ 42541-1	The Rising Tide	2000	$40
SUNNYLAND SLIM			
BLUESVILLE			
❏ BVLP-1016 [M]	Slim's Shout	1961	$120
—Blue label, silver print			
❏ BVLP-1016 [M]	Slim's Shout	1964	$30
—Blue label, trident logo at right			
PRESTIGE			
❏ PRST-7723	Slim's Shout	1969	$25
WORLD PACIFIC			
❏ WPS-21890	Slim's Got His Thing Goin' On	1969	$25
SUNRAYS, THE			
TOWER			
❏ T5017 [M]	Andrea	1966	$50
❏ ST5017 [S]	Andrea	1966	$75
SUNSET DRAGSTERS, THE			
PALACE			
❏ M-775 [M]	Hot Rod Rally	196?	$100
❏ PST-775 [S]	Hot Rod Rally	196?	$150
SUNSETS, THE (1)			
PALACE			
❏ M-752 [M]	Surfing with the Sunsets	1963	$40
❏ PST-752 [S]	Surfing with the Sunsets	1963	$50
SUNSHINE, MONTY			
STOMP OFF			
❏ SOS-1110	New Orleans Hula	1986	$25
SUNSHINE BOYS, THE			
DOT			
❏ DLP-3189 [M]	Sing Unto Him	1959	$30
❏ DLP-25189 [S]	Sing Unto Him	1959	$40
STARDAY			
❏ SLP-349 [M]	A Happy Home Up There	1965	$30
❏ SLP-113 [M]	America's Number One Gospel Group	1960	$40
❏ SLP-166 [M]	More Country Music Sing-Along	1962	$30
SUNSHINE COMPANY, THE			
IMPERIAL			
❏ LP-9359 [M]	Happy Is the Sunshine Company	1967	$25
❏ LP-12359 [S]	Happy Is the Sunshine Company	1967	$25
❏ LP-12399	Sunshine and Shadows	1969	$25
❏ LP-9368 [M]	The Sunshine Company	1968	$30
—Mono copies are promo only			
❏ LP-12368 [S]	The Sunshine Company	1968	$25
SUPER HEROINES, THE			
CLEOPATRA			
❏ 2243 [B]	L.A. Riot Grrrls - The Best Of 1982-1985		$25
SUPER STOCKS, THE			
CAPITOL			
❏ T1997 [M]	Hot Rod Rally	1963	$50
❏ ST1997 [S]	Hot Rod Rally	1963	$80

Number	Title	Yr	NM
❏ T2190 [M]	School Is a Drag	1964	$150
❏ ST2190 [S]	School Is a Drag	1964	$120
❏ T2113 [M]	Surf Route 101	1964	$150
—With bonus single, "Doin' the Surfink"/"Finksville, U.S.A." by Mr. Gasser and the Weirdos, in special pocket on front cover			
❏ T2113 [M]	Surf Route 101	1964	$150
—Without bonus single			
❏ ST2113 [S]	Surf Route 101	1964	$175
—With bonus single, "Doin' the Surfink"/"Finksville, U.S.A." by Mr. Gasser and the Weirdos, in special pocket on front cover			
❏ ST2113 [S]	Surf Route 101	1964	$150
—Without bonus single			
❏ T2060 [M]	Thunder Road	1964	$150
❏ ST2060 [S]	Thunder Road	1964	$150
❏ (S)T2060	Thunder Road Bonus Poster	1964	$50
SUPERBLUE			
BLUE NOTE			
❏ B1-91731	Superblue	1989	$35
SUPERCHUNK			
MERGE			
❏ MRG020 [B]	Tossing Seeds (Singles 89-91)	2016	$25
—180 gram			
SUPERFINE DANDELION, THE			
MAINSTREAM			
❏ 56102 [M]	The Superfine Dandelion	1967	$150
❏ S-6102 [S]	The Superfine Dandelion	1967	$75
SUPERSAX			
CAPITOL			
❏ ST-11177	Supersax Plays Bird	1973	$25
❏ ST-11271	Supersax Plays Bird, Volume 2/Salt Peanuts	1974	$25
❏ ST-11371	Supersax Plays Bird with Strings	1975	$25
COLUMBIA			
❏ FC44436	Stone Bird	1989	$30
❏ FC39140	Supersax and L.A. Voices	1984	$25
❏ FC39925	Supersax and L.A. Voices, Vol. 2	1985	$25
❏ FC40547	Supersax and L.A. Voices Volume 3: Straighten Up and Fly Right	1986	$25
MOBILE FIDELITY			
❏ 1-511	Supersax Plays Bird	1981	$40
—Audiophile vinyl			
PAUSA			
❏ 7038	Chasin' the Bird	1977	$25
❏ 7082	Dynamite!	1979	$25
❏ 9028	Supersax Plays Bird, Volume 2/Salt Peanuts	198?	$20
SUPERSISTER			
DWARF			
❏ PDLP-2001	Supersister	197?	$30
SUPERTRAMP			
A&M			
❏ SP-3708	Breakfast in America	1979	$10
❏ SP-3730 [PD]	Breakfast in America	1979	$500
—In-house picture discs featuring A&M staff members posing with the cover model			
❏ 2137081	Breakfast in America	2008	$25
❏ SP-5013	Brother Where You Bound	1985	$12
❏ SP-3647	Crime of the Century	1974	$15
❏ 2136471	Crime of the Century	2008	$25
❏ SP-4560	Crisis? What Crisis?	1975	$15
❏ SP-3214	Crisis? What Crisis?	1982	$10
—Budget-line reissue			
❏ SP-3215	Even in the Quietest Moments	1982	$10
—Budget-line reissue			
❏ SP-4634	Even in the Quietest Moments…	1977	$15
❏ SP-3732	…Famous Last Words…	1982	$12
❏ SP-3284	…Famous Last Words…	1986	$10
—Budget-line reissue			
❏ SP-5181	Free as a Bird	1987	$12
❏ SP-4311 [B]	Indelibly Stamped	1971	$30
—First edition with brown label			
❏ SP-3129	Indelibly Stamped	198?	$10
—Budget-line reissue			
❏ SP-4311	Indelibly Stamped	197?	$12
—Second edition with silverish label			
❏ SP-6702	Paris	1980	$15
❏ SP-4274 [B]	Supertramp	1970	$30
—First edition with brown label			
❏ SP-4665	Supertramp	1978	$15
—Reissue of 4274			
❏ SP-3149	Supertramp	198?	$10
—Budget-line reissue			
❏ SP-4274	Supertramp	197?	$12

Number	Title	Yr	NM
—Second edition with silverish label			
MOBILE FIDELITY			
❏ Jan-0045	Breakfast in America	1980	$75
—Audiophile vinyl			

Number	Title	Yr	NM
❏ Jan-005 [B]	Crime of the Century	1979	$80
—Audiophile vinyl			
❏ MFQR-005 [B]	Crime of the Century	1983	$175
—Ultra High Quality Recording; in box			
SWEET THUNDER			
❏ 5 [B]	Even in the Quietest Moments…	198?	$75
—Audiophile vinyl			
SUPREMES, THE, AND THE FOUR TOPS			
Also see each artist's individual listings.			
MOTOWN			
❏ MS745	Dynamite	1971	$18
❏ MS717	The Magnificent Seven	1970	$18
❏ M5-123V1A	The Magnificent Seven	1981	$15
—Reissue of Motown 717			
❏ MS736 [B]	The Return of the Magnificent Seven	1971	$18
SUPREMES, THE, DIANA ROSS AND, AND THE TEMPTATIONS			
Also see each artist's individual listings.			
MOTOWN			
❏ M679 [M]	Diana Ross and the Supremes Join the Temptations	1968	$30
❏ MS679 [S]	Diana Ross and the Supremes Join the Temptations	1968	$25
❏ M5-139V1	Diana Ross and the Supremes Join the Temptations	1981	$15
—Reissue of Motown 679			
❏ MS699	On Broadway	1969	$25
❏ MS682	TCB	1968	$25
❏ M5-171V1	TCB	1981	$15
—Reissue of Motown 682			
❏ MS692	Together	1969	$25
SUPREMES, THE			
DORAL			
❏ DRL104	Doral Presents Diana Ross and the Supremes	1971	$50
—Available through Doral cigarettes			
MOTOWN			
❏ 5381ML3	25th Anniversary	1986	$25
—By "Diana Ross and the Supremes			
❏ M623 [M]	A Bit of Liverpool	1964	$40
❏ MS623 [S]	A Bit of Liverpool	1964	$50
❏ M9-794L3	Anthology (1962-1969)	1974	$30
—By "Diana Ross and the Supremes			
❏ MT/MS637	A Tribute to the Girls	1965	$0
—Unreleased			
❏ 5278ML	Captured Live on Stage	1982	$10
—Reissue?			
❏ MS694	Cream of the Crop	1969	$25
❏ M663 [M]	Diana Ross and the Supremes Greatest Hits	1967	$50
❏ MS663 [S]	Diana Ross and the Supremes Greatest Hits	1967	$40
❏ MS702	Diana Ross and the Supremes Greatest Hits, Volume 3	1970	$25
❏ M5-203V1	Diana Ross and the Supremes Greatest Hits, Volume 3	1981	$15
—Reissue of Motown 702			
❏ MT/MS663	Diana Ross and the Supremes Greatest Hits Poster	1967	$12

Number	Title	Yr	NM
❑ 5371ML	Diana Ross and the Supremes Sing Motown	1985	$12
❑ MS708	Farewell	1970	$30
— By "Diana Ross and the Supremes			
❑ M751L	Floy Joy	1972	$18
❑ MS672 [S]	Funny Girl	1968	$25
— The above LP came out before Motown 670			
❑ M672 [M]	Funny Girl	1968	$30
— Mono appears to be promo only			
❑ M5-237V1	Greatest Hits	1982	$12
— Reissue (unknown if it's the complete 2-record set or an edited version)			
❑ 5313ML	Great Songs and Performances That Inspired the Motown 25th Anniversary TV Special	1983	$12
❑ M6-863S1	High Energy	1976	$18
❑ M643 [M]	I Hear a Symphony	1966	$30
❑ MS643 [S]	I Hear a Symphony	1966	$30
❑ M5-147V1	I Hear a Symphony	1981	$15
— Reissue of Motown 643			
❑ MS689	Let the Sunshine In	1969	$25
❑ 5305ML	Let the Sunshine In	1983	$10
— Reissue of MS 689			
❑ M676 [M]	Live at London's Talk of the Town	1968	$30
— Mono is promo only			
❑ MS676 [S]	Live at London's Talk of the Town	1968	$25
— The above LP came out before Motown 670 and 672			
❑ MS670	Love Child	1968	$25
❑ 5245ML	Love Child	1982	$10
— Reissue of MS 670			
❑ M6-873S1	Mary, Scherrie and Susaye	1976	$18
❑ M606 [M]	Meet the Supremes	1963	$900
— With group sitting on stools			
❑ M606 [M]	Meet the Supremes	1963	$30
— With close-up of group's faces			
❑ MS606 [S]	Meet the Supremes	1964	$40
— With close-up of group's faces			
❑ M5-223V1	Meet the Supremes	1982	$10
— Reissue of Motown 606			
❑ MT638 [M]	Merry Christmas	1965	$30
❑ MS638 [S]	Merry Christmas	1965	$40
— Same as above, but in stereo			
❑ 5252ML	Merry Christmas	1982	$12
— Reissue of MS 638			
❑ M627 [M]	More Hits by the Supremes	1965	$30
❑ MS627 [S]	More Hits by the Supremes	1965	$30
❑ 5361ML	Motown Legends	1985	$12
❑ MS720	New Ways But Love Stays	1970	$18
❑ MS746	Promises Kept	1972	$0
— Unreleased			
❑ MTMS648	Pure Gold	1966	$0
— Unreleased			
❑ M665 [M]	Reflections	1968	$30
❑ MS665 [S]	Reflections	1968	$25
❑ MS705	Right On	1970	$18
— By "The Supremes"; the first LP after Diana Ross left			
❑ M5-101V1	Superstar Series, Vol. 1	1981	$15
— By "Diana Ross and the Supremes			
❑ MT/MS628	There's a Place for Us	1965	$0
— Unreleased			
❑ M756L	The Supremes	1972	$18
❑ M6-828	The Supremes	1975	$18
❑ M649 [M]	The Supremes A' Go-Go	1966	$30
❑ MS649 [S]	The Supremes A' Go-Go	1966	$30
❑ M5-138V1	The Supremes A' Go-Go	1981	$15
— Reissue of Motown 649			
❑ M636 [M]	The Supremes at the Copa	1965	$30
❑ MS636 [S]	The Supremes at the Copa	1965	$30
❑ M5-162V1	The Supremes at the Copa	1981	$15
— Reissue of Motown 636			
❑ M7-904R1	The Supremes at Their Best	1978	$18
❑ MT/MS626	The Supremes Live! Live! Live!	1965	$0
— Unreleased			
❑ MT/MS610	The Supremes Sing Ballads and Blues	1963	$0
— Unreleased			
❑ MT-625 [M]	The Supremes Sing Country, Western & Pop	1965	$30
❑ MS625 [S]	The Supremes Sing Country, Western & Pop	1965	$30
❑ M5-158V1	The Supremes Sing Country Western and Pop	1981	$10
— Reissue of Motown 625			
❑ M650 [M]	The Supremes Sing Holland-Dozier-Holland	1967	$30
❑ MS650 [S]	The Supremes Sing Holland-Dozier-Holland	1967	$30
❑ M5-182V1	The Supremes Sing Holland-Dozier-Holland	1981	$15
— Reissue of Motown 650			
❑ M659 [M]	The Supremes Sing Rodgers & Hart	1967	$30
❑ MS659 [S]	The Supremes Sing Rodgers & Hart	1967	$30
❑ MS737	Touch	1971	$18
❑ PR-102 [DJ]	Touch Interview	1971	$30
❑ PR-102 [DJ]	Touch Interview	1971	$30
❑ M629 [M]	We Remember Sam Cooke	1965	$30

Number	Title	Yr	NM
❑ MS629 [S]	We Remember Sam Cooke	1965	$30
— The above LP came out before Motown 627			
❑ M621 [M]	Where Did Our Love Go	1964	$30
❑ MS621 [S]	Where Did Our Love Go	1964	$40
❑ 5270ML	Where Did Our Love Go	1982	$10
— Reissue of MS 621			

NATURAL RESOURCES

❑ NR4010	Merry Christmas	1978	$15
— Reissue of Motown 638			
❑ NR4006T1	Where Did Our Love Go	1978	$15
— Reissue of Motown 621			

PICKWICK

❑ SPC-3383	Baby Love	197?	$15
— Edited reissue of Motown 621			

UNIVERSAL MOTOWN

❑ 5315839	I Hear a Symphony	2009	$25

SURE!, AL B.
WARNER BROS.

❑ 25662	In Effect Mode	1988	$10
❑ 26005	Private Times...And the Whole 9!	1990	$15

SURF STOMPERS, THE
DEL-FI

❑ DFLP-1236 [M]	The Original Surfer Stomp	1963	$75
❑ DFST-1236 [S]	The Original Surfer Stomp	1963	$100
❑ DLF-1236	The Original Surfer Stomp	1997	$15

SURF TEENS, THE
SUTTON

❑ SU-339 [M]	Surf Mania	1963	$50
❑ SSU-339 [S]	Surf Mania	1963	$75

SURFARIS, THE (1)
DECCA

❑ DL4560 [M]	Fun City, U.S.A.	1964	$40
❑ DL74560 [S]	Fun City, U.S.A.	1964	$75
❑ DL4487 [M]	Hit City '64	1964	$40
❑ DL74487 [S]	Hit City '64	1964	$75
❑ DL4614 [M]	Hit City '65	1965	$40
❑ DL74614 [S]	Hit City '65	1965	$75
❑ DL4663 [M]	It Ain't Me, Babe	1965	$40
❑ DL74663 [S]	It Ain't Me, Babe	1965	$75
❑ DL4470 [M]	The Surfaris Play Wipe Out	1963	$40
❑ DL74470 [S]	The Surfaris Play Wipe Out	1963	$30

DOT

❑ DLP-3535 [M]	Wipe Out	1963	$50
— With back cover photo featuring five Surfaris			
❑ DLP-3535 [M]	Wipe Out	1963	$40
— With back cover photo featuring four Surfaris			
❑ DLP-3535 [M]	Wipe Out	1963	$30
— With no back cover photo of the Surfaris			
❑ DLP-25535 [S]	Wipe Out	1963	$100
— With back cover photo featuring five Surfaris			
❑ DLP-25535 [S]	Wipe Out	1963	$50
— With back cover photo featuring four Surfaris			
❑ DLP-25535 [S]	Wipe Out	1963	$40
— With no back cover photo of the Surfaris			

PICKWICK

❑ SPC-3636	Wipe Out and Surfer Joe	1978	$18

SURFARIS, THE (2)
DIPLOMAT

❑ D-2309 [M]	Wheels-Shorts-Hot Rods	1963	$30
— As "The Original Surfaris			
❑ DS-2309 [M]	Wheels-Shorts-Hot Rods	1963	$30
— As "The Original Surfaris			

SUNDAZED

❑ LP-5014	Bombora!	199?	$12
— As "The Original Surfaris			

SURFERS, THE
HIFI

❑ R-408 [M]	On the Rocks	1959	$120
❑ SR-408 [S]	On the Rocks	1959	$175

SURFRIDERS, THE
VAULT

❑ LP-105 [M]	Surfbeat, Volume 2	1963	$30
❑ VS-105 [S]	Surfbeat, Volume 2	1963	$40

SURFSIDERS, THE
DESIGN

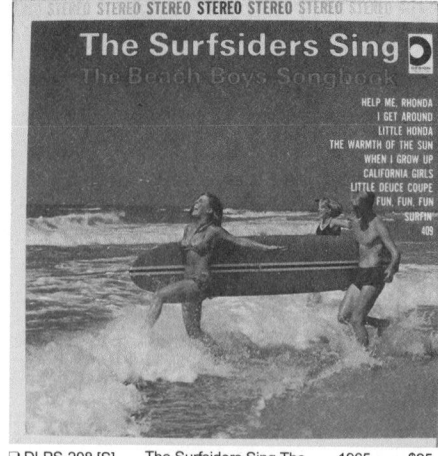

❑ DLPS-208 [S]	The Surfsiders Sing The Beach Boys Songbook	1965	$25
❑ DLP-208 [M]	The Surfsiders Sing The Beach Boys Songbook	1965	$18

SURMAN, JOHN
ANTILLES

❑ AN-7004	Morning Glory	197?	$30

ECM

❑ 1148	Reflection	197?	$30
❑ 23795	Such Winters of Memory	1983	$25
❑ 1193	The Amazing Adventures of Simon Simon	1981	$30
❑ 1295	Withholding Pattern	1986	$30

SURPRISE PACKAGE
LHI

❑ S-12005 [B]	Free Up	1968	$40

SURRATT, CECIL, AND SMITTY SMITH
AUDIO LAB

❑ AL-1565 [M]	Songs Everybody Knows	1961	$150

KING

❑ 860 [M]	Country Music from the Heart of the Country	1963	$50
❑ 966 [M]	Good Country Singin' and Pickin'	1966	$40

SURVIVOR
SCOTTI BROTHERS

❑ QZ38791	Caught in the Game	1983	$10
❑ FZ38062	Eye of the Tiger	1982	$10
❑ PZ38062	Eye of the Tiger	198?	$10
— Budget-line reissue with new prefix			
❑ ARZ37549	Premonition	1981	$12
❑ PZ37549	Premonition	198?	$10
— Budget-line reissue with new prefix			
❑ SB7107	Survivor	1980	$15
❑ OZ44282	Too Hot to Sleep	1988	$10
❑ FZ39578	Vital Signs	1984	$10
❑ FZ40457	When Seconds Count	1986	$10

SUSSMAN, RICHARD
INNER CITY

❑ IC-1045	Free Fall	1978	$30
❑ IC-1068	Tributaries	1979	$30

Number	Title	Yr	NM

SUTCH, SCREAMING LORD
COTILLION
❏ SD9049	Hands of Jack the Ripper	1972	$30
❏ SD9015	Lord Sutch and Heavy Friends	1970	$30

— With Jimmy Page, John Bonham and Jeff Beck

SUTHERLAND, JOAN
LONDON
❏ 5943 [M]	Joy of Christmas	1965	$15
❏ OS25943 [S]	Joy of Christmas	1965	$18

SUTHERLAND BROTHERS
COLUMBIA
❏ JC35293	Down to Earth	1978	$12
❏ JC35703	When the Night Comes Down	1979	$12
ISLAND
❏ SW-9315	The Sutherland Brothers Band	1972	$15

SUTHERLAND BROTHERS AND QUIVER
COLUMBIA
❏ PC33982	Reach for the Sky	1976	$12
❏ PC34376	Slipstream	1977	$12
ISLAND
❏ SW-9341	Dream Kid	1974	$12
❏ SW-9326	Lifeboat	1973	$12

SUTTON, DICK
JAGUAR
❏ JP-802 [10]	Jazz Idiom	1954	$100
❏ JP-804 [10]	Progressive Dixieland	1954	$100

SUTTON, GLENN
MERCURY
❏ SRM-1-5018	Close Encounters of the Sutton Kind	1979	$12

SUTTON, RALPH
ANALOGUE PRODUCTIONS
❏ AP 018	Partners in Crime	199?	$30

— Audiophile vinyl

AUDIOPHILE
❏ AP-163	Off the Cuff	198?	$25
CIRCLE
❏ L-413 [10]	Ralph Sutton	1951	$100
COLUMBIA
❏ CL6140 [10]	Piano Moods	1950	$100
COMMODORE
❏ XFL-16570	Bix Beiderbecke Suite and Jazz Portraits	198?	$25
❏ FL-30001 [M]	Ralph Sutton	1951	$100
DECCA
❏ DL5498 [10]	I Got Rhythm	1953	$175
DOWN HOME
❏ MGD-4 [M]	Backroom Piano: The Ragtime Piano of Ralph Sutton	1955	$85
❏ DH-1003 [10]	Ragtime Piano Solos	1953	$100
HARMONY
❏ HL7109 [M]	Tribute to Fats	1958	$30
JAZZ ARCHIVES
❏ JA-45	Ralph Sutton and the All-Stars	198?	$25
JAZZOLOGY
❏ JCE-92	Alligator Crawl	197?	$25
OMEGA
❏ OML-51 [M]	Jazz At the Olympics	196?	$35
❏ OSL-51 [S]	Jazz At the Olympics	196?	$25
PROJECT 3
❏ PR5040SD	Knocked Out Nocturne	1969	$30
RIVERSIDE
❏ RLP 12-212 [M]	Classic Jazz Piano	1956	$300
ROULETTE
❏ R-25232 [M]	Ragtime, U.S.A.	1963	$35
❏ SR-25232 [S]	Ragtime, U.S.A.	1963	$25
SACKVILLE
❏ 2012	Piano Solos	198?	$25
STORYVILLE
❏ 4013	Ralph Sutton Quartet	198?	$25
VERVE
❏ MGV-1004 [M]	Backroom Piano: The Ragtime Piano of Ralph Sutton	1956	$175

SUZUKI, PAT
RCA VICTOR
❏ LPM-1965 [M]	Broadway '59	1959	$25
❏ LSP-1965 [S]	Broadway '59	1959	$30
❏ LPM-2186 [M]	Looking at You	1960	$25
❏ LSP-2186 [S]	Looking at You	1960	$30
❏ LPM-2030 [M]	Pat Suzuki	1959	$25
❏ LSP-2030 [S]	Pat Suzuki	1959	$30
VIK
❏ LX-1147 [M]	Pat Suzuki	1958	$30
❏ LX-1127 [M]	The Many Sides of Pat Suzuki	1958	$30

SVENSSON, REINHOLD
PRESTIGE
❏ PRLP-155 [10]	New Sounds from Sweden, Volume 8	1953	$300
❏ PRLP-129 [10]	Reinhold Svensson, Volume 2: Favorites	1952	$350
❏ PRLP-106 [10]	Reinhold Svensson Piano	1951	$300

SVENSSON, REINHOLD/BENGT HALLBERG
PRESTIGE
❏ PRLP-174 [10]	Piano Moderns	1953	$300

SWAGGART, JIMMY
JIM
❏ 24-141	Silver Jubilee Album: The Very Best of Jimmy Swaggart	1981	$25

— One of the two records is a picture disc

SWAGMEN, THE
PARKWAY
❏ P-7015 [M]	Meet the Swagmen	1962	$40
❏ SP-7015 [S]	Meet the Swagmen	1962	$50

SWALLOW, STEVE
ECM
❏ 1160	Home	1979	$30

SWAMP DOGG
CANYON
❏ LP-7706	Total Destruction to Your Mind	1970	$30
ELEKTRA
❏ EKS-74089	Rat On	1971	$25

SWAMPWATER
KING
❏ KSD-1122	Swampwater	1971	$18
RCA VICTOR
❏ LSP-4572	Swampwater	1971	$18

SWAN, BILLY
A&M
❏ SP-4686	You're OK, I'm OK	1978	$12
COLUMBIA
❏ PZ34183	Billy Swan	1977	$10

— Reissue of Monument 34183

❏ PC34473	Four	1977	$12
❏ PZ33279	I Can Help	1977	$10

— Reissue of Monument 33279

❏ PZ33805	Rock 'n' Roll Moon	1977	$10

— Reissue of Monument 33805

EPIC
❏ FE37079	I'm Into Lovin' You	1981	$12
MONUMENT
❏ PZ34183	Billy Swan	1976	$12
❏ 7629	Billy Swan At His Best	1978	$12
❏ KZ33279	I Can Help	1974	$12
❏ PZ33805	Rock 'n' Roll Moon	1975	$12

SWAN SILVERTONES, THE
SPECIALTY
❏ SPS-2122	Love Lifted Me	1970	$25
❏ SPS-2148	My Rock	1971	$25
UPFRONT
❏ UPF-112	The Lord's Prayer	1968	$25
VEE JAY
❏ LP-5034 [M]	Blessed Assurance	1963	$30
❏ LP-5059 [M]	Let's Go to Church Together	1964	$30
❏ SR-5059 [S]	Let's Go to Church Together	1964	$30
❏ VJS-18008	Pray for Me	1975	$25
❏ LP-5013 [M]	Savior Pass Me Not	1962	$30
❏ LP-5006 [M]	Singing in My Soul	1960	$30
❏ LP-5052 [M]	The Best of the Swan Silvertones	1963	$30
❏ LP-5003 [M]	The Swan Silvertones	1959	$40

SWANN, BETTYE
ABET
❏ LP405 [B]	Make Me Yours	197?	$25
CAPITOL
❏ ST-270	Don't You Ever Get Tired of Hurting Me	1969	$50
❏ ST-190	The Soul View Now!	1969	$150

COLLECTABLES
❏ COL-5177	Make Me Yours	198?	$12
MONEY
❏ 1103 [M]	Make Me Yours	1967	$30
❏ S-1103 [S]	Make Me Yours	1967	$30

SWANSON, RIC
ARMERICAN GRAMAPHONE
❏ AG-600	Urban Surrender	1985	$25
OPTIMISM
❏ OP-3220	Renewal	198?	$30

SWARTZ, HARVIE
GRAMAVISION
❏ 8202	Underneath It All	198?	$25
❏ 18-8503-1	Urban Earth	1986	$25

SWEAT, ISAAC PAYTON
BELLAIRE
❏ LP1100	Cotton Eyed Joe/Shottish	1980	$15
PAID
❏ 2005	Cotton-Eyed Joe	1981	$15

SWEAT, KEITH
ELEKTRA
❏ 61707	Keith Sweat	1996	$15
❏ ED5872 [DJ]	Keith Sweat	1996	$18

— Promo-only sampler from LP of the same name

VINTERTAINMENT
❏ 60861	I'll Give All My Love to You	1990	$15
❏ 60763	Make It Last Forever	1987	$10

SWEATHOG
COLUMBIA
❏ KC31144	Hallelujah	1972	$15
❏ C30601	Sweathog	1971	$15

SWEDES FROM JAZZVILLE
EPIC
❏ LN3309 [M]	Swedes from Jazzville	195?	$150

SWEDISH JAZZ KINGS, THE
STOMP OFF
❏ SOS-1188	After Midnight	1987	$25
❏ SOS-1122	What Makes Me Love You So?	1986	$25

SWEENEY TODD
At different times, BRYAN ADAMS and NICK GILDER were in this group (Adams sings on album listed).
LONDON
❏ PS694	If Wishes Were Horses	1977	$75

— Possibly a Canadian import only

SWEET, MATTHEW
A&M
❏ SP-5233	Earth	1989	$18
COLUMBIA
❏ BFC40417	Inside	1986	$18
ZOO
❏ 31130	Blue Sky on Mars	1997	$18

— All copies authographed by Matthew Steel on the label

ZOO/CLASSIC
❏ 11081	100% Fun	1995	$25
❏ 11050 [B]	Altered Beast	1995	$30

— Audiophile vinyl pressing; released on CD in 1993

❏ 11015	Girlfriend	1995	$50

— Audiophile vinyl pressing; released on CD in 1991

SWEET, RACHEL
COLUMBIA
❏ FC38342	Blame It on Love	1982	$12
STIFF/COLUMBIA
❏ ARC37077	...And Then He Kissed Me	1981	$15
❏ JC36101	Fool Around	1979	$35
❏ NJC36337	Protect the Innocent	1980	$20
❏ JC36337	Protect the Innocent	1980	$20

SWEET, THE
CLEOPATRA
❏ 3955 [B]	Live In Denmark 1976		$25

SWEET, THE (1)
BEAT ROCKET
❏ BR125	Hell Raisers!	2000	$15
BELL
❏ 1125	The Sweet	1973	$30
CAPITOL
❏ ST-11929	Cut Above the Rest	1979	$15
❏ SN-16118	Cut Above the Rest	1980	$10

Number	Title	Yr	NM

—Budget-line reissue
❏ PRO-11929 [DJ] Cut Above the Rest 1979 $50
—Special promo box contains record, cassette, 8-track, photo, bio
❏ ST-11395 Desolation Boulevard 1975 $15
❏ SN-16287 Desolation Boulevard 1981 $10
—Budget-line reissue
❏ SPRO-8371/2 [DJ] For A.O.R. Radio Only 1976 $30
❏ ST-11496 Give Us a Wink 1976 $15
❏ SN-16115 Give Us a Wink 1980 $10
—Budget-line reissue
❏ SKAO-11744 Level Headed 1978 $15
❏ SN-16117 Level Headed 1980 $10
—Budget-line reissue
❏ STAO-11636 Off the Record 1977 $15
❏ SN-16116 Off the Record 1980 $10
—Budget-line reissue
❏ SPRO-8849 [DJ] Short and Sweet 1978 $30
❏ ST-12106 Sweet VI 1980 $15
KORY
❏ 3009 The Sweet 1977 $15
—Reissue of Bell LP

SWEET CREAM
SHADY BROOK
❏ SB-011 Sweet Cream and Other Delights 1978 $18

SWEET INSPIRATIONS, THE
ATLANTIC
❏ SD8182 Songs of Faith and Inspiration 1968 $25
❏ SD8253 Sweet, Sweet Soul 1970 $25
❏ SD8225 Sweets for My Sweet 1969 $25
❏ SD8155 The Sweet Inspirations 1968 $25
❏ 8201 [M] What the World Needs Now Is Love 1969 $50
—Mono is white label promo only; "d/j copy monaural" sticker on stereo cover
❏ SD8201 [S] What the World Needs Now Is Love 1969 $25
RSO
❏ RS-1-3058 Hot Butterfly 1979 $12
STAX
❏ STS-3017 Estelle, Myrna and Sylvia 1973 $25

SWEET PANTS
BARKLEY
❏ 1141 Fat Peter Presents Sweet Pants 1969 $250

SWEET RUSH
GUINNESS
❏ GNS36005 [B] Living on Giving 1977 $40

SWEET SENSATION (1)
PYE
❏ 12110 Sweet Sensation 1975 $12

SWEET SENSATION (2)
ATCO
❏ 90917 Take It While It's Hot 1988 $12
❏ 91722 Time to Jam! The Remix Album 1991 $18

SWEET THURSDAY
TETRAGRAMMATON
❏ T-112 Sweet Thursday 1969 $25

SWEET TOOTHE
DOMINION
❏ NR-7360 Testing 1974 $300

SWEETHEARTS OF THE RODEO
COLUMBIA
❏ FC40614 One Time, One Night 1988 $10
❏ B6C40406 Sweethearts of the Rodeo 1986 $10

SWEETWATER
REPRISE
❏ RS6417 Just for You 1970 $18
❏ RS6473 Melon 1971 $18
❏ RS6313 Sweetwater 1968 $18

SWENSON, INGA
LIBERTY
❏ LRP-3379 [M] I'm Old Fashioned 1964 $30
❏ LST-7379 [S] I'm Old Fashioned 1964 $30

SWIFT, DUNCAN
BLACK LION
❏ 301 Piano Ragtime: Joplin and Morton 197? $30

Number	Title	Yr	NM

SWIFT RAIN
HI
❏ SHL-32064 Coming Down 1971 $30

SWIMMING POOL Q'S, THE
A&M
❏ SP-5107 Blue Tomorrow 1986 $12
CAPITOL
❏ C1-91068 World War Two Point Five 1989 $15
DB
❏ 87 [EP] Firing Squad for God 1985 $10
❏ 55 The Deep End 1981 $18

SWING OUT SISTER
FONTANA
❏ 838293-1 Kaleidoscope World 1989 $15
MERCURY
❏ 832213-1 It's Better to Travel 1987 $12

SWINGIN' MEDALLIONS
SMASH
❏ MGS-27083 [M] Double Shot (Of My Baby's Love) 1966 $40
—First pressing contains the original 45 version of the title song
❏ MGS-27083 [M] Double Shot (Of My Baby's Love) 1966 $30
—Later pressings contain a "censored" version of the title song
❏ SRS-67083 [S] Double Shot (Of My Baby's Love) 1966 $50
—First pressing contains the original 45 version of the title song
❏ SRS-67083 [S] Double Shot (Of My Baby's Love) 1966 $40
—Later pressings contain a "censored" version of the title song

SWINGING BLUE JEANS, THE
IMPERIAL
❏ LP-9261 [M] Hippy Hippy Shake 1964 $150
❏ LP-12261 [R] Hippy Hippy Shake 1964 $150

SWINGING SWEDES, THE
TELEFUNKEN
❏ LGX-66050 [M] The Swinging Swedes 195? $150

SWINGING SWEDES, THE/THE COOL BRITONS
BLUE NOTE
❏ BLP-5019 [10] New Sounds from the Olde World 1951 $300

SWINGLE SINGERS, THE
COLUMBIA
❏ PC34194 Rags and All That Jazz 1976 $25
COLUMBIA MASTERWORKS
❏ M33013 Love Songs for Madrigals and Madriguys 1976 $25
MMG
❏ 1125 Folio 198? $20
❏ 1115 Swingle Skyliner 198? $20
PHILIPS
❏ PHM200149 [M] Anyone for Mozart? 1965 $25
❏ PHS600149 [S] Anyone for Mozart? 1965 $30
❏ PHS 2-5400 Bachanalia 1972 $30
—Reissue of 600-197 and 600-126 in same package
❏ PHM200097 [M] Bach's Greatest Hits 1963 $25
❏ PHS600097 [S] Bach's Greatest Hits 1963 $30
❏ PHS600288 Back to Bach 1968 $25
❏ PHM200225 [M] Encounter 1966 $30
—With the Modern Jazz Quartet
❏ PHS600225 [S] Encounter 1966 $35
—With the Modern Jazz Quartet
❏ PHM200191 [M] Getting Romantic 1965 $25
❏ PHS600191 [S] Getting Romantic 1965 $30
❏ PHM200126 [M] Going Baroque 1964 $25
❏ PHS600126 [S] Going Baroque 1964 $30
❏ 824544-1 Jazz Sebastian Bach 1985 $20
❏ 824545-1 Place Vendome 1985 $20
—With the Modern Jazz Quartet; reissue of 600-225
❏ PHM200214 [M] Rococo A-Go-Go 1966 $25
❏ PHS600214 [S] Rococo A-Go-Go 1966 $30
❏ PHM200261 [M] Spanish Masters 1967 $25
❏ PHS600261 [S] Spanish Masters 1967 $30
❏ PHS700004 The Joy of Singing 1973 $25

SWITCH
GORDY
❏ G8-993M1 Reaching for Tomorrow 1980 $15
❏ G7-980R1 Switch 1978 $15
❏ G7-988R1 Switch II 1979 $15
❏ G8-1007M1 Switch V 1981 $15
❏ G8-999M1 This Is My Dream 1980 $15
TOTAL EXPERIENCE
❏ TEL-8-5701 Am I Still Your Boyfriend? 1984 $12

Number	Title	Yr	NM

SWITTEL, JIMMY
DECCA
❏ DL8618 [M] Hymns to the Blessed Virgin Mary 1957 $25

SYKES, ROOSEVELT
BLUESVILLE
❏ BVLP-1014 [M] The Honeydripper 1961 $150
—Blue label, silver print
❏ BVLP-1014 [M] The Honeydripper 1964 $30
—Blue label, trident logo at right
❏ BVLP-1006 [M] The Return of Roosevelt Sykes 1960 $150
—Blue label, silver print
❏ BVLP-1006 [M] The Return of Roosevelt Sykes 1964 $30
—Blue label, trident logo at right
CROWN

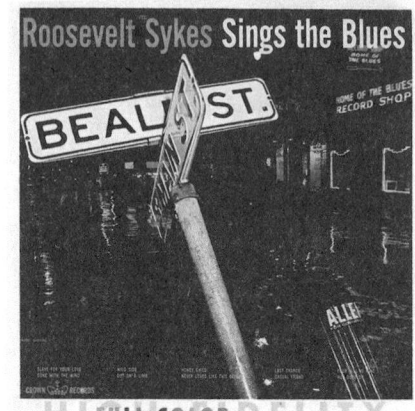

❏ CLP-5287 [M] Roosevelt Sykes Sings the Blues 1962 $50
❏ CST-287 [S] Roosevelt Sykes Sings the Blues 1962 $50
DELMARK
❏ DL-607 The Hard Driving Blues of Roosevelt Sykes 1963 $50

SYLVAIN SYLVAIN
NEY YORK DOLLS guitarist.
RCA VICTOR
❏ DJL1-4062 [DJ] RCA Special Radio Series XII 1981 $25
—Promo-only interviews and music
❏ AFL1-3913 Syl Sylvain and the Teardrops 1982 $15
❏ AFL1-3475 Sylvain Sylvain 1980 $15

SYLVERN, HANK
ABC-PARAMOUNT
❏ 146 [M] Christmas in Hi-Fi 1956 $30

SYLVERS, FOSTER
PRIDE
❏ 0027 Foster Sylvers 1973 $15

SYLVERS, THE
CAPITOL
❏ ST-11868 Best of the Sylvers 1978 $12
❏ ST-11705 New Horizons 1977 $12
❏ ST-11465 Showcase 1976 $12
❏ ST-11580 Something Special 1976 $12
CASABLANCA
❏ NBLP7151 Disco Fever 1979 $12
❏ NBLP7103 Forever Yours 1978 $12
GEFFEN
❏ GHS24039 Bizarre 1984 $12
MGM
❏ SE-4930 The Sylvers III 1974 $12
PRIDE
❏ 0007 The Sylvers 1972 $15
❏ 0026 The Sylvers II 1973 $15
SOLAR
❏ 22 Concept 1981 $12

SYLVESTER, TERRY
EPIC
❏ KE33076 Terry Sylvester 1974 $15

SYLVIA (1)
STANG
❏ 1010 Sylvia 197? $25

Number	Title	Yr	NM

SUGAR HILL
- 258 — Sylvia I — 1981 — $12

VIBRATION
- 143 — Brand New Funk — 197? — $15
- 131 — Lay It On Me — 1977 — $15
- 126 — Pillow Talk — 1973 — $18

SYLVIA (2)

RCA
- 5618-1-R — Greatest Hits — 1987 — $10

RCA VICTOR
- AHL1-3986 — Drifter — 1981 — $10
- AYL1-5154 — Drifter — 1984 — $10
- *— Best Buy Series" reissue*
- AHL1-4312 — Just Sylvia — 1982 — $10
- AHL1-5413 — One Step Closer — 1985 — $10
- AHL1-4672 — Snapshot — 1983 — $10
- AYL1-5439 — Snapshot — 1985 — $10
- *— Best Buy Series" reissue*
- AHL1-4960 — Surprise — 1984 — $10
- AYL1-7045 — Surprise — 1985 — $10
- *— Best Buy Series" reissue*

SYLVIAN, DAVID
Also see JAPAN.

VIRGIN
- 2167 [DJ] — Ink in the Well -- A Conversation — 1987 — $25
- *— Promo-only interview album*
- 90904 — Plight and Premonition — 1988 — $12
- *— With Holger Czukay*
- 90677 — Secrets of the Beehive — 1987 — $12

SYMPHONY JAZZ ENSEMBLE

QCA
- 364 — Carmen — 197? — $35
- 378 — Eastside Corridor — 197? — $35

SYMS, SYLVIA

20TH CENTURY FOX
- TFM-4123 [M] — The Fabulous Sylvia Syms — 1963 — $30
- TFS-4123 [S] — The Fabulous Sylvia Syms — 1963 — $30

ATLANTIC
- ALS-137 [10] — Songs by Sylvia Syms — 1952 — $350
- 1243 [M] — Songs by Sylvia Syms — 1956 — $300
- *— Black label*
- 1243 [M] — Songs by Sylvia Syms — 1960 — $300
- *— Multicolor label, white "fan" logo at right*

COLUMBIA
- CL1447 [M] — Torch Song — 1960 — $30
- *— Red and black label with six "eye" logos*
- CS8243 [S] — Torch Song — 1960 — $40
- *— Red and black label with six "eye" logos*

DECCA
- DL8639 [M] — Songs of Love — 1958 — $150
- *— Black label, silver print*
- DL8188 [M] — Sylvia Syms Sings — 1955 — $175
- *— Black label, silver print*

KAPP
- KL-1236 [M] — That Man -- Love Songs to Frank Sinatra — 1961 — $30
- KS-3236 [S] — That Man -- Love Songs to Frank Sinatra — 1961 — $40

MOVIETONE
- 2022 [M] — In a Sentimental Mood — 1967 — $25
- 72022 [S] — In a Sentimental Mood — 1967 — $35

PRESTIGE
- PRLP-7489 [M] — For Once in My Life — 1967 — $30
- PRST-7489 [S] — For Once in My Life — 1967 — $25
- PRLP-7439 [M] — Sylvia Is! — 1965 — $25
- PRST-7439 [S] — Sylvia Is! — 1965 — $30

VERSION
- VLP-103 [10] — After Dark — 1954 — $100

SYNDICATE OF SOUND

BELL
- 6001 [M] — Little Girl — 1966 — $50
- S-6001 [S] — Little Girl — 1966 — $100

SUNDAZED
- LP5051 — Little Girl — 2001 — $15
- *— Reissue on 180-gram vinyl*

SYNERGY

AUDION
- SYN204 — Metropolitan Suite — 1987 — $12

PASSPORT
- PB6005 — Audion — 1981 — $12
- PG-1 — Computer Experiments Volume One — 1981 — $18
- PB6000 — Cords — 1978 — $18
- *— First pressing on clear vinyl*
- PB6000 — Cords — 1978 — $12
- *— Later pressings on black vinyl*

- PPSD-98009 — Electronic Realizations for Rock Orchestra — 1975 — $15
- PB6001 — Electronic Realizations for Rock Orchestra — 1979 — $12
- *— Reissue of 98009*
- PB6003 — Games — 1979 — $12
- P2B11002 — Semi-Conductor — 1984 — $15
- PPSD-98014 — Sequencer — 1976 — $15
- PB6002 — Sequencer — 1979 — $12
- *— Reissue of 98014*

SYNTHESIS

CHIAROSCURO
- 172 — Six by Six — 197? — $30

SYREETA

MOTOWN
- M6-891 — Rich Love, Poor Love — 1977 — $12
- *— With G.C. Cameron*
- M6-808 — Stevie Wonder Presents Syreeta — 1974 — $12

MOWEST
- 113 — Syreeta — 1972 — $15

TAMLA
- T6-349 — One — 1977 — $12
- T8-376 — Set My Love in Motion — 1981 — $12
- T7-372 — Syreeta — 1980 — $12
- 6039TF — The Spell — 1983 — $12

SZABO, GABOR

ABC IMPULSE!
- AS-9105 — Gypsy 66 — 1968 — $30
- AS-9204 — His Great Hits — 1971 — $35
- AS-9128 — Jazz Raga — 1968 — $30
- AS-9159 — Light My Fire — 1968 — $35
- AS-9167 — More Sorcery — 1968 — $35
- AS-9123 — Spellbinder — 1968 — $30
- AS-9173 — The Best of Gabor Szabo — 1968 — $35
- AS-9146 — The Sorcerer — 1968 — $30
- AS-9151 — Wind, Sky and Diamonds — 1968 — $35

BLUE THUMB
- BTS-28 — High Contrast — 1972 — $30
- *— With Bobby Womack*
- 6014 — Live — 1974 — $30
- BTS-8823 — Magical Connection — 1971 — $30

BUDDAH
- 20-SK — Blowin' Some Old Smoke — 1971 — $30
- 18-SK — Watch What Happens — 1970 — $30

CTI
- 6026 — Mizrab — 1973 — $30
- 6035 — Rambler — 1974 — $30

GRP/IMPULSE!
- IMP-211 — The Sorcerer — 199? — $35
- *— Reissue on audiophile vinyl*

IMPULSE!
- A-9105 [M] — Gypsy 66 — 1966 — $250
- AS-9105 [S] — Gypsy 66 — 1966 — $250
- A-9128 [M] — Jazz Raga — 1967 — $250
- AS-9128 [S] — Jazz Raga — 1967 — $250
- A-9123 [M] — Spellbinder — 1966 — $250
- AS-9123 [S] — Spellbinder — 1966 — $250
- A-9146 [M] — The Sorcerer — 1967 — $250
- AS-9146 [S] — The Sorcerer — 1967 — $250
- AS-9151 — Wind, Sky and Diamonds — 1968 — $250
- *— This exists on the pre-ABC Impulse! label, though theoretically it shouldn't. Other titles may exist on that label also.*

MCA
- 4155 — His Great Hits — 198? — $30

MERCURY
- SRM-1-1141 — Faces — 1977 — $25
- SRM-1-1091 — Nightflight — 1976 — $25

PEPITA
- 707 — Femme Fatalo — 198? — $25

SALVATION
- 704 — Macho — 1975 — $30

SKYE
- SK-3 [S] — Bacchanal — 1968 — $35
- MK-3 [M] — Bacchanal — 1968 — $40
- *— Mono is promo only; "Monaural Promotion Copy" sticker on stereo cover*
- SK-7 — Dreams — 1969 — $35
- SK-9 — Gabor Szabo 1969 — 1969 — $35
- SK-15 — Lena & Gabor — 1970 — $35
- *— With Lena Horne*

SZABO, RICH

BBW
- 2001 — Best of Both Worlds — 198? — $30

SZAJNER, BOB

RMS
- 77004 — Afterthoughts — 198? — $30
- 77003 — Sound Ideas — 198? — $30

SEEDS & STEMS
- SSH-7802 — Jazz Opus 20/40 — 1979 — $30

SZAKCSI

GRP
- GR-9577 — Mystic Dreams — 1989 — $30
- GR-1045 — Sa-chi — 1988 — $25

SZERYNG, HENRYK

MERCURY LIVING PRESENCE
- SR90466 [S] — Bach: Violin Concertos in A and E; Double Concerto in D — 196? — $80
- *— Maroon label, with "Vendor: Mercury Record Corporation*
- SR90308 [S] — Brahms: Violin Concerto in D — 196? — $100
- *— With Antal Dorati/London Symphony Orchestra; maroon label, no "Vendor: Mercury Record Corporation*
- SR90308 [S] — Brahms: Violin Concerto in D — 196? — $30
- *— With Antal Dorati/London Symphony Orchestra; maroon label, with "Vendor: Mercury Record Corporation*
- SR90393 [S] — Khachaturian: Violin Concerto — 196? — $50
- *— With Antal Dorati/London Symphony Orchestra; maroon label, no "Vendor: Mercury Record Corporation*
- SR90393 [S] — Khachaturian: Violin Concerto — 196? — $40
- *— With Antal Dorati/London Symphony Orchestra; maroon label, with "Vendor: Mercury Record Corporation*
- SR90393 [S] — Khachaturian: Violin Concerto — 196? — $25
- *— With Antal Dorati/London Symphony Orchestra; third edition (dark red, not maroon, label)*
- SR90348 [S] — Kreisler: Caprice Viennois and 12 Others — 196? — $30
- *— Maroon label, no "Vendor: Mercury Record Corporation*
- SR90406 [S] — Mendelssohn: Violin Concerto in E; Schumann: Violin Concerto in D — 196? — $30
- *— With Antal Dorati/London Symphony Orchestra; maroon label, no "Vendor: Mercury Record Corporation*
- SR90367 [S] — Treasures — 196? — $30
- *— Maroon label, no "Vendor: Mercury Record Corporation*

RCA VICTOR RED SEAL
- LSC-2281 [S] — Brahms: Violin Concerto — 1959 — $175
- *— With Pierre Monteux/London Symphony Orchestra; original with "shaded dog" label*
- LSC-2421 [S] — In Recital — 1960 — $50
- *— Original with "shaded dog" label*
- LSC-2456 [S] — Lalo: Symphonie Espagnole — 1961 — $250
- *— With Walter Hendl/Chicago Symphony Orch.; original with "shaded dog" label*
- LSC-2363 [S] — Tchaikovsky: Violin Concerto in D — 1960 — $100
- *— With Charles Munch/Boston Symphony Orchestra; original with "shaded dog" label*

SZERYNG, HENRYK / ARTUR RUBENSTEIN

RCA VICTOR RED SEAL
- LSC-2377 [S] — Beethoven: Kreutzer and Spring Sonatas — 1960 — $40
- *— Original with "shaded dog" label*
- LSC-2620 [S] — Beethoven: Violin Sonata No. 8; Brahms: Violin Sonata No. 1 — 1962 — $50
- *— Original with "shaded dog" label*
- LSC-2619 [S] — Brahms: Violin Concertos 2 and 3 — 1962 — $50
- *— Original with "shaded dog" label*

SZIGETI, JOSEF; MIECZYSLAW HORSZOWSKI; JOHN BARROWS

MERCURY LIVING PRESENCE
- SR90210 [S] — Brahms: Horn Trio; Violin Sonata No. 2 — 196? — $180
- *— Maroon label, no "Vendor: Mercury Record Corporation*
- SR90210 [S] — Brahms: Horn Trio; Violin Sonata No. 2 — 196? — $80
- *— Maroon label, with "Vendor: Mercury Record Corporation*

SZIGETI, JOSEF

MERCURY LIVING PRESENCE
- SR90358 [S] — Beethoven: Violin Concerto in D — 196? — $150
- *— With Antal Dorati/London Symphony Orchestra; maroon label, no "Vendor: Mercury Record Corporation*
- SR90225 [S] — Brahms: Violin Concerto in D — 196? — $180
- *— Maroon label, no "Vendor: Mercury Record Corporation*
- SR90419 [S] — Prokofiev: Violin Concerto No. 1; Stravinsky: Duo Concertante — 196? — $30
- *— Maroon label, no "Vendor: Mercury Record Corporation*
- SR90419 [S] — Prokofiev: Violin Concerto No. 1; Stravinsky: Duo Concertante — 196? — $50
- *— Maroon label, with "Vendor: Mercury Record Corporation" (second edition is more sought after than the first)*
- SR90319 [S] — Prokofiev: Violin Sonatas No. 1 and 2 — 196? — $150
- *— Maroon label, no "Vendor: Mercury Record Corporation*
- SR90442 [S] — Violin Sonatas — 1965 — $50
- *— Maroon label, with "Vendor: Mercury Record Corporation*

SZOBEL, HERMANN

ARISTA
- AL4058 — Szobel — 1976 — $30

Number	Title	Yr	NM

T

T, JEAN-CLAUDE
PHILADELPHIA INT'L.
❑ PZ34246 [B]	The Bicentennial Poet	1976	$30

T. REX
CLEOPATRA
❑ 9625 [B]	Bang A Gong (Get It On)		$25
❑ 1987 [B]	Electric Suicide		$25

FAT POSSUM
❑ FP1244-1 [B]	Bolan's Zip Gun	2011	$30
❑ FP1238-1 [B]	Tanx	2011	$30
❑ FP1232-1 [B]	The Slider	2010	$30
❑ FP1242-1 [B]	Zinc Alloy And The Hidden Riders of Tomorrow	2011	$30

REPRISE
❑ PRO511 [DJ]	An Interview with Marc Bolan	1971	$175

T. REX
Featuring Marc Bolan.
A&M
❑ SP-3514	Tyrannosaurus Rex (A Beginning)	1972	$40

—Compilation of early LPs Prophets, Seers & Sages and My People Were Fair and Had Sky in Their Hair But Now They're Content to Wear Stars on Their Brows

BLUE THUMB

❑ BTS18 [B]	A Beard of Stars	1970	$85

—Add $5 for bonus single SP-6115/6, "Ride a White Swan"/"Is It Love." For reasons unknown, the single seems to be much more readily available than the LP

❑ BTS7 [B]	Unicorn	1969	$75

CASABLANCA
❑ NBLP7005	Light of Love	1974	$15

—Reissue of 9006

❑ NB9006	Light of Love	1974	$35

—Original, distributed by Warner Bros.

MARC ON WAX/RELATIVITY
❑ 8249	Bolan's Zip Gun	198?	$12
❑ 8251	Dandy in the Underworld	198?	$12
❑ 8252	Futuristic Dragon	198?	$12
❑ 8254	Tanx	198?	$12
❑ 8253	The Slider	198?	$12
❑ 8250	Zinc Alloy & The Hidden Riders of Tomorrow	198?	$12

REPRISE
❑ PRO511 [DJ]	An Interview with Marc Bolan	1971	$175
❑ RS6466 [B]	Electric Warrior	1971	$50
❑ MS2132 [B]	Tanx	1973	$35
❑ MS2095 [B]	The Slider	1972	$40
❑ RS6440	T. Rex	1971	$50

RHINO
❑ R1-76111	Electric Warrior	2003	$25

—Reissue on 180-gram vinyl

WARNER BROS.
❑ 25333	T. Rextasy: The Best of T. Rex, 1970-1973	1985	$12

T.A.T.U.
INTERSCOPE
❑ B0005382-01 [B]	Dangerous and Moving	2005	$50

T-BONES, THE
Members of this group later formed HAMILTON, JOE FRANK AND REYNOLDS.

LIBERTY
❑ LRP-3346 [M]	Boss Drag	1963	$75
❑ LST-7346 [S]	Boss Drag	1963	$150
❑ LRP-3363 [M]	Boss Drag at the Beach	1964	$75
❑ LST-7363 [S]	Boss Drag at the Beach	1964	$150
❑ LRP-3404 [M]	Doin' the Jerk	1965	$40
❑ LST-7404 [S]	Doin' the Jerk	1965	$75
❑ LRP-3471 [M]	Everyone's Gone to the Moon	1966	$35
❑ LST-7471 [S]	Everyone's Gone to the Moon	1966	$30
❑ LRP-3439 [M]	No Matter What Shape (Your Stomach's In)	1966	$25
❑ LST-7439 [S]	No Matter What Shape (Your Stomach's In)	1966	$30
❑ LRP-3446 [M]	Sippin' and Chippin'	1966	$25
❑ LST-7446 [S]	Sippin' and Chippin'	1966	$30

SUNSET
❑ SUM-1119 [M]	Shapin' Things Up	196?	$15
❑ SUS-5119 [S]	Shapin' Things Up	196?	$18

T.C. ATLANTIC
DOVE
❑ LP-4459	T.C. Atlantic	1966	$150

T.I.M.E.
LIBERTY
❑ LST-7605	Smooth Ball	1969	$30
❑ LST-7558	T.I.M.E.	1968	$30

T-MODEL FORD
FAT POSSUM
❑ 80303-1 [B]	Pee-Wee Get My Gun	1997	$18

T.S.O.L.
CLEOPATRA
❑ 5569 [B]	Code Blue		$25

T-SQUARE
PORTRAIT
❑ FR44193	Truth	1988	$25

T.V. AND THE TRIBESMEN
HANNA-BARBERA
❑ HLP-9507 [S]	Barefootin'	1966	$30

T2
LONDON
❑ PS583 [B]	It'll All Work Out in Boomland	1971	$150

TABACKIN, LEW
INNER CITY
❑ IC-1028	Dual Nature	1976	$30
❑ IC-6052	Rites of Pan	197?	$35
❑ IC-1038	Tabackin	1977	$30
❑ IC-6048	Tenor Gladness	197?	$35

JAM
❑ 5005	Black and Tan Fantasy	198?	$30

TABOR, ERON
STUDIO ONE
❑ S-104	Eron Tabor	196?	$25

TACO
RCA VICTOR
❑ AFL1-4818	After Eight	1983	$10
❑ CPL1-4920	Let's Face the Music	1984	$12

TACUMA, JAMAALADEEN
GRAMAVISION
❑ 18-8803	Jukebox	1988	$25
❑ 18-0(# unknown)	Music World	1986	$25
❑ GR-8308	Renaissance Man	1984	$25
❑ GR-8301	Showstopper	1983	$30

TAD
SUB POP
❑ 89 [B]	8-Way Santa	1991	$25
❑ 27 [B]	God's Balls	1989	$30

—Next 500 with "Manzine

❑ 27 [B]	God's Balls	1989	$30

—First 2,000 with gatefold cover

❑ 27 [B]	God's Balls	1989	$25

—Others in standard cover

❑ 49 [EP]	Salt Lick	1990	$30

TAFF, RUSS
HORIZON
❑ SP-751	Medals	198?	$15
❑ SP-671	Russ Taff	198?	$15

MYRRH
❑ 701-679206-4	Medals	1985	$15
❑ MSB-6706	Walls of Glass	1983	$15

TAILGATE RAMBLERS, THE
JAZZOLOGY
❑ J-32	Pause	1968	$30
❑ J-43	Swing	197?	$30

TALAS
Features bassist Billy Sheehan of DAVID LEE ROTH and MR. BIG fame.
COMBAT
❑ 8005	Live Speed On Ice	1984	$18

EVENFALL
❑ EF401 [B]	Talas	1979	$25

RELATIVITY
❑ EMCL8001	Sink Your Teeth Into That	1982	$16

TALBERT, THOMAS
ATLANTIC
❑ 1250 [M]	Bix Fats Duke Interpreted by Thomas Talbert	1957	$300

—Black label

❑ SD1250 [S]	Bix Fats Duke Interpreted by Thomas Talbert	1958	$300

—Green label

❑ 1250 [M]	Bix Fats Duke Interpreted by Thomas Talbert	1961	$300

—Multicolor label, white "fan" logo at right

❑ SD1250 [S]	Bix Fats Duke Interpreted by Thomas Talbert	1961	$300

—Multicolor label, white "fan" logo at right

SEA BREEZE
❑ SB-2038	Things As They Are	198?	$25

—As "Tom Talbert"

TALISMEN, THE
BLUE STAR
❑ M-6323 [M]	Treasury of American Railroad Songs and Ballads	1964	$25
❑ MS-6323 [S]	Treasury of American Railroad Songs and Ballads	1964	$30

PRESTIGE
❑ PRLP-7406 [M]	Folk Swingers Extraordinaire	1965	$25
❑ PRST-7406 [S]	Folk Swingers Extraordinaire	1965	$30

TALK TALK
EMI AMERICA
❑ ST-17113	It's My Life	1983	$12
❑ DLP-19001 [EP]	Talk Talk	1982	$12
❑ ST-17179	The Colour of Spring	1986	$12
❑ ST-17083	The Party's Over	1982	$12

EMI MANHATTAN
❑ E1-46977	Spirit of Eden	1988	$18
❑ SPRO 04172 [EP]	Spirit of Eden -- Let the Music Speak	1988	$25

—Promo-only sampler with edits of four of the six songs from the original LP on side 1 and the same four tracks again on Side 2

❑ E1-46366	The Party's Over	1988	$18

—Reissue of EMI America ST-17083; much scarcer than the original

TALKING HEADS
RHINO VINYL
❑ R1-70802	Remain in Light	2006	$18

—Reissue on 180-gram vinyl

SIRE
❑ SRK6076	Fear of Music	1979	$12
❑ R153839	Little Creatures	1985	$15

—RCA Music Service edition

❑ 25305	Little Creatures	1985	$12
❑ SR6058	More Songs About Buildings and Food	1978	$15
❑ SRK6058	More Songs About Buildings and Food	1979	$10

—Reissue with new prefix

❑ R153810	Naked	1988	$15

—BMG Direct Marketing edition

❑ 25654	Naked	1988	$12
❑ PRO01033 [DJ]	Psycho Killer/Life During Wartime/Take Me to the River/Houses in Motion	1982	$18

—Promo-only 4-song sampler

❑ SRK6095	Remain in Light	1981	$12
❑ R150102	Speaking in Tongues	1983	$15

—BMG Direct Marketing edition

❑ 23771 [B]	Speaking in Tongues	1983	$30

—Clear vinyl in oversize plastic container with Robert Rauschenberg artwork

❑ 23883	Speaking in Tongues	1983	$12

—Standard issue

❑ R124560	Stop Making Sense	1984	$15

—RCA Music Service edition

❑ 25121 [B]	Stop Making Sense (Soundtrack)	1984	$25

—First issue with booklet and black & white cover

❑ 25186	Stop Making Sense (Soundtrack)	1984	$12

TALKING HEADS (continued)

Number	Title	Yr	NM
— Second issue: No booklet, color cover			
PRO0930 [DJ]	Talking Heads	1980	$18
— Promo-only 4-song sampler from "Remain in Light			
PRO-A-930 [DJ]	Talking Heads	1980	$18
— Promo-only 4-song sampler from "Remain in Light			
SR6036	Talking Heads '77	1977	$15
2SR3590	The Name of This Band Is Talking Heads	1982	$25
PRO-A-1033 [DJ]	The Name of This Band Is Talking Heads Sampler	1982	$18
— Promo only			
25512	True Stories	1986	$12
WARNER BROS.			
WBMS-104 [DJ]	Talking Heads Live on Tour	1979	$30
— Part of "The Warner Bros. Music Show" series (has been counterfeited)			
WBMS-104 [DJ]	The Warner Bros. Music Show – Talking Heads Live on Tour	1979	$30
— Promo-only radio show (has been counterfeited)			

TALLEY, JAMES

Number	Title	Yr	NM
CAPITOL			
ST-11695	Ain't It Somethin'	1977	$12
ST-11605	Blackjack Choir	1977	$12
ST-11416	Got No Bread, No Milk, No Money, But We Sure Got a Lot of Love	1975	$15
ST-11494	Tryin' Like the Devil	1976	$12

TAMBA 4, THE

Number	Title	Yr	NM
A&M			
SP-3013	Samba Blim	1969	$30
SP-3004	We and the Sea	1968	$30

TAMPA RED

Number	Title	Yr	NM
BLUEBIRD			
AXM2-5501	Guitar Wizard	1975	$18
BLUES CLASSICS			
25	Guitar Wizard (1935-53)	197?	$15
BLUESVILLE			
BVLP-1043 [M]	Don't Jive Me	1962	$120
— Blue label, silver print			
BVLP-1043 [M]	Don't Jive Me	1963	$30
— Blue label, trident logo at right			

Number	Title	Yr	NM
BVLP-1030 [M]	Don't Tampa with the Blues	1961	$120
— Blue label, silver print			
BVLP-1030 [M]	Don't Tampa with the Blues	1963	$30
— Blue label, trident logo at right			
FANTASY			
OBC-516	Don't Tampa with the Blues	198?	$12
YAZOO			
1039	Bottleneck Guitar	197?	$15

TAMS, THE

Number	Title	Yr	NM
1-2-3			
ST-567	The Best of the Tams	1970	$25
ABC			
ABCS-627	A Little More Soul	1968	$30
ABCS-673	A Portrait of the Tams	1969	$30
ABCS-499 [S]	Hey Girl, Don't Bother Me	1964	$25
— Reissue of ABC-Paramount 499			
ABCS-481 [R]	Presenting the Tams	1968	$25
— Reissue of ABC-Paramount 481			
ABC-596 [M]	Time for the Tams	1967	$40
ABCS-596 [S]	Time for the Tams	1967	$30
ABC-PARAMOUNT			
ABC-499 [M]	Hey Girl, Don't Bother Me	1964	$30
ABCS-499 [S]	Hey Girl, Don't Bother Me	1964	$40
ABC-481 [M]	Presenting the Tams	1964	$50
ABCS-481 [R]	Presenting the Tams	1964	$30
CAPITOL			
SM-11839	The Best of the Tams	1979	$15
COMPLEAT			
CMLP-5001 [EP]	Beach Music from the Tams	198?	$10
SOUNDS SOUTH			
SO-16010	The Mighty, Mighty Tams	1977	$18

TANEGA, NORMA

Number	Title	Yr	NM
NEW VOICE			
NV-2001 [M]	Walkin' My Cat Named Dog	1966	$75
NVS-2001 [S]	Walkin' My Cat Named Dog	1966	$100

TANGERINE DREAM

Number	Title	Yr	NM
CAROLINE			
CAROL1349	Livemiles	1988	$15
CLEOPATRA			
CLO2318 [B]	Booster	2016	$50
— red, blue and white vinyl			
ELEKTRA			
5E-557	Exit	1981	$12
5E-521	Thief	1981	$12
EMI AMERICA			
ST-17141	Flashpoint	1984	$12
MCA			
6165	Legend	1986	$10
2277	Sorcerer	1977	$15
PRIVATE MUSIC			
2057-1-P	Lily on the Beach	1989	$18
2047-1-P	Miracle Mile	1989	$18
2042-1-P	Optical Race	1988	$18
RELATIVITY			
865618069	Alpha Centauri	1986	$15
865618071	Atam	1986	$15
865618068	Electronic Meditation	1986	$15
865618072	Green Desert	1986	$15
EMC8043	Le Parc	198?	$15
EMC8045	Poland	198?	$18
865618113	Underwater Sunlight	1986	$15
865618070	Zeit	1986	$18
VIRGIN			
PZG35014 [B]	Encore	1977	$30
VR 13-108 [B]	Phaedra	1974	$30
VR 13-116 [B]	Rubycon	1975	$30
PZ34427	Stratosfear	1976	$18
VIRGIN INTERNATIONAL			
VI2097 [B]	Cyclone	1979	$15
— Reissue			
VI2111	Force Majeure	1979	$15
VI2010	Phaedra	1979	$12
— Reissue			
VI2044 [B]	Ricochet	1975	$30
VI2025	Rubycon	1979	$12
— Reissue			
VI2068	Stratosfear	1979	$15
— Reissue of 34427			

TANGERINE ZOO, THE

Number	Title	Yr	NM
MAINSTREAM			
S-6116 [B]	Outside Looking In	1969	$85
S-6107 [B]	Tangerine Zoo	1968	$75

TAPSCOTT, HORACE

Number	Title	Yr	NM
FLYING DUTCHMAN			
FDS-107	The Giant Is Awakened	1969	$25
FD-10107	The Giant Is Awakened	197?	$35
INTERPLAY			
7724	Horace Tapscott in New York	197?	$30
7714	Songs of the Unsung	197?	$30

TARANTULA

Number	Title	Yr	NM
A&M			
SP-4202	Tarantula	1969	$25

TARIKA BLUE

Number	Title	Yr	NM
CHIAROSCURO			
141	Blue Path	197?	$35

TARRIERS, THE

Number	Title	Yr	NM
ATLANTIC			
8042 [M]	Tell the World	1960	$30
SD8042 [S]	Tell the World	1960	$40
DECCA			
DL4538 [M]	Gather 'Round	1964	$30
DL74538 [S]	Gather 'Round	1964	$30
DL4342 [M]	The Tarriers	1962	$30
DL74342 [S]	The Tarriers	1962	$30
GLORY			
PG-1200 [M]	The Tarriers	1958	$75
KAPP			
KL1349 [M]	The Original Tarriers	1963	$30
KS3349 [S]	The Original Tarriers	1963	$30
UNITED ARTISTS			
UAL-4033 [M]	Hard Travelin'	1959	$30
UAS-5033 [S]	Hard Travelin'	1959	$40

TASTE
RORY GALLAGHER was in this group.

Number	Title	Yr	NM
ATCO			
SD 33-322	On the Boards	1970	$30
SD 33-296	Taste	1969	$30

TASTE OF HONEY, A

Number	Title	Yr	NM
CAPITOL			
SOO-11951	Another Taste	1979	$15
ST-11754	A Taste of Honey	1978	$12
ST-12173	Ladies of the Eighties	1982	$15
ST-12089	Twice as Sweet	1980	$15

TATE, BABY

Number	Title	Yr	NM
BLUESVILLE			
BVLP-1072 [M]	What You Done	1963	$100
— Blue label, silver print			
BVLP-1072 [M]	What You Done	1963	$30
— Blue label, trident logo at right			

TATE, BUDDY, AND DOLLAR BRAND

Number	Title	Yr	NM
CHIAROSCURO			
165	Buddy Tate and Dollar Brand	1977	$30

TATE, BUDDY

Number	Title	Yr	NM
BASF			
20740	Unbroken	197?	$35
BLACK LION			
312	Kansas City Woman	197?	$35
CHIAROSCURO			
123	Buddy Tate and His Buddies	1973	$35
CONCORD JAZZ			
CJ-163	The Great Buddy Tate	1981	$25
FANTASY			
OJC-184	Tate-A-Tate	1985	$25
FELSTED			
7004 [M]	Swinging Like Tate	1958	$100
2004 [S]	Swinging Like Tate	1958	$100
MASTER JAZZ			
8127	Swinging Like Tate	197?	$30
8128	Texas Twister	197?	$30
MUSE			
MR-5198	Buddy Tate and the Muse All-Stars Live at Sandy's	1979	$25
MR-5249	Hard Blowin': Live at Sandy's	198?	$25
PAUSA			
7030	Unbroken	198?	$25
SACKVILLE			
3027	Buddy Tate Quartet	198?	$25
3017	Sherman Shuffle	198?	$25
3034	The Ballad of Artistry	198?	$25
SWINGVILLE			
SVLP-2029 [M]	Groovin' with Buddy Tate	1961	$50
— Purple label			
SVLP-2029 [M]	Groovin' with Buddy Tate	1965	$30
— Blue label, trident logo at right			
SVLP-2014 [M]	Tate-A-Tate	1960	$50
— Purple label			
SVLP-2014 [M]	Tate-A-Tate	1965	$30
— Blue label, trident logo at right			
SVLP-2003 [M]	Tate's Date	1960	$50
— Purple label			
SVLP-2003 [M]	Tate's Date	1965	$30
— Blue label, trident logo at right			

TATE, GRADY

Number	Title	Yr	NM
ABC IMPULSE!			
ASD-9330	The Master	197?	$30
BUDDAH			
BDS-5623	By Special Request	1973	$30
JANUS			
7010	Movin' Day	197?	$30
3050	She Is My Lady	197?	$30
SKYE			
SK-17	After the Long Ride Home	197?	$35
SK-1007	Feeling Life	197?	$35
SK-4	Windmills of My Mind	1969	$50

TATE, HOWARD

Number	Title	Yr	NM
ATLANTIC			
SD8303	Howard Tate	1971	$25
TURNTABLE			
5002	Reaction	1969	$25
VERVE			
V-5022 [M]	Get It While You Can	1967	$25
V6-5022 [S]	Get It While You Can	1967	$30

Number	Title	Yr	NM
TATRO, DUANE			
CONTEMPORARY			
❑ C-3514 [M]	Jazz for Moderns	1956	$250
TATUM, ART, AND BUDDY DEFRANCO			
AMERICAN RECORDING SOCIETY			
❑ G-412 [M]	The Art Tatum-Buddy DeFranco Quartet	1956	$40
CLEF			
❑ MGC-715 [M]	The Art Tatum-Buddy DeFranco Quartet	1955	$0
—Canceled			
VERVE			
❑ MGV-8229 [M]	The Art Tatum-Buddy DeFranco Quartet	1958	$175
❑ V-8229 [M]	The Art Tatum-Buddy DeFranco Quartet	1961	$75
TATUM, ART; BENNY CARTER; LOUIS BELLSON			
CLEF			
❑ MGC-643 [M]	Tatum-Carter-Bellson	1955	$250
VERVE			
❑ MGV-8227 [M]	Makin' Whoopee	1958	$120
❑ V-8227 [M]	Makin' Whoopee	1961	$25
❑ MGV-8013 [M]	The Three Giants	1957	$150
❑ V-8013 [M]	The Three Giants	1961	$25
TATUM, ART; ROY ELDRIDGE; ALVIN STOLLER; JOHN SIMMONS			
CLEF			
❑ MGC-679 [M]	The Art Tatum-Roy Eldridge-Alvin Stoller-John Simmons Quartet	1955	$300
VERVE			
❑ MGV-8064 [M]	The Art Tatum-Roy Eldridge-Alvin Stoller-John Simmons Quartet	1957	$150
❑ V-8064 [M]	The Art Tatum-Roy Eldridge-Alvin Stoller-John Simmons Quartet	1961	$75
TATUM, ART			
20TH CENTURY FOX			
❑ S-4162 [R]	This Is Art Tatum, Volume 1	196?	$30
❑ 3162 [M]	This Is Art Tatum, Volume 1	196?	$35
❑ S-4163 [R]	This Is Art Tatum, Volume 2	196?	$30
❑ 3163 [M]	This Is Art Tatum, Volume 2	196?	$35
20TH FOX			
❑ FTM-102-2 [M]	Piano Discoveries	1961	$250
❑ FTS-102-2 [R]	Piano Discoveries	1961	$250
❑ FTM-3029 [M]	Piano Discoveries Vol. I	1960	$250
❑ FTS-3029 [R]	Piano Discoveries Vol. I	1960	$250
❑ FTM-3033 [M]	Piano Discoveries Vol. II	1960	$250
❑ FTS-3033 [R]	Piano Discoveries Vol. II	1960	$250
AIRCHECK			
❑ 21	Radio Broadcasts	197?	$25
ASCH			
❑ ALP-356 [10]	Art Tatum	1950	$175
AUDIOPHILE			
❑ AP-88	The Remarkable Art Tatum	198?	$25
BOOK-OF-THE-MONTH			
❑ 51-5400	The One and Only	1980	$30
BRUNSWICK			
❑ BL58023 [10]	Art Tatum Piano Solos	1950	$150
❑ BL58013 [10]	Art Tatum Trio	1950	$150
❑ BL54004 [M]	Here's Art Tatum	1955	$120
CAPITOL			
❑ H216 [10]	Art Tatum	1950	$175
❑ T216 [M]	Art Tatum	1955	$175
—Turquoise label			
❑ M-11028	Art Tatum	1972	$30
❑ T216 [M]	Art Tatum	1959	$75
—Black colorband label, logo at left			
❑ T216 [M]	Art Tatum	196?	$50
—Black colorband label, logo at top			
❑ H269 [10]	Art Tatum Encores	1951	$175
❑ H408 [10]	Art Tatum Trio	1953	$175
CLEF			
❑ 0(no cat #) [M]	Art Tatum	1954	$350
—Boxed set with volumes 2, 3, 4 and 5 of The Genius of Art Tatum			
❑ MGC-746 [M]	Presenting the Art Tatum Trio	1955	$0
—Canceled			
❑ MGC-741 [M]	The Art Tatum Trio	1955	$0
—Canceled			
❑ MGC-612 [M]	The Genius of Art Tatum #1	1954	$250
❑ MGC-613 [M]	The Genius of Art Tatum #2	1954	$250
❑ MGC-614 [M]	The Genius of Art Tatum #3	1954	$250
❑ MGC-615 [M]	The Genius of Art Tatum #4	1954	$250
❑ MGC-618 [M]	The Genius of Art Tatum #5	1954	$250
❑ MGC-657 [M]	The Genius of Art Tatum #6	1955	$250
❑ MGC-658 [M]	The Genius of Art Tatum #7	1955	$250
❑ MGC-659 [M]	The Genius of Art Tatum #8	1955	$250
❑ MGC-660 [M]	The Genius of Art Tatum #9	1955	$250
❑ MGC-661 [M]	The Genius of Art Tatum #10	1955	$250

Number	Title	Yr	NM
❑ MGC-712 [M]	The Genius of Art Tatum #11	1956	$250
❑ MGC-616 [M]	The Genius of Art Tatum	1954	$0
—Canceled			
❑ MGC-617 [M]	The Genius of Art Tatum	1954	$0
—Canceled			
❑ MGC-619 [M]	The Genius of Art Tatum	1954	$0
—Canceled			
❑ MGC-620 [M]	The Genius of Art Tatum	1954	$0
—Canceled			
❑ MGC-621 [M]	The Genius of Art Tatum	1954	$0
—Canceled			
CMS/SAGA			
❑ 6915	The Rarest Solos	197?	$25
COLUMBIA			
❑ CL6301 [10]	An Art Tatum Concert	1954	$100
❑ GL101 [10]	Gene Norman Concert at Shrine Auditorium, May 1949	1952	$175
❑ CS9655 [S]	Piano Starts Here	1968	$25
—Red "360 Sound" label			
❑ CS9655	Piano Starts Here	1971	$25
—Orange label			
❑ PC9655	Piano Starts Here	198?	$20
—Reissue with new prefix			
❑ CS9655 [M]	Piano Starts Here	1968	$40
—Mono is white label promo only with stereo number; "Special Mono Radio Station Copy" sticker on cover			
❑ CL2565 [10]	The Tatum Touch	1956	$50
DECCA			
❑ DL5086 [10]	Art Tatum Piano Solos	1950	$175
❑ DL8715 [M]	The Art of Tatum	1958	$120
DIAL			
❑ LP-206 [10]	Art Tatum Trio	1950	$300
EMARCY			
❑ 826129-1	20th Century Piano Genius	1986	$30
FOLKWAYS			
❑ FL-33 [10]	Art Tatum Trio	1951	$150
❑ F-12293	Footnotes to Jazz	197?	$30
GNP CRESCENDO			
❑ GNP-9025	Art Tatum at the Crescendo, Vol. 1	197?	$25
❑ GNP-9026	Art Tatum at the Crescendo, Vol. 2	197?	$25
HARMONY			
❑ HL7006 [M]	An Art Tatum Concert	1957	$30
JAZZ MAN			
❑ 5030	Get Happy	198?	$25
❑ 5024	The Genius	198?	$25
JAZZZ			
❑ 101	Works of Art	197?	$30
MCA			
❑ 42327	Solos	1990	$30
❑ 4019	Tatum Masterpieces	197?	$30
MOVIETONE			
❑ 2021 [M]	The Legendary Art Tatum	1967	$35
❑ 72021 [R]	The Legendary Art Tatum	1967	$30
ONYX			
❑ 205	God Is in the House	197?	$30
PABLO			
❑ 2310887	The Best of Art Tatum	198?	$25
❑ 2405418	The Best of Art Tatum	198?	$25
❑ 2625706	The Tatum Group Masterpieces	197?	$75
—Boxed set with eight volumes (except 2310 775) included			
❑ 2310732	The Tatum Group Masterpieces with Benny Carter, Vol. 1	197?	$25
❑ 2310733	The Tatum Group Masterpieces with Benny Carter, Vol. 2	197?	$25
❑ 2310737	The Tatum Group Masterpieces with Ben Webster	197?	$25
❑ 2310736	The Tatum Group Masterpieces with Buddy DeFranco	197?	$25
❑ 2310735	The Tatum Group Masterpieces with Jo Jones	197?	$25
❑ 2310720	The Tatum Group Masterpieces with Lionel Hampton, Buddy Rich	197?	$25
❑ 2310775	The Tatum Group Masterpieces with Lionel Hampton, Buddy Rich, Vol. 2	198?	$25
❑ 2310731	The Tatum Group Masterpieces with Lionel Hampton, Sweets Edison, Barney Kessel	197?	$25
❑ 2310734	The Tatum Group Masterpieces with Roy Eldredge	197?	$25
❑ 2625703	The Tatum Solo Masterpieces	1974	$175
—Box set with all 13 volumes included			
❑ 2310723	The Tatum Solo Masterpieces, Vol. 1	197?	$25
❑ 2310729	The Tatum Solo Masterpieces, Vol. 2	197?	$25

Number	Title	Yr	NM
❑ 2310730	The Tatum Solo Masterpieces, Vol. 3	197?	$25
❑ 2310789	The Tatum Solo Masterpieces, Vol. 4	197?	$25
❑ 2310790	The Tatum Solo Masterpieces, Vol. 5	197?	$25
❑ 2310791	The Tatum Solo Masterpieces, Vol. 6	197?	$25
❑ 2310792	The Tatum Solo Masterpieces, Vol. 7	197?	$25
❑ 2310793	The Tatum Solo Masterpieces, Vol. 8	198?	$25
❑ 2310835	The Tatum Solo Masterpieces, Vol. 9	198?	$25
❑ 2310862	The Tatum Solo Masterpieces, Vol. 10	198?	$25
❑ 2310864	The Tatum Solo Masterpieces, Vol. 11	198?	$25
❑ 2310870	The Tatum Solo Masterpieces, Vol. 12	198?	$25
❑ 2310875	The Tatum Solo Masterpieces, Vol. 13	198?	$25
PAUSA			
❑ 9017	The Legend	198?	$25
REM HOLLYWOOD			
❑ LP-3 [10]	Piano Virtuoso	1950	$120
—The number "2" is on the front cover, but "LP-3" appears on the label			
STINSON			
❑ SLP-40 [M]	Art Tatum Solos and Trio	195?	$40
❑ SLP-40 [10]	Art Tatum Trio	1950	$175
STORYVILLE			
❑ 4108	Masters of Jazz, Vol. 8	199?	$30
TIME-LIFE			
❑ STL-J-24	Giants of Jazz	1982	$50
VARESE SARABANDE			
❑ VC81021	The Keystone Sessions	197?	$35
VERVE			
❑ MGV-8101-5 [M]	Art Tatum, Volume 1	1957	$300
—Boxed set with volumes 1-5 of The Genius of Art Tatum			
❑ MGV-8102-5 [M]	Art Tatum, Volume 2	1957	$300
—Boxed set with volumes 6-10 of The Genius of Art Tatum			
❑ MGV-8347 [M]	More of the Greatest Piano of Them All	1959	$150
❑ V-8347 [M]	More of the Greatest Piano of Them All	1961	$25
❑ MGV-8118 [M]	Presenting the Art Tatum Trio	1957	$150
❑ V-8118 [M]	Presenting the Art Tatum Trio	1961	$25
❑ MGV-8360 [M]	Still More of the Greatest Piano of Them All	1960	$100
❑ V-8360 [M]	Still More of the Greatest Piano of Them All	1961	$25
❑ VSP-33 [M]	The Art of Art	1966	$35
❑ VSPS-33 [R]	The Art of Art	1966	$30
❑ MGV-8220 [M]	The Art Tatum-Ben Webster Quartet	1958	$350
❑ V-8220 [M]	The Art Tatum-Ben Webster Quartet	1961	$75
❑ V-8433 [M]	The Essential Art Tatum	1962	$25
❑ MGV-8036 [M]	The Genius of Art Tatum #1	1957	$175
❑ V-8036 [M]	The Genius of Art Tatum #1	1961	$25
❑ MGV-8037 [M]	The Genius of Art Tatum #2	1957	$175
❑ V-8037 [M]	The Genius of Art Tatum #2	1961	$25
❑ MGV-8038 [M]	The Genius of Art Tatum #3	1957	$175
❑ V-8038 [M]	The Genius of Art Tatum #3	1961	$25
❑ MGV-8039 [M]	The Genius of Art Tatum #4	1957	$175
❑ V-8039 [M]	The Genius of Art Tatum #4	1961	$25
❑ MGV-8040 [M]	The Genius of Art Tatum #5	1957	$175
❑ V-8040 [M]	The Genius of Art Tatum #5	1961	$25
❑ MGV-8055 [M]	The Genius of Art Tatum #6	1957	$175
❑ V-8055 [M]	The Genius of Art Tatum #6	1961	$25
❑ MGV-8056 [M]	The Genius of Art Tatum #7	1957	$175
❑ V-8056 [M]	The Genius of Art Tatum #7	1961	$25
❑ MGV-8057 [M]	The Genius of Art Tatum #8	1957	$175
❑ V-8057 [M]	The Genius of Art Tatum #8	1961	$25
❑ MGV-8058 [M]	The Genius of Art Tatum #9	1957	$175
❑ V-8058 [M]	The Genius of Art Tatum #9	1961	$25
❑ MGV-8059 [M]	The Genius of Art Tatum #10	1957	$175
❑ V-8059 [M]	The Genius of Art Tatum #10	1961	$25
❑ MGV-8095 [M]	The Genius of Art Tatum #11	1957	$175
❑ V-8095 [M]	The Genius of Art Tatum #11	1961	$25
❑ MGV-8323 [M]	The Greatest Piano of Them All	1959	$50
❑ V-8323 [M]	The Greatest Piano of Them All	1961	$25
❑ MGV-8332 [M]	The Incomparable Music of Art Tatum	1959	$175
❑ V-8332 [M]	The Incomparable Music of Art Tatum	1961	$25
TATUM, ART/ERROLL GARNER			
JAZZTONE			
❑ J-1203 [M]	Kings of the Keyboard	1956	$40
ROOST			
❑ LP-2213 [M]	Giants of the Piano	1956	$50
TATUM, ART/JAMES P. JOHNSON			
MCA			
❑ 4112	Tatum Masterpieces Vol. 2/ Johnson Plays Fats Waller	197?	$30

Number	Title	Yr	NM

TATUM, ART/MARY LOU WILLIAMS
HALL OF FAME

❏ 607	King and Queen	197?	$25

JAZZTONE

| ❏ J-1280 [M] | The King and Queen | 1958 | $40 |

TAUPIN, BERNIE
ELTON JOHN's songwriting partner.
ASYLUM

| ❏ 6E-263 | He Who Rides the Tiger | 1980 | $15 |

ELEKTRA

| ❏ EKS-75020 | Bernie Taupin | 1972 | $18 |

RCA

❏ 6420RAB [DJ]	Interview Album	1987	$25
❏ 6420-1-RAB [DJ]	Interview Album	1987	$25
❏ 5922-1-R	Tribe	1987	$12

TAVARES
CAPITOL

❏ ST-11258	Check It Out	1973	$12
❏ SW-11719	Future Bound	1978	$12
❏ SN-16207	Future Bound	1981	$10
—Budget-line reissue			
❏ ST-11316	Hard Core Poetry	1974	$12
❏ ST-11396	In the City	1975	$12
❏ ST-12167	Loveline	1982	$12
❏ ST-11628	Love Storm	1977	$12
❏ SN-16206	Love Storm	1981	$10
—Budget-line reissue			
❏ ST-12117	Love Uprising	1981	$12
❏ SW-11874	Madam Butterfly	1979	$12
❏ ST-11533	Sky-High!	1976	$12
❏ ST-12026	Supercharged	1980	$12
❏ ST-11701	The Best of Tavares	1977	$12

RCA VICTOR

| ❏ AFL1-4357 | New Directions | 1982 | $12 |
| ❏ AFL1-4700 | Words and Music | 1983 | $12 |

TAVENER, JOHN
APPLE

| ❏ SMAS-3369 | The Whale | 1972 | $25 |

TAX FREE
POLYDOR

| ❏ 24-4053 [B] | Tax Free | 1971 | $30 |

TAXXI
FANTASY

❏ F-9603	Day for Night	1980	$18
❏ F-9628	Foreign Tongue	1983	$18
❏ F-9617	States of Emergency	1982	$25

MCA

| ❏ 5580 | Expose | 1985 | $12 |

TAYLES, THE
CINEVISTA

| ❏ US1001 | Who Are These Guys -- Live at the Nitty Gritty | 1972 | $100 |

TAYLOR, ALEX
CAPRICORN

| ❏ CP 0101 | Dinnertime | 1972 | $12 |
| ❏ 860 | With Friends and Neighbors | 1971 | $12 |

TAYLOR, ANDY
MCA

❏ R153322	Thunder	1987	$15
—BMG Direct Marketing edition			
❏ 5837	Thunder	1987	$12

TAYLOR, ART
BLUE NOTE

❏ BLP-4047 [M]	A.T.'s Delight	1960	$2000
—Deep groove" version (deep indentation under label on both sides)			
❏ BLP-4047 [M]	A.T.'s Delight	1960	$180
—Regular version, W. 63rd St. address on label			
❏ BST-84047 [S]	A.T.'s Delight	1960	$160
—W. 63rd St. address on label			
❏ BST-84047 [S]	A.T.'s Delight	1985	$1220
—The Finest in Jazz Since 1939" reissue			

FANTASY

| ❏ OJC-094 | Taylor's Wailers | 198? | $25 |

NEW JAZZ

❏ NJLP-8219 [M]	Taylor's Tenors	1959	$175
—Purple label			
❏ NJLP-8219 [M]	Taylor's Tenors	1965	$175
—Blue label, trident logo at right			

PRESTIGE

| ❏ PRLP-7117 [M] | Taylor's Wailers | 1957 | $650 |

Number	Title	Yr	NM

TAYLOR, BILLY
ABC IMPULSE!

| ❏ AS-71 [S] | My Fair Lady Loves Jazz | 1968 | $35 |

ABC-PARAMOUNT

❏ ABC-134 [M]	Billy Taylor At the London House	1956	$150
❏ ABC-162 [M]	Billy Taylor Introduces Ira Sullivan	1957	$150
❏ ABC-112 [M]	Evergreens	1956	$150
❏ ABC-177 [M]	My Fair Lady Loves Jazz	1957	$150
❏ ABC-226 [M]	The New Trio	1958	$150
❏ ABCS-226 [S]	The New Trio	1958	$40

ARGO

| ❏ LP-650 [M] | Taylor Made Flute | 1959 | $150 |
| ❏ LPS-650 [S] | Taylor Made Flute | 1959 | $40 |

ATLANTIC

❏ 1329 [M]	One for Fun	1960	$300
—Black label			
❏ SD1329 [S]	One for Fun	1960	$300
—Green label			
❏ ALR-113 [10]	Piano Panorama	1951	$300
❏ 1277 [M]	The Billy Taylor Touch	1958	$300
—Black label			
❏ 1277 [M]	The Billy Taylor Touch	1961	$300
—Multicolor label, white "fan" logo at right			

BELL

| ❏ S-6049 | OK Billy! | 1970 | $35 |

CAPITOL

❏ T2302 [M]	Midnight Piano	1965	$100
❏ ST2302 [S]	Midnight Piano	1965	$150
❏ T2039 [M]	Right Here, Right Now	1963	$100
❏ ST2039 [S]	Right Here, Right Now	1963	$150

CONCORD JAZZ

| ❏ CJ-145 | Where've You Been | 1981 | $25 |

FANTASY

| ❏ OJC-1730 | Cross Section | 198? | $25 |
| ❏ OJC-015 | The Billy Taylor Trio with Candido | 1982 | $25 |

IMPULSE!

| ❏ A-71 [M] | My Fair Lady Loves Jazz | 1965 | $250 |
| ❏ AS-71 [S] | My Fair Lady Loves Jazz | 1965 | $250 |

MERCURY

| ❏ MG-20722 [M] | Impromptu | 1962 | $150 |
| ❏ SR-60722 [S] | Impromptu | 1962 | $150 |

MONMOUTH-EVERGREEN

| ❏ 7089 | Jazz Alive | 1978 | $30 |

MOODSVILLE

❏ MVLP-16 [M]	Interlude	1961	$150
—Green label			
❏ MVLP-16 [M]	Interlude	1965	$75
—Blue label, trident logo at right			

NEW JAZZ

| ❏ NJLP-8313 [M] | Live! At Town Hall | 1963 | $0 |
| —Canceled; reassigned to Status | | | |

PAUSA

| ❏ 7096 | Sleeping Bee | 198? | $25 |

PRESTIGE

❏ PRLP-7001 [M]	A Touch of Taylor	1955	$300
❏ PRST-7664 [R]	A Touch of Taylor	1969	$35
❏ PRLP-184 [10]	Billy Taylor Trio	1954	$300
❏ PRLP-188 [10]	Billy Taylor Trio	1954	$300
❏ PRLP-139 [10]	Billy Taylor Trio, Volume 1	1953	$300
❏ PRLP-7015 [10]	Billy Taylor Trio, Volume 1	1956	$300
❏ PRLP-165 [10]	Billy Taylor Trio, Volume 2	1953	$300
❏ PRLP-7016 [10]	Billy Taylor Trio, Volume 2	1956	$300
❏ PRLP-168 [10]	Billy Taylor Trio, Volume 3	1953	$300
❏ PRLP-7093 [M]	Billy Taylor Trio at Town Hall	1957	$300
❏ PRLP-194 [10]	Billy Taylor Trio In Concert at Town Hall, December 17, 1954	1955	$300
❏ PRLP-7071 [M]	Cross Section	1956	$300
❏ 16-2 [M]	Let's Get Away from It All	1957	$500
— This album plays at 16 2/3 rpm and is marked as such; white label			
❏ PRLP-7051 [M]	The Billy Taylor Trio with Candido	1956	$300
❏ PRST-7762	Today!	1970	$35

RIVERSIDE

❏ RLP 12-319 [M]	Billy Taylor Trio Uptown	1960	$250
❏ RLP-1168 [S]	Billy Taylor Trio Uptown	1960	$50
❏ RLP 12-306 [M]	Billy Taylor with Four Flutes	1959	$300
❏ RLP-1151 [S]	Billy Taylor with Four Flutes	1959	$50
❏ RLP 12-339 [M]	Warming Up	1960	$250
❏ RLP-1195 [S]	Warming Up	1960	$50

ROOST

| ❏ R-406 [10] | Jazz at Storyville | 1952 | $250 |
| ❏ R-409 [10] | Taylor Made Jazz | 1952 | $250 |

SAVOY

| ❏ MG-9035 [10] | Billy Taylor Piano | 1953 | $250 |

SESAC

| ❏ N-3001 [M] | Custom Taylored | 1959 | $120 |
| ❏ SN-3001 [S] | Custom Taylored | 1959 | $150 |

STATUS

| ❏ ST-8313 [M] | Live! At Town Hall | 1965 | $40 |

Number	Title	Yr	NM

SURREY

| ❏ S-1033 [M] | Easy Life | 1966 | $75 |
| ❏ SS-1033 [S] | Easy Life | 1966 | $75 |

TOWER

| ❏ ST-5111 [S] | I Wish I Knew | 1968 | $75 |

WEST 54

| ❏ 8008 | Live at Storyville | 198? | $30 |

TAYLOR, BOBBY, AND THE VANCOUVERS
GORDY

❏ G-930 [M]	Bobby Taylor and the Vancouvers	1968	$100
—Mono is promo only			
❏ GS-930 [S]	Bobby Taylor and the Vancouvers	1968	$75
❏ GS-942	Taylor Made Soul	1969	$75

TAYLOR, BUCK
JPL

| ❏ 14098 | That Man from Gunsmoke | 197? | $40 |

TAYLOR, CARMOL
ELEKTRA

| ❏ 7E-1069 | Song Writer | 1976 | $15 |

TAYLOR, CATHIE
CAPITOL

❏ T1359 [M]	A Little Bit of Sweetness	1960	$25
❏ ST1359 [S]	A Little Bit of Sweetness	1960	$30
❏ T1448 [M]	The Tree Near My House	1961	$25
❏ ST1448 [S]	The Tree Near My House	1961	$30

TAYLOR, CECIL
A&M

| ❏ 7502152861 | In Florescence | 1990 | $30 |

AMERICAN RECORDING SOCIETY

| ❏ G-437 [M] | Modern Jazz | 195? | $40 |

ARISTA/FREEDOM

❏ AF1038	Indent	197?	$30
❏ AF1905	Nefertiti	197?	$35
❏ AF1005	Silent Tongues	1975	$30

BARNABY

| ❏ Z30562 | Cecil Taylor Quartet | 1971 | $35 |
| ❏ KZ31035 | New York City R&B | 1972 | $35 |

BLUE NOTE

❏ BLP-4260 [M]	Conquistador	1967	$75
❏ BST-84260 [S]	Conquistador	1967	$30
—With "A Division of Liberty Records" on label			
❏ B1-84260 [S]	Conquistador	1989	$30
—The Finest in Jazz Since 1939" reissue			
❏ BST-84260 [S]	Conquistador	197?	$20
—Reissue with newer label; with "A Division of United Artists Records" on label			
❏ BN-LA458-H2	In Transition	197?	$35
❏ BLP-4237 [M]	Unit Structures	1966	$75
❏ BST-84237 [S]	Unit Structures	1966	$30
—With "New York, USA" on label			
❏ BST-84237 [S]	Unit Structures	1967	$35
—With "A Division of Liberty Records" on label			

CANDID

| ❏ CD-8006 [M] | The World of Cecil Taylor | 1960 | $50 |

| ❏ CS-9006 [S] | The World of Cecil Taylor | 1960 | $40 |

CONTEMPORARY

| ❏ C-3562 [M] | Looking Ahead! | 1959 | $300 |
| ❏ S-7562 [S] | Looking Ahead! | 1959 | $300 |

FANTASY

❏ 6014 [M]	Live At the Café Montmarte	1964	$25
❏ 86014 [S]	Live At the Café Montmarte	1964	$30
❏ OJC-452	Looking Ahead	1990	$30

Number	Title	Yr	NM
HAT ART			
❏ 1993/4	Garden	1986	$35
— Reissue of Hat Hut 1993/4			
❏ 3011	One Too Many Salty Swift & Not Goodbye	1986	$25
— Reissue of Hat Hut 02			
❏ 2036	The Eight	1987	$35
HAT HUT			
❏ 3508	Calling It the 8th	1981	$30
❏ 1993/4	Garden	198?	$25
❏ 16	It Is In the Brewing Luminous	198?	$35
❏ 02	One Too Many Salty Swift & Not Goodbye	197?	$30
INNER CITY			
❏ IC-3021	Air Above Mountains (Buildings Within)	1977	$35
❏ IC-3001	The Dark to Themselves	197?	$35
JAZZ MAN			
❏ 5031	New York R & B	198?	$25
❏ 5026	The World of Cecil Taylor	198?	$25
JCOA			
❏ 1002	Cecil Taylor with the Jazz Composers Orchestra	197?	$35
MOSAIC			
❏ MR6-127	The Complete Candid Recordings of Cecil Taylor and Buell Neidlinger	199?	$150
NEW WORLD			
❏ 201	Cecil Taylor	1978	$30
❏ 303	Three Phasis	197?	$30
PAUSA			
❏ 7108	Fly! Fly! Fly!	198?	$25
❏ 7053	Live in the Black Forest	198?	$25
PRESTIGE			
❏ 34003	Great Concert	197?	$25
SOUL NOTE			
❏ 121150	For Olim	199?	$30
❏ SN-1089	Winged Serpent (Sliding Quadrants)	1986	$30
TRANSITION			
❏ TRLP-19 [M]	Jazz Advance	1956	$750
— With booklet (deduct 1/4 if missing)			
UNIT CORE			
❏ 30551	Spring of Two Blue-J's	197?	$25
UNITED ARTISTS			
❏ UAL-4014 [M]	Hard Driving Jazz	1959	$50
❏ UAL-4046 [M]	Love for Sale	1959	$50
❏ UAS-5046 [S]	Love for Sale	1959	$40
❏ UAS-5014 [S]	Stereo Drive	1959	$40

TAYLOR, CHET

Number	Title	Yr	NM
BRYLEN			
❏ BN-4408	Pretty Words	1982	$12

TAYLOR, CHIP

Number	Title	Yr	NM
BUDDAH			
❏ BDS-5118 [B]	Gasoline	1972	$18
CAPITOL			
❏ ST-11909	Saint Sebastian	1979	$12
COLUMBIA			
❏ KC34345	Somebody Shoot Out the Jukebox	1977	$12
WARNER BROS.			
❏ BS2718	Last Chance	1973	$15
❏ BS2824	Some of Us	1974	$15

TAYLOR, CREED

Number	Title	Yr	NM
ABC-PARAMOUNT			
❏ ABC-308 [M]	Lonelyville "The Nervous Beat	1960	$30
❏ ABCS-308 [S]	Lonelyville "The Nervous Beat	1960	$30
❏ ABC-259 [M]	Shock Music in Hi-Fi	1958	$40
❏ ABCS-259 [S]	Shock Music in Hi-Fi	1958	$75
❏ ABC-317 [M]	The Best of the Barracks Ballads	1960	$30
❏ ABCS-317 [S]	The Best of the Barracks Ballads	1960	$30

TAYLOR, DEBBIE

Number	Title	Yr	NM
TODAY			
❏ TLP-1007	Comin' Down on You	1972	$75
❏ TLP-1007	Comin' Down on You	1985	$50

TAYLOR, DICK

Number	Title	Yr	NM
SKYLARK			
❏ SKLP-18 [10]	Blue Moon	1954	$100

TAYLOR, EARL

Number	Title	Yr	NM
CAPITOL			
❏ T2090 [M]	Bluegrass Taylor-Made	1963	$40
❏ ST2090 [S]	Bluegrass Taylor-Made	1963	$50

Number	Title	Yr	NM
UNITED ARTISTS			
❏ UAL-3049 [M]	Folk Songs from the Bluegrass	1960	$30
❏ UAS-6049 [S]	Folk Songs from the Bluegrass	1960	$30

TAYLOR, HOUND DOG

Number	Title	Yr	NM
ALLIGATOR			
❏ 4701	Hound Dog Taylor	1971	$30
❏ 4704	Natural Boogie	1974	$25

TAYLOR, JAMES

Number	Title	Yr	NM
APPLE			
❏ SKAO3352	James Taylor	1969	$30
— With title in black print			
❏ SKAO3352	James Taylor	1970	$25
— With title in orange print			
COLUMBIA			
❏ TC37009	Dad Loves His Work	1981	$12
❏ PC37009	Dad Loves His Work	198?	$10
❏ HC47009	Dad Loves His Work	1983	$40
— Half-speed mastered edition			
❏ FC36058	Flag	1979	$12
❏ PC36058	Flag	198?	$10
❏ JC34811	JT	1977	$10
❏ PC34811	JT	198?	$10
❏ FC40851	Never Die Young	1988	$12
❏ FC40052	That's Why I'm Here	1985	$12
EUPHORIA			
❏ EST-2 [B]	James Taylor and the Original Flying Machine 1967	1971	$18
NAUTILUS			
❏ NR-29	Gorilla	1981	$40
— Audiophile pressing			
TRIP			
❏ TLP-9513	Rainy Day Man	197?	$12
— Reissue of Euphoria album			
WARNER BROS.			
❏ BS2866	Gorilla	1975	$12
— Burbank" label			
❏ BS2866	Gorilla	1979	$10
— Cream label			
❏ BS42866 [Q]	Gorilla	1975	$20
❏ BS2979	Greatest Hits	1976	$15
— This and other variations of this title have re-recorded versions of "Carolina in My Mind" and "Something in the Way She Moves."			
❏ BSK3113	Greatest Hits	1977	$12
— Burbank" label			
❏ BSK3113	Greatest Hits	1979	$10
— Cream label			
❏ BS2912	In the Pocket	1976	$12
— Burbank" label			
❏ BS2912	In the Pocket	1979	$10
— Cream label			
❏ BS2561	Mud Slide Slim and the Blue Horizon	1971	$12
— Green "WB" label			
❏ BS2561	Mud Slide Slim and the Blue Horizon	1973	$10
— Burbank" label or cream label			
❏ BS2660	One Man Dog	1972	$12
— Green "WB" label			
❏ BS2660	One Man Dog	1973	$10
— Burbank" label or cream label			
❏ BS42660 [Q]	One Man Dog	1975	$20
❏ WS1843	Sweet Baby James	1970	$30
— Very early pressings have green label with "W7" logo			
❏ WS1843	Sweet Baby James	1970	$18
— Green "WB" label with no reference to other songs on front cover			
❏ WS1843	Sweet Baby James	1970	$12
— Green "WB" label with "Contains Fire and Rain and Country Road" added to front cover			
❏ ST-93138	Sweet Baby James	1970	$25
— Capitol Record Club edition			
❏ WS1843	Sweet Baby James	1973	$10
— Burbank" label or cream label			
❏ 274300	Sweet Baby James	2007	$30
— Reissue on 180-gram vinyl with replica of original green "WB" label and lyric poster			
❏ BS2794	Walking Man	1973	$12
— Burbank" label			
❏ BS2794	Walking Man	1979	$10
— Cream label			

TAYLOR, JOE

Number	Title	Yr	NM
PROJAZZ			
❏ PAD-635	Mystery Walk	1988	$25

TAYLOR, JOHNNIE

Number	Title	Yr	NM
BEVERLY GLEN			
❏ 10001	Just Ain't Good Enough	1982	$15

Number	Title	Yr	NM
COLUMBIA			
❏ JC36548	A New Day	1980	$15
❏ PC33951	Eargasm	1976	$15
— Originals have no bar code			
❏ PCQ33951 [Q]	Eargasm	1976	$30
❏ PC33951	Eargasm	1986	$10
— Budget-line reissue with bar code			
❏ JC35340	Ever Ready	1978	$15
❏ PC34401	Rated Extraordinaire	1977	$15
❏ PCQ34401 [Q]	Rated Extraordinaire	1977	$30
❏ JC36061	She's Killing Me	1979	$15
❏ JC37127	The Best of Johnnie Taylor	1981	$15
ICHIBAN			
❏ ICH-1022	Stuck in the Mud	198?	$12
❏ ICH-1042	Ugly Man	198?	$12
MALACO			
❏ MAL-7452	Crazy 'Bout You	1989	$12
❏ MAL-7446	In Control	198?	$12
❏ MAL-7460	Just Can't Do Right	1991	$12
❏ MAL-7440	Lover Boy	198?	$12
❏ MAL-7463	The Best of Johnnie Taylor on Malaco, Vol. 1	1992	$12
❏ MAL-7421	This Is Your Night	198?	$12
❏ MAL-7431	Wall to Wall	198?	$12
STAX			
❏ 88001	Chronicle	1977	$25
❏ STS-2032	Johnnie Taylor's Greatest Hits	1970	$30
❏ MPS-8558	Little Bluebird	1988	$12
❏ STS-2030	One Step Beyond	1971	$30
❏ STS-2012	Rare Stamps	1969	$30
❏ STS-2008	Raw Blues	1969	$30
❏ MPS-8508	Raw Blues	1982	$12
❏ MPS-8520	Super Hits	1983	$12
❏ STS-5509	Super Taylor	1974	$25
❏ STS-3014	Taylored in Silk	1973	$25
❏ MPS-8537	Taylored in Silk	1987	$12
— Reissue of 3014			
❏ STS-5521	The Best of Johnnie Taylor	1975	$25
❏ STS-2023	The Johnnie Taylor Philosophy Continues	1969	$30
❏ ST-715 [M]	Wanted: One Soul Singer	1967	$50
❏ STS-715 [S]	Wanted: One Soul Singer	1967	$75
❏ STS-2005	Who's Making Love	1968	$40
❏ STX-4115	Who's Making Love	198?	$12
— Reissue of 2005			

TAYLOR, KATE

Number	Title	Yr	NM
COLUMBIA			
❏ JC36034	It's In There and It's Got to Come Out	1979	$12
❏ JC35089	Kate Taylor	1978	$12
COTILLION			
❏ SD9045	Sister Kate	1971	$12

TAYLOR, KINGSIZE, AND THE DOMINOES

Number	Title	Yr	NM
MIDNIGHT			
❏ HLP-2101 [M]	Real Gonk Man	1965	$50
❏ HST-2101 [S]	Real Gonk Man	1965	$150

TAYLOR, KOKO

Number	Title	Yr	NM
ALLIGATOR			
❏ AL4754	An Audience with the Queen	1987	$12
❏ AL4724	From the Heart of a Woman	1981	$12
❏ AL4706	I Got What It Takes	1976	$15
❏ AL4784	Junp for Joy	1990	$18
❏ AL4740	Queen of the Blues	1985	$12
❏ AL4711	The Earthshaker	1978	$15
CHESS			
❏ CH-50018 [B]	Basic Soul	1972	$35
❏ LPS-1532	Koko Taylor	1969	$30
❏ CH-9263	Koko Taylor	1987	$15
— Reissue of 1532			

TAYLOR, LAURA

Number	Title	Yr	NM
GOOD SOUNDS			
❏ GS-105	Dancin' in My Feet	1979	$30

TAYLOR, LITTLE JOHNNY, AND TED TAYLOR

Number	Title	Yr	NM
RONN			
❏ LSP-7533	The Super Taylors	1973	$25

TAYLOR, LITTLE JOHNNY

Number	Title	Yr	NM
FANTASY			
❏ MPF-4510	Little Johnny Taylor's Greatest Hits	1982	$12
GALAXY			
❏ 203 [M]	Little Johnny Taylor	1963	$150
❏ 8203 [S]	Little Johnny Taylor	1963	$175
❏ 207 [M]	Little Johnny Taylor's Greatest Hits	1964	$150
❏ 8207 [S]	Little Johnny Taylor's Greatest Hits	1964	$175
RONN			
❏ LPS-7530	Everybody Knows About My Good Thing	1972	$30
❏ LSP-7535	L.J.T.	1975	$25
❏ LSP-7532	Open House at My House	1973	$30

Number	Title	Yr	NM

TAYLOR, LIVINGSTON
ATCO
| ❏ SD 33-334 | Livingston Taylor | 1970 | $15 |

CAPRICORN
| ❏ 863 | Liv | 1971 | $12 |
| ❏ CP 0114 | Over the Rainbow | 1973 | $12 |

EPIC
| ❏ JE36153 | Man's Best Friend | 1979 | $12 |

TAYLOR, LYNN
GRAND AWARD
| ❏ GA-33-0(# unknown) [M] | Lynn Taylor Sings | 195? | $300 |

TAYLOR, MARTIN
CONCORD JAZZ
| ❏ CJ-184 | Skye Boat | 198? | $25 |

TAYLOR, MEL
WARNER BROS.
| ❏ W1624 [M] | Mel Taylor in Action | 1966 | $30 |
| ❏ WS1624 [S] | Mel Taylor in Action | 1966 | $40 |

TAYLOR, MICK
Also see THE ROLLING STONES.

COLUMBIA

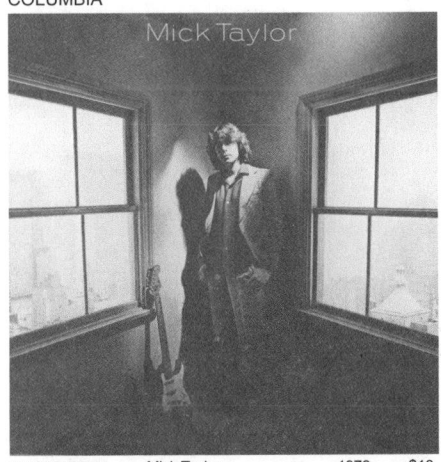

| ❏ JC35076 [B] | Mick Taylor | 1979 | $18 |

TAYLOR, R. DEAN
RARE EARTH
| ❏ RS-522 [B] | I Think, Therefore I Am | 1971 | $25 |

TAYLOR, RUSTY
STOMP OFF
❏ SOS-1082	Give Me a Call	1985	$25
❏ SOS-1028	Good Old Bad Old Days	198?	$25
❏ SOS-1186	Let's Misbehave	1988	$25

TAYLOR, SAM "THE MAN"
DECCA
❏ DL4417 [M]	It's a Blue World	1963	$35
❏ DL74417 [S]	It's a Blue World	1963	$25
❏ DL4302 [M]	Misty Mood	1962	$35
❏ DL74302 [S]	Misty Mood	1962	$25
❏ DL4573 [M]	Somewhere in the Night	1964	$35
❏ DL74573 [S]	Somewhere in the Night	1964	$25

LION
| ❏ L-70054 [M] | Sam "The Man" Taylor | 1958 | $30 |

METROJAZZ
| ❏ E-1008 [M] | Jazz for Commuters | 1958 | $120 |
| ❏ SE-1008 [S] | Jazz for Commuters | 1958 | $120 |

MGM
❏ E-3292 [M]	Blue Mist	1955	$85
— Yellow label			
❏ E-3973 [M]	Blue Mist	1961	$30
❏ SE-3973 [S]	Blue Mist	1961	$30
— Possibly a re-recording of 3292			
❏ E-3607 [M]	Lush Life	1957	$0
— Canceled			
❏ E-3783 [M]	More Blue Mist	1959	$30
❏ SE-3783 [S]	More Blue Mist	1959	$40
❏ E-3482 [M]	Music for Melancholy Babies	1957	$75
❏ E-293 [10]	Music with the Big Beat	195?	$150
❏ E-3473 [M]	Music with the Big Beat	1956	$100
— Yellow label			
❏ E-3380 [M]	Out of This World	1956	$75
— Yellow label			
❏ E-3573 [M]	Prelude to Blues	1957	$75
— Yellow label			

Number	Title	Yr	NM

❏ E-3553 [M]	Rockin' Sax and Rollin' Organ	1957	$75
— Yellow label			
❏ GAS-146	Sam "The Man" Taylor (Golden Archive Series)	1970	$35
❏ E-3967 [M]	Sam "The Man" Taylor Plays Hollywood	1960	$30
❏ SE-3967 [S]	Sam "The Man" Taylor Plays Hollywood	1960	$40

MOODSVILLE
❏ MVLP-24 [M]	The Bad and the Beautiful	1962	$50
— Green label			
❏ MVLP-24 [M]	The Bad and the Beautiful	1965	$30
— Blue label, trident logo at right			

TAYLOR, TED
SOLPUGIDS
| ❏ 101 | I Let You Hurt Me Too Long/ Pleading for Love | 198? | $10 |
| ❏ 102 | You're Tippin', She's Rippin'/ Little Red Rooster | 198? | $10 |

ALARM
| ❏ 1000 | 1976 | 1976 | $30 |

MCA
| ❏ 3059 | Keepin' My Head Above Water | 1978 | $15 |

OKEH
❏ OKM-12104 [M]	Be Ever Wonderful	1963	$30
❏ OKS-14104 [S]	Be Ever Wonderful	1963	$40
❏ OKM-12109 [M]	Blues and Soul	1965	$30
❏ OKS-14109 [S]	Blues and Soul	1965	$40
❏ OKM-12113 [M]	Ted Taylor's Greatest Hits	1966	$30
❏ OKS-14113 [S]	Ted Taylor's Greatest Hits	1966	$30

RONN
❏ LP-8003	Be Ever Wonderful	198?	$12
❏ LPS-7528	Shades of Blue	1969	$15
❏ LP-8004	Steal Away	198?	$12
❏ LPS-7531	Taylor Made	1972	$15
❏ LPS-7529	You Can Dig It!	197?	$15

SOLPUGIDS
| ❏ 1001 | Be Ever Wonderful | 198? | $18 |
| ❏ 1002 | Taylor Made for You | 198? | $18 |

TAYLOR, TUT
WORLD PACIFIC
❏ WP-1816 [M]	12 String Dobro	1964	$30
❏ ST-1816 [S]	12 String Dobro	1964	$100
— Red vinyl			
❏ ST-1816 [S]	12 String Dobro	1964	$30
— Black vinyl			
❏ WP-1829 [M]	Dobro Country	1964	$30
❏ ST-1829 [S]	Dobro Country	1964	$30

TAYLOR-GOOD, KAREN
MESA
| ❏ 1111 | Karen | 1984 | $15 |

TCHAIKOVSKY, ANDRE
RCA VICTOR RED SEAL
❏ LSC-2360 [S]	Chopin: Preludes; Barcarolle: Mazurkas, Etudes, Ballade 3	1960	$75
— Original with "shaded dog" label			
❏ LSC-2354 [S]	Mozart: Fantasia in C; Sonata in C, K. 457; Sonata in C, K. 330	1960	$80
— Original with "shaded dog" label			
❏ LSC-2287 [S]	Mozart: Piano Concerto No. 25	1959	$150
— With Fritz Reiner/Chicago Symphony Orchestra; original with "shaded dog" label			

TCHAIKOVSKY, BRAM/BENNY MARDONES
POLYDOR
| ❏ PRO129 [DJ] | Two Stars Are Better Than One | 1980 | $15 |
| — Promo-only sampler | | | |

TCHICAI, JOHN, AND PIERRE DERGE
STEEPLECHASE
| ❏ SCS-1174 | Ball at Louisiana | 1982 | $30 |

TCHICAI, JOHN
BLACK SAINT
| ❏ 120094 | Timo's Message | 1990 | $30 |

STEEPLECHASE
| ❏ SCS-1075 | The Real Tchical | 198? | $30 |

TE KANAWA, KIRI
PHILIPS
| ❏ 412629-1 | Ave Maria | 1984 | $12 |

TEA COMPANY, THE
SMASH
| ❏ SRS-67105 | Come and Have Some Tea | 1968 | $50 |

Number	Title	Yr	NM

TEAGARDEN, JACK
AIRCHECK
| ❏ 9 | Jack Teagarden and Frankie Trumbauer | 197? | $25 |
| ❏ 24 | Jack Teagarden on the Air | 198? | $25 |

BETHLEHEM
❏ BCP-32 [M]	Jazz Great	1955	$300
❏ BCP-6040	Meet Me Where They Play the Blues	1978	$30
— Distributed by Caytronics" reissue			

BIOGRAPH
| ❏ C-2 | Great Soloist | 197? | $25 |

BLUEBIRD
| ❏ 9986-1-RB | That's a Serious Thing | 1990 | $30 |

CAPITOL
❏ T1095 [M]	Big T's Dixieland Band	1959	$40
❏ ST1095 [S]	Big T's Dixieland Band	1959	$75
❏ T1143 [M]	Shades of Night	1959	$50
❏ ST1143 [S]	Shades of Night	1959	$75
❏ T820 [M]	Swing Low Sweet Spiritual	1957	$85
❏ T721 [M]	This Is Teagarden	1956	$85

COLUMBIA SPECIAL PRODUCTS
| ❏ JSN6044 [M] | King of the Blues Trombone | 197? | $30 |

COMMODORE
| ❏ 20015 [10] | Big T | 195? | $100 |

DECCA
❏ DL8304 [M]	Big T's Jazz	1956	$175
❏ DL4540 [M]	The Golden Horn of Jack Teagarden	1964	$35
❏ DL74540 [R]	The Golden Horn of Jack Teagarden	1964	$30

EPIC
❏ SN6044 [M]	King of the Blues Trombone	1963	$175
❏ LN24045 [M]	King of the Blues Trombone, Vol. 1	1963	$75
❏ LN24046 [M]	King of the Blues Trombone, Vol. 2	1963	$75
❏ LN24047 [M]	King of the Blues Trombone, Vol. 3	1963	$75

EVEREST ARCHIVE OF FOLK & JAZZ
| ❏ 352 | Big Band Jazz | 198? | $25 |
| ❏ FS-335 | Original Dixieland | 198? | $25 |

FOLKWAYS
| ❏ FJ-2819 | The Big Band Sound of Jack Teagarden and Bunny Berigan | 198? | $30 |

IAJRC
| ❏ LP-19 | Sincerely, Jack Teagarden | 198? | $35 |

JAZZTONE
| ❏ J-1222 [M] | Big T | 195? | $30 |
| — Reissue of Period material | | | |

JOLLY ROGER
| ❏ 5026 [10] | Jack Teagarden | 1955 | $75 |

MCA
| ❏ 227 | The Golden Horn of Jack Teagarden | 1973 | $25 |
| — Black rainbow label | | | |

MOSAIC
| ❏ MQ6-168 | The Complete Capitol Fifties Jack Teagarden Sessions | 199? | $175 |

PERIOD
| ❏ SLP-1106 [10] | Meet Me Where They Play the Blues | 1955 | $100 |
| ❏ SLP-1110 [10] | Original Dixieland | 1955 | $100 |

RCA VICTOR
| ❏ LPV-528 [M] | Jack Teagarden | 1965 | $25 |

RONDO-LETTE
| ❏ A-18 [M] | The Blues and Dixie | 1958 | $30 |

ROULETTE
❏ R-25177 [M]	Dixie Sound	1962	$35
❏ SR-25177 [S]	Dixie Sound	1962	$25
❏ R-25091 [M]	Jack Teagarden at the Round Table	1960	$35
❏ SR-25091 [S]	Jack Teagarden at the Round Table	1960	$25
❏ R-25119 [M]	Jazz Maverick	1961	$35
❏ SR-25119 [S]	Jazz Maverick	1961	$25
❏ R-25243 [M]	Portrait of Mr. T	1963	$35
❏ SR-25243 [S]	Portrait of Mr. T	1963	$25

ROYALE
| ❏ 18156 [10] | The Blues | 195? | $100 |

SAVOY JAZZ
| ❏ SJL-1162 | Varsity Sides | 1986 | $25 |

SOUNDS
| ❏ S-1203 | Jack Teagarden in Concert | 197? | $35 |

TIME-LIFE
| ❏ STL-J-08 | Giants of Jazz | 1979 | $50 |

TRIP
| ❏ 6 | Jack Teagarden | 197? | $25 |

URANIA
| ❏ UJLP-1002 [10] | Jack Teagarden Sings and Plays | 1954 | $300 |

Number	Title	Yr	NM
❏ UJLP-1001 [10]	Meet the New Jack Teagarden	1954	$300

VERVE

Number	Title	Yr	NM
❏ V-8495 [M]	Jack Teagarden!!	1962	$35
❏ V6-8495 [S]	Jack Teagarden!!	1962	$25
❏ V-8416 [M]	Mis'ry and the Blues	1961	$35
❏ V6-8416 [S]	Mis'ry and the Blues	1961	$25
❏ V-8465 [M]	Think Well of Me	1962	$35
❏ V6-8465 [S]	Think Well of Me	1962	$25

TEAGARDEN, JACK/BOBBY HACKETT
COMMODORE

Number	Title	Yr	NM
❏ FL-30012 [M]	Jack Teagarden and Bobby Hackett	1959	$30

TEAGARDEN, JACK/JONAH JONES
AAMCO

Number	Title	Yr	NM
❏ ALP-309 [M]	Two Boys from Dixieland	196?	$30

— *Reissue of Bethlehem material*

BETHLEHEM

Number	Title	Yr	NM
❏ BCP-6042 [M]	Dixieland	1959	$250

TEAGARDEN, JACK/MAX KAMINSKY
COMMODORE

Number	Title	Yr	NM
❏ XFL-14940	Big T and Mighty Max	198?	$25

HALL OF FAME

Number	Title	Yr	NM
❏ 616	Jack and Max	197?	$25

TEAGARDEN, JACK/PEE WEE RUSSELL
FANTASY

Number	Title	Yr	NM
❏ OJC-1708	Jack Teagarden's Big Eight / Pee Wee Russell's Rhythmakers	1985	$25

RIVERSIDE

Number	Title	Yr	NM
❏ RLP 12-141	Jack Teagarden's Big Eight / Pee Wee Russell's Rhythmakers	1956	$300

TEARDROP EXPLODES, THE
MERCURY

Number	Title	Yr	NM
❏ SRM-1-4016	Kilimanjaro	1981	$15
❏ SRM-1-4035	Wilder	1981	$15

TEARDROPS, THE (U)
20TH CENTURY FOX

Number	Title	Yr	NM
❏ FXG-5011 [M]	The Teardrops at Trinchi's	1963	$30

TEARS FOR FEARS
FONTANA

Number	Title	Yr	NM
❏ R133653	The Seeds of Love	1989	$15

— *BMG Direct Marketing edition*

Number	Title	Yr	NM
❏ 838730-1	The Seeds of Love	1989	$12

MERCURY

Number	Title	Yr	NM
❏ R143666	Songs from the Big Chair	1985	$15

— *BMG Direct Marketing edition*

Number	Title	Yr	NM
❏ 824300-1	Songs from the Big Chair	1985	$12
❏ 811039-1	The Hurting	1983	$18

— *Child on cover (original)*

Number	Title	Yr	NM
❏ 811039-1	The Hurting	1983	$12

— *Photo of group next to duck pond on cover (reissue)*

TEBALDI, RENATA
LONDON

Number	Title	Yr	NM
❏ OS26241	Christmas Festival	1971	$15

TECHNOTRONIC
SBK

Number	Title	Yr	NM
❏ K1-93422	Pump Up the Jam -- The Album	1989	$25
❏ K1-95028	Trip On This -- The Remixes	1990	$25

TEDDY AND THE PANDAS
TOWER

Number	Title	Yr	NM
❏ ST-5125	Basic Magnetism	1968	$30

TEDDY BEARS, THE
IMPERIAL

Number	Title	Yr	NM
❏ LP-9067 [M]	The Teddy Bears Sing!	1959	$400
❏ LP-12010 [S]	The Teddy Bears Sing!	1959	$1500

TEDESCO, TOMMY
DISCOVERY

Number	Title	Yr	NM
❏ 928	Hollywood Gypsy	1986	$12
❏ 851	My Desiree	1982	$12
❏ 789	When Do We Start	1978	$30

IMPERIAL

Number	Title	Yr	NM
❏ LP-9321 [M]	Calypso Soul	1966	$150
❏ LP-12321 [S]	Calypso Soul	1966	$175
❏ LP-9295 [M]	Guitars	1965	$150
❏ LP-12295 [S]	Guitars	1965	$175
❏ LP-9263 [M]	The Electric 12 String Guitar of Tommy Tedesco	1964	$150
❏ LP-12263 [S]	The Electric 12 String Guitar of Tommy Tedesco	1964	$175

TREND

Number	Title	Yr	NM
❏ TR-517	Alone at Last	1979	$25

— *Direct-to-disc recording*

Number	Title	Yr	NM
❏ TR-514	Autumn	1978	$25

— *Direct-to-disc recording*

Number	Title	Yr	NM
❏ TR-534 [B]	Carnival Time	1983	$15

TEE, WILLIE
CAPITOL

Number	Title	Yr	NM
❏ ST-199	I'm Only a Man	1969	$18

UNITED ARTISTS

Number	Title	Yr	NM
❏ UA-LA655-G	Anticipation	1976	$15

TEE SET, THE
COLOSSUS

Number	Title	Yr	NM
❏ CCS-1001 [B]	Ma Belle Amie	1970	$25

TEEGARDEN AND VAN WINKLE
ATCO

Number	Title	Yr	NM
❏ 33-272 [M]	An Evening at Home with Teegarden and Van Winkle	1968	$75

— *Mono is white label promo only*

Number	Title	Yr	NM
❏ SD 33-272 [S]	An Evening at Home with Teegarden and Van Winkle	1968	$18

WESTBOUND

Number	Title	Yr	NM
❏ 2003	But Anyhow	1969	$18
❏ 2010	On Our Way	1971	$18

TEEMATES, THE
AUDIO FIDELITY

Number	Title	Yr	NM
❏ AFLP-3042 [M]	Jet Set Dance Discotheque	1964	$40
❏ AFSD-7042 [S]	Jet Set Dance Discotheque	1964	$50

TEEN QUEENS, THE
CROWN

Number	Title	Yr	NM
❏ CLP-5022 [M]	Eddie My Love	1956	$300

— *Black label, all silver print*

Number	Title	Yr	NM
❏ CLP-5022 [M]	Eddie My Love	196?	$150

— *Black label, "CROWN" in alternating colored letters*

Number	Title	Yr	NM
❏ CLP-5373 [M]	The Teen Queens	1963	$50
❏ CST-373 [R]	The Teen Queens	1963	$30

RPM

Number	Title	Yr	NM
❏ LRP-3007 [M]	Eddie My Love	1956	$0

— *Canceled*

TEENA MARIE
EPIC

Number	Title	Yr	NM
❏ FE40318	Emerald City	1986	$12
❏ FE40318 [DJ]	Emerald City	1986	$25

— *Promo only on green vinyl*

Number	Title	Yr	NM
❏ FE40872	Naked to the World	1988	$12
❏ FE38882	Robbery	1983	$12
❏ FE39528	Starchild	1984	$12

GORDY

Number	Title	Yr	NM
❏ G8-997M1	Irons in the Fire	1980	$15
❏ G8-1004M1	It Must Be Magic	1981	$15
❏ G7-992R1	Lady T.	1980	$15
❏ G7-986R1	Wild and Peaceful	1979	$15

MOTOWN

Number	Title	Yr	NM
❏ 5370ML	Greatest Hits	1985	$12

TEENAGE JESUS AND THE JERKS
MIGRANE/LUST UNLUST

Number	Title	Yr	NM
❏ CC-336 [EP]	Teenage Jesus and the Jerks	1979	$75

— *Pink vinyl*

Number	Title	Yr	NM
❏ CC-336 [EP]	Teenage Jesus and the Jerks	1979	$50

— *Black vinyl*

TEENAGERS, THE
See FRANKIE LYMON AND THE TEENAGERS. These are records by the original group without FRANKIE LYMON.

TEITELBAUM, RICHARD
ARISTA/FREEDOM

Number	Title	Yr	NM
❏ AF1037	Time Zones	197?	$30

TELEVISION
Also see TOM VERLAINE.

4 MEN WITH BEARDS

Number	Title	Yr	NM
❏ 4M507LP [B]	Adventure		$25
❏ 4M533LP [B]	Television		$25

CAPITOL

Number	Title	Yr	NM
❏ SPRO-79456 [DJ]	Television	1992	$30

— *Promo-only vinyl release (stock copies on CD and cassette only)*

Number	Title	Yr	NM
❏ SPRO-79456 [DJ]	Television	1992	$30

— *Vinyl is promo only*

ELEKTRA

Number	Title	Yr	NM
❏ 6E-133 [B]	Adventure	1978	$25
❏ 7E-1098 [B]	Marquee Moon	1977	$30

RHINO

Number	Title	Yr	NM
❏ R11098 [B]	Marquee Moon	2015	$25

— *180g*

TEMIZ, OKAY
FINNADAR

Number	Title	Yr	NM
❏ 9032	Drummer of Two Worlds	198?	$35

TEMPERLEY, JOE, AND JIMMY KNEPPER
HEP

Number	Title	Yr	NM
❏ 2003	Just Friends	198?	$25

TEMPEST
WARNER BROS.

Number	Title	Yr	NM
❏ BS2682	Tempest	1973	$30

TEMPESTS, THE
SMASH

Number	Title	Yr	NM
❏ MGS-27098 [M]	Would You Believe?	1966	$30
❏ SRS-67098 [S]	Would You Believe?	1966	$30

TEMPLE, PICK
PRESTIGE INT'L.

Number	Title	Yr	NM
❏ PRLP-13008 [M]	Pick of the Crop	196?	$30

X

Number	Title	Yr	NM
❏ LXA-3022 [10]	Folk Songs of the People	1954	$50

TEMPLE, SHIRLEY
20TH CENTURY FOX

Number	Title	Yr	NM
❏ TFM-3102 [M]	The Best of Shirley Temple	1963	$30
❏ TFM-3172 [M]	The Best of Shirley Temple, Vol. 2	1965	$30

20TH FOX

Number	Title	Yr	NM
❏ FOX-3006 [M]	Little Miss Wonderful	1959	$40

— *Shirley Temple pictured as an adult on cover*

Number	Title	Yr	NM
❏ FOX-3006 [M]	Little Miss Wonderful	196?	$40

— *Shirley Temple pictured as a child on cover*

Number	Title	Yr	NM
❏ FOX-3045 [M]	More Little Miss Wonderful	1961	$40
❏ TCF-103 [M]	The Shirley Temple Songbook	1961	$50

MOVIETONE

Number	Title	Yr	NM
❏ MTM-71012 [M]	Curtain Call	1966	$25
❏ MTM-71001 [M]	On the Good Ship Lollipop	1966	$25

TEMPLETON, ALEC
ATLANTIC

Number	Title	Yr	NM
❏ 1222 [M]	The Magic Piano	1956	$300

— *Black label*

Number	Title	Yr	NM
❏ 1222 [M]	The Magic Piano	1961	$175

— *Multicolor label, white "fan" logo at right*

TEMPLIN, RAY
EUPHONIC

Number	Title	Yr	NM
❏ 1219	A Flash at the Piano	198?	$25

TEMPO, NINO, AND APRIL STEVENS
Also see each artist's individual listings.

ATCO

Number	Title	Yr	NM
❏ 33-156 [M]	Deep Purple	1963	$40
❏ SD 33-156 [S]	Deep Purple	1963	$50
❏ 33-180 [M]	Hey Baby	1966	$30
❏ SD 33-180 [S]	Hey Baby	1966	$40
❏ 33-162 [M]	Nino and April Sing the Great Songs	1964	$30
❏ SD 33-162 [S]	Nino and April Sing the Great Songs	1964	$40

RCA CAMDEN

Number	Title	Yr	NM
❏ CAL-824 [M]	A Nino Tempo/April Stevens Program	1964	$15

— *Actually contains solo recordings by each, packaged together to capitalize on the success of "Deep Purple"*

WHITE WHALE

Number	Title	Yr	NM
❏ WW-113 [M]	All Strung Out	1967	$25
❏ WWS-7113 [S]	All Strung Out	1967	$30

TEMPO, NINO
A&M

Number	Title	Yr	NM
❏ SP-3629	Come See Me 'Round Midnight	1974	$30

LIBERTY

Number	Title	Yr	NM
❏ LRP-3023 [M]	Rock 'n' Roll Beach Party	1958	$120

TEMPOS, THE
JUSTICE

Number	Title	Yr	NM
❏ JLP-104	Speaking of the Tempos	1966	$500

TEMPREES
WE PRODUCE

Number	Title	Yr	NM
❏ 1903	Love Maze	1973	$75
❏ 1901	Love Men	1972	$75
❏ 1905	Temprees 3	1974	$75

Number	Title	Yr	NM

TEMPTATIONS, THE
The famous Detroit/Motown male vocal group. Also see EDDIE KENDRICKS; DAVID RUFFIN; THE SUPREMES AND THE TEMPTATIONS.

ATLANTIC

Number	Title	Yr	NM
❏ SD19188	Bare Back	1978	$15
❏ SD19143	Hear to Tempt You	1977	$15

GORDY

Number	Title	Yr	NM
❏ G966V1	1990	1973	$18
❏ G962L	All Directions	1972	$25
❏ G6-969S1	A Song for You	1975	$18
❏ 6085GL	Back to Basics	1984	$15
❏ GS939	Cloud Nine	1969	$25
❏ G918 [M]	Gettin' Ready	1966	$30
❏ GS918 [S]	Gettin' Ready	1966	$30
—Script "Gordy" at top of label			
❏ GS918 [S]	Gettin' Ready	1967	$25
—Block "GORDY" inside "G" on left of label			
❏ G8-998M1	Give Love at Christmas	1980	$18
❏ G6-973S1	House Party	1975	$18
❏ GS953	Live at London's Talk of the Town	1970	$25
❏ GS938	Live at the Copa	1968	$25
❏ G965L	Masterpiece	1973	$25
❏ G911 [M]	Meet the Temptations	1964	$40
❏ GS911 [S]	Meet the Temptations	1964	$50
—Script "Gordy" at top of label			
❏ GS911 [S]	Meet the Temptations	1967	$30
—Block "GORDY" inside "G" on left of label			
❏ G8-994M1	Power	1980	$15
❏ GS947	Psychedelic Shack	1970	$25
❏ GS949	Puzzle People	1969	$25
❏ 6008GL	Reunion	1982	$15
❏ GS957	Sky's the Limit	1971	$25
❏ G961L	Solid Rock	1972	$25
❏ 6032GL	Surface Thrills	1983	$15
❏ GS954	Temptations Greatest Hits II	1970	$25
❏ G921 [M]	Temptations Live!	1967	$30
❏ GS921 [S]	Temptations Live!	1967	$30
—Script "Gordy" at top of label			
❏ GS921 [S]	Temptations Live!	1967	$30
—Block "GORDY" inside "G" on left of label			
❏ G914 [M]	Temptin' Temptations	1965	$30
❏ GS914 [S]	Temptin' Temptations	1965	$30
—Script "Gordy" at top of label			
❏ GS914 [S]	Temptin' Temptations	1967	$25
—Block "GORDY" inside "G" on left of label			
❏ G8-1006M1	The Temptations	1981	$15
❏ GS951	The Temptations' Christmas Card	1969	$30
❏ G7-975S1	The Temptations Do the Temptations	1976	$18
❏ G919 [M]	The Temptations' Greatest Hits	1966	$30
❏ GS919 [S]	The Temptations' Greatest Hits	1966	$30
—Script "Gordy" at top of label			
❏ GS919 [S]	The Temptations' Greatest Hits	1967	$25
—Block "GORDY" inside "G" on left of label			
❏ G924 [M]	The Temptations in a Mellow Mood	1967	$30
❏ GS924 [S]	The Temptations in a Mellow Mood	1967	$30
❏ GS933	The Temptations Show	1969	$25
❏ G912 [M]	The Temptations Sing Smokey	1965	$35
❏ GS912 [S]	The Temptations Sing Smokey	1965	$50
—Script "Gordy" at top of label			
❏ GS912 [S]	The Temptations Sing Smokey	1967	$25
—Block "GORDY" inside "G" on left of label			
❏ G927 [M]	The Temptations Wish It Would Rain	1968	$150
—Mono is white-label promo only			
❏ GS927 [S]	The Temptations Wish It Would Rain	1968	$25
❏ 6207GL	To Be Continued	1986	$15
❏ 6164GL	Touch Me	1986	$15
❏ 6119GL	Truly for You	1984	$15
❏ G6-971S1	Wings of Love	1976	$18
❏ G922 [M]	With a Lot o' Soul	1967	$30
❏ GS922 [S]	With a Lot o' Soul	1967	$30
—Script "Gordy" at top of label			
❏ GS922 [S]	With a Lot o' Soul	1967	$25
—Block "GORDY" inside "G" on left of label			

MOTOWN

Number	Title	Yr	NM
❏ 5389ML	25th Anniversary	1986	$18
❏ M5-212V1	All the Million Sellers	1982	$15
❏ M782	Anthology	1973	$30
❏ 5279ML	Give Love at Christmas	1983	$12
—Reissue of Gordy 998			
❏ M5-144V1	Masterpiece	1981	$15
—Reissue of Gordy 965			
❏ M5-140V1	Meet the Temptations	1981	$15
—Reissue of Gordy 911			
❏ M5-164V1	Psychedelic Shack	1981	$15
—Reissue of Gordy 947			
❏ M5-172V1	Puzzle People	1981	$15
—Reissue of Gordy 949			
❏ MOT-6275	Special	1989	$15

Number	Title	Yr	NM
❏ 5251ML	The Temptations Christmas Card	1982	$12
—Reissue of Gordy 951			
❏ M5-205V1	The Temptations Sing Smokey	1981	$15
—Reissue of Gordy 912			
❏ 6246ML	Together Again	1987	$15

NATURAL RESOURCES

Number	Title	Yr	NM
❏ NR4005T1	The Temptations in a Mellow Mood	1978	$15
—Reissue of Gordy 924			

PICKWICK

Number	Title	Yr	NM
❏ SPC-3540	Psychedelic Shack	197?	$15
—Reissue of Gordy 947			

UNIVERSAL MOTOWN

Number	Title	Yr	NM
❏ 5316011	Cloud Nine	2009	$25
—Reissue of Gordy 939			

10CC

MERCURY

Number	Title	Yr	NM
❏ SRM-1-3702 [B]	Deceptive Bends	1977	$20
❏ SRM-1-1061 [B]	How Dare You!	1976	$25
❏ SRM-2-8600	Live and Let Live	1977	$18
❏ SRM-1-1029 [B]	The Original Soundtrack	1975	$30

POLYDOR

Number	Title	Yr	NM
❏ PD-1-6161 [B]	Bloody Tourists	1978	$15
❏ PD-1-6244	Greatest Hits 1972-1978	1979	$12

U.K.

Number	Title	Yr	NM
❏ 53105 [B]	10cc	1973	$30

Number	Title	Yr	NM
❏ 53110 [B]	100cc	1975	$18
❏ AUKS53107 [B]	Sheet Music	1974	$30

WARNER BROS.

Number	Title	Yr	NM
❏ BSK3442	Look Hear?	1980	$12
❏ BSK3575	Ten Out of Ten	1981	$12

10,000 MANIACS

AUDIO FIDELITY

Number	Title	Yr	NM
❏ AFZTL1510 [B]	Our Time In Eden	2011	$30

CHRISTIAN BURIAL

Number	Title	Yr	NM
❏ P-2010 [EP]	Human Conflict #5	1983	$100
❏ P-3001	Secrets of the I Ching	1984	$120

ELEKTRA

Number	Title	Yr	NM
❏ R130236	Blind Man's Zoo	1989	$15
—BMG Direct Marketing edition			
❏ 60815	Blind Man's Zoo	1989	$15
❏ 60815 [DJ]	Blind Man's Zoo	1989	$18
—Promo-only audiophile pressing (white labels)			
❏ R100481	In My Tribe	1987	$15
—BMG Direct Marketing edition			
❏ 60738 [DJ]	In My Tribe	1987	$15
—Promo-only audiophile pressing			
❏ 60738	In My Tribe	1987	$12
❏ ED5270 [DJ]	Interview	1987	$30
—Lenny Kaye interviews Natalie Merchant; promo only			
❏ 60428	The Wishing Chair	1985	$15

MOBILE FIDELITY

Number	Title	Yr	NM
❏ MOFI1-013 [B]	In My Tribe	40	$

TEN WHEEL DRIVE
Featuring Genya Ravan.

CAPITOL

Number	Title	Yr	NM
❏ ST-11199	Ten Wheel Drive	1973	$12

POLYDOR

Number	Title	Yr	NM
❏ 24-4024	Brief Replies	1970	$15
❏ 24-4008	Construction #1	1969	$15
❏ 24-4062	Peculiar Friends	1971	$15

TEN YEARS AFTER
Also see ALVIN LEE.

Number	Title	Yr	NM

CHRYSALIS

Number	Title	Yr	NM
❏ F1-21722	About Time	1989	$15
❏ PV41001	A Space in Time	1987	$10
❏ F1-21001	A Space in Time	1989	$10
❏ CHS1084	Cricklewood Green	1975	$12
❏ PV41084	Cricklewood Green	1983	$10
❏ F1-21084	Cricklewood Green	1989	$10
❏ PV41573	Positive Vibrations	1987	$10
❏ F1-21573	Positive Vibrations	1989	$10
❏ FV41049	Recorded Live	1987	$12
❏ PV41009	Rock and Roll Music to the World	1987	$10
❏ F1-21009	Rock and Roll Music to the World	1989	$10
❏ CHS1083	Ssssh	1975	$12
❏ PV41083	Ssssh	1983	$10
❏ F1-21083	Ssssh	1989	$10
❏ FV41580	Universal	1988	$12
❏ F1-21580	Universal	1989	$10
❏ CHS1085	Watt	1975	$12
❏ PV41085	Watt	1983	$10
❏ F1-21085	Watt	1989	$10

COLUMBIA

Number	Title	Yr	NM
❏ KC30801	A Space in Time	1971	$15
❏ CQ30801 [Q]	A Space in Time	1973	$40
❏ PC30801	A Space in Time	1979	$10
❏ PC34366	Classic Performances of Ten Years After	1976	$12
❏ PC32851	Positive Vibrations	1974	$12
❏ C2X32288 [B]	Recorded Live	1973	$25
❏ KC31779	Rock and Roll Music to the World	1972	$15
❏ C31779	Rock and Roll Music to the World	197?	$12
—Reissue with new prefix			

DERAM

Number	Title	Yr	NM
❏ XDES18064	Alvin Lee and Company	1972	$15
❏ DES18038	Cricklewood Green	1970	$18
❏ DES18072	Goin' Home! Their Greatest Hits	1975	$15
❏ DES18029	Ssssh	1969	$18
❏ DES18021	Stonedhenge	1969	$18
❏ DES18009 [S]	Ten Years After	1968	$25
❏ DE16009 [M]	Ten Years After	1968	$175
❏ DES18016	Undead	1968	$18
❏ XDES18050	Watt	1970	$18
—With large "DERAM" on top half of label			
❏ SMAS-93428	Watt	1970	$25
—Capitol Record Club edition			
❏ XDES18050	Watt	1970	$30
—With "LONDON" under smaller "DERAM" at top of label			

LONDON

Number	Title	Yr	NM
❏ LC50008	Greatest Hits	1977	$12
❏ 820324-1	Greatest Hits	1986	$10

TERRACE, PETE

FANTASY

Number	Title	Yr	NM
❏ 3203 [M]	Going Loco	1956	$75
—Red vinyl			
❏ 3203 [M]	Going Loco	195?	$30
❏ 3215 [M]	Invitation to the Mambo	1956	$75
—Red vinyl			
❏ 3215 [M]	Invitation to the Mambo	195?	$30
❏ 3234 [M]	The Pete Terrace Quintet	1957	$75
—Red vinyl			
❏ 3234 [M]	The Pete Terrace Quintet	195?	$30

FORUM

Number	Title	Yr	NM
❏ F-9041 [M]	Cole Porter in Latin America	196?	$35
❏ SF-9041 [S]	Cole Porter in Latin America	196?	$30

TICO

Number	Title	Yr	NM
❏ LP-1023 [M]	A Night in Mambo Jazzland	1956	$40
❏ SLP-1082 [S]	Bella Pachanga	1961	$30
❏ LP-1082 [M]	Bella Pachanga	1961	$30
❏ LP-1036 [M]	Cha Cha Cha in New York	1957	$50
❏ LP-1063 [M]	Cole Porter in Latin America	1959	$30
❏ LP-1057 [M]	My One and Only Love	1959	$30
❏ LP-1050 [M]	Pete with a Latin Beat	1958	$30
❏ LP-1028 [M]	The Nearness of You	1956	$40

TERRACE, RAY

TOWER

Number	Title	Yr	NM
❏ ST-5105	The Home of Boogaloo	1968	$25

TERRELL, TAMMI

MOTOWN

Number	Title	Yr	NM
❏ MS-652	Irresistible Tammi	1969	$50
❏ M5-231V1	Irresistible Tammi	1982	$12

TERRY, AL

INDEX

Number	Title	Yr	NM
❏ 5001	This Is Al Terry	196?	$18

TERRY, BUDDY

MAINSTREAM

Number	Title	Yr	NM
❏ MRL-336	Awareness	1972	$35
❏ MRL-391	Lean On Him	1974	$30
❏ MRL-356	Pure Dynamite	1973	$35

PRESTIGE

Number	Title	Yr	NM
❏ PRLP-7525 [M]	Electric Soul	1967	$30

Number	Title	Yr	NM
❏ PRST-7525 [S]	Electric Soul	1967	$30
❏ PRLP-7541 [M]	Natural Soul	1967	$30
❏ PRST-7541 [S]	Natural Soul	1967	$30

TERRY, CLARK

20TH CENTURY FOX
❏ TFM-3137 [M]	What Makes Sammy Swing	1963	$25
❏ TFS-4137 [S]	What Makes Sammy Swing	1963	$30

ABC IMPULSE!
❏ AS-9157 [S]	It's What's Happenin'	1968	$250
❏ AS-9127 [S]	Spanish Rice	1968	$35
❏ AS-64 [S]	The Happy Horn of Clark Terry	1968	$35

ARGO
❏ LP-620 [M]	Out on a Limb	1957	$75

CAMEO
❏ CS-1064 [S]	More	1964	$40
❏ C-1064 [M]	More (Theme From Mondo Cane)	1964	$30
❏ C-1071 [M]	Tread Ye Lightly	1964	$30
❏ CS-1071 [S]	Tread Ye Lightly	1964	$40

CANDID
❏ CD-8009 [M]	Color Changes	1960	$50
❏ CS-9009 [S]	Color Changes	1960	$40

EMARCY
❏ MG-36007 [M]	Clark Terry	1955	$300
❏ MG-36093 [M]	The Jazz School	1956	$250

ETOILE
❏ CPR-1	Clark Terry's Big Bad Band	197?	$25

FANTASY
❏ OJC-229	Duke with a Difference	1990	$30
❏ OJC-302	In Orbit	1988	$30
❏ OJC-604	Memories of Duke	1991	$30
❏ OJC-066	Serenade to a Bus Seat	198?	$30

IMPULSE!
❏ A-9127 [M]	Spanish Rice	1966	$120
❏ AS-9127 [S]	Spanish Rice	1966	$120
❏ A-64 [M]	The Happy Horn of Clark Terry	1964	$120
❏ AS-64 [S]	The Happy Horn of Clark Terry	1964	$120

JAZZ MAN
❏ 5046	Color Changes	198?	$25

MAINSTREAM
❏ MRL-347	Angyumaluma	1972	$35
❏ MRL-373	Clark Terry and the W.B. Brookmeyer Quintet	1973	$35
❏ 56043 [M]	Clark Terry Tonight	1965	$25
❏ S-6043 [S]	Clark Terry Tonight	1965	$30
❏ S-6086	Clark Terry with Bob Brookmeyer	196?	$25
❏ 56066 [M]	Mumbles	1966	$25
❏ S-6066 [S]	Mumbles	1966	$30
❏ MRL-320	Straight No Chaser	1971	$35
❏ 56054 [M]	The Power of Positive Swinging	1965	$25
❏ S-6054 [S]	The Power of Positive Swinging	1965	$30
❏ MRL-803	What'd He Say	197?	$25

MILESTONE
❏ 47032	Cruising	197?	$35

MOODSVILLE
❏ MVLP-20 [M]	Everything's Mellow	1961	$50
—Green label			
❏ MVLP-20 [M]	Everything's Mellow	1965	$30
—Blue label, trident logo at right			
❏ MVLP-26 [M]	The Jazz Version of "All American	1962	$50
—Green label			
❏ MVLP-26 [M]	The Jazz Version of "All American	1965	$30
—Blue label, trident logo at right			

PABLO TODAY
❏ 2312105	Ain't Misbehavin'	1979	$30
❏ 2312118	Memories of Duke	1980	$30
❏ 2313127	Yes, the Blues	1981	$30

PAUSA
❏ 7131	Wham!	198?	$25

POLYDOR
❏ 24-5002	Clark Terry at Montreux Jazz Festival	1970	$35

RIVERSIDE
❏ 6167	Clark Terry and Thelonious Monk in Orbit	198?	$30
❏ RM-3009 [M]	C.T. Meets Monk	1967	$150
❏ RS-3009 [S]	C.T. Meets Monk	1967	$150
❏ RLP 12-246 [M]	Duke with a Difference	1957	$300
❏ RLP-1108 [S]	Duke with a Difference	1959	$300
❏ RLP 12-271 [M]	In Orbit	1958	$300
❏ RLP 12-237 [M]	Serenade to a Bus Seat	1957	$350
—White label, blue print			
❏ RLP 12-237 [M]	Serenade to a Bus Seat	1957	$350
—Blue label, microphone logo at top			
❏ 6209	Serenade to a Bus Seat	198?	$30
❏ RLP 12-295 [M]	Top and Bottom Brass	1959	$250
❏ RLP-1137 [S]	Top and Bottom Brass	1959	$250

SWING
❏ 8406	Paris 1960	1985	$25

TRIP
❏ 5528	Swahili	197?	$25

VANGUARD
❏ VSD-79365	Clark Terry and His Jolly Giants	197?	$30
❏ VSD-79373	Clark Terry Big Band Live at Buddy's Place	1976	$30
❏ VSD-79355	Clark Terry Big Band Live at Wichita Fest '74	1975	$30
❏ VSD-79393	Globetrotter	1977	$30

VERVE
❏ V6-8836	Previously Unreleased Recordings	197?	$35

WING
❏ MGW-60002 [M]	The Jazz School	1955	$100

TERRY, CLARK/COLEMAN HAWKINS

COLPIX
❏ CP-450 [M]	Eddie Costa Memorial Concert	1963	$300
❏ SCP-450 [S]	Eddie Costa Memorial Concert	1963	$50

TERRY, DON

COLUMBIA
❏ CL6288 [10]	Teen-Age Dance Session	1955	$50

TERRY, GORDON

LIBERTY
❏ LRP-3218 [M]	Liberty Square Dance Club	1962	$25
—With calls			
❏ LRP-3219 [M]	Liberty Square Dance Club	1962	$25
—Without calls			

PLANTATION
❏ 514	Disco Country	1977	$15

TERRY, LILLIAN

SOUL NOTE
❏ SN-1047	A Dream Comes True	198?	$30
❏ SN-1147	Oo-Shoo-Be-Doo-Be…Oo…Oo…Oo…Oo	1986	$30

TERRY, PAT, JR.

CIRCLE
❏ C-54	All Jazzed Up	1981	$25

TERRY, RON

WING
❏ MGW-12108 [M]	Polkas and Waltzes	1959	$18
❏ SRW-16108 [S]	Polkas and Waltzes	1959	$25

TERRY, SONNY, AND BROWNIE MCGHEE

A&M
❏ SP-4379	Sonny & Brownie	1973	$15

ARCHIVE OF FOLK MUSIC
❏ 242	Brownie & Sonny	198?	$15

BLUESVILLE
❏ BVLP-1020 [M]	Blues All Around My Head	1961	$100
—Bright blue label, no trident logo			
❏ BVLP-1020 [M]	Blues All Around My Head	1964	$30
—Blue label with trident logo on right			
❏ BVLP-1005 [M]	Blues and Folk	1960	$100
—Bright blue label, no trident logo			
❏ BVLP-1005 [M]	Blues and Folk	1964	$30
—Blue label with trident logo on right			
❏ BVLP-1033 [M]	Blues in My Soul	1961	$100
—Bright blue label, no trident logo			
❏ BVLP-1033 [M]	Blues in My Soul	1964	$30
—Blue label with trident logo on right			
❏ BVLP-1002 [M]	Down Home Blues	1960	$100
—Bright blue label, no trident logo			
❏ BVLP-1002 [M]	Down Home Blues	1964	$30
—Blue label with trident logo on right			
❏ BVLP-1058 [M]	Live at the Second Fret	1962	$100
—Bright blue label, no trident logo			
❏ BVLP-1058 [M]	Live at the Second Fret	1964	$30
—Blue label with trident logo on right			

BLUESWAY
❏ BLS-6059	Couldn't Believe My Eyes	1970	$18
❏ BLS-6028	Long Way from Home	1969	$18

COLLECTABLES
❏ COL-5198	Golden Classics: Blowin' the Fuses	198?	$12

EVEREST
❏ 242	Brownie McGhee and Sonny Terry	1969	$30
❏ 206	Sonny Terry	1968	$30

FANTASY
❏ 24708	Back to New Orleans	1972	$18
❏ F-3317 [M]	Blues and Shouts	1962	$175
—Red vinyl			

❏ F-3317 [M]	Blues and Shouts	1962	$40
—Black vinyl			
❏ OBC-505	Brownie's Blues	1984	$12
❏ 24723	California Blues	1981	$18
❏ F-3296 [M]	Just a Closer Walk with Thee	1962	$175
—Red vinyl			
❏ F-3296 [M]	Just a Closer Walk with Thee	1962	$40
—Black vinyl			
❏ 24721	Midnight Special	1977	$18
❏ F-3340 [M]	Sonny and Brownie at Sugar Hill	1962	$175
—Red vinyl			
❏ F-3340 [M]	Sonny and Brownie at Sugar Hill	1962	$40
—Black vinyl			
❏ FS-8091 [S]	Sonny and Brownie at Sugar Hill	1962	$175
—Blue vinyl			
❏ FS-8091 [S]	Sonny and Brownie at Sugar Hill	1962	$40
—Black vinyl			
❏ OBC-503	Sonny's Story	1984	$12
❏ F-3254 [M]	Sonny Terry & Brownie McGhee	1961	$175
—Red vinyl			
❏ F-3254 [M]	Sonny Terry & Brownie McGhee	1961	$40
—Black vinyl			

FOLKLORE
❏ FRLP-14013 [M]	Down Home Blues	1964	$40
❏ FRST-14013 [S]	Down Home Blues	1964	$50

FOLKWAYS
❏ FA-2327 [M]	Blues and Folk Songs	1960	$35
❏ F-2421 [M]	Traditional Blues, Volume 1	1961	$40
❏ FS-2421 [S]	Traditional Blues, Volume 1	1961	$40
❏ F-2422 [M]	Traditional Blues, Volume 2	1961	$40
❏ FS-2422 [S]	Traditional Blues, Volume 2	1961	$40

FONTANA
❏ SGF-67599	Where the Blues Begin	1969	$30

KIMBERLEY
❏ 2017 [M]	Southern Meetin'	1963	$25
❏ 11017 [S]	Southern Meetin'	1963	$30

MAINSTREAM
❏ M-6049 [M]	Hometown Blues	1966	$25
❏ MS-6049 [S]	Hometown Blues	1966	$30

MOBILE FIDELITY
❏ 1-233	Sonny and Brownie	1996	$25
—Audiophile vinyl			

MUSE
❏ 5117	Hootin'	198?	$15
❏ 5131	You Hear Me Talkin'	198?	$15

OLYMPIC
❏ 7108	Hootin' & Hollerin'	1972	$15

PRESTIGE
❏ PRLP-7715	Best of Sonny Terry and Brownie McGhee	1969	$18
❏ PRLP-7803	Live at the Second Fret	1970	$18

ROULETTE
❏ R-25074 [M]	The Folk Songs of Sonny & Brownie	1959	$50
❏ RS-25074 [S]	The Folk Songs of Sonny & Brownie	1959	$100

SAVOY
❏ SJL-1137	Climbin' Up	1984	$12
❏ 12218	Down Home Blues	1973	$15

SHARP
❏ 2003 [M]	Down Home Blues	195?	$175

SMASH
❏ MGS-27067 [M]	Brownie McGhee at the Bunkhouse	1965	$30
❏ SRS-67067 [S]	Brownie McGhee at the Bunkhouse	1965	$40

SMITHSONIAN/FOLKWAYS
❏ SF-40011	Sing	198?	$12

STORYVILLE
❏ 4007	Brownie & Sonny	1972	$15

TOPIC
❏ T-29 [M]	Songs	1958	$50

VEE JAY
❏ VJLP-1138	Coffee House Blues	198?	$12
—With Lightnin' Hopkins			

VERVE
❏ MGV3008 [M]	Blues Is My Companion	1961	$100

VERVE FOLKWAYS
❏ FV9010 [M]	Get Together	1965	$40
❏ FVS9010 [S]	Get Together	1965	$40
❏ FV9019 [M]	Guitar Highway	1965	$40
❏ FVS9019 [S]	Guitar Highway	1965	$40

WASHINGTON
❏ W-702 [M]	Talkin' 'Bout the Blues	1961	$50

WORLD PACIFIC
❏ WP-1294 [M]	Blues Is a Story	1960	$50

Number	Title	Yr	NM
❏ ST-1294 [S]	Blues Is a Story	1960	$100
❏ WP-1296 [M]	Down South Summit Meetin'	1960	$50
❏ ST-1296 [S]	Down South Summit Meetin'	1960	$100

TERRY, SONNY
ALLIGATOR
❏ AL-4734	Whoopin'	198?	$15

— With Johnny Winter, Willie Dixon and others

BLUE LABOR
❏ 101	Robbin' the Grave	197?	$15

BLUESVILLE
❏ BVLP-1069 [M]	Sonny Is King	1963	$100

— Bright blue label, no trident logo
❏ BVLP-1069 [M]	Sonny Is King	1964	$30

— Blue label with trident logo on right
❏ BVLP-1025 [M]	Sonny's Story	1961	$100

— Bright blue label, no trident logo
❏ BVLP-1025 [M]	Sonny's Story	1964	$30

— Blue label with trident logo on right

COLLECTABLES
❏ COL-5195	Chain Gang Blues	198?	$12
❏ COL-5307	Sonny Terry	198?	$12

ELEKTRA
❏ EKL-15 [10]	City Blues	1954	$175

— With Alec Stewart
❏ EKL-14 [10]	Folk Blues	1954	$175

FANTASY
❏ OBC-521	Sonny Is King	198?	$12

FOLKWAYS
❏ 3821	A New Sound	198?	$25
❏ FP-35 [10]	Harmonica and Vocal Solos	1952	$200
❏ FA-2035 [10]	Harmonica and Vocal Solos	1952	$1250
❏ FS-2369	On the Road	196?	$20
❏ FP-2006 [10]	Sonny Terry's Washboard Band	1950	$250

— Blue and white cover
❏ FA-2006 [10]	Sonny Terry's Washboard Band	195?	$175

— Black and white cover (reissue)

PRESTIGE
❏ PRST-7802	Sonny Is King	1970	$18

RIVERSIDE
❏ RLP-644 [M]	Sonny Terry and His Mouth Harp	195?	$100

STINSON
❏ SLP-55 [10]	Sonny Terry and His Mouth Harp	1950	$175
❏ 55	Sonny Terry and His Mouth Harp	197?	$15

— Reissue of 10-inch LP

TESCHEMACHER, FRANK
BRUNSWICK
❏ BL58017 [10]	Tesch Plays Jazz Classics	1950	$100

TIME-LIFE
❏ STL-J23	Giants of Jazz	1982	$25

TEX, JOE
ACCORD
❏ SN-7174	J.T.'s Funk	1982	$12

ATLANTIC
❏ SD8231	Buying a Book	1969	$25
❏ SD8292	From the Roots Came the Rapper	1972	$18
❏ SD8211	Happy Soul	1969	$25
❏ 8106 [M]	Hold What You've Got	1965	$40
❏ SD8106 [P]	Hold What You've Got	1965	$50
❏ 8133 [M]	I've Got to Do a Little Better	1966	$40
❏ SD8133 [S]	I've Got to Do a Little Better	1966	$50
❏ SD8254	Joe Tex Sings with Strings and Things	1970	$18
❏ SD8156	Live and Lively	1968	$25
❏ SD8187 [S]	Soul Country	1968	$25
❏ 8187 [M]	Soul Country	1968	$40

— Mono is white label promo only; "d/j copy monaural" sticker on cover
❏ 8144 [M]	The Best of Joe Tex	1967	$25
❏ SD8144 [P]	The Best of Joe Tex	1967	$30
❏ 81278	The Best of Joe Tex	1985	$12
❏ 8124 [M]	The Love You Save	1966	$40
❏ SD8124 [S]	The Love You Save	1966	$50
❏ 8115 [M]	The New Boss	1965	$40
❏ SD8115 [S]	The New Boss	1965	$50

CHECKER
❏ LP-2993 [M]	Hold On	1965	$175

DIAL
❏ DL6100	He Who Is Without Funk Cast the First Stone	1979	$12
❏ DL6002	I Gotcha	1972	$18
❏ DL6004	Joe Tex Spills the Beans	1973	$18

EPIC
❏ PE34666	Bumps and Bruises	1977	$15

KING
❏ 935 [M]	The Best of Joe Tex	1965	$150
❏ KS-935 [R]	The Best of Joe Tex	1965	$85

LONDON
❏ LC-50017	Super Soul	1977	$12

PARROT
❏ PA61002 [M]	The Best of Joe Tex	1965	$50
❏ PAS71002 [R]	The Best of Joe Tex	1965	$30

PRIDE
❏ PRD-0020	The History of Joe Tex	1973	$12

RHINO
❏ RNLP-70191	I Believe I'm Gonna Make It: The Best of Joe Tex 1964-1972	1988	$12

TEXAS PLAYBOYS, THE
CAPITOL
❏ ST-11725	Live and Kickin'	1978	$18
❏ ST-11612	Today	1977	$18

TEXAS RANGERS, THE
CUMBERLAND
❏ SRC-69505 [S]	The Best of Western Swing	1963	$30
❏ MGC-29507 [M]	The Best of Western Swing	1963	$25

TEXAS RUBY
KING
❏ 840 [M]	Texas Ruby Sings His Favorite Songs	1963	$50

TEXAS TROUBADOURS, THE
DECCA
❏ DL4644 [M]	Country Dance Time	1965	$25
❏ DL74644 [S]	Country Dance Time	1965	$30
❏ DL4745 [M]	Ernest Tubb's Fabulous Texas Troubadours	1966	$25
❏ DL74745 [S]	Ernest Tubb's Fabulous Texas Troubadours	1966	$30
❏ DL75017	The Terrific Texas Troubadours and Guests	1968	$25
❏ DL4459 [M]	The Texas Troubadours	1964	$30
❏ DL74459 [S]	The Texas Troubadours	1964	$30

THA ALKAHOLICS
LOUD/RCA
❏ 66280	21 & Over	1993	$18
❏ 66446	Coast II Coast	1995	$18
❏ 67345	Likwidation	1997	$15

THACKRAY, JAKE
PHILIPS
❏ PSH600-318 [B]	Jake's Progress	1969	$25
❏ PHS600-275 [B]	The Last Will and Testament of	1967	$30

THAT PETROL EMOTION
POLYDOR
❏ 833132-1	Babble	1987	$12

VIRGIN
❏ 91354	Chemicrazy	1990	$12
❏ 91019	End of the Millennium Psychosis Blues	1988	$12

THAXTON, LLOYD
DECCA
❏ DL4594 [M]	Lloyd Thaxton Presents	1964	$25
❏ DL74594 [S]	Lloyd Thaxton Presents	1964	$30

THE THE
EPIC
❏ BFE40471	Infected	1987	$15
❏ FE45241	Mindbomb	1989	$15
❏ BFE39266	Soul Mining	1985	$15

THE UGLY BEATS
❏ GH1170HCV [B]	Brand New Day	2014	$18

— 180-gram heavyweight orange vinyl. Housed in a full-color jacket and paper sleeve. Includes download card. New vinyl; retail value.

GET HIP RECORDINGS
❏ GH1170H [B]	Brand New Day	2014	$15

— 180-gram vinyl. Released June 24, 2014. Also released a CD (GH-1170CD) with a retail price of $12.99.
❏ GH1126 [S]	Bring on the Beats!	2011	$15

— Retail value of new LP. Also was released on CD.
❏ GH1156 [S]	Motor!	2010	$18

— 180-gram vinyl with free download code.
❏ GH1140 [S]	Take A Stand	2007	$15

THEE IMAGE
MANTICORE
❏ MA6506 [B]	Inside the Triangle	1975	$25
❏ MA6504S1 [B]	Thee Image	1975	$25

THEE MIDNITERS
CHATTAHOOCHIE
❏ C-1001 [M]	Thee Midniters	1965	$80
❏ CS-1001 [S]	Thee Midniters	1965	$125

WHITTIER
❏ W-5000 [M]	Bring You Love Special Delivery	1966	$40
❏ WS-5000 [S]	Bring You Love Special Delivery	1966	$50
❏ W-5002 [M]	Giants	1967	$40
❏ WS-5002 [S]	Giants	1967	$50
❏ W-5001 [M]	Unlimited	1966	$40
❏ WS-5001 [S]	Unlimited	1966	$50

ZYANYA/RHINO
❏ RNLP-063	The Best of Thee Midniters	1983	$15

THEE MUFFINS
(NO LABEL)
❏ 0(no cat #)	Thee Muffins Pop Up!	1967	$250

THEE PROPHETS
KAPP
❏ KS-3596	Playgirl	1969	$25

THEM
Also see BELFAST GYPSIES; VAN MORRISON.
HAPPY TIGER
❏ HT-1004	Them	1969	$50
❏ HT-1012	Them In Reality	1971	$120

LONDON
❏ PS639 [P]	Backtrackin'	1974	$12
❏ 820326-1	Them Featuring Van Morrison	1985	$12
❏ LC-50001 [R]	The Story of Them	1977	$12

PARROT
❏ PA61008 [M]	Them Again	1966	$150
❏ PAS71008 [R]	Them Again	1966	$50
❏ PA61005 [M]	Them Featuring "Gloria	1966	$75

— Same album as above, but with slightly different title
❏ PAS71005 [R]	Them Featuring "Gloria	1966	$40

— Same album as above, but with slightly different title
❏ PA61005 [M]	Them Featuring "Here Comes the Night	1965	$150
❏ PAS71005 [R]	Them Featuring "Here Comes the Night	1965	$80
❏ BP71053 [P]	Them Featuring Van Morrison	1972	$15

— Gloria," "Here Comes the Night," "If You and I Could Be as Two," "One More Time" and "One Two Brown Eyes" are true stereo.

TOWER
❏ T5104 [M]	Now and Them	1967	$75
❏ ST5104 [S]	Now and Them	1967	$100
❏ ST5116 [S]	Time Out! Time In for Them	1968	$150

THEODORE
CORAL
❏ CRL757322 [S]	Coral Records Presents Theodore in Stereo	1959	$150

THESAURUS RHYTHM MAKERS
SUNBEAM
❏ 101	The Thesaurus Rhythm Makers, Vol. 1	197?	$25
❏ 102	The Thesaurus Rhythm Makers, Vol. 2	197?	$25
❏ 103	The Thesaurus Rhythm Makers, Vol. 3	197?	$25

THESE TRAILS
Legendary psychedelic folk from Hawaii.
SINERGIA
❏ SR4059	These Trails	1973	$180

THESELIUS, GOSTA
BALLY
❏ BAL-12002 [M]	Swedish Jazz	1956	$50

THEUS, FATS
CTI
❏ 1005	Black Out	1972	$35

THEY MIGHT BE GIANTS
BAR NONE
❏ A-HAON 004 [EP]	Don't Let's Start	1987	$25
❏ A-HAON 005 [EP]	(She Was a) Hotel Detective	1988	$25
❏ A-HAON 002	They Might Be Giants	1986	$25

— Original edition contains lyric sheet and no mention of Restless Records

BAR NONE/RESTLESS
❏ 72605 [EP]	Don't Let's Start	1988	$18

— Reissue of A-HAON 004
❏ 72600	Lincoln	1988	$18
❏ 72611 [EP]	They'll Need a Crane	1989	$12
❏ A-HAON 002	They Might Be Giants	1988	$18

— With mention of Restless Records

ELEKTRA
❏ R114772	Flood	1990	$18

— BMG Music Service edition
❏ 60907	Flood	1990	$18

Number	Title	Yr	NM
❏ E1-60907	Flood	1990	$18

— Columbia House edition

THIELEMANS, TOOTS
A&M

Number	Title	Yr	NM
❏ SP-3613	Yesterday and Today	1974	$30

ABC-PARAMOUNT

❏ ABC-482 [M]	The Whistler and His Guitar	1965	$30
❏ ABCS-482 [S]	The Whistler and His Guitar	1965	$30

CHOICE

❏ 1007	Captured Alive	197?	$35

COLUMBIA

❏ CL658 [M]	The Sound	1955	$75

COMMAND

❏ RS 33-906 [M]	Contrasts	1967	$25
❏ RS906SD [S]	Contrasts	1967	$35
❏ RS 33-918 [M]	Guitars and Strings… And Things	1967	$25
❏ RS918SD [S]	Guitars and Strings… And Things	1967	$35
❏ RSSD978-2	The Salient One	1973	$35
❏ RS930SD	Toots!	1968	$35

CONCORD JAZZ

❏ CJ-355	Only Trust Your Heart	1988	$25

DECCA

❏ DL9204 [M]	Time Out for Toots	1958	$150
❏ DL79204 [S]	Time Out for Toots	1958	$150

FANTASY

❏ OJC-1738	Man Bites Harmonica	198?	$25

INNER CITY

❏ IC-1145	Live	198?	$30
❏ IC-1146	Live 2	198?	$30
❏ IC-1147	Live 3	198?	$30
❏ IC-1148	Spotlight	198?	$30

JAZZ MAN

❏ 5016	Slow Motion	198?	$25

RIVERSIDE

❏ RLP 12-257 [M]	Man Bites Harmonica	1958	$300

SIGNATURE

❏ SM-6006 [M]	The Soul of Toots Thielmans	1960	$100
❏ SS-6006 [S]	The Soul of Toots Thielmans	1960	$75

THIGPEN, ED
GNP CRESCENDO

❏ GNPS-2098	Action Re-Action	197?	$25

VERVE

❏ V-8663 [M]	Out of the Storm	1966	$25
❏ V6-8663 [S]	Out of the Storm	1966	$30

THILO, JESPER
STORYVILLE

❏ 4065	Swingin' Friends	198?	$25
❏ 4072	Tribute to Frog	198?	$25

THIN LIZZY
Also see PHIL LYNOTT; MOTORHEAD; WHITESNAKE.

FUTURE DAYS RECORDINGS

❏ FDR610 [B]	Shades of a Blue Orphanage	2015	$25

— 180g

❏ FDR611 [B]	Vagabonds of the Western World	2015	$25

LONDON

❏ LC-50004	The Rocker (1971-1974)	1977	$14
❏ PS594	Thin Lizzy	1971	$40
❏ PS636	Vagabonds of the Western World	1973	$30

MERCURY

❏ SRM-1-1186	Bad Reputation	1977	$15
❏ 5313416	Black Rose/A Rock Legend	2009	$25
❏ SRM-1-1108	Fighting	1976	$20

— Reissue of Vertigo 2005

❏ SRM-1-1081	Jailbreak	1976	$15
❏ 5310376	Jailbreak	2008	$25
❏ SRM-1-1119	Johnny the Fox	1976	$15
❏ SRM-1-1107	Night Life	1976	$15

— Reissue of Vertigo 2002

VERTIGO

❏ VEL-2005	Fighting	1975	$30
❏ VEL-2002	Night Life	1974	$18

VH1 CLASSICS

❏ VH132	Still Dangerous	2009	$25

WARNER BROS.

❏ BSK3338	Black Rose/A Rock Legend	1979	$12
❏ BSK3496	Chinatown	1980	$12
❏ 23986	Life" -- Live	1984	$18
❏ BS23213	Live and Dangerous	1978	$15
❏ BSK3622	Renegade	1982	$12
❏ 23831	Thunder and Lightning	1983	$12

Number	Title	Yr	NM

THINGS TO COME
SUNDAZED

❏ LP-5008	I Want Out	199?	$12

THINK
LAURIE

❏ SLLP-2052	Encounter	1972	$15

THINMAN, CARL
GUINNESS

❏ GNS36012 [B]	Carl Sings	1977	$50

THIRD ESTATE, THE
THIRD ESTATE

❏ LP-1000	Years Before the Wine	1976	$250

THIRD EYE BLIND
ELEKTRA

❏ 62415-1	Blue	1999	$75
❏ 62012-1	Third Eye Blind	1997	$40

THIRD POWER
VANGUARD

❏ VSD-6554 [B]	Believe	1970	$35

THIRD RAIL, THE
EPIC

❏ LN24327 [M]	Id Music	1967	$30
❏ BN26327 [S]	Id Music	1967	$40

THIRTEENTH FLOOR ELEVATORS, THE
INTERNATIONAL ARTISTS

❏ 8	13th Floor Elevators Live	1968	$150
❏ 8	13th Floor Elevators Live	1979	$30

— Repressing with "Masterfonics" in dead wax

❏ 9	Bull of the Woods	1968	$100
❏ 9	Bull of the Woods	1979	$30

— Repressing with "Masterfonics" in dead wax

❏ 5 [M]	Easter Everywhere	1968	$600

— Mono is promo only

❏ 5 [S]	Easter Everywhere	1968	$175

— With custom inner sleeve

❏ 5 [S]	Easter Everywhere	1968	$175

— Without custom inner sleeve

❏ 5 [S]	Easter Everywhere	1979	$30

— Repressing with "Masterfonics" in dead wax

❏ 1 [M]	Psychedelic Sounds	1967	$300

— Green and yellow label

❏ 1 [M]	Psychedelic Sounds	1968	$300

— All-yellow label

❏ 1 [S]	Psychedelic Sounds	1968	$250

— All-yellow label

❏ 1 [S]	Psychedelic Sounds	1979	$30

— Repressing with "Masterfonics" in dead wax

❏ 1 [S]	Psychedelic Sounds	1968	$250

— Aqua-blue label

SUNDAZED

❏ 5218 [B]	The Psychedelic Sounds of the Thirteenth Floor Elevators	2008	$

— reissued with same catalog number 2010

31ST OF FEBRUARY, THE
VANGUARD

❏ VSD-6503	The 31st of February	1969	$75

31 FLAVORS, THE
CROWN

❏ CST-592	Hair	1968	$50

.38 SPECIAL
A&M

❏ SP-17402 [DJ]	10 From 38	1986	$18

— Promo-only compilation

❏ SP-3164	.38 Special	198?	$10

— Budget-line reissue of 4638

❏ SP-4638	.38 Special	1977	$15
❏ SP-3910 [B]	Flashback	1987	$12

— Includes bonus 7-inch 33 1/3 rpm small hole single "Flashback Live EP"; deduct 40 percent if missing

❏ SP-5218	Rock & Roll Strategy	1988	$12
❏ SP-3216	Rockin' Into the Night	198?	$10

— Budget-line reissue of 4782

Number	Title	Yr	NM
❏ SP-4782 [B]	Rockin' Into the Night	1979	$15
❏ SP-3165	Special Delivery	198?	$10

— Budget-line reissue of 4684

❏ SP-4684	Special Delivery	1978	$15
❏ SP-3299	Special Forces	198?	$10

— Budget-line reissue of 4888

❏ SP-4888 [B]	Special Forces	1982	$12
❏ SP-5115	Strength in Numbers	1986	$12
❏ SP-3310	Tour de Force	198?	$10

— Budget-line reissue of 4971

❏ SP-4971	Tour de Force	1983	$12
❏ SP-3298	Wild-Eyed Southern Boys	198?	$10

— Budget-line reissue of 4835

❏ SP-4835	Wild-Eyed Southern Boys	1981	$12

THOMAS, B.J.
ABC

❏ ABCD-912	Help Me Make It to My Rockin' Chair	1976	$12
❏ ABDP-858	Reunion	1975	$12

ACCORD

❏ SN-7106	Lovin' You	198?	$12

BUCKBOARD

❏ 1023	B.J. Thomas Sings Hank Williams and Other Favorites	198?	$12

CLEVELAND INT'L.

❏ FC38561	New Looks	1983	$12
❏ PC38561	New Looks	1984	$10

— Budget-line reissue

❏ FC39337	Shining	1984	$12
❏ FC39111	The Great American Dream	1983	$12
❏ PC39111	The Great American Dream	1984	$10

— Budget-line reissue

❏ FC40157	Throwing Rocks at the Moon	1985	$12

COLUMBIA

❏ PC40148	All Is Calm, All Is Bright...	1985	$12
❏ PC38400	Love Shines	1984	$10

— Reissue of Priority 38400

❏ FC40496	Night Life	1986	$12

DORAL

❏ 0(# unknown)	Doral Presents B.J. Thomas	1971	$25

— Mail-order promotion from Doral cigarettes

EVEREST

❏ 4104	Golden Greats	1981	$12

HICKORY

❏ LPM-133 [M]	The Very Best of B.J. Thomas	1966	$25
❏ LPS-133 [S]	The Very Best of B.J. Thomas	1966	$30
❏ T90956 [M]	The Very Best of B.J. Thomas	1966	$30

— Capitol Record Club edition

❏ ST90956 [S]	The Very Best of B.J. Thomas	1966	$30

— Capitol Record Club edition

MCA

❏ 5296	As We Know Him	1982	$12
❏ 2286	B.J. Thomas	1977	$12
❏ 3035	Everybody Loves a Rain Song	1978	$12
❏ 746	Everybody Loves a Rain Song	1980	$10

— Budget-line reissue

❏ 3231	For the Best	1979	$12
❏ 5155	In Concert	1980	$12
❏ 27032	In Concert	198?	$10

— Reissue of MCA 5155

❏ 5195	Some Love Songs Never Die	1980	$12

MYRRH

❏ MSB-6593	A Happy Man	1979	$12
❏ MSB-6675	Amazing Grace	1981	$12
❏ WR-8200	Amazing Grace	1985	$10

— Reissue of 6675

Number	Title	Yr	NM
❏ MSB-6574	Home Where I Belong	1978	$12
❏ MSB-6705	Miracle	1983	$12
❏ WR-8153	Peace in the Valley	1985	$12
—Reissue of 6710			
❏ MSB-6710	Peace in the Valley	1983	$12
❏ MSB-6653	The Best of B.J. Thomas	1980	$12
❏ MSB-6725	The Best of B.J. Thomas, Volume 2	1984	$12
❏ MSB-6633	You Gave Me Love	1979	$12
PACEMAKER			
❏ PLP-3001 [M]	B.J. Thomas and the Triumphs	1965	$250
PAIR			
❏ PDL2-1099	Greatest Hits	1986	$15
PARAMOUNT			
❏ PAS-6052	B.J. Thomas Songs	1973	$15
❏ PAS1020	Longhorns & Londonbridges	1974	$15
PICKWICK			
❏ SPC-3623	The Best of B.J. Thomas	197?	$12
PRIORITY			
❏ JU38400	Love Shines	1982	$12
REPRISE			
❏ 25898	Midnight Minute	1989	$15
SCEPTER			
❏ 5101	Billy Joe Thomas	1972	$15
❏ 5108	B.J. Thomas Country	1972	$15
❏ SPS-582	Everybody's Out of Town	1970	$15
❏ SRM-561 [M]	For Lovers and Losers	1967	$25
❏ SPS-561 [S]	For Lovers and Losers	1967	$18
❏ 5112	Greatest All-Time Hits	1973	$18
❏ SPS-578	Greatest Hits, Volume 1	1969	$15
❏ SPS-597	Greatest Hits, Volume Two	1971	$15
❏ SRM-535 [M]	I'm So Lonesome I Could Cry	1966	$25
❏ SPS-535 [S]	I'm So Lonesome I Could Cry	1966	$30
❏ SPS-586	Most of All	1970	$15
❏ SPS-570 [S]	On My Way	1968	$18
❏ SRM-570 [M]	On My Way	1968	$30
—Mono appears to be white label promo only; in stereo cover with "Promotional DJ Copy Monaural Not for Sale" sticker on front			
❏ SPS-580	Raindrops Keep Fallin' on My Head	1970	$15
—Remixed version; trail-off wax number on Side 1 is "SPS-580-A-1C" or "SPS-580-A-1D" and on Side 2 is "SPS-580-B-1C"			
❏ SPS-580	Raindrops Keep Fallin' on My Head	1970	$18
—Original "muddy mix"; trail-off wax number on Side 1 is "SPS-580-A-1B" and on Side 2 is "SPS-580-B-1A"			
❏ SRM-556 [M]	Tomorrow Never Comes	1966	$18
❏ SPS-556 [S]	Tomorrow Never Comes	1966	$25
❏ SPS-576	Young and In Love	1969	$18
STARDAY			
❏ 992	The Best of B.J. Thomas	197?	$12
UNITED ARTISTS			
❏ UA-LA389-E	The Very Best of B.J. Thomas	1974	$15

THOMAS, CARLA, AND RUFUS THOMAS
See RUFUS AND CARLA.

THOMAS, CARLA
Also see OTIS AND CARLA; RUFUS AND CARLA.

Number	Title	Yr	NM
ATLANTIC			
❏ 8057 [M]	Gee Whiz	1961	$150
—With white "fan" logo			
❏ 8057 [M]	Gee Whiz	1963	$40
—With black "fan" logo			
❏ SD8057 [S]	Gee Whiz	1961	$175
—With white "fan" logo			
❏ SD8057 [S]	Gee Whiz	1963	$50
—With black "fan" logo			
❏ SD8232	The Best of Carla Thomas	1969	$30
STAX			
❏ 709 [M]	Carla	1966	$35
❏ 709 [S]	Carla	1966	$50
❏ 706 [M]	Comfort Me	1966	$35
❏ 706 [P]	Comfort Me	1966	$50
❏ STS-2044	Love Means Carla Thomas	1971	$35
❏ STS-2019	Memphis Queen	1969	$35
❏ MPS-8538	Memphis Queen	1987	$12
—Budget-line reissue			
❏ 718 [M]	The Queen Alone	1967	$35
❏ 718 [S]	The Queen Alone	1967	$50

THOMAS, DANNY

Number	Title	Yr	NM
COLUMBIA			
❏ XTV60818/9 [M]	An Evening with Danny Thomas	1960	$30
—Made for Post Cereals			
MGM			
❏ E-201 [10]	An Evening with Danny Thomas	1954	$150

Number	Title	Yr	NM
MYRRH			
❏ MST-6522	I'll Still Be Loving You	197?	$12
❏ MSA-6539	Jesus Is My Kind of People	197?	$12
❏ MST-6520	Tomorrow Belongs to You	1973	$12

THOMAS, DAVID

Number	Title	Yr	NM
STOMP OFF			
❏ SOS-1072	Through the Bottomlands	1984	$12

THOMAS, DYLAN

Number	Title	Yr	NM
CAEDMON			
❏ TC1002 [M]	A Child's Christmas in Wales and Five Poems (Dylan Thomas, Volume 1)	1957	$25
—Number stamped into dead wax; "New York, 1, New York" address on label and cover			

THOMAS, GARY

Number	Title	Yr	NM
ENJA			
❏ R1-79604	Code Violations	1989	$30
JMT			
❏ 834432-1	By Any Means Necessary	198?	$25

THOMAS, IAN

Number	Title	Yr	NM
ATLANTIC			
❏ SD19167	Still Here	1978	$12
CHRYSALIS			
❏ CHR1126	Goodnight Mrs. Calabash	1976	$15
JANUS			
❏ JLS-3058	Ian Thomas	1973	$15
❏ JXS-7005	Long Long Way	1974	$15
MERCURY			
❏ 826030-1	Add Water	1985	$15
❏ 822319-1	Riders on Dark Horses	1984	$12

THOMAS, IRMA

Number	Title	Yr	NM
BANDY			
❏ 70003	Irma Thomas Sings	197?	$30
FUNGUS			
❏ FB-25150	In Between Tears	1973	$40
IMPERIAL			
❏ LP-9302 [M]	Take a Look	1966	$50
❏ LP-12302 [S]	Take a Look	1966	$75
❏ LP-9266 [M]	Wish Someone Would Care	1964	$50
❏ LP-12266 [S]	Wish Someone Would Care	1964	$75
RCS			
❏ 1004	Safe with Me	1980	$30

THOMAS, JEANNIE

Number	Title	Yr	NM
STRAND			
❏ SL-1030 [M]	Jeannie Thomas Sings for the Boys	1961	$40
❏ SLS-1030 [S]	Jeannie Thomas Sings for the Boys	1961	$50

THOMAS, JOE (2), AND JAY MCSHANN

Number	Title	Yr	NM
UPTOWN			
❏ 2712	Blowin' In from Kansas City	198?	$30

THOMAS, JOE (2)

Number	Title	Yr	NM
UPTOWN			
❏ 271	Raw Meat	198?	$30

THOMAS, JOE (3), AND BILL ELLIOTT

Number	Title	Yr	NM
SUE			
❏ LP-1025 [M]	Speak Your Piece	1964	$50

THOMAS, JOE (3)

Number	Title	Yr	NM
CHIAROSCURO			
❏ 2018	Flash	1979	$30
GROOVE MERCHANT			
❏ 504	Joy of Cookin'	197?	$50
❏ 3310	Masada	197?	$35

THOMAS, JON

Number	Title	Yr	NM
ABC-PARAMOUNT			
❏ 351 [M]	Heartbreak	1960	$30
❏ S-351 [S]	Heartbreak	1960	$40
WING			
❏ MGW-12258 [M]	The Big Beat on the Organ	1963	$25
❏ SRW-16258 [R]	The Big Beat on the Organ	1963	$15

THOMAS, LEON

Number	Title	Yr	NM
FLYING DUTCHMAN			
❏ FD-10155	Blues and the Soulful Truth	197?	$35
❏ FD-10164	Facets	1973	$35
❏ FD-10167	Full Circle	197?	$35
❏ FD-10115	Spirits Known and Unknown	1969	$25
❏ FD-10132	The Leon Thomas Album	197?	$25
MEGA			
❏ M51-5003	Gold Sunrise on Magic Mountain	197?	$25

Number	Title	Yr	NM
PORTRAIT			
❏ FR44161	The Leon Thomas Blues Band	1988	$25

THOMAS, MARLO, AND FRIENDS

Number	Title	Yr	NM
A&M			
❏ SP-5196	Free to Be...A Family	1988	$15
—Includes a track by Soul Asylum			

THOMAS, PAT

Number	Title	Yr	NM
MGM			
❏ E-4103 [M]	Desafinado	1962	$35
❏ SE-4103 [S]	Desafinado	1962	$50
❏ E-4206 [M]	Moody's Mood	1964	$50
❏ SE-4206 [S]	Moody's Mood	1964	$75
STRAND			
❏ SL-1015 [M]	Jazz Patterns	1961	$40
❏ SLS-1015 [S]	Jazz Patterns	1961	$150

THOMAS, RAY
Also see THE MOODY BLUES.

Number	Title	Yr	NM
THRESHOLD			
❏ THS16	From Mighty Oaks	1975	$18
❏ THS17	Hopes Wishes & Dreams	1976	$18
❏ THSX-102 [DJ]	Ray Thomas Discusses The Recording of His First Solo Album From Mighty Oaks	1975	$50

THOMAS, RENE

Number	Title	Yr	NM
FANTASY			
❏ OJC-1725	Guitar Groove	198?	$25
JAZZLAND			
❏ JLP-27 [M]	Guitar Groove	1960	$30
❏ JLP-927 [S]	Guitar Groove	1960	$40

THOMAS, RUFUS

Number	Title	Yr	NM
ALLIGATOR			
❏ AV-4769	That Woman Is Poison	1988	$12
A.V.I.			
❏ 6046	I Ain't Gettin' Older, I'm Gettin' Better	1978	$18
❏ 6015	If There Were No Music	1977	$18
GUSTO			
❏ 0064	Rufus Thomas	1980	$12
STAX			
❏ STS-3008	Crown Prince of Dance	1973	$30
❏ STS-3004	Did You Hear Me	1972	$30
❏ STS-2028	Do the Funky Chicken	1970	$30
❏ STS-2039 [B]	Rufus Thomas Live/Doing the Push and Pull at P.J.'s	1971	$30
❏ ST-704 [M]	Walking the Dog	1963	$175

THOMAS, TIMMY

Number	Title	Yr	NM
GLADES			
❏ 33-6501	Why Can't We Live Together	1973	$18
GOLD MOUNTAIN			
❏ GM-80006	Gotta Give a Little Love	1984	$12

THOMAS, WALTER "FOOTS"

Number	Title	Yr	NM
PRESTIGE			
❏ PRST-7584	Walter "Foots" Thomas All-Stars	196?	$35

THOMPSON, BOB

Number	Title	Yr	NM
INTIMA			
❏ SJ-73284	7 In, 7 Out	1987	$25
—Reissue of Rainbow 2010			
❏ SJ-73238	Brother's Keeper	1987	$25
❏ D1-73331	Say What You Want	1988	$25
❏ D1-73519	Wilderness	1989	$30
RAINBOW			
❏ 2010	7 In, 7 Out	1986	$50

THOMPSON, BUTCH, AND CHET ELY

Number	Title	Yr	NM
JAZZOLOGY			
❏ J-79	Jelly Rolls On	197?	$25

THOMPSON, BUTCH, AND HAL SMITH

Number	Title	Yr	NM
STOMP OFF			
❏ SOS-1075	Echoes from Storyville, Vol. 1: If You Don't Shake	1985	$25
❏ SOS-1116	Echoes from Storyville, Vol. 2: Milenberg Joys	1986	$25

THOMPSON, BUTCH

Number	Title	Yr	NM
JAZZOLOGY			
❏ J-146	Butch Thompson and His Boys in Chicago	1986	$25
STOMP OFF			
❏ SOS-1037	A' Solas	198?	$25

THOMPSON, CHESTER

Number	Title	Yr	NM
BLACK JAZZ			
❏ 6	Powerhouse	197?	$30

Number	Title	Yr	NM

THOMPSON, DON
CONCORD JAZZ
| ❏ CJ-243 | Beautiful Friendship | 198? | $25 |

PM
| ❏ 08 | Country Place | 1976 | $30 |

THOMPSON, HANK
ABC
| ❏ AB-1095 | Brand New Hank | 1978 | $15 |

ABC DOT
❏ DOSD-2060	Back in the Swing of Things	1976	$15
❏ DO-2091	Doin' My Thing	1977	$15
❏ DOSD-2032	Hank Thompson Sings Nat King Cole	1975	$15
❏ DOSD-2003	Moving On	1974	$15
❏ DOSD-2069	The Thompson Touch	1977	$15

CAPITOL
❏ T1544 [M]	An Old Love Affair	1961	$30
— Black colorband label, logo at left			
❏ T1544 [M]	An Old Love Affair	1962	$18
— Black colorband label, logo at top			
❏ ST1544 [S]	An Old Love Affair	1961	$30
— Black colorband label, logo at left			
❏ ST1544 [S]	An Old Love Affair	1962	$25
— Black colorband label, logo at top			
❏ T2460 [M]	A Six Pack to Go	1966	$25
❏ ST2460 [S]	A Six Pack to Go	1966	$30
❏ T2274 [M]	Breakin' In Another Heart	1965	$25
❏ ST2274 [S]	Breakin' In Another Heart	1965	$30
❏ T2575 [M]	Breakin' the Rules	1966	$25
❏ ST2575 [S]	Breakin' the Rules	1966	$30
❏ T1775 [M]	Cheyenne Frontier Days	1962	$25
❏ ST1775 [S]	Cheyenne Frontier Days	1962	$30
❏ T1111 [M]	Favorite Waltzes	1959	$100
— Black colorband label, logo at left			
❏ T1111 [M]	Favorite Waltzes	1962	$25
— Black colorband label, logo at left			
❏ T2089 [M]	Golden Country Hits	1964	$25
❏ ST2089 [S]	Golden Country Hits	1964	$30
❏ T826 [M]	Hank!	1959	$30
— Black colorband label, logo at left			
❏ T826 [M]	Hank!	1962	$25
— Black colorband label, logo at top			
❏ T826 [M]	Hank!	1957	$100
— Turquoise or gray label			
❏ T1632 [M]	Hank Thompson at the Golden Nugget	1961	$30
— Black colorband label, logo at left			
❏ T1632 [M]	Hank Thompson at the Golden Nugget	1962	$18
— Black colorband label, logo at top			
❏ ST1632 [S]	Hank Thompson at the Golden Nugget	1961	$30
— Black colorband label, logo at left			
❏ ST1632 [S]	Hank Thompson at the Golden Nugget	1962	$25
— Black colorband label, logo at top			
❏ T1955 [M]	Hank Thompson at the State Fair of Texas	1963	$25
❏ ST1955 [S]	Hank Thompson at the State Fair of Texas	1963	$30
❏ T911 [M]	Hank Thompson Favorites	1957	$100
— Turquoise or gray label			
❏ T975 [M]	Hank Thompson's Dance Ranch	1958	$100
— Turquoise or gray label			
❏ T975 [M]	Hank Thompson's Dance Ranch	1959	$30
— Black colorband label, logo at left			
❏ T975 [M]	Hank Thompson's Dance Ranch	1962	$25
— Black colorband label, logo at top			
❏ T2154 [M]	It's Christmas Time	1963	$25
❏ ST2154 [S]	It's Christmas Time	1963	$30
❏ T2826 [M]	Just an Old Flame	1967	$30
❏ ST2826 [S]	Just an Old Flame	1967	$25
❏ T2342 [M]	Luckiest Heartache in Town	1965	$25
❏ ST2342 [S]	Luckiest Heartache in Town	1965	$30
❏ T1360 [M]	Most of All	1960	$30
— Black colorband label, logo at left			
❏ T1360 [M]	Most of All	1962	$25
— Black colorband label, logo at top			
❏ ST1360 [S]	Most of All	1960	$40
— Black colorband label, logo at left			
❏ ST1360 [S]	Most of All	1962	$30
— Black colorband label, logo at top			
❏ T729 [M]	New Recordings of Hank's All-Time Hits	1959	$30
— Black colorband label, logo at left			
❏ T729 [M]	New Recordings of Hank's All-Time Hits	1962	$25
— Black colorband label, logo at top			
❏ H729 [10]	New Recordings of Hank's All-Time Hits	195?	$120
❏ T729 [M]	New Recordings of Hank's All-Time Hits	1956	$100
— Turquoise or gray label			
❏ H618 [10]	North of the Rio Grande	1953	$120
❏ T618 [M]	North of the Rio Grande	1956	$100
— Turquoise or gray label			

Number	Title	Yr	NM
❏ T1246 [M]	Songs for Rounders	1959	$30
❏ ST1246 [S]	Songs for Rounders	1959	$40
❏ T418 [M]	Songs of the Brazos Valley	1959	$30
— Black colorband label, logo at left			
❏ T418 [M]	Songs of the Brazos Valley	1962	$25
— Black colorband label, logo at top			
❏ H418 [10]	Songs of the Brazos Valley	1953	$120
❏ T418 [M]	Songs of the Brazos Valley	1956	$100
— Turquoise or gray label			
❏ T1741 [M]	The #1 Country and Western Band	1962	$30
— Black colorband label, logo at left			
❏ T1741 [M]	The #1 Country and Western Band	1962	$25
— Black colorband label, logo at top			
❏ DT1741 [R]	The #1 Country and Western Band	1962	$25
— Black colorband label, logo at left			
❏ DT1741 [R]	The #1 Country and Western Band	1962	$15
— Black colorband label, logo at top			
❏ T1878 [M]	The Best of Hank Thompson	1963	$25
❏ ST1878 [S]	The Best of Hank Thompson	1963	$30
❏ T2661 [M]	The Best of Hank Thompson Vol. 2	1967	$30
❏ ST2661 [S]	The Best of Hank Thompson Vol. 2	1967	$25
❏ T1469 [M]	This Broken Heart of Mine	1960	$30
— Black colorband label, logo at left			
❏ T1469 [M]	This Broken Heart of Mine	1962	$25
— Black colorband label, logo at top			
❏ ST1469 [S]	This Broken Heart of Mine	1960	$40
— Black colorband label, logo at left			
❏ ST1469 [S]	This Broken Heart of Mine	1962	$30
— Black colorband label, logo at top			

DOT
❏ DOS-25996	Cab Driver (A Salute to the Mills Brothers)	1972	$18
❏ DOS 2-2000	Hank Thompson's 25th Anniversary Album	1971	$25
❏ DLP-25971	Hank Thompson Salutes Oklahoma	1969	$18
❏ DOS-26004	Hank Thompson's Greatest Hits Vol. 1	1972	$18
❏ DLP-25864	Hank Thompson Sings the Gold Standards	1968	$18
❏ DOS-26015	Kindly Keep It Country	1973	$18
❏ DLP-25991	Next Time I Fall in Love (I Won't)	1971	$18
❏ DLP-25894	On Tap, In the Can, or In the Bottle	1968	$18
❏ DLP-25932	Smoky the Bar	1969	$18

HILLTOP
| ❏ JS-6085 [S] | You Always Hurt the One You Love | 196? | $15 |
| *— Five tracks are rechanneled, five are true stereo* | | | |

MCA
| ❏ 689 | Brand New Hank | 198? | $10 |
| ❏ 3250 | Take Me Back to Tulsa | 1980 | $12 |

WARNER BROS.
❏ W1679 [M]	The Countrypolitan Sound of Hank Thompson	1967	$18
❏ WS1679 [S]	The Countrypolitan Sound of Hank Thompson	1967	$25
❏ W1686 [M]	The Gold Standard Collection of Hank Thompson	1967	$18
❏ WS1686 [S]	The Gold Standard Collection of Hank Thompson	1967	$25
❏ W1664 [M]	Where Is the Circus and Other Heart Breakin' Hits	1966	$18
❏ WS1664 [S]	Where Is the Circus and Other Heart Breakin' Hits	1966	$25

THOMPSON, HAYDEN
KAPP
| ❏ KL-1507 [M] | Here's Hayden Thompson | 1966 | $30 |
| ❏ KS-3507 [S] | Here's Hayden Thompson | 1966 | $40 |

THOMPSON, KAY
MGM
| ❏ E-3146 [M] | Kay Thompson Sings | 1955 | $30 |

SIGNATURE
| ❏ SM-1017 [M] | Let's Talk About Russia | 1959 | $30 |

THOMPSON, LES
RCA VICTOR
| ❏ LPT-3102 [10] | Gene Norman Presents "Just Jazz | 1952 | $175 |

THOMPSON, LINDA
WARNER BROS.
| ❏ 92 51641 [B] | One Clear Moment | 1985 | $25 |
| ❏ 1-25164 [B] | One Clear Moment | 1985 | $25 |

THOMPSON, LUCKY
51 WEST
| ❏ Q16072 | Back to the World | 198? | $30 |

Number	Title	Yr	NM

ABC IMPULSE!
| ❏ ASH-9307-2 | Dancing Sunbeam | 1975 | $75 |

ABC-PARAMOUNT
| ❏ ABC-111 [M] | Lucky Thompson Featuring Oscar Pettiford, Volume 1 | 1956 | $120 |
| ❏ ABC-171 [M] | Lucky Thompson Featuring Oscar Pettiford, Volume 2 | 1957 | $120 |

BIOGRAPH
| ❏ BLP-12061 | Lullaby in Rhythm | 1979 | $75 |

DAWN
| ❏ DLP-1113 [M] | Lucky Thompson | 1957 | $150 |

FANTASY
| ❏ OJC-194 | Lucky Strikes | 1985 | $30 |

GROOVE MERCHANT
❏ GM-508	Goodbye Yesterday	1973	$75
❏ GM-4411	Illuminations	197?	$30
❏ GM-517	I Offer You	1974	$75

INNER CITY
| ❏ IC-7016 | Lucky Thompson | 1976 | $35 |

LONDON
| ❏ D-93098 [10] | Recorded in Paris '56 | 1956 | $150 |

MOODSVILLE
❏ MVLP-39 [M]	Lucky Thompson Plays Jerome Kern and No More	1963	$75
— Green label			
❏ MVST-39 [S]	Lucky Thompson Plays Jerome Kern and No More	1963	$100
— Green label			
❏ MVLP-39 [M]	Lucky Thompson Plays Jerome Kern and No More	1965	$30
— Blue label, trident logo at right			
❏ MVST-39 [S]	Lucky Thompson Plays Jerome Kern and No More	1965	$40
— Blue label, trident logo at right			

NESSA
| ❏ N-13 | Body and Soul | 197? | $75 |

PRESTIGE
❏ PRLP-7394 [M]	Happy Days Are Here Again	1965	$50
— Blue label, trident logo at right			
❏ PRST-7394 [S]	Happy Days Are Here Again	1965	$75
— Blue label, trident logo at right			
❏ PRLP-7365 [M]	Lucky Strikes	1965	$50
— Blue label, trident logo at right			
❏ PRST-7365 [S]	Lucky Strikes	1965	$75
— Blue label, trident logo at right			

RIVOLI
❏ 44 [M]	Kinfolk's Corner	1965	$150
❏ S-44 [S]	Kinfolk's Corner	1965	$120
❏ 40 [M]	Lucky Is Back!	1965	$150
❏ S-40 [S]	Lucky Is Back!	1965	$120

SWING
| ❏ 8404 | Paris 1956, Vol. 1 | 1985 | $25 |

TOPS
| ❏ L-928 [10] | Jazz at the Auditorium | 1954 | $175 |

TRANSITION
| ❏ TRLP-21 [M] | Lucky Strikes | 1956 | $500 |
| *— With booklet (deduct 1/5 if missing)* | | | |

URANIA
| ❏ UJLP-1206 [M] | Accent on Tenor Sax | 1955 | $350 |

XANADU
| ❏ 204 | Brown Rose | 1985 | $35 |

THOMPSON, MALACHI
DELMARK
| ❏ DS-442 | Spirit | 1989 | $30 |

THOMPSON, MAYO
TEXAS REVOLUTION
| ❏ 2270 | Corky's Debt to His Father | 1969 | $100 |

THOMPSON, RICHARD
Also see FAIRPORT CONVENTION; RICHARD AND LINDA THOMPSON.
BONG LOAD
❏ BL52	Action Packed	2001	$18
— 1,000 copies pressed on "Coke-bottle green" vinyl			
❏ BL44 [B]	Mock Tudor	1999	$30

CAPITOL
| ❏ C1-48845 [B] | Amnesia | 1988 | $18 |
| ❏ C1-95713 [B] | Rumor & Sigh | 1991 | $18 |

CARTHAGE
❏ CGLP-4405 [B]	Henry the Human Fly	1983	$18
— Reissue of Reprise LP			
❏ CGLP-4413 [B]	Richard Thompson (Guitar/Vocal)	1983	$18
— Reissue of Island 9421 with original UK title			
❏ CGLP-4409 [B]	Strict Tempo	1983	$18

DIVERSE
| ❏ DIV 009 | Front Parlour Ballads | 2005 | $30 |

Number	Title	Yr	NM
HANNIBAL			
❏ HNLP-1313	Heart of Kindness	1983	$12
❏ HNLP-1316 [B]	Small Town Romance	1984	$18
POLYDOR			
❏ 825421-1 [B]	Across a Crowded Room	1985	$15
❏ 829728-1 [B]	Daring Adventures	1986	$18
REPRISE			
❏ MS2112 [B]	Henry the Human Fly	1972	$35

THOMPSON, RICHARD AND LINDA

Number	Title	Yr	NM
4 MEN WITH BEARDS			
❏ 4M139LP [B]	Shoot Out The Lights		$25
CARTHAGE			
❏ CGLP-4412 [B]	First Light	1983	$18
— Reissue of Chrysalis 1177			
❏ CGLP-4408 [B]	Hokey Pokey	1983	$18
— Reissue of Island 9305			
❏ CGLP-4407 [B]	I Want to See the Bright Lights Tonight	1983	$18
— Reissue of Island 9266 (UK)			
❏ CGLP-4404 [B]	Pour Down Like Silver	1983	$18
— Reissue of Island 9348			
❏ CGLP-4403 [B]	Sunnyvista	1983	$25
— First U.S. issue of this LP			
CHRYSALIS			
❏ CHR1177 [B]	First Light	1978	$30
❏ CHR1247	Sunnyvista	1979	$0
— Unreleased in U.S.			
HANNIBAL			
❏ HNBL1303 [B]	Shoot Out the Lights	1982	$18
ISLAND			
❏ ISLA9421 [B]	Bright Lights and Live! More or Less	1977	$40
— First U.S. issue of "I Want to See the Bright Lights Tonight" plus an LP of unreleased material			
❏ ILPS9305 [B]	Hokey Pokey	1974	$30
❏ ILPS9266	I Want to See the Bright Lights Tonight	1974	$0
— Unreleased in U.S. on this number			
❏ ILPS9348 [B]	Pour Down Like Silver	1975	$25

THOMPSON, SIR CHARLES

Number	Title	Yr	NM
AMERICAN RECORDING SOCIETY			
❏ G-447 [M]	Basically Swing	1957	$30
APOLLO			
❏ 103 [10]	Sir Charles Thompson and His All Stars	1951	$400
COLUMBIA			
❏ CL1663 [M]	Rockin' Rhythm	1961	$30
❏ CS8463 [S]	Rockin' Rhythm	1961	$30
❏ CL1364 [M]	Sir Charles Thompson and the Swing Organ	1959	$30
❏ CS8205 [S]	Sir Charles Thompson and the Swing Organ	1959	$30
EUPHONIC			
❏ 1221	The Neglected Professor	198?	$25
SACKVILLE			
❏ 3037	Portrait of a Piano	199?	$30
VANGUARD			
❏ VRS-8009 [10]	Sir Charles Thompson and His Band	1954	$175
❏ VRS-8006 [10]	Sir Charles Thompson Quartet	1954	$150
❏ VRS-8003 [10]	Sir Charles Thompson Sextet	1953	$150
❏ VRS-8018 [10]	Sir Charles Thompson Trio	1955	$120

THOMPSON, SONNY

Number	Title	Yr	NM
KING			
❏ 655 [M]	Mellow Blues	1959	$300
❏ 568 [M]	Moody Blues	1956	$500

THOMPSON, SUE

Number	Title	Yr	NM
HICKORY			
❏ H3G-4515	...And Love Me	1974	$18
❏ LPM-104 [M]	Meet Sue Thompson	1962	$50
❏ LPS-104 [S]	Meet Sue Thompson	1962	$100
❏ LPM-121 [M]	Paper Tiger	1965	$30
❏ LPS-121 [S]	Paper Tiger	1965	$40
❏ LPM-111 [M]	Sue Thompson's Golden Hits	1963	$30
❏ LPS-111 [S]	Sue Thompson's Golden Hits	1963	$40
❏ LPM-130 [M]	Sue Thompson with Strings Attached	1966	$30
❏ LPS-130 [S]	Sue Thompson with Strings Attached	1966	$40
❏ H3F-4511	Sweet Memories	1974	$18
❏ LPS-148	This Is Sue Thompson Country	1969	$25
❏ LPM-107 [M]	Two of a Kind	1962	$30
❏ LPS-107 [S]	Two of a Kind	1962	$40
WING			
❏ MGW-12317 [M]	The Country Side of Sue Thompson	1965	$25
❏ SRW-16317 [R]	The Country Side of Sue Thompson	1965	$18

THOMPSON TWINS

Number	Title	Yr	NM
ARISTA			
❏ R154479	Best of the Thompson Twins: Greatest Mixes	1988	$15
— BMG Direct Marketing edition			
❏ AL8542	Best of the Thompson Twins: Greatest Mixes	1988	$15
❏ R154307	Close to the Bone	1987	$15
— BMG Direct Marketing edition			
❏ AL-8449	Close to the Bone	1987	$12
❏ SP-137 [EP]	Extra Special Tuneful Twosome!	1982	$15
— Promo-only remixes; Side 1 is "Identical Twin Side" and Side 2 is "Fraternal Twin Side"			
❏ R144367	Here's to Future Days	1985	$15
— RCA Music Service edition			
❏ AL8-8276	Here's to Future Days	1985	$12
❏ ADP9586 [DJ]	Interview Sampler	1987	$25
— One side of interviews, the other of music; promo only			
❏ ADP9586 [DJ]	Interview Sampler	1987	$25
— One side of interviews, the other of music; promo only			
❏ AL6601	In the Name of Love	1982	$15
❏ ALB6-8309	In the Name of Love	1985	$10
— Reissue of AL8-8244			
❏ AL8-8244	In the Name of Love	1984	$12
— Reissue of AL 6601			
❏ R124567	Into the Gap	1984	$15
— RCA Music Service edition			
❏ AL8-8200	Into the Gap	1984	$12
❏ AL6607	Side Kicks	1983	$15
❏ ALB6-8310	Side Kicks	1985	$10
— Reissue of AL8-8002			
❏ AL9624	Side Kicks	1983	$12
— Reissue of 6607			
❏ AL8-8002	Side Kicks	1984	$10
— Reissue of 9624			
WARNER BROS.			
❏ 25921	Big Trash	1989	$12

THORINSHIELD

Number	Title	Yr	NM
PHILIPS			
❏ PHS600251 [B]	Thorinshield	1968	$30

THORNE, FRAN

Number	Title	Yr	NM
TRANSITION			
❏ TRLP-27 [M]	Piano Reflections	1956	$250
— With booklet (deduct 1/4 if missing)			

THORNHILL, CLAUDE

Number	Title	Yr	NM
CIRCLE			
❏ CLP-19	Claude Thornhill and His Orchestra 1941 & 1947	1981	$30
COLUMBIA			
❏ CL6164 [10]	Claude Thornhill Encores	1951	$100
❏ CL6050 [10]	Dance Parade	1949	$100
❏ CL709 [M]	Dancing After Midnight	1955	$50
❏ CL6035 [10]	Piano Reflections	1949	$100
❏ KG32906	The Memorable Claude Thornhill	1974	$35
— Original issue			
❏ PG32906	The Memorable Claude Thornhill	197?	$30
— Reissue with new prefix; some may have bar codes			
DECCA			
❏ DL8722 [M]	Claude on a Cloud	1958	$120
❏ DL78722 [S]	Claude on a Cloud	1958	$120
❏ DL8878 [M]	Dance to the Sound of Claude Thornhill	1958	$120
❏ DL78878 [S]	Dance to the Sound of Claude Thornhill	1958	$120
DESIGN			
❏ DLP-50 [M]	Sleepy Serenade	196?	$25
HARMONY			
❏ HL7088 [M]	The Thornhill Sound	1957	$30
HINDSIGHT			
❏ HSR-108	Claude Thornhill and His Orchestra 1947	198?	$30
INSIGHT			
❏ IN-207	Claude Thornhill and His Orchestra	198?	$30
KAPP			
❏ KL-1058 [M]	Two Sides of Claude Thornhill	1958	$30
❏ KS-3058 [S]	Two Sides of Claude Thornhill	1958	$30
MONMOUTH-EVERGREEN			
❏ 7024	Claude Thornhill at Glen Island Casino 1941	198?	$25
❏ MR-6606	Snowfall -- A Memory of Claude Thornhill	197?	$35
RCA CAMDEN			
❏ CAL-307 [M]	Dinner for Two	1958	$30

Number	Title	Yr	NM
TREND			
❏ TL-1002 [10]	Claude Thornhill Plays the Great Jazz Arrangements of Gerry Mulligan and Ralph Aldrich	1953	$120
❏ TL-1001 [10]	Dream Stuff	1953	$120

THORNTON, BIG MAMA

Number	Title	Yr	NM
ARHOOLIE			
❏ F-1039 [M]	Ball and Chain	1968	$30

Number	Title	Yr	NM
❏ F-1028 [M]	Big Mama Thornton in Europe	1966	$30
❏ F-1032 [M]	Chicago Blues: The Queen at Monterey	1967	$30
BACK BEAT			
❏ BLP-68	She's Back	1970	$75
MERCURY			
❏ SR-61225	Stronger Than Dirt	1969	$30
❏ SR-61249	The Way It Is	1970	$30
PENTAGRAM			
❏ PE-10005	Saved	1971	$25
VANGUARD			
❏ VSD-79351	Jail	1974	$18
❏ VSD-79354	Sassy Mama	1975	$18

THORNTON, CLIFFORD

Number	Title	Yr	NM
JCOA			
❏ 1008	Gardens of Harlem	197?	$35
THIRD WORLD			
❏ 12372	Communications Network	197?	$35
❏ 9636 [S]	Freedom and Unity	1969	$30

THORNTON, TERI

Number	Title	Yr	NM
COLUMBIA			
❏ CL2094 [M]	Open Highway	1963	$30
❏ CS8894 [S]	Open Highway	1963	$40
DAUNTLESS			
❏ DM-4306 [M]	Somewhere in the Night	1963	$30
❏ DS-6306 [S]	Somewhere in the Night	1963	$30
RIVERSIDE			
❏ RLP-352 [M]	Devil May Care	1961	$250
❏ RS-9352 [S]	Devil May Care	1961	$250
❏ 6142	Devil May Care	198?	$30
❏ RM-3525 [M]	Lullabye of the Leaves	1964	$175
❏ RS-93525 [S]	Lullabye of the Leaves	1964	$175

THOROGOOD, GEORGE, AND THE DESTROYERS

Number	Title	Yr	NM
EMI AMERICA			
❏ ST-17076	Bad to the Bone	1982	$12
❏ ST-17214	Live	1986	$12
❏ ST-17145	Maverick	1985	$12
EMI MANHATTAN			
❏ E1-46973	Born to Be Bad	1988	$12
MCA			
❏ 3091	Better Than the Rest	1979	$12
ROUNDER			
❏ 3013	George Thorogood and the Destroyers	1977	$15
❏ 3045	More George Thorogood and the Destroyers	1980	$12
❏ 3024	Move It On Over	1978	$15

THORPE, BILLY

Number	Title	Yr	NM
CAPRICORN			
❏ CPN 0221	Children of the Sun	1979	$25
ELEKTRA			
❏ 6E-294	21st Century Man	1980	$12
PASHA			
❏ BFZ40682	Children of the Sun... Revisited	1987	$12
❏ FZ38179	East of Eden's Gate	1982	$12
❏ ARZ37499	Stimulation	1981	$12

Number	Title	Yr	NM
POLYDOR			
❏ PD-1-6228	Children of the Sun	1979	$15
THRASHER BROTHERS, THE			
MCA			
❏ 5352	Country in My Soul	1983	$12
THREADGILL, HENRY			
ABOUT TIME			
❏ 1005	Just the Facts and Pass the Bucket	198?	$30
❏ 1004	When Was That?	198?	$30
NOVUS			
❏ 3025-1-N	Easily Slip Into Another World	1988	$25
❏ 3052-1-N	Rag, Bush and All	1989	$25
❏ 3013-1-N	You Know the Number	1987	$25
THREE			
STEEPLECHASE			
❏ SCS-1201	Three	198?	$30
— Khan Jamal; Johnny Dyani; Pierre Dorge			
THREE CATS AND A FIDDLE			
REPEAT			
❏ S-150 [M]	Three Cats and a Fiddle	1964	$18
THREE CHUCKLES, THE			
VIK			
❏ LX-1067 [M]	The Three Chuckles	1956	$300
THREE DEGREES, THE			
ARIOLA AMERICA			
❏ SW-50044	New Dimensions	1978	$12
❏ OL1501	Three D	1980	$12
EPIC			
❏ PE34385	Standing Up for Love	1977	$15
ICHIBAN			
❏ ICH-1041	Three Degrees...And Holding	198?	$12
PHILADELPHIA INT'L.			
❏ KZ33162	International	1975	$15
❏ KZ32406	The Three Degrees	1974	$15
❏ PZ33840	The Three Degrees Live	1975	$15
ROULETTE			
❏ SR-42050	Maybe	1970	$40
❏ 3015	So Much Love	1975	$12
THREE DEUCES, THE			
STOMP OFF			
❏ SOS-1185	Stompin' 'n' Slidin'	1988	$25
THREE DOG NIGHT			
ABC			
❏ 928	American Pastime	1976	$12
❏ 888	Coming Down Your Way	1975	$12
ABC COMMAND			
❏ CQD-40018 [Q]	Coming Down Your Way	1975	$30
❏ CQD-40014 [Q]	Hard Labor	1974	$30
ABC DUNHILL			
❏ DSY-50138	Around the World with Three Dog Night	1973	$18
❏ DSX-50158	Cyan	1973	$15
❏ DSX-50098	Golden Bisquits	1971	$15
— With detachable cardboard poster intact; interestingly, the label spells the LP title "Golden Biscuits			
❏ DSD-50168	Hard Labor	1974	$30
— With uncensored "childbirth" front cover			
❏ DSD-50168	Hard Labor	1974	$18
— With huge Band-Aid attached to jacket, covering the "childbirth			
❏ DSD-50168	Hard Labor	1974	$12
— With huge Band-Aid as part of the LP artwork			
❏ DSX-50108	Harmony	1971	$15
❏ DS-50078	It Ain't Easy	1970	$150
— Original cover with band members in the nude			
❏ DS-50078	It Ain't Easy	1970	$15
— Regular front cover with gatefold			
❏ SKAO-93211	It Ain't Easy	1970	$18
— Capitol Record Club edition			
❏ DSD-50178	Joy to the World: Their Greatest Hits	1974	$15
— With gatefold cover			
❏ DSD-50178	Joy to the World: Their Greatest Hits	1975	$12
— With standard cover			
❏ DSX-50088	Naturally	1970	$15
— With detachable cardboard poster intact			
❏ SMAS-93422	Naturally	1970	$18
— Capitol Record Club edition			
❏ DSD-50118	Seven Separate Fools	1972	$15
— With seven oversize playing cards included			
❏ SVAS-94772	Seven Separate Fools	1972	$18
— Capitol Record Club edition			

Number	Title	Yr	NM
❏ DS-50058	Suitable for Framing	1969	$15
❏ SKAO-92057	Suitable for Framing	1969	$18
— Capitol Record Club edition			
❏ DS-50048	Three Dog Night	1968	$18
❏ DS-50048	Three Dog Night "One	1969	$15
— Same album as above, but with revised title on cover			
❏ DS-50068	Three Dog Night Was Captured Live at the Forum	1969	$15
AT EASE			
❏ MD11109	Three Dog Night: Their Greatest Recordings	1978	$25
— This Album Compiled Exclusively for Military Personnel" by ABC			
COLUMBIA SPECIAL PRODUCTS			
❏ P14769	Three Dog Night	1978	$18
MCA			
❏ 37120	Joy to the World: Their Greatest Hits	1980	$10
❏ 6018	The Best of Three Dog Night	1982	$15
PASSPORT			
❏ PB5001 [EP]	It's a Jungle	1983	$10
PICKWICK			
❏ SPC-3664	Golden Greats of Three Dog Night	1979	$12
SESSIONS			
❏ ARI-1004	Sessions Presents Three Dog Night	1977	$15
THREE D'S, THE (2)			
CAPITOL			
❏ T2314 [M]	I Won't Be Worried Long	1965	$25
❏ ST2314 [S]	I Won't Be Worried Long	1965	$30
❏ T2171 [M]	New Dimensions in Folk Songs	1964	$25
❏ ST2171 [S]	New Dimensions in Folk Songs	1964	$30
THREE FACES WEST			
OUTPOST			
❏ 1000	Three Faces West	197?	$25
THREE FLAMES, THE			
MERCURY			
❏ MG-20239 [M]	At the Ben Soir	1957	$50
THREE JOLLY MINERS, THE			
HISTORICAL			
❏ 23 [M]	The Three Jolly Miners 1925-28	1968	$35
THREE MAN ARMY, THE			
KAMA SUTRA			
❏ KSBS-2044	A Third of a Lifetime	1971	$30
— Pink label, gatefold cover			
REPRISE			
❏ MS2150	Three Man Army	1973	$25
❏ MS2182	Three Man Army Two	1974	$25
311			
CAPRICORN			
❏ 536181-1 [B]	Transistor	1997	$15
THREE SOULS, THE			
ARGO			
❏ LP-4005 [M]	Almost Like Being In Love	1960	$0
— Canceled			
❏ LPS-4005 [S]	Almost Like Being In Love	1960	$0
— Canceled			
❏ LP-4036 [M]	Dangerous Dan Express	1964	$50
❏ LPS-4036 [S]	Dangerous Dan Express	1964	$75
❏ LP-4044 [M]	Soul Sounds	1965	$50
❏ LPS-4044 [S]	Soul Sounds	1965	$75
THREE SOUNDS, THE			
BLUE NOTE			
❏ BLP-4155 [M]	Black Orchid	1963	$75
❏ BST-84155 [S]	Black Orchid	1963	$30
— With "New York, USA" address on label			
❏ BST-84155 [S]	Black Orchid	1967	$35
— With "A Division of Liberty Records" on label			
❏ BLP-4014 [M]	Bottoms Up	1959	$300
— Deep groove" version (deep indentation under label on both sides)			
❏ BLP-4014 [M]	Bottoms Up	1959	$175
— Regular version, W. 63rd St. address on label			
❏ BST-4014 [S]	Bottoms Up	1959	$400
— Deep groove" version (deep indentation under label on both sides)			
❏ BST-4014 [S]	Bottoms Up	1959	$75
— Regular version, W. 63rd St. address on label			
❏ BLP-4014 [M]	Bottoms Up	1963	$75
— With "New York, USA" address on label			
❏ BST-4014 [S]	Bottoms Up	1963	$25
— With "New York, USA" address on label			

Number	Title	Yr	NM
❏ BST-84014 [S]	Bottoms Up	1967	$35
— With "A Division of Liberty Records" on label			
❏ BST-84285 [S]	Coldwater Flat	1968	$25
— With "A Division of Liberty Records" on label			
❏ BST-84301 [S]	Elegant Soul	1968	$25
— With "A Division of Liberty Records" on label			
❏ BLP-4072 [M]	Feelin' Good	1961	$175
— With W. 63rd St. address on label			
❏ BST-84072 [S]	Feelin' Good	1961	$50
— With W. 63rd St. address on label			
❏ BLP-4072 [M]	Feelin' Good	1963	$75
— With "New York, USA" address on label			
❏ BST-84072 [S]	Feelin' Good	1963	$25
— With "New York, USA" address on label			
❏ BST-84072 [S]	Feelin' Good	1967	$35
— With "A Division of Liberty Records" on label			
❏ BLP-4020 [M]	Good Deal	1959	$300
— Deep groove" version (deep indentation under label on both sides)			
❏ BLP-4020 [M]	Good Deal	1959	$175
— Regular version, W. 63rd St. address on label			
❏ BST-84020 [S]	Good Deal	1959	$50
— With W. 63rd St. address on label			
❏ BLP-4020 [M]	Good Deal	1963	$75
— With "New York, USA" address on label			
❏ BST-84020 [S]	Good Deal	1963	$25
— With "New York, USA" address on label			
❏ BST-84020 [S]	Good Deal	1967	$35
— With "A Division of Liberty Records" on label			
❏ BLP-4088 [M]	Here We Come	1961	$175
— With 61st St. address on label			
❏ BST-84088 [S]	Here We Come	1961	$50
— With 61st St. address on label			
❏ BLP-4088 [M]	Here We Come	1963	$75
— With "New York, USA" address on label			
❏ BST-84088 [S]	Here We Come	1963	$25
— With "New York, USA" address on label			
❏ BST-84088 [S]	Here We Come	1967	$35
— With "A Division of Liberty Records" on label			
❏ BLP-4102 [M]	Hey! There	1962	$75
❏ BST-84102 [S]	Hey! There	1962	$30
— With "New York, USA" address on label			
❏ BST-84102 [S]	Hey! There	1967	$35
— With "A Division of Liberty Records" on label			
❏ BLP-1600 [M]	Introducing the Three Sounds	1958	$300
— Deep groove" version (deep indentation under label on both sides)			
❏ BLP-1600 [M]	Introducing the Three Sounds	1958	$175
— Regular version, W. 63rd St. address on label			
❏ BST-1600 [S]	Introducing the Three Sounds	1959	$350
— Deep groove" version (deep indentation under label on both sides)			
❏ BST-1600 [S]	Introducing the Three Sounds	1959	$75
— Regular version, W. 63rd St. address on label			
❏ BLP-1600 [M]	Introducing the Three Sounds	1963	$75
— With "New York, USA" address on label			
❏ BST-1600 [S]	Introducing the Three Sounds	1963	$25
— With "New York, USA" address on label			
❏ BST-81600 [S]	Introducing the Three Sounds	1967	$35
— With "A Division of Liberty Records" on label			
❏ BLP-4120 [M]	It Just Got To Be	1963	$75
❏ BST-84120 [S]	It Just Got To Be	1963	$30
— With "New York, USA" address on label			
❏ BST-84120 [S]	It Just Got To Be	1967	$35
— With "A Division of Liberty Records" on label			
❏ BLP-4265 [M]	Live at the Lighthouse	1967	$75
❏ BST-84265 [S]	Live at the Lighthouse	1967	$25
— With "A Division of Liberty Records" on label			
❏ BLP-4044 [M]	Moods	1960	$400
— Deep groove" version (deep indentation under label on both sides)			
❏ BLP-4044 [M]	Moods	1960	$175
— Regular version, W. 63rd St. address on label			
❏ BST-84044 [S]	Moods	1960	$50
— With W. 63rd St. address on label			
❏ BLP-4044 [M]	Moods	1963	$75
— With "New York, USA" address on label			
❏ BST-84044 [S]	Moods	1967	$35
— With "A Division of Liberty Records" on label			
❏ BST-84044 [S]	Moods	1963	$25
— With "New York, USA" address on label			
❏ BLP-4197 [M]	Out of This World	1965	$75
❏ BST-84197 [S]	Out of This World	1965	$30
— With "New York, USA" address on label			
❏ BST-84197 [S]	Out of This World	1967	$35
— With "A Division of Liberty Records" on label			
❏ BST-84197 [S]	Out of This World	1970	$35
— With "Liberty/UA, Inc." on label			
❏ BST-84341 [S]	Soul Symphony	1969	$25

Number	Title	Yr	NM
— With "A Division of Liberty Records" on label			
❏ BLP-4248 [M]	Vibrations	1966	$75
❏ BST-84248 [S]	Vibrations	1966	$30
— With "New York, USA" address on label			
❏ BST-84248 [S]	Vibrations	1967	$35
— With "A Division of Liberty Records" on label			
LIMELIGHT			
❏ LM-82026 [M]	Beautiful Friendship	1965	$25
❏ LS-86026 [S]	Beautiful Friendship	1965	$30
❏ LM-82014 [M]	Three Moods	1965	$25
❏ LS-86014 [S]	Three Moods	1965	$30
MERCURY			
❏ MG-20776 [M]	Jazz On Broadway	1963	$150
❏ SR-60776 [S]	Jazz On Broadway	1963	$150
❏ MG-20921 [M]	Live at the Living Room	1963	$150
❏ SR-60921 [S]	Live at the Living Room	1963	$150
❏ MG-20839 [M]	Some Like It Modern	1963	$150
❏ SR-60839 [S]	Some Like It Modern	1963	$150
VERVE			
❏ V-8513 [M]	Blue Genes	1963	$30
❏ V6-8513 [S]	Blue Genes	1963	$30

THREE STOOGES, THE

Number	Title	Yr	NM
CORAL			
❏ CRL57289 [M]	Nonsense Song Book	1959	$100
❏ CRL757289 [S]	Nonsense Song Book	1959	$150
GOLDEN			
❏ GLP-43 [M]	Madcap Musical Nonsense	1962	$100
PETER PAN			
❏ 8098	The Three Stooges	1970	$30
VOCALION			
❏ VL3823 [M]	The Three Stooges Sing for Kids	196?	$25
❏ VL73823 [S]	The Three Stooges Sing for Kids	196?	$30

THREE SUNS, THE

Number	Title	Yr	NM
GOLDEN TONE			
❏ 14094	In Orbit	195?	$15
PICKWICK			
❏ SPC-3037	Twilight Time	197?	$12
RCA CAMDEN			
❏ CAL-633 [M]	The Sound of Christmas	1964	$15
❏ CAS-633(e) [R]	The Sound of Christmas	1964	$15
RCA VICTOR			
❏ LSP-2054 [S]	A Ding Dong Dandy Christmas!	1959	$30
❏ LPM-2054 [M]	A Ding Dong Dandy Christmas!	1959	$25
❏ LPM-2963 [M]	A Swingin' Thing	1964	$18
❏ LSP-2963 [S]	A Swingin' Thing	1964	$25
❏ LPM-3040 [10]	Busy Fingers	1952	$50
❏ LPM-52 [10]	Christmas Favorites	1951	$50
❏ LPM-3056 [10]	Christmas Party	1952	$50
❏ LPM-3354 [M]	Country Music Shindig	1965	$18
❏ LSP-3354 [S]	Country Music Shindig	1965	$25
❏ LPM-2307 [M]	Dancing on a Cloud	1961	$25
❏ LSP-2307 [S]	Dancing on a Cloud	1961	$30
❏ LPM-1316 [M]	Easy Listening	1956	$30
❏ LPM-2715 [M]	Everything Under the Sun	1963	$18
❏ LSP-2715 [S]	Everything Under the Sun	1963	$25
❏ LPM-2310 [M]	Fever and Smoke	1961	$25
❏ LSP-2310 [S]	Fever and Smoke	1961	$30
❏ LPM-2437 [M]	Fun in the Sun	1961	$25
❏ LSP-2437 [S]	Fun in the Sun	1961	$30
❏ LPM-28 [10]	Hands Across the Table	1951	$50
❏ LPM-1734 [M]	Having a Ball with the Three Suns	1959	$25
❏ LSP-1734 [S]	Having a Ball with the Three Suns	1959	$30
❏ LPM-1249 [M]	High Fi and Wide	1956	$30
❏ LPM-1578 [M]	Let's Dance with the Three Suns	1958	$25
❏ LSP-1578 [S]	Let's Dance with the Three Suns	1958	$30
❏ LPM-1669 [M]	Love in the Afternoon	1959	$25
❏ LSP-1669 [S]	Love in the Afternoon	1959	$30
❏ LPM-1220 [M]	Malaguena	1956	$30
❏ LPM-1333 [M]	Midnight for Two	1957	$30
❏ LPM-3125 [10]	Mods	1953	$50
❏ LPM-2532 [M]	Movin' 'N' Groovin'	1962	$25
❏ LSP-2532 [S]	Movin' 'N' Groovin'	1962	$30
❏ LPM-1173 [M]	My Reverie	1956	$30
❏ LPM-2235 [M]	On a Magic Carpet	1960	$25
❏ LSP-2235 [S]	On a Magic Carpet	1960	$30
❏ LPM-2904 [M]	One Enchanted Evening	1964	$18
❏ LSP-2904 [S]	One Enchanted Evening	1964	$25
❏ LPM-3146 [10]	Polka Time	1954	$50
❏ LPM-3113 [10]	Pops Concert Favorites	1953	$50
❏ ANL1-1779(e)	Pure Gold	1974	$12
❏ LPM-3174 [10]	Sacred Hymns	1954	$50
❏ LPM-3075 [10]	Slumbertime	1953	$50
❏ LPM-1219 [M]	Slumber Time	1956	$30
❏ LPM-1041 [M]	Soft and Sweet	1955	$30
❏ LPM-1132 [M]	Sounds of Christmas	1955	$30
❏ LPM-1964 [M]	Swingin' on a Star	1959	$25
❏ LSP-1964 [S]	Swingin' on a Star	1959	$30
❏ LPM-3447 [M]	The Best of the Three Suns	1965	$18
❏ LSP-3447 [S]	The Best of the Three Suns	1965	$25
❏ LPM-1543 [M]	The Things in Love in Hi-Fi	1958	$25
❏ LSP-1543 [S]	The Things in Love in Hi-Fi	1958	$30
❏ LPM-3034 [10]	The Three Suns Present	1952	$50

Number	Title	Yr	NM
❏ VPS-6075	This Is the Three Suns	1972	$18
❏ LPM-3 [10]	Three-Quarter Time	1951	$50
❏ LPM-3130 [10]	Top Pops	1953	$50
❏ LPM-2120 [M]	Twilight Memories	1960	$25
❏ LSP-2120 [S]	Twilight Memories	1960	$30
❏ LPM-3012 [10]	Twilight Moods	1952	$50
❏ LPM-1171 [M]	Twilight Time	1956	$30
❏ LPM-2617 [M]	Warm and Tender	1962	$25
❏ LSP-2617 [S]	Warm and Tender	1962	$30
ROYALE			
❏ 29 [10]	Midnight Time	1951	$50
❏ 1 [10]	Twilight Time	1951	$50
SEARS			
❏ SPS-437	Twilight Time	1969	$15
VARSITY			
❏ VLP-6048 [10]	Midnight Time	1950	$50
❏ VLP-6001 [10]	Twilight Time	1950	$50

THROCKMORTON, SONNY

Number	Title	Yr	NM
MERCURY			
❏ SRM-1-3736	Last Cheater's Waltz	1979	$12
WARNER BROS.			
❏ 25374	Southern Train	1986	$10

THROWING MUSES

Number	Title	Yr	NM
SIRE			
❏ 25710	House Tornado	1988	$12
❏ 25855	Hunkpapa	1989	$12
❏ 25640	The Fat Skier	1987	$12
❏ 26489	The Real Ramona	1991	$15

THUDPUCKER, JIMMY
Fictional singing star from Garry Trudeau's "Doonesbury" comic strip.

Number	Title	Yr	NM
WINDSONG			
❏ BXL1-2589	Greatest Hits	1977	$25

THUNDER, JOHNNY

Number	Title	Yr	NM
DIAMOND			
❏ D-5001 [M]	Loop De Loop	1963	$150
❏ DS-5001 [S]	Loop De Loop	1963	$175

THUNDER AND ROSES

Number	Title	Yr	NM
UNITED ARTISTS			
❏ UAS-6709	King of the Black Sunrise	1969	$30

THUNDERBIRDS, THE

Number	Title	Yr	NM
RED FEATHER			
❏ TH-1 [M]	Meet the Fabulous Thunderbirds	1964	$250

THUNDERCLAP NEWMAN

Number	Title	Yr	NM
MCA			
❏ 354	Hollywood Dream	1974	$12
— Reissue of Track 354			
TRACK			
❏ SD8264 [B]	Hollywood Dream	1970	$30
❏ 354	Hollywood Dream	1973	$15
— Reissue of Track 8264			

THUNDERKLOUD, BILLY, AND THE CHIEFTONES

Number	Title	Yr	NM
20TH CENTURY			
❏ T-452	Off the Reservation	1974	$15
❏ T-471	What Time of Day	1975	$15
SUPERIOR			
❏ SR-103	All Through the Night	197?	$18
❏ S-2010	Where Do I Begin to Tell the Story	1975	$18

THUNDERPUSSY

M.R.T.

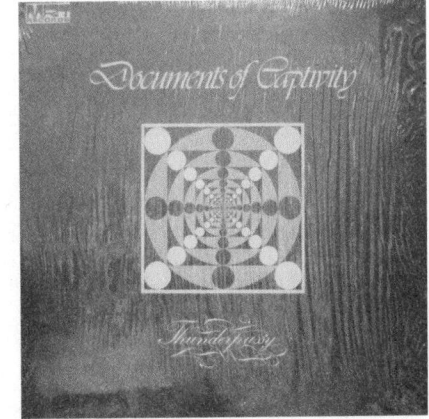

Number	Title	Yr	NM
❏ 31748 [B]	Documents of Captivity	1973	$175

THUNDERS, JOHNNY

Number	Title	Yr	NM
CLEOPATRA			
❏ 8200 [B]	Dawn Of The Dead: Live At Max's Kansas City (New York)		$30
— picture disc			
REAL			
❏ RR-1 [B]	So Alone	196?	$30
— ex-New York Dolls			

THUNDERTREE

Number	Title	Yr	NM
ROULETTE			
❏ SR-42038 [B]	Thundertree	1970	$35

THURSDAY GROUP, THE

Number	Title	Yr	NM
PATHFINDER			
❏ PTF-8307	The Thursday Group	198?	$30
❏ PTF-8807	Uncle Mean	198?	$30

TIBBETTS, STEVE

Number	Title	Yr	NM
ECM			
❏ 1218	Northern Song	198?	$25
❏ 25002	Safe Journey	1984	$25

TIBOR BROTHERS, THE

Number	Title	Yr	NM
JOMAR			
❏ S80-744-3631	The Tibor Brothers	1979	$18

TICHENOR, TREBOR

Number	Title	Yr	NM
DIRTY SHAME			
❏ 2001	King of Folk Ragtime	197?	$30

TIDE, THE

Number	Title	Yr	NM
MOUTH			
❏ 7237	Almost Live	1971	$50

TIDES, THE

Number	Title	Yr	NM
MERCURY			
❏ MG-20714 [M]	Limbo Rock	1962	$18
❏ SR-60714 [S]	Limbo Rock	1962	$25
WING			
❏ MGW-12265 [M]	Surf City and Other Surfin' Favorites	1963	$30
❏ SRW-16265 [S]	Surf City and Other Surfin' Favorites	1963	$30
❏ MGW-12248 [M]	The Best of Bossa Nova	1963	$18
❏ SRW-16248 [S]	The Best of Bossa Nova	1963	$25

TIEKEN, FREDDIE, AND THE ROCKERS

Number	Title	Yr	NM
I.T.			
❏ 2301 [M]	By Popular Demand	1957	$75
❏ 2304 [M]	Freddie Tieken and the Rockers	1958	$75

TIFFANY

Number	Title	Yr	NM
MCA			
❏ 6267	Hold an Old Friend's Hand	1988	$12
❏ 10030	New Inside	1990	$18
❏ 5793	Tiffany	1987	$10

TIFFANY SHADE, THE

Number	Title	Yr	NM
MAINSTREAM			
❏ S-6105	The Tiffany Shade	1968	$150

TIJUANA VOICES WITH BRASS

Number	Title	Yr	NM
PICKWICK			
❏ SPCX-1005	Tijuana Voices Sing Merry Christmas	1970	$15

TIKIS, THE
Probably two different groups.

Number	Title	Yr	NM
MINARET			
❏ TLP-7001 [M]	The Tikis	196?	$150
PHILIPS			
❏ PHM200043 [M]	The Tikis	1962	$30
❏ PHS600043 [S]	The Tikis	1962	$30

TIL, SONNY
Also see THE ORIOLES.

Number	Title	Yr	NM
DOBRE			
❏ 1026	Back to the Chapel	1978	$15
RCA VICTOR			
❏ LSP-4538	Old Gold/New Gold	1971	$18
❏ LSP-4451	Sonny Til Returns	1970	$25

'TIL TUESDAY

Number	Title	Yr	NM
EPIC			
❏ OE44041 [B]	Everything's Different Now	1988	$12
❏ EAS1350 [EP]	Everything's Different Now Sampler	1988	$15
— Promo only; four songs			
❏ BFE39458 [B]	Voices Carry	1985	$15
❏ FE39458	Voices Carry	1985	$10

Number	Title	Yr	NM
—Reissue wifh new prefix			
FE40314	Welcome Home	1986	$12

TILLES, NURIT
JAZZOLOGY

Number	Title	Yr	NM
JCE-87	Ragtime, Here and Now!	1982	$25

TILLIS, MEL, AND NANCY SINATRA
ELEKTRA

Number	Title	Yr	NM
5E-549	Mel and Nancy	1981	$15

TILLIS, MEL, AND SHERRY BRYCE
MGM

Number	Title	Yr	NM
SE-4937	Let's Go All the Way Tonight	1974	$18
SE-4800	Living and Learning/Take My Hand	1971	$18

TILLIS, MEL
COLUMBIA

Number	Title	Yr	NM
C30253	Heart Over Mind	1970	$15
CL1724 [M]	Heart Over Mind and Other Big Country Hits	1962	$30
CS8524 [S]	Heart Over Mind and Other Big Country Hits	1962	$40

ELEKTRA

Number	Title	Yr	NM
60016	It's a Long Way to Daytona	1982	$12
6E-236	Me and Pepper	1979	$12
60192	Mel Tillis' Greatest Hits	1982	$12
6E-310	Southern Rain	1980	$12
6E-271	Your Body Is an Outlaw	1980	$12

HARMONY

Number	Title	Yr	NM
KH31952	Mel	1972	$15
HS11170 [S]	The Great Mel Tillis Sings Walk On, Boy and Other Great Country Hits	196?	$15
HL7370 [M]	The Great Mel Tillis Sings Walk On, Boy and Other Great Country Hits	196?	$18

HILLTOP

Number	Title	Yr	NM
JS-6153	Detroit City	197?	$12

KAPP

Number	Title	Yr	NM
KS-3543	Let Me Talk to You	1968	$18
KL-1514 [M]	Life Turned Her That Way	1967	$18
KS-3514 [S]	Life Turned Her That Way	1967	$25
KS-3589	Mel Tillis' Greatest Hits	1969	$18
KS-3639	Mel Tillis In Person	1970	$18
KS-3609	Mel Tillis Sings Old Faithful	1969	$18
KS-3535 [S]	Mr. Mel	1967	$18
KL-1535 [M]	Mr. Mel	1967	$25
KS-3630	She'll Be Hanging 'Round Somewhere	1970	$18
KS-3570	Something Special	1968	$18
KL-1493 [M]	Stateside	1966	$18
KS-3493 [S]	Stateside	1966	$25
KS-3594	Who's Julie	1969	$18

MCA

Number	Title	Yr	NM
5378	After All This Time	1983	$10
3077	Are You Sincere	1979	$15
653	Are You Sincere	198?	$10
—Reissue of 3077			
2252	Heart Healer	1977	$15
650	Heart Healer	198?	$10
—Reissue of 2252			
2364	I Believe in You	1978	$15
652	I Believe in You	198?	$10
—Reissue of 2364			
2204	Love Revival	1976	$15
649	Love Revival	198?	$10
—Reissue of 2204			
2288	Love's Troubled Waters	1977	$15
651	Love's Troubled Waters	198?	$10
—Reissue of 2288			
66	Mel Tillis' Greatest Hits	1973	$15
—Reissue of Kapp 3589			
550	Mel Tillis In Person	197?	$12
—Reissue of Kapp 3639			
3208	M-M-Mel Live	1980	$15
789	M-M-Mel Live	198?	$10
—Reissue of 3208			
3167	Mr. Entertainer	1979	$15
37121	Mr. Entertainer	198?	$10
—Reissue of 3167			
5472	New Patches	1984	$10
4091	The Best of Mel Tillis	1975	$18
3274	The Very Best of Mel Tillis	1980	$12

MERCURY

Number	Title	Yr	NM
835310-1	Brand New Mister Me	1988	$10

MGM

Number	Title	Yr	NM
MG-2-5402	24 Great Hits	1977	$18
SE-4870	I Ain't Never/Neon Rose	1972	$18
MG-2-5404	Live at the Sam Houston Coliseum & Birmingham Municipal Auditorium	1978	$18
—Combines 4788 and 4889 in one package			
M3G-4987	Mel Tillis and the Statesiders	1975	$15
SE-4889	Mel Tillis and the Statesiders On Stage at the Birmingham Municipal Auditorium	1973	$18
M3G-4970	Mel Tillis' Greatest Hits	1974	$15
M3G-4981	Mel Tillis Time	1975	$0
—Canceled			
MG-1-5002	M-M-Mel	1975	$15
SE-4681	One More Time	1970	$18
SE-4788	Recorded Live at the Sam Houston Coliseum, Houston, Texas	1971	$18
SE-4907	Sawmill	1973	$18
M3F-4960	Stomp Them Grapes	1974	$15
SE-4757	The Arms of a Fool/Commercial Affection	1971	$18
MG-1-5021	The Best of Mel Tillis and the Statesiders	1976	$15
SE-4806	The Very Best of Mel Tillis and the Statesiders	1972	$18
MG-1-5022	Welcome to Mel Tillis Country	1976	$15
SE-4841	Would You Want Your World to End	1972	$18

POWER PAK

Number	Title	Yr	NM
PO-295	Mel Tillis & Friends	197?	$12

RCA VICTOR

Number	Title	Yr	NM
AHL1-5483	California Road	1985	$10

STARDAY

Number	Title	Yr	NM
SLP-471	Stateside	1972	$15

TIME-LIFE

Number	Title	Yr	NM
STW-111	Country Music	1981	$12

VOCALION

Number	Title	Yr	NM
VL73914	Big 'n' Country	1970	$15

TILLIS, PAM
WARNER BROS.

Number	Title	Yr	NM
23871	Above and Beyond the Doll of Cutey	1983	$30

TILLMAN, FLOYD
CIMARRON

Number	Title	Yr	NM
C-2003 [M]	Let's Make Memories	1962	$50

HARMONY

Number	Title	Yr	NM
HL7316 [M]	Floyd Tillman's Best	1964	$30
HS11297	I'll Still Be Lovin' You	1969	$30

HILLTOP

Number	Title	Yr	NM
JM-6017 [M]	Floyd Tillman Sings His Greatest Hits of Lovin'	196?	$18

MUSICOR

Number	Title	Yr	NM
MS-3157	Dream On	1968	$25
MM-2136 [M]	Floyd Tillman's Country	1967	$30
MS-3136 [S]	Floyd Tillman's Country	1967	$30

RCA VICTOR

Number	Title	Yr	NM
LPM-1686 [M]	Floyd Tillman's Greatest	1958	$75

STARDAY

Number	Title	Yr	NM
SLP-310 [M]	Let's Make Memories	1965	$30

TILLOTSON, JOHNNY
ACCORD

Number	Title	Yr	NM
SN-7194	Scrapbook	1982	$12

AMOS

Number	Title	Yr	NM
AAS7006	Tears on My Pillow	1969	$25

BARNABY

Number	Title	Yr	NM
BR-4007	Johnny Tillotson's Greatest	1977	$15

BUDDAH

Number	Title	Yr	NM
BDS-5112	Johnny Tillotson	1972	$18

CADENCE

Number	Title	Yr	NM
CLP-3058 [M]	It Keeps Right On a-Hurtin'	1962	$30
CLP-25058 [S]	It Keeps Right On a-Hurtin'	1962	$40
CLP-3052 [M]	Johnny Tillotson's Best	1961	$75
—Maroon and silver label			
CLP-3052 [M]	Johnny Tillotson's Best	1962	$30
—Red and black label			
CLP-25052 [P]	Johnny Tillotson's Best	1961	$50
—Maroon and silver label			
CLP-25052 [P]	Johnny Tillotson's Best	1962	$30
—Red and black label			
CLP-3067 [M]	You Can Never Stop Me Loving You	1963	$30
CLP-25067 [P]	You Can Never Stop Me Loving You	1963	$40

EVEREST

Number	Title	Yr	NM
4113	Johnny Tillotson's Greatest Hits	1982	$12

METRO

Number	Title	Yr	NM
M-561 [M]	Johnny Tillotson Sings Tillotson	1967	$18
MS-561 [S]	Johnny Tillotson Sings Tillotson	1967	$25

MGM

Number	Title	Yr	NM
E-4452 [M]	Here I Am	1967	$25
SE-4452 [S]	Here I Am	1967	$30
E-4395 [M]	No Love at All	1966	$25
SE-4395 [S]	No Love at All	1966	$30
E-4328 [M]	Our World	1965	$25
SE-4328 [S]	Our World	1965	$30
E-4270 [M]	She Understands Me	1965	$25
SE-4270 [S]	She Understands Me	1965	$30
E-4188 [M]	Talk Back Trembling Lips	1964	$25
SE-4188 [S]	Talk Back Trembling Lips	1964	$30
E-4302 [M]	That's My Style	1965	$25
SE-4302 [S]	That's My Style	1965	$30
SE-4532 [S]	The Best of Johnny Tillotson	1968	$25
E-4532 [M]	The Best of Johnny Tillotson	1968	$30
—May be promo only (yellow label)			
E-4402 [M]	The Christmas Touch	1966	$30
SE-4402 [S]	The Christmas Touch	1966	$30
E-4224 [M]	The Tillotson Touch	1964	$25
SE-4224 [S]	The Tillotson Touch	1964	$30
T90410 [M]	The Tillotson Touch	1965	$30
—Capitol Record Club edition			
ST90410 [S]	The Tillotson Touch	1965	$30
—Capitol Record Club edition			
SE-4814	The Very Best of Johnny Tillotson	1971	$15

UNITED ARTISTS

Number	Title	Yr	NM
UA-LA759-G	Johnny Tillotson	1977	$12

TIMBER CREEK
RENEGADE

Number	Title	Yr	NM
95014	Hellbound Highway	1975	$175

TIMBERLAKE, JUSTIN
JIVE

Number	Title	Yr	NM
82876-88062-1	Futuresex/Lovesounds	2006	$25
01241-41823-1	Justified	2002	$25

TIMBUK 3
I.R.S.

Number	Title	Yr	NM
42124	Eden Alley	1987	$12
82015	Edge of Allegiance	1989	$15
R143810	Greetings from Timbuk 3	1986	$16
—RCA Music Service edition			
5739	Greetings from Timbuk 3	1986	$14

TIMELESS ALL-STARS, THE
TIMELESS

Number	Title	Yr	NM
LPSJP-178	It's Timeless	1988	$25

TIMMENS, JIM, AND HIS JAZZ ALL-STARS
WARNER BROS.

Number	Title	Yr	NM
W1278 [M]	Gilbert and Sullivan Revisited	1958	$30
WS1278 [S]	Gilbert and Sullivan Revisited	1958	$30

TIMMONS, BOBBY
FANTASY

Number	Title	Yr	NM
OJC-364	Bobby Timmons In Person	198?	$25
OJC-104	This Here Is Bobby Timmons	198?	$25

MILESTONE

Number	Title	Yr	NM
MSP-9020	Do You Know the Way	1969	$25
MSP-9011	Got to Get It	1969	$25
47031	Moanin'	197?	$35

PRESTIGE

Number	Title	Yr	NM
PRLP-7429 [M]	Chicken and Dumplin's	1966	$30
PRST-7429 [S]	Chicken and Dumplin's	1966	$30
PRLP-7351 [M]	Chun-King	1965	$30
PRST-7351 [S]	Chun-King	1965	$30
PRLP-7414 [M]	Holiday Soul	1966	$30
PRST-7414 [S]	Holiday Soul	1966	$40
PRLP-7335 [M]	Little Barefoot Soul	1964	$30
PRST-7335 [S]	Little Barefoot Soul	1964	$30
PRLP-7483 [M]	Soul Food	1967	$75
PRST-7483 [S]	Soul Food	1967	$50
PRLP-7465 [M]	Soul Man	1967	$75
PRST-7465 [S]	Soul Man	1967	$50
PRST-7780	The Best of Soul Piano	1970	$50
PRLP-7387 [M]	Workin' Out	1966	$75
PRST-7387 [S]	Workin' Out	1966	$75

RIVERSIDE

Number	Title	Yr	NM
R-6110	Bobby Timmons In Person	197?	$35
RLP-468 [M]	Born to Be Blue!	1963	$175
RS-9468 [S]	Born to Be Blue!	1963	$175
RLP-363 [M]	Easy Does It	1961	$250
RS-9363 [S]	Easy Does It	1961	$250
RS-3053	From the Bottom	196?	$35
RLP-334 [M]	Soul Time	1960	$250
RS-9334 [S]	Soul Time	1960	$250
RLP-422 [M]	Sweet and Soulful Sounds	1962	$175
RS-9422 [S]	Sweet and Soulful Sounds	1962	$175
RLP-391 [M]	The Bobby Timmons Trio In Person -- Recorded "Live" at the Village Vanguard	1961	$250
RS-9391 [S]	The Bobby Timmons Trio In Person -- Recorded "Live" at the Village Vanguard	1961	$250
RLP 12-317 [M]	This Here Is Bobby Timmons	1960	$250
RLP-1164 [S]	This Here Is Bobby Timmons	1960	$250
R-6050	This Here Is Bobby Timmons	197?	$35

TIMOTHY
PEAR

Number	Title	Yr	NM
0(# unknown)	Strange But True	1972	$250

Number	Title	Yr	NM

TIN HOUSE
EPIC
❏ E30511 — Tin House — 1971 — $25

TIN HUEY
WARNER BROS.
❏ BSK3297 — Contents Dislodged During Shipment — 1979 — $15

TIN MACHINE
EMI
❏ R164054 — Tin Machine — 1989 — $14
— *BMG Direct Marketing edition*
❏ E1-91990 — Tin Machine — 1989 — $40
— *Featuring David Bowie*

TIN TIN
ATCO
❏ SD 33-370 — Astral Taxi — 1971 — $18
❏ SD 33-350 — Tin Tin — 1970 — $18

TINGLING MOTHER'S CIRCUS
MUSICOR
❏ MS-3167 — Circus of the Mind — 1968 — $30

TINO AND THE REVLONS
DEARBORN
❏ 1004 — By Request at the Sway-Zee — 1966 — $250

TINY TIM
BOUQUET
❏ SLP-711 [B] — Love and Kisses from Tiny Tim — 1968 — $25
REPRISE
❏ RS6351 — For All My Little Friends — 1969 — $18
❏ RS6292 [S] — God Bless Tiny Tim — 1968 — $18
❏ R6292 [M] — God Bless Tiny Tim — 1968 — $100
— *Mono copies may all be white label promos*
❏ RS6323 — Tiny Tim's Second Album — 1969 — $18

TIPPETTS, JULIE
UTOPIA
❏ BUL11248 [B] — Sunset Glow — 1975 — $30

TIPTON, CARL
SIMS
❏ LP-143 [M] — The Carl Tipton Show — 196? — $40

TIRABASSO, JOHN
DISCOVERY
❏ DS-884 — Live at Dino's — 198? — $25
DOBRE
❏ 1022 — Diamond Cuff Links and Mink — 197? — $35

TISO, WAGNER
PHILIPS
❏ 834632-1 — Manu Carue — 1989 — $30
VERVE
❏ 831819-1 — Giselle — 1987 — $25

TITANS, THE
MGM
❏ E-3992 [M] — Today's Teen Beat — 1961 — $30
❏ SE-3992 [S] — Today's Teen Beat — 1961 — $40

TITUS GROAN
JANUS
❏ JLS-3024 — Titus Groan — 1971 — $30

TITUS OATES
LIPS
❏ 0(no cat #) — Jungle Lady — 1974 — $250

TJADER, CAL, AND CARMEN MCRAE
CONCORD JAZZ
❏ CJ-189 — Heat Wave — 1982 — $25

TJADER, CAL, AND CHARLIE BYRD
FANTASY
❏ 9453 — Tambu — 1974 — $30

TJADER, CAL, AND STAN GETZ
Also see each artist's individual listings.
FANTASY
❏ 8348 [S] — Cal Tjader-Stan Getz Quartet — 1963 — $30
— *Reissue of 8005*
❏ 3266 [M] — Cal Tjader-Stan Getz Sextet — 1958 — $150
— *Red vinyl*
❏ 3266 [M] — Cal Tjader-Stan Getz Sextet — 1958 — $75

— *Black vinyl, red label, non-flexible vinyl*
❏ 3266 [M] — Cal Tjader-Stan Getz Sextet — 196? — $35
— *Black vinyl, red label, flexible vinyl*
❏ 3348 [M] — Cal Tjader-Stan Getz Sextet — 1963 — $35
— *Reissue of 3266*
❏ 8005 [S] — Cal Tjader-Stan Getz Sextet — 196? — $75
— *Blue vinyl*
❏ 8005 [S] — Cal Tjader-Stan Getz Sextet — 196? — $50
— *Black vinyl, blue label, non-flexible vinyl*
❏ 8005 [S] — Cal Tjader-Stan Getz Sextet — 196? — $30
— *Black vinyl, blue label, flexible vinyl*

TJADER, CAL
CONCORD JAZZ
❏ CJ-159 — The Shining Sea — 1981 — $25
CONCORD PICANTE
❏ CJP-176 — A Fuego Vivo — 1981 — $25
❏ CJP-247 — Good Vibes — 1983 — $25
❏ CJP-133 — Gozame! Pero Ya… — 1980 — $30
❏ CJP-113 — La Onda Va Bien — 1979 — $30
CRYSTAL CLEAR
❏ 8003 — Huracan — 1978 — $75
— *Direct-to-disc recording*
FANTASY
❏ 8416 — Agua Dulce — 1971 — $30
❏ 9502 — Amazonas — 1975 — $30
❏ 3283 [M] — A Night at the Blackhawk — 1959 — $150
— *Red vinyl*
❏ 3283 [M] — A Night at the Blackhawk — 1959 — $75
— *Black vinyl, red label, non-flexible vinyl*
❏ 3283 [M] — A Night at the Blackhawk — 196? — $35
— *Black vinyl, red label, flexible vinyl*
❏ 8026 [S] — A Night at the Blackhawk — 196? — $75
— *Blue vinyl*
❏ 8026 [S] — A Night at the Blackhawk — 196? — $50
— *Black vinyl, blue label, non-flexible vinyl*
❏ 8026 [S] — A Night at the Blackhawk — 196? — $30
— *Black vinyl, blue label, flexible vinyl*
❏ OJC-278 — A Night at the Blackhawk — 1987 — $25
— *Reissue of 8026*
❏ 9521 — At Grace Cathedral — 1977 — $30
❏ 3253 [M] — Cal Tjader — 1958 — $120
— *Red vinyl*
❏ 3253 [M] — Cal Tjader — 1958 — $40
— *Black vinyl, non-flexible vinyl*
❏ 3315 [M] — Cal Tjader Live and Direct — 1961 — $40
— *Red vinyl*
❏ 3315 [M] — Cal Tjader Live and Direct — 1961 — $75
— *Black vinyl, red label, non-flexible vinyl*
❏ 3315 [M] — Cal Tjader Live and Direct — 196? — $35
— *Black vinyl, red label, flexible vinyl*
❏ 8059 [S] — Cal Tjader Live and Direct — 1962 — $75
— *Blue vinyl*
❏ 8059 [S] — Cal Tjader Live and Direct — 1962 — $50
— *Black vinyl, blue label, non-flexible vinyl*
❏ 8059 [S] — Cal Tjader Live and Direct — 196? — $30
— *Black vinyl, blue label, flexible vinyl*
❏ 3330 [M] — Cal Tjader Plays the Harold Arlen Songbook — 1961 — $40
— *Red vinyl*
❏ 3330 [M] — Cal Tjader Plays the Harold Arlen Songbook — 1961 — $75
— *Black vinyl, red label, non-flexible vinyl*
❏ 3330 [M] — Cal Tjader Plays the Harold Arlen Songbook — 196? — $35
— *Black vinyl, red label, flexible vinyl*
❏ 8072 [S] — Cal Tjader Plays the Harold Arlen Songbook — 1962 — $75
— *Blue vinyl*
❏ 8072 [S] — Cal Tjader Plays the Harold Arlen Songbook — 1962 — $50
— *Black vinyl, blue label, non-flexible vinyl*
❏ 8072 [S] — Cal Tjader Plays the Harold Arlen Songbook — 196? — $30
— *Black vinyl, blue label, flexible vinyl*
❏ OJC-285 — Cal Tjader Plays the Harold Arlen Songbook — 1987 — $25
— *Reissue of 8072*
❏ 3227 [M] — Cal Tjader Quartet — 1956 — $200
— *Red vinyl*
❏ 3307 [M] — Cal Tjader Quartet — 1960 — $40
— *Red vinyl*
❏ 3307 [M] — Cal Tjader Quartet — 1960 — $75
— *Black vinyl, red label, non-flexible vinyl*
❏ 3307 [M] — Cal Tjader Quartet — 196? — $35
— *Black vinyl, red label, flexible vinyl*
❏ 8083 [R] — Cal Tjader Quartet — 1962 — $75
— *Blue vinyl*
❏ 8083 [R] — Cal Tjader Quartet — 1962 — $50
— *Black vinyl, blue label, non-flexible vinyl*
❏ 8083 [R] — Cal Tjader Quartet — 1962 — $30
— *Black vinyl, blue label, flexible vinyl*
❏ 3313 [M] — Cal Tjader Quintet — 1961 — $40
— *Red vinyl; evidently a different album than 3232*
❏ 3313 [M] — Cal Tjader Quintet — 1961 — $75

— *Black vinyl, red label, non-flexible vinyl*
❏ 3313 [M] — Cal Tjader Quintet — 196? — $35
— *Black vinyl, red label, flexible vinyl*
❏ 8084 [S] — Cal Tjader Quintet — 1962 — $75
— *Blue vinyl; stereo version of 3313*
❏ 8084 [S] — Cal Tjader Quintet — 1962 — $50
— *Black vinyl, blue label, non-flexible vinyl*
❏ 8084 [S] — Cal Tjader Quintet — 1962 — $30
— *Black vinyl, blue label, flexible vinyl*
❏ 3366 [M] — Cal Tjader's Greatest Hits — 1965 — $35
❏ 8366 [S] — Cal Tjader's Greatest Hits — 1965 — $30
❏ MPF-4527 — Cal Tjader's Greatest Hits — 1987 — $25
— *Reissue of 8366*
❏ 3374 [M] — Cal Tjader's Greatest Hits, Volume 2 — 1966 — $35
❏ 8374 [S] — Cal Tjader's Greatest Hits, Volume 2 — 1966 — $30
❏ MPF-4530 — Cal Tjader's Greatest Hits, Volume 2 — 1987 — $25
— *Reissue of 8374*
❏ 3275 [M] — Cal Tjader's Latin Concert — 1958 — $150
— *Red vinyl*
❏ 3275 [M] — Cal Tjader's Latin Concert — 1958 — $75
— *Black vinyl, red label, non-flexible vinyl*
❏ 3275 [M] — Cal Tjader's Latin Concert — 196? — $35
— *Black vinyl, red label, flexible vinyl*
❏ 8014 [S] — Cal Tjader's Latin Concert — 196? — $75
— *Blue vinyl*
❏ 8014 [S] — Cal Tjader's Latin Concert — 196? — $50
— *Black vinyl, blue label, non-flexible vinyl*
❏ 8014 [S] — Cal Tjader's Latin Concert — 196? — $30
— *Black vinyl, blue label, flexible vinyl*
❏ OJC-643 — Cal Tjader's Latin Concert — 1991 — $30
— *Reissue of 8014*
❏ 3295 [M] — Concert by the Sea — 1959 — $150
— *Red vinyl*
❏ 3295 [M] — Concert by the Sea — 1959 — $75
— *Black vinyl, red label, non-flexible vinyl*
❏ 3295 [M] — Concert by the Sea — 196? — $35
— *Black vinyl, red label, flexible vinyl*
❏ 8038 [S] — Concert by the Sea — 196? — $75
— *Blue vinyl*
❏ 8038 [S] — Concert by the Sea — 196? — $50
— *Black vinyl, blue label, non-flexible vinyl*
❏ 8038 [S] — Concert by the Sea — 196? — $30
— *Black vinyl, blue label, flexible vinyl*
❏ 3341 [M] — Concert by the Sea, Volume 2 — 1962 — $40
— *Red vinyl*
❏ 3341 [M] — Concert by the Sea, Volume 2 — 1962 — $75
— *Black vinyl, red label, non-flexible vinyl*
❏ 3341 [M] — Concert by the Sea, Volume 2 — 196? — $35
— *Black vinyl, red label, flexible vinyl*
❏ 8098 [S] — Concert by the Sea, Volume 2 — 1962 — $75
— *Blue vinyl*
❏ 8098 [S] — Concert by the Sea, Volume 2 — 1962 — $50
— *Black vinyl, blue label, non-flexible vinyl*
❏ 8098 [S] — Concert by the Sea, Volume 2 — 196? — $30
— *Black vinyl, blue label, flexible vinyl*
❏ 3299 [M] — Concert on the Campus — 1960 — $40
— *Red vinyl*
❏ 3299 [M] — Concert on the Campus — 1960 — $75
— *Black vinyl, red label, non-flexible vinyl*
❏ 3299 [M] — Concert on the Campus — 196? — $35
— *Black vinyl, red label, flexible vinyl*
❏ 8044 [S] — Concert on the Campus — 196? — $75
— *Blue vinyl*
❏ 8044 [S] — Concert on the Campus — 196? — $50
— *Black vinyl, blue label, non-flexible vinyl*
❏ 8044 [S] — Concert on the Campus — 196? — $30
— *Black vinyl, blue label, flexible vinyl*
❏ OJC-279 — Concert on the Campus — 1987 — $25
— *Reissue of 8044*
❏ 3309 [M] — Demasiado Caliente — 1960 — $40
— *Red vinyl*
❏ 3309 [M] — Demasiado Caliente — 1960 — $75
— *Black vinyl, red label, non-flexible vinyl*
❏ 3309 [M] — Demasiado Caliente — 196? — $35
— *Black vinyl, red label, flexible vinyl*
❏ 8053 [S] — Demasiado Caliente — 196? — $75
— *Blue vinyl*
❏ 8053 [S] — Demasiado Caliente — 196? — $50
— *Black vinyl, blue label, non-flexible vinyl*
❏ 8053 [S] — Demasiado Caliente — 196? — $30
— *Black vinyl, blue label, flexible vinyl*
❏ 9533 — Guarabe — 1977 — $30
❏ 3241 [M] — Jazz at the Blackhawk — 1957 — $150
— *Red vinyl*
❏ 3241 [M] — Jazz at the Blackhawk — 1957 — $75
— *Black vinyl, red label, non-flexible vinyl*
❏ 3241 [M] — Jazz at the Blackhawk — 196? — $35
— *Black vinyl, red label, flexible vinyl*

Number	Title	Yr	NM
❏ 8096 [R]	Jazz at the Blackhawk	1962	$75
—Blue vinyl			
❏ 8096 [R]	Jazz at the Blackhawk	1962	$50
—Black vinyl, blue label, non-flexible vinyl			
❏ 8096 [R]	Jazz at the Blackhawk	196?	$30
—Black vinyl, blue label, flexible vinyl			
❏ OJC-436	Jazz at the Blackhawk	1990	$25
—Reissue of 8096			
❏ 9446	Last Bolero in Berkeley	1974	$30
❏ 9482	Last Night When We Were Young	1975	$30
❏ 8019 [S]	Latin for Dancers	196?	$200
—Blue vinyl; the existence of this has been confirmed. Black vinyl copies of 8019 are unknown.			
❏ 8019 [S]	Latin for Dancers	196?	$250
—A red vinyl copy with this number is known to exist also, probably pressed in error			
❏ 3279 [M]	Latin for Lovers	1958	$150
—Red vinyl			
❏ 3279 [M]	Latin for Lovers	1958	$75
—Black vinyl, red label, non-flexible vinyl			
❏ 3279 [M]	Latin for Lovers	196?	$35
—Black vinyl, red label, flexible vinyl			
❏ 8016 [S]	Latin for Lovers	196?	$75
—Blue vinyl			
❏ 8016 [S]	Latin for Lovers	196?	$50
—Black vinyl, blue label, non-flexible vinyl			
❏ 8016 [S]	Latin for Lovers	196?	$30
—Black vinyl, blue label, flexible vinyl			
❏ 3250 [M]	Latin Kick	1957	$150
—Red vinyl			
❏ 3250 [M]	Latin Kick	1957	$75
—Black vinyl, red label, non-flexible vinyl			
❏ 3250 [M]	Latin Kick	196?	$35
—Black vinyl, red label, flexible vinyl			
❏ 8033 [S]	Latin Kick	196?	$75
—Blue vinyl			
❏ 8033 [S]	Latin Kick	196?	$50
—Black vinyl, blue label, non-flexible vinyl			
❏ 8033 [S]	Latin Kick	196?	$30
—Black vinyl, blue label, flexible vinyl			
❏ OJC-642	Latin Kick	1991	$30
—Reissue of 8033			
❏ 3339 [M]	Latino	1962	$40
—Red vinyl			
❏ 3339 [M]	Latino	1962	$75
—Black vinyl, red label, non-flexible vinyl			
❏ 3339 [M]	Latino	196?	$35
—Black vinyl, red label, flexible vinyl			
❏ 8079 [S]	Latino	1962	$75
—Blue vinyl			
❏ 8079 [S]	Latino	1962	$50
—Black vinyl, blue label, non-flexible vinyl			
❏ 8079 [S]	Latino	196?	$30
—Black vinyl, blue label, flexible vinyl			
❏ 9409	Live at the Funky Quarters	1970	$30
❏ 24712	Los Ritmos Caliente	197?	$35
❏ 3326 [M]	Mambo	1961	$40
—Red vinyl			
❏ 3326 [M]	Mambo	1961	$75
—Black vinyl, red label, non-flexible vinyl			
❏ 3326 [M]	Mambo	196?	$35
—Black vinyl, red label, flexible vinyl			
❏ 8057 [S]	Mambo	1962	$75
—Blue vinyl			
❏ 8057 [S]	Mambo	1962	$50
—Black vinyl, blue label, non-flexible vinyl			
❏ 8057 [S]	Mambo	196?	$30
—Black vinyl, blue label, flexible vinyl			
❏ 3202 [M]	Mambo with Tjader	1955	$200
—Red vinyl			
❏ 3202 [M]	Mambo with Tjader	1956	$150
—Black vinyl, red label, non-flexible vinyl			
❏ 3202 [M]	Mambo with Tjader	196?	$75
—Black vinyl, red label, flexible vinyl			
❏ 9424	Mambo with Tjader	1973	$30
❏ OJC-271	Mambo with Tjader	1987	$25
—Reissue of 3202			
❏ 3262 [M]	Mas Ritmo Caliente	1958	$150
—Red vinyl			
❏ 3262 [M]	Mas Ritmo Caliente	1958	$75
—Black vinyl, red label, non-flexible vinyl			
❏ 3262 [M]	Mas Ritmo Caliente	196?	$35
—Black vinyl, red label, flexible vinyl			
❏ 8003 [S]	Mas Ritmo Caliente	196?	$75
—Blue vinyl			
❏ 8003 [S]	Mas Ritmo Caliente	196?	$50
—Black vinyl, blue label, non-flexible vinyl			
❏ 8003 [S]	Mas Ritmo Caliente	196?	$30
—Black vinyl, blue label, flexible vinyl			
❏ 9422	Primo	1972	$30
❏ 9463	Puttin' It Together	1974	$30
❏ 3-17 [10]	Ritmo Caliente	1954	$175
—Any of various non-black vinyl pressings			
❏ 3-17 [10]	Ritmo Caliente	1954	$200

Number	Title	Yr	NM
—Black vinyl			
❏ 3216 [M]	Ritmo Caliente	1956	$200
—Red vinyl			
❏ 3216 [M]	Ritmo Caliente	1956	$150
—Black vinyl, red label, non-flexible vinyl			
❏ 3216 [M]	Ritmo Caliente	196?	$75
—Black vinyl, red label, flexible vinyl			
❏ 8077 [R]	Ritmo Caliente	1962	$75
—Blue vinyl			
❏ 8077 [R]	Ritmo Caliente	1962	$50
—Black vinyl, blue label, non-flexible vinyl			
❏ 8077 [R]	Ritmo Caliente	196?	$30
—Black vinyl, blue label, flexible vinyl			
❏ 3271 [M]	San Francisco Moods	1958	$150
—Red vinyl			
❏ 3271 [M]	San Francisco Moods	1958	$75
—Black vinyl, red label, non-flexible vinyl			
❏ 3271 [M]	San Francisco Moods	196?	$35
—Black vinyl, red label, flexible vinyl			
❏ 8017 [S]	San Francisco Moods	196?	$75
—Blue vinyl			
❏ 8017 [S]	San Francisco Moods	196?	$50
—Black vinyl, blue label, non-flexible vinyl			
❏ 8017 [S]	San Francisco Moods	196?	$30
—Black vinyl, blue label, flexible vinyl			
❏ OJC-277	San Francisco Moods	1987	$25
—Reissue of 8017			
❏ 3232 [M]	The Cal Tjader Quintet	1956	$200
—Red vinyl			
❏ 3232 [M]	The Cal Tjader Quintet	1956	$150
—Black vinyl, red label, non-flexible vinyl			
❏ 3232 [M]	The Cal Tjader Quintet	196?	$75
—Black vinyl, red label, flexible vinyl			
❏ 8085 [R]	The Cal Tjader Quintet	196?	$75
—Blue vinyl; stereo version of 3232			
❏ 8085 [R]	The Cal Tjader Quintet	196?	$50
—Black vinyl, blue label, non-flexible vinyl			
❏ 8085 [R]	The Cal Tjader Quintet	196?	$30
—Black vinyl, blue label, flexible vinyl			
❏ 3-9 [10]	The Cal Tjader Trio	1953	$300
—Any of various non-black vinyl pressings			
❏ 3-9 [10]	The Cal Tjader Trio	1953	$200
—Black vinyl			
❏ 8406	Tjader	1970	$30
❏ 3289 [M]	Tjader Goes Latin	1959	$150
—Red vinyl			
❏ 3289 [M]	Tjader Goes Latin	1959	$75
—Black vinyl, red label, non-flexible vinyl			
❏ 3289 [M]	Tjader Goes Latin	196?	$35
—Black vinyl, red label, flexible vinyl			
❏ 8030 [S]	Tjader Goes Latin	196?	$75
—Blue vinyl			
❏ 8030 [S]	Tjader Goes Latin	196?	$50
—Black vinyl, blue label, non-flexible vinyl			
❏ 8030 [S]	Tjader Goes Latin	196?	$30
—Black vinyl, blue label, flexible vinyl			
❏ 3221 [M]	Tjader Plays Mambo	1956	$200
—Red vinyl			
❏ 3221 [M]	Tjader Plays Mambo	1956	$150
—Black vinyl, red label, non-flexible vinyl			
❏ 3221 [M]	Tjader Plays Mambo	196?	$75
—Black vinyl, red label, flexible vinyl			
❏ OJC-274	Tjader Plays Mambo	1987	$25
—Reissue of 3221			
❏ 3-18 [10]	Tjader Plays Mambo	1954	$300
—Red vinyl			
❏ 3211 [M]	Tjader Plays Tjazz	1956	$200
—Red vinyl			
❏ 3211 [M]	Tjader Plays Tjazz	1956	$150
—Black vinyl, red label, non-flexible vinyl			
❏ 3278 [M]	Tjader Plays Tjazz	1958	$150
—Red vinyl; reissue of 3211			
❏ 3278 [M]	Tjader Plays Tjazz	1958	$30
—Black vinyl, red label, non-flexible vinyl			
❏ 3278 [M]	Tjader Plays Tjazz	196?	$35
—Black vinyl, red label, flexible vinyl			
❏ 8097 [R]	Tjader Plays Tjazz	1962	$75
—Blue vinyl			
❏ 8097 [R]	Tjader Plays Tjazz	1962	$50
—Black vinyl, blue label, non-flexible vinyl			
❏ 8097 [R]	Tjader Plays Tjazz	196?	$30
—Black vinyl, blue label, flexible vinyl			
❏ 3310 [M]	West Side Story	1960	$40
—Red vinyl			
❏ 3310 [M]	West Side Story	1960	$75
—Black vinyl, red label, non-flexible vinyl			
❏ 3310 [M]	West Side Story	196?	$35
—Black vinyl, red label, flexible vinyl			
❏ 8054 [S]	West Side Story	196?	$75
—Blue vinyl			
❏ 8054 [S]	West Side Story	196?	$50
—Black vinyl, blue label, non-flexible vinyl			
❏ 8054 [S]	West Side Story	196?	$30
—Black vinyl, blue label, flexible vinyl			

Number	Title	Yr	NM
❏ 8379	West Side Story	1967	$30
—Reissue of 8054			

GALAXY

Number	Title	Yr	NM
❏ 5107	Breathe Easy	1977	$30
❏ 5121	Here	1978	$30

MGM

❏ 10008	Sonido Nuevo	197?	$35

PRESTIGE

❏ 24026	The Monterey Concerts	1973	$35

SAVOY

❏ MG-9036 [10]	Cal Tjader -- Vibist	1954	$200

SKYE

❏ SK-10	Cal Tjader Plugs In	1969	$50
❏ SK-1	Solar Heat	1968	$50
❏ SK-19	Tjader-Ade	1970	$35

VERVE

❏ V-8671 [M]	Along Comes Cal	1966	$35
❏ V6-8671 [S]	Along Comes Cal	1966	$50
❏ V-8575 [M]	Breeze from the East	1964	$50
❏ V6-8575 [S]	Breeze from the East	1964	$75
❏ V-8651 [M]	El Soni Do Nuevo -- The New Soul Sound	1966	$35
❏ V6-8651 [S]	El Soni Do Nuevo -- The New Soul Sound	1966	$50
❏ V-8730 [M]	Hip Vibrations	1967	$50
❏ V6-8730 [S]	Hip Vibrations	1967	$35
❏ V-8419 [M]	In a Latin Bag	1961	$50
❏ V6-8419 [S]	In a Latin Bag	1961	$75
❏ V-8459 [M]	Saturday Night...Sunday Night at the Blackhawk	1962	$50
❏ V6-8459 [S]	Saturday Night...Sunday Night at the Blackhawk	1962	$75
❏ V-8507 [M]	Several Shades of Jade	1963	$50
❏ V6-8507 [S]	Several Shades of Jade	1963	$75
❏ V-8531 [M]	Sona Libre	1963	$50
❏ V6-8531 [M]	Sona Libre	1963	$75
❏ V-8626 [M]	Soul Bird: Whippenpoof	1965	$50
❏ V6-8626 [S]	Soul Bird: Whippenpoof	1965	$75
❏ V-8637 [M]	Soul Burst	1965	$50
❏ V6-8637 [S]	Soul Burst	1965	$75
❏ V-8614 [M]	Soul Sauce	1965	$50
❏ V6-8614 [S]	Soul Sauce	1965	$75
❏ 827756-1	Soul Sauce	1986	$25
—Reissue of 8614			
❏ V-8725 [M]	The Best of Cal Tjader	1967	$35
❏ V6-8725 [S]	The Best of Cal Tjader	1967	$50
❏ V-8470 [M]	The Contemporary Music of Mexico and Brazil	1962	$250
❏ V6-8470 [S]	The Contemporary Music of Mexico and Brazil	1962	$250
❏ V6-8769	The Prophet	1969	$35
❏ V-8585 [M]	Warm Wave	1964	$50
❏ V6-8585 [S]	Warm Wave	1964	$75

TJADER, CAL/DON ELLIOTT

SAVOY

❏ MG-12054 [M]	Vib-Rations	1956	$40
—Reissue of 9036 and 9033			

TLC

LAFACE

❏ LFL6155 [DJ]	Fanmail	1999	$18
—Promo-only "clean version" in company sleeve			
❏ 26055	Fanmail	1999	$15

TOAD HALL

LIBERTY

❏ LST-7580	Toad Hall	1968	$30

TOAD THE WET SPROCKET

COLUMBIA

❏ FC45326 [B]	Bread and Circus	1989	$18
❏ C47309	Fear	1991	$25
❏ C46060	Pale	1990	$30
—Marbled white (almost greenish) vinyl			

TOADS, THE

WIGGINS

❏ 64021 [M]	The Toads	1964	$300

TOBY BEAU

RCA VICTOR

❏ DJL1-2994 [DJ]	3 You Missed. 1 You Didn't	1978	$25
—Promo-only sampler			
❏ AFL1-3575	If You Believe	1980	$15
❏ AFL1-3119	More Than a Love Song	1979	$15
❏ AFL1-2771	Toby Beau	1978	$12

TODD, ART AND DOTTY

DART

❏ D-444 [M]	Black Velvet Eyes	1959	$40

DOT

❏ DLP-3742 [M]	Chanson d'Amour (Song of Love)	1966	$30
❏ DLP-25742 [S]	Chanson d'Amour (Song of Love)	1966	$30

Number	Title	Yr	NM

TODD, RICHARD
GM RECORDINGS

Number	Title	Yr	NM
❏ 2010	New Ideas	1986	$30

TOE FAT
RARE EARTH

| ❏ RS-511 | Toe Fat | 1970 | $30 |
| ❏ RS-525 | Toe Fat Two | 1971 | $30 |

TOGASHI, MASAHIKO
INNER CITY

| ❏ IC-6011 | Spiritual Nature | 197? | $35 |

TOGAWA, PAUL
MODE

| ❏ LP-104 [M] | Paul Togawa Quartet | 1957 | $100 |

TOKENS, THE
B.T. PUPPY

❏ BTPS-1014	December 5th	1971	$250
❏ BTPS-1012	Greatest Moments	1970	$30
❏ BTP-1000 [M]	I Hear Trumpets Blow	1966	$25
❏ BTPS-1000 [P]	I Hear Trumpets Blow	1966	$30
❏ BTPS-1027	Intercourse	1971	$600
❏ BTPS-1006	Tokens of Gold	1969	$30

BUDDAH

| ❏ BDS-5059 | Both Sides Now | 1971 | $18 |

DIPLOMAT

| ❏ D-2308 [M] | Kings of the Hot Rods | 196? | $30 |
| ❏ DS-2308 [S] | Kings of the Hot Rods | 196? | $30 |

RCA

| ❏ 8534-1-R | Re-Doo-Wopp | 1988 | $12 |

RCA VICTOR

❏ LPM-2514 [M]	The Lion Sleeps Tonight	1961	$100
❏ LSP-2514 [S]	The Lion Sleeps Tonight	1961	$175
❏ LPM-3685 [M]	The Tokens Again	1966	$40
❏ LSP-3685 [S]	The Tokens Again	1966	$50
❏ LPM-2631 [M]	We, The Tokens, Sing Folk	1962	$40
❏ LSP-2631 [S]	We, The Tokens, Sing Folk	1962	$50
❏ LPM-2886 [M]	Wheels	1964	$100
❏ LSP-2886 [S]	Wheels	1964	$150

WARNER BROS.

| ❏ W1685 [M] | It's a Happening World | 1967 | $30 |
| ❏ WS1685 [S] | It's a Happening World | 1967 | $25 |

TOKENS, THE AND THE HAPPENINGS
Also see each artist's individual listings.
B.T. PUPPY

| ❏ BTP-1002 [M] | Back to Back | 1967 | $25 |

— Half this LP is by the Tokens, the other half by the Happenings

| ❏ BTPS-1002 [S] | Back to Back | 1967 | $30 |

TOLBERT, ISRAEL
WARREN/STAX

| ❏ STS-2038 | Popper Stopper | 1971 | $30 |

— Cover says "Warren Records Distributed by Stax," label is Stax

TOLKIEN, J.R.R.
CAEDMON

| ❏ TC1478 | J.R.R. Tolkien Reads and Sings His "The Lord of the Rings | 1975 | $25 |

TOLLIVER, CHARLES
ARISTA/FREEDOM

| ❏ AF1002 | Paper Man | 1975 | $30 |
| ❏ AF1017 | The Ringer | 1975 | $30 |

STRATA-EAST

❏ SES-8001	Compassion	1980	$30
❏ SES-19757	Impact	1975	$35
❏ SES-1972	Live at Slugs'	1972	$25
❏ SES-19720	Live at Slugs', Vol. 2	1972	$25
❏ SES-19740/1	Live at the Loosdrecht Jazz Festival	1974	$30
❏ SES-19745	Live in Tokyo	1974	$25
❏ SES-1971	Music Inc.	1971	$25

TOLONEN, JUKKA
TERRA

| ❏ T-6 | Touch Wood | 1985 | $30 |

TOM AND JERRY (2)
Guitar duo of Tommy Tomlinson and Jerry Kennedy. No relation to the "Tom and Jerry" who recorded for Big and later became known as Simon and Garfunkel.
MERCURY

❏ MG-20626 [M]	Guitar's Greatest Hits	1961	$30
❏ SR-60626 [S]	Guitar's Greatest Hits	1961	$40
❏ MG-20756 [M]	Guitar's Greatest Hits, Vol. 2	1962	$30
❏ SR-60756 [S]	Guitar's Greatest Hits, Vol. 2	1962	$40
❏ MG-20671 [M]	Guitars Play the Sound of Ray Charles	1962	$30
❏ SR-60671 [S]	Guitars Play the Sound of Ray Charles	1962	$40

| ❏ MG-20842 [M] | Surfin' Hootenanny | 1963 | $40 |
| ❏ SR-60842 [S] | Surfin' Hootenanny | 1963 | $50 |

TOM TOM CLUB
SIRE

❏ 25888	Boom Boom Chi Boom Boom	1989	$12
❏ 23916	Close to the Bone	1983	$12
❏ SRK3628	Tom Tom Club	1981	$12

WARNER BROS.

| ❏ WBMS-120 [DJ] | Wordy Rapping with the Tom Tom Club | 1986 | $25 |

— Part of "The Warner Bros. Music Show"; promo only

TOMITA
RCA RED SEAL

❏ ARL1-4019	A Voyage Through His Greatest Hits, Vol. 2	1981	$12
❏ ARL1-5184	Canon of the 3 Stars	1984	$12
❏ ARL1-1312	Firebird	1976	$12
❏ ARD1-1312 [Q]	Firebird	1976	$40
❏ ARL1-4332	Grand Canyon Suite	1982	$12
❏ ARL1-3439	Greatest Hits	1980	$12
❏ ARL1-1919	Holst: The Planets	1976	$12
❏ ARL1-2616	Kosmos	1978	$12
❏ ARL1-5461	Live at Linz, 1984 -- The Mind of the Universe	1985	$12
❏ ARL1-0838	Moussorgsky: Pictures at an Exhibition	1975	$12
❏ ARD1-0838 [Q]	Moussorgsky: Pictures at an Exhibition	1975	$40
❏ ARL1-3412	Ravel: Bolero	1980	$12
❏ ARL1-0488	Snowflakes Are Dancing	1974	$12
❏ ATL1-4332	Snowflakes Are Dancing	1982	$15

— Reissue with die-cut cover and custom innersleeve

❏ ARD1-0488 [Q]	Snowflakes Are Dancing	1974	$40
❏ ARL1-5037	Spacewalk -- Impressions of an Astronaut	1984	$12
❏ ARL1-2885	The Bermuda Triangle	1979	$12

TOMLIN, LILY
ARISTA

| ❏ AB4142 | Lily Tomlin On Stage | 1977 | $15 |

POLYDOR

❏ PD5023	And That's the Truth	1972	$12
❏ PD6051	Modern Scream	1976	$15
❏ 24-4055	This Is a Recording	1971	$12

TOMMY AND THE TWISTERS
REGENT

| ❏ MG-6104 [M] | Let's All Do the Twist | 1961 | $40 |

TOMMY TUTONE
COLUMBIA

❏ FC38425	National Emotion	1983	$12
❏ JC36372	Tommy Tutone	1980	$15
❏ AS1461 [DJ]	Tommy Tutone	1982	$25

— Three tracks from "Tommy Tutone-2" and the same three tracks live; promo-only

| ❏ ARC37401 | Tommy Tutone-2 | 1981 | $15 |
| ❏ PC37401 | Tommy Tutone-2 | 198? | $10 |

— Budget-line reissue

TOMORROW
PARLOPHONE

| ❏ PPMC7042 [B] | Tomorrow | 2015 | $25 |

— Record Store Day

SIRE

| ❏ SES-97912 | Tomorrow | 1968 | $75 |

TOMPALL AND THE GLASER BROTHERS
DECCA

| ❏ DL4041 [M] | This Land Folk Songs | 1960 | $30 |
| ❏ DL74041 [S] | This Land Folk Songs | 1960 | $40 |

ELEKTRA

| ❏ 60148 | After All These Years | 1982 | $12 |
| ❏ 5E-542 | Lovin' Her Was Easier | 1981 | $12 |

MGM

❏ SE-4775	Award Winners	1971	$18
❏ SE-4888	Great Hits from Two Decades	1973	$18
❏ SE-4620	Now Country	1969	$18
❏ SE-4812	Rings and Things	1972	$18
❏ SE-4510	Through the Eyes of Love	1968	$18
❏ E-4465 [M]	Tompall & the Glaser Brothers	1967	$30
❏ SE-4465 [S]	Tompall & the Glaser Brothers	1967	$25
❏ SE-4976	Vocal Group of the Decade	1974	$18

TOMPKINS, FRED
FESTIVAL

| ❏ 9001 | Compositions | 197? | $30 |
| ❏ 9002 | Somesville | 1975 | $30 |

F.K.T.

❏ 103	Cecile	1980	$30
❏ 101	Compositions	1980	$25
❏ 102	Somesville	1980	$25

TOMPKINS, ROSS, AND JOE VENUTI
CONCORD JAZZ

| ❏ CJ-51 | Live '77 | 1978 | $30 |

TOMPKINS, ROSS
CONCORD JAZZ

❏ CJ-117	Festival Time	198?	$25
❏ CJ-46	Lost in the Stars	1977	$30
❏ CJ-65	Ross Tompkins and His Good Friends	1978	$30
❏ CJ-28	Scrimshaw	1976	$30

FAMOUS DOOR

❏ HL-153	In the Swing of Things	1987	$25
❏ HL-151	L.A. After Dark	1986	$25
❏ HL-143	Street of Dreams	198?	$25
❏ HL-146	Symphony	198?	$25

TOMS, GARY, EMPIRE
MCA

| ❏ 2289 | Turn It Out | 1977 | $12 |

MERCURY

| ❏ SRM-1-3731 | Do It Again | 1978 | $12 |

P.I.P.

| ❏ 6814 | 7-6-5-4-3-2-1 Blow Your Whistle | 1975 | $12 |

TONE LOC
DELICIOUS VINYL

| ❏ 314-510609-1 [B] | Cool Hand Loc | 1991 | $25 |
| ❏ DV3000 [B] | Loc-ed After Dark | 1989 | $30 |

TONEY, OSCAR, JR.
BELL

| ❏ 6006 [M] | For Your Precious Love | 1967 | $30 |
| ❏ S-6006 [S] | For Your Precious Love | 1967 | $30 |

TONGUE
HEMISPHERE

| ❏ HIS-101 | Tongue | 1970 | $30 |

TONGUE AND GROOVE
FONTANA

| ❏ SRF-67593 | Tongue and Groove | 1968 | $25 |

TONI AND TERRY
CAPITOL

| ❏ ST-11137 | Cross-Country | 1973 | $15 |

TONSBERG CHORAL CHOIR
HARMONY MUSIC

| ❏ LP-18 [M] | Christmas Songs from Norway | 196? | $18 |

TONTO'S EXPANDING HEAD BAND
EMBRYO

| ❏ SD732 [B] | Zero Time | 1971 | $35 |

TONY TONI TONE
WING

| ❏ 841902-1 | Revival | 1990 | $25 |
| ❏ 835549-1 | Who? | 1988 | $15 |

TOO MUCH JOY
ALIAS

| ❏ A-003 | Son of Sam I Am | 1988 | $12 |

GIANT

| ❏ PRO-A-5054 [DJ] | Besides | 1991 | $15 |

— Promo-only collection

STONEGARDEN

| ❏ SGN-901 | Green Eggs and Crack | 1987 | $250 |

TOOL
VOLCANO

| ❏ 31160-1 | Lateralus | 2005 | $40 |

— Two picture discs; CD version issued in 2001

ZOO

❏ 11087-1	Aenima	1996	$300
❏ 11027-1 [B]	Opiate	1992	$25
❏ 11052-1 RE	Undertow	1993	$30

TOOTS AND THE MAYTALS
ISLAND

| ❏ ILPS9330 [B] | Funky Kingston | 1975 | $18 |

MANGO

| ❏ MLPS9330 | Funky Kingston | 197? | $12 |

— Reissue of Island 9330

❏ MLPS9590	Just Like That	1980	$12
❏ MLPS9670	Knock Out	1982	$12
❏ MLPS9647	Live	1980	$15
❏ MLPS9534	Pass the Pipe	198?	$12
❏ MLPS9374	Reggae Got Soul	1976	$15
❏ 9781	Reggae Greats	198?	$12

Number	Title	Yr	NM

TOP DRAWER
WISH BONE
❏ 721207	Solid Oak	1969	$400

TOPSIDERS, THE
JOSIE
| ❏ JOZ-4000 [M] | Rock Goes Folk | 1963 | $30 |

TORFF, BRIAN
AUDIOPHILE
| ❏ AP-182 | Manhattan Hoe-Down | 1983 | $25 |
OPTIMISM
| ❏ OP-2601 | Hitchhiker of Karoo | 198? | $25 |

TORKANOWSKY, DAVID
ROUNDER
| ❏ 2090 | Steppin' Out | 198? | $25 |

TORME, MEL, AND BUDDY RICH
CENTURY
| ❏ 1100 | Together Again -- For the First Time | 1978 | $30 |
— Direct-to-disc recording
GRYPHON
| ❏ G-903 | Together Again -- For the First Time | 1978 | $25 |

TORME, MEL
ALLEGRO ELITE
| ❏ 4117 [10] | Mel Torme Sings | 195? | $30 |
ATLANTIC
❏ 8069 [M]	Comin' Home Baby	1962	$175
❏ SD8069 [S]	Comin' Home Baby	1962	$175
❏ SD18129	Live at the Maisonette	1975	$30
❏ 8066 [M]	Mel Torme at the Red Hill Inn	1962	$175
❏ SD8066 [S]	Mel Torme at the Red Hill Inn	1962	$175
❏ 80078	Songs of New York	1982	$12
❏ 8091 [M]	Sunday in New York	1963	$30
❏ SD8091 [S]	Sunday in New York	1963	$40
AUDIOPHILE
| ❏ 67 | Mel Torme Sings About Love | 198? | $25 |
BETHLEHEM
❏ BCP6016 [M]	California Suite	1957	$300
❏ BCP-34 [M]	It's a Blue World	1956	$300
❏ BCP-52 [M]	Mel Torme and the Marty Paich Dektette	1956	$300
❏ BCP6020 [M]	Mel Torme Live at the Crescendo	1958	$250
❏ BCP6013 [M]	Mel Torme Sings Fred Astaire	1957	$300
❏ BCP6031 [M]	Songs for Any Taste	1959	$250
❏ BCP6042	The Torme Touch	1978	$15
— Reissue of BCP 52
CAPITOL
❏ ST-313	A Time for Us	1969	$40
❏ P200 [M]	California Suite	1950	$175
❏ ST-430	Raindrops Keep Falling on My Head	1970	$15
COLUMBIA
❏ CL2535 [M]	Mel Torme Right Now	1966	$30
❏ CS9335 [S]	Mel Torme Right Now	1966	$35
❏ CL2318 [M]	That's All -- A Lush Romantic Album	1965	$35
❏ CS9118 [S]	That's All -- A Lush Romantic Album	1965	$25
COLUMBIA SPECIAL PRODUCTS
| ❏ P13090 | That's All | 1976 | $30 |
CONCORD JAZZ
| ❏ CJ-382 | In Concert Tokyo | 1989 | $25 |
— Above two with the Marty Paich Dek-Tette
| ❏ CJ-306 | Mel Torme with Rob McConnell and the Boss Brass | 1986 | $25 |
| ❏ CJ-360 | Reunion | 1988 | $25 |
CORAL
| ❏ CRL57012 [M] | Gene Norman Presents Mel Torme "Live" at the Crescendo | 1955 | $75 |
| ❏ CRL57044 [M] | Musical Sounds Are the Best Songs | 1956 | $50 |
DISCOVERY
| ❏ 910 | Sings His California Suite | 1986 | $12 |
— Reissue of Capitol 200
EVEREST ARCHIVE OF FOLK & JAZZ
| ❏ 324 | The Velvet Fog | 1976 | $12 |
FINESSE
| ❏ W2X37484 | Mel Torme & Friends Recorded at Marty's, New York City | 1981 | $15 |
GLENDALE
| ❏ 6018 | Easy to Remember | 1979 | $12 |
| ❏ 6007 | Mel Torme | 1978 | $12 |

GRYPHON
| ❏ G-916 | A New Album | 1980 | $12 |
LIBERTY
| ❏ LST-7560 [S] | A Day in the Life of Bonnie and Clyde | 1968 | $25 |
| ❏ LRP-3560 [M] | A Day in the Life of Bonnie and Clyde | 1968 | $40 |
— Stock copy mono inside stereo cover with "Audition Mono LP Not for Sale" sticker
METRO
| ❏ M-532 [M] | I Wished on the Moon | 1965 | $175 |
| ❏ MS-532 [S] | I Wished on the Moon | 1965 | $300 |
MGM
| ❏ E552 [10] | Mel Torme Sings | 1952 | $150 |
MUSICRAFT
❏ 2005	Gone with the Wind	1986	$12
❏ 510	It Happened in Monterey	1983	$12
❏ 508	Mel Torme, Volume 1	1983	$12
STASH
| ❏ ST-252 | 'Round Midnight | 1985 | $12 |
STRAND
| ❏ SL-1076 [M] | Mel Torme Sings | 1960 | $25 |
| ❏ SLS-1076 [S] | Mel Torme Sings | 1960 | $30 |
TIME-LIFE
| ❏ SLGD-13 | Legendary Singers: Mel Torme | 1986 | $20 |
TOPS
| ❏ L-1615 [M] | Prelude to a Kiss | 1958 | $75 |
VENISE
| ❏ 10021 [M] | The Touch of Your Lips | 196? | $25 |
— Yellow vinyl; reissue of Tops L-1615 without patter in between songs
VERVE
| ❏ MGV2120 [M] | Back in Town | 1959 | $175 |
| ❏ V-2120 [M] | Back in Town | 1961 | $25 |
— Reissue
| ❏ MGVS6063 [S] | Back in Town | 1960 | $175 |
| ❏ V6-2120 [S] | Back in Town | 1961 | $30 |
— Reissue
❏ UMV-2675	Back in Town	1982	$25
❏ MGV2146 [M]	Broadway, Right Now	1961	$50
❏ V-2146 [M]	Broadway, Right Now	1961	$25
— Reissue
| ❏ V6-2146 [S] | Broadway, Right Now | 1961 | $30 |
| ❏ MGV2153 [M] | I Dig the Duke! I Dig the Count! | 1961 | $0 |
— Canceled; moved to 8491
❏ V-8491 [M]	I Dig the Duke! I Dig the Count!	1962	$30
❏ V6-8491 [S]	I Dig the Duke! I Dig the Count!	1962	$30
❏ MGV2132 [M]	Mel Torme Swings Schubert Alley	1960	$150
❏ V-2132 [M]	Mel Torme Swings Shubert Alley	1961	$25
— Reissue
| ❏ MGVS6146 [S] | Mel Torme Swings Shubert Alley | 1960 | $150 |
| ❏ V6-2132 [S] | Mel Torme Swings Shubert Alley | 196? | $30 |
— Reissue of 62132
| ❏ UMV-2521 | Mel Torme Swings Shubert Alley | 1981 | $25 |
| ❏ MGVS62132 [S] | Mel Torme Swings Shubert Alley | 196? | $40 |
— Early reissue of 6146
❏ V-8440 [M]	My Kind of Music	1962	$30
❏ V6-8440 [S]	My Kind of Music	1962	$30
❏ MGV2117 [M]	Ole Torme! Mel Torme Goes South of the Border with Billy May	1959	$150
❏ V-2117 [M]	Ole Torme! Mel Torme Goes South of the Border with Billy May	1961	$25
— Reissue
| ❏ MGVS6058 [S] | Ole Torme! Mel Torme Goes South of the Border with Billy May | 1960 | $150 |
| ❏ V6-2117 [S] | Ole Torme! Mel Torme Goes South of the Border with Billy May | 1961 | $30 |
— Reissue
| ❏ MGV2144 [M] | Swingin' on the Moon | 1960 | $100 |
| ❏ V-2144 [M] | Swingin' on the Moon | 1961 | $25 |
— Reissue
| ❏ V6-2144 [S] | Swingin' on the Moon | 1961 | $30 |
— Reissue of 62144
| ❏ MGVS62144 [S] | Swingin' on the Moon | 1960 | $100 |
| ❏ 823248-1 | The Duke Ellington and Count Basie Songbooks | 1984 | $12 |
— Reissue of Verve 8491
| ❏ MGV2105 [M] | Torme | 1958 | $50 |
| ❏ V-2105 [M] | Torme | 1961 | $25 |
— Reissue
| ❏ MGVS6015 [S] | Torme | 1960 | $75 |
| ❏ V6-2105 [S] | Torme | 1961 | $30 |
— Reissue
| ❏ V-8593 [M] | Verve's Choice -- The Best of Mel Torme | 1964 | $30 |

| ❏ V6-8593 [S] | Verve's Choice -- The Best of Mel Torme | 1964 | $35 |
VOCALION
| ❏ VL73905 | The Velvet Fog | 197? | $25 |

TORMENTORS, THE
ROYAL
| ❏ RLP-111 [M] | Hanging Around | 1967 | $300 |

TORN, DAVID, AND GEOFFREY GORDON
ECM
| ❏ 1284 | Best Laid Plans | 1985 | $30 |

TORNADOES, THE (1)
LONDON
| ❏ LL3279 [M] | Telstar | 1963 | $250 |
| ❏ LL3293 [M] | The Sounds of the Tornadoes | 1963 | $250 |
— Basically the same album as above, but with a new cover, one different track and the song order shuffled.

TORNADOES, THE (2)
JOSIE
| ❏ J-4005 [M] | Bustin' Surfboards | 1963 | $250 |
| ❏ JS-4005 [S] | Bustin' Surfboards | 1963 | $300 |
SUNDAZED
| ❏ LP-5024 | Bustin' Surfboards | 1996 | $12 |

TOROK, MITCHELL
GUYDEN
| ❏ GLP-502 [M] | Caribbean | 1960 | $40 |
| ❏ ST-502 [S] | Caribbean | 1960 | $50 |
REPRISE
| ❏ R6223 [M] | Guitar Course | 1966 | $25 |
| ❏ RS6223 [S] | Guitar Course | 1966 | $30 |

TORQUES, THE
LEMCO
| ❏ 604 | The Torques Live | 1966 | $250 |
WIGGINS
| ❏ 64010 | Zoom! | 1967 | $250 |

TORRES, NESTOR
VERVE FORECAST
| ❏ 839387-1 | Morning Ride | 1989 | $30 |

TOTO
COLUMBIA
| ❏ 8C838685 [EP] | Africa/Rosanna | 1983 | $25 |
— Africa-shaped picture disc; numbered like an LP although it has only these two songs on it and is (approximately) 7 inches
❏ FC40273	Fahrenheit	1986	$12
❏ FC36229	Hydra	1979	$12
❏ PC36229	Hydra	198?	$10
— Budget-line reissue with new prefix
❏ 9C939911 [PD]	Isolation	1984	$25
❏ QC38962	Isolation	1984	$12
❏ C45369	Past to Present 1977-1990	1990	$30
— Vinyl available only from Columbia House
❏ AS577 [DJ]	Special Radio Interview	1979	$25
❏ FC40873	The Seventh One	1988	$12
❏ JC35317	Toto	1978	$12
❏ PC35317	Toto	198?	$10
— Budget-line reissue with new prefix
| ❏ HC47728 | Toto IV | 198? | $40 |
— Half-speed mastered edition
| ❏ FC37728 | Toto IV | 1982 | $12 |
| ❏ PD36813 [PD] | Turn Back | 1981 | $30 |
— Promo-only picture disc
| ❏ FC36813 | Turn Back | 1981 | $12 |
| ❏ PC36813 | Turn Back | 1984 | $10 |
— Budget-line reissue with new prefix
MOBILE FIDELITY
| ❏ 1-250 | Toto IV | 1996 | $40 |
— Audiophile vinyl

TOUCH, THE
COLISEUM
| ❏ DS-51004 | The Touch | 1968 | $30 |

TOUCH
GEAR FAB
| ❏ GF105 | Street Suite | 1999 | $30 |
— Reissue of rare album plus bonus tracks
MAINLINE
| ❏ 2001 | Street Suite | 1969 | $2000 |
— VG value 1000; VG+ value 1500

TOUCHSTONE
UNITED ARTISTS
| ❏ UAS-5563 | Tarot | 1972 | $30 |

Number	Title	Yr	NM

TOUFF, CY
ARGO
❏ LP-606 [M]	Doorway To Dixie	1956	$40
❏ LP-641 [M]	Touff Assignment	1959	$30
❏ LPS-641 [S]	Touff Assignment	1959	$30

PACIFIC JAZZ
❏ PJ-1211 [M]	Cy Touff, His Octet and Quintet	1956	$175
❏ PJ-42 [M]	Keester Parade	1962	$75

WORLD PACIFIC
❏ PJM-410 [M]	Havin' A Ball	1958	$250

TOURISTS, THE
EPIC
❏ NJE36757	Luminous Basement	1980	$18
❏ JE36386	Reality Effect	1980	$18
❏ PC39318	Should Have Been Greatest Hits	1984	$15

TOUSSAINT, ALLEN
4 MEN WITH BEARDS
❏ 4M213 [B]	Life, Love and Faith	2012	$25
❏ 4M214LP [B]	Southern Nights		$25

RCA VICTOR
❏ LPM-1767 [M]	The Wild Sounds of New Orleans	1958	$300

— As "Al Tousan

REPRISE
❏ MS2062	Life, Love and Faith	1972	$30

RHINO
❏ R1553408 [B]	Live in Philadelphia 1975	2016	$25

SCEPTER
❏ 24003	Toussaint	1971	$30

WARNER BROS.
❏ BSK3142	Motion	1978	$15

TOWER OF POWER
COLUMBIA
❏ PC34302	Ain't Nothin' Stoppin' Us Now	1976	$12

— No bar code on cover
❏ PC34302	Ain't Nothin' Stoppin' Us Now	198?	$10

— Budget-line reissue with bar code
❏ PCQ34302 [Q]	Ain't Nothin' Stoppin' Us Now	1976	$20
❏ JC35784	Back on the Streets	1979	$12
❏ JC34906	We Came to Play!	1978	$12

DIRECT DISC
❏ SD16601	Back to Oakland	1980	$30

— Audiophile vinyl

SAN FRANCISCO
❏ SD204	East Bay Grease	1971	$50

SHEFFIELD LABS
❏ 17	Direct	1982	$30

— Direct-to-disc recording

WARNER BROS.
❏ BS2749	Back to Oakland	1974	$18

— "Burbank" palm trees label
❏ BS2749	Back to Oakland	1979	$10

— White or tan label
❏ BS2616	Bump City	1972	$18

— Green "WB" label
❏ BS2880	In the Slot	1975	$18

— "Burbank" palm trees label
❏ BS2924	Live and In Living Color	1976	$18

— "Burbank" palm trees label
❏ BS2924	Live and In Living Color	1979	$10

— White or tan label
❏ BS2681	Tower of Power	1973	$18

— Green "WB" label
❏ BS2681	Tower of Power	1973	$15

— "Burbank" palm trees label
❏ BS2681	Tower of Power	1979	$10

— White or tan label
❏ BS2834	Urban Renewal	1975	$18

— "Burbank" palm trees label

TOWNER, RALPH, AND GARY BURTON
ECM
❏ 1056	Matchbook	1975	$30
❏ 25038	Slide Show	1986	$25

TOWNER, RALPH, AND GLEN MOORE
ECM
❏ 1025	Trios/Solos	197?	$30

TOWNER, RALPH, AND JOHN ABERCROMBIE
ECM
❏ 1207	Five Years Later	198?	$25

TOWNER, RALPH
ECM
❏ 1121	Batik	1978	$30
❏ 23788	Blue Sun	1983	$25
❏ 1032	Diary	1973	$35
❏ 1153	Old Friends, New Friends	197?	$25
❏ 1173	Solo Concert	1979	$25
❏ 1060	Solstice	197?	$30
❏ ECM-1-1095	Sound and Shadows	1977	$30

TOWNSEND, ED
CAPITOL
❏ T1214 [M]	Glad to Be Here	1959	$30
❏ ST1214 [S]	Glad to Be Here	1959	$30
❏ T1140 [M]	New in Town	1959	$30
❏ ST1140 [S]	New in Town	1959	$30

CURTOM
❏ 5006	Ed Townsend Now	1976	$15

TOWNSEND, HENRY
BLUESVILLE
❏ BVLP-1041 [M]	Tired Bein' Mistreated	1962	$120

— Blue label, silver print
❏ BVLP-1041 [M]	Tired Bein' Mistreated	1964	$30

— Blue label, trident logo at side

TOWNSHEND, PETE, AND RONNIE LANE
ATCO
❏ 90097	Rough Mix	1983	$10

— Reissue of MCA LP

MCA

❏ 2295 [B]	Rough Mix	1977	$12

TOWNSHEND, PETE
Also see THE WHO.
ATCO
❏ SD 38-149	All the Best Cowboys Have Chinese Eyes	1982	$12
❏ 90539	Another Scoop	1987	$15
❏ PR940 [EP]	Deep End Sampler	1986	$25

— Promo-only sampler from Deep End Live
❏ SD 32-100	Empty Glass	1980	$12
❏ 90553	Pete Townshend's Deep End Live!	1986	$12
❏ 90063	Scoop	1983	$15
❏ 90473	White City -- A Novel	1985	$12

ATLANTIC
❏ 81996	The Iron Man: The Musical by Pete Townshend	1989	$12

— Also includes tracks by John Lee Hooker, Simon Townshend, Nina Simone, The Who

DECCA
❏ 79189 [B]	Who Came First	1972	$35

— With poster (deduct 50% if missing). Evidently a near-simultaneous release with Track 79189

EEL PIE
❏ EPR-0007	Another Scoop	2002	$40

— Classic Records edition on "Quiex SV" vinyl
❏ EPR-0013	Scoop 3	2001	$50

— Classic Records edition on "Quiex SV" vinyl

MCA
❏ 2026	Who Came First	1973	$15

— Reissue of 79189

TRACK
❏ PR0160 [DJ]	Pete Townshend Talks To and About Thunderclap Newman	1970	$150

— One-sided promo-only interview record
❏ PR-A-160 [DJ]	Pete Townshend Talks To and About Thunderclap Newman	1970	$150

— One-sided promo-only interview record

❏ 79189 [B]	Who Came First	1972	$35

— With poster (deduct 50% if missing)

TOYS, THE
DYNOVOICE
❏ 9002 [M]	The Toys Sing "A Lover's Concerto" and "Attack!	1966	$40
❏ S-9002 [P]	The Toys Sing "A Lover's Concerto" and "Attack!	1966	$50

TRACEY, STAN, AND KEITH TIPPETT
EMANEM
❏ 3307	TNT	1975	$35

TRACEY, STAN
LONDON
❏ LL3107 [M]	Showcase	195?	$40

TRADE WINDS, THE
KAMA SUTRA
❏ KLP-8057 [M]	Excursions	1967	$35
❏ KLPS-8057 [S]	Excursions	1967	$30

TRADER HORNE
JANUS
❏ JLS-3012 [B]	Morning Way	1970	$100

TRAFFIC
Also see JIM CAPALDI; DAVE MASON; STEVE WINWOOD.
ASYLUM
❏ 7E-1020	When the Eagle Flies	1974	$15

ISLAND
❏ 90058	John Barleycorn Must Die	1983	$10

— Reissue
❏ 8427801	John Barleycorn Must Die	2008	$25
❏ 90060	Mr. Fantasy	1983	$10

— Reissue
❏ SW-9323	Shoot Out at the Fantasy Factory	1973	$18
❏ ILPS9224	Shoot Out at the Fantasy Factory	197?	$15

— Reissue
❏ 90027	Shoot Out at the Fantasy Factory	1983	$10

— Reissue
❏ SW-9306	The Low Spark of High Heeled Boys	1971	$18
❏ ILPS9180	The Low Spark of High Heeled Boys	197?	$15

— Reissue
❏ 90026	The Low Spark of High Heeled Boys	1983	$10

— Reissue
❏ 8427791	The Low Spark of High Heeled Boys	2008	$25
❏ 90059	Traffic	1983	$10

— Reissue
❏ SMAS-9336	Traffic -- On the Road	1973	$25
❏ ILSD2	Traffic -- On the Road	197?	$18

— Reissue
❏ 90028	Traffic -- On the Road	1983	$15

— Reissue

MOBILE FIDELITY
❏ 1-209	The Low Spark of High Heeled Boys	1994	$100

— Audiophile vinyl

UNITED ARTISTS
❏ UAS-5500	Best of Traffic	1969	$25

— Originals have pink and orange labels
❏ UAL-3651 [M]	Heaven Is In Your Mind	1967	$300
❏ UAS-6651 [S]	Heaven Is In Your Mind	1967	$50
❏ UA-LA421-G	Heavy Traffic	1975	$18
❏ UAS-5504	John Barleycorn Must Die	1970	$25

— Originals have black and orange labels
❏ UAS-6702	Last Exit	1969	$25

— Originals have purple and orange labels
❏ ST-92018	Last Exit	1969	$30

— Capitol Record Club edition; label is the old-style black with circles at the top!
❏ UA-LA526-G	More Heavy Traffic	1975	$18
❏ UAS-6651 [S]	Mr. Fantasy	1968	$35

— Retitled version of "Heaven Is In Your Mind" with old title still on back cover
❏ UAS-6651 [S]	Mr. Fantasy	1968	$30

— Retitled version of "Heaven Is In Your Mind" with green strip across top of back with song titles
❏ UAS-6676	Traffic	1968	$25

— Originals have purple and orange labels
❏ UAS-5550	Welcome to the Canteen	1971	$18

TRAILER, REX, AND THE PLAYBOYS
CROWN
❏ CLP-5158 [M]	Country & Western	1958	$30

TRAMLINE
A&M
❏ SP-4208	Somewhere Down the Line	1969	$25

Number	Title	Yr	NM

TRAMMELL, BOBBY LEE
ATLANTA
| ❏ 1503 [M] | Arkansas Twist | 1962 | $1000 |

SOUNCOT
| ❏ SC-1102 | I Dare America to Be Great | 1971 | $25 |
| ❏ SC-1141 | Love Isn't Love Till You Give It Away | 1972 | $18 |

TRAMMPS, THE
ATLANTIC
❏ SD18211	Disco Inferno	1977	$12
❏ SD19267	Mixin' It Up	1980	$12
❏ SD19290	Slipping Out	1981	$12
❏ SD19194	The Best of the Trammps	1978	$12
❏ SD19148	The Trammps III	1977	$12
❏ SD19210	The Whole World's Dancing	1979	$12
❏ SD18172	Where the Happy People Go	1976	$12

BUDDAH
| ❏ BDS-5641 | The Legendary Zing Album Featuring the Fabulous Trammps | 1975 | $15 |

GOLDEN FLEECE
| ❏ KZ33163 | Trammps | 1975 | $12 |

PHILADELPHIA INT'L.
| ❏ PZ33163 | Disco Champs | 1977 | $10 |
— Reissue of Golden Fleece LP

TRANSIENTS, THE
HORIZON
| ❏ WP-1633 [M] | The Funky 12 String Guitar | 1963 | $25 |
| ❏ WPS-1633 [S] | The Funky 12 String Guitar | 1963 | $30 |

TRANSVISION VAMP
UNI
| ❏ 5 | Pop Art | 1988 | $15 |
| ❏ 605 | Velveteen | 1989 | $15 |

TRAPEZE
Includes future JUDAS PRIEST drummer Dave Holland plus multi-band bassist/vocalist GLENN HUGHES.

PAID
| ❏ 2003 | Hold On | 1981 | $12 |

THRESHOLD
❏ THS4	Medusa	1971	$100
❏ THS11	The Final Swing	1974	$40
❏ THS2	Trapeze	1970	$40
❏ THS8	You Are the Music, We're Just the Band	1972	$40

WARNER BROS.
| ❏ BS2828 | Hot Wire | 1974 | $15 |
| ❏ BS2887 | Trapeze | 1975 | $15 |

TRAPP FAMILY SINGERS, THE
RCA CAMDEN
| ❏ CAL-209 [M] | The Trapp Family Singers Present Christmas and Folk Songs | 195? | $25 |

TRASHMEN, THE
BEAT ROCKET
| ❏ BR107 | Surfin' Bird | 1999 | $15 |
— Reissue on 180-gram vinyl

GARRETT
| ❏ GA-200 [M] | Surfin' Bird | 1964 | $300 |
| ❏ GAS-200 [R] | Surfin' Bird | 1964 | $350 |

SUNDAZED

THE TRASHMEN — GREAT LOST ALBUM!
UNRELEASED STUDIO RECORDINGS 1964-1966! FEATURING GHOST RIDERS IN THE SKY, WILD CAT, LOOSE IN TOWN, BIRD DIDDLEY BEAT, BE TRUE TO YOUR SCHOOL, HEARTBEAT, KEEP A KNOCKIN', STICK SHIFT, AND MORE!

| ❏ LP5003 [B] | Great Lost Album | 1991 | $12 |
| ❏ LP5002 | Live Bird '65-'67 | 1991 | $12 |

TRASK, DIANA
ABC
| ❏ ABDP-948 | Believe Me Now or Believe Me Later | 1976 | $15 |
| ❏ AC-30030 | The ABC Collection | 1976 | $15 |

ABC DOT
| ❏ DOSD-2007 | Diana Trask's Greatest Hits | 1974 | $15 |
| ❏ DOSD-2024 | The Mood I'm In | 1975 | $15 |

COLUMBIA
❏ CL1601 [M]	Diana Trask	1961	$30
❏ CS8401 [S]	Diana Trask	1961	$30
❏ CL1705 [M]	Diana Trask on TV	1961	$30
❏ CS8505 [S]	Diana Trask on TV	1961	$30

DOT
❏ DOS-25989	Diana's Country	1971	$18
❏ DOS-25999	Diana Trask Sings About Loving	1972	$18
❏ DLP-25957	From the Heart	1969	$18
❏ DOS-26016	It's a Man's World	1973	$18
❏ DOS-26022	Lean It All on Me	1974	$18
❏ DLP-25920	Miss Country Soul	1969	$18

PICKWICK/HILLTOP
| ❏ 6188 | Miss Country Soul | 197? | $12 |

TRAUT, ROSS
HEADFIRST
| ❏ 9709 | Ross Traut | 198? | $35 |

TRAUT/RODBY
COLUMBIA
| ❏ FC44472 | The Great Lawn | 1989 | $30 |

TRAVEL AGENCY, THE
VIVA
| ❏ V-36017 | The Travel Agency | 1968 | $30 |

TRAVELERS 3, THE
ELEKTRA
❏ EKL-236 [M]	Live! Live! Live!	1963	$30
❏ EKL-226 [M]	Open House	1963	$30
❏ EKL-216 [M]	The Travelers 3	1963	$30

TRAVELING WILBURYS
Also see BOB DYLAN; GEORGE HARRISON; JEFF LYNNE; ROY ORBISON; TOM PETTY AND THE HEARTBREAKERS.
WILBURY
| ❏ 26324 | Traveling Wilburys, Vol. 3 | 1990 | $25 |
| ❏ 25796 | Traveling Wilburys (Volume One) | 1988 | $25 |

TRAVELLERS, THE
KAPP
| ❏ KL-1157 [M] | Journey with the Travellers | 1960 | $30 |
| ❏ KS-3051 [S] | Journey with the Travellers | 1960 | $30 |

TRAVERS, MARY
CHRYSALIS
| ❏ CHR1168 | It's In Everyone of Us | 1978 | $12 |

WARNER BROS.
| ❏ BS2677 | All My Choices | 1973 | $15 |
— Green "WB" label
| ❏ BS2795 | Circles | 1974 | $15 |
— Burbank" palm-trees label
| ❏ WS1907 | Mary | 1971 | $15 |
— Green "WB" label
| ❏ BS2609 | Morning Glory | 1972 | $15 |
— Green "WB" label

TRAVERS, PAT
CLEOPATRA
| ❏ 9009 [B] | Blues On Fire | | $25 |

POLYDOR
❏ PD-16103 [B]	Makin' Magic	1977	$15
❏ PD-16079 [B]	Pat Travers	1976	$12
❏ PD-16121 [B]	Putting It Straight	1977	$12

TRAVIS, MERLE, AND JOE MAPHIS
CAPITOL
| ❏ T2102 [M] | Merle Travis and Joe Maphis | 1964 | $40 |
| ❏ ST2102 [S] | Merle Travis and Joe Maphis | 1964 | $50 |

TRAVIS, MERLE
CAPITOL
| ❏ T891 [M] | Back Home | 1957 | $150 |
— Turquoise or gray label
| ❏ T891 [M] | Back Home | 1959 | $30 |
— Black colorband label, logo at left
| ❏ T891 [M] | Back Home | 1962 | $25 |
— Black colorband label, logo at top
❏ T1956 [M]	Songs of the Coal Mines	1963	$40
❏ ST1956 [S]	Songs of the Coal Mines	1963	$50
❏ ST2938	Strictly Guitar	1968	$30
❏ T2662 [M]	The Best of Merle Travis	1967	$30
❏ DT2662 [R]	The Best of Merle Travis	1967	$25

| ❏ T650 [M] | The Merle Travis Guitar | 1956 | $120 |
— Turquoise or gray label
| ❏ T650 [M] | The Merle Travis Guitar | 1959 | $30 |
— Black colorband label, logo at left
| ❏ T650 [M] | The Merle Travis Guitar | 1962 | $25 |
— Black colorband label, logo at top
| ❏ T1664 [M] | Travis | 1962 | $40 |
— Black colorband label, logo at left
| ❏ T1664 [M] | Travis | 1962 | $25 |
— Black colorband label, logo at top
| ❏ ST1664 [S] | Travis | 1962 | $50 |
— Black colorband label, logo at left
| ❏ ST1664 [S] | Travis | 1962 | $30 |
— Black colorband label, logo at top
| ❏ T1391 [M] | Walkin' the Strings | 1960 | $100 |
— Black colorband label, logo at left
| ❏ T1391 [M] | Walkin' the Strings | 1962 | $25 |
— Black colorband label, logo at top

TRAVIS, NICK
RCA VICTOR
| ❏ LJM-1010 [M] | The Panic Is On | 1954 | $120 |

TRAVIS, RANDY
MUSIC VALLEY
| ❏ 0(# unknown) | Randy Ray Live at the Nashville Palace | 1982 | $300 |
— With no "Randy Travis" sticker on front cover
| ❏ 0(# unknown) | Randy Ray Live at the Nashville Palace | 1986 | $250 |
— With "Randy Travis" sticker on front cover; the records are the same as the first edition

WARNER BROS.
❏ 25568	Always & Forever	1987	$12
❏ 25972	An Old-Fashioned Christmas	1989	$15
❏ R174597	Heroes and Friends	1990	$25
— Only released on vinyl through BMG Direct Marketing
❏ 25988	No Holdin' Back	1989	$15
❏ 25738	Old 8x10	1988	$12
❏ 25435	Storms of Life	1986	$12

TRAVOLTA, JOHN
MIDLAND INT'L.
| ❏ BKL1-2211 | Can't Let You Go | 1977 | $15 |
| ❏ BKL1-1563 | John Travolta | 1976 | $15 |

MIDSONG INT'L.
| ❏ MTF 001 | Travolta Fever | 1978 | $18 |
— Reissue of his two LPs in one package

TREE
GOAT FARM
| ❏ 580 | Tree | 1970 | $80 |

TREMELOES, THE
DJM
| ❏ 2 | Shiner | 1974 | $15 |

EPIC
❏ LN24326 [M]	Even the Bad Times Are Good	1967	$40
❏ BN26326 [P]	Even the Bad Times Are Good	1967	$30
❏ LN24310 [M]	Here Comes My Baby	1967	$30
❏ BN26310 [R]	Here Comes My Baby	1967	$25
❏ LN24363 [M]	Suddenly You Love Me	1968	$30
❏ BN26363 [R]	Suddenly You Love Me	1968	$25
❏ BN26388 [S]	World Explosion '58/'68	1968	$30
❏ LN24388 [M]	World Explosion '58/'68	1968	$75
— White label promo only

TRENIERS, THE
DOT
| ❏ DLP-3257 [M] | Souvenir Album | 1960 | $150 |

EPIC
| ❏ LG3125 [M] | The Treniers on TV | 1955 | $250 |

TRENT, BUCK
ABC DOT
| ❏ DOSD-2058 | Bionic Banjo | 1976 | $12 |
| ❏ DO-2077 | Oh Yeah! | 1977 | $12 |

BOONE
| ❏ 1212 | Give Me Five | 1967 | $25 |

RCA VICTOR
| ❏ LSP-4705 | Sounds of Now and Beyond | 1972 | $15 |

SMASH
| ❏ MGS-27002 [M] | The Sound of a Bluegrass Banjo | 1962 | $25 |
— Smash LPs as "Charles Trent"
❏ SRS-67002 [S]	The Sound of a Bluegrass Banjo	1962	$30
❏ MGS-27017 [M]	The Sound of a Five String Banjo	1962	$25
❏ SRS-67017 [S]	The Sound of a Five String Banjo	1962	$30

Number	Title	Yr	NM

TRESVANT, RALPH
MCA

Number	Title	Yr	NM
❏ 10116	Ralph Tresvant	1990	$15

TREVOR, JEANNIE
MAINSTREAM

❏ 56075 [M]	Jeannie Trevor Sings!!	1965	$30
❏ S-6075 [S]	Jeannie Trevor Sings!!	1965	$30

TREVOR, VAN
BAND BOX

❏ 0(# unknown)	Come On Over to Our Side	1967	$25

DATE

❏ DES-4008	You've Been So Good to Me	1967	$18

ROYAL AMERICAN

❏ 2800	Funny Familiar Forgotten Feelings	1969	$18

TRIANGLE, THE
AMARET

❏ 5000 [B]	How Now Brown Cow	1969	$30

TRICHT, EVERT VAN
MERCURY LIVING PRESENCE

❏ SR90403 [S]	Oboe Concerti	196?	$30

—With Kurt Redel/Vienna Symphony Orchestra and Pro Arte Orchestra of Munich; maroon label, no "Vendor: Mercury Record Corporation"

TRICYCLE
ABC

❏ S-674	Tricycle	1969	$25

TRIGGER, VIC
SANCTUARY

❏ 12103	Electronic Wizard	1977	$150

TRIMBLE, BOBB
(NO LABEL)

❏ 0(no cat #)	Harvest of Dreams	1982	$175

VENGEANCE

❏ BT-8458	Iron Curtain Dream	1980	$800

TRIO, THE
SAVOY

❏ MG-12023 [M]	The Trio	1955	$150

TRIO
MERCURY

❏ 814320-1	Trio and Error	1983	$25
❏ MX-1-509 [EP]	Trio (Contains the Hit Da Da Da)	1982	$18

TRIPLETS, THE
ELEKTRA

❏ 60455 [EP]	Break the Silence	1986	$10

TRIPSICHORD MUSIC BOX, THE
JANUS

❏ JLS-3016	The Tripsichord Music Box	1971	$250

TRISTANO, LENNIE; JO BUSHKIN; BOBBY SCOTT; MARIAN MCPARTLAND
SAVOY

❏ MG-12043 [M]	The Jazz Keyboards of Lennie Tristano, Joe Bushkin, Bobby Scott & Marian McPartland	1955	$100

TRISTANO, LENNIE
ATLANTIC

❏ 1224 [M]	Lennie Tristano	1955	$300

—Black label

❏ 1224 [M]	Lennie Tristano	1960	$300

—Multicolor label, white "fan" logo at right

❏ 1224 [M]	Lennie Tristano	1964	$35

—Multicolor label, black "fan" logo at right

❏ SD 2-7006	Lennie Tristano Quartet	198?	$35
❏ SD 2-7003	Requiem	1980	$35
❏ 1357 [M]	The New Tristano	1960	$300

—Multicolor label, white "fan" logo at right

❏ 1357 [M]	The New Tristano	196?	$35

—Red and purple label, black "fan" logo at right

ELEKTRA/MUSICIAN

❏ 60264	New York Improvisations	1984	$30

INNER CITY

❏ IC-6002	Descent Into the Maelstrom	197?	$75

JAZZ

❏ JR-6	Continuity	1985	$30
❏ JR-1	Live at Birdland 1949	198?	$30
❏ JR-5	Live in Toronto 1952	198?	$30

Number	Title	Yr	NM

MOSAIC

❏ MQ10-174	The Complete Atlantic Recordings of Lennie Tristano, Lee Konitz and Warne Marsh	199?	$300

NEW JAZZ

❏ NJLP-101 [10]	Lennie Tristano with Lee Konitz	1950	$600

PRESTIGE

❏ PRLP-101 [10]	Lennie Tristano with Lee Konitz	1951	$500

TRISTANO, LENNIE/ARNOLD ROSS
EMARCY

❏ MG-26029 [10]	Holiday in Piano	1953	$400

TRISTANO, LENNIE/BUDDY DEFRANCO
CAPITOL

❏ M-11060	Cross Currents	1972	$150

—Capitol Jazz Classics, Vol. 14"; original edition does not have an "All Rights Reserved" disclaimer in the perimeter print

❏ M-11060	Cross Currents	1975	$35

—Capitol Jazz Classics, Voil. 14"; yellow label with "Capitol" at bottom; "All Rights Reserved" in perimeter print

TRITT, TRAVIS
WARNER BROS.

❏ W1-26589	It's All About to Change	1991	$25

—Vinyl available only from Columbia House

TRIUMPH
MCA

❏ MCA-5537 [B]	Thunder Seven	1984	$18

—Quiex II promo

TRIUMVIRAT
CAPITOL

❏ ST-11862	A La Carte	1978	$15
❏ SN-16123	A La Carte	1980	$10

—Budget-line reissue

❏ SN-16119	Illusions on a Double Dimple	1980	$10

—Budget-line reissue

❏ ST-11551	Old Loves Die Hard	1976	$15
❏ SN-16122	Old Loves Die Hard	1980	$10

—Budget-line reissue

❏ ST-11697	Pompeii	1977	$15
❏ SN-16120	Pompeii	1980	$10

—Budget-line reissue

❏ ST-11392	Spartacus	1975	$15
❏ SN-16121	Spartacus	1980	$10

—Budget-line reissue

HARVEST

❏ ST-11311	Illusions on a Double Dimple	1974	$18

TRIZO 50
CAVERN

❏ 740142	Trizo 50	197?	$300

TROGGS, THE
ATCO

❏ 33-193 [M]	Wild Thing	1966	$50
❏ SD 33-193 [R]	Wild Thing	1966	$40

FONTANA

❏ SRF67576 [R]	Love Is All Around	1968	$30
❏ MGF27556 [M]	Wild Thing/With a Girl Like You	1966	$40

—Contents identical to the Atco LP; two slightly different cover variations are known; record has mono number and plays mono; number "27556" in trail-off

❏ SRF67556 [R]	Wild Thing/With a Girl Like You	1966	$30

—Contents identical to the Atco LP; two slightly different cover variations are known

❏ MGF27556 [R]	Wild Thing/With a Girl Like You	1966	$30

—Contents identical to the Atco LP; two slightly different cover variations are known; record has mono number but plays in rechanneled stereo; number "2/67556" in trail-off

MKC

❏ 214	Live at Max's Kansas City	1980	$15

PRIVATE STOCK

❏ PS-2008 [B]	The Troggs Tapes	1976	$18

PYE

❏ 12112	The Troggs	1975	$15

RHINO

❏ RNLP-118	The Best of the Troggs	1985	$12
❏ R170118	The Best of the Troggs	1988	$10

SIRE

❏ SASH-3714	The Vintage Years	1976	$18

TROLL, THE
SMASH

❏ SRS-67114	Animated Music	1969	$50

Number	Title	Yr	NM

TROMBONES, INC., THE
WARNER BROS.

❏ W1272 [M]	They Met at the Continental Divide	1959	$50
❏ WS1272 [S]	They Met at the Continental Divide	1959	$75

TROMBONES UNLIMITED
LIBERTY

❏ LRP-3494 [M]	Big Boss Bones	1967	$25
❏ LST-7494 [S]	Big Boss Bones	1967	$20
❏ LST-7592	Grazing in the Grass	1968	$20
❏ LRP-3527 [M]	Holiday for Trombones	1967	$25
❏ LST-7527 [S]	Holiday for Trombones	1967	$20
❏ LRP-3549 [M]	One of Those Songs	1968	$30
❏ LST-7549 [S]	One of Those Songs	1968	$20
❏ LRP-3449 [M]	These Bones are Made for Walking	1966	$20
❏ LST-7449 [S]	These Bones are Made for Walking	1966	$25
❏ LRP-3472 [M]	You're Gonna Hear From Me	1966	$35
❏ LST-7472 [S]	You're Gonna Hear From Me	1966	$50

TROUBADOURS DE ROI BAUDOUIN
PHILIPS

❏ PCC606 [S]	Missa Luba	1963	$18

—Released in '63, this didn't chart until 1969

❏ PCC206 [M]	Missa Luba	1963	$18

TROUP, BOBBY
AUDIOPHILE

❏ AP-98	In a Class Beyond Compare	198?	$25

BETHLEHEM

❏ BCP-1030 [10]	Bobby Troup	1955	$300
❏ BCP-19 [M]	Bobby Troup Sings Johnny Mercer	1955	$300
❏ BCP-35 [M]	The Distinctive Style of Bobby Troup	1955	$300

CAPITOL

❏ H484 [10]	Bobby	1953	$175
❏ T484 [M]	Bobby	1955	$100

INTERLUDE

❏ MO-501 [M]	Cool	1959	$40
❏ ST-1001 [S]	Cool	1959	$40

LIBERTY

❏ LRP-3002 [M]	Bobby Troup and His Trio	1955	$75
❏ LRP-3026 [M]	Do Re Mi	1957	$50
❏ LRP-3078 [M]	Here's to My Lady	1958	$50

MODE

❏ LP-111 [M]	Bobby Swings Tenderly	1957	$150

PAUSA

❏ 9032	Bobby Troup	198?	$25

RCA VICTOR

❏ LPM-1959 [M]	Bobby Troup and His Jazz All-Stars	1959	$40
❏ LSP-1959 [S]	Bobby Troup and His Jazz All-Stars	1959	$50

TROWER, ROBIN
Also see JACK BRUCE/ROBIN TROWER; PROCOL HARUM.
ATLANTIC

❏ 82080	In the Line of Fire	1990	$15
❏ 81838	Take What You Need	1988	$12

CHRYSALIS

❏ FV41420	Back It Up	1983	$12
❏ PV41420	Back It Up	1986	$12

—Reissue

❏ CHR1324	B.L.T.	1981	$12
❏ PV41324	B.L.T.	1984	$10

—Reissue

❏ CHR1057	Bridge of Sighs	1974	$15

—Green label, "3300 Warner Blvd." address

❏ CHR1057	Bridge of Sighs	1977	$12

—Blue label, New York address

❏ FV41057	Bridge of Sighs	1984	$10

—Reissue

❏ PV41057	Bridge of Sighs	1986	$10

—Reissue

❏ CHR1189	Caravan to Midnight	1978	$15
❏ PV41189	Caravan to Midnight	1984	$10

—Reissue

❏ CHR1073	For Earth Below	1975	$15

—Green label, "3300 Warner Blvd." address

❏ CHR1073	For Earth Below	1977	$12

—Blue label, New York address

❏ PV41073	For Earth Below	1984	$10

—Reissue

❏ CHR1148 [B]	In City Dreams	1977	$15
❏ PV41148	In City Dreams	1984	$10

—Reissue

❏ CHR1107	Long Misty Days	1976	$15

—Green label, "3300 Warner Blvd." address

❏ CHR1107	Long Misty Days	1977	$12

—Blue label, New York address

❏ PV41107	Long Misty Days	1983	$10

—Reissue

Number	Title	Yr	NM
❏ CHR1089	Robin Trower Live!	1976	$15
— Green label, "3300 Warner Blvd." address			
❏ CHR1089	Robin Trower Live!	1977	$12
— Blue label, New York address			
❏ PV41089	Robin Trower Live!	1983	$10
— Reissue			
❏ CHR1039	Twice Removed from Yesterday	1973	$15
— Green label, "3300 Warner Blvd." address			
❏ CHR1039	Twice Removed from Yesterday	1977	$12
— Blue label, New York address			
❏ PV41039	Twice Removed from Yesterday	1983	$10
— Reissue			
❏ CHR1215	Victims of the Fury	1980	$15
❏ PV41215	Victims of the Fury	1983	$10
— Reissue			

GNP CRESCENDO
Number	Title	Yr	NM
❏ 2187	Passion	1986	$12

PASSPORT
Number	Title	Yr	NM
❏ PB-6049	Beyond the Mist	1985	$12

TROY, DORIS
APPLE
Number	Title	Yr	NM
❏ ST-3371	Doris Troy	1970	$30

ATLANTIC
Number	Title	Yr	NM
❏ 8088 [M]	Just One Look	1964	$30
❏ SD8088 [P]	Just One Look	1964	$50
— The title song is rechanneled			

TROYKA
COTILLION
Number	Title	Yr	NM
❏ SD9020 [B]	Troyka	1970	$40

TRUMAN, MARGARET
RCA VICTOR
Number	Title	Yr	NM
❏ LM-145 [10]	A Margaret Truman Program	1952	$100
❏ LM-57 [10]	American Songs	1951	$100

TRUMPET SUMMIT
PABLO TODAY
Number	Title	Yr	NM
❏ 2312114	Trumpet Summit Meets the Oscar Peterson Big 4	198?	$30

TRUMPETEERS, THE (1)
GRAND
Number	Title	Yr	NM
❏ 7701 [M]	The Last Supper	195?	$150

SCORE
Number	Title	Yr	NM
❏ SLP-4021 [M]	Milky White Way	1956	$300

TRYFOROS, BOB
PURITAN
Number	Title	Yr	NM
❏ 5002	Joplin on Guitar	197?	$30

TRYNIN, JENNIFER
PATHFINDER
Number	Title	Yr	NM
❏ PTF-8827 [EP]	Trespassing	1988	$20

SQUINT
Number	Title	Yr	NM
❏ JT-101	Cockamamie	1994	$15

T'SONGO
TIGER LILY
Number	Title	Yr	NM
❏ TL14042 [B]	T'songo	1976	$600

TUBB, ERNEST, AND LORETTA LYNN
DECCA
Number	Title	Yr	NM
❏ DL75115	If We Put Our Heads Together	1969	$30
❏ DL4639 [M]	Mr. and Mrs. Used to Be	1965	$30
❏ DL74639 [S]	Mr. and Mrs. Used to Be	1965	$40
❏ DL4872 [M]	Singin' Again	1967	$30
❏ DL74872 [S]	Singin' Again	1967	$30

MCA
Number	Title	Yr	NM
❏ 4000	The Ernest Tubb/Loretta Lynn Story	1973	$18

TUBB, ERNEST
CACHET
Number	Title	Yr	NM
❏ 33001	Ernest Tubb: The Legend and the Legacy, Volume One	1979	$15

DECCA

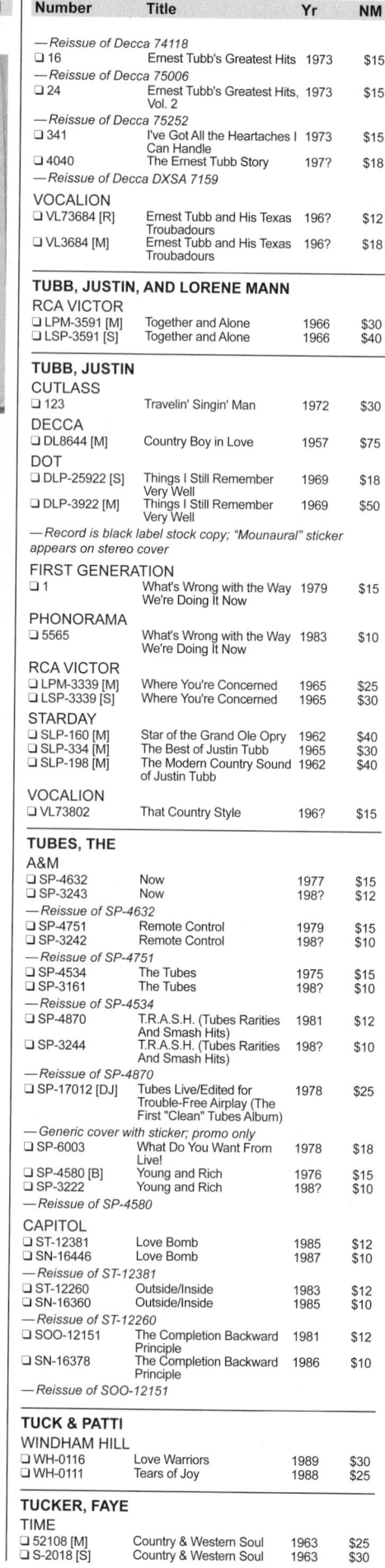

Number	Title	Yr	NM
❏ DL75222 [B]	A Good Year for the Wine	1970	$25
❏ DL4046 [M]	All Time Hits	1961	$30
❏ DL74046 [S]	All Time Hits	1961	$40
❏ DL4867 [M]	Another Story	1967	$30
❏ DL74867 [S]	Another Story	1967	$30
❏ DL75388	Baby, It's So Hard to Be Good	1972	$25
❏ DL4518 [M]	Blue Christmas	1963	$30
❏ DL74518 [S]	Blue Christmas	1963	$30
❏ DL4746 [M]	By Request	1966	$30
❏ DL74746 [S]	By Request	1966	$30
❏ DL75072	Country Hit Time	1968	$25
❏ DL5301 [10]	Ernest Tubb Favorites	1951	$175
❏ DL8291 [M]	Ernest Tubb Favorites	1955	$80
❏ DL4118 [M]	Ernest Tubb's Golden Favorites	1961	$30
❏ DL74118 [S]	Ernest Tubb's Golden Favorites	1961	$40
❏ DL75006 [S]	Ernest Tubb's Greatest Hits	1968	$30
❏ DL5006 [M]	Ernest Tubb's Greatest Hits	1968	$100
— White label promo only			
❏ DL75252	Ernest Tubb's Greatest Hits, Vol. 2	1970	$25
❏ DL4772 [M]	Ernest Tubb Sings Country Hits Old & New	1966	$30
❏ DL74772 [S]	Ernest Tubb Sings Country Hits Old & New	1966	$30
❏ DL4957 [M]	Ernest Tubb Sings Hank Williams	1968	$50
❏ DL74957 [S]	Ernest Tubb Sings Hank Williams	1968	$30
❏ DL4681 [M]	Hittin' the Road	1965	$30
❏ DL74681 [S]	Hittin' the Road	1965	$30
❏ DL5336 [10]	Jimmie Rodgers Songs Sung by Ernest Tubb	1951	$175
❏ DL4385 [M]	Just Call Me Lonesome	1962	$30
❏ DL74385 [S]	Just Call Me Lonesome	1962	$30
❏ DL75114	Let's Turn Back the Years	1969	$18
❏ DL4640 [M]	My Pick of the Hits	1965	$30
❏ DL74640 [S]	My Pick of the Hits	1965	$30
❏ DL75301	One Sweet Hello	1971	$25
❏ DL4321 [M]	On Tour	1962	$30
❏ DL74321 [S]	On Tour	1962	$30
❏ DL75122	Saturday Satan, Sunday Saint	1969	$25
❏ DL75345	Say Something Nice to Sarah	1972	$25
❏ DL5497 [10]	Sing a Song of Christmas	1954	$175
❏ DL4514 [M]	Thanks a Lot	1964	$30
❏ DL74514 [S]	Thanks a Lot	1964	$30
❏ DL8553 [M]	The Daddy of 'Em All	1956	$80
❏ DL4064 [M]	The Ernest Tubb Record Shop	1960	$40
❏ DL74064 [M]	The Ernest Tubb Record Shop	1960	$50
❏ DXA159 [M]	The Ernest Tubb Story	1959	$100
— Deduct 25 percent if book is missing			
❏ DXSA7159 [R]	The Ernest Tubb Story	196?	$30
— Deduct 25 percent if book is missing			
❏ DL4397 [M]	The Family Bible	1963	$30
❏ DL74397 [S]	The Family Bible	1963	$30
❏ DL8834 [M]	The Importance of Being Ernest	1959	$50
❏ DL78834 [S]	The Importance of Being Ernest	1959	$75
❏ DL5334 [10]	The Old Rugged Cross	1951	$175

FIRST GENERATION
Number	Title	Yr	NM
❏ LP-0002	The Legend and the Legacy	1979	$50
— No ads on back cover			
❏ LP-0002	The Legend and the Legacy	1979	$40
— With ad for Ernest Tubb Record Shop on back cover			
❏ TV-1033	The Legend and the Legacy	1979	$30
— Mail-order version			

MCA
Number	Title	Yr	NM
❏ 512	Baby, It's So Hard to Be Good	197?	$15
— Reissue of Decca 75388			
❏ 496	Ernest Tubb	1975	$15
❏ 84	Ernest Tubb's Golden Favorites	1973	$15

Number	Title	Yr	NM
— Reissue of Decca 74118			
❏ 16	Ernest Tubb's Greatest Hits	1973	$15
— Reissue of Decca 75006			
❏ 24	Ernest Tubb's Greatest Hits, Vol. 2	1973	$15
— Reissue of Decca 75252			
❏ 341	I've Got All the Heartaches I Can Handle	1973	$15
❏ 4040	The Ernest Tubb Story	197?	$18
— Reissue of Decca DXSA 7159			

VOCALION
Number	Title	Yr	NM
❏ VL73684 [R]	Ernest Tubb and His Texas Troubadours	196?	$12
❏ VL3684 [M]	Ernest Tubb and His Texas Troubadours	196?	$18

TUBB, JUSTIN, AND LORENE MANN
RCA VICTOR
Number	Title	Yr	NM
❏ LPM-3591 [M]	Together and Alone	1966	$30
❏ LSP-3591 [S]	Together and Alone	1966	$40

TUBB, JUSTIN
CUTLASS
Number	Title	Yr	NM
❏ 123	Travelin' Singin' Man	1972	$30

DECCA
Number	Title	Yr	NM
❏ DL8644 [M]	Country Boy in Love	1957	$75

DOT
Number	Title	Yr	NM
❏ DLP-25922 [S]	Things I Still Remember Very Well	1969	$18
❏ DLP-3922 [M]	Things I Still Remember Very Well	1969	$50
— Record is black label stock copy; "Mounaural" sticker appears on stereo cover			

FIRST GENERATION
Number	Title	Yr	NM
❏ 1	What's Wrong with the Way We're Doing It Now	1979	$15

PHONORAMA
Number	Title	Yr	NM
❏ 5565	What's Wrong with the Way We're Doing It Now	1983	$10

RCA VICTOR
Number	Title	Yr	NM
❏ LPM-3339 [M]	Where You're Concerned	1965	$25
❏ LSP-3339 [S]	Where You're Concerned	1965	$30

STARDAY
Number	Title	Yr	NM
❏ SLP-160 [M]	Star of the Grand Ole Opry	1962	$40
❏ SLP-334 [M]	The Best of Justin Tubb	1965	$30
❏ SLP-198 [M]	The Modern Country Sound of Justin Tubb	1962	$40

VOCALION
Number	Title	Yr	NM
❏ VL73802	That Country Style	196?	$15

TUBES, THE
A&M
Number	Title	Yr	NM
❏ SP-4632	Now	1977	$15
❏ SP-3243	Now	198?	$12
— Reissue of SP-4632			
❏ SP-4751	Remote Control	1979	$15
❏ SP-3242	Remote Control	198?	$10
— Reissue of SP-4751			
❏ SP-4534	The Tubes	1975	$15
❏ SP-3161	The Tubes	198?	$10
— Reissue of SP-4534			
❏ SP-4870	T.R.A.S.H. (Tubes Rarities And Smash Hits)	1981	$12
❏ SP-3244	T.R.A.S.H. (Tubes Rarities And Smash Hits)	198?	$10
— Reissue of SP-4870			
❏ SP-17012 [DJ]	Tubes Live/Edited for Trouble-Free Airplay (The First "Clean" Tubes Album)	1978	$25
— Generic cover with sticker; promo only			
❏ SP-6003	What Do You Want From Live!	1978	$18
❏ SP-4580 [B]	Young and Rich	1976	$15
❏ SP-3222	Young and Rich	198?	$10
— Reissue of SP-4580			

CAPITOL
Number	Title	Yr	NM
❏ ST-12381	Love Bomb	1985	$12
❏ SN-16446	Love Bomb	1987	$10
— Reissue of ST-12381			
❏ ST-12260	Outside/Inside	1983	$12
❏ SN-16360	Outside/Inside	1985	$10
— Reissue of ST-12260			
❏ SOO-12151	The Completion Backward Principle	1981	$12
❏ SN-16378	The Completion Backward Principle	1986	$10
— Reissue of SOO-12151			

TUCK & PATTI
WINDHAM HILL
Number	Title	Yr	NM
❏ WH-0116	Love Warriors	1989	$30
❏ WH-0111	Tears of Joy	1988	$25

TUCKER, FAYE
TIME
Number	Title	Yr	NM
❏ 52108 [M]	Country & Western Soul	1963	$25
❏ S-2018 [S]	Country & Western Soul	1963	$30

Number	Title	Yr	NM

TUCKER, MAUREEN
Also see THE VELVET UNDERGROUND..

50 SKIDILLION WATTS
❏ MOE7 [B]	Life in Exile After Abdication	1989	$30
❏ MOE1 [EP]	Moejadkatebarry	1987	$25

TRASH
❏ TLP-1001 [B]	Playin' Possum	1981	$35

TUCKER, MICKEY
MUSE
❏ MR-5174	Mister Mysterious	1978	$30
❏ MR-5223	The Crawl	1979	$30

XANADU
❏ 143	Sojourn	1977	$30
❏ 128	Triplicity	1976	$30

TUCKER, SOPHIE
COLUMBIA
❏ CL2604 [M]	Last of the Red Hot Mamas	1966	$35

DECCA
❏ DL5371 [10]	A Collection of Songs She Has Made Famous	1951	$250
❏ DL4942 [M]	Greatest Hits	1968	$75
❏ DL74942 [R]	Greatest Hits	1968	$30
❏ DL8355 [M]	The Great Sophie Tucker	195?	$75

MCA
❏ 263	Greatest Hits	1973	$25

MERCURY
❏ MG20267 [M]	Bigger and Better Than Ever	1957	$150
❏ MG20046 [M]	Cabaret Days	1955	$150
❏ MG20073 [M]	Her Latest and Greatest Spicy Songs	1956	$150
❏ MG20567 [M]	In Person -- Adults Only	1960	$150
❏ SR60227 [S]	In Person -- Adults Only	1960	$150
❏ MG20035 [M]	My Dream	1955	$150

WING
❏ MGW12176 [M]	Bigger and Better Than Ever	196?	$30
❏ MGW12213 [M]	Cabaret Days	196?	$30
❏ SRW16213 [R]	Cabaret Days	196?	$25
❏ MGW12167 [M]	Her Latest and Greatest Spicy Songs	196?	$30

TUCKER, TANYA
ARISTA
❏ AL9596	Changes	1982	$12
❏ AL8381	Changes	1984	$10
— Reissue of 9596			

CAPITOL
❏ ST-12474	Girls Like Me	1986	$12
❏ C1-91814	Greatest Hits	1989	$15
❏ CLT-46870	Love Me Like You Used To	1987	$12
❏ C1-48865	Strong Enough to Bend	1988	$12

CAPITOL NASHVILLE
❏ 1P8140	What Do I Do with Me	1991	$25
— Only available on vinyl through Columbia House			

COLUMBIA
❏ KC31742	Delta Dawn	1972	$18
❏ PC31742	Delta Dawn	198?	$10
❏ KC33355	Greatest Hits	1975	$15
— No bar code on cover			
❏ PC33355	Greatest Hits	197?	$10
— With bar code on cover			
❏ KC32272	What's Your Mama's Name	1973	$18
❏ KC32744	Would You Lay with Me (In a Field of Stone)	1974	$15
❏ PC32744	Would You Lay with Me (In a Field of Stone)	197?	$10
❏ PC34733	You Are So Beautiful	1977	$15
— No bar code on cover			
❏ PC34733	You Are So Beautiful	197?	$10
— With bar code on cover			

COLUMBIA SPECIAL PRODUCTS
❏ P15770	The Best of Tanya Tucker	1981	$15

MCA
❏ 5140	Dreamlovers	1980	$12
❏ 27030	Dreamlovers	198?	$10
— Reissue of 5140			
❏ 37225	Greatest Hits	1984	$10
— Reissue of 3032			
❏ 2213	Here's Some Love	1976	$15
❏ 656	Here's Some Love	1980	$10
— Reissue of 2213			
❏ 2167	Lovin' and Learnin'	1976	$15
❏ 655	Lovin' and Learnin'	1980	$10
— Reissue of 2167			
❏ 2253	Ridin' Rainbows	1977	$15
❏ 657	Ridin' Rainbows	1980	$10
— Reissue of 2253			
❏ 5228	Should I Do It	1981	$12
❏ 2141	Tanya Tucker	1975	$15
❏ 654	Tanya Tucker	1980	$10
— Reissue of 2141			
❏ 5299	Tanya Tucker Live	1982	$12
❏ 37242	Tanya Tucker Live	1984	$10
— Reissue of 5299			
❏ 3032	Tanya Tucker's Greatest Hits	1978	$15
❏ 5106	Tear Me Apart	1979	$12
❏ 37158	Tear Me Apart	1981	$10
— Reissue of 5106			
❏ 5357	The Best of Tanya Tucker	1983	$12
❏ 3066	TNT	1978	$15
— Original gatefold cover			
❏ 37075	TNT	1981	$10
— Reissue of 3066; gatefold removed			

TUCKER, TOMMY
CHECKER
❏ LP-2990 [M]	Hi-Heel Sneakers	1964	$300
— Black label			
❏ LP-2990 [M]	Hi-Heel Sneakers	1965	$120
— Blue label with checkers			

CIRCLE
❏ CLP-124	Tommy Tucker and His Californians 1933	1991	$30
❏ C-15	Tommy Tucker and His Orchestra 1942-1947	198?	$25

TUCKY BUZZARD
CAPITOL
❏ ST-787	Tucky Buzzard	1971	$16
❏ ST-864	Warm Slash	1972	$25

PASSPORT
❏ 97001	Alright in the Night	1973	$18
❏ 98002	Tucky Buzzard	1974	$18

TUDOR, DAVID
LOVELY
❏ VR1601 [B]	Pulsers / Untitled	1984	$100

ODYSSEY
❏ 32 16 0158 [S]	A Second Wind For Organ	1968	$40
❏ 32 16 0157 [M]	A Second Wind For Organ	1968	$25

TUFF DARTS
SIRE
❏ SRK6048	Tuff Darts!	1978	$15

TURBANS, THE
HERALD
❏ 5009	Presenting the Turbans	197?	$25
— No such album was released in the 1950s; this is a bootleg that has some collector value.			

LOST-NITE
❏ LLP-25 [10]	The Turbans	1981	$12
— Red vinyl			

RELIC
❏ 5009	The Turbans' Greatest Hits	198?	$15

TURNER, GRANT
CVS
❏ 8008	Grant Turner Remembers the Grand Ole Opry	197?	$18

TURNER, HANK
COLUMBIA
❏ CL1958 [M]	Golden Country and Western Hits	1963	$25
❏ CS8758 [S]	Golden Country and Western Hits	1963	$30

TURNER, IKE
Also see IKE AND TINA TURNER.
CROWN
❏ CLP-5367 [M]	Ike Turner Rocks the Blues	1963	$250
❏ CST-367 [R]	Ike Turner Rocks the Blues	1963	$150

FANTASY
❏ F-9597	The Edge	1980	$12

POMPEII
❏ SD6003	A Black Man's Soul	1969	$18

UNITED ARTISTS
❏ UA-LA087-F	Bad Dreams	1973	$18
❏ UAS-5576	Blues Roots	1972	$18

TURNER, IKE AND TINA
Also see IKE TURNER; TINA TURNER.
A&M
❏ SP-4178	River Deep -- Mountain High	1969	$30
— Official release of Philles 4011			
❏ SP-3179	River Deep -- Mountain High	1982	$12
— Budget-line reissue			

ABC
❏ 4014	16 Great Performances	1975	$15

ACCORD
❏ SN-7147	Hot and Sassy	1981	$12

BLUE THUMB
❏ BTS5	Outta Season	1968	$18
❏ BTS-8805	Outta Season	1971	$15
— Early reissue of Blue Thumb 5			
❏ BTS49	The Best of Ike & Tina Turner	1973	$15
❏ BTS11	The Hunter	1969	$18

CAPITOL
❏ ST-571	Her Man, His Woman	1971	$18

COLLECTABLES
❏ COL-5107	Golden Classics	198?	$12
❏ COL-5137	It's Gonna Work Out Fine	198?	$12

EMI AMERICA
❏ ST-17212	It's Gonna Work Out Fine	1986	$12
❏ SQ-17216	Workin' Together	1986	$12

HARMONY
❏ HS11360	Ooh Poo Pah Doo	1969	$18
❏ H30567	Something's Got a Hold on Me	1971	$18

KENT
❏ KST-538	Festival of Live Performances	1969	$30
❏ KST-550	Please Please Please	1971	$30
❏ K-5014 [M]	The Ike and Tina Turner Revue Live	1964	$30
❏ KST-514 [S]	The Ike and Tina Turner Revue Live	1964	$40
❏ K-5019 [M]	The Soul of Ike and Tina	1966	$30
❏ KST-519 [S]	The Soul of Ike and Tina	1966	$40

LIBERTY
❏ LT-917	Airwaves	1981	$10
❏ LST-7637	Come Together	1970	$18
❏ LO-51156	Get Back!	1985	$12
❏ LST-7650	Workin' Together	1970	$18

LOMA
❏ LS5904 [S]	Live! The Ike & Tina Turner Show, Vol. 2	1966	$30
— Reissue of Warner Bros. 1579?			
❏ L5904 [M]	Live! The Ike & Tina Turner Show Vol. 2	1966	$30

MINIT
❏ 24018	In Person	1969	$25

PHILLES
❏ PHLP4011 [M]	River Deep -- Mountain High	1967	$8000
— Value is for record alone; covers were not printed			

PICKWICK
❏ SPC-3284	Too Hot to Hold	197?	$12

POMPEII
❏ SD6004	Cussin', Cryin' and Carryin' On	1969	$30
❏ SD6006	Get It Together	1969	$30
❏ SD6000 [S]	So Fine	1968	$30
❏ 6000 [M]	So Fine	1968	$75
— Mono is white label promo only; fromt cover has "d/j copy monaural" sticker on it			

STRIPED HORSE
❏ SHL-2001	Golden Empire	1986	$12

SUE
❏ LP2005 [M]	Don't Play Me Cheap	1963	$400
❏ LP2004 [M]	Dynamite	1963	$400
❏ LP2003 [M]	Ike and Tina Turner's Kings of Rhythm Dance	1962	$400
— Despite the title, this is an all-instrumental album (Tina's vocals do not appear)			
❏ LP2007 [M]	It's Gonna Work Out Fine	1963	$400
❏ LP1038 [M]	The Greatest Hits of Ike and Tina Turner	1965	$300
❏ LP2001 [M]	The Soul of Ike and Tina Turner	1961	$400

SUNSET
❏ SUS-5286	Ike & Tima Turner's Greatest Hits	1969	$18
❏ SUS-5265	The Fantastic Ike & Tina Turner	1969	$18

UNART
❏ S21021	Greatest Hits	197?	$12

UNITED ARTISTS
❏ UA-LA917-H	Airwaves	1978	$15
❏ UA-LA707-G	Delilah's Power	1977	$15
❏ UA-LA592-G	Feel Good	1972	$15
❏ UAS-5598	Greatest Hits	1976	$15
❏ UAS-5667	Ike & Tina Turner's Greatest Hits	1972	$15
❏ UAS-5660	Let Me Touch Your Mind	1972	$15
❏ UAS-9953	Live at Carnegie Hall/What You Hear Is What You Get	1971	$18
❏ UAS-5530	'Nuff Said	1971	$15
❏ UA-LA180-F	Nutbush City Limits	1973	$15
❏ UA-LA312-G	Sweet Rhode Island Red	1974	$15
❏ UA-LA203-G	The Gospel According to Ike & Tina Turner	1974	$15
❏ UA-LA064-G	The World of Ike & Tina Live	1973	$18

WARNER BROS.
❏ WS1810	Ike & Tina Turner's Greatest Hits	1969	$30
❏ W1579 [M]	Live! The Ike & Tina Turner Show	1965	$30
❏ WS1579 [S]	Live! The Ike & Tina Turner Show	1965	$40

Number	Title	Yr	NM

TURNER, JIM
EUPHONIC

| ❏ 1222 | Old Fashioned Love: A Tribute to James P. Johnson | 198? | $25 |

TURNER, JOE, AND PETE JOHNSON
EMARCY

| ❏ MG-36014 [M] | Joe Turner and Pete Johnson | 1955 | $300 |

TURNER, JOE
ARHOOLIE

| ❏ 2004 [M] | Jumpin' the Blues | 1962 | $50 |

ATCO

| ❏ 33-376 [M] | Joe Turner -- His Greatest Recordings | 1971 | $35 |

ATLANTIC

❏ 8033 [M]	Big Joe Is Here	1959	$300
— Black label			
❏ 8033 [M]	Big Joe Is Here	1960	$300
— White "bullseye" label			
❏ 8033 [M]	Big Joe Is Here	1963	$50
— Black "fan" logo on label			
❏ 8033 [M]	Big Joe Is Here	1960	$300
— White "fan" logo on label			
❏ 1332 [M]	Big Joe Rides Again	1959	$300
— Black label			
❏ SD1332 [S]	Big Joe Rides Again	1959	$300
— Green label			
❏ 1332 [M]	Big Joe Rides Again	1963	$50
— Black "fan" logo on label			
❏ SD1332 [S]	Big Joe Rides Again	1963	$50
— Black "fan" logo on label			
❏ 1332 [M]	Big Joe Rides Again	1960	$300
— White "fan" logo on label			
❏ SD1332 [S]	Big Joe Rides Again	1960	$300
— White "fan" logo on label			
❏ SD8812	Boss of the Blues	1981	$25
— Reissue of 1234			
❏ 81752	Greatest Hits	1987	$25
❏ 8005 [M]	Joe Turner	1957	$300
— Black label			
❏ 8005 [M]	Joe Turner	1963	$50
— Black "fan" logo on label			
❏ 8005 [M]	Joe Turner	1961	$175
— White "fan" logo on label			
❏ 8023 [M]	Rockin' the Blues	1958	$300
— Black label			
❏ 8023 [M]	Rockin' the Blues	1963	$35
— Black "fan" logo on label			
❏ 8023 [M]	Rockin' the Blues	1960	$300
— White "fan" logo on label			
❏ 8081 [M]	The Best of Joe Turner	1963	$150
❏ 1234 [M]	The Boss of the Blues	1956	$300
— Black label			
❏ SD1234 [S]	The Boss of the Blues	1959	$300
— Green label			
❏ 1234 [M]	The Boss of the Blues	1960	$300
— White "bullseye" label			
❏ SD1234 [S]	The Boss of the Blues	1960	$400
— White "bullseye" label			
❏ 1234 [M]	The Boss of the Blues	1963	$50
— Black "fan" logo on label			
❏ SD1234 [S]	The Boss of the Blues	1963	$50
— Black "fan" logo on label			
❏ 1234 [M]	The Boss of the Blues	1961	$300
❏ SD1234 [S]	The Boss of the Blues	1961	$175
— White "fan" logo on label			

BLUES SPECTRUM

| ❏ BS-104 | Great Rhythm and Blues Oldies Vol. 4 | 197? | $35 |

BLUESTIME

| ❏ 9002 [M] | The Real Boss of the Blues | 196? | $40 |
| ❏ 29002 [S] | The Real Boss of the Blues | 196? | $75 |

BLUESWAY

❏ S-6060	Roll 'Em	1973	$35
❏ BL6006 [M]	Singing the Blues	1967	$50
❏ BLS-6006 [S]	Singing the Blues	1967	$75

DECCA

| ❏ DL8044 [M] | Joe Turner Sings Kansas City Jazz | 1953 | $300 |

FANTASY

| ❏ OJC-497 | Trumpet Kings Meet Joe Turner | 1991 | $30 |

INTERMEDIA

❏ QS-5036	Everyday I Have the Blues	198?	$25
❏ QS-5008	Rock This Joint	198?	$25
❏ QS-5043	Roll Me Baby	198?	$25
❏ QS-5030	The Blues Boss – Live	198?	$25
❏ QS-5026	The Very Best of Joe Turner – Live	198?	$25

KENT

| ❏ KST-542 | Joe Turner Turns On the Blues | 1973 | $35 |

MCA

| ❏ 1325 | Early Big Joe | 198? | $25 |

MUSE

| ❏ MR-5293 | Blues Train | 198? | $25 |
| — With Roomful of Blues and Dr. John | | | |

PABLO

❏ 2310818	Every Day I Have the Blues	198?	$30
❏ 2310937	Flip, Flop and Fly	1989	$30
❏ 2310863	Have No Fear, Joe Turner Is Here	1983	$30
❏ 2310776	In the Evening	197?	$30
❏ 2310760	Nobody in Mind	197?	$30
❏ 2310913	Patcha, Patcha, All Night Long	198?	$30
❏ 2310883	Singing the Same, Sad, Happy, Forever Blues	1983	$30
❏ 2405404	The Best of "Big" Joe Turner	198?	$30
❏ 2310848	The Best of Joe Turner	1980	$30
❏ 2310800	Things That I Used to Do	197?	$30
❏ 2310717	Trumpet Kings Meet Joe Turner	197?	$30

SAVOY

| ❏ MG-14012 [M] | Blues'll Make You Happy | 1958 | $300 |
| ❏ MG-14106 [M] | Careless Love | 1963 | $175 |

SAVOY JAZZ

❏ SJC-406	Blues'll Make You Happy	1985	$25
— Reissue of Savoy 14012			
❏ SJL-2223	Have No Fear	197?	$35

TURNER, JOE (2)
CHIAROSCURO

| ❏ 147 | King of Stride | 1976 | $35 |

CLASSIC JAZZ

| ❏ 138 | Effervescent | 1976 | $35 |

PABLO

| ❏ 2310763 | Another Epoch Stride Piano | 197? | $30 |

TURNER, NIK
CLEOPATRA

| ❏ CLP0661 [B] | Space Gypsy | 2013 | $30 |

TURNER, RAY
CAPITOL

| ❏ H306 [10] | Kitten on the Keys | 1952 | $100 |

TURNER, SAMMY
BIG TOP

| ❏ 12-1301 [M] | Lavender Blue Moods | 1959 | $300 |
| — May not exist in stereo | | | |

TURNER, SPYDER
MGM

| ❏ E-4450 [M] | Stand By Me | 1967 | $30 |
| ❏ SE-4450 [S] | Stand By Me | 1967 | $30 |

WHITFIELD

| ❏ BSK3124 | Music Web | 1978 | $12 |
| ❏ BSK3397 | Only Love | 1979 | $12 |

TURNER, TINA
Also see IKE AND TINA TURNER.
CAPITOL

❏ PJ-12530	Break Every Rule	1986	$10
❏ C1-91873	Foreign Affair	1989	$10
❏ ST-12330	Private Dancer	1984	$10
❏ 1P8192	Simply the Best	1991	$25
— Columbia House edition (only US vinyl version)			
❏ C1-90126	Tina Live in Europe	1988	$15

FANTASY

| ❏ MFP-4520 [EP] | Mini | 1984 | $10 |

SPRINGBOARD

| ❏ SPB-4033 | The Queen | 1972 | $12 |

UNITED ARTISTS

❏ UA-LA495-G	Acid Queen	1975	$15
❏ UA-LA919-G	Rough	1978	$15
❏ UA-LA200-F	Tina Turns the Country On	1973	$18

WAGNER

| ❏ 14108 | Good Hearted Woman | 1979 | $15 |

TURNER, TITUS
JAMIE

| ❏ JLP-3018 [M] | Sound Off | 1961 | $25 |
| ❏ JLPS-3018 [S] | Sound Off | 1961 | $30 |

TURNER, VELVERT, GROUP
FAMILY PRODUCTIONS

| ❏ FPS-2704 [B] | Velvert Turner Group | 1972 | $75 |

TURNER, ZEB
AUDIO LAB

| ❏ AL-1537 [M] | Country Music in the Turner Style | 1959 | $175 |

TURNQUIST REMEDY
PENTAGRAM

| ❏ PE-10004 [B] | Turnquist Remedy | 1970 | $35 |

TURRE, STEVE
STASH

| ❏ ST-275 | Fire and Ice | 1988 | $25 |
| ❏ ST-270 | Viewpoint | 1987 | $25 |

TURRENTINE, STANLEY
BAINBRIDGE

| ❏ BT-1038 | Stan the Man | 1981 | $30 |

BLUE NOTE

❏ BLP-4150 [M]	A Chip Off the Old Block	1963	$120
❏ BST-84150 [S]	A Chip Off the Old Block	1963	$250
— With New York, USA address on label			
❏ BST-84150 [S]	A Chip Off the Old Block	1967	$175
— With "A Division of Liberty Records" on label			
❏ LT-1095	Ain't No Way	1981	$35
❏ BST-84298	Always Something There	1968	$40
— A Division of Liberty Records" on label			
❏ BST-84336	Another Story	1969	$40
— A Division of Liberty Records" on label			
❏ BLP-4057 [M]	Blue Hour	1961	$300
— With W. 63rd St. addresss on label			
❏ BLP-4057 [M]	Blue Hour	1963	$100
— With New York, USA address on label			
❏ BST-84057 [S]	Blue Hour	1961	$250
— With W. 63rd St. addresss on label			
❏ BST-84057 [S]	Blue Hour	1963	$40
— With New York, USA address on label			
❏ BST-84057 [S]	Blue Hour	1967	$75
— With "A Division of Liberty Records" on label			
❏ BST-84057 [S]	Blue Hour	1971	$50
— With "A Division of United Artists" on label			
❏ BST-84057	Blue Hour	1986	$30
— The Finest in Jazz Since 1939' label reissue			
❏ B1-84065	Comin' Your Way	1988	$35
— The Finest in Jazz Since 1939' label; first issue of LP			
❏ BLP-4065 [M]	Comin' Your Way	1961	$0
— Canceled			
❏ BST-84065 [S]	Comin' Your Way	1961	$0
— Canceled			
❏ BST-84315	Common Touch!	1969	$75
— A Division of Liberty Records" on label			
❏ BLP-4081 [M]	Dearly Beloved	1961	$250
— With W. 63rd St. address on label			
❏ BLP-4081 [M]	Dearly Beloved	1963	$100
— With New York, USA address on label			
❏ BST-84081 [S]	Dearly Beloved	1961	$250
— With W. 63rd St. address on label			
❏ BST-84081 [S]	Dearly Beloved	1963	$150
— With New York, USA address on label			
❏ BST-84081 [S]	Dearly Beloved	1967	$75
— With "A Division of Liberty Records" on label			
❏ BLP-4268 [M]	Easy Walker	1967	$200
— A Division of Liberty Records" on label			
❏ BST-84268 [S]	Easy Walker	1967	$150
— A Division of Liberty Records" on label			
❏ BLP-4162 [M]	Hustlin'	1964	$120
❏ BST-84162 [M]	Hustlin'	1964	$120
— With New York, USA address on label			
❏ BST-84162 [S]	Hustlin'	1967	$75
— With "A Division of Liberty Records" on label			
❏ BST-84162 [S]	Hustlin'	1970	$35
— With "A Division of United Artists" on label			
❏ LT-1037	In Memory Of...	1980	$75
❏ BLP-4201 [M]	Joyride	1965	$250
❏ BST-84201 [S]	Joyride	1964	$120
— With New York, USA address on label			
❏ BST-84201 [S]	Joyride	1967	$75
— With "A Division of Liberty Records" on label			
❏ BST-84201	Joyride	1984	$30
— The Finest in Jazz Since 1939" label reissue			
❏ BLP-4122 [M]	Jubilee Shout!!!	1963	$0
— Canceled			
❏ BN-LA883-4047	Jubilee Shout!!	1977	$75
❏ BST-84122	Jubilee Shout!!	1986	$35
— The Finest in Jazz Since 1939' label; first issue of LP			
❏ B1-90261	La Place	1989	$35
— The Finest in Jazz Since 1939" on label			
❏ BLP-4039 [M]	Look Out!	1960	$400
— Deep groove" version; W. 63rd St. address on label			
❏ BLP-4039 [M]	Look Out!	1960	$175
— Regular version with W. 63rd St. address on label			
❏ BLP-4039 [M]	Look Out!	1963	$100
— With New York, USA address on label			
❏ BST-84039 [S]	Look Out!	1960	$120
— With W. 63rd St. addresss on label			
❏ BST-84039 [S]	Look Out!	1963	$40
— With New York, USA address on label			
❏ BST-84039 [S]	Look Out!	1967	$75
— With "A Division of Liberty Records" on label			
❏ LT-1075	Mr. Natural	1980	$35

Number	Title	Yr	NM
❏ BLP-4129 [M]	Never Let Me Go	1963	$120
❏ BST-84129 [S]	Never Let Me Go	1963	$120
— With New York, USA address on label			
❏ BST-84129 [S]	Never Let Me Go	1967	$75
— With "A Division of Liberty Records" on label			
❏ LT-993	New Time Shuffle	1979	$35
❏ BLP-4240 [M]	Rough 'n Tumble	1966	$250
❏ BST-84240 [S]	Rough 'n Tumble	1966	$150
— With New York, USA address on label			
❏ BST-84240 [S]	Rough 'n Tumble	1967	$75
— With "A Division of Liberty Records" on label			
❏ BLP-4234 [M]	Stanley Turrentine	1965	$0
— Canceled			
❏ BST-84234 [S]	Stanley Turrentine	1965	$0
— Canceled			
❏ BN-LA394-H2	Stanley Turrentine	1975	$50
❏ BT-85105	Straight Ahead	1984	$30
— The Finest in Jazz Since 1939" on label			
❏ BLP-4096 [M]	That's Where It's At	1962	$250
— With W. 63rd St. address on label			
❏ BLP-4096 [M]	That's Where It's At	1963	$120
— With New York, USA address on label			
❏ BST-84096 [S]	That's Where It's At	1962	$250
— With W. 63rd St. address on label			
❏ BST-84096 [S]	That's Where It's At	1963	$150
— With New York, USA address on label			
❏ BST-84096 [S]	That's Where It's At	1967	$75
— With "A Division of Liberty Records" on label			
❏ BST-84096	That's Where It's At	1986	$30
— The Finest in Jazz Since 1939" reissue			
❏ B1-93201	The Best of Stanley Turrentine	1989	$35
— The Finest in Jazz Since 1939" on label			
❏ BST-84286	The Look of Love	1968	$75
— With "A Division of Liberty Records" on label			
❏ BST-84286	The Look of Love	1971	$50
— With "A Division of United Artists" on label			
❏ BLP-4256 [M]	The Spoiler	1967	$175
— A Division of Liberty Records" on label			
❏ BST-84256 [S]	The Spoiler	1967	$40
— A Division of Liberty Records" on label			
❏ BLP-4069 [M]	Up at Minton's, Volume 1	1961	$250
— With W. 63rd St. addressb on label			
❏ BLP-4069 [M]	Up at Minton's, Volume 1	1963	$100
— With New York, USA address on label			
❏ BST-84069 [S]	Up at Minton's, Volume 1	1961	$250
— With W. 63rd St. addressb on label			
❏ BST-84069 [S]	Up at Minton's, Volume 1	1963	$40
— With New York, USA address on label			
❏ BST-84069 [S]	Up at Minton's, Volume 1	1967	$75
— With "A Division of Liberty Records" on label			
❏ BLP-4070 [M]	Up at Minton's, Volume 2	1961	$250
— With W. 63rd St. addressb on label			
❏ BLP-4070 [M]	Up at Minton's, Volume 2	1963	$100
— With New York, USA address on label			
❏ BST-84070 [S]	Up at Minton's, Volume 2	1961	$250
— With W. 63rd St. addressb on label			
❏ BST-84070 [S]	Up at Minton's, Volume 2	1963	$40
— With New York, USA address on label			
❏ BST-84070 [S]	Up at Minton's, Volume 2	1967	$75
— With "A Division of Liberty Records" on label			
❏ BT-85140	Wonderland	1987	$30
— The Finest in Jazz Since 1939" on label			
❏ BST-84424	Z.T.'s Blues	1985	$30
— The Finest in Jazz Since 1939" on label			

CTI

Number	Title	Yr	NM
❏ 6017	Cherry	1972	$50
❏ 8010	Cherry	1981	$30
— Reissue of 6017			
❏ 6030	Don't Mess with Mister T.	1973	$35
❏ 8011	Don't Mess with Mister T.	1981	$30
— Reissue of 6030			
❏ CTSQ-6030 [Q]	Don't Mess with Mister T.	1973	$175
❏ 6010	Salt Song	1971	$50
❏ 8008	Salt Song	1981	$30
— Reissue of 6010			
❏ 6005	Sugar	1971	$50
❏ 8006	Sugar	1981	$30
— Reissue of 6005			
❏ 6048	The Baddest Turrentine	1974	$35
❏ 6052	The Sugar Man	1975	$50

ELEKTRA

Number	Title	Yr	NM
❏ 6E-217	Betcha	1979	$25
❏ 60201	Home Again	1982	$30
❏ 6E-269	Inflation	1980	$25
❏ 5E-534	Tender Togetherness	1981	$30

FANTASY

Number	Title	Yr	NM
❏ F-9508	Everybody Come On Out	1976	$35
❏ F-9493	Have You Ever Seen the Rain	1975	$35
❏ F-9478	In the Pocket	1975	$35
❏ F-9534	Nightwings	1977	$35
❏ FPM-4002 [Q]	Pieces of Dreams	1974	$40
❏ F-9465	Pieces of Dreams	1974	$35
❏ F-9519	The Man with the Sad Face	1976	$35
❏ F-9604	Use the Stairs	1980	$30

Number	Title	Yr	NM
❏ F-9548	West Side Highway	1978	$35
❏ F-9563	What About You!	1978	$30

IMPULSE!

Number	Title	Yr	NM
❏ AS-9115 [B]	Let It Go	1967	$120

MAINSTREAM

| ❏ 56041 [M] | Tiger Tail | 1965 | $40 |
| ❏ S-6041 [S] | Tiger Tail | 1965 | $150 |

PHOENIX 10

| ❏ PHX-317 | Yester-Me, Yester-You | 198? | $30 |

SUNSET

| ❏ SUS-5255 | The Soul of Stanley Turrentine | 196? | $30 |

TIME

| ❏ 52086 [M] | Stan the Man | 1962 | $200 |
| ❏ S-2086 [S] | Stan the Man | 1962 | $250 |

TRIP

| ❏ TLX-5006 | Yester-Me, Yester-You | 197? | $35 |

UPFRONT

| ❏ UPF-147 | Stanley Turrentine | 197? | $30 |

TURRENTINE, TOMMY

BAINBRIDGE

| ❏ BT-1047 | Tommy Turrentine | 198? | $30 |

TIME

❏ T-70008 [M]	Tommy Turrentine	1960	$100
— Reproductions exist			
❏ ST-70008 [S]	Tommy Turrentine	1960	$150

TURTLE ISLAND STRING QUARTET

WINDHAM HILL

| ❏ WH-0114 | Metropolis | 1989 | $30 |
| ❏ WH-0110 | Turtle Island String Quartet | 1988 | $25 |

TURTLES, THE
Also see FLO AND EDDIE.

RHINO

Number	Title	Yr	NM
❏ RNPD901 [PD]	1968	1984	$15
❏ RNPD900	1968	1984	$10
❏ RNLP70155	Chalon Road	1986	$12
❏ RNLP160	Greatest Hits	1983	$12
❏ RNLP152	Happy Together	1983	$12
❏ RNLP151	It Ain't Me Babe	1983	$12
❏ RNLP70158	Shell Shock	1986	$12
❏ RNLP70177	The Best of the Turtles (Golden Archives Series)	1987	$12
❏ RNLP70156	The Turtles Present the Battle of the Bands	1986	$12
❏ RNDF280 [EP]	Turtle-Sized	1984	$15
— Green vinyl turtle-shaped EP			
❏ RNLP70157	Turtle Soup	1986	$12
❏ RNLP70159	Turtle Wax: The Best of the Turtles, Vol. 2	1988	$12
❏ RNLP154	Wooden Head	1983	$12
❏ RNLP153	You Baby	1983	$12

SIRE

| ❏ SASH-3703 | The Turtles' Greatest Hits/ Happy Together Again | 1974 | $25 |

WHITE WHALE

❏ WW114 [M]	Happy Together	1967	$50
❏ WWS7114 [S]	Happy Together	1967	$30
❏ WW111 [M]	It Ain't Me Babe	1965	$40
❏ WWS7111 [S]	It Ain't Me Babe	1965	$40
❏ WW115 [M]	The Turtles! Golden Hits	1967	$75
❏ WWS7115 [S]	The Turtles! Golden Hits	1967	$25
❏ WW7127	The Turtles! More Golden Hits	1970	$25

Number	Title	Yr	NM
❏ WWS7118 [B]	The Turtles Present the Battle of the Bands	1968	$30
❏ WW7124	Turtle Soup	1969	$30
❏ WW7133	Wooden Head	1970	$25
❏ WW112 [M]	You Baby	1966	$40
❏ WWS7112 [S]	You Baby	1966	$40

TUSA, FRANK

ENJA

| ❏ 2056 | Father Time | 197? | $35 |

TUSKEGEE INSTITUTE CHOIR

WESTMINSTER

| ❏ XWM-18080 [M] | Spirituals | 195? | $50 |

TUXEDOMOON

RALPH

❏ TX8354	A Thousand Lives by Picture	1983	$15
❏ TX8104	Desire	1981	$15
❏ TX8004-L	Half-Mute	1980	$15

TUXEDOMOON

| ❏ EP79 [EP] | Scream with a View | 1979 | $25 |
| ❏ EP45 [EP] | Tuxedomoon | 1978 | $25 |

TV ON THE RADIO

DGC

| ❏ 1188201 | Dear Science | 2008 | $25 |

TV SMITH'S EXPLORERS

EPIC

| ❏ ARE37432 [B] | The Last Words of the Great Explorer | 1981 | $30 |
| — promo | | | |

TWARDZIK, RICHARD

PACIFIC JAZZ

| ❏ PJ-37 [M] | The Last Set | 1962 | $75 |

TWENTIETH CENTURY ZOO, THE

VAULT

| ❏ LPS-122 | Thunder on a Clear Day | 1968 | $75 |

21ST CENTURY, THE

RCA VICTOR

| ❏ APL1-1189 | Ahead of Our Time | 1975 | $30 |

TWENTY MILES

FAT POSSUM

| ❏ 80302-1 [B] | Twenty Miles | 1997 | $18 |

$27 SNAP-ON FACE

HETERODYNE

| ❏ 01 [B] | $27 Snap-On Face | 1977 | $150 |
| — Blue vinyl; with lyric sheet | | | |

TWIGGY

MERCURY

| ❏ SRM-1-1138 | Please Get My Name Right | 1977 | $15 |
| ❏ SRM-1-1093 | Twiggy | 1976 | $15 |

TWILLEY, DWIGHT

ARISTA

❏ AB4251	Blueprint	1980	$0
— Unreleased			
❏ AB4214	Twilley	1979	$12
❏ AB4140	Twilley Don't Mind	1977	$12

CBS ASSOCIATED

| ❏ BFZ40266 | Wild Dogs | 1986 | $10 |

EMI AMERICA

| ❏ ST-17107 | Jungle | 1984 | $12 |
| ❏ ST-17064 | Scuba Divers | 1982 | $12 |

Number	Title	Yr	NM

MCA

❏ 688	Sincerely	1981	$10

—Reissue of Shelter LP

SHELTER

| ❏ SA-52001 | Sincerely | 1976 | $12 |

TWIN CITIES CATHOLIC CHORALE, THE

WANDERER FORUM

| ❏ WFR103 | Every Year at Christmas Comes the Holy Child | 197? | $15 |

TWINK
Of PINK FAIRIES fame.

SIRE

| ❏ SES-97022 [B] | Think Pink | 1970 | $300 |

TWINS, THE

RCA VICTOR

| ❏ LPM-1708 [M] | Teenagers Love the Twins | 1958 | $50 |

TWISTED SISTER
Bassist Mark "The Animal" Mendoza was also in THE DICTATORS.

ATLANTIC

❏ 81275	Come Out and Play	1985	$10
❏ 81772	Love Is for Suckers	1987	$10
❏ 80156	Stay Hungry	1984	$10
❏ 81256	Under the Blade	1985	$10
❏ 80074	You Can't Stop Rock 'n' Roll	1983	$10

SECRET

| ❏ SHH13712 [EP] | Ruff Cuts | 1981 | $18 |

—UK import

| ❏ SECX9 | Under the Blade | 1982 | $15 |

—UK import

| ❏ SECXP9 [PD] | Under the Blade | 1982 | $25 |

—UK import

TWISTERS, THE

TREASURE

| ❏ TLP-890 [M] | Doin' the Twist | 1962 | $30 |

TWISTIN' KINGS

MOTOWN

| ❏ M-601 [M] | Twistin' the World Around | 1961 | $300 |

TWITTY, CONWAY, AND LORETTA LYNN
Also see each artist's individual listings.

DECCA

| ❏ DL75326 | Lead Me On | 1972 | $25 |
| ❏ DL75251 | We Only Make Believe | 1971 | $25 |

HEARTLAND

| ❏ HL-1059/60 | The Best of Conway and Loretta | 1987 | $25 |

MCA

| ❏ 427 | Country Partners | 1974 | $18 |
| ❏ 2354 | Country Partners | 1978 | $12 |

—Reissue of MCA 427

| ❏ 3190 | Diamond Duet | 1979 | $15 |
| ❏ 723 | Diamond Duet | 198? | $12 |

—Reissue of MCA 3190

❏ 2278	Dynamic Duo	1977	$15
❏ 2143	Feelins'	1975	$18
❏ 2372	Honky Tonk Heroes	1978	$15
❏ 722	Honky Tonk Heroes	198?	$12

—Reissue of MCA 2372

| ❏ 9 | Lead Me On | 1973 | $15 |

—Reissue of Decca 75326

❏ 335	Louisiana Woman, Mississippi Man	1973	$18
❏ 42216	Making Believe	1988	$10
❏ 3164	The Very Best of Loretta and Conway	1979	$15
❏ 37237	The Very Best of Loretta and Conway	1983	$10

—Budget-line reissue

❏ 5178	Two's a Party	1981	$15
❏ 2209	United Talent	1976	$18
❏ 629	United Talent	198?	$12

—Reissue of MCA 2209

| ❏ 8 | We Only Make Believe | 1973 | $15 |

—Reissue of Decca 75251

MCA CORAL

| ❏ CDL-8006 | Never Ending Song of Love | 1973 | $15 |

TWITTY, CONWAY

ACCORD

| ❏ SN-7169 | Early Favorites | 1982 | $15 |

ALLEGIANCE

| ❏ AV-5012 | You Made Me What I Am | 1983 | $18 |

DECCA

❏ DL4913 [M]	Conway Twitty Country	1967	$30
❏ DL74913 [S]	Conway Twitty Country	1967	$30
❏ DL75352	Conway Twitty's Greatest Hits Vol. I	1972	$25

Number	Title	Yr	NM
❏ DL4724 [M]	Conway Twitty Sings	1965	$30
❏ DL74724 [S]	Conway Twitty Sings	1965	$30
❏ DL75105	Darling, You Know I Wouldn't Lie	1968	$25
❏ DL75248	Fifteen Years Ago	1970	$25
❏ DL75209	Hello Darlin'	1970	$25
❏ DL4990 [M]	Here's Conway Twitty	1968	$50
❏ DL74990 [S]	Here's Conway Twitty	1968	$30
❏ DL75276	How Much More Can She Stand	1971	$25
❏ ST-93776	How Much More Can She Stand	1971	$30

—Capitol Record Club edition

❏ DL75335	I Can't See Me Without You	1972	$25
❏ DL75361	I Can't Stop Loving You/ Last Date	1972	$25
❏ DL75131	I Love You More Today	1969	$25
❏ DL75292	I Wonder What She'll Think About Me Leaving	1971	$25
❏ DL4828 [M]	Look Into My Teardrops	1966	$30
❏ DL74828 [S]	Look Into My Teardrops	1966	$30
❏ DL75062 [B]	Next in Line	1968	$30
❏ DL75172	To See My Angel Cry	1970	$25

ELEKTRA

❏ 60115 [B]	#1 Classics, Volume 1	1982	$12
❏ 60209	#1 Classics, Volume 2	1982	$12
❏ 60182	Dream Maker	1982	$12
❏ 60005	Southern Comfort	1982	$12

HEARTLAND

| ❏ HL-1088/9 | The Very Best of Conway Twitty | 1989 | $25 |

MCA

❏ 5817	A Night with Conway Twitty	1986	$10
❏ 5969	Borderline	1987	$10
❏ 5424	Classic Conway	1983	$12
❏ 376	Clinging to a Saving Hand	1973	$75
❏ 3063	Conway	1978	$15
❏ 702	Conway	197?	$12

—Reissue of MCA 3063

| ❏ 52 | Conway Twitty's Greatest Hits | 1973 | $15 |

—Reissue of Decca 75352

| ❏ 2345 | Conway Twitty's Greatest Hits, Vol. 1 | 1978 | $15 |

—Reissue of Decca 75352

| ❏ 37229 | Conway Twitty's Greatest Hits, Vol. 1 | 1983 | $10 |

—Budget-line reissue

❏ 2235	Conway Twitty's Greatest Hits, Vol. 2	1976	$18
❏ 3086	Cross Winds	1979	$15
❏ 37163	Cross Winds	198?	$10

—Budget-line reissue

| ❏ 2328 | Georgia Keeps Pullin' on My Ring | 1978 | $15 |
| ❏ 37081 | Georgia Keeps Pullin' on My Ring | 198? | $10 |

—Budget-line reissue

| ❏ 3210 | Heart and Soul | 1980 | $15 |
| ❏ 37227 | Heart and Soul | 1983 | $10 |

—Budget-line reissue

| ❏ 19 | Hello Darlin' | 1973 | $15 |

—Reissue of Decca 75209

| ❏ 625 | High Priest of Country | 197? | $12 |

—Reissue of MCA 2144

❏ 2144	High Priest of Country Music	1975	$18
❏ 406	Honky Tonk Angel	1974	$18
❏ 42297	House on Old Lonesome Road	1989	$15
❏ 53	I Can't Stop Loving You/ Last Date	1973	$15

—Reissue of Decca 75361

❏ 441	I'm Not Through Loving You Yet	1974	$18
❏ 2293	I've Already Loved You in My Mind	1977	$15
❏ 469	Linda on My Mind	1975	$18
❏ 5204	Mr. T.	1981	$15
❏ 2206	Now and Then	1976	$18
❏ 5318	Number Ones	1982	$15
❏ 2262	Play Guitar Play	1977	$15
❏ 5138	Rest Your Love on Me	1980	$15
❏ 37228	Rest Your Love on Me	1983	$10

—Budget-line reissue

❏ 303	She Needs Someone to Hold Her (When She Cries)	1973	$18
❏ 5700	Songwriter	1986	$10
❏ 42115	Still in Your Dreams	1988	$10
❏ 3043	The Very Best of Conway Twitty	1978	$15
❏ 18	To See My Angel Cry	1973	$15

—Reissue of Decca 75172

| ❏ 2176 | Twitty (This Time I've Hurt Her More Than She Loves Me) | 1975 | $18 |
| ❏ 359 | You've Never Been This Far Before/Baby's Gone | 1973 | $18 |

MCA CORAL

| ❏ CB-20000 | I'm So Used to Loving You | 1973 | $15 |

METRO

| ❏ M-512 [M] | It's Only Make Believe | 1966 | $18 |
| ❏ MS-512 [S] | It's Only Make Believe | 1966 | $25 |

Number	Title	Yr	NM

MGM

❏ SES-4844	20 Great Hits by Conway Twitty	1973	$25
❏ GAS-110	Conway Twitty (Golden Archive Series)	1970	$25
❏ SE-4799	Conway Twitty Hits	1971	$18
❏ E-3849 [M]	Conway Twitty's Greatest Hits	1960	$80

—With poster

| ❏ E-3849 [M] | Conway Twitty's Greatest Hits | 1960 | $40 |

—Without poster

| ❏ SE-3849 [P] | Conway Twitty's Greatest Hits | 1960 | $100 |

—With poster

| ❏ SE-3849 [P] | Conway Twitty's Greatest Hits | 1960 | $50 |

—Without poster

| ❏ E-3744 [M] | Conway Twitty Sings | 1959 | $150 |

—Yellow label

| ❏ E-3744 [M] | Conway Twitty Sings | 1960 | $40 |

—Black label

| ❏ E-3744 [M] | Conway Twitty Sings | 196? | $300 |

—Reissue with orange cover and a clean-cut photo of Conway

| ❏ SE-3744 [S] | Conway Twitty Sings | 1959 | $175 |

—Yellow label

| ❏ SE-3744 [S] | Conway Twitty Sings | 1960 | $50 |

—Black label

| ❏ SE-3744 [S] | Conway Twitty Sings | 196? | $300 |

—Reissue with orange cover and a clean-cut photo of Conway

❏ SE-4837	Conway Twitty Sings the Blues	1972	$18
❏ E-4217 [M]	Hit the Road	1964	$30
❏ SE-4217 [S]	Hit the Road	1964	$30
❏ E-3818 [M]	Lonely Blue Boy	1960	$80
❏ SE-3818 [S]	Lonely Blue Boy	1960	$150
❏ E-4019 [M]	Portrait of a Fool and Others	1962	$40
❏ SE-4019 [S]	Portrait of a Fool and Others	1962	$50
❏ E-4089 [M]	R & B '63	1963	$40
❏ SE-4089 [S]	R & B '63	1963	$50
❏ E-3786 [M]	Saturday Night with Conway Twitty	1960	$80
❏ SE-3786 [S]	Saturday Night with Conway Twitty	1960	$150
❏ E-3943 [M]	The Conway Twitty Touch	1961	$50
❏ SE-3943 [S]	The Conway Twitty Touch	1961	$100
❏ E-3907 [M]	The Rock and Roll Story	1961	$50
❏ SE-3907 [S]	The Rock and Roll Story	1961	$100
❏ SE-4650	You Can't Take the Country Out of Conway	1969	$18

PICKWICK

| ❏ SPC-3360 | Shake It Up | 1973 | $15 |

TEE VEE

| ❏ TV-1009 | 20 Certified #1 Hits | 1978 | $18 |

—Alternate number is MCA Special Markets MSM-35003

WARNER BROS.

| ❏ 60115 | #1 Classics, Volume 1 | 1983 | $10 |

—Reissue of Elektra LP

| ❏ 60209 | #1 Classics, Volume 2 | 1983 | $10 |

—Reissue of Elektra LP

❏ 25777	#1's – The Warner Bros. Years	1988	$10
❏ 25078	By Heart	1984	$12
❏ 25294	Chasin' Rainbows	1985	$12
❏ 25170	Conway's Latest Greatest Hits	1984	$12
❏ 25207	Don't Call Him a Cowboy	1985	$12
❏ 60182	Dream Maker	1983	$10

—Reissue of Elektra LP

❏ 25406	Fallin' for You for Years	1986	$12
❏ 23869	Lost in the Feeling	1983	$12
❏ 23971	Merry Twismas	1983	$25

2 LIVE CREW, THE

EFFECT

| ❏ E3003 | Live in Concert | 1990 | $12 |

LIL' JOE

❏ 286	Essential DJ 12" and Mega Mixes	2002	$12
❏ XR-238	Greatest Hits Vol. 2	1999	$18
❏ XR-239	Greatest Hits Vol. 2/Edit	1999	$18
❏ 264	Private Personal Parts	2000	$15
❏ XR-215	Shake a Lil' Somethin'	1996	$18
❏ XR-227	The 2 Live Crew Goes to the Movies -- A Decade of Hits	1997	$15
❏ XR-231	The Real One	1998	$15

LUKE

| ❏ 208 | Back At You for '94 | 1994 | $25 |

—As "The New 2 Live Crew"; edited version

| ❏ 207 | Back at Your Ass for the Nine-4 | 1994 | $25 |

—As "The New 2 Live Crew"

| ❏ 91424 | Banned in the U.S.A. | 1990 | $18 |

—As "Luke Featuring The 2 Live Crew"

❏ 122	Greatest Hits	1992	$25
❏ 123	Greatest Hits/Edit	1992	$25
❏ DMD1760	Sports Weekend (As Nasty As They Wanna Be Part II)	1991	$18

—Promo-only vinyl issue in generic black cardboard sleeve

Number	Title	Yr	NM

LUKE SKYYWALKER

❏ XR-108	As Clean As They Wanna Be	1989	$18

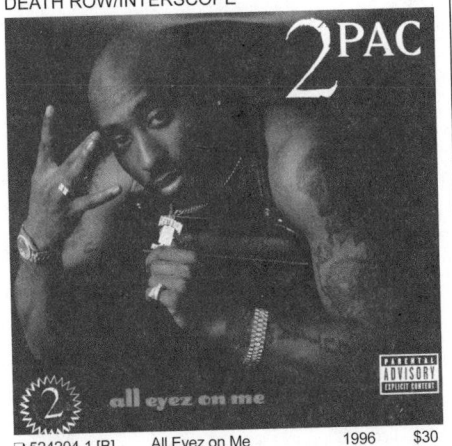

❏ XR-107 [B]	As Nasty As They Wanna Be	1989	$18
❏ XR-101	Move Somethin'	1988	$15
❏ XR-100	The 2 Live Crew "Is What We Are	1987	$18

2PAC
Includes records as "Makaveli."

AMARU/JIVE

❏ 41628	R U Still Down? (Remember Me)	1997	$30

DEATH ROW

❏ 63008	All Eyez on Me	2001	$25
— *Reissue*
| ❏ 63012 | The Don Killuminati -- The 7 Day Theory | 2001 | $18 |

— *As "Makaveli"; reissue*

DEATH ROW/INTERSCOPE

❏ 524204-1 [B]	All Eyez on Me	1996	$30
❏ INT4-90301	Greatest Hits	1998	$30
❏ 490413-1	Still I Rise	1999	$18
— *As "2Pac + Outlawz*
| ❏ INT2-90039 | The Don Killuminati -- The 7 Day Theory | 1996 | $18 |

— *As "Makaveli*
| ❏ 490840-1 | Until the End of Time | 2001 | $30 |

INTERSCOPE

❏ 91767 [B]	2Pacalypse Now	1991	$25
❏ 92399	Me Against the World	1995	$25

RESTLESS

❏ 72737	Strictly 4 My N.I.G.G.A.Z.	1998	$18
— *Vinyl reissue of 1993 album (we can't prove or disprove the existence of the original Interscope edition on vinyl)*

TYLE, TEDDY

GOLDEN CREST

❏ GC-3060 [M]	Moon Shot	1959	$40

TYLER, ALVIN "RED

ACE

❏ LP-1006 [M]	Rockin' and Rollin'	1960	$175
❏ LP-1021 [M]	Twistin' with Mr. Sax	1962	$120

ROUNDER

❏ 2061	Graciously	1987	$25
❏ 2047	Heritage	1986	$30

TYLER, BONNIE

CHRYSALIS

❏ CHR-1140	The World Starts Tonight	1976	$18
❏ PV41140	The World Starts Tonight	1983	$12
— *Reissue of 1140*

COLUMBIA

❏ BFC38710	Faster Than the Speed of Night	1983	$18
— *Silver print on front cover*
| ❏ FC38710 | Faster Than the Speed of Night | 1983 | $10 |
— *Blue-green print on front cover*
| ❏ FC44163 | Notes from America | 1988 | $15 |
| ❏ OC40312 | Secret Dreams and Forbidden Fire | 1986 | $10 |

RCA VICTOR

❏ AFL1-3072	Diamond Cut	1979	$12
❏ AFL1-2821	It's a Heartache	1978	$12
❏ AYL1-4110	It's a Heartache	1984	$10
— *Best Buy Series" reissue*

TYLER, CHARLES

ADELPHI

❏ 5011	Sixty Minute Man	1980	$30

ESP-DISK'

❏ S-1059 [S]	Eastern Man Alone	1968	$150
❏ 1029 [M]	The Charles Tyler Ensemble	1966	$150
❏ S-1029 [S]	The Charles Tyler Ensemble	1966	$150

NESSA

❏ N-16	Saga of the Outlaws	197?	$35

SILKHEART

❏ SH-118	Autumn in Paris	199?	$30

STORYVILLE

❏ 4098	Definite, Vol. 1	198?	$25

TYLER, T. TEXAS

CAPITOL

❏ T1662 [M]	Salvation	1962	$30
❏ ST1662 [S]	Salvation	1962	$30
❏ T2344 [M]	The Hits of T. Texas Tyler	1965	$25
❏ ST2344 [S]	The Hits of T. Texas Tyler	1965	$30

KING

❏ 734 [M]	Songs Along the Way	1962	$100
❏ 689 [M]	The Great Texan	1960	$120
❏ 664 [M]	T. Texas Tyler	1959	$120
❏ 721 [M]	T. Texas Tyler	1961	$100

SOUND

❏ 607 [M]	Deck of Cards	1958	$100

STARDAY

❏ SLP-379 [M]	The Man with a Million Friends	1966	$30

WRANGLER

❏ W-1002 [M]	T. Texas Tyler	1962	$40
❏ W-31002 [S]	T. Texas Tyler	1962	$50

TYLER, WILLIE, AND LESTER

TAMLA

❏ TM-265 [M]	Hello Dummy	1965	$250

TYMES, THE

ABKCO

❏ 4228	The Best of Tymes	1973	$15

COLUMBIA

❏ CS9778	People	1969	$18

PARKWAY

❏ P7049 [M]	18 Greatest Hits	1964	$40
❏ P7039 [M]	Somewhere	1964	$50
— *Includes bonus single 7039 (deduct 20 percent if missing)*
| ❏ P7032 [M] | So Much in Love | 1963 | $40 |
— *With group standing in front-cover photo*
| ❏ P7032 [M] | So Much in Love | 1963 | $250 |
— *With head-and-shoulders group photo on front cover*
| ❏ P7038 [M] | The Sound of the Wonderful Tymes | 1963 | $40 |
| ❏ SP7038 [S] | The Sound of the Wonderful Tymes | 1963 | $50 |

RCA VICTOR

❏ APL1-2406	Diggin' Their Roots	1977	$15
❏ APL1-0727	Trustmaker	1974	$15
❏ APL1-1835	Turning Point	1976	$15

TYNER, MCCOY

ABC IMPULSE!

❏ IA-9338	Early Trios	1978	$35
❏ AS-18	Inception	1968	$30
❏ AS-48	McCoy Tyner Live at Newport	1968	$30
❏ AS-79	McCoy Tyner Plays Duke Ellington	1968	$30
❏ AS-39	Nights of Ballads and Blues	1968	$30
❏ AS-33	Reaching Fourth	1968	$30
❏ IA-9235	Reevaluation: The Impulse! Years	197?	$35
❏ AS-63	Today and Tomorrow	1968	$30

Number	Title	Yr	NM

BLUE NOTE

❏ BN-LA223-G	Asante	1974	$35
❏ BST-84338	Expansions	1969	$50
— *With "A Division of Liberty Records" on label*
| ❏ BST-84338 | Expansions | 1970 | $30 |
— *With United Artists distribution*
| ❏ BST-84338 | Expansions | 1984 | $25 |
— *The Finest in Jazz Since 1939" label*
❏ BN-LA022-F	Extensions	1973	$35
❏ B1-91651	Revelations	1989	$30
❏ BST-84275	Tender Moments	1968	$50
— *With "A Division of Liberty Records" on label*
| ❏ BST-84275 | Tender Moments | 1970 | $30 |
— *With United Artists distribution*
| ❏ BST-84275 | Tender Moments | 1985 | $25 |
— *The Finest in Jazz Since 1939" label*
| ❏ BLP-4264 [M] | The Real McCoy | 1967 | $150 |
| ❏ BST-84264 [S] | The Real McCoy | 1967 | $50 |
— *With "A Division of Liberty Records" on label*
| ❏ BST-84264 | The Real McCoy | 1970 | $30 |
— *With United Artists distribution*
| ❏ BLP-84264 | The Real McCoy | 1987 | $75 |
— *The Finest in Jazz Since 1939" label*
| ❏ BST-84307 | Time for Tyner | 1969 | $50 |
— *With "A Division of Liberty Records" on label*
| ❏ BLP-84307 | Time for Tyner | 1987 | $75 |
— *The Finest in Jazz Since 1939" label*

COLUMBIA

❏ FC37375	La Leyenda de la Hora (The Legend of the Hour)	1981	$25
❏ FC38053	Looking Out	1982	$25

ELEKTRA/MUSICIAN

❏ 60350	Dimensions	1984	$25

FANTASY

❏ OJC-650	Echoes of a Friend	1991	$25
— *Reissue of Milestone 9055*
| ❏ OJC-311 | Sahara | 1988 | $25 |
— *Reissue of Milestone 9039*
| ❏ OJC-313 | Song for My Lady | 1988 | $25 |
— *Reissue of Milestone 9044*
| ❏ OJC-618 | Song of the New World | 1991 | $25 |
— *Reissue of Milestone 9049*

GRP/IMPULSE!

❏ 220	Inception	1997	$250
— *Reissue on audiophile vinyl*
| ❏ 216 | McCoy Tyner Plays Duke Ellington | 1997 | $250 |
— *Reissue on audiophile vinyl*
| ❏ 221 | Nights of Ballads and Blues | 1997 | $250 |
— *Reissue on audiophile vinyl*

IMPULSE!

❏ A-18 [M]	Inception	1962	$250
❏ AS-18 [S]	Inception	1962	$250
❏ A-48 [M]	McCoy Tyner Live at Newport	1963	$250
❏ AS-48 [S]	McCoy Tyner Live at Newport	1963	$250
❏ A-79 [M]	McCoy Tyner Plays Duke Ellington	1965	$250
❏ AS-79 [S]	McCoy Tyner Plays Duke Ellington	1965	$250
❏ A-39 [M]	Nights of Ballads and Blues	1963	$250
❏ AS-39 [S]	Nights of Ballads and Blues	1963	$250
❏ A-33 [M]	Reaching Fourth	1963	$250
❏ AS-33 [S]	Reaching Fourth	1963	$250
❏ A-63 [M]	Today and Tomorrow	1964	$250
❏ AS-63 [S]	Today and Tomorrow	1964	$250

MCA

❏ 4157	Early Trios	1981	$30
— *Reissue of Impulse! 9338*
| ❏ 4126 | Great Moments with McCoy Tyner | 1981 | $30 |
| ❏ 4156 | Reevaluation: The Impulse Years | 1981 | $30 |
— *Reissue of Impulse! 9235*

MILESTONE

❏ 55007	4 x 4	1980	$30
❏ 9102	13th House	1981	$25
❏ 55002	Atlantis	1975	$30
❏ 9055	Echoes of a Friend	1974	$25
❏ 55001	Enlightenment	1973	$30
❏ 9067	Fly with the Wind	1976	$25
❏ 9072	Focal Point	1977	$25
❏ 9094	Horizon	1980	$25
❏ 9079	Inner Voices	1978	$25
❏ 9091	Passion Dance	1979	$25
❏ M-47062	Reflections	1981	$25
❏ 9039	Sahara	197?	$25
❏ 9056	Sama Layuca	1974	$25
❏ 9044	Song for My Lady	197?	$25
❏ FPM-4006 [Q]	Song of the New World	197?	$75
❏ 9049	Song of the New World	197?	$25
❏ 55003	Supertrios	1977	$30
❏ 9085	The Greeting	1978	$25
❏ 9087	Together	1979	$25
❏ 9063	Trident	1975	$25
❏ 9167	Uptown/Downtown	1988	$25

Number	Title	Yr	NM

PALO ALTO

Number	Title	Yr	NM
❑ PA-8083	Just Feelin'	1985	$25

PAUSA

| ❑ 9007 | Time for Tyner | 198? | $20 |
—*Reissue of Blue Note 84307*

QUICKSILVER

| ❑ QS-4010 | Just Feelin' | 1990 | $25 |
—*Reissue of Palo Alto LP*

TIMELESS

| ❑ SJP-260 | Bon Voyage | 1990 | $25 |

TYRANNOSAURUS REX
See T. REX.

U

U-GOD
PRIORITY

| ❑ 50086 | Golden Arms Redemption | 1999 | $18 |

U.K.
Prog rock supergroup.
POLYDOR

❑ PD-1-6194 [B]	Danger Money	1979	$12
❑ PD-1-6234	Night After Night	1979	$12
❑ PD-1-6146	U.K.	1978	$12

U.K. SUBS
CLEOPATRA

| ❑ 9860 [B] | Endangered Species | | $25 |
| ❑ 2970 [B] | Punk As Fuck | | $25 |

LET THEM EAT VINYL

| ❑ LETV397LP [B] | Violent State + The Revolution's Here | 2016 | $20 |
—*red vinyl*

U-KREW, THE
ENIGMA

| ❑ 7735241 | The U-Krew | 1990 | $18 |

U-MEN
BLACK LABEL

| ❑ BLR 002 [B] | Step on a Bug The Red Toad Speaks | 1988 | $30 |

HOMESTEAD

| ❑ HMS 024 [EP] | Stop Spinning | 1985 | $30 |

U2
INTERSCOPE

| ❑ 1263001 | No Line on the Horizon | 2009 | $30 |

ISLAND

| ❑ 510347-1 [B] | Achtung Baby | 1991 | $150 |
—*U.S. LP covers are uncensored (Adam Clayton appears naked without any "X" or shamrock over his appendage)*
| ❑ R144636 | Boy | 1983 | $15 |
—*RCA Music Service edition*
| ❑ ILPS9646 | Boy | 1980 | $18 |
| ❑ 842296-1 | Boy | 1990 | $10 |
—*Reissue; sticker with new number placed over bar code of leftover 90040 pressings*
| ❑ 90040 | Boy | 1983 | $15 |
—*Reissue; first pressings have dark purple labels*
| ❑ 90040 [B] | Boy | 1983 | $12 |
—*Second pressings have light blue labels*
| ❑ 90040 [B] | Boy | 1983 | $10 |
—*Third pressings have black labels*
| ❑ 1084301 | Boy | 2008 | $25 |
| ❑ R114632 | October | 1983 | $15 |
—*RCA Music Service edition*
| ❑ ILPS9680 | October | 1981 | $15 |
—*Back cover has engineering credits, etc., in upper left*
| ❑ 842297-1 | October | 1990 | $10 |
—*Reissue; sticker with new number placed over bar code of leftover 90092 pressings*
| ❑ 90092 | October | 1983 | $12 |
—*Reissue; first pressings have dark purple labels*
| ❑ ILPS9680 | October | 1981 | $18 |
—*Back cover is blank (no engineering credits, etc.) in upper left*

U2 OCTOBER

Number	Title	Yr	NM
❑ 90092 [B]	October	1983	$12
—*Second pressings have light blue labels*
| ❑ 90092 [B] | October | 1983 | $10 |
—*Third pressings have black labels*
❑ 1082901	October	2008	$25
❑ 524334-1 [B]	Pop	1997	$50
❑ PR127545-1 [B]	PopMart Sampler	1997	$100
—*Promo-only 8-song collection of old and new U2 material*
| ❑ R200596 | Rattle and Hum | 1988 | $18 |
—*BMG Direct Marketing edition*
| ❑ 91003 | Rattle and Hum | 1988 | $18 |
| ❑ 842299-1 | Rattle and Hum | 1990 | $15 |
—*Reissue; sticker with new number placed over bar code of leftover 91003 pressings*
| ❑ R153501 | The Joshua Tree | 1987 | $15 |
—*RCA Music Service edition; no lyric sheet*
| ❑ 90581 | The Joshua Tree | 1987 | $12 |
—*With lyric sheet*
| ❑ 842298-1 | The Joshua Tree | 1990 | $10 |
—*Reissue; sticker with new number placed over bar code of leftover 90581 pressings*
| ❑ PR2049 [DJ] | The Joshua Tree Interview... Their Words and Music | 1987 | $40 |
| ❑ R154515 | The Unforgettable Fire | 1985 | $15 |
—*RCA Music Service edition*
| ❑ 822898-1 | The Unforgettable Fire | 1990 | $10 |
—*Reissue; new sticker placed on leftover Island/Atco pressings*
| ❑ 90231 | The Unforgettable Fire | 1984 | $12 |
| ❑ R153598 [EP] | Under a Blood Red Sky | 1983 | $12 |
—*BMG Direct Marketing edition*
| ❑ 90127-1-B [EP] | Under a Blood Red Sky | 1983 | $30 |
—*White labels with "Mini LP" logo; with version of "The Electric Co." in which Bono sings snippets of "A-Me-Ri-Ca" from West Side Story and "Send In The Clowns" during the instrumental break.*
| ❑ 818008-1 [EP] | Under a Blood Red Sky | 1990 | $10 |
—*Reissue; sticker with new number placed over bar code of leftover 90127 pressings*
| ❑ 90127-1-B [EP] | Under a Blood Red Sky | 1983 | $12 |
—*White labels with "Mini LP" logo; edited version of "The Electric Co.*
| ❑ 1095001 [EP] | Under a Blood Red Sky | 2008 | $25 |
| ❑ R124619 | War | 1983 | $15 |
—*BMG Direct Marketing edition*
| ❑ 90067 [B] | War | 1983 | $15 |
—*Original pressings have dark purple labels*
| ❑ 811148-1 | War | 1990 | $10 |
—*Reissue; sticker with new number placed over bar code of leftover 90067 pressings*
| ❑ 90067 [B] | War | 1983 | $12 |
—*Second pressings have light blue labels*
| ❑ 90067 [B] | War | 1983 | $10 |
—*Third pressings have black labels*
| ❑ 1083201 | War | 2008 | $25 |
| ❑ R140642 [EP] | Wide Awake in America | 1985 | $15 |
—*RCA Music Service edition*
| ❑ 90279-1-A [EP] | Wide Awake in America | 1985 | $12 |
| ❑ 842479-1 [EP] | Wide Awake in America | 1990 | $10 |
—*Reissue; sticker with new number placed over bar code of leftover 90279 pressings*
| ❑ 518047-1 [B] | Zooropa | 1993 | $35 |
—*All "U.S." copies actually are British imports*

MOBILE FIDELITY

| ❑ 1-207 | The Unforgettable Fire | 1994 | $75 |
—*Audiophile vinyl*

WARNER BROS.

| ❑ WBMS-117 [DJ] | Two Sides Live | 1981 | $250 |
—*Promo only, part of "The Warner Bros. Music Show"; legitimate copies are on black vinyl*

UB40
A&M

| ❑ R144329 | CCCP/Live in Moscow | 1987 | $15 |
—*BMG Direct Marketing edition*

Number	Title	Yr	NM
❑ SP-5168	CCCP/Live in Moscow	1987	$12
❑ SP-5033	Geffery Morgan	1984	$12
❑ R100677	Labour of Love	1986	$15
—*BMG Direct Marketing edition*
| ❑ SP-6-4980 | Labour of Love | 1983 | $12 |
| ❑ SP-4980 | Labour of Love | 198? | $10 |
—*Reissue with altered prefix*
| ❑ SP-6-5090 [EP] | Little Baggariddim | 1985 | $12 |
—*Original copies are in a clear plastic sleeve*
| ❑ SP-5090 [EP] | Little Baggariddim | 1985 | $10 |
—*Second printings are in standard album cover*
| ❑ R134092 | Rat in the Kitchen | 1986 | $15 |
—*RCA Music Service edition*
| ❑ SP-5137 | Rat in the Kitchen | 1986 | $12 |
| ❑ R100479 | UB40 | 1988 | $15 |
—*BMG Direct Marketing edition*
| ❑ SP-5213 | UB40 | 1988 | $12 |
| ❑ SP-4955 | UB40 1980-83 | 1983 | $15 |

VIRGIN

| ❑ 91324 | Labour of Love II | 1989 | $25 |

UBC, THE
EMI

| ❑ E1-93919 | 2 All Serious Thinkers | 1990 | $18 |

UBIQUITY
ELEKTRA

| ❑ 6E-120 | Starbooty | 1978 | $15 |

UFO
LONE STAR, MICHAEL SCHENKER GROUP, WAYSTED, GARY MOORE related.
CHRYSALIS

❑ CHR1074	Force It	1975	$15
❑ PV41074	Force It	1983	$10
❑ CHR1127	Lights Out	1977	$15
❑ FV41127	Lights Out	1983	$10
❑ PV41127	Lights Out	1986	$10
—*Reissue of FV 41127*
| ❑ FV41402 | Making Contact | 1983 | $12 |
| ❑ PV41402 | Making Contact | 1986 | $10 |
—*Reissue of FV 41402*
❑ CHR1360	Mechanix	1982	$15
❑ PV41360	Mechanix	1983	$10
❑ BFV41518	Misdemeanor	1986	$12
❑ CHR1103	No Heavy Petting	1976	$15
❑ PV41103	No Heavy Petting	1983	$10
❑ CHR1239	No Place to Run	1980	$15
❑ PV41239	No Place to Run	1983	$10
❑ CHR1182	Obsession	1978	$15
❑ PV41182	Obsession	1983	$10
❑ CHR1059	Phenomenon	1974	$18
—*Green label*
| ❑ PV41059 | Phenomenon | 1983 | $10 |
| ❑ CHR1059 | Phenomenon | 1977 | $15 |
—*Fading blue label*
❑ CHR1209	Strangers in the Night	1979	$18
❑ V2X41209	Strangers in the Night	1983	$14
❑ FV41644	The Best of the Rest	1988	$15
❑ CHR1307	The Wild, the Willing and the Innocent	1981	$15
❑ PV41307	The Wild, the Willing and the Innocent	1983	$10

METAL BLADE/ENIGMA

| ❑ 7734041 [EP] | Ain't Misbehavin' | 1989 | $12 |

RARE EARTH

| ❑ RS624 | UFO 1 | 1971 | $30 |

UGGAMS, LESLIE
ATLANTIC

❑ SD8241	Just to Satisfy You	1969	$18
❑ 8128 [M]	Time to Love	1967	$18
❑ SD8128 [S]	Time to Love	1967	$25
❑ SD8196 [S]	What's an Uggams?	1968	$18
❑ 8196 [M]	What's an Uggams?	1968	$40
—*Mono is white label promo only; cover has "d/j copy monaural" sticker on front*

COLUMBIA

❑ CS9936	Leslie	1970	$15
❑ CL1706 [M]	Leslie Uggams on TV	1962	$18
❑ CS8506 [S]	Leslie Uggams on TV	1962	$25
❑ CS8665 [S]	More Leslie Uggams on TV	1963	$25
❑ CL1865 [M]	More Leslie Uggams on TV	1963	$18
❑ CL2071 [M]	So in Love	1963	$18
❑ CS8871 [S]	So in Love	1963	$25

MOTOWN

| ❑ M6-846 | Leslie Uggams | 1975 | $15 |

SONDAY

| ❑ 8000 | Try to See It My Way | 1972 | $15 |

ULANO, SAM
Drummer.
LANE

| ❑ LP-140 [M] | Sam Ulano | 195? | $50 |
| ❑ LP-151 [M] | Sam Ulano Is Mr. Rhythm | 195? | $50 |

Number	Title	Yr	NM
ULLMAN, TRACEY			
MCA			
❏ 5471	You Broke My Heart in 17 Places	1984	$12
ULMER, JAMES "BLOOD			
ARTISTS HOUSE			
❏ 13	Are You Glad to Be in America?	1980	$50
❏ AH9407 [B]	Tales of Captain Black	1979	$25
BLUE NOTE			
❏ BT-85136	America -- Do You Remember the Love?	1987	$30
CARAVAN OF DREAMS			
❏ CDP85004	Live at the Caravan of Dreams	1986	$35
COLUMBIA			
❏ ARC38285	Black Rock	1982	$50
❏ ARC37493 [B]	Free Lancing	1981	$25
❏ BFC38900	Odyssey	1983	$30
IN+OUT			
❏ 7007	Revealing	1990	$30
ULTIMATE			
CASABLANCA			
❏ NBLP-7128	Ultimate	1979	$18
❏ NBLP-7208	Ultimate	1980	$15
— These are different albums			
ULTIMATE SPINACH			
MGM			
❏ E-4570 [M]	Behold & See	1968	$150
— Mono is promo only (yellow label)			
❏ SE-4570 [S]	Behold & See	1968	$30
❏ E-4518 [M]	Ultimate Spinach	1968	$75
❏ SE-4518 [S]	Ultimate Spinach	1968	$30
❏ SE-4600	Ultimate Spinach	1969	$30
ULTRA VIOLET			
CAPITOL			
❏ ST-11244	Ultra Violet	1973	$30
ULTRAMAGNETIC MC'S, THE			
MERCURY			
❏ 510893-1	Funk Your Head Up	1991	$25
NEXT PLATEAU			
❏ 5482	B-Sides Companion	1997	$18
❏ 1013	Critical Beatdown	1988	$30
❏ 5496	Critical Beatdown	199?	$15
— Reissue			
TUFF CITY			
❏ 4023	Mo Love's Basement Tapes	1996	$18
— Compilation of older material			
❏ 4021	New York What Is Funky	1996	$18
— Compilation of older material			
❏ 624	Smack My Bitch Up	1998	$25
— Compilation of older material			
❏ 618	The Basement Tapes 1984-1990	1994	$18
— Compilation of older material			
WILD PITCH			
❏ WP2010	The Four Horsemen	199?	$18
— Reissue			
❏ E1-89917	The Four Horsemen	1993	$25
ULTRAVOX			
ANTILLES			
❏ AN7069	Systems of Romance	1978	$18
❏ AN7079	Three Into One	1980	$18
CHRYSALIS			
❏ FV41459	Lament	1984	$12
❏ B6V41394	Quartet	1983	$12
❏ CHR1338	Rage in Eden	1981	$12
❏ FV41490	The Collection	1984	$12
❏ CHR1296 [B]	Vienna	1980	$18
❏ FV41296	Vienna	198?	$10
— Reissue			
ISLAND			
❏ ILPS9449 [B]	Ultravox!	1977	$18
UMEKI, MIYOSHI			
MERCURY			
❏ MG-20568 [M]	Miyoshi	1958	$25
❏ SR-60228 [S]	Miyoshi	1959	$30
UNBEATABLES, THE			
DAWN			
❏ 5050 [M]	Live at Palisades Park	1964	$175
UNCLE DOG			
MCA			
❏ 302 [B]	Old Hat	1973	$25

Number	Title	Yr	NM
UNCLE FESTIVE			
NOVA			
❏ 8703-1	Money's No Object	198?	$25
OPTIMISM			
❏ OP-3107	Say Uncle	1988	$25
UNCLE JOSH AND COUSIN JAKE			
COTTON TOWN			
❏ 101 [M]	Just Joshing	1958	$150
UNCLE KRACKER			
ATLANTIC			
❏ 83279-1 [B]	Double Wide	2000	$25
❏ 83542-1	No Stranger to Shame	2002	$18
UNCLE LAR' AND LIL' TOMMY			
WLS			
❏ WLS-890	Animal Stories	1981	$25
❏ WLS-947	Animal Stories Volume Three	1983	$25
❏ WLS-1000	Animal Stories Volume Two	1982	$25
UNCLE LOUIE			
MARLIN			
❏ 2228	Unclue Louie's Here	1979	$25
UNCLE TUPELO			
Also see WILCO.			
ROCKVILLE			

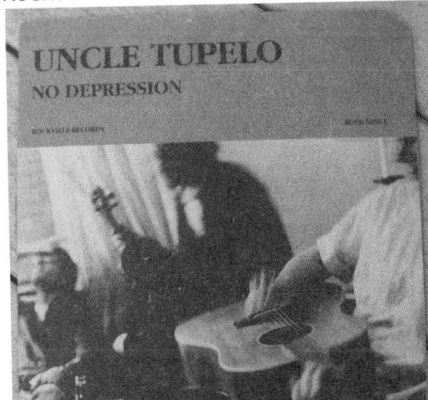

Number	Title	Yr	NM
❏ 6050-1 [B]	No Depression	1990	$75
❏ 6110-1	Still Feel Gone/March 16-20, 1992	1992	$175
SUNDAZED			
❏ LP-5153	89/93: An Anthology	2002	$30
UNDEAD			
POST MORTEM			
❏ LP 002	Act Your Rage	1989	$25
— Pink (white with red accents) vinyl			
❏ LP 002	Act Your Rage	1989	$25
— Teal (white with blue accents) vinyl			
❏ LP 002	Act Your Rage	1989	$30
— Blue vinyl			
❏ LP 002	Act Your Rage	1989	$30
— Yellow vinyl			
❏ LP 002	Act Your Rage	1989	$30
— Red vinyl			
❏ LP 002	Act Your Rage	1989	$50
— Clear vinyl			
❏ LP 002	Act Your Rage	1989	$150
— Green vinyl			
❏ LP 002	Act Your Rage	1989	$150
— Orange vinyl			
❏ LP 002	Act Your Rage	1989	$18
— Black vinyl			
❏ SHAG1001	Dawn of the Undead	1991	$30
❏ LP 001 [EP]	Never Say Die!	1989	$30
SKYCLAD/SKREAMIN' SKULL			
❏ LIVE119 [B]	Live Slayer	1992	$18
UNDERWORLD			
❏ UWR 008	'Til Death!	1998	$12
— Pressed on four different colors of vinyl (blue, green, yellow, red), each of equal value			
UNDERGRADS, THE			
SOMERSET			
❏ P-21600 [M]	Bluegrass Hoot on Campus	1963	$12
❏ SF-21600 [S]	Bluegrass Hoot on Campus	1963	$15

Number	Title	Yr	NM
UNDERGROUND, THE			
WING			
❏ MGW-12337 [M]	Psychedelic Visions	1967	$100
❏ SRW-16337 [S]	Psychedelic Visions	1967	$150
UNDERGROUND KINGZ			
JIVE			
❏ 41502	Too Hard to Swallow	1992	$18
— Issued in generic black cover			
UNDERGROUND SUNSHINE			
INTREPID			
❏ IT-74003	Let There Be Light	1969	$30
UNDERTONES, THE			
CAPITOL			
❏ ST-12358	All Wrapped Up	1983	$18
HARVEST			
❏ ST-12159 [B]	Positive Touch	1981	$18
SIRE			
❏ SRK6088	Hypnotised	1980	$15
❏ SRK6071	The Undertones	1979	$15
UNDERWOOD, VERONICA			
PHILLY WORLD			
❏ 90297	Veronica Underwood	1985	$12
UNDERWORLD			
SIRE			
❏ 25945	Change the Weather!	1989	$12
❏ 25627	Underneath the Radar	1988	$15
UNDISPUTED TRUTH, THE			
GORDY			
❏ G6-970	Cosmic Truth	1975	$25
❏ G6-968	Down to Earth	1974	$25
❏ G5-959	Face to Face with the Truth	1972	$25
❏ G6-972	Higher Than High	1975	$25
❏ G5-963	Law of the Land	1973	$25
❏ G955L	The Undisputed Truth	1971	$30
WHITFIELD			
❏ BS2967	Method to the Madness	1977	$25
❏ BSK3202	Smokin'	1979	$18
UNFOLDING			
AUDIO FIDELITY			
❏ AFLP-2184 [M]	How to Blow Your Mind and Have a Freak-Out Party	1967	$80
❏ AFSD-6184 [S]	How to Blow Your Mind and Have a Freak-Out Party	1967	$150
UNFORGIVEN, THE			
ELEKTRA			
❏ 60461	The Unforgiven	1986	$12
UNHOLY SWILL			
NOISEVILLE			
❏ 30	Oniontown Is the Place to Be	199?	$15
UNICORN			
CAPITOL			
❏ ST-11334 [B]	Blue Pine Trees	1974	$18
— Produced by David Gilmour (Pink Floyd)			
❏ ST-11692	One More Tomorrow	1977	$12
❏ ST-11453 [B]	Unicorn 2	1976	$18
UNIFICS, THE			
KAPP			
❏ KS-3582 [B]	Sittin' In at the Court of Love	1968	$30
UNIPOP			
KAT FAMILY			
❏ FZ38288	Unilove	1982	$12
UNIQUES, THE (1)			
PAULA			
❏ LPS-2208	Golden Hits	1970	$30
❏ LP-2194 [M]	Happening Now	1967	$30
❏ LPS-2194 [S]	Happening Now	1967	$30
❏ LP-2199 [M]	Playtime	1968	$30
❏ LPS-2199 [S]	Playtime	1968	$30
❏ LPS-2204	The Uniques	1969	$30
❏ LP-2190 [M]	Uniquely Yours	1966	$30
❏ LPS-2190 [S]	Uniquely Yours	1966	$30
UNIT 5			
CLONE			
❏ CL-014 [B]	Scared of the Dark	1981	$30
UNIT FOUR PLUS TWO			
LONDON			
❏ LL3427 [M]	Unit Four Plus Two #1	1965	$100
❏ PS427 [P]	Unit Four Plus Two #1	1965	$75

Number	Title	Yr	NM

UNITED STATES DOUBLE QUARTET
B.T. PUPPY
| ❏ BTS-1005 | Life Is Groovy | 1969 | $50 |

UNITED STATES OF AMERICA, THE
COLUMBIA
| ❏ CL2814 [M] | The United States of America | 1968 | $150 |

— Mono is promo only
| ❏ CS9614 [S] | The United States of America | 1968 | $100 |

— With outer bag
| ❏ CS9614 [S] | The United States of America | 1968 | $40 |

— Without outer bag

UNIVERSAL ROBOT BAND
RED GREG
| ❏ 1003 | Freak in the Light of the Moon | 1978 | $25 |

UNREST
MATADOR
| ❏ OLE 024 | Fuck Pussy Galore (And All Her Friends) | 1993 | $12 |

TEEN BEAT
❏ 77 [B]	Imperial FFRR	1992	$18
❏ 35	Kustom Karnal Blackxploitation	1990	$18
❏ 21	Malcolm X Park	1988	$18
❏ 14	Tink of S.E.	1987	$18

UNSANE
AMPHETAMINE REPTILE
| ❏ Amrep 039 | Scattered, Smothered and Covered | 1995 | $18 |

MATADOR
❏ OLE 074	Peel Sessions	1994	$18
❏ OLE 047	Singles '89-'92	1993	$18
❏ OLE 070	Total Destruction	1994	$18
❏ OLE 009	Unsane	1991	$18
❏ OLE 009	Unsane for Tennis	1991	$150

— Original title of this LP with a different cover; quickly pulled from release and replaced with a "less offensive" cover

RELAPSE
| ❏ RR6976 | Occupational Hazard | 1998 | $18 |
— Picture disc

UNSPOKEN WORD, THE
ASCOT
| ❏ AS16028 | Tuesday, April 19th | 1968 | $25 |

UNTAMED YOUTH, THE
ESTRUS
| ❏ ES1223 | Live in Las Vegas | 1995 | $15 |
| ❏ ES1231 | Planet Mace | 1997 | $15 |

NORTON
❏ ED215	More Gone Gassers	1990	$10
❏ ED207	Some Kinda Fun!!	1989	$12
❏ ED223	The Untamed Youth Are the Sophisticated International Playboys	1992	$50
❏ ED263	Youth Runs Wild!	199?	$12

UNTOUCHABLES, THE
ENIGMA
| ❏ E1102 | Live and Let Dance | 1984 | $15 |

MCA/STIFF
| ❏ 36106 [EP] | Dance Party | 1986 | $25 |
| ❏ 5634 | Wild Child | 1985 | $20 |

RESTLESS
| ❏ 72342 | Agent Double O Soul | 1988 | $12 |

UNUSUAL WE
PULSAR
| ❏ 10608 [B] | Unusual We | 1969 | $35 |

UPCHURCH, PHIL
BLUE THUMB
| ❏ BTS-6005 | Darkness, Darkness | 1971 | $50 |
| ❏ BTS-59 | Lovin' Feelin' | 1973 | $30 |

BOYD
| ❏ B-398 [M] | You Can't Sit Down | 1961 | $175 |
| ❏ BS-398 [S] | You Can't Sit Down | 1961 | $200 |

CADET
| ❏ LPS-840 | The Way I Feel | 1970 | $35 |
| ❏ LPS-826 | Upchurch | 1969 | $35 |

JAM
| ❏ 07 | Free and Easy | 198? | $30 |

KUDU
| ❏ 22 | Phil Upchurch and Tennyson Stevens | 1975 | $30 |

MARLIN
| ❏ 2209 | Phil Upchurch | 1978 | $30 |

MILESTONE
| ❏ MSP-9010 | Feeling Blue | 1968 | $35 |

UNITED ARTISTS
❏ UAL-3175 [M]	Big Hit Dances	1962	$75
❏ UAS-6175 [S]	Big Hit Dances	1962	$75
❏ UAL-3162 [M]	You Can't Sit Down, Part 2	1961	$75
❏ UAS-6162 [S]	You Can't Sit Down, Part 2	1961	$40

UPSET, THE
GUINNESS
| ❏ GNS36058 [B] | Midsummer Night | 1977 | $150 |
| ❏ GNS36057 [B] | Sunshine | 1977 | $25 |

UPTOWN LOWDOWN JAZZ BAND
GHB
| ❏ GHB-159 | Hauling Ash | 1981 | $25 |
| ❏ GHB-149 | Uptown Lowdown Jazz Band | 1979 | $25 |

STOMP OFF
| ❏ SOS-1030 | Uptown Lowdown Jazz Band in Colonial York, Pa. | 1982 | $25 |

ULJB
❏ UL-0(# unknown)	Jingle Jazz	1989	$25
❏ UL-0(# unknown)	Seattle Style	1985	$25
❏ UL-101	Uptown Lowdown Jazz Band	197?	$25

UPTOWN STRING QUARTET, THE
PHILIPS
| ❏ 838358-1 | Max Roach Presents the Uptown String Quartet | 1989 | $30 |

URBAN DANCE SQUAD
ARISTA
| ❏ ADP2099 [DJ] | Hollywood Live July 24, 1990/Pinkpop Live June 4, 1990 | 1990 | $18 |
| ❏ AL8640 | Mental Floss for the Globe | 1990 | $18 |

URBAN EARTH FEATURING HARVIE SWARTZ
BLUEMOON
| ❏ R1-79150 | Full Moon Dancer | 1989 | $15 |

URBANIAK, MICHAL
ARISTA
| ❏ AL4086 | Body English | 1976 | $30 |

CATALYST
| ❏ 7909 | Beginning | 197? | $35 |

COLUMBIA
❏ KC33184	Atma	1975	$30
❏ KC32852	Fusion	1974	$30
❏ PC33542	Fusion III	1975	$30

EASTWEST
| ❏ 90992 | Urban Express | 1989 | $30 |

INNER CITY
| ❏ IC-1036 | Urbaniak | 1977 | $30 |

JAM
| ❏ 5004 | Jam at Sandy's | 198? | $30 |

OPTIMISM
| ❏ OP-5012 | Milky Way | 198? | $25 |

PAUSA
| ❏ 7114 | Daybreak | 198? | $25 |
| ❏ 7047 | Heritage | 197? | $25 |

STEEPLECHASE
| ❏ SCS-1159 | My One and Only Love | 1981 | $30 |
| ❏ SCS-1195 | Take Good Care of My Heart | 198? | $30 |

URE, MIDGE
CHRYSALIS
| ❏ FV41649 | Answers to Nothing | 1988 | $12 |
| ❏ BFV41508 | The Gift | 1985 | $12 |

URGE OVERKILL
GEFFEN
| ❏ GEF-24818 | Exit the Dragon | 1995 | $18 |
| ❏ GEF-24529 | Saturation | 1993 | $15 |
— All copies on orange vinyl

TOUCH & GO
❏ 52	Americruiser	1990	$15
❏ 37	Jesus Urge Superstar	1989	$15
❏ 86 [10]	Stull	1992	$35
— Whitish vinyl original
| ❏ 86 [10] | Stull | 1992 | $12 |
— Black vinyl

| ❏ 70 [B] | The Supersonic Storybook | 1991 | $15 |

URGENT
MANHATTAN
| ❏ ST-53004 | Cast the First Stone | 1984 | $12 |
| ❏ MLT-46680 | Thinking Out Loud | 1987 | $15 |

URIAH HEEP
CHRYSALIS
| ❏ CHR1204 [B] | Fallen Angel | 1978 | $12 |

COLUMBIA
| ❏ BFC40132 | Equator | 1985 | $10 |

MERCURY
❏ SRM-1-4057	Abominog	1982	$10
❏ SRM-1-630 [B]	Demons and Wizards	1972	$18
❏ 812313-1	Head First	1983	$10
❏ SRM-1-614	Look at Yourself	1971	$12
❏ SR-61319	Salisbury	1970	$15
❏ SRM-1-1070	The Best of Uriah Heep	1976	$10
❏ 822476-1	The Best of Uriah Heep	1986	$10
— Reissue of Mercury 1070
❏ SRM-1-652 [B]	The Magician's Birthday	1972	$18
❏ SR-61294	Uriah Heep	1970	$18
❏ SRM-2-7503 [B]	Uriah Heep Live	1973	$25

WARNER BROS.
❏ BS3013 [B]	Firefly	1977	$12
❏ BS2949	High and Mighty	1976	$12
❏ BSK3145	Innocent Victim	1978	$12
❏ BS2869	Return to Fantasy	1975	$12
❏ BS2724	Sweet Freedom	1973	$12
❏ W2800	Wonderworld	1974	$12

URSO, PHIL
REGENT
| ❏ MG-6003 [M] | Sentimental Journey | 1956 | $50 |

SAVOY
| ❏ MG-15041 [10] | Bob Brookmeyer with Phil Urso | 1954 | $175 |
| ❏ MG-12056 [M] | The Philosophy of Urso | 1956 | $50 |

US3
BLUE NOTE
| ❏ B1-30027 | Broadway & 52nd | 1997 | $18 |
| ❏ B1-80883 | Hand on the Torch | 1993 | $18 |

USA-EUROPEAN CONNECTION
MARLIN
| ❏ 2212 | Come Into My Heart | 1978 | $15 |
| ❏ 2231 | USA-European Connection | 1979 | $15 |

USA FOR AFRICA
COLUMBIA
| ❏ USA40043 | We Are the World | 1985 | $15 |
— Actually a various-artists LP, but listed here because it was credited to "USA For Africa"

USHER
ARISTA
| ❏ 14715 | 8701 | 2001 | $18 |

LAFACE
| ❏ 26082 | All About U | 2000 | $0 |
— Canceled
| ❏ LFPL6043 [DJ] | My Way | 1997 | $18 |
— Promo-only "clean" version
| ❏ 26008 | Usher | 1994 | $15 |

USSELTON, BILLY
KAPP
| ❏ KL-1051 [M] | Bill Usselton -- His First Album | 1957 | $50 |

Number	Title	Yr	NM
UTFO			
JIVE			
❑ 1326	Bag It and Bone It	1991	$25
SELECT			
❑ 21629	Doin' It!	1989	$15
❑ 21619	Lethal	1987	$15
❑ 21616	Skeezer Pleezer	1986	$15
❑ 21614	UTFO	1985	$30

UTOPIA
Also see TODD RUNDGREN.

Number	Title	Yr	NM
BEARSVILLE			
❑ BRK6991	Adventures in Utopia	1979	$15
❑ BRK3487	Deface the Music	1980	$15
❑ BRK6970 [B]	Oops! Wrong Planet	1977	$15
❑ BR6965	RA	1977	$15
❑ BRK3666	Swing to the Right	1982	$15
❑ BR6954	Todd Rundgren's Utopia	1974	$15
❑ BR6961	Todd Rundgren's Utopia/ Another Live	1975	$15
NETWORK			
❑ 60183	Utopia	1982	$18

— *The second record has the same five songs on both sides*

Number	Title	Yr	NM
PASSPORT			
❑ PB6029	Oblivion	1984	$12
❑ PB6044	POV	1985	$12
❑ PB6053	Trivia	1986	$12
RHINO			
❑ RNLP70872	Adventures in Utopia	1987	$10
❑ R1-70892	Anthology (1974-1985)	1989	$12
❑ RNLP70873	Deface the Music	1987	$10
❑ RNLP70870	Oops! Wrong Planet	1987	$10
❑ RNLP70869	RA	1987	$10
❑ RNLP70875	Swing to the Right	1987	$10
❑ RNLP70865	Todd Rundgren's Utopia	1987	$10
❑ RNLP70867	Todd Rundgren's Utopia/ Another Live	1987	$10

Number	Title	Yr	NM
UZI			
HOMESTEAD			
❑ HMS055 [B]	Sleep Asylum	1986	$18
MATADOR			
❑ OLE073-1 [B]	Sleep Asylum	1993	$15

V

Number	Title	Yr	NM
VACHE, ALLAN, AND CHUCK HUGHES			
JAZZOLOGY			
❑ J-131	Clarinet Climax	198?	$25

Number	Title	Yr	NM
VACHE, ALLAN			
AUDIOPHILE			
❑ AP-192	High Speed Swing	1986	$25
❑ AP-176	Vache's Jazz Moods	1983	$25

Number	Title	Yr	NM
VACHE, WARREN			
AUDIOPHILE			
❑ AP-196	First Time Out	1986	$25
CONCORD JAZZ			
❑ CJ-323	Easy Going	1987	$25
❑ CJ-153	Iridescence	1981	$25
❑ CJ-87	Jillian	1979	$25
❑ CJ-203	Midtown Jazz	1982	$25
❑ CJ-98	Polished Brass	1980	$25
❑ CJ-392	Warm Evenings	1989	$30
DREAMSTREET			
❑ 101	Blues Walk	197?	$35
MONMOUTH-EVERGREEN			
❑ 7081	First Time Out	197?	$35

Number	Title	Yr	NM
VAGABONDS, THE			
UNIQUE			
❑ LP-112 [M]	The Vagabonds	1957	$30

Number	Title	Yr	NM
VAGRANTS, THE			
ARISTA			
❑ AL-8459	The Great Lost Vagrants Album	1987	$25

Number	Title	Yr	NM
VALE, JERRY			
COLUMBIA			
❑ KG31543	All-Time Greatest Hits	1972	$15
❑ KC31716	Alone Again (Naturally)	1972	$12
❑ CL1955 [M]	Arrivederci, Roma	1963	$15
❑ CS8755 [S]	Arrivederci, Roma	1963	$18
❑ CL2181 [M]	Be My Love	1964	$15
❑ CS8981 [S]	Be My Love	1964	$18
❑ CL2225 [M]	Christmas Greetings from Jerry Vale	1964	$15
❑ CS9025 [S]	Christmas Greetings from Jerry Vale	1964	$18
❑ CL2530 [M]	Everybody Loves Somebody	1966	$15
❑ KC32829	Free As the Wind	1974	$12

Number	Title	Yr	NM
❑ KG31938	Great Italian Hits	1973	$15
❑ CL2489 [M]	Great Moments on Broadway	1966	$15
❑ CS9289 [S]	Great Moments on Broadway	1966	$18
❑ CL2313 [M]	Have You Looked Into Your Heart	1965	$15
❑ CS9113 [S]	Have You Looked Into Your Heart	1965	$18
❑ C30799	I Don't Know How to Love Her	1971	$12
❑ CL1797 [M]	I Have But One Heart	1962	$15
❑ CS8597 [S]	I Have But One Heart	1962	$18
❑ CS9634	I Hear a Rhapsody	1968	$18
❑ CL1114 [M]	I Remember Buddy	1958	$18
❑ CS8069 [S]	I Remember Buddy	1959	$25

— *Originals have red and black "6 eye" labels*

Number	Title	Yr	NM
❑ CL1164 [M]	I Remember Russ	1958	$18
❑ CS8016 [S]	I Remember Russ	1958	$25

— *Originals have red and black "6 eye" labels*

Number	Title	Yr	NM
❑ CL2444 [M]	It's Magic	1966	$15
❑ CS9244 [S]	It's Magic	1966	$18
❑ CL1529 [M]	Jerry Vale's Greatest Hits	1961	$18
❑ CS8778 [R]	Jerry Vale's Greatest Hits	1963	$15
❑ CS9982	Jerry Vale Sings 16 Greatest Hits of the 60's	1970	$15
❑ C31147	Jerry Vale Sings the Great Hits of Nat King Cole	1972	$15
❑ KG32083	Jerry Vale Sings the Great Love Songs	1973	$15
❑ KC32454	Jerry Vale's World	1973	$12
❑ CS1021	Let It Be	1970	$15
❑ C32238	Love Is a Many-Splendored Thing	1973	$12
❑ CL2371 [M]	Moonlight Becomes You	1965	$15
❑ CS9171 [S]	Moonlight Becomes You	1965	$18
❑ CL2659 [M]	More Jerry Vale's Greatest Hits	1967	$18
❑ CS9459 [S]	More Jerry Vale's Greatest Hits	1967	$15
❑ CL2273 [M]	Standing Ovation!	1965	$15
❑ CS9073 [S]	Standing Ovation!	1965	$18
❑ CL2583 [M]	The Impossible Dream	1967	$15
❑ CS9383 [S]	The Impossible Dream	1967	$18
❑ C30389	The Italian Album	1970	$12
❑ CG33615	The Italian Album/Arrivederci, Roma	1974	$15
❑ CL2043 [M]	The Language of Love	1963	$15
❑ CS8843 [S]	The Language of Love	1963	$18
❑ CL2387 [M]	There Goes My Heart	1965	$15
❑ CS9187 [S]	There Goes My Heart	1965	$18
❑ CS8175 [S]	The Same Old Moon	1960	$18
❑ CL1380 [M]	The Same Old Moon	1959	$18
❑ CS9694	This Guy's in Love with You	1968	$18
❑ CS9757	Till	1969	$18
❑ CL2116 [M]	Till the End of Time	1964	$15
❑ CS8916 [S]	Till the End of Time	1964	$18
❑ CL2684 [M]	Time Alone Will Tell	1967	$15
❑ CS9484 [S]	Time Alone Will Tell	1967	$18
❑ C30104	We've Only Just Begun	1971	$12
❑ CS9838	Where's the Playground Susie?	1969	$18
❑ GP16	With Love, Jerry Vale	1969	$18
❑ CL2774 [M]	You Don't Have to Say You Love Me	1968	$18
❑ CS9574 [S]	You Don't Have to Say You Love Me	1968	$18

Number	Title	Yr	NM
COLUMBIA LIMITED EDITION			
❑ LE10164	Christmas Greetings from Jerry Vale	197?	$12

— *Reissue*

Number	Title	Yr	NM
❑ LE10058	Till	197?	$12

— *Reissue of 9757*

Number	Title	Yr	NM
HARMONY			
❑ HS11298	As Long As She Needs Me	1969	$12
❑ KH30345	Born Free	1971	$12
❑ HS11376	Hey Look Me Over	1970	$12
❑ KH30759	More	1971	$12
❑ KH32478	What a Wonderful World	1973	$12

Number	Title	Yr	NM
VALE, RICKY, AND THE SURFERS			
STRAND			
❑ SL-1104 [M]	Everybody's Surfin'	1963	$40
❑ SLS-1104 [S]	Everybody's Surfin'	1963	$50

Number	Title	Yr	NM
VALENS, RITCHIE			
DEL-FI			
❑ DFLP1225 [M]	His Greatest Hits	1963	$350

— *Black cover*

RITCHIE VALENS — HIS GREATEST HITS
HIS INCOMPARABLE NEVER TO BE FORGOTTEN PERFORMANCES
DONNA · LA BAMBA · COME ON LET'S GO · WE BELONG TOGETHER · BLUEBIRDS OVER THE MOUNTAIN · IN A TURKISH TOWN · STAY BESIDE ME · CRY, CRY, CRY · HURRY UP · ROCKIN' ALL NIGHT · FROM BEYOND · MALAGUENA

Number	Title	Yr	NM
❑ DFLP1225 [M]	His Greatest Hits	1963	$175

— *White cover*

Number	Title	Yr	NM
❑ DFLP1247 [M]	His Greatest Hits, Volume 2	1965	$250
❑ DFLP1214 [M]	In Concert at Pacoima Jr. High	1960	$300
❑ DFLP1206 [M]	Ritchie	1959	$175
❑ DFLP1201 [M]	Ritchie Valens	1959	$300

— *Blue label with black border*

Number	Title	Yr	NM
❑ DFLP1201 [M]	Ritchie Valens	1959	$175

— *Black label with "diamonds" border*

Number	Title	Yr	NM
GUEST STAR			
❑ GS-1484 [M]	The Original La Bamba	1963	$30
❑ GSS-1484 [R]	The Original La Bamba	1963	$25
❑ GS-1469 [M]	The Original Ritchie Valens	1963	$30
❑ GSS-1469 [R]	The Original Ritchie Valens	1963	$25
MGM			
❑ GAS-117	Ritchie Valens (Golden Archive Series)	1970	$30
RHINO			
❑ RNLP-70233	In Concert at Pacoima Jr. High	1987	$12
❑ RNLP-70232	Ritchie	1987	$12
❑ RNLP-70231	Ritchie Valens	1987	$12
❑ RNDF-200	The Best of Ritchie Valens	1981	$15
❑ RNLP-70178	The Best of Ritchie Valens (Golden Archive Series)	1987	$12
❑ RNBC-2798	The History of Ritchie Valens	198?	$30

Number	Title	Yr	NM
VALENS, RITCHIE / JERRY KOLE			
CROWN			
❑ CLP-5336 [M]	Ritchie Valens and Jerry Kole	1963	$30

Number	Title	Yr	NM
VALENTE, BENITA, AND THE PHILADELPHIA SINGERS			
RCA RED SEAL			
❑ 6559-1-RC	Gloria! Gloria! Christmas with Benita Valente	1987	$12

Number	Title	Yr	NM
VALENTE, CATERINA			
DECCA			
❑ DL4051 [M]	Arriba	1959	$30
❑ DL8755 [M]	A Toast to the Girls	1958	$30
❑ DL4052 [M]	Catarina: The Greatest in Any Language	1959	$30
❑ DL4050 [M]	Catarina A La Carte	1959	$30
❑ DL4504 [M]	Golden Favorites	1964	$25
❑ DL74504 [R]	Golden Favorites	1964	$15
❑ DL4035 [M]	More Schlagerparade	1959	$30
❑ DL8436 [M]	Ole Caterina	1957	$30
❑ DL8440 [M]	Plenty Valente!	1957	$30
❑ DL8852 [M]	Schlagerparade	1958	$25
❑ DL8203 [M]	The Hi-Fi Nightingale	1956	$30
LONDON			
❑ LL3441 [M]	Caterina Valente's Greatest Hits	1965	$15
❑ PS441 [S]	Caterina Valente's Greatest Hits	1965	$18
❑ ST-93108 [S]	Caterina Valente's Greatest Hits	196?	$25

— *Capitol Record Club edition*

Number	Title	Yr	NM
❑ TW91198 [M]	Continental Favorites	196?	$18
❑ TW91253 [M]	Fire and Frenzy	196?	$18

— *With Edmundo Ros*

Number	Title	Yr	NM
❑ SW99019 [S]	Fire and Frenzy	196?	$25

— *With Edmundo Ros*

Number	Title	Yr	NM
❑ SW99025 [S]	German Evergreens	196?	$25

— *With Silvio Francesco*

Number	Title	Yr	NM
❑ TW91267 [M]	German Evergreens	196?	$18

— *With Silvio Francesco*

Number	Title	Yr	NM
❑ LL3471 [M]	Go Latin!	196?	$15

— *With Silvio Francesco*

Number	Title	Yr	NM
❑ PS471 [S]	Go Latin!	196?	$18

— *With Silvio Francesco*

Number	Title	Yr	NM
❑ LL3362 [M]	I Happen to Like New York	196?	$15

VALENTE, CATERINA (continued)

Number	Title	Yr	NM
❑ PS362 [S]	I Happen to Like New York	196?	$18
❑ PS473 [S]	Intimate Valente	196?	$18
❑ LL3473 [M]	Intimate Valente	196?	$15
❑ PS275 [S]	I Wish You Love	196?	$18
— With Stanley Black			
❑ LL3275 [M]	I Wish You Love	196?	$15
— With Stanley Black			
❑ TW91260 [M]	Miss Personality	196?	$18
❑ LL3355 [M]	Songs I've Sung on the Perry Como Show	196?	$15
❑ PS355 [S]	Songs I've Sung on the Perry Como Show	196?	$18
❑ SW99292 [S]	South of the Border	196?	$25
❑ TW91292 [M]	South of the Border	196?	$18
❑ LL3307 [M]	Strictly U.S.A.	196?	$15
❑ PS307 [S]	Strictly U.S.A.	196?	$18
❑ PS536	Sweet Beat	1969	$18
❑ LL3363 [M]	Valente and Violins	196?	$15
❑ PS363 [S]	Valente and Violins	196?	$18

LONDON PHASE 4
Number	Title	Yr	NM
❑ SP-44181	Love	197?	$30
❑ SP-44125	Silk and Latin	197?	$30

PETERS INT'L.
Number	Title	Yr	NM
❑ PLD-7046	Caterina Valente	197?	$15
❑ PLD-7021	Golden Days	197?	$15

RCA VICTOR
Number	Title	Yr	NM
❑ LPM-2119 [M]	Classics with a Chaser	1960	$25
❑ LSP-2119 [S]	Classics with a Chaser	1960	$30
❑ LPM-2241 [M]	Superfonics	1961	$25
❑ LSP-2241 [S]	Superfonics	1961	$30

VALENTI, DINO
EPIC
Number	Title	Yr	NM
❑ LN24335 [M]	Dino Valenti	1967	$25
❑ BN26335 [S]	Dino Valenti	1967	$25

VALENTIN, DAVE
GRP
Number	Title	Yr	NM
❑ GR-1004	Flute Juice	198?	$12
❑ GR-1016	Jungle Garden	198?	$25
❑ GR-1009	Kalahari	198?	$25
❑ GR-1028	Light Struck	198?	$25
❑ GR-9568	Live at the Blue Note	1988	$25
❑ GR-1043	Mind Time	1988	$25

GRP/ARISTA
Number	Title	Yr	NM
❑ GL5006	Hawk	1979	$25
❑ GL5511	In Love's Time	198?	$25
❑ GL5001	Legends	1978	$30
❑ GL5505	Pied Piper	198?	$25

VALENTINE, HILTON
Former member of THE ANIMALS.
CAPITOL
Number	Title	Yr	NM
❑ ST-330 [B]	All in Your Head	1969	$35

VALENTINE, JIMMIE
JUBILEE
Number	Title	Yr	NM
❑ LP-9 [10]	Music to Beat By	1954	$40

VALENTINO, MARK
SWAN
Number	Title	Yr	NM
❑ SLP-508 [M]	Mark Valentino	1963	$50

VALENTYNE, RUDY
ROULETTE
Number	Title	Yr	NM
❑ R-25299 [M]	And Now... Rudy Valentyne	1965	$25
❑ SR-25299 [S]	And Now... Rudy Valentyne	1965	$30

VALHALLA
UNITED ARTISTS
Number	Title	Yr	NM
❑ UAS-6730 [B]	Valhalla	1969	$30

VALIDS, THE
AMBER
Number	Title	Yr	NM
❑ 802 [M]	Accapella	1966	$30

VALJEAN
CARLTON
Number	Title	Yr	NM
❑ LP-146 [M]	Mashin' the Classics	1963	$25
❑ STLP-146 [S]	Mashin' the Classics	1963	$30
❑ LP-143 [M]	The Theme from Ben Casey	1962	$25
❑ STLP-143 [S]	The Theme from Ben Casey	1962	$30

VALLEE, RUDY
RCA VICTOR
Number	Title	Yr	NM
❑ LPM-2507 [M]	Young Rudy Vallee	1961	$30
❑ LSP-2507 [R]	Young Rudy Vallee	196?	$25

VALLEY, JIM
FIRST AMERICAN
Number	Title	Yr	NM
❑ 7710	Dance Inside Your Head	1977	$18

LIGHT
Number	Title	Yr	NM
❑ LS-5564	Family	197?	$18

PANORAMA
Number	Title	Yr	NM
❑ 104-S	Jim "Harpo" Valley	1968	$40

VALLI, FRANKIE, AND THE FOUR SEASONS
See THE FOUR SEASONS.

VALLI, FRANKIE
Includes records under numerous pseudonyms. Also see THE FOUR LOVERS; THE FOUR SEASONS.

MCA
Number	Title	Yr	NM
❑ 5134	Heaven Above Me	1979	$12
❑ 743	Heaven Above Me	1982	$10
— Reissue of 5134			
❑ 3198	The Very Best of Frankie Valli	1980	$12
❑ 756	The Very Best of Frankie Valli	1982	$10
— Reissue of 3198			

MOTOWN
Number	Title	Yr	NM
❑ M6-852	Inside You	1975	$18
❑ M5-104V1	Motown Superstar Series, Vol. 4	1981	$12

PHILIPS
Number	Title	Yr	NM
❑ PHM200247 [M]	Frankie Valli -- Solo	1967	$40
❑ PHS600247 [S]	Frankie Valli -- Solo	1967	$30
❑ PHS600274	Timeless	1968	$30

PRIVATE STOCK
Number	Title	Yr	NM
❑ PS-2000	Closeup	1975	$15
❑ PS-2001	Frankie Valli Gold	1975	$15
❑ PS-7012	Hits	1978	$15
❑ PS-7002 [B]	Lady Put the Light Out	1977	$15
❑ PS-2006	Our Day Will Come	1975	$15
❑ PS-2017	Valli	1976	$15

WARNER BROS.
Number	Title	Yr	NM
❑ BSK3233	Frankie Valli…Is the Word	1978	$12

VALLI, JUNE
AUDIO FIDELITY
Number	Title	Yr	NM
❑ AFSD-6214 [S]	June Valli Today	1969	$25

MERCURY
Number	Title	Yr	NM
❑ SR-60145 [S]	Do-It-Yourself Wedding Album	1959	$30
❑ MG-20463 [M]	Do-It-Yourself Wedding Album	1959	$25

RCA VICTOR
Number	Title	Yr	NM
❑ LPM-1120 [M]	The Torch	1955	$40

VAMPIRES, THE
UNITED ARTISTS
Number	Title	Yr	NM
❑ UAL-3378 [M]	The Vampires at the Monster Ball	1964	$30
❑ UAS-6378 [S]	The Vampires at the Monster Ball	1964	$30

VAN DAMME, ART
BASF
Number	Title	Yr	NM
❑ 22016	Invitation	197?	$35
❑ 21755	Squeezing Art and Tender Flutes	197?	$35
❑ 25257	Star Spangled Rhythm	197?	$25
❑ 25113	The Many Moods of Art Van Damme	197?	$25

CAPITOL
Number	Title	Yr	NM
❑ H178 [10]	Cocktail Capers	1950	$100
❑ T178 [M]	Cocktail Capers	1954	$75
❑ L300 [10]	More Cocktail Capers	1952	$100
❑ T300 [M]	More Cocktail Capers	1954	$85

COLUMBIA
Number	Title	Yr	NM
❑ CL1563 [M]	Accordion A La Mode	1960	$30
❑ CS8363 [S]	Accordion A La Mode	1960	$30
❑ CL2013 [M]	A Perfect Match	1963	$35
❑ CS8813 [S]	A Perfect Match	1963	$25
❑ CL1794 [M]	Art Van Damme Swings Sweetly	1962	$35
❑ CS8594 [M]	Art Van Damme Swings Sweetly	1962	$25
❑ CL1382 [M]	Everything's Coming Up Music	1959	$30
❑ CS8177 [S]	Everything's Coming Up Music	1959	$30
❑ CL801 [M]	Manhattan Time	1956	$30
❑ CL6265 [10]	Martini Time	1953	$40
❑ CL630 [M]	Martini Time	1955	$40
❑ CL876 [M]	The Art of Van Damme	1956	$30
❑ CL2585 [10]	The Art Van Damme Quintet	1956	$40
❑ CL2192 [M]	The New Sound Of the Art Van Damme Septet	1964	$30
❑ CS8992 [S]	The New Sound Of the Art Van Damme Septet	1964	$35
❑ CL544 [M]	The Van Damme Sound	1955	$40
❑ C2L7 [M]	They're Playing Our Song	1958	$40

DESIGN
Number	Title	Yr	NM
❑ DLP-905 [M]	3 of a Kind	196?	$30
❑ SDLP-905 [R]	3 of a Kind	196?	$20

HARMONY
Number	Title	Yr	NM
❑ HL-7439 [M]	Music for Lovers	196?	$30
❑ HS-11439 [S]	Music for Lovers	196?	$25

PAUSA
Number	Title	Yr	NM
❑ 7151	Art Van Damme and Friends	198?	$25
❑ 7027	Blue World	197?	$25

Number	Title	Yr	NM
❑ 7066	Invitation	197?	$25
❑ 7104	Keep Going	198?	$25
❑ 7126	Squeezing Art and Tender Flutes	198?	$25

PICKWICK
Number	Title	Yr	NM
❑ PC-3009 [M]	Lover Man!	196?	$30
❑ PCS-3009 [R]	Lover Man!	196?	$20

SONIC ARTS
Number	Title	Yr	NM
❑ 12	By Request	1980	$30

VAN DER GELD, TOM
ECM
Number	Title	Yr	NM
❑ 1134	Path	1979	$30
❑ 1113	Patience	1977	$30

VAN DER GRAAF GENERATOR
Featuring Peter Hammill.
4 MEN WITH BEARDS
Number	Title	Yr	NM
❑ 4M217LP [B]	H To He, Who Am The Only One		$25
❑ 4M218LP [B]	Pawn Hearts		$25
❑ 4M216LP [B]	The Least We Can Do Is Wave To Each Other		$25

ABC DUNHILL
Number	Title	Yr	NM
❑ DS50097	H to He Who Am the Only One	1971	$30

CHARISMA
Number	Title	Yr	NM
❑ CAS-1051 [B]	Pawn Hearts	1971	$30

MERCURY
Number	Title	Yr	NM
❑ SRM-1-1069 [B]	Godbluff	1975	$25
❑ SRM-1-1096 [B]	Still Life	1976	$25
❑ SR-61238	The Aerosol Grey Machine	1969	$150
❑ SRM-1-1116 [B]	World Record	1976	$25

PROBE
Number	Title	Yr	NM
❑ CPLP-4515	The Least We Can Do Is Wave to Each Other	1970	$30

PVC
Number	Title	Yr	NM
❑ 9901 [B]	Vital	1979	$30

VAN DERBUR, MARILYN
DECCA
Number	Title	Yr	NM
❑ DL8770 [M]	Miss America	1958	$40

VAN DYKE, DICK
COMMAND
Number	Title	Yr	NM
❑ RS860SD [S]	Songs I Like	1963	$30

Number	Title	Yr	NM
❑ RS 33-860 [M]	Songs I Like	1963	$30

VAN DYKE, EARL, AND THE SOUL BROTHERS
MOTOWN
Number	Title	Yr	NM
❑ M-631 [M]	The Motown Sound	1965	$40
❑ MS-631 [S]	The Motown Sound	1965	$50

SOUL
Number	Title	Yr	NM
❑ SS-715	The Earl of Funk	1970	$40

VAN DYKE, LEROY
DOT
Number	Title	Yr	NM
❑ DLP3693 [M]	Auctioneer	1966	$25

HARMONY
Number	Title	Yr	NM
❑ HS11308	I've Never Been Loved	196?	$15

KAPP
Number	Title	Yr	NM
❑ KS-3605	Greatest Hits	1969	$18
❑ KS-3607	Just a Closer Walk with Thee	1969	$18
❑ KS-3571	Lonesome Is	1968	$18

MCA
Number	Title	Yr	NM
❑ 145	Greatest Hits	1973	$15

MERCURY
Number	Title	Yr	NM
❑ MG-20950 [M]	Leroy Van Dyke at the Tradewinds	1964	$12

Number	Title	Yr	NM
❏ SR-60950 [S]	Leroy Van Dyke at the Tradewinds	1964	$30
❏ MG-20716 [M]	Movin' Van Dyke	1963	$25
❏ SR-60716 [S]	Movin' Van Dyke	1963	$30
❏ MG-20922 [M]	Songs for Mom and Dad	1964	$25
❏ SR-60922 [S]	Songs for Mom and Dad	1964	$30
❏ MG-20802 [M]	The Great Hits of Leroy Van Dyke	1963	$25
❏ SR-60802 [S]	The Great Hits of Leroy Van Dyke	1963	$30
❏ MG-20682 [M]	Walk On By	1962	$25
❏ SR-60682 [S]	Walk On By	1962	$30

PLANTATION

❏ 516	Gospel Greats	1977	$15

SUN

❏ 131	Golden Hits	1974	$15

WARNER BROS.

❏ W1652 [M]	Country Hits	1966	$18
❏ WS1652 [S]	Country Hits	1966	$25
❏ W1618 [M]	The Leroy Van Dyke Show	1965	$18
❏ WS1618 [S]	The Leroy Van Dyke Show	1965	$25

WING

❏ MGW-12322 [M]	Movin'	196?	$15
❏ SRW-16322 [S]	Movin'	196?	$18
❏ MGW-12302 [M]	Out of Love	196?	$15
❏ SRW-16302 [S]	Out of Love	196?	$18

VAN DYKE, LOUIS
COLUMBIA MASTERWORKS

❏ M34511	'Round Midnight	1977	$25

VAN DYKES, THE (2)
BELL

❏ 6004 [M]	Tellin' It Like It Is	1967	$50
❏ S-6004 [S]	Tellin' It Like It Is	1967	$75

VAN EATEN, LON AND DERREK
A&M

❏ SP-4507	Who Do You Outdo	1975	$12

APPLE

❏ SMAS-3390	Brother	1972	$18

VAN EPS, GEORGE
CAPITOL

❏ T2533 [M]	My Guitar	1966	$50
❏ ST2533 [S]	My Guitar	1966	$40
❏ ST2783	Seven String Guitar	1968	$50
❏ ST-267	Soliloquy	1969	$50

COLUMBIA

❏ CL929 [M]	Mellow Guitar	1956	$40

CORINTHIAN

❏ 121	Mellow Guitar	198?	$25

VAN HALEN
Also see SAMMY HAGAR; DAVID LEE ROTH; CHICKENFOOT.

DCC COMPACT CLASSICS

❏ LPZ-2066	Van Halen	1998	$40

— *Audiophile vinyl*

WARNER BROS.

❏ 23985 [DJ]	1984	1984	$40

— *Promo on Quiex II vinyl*

❏ 23985 [B]	1984	1984	$12
❏ 25394 [B]	5150	1986	$12
❏ 45760	Balance	1995	$30
❏ BSK3677 [B]	Diver Down	1982	$12
❏ HS3540	Fair Warning	1981	$12
❏ W1-26594	For Unlawful Carnal Knowledge	1991	$30

— *The only U.S. vinyl version was released through Columbia House*

❏ PRO705 [DJ]	Looney Tunes	1978	$150

— *Promo-only EP on red vinyl*

Number	Title	Yr	NM
❏ 25732	OU812	1988	$12
❏ BSK3075	Van Halen	1978	$15

— *Early pressings have "Burbank" labels*

❏ BSK3075	Van Halen	1979	$12

— *White/cream labels*

❏ HS3312	Van Halen II	1979	$12
❏ HS3415	Women and Children First	1980	$12

VAN HEUSEN, JIMMY
UNITED ARTISTS

❏ UAL-3494 [M]	Van Heusen Plays Van Heusen	1966	$25
❏ UAS-6494 [S]	Van Heusen Plays Van Heusen	1966	$30

VAN RONK, DAVE
CADET

❏ CA-50044	Songs for Aging Children	1973	$25

FANTASY

❏ 24710	Dave Van Ronk	1972	$25

FOLKLORE

❏ FRLP-14012 [M]	Dave Van Ronk, Folksinger	1963	$30
❏ FRST-14012 [S]	Dave Van Ronk, Folksinger	1963	$40
❏ FRLP-14025 [M]	Inside Dave Van Ronk	1964	$30
❏ FRST-14025 [S]	Inside Dave Van Ronk	1964	$40
❏ FRLP-14001 [M]	In the Tradition	1963	$30
❏ FRST-14001 [S]	In the Tradition	1963	$40

FOLKWAYS

❏ FTS31020	Black Mountain Blues	1968	$35
❏ FS-3818 [M]	Dave Van Ronk Sings Ballads, Blues and Spirituals	1959	$50
❏ FA-2383 [M]	Dave Van Ronk Sings Earthy Ballads and Blues	1961	$50

MERCURY

❏ MG-20864 [M]	Dave Van Ronk and the Ragtime Jug Stompers	1964	$30
❏ SR-60864 [S]	Dave Van Ronk and the Ragtime Jug Stompers	1964	$30
❏ MG-20908 [M]	Just Dave Van Ronk	1964	$30
❏ SR-60908 [S]	Just Dave Van Ronk	1964	$30

POLYDOR

❏ 24-4052	Van Ronk	1972	$25

VERVE FOLKWAYS

❏ FV-9006 [M]	Dave Van Ronk Sings the Blues	1965	$50
❏ FVS-9006 [S]	Dave Van Ronk Sings the Blues	1965	$50
❏ FV-9017 [M]	Gambler's Blues	1965	$50
❏ FVS-9017 [S]	Gambler's Blues	1965	$50

VERVE FORECAST

❏ FTS-3041 [M]	Dave Van Ronk and the Hudson Dusters	1968	$30
❏ FT-3009 [M]	No Dirty Names	1967	$30
❏ FTS-3009 [S]	No Dirty Names	1967	$30

VAN VOOREN, MONIQUE
RCA VICTOR

❏ LPM-1553 [M]	Mink in Hi-Fi	1958	$30

VAN ZANDT, TOWNES
POPPY

❏ PYS-40012	Delta Momma Blues	1970	$18
❏ PYS-40001	For the Sake of a Song	1968	$30
❏ PYS-5700	High, Low and In Between	1972	$18
❏ PYS-40004	Our Mother, The Mountain	1969	$18
❏ PP-LA004-F	The Late Great Townes Van Zandt	1973	$18
❏ PYS-40007	Townes Van Zandt	1969	$18

SUGAR HILL

❏ SH-1020	At My Window	1987	$12
❏ SH-1026	Live and Obscure	1989	$12

TOMATO

❏ 7013	Delta Momma Blues	1978	$15

— *Reissue of Poppy 40012*

❏ 7017 [B]	Flyin' Shoes	1978	$15
❏ 7012	High, Low and In Between	1978	$15

— *Reissue of Poppy 5700*

❏ 7001	Live at the Old Quarter, Houston, Texas	1977	$18
❏ 7015	Our Mother, The Mountain	1978	$15

— *Reissue of Poppy 40004*

❏ 7011	The Late Great Townes Van Zandt	1978	$15

— *Reissue of Poppy 004*

❏ 7014	Townes Van Zandt	1978	$15

— *Reissue of Poppy 40007*

VANCE, PAUL
SCEPTER

❏ SRM-557 [M]	Ma Vie (My Life)	1966	$18
❏ SPS-557 [S]	Ma Vie (My Life)	1966	$25

VANDALS, THE
KUNG FU

❏ 78762	Christmas with the Vandals: Oi to the World!	1996	$12

VANDROSS, LUTHER
COTILLION

❏ SD9907	Luther	1976	$50

— *As "Luther*

❏ SD9916	This Close to You	1977	$150

— *As "Luther*

EPIC

❏ FE44308	Any Love	1988	$10
❏ FE39196 [B]	Busy Body	1983	$12
❏ FE38235	Forever, For Always, For Love	1982	$12
❏ FE40415	Give Me the Reason	1986	$10
❏ HE47451	Never Too Much	198?	$30

— *Half-speed mastered edition*

❏ FE37451	Never Too Much	1981	$12
❏ E46789	Power of Love	1991	$15
❏ E57775	Songs	1994	$18
❏ E245320	The Best of Luther Vandross... The Best of Love	1989	$15
❏ FE39882	The Night I Fell in Love	1985	$10
❏ E57795	This Is Christmas	1995	$15
❏ E67553	Your Secret Love	1996	$15

VANGELIS
ARISTA

❏ AL-8545	Direct	1988	$12

DEUTSCHE GRAMMAPHON

❏ 415196-1	Invisible Connections	1985	$18

— *All copies for U.S. distribution were pressed in West Germany*

POLYDOR

❏ 815732-1	Antarctica	198?	$18

— *Most copies may be imports*

❏ PD-1-6335	Chariots of Fire	1981	$12
❏ 825384-1	Chariots of Fire	1985	$10

— *Reissue*

❏ PD-1-6199	China	1979	$12
❏ 825245-1	Mask	1985	$12
❏ 829663-1	Opera Sauvage	1986	$10

— *Reissue*

❏ 823396-1	Soil Festivities	1984	$12
❏ 839518-1	Themes	1989	$18

RCA VICTOR

❏ LPL1-5136	Albedo 0.39	1976	$12

— *Original prefix*

❏ AFL1-5136	Albedo 0.39	197?	$10

— *Reissue prefix*

❏ AFL1-3020	Beaubourg	1978	$15
❏ AYL1-4387	Beaubourg	1982	$10

— *Best Buy Series" reissue*

❏ LPL1-5110	Heaven and Hell	1976	$12

— *Original prefix; tan label*

❏ AFL1-5110	Heaven and Hell	197?	$10

— *Reissue prefix; black label, dog near top*

❏ AFL1-2627	Spiral	1977	$12
❏ DJL1-1849 [DJ]	The Vangelis Radio Special	1976	$150

— *Promo only music and interviews*

❏ AFL1-4397	To the Unknown Man	1982	$10

VERTIGO

❏ VEL-1019	Earth	1974	$300

— *As "Vangelis O.*

VANILLA FUDGE
Also see CACTUS, BECK, BOGERT & APPICE.

ATCO

❏ 90149	Mystery	1984	$15
❏ SD 33-278	Near the Beginning	1969	$18
❏ SD 33-244	Renaissance	1968	$25

— *Purple and brown label*

❏ SD 33-244	Renaissance	1969	$15

— *Yellow label*

❏ SD 33-303 [B]	Rock 'N' Roll	1969	$18

— *add 50% for white label mono promo*

❏ SD 33-237	The Beat Goes On	1968	$25

— *Purple and brown label*

❏ SD 33-237	The Beat Goes On	1969	$15

— *Yellow label*

❏ 33-237 [M]	The Beat Goes On	1968	$150
❏ 90006	The Best of Vanilla Fudge	1982	$12
❏ 33-224 [M]	Vanilla Fudge	1967	$75
❏ SD 33-224 [S]	Vanilla Fudge	1967	$25

— *Purple and brown label*

❏ SD 33-224 [S]	Vanilla Fudge	1969	$15

— *Yellow label*

❏ SD 33-224	Vanilla Fudge	197?	$10

— *Any later label*

SUNDAZED

❏ LP5168 [M]	Vanilla Fudge	2004	$18

— *Reissue on 180-gram vinyl*

VANILLA ICE
ULTRA

❏ ULT4019	Hooked	1990	$40

— *Basically the same album as "To the Extreme," which was not issued on vinyl in the United States*

Number	Title	Yr	NM

VANITY FARE
PAGE ONE
| ❏ 2502 [B] | Early in the Morning | 1970 | $35 |

VANNELLI, GINO
A&M
❏ SP-4664	A Pauper in Paradise	1977	$12
❏ SP-4722	Brother to Brother	1978	$12
❏ SP-3170	Brother to Brother	1981	$10
—Reissue of 4722			
❏ SP-3139	Crazy Life	1981	$10
—Reissue of 4395			
❏ SP-4395	Crazy Life	1973	$15
❏ SP-3630	Powerful People	1974	$12
❏ SP-3120	Powerful People	1981	$10
—Reissue of 3630			
❏ SP-4533 [B]	Storm at Sunup	1975	$12
❏ SP-3729	The Best of Gino Vannelli	1981	$12
❏ SP-3260	The Best of Gino Vannelli	1982	$10
—Reissue of 3729			
❏ SP-4596	The Gist of the Gemini	1976	$12
❏ SP-3112	The Gist of the Gemini	1981	$10
—Reissue of 4596			
ARISTA
| ❏ AB9539 | Nightwalker | 1981 | $12 |
CBS ASSOCIATED
| ❏ BFZ40337 | Big Dreamers Never Sleep | 1987 | $12 |
HME
| ❏ FZ40077 | Black Cars | 1985 | $12 |
MOBILE FIDELITY
| ❏ Jan-0041 | Powerful People | 1980 | $25 |
| —Audiophile vinyl | | | |
NAUTILUS
| ❏ NR-35 | Brother to Brother | 198? | $30 |
| —Audiophile vinyl | | | |

VAN'T HOF, JASPER
PAUSA
| ❏ 7084 | Live in Montreux | 1979 | $25 |

VANWARMER, RANDY
16TH AVENUE
| ❏ D1-70553 | I Am/Randy Vanwarmer | 1988 | $12 |
BEARSVILLE
| ❏ BRK3561 | The Beat of Love | 1981 | $12 |
| ❏ BRK6988 | Warmer | 1979 | $12 |

VAPORS, THE
LIBERTY
❏ LT-1090	Magnets	1981	$12
❏ LT-1049	New Clear Days	1981	$12
—Reissue			
UNITED ARTISTS
| ❏ LT-1049 | New Clear Days | 1980 | $18 |

VARIATIONS, THE
JUSTICE
| ❏ JLP-212 | Dig 'Em Up | 196? | $400 |

VARNER, TOM
SOUL NOTE
| ❏ SN-1067 | Motion/Stillness | 198? | $30 |
| ❏ SN-1017 | TV | 198? | $30 |

VASCONCELOS, NANA
ANTILLES
| ❏ 90698 | Bush Dance | 1987 | $25 |
ECM
| ❏ 1147 | Saudades | 1979 | $30 |

VAUGHAN, DENNY
BEVERLY HILLS
| ❏ BHS-19 | Aberga-Denny | 1969 | $18 |
CORAL
| ❏ CRL56038 [10] | Moonlight and Roses | 1951 | $50 |

VAUGHAN, FRANKIE
PHILIPS
| ❏ PHM200006 [M] | Singin' Happy | 1962 | $25 |
| ❏ PHS600006 [S] | Singin' Happy | 1962 | $30 |

VAUGHAN, SARAH, AND BILLY ECKSTINE
Also see each artist's individual listings.
EMARCY
| ❏ 822526-1 | The Irving Berlin Songbook | 1984 | $25 |
LION
| ❏ L-70088 [M] | Billy and Sarah | 195? | $30 |

MERCURY
| ❏ MG-20316 [M] | Sarah Vaughan and Billy Eckstine Sing the Best of Irving Berlin | 1959 | $150 |
| ❏ SR-60002 [S] | Sarah Vaughan and Billy Eckstine Sing the Best of Irving Berlin | 1959 | $150 |

VAUGHAN, SARAH, AND COUNT BASIE
Also see each artist's individual listings.
PABLO
| ❏ 2312130 | Send In the Clowns | 1980 | $25 |
ROULETTE
❏ R52061 [M]	Count Basie and Sarah Vaughan	1960	$75
❏ SR52061 [S]	Count Basie and Sarah Vaughan	1960	$75
❏ SR42018	Count Basie and Sarah Vaughan	1968	$35

VAUGHAN, SARAH; DINAH WASHINGTON; JOE WILLIAMS
ROULETTE
| ❏ R52108 [M] | We Three | 1964 | $35 |
| ❏ SR52108 [S] | We Three | 1964 | $50 |

VAUGHAN, SARAH
ACCORD
| ❏ SN-7195 | Simply Divine | 1981 | $25 |
ALLEGRO
❏ 3080 [10]	Early Sarah	195?	$100
❏ 1592 [M]	Sarah Vaughan	1955	$150
❏ 1608 [M]	Sarah Vaughan	1955	$150
ALLEGRO ELITE
| ❏ 4106 [10] | Sarah Vaughan Sings | 195? | $30 |
ATLANTIC
| ❏ SD16037 | Songs of the Beatles | 1981 | $30 |
BRYLEN
| ❏ BN4411 | Desires | 198? | $25 |
| —Last name is misspelled "Vaughn" | | | |
CBS MASTERWORKS
❏ FM42519	Brazilian Romance	1987	$25
❏ FM37277	Gershwin Live!	1982	$25
—With the Los Angeles Philharmonic Orchestra			
COLUMBIA
❏ CL660 [M]	After Hours with Sarah Vaughan	1955	$150
❏ CL914 [M]	Linger Awhile	1956	$150
❏ CL6133 [10]	Sarah Vaughan	1950	$250
❏ CL745 [M]	Sarah Vaughan in Hi-Fi	1956	$150
COLUMBIA SPECIAL PRODUCTS
❏ P14364	Linger Awhile	1978	$25
—Reissue of Columbia 914			
❏ P13084	Sarah Vaughan in Hi-Fi	1976	$25
—Reissue of Columbia 745			
CONCORD
| ❏ 3018 [M] | Sarah Vaughan Concert | 1957 | $75 |
CORONET
| ❏ 277 | Sarah Vaughan Belts the Hits | 196? | $35 |
EMARCY
❏ MG-26005 [10]	Images	1954	$250
❏ MG-36058 [M]	In the Land of Hi-Fi	1956	$250
❏ 826454-1	In the Land of Hi-Fi	1986	$25
—Reissue of 36058			
❏ MG-36004 [M]	Sarah Vaughan	1955	$250
❏ EMS-2-412	Sarah Vaughan Live	197?	$30
❏ MG-36089 [M]	Sassy	1956	$250
❏ MG-36109 [M]	Swingin' Easy	1957	$250
❏ 814187-1	The George Gershwin Songbook	1983	$30
❏ 824864-1	The Rodgers & Hart Songbook	1985	$25
EVEREST ARCHIVE OF FOLK & JAZZ
❏ 250	Sarah Vaughan	197?	$25
❏ 271	Sarah Vaughan, Volume 2	1973	$25
❏ 325	Sarah Vaughan, Volume 3	197?	$25
FORUM
| ❏ F-9034 [M] | Dreamy | 196? | $30 |
| ❏ SF-9034 [S] | Dreamy | 196? | $18 |
HARMONY
| ❏ HL7158 [M] | The Great Sarah Vaughan | 196? | $30 |
LION
| ❏ L70052 [M] | Tenderly | 1958 | $75 |
MAINSTREAM
❏ MRL379	Feelin' Good	1973	$35
❏ MRL419	More Sarah Vaughan from Japan	1974	$35
❏ MRL404	Sarah Vaughan and the Jimmy Rowles Quintet	1974	$35
❏ MRL2401	Sarah Vaughan "Live" In Japan	1973	$50
❏ MRL361	Sarah Vaughan/Michel Legrand	1972	$35
❏ MRL412 [B]	Send In the Clowns	1974	$18
❏ MRL340	Time in My Life	1972	$35

MASTERSEAL
| ❏ MS-55 [M] | Sarah Vaughan Sings | 195? | $30 |
MERCURY
❏ SR-60020 [S]	After Hours at the London House	1959	$175
❏ MG-20383 [M]	After Hours at the London House	1958	$175
❏ MG-20580 [M]	Close to You	1960	$150
❏ SR-60240 [S]	Close to You	1960	$150
❏ MG-25188 [10]	Divine Sarah	1955	$300
❏ MGP-2-100 [M]	Great Songs from Hit Shows	1957	$250
❏ MG-20244 [M]	Great Songs from Hit Shows, Vol. 1	1958	$150
❏ SR-60041 [S]	Great Songs from Hit Shows, Vol. 1	1959	$150
❏ MG-20245 [M]	Great Songs from Hit Shows, Vol. 2	1958	$150
❏ SR-60078 [S]	Great Songs from Hit Shows, Vol. 2	1959	$150
❏ MG-20223 [M]	In a Romantic Mood	1957	$150
❏ MG-21122 [M]	It's a Man's World	1967	$150
❏ SR-61122 [S]	It's a Man's World	1967	$150
❏ MG-20617 [M]	My Heart Sings	1961	$150
❏ SR-60617 [S]	My Heart Sings	1961	$150
❏ MG-20441 [M]	No 'Count Sarah	1959	$150
❏ SR-60116 [S]	No 'Count Sarah	1959	$150
❏ MG-21069 [M]	Pop Artistry	1966	$150
❏ SR-61069 [S]	Pop Artistry	1966	$150
❏ MG-20326 [M]	Sarah Vaughan and Her Trio at Mr. Kelly's	1958	$150
❏ MG-20094 [M]	Sarah Vaughan at the Blue Note	1956	$150
❏ MG-20645 [M]	Sarah Vaughan's Golden Hits	1961	$150
❏ SR-60645 [S]	Sarah Vaughan's Golden Hits	1961	$150
—Original black label version			
❏ SR-60645 [S]	Sarah Vaughan's Golden Hits	1965	$150
—Red label version with white "MERCURY" alone at top			
❏ SR-60645 [S]	Sarah Vaughan's Golden Hits	1968	$150
—Red label with multiple Mercury logos along the label edge			
❏ MGP-2-101 [M]	Sarah Vaughan Sings George Gershwin	1957	$250
❏ MG-20310 [M]	Sarah Vaughan Sings George Gershwin, Vol. 1	1958	$150
❏ SR-60045 [S]	Sarah Vaughan Sings George Gershwin, Vol. 1	1959	$150
❏ MG-20311 [M]	Sarah Vaughan Sings George Gershwin, Vol. 2	1958	$150
❏ SR-60046 [S]	Sarah Vaughan Sings George Gershwin, Vol. 2	1959	$150
❏ MG-21009 [M]	Sarah Vaughan Sings the Mancini Songbook	1965	$150
❏ SR-61009 [S]	Sarah Vaughan Sings the Mancini Songbook	1965	$150
❏ MG-21116 [M]	Sassy Swings Again	1967	$150
❏ SR-61116 [S]	Sassy Swings Again	1967	$150
❏ MG-20831 [M]	Sassy Swings the Tivoli	1962	$150
❏ SR-60831 [S]	Sassy Swings the Tivoli	1962	$150
❏ 826320-1	The Complete Sarah Vaughan on Mercury Vol. 1: Great Jazz years (1954-56)	1986	$40
❏ 826327-1	The Complete Sarah Vaughan on Mercury Vol. 2: Great American Songs (1956-57)	1986	$40
❏ 826333-1	The Complete Sarah Vaughan on Mercury Vol. 3: Great Show on Stage (1954-56)	1986	$40
❏ 830721-1	The Complete Sarah Vaughan on Mercury Vol. 4 Part 1: Live in Europe (1963-64)	1987	$40
❏ 830726-1	The Complete Sarah Vaughan on Mercury Vol. 4 Part 2: Sassy Swings Again	1987	$40
❏ MG-25213 [10]	The Divine Sarah Sings	1955	$300
❏ MG-20540 [M]	The Divine Sarah Vaughan	1960	$150
❏ SR-60255 [S]	The Divine Sarah Vaughan	1960	$150
❏ MG-20438 [M]	The Magic of Sarah Vaughan	1959	$150
❏ SR-60110 [S]	The Magic of Sarah Vaughan	1959	$150
❏ MG-21079 [M]	The New Scene	1966	$150
❏ SR-61079 [S]	The New Scene	1966	$150
❏ MG-20370 [M]	Vaughan and Violins	1958	$150
❏ SR-60038 [S]	Vaughan and Violins	1959	$150
❏ MG-20882 [M]	Vaughan with Voices	1963	$150
❏ SR-60882 [S]	Vaughan with Voices	1963	$150
❏ MG-20941 [M]	Viva Vaughan	1964	$150
❏ SR-60941 [S]	Viva Vaughan	1964	$150
❏ MG-20219 [M]	Wonderful Sarah	1957	$150
METRO
| ❏ M-539 [M] | Tenderly | 1965 | $175 |
| ❏ MS-539 [S] | Tenderly | 1965 | $300 |
MGM
❏ E-3274 [M]	My Kinda Love	1955	$75
—Combination of two 10-inch LPs on one 12-inch LP			
❏ E-544 [10]	Sarah Vaughan Sings	1951	$250
❏ E-165 [10]	Tenderly	1950	$250
MUSICRAFT
❏ 504	Divine Sarah	197?	$25
❏ MVS-2006	Lover Man	1986	$25
❏ MVS-2002	The Man I Love	1986	$25

Number	Title	Yr	NM
PABLO			
❏ 2312125	Copacabana	1981	$25
❏ 2310821	How Long	1978	$25
❏ 2312101	I Love Brazil	1978	$25
❏ 2310885	The Best of Sarah Vaughan	1983	$25
❏ 2405416	The Best of Sarah Vaughan	1990	$25
❏ 2312111	The Duke Ellington Songbook One	1979	$25
❏ 2312116	The Duke Ellington Songbook Two	1980	$25
PABLO TODAY			
❏ 2312137	Crazy and Mixed Up	1982	$25
PALACE			
❏ 5191 [M]	Sarah Vaughan Sings	195?	$30
PICKWICK			
❏ PCS-3035	Fabulous Sarah Vaughan	197?	$25
REMINGTON			
❏ RLP-1024 [10]	Hot Jazz	1953	$250
RIVERSIDE			
❏ RLP2511 [10]	Sarah Vaughan Sings with John Kirby	1955	$300
RONDO-LETTE			
❏ A-53 [M]	Sarah Vaughan Sings	1959	$75
❏ A-35 [M]	Songs of Broadway	1958	$75
ROULETTE			
❏ R52070 [M]	After Hours	1961	$75
❏ SR52070 [S]	After Hours	1961	$75
❏ R52060 [M]	Divine One	1960	$75
❏ SR52060 [S]	Divine One	1960	$75
❏ R52046 [M]	Dreamy	1960	$75
❏ SR52046 [S]	Dreamy	1960	$40
❏ RE-103	Echoes of an Era: The Sarah Vaughan Years	197?	$35
❏ R52104 [M]	Lonely Hours	1963	$35
❏ SR52104 [S]	Lonely Hours	1963	$50
❏ R52118 [M]	Sarah Plus Two	1965	$35
❏ SR52118 [S]	Sarah Plus Two	1965	$50
❏ R52116 [M]	Sarah Sings Soulfully	1965	$35
❏ SR52116 [S]	Sarah Sings Soulfully	1965	$50
❏ R52123 [M]	Sarah Slightly Classical	1966	$35
❏ SR52123 [S]	Sarah Slightly Classical	1966	$50
❏ R52091 [M]	Snowbound	1962	$50
❏ SR52091 [S]	Snowbound	1962	$75
❏ R52100 [M]	Star Eyes	1963	$35
❏ SR52100 [S]	Star Eyes	1963	$50
❏ R52112 [M]	Sweet 'N Sassy	1964	$35
❏ SR52112 [S]	Sweet 'N Sassy	1964	$50
❏ R52092 [M]	The Explosive Side of Sarah	1962	$50
❏ SR52092 [S]	The Explosive Side of Sarah	1962	$75
❏ K-105 [M]	The Sarah Vaughan Years	196?	$50
❏ SK-105 [S]	The Sarah Vaughan Years	196?	$75
❏ K-105 [M]	The Sarah Vaughan Years	196?	$50
❏ R52109 [M]	The World of Sarah Vaughan	1964	$35
❏ SR52109 [S]	The World of Sarah Vaughan	1964	$50
❏ R52082 [M]	You're Mine	1962	$75
❏ SR52082 [S]	You're Mine	1962	$75
—Black vinyl			
❏ SR52082 [S]	You're Mine	1962	$120
—Red vinyl			
ROYALE			
❏ 18129 [10]	Sarah Vaughan and Orchestra	195?	$30
❏ 18149 [10]	Sarah Vaughan and Orchestra	195?	$30

—Includes recordings made on the Musicraft label in the 1940s

Number	Title	Yr	NM
SCEPTER CITATION			
❏ CTN-18029	The Best of Sarah Vaughan	1972	$30
SPIN-O-RAMA			
❏ 73 [M]	Sweet, Sultry and Swinging	196?	$40
❏ S-73 [S]	Sweet, Sultry and Swinging	196?	$150
❏ 114 [M]	The Divine Sarah Vaughan	196?	$40
❏ S-114 [S]	The Divine Sarah Vaughan	196?	$150
TIME-LIFE			
❏ SLGD-09	Legendary Singers: Sarah Vaughan	1985	$35
TRIP			
❏ 5523	In the Land of Hi-Fi	197?	$25
❏ 5501	Sarah Vaughan	197?	$25
❏ 5517	Sassy	197?	$25
❏ 5551	Swingin' Easy	197?	$25
WING			
❏ MGW-12123 [M]	All Time Favorites	1963	$30
❏ SRW-16123 [S]	All Time Favorites	1963	$35
❏ MGW-12280 [M]	The Magic of Sarah Vaughan	1964	$30
❏ SRW-16280 [S]	The Magic of Sarah Vaughan	1964	$35

VAUGHAN, STEVIE RAY

Number	Title	Yr	NM
EPIC			
❏ 8.00E+0839609 [PD]	Couldn't Stand the Weather	1984	$250
❏ FE39304 [B]	Couldn't Stand the Weather	1984	$18
❏ E66217	Greatest Hits	1995	$18

Number	Title	Yr	NM
❏ FE45024 [B]	In Step	1989	$18
❏ E240511 [B]	Live Alive	1986	$25
❏ FE40036 [B]	Soul to Soul	1985	$18
❏ BFE38734 [B]	Texas Flood	1983	$18
❏ E47390	The Sky Is Crying	1991	$30

VAUGHAN BROTHERS, THE

Number	Title	Yr	NM
CBS ASSOCIATED			
❏ Z46625	Family Style	1990	$25

VAUGHN, BILLY

Number	Title	Yr	NM
ABC			
❏ 4005	16 Great Performances	1974	$12
DOT			
❏ DLP3625 [M]	12 Golden Hits from Latin America	1965	$15
❏ DLP25625 [S]	12 Golden Hits from Latin America	1965	$18
❏ DLP3497 [M]	1962's Greatest Hits	1963	$15
❏ DLP25497 [S]	1962's Greatest Hits	1963	$18
❏ DLP25882	A Current Set of Standards	1968	$12
❏ DLP3751 [M]	Alfie	1966	$15
❏ DLP25751 [S]	Alfie	1966	$18
❏ DLP-25897	Alone with Today	1968	$12
❏ DLP3593 [M]	Another Hit Album!	1964	$15
❏ DLP25593 [S]	Another Hit Album!	1964	$18
❏ DLP25841	As Requested	1968	$12
❏ DLP3458 [M]	A Swingin' Safari	1962	$18
❏ DLP25458 [S]	A Swingin' Safari	1962	$25
❏ DLP3396 [M]	Berlin Melody	1961	$18
❏ DLP25396 [S]	Berlin Melody	1961	$25
❏ DLP3156 [M]	Billy Vaughn Plays	1959	$18
❏ DLP25156 [S]	Billy Vaughn Plays	1959	$25
❏ DLP3260 [M]	Billy Vaughn Plays Stephen Foster	1960	$18
❏ DLP25260 [S]	Billy Vaughn Plays Stephen Foster	1960	$25
❏ DLP3119 [M]	Billy Vaughn Plays the Million Sellers	1958	$18
❏ DLP25119 [S]	Billy Vaughn Plays the Million Sellers	1959	$25
❏ DLP3800 [M]	Billy Vaughn Presents Friends from Rio Playing "Something Stupid"	1967	$15
❏ DLP25800 [S]	Billy Vaughn Presents Friends from Rio Playing "Something Stupid"	1967	$12
❏ DLP3165 [M]	Blue Hawaii	1959	$18
❏ DLP25165 [S]	Blue Hawaii	1959	$25
❏ DLP3559 [M]	Blue Velvet & 1963's Great Hits	1964	$15
❏ DLP25559 [S]	Blue Velvet & 1963's Great Hits	1964	$18
❏ DLP3424 [M]	Chapel by the Sea	1962	$18
❏ DLP25424 [S]	Chapel by the Sea	1962	$25
❏ DLP3148 [M]	Christmas Carols	1958	$18
❏ DLP25985	Everything Is Beautiful	1970	$12
❏ DLP3578 [M]	Forever	1964	$15
❏ DLP25578 [S]	Forever	1964	$18
❏ DLP3201 [M]	Golden Hits	1959	$18
❏ DLP25201 [S]	Golden Hits	1959	$25
❏ DLP3811 [M]	Golden Hits/The Best of Billy Vaughn	1967	$15
❏ DLP25811 [S]	Golden Hits/The Best of Billy Vaughn	1967	$12
❏ DLP3205 [M]	Golden Saxophones	1959	$18
❏ DLP25205 [S]	Golden Saxophones	1959	$25
❏ DLP3280 [M]	Golden Waltzes	1961	$18
❏ DLP25280 [S]	Golden Waltzes	1961	$25
❏ DLP3698 [M]	Great Country Hits	1966	$15
❏ DLP25698 [S]	Great Country Hits	1966	$18
❏ DLP3558 [M]	Greatest Boogie Woogie Hits	1963	$15
❏ DLP25558 [S]	Greatest Boogie Woogie Hits	1963	$18
❏ DLP3409 [M]	Greatest String Band Hits	1962	$18
❏ DLP25409 [S]	Greatest String Band Hits	1962	$25
❏ DLP3288 [M]	Great Golden Hits	1960	$18
❏ DLP25288 [S]	Great Golden Hits	1960	$25
❏ DLP3899	Have Yourself a Merry Merry Christmas	1968	$15
❏ DLP3813 [M]	I Love You	1967	$15

Number	Title	Yr	NM
❏ DLP25813 [S]	I Love You	1967	$12
❏ DLP3045 [M]	Instrumental Souvenirs	1957	$18
❏ DLP3796 [M]	Josephine	1967	$15
❏ DLP25796 [S]	Josephine	1967	$12
❏ DLP3140 [M]	La Paloma	1959	$18
❏ DLP25140 [S]	La Paloma	1959	$25
❏ DLP3275 [M]	Linger Awhile	1960	$18
❏ DLP25275 [S]	Linger Awhile	1960	$25
❏ DLP3322 [M]	Look for a Star	1960	$18
❏ DLP25322 [S]	Look for a Star	1960	$25
❏ DLP3064 [M]	Melodies in Gold	1957	$18
❏ DLP25064 [R]	Melodies in Gold	196?	$12
❏ DLP3628 [M]	Mexican Pearls	1965	$15
❏ DLP25628 [S]	Mexican Pearls	1965	$18
❏ DLP3679 [M]	Michelle	1966	$15
❏ DLP25679 [S]	Michelle	1966	$18
❏ DLP3654 [M]	Moon Over Naples	1965	$15
❏ DLP25654 [S]	Moon Over Naples	1965	$18
❏ DLP3086 [M]	Music for the Golden Hours	1958	$18
❏ DLP25086 [R]	Music for the Golden Hours	196?	$12
❏ DLP25911	Nashville Saxophones	1969	$12
❏ DLP3540 [M]	Number One Hits, Vol. #1	1963	$15
❏ DLP25540 [S]	Number One Hits, Vol. #1	1963	$18
❏ DLP3828 [M]	Ode to Billy Joe	1967	$15
❏ DLP25828 [S]	Ode to Billy Joe	1967	$12
❏ DLP3366 [M]	Orange Blossom Special and Wheels	1961	$18
❏ DLP25366 [S]	Orange Blossom Special and Wheels	1961	$25
❏ DLP3605 [M]	Pearly Shells	1965	$15
❏ DLP25605 [S]	Pearly Shells	1965	$18
❏ DLP25837	Pretty Country	1968	$12
❏ DLP5857	Quietly Wild	1968	$12
❏ DLP3100 [M]	Sail Along Silv'ry Moon	1958	$18
❏ DLP25100 [S]	Sail Along Silv'ry Moon	1959	$25
❏ DLP3523 [M]	Sukiyaki and 11 Hawaiian Hits	1963	$15
❏ DLP25523 [S]	Sukiyaki and 11 Hawaiian Hits	1963	$18
❏ DLP3782 [M]	Sweet Maria	1967	$15
❏ DLP25782 [S]	Sweet Maria	1967	$12
❏ DLP3001 [M]	Sweet Music and Memories	1955	$30
—Maroon label			
❏ DLP3001 [M]	Sweet Music and Memories	1957	$18
—Black label			
❏ DLP25001 [R]	Sweet Music and Memories	196?	$12
❏ DLP3788 [M]	That's Life & Pineapple Market	1967	$15
❏ DLP25788 [S]	That's Life & Pineapple Market	1967	$12
❏ DLP3016 [M]	The Golden Instrumentals	1956	$30
—Maroon label			
❏ DLP3016 [M]	The Golden Instrumentals	1957	$18
—Black label			
❏ DLP25016 [R]	The Golden Instrumentals	196?	$12
❏ DLP3276 [M]	Theme from A Summer Place	1960	$18
❏ DLP25276 [S]	Theme from A Summer Place	1960	$25
❏ DLP3349 [M]	Theme from The Sundowners	1960	$18
❏ DLP25349 [S]	Theme from The Sundowners	1960	$25
❏ DLP3442 [M]	The Shifting, Whispering Sands	1962	$18
❏ DLP25442 [S]	The Shifting, Whispering Sands	1962	$25
❏ DLP25937	The Windmills of Your Mind	1969	$12
❏ DLP25969	True Grit	1969	$12
❏ DLP25975	Winter World of Love	1970	$12
HAMILTON			
❏ HLP113 [M]	Golden Gems	196?	$15
❏ HLP12113 [S]	Golden Gems	196?	$15
❏ HLP162 [M]	Songs I Wrote	196?	$15
❏ HLP12162 [S]	Songs I Wrote	196?	$15
❏ HLP147 [M]	Strauss Waltz Concert	196?	$15
❏ HLP12147 [S]	Strauss Waltz Concert	196?	$15
MCA			
❏ 27018	Blue Hawaii	198?	$10
—Budget-line reissue			
❏ 801	La Paloma	198?	$10
—Budget-line reissue			
❏ 4164	The Best of Billy Vaughn	198?	$15
PARAMOUNT			
❏ PAS-6025	An Old Fashioned Love Song	1972	$12
❏ PAS-1031	Billy Vaughn Plays His Greatest Hits	1974	$15
❏ PAS-6044	Country's Greatest Hits	1973	$12
❏ PAS-1033	Electrified	1974	$12
❏ PAS-5037	I Don't Know How to Love Him	1971	$12
❏ PAS-6035	Soundstage!	1972	$12
❏ PAS-5032	Theme from Love Story	1971	$12
PICKWICK			
❏ SPC-3093	Embraceable You	197?	$12
❏ SPC-3213	Moon River	197?	$12
❏ SPC-3146	Up, Up and Away	197?	$12
RANWOOD			
❏ 7025	Billy Vaughn and His Orchestra Play 22 Greatest Hits	1982	$15

Number	Title	Yr	NM

VAUGHN, FATHER TOM
CONCORD JAZZ
| ❏ CJ-16 | Joyful Jazz | 1976 | $30 |

RCA VICTOR
❏ LPM-3708 [M]	Cornbread (Meat Loaf, Greens and Deviled Eggs)	1967	$50
❏ LSP-3708 [S]	Cornbread (Meat Loaf, Greens and Deviled Eggs)	1967	$35
❏ LPM-3577 [M]	Jazz In Concert at the Village Gate	1966	$35
❏ LSP-3577 [S]	Jazz In Concert at the Village Gate	1966	$50
❏ LPM-3845 [M]	Motor City Soul	1967	$50
❏ LSP-3845 [S]	Motor City Soul	1967	$35

VAUGHN, ROBERT
MGM
| ❏ E-4488 [M] | Readings from Hamlet | 1962 | $30 |
| ❏ SE-4488 [S] | Readings from Hamlet | 1962 | $30 |

VAUGHT, BOB, AND THE RENEGADES
GNP CRESCENDO
| ❏ GNP-83 [M] | Surf Crazy | 1963 | $30 |
| ❏ GNPS-83 [S] | Surf Crazy | 1963 | $40 |

VAZQUEZ, ROLAND
GRP/ARISTA
| ❏ GL5002 | Roland Vazquez and the Urban Ensemble | 1978 | $35 |

HEADFIRST
| ❏ 9710 | Feel Your Dream | 198? | $30 |

SOUNDWINGS
| ❏ SW-2106 | The Tides of Time | 1988 | $25 |

VEE, BOBBY
LIBERTY
❏ LRP-3385 [M]	30 Big Hits From the 60's	1964	$30
❏ LST-7385 [S]	30 Big Hits From the 60's	1964	$30
❏ LRP-3448 [M]	30 Big Hits From the 60's	1966	$30
❏ LST-7448 [S]	30 Big Hits From the 60's, Volume 2	1966	$30
❏ LRP-3232 [M]	A Bobby Vee Recording Session	1962	$30

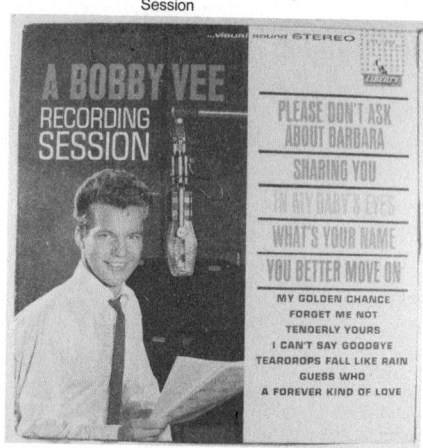

❏ LST-7232 [S]	A Bobby Vee Recording Session	1962	$40
❏ LRP-3181 [M]	Bobby Vee	1961	$40
❏ LST-7181 [S]	Bobby Vee	1961	$50
❏ LRP-3393 [M]	Bobby Vee Live on Tour	1965	$30
❏ LST-7393 [S]	Bobby Vee Live on Tour	1965	$30
❏ LRP-3228 [M]	Bobby Vee Meets the Crickets	1962	$40
❏ LST-7228 [S]	Bobby Vee Meets the Crickets	1962	$50
❏ LRP-3289 [M]	Bobby Vee Meets the Ventures	1963	$40
❏ LST-7289 [S]	Bobby Vee Meets the Ventures	1963	$50
❏ LRP-3245 [M]	Bobby Vee's Golden Greats	1962	$30
❏ LST-7245 [S]	Bobby Vee's Golden Greats	1962	$40
❏ LM-51008	Bobby Vee's Golden Greats	198?	$10
❏ LRP-3464 [M]	Bobby Vee's Golden Greats, Volume 2	1966	$25
❏ LST-7464 [S]	Bobby Vee's Golden Greats, Volume 2	1966	$30
❏ LRP-3205 [M]	Bobby Vee Sings Hits of the Rockin' 50's	1961	$40
❏ LST-7205 [S]	Bobby Vee Sings Hits of the Rockin' 50's	1961	$50
❏ LRP-3352 [M]	Bobby Vee Sings the New Sound from England!	1964	$30
❏ LST-7352 [S]	Bobby Vee Sings the New Sound from England!	1964	$30
❏ LRP-3165 [M]	Bobby Vee Sings Your Favorites	1960	$50
❏ LST-7165 [S]	Bobby Vee Sings Your Favorites	1960	$100
❏ LRP-3186 [M]	Bobby Vee With Strings and Things	1961	$40

Number	Title	Yr	NM
❏ LST-7186 [S]	Bobby Vee With Strings and Things	1961	$50
❏ LRP-3534 [M]	Come Back When You Grow Up	1967	$25
❏ LST-7534 [S]	Come Back When You Grow Up	1967	$30
❏ LST-7592	Do What You Gotta Do	1968	$30
❏ LST-7612	Gates, Grills and Railings	1969	$30
❏ LRP-3336 [M]	I Remember Buddy Holly	1963	$40
❏ LST-7336 [S]	I Remember Buddy Holly	1963	$50
❏ LN-10223	I Remember Buddy Holly	198?	$10
❏ LST-7554 [S]	Just Today	1968	$30
❏ LST-3554 [M]	Just Today	1968	$40

—Cover is stereo with "Audition Mono Not for Sale" sticker, but the label is regular stock mono

❏ LRP-3480 [M]	Look at Me Girl	1966	$25
❏ LST-7480 [S]	Look at Me Girl	1966	$30
❏ LRP-3267 [M]	Merry Christmas from Bobby Vee	1962	$30
❏ LST-7267 [S]	Merry Christmas from Bobby Vee	1962	$40
❏ LRP-3211 [M]	Take Good Care of My Baby	1962	$30
❏ LST-7211 [S]	Take Good Care of My Baby	1962	$40
❏ LRP-3285 [M]	The Night Has a Thousand Eyes	1963	$30
❏ LST-7285 [S]	The Night Has a Thousand Eyes	1963	$40

SUNSET
❏ SUM-1162 [M]	A Forever Kind of Love	1967	$12
❏ SUS-5162 [S]	A Forever Kind of Love	1967	$15
❏ SUM-1111 [M]	Bobby Vee	1966	$12
❏ SUS-5111 [S]	Bobby Vee	1966	$15
❏ SUM-1186 [M]	The Christmas Album	1967	$15

—Reissue of Liberty album with two fewer tracks

| ❏ SUS-5186 [S] | The Christmas Album | 1967 | $15 |

UNITED ARTISTS
| ❏ LT-1008 | Bobby Vee's Golden Greats | 1980 | $12 |
| ❏ UA-LA025-G2 | Legendary Masters Series | 1973 | $300 |

—Withdrawn before release, but a few copies survived

❏ UAS-5656	Nothin' Like a Sunny Day	1972	$15
❏ UA-LA085-G	Robert Thomas Velline	1973	$25
❏ UA-LA332-E	The Very Best of Bobby Vee	1975	$15

VEGA, AL
PRESTIGE
| ❏ PRLP-152 [10] | Al Vega Piano Solos With Bongos | 1953 | $300 |

VEGA, SUZANNE
A&M
| ❏ 7502152931 | Days of Open Hand | 1990 | $15 |
| ❏ SP-17472 [DJ] | Portrait of an Artist | 1987 | $18 |

—Promo-only 7-song sampler

| ❏ SP-5136 | Solitude Standing | 1987 | $10 |
| ❏ SP-6-5072 | Suzanne Vega | 1985 | $12 |

VEGA, TATA
TAMLA
❏ T6-347S1	Full Speed Ahead	1976	$18
❏ T8-370M1	Givin' All My Love	1980	$30
❏ T6-353S1	Totally Tata	1977	$18
❏ T7-360R1	Try My Love	1978	$18

VEGA BROTHERS, THE
MCA
| ❏ 5686 | The Vega Brothers | 1986 | $10 |

VEGAS, PAT AND LOLLY
Also see REDBONE.
MERCURY
| ❏ MG-21059 [M] | At the Haunted House | 1966 | $30 |
| ❏ SR-61059 [S] | At the Haunted House | 1966 | $40 |

VELASCO, VI
VEE JAY
| ❏ VJ-1135 [M] | The Vi Velasco Album | 1965 | $25 |

VELEZ, GLEN
CMP
❏ CMP-42-ST	Assyrian Rose	1989	$25
❏ CMP-23-ST	Internal Combustion	1987	$25
❏ CMP-30-ST	Seven Heaven	1988	$25

VELEZ, MARTHA
POLYDOR
| ❏ PD5034 | Hypnotized | 1972 | $18 |
SIRE
| ❏ SR6040 | American Heartbeat | 1977 | $12 |
| ❏ SASD-7515 | Escape from Babylon | 1976 | $12 |

—Produced by Bob Marley

| ❏ SES-97008 | Fiends and Angels | 1969 | $30 |
| ❏ SES-7409 | Matinee Weepers | 1973 | $18 |

VELVET, JIMMY
UNITED ARTISTS
| ❏ UAS-6653 | A Touch of Velvet | 1968 | $30 |
VELVET TONE
| ❏ 501 | A Touch of Velvet | 1968 | $75 |

Number	Title	Yr	NM

VELVET ELVIS
ENIGMA
| ❏ 73300 [B] | Velvet Elvis | 1988 | $15 |

VELVET MONKEYS
ROUGH TRADE
| ❏ RUS102 | Rake | 1990 | $15 |

—Band includes Thurston Moore (Sonic Youth), J Mascis (Dinosaur Jr), etc.

VELVET NIGHT
METROMEDIA
| ❏ MD-1028 | Velvet Night | 1970 | $30 |

VELVET REVOLVER
Consists of members of GUNS N' ROSES and STONE TEMPLE PILOTS.
RCA
| ❏ 59794-1 | Contraband | 2004 | $30 |

VELVET UNDERGROUND, THE
Includes releases with NICO. Also see JOHN CALE; LOU REED.
4 MEN WITH BEARDS
❏ 4M137LP [B]	Another View		$25
❏ 4M154LP [B]	The Velvet Underground & Nico		$25
❏ 4M156LP [B]	Velvet Underground		$25
❏ 4M136LP [B]	VU: A Collection of Previously Unreleased Recordings		$25
❏ 4M155LP [B]	White Light/White Heat		$25

COTILLION
| ❏ SD9500 [DJ] | Live at Max's Kansas City | 1972 | $85 |

—White label promo with "d/j copy monaural" sticker on front cover, which in this case is odd because all copies are mono!

| ❏ SD9500 | Live at Max's Kansas City | 1972 | $25 |

—Original pressing has a light blue label

| ❏ SD9500 | Live at Max's Kansas City | 197? | $18 |

—Reissue with purplish label

| ❏ SD9500 | Live at Max's Kansas City | 198? | $15 |

—Reissue with purplish label and bar code on back cover

| ❏ SD9500 | Live at Max's Kansas City | 2001 | $12 |

—Rhino/Scorpio reissue; light blue label

| ❏ SD9034 [S] | Loaded | 1970 | $175 |

—White label promo; not the monaural version, this one has no sticker on the cover and has the "SD" prefix on the label

| ❏ SD9034 [S] | Loaded | 1970 | $25 |

—Original pressing has a light blue label

| ❏ SD9034 [S] | Loaded | 197? | $18 |

—Reissue with purplish label

| ❏ SD9034 [S] | Loaded | 198? | $15 |

—Reissue with purplish label and bar code on back cover

| ❏ 9034 [M] | Loaded | 1970 | $1250 |

—Mono is white label promo only; "d/j copy monaural" sticker on front cover; no "SD" prefix on label

| ❏ SD9034 [S] | Loaded | 2001 | $12 |

—Rhino/Scorpio reissue; purplish label

| ❏ R19034 [B] | Loaded | 2014 | $40 |

MERCURY
| ❏ SRM-2-7504 [B] | 1969 (Live) | 1974 | $18 |

—Reissues with Chicago skyline labels

| ❏ SRM-2-7504 | 1969 (Live) | 1974 | $50 |

—Originals with red labels

| ❏ SRM-2-7504 [DJ] | 1969 (Live) | 1974 | $150 |

—White label promo

| ❏ SRM-2-7504 | 1969 (Live) | 1983 | $25 |

—Reissue with black labels; non-gatefold cover; no bar code on back

MGM
| ❏ M3G4950 | Archetypes | 1974 | $25 |
| ❏ M3G4950 [DJ] | Archetypes | 1974 | $40 |

—White label promo

| ❏ SW-95722 | Archetypes | 1974 | $30 |

—Longines Symphonette edition

| ❏ SE-4617 | The Velvet Underground | 1969 | $50 |

—With "BMI" publishing credit

| ❏ SE-4617 [DJ] | The Velvet Underground | 1969 | $400 |

—Yellow label promo

| ❏ SE-4617 [DJ] | The Velvet Underground | 1969 | $300 |

—White label promo

| ❏ SE-4617 | The Velvet Underground | 1971 | $40 |

—With "ASCAP" publishing credit

| ❏ GAS-131 | The Velvet Underground (Golden Archive Series) | 1970 | $40 |

—Blue and gold label stock copy

| ❏ GAS-131 [DJ] | The Velvet Underground (Golden Archive Series) | 1970 | $150 |

—Yellow label promo

| ❏ GAS-131 [DJ] | The Velvet Underground (Golden Archive Series) | 1970 | $150 |

—White label promo

POLYDOR
| ❏ B0017649-01 [B] | Scepter Studios Sessions | 2012 | $30 |
| ❏ 8232901 [S] | The Velvet Underground and Nico | 2008 | $25 |

Number	Title	Yr	NM
❏ B0022028-01 [B]	Velvet Underground	2015	$25
PRIDE			
❏ 0022	Lou Reed and the Velvet Underground	1973	$18

—Tan label; label calls this "That's the Story of My Life

❏ 0022 [DJ]	Lou Reed and the Velvet Underground	1973	$50

—White label; label calls this "That's the Story of My Life

SUNDAZED			
❏ VU4002 [M]	The Quine Tapes	2010	$250
❏ VU4003 [B]	The Verve/MGM Albums	2012	$250
❏ LP5466 [B]	Velvet Underground	2014	$30
VERVE			
❏ 826284-1	1969 (Live)	1985	$15

—Reissue of Mercury SRM-2-7504

❏ 829405-1	Another View	1986	$15
❏ 815454-1	The Velvet Underground	1985	$15

—Reissue of MGM SE-4617

❏ V-5008 [M]	The Velvet Underground and Nico	1967	$500

—Version 1: With peel-off banana peel, photo of band framed by a male torso (deduct 50% if banana sticker is gone)

❏ V-5008 [M]	The Velvet Underground and Nico	1967	$800

—Version 2: With peel-off banana peel, photo of torso obscured by a large black sticker (deduct 50% if stickers removed)

❏ V-5008 [M]	The Velvet Underground and Nico	1967	$500

—Version 3: With peel-off banana peel, torso is airbrushed off the cover (deduct 50% if banana sticker removed)

❏ V6-5008 [S]	The Velvet Underground and Nico	1967	$600

—Version 1: With peel-off banana peel, photo of band framed by a male torso (deduct 50% if banana sticker is gone)

❏ V6-5008 [S]	The Velvet Underground and Nico	1967	$250

—Version 2: With peel-off banana peel, photo of torso obscured by a sticker (deduct 50% if stickers removed)

❏ V6-5008 [S]	The Velvet Underground and Nico	1967	$175

—Version 3: With peel-off banana peel, torso is airbrushed off the cover, publishing on label is credited to "Three Prong Music" (deduct 50% if banana sticker removed)

❏ V6-5008 [S]	The Velvet Underground and Nico	1970	$100

—Version 5: With peel-off banana; blue label with silver "T" shape on it; publishing on the label is credited to "Oakfield Avenue Music"

❏ 823290-1	The Velvet Underground and Nico	1985	$15

—Reissue of Verve V6-5008

❏ V-5008 [M]	The Velvet Underground and Nico	1967	$2000

—Promo copy; white label

❏ V-5008 [M]	The Velvet Underground and Nico	1967	$2000

—Promo copy; yellow label

❏ V6-5008 [S]	The Velvet Underground and Nico	1968	$150

—Version 4: With peel-off banana peel, torso is airbrushed off the cover, publishing on label is credited to "Oakfield Avenue Music," Side 2 trail-off wax has an "RE-1" (deduct 50% if banana sticker removed)

❏ V6-5008 [S]	The Velvet Underground and Nico	1973	$80

—Version 6: Same as Version 5 except the label is now white with "MGM" at left and "Verve" at right

❏ V6-5008 [S]	The Velvet Underground and Nico	1975	$50

—Version 7: Same as Version 5, but the label is now black with silver T-shape

❏ V6-5008 [S]	The Velvet Underground and Nico	1978	$30

—Version 8: The cover is no longer a gatefold

❏ 823721-1	VU	1985	$15
❏ V-5046 [M]	White Light/White Heat	1967	$2000

—White label promo

❏ V-5046 [M]	White Light/White Heat	1967	$1200

—Version 1: "Skeleton" cover -- a black-on-black skeleton is visible when cover is viewed at an angle

❏ V-5046 [M]	White Light/White Heat	1967	$1000

—Version 2: No "skeleton" on cover

❏ V6-5046 [S]	White Light/White Heat	1967	$300

—Yellow label promo

❏ V6-5046 [S]	White Light/White Heat	1967	$40

—Version 2: No "skeleton" on cover; publishing on label is credited to "Three Prong Music

❏ V6-5046 [S]	White Light/White Heat	1967	$100

—Version 1: "Skeleton" cover -- a black-on-black skeleton is visible when cover is viewed at an angle

❏ 825119-1	White Light/White Heat	1985	$15

—Reissue of Verve V6-5046

❏ V-5046 [M]	White Light/White Heat	1967	$1500

—Yellow label promo

❏ V6-5046 [S]	White Light/White Heat	1968	$30

—Version 3: No "skeleton" on cover; publishing on label is credited to "Oakfield Avenue Music

Number	Title	Yr	NM
VENTURA, CAROL			
PRESTIGE			
❏ PRLP-7358 [M]	Carol!	1965	$30
❏ PRST-7358 [S]	Carol!	1965	$30
❏ PRLP-7405 [M]	I Love to Sing!	1965	$30
❏ PRST-7405 [S]	I Love to Sing!	1965	$30

VENTURA, CHARLIE, AND MARY ANN MCCALL

NORGRAN			
❏ MGN-20 [10]	An Evening with Mary Ann McCall and Charlie Ventura	1954	$250
❏ MGN-1053 [M]	An Evening with Mary Ann McCall and Charlie Ventura	1955	$250
❏ MGN-1013 [M]	Another Evening with Charlie Ventura and Mary Ann McCall	1954	$300
VERVE			
❏ MGV-8143 [M]	An Evening with Mary Ann McCall and Charlie Ventura	1957	$150
❏ V-8143 [M]	An Evening with Mary Ann McCall and Charlie Ventura	1961	$30

VENTURA, CHARLIE

BATON			
❏ 1202 [M]	New Charlie Ventura in Hi-Fi	1957	$50
BRUNSWICK			
❏ BL54025 [M]	Here's Charlie	1957	$100
CLEF			
❏ MGC-117 [10]	Charlie Ventura Collates	1953	$350
CORAL			
❏ CRL56067 [10]	Open House	1952	$175
CRAFTSMAN			
❏ 8039 [M]	Charlie Ventura Plays for the People	1960	$30
CRYSTALETTE			
❏ 5000 [10]	Stomping With the Sax	1950	$250
DECCA			
❏ DL8046 [M]	Charlie Ventura Concert	1954	$150
EMARCY			
❏ MG-26028 [10]	F.Y.I. Ventura	1954	$250
❏ MG-36015 [M]	Jumping with Ventura	1955	$250
FAMOUS DOOR			
❏ 115	Chazz '77	1977	$25
GENE NORMAN			
❏ GNP-1 [M]	Charlie Ventura In Concert	1954	$150
GNP CRESCENDO			
❏ GNP-1 [M]	Charlie Ventura In Concert	196?	$30
❏ GNPS-1 [R]	Charlie Ventura In Concert	196?	$25
HALL OF FAME			
❏ 605	Charlie Ventura Quintet	197?	$25
IMPERIAL			
❏ IM-3002 [10]	Charlie Ventura and His Sextet	1953	$300
KING			
❏ 543 [M]	Adventure with Charlie Ventura	1958	$100
MCA			
❏ 42330	Gene Norman Presents a Charlie Ventura Concert	1990	$30
MERCURY			
❏ MGC-117 [10]	Charlie Ventura Collates	1952	$300
MOSAIC			
❏ MQ9-182	The Complete Verve/Clef Charlie Ventura/Flip Phillips Studio Sessions	199?	$300
NORGRAN			
❏ MGN-1075 [M]	Blue Saxophone	1956	$100
❏ MGN-1103 [M]	Charley's Parley	1956	$250
❏ MGN-1073 [M]	Charlie Ventura in a Jazz Mood	1956	$250
❏ MGN-8 [10]	Charlie Ventura Quartet	1953	$300
❏ MGN-1041 [M]	Charlie Ventura's Carnegie Hall Concert	1955	$250
PHOENIX			
❏ 6	Charlie Boy	197?	$25
RCA VICTOR			
❏ LPM-1135 [M]	It's All Bop to Me	1955	$120
REGENT			
❏ MG-6064 [M]	East of Suez	1958	$50
SAVOY JAZZ			
❏ SJL-2243	Euphoria	198?	$30
TOPS			
❏ L-1528 [M]	Charlie Ventura Plays Hi-Fi Jazz	1958	$30
TRIP			
❏ 5536	Jumping with Ventura	197?	$25
VERVE			
❏ V-8165 [M]	Blue Saxophone	1961	$30
❏ MGV-8165 [M]	Blue Saxophone	1957	$175
❏ V-8132 [M]	Charlie Ventura'a Carnegie Hall Concert	1961	$30
❏ MGV-8163 [M]	Charlie Ventura in a Jazz Mood	1957	$175

Number	Title	Yr	NM
❏ V-8163 [M]	Charlie Ventura in a Jazz Mood	1961	$30
❏ MGV-8132 [M]	Charlie Ventura's Carnegie Hall Concert	1957	$175
ZIM			
❏ 1004	Charlie Ventura in Chicago	197?	$25

VENTURA, CHARLIE/CHARLIE KENNEDY

REGENT			
❏ MG-6047 [M]	Crazy Rhythms	1957	$75
SAVOY			
❏ MG-12200	Crazy Rhythms	197?	$30

VENTURA, RAY

ATLANTIC			
❏ 8011 [M]	Hi-Fi Music for Young Parisians	1956	$50

—Black label

DOT			
❏ DLP-3120 [M]	La Belle Bardot	1958	$50

—Brigitte Bardot is the cover model

VENTURAS, THE

DRUM BOY			
❏ DBM-1003 [M]	Here They Are	1964	$250
❏ DBS-1003 [S]	Here They Are	1964	$300

VENTURES, THE

COMPLEAT			
❏ 672013-1	The Best of the Ventures	1986	$12
DOLTON			
❏ BLP2006 [M]	Another Smash!!!	1961	$150

—Pale blue label with dolphins on top

❏ BLP2006 [M]	Another Smash!!!	1963	$50

—Dark label, logo on left

❏ BST8006 [S]	Another Smash!!!	1961	$75

—Pale blue label with dolphins on top

❏ BST8006 [S]	Another Smash!!!	1963	$30

—Dark label, logo on left

❏ BLP2016 [M]	Beach Party	1963	$50

—Retitled version of "Mashed Potatoes and Gravy

❏ BST8016 [S]	Beach Party	1963	$30

—Retitled version of "Mashed Potatoes and Gravy

❏ BLP2010 [M]	Dance!	1963	$50

—Dark label, logo on left; retitled version of "Twist with the Ventures

❏ BST8010 [S]	Dance!	1963	$30

—Dark label, logo on left; retitled version of "Twist with the Ventures

❏ BLP2014 [M]	Dance with the Ventures	1963	$50

—Dark label, logo on left' retitled version of "The Ventures' Twist Party, Vol. 2

❏ BST8014 [S]	Dance with the Ventures	1963	$30

—Dark label, logo on left' retitled version of "The Ventures' Twist Party, Vol. 2

❏ BLP2017 [M]	Going to the Ventures Dance Party!	1962	$75
❏ BST8017 [S]	Going to the Ventures Dance Party!	1962	$40
❏ BLP2045 [M]	Go with the Ventures!	1966	$50
❏ BST8045 [S]	Go with the Ventures!	1966	$30
❏ BLP2050 [M]	Guitar Freakout	1967	$50
❏ BST8050 [S]	Guitar Freakout	1967	$30
❏ BLP2024 [M]	Let's Go!	1963	$75
❏ BST8024 [S]	Let's Go!	1963	$30
❏ BLP2016 [M]	Mashed Potatoes and Gravy	1962	$75
❏ BST8016 [S]	Mashed Potatoes and Gravy	1962	$40
❏ BLP16501 [M]	Play Guitar with the Ventures	1965	$75
❏ BST17501 [S]	Play Guitar with the Ventures	1965	$30
❏ BLP16502 [M]	Play Guitar with the Ventures, Vol. 2	196?	$75
❏ BST17502 [S]	Play Guitar with the Ventures, Vol. 2	196?	$30
❏ BLP16503 [M]	Play Guitar with the Ventures, Vol. 3	196?	$75
❏ BST17503 [S]	Play Guitar with the Ventures, Vol. 3	196?	$30
❏ BLP16504 [M]	Play Guitar with the Ventures, Vol. 4	196?	$75
❏ BST16504 [S]	Play Guitar with the Ventures, Vol. 4	196?	$30
❏ BLP2022 [M]	Surfing	1963	$75
❏ BST8022 [S]	Surfing	1963	$30
❏ BLP2008 [M]	The Colorful Ventures	1961	$150

—Pale blue label with dolphins on top

❏ BLP2008 [M]	The Colorful Ventures	1963	$50

—Dark label, logo on left

❏ BST8008 [S]	The Colorful Ventures	1961	$75

—Pale blue label with dolphins on top

❏ BST8008 [S]	The Colorful Ventures	1963	$30

—Dark label, logo on left

❏ BLP2029 [M]	The Fabulous Ventures	1964	$75
❏ BST8029 [S]	The Fabulous Ventures	1964	$30
❏ BLP2004 [M]	The Ventures	1961	$150

—Pale blue label with dolphins on top

❏ BLP2004 [M]	The Ventures	1963	$25

Number	Title	Yr	NM

—Dark label, logo on left
| ❑ BST8004 [S] | The Ventures | 1961 | $75 |

—Pale blue label with dolphins on top
| ❑ BST8004 [S] | The Ventures | 1963 | $30 |

—Dark label, logo on left
❑ BLP2037 [M]	The Ventures A-Go-Go	1965	$75
❑ BST8037 [S]	The Ventures A-Go-Go	1965	$30
❑ BLP2042 [M]	The Ventures/Batman Theme	1966	$75
❑ BST8042 [S]	The Ventures/Batman Theme	1966	$40
❑ BLP-2038 [M]	The Ventures' Christmas Album	1965	$75
❑ BST-8038 [S]	The Ventures' Christmas Album	1965	$25
❑ BLP2027 [M]	(The) Ventures in Space	1964	$100
❑ BST8027 [S]	(The) Ventures in Space	1964	$50
❑ BLP2033 [M]	The Ventures Knock Me Out!	1965	$75
❑ BST8033 [S]	The Ventures Knock Me Out!	1965	$30
❑ BLP2035 [M]	The Ventures on Stage	1965	$75
❑ BST8035 [S]	The Ventures on Stage	1965	$30
❑ BLP2019 [M]	The Ventures Play Telstar, The Lonely Bull	1962	$75
❑ BST8019 [S]	The Ventures Play Telstar, The Lonely Bull	1962	$40
❑ BLP2023 [M]	The Ventures Play the Country Classics	1963	$75
❑ BST8023 [S]	The Ventures Play the Country Classics	1963	$30
❑ BLP2014 [M]	The Ventures' Twist Party, Vol. 2	1962	$150

—Pale blue label with dolphins on top
| ❑ BST8014 [S] | The Ventures' Twist Party, Vol. 2 | 1962 | $75 |

—Pale blue label with dolphins on top
| ❑ BLP2010 [M] | Twist with the Ventures | 1962 | $150 |

—Pale blue label with dolphins on top
| ❑ BST8010 [S] | Twist with the Ventures | 1962 | $75 |

—Pale blue label with dolphins on top
❑ BLP2031 [M]	Walk, Don't Run, Vol. 2	1964	$75
❑ BST8031 [S]	Walk, Don't Run, Vol. 2	1964	$30
❑ BLP2003 [M]	Walk Don't Run	1960	$150

—Pale blue label with dolphins on top
| ❑ BLP2003 [M] | Walk Don't Run | 1963 | $25 |

—Dark label, logo on left
| ❑ BST8003 [S] | Walk Don't Run | 1960 | $75 |

—Pale blue label with dolphins on top

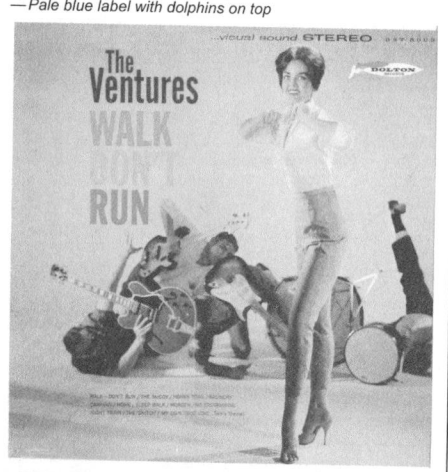

| ❑ BST8003 [S] | Walk Don't Run | 1963 | $30 |

—Dark label, logo on left
❑ BLP2040 [M]	Where the Action Is	1966	$25
❑ BST8040 [S]	Where the Action Is	1966	$30
❑ BLP2047 [M]	Wild Things!	1966	$25
❑ BST8047 [S]	Wild Things!	1966	$30

LIBERTY
❑ LRP-2054 [M]	$1,000,000.00 Weekend	1967	$35
❑ LST-8054 [S]	$1,000,000.00 Weekend	1967	$25
❑ LST-8052 [S]	Changing Times	1970	$40
—Reissue of "Super Psychedelics"
❑ LRP-2055 [M]	Flights of Fancy	1968	$30
❑ LST-8055 [S]	Flights of Fancy	1968	$25
❑ LRP-2053 [M]	Golden Greats by the Ventures	1967	$25
❑ LST-8053 [S]	Golden Greats by the Ventures	1967	$25
❑ LTAO-8053	Golden Greats by the Ventures	1981	$10
❑ LST-8061	Hawaii Five-O	1969	$18
❑ LST-8023	I Walk the Line and Other Giant Hits	1970	$25
—Reissue of "The Ventures Play the Country Classics"
| ❑ LST-8060 | More Golden Greats | 1970 | $18 |
| ❑ LST-8057 | On the Scene | 1970 | $18 |
—Reissue of "The Horse"
| ❑ LST-8050 | Revolving Sounds | 1970 | $30 |
—Reissue of "Guitar Freakout"
| ❑ LRP-2052 [M] | Super Psychedelics | 1967 | $25 |
| ❑ LST-8052 [S] | Super Psychedelics | 1967 | $30 |

Number	Title	Yr	NM
❑ LST-8062 [B]	Swamp Rock	1969	$18
❑ LST-8057	The Horse	1968	$25
❑ LN-10203	The Ventures	1984	$10
❑ LST-35000	The Ventures 10th Anniversary Album	1970	$25
❑ LN-10190	(The) Ventures in Space	1984	$10
❑ LN-10155	The Ventures Play Telstar, The Lonely Bull	1981	$10
❑ LN-10156	The Ventures Play the Country Classics	1981	$10
❑ LN-10122	The Very Best of the Ventures	1981	$10
❑ LN-10224	TV Themes	1984	$10
❑ LST-8059	Underground Fire	1969	$25
❑ LST-8031	Walk, Don't Run, Vol. 2	1970	$30
—Reissue of Dolton 8031 with new cover
| ❑ LN-10188 | Walk, Don't Run, Vol. 2 | 1984 | $10 |
| ❑ LST-8003 [B] | Walk Don't Run | 1970 | $18 |
—Reissue of Dolton 8003 with new front cover, original back cover
| ❑ LST-8003 | Walk Don't Run | 1970 | $25 |
—Reissue of Dolton 8003 with new front and back covers
| ❑ LT-8003 | Walk Don't Run | 1981 | $10 |

SUNDAZED
❑ LP5398 [B]	Another Smash	2013	$25
❑ LP5400 [B]	Mashed Potatoes and Gravy	2013	$25
❑ LP5399 [B]	The Colorful Ventures	2013	$25
❑ LP5397 [B]	The Ventures	2013	$25
❑ LP5396 [B]	Walk Don't Run	2013	$25

SUNSET
❑ SUS-5317	A Decade with the Ventures	1970	$15
❑ SUS-5270	Super Group	1969	$15
❑ SUM-1160 [M]	The Guitar Genius of the Ventures	1967	$15
❑ SUS-5160 [S]	The Guitar Genius of the Ventures	1967	$18

UNITED ARTISTS
❑ UAS-5575	Joy/The Ventures Play the Classics	1972	$15
❑ UAS-6796	New Testament	1971	$15
❑ UA-LA147-G	Only Hits	1973	$18
❑ UAS-5649	Rock and Roll Forever	1972	$15
❑ UA-LA586-F	Rocky Road	1976	$15
❑ UA-LA217-E	The Jim Croce Songbook	1973	$15
❑ UAS-5547	Theme from Shaft	1971	$15
❑ UXS-80	The Ventures	1971	$18
❑ UA-LA331-E	The Very Best of the Ventures	1974	$15
❑ UA-LA717-F	TV Themes	1977	$30

VENUTA, BENAY
MERCURY
| ❑ MG-25006 [10] | Old Time Favorites | 1949 | $80 |

VENUTI, JOE, AND DAVE MCKENNA
CHIAROSCURO
| ❑ 160 | Alone at the Palace | 1977 | $30 |

VENUTI, JOE, AND EARL HINES
CHIAROSCURO
| ❑ 145 | Hot Sonatas | 1975 | $30 |

VENUTI, JOE, AND GEORGE BARNES
CONCORD JAZZ
| ❑ CJ-14 | Gems | 197? | $30 |
| ❑ CJ-30 | Live at the Concord Summer Festival | 197? | $30 |

VENUTI, JOE, AND LOUIS PRIMA
DESIGN
| ❑ DLP-54 [M] | Hi-Fi Lootin' | 195? | $25 |

VENUTI, JOE, AND MARIAN MCPARTLAND
HALCYON
| ❑ 112 | Maestro and Friend | 197? | $30 |

VENUTI, JOE, AND ZOOT SIMS
CHIAROSCURO
| ❑ 128 | Joe and Zoot | 197? | $35 |
| ❑ 142 | Joe Venuti and Zoot Sims | 1975 | $30 |

VENUTI, JOE
AUDIOPHILE
| ❑ AP-118 | Incredible | 197? | $25 |
CHIAROSCURO
| ❑ 134 | Blue Four | 1975 | $30 |
| ❑ 203 | The Best of Joe Venuti | 1979 | $25 |
EVEREST ARCHIVE OF FOLK & JAZZ
| ❑ 349 | Joe Venuti and the Dutch Swing College Band | 197? | $25 |
FLYING FISH
| ❑ FF-077 | Joe in Chicago, 1978 | 1979 | $30 |
GOLDEN CREST
| ❑ GC-3100 [M] | Joe Venuti Plays Gershwin | 1959 | $30 |
| ❑ GC-3101 [M] | Joe Venuti Plays Jerome Kern | 1959 | $30 |

Number	Title	Yr	NM
GRAND AWARD
| ❑ GA-33-351 [M] | Fiddle on Fire | 1956 | $40 |
PAUSA
| ❑ 7034 | Doin' Things | 197? | $25 |
TOPS
| ❑ L923 [10] | Twilight on the Trail | 195? | $30 |
VANGUARD
| ❑ VSD-79405 | Jazz Violin | 197? | $25 |
| ❑ VSD-79396 | Joe Venuti in Milan | 197? | $25 |
YAZOO
| ❑ 1062 | Violin Jazz | 198? | $25 |

VENUTI, JOE/EDDIE LANG
COLUMBIA
| ❑ C2L24 [M] | Swinging the Blues | 1965 | $25 |
—Red labels with "360 Sound Mono" on labels
| ❑ C2L24 [M] | Swinging the Blues | 1963 | $30 |
—Guaranteed High Fidelity" on labels
COLUMBIA SPECIAL PRODUCTS
| ❑ JC2L24 [M] | Swinging the Blues | 1975 | $35 |
—Reissue of C2L 24
X
| ❑ LVA-3036 [M] | Joe Venuti and Eddie Lang | 1955 | $50 |

VER PLANCK, BILLY
SAVOY
| ❑ MG-12101 [M] | Dancing Jazz | 1957 | $40 |
| ❑ MG-12121 [M] | Jazz for Playgirls | 1957 | $40 |

VER PLANCK, MARLENE
AUDIOPHILE
❑ AP-160	A New York Singer	1980	$25
❑ AP-169	A Warmer Place	1981	$25
❑ AP-186	I Like to Sing	1984	$25
❑ AP-138	Marlene Ver Planck Loves Johnny Mercer	197?	$25
❑ AP-218	Marlene Ver Planck Sings Alec Wilder	1986	$25
❑ AP-235	Pure and Natural	1988	$25
❑ AP-121	You'd Better Love Me	197?	$25
MOUNTED
| ❑ 108 | A Breath of Fresh Air | 1968 | $35 |
| ❑ 114 | This Happy Feeling | 197? | $35 |
SAVOY
| ❑ MG-12058 [M] | I Think of You with Every Breath I Take | 1956 | $150 |
—As "Marlene

VERA, BILLY, AND JUDY CLAY
ATLANTIC
| ❑ 8174 [M] | Storybook Children | 1967 | $30 |
| ❑ SD8174 [S] | Storybook Children | 1967 | $30 |

VERA, BILLY
ALFA
| ❑ 10001 | Billy and the Beaters | 1981 | $18 |
| ❑ 10012 | Billy Vera | 1982 | $15 |
ATLANTIC
| ❑ SD8197 [S] | With Pen in Hand | 1968 | $30 |
| ❑ 8197 [M] | With Pen in Hand | 1968 | $40 |
CAPITOL
| ❑ C1-46948 | Retro Nuevo | 1988 | $12 |
MACOLA
| ❑ 0961 | The Billy Vera Album | 1987 | $12 |
—Reissue of Midsong Int'l. LP
MIDSONG INT'L.
| ❑ BKL1-2219 | Out of the Darkness | 1977 | $15 |
RHINO
| ❑ RNLP70858 | By Request -- The Best of Billy Vera and the Beaters | 1986 | $15 |
| ❑ RNLP70185 | The Atlantic Years | 1987 | $12 |
THUNDER
| ❑ TVLP 0018 | The Hollywood Sessions | 1987 | $12 |

VERDON, GWEN
RCA VICTOR
| ❑ LPM-1152 [M] | The Girl I Left Home For | 1956 | $40 |

VERGARI, MADELINE
SEA BREEZE
| ❑ SB-108 | This Is My Lucky Day | 198? | $25 |

VERHEYEN, CARL
CMG
| ❑ CML-8012 | No Borders | 198? | $25 |

VERITY, JOHN, BAND
ABC DUNHILL
| ❑ DSX-50170 | The John Verity Band | 1974 | $25 |

Number	Title	Yr	NM
VERLAINE, TOM			
Also see TELEVISION.			
ELEKTRA			
6E-216	Tom Verlaine	1979	$18
I.R.S.			
42050	Flash Light	1987	$12
WARNER BROS.			
25144	Cover	1984	$12
BSK3539	Dreamtime	1981	$12
BSK3685 [B]	Words from the Front	1982	$12
VERNE, LARRY			
ERA			
104 [M]	Mister Larry Verne	1961	$75
VERNON, KENNY			
CAPITOL			
ST-11227	Loversville	1973	$15
CHART			
CHS-1018	Country Happening	1969	$18
CHS-1038	Nashville Union Station Depot	1971	$18
MERCURY			
SRM-1-606	Country Giants	1970	$18
VERNON, MILLI			
AUDIOPHILE			
AP-178 [B]	Old Shoes	1989	$12
— As "Millie Vernon"			
STORYVILLE			
STLP-910 [M]	Introducing Milli Vernon	1956	$300
VERSATONES, THE			
RCA VICTOR			
LPM-1538 [M]	The Versatones	1957	$150
VERUCA SALT			
BEYOND			
78103	Resolver	2000	$15
GEFFEN			
22121 [EP]	Blow It Out Your Ass, It's Veruca Salt	1996	$15
MINTY FRESH			
MF-7 [B]	American Thighs	1994	$25
MF-19	Eight Arms to Hold You	1997	$18
MF-9 [10]	Nunber One Blind	1995	$15
— Pink vinyl			
VERY SPECIAL ENVOY			
ROULETTE			
SR-42003	Very Special Envoy	1968	$25
VESALA, EDWARD			
ECM			
1088	Satu	197?	$30
VETTES, THE			
MGM			
E-4193 [M]	Rev-Up	1963	$150
SE-4193 [S]	Rev-Up	1963	$120
VIBRATION SOCIETY, THE			
STASH			
ST-261	The Music of Rahsaan Roland Kirk	1986	$25
VIBRATIONS, THE			
CHECKER			
LP-2978 [M]	The Watusi	1961	$250
GUINNESS			
GNS36045 [B]	Good Vibrations	1977	$35
MANDALA			
3006	Taking a New Step	1972	$25
OKEH			
OKM-12112 [M]	Misty	1966	$30
OKS-14112 [S]	Misty	1966	$40
OKM-12114 [M]	New Vibrations	1967	$30
OKS-14114 [S]	New Vibrations	1967	$40
OKM-12111 [M]	Shout	1965	$30
OKS-14111 [S]	Shout	1965	$40
OKS-14129	The Vibrations' Greatest Hits	1969	$30
VIBRATORS, THE			
CLEOPATRA			
9152 [B]	Alaska 127		$25
3670 [B]	Garage Punk		$25
8201 [B]	Pure Mania		$30
— picture disc			
6453 [B]	Pure Mania		$25
7061 [B]	V2		$25

Number	Title	Yr	NM
VICE SQUAD			
CLEOPATRA			
3830 [B]	Fuck Authority		$25
VICEROYS, THE (3)			
BOLO			
BLP-8000 [M]	The Viceroys at Granny's Pad	1963	$100
VICK, HAROLD			
BLUE NOTE			
BLP-4138 [M]	Steppin' Out	1963	$100
BST-84138 [S]	Steppin' Out	1963	$50
— With "New York, USA" address on label			
BST-84138 [S]	Steppin' Out	196?	$35
— With "A Division of Liberty Records" on label			
MUSE			
MR-5054	Commitment	197?	$30
RCA VICTOR			
LPM-3761 [M]	Straight Up	1967	$25
LSP-3761 [S]	Straight Up	1967	$35
LPM-3677 [M]	The Caribbean Suite	1966	$35
LSP-3677 [S]	The Caribbean Suite	1966	$25
STRATA-EAST			
SES-7431	Don't Look Back	197?	$25
VICKERY, MACK			
MEGA			
31-1002	Mack Vickery at the Alabama Women's Prison	1970	$18
VICTIMS OF CHANCE, THE			
CRESTVIEW			
CRS-3052	The Victims of Chance	197?	$75
VICTORIA, C.B.			
JANUS			
JXS-7029	Dawning Day	1976	$15
VIDEO ALL STARS, THE			
SOMERSET			
SF-8800 [M]	The Video All Stars Play TV Jazz Themes	1956	$120
VIENNA ART ORCHESTRA			
HAT HUT			
1980/1	Concerto Piccolo	1980	$50
1999/2000	From No Time to Rag Time	1982	$50
2024	Perpetuum Mobile	1985	$35
1991/2	Suite for the Green Eighties	1981	$50
2005	The Minimalism of Erik Satie	1984	$35
VIENNA BOYS CHOIR			
CAPITOL			
T10164 [M]	Christmas in Austria	1959	$18
— As "Wiener Sangerknaben"			
VIENNA CHOIR BOYS, THE, AND HERMANN PREY			
RCA RED SEAL			
ARL1-2939	Christmas with the Vienna Choir Boys and Hermann Prey	1978	$12
VIENNA CHOIR BOYS			
RCA RED SEAL			
ARL1-3437	Britten: A Ceremony of Carols/Seven English Christmas Carols	1979	$12
VIENNA PHILHARMONIC ORCHESTRA (FRITZ REINER, CONDUCTOR)			
RCA VICTOR RED SEAL			
LSC-2077 [S]	Strauss: Till Eulenspiegel	1959	$150
— Original with "shaded dog" label			
LSC-2077 [S]	Strauss: Till Eulenspiegel	199?	$30
— Classic Records reissue			
VIENNA PHILHARMONIC ORCHESTRA (PIERRE MONTEUX, CONDUCTOR)			
RCA VICTOR RED SEAL			
LSC-2491 [S]	Beethoven: Symphonies No. 1 and 8	1961	$40
— Original with "shaded dog" label			
LSC-2316 [S]	Beethoven: Symphony No. 6	1959	$50
— Original with "shaded dog" label			
LSC-2362 [S]	Berlioz: Symphonie Fantastique	1960	$40
— Original with "shaded dog" label			
LSC-2394 [S]	Haydn: Symphonies No. 94 and 101	1960	$30
— Original with "shaded dog" label			

Number	Title	Yr	NM
VIENNA PHILHARMONIC ORCHESTRA (WILHELM FURTWANGLER, CONDUCTOR)			
URANIA			
URLP-7095 [M]	Beethoven: Symphony No. 3	195?	$600
— Withdrawn from the market when it was discovered that the record had been mastered slightly fast			
VIG, TOMMY			
DISCOVERY			
780	Encounter with Time	197?	$25
DOBRE			
1015		1978	$30
MILESTONE			
MSP-9007	Sounds of the Seventies	1968	$25
VIGRASS AND OSBORNE			
EPIC			
KE33077	Steppin' Out	1975	$15
UNI			
73129	Queues	1971	$18
VIKEN, HOWARD, WITH EDITH NORBERG'S CARILLON CHORISTERS			
PERSONALITY PRODUCTS			
S80-178-1781S	In a Holiday Mood	19??	$15
VILLA, PEPE			
KING			
660 [M]	Music of Mexico	1959	$30
VILLAGE PEOPLE			
CASABLANCA			
NBLP-7220	Can't Stop the Music (Soundtrack)	1980	$12
— Also includes one song by the Ritchie Family and one song by David London			
NBLP-7118	Cruisin'	1978	$12
NBPIX-7118 [PD]	Cruisin'	1978	$25
NBLP-7144	Go West	1979	$12
NBLP-7183 [PD]	Live and Sleazy	1979	$15
NBLP-7096	Macho Man	1978	$12
NBPIX-7096 [PD]	Macho Man	1978	$25
NBLP-7064	Village People	1977	$12
NBPIX-7064 [PD]	Village People	1978	$25
RCA VICTOR			
AFL1-4105	Renaissance	1981	$15
RHINO			
R1-70167	Greatest Hits	1988	$18
VILLAGE STOMPERS, THE			
EPIC			
LN24109 [M]	Around the World with the Village Stompers	1964	$75
BN26109 [S]	Around the World with the Village Stompers	1964	$75
LN24180 [M]	A Taste of Honey	1965	$75
BN26180 [S]	A Taste of Honey	1965	$85
LN24090 [M]	More Sounds of Washington Square	1964	$85
BN26090 [S]	More Sounds of Washington Square	1964	$150
LN24129 [M]	New Beat on Broadway!	1964	$75
BN26129 [S]	New Beat on Broadway!	1964	$85
LN24235 [M]	One More Time	1966	$75
BN26235 [S]	One More Time	1966	$85
LN24161 [M]	Some Folk, a Bit of Country and a Whole Lot of Dixie	1965	$75
BN26161 [S]	Some Folk, a Bit of Country and a Whole Lot of Dixie	1965	$85
LN24318 [M]	The Village Stompers' Greatest Hits	1967	$75
BN26318 [S]	The Village Stompers' Greatest Hits	1967	$85
LN24078 [M]	Washington Square	1963	$85
BN26078 [S]	Washington Square	1963	$150
VILLEGAS			
COLUMBIA			
CL787 [M]	Introducing Villegas	1956	$30
CL877 [M]	Very, Very Villegas	1956	$30
VINCENT, GENE			
CAPITOL			
T1059 [M]	A Gene Vincent Record Date	1958	$1500
— Yellow label promo			
T1059 [M]	A Gene Vincent Record Date	1958	$1500
— Black label promo			
T1059 [M]	A Gene Vincent Record Date	1958	$400
— Turquoise label stock copy			
T764 [M]	Bluejean Bop!	1957	$1000
— Yellow label promo			
T764 [M]	Bluejean Bop!	1957	$1000
— Black label promo			
T764 [M]	Bluejean Bop!	1957	$600

VINCENT, GENE

Number	Title	Yr	NM
— Turquoise label stock copy			
T1342	Crazy Times	1960	$300
— Black label with colorband, Capitol logo at left			
ST1342 [S]	Crazy Times	1960	$500
— Black label with colorband, Capitol logo at left			
T811 [M]	Gene Vincent and the Blue Caps	1957	$1000
— Yellow label promo			
T811 [M]	Gene Vincent and the Blue Caps	1957	$1000
— Black label promo			
T811 [M]	Gene Vincent and the Blue Caps	1957	$500
— Turquoise label stock copy			
T970 [M]	Gene Vincent Rocks! And the Blue Caps Roll	1958	$1000
— Yellow label promo			
T970 [M]	Gene Vincent Rocks! And the Blue Caps Roll	1958	$1500
— Black label promo			
T970 [M]	Gene Vincent Rocks! And the Blue Caps Roll	1958	$500
— Turquoise label stock copy			
DKAO-380 [R]	Gene Vincent's Greatest	1969	$50
SM-380 [R]	Gene Vincent's Greatest	197?	$18
— Abridged reissue of DKAO-380			
N-16208	Gene Vincent's Greatest	198?	$15
— Budget-line reissue			
T1207 [M]	Sounds Like Gene Vincent	1959	$300
— Black label with colorband, Capitol logo at left			
SM-11287	The Bop That Just Won't Stop	1974	$18
N-16209 [B]	The Bop That Just Won't Stop	198?	$18
— Budget-line reissue			

DANDELION
Number	Title	Yr	NM
9-102	I'm Back and I'm Proud	1970	$50

INTERMEDIA
QS-5074	Rockabilly Fever	198?	$15

KAMA SUTRA
KSBS2019	Gene Vincent	1970	$50
KSBS2027	The Day the World Turned Blue	1971	$50

ROLLIN' ROCK
022	Forever	1981	$18

VINEGAR JOE
ATCO
Number	Title	Yr	NM
SD7016	Rock 'n Roll Gypsies	1973	$18
SD7007	Vinegar Joe	1972	$18

VINNEGAR, LEROY
CONTEMPORARY
Number	Title	Yr	NM
C-3542 [M]	Leroy Walks!	1957	$300
S-7003 [S]	Leroy Walks!	1959	$300
S-7542 [S]	Leroy Walks!	197?	$30
M-3608 [M]	Leroy Walks Again!	1962	$250
S-7608 [S]	Leroy Walks Again!	1962	$250

FANTASY
OJC-160	Leroy Walks!	198?	$25
OJC-454	Leroy Walks Again!	1990	$25

LEGEND
1001	Glass of Water	197?	$35

PBR
6	The Kid	197?	$30

STEREO RECORDS
S-7003 [S]	Leroy Walks!	1958	$75

VEE JAY
LP-2502 [M]	Jazz's Great Walker	1964	$30
LPS-2502 [S]	Jazz's Great Walker	1964	$30

VINSON, EDDIE "CLEANHEAD"/JIMMY WITHERSPOON
KING
634 [M]	Battle of the Blues, Volume 3	1960	$1500

VINSON, EDDIE "CLEANHEAD
AAMCO
312 [M]	Cleanhead's Back in Town	196?	$40

BETHLEHEM
BCP-6036	Back in Town	1978	$35
BCP-5005 [M]	Eddie "Cleanhead" Vinson Sings	1957	$300

BLUESWAY
BL-6007 [M]	Cherry Red	1967	$75
BLS-6007 [S]	Cherry Red	1967	$75

CIRCLE
CLP-57	Kidney Stew	1983	$30

DELMARK
631	Old Kidney Stew Is Fine	1980	$30

FLYING DUTCHMAN
31-1012	You Can't Make Love Alone	197?	$35

KING
KS-1087	Cherry Red	1969	$75

MUSE
Number	Title	Yr	NM
MR-5282	Cleanhead and Roomful of Blues	1982	$30
MR-5243	Eddie "Cleanhead" Vinson and the Muse All-Stars: Hold It Right There	198?	$30
MR-5208	Eddie "Cleanhead" Vinson and the Muse All-Stars: Live at Sandy's	1979	$30
MR-5310	Eddie "Cleanhead" Vinson Sings the Blues	198?	$30
MR-5116	The Clean Machine	1978	$35

PABLO
2310866	I Want a Little Girl	198?	$30

REGGIES
1000	Rollin' Over the Devil	1981	$30

RIVERSIDE
RLP-502 [M]	Back Door Blues	1965	$175
RLS-9502 [S]	Back Door Blues	1965	$175

VINTON, BOBBY
EPIC
Number	Title	Yr	NM
5-26341 [PS]	Please Love Me Forever	1967	$12
5-26341	Please Love Me Forever/It's All in the Game/Love Me with All Your Heart//Just As Much As Ever/P.S. I Love You/My Song of Love	1967	$10
— Stereo jukebox issue; small hole, plays at 33 1/3 rpm			
7-26081 [PS]	There! I've Said It Again	1964	$15
— Slightly different cover than on N7-26081			
7-26081	You're Nobody 'Til Somebody Loves You/Trying/Unchained Melody//To Each His Own/I Can Dream, Can't I/My Foolish Heart	1964	$15
— Jukebox issue; small hole, plays at 33 1/3 rpm; original edition			

ABC
D-891	Heart of Hearts	1975	$12
X-851	Melodies of Love	1974	$12
D-957	Serenades of Love	1976	$12
D-924	The Bobby Vinton Show	1975	$12
AB-981	The Name Is Love	1977	$12

COLUMBIA LIMITED EDITION
LE10016	Big Ones	197?	$12
LE10140	Blue Velvet	197?	$12
— Reissue of Epic 26068			
LE10052	Please Love Me Forever	197?	$12
LE10139	Roses Are Red	197?	$12

COLUMBIA MUSICAL TREASURY
6P6035	The Bobby Vinton Treasury	197?	$30
— Columbia House" logo on upper right back cover			

EPIC
Number	Title	Yr	NM
JE35605	Autumn Memories	1979	$12
LN24122 [M]	A Very Merry Christmas	1964	$15
BN26122 [S]	A Very Merry Christmas	1964	$18
LN24068 [M]	Blue On Blue	1963	$175
— Promo only on blue vinyl			
LN24068 [M]	Blue On Blue	1963	$30
— Stock copy on black vinyl			
BN26068 [S]	Blue On Blue	1963	$30
LN24068 [M]	Blue Velvet	1963	$18
— Retitled version of "Blue On Blue"			
BN26068 [S]	Blue Velvet	1963	$25
— Retitled version of "Blue On Blue"			
KEG31487	Bobby Vinton's All-Time Greatest Hits	1972	$18
PEG31487	Bobby Vinton's All-Time Greatest Hits	197?	$15
— Reissue			
LN24098 [M]	Bobby Vinton's Greatest Hits	1964	$15
— Despite lower number, this came out after "Tell Me Why			
BN26098 [S]	Bobby Vinton's Greatest Hits	1964	$18
— Despite lower number, this came out after "Tell Me Why			
PE26098	Bobby Vinton's Greatest Hits	198?	$10
— Budget-line reissue			
BN26517	Bobby Vinton's Greatest Hits of Love	1970	$18
LN24154 [M]	Bobby Vinton Sings for Lonely Nights	1965	$15
BN26154 [S]	Bobby Vinton Sings for Lonely Nights	1965	$18
LN24035 [M]	Bobby Vinton Sings the Big Ones	1962	$18
BN26035 [S]	Bobby Vinton Sings the Big Ones	1962	$25
KEG33468	Bobby Vinton Sings the Golden Decade of Love	1975	$15
LN24245 [M]	Bobby Vinton's Newest Hits	1967	$15
BN26245 [S]	Bobby Vinton's Newest Hits	1967	$18
LN24188 [M]	Country Boy	1966	$15
BN26188 [S]	Country Boy	1966	$18
LN3727 [M]	Dancing at the Hop	1961	$30
BN579 [S]	Dancing at the Hop	1961	$50
LN24170 [M]	Drive-In Movie Time	1965	$15
BN26170 [S]	Drive-In Movie Time	1965	$18
KE31286	Ev'ry Day of My Life	1972	$15
KEG33767	Greatest Hits/Greatest Hits of Love	1976	$15
BN26437	I Love How You Love Me	1968	$18
LN24203 [M]	Live at the Copa	1967	$15
BN26203 [S]	Live at the Copa	1967	$18
LN24187 [M]	More of Bobby Vinton's Greatest Hits	1966	$15
BN26187 [S]	More of Bobby Vinton's Greatest Hits	1966	$18
LN24136 [M]	Mr. Lonely	1965	$15
BN26136 [S]	Mr. Lonely	1965	$18
BN26540	My Elusive Dreams	1970	$18
LN24341 [M]	Please Love Me Forever	1967	$18
BN26341 [S]	Please Love Me Forever	1967	$18
LN24020 [M]	Roses Are Red	1962	$18
BN26020 [S]	Roses Are Red	1962	$25
LN24182 [M]	Satin Pillows and Careless	1966	$15
BN26182 [S]	Satin Pillows and Careless	1966	$18
KE31642	Sealed with a Kiss	1972	$15
JE35998	Spring Sensations	1979	$12
JE35999	Summer Serenade	1979	$12
BN26382	Take Good Care of My Baby	1968	$18
LN24113 [M]	Tell Me Why	1964	$15
BN26113 [S]	Tell Me Why	1964	$18
LN24049 [M]	The Greatest Hits of the Greatest Groups	1963	$18
BN26049 [S]	The Greatest Hits of the Greatest Groups	1963	$25
LN24081 [M]	There! I've Said It Again	1964	$18
BN26081 [S]	There! I've Said It Again	1964	$25
BN26471	Vinton	1969	$18
PE32921	With Love	1974	$12
LN3780 [M]	Young Man with a Big Band	1961	$30
BN597 [S]	Young Man with a Big Band	1961	$50

HARMONY
KH11402	Vinton Sings Vinton	197?	$12

PICKWICK
SPC-3353	Melodies of Love	197?	$10

TAPESTRY
TRS-1001 [EP]	Santa Must Be Polish	1987	$12

VIOLA, AL
LEGEND
1002	Alone Again	197?	$35

MODE
LP-121 [M]	Solo Guitar	1957	$100

PBR
11	Prelude to a Kiss	197?	$30
7	Salutations F.S.	197?	$30

VIOLENT FEMMES
RHINO
R1-79951 [B]	Violent Femmes	2003	$18
— Reissue on 180-gram vinyl			

SLASH
25819	3	1988	$12
25094	Hallowed Ground	1984	$15
25340	The Blind Leading the Naked	1986	$12
23845	Violent Femmes	1983	$18

WARNER BROS.
PRO-A-3519 [DJ]	3 On 3	1989	$30
— Promo-only interviews and music			

VIOLINAIRES, THE
CHECKER
Number	Title	Yr	NM
LP-10060	At His Command	1970	$25
LPS-10057	God's Creation	1969	$25
CK-10067	Groovin' with Jesus	197?	$25
LPS-10020 [S]	I'm Going to Serve the Lord	196?	$30
LP-10020	I'm Going to Serve the Lord	196?	$25
LPS-10045 [S]	Live the Right Way	196?	$30
LP-10045	Live the Right Way	196?	$30
LPS-10030 [S]	Move On Up	196?	$30
LP-10030	Move On Up	196?	$25
2CK-10065	Please Answer This Prayer	197?	$30
LPS-10040 [S]	Shout!	196?	$30
LP-10040	Shout!	196?	$25
LP-10011 [M]	Stand By Me	1965	$30
LP-10017 [M]	The Fantastic Violinaires	1966	$30
LPS-10053	The Violinaires in Concert	1968	$25

VIRGIN INSANITY
FUNKY
71411	Illusions of the Maintenance Man	1970	$250

VIRGINIANS, THE
MONUMENT
MLP-8031 [M]	Ballads and Bluegrass	1965	$25
SLP-18031 [S]	Ballads and Bluegrass	1965	$30

UNITED ARTISTS
UAL-3293 [M]	The Wonderful World of Bluegrass Music	1963	$25
UAS-6293 [M]	The Wonderful World of Bluegrass Music	1963	$30

Number	Title	Yr	NM

VIRTUES, THE
FAYETTE
❏ 1816 [M]	Frank Virtue and the Virtues	1964	$75
—Blue cover			
❏ 1816 [M]	Frank Virtue and the Virtues	1964	$40
—White cover			
STRAND
❏ L-1061 [M]	Guitar Boogie Shuffle	1960	$30
❏ SL-1061 [S]	Guitar Boogie Shuffle	1960	$40
WYNNE
❏ WLP-111 [M]	Guitar Boogie Shuffle	1960	$120
❏ WLP-711 [S]	Guitar Boogie Shuffle	1960	$180

VISAGE
POLYDOR
❏ 823052-1	Beat Boy	1984	$15
❏ 815347-1	Fade to Grey -- The Singles Collection	1983	$15
❏ PD1-6350	The Anvil	1982	$15
❏ PD1-6304	Visage	1981	$15
❏ PX1-501 [EP]	Visage	1981	$15

VISCOUNTS, THE (1)
AMY
| ❏ 8008 [M] | Harlem Nocturne | 1965 | $40 |
| ❏ S-8008 [S] | Harlem Nocturne | 1965 | $50 |
MADISON

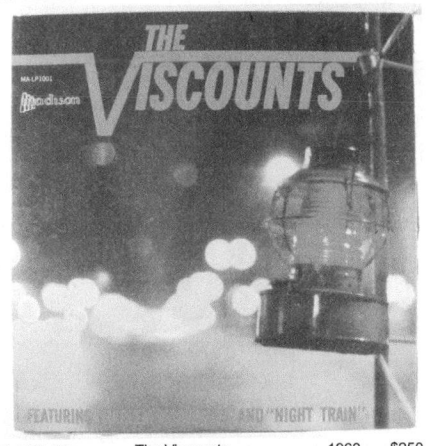

| ❏ 1001 [M] | The Viscounts | 1960 | $250 |

VISION
MUSIC IS MEDICINE
| ❏ 9027 | Vision | 198? | $30 |

VISION OF SUNSHINE
AVCO EMBASSY
| ❏ 33007 | Vision of Sunshine | 1970 | $30 |

VISITORS, THE
COBBLESTONE
| ❏ 9010 | Neptune | 197? | $25 |
MUSE
❏ MR-5024	In My Youth	197?	$30
❏ MR-5094	Motherland	1976	$30
❏ MR-5195	Neptune	197?	$25
❏ MR-5047	Rebirth	197?	$30

VITALE, JOE
ASYLUM
| ❏ 5E-529 | Plantation Harbor | 1981 | $12 |
ATLANTIC
| ❏ SD18114 | Rollercoaster Weekend | 1975 | $12 |

VITOUS, MIROSLAV
ARISTA
| ❏ AL4099 | Majesty Music | 197? | $25 |
ARISTA/FREEDOM
| ❏ AF1040 | Vitous | 1976 | $30 |
ATLANTIC
| ❏ SD1622 | Mountain in the Clouds | 1972 | $30 |
ECM
| ❏ 1145 | First Meeting | 1979 | $30 |
| ❏ 1185 | Miroslav Vitous Group | 198? | $30 |
EMBRYO
| ❏ SD524 | Infonite Search | 1970 | $35 |
WARNER BROS.
| ❏ BS2925 | Magical | 1976 | $25 |

VITRO, ROSEANNA
SKYLINE
| ❏ SKYP-1001 | A Quiet Place | 1987 | $25 |
TEXAS ROSE
| ❏ TRM-1001 | Listen Here | 1984 | $25 |

VIZZUTTI, ALLEN
BAINBRIDGE
| ❏ 6246 | Red Metal | 198? | $25 |
HEADFIRST
| ❏ 9700 | Vizzutti | 198? | $30 |

VOCAL JAZZ INCORPORATED
GRAPEVINE
| ❏ 3310 | Vocal Jazz Incorporated | 197? | $30 |

VOGUES, THE
CO & CE
❏ LP-1230 [M]	Five O'Clock World	1966	$50
—Stereo pressings of these two albums are not known to exist!			
❏ LP-1229 [M]	Meet the Vogues	1965	$50
PICKWICK
❏ SPC-3214 [R]	A Lover's Concerto	1971	$12
❏ SPC-3188 [R]	Five O'Clock World	1971	$12
REPRISE
❏ RS6347	Memories	1969	$18
—With "W7" and "r:" logos on two-tone orange label			
❏ RS6371	The Vogues' Greatest Hits	1969	$18
—With "W7" and "r:" logos on two-tone orange label			
❏ SW-93040	The Vogues' Greatest Hits	1970	$25
—Capitol Record Club edition			
❏ RS6395	The Vogues Sing the Good Old Songs	1970	$15
❏ RS6326 [B]	Till	1969	$18
—With "W7" and "r:" logos on two-tone orange label			
❏ RS6314	Turn Around, Look at Me	1968	$18
—With "W7" and "r:" logos on two-tone orange label			
❏ ST-91559	Turn Around, Look at Me	1968	$25
—Capitol Record Club edition			
SSS INTERNATIONAL
❏ 34	The Vogues' Greatest Hits	1977	$12

VOICE OF THE BEEHIVE
LONDON
| ❏ 828100-1 [B] | Let It Bee | 1988 | $18 |
| *—issue of Custom LP* | | | |

VOICES OF EAST HARLEM, THE
ELEKTRA
| ❏ EKS-74080 [B] | Right On Be Free | 1970 | $18 |
JUST SUNSHINE
| ❏ 3504 | Can You Feel It? | 1974 | $12 |
| ❏ 7 [B] | Voices of East Harlem | 1973 | $15 |

VOLLENWEIDER, ANDREAS
CBS/FM
| ❏ FM42255 | Down to the Moon | 1986 | $25 |
| ❏ FM39963 | White Winds | 1985 | $25 |
CBS MASTERWORKS
| ❏ FM37793 | ...Behind the Gardens... Behind the Wall...Under the Tree... | 1984 | $25 |
| ❏ FM37827 | Caverna Magica (...Under the Tree-In the Cave...) | 1984 | $25 |
COLUMBIA
| ❏ OC45154 | Dancing with the Lion | 1989 | $30 |

VOLTAGE BROTHERS, THE
LIFESONG
| ❏ JZ35042 | The Voltage Brothers | 1978 | $25 |
| ❏ JZ35653 | Throw Down | 1978 | $25 |
MTM
| ❏ ST-71055 | The Voltage Brothers | 1986 | $18 |

VON OHLEN, JOHN "THE BARON
CREATIVE WORLD
| ❏ ST-3001 | The Baron | 197? | $25 |

VON SCHLIPPENBACH, ALEXANDER
ENJA
| ❏ 2012 | Payan | 197? | $35 |

VON SCHMIDT, ERIC
FOLKLORE
| ❏ FRLP-14005 [M] | Folk Blues | 1964 | $30 |
| ❏ FRST-14005 [S] | Folk Blues | 1964 | $40 |
PRESTIGE
| ❏ PRLP-7384 [M] | Eric Sings Von Schmidt | 1966 | $25 |
| ❏ PRST-7384 [S] | Eric Sings Von Schmidt | 1966 | $30 |

SMASH
| ❏ SRS-67124 | Who Knocked the Brains Out of the Sky? | 1969 | $25 |

VRONSKY AND BABIN
RCA VICTOR RED SEAL
| ❏ LSC-2417 [S] | 178 Keys | 1960 | $30 |
| *—Original with "shaded dog" label* | | | |

VUCKOVICH, LARRY
INNER CITY
| ❏ IC-1096 | Blue Balkan | 198? | $30 |
PALO ALTO
| ❏ PA-8012 | City Sounds | 1981 | $25 |

W

WACKER, FRED
CADET
| ❏ LPS-4050 [S] | Fred Wacker Swings Cool | 1966 | $35 |
| ❏ LP-4050 [M] | Fred Wacker Swings Cool | 1966 | $30 |
DOLPHIN
| ❏ 9 [M] | Freddy Wacker and His Windy City Seven | 195? | $50 |

WADDELL, STEVE
STOMP OFF
| ❏ SOS-1172 | Frisco Comes to Melbourne | 1987 | $25 |

WADE, ADAM
COED
❏ LPC-903 [M]	Adam and Evening	1961	$50
❏ LPCS-903 [S]	Adam and Evening	1961	$75
❏ LPC-902 [M]	And Then Came Adam	1960	$50
❏ LPCS-902 [S]	And Then Came Adam	1960	$75
EPIC
❏ LN24019 [M]	Adam Wade's Greatest Hits	1962	$30
❏ BN26019 [S]	Adam Wade's Greatest Hits	1962	$30
❏ LN24056 [M]	A Very Good Year for Girls	1963	$30
❏ BN26056 [S]	A Very Good Year for Girls	1963	$30
❏ LN24026 [M]	One Is a Lonely Number	1962	$30
❏ BN26026 [S]	One Is a Lonely Number	1962	$30
❏ LN24044 [M]	What Kind of Fool Am I?	1963	$30
❏ BN26044 [S]	What Kind of Fool Am I?	1963	$30
KIRSHNER
❏ PZ34919	Adam Wade	1977	$15

WADSWORTH MANSION
SUSSEX
❏ SXBS-7008	Wadsworth Manison	1971	$30
—Some copies of this LP have the above typographical error			
❏ SXBS-7008	Wadsworth Mansion	1971	$25

WADUD, ABDUL
RED RECORD
| ❏ VPA-147 | Straight Ahead/Free at Last | 198? | $30 |

WAGNER, DANNY, AND KINDRED SOUL
IMPERIAL
| ❏ LP-12405 | The Kindred Soul of Danny Wagner | 1968 | $30 |

WAGNER, JACK
QWEST
❏ 25089 [EP]	All I Need	1984	$10
—Version with five songs on it			
❏ 25214	All I Need	1985	$10
—Version with 10 songs on it			
❏ 25562	Don't Give Up Your Day Job	1987	$10
❏ 25318	Lighting Up the Night	1985	$10

WAGNER, LARRY
A44
| ❏ AP-501 [10] | Larry Wagner | 1954 | $75 |

WAGNER, ROGER, CHORALE
CAPITOL
❏ P8332 [M]	Folk Songs of the Frontier	195?	$30
❏ P8324 [M]	Folk Songs of the New World	195?	$30
❏ PBR8345 [M]	Folk Songs of the Old World	195?	$40
❏ P8387 [M]	Folk Songs of the World	195?	$25
❏ STBB-488	Great Choral Music of Christmas	1970	$18
❏ P8353 [M]	Joy to the World!	195?	$18
—Original labels are green and gold			
❏ SP8353 [S]	Joy to the World!	195?	$30
❏ P8267 [M]	Songs of Stephen Foster	195?	$30
❏ T2591 [M]	The Best of the Roger Wagner Chorale Christmas Carols	1966	$15

Number	Title	Yr	NM
❑ ST2591 [S]	The Best of the Roger Wagner Chorale Christmas Carols	1966	$18

— Originals have black "The Star Line" labels

WAGONEERS

A&M
Number	Title	Yr	NM
❑ SP-5200	Stout and High	1988	$10

WAGONER, PORTER, AND DOLLY PARTON
Also see each artist's individual listings.

PAIR
Number	Title	Yr	NM
❑ PDL1-1013	Sweet Harmony	1986	$15

RCA VICTOR
Number	Title	Yr	NM
❑ LSP-4186	Always, Always	1969	$25
❑ LPM-3926 [M]	Just Between You and Me	1968	$150
❑ LSP-3926 [S]	Just Between You and Me	1968	$25
❑ LSP-4039	Just the Two of Us	1968	$25
❑ APL1-0248	Love and Music	1973	$18
❑ LSP-4388	Once More	1970	$25
❑ APL1-0646	Porter 'N' Dolly	1974	$18
❑ AHL1-3700	Porter Wagoner and Dolly Parton	1980	$15
❑ AYL1-4251	Porter Wagoner and Dolly Parton	1982	$10

— Best Buy Series" reissue

Number	Title	Yr	NM
❑ LSP-4305	Porter Wayne and Dolly Rebecca	1970	$25
❑ APL1-1116	Say Forever	1975	$18
❑ LSP-4556	The Best of Porter Wagoner and Dolly Parton	1971	$25
❑ AHL1-4556	The Best of Porter Wagoner and Dolly Parton	1983	$12
❑ LSP-4628	The Right Combination/ Burning the Midnight Oil	1972	$18
❑ LSP-4761	Together Always	1972	$18
❑ LSP-4490	Two of a Kind	1971	$25
❑ LSP-4841	We Found It	1973	$18

WAGONER, PORTER, AND SKEETER DAVIS
Also see each artist's individual listings.

RCA VICTOR
Number	Title	Yr	NM
❑ LPM-2529 [M]	Porter Wagoner and Skeeter Davis Sing Duets	1962	$30
❑ LSP-2529 [S]	Porter Wagoner and Skeeter Davis Sing Duets	1962	$30

WAGONER, PORTER

ACCORD
Number	Title	Yr	NM
❑ SN-7179	Down Home Country	1982	$15

DOT/MCA
Number	Title	Yr	NM
❑ 39053	Porter Wagoner	1986	$12

RCA CAMDEN
Number	Title	Yr	NM
❑ CAL-861 [M]	An Old Log Cabin for Sale	1965	$15
❑ CAS-861 [S]	An Old Log Cabin for Sale	1965	$15
❑ CAL-769 [M]	A Satisfied Mind	1963	$15
❑ CAS-769(e) [R]	A Satisfied Mind	1963	$12
❑ CXS-9010	Blue Moon of Kentucky	1971	$18
❑ CAS-2321	Country Feeling	1968	$15
❑ CAL-2191 [M]	Green, Green Grass of Home	1967	$15
❑ CAS-2191 [S]	Green, Green Grass of Home	1967	$15
❑ CAS-2409	Howdy Neighbor	1970	$15
❑ CAL-2116 [M]	I'm Day Dreamin' Tonight	1967	$15
❑ CAS-2116 [S]	I'm Day Dreamin' Tonight	1967	$15
❑ CAS-2478	Porter Wagoner Country	1971	$15
❑ CAS-2588	The Silent Kind	1972	$15
❑ CAL-942 [M]	Your Old Love Letters" And Other Country Hits	1966	$15
❑ CAS-942 [S]	Your Old Love Letters" And Other Country Hits	1966	$15

RCA VICTOR
Number	Title	Yr	NM
❑ LPM-1358 [M]	A Satisfied Mind	1956	$250
❑ LPM-2447 [M]	A Slice of Life -- Songs Happy 'N' Sad	1962	$30
❑ LSP-2447 [S]	A Slice of Life -- Songs Happy 'N' Sad	1962	$30
❑ LSP-4734	Ballads of Love	1972	$18
❑ AHL1-7000	Collector's Series	1985	$12
❑ LPM-3593 [M]	Confessions of a Broken Man	1966	$25
❑ LSP-3593 [S]	Confessions of a Broken Man	1966	$30
❑ LSP-4386	Down in the Alley	1970	$25
❑ LSP-4034	Gospel Country	1968	$25
❑ LPM-3488 [M]	Grand Old Gospel	1966	$25
❑ LSP-3488 [S]	Grand Old Gospel	1966	$30
❑ APL1-0713	Highway Headin' South	1974	$18
❑ APL1-0142	I'll Keep on Lovin' You	1973	$18
❑ LPM-2840 [M]	In Person	1964	$30
❑ LSP-2840 [S]	In Person	1964	$30
❑ LSP-4181	Me and My Boys	1969	$25
❑ LPM-3855 [M]	More Grand Old Gospel	1967	$30
❑ LSP-3855 [S]	More Grand Old Gospel	1967	$25
❑ LPM-3509 [M]	On the Road	1966	$25
❑ LSP-3509 [S]	On the Road	1966	$30
❑ AHL1-2432	Porter	1977	$15
❑ LSP-4586	Porter Wagoner Sings His Own	1971	$18
❑ LSP-4508	Simple As I Am	1971	$25
❑ APL1-1056	Sing Love	1975	$18
❑ LPM-3683 [M]	Soul of a Convict	1967	$30
❑ LSP-3683 [S]	Soul of a Convict	1967	$25
❑ LPM-3560 [M]	The Best of Porter Wagoner	1966	$25
❑ LSP-3560 [S]	The Best of Porter Wagoner	1966	$30
❑ ANL1-1213	The Best of Porter Wagoner	1975	$15
❑ LSP-4321	The Best of Porter Wagoner, Volume 2	1970	$25
❑ LPM-2960 [M]	The Bluegrass Story	1964	$25
❑ LSP-2960 [S]	The Bluegrass Story	1964	$30
❑ LPM-3968 [M]	The Bottom of the Bottle	1968	$150
❑ LSP-3968 [S]	The Bottom of the Bottle	1968	$25
❑ LSP-4116	The Carroll County Accident	1969	$25
❑ LPM-3797 [M]	The Cold Hard Facts of Life	1967	$30
❑ LSP-3797 [S]	The Cold Hard Facts of Life	1967	$25
❑ APL1-0346	The Farmer	1974	$18
❑ LSP-4810	The Porter Wagoner Experience	1973	$18
❑ LPM-2650 [M]	The Porter Wagoner Show	1963	$30
❑ LSP-2650 [S]	The Porter Wagoner Show	1963	$30
❑ LPM-3389 [M]	The Thin Man from West Plains	1965	$25
❑ LSP-3389 [S]	The Thin Man from West Plains	1965	$30
❑ APL1-0496	Tore Down	1974	$18
❑ LSP-4661	What Ain't to Be	1972	$18
❑ LPM-2706 [M]	Y'All Come	1963	$30
❑ LSP-2706 [S]	Y'All Come	1963	$30
❑ LSP-4286	You Got-ta Have a License	1970	$25

WARNER BROS.
Number	Title	Yr	NM
❑ 23783	Viva Porter Wagoner!	1983	$12

WAIKIKIS, THE

KAPP
Number	Title	Yr	NM
❑ KL-1484 [M]	A Taste of Hawaii	1966	$18
❑ KS-3484 [S]	A Taste of Hawaii	1966	$25
❑ KL-1437 [M]	Beach Party	1965	$18
❑ KS-3437 [S]	Beach Party	1965	$25
❑ KS-3612	Greatest Hits	1970	$15
❑ KL-1432 [M]	Hawaii Honeymoon	1965	$18
❑ KS-3432 [S]	Hawaii Honeymoon	1965	$25
❑ KL-1366 [M]	Hawaii Tattoo	1964	$18
❑ KS-3366 [S]	Hawaii Tattoo	1964	$25
❑ KL-1473 [M]	Lollipops and Roses	1966	$18
❑ KS-3473 [S]	Lollipops and Roses	1966	$25
❑ KS-3575	Midnight Luau	1969	$18
❑ KS-3593	Moonlight on Diamond Head	1969	$18
❑ KL-1555 [M]	Pearly Shells from Hawaii	1968	$30

— White label promo in stereo cover, "Mono" sticker on front

Number	Title	Yr	NM
❑ KS-3555 [S]	Pearly Shells from Hawaii	1968	$18

MCA
Number	Title	Yr	NM
❑ 547	Greatest Hits	197?	$12
❑ 544	Pearly Shells from Hawaii	197?	$12

WAILERS, THE

BELL
Number	Title	Yr	NM
❑ 6016	Walk Thru the People	1969	$30

ETIQUETTE
Number	Title	Yr	NM
❑ ALB-026 [M]	Out of Our Tree	1966	$250
❑ ALB-01 [M]	The Fabulous Wailers at the Castle	196?	$250
❑ ALB-022 [M]	The Wailers and Company	196?	$140
❑ 22296/7 [B]	The Wailers and Their Greatest Hits	1979	$30
❑ ALB-023 [M]	Wailers, Wailers, Everywhere	196?	$250

GOLDEN CREST
Number	Title	Yr	NM
❑ CR-3075 [M]	Fabulous Wailers	1959	$300

— Full-color photo on cover

Number	Title	Yr	NM
❑ CR-3075 [M]	Fabulous Wailers	1962	$300

— Black and white photo on cover

Number	Title	Yr	NM
❑ CR-3075 [M]	Fabulous Wailers	196?	$100

— Title, no photo, on cover

IMPERIAL

Number	Title	Yr	NM
❑ LP-9262 [M]	Tall Cool One	1964	$100
❑ LP-12262 [S]	Tall Cool One	1964	$120

UNITED ARTISTS
Number	Title	Yr	NM
❑ UAL-3557 [M]	Outburst!	1966	$100
❑ UAS-6557 [S]	Outburst!	1966	$120

WAINWRIGHT, LOUDON, III

ARISTA
Number	Title	Yr	NM
❑ AB4173	Final Exam	1978	$15
❑ AL4063	T Shirt	1976	$15

ATLANTIC
Number	Title	Yr	NM
❑ SD8291	Album II	1971	$25
❑ SD8260	Loudon Wainwright III	1970	$25

COLUMBIA
Number	Title	Yr	NM
❑ KC31462	Album III	1972	$18
❑ PC31462 [B]	Album III	198?	$10

— Budget-line reissue

Number	Title	Yr	NM
❑ KC32710	Attempted Mustache	1973	$18
❑ PC32710 [B]	Attempted Mustache	198?	$10

— Budget-line reissue

Number	Title	Yr	NM
❑ PC33369	Unrequited	1975	$15

— No bar code on cover

Number	Title	Yr	NM
❑ PC33369	Unrequited	198?	$10

— Budget-line reissue with bar code

ROUNDER
Number	Title	Yr	NM
❑ 3050	A Live One	1979	$15
❑ 3076	Fame and Wealth	1983	$15
❑ 3096	I'm Alright	1986	$12
❑ 3106	More Love Songs	1987	$12

SILVERTONE
Number	Title	Yr	NM
❑ 1203-1-J	Therapy	1989	$15

WAITE, GENEVIEVE

PARAMOUR
Number	Title	Yr	NM
❑ 5088 [B]	Romance Is on the Rise	1974	$30

WAITE, JOHN

CHRYSALIS
Number	Title	Yr	NM
❑ CHR-1376	Ignition	1982	$12
❑ FV41376	Ignition	1983	$10

— Reissue of 1376

EMI AMERICA
Number	Title	Yr	NM
❑ ST-17164	Mask of Smiles	1985	$10
❑ ST-517164	Mask of Smiles	1985	$12

— Columbia House edition

Number	Title	Yr	NM
❑ ST-17124	No Brakes	1984	$10
❑ ST-517124	No Brakes	1984	$12

— Columbia House edition

Number	Title	Yr	NM
❑ PW-17227	Rover's Return	1987	$10

WAITRESSES, THE

POLYDOR
Number	Title	Yr	NM
❑ 810980-1	Bruiseology	1983	$12
❑ 810980-1 [DJ]	Bruiseology	1983	$30

— Promo only on purpleish vinyl

Number	Title	Yr	NM
❑ PX-1-507 [EP]	I Could Rule the World If I Could Only Get the Parts	1982	$12
❑ PD-1-6346	Wasn't Tomorrow Wonderful?	1982	$12

WAITS, TOM

ASYLUM

Number	Title	Yr	NM
❑ 6E-162 [B]	Blue Valentine	1978	$12
❑ SD5061	Closing Time	1973	$15
❑ 7E-1117	Foreign Affairs	1977	$12
❑ 6E-295	Heartattack and Vine	1980	$12
❑ 7E-2008	Nighthawks at the Diner	1975	$15
❑ 7E-1078 [B]	Small Change	1976	$15
❑ 7E-1015	The Heart of Saturday Night	1974	$15

— Original "clouds" label, no Warner Communications logo

Number	Title	Yr	NM
❑ 7E-1015	The Heart of Saturday Night	1984	$10

— Reissue with black and yellow label

ELEKTRA
Number	Title	Yr	NM
❑ 60416	Anthology of Tom Waits	1985	$12

EPITAPH
Number	Title	Yr	NM
❑ 86547	Mule Variations	1999	$15

Number	Title	Yr	NM

ISLAND
❑ 90987	Big Time	1988	$12
❑ 90572	Franks Wild Years	1987	$12
❑ 90299	Rain Dogs	1985	$12
❑ 90095	Swordfishtrombones	1983	$15
❑ 424691	Swordfishtrombones	2009	$25

WAKEFIELD SUN
MGM
❑ SE-4626	Wakefield Sun	1969	$30

WAKELY, JIMMY
CAPITOL
❑ H-9004 [10]	Christmas on the Range	1950	$175
❑ H4008 [10]	Songs of the West	195?	$120

DECCA
❑ DL8680 [M]	Enter and Rest and Pray	1957	$75
❑ DL75077	Heartaches	1969	$18
❑ DL75192	Now and Then	1970	$18
❑ DL8409 [M]	Santa Fe Trail	1956	$100

DOT
❑ DLP-3754 [M]	Christmas with Jimmy Wakely	1966	$25
❑ DLP-25734 [S]	Christmas with Jimmy Wakely	1966	$30
❑ DLP-3711 [M]	Slippin' Around	1966	$25
❑ DLP-25711 [S]	Slippin' Around	1966	$30

MCA CORAL
❑ 20033	Blue Shadows	1973	$12

MCR
❑ 1254	Jimmy Wakely Revisits Country Western Swing with the Big Band Sound	1974	$18
❑ 1250	Jimmy Wakely Sings a Tribute to Bob Wills	1974	$18

SHASTA
❑ 501	Country Million Sellers	195?	$18
❑ 505	Jimmy Wakely Sings	196?	$18
❑ 528	J.W. Country	196?	$18
❑ 502	Merry Christmas	1959	$18
❑ 512	The Jimmy Wakely Family Show	196?	$18

TOPS
❑ L-1601 [M]	A Cowboy Serenade	195?	$30

VOCALION
❑ VL73904	Big Country Songs	1970	$15
❑ VL73857	Here's Jimmy Wakely	1968	$15

WAKEMAN, RICK
Also see YES.
A&M
❑ SP-3621	Journey to the Centre of the Earth	1974	$15
❑ QU-53621 [Q]	Journey to the Centre of the Earth	1974	$50
❑ SP-3156	Journey to the Centre of the Earth	198?	$10
— Budget-line reissue of 3621			
❑ SP-4583	No Earthly Connection	1976	$15
❑ SP-6501 [B]	Rhapsodies	1979	$25
❑ SP-4660	Rick Wakeman's Criminal Record	1977	$15
❑ SP-4515	The Myths and Legends of King Arthur and the Knights of the Round Table	1975	$15
❑ QU-54515 [Q]	The Myths and Legends of King Arthur and the Knights of the Round Table	1975	$50
❑ SP-3230	The Myths and Legends of King Arthur and the Knights of the Round Table	1984	$10
— Budget-line reissue of 4515			
❑ SP-4361	The Six Wives of Henry VIII	1973	$15
— Originals have brown labels			
❑ QU-54361 [Q]	The Six Wives of Henry VIII	1974	$50
❑ SP-4361	The Six Wives of Henry VIII	1974	$12
— Silver label with "fading" A&M logo			
❑ SP-3229	The Six Wives of Henry VIII	1984	$10
— Budget-line reissue of 4361			
❑ SP-4614	White Rock	1977	$15

MOBILE FIDELITY
❑ 1-230	Journey to the Centre of the Earth	1995	$75
— Audiophile vinyl			

SWEET THUNDER
❑ 1	Journey to the Centre of the Earth	1981	$50
— Audiophile vinyl			

VARESE SARABANDE
❑ STV-81162 [B]	The Burning (Soundtrack)	1982	$25

WALCOTT, COLLIN
ECM
❑ 1062	Cloud	1976	$30
❑ 1096	Grazing	1977	$30

WALD, JERRY
KAPP
❑ KL-1043 [M]	Listen to the Music of Jerry Wald	1956	$40

LION
❑ L-70014 [M]	Tops in Pops -- Designed for Dancing	1958	$30

WALDEN, NARADA MICHAEL
ATLANTIC
❑ SD19222	Awakening	1979	$25
❑ SD19351	Confidence	1981	$25
❑ SD19141	I Cry, I Smile	1978	$25
❑ SD19259	The Dance of Life	1979	$25
❑ SD19279	Victory	1980	$25
❑ 80058	You, Looking at Me	1982	$25

REPRISE
❑ 25694	Divine Emotion	1988	$25

WARNER BROS.
❑ 25176	The Nature of Things	1984	$25

WALDO, TERRY
DIRTY SHAME
❑ 1237	Snookums Rag	197?	$30

STOMP OFF
❑ SOS-1120	Terry Waldo and the Gotham City Band	1987	$25
❑ SOS-1002	Wizard of the Keyboard	198?	$25

WALDO'S GUTBUCKET SYNCOPATORS
BLACKBIRD
❑ 12009	Jazz in the Afternoon	197?	$30
❑ 6002	Ohio Theatre Concert	197?	$25

STOMP OFF
❑ SOS-1001	Feelin' Devilish	198?	$25
❑ SOS-1036	Presents	198?	$25

WALDO'S RAGTIME ORCHESTRA
STOMP OFF
❑ SOS-1007	Smiles and Chuckles	198?	$25
❑ SOS-1069	Spectacular Ragtime	198?	$25

WALDRON, MAL, AND GARY PEACOCK
CATALYST
❑ 7906	First Encounter	197?	$30

WALDRON, MAL, AND STEVE LACY
HAT ART
❑ 2038	Let's Call This	1987	$35

INNER CITY
❑ IC-3010	One-upsmanship	197?	$30

SOUL NOTE
❑ 121170	Sempre Amore	1990	$35

WALDRON, MAL
ARISTA/FREEDOM
❑ AF1013	Blues for Lady Day	1975	$30
❑ AF1042	Signals	1977	$30

BETHLEHEM

❑ BCP-6045 [M]	Left Alone	1960	$1200
— maroon label, deep groove			
❑ SBCP-6045 [S]	Left Alone	1960	$300

ENJA
❑ 2004	Black Glory	197?	$35
❑ 2050	Hard Talk	197?	$35
❑ 3075	Mingus Lives	198?	$30
❑ 2034	Up Popped the Devil	197?	$35
❑ 4010	What It Is	198?	$30

FANTASY
❑ OJC-132	Impressions	198?	$25
❑ OJC-611	Mal/1	1991	$30
❑ OJC-082	The Quest	198?	$25

INNER CITY
❑ IC-3018	Moods	1979	$35

MUSE
❑ MR-5305	Encounters	198?	$25

MUSIC MINUS ONE
❑ 4005 [M]	Blue Drums	1961	$25
❑ 4007 [M]	For Pianists Only	1961	$25
❑ 1018 [M]	For Singers 'N Singer	1960	$25
❑ 175 [M]	Fun With Brushes	1960	$25
❑ 1017 [M]	Mal Waldron	1960	$25
❑ 1012 [M]	Moonglow and Stardust	1960	$25
❑ 1015 [M]	Music of Duke Ellington	1960	$25
❑ 1016 [M]	Music of McHugh	1960	$25
❑ 4008 [M]	They Laughed When I Sat Down to Play	1961	$25

NEW JAZZ
❑ NJLP-8242 [M]	Impressions	1960	$175
— Purple label			
❑ NJLP-8242 [M]	Impressions	1965	$175
— Blue label, trident logo at right			
❑ NJLP-8201 [M]	Mal/3: Sounds	1958	$175
— Purple label			
❑ NJLP-8201 [M]	Mal/3: Sounds	1958	$250
— Yellow label			
❑ NJLP-8201 [M]	Mal/3: Sounds	1965	$175
— Blue label, trident logo at right			
❑ NJLP-8208 [M]	Mal/4: Trio	1958	$175
— Purple label			
❑ NJLP-8208 [M]	Mal/4: Trio	1965	$175
— Blue label, trident logo at right			
❑ NJLP-8316 [M]	The Dealers	1963	$0
— Canceled; reassigned to Status			
❑ NJLP-8269 [M]	The Quest	1962	$175
— Purple label			
❑ NJLP-8269 [M]	The Quest	1965	$175
— Blue label, trident logo at right			

PALO ALTO
❑ PA-8014	One Entrance, Many Exits	1982	$25

PAULA
❑ LPS-4000	Mal Waldron on the Steinway	197?	$30

PRESTIGE
❑ 24107	After Hours	197?	$35
❑ PRLP-7090 [M]	Mal/1	1957	$300
❑ PRLP-7111 [M]	Mal/2	1957	$650
❑ 24068	Mal Waldron/1 and 2	197?	$35
❑ PRST-7579 [S]	The Quest	1969	$25

SOUL NOTE
❑ 121118	The Go-Go -- Live at the Vilalge Gate	1989	$30
❑ 121148	The Seagulls of Kristiansund	1990	$35
❑ 121130	Update	1989	$30

STATUS
❑ ST-8316 [M]	The Dealers	1965	$40

WEST 54
❑ 8010	Live/Left Alone	1980	$30

WALES, HOWARD, AND JERRY GARCIA
DOUGLAS
❑ Z30589	Hooteroll	1971	$40

WALI AND THE AFRO-CARAVAN
SOLID STATE
❑ SS-18065	Home Lost and Found	1969	$25

WALKER, BILLY
COLUMBIA
❑ CL1935 [M]	Billy Walker's Greatest Hits	1963	$18
❑ CS8735 [S]	Billy Walker's Greatest Hits	1963	$25
❑ CS9798	Billy Walker's Greatest Hits, Volume 2	1969	$18
❑ CL1624 [M]	Everybody's Hits But Mine	1961	$25
❑ CS8424 [S]	Everybody's Hits But Mine	1961	$30
❑ C30226	Goodnight	1971	$15
❑ CL2206 [M]	Thank You for Calling	1964	$18
❑ CS9006 [S]	Thank You for Calling	1964	$25
❑ CL2331 [M]	The Gun, the Gold and the Girl/Cross the Brazos at Waco	1965	$18
❑ CS9131 [S]	The Gun, the Gold and the Girl/Cross the Brazos at Waco	1965	$25

HARMONY
❑ HL7306 [M]	Anything Your Heart Desires	1964	$18
❑ HL7410 [M]	Big Country Hits	1967	$18
❑ HS11210 [S]	Big Country Hits	1967	$15
❑ HS11414	Charlie's Shoes	1970	$15
❑ H31177	There May Be No Tomorrow	1972	$12

MGM
❑ SE-4887	Billy Walker's All Time Greatest Hits	1972	$15

WALKER, BILLY

Number	Title	Yr	NM
❏ SE-4756	I'm Gonna Keep On Lovin' You/She Goes Walking Through My Mind	1971	$18
❏ SE-4789	Live!	1972	$18
❏ SE-4863	The Billy Walker Show	1973	$15
❏ SE-4938 [B]	Too Many Memories	1974	$15
❏ SE-4682	When a Man Loves a Woman (The Way That I Love You)	1970	$18

MONUMENT

Number	Title	Yr	NM
❏ MLP-8047 [M]	A Million and One	1966	$15
❏ SLP-18047 [S]	A Million and One	1966	$18
❏ SLP-18101	Billy Walker Salutes the Country Music Hall of Fame	1969	$18
❏ KZ31912	Billy Walker's Greatest Hits	1972	$15
❏ 6641	Billy Walker's Greatest Hits	1976	$12
❏ SLP-18143	Darling Days	1970	$18
❏ SLP-18090	I Taught Her Everything She Knows	1968	$18
❏ SLP-18116	Portrait of Billy	1969	$18
❏ MLP-8072 [M]	The Walker Way	1967	$25
❏ SLP-18072 [S]	The Walker Way	1967	$18

RCA VICTOR

Number	Title	Yr	NM
❏ APL1-1489	Alone Again	1976	$15
❏ APL1-1160	Lovin' and Losin'	1975	$15

WALKER, CHARLIE

COLUMBIA

Number	Title	Yr	NM
❏ CL1691 [M]	Charlie Walker's Greatest Hits	1961	$25
❏ CS8491 [S]	Charlie Walker's Greatest Hits	1961	$30

EPIC

Number	Title	Yr	NM
❏ LN24153 [M]	Born to Lose	1965	$18
❏ BN26153 [S]	Born to Lose	1965	$25
❏ BN26343 [S]	Charlie Walker's Greatest Hits	1968	$18
❏ LN24343 [M]	Charlie Walker's Greatest Hits	1968	$40
❏ LN24137 [M]	Close All the Honky Tonks	1965	$18
❏ BN26137 [S]	Close All the Honky Tonks	1965	$25
❏ LN24328 [M]	Don't Squeeze My Sharmon	1967	$30
❏ BN26328 [S]	Don't Squeeze My Sharmon	1967	$25
❏ BN26424	He Is My Everything	1969	$18
❏ E30660	Honky Tonkin'	1971	$18
❏ BN26483	Recorded Live in Dallas	1969	$18
❏ LN24209 [M]	Wine, Women and Walker	1966	$18
❏ BN26209 [S]	Wine, Women and Walker	1966	$25

HARMONY

Number	Title	Yr	NM
❏ HL7415 [M]	Golden Hits	1967	$18
❏ HS11215 [S]	Golden Hits	1967	$15

PLANTATION

Number	Title	Yr	NM
❏ 535	Golden Hits	1978	$12

RCA VICTOR

Number	Title	Yr	NM
❏ APL1-0181	Break Out the Bottle	1973	$15
❏ LSP-4737	Charlie Walker	1972	$18

VOCALION

Number	Title	Yr	NM
❏ VL73814	The Style of Charlie Walker	1968	$15

WALKER, CINDY

MONUMENT

Number	Title	Yr	NM
❏ MLP-8020 [M]	Words and Music by Cindy Walker	1964	$25
❏ SLP-18020 [S]	Words and Music by Cindy Walker	1964	$30

WALKER, CLINT

WARNER BROS.

Number	Title	Yr	NM
❏ W1343 [M]	Inspiration	1959	$30
❏ WS1343 [S]	Inspiration	1959	$40

WALKER, DAVID T.

ODE

Number	Title	Yr	NM
❏ SP-77011	David T. Walker	1971	$12
❏ SP-77035	On Love	1976	$12
❏ SP-77020	Press On	1974	$12

ZEA

Number	Title	Yr	NM
❏ 1000	Plum Happy	1970	$18

WALKER, JERRY JEFF

Also see CIRCUS MAXIMUS.

ATCO

Number	Title	Yr	NM
❏ SD 33-336	Bein' Free	1970	$25
❏ SD 33-297	Five Years Gone	1969	$30
❏ SD 33-259 [B]	Mr. Bojangles	1968	$30

BAINBRIDGE

Number	Title	Yr	NM
❏ 6222	Mr. Bojangles	198?	$12

DECCA

Number	Title	Yr	NM
❏ DL75384	Jerry Jeff Walker	1972	$18

ELEKTRA

Number	Title	Yr	NM
❏ 6E-163	Jerry Jeff	1978	$12
❏ 6E-239	Too Old to Change	1980	$12

MCA

Number	Title	Yr	NM
❏ 8013	A Man Must Carry On	1977	$15
❏ 6003	A Man Must Carry On	198?	$12
—Budget-line reissue			
❏ 3041	Contrary to Ordinary	1978	$12
❏ 37162	Contrary to Ordinary	198?	$10
—Budget-line reissue			
❏ 5355	Cowjazz	1983	$12
❏ 2202	It's a Good Night for Singin'	1976	$12
❏ 27026	It's a Good Night for Singin'	198?	$10
—Budget-line reissue			
❏ 510	Jerry Jeff Walker	1975	$12
—Reissue of Decca LP			
❏ 2358	Jerry Jeff Walker	1977	$10
—Reissue of MCA 510			
❏ 37004	Jerry Jeff Walker	198?	$10
—Budget-line reissue			
❏ 2156	Ridin' High	1975	$12
❏ 37006	Ridin' High	198?	$10
—Budget-line reissue			
❏ 5128	The Best of Jerry Jeff Walker	1980	$12
❏ 382	Viva Terlingua!	1973	$12
❏ 2350	Viva Terlingua!	1977	$10
—Reissue of MCA 382			
❏ 37005	Viva Terlingua!	198?	$10
—Budget-line reissue			
❏ 450	Walker's Collectibles	1974	$12
❏ 2355	Walker's Collectibles	1977	$10
—Reissue of MCA 450			
❏ 27027	Walker's Collectibles	198?	$10
—Budget-line reissue			

SOUTHCOAST

Number	Title	Yr	NM
❏ 5199	Reunion	1981	$12

VANGUARD

Number	Title	Yr	NM
❏ VSD-6521	Driftin' Way of Life	1969	$25
❏ VMS-73124	Driftin' Way of Life	1985	$10
—Reissue of 6521			

WALKER, JIMMIE

BUDDAH

Number	Title	Yr	NM
❏ BDS5635 [B]	Dyn-O-Mite	1975	$15

WALKER, JR., AND THE ALL STARS

MOTOWN

Number	Title	Yr	NM
❏ 5297ML	All the Great Hits of Jr. Walker and the All Stars	1984	$12
❏ M7-786	Anthology	1974	$25
❏ 6053ML	Blow the House Down	1983	$12
❏ M5-208V1	Greatest Hits	1981	$12
—Reissue of Soul 718			
❏ M5-105V1	Motown Superstar Series, Vol. 5	1981	$12
❏ M5-141V1	Shotgun	1981	$12
—Reissue of Soul 701			

PICKWICK

Number	Title	Yr	NM
❏ SPC-3391	Shotgun	197?	$15

SOUL

Number	Title	Yr	NM
❏ SS-726	A Gassss	1970	$18
❏ SS-721	Gotta Hold on to This Feeling	1969	$30
❏ SS-718	Greatest Hits	1969	$25
❏ SS-710	Home Cookin'	1969	$25
❏ S6-745	Hot Shot	1976	$18
❏ S6-742	Jr. Walker and the All Stars	1973	$0
—Canceled			
❏ 705 [M]	Live	1967	$25
❏ SS-705 [S]	Live	1967	$30
❏ SS-733	Moody Jr.	1971	$18
❏ SS-738	Peace and Understanding Is Hard to Find	1973	$18
❏ S-732L	Rainbow Funk	1971	$18
❏ 703 [M]	Road Runner	1966	$25
❏ SS-703 [S]	Road Runner	1966	$30
❏ S6-747	Sax Appeal	1976	$18
❏ 701 [M]	Shotgun	1965	$75
—Mostly white label with vertical "Soul" at left			
❏ 701 [M]	Shotgun	1965	$25
—Purple swirl label with "Soul" at top			
❏ SS-701 [S]	Shotgun	1965	$30
❏ S7-750	Smooth	1978	$18
❏ 702 [M]	Soul Session	1966	$75
—Mostly white label with vertical "Soul" at left			
❏ 702 [M]	Soul Session	1966	$25
—Purple swirl label with "Soul" at top			
❏ SS-702 [S]	Soul Session	1966	$30
❏ SS-721	What Does It Take to Win Your Love	1970	$25
—Retitled version of above			
❏ S6-748	Whopper Bopper Show Stopper	1977	$18

WHITFIELD

Number	Title	Yr	NM
❏ WHK3331	Back Street Boogie	1980	$15

WALKER, KIT

WINDHAM HILL

Number	Title	Yr	NM
❏ WH-0109	Dancing on the Edge of the World	1987	$25
❏ WH-0117	Fire in the Lake	1989	$30

WALKER, MARTIN

ABC-PARAMOUNT

Number	Title	Yr	NM
❏ ABC-483 [M]	From Scotland with Love	1964	$18
❏ ABCS-483 [S]	From Scotland with Love	1964	$25

WALKER, NANCY

RCA CAMDEN

Number	Title	Yr	NM
❏ CAL-561 [M]	I Hate Men	1960	$30
❏ CAS-561 [S]	I Hate Men	1960	$30

WALKER, PETER

VANGUARD

Number	Title	Yr	NM
❏ VSD-79282	Second Poem to Karmela	1968	$25

WALKER, SCOTT

Also see THE WALKER BROTHERS.

4 MEN WITH BEARDS

Number	Title	Yr	NM
❏ 4M149LP [B]	Scott		$25
❏ 4M150LP [B]	Scott 2		$25
❏ 4M151LP [B]	Scott 3		$25
❏ 4M152LP [B]	Scott 4		$25

SMASH

Number	Title	Yr	NM
❏ SRS-67099	Aloner	1968	$25
❏ SRS-67106	Scott, Volume 2	1968	$25
❏ SRS-67121	Scott Walker 3	1969	$25

WALKER, T-BONE

ATLANTIC

Number	Title	Yr	NM
❏ 8020 [M]	T-Bone Blues	1959	$300
—Black label			
❏ 8020 [M]	T-Bone Blues	1960	$150
—Red and purple label			
❏ SD8256	T-Bone Blues	1970	$50

BLUE NOTE

Number	Title	Yr	NM
❏ BN-LA533-H2	Classics	1975	$50

BLUESTIME

Number	Title	Yr	NM
❏ 29010	Blue Rocks	1969	$75
❏ 29004	Everyday I Have the Blues	1968	$75

BLUESWAY

Number	Title	Yr	NM
❏ BLS-6058	Dirty Mistreater	1973	$35
❏ BLS-6014	Funky Town	1968	$75
❏ BLS-6008 [B]	Stormy Monday Blues	1968	$40
—Reissue of Wet Soul LP?			

BRUNSWICK

Number	Title	Yr	NM
❏ BL754126	The Truth	1968	$75

CAPITOL

Number	Title	Yr	NM
❏ H370 [10]	Classics in Jazz	1953	$1000
❏ T370 [M]	Classics in Jazz	1953	$350
❏ T1958 [M]	Great Blues Vocal and Guitar	1963	$250
—Black "The Star Line" label (existence of black colorband label not confirmed)			

DELMARK

Number	Title	Yr	NM
❏ D-633 [M]	I Want a Little Girl	1967	$40
❏ DS-633 [S]	I Want a Little Girl	1967	$150

IMPERIAL

Number	Title	Yr	NM
❏ LP-9146 [M]	I Get So Weary	1961	$300
❏ LP-9116 [M]	Singing the Blues	1960	$300
❏ LP-9098 [M]	T-Bone Walker Sings the Blues	1959	$300

MOSAIC

Number	Title	Yr	NM
❏ MR9-130	The Complete Recordings of T-Bone Walker 1940-1954	199?	$300
—Limited edition of 7,500			

POLYDOR

Number	Title	Yr	NM
❏ PD-5521 [B]	Fly Walker Airlines	1973	$25
❏ 24-4502 [B]	Good Feelin'	1972	$25

REPRISE

Number	Title	Yr	NM
❏ 2RS6483	Very Rare	1973	$50

WET SOUL

Number	Title	Yr	NM
❏ 1002	Stormy Monday Blues	1967	$150

WALKER BROTHERS, THE

SMASH

Number	Title	Yr	NM
❏ MGS-27076 [M]	Introducing the Walker Brothers	1965	$80
❏ SRS-67076 [R]	Introducing the Walker Brothers	1965	$50
❏ MGS-27082 [M]	The Sun Ain't Gonna Shine (Anymore)	1966	$50
❏ SRS-67082 [P]	The Sun Ain't Gonna Shine (Anymore)	1966	$75
—"The Sun Ain't Gonna Shine (Anymore)" and "When the Lights Go Out" are rechanneled.			

TOWER

Number	Title	Yr	NM
❏ T5026 [M]	I Only Came to Dance with You	1966	$30
—As "Scott Engel and John Stewart"			
❏ ST5026 [S]	I Only Came to Dance with You	1966	$25
—As "Scott Engel and John Stewart"			

WALL, DAN

AUDIOPHILE

Number	Title	Yr	NM
❏ AP-143	Dan Wall Trio	198?	$25

PROGRESSIVE

Number	Title	Yr	NM
❏ PRO-7016	The Trio	198?	$30

Number	Title	Yr	NM

WALL OF VOODOO

INDEX/I.R.S.
❏ SP-70401 [EP]	Wall of Voodoo	1980	$15

I.R.S.
❏ SP-70026	Call of the West	1982	$15
❏ SP-70022	Dark Continent	1981	$15
❏ 5997	Happy Planet	1987	$12
❏ 5662	Seven Days in Sammystown	1985	$15
❏ 42140	The Ugly American in Australia	1988	$12

WALLACE, BENNIE

AUDIOQUEST
❏ AQLP-1017	The Old Songs	1993	$35

BLUE NOTE
❏ BT-48014	Border Town	1988	$30
❏ BT-85107	Twilight Time	198?	$30

ENJA
❏ 4028	Bennie Wallace and Chick Corea	1982	$30
❏ 4046	Big Jim's Tango	1982	$30
❏ 3091	Wallace Plays Monk	198?	$30

INNER CITY
❏ IC-3025	Fourteen Bar Blues	1979	$30
❏ IC-3034	Live at the Public Theater	1979	$30

WALLACE, GEORGE, JR.

PORTRAIT
❏ JR36579	Heroes Like You and Me	1981	$30

WALLACE, JERRY

CHALLENGE
❏ 2002	Greatest Hits	1969	$18
❏ CH619 [M]	In the Misty Moonlight	1964	$25
❏ CHS619 [S]	In the Misty Moonlight	1964	$30
❏ CHL606 [M]	Just Jerry	1959	$75
❏ CH616 [M]	Shutters and Boards	1962	$30
❏ CHS616 [S]	Shutters and Boards	1962	$40
❏ CH612 [M]	There She Goes	1961	$30
❏ CHS612 [S]	There She Goes	1961	$40

DECCA
❏ DL75294	This Is Jerry Wallace	1971	$18
❏ DL75349	To Get to You	1972	$18

LIBERTY
❏ LST-7564	Another Time, Another World	1968	$25
❏ LST-7597	Sweet Child of Sunshine	1968	$25
❏ LRP-3545 [M]	This One's on the House	1967	$40

— *Stock copy inside stereo cover; "Audition Mono LP Not for Sale" sticker on front*

❏ LST-7545 [S]	This One's on the House	1967	$25

MCA
❏ 301 [B]	Do You Know What It's Like to Be Lonesome?	1973	$15
❏ 408	For Wives and Lovers	1974	$15
❏ 462	I Wonder Whose Baby (You Are Now)/Make Hay While the Sun Shines	1975	$15
❏ 366	Primrose Lane/Don't Give Up on Me	1973	$15

MERCURY
❏ MG-21072 [M]	The Best of Jerry Wallace	1966	$18
❏ SR-61072 [S]	The Best of Jerry Wallace	1966	$25

MGM
❏ M3G-4995	Comin' Home to You	1976	$15
❏ M3G-4990	Greatest Hits	1975	$12
❏ M3G-5007	Jerry Wallace	1976	$12

SUNSET
❏ SUS-5294	Primrose Lane	1969	$15

UNITED ARTISTS
❏ UXS-95	Jerry Wallace Superpak	1972	$25

WALLACE BROTHERS, THE

SIMS
❏ LP-128 [M]	Soul, Soul and More Soul	1965	$250
❏ LPS-128 [S]	Soul, Soul and More Soul	1965	$300

WALLER, FATS

BIOGRAPH
❏ 1002	Rare Piano Rolls	197?	$25
❏ 1005	Rare Piano Rolls, Volume 2	197?	$25
❏ 1015	Rare Piano Rolls, Volume 3	197?	$25

BLUEBIRD
❏ AXM2-5518	Piano Solos	197?	$35
❏ AXM2-5511	The Complete Fats Waller, Volume 1	197?	$35
❏ AXM2-5575	The Complete Fats Waller, Volume 2	198?	$35
❏ AXM2-5583	The Complete Fats Waller, Volume 3	198?	$35
❏ 5905-1-RB	The Complete Fats Waller, Volume 4	1987	$35
❏ 6288-1-RB	The Joint Is Jumpin'	1987	$25
❏ 9983-1-RB	The Last Years: Fats Waller and His Rhythm, 1940-1943	198?	$30

BULLDOG
❏ BDL-2004	20 Golden Pieces of Fats Waller	198?	$25

EVEREST ARCHIVE OF FOLK & JAZZ
❏ 337	Ain't Misbehavin'	197?	$25
❏ 319	Fats Waller Plays Fats Waller	197?	$25

GIANTS OF JAZZ
❏ GOJ-1035	Live, Volume 2	198?	$25
❏ GOJ-1029	Live at the Yacht Club	198?	$25

MUSICAL HERITAGE SOCIETY
❏ MHS4937	Fats" Waller at the Organ	1981	$25

RCA VICTOR
❏ LPV-562 [M]	African Ripples	1969	$25
❏ LPM-1246 [M]	Ain't Misbehavin'	1956	$50
❏ CPL1-2904	A Legendary Performer	1979	$25
❏ LPM-6000 [M]	Fats	1960	$100
❏ LPT-8 [10]	Fats Waller 1934-42	1951	$175
❏ LPV-516 [M]	Fats Waller '34/'35	1965	$25
❏ LPT-14 [10]	Fats Waller Favorites	1951	$175
❏ LPT-1001 [M]	Fats Waller Plays and Sings	1954	$100
❏ LPT-6001 [M]	Fats Waller Radio Transcriptions	1954	$120

— *Boxed set with booklet*

❏ LPM-1502 [M]	Handful of Keys	1957	$50
❏ LPM-1503 [M]	One Never Knows, Do One?	1959	$50
❏ LPV-550 [M]	Smashing Thirds	1968	$25
❏ LPT-3040 [10]	Swingin' the Organ	1953	$120
❏ LPV-473 [M]	The Real Fats Waller	1965	$30
❏ LPV-525 [M]	Valentine Stomp	1966	$25

RIVERSIDE
❏ RLP-1021 [10]	Fats Waller at the Organ	1953	$300
❏ RLP-1010 [10]	Rediscovered Fats Waller Piano Solos	1953	$300
❏ RLP 12-109 [M]	The Amazing Mr. Waller	1955	$300
❏ RLP-1022 [10]	The Amazing Mr. Waller Vol. 2: Jivin' with Fats	1953	$175

— *Black vinyl*

❏ RLP-1022 [10]	The Amazing Mr. Waller Vol. 2: Jivin' with Fats	1953	$350

— *Red vinyl*

❏ RLP 12-103 [M]	The Young Fats Waller	1955	$300

STANYAN
❏ 10057	The Undiscovered Fats Waller	197?	$25

SWING
❏ SW-8442/3	Fats Waller in London	198?	$30

TIME-LIFE
❏ STL-J-15	Giants of Jazz	1980	$50

TRIP
❏ 5042	A Legend in His Lifetime	197?	$30
❏ J-4	Fats Waller on the Air	197?	$25

X
❏ LVA-3035 [10]	The Young Fats Waller	1955	$175

WALLER, GORDON

ABC
❏ X-749	And Gordon	1972	$18

WALLER, JIM, AND THE DELTAS

ARVEE
❏ A-432 [M]	Surfin' Wild	1963	$100
❏ AS-432 [S]	Surfin' Wild	1963	$150

WALLINGTON, GEORGE

ATLANTIC
❏ 1275 [M]	Knight Music	1958	$300

— *Black label*

❏ SD1275 [S]	Knight Music	1958	$300

— *Green label*

❏ 1275 [M]	Knight Music	1961	$175

— *Multicolor label, white "fan" logo at right*

❏ SD1275 [S]	Knight Music	1961	$175

— *Multicolor label, white "fan" logo at right*

BLUE NOTE
❏ BLP-5045 [10]	George Wallington and His All-Star Band	1954	$1000

EAST-WEST
❏ 4004 [M]	The Prestidigitator	1958	$300

FANTASY
❏ OJC-1704	Jazz for the Carriage Trade	1985	$30
❏ OJC-1754	The George Wallington Trios	198?	$30

NEW JAZZ
❏ NJLP-8207 [M]	The New York Scene	1958	$900

— *Purple label*

❏ NJLP-8207 [M]	The New York Scene	1965	$175

— *Blue label, trident logo at right*

NORGRAN
❏ MGN-1010 [M]	George Wallington with Strings	1954	$300
❏ MGN-24 [10]	The Workshop of the George Wallington Trio	1954	$250

PRESTIGE
❏ PRST-7820	At Café Bohemia '55	1971	$35

❏ PLP-1001 [M]	George Wallington Quintet at the Bohemia	1955	$1500
❏ PRLP-7032 [M]	Jazz for the Carriage Trade	1956	$800
❏ P-24093	Our Delight	197?	$35
❏ PRLP-136 [10]	The George Wallington Trio	1952	$500
❏ PRLP-158 [10]	The George Wallington Trio, Volume 2	1953	$500
❏ PRST-7587 [R]	The George Wallington Trios	1968	$30

PROGRESSIVE
❏ PRO-7001	The George Wallington Quintet at the Café Bohemia, 1955	198?	$25
❏ PLP-3001 [10]	The George Wallington Trio	1952	$500

SAVOY
❏ MG-12122 [M]	Jazz at Hotchkiss	1957	$150
❏ MG-15037 [10]	The George Wallington Trio	1954	$175
❏ MG-12081 [M]	The George Wallington Trio	1956	$150

SAVOY JAZZ
❏ SJL-1122	Dance of the Infidels	198?	$30

VERVE
❏ MGV-2017 [M]	Variations	1956	$250

WALLIS, RUTH

JUBILEE
❏ JGM-2050 [M]	Ruth Wallis Sings The Spice Is Right	1963	$25

KING
❏ 993 [M]	Bahama Mama	1966	$30
❏ 987 [M]	Davy's Little Dinghy	1966	$30
❏ 986 [M]	Here's Looking Up Your Hatch	1966	$30
❏ 992 [M]	He Wants a Little...Pizza	1966	$30
❏ 265-9 [10]	House Party	1952	$120
❏ 395-507 [M]	House Party	1956	$150
❏ 988 [M]	Marry Go Round	1966	$30
❏ 991 [M]	Oil Man from Texas	1966	$30
❏ 989 [M]	Red Lights	1966	$30
❏ 265-6 [10]	Rhumba Party	1952	$120
❏ 904 [M]	Saucy Hit Parade	1964	$30
❏ 990 [M]	Ubangi Me	1966	$30

MERCURY
❏ SR-61210	How to Stay Sexy Tho' Married	1969	$25

WALLIS ORIGINAL
❏ W-3 [10]	Cafe Party	195?	$40
❏ WLP-15 [M]	Cruise Party	195?	$30
❏ WLP-13 [M]	For Sophisticates Only	195?	$30
❏ WLP-14 [M]	French Postcards Set to Music	195?	$30
❏ W-5 [10]	Holiday Party	195?	$40

— *Black vinyl*

❏ W-5 [10]	Holiday Party	195?	$75

— *Red vinyl*

❏ WLP-18 [M]	Hot Songs for Cool Knights	195?	$30
❏ W-6 [10]	Life of the Party	195?	$40
❏ WLP-17 [M]	Love Is for the Birds	195?	$30
❏ W-9 [M]	Men and Memories	195?	$40
❏ W-2 [M]	Ruth Wallis	195?	$40
❏ W-1 [10]	Ruth Wallis' Old Party Favorites	195?	$40
❏ WLP-16 [M]	Salty Songs for Underwater Listening	195?	$30
❏ WLP-11 [M]	Saucy Hit Parade	195?	$30
❏ W-4 [10]	Senorita Ruth Wallis and Her Latin Party Rhythms	195?	$40
❏ WLP-12 [M]	That Saucy Redhead	195?	$30
❏ WLP-10 [M]	Wallis on the Party Line	195?	$30

WALLOWITCH, JOHN

SERENUS
❏ 22015 [B]	Now Appearing At The Dreamland Memory Ballroom	197?	$40
❏ SEP2005 [B]	This Is	1964	$300

— *Andy Warhol cover.*

❏ SEP2006 [B]	This Is The Other Side Of	1975	$300

— *Andy Warhol cover utilized same artwork as SEP 2005 but placed on the back cover - "the other side".*

Number	Title	Yr	NM
WALRATH, JACK			
BLUE NOTE			
❏ BT-46905	Master of Suspense	1987	$30
❏ B1-91101	Neohippus	1989	$30
GATEMOUTH			
❏ 1002	Demons in Pursuit	1979	$30
MUSE			
❏ MR-5362	Wholly Trinity	198?	$25
RED RECORD			
❏ VPA-182	Live at Umbria Jazz Festival, 1986 Vol. 1	1986	$30
❏ VPA-186	Live at Umbria Jazz Festival, 1986 Vol. 2	1986	$30
STASH			
❏ ST-223	A Plea for Sanity	198?	$25
❏ ST-221	Revenge of the Fat People	198?	$25
STEEPLECHASE			
❏ SCS-1172	Jack Walrath in Europe	1982	$30
WALSH, JOE			
Also see EAGLES; THE JAMES GANG (1)			
ABC			
❏ AA-1083	The Best of Joe Walsh	1978	$12
—Also contains two James Gang tracks			
❏ ABCD-932	You Can't Argue with a Sick Mind	1976	$12
ABC COMMAND			
❏ QD-40017 [Q]	So What	1975	$0
—Not released			
❏ QD-40016 [Q]	The Smoker You Drink, the Player You Get	1974	$30
ABC DUNHILL			
❏ DS-50130	Barnstorm	1972	$12
—Of the James Gang and the Eagles			
❏ DS-51071	So What	1974	$12
❏ DS-50140 [B]	The Smoker You Drink, the Player You Get	1973	$12
ASYLUM			
❏ 6E-141	But Seriously, Folks…	1978	$12
❏ 5E-523	There Goes the Neighborhood	1981	$10
MCA			
❏ 37053	Barnstorm	1979	$10
—Reissue of ABC Dunhill 50130			
❏ 37055	So What	1979	$10
—Reissue of ABC Dunhill 50171			
❏ 37052	The Best of Joe Walsh	1979	$10
—Reissue of ABC 1083			
❏ 37054	The Smoker You Drink, the Player You Get	1979	$10
—Reissue of ABC Dunhill 50140			
❏ 37051	You Can't Argue with a Sick Mind	1979	$10
—Reissue of ABC 932			
WARNER BROS.			
❏ 25606	Got Any Gum?	1987	$10
❏ 25281	The Confessor	1985	$10
❏ 25281 [DJ]	The Confessor	1985	$18
—Promo only on Quiex II vinyl			
❏ 23884	You Bought It -- You Name It	1983	$10
WALSTON, RAY			
VEE JAY			
❏ LP-1110 [M]	My Favorite Songs from "Mary Poppins" and Other Songs to Delight	1965	$30
❏ SR-1110 [S]	My Favorite Songs from "Mary Poppins" and Other Songs to Delight	1965	$30
WALT, SHERMAN			
RCA VICTOR RED SEAL			
❏ LSC-2353 [S]	Vivaldi: The Four Seasons Concertos	1960	$30
— Original with "shaded dog" label			
WALTER, CY			
ATLANTIC			
❏ 1236 [M]	Rodgers Revisited	1956	$300
—Black label			
❏ 1236 [M]	Rodgers Revisited	1961	$175
—Multicolor label, white "fan" logo at right			
MGM			
❏ E-4393 [M]	Cy Walter at the Drake	1966	$30
❏ SE-4393 [S]	Cy Walter at the Drake	1966	$35
WESTMINSTER			
❏ WP-6120 [M]	Dry Martini, Please	195?	$30
❏ WST-15054 [S]	Dry Martini, Please	195?	$30
WALTON, CEDAR, AND HANK MOBLEY			
MUSE			
❏ MR-5132	Breakthrough	197?	$30

Number	Title	Yr	NM
WALTON, CEDAR			
CLEAN CUTS			
❏ 704	Solos	1980	$35
COBBLESTONE			
❏ 9011	Breakthrough	197?	$35
COLUMBIA			
❏ JC36285	Soundscapes	1980	$25
FANTASY			
❏ OJC-462	Cedar!	1990	$25
❏ OJC-6002	Cedar Walton Plays Cedar Walton	1988	$25
INNER CITY			
❏ IC-6019	Pit Inn	198?	$30
❏ IC-6009	The Pentagon	197?	$30
MUSE			
❏ MR-5010	A Night at Boomer's, Vol. 1	1973	$30
❏ MR-5022	A Night at Boomer's, Vol. 2	1973	$30
❏ MR-5059	Firm Roots	197?	$35
❏ MR-5244	The Maestro	1981	$25
PRESTIGE			
❏ PRLP-7519 [M]	Cedar!	1967	$30
❏ PRST-7519 [S]	Cedar!	1967	$25
❏ PRST-7693	Soul Cycle	1970	$25
❏ PRST-7591	Spectrum	1968	$25
❏ PRST-7618	The Electric Boogaloo Song	1969	$25
RCA VICTOR			
❏ APL1-1435	Beyond Mobius	1976	$25
❏ APL1-1009 [B]	Mobius	1975	$25
RED RECORD			
❏ VPA-179	Cedar's Blues	1986	$30
STEEPLECHASE			
❏ SCS-1085	First Set	198?	$30
❏ SCS-1179	Third Set	198?	$30
WALTON, FRANK			
DELMARK			
❏ DS-436	Reality	197?	$25
WALTON, JON			
GATEWAY			
❏ 7006	Jon Walton Swings Again	1964	$35
WALTON, WADE			
BLUESVILLE			
❏ BVLP-1060 [M]	Shake 'Em on Down	1963	$150
—Blue label, silver print			
❏ BVLP-1060 [M]	Shake 'Em on Down	1964	$30
—Blue label, trident logo at right			
WALTONS, THE			
See VARIOUS ARTISTS COMPILATIONS in back.			
WANDERERS THREE, THE			
DOLTON			
❏ BLP2021 [M]	We Sing Folk Songs	1963	$25
❏ BST8021 [S]	We Sing Folk Songs	1963	$30
WANDERLEY, WALTER			
A&M			
❏ SP-3022	Moondreams	1969	$30
❏ SP-3018	When It Was Done	1969	$30
CANYON			
❏ 7711	Return of the Original Sound	196?	$30
GNP CRESCENDO			
❏ GNPS-2137	Brazil's Greatest Hits	197?	$25
❏ GNPS-2142	Perpetual Motion Love	197?	$25
MGM LATINO SERIES			
❏ LAT10010 [S]	Cheganca	197?	$35
—Reissue of Verve V6-8676			
PHILIPS			
❏ PHM200227 [M]	Brazilian Blend	1967	$30
❏ PHS600227 [S]	Brazilian Blend	1967	$35
❏ PHM200233 [M]	Organ-ized	1967	$30
❏ PHS600233 [S]	Organ-ized	1967	$35
TOWER			
❏ T5047 [M]	From Rio with Love	1966	$35
❏ ST5047 [S]	From Rio with Love	1966	$35
❏ T5058 [M]	Murmurio	1967	$35
❏ ST5058 [S]	Murmurio	1967	$35
VERVE			
❏ V-8706 [M]	Batucada	1967	$50
❏ V6-8706 [S]	Batucada	1967	$35
❏ V-8676 [M]	Cheganca	1966	$35
❏ V6-8676 [S]	Cheganca	1966	$50
❏ V-8739 [M]	Kee-Ka-Roo	1967	$50
❏ V6-8739 [S]	Kee-Ka-Roo	1967	$35
❏ V-8658 [M]	Rain Forest	1966	$18
❏ V6-8658 [S]	Rain Forest	1966	$50
WORLD PACIFIC			
❏ WP-1866 [M]	Quarteto Bossamba	1967	$175
❏ ST-21866 [S]	Quarteto Bossamba	1967	$150
❏ WP-1856 [M]	Samba So!	1967	$175
❏ ST-21856 [S]	Samba So!	1967	$150

Number	Title	Yr	NM
WANG CHUNG			
ARISTA			
❏ AL6603	Huang Chung	1982	$18
—As "Huang Chung			
GEFFEN			
❏ R163751	Mosaic	1986	$15
—RCA Music Service edition			
❏ GHS24115	Mosaic	1986	$12
❏ R144369	Points on the Curve	1983	$15
—RCA Music Service edition			
❏ GHS4004	Points on the Curve	1983	$12
❏ R101063	The Warmer Side of Cool	1989	$15
—BMG Direct Marketing edition			
❏ GHS24222	The Warmer Side of Cool	1989	$12
WAR			
Also see ERIC BURDON AND WAR.			
AVENUE			
❏ R171706	Peace Sign	1994	$18
BLUE NOTE			
❏ BN-LA690-G [B]	Platinum Jazz	1977	$18
LAX			
❏ PW37111	All Day Music	1981	$12
—Reissue of United Artists 5546			
❏ PW37112	The World Is a Ghetto	1981	$12
—Reissue of United Artists 5652			
❏ PW37113	Why Can't We Be Friends?	1981	$12
—Reissue of United Artists 441			
MCA			
❏ 5362	Best of the Music Band	1982	$12
❏ 3030	Galaxy	1977	$12
❏ 745	Galaxy	1983	$10
—Reissue of MCA 3030			
❏ 5411	Music Band Jazz	1983	$12
❏ 3085	The Music Band	1979	$12
❏ 747	The Music Band	1983	$10
—Reissue of MCA 3085			
❏ 3193	The Music Band 2	1979	$12
❏ 751	The Music Band 2	1983	$10
—Reissue of MCA 3193			
❏ 5156	The Music Band Live	1980	$12
PRIORITY			
❏ SL9467	The Best of War…And More	1987	$12
RCA VICTOR			
❏ AFL1-4598	Life (Is So Strange)	1983	$12
❏ AFL1-4208	Outlaw	1982	$12
UNITED ARTISTS			

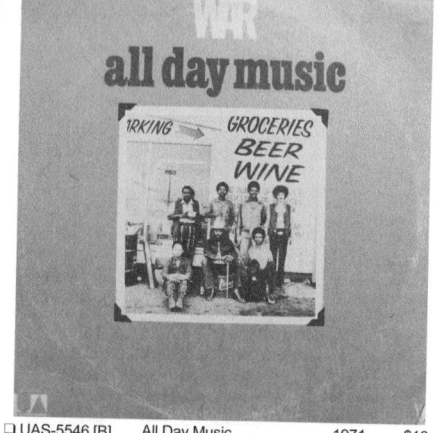

❏ UAS-5546 [B]	All Day Music	1971	$18
❏ UA-LA128-F [B]	Deliver the Word	1973	$18
❏ UA-LA648-G	Greatest Hits	1976	$12
❏ SP-103 [DJ]	Radio Free War	1974	$30
—Promo only on blue vinyl			
❏ UAS-5652	The World Is a Ghetto	1972	$15
❏ UAS-5508	War	1971	$18
❏ UA-LA193-J [B]	War Live!	1974	$25
❏ UA-LA441-G	Why Can't We Be Friends?	1975	$12
WARBURTON, PAUL, AND DALE BRUNING			
CAPRI			
❏ 7986	Our Delight	198?	$25
WARD, ALAN			
RCA VICTOR RED SEAL			
❏ LSC-2302 [S]	Gilbert and Sullivan Overtures	1959	$25
—Original with "shaded dog" label			
WARD, ANITA			
JUANA			
❏ 200,004	Songs of Love	1979	$12
❏ 200,006	Sweet Surrender	1979	$12

Number	Title	Yr	NM

WARD, BILLY, AND THE DOMINOES
DECCA

Number	Title	Yr	NM
❑ DL8621 [M]	Billy Ward and the Dominoes	1958	$300

FEDERAL
| ❑ 295-94 [10] | Billy Ward and His Dominoes | 1955 | $15000 |

— VG value 6000; VG+ value 9500

| ❑ 548 [M] | Billy Ward and His Dominoes | 1958 | $1500 |
| ❑ 559 [M] | Clyde McPhatter with Billy Ward and His Dominoes | 1958 | $1200 |

KING
❑ 5005	14 Hits	197?	$15
❑ 5008	21 Hits	197?	$15
❑ 952 [M]	24 Songs	1966	$50
❑ 548 [M]	Billy Ward and His Dominoes	1958	$0

— Unknown

| ❑ 733 [M] | Billy Ward and His Dominoes Featuring Clyde McPhatter and Jackie Wilson | 1961 | $600 |
| ❑ 559 [M] | Clyde McPhatter with Billy Ward and His Dominoes | 1958 | $600 |

— Yellow cover

| ❑ 559 [M] | Clyde McPhatter with Billy Ward and His Dominoes | 196? | $300 |

— Pink cover

LIBERTY
❑ LRP-3113 [M]	Pagan Love Song	1959	$75
❑ LST-7113 [S]	Pagan Love Song	1959	$150
❑ LRP-3056 [M]	Sea of Glass	1957	$75
❑ LRP-3083 [M]	Yours Forever	1958	$75

WARD, HELEN
COLUMBIA
| ❑ CL-6271 [10] | It's Been So Long | 1954 | $50 |

PAX
| ❑ 6004 [10] | Wild Bill Davison with Helen Ward | 1954 | $120 |

RCA VICTOR
| ❑ LPM-1464 [M] | With a Little Bit of Swing | 1957 | $40 |

WARD, JACKY
ASYLUM
| ❑ 60013 | Night After Night | 1982 | $10 |

MERCURY
❑ SRM-1-5009	A Lover's Question	1978	$12
❑ SRM-1-1170	Jacky Ward	1977	$15
❑ SRM-1-5030	More!	1980	$12
❑ SRM-1-5013	Rainbow	1978	$12
❑ SRM-1-5021	The Best of Jacky Ward ... Up 'Til Now	1979	$12

SUNBIRD
| ❑ SN50103 | Big Blue Diamond | 1980 | $15 |

TARGET
| ❑ 1315 | Big Blue Diamond | 1972 | $15 |

WARD, ROBIN
DOT
| ❑ DLP3555 [M] | Wonderful Summer | 1963 | $250 |
| ❑ DLP25555 [S] | Wonderful Summer | 1963 | $300 |

WARDELL, ROOSEVELT
RIVERSIDE
| ❑ RLP-350 [M] | The Revelation | 1960 | $250 |
| ❑ RS-9350 [S] | The Revelation | 1960 | $250 |

WARE, DAVID S.
HAT HUT
| ❑ W | Birth of a Being | 1978 | $35 |

Number	Title	Yr	NM

WARE, WILBUR; JOHNNY GRIFFIN; JUNIOR MANCE
JAZZLAND
| ❑ JLP-12 [M] | The Chicago Cookers | 1960 | $40 |

WARE, WILBUR
FANTASY
| ❑ OJC-1737 | The Chicago Sound | 198? | $25 |

RIVERSIDE
| ❑ RLP 12-252 [M] | The Chicago Sound | 1957 | $400 |
| ❑ 6048 | The Chicago Sound | 197? | $30 |

WARFIELD, WILLIAM
COLUMBIA MASTERWORKS
| ❑ ML2206 [M] | Old American Songs and Five Sea Chanties | 195? | $50 |

WARHORSE
CLEOPATRA
| ❑ CLP2071 [B] | Warhorse | 2015 | $25 |

— white vinyl

WARINER, STEVE
ARISTA
| ❑ AL8691 | I Am Ready | 1992 | $25 |

— Vinyl version available only from Columbia House

MCA
❑ 42032	Greatest Hits	1987	$10
❑ 42272	I Got Dreams	1989	$12
❑ 42130	I Should Be with You	1988	$10
❑ 5926	It's a Crazy World	1987	$10
❑ 5672	Life's Highway	1985	$10
❑ 5545	One Good Night Deserves Another	1985	$10

RCA VICTOR
❑ AHL1-7164	Down in Tennessee	1986	$10
❑ AHL1-5326	Greatest Hits	1985	$10
❑ AHL1-4859	Midnight Fire	1983	$12
❑ AHL1-4154	Steve Wariner	1982	$12
❑ AYL1-5440	Steve Wariner	1985	$10

— Best Buy Series" reissue

WARING, FRED, AND THE PENNSYLVANIANS
CAPITOL
| ❑ T936 [M] | All Through the Night | 1959 | $18 |

— Black colorband label, logo at left

| ❑ ST936 [S] | All Through the Night | 1958 | $25 |
| ❑ T936 [M] | All Through the Night | 1958 | $25 |

— Turquoise label

❑ T1949 [M]	Alma Mater Memories	1963	$15
❑ ST1949 [S]	Alma Mater Memories	1963	$18
❑ WBO1079 [M]	Broadway Cavalcade	1958	$30

— Black colorband labels, logo at left

| ❑ SWBO1079 [S] | Broadway Cavalcade | 1959 | $30 |

— Black colorband labels, logo at left

| ❑ T1389 [M] | Broadway Cavalcade, Volume 1 | 1960 | $18 |

— Reissue of Side 1 and Side 2 of WBO 1079; black colorband label, logo at left

| ❑ T1389 [M] | Broadway Cavalcade, Volume 1 | 1963 | $12 |

— Black colorband label, logo at top

| ❑ ST1389 [S] | Broadway Cavalcade, Volume 1 | 1960 | $25 |

— Reissue of Side 1 and Side 2 of SWBO 1079; black colorband label, logo at left

| ❑ ST1389 [S] | Broadway Cavalcade, Volume 1 | 1963 | $15 |

— Black colorband label, logo at top

| ❑ T1390 [M] | Broadway Cavalcade, Volume 1 | 1960 | $18 |

— Reissue of Side 3 and Side 4 of WBO 1079; black colorband label, logo at left

| ❑ ST1390 [S] | Broadway Cavalcade, Volume 2 | 1960 | $25 |

— Reissue of Side 3 and Side 4 of SWBO 1079; black colorband label, logo at left

| ❑ STBB-347 | Christmas Magic | 1969 | $18 |

— Collects ST 1260 and ST 1610 in one package; green label original

| ❑ STBB-347 | Christmas Magic | 1972 | $15 |

— Orange label reissue

| ❑ T1208 [M] | Do You Remember? | 1959 | $18 |

— Black colorband label, logo at left

| ❑ ST1208 [S] | Do You Remember? | 1959 | $25 |

— Black colorband label, logo at left

| ❑ W845 [M] | Fred Waring and the Pennsylvanians in Hi-Fi | 1957 | $30 |

— Gray label (original)

| ❑ W845 [M] | Fred Waring and the Pennsylvanians in Hi-Fi | 1959 | $18 |

— Black colorband label, logo at left

| ❑ SW845 [S] | Fred Waring and the Pennsylvanians in Hi-Fi | 1958 | $25 |

— Black colorband label, logo at left; does not include "Way Back Home" or "So Beats My Heart for You," which are on

---

Number	Title	Yr	NM

mono versions

| ❑ T1452 [M] | Keyboard Chorale | 1960 | $18 |

— Black colorband label, logo at left

| ❑ ST1452 [S] | Keyboard Chorale | 1960 | $25 |

— Black colorband label, logo at left

| ❑ TAO1504 [M] | Let Freedom Sing: An Album for Americans | 1961 | $25 |

— Includes booklet; black colorband label, logo at left

| ❑ STAO1504 [S] | Let Freedom Sing: An Album for Americans | 1961 | $30 |

— Includes booklet; black colorband label, logo at left

| ❑ T896 [M] | Now Is the Caroling Season | 1957 | $25 |

— Originals have turquoise labels

| ❑ ST896 [S] | Now Is the Caroling Season | 1959 | $18 |

— Black colorband label, logo at left

| ❑ T896 [M] | Now Is the Caroling Season | 1959 | $18 |

— Black colorband label, logo at left

| ❑ T896 [M] | Now Is the Caroling Season | 1962 | $15 |

— Black colorband label, logo at top

| ❑ ST896 [S] | Now Is the Caroling Season | 1962 | $15 |

— Black colorband label, logo at top

| ❑ T1122 [M] | Praise Him | 1959 | $18 |

— Black colorband label, logo at left

| ❑ ST1122 [S] | Praise Him | 1959 | $25 |

— Black colorband label, logo at left

| ❑ T1396 [M] | Rise Up Singin' | 1960 | $18 |

— Black colorband label, logo at left

| ❑ ST1396 [S] | Rise Up Singin' | 1960 | $25 |

— Black colorband label, logo at left

| ❑ T989 [M] | Selections from "The Music Man | 1958 | $25 |

— Turquoise label

| ❑ ST989 [S] | Selections from "The Music Man | 1959 | $25 |

— Black colorband label, logo at left

❑ T2625 [M]	The Best of Fred Waring and the Pennsylvanians	1967	$15
❑ ST2625 [S]	The Best of Fred Waring and the Pennsylvanians	1967	$18
❑ T1610 [M]	The Meaning of Christmas	1963	$18

— Black colorband label, logo at left

| ❑ ST1610 [S] | The Meaning of Christmas | 1963 | $25 |

— Black colorband label, logo at left

| ❑ SM-1610 | The Meaning of Christmas | 197? | $10 |

— Reissue of ST 1610 with same contents

| ❑ ST1610 [S] | The Meaning of Christmas | 1963 | $15 |

— Black colorband label, logo at top

| ❑ ST1610 [S] | The Meaning of Christmas | 1963 | $18 |

— Black colorband label, logo at top

| ❑ T1260 [M] | The Sounds of Christmas | 1959 | $18 |

— Black colorband label, logo at left

| ❑ ST1260 [S] | The Sounds of Christmas | 1959 | $25 |

— Black colorband label, logo at left

| ❑ T1298 [M] | The Time, the Place, the Girl | 1960 | $18 |

— Black colorband label, logo at left

| ❑ ST1298 [S] | The Time, the Place, the Girl | 1960 | $25 |

— Black colorband label, logo at left

❑ T1764 [M]	The Waring Blend	1962	$15
❑ ST1764 [S]	The Waring Blend	1962	$18
❑ T2054 [M]	This I Believe	1964	$15
❑ ST2054 [S]	This I Believe	1964	$18

CAPITOL CREATIVE PRODUCTS
| ❑ L-6550 [M] | Fred Waring and the Pennsylvanians Sing of Faith, Home and Christmas | 1967 | $18 |

— Compiled for the E.F. MacDonald Company, Dayton, Ohio

CAPITOL PICKWICK SERIES
❑ PC-3454 [M]	Some Enchanted Evening	196?	$12
❑ SPC-3454 [S]	Some Enchanted Evening	196?	$15
❑ PC-3451 [M]	The Romantic Sound	196?	$12
❑ SPC-3451 [S]	The Romantic Sound	196?	$15

DECCA
❑ DL4809 [M]	A-Caroling We Go	1966	$15
❑ DL74809 [S]	A-Caroling We Go	1966	$18
❑ DL4875 [M]	Barbershop Sing	1967	$15
❑ DL74875 [S]	Barbershop Sing	1967	$15
❑ DL8172 [M]	Christmas Time	1955	$25
❑ DL78172 [R]	Christmas Time	196?	$15
❑ DL5295 [10]	Christmas Time	1950	$40
❑ DLP5005 [10]	Cole Porter Songs	1950	$50
❑ DL8222 [M]	College Memories	1956	$18
❑ DL5202 [10]	Columbia, the Gem of the Ocean (Patriotic and Service Songs)	1950	$40
❑ DL8708 [M]	Excerpts from Carousel and Oklahoma	1958	$18
❑ DL8082 [M]	For Listening Only	1954	$30
❑ DL4753 [M]	Fred Waring Showcase	1966	$12
❑ DL74753 [S]	Fred Waring Showcase	1966	$15
❑ DL4345 [M]	God's Trombones	1962	$15
❑ DL74345 [S]	God's Trombones	1962	$18
❑ DL8047 [M]	God's Trombones and Other Spirituals	195?	$30
❑ DL8335 [M]	Harmonizin' the Old Songs	1956	$18
❑ DL9031 [M]	Hear, Hear	195?	$18
❑ DLP5004 [10]	Jerome Kern Songs	1950	$50
❑ DL8005 [M]	Listening Time	1950	$40
❑ DL8110 [M]	Lullaby Time	1955	$25
❑ DL4759 [M]	Magic Music	1966	$12
❑ DL74759 [S]	Magic Music	1966	$15

Number	Title	Yr	NM
❏ DL8829	Memorable Moments from Broadway Musicals	1959	$18
❏ DLP5036 [10]	Pleasure Time	1951	$40
❏ DL8026 [M]	Program Time	1950	$30
❏ DL5292 [10]	Richard Rodgers and Oscar Hammerstein II Songs, Vol. 1	1950	$40
❏ DL5293 [10]	Richard Rodgers and Oscar Hammerstein II Songs, Vol. 2	1950	$40
❏ DLP5009 [10]	Selections from Miss Liberty	1950	$50
❏ DL8033 [M]	Song of America	195?	$40
❏ DL8084 [M]	Song of Christmas	1954	$30
❏ DL4511 [M]	Song of Easter	1965	$12
❏ DL74511 [S]	Song of Easter	1965	$15
❏ DL8111 [M]	Songs in Reverence	1955	$25
❏ DL8670 [M]	Songs of Devotion	1958	$18
❏ DL5061 [10]	Songs of Devotion, Vol. 1	1950	$40
❏ DL5062 [10]	Songs of Devotion, Vol. 2	1950	$40
❏ DL4234 [M]	Songs of Faith	1962	$15
❏ DL74234 [S]	Songs of Faith	1962	$18
❏ DL8039 [M]	Songs of Faith, Vols. 1 and 2	195?	$30
❏ DL8709 [M]	Songs of Inspiration	1958	$18
❏ DL8710 [M]	Stars and Stripes Forever	1958	$18
❏ DBX186 [M]	The Best of Fred Waring	1965	$18
❏ DXSB7186 [S]	The Best of Fred Waring	1965	$18
❏ DL4158 [M]	This Is My Country	1961	$15
❏ DL74158 [S]	This Is My Country	1961	$18
❏ DL5141 [10]	This Is My Country	1950	$40
❏ DL8171 [M]	'Twas the Night Before Christmas	1955	$25
❏ DL78171 [R]	'Twas the Night Before Christmas	196?	$15
❏ DLP5021 [10]	'Twas the Night Before Christmas	1950	$50
❏ DL75007	Two Sides of Fred Waring and the Pennsylvanians	1968	$15

HARMONY
❏ HS11363	In Concert	1970	$12

MCA
❏ 15009	A-Caroling We Go	1973	$12

—Reissue of DL 74809; black label with rainbow
❏ 15009	A-Caroling We Go	1980	$10

—Blue label with rainbow
❏ 15011	Christmas Time	1973	$12

—Reissue of DL 78172; black label with rainbow
❏ 15011	Christmas Time	1980	$10

—Blue label with rainbow
❏ 207	God's Trombones	1973	$10

—Reissue of Decca 74345
❏ 4008	The Best of Fred Waring and the Pennsylvanians	1973	$15

—Reissue of Decca 7186; black labels with rainbow
❏ 193	This Is My Country	1973	$10

—Reissue of Decca 74158
❏ 15016	'Twas the Night Before Christmas	197?	$12

—Reissue of MCA 517; black label with rainbow
❏ 15016	'Twas the Night Before Christmas	1980	$10

—Blue label with rainbow
❏ 517	'Twas the Night Before Christmas	1974	$15

—Black rainbow label

MEGA
❏ 31-1005	Nashville	1971	$12

REPRISE
❏ R6148 [M]	Fred Waring and the Pennsylvanians in Concert	1964	$15
❏ RS6148 [S]	Fred Waring and the Pennsylvanians in Concert	1964	$18
❏ R6137 [M]	To You...Forever	1964	$15
❏ RS6137 [S]	To You...Forever	1964	$18

STASH
❏ 126	Memorial Album	1985	$12

WARLAND, DALE, SINGERS
AUGSBURG
❏ 23-1317	Carols of Christmas	1981	$12
❏ 23-1621	Echoes of Christmas	1979	$12

WARNES, JENNIFER
Includes records as "Jennifer." Also see JOE COCKER; BILL MEDLEY.

ARISTA
❏ AL4062	Jennifer Warnes	1977	$12

Number	Title	Yr	NM
❏ AB4217 [B]	Shot Through the Heart	1979	$12
❏ AL9560	The Best of Jennifer Warnes	1982	$10

CYPRESS
❏ 661111-1 [B]	Famous Blue Raincoat	1987	$40

PARROT
❏ PAS-71020 [B]	I Can Remember Anything	1968	$30

—As "Jennifer
❏ PAS-71034 [B]	See Me	1970	$30

—As "Jennifer

ROCK THE HOUSE
❏ RTH5052	Famous Blue Raincoat	1996	$50

—Classic Records reissue

WARRANT
COLUMBIA
❏ C45487	Cherry Pie	1990	$18
❏ FC44383	Dirty Rotten Filthy Stinking Rich	1988	$10

WARREN, EARLE
MUSE
❏ MR-5312	Earle Warren and the Count's Men	198?	$25

WARREN, FRAN
AUDIO FIDELITY
❏ AFSD-6207	Come Into My World	1968	$30

MGM
❏ E-3394 [M]	Mood Indigo	1956	$50

—Yellow label

TOPS
❏ L-1585 [M]	Hey There	195?	$25

VENISE
❏ 7019 [M]	Come Rain or Come Shine	195?	$30
❏ 10019 [S]	Come Rain or Come Shine	195?	$50

—Yellow vinyl

WARWICK
❏ W-2012 [M]	Something's Coming	1960	$30

WARREN, PETER
ENJA
❏ 2018	Bass Is	197?	$35

WARREN, RUSTY
JUBILEE
❏ EP-45-2049	Roll Me Over//Do It Now/ Twist Blues	1963	$20
❏ EP-45-2049 [PS]	Rusty Warren Sings	1963	$20

GNP CRESCENDO
❏ 2103	Bottoms Up!	1976	$15
❏ 2088	Knockers Up! '76	1976	$15
❏ 2079	Knockers Up!/Songs for Sinners	1975	$18
❏ 2080	Rusty Warren Bounces Back/Sin-Sational	1975	$18
❏ 2081	Rusty Warren Lays It on the Line	1975	$15
❏ 2114	Sexplosion	1977	$15

JUBILEE
❏ JLP2049 [M]	Banned in Boston?	1963	$30
❏ JGM2069 [M]	Bottoms Up!	1967	$25
❏ JGS2069 [S]	Bottoms Up!	1967	$25
❏ JGM-2029 [M]	Knockers Up!	1960	$30
❏ JGM2074	Look What I've Got for You	1967	$25
❏ JGM-2059 [M]	More Knockers Up!	1965	$30
❏ JLP5025 [M]	Portrait of Life	196?	$25
❏ JLPS5025 [S]	Portrait of Life	196?	$25
❏ JGM-2064 [M]	Rusty Rides Again	1966	$30
❏ JGM2039 [M]	Rusty Warren Bounces Back	1961	$30
❏ JGM2044 [M]	Rusty Warren in Orbit	1962	$30
❏ JGM-2054 [M]	Sex-X-Ponent	1964	$30

—Cover has JGM prefix; label has JG prefix

Number	Title	Yr	NM
❏ JLP2034 [M]	Sin-Sational	1961	$30
❏ JGM-2024 [M]	Songs for Sinners	1960	$30

WARWICK, DEE DEE
ATCO
❏ SD 33-337	Turnin' Around	1970	$30

MERCURY
❏ SR-61221	Foolish Fool	1968	$30
❏ MG-21100 [M]	I Want to Be with You	1967	$30
❏ SR-61100 [S]	I Want to Be with You	1967	$30

WARWICK, DIONNE
ARISTA
❏ AB4230 [B]	Dionne	1979	$12
❏ AL8295	Dionne	1985	$10

—Budget-line reissue
❏ AL8573	Dionne Warwick Sings Cole Porter	1990	$15
❏ AL8262	Finder of Lost Loves	1985	$12
❏ AL8398	Friends	1985	$12
❏ AL9585	Friends in Love	1982	$12
❏ AL8358	Friends in Love	1985	$10

—Budget-line reissue
❏ AL8540	Greatest Hits 1979-1990	1989	$15
❏ AL9609	Heartbreaker	1982	$12
❏ AL8338 [B]	Heartbreaker	1985	$10

—Budget-line reissue
❏ A2L8605	Hot! Live and Otherwise	1981	$15
❏ A2L8111	Hot! Live and Otherwise	1983	$12

—Budget-line reissue
❏ AL8104	How Many Times Can We Say Goodbye	1983	$12
❏ AL9526	No Night So Long	1980	$12
❏ AL8446	Reservations for Two	1987	$12

EVEREST
❏ 4103	Dionne Warwick	1981	$12

MOBILE FIDELITY
❏ Feb-0098	Hot! Live and Otherwise	1982	$75

—Audiophile vinyl

MUSICOR
❏ 2501	Only Love Can Break a Heart	1977	$15

PAIR
❏ PDL2-1098	Masterpieces	1986	$15
❏ PDL2-1043	The Dynamic Dionne Warwick	1986	$15

PICKWICK
❏ PTP-2056	Alfie	1973	$15

—As "Dionne Warwicke

RHINO
❏ RNDA-1100	Anthology 1962-1971	1985	$18

SCEPTER
❏ S-517 [M]	Anyone Who Had a Heart	1964	$18
❏ SS-517 [S]	Anyone Who Had a Heart	1964	$25
❏ P2M5139 [M]	Dionne!	1967	$25

—Columbia Record Club exclusive
❏ P2S5140 [S]	Dionne!	1967	$25

—Columbia Record Club exclusive
❏ SRM-534 [M]	Dionne Warwick in Paris	1966	$15
❏ SPS-534 [S]	Dionne Warwick in Paris	1966	$18
❏ SPS-577	Dionne Warwick's Golden Hits, Part 2	1969	$18
❏ SRM-565 [M]	Dionne Warwick's Golden Hits, Part One	1967	$25
❏ SPS-565 [S]	Dionne Warwick's Golden Hits, Part One	1967	$18
❏ SPS-575	Dionne Warwick's Greatest Motion Picture Hits	1969	$18
❏ SPS-598	From Within	1972	$25

—As "Dionne Warwicke
❏ SRM-531 [M]	Here I Am	1965	$18
❏ SPS-531 [S]	Here I Am	1965	$25
❏ SRM-555 [M]	Here Where There Is Love	1966	$15
❏ SPS-555 [S]	Here Where There Is Love	1966	$18
❏ ST-91010 [S]	Here Where There Is Love	1966	$25

—Capitol Record Club edition
❏ SPS-581	I'll Never Fall in Love Again	1970	$18
❏ LP-523 [M]	Make Way for Dionne Warwick	1964	$18
❏ SPS-523 [S]	Make Way for Dionne Warwick	1964	$25
❏ SRM-559 [M]	On Stage and in the Movies	1967	$15
❏ SPS-559 [S]	On Stage and in the Movies	1967	$18
❏ ST-91099 [S]	On Stage and in the Movies	1967	$25

—Capitol Record Club edition
❏ S-508 [M]	Presenting Dionne Warwick	1963	$18
❏ SS-508 [S]	Presenting Dionne Warwick	1963	$25
❏ SPS-571	Promises, Promises	1968	$18
❏ SPS-573	Soulful	1969	$18
❏ SPS 2-596	The Dionne Warwicke Story	1971	$25

—As "Dionne Warwicke
❏ SRM-567 [M]	The Magic of Believing	1968	$30
❏ SPS-567 [S]	The Magic of Believing	1968	$25
❏ LP-528 [M]	The Sensitive Sound of Dionne Warwick	1965	$18
❏ SPS-528 [S]	The Sensitive Sound of Dionne Warwick	1965	$25
❏ SRM-563 [M]	The Windows of the World	1967	$15
❏ SPS-563 [S]	The Windows of the World	1967	$18
❏ SRM-568 [M]	Valley of the Dolls	1968	$50

Number	Title	Yr	NM
— May only exist as a white label promo			
SPS-568 [S]	Valley of the Dolls	1968	$18
SPS-587 [B]	Very Dionne	1970	$18
SPRINGBOARD			
SPS-4002	Dionne Warwicke Sings Her Very Best	1972	$12
— As "Dionne Warwicke			
SPS-4032	Greatest Hits, Vol. 2	197?	$12
SPS-4003	One Hit After Another	1972	$12
— As "Dionne Warwicke			
SPS-4001	The Golden Voice of Dionne Warwicke	1972	$12
— As "Dionne Warwicke			
TIME-LIFE			
SLGD-18	Legendary Singers: Dionne Warwick	1987	$18
UNITED ARTISTS			
UA-LA337-G	The Very Best of Dionne Warwicke	1974	$15
— As "Dionne Warwicke			
WARNER BROS.			
BS2585	Dionne	1971	$15
— As "Dionne Warwicke			
BS2658	Just Being Myself	1973	$15
— As "Dionne Warwicke			
BS3119	Love at First Sight	1976	$15
BS2846	Then Came You	1975	$15
— As "Dionne Warwicke			
BS42846 [Q]	Then Came You	1975	$30
— As "Dionne Warwicke			
BS2893	Track of the Cat	1975	$15

WAS (NOT WAS)

Number	Title	Yr	NM
CHRYSALIS			
R100615	What's Up Dog?	1988	$15
— BMG Direct Marketing edition			
FV41664 [B]	What's Up Dog?	1988	$15
GEFFEN			
GHS4016	Born to Laugh at Tornadoes	1983	$12
PRO-A-2079 [DJ]	Shake Your Head + 3	1983	$18
— Promo-only sampler from Born to Laugh at Tornadoes			
ISLAND			
ILPS9666	Was (Not Was)	1981	$15

WASHBOARD SAM

Number	Title	Yr	NM
RCA VICTOR			
LPV-577 [M]	Feeling Lowdown	196?	$30

WASHINGTON, BABY

Number	Title	Yr	NM
AVI			
AV-6038	I Wanna Dance	1978	$12
COLLECTABLES			
COL-5108	Only Those in Love	198?	$12
COL-5124	That's How Heartaches Are Made	198?	$12
COL-5040	The Best of Baby Washington	198?	$12
SUE			
LP-1042 [M]	Only Those in Love	1965	$175
LPS-1042 [S]	Only Those in Love	1965	$300
LP-1014 [M]	That's How Heartaches Are Made	1963	$175
TRIP			
8009	The One and Only Baby Washington	1971	$18
VEEP			
VPS-16528	With You in Mind	1968	$30

WASHINGTON, DINAH, AND BROOK BENTON

Number	Title	Yr	NM
MERCURY			
MG-20588 [M]	The Two of Us	1960	$150
SR-60244 [S]	The Two of Us	1960	$150
824823-1	The Two of Us	1985	$20
— Reissue			

WASHINGTON, DINAH

Number	Title	Yr	NM
ACCORD			
SN-7207	Retrospective	1982	$25
COLLECTABLES			
COL-5200	Golden Classics	1989	$25
DELMARK			
DL-451	Mellow Mama	1992	$50
EMARCY			
MG-26032 [10]	After Hours with Miss D	1954	$300
MG-36028 [M]	After Hours with Miss D	1955	$300
— Reissue of 26032			
MG-36065 [M]	Dinah	1956	$250
MG-36000 [M]	Dinah Jams	1955	$300
MG-36130 [M]	Dinah Washington Sings Bessie Smith	1957	$250
MG-36119 [M]	Dinah Washington Sings Fats Waller	1957	$250
MG-36011 [M]	For Those in Love	1955	$300
MG-36073 [M]	In the Land of Hi-Fi	1956	$75
826453-1	In the Land of Hi-Fi	1986	$25
EMS-2-401	Jazz Sides	197?	$35
824883-1	Jazz Sides	198?	$30
— Reissue of 401			
MG-36141 [M]	Newport '58	1958	$250
814184-1	Slick Chick (On the Mellow Side)	1983	$30
MG-36104 [M]	The Swingin' Miss "D	1956	$250
EVEREST ARCHIVE OF FOLK & JAZZ			
FS-297	Dinah Washington	197?	$30
GRAND AWARD			
GA 33-318 [M]	Dinah Washington Sings the Blues	1955	$150
— Add 50% if removable wrap-around cover is still there			
HARLEM HIT PARADE			
8002	Finer Dinah	197?	$25
MERCURY			
MG-25140 [10]	Blazing Ballads	1952	$300
MG-21119 [M]	Dinah Discovered	1967	$150
SR-61119 [S]	Dinah Discovered	1967	$150
MG-25060 [10]	Dinah Washington	1950	$300
MG-20525 [M]	Dinah Washington Sings Fats Waller	1960	$175
— Reissue of EmArcy 36119			
SR-60202 [S]	Dinah Washington Sings Fats Waller	1960	$150
MG-25138 [10]	Dynamic Dinah	1952	$300
MG-20614 [M]	For Lonely Lovers	1961	$150
SR-60614 [S]	For Lonely Lovers	1961	$150
MG-20604 [M]	I Concentrate on You	1961	$150
SR-60604 [S]	I Concentrate on You	1961	$150
MG-20729 [M]	I Wanna Be Loved	1962	$150
SR-60729 [S]	I Wanna Be Loved	1962	$150
MG-20119 [M]	Music for a First Love	1957	$50
MG-20120 [M]	Music for Late Hours	1957	$175
MG-20523 [M]	Newport '58	1960	$175
— Reissue of EmArcy 36141			
SR-60200 [S]	Newport '58	1960	$150
MG-20638 [M]	September in the Rain	1961	$150
SR-60638 [S]	September in the Rain	1961	$150
MG-20661 [M]	Tears and Laughter	1962	$150
SR-60661 [S]	Tears and Laughter	1962	$150
MG-20247 [M]	The Best in Blues	1958	$175
MG-20829 [M]	The Good Old Days	1963	$150
SR-60829 [S]	The Good Old Days	1963	$150
MG-20439 [M]	The Queen	1959	$150
SR-60111 [S]	The Queen	1959	$150
MG-20928 [M]	The Queen and Quincy	1965	$150
SR-60928 [S]	The Queen and Quincy	1965	$150
MGP-2-103	This Is My Story	1963	$150
— Combines 20788 and 20789 in one package			
MGP-2-603 [S]	This Is My Story	1963	$150
— Combines 60788 and 60789 in one package			
MG-20788 [M]	This Is My Story -- Dinah Washington's Golden Hits, Volume 1	1963	$150
SR-60788 [S]	This Is My Story -- Dinah Washington's Golden Hits, Volume 1	1963	$150
822867-1	This Is My Story -- Dinah Washington's Golden Hits, Volume 1	1985	$20
— Reissue			
MG-20789 [M]	This Is My Story -- Dinah Washington's Golden Hits, Volume 2	1963	$150
SR-60789 [S]	This Is My Story -- Dinah Washington's Golden Hits, Volume 2	1963	$150
MG-20572 [M]	Unforgettable	1961	$150
SR-60232 [S]	Unforgettable	1961	$150
MG-20479 [M]	What a Diff'rence a Day Makes!	1960	$150
SR-60158 [S]	What a Diff'rence a Day Makes!	1960	$150
818815-1	What a Diff'rence a Day Makes!	198?	$20
— Reissue			
PICKWICK			
SPC-3043	Dinah Washington	196?	$25
SPC-3536	Greatest Hits	197?	$25
SPC-3230	I Don't Hurt Anymore	197?	$25
ROULETTE			
R25253 [M]	A Stranger on Earth	1964	$35
SR25253 [S]	A Stranger on Earth	1964	$50
R25189 [M]	Back to the Blues	1963	$35
SR25189 [S]	Back to the Blues	1963	$50
R25170 [M]	Dinah '62	1962	$35
SR25170 [S]	Dinah '62	1962	$50
R25220 [M]	Dinah '63	1963	$35
SR25220 [S]	Dinah '63	1963	$50
R25269 [M]	Dinah Washington	1964	$35
SR25269 [S]	Dinah Washington	1964	$50
R25183 [M]	Drinking Again	1962	$35
SR25183 [S]	Drinking Again	1962	$50
RE104	Echoes of an Era	196?	$35
R25180 [M]	In Love	1962	$35
SR25180 [S]	In Love	1962	$50
R25244 [M]	In Tribute	1963	$35
SR25244 [S]	In Tribute	1963	$50
RE117	Queen of the Blues	1971	$35
R25289 [M]	The Best of Dinah Washington	1965	$35
SR25289 [S]	The Best of Dinah Washington	1965	$50
42014	The Best of Dinah Washington	1968	$30
— Reissue of 25289			
RE125	The Immortal Dinah Washington	1973	$35
TRIP			
5516	After Hours	1973	$25
5500	Dinah Jams	1973	$25
5556	Dinah Washington Sings Bessie Smith	197?	$25
TLX9505	Sad Songs -- Blue Songs	197?	$30
5524	Tears and Laughter	1974	$25
5565	The Swingin' Miss D	197?	$25
VERVE			
818930-1	The Fats Waller Songbook	1984	$25
WING			
MGW-12271 [M]	Dinah Washington Sings Fats Waller	1964	$30
SRW-16271 [S]	Dinah Washington Sings Fats Waller	1964	$30
MGW-12140 [M]	The Late Late Show	1963	$30
SRW-16140 [S]	The Late Late Show	1963	$30
PKW-2-121	The Original Queen of Soul	1969	$50
SRW-16386	The Original Soul Sister	196?	$30

WASHINGTON, EARL

Number	Title	Yr	NM
JAZZ WORKSHOP			
JWS-202 [M]	All Star Jazz	1963	$75
JWS-213 [M]	Reflections	1963	$75

WASHINGTON, ERNESTINE

Number	Title	Yr	NM
DISC			
DLP-712 [10]	Ernestine Washington with Bunk Johnson	195?	$250

WASHINGTON, GINO

Number	Title	Yr	NM
ATAC			
2730	Gino Washington's Golden Hits	1969	$30
KAPP			
KL-1415 [M]	Gino Washington's Ram Jam Band	1967	$100
KS-3415 [S]	Gino Washington's Ram Jam Band	1967	$30

WASHINGTON, GROVER, JR.

Number	Title	Yr	NM
COLUMBIA			
C48530	Next Exit	1992	$50
FC40510	Strawberry Moon	1987	$25
OC44256	Then and Now	1988	$25
OC45253	Time Out of Mind	1989	$25
ELEKTRA			
60415	Anthology of Grover Washington, Jr.	1985	$25
5E-562	Come Morning	1981	$25
60318	Inside Moves	1984	$25
6E-182	Paradise	1979	$25
60215	The Best Is Yet to Come	1982	$25
6E-305	Winelight	1980	$25
KUDU			
KU-07	All the King's Horses	1972	$30
KU-32	A Secret Place	1976	$30
KU-24	Feels So Good	1975	$30
KU-03	Inner City Blues	1971	$30
KUX-3637	Live at the Bijou	1977	$35
KU-20	Mister Magic	1975	$30
KUX-1213	Soul Box	1973	$35
— The two records also were issued separately			
KSQX-1213 [Q]	Soul Box	1973	$40
KU-12 [B]	Soul Box, Vol. 1	1973	$15
KU-13	Soul Box, Vol. 2	1973	$30
MOTOWN			
M5-186V1	All the King's Horses	1981	$20
— Reissue of Kudu 07			

Number	Title	Yr	NM
❑ M9-961A2	Anthology	1981	$35
❑ M5-165V1	A Secret Place	1981	$20
—Reissue of Kudu 32			
❑ M9-940	Baddest	1980	$35
❑ M5-177V1	Feels So Good	1981	$20
—Reissue of Kudu 24			
❑ 5307ML	Greatest Performances	1983	$25
❑ 6126ML	Grover Washington Jr. at His Best	198?	$25
❑ M5-189V1	Inner City Blues	1981	$20
—Reissue of Kudu 03			
❑ M8-239	Live at the Bijou	1982	$30
—Reissue			
❑ M5-175V1	Mister Magic	1981	$20
—Reissue of Kudu 20			
❑ M7-910	Reed Seed	1978	$25
❑ 5236ML	Reed Seed	1982	$20
—Reissue of 910			
❑ M7-933	Skylarkin'	1980	$25
❑ 5232ML	Skylarkin'	1982	$20
—Reissue of 933			
❑ M5-184V1	Soul Box, Vol. 1	1981	$20
—Reissue of half of Kudu 1213			
❑ M5-187V1	Soul Box, Vol. 2	1981	$20
—Reissue of half of Kudu 1213			
NAUTILUS			
❑ NR-39	Winelight	1981	$150
—Audiophile vinyl			

WASHINGTON, TUTS
ROUNDER

Number	Title	Yr	NM
❑ 2041	New Orleans Piano Professor	198?	$25

WASHINGTON, TYRONE
BLUE LABOR

Number	Title	Yr	NM
❑ 102	Do Right	197?	$25
BLUE NOTE			
❑ BST-84274	Natural Essence	1968	$30

WASSERMAN, ROB
MCA

Number	Title	Yr	NM
❑ 42131	Duets	1988	$25
ROUNDER			
❑ 0179	Solo	198?	$30

WATANABE, KAZUMI
GRAMAVISION

Number	Title	Yr	NM
❑ R1-79415	Kilowatt	1989	$30
❑ 18-8506	Mobo Club	1985	$25
❑ GR-8404	Mobo I	1984	$30
❑ GR-8406	Mobo II	1984	$30
❑ 18-8602	Mobo Splash	1986	$25
❑ 18-8706	Spice of Life	1987	$25
❑ 18-8810	Spice of Life Too	1988	$25
INNER CITY			
❑ IC-6071	Mermaid Boulevard	198?	$30

WATANABE, SADAO
CATALYST

Number	Title	Yr	NM
❑ 7911	Sadao Watanabe and Charlie Mariano	197?	$30
COLUMBIA			
❑ C2X36818	How's Everything	1980	$30
❑ FC37433	Orange Express	1981	$25
ELEKTRA			
❑ 60748	Birds of Passage	1987	$25
❑ 60816	Elis	1988	$25
❑ 60906	Front Seat	1989	$30
❑ 60431	Maisha	1986	$25
❑ 60475	Parker's Mood	1986	$25
❑ 60803	Selected Sadao Watanabe	1989	$35
ELEKTRA/MUSICIAN			
❑ 60297	Fill Up the Night	1984	$25
❑ 60371	Rendezvous	1985	$25
INNER CITY			
❑ IC-6064	Autumn Blow	198?	$30
❑ IC-6061	Bird of Paradise	198?	$30
❑ IC-6062	California Shower	197?	$30
❑ IC-6015	I'm Old Fashioned	1978	$30
❑ IC-6060	Morning Island	198?	$30
❑ IC-6063	My Dear Life	198?	$30
VANGUARD			
❑ VSD-79344	Round Trip	1974	$30

WATERBOYS, THE
CHRYSALIS

Number	Title	Yr	NM
❑ PV41542	A Pagan Place	1986	$10
—Reissue			
❑ FV41589	Fisherman's Blues	1988	$12
❑ PV41541	The Waterboys	1986	$10
—Reissue of first U.K. LP			
❑ FV41543	This Is the Sea	1986	$12
—Reissue			

ISLAND

Number	Title	Yr	NM
❑ 90190	A Pagan Place	1984	$18
❑ 90147 [EP]	The Waterboys	1983	$12
❑ 90457	This Is the Sea	1985	$15

WATERGATE SEVEN PLUS ONE, THE
STOMP OFF

Number	Title	Yr	NM
❑ SOS-1165	Ostrich Walk and Alligator Crawl	1989	$25

WATERS, BENNY
MUSE

Number	Title	Yr	NM
❑ MR-5340	From Paradise (Small's) to Shangri-La	1987	$25
STOMP OFF			
❑ SOS-1210	Memories of the Twenties	1991	$25

WATERS, CRYSTAL
MERCURY

Number	Title	Yr	NM
❑ 848894-1	Surprise	1991	$15

WATERS, ETHEL
BIOGRAPH

Number	Title	Yr	NM
❑ 12022	Ethel Waters 1921/24	197?	$25
❑ 12025	Jazzin' Babies Blues	197?	$25
COLUMBIA			
❑ KG31571	Her Greatest Years	1972	$35
❑ PG31571	Her Greatest Years	197?	$30
—Reissue with new prefix			
❑ CL2792 [M]	On Stage and Screen 1925-1940	1968	$35
GLENDALE			
❑ GL-9011	Ethel Waters	198?	$25
MERCURY			
❑ MG-20051 [M]	Ethel Waters	1954	$150
MONMOUTH-EVERGREEN			
❑ 6812	Miss Ethel Waters	1968	$30
REMINGTON			
❑ RLP-1025 [10]	Ethel Waters	1950	$50
WORD			
❑ WST-8044	His Eye Is On the Sparrow	197?	$30
❑ W-3100LP [M]	His Eye Is On the Sparrow	196?	$35
X			
❑ LVA-1009 [M]	Ethel Waters	1955	$75

WATERS, JOE
NEW COLONY

Number	Title	Yr	NM
❑ 831	Harvest Moon	1983	$12

WATERS, KIM
WARLOCK

Number	Title	Yr	NM
❑ WAR-2720	All Because of You	1990	$30
❑ WAR-2713	Sweet and Saxy	1989	$30

WATERS, MUDDY, AND HOWLIN' WOLF
CHESS

Number	Title	Yr	NM
❑ CH-9100	Muddy and The Wolf	1985	$15

WATERS, MUDDY
BLUE SKY

Number	Title	Yr	NM
❑ PZ34449	Hard Again	1977	$15
—No bar code on cover			
❑ PZ34449 [B]	Hard Again	198?	$10
—Budget-line reissue with bar code			
❑ JZ34928	I'm Ready	1978	$15
❑ PZ34928	I'm Ready	198?	$10
—Budget-line reissue			
❑ JZ37064	King Bee	1981	$15
❑ PZ37064	King Bee	198?	$10
—Budget-line reissue			
❑ JZ35712	Muddy "Missisiippi" Waters Live	1980	$15
❑ PZ35712	Muddy "Missisiippi" Waters Live	198?	$10
—Budget-line reissue			
CADET CONCEPT			
❑ CS-320	After the Rain	1969	$30
❑ CS-314	Electric Mud	1968	$30
CHESS			
❑ LP-1533 [M]	Blues from Big Bill's Copacabana	1968	$50
❑ CH-50023	Can't Get No Grindin'	1973	$25
❑ CH-9319	Can't Get No Grindin'	1990	$12
—Reissue of 50023			
❑ 127	Fathers and Sons	1969	$30
❑ 2CH-50033	Fathers and Sons	1974	$25
—Reissue of 127			
❑ LP-1483 [M]	Folk Singer	1964	$120
❑ CH-9261	Folk Singer	1987	$12
—Reissue of 1483			
❑ CH-60026	London Revisited	1974	$18
❑ 2CH-60006	McKinley Morganfield, A.K.A. Muddy Waters	1971	$30

Number	Title	Yr	NM
❑ LP-1511 [M]	More Real Folk Blues	1967	$50
❑ LPS-1511 [S]	More Real Folk Blues	1967	$40
❑ CH-9278	More Real Folk Blues	1988	$12
—Reissue of 1511			
❑ LP-1507 [M]	Muddy, Brass and Blues	1966	$40
❑ LPS-1507 [S]	Muddy, Brass and Blues	1966	$50
❑ CH-9286	Muddy, Brass and the Blues	1989	$12
—Reissue of 1507			

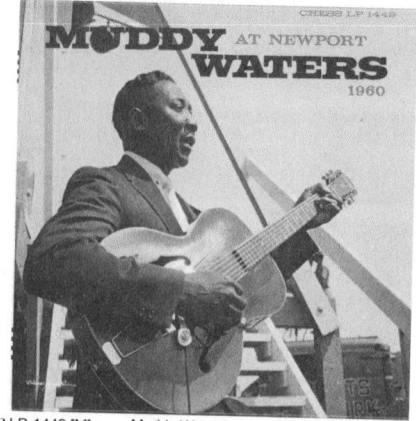

Number	Title	Yr	NM
❑ LP-1449 [M]	Muddy Waters at Newport	1962	$120
❑ CH-9198	Muddy Waters at Newport	1986	$12
—Reissue of 1449			
❑ CH-50012	Muddy Waters Live	1972	$25
❑ LP-1444 [M]	Muddy Waters Sings Big Bill	1960	$300
❑ LP-1444 [DJ]	Muddy Waters Sings Big Bill	1960	$1000
—White label promo			
❑ CH-9197	Muddy Waters Sings Big Bill	1986	$12
—Reissue of 1444			
❑ LPS-1444 [R]	Muddy Waters Sings Big Bill	196?	$18
—Rechanneled stereo reissue			
❑ CH-9180	Rare and Unissued	1986	$15
❑ CH-9101	Rolling Stone	1985	$25
❑ LPS-1539	Sail On	1969	$30
❑ LP-1427 [M]	The Best of Muddy Waters	1957	$500
—Black label			
❑ LP-1427 [DJ]	The Best of Muddy Waters	1957	$1500
—White label promo; VG value 500; VG+ value 1000			
❑ CH-9255	The Best of Muddy Waters	1987	$12
—Reissue of 1427			
❑ LPS-1427 [R]	The Best of Muddy Waters	196?	$15
—Black label			
❑ CH6-80002	The Chess Box	1990	$50
❑ CH-60013	The London Muddy Waters Sessions	1972	$25
❑ CH-9298	The London Muddy Waters Sessions	1989	$12
—Reissue of 60013			
❑ CH-50035	The Muddy Waters Woodstock Album	1976	$18
❑ LP-1501 [M]	The Real Folk Blues of Muddy Waters	1965	$75
❑ CH-9274	The Real Folk Blues of Muddy Waters	1987	$12
—Reissue of 1501			
❑ LPS-1553	They Call Me Muddy Waters	1971	$25
❑ CH-9299	They Call Me Muddy Waters	1989	$12
—Reissue of 1553			
❑ CH-9291	Trouble No More: Singles 1955-1959	1989	$15
❑ CH-60031	Unk" in Funk	1975	$18
INTERMEDIA			
❑ QS-5071	Sweet Home Chicago	198?	$12
MOBILE FIDELITY			
❑ 1-201	Folk Singer	1994	$50
—Audiophile vinyl			
MUSE			
❑ MR-5008	Mud in Your Ear	198?	$15
TESTAMENT			
❑ 2210	Stovall's Plantation	197?	$15

WATERS, PATTY
ESP-DISK'

Number	Title	Yr	NM
❑ 1055 [S]	Patty Waters College Tour	1968	$150
❑ 1025 [M]	Patty Waters Sings	1966	$150
❑ S-1025 [S]	Patty Waters Sings	1966	$150

WATERS, ROGER
Also see PINK FLOYD.
COLUMBIA

Number	Title	Yr	NM
❑ FC40795 [B]	Radio K.A.O.S.	1987	$18
❑ FC39290 [B]	The Pros and Cons of Hitch Hiking	1984	$30
—Original nude cover			
❑ FC39290 [B]	The Pros and Cons of Hitch Hiking	1984	$15
—Revised cover with black rectangle over woman's naked rear end			

Number	Title	Yr	NM
❏ PC39290	The Pros and Cons of Hitch Hiking	1986	$12

—*Budget-line reissue with new prefix*

MERCURY

❏ R209833 [B]	The Wall -- Live in Berlin	1990	$30

—*BMG Direct Marketing version*

❏ 846611-1 [B]	The Wall -- Live in Berlin	1990	$35

WATKINS, DOUG

NEW JAZZ

❏ NJLP-8238 [M]	Soulnik	1960	$175

—*Purple label*

❏ NJLP-8238 [M]	Soulnik	1965	$175

—*Blue label, trident logo at right*

PHILIPS

❏ PHM200001 [M]	French Horns for My Lady	1962	$25
❏ PHS600001 [S]	French Horns for My Lady	1962	$30

TRANSITION

❏ TRLP-20 [M]	Watkins at Large	1956	$1200

—*Deduct 1/10 if booklet is missing*

WATKINS, JOE

GHB

❏ GHB-74	Last Will and Testament	197?	$25

WATKINS, JULIUS

BLUE NOTE

❏ BLP-5053 [10]	Julius Watkins Sextet	1954	$400
❏ BLP-5064 [10]	Julius Watkins Sextet, Volume 2	1955	$400

WATKINS, LOVELACE

MGM

❏ E-3831 [M]	The Voice of Lovelace Watkins	1960	$30
❏ SE-3831 [S]	The Voice of Lovelace Watkins	1960	$40

WATKINS, MARY

OLIVIA

❏ LF-919	Something Moving	198?	$25

PALO ALTO

❏ PA-8030	Wind of Change	198?	$25

REDWOOD

❏ R-8506	Spiritsong	1985	$25

WATKINS, MITCH

ENJA

❏ R1-79603	Underneath It All	1989	$30

WATLEY, JODY

ATLANTIC

❏ 83087	Flower	1998	$18

MCA

❏ 10355	Affairs of the Heart	1991	$15
❏ 5898	Jody Watley	1987	$12
❏ 6276	Larger Than Life	1989	$12
❏ 6343	You Wanna Dance with Me?	1989	$15

SOLAR

❏ D1-72561	Beginnings	1988	$12

WATROUS, BILL

COLUMBIA

❏ PC36977	Bill Watrous	1981	$30
❏ KC33090	Manhattan Wildlife Refuge	1974	$50
❏ PC33701	Tiger of San Pedro	1975	$50

FAMOUS DOOR

❏ HL-101	Bone Straight Ahead	1973	$75
❏ HL-136	Coronary Trombossa	1981	$25
❏ HL-134	I'll Play for You	1980	$30
❏ HL-137	La Zorra	1981	$25
❏ HL-144	Roarin' Back Into New York	1982	$25
❏ HL-147	The Best of Bill Watrous	198?	$25
❏ HL-127	Watrous in Hollywood	1979	$30

SOUNDWINGS

❏ SW-2104	Reflections	1987	$35
❏ SW-2100	Someplace Else	1986	$35

WATSON, BOBBY

BLUE NOTE

❏ B1-90262	No Question About It	1988	$30
❏ B1-91915	The Inventor	1990	$30

RED RECORD

❏ VPA-184	Appointment in Milano	1986	$30
❏ VPA-173	Perpetual Groove (Live in Europe)	198?	$30

WATSON, DOC
Includes records by the father-son duo of "Doc and Merle Watson."

FLYING FISH

❏ FF-301	Guitar Album	1983	$15
❏ FF-352	Pickin' the Blues	1985	$12

Number	Title	Yr	NM
❏ FF-252	Red Rocking Chair	1981	$15

FOLKWAYS

❏ FA-2366 [M]	Doc Watson and Family	1963	$35
❏ FA-31021 [S]	Doc Watson and Family	196?	$20

INTERMEDIA

❏ QS-5031	Out in the Country	198?	$12

LIBERTY

❏ LW-601	Doc and the Boys	1981	$12

—*Reissue of United Artists 601*

❏ LT-943	Live and Pickin'	1981	$12

—*Reissue of United Artists 943*

❏ LN-10027	Lonesome Road	1981	$10

—*Budget-line reissue*

❏ LT-887	Look Away!	1981	$12

—*Reissue of United Artists 887*

DOC WATSON *MEMORIES*

❏ LWB-423 [B]	Memories	1981	$15

—*Reissue of United Artists 423*

POPPY

❏ PYS-5703	The Elementary Doc Watson	1972	$18
❏ PP-LA022-F	Then and Now	1973	$18
❏ PP-LA210-G	Two Days in November	1974	$18

SMITHSONIAN/FOLKWAYS

❏ SF-40012	The Doc Watson Family	1990	$15

—*Reissue of Folkways LP*

SUGAR HILL

❏ SH-3742	Down South	1985	$12
❏ SH-3759	Portrait	1987	$12
❏ SH-3752	Riding the Midnight Train	1986	$12

UNITED ARTISTS

❏ UA-LA601-G	Doc and the Boys	1976	$15
❏ UA-LA943-H	Live and Pickin'	1979	$15
❏ UA-LA725-G	Lonesome Road	1977	$15
❏ UA-LA887-H	Look Away!	1978	$15
❏ UA-LA423-G	Memories	1975	$18

VANGUARD

❏ VSD-6576	Ballads from Deep Gap	1971	$18
❏ VRS-9152 [M]	Doc Watson	1964	$40
❏ VSD-79152 [S]	Doc Watson	1964	$40
❏ VRS-9170 [M]	Doc Watson and Son	1965	$30
❏ VSD-79170 [S]	Doc Watson and Son	1965	$35
❏ VSD-9/10	Doc Watson on Stage	1970	$25
❏ VSD-79276	Good Deal	1968	$18
❏ VRS-9239 [M]	Home Again	1967	$18
❏ VSD-79239 [S]	Home Again	1967	$25
❏ VSD107/8	Old Timey Concert	1977	$25
❏ VRS-9213 [M]	Southbound	1966	$18
❏ VSD-79213 [S]	Southbound	1966	$25
❏ VSD79213 [B]	Southbound	2014	$30
❏ VSD45/46	The Essential Doc Watson	1973	$25
❏ VMS-73108	The Essential Doc Watson, Vol. 1	1985	$12
❏ VMS-73121	The Essential Doc Watson, Vol. 2	1985	$12

WATSON, GENE

CAPITOL

❏ ST-11715	Beautiful Country	1977	$15
❏ ST-11529	Because You Believe in Me	1976	$15
❏ ST-11443	Love in the Hot Afternoon	1975	$15
❏ ST-12102	No One Will Ever Know	1980	$15
❏ ST-11597	Paper Rosie	1977	$15
❏ SN-16124	Paper Rosie	198?	$10

—*Budget-line reissue*

❏ SW-11805	Reflections	1978	$15
❏ SN-16304	Reflections	198?	$10

—*Budget-line reissue*

❏ ST-11947	Should I Come Home	1979	$15
❏ ST-11782	The Best of Gene Watson	1978	$15
❏ C1-91641	The Best of Gene Watson	1989	$15
❏ SN-16241	The Best of Gene Watson, Vol. 2	198?	$10

EPIC

❏ FE40644	Honky Tonk Crazy	1987	$10

Number	Title	Yr	NM
❏ BFE40076	Memories to Burn	1985	$10
❏ FE40306	Starting New Memories	1986	$10

MCA

❏ 5170	Between This Time and the Next Time	1981	$12
❏ 5572	Greatest Hits	1985	$10
❏ 5440	Little by Little	1984	$12
❏ 951	Little by Little	1985	$10

—*Reissue of 5440*

❏ 5241	Old Loves Never Die	1981	$12
❏ 5384	Sometimes I Get Lucky	1983	$12
❏ 950	Sometimes I Get Lucky	1985	$10

—*Reissue of 5384*

❏ 5302	This Dream's on Me	1982	$12

MCA CURB

❏ 5520	Heartaches, Love and Stuff	1984	$10
❏ 5670	Texas Saturday Night	1985	$10

WARNER BROS.

❏ 25832	Back in the Fire	1989	$12

WATSON, JOHNNY "GUITAR", AND LARRY WILLIAMS

OKEH

❏ OKM12122 [M]	Two for the Price of One	1967	$40
❏ OKS14122 [S]	Two for the Price of One	1967	$75

WATSON, JOHNNY "GUITAR"

A&M

❏ SP-4880	That's What Time It Is	1981	$12

CADET

❏ LP-4056 [M]	I Cried for You	1967	$30
❏ LPS-4056 [S]	I Cried for You	1967	$30

CHESS

❏ LP-1490 [M]	Blues Soul	1965	$80
❏ LPS-1490 [S]	Blues Soul	1965	$100

DJM

❏ 3	Ain't That a Bitch	1976	$12
❏ 7	A Real Mother for Ya	1977	$12
❏ 27 [B]	E.D.P. Extra Disco Perception	1979	$12

—*As "Watsonian Institute*

❏ 714 [B]	Funk Beyond the Call of Duty	1977	$12
❏ 19	Giant	1978	$12
❏ 501	Johnny "Guitar" Watson and the Family Clone	1981	$12
❏ 31	Love Jones	1980	$12
❏ 13	Master Funk	1978	$12

—*As "Watsonian Institute*

❏ 24	What the Hell Is This?	1979	$12

FANTASY

❏ MPF-4503	Greatest Hits	1981	$12
❏ 9484	I Don't Want to Be Alone Stranger	1975	$15
❏ 9437	Listen	1973	$15

KING

❏ 857 [M]	Johnny Guitar Watson	1963	$400

MCA

❏ 5273	The Very Best of Johnny "Guitar" Watson	1981	$12

OKEH

❏ OKM12118 [M]	Bad	1967	$30
❏ OKS14118 [S]	Bad	1967	$40
❏ OKM12124 [M]	In the Fats Bag	1967	$30
❏ OKS14124 [S]	In the Fats Bag	1967	$40

POWER PAK

❏ 306	Gangster of Love	1978	$12

WATSON, ROBERT

ROULETTE

❏ SR-5009	Estimated Time of Arrival	1977	$15

WATSONIAN INSTITUTE
See JOHNNY "GUITAR"

WATT, MIKE
Also see MINUTEMEN; FIREHOSE. Watt also played bass for JANE'S ADDICTION and THE STOOGES.

COLUMBIA

❏ C66464	Ball-Hog Or Tugboat?	1995	$15

WATT, TOMMY

BETHLEHEM

❏ BCP-6052 [M]	Watts Cooking	1961	$250

WATTERS, LU

CLEF

❏ MGC-103 [10]	Lu Watters Jazz	1954	$0

—*Canceled*

❏ MGC-503 [10]	Lu Watters Jazz	1954	$300

DOWN HOME

❏ MGD-5 [10]	Lu Watters and His Yerba Buena Jazz Band	1955	$85

Number	Title	Yr	NM

GOOD TIME JAZZ
Number	Title	Yr	NM
❑ L-12007 [M]	1942 Series	1955	$50
❑ L-12001 [M]	Dawn Club Favorites	1954	$40
❑ L-8 [10]	Lu Watters and His Yerba Buena Jazz Band	1952	$50
❑ L-12002 [M]	Originals and Ragtime	1954	$40
❑ L-0A [M]	San Francisco Style	195?	$75
❑ L-12003 [M]	Stomps, Etc. and the Blues	1954	$40

HOMESPUN
❑ 103	Live Recordings from Hambone Kelly's	197?	$25
❑ 107	Lu Watters and the Yerba Buena Jazz Band, 1941	197?	$25
❑ 101	Lu Watters and the Yerba Buena Jazz Band, Vol. 1	197?	$25
❑ 102	Lu Watters and the Yerba Buena Jazz Band, Vol. 2	197?	$25
❑ 104	Lu Watters and the Yerba Buena Jazz Band, Vol. 4	197?	$30
❑ 106	Lu Watters and the Yerba Buena Jazz Band, Vol. 6	197?	$25
❑ 105	Memories of the Bodega Battle	197?	$30

MERCURY
❑ MGC-510 [10]	Lu Watters and His Yerba Buena Jazz Band	1952	$250
❑ MG-35013 [10]	Lu Watters and His Yerba Buena Jazz Band	1950	$300
❑ MGC-103 [10]	Lu Watters and His Yerba Buena Jazz Band	1950	$250
❑ MGC-503 [10]	Lu Watters Jazz	1951	$250

RIVERSIDE
❑ RLP-2513 [10]	Lu Watters 1947	1955	$300
❑ RLP 12-213 [M]	San Francisco Style	1956	$300

VERVE
❑ MGV-1005 [M]	Lu Watters and His Yerba Buena Jazz Band	1956	$250
❑ V-1005 [M]	Lu Watters and His Yerba Buena Jazz Band	1961	$25

WATTERS, LU/SANTO PECORA
VERVE
❑ MGV-1008 [M]	Dixieland Jamboree	1956	$175
❑ V-1008 [M]	Dixieland Jamboree	1961	$30

WATTS, ALAN
ASCENSION
❑ 0(# unknown)	Dhyana: of the Art of Meditation, Vol. 1	1970	$30
❑ 0(# unknown)	Dhyana: of the Art of Meditation, Vol. 2	1970	$30

MEA
❑ LP-1001 [M]	Haiku Poems	1962	$50
❑ LP-1007 [M]	This Is It	1962	$75
❑ LP-1002 [M]	Zen and Senryu	1962	$50

TOGETHER
❑ 1025	Why Not Now	1970	$30

WARNER BROS.
❑ W1923	The Sounds of Hinduism	1968	$30

WATTS, CHARLIE
Also see THE ROLLING STONES.
COLUMBIA
❑ FC40570	The Charlie Watts Orchestra Live Fulham Town Hall	1986	$35

CONTINUUM
❑ 19308	From One Charlie	1990	$75
— Box set with LP, book ("Ode to a High Flying Bird") and photo of Charlie Parker

WATTS, ERNIE
ELEKTRA
❑ 6E-285	Look in Your Heart	1980	$25

PACIFIC JAZZ
❑ PJ-20155	Planet Love	1969	$30

QWEST
❑ 25283	Musician	1985	$25

VAULT
❑ LP-9011	Wonderbag	1968	$50

WATTS, MARZETTE
ESP-DISK'
❑ 1044 [S]	Marzette Watts and Company	1971	$85

SAVOY
❑ MG-12193 [M]	The Marzette Watts Ensemble	1968	$25

WAVE, THE
ATLANTIC
❑ 81883	Second Wave	1988	$25

WAVE CRESTS, THE
VIKING
❑ VKL-6606 [M]	Surftime U.S.A.	1963	$75
❑ VKS-6606 [S]	Surftime U.S.A.	1963	$150

WAVERLY CONSORT, THE
COLUMBIA MASTERWORKS
❑ M34554	A Renaissance Christmas Celebration	1977	$15

WAYBILL, FEE
CAPITOL
❑ ST-12369 [B]	Read My Lips	1984	$15

WAYFARERS, THE
RCA VICTOR
❑ LPM-2666 [M]	Come Along with the Wayfarers	1963	$30
❑ LSP-2666 [S]	Come Along with the Wayfarers	1963	$30
❑ LPM-1213 [M]	The Wayfarers	1956	$50
❑ LPM-2735 [M]	The Wayfarers at the Hungry I	1963	$30
❑ LSP-2735 [S]	The Wayfarers at the Hungry I	1963	$30
❑ LPM-2946 [M]	The Wayfarers at the World's Fair	1964	$30
❑ LSP-2946 [S]	The Wayfarers at the World's Fair	1964	$40

WAYLAND QUARTET, THE
4 CORNERS OF THE WORLD
❑ FCS-4249	Jazz Bach	1968	$35

WAYLON AND JESSI
RCA VICTOR
❑ AAL1-3931	Leather and Lace	1981	$12

WAYLON AND WILLIE
For convenience's sake, we've listed all the variations of their credits here, including "Willie Nelson and Waylon Jennings." Also see WAYLON JENNINGS; WILLIE NELSON.
COLUMBIA
❑ FC38562	Take It to the Limit	1983	$12

RCA VICTOR
❑ AFL1-2686	Waylon and Willie	1978	$12
❑ AAL1-2686	Waylon and Willie	198?	$10
— Reissue with new prefix
| ❑ AYL1-5134 | Waylon and Willie | 198? | $10 |
— Best Buy Series" reissue
| ❑ AFL1-2686 [DJ] | Waylon and Willie | 1978 | $30 |
— Promo only on gold vinyl
| ❑ AHL1-4455 | WW II | 1982 | $12 |
| ❑ AYL1-5138 | WW II | 198? | $10 |
— Best Buy Series" reissue

WAYNE, CHUCK, AND JOE PUMA
CHOICE
❑ 1004	Interactions	197?	$30

WAYNE, CHUCK
FOCUS
❑ FL-333 [M]	Tapestry	1964	$30
❑ FS-333 [M]	Tapestry	1964	$30

PRESTIGE
❑ PRLP-7367 [M]	Morning Mist	1965	$25
❑ PRST-7367 [S]	Morning Mist	1965	$30

PROGRESSIVE
❑ 3003 [10]	The Chuck Wayne Quintet	1953	$250
❑ PRO-7008	Traveling	1976	$30

SAVOY
❑ MG-12077 [M]	The Jazz Guitarist	1956	$50

SAVOY JAZZ
❑ SJL-1144	Tasty Pudding	198?	$25

VIK
❑ LX-1098 [M]	String Fever	1957	$50

WAYNE, FRANCES
ATLANTIC
❑ 1263 [M]	The Warm Sound	1957	$300
— Black label
| ❑ 1263 [M] | The Warm Sound | 1961 | $175 |
— White "fan" logo at right of label

BRUNSWICK
❑ BL54022 [M]	Frances Wayne	1958	$40

CORAL
❑ CRL56019 [10]	Salute to Ethel Waters	195?	$75

EPIC
❑ LN3222 [M]	Songs for My Man	1956	$150

WAYNE, JOHN
RCA VICTOR
❑ LSP-4828	America, Why I Love Her	1973	$30
❑ AFL1-3484	America, Why I Love Her	1979	$12
— Reissue of 4828
| ❑ AYL1-3959 | America, Why I Love Her | 1981 | $10 |
— Best Buy Series" reissue

WAYNE, NANCY
20TH CENTURY
❑ T-442	Cheatin' Was the Last Thing on My Mind	1974	$15
❑ T-472	I Wanna Kiss You	1975	$15

WAYNE, WEE WILLIE
IMPERIAL
❑ LP-9144 [M]	Travelin' Mood	1961	$500

WAZOO
ZIG ZAG
❑ 217	Wazoo	197?	$30

WE FIVE
A&M
❑ SP-138 [M]	Make Someone Happy	1967	$25
❑ SP-4138 [S]	Make Someone Happy	1967	$18
❑ SP-4168	The Return of We Five	1969	$18
❑ SP-111 [M]	You Were On My Mind	1965	$18
❑ SP-4111 [S]	You Were On My Mind	1965	$25

VAULT
❑ 136	Catch the Wind	1970	$18

WEASELS, THE
WING
❑ MGW-12282 [M]	The Liverpool Beat	1964	$30
❑ SRW-16282 [S]	The Liverpool Beat	1964	$30

WEATHER REPORT
ARC
❑ PC236030	8:30	1979	$35
❑ JC35358	Mr. Gone	1978	$25
— Original issue; no bar code on cover
| ❑ PC35358 | Mr. Gone | 1980 | $20 |
— Budget-line reissue; bar code on back cover
| ❑ JC36793 | Night Passage | 1980 | $25 |
| ❑ PC36793 | Night Passage | 198? | $20 |
— Budget-line reissue
| ❑ FC37616 | Weather Report | 1982 | $25 |
| ❑ HC47616 | Weather Report | 1982 | $40 |
— Half Speed Mastered" on cover
| ❑ PC37616 | Weather Report | 198? | $20 |
— Budget-line reissue

COLUMBIA
❑ PC34099	Black Market	1976	$30
— No bar code on cover
| ❑ PC34099 | Black Market | 1980 | $20 |
— With bar code on cover
| ❑ FC39147 | Domino Theory | 1984 | $25 |
| ❑ PC34418 | Heavy Weather | 1977 | $25 |
— No bar code on cover
| ❑ PC34418 | Heavy Weather | 198? | $20 |
— Budget-line reissue; bar code on back cover
| ❑ HC44418 | Heavy Weather | 198? | $40 |
— Half-Speed Mastered" on cover
| ❑ KC31352 | I Sing the Body Electric | 1972 | $30 |
— Original edition; no bar code on cover
| ❑ PC31352 | I Sing the Body Electric | 1977 | $20 |
— Reissue; with or without bar code on cover
| ❑ KC32494 | Mysterious Traveller | 1974 | $30 |
— Original issue; no bar code on cover
| ❑ PC32494 | Mysterious Traveller | 1977 | $20 |
— Reissue; with or without bar code on cover
❑ CQ32494 [Q]	Mysterious Traveller	1974	$40
❑ FC38427	Procession	1983	$25
❑ FC39908	Sportin' Life	1985	$25
❑ KC32210	Sweetnighter	1973	$30
— Original edition; no bar code on back cover
| ❑ PC32210 | Sweetnighter | 1977 | $20 |
— Reissue with new prefix; with or without bar code on cover
| ❑ PC33417 | Tale Spinnin' | 1975 | $30 |
— Original edition; no bar code on cover
| ❑ PC33417 | Tale Spinnin' | 1977 | $20 |
— Budget-line reissue; with or without bar code
❑ PCQ33417 [Q]	Tale Spinnin'	1975	$40
❑ FC40280	This Is This	1986	$30
❑ C30661	Weather Report	1971	$30
— Original edition; no bar code on cover
| ❑ KC30661 | Weather Report | 1974 | $25 |
— Reissue of C 30661
| ❑ PC30661 | Weather Report | 1977 | $20 |
— Reissue; with or without bar code on cover

FRIDAY MUSIC
❑ 213441 [B]	Heavy Weather	2015	$25
— 180g
| ❑ FRM32210 [B] | Sweetnighter | 2015 | $25 |

WEATHERBIRD JAZZ BAND, THE
STOMP OFF
❑ SOS-1034	Fireworks	198?	$25

Number	Title	Yr	NM

WEATHERBURN, RONN
STOMP OFF
| SOS-1107 | After the Ball | 198? | $25 |

WEATHERLY, JIM
ABC
| ABCD-982 | Pictures and Rhymes | 1977 | $12 |
| ABCD-937 | The People Some People Choose to Love | 1976 | $12 |
BUDDAH
| BDS-5637 | Magnolias & Misfits | 1975 | $12 |
| BDS-5608 | The Songs of Jim Weatherly | 1974 | $12 |
RCA VICTOR
APL1-0090	A Simpler Time	1973	$15
APL1-0267	Jim Weatherly	1974	$15
LSP-4747	Weatherly	1972	$15

WEAVER, CHARLIE
COLUMBIA
| CL1345 [M] | Charlie Weaver Sings for His People | 1959 | $30 |
STARLITE
| 6003 [10] | Charlie Weaver Sings | 1954 | $50 |

WEAVER, DENNIS
ABC
| DP-847 | People Songs | 1974 | $15 |
IM'PRESS
| 1614 | Dennis Weaver | 1972 | $18 |
OVATION
| OVOD-1440 | One More Road | 1975 | $15 |

WEAVERS, THE
ANALOGUE PRODUCTIONS
| 005 | Reunion at Carnegie Hall, 1963 | 199? | $30 |
— Audiophile vinyl
DECCA
DL8909 [M]	Folk Songs Around the World	1959	$40
DL8893 [M]	Folk Songs Made Famous by the Weavers	196?	$25
DL78893 [R]	Folk Songs Made Famous by the Weavers	196?	$18
DL5285 [10]	Folk Songs of America and Other Lands	1951	$150
DL8893 [M]	The Best of the Weavers	1959	$40
— Black label, silver print
DXB173 [M]	The Best of the Weavers	1965	$30
DXSB7173 [R]	The Best of the Weavers	1965	$25
DL75169 [R]	The Weavers' Greatest Hits	1971	$15
DL4277 [M]	Weavers' Gold	1962	$25
DL74277 [R]	Weavers' Gold	1962	$18
DL-5373 [10]	We Wish You a Merry Christmas	1952	$150
MCA
| 4052 | The Best of the Weavers | 197? | $18 |
— Reissue of Decca 7173; black rainbow labels
| 4052 | The Best of the Weavers | 1980 | $15 |
— Blue rainbow labels
VANGUARD

VRS9100 [M]	Almanac	1961	$50
VSD2101 [S]	Almanac	1961	$75
VMS-73122	Classics	1985	$12
VRS9130 [M]	Reunion at Carnegie Hall, 1963	1963	$25
VSD2150 [S]	Reunion at Carnegie Hall, 1963	1963	$30
VRS9161 [M]	Reunion at Carnegie Hall, Part 2	1965	$25
VSD79161 [S]	Reunion at Carnegie Hall, Part 2	1965	$30
VRS9010 [M]	The Weavers at Carnegie Hall	1957	$75
VRS-6533 [R]	The Weavers at Carnegie Hall	1970	$15
VMS-73101	The Weavers at Carnegie Hall	1984	$10
— Reissue of 6533
VRS9075 [M]	The Weavers at Carnegie Hall, Vol. 2	1960	$40
VSD2069 [S]	The Weavers at Carnegie Hall, Vol. 2	1960	$50
VRS9024 [M]	The Weavers at Home	1959	$50
VSD2030 [S]	The Weavers at Home	1959	$75
VSD-15/16	The Weavers' Greatest Hits	1971	$18
VRS9013 [M]	The Weavers on Tour	1957	$75
VRS-6537 [R]	The Weavers on Tour	1970	$15
VMS-73116	The Weavers on Tour	1985	$10
— Reissue of 6537
SRV-3001 [M]	The Weavers Song Bag	1967	$25
SRV-73001 [S]	The Weavers Song Bag	1967	$30
VRS9043 [M]	Travelling on with the Weavers	1959	$50
VSD2022 [S]	Travelling on with the Weavers	1959	$75

WEB, THE
DERAM
| DES18018 [B] | Fully Interlocking | 1968 | $40 |

WEBB, ART
ATLANTIC
| SD18226 | Love Eyes | 197? | $25 |
| SD18212 | Mr. Flute | 197? | $25 |

WEBB, CHICK
CIRCLE
| CLP-81 | Stompin' at the Savoy, 1936 | 198? | $25 |
COLUMBIA
| CL2639 [M] | The Immortal Chick Webb | 1967 | $30 |
| CS9439 [R] | The Immortal Chick Webb | 1967 | $30 |
DECCA
| DL9223 [M] | Chick Webb 1937-39 | 1958 | $120 |
| DL79223 [R] | Chick Webb 1937-39 | 1958 | $120 |
FOLKWAYS
| FJ-2818 | Chick Webb Featuring Ella Fitzgerald | 197? | $30 |
MCA
1327	Ella Swings the Band	198?	$25
1303	Legend	198?	$25
1348	Princess of the Savoy	198?	$25
4107	The Best of Chick Webb	197?	$30
TRIP
| J-5 | On the Air | 197? | $25 |

WEBB, GEORGE
JAZZOLOGY
| J-122 | George Webb's Dixielanders | 1985 | $25 |

WEBB, JACK
RCA VICTOR
| LPM-3199 [10] | Dragnet -- The Christmas Story | 1954 | $175 |
| LPM-1126 [M] | Pete Kelly's Blues | 1955 | $50 |
— Webb narrates; jazz combo plays
| LPM-2053 [M] | Pete Kelly's Blues | 1959 | $30 |
— Reissue of 1126
| LSP-2053(e) [R] | Pete Kelly's Blues | 1959 | $25 |
WARNER BROS.
W1207 [M]	You're My Girl	1958	$30
WS1207 [S]	You're My Girl	1958	$40
W1207 [M]	You're My Girl	1958	$30
WS1207 [S]	You're My Girl	1958	$40

WEBB, JAY LEE
DECCA
DL4933 [M]	I Come Home a-Drinkin'	1967	$30
DL74933 [S]	I Come Home a-Drinkin'	1967	$25
DL75121	She's Looking Better by the Minute	1969	$25

WEBB, JIMMY
ASYLUM
| SD5070 | Land's End | 1974 | $18 |
ATLANTIC
| SD18218 [B] | El Mirage | 1977 | $15 |
EPIC
| BN26401 | Jim Webb Sings Jim Webb | 1968 | $25 |
LORIMAR
| FC37695 | Angel Heart | 1982 | $15 |
REPRISE
RS6448	And So: On	1971	$18
MS2055	Letters	1972	$18
RS6421	Words and Music	1970	$18

WEBB, ROGER
SWAN
| SLP-516 [M] | John, Paul and All That Jazz | 1964 | $30 |

WEBER, EBERHARD
ECM
1288	Chorus	1985	$30
1042	Colours of Chloe	197?	$35
1137	Fluid Rustle	1979	$25
1086	Following Morning	197?	$30
1231	Later That Evening	198?	$25
1188	Little Movements	1980	$25
1107	Silent Feet	1978	$25
1066	Yellow Fields	197?	$30

WEBER, HAJO, AND ULRICH INGENBOLD
ECM
| 1235 | Winterreise | 198? | $30 |

WEBSTER, BEN, AND COLEMAN HAWKINS
COLUMBIA
| KG32774 | Giants of the Tenor Saxophone | 1973 | $35 |
VERVE
| VE-2-2520 | Tenor Giants | 197? | $35 |

WEBSTER, BEN, AND DON BYAS
COMMODORE
| XFL-14938 | Kings of Tenor Sax | 198? | $25 |

WEBSTER, BEN, AND HARRY "SWEETS" EDISON
COLUMBIA
| CL1891 [M] | Ben Webster-Sweets Edison | 1962 | $30 |
| CS8691 [S] | Ben Webster-Sweets Edison | 1962 | $30 |
COLUMBIA JAZZ MASTERPIECES
| CJ40853 | Ben and "Sweets" | 1987 | $25 |
COLUMBIA JAZZ ODYSSEY
| PC37036 | Ben and "Sweets" | 1981 | $25 |

WEBSTER, BEN, AND JOE ZAWINUL
FANTASY
| OJC-109 | Soulmates | 198? | $25 |
MILESTONE
| 47056 | Trav'lin' Light | 198? | $30 |
RIVERSIDE
| RLP-476 [M] | Soulmates | 1964 | $175 |
| RS-9476 [S] | Soulmates | 1964 | $175 |

WEBSTER, BEN
ABC IMPULSE!
| AS-65 [S] | See You at the Fair | 1968 | $35 |
ANALOGUE PRODUCTIONS
| AP 011 | Ben Webster at the Renaissance | 199? | $30 |
BASF
| 20658 [B] | Ben Webster Meets Don Byas | 197? | $175 |
BLACK LION
111	Atmosphere for Lovers and Thieves	197?	$35
190	Duke's in Bed!	197?	$30
302	Saturday Montmartre	197?	$30
BRUNSWICK
| BL58031 [10] | Tenor Sax Stylings | 1952 | $600 |
CIRCLE
| 41 | The Horn | 198? | $25 |
| 42 | The Horn -- Alternate Takes | 198? | $25 |
DISCOVERY
| 818 | The Warm Moods of Ben Webster | 198? | $25 |
EMARCY
| MG-26006 [10] | The Big Tenor | 1954 | $300 |
| 824836-1 | The Complete Ben Webster on EmArcy | 1986 | $35 |
ENJA
| 2038 | Live at Pio's | 197? | $30 |
FIDELIO
| FL-4475 | Gentle Ben | 198? | $25 |
IMPULSE!
| A-65 [M] | See You at the Fair | 1964 | $120 |
| AS-65 [S] | See You at the Fair | 1964 | $120 |
INNER CITY
| IC-2008 | My Man | 197? | $35 |
JAZZ ARCHIVES
| JA-15 | Ben: A Tribute to a Great Jazzman | 198? | $25 |
| JA-35 | Ben and the Boys | 198? | $25 |
JAZZ MAN
| 5007 | Atmosphere for Lovers | 198? | $25 |
NESSA
| N-8 | Did You Call? | 197? | $25 |
NORGRAN
| MGN-1039 [M] | Ben Webster Plays Music with Feeling | 1955 | $250 |
| MGN-1089 [M] | King of the Tenors | 1956 | $300 |

WEBSTER, BEN

Number	Title	Yr	NM
❏ MGN-1018 [M]	Music for Loving	1955	$300
❏ MGN-1001 [M]	The Consummate Artistry of Ben Webster	1954	$400

PRESTIGE
❏ 24031	At Work in Europe	197?	$35

REPRISE
❏ R-2001 [M]	The Warm Moods of Ben Webster	1961	$30
❏ R9-2001 [S]	The Warm Moods of Ben Webster	1961	$30

STEEPLECHASE
❏ SCS-1008	My Man	198?	$30

TIME-LIFE
❏ STL-J-21	Giants of Jazz	1981	$50

VERVE
❏ VE-2-2530	Ballads	197?	$35
❏ 833550-1	Ballads	198?	$30
❏ MGV-8318 [M]	Ben Webster and Associates	1959	$175
❏ MGVS-6056 [S]	Ben Webster and Associates	1959	$175
❏ V-8318 [M]	Ben Webster and Associates	1961	$30
❏ V6-8318 [S]	Ben Webster and Associates	1961	$25
❏ UMV-2515	Ben Webster and Associates	198?	$30
❏ MGV-8349 [M]	Ben Webster Meets Oscar Peterson	1959	$175

❏ MGVS-6114 [S]	Ben Webster Meets Oscar Peterson	1960	$40
❏ V-8349 [M]	Ben Webster Meets Oscar Peterson	1961	$30
❏ V6-8349 [S]	Ben Webster Meets Oscar Peterson	1961	$25
❏ MGV-8020 [M]	King of the Tenors	1957	$175
❏ V-8020 [M]	King of the Tenors	1961	$30
❏ UMV-2081	King of the Tenors	198?	$25
❏ MGV-8130 [M]	Music with Feeling -- Ben Webster with Strings	1957	$175
❏ V-8130 [M]	Music with Feeling -- Ben Webster with Strings	1961	$30
❏ MGV-2026 [M]	Sophisticated Lady -- Ben Webster with Strings	1956	$250
❏ V-2026 [M]	Sophisticated Lady -- Ben Webster with Strings	1961	$30
❏ MGV-8274 [M]	Soulville	1958	$450
❏ V-8274 [M]	Soulville	1961	$30
❏ VE-2-2536	Soulville	1980	$35
❏ 833551-1	Soulville	198?	$30
❏ MGV-8359 [M]	The Soul of Ben Webster	1960	$50
❏ MGVS-6124 [S]	The Soul of Ben Webster	1960	$0
—Canceled			
❏ V-8359 [M]	The Soul of Ben Webster	1961	$30

WEBSTER, MAMIE

CUB
❏ 8002 [M]	The Blues	1959	$175

WECHTER, JULIUS

JAZZ: WEST
❏ LP-9 [M]	Linear Sketches	1956	$250

WEDGES, THE

TIME
❏ 52090 [M]	Hang Ten (For Surfers Only)	1963	$50
❏ S-2090 [S]	Hang Ten (For Surfers Only)	1963	$80

WEED, BUDDY

COLUMBIA
❏ CL6160 [10]	Piano Moods	1951	$50

CORAL
❏ CRL57087 [M]	Piano Solos with Rhythm Accompaniment	1957	$40

WEEKS, ANSON

FANTASY
❏ 3306 [M]	Cruisin' with Anson	1960	$30
—Red vinyl			
❏ 3306 [M]	Cruisin' with Anson	1960	$35
—Black vinyl			

Number	Title	Yr	NM
❏ 8051 [S]	Cruisin' with Anson	1960	$30
—Blue vinyl			
❏ 8051 [S]	Cruisin' with Anson	1960	$30
—Black vinyl			
❏ 3333 [M]	Dancin' at Anson's	1961	$15
—Black vinyl			
❏ 8076 [S]	Dancin' at Anson's	1961	$25
—Black vinyl			
❏ 3333 [M]	Dancin' at Anson's	1961	$75
—Red vinyl			
❏ 8076 [S]	Dancin' at Anson's	1961	$75
—Blue vinyl			
❏ 3258 [M]	Dancin' with Anson	1958	$30
—Red vinyl			
❏ 3258 [M]	Dancin' with Anson	1958	$35
—Black vinyl			
❏ 8001 [S]	Dancin' with Anson	1960	$30
—Blue vinyl			
❏ 8001 [S]	Dancin' with Anson	1960	$30
—Black vinyl			
❏ 8001 [S]	Dancin' with Anson	1960	$30
—Red vinyl (error pressing?)			
❏ 3269 [M]	Memories	1958	$30
—Red vinyl			
❏ 3269 [M]	Memories	1958	$35
—Black vinyl			
❏ 8006 [S]	Memories	1960	$30
—Blue vinyl			
❏ 8006 [S]	Memories	1960	$30
—Black vinyl			
❏ 3297 [M]	More Dancin' with Anson	1959	$30
—Red vinyl			
❏ 3297 [M]	More Dancin' with Anson	1959	$35
—Black vinyl			
❏ 8043 [S]	More Dancin' with Anson	1960	$30
—Blue vinyl			
❏ 8043 [S]	More Dancin' with Anson	1960	$30
—Black vinyl			
❏ 3338 [M]	Old Favorites and New	1962	$30
—Red vinyl			
❏ 3338 [M]	Old Favorites and New	1962	$30
—Black vinyl			
❏ 8090 [S]	Old Favorites and New	1962	$30
—Blue vinyl			
❏ 8090 [S]	Old Favorites and New	1962	$35
—Black vinyl			
❏ 8355 [S]	Reminiscing at the Mark	1964	$35
❏ 3355 [M]	Reminiscing at the Mark	1964	$30

HINDSIGHT
❏ HSR-146	Anson Weeks and the Hotel Mark Hopkins Orchestra 1932	198?	$25

WEEN

GRAND ROYAL
❏ GR 010 [B]	Chocolate and Cheese	1994	$30
—Cassette and CD on Elektra 61639			

PLAIN
❏ 142 [B]	12 Golden Country Greats	2016	$25
❏ PLAIN143 [B]	The Mollusk	2016	$25

WEEZER

DGC
❏ DGC-25007 [B]	Pinkerton	1996	$50

GEFFEN
❏ B0004520-01	Make Believe	2005	$18

❏ 069-493241-1 [B]	Maladroit	2002	$18
❏ 069-493045-1	Weezer	2001	$25
—Green vinyl			
❏ 069-493045-1	Weezer	2001	$18
—Black vinyl			

Number	Title	Yr	NM

WEIGAND, JACK

CAMEO
❏ C-1012 [M]	Stairway to the Stars	1961	$15
❏ SC-1012 [S]	Stairway to the Stars	1961	$18

WYNCOTE
❏ SW-9017 [S]	Shangri-La and Other Favorites	1964	$15
❏ W-9017 [M]	Shangri-La and Other Favorites	1964	$12

WEIN, GEORGE

ATLANTIC
❏ SD1533 [S]	George Wein and the Newport All-Stars	1969	$35
❏ 1221 [M]	Wein, Women and Song	1955	$300
—Black label			
❏ 1221 [M]	Wein, Women and Song	1961	$175
—Multicolor label, white "fan" logo at right			

BETHLEHEM
❏ BCP-6050 [M]	George Wein and the Storyville Sextet -- Jazz at the Modern	1960	$300
❏ SBCP-6050 [S]	George Wein and the Storyville Sextet -- Jazz at the Modern	1960	$300

COLUMBIA
❏ CS9631 [S]	Alive and Well in Mexico	1968	$35

IMPULSE!
❏ A-31 [M]	George Wein and the Newport All-Stars	1963	$250

❏ AS-31 [S]	George Wein and the Newport All-Stars	1963	$120

RCA VICTOR
❏ LPM-1332 [M]	The Magic Horn of George Wein	1956	$40

WEINER SANGERKNABEN

CAPITOL
❏ T10164 [M]	Christmas in Austria	196?	$18

WEIR, BOB
Also see THE GRATEFUL DEAD.

ARISTA
❏ AL9568	Bobby and the Midnites	1981	$12
❏ AL8367	Bobby and the Midnites	1985	$10
—Budget-line reissue			
❏ AL4155 [B]	Heaven Help the Fool	1978	$12
❏ AL8366	Heaven Help the Fool	1985	$10
—Budget-line reissue			

WARNER BROS.
❏ BS2627	Ace	1972	$40
—Color photo on back cover			
❏ BS2627	Ace	1972	$30
—Black and white photo on back cover			

WEIRD-OHS, THE

MERCURY
❏ MG-20976 [M]	The Sounds of the Weird-Ohs	1964	$175
❏ SR-60976 [S]	The Sounds of the Weird-Ohs	1964	$250

WEIRDOS

BOMP!
❏ 4007 [EP]	Who? What? When? Where? Why?	1979	$18

FRONTIER
❏ 4623-1-L [B]	Condor	1990	$15
❏ 4630-1-L [B]	Weird World	1991	$25

OUT OF DARKNESS
❏ OTD 001 [DJ]	Message from the Underworld	198?	$40
—Promo-only release			

RHINO
❏ RNEP508 [EP]	Action Design	1980	$25

Number	Title	Yr	NM

WEISBERG, TIM

A&M

Number	Title	Yr	NM
❑ SP-3045	Dreamspeaker	1973	$25
❑ SP-4352	Hurtwood Edge	1972	$30
❑ SP-4545	Listen to the City	1975	$25
❑ SP-4600	Live at Last!	1976	$25
❑ SP-4749	Smile/The Best of Tim Weisberg	1979	$25
❑ SP-3261	Smile/The Best of Tim Weisberg	198?	$20

— Budget-line reissue

❑ SP-3039	Tim Weisberg	1971	$30
❑ SP-3658	Tim Weisberg 4	1974	$25
❑ SP-3121	Tim Weisberg 4	198?	$20

— Budget-line reissue

CYPRESS

| ❑ 661112-1 | High Risk | 1986 | $25 |
| ❑ YL-0123 | Outrageous Temptations | 1989 | $30 |

DESERT ROCK

| ❑ DR-001 | High Risk | 1985 | $35 |

LIBERTY

| ❑ LN-10029 | Rotations | 198? | $20 |

— Budget-line reissue

| ❑ LN-10031 | The Tim Weisberg Band | 198? | $20 |

— Budget-line reissue

MCA

❑ 3084	Night-Rider!	1979	$25
❑ 5125	Party of One	1980	$25
❑ 5245	Travelin' Light	1981	$25

NAUTILUS

| ❑ NR-7 [B] | Tip of the Weisberg | 1980 | $30 |

— Audiophile vinyl

UNITED ARTISTS

| ❑ UA-LA857-H | Rotations | 1978 | $25 |
| ❑ UA-LA773-G | The Tim Weisberg Band | 1977 | $25 |

WEISS, LARRY

20TH CENTURY

| ❑ T-428 | Black and Blue Suite | 1974 | $18 |

WEISSBERG, ERIC, AND DELIVERANCE

WARNER BROS.

| ❑ BS2720 | Rural Free Delivery | 1973 | $12 |

WEISSBERG, ERIC, AND MARSHALL BRICKMAN

ELEKTRA

| ❑ EKL-238 [M] | New Dimensions in Banjo and Bluegrass | 1963 | $25 |
| ❑ EKS-7238 [S] | New Dimensions in Banjo and Bluegrass | 1963 | $30 |

— Mandolin-player label

| ❑ EKS-7238 [S] | New Dimensions in Banjo and Bluegrass | 1967 | $25 |

— Tan label with large stylized "E" at top

| ❑ EKS-7238 [S] | New Dimensions in Banjo and Bluegrass | 1969 | $18 |

— Red label with large stylized "E" at top

| ❑ EKS-7238 [S] | New Dimensions in Banjo and Bluegrass | 1971 | $15 |

— Butterfly label

| ❑ EKS-7238 [S] | New Dimensions in Banjo and Bluegrass | 1980 | $12 |

— Red label with Warner Communications logo in lower right

WEISSBERG, ERIC, AND STEVE MANDELL

WARNER BROS.

| ❑ BS2683 | Dueling Banjos from Deliverance | 1973 | $12 |

— Except for the title song and "End of a Dream," this is actually a reissue of Elektra 7238; green label

| ❑ BS2683 | Dueling Banjos from Deliverance | 1973 | $10 |

— Burbank" palm trees label

| ❑ BS2683 | Dueling Banjos from Deliverance | 1979 | $10 |

— Tan or white label

WELCH, ELISABETH

DRG

| ❑ SL-5202 | Where Have You Been? | 1987 | $25 |

WELCH, LENNY

CADENCE

| ❑ CLP3068 [M] | Since I Fell for You | 1963 | $30 |
| ❑ CLP25068 [S] | Since I Fell for You | 1963 | $50 |

COLUMBIA

| ❑ CL2430 [M] | Since I Fell for You | 1965 | $25 |

— Reissue of Cadence 3068

Number	Title	Yr	NM
❑ CS9230 [S]	Since I Fell for You	1965	$30

— Reissue of Cadence 25068

KAPP

❑ KL-1517 [M]	Lenny	1967	$18
❑ KS-3517 [S]	Lenny	1967	$25
❑ KL-1481 [M]	Rags to Riches	1966	$18
❑ KS-3481 [S]	Rags to Riches	1966	$25
❑ KL-1457 [M]	Two Different Worlds	1965	$18
❑ KS-3457 [S]	Two Different Worlds	1965	$25

WELCH CHORALE, THE

VANGUARD

| ❑ VRS428 [M] | A Music Box of Christmas Carols | 1954 | $25 |

— With Music Boxes from the Bornand Collection

WELDON, MAXINE

MAINSTREAM

| ❑ MRL-339 | Chilly Wind | 1972 | $30 |
| ❑ MRL-319 | Right On | 1971 | $30 |

WELK, LAWRENCE

CORAL

❑ CRL57038 [M]	Bubbles in the Wine	1956	$25
❑ CRL57226 [M]	Champagne Dancing Party	1958	$18
❑ CRL757226 [S]	Champagne Dancing Party	1958	$25
❑ CRL57078 [M]	Champagne Pops Parade	1956	$25
❑ CRL57186 [M]	Jingle Bells	1957	$25
❑ CRL757186 [R]	Jingle Bells	196?	$15
❑ CRL57011 [M]	Lawrence Welk and His Sparkling Strings	1955	$25
❑ CRL57066 [M]	Lawrence Welk at Madison Square Garden	1956	$25
❑ CRL57262 [M]	Lawrence Welk Featuring Larry Hooper	1959	$18
❑ CRL57260 [M]	Lawrence Welk Featuring the Lennon Sisters	1959	$18
❑ CRL57023 [M]	Lawrence Welk Introduces the Girl Friends	1955	$30
❑ CRL57146 [M]	Lawrence Welk Plays Dixieland	1957	$25
❑ CRL57214 [M]	Lawrence Welk Presents Keyboard Kapers	1958	$18
❑ CRL57383 [M]	Lawrence Welk Showcase	1962	$15
❑ CRL757383 [S]	Lawrence Welk Showcase	1962	$15
❑ CRL57093 [M]	Merry Christmas from Lawrence Welk	1956	$25
❑ CRL757093 [R]	Merry Christmas from Lawrence Welk	196?	$15
❑ CRL57068 [M]	Moments to Remember	1956	$25
❑ CRL57353 [M]	My Golden Favorites	1961	$15
❑ CRL757353 [S]	My Golden Favorites	1961	$15
❑ CRL57178 [M]	Nimble Fingers	1957	$25
❑ CRL56101 [10]	Nimble Fingers	195?	$30
❑ CRL56043 [10]	On Moonlight Bay	195?	$30
❑ CRL57067 [M]	Pick-A-Polka!	1956	$25
❑ CRL757067 [R]	Pick-A-Polka!	1959	$15
❑ CRL57041 [R]	Say It With Music	196?	$15
❑ CRL57041 [M]	Say It With Music	1956	$25
❑ CRL57036 [M]	Shamrocks and Champagne	1955	$25
❑ CRL757036 [R]	Shamrocks and Champagne	196?	$15
❑ CRL57111 [M]	Show Time	1957	$25
❑ CRL56045 [10]	Songs About My Extraordinary Gal and Her Friends	195?	$30
❑ CRL57439 [M]	Songs Everybody Knows	1964	$15
❑ CRL757439 [S]	Songs Everybody Knows	1964	$15
❑ CRL57191 [M]	Songs of Faith	1958	$18
❑ CRL56088 [10]	Souvenir Album	195?	$30
❑ CXB5 [M]	The Best of Lawrence Welk	196?	$25
❑ 7CXSB5 [S]	The Best of Lawrence Welk	196?	$18
❑ CRL57113 [M]	The World's Finest Music	1957	$25
❑ CRL757113 [R]	The World's Finest Music	196?	$15
❑ CRL57025 [M]	TV Favorites	1955	$25
❑ CRL57267 [M]	TV Western Theme Songs	1959	$18
❑ CRL757267 [S]	TV Western Theme Songs	1959	$25
❑ CRL56120 [10]	Viennese Waltzes for Dancing	1954	$30
❑ CRL57119 [M]	Waltz with Lawrence Welk	1957	$25

CORONET

| ❑ 275 | Lawrence Welk and His Orchestra | 196? | $12 |

DECCA

❑ DL8323 [M]	Around We Go	1956	$18
❑ DL8213 [M]	Lawrence Welk's Polka Party	1956	$18
❑ DL8324 [M]	Welktime	1956	$18

DESIGN

| ❑ 200 | Champagne Time | 196? | $12 |
| ❑ 912 | Three of a Kind | 196? | $12 |

DOT

❑ DLP3510 [M]	1963's Early Hits	1963	$12
❑ DLP25510 [S]	1963's Early Hits	1963	$15
❑ DLP3629 [M]	Apples and Bananas	1965	$12
❑ DLP25629 [S]	Apples and Bananas	1965	$15
❑ DLP3544 [M]	A Tribute to the All-Time Greats	1963	$12
❑ DLP25544 [S]	A Tribute to the All-Time Greats	1963	$15
❑ DLP3457 [M]	Baby Elephant Walk and Theme from The Brothers Grimm	1962	$12
❑ DLP25457 [S]	Baby Elephant Walk and Theme from The Brothers Grimm	1962	$15
❑ DLP3489 [M]	Bubbles in the Wine	1962	$12
❑ DLP25489 [S]	Bubbles in the Wine	1962	$15
❑ DLP3359 [M]	Calcutta!	1961	$12
❑ DLP25359 [S]	Calcutta!	1961	$15
❑ DLP3688 [M]	Champagne on Broadway	1966	$12
❑ DLP25688 [S]	Champagne on Broadway	1966	$15
❑ DLP3224 [M]	Dance with Lawrence Welk	1959	$15
❑ DLP25224 [S]	Dance with Lawrence Welk	1959	$18
❑ DLP3395 [M]	Diamond Jubilee	1961	$12
❑ DLP25395 [S]	Diamond Jubilee	1961	$15
❑ DLP3318 [M]	Double Shuffle	1960	$12
❑ DLP25318 [S]	Double Shuffle	1960	$15
❑ DLP3572 [M]	Early Hits of 1964	1964	$12
❑ DLP25572 [S]	Early Hits of 1964	1964	$15
❑ DLP3812 [M]	Golden Hits/The Best of Lawrence Welk	1967	$15
❑ DLP25812 [S]	Golden Hits/The Best of Lawrence Welk	1967	$12
❑ DLP3779 [M]	Hymns We Love	1967	$12
❑ DLP25779 [S]	Hymns We Love	1967	$15
❑ DLP3248 [M]	I'm Forever Blowing Bubbles	1960	$12
❑ DLP25248 [S]	I'm Forever Blowing Bubbles	1960	$15
❑ DLP3350 [M]	Last Date	1960	$12
❑ DLP25350 [S]	Last Date	1960	$15
❑ DLP3317 [M]	Lawrence in Dixieland	1960	$12
❑ DLP25317 [S]	Lawrence in Dixieland	1960	$15
❑ DLP3238 [M]	Lawrence Welk Presents Great American Composers	1960	$12
❑ DLP25238 [S]	Lawrence Welk Presents Great American Composers	1960	$15
❑ DLP3247 [M]	Lawrence Welk Presents Great Overtures in Dance Time	1960	$12
❑ DLP25247 [S]	Lawrence Welk Presents Great Overtures in Dance Time	1960	$15
❑ DLP3790 [M]	Lawrence Welk's "Hits of Our Time	1967	$15
❑ DLP25790 [S]	Lawrence Welk's "Hits of Our Time	1967	$15
❑ DLP3412 [M]	Moon River	1961	$12
❑ DLP25412 [S]	Moon River	1961	$15
❑ DLP3164 [M]	Mr. Music Maker	1959	$15
❑ DLP25164 [S]	Mr. Music Maker	1959	$18
❑ DLP3616 [M]	My First of 1965	1965	$12
❑ DLP25616 [S]	My First of 1965	1965	$15
❑ DLP3302 [M]	Polkas	1960	$12
❑ DLP25302 [S]	Polkas	1960	$15
❑ DLP3528 [M]	Scarlett O'Hara	1963	$12
❑ DLP25528 [S]	Scarlett O'Hara	1963	$15
❑ DLP3397 [M]	Silent Night and 13 Other Best-Loved Christmas Songs	1961	$15
❑ DLP25397 [S]	Silent Night and 13 Other Best-Loved Christmas Songs	1961	$18
❑ DLP3432 [M]	Sing-a-Long Party	1962	$12
❑ DLP25432 [S]	Sing-a-Long Party	1962	$15
❑ DLP3251 [M]	Songs of the Islands	1960	$12
❑ DLP25251 [S]	Songs of the Islands	1960	$15
❑ DLP3274 [M]	Strictly for Dancing	1960	$12
❑ DLP25274 [S]	Strictly for Dancing	1960	$15
❑ DLP3296 [M]	Sweet and Lovely	1960	$12
❑ DLP25296 [S]	Sweet and Lovely	1960	$15
❑ DLP3342 [M]	The Champagne Music of Lawrence Welk	1960	$12
❑ DLP25342 [S]	The Champagne Music of Lawrence Welk	1960	$15
❑ DLP3611 [M]	The Golden Millions	1964	$12
❑ DLP25611 [S]	The Golden Millions	1964	$15
❑ DLP3653 [M]	The Happy Wanderer	1966	$12
❑ DLP25653 [S]	The Happy Wanderer	1966	$15
❑ DLP3218 [M]	The Lawrence Welk Glee Club	1959	$15
❑ DLP25218 [S]	The Lawrence Welk Glee Club	1959	$18
❑ DLP3591 [M]	The Lawrence Welk Television Show 10th Anniversary	1964	$12
❑ DLP25591 [S]	The Lawrence Welk Television Show 10th Anniversary	1964	$15
❑ DLP3200 [M]	The Voices and Strings of Lawrence Welk	1959	$15
❑ DLP3663 [M]	Today's Great Hits	1966	$12

Number	Title	Yr	NM
DLP25663 [S]	Today's Great Hits	1966	$15
DLP3284 [M]	To Mother	1960	$12
DLP25284 [S]	To Mother	1960	$15
DLP25200 [S]	Voices and Strings	1959	$18
DLP3499 [M]	Waltz Time	1963	$12
DLP25499 [S]	Waltz Time	1963	$15
DLP3774 [M]	Winchester Cathedral	1966	$12
DLP25774 [S]	Winchester Cathedral	1966	$15
DLP3552 [M]	Wonderful! Wonderful!	1963	$12
DLP25552 [S]	Wonderful! Wonderful!	1963	$15
DLP3389 [M]	Yellow Bird	1961	$12
DLP25389 [S]	Yellow Bird	1961	$15
DLP3428 [M]	Young World	1962	$12
DLP25428 [S]	Young World	1962	$15

HAMILTON
Number	Title	Yr	NM
HLP152 [M]	Mary Poppins	1965	$12
HLP12152 [S]	Mary Poppins	1965	$15

HARMONY
Number	Title	Yr	NM
HS11301	Champagne Dance Party	1969	$12
HL7394 [M]	Vintage Champagne	1966	$15
HS11194 [S]	Vintage Champagne	1966	$15

HEARTLAND
Number	Title	Yr	NM
1006	Musical Family Reunion	198?	$12

MCA
Number	Title	Yr	NM
733	Polka and Waltz Time	197?	$10
— Reissue of Vocalion 73670
4044	The Best of Lawrence Welk	197?	$15
4026	The Best of Lawrence Welk, Volume 2	197?	$15
4104	The Best Polkas	197?	$15

MCA CORAL
Number	Title	Yr	NM
20100	Champagne Music	197?	$10

MERCURY
Number	Title	Yr	NM
MG-20092 [M]	Dance Party	1956	$18

MISTLETOE
Number	Title	Yr	NM
MLP-1215	Christmas with Lawrence Welk	197?	$12

PICKWICK
Number	Title	Yr	NM
SPC-3157	As Time Goes By	196?	$12
SPC-3212	Blue Hawaii	197?	$12
SPC-3143	If You Were the Only One	196?	$12
SPC-3092	I'll See You Again	196?	$12
SPC-3196	Love Is a Many-Splendored Thing	197?	$12
SPC-3252	Polkas!	197?	$12
SPC-3070	Save the Last Dance for Me	196?	$12
SPC-1019	The Christmas Song	197?	$12
— Reissue of Coral LP "Jingle Bells" with shuffled running order
| SPC-3116 | You'll Never Walk Alone | 196? | $12 |

PREMIER
Number	Title	Yr	NM
9043	Lawrence Welk	196?	$12

RANWOOD
Number	Title	Yr	NM
7023	22 All-Time Big Band Favorites	1983	$15
7028	22 All-Time Favorite Waltzes	198?	$15
7009	22 Great Songs for Dancing	1978	$15
7016	22 Great Songs for Easy Listening	198?	$15
7004	22 Great Waltzes	1977	$15
7029	22 Merry Christmas Favorites	198?	$15
5005	24 of the World's Greatest Polkas	197?	$15
— With Myron Floren
8145	25 Years on Television	1975	$12
7002	200 Years of American Music	1976	$15
8024	Calcutta!	1968	$10
— Reissue of Dot 25359
8083	Candida	1970	$12
8079	Champagne Strings	1970	$12
8211	Come Waltz with Me	1984	$10
8027	Country Music's Great Hits	1968	$12
8049	Galveston	1969	$12
8091	Go Away Little Girl	1971	$12
8028	Golden Hits/The Best of Lawrence Welk	1968	$10
— Reissue of Dot 25812
| 8184 | Hallelujah! | 1978 | $12 |
| 8042 | Hymns We Love | 1968 | $10 |
— Reissue of Dot 25779
| 2009 | Hymns We Love | 197? | $10 |
— Reissue of Ranwood 8042
8060	Jean	1969	$12
6002	Lawrence Welk and His Musical Family Celebrate 50 Years in Music	1974	$12
6001	Lawrence Welk and His Musical Family in Concert	1973	$15
8194	Lawrence Welk Plays Dixieland	1980	$12
8130	Lawrence Welk Plays From That's Entertainment	1974	$12
8053	Lawrence Welk Plays I Love You Truly and Other Songs of Love	1969	$12
8201	Lawrence Welk Presents Anacani	1982	$12
10001	Live at Lake Tahoe	1978	$15
8003	Love Is Blue	1968	$12
8044	Memories	1969	$12

Number	Title	Yr	NM
2010	Memories	197?	$10
— Reissue of Ranwood 8044
| 2000 | Merry Christmas | 197? | $12 |
| 8016 | Moon River | 1968 | $10 |
— Reissue of Dot 25412
| 2005 | Moon River | 197? | $10 |
— Reissue of Ranwood 8016
8109	(More of) The Big Band Sound	1972	$12
8140	Most Requested TV Favorites	1974	$12
8210	Musical Memories with Lawrence Welk	1984	$10
8183	My Personal Favorites	1978	$12
8165	Nadia's Theme	1976	$12
8087	No, No, Nanette	1971	$12
4100	On Tour, Volume 1	198?	$10
4101	On Tour, Volume 2	198?	$10
2004	Polkas	197?	$10
— With Myron Floren
8191	Remembering the Sweet and Swing Band Era, Vol. 1	1979	$12
8192	Remembering the Sweet and Swing Band Era, Vol. 2	1979	$12
5001	Reminiscing	1972	$15
8195	Reminiscing, Vol. 2	1980	$15
8020	Silent Night and 13 Other Best-Loved Christmas Songs	1968	$10
— Reissue of Dot 25397
| 8022 | Songs of the Islands | 1968 | $10 |
— Reissue of Dot 25251
| 2007 | Songs of the Islands | 197? | $10 |
— Reissue of Ranwood 8022
8162	The Best of Lawrence Welk: 20 Great Hits	1976	$12
8077	The Big Band Sound	1970	$12
8023	The Champagne Music of Lawrence Welk	1968	$10
— Reissue of Dot 25342
8068	The Golden 60's	1970	$12
8114	The Good Life	1973	$12
8034	The Lawrence Welk Singers and Orchestra	1968	$12
8026	The Lawrence Welk Television Show	1968	$10
— Reissue of Dot 25591
10002	The Sweet and Swing Band Era	1979	$15
8030	To America with Love	1968	$12
8025	Waltz Time	1968	$10
— Reissue of Dot 25499
| 2008 | Waltz Time | 197? | $10 |
— Reissue of Ranwood 8025
| 8017 | Winchester Cathedral | 1968 | $10 |
— Reissue of Dot 25774
| 8021 | Yellow Bird | 1968 | $10 |
— Reissue of Dot 25389
| 2006 | Yellow Bird | 197? | $10 |
— Reissue of Ranwood 8021

READER'S DIGEST
Number	Title	Yr	NM
RDA156	Champagne Dance Time with Lawrence Welk	196?	$12
RDA95	Champagne Music Varieties	196?	$30
RDA-07-A	Merry Christmas from Lawrence Welk and His Champagne Music Makers	1970	$30

SUNNYVALE
Number	Title	Yr	NM
SVL-1015	Silent Night and 13 Other Best-Loved Christmas Songs	1978	$10
— Same contents as Dot 25397

THOMAS
Number	Title	Yr	NM
20052	The Magic of Color-Glo	196?	$15

VOCALION
Number	Title	Yr	NM
VL73865	Champagne Polkas	1969	$12
VL3671 [M]	Lawrence Welk and His Champagne Music	196?	$12
VL73671 [R]	Lawrence Welk and His Champagne Music	196?	$12
VL73783 [R]	Lawrence Welk and His Champagne Music Makers Play for You	1967	$12
VL3783 [M]	Lawrence Welk and His Champagne Music Makers Play for You	1967	$15
VL3670 [M]	Polka and Waltz Time	196?	$12
VL73670 [R]	Polka and Waltz Time	196?	$12
VL73888	Til the End of Time	1969	$12
VL73921	Wonderful Music	1970	$12

WING
Number	Title	Yr	NM
MGW-12214 [M]	Aragon Trianon Memories	196?	$15
SRW-16214 [R]	Aragon Trianon Memories	196?	$12
MGW-12119 [M]	Dance Party	196?	$15
SRW-16210 [S]	Music for Polka Lovers	196?	$12
MGW-12210 [M]	Music for Polka Lovers	196?	$15
SRW-16379	The Best of Welk	196?	$12
PKW-2-114	With a-One and a-Two	1969	$18

WELLER, FREDDY
ABC DOT
Number	Title	Yr	NM
DOSD-2026	Love You Back to Georgia	1975	$15

COLUMBIA
Number	Title	Yr	NM
CS9904	Games People Play/These Are Not My People	1969	$18
KC33883	Greatest Hits	1975	$15
KC34244	Liquor, Love and Life	1976	$12
CS1036	Listen to the Young Folks	1970	$18
KC35658	Love Got in the Way	1979	$12
PC34709	One Man Show	1977	$12
C30638	Promised Land	1971	$15
KC31769	Roadmaster	1972	$15
KC32958	Sexy Lady	1974	$15
KC32218	Too Much Monkey Business	1973	$15

HARMONY
Number	Title	Yr	NM
KH31784	Country Collection	1972	$12

WELLES, ORSON
AUDIO FIDELITY
Number	Title	Yr	NM
W-90366	War of the Worlds	1964	$18
— Capitol Record Club edition; same edited version as Audio Rarities LPA 2355

AUDIO RARITIES
Number	Title	Yr	NM
LPA2355 [B]	War of the Worlds	1955	$30
— Edited version of the October 30, 1938 Mercury Theatre radio broadcast

EVOLUTION
Number	Title	Yr	NM
2 LPS4001 [B]	War of the Worlds	1971	$30
— Complete version of the October 30, 1938 Mercury Theatre radio broadcast

LONGINES SYMPHONETTE
Number	Title	Yr	NM
SY-5251	War of the Worlds	197?	$18
— Complete version of the October 30, 1938 Mercury Theatre radio broadcast, but on one record

MEDIARTS
Number	Title	Yr	NM
41-2	The Begatting of the President	1970	$18

MURRAY HILL
Number	Title	Yr	NM
S44217	War of the Worlds	197?	$15
— Complete version of the October 30, 1938 Mercury Theatre radio broadcast; reissue of Evolution LP

UNITED ARTISTS
Number	Title	Yr	NM
UAS-5521	The Begatting of the President	1971	$15
— Reissue of Mediarts LP

WELLS, DICKY
FELSTED
Number	Title	Yr	NM
FAJ-7006 [M]	Bones for the King	1958	$40
SJA-2006 [S]	Bones for the King	1958	$40
FAJ-7009 [M]	Trombone Four in Hand	1958	$40
SJA-2009 [S]	Trombone Four in Hand	1958	$40

MASTER JAZZ
Number	Title	Yr	NM
8118	Trombone Four-in-Hand	197?	$30

PRESTIGE
Number	Title	Yr	NM
PRST-7593 [R]	Dicky Wells in Pais 1937	1968	$30

UPTOWN
Number	Title	Yr	NM
277	Lonesome Road	198?	$25

WELLS, JUNIOR
BLUE ROCK
Number	Title	Yr	NM
64003	Live at the Golden Bear	1969	$30
64002	You're Tuff Enough	1968	$30

DELMARK
Number	Title	Yr	NM
DS-640	Blue Hit Big Towns	1969	$30
DS-640	Blues Hit the Big Town	1969	$30

Number	Title	Yr	NM
DL-612 [M]	Hoodoo Man Blues	1966	$40
DS-612 [S]	Hoodoo Man Blues	1966	$50
DS-628 [B]	Southside Blues Jam	1967	$30

VANGUARD
Number	Title	Yr	NM
VSD-79262	Comin' At You	1968	$30
VRS-9231 [M]	It's My Life Baby	1966	$50
VSD-79231 [S]	It's My Life Baby	1966	$75

Number	Title	Yr	NM

WELLS, KITTY, AND JOHNNY WRIGHT
DECCA
| ❏ DL75028 [S] | We'll Stick Together | 1968 | $30 |
| ❏ DL5028 [M] | We'll Stick Together | 1968 | $50 |
| — Mono appears to be white label promo only |

WELLS, KITTY, AND RED FOLEY
Also see each artist's individual listings.
DECCA
❏ DL4109 [M]	Golden Favorites	1961	$30
❏ DL74109 [S]	Golden Favorites	1961	$40
❏ DL4906 [M]	Together Again	1967	$30
❏ DL74906 [S]	Together Again	1967	$30

WELLS, KITTY
DECCA
| ❏ DL8888 [M] | After Dark | 1959 | $75 |
| — Black label, silver print |
| ❏ DL8888 [M] | After Dark | 1961 | $30 |
| — Black label with color bars |
❏ DL75164	Bouquet of Country Hits	1969	$25
❏ DL4612 [M]	Burning Memories	1965	$30
❏ DL74612 [S]	Burning Memories	1965	$30
❏ DL4349 [M]	Christmas Day with Kitty Wells	1962	$30
❏ DL74349 [S]	Christmas Day with Kitty Wells	1962	$30
❏ DL4776 [M]	Country All the Way	1966	$30
❏ DL74776 [S]	Country All the Way	1966	$30
❏ DL4554 [M]	Country Music Time	1964	$30
❏ DL74554 [S]	Country Music Time	1964	$30
❏ DL75067	Cream of Country Hits	1968	$30
❏ DL8858 [M]	Dust on the Bible	1959	$75
— Black label, silver print
❏ DL8858 [M]	Dust on the Bible	1961	$30
— Black label with color bars
❏ DL78858 [R]	Dust on the Bible	196?	$25
❏ DL4493 [M]	Especially for You	1964	$30
❏ DL74493 [S]	Especially for You	1964	$30
❏ DL4679 [M]	Family Gospel Sing	1965	$30
❏ DL74679 [S]	Family Gospel Sing	1965	$30
❏ DL75098	Guilty Street	1969	$30
❏ DL4141 [M]	Heartbreak U.S.A.	1961	$30
❏ DL74141 [S]	Heartbreak U.S.A.	1961	$40
❏ DL75325	Heartwarming Gospel Songs	1972	$25
❏ DL75382	I've Got Yesterday	1972	$25
❏ DL8979 [M]	Kitty's Choice	1960	$50
— Black label, silver print
❏ DL78979 [S]	Kitty's Choice	1960	$75
— Maroon label, silver print
❏ DL8979 [M]	Kitty's Choice	1961	$30
— Black label with color bars
❏ DL78979 [S]	Kitty's Choice	1961	$30
— Black label with color bars
❏ DL8293 [M]	Kitty Wells' Country Hit Parade	1956	$75
— Black label, silver print
❏ DL8293 [M]	Kitty Wells' Country Hit Parade	1961	$30
— Black label with color bars
❏ DL78293 [R]	Kitty Wells' Country Hit Parade	196?	$25
❏ DL4108 [M]	Kitty Wells' Golden Favorites	1961	$30
❏ DL74108 [R]	Kitty Wells' Golden Favorites	196?	$25
❏ DL5001 [M]	Kitty Wells' Greatest Hits	1968	$50
— White label promo only
❏ DL75001 [S]	Kitty Wells' Greatest Hits	1968	$30
❏ DL74961	Kitty Wells Showcase	1968	$30
❏ DL4741 [M]	Kitty Wells Sings Songs Made Famous by Jim Reeves	1966	$30
❏ DL74741 [S]	Kitty Wells Sings Songs Made Famous by Jim Reeves	1966	$30
❏ DL8732 [M]	Lonely Street	1958	$75
— Black label, silver print
❏ DL8732 [M]	Lonely Street	1961	$30
— Black label with color bars
❏ DL78732 [R]	Lonely Street	196?	$25
❏ DL4658 [M]	Lonesome Sad and Blue	1965	$30
❏ DL74658 [S]	Lonesome Sad and Blue	1965	$30
❏ DL4857 [M]	Love Makes the World Go Around	1967	$30
❏ DL74857 [S]	Love Makes the World Go Around	1967	$30
❏ DL75313	Pledging My Love	1971	$25
❏ DL4197 [M]	Queen of Country Music	1962	$30
❏ DL74197 [S]	Queen of Country Music	1962	$40
❏ DL4929 [M]	Queen of Honky Tonk Street	1967	$40
❏ DL74929 [S]	Queen of Honky Tonk Street	1967	$30
❏ DL4075 [M]	Seasons of My Heart	1961	$30
❏ DL74075 [S]	Seasons of My Heart	1961	$40
❏ DL75350	Sincerely	1972	$25
❏ SW-94491	Sincerely	1972	$30
— Capitol Record Club edition
❏ DL75221	Singin' 'Em Country	1970	$25
❏ DL4270 [M]	Singing on Sunday	1962	$30
❏ DL74270 [S]	Singing on Sunday	1962	$40
❏ DL4831 [M]	The Kitty Wells Show	1966	$30
❏ DL74831 [S]	The Kitty Wells Show	1966	$30
❏ DXB174 [M]	The Kitty Wells Story	1963	$30
❏ DXSB7174 [P]	The Kitty Wells Story	1963	$40

| ❏ DL75277 | They're Stepping All Over My Heart | 1971 | $25 |
| ❏ DL8552 [M] | Winner of Your Heart | 1957 | $75 |
| — Black label, silver print |
| ❏ DL8552 [M] | Winner of Your Heart | 1961 | $30 |
| — Black label with color bars |
| ❏ DL78552 [R] | Winner of Your Heart | 196? | $25 |
| ❏ DL75245 | Your Love Is the Way | 1970 | $25 |

WELLS, MARY
20TH FOX
❏ TFM3178 [M]	Love Songs to the Beatles	1965	$100
❏ TFS4178 [S]	Love Songs to the Beatles	1965	$150
❏ ST-90790 [S]	Love Songs to the Beatles	1965	$175
— Capitol Record Club edition
❏ TFM3171 [M]	Mary Wells	1965	$40
❏ TFS4171 [S]	Mary Wells	1965	$75
ALLEGIANCE
| ❏ AV-444 | The Old, the New, and the Best of Mary Wells | 1984 | $12 |
ATCO
| ❏ 33-199 [M] | Two Sides of Mary Wells | 1966 | $30 |
| ❏ SD 33-199 [S] | Two Sides of Mary Wells | 1966 | $30 |
EPIC
| ❏ ARE37540 | In and Out of Love | 1981 | $18 |
JUBILEE
| ❏ JGS-8018 | Servin' Up Some Soul | 1968 | $30 |
MOTOWN
| ❏ MLP-600 [M] | Bye Bye Baby/I Don't Want to Take a Chance | 1961 | $300 |
| — White label stock copy |
| ❏ MLP-600 [M] | Bye Bye Baby/I Don't Want to Take a Chance | 1962 | $300 |
| — With map; label address above the center hole |
❏ M5-161V1	Bye Bye Baby/I Don't Want to Take a Chance	1981	$12
❏ M616 [M]	Greatest Hits	1964	$40
❏ MS616 [S]	Greatest Hits	1964	$40
❏ 5233ML	Greatest Hits	1982	$12
❏ M617 [M]	Mary Wells Sings My Guy	1964	$50
❏ M5-167V1	Mary Wells Sings My Guy	1981	$12
❏ M611 [M]	Recorded Live on Stage	1963	$120
— With map; label address above the center hole
❏ M611 [M]	Recorded Live on Stage	1964	$40
— With map; label address around lower part of label
❏ M612	Second Time Around	1963	$0
— Canceled
❏ M605 [M]	The One Who Really Loves You	1962	$160
— With map; label address above the center hole
❏ M605 [M]	The One Who Really Loves You	1964	$40
— With map; label address around lower part of label
❏ M5-221V1	Two Lovers	1981	$12
❏ M607 [M]	Two Lovers and Other Great Hits	1963	$120
— With map; label address above the center hole
❏ M607 [M]	Two Lovers and Other Great Hits	1964	$40
— With map; label address around lower part of label
❏ M653 [M]	Vintage Stock	1967	$50
❏ MS653 [S]	Vintage Stock	1967	$50
MOVIETONE
| ❏ 71010 [M] | Ooh | 1966 | $30 |
| ❏ 72010 [S] | Ooh | 1966 | $30 |

WELLSTOOD, DICK, AND CLIFF JACKSON
SWINGVILLE
| ❏ SVLP-2026 [M] | Uptown and Downtown | 1961 | $50 |
| — Purple label |
| ❏ SVLP-2026 [M] | Uptown and Downtown | 1965 | $30 |
| — Blue label, trident logo at right |

WELLSTOOD, DICK
CHIAROSCURO
❏ 129	Dick Wellstood Featuring Kenny Davern	197?	$30
❏ 109	From Ragtime On	197?	$30
❏ 139	One-Man Jazz Machine	1975	$30
CLASSIC JAZZ
| ❏ 10 | From Dixie to Swing | 197? | $25 |
JAZZOLOGY
| ❏ JCE-73 | Alone | 197? | $25 |
PICKWICK
| ❏ SPC-3376 | Music from "The Sting" | 197? | $25 |
| ❏ SPC-3575 | Ragtime Music of Scott Joplin | 197? | $25 |
RIVERSIDE
| ❏ RLP-2506 [10] | Dick Wellstood | 1955 | $300 |

WERNER, KEN
FINNADAR
| ❏ SR9019 | The Piano Music of Bix Beiderbecke - Duke Ellington - George Gershwin - James P. Johnson | 1978 | $25 |

INNER CITY
| ❏ IC-3036 | Beyond the Forest of Mirkwood | 198? | $30 |

WESLEY, FRED
ATLANTIC
| ❏ SD18214 | A Blow for Me, A Toot to You | 1977 | $15 |
| ❏ SD19254 | Say Blow by Blow Backwards | 1979 | $15 |
PEOPLE
❏ PE-6604	Breakin' Bread	1974	$25
❏ PE-6602	Damn Right I Am Somebody	1974	$25
❏ PE-5603	Doing It to Death	1973	$100
❏ PE-5601	Food for Thought	1972	$100

WESS, FRANK, AND JOHNNY COLES
UPTOWN
| ❏ 2714 | Two at the Top | 198? | $25 |

WESS, FRANK, AND KENNY BURRELL
PRESTIGE
| ❏ PRLP-7278 [M] | Steamin' | 1963 | $40 |
| ❏ PRST-7278 [R] | Steamin' | 1963 | $30 |

WESS, FRANK, AND THAD JONES
NEW JAZZ
| ❏ NJLP-8310 [M] | Touche | 1963 | $0 |
| — Canceled; reassigned to Status |
STATUS
| ❏ ST-8310 [M] | Touche | 1965 | $40 |

WESS, FRANK
COMMODORE
| ❏ FL-20032 [10] | Frank Wess | 1952 | $120 |
| ❏ FL-20031 [10] | Frank Wess Quintet | 1952 | $120 |
ENTERPRISE
| ❏ 5001 | To Memphis | 197? | $35 |
MAINSTREAM
| ❏ 56033 [M] | Award Winner | 1965 | $30 |
| ❏ S-6033 [R] | Award Winner | 1965 | $30 |
MOODSVILLE
| ❏ MVLP-8 [M] | Frank Wess Quartet | 1960 | $50 |
| — Green label |
| ❏ MVLP-8 [M] | Frank Wess Quartet | 1965 | $30 |
| — Blue label, trident logo at right |
PRESTIGE
❏ PRLP-7231 [M]	Southern Comfort	1962	$175
❏ PRST-7231 [S]	Southern Comfort	1962	$175
❏ PRLP-7266 [M]	Yo Ho! Poor You, Little Me	1963	$40
❏ PRST-7266 [S]	Yo Ho! Poor You, Little Me	1963	$150
PROGRESSIVE
| ❏ PRO-7057 | Flute Juice | 198? | $25 |
SAVOY
❏ MG-12022 [M]	Flutes and Reeds	1955	$100
❏ MG-12095 [M]	Jazz for Playboys	1956	$100
❏ MG-12072 [M]	North, South, East, Wess	1956	$100
SAVOY JAZZ
| ❏ SJL-1136 | I Hear Ya Talkin' | 198? | $25 |
STATUS
| ❏ ST-7266 [S] | Yo Ho! Poor You, Little Me | 1965 | $50 |

WEST, ALVY
COLUMBIA
| ❏ CL6062 [10] | Alvy West and His Little Band | 1949 | $75 |

WEST, BRUCE & LAING
Also see JACK BRUCE; LESLIE WEST; MOUNTAIN.
WINDFALL
❏ KC32899	Live 'N' Kickin'	1974	$15
❏ KC32216	Whatever Turns You On	1973	$15
❏ CQ32216 [Q]	Whatever Turns You On	1973	$30
❏ KC31929	Why Dontcha	1972	$15
❏ CQ31929 [Q]	Why Dontcha	1972	$30

WEST, DOTTIE, AND DON GIBSON
RCA VICTOR
| ❏ LSP-4131 | Dottie and Don | 1969 | $25 |

WEST, DOTTIE
LIBERTY
| ❏ LT-860 | Dottie | 1981 | $10 |
| — Reissue of United Artists 860 |
❏ LT-51129	Full Circle	1982	$12
❏ LT-51155	Greatest Hits	1984	$12
❏ LT-51114	High Times	1982	$12
❏ LT-51145	New Horizons	1983	$12
❏ LT-1000	Special Delivery	1981	$10
— Reissue of United Artists 1000
❏ LT-740	When It's Just You and Me	1981	$10
— Reissue of United Artists 740
❏ LT-1062	Wild West	1981	$12

Number	Title	Yr	NM
POWER PAK			
❏ 274	Country Girl Singing Sensation	197?	$12
RCA CAMDEN			
❏ CAS-2454	A Legend in My Time	1971	$15
❏ ACL1-0482	Loving You	1974	$12
❏ CAL-2155 [M]	The Sound of Country Music	1967	$18
❏ CAS-2155 [S]	The Sound of Country Music	1967	$15
❏ ACL1-0125	Would You Hold It Against Me	1973	$12
RCA VICTOR			
❏ LSP-4482	Careless Hands	1971	$18
❏ APL1-1041	Carolina Cousins	1975	$15
❏ CPL1-7047	Collector's Series	1985	$12
❏ LSP-4332	Country and West	1970	$25
❏ LSP-4004	Country Girl	1968	$30
❏ APL1-0344	Country Sunshine	1973	$15
❏ ANL1-2327	Country Sunshine	1977	$12
—Reissue of APL1-0344			
❏ LSP-4154	Dottie Sings Eddy	1969	$25
❏ LPM-3490 [M]	Dottie West Sings	1966	$30
❏ LSP-3490 [S]	Dottie West Sings	1966	$30
❏ LPM-3784 [M]	Dottie West Sings Sacred Ballads	1967	$30
❏ LSP-3784 [S]	Dottie West Sings Sacred Ballads	1967	$30
❏ LSP-4095	Feminine Fancy	1969	$25
❏ LSP-4433	Forever Yours	1970	$25
❏ LSP-4606	Have You Heard	1971	$18
❏ LPM-3368 [M]	Here Comes My Baby	1965	$30
❏ LSP-3368 [S]	Here Comes My Baby	1965	$30
❏ APL1-0543	House of Love	1974	$15
❏ APD1-0151 [Q]	If It's All Right with You/Just What I've Been Looking For	1973	$30
❏ APL1-0151	If It's All Right with You/Just What I've Been Looking For	1973	$15
❏ LPM-3830 [M]	I'll Help You Forget Her	1967	$30
❏ LSP-3830 [S]	I'll Help You Forget Her	1967	$30
❏ LSP-4704	I'm Only a Woman	1972	$18
❏ LSP-4276	Makin' Memories	1970	$25
❏ AYL1-4302	Once You Were Mine	1982	$10
❏ AHL1-4117	Once You Were Mine	1981	$12
❏ LPM-3587 [M]	Suffer Time	1966	$30
❏ LSP-3587 [S]	Suffer Time	1966	$30
❏ LSP-4811	The Best of Dottie West	1973	$18
❏ LPM-3932 [M]	What I'm Cut Out to Be	1968	$50
❏ LSP-3932 [S]	What I'm Cut Out to Be	1968	$30
❏ LPM-3693 [M]	With All My Heart and Soul	1967	$30
❏ LSP-3693 [S]	With All My Heart and Soul	1967	$30
STARDAY			
❏ SLP-302 [M]	Country Girl Singing Sensation	1964	$40
UNITED ARTISTS			
❏ UA-LA860-G	Dottie	1978	$12
❏ LT-1000	Special Delivery	1980	$12
❏ UA-LA740-G	When It's Just You and Me	1977	$12

WEST, HEDY

Number	Title	Yr	NM
VANGUARD			
❏ VRS-9126 [M]	Hedy West, Volume 2	1963	$25
❏ VSD-2126 [S]	Hedy West, Volume 2	1963	$30
❏ VRS-9124 [M]	Hedy West Accompanying Herself on the 5-String Banjo	1963	$25
❏ VSD-2124 [S]	Hedy West Accompanying Herself on the 5-String Banjo	1963	$30

WEST, KANYE

Number	Title	Yr	NM
DEF JAM			
❏ 1219801	808s & Heartbreak	2008	$30

WEST, LESLIE

Number	Title	Yr	NM
I.R.S.			
❏ 82016	Alligator	1989	$18
PASSPORT			
❏ PB-6061	Theme	1987	$15
PHANTOM			
❏ BPL1-0954	The Great Fatsby	1975	$15
❏ BPL1-1258	The Leslie West Band	1976	$15
WINDFALL			
❏ 4500	Mountain	1969	$18

WEST, LUCRETIA

Number	Title	Yr	NM
WESTMINSTER			
❏ WP-6063 [M]	Spirituals	1957	$40

WEST, MAE

Number	Title	Yr	NM
DAGONET			
❏ DG-4 [M]	Wild Christmas	1966	$30
❏ DGS-4 [S]	Wild Christmas	1966	$40
DECCA			
❏ DL9016 [M]	The Fabulous Mae West	1955	$75
—All-black label with silver print			
❏ DL9016 [M]	The Fabulous Mae West	1960	$30
—Black label with colorband			
❏ DL79016 [R]	The Fabulous Mae West	1960	$18
❏ DL79176	The Original Voice Tracks from Her Greatest Movies	1970	$18

Number	Title	Yr	NM
MCA			
❏ 2053	The Fabulous Mae West	1974	$15
—Reissue of Decca LP			
MEZZOTONE			
❏ 1 [10]	Mae West Songs, Vol. 1	1952	$150
❏ 2 [10]	Mae West Songs, Vol. 2	1952	$150
MGM			
❏ SE-4869	Great Balls of Fire	1972	$25
ROUND			
❏ RS-100	Under the Mistletoe with Mae West	1977	$25
TOWER			
❏ T5028 [M]	Way Out West	1966	$30

❏ ST5028 [S]	Way Out West	1966	$40

WEST, SHELLY

Number	Title	Yr	NM
VIVA			
❏ 25189	Don't Make Me Wait on the Moon	1985	$10
❏ 23983	Red Hot	1983	$10
WARNER BROS.			
❏ 23775	West by West	1983	$10

WEST, SPEEDY, AND JIMMY BRYANT

Number	Title	Yr	NM
CAPITOL			
❏ H520 [10]	Two Guitars Country Style	1954	$250
❏ T520 [M]	Two Guitars Country Style	1954	$120

WEST, SPEEDY

Number	Title	Yr	NM
CAPITOL			
❏ T1835 [M]	Guitar Spectacular	1962	$30
❏ ST1835 [S]	Guitar Spectacular	1962	$40
❏ T1341 [M]	Steel Guitar	1960	$40
❏ ST1341 [S]	Steel Guitar	1960	$75
❏ T956 [M]	West of Hawaii	1958	$100

WEST

Number	Title	Yr	NM
EPIC			
❏ BN26433	Bridges	1969	$25
❏ BN26380	West	1968	$25

WEST COAST POP ART EXPERIMENTAL BAND, THE

Number	Title	Yr	NM
AMOS			
❏ AAS-7004	Where's My Daddy	1969	$50
FIFO			
❏ M101	West Coast Pop Art Experimental Band	1966	$2000
—With regular cover; VG value 1000; VG+ value 1500			
❏ M101	West Coast Pop Art Experimental Band	1966	$500
—With plain cardboard cover			
RAZZBERRY SAWFLY			
❏ 800	West Coast Pop Art Experimental Band	1980	$150
—Reissue of Fifo LP			
REPRISE			
❏ R6247 [M]	The West Coast Pop Art Experimental Band, Part One	1967	$250
❏ RS6247 [S]	The West Coast Pop Art Experimental Band, Part One	1967	$150
❏ R6270 [M]	The West Coast Pop Art Experimental Band, Vol. 2	1967	$300
❏ RS6270 [S]	The West Coast Pop Art Experimental Band, Vol. 2	1967	$150
❏ R6298 [M]	Vol. 3: A Child's Guide to Good and Evil	1968	$250
—May exist only as a white label promo			
❏ RS6298 [S]	Vol. 3: A Child's Guide to Good and Evil	1968	$150

Number	Title	Yr	NM
SUNDAZED			
❏ LP5036	West Coast Pop Art Experimental Band, Volume One	1997	$18

WEST END JAZZ BAND

Number	Title	Yr	NM
STOMP OFF			
❏ SOS-1085	Chicago Breakdown	1985	$25
❏ SOS-1042	Red Hot Chicago	1982	$25

WESTBROOK, FORREST

Number	Title	Yr	NM
REVELATION			
❏ REV-11	This Is Their Time, Oh Yes	197?	$35

WESTBROOK, MIKE

Number	Title	Yr	NM
HAT ART			
❏ 2031	Love for Sale	198?	$35
❏ 2012	On Duke's Birthday	1986	$35
❏ 2040	Westbrook-Rossini	1987	$35

WESTCHESTER WORKSHOP, THE

Number	Title	Yr	NM
UNIQUE			
❏ LP-103 [M]	Unique Jazz	1957	$50

WESTERN, JOHNNY

Number	Title	Yr	NM
COLUMBIA			
❏ CL1788 [M]	Have Gun, Will Travel	1962	$40
❏ CS8588 [S]	Have Gun, Will Travel	1962	$50
❏ 79053	An Old-Fashioned Christmas: Caroling with the Western Wind	1983	$12

WESTON, KIM

Number	Title	Yr	NM
MGM			
❏ E-4477 [M]	For the First Time	1967	$30
❏ SE-4477 [S]	For the First Time	1967	$40
❏ SE-4561	This Is America	1968	$40
VOLT			
❏ VOS-6014	Kim, Kim, Kim	1971	$30

WESTON, PAUL

Number	Title	Yr	NM
CAPITOL			
❏ T1153 [M]	Floatin' Like a Feather	1959	$100
❏ T1154 [M]	Music for Dreaming	1959	$50
❏ ST1154 [S]	Music for Dreaming	1959	$40
❏ H222 [10]	Music for Dreaming	195?	$85
❏ T1222 [M]	Music for Memories	1959	$50
❏ ST1222 [S]	Music for Memories	1959	$40
❏ T1563 [M]	Music for My Love	1961	$50
❏ ST1563 [S]	Music for My Love	1961	$40
❏ T1192 [M]	Music for the Fireside	1959	$40
❏ ST1192 [S]	Music for the Fireside	1959	$40
❏ ST-91212	Romantic Reflections	196?	$40
—Capitol Record Club exclusive			
COLUMBIA			
❏ CL572 [M]	Caribbean Cruise	1955	$40
❏ CL977 [M]	Crescent City	1956	$30
❏ CL1112 [M]	Hollywood	1958	$30
❏ CL794 [M]	Love Music from Hollywood	1956	$30
❏ CL693 [M]	Mood for 12	1955	$40
❏ CL909 [M]	Moonlight Becomes You	1956	$30
❏ CL879 [M]	Solo Mood	1956	$30
❏ CL6232 [10]	Whispers in the Dark	195?	$40
CORINTHIAN			
❏ 107	Cinema Cameos	198?	$10
❏ 116	Crescent City	198?	$10
❏ 109	Easy Jazz	198?	$10
HARMONY			
❏ KH31578	Paul Weston Plays Jerome Kern	1972	$12
❏ KH31603	Paul Weston Plays Jerome Kern, Vol. 2	1972	$12

WESTON, RANDY, AND CECIL PAYNE

Number	Title	Yr	NM
JAZZLAND			
❏ JLP-13 [M]	Greenwich Village Jazz	1960	$40

WESTON, RANDY

Number	Title	Yr	NM
1750 ARCH			
❏ 1802	Blue	198?	$30
ARISTA/FREEDOM			
❏ AF1026	Berkshire Blues	197?	$30
❏ AF1014	Blues Africa	197?	$30
❏ AF1004	Carnival	1975	$30
ATLANTIC			
❏ SD1609	African Cookbook	197?	$35
COLPIX			
❏ CP-456 [M]	Highlight	1963	$30
❏ SCP-456 [S]	Highlight	1963	$75
CTI			
❏ 6016	Blue Moses	197?	$30
DAWN			
❏ DLP-1116 [M]	The Modern Art of Jazz	1957	$300
FANTASY			
❏ OJC-1747	Jazz A La Bohemia	1990	$25

Number	Title	Yr	NM
INNER CITY			
❏ IC-1013	African Nite	1975	$30
JAZZLAND			
❏ JLP-4 [M]	Zulu!	1960	$40
JUBILEE			
❏ JLP-1060 [M]	Piano A La Mode	1957	$40
MILESTONE			
❏ 7206	Zulu	197?	$35
PAUSA			
❏ PR7017	Randy Weston	198?	$35
POLYDOR			
❏ PD-5055	Tanjah	197?	$30
RIVERSIDE			
❏ RLP-2508 [10]	Cole Porter in a Modern Mood	1954	$300
❏ RLP 12-203 [M]	Get Happy	1956	$300
❏ 6063	Get Happy	197?	$30
❏ RLP 12-232 [M]	Jazz A La Bohemia	1957	$300
❏ RLP-2515 [10]	Randy Weston Trio	1955	$300
❏ RLP 12-227 [M]	Randy Weston Trio and Solo	1957	$350
❏ 6208	Trio and Solo	198?	$25
❏ RLP 12-214 [M]	With These Hands…	1956	$300
ROULETTE			
❏ R-65001 [M]	Uhuru Afrika	1960	$150
❏ RS-65001 [S]	Uhuru Afrika	1960	$120
TRIP			
❏ 5033	Blues	197?	$25
UNITED ARTISTS			
❏ UAL-4045 [M]	Destry Rides Again	1959	$40
❏ UAS-5045 [S]	Destry Rides Again	1959	$50
❏ UAL-4011 [M]	Little Niles	1959	$40
❏ UAS-5011 [S]	Little Niles	1959	$50
❏ UAL-4066 [M]	Live at the Five Spot	1959	$40
❏ UAS-5066 [S]	Live at the Five Spot	1959	$50

WESTON, RANDY/LEM WINCHESTER

Number	Title	Yr	NM
METROJAZZ			
❏ E-1005 [M]	New Faces at Newport	1958	$50
❏ SE-1005 [S]	New Faces at Newport	1958	$120

WET WET WET

Number	Title	Yr	NM
UNI			
❏ 5000	Popped In Souled Out	1987	$12

WET WILLIE

Number	Title	Yr	NM
CAPRICORN			
❏ CP 0149	Dixie Rock	1975	$12
❏ CP 0113	Drippin' Wet/Live	1973	$15
❏ CP 0200	Greatest Hits	1978	$12
❏ CP 0128	Keep on Smilin'	1974	$12
❏ CP 0182	Left Coast Live	1977	$12
❏ CP 0166	The Wetter the Better	1976	$12
❏ SD861	Wet Willie	1971	$18
❏ CP 0138	Wet Willie	1974	$12
—Reissue of 861			
❏ CP 0109	Wet Willie II	1972	$15
EPIC			
❏ JE34983	Manorisms	1977	$12
❏ JE35794	Which One's Willie?	1979	$12

WETMORE, DICK

Number	Title	Yr	NM
BETHLEHEM			
❏ BCP-1035 [10]	Dick Wetmore	1955	$300

WETTLING, GEORGE

Number	Title	Yr	NM
COLUMBIA			
❏ CL2559 [10]	George Wettling's Jazz Band	1956	$50
—House Party Series" issue			
❏ CL6189 [10]	George Wettling's Jazz Band	1951	$100
—Original issue			
HARMONY			
❏ HL7080 [M]	Dixieland in Hi-Fi	1957	$30
KAPP			
❏ KL-1028 [M]	Jazz Trios	1956	$40
❏ KL-1005 [M]	Ragtime Duo	1955	$50
WEATHERS INDUSTRIES			
❏ 5501 [M]	High Fidelity Rhythms	1955	$50

WHALEFEATHERS, THE

Number	Title	Yr	NM
NASCO			
❏ 9005	The Whalefeathers	1970	$150
❏ 9003	The Whalefeathers Declare	1969	$150

WHALUM, KIRK

Number	Title	Yr	NM
COLUMBIA			
❏ FC40812	And You Know That!	1988	$25
❏ FC40221	Floppy Disk	1985	$25
❏ FC45215	The Promise	1989	$30

WHAM!
Also see GEORGE MICHAEL.

Number	Title	Yr	NM
COLUMBIA			
❏ BFC38911	Fantastic	1983	$18
—Cover and label list artist as "Wham! U.K.			

❏ FC38911 [B]	Fantastic	1985	$12
—Reissue; cover and label list artist as "Wham!			
❏ 9C940062 [PD]	Make It Big	1985	$30
—Picture disc			
❏ FC39595	Make It Big	1984	$12
❏ OC40285	Music from the Edge of Heaven	1986	$12
—With "removable sticker" list of song titles still on front cover			

WHAT IS THIS

Number	Title	Yr	NM
MCA			
❏ 39041	3 Out of 5 Live	1985	$10
❏ L33-1174 [EP]	What Is This	1985	$18
—Promo-only version with custom labels and sleeve			
❏ 5598	What Is This	1985	$12

WHATNAUTS, THE

Number	Title	Yr	NM
STANG			
❏ 1005	The Whatnauts	1970	$25

WHEELER, BILLY EDD

Number	Title	Yr	NM
FLYING FISH			
❏ FF-085	Wild Mountain Flowers	1979	$15
FOLKWAYS			
❏ 31014	When Kentucky Had No Union Men	196?	$25
KAPP			
❏ KL-1351 [M]	A New Bag of Songs Written and Sung by Billy Edd Wheeler	1964	$18
❏ KS-3351 [S]	A New Bag of Songs Written and Sung by Billy Edd Wheeler	1964	$25
❏ KL-1479 [M]	Goin' Town and Country	1966	$18
❏ KS-3479 [S]	Goin' Town and Country	1966	$25
❏ KS-3567	I Ain't the Worryin' Kind	1968	$18
❏ KL-1425 [M]	Memories of America/Ode to the Little Brown Shack Out Back	1965	$18
❏ KS-3425 [S]	Memories of America/Ode to the Little Brown Shack Out Back	1965	$25
❏ KL-1533 [M]	Paper Birds	1967	$25
❏ KS-3533 [S]	Paper Birds	1967	$18
❏ KL-1443 [M]	Wheeler Man	1965	$18
❏ KS-3443 [S]	Wheeler Man	1965	$25
MONITOR			
❏ MF-367 [M]	Billy Edd and Bluegrass	1962	$30
❏ MF-354 [M]	Billy Edd U.S.A.	1961	$30
RCA VICTOR			
❏ LSP-4491	Love	1971	$18
UNITED ARTISTS			
❏ UAS-6711	Nashville Zodiac	1969	$18

WHEELER, CLARENCE

Number	Title	Yr	NM
ATLANTIC			
❏ SD1551	Doin' What We Wanna	1970	$150
❏ SD1636	New Chicago Blues	1973	$50
❏ SD1585	The Love I've Been Looking For	1971	$75

WHEELER, KENNY

Number	Title	Yr	NM
ECM			
❏ 1156	Around 6	1979	$25
❏ 1102	Deer Wan	1977	$25
❏ 25000	Double, Double You	1984	$25
❏ 1069	Gnu High	197?	$30

WHEELS, BURT, AND THE SPEEDSTERS

Number	Title	Yr	NM
CORONET			
❏ CX-216 [M]	Sounds of the Big Racers	1964	$30
❏ CXS-216 [S]	Sounds of the Big Racers	1964	$30

WHEELS, THE

Number	Title	Yr	NM
MONTGOMERY WARD			
❏ 010	Sounds of the Hot Rods	196?	$120

WHEN IN ROME

Number	Title	Yr	NM
VIRGIN			
❏ 90994	When in Rome	1988	$12

WHIGHAM, JIGGS

Number	Title	Yr	NM
PAUSA			
❏ 7134	Hope	198?	$25

WHISPERS, THE

Number	Title	Yr	NM
ACCORD			
❏ SN-7100	I Can Remember	1981	$12
ALLEGIANCE			
❏ AV-5004	Excellence	1985	$12
CAPITOL			
❏ C1-92957	More of the Night	1990	$15
DORE			
❏ 338	Shhh	197?	$15
INTERMEDIA			
❏ QS-5075	Doctor Love	198?	$12
JANUS			
❏ 7006	Bingo	1974	$40
❏ 7013	Greatest Hits	1975	$30
❏ JLS-3046	Life and Breath	1973	$40
❏ JLS-3041	The Whispers' Love Story	1972	$50
SOLAR			
❏ 60451 [B]	Happy Holidays to You	1985	$15
❏ BXL1-2774	Headlights	1978	$15
❏ BXL1-3578	Imagination	1980	$15
❏ ST-72554	Just Gets Better with Time	1987	$12
❏ 60216	Love for Love	1983	$12
❏ S-27	Love Is Where You Find It	1982	$12
❏ BXL1-2270	Open Up Your Love	1978	$15
—Reissue of Soul Train 2270			
❏ AYL1-3839	Open Up Your Love	1981	$10
—Best Buy Series" reissue			
❏ 60356	So Good	1984	$12
❏ BXL1-4242	The Best of the Whispers	1982	$15
❏ BXL1-3521	The Whspers	1979	$15
❏ BXL1-3976	This Kind of Lovin'	1981	$15
❏ PZ75306	Vintage Whispers	1989	$15
❏ BXL1-3105	Whisper in Your Ear	1979	$15
SOUL CLOCK			
❏ 22001	Planets of Life	1969	$150
SOUL TRAIN			
❏ BVL1-1450	One for the Money	1976	$18
❏ BVL1-2270	Open Up Your Love	1977	$18

WHITCOMB, IAN, AND DICK ZIMMERMAN

Number	Title	Yr	NM
AUDIOPHILE			
❏ AP-225	Steppin' Out	1987	$25
STOMP OFF			
❏ SOS-1017	Don't Say Goodbye Miss Ragtime	198?	$30
❏ SOS-1049	My Wife Is Dancing Mad	198?	$30

WHITCOMB, IAN

Number	Title	Yr	NM
AUDIOPHILE			
❏ AP-147	At the Ragtime Ball	1983	$30
❏ AP-115	Treasures of Tin Pan Alley	197?	$30
FIRST AMERICAN			
❏ 7704	Crooner Tunes	1979	$25
❏ 7789	In Hollywood	1982	$25
❏ 7751	Instrumentals	1981	$25
❏ 7725	Red Hot "Blue Heaven	1980	$25
❏ 7729	The Rock and Roll Years	1981	$25
RHINO			
❏ RNLP-127	The Best of Ian Whitcomb (1964-1968)	1986	$20
SIERRA			
❏ 8708	Pianomelt	1980	$25
TOWER			
❏ T5042 [M]	Mod, Mod Music Hall	1966	$35
❏ ST5042 [S]	Mod, Mod Music Hall	1966	$50
❏ ST5100	Sock Me Some Rock	1968	$50
❏ T5071 [M]	Yellow Underground	1967	$35
❏ ST5071 [S]	Yellow Underground	1967	$50
❏ T5004 [M]	You Turn Me On	1965	$75

Number	Title	Yr	NM

❑ DT5004 [R]	You Turn Me On	1965	$50

UNITED ARTISTS

❑ UA-LA021-F	Under the Ragtime Moon	1972	$25

WHITE, ANDREW
Tenor saxophone player who, in addition to his vast catalog on his own label, has transcribed and published the solos of JOHN COLTRANE and ERIC DOLPHY in book form. Also see THE J.F.K. QUINTET.

ANDREW'S MUSIC

❑ AM-1	Andrew Nathaniel White III	197?	$50
❑ AM-33	Bionic Saxophone	1978	$30
❑ AM-14	Collage	1975	$35
❑ AM-25	Countdown	1976	$35
❑ AM-28	Ebony Glaze	1977	$30
❑ AM-8	Live at the Foolery, Vol. 1	1975	$35
❑ AM-9	Live at the Foolery, Vol. 2	1975	$35
❑ AM-10	Live at the Foolery, Vol. 3	1975	$35
❑ AM-11	Live at the Foolery, Vol. 4	1975	$35
❑ AM-12	Live at the Foolery, Vol. 5	1975	$35
❑ AM-13	Live at the Foolery, Vol. 6	1975	$35
❑ AM-2	Live at the "New Thing"	197?	$75
❑ AM-3	Live in Bucharest	197?	$50
❑ AM-31	Live in New York Vol. 1	1977	$30
❑ AM-32	Live in New York Vol. 2	1977	$30
❑ AM-15	Marathon' 75, Vol. 1	1976	$35
❑ AM-16	Marathon' 75, Vol. 2	1976	$35
❑ AM-17	Marathon' 75, Vol. 3	1976	$35
❑ AM-18	Marathon' 75, Vol. 4	1976	$35
❑ AM-19	Marathon' 75, Vol. 5	1976	$35
❑ AM-20	Marathon' 75, Vol. 6	1976	$35
❑ AM-21	Marathon' 75, Vol. 7	1976	$35
❑ AM-22	Marathon' 75, Vol. 8	1976	$35
❑ AM-23	Marathon' 75, Vol. 9	1976	$35
❑ AM-29	Miss Ann	1977	$30
❑ AM-5	Passion Flower	197?	$50
❑ AM-42	Profile: White	1983	$30
❑ AM-26	Red Top	1977	$30
❑ AM-36	Saxophonitis	1979	$30
❑ AM-30	Seven Giant Steps for Coltrane	1977	$35
❑ AM-6	Songs for a French Lady	197?	$50
❑ AM-24	Spotts, Maxine and Brown	1976	$35
❑ AM-7	Theme	1975	$50
❑ AM-27	Trinkle, Trinkle	1977	$30
❑ AM-37	Weekend at One Step, Vol. 1: Fonk Update	1980	$30
❑ AM-38	Weekend at One Step, Vol. 2: I Love Japan	1980	$30
❑ AM-39	Weekend at One Step, Vol. 3: Have Band Will Travel	1980	$30
❑ AM-4	Who Got Da Funk?	197?	$50

WHITE, BARRY
20TH CENTURY

❑ T-493	Barry White's Greatest Hits	1975	$12
❑ T-599	Barry White's Greatest Hits, Volume 2	1981	$12
❑ T-543	Barry White Sings for Someone You Love	1977	$12
❑ T-571	Barry White The Man	1978	$12
❑ T-444	Can't Get Enough	1974	$12
❑ T-590	I Love to Sing the Songs I Sing	1979	$12
❑ T-516	Is This Whatcha Wont?	1976	$12
❑ T-407	I've Got So Much to Give	1973	$12
❑ T-466	Just Another Way to Say I Love You	1975	$12
❑ T-502	Let the Music Play	1976	$12
❑ T-423	Stone Gon'	1973	$12

A&M

❑ 7502153771	Put Me in Your Mix	1991	$15
❑ SP-5256	The Man Is Back!	1990	$12
❑ SP-5154	The Right Night and Barry White	1987	$12

AUDIO FIDELITY

❑ AFZLP169 [B]	Can't Get Enough	2014	$30

CASABLANCA

❑ 822782-1	Barry White's Greatest Hits	1984	$10
❑ 822783-1	Barry White's Greatest Hits, Volume 2	1984	$10

SUPREMACY

❑ SUP-8002	No Limit on Love	1974	$15

—Compilation of older material

UNLIMITED GOLD

❑ FZ36208	Barry White's Sheet Music	1980	$12
❑ FZ37176	Beware	1982	$12
❑ FZ38048	Change	1982	$12
❑ FZ38711	Dedicated	1983	$12
❑ Z2X36957	The Best of Our Love	1981	$15
❑ JZ35763	The Message Is Love	1979	$12

WHITE, BARRY AND GLODEAN
UNLIMITED GOLD

❑ FZ37054	Barry and Glodean White	1981	$12

WHITE, BRIAN, AND ALAN GRESTY
JAZZOLOGY

❑ J-116	Muggsy Remembered	1988	$25

WHITE, BUKKA
ARHOOLIE

❑ 1019 [M]	Sky Songs, Volume 1	1966	$30
❑ 1020 [M]	Sky Songs, Volume 2	1966	$30

BLUE HORIZON

❑ 4604	Blues Masters, Volume 4	1970	$30

CLEOPATRA

❑ 9492 [B]	Aberdeen, Mississippi Blues		$25

HERWIN

❑ 201	Sic 'em Dogs	196?	$30

TAKOMA

❑ C-1001 [M]	Mississippi Blues	196?	$35

WHITE, CARLA
STASH

❑ ST-237	Andruline	1983	$25

WHITE, DANNY
GRAND PRIX

❑ 101	Danny White Sings Country	1983	$30

WHITE, JOHN
MAINSTREAM

❑ MRL-330	John White	1972	$30

WHITE, JOSH
ABC-PARAMOUNT

❑ ABC-407 [M]	Josh White -- Live!	1962	$30
❑ ABCS-407 [S]	Josh White -- Live!	1962	$40
❑ T-90190 [M]	Josh White -- Live!	1964	$30

—Capitol Record Club edition

❑ ABC-124 [M]	Josh White Stories, Vol. 1	1956	$75
❑ ABC-166 [M]	Josh White Stories, Vol. 2	1957	$75

DECCA

❑ DL5062 [10]	Ballads and Blues	1949	$175
❑ DL5247 [10]	Ballads and Blues, Vol. 2	195?	$120
❑ DL8665 [M]	Josh White	1958	$40

—Black label, silver print

ELEKTRA

❑ EKL-123 [M]	25th Anniversary Album	1957	$40
❑ EKL-158 [M]	Chain Gang Songs	1958	$100
❑ EKS-7158 [S]	Chain Gang Songs	195?	$150
❑ EKL-211 [M]	Empty Bed Blues	1962	$30
❑ EKS-7211 [S]	Empty Bed Blues	1962	$30
❑ EKL-114 [M]	Josh, Ballads and Blues	1957	$40
❑ EKL-102 [M]	Josh at Midnight	1956	$40
❑ EKL-193 [M]	Spirituals and Blues	1960	$30
❑ EKS-7193 [S]	Spirituals and Blues	1960	$40
❑ EKL-203 [M]	The House I Live In	1961	$30
❑ EKS-7203 [S]	The House I Live In	1961	$40
❑ EKL-701 [10]	The Story of John Henry/ Ballads, Blues and Other Songs	1955	$50

EMARCY

❑ MG-26010 [10]	Strange Fruit	1954	$120

LONDON

❑ LPB-338 [10]	A Josh White Program	195?	$120
❑ LL1147 [M]	A Josh White Program	1956	$50
❑ LPB-341 [10]	A Josh White Program, Vol. 2	195?	$120
❑ LL1341 [M]	A Josh White Program, Vol. 2	195?	$50

MERCURY

❑ MG-21022 [M]	I'm on My Own Way	1963	$30
❑ SR-61022 [R]	I'm on My Own Way	1963	$25
❑ MG-20203 [M]	Josh White's Blues	1957	$75
❑ MG-25014 [10]	Josh White Sings Blues	1949	$175
❑ MG-20821 [M]	The Beginning	1963	$30
❑ SR-60821 [R]	The Beginning	1963	$25

PERIOD

❑ SLP-1115 [10]	Josh White Comes a-Visiting	1956	$75

STINSON

❑ SLP-15 [10]	Josh White Sings Folk Songs	1950	$120
❑ SLP-14 [10]	Josh White Sings the Blues	1950	$120

WHITE, KITTY
EMARCY

❑ MG-36020 [M]	A New Voice in Jazz	1955	$250
❑ MG-36068 [M]	Kitty White	1955	$250

PACIFICA

❑ PL-802 [10]	Kitty White	1955	$150

WHITE, LENNY
ELEKTRA

❑ 6E-121	Adventures of Astral Pirates	1978	$25
❑ 6E-223	Best of Friends	1979	$25
❑ 5E-551	Just Like Dreamin'	1981	$25
❑ 6E-164	Streamline	1978	$25
❑ 6E-304	Twennynine with Lenny White	1980	$25

NEMPEROR

❑ SD441	Big City	1977	$30
❑ SD435	Venusian Summer	1975	$30

WHITE, MACK
COMMERCIAL

❑ 782	Lonely in the Crowd	197?	$18

WHITE, MAURICE
COLUMBIA

❑ FC39883	Maurice White	1985	$12

WHITE, MICHAEL
ABC IMPULSE!

❑ AS-9268	Father Music, Mother Dance	1974	$35
❑ ASD-9281	Go with the Flow	1974	$35
❑ AS-9241	Land of Spirit and Light	1973	$35
❑ AS-9221	Pneuma	197?	$35
❑ AS-9215	Spirit Dance	197?	$35

ELEKTRA

❑ 6E-138	X Factor	1978	$25

WHITE, MIKE
SEECO

❑ SLP-442 [M]	Dixieland Jazz	1960	$150
❑ SLP-4420 [S]	Dixieland Jazz	1960	$150

WHITE, STEVE
LIBERTY

❑ LJH-6006 [M]	Jazz Mad -- The Unpredictable Steve White	1955	$75

WHITE, TONY JOE
20TH CENTURY

❑ T-523	Eyes	1977	$15

CASABLANCA

❑ NBLP7233	Real Thang	1980	$12

COLUMBIA

❑ FC38817	Dangerous	1983	$12

MONUMENT

❑ SLP-18114	Black and White	1969	$18
❑ SLP-18133	…Continued	1969	$18
❑ SLP-18142	Tony Joe	1970	$18

WARNER

❑ MOVLP1073 [B]	Tony Joe White	2014	$30

WARNER BROS.

❑ BS2708	Homemade Ice Cream	1973	$15
❑ BS2580	The Train I'm On	1972	$15
❑ WS1900	Tony Joe White	1971	$15

WHITE BOY
TRADEWIND

❑ MM-11761	The Average Rat Band	1976	$175

WHITE EAGLE JAZZ BAND, THE
GHB

❑ GHB-204	The White Eagle Jazz Band	1988	$25

WHITE LIGHT
CENTURY

❑ 39955	White Light	1968	$300

WHITE LIGHTNIN'
ABC

❑ S-690	File Under Rock	1969	$25

WHITE NOISE
ANTILLES

❑ AN-7011 [B]	An Electric Storm	1973	$30

WHITE PLAINS
DERAM

❑ DES18045 [B]	My Baby Loves Lovin'	1970	$25

WHITE TIGER
With Mark St. John, who was briefly a member of KISS.

Number	Title	Yr	NM
E.M.C.			
❏ EMC-3653	White Tiger	1986	$25
WHITE WITCH			
CAPRICORN			
❏ CP 0129 [B]	A Spiritual Greeting	1974	$30
❏ CP 0107 [B]	White Witch	1973	$30
WHITE ZOMBIE			
Featuring Rob Zombie.			
CAROLINE			
❏ 1362	Make Them Die Slowly	1989	$25
❏ 1350	Soul Crusher	1988	$25
GEFFEN			
❏ GEF24806	Astro-Creep: 2000	1995	$18
❏ Numero NUM204 [B]	It Came From N.Y.C.	2016	$250
— white vinyl			
SILENT EXPLOSION			
❏ 0(# unknown) [EP]	Psycho-Head Blowout	1986	$75
❏ SE 002	Soul Crusher	1987	$75
WHITEMAN, PAUL, ORCHESTRA			
MONMOUTH-EVERGREEN			
❏ 7078	Live in '75	1975	$30
❏ 7074	The Classic Arrangements of Challis, Satterfield, Hayton	197?	$30
WHITEMAN, PAUL			
CAPITOL			
❏ T622 [M]	Classics in Jazz	1955	$100
❏ T1678 [M]	Paul Whiteman Conducts George Gershwin	1962	$50
❏ DT1678 [R]	Paul Whiteman Conducts George Gershwin	1962	$75
COLUMBIA			
❏ CL2830 [M]	Paul Whiteman Featuring Bing Crosby	1968	$35
CORAL			
❏ CRL57021 [M]	The Great Gershwin	1955	$40
GRAND AWARD			
❏ GA-33-412 [M]	Cavalcade of Music	1960	$25
❏ GA-244SD [S]	Cavalcade of Music	1960	$30
❏ GA-33-351 [M]	Fiddle on Fire	195?	$30
❏ GA-33-502 [M]	Great Whiteman Hits	195?	$30
❏ GA-33-356 [M]	Hawaiian Magic	1958	$30
❏ GA-208SD [S]	Hawaiian Magic	1958	$30
❏ GA-33-901 [M]	Paul Whiteman/50th Anniversary	1956	$50
❏ GA-33-503 [M]	The Greatest Stars of My Life	195?	$50
— In red velvet jacket			
❏ GA-33-409 [M]	The Night I Played at 666 Fifth Ave.	1960	$25
❏ GA-241SD [S]	The Night I Played at 666 Fifth Ave.	1960	$30
MARK 56			
❏ 761 [M]	Tribute to Gershwin 1936	197?	$30
RCA VICTOR			
❏ LPV-555 [M]	Paul Whiteman, Volume 1	195?	$35
SUNBEAM			
❏ 18 [M]	In Concert 1927-32	197?	$30
X			
❏ LVA-3040 [10]	Paul Whiteman's Orchestra Featuring Bix Beiderbecke	1955	$100
WHITES, THE			
MCA CURB			
❏ 5820	Ain't No Binds	1987	$10
❏ 5490	Forever You	1984	$10
❏ 5717	Greatest Hits	1986	$10
❏ 5562	Whole New World	1985	$10
WARNER BROS.			
❏ 23872	Old Familiar Feeling	1983	$10
WHITESNAKE			
Also see DEEP PURPLE; THIN LIZZY.			
GEFFEN			
❏ GHS24167	Come an' Get It	1987	$12
— Reissue of Mirage 16043			
❏ GHS24168	Live... In the Heart of the City	1987	$12
— Reissue of Mirage 19292			
❏ GHS24176	Lovehunter	1988	$12
— Reissue of United Artists 981			
❏ GHS24173	Saints & Sinners	1988	$12
— First U.S. issue of 1982 U.K. LP			
❏ GHS4018 [B]	Slide It In	1984	$12
❏ GHS24249	Slip of the Tongue	1989	$12
❏ GHS24174	Snakebite	1988	$12
— Reissue of United Artists 915			
❏ GHS24175	Trouble	1988	$12
— Reissue of United Artists 937			
❏ GHS24099	Whitesnake	1987	$12

Number	Title	Yr	NM
❏ R163629	Whitesnake	1987	$15
— BMG Direct Marketing version			
MIRAGE			
❏ WTG16043	Come an' Get It	1981	$15
❏ WTG19292	Live... In the Heart of the City	1980	$15
❏ WTG19276	Ready an' Willing	1980	$15
PARLOPHONE			
❏ UAGR30305 [B]	Trouble	2014	$30
UNITED ARTISTS			
❏ LT-981	Lovehunter	1979	$15
❏ UA-LA915-H	Snakebite	1978	$15
— As "David Coverdale's Whitesnake"			
❏ UA-LA937-H	Trouble	1978	$15
WHITING, MARGARET, AND JIMMY WAKELY			
HILLTOP			
❏ JM-6053 [M]	I'll Never Slip Around Again	196?	$30
❏ JS-6053 [R]	I'll Never Slip Around Again	196?	$30
WHITING, MARGARET			
AUDIOPHILE			
❏ AP-173	Come a Little Closer	198?	$25
❏ AP-207	This Lady's in Love with You	1986	$25
❏ AP-152	Too Marvelous for Words	198?	$25
CAPITOL			
❏ T685 [M]	For the Starry-Eyed	1955	$85
❏ T410 [M]	Love Songs	1954	$85
❏ H209 [10]	Margaret Whiting Sings Rodgers and Hart	1950	$175
❏ H234 [10]	Songs	1950	$175
❏ H163 [10]	South Pacific	1950	$175
DOT			
❏ DLP3072 [M]	Goin' Places	1957	$175
❏ DLP3337 [M]	Just a Dream	1960	$85
❏ DLP25337 [S]	Just a Dream	1960	$150
❏ DLP3113 [M]	Margaret	1958	$85
❏ DLP25113 [S]	Margaret	1958	$150
❏ DLP3176 [M]	Margaret Whiting's Great Hits	1959	$85
❏ DLP25176 [S]	Margaret Whiting's Great Hits	1959	$150
❏ DLP3235 [M]	Ten Top Hits	1960	$85
❏ DLP25235 [S]	Ten Top Hits	1960	$150
HAMILTON			
❏ HLP143 [M]	My Ideal	196?	$30
❏ HLP12143 [S]	My Ideal	196?	$35
LONDON			
❏ LL3510 [M]	Maggie Isn't Margaret Anymore	1967	$50
❏ PS510 [S]	Maggie Isn't Margaret Anymore	1967	$35
❏ PS527	Pop Country	1968	$35
❏ LL3497 [M]	The Wheel of Hurt	1967	$50
❏ PS497 [S]	The Wheel of Hurt	1967	$35
MGM			
❏ E-4006 [M]	Past Midnight	1961	$35
❏ SE-4006 [S]	Past Midnight	1961	$50
VERVE			
❏ V-4038 [M]	The Jerome Kern Song Book	1960	$150
❏ V6-4038 [S]	The Jerome Kern Song Book	1960	$150
WHITLEY, KEITH			
RCA			
❏ 6494-1-R	Don't Close Your Eyes	1988	$12
❏ 9809-1-R	I Wonder Do You Think of Me	1989	$15
RCA VICTOR			
❏ MHL1-8525 [EP]	A Hard Act to Follow	1984	$15
❏ AHL1-7043	L.A. to Miami	1986	$18
— Original issue, has 7 tracks			
❏ AEL1-5870	L.A. to Miami	1986	$12
— Reissue of 7043, has 10 tracks			
WHITLOCK, BOBBY			
ABC DUNHILL			
❏ DS-50121	Bobby Whitlock	1972	$15
❏ DSX-50131	Raw Velvet	1972	$15
CAPRICORN			
❏ CP 0160 [B]	One of a Kind	1975	$12
❏ CP 0168	Rock Your Sox Off	1976	$12
WHITMAN, SLIM			
CLEVELAND INT'L.			
❏ JE36847	Christmas with Slim Whitman	1980	$15
❏ FE37403	Mr. Songman	1982	$12
❏ JE36768	Songs I Love to Sing	1980	$12
❏ AS99-875 [DJ]	Songs I Love to Sing	1980	$40
— Promo-only picture disc			
COLUMBIA SPECIAL PRODUCTS			
❏ P16323	Christmas with Slim Whitman	1981	$12

Number	Title	Yr	NM
EPIC			
❏ PE36847	Christmas with Slim Whitman	1981	$10
— Reissue of Cleveland Int'l. JE 36847			
❏ PE36768	Songs I Love to Sing	198?	$10
— Reissue of Cleveland Int'l. JE 36768			
IMPERIAL			
❏ LP-9342 [M]	15th Anniversary	1967	$25
❏ LP-12342 [S]	15th Anniversary	1967	$15
❏ LP-9252 [M]	All-Time Favorites	1964	$30
— Black label with stars on top			
❏ LP-9252 [M]	All-Time Favorites	1964	$18
— Black and pink label			
❏ LP-9252 [M]	All-Time Favorites	1966	$15
— Black and green label			
❏ LP-3004 [10]	America's Favorite Folk Artist	1954	$600
❏ LP-9333 [M]	A Time for Love	1966	$15
❏ LP-12333 [S]	A Time for Love	1966	$18
❏ LP-9313 [M]	A Travelin' Man	1966	$15
❏ LP-12313 [S]	A Travelin' Man	1966	$18
❏ LP-9356 [M]	Country Memories	1967	$15
❏ LP-12356 [S]	Country Memories	1967	$15
❏ LP-9268 [M]	Country Songs/City Hits	1964	$18
— Black and pink label			
❏ LP-9268 [M]	Country Songs/City Hits	1966	$15
— Black and green label			
❏ LP-12268 [S]	Country Songs/City Hits	1964	$25
— Black and pink label			
❏ LP-12268 [S]	Country Songs/City Hits	1966	$18
— Black and green label			
❏ LP-9003 [M]	Favorites	1956	$50
— Maroon label			
❏ LP-9003 [M]	Favorites	1958	$30
— Black label with stars on top			
❏ LP-9003 [M]	Favorites	1964	$25
— Black and pink label			
❏ LP-9003 [M]	Favorites	1966	$18
— Black and green label			
❏ LP-9171 [M]	Forever	1961	$30
— Black label with stars on top			
❏ LP-9171 [M]	Forever	1964	$18
— Black and pink label			
❏ LP-9171 [M]	Forever	1966	$15
— Black and green label			
❏ LP-9308 [M]	God's Hand in Mine	1966	$15
❏ LP-12411	Happy Street	1969	$15
❏ LP-9209 [M]	Heart Songs and Love Songs	1962	$30
— Black label with stars on top			
❏ LP-9209 [M]	Heart Songs and Love Songs	1964	$18
— Black and pink label			
❏ LP-9209 [M]	Heart Songs and Love Songs	1966	$15
— Black and green label			
❏ LP-9088 [M]	I'll Walk with God	1960	$30
— Black label with stars on top			
❏ LP-9088 [M]	I'll Walk with God	1964	$25
— Black and pink label			
❏ LP-9088 [M]	I'll Walk with God	1966	$18
— Black and green label			
❏ LP-12032 [S]	I'll Walk with God	1959	$40
— Black label with silver top			
❏ LP-12032 [S]	I'll Walk with God	1964	$30
— Black and pink label			
❏ LP-12032 [S]	I'll Walk with God	1966	$25
— Black and green label			
❏ LP-9226 [M]	I'm a Lonely Wanderer	1963	$30
— Black label with stars on top			
❏ LP-9226 [M]	I'm a Lonely Wanderer	1964	$18
— Black and pink label			
❏ LP-9226 [M]	I'm a Lonely Wanderer	1966	$15
— Black and green label			
❏ LP-12375	In Love, The Whitman Way	1968	$15
❏ LP-9245 [M]	Irish Songs The Whitman Way	1963	$30
— Black label with stars on top			
❏ LP-9245 [M]	Irish Songs The Whitman Way	1964	$18
— Black and pink label			
❏ LP-9245 [M]	Irish Songs The Whitman Way	1966	$15
— Black and green label			
❏ LP-9137 [M]	Just Call Me Lonesome	1961	$30
— Black label with stars on top			
❏ LP-9137 [M]	Just Call Me Lonesome	1964	$18
— Black and pink label			
❏ LP-9137 [M]	Just Call Me Lonesome	1966	$15
— Black and green label			
❏ LP-9277 [M]	Love Song of the Waterfall	1964	$18
— Black and pink label			
❏ LP-9277 [M]	Love Song of the Waterfall	1966	$15
— Black and green label			
❏ LP-12277 [S]	Love Song of the Waterfall	1964	$25
— Black and pink label			
❏ LP-12277 [S]	Love Song of the Waterfall	1966	$18

Number	Title	Yr	NM
—Black and green label			
❏ LP-9102 [M]	Million Record Hits	1960	$30
—Black label with stars on top			
❏ LP-9303 [M]	More Than Yesterday	1965	$18
—Black and pink label			
❏ LP-9303 [M]	More Than Yesterday	1966	$15
—Black and green label			
❏ LP-12303 [S]	More Than Yesterday	1965	$25
—Black and pink label			
❏ LP-12303 [S]	More Than Yesterday	1966	$18
—Black and green label			
❏ LP-9156 [M]	Once in a Lifetime	1961	$30
—Black label with stars on top			
❏ LP-9156 [M]	Once in a Lifetime	1964	$18
—Black and pink label			
❏ LP-9156 [M]	Once in a Lifetime	1966	$15
—Black and green label			
❏ LP-9288 [M]	Reminiscing	1965	$18
—Black and pink label			
❏ LP-9288 [M]	Reminiscing	1966	$15
—Black and green label			
❏ LP-12288 [S]	Reminiscing	1965	$25
—Black and pink label			
❏ LP-12288 [S]	Reminiscing	1966	$18
—Black and green label			
❏ LP-12436	Slim	1969	$15
❏ LP-12100 [R]	Slim Whitman	1964	$18
—Black and pink label			
❏ LP-12100 [R]	Slim Whitman	1966	$15
—Black and green label			
❏ LP-9135 [M]	Slim Whitman's First Visit to Britain	1960	$30
—Black label with stars on top			
❏ LP-9135 [M]	Slim Whitman's First Visit to Britain	1964	$18
—Black and pink label			
❏ LP-9135 [M]	Slim Whitman's First Visit to Britain	1966	$15
—Black and green label			
❏ LP-9026 [M]	Slim Whitman Sings	1957	$50
—Maroon label			
❏ LP-9026 [M]	Slim Whitman Sings	1958	$30
—Black label with stars on top			
❏ LP-9026 [M]	Slim Whitman Sings	1964	$25
—Black and pink label			
❏ LP-9026 [M]	Slim Whitman Sings	1966	$18
—Black and green label			
❏ LP-9056 [M]	Slim Whitman Sings	1958	$50
—Maroon label			
❏ LP-9056 [M]	Slim Whitman Sings	1958	$30
—Black label with stars on top			
❏ LP-9056 [M]	Slim Whitman Sings	1964	$25
—Black and pink label			
❏ LP-9056 [M]	Slim Whitman Sings	1966	$18
—Black and green label			
❏ LP-9064 [M]	Slim Whitman Sings	1959	$30
—Black label with stars on top			
❏ LP-9064 [M]	Slim Whitman Sings	1964	$25
—Black and pink label			
❏ LP-9064 [M]	Slim Whitman Sings	1966	$18
—Black and green label			
❏ LP-9194 [M]	Slim Whitman Sings	1962	$30
—Black label with stars on top			
❏ LP-9194 [M]	Slim Whitman Sings	1964	$18
—Black and pink label			
❏ LP-9194 [M]	Slim Whitman Sings	1966	$15
—Black and green label			
❏ LP-12194 [S]	Slim Whitman Sings	1962	$30
—Black label with silver top			
❏ LP-12194 [S]	Slim Whitman Sings	1964	$25
—Black and pink label			
❏ LP-12194 [S]	Slim Whitman Sings	1966	$18
—Black and green label			
❏ LP-9163 [M]	Slim Whitman Sings Annie Laurie	1961	$30
—Black label with stars on top			
❏ LP-9163 [M]	Slim Whitman Sings Annie Laurie	1964	$18
—Black and pink label			
❏ LP-9163 [M]	Slim Whitman Sings Annie Laurie	1966	$15
—Black and green label			
❏ LP-12077 [S]	Slim Whitman Sings Annie Laurie	1961	$30
—Black label with silver top			
❏ LP-12077 [S]	Slim Whitman Sings Annie Laurie	1964	$25
—Black and pink label			
❏ LP-12077 [S]	Slim Whitman Sings Annie Laurie	1966	$18
—Black and green label			
❏ LP-9102 [M]	Song of the Old Waterwheel	1964	$25
—Black and pink label; title changed			
❏ LP-9102 [M]	Song of the Old Waterwheel	1966	$18
—Black and green label			
❏ LP-12102 [R]	Song of the Old Waterwheel	1964	$18

Number	Title	Yr	NM
—Black and pink label			
❏ LP-12102 [R]	Song of the Old Waterwheel	1966	$15
—Black and green label			
❏ LP-12448	The Slim Whitman Christmas Album	1969	$18
❏ LP-9235 [M]	Yodeling	1963	$30
—Black label with stars on top			
❏ LP-9235 [M]	Yodeling	1964	$18
—Black and pink label			
❏ LP-9235 [M]	Yodeling	1966	$15

LIBERTY

Number	Title	Yr	NM
❏ SL-8128	All My Best	1981	$15
—Mail-order album			
❏ LN-10153	Country Songs/City Hits	1981	$10
—Budget-line reissue			
❏ LN-10124	Ghost Riders in the Sky	1981	$10
—Budget-line reissue			
❏ LN-10152	God's Hand in Mine	1981	$10
—Budget-line reissue			
❏ LN-10033	Red River Valley	1981	$10
—Budget-line reissue			
❏ LN-10125	The Best of Slim Whitman, Vol. 2	1981	$10
—Budget-line reissue			
❏ LM-1067	The Slim Whitman Christmas Album	1980	$10
—Abridged reissue of Imperial 12448			
❏ LM-1005	The Very Best of Slim Whitman	1981	$10
—Reissue of United Artists 1005			
❏ LN-10123	Till We Meet Again	1981	$10
—Budget-line reissue			

PAIR

Number	Title	Yr	NM
❏ PDL2-1085	One of a Kind	1986	$15

PICKWICK

Number	Title	Yr	NM
❏ SPC-3590	Happy Anniversary	1978	$12

RCA CAMDEN

Number	Title	Yr	NM
❏ CAL-954 [M]	Birmingham Jail	1966	$25
❏ CAS-954(e) [R]	Birmingham Jail	1966	$15

RCA VICTOR

Number	Title	Yr	NM
❏ AYL1-3774	Birmingham Jail	1980	$10
—Best Buy Series" reissue			
❏ LPM-3217 [10]	Slim Whitman Sings and Yodels	1954	$300

SUNSET

Number	Title	Yr	NM
❏ SUM-1167 [M]	Lonesome Heart	1967	$15
❏ SUS-5167 [R]	Lonesome Heart	1967	$15
❏ SUS-5320	Ramblin' Rose	1970	$12
❏ SUS-5267	Slim Whitman	1969	$15
❏ SUM-1112 [M]	Unchain Your Heart	1966	$15
❏ SUS-5112 [R]	Unchain Your Heart	1966	$15

UNITED ARTISTS

Number	Title	Yr	NM
❏ UA-LA513-G	Everything Leads Back to You	1975	$12
❏ UAS-6783	Guess Who	1970	$15
❏ UA-LA319-G	Happy Anniversary	1974	$12
❏ UA-LA787-G	Home on the Range	1978	$12
❏ UA-LA046-F	I'll See You When I Get There	1973	$12
❏ UAS-6819	It's a Sin to Tell a Lie	1971	$15
❏ UA-LA752-G	Red River Valley	1977	$12
❏ UAS-6832	The Best of Slim Whitman	1972	$15
❏ UA-LA245-G	The Very Best of Slim Whitman	1974	$12
❏ LM-1005	The Very Best of Slim Whitman	1980	$12
❏ UA-LA386-E	The Very Best of Slim Whitman	1974	$12
❏ UAS-6763	Tomorrow Never Comes	1970	$15

WHITNEY, MARVA

KING

Number	Title	Yr	NM
❏ KS-1053	I Sing Soul	1969	$120
❏ KS-1062	It's My Thing	1969	$120
❏ KS-1079	Live and Lowdown at the Apollo	1970	$250

WHITTAKER, ROGER

CAPITOL NASHVILLE

Number	Title	Yr	NM
❏ C1594058	World's Most Beautiful Christmas Songs	1990	$18
—Available on vinyl through Columbia House only			

PAIR

Number	Title	Yr	NM
❏ PDL2-1111	Fire and Rain	1986	$15
❏ PDL2-1039	Golden Tones	1986	$15

RCA VICTOR

Number	Title	Yr	NM
❏ LSP-4505	A Special Kind of Man	1971	$18
❏ AFL1-4505	A Special Kind of Man	1978	$12
—Reissue of LSP-4505			
❏ AYL1-3946	A Special Kind of Man	1981	$10
—Best Buy Series" reissue			
❏ AFL1-4129	Changes	1982	$12
❏ AFL1-2525	Folk Songs	1978	$15
❏ AQL1-2525	Folk Songs	198?	$12
—Reissue of AFL1-2525			
❏ LSP-4405	I Don't Believe in It Any More	1970	$18

Number	Title	Yr	NM
❏ AFL1-4405	I Don't Believe in It Any More	1978	$12
—Reissue of LSP-4405			
❏ AYL1-4177	I Don't Believe in It Any More	1982	$10
—Best Buy Series" reissue			
❏ AFL1-3077	Imagine	1978	$15
❏ AQL1-3077	Imagine	198?	$10
—Reissue of AFL1-3077			
❏ APL1-0855	Last Farewell" and Other Hits, The	1975	$15
❏ AFL1-0855	Last Farewell" and Other Hits, The	1978	$12
—Reissue of APL1-0855			
❏ AQL1-0855	Last Farewell" and Other Hits, The	198?	$10
—Reissue of AFL1-0855			
❏ CPL2-4057	Live in Concert	1981	$15
❏ LSP-4652	Loose and Fiery	1972	$18
❏ AFL1-3501	Mirrors of My Mind	1979	$12
❏ AQL1-3501	Mirrors of My Mind	198?	$10
—Reissue of AFL1-3501			
❏ LSP-4340	New World in the Morning	1970	$18
❏ AFL1-4340	New World in the Morning	1978	$12
—Reissue of LSP-4340			
❏ AYL1-4178	New World in the Morning	1982	$10
—Best Buy Series" reissue			
❏ APL1-1853	Reflections of Love	1976	$15
❏ AFL1-1853	Reflections of Love	1978	$12
—Reissue of APL1-1853			
❏ ANL1-1405	Roger Whittaker	1976	$15
❏ NFL1-8047	Take a Little -- Give a Little	1985	$12
❏ APL1-2255	The Best of Roger Whittaker	1977	$15
❏ AFL1-2255	The Best of Roger Whittaker	1978	$12
—Reissue of APL1-2255			
❏ AQL1-2255	The Best of Roger Whittaker	198?	$10
—Reissue of AFL1-2255			
❏ AYL1-5166	The Best of Roger Whittaker	1985	$10
—Best Buy Series" reissue			
❏ AFL1-5803	The Genius of Love	1986	$12
❏ APL1-1313	The Magical World of Roger Whittaker	1976	$15
❏ AFL1-1313	The Magical World of Roger Whittaker	1978	$12
—Reissue of APL1-1313			
❏ AYL1-3670	The Magical World of Roger Whittaker	1980	$10
—Best Buy Series" reissue			
❏ ANL1-2933	The Roger Whittaker Christmas Album	1978	$15
❏ AFL1-4321	The Wind Beneath My Wings	1983	$12
❏ AFL1-0078	Traveling with Roger Whittaker	1978	$12
—Reissue of APL1-0078			
❏ APL1-0078	Traveling with Roger Whittaker	1973	$18
❏ AFL1-3518	Voyager	1980	$12
❏ AQL1-3518	Voyager	198?	$10
—Reissue of AFL1-3518			
❏ AFL1-3355	When I Need You	1979	$12
❏ AYL1-3911	When I Need You	1981	$10
—Best Buy Series" reissue			
❏ AFL1-3778	With Love	1980	$12

WHO, THE
Also see ROGER DALTREY; JOHN ENTWISTLE; KEITH MOON; PETE TOWNSHEND.

DECCA

Number	Title	Yr	NM
❏ DL4892 [M]	Happy Jack	1967	$150
❏ DL4892 [M]	Happy Jack	1967	$250
—White label promo			

Number	Title	Yr	NM
❏ DL74892 [P]	Happy Jack	1967	$75
—All stereo except that "Happy Jack" and "Don't Look Away" are rechanneled			
❏ DL74892 [P]	Happy Jack	1967	$180
—White label promo			

Number	Title	Yr	NM
DL79175	Live at Leeds	1970	$40

— *With gatefold cover and numerous inserts*

Number	Title	Yr	NM
DL5064 [M]	Magic Bus -- The Who on Tour	1968	$300

— *White label promo; no stock copies were released in mono*

DL75064 [P]	Magic Bus -- The Who on Tour	1968	$50

— *All rechanneled except "Magic Bus" and "I Can't Reach You," which are true stereo.*

DL75064 [P]	Magic Bus -- The Who on Tour	1968	$175

— *White label promo*

DL79184 [B]	Meaty Beaty Big and Bouncy	1971	$30

— *With poster (deduct 1/3 if missing)*

DL4950 [M]	The Who Sell Out	1967	$175
DL4950 [M]	The Who Sell Out	1967	$300

— *White label promo with songs in the same order as the stock copy*

DL4950 [M]	The Who Sell Out	1967	$500

— *White label promo with side 1 banded for airplay and all the commercials on one side*

DL74950 [S]	The Who Sell Out	1967	$50
DL74950 [S]	The Who Sell Out	1967	$300

— *White label promo with songs in the same order as the stock copy*

DL74950 [S]	The Who Sell Out	1967	$400

— *White label promo with side 1 banded for airplay and all the commercials on one side*

DL4664 [M]	The Who Sing My Generation	1966	$175
DL4664 [M]	The Who Sing My Generation	1966	$300

— *White label promo*

DL74664 [R]	The Who Sing My Generation	1966	$75
DL74664 [R]	The Who Sing My Generation	1966	$250

— *White label promo*

DL734586 [B]	The Who/The Strawberry Alarm Clock	1969	$175

— *Special Products release for Philco. One side has Who songs, the other, Strawberry Alarm Clock songs.*

DXSW7205 [B]	Tommy	1969	$75

— *With booklet*

DXSW7205 [DJ]	Tommy	1969	$250

— *White label promo*

DL79182	Who's Next	1971	$30

DIRECT DISC
SD16610 [B]	Who Are You	1980	$50

— *Audiophile vinyl*

GEFFEN
B0022555-1 [M]	A Quick One	2015	$25
B0022558 [B]	My Generation	2015	$20
2256001 [B]	Who Are You	2015	$25

— *180g*

8136511	Who's Next	2008	$25

LIFE
DL74664 [R]	The Who Sing My Generation	1967	$175

MCA
2-4067 [P]	A Quick One/The Who Sell Out	1976	$25

— *Black labels with rainbow*

2-4067 [P]	A Quick One/The Who Sell Out	1978	$18

— *Tan labels*

2-4067 [P]	A Quick One/The Who Sell Out	1980	$15

— *Blue labels with rainbow*

25987	Face Dances	1989	$10
2045 [P]	Happy Jack	1974	$50
2-12001	Hooligans	1981	$12
25986	It's Hard	1989	$10
3-19501	Join Together	1990	$25

— *Box set with booklet*

2022	Live at Leeds	1973	$15
3023	Live at Leeds	1977	$12
37000	Live at Leeds	1979	$10
1577	Live at Leeds	1988	$10
2-4068 [P]	Magic Bus/The Who Sing My Generation	1976	$25

— *Black labels with rainbow*

2-4068 [P]	Magic Bus/The Who Sing My Generation	1978	$18

— *Tan labels*

2-4068 [P]	Magic Bus/The Who Sing My Generation	1980	$15

— *Blue labels with rainbow*

2025	Meaty Beaty Big and Bouncy	1973	$15
3025	Meaty Beaty Big and Bouncy	1977	$12
37001	Meaty Beaty Big and Bouncy	1979	$10
1578	Meaty Beaty Big and Bouncy	1988	$10
37169	Odds and Sods	1980	$10
2-10004 [B]	Quadrophenia	1973	$25

— *Black labels with rainbow*

8310741	Quadrophenia	2008	$30

— *Tan labels*

Number	Title	Yr	NM
6895 [B]	Quadrophenia	1980	$18
2-11005	The Kids Are Alright	1979	$15
6899	The Kids Are Alright	1980	$12

— *Early versions have number stamped in gold on cover with 11005 records. No difference in value.*

2161	The Who By Numbers	1975	$15
3026	The Who By Numbers	1977	$12
37002	The Who By Numbers	1979	$10
1579	The Who By Numbers	1988	$10
2044 [R]	The Who Sing My Generation	1974	$50
2-10005	Tommy	1973	$18

— *Black labels with rainbow*

2-10005	Tommy	1978	$15

— *Tan labels*

2-10005	Tommy	1980	$12

— *Blue labels with rainbow*

5712	Two's Missing	1987	$12
3050	Who Are You	1978	$12
L33-1987 [DJ]	Who Are You	1978	$30

— *White label promo with sticker "Who Are You Edited for Broadcast" on cover -- the line "Who the fuck are you?" is deleted twice.*

14950 [PD]	Who Are You	1978	$18

— *Picture disc*

37003	Who Are You	1979	$10
1580	Who Are You	1988	$10
8031	Who's Better, Who's Best	1989	$18
5408	Who's Greatest Hits	1983	$10
1496	Who's Greatest Hits	1987	$10
8018	Who's Last	1984	$12
5641	Who's Missing	1986	$12
2023	Who's Next	1973	$15
3024	Who's Next	1977	$12
5220	Who's Next	1979	$10
11164	Who's Next	1995	$30

— *Heavy Vinyl" reissue on 180-gram vinyl with gatefold cover*

MOBILE FIDELITY
1-115	Face Dances	1984	$50

— *Audiophile vinyl*

TRACK
2-4067 [P]	A Quick One/The Who Sell Out	1974	$40
2-4068 [P]	Magic Bus/The Who Sing My Generation	1974	$40
2126 [B]	Odds and Sods	1974	$30
2-10004	Quadrophenia	1973	$25

WARNER BROS.
HS3516	Face Dances	1981	$10
WBMS-116 [DJ]	Filling In the Gaps	1981	$100

— *With drawing on cover*

WBMS-116 [DJ]	Filling In the Gaps	1981	$50

— *With generic "Warner Bros. Music Show" cover*

23731 [DJ]	It's Hard	1982	$35

— *Promo version on Quiex II vinyl*

23731	It's Hard	1982	$10

WHYTE, RONNIE
AUDIOPHILE
AP-127	I Love a Piano	198?	$25
AP-151	Ronnie Whyte at the Conservatory	198?	$25
AP-204	Soft Whyte	1986	$25

MONMOUTH-EVERGREEN
7088	New York State of Mind	197?	$30

PROGRESSIVE
PRO-7075	Something Wonderful	1986	$25

WICHITA TRAIN WHISTLE, THE
DOT
DLP-25861 [B]	Mike Nesmith Presents/The Wichita Train Whistle Sings	1968	$50

WIDESPREAD DEPRESSION ORCHESTRA, THE
STASH
ST-206	Boogie in the Barnyard	1980	$25
ST-203	Downtown Uproar	1979	$25
ST-212	Time to Jump and Shout	198?	$25

WIDESPREAD JAZZ ORCHESTRA
ADELPHI
5015	Swing Is the Thing	198?	$25

COLUMBIA
FC40034	Paris Blues	1985	$25

WIEDLIN, JANE
EMI MANHATTAN
R152262	Fur	1988	$15

— *BMG Direct Marketing edition*

E1-48683	Fur	1988	$12

I.R.S.
5638	Jane Wiedlin	1985	$12

WIER, RUSTY
20TH CENTURY
Number	Title	Yr	NM
T-469	Don't It Make You Wanna Dance?	1975	$12
T-495	Rusty Wier	1975	$12

ABC
D-820	Stoned, Slow and Rugged	1974	$15

COLUMBIA
KC34319	Black Hat Saloon	1976	$12
PC34775	Stacked Deck	1977	$12

MCA
820	Stoned, Slow and Rugged	1980	$10

— *Reissue of ABC 820*

WIGGINS, GERALD
CHALLENGE
CHP-604 [M]	The King and I	1957	$75

CLASSIC JAZZ
117	Wig Is Here	198?	$25

CONTEMPORARY
M-3595 [M]	Relax and Enjoy It	1961	$250
S-7595 [S]	Relax and Enjoy It	1961	$250

DIG
LP-102 [M]	Gerald Wiggins Trio	1956	$75

DISCOVERY
DL-2003 [10]	Gerald Wiggins Trio	1953	$300

FANTASY
OJC-173	Relax and Enjoy It	198?	$25

HIFI
J-618 [M]	Wiggin' Out	1961	$75
JS-618 [S]	Wiggin' Out	1961	$40

MOTIF
504 [M]	Reminiscin' with Wig	1956	$75

SPECIALTY
SP-2101 [S]	Around the World	1969	$25

TAMPA
TP-33 [M]	Gerald Wiggins Trio	1957	$250

— *Colored vinyl*

TP-33 [M]	Gerald Wiggins Trio	1958	$175

— *Black vinyl*

TP-1 [M]	The Loveliness of You	1957	$250

— *Colored vinyl*

TP-1 [M]	The Loveliness of You	1958	$175

— *Black vinyl*

WIGGINS, ROY
DIPLOMAT
DPL2615 [M]	Songs I Played for Eddy Arnold	196?	$18

STARDAY
SLP-188 [M]	Mister Steel Guitar	1962	$30
SLP-392 [M]	Nashville Steel Guitar	1965	$30
SLP-259 [M]	The Fabulous Steel Guitar Artistry of Roy Wiggins	1963	$30

WIGGS, JOHNNY, AND RAYMOND BURKE
S/D
LP-1001 [10]	Chamber Jazz	1955	$75

WIGGS, JOHNNY
GHB
GHB-100	Johnny Wiggs and the New Orleans Kids	197?	$25

NEW ORLEANS
7206	Congo Square	197?	$25
47045	Congo Square	197?	$25

PARAMOUNT
CJS107 [10]	Johnny Wiggs' New Orleanians Playing Jazz Favorites and Featuring Ray Burke	195?	$75

SOUTHLAND
LP-200 [10]	Johnny Wiggs	1954	$50
LP-200 [M]	Johnny Wiggs	195?	$30

WIGWAM
VERVE FORECAST
FTS-3089 [B]	Tombstone Valentine	1970	$30

WILBER, BOB, AND KENNY DAVERN
WORLD JAZZ
WJLP-S-5	Soprano Summit	1974	$35

WILBER, BOB, AND SCOTT HAMILTON
CHIAROSCURO
171	Bob Wilber and Scott Hamilton	1977	$30

Number	Title	Yr	NM

WILBER, BOB

CIRCLE
❑ L-406 [10]	Bob Wilbur Jazz Band	1951	$50
❑ CLP-98	Reflections	1986	$25

CLASSIC JAZZ
❑ 9	Blowin' the Blues Away	197?	$25
❑ 8	New Clarinet in Town	197?	$25
❑ 5	Spreadin' Joy	197?	$25

JAZZOLOGY
❑ J-44	Bob Wilber and His Famous Jazz Band	198?	$25
❑ J-141	Live at Bechet's	1986	$25
❑ J-142	Ode to Bechet	1986	$25

MONMOUTH-EVERGREEN
❑ 6917	The Music of Hoagy Carmichael	197?	$30

RIVERSIDE
❑ RLP-2501 [10]	Young Men With Horns	1952	$300

WILBURN BROTHERS, THE

DECCA
❑ DL4211 [M]	City Limits	1961	$30
❑ DL74211 [S]	City Limits	1961	$40
❑ DL4871 [M]	Cool	1967	$30
❑ DL74871 [S]	Cool	1967	$25
❑ DL4615 [M]	Country Gold	1965	$25
❑ DL74615 [S]	Country Gold	1965	$30
❑ DL4225 [M]	Folk Songs	1962	$25
❑ DL74225 [S]	Folk Songs	1962	$30
❑ DL4645 [M]	I'm Gonna Tie One on Tonight	1965	$25
❑ DL74645 [S]	I'm Gonna Tie One on Tonight	1965	$30
❑ DL4954 [M]	It's Another World	1968	$40
❑ DL74954 [S]	It's Another World	1968	$25
❑ DL4764 [M]	Let's Go Country	1966	$25
❑ DL74764 [S]	Let's Go Country	1966	$30
❑ DL75173	Little Johnny from Down the Street	1970	$25
❑ DL8959 [M]	Livin' in God's Country	1959	$40
❑ DL78959 [S]	Livin' in God's Country	1959	$75
❑ DL4544 [M]	Never Alone	1964	$25
❑ DL74544 [S]	Never Alone	1964	$30
❑ DL8774 [M]	Side by Side	1958	$40
❑ DL78774 [S]	Side by Side	1959	$75
❑ DL75214	Sing Your Heart Out Country Boy	1971	$25
❑ DL4464 [M]	Take Up Thy Cross	1964	$25
❑ DL74464 [S]	Take Up Thy Cross	1964	$30
❑ DL75291	That She's Leaving Feeling	1972	$25
❑ DL4058 [M]	The Big Heartbreak	1960	$30
❑ DL74058 [S]	The Big Heartbreak	1960	$40
❑ DL8576 [M]	The Wilburn Brothers	1957	$40

❑ DL4721 [M]	The Wilburn Brothers Show	1966	$75

—With guests Loretta Lynn, Ernest Tubb, Harold Morrison

❑ DL74721 [S]	The Wilburn Brothers Show	1966	$100

—With guests Loretta Lynn, Ernest Tubb, Harold Morrison

❑ DL4142 [M]	The Wilburn Brothers Sing	1961	$30
❑ DL74142 [S]	The Wilburn Brothers Sing	1961	$40
❑ DL4391 [M]	Trouble's Back in Town	1963	$25
❑ DL74391 [S]	Trouble's Back in Town	1963	$30
❑ DL4824 [M]	Two for the Show	1967	$30
❑ DL74824 [S]	Two for the Show	1967	$25

KING
❑ 746 [M]	The Wonderful Wilburn Brothers	1961	$150

MCA
❑ 4011	Portrait	197?	$18

MCA CORAL
❑ 20058	That Country Feeling	1973	$12

VOCALION
❑ VL3691 [M]	Carefree Moments	1962	$18
❑ VL73691 [S]	Carefree Moments	1962	$18
❑ VL73889	I Walk the Line	197?	$15
❑ VL73876	That Country Feeling	197?	$15

WILCO
Also see UNCLE TUPELO.

REPRISE
❑ 46236-1 [B]	Being There	1996	$30

RHINO VINYL
❑ RI-76492	A Ghost is Born	2005	$30

SIRE
❑ 45857	A.M.	1995	$100

—Red vinyl in generic plastic sleeve with sticker in upper left corner

SUNDAZED
❑ LP5161	Yankee Hotel Foxtrot	2002	$30

WILCOX, HARLOW

PLANTATION
❑ PLP-12	Cripple Cricket and Other Country Critters	1971	$18
❑ PLP-7	Groovy Grubworm and Other Golden Guitar Greats	1970	$18

WILCOX, LARRY

COLUMBIA
❑ CL2147 [M]	Hot Rod Jazz	1964	$30
❑ CS8947 [S]	Hot Rod Jazz	1964	$40

COLUMBIA SPECIAL PRODUCTS
❑ CSRP8947 [M]	Hot Rod Jazz	196?	$25

WILCOX THREE, THE

RCA CAMDEN
❑ CAL-669 [M]	The Greatest Folk Songs Ever Sung	1961	$25

WILD, JACK

BUDDAH
❑ BDS-5110	A Beautiful World	1972	$30
❑ BDS-5083	Everything's Coming Up Roses	1971	$30

CAPITOL
❑ SKAO-545	The Jack Wild Album	1970	$30

WILD-CATS, THE

UNITED ARTISTS
❑ UAL-3031 [M]	Bandstand Record Hop	1958	$50

WILD BUTTER

UNITED ARTISTS
❑ UAS-6766	Wild Butter	1970	$30

WILD CHERRY

EPIC
❑ PE34462	Electrified Funk	1977	$12
❑ JE35011	I Love My Music	1978	$12
❑ JE35760	Only the Wild	1979	$12

❑ PE34195 [B]	Wild Cherry	1976	$15

WILD COUNTRY
See ALABAMA.

WILD MAN STEVE

DEALER'S CHOICE
❑ 780	Did He Really Say That	198?	$18
❑ 777	Is It Good Baby	198?	$18

DICK-ER
❑ D70	Do Not Disturb	1972	$25

LAFF
❑ 181	Eatin' Ain't Cheatin'	1973	$15
❑ 191	When You're Hot You're Hot	1976	$15

RAW
❑ 7002	King of Them All	1971	$18

❑ 7000	My Man! Wild Man!	1969	$18
❑ 7001	Wild! Wild! Wild! Wild!	1970	$18

WILD ONES, THE (1)

UNITED ARTISTS
❑ UAL-3450 [M]	The Arthur Sound	1965	$30
❑ UAS-6450 [S]	The Arthur Sound	1965	$30

WILD TURKEY

CHRYSALIS
❑ CHR1010	Turkey	1973	$12

REPRISE
❑ MS2070	Battle Hymn	1972	$15

WILDE, KIM

EMI AMERICA
❑ SN-16351	Kids in America	198?	$15

—Budget-line reissue of first LP

❑ ST-17065	Kim Wilde	1981	$12
❑ ST-517065	Kim Wilde	1981	$15

—Columbia House edition

MCA
❑ 5903	Another Step	1987	$12
❑ 42230	Close	1988	$12
❑ 5550	Teases and Dares	1985	$12

WILDE, MARTY

EPIC
❑ LN3686 [M]	Bad Boy	1960	$100
❑ LN3711 [M]	Wilde About Marty	1960	$100
❑ BN575 [S]	Wilde About Marty	1960	$150

WILDER, ALEC

COLUMBIA
❑ CL6181 [10]	Alec Wilder Octet	1951	$75

MERCURY
❑ MG25008 [10]	Alec Wilder and His Octet	1949	$150

WILDER, JOE

COLUMBIA
❑ CL1319 [M]	Jazz from "Peter Gunn"	1959	$40

—Red and black label with six "eye" logos

❑ CS8121 [S]	Jazz from "Peter Gunn"	1959	$75

—Red and black label with six "eye" logos

❑ CL1372 [M]	The Pretty Sound of Joe Wilder	1959	$50

—Red and black label with six "eye" logos

❑ CS8173 [S]	The Pretty Sound of Joe Wilder	1959	$150

—Red and black label with six "eye" logos

SAVOY
❑ MG-12063 [M]	'N' Wilder...	1956	$50

SAVOY JAZZ
❑ SJL-1191	Softly with Feeling	1989	$30

WILDER, MATTHEW

PRIVATE I
❑ FZ39879	Bouncin' Off the Walls	1984	$12
❑ BFZ39112	I Don't Speak the Language	1983	$12
❑ FZ39112	I Don't Speak the Language	1984	$10

—Reissue with new prefix

WILDERNESS ROAD

COLUMBIA
❑ C31118	Wilderness Road	1972	$25

REPRISE
❑ MS2125	Sold for the Prevention of Disease Only	1973	$25

WILDWEEDS, THE

VANGUARD
❑ VSD-6552	The Wildweeds	1970	$30

WILEY, LEE

ALLEGRO ELITE
❑ 4019 [10]	Lee Wiley Sings -- Lennie Tristano Plays	195?	$150

AUDIOPHILE
❑ AP-1	Lee Wiley Sings Ira and George Gershwin and Cole Porter	1986	$25
❑ AP-10	Lee Wiley Sings the Songs of Richard Rodgers and Lorenz Hart and Harold Arlen	1990	$30

COLUMBIA
❑ CL6216 [10]	Lee Wiley Sings Irving Berlin	1952	$150
❑ CL6215 [10]	Lee Wiley Sings Vincent Youmans	1952	$150
❑ CL6169 [10]	Night in Manhattan	1951	$120
❑ CL656 [M]	Night in Manhattan	1955	$100

Number	Title	Yr	NM
JAZZTONE			
❏ J-1248 [M]	The Songs of Rodgers and Hart -- Intimate Jazz	1956	$50
JJC			
❏ M-2003 [M]	The Classic Interpretations of the Immortal Cole Porter	195?	$50
❏ M-2002 [M]	The One and Only Lee Wiley	195?	$50
LIBERTY MUSIC SHOP			
❏ 1003 [10]	Cole Porter Songs by Lee Wiley	195?	$300
❏ 1004 [10]	George Gershwin Songs by Lee Wiley	195?	$300
MONMOUTH-EVERGREEN			
❏ 7041	Back Home Again	1971	$30
❏ 6807	Lee Wiley Plays Rodgers & Hart/Harold Arlen	1968	$35
❏ 7034	Lee Wiley Sings Gershwin & Porter	1970	$30
RCA VICTOR			
❏ LPM-1566 [M]	Touch of the Blues	1957	$75
❏ LPM-1408 [M]	West of the Moon	1957	$100
RIC			
❏ M-2002 [M]	The One and Only Lee Wiley	1964	$25
❏ S-2002 [S]	The One and Only Lee Wiley	1964	$30
STORYVILLE			
❏ STLP-312 [10]	Lee Wiley Sings Rodgers and Hart	1954	$250
TOTEM			
❏ 1021	Lee Wiley on the Air	197?	$25
❏ 1033	Lee Wiley on the Air, Vol. 2	198?	$25

WILKERSON, DON

Number	Title	Yr	NM
BLUE NOTE			
❏ BLP-4121 [M]	Elder Don	1963	$75
❏ BST-84121 [S]	Elder Don	1963	$40
— With "New York, USA" address on label			
❏ BST-84121 [S]	Elder Don	1967	$25
— With "A Division of Liberty Records" on label			
❏ BLP-4107 [M]	Preach, Brother!	1962	$75
❏ BST-84107 [S]	Preach, Brother!	1962	$40
— With "New York, USA" address on label			
❏ BST-84107 [S]	Preach, Brother!	1967	$25
— With "A Division of Liberty Records" on label			
❏ BLP-4145 [M]	Shoutin'	1963	$75
❏ BST-84145 [S]	Shoutin'	1963	$40
— With "New York, USA" address on label			
❏ BST-84145 [S]	Shoutin'	1967	$25
— With "A Division of Liberty Records" on label			
RIVERSIDE			
❏ RLP-332 [M]	Texas Twister	1960	$250
❏ RLP-1186 [S]	Texas Twister	1960	$250

WILKES, RAY

Number	Title	Yr	NM
INNER CITY			
❏ IC-1051	Dark Blue Man	197?	$30

WILKINS, ERNIE

Number	Title	Yr	NM
EVEREST			
❏ LPBR-5077 [M]	Here Comes the Swingin' Mr. Wilkins	1959	$30
❏ SDBR-1077 [S]	Here Comes the Swingin' Mr. Wilkins	1959	$30
❏ LPBR-5104 [M]	The Big New Band of the '60s	1960	$30
❏ SDBR-1104 [S]	The Big New Band of the '60s	1960	$30
MAINSTREAM			
❏ MRL-305	Hard Mother Blues	1971	$35
❏ MRL-806	Screaming Mothers	197?	$35
RCA CAMDEN			
❏ CAL-543 [M]	The Greatest Songs Ever Swung	195?	$35
SAVOY			
❏ MG-12044 [M]	Top Brass Featuring 5 Trumpets	1955	$85
STEEPLECHASE			
❏ SCS-1190	Montreux	198?	$30
STORYVILLE			
❏ 4051	Ernie Wilkins and the Almost Big Band	198?	$25

WILKINS, JACK

Number	Title	Yr	NM
CHIAROSCURO			
❏ 156	Merge	1977	$30
❏ 185	You Can't Live Without It	1978	$30
MAINSTREAM			
❏ MRL-396	Windows	197?	$30

WILKINS, LITTLE DAVID

Number	Title	Yr	NM
MCA			
❏ 2215	King of All the Taverns	1976	$15
❏ 445	Little David Wilkins	1974	$15

Number	Title	Yr	NM
PLAYBOY			
❏ KZ35028	New Horizons	1977	$15

WILKINSON TRI-CYCLE

Number	Title	Yr	NM
DATE			
❏ TES4016 [B]	Wilkinson Tri-Cycle	1969	$75

WILL TO POWER

Number	Title	Yr	NM
EPIC			
❏ E46051	Journey Home	1991	$15
❏ FE40940	Will to Power	1988	$12

WILLET, SLIM

Number	Title	Yr	NM
AUDIO LAB			
❏ AL-1542 [M]	Slim Willet	1959	$150

WILLETTE, BABY FACE

Number	Title	Yr	NM
ARGO			
❏ LP-749 [M]	Behind the 8-Ball	1965	$30
❏ LPS-749 [S]	Behind the 8-Ball	1965	$30
❏ LP-739 [M]	No Rock	1964	$30
❏ LPS-739 [S]	No Rock	1964	$30
BLUE NOTE			
❏ BLP-4068 [M]	Face to Face	1961	$175
— With W. 63rd St. address on label			
❏ BST-84068 [S]	Face to Face	1961	$120
— With W. 63rd St. address on label			
❏ BLP-4068 [M]	Face to Face	1963	$75
— With "New York, USA" address on label			
❏ BST-84068 [S]	Face to Face	1963	$25
— With "New York, USA" address on label			
❏ BST-84068 [S]	Face to Face	1967	$35
— With "A Division of Liberty Records" on label			
❏ BLP-4084 [M]	Stop and Listen	1962	$120
— With 61st St. address on label			
❏ BST-84084 [S]	Stop and Listen	1962	$150
— With 61st St. address on label			
❏ BLP-4084 [M]	Stop and Listen	1963	$75
— With "New York, USA" address on label			
❏ BST-84084 [S]	Stop and Listen	1963	$25
— With "New York, USA" address on label			
❏ BST-84084 [S]	Stop and Listen	1967	$35
— With "A Division of Liberty Records" on label			
CADET			
❏ LP-749 [M]	Behind the 8-Ball	1966	$30
❏ LPS-749 [S]	Behind the 8-Ball	1966	$35
❏ LPS-739 [S]	No Rock	1966	$35
❏ LP-739 [M]	No Rock	1966	$30

WILLIAMS, AL

Number	Title	Yr	NM
RENAISSANCE			
❏ 9565	Sandance	1976	$30

WILLIAMS, ANDRE

Number	Title	Yr	NM
SDEG			
❏ 4020	Directly from the Streets	198?	$12

WILLIAMS, ANDY

Number	Title	Yr	NM
ATCO			
❏ 90561	Close Enough for Love	1987	$12
CADENCE			
❏ CLP1018 [M]	Andy Williams	1957	$50
❏ CLP3002 [M]	Andy Williams	1958	$50
— Cover depicts Andy standing			
❏ CLP3002 [M]	Andy Williams	1960	$25
— Cover depicts Andy reclining			
❏ CLP3054 [M]	Andy Williams' Best	1962	$25
❏ CLP25054 [S]	Andy Williams' Best	1962	$30
❏ CLP3005 [M]	Andy Williams Sings Rodgers and Hammerstein	1958	$40
— Cover depicts a café scene			
❏ CLP3005 [M]	Andy Williams Sings Rodgers and Hammerstein	1960	$25
— Cover depicts a close-up of Andy's face			
❏ CLP3027 [M]	Andy Williams Sings... Steve Allen	1959	$25
❏ CLP25027 [R]	Andy Williams Sings... Steve Allen	1959	$18
❏ CLP3030 [M]	Lonely Street	1960	$25
❏ CLP25030 [S]	Lonely Street	1960	$30
❏ CLP3061 [M]	Million Seller Songs	1962	$25
❏ CLP25061 [S]	Million Seller Songs	1962	$30
❏ CLP3038 [M]	The Village of St. Bernadette	1960	$25
❏ CLP25038 [S]	The Village of St. Bernadette	1960	$30

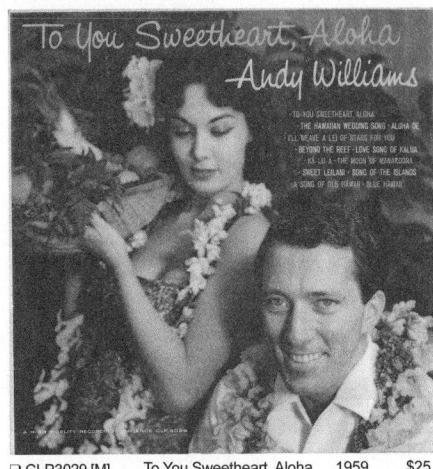

Number	Title	Yr	NM
❏ CLP3029 [M]	To You Sweetheart, Aloha	1959	$25
❏ CLP25029 [S]	To You Sweetheart, Aloha	1959	$30
❏ CLP3026 [M]	Two Time Winners	1959	$25
❏ CLP25026 [S]	Two Time Winners	1959	$30
— Black vinyl			
❏ CLP25026 [S]	Two Time Winners	1959	$100
— Red vinyl			
❏ CLP3047 [M]	Under Paris Skies	1961	$25
❏ CLP25047 [S]	Under Paris Skies	1961	$30
CAPITOL			
❏ ST-12387	Greatest Love Classics	1984	$12
COLUMBIA			
❏ KC31625	Alone Again (Naturally)	1972	$12
❏ CQ31625 [Q]	Alone Again (Naturally)	1972	$20
❏ PC34299	Andy	1976	$12
❏ PCQ34299 [Q]	Andy	1976	$20
❏ KCS9979	Andy Williams' Greatest Hits	1970	$15
❏ KC32384	Andy Williams' Greatest Hits, Vol. 2	1973	$12
❏ CL2383 [M]	Andy Williams' Newest Hits	1966	$15
❏ CS9183 [S]	Andy Williams' Newest Hits	1966	$18
❏ CL2680 [M]	Born Free	1967	$15
❏ CS9480 [S]	Born Free	1967	$18
❏ CL2324 [M]	Canadian Sunset	1965	$15
— Reissue of Cadence 3054			
❏ CS9124 [S]	Canadian Sunset	1965	$18
— Reissue of Cadence 25054			
❏ C33191	Christmas Present	1974	$12
❏ CL1751 [M]	Danny Boy And Other Songs I Love to Sing	1962	$18
❏ CS8551 [S]	Danny Boy And Other Songs I Love to Sing	1962	$25
❏ CL2015 [M]	Days of Wine and Roses	1963	$15
❏ CS8815 [S]	Days of Wine and Roses	1963	$18
❏ CL2338 [M]	Dear Heart	1965	$15
❏ CS9138 [S]	Dear Heart	1965	$18
❏ CS9922	Get Together with Andy Williams	1969	$18
— The Osmonds appear on three tracks			
❏ CS9844	Happy Heart	1969	$15
❏ CL2323 [M]	Hawaiian Wedding Song	1965	$15
— Reissue of Cadence 3029			
❏ CS9123 [S]	Hawaiian Wedding Song	1965	$18
— Reissue of Cadence 25029			
❏ CS9662 [S]	Honey	1968	$15
❏ CS2862 [M]	Honey	1968	$25
❏ CL2533 [M]	In the Arms of Love	1967	$15
❏ CS9333 [S]	In the Arms of Love	1967	$18
❏ CL2766 [M]	Love, Andy	1967	$18
❏ CS9566 [S]	Love, Andy	1967	$15
❏ KC30497	Love Story	1971	$12
❏ CQ30497 [Q]	Love Story	1972	$20
❏ CG33597	Love Story/Born Free	1975	$15
❏ KC31303	Love Theme from "The Godfather"	1972	$12
❏ CQ31303 [Q]	Love Theme from "The Godfather"	1972	$20
❏ CL2420 [M]	Merry Christmas	1965	$15
❏ CS9220 [S]	Merry Christmas	1965	$15
❏ CL1809 [M]	Moon River and Other Great Movie Themes	1962	$15
❏ CS8609 [S]	Moon River and Other Great Movie Themes	1962	$18
❏ CG33600	Moon River/Days of Wine and Roses	1975	$15
❏ CS9896	Raindrops Keep Fallin' on My Head	1970	$15
❏ KC32383	Solitaire	1973	$12
❏ CL2171 [M]	The Academy Award Winning "Call Me Irresponsible" and Other Hits Songs from the Movies	1964	$15
❏ CS8971 [S]	The Academy Award Winning "Call Me Irresponsible" and Other Hits Songs from the Movies	1964	$18
❏ CL2087 [M]	The Andy Williams Christmas Album	1963	$15
❏ CS8887 [S]	The Andy Williams Christmas Album	1963	$15
❏ KC30105	The Andy Williams Show	1970	$12

Number	Title	Yr	NM
❏ GP5	The Andy Williams Sound of Music	1969	$25
❏ CL2205 [M]	The Great Songs from "My Fair Lady" and Other Broadway Hits	1964	$15
❏ CS9005 [S]	The Great Songs from "My Fair Lady" and Other Broadway Hits	1964	$18
❏ CG31064	The Impossible Dream	1971	$18
❏ PC33563	The Other Side of Me	1975	$12
❏ CL2499 [M]	The Shadow of Your Smile	1966	$15
❏ CS9299 [S]	The Shadow of Your Smile	1966	$18
❏ KC32949	The Way We Were	1974	$12
❏ CL2137 [M]	The Wonderful World of Andy Williams	1964	$15
❏ CS8937 [S]	The Wonderful World of Andy Williams	1964	$18
❏ CL1879 [M]	Warm and Willing	1962	$15
❏ CS8679 [S]	Warm and Willing	1962	$18
❏ KC33234	You Lay So Easy on My Mind	1974	$12
❏ KC30797	You've Got a Friend	1971	$12
❏ CQ30797 [Q]	You've Got a Friend	1971	$20

COLUMBIA SPECIAL PRODUCTS

❏ CSS966	Andy... & Company	1969	$15

—*Side 1 is Andy Williams; Side 2 has tracks by the Williams Brothers, Claudine Longet and the Osmond Brothers; sold only at Woolworth's*

HARMONY

❏ KH30133	Andy Williams	1970	$12

PAIR

❏ PDL2-1103	The Best of Andy Williams	1986	$15

TIME-LIFE

❏ SLGD-11	Legendary Singers: Andy Williams	1986	$18

WILLIAMS, ANN

CHARLIE PARKER

❏ PLP-807 [M]	First Time Out	1963	$40
❏ PLP-807S [S]	First Time Out	1963	$40

WILLIAMS, BETTY VAIDEN

VANGUARD

❏ VRS-9028 [M]	Folk Songs and Ballads of North Carolina	195?	$30

WILLIAMS, BIG JOE

BLUESVILLE

❏ BVLP-1067 [M]	Big Joe Williams at Folk City	1963	$150

—*Blue label, silver print*

❏ BVLP-1067 [M]	Big Joe Williams at Folk City	1964	$30

—*Blue label with trident logo*

❏ BVLP-1056 [M]	Blues for 9 Strings	1962	$150

—*Blue label, silver print*

❏ BVLP-1056 [M]	Blues for 9 Strings	1964	$30

—*Blue label with trident logo*

❏ BVLP-1083 [M]	Studio Blues	1964	$150

—*Blue label, silver print*

❏ BVLP-1083 [M]	Studio Blues	1964	$30

—*Blue label with trident logo*

DELMARK

❏ DL-604 [M]	Blues on Highway 49	1962	$75
❏ DL-609 [M]	Starvin' Chain Blues	1966	$30

FOLKWAYS

❏ FA-3820 [M]	Mississippi's Big Joe Williams	1962	$40
❏ FAS-3820 [R]	Mississippi's Big Joe Williams	1962	$25

MILESTONE

❏ 3001 [M]	Classic Delta Blues	1966	$30

WILLIAMS, BILLY

CORAL

❏ CRL57184 [M]	Billy Williams	1957	$120
❏ CRL57251 [M]	Half Sweet, Half Beat	1959	$150
❏ CRL757251 [S]	Half Sweet, Half Beat	1959	$175
❏ CRL57343 [M]	The Billy Williams Revue	1960	$150
❏ CRL757343 [S]	The Billy Williams Revue	1960	$120

MERCURY

❏ MG20317 [M]	Oh Yeah!	1958	$250

MGM

❏ E-3400 [M]	The Billy Williams Quartet	1957	$120

WING

❏ MGW-12131 [M]	Vote for Billy Williams	1959	$40

WILLIAMS, BILLY DEE
PRESTIGE LIVELY ARTS

❏ 30001 [M]	Let's Misbehave	1962	$40

WILLIAMS, BUSTER

BUDDAH

❏ BDS-5728	Dreams Come True	1980	$30

MUSE

❏ MR-5171	Heartbeat	1979	$30
❏ MR-5080	Pinnacle	1975	$30
❏ MR-5101	Reflections	1976	$30

WILLIAMS, CAMILLA

MGM

❏ E-156 [10]	Spirituals	1952	$150

WILLIAMS, CHARLES

MAINSTREAM

❏ MRL-312	Charles Williams	1971	$15
❏ MRL-381	Stickball	1973	$30
❏ MRL-345	Trees and Grass and Things	1972	$30

WILLIAMS, CLARENCE

BIOGRAPH

❏ 12038	Clarence Williams Volume 1, 1927-28	197?	$25
❏ 12006	Clarence Williams Volume 1, 1927-29	197?	$25

MCA

❏ 1349	Music Mann	198?	$25

RIVERSIDE

❏ RLP-1033 [10]	Clarence Williams and Orchestra	1954	$300

WILLIAMS, CLAUDE

CLASSIC JAZZ

❏ 135	Fiddler's Dream	198?	$25

WILLIAMS, COOTIE

HALL OF FAME

❏ 602	The Big Challenge	197?	$25

JARO

❏ JAM-5001 [M]	Around Midnight	1959	$150
❏ JAS-8001 [S]	Around Midnight	1959	$100

MOODSVILLE

❏ MVLP-27 [M]	The Solid Trumpet of Cootie Williams	1962	$50

—*Green label*

❏ MVLP-27 [M]	The Solid Trumpet of Cootie Williams	1965	$30

—*Blue label, trident logo at right*

PHOENIX

❏ 1	Cootie Williams Sextet and Orchestra	197?	$25

RCA VICTOR

❏ LPM-1718 [M]	Cootie Williams in Hi-Fi	1958	$100
❏ LSP-1718 [S]	Cootie Williams in Stereo	1958	$175

WARWICK

❏ W-2027 [M]	Do Nothing Till You Hear From Me	1960	$40
❏ W-2027ST [S]	Do Nothing Till You Hear From Me	1960	$75

WILLIAMS, COOTIE/JIMMY PRESTON
ALLEGRO ELITE

❏ 4109 [10]	Rock 'N' Roll	195?	$50

WILLIAMS, DANNY
UNITED ARTISTS

❏ UAL-3493 [M]	Magic Town	1966	$18

❏ UAS-6493 [S]	Magic Town	1966	$25
❏ UAL-3297 [M]	The Exciting Danny Williams	1963	$18
❏ UAS-6297 [S]	The Exciting Danny Williams	1963	$25
❏ UAL-3359 [M]	White on White	1964	$18
❏ UAS-6359 [S]	White on White	1964	$25
❏ UAL-3380 [M]	With You in Mind	1964	$18
❏ UAS-6380 [S]	With You in Mind	1964	$25

WILLIAMS, DAVID "FAT MAN"
NEW ORLEANS

❏ 7204	Apple Tree	197?	$25

WILLIAMS, DENIECE

ARC

❏ FC37048	My Melody	1981	$12
❏ PC37048	My Melody	198?	$10

—*Budget-line reissue*

❏ FC37952	Niecy	1982	$12
❏ HC47952	Niecy	1983	$50

—*Half-speed mastered edition*

❏ PC37952	Niecy	198?	$10

—*Budget-line reissue*

❏ AS1432 [DJ]	Niecy	1982	$30

—*Promo-only picture disc*

❏ JC35568 [B]	When Love Comes Calling	1979	$15

COLUMBIA

❏ FC44322	As Good As It Gets	1989	$12
❏ FC40084	Hot on the Trail	1986	$12
❏ FC38622 [B]	I'm So Proud	1983	$12
❏ PC38622	I'm So Proud	198?	$10

—*Budget-line reissue*

❏ FC39366	Let's Hear It for the Boy	1984	$12
❏ JC34911	Song Bird	1977	$12
❏ PC34911	Song Bird	198?	$10

—*Budget-line reissue*

❏ PC34242	This Is Niecy	1976	$15

—*No bar code on cover*

❏ PC34242	This Is Niecy	198?	$10

—*Reissue with bar code on cover*

❏ FC40486	Water Under the Bridge	1987	$12

MCA

❏ 6338	Special Love	1989	$12

SPARROW

❏ SPR-1256	From the Beginning	1990	$18
❏ ST-41039	So Glad I Know	198?	$15

—*Reissue of 1121?*

❏ SPR-1121	So Glad I Know	1986	$15
❏ SPR-1174	Special Love	1989	$15

WILLIAMS, DIANA
CAPITOL

❏ ST-11587	Diana Williams	1976	$15

WILLIAMS, DON
Also see EMMYLOU HARRIS; THE POZO-SECO SINGERS.

ABC

❏ AA-1069 [B]	Expressions	1978	$15

ABC/DOT

❏ DOSD-2018	Don Williams, Vol. 2	1974	$15

—*Reissue of JMI 4006*

❏ DOSD-2004	Don Williams, Vol. III	1974	$15
❏ DOSD-2014	Don Williams, Volume One	1974	$15

—*Reissue of JMI 4004*

❏ DO-2035	Greatest Hits	1975	$15
❏ DO-2049	Harmony	1976	$15
❏ DO-2088	I'm Just a Country Boy	1977	$15
❏ DO-2064	Visions	1976	$15
❏ DOSD-2021	You're My Best Friend	1975	$15

CAPITOL

❏ ST-12440	New Moves	1987	$10
❏ C1-91444	Prime Cuts	1989	$10
❏ CLT-48034	Traces	1988	$10

Number	Title	Yr	NM
JMI			
❏ 4006	Don Williams, Volume 2	1974	$25
❏ 4004	Don Williams, Volume One	1973	$30
MCA			
❏ 5493	Café Carolina	1984	$12
❏ 5697	Don Williams Sings Bob McDill	1986	$12
❏ 5210	Especially for You	1981	$12
❏ 37233	Especially for You	198?	$10
—Budget-line reissue			
❏ 3279	Expressions	1980	$10
—Reissue of ABC 1069			
❏ 37135	Greatest Hits	198?	$10
—Budget-line reissue			
❏ 5133	I Believe in You	1980	$12
❏ 37234	I Believe in You	198?	$10
—Budget-line reissue			
❏ 37232	I'm Just a Country Boy	198?	$10
—Budget-line reissue			
❏ 5306	Listen to the Radio	1982	$12
❏ 5803	Lovers and Best Friends	1986	$12
❏ 3192	Portrait	1980	$12
❏ 37231	Portrait	198?	$10
—Budget-line reissue			
❏ 3096	The Best of Don Williams, Vol. 2	1979	$12
❏ 37155	The Best of Don Williams, Vol. 2	198?	$10
—Budget-line reissue			
❏ 5465	The Best of Don Williams, Vol. 3	1984	$12
❏ 1442	The Best of Don Williams, Vol. 3	1985	$10
—Budget-line reissue			
❏ 5671	The Best of Don Williams, Vol. 4	1985	$12
❏ 37230	Visions	198?	$10
—Budget-line reissue			
❏ 5407	Yellow Moon	1983	$12
RCA			
❏ 9656-1-R	One Good Well	1989	$12
❏ R124814	True Love	1990	$18
—BMG Music Service pressing; only US vinyl edition			

WILLIAMS, GEORGE
BRUNSWICK

Number	Title	Yr	NM
❏ BL54020 [M]	The Fox	1957	$50
RCA VICTOR			
❏ LPM-1301 [M]	Rhythm Was His Business	1956	$40
❏ LPM-1205 [M]	We Could Make Such Beautiful Music	1956	$40

WILLIAMS, GRIFF
HINDSIGHT

Number	Title	Yr	NM
❏ HSR-175	Griff Williams and His Orchestra 1946-1951	198?	$25

WILLIAMS, HANK, AND HANK WILLIAMS, JR.
Also see each artist's individual listings.

MGM

Number	Title	Yr	NM
❏ E-4378 [M]	Again	1966	$25
❏ SE-4378 [S]	Again	1966	$30
❏ E-4276 [M]	Father and Son	1965	$30
❏ SE-4276 [S]	Father and Son	1965	$30
❏ 2SES-4865	Hank Williams: The Legend in Story and Song	1973	$18
❏ M3HB4975	Insights Into Hank Williams in Song and Story	1974	$18

WILLIAMS, HANK, JR., AND LOIS JOHNSON
MGM

Number	Title	Yr	NM
❏ SE-4750	All for the Love of Sunshine	1971	$25
❏ SE-4721	Removing the Shadow	1971	$18
—The label has the word "Shadows" instead of "Shadow"			
❏ SE-4857	Send Me Some Lovin'/ Whole Lotta Lovin'	1972	$25

WILLIAMS, HANK, JR.
CAPRICORN

Number	Title	Yr	NM
❏ W1-26806	Maverick	1992	$25
—Columbia House edition (only U.S. vinyl release)			
ELEKTRA			
❏ 6E-194	Family Tradition	1979	$15
❏ 6E-278	Habits Old and New	1980	$12
❏ 60193	Hank Williams, Jr.'s, Greatest Hits	1982	$12
❏ 60100	High Notes	1982	$12
❏ 5E-538	One Night Stands	1982	$12
—Reissue			
❏ 6E-330	Rowdy	1981	$12
❏ 60223 [B]	Strong Stuff	1983	$18
❏ 5E-539	The New South	1982	$12
—Reissue			
❏ 5E-535	The Pressure Is On	1981	$12
❏ 6E-237	Whiskey Bent and Hell Bound	1979	$12

Number	Title	Yr	NM
MGM			
❏ MG-1-5020	14 Greatest Hits	1976	$15
❏ SE-4862	After You/Pride's Not Hard to Swallow	1973	$15
❏ SE-4540	A Time to Sing	1968	$30
❏ E-4316 [M]	Ballads of the Hills and Plains	1965	$25
❏ SE-4316 [S]	Ballads of the Hills and Plains	1965	$30
❏ E-4344 [M]	Blues My Name	1966	$25
❏ SE-4344 [S]	Blues My Name	1966	$30
❏ T-90695 [M]	Blues My Name	1966	$30
—Capitol Record Club edition			
❏ ST-90695 [S]	Blues My Name	1966	$30
—Capitol Record Club edition			
❏ M3G-4988	Bocephus	1974	$15
❏ E-4391 [M]	Country Shadows	1966	$25
❏ SE-4391 [S]	Country Shadows	1966	$30
❏ T-90925 [M]	Country Shadows	1966	$30
—Capitol Record Club edition			
❏ SE-4843	Eleven Roses	1972	$15
❏ MG-1-5009	Hank Williams, Jr., and Friends	1975	$40
❏ SE-4675	Hank Williams, Jr., Singing My Songs (Johnny Cash)	1970	$18
❏ GAS-119	Hank Williams, Jr. (Golden Archive Series)	1970	$18
❏ SE-4656	Hank Williams, Jr.'s Greatest Hits	1970	$18
❏ SE-4822	Hank Williams, Jr.'s Greatest Hits, Volume 2	1972	$15
❏ SE-4774	I've Got a Right to Cry/They All Used to Belong to Me	1971	$18
❏ SE-4906	Just Pickin' -- No Singin'	1973	$15
❏ SE-4644	Live at Cobo Hall, Detroit	1969	$25
❏ M3G-4971	Living Proof	1974	$15
❏ SE-4559	Luke the Drifter, Jr.	1969	$25
❏ SE-4632	Luke the Drifter, Jr. (Vol. 2)	1969	$25
❏ SE-4673	Luke the Drifter, Jr. (Vol. 3)	1970	$18
❏ E-4428 [M]	My Own Way	1967	$25
❏ SE-4428 [S]	My Own Way	1967	$30
❏ E-4527 [M]	My Songs	1968	$40
❏ SE-4527 [S]	My Songs	1968	$30
❏ E-4213 [M]	Sings the Songs of Hank Williams	1964	$25
❏ SE-4213 [S]	Sings the Songs of Hank Williams	1964	$30
❏ SE-4621	Songs My Father Left Me	1969	$25
❏ SE-4657	Sunday Morning	1970	$18
❏ SE-4798	Sweet Dreams	1972	$15
—With the Mike Curb Congregation			
❏ E-4513 [M]	The Best of Hank Williams, Jr.	1967	$25
❏ SE-4513 [S]	The Best of Hank Williams, Jr.	1967	$30
❏ SE-4936	The Last Love Song	1973	$15
❏ E-4260 [M]	Your Cheatin' Heart	1964	$25
❏ SE-4260 [S]	Your Cheatin' Heart	1964	$30
PAIR			
❏ PDL2-1164	I'm Walkin'	1987	$15
POLYDOR			
❏ 825091-1	14 Greatest Hits	1985	$10
❏ 833069-1	Blues My Name	1987	$10
❏ 833070-1	Eleven Roses	1987	$10
❏ 831575-1	Hank Williams, Jr., and Friends	1987	$15
❏ 811903-1	Hank Williams, Jr.'s Greatest Hits	1983	$10
❏ 811906-1	Hank Williams, Jr.'s Greatest Hits, Volume 2	1983	$10
❏ 811902-1	Live at Cobo Hall, Detroit	1983	$10
—Reissue			
❏ 835132-1	Standing in the Shadows	1988	$10
WARNER BROS.			
❏ R120612	America (The Way I See It)	1990	$25
—BMG Music Service edition (no regular vinyl release)			
❏ 25593	Born to Boogie	1987	$10
❏ 6E-194	Family Tradition	1983	$10
❏ 25267	Five-O	1985	$12
❏ 25834	Greatest Hits III	1989	$10
❏ 25328	Greatest Hits -- Volume 2	1985	$10
❏ 6E-278	Habits Old and New	1983	$10
❏ 25538	Hank "Live"	1987	$10
❏ 60193	Hank Williams, Jr.'s, Greatest Hits	1983	$10
❏ 60100	High Notes	1983	$10
❏ 26090	Lone Wolf	1990	$15
❏ 25088	Major Moves	1984	$12
❏ 23924	Man of Steel	1983	$12
❏ 25412	Montana Café	1986	$10
❏ 5E-538	One Night Stands	1983	$10
❏ BS2988	One Night Stands	1977	$15
❏ R160351	Pure Hank	1991	$25
—BMG Music Service edition (no regular vinyl release)			
❏ 6E-330	Rowdy	1983	$10
❏ 60223 [B]	Strong Stuff	1983	$12
❏ 25514	The Early Years	1984	$15
❏ PRO-A-2092 [DJ]	The Hank Williams, Jr., Interview	1983	$30
❏ 5E-539	The New South	1983	$10
❏ BS3127	The New South	1977	$15
❏ 5E-535	The Pressure Is On	1983	$10
❏ 6E-237	Whiskey Bent and Hell Bound	1983	$10
❏ 25725	Wild Streak	1988	$10

WILLIAMS, HANK
CANDELITE MUSIC

Number	Title	Yr	NM
❏ CMI-1951/2	The Golden Dream of Hank Williams	1976	$18
COUNTRY MUSIC FOUNDATION			
❏ CMF-006	Just Me and My Guitar	198?	$12
❏ CMF-007	The First Recordings	198?	$12
METRO			
❏ M-509 [M]	Hank Williams	1966	$25
❏ MS-509 [R]	Hank Williams	1966	$15
❏ M-547 [M]	Mr. and Mrs. Hank Williams	1966	$25

Number	Title	Yr	NM
❏ MS-547 [R]	Mr. and Mrs. Hank Williams	1966	$15
❏ M-602 [M]	The Immortal Hank Williams	1967	$25
❏ MS-602 [R]	The Immortal Hank Williams	1967	$15
MGM			
❏ E-4040 [M]	14 More of Hank Williams' Greatest Hits -- Vol. II	1962	$40
❏ SE-4040 [S]	14 More of Hank Williams' Greatest Hits -- Vol. II	1963	$18
—Black label			
❏ E-4140 [M]	14 More of Hank Williams' Greatest Hits (Volume 3)	1963	$30
❏ SE-4140 [S]	14 More of Hank Williams' Greatest Hits (Volume 3)	1963	$18
—Black label			
❏ SE-4140 [R]	14 More of Hank Williams' Greatest Hits (Volume 3)	1968	$15
—Blue and gold label			
❏ SE-4755-2	24 Greatest Hits	1971	$18
❏ MG-2-5401	24 Greatest Hits, Volume 2	197?	$18
❏ SE240-2	24 Karat Hits	1969	$30
❏ 3E-2 [M]	36 of His Greatest Hits	1957	$300
—Yellow labels			
❏ 3E-2 [M]	36 of His Greatest Hits	1960	$175
—Black labels			
❏ M3G-4954	Archetypes	1974	$15
❏ E-4138 [M]	Beyond the Sunset	1963	$30
❏ SE-4138 [R]	Beyond the Sunset	1963	$18
—Black label			
❏ SE-4651	Essential Hank Williams	1969	$15
❏ E-3928 [M]	First, Last and Always	1961	$40
—Reissue of E-3605			
❏ SE-3928 [R]	First, Last and Always	1968	$15
—Blue and gold label			
❏ MG-1-5019	Hank Williams, Sr., Live at the Grand Old Opry	1976	$15
❏ E-4529 [M]	Hank Williams and Strings, Volume 3	1968	$40
❏ SE-4529 [S]	Hank Williams and Strings, Volume 3	1968	$25
❏ E-203 [10]	Hank Williams as Luke the Drifter	1953	$500
❏ E-3267 [M]	Hank Williams as Luke the Drifter	1955	$150
—Yellow label			
❏ E-3267 [M]	Hank Williams as Luke the Drifter	1960	$40
—Black label			
❏ E-3927 [M]	Hank Williams as Luke the Drifter	1961	$40
—Reissue of E-3267			
❏ SE-3927 [R]	Hank Williams as Luke the Drifter	1968	$15
—Blue and gold label			
❏ E-3918 [M]	Hank Williams' Greatest Hits	1961	$40
❏ SE-3918 [R]	Hank Williams' Greatest Hits	1963	$25
—Black label			
❏ SE-3918 [R]	Hank Williams' Greatest Hits	1968	$15
—Blue and gold label			
❏ SE-4040 [R]	Hank Williams' Greatest Hits, Volume 2	1968	$15
—Blue and gold label			
❏ E-4576 [M]	Hank Williams in the Beginning	1968	$40
❏ SE-4576 [R]	Hank Williams in the Beginning	1968	$18
❏ E-3923 [M]	Hank Williams Lives Again	1961	$40
—Reissue of E-3272 with new title			

Number	Title	Yr	NM
❏ SE-3923 [R]	Hank Williams Lives Again	1968	$15
— Blue and gold label			
❏ E-3999 [M]	Hank Williams on Stage Recorded Live	1962	$40
— Note revised title			
❏ SE-3999 [R]	Hank Williams on Stage Recorded Live	1968	$15
— Blue and gold label			
❏ E-107 [10]	Hank Williams Sings	1952	$500
❏ 3E-4 [M]	Hank Williams Sings 36 More of His Greatest Hits	1958	$300
— Yellow labels			
❏ 3E-4 [M]	Hank Williams Sings 36 More of His Greatest Hits	1960	$175
— Black labels			
❏ E-242 [10]	Honky Tonkin'	1954	$500
❏ E-3412 [M]	Honky Tonkin'	1957	$150
— Yellow label			
❏ E-3412 [M]	Honky Tonkin'	1960	$50
— Black label			
❏ E-3926 [M]	I'm Blue Inside	1961	$40
— Reissue of E-3330			
❏ SE-3926 [R]	I'm Blue Inside	1968	$15
— Blue and gold label			
❏ E-243 [10]	I Saw the Light	1954	$500
❏ E-3331 [M]	I Saw the Light	1956	$300
— Yellow label; green cover			
❏ E-3331 [M]	I Saw the Light	1959	$150
— Yellow label; church on cover			
❏ E-3331 [M]	I Saw the Light	1960	$40
— Black label			
❏ SE-3331 [R]	I Saw the Light	1968	$15
— Blue and gold label			
❏ E-4481 [M]	I Won't Be Home No More	1967	$30
❏ SE-4481 [S]	I Won't Be Home No More	1967	$25
— Black label			
❏ SE-4481 [S]	I Won't Be Home No More	1968	$18
— Blue and gold label			
❏ E-4300 [M]	Kaw-Liga and Other Humorous Songs	1965	$30
❏ SE-4300 [R]	Kaw-Liga and Other Humorous Songs	1965	$18
— Black label			
❏ SE-4300 [R]	Kaw-Liga and Other Humorous Songs	1968	$15
— Blue and gold label			
❏ E-3924 [M]	Let Me Sing a Blue Song	1961	$40
— Reissue of E-3560			
❏ SE-3924 [R]	Let Me Sing a Blue Song	1968	$15
— Blue and gold label			
❏ SE-4680	Life to Legend	1970	$15
❏ E-4254 [M]	Lost Highway (and Other Folk Ballads)	1964	$40
❏ SE-4254 [R]	Lost Highway (and Other Folk Ballads)	1964	$25
— Black label			
❏ SE-4254 [R]	Lost Highway (and Other Folk Ballads)	1968	$15
— Blue and gold label			
❏ E-202 [10]	Memorial Album	1953	$500
❏ E-3272 [10]	Memorial Album	1955	$150
— Yellow label			
❏ E-3272 [M]	Memorial Album	1960	$40
— Black label			
❏ E-3272 [M]	Memorial Album	1968	$25
— Blue and gold label			
❏ E-168 [10]	Moanin' the Blues	1952	$500
❏ E-3330 [10]	Moanin' the Blues	1956	$150
— Yellow label			
❏ E-3330 [M]	Moanin' the Blues	1960	$40
— Black label			
❏ E-4429 [M]	More Hank Williams and Strings	1966	$25
❏ SE-4429 [S]	More Hank Williams and Strings	1966	$30
— Black label			
❏ SE-4429 [S]	More Hank Williams and Strings	1968	$18
— Blue and gold label			
❏ E-4380 [M]	Movin' on -- Luke the Drifter	1966	$30
❏ SE-4380 [R]	Movin' on -- Luke the Drifter	1968	$15
— Blue and gold label			
❏ ST-90884 [R]	Movin' on -- Luke the Drifter	1968	$18
— Capitol Record Club edition; blue and gold label			
❏ E-3999 [M]	On Stage! Hank Williams Recorded Live	1962	$75
❏ SE-3999 [R]	On Stage! Hank Williams Recorded Live	196?	$25
— Black label			
❏ E-4109 [M]	On Stage Volume II/Hank Williams	1963	$40
❏ SE-4109 [R]	On Stage Volume II/Hank Williams	1963	$25
— Black label			
❏ SE-4109 [R]	On Stage Volume II/Hank Williams	1968	$15
— Blue and gold label			
❏ E-291 [10]	Ramblin' Man	1954	$500
❏ E-3219 [M]	Ramblin' Man	1955	$250
— Yellow label			

Number	Title	Yr	NM
❏ E-3219 [M]	Ramblin' Man	1960	$40
— Black label			
❏ PRO-912 [DJ]	Reflections of Those Who Loved Him	1975	$300
— Promo-only box set			
❏ E-3560 [M]	Sing Me a Blue Song	1957	$150
— Yellow label			
❏ E-3560 [M]	Sing Me a Blue Song	1960	$50
— Black label			
❏ E-4267-4 [M]	The Hank Williams Story	1965	$75
❏ E-3605 [M]	The Immortal Hank Williams	1958	$150
— Yellow label			
❏ E-3605 [M]	The Immortal Hank Williams	1960	$40
— Black label			
❏ E-4377 [M]	The Legend Lives Anew -- Hank Williams with Strings	1966	$25
❏ SE-4377 [S]	The Legend Lives Anew -- Hank Williams with Strings	1966	$30
— Black label			
❏ SE-4377 [S]	The Legend Lives Anew -- Hank Williams with Strings	1968	$18
— Blue and gold label			
❏ ST-91115 [S]	The Legend Lives Anew -- Hank Williams with Strings	1968	$25
— Capitol Record Club edition; blue and gold label			
❏ E-3803 [M]	The Lonesome Sound of Hank Williams	1960	$40
❏ E-3955 [M]	The Spirit of Hank Williams	1961	$40
❏ SE-3955 [R]	The Spirit of Hank Williams	1968	$15
— Blue and gold label			
❏ E-3733 [M]	The Unforgettable Hank Williams	1959	$150
— Yellow label			
❏ E-3733 [M]	The Unforgettable Hank Williams	1960	$40
— Black label			
❏ SE-3733 [R]	The Unforgettable Hank Williams	1968	$15
— Blue and gold label			
❏ T-90511 [M]	The Very Best of Hank Williams	1965	$40
— Capitol Record Club edition			
❏ ST-90511 [R]	The Very Best of Hank Williams	1965	$25
— Capitol Record Club edition			
❏ E-4168 [M]	The Very Best of Hank Williams	1963	$30
❏ SE-4168 [R]	The Very Best of Hank Williams	1963	$18
— Black label			
❏ SE-4168 [R]	The Very Best of Hank Williams	1968	$15
— Blue and gold label			
❏ E-4227 [M]	The Very Best of Hank Williams, Volume 2	1964	$30
❏ SE-4227 [R]	The Very Best of Hank Williams, Volume 2	1964	$18
— Black label			
❏ SE-4227 [R]	The Very Best of Hank Williams, Volume 2	1968	$15
— Blue and gold label			
❏ E-3850 [M]	Wait for the Light to Shine	1960	$40
❏ SE-3850 [R]	Wait for the Light to Shine	1968	$15
— Blue and gold label			
❏ E-3925 [M]	Wanderin' Around	1961	$40
— Reissue of E-3219			
❏ SE-3925 [R]	Wanderin' Around	1968	$15
— Blue and gold label			

POLYDOR

Number	Title	Yr	NM
❏ 823293-1	24 Greatest Hits	1984	$15
❏ 823294-1	24 Greatest Hits, Volume 2	1984	$15
❏ 821233-1	40 Greatest Hits	1984	$18
❏ 831574-1	Beyond the Sunset	1987	$12
❏ 823291-1	Hank Williams' Greatest Hits	1984	$10
❏ 831634-1	Hey, Good Lookin'	1987	$12
❏ 825548-1	I Ain't Got Nothin' But Time	1985	$12
❏ 825557-1	I'm So Lonesome I Could Cry	1986	$12
❏ 833752-1	I Won't Be Home No More	1988	$12
❏ 833749-1	Let's Turn Back the Years	1988	$12
❏ 831633-1	Long Gone Lonesome Blues	1987	$12
❏ 825554-1	Lost Highway	1986	$12
❏ 825551-1	Lovesick Blues	1985	$12
❏ 825531-1	On the Air	1985	$12
❏ 823695-1	Rare Takes and Radio Cuts	1984	$12
❏ 823292-1	The Very Best of Hank Williams	1984	$10
❏ SE-4168	The Very Best of Hank Williams	1976	$10
— Reissue of MGM SE-4168			

TIME-LIFE

Number	Title	Yr	NM
❏ TLCW-01	Country and Western Classics	1981	$30
❏ STW-118	Country Music	1981	$12

WILLIAMS, HANK /ROY ACUFF

LAMB AND LION

Number	Title	Yr	NM
❏ LL-706	Hank Williams, Sr./Roy Acuff "Collector's Item!	197?	$40
— Sides 1-4 are reissues of Hank Williams; side 5-6 are Roy Acuff			

WILLIAMS, HERBIE
WORKSHOP JAZZ

Number	Title	Yr	NM
❏ WSJ-216 [M]	The Soul and Sound of Herbie Williams	1963	$75

WILLIAMS, JAMES
CONCORD JAZZ

Number	Title	Yr	NM
❏ CJ-104	Everything I Love	1980	$25
❏ CJ-140	Images (Of the Things to Come)	1981	$25
❏ CJ-192	The Arioso Touch	1982	$25

EMARCY

Number	Title	Yr	NM
❏ 834368-1	Magical Trio 2	1989	$30
❏ 832859-1	The Magical Trio	1988	$25

SUNNYSIDE

Number	Title	Yr	NM
❏ SSC-1007	Alter Ego	1985	$25
❏ SSC-1012	Progress Report	1986	$25

ZIM

Number	Title	Yr	NM
❏ 2005	Flying Colors	1977	$30

WILLIAMS, JASON D.
RCA

Number	Title	Yr	NM
❏ 9782-1-R	Tore Up	1989	$15

WILLIAMS, JESSICA
ADELPHI

Number	Title	Yr	NM
❏ 5005	Portraits	197?	$35
❏ 5003	The Portal of Antrim	1976	$35

BLACKHAWK

Number	Title	Yr	NM
❏ BKH-51301	Nothin' But the Truth	1986	$25

CLEAN CUTS

Number	Title	Yr	NM
❏ 703	Orgonomic Music	198?	$30
❏ 701	Rivers of Memory	1979	$30
❏ 706	Update	1982	$30

WILLIAMS, JOE
BLUEBIRD

Number	Title	Yr	NM
❏ 6464-1-RB	The Overwhelming Joe Williams	1988	$25

BLUE NOTE

Number	Title	Yr	NM
❏ BST-84355	Worth Waiting For	1970	$35

DELOS

Number	Title	Yr	NM
❏ DMS-4001	Nothin' But the Blues	1984	$30

FANTASY

Number	Title	Yr	NM
❏ F-9441	Joe Williams Live	1974	$30
❏ OJC-438	Joe Williams Live	1990	$25

FORUM

Number	Title	Yr	NM
❏ F-9033 [M]	That Kind of Woman	196?	$30
❏ SF-9033 [S]	That Kind of Woman	196?	$35

JASS

Number	Title	Yr	NM
❏ J-6	Chains of Love	198?	$25

PAUSA

Number	Title	Yr	NM
❏ PR9008	Worth Waiting For	1982	$25

RCA VICTOR

Number	Title	Yr	NM
❏ LPM-2762 [M]	Joe Williams at Newport '63	1963	$30
❏ LSP-2762 [S]	Joe Williams at Newport '63	1963	$30
❏ LPM-2713 [M]	Jump for Joy	1963	$30
❏ LSP-2713 [S]	Jump for Joy	1963	$30
❏ LPM-2879 [M]	Me and the Blues	1964	$30
❏ LSP-2879 [S]	Me and the Blues	1964	$30
❏ LPM-3461 [M]	The Exciting Joe Williams	1965	$25
❏ LSP-3461 [S]	The Exciting Joe Williams	1965	$30
❏ LPM-3433 [M]	The Song Is You	1965	$25
❏ LSP-3433 [S]	The Song Is You	1965	$30

REGENT

Number	Title	Yr	NM
❏ MG-6002 [M]	Everyday	1956	$50

ROULETTE

Number	Title	Yr	NM
❏ R-52005 [M]	A Man Ain't Supposed to Cry	1958	$30
❏ SR-52005 [S]	A Man Ain't Supposed to Cry	1958	$40
❏ SR-42016	A Man Ain't Supposed to Cry	1968	$35
❏ R-52071 [M]	Have a Good Time with Joe Williams	1961	$30
❏ SR-52071 [S]	Have a Good Time with Joe Williams	1961	$40
❏ R-52030 [M]	Joe Williams Sings About You!	1959	$30
❏ SR-52030 [S]	Joe Williams Sings About You!	1959	$40
❏ R-52105 [M]	New Kind of Love	1964	$30
❏ SR-52105 [S]	New Kind of Love	1964	$30
❏ R-52102 [M]	One Is a Lonesome Number	1963	$30
❏ SR-52102 [S]	One Is a Lonesome Number	1963	$30
❏ R-52066 [M]	Sentimental and Melancholy	1961	$30
❏ SR-52066 [S]	Sentimental and Melancholy	1961	$40
❏ R-52085 [M]	Swingin' Night at Birdland	1962	$30
❏ SR-52085 [S]	Swingin' Night at Birdland	1962	$30
❏ R-52039 [M]	That Kind of Woman	1960	$30
❏ SR-52039 [S]	That Kind of Woman	1960	$40
❏ R-52069 [M]	Together	1961	$30
❏ SR-52069 [S]	Together	1961	$40
— With Harry "Sweets" Edison			

SAVOY

Number	Title	Yr	NM
❏ MG-12216 [M]	Joe Williams Sings	196?	$35
— Reissue of Regent LP			

Number	Title	Yr	NM
SAVOY JAZZ			
☐ SJL-1140	Everyday I Have the Blues	198?	$25
SHEBA			
☐ 102	Heart and Soul	197?	$30
SOLID STATE			
☐ SM-17008 [M]	Presenting Joe Williams and the Jazz Orchestra	1967	$30
☐ SS-18008 [S]	Presenting Joe Williams and the Jazz Orchestra	1967	$25
☐ SS-18015 [S]	Something Old, New and Blue	1968	$25
TEMPONIC			
☐ 29561	With Love	197?	$35
VERVE			
☐ 833236-1	Every Night	1987	$25
☐ 837932-1	In Good Company	1989	$30

WILLIAMS, JOHN

Number	Title	Yr	NM
EMARCY			
☐ MG-26047 [10]	John Williams	1955	$250
☐ MG-36061 [M]	John Williams Trio	1956	$250

WILLIAMS, JOHN TOWNER

Number	Title	Yr	NM
BETHLEHEM			
☐ BCP-6025 [M]	World on a String	1958	$250

WILLIAMS, KEITH

Number	Title	Yr	NM
EDISON INTERNATIONAL			
☐ SDP-501 [S]	Big Band Jazz Themes	1960	$30
☐ 501 [M]	Big Band Jazz Themes	1960	$25
LIBERTY			
☐ LRP-3040 [M]	The Dazzling Sound	1957	$30

WILLIAMS, LARRY

Number	Title	Yr	NM
CHESS			
☐ LP-1457 [M]	Larry Williams	1961	$250
OKEH			
☐ OKM-12123 [M]	Larry Williams' Greatest Hits	1967	$30
☐ OKS-14123 [S]	Larry Williams' Greatest Hits	1967	$40
SPECIALTY			
☐ SP-7002	Bad Boy	1990	$25
☐ SP-2109 [M]	Here's Larry Williams	1959	$250

— Original pressing on thick vinyl with no copyright information on back cover

☐ SP-2109 [M]	Here's Larry Williams	198?	$12

— Reissue with thinner vinyl and copyright information on back

WILLIAMS, LAWTON

Number	Title	Yr	NM
MEGA			
☐ 1004	Between Truck Stops	1971	$15

WILLIAMS, LENNY

Number	Title	Yr	NM
ABC			
☐ AB-1023	Choosing You	1977	$12
☐ AA-1073	Spark of Love	1978	$12
MCA			
☐ 5147	Let's Do It Today	1980	$12
☐ 3155	Love Current	1979	$12
☐ 5253	Taking Chances	1982	$12
MOTOWN			
☐ M6-843	Rise Sleeping Beauty	1975	$15

WILLIAMS, LEONA

Number	Title	Yr	NM
HICKORY			
☐ LPS-151	That Williams Girl	1971	$18
☐ LPS-165	The Best of Leona Williams	1972	$18
MCA			
☐ 2212	San Quentin's First Lady	1976	$15
MERCURY			
☐ 822424-1	Someday When Things Are Good	1984	$10

WILLIAMS, LOIS

Number	Title	Yr	NM
STARDAY			
☐ SLP-448	A Girl Named Sam	1970	$25

WILLIAMS, LUCINDA

Number	Title	Yr	NM
FOLKWAYS			
☐ 31067	Happy Woman Blues	1980	$300

— As "Lucinda"

☐ 31066	Ramblin' on My Mind	1979	$300

— As "Lucinda"

LOST HIGHWAY			
☐ B0002368-01	Live @ the Fillmore	2005	$25

Number	Title	Yr	NM
☐ B0006398-01 [B]	West	2007	$18
☐ 088170255-1	World Without Tears	2003	$18
ROUGH TRADE			
☐ 66 [EP]	Passionate Kisses	1989	$12
SMITHSONIAN/FOLKWAYS			
☐ 40003	Happy Woman Blues	1990	$25

— Reissue

WILLIAMS, MARY LOU, AND CECIL TAYLOR

Number	Title	Yr	NM
PABLO LIVE			
☐ 2620108	Embraced	1978	$35

WILLIAMS, MARY LOU, AND DON BYAS

Number	Title	Yr	NM
GNP CRESCENDO			
☐ GNP-9030	Mary Lou Williams and Don Byas	197?	$25

WILLIAMS, MARY LOU, AND DON BYAS/BUCK CLAYTON AND ALIX COMBELLE

Number	Title	Yr	NM
STORYVILLE			
☐ STLP-906 [M]	Messin' 'Round in Montmarte	1956	$50

WILLIAMS, MARY LOU

Number	Title	Yr	NM
ASCH			
☐ ALP-345 [10]	Mary Lou Williams Trio	1950	$250
ATLANTIC			
☐ ALR-114 [10]	Piano Panorama, Volume 2	1951	$300
AUDIOPHILE			
☐ AP-8 [M]	Roll 'Em	1988	$25
CHIAROSCURO			
☐ 103	From the Heart	197?	$30
☐ 146	Live at the Cookery	197?	$30
CIRCLE			
☐ 412 [10]	Piano Contempo	1951	$120
CONCERT HALL JAZZ			
☐ 1007 [10]	A Keyboard History	1955	$75
CONTEMPORARY			
☐ C-2507 [10]	Piano '53	1953	$300
EMARCY			
☐ MG-26033 [10]	Mary Lou	1954	$250
FOLKWAYS			
☐ FS-2860 [M]	History of Jazz	197?	$30
☐ FS-32843 [R]	Mary Lou Williams	196?	$30
☐ FS-2843 [M]	Mary Lou Williams	196?	$40
☐ FP-32 [10]	Rehearsal -- Jazz Session/ Footnotes to Jazz, Vol. 3	1951	$120
☐ FJ-2966	The Asch Recordings 1944-1947	197?	$35
☐ FJ-32844	Zodiac Suite	196?	$30
GNP CRESCENDO			
☐ GNPS-9029	Mary Lou Williams in London	198?	$25
INNER CITY			
☐ IC-2043	Free Spirits	197?	$35
JAZZTONE			
☐ J-1206 [M]	A Keyboard History	1955	$50
KING			
☐ 295-85 [10]	Progressive Piano Stylings	1953	$175
MARY			
☐ 32843 [M]	Black Christ of the Andes	1964	$30
☐ 32843 [S]	Black Christ of the Andes	1964	$30
☐ 101	Black Christ of the Andes	197?	$35

— Reissue with new number

☐ 102	Mary Lou's Mass	197?	$35
☐ 282489 [M]	Music for Peace	1964	$30
☐ 282489 [S]	Music for Peace	1964	$30
☐ 103	Zoning	1974	$35

Number	Title	Yr	NM
PABLO			
☐ 2310819	My Mama Pinned a Rose	1978	$30
☐ 2405412	The Best of Mary Lou Williams	198?	$25
PABLO LIVE			
☐ 2308218	Solo Recital/Montreux Jazz Festival 1978	1979	$30
STEEPLECHASE			
☐ SCS-1043	Free Spirits	198?	$30
STINSON			
☐ SLP-29 [10]	Jazz Variation	1950	$175
☐ SLP-24 [M]	Mary Lou Williams	195?	$30
☐ SLP-24 [10]	Mary Lou Williams	1950	$175

WILLIAMS, MARY LOU/JUTTA HIPP

Number	Title	Yr	NM
SAVOY JAZZ			
☐ SJL-1202	First Ladies of Jazz	1990	$30

WILLIAMS, MARY LOU/RALPH BURNS

Number	Title	Yr	NM
JAZZTONE			
☐ J-1255 [M]	Composers -- Pianists	1956	$40

WILLIAMS, MASON

Number	Title	Yr	NM
AMERICAN GRAMAPHONE			
☐ AG-800	Classical Gas	1987	$12

— With Mannheim Steamroller

EVEREST			
☐ 3265	Listening Matter	1969	$15
FLYING FISH			
☐ FF-059	Fresh Fish	1978	$12
VEE JAY			
☐ VJ-1103 [M]	Them Poems and Things	1964	$25
☐ VJS-1103 [S]	Them Poems and Things	1964	$30
WARNER BROS.			
☐ WS1838	Hand Made	1970	$15
☐ WS1788	Music by Mason Williams	1969	$15
☐ WS1941	Sharepickers	1971	$15
☐ WS1776	The Mason Williams Ear Show	1968	$15
☐ WS1729 [S]	The Mason Williams Phonograph Record	1968	$15

— Green label with "W7" logo

☐ WS1729	The Mason Williams Phonograph Record	1979	$10

— White or tan label

☐ WS1729	The Mason Williams Phonograph Record	1973	$10

— Burbank" palm trees label

☐ WS1729	The Mason Williams Phonograph Record	1970	$12

— Green label with "WB" logo

☐ W1729 [M]	The Mason Williams Phonograph Record	1968	$30

— Mono is white label promo only

WILLIAMS, MAURICE, AND THE ZODIACS

Number	Title	Yr	NM
COLLECTABLES			
☐ COL-5021	The Best of Maurice Williams and the Zodiacs	198?	$12
HERALD			
☐ HLP-1014 [M]	Stay	1961	$500
RELIC			
☐ 5017	Greatest Hits	197?	$18
SNYDER			
☐ 5586 [M]	At the Beach	196?	$150
SPHERE SOUND			
☐ SR-7007 [M]	Stay	1965	$120

☐ SSR-7007 [R]	Stay	1965	$100

WILLIAMS, MEL

DIG

Number	Title	Yr	NM
LP-103 [M]	All Thru the Night	1956	$600

WILLIAMS, NORMAN

THERESA

Number	Title	Yr	NM
105	One for Bird	1980	$30
101	The Bishop	1979	$30
102	The Bishop's Bag	1979	$30

WILLIAMS, OTIS, AND HIS CHARMS

DELUXE

Number	Title	Yr	NM
570 [M]	Their All Time Hits	1957	$1000

KING

Number	Title	Yr	NM
570 [M]	Their All Time Hits	1957	$600
614 [M]	This Is Otis Williams and His Charms	1959	$400

STOP

Number	Title	Yr	NM
STLP-1022	Otis Williams and the Midnight Cowboys	1971	$30

WILLIAMS, PATRICK

ALLEGIANCE

Number	Title	Yr	NM
AV-443	Dreams and Themes	1985	$25

—Reissue of PCM album

CAPITOL

Number	Title	Yr	NM
ST-11242	Threshold	1974	$25

COLUMBIA

Number	Title	Yr	NM
JC36318	An American Concerto	1979	$25

PAUSA

Number	Title	Yr	NM
7060	Theme	1980	$25

PCM

Number	Title	Yr	NM
PAA1001	Dreams and Themes	1984	$30

SOUNDWINGS

Number	Title	Yr	NM
SW-2103	10th Avenue	1987	$25
SW-2107	Threshold	1988	$25

WILLIAMS, PAUL

A&M

Number	Title	Yr	NM
SP-3655	A Little Bit of Love	1974	$12
SP-4701	Classics	1977	$12
SP-3606	Here Comes Inspiration	1974	$12
SP-4327	Just an Old Fashioned Love Song	1971	$12
SP-3131	Just an Old Fashioned Love Song	198?	$10

—Budget-line reissue

Number	Title	Yr	NM
SP-4367	Life Goes On	1972	$12
SP-4550	Ordinary Fool	1975	$12

PORTRAIT

Number	Title	Yr	NM
JR35610	Windy Side	1979	$12

REPRISE

Number	Title	Yr	NM
RS6401	Someday Man	1970	$15

WILLIAMS, RICHARD

BARNABY

Number	Title	Yr	NM
BR-5014	New Horn in Town	197?	$25

CANDID

Number	Title	Yr	NM
CD-8003 [M]	New Horn in Town	1960	$40
CS-9003 [S]	New Horn in Town	1960	$50

WILLIAMS, ROBERT PETE

BLUESVILLE

Number	Title	Yr	NM
BVLP-1026 [M]	Free Again	1961	$150

—Blue label, silver print

Number	Title	Yr	NM
BVLP-1026 [M]	Free Again	1964	$30

—Blue label with trident logo

FOLK/LYRIC

Number	Title	Yr	NM
FL-109 [M]	Prison Blues	1960	$150

WILLIAMS, ROD

MUSE

Number	Title	Yr	NM
MR-5380	Hanging in the Balance	198?	$25

WILLIAMS, ROGER

BAINBRIDGE

Number	Title	Yr	NM
8002	Ivory Impact	1982	$15
6265	Somewhere in Time	1986	$12

HOLIDAY

Number	Title	Yr	NM
HDY1927	Golden Christmas	1981	$10

KAPP

Number	Title	Yr	NM
KLE-1 [M]	10th Anniversary/Limited Edition	1964	$25

—Reissue of Kapp 1088, 1130 and 1172 in one package

Number	Title	Yr	NM
SKLE-1 [S]	10th Anniversary/Limited Edition	1964	$30
KL-1406 [M]	Academy Award Winners	1964	$12
KS-3406 [S]	Academy Award Winners	1964	$15
KL-1483 [M]	Academy Award Winners, Vol. 2	1966	$12
KS-3483 [S]	Academy Award Winners, Vol. 2	1966	$15
KL-1063 [M]	Almost Paradise	1957	$18

—Maroon and silver (or blue and silver) label

Number	Title	Yr	NM
KL-1063 [M]	Almost Paradise	1962	$15

—Any later label variation

Number	Title	Yr	NM
KL-1172 [M]	Always	1960	$18

—Maroon and silver (or blue and silver) labels

Number	Title	Yr	NM
KL-1172 [M]	Always	1962	$15

—Any later label variation

Number	Title	Yr	NM
KS-3056 [S]	Always	1960	$25

—Maroon and silver (or blue and silver) labels

Number	Title	Yr	NM
KS-3056 [S]	Always	1962	$18

—Any later label variation

Number	Title	Yr	NM
KS-3549	Amore	1968	$15
KL-1012 [M]	Autumn Leaves	1956	$25

—Retitled version of above; maroon and silver (or blue and silver) label

Number	Title	Yr	NM
KL-1012 [M]	Autumn Leaves	1962	$15

—Any later label variation

Number	Title	Yr	NM
KL-1452 [M]	Autumn Leaves -- 1965	1965	$12
KS-3452 [S]	Autumn Leaves -- 1965	1965	$15
KL-1501 [M]	Born Free	1966	$12
KS-3501 [S]	Born Free	1966	$15
KL-3 [M]	By Special Request	196?	$15

—Columbia Record Club exclusive

Number	Title	Yr	NM
KL-4 [M]	By Special Request, Vol. 2	196?	$15

—Columbia Record Club exclusive

Number	Title	Yr	NM
KL-1164 [M]	Christmas Time	1959	$18

—Merry Christmas" silver, red and green label

Number	Title	Yr	NM
KL-1164 [M]	Christmas Time	1962	$15

—Any later label variation

Number	Title	Yr	NM
KS-3164 [S]	Christmas Time	196?	$15

—Reissue of KS-3048 (new cover, no gatefold)

Number	Title	Yr	NM
KS-3048 [S]	Christmas Time	1959	$25
KL-1305 [M]	Country Style	1963	$15
KS-3305 [S]	Country Style	1963	$18
KL-1031 [M]	Daydreams	1956	$18

—Maroon and silver (or blue and silver) label

Number	Title	Yr	NM
KL-1031 [M]	Daydreams	1962	$15

—Any later label variation

Number	Title	Yr	NM
KL-1395 [M]	Family Album of Hymns	1964	$12
KS-3395 [S]	Family Album of Hymns	1964	$15
KL-1336 [M]	For You	1963	$15
KS-3336 [S]	For You	1963	$18
KL-1260 [M]	Greatest Hits	1962	$15
KS-3260 [S]	Greatest Hits	1962	$18
KS-3595	Happy Heart	1969	$15
KL-1470 [M]	I'll Remember You	1966	$12
KS-3470 [S]	I'll Remember You	1966	$15
KL-1008 [M]	It's a Big, Wide, Wonderful World	1955	$30

—Maroon and silver (or blue and silver) labels

Number	Title	Yr	NM
KL-1008 [M]	It's a Big, Wide, Wonderful World	1962	$15

—Any later label variation

Number	Title	Yr	NM
KS-3645	Love Story	1971	$12
KS-3610	Love Theme from "Romeo and Juliet"	1969	$15
KS-3665	Love Theme from "The Godfather"	1972	$12
KL-1266 [M]	Maria	1962	$15
KS-3266 [S]	Maria	1962	$18
KL-1130 [M]	More Songs of the Fabulous Fifties	1959	$18

—Maroon and silver (or blue and silver) labels

Number	Title	Yr	NM
KL-1130 [M]	More Songs of the Fabulous Fifties	1962	$15

—Any later label variation

Number	Title	Yr	NM
KS-3013 [S]	More Songs of the Fabulous Fifties	1959	$25

—Maroon and silver (or blue and silver) labels

Number	Title	Yr	NM
KS-3013 [S]	More Songs of the Fabulous Fifties	1962	$18

—Any later label variation

Number	Title	Yr	NM
KS-3550	More Than a Miracle	1968	$15
KL-1290 [M]	Mr. Piano	1962	$15
KS-3290 [S]	Mr. Piano	1962	$18
KL-1112 [M]	Near You	1959	$18

—Maroon and silver (or blue and silver) labels

Number	Title	Yr	NM
KL-1112 [M]	Near You	1962	$15

—Any later label variation

Number	Title	Yr	NM
KS-3112 [S]	Near You	1959	$25

—Maroon and silver (or blue and silver) labels

Number	Title	Yr	NM
KS-3112 [S]	Near You	1962	$18

—Any later label variation

Number	Title	Yr	NM
KS-3565	Only for Lovers	1969	$15
KS-3671	Play Me	1972	$12
KL-1512 [M]	Roger!	1967	$12
KS-3512 [S]	Roger!	1967	$15
KL-1012 [M]	Roger Williams	1956	$30
KL-1530 [M]	Roger Williams/Golden Hits	1967	$15
KS-3530 [S]	Roger Williams/Golden Hits	1967	$15
KS-3638	Roger Williams/Golden Hits, Volume 2	1970	$15
KL-1222 [M]	Roger Williams Invites You to Dance	1961	$18
KS-3222 [S]	Roger Williams Invites You to Dance	1961	$25
KL-1062 [M]	Roger Williams Plays Beautiful Waltzes	1962	$15

—Any later label variation

Number	Title	Yr	NM
KL-1062 [M]	Roger Williams Plays Beautiful Waltzes	1957	$18

—Maroon and silver (or blue and silver) label

Number	Title	Yr	NM
KL-1042 [M]	Roger Williams Plays Christmas Songs	1956	$18

—Maroon and silver label; unbanded

Number	Title	Yr	NM
KL-1088 [M]	Roger Williams Plays Gershwin	1958	$18

—Maroon and silver (or blue and silver) labels

Number	Title	Yr	NM
KL-1088 [M]	Roger Williams Plays Gershwin	1962	$15

—Any later label variation

Number	Title	Yr	NM
KL-1414 [M]	Roger Williams Plays the Hits	1965	$12
KS-3414 [S]	Roger Williams Plays the Hits	1965	$15
KL-1040 [M]	Roger Williams Plays the Wonderful Music of the Masters	1956	$18

—Maroon and silver (or blue and silver) label

Number	Title	Yr	NM
KL-1040 [M]	Roger Williams Plays the Wonderful Music of the Masters	1962	$15

—Any later label variation

Number	Title	Yr	NM
KW-900 [M]	Roger Williams Showcase	196?	$15
SKW-900 [S]	Roger Williams Showcase	196?	$18
KXL-5005 [M]	Songs of the Fabulous Century	195?	$25

—Maroon and silver (or blue and silver) labels

Number	Title	Yr	NM
KXL-5005 [M]	Songs of the Fabulous Century	1962	$18

—Any later label variation

Number	Title	Yr	NM
KXS-5005 [S]	Songs of the Fabulous Century	1959	$30

—Maroon and silver (or blue and silver) labels

Number	Title	Yr	NM
KXS-5005 [S]	Songs of the Fabulous Century	1962	$25

—Any later label variation

Number	Title	Yr	NM
KL-1211 [M]	Songs of the Fabulous Century, Volume 1	1960	$15
KS-3211 [S]	Songs of the Fabulous Century, Volume 1	1960	$18
KL-1212 [M]	Songs of the Fabulous Century, Volume 2	1960	$15
KS-3212 [S]	Songs of the Fabulous Century, Volume 2	1960	$18
KXL-5000 [M]	Songs of the Fabulous Fifties	1957	$25

—Maroon and silver (or blue and silver) labels

Number	Title	Yr	NM
KXL-5000 [M]	Songs of the Fabulous Fifties	1962	$18

—Any later label variation

Number	Title	Yr	NM
KXS-5000 [S]	Songs of the Fabulous Fifties	1959	$30

—Maroon and silver (or blue and silver) labels

Number	Title	Yr	NM
KXS-5000 [S]	Songs of the Fabulous Fifties	1962	$25

—Any later label variation

Number	Title	Yr	NM
KL-1209 [M]	Songs of the Fabulous Fifties, Volume 1	1960	$15
KS-3209 [S]	Songs of the Fabulous Fifties, Volume 1	1960	$18
KL-1210 [M]	Songs of the Fabulous Fifties, Volume 2	1960	$15
KS-3210 [S]	Songs of the Fabulous Fifties, Volume 2	1960	$18
KXL-5003 [M]	Songs of the Fabulous Forties	1957	$25

—Maroon and silver (or blue and silver) labels

Number	Title	Yr	NM
KXL-5003 [M]	Songs of the Fabulous Forties	1962	$18

—Any later label variation

Number	Title	Yr	NM
KXS-5003 [S]	Songs of the Fabulous Forties	1959	$30

—Maroon and silver (or blue and silver) labels

Number	Title	Yr	NM
KXS-5003 [S]	Songs of the Fabulous Forties	1962	$25

—Any later label variation

Number	Title	Yr	NM
KL-1207 [M]	Songs of the Fabulous Forties, Volume 1	1960	$15
KS-3207 [S]	Songs of the Fabulous Forties, Volume 1	1960	$18
KL-1208 [M]	Songs of the Fabulous Forties, Volume 2	1960	$15
KS-3208 [S]	Songs of the Fabulous Forties, Volume 2	1960	$18
KL-1251 [M]	Songs of the Soaring '60s	1961	$18
KS-3251 [S]	Songs of the Soaring '60s	1961	$25
KS-3650	Summer of '42	1971	$12
KL-1434 [M]	Summer Wind	1965	$12
KS-3434 [S]	Summer Wind	1965	$15
KL-1217 [M]	Temptation	1960	$18

—Maroon and silver (or blue and silver) labels

Number	Title	Yr	NM
KL-1217 [M]	Temptation	1962	$15

—Any later label variation

Number	Title	Yr	NM
KS-3217 [S]	Temptation	1960	$25
KL-1003 [M]	The Boy Next Door	1955	$30

—Maroon and silver (or blue and silver) labels

Number	Title	Yr	NM
KL-1003 [M]	The Boy Next Door	1962	$15

—Any later label variation

Number	Title	Yr	NM
KS-3629	Themes from Great Movies	1970	$15
KL-1354 [M]	The Solid Gold Steinway	1964	$15
KS-3354 [S]	The Solid Gold Steinway	1964	$18
KL-1081 [M]	Till	1962	$15

—Any later label variation

Number	Title	Yr	NM
KL-1081 [M]	Till	1958	$18

—Maroon and silver (or blue and silver) label

Number	Title	Yr	NM
K-1081-S [S]	Till	1959	$25

Number	Title	Yr	NM

Number	Title	Yr	NM
—Maroon and silver (or blue and silver) labels			
❏ KS-1081 [S]	Till	1962	$18
—Any later label variation			
❏ KXL-5008 [M]	Tonight! Roger Williams at Town Hall	196?	$25
❏ KXS-5008 [S]	Tonight! Roger Williams at Town Hall	196?	$30
❏ KS-3000 [S]	Waltzes in Stereo	1959	$25
—Maroon and silver (or blue and silver) labels			
❏ KS-3000 [S]	Waltzes in Stereo	1962	$18
—Any later label variation			
❏ KL-1147 [M]	With These Hands	1959	$18
—Maroon and silver (or blue and silver) labels			
❏ KL-1147 [M]	With These Hands	1962	$15
—Any later label variation			
❏ KS-3030 [S]	With These Hands	1959	$25
—Maroon and silver (or blue and silver) labels			
❏ KS-3030 [S]	With These Hands	1962	$18
—Any later label variation			
❏ KL-1244 [M]	Yellow Bird	1961	$18
❏ KS-3244 [S]	Yellow Bird	1961	$25
MCA			
❏ 20202	Autumn Leaves	198?	$10
—Reissue of Kapp material			
❏ 15005	Christmas Time	197?	$10
—Reissue of Kapp material			
❏ 2279	Evergreen	1977	$12
❏ 539	Family Album of Hymns	1975	$10
—Reissue of Kapp 3395			
❏ 63	Greatest Hits	1973	$10
—Reissue of Kapp 3260			
❏ 438	I Honestly Love You	1974	$12
❏ 324	Last Tango in Paris	1973	$12
❏ 378	Live	1973	$12
❏ 2237	Nadia's Theme	1976	$12
❏ 76	Play Me	1973	$10
—Reissue of Kapp 3671			
❏ 64	Roger Williams/Golden Hits	1973	$10
—Reissue of Kapp 3530			
❏ 68	Roger Williams/Golden Hits, Volume 2	1973	$10
—Reissue of Kapp 3638			
❏ 71	Somewhere My Love	1973	$10
—Retitled reissue of unknown Kapp LP			
❏ 542	Somewhere My Love	1975	$10
—Reissue of MCA 71			
❏ 4106	The Best of Roger Williams	197?	$15
❏ 403	The Way We Were	1974	$12
❏ 5574	To Amadeus With Love	1985	$12
❏ 2175	Virtuoso	1975	$12
PICKWICK			
❏ PTP-2086	Roger Williams at the Piano	197?	$15
❏ SPC-3367	Spanish Eyes	197?	$10
❏ SPC-3511	Sunrise, Sunset	197?	$10
VOCALION			
❏ VL73918	Moments to Remember	1970	$12

WILLIAMS, TEX

Number	Title	Yr	NM
BOONE			
❏ LP-1210 [M]	The Two Sides of Tex Williams	1966	$25
❏ LSP-1210 [S]	The Two Sides of Tex Williams	1966	$30
CAPITOL			
❏ T1463 [M]	Smoke! Smoke! Smoke!	1960	$30
❏ ST1463 [S]	Smoke! Smoke! Smoke!	1960	$40
DECCA			
❏ DL4295 [M]	Country Music Time	1962	$25
❏ DL74295 [S]	Country Music Time	1962	$30
❏ DL5565 [10]	Dance-O-Rama #5	1955	$300
IMPERIAL			
❏ LP-9309 [M]	The Voice of Authority	1966	$25
❏ LP-12309 [S]	The Voice of Authority	1966	$30
LIBERTY			
❏ LRP-3304 [M]	Tex Williams in Las Vegas	1963	$25
❏ LST-7304 [S]	Tex Williams in Las Vegas	1963	$30
MONUMENT			
❏ Z30909	A Man Called Tex	1971	$25
RCA CAMDEN			
❏ CAL-363 [M]	Tex Williams' Best	1958	$30

WILLIAMS, TONY
Also see THE PLATTERS.

Number	Title	Yr	NM
MERCURY			
❏ MG-20454 [M]	A Girl Is a Girl Is a Girl	1959	$50
❏ SR-60138 [S]	A Girl Is a Girl Is a Girl	1959	$75
PHILIPS			
❏ PHM200051 [M]	The Magic Touch of Tony	1962	$30
❏ PHS600051 [S]	The Magic Touch of Tony	1962	$30
REPRISE			
❏ R-6006 [M]	His Greatest Hits	1961	$30
❏ R9-6006 [S]	His Greatest Hits	1961	$30

WILLIAMS, TONY (2)
Drummer. Not to be confused with the Tony Williams who was one of the lead voices in the R&B group The Platters in the 1950s and early 1960s.

Number	Title	Yr	NM
BLUE NOTE			
❏ BT-48494	Angel Street	1988	$30
❏ BT-85138	Civilization	1987	$30
❏ BT-85119	Foreign Intrigue	198?	$30
❏ BLP-4180 [M]	Life Time	1964	$75
❏ BST-84180 [S]	Life Time	1964	$30
—With "New York, USA" address on label			
❏ BST-84180 [S]	Life Time	1967	$35
—With "A Division of Liberty Records" on label			
❏ B1-93170	Native Heart	1990	$30
❏ BLP-4216 [M]	Spring	1965	$75
❏ BST-84216 [S]	Spring	1965	$30
—With "New York, USA" address on label			
❏ BST-84216 [S]	Spring	1967	$35
—With "A Division of Liberty Records" on label			
❏ BST-84216 [S]	Spring	1985	$25
—The Finest in Jazz Since 1939" reissue			
COLUMBIA			
❏ PC33836	Believe It	1975	$25
❏ HC45705	Joy of Flying	198?	$50
—Half-speed mastered edition			
❏ JC35705	Joy of Flying	1979	$25
❏ PC34263	Million Dollar Legs	1976	$25
❏ JC36397	The Best of Tony Williams	1980	$25
POLYDOR			
❏ PD-4065	Ego	197?	$30
❏ 25-3001	Emergency	1969	$50
❏ PD-4017	Emergency, Vol. 1	197?	$30
❏ PD-5040	The Old Bum's Rush	1973	$30
❏ PD-4021	Turn It Over	197?	$30
VERVE			
❏ VE-2-2541	Once in a Lifetime	198?	$30

WILLIAMS, VALDO

Number	Title	Yr	NM
SAVOY			
❏ MG-12188 [M]	New Advanced Jazz	1967	$30

WILLIAMS, WENDY O.

Number	Title	Yr	NM
PASSPORT			
❏ PB-6034	W.O.W.	1984	$15
PROFILE			
❏ PAL1230	Maggots: The Record	1987	$18

WILLIAMSON, CLAUDE

Number	Title	Yr	NM
BETHLEHEM			
❏ BCP-54 [M]	Claude Williamson	1956	$250
❏ BCP-69 [M]	'Round Midnight	1957	$300
CAPITOL			
❏ H6502 [10]	Claude Williamson	1954	$250
❏ H6511 [10]	Keys West	1955	$250
❏ T6511 [M]	Keys West	1956	$175
—Turquoise label			
CONTRACT			
❏ 15003 [M]	Theatre Party	196?	$30
❏ 15001 [M]	The Fabulous Claude Williamson Trio	196?	$30
CRITERION			
❏ 601 [M]	Claude Williamson Mulls the Mulligan Scene	1958	$100
DISCOVERY			
❏ 862	La Fiesta	198?	$25
INTERPLAY			
❏ 7708	Holography	1977	$30
❏ 7727	La Fiesta	1979	$30
❏ 7717	New Departure	1978	$30

WILLIAMSON, SONNY BOY (1)

Number	Title	Yr	NM
BLUES CLASSICS			
❏ 3	Blues Classics by Sonny Boy Williamson	196?	$30
❏ 20	Blues Classics by Sonny Boy Williamson, Vol. 2	196?	$30
❏ BC24	Blues Classics by Sonny Boy Williamson, Volume 3	196?	$30

WILLIAMSON, SONNY BOY (2), AND THE YARDBIRDS

Number	Title	Yr	NM
MERCURY			
❏ SR-61271 [R]	Eric Clapton and the Yardbirds Live with Sonny Boy Williamson	1970	$25
—Reissue			
❏ MG-21071 [M]	Sonny Boy Williamson and the Yardbirds	1965	$150
❏ SR-61071 [R]	Sonny Boy Williamson and the Yardbirds	1965	$50
—First cover with a picture of the bluesman and the band			
❏ SR-61071 [R]	Sonny Boy Williamson and the Yardbirds	196?	$30
—Later cover with cartoon artwork on the cover			

WILLIAMSON, SONNY BOY (2)

Number	Title	Yr	NM
ALLIGATOR			
❏ AL-4787	Keep It To Ourselves	1990	$15
ARHOOLIE			
❏ 2020 [B]	King Biscuit Time	197?	$15
CHECKER			
❏ LP-1437 [M]	Down and Out Blues	1959	$350
CHESS			
❏ LPS-1536	Bummer Road	1969	$30
❏ CH-9257	Down and Out Blues	1988	$12
❏ LP-1509 [M]	More Real Folk Blues	1966	$100
❏ CH-9277	More Real Folk Blues	1988	$12
❏ CHV-417	One Way Out	1975	$18
❏ CH-9116	One Way Out	198?	$12
❏ 2ACMB-206	Sonny Boy Williamson	1976	$25
—Reissue of 50027			
❏ LP-1503 [M]	The Real Folk Blues	1966	$100
❏ CH-9272	The Real Folk Blues	1988	$12
❏ 2CH-50027	This Is My Story	1972	$30
GNP CRESCENDO			
❏ GNPS-10003	Sonny Boy Williamson in Chicago	198?	$12
STORYVILLE			
❏ 4016	A Portrait in Blues	197?	$15
❏ 4062	The Blues of Sonny Boy Williamson	197?	$15

WILLIAMSON, STU

Number	Title	Yr	NM
BETHLEHEM			
❏ BCP-55 [M]	Stu Williamson	1956	$300
❏ BCP-1024 [10]	Stu Williamson Plays	1955	$300
❏ BCP-31 [M]	Stu Williamson Plays	1955	$300

WILLING, FOY, AND THE RIDERS OF THE PURPLE SAGE

Number	Title	Yr	NM
CROWN			
❏ CLP-5306 [M]	Cool Water	196?	$15
❏ CST-582 [S]	Country & Western Favorites	196?	$12
CUSTOM			
❏ CS1017	Cool, Cool Water	197?	$12
JUBILEE			
❏ JL-5028 [M]	The New Sound of American Folk	1962	$25
❏ JLS-5028 [S]	The New Sound of American Folk	1962	$30
ROULETTE			
❏ R-25035 [M]	Cowboy	1958	$40
ROYALE			
❏ 6032 [10]	The Riders of the Purple Sage	1952	$150
VARSITY			
❏ 6032 [10]	The Riders of the Purple Sage	1950	$120

WILLIS, CHUCK

Number	Title	Yr	NM
ATLANTIC			
❏ 8079 [M]	I Remember Chuck Willis	1963	$175
❏ SD8079 [P]	I Remember Chuck Willis	1963	$250
❏ 8018 [M]	The King of the Stroll	1958	$300
—Black label			
❏ 8018 [M]	The King of the Stroll	1960	$175
—Purple and orange label			
EPIC			
❏ LN3728 [M]	A Tribute to Chuck Willis	1960	$300
❏ LN3425 [M]	Chuck Willis Wails the Blues	1958	$500

WILLIS, LARRY

Number	Title	Yr	NM
GROOVE MERCHANT			
❏ 514	Inenr Crisis	197?	$35

WILLIS, PETE

Number	Title	Yr	NM
CIRCLE			
❏ C-45	The One and Only Pete Willis	1982	$25
PROGRESSIVE			
❏ PRO-7013	The One and Only Pete Willis	198?	$25

WILLIS BROTHERS, THE

Number	Title	Yr	NM
STARDAY			
❏ SLP-403 [M]	Bob	1967	$30
❏ SLP-442	Bummin' Around	1969	$30
❏ SLP-229 [M]	Code of the West	1963	$50
❏ SLP-472	For the Good Times	1971	$25
❏ SLP-323 [M]	Give Me 40 Acres	1965	$40
❏ SLP-387 [M]	Goin' to Town	1966	$30
❏ SLP-428	Hey, Mister Truck Driver	1968	$30
❏ SLP-306 [M]	Let's Hit the Road	1965	$40

Number	Title	Yr	NM

Number	Title	Yr	NM
□ SLP-353 [M]	Road Stop Juke Box Hits	1966	$30
□ SLP-466	The Best of the Willis Brothers	1970	$25
□ SLP-369 [M]	The Wild Side of Life	1966	$30
□ SLP-163 [M]	The Willis Brothers in Action	1962	$75

WILLOUGHBY, LARRY
ATLANTIC AMERICA
□ 90112	Building Bridges	1983	$12

WILLS, BOB
ANTONES
□ 6000 [10]	Old Time Favorites	195?	$500

—Fan club release
□ 6010 [10]	Old Time Favorites	195?	$500

—Fan club release
CAPITOL
□ SKBB-11550	Bob Wills and His Texas Playboys in Concert	1976	$25

COLUMBIA
□ KG32416	Anthology	1973	$25
□ CL9003 [10]	Bob Wills Round-Up	1949	$300

DECCA
□ DL8727 [M]	Bob Wills and His Texas Playboys	1957	$175

—Black label, silver print
□ DL8727 [M]	Bob Wills and His Texas Playboys	1961	$40

—Black label with color bars
□ DL78727 [R]	Bob Wills and His Texas Playboys	196?	$25
□ DL5562 [10]	Dance-O-Rama #2	1955	$300

DELTA
□ DLP-1149	Bob Wills and His Texas Playboys On Stage	1982	$12

HARMONY
□ HL7036 [M]	Bob Wills Special	1957	$40

—Maroon label
□ HL7036 [M]	Bob Wills Special	196?	$25

—Black label
□ HL7304 [M]	The Best of Bob Wills	1963	$30
□ HL7345 [M]	The Great Bob Wills	1965	$25

KAPP
□ KS-3639	Bob Wills in Person	1970	$25
□ KL-1506 [M]	From the Heart of Texas	1966	$25
□ KS-3506 [S]	From the Heart of Texas	1966	$30
□ KL-1542 [M]	Here's That Man Again	1968	$50

—Mono is white label promo only; in stereo cover with "Mono" sticker
□ KS-3542 [S]	Here's That Man Again	1968	$30
□ KL-1523 [M]	King of Western Swing	1967	$30
□ KS-3523 [S]	King of Western Swing	1967	$30
□ KS-3641	The Best of Bob Wills	1971	$25
□ KS-3601	The Greatest String Band Hits	1969	$25
□ KS-3587	The Living Legend	1969	$25
□ KS-3569	Time Changes Everything	1969	$25

LIBERTY
□ LRP-3303 [M]	Bob Wills Sings and Plays	1963	$30
□ LST-7303 [S]	Bob Wills Sings and Plays	1963	$40
□ LRP-3182 [M]	Living Legend	1961	$30
□ LST-7182 [S]	Living Legend	1961	$40
□ LRP-3194 [M]	Mr. Words and Mr. Music	1961	$30
□ LST-7194 [S]	Mr. Words and Mr. Music	1961	$40
□ LRP-3173 [M]	Together Again	1960	$30
□ LST-7173 [S]	Together Again	1960	$40

LONGHORN
□ LP-001 [M]	My Keepsake Album	1965	$100

MGM
□ GAS-141	A Tribute (Golden Archive Series)	1971	$30
□ E-91 [10]	Ranch House Favorites	1951	$300
□ E-3352 [M]	Ranch House Favorites	1956	$175

STARDAY
□ SLP-375 [M]	San Antonio Rose	1965	$40

TIME-LIFE
□ STW-119	Country Music	1981	$12

UNITED ARTISTS
□ LST-7303 [S]	Bob Wills Sings and Plays	1978	$20

—Reissue of Liberty 7303 on "sunrise" label; tan label variations may exist but are unconfirmed
□ UA-LA216-J [B]	For the Last Time	1974	$40

—Box set with booklet
□ UAS-9962	Legendary Masters	1971	$30

VOCALION
□ VL3735 [M]	Western Swing Band	1965	$25

WILLS, DAVID
EPIC
□ KE33353	Barrooms to Bedrooms	1975	$15
□ KE33548	Everybody's Country	1975	$15

RCA VICTOR
□ MHL1-8516 [EP]	New Beginnings	1984	$10

WILLS, JOHNNIE LEE
FLYING FISH
□ FF-069	Reunion	1978	$15

ROUNDER
□ 1027 [B]	Tulsa Swing	1978	$15

SIMS
□ LP-108 [M]	Johnny Lee Wills at the Tulsa Stampede	1963	$30
□ LPS-108 [S]	Johnny Lee Wills at the Tulsa Stampede	1963	$50
□ LP-101 [M]	Where There's a Wills, There's a Way	1962	$40
□ LPS-101 [S]	Where There's a Wills, There's a Way	1962	$75

WILMER AND THE DUKES
APHRODISIAC
□ 6001 [B]	Wilmer and the Dukes	1969	$30

WILSON, AL
PLAYBOY
□ PB410	I've Got a Feeling	1976	$15
□ JZ34744	I've Got a Feeling	1977	$12

—Reissue of 410
ROCKY ROAD
□ 3700 [B]	La La Peace Song	1974	$18
□ RR-3601	Show and Tell	1973	$18
□ RR-3600	Weighing In	1973	$18

SOUL CITY
□ SCS-92006	Searching for the Dolphins	1969	$30

WILSON, BRIAN
Also see THE BEACH BOYS.
ARISTA
□ 82876-70300-1	What I Really Want for Christmas	2005	$15

RHINO
□ RI-76582	Brian Wilson Presents Smile	2004	$30
□ RI-76471	Gettin' In Over My Head	2004	$25

SIRE
□ 25669	Brian Wilson	1988	$12
□ PRO-A-3248 [DJ]	Words and Music	1988	$30

—Promo-only music and interview
WILSON, CARL
Also see THE BEACH BOYS.
CARIBOU
□ NJZ37010	Carl Wilson	1981	$25
□ ARZ37970	Youngblood	1982	$25

WILSON, CASSANDRA
JMT
□ 834419-1	Blue Skies	1988	$25
□ 834412-1	Days Aweigh	1987	$25
□ 860004-1	Point of View	1986	$35

—Original edition
□ 834404-1	Point of View	1987	$25

WILSON, CLIVE
NEW ORLEANS
□ NOR-7210	Clive Wilson Plays New Orleans Jazz	1986	$25

WILSON, DENNIS
Also see THE BEACH BOYS.

CARIBOU

Number	Title	Yr	NM
□ PZ34354 [B]	Pacific Ocean Blue	1977	$30

WILSON, FLIP
ATLANTIC
□ 8149 [M]	Cowboys and Colored People	1967	$30
□ SD8149 [S]	Cowboys and Colored People	1967	$18

—Green and blue label
□ SD8149 [S]	Cowboys and Colored People	1969	$15

—Red and green label
□ SD8179	You Devil You	1968	$18

—Green and blue label
□ SD8179	You Devil You	1969	$15

—Red and green label
IMPERIAL
□ LP-9155 [M]	Flippin'	1961	$30

LITTLE DAVID
□ LD1001 [M]	Geraldine/Don't Fight the Feeling	1972	$30

—White label promo only; sticker on cover says "Promotional DJ Copy Monaural Not for Sale
□ LD1001 [S]	Geraldine/Don't Fight the Feeling	1972	$15
□ LD1000	The Devil Made Me Buy This Dress	1970	$15
□ LD2000	The Flip Wilson Show	1970	$15

MINIT
□ 24012	Flippin'	1968	$18

—Reissue of Imperial LP
SCEPTER
□ S-520	Flip Wilson's Pot Luck	1964	$25

SPRINGBOARD
□ SPB-4004	Funny and Live at the Village Gate	1972	$15

—Reissue of Scepter LP
SUNSET
□ SUS-5297	Flipped Out	1970	$15

—Reissue of Minit LP
WILSON, GERALD
AUDIO LAB
□ AL-1538 [M]	Big Band Modern	1959	$175

DISCOVERY
□ 872	Corcovado	1983	$25
□ 833	Lomelin	1981	$25

FEDERAL
□ 295-93 [10]	Gerald Wilson	1953	$300

PACIFIC JAZZ
□ ST-20135 [S]	California Soul	1969	$35
□ ST-20160 [S]	Eternal Equinox	1969	$35
□ ST-20132 [S]	Everywhere	1968	$35
□ PJ-10099 [M]	Feelin' Kinda Blue	1964	$35
□ ST-20099 [S]	Feelin' Kinda Blue	1966	$25
□ LN-10101	Feelin' Kinda Blue	1981	$20

—Budget-line reissue
□ PJ-88 [M]	Gerald Wilson on Stage	1964	$30
□ ST-88 [S]	Gerald Wilson on Stage	1964	$30
□ LN-10100	Gerald Wilson on Stage	1981	$20

—Budget-line reissue
□ PJ-10111 [M]	Golden Sword	1966	$35
□ ST-20111 [S]	Golden Sword	1966	$25
□ PJ-10118 [M]	Live and Swinging	1967	$25
□ ST-20118 [S]	Live and Swinging	1967	$35
□ PJ-61 [M]	Moment of Truth	1962	$30
□ ST-61 [S]	Moment of Truth	1962	$30
□ LN-10098	Moment of Truth	1981	$20

—Budget-line reissue
□ PJ-80 [M]	Portraits	1964	$30

Number	Title	Yr	NM
❑ ST-80 [S]	Portraits	1964	$30
❑ ST-20174	The Best of Gerald Wilson	1970	$35
❑ PJ-LA889-H	The Best of the Gerald Wilson Orchestra	1978	$25
❑ PJ-34 [M]	You Better Believe It	1961	$75
❑ ST-34 [S]	You Better Believe It	1961	$75
❑ LN-10097	You Better Believe It	1981	$20
—Budget-line reissue			

TREND

❑ TR-537	Calafia	1985	$30

WILSON, GLENN

CADENCE JAZZ

❑ CJR-1023	Impasse	198?	$25

SUNNYSIDE

❑ SSC-1030	Elusive	1988	$25

WILSON, J. FRANK, AND THE CAVALIERS

JOSIE

❑ JM-4006 [M]	Last Kiss	1964	$85
❑ JS-4006 [S]	Last Kiss	1964	$150

WILSON, JACK

ATLANTIC

❑ 1406 [M]	Jack Wilson Quartet	1963	$50
❑ SD1406 [S]	Jack Wilson Quartet	1963	$50
❑ 1427 [M]	The Two Sides of Jack Wilson	1964	$30
❑ SD1427 [S]	The Two Sides of Jack Wilson	1964	$40

BLUE NOTE

❑ BST-84270 [S]	Easterly Winds	1968	$25
— With "A Division of Liberty Records" on label			
❑ BLP-4251 [M]	Something Personal	1967	$100
❑ BST-84251 [S]	Something Personal	1967	$30
— With "New York, USA" address on label			
❑ BST-84251 [S]	Something Personal	1967	$25
— With "A Division of Liberty Records" on label			
❑ BST-84328 [S]	Song for My Daughter	1969	$25
— With "A Division of Liberty Records" on label			

DISCOVERY

❑ 872	Corcovado	198?	$25
❑ 777	Innovations	1977	$35
❑ 805	Margo's Theme	1979	$30

VAULT

❑ LP-9001 [M]	Brazilian Mancini	1964	$30
❑ LPS-9001 [S]	Brazilian Mancini	1964	$30
❑ LP-9008 [M]	Jazz Organs	1965	$30
❑ LPS-9008 [S]	Jazz Organs	1965	$30
❑ LP-9002 [M]	Ramblin'	1964	$30
❑ LPS-9002 [S]	Ramblin'	1964	$30

WILSON, JACKIE

BRUNSWICK

❑ BL54059 [M]	A Woman, a Lover, a Friend	1961	$50
—All-black label			
❑ BL754059 [S]	A Woman, a Lover, a Friend	1961	$100
—All-black label			
❑ BL54059 [M]	A Woman, a Lover, a Friend	1964	$25
— Black label with color bars			
❑ BL754059 [S]	A Woman, a Lover, a Friend	1964	$30
— Black label with color bars			
❑ BL54110 [M]	Baby Workout	1963	$50
—All-black label			
❑ BL754110 [S]	Baby Workout	1963	$100
—All-black label			
❑ BL54110 [M]	Baby Workout	1963	$25
— Black label with color bars			
❑ BL754110 [S]	Baby Workout	1963	$30
— Black label with color bars			
❑ BL754185 [B]	Beautiful Day	1972	$18
❑ BL54105 [M]	Body and Soul	1962	$50
—All-black label			
❑ BL754105 [S]	Body and Soul	1962	$100
—All-black label			
❑ BL54105 [M]	Body and Soul	1964	$25
— Black label with color bars			
❑ BL754105 [S]	Body and Soul	1964	$30
— Black label with color bars			
❑ BL54101 [M]	By Special Request	1961	$50
—All-black label			
❑ BL754101 [S]	By Special Request	1961	$100
—All-black label			
❑ BL54101 [M]	By Special Request	1964	$25
— Black label with color bars			
❑ BL754101 [S]	By Special Request	1964	$30
— Black label with color bars			
❑ BL754154	Do Your Thing	1969	$25
❑ BL54042 [M]	He's So Fine	1959	$120
—All-black label			

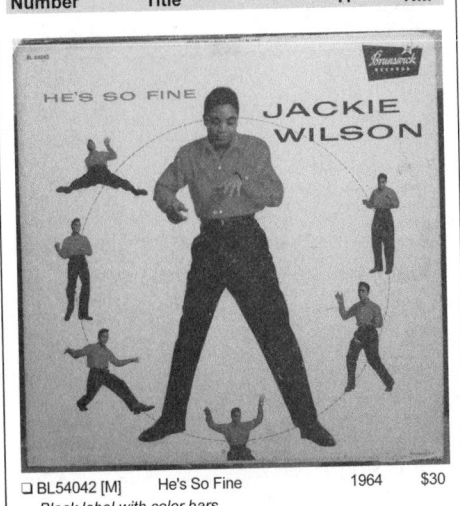

❑ BL54042 [M]	He's So Fine	1964	$30
— Black label with color bars			
❑ BL54130 [M]	Higher and Higher	1967	$30
❑ BL754130 [S]	Higher and Higher	1967	$30
❑ BL754138 [S]	I Get the Sweetest Feeling	1968	$25
❑ BL54138 [M]	I Get the Sweetest Feeling	1968	$175
— Yellow label promo only; "Monaural" sticker over the word "Stereo" on cover			
❑ BL754158	It's All a Part of Love	1970	$25
❑ BL54055 [M]	Jackie Sings the Blues	1960	$175
—All-black label			
❑ BL754055 [S]	Jackie Sings the Blues	1960	$250
—All-black label			
❑ BL54055 [M]	Jackie Sings the Blues	1964	$25
— Black label with color bars			
❑ BL754055 [S]	Jackie Sings the Blues	1964	$30
— Black label with color bars			
❑ BL54108 [M]	Jackie Wilson at the Copa	1962	$50
—All-black label			
❑ BL754108 [S]	Jackie Wilson at the Copa	1962	$100
—All-black label			
❑ BL54108 [M]	Jackie Wilson at the Copa	1964	$25
— Black label with color bars			
❑ BL754108 [S]	Jackie Wilson at the Copa	1964	$30
— Black label with color bars			
❑ BL754140	Jackie Wilson's Greatest Hits	1969	$25
❑ BL54045 [M]	Lonely Teardrops	1959	$175
—All-black label			
❑ BL54045 [M]	Lonely Teardrops	1964	$30
— Black label with color bars			
❑ BL54134 [M]	Manufacturers of Soul	1968	$50
— With Count Basie			
❑ BL754134 [S]	Manufacturers of Soul	1968	$25
— With Count Basie			
❑ BL54112 [M]	Merry Christmas from Jackie Wilson	1963	$30
❑ BL754112 [S]	Merry Christmas from Jackie Wilson	1963	$40
❑ BL54058 [M]	My Golden Favorites	1960	$75
—All-black label			
❑ BL54058 [M]	My Golden Favorites	1964	$30
— Black label with color bars			
❑ BL54115 [M]	My Golden Favorites, Volume 2	1964	$30
❑ BL754115 [S]	My Golden Favorites, Volume 2	1964	$30
❑ BL754212	Nobody But You	1977	$18
❑ BL754199	Nowstalgia	1974	$18
❑ BL54113 [M]	Shake a Hand	1964	$30
❑ BL754113 [S]	Shake a Hand	1964	$30
❑ BL54117 [M]	Somethin' Else	1964	$30
❑ BL754117 [S]	Somethin' Else	1964	$30
❑ BL54050 [M]	So Much	1960	$150
—All-black label			
❑ BL754050 [S]	So Much	1960	$175
—All-black label			
❑ BL54050 [M]	So Much	1964	$25
— Black label with color bars			
❑ BL754050 [S]	So Much	1964	$30
— Black label with color bars			
❑ BL54120 [M]	Soul Galore	1966	$30
❑ BL754120 [S]	Soul Galore	1966	$30
❑ BL54118 [M]	Soul Time	1965	$30
❑ BL754118 [S]	Soul Time	1965	$30
❑ BL54119 [M]	Spotlight on Jackie	1965	$30
❑ BL754119 [S]	Spotlight on Jackie	1965	$30
❑ BL54106 [M]	The World's Greatest Melodies	1962	$50
—All-black label			
❑ BL754106 [S]	The World's Greatest Melodies	1962	$100
—All-black label			
❑ BL54106 [M]	The World's Greatest Melodies	1964	$25
— Black label with color bars			

❑ BL754106 [S]	The World's Greatest Melodies	1964	$30
— Black label with color bars			
❑ BL754167	This Love Is Real	1971	$25
❑ BL54122 [M]	Whispers	1966	$30
❑ BL754122 [S]	Whispers	1966	$30
❑ BL54100 [M]	You Ain't Heard Nothin' Yet	1961	$50
—All-black label			
❑ BL754100 [S]	You Ain't Heard Nothin' Yet	1961	$100
—All-black label			
❑ BL54100 [M]	You Ain't Heard Nothin' Yet	1964	$25
— Black label with color bars			
❑ BL754100 [S]	You Ain't Heard Nothin' Yet	1964	$30
— Black label with color bars			
❑ BL754172	You Got Me Walking	1971	$25

COLUMBIA

❑ FC40866	Reet Petite: The Best of Jackie Wilson	1987	$15

EPIC

❑ EG38623	The Jackie Wilson Story	1983	$25
❑ FE39408	The Jackie Wilson Story, Vol. 2	1985	$15
❑ PE39408	The Jackie Wilson Story, Vol. 2	198?	$10
—Budget-line reissue			

RHINO

❑ RNLP-70230	Through the Years: A Collection of Rare Album Tracks and Single Sides	1987	$15

WILSON, JOE LEE

INNER CITY

❑ IC-1042	Secrets from the Sun	197?	$30
❑ IC-1064	Without a Song	197?	$30

OBLIVION

❑ 5	Livin' High Off Nickels and Dimes	197?	$35

SURVIVAL

❑ 110	What Would It Be	1975	$30

WILSON, JOEMY

DARGASON

❑ DM-105	Gifts II: Traditional Christmas Carols	1987	$12

WILSON, JULIE

ARDEN

❑ B&S-1	Julie Wilson at Brothers and Sisters, Vol. 1	1976	$25
❑ B&S-2	Julie Wilson at Brothers and Sisters, Vol. 2	1976	$25

CAMEO

❑ C-1021 [M]	Meet Julie Wilson	1962	$30

DOLPHIN

❑ 6 [M]	Love	1956	$50

VIK

❑ LX-1118 [M]	Julie Wilson at the St. Regis	1958	$30
❑ LX-1095 [M]	My Old Flame	1957	$30

WILSON, LARRY JON

MONUMENT

❑ KZ34041	Let Me Sing My Song to You	1976	$12
❑ 7615	Loose Change	1978	$12
❑ KZ33382	New Beginnings	1975	$12

WILSON, LESETTE

HEADFIRST

❑ 9708	Now That I've Got Your Attention	198?	$30

WILSON, LONNIE

STARDAY

❑ SLP-217 [M]	The Playboy Farmer	196?	$30

WILSON, MARIE

DESIGN

❑ DLP-76 [M]	Gentlemen Prefer Marie Wilson	1959	$40

STASH

❑ ST-250	I Thought About You	1985	$25

WILSON, MARTY

20TH CENTURY FOX

❑ TF-3101 [M]	Young America Dances to Golden Goodies	1963	$25
❑ TFS-4101 [S]	Young America Dances to Golden Goodies	1963	$30

WILSON, MERI

GRT

❑ 8023	First Take	1977	$18

WILSON, MURRY
Father of Brian, Carl and Dennis Wilson of the Beach Boys.

Number	Title	Yr	NM

CAPITOL

| ❏ T2819 [M] | The Many Moods of Murry Wilson | 1967 | $75 |
| ❏ ST2819 [S] | The Many Moods of Murry Wilson | 1967 | $50 |

WILSON, NANCY, AND CANNONBALL ADDERLEY

CAPITOL

| ❏ T1657 [M] | Nancy Wilson/Cannonball Adderley | 1962 | $150 |

—*Black label with colorband, Capitol logo on left*

| ❏ ST1657 [S] | Nancy Wilson/Cannonball Adderley | 1962 | $150 |

—*Black label with colorband, Capitol logo on left*

| ❏ ST1657 [S] | Nancy Wilson/Cannonball Adderley | 1962 | $100 |

—*Black label with colorband, Capitol logo on top*

| ❏ T1657 [M] | Nancy Wilson/Cannonball Adderley | 1962 | $50 |

—*Black label with colorband, Capitol logo on top*

| ❏ SM-1657 | Nancy Wilson/Cannonball Adderley | 197? | $25 |

—*Reissue*

WILSON, NANCY

CAPITOL

❏ ST-11317	All in Love Is Fair	1974	$30
❏ T2495 [M]	A Touch of Today	1966	$50
❏ ST2495 [S]	A Touch of Today	1966	$100
❏ SM-2495	A Touch of Today	197?	$25

—*Reissue*

❏ T1828 [M]	Broadway My Way	1963	$85
❏ ST1828 [S]	Broadway My Way	1963	$100
❏ SM-1828	Broadway My Way	197?	$25

—*Reissue*

| ❏ SY-4575 | Broadway My Way | 197? | $25 |

—*Odd reissue*

| ❏ ST-798 | But Beautiful | 1971 | $35 |
| ❏ SM-798 | But Beautiful | 197? | $25 |

—*Reissue*

| ❏ ST-429 | Can't Take My Eyes Off You | 1970 | $35 |
| ❏ SM-12031 | Can't Take My Eyes Off You | 1980 | $25 |

—*Reissue of 429*

| ❏ SWBB-256 | Close-Up | 1969 | $100 |

—*Combines 1828 and 1934 into one package*

| ❏ ST-11386 | Come Get to This | 1975 | $30 |
| ❏ SM-11819 | Come Get to This | 1978 | $25 |

—*Reissue of 11386*

| ❏ ST2909 | Easy | 1968 | $85 |
| ❏ SM-11802 | Easy | 1978 | $25 |

—*Reissue of 2909*

❏ STBB-727	For Once in My Life/Who Can I Turn To	1971	$100
❏ T2433 [M]	From Broadway with Love	1966	$85
❏ ST2433 [S]	From Broadway with Love	1966	$100
❏ T2351 [M]	Gentle Is My Love	1965	$85
❏ ST2351 [S]	Gentle Is My Love	1965	$100
❏ T1767 [M]	Hello Young Lovers	1962	$100
❏ ST1767 [S]	Hello Young Lovers	1962	$150
❏ T1934 [M]	Hollywood My Way	1963	$85
❏ ST1934 [S]	Hollywood My Way	1963	$100
❏ SM-1934	Hollywood My Way	197?	$25

—*Reissue*

❏ T2155 [M]	How Glad I Am	1964	$85
❏ ST2155 [S]	How Glad I Am	1964	$100
❏ SM-11767	How Glad I Am	1978	$25

—*Reissue of 2155*

❏ ST-353	Hurt So Bad	1969	$85
❏ ST-11131	I Know I Love Him	1972	$30
❏ ST-11659	I've Never Been to Me	1977	$30
❏ T2712 [M]	Just for Now	1967	$75
❏ ST2712 [S]	Just for Now	1967	$100
❏ ST-842	Kaleidoscope	1971	$35
❏ ST-11943	Life, Love and Happiness	1979	$30
❏ T1319 [M]	Like in Love	1960	$150

—*Black label with colorband, Capitol logo on left*

| ❏ ST1319 [S] | Like in Love | 1960 | $150 |

—*Black label with colorband, Capitol logo on left*

| ❏ T1319 [M] | Like in Love | 1960 | $85 |

—*Black label with colorband, Capitol logo on top*

| ❏ ST1319 [S] | Like in Love | 1960 | $100 |

—*Black label with colorband, Capitol logo on top*

❏ T2757 [M]	Lush Life	1967	$100
❏ ST2757 [S]	Lush Life	1967	$85
❏ SMAS-11786	Music on My Mind	1978	$30
❏ ST-148	Nancy	1969	$50
❏ T2634 [M]	Nancy -- Naturally	1967	$50
❏ ST2634 [S]	Nancy -- Naturally	1967	$100
❏ SM-11884	Nancy -- Naturally	1979	$25

—*Reissue of 2634*

| ❏ ST-541 | Now I'm a Woman | 1970 | $50 |
| ❏ T1440 [M] | Something Wonderful | 1960 | $150 |

—*Black label with colorband, Capitol logo on left*

| ❏ ST1440 [S] | Something Wonderful | 1960 | $150 |

—*Black label with colorband, Capitol logo on left*

| ❏ T1440 [M] | Something Wonderful | 1960 | $50 |

—*Black label with colorband, Capitol logo on top*

CAPITOL FULL DIMENSIONAL STEREO

something wonderful
Nancy Wilson

| ❏ ST1440 [S] | Something Wonderful | 1960 | $25 |

—*Black label with colorband, Capitol logo on top*

❏ ST-234	Son of a Preacher Man	1969	$50
❏ ST-12055	Take My Love	1980	$30
❏ T2555 [M]	Tender Loving Care	1966	$50
❏ ST2555 [S]	Tender Loving Care	1966	$100
❏ SKAO2947	The Best of Nancy Wilson	1968	$85
❏ SN-16128	The Best of Nancy Wilson	198?	$20

—*Budget-line reissue*

❏ KAO2136 [M]	The Nancy Wilson Show!	1965	$50
❏ SKAO2136 [S]	The Nancy Wilson Show!	1965	$100
❏ ST-763	The Right to Love	1971	$50

—*Retitled reissue of 2757*

| ❏ ST2970 | The Sound of Nancy Wilson | 1968 | $50 |
| ❏ T1524 [M] | The Swingin's Mutual | 1961 | $150 |

—*Black label with colorband, Capitol logo on left*

| ❏ ST1524 [S] | The Swingin's Mutual | 1961 | $150 |

—*Black label with colorband, Capitol logo on left*

| ❏ T1524 [M] | The Swingin's Mutual | 1961 | $50 |

—*Black label with colorband, Capitol logo on top*

| ❏ ST1524 [S] | The Swingin's Mutual | 1961 | $100 |

—*Black label with colorband, Capitol logo on top*

| ❏ SM-1524 [S] | The Swingin's Mutual | 1976 | $25 |

—*With George Shearing; reissue*

❏ ST-11518	This Mother's Daughter	1976	$30
❏ T2082 [M]	Today, Tomorrow, Forever	1964	$50
❏ ST2082 [S]	Today, Tomorrow, Forever	1964	$100
❏ T2321 [M]	Today -- My Way	1965	$50
❏ ST2321 [S]	Today -- My Way	1965	$100
❏ T2844 [M]	Welcome to My Love	1968	$150
❏ ST2844 [S]	Welcome to My Love	1968	$75
❏ T2012 [M]	Yesterday's Love Songs/Today's Blues	1964	$75
❏ ST2012 [S]	Yesterday's Love Songs/Today's Blues	1964	$100

COLUMBIA

❏ FC40787	Forbidden Lover	1987	$25
❏ FC40330	Keep You Satisfied	1986	$25
❏ FC44464	Nancy Now!	1989	$25

PAUSA

| ❏ PR-9041 | Nancy -- Naturally | 1985 | $25 |

PICKWICK

| ❏ SPC-3273 | Goin' Out of My Head | 197? | $25 |
| ❏ SPC-3348 | The Good Life | 197? | $25 |

WILSON, NANCY AND CANNONBALL ADDERLEY
Also see each artist's individual listings.

WILSON, NORRO

SMASH

| ❏ SRS-67116 | Dedicated to: Only You | 1969 | $18 |

WILSON, PHIL, AND RICH MATTESON

ASI

| ❏ 203 | Sound of Wasp | 197? | $30 |
| ❏ 5000 | Sound of Wasp | 197? | $25 |

—*Reissue of 203*

WILSON, PHIL

FAMOUS DOOR

| ❏ HL-133 | Boston-New York Axis | 1980 | $30 |
| ❏ HL-109 | That's All | 197? | $30 |

OUTRAGEOUS

| ❏ 1 | Getting It All Together | 197? | $35 |

WILSON, PHILLIP

HAT HUT

| ❏ 0Q | Esoteric | 197? | $35 |

WILSON, REG

HERALD

| ❏ HLP-0104 [M] | All By Himself | 1956 | $50 |

WILSON, REUBEN

BLUE NOTE

❏ BST-84343	Blue Mode	1970	$30
❏ BST-84365	Groovy Situation	1971	$30
❏ BST-84317	Love Bug	1969	$30

—*With "A Division of Liberty Records" on label*

| ❏ BST-84295 | On Broadway | 1968 | $30 |

—*With "A Division of Liberty Records" on label*

| ❏ BST-84377 | Set Us Free | 1972 | $30 |

CADET

| ❏ CA-60033 | Got to Get Your Own | 1975 | $35 |

GROOVE MERCHANT

❏ 4404	Bad Stuff	197?	$25
❏ 511	Sweet Life	1973	$25
❏ 523	The Cisco Kid	1974	$35

WILSON, TEDDY, AND MARIAN MCPARTLAND

HALCYON

| ❏ 106 | Elegant Piano | 197? | $30 |

WILSON, TEDDY

ALLEGRO

| ❏ 4024 [10] | All Star Sextet | 1954 | $150 |
| ❏ 4031 [10] | All Star Sextet | 1954 | $150 |

BLACK LION

❏ 177	Moonglow	197?	$30
❏ 209	Runnin' Wild Montreux	197?	$30
❏ 308	Striding After Fats	197?	$30

CAMEO

| ❏ C-1059 [M] | Teddy Wilson 1964 | 1964 | $30 |
| ❏ SC-1059 [S] | Teddy Wilson 1964 | 1964 | $30 |

CHIAROSCURO

❏ 168	Teddy Martin Revamps Rodgers and Hart	197?	$30
❏ 150	Teddy Wilson and the All-Stars	197?	$30
❏ 111	With Billie in Mind	1973	$30

CLASSIC JAZZ

| ❏ 32 | Live at Santa Tecla | 1976 | $25 |
| ❏ 101 | Three Little Words | 197? | $25 |

CLEF

| ❏ MGC-156 [10] | Soft Moods with Teddy Wilson | 1954 | $350 |
| ❏ MGC-140 [10] | The Didactic Mr. Wilson | 1953 | $350 |

COLUMBIA

❏ CL1442 [M]	And Then They Wrote	1960	$30
❏ CS8242 [S]	And Then They Wrote	1960	$40
❏ CS8160 [S]	Gypsy	1959	$40
❏ CL1352 [M]	Gypsy in Jazz	1959	$30
❏ CL748 [M]	Mr. Wilson	1956	$75
❏ CL1318 [M]	Mr. Wilson and Mr. Gershwin	1959	$40
❏ CL6153 [10]	Piano Moods	1950	$120
❏ KG31617	Teddy Wilson and His All-Stars	1973	$35
❏ CL6098 [10]	Teddy Wilson and His Piano	1950	$300
❏ CL6040 [10]	Teddy Wilson Featuring Billie Holiday	1949	$400

COMMODORE

| ❏ FL-20029 [10] | Town Hall Concert | 1952 | $250 |

DIAL

| ❏ LP-213 [10] | Teddy Wilson All Stars | 1950 | $300 |

GNP CRESCENDO

| ❏ GNP-9014 | Teddy Wilson | 197? | $25 |

JAZZ ARCHIVES

| ❏ JA-28 | Teddy Wilson Sextet 1944, Vol. 1 | 198? | $25 |
| ❏ JA-36 | Teddy Wilson Sextet 1944, Vol. 2 | 198? | $25 |

JAZZOLOGY

| ❏ J-86 | Teddy's Choice | 198? | $25 |

MERCURY

| ❏ MG-25172 [10] | Piano Pastries | 1953 | $250 |

MGM

| ❏ E-129 [10] | Runnin' Wild | 1951 | $250 |

MOSAIC

| ❏ MQ8-173 | The Complete Verve Recordings of the Teddy Wilson Trio | 199? | $175 |

MUSICRAFT

❏ 2007	As Time Goes By	1986	$25
❏ 2008	Sunny Morning	1986	$25
❏ 502	Teddy Wilson and His All Stars, Vol. 1	198?	$25

NORGRAN

| ❏ MGN-1019 [M] | The Creative Teddy Wilson | 1955 | $250 |

PRESTIGE

| ❏ PRST-7696 [S] | The Teddy Wilson Trio in Europe | 1969 | $35 |

QUICKSILVER

| ❏ QS-9002 | Into the Sky | 198? | $25 |

ROYALE

| ❏ 18169 [10] | Teddy Wilson and His All Stars | 195? | $150 |

Number	Title	Yr	NM
SACKVILLE			
❏ 2005	Teddy Wilson in Tokyo	198?	$25
STORYVILLE			
❏ 4046	Teddy Wilson Revisits the Goodman Years	198?	$25
TIME-LIFE			
❏ STL-J-20	Giants of Jazz	1981	$75
VERVE			
❏ MGV-2029 [M]	For Quiet Lovers	1956	$175
❏ V-2029 [M]	For Quiet Lovers	1961	$30
❏ MGV-2073 [M]	I Got Rhythm	1957	$175
❏ V-2073 [M]	I Got Rhythm	1961	$25
❏ MGV-2011 [M]	Intimate Listening	1956	$250
❏ V-2011 [M]	Intimate Listening	1961	$25
❏ MGV-8272 [M]	The Impeccable Mr. Teddy Wilson	1958	$120
❏ V-8272 [M]	The Impeccable Mr. Teddy Wilson	1961	$25
❏ MGV-8299 [M]	These Tunes Remind Me of You	1959	$150
❏ V-8299 [M]	These Tunes Remind Me of You	1961	$25
❏ MGV-8330 [M]	The Touch of Teddy Wilson	1959	$150
❏ V-8330 [M]	The Touch of Teddy Wilson	1961	$25
WHO'S WHO IN JAZZ			
❏ 21009	Lionel Hampton Presents Teddy Wilson	1979	$25
WILSON, TEDDY/GERRY MULLIGAN			
VERVE			
❏ V6-8827	Newport Years	197?	$30
❏ MGV-8235 [M]	The Teddy Wilson Trio and the Gerry Mulligan Quartet at Newport	1958	$175
❏ V-8235 [M]	The Teddy Wilson Trio and the Gerry Mulligan Quartet at Newport	1961	$25
❏ UMV-2622 [M]	The Teddy Wilson Trio and the Gerry Mulligan Quartet at Newport	198?	$30
WILSON PHILLIPS			
SBK			
❏ 1P-8219	Shadows and Light	1992	$75
— Only U.S. vinyl release was through Columbia House			
❏ K1-93745	Wilson Phillips	1990	$15
WINCHESTER, JESSE			
AMPEX			
❏ A10104	Jesse Winchester	1970	$25
BEARSVILLE			
❏ BRK6984	A Touch on the Rainy Side	1978	$12
❏ BR2045	Jesse Winchester	1971	$18
— Reissue of Ampex LP			
❏ BR6953	Learn to Love It	1974	$15
❏ BR6964	Let the Rough Side Drag	1976	$15
❏ PRO-A-693 [DJ]	Live at the Bijou Café Plus a Live Interview at Media College in Montreal	1977	$40
❏ BR6968	Nothing But a Breeze	1977	$12
❏ BRK6989	Talk Memphis	1981	$12
❏ PRO560 [DJ]	The Jesse Winchester Radio Show	1976	$40
❏ BR2102	Third Down, 110 to Go	1972	$18
RHINO			
❏ RNLP-70885	Jesse Winchester	1988	$12
❏ R1-70085	The Best of Jesse Winchester	1989	$12
❏ RNLP-70886	Third Down, 110 to Go	1988	$12
SUGAR HILL			
❏ SH-1023	Humour Me	1988	$15
WINCHESTER, LEM			
ARGO			
❏ LPS-642 [S]	Lem Winchester with the Ramsey Lewis Trio	1959	$40
❏ LP-642 [M]	Lem Winchester with the Ramsey Lewis Trio	1959	$50
FANTASY			
❏ OJC-1719	Winchester Special	198?	$25
METROJAZZ			
❏ E-1005 [M]	New Faces at Newport	1958	$120
MOODSVILLE			
❏ MVLP-11 [M]	Lem Winchester with Feeling	1960	$50
— Green label			
❏ MVLP-11 [M]	Lem Winchester with Feeling	1965	$30
— Blue label, trident logo at right			
NEW JAZZ			
❏ NJLP-8244 [M]	Another Opus	1960	$175
— Purple label			
❏ NJLP-8244 [M]	Another Opus	1965	$175
— Blue label, trident logo at right			
❏ NJLP-8239 [M]	Lem's Beat	1960	$175
— Purple label			
❏ NJLP-8239 [M]	Lem's Beat	1965	$175
— Blue label, trident logo at right			

Number	Title	Yr	NM
❏ NJLP-8223 [M]	Winchester Special	1959	$250
— Purple label			
❏ NJLP-8223 [M]	Winchester Special	1965	$175
— Blue label, trident logo at right			
WIND			
TONY ORLANDO was in this group.			
LIFE			
❏ LLPS-2000	Make Believe	1969	$25
WIND CHILL FACTOR			
QCA			
❏ 372	City Streets	1978	$30
WIND HARP, THE			
UNITED ARTISTS			
❏ UAS-9963	Song from the Hill	1972	$25
WIND IN THE WILLOWS, THE			
With Debbie Harry, later of Blondie.			
CAPITOL			
❏ SKAO2956 [B]	The Wind in the Willows	1968	$150
WINDHURST, JOHNNY			
JAZZOLOGY			
❏ J-3	The Imaginative Johnny Windhurst	1963	$35
TRANSITION			
❏ TRLP-2 [M]	Jazz at Columbus Ave.	1956	$250
— Deduct 1/4 if booklet is missing			
WINDING, KAI, AND SONNY STITT			
HALL OF FAME			
❏ 612	Early Modern	197?	$25
WINDING, KAI			
A&M			
❏ SP-3008	Israel	1969	$30
ABC IMPULSE!			
❏ AS3 [S]	The Incredible Kai Winding Trombones	1968	$30
— Black and red label			
COLUMBIA			
❏ CL1329 [M]	Dance to the City Beat	1959	$40
❏ CS8136 [S]	Dance to the City Beat	1959	$75
❏ CL1264 [M]	Swingin' State	1958	$150
❏ CS8062 [S]	Swingin' State	1958	$40
❏ CL999 [M]	Trombone Panorama	1957	$150
❏ CL936 [M]	Trombone Sound	1956	$150
GATEWAY			
❏ 7022	Jazz Showcase	1979	$25
GLENDALE			
❏ 6004	Caravan	1977	$25
❏ 6003	Danish Blue	1976	$25
HARMONY			
❏ HL7341 [M]	The Great Kai Winding Sound	1962	$35
IMPULSE!			
❏ A3 [M]	The Incredible Kai Winding Trombones	1960	$250
❏ AS3 [S]	The Incredible Kai Winding Trombones	1960	$250
— Orange and black label			
MCA			
❏ 29062	Incredible Kai Winding Trombones	198?	$25
— Reissue of Impulse! 3			
PICKWICK			
❏ SPC-3004	Trombones	196?	$30
RED RECORD			
❏ VPA-143	Duo Bones	198?	$30
ROOST			
❏ LP408 [10]	Kai Winding All Stars	1952	$250
SAVOY			
❏ MG-12119 [M]	In the Beginning	196?	$35
❏ MG-9017 [10]	New Trends Of Jazz	1952	$250
VERVE			
❏ V-8661 [M]	Dirty Dog	1966	$30
❏ V6-8661 [S]	Dirty Dog	1966	$35
❏ V-8427 [M]	Kai Ole	1962	$75
❏ V6-8427 [S]	Kai Ole	1962	$75
❏ V-8525 [M]	Kai Winding Solo	1963	$75
❏ V6-8525 [S]	Kai Winding Solo	1963	$75
❏ V-8602 [M]	Modern Country	1964	$175
❏ V6-8602 [S]	Modern Country	1964	$175
❏ V-8573 [M]	Mondo Cane #2	1964	$75
❏ V6-8573 [S]	Mondo Cane #2	1964	$75
❏ V-8551 [M]	More!!!	1963	$75
❏ V6-8551 [S]	More!!!	1963	$75
❏ V-8657 [M]	More Brass	1966	$30
❏ V6-8657 [S]	More Brass	1966	$35
❏ V-8691 [M]	Penny Lane and Time	1967	$35
❏ V6-8691 [S]	Penny Lane and Time	1967	$30

Number	Title	Yr	NM
❏ V-8620 [M]	Rainy Day	1965	$35
❏ V6-8620 [S]	Rainy Day	1965	$50
❏ V-8493 [M]	Suspense Themes in Jazz	1962	$75
❏ V6-8493 [S]	Suspense Themes in Jazz	1962	$75
❏ V-8639 [M]	The "In" Instrumentals	1965	$35
❏ V6-8639 [S]	The "In" Instrumentals	1965	$50
❏ V-8556 [M]	The Lonely One	1963	$75
❏ V6-8556 [S]	The Lonely One	1963	$75
WHO'S WHO IN JAZZ			
❏ 21001	Lionel Hampton Presents Kai Winding	1978	$25
WINDMILL SAXOPHONE QUARTET			
PATHFINDER			
❏ PTF-8801	Very Scary	1988	$25
WINDOWS			
CYPRESS			
❏ YL-0214	The French Laundry	1989	$30
INTIMA			
❏ SJ-73218	Is It Safe	1987	$25
❏ D1-73298	Mr. Bongo	1988	$25
❏ SJ-73219	Windows	1987	$25
— Reissue of self-titled debut album			
(LABEL UNKNOWN)			
❏ 0(# unknown)	Windows	1985	$50
WINDY CITY BANJO BAND, THE			
PINNACLE			
❏ 107	The Windy City Banjo Band	1963	$35
WINGFIELD, PETE			
ISLAND			
❏ ILPS9333	Breakfast Special	1975	$15
WINGS			
See PAUL McCARTNEY.			
WINKLER, MARK			
CMG			
❏ CML-7207	Ebony Rain	1988	$25
❏ CML-8021	Hottest Night of the Year	1989	$30
WINNERS, THE			
CROWN			
❏ CLP-5394 [M]	Checkered Flag	1963	$30
❏ CST-394 [S]	Checkered Flag	1963	$30
WINSTON, GEORGE			
LOST LAKE ARTS			
❏ LL-0081	Ballads and Blues 1972	1981	$40
— Reissue of Takoma recordings			
TAKOMA			
❏ 9016	Piano Solos	1973	$40
WINDHAM HILL			
❏ WH-1012	Autumn	1984	$25
— Reissue with A&M distribution			
❏ C-1012	Autumn	1980	$30
— Original issue			
❏ WH-1025	December	1984	$25
— Distributed by A&M Records; "December" in raised white letters			
❏ C-1025	December	1982	$35
— NOT distributed by A&M Records; "December" in black letters			
❏ WH-1019	Winter Into Spring	1984	$25
— Reissue, distributed by A&M Records			
❏ C-1019	Winter Into Spring	1982	$30
— Original issue			
WINSTON, MURIEL			
STRATA-EAST			
❏ SES-7411	A Fresh Viewpoint	197?	$35
WINSTON, SHERRY			
HEADFIRST			
❏ 634	Do It for Love	198?	$25
WARLOCK			
❏ WAR-2724	Love Is	1991	$30
WINSTONS, THE			
METROMEDIA			
❏ MD-1010	Color Him Father	1969	$50
WINTER, EDGAR			
BLUE SKY			
❏ PZ33483 [B]	Jasmine Nightdreams	1975	$15
❏ PZQ33483 [Q]	Jasmine Nightdreams	1975	$40
❏ PZ34858	Re-Cycled	1977	$15
❏ JZ36494	Standing on Rock	1981	$15
❏ PZ33798	The Edgar Winter Group with Rick Derringer	1975	$15

Number	Title	Yr	NM
❏ PZQ33798 [Q]	The Edgar Winter Group with Rick Derringer	1975	$40
❏ JZ35989	The Edgar Winter Album	1979	$15

EPIC

Number	Title	Yr	NM
❏ E30512	Edgar Winter's White Trash	1971	$18
— Yellow label			
❏ KE30512	Edgar Winter's White Trash	1973	$15
— Orange label			
❏ PE30512	Edgar Winter's White Trash	1985	$10
— Budget-line reissue; dark blue label			
❏ BN26503	Entrance	1970	$18
— Yellow label			
❏ BN26503 [B]	Entrance	1973	$15
— Orange label			
❏ BG33770	Entrance/White Trash	1975	$18
— Combines 26503 and 30512 into one package			
❏ KEG31249	Roadwork	1972	$25
— Yellow labels			
❏ KEG31249	Roadwork	1973	$18
— Orange labels			
❏ EG31249	Roadwork	1987	$12
— Budget-line reissue; dark blue labels			
❏ PE32461	Shock Treatment	1974	$18
— Orange label			
❏ PEQ32461 [Q]	Shock Treatment	1974	$50
❏ PE32461	Shock Treatment	1985	$10
— Budget-line reissue; dark blue label			
❏ KE31584	They Only Come Out at Night	1972	$18
— Yellow label			
❏ KE31584	They Only Come Out at Night	1973	$15
— Orange label			
❏ EQ31584 [Q]	They Only Come Out at Night	1973	$50
❏ PE31584	They Only Come Out at Night	197?	$12
— Reissue with new prefix; orange label			
❏ PE31584	They Only Come Out at Night	1979	$10
— Budget-line reissue; dark blue label			

RHINO

Number	Title	Yr	NM
❏ R1-70709	Mission Earth	1989	$15
❏ R1-70895	The Edgar Winter Collection	1989	$12

WINTER, JOHNNY

ACCORD

Number	Title	Yr	NM
❏ SN-7135	Ready for Winter	1981	$12

ALLIGATOR

Number	Title	Yr	NM
❏ 4735	Guitar Slinger	1984	$12
❏ 4742	Serious Business	1985	$12
❏ 4748	Third Degree	1986	$12

BLUE SKY

Number	Title	Yr	NM
❏ PZ33944	Captured Live	198?	$10
— Budget-line reissue with bar code on cover			
❏ PZ33944	Captured Live!	1976	$15
— No bar code on cover			
❏ PZQ33292 [Q]	John Dawson Winter III	1974	$30
❏ PZ33292	John Dawson Winter III	1974	$15
❏ PZ34813	Nothin' But the Blues	1977	$15
— No bar code on cover			
❏ PZ34813	Nothin' But the Blues	198?	$10
— Budget-line reissue with bar code on cover			
❏ JZ36343 [B]	Raisin' Cain	1980	$15
❏ JZ35475	White, Hot and Blue	1978	$15

BUDDAH

Number	Title	Yr	NM
❏ BDS-7513	First Winter	1969	$25

COLUMBIA

Number	Title	Yr	NM
❏ CS9826	Johnny Winter	1969	$25
— 360 Sound" label			
❏ CS9826	Johnny Winter	1970	$15
— Orange label			
❏ PC9826	Johnny Winter	198?	$10
— Budget-line reissue			
❏ C30221	Johnny Winter And	1970	$25
— 360 Sound" label			
❏ C30221	Johnny Winter And	1970	$15
— Orange labels			
❏ PC30221	Johnny Winter And	198?	$10
— Budget-line reissue			
❏ CG33651	Johnny Winter And//Live/ Johnny Winter And	1975	$18
❏ C30475	Live/Johnny Winter And	1971	$18
❏ PC30475	Live/Johnny Winter And	198?	$10
— Budget-line reissue			
❏ CQ32715 [Q]	Saints and Sinners	1974	$40
❏ KC32715	Saints and Sinners	1974	$18
❏ PC32715	Saints and Sinners	197?	$10
— Budget-line reissue			
❏ KCS9947	Second Winter	1969	$30
— 360 Sound" labels; record 2 has music on only one side (other side is blank)			
❏ KCS9947	Second Winter	1970	$18
— Orange labels			
❏ PC9947	Second Winter	198?	$12

Number	Title	Yr	NM
— Budget-line reissue			
❏ KC32188	Still Alive and Well	1973	$18
❏ CQ32188 [Q]	Still Alive and Well	1973	$40
❏ PC32188	Still Alive and Well	198?	$10
— Budget-line reissue			

FRIDAY MUSIC

Number	Title	Yr	NM
❏ FRM41914 [B]	Live Bootleg Special Edition	2014	$30

GRT

Number	Title	Yr	NM
❏ 10010	The Johnny Winter Story	1969	$25

IMPERIAL

Number	Title	Yr	NM
❏ LP-12431	The Progressive Blues Experiment	1969	$50

JANUS

Number	Title	Yr	NM
❏ 3008	About Blues	1970	$25
❏ 3056	Before the Storm	197?	$25
❏ 3023	Early Times	1970	$30

LIBERTY

Number	Title	Yr	NM
❏ LN-10294	The Progressive Blues Experiment	1986	$12
— Reissue of Imperial LP			
❏ MVD8129LP [B]	Live in Sweden 1987 (with Dr John)	2016	$25

MCA/VOYAGER

Number	Title	Yr	NM
❏ 42241	The Winter of '88	1988	$12

SONOBEAT

Number	Title	Yr	NM
❏ RS-1002	The Progressive Blues Experiment	1968	$300
— Released in plain white cardboard jacket			

UNITED ARTISTS

Number	Title	Yr	NM
❏ UA-LA139-F	Austin, Tex.	1974	$18

WINTER, JOHNNY AND EDGAR
Also see each artist's individual listings.

BLUE SKY

Number	Title	Yr	NM
❏ ASZ242 [DJ]	Johnny and Edgar Winter Discuss Together	1976	$30
— Promo-only interview album			
❏ PZ34033	Together	1976	$15

WINTER, PAUL, AND PAUL HALLEY

LIVING MUSIC

Number	Title	Yr	NM
❏ LM-0013	Whales Alive!	1987	$25

WINTER, PAUL

A&M

Number	Title	Yr	NM
❏ SP-4698	Common Ground	1978	$15
❏ SP-4653	Earthdance	1977	$15
❏ SP-4207	Something in the Wind	1969	$35
❏ SP-4279	The Road	1970	$35
❏ SP-4170	The Winter Consort	1968	$35

COLUMBIA

Number	Title	Yr	NM
❏ CL1925 [M]	Jazz Meets the Bossa Nova	1962	$35
❏ CS8725 [S]	Jazz Meets the Bossa Nova	1962	$25
❏ CL2155 [M]	Jazz Meets the Folk Song	1964	$35
❏ CS8955 [S]	Jazz Meets the Folk Song	1964	$25
❏ CL1997 [M]	Jazz Premiere: Washington	1963	$35
❏ CS8797 [S]	Jazz Premiere: Washington	1963	$25
❏ CL2064 [M]	New Jazz on Campus	1963	$35
❏ CS8864 [S]	New Jazz on Campus	1963	$25
❏ CL2315 [M]	Rio	1965	$35
❏ CS9115 [S]	Rio	1965	$25
❏ CL2272 [M]	The Sound of Ipanema	1965	$35
❏ CS9072 [S]	The Sound of Ipanema	1965	$25

EPIC

Number	Title	Yr	NM
❏ KE31643	Icarus	1972	$75
❏ PE31643	Icarus	197?	$25
— Reissue			

LIVING MUSIC

Number	Title	Yr	NM
❏ LMR-1	Callings	1980	$25
— With 20-page booklet			
❏ LM-0001	Callings	198?	$20
— Reissue of LMR-1			
❏ LMR-6	Canyon	1986	$15
❏ LMR-5	Concert for the Earth Live at the United Nations	1985	$15
❏ LM-0015	Earthbeat	1987	$12
❏ LMR-4	Icarus	1985	$25
— Reissue of Epic LP			
❏ LM-0004	Icarus	198?	$12
— Reissue of LMR-4			
❏ LMR-2	Missa Gaia/Earth Mass	1983	$25
❏ LMR-3	Sun Singer	1984	$15
❏ LM-0003	Sun Singer	198?	$12
— Reissue of LMR-3			
❏ LM-0012	Wintersong	1986	$25

WINTER, RAYMOND

INNER CITY

Number	Title	Yr	NM
❏ IC-1135	Tropic Woods	198?	$30

WINTERHALTER, HUGO

ABC-PARAMOUNT

Number	Title	Yr	NM
❏ ABCS-447 [S]	Season for My Beloved	1963	$18
❏ ABC-447 [M]	Season for My Beloved	1963	$15

HARMONY

Number	Title	Yr	NM
❏ HL7078 [M]	Music, Music, Music	195?	$18

KAPP

Number	Title	Yr	NM
❏ KS3407 [S]	Best of '64, The	1964	$18
❏ KL1407 [M]	Best of '64, The	1964	$15
❏ KL1429 [M]	Big Hits of 1965	1965	$15
❏ KS3429 [S]	Big Hits of 1965	1965	$18
❏ KL-1426 [M]	Semi-Classical Favorites	196?	$15
❏ KS-3426 [S]	Semi-Classical Favorites	196?	$18

MUSICOR

Number	Title	Yr	NM
❏ MDS-1036	Airport Love Theme	197?	$12
❏ M2S3160	All Time Movie Greats	196?	$18
❏ MS3190	Applause	1971	$15
❏ MDS-1042	Best of the Motion Picture Hits	197?	$15
❏ MS-3170	Classical Gas	1970	$12
❏ MS-3196	Love Story	1971	$12
❏ MDS-1029	Midnight Cowboy	197?	$15
❏ MS-3184	My Favorite Broadway and Hollywood Music	197?	$12
❏ MDS-1013	Pop Parade	197?	$15
❏ M2S3168	Romanceable and Danceable	196?	$18
❏ M2S3178	Your Favorite Motion Picture Music	197?	$18

PICKWICK

Number	Title	Yr	NM
❏ CAS-2309	Hawaiian Wedding Song	197?	$10
— Black label, multi-color "P" logo			

RCA CAMDEN

Number	Title	Yr	NM
❏ CAL-443 [M]	Big and Sweet with a Beat	1958	$18
❏ CAL-449 [M]	Christmas Magic	1958	$18
— Reissue of RCA Victor 3132 with two extra tracks			
❏ CAS-2309	Hawaiian Wedding Song	1969	$12
❏ CAS-2546	Latin Gold	1972	$12
❏ CAL-379 [M]	Magic Touch	195?	$18

RCA VICTOR

Number	Title	Yr	NM
❏ LPM-1179 [M]	Always	1955	$25
❏ LPM-3132 [10]	Christmas Magic	1954	$30
❏ LPM-1020 [M]	Great Music Themes of TV	1954	$30
❏ LPM-1400 [M]	Happy Hunting	1956	$25
❏ LPM-2482 [M]	Hugo Winterhalter Goes... Continental	1961	$18
❏ LSP-2482 [S]	Hugo Winterhalter Goes... Continental	1961	$25
❏ LPM-2167 [M]	Hugo Winterhalter Goes... Gypsy	1960	$18
❏ LSP-2167 [S]	Hugo Winterhalter Goes... Gypsy	1960	$25
❏ LPM-2417 [M]	Hugo Winterhalter Goes... Hawaiian	1961	$18
❏ LSP-2417 [S]	Hugo Winterhalter Goes... Hawaiian	1961	$25
❏ LPM-1677 [M]	Hugo Winterhalter Goes... Latin	1957	$25
❏ LSP-1677 [S]	Hugo Winterhalter Goes... Latin	1958	$30
❏ LPM-2271 [M]	Hugo Winterhalter Goes... South of the Border	1960	$18
❏ LSP-2271 [S]	Hugo Winterhalter Goes... South of the Border	1960	$25
❏ LSP-2645 [S]	I Only Have Eyes for You	1964	$18
❏ LPM-2645 [M]	I Only Have Eyes for You	1964	$15
❏ LPM-3051 [10]	Music by Starlight	195?	$30
❏ LPM-1185 [M]	Music by Starlight	1955	$25
❏ ANL1-2483	Pure Gold	1977	$12
❏ LPM-3050 [10]	Reminiscing	195?	$30
❏ LPM-3101 [10]	Song Hits from "Peter Pan" and "Hans Christian Andersen	195?	$30
❏ LPM-3379 [M]	The Best of Hugo Winterhalter	1965	$15
❏ LSP-3379 [S]	The Best of Hugo Winterhalter	1965	$18
❏ LPM-1338 [M]	The Eyes of Love	1956	$25
❏ LPM-1905 [M]	Two Sides of Hugo Winterhalter	1958	$25
❏ LSP-1905 [S]	Two Sides of Hugo Winterhalter	1958	$30
❏ LPM-3100 [10]	Winterhalter Magic	195?	$30
❏ LPM-1904 [M]	Wish You Were Here	1958	$25
❏ LSP-1904 [S]	Wish You Were Here	1958	$30

WINTERS, JERRI

BETHLEHEM

Number	Title	Yr	NM
❏ BCP-76 [M]	Somebody Loves Me	1957	$300

FRATERNITY

Number	Title	Yr	NM
❏ F-1001 [M]	Winter's Here	1955	$120

WINTERS, JONATHAN

COLUMBIA

Number	Title	Yr	NM
❏ KG31985	Jonathan Winters Laughs Live	1972	$25
— Reissue of 9611 and 9799 in one package			
❏ PG31985	Jonathan Winters Laughs Live	197?	$15
— Reissue with new prefix			
❏ CL2811 [M]	Jonathan Winters Wings It!	1968	$30
❏ CS9611 [S]	Jonathan Winters Wings It!	1968	$18
❏ CS9799	Stuff 'N' Nonsense	1969	$18

VERVE

Number	Title	Yr	NM
❏ V-15032 [M]	Another Day, Another World	1962	$30
❏ V6-15032 [R]	Another Day, Another World	196?	$15

Number	Title	Yr	NM
❑ MGV-15011 [M]	Down to Earth	1960	$30
❑ MGVS-6155 [S]	Down to Earth	1960	$30
❑ V-15011 [M]	Down to Earth	1961	$25
❑ V6-15011 [S]	Down to Earth	1961	$25
—Reissue of 6155			
❑ V-15047 [M]	Great Moments in Comedy	1965	$25
❑ V6-15047 [R]	Great Moments in Comedy	196?	$15
❑ V-15025 [M]	Here's Jonathan	1961	$30
❑ V6-15025 [S]	Here's Jonathan	1961	$30
❑ V-15035 [M]	Humor As Seen Through the Eyes of Jonathan Winters	1963	$30
❑ V6-15035 [S]	Humor As Seen Through the Eyes of Jonathan Winters	1963	$30
❑ V-15041 [M]	Jonathan Winters' Mad, Mad, Mad, Mad World	1964	$25

Number	Title	Yr	NM
❑ V6-15041 [R]	Jonathan Winters' Mad, Mad, Mad, Mad World	196?	$15
❑ V-15057 [M]	Movies Are Better Than Ever	1967	$25
❑ V6-15057 [R]	Movies Are Better Than Ever	196?	$15
❑ V-15052 [M]	The Best of Frickert and Suggins	1966	$25
❑ V6-15052 [R]	The Best of Frickert and Suggins	196?	$15
❑ MGV-15009 [M]	The Wonderful World of Jonathan Winters	1960	$30
❑ MGVS-6099 [S]	The Wonderful World of Jonathan Winters	1960	$30
❑ V-15009 [M]	The Wonderful World of Jonathan Winters	1961	$25
❑ V6-15009 [S]	The Wonderful World of Jonathan Winters	1961	$25
—Reissue of 6099			
❑ V-15037 [M]	Whistle Stopping with Jonathan Winters	1964	$25
❑ V6-15037 [R]	Whistle Stopping with Jonathan Winters	196?	$15

WINTERS, PINKY
ARGO
Number	Title	Yr	NM
❑ LP-604 [M]	Lonely One	1956	$650

CREATIVE
| ❑ LP-604 [M] | Lonely One | 1956 | $75 |

VANTAGE
| ❑ VLP-3 [10] | Pinky Winters | 1954 | $1000 |

WINTERS, SMILEY
ARHOOLIE
| ❑ 8004/5 | Smiley Etc. | 1969 | $25 |

WINWOOD, STEVE
Also see BLIND FAITH; THE SPENCER DAVIS GROUP; TRAFFIC.

ISLAND
Number	Title	Yr	NM
❑ ILPS9576	Arc of a Diver	1981	$12
❑ 5317713	Arc of a Diver	2009	$25
❑ 25448	Back in the High Life	1986	$10
❑ 25660	Chronicles	1987	$10
❑ ILPS9387	Go	1976	$15
—With Stomo Yamahita and Michael Shrieve			
❑ ILPS9494	Steve Winwood	1977	$12
❑ ILPS9777	Talking Back to the Night	1982	$12

SPRINGBOARD
| ❑ SPB-4040 | Winwood & Friends | 197? | $18 |
| —Budget release with Winwood material on Side 1 and a collection of tracks Winwood recorded with Jeff Beck, Yardbirds, Long John Baldry and Jack Bruce/Ginger Baker material on Side 2 | | | |

UNITED ARTISTS
❑ UAS-9950	Winwood	1971	$18
—Collection of tracks Winwood recorded with the Spencer Davis Group, Traffic and Blind Faith; without booklet			
❑ UAS-9950	Winwood	1971	$30
—Collection of tracks Winwood recorded with the Spencer Davis Group, Traffic and Blind Faith; with booklet			

VIRGIN
| ❑ 91405 | Refugees of the Heart | 1990 | $18 |

Number	Title	Yr	NM
❑ 90946	Roll With It	1988	$10
❑ R154633	Roll With It	1988	$12
—BMG Direct Marketing edition			

WIPERS, THE
PARK AVE.
| ❑ 0(# unknown) | Is This Real? | 1980 | $50 |
| ❑ 82802 | Youth of America | 1981 | $50 |

RESTLESS
❑ 72194	Follow Blind	1987	$15
❑ 72094	Land of the Lost	1986	$15
❑ 72187	Over the Edge	1987	$15
—Reissue			
❑ 72026	Wipers Live	1985	$15

TIM/KERR
| ❑ 31 [B] | Silver Sail | 1993 | $25 |

WIRE
4 MEN WITH BEARDS
❑ 4M510LP [B]	154		$25
❑ 4M509LP [B]	Chairs Missing		$25
❑ 4M508LP [B]	Pink Flag		$25

HARVEST
| ❑ ST-11757 [B] | Pink Flag | 1977 | $30 |

MUTE/ENIGMA
❑ D1-73314 [B]	A Bell Is a Cup Until It Is Struck	1988	$18
❑ D1-73516 [B]	It's Beginning to and Back Again	1989	$18
❑ MLP-73273 [EP]	Snakedrill	1987	$18
❑ SWAO-73270 [B]	The Ideal Copy	1987	$18

PINK FLAG
| ❑ 5024545743012 [B] | Nocturnal Koreans | 2016 | $25 |

WARNER BROS.
| ❑ BSK3398 [B] | 154 | 1979 | $25 |

WISE, CHUBBY, AND MAC WISEMAN
GILLEY'S
| ❑ 500 | Give Me My Smokies and The Tennessee Waltz | 197? | $25 |

WISE, CHUBBY
STARDAY
| ❑ SLP-154 [M] | The Tennessee Fiddler | 1961 | $50 |

WISEMAN, MAC
ABC
Number	Title	Yr	NM
❑ 4009	16 Great Performances	1974	$15
❑ AC-30033	The ABC Collection	1976	$15

CAPITOL
| ❑ T1800 [M] | Bluegrass Favorites | 1962 | $30 |
| ❑ ST1800 [S] | Bluegrass Favorites | 1962 | $40 |

CMH
❑ 6202	Country Memories	197?	$15
❑ 4502	Greatest Bluegrass Hits	198?	$12
❑ 6217	Mac Wiseman Sings Gordon Lightfoot	197?	$15
❑ 9021	Songs That Made the Juke Box Play	197?	$18
❑ 9001	The Mac Wiseman Story	197?	$18

DOT
❑ DLP-3313 [M]	12 Great Hits	1960	$30
❑ DLP-25313 [S]	12 Great Hits	1960	$40
❑ DLP-3730 [M]	A Master at Work	1966	$25
❑ DLP-25730 [S]	A Master at Work	1966	$30
❑ DLP-3135 [M]	Beside the Still Waters	1959	$30
❑ DLP-25135 [S]	Beside the Still Waters	1959	$40
❑ DLP-3373 [M]	Best Loved Gospel Hymns	1961	$30
❑ DLP-25373 [S]	Best Loved Gospel Hymns	1961	$40
❑ DLP-3731 [M]	Bluegrass	1966	$25
❑ DLP-25731 [S]	Bluegrass	1966	$30
❑ DLP-3408 [M]	Fireball Mail	1961	$40
❑ DLP-25408 [R]	Fireball Mail	196?	$25
❑ DLP-25896	Golden Hits of Mac Wiseman	1968	$25
❑ DLP-3213 [M]	Great Folk Ballads	1959	$30
❑ DLP-25213 [S]	Great Folk Ballads	1959	$40
❑ DLP-3336 [M]	Keep on the Sunny Side	1960	$40
❑ DLP-25336 [R]	Keep on the Sunny Side	196?	$25
❑ DLP-3697 [M]	This Is Mac Wiseman	1966	$25
❑ DLP-25697 [S]	This Is Mac Wiseman	1966	$30
❑ DLP-3084 [M]	Tis Sweet to Be Remembered	1958	$50
❑ DLP-25084 [R]	Tis Sweet to Be Remembered	196?	$25

HAMILTON
| ❑ HLP-12130 [M] | Sincerely | 1964 | $25 |
| ❑ HLP-12167 [M] | Songs of the Dear Old Days | 1965 | $25 |

HILLTOP
| ❑ JM-6047 [M] | Mac Wiseman | 1967 | $18 |
| ❑ JS-6047 [R] | Mac Wiseman | 1967 | $15 |

MCA
| ❑ 4009 | 16 Great Performances | 198? | $10 |
| —Reissue of ABC 4009 | | | |

RCA VICTOR
Number	Title	Yr	NM
❑ LSP-4845	Concert Favorites	1972	$18
❑ ANL1-1208	Concert Favorites	1975	$12
—Reissue of 4845			
❑ LSP-4336	Johnny's Cash and Charley's Pride	1970	$18

VETCO
| ❑ 508 | New Traditions, Vol. 1 | 197? | $18 |
| ❑ 509 | New Traditions, Vol. 2 | 197? | $18 |

WISHBONE ASH
ATLANTIC
| ❑ SD18164 | Locked In | 1976 | $12 |
| ❑ SD18200 | New England | 1976 | $12 |

DECCA
❑ DL75437 [B]	Argus	1972	$25
❑ DL75295	Pilgrimage	1971	$18
❑ DL75249	Wishbone Ash	1971	$18

FANTASY
| ❑ 9629 | Twin Barrels Burning | 1983 | $12 |

I.R.S.
| ❑ 82006 | Here to Hear | 1989 | $15 |
| ❑ 42101 | Nouveau Calls | 1988 | $15 |

MCA
❑ 49	Argus	1973	$15
—Reissue of Decca 75437			
❑ 2344	Argus	1978	$12
—Reissue of MCA 49			
❑ 787	Argus	198?	$10
—Reissue			
❑ 2311	Front Page News	1977	$12
❑ 5283	Hot Ash	1981	$12
❑ 3221	Just Testing	1980	$12
❑ 770	Just Testing	198?	$10
—Reissue			
❑ 8006	Live Dates	1973	$18
❑ 3060	No Smoke Without Fire	1978	$12
❑ 769	No Smoke Without Fire	198?	$10
—Reissue			
❑ 36	Pilgrimage	1973	$15
—Reissue of Decca 75295			
❑ 464	There's the Rub	1974	$15
❑ 2343	Wishbone Ash	1978	$12
—Reissue of Decca 75249			
❑ 327	Wishbone Four	1973	$15
❑ 2348	Wishbone Four	1978	$12
—Reissue of MCA 327			
❑ 786	Wishbone Four	198?	$10
—Reissue			

WISHFUL THINKING
PAUSA
| ❑ 7205 | Think Again | 1987 | $30 |
| ❑ 7187 | Wishful Thinking | 1986 | $25 |

SOUNDWINGS
| ❑ SW-2109 | Way Down West | 1988 | $25 |

WISNER, JIMMY
CHANCELLOR
| ❑ CHJ-5014 [M] | Aper-Sepshun | 1960 | $75 |
| ❑ CHJS-5014 [S] | Aper-Sepshun | 1960 | $75 |

COLUMBIA
| ❑ CS9837 | Love Theme from "Romeo and Juliet | 1969 | $12 |

FELSTED
| ❑ FL-7509 [M] | Blues for Harvey | 1962 | $75 |
| ❑ FL-2509 [S] | Blues for Harvey | 1962 | $75 |

WYNCOTE
| ❑ W-9103 [M] | Cast Your Fate to the Wind | 1965 | $12 |
| ❑ SW-9103 [S] | Cast Your Fate to the Wind | 1965 | $15 |

WITHERS, BILL
COLUMBIA
❑ FC37199	Bill Withers' Greatest Hits	1981	$12
—Re-release of 36877 with "Just the Two of Us" added			
❑ JC35596	'Bout Love	1979	$12
❑ PC40178	Just As I Am	1985	$10
—Reissue of Sussex 7006			
❑ PC33704	Making Music	1975	$12
❑ JC34903	Menagerie	1977	$12
❑ PC34327	Naked and Warm	1976	$12
❑ PC40177	Still Bill	1985	$10
—Reissue of Sussex 7014			
❑ JC36877	The Best of Bill Withers	1981	$0
—Canceled?			
❑ FC39887	Watching You Watching Me	1985	$12

MOBILE FIDELITY
| ❑ MFSL20446 [B] | Bill Withers Live At Carnegie Hall | 2014 | $40 |

SUSSEX
| ❑ SXBS-7025-2 | Bill Withers Live at Carnegie Hall | 1973 | $25 |
| ❑ SUX-8032 | +'Justments | 1974 | $18 |

Number	Title	Yr	NM

Number	Title	Yr	NM
❏ SXBS-7006 [B]	Just As I Am	1971	$25
❏ SXBS-7014	Still Bill	1972	$25
❏ SUX-8037	The Best of Bill Withers	1975	$18

WITHERSPOON, JIMMY, AND BEN WEBSTER
VERVE
❏ V6-8835	Previously Unreleased Recordings	197?	$35

WITHERSPOON, JIMMY, AND GERRY MULLIGAN
EVEREST ARCHIVE OF FOLK & JAZZ
❏ 264	Jimmy Witherspoon and Gerry Mulligan	197?	$30

WITHERSPOON, JIMMY, AND RICHARD "GROOVE" HOLMES
OLYMPIC GOLD MEDAL
❏ 7107	Groovin' and Spoonin'	1974	$30

SURREY
❏ S-1106 [M]	Blues for Spoon and Groove	1965	$75
❏ SS-1106 [S]	Blues for Spoon and Groove	1965	$75

WITHERSPOON, JIMMY
ABC
❏ 717	Handbags and Gladrags	1970	$75

ANALOGUE PRODUCTIONS
❏ APR3008	Evenin' Blues	199?	$35

BLUE NOTE
❏ BN-LA534-G	Spoonful	1976	$30

BLUESWAY
❏ BLS-6026	Blues Singer	1969	$75
❏ BLS-6040	Hunh	1970	$75
❏ BLS-6051	The Best of Jimmy Witherspoon	1970	$75

CAPITOL
❏ ST-11360	Love Is a Five Letter Word	1975	$30

CHESS
❏ CH-93003	Spoon So Easy: The Chess Years	1990	$30

CONSTELLATION
❏ CM1422 [M]	Take This Hammer	1964	$150
❏ CMS1422 [R]	Take This Hammer	1964	$75

CROWN
❏ CLP-5156 [M]	Jimmy Witherspoon	1959	$175

— Black label, silver print
❏ CLP-5156 [M]	Jimmy Witherspoon	1961	$75

— Gray label, black print
❏ CLP-5192 [M]	Jimmy Witherspoon Sings the Blues	1959	$175

— Black label, silver print
❏ CLP-5192 [M]	Jimmy Witherspoon Sings the Blues	1961	$75

— Gray label, black print
❏ CST-215 [S]	Jimmy Witherspoon Sings the Blues	1961	$175

— Red vinyl; contrary to prior reports, this album -- at least the red vinyl version -- is in true stereo!
❏ CST-215 [S]	Jimmy Witherspoon Sings the Blues	1961	$200

— Black vinyl; this value assumes that this is in true stereo, as the red vinyl version is, but this has not been confirmed

FANTASY
❏ OBC-527	Baby, Baby, Baby	1990	$30

— Reissue of Prestige 7290
❏ OBC-511	Evenin' Blues	1988	$30

— Reissue of Prestige 7300
❏ 9660	Rockin' L.A.	1989	$30
❏ 24701	The 'Spoon Concerts	1972	$50

HIFI
❏ R-421 [M]	At the Monterey Jazz Festival	1959	$200
❏ SR-421 [S]	At the Monterey Jazz Festival	1959	$120
❏ R-422 [M]	Feelin' the Spirit	1959	$200
❏ SR-422 [S]	Feelin' the Spirit	1959	$120
❏ R-426 [M]	Jimmy Witherspoon at the Renaissance	1959	$200
❏ SR-426 [S]	Jimmy Witherspoon at the Renaissance	1959	$120

JAZZ MAN
❏ 5013	Jimmy Witherspoon Sings the Blues	1980	$30

LAX
❏ PW37115	Love Is a Five Letter Word	1981	$25

— Reissue of Capitol LP

MUSE
❏ MR-5288	Jimmy Witherspoon Sings the Blues	1983	$25
❏ MR-5327	Midnight Lady Called the Blues	1986	$25

PRESTIGE
❏ PRLP-7290 [M]	Baby, Baby, Baby	1963	$40
❏ PRST-7290 [S]	Baby, Baby, Baby	1963	$40
❏ PRLP-7314 [M]	Blues Around the Clock	1964	$40
❏ PRST-7314 [S]	Blues Around the Clock	1964	$40
❏ PRLP-7475 [M]	Blues for Easy Livers	1967	$75
❏ PRST-7475 [S]	Blues for Easy Livers	1967	$50
❏ PRLP-7327 [M]	Blue Spoon	1964	$40
❏ PRST-7327 [S]	Blue Spoon	1964	$40
❏ PRLP-7300 [M]	Evenin' Blues	1964	$40
❏ PRST-7300 [S]	Evenin' Blues	1964	$40
❏ 7855	Mean Old Frisco	1974	$35
❏ PRLP-7356 [M]	Some of My Best Friends Are the Blues	1965	$75
❏ PRST-7356 [S]	Some of My Best Friends Are the Blues	1965	$75
❏ PRLP-7418 [M]	Spoon in London	1966	$75
❏ PRST-7418 [S]	Spoon in London	1966	$75
❏ PRST-7713	The Best of Jimmy Witherspoon	1969	$50

RCA VICTOR
❏ LPM-1639 [M]	Goin' to Kansas City Blues	1957	$200
❏ ANL1-1048	Goin' to Kansas City Blues	1976	$25

— Reissue

REPRISE
❏ R-6012 [M]	Hey, Mrs. Jones	1961	$40
❏ R9-6012 [S]	Hey, Mrs. Jones	1961	$120
❏ R-6059 [M]	Roots	1962	$40
❏ R9-6059 [S]	Roots	1962	$120
❏ R-2008 [M]	Spoon	1961	$40
❏ R9-2008 [S]	Spoon	1961	$120

UNITED
❏ 7715	A Spoonful of Blues	197?	$30

VERVE
❏ V-5050 [M]	A Spoonful of Soul	1968	$75
❏ V6-5050 [S]	A Spoonful of Soul	1968	$50
❏ V-5007 [M]	Blue Point of View	1966	$50
❏ V6-5007 [S]	Blue Point of View	1966	$75
❏ V-5030 [M]	Blues Is Now	1967	$75
❏ V6-5030 [S]	Blues Is Now	1967	$50

WORLD PACIFIC
❏ WP-1267 [M]	Singin' the Blues	1959	$300
❏ WP-1402 [M]	There's Good Rockin' Tonight	1961	$300

— Reissue of 1267

WITTWER, JOHNNY
STINSON
❏ SLP-58	Piano Rags	195?	$25

— reissue with new prefix and label

WIZARD
PEON
❏ 1069	Original Wizard	1971	$250

WIZARDS FROM KANSAS, THE
MERCURY
❏ SR-61309	The Wizards from Kansas	1970	$250

WOFFORD, MIKE
DISCOVERY
❏ 784	Afterthoughts	1978	$35
❏ 778	Bird of Paradise	1977	$35
❏ 808	Mike Wofford Plays Jerome Kern	1979	$25
❏ 816	Mike Wofford Plays Jerome Kern, Volume 2	1980	$25
❏ 827	Mike Wofford Plays Jerome Kern, Volume 3	198?	$25

EPIC
❏ LN24225 [M]	Strawberry Wine	1967	$40
❏ BN26225 [S]	Strawberry Wine	1967	$85

FLYING DUTCHMAN
❏ BDL1-1372	Joplin: Interpretations '76	1976	$30

MILESTONE
❏ MPS-9012	Summer Night	1968	$25

TREND
❏ TR-552	Funkalero	1988	$25

WOFSEY, GARY
AMBI
❏ 1521	Kef's Pool	198?	$30
❏ 1520	Mel	198?	$30
❏ 1519	My Grandfather's Clock	198?	$30

WOLFE, NEIL, AND NOAH YOUNG
WK
❏ 101	I Am Music/I Am Song	197?	$35

WOLFE, NEIL
COLUMBIA
❏ CL2378 [M]	Out of This World	1965	$30
❏ CS9178 [S]	Out of This World	1965	$35
❏ CS9600	Piano for Barbra	1968	$30
❏ CL2239 [M]	Piano -- My Way	1964	$30
❏ CS9039 [S]	Piano -- My Way	1964	$35

IMPERIAL
❏ LP-9169 [M]	Neil Swings Nicely	1962	$175
❏ LP-12084 [S]	Neil Swings Nicely	1962	$175
❏ LP-9192 [M]	One Order of Blues	1962	$175
❏ LP-12192 [S]	One Order of Blues	1962	$175

WOLFE, STEVE, AND NANCY KING
INNER CITY
❏ IC-1049	First Date	197?	$30

WOLFMAN JACK
BREAD
❏ 0170	Wolfman Jack and the Wolf Pack	1965	$400

WOODEN NICKEL
❏ BWS1-0119	Fun and Romance Through the Ages	1974	$30
❏ WNS-1009	Wolfman Jack	1972	$30

WOLLMAN, TERRY
NOVA
❏ 8706	Bimini	1987	$25

WOMACK, BOBBY
ARISTA
❏ AB4222 [B]	Roads of Life	1979	$15

BEVERLY GLEN
❏ 10000	The Poet	1981	$12
❏ 10003	The Poet II	1984	$12

COLUMBIA
❏ PC34384	Home Is Where the Heart Is	1977	$12
❏ JC35083	Pieces	1978	$12

LIBERTY
❏ LN-10171	Bobby Womack's Greatest Hits	198?	$10

— Budget-line reissue of United Artists 346
❏ LST-7645	The Womack "Live	1971	$15

MCA
❏ 5617	So Many Rivers	1985	$10

MINIT
❏ 24014	Fly Me to the Moon	1968	$30
❏ 24027	My Prescription	1969	$30

UNITED ARTISTS
❏ UAS-5225	Across 110th Street	1972	$15
❏ UA-LA346-G	Bobby Womack's Greatest Hits	1974	$15
❏ UA-LA638-G	B.W. Goes C and W	1976	$15
❏ UAS-5539	Communication	1971	$15
❏ UA-LA043-F [B]	Facts of Life	1973	$18
❏ UA-LA353-G	I Don't Know What the World Is Coming To	1975	$15
❏ UA-LA199-G	Lookin' for a Love Again	1974	$15
❏ UA-LA544-G	Safety Zone	1975	$15
❏ UAS-5577	Understanding	1972	$15
❏ LM-1002	Understanding	1980	$10

— Reissue of 5577

WOMB
DOT
❏ DLP-25959 [B]	Overdub	1969	$30
❏ DLP-25933 [B]	Womb	1969	$30

WOMBLES, THE
COLUMBIA
❏ KC33140	Remember You're a Womble	1974	$15

HALLMARK
❏ SHM977	The Wombles Christmas Party	197?	$0

— UK import; only one Christmas song despite the LP title

WOMENFOLK, THE
RCA VICTOR
❏ LPM-3527 [M]	Man Oh Man	1966	$15
❏ LSP-3527 [S]	Man Oh Man	1966	$18

Number	Title	Yr	NM
❏ LPM-2919 [M]	Never Underestimate the Power of the Womenfolk	1964	$15
❏ LSP-2919 [S]	Never Underestimate the Power of the Womenfolk	1964	$18
❏ LPM-2832 [M]	The Womenfolk	1964	$15
❏ LSP-2832 [S]	The Womenfolk	1964	$18
❏ LPM-2991 [M]	The Womenfolk at the Hungry I	1965	$15
❏ LSP-2991 [S]	The Womenfolk at the Hungry I	1965	$18

WONDER, STEVIE
GORDY
❏ GS932 [B]	Eivets Rednow	1968	$40

— *As "Eivets Rednow*

JOBETE
❏ JSA-6253 [DJ]	The Wonder of Stevie	1988	$40

— *Publisher's demo with excerpts of 105 (!) Stevie Wonder songs*

MOTOWN
❏ 6248ML	Characters	1987	$12
❏ 31453 0238-1 [DJ]	Conversation Peace	1995	$30

— *Vinyl is promo only; white cover with custom sticker*

❏ M5-166V1	Down to Earth	1981	$15

— *Reissue of Tamla 272*

❏ M9-804A3	Looking Back	1977	$30

— *Withdrawn after Stevie Wonder objected to its release*

❏ 6291ML	Music from the Movie Jungle Fever	1991	$25
❏ 10903141	Music of My Mind	2008	$25
❏ M5-179V1	My Cherie Amour	1981	$15

— *Reissue of Tamla 296*

❏ M5-131V1	Recorded Live/Little Stevie Wonder/The 12 Year Old Genius	1981	$15

— *Reissue of Tamla 240*

❏ M5-176V1	Signed, Sealed and Delivered	1981	$15

— *Reissue of Tamla 304*

❏ 5255ML	Someday at Christmas	1982	$12

— *Reissue of Tamla 281*

❏ M5-219V1	The Jazz Soul of Little Stevie	1981	$15

— *Reissue of Tamla 233*

❏ 6108ML	The Woman in Red	1984	$15

— *With no sticker proclaiming "New Stevie Wonder Album*

❏ 6108ML	The Woman in Red	1984	$12

— *With sticker at top proclaiming "New Stevie Wonder Album*

❏ M5-173V1	Tribute to Uncle Ray	1981	$15

— *Reissue of Tamla 232*

❏ M5-183V1	Up-Tight Everything's Alright	1981	$15

— *Reissue of Tamla 268*

❏ M5-150V1	With a Song in My Heart	1981	$15

— *Reissue of Tamla 250*

TAMLA
❏ T272 [M]	Down to Earth	1966	$25
❏ TS272 [S]	Down to Earth	1966	$30
❏ TS291	For Once in My Life	1968	$25
❏ T6-332S1	Fulfillingness' First Finale	1974	$18
❏ T282 [M]	Greatest Hits	1968	$30
❏ TS282 [S]	Greatest Hits	1968	$25
❏ T8-373S1	Hotter Than July	1980	$15
❏ T326L	Innervisions	1973	$18
❏ 6134TL	In Square Circle	1985	$12

❏ T279 [M]	I Was Made to Love Her	1967	$25
❏ TS279 [S]	I Was Made to Love Her	1967	$30
❏ T13-371C2	Journey Through the Secret Life of Plants	1979	$18
❏ T314L	Music of My Mind	1972	$25
❏ TS296	My Cherie Amour	1969	$25
❏ T240 [M]	Recorded Live/Little Stevie Wonder/The 12 Year Old Genius	1963	$175

— *The above three LPs as "Little Stevie Wonder*

Number	Title	Yr	NM
❏ TS304	Signed Sealed and Delivered	1970	$25
❏ T281 [M]	Someday at Christmas	1967	$30
❏ TS281 [S]	Someday at Christmas	1967	$40
❏ T7-362R1	Someday at Christmas	1978	$25

— *Unusual reissue of 281*

❏ T13-340C2	Songs in the Key of Life	1976	$25

— *With booklet and bonus 7-inch EP (deduct 25% if missing)*

❏ T255 [M]	Stevie at the Beach	1964	$100
❏ TS298	Stevie Wonder Live	1970	$25
❏ T313L	Stevie Wonder's Greatest Hits Vol. 2	1971	$25

— *Some, if not all, LP covers have the title mis-punctuated as "Stevie Wonders' Greatest Hits Vol. 2*

❏ 6002TL2	Stevie Wonder's Original Musiquarium I	1982	$18
❏ T319L [B]	Talking Book	1972	$30

— *Original pressings have a braille note on cover*

❏ T319L	Talking Book	1973	$12

— *No braille note on cover*

❏ T233 [M]	The Jazz Soul of Little Stevie	1962	$250
❏ T232 [M]	Tribute to Uncle Ray	1962	$250
❏ T268 [M]	Up-Tight Everything's Alright	1966	$30
❏ TS268 [S]	Up-Tight Everything's Alright	1966	$30
❏ TS308	Where I'm Coming From	1971	$25
❏ T250 [M]	With a Song in My Heart	1964	$100
❏ T248 [M]	Workout Stevie, Workout	1963	$1000

— *Canceled; test pressings or acetates may exist*

UNIVERSAL MOTOWN
❏ 5316422	Songs in the Key of Life	2009	$30

— *Two LP plus 7*

WONDERLAND BAND, THE
ROADSHOW
❏ BXL1-3390	Wonderwoman	1979	$18

WOOD, BOBBY
JOY
❏ JL1001 [M]	Bobby Wood	1964	$40

WOOD, BOOTY
MASTER JAZZ
❏ 8102	Hang In There	197?	$35

WOOD, BRENTON
BRENT
❏ 5100 [M]	Introducing Brenton Wood! Boogaloo	1967	$40
❏ S-100 [S]	Introducing Brenton Wood! Boogaloo	1967	$75

— *Four tracks by Brenton Wood, six by other artists*

CREAM
❏ 1006	Come Softly	1977	$18

DOUBLE SHOT
❏ 1003 [M]	Baby You Got It	1967	$30
❏ 5003 [S]	Baby You Got It	1967	$30

— *Black vinyl*

❏ 5003 [S]	Baby You Got It	1967	$250

— *Multi-color vinyl*

❏ 1002 [M]	Oogum Boogum	1967	$30
❏ 5002 [S]	Oogum Boogum	1967	$30

RHINO
❏ RNLP-70223	The Best of Brenton Wood	1986	$12

WOOD, DEL
COLUMBIA
❏ CL2539 [M]	Upright, Low Down and Honky Tonk	1966	$15
❏ CS9339 [S]	Upright, Low Down and Honky Tonk	1966	$18

LAMB & LION
❏ 1009	Rag Time Glory Special	197?	$15

MERCURY
❏ MG-20804 [M]	Piano Roll Blues	1963	$15
❏ SR-60804 [S]	Piano Roll Blues	1963	$18
❏ MG-20713 [M]	Ragtime Goes International	1962	$15
❏ SR-60713 [S]	Ragtime Goes International	1962	$18
❏ SR-60678 [S]	Ragtime Goes South of the Border	1962	$18
❏ MG-20678 [M]	Ragtime Goes South of the Border	1962	$15
❏ MG-20978 [M]	Roll Out the Piano	1964	$15
❏ SR-60978 [S]	Roll Out the Piano	1964	$18

RCA CAMDEN
❏ CAL-684 [M]	Honky Tonk Piano	1962	$15
❏ CAS-684 [R]	Honky Tonk Piano	1962	$12
❏ CAL-796 [M]	It's Honky Tonk Time	1964	$15
❏ CAS-796 [R]	It's Honky Tonk Time	1964	$12

RCA VICTOR
❏ LPM-2240 [M]	Buggies, Bustles and Barrelhouse	1960	$18
❏ LSP-2240 [S]	Buggies, Bustles and Barrelhouse	1960	$25
❏ LPM-1129 [M]	Down Yonder	1955	$25
❏ LPM-2203 [M]	Flivvers, Flappers and Fox Trots	1960	$18

Number	Title	Yr	NM
❏ LSP-2203 [S]	Flivvers, Flappers and Fox Trots	1960	$25
❏ LPM-1437 [M]	Hot, Happy and Honky	1957	$25
❏ LPM-2091 [M]	Mississippi Show Boat	1959	$18
❏ LSP-2091 [S]	Mississippi Show Boat	1959	$25
❏ LPM-1633 [M]	Rags to Riches	1958	$18
❏ LSP-1633 [S]	Rags to Riches	1958	$25
❏ LPM-3907 [M]	The Best of Del Wood	1968	$30
❏ LSP-3907 [S]	The Best of Del Wood	1968	$15

VOCALION
❏ VL3609 [M]	There's a Tavern in the Town	196?	$15

WOOD, HALLY
ELEKTRA
❏ EKL-10 [10]	O Lovely Appearance of Death	1953	$50

WOOD, JOHN
LOS ANGELES
❏ 1001	Freeway of Love	197?	$35
❏ 1002	Until Goodbye	1976	$35

RANWOOD
❏ RLP-8036	Introducing the John Wood Trio	1969	$35

WOOD, RONNIE
Also see FACES; THE ROLLING STONES.
COLUMBIA
❏ FC37473	1234	1981	$18
❏ JC35702	Gimme Some Neck	1979	$18
❏ PC35702 [B]	Gimme Some Neck	198?	$10

— *Budget-line reissue*

WARNER BROS.
❏ BS2819	I've Got My Own Album to Do	1974	$25
❏ BS2872	Now Look	1975	$18

WOOD, ROY
Also see ELECTRIC LIGHT ORCHESTRA; THE MOVE.
TOWNHOUSE
❏ SN-7127	One Man Band	1981	$15

UNITED ARTISTS
❏ UA-LA168-F [B]	Boulders	1973	$18
❏ 0(# unknown) [DJ]	Boulders Folder	1973	$40

— *Promo version of 168 in 13x13 folder with press kit and postcards*

❏ UA-LA219-G [B]	Introducing Eddy and the Falcons	1974	$15
❏ UA-LA575-G [B]	Mustard	1976	$15
❏ UA-LA042-F [B]	Wizzard's Brew	1973	$15

WARNER BROS.
❏ BSK3247 [B]	On the Road Again	1979	$15
❏ BS3065 [B]	Super Active Wizzo	1977	$15

WOODARD, LYMAN
STRATA
❏ 105-75	Saturday Night Special	197?	$35

WOODBURY, WOODY
STEREODDITIES
❏ 0BITOA	Booze Is the Only Answer	1961	$40

— *With record, paperback book and smaller booklets*

❏ MW6	The Best of Woody Woodbury	1963	$25
❏ MW5	The Spice Is Right	1962	$30
❏ MW7	Through the Keyhole	1964	$25
❏ MW1	Woody Woodbury Looks at Love and Life	1960	$30
❏ MW3	Woody Woodbury's Concert in Comedy	1961	$30
❏ MW2	Woody Woodbury's Laughing Room	1960	$30
❏ MW4	Woody Woodbury's Saloonatics	1961	$30

WOODEN GLASS FEATURING BILLY WOOTEN
INTERIM
❏ 2546 [B]	Recorded Live	1972	$100

WOODING, SAM
BIOGRAPH
❏ 12026	Chocolate Dandies	197?	$25

WOODS, BILL
COUNTRY TOWN
❏ CTR-24803 [M]	Bill Woods from Bakersfield	196?	$120

WOODS, CHRIS
DELMARK
❏ DS-437	Modus Operandi	1979	$25
❏ DS-434	Somebody Stole My Blues	197?	$30

Number	Title	Yr	NM

WOODS, JIMMY

CAPITOL
❑ ST-654	Essence	1971	$20

CONTEMPORARY
❑ M-3605 [M]	Awakening	1962	$250
❑ S-7605 [S]	Awakening	1962	$250
❑ M-3612 [M]	Conflict	1963	$250
❑ S-7612 [S]	Conflict	1963	$250

WOODS, MACEO

VEE JAY
❑ LP-5001 [M]	Amazing Grace	1959	$30
—Maroon label			
❑ LP-5001 [M]	Amazing Grace	1961	$25
—Black colorband label			
❑ LP-5053 [M]	Garden of Prayer	1963	$25
❑ SR-5053 [S]	Garden of Prayer	1963	$30
❑ VJS-18002	Seeking Salvation	1975	$18
❑ LP-5010 [M]	The Lord Will Make a Way	1960	$30
—Maroon label			
❑ LP-5010 [M]	The Lord Will Make a Way	1961	$25
—Black colorband label			

VOLT
❑ VOS-6009	Hello Sunshine	1970	$25
❑ VOS-6013	Step to Jesus	1971	$25

WOODS, PHIL, AND CHRIS SWANSON

SEA BREEZE
❑ SB-2008	Crazy Horse	198?	$25
❑ SB-2019	Piper at the Gates of Dawn	1984	$25

WOODS, PHIL, AND GENE QUILL

COLUMBIA JAZZ ODYSSEY
❑ PC36806	Phil Talks with Quill	1980	$25

EPIC
❑ LN3521 [M]	Phil Talks with Quill	1959	$150
❑ BN554 [S]	Phil Talks with Quill	1959	$100
❑ BN554 [S]	Phil Talks with Quill	199?	$75
—Classic Records reissue on audiophile vinyl			

FANTASY
❑ OJC-215	Phil and Quill with Prestige	198?	$25

PRESTIGE
❑ 2508	Four Altos	198?	$30
❑ PRLP-7115 [M]	Phil and Quill with Prestige	1957	$300

RCA VICTOR
❑ LPM-1284 [M]	The Woods-Quill Sextet	1956	$100

WOODS, PHIL, AND GENE QUILL/JACKIE MCLEAN AND JOHN JENKINS/HAL MCKUSICK

NEW JAZZ
❑ NJLP-8204 [M]	Bird Feathers	1958	$350
— Yellow Prestige label			
❑ NJLP-8204 [M]	Bird Feathers	1959	$175
—Purple label			
❑ NJLP-8204 [M]	Bird Feathers	1965	$175
—Blue label, trident logo at right			

WOODS, PHIL, AND LEW TABACKIN

OMNISOUND
❑ 1033	Phil Woods and Lew Tabackin	198?	$25

WOODS, PHIL

ABC IMPULSE!
❑ AS-9143 [S]	Greek Cooking	1968	$35

ADELPHI
❑ 5010	More Live	198?	$25

ANTILLES
❑ AN-1013	At the Vanguard	198?	$25
❑ AN-1006	Birds of a Feather	1982	$25

BARNABY
❑ KZ31036	Rights of Swing	1972	$30
❑ BR-5016	Rights of Swing	197?	$25
—Reissue			

BLACKHAWK
❑ BKH-50401	Heaven	1986	$25

CANDID
❑ CD-8016 [M]	Rights of Swing	1960	$40
❑ CS-9016 [S]	Rights of Swing	1960	$50

CENTURY
❑ 1050	Songs for Sisyphus	197?	$25

CLEAN CUTS
❑ 702	Phil Woods Quartet, Vol. 1	1979	$30

CONCORD JAZZ
❑ CJ-345	Bop Stew	1988	$25
❑ CJ-377	Bouquet	1989	$30
❑ CJ-361	Evolution	1988	$25

EMBRYO
❑ SD530	Phil Woods at the Frankfurt Jazz Festival	197?	$35

ENJA
❑ 3081	Three for All	1981	$30

EPIC
❑ LN3436 [M]	Warm Woods	1958	$600

FANTASY
❑ OJC-1735	Bird Feathers	198?	$30
❑ OJC-092	Paring Off	198?	$30
❑ OJC-1732	The Young Bloods	198?	$30
❑ OJC-052	Woodlore	1982	$30

GRYPHON
❑ 788	I Remember	1979	$30
❑ 782	Sisyphus	1978	$30

IMPULSE!
❑ A-9143 [M]	Greek Cooking	1967	$75
❑ AS-9143 [S]	Greek Cooking	1967	$75

INNER CITY
❑ IC-1002	European Rhythm Machine	197?	$35

JAZZ MAN
❑ 5001	Rights of Swing	1982	$25

MGM
❑ SE-4695	Phil Woods at the Montreux Jazz Festival	197?	$35

MOSAIC
❑ MQ7-159	The Phil Woods Quartet/ Quintet 20th Anniversary Set	199?	$120

MUSE
❑ MR-5037	Musique de Bois	1974	$30

NEW JAZZ
❑ NJLP-1104 [10]	Phil Woods New Jazz Quintet	1954	$500
❑ NJLP-8291 [M]	Pot Pie	1962	$250
—Purple label			
❑ NJLP-8291 [M]	Pot Pie	1965	$175
—Blue label, trident logo at right			
❑ NJLP-8304 [M]	Sugan	1963	$0
—Canceled, reassigned to Status			

PALO ALTO/TBA
❑ PA-8084	Live from New York	1985	$25

PRESTIGE
❑ 24065	Altology	197?	$35
❑ PRST-7673 [R]	Early Quintets	1969	$35
❑ PRLP-7046 [M]	Paring Off	1956	$400
❑ PRLP-191 [10]	Phil Woods New Jazz Quartet	1954	$400
❑ PRLP-204 [10]	Phil Woods New Jazz Quintet	1955	$400
❑ PRLP-7080 [M]	The Young Bloods	1957	$300
❑ PRLP-7018 [M]	Woodlore	1956	$500
—Yellow label with W. 50th St. address			

QUICKSILVER
❑ QS-4011	Live from New York	1991	$30

RCA VICTOR
❑ BGL1-1800	Floresta	1976	$30
❑ BXL1-1800	Floresta	1978	$25
—Reissue with new prefix			
❑ BGL1-1027	Images	1975	$30
❑ BXL1-1027	Images	1978	$25
—Reissue with new prefix			
❑ BGL2-2202	Live from the Showboat	1977	$35
❑ BGL1-1391	The New Album	1976	$30
❑ BXL1-1391	The New Album	1978	$25
—Reissue with new prefix			

RED RECORD
❑ VPA-163	European Tour Live	198?	$30
❑ VPA-177	Integrity	1985	$35

SAVOY JAZZ
❑ SJL-1179	Bird Calls: Vol. 1	1987	$25

STATUS
❑ ST-8304 [M]	Sugan	1965	$40

TESTAMENT
❑ 4402	New Music	197?	$35

VERVE
❑ V6-8791	Round Trip	1969	$35

WOODY, BILL

ABC HICKORY
❑ HB-44009	Just for You Babe	1977	$15
—As "Woody			

MCA
❑ 3095	Organized Noise	1979	$12

WOODY'S TRUCK STOP

SMASH

❑ SRS-67111 [B]	Woody's Truck Stop	1969	$30

WOOFERS, THE

WYNCOTE
❑ W9011 [M]	Dragsville	1964	$40
❑ SW9011 [S]	Dragsville	1964	$50

WOOLEY, AMY

MCA
❑ 5240	Amy Wooley	1981	$12

WOOLEY, SHEB
Includes records by his comedic alter ego, "Ben Colder."

GUSTO
❑ GTV-110	Greatest Hits of Sheb Wooley Or Do You Say Ben Colder	1979	$15

MGM
❑ E-4173 [M]	Ben Colder	1963	$30
❑ SE-4173 [S]	Ben Colder	1963	$40
—MGM 4173 as "Ben Colder			
❑ GAS-139	Ben Colder (Golden Archive Series)	1970	$18
—As "Ben Colder			
❑ E-4421 [M]	Big Ben Strikes Again	1967	$25
❑ SE-4421 [S]	Big Ben Strikes Again	1967	$25
—MGM 4421 as "Ben Colder			
❑ SE-4614	Harper Valley P.T.A.	1968	$25
—As "Ben Colder			
❑ SE-4629	Have One On	1969	$18
—As "Ben Colder			
❑ E-4325 [M]	It's a Big Land	1965	$25
❑ SE-4325 [S]	It's a Big Land	1965	$30
❑ SE-4758	Live and Loaded	1971	$18
—As "Ben Colder			
❑ E-3299 [M]	Sheb Wooley	1956	$175
❑ E-3904 [M]	Songs from the Days of Rawhide	1961	$40
❑ SE-3904 [S]	Songs from the Days of Rawhide	1961	$50
❑ E-4117 [M]	Spoofing the Big Ones	1961	$40
❑ SE-4117 [S]	Spoofing the Big Ones	1961	$50
—MGM 4117 as "Ben Colder			
❑ E-4136 [M]	Tales of How the West Was Won	1963	$30
❑ SE-4136 [S]	Tales of How the West Was Won	1963	$40
❑ E-4026 [M]	That's My Ma and That's My Pa	1962	$30
❑ SE-4026 [S]	That's My Ma and That's My Pa	1962	$40
❑ SE-4530	The Best of Ben Colder	1968	$25
—As "Ben Colder			
❑ E-4275 [M]	The Very Best of Sheb Wooley	1965	$25
❑ SE-4275 [S]	The Very Best of Sheb Wooley	1965	$30
❑ SE-4876	The Wacky World of Ben Colder	1973	$18
—As "Ben Colder			
❑ SE-4615	Warm and Wooley	1969	$25
❑ SE-4807	Warming Up to Colder	1972	$18
—As "Ben Colder			
❑ SE-4674	Wild Again	1970	$18
—As "Ben Colder			
❑ E-4482 [M]	Wine, Women and Song	1967	$25
❑ SE-4482 [S]	Wine, Women and Song	1967	$25
—MGM 4482 as "Ben Colder			

WOOLIES, THE

SPIRIT
❑ 9645-2001	Basic Rock	1971	$40
❑ 9645-2005	Live at Lizards	1973	$40

WOOLLEY, BRUCE, AND THE CAMERA CLUB
COLUMBIA
Number	Title	Yr	NM
□ NJC36301	Bruce Woolley and the Camera Club	1980	$18

WORLD BASS VIOLIN ENSEMBLE
BLACK SAINT
Number	Title	Yr	NM
□ BSR-0063	Basically Yours	198?	$30

WORLD FAMOUS CHORUS, A
KAYBANK-MUSICMASTERS
| □ KB2698 | Seasons Greetings | 197? | $15 |

WORLD OF OZ, THE
DERAM
| □ DES18022 [B] | The World of Oz | 1969 | $75 |

WORLD PARTY
CHRYSALIS
| □ F1-21654 | Goodbye Jumbo | 1990 | $15 |
| □ R134261 | Private Revolution | 1987 | $15 |

—RCA Music Service edition
| □ BFV41552 | Private Revolution | 1986 | $12 |

WORLD RHYTHM BAND
DISCOVERY
| □ 865 | Ibex | 198? | $25 |

WORLD SAXOPHONE QUARTET
BLACK SAINT
□ BSR-0077	Live in Zurich	198?	$30
□ BSR-0056	Revue	198?	$30
□ BSR-0027	Steppin'	198?	$30
□ BSR-0046	W.S.Q.	198?	$30

ELEKTRA/MUSICIAN
| □ 60864 | Rhythm and Blues | 1989 | $30 |

ELEKTRA/NONESUCH
| □ 79164 | Dances and Ballads | 1988 | $25 |
| □ 79137 | World Saxophone Quartet Plays Duke Ellington | 1987 | $25 |

WORLD'S GREATEST JAZZ BAND, THE
EVEREST ARCHIVE OF FOLK & JAZZ
| □ 314 | The World's Greatest Jazz Band | 197? | $25 |

FLYING DUTCHMAN
| □ BDL1-1371 | The World's Greatest Jazz Band In Concert | 1976 | $30 |

WORLD JAZZ
□ 1	Century Plaza	197?	$30
□ 2	Hark the Herald Angels Swing	197?	$30
□ 3	The World's Greatest Jazz Band in Concert, Vol. 1	197?	$30
□ 4	The World's Greatest Jazz Band in Concert, Vol. 2	197?	$30
□ 8	The World's Greatest Jazz Band On Tour	197?	$30
□ 10	The World's Greatest Jazz Band On Tour II	197?	$30
□ 6	The World's Greatest Jazz Band Plays Cole Porter	197?	$30
□ 9	The World's Greatest Jazz Band Plays Duke Ellington	197?	$30
□ 11	The World's Greatest Jazz Band Plays George Gershwin	1978	$30
□ 7	The World's Greatest Jazz Band Plays Rodgers and Hart	197?	$30

WORTH, MARION, AND GEORGE MORGAN
Also see each artist's individual listings.
COLUMBIA
| □ CL2197 [M] | Slippin' Around | 1964 | $25 |
| □ CS8997 [S] | Slippin' Around | 1964 | $30 |

WORTH, MARION
COLUMBIA
□ CL2011 [M]	Marion Worth's Greatest Hits	1963	$25
□ CS8811 [S]	Marion Worth's Greatest Hits	1963	$30
□ CL2287 [M]	Marion Worth Sings Marty Robbins	1964	$25
□ CS9087 [S]	Marion Worth Sings Marty Robbins	1964	$30

DECCA
| □ DL4936 [M] | A Woman Needs Love | 1967 | $30 |
| □ DL74936 [S] | A Woman Needs Love | 1967 | $25 |

WOULD
PERCEPTION
| □ 24 | Would | 1972 | $30 |

WRAY, LINK
EPIC
| □ LN3661 [M] | Link Wray and the Waymen | 1960 | $300 |

NORTON
□ 211	Big City After Dark (Missing Links Vol. 2)	199?	$12
□ 210	Hillbilly Wolf (Missing Links Vol. 1)	199?	$12
□ 212	Some Kinda Nut (Missing Links Vol. 3)	199?	$12
□ 253	Streets of Chicago (Missing Links Vol. 4)	1995	$12

POLYDOR
□ PD-5047	Be What You Want To	1972	$25
□ 24-4064	Link Wray	1971	$25
□ PD-6025	The Link Wray Rumble	1974	$25

RECORD FACTORY
| □ 1929 | Yesterday and Today | 1969 | $100 |

SWAN
| □ SLP-510 [M] | Jack the Ripper | 1963 | $175 |

VERMILLION
| □ 1924 [M] | Great Guitar Hits | 196? | $100 |
| □ 1925 [M] | Link Wray Sings and Plays Guitar | 196? | $100 |

VISA
| □ 7009 | Bullshot | 1979 | $15 |
| □ 7010 | Live at the Paradiso | 1980 | $15 |

WRAY, VERNON
VERMILLION
| □ 1972 | Wasted | 1972 | $150 |

WRECKLESS ERIC & AMY RIGBY
SOUTHERN DOMESTIC
| □ SD005LP [B] | A Working Museum | 2012 | $25 |

WRECKLESS ERIC
STIFF
| □ USE1 [B] | Whole Wide World | 1979 | $25 |

STIFF/EPIC
| □ E236463 [B] | Big Smash | 1980 | $35 |
| □ AS785 [EP] | Wreckless Eric | 1980 | $25 |

—Promo-only 5-song sample from E2 36463

WRICE, LARRY "WILD"
PACIFIC JAZZ
| □ PJ-24 [M] | Wild! | 1961 | $75 |
| □ ST-24 [S] | Wild! | 1961 | $75 |

WRIGHT, BERNARD
ARISTA
| □ ALB8-8103 | Funky Beat | 198? | $25 |

GRP/ARISTA
| □ GL5011 | 'Nard | 1980 | $30 |

MANHATTAN
| □ ST-53014 | Mr. Wright | 1985 | $25 |

WRIGHT, BETTY
ALSTON
□ 4410	Betty Travelin' in the Wright Circle	1979	$15
□ 4408	Betty Wright Live	1978	$15
□ 4400 [B]	Danger High Voltage	1974	$15
□ SD7026	Hard to Stop	1973	$18
□ SD 33-388 [B]	I Love the Way You Love	1972	$18
□ 4406	This Time for Real	1977	$15

ATCO
| □ SD 33-260 | My First Time Around | 1968 | $30 |

COLLECTABLES
| □ COL-5118 | Golden Classics | 198? | $12 |

EPIC
| □ JE36879 | Betty Wright | 1981 | $12 |
| □ FE38558 | Wright Back at You | 1983 | $12 |

FANTASY
| □ 9644 | Sevens | 1986 | $12 |

MS. B.
| □ 3301 | Mother Wit | 1988 | $12 |
| □ 3318 | Passion and Compassion | 198? | $18 |

WRIGHT, BOBBY
ABC
| □ ABCD-842 | Seasons of Love | 1974 | $15 |

DECCA
| □ DL75319 | Here I Go Again | 1971 | $18 |

WRIGHT, CHARLES, AND THE WATTS 103RD STREET RHYTHM BAND
ABC
| □ D-887 | Lil' Encouragement | 1975 | $15 |

ABC DUNHILL
| □ DS-50162 | Doin' What Comes Naturally | 1973 | $18 |
| □ DS-50187 | Ninety Day Cycle People | 1974 | $15 |

WARNER BROS.
| □ WS1864 | Express Yourself | 1970 | $18 |
| □ WS1801 | In the Jungle, Babe | 1969 | $25 |

—Green label with "W7" logo
| □ WS1801 | In the Jungle, Babe | 1970 | $18 |

—Green label with "WB" logo
| □ BS2620 | Rhythm and Poetry | 1972 | $18 |

—Green label with "WB" logo
| □ BS2620 | Rhythm and Poetry | 1973 | $15 |

—Burbank" palm-trees logo
| □ WS1741 | The Watts 103rd Street Rhythm Band | 1968 | $25 |

—Green label with "W7" logo
| □ WS1761 | Together | 1969 | $25 |

—Green label with "W7" logo
| □ WS1761 | Together | 1970 | $18 |

—Green label with "WB" logo
| □ WS1904 | You're So Beautiful | 1971 | $18 |

WRIGHT, DEMPSEY
ANDEX
| □ A-3006 [M] | The Wright Approach | 1958 | $75 |
| □ AS-3006 [S] | The Wright Approach | 1958 | $50 |

WRIGHT, FRANK
CHIAROSCURO
| □ 2014 | Kevin, My Dear Son | 1979 | $30 |

ESP-DISK'
□ 1023 [M]	Frank Wright Trio	1966	$150
□ S-1023 [S]	Frank Wright Trio	1966	$150
□ 1053 [S]	Your Prayer	1968	$150

WRIGHT, GARY
A&M
□ SP-4277	Extraction	1970	$18
□ SP-4296	Footprint	1971	$18
□ SP-3528	That Was Only Yesterday	1976	$18

—By "Gary Wright/Spooky Tooth"
CYPRESS
| □ 0111 | Who I Am | 1988 | $15 |

WARNER BROS.
□ BSK3244	Headin' Home	1979	$12
□ BS2868	The Dream Weaver	1975	$12
□ BS2951	The Light of Smiles	1976	$12
□ BSK3511	The Right Place	1981	$12
□ BSK3137	Touch and Gone	1977	$12

WRIGHT, GEORGE
ABC/WESTMINSTER GOLD
| □ WGDP-8305 | The Christmas Album | 1974 | $12 |

—Reissue of Dot 25479
DOT
| □ DLP3479 [M] | Christmas Time | 1962 | $15 |
| □ DLP25479 [S] | Christmas Time | 1962 | $18 |

HIFI
| □ R-706 [M] | Merry Christmas | 195? | $18 |
| □ R-705 [M] | Music for Christmas | 195? | $18 |

WRIGHT, JOHN
FANTASY
| □ OJC-1743 | South Side Soul | 1990 | $30 |

NEW JAZZ
| □ NJLP-8322 [M] | The Last Amen | 196? | $0 |

—Canceled; reassigned to Status
PRESTIGE
□ PRLP-7212 [M]	Makin' Out	1961	$250
□ PRLP-7233 [M]	Mr. Soul	1962	$175
□ PRST-7233 [S]	Mr. Soul	1962	$175
□ PRLP-7197 [M]	Nice 'N' Nasty	1961	$250
□ PRLP-7190 [M]	South Side Soul	1960	$250

STATUS
| □ ST-8322 [M] | The Last Amen | 1965 | $100 |

WRIGHT, JOHNNY
DECCA
□ DL4770 [M]	Country Music Special	1966	$30
□ DL74770 [S]	Country Music Special	1966	$30
□ DL4846 [M]	Country the Wright Way	1967	$30
□ DL74846 [S]	Country the Wright Way	1967	$25
□ DL4698 [M]	Hello Vietnam	1965	$30
□ DL74698 [S]	Hello Vietnam	1965	$30
□ DL75019	Johnny Wright Sings Country Favorites	1968	$25

WRIGHT, LEO
ATLANTIC
| □ 1358 [M] | Blues Shout | 1960 | $300 |

—Multicolor label, white "fan" logo at right
| □ SD1358 [S] | Blues Shout | 1960 | $300 |

—Multicolor label, white "fan" logo at right
| □ 1358 [M] | Blues Shout | 196? | $35 |

—Multicolor label, black "fan" logo at right
| □ SD1358 [S] | Blues Shout | 196? | $25 |

Number	Title	Yr	NM
—Multicolor label, black "fan" logo at right			
❏ 1393 [M]	Suddenly the Blues	1962	$175
—Multicolor label, black "fan" logo at right			
❏ SD1393 [S]	Suddenly the Blues	1962	$175
—Multicolor label, black "fan" logo at right			

ROULETTE

Number	Title	Yr	NM
❏ SR-5007	Evening Breeze	1977	$25

VORTEX

Number	Title	Yr	NM
❏ 2011	Soul Talk	197?	$25

WRIGHT, MARVIN "LEFTY"

X

Number	Title	Yr	NM
❏ LXA-3028 [10]	Boogie Woogie Piano	1954	$75

WRIGHT, NAT

WARWICK

Number	Title	Yr	NM
❏ W-2040 [M]	The Biggest Voice in Jazz	1961	$50
❏ W-2040ST [S]	The Biggest Voice in Jazz	1961	$100

WRIGHT, O.V.

BACK BEAT

Number	Title	Yr	NM
❏ 70	A Nickel and a Nail and Ace of Spade	1971	$75
❏ 66	Eight Men, Four Women	1968	$75
❏ 61 [M]	If It's Only for Tonight	1965	$150
❏ S-61 [S]	If It's Only for Tonight	1965	$175
❏ 72	Memphis Unlimited	1973	$50

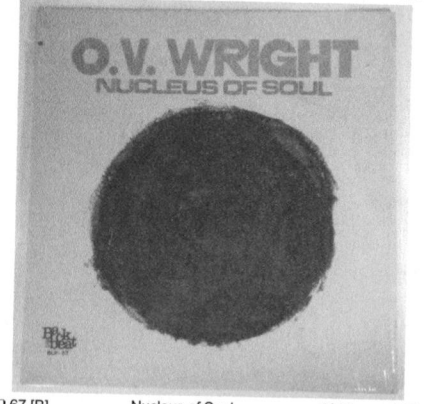

Number	Title	Yr	NM
❏ 67 [B]	Nucleus of Soul	1969	$75

HI

Number	Title	Yr	NM
❏ 6008	Bottom Line	1978	$30
❏ 6001	Into Something	1977	$30
❏ 6011	We're Still Together	1979	$30

WRIGHT, RICHARD
Also see PINK FLOYD.

COLUMBIA

Number	Title	Yr	NM
❏ JC35559 [B]	Wet Dream	1978	$30

WRIGHT, SONNY (2)

KAPP

Number	Title	Yr	NM
❏ KS-3614	I Love You, Loretta Lynn	1968	$25

WRIGHT, WILLIE

ARGO

Number	Title	Yr	NM
❏ LP-4024 [M]	I'm on My Way	1963	$25
❏ LPS-4024 [S]	I'm on My Way	1963	$30

CONCERT DISC

Number	Title	Yr	NM
❏ 45 [S]	I Sing Folk Songs	1960	$40
❏ 1045 [M]	I Sing Folk Songs	1960	$30

WRIGHT BROTHERS, THE

MERCURY

Number	Title	Yr	NM
❏ 818654-1	Easy Street	1984	$10

WARNER BROS.

Number	Title	Yr	NM
❏ 23736	Made in the U.S.A.	1982	$12

WYLER, GRETCHEN

JUBILEE

Number	Title	Yr	NM
❏ JLP-1100 [M]	Wild, Wyler, Wildest	1959	$30
❏ SDJLP-1100 [S]	Wild, Wyler, Wildest	1959	$30

WYLIE, RICHARD "POPCORN

ABC

Number	Title	Yr	NM
❏ ABCD-834	E.S.P.	1974	$75

WYMAN, BILL
Also see THE ROLLING STONES.

ROLLING STONES

Number	Title	Yr	NM
❏ COC59102 [B]	Monkey Grip	1974	$25
❏ COC79100 [B]	Monkey Grip	1974	$30
—Reissue of 59102			

Number	Title	Yr	NM
❏ QD79100 [Q]	Monkey Grip	1974	$40
❏ COC79103	Stone Alone	1976	$25
❏ QD79103 [Q]	Stone Alone	1976	$40

WYNDER K. FROG

UNITED ARTISTS

Number	Title	Yr	NM
❏ UAS-5740 [B]	Into the Fire	1971	$18
❏ UAS-6695 [B]	Out of the Frying Pan	1970	$18

WYNETTE, TAMMY
Also see DAVID HOUSTON AND TAMMY WYNETTE; GEORGE JONES AND TAMMY WYNETTE.

COLUMBIA LIMITED EDITION

Number	Title	Yr	NM
❏ LE10194	Tammy's Touch	197?	$15
❏ LE10049	The First Lady	197?	$15
❏ LE10193	The Ways to Love a Man	197?	$15
❏ LE10195	We Sure Can Love Each Other	197?	$15

COLUMBIA SPECIAL PRODUCTS

Number	Title	Yr	NM
❏ P13261	Bedtime Story	1976	$15
❏ P13259	My Man	1976	$15
❏ P11228	Take Me to Your World	1973	$15
❏ P13256	The Ways to Love a Man	1976	$15
❏ P13611	Twenty Big Hits of Tammy Wynette	197?	$18
❏ P11519	Your Good Girl's Gonna Go Bad	1973	$15

EPIC

Number	Title	Yr	NM
❏ EG40625	Anniversary: 20 Years of Hits	1987	$18
❏ KE32745	Another Lonely Song	1974	$15
❏ KE31285	Bedtime Story	1972	$18
❏ FE38312	Biggest Hits	1984	$12
❏ E30343	Christmas with Tammy	1970	$25
❏ BN26392 [S]	D-I-V-O-R-C-E	1968	$25
❏ LN24392 [M]	D-I-V-O-R-C-E	1968	$50
—This has been confirmed to exist on yellow label stock copies			
❏ FE37344	Encore	1981	$12
❏ PE37344	Encore	198?	$10
—Budget-line reissue			
❏ FE38744	Even the Strong Get Lonely	1983	$12
❏ FE38372	Good Love and Heartbreak	1983	$12
❏ FE40832	Higher Ground	1987	$12
❏ BN26423	Inspiration	1969	$25
❏ KE33582	I Still Believe in Fairy Tales	1975	$15
❏ KE36013	Just Tammy	1979	$15
❏ KE31937	Kids Say the Darndest Things	1973	$18
❏ PE34694	Let's Get Together One Last Time	1977	$15
❏ KE31717	My Man	1972	$18
❏ FE44498	Next to You	1989	$15
❏ KE35044	One of a Kind	1977	$15
❏ JE36485	Only Lonely Sometimes	1980	$12
❏ FE37980	Soft Touch	1982	$12
❏ FE39971	Sometimes When We Touch	1985	$12
❏ BN26451	Stand By Your Man	1969	$25
❏ BG33773	Stand By Your Man/Bedtime Story	1976	$18
❏ LN24353 [M]	Take Me to Your World/I Don't Wanna Play House	1968	$40
—May exist only as a white label promo			
❏ BN26353 [S]	Take Me to Your World/I Don't Wanna Play House	1968	$25
❏ BN26486	Tammy's Greatest Hits	1969	$25
❏ PE26486	Tammy's Greatest Hits	198?	$10
—Budget-line reissue			
❏ E30733	Tammy's Greatest Hits, Volume II	1971	$25
❏ PE30733	Tammy's Greatest Hits, Volume II	198?	$10
—Budget-line reissue			
❏ KE33396	Tammy's Greatest Hits, Volume III	1975	$15
❏ PE33396	Tammy's Greatest Hits, Volume III	198?	$10
—Budget-line reissue			
❏ KE35630	Tammy's Greatest Hits, Volume IV	1978	$15
❏ BN26549	Tammy's Touch	1970	$25

Number	Title	Yr	NM
❏ E30213 [B]	The First Lady	1970	$25
❏ KEG30358	The First Songs of the First Lady	1970	$25
❏ BN26519	The Ways to Love a Man	1970	$25
❏ EGP503	The World of Tammy Wynette	1970	$30
❏ PE34075	'Til I Can Make It on My Own	1976	$15
❏ E30658	We Sure Can Love Each Other	1971	$25
❏ EQ30658 [Q]	We Sure Can Love Each Other	1972	$40
❏ KE35442	Womanhood	1978	$15
❏ KE33246	Woman to Woman	1975	$15
❏ PE34289	You and Me	1976	$15
❏ FE37104	You Brought Me Back	1981	$12
❏ LN24305 [M]	Your Good Girl's Gonna Go Bad	1967	$30
❏ BN26305 [S]	Your Good Girl's Gonna Go Bad	1967	$25

HARMONY

Number	Title	Yr	NM
❏ KH30914	Just a Matter of Time	1971	$15
❏ KH30096	Send Me No Roses	1970	$15

PAIR

Number	Title	Yr	NM
❏ PDL2-1073	From the Bottom of My Heart	1986	$15

REALM

Number	Title	Yr	NM
❏ 2V8047	The Queen Volume 1	1976	$18
❏ 1V8048	The Queen Volume 2	1976	$12

TIME-LIFE

Number	Title	Yr	NM
❏ STW-116	Country Music	1981	$15

WYNN, ALBERT

RIVERSIDE

Number	Title	Yr	NM
❏ RLP-426 [M]	Albert Wynn and His Gutbucket Seven	1962	$250
❏ RS-9426 [R]	Albert Wynn and His Gutbucket Seven	1962	$250

WYNONNA
See WYNONNA JUDD.

WYNTERS, GAIL

HICKORY

Number	Title	Yr	NM
❏ LPS-138 [S]	A Girl for All Seasons	1967	$18
❏ LPM-138 [M]	A Girl for All Seasons	1967	$25

RCA VICTOR

Number	Title	Yr	NM
❏ APL1-2285	Let the Lady Sing	1977	$25

X

X-RAY SPEX

BLUE PLATE

Number	Title	Yr	NM
❏ CAROL-1813-1	Germ Free Adolescents	1992	$25
—Recorded in 1978, this is this classic new wave LP's first American issue			

EMI

Number	Title	Yr	NM
❏ INS-3023	Germ Free Adolescents	1978	$35
—British release only, no U.S. version until 1992			

X

ELEKTRA

Number	Title	Yr	NM
❏ 60430	Ain't Love Grand	1985	$15
❏ 60788	Live at the Whiskey A-Go-Go on the Fabulous Sunset Strip	1988	$18
❏ 60283	More Fun in the New World	1983	$15
❏ 60492	See How We Are	1987	$12
❏ 60150 [B]	Under the Big Black Sun	1982	$18

RHINO

Number	Title	Yr	NM
❏ R1-74370	Los Angeles	2003	$25
—Reissue on 180-gram vinyl			

SLASH

Number	Title	Yr	NM
❏ SR-104 [B]	Los Angeles	1980	$30
❏ 23930	Los Angeles	1983	$15
—Reissue of Slash 104			
❏ SR-107 [B]	Wild Gift	1981	$30
❏ 23931	Wild Gift	1983	$15
—Reissue of Slash 107			

X CLAN

4TH & B'WAY

Number	Title	Yr	NM
❏ 444019-1	To the East Blackwards	1990	$18

POLYDOR

Number	Title	Yr	NM
❏ 513225-1	Xodus — The New Testament	1992	$18

XAVIER

LIBERTY

Number	Title	Yr	NM
❏ LT-51116	Point of Pleasure	1981	$18

XAVION

ASYLUM

Number	Title	Yr	NM
❏ 60375	Burnin' Hot	1984	$18

Number	Title	Yr	NM

XIT
CANYON
❏ 7114	Entrance	197?	$50
❏ C-7121	Relocation	1977	$40

RARE EARTH
❏ R-536	Plight of the Redman	1972	$30
❏ R-545 [B]	Silent Warrior	1973	$30

WARRIOR
❏ WAR49	Plight of the Redman	1981	$18

— *Reissue of Rare Earth 536*

XSCAPE
SO SO DEF
❏ C57107	Hummin' Comin' At Cha	1993	$15
❏ C67022	Off the Hook	1995	$15

XTC
GEFFEN
❏ GHS4035	Black Sea	1984	$12

— *Reissue of Virgin/Epic 38150*

❏ GHS4034	Drums and Wires	1984	$12

— *Reissue of Virgin/Epic 38151*

❏ GHS4036	English Settlement	1984	$18

— *First release of British version of this album in U.S.*

❏ GHS4033	Go2	1984	$12

— *Reissue of Virgin/Epic 38152*

❏ GHS4027	Mummer	1983	$12
❏ R201086 [B]	Oranges and Lemons	1989	$18

— *BMG Direct Marketing edition*

❏ GHS24218	Oranges and Lemons	1989	$18
❏ GHS24169	Psonic Psunspot	1987	$18

— *As "The Dukes of Stratosphear"*

❏ GHS24117	Skylarking	1986	$18

— *First pressing, with "Mermaid Smiled" and without "Dear God"*

❏ GHS24117	Skylarking	1986	$12

— *Second pressing, with "Dear God" and without "Mermaid Smiled"*

❏ GHS24054	The Big Express	1984	$12
❏ GHS4037	Waxworks (Some Singles, 1977-82)	1984	$15
❏ GHS4032	White Music	1984	$12

— *Reissue of Virgin/Epic 38153*

VIRGIN
❏ VA13147	Black Sea	1980	$30

— *Promo only; label, jacket and innersleeve ALL must have this number*

❏ VA13134 [B]	Drums and Wires	1979	$35

— *With bonus 7-inch record (PR 344) enclosed -- deduct 40 percent if missing*

VIRGIN/EPIC
❏ PE38150	Black Sea	1982	$12

— *Reissue of Virgin/RSO 1001*

❏ PE38151	Drums and Wires	1982	$12

— *Reissue of Virgin 13134*

❏ ARE37943	English Settlement	1982	$12

— *Drastically edited version of U.K. original, which was a 2-record set*

❏ PE38152	Go2	1982	$12

— *Reissue of Virgin International VI-2108*

❏ PE38153	White Music	1982	$12

— *Reissue of Virgin International VI-2095*

VIRGIN INTERNATIONAL
❏ VI-2108	Go2	1979	$18
❏ VI-2095 [B]	White Music	1979	$25

VIRGIN/RSO
❏ VR-1-1000	Black Sea	1980	$25

— *With green outer bag and "VA 13147" on innersleeve*

❏ VR-1-1000	Black Sea	1980	$15

— *Without green outer bag; innersleeves may or may not have "VA 13147" reference*

WARNER BROS.
❏ WBMS-146 [DJ]	Skylarking Interview with Andy Partridge	1986	$30

— *Part of "The Warner Bros. Music Show" series*

Number	Title	Yr	NM

XYMOX
RELATIVITY
❏ EMC8037	The Clan of Xymox	1985	$30

WING
❏ 848516-1	Phoenix	1991	$15
❏ 839233-1	Twist of Shadows	1989	$15

XYZ
ENIGMA
❏ 7735251	XYZ	1989	$12

XZIBIT
LOUD
❏ 1885	Restless	2001	$18

LOUD/RCA
❏ 67578	40 Dayz & 40 Nightz	1998	$18
❏ 66816-1	At the Speed of Life	1996	$18

Y

Y KANT TORI READ
Lead singer is Tori Amos.
ATLANTIC
❏ 81845	Y Kant Tori Read	1989	$250

— *Deduct 20% for albums with a gold promo stamp and cut-out mark. Also, any picture disc of this album is a bootleg, no matter what it claims to be*

YA HO WA 13
HIGHER KEY
❏ 3304	All or Nothing at All	1974	$400

— *Above 4 as "Father Yod and the Spirit of '76*

❏ 3302	Contraction	1974	$500
❏ 3303	Expansion	1974	$500
❏ 3308	I'm Gonna Take You Home	1975	$800
❏ 3301	Kohoutek	1973	$300
❏ 3307	Penetration: An Aquarian Symphony	1974	$400
❏ 3306	The Savage Sons of Ya Ho Wa	1974	$400
❏ 3309	To the Principles for the Children	1975	$800
❏ 3305	Ya Ho Wa 13	1974	$500

YACHTSMEN, THE
BUENA VISTA
❏ BV-3310 [M]	High and Dry with the Yachtsmen	1961	$30

YAGED, SOL
HERALD
❏ HLP-0103 [M]	It Might As Well Be Swing	1956	$50

LANE
❏ LP-149 [M]	Live at the Gaslight Club	195?	$50
❏ LP-154 [M]	One More Time	195?	$50
❏ LPS-154 [S]	One More Time	195?	$50
❏ LP-155 [M]	Sol Yaged at the Gaslight Club	195?	$50
❏ LPS-155 [S]	Sol Yaged at the Gaslight Club	195?	$50

PHILIPS
❏ PHM200002 [M]	Jazz at the Metropole	1961	$35
❏ PHS600002 [S]	Jazz at the Metropole	1961	$25

YALE DIXIELAND BAND, THE
COLUMBIA
❏ CL736 [M]	Eli's Chosen Six	1955	$50

YAMA AND THE KARMA DUSTERS
MANHOLE

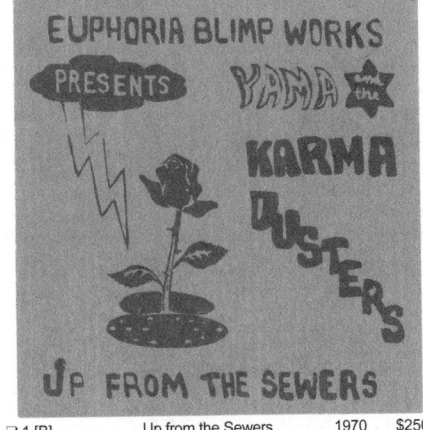

❏ 1 [B]	Up from the Sewers	1970	$250

Number	Title	Yr	NM

YAMA YAMA JAZZ BAND, THE
JAZZOLOGY
❏ J-78	New Orleans Jazz -- Australian Style, Vol. 1	198?	$25
❏ J-79	New Orleans Jazz -- Australian Style, Vol. 2	198?	$25

YAMAMOTO, TSUYOSHI
CONCORD JAZZ
❏ CJ-218	Zephyr	1981	$25

THREE BLIND MICE
❏ TBM-23	Midnight Sugar	1995	$30

— *Audiophile vinyl*

❏ TBM-30	Misty	199?	$30

— *Audiophile vinyl*

YAMASHITA, STOMU
KUCKUCK
❏ KU-072	Sea and Sky	198?	$30

YANCEY, JIMMY
ATLANTIC
❏ ALS-134 [10]	Piano Solos	1952	$350
❏ 1283 [M]	Pure Blues	1958	$300

— *Black label*

❏ 1283 [M]	Pure Blues	1961	$175

— *Multicolor label, white "fan" logo at right*

❏ 1283 [M]	Pure Blues	1964	$35

— *Multicolor label, black "fan" logo at right*

❏ ALS-103 [10]	Yancey Special	1950	$300
❏ ALS-130 [10]	Yancey Special	1952	$350

JAZZOLOGY
❏ J-51	In the Beginning	197?	$25

PARAMOUNT
❏ CJS-101 [10]	Yancey Special	1951	$200

PAX
❏ LP-6011 [10]	1943 Mixture	1954	$100
❏ LP-6012 [10]	Evening With the Yanceys	1954	$100

RIVERSIDE
❏ RLP-1028 [10]	Lost Recording Date	1954	$300
❏ RLP 12-124 [M]	Yancey's Getaway	1956	$300

X
❏ LX-3000 [10]	Blues and Boogie	1954	$150

YANCEY, MAMA, AND ART HODES
VERVE FOLKWAYS
❏ FVS-9015 [S]	Blues	1965	$35
❏ FV-9015 [M]	Blues	1965	$35

YANCY DERRINGER
HEMISPHERE
❏ H-15104	Openers	1975	$50

YANKEE DOLLAR, THE
DOT
❏ DLP-25874 [B]	The Yankee Dollar	1968	$120

YANKEE RHYTHM KINGS
GHB
❏ GHB-151	Classic Jazz of the 20s	1980	$25
❏ GHB-97	Classic Jazz of the 20s	1978	$25
❏ GHB-83	Yankee Rhythm Kings, Vol. 1	197?	$25

YANKOVIC, "WEIRD AL"
ROCK N ROLL
❏ FZ40033	Dare to Be Stupid	1985	$12
❏ FZ44149	Even Worse	1988	$12
❏ FZ39221	In 3-D	1984	$12
❏ BFZ38679	Weird Al	1983	$12
❏ PZ38679	Weird Al	1985	$10

— *Budget-line reissue*

YANKOVIC, FRANKIE
COLUMBIA
❏ CL2253 [M]	Christmas Party	1964	$15
❏ CS9053 [S]	Christmas Party	1964	$18

SMASH
❏ 830396-1	Christmas Memories	198?	$12

YANOVSKY, ZALMAN
Also see THE LOVIN' SPOONFUL.

BUDDAH
❏ BDS-5019	Alive and Well in Argentina	1968	$40

KAMA SUTRA
❏ KSBS-2030	Alive and Well in Argentina	1971	$25

YARBROUGH, BOB
SUGAR HILL
❏ 002	Because You're Just More a Woman	1971	$18

Number	Title	Yr	NM

YARBROUGH, CAMILLE
VANGUARD
| ❏ VSD-79356 | The Iron Pot Cooker | 197? | $30 |

YARBROUGH, GLENN
ELEKTRA
| ❏ EKL-135 [M] | Here We Go, Baby | 1957 | $40 |

FIRST AMERICAN
| ❏ 7766 | Just a Little Love | 1981 | $12 |

RCA VICTOR
❏ LPM-3422 [M]	Baby the Rain Must Fall	1965	$15
❏ LSP-3422 [S]	Baby the Rain Must Fall	1965	$18
❏ ANL1-2138	Baby the Rain Must Fall	1977	$12

—Reissue of LSP-3422

❏ LPM-3301 [M]	Come Share My Life	1965	$18
❏ LSP-3301 [S]	Come Share My Life	1965	$25
❏ LPM-3801 [M]	For Emily, Whenever I May Find Her	1967	$18
❏ LSP-3801 [S]	For Emily, Whenever I May Find Her	1967	$18
❏ VPS-6018	Glenn Yarbrough Sings the Rod McKuen Songbook	1969	$18
❏ LPM-3860 [M]	Honey and Wine	1967	$25
❏ LSP-3860 [S]	Honey and Wine	1967	$18
❏ LPM-3472 [M]	It's Gonna Be Fine	1965	$15
❏ LSP-3472 [S]	It's Gonna Be Fine	1965	$18
❏ LPM-3661 [M]	Live at the Hungry I	1966	$15
❏ LSP-3661 [S]	Live at the Hungry I	1966	$18
❏ LPM-2905 [M]	One More Round	1964	$18
❏ LSP-2905 [S]	One More Round	1964	$25
❏ LSP-4349	The Best of Glenn Yarbrough	1970	$15
❏ LPM-3951 [M]	The Bitter and the Sweet	1968	$30
❏ LSP-3951 [S]	The Bitter and the Sweet	1968	$18
❏ LPM-3539 [M]	The Lonely Things	1966	$15
❏ LSP-3539 [S]	The Lonely Things	1966	$18
❏ LPM-2836 [M]	Time to Move On	1964	$25
❏ LSP-2836 [S]	Time to Move On	1964	$18
❏ LSP-4047	We Survived the Madness	1968	$18

STAX
| ❏ STX-5506 | My Sweet Lady | 1975 | $12 |

TRADITION
❏ 1019 [M]	Come Sit By My Side	195?	$25
❏ 2095	Looking Back	1970	$15
❏ 2054	The Best of Glenn Yarbrough	1967	$18

WARNER BROS.
❏ WS1911	Bend Down and Touch Me	1971	$15
❏ WS1736	Each of Us Alone: Glenn Yarbrough Sings the Words and Music of Rod McKuen	1968	$15
❏ WS1876	Jubilee	1970	$15
❏ WS1832	Let Me Choose Life	1969	$15
❏ WS1782	Somehow, Someway	1969	$15
❏ WS1817	Yarbrough Country	1969	$15

YARDBIRDS, THE
Also see JEFF BECK; ERIC CLAPTON; JIMMY PAGE; KEITH RELF; SONNY BOY WILLIAMSON (2). Ex-members of the group formed LED ZEPPELIN and RENAISSANCE.

ACCORD
| ❏ SN-7143 [S] | For Your Love | 1981 | $10 |
| ❏ SN-7237 [R] | Having a Rave Up with the Yardbirds | 1981 | $10 |

COLUMBIA SPECIAL PRODUCTS
| ❏ P13311 [S] | Live Yardbirds Featuring Jimmy Page | 1976 | $100 |

COMPLEAT
| ❏ CPL-2-2002 | A Compleat Collection | 1984 | $15 |

EPIC
| ❏ LN24167 [DJ] | For Your Love | 1965 | $400 |

—White label promo

| ❏ LN24167 [M] | For Your Love | 1965 | $400 |

| ❏ BN26167 [P] | For Your Love | 1965 | $250 |

—The album is in true stereo except for "Sweet Music

| ❏ PE34491 [R] | Great Hits | 1977 | $12 |
| ❏ LN24177 [DJ] | Having a Rave Up with the Yardbirds | 1965 | $400 |

—White label promo

Number	Title	Yr	NM

❏ LN24177 [M]	Having a Rave Up with the Yardbirds	1965	$100
❏ BN26177 [R]	Having a Rave Up with the Yardbirds	1965	$50
❏ BN26177 [R]	Having a Rave Up with the Yardbirds	1973	$30

—Reissue with orange label

| ❏ LN24313 [DJ] | Little Games | 1967 | $400 |
| ❏ LN24313 [M] | Little Games | 1967 | $350 |

—Some copies with this number are stereo; look for the "XSB" prefix before the master number

❏ BN26313 [S]	Little Games	1967	$50
❏ E30615 [S]	Live Yardbirds Featuring Jimmy Page	1971	$300
❏ LN24210 [DJ]	Over Under Sideways Down	1966	$500

—White label promo

| ❏ LN24210 [M] | Over Under Sideways Down | 1966 | $75 |
| ❏ BN26210 [P] | Over Under Sideways Down | 1966 | $100 |

—Over Under Sideways Down" is rechanneled

| ❏ EG30135 | The Yardbirds Featuring Performances by Jeff Beck, Eric Clapton, Jimmy Page | 1970 | $50 |
| ❏ LN24246 [DJ] | The Yardbirds' Greatest Hits | 1966 | $300 |

—White label promo

❏ LN24246 [M]	The Yardbirds' Greatest Hits	1966	$50
❏ BN26246 [P]	The Yardbirds' Greatest Hits	1966	$30
❏ PE34490 [P]	Yardbirds Favorites	1977	$12
❏ FE38455	Yardbirds (Roger the Engineer)	1982	$30
❏ HE48455	Yardbirds (Roger the Engineer)	1982	$300

—Half-Speed Mastered" edition

PAIR
| ❏ PDL2-1151 | Best of British Rock | 1988 | $15 |

PARLOPHONE
| ❏ 825646335404 [B] | Little Games | 2014 | $30 |

RHINO
❏ RNDF253 [PD]	Afternoon Tea	1982	$18
❏ RNLP70189 [M]	Five Live Yardbirds	1986	$10
❏ RNLP70128 [M]	Greatest Hits, Volume 1: 1964-1966	1986	$10

SPRINGBOARD
| ❏ SPB-4036 [R] | Eric Clapton and the Yardbirds | 1972 | $12 |
| ❏ SPB-4039 [R] | Shapes of Things | 1972 | $12 |

SUNDAZED
| ❏ 5368 [M] | Little Games | 2010 | $25 |
| ❏ LP5181 | Live! Blueswailing July '64 | 2004 | $15 |

YARROW, PETER
WARNER BROS.
❏ BS2860	Hard Times	1975	$15
❏ BS2599	Peter	1972	$15
❏ BS2891	Peter Yarrow	1975	$15
❏ BS2730	That's Enough for Me	1973	$15

YATES, LORI
COLUMBIA
| ❏ FC44278 | Can't Stop the Girl | 1988 | $10 |

YAZ-KAZ
GRAMAVISION
| ❏ 18-7013 | Jonon-Sho | 198? | $30 |

YAZ
SIRE
| ❏ 23737 | Upstairs at Eric's | 1982 | $25 |

—As "Yazoo

| ❏ 23737 | Upstairs at Eric's | 1982 | $12 |

—As "Yaz

| ❏ 23903 | You and Me Both | 1983 | $12 |

YEARWOOD, TRISHA
MCA
| ❏ 1P-8161 | Trisha Yearwood | 1991 | $30 |

—Vinyl edition available only from Columbia House

YELL CHASERS, THE
REALTIME
| ❏ 822 | I've Got My Fingers | 197? | $25 |

—Direct-to-disc recording; plays at 45 rpm

YELLIN, PETE
MAINSTREAM
| ❏ MRL-363 | Dance of Allegra | 197? | $35 |
| ❏ MRL-397 | It's the Right Thing | 1974 | $35 |

YELLO
ELEKTRA
| ❏ 60401 | Stella | 1985 | $15 |
| ❏ 60271 | You Gotta Say Yes to Another Excess | 1983 | $15 |

MERCURY
| ❏ 818340-1 | Claro Que Si | 1988 | $10 |

—Reissue

| ❏ 836426-1 | Flag | 1989 | $15 |

Number	Title	Yr	NM

| ❏ 832675-1 | One Second | 1987 | $15 |
| ❏ 818339-1 | Solid Pleasure | 1988 | $10 |

—Reissue

| ❏ 822820-1 | Stella | 1988 | $10 |

—Reissue

| ❏ 812166-1 | You Gotta Say Yes to Another Excess | 1988 | $10 |

—Reissue

RALPH
| ❏ YL8159 | Claro Que Si | 1981 | $25 |
| ❏ YL8059-L | Solid Pleasure | 1980 | $25 |

YELLOW BALLOON, THE
CANTERBURY
| ❏ CLPM-1502 [M] | The Yellow Balloon | 1967 | $30 |
| ❏ CLPS-1502 [S] | The Yellow Balloon | 1967 | $30 |

YELLOW PAYGES, THE
UNI
| ❏ 73045 | The Yellow Payges, Volume 1 | 1969 | $30 |

YELLOW SUNSHINE
GAMBLE
| ❏ KZ32405 [B] | Yellow Sunshine | 1973 | $50 |

YELLOWJACKETS
MCA
❏ 5994	Four Corners	1987	$25
❏ 6236	Politics	1988	$25
❏ 5752	Shades	1986	$25
❏ 6304	The Spin	1989	$30

WARNER BROS.
❏ 23813	Mirage A Trois	1983	$25
❏ 25204	Samurai Samba	1985	$25
❏ BSK3573	The Yellowjackets	1982	$25

YES
Also see JON ANDERSON; ANDERSON BRUFORD WAKEMAN HOWE; THE BUGGLES; STEVE HOWE; CHRIS SQUIRE; CHRIS SQUIRE AND ALAN WHITE; RICK WAKEMAN; ALAN WHITE.

ARISTA
| ❏ AL8643 | Union | 1991 | $30 |

—U.S. vinyl available only through Columbia House

ATCO
❏ 90125 [B]	90125	1983	$10
❏ 90474	9012Live: The Solos	1985	$10
❏ 90522	Big Generator	1987	$10

ATLANTIC
| ❏ SD19320 [B] | Classic Yes | 1982 | $30 |

—Original copies include a bonus 7-inch promo single

| ❏ SD19320 | Classic Yes | 1982 | $12 |

—With bonus single missing

❏ SD7244	Close to the Edge	1972	$15
❏ SD19133	Close to the Edge	1977	$10
❏ 7244 [DJ]	Close to the Edge	1972	$100

—White label mono copies banded for airplay

| ❏ SD16019 | Drama | 1980 | $12 |
| ❏ R182685 [B] | Drama | 2016 | $25 |

—180 gram

❏ SD7211	Fragile	1972	$15
❏ SD19132	Fragile	1977	$10
❏ SD19106	Going for the One	1977	$12
❏ SD18122	Relayer	1974	$12
❏ SD18122 [DJ]	Relayer	1974	$25

—Promo copies banded for airplay

❏ SD19135	Relayer	1977	$10
❏ SD 2-908	Tales from Topographic Oceans	1974	$18
❏ SD 2-908 [DJ]	Tales from Topographic Oceans	1974	$30

—Promo copies banded for airplay

❏ SD8283	The Yes Album	1971	$15
❏ SD19131	The Yes Album	1977	$10
❏ 8283 [M]	The Yes Album	1971	$300

—White label promo only; "DJ Copy Monaural" sticker on cover

❏ SD8273	Time and a Word	1970	$15
❏ SD19202 [B]	Tormato	1978	$12
❏ SD8243	Yes	1969	$15
❏ PR285 [DJ]	Yes Music: An Evening with Jon Anderson	1977	$50
❏ SD 2-510	Yesshows	1980	$15
❏ PR260 [DJ]	Yes Solo LP Sampler	1976	$35
❏ SD 3-100 [B]	Yessongs	1973	$30
❏ SD18103	Yesterdays	1975	$12
❏ SD19134	Yesterdays	1977	$10

CLEOPATRA
| ❏ 8169 [B] | The BBC Recordings 1969-1970 | | $30 |

FRIDAY MUSIC
| ❏ 219004 | Close to the Edge | 2008 | $30 |

MOBILE FIDELITY
| ❏ Jan-0077 | Close to the Edge | 1982 | $100 |

—Audiophile vinyl

Number	Title	Yr	NM

RHINO
☐ R1-73788 · The Yes Album · 2003 · $25
— *Reissue on 180-gram vinyl*

YESTERDAY'S CHILDREN
MAP CITY
☐ 3012 · Yesterday's Children · 1969 · $85

YESTERDAY'S FOLK
BUDDAH
☐ BDS-5035 · U.S. 69 · 1969 · $25

YETTI-MEN, THE / THE UPPA TRIO
KAL
☐ KB-4348 · The Yetti-Men/The Uppa Trio · 1967 · $600

YOAKAM, DWIGHT
OAK
☐ OR2356 [EP] · Guitars, Cadillacs, Etc., Etc. · 1984 · $100
— *Six-song EP; cover is in black and white; the song "Guitars, Cadillacs" does NOT appear on this release*

REPRISE
☐ R100009 · Buenas Noches from a Lonely Room · 1988 · $15
— *BMG Direct Marketing edition*
☐ 25749 · Buenas Noches from a Lonely Room · 1988 · $12
☐ W1-25749 · Buenas Noches from a Lonely Room · 1988 · $15
— *Columbia House edition*
☐ R150223 · Guitars, Cadillacs, Etc., Etc. · 1986 · $15
— *RCA Music Service edition*

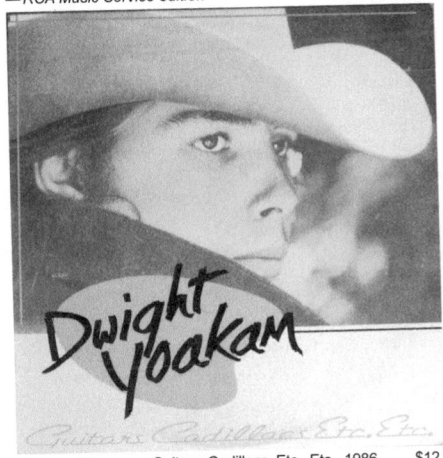

☐ 25372 [B] · Guitars, Cadillacs, Etc., Etc. · 1986 · $12
— *LP has 10 songs rather than the six on the Oak EP; front cover has color on it*
☐ W1-25372 · Guitars, Cadillacs, Etc., Etc. · 1986 · $15
— *Columbia House edition*
☐ R164146 · Hillbilly Deluxe · 1987 · $15
— *BMG Direct Marketing edition*
☐ 25567 · Hillbilly Deluxe · 1987 · $12
☐ W1-25567 · Hillbilly Deluxe · 1987 · $15
— *Columbia House edition*
☐ R164310 · If There Was a Way · 1990 · $25
— *BMG Direct Marketing edition; only U.S. vinyl version*
☐ 25989 · Just Lookin' for a Hit · 1989 · $12
☐ W1-25989 · Just Lookin' for a Hit · 1989 · $15
— *Columbia House edition*
☐ R174052 · Just Lookin' for a Hit · 1989 · $15
— *BMG Direct Marketing edition*

YOBS, THE
SAFARI
☐ RUDE1 · Christmas Album · 1980 · $0
— *U.K. import*

YORK, BETH
LADYSLIPPER
☐ LR-104 · Transformations · 1986 · $30

YORK BROTHERS, THE
KING
☐ 820 [M] · 16 Great Country and Western Hits · 1963 · $100
☐ 581 [M] · The York Brothers · 1958 · $150
☐ 586 [M] · The York Brothers, Volume 2 · 1958 · $150

YOST, PHIL
TAKOMA
☐ C-1016 · Bent City · 196? · $50
☐ C-1021 · Fog-Hat Ramble · 196? · $50

YOSUKA, YAMASHITA
WEST 54
☐ 8009 · Breathtake · 1980 · $30

YOU KNOW WHO GROUP, THE
INTERNATIONAL ALLIED
☐ 420 [M] · The "You Know Who" Group · 1965 · $50

YOUNG, BARRY
DOT
☐ DLP3672 [M] · One Has My Name · 1965 · $25
☐ DLP25672 [S] · One Has My Name · 1965 · $30

YOUNG, CATHY
MAINSTREAM
☐ S-6121 · A Spoonful of Cathy Young · 1968 · $40

YOUNG, CECIL
AUDIO LAB
☐ AL-1516 [M] · Jazz on the Rocks · 1959 · $100
KING
☐ 295-1 [10] · A Concert of Cool Jazz · 1952 · $150

YOUNG, DAVID
MAINSTREAM
☐ MRL-323 · David Young · 1972 · $35

YOUNG, ELDEE
ARGO
☐ LP-1003 [M] · Eldee Young and Company · 1962 · $30
☐ LPS-1003 [S] · Eldee Young and Company · 1962 · $30
☐ LP-699 [M] · Just for Kicks · 1962 · $25
☐ LPS-699 [S] · Just for Kicks · 1962 · $25

YOUNG, FARON
ALLEGIANCE
☐ AV-5008 · The Sheriff · 198? · $12
CAPITOL
☐ T2307 [M] · Falling in Love · 1965 · $25
☐ ST2307 [S] · Falling in Love · 1965 · $30
☐ T2037 [M] · Faron Young's Memory Lane · 1964 · $30
☐ DT2037 [R] · Faron Young's Memory Lane · 1964 · $25
☐ T1528 [M] · Hello Walls · 1961 · $30
☐ ST1528 [S] · Hello Walls · 1961 · $40
☐ T2536 [M] · If You Ain't Lovin' You Ain't Livin' · 1966 · $30
☐ DT2536 [R] · If You Ain't Lovin' You Ain't Livin' · 1966 · $25
☐ T1185 [M] · My Garden of Prayer · 1959 · $40
☐ T778 [M] · Sweethearts or Strangers · 1957 · $75
— *Turquoise or gray label*
☐ T778 [M] · Sweethearts or Strangers · 1959 · $30
— *Black colorband label, logo at left*
☐ T1245 [M] · Talk About Hits · 1959 · $30
☐ ST1245 [S] · Talk About Hits · 1959 · $40
☐ T1876 [M] · The All-Time Great Hits of Faron Young · 1963 · $30
☐ DT1876 [P] · The All-Time Great Hits of Faron Young · 1963 · $25
☐ T1450 [M] · The Best of Faron Young · 1960 · $30
☐ ST1450 [S] · The Best of Faron Young · 1960 · $40
☐ T1004 [M] · The Object of My Affection · 1958 · $50
☐ T1634 [M] · The Young Approach · 1961 · $30
☐ ST1634 [S] · The Young Approach · 1961 · $40
☐ T1096 [M] · This Is Faron Young · 1959 · $50
HILLTOP
☐ JM-6037 [M] · Faron Young · 1966 · $18
☐ JS-6037 [S] · Faron Young · 1966 · $15
☐ JS-6073 · I'll Be Yours · 1968 · $15
MARY CARTER
☐ MC1000 [M] · Faron Young Sings on Stage for Mary Carter Paints · 196? · $75
— *Promotional item for sponsor of The Faron Young Show*
MCA
☐ 3092 · Chapter Two · 1979 · $15
☐ 757 · Chapter Two · 198? · $10
— *Budget-line reissue of 3092*
☐ 3212 · Free and Easy · 1980 · $15
MERCURY
☐ SRM-1-1016 · A Man and His Music · 1974 · $15
☐ MG20931 [M] · Country Dance Favorites · 1964 · $25
☐ SR60931 [S] · Country Dance Favorites · 1964 · $30
☐ SR61359 · Evening · 1972 · $25
— *Original title?*
☐ MG20840 [M] · Faron Young Aims at the West · 1963 · $25
☐ SR60840 [S] · Faron Young Aims at the West · 1963 · $30
☐ MG21047 [M] · Faron Young's Greatest Hits · 1965 · $25
☐ SR61047 [S] · Faron Young's Greatest Hits · 1965 · $30
☐ SR61354 · Faron Young Sings "Leavin' and Sayin' Goodbye" · 1971 · $18
☐ SR61275 · Faron Young Sings "Occasional Wife" and "If I Ever Fall in Love with a Honky Tonk Girl" · 1970 · $25
☐ SRM-1-698 · Faron Young Sings "Some Kind of a Woman" · 1974 · $18

Number	Title	Yr	NM

☐ MG21058 [M] · Faron Young Sings the Best of Jim Reeves · 1966 · $25
☐ SR61058 [S] · Faron Young Sings the Best of Jim Reeves · 1966 · $30
☐ SR61364 · Faron Young Sings This Little Girl of Mine · 1972 · $18
☐ SR61143 · Greatest Hits Vol. 2 · 1968 · $25
☐ SR61174 · Here's Faron Young · 1968 · $25
☐ SRM-1-1075 · I'd Just Be Fool Enough · 1976 · $15
☐ SR61359 · It's Four in the Morning · 1972 · $18
— *Revised title to reflect the hit?*
☐ SR61212 · I've Got Precious Memories · 1969 · $25
☐ SRM-1-674 · Just What I Had in Mind · 1973 · $18
☐ MG21007 [M] · Pen and Paper · 1965 · $25
☐ SR61007 [S] · Pen and Paper · 1965 · $30
☐ SR61337 · Step Aside · 1971 · $25
☐ MG20896 [M] · Story Songs for Country Folks · 1964 · $25
☐ SR60896 [S] · Story Songs for Country Folks · 1964 · $30
☐ MG20971 [M] · Story Songs of Mountains and Valleys · 1965 · $25
☐ SR60971 [S] · Story Songs of Mountains and Valleys · 1965 · $30
☐ SR61267 · The Best of Faron Young · 1970 · $25
☐ SRM-1-1130 · The Best of Faron Young, Vol. 2 · 1977 · $15
☐ MG20785 [M] · This Is Faron · 1963 · $25
☐ SR60785 [S] · This Is Faron · 1963 · $30
☐ SR61376 [B] · This Time the Hurtin's on Me · 1973 · $18
☐ MG21110 [M] · Unmitigated Gall · 1967 · $30
☐ SR61110 [S] · Unmitigated Gall · 1967 · $25
☐ SR61241 · Wine Me Up · 1969 · $25
☐ SRM-1-5005 · Young Feelin' · 1978 · $15
PICCADILLY
☐ 3547 · Hello Walls · 198? · $12
SEARS
☐ SPS-124 · Candy Kisses · 1969 · $30
SESAC
☐ (# unknown) [DJ] · Church Songs · 196? · $100
TOWER
☐ T5022 [M] · It's a Great Life · 1966 · $25
☐ DT5022 [R] · It's a Great Life · 1966 · $15
☐ DT5121 · The World of Faron Young · 1968 · $18

YOUNG, JESSE COLIN
Also see THE YOUNGBLOODS.
CAPITOL
☐ T2070 [M] · The Soul of a City Boy · 1964 · $50
☐ ST-11267 · The Soul of a City Boy · 1974 · $15
— *Reissue of 2070*
☐ N-16129 · The Soul of a City Boy · 1981 · $10
— *Budget-line reissue*
CYPRESS
☐ 0103 · The Highway Is for Heroes · 1987 · $12
ELEKTRA
☐ 6E-157 · American Dreams · 1978 · $12
MERCURY
☐ MG21005 [M] · Young Blood · 1965 · $30
☐ SR61005 [S] · Young Blood · 1965 · $40
RACCOON
☐ BS2588 · Together · 1972 · $15
WARNER BROS.
☐ BS2790 · Light Shine · 1974 · $12
☐ BS3033 · Love on the Wing · 1977 · $12
☐ BS2913 · On the Road · 1976 · $12
☐ BS2845 · Songbird · 1975 · $12
☐ BS2734 · Song for Juli · 1973 · $12

YOUNG, JOHN
ARGO
☐ LP-713 [M] · A Touch of Pepper · 1962 · $30
☐ LPS-713 [S] · A Touch of Pepper · 1962 · $30
☐ LP-692 [M] · Themes and Things · 1962 · $30
☐ LPS-692 [S] · Themes and Things · 1962 · $30
☐ LP-612 [M] · Young John Young · 1957 · $40
CADET
☐ LPS-692 [S] · Themes and Things · 1966 · $35
☐ LP-692 [M] · Themes and Things · 1966 · $30
DELMARK
☐ DL-403 [M] · The John Young Trio · 1961 · $30
☐ DS-403 [S] · The John Young Trio · 1961 · $40
VEE JAY
☐ VJS-3060 · Opus de Funk · 1974 · $25

YOUNG, JOHNNY
ARHOOLIE
☐ F-1037 · Chicago Blues · 1966 · $30
☐ F-1029 · Johnny Williams and His Chicago Blues Band · 1965 · $30
BLUE HORIZON
☐ BH-4609 · Blues Masters, Volume 9 · 1969 · $25

YOUNG, KATHY, AND THE INNOCENTS
INDIGO
☐ LP-504 [M] · The Sound of Kathy Young · 1961 · $300

YOUNG, LAMONTE

GRAMAVISION

Number	Title	Yr	NM
❏ 188701 [B]	The Well-Tuned Piano 81 X 25 6:17:50 - 11:18:59 PM NYC	1987	$1000

YOUNG, LARRY

ARISTA

Number	Title	Yr	NM
❏ AL4072	Spaceball	1976	$30

BLUE NOTE

Number	Title	Yr	NM
❏ BLP-4266 [S]	Contrasts	1967	$100
❏ BST-84266 [S]	Contrasts	1967	$30

— With "A Division of Liberty Records" on label

| ❏ BST-84304 [S] | Heaven on Earth | 1968 | $30 |

— With "A Division of Liberty Records" on label

| ❏ BLP-4187 [M] | Into Somethin' | 1964 | $75 |
| ❏ BST-84187 [S] | Into Somethin' | 1964 | $40 |

— With "New York, USA" address on label

| ❏ BST-84187 [S] | Into Somethin' | 1967 | $25 |

— With "A Division of Liberty Records" on label

❏ LT-1038	Mother Ship	1980	$30
❏ BLP-4242 [M]	Of Love and Peace	1966	$75
❏ BST-84242 [S]	Of Love and Peace	1966	$40

— With "New York, USA" address on label

| ❏ BST-84242 [S] | Of Love and Peace | 1967 | $25 |

— With "A Division of Liberty Records" on label

| ❏ BLP-4221 [M] | Unity | 1966 | $75 |
| ❏ BST-84221 [S] | Unity | 1966 | $40 |

— With "New York, USA" address on label

| ❏ BST-84221 [S] | Unity | 1967 | $25 |

— With "A Division of Liberty Records" on label

| ❏ BST-84221 | Unity | 198? | $25 |

— The Finest in Jazz Since 1939" reissue

MOSAIC

| ❏ MR9-137 | The Complete Blue Note
Recordings of Larry Young | 199? | $250 |

NEW JAZZ

| ❏ NJLP-8249 [M] | Testifying | 1960 | $175 |

— Purple label

| ❏ NJLP-8249 [M] | Testifying | 1965 | $175 |

— Blue label, trident logo at right

| ❏ NJLP-8264 [M] | Young Blues | 1961 | $250 |

— Purple label

| ❏ NJLP-8264 [M] | Young Blues | 1965 | $175 |

— Blue label, trident logo at right

PRESTIGE

| ❏ PRLP-7237 [M] | Groove Street | 1962 | $175 |
| ❏ PRST-7237 [S] | Groove Street | 1962 | $175 |

YOUNG, LEON

ATCO

| ❏ 33-163 [M] | Liverpool Sound for Strings | 1964 | $30 |
| ❏ SD 33-163 [S] | Liverpool Sound for Strings | 1964 | $30 |

YOUNG, LESTER, AND PAUL QUINICHETTE

EMARCY

| ❏ MG-26021 [10] | Pres Meets Vice-Pres | 1954 | $300 |

YOUNG, LESTER; ROY ELDRIDGE; HARRY "SWEETS" EDISON

VERVE

❏ MGV-8298 [M]	Going for Myself	1959	$150
❏ V-8298 [M]	Going for Myself	1961	$30
❏ MGV-8316 [M]	Laughin' to Keep from Cryin'	1960	$150
❏ V-8316 [M]	Laughin' to Keep from Cryin'	1961	$30
❏ MGVS-6054 [S]	Laughin' to Keep from Cryin'	1960	$175
❏ V6-8316 [S]	Laughin' to Keep from Cryin'	1961	$30
❏ UMV-2694	Laughin' to Keep from Cryin'	198?	$25
❏ MGVS-6054 [S]	Laughin' to Keep from Cryin'	199?	$30

— Classic Records reissue on audiophile vinyl

YOUNG, LESTER

ALADDIN

Number	Title	Yr	NM
❏ LP-706 [10]	Easy Does It	1954	$700
❏ LP-801 [M]	Lester Young and His Tenor Sax, Volume 1	1956	$400
❏ LP-802 [M]	Lester Young and His Tenor Sax, Volume 2	1956	$300
❏ LP-705 [M]	Lester Young Trio	1953	$300

AMERICAN RECORDING SOCIETY

| ❏ G-417 [M] | Pres and Teddy | 1957 | $50 |

BLUE NOTE

| ❏ BN-LA456-H2 | Pres: The Aladdin Sessions | 1975 | $35 |

CHARLIE PARKER

| ❏ CLP-402 [M] | Pres | 1961 | $50 |
| ❏ CLP-405 [M] | Pres Is Blue | 1961 | $50 |

CLEF

| ❏ MGC-108 [10] | Lester Young Collates | 1953 | $350 |
| ❏ MGC-124 [10] | Lester Young Collates No. 2 | 1953 | $350 |

— Some copies of this have Mercury covers; no difference in value

| ❏ MGC-104 [10] | The Lester Young Trio | 1953 | $350 |
| ❏ MGC-135 [10] | The Lester Young Trio No. 2 | 1953 | $350 |

COLUMBIA

❏ JG33502	The Lester Young Story, Vol. 1	1975	$35
❏ JG34837	The Lester Young Story, Vol. 2: Romance	1976	$35
❏ JG34840	The Lester Young Story, Vol. 3: Enter Count	1976	$35

COMMODORE

❏ XFL-15352	A Complete Session	198?	$25
❏ FL-20021 [10]	Kansas City Style	1952	$300
❏ FL-30014 [M]	Kansas City Style	1959	$150
❏ XFL-14937	The Kansas City Six and Five	198?	$25

CROWN

| ❏ CLP-5305 [M] | Nat "King" Cole Meets
Lester Young | 196? | $30 |
| ❏ CST-305 [R] | Nat "King" Cole Meets
Lester Young | 196? | $30 |

EMARCY

| ❏ SRE-66010 | Lester Young At His Very
Best | 1967 | $150 |

EPIC

❏ LN3107 [M]	Lester Leaps In	1956	$250
❏ SN6031 [M]	Lester Young Memorial Album	1959	$300
❏ LN3576 [M]	Lester Young Memorial Album, Volume 1	1959	$150
❏ LN3577 [M]	Lester Young Memorial Album, Volume 2	1959	$150
❏ LN3168 [M]	Let's Go to Pres	1956	$250

EVEREST ARCHIVE OF FOLK & JAZZ

| ❏ 287 | Pres | 197? | $25 |

IMPERIAL

❏ LP-9187-A [M]	The Great Lester Young, Volume 2	1962	$200
❏ LP-12187-A [R]	The Great Lester Young, Volume 2	196?	$175
❏ LP-9181-A [M]	The Immortal Lester Young	1962	$200
❏ LP-12181-A [R]	The Immortal Lester Young	196?	$175

INTRO

| ❏ LP-602 [M] | Swinging Lester Young | 1957 | $150 |
| ❏ LP-603 [M] | The Greatest | 1957 | $150 |

JAZZ ARCHIVES

❏ JA-18	Jammin' with Lester, Vol. 1	198?	$25
❏ JA-34	Jammin' with Lester, Vol. 2	198?	$25
❏ JA-42	Lester Young and Charlie Christian 1939-40	198?	$25

MAINSTREAM

❏ 56009 [M]	52nd Street	1965	$30
❏ S-6009 [R]	52nd Street	1965	$30
❏ 56008 [M]	Chairman of the Board	1965	$30
❏ S-6008 [R]	Chairman of the Board	1965	$30
❏ 56012 [M]	Prez	1965	$30
❏ S-6012 [R]	Prez	1965	$30
❏ 56002 [M]	The Influence of Five	1965	$30
❏ S-6002 [R]	The Influence of Five	1965	$30
❏ 56004 [M]	Town Hall Concert	1965	$30
❏ S-6004 [R]	Town Hall Concert	1965	$30

MERCURY

| ❏ MGC-108 [10] | Lester Young Collates | 1951 | $300 |
| ❏ MGC-124 [10] | Lester Young Collates No. 2 | 1953 | $0 |

— Canceled

| ❏ MGC-104 [10] | The Lester Young Trio | 1951 | $300 |

NORGRAN

❏ MGN-1071 [M]	Lester's Here	1956	$250
❏ MGN-1093 [M]	Lester Swings Again	1956	$250
❏ MGN-1022 [M]	Lester Young	1955	$250
❏ MGN-1100 [M]	Lester Young	1956	$250
❏ MGN-1074 [M]	Lester Young and the Buddy Rich Trio	1956	$250
❏ MGN-5 [10]	Lester Young with the Oscar Peterson Trio	1954	$500
❏ MGN-6 [10]	Lester Young with the Oscar Peterson Trio No. 2	1954	$500
❏ MGN-1072 [M]	Pres	1956	$150
❏ MGN-1043 [M]	Pres and Sweets	1955	$250
❏ MGN-1005 [M]	The President	1954	$350
❏ MGN-1054 [M]	The President Plays with the Oscar Peterson Trio	1955	$150

ONYX

Number	Title	Yr	NM
❏ 218	Prez in Europe	197?	$30

PABLO

| ❏ 2405420 | The Best of Lester Young | 198? | $25 |

PABLO LIVE

❏ 2308219	Lester Young in Washington, D.C., at Olivia Davis', Vol. 1	1979	$30
❏ 2308225	Lester Young in Washington, D.C., at Olivia Davis', Vol. 2	1980	$30
❏ 2308228	Lester Young in Washington, D.C., at Olivia Davis', Vol. 3	198?	$25
❏ 2308230	Lester Young in Washington, D.C., at Olivia Davis', Vol. 4	198?	$25

PICKWICK

| ❏ SPC-5015 | Prez Leaps Again | 197? | $25 |

SAVOY

❏ MG-12068 [M]	Blue Lester	1956	$100
❏ MG-9002 [10]	Lester Young (All Star Be Bop)	1951	$300
❏ MG-12155 [M]	The Immortal Lester Young	1959	$75
❏ MG-12071 [M]	The Master's Touch	1956	$100

SAVOY JAZZ

❏ SJL-1133	Master Takes	198?	$25
❏ SJL-1109	Pres Lives	1977	$25
❏ SJL-2202	The Complete Lester Younbg (1944-49)	197?	$35

SCORE

❏ SLP-4019 [M]	Lester Young / The King Cole Trio	1958	$100
❏ SLP-4028 [M]	Swinging Lester Young	1958	$100
❏ SLP-4029 [M]	The Great Lester Young	1958	$100

SUNSET

| ❏ SUS-5181 | Giant of Jazz | 1967 | $30 |

TIME-LIFE

| ❏ STL-J-13 | Giants of Jazz | 1980 | $50 |

TRIP

| ❏ 5519 | Pres at His Best | 197? | $25 |

VERVE

| ❏ VSP-30 [M] | Giants 3 | 1966 | $30 |

— With Buddy Rich and Nat King Cole

❏ VSPS-30 [R]	Giants 3	1966	$30
❏ MGV-8187 [M]	It Don't Mean a Thing (If It Ain't Got That Swing)	1957	$175
❏ V-8187 [M]	It Don't Mean a Thing (If It Ain't Got That Swing)	1961	$30
❏ VE-2-2527	Jazz Giants '56	197?	$35
❏ MGV-8161 [M]	Lester's Here	1957	$175
❏ V-8161 [M]	Lester's Here	1961	$30
❏ VE-2-2516	Lester Swings	197?	$35
❏ 833554-1	Lester Swings	198?	$30
❏ MGV-8181 [M]	Lester Swings Again	1957	$175
❏ V-8181 [M]	Lester Swings Again	1961	$30
❏ MGV-8164 [M]	Lester Young and the Buddy Rich Trio	1957	$175
❏ V-8164 [M]	Lester Young and the Buddy Rich Trio	1961	$30
❏ VSPS-41 [R]	Lester Young at J.A.T.P.	196?	$30
❏ VSP-41 [M]	Lester Young at J.A.T.P.	196?	$35
❏ MGV-8378 [M]	Lester Young in Paris	1960	$150
❏ V-8378 [M]	Lester Young in Paris	1961	$30
❏ VE-2-2538	Mean to Me	197?	$35
❏ VE-2-2502	Pres & Teddy & Oscar	197?	$35
❏ MGV-8162 [M]	Pres	1957	$150
❏ V-8162 [M]	Pres	1961	$30
❏ UMV-2672	Pres	198?	$25
❏ VSP-27 [M]	Pres and His Cabinet	1966	$30
❏ VSPS-27 [R]	Pres and His Cabinet	1966	$30
❏ MGV-8134 [M]	Pres and Sweets	1957	$150
❏ V-8134 [M]	Pres and Sweets	1961	$30
❏ UMV-2528	Pres and Sweets	198?	$25
❏ MGV-8205 [M]	Pres and Teddy	1957	$150
❏ V-8205 [M]	Pres and Teddy	1961	$30
❏ MGV-8398 [M]	The Essential Lester Young	1961	$75
❏ V-8398 [M]	The Essential Lester Young	1961	$30
❏ MGV-8308 [M]	The Lester Young Story	1959	$150
❏ V-8308 [M]	The Lester Young Story	1961	$30
❏ MGV-8144 [M]	The President Plays with the Oscar Peterson Trio	1957	$150
❏ V-8144 [M]	The President Plays with the Oscar Peterson Trio	1961	$30

YOUNG, LESTER/CHU BERRY

JAZZTONE

| ❏ J-1218 [M] | Tops on Tenor: Pres and
Chu | 1956 | $150 |

YOUNG, LESTER/COUNT BASIE

MERCURY

| ❏ MG-25015 [10] | Lester Young Quartet/Count
Basie Seven | 1950 | $300 |

YOUNG, NEIL

Also see BUFFALO SPRINGFIELD; CROSBY, STILLS, NASH AND YOUNG; THE STILLS-YOUNG BAND.

GEFFEN

| ❏ GHS4013 [B] | Everybody's Rockin' | 1983 | $50 |

— Promo on Quiex II audiophile vinyl

| ❏ GHS4013 | Everybody's Rockin' | 1983 | $12 |
| ❏ R134125 | Landing on Water | 1986 | $18 |

— RCA Music Service edition

| ❏ GHS24109 | Landing on Water | 1986 | $15 |

Number	Title	Yr	NM
R144439	Life	1987	$18

— BMG Direct Marketing edition

| GHS24154 | Life | 1987 | $15 |
| R163233 | Old Ways | 1985 | $18 |

— RCA Music Service edition

| GHS24068 | Old Ways | 1985 | $15 |
| GHS2018 [DJ] | Trans | 1982 | $40 |

— Promo on Quiex II audiophile vinyl

| GHS2018 [B] | Trans | 1982 | $35 |

— First pressings have a sticker on rear cover explaining the absence of "If You've Got Love"

| GHS2018 | Trans | 1982 | $12 |

— Later pressings have neither sticker nor title of absent song

MOBILE FIDELITY

| 1-252 | Old Ways | 1996 | $80 |

— Audiophile vinyl

NAUTILUS

| NR-44 [B] | Harvest | 1982 | $250 |

— Audiophile vinyl

REPRISE

| RS6383 [B] | After the Gold Rush | 1970 | $75 |

— Brown and orange label; photo of Marc Bolan (of T. Rex) appears erroneously in gatefold

| RS6383 | After the Gold Rush | 1970 | $35 |

— Brown and orange label; photo of Neil Young appears erroneously printed upside down in gatefold

| RS6383 | After the Gold Rush | 1970 | $18 |

— Brown and orange label; all photos correct

| RS6383 | After the Gold Rush | 1970 | $12 |

— Brown "Reprise" label

| MSK2283 | After the Gold Rush | 1978 | $40 |

— Contains remixed extended version of "When You Dance I Can Really Love." Title on cover in red, "RE 2" in trail-off vinyl

531195-1 [B]	Americana	2012	$50
MSK2261	American Stars 'N' Bars	1977	$12
527650-1 [B]	A Treasure	2011	$50
46291	Broken Arrow	1996	$40
311932-1 [B]	Chrome Dreams II	2007	$75
MSK2266	Comes A Time	1978	$12

— With "Peace of Mind" as the last song on side 1. Covers can list either "Lotta Love" or "Peace of Mind."

| MSK2266 | Comes A Time | 1978 | $85 |

— With "Lotta Love" listed and playing as the last song on side 1

| MSK2266 [B] | Comes A Time | 1978 | $15 |

— white label promo with printed sheet advising change of title from the earlier Give To The Wind

| 3RS2257 [DJ] | Decade | 1977 | $500 |

— Test pressing; "Campaigner" contains extra verse deleted from the final version

| 3RS2257 [DJ] | Decade | 1977 | $500 |

— Test pressing; "Campaigner" contains extra verse deleted from the final version

3RS2257	Decade	1977	$25
511277-1 [B]	Dreamin' Man Live '92	2009	$30
RS6349 [DJ]	Everybody Knows This Is Nowhere	1969	$85

— White label promo

| RS6349 [DJ] | Everybody Knows This Is Nowhere | 1969 | $85 |

— White label promo

| RS6349 | Everybody Knows This Is Nowhere | 1969 | $30 |

— Brown and orange "Reprise/W7" label

| RS6349 | Everybody Knows This Is Nowhere | 1970 | $18 |

— Brown "Reprise" label

| MSK2282 | Everybody Knows This Is Nowhere | 1978 | $10 |

— Brown "Reprise" label; new number

518040-1 [B]	Fork In The Road	2009	$30
25899	Freedom	1989	$18
MSK2266 [DJ]	Give to the Wind	1978	$1000

— Test pressing; plain white jacket with inserts and STOCK COPY LABEL. Title changed to "Comes A Time" for commercial release.

| 48935-1 | Greatest Hits | 2005 | $40 |

— Distributed by Classic Records; 200-gram vinyl; with poster; also includes a bonus 7-inch single of "The Loner"/"Sugar Mountain" on either red, white or blue vinyl (not marked on packaging which color is inside; no difference in value)

| R113998 | Harvest | 1972 | $15 |

— RCA Music Service edition

| MS2032 | Harvest | 1972 | $18 |

— First pressings have textured cover and lyric insert

| MS2032 | Harvest | 1972 | $12 |
| MSK2277 | Harvest | 1978 | $10 |

— Brown "Reprise" label; new number

| SMAS-94285 | Harvest | 1972 | $30 |

— Capitol Record Club edition

HS2297	Hawks and Doves	1980	$12
2XS6480	Journey Through the Past (Soundtrack)	1972	$25
525956-1 [B]	Le Noise	2010	$30
525956-1 [B]	Le Noise	2013	$30
43328	Live at Massey Hall	2008	$30
44429-1 [B]	Live At The Fillmore East	2006	$30

Number	Title	Yr	NM
2RX2296	Live Rust	1979	$18
44335-1 [B]	Living With War	2006	$30
44335-1	Living With War	2006	$30

— Distributed by Classic Records; 200-gram vinyl

43265-1 [B]	Living With War "In The Beginning"	2007	$30
43328-1 [B]	Massey Hall 1971	2008	$50
45934 [B]	Mirror Ball	1995	$25

— With Pearl Jam (uncredited)

| RS6317 | Neil Young | 1968 | $250 |

— Brown and orange "Reprise/W7" label, no name on front cover, no "RE-1" in trail-off wax

| RS6317 | Neil Young | 1969 | $75 |

— Re-release: Brown and orange "Reprise/W7" label, no name on front cover, four tracks remixed ("RE 1" in trail-off wax)

| RS6317 | Neil Young | 1970 | $18 |

— Reissue: Brown "Reprise" label, Neil Young's name is now on front cover

| MSK2266 [DJ] | Ode to the Wind | 1978 | $1000 |

— Test pressing; plain white jacket with inserts. Title changed to "Comes A Time" for commercial release

| R2180 | On the Beach | 1974 | $25 |
| 49593-1 | Prairie Wind | 2005 | $40 |

— Distributed by Classic Records; 200-gram vinyl

49593-1	Prairie Wind	2005	$30
531980 [B]	Psychedelic Pill	2012	$100
26315	Ragged Glory	1990	$25

re·ac·tor — neil young crazy horse

HS2304 [B]	Re-Ac-Tor	1981	$12
HS2295	Rust Never Sleeps	1979	$12
45749 [B]	Sleeps with Angels	1994	$30
512563-1 [B]	Sugar Mountain - Live At Canterbury House 1968	2009	$75
R154182	This Note's for You	1987	$15

— BMG Direct Marketing edition

| 25719 | This Note's for You | 1988 | $15 |
| MS2151 [S-DJ] | Time Fades Away | 1973 | $250 |

— With a cardboard inner sleeve, withdrawn after the earliest pressing.

| M2151 [M] | Time Fades Away | 1973 | $500 |

— Special mono pressing for radio stations only

| MS2151 [S] | Time Fades Away | 1973 | $250 |

— With a cardboard inner sleeve, withdrawn after the earliest pressing

MS2151	Time Fades Away	1973	$12
MS2221	Tonight's the Night	1975	$12
46652 [B]	Year of the Horse	1997	$50
MS2242	Zuma	1975	$12

THIRD MAN

| TMR245 [B] | A Letter Home | 2014 | $30 |

VAPOR

48111	Are You Passionate?	2002	$30
46171	Dead Man (Soundtrack)	1996	$15
VAP-1001	Greendale	2005	$50

— Distributed by Classic Records; 140-gram vinyl with bonus 7-inch single, book, bumper sticker and stage bill

| VAP-1001 | Greendale | 2005 | $100 |

— Distributed by Classic Records; 200-gram vinyl with bonus 7-inch single, book, bumper sticker and stage bill

WARNER BROS.

| WBMS-107 [DJ] | The Warner Bros. Music Show | 1979 | $50 |

— Promo-only interview album

| WBMS-107 [DJ] | The Warner Bros. Music Show | 1979 | $50 |

— Promo-only interview album

YOUNG, NOAH

LAUGHING ANGEL

| LAR33 | Unicorn Dream | 1981 | $35 |

YOUNG, PAUL

COLUMBIA

| FC40543 | Between Two Fires | 1986 | $10 |

Number	Title	Yr	NM
BFC38976	No Parlez	1984	$12
FC38976	No Parlez	1985	$10

— Reissue with new prefix

| BFC39957 | The Secret of Association | 1985 | $12 |
| FC39957 | The Secret of Association | 1985 | $10 |

— Reissue with new prefix

COMPLEAT

| 672006-1 | London Dilemma | 1986 | $18 |

— As "Paul Young and Street Band"

YOUNG, SNOOKY

CONCORD JAZZ

| CJ-91 | Horn of Plenty | 1979 | $30 |
| CJ-55 | The Snooky Young/Marshal Royal Album | 1977 | $30 |

MASTER JAZZ

| 8130 | Dayton | 197? | $30 |

YOUNG, STERLING

HINDSIGHT

| HSR-113 | Sterling Young and His Orchestra 1939-1949 | 198? | $25 |

YOUNG, STEVE

BLUE CANYON

| 505 | Seven Bridges Road | 197? | $18 |

MOUNTAIN RAILROAD

| 52776 | Honky-Tonk Man | 197? | $18 |

RCA VICTOR

| APL1-2510 | No Place to Fall | 1978 | $18 |
| APL1-1759 | Renegade Picker | 1976 | $18 |

REPRISE

| MS2081 | Seven Bridges Road | 1972 | $18 |

ROUNDER

3087	Honky-Tonk Man	198?	$12
3058	Seven Bridges Road	198?	$12
3057	To Satisfy You	198?	$12

YOUNG, WEBSTER

FANTASY

| OJC-1716 | For Lady | 198? | $25 |

PRESTIGE

| PRLP-7106 [M] | For Lady | 1957 | $650 |

YOUNG-HOLT UNLIMITED

ATLANTIC

| SD1634 | Oh Girl | 1973 | $30 |

BRUNSWICK

BL754141	Funky But!	1968	$50
BL754150	Just a Melody	1969	$35
BL54125 [M]	On Stage	1967	$50

— As "Young-Holt Trio"

| BL754125 [S] | On Stage | 1967 | $50 |

— As "Young-Holt Trio"

BL754144	Soulful Strut	1968	$35
BL54128 [M]	The Beat Goes On	1967	$75
BL754128 [S]	The Beat Goes On	1967	$50
BL54121 [M]	Wack-Wack	1966	$50

— As "Young-Holt Trio"

| BL754121 [S] | Wack-Wack | 1966 | $50 |

— As "Young-Holt Trio"

CADET

| LPS-791 [S] | Feature Spot | 1967 | $50 |

— As "Eldee Young and Red Holt (of the Ramsey Lewis Trio)

| LP-791 [M] | Feature Spot | 1967 | $75 |

COTILLION

| SD18004 | Born Again | 1972 | $30 |
| SD18001 | Mellow Dreamin' | 1971 | $30 |

PAULA

| LPS-4002 | Super Fly | 1973 | $50 |

YOUNG AMERICANS, THE

ABC

S-626 [B]	The Wonderful World of the Young	1968	$25
S-659 [B]	Time for Livin'	1969	$18
586 [M]	While We're Young	1967	$30
S-586 [S]	While We're Young	1967	$25

YOUNG HEARTS, THE

MINIT

| LP-40016 [M] | Sweet Soul Shakin'! | 1968 | $30 |
| LP-24016 [S] | Sweet Soul Shakin'! | 1968 | $30 |

YOUNG LIONS, THE (1)

TRIP

| 5011 | Lions of Jazz | 197? | $30 |

VEE JAY

| VJS-3013 [S] | The Young Lions | 197? | $25 |

— Reissue on thinner, more flexible vinyl

| LP-3013 [M] | The Young Lions | 1960 | $40 |
| SR-3013 [S] | The Young Lions | 1960 | $50 |

Number	Title	Yr	NM

YOUNG LIONS, THE (2)
ELEKTRA/MUSICIAN
☐ 60196	The Young Lions	1984	$30

YOUNG MEN FROM MEMPHIS
UNITED ARTISTS
☐ UAL-4029 [M]	Down Home Reunion	1959	$50
☐ UAS-5029 [S]	Down Home Reunion	1959	$40

YOUNG RASCALS, THE
See THE RASCALS.

YOUNG TUXEDO BRASS BAND, THE
ATLANTIC
☐ 1297 [M]	Jazz Begins	1958	$300
—Black label			
☐ SD-1297 [M]	Jazz Begins	1958	$300
—Green label			
☐ 1297 [M]	Jazz Begins	1961	$175
—Multicolor label, white "fan" logo at right			
☐ SD-1297 [M]	Jazz Begins	1961	$175
—Multicolor label, white "fan" logo at right			
☐ 1297 [M]	Jazz Begins	1964	$35
—Multicolor label, black "fan" logo at right			
☐ SD-1297 [M]	Jazz Begins	1964	$30
—Multicolor label, black "fan" logo at right			

YOUNGBLOOD, LONNIE
RADIO
☐ RR16045	Lonnie Youngblood	1981	$18
TURBO
☐ TU7019	Lonnie Youngblood	1977	$25
☐ TU7011	Sweet Sweet Tootie	1972	$50

YOUNGBLOODS, THE
Also see JESSE COLIN YOUNG.
MERCURY
☐ SR-61273	Two Trips	1970	$30
—Gold border on cover			
☐ SR-61273	Two Trips	1971	$25
—Red border on cover			
RACCOON
☐ BS2566	Good and Dusty	1971	$15
☐ BS2653	High on a Ridge Top	1972	$15
☐ BS2563	Ride the Wind	1971	$15
☐ WS1878	Rock Festival	1970	$15
RCA VICTOR
☐ LPM-3865 [M]	Earth Music	1968	$50
☐ LSP-3865 [S]	Earth Music	1968	$30
☐ LSP-4150 [B]	Elephant Mountain	1969	$18
—Orange label			
☐ AFL1-4150	Elephant Mountain	1977	$12
—Reissue of LSP-4150			
☐ LSP-4150 [B]	Elephant Mountain	1975	$15
—Tan label			
☐ LSP-3724	Get Together	1969	$18
—Retitled version of "The Youngbloods"			
☐ LSP-4561	Sunlight	1971	$15
☐ LSP-4399	The Best of the Youngbloods	1970	$18
☐ AFL1-4399	The Best of the Youngbloods	1977	$12
—Reissue of LSP-4399			
☐ AYL1-3680	The Best of the Youngbloods	1980	$10
—Best Buy Series" reissue			
☐ LPM-3724 [M]	The Youngbloods	1967	$40
☐ LSP-3724 [S]	The Youngbloods	1967	$30
☐ VPS-6051	This Is the Youngbloods	1972	$18

YOUNGER, JAMES AND MICHAEL
MCA
☐ 5391	James and Michael Younger	1983	$12
☐ 900	James and Michael Younger	198?	$10
—Budget-line reissue of 5391			

YOUNGER BROTHERS BAND, THE
HME
☐ FW39978	The Younger Brothers Band	1985	$10

YOUNGMAN, HENNY
URANIA
☐ UR-9014 [M]	The Horse and Auto Race Game	195?	$50

YUM YUM KIDS, THE
MGM
☐ E-4396 [M]	Yummy in Your Tummy	1966	$18
☐ SE-4396 [S]	Yummy in Your Tummy	1966	$25

YURO, TIMI
LIBERTY
☐ LRP-3208 [M]	Hurt	1961	$40
☐ LST-7208 [S]	Hurt	1961	$50
☐ LRP-3234 [M]	Let Me Call You Sweetheart	1962	$18
☐ LST-7234 [S]	Let Me Call You Sweetheart	1962	$25
☐ LRP-3319 [M]	Make the World Go Away	1963	$18
☐ LST-7319 [S]	Make the World Go Away	1963	$25
☐ LST-7594	Something Bad on My Mind	1968	$15
☐ LRP-3212 [M]	Soul	1962	$18
☐ LST-7212 [S]	Soul	1962	$25
☐ LRP-3286 [M]	The Best of Timi Yuro	1963	$18
☐ LST-7286 [S]	The Best of Timi Yuro	1963	$25
☐ LRP-3263 [M]	What's a Matter Baby?	1963	$18
☐ LST-7263 [S]	What's a Matter Baby?	1963	$25
MERCURY
☐ MG-20963 [M]	The Amazing Timi Yuro	1964	$15
☐ SR-60963 [S]	The Amazing Timi Yuro	1964	$18
SUNSET
☐ SUM-1107 [M]	Timi Yuro	1966	$12
☐ SUS-5107 [S]	Timi Yuro	1966	$15
UNITED ARTISTS
☐ UA-LA429-E	The Very Best of Timi Yuro	1974	$15

YUTAKA
GRP
☐ GR-1046	Yutaka	1988	$25

Z

ZABACH, FLORIAN
DECCA
☐ DL8158 [M]	Dream of Romance	195?	$30
—Black label, silver print			
☐ DL8239 [M]	Hi-Fi Fiddle	195?	$30
—Black label, silver print			
☐ DL8086 [M]	Hour of Love	195?	$30
—Black label, silver print			
☐ DL5367 [10]	The Hot Canary	1951	$75
☐ DL4425 [M]	The Hot Canary	196?	$18
MERCURY
☐ SR60145 [S]	Do-It-Yourself Wedding Album	1959	$30
☐ MG20463 [M]	Do-It-Yourself Wedding Album	1959	$25
☐ MG20436 [M]	It's Easy to Dance with Florian Zabach	1959	$25
☐ SR60107 [S]	It's Easy to Dance with Florian Zabach	1959	$30
☐ MG20305 [M]	Till the End of Time	1958	$18
☐ SR60084 [S]	Till the End of Time	1958	$25
VOCALION
☐ VL3701 [M]	String Along	196?	$15
WING
☐ MGW12172 [M]	Golden Strings	196?	$15
☐ SRW16172 [S]	Golden Strings	196?	$18
☐ MGW12245 [M]	Till the End of Time	196?	$15
☐ SRW16245 [S]	Till the End of Time	196?	$18

ZACHERLEY, JOHN
CRESTVIEW
☐ CR803 [M]	Zacherle's Monster Gallery	1963	$40
☐ CRS7803 [S]	Zacherle's Monster Gallery	1963	$50
ELEKTRA
☐ EKL-190 [M]	Spook Along with Zacherle	1960	$75
☐ EKS-7190 [S]	Spook Along with Zacherle	1960	$100
PARKWAY
☐ P7018 [M]	Monster Mash	1962	$75
☐ P7023 [M]	Scary Tales	1963	$75

ZACK, GEORGE
COMMODORE
☐ FL-20001 [10]	Party Piano of the Roaring '20s	1950	$50

ZADORA, PIA
CBS ASSOCIATED
☐ BFZ40533	I Am What I Am	1986	$12
☐ FZ40259	Pia and Phil	1986	$10
☐ FZ45273	Pia Z.	1989	$18
ELEKTRA
☐ 60109	Pia	1982	$15

ZAGER, MICHAEL
COLUMBIA
☐ JC35771	Life's a Party	1979	$12
☐ JC36348	Zager	1980	$12
PRIVATE STOCK
☐ PS7013	Let's All Chant	1978	$12

ZAGER AND EVANS
RCA VICTOR
☐ LSP-4214 [B]	2525 (Exordium and Terminus)	1969	$25
☐ ANL1-1077	2525 (Exordium and Terminus)	1975	$12
—Reissue of 4214			
☐ LSP-4302	Zager and Evans	1970	$25

VANGUARD
☐ VSD-6568	Food for the Mind	1971	$18
WHITE WHALE
☐ WWS-7123	The Early Writings of Zager and Evans (And Others)	1969	$25
—Actually doesn't contain any music by Zager or Evans, but only songs they wrote; it remains here as it's usually considered a "Zager and Evans" LP			

ZAHARA
ANTILLES
☐ AN-1011	Flight of the Spirit	198?	$30

ZAHAROFF, PETE
GUINNESS
☐ GNS36063 [B]	Tiger Rose	1977	$25

ZAMFIR
MERCURY
☐ 822571-1	Christmas with Zamfir	1984	$12

ZANIES, THE
DORE
☐ 321	The Zanies	1969	$30
☐ 337	The Zanies	1979	$18

ZAPP
REPRISE
☐ 25807	Zapp V (Vibe)	1989	$15
WARNER BROS.
☐ 25327	The New Zapp IV U	1985	$10
☐ BSK3463	Zapp	1980	$12
☐ 23583	Zapp II	1982	$12
☐ 23875	Zapp III	1983	$12

ZAPPA, DWEEZIL
BARKING PUMPKIN
☐ ST-74204	Havin' a Bad Day	1987	$12
—Reissue of Chrysalis 41581			
CHRYSALIS
☐ BFV41581	Havin' a Bad Day	1986	$15
☐ BFV41633	My Guitar Wants to Kill Your Mama	1988	$12

ZAPPA, FRANK
Includes his work leading The Mothers of Invention. The label credit, if other than "Frank Zappa," is listed under each record. Also see BABY RAY AND THE FERNS; BOB GUY; ADRIAN BELEW.
ANGEL
☐ DS-38170	Boulez Conducts Zappa: The Perfect Stranger	1983	$30
BARKING PUMPKIN
☐ BPRP-1115 [PD]	Baby Snakes	1983	$30
—Picture disc			
☐ D1-74218	Broadway the Hard Way	1988	$25
☐ ST-74202	Francesco Zappa	1985	$25
☐ ST-74203	Frank Zappa Meets the Mothers of Prevention	1985	$25
☐ D1-74212	Guitar	1988	$25
☐ ST-74205	Jazz from Hell	1986	$25
☐ 74206	Joe's Garage, Acts 1, 2 and 3	1986	$150
—Box set, two gatefolds, with insert			
☐ FW38820	London Symphony Orchestra	1983	$30
☐ SJ-74207	London Symphony Orchestra, Volume 2	1987	$25
☐ FW38403	Man from Utopia	1983	$30
☐ BPR-1113 [B]	Return of the Son of Shut Up 'N' Play Yer Guitar	1981	$40
—Mail-order item only			
☐ FW38066	Ship Arriving Too Late to Save a Drowning Witch	1982	$30
☐ BPR-1111 [B]	Shut Up 'N' Play Yer Guitar	1981	$40
—Mail-order item only			
☐ W3X-38289 [B]	Shut Up 'N' Play Yer Guitar	1982	$50
—Box set containing all three "Shut Up 'N' Play Yer Guitar" albums			
☐ BPR-1112 [B]	Shut Up 'N' Play Yer Guitar Some More	1981	$40
—Mail-order item only			
☐ SVBO-74200	Them Or Us	1984	$35
☐ 7777 [B]	The Old Masters, Box 1	1984	$100
—Boxed set			
☐ 8888 [B]	The Old Masters, Box 2	1986	$100
—Another boxed set			
☐ 9999 [B]	The Old Masters, Box 3	1987	$100
—Still another boxed set			
☐ 7X4-1 [B]	The Old Masters Sampler	1984	$40
☐ 8888X [B]	The Old Masters Sampler 2	1986	$40
☐ SWCO-74201	Thing-Fish	1984	$50
☐ PW237336	Tinsel Town Rebellion	1981	$50
☐ AS995 [DJ]	Tinsel Town Rebellion	1981	$50
—Promo-only sampler			
☐ PW237537	You Are What You Is	1981	$50
☐ AS1294 [DJ]	You Are What You Is Special Clean Cuts Edition	1981	$50

Number	Title	Yr	NM
❏ R174213	You Can't Do That on Stage Anymore Sampler	1988	$30
❏ D1-74213	You Can't Do That on Stage Anymore Sampler	1988	$25
❏ D1-74217	You Can't Do That on Stage Anymore Vol. 2	1988	$25
❏ BPRP-1114 [PD]	Zappa	1982	$30

— Picture disc with two songs

BIZARRE

Number	Title	Yr	NM
❏ RS-6370 [B]	Burnt Weenie Sandwich	1970	$30

— Blue label original; with booklet

| ❏ RS-6370 [B] | Burnt Weenie Sandwich | 1973 | $18 |

— Reissue with brown Reprise label

| ❏ MS2030 [DJ] | Chunga's Revenge | 1970 | $75 |

— White label promo

| ❏ MS-2030 | Chunga's Revenge | 1970 | $75 |

— Blue label original

| ❏ MS-2030 | Chunga's Revenge | 1973 | $35 |

— Reissue with brown Reprise label

| ❏ MS-2042 [B] | Fillmore East, June 1971 | 1971 | $30 |

— Blue label original

| ❏ MS-2042 | Fillmore East, June 1971 | 1973 | $35 |

— Reissue with brown Reprise label

| ❏ RS-6356 | Hot Rats | 1969 | $150 |

— Blue label original

| ❏ RS-6356 | Hot Rats | 1973 | $35 |

— Reissue with brown Reprise label

| ❏ MS2075 [B] | Just Another Band from L.A. | 1972 | $40 |

— Blue label original

| ❏ MS2075 | Just Another Band from L.A. | 1973 | $35 |

— Reissue with brown Reprise label

| ❏ MS2093 [B] | The Grand Wazoo | 1972 | $30 |

— Blue label original

| ❏ MS2093 | The Grand Wazoo | 1973 | $35 |

— Reissue with brown Reprise label

| ❏ MS-2024 [B] | Uncle Meat | 1969 | $75 |

— Originals come with a booklet; blue label

| ❏ MS-2024 | Uncle Meat | 1973 | $50 |

— Reissue with brown Reprise label

| ❏ MS2094 [B] | Waka/Jawaka | 1972 | $30 |

— Blue label original

| ❏ MS2094 [B] | Waka/Jawaka | 1973 | $18 |

— Reissue with brown Reprise label

| ❏ MS-2028 [B] | Weasels Ripped My Flesh | 1970 | $30 |

— Blue label original

| ❏ MS-2028 [B] | Weasels Ripped My Flesh | 1973 | $18 |

— Reissue with brown Reprise label

COLUMBIA

| ❏ (no #) [DJ] | Lather | 1977 | $750 |

— Test pressing only; parts of this LP are on DSK 2291, 2292 and 2294; released as a whole only after Zappa's death, with vinyl only coming out in Japan

DISCREET

Number	Title	Yr	NM
❏ DS2175	Apostrophe (')	1974	$35
❏ DS42175 [Q]	Apostrophe (')	1974	$150
❏ DS2175	Apostrophe (')	1974	$150

— White label promo

| ❏ DSK2289 | Apostrophe (') | 1977 | $30 |

— Reissue with new number

❏ DS2234	Bongo Fury	1975	$35
❏ DS2216	One Size Fits All	1975	$35
❏ DSK2294	Orchestral Favorites	1978	$35
❏ MS2149 [B]	Over-Nite Sensation	1973	$40
❏ MS42149 [Q]	Over-Nite Sensation	1973	$150
❏ DSK2288	Over-Nite Sensation	1977	$30

— Reissue of DiscReet 2149 with new number

❏ 2DS2202	Roxy and Elsewhere	1974	$75
❏ DSK2292	Sleep Dirt	1978	$35
❏ DSK2291	Studio Tan	1978	$35
❏ 2D2290 [DJ]	Zappa in New York	1978	$400

— Test pressing with "Punky's Whips"

| ❏ 2D2290 | Zappa in New York | 1978 | $300 |

— Stock copy with "Punky's Whips" erroneously listed on jacket

Number	Title	Yr	NM
❏ 2D2290	Zappa in New York	1978	$50

FOO-EEE

| ❏ R1-70372 [B] | Beat the Boots #2 | 1992 | $175 |

— Legitimate box-set release by Rhino of 11 bootlegged concerts

| ❏ R1-70907 [B] | Beat the Boots | 1991 | $350 |

— Legitimate box-set release by Rhino of eight bootlegged concerts

MCA

| ❏ 4183 | 200 Motels (movie soundtrack) | 1986 | $35 |

— Reissue

MGM

| ❏ GAS-112 [DJ] | The Mothers of Invention | 1970 | $200 |

— Yellow label promo

| ❏ GAS-112 | The Mothers of Invention | 1970 | $150 |
| ❏ SE-4754 [DJ] | The Worst of the Mothers | 1971 | $300 |

— Yellow label promo

| ❏ SE-4754 | The Worst of the Mothers | 1971 | $150 |

RHINO/DEL-FI

| ❏ RNEP-604 | Rare Meat: The Early Productions of Frank Zappa | 1984 | $40 |

— With original cover

RYKO ANALOGUE

| ❏ RALP40500 [B] | Strictly Commercial: The Best of Frank Zappa | 1995 | $40 |

— Issued with obi

| ❏ RALP10503 [B] | We're Only in It for the Money | 1995 | $75 |

— Vinyl reissue; Frank Zappa/The Mothers of Invention

UNITED ARTISTS

| ❏ UAS-9956 | 200 Motels (movie soundtrack) | 1971 | $150 |

VERVE

| ❏ V-5013 [M] | Absolutely Free | 1967 | $350 |

— White label promo

❏ V-5013 [M]	Absolutely Free	1967	$400
❏ V6-5013 [S]	Absolutely Free	1967	$100
❏ V6-5055 [DJ]	Cruising with Ruben and the Jets	1968	$250

— Yellow label promo

| ❏ V6-5055 | Cruising with Ruben and the Jets | 1968 | $120 |
| ❏ V-5005-2 [M] | Freak Out! | 1966 | $400 |

— White label promo

| ❏ V-5005-2 [M] | Freak Out! | 1966 | $250 |

— Cover version 1: Has blurb on inside gatefold on how to get a map of "freak-out hot spots" in L.A.

| ❏ V-5005-2 [M] | Freak Out! | 1966 | $300 |

— Cover version 2: Has no blurb inside on getting a map of "freak-out hot spots"

| ❏ V6-5005-2 [S] | Freak Out! | 1966 | $300 |

— Yellow label promo

| ❏ V6-5005-2 [S] | Freak Out! | 1966 | $100 |

— Cover version 2: Has no blurb inside on getting a map of "freak-out hot spots"

| ❏ V6-5005-2 [S] | Freak Out! | 1966 | $175 |

— Cover version 1: Has blurb on inside gatefold on how to get a map of "freak-out hot spots" in L.A.

| ❏ V6-8741 [DJ] | Lumpy Gravy | 1968 | $250 |

— Yellow label promo

| ❏ V6-8741 [B] | Lumpy Gravy | 1968 | $75 |
| ❏ V-8741 [M] | Lumpy Gravy | 1968 | $350 |

— Yellow label promo; no stock copies were issued in mono

| ❏ V6-5068 [DJ] | Mothermania – The Best of the Mothers | 1969 | $175 |

— Yellow label promo

| ❏ V6-5068 [B] | Mothermania – The Best of the Mothers | 1969 | $100 |
| ❏ V6-5074 [DJ] | The XXXX of the Mothers | 1969 | $300 |

— Yellow label promo

| ❏ V6-5074 | The XXXX of the Mothers | 1969 | $150 |
| ❏ V-5045 [M] | We're Only in It for the Money | 1968 | $1000 |

— White label promo

| ❏ V-5045 [M] | We're Only in It for the Money | 1968 | $800 |

— With sheet of cut-outs a la "Sgt. Pepper's Lonely Hearts Club Band"

| ❏ V6-5045 [S] | We're Only in It for the Money | 1968 | $120 |

— Un-censored version, with cut-outs

| ❏ V6-5045 [S] | We're Only in It for the Money | 1968 | $250 |

— Censored version: the songs "Who Needs the Peace Corps?" and "Let's Make the Water Turn Black" have lines deleted

WARNER BROS.

| ❏ BS-2970 | Zoot Allures | 1976 | $35 |

ZAPPA

Number	Title	Yr	NM
❏ SRZ-1-1603	Joe's Garage, Act I	1979	$35
❏ SRZ-2-1502	Joe's Garage, Acts II and III	1980	$50
❏ MK-129 [DJ]	Joe's Garage Acts I, II and III Sampler	1980	$175
❏ SRZ-2-1501	Sheik Yerbouti	1979	$50
❏ MK-78 [DJ]	Sheik Yerbouti Clean Cuts	1979	$175

ZAWINUL, JOE

ATLANTIC

Number	Title	Yr	NM
❏ SD1694	Concerto	1976	$35
❏ 3004 [M]	Money in the Pocket	1966	$50
❏ SD3004 [S]	Money in the Pocket	1966	$75
❏ SD1579	Zawinul	1970	$50

COLUMBIA

❏ FC44316	Black Water	1989	$30
❏ FC40081	Dialects	1986	$25
❏ FC40969	Immigrants	1988	$25

VORTEX

| ❏ 2002 [S] | The Rise and Fall of the 3rd Stream | 1968 | $50 |

ZAZU

WOODEN NICKEL

| ❏ BWL1-0791 [B] | Zazu | 1975 | $25 |

ZEBRA

ATLANTIC

| ❏ 81692 [B] | 3.V | 1986 | $12 |
| ❏ PR1028 [DJ] | Interview/Questions and Answers | 1987 | $25 |

— Promo-only music and interviews

| ❏ 80159 [B] | No Tellin' Lies | 1984 | $10 |
| ❏ 80054 | Zebra | 1983 | $10 |

ZEITLIN, DENNY, AND CHARLIE HADEN

ECM

| ❏ 1239 | Time Remembers One Time Once | 1981 | $30 |

ZEITLIN, DENNY

1750 ARCH

❏ 1758	Expansions	197?	$35
❏ 1770	Soundings	1979	$35
❏ 1759	Syzygy	197?	$35

COLUMBIA

❏ CL2340 [M]	Carnival	1965	$25
❏ CS9140 [S]	Carnival	1965	$30
❏ CL2182 [M]	Cathexis	1964	$25
❏ CS8982 [S]	Cathexis	1964	$30
❏ CL2463 [M]	My Shining Hour	1966	$35
❏ CS9263 [S]	My Shining Hour	1966	$25
❏ CL2748 [M]	Zeitgeist	1966	$35
❏ CS9548 [S]	Zeitgeist	1966	$50

LIVING MUSIC

| ❏ LM-0011 | Homecoming | 1986 | $25 |

WINDHAM HILL

| ❏ WH-0112 | Denny Zeitlin Trio | 1988 | $25 |
| ❏ WH-0121 | In the Moment | 1989 | $30 |

ZELL, JOHNNY

MANNA

| ❏ MS-2065 | Heralding Christmas | 1979 | $12 |

ZENITH HOT STOMPERS, THE

STOMP OFF

| ❏ SOS-1191 | 20th Anniversary Album | 1991 | $30 |

ZENITH SIX, THE

GHB

| ❏ GHB-12 | The Zenith Six, Vol. 1 | 196? | $30 |
| ❏ GHB-13 | The Zenith Six, Vol. 2 | 196? | $30 |

ZENITHS, THE

ATLANTIC

| ❏ 8043 [M] | Makin' the Scene | 1960 | $150 |
| ❏ SD8043 [S] | Makin' the Scene | 1960 | $175 |

ZENTNER, SI

LIBERTY

Number	Title	Yr	NM
❏ LMM-13009 [M]	A Great Band with Great Voices	1961	$30
❏ LSS-14009 [S]	A Great Band with Great Voices	1961	$35
❏ LMM-13017 [M]	A Great Band with Great Voices Swing the Great Voices of the Great Bands	1962	$30
❏ LSS-14017 [S]	A Great Band with Great Voices Swing the Great Voices of the Great Bands	1962	$35
❏ LRP-3197 [M]	Big Band Plays the Big Hits	1961	$30
❏ LST-7197 [S]	Big Band Plays the Big Hits	1961	$35
❏ LRP-3350 [M]	Big Big Band Hits	1964	$30
❏ LST-7350 [S]	Big Big Band Hits	1964	$35
❏ LRP-3273 [M]	Desafinado	1963	$30
❏ LST-7273 [S]	Desafinado	1963	$35
❏ LRP-3353 [M]	From Russia with Love	1964	$30
❏ LST-7353 [S]	From Russia with Love	1964	$35
❏ LRP-3326 [M]	More	1963	$30
❏ LST-7326 [S]	More	1963	$35
❏ LRP-3457 [M]	The Best of Si Zentner	1966	$30
❏ LST-7457 [S]	The Best of Si Zentner	1966	$30
❏ LRP-3247 [M]	The Stripper and Other Big Band Hits	1962	$30
❏ LST-7247 [S]	The Stripper and Other Big Band Hits	1962	$35

Number	Title	Yr	NM
❑ LRP-3216 [M]	Up a Lazy River (Big Band Plays the Big Hits: Vol. 2)	1962	$30
❑ LST-7216 [S]	Up a Lazy River (Big Band Plays the Big Hits: Vol. 2)	1962	$35
❑ LRP-3284 [M]	Waltz in Jazz Time	1963	$30
❑ LST-7284 [S]	Waltz in Jazz Time	1963	$35

SMASH

❑ MGS-27007 [M]	Presenting Si Zentner	1961	$35
❑ SRS-67007 [S]	Presenting Si Zentner	1961	$50
❑ MGS-27013 [M]	Swing Fever	1962	$35
❑ SRS-67013 [S]	Swing Fever	1962	$50

SUNSET

❑ SUM-1110 [M]	Big Band Brilliance	196?	$25
❑ SUS-5110 [S]	Big Band Brilliance	196?	$30

ZEPHYR
PROBE

❑ 4510 [B]	Zephyr	1969	$75

WARNER BROS.

❑ WS1897 [B]	Goin' Back to Colorado	1971	$50
❑ BS2603 [B]	Sunset Ride	1972	$30

ZERFAS
700 WEST

❑ 730710	Zerfas	1973	$800

ZERO BOYS
LOOKOUT!

❑ LK-253	Vicious Circle	2000	$12

—*Same reissue as on Panic Button except for the label and number*

NIMROD

❑ 1	Vicious Circle	1982	$150

PANIC BUTTON

❑ PB286	Vicious Circle	2000	$15

—*Reissue of Nimrod release with two bonus tracks*

TOXIC SHOCK

❑ TXLP11 [B]	Vicious Circle	1987	$30

—*Reissue of Nimrod release*

ZEROS
BOMP!

❑ BLP4035 [B]	Don't Push Me Around	1991	$50
❑ BLP4074	Right Now!	1999	$12

ZETTERLUND, MONICA
INNER CITY

❑ IC-1082	It Only Happens Every Time	197?	$35

ZEVON, WARREN
ARTEMIS

❑ 51156	The Wind	2004	$25

—*180-gram version; CD was issued in 2003*

ASYLUM

❑ 60503	A Quiet Normal Life: The Best of Warren Zevon	1987	$12
❑ 5E-509	Bad Luck Streak in Dancing School	1980	$12

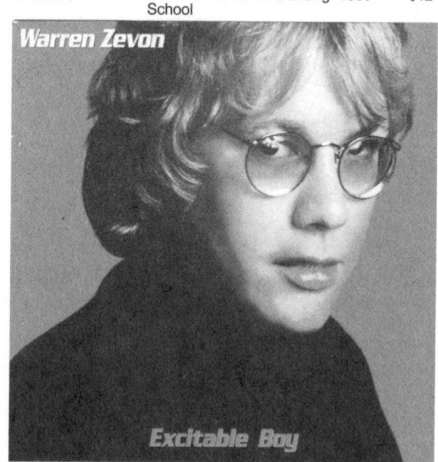

Warren Zevon — *Excitable Boy*

❑ 6E-118 [B]	Excitable Boy	1978	$12
❑ 5E-519	Stand in the Fire	1980	$12
❑ 60159	The Envoy	1982	$12
❑ 7E-1060	Warren Zevon	1976	$12

IMPERIAL

❑ LP-12456	Wanted Dead or Alive	1970	$50

—*As "Zevon*

PICKWICK

❑ SPC-3715	Wanted Dead or Alive	1979	$18

—*Reissue of Imperial album*

VIRGIN

❑ 90603	Sentimental Hygiene	1987	$12
❑ 91068 [B]	Transverse City	1989	$12

ZIG ZAG PEOPLE, THE
DECCA

❑ DL75110 [B]	The Zig Zag People Take Bubble Gum Music Underground	1969	$30

ZINGARA
WHEEL

❑ 10001	Zingara	1981	$18

ZINN'S RAGTIME STRING QUARTET
CLASSIC JAZZ

❑ 13	Zinn's Ragtime String Quartet	197?	$25

ZIP CODES, THE
LIBERTY

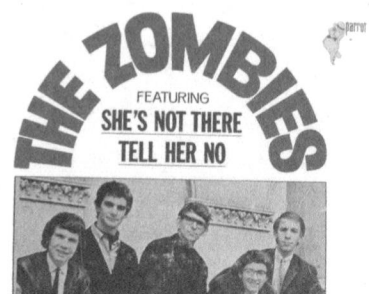

❑ LRP-3367 [M]	Mustang	1964	$175
❑ LST-7367 [S]	Mustang	1964	$250

ZIPPERS, THE
RHINO

❑ RNEP601 [EP]	Six Song Mini Album	1981	$30

ZIRCONS, THE
SNOWFLAKE

❑ 1003	The Crown Kings of Acappella	196?	$75

ZITO, PHIL
COLUMBIA

❑ CL6110 [10]	International City Dixielanders	1950	$50

ZITRO, JAMES
ESP-DISK'

❑ 1052 [S]	Zitro	1968	$120

Z'LOOKE
ORPHEUS

❑ D1-75600	Take U Back to My Place	1988	$15

ZODIAC MINDWARP & THE LOVE REACTION
VERTIGO

❑ 832729-1	Tattooed Beat Messiah	1988	$15

ZOLLER, ATTILA
EMARCY

❑ SPE-66013 [S]	The Horizon Beyond	1968	$150

EMBRYO

❑ SD523 [B]	Gypsy Cry	1970	$25

INNER CITY

❑ IC-3008	Dream Bells	1976	$20

ZOMBIE, ROB
1500 RECORDS

❑ 497201-1 [EP]	Remix-A-Go-Go	2000	$10

—*Five-song remix EP in generic black sleeve with sticker*

GEFFEN

❑ 069490349-1	American Made Music to Strip By	1999	$50
❑ GEF25212	Hellbilly Deluxe	1998	$40

—*Picture disc in plastic sleeve with sticker*

❑ 0694931471 [B]	The Sinister Urge	2001	$50

ZODIAC SWAN

❑ B002473901 [B]	The Electric Warlock Acid Witch Satanic Orgy Celebration Dispenser	2016	$25

ZOMBIES, THE
DATE

❑ TES-4013	Odessey and Oracle	1968	$30

—*With no mention of "Time of the Season" on front cover*

❑ TES-4013 [B]	Odessey and Oracle	1969	$25

—*With "Time of the Season" mentioned on front cover*

EPIC

❑ KEG32861 [B]	Time of the Zombies	1974	$25

—*Record 1 is mono; Record 2 is stereo; orange labels*

❑ PEG32861 [B]	Time of the Zombies	1979	$18

—*Later edition with blue labels*

LONDON

❑ PS557 [P]	Early Days	1969	$25

—*All tracks in true stereo except "Tell Her No*

PARROT

❑ PA61001 [M]	The Zombies	1965	$80

❑ PAS71001 [R]	The Zombies	1965	$40

RHINO

❑ RNLP-120	Live on the BBC, 1965-67	1985	$12
❑ RNLP70186 [S]	Odessy and Oracle	1986	$10

THE END

❑ TE7081 [B]	Still Got That Hunger	2016	$25

VARESE SARABANDE

❑ 302 066 254 3 [B]	Odessey and Oracle	2015	$25
❑ 302 066 436 1 [B]	The Zombies	2013	$30

VARESE VINTAGE

❑ 302 067 266 1 [B]	R.I.P.	2015	$25

—*Record Store day ltd edition*

ZONJIC, ALEXANDER
OPTIMISM

❑ OP-3206	Elegant Evening	198?	$25
❑ OP-3207	Romance with You	198?	$25
❑ OP-3102	When Is It Real	198?	$25

ZOO, THE (1)
MERCURY

❑ SR-61300	The Zoo	1970	$25

SUNBURST

❑ 7500 [B]	The Zoo Presents the Chocolate Moose	1968	$50

ZOOM
MCA

❑ 5420	Blasting Off	1983	$18

POLYDOR

❑ PD-1-6343	Saturday, Saturday Night	1981	$25

ZORN, JOHN
ELEKTRA

❑ 60844	Spy vs. Spy	1989	$30

ELEKTRA/NONESUCH

❑ 79238	Naked City	1990	$30
❑ 79172	Spillane/Two-Lane Highway/ Forbidden Fruit	1987	$25
❑ 79139	The Big Gundown	1987	$25

HAT ART

❑ 2034	Cobra	1987	$35

ZOTTOLA, GLENN
DREAMSTREET

❑ 105	Live at Eddie Condon's	1980	$30
❑ 107	Steamin' Mainstream	1986	$25

FAMOUS DOOR

❑ HL-141	Secret Love	1981	$30
❑ HL-149	Stardust	1983	$30

Number	Title	Yr	NM

ZULEMA
LEJOINT
☐ LEJ17000 — Z-Licious — 1978 — $18
RCA VICTOR
☐ APL1-1152 — R.S.V.P. — 1975 — $18
☐ APL1-1423 — Suddenly There Was You — 1976 — $18
☐ APL1-0819 — Zulema — 1975 — $18
SUSSEX
☐ SRA8029 — Ms. Z. — 1973 — $18
☐ SXBS7015 — Zulema — 1972 — $18

ZUNIGER, RICK
HEADFIRST
☐ 675 — New Frontier — 198? — $30

ZURKE, BOB
RCA VICTOR
☐ LPM-1013 [M] — The Tom Cat on the Keys — 1955 — $100

ZWOL
EMI AMERICA
☐ SW-17014 — Effective Immediately — 1979 — $12
☐ SW-17005 — Zwol — 1978 — $12

ZYTRON
PACIFIC ARTS
☐ B7-120 — New Moon in Zytron — 197? — $35

ZZ TOP
LONDON
☐ PS656 — Fandango! — 1975 — $15
☐ PS612 — Rio Grande Mud — 1972 — $15
☐ PS-X-1001 [DJ] — Takin' Texas to the People — 1976 — $75
☐ PS680 — Tejas — 1977 — $15
☐ PS706 — The Best of ZZ Top — 1977 — $15
☐ XPS631 [B] — Tres Hombres — 1973 — $15
☐ PS584 — ZZ Top's First Album — 1971 — $15
RHINO/WARNER BROS.
☐ 306172 — Fandango! — 2008 — $25
WARNER BROS.
☐ 25342 [B] — Afterburner — 1985 — $10
☐ HS3361 — Deguello — 1979 — $12
☐ 23774 — Eliminator — 1983 — $10

☐ BSK3593 [B] — El Loco — 1981 — $12
☐ BSK3271 — Fandango! — 1979 — $10
☐ 26846 — Greatest Hits — 1992 — $25
— U.S. vinyl available only through Columbia House
☐ 26265 — Recycler — 1990 — $18
☐ BSK3269 — Rio Grande Mud — 1979 — $10
☐ BSK3272 — Tejas — 1979 — $10
☐ BSK3273 — The Best of ZZ Top — 1979 — $10
☐ BSK3270 — Tres Hombres — 1979 — $10
☐ 274492 — Tres Hombres — 2007 — $30
— Reissue on 180-gram vinyl with gatefold, replica of "Burbank" WB label and insert
☐ MOVLP1142 [B] — Tres Hombres — 2014 — $30
☐ BSK3268 — ZZ Top's First Album — 1979 — $10

ORIGINAL CAST RECORDINGS

*A WONDERFUL GUY/SOME ENCHANTED EVENING/YOUNGER THAN SPRINGTIME/I'M GONNA WASH THAT MAN RIGHT OUTA MY HAIR
☐ Columbia Masterworks A-1723 — 195? — 15.00
— Tracks by (not necessarily in this order) Mary Martin, Ezio Pinza and William Tabbert

*A WONDERFUL GUY/SOME ENCHANTED EVENING/YOUNGER THAN SPRINGTIME/I'M GONNA WASH THAT MAN RIGHT OUT OF MY HAIR
☐ Columbia B-2579 — 195? — 10.00
— Track 1 and 4 by Mary Martin; track 2 by Ezio Pinza; track 3 by William Tabbert

AIN'T MISBEHAVIN'
☐ RCA Victor CBL2-2965 — 1978 — 15.00
— New recordings of the music of Fats Waller

ALL AMERICAN
☐ Columbia Masterworks KOL5760 [M] — 1962 — 30.00
☐ Columbia Masterworks KOS2160 [S] — 1962 — 30.00

ALL NIGHT STRUT!
☐ Playhouse Square PHS-CLE 1S-1001 — 1976 — 100.00

ANKLES AWEIGHT
☐ Decca DL9025 [M] — 1955 — 40.00

ANNIE
☐ CBS Masterworks JS34712 — 197? — 10.00

Number	Title	Yr	NM

— Reissue; cover is basically the same, but label has "CBS Masterworks" along the outer edge
☐ Columbia Masterworks JS34712 — 1977 — 12.00
— Original; labels have "Columbia" circling the perimeter of the label

ANNIE GET YOUR GUN
☐ Decca DL8001 [M] — 1949 — 50.00
— Original LP issue of the Broadway cast
☐ Decca DL9018 [M] — 1955 — 40.00
— Early reissue of DL 8001; black label with silver print
☐ Decca DL79018 [R] — 196? — 15.00
☐ RCA Victor LOC-1124 [M] — 1966 — 15.00
☐ RCA Victor LSO-1124 [M] — 1966 — 18.00
— Revival cast; black label, dog on top, "Stereo Dynagroove" at bottom
☐ RCA Victor LSO-1124 [S] — 1969 — 12.00
— Revival cast; orange, tan or black "dog near top" label

ANNIE'S CHRISTMAS
☐ Columbia CC38361 — 1982 — 15.00
— Based on the characters in the "Annie" Broadway play

ANYA
☐ United Artists UAL-4133 [M] — 1965 — 25.00
☐ United Artists UAS-5133 [S] — 1965 — 50.00

APPLAUSE
☐ ABC ABCS-OC-11 — 1970 — 25.00

THE APPLE TREE
☐ Columbia Masterworks KOL6620 [M] — 1966 — 25.00
☐ Columbia Masterworks KOS3020 [S] — 1966 — 30.00

ARABIAN NIGHTS
☐ Decca DL9013 [M] — 1954 — 100.00

THE ATHENIAN TOUCH
☐ Broadway East OCM-101 [M] — 1964 — 175.00
☐ Broadway East OCS-101 [S] — 1964 — 250.00

BAJOUR
☐ Columbia Masterworks KOL6300 [M] — 1964 — 30.00
☐ Columbia Masterworks KOS2700 [S] — 1964 — 30.00

BAKER STREET (A MUSICAL ADVENTURE OF SHERLOCK HOLMES)
☐ MGM E-7000 [M] — 1965 — 30.00
☐ MGM SE-7000 [S] — 1965 — 30.00

A BALLAD FOR BIMSHIRE
☐ London AM48002 [M] — 1963 — 40.00
☐ London AMS78002 [S] — 1963 — 100.00

THE BALLAD OF BABY DOE
☐ MGM 3GC-1 [M] — 1958 — 175.00
— Box set

THE BAND WAGON
☐ X LVA-1001 [M] — 1955 — 80.00

BELLS ARE RINGING
☐ Columbia Masterworks OL5170 [M] — 1957 — 30.00
— Gray and black label with six "eye" logos
☐ Columbia Masterworks OS2006 [S] — 1959 — 30.00
— Re-recording in stereo of OL 5170

BEN FRANKLIN IN PARIS
☐ Capitol VAS2191 [M] — 1964 — 30.00
☐ Capitol SVAS2191 [S] — 1964 — 30.00

BEST FOOT FORWARD
☐ Cadence CLP-4012 [M] — 1963 — 25.00
☐ Cadence CLP-24012 [S] — 1963 — 30.00
— 1963 revival of 1941 play

THE BEST LITTLE WHOREHOUSE IN TEXAS
☐ MCA 3049 — 1978 — 15.00
— Tan label original
☐ MCA 37218 — 1980 — 10.00
— Reissue of MCA 3049

BEYOND THE FRINGE
☐ Capitol W1792 [M] — 1962 — 30.00
☐ Capitol SW1792 [S] — 1962 — 30.00

BEYOND THE FRINGE '64
☐ Capitol W2072 [M] — 1964 — 25.00
☐ Capitol SW2072 [S] — 1964 — 30.00

BIG RIVER
☐ MCA 6147 — 1985 — 12.00
— Music written by Roger Miller

THE BIRTHDAY OF A KING
☐ Hal Leonard Publishing HLP-42 — 1986 — 15.00
— Composers: John Jacobson and Ed Lojeski

THE BOY FRIEND
☐ RCA Victor LOC-1018 [M] — 1954 — 30.00
— Originals have green labels

THE BOYS IN THE BAND
☐ A&M SP-6001 — 1969 — 30.00

BRAVO, GIOVANNI
☐ Columbia Masterworks KOL5800 [M] — 1962 — 18.00
☐ Columbia Masterworks KOS2200 [S] — 1962 — 25.00

BRIGADOON
☐ RCA Victor LOC-1001 [M] — 1951 — 30.00
— Green front cover; green label

Number	Title	Yr	NM

☐ RCA Victor LOC-1001 [M] — 195? — 25.00
— Photos of kilted dancers on front cover; black "Long Play" label
☐ RCA Victor LOC-1001 [M] — 1963 — 18.00
— Drawing of kilted dancers on front cover; black "Mono" label
☐ RCA Victor LSO-1001(e) [R] — 1963 — 15.00
— Black label, dog on top

BYE BYE BIRDIE
☐ Columbia Masterworks KOL5510 [M] — 1960 — 30.00
— Gray and black label with six "eye" logos; with gatefold cover
☐ Columbia Masterworks OL5510 [M] — 196? — 25.00
— Gray and black label with six "eye" logos; with regular cover
☐ Columbia Masterworks KOS2025 [S] — 1960 — 30.00
— Gray and black label with six "eye" logos; with gatefold cover
☐ Columbia Masterworks OS2025 [S] — 196? — 30.00
— Gray and black label with six "eye" logos; with regular cover

BY JUPITER
☐ RCA Victor LOC-1137 [M] — 1967 — 40.00
☐ RCA Victor LSO-1137 [S] — 1967 — 85.00
— Above is by a revival cast

BY THE BEAUTIFUL SEA
☐ Capitol S531 [M] — 1954 — 80.00

CABARET
☐ Columbia Masterworks KOL6640 [M] — 1966 — 18.00
☐ Columbia Masterworks KOS3040 [S] — 1966 — 25.00

CABIN IN THE SKY
☐ Capitol W2073 [M] — 1964 — 30.00
☐ Capitol SW2073 [S] — 1964 — 50.00
— Above is by a revival cast

CALL ME MADAM
☐ RCA Victor LOC-1000 [M] — 1950 — 100.00
— Dinah Shore sings Ethel Merman's part for contractual reasons, otherwise it's by the entire original cast

CAMELOT
☐ Columbia Masterworks KOL5620 [M] — 1960 — 25.00
— Gray and black label with six "eye" logos
☐ Columbia Masterworks KOS2031 [S] — 1960 — 30.00
— Gray and black label with six "eye" logos; gatefold cover

CAN-CAN
☐ Capitol S452 [M] — 1953 — 30.00
— Originals have red labels with Capitol logo at top
☐ Capitol W452 [M] — 195? — 18.00
☐ Capitol DW452 [R] — 196? — 15.00

CANTERBURY TALES
☐ Capitol SW-229 — 1969 — 30.00

CAPTAIN JINKS OF THE HORSE MARINES
☐ RCA Victor ARL2-1727 — 1975 — 30.00
— Box set

CARMEN JONES
☐ Decca DL8014 [M] — 1949 — 40.00
— Black label, gold print
☐ Decca DL9021 [M] — 1955 — 25.00
— Reissue of 8014; black label, silver print

CARNIVAL
☐ MGM E-3946 [M] — 1961 — 25.00
☐ MGM SE-3946 [S] — 1961 — 30.00
— Black label
☐ MGM SE-3946 [S] — 1968 — 12.00
— Blue and gold label

CAROUSEL
☐ Command RS 33-843 [M] — 1962 — 18.00
— Studio cast
☐ Command RS-843SD [M] — 1962 — 25.00
— Studio cast witrh Alfred Drake and Roberta Peters, and Enoch Light's orchestra
☐ Decca DL8003 [M] — 1949 — 40.00
— Original LP issue of the Broadway cast
☐ Decca DL9020 [M] — 1955 — 30.00
— Early reissue of DL 8003; black label with silver print
☐ Decca DL79020 [R] — 196? — 12.00
☐ MCA 1627 [R] — 198? — 10.00
— Reissue of MCA 37093
☐ MCA 37093 [R] — 1980 — 10.00
— Reissue of MCA 2033
☐ MCA 2033 [R] — 1973 — 10.00
— Reissue of Decca 79020; black label with rainbow

CELEBRATE THE KING
☐ John W. Peterson Music JPLP 07013 — 1986 — 15.00
— A Christmas Musical by John W. Peterson," who composed it

A CHORUS LINE
☐ Columbia PS33581 — 1975 — 15.00
— Original edition; no bar code on back cover
☐ Columbia PSQ33581 [Q] — 1976 — 30.00
☐ Columbia JS33581 — 197? — 12.00
— Second issue with new prefix; no bar code
☐ Columbia JS33581 — 1981 — 10.00
— Third edition; bar code added to back cover

Number	Title	Yr	NM
❑ Columbia HS43581		1981	40.00
—Half-speed mastered edition			
CHRISTINE			
❑ Columbia Masterworks OL5520 [M]		1960	75.00
❑ Columbia Masterworks OS2026 [S]		1960	150.00
CHRISTMAS FEVER			
❑ Lillenas L-9022		1981	12.00
CHRISTMAS…IN SPLENDOR AND MAJESTY			
❑ Light LS5833		1984	15.00
—Composed by Otis Skillings			
CINDY			
❑ ABC-Paramount ABC-OC-2 [M]		1964	30.00
❑ ABC-Paramount ABC-OCS-2 [S]		1964	50.00
CLARA (BEG, BORROW OR STEAL)			
❑ Commentary CYN-02 [M]		1960	120.00
CLOWNAROUND			
❑ RCA Victor LSP-4741		1972	300.00
CLUB 15			
❑ Decca DL5155 [10]		1949	75.00
THE COACH WITH THE SIX INSIDES			
❑ ESP-Disk' 1019 [M]		1967	30.00
COCO			
❑ Paramount PMS-1002		1969	30.00
COME CELEBRATE JESUS: A CHRISTMAS INVITATION			
❑ Word 7-01-896610-8		1985	15.00
—By Don Marsh and Claire Cloninger," the composers			
THE COMMITTEE			
❑ Reprise F-2023 [M]		1964	30.00
❑ Reprise FS-2023 [S]		1964	40.00
COMPANY			
❑ Columbia Masterworks SQ30993 [Q]		1971	40.00
—Quadraphonic version has substantially different mixes than the original stereo LP			
❑ Columbia Masterworks OS3550		1970	15.00
THE CRADLE WILL ROCK			
❑ MGM E-4289-2 [M]		1964	30.00
❑ MGM SE-4289-2 [S]		1964	30.00
—The above is by a revival cast			
THE CRITIC			
❑ Decca DL9154 [M]		1967	25.00
❑ Decca DL79154 [S]		1967	25.00
CRY FOR US ALL			
❑ Project 3 TS-1000SD		1970	40.00
DAMES AT SEA			
❑ Columbia Masterworks OS3550		1969	25.00
DAMN YANKEES			
❑ RCA Victor LOC-1021 [M]		1955	30.00
—Green cover			
❑ RCA Victor LOC-1021 [M]		195?	25.00
—Orange cover			
❑ RCA Victor LSO-1021(e) [R]		1965	18.00
—Black label, dog on top, "Stereo Electronically Reprocessed" at bottom			
❑ RCA Victor AYL1-3948		1980	10.00
—Best Buy Series" reissue			
THE DANCERS OF BALI			
❑ Columbia Masterworks ML4618 [M]		1952	40.00
DARLING OF THE DAY			
❑ RCA Victor LOC-1149 [M]		1968	40.00
❑ RCA Victor LSO-1149 [S]		1968	75.00
DEAR WORLD			
❑ Columbia Masterworks BOS3260		1969	25.00
DEATH OF A SALESMAN			
❑ Decca DX102 [M]		1951	40.00
—Two-record boxed set with contents of 9007 and 9008			
DEATH OF A SALESMAN (PART 1)			
❑ Decca DL9006 [M]		1951	30.00
—Black label, gold print			
DEATH OF A SALESMAN (PART 2)			
❑ Decca DL9007 [M]		1951	30.00
—Black label, gold print			
DESTRY RIDES AGAIN			
❑ Decca DL9075 [M]		1959	30.00
❑ Decca DL79075 [S]		1959	40.00
DOCTOR SELAVY'S MAGIC THEATRE			
❑ United Artists UA-LA196-G		1974	30.00
DO I HEAR A WALTZ?			
❑ Columbia Masterworks KOL6370 [M]		1965	18.00
❑ Columbia Masterworks KOS2770 [S]		1965	25.00
DONNYBROOK!			
❑ Kapp KDL-8500 [M]		1961	25.00
❑ Kapp KD-8500-S [S]		1961	30.00
DO RE MI			
❑ RCA Victor LOCD-2002 [M]		1961	30.00
—In black box with orange sleeve			

Number	Title	Yr	NM
❑ RCA Victor LSOD-2002 [S]		1961	40.00
—In black box with orange sleeve			
❑ RCA Victor LOC-1105 [M]		1965	18.00
—Reissue of 2002 with standard red cover			
❑ RCA Victor LSO-1105 [S]		1965	25.00
—Reissue of 2002 with standard red cover			
DRESSED TO THE NINES			
❑ MGM E-3914 [M]		1960	30.00
❑ MGM SE-3914 [S]		1960	40.00
THE EARL OF RUSTON			
❑ Capitol ST-465		1971	40.00
ERNEST IN LOVE			
❑ Columbia Masterworks OL5530 [M]		1960	75.00
❑ Columbia Masterworks OS2027 [S]		1960	150.00
AN EVENING WITH RICHARD NIXON			
❑ Ode SP-77015		1972	30.00
EVERLASTING LIGHT: A CHRISTMAS CAROL FOR A DARK WORLD			
❑ Word 7-01-900810-0		1986	15.00
—By Claire Cloninger and Mark Hayes," the composers			
EVITA			
❑ MCA 2-11003		1976	25.00
—London cast; white cover; with booklet			
❑ MCA 2-11007		1979	18.00
—New York cast; mostly black cover; with booklet			
FADE OUT-FADE IN			
❑ ABC-Paramount ABC-OC-3 [M]		1964	30.00
❑ ABC-Paramount ABCS-OC-3 [S]		1964	30.00
A FAMILY AFFAIR			
❑ United Artists UAL-4099 [M]		1962	30.00
❑ United Artists UAS-5099 [S]		1962	50.00
FANNY			
❑ RCA Victor LOC-1015 [M]		1954	30.00
—"Long Play" on label			
❑ RCA Victor LOC-1015 [M]		196?	18.00
—"Mono" on label			
❑ RCA Victor LSO-1015(e) [R]		196?	15.00
—Stereo Electronically Reprocessed" on label			
THE FANTASTICKS			
❑ MGM E-3872 [M]		1963	25.00
—Original non-gatefold cover			
❑ MGM SE-3872 [S]		1963	30.00
—Original non-gatefold cover			
❑ MGM E-3872 [M]		196?	12.00
—White gatefold cover			
❑ MGM SE-3872 [S]		196?	15.00
—White gatefold cover			
❑ MGM SE-3872 [S]		196?	12.00
—Black gatefold cover			
FIDDLER ON THE ROOF			
❑ RCA Victor LOC-1093 [M]		1964	18.00
❑ RCA Victor LSO-1093 [S]		1964	25.00
—Black label, dog on top			
FINIAN'S RAINBOW			
❑ Columbia Masterworks ML4062 [M]		1948	30.00
—Original cover with no photo; green label			
❑ Columbia Masterworks OL4062 [M]		196?	15.00
—Reissue cover, either pink or green; gray label			
❑ Columbia Masterworks OS2080 [R]		1963	15.00
❑ RCA Victor LOC-1057 [M]		1960	15.00
—Revival cast; "pot of gold" cover			
❑ RCA Victor LOC-1057 [M]		1960	12.00
—Revival cast; cover shows co-stars hiding in the trees			
❑ RCA Victor LSO-1057 [S]		1960	18.00
—Revival cast; "pot of gold" cover			
❑ RCA Victor LSO-1057 [S]		1960	15.00
—Revival cast; cover shows co-stars hiding in the trees			
FIORELLO!			
❑ Capitol WAO1321 [M]		1959	25.00
❑ Capitol SWAO1321 [S]		1959	30.00
FIRST IMPRESSIONS			
❑ Columbia Masterworks OL5400 [M]		1959	30.00
❑ Columbia Masterworks OS2014 [S]		1959	75.00
FLAHOOLEY			
❑ Capitol S284 [M]		1951	175.00
❑ Capitol T-11649 [M]		1977	18.00
FLORA, THE RED MENACE			
❑ RCA Victor LOC-1111 [M]		1965	30.00
❑ RCA Victor LSO-1111 [S]		1965	30.00
FLOWER DRUM SONG			
❑ Columbia Masterworks OL5350 [M]		1958	25.00
—Gray and black label with six "eye" logos			
❑ Columbia Masterworks OS2009 [S]		1958	30.00
—Gray and black label with six "eye" logos			
FLY BLACKBIRD			
❑ Mercury OCM-2206 [M]		1962	30.00
❑ Mercury OCS-6206 [S]		1962	75.00
FUNNY GIRL			
❑ Capitol VAS2059 [M]		1964	18.00

Number	Title	Yr	NM
❑ Capitol SVAS2059 [S]		1964	25.00
—Both Barbra Streisand and Sydney Chaplin are pictured on the back cover			
❑ Capitol STAO2059 [S]		196?	15.00
—Only Barbra Streisand is pictured on the back cover			
A FUNNY THING HAPPENED ON THE WAY TO THE FORUM			
❑ Capitol WAO1717 [M]		1962	18.00
—Gatefold cover			
❑ Capitol SWAO1717 [S]		1962	25.00
—Gatefold cover			
THE GAY LIFE			
❑ Capitol WAO1560 [M]		1961	30.00
❑ Capitol SWAO1560 [S]		1961	50.00
GENTLEMEN PREFER BLONDES			
❑ Columbia Masterworks ML4290 [M]		1949	30.00
—Original with green label			
❑ Columbia Masterworks OL4290 [M]		196?	18.00
—Reissue with new prefix and various gray labels			
❑ Columbia Masterworks OS2310 [R]		1963	12.00
—Gray label			
❑ Columbia Masterworks S32610 [R]		1973	10.00
GEORGE M!			
❑ Columbia Masterworks KOL6800 [M]		1968	30.00
❑ Columbia Masterworks KOS3200 [S]		1968	25.00
THE GIRL IN PINK TIGHTS			
❑ Columbia Masterworks ML4890 [M]		1954	75.00
THE GIRL WHO CAME TO SUPPER			
❑ Columbia Masterworks KOL6020 [M]		1963	30.00
❑ Columbia Masterworks KOS2420 [S]		1963	30.00
GIVE 'EM HELL, HARRY!			
❑ United Artists UA-LA540-H2		1975	25.00
THE GLORY OF CHRISTMAS			
❑ Light LS-5775		1980	15.00
—A Cantata byt Jimmy & Carol Owens"; narrated by Efrem Zimbalist, Jr.			
THE GOLDEN APPLE			
❑ RCA Victor LOC-1014 [M]		1954	150.00
GOLDEN BOY			
❑ Capitol VAS2124 [M]		1964	30.00
❑ Capitol SVAS2124 [S]		1964	30.00
GOLDILOCKS			
❑ Columbia Masterworks OL5340 [M]		1958	30.00
❑ Columbia Masterworks OS2007 [S]		1958	75.00
GOODTIME CHARLEY			
❑ RCA Victor ARL1-1011		1975	30.00
GREASE			
❑ MGM 1SE-34		1972	15.00
THE GREAT WALTZ			
❑ Capitol VAS2426 [M]		1965	25.00
❑ Capitol SVAS2426 [S]		1965	30.00
GREENWICH VILLAGE U.S.A.			
❑ 20th Fox TCF-105-2 [M]		1960	75.00
—With complete show			
❑ 20th Fox TCF-105-2S [S]		1960	150.00
—With complete show			
❑ 20th Fox FOX-4005 [M]		1960	40.00
—With excerpts from the show			
❑ 20th Fox SFX-4005 [S]		1960	50.00
—With excerpts from the show			
GREENWILLOW			
❑ RCA Victor LOC-2001 [M]		1960	25.00
❑ RCA Victor LSO-2001 [S]		1960	50.00
GUYS AND DOLLS			
❑ Decca DL8036 [M]		1950	30.00
❑ Decca DL9023 [M]		1955	25.00
—Reissue of 8036			
❑ Decca DL79023 [R]		196?	15.00
❑ MCA 2034		1973	12.00
—Reissue of 79023			
❑ MCA 37094		198?	10.00
—Reissue of 2034			
❑ MCA 1628		198?	10.00
—Reissue of 37094			
GYPSY			
❑ Columbia Masterworks OL5420 [M]		1959	25.00
—Original covers are white with drawings			
❑ Columbia Masterworks OS2017 [S]		1959	30.00
—Original covers are white with drawings			
❑ Columbia Masterworks OL5420 [M]		1962	15.00
—Reissue covers are brown with show photos			
❑ Columbia Masterworks OS2017 [S]		1962	18.00
—Reissue covers are brown with show photos			
HAIR			
❑ Atco SD7002		1969	30.00
—Original London cast			
❑ Philips PHS600329		1969	30.00
—Original French cast			
❑ RCA Victor LOC-1143 [M]		1967	30.00

Number	Title	Yr	NM
—Off-Broadway cast			
❑ RCA Victor LSO-1143 [S]		1967	15.00
—Off-Broadway cast; black label, dog at top, "Stereo" at bottom			
❑ RCA Victor LOC-1150 [M]		1968	30.00
—Broadway cast			
❑ RCA Victor LSO-1150 [S]		1968	25.00
—Broadway cast; black label, dog on top, "Stereo" at bottom			
❑ RCA Victor LSO-1150 [S]		1968	12.00
—Broadway cast; orange label			
❑ RCA Victor ANL1-0986		1974	12.00
—Off-Broadway cast; reissue with new number			
❑ RCA Victor ABD1-0245 [Q]		1973	30.00
—Broadway cast; quadraphonic remix			

HALF A SIXPENCE
| ❑ RCA Victor LOC-1110 [M] | | 1965 | 25.00 |
| ❑ RCA Victor LSO-1110 [S] | | 1965 | 30.00 |

HALF PAST WEDNESDAY
| ❑ Columbia CL1917 [M] | | 1962 | 30.00 |
| ❑ Columbia CS8717 [S] | | 1962 | 40.00 |

HAMLET
❑ Columbia Masterworks DOL302 [M]		1964	30.00
—Boxed set with entire play (Broadway revival)			
❑ Columbia Masterworks DOS702 [M]		1964	30.00
—Boxed set with entire play (Broadway revival)			
❑ Columbia Masterworks OL6220 [M]		1964	18.00
—Highlights from the box set			
❑ Columbia Masterworks OS2620 [S]		1964	18.00
—Highlights from the box set			

THE HAPPIEST GIRL IN THE WORLD
❑ Columbia Masterworks KOL5650 [M]		1961	40.00
—Original covers are yellow			
❑ Columbia Masterworks KOL5650 [M]		1961	30.00
— Second covers are white			
❑ Columbia Masterworks KOS2050 [S]		1961	75.00
—Original covers are yellow			
❑ Columbia Masterworks KOS2050 [S]		1961	40.00
— Second covers are white			

HAPPY HUNTING
| ❑ RCA Victor LOC-1026 [M] | | 1956 | 40.00 |

HEAR! HEAR!
| ❑ Decca DL9031 [M] | | 1955 | 50.00 |

HELLO, DOLLY!
❑ RCA Victor LOCD-1087 [M]		1964	30.00
—Original cover is black and white on back and spotlights "Come and Be My Butterfly"; this song was deleted from the show, so the cover was changed			
❑ RCA Victor LOCD-1087 [M]		1964	18.00
—New back cover is in color and has a photo of Carol Channing; "RE" is on cover			
❑ RCA Victor LSOD-1087 [S]		1964	30.00
—Original cover is black and white on back and spotlights "Come and Be My Butterfly"; this song was deleted from the show, so the cover was changed			
❑ RCA Victor LSOD-1087 [S]		1964	25.00
—New back cover is in color and has a photo of Carol Channing; "RE" is on cover; black label, dog on top			
❑ RCA Victor LSOD-1087 [S]		1969	12.00
— Orange or tan label			

HENRY, SWEET HENRY
| ❑ ABC ABC-OC-4 [M] | | 1967 | 30.00 |
| ❑ ABC ABCS-OC-4 [S] | | 1967 | 50.00 |

HERE'S LOVE
| ❑ Columbia Masterworks KOL6000 [M] | | 1963 | 30.00 |
| ❑ Columbia Masterworks KOS2400 [S] | | 1963 | 40.00 |

HIGH BUTTON SHOES
❑ RCA Camden CAL-457 [M]		1958	30.00
❑ RCA Victor LOC-1107 [M]		1964	40.00
❑ RCA Victor LSO-1107 [R]		1964	30.00

HIGH SPIRITS
| ❑ ABC-Paramount ABC-OC-1 [M] | | 1964 | 30.00 |
| ❑ ABC-Paramount ABCS-OC-1 [S] | | 1964 | 30.00 |

HOUSE OF FLOWERS
❑ Columbia Masterworks ML4969 [M]		1954	40.00
—Blue label original			
❑ United Artists UAS-5180		1968	40.00
—Revival cast			

HOW NOW, DOW JONES
| ❑ RCA Victor LOC-1142 [M] | | 1967 | 30.00 |
| ❑ RCA Victor LSO-1142 [S] | | 1967 | 30.00 |

HOW TO SUCCEED IN BUSINESS WITHOUT REALLY TRYING
❑ RCA Victor LOC-1066 [M]		1961	25.00
❑ RCA Victor LSO-1066 [S]		1961	30.00
—Black label, dog on top			
❑ RCA Victor LSO-1066 [S]		1969	12.00
— Orange or tan label			

HUGHIE
| ❑ Columbia Masterworks OL6260 [M] | | 1965 | 30.00 |
| ❑ Columbia Masterworks OS2760 [S] | | 1965 | 30.00 |

I CAN GET IT FOR YOU WHOLESALE
| ❑ Columbia Masterworks KOL5780 [M] | | 1962 | 30.00 |
| ❑ Columbia Masterworks KOS2180 [S] | | 1962 | 30.00 |

ICE FOLLIES
| ❑ Dot DLP-3757 [M] | | 1967 | 30.00 |
| ❑ Dot DLP-25757 [S] | | 1967 | 30.00 |

I DO! I DO!
❑ RCA Victor LOC-1128 [M]		1966	18.00
❑ RCA Victor LSO-1128 [S]		1966	25.00
—Black label, dog on top			

I HAD A BALL
❑ Mercury OCM-2210 [M]		1964	25.00
❑ Mercury OCS-6210 [S]		1964	30.00
❑ Mercury OCM-2210 [M]		1964	40.00
—Promo-only two-record set with bonus interview record MGD-2-24			

ILLYA DARLING
| ❑ United Artists UAL-8901 [M] | | 1967 | 25.00 |
| ❑ United Artists UAS-9901 [S] | | 1967 | 25.00 |

I LOVE MY WIFE
| ❑ Atlantic SD19107 | | 1977 | 12.00 |

INTO THE WOODS
| ❑ RCA 6796-1-RC | | 1988 | 25.00 |

IRMA LA DOUCE
| ❑ Columbia Masterworks OL5560 [M] | | 1960 | 25.00 |
| ❑ Columbia Masterworks OS2029 [S] | | 1960 | 30.00 |

JACQUES BREL IS ALIVE AND WELL AND LIVING IN PARIS
| ❑ Columbia Masterworks D2S779 | | 1968 | 25.00 |
| *—Box set; gray "360 Sound" labels* | | | |

J.B.
| ❑ RCA Victor LD-6075 [M] | | 1959 | 75.00 |
| ❑ RCA Victor LDS-6075 [S] | | 1959 | 80.00 |

JENNIE
| ❑ RCA Victor LOC-1083 [M] | | 1963 | 30.00 |
| ❑ RCA Victor LSO-1083 [S] | | 1963 | 50.00 |

JESUS CHRIST SUPERSTAR
❑ Decca DL71503		1971	25.00
—From the Broadway production; also see listings for this title in the VARIOUS ARTISTS COLLECTIONS sections.			
❑ MCA 5000		1973	15.00
—From the Broadway production; reissue			

JOSEPH AND THE AMAZING TECHNICOLOR DREAMCOAT
❑ Scepter SPS-588X		1968	25.00
—With gatefold cover and libretto			
❑ Scepter SMAS-93738		197?	30.00
—Capitol Record Club edition			

JOY
| ❑ RCA Victor LSO-1166 | | 1970 | 25.00 |

JUNO
| ❑ Columbia Masterworks OL5380 [M] | | 1959 | 40.00 |
| ❑ Columbia Masterworks OS2013 [S] | | 1959 | 80.00 |

KEAN
| ❑ Columbia Masterworks KOL5720 [M] | | 1961 | 30.00 |
| ❑ Columbia Masterworks KSO2120 [S] | | 1961 | 40.00 |

THE KING AND I
❑ Decca DL9008 [M]		1951	30.00
—Black label, gold print			
❑ Decca DL9008 [M]		195?	40.00
—Drawing of Gertrude Lawrence and Yul Brynner on cover, with title on three lines			
❑ Decca DL9008 [M]		195?	15.00
—Drawing of Gertrude Lawrence and Yul Brynner on cover, with title on two lines			
❑ Decca DL79008 [R]		196?	12.00

KWAMINA
| ❑ Capitol W1645 [M] | | 1962 | 30.00 |
| ❑ Capitol SW1645 [S] | | 1962 | 50.00 |

THE LADY'S NOT FOR BURNING
| ❑ Decca DL9508/9 [M] | | 1951 | 50.00 |
| *—Oversize box set* | | | |

LAGINAPPE '59 PRESENTS BE MY GUEST
| ❑ (no label) XCTV-10303 [M] | | 1959 | 300.00 |
| *— Custom pressing for New Trier High School, Illinois. Collectible because the future Ann-Margret sings one track on the LP!* | | | |

LEGS DIAMOND
| ❑ RCA 7983-1-RC | | 1989 | 30.00 |

LES MISERABLES
❑ Geffen GHS24151		1987	18.00
— Original Broadway cast recording			
❑ Relativity 88561-8140-1		1985	25.00
— Original London cast recording			

LET IT RIDE
| ❑ RCA Victor LOC-1064 [M] | | 1961 | 25.00 |
| ❑ RCA Victor LSO-1064 [S] | | 1961 | 40.00 |

LI'L ABNER
| ❑ Columbia Masterworks OL5150 [M] | | 1956 | 30.00 |

LITTLE ME
| ❑ RCA Victor LOC-1078 [M] | | 1962 | 25.00 |
| ❑ RCA Victor LSO-1078 [S] | | 1962 | 30.00 |

LITTLE SHOP OF HORRORS
| ❑ Geffen GHSP-2020 | | 1982 | 30.00 |

LOOK MA, I'M DANCIN'!
| ❑ Decca DL5231 [M] | | 1950 | 150.00 |

LORELEI
❑ MGM M3G-55		1974	30.00
— Second version, recorded with Broadway cast			
❑ Verve MV-5097-OC		1974	30.00
— First version, recorded before the show hit Broadway			

LOST IN THE STARS
❑ Decca DL8028 [M]		1949	50.00
❑ Decca DL9120 [M]		1965	18.00
—Reissue of 8028			

THE MAD SHOW
| ❑ Columbia Masterworks OL6530 [M] | | 1965 | 50.00 |
| ❑ Columbia Masterworks OS2930 [S] | | 1965 | 150.00 |

MAGGIE FLYNN
| ❑ RCA Victor LSOD-2009 | | 1968 | 30.00 |
| ❑ RCA Victor LSOD-2009 | | 1968 | 25.00 |

THE MAGIC SHOW
| ❑ Bell 9003 | | 1974 | 25.00 |

MAKE A WISH
| ❑ RCA Victor LOC-1002 [M] | | 1951 | 175.00 |

MAME
❑ Columbia Masterworks KOS3000 [S]		1966	25.00
— Gray label with "360 Sound Stereo			
❑ Columbia Masterworks KOL6600 [M]		1966	18.00
❑ Columbia Masterworks KOS3000 [S]		1970	15.00
— Olive label with orange "Columbia" around outside			

MAN OF LA MANCHA
| ❑ Kapp KRL-4505 [M] | | 1965 | 18.00 |
| ❑ Kapp KRS-4505 [S] | | 1965 | 25.00 |

MARK TWAIN TONIGHT!
| ❑ Columbia Masterworks OL5440 [M] | | 1959 | 15.00 |
| ❑ Columbia Masterworks OS2019 [S] | | 1959 | 18.00 |

ME AND JULIET
| ❑ RCA Victor LOC-1012 [M] | | 1953 | 80.00 |

MEDEA
| ❑ Decca DLP9000 [M] | | 1949 | 30.00 |

MEGILLA OF ITZIG MANGER
| ❑ Columbia Masterworks OS3270 | | 1968 | 40.00 |

MERRILY WE ROLL ALONG
| ❑ RCA Victor CBL1-4197 | | 1981 | 30.00 |

THE MERRY WIDOW
| ❑ RCA Victor LOC-1094 [M] | | 1964 | 25.00 |
| ❑ RCA Victor LSO-1094 [S] | | 1964 | 30.00 |

MESSIAH, BRIGHT MORNING STAR
| ❑ Light LS5811 | | 1982 | 15.00 |
| *— Composers: Reba Rambo & Dony McGuire* | | | |

MEXICAN HAYRIDE
| ❑ Decca DL5232 [10] | | 1950 | 120.00 |

MILK AND HONEY
❑ RCA Victor LOC-1065 [M]		1961	30.00
— With only credits (no picture) on front cover			
❑ RCA Victor LOC-1065 [M]		1961	25.00
— With picture of Tommy Rall and two dancers on front cover			
❑ RCA Victor LSO-1065 [S]		1961	30.00
— With only credits (no picture) on front cover			
❑ RCA Victor LSO-1065 [S]		1961	30.00
— With picture of Tommy Rall and two dancers on front cover			

MISS LIBERTY
| ❑ Columbia Masterworks ML4220 [M] | | 1949 | 30.00 |
| *—Originals have green labels* | | | |

MISS SAIGON
| ❑ Geffen GHS24271 | | 1990 | 25.00 |

THE MOST HAPPY FELLA
❑ Columbia Masterworks OL5118 [M]		1956	30.00
— Gray and black label with six "eye" logos			
❑ Columbia Masterworks OS2330 [R]		196?	18.00
❑ Columbia Masterworks O3L240 [M]		1956	50.00
— Box set with entire show			

MR. PRESIDENT
❑ Columbia Masterworks KOL5870 [M]		1962	25.00
— Gatefold with shiny silver cover			
❑ Columbia Masterworks KOS2270 [S]		1962	30.00
— Gatefold with shiny silver cover			

MRS. PATTERSON
| ❑ RCA Victor LOC-1017 [M] | | 1954 | 175.00 |

MR. WONDERFUL
| ❑ Decca DL9032 [M] | | 1956 | 50.00 |

Number / Title	Yr	NM
THE MUSIC MAN		
Capitol WAO990 [M]	1957	25.00
—Gatefold cover, white with credits and drawing on front; gray label		
Capitol SWAO990 [S]	1957	30.00
—Gatefold cover, white with credits and drawing on front; gray label		
Capitol W990 [M]	196?	15.00
—Regular cover with photo of Robert Preston as Harold Hill		
Capitol SW990 [S]	196?	18.00
—Regular cover with photo of Robert Preston as Harold Hill		
MY FAIR LADY		
Columbia Masterworks OL5090 [M]	1956	30.00
—Gray and black label with six "eye" logos		
Columbia Masterworks OS2015 [S]	1959	25.00
—Gray and black label with six "eye" logos; original London cast		
Columbia Masterworks OL5090 [M]	1963	18.00
—Gray label with "Guaranteed High Fidelity" at bottom		
Columbia Masterworks OL5090 [M]	1956	12.00
—Gray label, "Mono" at bottom		
Columbia Masterworks OS2015 [S]	1959	15.00
—Gray label, "Stereo" at bottom; original London cast		
Columbia Masterworks PS2015 [S]	198?	10.00
—Budget-line reissue with new prefix		
Columbia Masterworks PS34197	1976	12.00
—Revival cast		
MY PEOPLE		
Contact C-1 [M]	1966	50.00
Contact CS-1 [S]	1966	75.00
THE NERVOUS SET		
Columbia Masterworks OL5430 [M]	1959	30.00
Columbia Masterworks OS2018 [S]	1959	75.00
NEW FACES OF 1952		
RCA Victor LOC-1008 [M]	1952	30.00
NEW FACES OF 1956		
RCA Victor LOC-1025 [M]	1956	50.00
NEW FACES OF 1968		
Warner Bros. BS2551	1968	30.00
THE NEW GIRL IN TOWN		
RCA Victor LOC-1027 [M]	1957	25.00
RCA Victor LSO-1027 [S]	1958	50.00
RCA Victor LOC-1106 [M]	1965	25.00
RCA Victor LSC-1106 [S]	1965	30.00
THE NINA, THE PINTA AND THE SANTA MARIA		
Dot DLP-9009 [M]	1960	40.00
Dot DLP-29009 [S]	1960	50.00
NO STRINGS		
Capitol O1695 [M]	1962	25.00
Capitol SO1695 [S]	1962	40.00
OF THEE I SING		
Capitol S350 [M]	1952	175.00
OH, KAY!		
20th Fox FOX-4003 [M]	1960	30.00
20th Fox SFX-4003 [S]	1960	50.00
OKLAHOMA!		
Decca DLP8000 [M]	1949	30.00
—Black label, gold print; the first 12-inch LP on Decca		
Decca DL9017 [M]	1955	25.00
—Reissue of 8000		
Decca DL9017 [M]	196?	25.00
—Reissue with new cover art		
Decca DL79017 [R]	196?	18.00
Decca DL79017 [R]	1968	25.00
—Special 25th Anniversary edition; cover has yellow drawing, inner sleeve has liner notes		
MCA 2030	1973	10.00
—Reissue of 79017; black label with rainbow		
MCA 37096	198?	10.00
—Reissue of 2030		
OLIVER!		
RCA Victor LOCD-2004 [M]	1962	18.00
RCA Victor LSOD-2004 [S]	1962	25.00
ON A CLEAR DAY YOU CAN SEE FOREVER		
RCA Victor LOCD-2006 [M]	1965	25.00
RCA Victor LSOD-2006 [S]	1965	30.00
ONCE UPON A MATTRESS		
Kapp KDL-7004 [M]	1959	30.00
Kapp KDL-7004-S [S]	1959	30.00
110 IN THE SHADE		
RCA Victor LOC-1085 [M]	1963	30.00
RCA Victor LSO-1085 [S]	1963	40.00
ONE TOUCH OF VENUS		
Decca DL9122 [M]	1965	30.00
Decca DL79122 [R]	1965	30.00
ON YOUR TOES		
Decca DL9015 [M]	1954	85.00
OVER HERE!		
Columbia Masterworks KS32961	1974	25.00
Columbia Masterworks SQ32961 [Q]	1974	40.00

Number / Title	Yr	NM
PAINT YOUR WAGON		
RCA Victor LOC-1006 [M]	1951	30.00
—Green label		
RCA Victor LOC-1006 [M]	1955	25.00
—Black label, dog on top, "Long Play" at bottom		
RCA Victor LOC-1006 [M]	1965	18.00
—Black label, dog on top, "Mono" at bottom		
RCA Victor LSO-1006 [R]	1965	15.00
—Black label, dog on top		
RCA Victor LSO-1006 [R]	1969	12.00
—Orange or tan label		
PARADE		
Kapp KDL-7005 [M]	1960	250.00
Kapp KDS-7005 [S]	1960	300.00
PARIS '90		
Columbia Masterworks ML4619 [M]	1952	175.00
PEACE		
Metromedia MP-33001	1969	30.00
PETER PAN		
RCA Victor LOC-1019 [M]	1954	40.00
RCA Victor LSO-1019 [R]	196?	15.00
RCA Victor AYL1-3762 [R]	1980	10.00
THE PHANTOM OF THE OPERA		
Polydor 831273-1	1987	25.00
—With libretto		
Polydor 831563-1	1987	12.00
—One-record "highlights" release		
PIPE DREAM		
RCA Victor LOC-1023 [M]	1955	80.00
—With "Special Advance Edition" sticker on cover		
RCA Victor LOC-1023 [M]	1955	50.00
—Without "Special Advance Edition" sticker on cover		
PLAIN AND FANCY		
Capitol S603 [M]	1955	30.00
—Red label		
PLAYGIRLS		
Warner Bros. W1530 [M]	1964	30.00
Warner Bros. WS1530 [S]	1964	30.00
PORGY AND BESS		
Decca DL7006 [10]	1950	30.00
—Reissue of material first released on 78s		
Decca DL8042 [M]	1950	30.00
Decca DL9024 [M]	1955	30.00
—Reissue of 8042; drawing of Catfish Row on cover		
Decca DL9024 [M]	196?	18.00
—Photo of cast members on cover		
Decca DL79024 [R]	196?	12.00
—Photo of cast members on cover		
MCA 2035 [R]	1973	10.00
—Reissue of 79024; black label with rainbow		
MCA 1631 [R]	198?	10.00
—Reissue of 2035		
THE PREMISE		
Vanguard VRS-9092 [M]	1960	50.00
PUMP BOYS AND DINETTES		
CBS FM37790	1982	18.00
PURLIE		
Ampex A-40101	1970	30.00
RASHOMON		
Carlton LPX-5000 [M]	1959	30.00
Carlton STLPX-5000 [S]	1959	30.00
—Not actually the original cast recording, but the play's incidental music		
REDHEAD		
RCA Victor LOC-1048 [M]	1959	25.00
RCA Victor LSO-1048 [S]	1959	50.00
—Without "Essie's Vision"		
RCA Victor LOC-1104 [M]	1959	18.00
—Reissue of 1048		
RCA Victor LSO-1104 [S]	1965	30.00
—Reissue adds "Essie's Vision" to stereo version		
THE RIVER WIND		
London AM-48001 [M]	1962	40.00
London AMS-78001 [S]	1962	100.00
THE ROAR OF THE GREASEPAINT -- THE SMELL OF THE CROWD		
RCA Victor LOC-1109 [M]	1965	18.00
RCA Victor LSO-1109 [S]	1965	25.00
THE ROTHSCHILDS		
Columbia Masterworks S30337	1970	30.00
SAIL AWAY		
Capitol WAO1643 [M]	1961	25.00
Capitol SWAO1643 [S]	1961	30.00
SARATOGA		
RCA Victor LOC-1051 [M]	1959	30.00
RCA Victor LSO-1051 [S]	1959	50.00
SAY, DARLING		
RCA Victor LOC-1045 [M]	1958	40.00
RCA Victor LSO-1045 [S]	1958	75.00

Number / Title	Yr	NM
SELMA		
Cotillion SD 2-110	1976	25.00
SEVENTEEN		
RCA Victor LOC-1003 [M]	1951	175.00
1776		
Columbia Masterworks BOS3310	1969	30.00
—The first edition has Howard DaSilva shown as Ben Franklin in credits and synopsis, though he does not appear on the LP		
Columbia Masterworks BOS3310	1969	15.00
—Revised (correct) edition has Rex Everhart shown as Ben Franklin in credits and synopsis		
SEVENTH HEAVEN		
Decca DL9001 [M]	1955	175.00
70 GIRLS, 70		
Columbia Masterworks S30589	1971	50.00
SHE LOVES ME		
MGM E4118OC-2 [M]	1963	40.00
MGM SE4118OC-2 [S]	1963	50.00
SHOW BIZ (FROM VAUDE TO VIDEO)		
RCA Victor LOC-1011 [M]	1954	40.00
SHOW BOAT		
Columbia Masterworks ML4058 [M]	1948	30.00
—From the 1946 revival; paper envelope jacket with its opening on top		
Columbia Masterworks OL4058 [M]	195?	25.00
—From the 1946 revival; reissue of ML 4058		
SHOW GIRL		
Roulette R-80001 [M]	1961	25.00
Roulette SR-80001 [S]	1961	30.00
SIDE BY SIDE BY SONDHEIM		
RCA Victor CBL2-1851	1976	25.00
SILK STOCKINGS		
RCA Victor LOC-1016 [M]	1955	40.00
RCA Victor LOC-1102 [M]	1965	25.00
—Reissue; regular cover		
RCA Victor LSO-1102 [S]	1965	25.00
SIMPLY HEAVENLY		
Columbia Masterworks OL5240 [M]	1957	30.00
SING OUT, SWEET LAND!		
Decca DL8023 [M]	1950	50.00
Decca DL4304 [M]	1963	25.00
Decca DL74304 [R]	1963	25.00
SKYSCRAPER		
Capitol VAS2422 [M]	1965	25.00
Capitol SVAS2422 [S]	1965	30.00
SNOW WHITE AND THE SEVEN DWARFS		
Buena Vista STER-5009	1979	30.00
SONDHEIM: A MUSICAL TRIBUTE		
Warner Bros. 2WS2705	1973	25.00
SONG OF NORWAY		
Columbia CL1328 [M]	1959	25.00
—1958 revival cast		
Columbia CS8135 [S]	1959	50.00
—1958 revival cast		
Decca DL8002 [M]	1949	30.00
Decca DL9019 [M]	1955	25.00
Decca DL79019 [R]	196?	15.00
MCA 2032 [R]	1973	12.00
—Reissue of 79019; black label with rainbow		
THE SOUND OF MUSIC		
Capitol DT91034 [R]	1966	15.00
—Original London cast; Capitol Record Club exclusive		
Columbia Masterworks KOL5450 [M]	1959	25.00
—Gray and black label with six "eye" logos		
Columbia Masterworks KOS2020 [S]	1959	30.00
—Gray and black label with six "eye" logos		
Columbia Masterworks KOL5450 [M]	1963	15.00
—Gray label with "Guaranteed High Fidelity" or "360 Sound Mono" on label		
Columbia Masterworks KOS2020 [S]	1959	15.00
—Gray label with "360 Sound Stereo" at bottom		
Columbia Masterworks S32601 [S]	1973	12.00
—Reissue of 2020		
SOUTH PACIFIC		
Columbia Masterworks ML4180 [M]	1949	30.00
—Green or blue label; large anchor on front cover		
Columbia Masterworks OL4180 [M]	195?	18.00
—Gray and black label with six "eye" logos; large anchor on front cover		
Columbia Masterworks OL4180 [M]	195?	15.00
—Gray and black label with six "eye" logos; glossy gatefold cover with Ezio Pinza and Mary Martin pictured		
Columbia Masterworks OL4180 [M]	1963	12.00
—Gray label with "Guaranteed High Fidelity" or "360 Sound Mono		
Columbia Masterworks OS2040 [R]	196?	12.00
—Gray label with "360 Sound Stereo		
Columbia Masterworks S32604 [R]	1973	10.00
—Reissue of 2040		

Number	Title	Yr	NM
SOUTH PACIFIC, HITS FROM			
❏ Columbia Masterworks A-1723 [PS]		195?	15.00
SOUTH PACIFIC, HITS FROM, VOL. 1 (HALL OF FAME SERIES)			
❏ Columbia B-2579 [PS]		195?	12.00
ST. LOUIS WOMAN			
❏ Capitol L355 [10]		1952	100.00
STOP THE WORLD-I WANT TO GET OFF			
❏ London AM58001 [M]		1962	18.00
❏ London AMS88001 [S]		1962	25.00
STREET SCENE			
❏ Columbia Masterworks ML4139 [M]		1949	30.00
—Paper envelope jacket with its opening on top			
THE SUBJECT WAS ROSES			
❏ Columbia Masterworks DOL308 [M]		1964	25.00
❏ Columbia Masterworks DOS708 [S]		1964	30.00
SUBWAYS ARE FOR SLEEPING			
❏ Columbia Masterworks KOL5730 [M]		1962	30.00
❏ Columbia Masterworks KOS2130 [S]		1962	40.00
THE SURVIVAL OF ST. JOAN			
❏ Paramount PAS-9000		1971	30.00
SWEENEY TODD-THE DEMON BARBER OF FLEET STREET			
❏ RCA Victor CBL2-3379		1979	25.00
SWEET CHARITY			
❏ Columbia Masterworks KOL6500 [M]		1966	18.00
❏ Columbia Masterworks KOS2900 [S]		1966	25.00
TAKE ME ALONG			
❏ RCA Victor LOC-1050 [M]		1959	18.00
❏ RCA Victor LSO-1050 [S]		1959	25.00
—Black label			
TAMALPAIS EXCHANGE			
❏ Atlantic SD8263		1970	30.00
TAROT			
❏ United Artists UAS-5563		1970	25.00
TENDERLOIN			
❏ Capitol WAO1492 [M]		1960	30.00
—With program			
❏ Capitol SWAO1492 [S]		1960	40.00
—With program			
TEVYA AND HIS DAUGHTERS			
❏ Columbia Masterworks OL5225 [M]		1957	30.00
TEXAS, LI'L DARLIN'			
❏ Decca DL5188 [10]		1950	100.00
THIS IS THE ARMY			
❏ Decca DL5108 [10]		1950	150.00
THIS WAS BURLESQUE			
❏ Roulette R-25185 [M]		1962	30.00
❏ Roulette SR-25186 [S]		1962	30.00
THE THREEPENNY OPERA			
❏ Columbia Masterworks PS34326		1976	25.00
—Another revival cast			
❏ MGM E-3121 [M]		1954	30.00
—Revival cast; yellow label			
❏ MGM E-3121 [M]		1959	18.00
—Revival cast; black label			
❏ MGM SE-3121 [R]		196?	15.00
—Revival cast; rechanneled stereo			
❏ Polydor 820260-1		198?	10.00
—Revival cast; reissue			
THREE TO MAKE MUSIC			
❏ RCA Victor LPM-2012 [M]		1958	30.00
❏ RCA Victor LSP-2012 [S]		1958	30.00
THREE WISHES FOR JAMIE			
❏ Capitol S317 [M]		1952	120.00
TIME CHANGES			
❏ ABC ABCS-681		1969	30.00
A TIME FOR SINGING			
❏ Warner Bros. W1639 [M]		1966	40.00
❏ Warner Bros. WS1639 [S]		1966	75.00
A TIME REMEMBERED			
❏ Mercury MG-20380 [M]		1957	30.00
❏ Mercury SR-60023 [S]		1957	40.00
—Music from the dramatic play			
TO BROADWAY WITH LOVE			
❏ Columbia Masterworks OL6030 [M]		1964	30.00
❏ Columbia Masterworks OS2630 [S]		1964	50.00
TOP BANANA			
❏ Capitol S308 [M]		1952	150.00
TOVARICH			
❏ Capitol TAO1940 [M]		1963	25.00
❏ Capitol STAO1940 [S]		1963	30.00
A TREE GROWS IN BROOKLYN			
❏ Columbia Masterworks ML4405 [M]		1951	30.00
—Blue label			

Number	Title	Yr	NM
TWO BY TWO			
❏ Columbia Masterworks S30338		1970	25.00
TWO ON THE AISLE			
❏ Decca DL8040 [M]		1951	150.00
—Black label, gold print			
❏ Decca DL8040 [M]		1955	75.00
—Black label, silver print			
❏ Decca DL8040 [M]		196?	75.00
—Black label with color bars			
TWO'S COMPANY			
❏ RCA Victor LOC-1009 [M]		1952	150.00
THE UNSINKABLE MOLLY BROWN			
❏ Capitol WAO1509 [M]		1960	25.00
❏ Capitol SWAO1509 [S]		1960	30.00
UP IN CENTRAL PARK			
❏ Decca DL8016 [M]		1950	40.00
—Black label, gold print			
❏ Decca DL8016 [M]		1955	30.00
—Black label, silver print			
WAITING FOR GODOT			
❏ Columbia Masterworks O2L238 [M]		1956	30.00
WEST SIDE STORY			
❏ Columbia Masterworks OL5230 [M]		1958	30.00
—Gray and black label with six "eye" logos			
❏ Columbia Masterworks OS2001 [S]		1958	30.00
—Gray and black label with six "eye" logos			
❏ Columbia Masterworks OL5230 [M]		1963	15.00
—Gray label with "Guaranteed High Fidelity" or "360 Sound Mono			
❏ Columbia Masterworks OS2001 [S]		1963	18.00
—Gray label with "360 Sound Stereo			
❏ Columbia Masterworks S32603 [S]		1973	12.00
—Reissue with new number			
WHAT MAKES SAMMY RUN?			
❏ Columbia Masterworks KOL6040 [M]		1964	30.00
❏ Columbia Masterworks KSO2440 [S]		1964	40.00
WILDCAT			
❏ RCA Victor LOC-1060 [M]		1961	30.00
❏ RCA Victor LSO-1060 [S]		1961	40.00
WISH YOU WERE HERE			
❏ RCA Victor LOC-1007 [M]		1952	75.00
WONDERFUL TOWN			
❏ Decca DL9010 [M]		1953	30.00
—Black label, gold print			
WORDS AND MUSIC			
❏ RCA Victor LRL1-5079		1974	25.00
YOU'RE A GOOD MAN, CHARLIE BROWN			
❏ MGM 1E-9 [M]		1967	25.00
❏ MGM S1E-9 [S]		1967	25.00
YOUR OWN THING			
❏ RCA Victor LOC-1148 [M]		1968	30.00
❏ RCA Victor LSO-1148 [S]		1968	25.00
ZORBA			
❏ Capitol SO-118		1969	25.00

SOUNDTRACKS

Number	Title	Yr	NM
AARON SLICK FROM PUNKIN CRICK			
❏ RCA Victor LPM-3006 [10]		1952	175.00
ABOUT LAST NIGHT...			
❏ EMI America SV-17210		1986	12.00
ABSOLUTE BEGINNERS			
❏ EMI America SV-17182		1986	15.00
❏ EMI America SV-517182		1986	15.00
—Columbia House record club edition			
ADVENTURES IN PARADISE			
❏ ABC-Paramount ABC-329 [M]		1960	30.00
❏ ABC-Paramount ABCS-329 [S]		1960	40.00
ADVISE AND CONSENT			
❏ RCA Victor LOC-1068 [M]		1962	30.00
❏ RCA Victor LSO-1068 [S]		1962	75.00
AN AFFAIR TO REMEMBER			
❏ Columbia CL1013 [M]		1957	40.00
AFRICA ADDIO			
❏ United Artists UAL-4141 [M]		1966	25.00
❏ United Artists UAS-5141 [S]		1966	30.00
AGAINST ALL ODDS			
❏ Atlantic 80152-1-E		1984	12.00
THE AGONY AND THE ECSTASY			
❏ Capitol MAS2427 [M]		1965	75.00
❏ Capitol SMAS2427 [S]		1965	100.00
AIRPORT			
❏ Decca DL79173		1970	30.00
ALAKAZAM THE GREAT			
❏ Vee Jay LP-6000 [M]		1961	100.00

Number	Title	Yr	NM
THE ALAMO			
❏ Columbia CL1558 [M]		1960	25.00
❏ Columbia CS8358 [S]		1960	30.00
ALBERT PECKINPAW'S REVENGE			
❏ Sidewalk T5907 [M]		1967	30.00
❏ Sidewalk ST5907 [S]		1967	30.00
ALEXANDER			
❏ Polydor 24-7001		1970	40.00
ALEXANDER THE GREAT			
❏ Mercury MG-20148 [M]		1956	300.00
ALFIE			
❏ ABC Impulse! AS-9111 [S]		1968	35.00
❏ Impulse! A-9111 [M]		1966	120.00
❏ Impulse! AS-9111 [S]		1966	120.00
ALIEN			
❏ 20th Century T-593		1979	30.00
ALIENS			
❏ Varese Sarabande STV-81283		1986	30.00
ALIKI, MY LOVE			
❏ Fontana MGF-27523 [M]		1963	30.00
❏ Fontana SRF-67523 [S]		1963	30.00
THE ALLNIGHTER			
❏ Chameleon CHST9601		1987	18.00
❏ Chameleon CHPD9601 [PD]		1987	30.00
—Picture disc			
ALL NIGHT LONG			
❏ Epic LA16032 [M]		1962	100.00
❏ Epic BA17032 [S]		1962	250.00
ALL THAT JAZZ			
❏ Casablanca NBLP-7198		1979	12.00
ALL THE LOVING COUPLES			
❏ GNP Crescendo GNPS-2051		1969	40.00
ALL THE RIGHT MOVES			
❏ Casablanca 814449-1		1983	15.00
ALL THE RIGHT NOISES			
❏ Buddah BDS-5132		1971	30.00
ALL THIS AND WORLD WAR II			
❏ 20th Century 2T-522 [B]		1976	35.00
—Box set with booklet and flyer			
ALMOST FAMOUS			
❏ Dreamworks RTH-2001		2001	40.00
—Album is called "Untitled"; contains five songs by Stillwater not on the CD version; 180-gram vinyl; with poster			
ALMOST SUMMER			
❏ MCA 3037		1978	30.00
ALWAYS			
❏ MCA 8036		1990	18.00
AMATEUR			
❏ Matador OLE 098-1		1995	15.00
AMERICA, AMERICA			
❏ Warner Bros. W1527 [M]		1963	25.00
❏ Warner Bros. WS1527 [S]		1963	30.00
AMERICAN ANTHEM			
❏ Atlantic 81661		1986	12.00
AMERICAN FLYERS			
❏ GRP 2001		1985	15.00
AMERICAN GIGOLO			
❏ Polydor PD1-6259		1980	15.00
AMERICAN HOT WAX			
❏ A&M SP-6500		1978	25.00
AN AMERICAN IN PARIS			
❏ MGM E-93 [10]		1951	40.00
AMERICAN POP			
❏ MCA 5201		1981	30.00
AN AMERICAN TAIL			
❏ MCA 39096		1986	18.00
AMERICATHON			
❏ Lorimar JS36174		1979	15.00
THE AMOROUS ADVENTURES OF MOLL FLANDERS			
❏ RCA Victor LOC-1113 [M]		1965	40.00
❏ RCA Victor LSO-1113 [S]		1965	100.00
ANASTASIA			
❏ Decca DL8460 [M]		1956	30.00
ANATOMY OF A MURDER			
❏ Columbia CL1360 [M]		1959	40.00
❏ Columbia CS8166 [S]		1959	150.00
AND GOD CREATED WOMAN			
❏ Decca DL8685 [M]		1957	120.00
THE ANDROMEDA STRAIN			
❏ Kapp KRS-5513		1971	40.00
—Regular cover			
❏ Kapp KRS-5513		1971	150.00
—Hexagonal cover glued onto silver cardboard			

Number Title	Yr	NM
ANGEL, ANGEL, DOWN WE GO		
❏ Tower ST-5161	1970	30.00
ANGELS DIE HARD		
❏ Uni 73091	1971	30.00
ANGELS FROM HELL		
❏ Tower ST5128	1968	75.00
ANNIE		
❏ CBS Masterworks JS38000	1982	12.00
THE ANONYMOUS VENETIAN		
❏ United Artists UAS-5218	1971	30.00
ANOTHER TIME, ANOTHER PLACE		
❏ Columbia CL1180 [M]	1958	40.00
ANY WEDNESDAY		
❏ Warner Bros. W1669 [M]	1966	30.00
❏ Warner Bros. WS1669 [S]	1966	40.00
ANY WHICH WAY YOU CAN		
❏ Warner Bros. HS3499	1980	12.00
THE APARTMENT		
❏ United Artists UAL-3105 [M]	1960	30.00
❏ United Artists UAS-6105 [S]	1960	40.00
APOCALYPSE NOW		
❏ Elektra DP-90001	1979	30.00
THE APPLE		
❏ Cannon 1001	1980	80.00
APRIL LOVE		
❏ Dot DLP-9000 [M]	1957	25.00
ARMED AND DANGEROUS		
❏ Manhattan SJ-53041	1986	12.00
—Includes Sigue Sigue Sputnik		
ARMS AND THE GIRL		
❏ Decca DL5200 [10]	1950	150.00
AROUND THE WORLD IN 80 DAYS		
❏ Decca DL9046 [M]	1957	30.00
—Black label, silver print		
❏ Decca DL79046 [M]	1959	40.00
—Maroon label, silver print; cover has "Full Stereo" banner		
❏ Decca DL79046 [S]	196?	15.00
—Black label with color bars		
❏ Decca SW-94840 [S]	1972	18.00
—Capitol Record Club edition		
❏ MCA 2062 [S]	1973	12.00
—Reissue of 79046; black label with rainbow		
❏ MCA 37086 [S]	198?	10.00
—Reissue of 2062		
AROUND THE WORLD UNDER THE SEA		
❏ Monument MLP-8050 [M]	1966	30.00
❏ Monument SLP-18050 [S]	1966	50.00
ARRIVIDERCI, BABY!		
❏ RCA Victor LOC-1132 [M]	1966	25.00
❏ RCA Victor LSO-1132 [S]	1966	40.00
ARTHUR		
❏ Warner Bros. BSK3582	1980	12.00
ARTHUR 2: ON THE ROCKS		
❏ A&M SP-3916	1988	12.00
ATHENA		
❏ Mercury MG-25202 [10]	1954	175.00
ATHENS, GA. -- INSIDE/OUT		
❏ I.R.S. 6185	1987	12.00
—Includes R.E.M. (2), Dreams So Real		
AT LONG LAST LOVE		
❏ RCA Victor ABL2-0967	1975	25.00
AVIATOR		
❏ Varese Sarabande STV-81240	1985	25.00
BABES IN TOYLAND		
❏ Buena Vista BV-4022 [M]	1961	30.00
❏ Buena Vista STER-4022 [S]	1961	40.00
BABY, THE RAIN MUST FALL		
❏ Ava A-53 [M]	1965	40.00
❏ Ava AS-53 [S]	1965	50.00
❏ Mainstream 56056 [M]	1965	30.00
—Reissue of Ava A-53		
❏ Mainstream S-6056 [S]	1965	40.00
—Reissue of Ava AS-53		
BABY DOLL		
❏ Columbia CL958 [M]	1956	120.00
—Ads for other Columbia LPs on back cover		
❏ Columbia CL958 [M]	195?	50.00
—No ads for LPs on back cover		
BABY FACE NELSON		
❏ Jubilee JLP-2021 [M]	1957	120.00
BACHELOR PARTY		
❏ I.R.S. SP-70047	1984	15.00
—Includes R.E.M., Oingo Boingo (2), The Fleshtones, The Alarm		

Number Title	Yr	NM
BACK STREET		
❏ Decca DL9097 [M]	1961	40.00
❏ Decca DL79097 [S]	1961	100.00
BACK TO SCHOOL		
❏ MCA 6175	1986	15.00
BACK TO THE BEACH		
❏ Columbia SC40892	1987	12.00
BACK TO THE FUTURE		
❏ MCA 6144	1985	12.00
—Original issue		
❏ MCA 39300	198?	10.00
—Second edition; includes copies with 6144 labels and this number stamped on the front cover		
BACK TO THE FUTURE PART II		
❏ MCA 6361	1989	18.00
THE BAD SEED		
❏ RCA Victor LPM-1395 [M]	1956	300.00
BAND OF ANGELS		
❏ RCA Victor LPM-1557 [M]	1957	150.00
BAND OF THE HAND		
❏ MCA 6187	1986	15.00
—Includes Andy Summers		
THE BAND WAGON		
❏ MGM E-3051 [M]	1953	30.00
—Yellow label		
❏ MGM E-3051 [M]	1960	25.00
—Black label		
THE BANJOMAN		
❏ Sire SA-7527	1977	25.00
BARABBAS		
❏ Colpix CP510 [M]	1962	40.00
❏ Colpix SCP510 [S]	1962	100.00
BARBARELLA		
❏ Dyno Voice DV-31908	1968	50.00
THE BARBARIAN AND THE GEISHA		
❏ 20th Fox FOX-3004 [M]	1958	300.00
BAREFOOT ADVENTURE		
❏ Pacific Jazz PJ-35 [M]	1961	40.00
❏ Pacific Jazz ST-35 [S]	1961	120.00
BAREFOOT IN THE PARK		
❏ Dot DLP-3803 [M]	1967	25.00
❏ Dot DLP-25803 [S]	1967	30.00
THE BARKLEYS OF BROADWAY		
❏ MGM E-503 [10]	1949	100.00
BARRY LYNDON		
❏ Warner Bros. BS2903	1975	18.00
BATMAN		
❏ Warner Bros. 25977	1989	25.00
—Music composed and conducted by Danny Elfman		
BATMAN FOREVER		
❏ Atlantic PR6339 [DJ]	1995	30.00
—Promo only; generic white cover with sticker		
BATTLE OF THE BULGE		
❏ Warner Bros. W1617 [M]	1965	40.00
❏ Warner Bros. WS1617 [S]	1965	40.00
BEACH BLANKET BINGO		
❏ Capitol T2323 [M]	1965	30.00
❏ Capitol ST2323 [S]	1965	75.00
BEAT STREET		
❏ Atlantic 80154	1984	18.00
❏ Atlantic 80158	1984	30.00
—Album called "Beat Street, Volume 2		
BEAU JAMES		
❏ Imperial LP-9041 [M]	1957	40.00
BECKET		
❏ Decca DL9117 [M]	1964	30.00
❏ Decca DL79117 [S]	1964	50.00
BEDAZZLED		
❏ London MS-82009	1967	100.00
BEETLEJUICE		
❏ Geffen R174166	1988	18.00
—BMG Direct Marketing edition		
❏ Geffen GHS24204	1988	15.00
—Music composed and conducted by Danny Elfman		
BEHOLD A PALE HORSE		
❏ Colpix CP519 [M]	1964	50.00
❏ Colpix SCP519 [S]	1964	80.00
THE BELIEVERS		
❏ Varese Sarabande STV-81328	1987	25.00
BELL, BOOK AND CANDLE		
❏ Colpix CP502 [M]	1959	75.00
BELLS ARE RINGING		
❏ Capitol W1435 [M]	1960	30.00
❏ Capitol SW1435 [S]	1960	30.00
BELLY		
❏ Def Jam 314-558925-1	1998	18.00

Number Title	Yr	NM
BENEATH THE PLANET OF THE APES		
❏ Amos AAS-8001	1970	40.00
BEN-HUR		
❏ MGM 1E1 [M]	1959	40.00
—Boxed edition with hardcover book		
❏ MGM S-1E1 [S]	1959	50.00
—Boxed edition with hardcover book		
❏ MGM 1E1 [M]	196?	15.00
—Gatefold cover, no book		
❏ MGM S-1E1 [S]	196?	18.00
—Gatefold cover, no book; black label		
❏ MGM S-1E1 [S]	196?	12.00
—Gatefold cover, no book; blue and gold label		
THE BEST LITTLE WHOREHOUSE IN TEXAS		
❏ MCA 6112	1982	12.00
❏ MCA 1499	198?	10.00
—Reissue of 6112		
BEST OF THE BEST		
❏ Relativity 88561 0341	1989	25.00
BETRAYED		
❏ Varese Sarabande 704.700	1988	30.00
BEVERLY HILLS COP		
❏ MCA 5553	1984	12.00
—Includes Danny Elfman		
BEVERLY HILLS COP II		
❏ MCA R123346	1987	12.00
—Includes George Michael ("I Want Your Sex")		
❏ MCA 6207	1987	10.00
—Includes George Michael		
BEYOND THE GREAT WALL		
❏ Capitol T10401 [M]	1965	50.00
BEYOND THE VALLEY OF THE DOLLS		
❏ 20th Century Fox TFS-4211	1970	250.00
THE BIBLE		
❏ 20th Century Fox TF-3184 [M]	1966	25.00
❏ 20th Century Fox TFS-4184 [S]	1966	30.00
THE BIG CHILL		
❏ Motown 6062ML	1983	12.00
❏ Motown 6094ML	1983	12.00
—Subtitled "More Songs from the Original Soundtrack		
THE BIG COUNTRY		
❏ United Artists UAL-4004 [M]	1958	30.00
❏ United Artists UAS-5004 [S]	1958	50.00
THE BIG EASY		
❏ Antilles AN-7087	1987	12.00
THE BIGGEST BUNDLE OF THEM ALL		
❏ MGM E-4446 [M]	1967	25.00
❏ MGM SE-4446 [S]	1967	30.00
THE BIG GUNDOWN		
❏ United Artists UAS-5190	1967	40.00
BILL & TED'S EXCELLENT ADVENTURE		
❏ A&M SP-3915	1989	18.00
BILLIE		
❏ United Artists UAL-4131 [M]	1965	25.00
❏ United Artists UAS-5131 [S]	1965	30.00
THE BILLION DOLLAR BRAIN		
❏ United Artists UAL-4174 [M]	1967	18.00
❏ United Artists UAS-5174 [S]	1967	25.00
BILLY JACK		
❏ Warner Bros. WS1926	1971	30.00
—Original; green "WB" label		
❏ Warner Bros. BJS-1001	1973	20.00
—Reissue; "Burbank" palm trees label		
BIRD		
❏ Columbia SC44299	1988	20.00
THE BIRD WITH THE CRYSTAL PLUMAGE		
❏ Capitol ST-642	1970	150.00
BLACK AND WHITE IN COLOR		
❏ Buddah BDS-5698	1977	40.00
BLACKBIRDS OF 1928		
❏ Columbia Masterworks OL6770 [M]	1968	35.00
❏ Revue 1 [M]	196?	75.00
❏ Sutton SU-270 [M]	196?	50.00
❏ Sutton SSU-270 [R]	196?	30.00
BLACK GIRL		
❏ Fantasy F-9420	1973	80.00
THE BLACK HOLE		
❏ Buena Vista STER-5008	1979	50.00
THE BLACK ORCHID		
❏ Dot DLP-3178 [M]	1959	40.00
❏ Dot SLP-25178 [S]	1959	50.00
BLACK ORPHEUS		
❏ Epic LN3672 [M]	1959	100.00
❏ Fontana MGF-27520 [M]	1963	50.00
❏ Fontana SRF-67520 [R]	1963	35.00

Number	Title	Yr	NM

BLACK RAIN
❏ Virgin 91292 — 1989 — 12.00
—*Includes UB40, Iggy Pop*

BLACULA
❏ RCA Victor LSP-4806 — 1972 — 75.00

BLADE RUNNER
❏ Full Moon/Warner Bros. 23748 — 1982 — 25.00

BLESS THE BEASTS AND CHILDREN
❏ A&M SP-4322 — 1971 — 30.00

BLOOD AND SAND
❏ Decca DL5380 [10] — 1952 — 100.00

BLOOMER GIRL
❏ Decca DL8015 [M] — 1950 — 30.00

BLOW-UP
❏ MGM E-4447 [M] — 1967 — 40.00
❏ MGM SE-4447 [S] — 1967 — 150.00

THE BLUE MAX
❏ Mainstream 56081 [M] — 1966 — 40.00
❏ Mainstream S-6081 [S] — 1966 — 100.00

BLUE VELVET
❏ Varese Sarabande STV-81292 — 1986 — 30.00

BOBO
❏ Warner Bros. W1711 [M] — 1967 — 25.00
❏ Warner Bros. WS1711 [S] — 1967 — 25.00

THE BODYGUARD
❏ Arista 18699 — 1992 — 15.00

BODY HEAT
❏ Label X LXSE-1-002 — 1983 — 120.00

BOEING, BOEING
❏ RCA Victor LOC-1121 [M] — 1965 — 30.00
❏ RCA Victor LSO-1121 [S] — 1965 — 30.00

BONNIE AND CLYDE
❏ Warner Bros. W1742 [M] — 1968 — 40.00
❏ Warner Bros. WS1742 [S] — 1968 — 30.00
—*Originals have green labels with "W7" logo in a square at top*
❏ Warner Bros. ST-91414 [S] — 1968 — 30.00
—*Capitol Record Club issue*

BORA, BORA
❏ American Int'l. STA-1029 — 1970 — 30.00

BORDER RADIO
❏ Enigma ST-73221 — 1987 — 15.00
—*Includes John Doe*

BORN FREE
❏ MGM E-4368 [M] — 1966 — 18.00
❏ MGM SE-4368 [S] — 1966 — 25.00

BORN ON THE FOURTH OF JULY
❏ MCA 6340 — 1989 — 15.00
—*Includes Edie Brickell and New Bohemians*

BORSALINO
❏ Paramount PAS-5019 — 1970 — 30.00

THE BOY FRIEND
❏ MGM 1SE-32 — 1971 — 25.00

A BOY NAMED CHARLIE BROWN
❏ Columbia Masterworks OS3500 — 1970 — 50.00

BOY ON A DOLPHIN
❏ Decca DL8580 [M] — 1957 — 75.00
—*Black label with silver print, or pink label with black print (promo)*
❏ Decca DL8580 [M] — 196? — 25.00
—*Black label with color bars*

THE BOYS FROM SYRACUSE
❏ Capitol TAO1933 [M] — 1963 — 30.00
❏ Capitol STAO1933 [S] — 1963 — 30.00

THE BOY WHO COULD FLY
❏ Varese Sarabande STV-81299 — 1986 — 25.00

BOYZ 'N THE HOOD
❏ Warner Bros. PRO-A-4996 [DJ] — 1991 — 25.00
—*Promo-only vinyl release*

THE BRAVE ONE
❏ Decca DL8344 [M] — 1956 — 40.00

BREAKIN'
❏ Polydor 821919-1 — 1984 — 12.00
—*Includes Re-Flex*

BRIGHT LIGHTS, BIG CITY
❏ Warner Bros. R100483 — 1988 — 15.00
—*Includes M/A/R/R/S, Depeche Mode, New Order, Prince; BMG Direct Marketing edition*
❏ Warner Bros. 25688 — 1988 — 12.00
—*Includes M/A/R/R/S, Depeche Mode, New Order, Prince*

BRIMSTONE & TREACLE
❏ A&M SP-4915 — 1982 — 12.00
—*Includes Sting, The Police, Go-Go's, Squeeze*

BRONCO BILLY
❏ Elektra 5E-512 — 1980 — 12.00

BROTHER ON THE RUN
❏ Perception PLP-45 — 1973 — 40.00

THE BROTHERS
❏ Warner Bros. 48058-1 — 2001 — 25.00

BUCCANEER
❏ Columbia CL1278 [M] — 1958 — 30.00
❏ Columbia CS8096 [S] — 1958 — 40.00

BULL DURHAM
❏ Capitol C1-90586 — 1988 — 12.00
—*Includes Los Lobos, The Blasters, House of Schock*

BULLITT
❏ Warner Bros. WS1777 — 1968 — 75.00

BUNDLE OF JOY
❏ RCA Victor LPM-1399 [M] — 1956 — 40.00

BUNNY LAKE IS MISSING
❏ RCA Victor LOC-1115 [M] — 1965 — 40.00
❏ RCA Victor LSO-1115 [S] — 1965 — 80.00

BUNNY O'HARE
❏ American Int'l. STA-1041 — 1971 — 25.00

BUONA SERA, MRS. CAMPBELL
❏ United Artists UAS-5192 — 1969 — 30.00

BURGLAR
❏ MCA 6201 — 1987 — 12.00
—*Includes Belinda Carlisle, The Belle Stars, The Smithereens*

THE BURGLARS
❏ Bell 1105 — 1971 — 40.00

BUSTER
❏ Atlantic 81905 — 1988 — 12.00
—*Includes The Searchers ("Sweets for My Sweet")*

BUTTERFIELD-8
❏ MGM E-3952 [M] — 1960 — 25.00
❏ MGM SE-3952 [S] — 1960 — 30.00

BYE BYE BIRDIE
❏ RCA Victor LOC-1081 [M] — 1963 — 30.00
—*First cover without Ann-Margret on the front*
❏ RCA Victor LOC-1081 [M] — 196? — 25.00
—*Second cover with Ann-Margret on front, but with no credits underneath*
❏ RCA Victor LOC-1081 [M] — 196? — 18.00
—*Third cover with Ann-Margret on front and with credits underneath*
❏ RCA Victor LSO-1081 [S] — 1963 — 30.00
—*First cover without Ann-Margret on the front*
❏ RCA Victor LSO-1081 [S] — 196? — 30.00
—*Second cover with Ann-Margret on front, but with no credits underneath*
❏ RCA Victor LSO-1081 [S] — 196? — 25.00
—*Third cover with Ann-Margret on front and with credits underneath*
❏ RCA Victor AYL1-3947 [S] — 1980 — 10.00
—*Best Buy Series" reissue*

CABARET
❏ ABC ABCD-752 — 1972 — 25.00
❏ MCA 37125 — 198? — 10.00
—*Reissue; blue label with rainbow*

THE CAINE MUTINY
❏ RCA Victor LOC-1013 [M] — 1954 — 10000.00
—*VG value 4000; VG+ value 7000*
❏ RCA Victor LOC-1013 [M] — 1993 — 250.00
—*Very limited edition (100 copies) reproduction of the original LP*

CALIFORNIA SUITE
❏ Columbia JC35727 — 1978 — 12.00
—*Full name: "Neil Simon's California Suite*

CALL ME MADAM
❏ Decca DL5465 [10] — 1953 — 50.00

CALL ME MISTER
❏ Decca DLP7005 [10] — 1950 — 150.00

CAMELOT
❏ Warner Bros. B1712 [M] — 1967 — 30.00
❏ Warner Bros. BS1712 [S] — 1967 — 25.00
—*Gold label original*
❏ Warner Bros. SW-91347 — 1968 — 30.00
—*Capitol Record Club edition*
❏ Warner Bros. BS1712 [S] — 1968 — 18.00
—*Green label, "W7" box logo at top*
❏ Warner Bros. BS1712 [S] — 1970 — 15.00
—*Green label, "WB" shield logo at top*
❏ Warner Bros. BS1712 [S] — 1973 — 12.00
—*Burbank" palm trees label*
❏ Warner Bros. BSK3102 [S] — 1977 — 10.00
—*Reissue with new number*

CAN-CAN
❏ Capitol W1301 [M] — 1960 — 25.00
❏ Capitol SW1301 [S] — 1960 — 30.00

CANDY
❏ ABC ABCS-OC-9 — 1968 — 30.00

CAPTIVE
❏ Virgin 90609 — 1987 — 18.00
—*Music by The Edge and Larry Mullen of U2*

THE CARDINAL
❏ RCA Victor LOC-1084 [M] — 1963 — 40.00
❏ RCA Victor LSO-1084 [S] — 1963 — 75.00

THE CARE BEARS MOVIE
❏ Kid Stuff 3901 — 1985 — 25.00

THE CARETAKERS
❏ Ava A-31 [M] — 1963 — 25.00
❏ Ava AS-31 [S] — 1963 — 30.00

CAROUSEL
❏ Capitol W694 [M] — 1956 — 30.00
—*Gray label*
❏ Capitol W694 [M] — 1959 — 25.00
—*Black colorband label, logo at left*
❏ Capitol W694 [M] — 1962 — 18.00
—*Black colorband label, logo at top*
❏ Capitol SW694 [S] — 1962 — 25.00
—*Black colorband label*
❏ Capitol SW694 [S] — 1969 — 18.00
—*Lime green label*
❏ Capitol SW694 [S] — 1973 — 15.00
—*Orange label*

THE CARPETBAGGERS
❏ Ava A-45 [M] — 1964 — 30.00
❏ Ava AS-45 [S] — 1964 — 40.00

CARRY IT ON
❏ Vanguard VSD-79313 — 1971 — 30.00

CASINO ROYALE
❏ Colgems COMO-5005 [M] — 1967 — 30.00
❏ Colgems COSO-5005 [S] — 1967 — 150.00
❏ Colgems COSO-5005 [S] — 1999 — 30.00
—*Classic Records reissue on audiophile vinyl*
❏ Colgems COSO-5005-45 — 199? — 40.00
—*Classic Records reissue on four 12-inch 45 rpm records*

THE CATHERINE WHEEL
❏ Sire SRK3645 — 1981 — 15.00
—*Includes David Byrne, who also composed all the music*

CAT PEOPLE
❏ Backstreet BSR6107 — 1982 — 25.00

A CERTAIN SMILE
❏ Columbia CL1194 [M] — 1958 — 40.00
❏ Columbia CS8068 [S] — 1958 — 100.00

THE CHAIRMAN
❏ Tetragrammaton T-5007 — 1969 — 30.00

CHARLOTTE'S WEB
❏ Paramount PAS-1008 — 1973 — 30.00

THE CHASE
❏ Columbia Masterworks OL6560 [M] — 1966 — 40.00
❏ Columbia Masterworks OS2960 [S] — 1966 — 75.00

CHINATOWN
❏ ABC ABDP-848 — 1974 — 40.00

CHITTY CHITTY BANG BANG
❏ United Artists UAS-5188 — 1968 — 30.00

CHRISTIANE F.
❏ RCA ABL1-4239 — 1981 — 40.00
—*Includes David Bowie ("Helgen (Heroes)")*

THE CHRISTMAS RACCOONS
❏ Starland Music 1031 — 1982 — 15.00
—*Story record with Rich Little, Rita Coolidge and Rupert Holmes as the star voices*

THE CHRISTMAS THAT ALMOST WASN'T
❏ RCA Camden CAL-1086 [M] — 1966 — 30.00
❏ RCA Camden CAS-1086 [S] — 1966 — 40.00

CINDERELLA
❏ Disneyland WDL-4007 [M] — 1957 — 250.00
—*Original issue, gatefold cover*
❏ Disneyland DQ-1207 [M] — 1959 — 40.00
—*Second issue, white back cover with ads for nine other LPs*
❏ Disneyland DQ-1207 [M] — 1963 — 30.00
—*Third issue, pink back cover*
❏ Disneyland DQ-1207 [M] — 1987 — 30.00
—*Fifth issue, high gloss cover with prince putting slipper on Cinderella's foot*
❏ Disneyland 3107 [PD] — 1981 — 30.00
—*Fourth issue, picture disc*

CINDERFELLA
❏ Dot DLP-8001 [M] — 1960 — 75.00
❏ Dot SLP-38001 [S] — 1960 — 150.00
—*Gatefold cover with many extras including game board, spinner, booklet, music stand.*

CITY HEAT
❏ Warner Bros. 25219 — 1984 — 15.00
—*Incidental music by Lennie Niehaus*

CLEOPATRA
❏ 20th Century Fox FXG-5008 [M] — 1963 — 30.00
❏ 20th Century Fox SXG-5008 [S] — 1963 — 40.00

Number	Title	Yr	NM

CLEOPATRA JONES
❏ Warner Bros. BS2719 — 1973 — 30.00

CLOCKERS
❏ MCA 11304 — 1995 — 12.00
—Includes Seal

CLOSE ENCOUNTERS OF THE THIRD KIND
❏ Arista AL9500 — 1977 — 30.00
—Includes one 12-inch record and one 7-inch record. Deduct 50 percent if the 7-inch record is missing.

THE CLOWNS
❏ Columbia S30772 — 1971 — 40.00

C'MON, LET'S LIVE A LITTLE
❏ Liberty LRP-3430 [M] — 1966 — 30.00
❏ Liberty LST-7430 [S] — 1966 — 30.00

COAL MINER'S DAUGHTER
❏ MCA 5107 — 1980 — 18.00

COFFY
❏ Polydor PD-5048 — 1973 — 150.00

THE COLLECTOR
❏ Mainstream 56053 [M] — 1965 — 30.00
❏ Mainstream S-6053 [S] — 1965 — 50.00

COLLEGE CONFIDENTIAL
❏ Chancellor CHL-5016 [M] — 1960 — 40.00
❏ Chancellor CHLS-5016 [S] — 1960 — 150.00

THE COLOR PURPLE
❏ Qwest 25336 — 1985 — 25.00
—Regular gatefold edition; records are still on purple vinyl
❏ Qwest 25289 — 1985 — 30.00
—Box set "limited edition" on purple vinyl with booklet

COLORS
❏ Sire R154136 — 1988 — 15.00
—Includes Ice-T ("Colors")
❏ Warner Bros. 25713 — 1988 — 12.00
—Includes Ice-T, Salt-N-Pepa

COMANCHE
❏ Coral CRL57046 [M] — 1956 — 400.00

COME BACK CHARLESTON BLUE
❏ Atco SD7010 — 1972 — 30.00

COME BLOW YOUR HORN
❏ Reprise R-6071 [M] — 1963 — 30.00
❏ Reprise R9-6071 [S] — 1963 — 50.00

COMETOGETHER
❏ Apple SW-3377 — 1971 — 25.00

THE CONNECTION
❏ Charlie Parker PLP-806 [M] — 1962 — 75.00
❏ Charlie Parker PLP-806S [S] — 1962 — 40.00
❏ Felsted 7512 [M] — 1960 — 250.00
❏ Felsted 2512 [S] — 1960 — 300.00

CONVOY
❏ United Artists UA-LA910-H — 1978 — 15.00

COOLEY HIGH
❏ Motown M7-840R2 — 1975 — 25.00

THE CORRUPT ONES
❏ United Artists UAL-4158 [M] — 1967 — 40.00
❏ United Artists UAS-5158 [S] — 1967 — 40.00

COTTON COMES TO HARLEM
❏ United Artists UAS-5211 — 1970 — 30.00

COURIER
❏ Virgin 90954 — 1989 — 15.00
—Includes U2, Elvis Costello (as Declan MacManus), Hothouse Flowers

THE COURT JESTER
❏ Decca DL8212 [M] — 1956 — 80.00
—Black label, silver print, or pink label, black print promo copy
❏ Decca DL8212 [M] — 196? — 30.00
—Black label with color bars

THE COWBOY
❏ Decca DL8684 [M] — 1958 — 75.00
—Black label, silver print, or pink label, black print promo copy
❏ Decca DL8684 [M] — 196? — 25.00
—Black label with color bars

CRADLE 2 THE GRAVE
❏ Def Jam 44063615-1 — 2002 — 25.00

CRIME IN THE STREETS
❏ Decca DL8376 [M] — 1956 — 75.00
—Black label, silver print, or pink label, black print promo copy
❏ Decca DL8376 [S] — 196? — 30.00
—Black label with color bars

THE CROSS AND THE SWITCHBLADE
❏ Light LS-5550 — 1970 — 30.00

CRUISING
❏ Columbia JS36410 — 1980 — 40.00

CUSTER OF THE WEST
❏ ABC ABC-OC-5 [M] — 1968 — 100.00
❏ ABC ABCS-OC-5 [S] — 1968 — 150.00

CYCLE SAVAGES
❏ American Int'l. STA-1033 — 1970 — 30.00

CYRANO DE BERGERAC
❏ Capitol S283 [M] — 1951 — 30.00
—Originals have red labels with Capitol logo at top

DAKTARI
❏ Leo the Lion CH-1043 [M] — 1967 — 50.00
❏ MGM CH-1043 [M] — 1967 — 50.00

THE DAMNED
❏ Warner Bros. WS1829 — 1969 — 30.00

DAMN THE DEFIANT!
❏ Colpix CP511 [M] — 1962 — 30.00
❏ Colpix SCP511 [S] — 1962 — 75.00

DAMN YANKEES
❏ RCA Victor LOC-1047 [M] — 1958 — 40.00
—Original pressing with "Long Play" on label

DANCE CRAZE
❏ Chrysalis CHR1299 — 1981 — 25.00
—Includes The Specials, The Selecter, Bad Manners, Madness, The English Beat, The Bodysnatchers; a great introduction to 2-Tone ska

DANGEROUSLY CLOSE
❏ Enigma SJ-73204 — 1986 — 12.00
—Includes The Smithereens, Lords of the New Church

DARKMAN
❏ MCA 10094 — 1990 — 15.00
—Composed and conducted by Danny Elfman

THE DARK OF THE SUN
❏ MGM SE-4544 — 1968 — 40.00

DARLING LILI
❏ RCA Victor LSPX-1000 — 1969 — 25.00

DAWN OF THE DEAD
❏ Varese Sarabande VC-81106 — 1979 — 30.00

DAYDREAMER
❏ Columbia Masterworks OL6540 [M] — 1966 — 30.00
❏ Columbia Masterworks OS2940 [S] — 1966 — 40.00

DAY OF ANGER
❏ RCA Victor LSO-1165 — 1969 — 25.00

THE DAY OF THE DOLPHIN
❏ Avco AV-11014 — 1973 — 30.00

DAYS OF HEAVEN
❏ Pacific Arts PAC8-128 — 1978 — 40.00

DAYS OF THUNDER
❏ DGC 24294 — 1990 — 25.00

THE DAY THE FISH CAME OUT
❏ 20th Century Fox TF-3194 [M] — 1967 — 30.00
❏ 20th Century Fox TFS-4194 [S] — 1967 — 40.00

DEADFALL
❏ 20th Century Fox S-4203 — 1968 — 75.00

THE DEADLY AFFAIR
❏ Verve V-8679 [M] — 1966 — 75.00
❏ Verve V6-8679 [S] — 1966 — 75.00

DEAD MAN WALKING
❏ Columbia C367989 — 1997 — 250.00

DEAR JOHN
❏ Dunhill OCD-55001 [M] — 1966 — 25.00
❏ Dunhill OCDS-55001 [S] — 1966 — 30.00

THE DECLINE OF WESTERN CIVILIZATION
❏ Slash 105 — 1981 — 25.00

THE DEEP
❏ Casablanca NBLP-7060 — 1977 — 18.00
—Blue vinyl

DEEP IN MY HEART
❏ MGM E-3153 [M] — 1955 — 40.00
❏ MGM E-3153 [M] — 1955 — 50.00

DE SADE
❏ Tower ST-5170 — 1969 — 30.00

DESIRE UNDER THE ELMS
❏ Dot DLP-3095 [M] — 1958 — 150.00

DESTINATION MOON
❏ Columbia CL6151 [10] — 1950 — 250.00
❏ Omega OL-3 [M] — 1959 — 40.00
❏ Omega OSL-3 [S] — 196? — 175.00

THE DEVIL AT 4 O'CLOCK
❏ Colpix CP509 [M] — 1962 — 40.00
❏ Colpix SCP509 [S] — 1962 — 80.00

THE DEVIL IN MISS JONES
❏ Janus JLS-3059 — 1973 — 30.00

THE DEVIL'S BRIGADE
❏ United Artists UAS-6654 — 1968 — 25.00

DIAMOND HEAD
❏ Colpix CP-440 [M] — 1963 — 30.00
❏ Colpix SCP440 [S] — 1963 — 75.00

DIAMONDS ARE FOREVER
❏ United Artists UAS-5520 — 1971 — 25.00
❏ United Artists UA-LA301-G — 1974 — 15.00
—Reissue of 5520

THE DIARY OF ANNE FRANK
❏ 20th Fox FOX-3012 [M] — 1959 — 50.00
❏ 20th Fox SFX-3012 [S] — 1959 — 100.00

DIRTY DANCING
❏ RCA 6408-1-R — 1987 — 12.00
❏ RCA 6965-1-R — 1988 — 18.00
—Album's title is "More Dirty Dancing"; original editions of the LP have instrumental selections entitled "Baby's Walk" and "The Lifts in the Lake Theme (Finale)
❏ RCA 6965-1-R-A — 1988 — 12.00
—Album's title is "More Dirty Dancing"; revised editions of the LP have the two instrumental selections, but they are retitled "(I've Had) The Time of My Life (Instrumental Version)"

DIRTY GAME
❏ Laurie LLP-2034 [M] — 1966 — 30.00
❏ Laurie SLP-2034 [S] — 1966 — 30.00

DIVORCE AMERICAN STYLE
❏ United Artists UAL-4163 [M] — 1967 — 25.00
❏ United Artists UAS-5163 [S] — 1967 — 25.00

DIVORCE ITALIAN STYLE
❏ United Artists UAL-4106 [M] — 1962 — 40.00
❏ United Artists UAS-5106 [S] — 1962 — 50.00

D.O.A.
❏ Varese Sarabande 704.610 — 1988 — 40.00

DOCTOR DETROIT
❏ Backstreet 6120 — 1983 — 12.00
—Includes Devo (2)

DOCTOR DOLITTLE
❏ 20th Century Fox TCF-5101 [M] — 1967 — 25.00
❏ 20th Century Fox TCS-5101 [S] — 1967 — 25.00

DOCTOR GOLDFOOT AND THE GIRL BOMBS
❏ Tower T5053 [M] — 1966 — 25.00
❏ Tower DT5053 [R] — 1966 — 30.00

DOCTOR ZHIVAGO
❏ MCA 39042 — 198? — 10.00
—Reissue
❏ MGM 1E-6 [M] — 1965 — 18.00
❏ MGM S1E-6ST [S] — 1965 — 25.00
❏ MGM SWAE-90620 [S] — 1965 — 25.00
—Capitol Record Club issue

A DOG OF FLANDERS
❏ 20th Fox FOX-3026 [M] — 1959 — 100.00
❏ 20th Fox SFX-3026 [S] — 1959 — 300.00

DOGS IN SPACE
❏ Atlantic 81789 — 1987 — 30.00
—Includes Iggy Pop, Michael Hutchense (of INXS), Brian Eno, etc.

$ (DOLLARS)
❏ Reprise MS2051 — 1971 — 25.00

DON'T MAKE WAVES
❏ MGM E-4483 [M] — 1967 — 30.00
❏ MGM SE-4483 [S] — 1967 — 30.00

THE DOORS
❏ Elektra E1-61047 — 1991 — 150.00
—Only vinyl edition in US released through Columbia House

DO THE RIGHT THING
❏ Motown 6272 — 1989 — 12.00
—Includes Public Enemy

DOWN AND OUT IN BEVERLY HILLS
❏ MCA 6160 — 1986 — 12.00
—Includes Andy Summers (6)

DRAGNET
❏ MCA 6210 — 1987 — 12.00
—Includes Art of Noise

DRANGO
❏ Liberty LRP-3036 [M] — 1957 — 175.00

A DREAM OF KINGS
❏ National General NG-1000 — 1969 — 30.00

DR. NO
❏ Liberty LT-50275 — 1981 — 10.00
—Reissue of United Artists 275
❏ United Artists UAL-4108 [M] — 1963 — 40.00
❏ United Artists UAS-5108 [S] — 1963 — 50.00
❏ United Artists UA-LA275-G — 1974 — 12.00
—Reissue of 5108

DR. PHIBES
❏ American Int'l. A-1040 — 1971 — 75.00

DUCK, YOU SUCKER
❏ United Artists UAS-5221 — 1972 — 40.00

DUDES
❏ MCA 6212 — 1987 — 12.00
—Includes Jane's Addiction

Number Title	Yr	NM
DUEL AT DIABLO		
❑ United Artists UAL-4139 [M]	1966	30.00
❑ United Artists UAS-5139 [S]	1966	30.00
DUMBO		
❑ Disneyland WDL-4013 [M]	1957	250.00
—Original issue, gatefold cover		
❑ Disneyland DQ-1204 [M]	1959	30.00
—Second issue, back cover has ads for nine other LPs		
❑ Disneyland DQ-1204 [M]	1963	18.00
—Third issue, four black & white photos on back cover		
❑ Disneyland 1204 [M]	197?	12.00
—Fourth issue, yellow rainbow label, flying Dumbo on back cover		
❑ Disneyland ST-4904 [M]	1963	250.00
—Special issue with pop-up figures in gatefold		
DUNE		
❑ Polydor 823770-1	1984	30.00
THE DUNWICH HORROR		
❑ American Int'l. STA-1028	1970	40.00
EARTH GIRLS ARE EASY		
❑ Sire 25835	1989	12.00
—Includes The B-52's, Depeche Mode, The Jesus and Mary Chain, Julie Brown (2), Stewart Copeland		
EASTER PARADE		
❑ MGM E-502 [10]	1950	100.00
EAST SIDE, WEST SIDE		
❑ Columbia CL2123 [M]	1963	175.00
❑ Columbia CS8923 [S]	1963	175.00
EASY MONEY		
❑ Columbia JS38968	1983	12.00
—Includes Nick Lowe		
EASY RIDER		
❑ ABC Dunhill DSX-50063	1969	30.00
EATING RAOUL		
❑ Varese Sarabande STV81164	1982	15.00
—Includes Los Lobos		
ECCO		
❑ Warner Bros. W1600 [M]	1965	30.00
❑ Warner Bros. WS1600 [S]	1965	30.00
THE EDDY DUCHIN STORY		
❑ Decca DL8289 [M]	1956	40.00
—Original cover with Tyrone Power and Kim Novak at a piano		
❑ Decca DL8289 [M]	1959	25.00
—Reissue cover with Tyrone Power and Kim Novak kissing		
❑ Decca DL78289 [S]	1959	30.00
—Maroon label, silver print, "Full Stereo" on front cover		
❑ Decca DL9121 [M]	196?	15.00
—Reissue of 8289		
❑ Decca DL79121 [S]	196?	18.00
—Reissue of 78289		
❑ MCA 2041	1973	12.00
—Reissue of 79121; black label with rainbow		
❑ MCA 37088	198?	10.00
—Reissue of 2041		
THE EDUCATION OF SONNY CARSON		
❑ Paramount PAS-1045	1974	25.00
THE EGYPTIAN		
❑ Decca DL9014 [M]	1954	75.00
❑ Decca DL79014 [R]	196?	25.00
EIGHT MEN OUT		
❑ Varese Sarabande 704.600	1988	30.00
8 MILE, MORE MUSIC FROM		
❑ Shady/Interscope 004450979-1	2002	30.00
—U.S. edition comes in generic black sleeve with center hole and sticker across top of cover		
84 CHARING CROSS ROAD		
❑ Varese Sarabande STV81306	1987	15.00
EL CID		
❑ MGM E-3977 [M]	1962	40.00
❑ MGM SE-3977 [S]	1962	50.00
EL DORADO		
❑ Epic FLM-13114 [M]	1967	50.00
❑ Epic LFS-15114 [S]	1967	80.00
ELECTRA GLIDE IN BLUE		
❑ United Artists UA-LA062-H	1973	40.00
—With booklet and two posters		
ELEPHANT STEPS		
❑ Columbia Masterwords M2X33044	1975	25.00
ELMER GANTRY		
❑ United Artists UAL-4069 [M]	1960	40.00
❑ United Artists UAS-5069 [S]	1960	50.00
EL TOPO		
❑ Apple SWAO-3388	1972	40.00
THE EMPIRE STRIKES BACK		
❑ RSO RS-2-4201	1980	25.00
—With booklet		

Number Title	Yr	NM
ENTER THE DRAGON		
❑ Warner Bros. BS2727	1973	75.00
E.T. THE EXTRA-TERRESTRIAL		
❑ MCA 6109	1982	12.00
❑ MCA 6113 [PD]	1982	30.00
—Picture disc in plastic envelope		
❑ MCA 16014	1982	40.00
—Audiophile edition		
❑ MCA 70000	1982	100.00
—Boxed version with booklet; story narrated by Michael Jackson		
EVERYTHING I HAVE IS YOURS		
❑ MGM E-187 [10]	1953	40.00
EVERY WHICH WAY BUT LOOSE		
❑ Elektra 5E-503	1978	15.00
EVIL DEAD		
❑ Varese Sarabande STV-81199	1984	25.00
EXODUS		
❑ RCA Victor LOC-1058 [M]	1960	25.00
—"Long Play" on label		
❑ RCA Victor LSO-1058 [S]	1960	30.00
—"Living Stereo" on label		
THE EXORCIST		
❑ Warner Bros. W2774	1974	30.00
A FACE IN THE CROWD		
❑ Capitol W872 [M]	1957	50.00
THE FALCON AND THE SNOWMAN		
❑ EMI America SV-17150	1985	25.00
—Includes David Bowie ("This Is Not America")		
THE FALL OF THE ROMAN EMPIRE		
❑ Columbia Masterworks OL6060 [M]	1964	40.00
❑ Columbia Masterworks OS2460 [S]	1964	75.00
THE FAMILY WAY		
❑ London M76007 [M]	1967	150.00
—No promo sticker on front cover (deduct 20 percent for promo)		
❑ London ST82007 [S]	1967	120.00
—No promo sticker on front cover (deduct 20 percent for promo)		
FANNY		
❑ Warner Bros. W1416 [M]	1961	30.00
❑ Warner Bros. WS1416 [S]	1961	30.00
FANTASIA		
❑ Buena Vista WDX-101 [M]	1961	30.00
—Second issue, blue labels, includes 24-page booklet		
❑ Buena Vista STER-101 [S]	1961	40.00
—First stereo issue, black and yellow rainbow labels, includes 24-page booklet		
❑ Buena Vista 101 [S]	1982	25.00
—Stereo reissue, two records, no booklet		
❑ Buena Vista V-104	1982	30.00
—Digitally re-recorded music track, Mickey Mouse as The Sorcerer on cover		
❑ Disneyland WDX-101	1957	75.00
—Original issue, maroon/red labels, includes 24-page booklet		
FANTASIA: NIGHT ON BALD MOUNTAIN; PASTORAL SYMPHONY; AVE MARIA		
❑ Disneyland WDL-4101C [M]	1958	25.00
❑ Disneyland STER-4101C [S]	1958	30.00
FANTASIA: RITE OF SPRING; TOCCATA AND FUGUE		
❑ Disneyland WDL-4101A [M]	1958	25.00
❑ Disneyland STER-4101A [S]	1959	30.00
FANTASIA: THE NUTCRACKER SUITE; DANCE OF THE HOURS		
❑ Disneyland WDL-4101B [M]	1958	25.00
❑ Disneyland STER-4101B [S]	1959	30.00
THE FANTASTIC PLASTIC MACHINE		
❑ Epic BN26469	1969	30.00
A FAREWELL TO ARMS		
❑ Capitol W918 [M]	1957	50.00
FAR FROM THE MADDING CROWD		
❑ MGM 1E-11 [M]	1967	30.00
❑ MGM S1E-11 [S]	1967	30.00
THE FASTEST GUITAR ALIVE		
❑ MGM SE-4475	1968	30.00
FAST TIMES AT RIDGEMONT HIGH		
❑ Full Moon/Asylum 60158	1982	18.00
—Includes Go-Go's, Oingo Boingo		
FATHOM		
❑ 20th Century Fox TFM-4195 [M]	1967	40.00
❑ 20th Century Fox TFS-4195 [S]	1967	50.00
FELLINI SATYRICON		
❑ United Artists UAS-5208	1969	30.00
FELLINI'S ROMA		
❑ United Artists UA-LA052-F	1972	30.00

Number Title	Yr	NM
THE FEMALE PRISONER		
❑ Columbia Masterworks OS3320	1969	30.00
FIDDLER ON THE ROOF		
❑ United Artists UAS-10900	1971	25.00
—With booklet		
55 DAYS AT PEKING		
❑ Columbia CL2028 [M]	1963	40.00
❑ Columbia CS8828 [S]	1963	80.00
THE FIGHTER		
❑ Decca DL5414 [10]	1952	100.00
THE FINAL COUNTDOWN		
❑ Casablanca NBLP-7232	1980	40.00
A FINE MESS		
❑ Motown 6180	1986	12.00
—Includes Los Lobos		
FINIAN'S RAINBOW		
❑ Warner Bros. BS2550	1968	25.00
FIRE DOWN BELOW		
❑ Decca DL8597 [M]	1957	80.00
FIRSTBORN		
❑ EMI America ST-517144	1984	15.00
—Includes Wang Chung, Talk Talk, Re-Flex; Columbia House edition		
❑ EMI America ST-17144	1984	12.00
—Includes Wang Chung, Talk Talk, Re-Flex		
A FISTFUL OF DOLLARS		
❑ RCA Victor LOC-1135 [M]	1967	25.00
❑ RCA Victor LSO-1135 [S]	1967	30.00
—Black label, dog on top		
❑ RCA Victor LSO-1135 [S]	1969	15.00
—Orange label, tan label, or black label with dog at 1 o'clock		
FITZWILLY		
❑ United Artists UAL-4173 [M]	1967	25.00
❑ United Artists UAS-5173 [S]	1967	30.00
FIVE EASY PIECES		
❑ Epic KE30456	1971	30.00
THE FIVE PENNIES		
❑ Dot DLP-9500 [M]	1959	175.00
❑ Dot DLP-29500 [S]	1959	250.00
THE FLAMINGO KID		
❑ Motown 6131ML	1984	12.00
—Commonly distributed issue		
❑ Varese Sarabande STV-81232	1984	40.00
—Original issue		
FLASHDANCE		
❑ Casablanca 811492-1	1983	12.00
A FLEA IN HER EAR		
❑ 20th Century Fox TFS-4200	1968	30.00
FLETCH		
❑ MCA 6142	1985	12.00
—Includes The Fixx, Kim Wilde		
FLOWER DRUM SONG		
❑ Decca DL9098 [M]	1961	25.00
❑ Decca DL79098 [S]	1961	30.00
❑ MCA 2069	1973	12.00
—Reissue; black label with rainbow		
THE FOG		
❑ Varese Sarabande STV-81191	1980	30.00
FOLIES BERGERE		
❑ Decca DL8571 [M]	1958	30.00
FOLLOW ME		
❑ Uni 73056	1969	30.00
FOOTLOOSE		
❑ Columbia JS39242	1984	12.00
❑ Columbia 9C939404 [PD]	1984	25.00
—Picture disc version		
FOR A FEW DOLLARS MORE		
❑ United Artists UAL-3608 [M]	1967	25.00
❑ United Artists UAS-6608 [S]	1967	30.00
FORBIDDEN ZONE		
❑ Varese Sarabande STV81170	1983	15.00
—Includes Oingo Boingo (as The Mystical Knights of the Oingo Boingo); composed by Danny Elfman		
FOR LOVE OF IVY		
❑ ABC SOC-7	1968	30.00
FOR THE FIRST TIME		
❑ RCA Victor Red Seal LSC-2338 [S]	1959	25.00
—"Shaded dog" and smaller "RCA Victor" lettering		
❑ RCA Victor Red Seal LSC-2338 [S]	1965	18.00
—"White dog" and larger "RCA Victor" lettering		
❑ RCA Victor Red Seal LSC-2338 [S]	1969	15.00
—Red label, no dog		
❑ RCA Victor Red Seal LM-2338 [M]	1959	18.00
40 POUNDS OF TROUBLE		
❑ Mercury MG-20784 [M]	1963	30.00
❑ Mercury SR-60784 [S]	1963	40.00

Number	Title	Yr	NM

FOR YOUR EYES ONLY
❏ Liberty LOO-1109 — 1981 — 30.00

THE FOUR HORSEMEN OF THE APOCALYPSE
❏ MGM E-3993 [M] — 1962 — 25.00
❏ MGM SE-3993 [S] — 1962 — 30.00

FOUR IN THE MORNING
❏ Roulette OS805 [M] — 1966 — 40.00
❏ Roulette OSS805 [S] — 1966 — 50.00

THE FOX
❏ Warner Bros. W1738 [M] — 1968 — 40.00
❏ Warner Bros. WS1738 [S] — 1968 — 30.00

THE FOX AND THE HOUND
❏ Disneyland 3106 [PD] — 1981 — 30.00
—*Disney Picture Disc" series*
❏ Disneyland ST-3823 — 1981 — 25.00
—*Non-picture disc version*

FOXY BROWN
❏ Motown M7-811 — 1974 — 25.00

FRANCIS OF ASSISI
❏ 20th Fox FOX-3053 [M] — 1961 — 250.00
❏ 20th Fox SFX-3053 [S] — 1961 — 300.00

THE FRENCH LINE
❏ Mercury MG-25182 [10] — 1954 — 100.00

FRIDAY
❏ Priority P1-53959 — 1995 — 18.00
—*Includes Ice Cube, Dr. Dre, other gangsta rappers*

FRIENDLY PERSUASION
❏ RKO Unique LP-110 [M] — 1956 — 85.00

FRIGHT NIGHT
❏ Private I SZ40087 — 1985 — 15.00
—*Includes Devo ("Let's Talk")*

FRITZ THE CAT
❏ Fantasy F-9406 — 1972 — 30.00

FROM RUSSIA WITH LOVE
❏ United Artists UAL-4114 [M] — 1964 — 25.00
❏ United Artists UAS-5114 [S] — 1964 — 30.00

THE FUGITIVE KIND
❏ United Artists UAL-4065 [M] — 1959 — 150.00
❏ United Artists UAS-5065 [S] — 1959 — 140.00

FUNERAL IN BERLIN
❏ RCA Victor LOC-1136 [M] — 1966 — 30.00
❏ RCA Victor LSO-1136 [S] — 1966 — 50.00

FUNNY GIRL
❏ Columbia Masterworks SQ30992 [Q] — 1971 — 50.00
❏ Columbia Masterworks BOS3220 — 1968 — 18.00
—*Gray "360 Sound" label; record is removed from inside the gatefold; liner notes on a black background*
❏ Columbia Masterworks BOS3220 — 1968 — 15.00
—*Gray "360 Sound" label; record is removed from inside the gatefold; liner notes on a tan background*
❏ Columbia Masterworks BOS3220 — 1970 — 12.00
—*Olive label with "Columbia" encircling the edge*

A FUNNY THING HAPPENED ON THE WAY TO THE FORUM
❏ United Artists UAL-4144 [M] — 1966 — 15.00
❏ United Artists UAS-5144 [S] — 1966 — 18.00
❏ United Artists UA-LA284-G — 1974 — 12.00
—*Reissue of 5144*

GAILY, GAILY
❏ United Artists UAS5202 — 1969 — 30.00

THE GAME IS OVER
❏ Atco 33-205 [M] — 1967 — 25.00
❏ Atco SD 33-205 [S] — 1967 — 30.00

THE GAMES
❏ Viking LPS-105 — 1970 — 250.00

GAY PURR-EE
❏ Warner Bros. B1479 [M] — 1963 — 25.00
❏ Warner Bros. BS1479 [S] — 1963 — 30.00

GEISHA BOY
❏ Jubilee JLP-1096 [M] — 1958 — 50.00
❏ Jubilee JGS-1096 [S] — 1959 — 100.00

THE GENE KRUPA STORY
❏ Verve MGV-15010 [M] — 1959 — 150.00
❏ Verve MGVS-6105 [S] — 1959 — 200.00
—*Original issue*
❏ Verve V6-15010 [S] — 1963 — 175.00
—*Early reissue*
❏ Verve V-15010 [M] — 1961 — 50.00

GENGHIS KHAN
❏ Liberty LRP-3412 [M] — 1965 — 40.00
❏ Liberty LST-7412 [S] — 1965 — 75.00

GENTLEMEN MARRY BRUNETTES
❏ Coral CRL57013 [M] — 1955 — 80.00

GENTLEMEN PREFER BLONDES
❏ MGM E-208 [M] — 1953 — 120.00

THE GENTLE RAIN
❏ Mercury MG-21016 [M] — 1966 — 150.00
❏ Mercury SR-61016 [S] — 1966 — 150.00

GET CRAZY
❏ Morocco 6065 — 1983 — 14.00
—*Includes Ramones, Marshall Crenshaw, Lou Reed, Fear*

GETTING STRAIGHT
❏ Colgems COSO-5010 — 1970 — 30.00

GET YOURSELF A COLLEGE GIRL
❏ MGM E-4273 [M] — 1965 — 25.00
❏ MGM SE-4273 [S] — 1965 — 40.00

GHOSTBUSTERS
❏ Arista AL8-8246 — 1984 — 18.00
—*First pressing has smaller print on front and eight photos on back*
❏ Arista AL8-8246 — 1984 — 12.00
—*Later pressings have large print on front and seven photos on back*

GHOSTBUSTERS II
❏ MCA R151964 — 1989 — 15.00
—*BMG Direct Marketing edition*
❏ MCA 6306 — 1989 — 12.00

GIANT
❏ Capitol W773 [M] — 1956 — 40.00
—*Turquoise or gray label*
❏ Capitol W773 [M] — 1959 — 30.00
—*Black colorband label, logo at left*
❏ Capitol W773 [M] — 1962 — 18.00
—*Black colorband label, logo at top*
❏ Capitol DW773 [R] — 196? — 15.00

GIDGET GOES HAWAIIAN
❏ Colpix CP418 [M] — 1961 — 50.00

GIGI
❏ MCA 39045 — 1986 — 10.00
—*Reissue*
❏ MGM W90523 [M] — 1965 — 15.00
—*Capitol Record Club edition*
❏ MGM SW90523 [S] — 1965 — 18.00
❏ MGM E-3641 [M] — 1958 — 25.00
—*Yellow label*
❏ MGM SE-3641 [S] — 1959 — 30.00
—*Yellow label*
❏ MGM E-3641 [M] — 1960 — 15.00
—*Black label*
❏ MGM SE-3641 [S] — 1960 — 18.00
—*Black label*
❏ MGM SE-3641 [S] — 1968 — 15.00
—*Blue and gold label*

GIGOT
❏ Capitol W1754 [M] — 1962 — 30.00
❏ Capitol SW1754 [S] — 1962 — 40.00

THE GIRL IN THE BIKINI
❏ Poplar PLP 33-1002 [M] — 1952 — 400.00

THE GIRL MOST LIKELY
❏ Capitol W930 [M] — 1957 — 75.00

GIRL ON A MOTORCYCLE
❏ Tetragrammaton T-5000 — 1969 — 30.00

GIRLS JUST WANT TO HAVE FUN
❏ Mercury 824510-1 — 1985 — 12.00
—*Includes Animotion*

THE GLENN MILLER STORY
❏ Decca DL5519 [10] — 1954 — 175.00
❏ Decca DL8226 [M] — 1956 — 175.00
❏ Decca DL9123 [M] — 196? — 50.00
—*Reissue of 8226*
❏ Decca DL79123 [R] — 196? — 35.00
❏ MCA 2036 — 1973 — 25.00
❏ MCA 1624 — 198? — 35.00
—*This reissue is a bit more desirable because it was issued in true stereo*

GLORY
❏ Virgin 91329 — 1989 — 30.00
❏ Virgin 91329 — 1998 — 25.00
—*Classic Records edition; audiophile reissue; cover is noticeably less sharp than the originals*

THE GLORY STOMPERS
❏ Sidewalk DT5910 [R] — 1968 — 50.00

GO, GO, GO WORLD
❏ Musicor MM-2059 [M] — 1965 — 40.00
❏ Musicor MS-3059 [S] — 1965 — 75.00

GO, JOHNNY, GO!
❏ (no label) (no number) [DJ] — 1959 — 1000.00
—*Only exists as a promo*

THE GODFATHER
❏ Paramount PAS-1003 — 1972 — 25.00
—*Original cover with triple gatefold*

THE GODFATHER PART II
❏ ABC ABDP-856 — 1975 — 25.00

THE GODFATHER PART III
❏ Columbia C47078 — 1990 — 25.00

GOD'S LITTLE ACRE
❏ United Artists UAL-4002 [M] — 1958 — 175.00

GOLD
❏ ABC ABCD-855 — 1975 — 30.00

GOLDEN BOY
❏ Colpix CP-478 [M] — 1964 — 50.00
❏ Colpix SCP-478 [S] — 1964 — 75.00

THE GOLDEN BREED
❏ Capitol ST2886 — 1967 — 30.00

THE GOLDEN CHILD
❏ Capitol SJ-12544 — 1986 — 12.00
—*Includes Martha Davis*

THE GOLDEN COACH
❏ MGM E-3111 [M] — 1954 — 175.00

THE GOLDEN SCREW
❏ Atco 33-208 [M] — 1967 — 30.00
❏ Atco SD 33-208 [S] — 1967 — 40.00

GOLDFINGER
❏ United Artists UAL-4117 [M] — 1964 — 18.00
❏ United Artists UAS-5117 [S] — 1964 — 25.00

GOLIATH AND THE BARBARIANS
❏ American Int'l. 1001-M [M] — 1960 — 40.00
❏ American Int'l. 1001#NAME? [S] — 1960 — 80.00

GONE WITH THE WAVE
❏ Colpix CP-492 [M] — 1965 — 40.00
❏ Colpix SCP-492 [S] — 1965 — 120.00

GONE WITH THE WIND
❏ MGM 1E-10 [M] — 1967 — 25.00
—*Gatefold edition with 32-page booklet*
❏ MGM S1E-10 [S] — 1967 — 25.00
—*Gatefold edition with 32-page booklet*

GOODBYE, CHARLIE
❏ 20th Century Fox TFM-3165 [M] — 1964 — 30.00
❏ 20th Century Fox TFS-4165 [S] — 1964 — 30.00

GOODBYE, MR. CHIPS
❏ MCA 39006 — 1986 — 10.00
—*Reissue*
❏ MGM 1SE-19 — 1969 — 25.00

GOODBYE AGAIN
❏ United Artists UAL-4091 [M] — 1961 — 30.00
❏ United Artists UAS-5091 [S] — 1961 — 40.00

GOOD MORNING, VIETNAM
❏ A&M R154001 — 1987 — 15.00
—*Includes The Searchers; BMG Direct Marketing edition*

GOOD NEWS
❏ MGM E-504 [10] — 1950 — 50.00

THE GOONIES
❏ Epic SE40067 — 1985 — 12.00
—*Includes Cyndi Lauper (2), Bangles*

GORDON'S WAR
❏ Buddah BDS-5137 — 1973 — 40.00

THE GOSPEL ACCORDING TO ST. MATTHEW
❏ Mainstream 54000 [M] — 1966 — 30.00
❏ Mainstream S-4000 [S] — 1966 — 150.00

GOTCHA!
❏ MCA Curb 5596 — 1985 — 15.00
—*Includes Joan Jett and the Blackhearts, Bronski Beat*

GOTHIC
❏ Virgin 90607 — 1987 — 25.00

GOYA
❏ Decca DL8236 [M] — 1959 — 175.00

THE GRADUATE
❏ CBS Masterworks JS3180 [S] — 198? — 10.00
—*CBS Masterworks" replaces "Columbia" along outer edge of label*
❏ Columbia Masterworks OS3180 [S] — 1968 — 15.00
—*Original stereo edition: Gray label, "360 Sound Stereo" in white*
❏ Columbia Masterworks OL6780 [M] — 1968 — 50.00
—*Mono" on label*
❏ Columbia Masterworks OS3180 [S] — 1971 — 12.00
—*Olive label, "Columbia" along outer edge*
❏ Columbia Masterworks JS3180 [S] — 197? — 10.00
—*Reissue with new prefix*

GRAND PRIX
❏ MGM 1E-8 [M] — 1967 — 25.00
❏ MGM 1SE-8 [S] — 1967 — 30.00

THE GREAT ESCAPE
❏ United Artists UAL-4107 [M] — 1963 — 30.00
❏ United Artists UAS-5107 [S] — 1963 — 30.00

THE GREATEST SHOW ON EARTH
❏ RCA Victor LPM-3018 [10] — 1952 — 250.00

THE GREATEST STORY EVER TOLD
❏ United Artists UAL-4120 [M] — 1965 — 30.00
❏ United Artists UAS-5120 [S] — 1965 — 30.00

THE GREAT GATSBY
❏ Paramount 2-3001 — 1974 — 25.00

Number	Title	Yr	NM

THE GREAT OUTDOORS
❏ Atlantic 81859 — 1988 — 12.00
— *Includes Pop Will Eat Itself*

GREMLINS
❏ Geffen GHSP24044 [EP] — 1984 — 12.00
— *Includes Peter Gabriel*

GROUNDS FOR MARRIAGE
❏ MGM E-536 [M] — 1950 — 100.00

GUESS WHO'S COMING TO DINNER
❏ Colgems COM-108 [M] — 1968 — 30.00
❏ Colgems COS-108 [S] — 1968 — 30.00

GULLIVER'S TRAVELS BEYOND THE MOON
❏ Mainstream 54001 [M] — 1965 — 30.00
❏ Mainstream S-4001 [S] — 1965 — 40.00

GUNS FOR SAN SEBASTIAN
❏ MGM SE-4565 — 1968 — 75.00

THE GUNS OF NAVARONE
❏ Columbia CL1655 [M] — 1961 — 25.00
❏ Columbia CS8455 [S] — 1961 — 50.00

GURU
❏ RCA Victor LSO-1158 — 1969 — 25.00

GYPSY
❏ Warner Bros. B1480 [M] — 1962 — 25.00
❏ Warner Bros. BS1480 [S] — 1962 — 30.00

GYPSY GIRL
❏ Mainstream 56090 [M] — 1966 — 30.00
❏ Mainstream S-6090 [S] — 1966 — 40.00

HALLELUJAH THE HILLS
❏ Fontana MGF-27524 [M] — 1964 — 30.00
❏ Fontana SRF-67524 [S] — 1964 — 30.00

THE HALLELUJAH TRAIL
❏ United Artists UAL-4127 [M] — 1965 — 25.00
❏ United Artists UAS-5127 [S] — 1965 — 30.00

HAMMERHEAD
❏ Colgems COS-110 — 1968 — 40.00

HAMMERSMITH IS OUT
❏ Capitol SW-861 — 1972 — 30.00

HANG 'EM HIGH
❏ United Artists UAS-5179 — 1968 — 30.00

THE HAPPENING
❏ Colgems COMO-5006 [M] — 1967 — 30.00
❏ Colgems COSO-5006 [S] — 1967 — 50.00

THE HAPPIEST MILLIONAIRE
❏ Buena Vista BV-5001 [M] — 1967 — 18.00
❏ Buena Vista STER-5001 [S] — 1967 — 25.00

HARD COUNTRY
❏ Epic SE37367 — 1981 — 12.00

THE HARD RIDE
❏ Paramount PAS-6005 — 1971 — 30.00

HARPER
❏ Mainstream 56078 [M] — 1966 — 25.00
❏ Mainstream S-6078 [S] — 1966 — 30.00

THE HARRAD EXPERIMENT
❏ Capitol ST-11182 — 1973 — 30.00

HARRAD SUMMER
❏ Capitol ST-11338 — 1974 — 30.00

HAWAII
❏ United Artists UAL-4143 [M] — 1966 — 25.00
❏ United Artists UAS-5143 [S] — 1966 — 30.00
❏ United Artists SW-90935 [S] — 1966 — 30.00
— *Capitol Record Club issue*

THE HEART IS A LONELY HUNTER
❏ Warner Bros. WS1759 — 1968 — 30.00

HEART OF DIXIE
❏ A&M SP-3930 — 1989 — 25.00

HEAVENLY BODIES
❏ Private I SZ39930 — 1985 — 12.00
— *Includes The Tubes*

HEAVENLY BODIES SAMPLER
❏ Private I AS1965 [DJ] — 1984 — 10.00
— *Includes The Tubes; promo-only 4-song sampler*

HEAVY METAL
❏ Full Moon/Asylum DP-90004 — 1981 — 25.00
— *Contains two LPs of pop/rock music*

HEAVY METAL, THE SCORE
❏ Full Moon/Asylum 5E-547 — 1981 — 50.00
— *Contains Elmer Bernstein's instrumental music*

HEAVY TRAFFIC
❏ Fantasy F-9436 — 1973 — 75.00

HEIDI'S SONG
❏ K-Tel NU5310 — 1982 — 25.00

THE HELEN MORGAN STORY
❏ RCA Victor LOC-1030 [M] — 1957 — 75.00

HELLCATS
❏ Tower ST5124 — 1968 — 30.00

HELLO-GOODBYE
❏ 20th Century Fox S-4210 — 1970 — 40.00

HELL'S ANGELS '69
❏ Capitol SKAO-303 — 1969 — 30.00

HELL'S ANGELS ON WHEELS
❏ Smash MGS-27094 [M] — 1967 — 30.00
❏ Smash SRS-67094 [S] — 1967 — 30.00

HELL'S BELLS
❏ Sidewalk ST5919 — 1969 — 30.00

HELL TO ETERNITY
❏ Warwick W2030 [M] — 1960 — 250.00
❏ Warwick WST2030 [S] — 1960 — 250.00

HELL UP IN HARLEM
❏ Motown M802V1 — 1974 — 30.00

HEMINGWAY'S ADVENTURES OF A YOUNG MAN
❏ RCA Victor LOC-1074 [M] — 1962 — 40.00
❏ RCA Victor LSO-1074 [S] — 1962 — 80.00

HERCULES
❏ Varese Sarabande STV-81187 — 1983 — 25.00

THE HERO
❏ Capitol SW-11098 — 1972 — 25.00

A HERO AIN'T NOTHIN' BUT A SANDWICH
❏ Columbia PS35046 — 1978 — 25.00

HEROES OF TELEMARK
❏ Mainstream 56064 [M] — 1965 — 25.00
❏ Mainstream S-6064 [S] — 1965 — 30.00

HEY, LET'S TWIST
❏ Roulette R-25168 [M] — 1962 — 30.00
❏ Roulette SR-25168 [S] — 1962 — 30.00

HEY THERE, IT'S YOGI BEAR!
❏ Colpix CP-472 [M] — 1964 — 50.00
❏ Colpix SCP-472 [S] — 1964 — 100.00

HIDING OUT
❏ Virgin R163706 — 1987 — 12.00
— *Includes Pretty Poison ("Catch Me I'm Falling"), Boy George ("Live My Life"); Public Image Ltd. ("Seattle")*
❏ Virgin 90661 — 1987 — 10.00
— *Includes Pretty Poison ("Catch Me I'm Falling"), Boy George ("Live My Life"); Public Image Ltd. ("Seattle")*

HIGH SOCIETY
❏ Capitol W750 [M] — 1956 — 30.00
— *Gray label original*
❏ Capitol W750 [M] — 1959 — 25.00
— *Black colorband label, logo at left*
❏ Capitol W750 [M] — 1962 — 18.00
— *Black colorband label, logo at top*
❏ Capitol SW750 [S] — 1959 — 30.00
— *Black colorband label, logo at left*
❏ Capitol SW750 [S] — 1962 — 25.00
— *Black colorband label, logo at top*

THE HOBBIT
❏ Buena Vista 103 — 1977 — 30.00
❏ Buena Vista 103A — 1977 — 40.00
— *Special edition sold at Sears stores, with four decals and poster*
❏ Disneyland ST-3819 — 1978 — 30.00

HOLIDAY INN
❏ Decca DL4256 — 1962 — 30.00
❏ MCA 25205 — 1987 — 10.00
— *Reissue of Decca LP*

HOMER AND EDDIE
❏ Apache D1-71654 — 1989 — 30.00

HONKYTONK MAN
❏ Warner Bros. 23739 — 1982 — 12.00

HOOSIERS
❏ Polydor 831475-1 — 1987 — 30.00

HOOTENANNY HOOT
❏ MGM E-4172 [M] — 1963 — 25.00
❏ MGM SE-4172 [S] — 1963 — 30.00

THE HORSEMEN
❏ Sunflower SNF-5007 — 1971 — 40.00

THE HORSE SOLDIERS
❏ United Artists UAL-4035 [M] — 1959 — 75.00
❏ United Artists UAS-5035 [S] — 1959 — 175.00

HOTEL PARADISO
❏ MGM E-4419 [M] — 1966 — 25.00
❏ MGM SE-4419 [S] — 1966 — 30.00

THE HOT ROCK
❏ Prophesy SD8055 — 1972 — 25.00

HOT ROD RUMBLE
❏ Liberty LRP-3048 [M] — 1957 — 175.00

THE HOUR OF THE GUN
❏ United Artists UAL-4166 [M] — 1967 — 40.00
❏ United Artists UAS-5166 [S] — 1967 — 80.00

HOUSEBOAT
❏ Columbia CL1222 [M] — 1958 — 50.00

A HOUSE IS NOT A HOME
❏ Ava A-50 [M] — 1964 — 30.00
❏ Ava AS-50 [S] — 1964 — 30.00

HOUSE PARTY
❏ Motown 9296 — 1990 — 15.00
— *Includes L.L. Cool J, Flavor Flav (of Public Enemy)*

HOWARD THE DUCK
❏ MCA 6173 — 1986 — 25.00

HOW SWEET IT IS
❏ RCA Victor LSP-4037 — 1968 — 25.00

HOW THE WEST WAS WON
❏ MCA 39043 — 1986 — 10.00
— *Reissue*
❏ MGM 1E-5 [M] — 1963 — 18.00
❏ MGM 1SE-5 [S] — 1963 — 25.00

HOW TO BEAT THE HIGH COST OF LIVING
❏ Columbia JS36741 — 1981 — 35.00

HOW TO MURDER YOUR WIFE
❏ United Artists UAL-4119 [M] — 1965 — 18.00
❏ United Artists UAS-5119 [S] — 1965 — 25.00

HOW TO SAVE A MARRIAGE AND RUIN YOUR LIFE
❏ Columbia Masterworks OS3140 — 1968 — 25.00

HOW TO STEAL A MILLION
❏ 20th Century Fox TFM-3183 [M] — 1966 — 40.00
❏ 20th Century Fox TFS-4183 [S] — 1966 — 50.00

HOW TO STUFF A WILD BIKINI
❏ Wand 671 [M] — 1965 — 30.00
❏ Wand S-671 [S] — 1965 — 40.00

HOW TO SUCCEED IN BUSINESS WITHOUT REALLY TRYING
❏ United Artists UAL-4151 [M] — 1967 — 25.00
❏ United Artists UAS-5151 [S] — 1967 — 30.00

HUGO THE HIPPO
❏ United Artists UA-LA637-G — 1976 — 25.00

THE HUNGER
❏ Varese Sarabande STV-81184 — 1984 — 15.00
— *Includes David Bowie*
❏ Varese Sarabande STV-81184 — 1983 — 25.00

THE HUNT FOR RED OCTOBER
❏ MCA 6428 — 1990 — 30.00

HURRICANE
❏ Elektra 5E-504 — 1979 — 25.00

HURRY SUNDOWN
❏ RCA Victor LOC-1133 [M] — 1967 — 30.00
❏ RCA Victor LSO-1133 [S] — 1967 — 40.00

THE HUSTLER
❏ Kapp KL-1264 [M] — 1961 — 75.00
❏ Kapp KS-3264 [S] — 1961 — 120.00

ICEMAN
❏ Southern Cross SCRS-1006 — 1983 — 25.00

ICE STATION ZEBRA
❏ MGM S1E-14ST — 1968 — 40.00

IF HE HOLLERS, LET HIM GO
❏ Tower ST5152 — 1968 — 40.00

I'LL NEVER FORGET WHAT'S 'IS NAME
❏ Decca DL9163 [M] — 1967 — 30.00
❏ Decca DL79163 [S] — 1967 — 30.00

I LOVE MELVIN
❏ MGM E-190 [10] — 1953 — 50.00

I'M GONNA GIT YOU SUCKA
❏ Arista AL-8574 — 1988 — 12.00
— *Includes Fishbone (with Curtis Mayfield)*

IMITATION OF LIFE
❏ Decca DL8879 [M] — 1959 — 50.00
❏ Decca DL78879 [S] — 1959 — 100.00

IN A SHALLOW GRAVE
❏ Varese Sarabande STV-81359 — 1988 — 40.00

INCHON
❏ Regency RI-8502 — 1982 — 30.00

INDIANA JONES AND THE TEMPLE OF DOOM
❏ Polydor 821592-1 — 1984 — 25.00

THE INDISCRETION OF AN AMERICAN WIFE
❏ Columbia CL6277 [10] — 1954 — 100.00

I NEVER SANG FOR MY FATHER
❏ Bell 1204 — 1970 — 40.00

IN HARM'S WAY
❏ RCA Victor LOC-1100 [M] — 1965 — 40.00
❏ RCA Victor LSO-1100 [S] — 1965 — 100.00

IN LIKE FLINT
❏ 20th Century Fox 4193 [M] — 1967 — 40.00
❏ 20th Century Fox S-4193 [S] — 1967 — 100.00

INNERSPACE
❏ Geffen GHS24161 — 1987 — 12.00
— *Includes Wang Chung, Berlin*

Number / Title	Yr	NM
THE INN OF THE SIXTH HAPPINESS		
❏ 20th Century Fox FOX-3011 [M]	1958	50.00
❏ 20th Century Fox SFX-3011 [S]	1958	80.00
IN SEARCH OF THE CASTAWAYS		
❏ Disneyland ST-3916 [M]	1962	80.00
INSIDE DAISY CLOVER		
❏ Warner Bros. W1616 [M]	1965	25.00
❏ Warner Bros. WS1616 [S]	1965	30.00
INSPECTOR CLOUSEAU		
❏ MCA 25107	1986	10.00
—Reissue		
❏ United Artists UAS-5186	1968	30.00
INTERLUDE		
❏ Colgems COSO-5007	1968	40.00
THE INTERNS		
❏ Colpix CP427 [M]	1962	75.00
❏ Colpix SCP427 [S]	1962	40.00
IN THE GOOD OLD SUMMERTIME		
❏ MGM E-169 [10]	1949	150.00
IN THE HEAT OF THE NIGHT		
❏ United Artists UAL-4160 [M]	1967	18.00
❏ United Artists UAS-5160 [S]	1967	25.00
INVITATION TO THE DANCE		
❏ MGM E-3207 [M]	1956	50.00
THE IPCRESS FILE		
❏ Decca DL9124 [M]	1965	30.00
❏ Decca DL79124 [S]	1965	40.00
IRMA LA DOUCE		
❏ United Artists UAL-4109 [M]	1963	25.00
❏ United Artists UAS-5109 [S]	1963	30.00
THE ISLAND		
❏ Varese Sarabande VC-81147	1979	25.00
THE ISLAND AT THE TOP OF THE WORLD		
❏ Disneyland ST-3814	1974	30.00
ISLAND IN THE SKY		
❏ Decca DL7029 [10]	1953	300.00
IS PARIS BURNING?		
❏ Columbia Masterworks OL6630 [M]	1966	30.00
❏ Columbia Masterworks OS3030 [S]	1966	40.00
THE ITALIAN JOB		
❏ Paramount PAS-5007	1969	40.00
IT'S ALWAYS FAIR WEATHER		
❏ MCA 25018	1986	12.00
—Reissue		
❏ MGM E-3241 [M]	1955	50.00
IT'S A MAD, MAD, MAD, MAD WORLD		
❏ MCA 39076	198?	10.00
—Reissue of United Artists 276		
❏ United Artists UAL-4110 [M]	1963	25.00
❏ United Artists UAS-5110 [S]	1963	30.00
❏ United Artists UA-LA276-G	1974	12.00
—Reissue of 5110		
IT STARTED IN NAPLES		
❏ Dot DLP-3324 [M]	1960	75.00
❏ Dot DLP-25324 [S]	1960	150.00
❏ Varese Sarabande STV-81122	1982	18.00
—Reissue of Dot 25324		
I WANT TO LIVE		
❏ United Artists UAL-4005 [M]	1958	75.00
—Orchestral music by Johnny Mandel		
❏ United Artists UAS-4005 [S]	1958	40.00
—Orchestral music by Johnny Mandel		
❏ United Artists UAL-4006 [M]	1958	75.00
—Jazz music by Gerry Mulligan, Shelly Manne and Art Farmer		
❏ United Artists UAS-4006 [S]	1958	40.00
—Jazz music by Gerry Mulligan, Shelly Mann and Art Farmer		
❏ United Artists UXL1 [M]	1958	120.00
—Combines 4005 and 4006 into one package		
❏ United Artists UXS51 [S]	1958	175.00
—Combines 5005 and 5006 into one package		
I WAS A TEENAGE ZOMBIE		
❏ Enigma SJ-73296	1987	15.00
—Includes The Fleshtones, The Del Fuegos, the dB's, The Dream Syndicate, Violent Femmes, The Waitresses, The Smithereens, Los Lobos		
JACK THE RIPPER		
❏ RCA Victor LPM-2199 [M]	1960	30.00
❏ RCA Victor LSP-2199 [S]	1960	50.00
JAMBOREE!		
❏ Warner Bros. (no #) [M]	1957	1200.00
—Album has been counterfeited. Originals have front cover slicks and back cover notes printed on the cardboard, and the records have "Jam 1" and "Jam 2" stamped (not etched) in the dead wax.		
THE JAMES DEAN STORY		
❏ Capitol W881 [M]	1957	250.00
❏ Kimberly 2016 [M]	1960	40.00
❏ Kimberly 11016 [S]	1960	250.00
—Reissue of World Pacific 2005		
❏ World Pacific P-2005 [M]	1958	300.00

Number / Title	Yr	NM
JAWS		
❏ MCA 2087	1975	25.00
❏ MCA 1660	198?	10.00
—Reissue of 2087		
JEAN DE FLORETTE		
❏ TVT 3004	1986	25.00
JEREMIAH JOHNSON		
❏ Warner Bros. BS2902	1972	25.00
—Green label		
JESSICA		
❏ United Artists UAL-4096 [M]	1962	25.00
❏ United Artists UAS-5096 [S]	1962	30.00
THE JOE LOUIS STORY		
❏ MGM E-221 [10]	1953	100.00
JOHNNY COOL		
❏ United Artists UAL-4111 [M]	1963	25.00
❏ United Artists UAS-5111 [S]	1963	30.00
JOHNNY TREMAIN		
❏ Disneyland WDL-4014 [M]	1957	50.00
JOHN PAUL JONES		
❏ Varese Sarabande STV-81146	1981	18.00
—Reissue of Warner Bros. WS 1293		
❏ Warner Bros. W1293 [M]	1959	75.00
❏ Warner Bros. WS1293 [S]	1959	120.00
JUD		
❏ Ampex A-50101	1971	25.00
JUDGMENT AT NUREMBERG		
❏ MCA 39055	198?	12.00
—Reissue of United Artists 5095		
❏ United Artists UAL-4095 [M]	1961	25.00
❏ United Artists UAS-5095 [S]	1961	50.00
JUDITH		
❏ RCA Victor LOC-1119 [M]	1966	18.00
❏ RCA Victor LSO-1119 [S]	1966	30.00
JUICE		
❏ MCA 10577	1992	12.00
—Includes Naughty By Nature, others; issude in generic sleeve with sticker		
JULIET OF THE SPIRITS		
❏ Mainstream 56062 [M]	1965	30.00
❏ Mainstream S-6062 [S]	1965	75.00
JULIUS CAESAR		
❏ MGM E-3033 [M]	1953	40.00
JUMBO (BILLY ROSE'S)		
❏ Columbia Masterworks OL5860 [M]	1962	25.00
❏ Columbia Masterworks OS2260 [S]	1962	30.00
JUMPIN' JACK FLASH		
❏ Mercury 830545-1	1986	12.00
—Includes Bananarama		
THE JUNGLE BOOK		
❏ Buena Vista BV-4041 [M]	1967	18.00
❏ Buena Vista STER-4041 [S]	1967	30.00
❏ Disneyland 3105 [PD]	1981	30.00
—Disney Picture Disc" series		
JURASSIC PARK		
❏ MCA/BMG (no #) [PD]	1993	1500.00
—Custom-made picture disc; promo only		
JUSTINE		
❏ Monument SLP-18123	1969	30.00
JUST ONE OF THE GUYS		
❏ Elektra 60426	1985	12.00
—Includes Berlin		
KALEIDOSCOPE		
❏ Warner Bros. W1663 [M]	1966	25.00
❏ Warner Bros. WS1663 [S]	1966	30.00
THE KARATE KID		
❏ Casablanca 822213-1	1984	15.00
—Includes The Flirts (with Jan & Dean), Gang of Four		
KELLY'S HEROES		
❏ MGM S1E-23	1970	30.00
THE KEY		
❏ Columbia CL1185 [M]	1958	100.00
KILLERS THREE		
❏ Tower ST-5141	1968	25.00
THE KING AND I		
❏ Capitol W740 [M]	1956	30.00
—Gray label		
❏ Capitol W740 [M]	1959	18.00
—Black colorband label, logo at left		
❏ Capitol W740 [M]	1962	15.00
—Black colorband label, logo at top		
❏ Capitol SW740 [S]	1959	25.00
—Black colorband label, logo at left		
❏ Capitol SW740 [S]	1962	18.00
—Black colorband label, logo at top		
❏ Capitol SW740 [S]	1969	15.00
—Lime green label		

Number / Title	Yr	NM
❏ Capitol SW740 [S]	1973	12.00
—Orange label		
❏ Capitol SW740 [S]	1978	10.00
—Purple label		
KING KONG		
❏ Reprise MS2260	1976	25.00
KING KONG LIVES		
❏ MCA 6203	1987	30.00
THE KING OF COMEDY		
❏ Warner Bros. 23765	1983	12.00
—Includes The Pretenders ("Back on the Chain Gang"), Talking Heads, Ric Ocasek		
KING OF KINGS		
❏ MCA 39056	198?	10.00
—Reissue of MGM S1E-2		
❏ MGM 1E-2 [M]	1961	30.00
—Boxed version with hardbound book and four 8x10 photos		
❏ MGM S1E-2 [S]	1961	40.00
—Boxed version with hardbound book and four 8x10 photos		
❏ MGM 1E-2 [M]	1961	18.00
—Standard cover		
❏ MGM S1E-2 [S]	1961	25.00
—Standard cover		
KING RAT		
❏ Mainstream 56061 [M]	1965	30.00
❏ Mainstream S-6061 [S]	1965	50.00
KINGS GO FORTH		
❏ Capitol W1063 [M]	1958	175.00
KING SOLOMON'S MINES		
❏ Restless 72106	1985	25.00
KISMET		
❏ MCA 1424	198?	10.00
—Reissue of MGM 3281		
❏ Metro M-526 [M]	1965	15.00
—Reissue of MGM E-3281 with one fewer track		
❏ Metro MS-526 [R]	1955	12.00
—Rechanneled reissue of MGM E-3281 with one fewer track		
❏ MGM E-3281 [M]	1955	25.00
—Yellow label		
❏ MGM E-3281 [M]	1960	18.00
—Black label		
KISS ME, KATE		
❏ MCA 25003	1986	12.00
—Reissue of MGM 3077		
❏ Metro M-525 [M]	1965	15.00
—Reissue of MGM 3077, but with only 10 songs		
❏ Metro MS-525 [R]	1965	12.00
—Rechanneled reissue of MGM 3077, but with only 10 songs		
❏ MGM E-3077 [M]	1953	25.00
—Yellow label		
❏ MGM E-3077 [M]	1959	18.00
—Black label		
KRULL		
❏ Southern Cross SCRS-1004	1983	25.00
KRUSH GROOVE		
❏ Warner Bros. 25295	1985	12.00
—Includes Beastie Boys, L.L. Cool J, Krush Groove All-Stars, Debbie Harry		
KWAMINA		
❏ Mercury MG-20654 [M]	1961	150.00
❏ Mercury SR-60654 [S]	1961	150.00
LA BAMBA		
❏ Slash/Warner Bros. R120062	1987	15.00
—BMG Direct Marketing version		
❏ Slash/Warner Bros. 25605	1987	12.00
LABYRINTH		
❏ EMI America SV-17206	1986	25.00
—Includes David Bowie		
LADY AND THE TRAMP		
❏ Decca DL5557 [10]	1955	75.00
❏ Decca DL8462 [M]	1957	80.00
❏ Disneyland 3103 [PD]	1981	30.00
—Disney Picture Disc" edition		
LADYHAWKE		
❏ Atlantic 81248	1985	25.00
THE LANDLORD		
❏ United Artists UAS-5209	1970	25.00
THE LAST AMERICAN VIRGIN		
❏ Columbia JS38279	1982	40.00
THE LAST EMBRACE		
❏ Varese Sarabande STV-81166	1983	25.00
THE LAST EMPEROR		
❏ Virgin 90690	1987	12.00
—One side of music by David Byrne		
THE LAST OF THE SECRET AGENTS		
❏ Dot DLP-3714 [M]	1966	25.00
❏ Dot DLP-25714 [S]	1966	30.00

Number	Title	Yr	NM

THE LAST RUN
❑ MCA 25116 — 1986 — 10.00
— *Reissue of MGM 1SE-30*
❑ MGM 1SE-30 — 1971 — 30.00

THE LAST STARFIGHTER
❑ Southern Cross SCRS-1007 — 1984 — 30.00

LAST SUMMER
❑ Warner Bros. WS1791 — 1969 — 25.00

THE LAST VALLEY
❑ ABC-Dunhill DSX-50102 — 1971 — 40.00

LAWRENCE OF ARABIA
❑ Arista ABM-4009 — 1975 — 12.00
— *Reissue of Bell 1205*
❑ Bell 1205 — 1971 — 12.00
— *Reissue of Colgems COSO-5004*
❑ Colgems COMO-5004 [M] — 1967 — 15.00
— *Reissue of Colpix CP-514*
❑ Colgems COSO-5004 [S] — 1967 — 18.00
— *Reissue of Colpix SCP-514*
❑ Colpix CP-514 [M] — 1962 — 25.00
❑ Colpix SCP-514 [S] — 1962 — 30.00

LEAN ON ME
❑ Warner Bros. 25843 — 1987 — 12.00
— *Includes Guns N' Roses ("Welcome to the Jungle")*

LENNY
❑ United Artists UA-LA359#NAME? — 1974 — 50.00

THE LEOPARD
❑ 20th Century Fox FXG-5015 [M] — 1963 — 30.00
❑ 20th Century Fox SXG-5015 [S] — 1963 — 40.00
❑ Varese Sarabande STV-81190 — 1982 — 18.00
— *Reissue of 20th Century Fox SXG-5015*

LES LIAISONS DANGEREUSES
❑ Charlie Parker PLP-813 [M] — 1962 — 75.00
❑ Charlie Parker PLP-813S [S] — 1962 — 75.00
❑ Epic LA16022 [M] — 1961 — 100.00
❑ Epic BA17022 [S] — 1961 — 150.00
❑ Fontana MGF-27539 [M] — 1965 — 50.00
❑ Fontana SRF-67539 [R] — 1965 — 35.00

LESS THAN ZERO
❑ Def Jam SC44042 — 1987 — 12.00
— *Includes Bangles, Joan Jett and the Blackhearts, Glenn Danzig, Publ;ic Enemy, L.L. Cool J, Oran "Juice" Jones*

LETHAL WEAPON
❑ Warner Bros. 25561 — 1987 — 12.00
— *Includes Honeymoon Suite*

LET'S MAKE LOVE
❑ Columbia CL1527 [M] — 1960 — 30.00
❑ Columbia CS8327 [S] — 1960 — 50.00

LETTER TO BREZHNEV
❑ MCA/London 6162 — 1985 — 12.00
— *Includes Fine Young Cannibals, Bronski Beat*

LET THE GOOD TIMES ROLL
❑ Bell 9002 — 1973 — 30.00

LEVIATHAN
❑ Varese Sarabande VS-5226 — 1989 — 25.00

THE LIFE AND TIMES OF JUDGE ROY BEAN
❑ Columbia Masterworks S31948 — 1972 — 30.00

LIFEFORCE
❑ Varese Sarabande STV-81249 — 1985 — 30.00

LIGHT FANTASTIC
❑ 20th Century Fox FXG-5016 [M] — 1963 — 25.00
❑ 20th Century Fox SXG-5016 [S] — 1963 — 30.00

LIGHT OF DAY
❑ Blackheart SZ40654 — 1986 — 15.00
— *Includes The Barbusters (Joan Jett and the Blackhearts), Dave Edmunds*

LI'L ABNER
❑ Columbia Masterworks OL5460 [M] — 1959 — 30.00
— *Credits within photo*
❑ Columbia Masterworks OL5460 [M] — 196? — 25.00
— *Credits in red strip at bottom of photo*
❑ Columbia Masterworks OS2021 [S] — 1959 — 40.00
— *Credits within photo*
❑ Columbia Masterworks OS2021 [S] — 196? — 30.00
— *Credits in red strip at bottom of photo*

LILIES OF THE FIELD
❑ Epic LN24094 [M] — 1964 — 25.00
❑ Epic BN26094 [S] — 1964 — 30.00

THE LION
❑ London M-76001 [M] — 1962 — 400.00

LIONHEART
❑ Varese Sarabande STV-81304 — 1987 — 25.00

LIONHEART (MORE MUSIC FROM THE FILM)
❑ Varese Sarabande STV-81311 — 1987 — 50.00

THE LION IN WINTER
❑ Columbia Masterworks OS3250 — 1969 — 25.00

LITTLE BIG MAN
❑ Columbia Masterworks S30545 — 1970 — 25.00

LITTLE SHOP OF HORRORS
❑ Geffen GHS-24125 — 1986 — 25.00

LIVE AND LET DIE
❑ Liberty LMAS-100 — 1981 — 15.00
— *Gray label; reissue of United Artists 100 with gatefold cover*
❑ Liberty LT-50100 — 1982 — 15.00
— *Gray label; reissue of Liberty 100 with standard cover*
❑ United Artists UA-LA100-G — 1973 — 25.00
— *Tan label; cover corner is not clipped off*
❑ United Artists SWAO-95120 — 1973 — 30.00
— *Longines (formerly Capitol) Record Club edition*
❑ United Artists UA-LA100-G — 1973 — 12.00
— *Tan label; cover corner is clipped*
❑ United Artists UA-LA100-G — 1977 — 12.00
— *Sunrise" label with this number on both jacket and label*
❑ United Artists LMAS-100 — 1979 — 12.00
— *Sunrise" label with this number on label (jacket still has UA-LA100-G)*

LIVE FOR LIFE
❑ United Artists UAL-4165 [M] — 1967 — 25.00
❑ United Artists UAS-5165 [S] — 1967 — 25.00

THE LIVELY SET
❑ Decca DL9119 [M] — 1964 — 30.00
❑ Decca DL79119 [S] — 1964 — 40.00

LOGAN'S RUN
❑ MGM MG-1-5302 — 1976 — 30.00

LOLITA
❑ MCA 39067 — 198? — 10.00
— *Reissue of MGM SE-4050*
❑ MGM E-4050 [M] — 1962 — 25.00
❑ MGM SE-4050 [S] — 1962 — 30.00

THE LOLLIPOP COVER
❑ Mainstream 56067 [M] — 1966 — 25.00
❑ Mainstream S-6067 [S] — 1966 — 30.00

THE LONGEST DAY
❑ 20th Century Fox FXG-5007 [M] — 1962 — 25.00
❑ 20th Century Fox SXG-5007 [S] — 1962 — 30.00

THE LONG HOT SUMMER
❑ Roulette R-25026 [M] — 1958 — 85.00

LONG JOHN SILVER
❑ RCA Victor LPM-3279 [10] — 1954 — 300.00

THE LONG SHIPS
❑ Colpix CP-517 [M] — 1964 — 50.00
❑ Colpix SCP-517 [S] — 1964 — 75.00

LORD JIM
❑ Colpix CP-521 [M] — 1965 — 30.00
❑ Colpix SCP-521 [S] — 1965 — 40.00

LORD LOVE A DUCK
❑ United Artists UAL-4137 [M] — 1966 — 25.00
❑ United Artists UAS-5137 [S] — 1966 — 30.00

THE LORD OF THE RINGS
❑ Fantasy LOR-1 — 1978 — 25.00
❑ Fantasy LOR-PD2 — 1978 — 30.00
— *Two picture discs*

THE LORDS OF FLATBUSH
❑ ABC ABCD-828 — 1974 — 30.00

A LOSS OF INNOCENCE
❑ Colpix CP-508 [M] — 1961 — 40.00

LOST ANGELS
❑ A&M SP-3926 — 1989 — 15.00
— *Includes The Cure, Soundgarden, The Pogues, Soul Ayslum, Happy Mondays*

THE LOST BOYS
❑ Atlantic 81767 — 1987 — 12.00
— *Includes INXS and Jimmy Barnes, Echo and the Bunnymen*

THE LOST CONTINENT
❑ MGM E-3635 [M] — 1957 — 250.00

LOVE IN 4 DIMENSIONS
❑ Request RLP-8090 [M] — 1966 — 30.00
❑ Request SRLP-8090 [S] — 1966 — 30.00

LOVE LIFE
❑ Heritage 600 [M] — 195? — 75.00

LOVERS AND OTHER STRANGERS
❑ ABC ABCS-OC-15 — 1970 — 25.00
❑ ABC SW-93479 — 1971 — 30.00
— *Capitol Record Club edition*

M*A*S*H
❑ Columbia Masterworks OS3520 — 1970 — 50.00
— *Original copies do not have the theme song done by Ahmad Jamal*
❑ Columbia Masterworks S32753 — 1973 — 25.00
— *Reissue with the movie's theme performed by Ahmad Jamal*

MACARTHUR
❑ MCA 2287 — 1977 — 25.00

THE MAD ADVENTURES OF RABBI JACOB
❑ London PS652 — 1974 — 25.00
— *Cover is intact with no cut-out markings*
❑ London PS652 — 1974 — 12.00
— *Cover has cut-out markings (usually a hole punch or a cut-off corner)*

MADAME BOVARY
❑ MGM E-3507 [M] — 195? — 175.00

MADE IN USA
❑ Chrysalis OV41566 — 1987 — 12.00
— *Includes Timbuk 3, World Party, Sonic Youth, Mojo Nixon & Skid Roper*

THE MAGIC CHRISTIAN
❑ Commonwealth United CU-6004 — 1970 — 30.00

MAGNIFICENT OBSESSION
❑ Decca DL8078 [M] — 1954 — 75.00
— *Black label, gold print*
❑ Decca DL8078 [M] — 1955 — 50.00
— *Black label, silver print*
❑ Decca DL8078 [M] — 196? — 30.00
— *Black label with color bars*
❑ Varese Sarabande STV-81118 — 1981 — 15.00
— *Reissue of Decca 8078*

MAJOR DUNDEE
❑ Columbia Masterworks OL6380 [M] — 1965 — 25.00
❑ Columbia Masterworks OS2780 [S] — 1965 — 30.00

MAJOR LEAGUE
❑ Curb 10402 — 1989 — 15.00
— *Includes X, Beat Farmers, Lyle Lovett*

MALAMONDO
❑ Epic LN24126 [M] — 1964 — 30.00
❑ Epic BN26126 [S] — 1964 — 40.00

MALLRATS
❑ MCA 11294 — 1995 — 12.00
— *Includes Weezer, Elastica, Belly, etc.*

MAME
❑ Warner Bros. W2773 — 1974 — 18.00
❑ Warner Bros. PRO509 [DJ] — 1973 — 50.00
— *Promo-only gatefold edition with Lucille Ball in Christmas hat on the cover*

A MAN AND A WOMAN (UN HOMME ET UNE FEMME)
❑ United Artists UAL-4147 [M] — 1966 — 18.00
❑ United Artists UAS-5147 [S] — 1966 — 25.00
❑ United Artists SW-91032 [S] — 1967 — 30.00
— *Capitol Record Club edition*

A MAN CALLED ADAM
❑ Reprise R6180 [M] — 1966 — 35.00
❑ Reprise RS6180 [S] — 1966 — 50.00

A MAN CALLED DAGGER
❑ MGM E-4516 [M] — 1967 — 18.00
❑ MGM SE-4516 [S] — 1967 — 25.00

A MAN CALLED FLINTSTONE
❑ Hanna-Barbera HLP-2055 [M] — 1967 — 150.00

A MAN COULD GET KILLED
❑ Decca DL4750 [M] — 1966 — 18.00
❑ Decca DL74750 [S] — 1966 — 25.00

A MAN FOR ALL SEASONS
❑ RCA Victor VDM-116 [M] — 1966 — 30.00

MAN FROM SHAFT
❑ MGM SE-4836 — 1972 — 30.00

MANIAC
❑ Varese Sarabande STV-81143 — 1980 — 25.00

MAN IN THE MIDDLE
❑ 20th Century Fox TFM-3128 [M] — 1965 — 30.00
❑ 20th Century Fox TFS-4128 [S] — 1965 — 50.00

THE MAN OF A THOUSAND FACES
❑ Decca DL8623 [M] — 1957 — 50.00
— *Black label, silver print, or pink label, black print promos*
❑ Decca DL8623 [M] — 196? — 30.00
— *Black label with color bars*
❑ Varese Sarabande STV-81121 — 1981 — 15.00
— *Reissue of Decca 8623*

MAN OF LA MANCHA
❑ United Artists UAS-9906 — 1972 — 25.00
— *Cover is intact with no cut corners*
❑ United Artists UAS-9906 — 1972 — 12.00
— *Cover has cut-out marking such as a cut-off corner*

THE MAN WHO WOULD BE KING
❑ Capitol SW-11474 — 1975 — 25.00

THE MAN WITH THE GOLDEN ARM
❑ Decca DL8257 [M] — 1956 — 120.00
❑ Decca DL78257 [R] — 196? — 50.00
❑ MCA 2043 [R] — 1973 — 25.00
— *Reissue of Decca 78257; black label with rainbow*
❑ MCA 1528 — 198? — 10.00
— *Reissue of MCA 2043*

Number	Title	Yr	NM

THE MAN WITH THE GOLDEN GUN
- ❏ United Artists UA-LA358-G — 1974 — 25.00

MARACAIBO
- ❏ Decca DL8756 [M] — 1958 — 40.00
- —*Black label, silver print, or pink label, black print promos*
- ❏ Decca DL8756 [M] — 196? — 25.00
- —*Black label with color bars*

MARCO THE MAGNIFICENT
- ❏ Columbia Masterworks OS2870 [S] — 1966 — 40.00
- ❏ Columbia Masterworks OL6470 [M] — 1966 — 30.00

MARIE WARD
- ❏ Varese Sarabande STV-81268 — 1985 — 50.00

MARJORIE MORNINGSTAR
- ❏ RCA Victor LOC-1044 [M] — 1958 — 40.00
- —*RE" next to label number*
- ❏ RCA Victor LOC-1044 [M] — 1958 — 75.00
- —*An Original Soundtrack Recording" on spine*

MARRIED TO THE MOB
- ❏ Reprise 25763 — 1988 — 30.00
- —*Includes New Order, Sinead O'Connor, Chris Isaak, Debbie Harry, Brian Eno, The Feelies, Tom Tom Club*

MARRY ME, MARRY ME
- ❏ RCA Victor LSO-1160 — 1969 — 25.00

MARY, QUEEN OF SCOTS
- ❏ Decca DL79186 — 1972 — 30.00

MARY POPPINS
- ❏ Buena Vista BV-4026 [M] — 1964 — 15.00
- —*Originals have gatefold covers*
- ❏ Buena Vista STER-4026 [S] — 1964 — 18.00
- —*Originals have gatefold covers*
- ❏ Buena Vista STER-5005 [S] — 1973 — 12.00
- —*Reissue with new number and no gatefold*
- ❏ RCA Victor COP-111 [M] — 1964 — 18.00
- —*With gatefold; RCA Record Club edition*
- ❏ RCA Victor CSO-111 [S] — 1964 — 25.00
- —*With gatefold; RCA Record Club edition*

THE MASK
- ❏ Chaos 6455 [DJ] — 1994 — 25.00
- —*Generic cover; no other U.S. vinyl*

MASKED AND ANONYMOUS
- ❏ Columbia CSK90618-1 — 2006 — 30.00
- —*Classic Records issue on 140-gram vinyl; CD issued in 2003*

MASTER OF THE WORLD
- ❏ Varese Sarabande VC-81070 — 1978 — 18.00
- —*Reissue of Vee Jay 4000*
- ❏ Vee Jay LP-4000 [M] — 1961 — 30.00
- ❏ Vee Jay SR-4000 [S] — 1961 — 40.00

MASTERS OF THE UNIVERSE
- ❏ Varese Sarabande STV-81333 — 1987 — 25.00

MCLINTOCK!
- ❏ United Artists UAL-4112 [M] — 1963 — 75.00
- ❏ United Artists UAS-5112 [S] — 1963 — 100.00

ME AND THE COLONEL
- ❏ RCA Victor LOC-1046 [M] — 1958 — 50.00

MEDITERRANEAN HOLIDAY
- ❏ London M-76003 [M] — 1964 — 50.00
- ❏ London MS-82003 [S] — 1964 — 100.00

MEET ME IN ST. LOUIS
- ❏ AEI 3101 — 1978 — 15.00
- —*Reissue of Decca LP*
- ❏ Decca DL8498 [M] — 1957 — 30.00
- —*LP reissue of 78 rpm album from 1944; B-side of LP is "The Harvey Girls."*

MEMORIES AUX BRUXELLES
- ❏ Carlton LP-112 [M] — 1959 — 30.00
- ❏ Carlton LP-12112 [S] — 1959 — 40.00

MENACE II SOCIETY
- ❏ Jive 41522 [DJ] — 1993 — 25.00
- —*Vinyl is promo only*

MEN IN WAR
- ❏ Imperial LP-9032W [M] — 1957 — 175.00

MERRY ANDREW
- ❏ Capitol T1016 [M] — 1958 — 50.00

MERRY CHRISTMAS, MR. LAWRENCE
- ❏ MCA 6125 — 1983 — 15.00
- —*Includes David Sylvian*
- ❏ MCA 6125 — 1983 — 20.00
- —*Music by Ryuichi Sakamoto. David Bowie stars in the movie, but does not sing on the LP.*

METROPOLIS
- ❏ Columbia JS39526 — 1984 — 12.00
- —*Includes Adam Ant*

MICKEY ONE
- ❏ MGM E-4312 [M] — 1965 — 50.00
- ❏ MGM SE-4312 [S] — 1965 — 75.00

MIDNIGHT COWBOY
- ❏ United Artists UAS-5198 — 1969 — 25.00

MIDNIGHT EXPRESS
- ❏ Casablanca NBLP-7114 — 1978 — 25.00

THE MIGHTY QUINN
- ❏ A&M SP-3924 — 1989 — 12.00
- —*Includes UB40, Yello*

A MILANESE STORY
- ❏ Atlantic 1388 [M] — 1962 — 175.00
- ❏ Atlantic SD1388 [S] — 1962 — 175.00

THE MINX
- ❏ Amsterdam 12007 — 1970 — 120.00

THE MISFITS
- ❏ United Artists UAL-4087 [M] — 1961 — 50.00
- ❏ United Artists UAS-5087 [S] — 1961 — 150.00
- ❏ United Artists UA-LA273-G [S] — 1974 — 15.00
- —*Reissue of 5087*

THE MISSOURI BREAKS
- ❏ MCA 25113 — 1986 — 12.00
- —*Reissue of United Artists UA-LA623-G*
- ❏ United Artists UA-LA623-G — 1976 — 30.00

MISS SADIE THOMPSON
- ❏ Mercury MG-25181 [10] — 1954 — 85.00
- ❏ Mercury MG-20123 [M] — 1956 — 175.00

MOBY DICK
- ❏ RCA Victor LPM-1247 [M] — 1956 — 120.00

MODERN GIRLS
- ❏ Warner Bros. 25526 — 1986 — 12.00
- —*Includes Depeche Mode, Toni Basil, Icehouse, The Jesus and Mary Chain*

MODERN TIMES
- ❏ United Artists UAL-4049 [M] — 1959 — 30.00
- ❏ United Artists UAS-5049 [R] — 196? — 25.00

MODESTY BLAISE
- ❏ 20th Century Fox TFM-3182 [M] — 1966 — 30.00
- ❏ 20th Century Fox TFS-4182 [S] — 1966 — 50.00

MOHAMMAD, MESSENGER OF GOD
- ❏ Namara 79001 — 1977 — 30.00

MONDO CANE
- ❏ United Artists UAL-4105 [M] — 1963 — 18.00
- ❏ United Artists UAS-5105 [S] — 1963 — 25.00

MONDO CANE NO. 2
- ❏ 20th Century Fox TFM-3147 [M] — 1964 — 30.00
- ❏ 20th Century Fox TFS-4147 [S] — 1964 — 40.00

MOON OVER PARADOR
- ❏ MCA 6249 — 1988 — 30.00

THE MOON SPINNERS
- ❏ Buena Vista BV-3323 [M] — 1964 — 40.00

MORE AMERICAN GRAFFITI
- ❏ MCA MCA2-11006 — 1979 — 25.00
- —*Tan labels*

MR. BUDDWING
- ❏ Verve V-8638 [M] — 1965 — 35.00
- ❏ Verve V6-8638 [S] — 1965 — 75.00

MR. MAGOO: 1001 ARABIAN NIGHTS
- ❏ Colpix CP-410 [M] — 1959 — 50.00
- ❏ Colpix SCP-410 [S] — 1959 — 175.00

MURDER INC.
- ❏ Canadian American CALP-1003 [M] — 1960 — 150.00

MUSCLE BEACH PARTY PLUS MERLIN JONES AND THE SCRAMBLED EGGHEAD
- ❏ Buena Vista BV-3314 [M] — 1964 — 75.00
- ❏ Buena Vista STER-3314 [S] — 1964 — 120.00

THE MUSIC MAN
- ❏ Warner Bros. B1459 [M] — 1962 — 18.00
- ❏ Warner Bros. BS1459 [S] — 1962 — 25.00
- —*Gold label originals*
- ❏ Warner Bros. BS1459 [S] — 1968 — 15.00
- —*Green label with "W7" box logo at top*
- ❏ Warner Bros. BS1459 [S] — 1970 — 12.00
- —*Green label with "WB" shield logo at top*
- ❏ Warner Bros. BS1459 [S] — 1973 — 10.00
- —*Burbank" palm trees label or later white label*

MUTINY ON THE BOUNTY
- ❏ MCA 25007 — 1986 — 10.00
- —*Reissue of MGM 1SE-4*
- ❏ MGM 1E-4 [M] — 1962 — 30.00
- —*Boxed set with book and painting*
- ❏ MGM S1E-4 [S] — 1962 — 40.00
- —*Boxed set with book and painting*
- ❏ MGM 1E-4 [M] — 196? — 15.00
- —*Standard cover*
- ❏ MGM S1E-4 [S] — 196? — 18.00
- —*Standard cover*

MY FAIR LADY
- ❏ Columbia Masterworks KOL8000 [M] — 1964 — 50.00
- —*Purple vinyl with letter from the vice-president of Columbia*

Records, stating that this is one of 8,475 copies distributed to radio station owners.
- ❏ Columbia Masterworks KOS2600 [S] — 1964 — 18.00

MY GEISHA
- ❏ RCA Victor LOC-1070 [M] — 1962 — 50.00
- ❏ RCA Victor LSO-1070 [S] — 1962 — 150.00

MY SIDE OF THE MOUNTAIN
- ❏ Capitol ST-245 — 1969 — 30.00

MY STEPMOTHER IS AN ALIEN
- ❏ Polydor 837798-1 — 1988 — 12.00
- —*Includes Animotion, M/A/R/R/S*

MY WILD IRISH ROSE
- ❏ RCA Victor LPM-3036 [10] — 1952 — 40.00

NAKED ANGELS
- ❏ Straight STS-1056 — 1969 — 30.00

THE NAKED MAJA
- ❏ United Artists UAL-4031 [M] — 1959 — 30.00
- ❏ United Artists UAS-5031 [S] — 1959 — 40.00

NANCY GOES TO RIO
- ❏ MGM E-508 [10] — 1950 — 75.00

NASHVILLE
- ❏ ABC ABCD-893 — 1975 — 25.00

NATIONAL LAMPOON'S ANIMAL HOUSE
- ❏ MCA 3046 — 1978 — 15.00
- —*Tan label original*
- ❏ MCA 3046 — 1980 — 12.00
- —*Blue label with rainbow*
- ❏ MCA 1692 — 198? — 10.00
- —*Reissue; blue label with rainbow*

NATIONAL LAMPOON'S VACATION
- ❏ Warner Bros. 23909 — 1983 — 25.00

NATIVE SON
- ❏ MCA 6198 — 1986 — 25.00

NAVAJO JOE
- ❏ United Artists UA-LA292-G — 1974 — 30.00

NED KELLY
- ❏ United Artists UAS-5213 — 1970 — 30.00
- ❏ United Artists UA-LA300-G — 1974 — 15.00
- —*Reissue of 5213*

NEVADA SMITH
- ❏ Dot DLP-3718 [M] — 1966 — 30.00
- ❏ Dot DLP-25718 [S] — 1966 — 40.00

THE NEVER ENDING STORY
- ❏ EMI America ST-17139 — 1984 — 25.00

NEVER ON SUNDAY
- ❏ United Artists UAL-4070 [M] — 1960 — 18.00
- ❏ United Artists UAS-5070 [S] — 1960 — 25.00
- ❏ United Artists SW-90834 [S] — 196? — 25.00
- —*Capitol Record Club edition*

THE NEW INTERNS
- ❏ Colpix CP-473 [M] — 1964 — 30.00
- ❏ Colpix SCP-473 [S] — 1964 — 40.00

NEW JACK CITY
- ❏ Giant 24409 — 1991 — 15.00
- —*Includes Ice-T*

A NEW KIND OF LOVE
- ❏ Mercury MG-20859 [M] — 1963 — 150.00
- ❏ Mercury SR-60859 [S] — 1963 — 150.00

THE NEW MESSIAH
- ❏ Columbia KC31713 — 1972 — 25.00

NEW YORK STORIES
- ❏ Elektra Musician 60857 — 1988 — 15.00
- —*Includes Kid Creole and the Coconuts, Transvision Vamp*

NICHOLAS AND ALEXANDRA
- ❏ Bell 1103 — 1971 — 30.00

A NIGHT IN HEAVEN
- ❏ A&M SP-4966 — 1983 — 15.00
- —*Includes The English Beat*

A NIGHTMARE ON ELM STREET
- ❏ Varese Sarabande STV-81236 — 1984 — 18.00

A NIGHTMARE ON ELM STREET 2: FREDDY'S REVENGE
- ❏ Varese Sarabande STV-81275 — 1986 — 15.00

A NIGHTMARE ON ELM STREET 3: DREAM WARRIORS
- ❏ Varese Sarabande STV-81314 — 1987 — 18.00

A NIGHTMARE ON ELM STREET 4: THE DREAM MASTER
- ❏ Chrysalis R100504 — 1988 — 18.00
- —*BMG Direct Marketing edition*
- ❏ Chrysalis OV41673 — 1988 — 18.00
- —*Various-artists song collection*
- ❏ Varese Sarabande VS-5203 — 1988 — 18.00
- —*Orchestral and incidental music*

Number Title	Yr	NM
A NIGHTMARE ON ELM STREET 5: THE DREAM CHILD		
❑ Jive 1258-1-J	1989	15.00
—Various-artists song collection		
NIGHT OF THE GENERALS		
❑ Colgems COMO-5002 [M]	1967	40.00
❑ Colgems COSO-5002 [S]	1967	80.00
THE NIGHT OF THE HUNTER		
❑ RCA Victor LPM-1136 [M]	1955	300.00
THE NIGHT THE LIGHTS WENT OUT IN GEORGIA		
❑ Mirage SD16051	1981	12.00
9 1/2 WEEKS		
❑ Capitol SV-12470	1986	12.00
❑ Capitol SV-512470	1986	18.00
—Columbia House edition		
NINE HOURS TO RAMA		
❑ London M-76002 [M]	1963	300.00
1969		
❑ Polydor R100724	1988	12.00
—Includes Pretenders ("Windows of the World")		
9 TO 5		
❑ 20th Century T-627	1980	12.00
NOTHING BUT THE BEST		
❑ Colpix CP-477 [M]	1964	25.00
❑ Colpix SCP-477 [S]	1964	30.00
NOT WITH MY WIFE, YOU DON'T		
❑ Warner Bros. W1668 [M]	1966	18.00
❑ Warner Bros. WS1668 [S]	1966	25.00
NO WAY TO TREAT A LADY		
❑ Dot DLP-25846	1968	30.00
A NUN'S STORY		
❑ Warner Bros. B1306 [M]	1959	75.00
❑ Warner Bros. BS1306 [S]	1959	150.00
O BROTHER, WHERE ART THOU?		
❑ Lost Highway 088170069-1	2003	25.00
OBSESSION		
❑ London Phase 4 SPC-21160	1976	30.00
OCTOPUSSY		
❑ A&M SP-4967	1983	25.00
THE ODD COUPLE		
❑ Dot DLP-25862	1968	25.00
ODDS AGAINST TOMORROW		
❑ United Artists UAL-4061 [M]	1959	75.00
❑ United Artists UAS-5061 [S]	1959	150.00
OF LOVE AND DESIRE		
❑ 20th Century Fox FXG-5014 [M]	1963	30.00
❑ 20th Century Fox SXG-5014 [S]	1963	30.00
OH, ROSALINDA!		
❑ Mercury MG-20145 [M]	1957	50.00
OH DAD, POOR DAD, MAMMA'S HUNG YOU IN THE CLOSET AND I'M FEELIN' SO SAD		
❑ RCA Victor LPM-3750 [M]	1967	25.00
❑ RCA Victor LSP-3750 [S]	1967	30.00
OIL TOWN, U.S.A.		
❑ RCA Victor LFM-2000 [10]	1953	75.00
OKLAHOMA!		
❑ Capitol WAO595 [M]	1955	30.00
—Purple or dark red label		
❑ Capitol WAO595 [M]	1956	25.00
—Gray label		
❑ Capitol WAO595 [M]	1959	18.00
—Black colorband label, logo at left		
❑ Capitol WAO595 [M]	1962	15.00
—Black colorband label, logo at top		
❑ Capitol SWAO595 [S]	1959	25.00
—Black colorband label, logo at left		
❑ Capitol SWAO595 [S]	1962	18.00
—Black colorband label, logo at top		
❑ Capitol SWAO595 [S]	1969	15.00
—Lime green label		
❑ Capitol SWAO595 [S]	1973	12.00
—Orange label		
OLD BOYFRIENDS		
❑ Columbia Masterworks JS36072	1979	50.00
THE OLD MAN AND THE SEA		
❑ Columbia CL1183 [M]	1958	30.00
❑ Columbia CS8013 [S]	1958	75.00
OLD YELLER		
❑ Disneyland WDL-3024 [M]	1957	50.00
—First edition		
❑ Disneyland WDL-1024 [M]	1960	40.00
—Second edition		
❑ Disneyland 1024 [M]	1974	30.00
—Reissue with no prefix		
OLIVER AND COMPANY		
❑ Disney 64101	1988	30.00

Number Title	Yr	NM
ONCE UPON A TIME IN THE WEST		
❑ RCA Victor LSP-4736	1969	30.00
THE ONE AND ONLY, GENUINE, ORIGINAL FAMILY BAND		
❑ Buena Vista BV-5002 [M]	1968	18.00
❑ Buena Vista STER-5002 [S]	1968	25.00
THE ONE-EYED JACKS		
❑ Liberty LOM-16001 [M]	1961	30.00
❑ Liberty LOS-17001 [S]	1961	50.00
ONE FLEW OVER THE CUCKOO'S NEST		
❑ Fantasy F-9500	1975	25.00
❑ Fantasy MPF-4531	198?	12.00
—Budget-line reissue of 9500		
101 DALMATIONS		
❑ Disneyland ST-4903 [M]	1963	175.00
—Gatefold cover with pop-up scene in center		
❑ Disneyland ST-3931 [M]	1965	40.00
❑ Disneyland DQ-1308 [M]	1966	25.00
❑ Disneyland ST-1908 [M]	1960	30.00
ON HER MAJESTY'S SECRET SERVICE		
❑ United Artists UAS-5204	1969	25.00
❑ United Artists UA-LA299-G	1974	15.00
—Reissue of 5204		
ON THE BEACH		
❑ Roulette R-25098 [M]	1959	100.00
❑ Roulette SR-25098 [S]	1959	175.00
THE OPTIMISTS		
❑ Paramount PAS-1015	1973	30.00
ORCHESTRA WIVES		
❑ RCA Victor LPT-3065 [10]	1954	120.00
THE OSCAR		
❑ Columbia Masterworks OL6550 [M]	1966	25.00
❑ Columbia Masterworks OS2950 [S]	1966	30.00
OTLEY		
❑ Colgems COS-112	1969	30.00
OUR MAN FLINT		
❑ 20th Century Fox TFM-3179 [M]	1966	40.00
❑ 20th Century Fox TFS-4179 [S]	1966	75.00
OUTLAND		
❑ Warner Bros. HS3551	1981	30.00
OUTLAW BLUES		
❑ Capitol ST-11691	1977	18.00
THE OUTLAW JOSEY WALES		
❑ Warner Bros. BS2956	1976	30.00
THE OUTLAW RIDERS		
❑ MGM 1SE-26	1970	25.00
OUT OF AFRICA		
❑ MCA 6158	1985	25.00
❑ MCA 11327	1995	25.00
—Limited edition on "Heavy Vinyl"		
OUT OF SIGHT		
❑ Decca DL4751 [M]	1966	25.00
❑ Decca DL74751 [S]	1966	30.00
OVER THE EDGE		
❑ Warner Bros. HS3335	1979	12.00
—Includes The Ramones, The Cars		
PAGAN LOVE SONG		
❑ MGM E-534 [M]	1950	40.00
PAINT YOUR WAGON		
❑ MCA 37099	198?	10.00
—Reissue of Paramount 1001		
❑ Paramount PMS-1001	1969	25.00
—With booklet		
THE PAJAMA GAME		
❑ Columbia Masterworks OL5210 [M]	1957	30.00
—Gray and black label with six "eye" logos		
PAL JOEY		
❑ Capitol W912 [M]	1957	25.00
—Gray label		
❑ Capitol W912 [M]	1959	18.00
—Black colorband label, logo at left		
❑ Capitol W912 [M]	1962	15.00
—Black colorband label, logo on top		
❑ Capitol DW912 [R]	196?	12.00
—Black colorband label		
❑ Capitol SM-912 [R]	1977	10.00
—Reissue with new prefix		
PANIC BUTTON		
❑ Musicor MM-2026 [M]	1964	100.00
❑ Musicor MS-3026 [S]	1964	120.00
PAPER MOON		
❑ Paramount PAS-1012	1973	50.00
PAPER TIGER		
❑ Capitol SW-11475	1975	25.00
PAPILLON		
❑ Capitol ST-11260	1973	25.00

Number Title	Yr	NM
THE PARENT TRAP!		
❑ Buena Vista BV-3309 [M]	1961	40.00
❑ Buena Vista STER-3309 [S]	1961	75.00
—B-side of the above two: Camerata Conducts Themes from Great Motion Pictures		
PARIS BLUES		
❑ United Artists UAL-4092 [M]	1961	75.00
❑ United Artists UAS-5092 [S]	1961	75.00
PARIS HOLIDAY		
❑ United Artists UAL-4001 [M]	1958	50.00
PARIS WHEN IT SIZZLES		
❑ Reprise R6113 [M]	1964	30.00
❑ Reprise RS6113 [S]	1964	40.00
PARRISH		
❑ Warner Bros. W1413 [M]	1961	30.00
❑ Warner Bros. WS1413 [S]	1961	100.00
—B-side of the above two: Popular Piano Concertos by George Greeley		
PARTY PARTY		
❑ A&M SP-3212	1982	18.00
—Includes Elvis Costello, Dave Edmunds ("Run Rudolph Run"), Bananarama, Midge Ure, Bad Manners, etc.		
A PATCH OF BLUE		
❑ Mainstream 56068 [M]	1965	25.00
❑ Mainstream S-6068 [S]	1965	30.00
❑ Mainstream ST-90805 [S]	1965	30.00
—Capitol Record Club edition		
PATTON		
❑ 20th Century Fox S-4208	1970	25.00
PATTY		
❑ Stang 1026	1976	25.00
PENELOPE		
❑ MGM E-4426 [M]	1966	25.00
❑ MGM SE-4426 [S]	1966	30.00
PENTHOUSE		
❑ United Artists UAL-4170 [M]	1967	25.00
❑ United Artists UAS-5170 [S]	1967	25.00
THE PEOPLE NEXT DOOR		
❑ Avco AV-11002	1970	30.00
PEPE		
❑ Colpix CP-507 [M]	1960	25.00
❑ Colpix SCP-507 [S]	1960	30.00
PERFECT		
❑ Arista R163614	1985	15.00
—Includes Wham! ("Wham Rap")		
❑ Arista AL98278	1985	12.00
—Includes Wham! ("Wham Rap")		
PERFORMANCE		
❑ Warner Bros. WS1846	1970	1500.00
—Original issue; has a completely different cover to the more common 2554		
❑ Warner Bros. BS2554	1970	25.00
—Second issue		
PERMANENT RECORD		
❑ Epic E40879	198?	15.00
—Includes Joe Strummer (5 tracks), Lou Reed, The Stranglers		
PETE KELLY'S BLUES		
❑ Columbia CL690 [M]	1955	50.00
❑ Decca DL8166 [M]	1955	175.00
—Black label, silver print		
PETE'S DRAGON		
❑ Capitol SW-11704	1977	25.00
PET SEMATARY		
❑ Varese Sarabande VS-5227	1989	18.00
PETULIA		
❑ Warner Bros. WS1755	1968	30.00
PEYTON PLACE		
❑ RCA Victor LOC-1042 [M]	1958	30.00
—"Long Play" at bottom of label		
❑ RCA Victor LOC-1042 [M]	1965	30.00
—"Monaural" at bottom of label		
❑ RCA Victor LSO-1042 [S]	1958	150.00
—"Living Stereo" at bottom of label		
❑ RCA Victor LSO-1042 [S]	1965	75.00
—"Stereo" at bottom of label		
PHAEDRA		
❑ United Artists UAL-4102 [M]	1962	25.00
❑ United Artists UAS-5102 [S]	1962	30.00
THE PHILADELPHIA EXPERIMENT		
❑ Rhino RNSP-306	1984	30.00
PICNIC		
❑ Decca DL8320 [M]	1956	30.00
—Black label, silver print		
❑ Decca DL8320 [M]	196?	18.00
—Black label with color bars		
❑ Decca DL78320 [S]	1959	30.00
—Maroon or all-black label		

Number	Title	Yr	NM
❑ Decca DL78320 [S]		196?	18.00
— Black label with color bars			
❑ MCA 2049		1973	12.00
— Reissue of Decca 78320; black label with rainbow			
❑ MCA 1527		198?	10.00
— Reissue of 2049			
A PIECE OF THE ACTION			
❑ Curtom CU5019		1977	25.00
PINK CADILLAC			
❑ Warner Bros. 25922		1989	12.00
PINOCCHIO			
❑ Disneyland WDL-4002 [M]		1956	300.00
— Original edition			
❑ Disneyland ST-4905 [M]		1963	175.00
— Gatefold cover with pop-up center graphics			
❑ Disneyland DQ-1202 [M]		1959	30.00
— Second edition			
❑ Disneyland DQ-1202MO [M]		1963	25.00
— Third edition			
❑ Disneyland 3102 [PD]		1981	30.00
— Disney Picture Disc" edition			
PIRANHA			
❑ Varese Sarabande STV-81126		1979	25.00
THE PIRATE			
❑ MGM E-21 [10]		1951	80.00
PLANET OF THE APES			
❑ Project 3 PR-5023SD		1968	30.00
— Gatefold cover			
❑ Project 3 PR-5023SD		1968	25.00
— Regular cover			
PLAYING FOR KEEPS			
❑ Atlantic 81678		1986	12.00
— Includes Arcadia			
THE PLEASURE SEEKERS			
❑ RCA Victor LOC-1101 [M]		1964	50.00
❑ RCA Victor LSO-1101 [S]		1964	150.00
POLLYANNA			
❑ Disneyland ST-1906 [M]		1960	50.00
❑ Disneyland DQ-1307 [M]		1967	30.00
POLTERGEIST			
❑ MGM MG-1-5408		1982	40.00
POLTERGEIST III			
❑ Varese Sarabande 704620		1988	100.00
PORGY AND BESS			
❑ Columbia Masterworks OL5410 [M]		1959	18.00
❑ Columbia Masterworks OS2016 [S]		1959	25.00
PORKY'S REVENGE			
❑ Columbia CAS2034 [DJ]		1985	15.00
— Promo-only sampler; includes Dave Edmunds, Jeff Beck and George Harrison			
❑ Columbia JS39983		1985	15.00
— Includes Dave Edmunds			
THE POWER			
❑ Cerberus CST-0211		1984	25.00
PRET-A-PORTER			
❑ Miramax CAS6700 [DJ]		1994	30.00
— Promo only vinyl			
PRETTY BOY FLOYD			
❑ Audio Fidelity AFLP-1936 [M]		1960	75.00
❑ Audio Fidelity AFSD-5936 [S]		1960	100.00
PRETTY IN PINK			
❑ A&M R144487		1986	12.00
— Includes Orchestral Manoeuvres in the Dark ("If You Leave"); Psychedelic Furs ("Pretty in Pink"); etc.			
PRETTY WOMAN			
❑ EMI E1-93492		1990	15.00
— Includes David Bowie, Go West, Red Hot Chili Peppers, Jane Wiedlin			
THE PRIDE AND THE PASSION			
❑ Capitol W873 [M]		1957	75.00
THE PRINCESS BRIDE			
❑ Warner Bros. 25610		1987	25.00
THE PRISONER OF ZENDA			
❑ United Artists UA-LA374-G		1974	25.00
PRIVATE HELL 36			
❑ Coral CRL56122 [10]		1954	200.00
THE PRODUCERS			
❑ RCA Victor LPM-4008 [M]		1968	50.00
❑ RCA Victor LSP-4008 [S]		1968	30.00
❑ RCA Victor ANL1-1132		1975	12.00
— Reissue of LSP-4008			
THE PROFESSIONALS			
❑ Colgems COMO-5001 [M]		1966	75.00
❑ Colgems COSO-5001 [S]		1966	175.00
A PROMISE AT DAWN			
❑ Polydor 24-5502		1970	30.00

Number	Title	Yr	NM
THE PROPER TIME			
❑ Contemporary M-3587 [M]		1960	250.00
❑ Contemporary S-7587 [S]		1960	250.00
PROVIDENCE			
❑ DRG SL-9502		1977	25.00
PRUDENCE AND THE PILL			
❑ 20th Century Fox S-4199		1968	25.00
PSYCHO II			
❑ MCA 6119		1983	25.00
Q THE WINGED SERPENT			
❑ Cerberus CST-0206		1983	25.00
QUEST FOR FIRE			
❑ RCA Victor ABL1-4274		1982	25.00
THE QUIET MAN			
❑ Decca DL5411 [10]		1952	120.00
THE QUILLER MEMORANDUM			
❑ Columbia Masterworks OL6660 [M]		1966	30.00
❑ Columbia Masterworks OS3060 [S]		1966	75.00
QUO VADIS?			
❑ MCA 39075		198?	10.00
— Reissue of MGM 3524			
❑ MGM E-103 [10]		1951	40.00
— Music soundtrack only			
❑ MGM E-134 [10]		1951	75.00
— Box set of two discs; includes dialogue			
❑ MGM E-3524 [M]		1957	30.00
— Yellow label; has both music and dialogue			
RAGTIME			
❑ Elektra 5E-565		1981	25.00
RAIDERS OF THE LOST ARK			
❑ Columbia JS37373		1981	15.00
— Original issue; music only			
❑ Columbia JS37696		1981	15.00
— Music and dialogue			
❑ DCC Compact Classics LPZ 2-2009		1995	30.00
— Audiophile edition; includes music not on other releases of the soundtrack			
❑ Polydor 821583-1		1984	12.00
— Reissue			
THE RAILWAY CHILDREN			
❑ Capitol SW-871		1972	25.00
THE RAINMAKER			
❑ RCA Victor LPM-1434 [M]		1956	150.00
RAINTREE COUNTY			
❑ RCA Victor LOC-6000 [M]		1957	120.00
❑ RCA Victor LOC-1038 [M]		1958	30.00
❑ RCA Victor LSO-1038 [S]		1958	50.00
RAN			
❑ Fantasy FSP-21004		1985	25.00
THE RAT RACE			
❑ Dot DLP-3306 [M]		1960	100.00
❑ Dot DLP-25306 [S]		1960	250.00
RED DAWN			
❑ Intrada RVF-6001		1985	40.00
RED GARTERS			
❑ Columbia CL6282 [10]		1954	50.00
RED HEAT			
❑ Virgin Movie Music 90891		1988	30.00
THE RED PONY			
❑ Columbia Masterworks ML5983 [M]		196?	30.00
❑ Columbia Masterworks MS6583 [R]		196?	30.00
❑ Varese Sarabande STV-81259		1986	30.00
REDS			
❑ Columbia Masterworks BJS37960		1981	25.00
THE RED TENT			
❑ Paramount PAS-6019		1971	30.00
RENT-A-COP			
❑ Intrada MAS-7002		1988	25.00
THE REPORTER			
❑ Columbia CL2269 [M]		1963	75.00
❑ Columbia CS9069 [S]		1963	40.00
THE RESCUERS			
❑ Disneyland ST-3816		1977	25.00
RETURN OF SUPERFLY			
❑ Capitol C1-94244		1990	15.00
— Includes Ice-T			
RETURN TO PARADISE			
❑ Decca DL5489 [10]		1953	250.00
THE REVOLUTION			
❑ United Artists UAS-5185		1968	30.00
❑ United Artists UA-LA296-G		1974	15.00
— Reissue of 5185			
RHAPSODY OF STEEL			
❑ U.S. Steel JB-502/3		1958	150.00
RICH, YOUNG AND PRETTY			
❑ MGM E-86 [10]		1951	40.00

Number	Title	Yr	NM
RIDER ON THE RAIN			
❑ Capitol ST-584		1970	30.00
RIKKI AND PETE			
❑ DRG SBL-12593		1988	15.00
— Includes Crowded House			
RIOT ON SUNSET STRIP			
❑ Tower T5065 [M]		1967	25.00
❑ Tower DT5065 [R]		1967	30.00
ROADIE			
❑ Warner Bros. 2HS3441		1980	18.00
— Includes Blondie			
ROAD TO HONG KONG			
❑ Liberty LOM-16002 [M]		1962	25.00
❑ Liberty LOS-17002 [S]		1962	40.00
THE ROBE			
❑ Decca DL9012 [M]		1953	30.00
— Maroon label			
❑ Decca DL79012 [R]		196?	15.00
❑ MCA 1529		198?	10.00
— Reissue of MCA 2052			
❑ MCA 2052		1973	12.00
— Reissue of Decca 79012; black label with rainbow			
ROBIN AND THE SEVEN HOODS			
❑ Reprise F2021 [M]		1964	50.00
❑ Reprise FS2021 [S]		1964	75.00
ROBIN HOOD			
❑ Disneyland ST-3810		1973	30.00
ROCK, PRETTY BABY			
❑ Decca DL8429 [M]		1957	120.00
— Black label, silver print; also includes pink label promo			
❑ Decca DL8429 [M]		196?	30.00
— Black label with color bars			
ROCK, ROCK, ROCK			
❑ Chess LP-1425 [M]		1958	250.00
❑ (no label) (no #)		1958	1500.00
— Demo version, 20 tracks			
ROCK ALL NIGHT			
❑ Mercury MG-20293 [M]		1957	150.00
ROCK 'N' ROLL HIGH SCHOOL			
❑ Sire QSR-6070		1980	18.00
— Includes The Ramones (title song), Devo			
ROMANCE OF A HORSETHIEF			
❑ Allied Artists AAS-110-100		1971	50.00
ROME ADVENTURE			
❑ Warner Bros. W1458 [M]		1962	25.00
❑ Warner Bros. WS1458 [S]		1962	30.00
ROMEO AND JULIET			
❑ Capitol SWDR-289		1969	30.00
— From the 1968 Franco Zeffirelli remake; contains dialogue and music			
❑ Capitol ST-2993		1968	15.00
— From the 1968 Franco Zeffirelli remake; contains the music; black label with colorband			
❑ Capitol ST-400		1970	18.00
— From the 1968 Franco Zeffirelli remake; edited version of 289			
❑ Epic LC3126 [M]		1954	75.00
❑ Epic FLM13104 [M]		1966	30.00
— Reissue of 3126			
❑ Epic FLS15104 [R]		1966	30.00
ROOTS OF HEAVEN			
❑ 20th Fox FOX-3005 [M]		1958	300.00
ROSE MARIE			
❑ MGM E-229 [10]		1954	40.00
ROSEMARY'S BABY			
❑ Dot DLP-25875		1968	25.00
THE ROSE TATTOO			
❑ Columbia CL727 [M]		1955	50.00
THE ROYAL WEDDING			
❑ MGM E-543 [10]		1951	50.00
THE RULING CLASS			
❑ Avco AV-11003		1972	30.00
RUMBLE FISH			
❑ A&M SP-6-4983		1983	12.00
— Includes Stewart Copeland (ex-Police)			
RUN, ANGEL, RUN			
❑ Epic BN26474		1969	25.00
THE RUN OF THE ARROW			
❑ Decca DL8620 [M]		1957	75.00
— Black label, silver print, or pink label, black print promo			
❑ Decca DL8620 [M]		196?	30.00
— Black label with color bars			
RUN WILD, RUN FREE			
❑ SGC SD5003		1969	25.00
RUSTLERS' RHAPSODY			
❑ Warner Bros. 25284		1985	12.00

Number	Title	Yr	NM

RYAN'S DAUGHTER
- ❏ MGM 1SE-27 — 1970 — 30.00

SACCO AND VANZETTI
- ❏ RCA Victor LSP-4612 — 1971 — 25.00

THE SACRED IDOL
- ❏ Capitol T1293 [M] — 1960 — 30.00
- ❏ Capitol ST1293 [S] — 1960 — 30.00

THE SAINT
- ❏ Virgin SPRO-12261 [DJ] — 1997 — 30.00

SAINT JOAN
- ❏ Capitol W865 [M] — 1957 — 30.00

SALLAH
- ❏ Philips PHM200177 [M] — 1965 — 25.00
- ❏ Philips PHS600177 [S] — 1965 — 30.00

SALOME
- ❏ Decca DL6026 [10] — 1953 — 120.00

SALVATION
- ❏ Giant GR-16002 — 1988 — 15.00
- — Includes New Order, Cabaret Voltaire

SAMSON AND DELILAH
- ❏ Decca DL6007 [10] — 1952 — 75.00

THE SAND CASTLE
- ❏ Columbia CL1455 [M] — 1961 — 18.00
- ❏ Columbia CS8249 [S] — 1961 — 25.00

THE SAND PEBBLES
- ❏ 20th Century Fox 3189 [M] — 1966 — 30.00
- ❏ 20th Century Fox S-4189 [S] — 1966 — 50.00

THE SANDPIPER
- ❏ Mercury MG-21032 [M] — 1965 — 30.00
- ❏ Mercury SR-61032 [S] — 1965 — 30.00

SANTA AND THE 3 BEARS
- ❏ Mr. Pickwick SPC1501 — 196? — 25.00
- — With "Santa" cutout intact

SANTA CLAUS THE MOVIE
- ❏ EMI America SJ-17177 — 1985 — 12.00

SATAN IN HIGH HEELS
- ❏ Charlie Parker PLP-406 [M] — 1962 — 150.00
- — Gatefold cover
- ❏ Charlie Parker PLP-406S [S] — 1962 — 120.00
- — Gatefold cover
- ❏ Charlie Parker PLP-406 [M] — 1962 — 75.00
- — Standard cover
- ❏ Charlie Parker PLP-406S [S] — 1962 — 40.00
- — Standard cover

SATAN'S SADISTS
- ❏ Smash SRS-67127 — 1969 — 30.00

SATURDAY NIGHT FEVER
- ❏ RSO RS-2-4001 — 1977 — 18.00
- — First editions have the studio version of "Jive Talkin'" by the Bee Gees on side 3
- ❏ RSO RS-2-4001 — 1978 — 15.00
- — Later editions have a live version of "Jive Talkin'" by the Bee Gees on side 3 ("REV" is in the Side 3 trail-off wax)
- ❏ RSO 825389-1 — 198? — 12.00
- — Reissue with new number

SATURDAY NIGHT FEVER/GREASE
- ❏ RSO RPO1011 [DJ] — 1978 — 30.00
- — Side 1 has "The Best of Saturday Night Fever" (side 1 of original LP); Side 2 has "The Best of Grease" (side 1 of original LP)

THE SAVAGE SEVEN
- ❏ Atco 33-245 [M] — 1968 — 30.00
- ❏ Atco SD 33-245 [S] — 1968 — 30.00

SAVAGE WILD
- ❏ American Int'l. STA-1032 — 1970 — 25.00

SAYONARA
- ❏ RCA Victor LOC-1041 [M] — 1957 — 50.00
- ❏ RCA Victor LSO-1041 [S] — 1957 — 80.00

SAY ONE FOR ME
- ❏ Columbia CL1337 [M] — 1959 — 40.00
- ❏ Columbia CS8147 [S] — 1959 — 100.00

THE SCALPHUNTERS
- ❏ MCA 25042 — 1986 — 12.00
- — Reissue of United Artists 5176
- ❏ United Artists UAL-4176 [M] — 1968 — 30.00
- ❏ United Artists UAS-5176 [S] — 1968 — 40.00

SCARFACE
- ❏ MCA 6126 — 1984 — 25.00

THE SCARLET AND THE BLACK
- ❏ Cerberus CEM-0120 — 1983 — 30.00

SCENT OF MYSTERY
- ❏ Ramrod T-6001 [M] — 1960 — 50.00
- ❏ Ramrod ST-6001 [S] — 1960 — 150.00

SCROOGE
- ❏ Columbia Masterworks S30258 — 1970 — 30.00
- ❏ Columbia Special Products P14077 — 1977 — 15.00
- — Special Products reissue

SCROOGED
- ❏ A&M SP-3921 — 1988 — 12.00
- — Includes the following Christmas songs:

SEARCH FOR PARADISE
- ❏ RCA Victor LOC-1034 [M] — 1957 — 40.00

SEASIDE SWINGERS
- ❏ Mercury MG-21031 [M] — 1965 — 25.00
- ❏ Mercury SR-61031 [S] — 1965 — 30.00

SEBASTIAN
- ❏ Dot DLP-3845 [M] — 1968 — 50.00
- ❏ Dot DLP-25845 [S] — 1968 — 25.00

THE SECRET OF SANTA VITTORIA
- ❏ MCA 25034 — 1986 — 12.00
- — Reissue of United Artists 5200
- ❏ United Artists UAS-5200 — 1969 — 30.00

SERGEANTS 3
- ❏ Reprise R-2013 [M] — 1962 — 30.00
- ❏ Reprise RS-2013 [S] — 1962 — 50.00

THE SERPENT AND THE RAINBOW
- ❏ Varese Sarabande STV-81362 — 1988 — 40.00

SERPICO
- ❏ Paramount PAS-1016 — 1973 — 30.00

SEVEN BRIDES FOR SEVEN BROTHERS
- ❏ MGM E-244 [10] — 1954 — 40.00

SEVEN GOLDEN MEN
- ❏ United Artists UAS-5193 — 1969 — 30.00

THE SEVEN LITTLE FOYS
- ❏ RCA Victor LPM-3275 [10] — 1955 — 80.00

1776
- ❏ Columbia S31741 — 1972 — 25.00

THE SEVENTH DAWN
- ❏ United Artists UAL-4115 [M] — 1964 — 30.00

THE 7TH DAWN
- ❏ United Artists UAL-4115 [M] — 1964 — 30.00

THE SEVENTH DAWN
- ❏ United Artists UAS-5115 [S] — 1964 — 40.00

THE 7TH DAWN
- ❏ United Artists UAS-5115 [S] — 1964 — 40.00

THE 7TH VOYAGE OF SINBAD
- ❏ Colpix CP-504 [M] — 1958 — 250.00
- ❏ Varese Sarabande STV-81135 — 1983 — 25.00

SEX AND THE SINGLE GIRL
- ❏ Warner Bros. W1572 [M] — 1964 — 18.00
- ❏ Warner Bros. WS1572 [S] — 1964 — 25.00

SHAFT IN AFRICA
- ❏ ABC ABCX-793 — 1973 — 30.00

SHAFT'S BIG SCORE
- ❏ MGM 1SE-36 — 1972 — 30.00

SHAG
- ❏ Sire 25800 — 1989 — 12.00
- — Includes k.d. lang, Chris Isaak

SHAKE HANDS WITH THE DEVIL
- ❏ United Artists UAL-4043 [M] — 1959 — 30.00
- ❏ United Artists UAS-5043 [S] — 1959 — 50.00

SHALAKO
- ❏ Philips PHS600286 — 1968 — 30.00

SHEBA BABY
- ❏ Buddah BDS-5634 — 1975 — 30.00

SHE-DEVIL
- ❏ Polydor 841583-1 — 1989 — 30.00

SHENANDOAH
- ❏ Decca DL9125 [M] — 1965 — 30.00
- ❏ Decca DL79125 [S] — 1965 — 40.00

SHE'S OUT OF CONTROL
- ❏ MCA 6281 — 1989 — 12.00
- — Includes Oingo Boingo

THE SHINING
- ❏ Warner Bros. HS3449 — 1980 — 25.00

THE SHOP ON MAIN STREET
- ❏ Mainstream 56082 [M] — 1966 — 30.00
- ❏ Mainstream S-6082 [S] — 1966 — 40.00

SHORT EYES
- ❏ Curtom CU5017 — 1977 — 30.00

THE SHOW
- ❏ Def Jam 529021-1 — 1995 — 15.00
- — Includes L.L. Cool J, etc.

SHOW BOAT
- ❏ MGM E-559 [10] — 1951 — 30.00

THE SICILIAN CLAN
- ❏ 20th Century Fox S-4209 — 1970 — 50.00

SID & NANCY
- ❏ MCA 6181 — 1986 — 12.00
- — Includes Joe Strummer (ex-Clash), John Cale, The Pogues, Steve Jones (ex-Pistols)

THE SIDEHACKERS
- ❏ Amaret ST-5004 — 1969 — 25.00

THE SILENCERS
- ❏ RCA Victor LOC-1120 [M] — 1966 — 30.00
- ❏ RCA Victor LSO-1120 [S] — 1966 — 50.00

SILENT RUNNING
- ❏ Decca DL79188 — 1972 — 40.00
- ❏ Varese Sarabande STV-81072 — 1980 — 18.00
- — Reissue

SILK STOCKINGS
- ❏ MCA 39074 — 198? — 12.00
- — Reissue
- ❏ MGM E-3542 [M] — 1957 — 30.00

SILVERADO
- ❏ Geffen GHS24080 — 1985 — 25.00

SINGIN' IN THE RAIN
- ❏ MCA 39044 — 198? — 12.00
- ❏ Metro M-599 [M] — 1966 — 18.00
- — Reissue of MGM LP
- ❏ Metro MS-599 [R] — 1966 — 15.00
- ❏ MGM E-113 [10] — 1952 — 30.00

SINGLE ROOM FURNISHED
- ❏ Sidewalk ST-5917 — 1968 — 40.00

THE 633 SQUADRON
- ❏ United Artists UA-LA305-G — 1974 — 30.00

SKATEDANCER
- ❏ Mira LP-3004 [M] — 1966 — 25.00
- ❏ Mira LPS-3004 [S] — 1966 — 30.00

SKI ON THE WILD SIDE
- ❏ MGM E-4439 [M] — 1967 — 30.00
- ❏ MGM SE-4439 [S] — 1967 — 50.00

SLAUGHTERHOUSE-FIVE
- ❏ Columbia Masterworks S31333 — 1972 — 30.00

SLAUGHTER ON 10TH AVENUE
- ❏ Decca DL8657 [M] — 1957 — 30.00
- — Black label, silver print
- ❏ Decca DL78657 [S] — 1957 — 30.00
- — Black label, silver print
- ❏ Decca DL8657 [M] — 1960 — 15.00
- — Black label with color bars
- ❏ Decca DL78657 [S] — 1960 — 18.00
- — Black label with color bars

SLAVES
- ❏ Skye SK-11 — 1969 — 75.00

THE SLAVE TRADE IN THE WORLD TODAY
- ❏ London M-76006 [M] — 1964 — 250.00

SLEEPING BEAUTY
- ❏ Disneyland WDL-4018 [M] — 1959 — 30.00
- ❏ Disneyland STER-4018 [S] — 1959 — 40.00
- ❏ Disneyland STER-4036 [S] — 1970 — 25.00
- — Reissue of STER-4018

SLEUTH
- ❏ Columbia Masterworks S32154 — 1973 — 25.00

SLIPPERY WHEN WET
- ❏ World Pacific WP-1265 [M] — 1959 — 250.00

SLUMBER PARTY '57
- ❏ Mercury SRM-1-1097 — 1976 — 30.00

A SMASHING TIME
- ❏ ABC ABC-OC-6 [M] — 1967 — 25.00
- ❏ ABC ABCS-OC-6 [S] — 1967 — 30.00
- ❏ ABC SW-91399 [S] — 1967 — 30.00
- — Capitol Record Club edition

SMOKEY AND THE BANDIT
- ❏ MCA 2099 — 1977 — 15.00

SMOKEY AND THE BANDIT 2
- ❏ MCA 6101 — 1980 — 12.00

SMOKEY AND THE BANDIT 3
- ❏ MCA 36006 — 1983 — 12.00

SNOOPY COME HOME
- ❏ Columbia Masterworks S31451 — 1972 — 25.00

THE SNOW QUEEN
- ❏ Decca DL8977 [M] — 1959 — 40.00
- ❏ Decca DL78977 [S] — 1959 — 75.00

SNOW WHITE AND THE SEVEN DWARFS
- ❏ Buena Vista 102 — 1975 — 50.00
- — Entire movie on three LPs; TV mail-order item
- ❏ Disneyland WDL-4005 [M] — 1956 — 250.00
- — Gatefold cover
- ❏ Disneyland DQ-1201 [M] — 1959 — 50.00
- — Reissue of 4005; whirlpool-like designs on cover
- ❏ Disneyland DQ-1201 [M] — 1968 — 30.00
- — Reissue; with same cover as 4005, but no gatefold
- ❏ Disneyland DQ-1201 [M] — 197? — 30.00
- — Reissue; high-gloss cover with cel photos on back
- ❏ Disneyland 3101 [PD] — 1981 — 30.00
- — Disney Picture Disc" edition

Number	Title	Yr	NM
SNOW WHITE AND THE THREE STOOGES			
❏ Columbia CL1650 [M]		1961	75.00
❏ Columbia CS8450 [S]		1961	150.00
SODOM AND GOMORRAH			
❏ RCA Victor LOC-1076 [M]		1963	100.00
❏ RCA Victor LSO-1076 [S]		1963	150.00
SOL MADRID			
❏ MGM SE-4541ST		1968	30.00
SOLOMON AND SHEBA			
❏ MCA 1425		198?	10.00
— Reissue			
❏ United Artists UAL-4051 [M]		1959	50.00
— First cover with silky finish			
❏ United Artists UAL-4051 [M]		1959	30.00
— Second, regular cover			
❏ United Artists UAS-5051 [S]		1959	120.00
— First cover with silky finish			
❏ United Artists UAS-5051 [S]		1959	75.00
— Second, regular cover			
SOMEBODY LOVES ME			
❏ RCA Victor LPM-3097 [10]		1952	50.00
SOME CAME RUNNING			
❏ Capitol W1109 [M]		1958	30.00
❏ Capitol SW1109 [S]		1958	100.00
SOME LIKE IT HOT			
❏ United Artists UAL-4030 [M]		1959	50.00
❏ United Artists UAS-5030 [S]		1959	85.00
❏ United Artists UA-LA272-G		1974	15.00
— Reissue of 5030			
SOMETHING WILD			
❏ MCA 6194		1986	12.00
— Includes New Order			
SOMEWHERE IN TIME			
❏ MCA 5154		1980	25.00
SONG OF THE SOUTH			
❏ Disneyland WDL-4001 [M]		1956	300.00
— Yellow label (first pressing)			
❏ Disneyland WDL-4001 [M]		1957	250.00
— Red/maroon label (second pressing)			
SONG OF THE SOUTH (UNCLE REMUS)			
❏ Disneyland DQ-1205 [M]		1959	30.00
SONG WITHOUT END			
❏ Colpix CP-506 [M]		1960	25.00
❏ Colpix SCP-506 [S]		1960	30.00
THE SONS OF KATIE ELDER			
❏ Columbia Masterworks OL6420 [M]		1965	50.00
❏ Columbia Masterworks OS2820 [S]		1965	150.00
SO THIS IS LOVE			
❏ RCA Victor LOC-3000 [10]		1953	100.00
SO THIS IS PARIS			
❏ Decca DL5553 [10]		1955	50.00
SOUL MAN			
❏ A&M SP-3903		1986	10.00
— Includes Lou Reed, Martha Davis			
THE SOUL OF NIGGER CHARLEY			
❏ MGM 1SE-46		1973	25.00
THE SOUND AND THE FURY			
❏ Decca DL8885 [M]		1959	30.00
❏ Decca DL78885 [S]		1959	80.00
THE SOUND OF MUSIC			
❏ RCA Victor LOCD-2005 [M]		1965	18.00
— With booklet; back cover lists "I Have Confidence" as "I Have Confidence in Me			
❏ RCA Victor LSOD-2005 [S]		1965	25.00
— With booklet; back cover lists "I Have Confidence" as "I Have Confidence in Me			
❏ RCA Victor LOCD-2005 [M]		1965	15.00
— With booklet; back cover lists "I Have Confidence" correctly			
❏ RCA Victor LSOD-2005 [S]		1965	18.00
— With booklet; back cover lists "I Have Confidence" correctly			
❏ RCA Victor LSOD-2005 [S]		1969	15.00
— No booklet; gatefold cover, record comes out from inside; orange or tan label			
❏ RCA Victor LSOD-2005 [S]		1977	12.00
— Gatefold cover, record comes out from outside; black label with dog at 1 o'clock			
SOUTH CENTRAL			
❏ Hollywood 61403 [DJ]		1992	25.00
— Vinyl is promo only			
SOUTHERN STAR			
❏ Colgems COSO-5009		1969	75.00
SOUTH PACIFIC			
❏ RCA Victor LOC-1032 [M]		1958	25.00
— Long Play" on label; no "Academy Award Winner" on front cover			
❏ RCA Victor LSO-1032 [S]		1958	30.00
— Living Stereo" on label; no "Academy Award Winner" on front cover			

Number	Title	Yr	NM
❏ RCA Victor LOCD-2000 [M]		1958	40.00
— Gatefold cover with photos inside			
❏ RCA Victor LOC-1032 [M]		196?	15.00
— Long Play" or "Mono" on label; with "Academy Award Winner" on front cover			
❏ RCA Victor LSO-1032 [S]		196?	18.00
— Living Stereo" or "Stereo" on black label; with "Academy Award Winner" on front cover			
❏ RCA Victor LSO-1032 [S]		1958	15.00
— Orange label			
❏ RCA Victor AYL1-3681		1981	10.00
— Best Buy Series" reissue			
SPACEBALLS			
❏ Atlantic 81770		1987	12.00
— Includes Berlin			
SPACECAMP			
❏ RCA Victor ABL1-5856		1986	40.00
SPACE JAM, MUSIC FROM AND INSPIRED BY			
❏ Warner Sunset/Atlantic 82961		1997	18.00
A SPANISH AFFAIR			
❏ Dot DLP-3078 [M]		1958	150.00
SPARKLE			
❏ Atlantic SD18176		1976	25.00
SPARTACUS			
❏ Decca DL9092 [M]		1960	25.00
— Black label, silver print			
❏ Decca DL79092 [S]		1960	30.00
— Maroon label, silver print			
❏ Decca DL9092 [M]		1961	15.00
— Black label with color bars			
❏ Decca DL79092 [S]		1961	18.00
— Black label with color bars			
❏ MCA 2068		1973	15.00
— Reissue of 79092; black label with rainbow			
❏ MCA 1534		198?	12.00
— Reissue of 2068			
THE SPIRIT OF ST. LOUIS			
❏ RCA Victor LPM-1472 [M]		1957	50.00
SPLASH			
❏ Cherry Lane 00301		1984	30.00
— With poster of Daryl Hannah			
THE SPY WHO CAME IN FROM THE COLD			
❏ RCA Victor LOC-1118 [M]		1965	25.00
❏ RCA Victor LSO-1118 [S]		1965	40.00
THE SPY WITH A COLD NOSE			
❏ Columbia Masterworks OL6670 [M]		1966	25.00
❏ Columbia Masterworks OS3070 [S]		1966	30.00
STAGECOACH			
❏ Mainstream 56077 [M]		1966	25.00
❏ Mainstream S-6077 [S]		1966	30.00
❏ Mainstream T-90802 [M]		1966	30.00
— Capitol Record Club edition			
❏ Mainstream ST-90802 [S]		1966	30.00
— Capitol Record Club edition			
STAR!			
❏ 20th Century Fox DTCS-5102		1968	25.00
THE STARS AND STRIPES FOREVER			
❏ MGM E-176 [10]		1952	30.00
STAR TREK -- THE MOTION PICTURE			
❏ Columbia JS36334		1979	25.00
STATE FAIR			
❏ Dot DLP-9011 [M]		1962	30.00
❏ Dot DLP-29011 [S]		1962	30.00
THE STERILE CUCKOO			
❏ Paramount PAS-5009		1970	25.00
STILETTO			
❏ Columbia Masterworks OS3360		1969	25.00
THE STING			
❏ MCA 2040		197?	25.00
❏ MCA 37091		1981	20.00
❏ MCA 390		1973	30.00
— Original edition			
ST. LOUIS BLUES			
❏ Capitol W993 [M]		1958	175.00
— Turquoise or gray label			
❏ Capitol W993 [M]		1959	150.00
— Black colorband label, logo at left			
❏ Capitol W993 [M]		196?	100.00
— Black colorband label, logo at top			
ST. LOUIS WOMAN			
❏ Capitol L355 [10]		1955	300.00
THE STRANGE ONE			
❏ Coral CRL57132 [M]		1957	140.00
THE STRAWBERRY STATEMENT			
❏ MGM 2SE-14		1970	30.00
A STREETCAR NAMED DESIRE			
❏ Capitol L289 [10]		1951	50.00

Number	Title	Yr	NM
STREETS OF FIRE			
❏ MCA 5492		1984	12.00
— Includes The Fixx, The Blasters			
STRICTLY BUSINESS			
❏ MCA 10428		1991	12.00
— Includes L.L. Cool J			
A STUDY IN TERROR			
❏ Roulette OS-801 [M]		1965	40.00
❏ Roulette OSS-801 [S]		1965	100.00
THE STUNT MAN			
❏ 20th Century T-626		1980	30.00
THE SUBTERRANEANS			
❏ MGM E-3812ST [M]		1960	40.00
❏ MGM SE-3812ST [S]		1960	100.00
SUMMER AND SMOKE			
❏ RCA Victor LOC-1067 [M]		1961	50.00
❏ RCA Victor LSO-1067 [S]		1961	80.00
SUMMER HOLIDAY			
❏ Epic LN24063 [M]		1963	30.00
❏ Epic BN26063 [S]		1963	30.00
SUMMER LOVE			
❏ Decca DL8714 [M]		1958	75.00
— Black label, silver print, or pink label, black print promo			
❏ Decca DL8714 [M]		196?	30.00
— Black label with color bars			
SUMMER MAGIC			
❏ Buena Vista BV-4025 [M]		1963	40.00
❏ Buena Vista STER-4025 [S]		1963	75.00
SUMMER STOCK			
❏ MGM E-519 [10]		1950	40.00
THE SUN ALSO RISES			
❏ Kapp KDL-7001 [M]		1957	75.00
THE SUNNY SIDE OF THE STREET			
❏ Mercury MG-25100 [10]		1951	75.00
SUN VALLEY SERENADE			
❏ RCA Victor LPT-3064 [10]		1954	120.00
SURFER GIRLS			
❏ Oakwood SUS-1001		1978	150.00
SURF PARTY			
❏ 20th Century Fox TFM-3131 [M]		1964	30.00
❏ 20th Century Fox TFS-4131 [S]		1964	30.00
THE SWAN			
❏ MCA 25086		1986	12.00
— Reissue of MGM 3399			
❏ MGM E-3399 [M]		1956	80.00
THE SWARM			
❏ Warner Bros. BSK3208		1978	30.00
SWEDISH HEAVEN AND HELL			
❏ Ariel ARS-15000		1969	30.00
SWEET CHARITY			
❏ Decca DL71502		1969	25.00
SWEET LOVE, BITTER			
❏ ABC Impulse! AS-9141 [S]		1968	35.00
❏ Impulse! A-9141 [M]		1967	160.00
❏ Impulse! AS-9141 [S]		1967	120.00
THE SWEET RIDE			
❏ 20th Century Fox S-4198		1968	25.00
THE SWEET SMELL OF SUCCESS			
❏ Decca DL8610 [M]		1957	120.00
SWEET SWEETBACK'S BADASSSSSS SONG			
❏ Stax STS-3001		1971	30.00
SWEPT AWAY			
❏ Peters International PLD1005		1957	40.00
THE SWIMMER			
❏ Columbia Masterworks OS3210		1968	30.00
SWINGER'S PARADISE			
❏ Epic LN24145 [M]		1965	25.00
❏ Epic BN26145 [S]		1965	30.00
A SWINGIN' SUMMER			
❏ Hanna-Barbera HLP-8500 [M]		1966	30.00
❏ Hanna-Barbera HST-9500 [S]		1966	30.00
SYLVIA			
❏ Mercury MG-21004 [M]		1965	25.00
❏ Mercury SR-61004 [S]		1965	30.00
TAKE THIS JOB AND SHOVE IT!			
❏ Epic SE37177		1981	15.00
TAPEHEADS			
❏ Island 91030		1988	12.00
— Includes Devo ("Baby Doll" sung in Swedish!), Fishbone			
TARAS BULBA			
❏ United Artists UAL-4100 [M]		1962	30.00
❏ United Artists UAS-5100 [S]		1962	50.00
TAXI DRIVER			
❏ Arista AL4079		1976	25.00
❏ Arista AL8179		198?	18.00
— Reissue of 4079			

Number	Title	Yr	NM

TEENAGE CRUISERS
- ❑ Rhino RNLP-016 — 197? — 18.00
- *— Includes The Blasters, many others*

TEENAGE REBELLION
- ❑ Sidewalk T-5903 [M] — 1967 — 25.00
- ❑ Sidewalk ST-5903 [S] — 1967 — 30.00

TELL ME THAT YOU LOVE ME, JUNIE MOON
- ❑ Columbia Masterworks OS3540 — 1970 — 25.00

THE TEN COMMANDMENTS
- ❑ Dot DLP-3054 [M] — 1956 — 40.00
- ❑ Dot DLP-25054 [S] — 1959 — 30.00
- *— Re-recording of the original soundtrack in stereo*
- ❑ MCA 4159 — 198? — 18.00
- *— Reissue of Paramount set*
- ❑ Paramount PAS-1006 — 1973 — 25.00
- *— Reissue of Dot 25054*

TENDER IS THE NIGHT
- ❑ 20th Century Fox FOX-3054 [M] — 1962 — 175.00
- ❑ 20th Century Fox SFX-3054 [S] — 1962 — 250.00

THE TENTH VICTIM
- ❑ Mainstream 56071 [M] — 1965 — 40.00
- ❑ Mainstream S-6071 [S] — 1965 — 50.00

TEQUILA SUNRISE
- ❑ Capitol C1-91185 — 1988 — 15.00
- *— Includes Crowded House, Duran Duran*

THANK GOD IT'S FRIDAY
- ❑ Casablanca NBLP-7099-3 — 1978 — 25.00
- *— Two full-length LPs plus a bonus 12-inch single by Donna Summer with blank B-side*

THAT DARN CAT
- ❑ Buena Vista BV-3334 [M] — 1965 — 25.00
- ❑ Buena Vista STER-3334 [S] — 1965 — 30.00

THAT MAN IN ISTANBUL
- ❑ Mainstream 56072 [M] — 1966 — 25.00
- ❑ Mainstream S-6072 [S] — 1966 — 30.00

THAT'S ENTERTAINMENT!
- ❑ MCA 11002 — 1974 — 25.00
- *— Film credits in small print on back cover, and list of songs omits "That's Entertainment"*
- ❑ MCA 11002 — 1976 — 18.00
- *— Film credits in larger print on back cover, and list of songs includes "That's Entertainment"*

THERE'S NO BUSINESS LIKE SHOW BUSINESS
- ❑ Decca DL8091 [M] — 196? — 25.00
- *— Black label with color bars*
- ❑ Decca DL8091 [M] — 1954 — 30.00
- *— Black label with silver print*

THEY CALL IT AN ACCIDENT
- ❑ Island ILPS9757 — 1982 — 12.00
- *— Includes U2 (two versions of "October")*

THEY SHOOT HORSES, DON'T THEY?
- ❑ ABC ABCS-OC-10 — 1969 — 25.00

THIEF OF HEARTS
- ❑ Casablanca 822942-1 — 1984 — 25.00

THE THIN BLUE LINE
- ❑ Nonesuch 79209-1 — 1988 — 25.00

THIS COULD BE THE NIGHT
- ❑ MGM E-3530 [M] — 1957 — 50.00

THIS EARTH IS MINE
- ❑ Decca DL8915 [M] — 1959 — 100.00
- ❑ Decca DL78915 [S] — 1959 — 150.00
- ❑ Varese Sarabande VC-81076 — 1979 — 18.00
- *— Reissue of Decca 78915*

THIS PROPERTY IS CONDEMNED
- ❑ Verve V-8664 [M] — 1966 — 50.00
- ❑ Verve V6-8664 [S] — 1966 — 75.00

THE THOMAS CROWN AFFAIR
- ❑ United Artists UAS-5182 — 1968 — 25.00
- ❑ United Artists UA-LA295-G — 1974 — 15.00
- *— Reissue of 5182*

THOROUGHLY MODERN MILLIE
- ❑ Decca DL1500 [M] — 1967 — 25.00
- *— With bound-in booklet*
- ❑ Decca DL71500 [S] — 1967 — 25.00
- *— With bound-in booklet*

THOSE GLORIOUS MGM MUSICALS: DEEP IN MY HEART/WORDS AND MUSIC
- ❑ MGM 2-SES-54-ST — 1973 — 25.00

THOSE GLORIOUS MGM MUSICALS: EVERYTHING I HAVE IS YOURS/SUMMER STOCK/I LOVE MELVIN
- ❑ MGM 2-SES-52-ST — 1973 — 25.00

THOSE GLORIOUS MGM MUSICALS: GOOD NEWS/IN THE GOOD OLD SUMMERTIME/TWO WEEKS WITH LOVE
- ❑ MGM 2-SES-49-ST — 1973 — 25.00

THOSE GLORIOUS MGM MUSICALS: LOVELY TO LOOK AT/BRIGADOON
- ❑ MGM 2-SES-50-ST — 1973 — 25.00

THOSE GLORIOUS MGM MUSICALS: NANCY GOES TO RIO/RICH, YOUNG AND PRETTY/ROYAL WEDDING
- ❑ MGM 2-SES-53-ST — 1973 — 25.00

THOSE GLORIOUS MGM MUSICALS: ROSE MARIE/SEVN BRIDES FOR SEVEN BROTHERS
- ❑ MGM 2-SES-41-ST — 1973 — 25.00

THOSE GLORIOUS MGM MUSICALS: SHOW BOAT/ANNIE GET YOUR GUN
- ❑ MGM 2-SES-42-ST — 1973 — 25.00

THOSE GLORIOUS MGM MUSICALS: SINGIN' IN THE RAIN/EASTER PARADE
- ❑ MGM 2-SES-40-ST — 1973 — 25.00

THOSE GLORIOUS MGM MUSICALS: THE BAND WAGON/KISS ME, KATE
- ❑ MGM 2-SES-44-ST — 1973 — 25.00

THOSE GLORIOUS MGM MUSICALS: THE BARKLEYS OF BROADWAY/LES GIRLS
- ❑ MGM 2-SES-51-ST — 1973 — 25.00

THOSE GLORIOUS MGM MUSICALS: THE PIRATE/PAGAN LOVE SONG/HIT THE DECK
- ❑ MGM 2-SES-43-ST — 1973 — 40.00

THOSE GLORIOUS MGM MUSICALS: TILL THE CLOUDS ROLL BY/THREE LITTLE WORDS
- ❑ MGM 2-SES-45-ST — 1973 — 25.00

THREE BITES OF THE APPLE
- ❑ MCA 25010 — 198? — 10.00
- *— Reissue of MGM SE-4444*
- ❑ MGM E-4444 [M] — 1967 — 30.00
- ❑ MGM SE-4444 [S] — 1967 — 25.00

THREE FOR THE SHOW
- ❑ Mercury MG-25204 [M] — 1955 — 75.00

THREE IN THE ATTIC
- ❑ Sidewalk ST-5918 — 1968 — 30.00

THREE LITTLE WORDS
- ❑ MGM E-516 [10] — 1959 — 75.00

THE THREEPENNY OPERA
- ❑ RCA Victor LOC-1086 [M] — 1964 — 175.00
- *— With rare original cover: White background, pink and black drawing, characters underneath*
- ❑ RCA Victor LOC-1086 [M] — 1964 — 18.00
- *— Reissue cover: White background, orange drawing, Sammy Davis Jr. in foreground, "RE" at bottom*
- ❑ RCA Victor LSO-1086 [S] — 1964 — 250.00
- *— With rare original cover: White background, pink and black drawing, characters underneath*
- ❑ RCA Victor LSO-1086 [S] — 1964 — 25.00
- *— Reissue cover: White background, orange drawing, Sammy Davis Jr. in foreground, "RE" at bottom*

THE THREE WORLDS OF GULLIVER
- ❑ Colpix CP-414 [M] — 1960 — 75.00

THUNDER ALLEY
- ❑ Sidewalk T-5902 [M] — 1967 — 25.00
- ❑ Sidewalk ST-5902 [S] — 1967 — 30.00

THUNDERBALL
- ❑ United Artists UAL-4132 [M] — 1965 — 25.00
- ❑ United Artists UAS-5132 [S] — 1965 — 30.00
- ❑ United Artists SW-90820 [S] — 1965 — 40.00
- *— Capitol Record Club edition*

TICK…TICK…TICK
- ❑ MGM SE-4667 [M] — 1970 — 30.00

TILL THE CLOUDS ROLL BY
- ❑ MCA 25000 — 1986 — 12.00
- ❑ Metro M-578 [M] — 1966 — 15.00
- *— Reissue of MGM 501*
- ❑ Metro MS-578 [R] — 1966 — 12.00
- ❑ MGM E-501 [10] — 1950 — 50.00

TIMES SQUARE
- ❑ RSO RS-2-4203 — 1980 — 18.00
- *— Includes The Ramones ("I Wanna Be Sedated"), Talking Heads ("Life During Wartime"), XTC, Patti Smith, The Cure, etc.*

TIMES SQUARE SAMPLER
- ❑ RSO RPO1026 [DJ] — 1980 — 15.00
- *— Includes Talking Heads, Roxy Music, Pretenders, two others*

A TIME TO LOVE AND A TIME TO DIE
- ❑ Decca DL8778 [M] — 1958 — 150.00
- ❑ Varese Sarabande VC-81075 — 1979 — 18.00
- *— Reissue of Decca 8778*

TO BED… OR NOT TO BED
- ❑ London M-76005 [M] — 1963 — 40.00

TO KILL A MOCKINGBIRD
- ❑ Ava A-20 [M] — 1962 — 30.00
- ❑ Ava AS-20 [S] — 1962 — 30.00

TOKYO OLYMPIAD
- ❑ Monument MLP-8046 [M] — 1966 — 18.00
- ❑ Monument SLP-18046 [S] — 1966 — 25.00

TOM JONES
- ❑ United Artists UAL-4113 [M] — 1963 — 25.00
- ❑ United Artists UAS-5113 [S] — 1963 — 30.00

TOMMY
- ❑ Polydor PD 2-9502 — 1975 — 25.00

TOM SAWYER
- ❑ United Artists UA-LA057-F — 1973 — 25.00

TOO MUCH TOO SOON
- ❑ Mercury MG-20381 [M] — 1958 — 30.00
- ❑ Mercury SR-60019 [S] — 1958 — 100.00

TOP GUN
- ❑ Columbia SC40323 — 1986 — 12.00

TOPKAPI
- ❑ MCA 25118 — 1986 — 12.00
- ❑ United Artists UAL-4118 [M] — 1964 — 25.00
- ❑ United Artists UAS-5118 [S] — 1964 — 30.00

TO SIR, WITH LOVE
- ❑ Fontana MGF-27569 [M] — 1967 — 25.00
- ❑ Fontana SRF-67569 [S] — 1967 — 30.00

THE TOUCHABLES
- ❑ 20th Century Fox S-4206 — 1969 — 25.00

TO WONG FOO, THANKS FOR EVERYTHING! JULIE NEWMAR
- ❑ MCA 11231 — 1995 — 15.00
- *— Includes Cyndi Lauper, Salt-N-Pepa*

THE TRAIN
- ❑ United Artists UAL-4122 [M] — 1965 — 25.00
- ❑ United Artists UAS-5122 [S] — 1965 — 40.00

TRANSYLVANIA 6-5000
- ❑ Varese Sarabande STV-81267 — 1985 — 25.00

THE TRAP
- ❑ Atco 33-204 [M] — 1966 — 40.00
- ❑ Atco SD 33-204 [S] — 1966 — 80.00

TRAPEZE
- ❑ Columbia CL870 [M] — 1956 — 30.00

THE TRAPP FAMILY
- ❑ 20th Fox FOX-3044 [M] — 1961 — 30.00
- ❑ 20th Fox STX-3044 [S] — 1961 — 40.00

THE TREASURE OF SAN GENNARO
- ❑ Buddah BDS-5011 — 1968 — 40.00

THE TRIP
- ❑ Sidewalk T-5908 [M] — 1967 — 30.00
- ❑ Sidewalk ST-5908 [S] — 1967 — 40.00

TRIPLE CROSS
- ❑ United Artists UAL-4162 [M] — 1967 — 25.00
- ❑ United Artists UAS-5162 [S] — 1967 — 30.00

TROUBLE IN MIND
- ❑ Island 90501 — 1986 — 12.00
- *— Includes Marianne Faithfull*

THE TROUBLE WITH ANGELS
- ❑ Mainstream 56073 [M] — 1966 — 40.00
- ❑ Mainstream S-6073 [S] — 1966 — 100.00

TRUE GRIT
- ❑ Capitol ST-263 — 1969 — 30.00
- ❑ Capitol ST-8-0263 — 1969 — 40.00
- *— Capitol Record Club edition*

TRUE LIFE ADVENTURES
- ❑ Disneyland WDL-4011 [M] — 1957 — 80.00

TRUE STORIES, SOUNDS FROM
- ❑ Sire 25515 — 1986 — 12.00
- *— Includes individual members of Talking Heads…not to be confused with the Talking Heads album True Stories.*

THE TRUE STORY OF THE CIVIL WAR
- ❑ Coral CRL59100 [M] — 1958 — 100.00

TWO MULES FOR SISTER SARA
- ❑ Kapp KRS-5512 — 1970 — 30.00

TWO WEEKS WITH LOVE
- ❑ MGM E-530 [10] — 1950 — 40.00

ULYSSES
- ❑ RCA Victor LOC-1138 [M] — 1967 — 30.00
- ❑ RCA Victor LSO-1138 [S] — 1967 — 30.00

THE UMBRELLAS OF CHERBOURG (LES PARAPLUIES DE CHERBOURG)
- ❑ Philips PCC216 [M] — 1965 — 25.00
- ❑ Philips PCC616 [S] — 1965 — 30.00

THE UNBEARABLE LIGHTNESS OF BEING
- ❑ Fantasy FSP-21006 — 1988 — 25.00

UNCLE TOM'S CABIN
- ❑ Philips PHS600272 — 1968 — 40.00

Number	Title	Yr	NM
THE UNFORGIVEN			
❏ United Artists UAL-4068 [M]		1960	40.00
❏ United Artists UAS-5068 [S]		1960	80.00
THE UNSINKABLE MOLLY BROWN			
❏ MCA 25011		1986	12.00
—Reissue of MGM 4232			
❏ MGM E-4232 [M]		1964	18.00
❏ MGM SW-90048 [S]		1964	18.00
—Capitol Record Club edition			
❏ MGM W-90048 [M]		1964	15.00
—Capitol Record Club edition			
❏ MGM SE-4232 [S]		1964	25.00
UP IN THE CELLAR			
❏ American Int'l. A-1036		1970	25.00
UP THE DOWN STAIRCASE			
❏ United Artists UAL-4169 [M]		1967	25.00
❏ United Artists UAS-5169 [S]		1967	40.00
UP THE JUNCTION			
❏ Mercury SR-61159		1968	30.00
URBAN COWBOY			
❏ Full Moon/Asylum DP-90002		1980	15.00
URBAN COWBOY II (MORE MUSIC FROM THE ORIGINAL SOUNDTRACK)			
❏ Full Moon/Epic SE36291		1980	12.00
URGH! A MUSIC WAR			
❏ A&M SP-6019		1981	15.00
—Includes live tracks by The Police, Joan Jett and the Blackhearts, Wall of Voodoo, XTC, Go-Go's, Orchestral Manouvres in the Dark, Pere Ubu, Devo, Gary Numan, X, Gang of Four, The Cramps, etc.			
VALENTINO			
❏ United Artists UA-LA810-H		1977	30.00
VALLEY GIRL			
❏ Epic FE38623		1983	100.00
❏ Roadshow RS-101		1983	120.00
VALLEY OF THE DOLLS			
❏ 20th Century Fox TF-4196 [M]		1968	30.00
❏ 20th Century Fox TFS-4196 [S]		1968	30.00
❏ 20th Century Fox SW-91374 [S]		1968	30.00
—Capitol Record Club edition			
VANILLA SKY			
❏ Reprise RTH-2002		2002	40.00
—Classic Records edition on 180-gram vinyl ; contains a packet with a piece of film from the movie			
THE VANISHING POINT			
❏ Amos AAS-8002		1971	25.00
THE VANISHING PRAIRIE			
❏ Columbia CL6332 [10]		1954	100.00
VERTIGO			
❏ Mercury MG-20384 [M]		1958	175.00
THE VICTORS			
❏ Colpix CP-516 [M]		1963	25.00
❏ Colpix SCP-516 [S]		1963	30.00
VICTOR/VICTORIA			
❏ MGM MG-1-5407		1982	30.00
❏ Polydor MG-1-5407		198?	12.00
—Reissue of MGM release			
A VIEW TO A KILL			
❏ Capitol SJ-12413		1985	25.00
THE VIKINGS			
❏ United Artists UAL-4003 [M]		1958	30.00
❏ United Artists UAS-5003 [S]		1958	40.00
VILLA RIDES!			
❏ Dot DLP-25870		1968	40.00
THE V.I.P.S			
❏ MGM E-4184 [M]		1963	50.00
❏ MGM SE-4184 [S]		1963	75.00
—Music by Bill Evans			
VISION QUEST			
❏ Geffen R153920		1985	12.00
—Includes Madonna ("Crazy for You," "Gambler")			
VIVA MARIA!			
❏ United Artists UAL-4135 [M]		1965	25.00
❏ United Artists UAS-5135 [S]		1965	30.00
VIVA MAX!			
❏ RCA Victor LSP-4275		1969	25.00
THE VIXEN			
❏ Beverly Hills BHS-22		1968	50.00
VOYAGE EN BALLON			
❏ Philips PHM200029 [M]		1960	30.00
❏ Philips PHS600029 [S]		1960	40.00
WALK DON'T RUN			
❏ Mainstream 56080 [M]		1966	25.00
❏ Mainstream S-6080 [S]		1966	40.00
WALK ON THE WILD SIDE			
❏ Ava A-4-ST [M]		1962	25.00
❏ Ava AS-4-ST [S]		1962	40.00
❏ Choreo A-4-ST [M]		1962	30.00

Number	Title	Yr	NM
❏ Choreo AS-4-ST [S]		1962	50.00
A WALK WITH LOVE AND DEATH			
❏ Citadel CT-6025		1969	100.00
THE WANDERERS			
❏ Warner Bros. BSK3359		1979	30.00
WAR AND PEACE			
❏ Columbia CL930 [M]		1956	30.00
❏ Melodiya/Capitol SWAO2918		1968	40.00
THE WARLOCK			
❏ Intrada MAF-7003		1990	25.00
THE WAR LORD			
❏ Decca DL9149 [M]		1965	30.00
❏ Decca DL79149 [S]		1965	50.00
WARNING SHOT			
❏ Liberty LRP-3498 [M]		1967	30.00
❏ Liberty LST-7498 [S]		1967	40.00
WATERLOO			
❏ Paramount PAS-6003		1971	30.00
❏ Paramount SW-93729		1971	30.00
—Capitol Record Club edition			
WATERMELON MAN			
❏ Beverly Hills BHS-26		1970	30.00
WATERSHIP DOWN			
❏ Columbia JS35707		1978	30.00
WAY…WAY OUT			
❏ 20th Century Fox 3192 [M]		1966	30.00
❏ 20th Century Fox S-4192 [S]		1966	40.00
WEDDING IN MONACO			
❏ Mercury MG-20149 [M]		1956	300.00
WEST SIDE STORY			
❏ Columbia Masterworks OL5670 [M]		1961	25.00
—Originals have gatefold covers and gray and black labels with six "eye" logos			
❏ Columbia Masterworks OS2070 [S]		1961	30.00
—Originals have gatefold covers and gray and black labels with six "eye" logos			
❏ Columbia Masterworks OS2070 [S]		1963	18.00
—Gatefold cover; gray "360 Sound Stereo" label			
❏ Columbia Masterworks OS2070 [S]		196?	15.00
—Regular cover; gray "360 Sound Stereo" label			
❏ Columbia Masterworks OS2070 [S]		1971	12.00
—Regular cover; olive label with "Columbia" continuously around edge			
❏ Columbia Masterworks OL5670 [M]		1963	15.00
—Gatefold cover; gray "360 Sound Stereo" label			
❏ Columbia Masterworks OL5670 [M]		196?	12.00
—Regular cover; gray "360 Sound Stereo" label			
WHAT A WAY TO GO!			
❏ 20th Century Fox TFM-3143 [M]		1964	25.00
❏ 20th Century Fox TFS-4143 [S]		1964	40.00
WHAT'S NEW PUSSYCAT?			
❏ United Artists UAL-4128 [M]		1965	25.00
❏ United Artists UAS-5128 [S]		1965	30.00
❏ United Artists UA-LA278-G		1974	15.00
—Reissue of 5128			
WHEN HARRY MET SALLY…			
❏ Columbia SC45319		1989	15.00
WHEN THE BOYS MEET THE GIRLS			
❏ MCA 25013		1986	12.00
—Reissue of MGM 4334			
❏ MGM E-4334 [M]		1965	18.00
❏ MGM SE-4334 [S]		1965	30.00
WHEN THE WIND BLOWS			
❏ Virgin 90599		1987	12.00
—Includes David Bowie, Squeeze			
WHERE EAGLES DARE			
❏ MCA 25082		1986	12.00
—Reissue of MGM S1E-16			
❏ MGM S1E-16ST		1969	30.00
WHERE'S JACK?			
❏ Paramount PAS-5005		1969	30.00
WHERE'S POPPA?			
❏ United Artists UAS-5216		1970	30.00
WHERE THE BUFFALO ROAM			
❏ Backstreet 5126		1980	15.00
—Includes Neil Young			
THE WHISPERERS			
❏ MCA 25041		1986	12.00
—Reissue of United Artists 5161			
❏ United Artists UAL-4161 [M]		1967	25.00
❏ United Artists UAS-5161 [S]		1967	30.00
WHITE CHRISTMAS			
❏ Decca DL8083		1954	50.00
❏ Decca ED819 [PS]		1954	12.00
—Box for 3-EP set			
WHITE CHRISTMAS (PART 1)			
❏ Decca (# unknown)		1954	10.00
—Contents unknown			

Number	Title	Yr	NM
WHITE CHRISTMAS (PART 2)			
❏ Decca (# unknown)		1954	10.00
—Contents unknown			
WHITE CHRISTMAS (PART 3)			
❏ Decca (# unknown)		1954	10.00
—Contents unknown			
WHO FRAMED ROGER RABBIT?			
❏ Buena Vista 64100		1988	25.00
WHO'S AFRAID OF VIRGINIA WOOLF?			
❏ Warner Bros. B1656 [M]		1966	30.00
❏ Warner Bros. BS1656 [S]		1966	30.00
❏ Warner Bros. 2B1657 [M]		1966	40.00
—Above (1657) is the complete film, not just the music and some dialogue			
WHO'S THAT GIRL			
❏ Sire R100761		1987	12.00
—Includes Madonna ("Who's That Girl," "Causing a Commotion," "The Look of Love," "Can't Stop"); Scritti Politti ("Best Thing Ever")			
WILD, WILD WINTER			
❏ Decca DL4699 [M]		1966	25.00
❏ Decca DL74699 [S]		1966	30.00
THE WILD BUNCH			
❏ Varese Sarabande STV-81145		1981	18.00
—Reissue of Warner Bros. 1814			
❏ Warner Bros. WS1814		1969	150.00
THE WILD EYE			
❏ RCA Victor LSP-4003		1968	30.00
WILD GEESE			
❏ A&M SP-4730		1978	25.00
WILD IN THE STREETS			
❏ Tower SKAO5099		1968	30.00
WILD IS THE WIND			
❏ Columbia CL1090 [M]		1957	30.00
THE WILD ONE			
❏ Decca DL5515 [10]		1954	175.00
❏ Decca DL8349 [M]		1956	175.00
WILD ON THE BEACH			
❏ RCA Victor LPM-3441 [M]		1965	30.00
❏ RCA Victor LSP-3441 [S]		1965	40.00
THE WILD RACERS			
❏ Sidewalk ST-5914		1968	30.00
WILD WHEELS			
❏ RCA Victor LSO-1156		1969	25.00
WILLIE DYNAMITE			
❏ MCA 393		1974	25.00
WILLOW			
❏ Virgin Movie Music 90939		1988	30.00
WILLY WONKA AND THE CHOCOLATE FACTORY			
❏ MCA 37124		198?	12.00
—Reissue of Paramount 6012			
❏ Paramount PAS-6012		1971	40.00
THE WITCHES OF EASTWICK			
❏ Warner Bros. 25607		1987	30.00
WITH A SONG IN MY HEART			
❏ Capitol L309 [10]		1952	40.00
❏ Capitol T309 [M]		195?	30.00
THE WIZARD OF OZ			
❏ MCA 39046		198?	12.00
—Reissue of MGM 3996			
❏ MGM E-3464 [M]		1956	50.00
—Yellow label			
❏ MGM E-3996 [M]		1962	18.00
—Gatefold cover, black label			
❏ MGM SE-3996 [R]		196?	18.00
—Gatefold cover, black label			
WOMEN OF THE WORLD			
❏ Decca DL9112 [M]		1963	25.00
❏ Decca DL79112 [S]		1963	30.00
WONDERFUL COUNTRY			
❏ United Artists UAL-4050 [M]		1959	50.00
❏ United Artists UAS-5050 [S]		1959	150.00
WONDERFUL TO BE YOUNG			
❏ Dot DLP-3474 [M]		1962	30.00
❏ Dot DLP-25474 [S]		1962	40.00
THE WONDERFUL WORLD OF THE BROTHERS GRIMM			
❏ MGM 1E-3 [M]		1962	30.00
—With box and hardback book			
❏ MGM S1E-3 [S]		1962	40.00
—With box and hardback book			
WORDS AND MUSIC			
❏ MCA 25029		1986	15.00
—Reissue of MGM 505 with the addition of "Slaughter on Tenth Avenue," which does not appear on either the 10-inch LP or the budget-line Metro reissues			
❏ Metro M-580 [M]		1966	15.00

Number	Title	Yr	NM

❏ Metro MS-580 [R] — 1966 — 12.00
❏ MGM E-505 [10] — 1950 — 50.00

THE WORLD OF SUZIE WONG
❏ RCA Victor LOC-1059 [M] — 1960 — 25.00
❏ RCA Victor LSO-1059 [S] — 1960 — 50.00

THE WRAITH
❏ Scotti Bros. SZ40429 — 1986 — 12.00
— Includes Honeymoon Suite

WRITTEN ON THE WIND
❏ Decca DL8424 [M] — 1956 — 40.00
— Black label, silver print, or pink label, black print promo
❏ Decca DL8424 [M] — 196? — 25.00
— Black label with color bars
❏ Varese Sarabande VC-81074 — 1979 — 15.00
— Reissue of Decca 8424

THE WRONG BOX
❏ Mainstream 56088 [M] — 1966 — 150.00
❏ Mainstream S-6088 [S] — 1966 — 175.00

WUTHERING HEIGHTS
❏ American Int'l. A-1039 — 1971 — 30.00

W.W. AND THE DIXIE DANCEKINGS
❏ 20th Century ST-103 — 1975 — 30.00

THE YELLOW CANARY
❏ Verve V-8548 [M] — 1963 — 50.00
❏ Verve V6-8548 [S] — 1963 — 75.00

THE YELLOW ROLLS-ROYCE
❏ MGM T90424 [M] — 1965 — 18.00
— Capitol Record Club edition
❏ MGM ST90424 [S] — 1965 — 18.00
— Capitol Record Club edition
❏ MGM E-4292 [M] — 1965 — 25.00
❏ MGM SE-4292 [S] — 1965 — 30.00

YES, GEORGIO
❏ London PDV9001 — 1982 — 12.00
— Contains one Christmas song:

YESTERDAY, TODAY AND TOMORROW
❏ Warner Bros. W1552 [M] — 1964 — 40.00
❏ Warner Bros. WS1552 [S] — 1964 — 50.00

YOJIMBO
❏ MGM E-4096 [M] — 1962 — 150.00
❏ MGM SE-4096 [S] — 1962 — 175.00

YOU ARE WHAT YOU EAT
❏ Columbia Masterworks OS3240 — 1968 — 25.00

YOUNG BILLY YOUNG
❏ MCA 25031 — 1986 — 25.00
— Reissue of United Artists 5199
❏ United Artists UAS-5199 — 1969 — 75.00

YOUNG DOCTORS IN LOVE
❏ Regency RI-8501 — 1982 — 25.00

YOUNG FRANKENSTEIN
❏ ABC ABCD-870 — 1975 — 25.00

THE YOUNG GIRLS OF ROCHEFORT
❏ Philips PCC 2-226 [M] — 1968 — 25.00
❏ Philips PCC 2-626 [S] — 1968 — 30.00

THE YOUNG LIONS
❏ Decca DL8719 [M] — 1958 — 30.00
❏ Decca DL78719 [S] — 1958 — 100.00
❏ Varese Sarabande STV-81115 — 1981 — 18.00
— Reissue of Decca 78719

YOUNG LOVERS
❏ Columbia Masterworks OL7010 [M] — 1964 — 25.00
❏ Columbia Masterworks OS2510 [S] — 1964 — 30.00

YOUNG MAN WITH A HORN
❏ Columbia CL6106 [10] — 1950 — 200.00
❏ Columbia CL582 [M] — 1950 — 40.00

THE YOUNG SAVAGES
❏ Columbia CL1672 [M] — 1961 — 30.00
❏ Columbia CS8472 [S] — 1961 — 150.00

YOUNG WINSTON
❏ Angel SFO-36901 — 1972 — 30.00

YOU ONLY LIVE TWICE
❏ United Artists UAL-4155 [M] — 1967 — 25.00
❏ United Artists UAS-5155 [S] — 1967 — 30.00
❏ United Artists UA-LA289-G — 1974 — 15.00
— Reissue of 5155

YOURS, MINE AND OURS
❏ MCA 1434 — 198? — 10.00
— Reissue of United Artists 5181
❏ United Artists UAS-5181 — 1968 — 25.00

Z
❏ Columbia Masterworks OS3370 — 1970 — 25.00

ZABRISKIE POINT
❏ MCA 25032 — 1986 — 12.00
— Reissue of MGM 4468
❏ MGM SE-4468 — 1970 — 25.00

ZACHARIAH
❏ ABC ABCS-OC-13 — 1970 — 30.00

ZOOT SUIT
❏ MCA 5267 — 1981 — 25.00

ZORBA THE GREEK
❏ 20th Century T-903 — 1973 — 15.00
— Reissue of 20th Century Fox 4167
❏ 20th Century Fox TFM-3167 [M] — 1965 — 25.00
❏ 20th Century Fox TFS-4167 [S] — 1965 — 30.00
❏ Casablanca 826245-1 — 198? — 10.00
— Reissue of 20th Century 903

ZULU
❏ United Artists UAL-4116 [M] — 1964 — 40.00
❏ United Artists UAS-5116 [S] — 1964 — 80.00

VARIOUS ARTISTS COLLECTIONS

ACCENT ON TROMBONE
❏ Urania UJLP-1205 [M] — 1955 — 175.00

AC-DC BLUES
❏ Stash ST-106 — 197? — 25.00

ADD-A-PART JAZZ
❏ Columbia CL908 [M] — 1956 — 75.00

AFRO-COOL
❏ GNP Crescendo GNP-48 [M] — 1959 — 50.00

AFRO-CUBAN JAZZ
❏ Verve 833561-1 — 198? — 30.00
❏ Verve VE-2-2522 — 197? — 35.00

AFRO SUMMIT
❏ BASF 20675 — 197? — 50.00
❏ Pausa 7026 — 198? — 25.00

AFTER HOUR JAZZ
❏ Epic LN(# unk) [M] — 1955 — 150.00

AFTER HOURS BLUES, 1949
❏ Biograph 12010 — 1969 — 30.00

ALIVEMUTHERFORYA
❏ Columbia JC35349 — 1977 — 30.00
— With Billy Cobham, Alphonso Johnson, Steve Khan, Tom Scott

ALL DAY LONG
❏ Prestige PRLP-7081 [M] — 1957 — 300.00
— Reissued as Prestige 7277; see KENNY BURRELL.

ALL NIGHT LONG
❏ Prestige PRLP-7073 [M] — 1957 — 300.00
— Reissued as Prestige 7289; see KENNY BURRELL.

ALL-STAR DATES
❏ RCA Victor LPT-21 [10] — 1951 — 150.00

ALL STAR JAZZ
❏ Halo 50223 [M] — 195? — 30.00

ALL STAR SESSIONS
❏ Capitol M-11031 — 1973 — 30.00

ALL-STAR STOMPERS
❏ Circle L-402 [M] — 1951 — 40.00

ALL STAR SWING GROUPS
❏ Savoy Jazz SJL-2218 — 198? — 30.00

ALL STAR TRIBUTE TO TATUM
❏ American Recording Society G-424 [M] — 1957 — 75.00

ALTO ALTITUDE
❏ EmArcy MG-36018 [M] — 1955 — 300.00

ALTO ARTISTRY
❏ Trip 5543 — 197? — 25.00

ALTO SAXES
❏ Norgran MGN-1035 [M] — 1955 — 300.00
❏ Verve MGV-8126 [M] — 1957 — 175.00
❏ Verve V-8126 [M] — 1961 — 75.00

ALTO SUMMIT
❏ Prestige PRLP-7684 — 1969 — 35.00

AMERICANS ABROAD, VOL. 1
❏ Pax LP-6009 [10] — 1955 — 80.00

AMERICANS ABROAD, VOL. 2
❏ Pax LP-6015 [10] — 1955 — 80.00

AMERICANS IN EUROPE, VOL. 1
❏ ABC Impulse! AS-36 [S] — 1968 — 30.00
❏ Impulse! A-36 [M] — 1963 — 150.00
❏ Impulse! AS-36 [S] — 1963 — 120.00

AMERICANS IN EUROPE, VOL. 2
❏ ABC Impulse! AS-37 [S] — 1968 — 30.00
❏ Impulse! A-37 [M] — 1963 — 150.00
❏ Impulse! AS-37 [S] — 1963 — 120.00

AMERICA'S GREATEST JAZZMEN PLAY COLE PORTER
❏ Moodsville MVLP-34 [M] — 1963 — 40.00
— Green label
❏ Moodsville MVST-34 [S] — 1963 — 40.00

— Green label
❏ Moodsville MVLP-34 [M] — 1965 — 50.00
— Blue label, trident logo at right
❏ Moodsville MVST-34 [S] — 1965 — 50.00
— Blue label, trident logo at right

AMERICA'S GREATEST JAZZMEN PLAY GEORGE GERSHWIN
❏ Moodsville MVLP-33 [M] — 1963 — 40.00
— Green label
❏ Moodsville MVST-33 [S] — 1963 — 40.00
— Green label
❏ Moodsville MVLP-33 [M] — 1965 — 50.00
— Blue label, trident logo at right
❏ Moodsville MVST-33 [S] — 1965 — 50.00
— Blue label, trident logo at right

AMERICA'S GREATEST JAZZMEN PLAY RICHARD RODGERS
❏ Moodsville MVLP-35 [M] — 1963 — 40.00
— Green label
❏ Moodsville MVST-35 [S] — 1963 — 40.00
— Green label
❏ Moodsville MVLP-35 [M] — 1965 — 50.00
— Blue label, trident logo at right
❏ Moodsville MVST-35 [S] — 1965 — 50.00
— Blue label, trident logo at right

AMERICA'S GREATEST JAZZMEN PLAY THE BROADWAY SCENE
❏ Moodsville MVLP-38 [M] — 1963 — 40.00
— Green label
❏ Moodsville MVST-38 [S] — 1963 — 40.00
— Green label
❏ Moodsville MVLP-38 [M] — 1965 — 50.00
— Blue label, trident logo at right
❏ Moodsville MVST-38 [S] — 1965 — 50.00
— Blue label, trident logo at right

ANNIVERSARY
❏ Xanadu 201 — 1986 — 25.00

ANOTHER MONDAY NIGHT AT BIRDLAND
❏ Roulette R52022 [M] — 1959 — 75.00
❏ Roulette SR52022 [S] — 1959 — 75.00

AN ANTHOLOGY OF CALIFORNIA MUSIC
❏ Jazz: West Coast JWC-500 [M] — 1955 — 300.00

AN ANTHOLOGY OF CALIFORNIA MUSIC, VOL. 2
❏ Jazz: West Coast JWC-501 [M] — 1956 — 300.00

ANTHROPOLOGY
❏ Zim 1002 — 197? — 30.00

THE ART OF JAZZ PIANO
❏ Epic LN3295 [M] — 1956 — 150.00

THE ART OF THE BALLAD
❏ Verve VSP-17 [M] — 1966 — 35.00
❏ Verve VSPS-17 [R] — 1966 — 25.00

THE ART OF THE BALLAD 2
❏ Verve VSP-38 [M] — 1966 — 35.00
❏ Verve VSPS-38 [R] — 1966 — 25.00

THE ART OF THE JAM SESSION: MONTREUX '77
❏ Pablo Live 2620106 — 1978 — 150.00

ASIAN JOURNAL
❏ Music of the World H-303 — 198? — 25.00

ASSORTED FLAVORS OF PACIFIC JAZZ
❏ Pacific Jazz HFS-1 [M] — 1956 — 150.00

THE ATLANTIC FAMILY LIVE AT MONTREUX
❏ Atlantic SD-2-3000 — 1977 — 35.00

ATLANTIC JAZZ
❏ Atlantic 81712 — 1987 — 300.00
— Boxed set with 12 volumes in 15 records, liner notes and credits

ATLANTIC JAZZ: BEBOP
❏ Atlantic 81702 — 1987 — 25.00

ATLANTIC JAZZ: FUSION
❏ Atlantic 81711 — 1987 — 25.00

ATLANTIC JAZZ: INTROSPECTION
❏ Atlantic 81710 — 1987 — 25.00

ATLANTIC JAZZ: KANSAS CITY
❏ Atlantic 81701 — 1987 — 25.00

ATLANTIC JAZZ: MAINSTREAM
❏ Atlantic 81704 — 1987 — 25.00

ATLANTIC JAZZ: NEW ORLEANS
❏ Atlantic 81700 — 1987 — 25.00

ATLANTIC JAZZ: PIANO
❏ Atlantic 81707 — 1987 — 30.00

ATLANTIC JAZZ: POST BOP
❏ Atlantic 81705 — 1987 — 25.00

ATLANTIC JAZZ: SINGERS
❏ Atlantic 81706 — 1987 — 30.00

ATLANTIC JAZZ: SOUL
❏ Atlantic 81708 — 1987 — 30.00

Number	Title	Yr	NM

ATLANTIC JAZZ: THE AVANT-GARDE
❑ Atlantic 81709 — 1987 — 25.00

ATLANTIC JAZZ: WEST COAST
❑ Atlantic 81703 — 1987 — 25.00

ATLANTIC RECORDS: GREAT MOMENTS IN JAZZ
❑ Atlantic 81907 — 1989 — 30.00

AUDIO MASTER PLUS SAMPLER
❑ A&M SP6-3021 — 1983 — 30.00

AUDIO MASTER PLUS SAMPLER II
❑ A&M SP6-3021 — 1984 — 30.00

AUTOBIOGRAPHY IN JAZZ
❑ Debut DEB-198 [M] — 1955 — 350.00
❑ Fantasy OJC-115 — 198? — 12.00

AWARD ALBUM JAZZ VOCALS
❑ Bethlehem BCP-6060 [M] — 1961 — 300.00

BACKGROUNDS OF JAZZ, VOL. 1: THE JUG BANDS
❑ X LX-3009 [10] — 1954 — 175.00

BACKGROUNDS OF JAZZ, VOL. 2: COUNTRY & URBAN BLUES
❑ X LVA-3016 [10] — 1954 — 175.00

BACKGROUNDS OF JAZZ, VOL. 3: KINGS OF THE BLUES
❑ X LVA-3032 [10] — 1955 — 175.00

BACKWOOD BLUES
❑ Riverside RLP-1039 [10] — 1954 — 300.00

BALLROOM BANDSTAND
❑ Columbia CL611 [M] — 1955 — 85.00

BARGAIN DAY
❑ EmArcy MG-36087 [M] — 1956 — 250.00

BARRELHOUSE BOOGIE
❑ Bluebird 8334#NAME? — 198? — 25.00

BARREL HOUSE PIANO
❑ Brunswick BL58022 [10] — 1951 — 120.00

BARRELHOUSE PIANO 1927-36
❑ Yazoo 1028 — 197? — 25.00

THE BASS
❑ ABC Impulse! AS-9284 — 197? — 150.00

BATTLE OF BANDS
❑ Capitol H235 [10] — 1950 — 175.00

BATTLE OF JAZZ, VOL. 3
❑ Brunswick BL58039 [10] — 1953 — 150.00

BATTLE OF THE BIG BANDS
❑ Capitol T667 [M] — 1956 — 150.00
❑ Trip 5527 — 197? — 25.00

BATTLE OF THE SAXES-TENOR ALL STARS
❑ EmArcy MG-36023 [M] — 1955 — 300.00

BEBOP BOYS
❑ Savoy Jazz SJL-2225 — 198? — 30.00

THE BEBOP ERA
❑ Columbia Jazz Masterpieces CJ40972 — 1988 — 25.00

THE BE-BOP ERA
❑ RCA Victor LPV-519 — 1965 — 50.00

BE-BOP SINGERS
❑ Prestige PRST-7828 — 1971 — 30.00

BE OUR GUEST
❑ Gene Norman GNP-20 [M] — 1955 — 85.00

BEST COAST JAZZ
❑ EmArcy MG-36039 [M] — 1955 — 300.00

BEST FROM THE WEST: MODERN SOUNDS FROM CALIFORNIA, VOL. 1
❑ Blue Note BLP-5059 [10] — 1955 — 250.00

BEST FROM THE WEST: MODERN SOUNDS FROM CALIFORNIA, VOL. 2
❑ Blue Note BLP-5060 [10] — 1955 — 250.00

THE BEST OF ARGO JAZZ
❑ Argo ALPS-1 [M] — 1961 — 75.00

THE BEST OF BLUE NOTE, VOL. 1
❑ Blue Note BST-84429 — 197? — 50.00

THE BEST OF BLUE NOTE, VOL. 2
❑ Blue Note BST-84433 — 197? — 50.00

BEST OF DIXIELAND
❑ RCA Victor ANL1-1431 — 1976 — 12.00

THE BEST OF DIXIELAND
❑ RCA Victor LPM-2982 [M] — 1965 — 50.00
❑ RCA Victor LSP-2982 [R] — 1965 — 30.00

BEST OF THE BIG NAME BANDS
❑ RCA Camden CAL-368 [M] — 1958 — 75.00

BETHLEHEM'S BEST
❑ Bethlehem EXLP-6 [M] — 1958 — 400.00
— Box set of 82, 83, and 84

BETHLEHEM'S BEST, VOLUME 1
❑ Bethlehem BCP-82 [M] — 1958 — 300.00

BETHLEHEM'S BEST, VOLUME 2
❑ Bethlehem BCP-83 [M] — 1958 — 300.00

BETHLEHEM'S BEST, VOLUME 3
❑ Bethlehem BCP-84 [M] — 1958 — 300.00

BETHLEHEM'S GRAB BAG
❑ Bethlehem EXLP-2 [M] — 1958 — 250.00

THE BIG 18 -- LIVE ECHOES OF THE SWINGING BANDS
❑ RCA Victor LSP-1921 [S] — 1959 — 50.00
❑ RCA Victor LPM-1921 [M] — 1959 — 40.00

BIG BAND CONTRAST
❑ Bethlehem BCP-6037 [M] — 1960 — 250.00

BIG BAND JAZZ
❑ Brunswick BL58050 [10] — 1953 — 150.00

BIG BAND JAZZ: TULSA TO HARLEM
❑ Delmark DL-439 — 1989 — 25.00

BIG BANDS
❑ Capitol STFL-293 — 1969 — 150.00
— One album each by Les Brown, Glen Gray, Duke Ellington, Benny Goodman, Harry James and Woody Herman

BIG BANDS!
❑ Onyx 202 — 197? — 30.00

BIG BANDS: BIG BAND BASH
❑ Time-Life STBB-15 — 1984 — 20.00

BIG BANDS: ON THE ROAD
❑ Time-Life STBB-18 — 1985 — 20.00

BIG BANDS: THE SMALL GROUPS
❑ Time-Life STBB-21 — 1985 — 20.00

BIG BANDS: UPTOWN
❑ Time-Life STBB-20 — 1985 — 20.00

BIG BANDS: WORLD WAR II
❑ Time-Life STBB-28 — 1986 — 20.00

THE BIG BANDS 1933
❑ Prestige PRLP-7645 — 1969 — 35.00

BIG BANDS ARE BACK
❑ Commodore J2-15596 — 198? — 30.00

BIG BANDS' GREATEST HITS
❑ Columbia G30009 — 1970 — 50.00
— Red "360 Sound" labels
❑ Columbia G30009 — 1970 — 35.00
— Orange labels
❑ Columbia CG30009 — 197? — 30.00
— CG" prefix is a reissue of "G

BIG BANDS' GREATEST HITS, VOL. 2
❑ Columbia G31213 — 1972 — 35.00
❑ Columbia CG31213 — 197? — 30.00
— CG" prefix is a reissue of "G

BIG BANDS OF THE SINGING YEARS, VOLUME 1
❑ Collectables COL-5096 — 198? — 25.00

BIG BANDS OF THE SINGING YEARS, VOLUME 2
❑ Collectables COL-5097 — 198? — 25.00

BIG BANDS OF THE SWING YEARS
❑ Everest Archive of Folk & Jazz 359 — 198? — 25.00

BIG BAND STEREO
❑ Capitol SW1055 [S] — 1959 — 150.00

BIG BANDS UPTOWN
❑ MCA 1323 — 198? — 25.00

BIG BANDS UPTOWN, VOL. 1
❑ Decca DL79242 — 1969 — 30.00

THE BIG BEAT
❑ Milestone 47016 — 1990 — 35.00

BIG LITTLE BANDS
❑ Onyx 220 — 197? — 30.00

BIG NAME DIXIE
❑ Score SLP-4024 [M] — 1958 — 150.00

BILL EVANS: A TRIBUTE
❑ Palo Alto PA-8028 — 1982 — 35.00

BILLIE, ELLA, LENA, SARAH!
❑ Columbia Jazz Odyssey PC36811 — 198? — 25.00

BILLIE HOLIDAY REVISITED
❑ Mainstream MRL-409 — 197? — 30.00

BIRDLAND ALL STARS AT CARNEGIE HALL
❑ Roulette RE-127 — 197? — 30.00

BIRDLANDERS
❑ Everest Archive of Folk & Jazz 275 — 197? — 25.00

THE BIRDLAND STARS ON TOUR, VOL. 1
❑ RCA Victor LPM-1327 [M] — 1956 — 40.00

THE BIRDLAND STARS ON TOUR, VOL. 2
❑ RCA Victor LPM-1328 [M] — 1956 — 40.00

THE BIRDLAND STORY
❑ Roulette RB-2 [M] — 1961 — 40.00
❑ Roulette SRB-2 [S] — 1961 — 40.00

BIRD'S NIGHT: A CELEBRATION OF THE MUSIC OF CHARLIE PARKER, LIVE AT THE FIVE SPOT
❑ Savoy Jazz SJL-2257 — 198? — 30.00

BIRD'S NIGHT -- THE MUSIC OF CHARLIE PARKER
❑ Savoy MG-12138 [M] — 1958 — 150.00

THE BIRTH OF BOP, VOL. 1
❑ Savoy MG-9022 [10] — 1953 — 300.00

THE BIRTH OF BOP, VOL. 2
❑ Savoy MG-9023 [10] — 1953 — 300.00

THE BIRTH OF BOP, VOL. 3
❑ Savoy MG-9024 [10] — 1953 — 300.00

THE BIRTH OF BOP, VOL. 4
❑ Savoy MG-9025 [10] — 1953 — 300.00

THE BIRTH OF BOP, VOL. 5
❑ Savoy MG-9026 [10] — 1953 — 300.00

BLACK AND WHITE RAGTIME, 1921-39
❑ Biograph 12047 — 197? — 30.00

BLACKBERRY JAM 1943-45
❑ Sunbeam 214 — 197? — 25.00

BLACK CALIFORNIA, VOL. 1
❑ Savoy Jazz SJL-2215 — 198? — 30.00

BLACK CALIFORNIA, VOL. 2
❑ Savoy Jazz SJL-2242 — 198? — 30.00

BLACK GIANTS
❑ Columbia CG33402 — 197? — 35.00

BLACK LION AT MONTREUX
❑ Black Lion 213 — 197? — 35.00

THE BLACK SWING TRADITION
❑ Savoy Jazz SJL-2246 — 198? — 30.00

BLOWIN' SESSIONS
❑ Blue Note BN-LA521#VALUE! — 1975 — 50.00

BLOWOUT AT MARDI GRAS
❑ Cook LP-1084 [M] — 1955 — 50.00

THE BLUE NOTE 50TH ANNIVERSARY COLLECTION VOL. 1: FROM BOOGIE TO BOP, 1939-1956
❑ Blue Note B1-92465 — 1989 — 35.00

THE BLUE NOTE 50TH ANNIVERSARY COLLECTION VOL. 2: THE JAZZ MESSAGE, 1956-1965
❑ Blue Note B1-92468 — 1989 — 35.00

THE BLUE NOTE 50TH ANNIVERSARY COLLECTION VOL. 3: FUNK AND BLUES, 1956-1967
❑ Blue Note B1-92471 — 1989 — 35.00

THE BLUE NOTE 50TH ANNIVERSARY COLLECTION VOL. 4: OUTSIDE IN, 1964-1989
❑ Blue Note B1-92474 — 1989 — 35.00

THE BLUE NOTE 50TH ANNIVERSARY COLLECTION VOL. 5: LIGHTING THE FUSE, 1970-1989
❑ Blue Note B1-92477 — 1989 — 35.00

BLUE NOTE '86: A GENERATION OF JAZZ
❑ Blue Note BQ-85127 — 1986 — 30.00

BLUE NOTE CLASSICS
❑ Blue Note B-6509 [M] — 1969 — 35.00

BLUE NOTE LIVE AT THE ROXY
❑ Blue Note BN-LA663-4047 — 1976 — 35.00

BLUE NOTE MEETS THE L.A. PHILHARMONIC
❑ Blue Note BN-LA870#NAME? — 1977 — 35.00

THE BLUES, VOL. 2
❑ Pacific Jazz JWC-502 [M] — 1956 — 150.00
❑ World Pacific JWC-502 [M] — 1958 — 175.00

THE BLUES, VOL. 2: HAVE BLUES, WILL TRAVEL
❑ World Pacific JWC-509 [M] — 1958 — 175.00

THE BLUES, VOL. 3: BLOWIN' THE BLUES
❑ World Pacific JWC-512 [M] — 1958 — 175.00
❑ World Pacific ST-1029 [S] — 1959 — 175.00

THE BLUES AND ALL THAT JAZZ
❑ MCA 1353 — 198? — 25.00

BLUES FOR TOMORROW
❑ Fantasy OJC-030 — 1982 — 12.00
❑ Riverside RLP 12-243 [M] — 1957 — 300.00

BLUES IN CONCERT
❑ Groove Merchant 4405 — 197? — 25.00

THE BLUES IN MODERN JAZZ
❑ Atlantic 1337 [M] — 1961 — 300.00
— Multicolor label, white "fan" logo at right
❑ Atlantic 1337 [M] — — 50.00
— Multicolor label, black "fan" logo at right
❑ Atlantic SD1337 [R] — 1969 — 30.00

THE BLUES IN STEREO
❑ World Pacific ST-1021 [S] — 1959 — 175.00

Number	Title	Yr	NM

BODY AND SOUL
❏ RCA Victor LPV-501 — 1964 — 50.00

BONING UP ON 'BONES
❏ EmArcy MG-36038 [M] — 1955 — 300.00

BOOGIE WOOGIE
❏ Decca DL5248 [10] — 1950 — 175.00

BOOGIE WOOGIE KINGS AND QUEENS
❏ Decca DL5249 [10] — 1950 — 175.00

BOOGIE WOOGIE PIANO
❏ Brunswick BL58018 [10] — 1950 — 120.00

BOOGIE WOOGIE PIANOS
❏ Columbia KC32708 — 197? — 25.00

BOOGIE WOOGIE RARITIES (1927-43)
❏ Milestone M-2009 — 197? — 30.00

BOOGIE WOOGIE TRIO
❏ Storyville 4006 — 198? — 25.00

BOOTY
❏ Mainstream MRL-413 — 1974 — 75.00

BOP CITY: EVIDENCE
❏ Boplicity BOPM-12 — 198? — 25.00

BOP CITY: MIDNIGHT
❏ Boplicity BOPM-9 — 198? — 25.00

BOP CITY: STRAIGHT AHEAD
❏ Boplicity BOPM-10 — 198? — 25.00

BOP CITY: THINGS ARE GETTING BETTER
❏ Boplicity BOPM-11 — 198? — 25.00

BOP LIVES
❏ Pickwick SPC-5011 — 197? — 25.00

BRASS FEVER
❏ ABC Impulse! AS-9308 — 1975 — 35.00

BRASS FEVER: TIME IS RUNNING OUT
❏ ABC Impulse! AS-9319 — 197? — 35.00

BRITISH FESTIVAL OF JAZZ CONCERT
❏ Decca DL5422 [10] — 1952 — 250.00

BRITISH JAZZ FESTIVAL
❏ Decca DL5424 [10] — 1952 — 250.00

BROTHERS AND OTHER MOTHERS
❏ Savoy Jazz SJL-2210 — 198? — 30.00

BROTHERS AND OTHER MOTHERS, VOL. 2
❏ Savoy Jazz SJL-2236 — 198? — 30.00

BUSHKIN-SAFRANSKI-WILSON GROUPS
❏ Allegro 1590 [10] — 1955 — 150.00

CAFÉ SOCIETY
❏ Onyx 210 — 197? — 30.00

CALIFORNIA CONCERT
❏ CTI CTX22 — 197? — 35.00

CATS AND JAMMER KIDS
❏ Angel ANG-60007 [10] — 1955 — 150.00

CATS VS. CHICKS
❏ MGM E-255 [10] — 1954 — 150.00

A CELEBRATION OF DUKE
❏ Fantasy OJC-605 — 1991 — 30.00
❏ Pablo Today 2312119 — 197? — 35.00

CENTRAL AVENUE BREAKDOWN, VOL. 1
❏ Onyx 212 — 197? — 30.00

CENTRAL AVENUE BREAKDOWN, VOL. 2
❏ Onyx 215 — 197? — 30.00

THE CHANGING FACE OF HARLEM
❏ Savoy Jazz SJL-2208 — 198? — 30.00

THE CHANGING FACE OF HARLEM, VOL. 2
❏ Savoy Jazz SJL-2224 — 198? — 30.00

CHARLIE PARKER 10TH MEMORIAL CONCERT
❏ Limelight LM-82017 [M] — 1965 — 35.00
❏ Limelight LS-86017 [S] — 1965 — 50.00
❏ Trip 5510 — 197? — 25.00

CHARLIE PARKER MEMORIAL CONCERT
❏ Cadet 2CA-60002 — 1971 — 50.00
❏ Chess CH-92510 — 198? — 15.00

CHICAGO: THE LIVING LEGENDS, VOL. 1
❏ Riverside RLP-389 [M] — 196? — 50.00
❏ Riverside RS-9389 [R] — 196? — 30.00

CHICAGO: THE LIVING LEGENDS, VOL. 2
❏ Riverside RLP-390 [M] — 196? — 50.00
❏ Riverside RS-9390 [R] — 196? — 30.00

CHICAGO AND ALL THAT JAZZ!
❏ Verve V-8441 [M] — 1961 — 75.00
❏ Verve V6-8441 [S] — 1962 — 75.00

THE CHICAGOANS
❏ Decca DL79231 — 1968 — 30.00

CHICAGO / AUSTIN HIGH SCHOOL
❏ RCA Victor LPM-1508 [M] — 1957 — 75.00

CHICAGO JAZZ, 1923-29
❏ Biograph 12005 — 1968 — 30.00

CHICAGO JAZZ, VOLUME 2, 1925-29
❏ Biograph 12043 — 197? — 30.00

CHICAGO JAZZ ALBUM
❏ Decca DL8029 [M] — 1954 — 175.00

CHICAGO'S BOSS TENORS
❏ Chess CHV-414 — 1970 — 35.00

CHICAGO SOUTH SIDE
❏ Historical 10 — 1968 — 25.00

CHICAGO SOUTH SIDE, VOL. 2
❏ Historical 30 — 1969 — 25.00

CHOCOLATE DANDIES, 1928-1933
❏ Swing SW-8448 — 198? — 25.00

CLAMBAKE ON BOURBON STREET
❏ Cook LP-1085 [10] — 1955 — 150.00

CLASSIC BLUES ACCOMPANISTS
❏ Riverside RLP-1052 [10] — 1955 — 300.00

CLASSIC CAPITOL JAZZ SESSIONS
❏ Mosaic MQ19-170 — 199? — 400.00

THE CLASSIC COLLECTION -- CONTEMPORARY: THE GREAT JAZZ MEN/VOL. 2
❏ Dot DLP-25879 — 1968 — 85.00

THE CLASSIC COLLECTION -- TRADITIONAL: THE GREAT JAZZ MEN/VOL. 1
❏ Dot DLP-25878 — 1968 — 85.00

CLASSIC JAZZ PIANO STYLES
❏ RCA Victor LPV-544 [M] — 1967 — 50.00

CLASSIC PIANOS
❏ Doctor Jazz FW38851 — 198? — 25.00

CLASSICS IN JAZZ
❏ Capitol T320 [M] — 1954 — 75.00

CLASSICS IN JAZZ: COOL AND QUIET
❏ Capitol H371 [10] — 1953 — 175.00

CLASSICS IN JAZZ: DIXIELAND STYLISTS
❏ Capitol H321 [10] — 1952 — 175.00

CLASSICS IN JAZZ: SMALL COMBOS
❏ Capitol H322 [10] — 1952 — 175.00

CLASSIC TENORS, VOL. 2
❏ Doctor Jazz FW39519 — 198? — 25.00

COLLECTORS' ITEMS, 1922-30
❏ Historical 11 — 1967 — 25.00

COLLECTORS' ITEMS, 1925-29
❏ Historical 20 — 1968 — 25.00

COLLECTORS ITEMS, VOL. 2
❏ Riverside RLP-1040 [10] — 1954 — 300.00

COLLECTOR'S JACKPOT, VOL. 1
❏ Jazz Archives JA-21 — 198? — 25.00

COLLECTOR'S JACKPOT, VOL. 2
❏ Jazz Archives JA-40 — 198? — 25.00

COLLEGE JAZZ: DIXIELAND
❏ Columbia CL736 [M] — 1956 — 50.00

COLORADO JAZZ PARTY
❏ BASF 25099 — 197? — 50.00

COLUMBIA JAZZ FESTIVAL
❏ Columbia JJ-1 [M] — 1959 — 75.00

COLUMBIA'S ALL NEW TIME-RELEASE CAPSULE
❏ Columbia AS247 [DJ] — 1977 — 35.00
— *Promo-only sampler*

COMBO JAZZ
❏ Jazztone J-1221 [M] — 1956 — 75.00

COMPARATIVE BLUES
❏ Hall of Fame 603 — 197? — 25.00
❏ Jazztone J-1258 [M] — 1957 — 75.00

THE COMPLETE COMMODORE JAZZ RECORDINGS, VOLUME I
❏ Mosaic M23-123 — 199? — 400.00

THE COMPLETE COMMODORE JAZZ RECORDINGS, VOLUME II
❏ Mosaic M23-128 — 199? — 400.00

THE COMPLETE COMMODORE JAZZ RECORDINGS, VOLUME III
❏ Mosaic M20-134 — 199? — 300.00

THE COMPLETE KEYNOTE COLLECTION
❏ Keynote 830121-1 — 1986 — 300.00

THE COMPLETE MASTER JAZZ PIANO SERIES
❏ Mosaic M6-140 — 199? — 150.00

COMPOSERS AT PLAY: HAROLD ARLEN AND COLE PORTER
❏ X LVA-1003 [M] — 1955 — 50.00

THE COMPOSITIONS OF BENNY GOLSON
❏ Riverside RLP-3505 [M] — 1962 — 250.00
❏ Riverside RS-93505 [S] — 1962 — 250.00

THE COMPOSITIONS OF BOBBY TIMMONS
❏ Riverside RLP-3512 [M] — 1962 — 250.00
❏ Riverside RS-93512 [S] — 1962 — 250.00

THE COMPOSITIONS OF CHARLIE PARKER
❏ Riverside RLP-3506 [M] — 1962 — 250.00
❏ Riverside RS-93506 [S] — 1962 — 250.00

THE COMPOSITIONS OF COLE PORTER
❏ Riverside RM-3515 [M] — 1963 — 175.00
❏ Riverside RS-93515 [S] — 1963 — 175.00

THE COMPOSITIONS OF DIZZY GILLESPIE
❏ Riverside RLP-3508 [M] — 1962 — 250.00
❏ Riverside RS-93508 [S] — 1962 — 250.00

THE COMPOSITIONS OF DUKE ELLINGTON
❏ Riverside RLP-3507 [M] — 1962 — 250.00
❏ Riverside RS-93507 [S] — 1962 — 250.00

THE COMPOSITIONS OF DUKE ELLINGTON, VOL. 2
❏ Riverside RLP-3510 [M] — 1962 — 250.00
❏ Riverside RS-93510 [S] — 1962 — 250.00

THE COMPOSITIONS OF GEORGE GERSHWIN
❏ Riverside RM-3517 [M] — 1963 — 175.00
❏ Riverside RS-93517 [S] — 1963 — 175.00

THE COMPOSITIONS OF HAROLD ARLEN
❏ Riverside RM-3518 [M] — 1963 — 175.00
❏ Riverside RS-93518 [S] — 1963 — 175.00

THE COMPOSITIONS OF HORACE SILVER
❏ Riverside RLP-3509 [M] — 1962 — 250.00
❏ Riverside RS-93509 [S] — 1962 — 250.00

THE COMPOSITIONS OF IRVING BERLIN
❏ Riverside RM-3519 [M] — 1963 — 175.00
❏ Riverside RS-93519 [S] — 1963 — 175.00

THE COMPOSITIONS OF JEROME KERN
❏ Riverside RM-3516 [M] — 1963 — 175.00
❏ Riverside RS-93516 [S] — 1963 — 175.00

COMPOSITIONS OF LIONEL HAMPTON
❏ Crown CLP-5107 [M] — 195? — 30.00

THE COMPOSITIONS OF MILES DAVIS
❏ Riverside RLP-3504 [M] — 1962 — 250.00
❏ Riverside RS-93504 [S] — 1962 — 250.00

THE COMPOSITIONS OF RICHARD RODGERS
❏ Riverside RM-3514 [M] — 1963 — 175.00
❏ Riverside RS-93514 [S] — 1963 — 175.00

THE COMPOSITIONS OF TADD DAMERON
❏ Riverside RLP-3511 [M] — 1962 — 250.00
❏ Riverside RS-93511 [S] — 1962 — 250.00

THE COMPOSITIONS OF THELONIOUS MONK
❏ Riverside RLP-3503 [M] — 1962 — 250.00
❏ Riverside RS-93503 [S] — 1962 — 250.00

CONCEPTION
❏ Prestige PRLP-7013 [M] — 1956 — 300.00

CONCERT IN ARGENTINA
❏ Halcyon 113 — 197? — 35.00

CONCERT IN JAZZ
❏ Tops L-1532 [M] — 1958 — 50.00

CONCERT JAZZ
❏ Brunswick BL54027 [M] — 1956 — 75.00

A CONCORD JAM
❏ Concord Jazz CJ-142 — 1981 — 25.00

A CONCORD JAM, VOL. 2
❏ Concord Jazz CJ-180 — 1982 — 25.00

A CONCORD JAM, VOL. 3: A GREAT AMERICAN EVENING
❏ Concord Jazz CJ-220 — 1984 — 25.00

CONCORD JAZZ GUITAR COLLECTION, VOL. 1 AND 2
❏ Concord Jazz CJ-160 — 198? — 30.00

THE CONCORD SOUND, VOL. 1
❏ Concord Jazz CJ-278 — 1985 — 25.00

COOL AND CAREFREE
❏ Columbia Special Products CSP119 [M] — 1963 — 30.00
— *Sold only by Carrier air conditioner dealers*

COOL CALIFORNIA
❏ Savoy Jazz SJL-2254 — 198? — 30.00

COOL EUROPE
❏ MGM E-3157 [M] — 1955 — 85.00

COOLIN'
❏ New Jazz NJLP-8216 [M] — 1959 — 250.00
— *Purple label*
❏ New Jazz NJLP-8216 [M] — 1965 — 175.00
— *Blue label, trident logo at right*

COOL JAZZ
❏ Seeco CELP-465 [M] — 1960 — 150.00

COOL JAZZ FROM HOLLAND
❏ Epic LN1126 [10] — 1955 — 100.00

COPULATIN' BLUES
❏ Stash ST-101 — 197? — 35.00

COPULATIN' BLUES, VOL. 2
❏ Stash ST-122 — 198? — 35.00

Number	Title	Yr	NM
COPULATIN' RHYTHM			
❑ Jass J-3		198?	35.00
COPULATIN' RHYTHM, VOL. 2			
❑ Jass J-5		198?	35.00
THE CORE OF JAZZ			
❑ MGM SE-4737		1970	30.00
COTTON CLUB STARS			
❑ Stash ST-124		198?	30.00
CRITICS' CHOICE			
❑ Dawn DLP-1123 [M]		1958	175.00
CRUISIN'			
❑ Jazzland JLP-7 [M]		1960	75.00
❑ Jazzland JLP-97 [S]		1960	75.00
CTI SUMMER JAZZ AT THE HOLLYWOOD BOWL: LIVE ONE			
❑ CTI 7076		197?	30.00
CTI SUMMER JAZZ AT THE HOLLYWOOD BOWL: LIVE THREE			
❑ CTI 7078		197?	30.00
CTI SUMMER JAZZ AT THE HOLLYWOOD BOWL: LIVE TWO			
❑ CTI 7077		197?	30.00
CYLINDER JAZZ			
❑ Saydisc SDL-334		198?	25.00
DANCE, BE HAPPY!			
❑ Columbia CL967 [M]		1957	50.00
DANCE BAND HITS			
❑ RCA Victor LPT-2 [10]		1951	40.00
DANCE TO THE BANDS			
❑ Capitol TBO727 [M]		1956	75.00
❑ Capitol T977 [M]		1958	100.00
DANCING WITH THE STARS			
❑ Epic LN3136 [M]		1955	150.00
DAS IS JAZZ!			
❑ Decca DL8229 [M]		1956	175.00
A DATE WITH GREATNESS			
❑ Imperial LP-12188A [R]		1962	200.00
❑ Imperial LP-9188A [M]		1962	300.00
—Features Aladdin tracks by Coleman Hawkins, Howard McGhee and Lester Young			
A DATE WITH RIVERSIDE			
❑ Riverside S-4 [M]		195?	40.00
DECADE OF JAZZ, VOLUME 1, 1939-49			
❑ Blue Note BN-LA158#VALUE!		1974	35.00
DECADE OF JAZZ, VOLUME 2, 1949-59			
❑ Blue Note BN-LA159#VALUE!		1974	35.00
DECADE OF JAZZ, VOLUME 3, 1959-69			
❑ Blue Note BN-LA160#VALUE!		1974	35.00
THE DEFINITIVE JAZZ SCENE, VOL. 1			
❑ ABC Impulse! AS-99 [S]		1968	30.00
❑ Impulse! A-99 [M]		1966	35.00
❑ Impulse! AS-99 [S]		1966	150.00
THE DEFINITIVE JAZZ SCENE, VOL. 2			
❑ ABC Impulse! AS-100 [S]		1968	30.00
❑ Impulse! A-100 [M]		1966	35.00
❑ Impulse! AS-100 [S]		1966	150.00
THE DEFINITIVE JAZZ SCENE, VOL. 3			
❑ ABC Impulse! AS-9101 [S]		1968	30.00
❑ Impulse! A-9101 [M]		1966	35.00
❑ Impulse! AS-9101 [S]		1966	150.00
DIGITAL III AT MONTREUX			
❑ Pablo Live 2308223		1980	30.00
DIXIE, LONDON STYLE			
❑ London LL1337 [M]		1956	50.00
DIXIELAND AT CARNEGIE HALL			
❑ Forum SF-9011 [S]		196?	75.00
❑ Forum F-9011 [M]		196?	50.00
❑ Roulette R25038 [M]		1958	75.00
—Originals have a black label			
❑ Roulette R25038 [M]		1959	50.00
—Second pressings have a white label with colored spokes			
DIXIELAND AT ITS BEST			
❑ RCA Camden CAL-838 [M]		1964	30.00
❑ RCA Camden CAS-838 [R]		1964	25.00
DIXIELAND AT JAZZ, LTD.			
❑ Atlantic 1261 [M]		1957	300.00
—Black label			
❑ Atlantic 1261 [M]		1961	175.00
—Multicolor label, white "fan" logo at right			
DIXIELAND AT JAZZ, LTD., VOL. 1			
❑ Atlantic ALS-139 [10]		1952	300.00
DIXIELAND AT JAZZ, LTD., VOL. 2			
❑ Atlantic ALS-140 [10]		1952	300.00
DIXIELAND CLASSICS			
❑ Jazztone J-1216 [M]		1956	75.00

Number	Title	Yr	NM
DIXIELAND CONTRASTS			
❑ Jazzman LJ-334 [M]		1954	75.00
DIXIELAND FESTIVAL, VOL. 1			
❑ Vik LX-1057 [M]		1956	75.00
DIXIELAND HITS			
❑ Swingville SVLP-2040 [M]		1962	40.00
—Purple label			
❑ Swingville SVLP-2040 [M]		1965	50.00
—Blue label, trident logo at right			
DIXIELAND IN OLD NEW ORLEANS			
❑ Golden Crest GC-3021 [M]		1958	50.00
DIXIELAND JAZZ			
❑ Audiophile XL-325 [M]		1954	75.00
❑ Audiophile XL-330 [M]		1954	75.00
❑ Grand Award GA 33-310 [M]		1955	120.00
—With wrap-around outer cover			
❑ Grand Award GA 33-310 [M]		1955	85.00
—Without wrap-around outer cover			
DIXIELAND JAZZ CLASSICS			
❑ Herwin H-116		1980	30.00
DIXIELAND JAZZ GEMS			
❑ Commodore FL-20010 [10]		1950	150.00
DIXIELAND MAIN STREAM			
❑ Savoy MG-12213 [M]		196?	50.00
DIXIELAND -- NEW ORLEANS			
❑ Mainstream 56003 [M]		1965	75.00
❑ Mainstream S-6003 [R]		1965	30.00
DIXIELAND RHYTHM KINGS			
❑ Paradox LP-6002 [10]		1951	150.00
DIXIELAND SERIES, VOL. 1			
❑ Savoy MG-15005 [10]		1952	175.00
DIXIELAND SERIES, VOL. 2			
❑ Savoy MG-15009 [10]		1952	175.00
DIXIE LAND U.S.A.			
❑ Promenade 2134 [M]		195?	20.00
DIXIELAND VS. BIRDLAND			
❑ MGM E-231 [10]		1954	175.00
DIZZY ATMOSPHERE			
❑ Specialty LP-2110 [M]		1957	40.00
—Original edition, heavier vinyl			
❑ Specialty LP-2110 [M]		198?	50.00
—Reissue on lighter vinyl			
DOUBLE BARREL JAZZ			
❑ Bethlehem BCP-87 [M]		1958	250.00
DOWN BEAT JAZZ CONCERT			
❑ Dot DLP-9003 [M]		1958	175.00
❑ Dot DLP-29003 [S]		1958	175.00
DOWN BEAT JAZZ CONCERT, VOL. 2			
❑ Dot DLP-3188 [M]		1959	175.00
❑ Dot DLP-25188 [S]		1959	175.00
DOWN BEAT'S HALL OF FAME, VOL. 1			
❑ Verve MGV-8320 [M]		1959	150.00
❑ Verve V-8320 [M]		1961	50.00
DREAMING ON THE RIVER TO NEW ORLEANS			
❑ Southland SLP-238		1963	35.00
THE DRUMS			
❑ ABC Impulse! AS-9272		197?	150.00
THE EARL BAKER CYLINDERS			
❑ Jazz Archives JA-43		198?	25.00
EARLY AND RARE: CLASSIC JAZZ "COLLECTORS ITEMS			
❑ Riverside RLP 12-134 [M]		1957	300.00
EARLY JAZZ GREATS, VOL. 1			
❑ Jazztone J-1249 [M]		1957	75.00
EARLY JAZZ GREATS, VOL. 2			
❑ Jazztone J-1252 [M]		1957	75.00
EARLY MODERN			
❑ Milestone M-9035		197?	30.00
EARLY VIPER JIVE			
❑ Stash ST-105		197?	25.00
EARTHY!			
❑ Prestige PRLP-7102 [M]		1957	500.00
THE EAST COAST JAZZ SCENE, VOL. 1			
❑ Coral CRL57035 [M]		1956	150.00
EASY LISTENING			
❑ Audiophile AP-27 [M]		1953	75.00
❑ Audiophile AP-38 [M]		1953	75.00
❑ Audiophile XL-327 [M]		1954	75.00
ECHOES OF AN ERA			
❑ Elektra 60021		1982	25.00
—With Stanley Clarke, Chick Corea, Chaka Khan and Joe Henderson			
ECHOES OF AN ERA VOLUME 2: THE CONCERT			
❑ Elektra/Musician 60165		1983	25.00

Number	Title	Yr	NM
ECHOES OF ENJA			
❑ Enja 4000		197?	30.00
ECHOES OF NEW ORLEANS			
❑ Southland SLP-239		1963	35.00
EIGHT WAYS TO JAZZ			
❑ Riverside RLP 12-272 [M]		1958	300.00
THE ELVIS PRESLEY YEARS			
❑ Reader's Digest RBA-236A		1991	150.00
ENCYCLOPEDIA OF JAZZ IN THE '60'S, VOL. 1			
❑ Verve V-8677 [M]		1966	35.00
❑ Verve V6-8677 [S]		1966	50.00
THE ENCYCLOPEDIA OF JAZZ IN THE 70S			
❑ RCA Victor APL2-1984		197?	35.00
THE ENCYCLOPEDIA OF JAZZ ON RECORDS			
❑ Decca DXF140 [M]		1957	275.00
—Box set; individually issued as Decca 8398, 8399, 8400 and 8401			
THE ENCYCLOPEDIA OF JAZZ ON RECORDS, VOL. 1: JAZZ OF THE TWENTIES			
❑ Decca DL8398 [M]		1957	175.00
THE ENCYCLOPEDIA OF JAZZ ON RECORDS, VOL. 1 AND 2: JAZZ OF THE TWENTIES/JAZZ OF THE THIRTIES			
❑ MCA 4061		197?	20.00
THE ENCYCLOPEDIA OF JAZZ ON RECORDS, VOL. 2: JAZZ OF THE THIRTIES			
❑ Decca DL8399 [M]		1957	175.00
THE ENCYCLOPEDIA OF JAZZ ON RECORDS, VOL. 3: JAZZ OF THE FORTIES			
❑ Decca DL8400 [M]		1957	175.00
THE ENCYCLOPEDIA OF JAZZ ON RECORDS, VOL. 3 AND 4: JAZZ OF THE FORTIES/JAZZ OF THE FIFTIES			
❑ MCA 4062		197?	20.00
THE ENCYCLOPEDIA OF JAZZ ON RECORDS, VOL. 4: JAZZ OF THE FIFTIES			
❑ Decca DL8401 [M]		1957	175.00
THE ENCYCLOPEDIA OF JAZZ ON RECORDS, VOL. 5: JAZZ OF THE SIXTIES			
❑ MCA 4063		197?	20.00
ENERGY ESSENTIALS			
❑ ABC Impulse! ASD-9228		197?	150.00
ERA OF THE CLARINET			
❑ Mainstream S-6011 [R]		1965	30.00
❑ Mainstream 56011 [M]		1965	75.00
ESCAPADE REVIEWS THE JAZZ SCENE			
❑ Liberty SL-9005 [M]		1957	75.00
ESCAPE			
❑ Gene Norman GNP-27 [M]		1958	75.00
ESQUIRE'S 2ND ANNUAL ALL-AMERICAN JAZZ CONCERT			
❑ Sunbeam 219		197?	30.00
ESQUIRE'S ALL-AMERICAN HOT JAZZ			
❑ RCA Victor LPV-544 [M]		1967	50.00
ESQUIRE'S WORLD OF JAZZ			
❑ Capitol TBO1970 [M]		1963	100.00
❑ Capitol STBO1970 [S]		1963	100.00
THE ESSENTIAL JAZZ VOCALS			
❑ Verve V-8505 [M]		1963	50.00
❑ Verve V6-8505 [R]		1963	30.00
AN EVENING OF JAZZ			
❑ Norgran MGN-1065 [M]		1956	300.00
❑ Verve MGV-8155 [M]		1957	150.00
❑ Verve V-8155 [M]		1961	50.00
FANTASY SAMPLER			
❑ Fantasy FS-654 [M]		195?	25.00
—Red vinyl			
THE FEMININE TOUCH			
❑ Decca DL5486 [10]		1953	175.00
❑ Decca DL8316 [M]		1956	175.00
FESTIVAL JAZZ, VOL. 1			
❑ Jim Taylor Presents 106		197?	30.00
FESTIVAL JAZZ, VOL. 2			
❑ Jim Taylor Presents 107		197?	30.00
FIFTEEN STAR SAXOPHONES			
❑ Bethlehem BCP-6035 [M]		1959	250.00
52ND STREET, VOL. 1			
❑ Onyx 203		197?	30.00
52ND STREET, VOL. 2			
❑ Onyx 217		197?	30.00
52ND STREET JAZZ			
❑ Waldorf Music Hall MH 33-148 [10]		195?	200.00
50 YEARS OF JAZZ GREATS			
❑ Columbia Musical Treasury P3S5932		197?	50.00

Number / Title	Yr	NM
50 YEARS OF JAZZ GUITAR		
❑ Columbia CG33566	1973	35.00
FILL YOUR HEAD WITH JAZZ		
❑ Columbia G30217	1971	35.00
FIRE INTO MUSIC		
❑ CTI CTS-2	197?	35.00
FIRST ALBUM OF JAZZ		
❑ Folkways FP-712 [10]	1951	120.00
FIVE BIRDS AND A MONK		
❑ Galaxy 5134	1979	30.00
FIVE FEET OF SWING		
❑ Decca DL8045 [M]	1954	175.00
FOOTNOTES TO JAZZ, VOL. 2: ANATOMY OF A		
JAZZ COMPOSITION		
❑ Folkways FP-31 [10]	1951	120.00
FOR DANCERS ONLY		
❑ Epic LN3120 [M]	1955	150.00
FOREMOST!		
❑ Onyx 201	197?	30.00
FOR JAZZ LOVERS		
❑ EmArcy MG-36086 [M]	1956	250.00
FOUNDATIONS		
❑ MCA 4153	198?	30.00
FOUNDATIONS OF MODERN JAZZ		
❑ Everest Archive of Folk & Jazz 229	196?	25.00
FOUR ALTOS		
❑ Prestige PRLP-7116 [M]	1957	300.00
FOUR DECADES OF JAZZ		
❑ Xanadu 5001	197?	35.00
FOUR FRENCH HORNS		
❑ Savoy MG-12173 [M]	1961	150.00
THE FOUR MOST GUITARS		
❑ ABC-Paramount ABC-109 [M]	1956	75.00
❑ Paramount LP-109 [10]	1954	120.00
THE FOUR ROSES DANCE PARTY		
❑ Columbia Special Products XTV68933/4 [M]	1961	35.00
FOUR TO GO		
❑ Columbia CL2018 [M]	1963	50.00
❑ Columbia CS8818 [S]	1963	75.00
FOUR TROMBONES... THE DEBUT RECORDINGS		
❑ Prestige 24097	197?	175.00
FRANK BULL AND GENE NORMAN PRESENT		
DIXIELAND JUBILEE		
❑ Decca DL7022 [10]	1952	175.00
FRENCH FESTIVAL		
❑ Classic Jazz 133	197?	30.00
FRENCH TOAST		
❑ Angel ANG-60009 [10]	1956	150.00
FRIDAY THE 13TH, COOK COUNTY JAIL		
❑ Groove Merchant 515	197?	35.00
FROM CANADA WITH LOVE		
❑ PM 011	198?	25.00
FROM SPIRITUALS TO SWING		
❑ Vanguard VMS-73131	197?	25.00
❑ Vanguard VSD-47/48	197?	35.00
FUNKY BLUES NO. 2		
❑ American Recording Society G-404 [M]	1956	75.00
FUN ON THE FRETS: EARLY JAZZ GUITAR		
❑ Yazoo 1061	197?	25.00
GARY MOORE PRESENTS "MY KIND OF MUSIC		
❑ Columbia CL717	1956	75.00
GEMS OF JAZZ, VOL. 1		
❑ Decca DL5133 [10]	1950	175.00
❑ Decca DL8039 [M]	1954	175.00
GEMS OF JAZZ, VOL. 2		
❑ Decca DL5134 [10]	1950	175.00
❑ Decca DL8040 [M]	1954	175.00
GEMS OF JAZZ, VOL. 3		
❑ Decca DL5383 [10]	1952	175.00
❑ Decca DL8041 [M]	1954	175.00
GEMS OF JAZZ, VOL. 4		
❑ Decca DL5384 [10]	1952	175.00
❑ Decca DL8042 [M]	1954	175.00
GEMS OF JAZZ, VOL. 5		
❑ Decca DL8043 [M]	1954	175.00
GET IT TOGETHER		
❑ Mainstream MRL-350	197?	30.00
GIANTS OF BOOGIE WOOGIE		
❑ Riverside RLP 12-106 [M]	1956	300.00
GIANTS OF JAZZ		
❑ American Recording Society G-401 [M]	1956	75.00
THE GIANTS OF JAZZ		
❑ Columbia CL1970 [M]	1963	75.00
GIANTS OF JAZZ		
❑ George Wein Collection GW-3004	198?	25.00
GIANTS OF JAZZ, VOL. 2		
❑ Who's Who in Jazz 21014	197?	25.00
GIANTS OF JAZZ, VOLUME 1		
❑ Who's Who in Jazz WWLP21012	1977	25.00
GIANTS OF JAZZ: THE GUITARISTS		
❑ Time-Life STL-J-12	1980	35.00
GIANTS OF JAZZ ORGAN		
❑ King 837 [M]	1963	250.00
GIANTS OF JAZZ VOL. 2		
❑ American Recording Society G-444 [M]	1957	75.00
GIANTS OF SMALL BAND SWING, VOL. 1		
❑ Fantasy OJC-1723	1990	12.00
❑ Riverside RLP 12-143 [M]	1957	300.00
GIANTS OF SMALL BAND SWING, VOL. 2		
❑ Fantasy OJC-1724	1990	12.00
❑ Riverside RLP 12-145 [M]	1957	300.00
GIANTS OF THE BLUES TENOR SAX		
❑ Prestige 24101	197?	35.00
GIANTS OF THE FUNK TENOR SAX		
❑ Prestige 24102	197?	35.00
GIANTS OF TRADITIONAL JAZZ		
❑ Savoy Jazz SJL-2251	198?	30.00
THE GIRLS SING		
❑ Savoy MG-12220 [M]	196?	50.00
GOD REST YE MERRY, JAZZMEN		
❑ Columbia FC37551	1981	30.00
—7-inch 33 1/3 rpm single with small hole; distributed by various banks		
❑ Columbia PC37551	198?	20.00
—Budget-line reissue		
THE GOLDEN ERA OF JAZZ, VOL. 1		
❑ Savoy MG-15015 [10]	1952	175.00
THE GOLDEN ERA OF JAZZ, VOL. 2		
❑ Savoy MG-15018 [10]	1952	175.00
GOLDEN JAZZ INTRSUMENTALS		
❑ Bethlehem BCP-6065 [M]	1962	250.00
THE GREAT BAND ERA		
❑ Reader's Digest RD-25 [M]	1965	50.00
—Box set with flip-open top		
❑ Reader's Digest RD-25 [R]	1965	35.00
—Box set with flip-open top		
THE GREAT BANDS		
❑ Columbia Musical Treasury P2M5267	1968	50.00
GREAT BLUES		
❑ Riverside RLP-1074 [10]	1955	300.00
GREAT BLUES SINGERS		
❑ Riverside RLP 12-121 [M]	1957	300.00
THE GREAT BLUES SINGERS		
❑ Riverside RLP-1032 [10]	1954	300.00
GREATEST HITS		
❑ Harmony HL7255 [M]	1960	35.00
THE GREATEST JAZZ CONCERT EVER		
❑ Prestige 24024	197?	35.00
THE GREATEST JAZZ CONCERT IN THE WORLD		
❑ Pablo 2625704	197?	30.00
THE GREATEST NAMES IN JAZZ		
❑ Verve PR2-3	196?	50.00
—Box set		
GREAT GUITARS AT THE WINERY		
❑ Concord Jazz CJ-131	1980	30.00
—Original issue		
GREAT GUITARS OF JAZZ		
❑ MGM SE-4691	1970	30.00
GREAT JAZZ		
❑ Rondo-lette A-31	195?	30.00
THE GREAT JAZZ ALBUM		
❑ Project 3 PR6009/10	197?	35.00
THE GREAT JAZZ ALBUM, VOLUME 2		
❑ Project 3 PR6023/24	197?	35.00
GREAT JAZZ BRASS		
❑ RCA Camden CAL-383 [M]	1958	75.00
GREAT JAZZ PIANISTS		
❑ RCA Camden CAL-328 [M]	1958	75.00
GREAT JAZZ PIANISTS OF OUR TIME		
❑ RCA Camden CAL-882 [M]	1965	35.00
❑ RCA Camden CAS-882 [R]	1965	25.00
GREAT JAZZ REEDS		
❑ RCA Camden CAL-339 [M]	1958	75.00
THE GREAT JAZZ SINGERS		
❑ Halo 50269 [M]	1957	35.00
THE GREAT SWING BANDS		
❑ Jazztone J-1245 [M]	1957	75.00
GREAT SWING BANDS OF THE FORTIES		
❑ Audio Lab AL-1530 [M]	1959	175.00
THE GREAT TENOR JAZZMEN		
❑ Allegro 1634 [M]	195?	40.00
GREAT TRUMPET ARTISTS		
❑ RCA Victor LPT-26 [10]	1951	150.00
❑ RCA Victor LPT-35 [10]	1952	150.00
GRETSCH DRUM NIGHT, VOLUME 2		
❑ Roulette R52067 [M]	1961	75.00
❑ Roulette SR52067 [S]	1961	75.00
GRETSCH DRUM NIGHT AT BIRDLAND		
❑ Roulette R52049 [M]	1960	75.00
❑ Roulette SR52049 [S]	1960	75.00
THE GRIFFITH PARK COLLECTION		
❑ Elektra/Musician 60025	1982	25.00
—All-star session with STANLEY CLARKE; CHICK COREA; JOE HENDERSON; FREDDIE HUBBARD; LENNY WHITE		
THE GRIFFITH PARK COLLECTION VOL. 2: THE		
CONCERT		
❑ Elektra/Musician 60262	198?	30.00
A GRP CHRISTMAS COLLECTION		
❑ GRP GR-9574	1988	30.00
GRP LIVE IN SESSION		
❑ GRP GR-1023	1985	25.00
GRP SAMPLER, VOL. 1		
❑ GRP F-7701	198?	25.00
GRP SUPER LIVE IN CONCERT		
❑ GRP GR-2-1650	1988	30.00
GUIDE TO JAZZ		
❑ RCA Victor LPM-1393 [M]	1956	75.00
GUITAR PLAYER		
❑ MCA 6002	197?	35.00
❑ MCA 8012	197?	35.00
GUITAR PLAYER PRESENTS JAZZ GUITAR		
CLASSICS		
❑ Fantasy OJC-6012	1990	35.00
GUITAR PLAYERS		
❑ Mainstream MRL-410	197?	30.00
GUITAR SESSION		
❑ Inner City IC-6050	198?	30.00
GUITAR WORKSHOP		
❑ Pausa 7089	198?	25.00
HANDFUL OF COOL JAZZ		
❑ Bethlehem BCP-90 [M]	1959	250.00
HAPPY JAZZ		
❑ Jazztone J-1215 [M]	1956	75.00
THE HARD SWING		
❑ Pacific Jazz JWC-508 [M]	1957	150.00
❑ World Pacific JWC-508 [M]	1958	175.00
HARLEM COMES TO LONDON		
❑ Swing SW-8444	198?	25.00
HARLEM JAZZ 1930		
❑ Brunswick BL58024 [10]	1951	150.00
HARLEN ODYSSEY		
❑ Xanadu 112	197?	25.00
HEAD START -- BOB THIELE EMERGENCY		
❑ Flying Dutchman FDS-104	1969	30.00
HERE AND NOW		
❑ Catalyst 7613	197?	25.00
HERE COME THE GIRLS		
❑ Verve MGV-2036 [M]	1956	250.00
❑ Verve V-2036 [S]	1961	50.00
HERE COME THE SWINGING BANDS		
❑ Verve MGV-8207 [M]	1957	175.00
❑ Verve V-8207 [M]	1961	50.00
HI-FI JAZZ		
❑ Brunswick BL58058 [10]	1954	150.00
HI-FI JAZZ SESSION		
❑ Masterseal MSLP5013 [M]	1957	75.00
A HI-FI SALUTE TO THE GREAT ONES		
❑ MGM E-3325 [M]	1956	75.00
A HI-FI SALUTE TO THE GREAT ONES, VOL. 2		
❑ MGM E-3354 [M]	1956	75.00
HIGHLIGHTS IN JAZZ: TWELFTH ANNIVERSARY		
CONCERT		
❑ Stash ST-254	1985	25.00
THE HISTORIC DONAUESCHINGEN JAZZ		
CONCERT 1957		
❑ Pausa 7081	198?	25.00
HISTORIC JAZZ CONCERT AT MUSIC INN		
❑ Atlantic 1298 [M]	1958	300.00
—Black label		
❑ Atlantic 1298 [M]	1961	175.00
—Multicolor label, white "fan" logo at right		
❑ Atlantic 1298 [M]	1963	50.00

Number	Title	Yr	NM

—Multicolor label, black "fan" logo at right

HISTORY OF CLASSIC JAZZ
❏ Riverside SDP-11 [M] — 1956 — 300.00
—Five-record set in leatherette album with booklet; records were available separately as Riverside 112, 113, 114, 115 and 116.

HISTORY OF CLASSIC JAZZ, VOL. 1
❏ Riverside RLP 12-112 [M] — 1957 — 300.00

HISTORY OF CLASSIC JAZZ, VOL. 2
❏ Riverside RLP 12-113 [M] — 1957 — 300.00

HISTORY OF CLASSIC JAZZ, VOL. 3
❏ Riverside RLP 12-114 [M] — 1957 — 300.00

HISTORY OF CLASSIC JAZZ, VOL. 4
❏ Riverside RLP 12-115 [M] — 1957 — 300.00

HISTORY OF CLASSIC JAZZ, VOL. 5
❏ Riverside RLP 12-116 [M] — 1957 — 300.00

HISTORY OF JAZZ, VOL. 1: NEW ORLEANS ORIGINS
❏ Capitol T793 [M] — 1956 — 150.00

HISTORY OF JAZZ, VOL. 1: THE SOLID SOUTH
❏ Capitol H239 [10] — 1950 — 175.00

HISTORY OF JAZZ, VOL. 2: THE GOLDEN ERA
❏ Capitol H240 [10] — 1950 — 175.00

HISTORY OF JAZZ, VOL. 2: THE TURBULENT '20S
❏ Capitol T794 [M] — 1956 — 150.00

HISTORY OF JAZZ, VOL. 3: EVERYBODY SWINGS
❏ Capitol T795 [M] — 1956 — 150.00

HISTORY OF JAZZ, VOL. 3: THEN CAME SWING
❏ Capitol H241 [10] — 1950 — 175.00

HISTORY OF JAZZ, VOL. 4: ENTER THE COOL
❏ Capitol H242 [10] — 1950 — 175.00
❏ Capitol T796 [M] — 1956 — 150.00

THE HITS ARE ON VERVE
❏ Verve V-201 [M] — 1964 — 35.00
❏ Verve V6-201 [S] — 1964 — 50.00

HODGE PODGE OF OFF-BEAT JAZZ
❏ Sunbeam 1 — 197? — 25.00

HODGE PODGE OF OFF-BEAT JAZZ, VOL. 2
❏ Sunbeam 5 — 197? — 25.00

HOLIDAY IN SAX
❏ EmArcy MG-26019 [10] — 1954 — 250.00

HOLIDAY IN TRUMPET
❏ EmArcy MG-26015 [10] — 1954 — 250.00

HONKERS AND BAR WALKERS
❏ Delmark DL-438 — 198? — 25.00

HOT CANARIES
❏ Columbia CL2534 [10] — 1954 — 75.00

HOT CLARINETS
❏ Historical 25 — 1969 — 25.00

THE HOT ONES
❏ Columbia Special Products CSP-107 [M] — 1963 — 50.00
—Available only from Johnson Sea Horse boat dealers

HOT PIANOS
❏ Historical 29 — 1969 — 25.00

HOT TRUMPETS
❏ Historical 28 — 1969 — 25.00

HOT VS. COOL: A BATTLE OF JAZZ
❏ MGM E-211 [10] — 1953 — 150.00

HOUSE RENT PARTY
❏ Savoy MG-12199 [M] — 1961 — 150.00

HOW BLUE CAN YOU GET? GREAT BLUES VOCALS IN THE JAZZ TRADITION
❏ Bluebird 6758#NAME? — 1989 — 30.00

HOW HIGH THE MOON
❏ Clef MGC-Vol.1 [M] — 1955 — 300.00
—Reissue of 608
❏ Clef MGC-608 [M] — 1955 — 300.00
—Reissue of Mercury 608
❏ Mercury MGC-608 [M] — 1953 — 300.00
—Reissue of Vol. 1
❏ Mercury MG-35001 [10] — 1950 — 300.00
❏ Mercury MGC-Vol.1 [10] — 1951 — 250.00
—Reissue of 35001

(I GOT NO KICK AGAINST) MODERN JAZZ
❏ GRP GR-9827 — 1995 — 35.00
—Jazz artists do songs made famous by the Beatles

I LIKE JAZZ!
❏ Columbia JZ1 [M] — 1955 — 85.00

IMPULSE ARTISTS ON TOUR
❏ ABC Impulse! AS-9264 — 197? — 30.00

IMPULSIVELY!
❏ ABC Impulse! AS-9266 — 197? — 35.00

I'M WILD ABOUT MY LOVIN'
❏ Historical 32 — 1969 — 25.00

IN CONCERT, VOL. 2
❏ CTI 6049 — 197? — 30.00

INDIVIDUALS
❏ Columbia CG36213 — 197? — 30.00

INFORMAL SESSION AT SQUIRREL'S BY THE SONS OF BIX
❏ Paramount LP-104 [10] — 1954 — 175.00

IN FROM THE STORM: THE MUSIC OF JIMI HENDRIX
❏ RCA Victor 68233-1 [PD] — 1995 — 30.00
—Includes Sting (with many jazz and rock musicians); limited edition picture disc (no regular U.S. vinyl exists)

INTERCOLLEGIATE MUSIC FESTIVAL, VOL. 1
❏ ABC Impulse! AS-9145 [S] — 1968 — 30.00
❏ Impulse! A-9145 [M] — 1967 — 150.00
❏ Impulse! AS-9145 [S] — 1967 — 35.00

INTERNATIONAL JAM SESSIONS
❏ Xanadu 122 — 197? — 25.00

INTERNATIONAL JAZZ WORKSHOP
❏ EmArcy MGE-26002 [M] — 1964 — 150.00
❏ EmArcy SRE-66002 [S] — 1964 — 150.00

INTERPLAY FOR TWO TRUMPETS AND TWO TENORS
❏ Fantasy OJC-292 — 1988 — 25.00
❏ Prestige PRLP-7112 [M] — 1957 — 300.00

INTRODUCTION TO JAZZ
❏ Decca DL8244 [M] — 1956 — 175.00

I REMEMBER BEBOP
❏ Columbia C235381 — 197? — 35.00

IRREPRESSIBLE IMPULSES
❏ ABC Impulse! IMP-1972 — 1972 — 35.00

ISLES OF JAZZ
❏ Discovery DL-2010 [10] — 1954 — 300.00

ITALIAN JAZZ STARS
❏ Angel ANG-60001 [10] — 1955 — 150.00

IVY LEAGUE JAZZ
❏ Decca DL8282 [M] — 1956 — 175.00
❏ Golden Crest GC-3039 [M] — 1958 — 50.00

JAMMING AT RUDI'S, VOL. 1
❏ Circle L-407 [M] — 1951 — 40.00

JAMMING AT RUDI'S, VOL. 2
❏ Circle L-410 [M] — 1951 — 40.00

JAMMIN' IN SWINGVILLE
❏ Prestige 24051 — 197? — 35.00

JAM SESSION #1
❏ Clef MGC-4001 [M] — 1953 — 300.00
❏ Clef MGC-601 [M] — 1954 — 250.00
❏ Clef MGC-651 [M] — 1955 — 250.00
—Reissue of 4001
❏ Mercury MGC-601 [M] — 1953 — 300.00
❏ Verve MGV-8049 [M] — 1956 — 350.00
—Reissue of Clef 651

JAM SESSION #2
❏ Clef MGC-4002 [M] — 1953 — 300.00
❏ Clef MGC-652 [M] — 1955 — 250.00
—Reissue of 4002
❏ Clef MGC-602 [M] — 1954 — 250.00
❏ Mercury MGC-602 [M] — 1953 — 300.00
❏ Verve MGV-8050 [M] — 1956 — 350.00
—Reissue of Clef 652

JAM SESSION #3
❏ Clef MGC-653 [M] — 1955 — 250.00
—Reissue of 4003
❏ Clef MGC-4003 [M] — 1953 — 300.00
❏ Verve MGV-8051 [M] — 1956 — 350.00
—Reissue of Clef 653

JAM SESSION #4
❏ Clef MGC-654 [M] — 1955 — 250.00
—Reissue of 4004
❏ Clef MGC-4004 [M] — 1953 — 300.00
❏ Verve MGV-8052 [M] — 1956 — 350.00
—Reissue of Clef 654

JAM SESSION #5
❏ Clef MGC-655 [M] — 1955 — 250.00
—Reissue of 4005
❏ Clef MGC-4005 [M] — 1953 — 300.00
❏ Verve MGV-8053 [M] — 1956 — 350.00
—Reissue of Clef 655

JAM SESSION #6
❏ Clef MGC-656 [M] — 1955 — 250.00
—Reissue of 4006
❏ Clef MGC-4006 [M] — 1953 — 300.00
❏ Verve MGV-8054 [M] — 1956 — 350.00
—Reissue of Clef 656

JAM SESSION #7
❏ Clef MGC-677 [M] — 1955 — 250.00
❏ Verve MGV-8062 [M] — 1957 — 300.00
—Reissue of Clef 677

JAM SESSION #8
❏ Clef MGC-711 [M] — 1955 — 250.00
❏ Verve MGV-8094 [M] — 1957 — 300.00
—Reissue of Clef 711

JAM SESSION #9
❏ Verve MGV-8196 [M] — 1957 — 175.00

JAM SESSION
❏ Clef MGC-4001/7 [M] — 1953 — 350.00
—Boxed set containing 4001-4007
❏ EmArcy MG-36002 [M] — 1954 — 250.00

JAM SESSION, VOL. 2
❏ Skylark SKLP-12 [10] — 1954 — 300.00

JAM SESSION AT CARNEGIE HALL
❏ Columbia CL557 [M] — 1954 — 75.00

JAM SESSION AT COMMODORE
❏ Commodore FL-30006 [M] — 1951 — 40.00

JAM SESSION COAST TO COAST
❏ Columbia CL547 [M] — 1954 — 75.00

THE JAM SESSIONS: MONTREUX '77
❏ Fantasy OJC-385 — 1989 — 25.00
❏ Pablo Live 2620105 — 1978 — 35.00

THE JATP ALL-STARS: FUNKY BLUES
❏ Verve V-8486 [M] — 1962 — 50.00
❏ Verve V6-8486 [S] — 1962 — 75.00

THE JATP ALL STARS: HOW HIGH THE MOON
❏ Verve VSP-15 [M] — 1966 — 30.00
❏ Verve VSPS-15 [R] — 1966 — 20.00

THE JATP ALL-STARS: PERDIDO
❏ Verve VSP-16 [M] — 1966 — 30.00
❏ Verve VSPS-16 [R] — 1966 — 20.00

THE JATP ALL-STARS AT THE OPERA HOUSE
❏ Verve MGV-8267 [M] — 1958 — 120.00
❏ Verve MGVS-6029 [S] — 1960 — 150.00
❏ Verve V-8267 [M] — 1961 — 40.00
❏ Verve V6-8267 [S] — 1961 — 30.00
❏ Verve V-8489 [M] — 1962 — 50.00
❏ Verve V6-8489 [S] — 1962 — 75.00

JAZZ
❏ Halo 50242 [M] — 1957 — 35.00
❏ Mainstream MRL-408 — 197? — 30.00
❏ Royale 1883 [10] — 195? — 30.00

JAZZ, SKIFFLE AND JUG STYLE
❏ Herwin 113 — 197? — 30.00

JAZZ, VOL. 1: THE SOUTH
❏ Folkways FP-53/4 [M] — 1951 — 175.00
❏ Folkways FJ-2801 [M] — 197? — 30.00

JAZZ, VOL. 2: THE BLUES
❏ Folkways FP-55/6 [M] — 1951 — 40.00
❏ Folkways FJ-2802 [M] — 197? — 30.00

JAZZ, VOL. 3: NEW ORLEANS
❏ Folkways FP-57/8 [M] — 1951 — 40.00
❏ Folkways FJ-2803 [M] — 197? — 30.00

JAZZ, VOL. 4: JAZZ SINGERS
❏ Folkways FP-59/60 [M] — 1951 — 40.00
❏ Folkways FJ-2804 [M] — 197? — 30.00

JAZZ, VOL. 5: CHICAGO
❏ Folkways FP-63/4 [M] — 1951 — 40.00
❏ Folkways FJ-2805 [M] — 197? — 30.00

JAZZ, VOL. 6: CHICAGO #2
❏ Folkways FP-65/6 [M] — 1951 — 40.00
❏ Folkways FJ-2806 [M] — 197? — 30.00

JAZZ, VOL. 7: NEW YORK 1922-1934
❏ Folkways FP-67/8 [M] — 1951 — 40.00
❏ Folkways FJ-2807 [M] — 197? — 30.00

JAZZ, VOL. 8: BIG BANDS BEFORE 1938
❏ Folkways FP-69/70 [M] — 1951 — 40.00
❏ Folkways FJ-2808 [M] — 197? — 30.00

JAZZ, VOL. 9: PIANO
❏ Folkways FP-71/2 [M] — 1951 — 40.00
❏ Folkways FJ-2809 [M] — 197? — 30.00

JAZZ, VOL. 10: BOOGIE WOOGIE, JUMP, KANSAS CITY
❏ Folkways FP-73/4 [M] — 1951 — 40.00
❏ Folkways FJ-2810 [M] — 197? — 30.00

JAZZ, VOL. 11: ADDENDA
❏ Folkways FP-75/6 [M] — 1951 — 40.00
❏ Folkways FJ-2811 [M] — 197? — 30.00

JAZZ: THE 60S, VOLUME 1
❏ Pacific Jazz PJ-LA893#NAME? — 1977 — 25.00

JAZZ: THE 60S, VOLUME 2
❏ Pacific Jazz PJ-LA895#NAME? — 1977 — 25.00

JAZZ A LA MIDNIGHT
❏ Hall of Fame 608 — 197? — 12.00
❏ Jazztone J-1282 [M] — 1957 — 75.00

JAZZ A LA MOOD
❏ Jazztone J-1254 [M] — 1957 — 75.00

JAZZ ALL STARS, VOL. 1
❏ Who's Who in Jazz 21010 — 197? — 30.00

Number Title	Yr	NM
JAZZ AMERICANA		
☐ Tampa TP-11 [M]	1957	300.00
—Colored vinyl		
☐ Tampa TP-11 [M]	1958	175.00
—Black vinyl		
JAZZ AND POPS FROM THE SOVIET UNION		
☐ Colosseum CRLP-171 [M]	1955	40.00
JAZZ ANTHOLOGY OF WEST COAST JAZZ		
☐ Jazztone J-1243 [M]	1957	300.00
JAZZ AT CARNEGIE HALL		
☐ Arco AL-4 [10]	1950	175.00
☐ Mercury MG-35002 [10]	1950	300.00
—Reissue of Arco 4		
JAZZ AT CARNEGIE HALL, VOLUME 2		
☐ Arco AL-8 [10]	195?	100.00
JAZZ AT COLUMBIA -- COLLECTORS ITEMS		
☐ Columbia CB-16 [M]	195?	25.00
—Columbia Record Club "bonus record" in generic sleeve with die-cut circle in middle		
JAZZ AT COLUMBIA -- DIXIELAND		
☐ Columbia CB-8 [M]	195?	25.00
—Columbia Record Club "bonus record" in generic sleeve with die-cut circle in middle		
JAZZ AT JAZZ LTD.		
☐ Atlantic 1338 [M]	1961	175.00
—Multicolor label, white "fan" logo at right		
JAZZ AT PRESERVATION HALL		
☐ Atlantic 1408 [M]	1964	30.00
☐ Atlantic SD1408 [S]	1964	35.00
JAZZ AT PRESERVATION HALL, VOL. 2		
☐ Atlantic 1409 [M]	1964	30.00
☐ Atlantic SD1409 [S]	1964	35.00
JAZZ AT PRESERVATION HALL, VOL. 3		
☐ Atlantic 1410 [M]	1964	30.00
☐ Atlantic SD1410 [S]	1964	35.00
JAZZ AT STORYVILLE		
☐ Paradox LP-6003 [10]	1951	150.00
☐ Savoy MG-15001 [10]	1952	175.00
☐ Savoy MG-15014 [10]	1952	175.00
☐ Storyville STLP-319 [10]	1955	175.00
JAZZ AT STORYVILLE, VOL. 2		
☐ Savoy MG-15016 [10]	1952	175.00
JAZZ AT STORYVILLE, VOL. 3		
☐ Savoy MG-15019 [10]	1953	175.00
JAZZ AT STORYVILLE, VOL. 4		
☐ Savoy MG-15020 [10]	1953	175.00
JAZZ AT THE BOSTON ARTS FESTIVAL		
☐ Storyville STLP-311 [10]	1954	175.00
JAZZ AT THE HOLLYWOOD BOWL		
☐ Verve MGV-8231-2 [M]	1958	150.00
☐ Verve V-8231-2 [M]	1961	75.00
JAZZ AT THE NEW SCHOOL		
☐ Chiaroscuro 110	197?	35.00
JAZZ AT THE PHILHARMONIC		
☐ Stinson SLP-23 [10]	195?	100.00
—Black vinyl		
☐ Stinson SLP-23 [10]	195?	100.00
—Opaque red vinyl		
☐ Stinson SLP-23 [10]	1950	250.00
—See-through red vinyl; the first pressing of the first volume to be issued		
☐ Stinson SLP-23 [M]	195?	25.00
JAZZ AT THE PHILHARMONIC, NEW VOLUME 2		
☐ Clef MGC-Vol.2 [M]	1955	300.00
—Side 1 is the 10-inch Vol. 2; Side 2 is the 10-inch Vol. 3		
JAZZ AT THE PHILHARMONIC, NEW VOLUME 3		
☐ Clef MGC-Vol.3 [M]	1955	300.00
—Side 1 is the 10-inch Vol. 4; Side 2 is the 10-inch Vol. 5		
JAZZ AT THE PHILHARMONIC, NEW VOLUME 4		
☐ Clef MGC-Vol.4 [M]	1955	300.00
—Combines the 10-inch Vol. 6 and Vol. 14 on one record		
JAZZ AT THE PHILHARMONIC, NEW VOLUME 5		
☐ Clef MGC-Vol.5 [M]	1955	300.00
—Combines the 10-inch Vol. 7, 10 and 11 on one record		
JAZZ AT THE PHILHARMONIC, NEW VOLUME 6		
☐ Clef MGC-Vol.6 [M]	1955	300.00
—Combines the 10-inch Vol. 8 and Vol. 9 on one record		
JAZZ AT THE PHILHARMONIC, NEW VOLUME 7		
☐ Clef MGC-Vol.7 [M]	1955	300.00
—Combines the 10-inch Vol. 12 and 13 on one record		
JAZZ AT THE PHILHARMONIC, VOL. 2		
☐ Verve MGV-Vol.2 [M]	1957	300.00
—Reissue of 12-inch Clef Vol. 2		
JAZZ AT THE PHILHARMONIC, VOL. 3		
☐ Verve MGV-Vol.3 [M]	1957	300.00
—Reissue of 12-inch Clef Vol. 3		
JAZZ AT THE PHILHARMONIC, VOL. 4		
☐ Verve MGV-Vol.4 [M]	1957	300.00
—Reissue of 12-inch Clef Vol. 4		
JAZZ AT THE PHILHARMONIC, VOL. 5		
☐ Verve MGV-Vol.5 [M]	1957	300.00
—Reissue of 12-inch Clef Vol. 5		
JAZZ AT THE PHILHARMONIC, VOL. 6		
☐ Verve MGV-Vol.6 [M]	1957	300.00
—Reissue of 12-inch Clef Vol. 6		
JAZZ AT THE PHILHARMONIC, VOL. 7		
☐ Verve MGV-Vol.7 [M]	1957	300.00
—Reissue of 12-inch Clef Vol. 7		
JAZZ AT THE PHILHARMONIC, VOL. 8		
☐ Verve MGV-Vol.8 [M]	1957	300.00
—Reissue of Clef Vol. 15		
JAZZ AT THE PHILHARMONIC, VOL. 9		
☐ Verve MGV-Vol.9 [M]	1957	300.00
—Reissue of Clef Vol. 16		
JAZZ AT THE PHILHARMONIC, VOL. 10		
☐ Verve MGV-Vol.10 [M]	1957	300.00
—Reissue of Clef Vol. 17		
JAZZ AT THE PHILHARMONIC, VOL. 11		
☐ Verve MGV-Vol.11 [M]	1957	300.00
—Reissue of Clef Vol. 18		
JAZZ AT THE PHILHARMONIC, VOLUME 2		
☐ Arco AL-1 [10]	1950	175.00
☐ Clef MGC-Vol.2 [10]	1953	350.00
—Reissue of Mercury Vol. 2		
☐ Mercury MGC-Vol.2 [10]	1951	250.00
—Reissue of 35003		
☐ Mercury MG-35003 [10]	1950	300.00
—Reissue of Arco 1		
JAZZ AT THE PHILHARMONIC, VOLUME 3		
☐ Arco AL-2 [10]	1950	175.00
☐ Clef MGC-Vol.3 [10]	1953	350.00
—Reissue of Mercury Vol. 3		
☐ Mercury MGC-Vol.3 [10]	1951	250.00
—Reissue of 35004		
☐ Mercury MG-35004 [10]	1950	300.00
—Reissue of Arco 2		
JAZZ AT THE PHILHARMONIC, VOLUME 4		
☐ Clef MGC-Vol.4 [10]	1953	350.00
—Reissue of Mercury Vol. 4		
☐ Mercury MGC-Vol.4 [10]	1951	250.00
—Reissue of 35005		
☐ Mercury MG-35005 [10]	1950	300.00
JAZZ AT THE PHILHARMONIC, VOLUME 5		
☐ Clef MGC-Vol.5 [10]	1953	350.00
—Reissue of Mercury Vol. 5		
☐ Mercury MGC-Vol.5 [10]	1951	250.00
—Reissue of 35006		
☐ Mercury MG-35006 [10]	1950	300.00
JAZZ AT THE PHILHARMONIC, VOLUME 6		
☐ Clef MGC-Vol.6 [10]	1953	350.00
—Reissue of Mercury Vol. 6		
☐ Mercury MGC-Vol.6 [10]	1951	250.00
—Reissue of 35007		
☐ Mercury MG-35007 [10]	1950	300.00
JAZZ AT THE PHILHARMONIC, VOLUME 7		
☐ Clef MGC-Vol.7 [10]	1953	350.00
—Reissue of Mercury Vol. 7		
☐ Mercury MGC-Vol.7 [10]	1951	250.00
—Reissue of 35008		
☐ Mercury MG-35008 [10]	1950	300.00
JAZZ AT THE PHILHARMONIC, VOLUME 8		
☐ Clef MGC-Vol.8 [10]	1953	350.00
—Reissue of Mercury Vol. 8		
☐ Mercury MGC-Vol.8 [10]	1951	250.00
—Reissue of 35000		
☐ Mercury MG-35000 [10]	1950	300.00
JAZZ AT THE PHILHARMONIC, VOLUME 9		
☐ Clef MGC-Vol.9 [10]	1953	350.00
—Reissue of Mercury Vol. 9		
☐ Mercury MGC-Vol.9 [10]	1951	250.00
—Reissue of 35009		
☐ Mercury MG-35009 [10]	1950	300.00
JAZZ AT THE PHILHARMONIC, VOLUME 10		
☐ Clef MGC-Vol.10 [10]	1953	350.00
—Reissue of Mercury Vol. 10		
☐ Mercury MGC-Vol.10 [10]	1951	250.00
—Reissue of 35010		
☐ Mercury MG-35010 [10]	1950	300.00
JAZZ AT THE PHILHARMONIC, VOLUME 11		
☐ Clef MGC-Vol.11 [10]	1953	350.00
—Reissue of Mercury Vol. 11		
☐ Mercury MGC-Vol.11 [10]	1951	250.00
—Reissue of 35011		
☐ Mercury MG-35011 [10]	1950	300.00
JAZZ AT THE PHILHARMONIC, VOLUME 12		
☐ Clef MGC-Vol.12 [10]	1953	350.00
—Reissue of Mercury Vol. 12		
☐ Mercury MGC-Vol.12 [10]	1951	250.00
JAZZ AT THE PHILHARMONIC, VOLUME 13		
☐ Clef MGC-Vol.13 [10]	1953	350.00
—Reissue of Mercury Vol. 13		
☐ Mercury MGC-Vol.13 [10]	1951	250.00
JAZZ AT THE PHILHARMONIC, VOLUME 14		
☐ Clef MGC-Vol.14 [10]	1953	350.00
—Reissue of Mercury Vol. 14		
☐ Mercury MGC-Vol.14 [10]	1951	250.00
JAZZ AT THE PHILHARMONIC, VOLUME 15		
☐ Clef MGC-Vol.15 [M]	1954	300.00
—Boxed set of new material with program		
☐ Clef MGC-Vol.15 [10]	1953	350.00
—Reissue of Mercury Vol. 15		
☐ Mercury MGC-Vol.15 [10]	1951	250.00
JAZZ AT THE PHILHARMONIC, VOLUME 16		
☐ Clef MGC-Vol.16 [M]	1954	300.00
—Boxed set of new material with program		
JAZZ AT THE PHILHARMONIC, VOLUME 17		
☐ Clef MGC-Vol.17 [M]	1955	300.00
—Boxed set of new material with photo booklet		
JAZZ AT THE PHILHARMONIC, VOLUME 18		
☐ Clef MGC-Vol.18 [M]	1955	300.00
—Boxed set of new material with booklet		
JAZZ AT THE PHILHARMONIC: BIRD & PRES, CARNEGIE HALL 1949		
☐ Verve 815150-1	1984	25.00
JAZZ AT THE PHILHARMONIC: BIRD & PRES, THE '46 CONCERTS		
☐ Verve 833565-1	198?	30.00
☐ Verve VE-2-2518	197?	35.00
JAZZ AT THE PHILHARMONIC: BLUES IN CHICAGO, 1955		
☐ Verve 815155-1	1984	25.00
JAZZ AT THE PHILHARMONIC: CARNEGIE BLUES		
☐ Verve 825101-1	1985	25.00
JAZZ AT THE PHILHARMONIC: HARTFORD 1953		
☐ Pablo Live 2308240	198?	25.00
JAZZ AT THE PHILHARMONIC: HISTORIC RECORDINGS		
☐ Verve VE-2-2504	197?	35.00
JAZZ AT THE PHILHARMONIC: IN TOKYO 1983		
☐ Pablo Live 2620117	1984	25.00
JAZZ AT THE PHILHARMONIC: LONDON 1969		
☐ Pablo Live 2620119	198?	30.00
JAZZ AT THE PHILHARMONIC: MONTREUX '75		
☐ Pablo 2310748	197?	35.00
JAZZ AT THE PHILHARMONIC: NORGRAN BLUES 1950		
☐ Verve 815151-1	1984	25.00
JAZZ AT THE PHILHARMONIC: ONE O'CLOCK JUMP 1953		
☐ Verve 815153-1	1984	25.00
JAZZ AT THE PHILHARMONIC: THE 1940S		
☐ Verve UMV-9070/2	197?	30.00
JAZZ AT THE PHILHARMONIC: THE CHALLENGES, 1954		
☐ Verve 815154-1	1984	25.00
JAZZ AT THE PHILHARMONIC: THE COLEMAN HAWKINS SET		
☐ Verve 815148-1	1984	25.00
JAZZ AT THE PHILHARMONIC: THE DRUM BATTLE		
☐ Verve 815146-1	1984	25.00
JAZZ AT THE PHILHARMONIC: THE ELLA FITZGERALD SET		
☐ Verve 815147-1	1984	25.00
JAZZ AT THE PHILHARMONIC: THE EXCITING BATTLE -- STOCKHOLM '55		
☐ Pablo 2310713	197?	30.00
JAZZ AT THE PHILHARMONIC: THE GETZ & J.J. SET		
☐ Verve 825100-1	1985	25.00
JAZZ AT THE PHILHARMONIC: THE OSCAR PETERSON SET		
☐ Verve 825099-1	1985	25.00
JAZZ AT THE PHILHARMONIC: THE RAREST CONCERTS		
☐ Verve 815149-1	1984	25.00
JAZZ AT THE PHILHARMONIC: TRUMPET BATTLE, 1952		
☐ Verve 815152-1	1984	25.00

Number	Title	Yr	NM
JAZZ AT THE PHILHARMONIC ALL STARS			
❑ American Recording Society G-416 [M]		1957	75.00
JAZZ AT THE PHILHARMONIC IN EUROPE			
❑ Verve V6-8823		197?	50.00
JAZZ AT THE PHILHARMONIC IN EUROPE, VOL. 1			
❑ Verve V-8539 [M]		1963	40.00
❑ Verve V6-8539 [S]		1963	50.00
JAZZ AT THE PHILHARMONIC IN EUROPE, VOL. 2			
❑ Verve V-8540 [M]		1963	40.00
❑ Verve V6-8540 [S]		1963	50.00
JAZZ AT THE PHILHARMONIC IN EUROPE, VOL. 3			
❑ Verve V-8541 [M]		1963	40.00
❑ Verve V6-8541 [S]		1963	50.00
JAZZ AT THE PHILHARMONIC IN EUROPE, VOL. 4			
❑ Verve V-8542 [M]		1963	40.00
❑ Verve V6-8542 [S]		1963	50.00
JAZZ AT THE PHILHARMONIC IN TOKYO			
❑ Pablo Live 2620104		198?	30.00
JAZZ AT THE SANTA MONICA CIVIC '72			
❑ Pablo 2625701		197?	30.00
JAZZ BAND BALL			
❑ Good Time Jazz L-12005 [M]		1954	50.00
JAZZ BANDS 1926-30			
❑ Historical 16		1967	25.00
JAZZ CITY PRESENTS			
❑ Bethlehem BCP-80 [M]		1957	300.00
JAZZ COMMITTEE FOR LATIN AMERICAN AFFAIRS			
❑ FM LP-303 [M]		1963	150.00
❑ Vee-Jay LP-303 [S]		196?	50.00
—All-black label with Vee Jay "brackets" logo and "STEREO" on label; most likely a reissue			
JAZZ CONCERT			
❑ Jazztone J-1219 [M]		1956	75.00
❑ Mercury MGJC-1 [M]		1953	300.00
—Combines 601 and 602 in a box			
❑ Norgran MGN-3501-2 [M]		1956	300.00
—Reissue of Mercury MGJC-1			
JAZZ CONCERT WEST COAST			
❑ Savoy MG-12012 [M]		1955	175.00
❑ Savoy MG-12196 [M]		1961	150.00
JAZZ CONFIDENTIAL			
❑ Crown CLP-5056 [M]		1959	50.00
JAZZ CORNUCOPIA			
❑ Coral CRL57149 [M]		1958	75.00
JAZZ CRITICS' CHOICE			
❑ Columbia Jazz Odyssey PC36807		198?	25.00
JAZZ CRITICS' CHOICE: GREAT JAZZ CRITICS CHOOSE HISTORIC PERFORMANCES			
❑ Columbia CL2126 [M]		1964	30.00
JAZZ CRYSTALLIZATIONS			
❑ Pausa 7020		198?	25.00
JAZZ DANCE			
❑ Jaguar JP-801 [10]		1954	150.00
JAZZ DUPLEX			
❑ Pax LP-6006 [10]		1954	75.00
JAZZ FESTIVAL			
❑ Imperial LP-9233 [M]		1963	200.00
❑ Imperial LP-12233 [S]		1963	200.00
❑ Kapp KS-1 [M]		1956	50.00
JAZZ FESTIVAL, VOLUME 2			
❑ Imperial LP-9238 [M]		1963	200.00
❑ Imperial LP-12238 [S]		1963	200.00
JAZZ FESTIVAL IN HI-FI: NEAR IN AND FAR OUT			
❑ Warner Bros. W1281 [M]		1959	75.00
JAZZ FESTIVAL IN STEREO: NEAR IN AND FAR OUT			
❑ Warner Bros. WS1281 [S]		1959	75.00
JAZZ FOR ART'S SAKE			
❑ Dotted Eighth 101 [M]		195?	40.00
JAZZ FOR A SUNDAY AFTERNOON			
❑ Solid State SS-18027		1968	35.00
JAZZ FOR A SUNDAY AFTERNOON, VOL. 2			
❑ Solid State SS-18028		1968	35.00
JAZZ FOR A SUNDAY AFTERNOON, VOL. 3			
❑ Solid State SS-18037		1968	35.00
JAZZ FOR A SUNDAY AFTERNOON, VOL. 4			
❑ Solid State SS-18052		1969	35.00
JAZZ FOR HI-FI LOVERS			
❑ Dawn DLP-1124 [M]		1958	175.00
JAZZ FOR LOVERS			
❑ Riverside RLP 12-244 [M]		1957	300.00
JAZZ FOR PEOPLE WHO HATE JAZZ			
❑ RCA Victor LJM-1008 [M]		1954	150.00
JAZZ FOR PLAYBOYS			
❑ Savoy Jazz SJC-412		1985	25.00

Number	Title	Yr	NM
JAZZ FOR PLAYGIRLS			
❑ Savoy Jazz SJC-413		1985	25.00
JAZZ FOR SURF-NIKS			
❑ Bethlehem BCP-6073 [M]		1961	300.00
JAZZ FROM DOWN UNDER			
❑ Jaguar JP-803 [10]		1954	150.00
JAZZ FROM NEW YORK, 1928-32			
❑ Historical 33		1969	25.00
JAZZ FROM SWEDEN			
❑ Discovery DL-2002 [10]		1953	300.00
JAZZ FROM THE FAMOUS DOOR			
❑ GHB GHB-116		197?	25.00
JAZZ GALA CONCERT			
❑ Atlantic SD1693		197?	30.00
JAZZ GIANTS			
❑ Biograph 3002		196?	30.00
THE JAZZ GIANTS			
❑ Norgran MGN-1056 [M]		1956	500.00
JAZZ GIANTS, VOL. 1			
❑ EmArcy MG-36048 [M]		1955	250.00
❑ Trip 5504		197?	25.00
JAZZ GIANTS, VOL. 2: THE PIANO PLAYERS			
❑ EmArcy MG-36049 [M]		1955	250.00
JAZZ GIANTS, VOL. 2 (REEDS)			
❑ Trip 5518		197?	25.00
JAZZ GIANTS, VOL. 3			
❑ Trip 5538		197?	25.00
JAZZ GIANTS, VOL. 3: REEDS, PART 1			
❑ EmArcy MG-36050 [M]		1955	250.00
JAZZ GIANTS, VOL. 3: REEDS, PART 2			
❑ EmArcy MG-36051 [M]		1955	250.00
JAZZ GIANTS, VOL. 3 (REEDS)			
❑ Trip 5555		197?	25.00
JAZZ GIANTS, VOL. 4: FOLK BLUES			
❑ EmArcy MG-36052 [M]		1955	250.00
JAZZ GIANTS, VOL. 5: BRASS			
❑ EmArcy MG-36053 [M]		1955	250.00
JAZZ GIANTS, VOL. 6: MODERN SWEDES			
❑ EmArcy MG-36054 [M]		1955	250.00
JAZZ GIANTS, VOL. 7: DIXIELAND			
❑ EmArcy MG-36055 [M]		1955	250.00
JAZZ GIANTS, VOL. 8: DRUM ROLE			
❑ EmArcy MG-36071 [M]		1956	250.00
JAZZ GIANTS '56			
❑ Verve UMV-2511		197?	15.00
THE JAZZ GIANTS '56			
❑ Verve MGV-8146 [M]		1957	175.00
❑ Verve V-8146 [M]		1961	50.00
JAZZ GIANTS '58			
❑ Verve MGV-8248 [M]		1958	150.00
❑ Verve V-8248 [M]		1961	75.00
❑ Verve UMV-2540		197?	30.00
JAZZ GOES TO BROADWAY			
❑ Kapp KL-1007 [M]		1956	50.00
JAZZ GREATS			
❑ Gateway 10111		197?	30.00
❑ Tops L-1508 [M]		1958	50.00
JAZZ GREATS!			
❑ Allegro 737 [M]		1958	75.00
JAZZ GREATS, VOL. 2			
❑ Columbia Special Products P13230		1976	25.00
—Custom manufactured for Radio Shack			
JAZZ GREATS 2			
❑ Gateway 10112		197?	30.00
JAZZ GREATS 3			
❑ Gateway 10113		197?	30.00
JAZZ HALL OF FAME, VOL. 2			
❑ Design DLP-113 [M]		196?	50.00
A JAZZ HOLIDAY			
❑ MCA MCA2-4018		1973	35.00
—Black label with rainbow			
THE JAZZ HOUR			
❑ Savoy MG-12126 [M]		1957	150.00
JAZZ IN A VERTICAL GROOVE, 1925-28			
❑ Biograph 12057		197?	25.00
JAZZ IN HOLLYWOOD			
❑ Liberty LJH-6001 [M]		1955	85.00
JAZZ INTERPLAY			
❑ Prestige PRLP-7341 [M]		1964	40.00
❑ Prestige PRLP-7341 [R]		1964	75.00
JAZZ IN THE THIRTIES			
❑ Swing SW-8457/8		198?	30.00
JAZZ IN TRANSITION			
❑ Transition TRLP-30 [M]		1956	250.00

Number	Title	Yr	NM
—With booklet (deduct 1/4 if missing)			
JAZZ IS BUSTING OUT ALL OVER			
❑ Savoy MG-12123 [M]		1957	150.00
❑ Savoy MG-12123 [M]		198?	12.00
JAZZ JAMBOREE			
❑ Halo 50229 [M]		1957	50.00
JAZZ LAB			
❑ Starlite ST-7003 [M]		1955	150.00
THE JAZZ LIFE			
❑ Candid CD-8019 [M]		1960	40.00
❑ Candid CS-9019 [S]		1960	75.00
JAZZ LIFE!			
❑ Barnaby BR-5021		197?	30.00
JAZZ LTD.			
❑ Regal LP-11 [10]		1951	150.00
THE JAZZ MAKERS			
❑ Columbia CL1036 [M]		1957	50.00
JAZZMEN -- DETROIT			
❑ Savoy MG-12083 [M]		1956	175.00
JAZZ MONTAGE			
❑ Liberty LRP-3292 [M]		1963	35.00
❑ Liberty LST-7292 [S]		1963	50.00
JAZZ MUSIC FOR BIRDS			
❑ Bethlehem BCP-6039 [M]		1959	250.00
JAZZ MUSIC FOR PEOPLE WHO DON'T CARE ABOUT MONEY			
❑ Bethlehem BCP-88 [M]		1958	250.00
JAZZ ODYSSEY: THE SOUND OF CHICAGO			
❑ Columbia C3L32 [M]		1964	40.00
JAZZ ODYSSEY: THE SOUND OF HARLEM			
❑ Columbia C3L33 [M]		1964	40.00
JAZZ ODYSSEY: THE SOUND OF NEW ORLEANS			
❑ Columbia C3L30 [M]		1964	40.00
JAZZ OFF THE AIR, VOL. 1			
❑ Esoteric ESJ-2 [10]		1952	175.00
JAZZ OFF THE AIR, VOL. 2			
❑ Esoteric ESJ-3 [10]		1952	175.00
JAZZ OF THE FORTIES, VOL. 1			
❑ Folkways FJ-2841		197?	30.00
JAZZ OF THE ROARING 20'S			
❑ Riverside RLP 12-801 [M]		195?	50.00
JAZZ OF THE ROARING TWENTIES: DANCE MUSIC OF THE CHARLESTON ERA			
❑ Riverside RLP 12-108 [M]		1956	300.00
JAZZ OF THE SIXTIES			
❑ Vee Jay VJS-2-1008		1974	50.00
JAZZ OF TWO DECADES			
❑ EmArcy DEM-2 [M]		1956	250.00
THE JAZZOLOGY POLL WINNERS 1964			
❑ GHB GHB-200		1986	25.00
JAZZ OMNIBUS			
❑ Columbia CL1020 [M]		1957	50.00
JAZZ ON THE AIR			
❑ Brunswick BL58048 [10]		1953	150.00
JAZZ ON THE SCREEN			
❑ Fontana MGF-27532 [M]		1965	40.00
❑ Fontana SRF-67532 [S]		1965	40.00
JAZZ PIANISTS GALORE			
❑ Jazz: West Coast JWC-506 [M]		1956	175.00
THE JAZZ PIANO			
❑ RCA Victor LPM-3499 [M]		1966	50.00
❑ RCA Victor LSP-3499 [S]		1966	75.00
A JAZZ PIANO ANTHOLOGY			
❑ Columbia PG32355		197?	35.00
JAZZ PIANO GREATS			
❑ Folkways FJ-2852		197?	30.00
JAZZ PIONEERS 1933-36			
❑ Prestige PRLP-7647		1969	35.00
JAZZ POLL WINNERS			
❑ Columbia CL1610 [M]		1960	50.00
JAZZ POTPOURRI			
❑ Audiophile AP-24 [M]		1953	75.00
THE JAZZ RECORD STORY			
❑ Jazzology J-82		197?	25.00
THE JAZZ-ROCK-SOUL PROJECT			
❑ Riverside 3048		197?	50.00
THE JAZZ ROUND			
❑ Verve VSP-24 [M]		1966	35.00
❑ Verve VSPS-24 [R]		1966	25.00
A JAZZ SALUTE TO FREEDOM			
❑ Core 100		196?	75.00
THE JAZZ SCENE			
❑ American Recording Society G-419 [M]		1957	75.00
❑ Clef MGC-674 [M]		1955	250.00

Number	Title	Yr	NM

Number / Title	Yr	NM
—Reissue of 4007		
❏ Clef MGC-4007 [M]	1953	300.00
❏ Clef Special Edition (no #) [10]	1953	350.00
—Two 10-inch LPs in box. Buyers had the option of purchasing a collection of photos that had been used in the original 78 rpm album; add another 50 percent if these photos are included		
❏ Verve MGV-8060 [M]	1957	300.00
—Reissue of Clef 674		
❏ Verve V-8060 [M]	1961	40.00
JAZZ SET		
❏ Columbia Special Products CSP-217S [S]	1965	25.00
—Special item for Zenith		
❏ Columbia Special Products CSP-217M [M]	1965	30.00
THE JAZZ SINGERS		
❏ Prestige 24113	197?	35.00
JAZZ SOUL OF "CLEOPATRA"		
❏ New Jazz NJLP-8292 [M]	1962	175.00
—Purple label		
❏ New Jazz NJLP-8292 [M]	1965	175.00
—Blue label, trident logo at right		
THE JAZZ SOUND		
❏ Columbia Special Products CSP298 [M]	1966	25.00
THE JAZZ STORY		
❏ Coral CJE-100 [M]	195?	150.00
—Box set; narrated by Steve Allen		
JAZZ SUPER HITS		
❏ Atlantic SD1528	1969	75.00
JAZZ SUPER HITS, VOL. 2		
❏ Atlantic SD1559	1970	50.00
JAZZ SURPRISE		
❏ Crown CLP-5008 [M]	1957	50.00
JAZZ SWINGS BROADWAY		
❏ Pacific Jazz PJM-404 [M]	1956	150.00
❏ World Pacific PJM-404 [M]	1958	175.00
JAZZTIME, U.S.A.		
❏ MCA 4113	197?	30.00
JAZZ TIME U.S.A. -- VOLUME 1		
❏ Brunswick BL54000 [M]	1952	75.00
JAZZ TIME U.S.A. -- VOLUME 2		
❏ Brunswick BL54001 [M]	1953	75.00
JAZZ TIME U.S.A. -- VOLUME 3		
❏ Brunswick BL54002 [M]	1954	75.00
JAZZTONE SAMPLER		
❏ Jazztone J-SPEC-100 [10]	1955	150.00
—With booklet		
JAZZ TRUMPET, VOL. 1		
❏ Prestige 24111	198?	35.00
THE JAZZ TRUMPET, VOL. 2		
❏ Prestige 24112	198?	35.00
JAZZ VARIATIONS, VOL. 1		
❏ Stinson SLP-20 [10]	195?	75.00
❏ Stinson SLP-20 [M]	196?	75.00
JAZZ VARIATIONS, VOL. 2		
❏ Stinson SLP-29 [M]	196?	75.00
JAZZVILLE, VOL. 1		
❏ Dawn DLP-1101 [M]	1956	175.00
JAZZ VIOLINS OF THE 40S		
❏ Folkways FJ-2854	197?	30.00
JAZZVISIONS: ALL STRINGS ATTACHED		
❏ Verve 841291-1	1989	30.00
JAZZVISIONS: BRIZILIAN KNIGHTS AND A LADY		
❏ Verve 841292-1	1989	30.00
JAZZVISIONS: ECHOES OF ELLINGTON, VOL. 1		
❏ Verve 841288-1	1989	30.00
JAZZVISIONS: ECHOES OF ELLINGTON, VOL. 2		
❏ Verve 841289-1	1989	30.00
JAZZVISIONS: JUMP THE BLUES AWAY		
❏ Verve 841287-1	1989	30.00
JAZZVISIONS: LATIN FAMILIA		
❏ Verve 841290-1	1989	30.00
JAZZVISIONS: RIO REVISITED		
❏ Verve 841286-1	1989	30.00
JAZZVISIONS: THE MANY FACES OF BIRD		
❏ Verve 841285-1	1989	30.00
JAZZ VOCALS AWARD ALBUM		
❏ Bethlehem BCP-6068 [M]	1963	250.00
JAZZ WEST COAST, VOL. 1		
❏ Pacific Jazz JWC-500 [M]	1956	150.00
❏ World Pacific JWC-500 [M]	1958	175.00
JAZZ WEST COAST, VOL. 2		
❏ Pacific Jazz JWC-501 [M]	1956	150.00
❏ World Pacific JWC-501 [M]	1958	175.00
JAZZ WEST COAST, VOL. 3		
❏ Pacific Jazz JWC-507 [M]	1957	150.00
❏ World Pacific JWC-507 [M]	1958	175.00

Number / Title	Yr	NM
JAZZ WEST COAST, VOL. 4		
❏ World Pacific JWC-510 [M]	1958	175.00
❏ World Pacific ST-1009 [S]	1959	175.00
JAZZ WEST COAST, VOL. 5		
❏ World Pacific JWC-511 [M]	1958	175.00
JAZZ -- WEST COAST VOL. III		
❏ Jazztone J-1274 [M]	195?	30.00
JAZZ WIZARDS, VOL. 1		
❏ Herwin 106	197?	30.00
JAZZ WIZARDS, VOL. 2		
❏ Herwin 107	197?	30.00
JAZZ WOMEN: A FEMINIST RETROSPECTIVE		
❏ Stash ST-109	197?	35.00
THE JAZZ WORLD		
❏ Columbia Special Products CSS524 [S]	1967	25.00
JAZZ YEARS: 25TH ANNIVERSARY		
❏ Atlantic SD-2-316	197?	35.00
A JAZZY WONDERLAND		
❏ Columbia 1P8120	1990	35.00
—Available on vinyl through Columbia House only		
JINGLE BELL JAZZ		
❏ Columbia CL1893 [M]	1962	50.00
❏ Columbia CS8693 [S]	1962	35.00
❏ Columbia PC36803	1980	12.00
—Reissue of Harmony KH 32529 on the "Jazz Odyssey" series		
❏ Harmony KH32529	1973	30.00
—Reissue of CS 8693 with one track changed		
JOHN COLTRANE IN THE WINNER'S CIRCLE		
❏ Bethlehem BCP-6066 [M]	1961	175.00
—Reissue of 6024 with new title		
JOHN HAMMOND PRESENTS "FROM SPIRITUALS TO SWING" AT CARNEGIE HALL 1938		
❏ Vanguard VRS-8523 [M]	1959	120.00
JOHN HAMMOND PRESENTS "FROM SPIRITUALS TO SWING" AT CARNEGIE HALL 1939		
❏ Vanguard VRS-8524 [M]	1959	120.00
JOURNEYS INTO JAZZ, VOL. 1		
❏ GHB GHB-65	197?	25.00
JOURNEYS INTO JAZZ, VOL. 2		
❏ GHB GHB-66	197?	25.00
JUST JAZZ		
❏ Imperial LP-9246 [M]	1963	200.00
❏ Imperial LP-12246 [S]	1963	200.00
KANSAS CITY IN THE '30S		
❏ Capitol T1057 [M]	1958	150.00
KANSAS CITY JAZZ		
❏ Decca DL8044 [M]	1954	175.00
KANSAS CITY PIANO		
❏ Decca DL9226 [M]	1967	75.00
❏ Decca DL79226 [R]	1967	30.00
KBIG CHOICES		
❏ World Pacific KBIG-1 [S]	1964	175.00
KELLOGG'S PRESENTS...BIG BAND CLASSICS		
❏ RCA Special Products DPL1-0438(e)	1980	25.00
KEYBOARD KINGS		
❏ MGM E-100 [10]	1951	150.00
KEYBOARD KINGS OF JAZZ		
❏ RCA Victor LPT-4 [10]	1951	40.00
KINGS AND QUEENS OF IVORY		
❏ MCA 1329	198?	25.00
KINGS OF CLASSIC JAZZ		
❏ Riverside RLP 12-131 [M]	1957	300.00
KINGS OF SWING		
❏ Pickwick PTP-2072	197?	30.00
KINGS OF THE KEYBOARD		
❏ American Recording Society G-406 [M]	1956	75.00
KNOW YOUR JAZZ		
❏ ABC-Paramount ABC-115 [M]	1956	75.00
LEGENDARY BLACK JAZZ STARS IN THEIR FIRST FILMS		
❏ Biograph M-3	198?	25.00
LENNY TRISTANO MEMORIAL CONCERT		
❏ Jazz Records JR-3	198?	40.00
LEONARD FEATHER'S ENCYCLOPEDIA OF JAZZ		
❏ Vee Jay VJSP-400	1977	30.00
LEONARD FEATHER'S ENCYCLOPEDIA OF JAZZ, VOLUME ONE: GIANTS OF THE SAXOPHONE		
❏ Vee Jay LP-2501 [M]	1964	50.00
❏ Vee Jay VJS-2501 [S]	1964	75.00
LEONARD FEATHER'S ENCYCLOPEDIA OF JAZZ OF THE '60S: BLUES BAG		
❏ Vee Jay LP-2506 [M]	1964	50.00

Number / Title	Yr	NM
LIGHTS OUT SAN FRANCISCO		
❏ Blue Thumb BT6004	1970	75.00
LISTEN TO OUR STORY		
❏ Brunswick BL59001 [10]	1950	120.00
LISTEN TO OUR VISION		
❏ Gramavision 18-8509	1986	25.00
LIVE AT THE FESTIVAL		
❏ Enja 2030	197?	35.00
THE LIVELY SOUND OF UNIVERSITY		
❏ Capitol Custom (no #)	1966	100.00
—Mustang Sweepstakes Prize Winner" on front cover		
LIVING MUSIC COLLECTION '86		
❏ Living Music LM-0006	1986	25.00
LOADED		
❏ Savoy MG-12074 [M]	1956	150.00
LONDON BROIL		
❏ Angel ANG-60004 [10]	1955	150.00
A LOOK AT YESTERDAY		
❏ Mainstream 56025 [M]	1965	75.00
❏ Mainstream S-6025 [R]	1965	30.00
A LOT OF YARN BUT A WELL-KNITTED JAZZ ALBUM		
❏ Bethlehem BCP-91 [M]	1958	250.00
LULLABY OF BIRDLAND		
❏ RCA Victor LPM-1146 [M]	1955	150.00
LUSTY MOODS		
❏ Moodsville MVLP-37 [M]	1963	40.00
—Green label		
❏ Moodsville MVST-37 [S]	1963	40.00
—Green label		
❏ Moodsville MVLP-37 [M]	1965	50.00
—Blue label, trident logo at right		
❏ Moodsville MVST-37 [S]	1965	50.00
—Blue label, trident logo at right		
❏ Status ST-8319 [M]	1965	75.00
THE MAGIC HORN		
❏ RCA Victor LPM-1332 [M]	1956	40.00
MAGNAVOX PRESENTS A REPRISE OF GREAT HITS		
❏ Reprise PRO578	1973	25.00
MAMBO JAZZ		
❏ Prestige PRLP-135 [10]	1952	300.00
MANASSAS JAZZ FESTIVAL		
❏ Jazzology J-17	196?	25.00
THE MAN WITH A HORN		
❏ Decca DL5191 [10]	1950	150.00
THE MANY FACES OF THE BLUES		
❏ Savoy MG-12125 [M]	1957	150.00
MASTER JAZZ PIANO		
❏ Master Jazz 8105	197?	30.00
MASTER JAZZ PIANO, VOL. 2		
❏ Master Jazz 8108	197?	30.00
MASTER JAZZ PIANO, VOL. 3		
❏ Master Jazz 8117	197?	30.00
MASTER JAZZ PIANO, VOL. 4		
❏ Master Jazz 8129	197?	30.00
MASTERS OF THE MODERN PIANO		
❏ Verve VE-2-2514	197?	35.00
THE MELLOW MOODS		
❏ RCA Victor LPM-1365 [M]	1956	40.00
MELLOW THE MOOD/JAZZ IN A MELLOW MOOD		
❏ Blue Note BLP-5001 [10]	1951	250.00
MEMORABLE SESSIONS IN JAZZ		
❏ Blue Note BLP-5026 [10]	1953	250.00
MEMPHIS JAZZ FESTIVAL		
❏ Jazzology J-134	198?	25.00
THE MERCURY 40TH ANNIVERSARY V.S.O.P. ALBUM		
❏ Mercury 824116-1	1985	150.00
THE METRONOME ALL-STARS		
❏ Columbia CL2528 [10]	1954	75.00
METRONOME ALL-STARS		
❏ Harmony HL7044 [M]	1957	75.00
❏ RCA Camden CAL-426 [M]	1958	75.00
METRONOME ALL STARS 1956		
❏ Clef MGC-743 [M]	1956	250.00
❏ Verve MGV-8030 [M]	1957	175.00
❏ Verve V-8030 [M]	1961	50.00
MIDNIGHT JAZZ AT CARNEGIE HALL		
❏ Verve MGV-8189-2 [M]	1957	175.00
❏ Verve V-8189-2 [M]	1961	75.00
MILESTONE JAZZSTARS IN CONCERT		
❏ Milestone M-55006	198?	35.00
MILESTONE TWOFER GIANTS		
❏ Milestone MSP-1	197?	35.00

Number	Title	Yr	NM
MISSING LINKS			
❏ MCA 42206		1988	25.00
THE MODERN IDIOM			
❏ Capitol H325 [10]		1952	250.00
MODERN JAZZ			
❏ London LL1185 [M]		1955	300.00
❏ Tops L-1521 [M]		1958	300.00
MODERN JAZZ CONCERT			
❏ Adventures in Sound WL-127 [M]		1958	300.00
MODERN JAZZ FESTIVAL			
❏ Harmony HL7196 [M]		1958	300.00
MODERN JAZZ GALLERY			
❏ Kapp KXL-5001 [M]		195?	25.00
MODERN JAZZ GREATS			
❏ Crown CLP-5212 [M]		196?	35.00
MODERN JAZZ HALL OF FAME			
❏ Design DLP-29 [M]		196?	30.00
❏ Design DLPS-29 [R]		196?	20.00
MODERN JAZZ PIANO			
❏ RCA Camden CAL-384 [M]		1958	300.00
MODERN JAZZ PIANO ALBUM			
❏ Savoy Jazz SJL-2247		198?	30.00
MODERN JAZZ SPECTACULAR			
❏ Jazztone J-1231 [M]		1956	250.00
MODERN JAZZ SURVEY 1: NEW YORK JAZZ			
❏ Prestige 16-5		1957	600.00
—This album plays at 16 2/3 rpm and is marked as such; white label			
MODERN JAZZ SURVEY 2: BARITONES AND FRENCH HORNS			
❏ Prestige 16-6		1957	600.00
—This album plays at 16 2/3 rpm and is marked as such; white label			
MODERN JAZZ TRUMPETS			
❏ Prestige PRLP-113 [10]		1951	300.00
MODERN MOODS			
❏ Moodsville MVLP-2 [M]		1961	175.00
—Green label			
❏ Moodsville MVLP-2 [M]		1965	100.00
—Blue label, trident logo at right			
MONARCH ALL STAR JAZZ, VOL. 1			
❏ Monarch LP-201 [10]		1952	150.00
MONARCH ALL STAR JAZZ, VOL. 2			
❏ Monarch LP-202 [10]		1952	150.00
MONARCH ALL STAR JAZZ, VOL. 3			
❏ Monarch LP-203 [10]		1952	150.00
MONARCH ALL STAR JAZZ, VOL. 4			
❏ Monarch LP-204 [10]		1952	150.00
MONARCH ALL STAR JAZZ, VOL. 5			
❏ Monarch LP-205 [10]		1952	150.00
MONDAY NIGHT AT BIRDLAND			
❏ Roulette R52015 [M]		1958	75.00
❏ Roulette SR52015 [S]		1959	75.00
MONTAGE			
❏ Savoy MG-12029 [M]		1955	175.00
THE MONTREUX '77 COLLECTION			
❏ Pablo Live 2620107		1978	150.00
THE MONTREUX COLLECTION			
❏ Pablo 2625707		197?	35.00
MONTREUX SUMMIT			
❏ Columbia JG35005		1978	35.00
MONTREUX SUMMIT, VOLUME 2			
❏ Columbia JG35090		1978	35.00
MOOD IN BLUE			
❏ Urania UJLP-1209 [M]		1955	175.00
MOOD TO BE WOOED			
❏ Cadet LP-784 [M]		1967	50.00
❏ Cadet LPS-784 [S]		1967	35.00
MORE DRUMS ON FIRE			
❏ World Pacific WP-1261 [M]		1960	175.00
❏ World Pacific ST-1022 [S]		1960	175.00
MORE LIVE ECHOES OF THE SWINGING BANDS			
❏ RCA Victor LSP-1983 [S]		1959	150.00
❏ RCA Victor LPM-1983 [M]		1959	40.00
THE MOST			
❏ Forum Circle FC-9079 [M]		1963	30.00
❏ Forum Circle FCS-9079 [S]		1963	30.00
THE MOST, VOLUME 1			
❏ Roulette R52050 [M]		1960	50.00
❏ Roulette SR52050 [S]		1960	75.00
THE MOST, VOLUME 2			
❏ Roulette R52053 [M]		1960	50.00
❏ Roulette SR52053 [S]		1960	75.00
THE MOST, VOLUME 3			
❏ Roulette R52057 [M]		1961	50.00
❏ Roulette SR52057 [S]		1961	75.00

Number	Title	Yr	NM
THE MOST, VOLUME 4			
❏ Roulette R52062 [M]		1961	50.00
❏ Roulette SR52062 [S]		1961	75.00
THE MOST, VOLUME 5			
❏ Roulette R52075 [M]		1961	50.00
❏ Roulette SR52075 [S]		1961	75.00
MOTOR CITY SCENE			
❏ Bethlehem BCP-6056 [M]		1961	250.00
A MUSICAL HISTORY OF JAZZ			
❏ Grand Award GA 33-322 [M]		1955	75.00
MUSIC FOR THE BOY FRIEND…HE REALLY DIGS JAZZ			
❏ Decca DL8314 [M]		1956	120.00
MUSIC FROM THE DANCING YEARS			
❏ RCA Victor PR-112 [M]		1961	35.00
—Created for Dole Pineapple			
MUSIC FROM THE SOUTH, VOL. 1: COUNTRY BRASS BANDS			
❏ Folkways FA-2650 [M]		195?	30.00
THE MUSIC OF NEW ORLEANS, VOL. 1			
❏ Folkways FA-2461 [M]		1959	75.00
THE MUSIC OF NEW ORLEANS, VOL. 2			
❏ Folkways FA-2462 [M]		1959	75.00
THE MUSIC OF NEW ORLEANS, VOL. 3: DANCE HALLS			
❏ Folkways FA-2463 [M]		1959	75.00
THE MUSIC OF NEW ORLEANS, VOL. 4: THE BIRTH OF JAZZ			
❏ Folkways FA-2464 [M]		1959	75.00
THE MUSIC OF NEW ORLEANS, VOL. 5: NEW ORLEANS JAZZ			
❏ Folkways FA-2465 [M]		1959	75.00
❏ Status ST-8315 [M]		1965	75.00
THE NAMES OF DIXIELAND			
❏ Baronet B-108 [M]		195?	25.00
NATIVE NEW ORLEANS JAZZ			
❏ Dot DLP-3009 [M]		1956	200.00
NEW AMERICAN MUSIC VOL. 1: JAZZ			
❏ Folkways FA-33901		197?	30.00
NEW BLUE HORNS			
❏ Fantasy OJC-256		198?	25.00
❏ Riverside RLP 12-294 [M]		1958	300.00
THE NEW BREED			
❏ ABC Impulse! IA-9339		197?	35.00
NEW CHAMBER JAZZ			
❏ Epic LN1124 [10]		1955	150.00
NEW FACES AT NEWPORT			
❏ Metrojazz E-1005 [M]		1958	175.00
❏ Metrojazz SE-1005 [S]		1958	120.00
NEW MUSIC: SECOND WAVES			
❏ Savoy Jazz SJL-2235		198?	30.00
NEW ORLEANS: THE LIVING LEGENDS			
❏ Riverside RLP-356/7 [M]		196?	150.00
—Two records in gatefold jacket			
NEW ORLEANS: THE LIVING LEGENDS, VOL. 1			
❏ Riverside RLP-356 [M]		196?	50.00
❏ Riverside RS-9356 [R]		196?	30.00
NEW ORLEANS: THE LIVING LEGENDS, VOL. 2			
❏ Riverside RLP-357 [M]		196?	50.00
❏ Riverside RS-9357 [R]		196?	30.00
NEW ORLEANS ALL-STARS			
❏ GHB GHB-35		196?	30.00
NEW ORLEANS BRASS BANDS: DOWN YONDER			
❏ Rounder 2062		198?	25.00
NEW ORLEANS DIXIELAND			
❏ Southland SLP-216 [M]		1955	85.00
NEW ORLEANS ENCORE			
❏ Riverside RLP-2503 [M]		1954	300.00
NEW ORLEANS EXPRESS			
❏ EmArcy MG-36022 [M]		1955	250.00
NEW ORLEANS HORNS			
❏ Riverside RLP-1005 [10]		1953	300.00
NEW ORLEANS JAZZ			
❏ Decca DL5483 [10]		1953	175.00
❏ Decca DL8283 [M]		1956	120.00
NEW ORLEANS JAZZ AND HERITAGE FESTIVAL, 10TH ANNIVERSARY			
❏ Flying Fish FF-089		198?	25.00
NEW ORLEANS JAZZ AND HERITAGE FESTIVAL, 1976			
❏ Rhino R1-71111		1989	35.00
NEW ORLEANS JAZZ AT THE KITTY HALLS			
❏ Arhoolie 1013		198?	25.00

Number	Title	Yr	NM
NEW ORLEANS JAZZ BABIES			
❏ Southland SLP-214 [M]		1955	85.00
NEW ORLEANS JAZZ KINGS			
❏ Southland SLP-217 [M]		1955	85.00
NEW ORLEANS JAZZ STARS			
❏ Southland SLP-211 [M]		1955	85.00
NEW ORLEANS LEGENDS			
❏ Riverside RLP 12-119 [M]		1957	350.00
NEW ORLEANS REVIVAL			
❏ Riverside RLP-1047 [10]		1954	300.00
NEW ORLEANS RHYTHM KINGS			
❏ Riverside RLP 12-102 [M]		195?	75.00
—Also see NEW ORLEANS RHYTHM KINGS in the main A-Z listings.			
NEW ORLEANS STYLE			
❏ X LVA-3029 [10]		1954	175.00
NEW ORLEANS TO LOS ANGELES			
❏ Southland SLP-215 [M]		1955	85.00
NEWPORT JAZZ FESTIVAL			
❏ RCA Victor LPM-3369 [M]		1965	35.00
❏ RCA Victor LSP-3369 [S]		1965	50.00
NEWPORT JAZZ FESTIVAL: LIVE			
❏ Columbia C238262		198?	30.00
NEWPORT JAZZ FESTIVAL ALL STARS			
❏ Atlantic SD1331 [S]		1961	175.00
—Multicolor label, white "fan" logo at right			
NEWPORT JAZZ FESTIVAL ALL-STARS			
❏ Atlantic 1331 [M]		1961	175.00
—Multicolor label, white "fan" logo at right			
NEW SOUNDS FROM SWEDEN, VOL. 1: THE DARING YOUNG SWEDES			
❏ Prestige PRLP-119 [10]		1951	400.00
A NEW VISION FROM GRAMAVISION			
❏ Gramavision 18-8510		1986	25.00
NEW VOICES			
❏ Dawn DLP-1125 [M]		1956	175.00
THE NEW WAVE IN JAZZ			
❏ ABC Impulse! AS-90 [S]		1968	30.00
❏ Impulse! A-90 [M]		1966	35.00
❏ Impulse! AS-90 [S]		1966	150.00
NEW YORK JAZZ OF THE TWENTIES			
❏ Riverside RLP-1048 [10]		1954	300.00
THE 1930S, VOL. 1			
❏ Aircheck 1		197?	25.00
1944 ESQUIRE JAZZ ALL-STARS			
❏ Aircheck 27		197?	25.00
1947 WNEW SATURDAY NIGHT SWING SESSION			
❏ Everest Archive of Folk & Jazz 231		196?	25.00
1959 MONTEREY JAZZ FESTIVAL			
❏ Everest Archive of Folk & Jazz 239		196?	25.00
NO 'COUNT			
❏ Savoy MG-12078 [M]		1956	120.00
NO ENERGY CRISIS			
❏ ABC Impulse! AS-9267		1974	150.00
NORMAN GRANZ JAM SESSION			
❏ Verve VE-2-2508		197?	35.00
NORMAN GRANZ JAZZ CONCERT			
❏ Norgran MGN-2502 [M]		1954	300.00
❏ Norgran MGN-2501 [M]		1954	300.00
NO SOUR GRAPES, JUST PURE JAZZ			
❏ Bethlehem BCP-92 [M]		1958	250.00
NOTHING CHEESY ABOUT THIS JAZZ			
❏ Bethlehem BCP-85 [M]		1958	250.00
THE OFFICIAL GRAMMY AWARDS ARCHIVE COLLECTION (JAZZ VOCALISTS)			
❏ Franklin Mint GRAM-13		1985	75.00
THE OFFICIAL GRAMMY AWARDS ARCHIVE COLLECTION (THE BIG BAND SOUND)			
❏ Franklin Mint GRAM-7		1985	75.00
OLEO			
❏ Pausa 7025		198?	25.00
OLIO			
❏ Prestige PRLP-7084 [M]		1957	500.00
—Yellow label with W. 50th St. address			
ONE NIGHT STAND: A KEYBOARD EVENT			
❏ Columbia KC237100		198?	15.00
—Half-Speed Mastered" edition			
❏ Columbia HC247100		198?	50.00
ONE NIGHT WITH BLUE NOTE PRESERVED			
❏ Blue Note BTDK-85117		1985	75.00
ONE NIGHT WITH BLUE NOTE PRESERVED, VOL. 1			
❏ Blue Note BT-85113		1985	30.00
ONE NIGHT WITH BLUE NOTE PRESERVED, VOL. 2			
❏ Blue Note BT-85114		1985	30.00

Number / Title	Yr	NM
ONE NIGHT WITH BLUE NOTE PRESERVED, VOL. 3		
❏ Blue Note BT-85115	1985	30.00
ONE NIGHT WITH BLUE NOTE PRESERVED, VOL. 4		
❏ Blue Note BT-85116	1985	30.00
—*Box set containing all 4 volumes*		
ONE WORLD JAZZ		
❏ Adventures in Sound WL-162 [M]	1959	150.00
❏ Adventures in Sound WS-314 [S]	1959	40.00
ON-THE-ROAD JAZZ		
❏ Riverside RLP 12-127 [M]	1957	350.00
ON THE TRAIL		
❏ Pausa 7024	198?	25.00
OPUS DE BLUES		
❏ Savoy MG-12142 [M]	1959	120.00
OPUS DE JAZZ		
❏ Savoy MG-12036 [M]	1955	175.00
OPUS IN SWING		
❏ Savoy MG-12085 [M]	1956	120.00
THE ORCHESTRA "HOUSE OF SOUND		
❏ Brunswick BL54003 [M]	1954	75.00
ORIGINAL BLUE NOTE JAZZ, VOL. 1		
❏ Blue Note B-6504	1969	50.00
ORIGINAL BLUE NOTE JAZZ, VOL. 2		
❏ Blue Note B-6506	1970	50.00
THE ORIGINAL SOUND OF THE 20'S		
❏ Columbia C3L35	1965	40.00
OUR BEST		
❏ Clef MGC-639 [M]	1955	300.00
❏ Norgran MGN-1021 [M]	1955	300.00
OUT CAME THE BLUES		
❏ MCA 1352	198?	25.00
PABLO ALL-STARS JAM: MONTREUX '77		
❏ Fantasy OJC-380	1989	25.00
❏ Pablo Live 2308210	197?	35.00
PANORAMA OF BRITISH JAZZ		
❏ Discovery DL-2001 [10]	1953	300.00
PARAMOUNT CORNET BLUES RARITIES CHICAGO 1924-27		
❏ Herwin 111	197?	30.00
PARAMOUNT HOT JAZZ RARITIES 1926-28		
❏ Herwin 110	197?	30.00
PARLOR PIANO: BLUES AND STOMPS		
❏ Biograph 1001	197?	25.00
PARTY AFTER HOURS		
❏ Aladdin LP-703 [10]	1950	8000.00
—*Red vinyl*		
❏ Aladdin LP-703 [10]	1950	4000.00
—*Black vinyl*		
PERCUSSION PROFILES		
❏ ECM 19002	1977	30.00
PERCUSSION UNABRIDGED		
❏ Kimberly 2022 [M]	1963	50.00
❏ Kimberly 11022 [S]	1963	75.00
PERFECT FOR DANCING: ALL TEMPOS		
❏ RCA Victor LPM-1072 [M]	1954	75.00
PERFECT FOR DANCING: FOX TROTS		
❏ RCA Victor LPM-1070 [M]	1954	75.00
PERFECT FOR DANCING: JITTERBUG OR LINDY		
❏ RCA Victor LPM-1071 [M]	1954	75.00
PERIOD'S JAZZ DIGEST		
❏ Period SPL-302 [M]	1956	150.00
PERIOD'S JAZZ DIGEST VOL. 2		
❏ Period SPL-304 [M]	1955	150.00
PIANISTS GALORE		
❏ Pacific Jazz JWC-506 [M]	1957	150.00
❏ World Pacific JWC-506 [M]	1958	175.00
PIANO ARTISTRY		
❏ Audiophile AP-28 [M]	1953	75.00
PIANO GIANTS		
❏ Prestige 24052	197?	20.00
PIANO IN STYLE		
❏ MCA 1332	198?	12.00
PIANO INTERPRETATIONS		
❏ Norgran MGN-1036 [M]	1955	300.00
❏ Verve MGV-8125 [M]	1957	175.00
❏ Verve V-8125 [M]	1961	50.00
PIANO JAZZ, VOLUME 1		
❏ Brunswick BL54014 [M]	1955	85.00
PIANO JAZZ, VOLUME 2		
❏ Brunswick BL54015 [M]	1955	85.00
PIANO MODERN		
❏ Verve VSP-13 [M]	1966	35.00
❏ Verve VSPS-13 [R]	1966	25.00
PIANO MUSIC FOR PARTIES		
❏ Columbia CL603 [M]	1955	85.00

Number / Title	Yr	NM
PIANO MUSIC FOR TWO		
❏ Columbia CL602 [M]	1955	85.00
PIANO ONE		
❏ Private Music 2004#NAME?	1986	25.00
THE PIANO PLAYERS		
❏ Xanadu 171	197?	30.00
PIANO RAGTIME OF THE FORTIES		
❏ Herwin 403	197?	30.00
PIANO RAGTIME OF THE TEENS, TWENTIES AND THIRTIES		
❏ Herwin 402	197?	30.00
PIANO RAGTIME OF THE TEENS, TWENTIES AND THIRTIES, VOL. 2		
❏ Herwin 405	197?	30.00
PIANO RAGTIME OF THE TEENS, TWENTIES AND THIRTIES, VOL. 3		
❏ Herwin 406	197?	30.00
PIANO ROLL HALL OF FAME		
❏ Sounds 1202	196?	30.00
PIANO ROLL TRANSCRIPTIONS		
❏ Riverside RLP 12-110 [M]	1956	300.00
❏ Riverside RLP 12-126 [M]	1957	350.00
PIANO STYLISTS		
❏ Capitol H323 [10]	1952	175.00
PIANO TWO		
❏ Private Music 2027#NAME?	1988	25.00
PICK UP THE BEAT		
❏ Epic LN3127 [M]	1955	150.00
PIONEERS OF BOOGIE WOOGIE		
❏ Riverside RLP-1009 [10]	1953	300.00
PIONEERS OF BOOGIE WOOGIE, VOL. 2		
❏ Riverside RLP-1034 [10]	1954	300.00
PIONEERS OF THE JAZZ GUITAR		
❏ Yazoo 1057	197?	25.00
PLAYBOY ALL STARS VOLUME 1		
❏ Playboy PB-1957 [M]	1957	40.00
PLAYBOY ALL STARS VOLUME 2		
❏ Playboy PB-1958 [M]	1958	40.00
PLAYBOY ALL STARS VOLUME 3		
❏ Playboy PB-1959 [M]	1959	120.00
THE PLAYERS' ASSOCIATION		
❏ Vanguard VSD-79384	197?	30.00
POP PARADE		
❏ MGM E-194 [10]	1953	150.00
POPULAR FAVORITES		
❏ Columbia CL6057 [10]	1949	40.00
PORGY AND BESS		
❏ Bethlehem EXLP-1 [M]	1956	300.00
❏ Bethlehem BCP-6040 [M]	1959	250.00
PORTRAITS IN JAZZ		
❏ Reprise R-6084 [M]	1963	30.00
❏ Reprise R9-6084 [S]	1963	35.00
POT, SPOON, PIPE AND JUG		
❏ Stash ST-102	197?	25.00
A POTPOURRI OF JAZZ		
❏ Verve MGV-2032 [M]	1956	250.00
❏ Verve V-2032 [M]	1961	50.00
POWER, GLORY AND MUSIC		
❏ Salvation 1000	197?	35.00
PRESTIGE CLASSIC JAM SESSIONS, VOL. 1		
❏ Prestige 24107	198?	35.00
PRESTIGE GROOVY GOODIES, VOL. 1		
❏ Prestige PRLP-7298 [M]	1964	75.00
❏ Prestige PRST-7298 [R]	1964	50.00
PRESTIGE SOUL MASTERPIECES		
❏ Fantasy OJC-1201	1988	30.00
PRESTIGE TWOFER GIANTS, VOL. 1		
❏ Prestige PRP-1	197?	35.00
PRESTIGE TWOFER GIANTS, VOL. 2		
❏ Prestige PRP-2	197?	35.00
PRIMITIVE PIANO		
❏ Tone 1 [M]	195?	30.00
PROGRESSIVE PIANO		
❏ RCA Victor LJM-3001 [10]	1952	150.00
THE PROGRESSIVE RECORDS ALL STAR TENOR SAX SPECTACULAR		
❏ Progressive PRO-7019	1978	30.00
THE PROGRESSIVE RECORDS ALL STAR TROMBONE SPECTACULAR		
❏ Progressive PRO-7018	1978	30.00
THE PROGRESSIVE RECORDS ALL STAR TRUMPET SPECTACULAR		
❏ Progressive PRO-7015	1978	30.00

Number / Title	Yr	NM
THE PROGRESSIVE RECORDS ALL STAR TRUMPET SPECTACULAR, VOL. 2		
❏ Progressive PRO-7017	1978	30.00
THE PROGRESSIVES		
❏ Columbia KG31574	1973	50.00
❏ Columbia CG31574	197?	30.00
—*CG" prefix is a reissue of "KG*		
RAGTIME PIANO ROLL, VOL. 1		
❏ Riverside RLP-1006 [10]	1953	300.00
RAGTIME PIANO ROLL, VOL. 2		
❏ Riverside RLP-1025 [10]	1954	300.00
RAGTIME PIANO ROLL, VOL. 3		
❏ Riverside RLP-1049 [10]	1954	300.00
RAGTIMERS' IMMORTAL PERFORMANCES		
❏ RCA Victor LPT-1000 [M]	1954	75.00
RARE BANDS OF THE 20S, VOL. 1		
❏ Historical ASC-3	1966	30.00
RARE BANDS OF THE 20S, VOL. 2		
❏ Historical ASC-6	1966	30.00
RARE BANDS OF THE 20S, VOL. 3		
❏ Historical ASC-7	1966	30.00
RARE HOT CHICAGO JAZZ		
❏ Herwin 109	197?	30.00
RARE VERTICAL JAZZ		
❏ Historical ASC-8	1966	30.00
THE RCA VICTOR ENCYCLOPEDIA OF RECORDED JAZZ, ALBUM 1		
❏ RCA Victor LEJ-1 [10]	1956	40.00
THE RCA VICTOR ENCYCLOPEDIA OF RECORDED JAZZ, ALBUM 2		
❏ RCA Victor LEJ-2 [10]	1956	40.00
THE RCA VICTOR ENCYCLOPEDIA OF RECORDED JAZZ, ALBUM 3		
❏ RCA Victor LEJ-3 [10]	1956	40.00
THE RCA VICTOR ENCYCLOPEDIA OF RECORDED JAZZ, ALBUM 4		
❏ RCA Victor LEJ-4 [10]	1956	40.00
THE RCA VICTOR ENCYCLOPEDIA OF RECORDED JAZZ, ALBUM 5		
❏ RCA Victor LEJ-5 [10]	1956	40.00
THE RCA VICTOR ENCYCLOPEDIA OF RECORDED JAZZ, ALBUM 6		
❏ RCA Victor LEJ-6 [10]	1956	40.00
THE RCA VICTOR ENCYCLOPEDIA OF RECORDED JAZZ, ALBUM 7		
❏ RCA Victor LEJ-7 [10]	1956	40.00
THE RCA VICTOR ENCYCLOPEDIA OF RECORDED JAZZ, ALBUM 8		
❏ RCA Victor LEJ-8 [10]	1956	40.00
THE RCA VICTOR ENCYCLOPEDIA OF RECORDED JAZZ, ALBUM 9		
❏ RCA Victor LEJ-9 [10]	1956	40.00
THE RCA VICTOR ENCYCLOPEDIA OF RECORDED JAZZ, ALBUM 10		
❏ RCA Victor LEJ-10 [10]	1956	40.00
THE RCA VICTOR ENCYCLOPEDIA OF RECORDED JAZZ, ALBUM 11		
❏ RCA Victor LEJ-11 [10]	1956	40.00
THE RCA VICTOR ENCYCLOPEDIA OF RECORDED JAZZ, ALBUM 12		
❏ RCA Victor LEJ-12 [10]	1956	40.00
THE REAL AMBASSADORS		
❏ Columbia CL5850 [M]	1962	50.00
❏ Columbia OS2250 [S]	1962	75.00
REBIRTH OF BEALE STREET		
❏ Beale Street BS-1	1983	250.00
—*Limited edition of 1,000 made for the city of Memphis*		
RECORDED IN NEW ORLEANS, VOL. 1		
❏ Good Time Jazz L-12019 [M]	1955	75.00
RECORDED IN NEW ORLEANS, VOL. 2		
❏ Good Time Jazz L-12020 [M]	1955	75.00
RECORDED ON LOCATION AT THE FIVE SPOT CAFE IN NEW YORK CITY...A MEMORIAL CONCERT DEDICATED TO THE MUSIC OF CHARLIE PARKER		
❏ Signal S-1204 [M]	1957	250.00
RECORD HOP		
❏ Decca DL8067 [M]	1955	175.00
RED HOT AND BLUE JAZZ		
❏ Waldorf Music Hall MH 33-141 [10]	195?	250.00
REEFER SONGS		
❏ Stash ST-100	197?	35.00

Number	Title	Yr	NM
RELAXED SAXOPHONE MOODS			
❏ Prestige PRLP-141 [10]		1953	300.00
REMEMBERING CHRISTMAS WITH THE BIG BANDS			
❏ RCA Special Products DPM1-0506 [M]		1981	30.00
REQUESTED BY YOU			
❏ Columbia CL607 [M]		1955	85.00
RHYTHM & BLUES			
❏ RCA Camden CAL-371 [M]		1958	75.00
RHYTHM, BLUES AND BOOGIE-WOOGIE			
❏ Decca DL4011 [M]		1960	75.00
RHYTHM AND BLUES			
❏ Savoy MG-15008 [10]		1952	175.00
RHYTHM PLUS ONE			
❏ Epic LN3297 [M]		1956	150.00
THE RHYTHM SECTION			
❏ Epic LN3271 [M]		1956	150.00
RIDIN' IN RHYTHM			
❏ Swing SW-8453/4		198?	30.00
RINGSIDE AT CONDON'S			
❏ Savoy MG-15029 [10]		1954	175.00
RINGSIDE AT CONDON'S VOL. 2			
❏ Savoy MG-15030 [10]		1954	175.00
RIVERBOAT JAZZ			
❏ Brunswick BL58026 [10]		1951	150.00
RIVERSIDE DRIVE			
❏ Riverside RLP 12-267 [M]		1958	300.00
RIVERSIDE MODERN JAZZ SAMPLER			
❏ Riverside S-3 [M]		1956	300.00
THE ROARING 20'S			
❏ Saydisc SDL-344		198?	25.00
—*Compilation of seven versions of the title song, released not long after the movie of the same name*			
RODGERS AND HART GEMS			
❏ Pacific Jazz JWC-504 [M]		1956	150.00
❏ World Pacific JWC-504 [M]		1958	175.00
ROOST 5TH ANNIVERSARY ALBUM			
❏ Roost RST-1201 [M]		1955	150.00
THE ROOTS OF DIXIELAND JAZZ			
❏ Everest Archive of Folk & Jazz 274		197?	25.00
THE ROOTS OF DIXIELAND JAZZ, VOL. 2			
❏ Everest Archive of Folk & Jazz 320		198?	25.00
'ROUND MIDNIGHT			
❏ Milestone M-9144		1986	30.00
SAXES, INC.			
❏ Warner Bros. W1336 [M]		1959	150.00
❏ Warner Bros. WS1336 [S]		1959	175.00
SAX GREATS			
❏ Everest Archive of Folk & Jazz 331		198?	25.00
THE SAXOPHONE			
❏ ABC Impulse! AS-9253		197?	150.00
SAXOPHONE REVOLT			
❏ Riverside RLP 12-284 [M]		1958	300.00
THE SAX SECTION			
❏ Epic LN3278 [M]		1956	100.00
SAX STYLISTS			
❏ Capitol H328 [10]		1952	175.00
A SCRAPBOOK OF BRITISH JAZZ, 1926-1956			
❏ London LL1444 [M]		1956	50.00
SECOND SESSION AT SQUIRREL'S			
❏ Paramount LP-108 [10]		1954	120.00
SESSION AT MIDNIGHT			
❏ Capitol T707 [M]		1956	150.00
SESSION AT RIVERSIDE			
❏ Capitol T761 [M]		1956	300.00
THE SEVEN AGES OF JAZZ			
❏ Metrojazz 2-E-1009 [M]		1959	200.00
❏ Metrojazz 2-SE-1009 [S]		1959	175.00
THE 77 SESSIONS			
❏ GHB GHB-250		198?	25.00
SHADES OF NEW ORLEANS			
❏ GHB GHB-140		198?	25.00
❏ Southland SLP-240		1963	35.00
SHOUTIN', SWINGIN' AND MAKIN' LOVE			
❏ Chess CHV-412		1970	35.00
SIGNALS			
❏ Savoy Jazz SJL-2231		198?	30.00
SILVER BLUE			
❏ Xanadu 137		197?	30.00
THE SILVER YEARS: COMMEMORATING CAPITOL'S 25 YEARS IN THE RECORDING INDUSTRY			
❏ Capitol SNP-91097 [S]		1967	75.00
—*Custom silver label*			

Number	Title	Yr	NM
❏ Capitol NP-91097 [M]		1967	75.00
—*Custom silver label*			
❏ Savoy MG-12217 [M]		196?	50.00
SINGIN' THE BLUES			
❏ MCA 4064		197?	30.00
SITTIN' IN			
❏ Verve MGV-8225 [M]		1958	150.00
❏ Verve V-8225 [M]		1961	75.00
SMALL COMBO HITS			
❏ RCA Victor LPT-3 [10]		1951	40.00
SMART, LUSCIOUS, BEAUTIFUL			
❏ Bethlehem BCP-6034 [M]		1960	300.00
THE SMITHSONIAN COLLECTION OF CLASSIC JAZZ			
❏ Smithsonian/CSP P611891		1973	40.00
❏ Smithsonian/CSP P719477		1987	40.00
—*Revised version of 1973 original*			
SMOKE RINGS			
❏ RCA Victor LPT-13 [10]		1951	40.00
SMOOTH & SWINGING JAZZ			
❏ Verve PM-12 [M]		1964	35.00
—*Custom edition for Whyte & Mackay's Blended Scotch Whiskey*			
SOFT PEDAL			
❏ Columbia CL2511 [10]		1954	75.00
SOLID STATE DEMONSTRATION RECORD			
❏ Solid State SS93 [DJ]		1966	35.00
—*Sampler from six Solid State LP releases*			
SOLO FLIGHT			
❏ Pacific Jazz JWC-505 [M]		1956	150.00
❏ World Pacific JWC-505 [M]		1958	175.00
SOME LIKE IT COOL			
❏ United Artists X-71 [M]		1959	40.00
❏ United Artists SX-71 [S]		1959	40.00
SOMETHING FOR BOTH EARS			
❏ World Pacific HFS-2 [S]		1958	175.00
—*Stereo sampler*			
SOMETHING NEW, SOMETHING BLUE			
❏ Columbia CL1388 [M]		1959	50.00
SONGS BY RODGERS AND HART AND JOHNNY GREEN			
❏ Discovery DL-3014 [10]		1951	300.00
SOUL JAZZ, VOL. 1			
❏ Bluesville BVLP-1009 [M]		1960	150.00
—*Blue label, silver print*			
❏ Bluesville BVLP-1009 [M]		1965	75.00
—*Blue label, trident logo at right*			
SOUL JAZZ, VOL. 2			
❏ Bluesville BVLP-1010 [M]		1960	150.00
—*Blue label, silver print*			
❏ Bluesville BVLP-1010 [M]		1965	75.00
—*Blue label, trident logo at right*			
SOUL JAZZ GIANTS			
❏ Prestige PRST-7791		1970	35.00
THE SOUL OF JAZZ			
❏ Riverside S-5 [M]		1957	300.00
❏ World Wide MGS-20002 [S]		1958	175.00
THE SOUL OF JAZZ PERCUSSION			
❏ Warwick W5003 [M]		1961	75.00
❏ Warwick W5003ST [S]		1961	40.00
THE SOUL OF JAZZ PIANO			
❏ Riverside 9S-7 [S]		196?	75.00
THE SOUND OF BIG BAND JAZZ IN HI-FI			
❏ World Pacific WP-1257 [M]		1960	175.00
THE SOUND OF BIG BAND JAZZ IN STEREO			
❏ World Pacific ST-1015 [S]		1960	175.00
THE SOUND OF PICANTE			
❏ Concord Picante CJP-295		1986	25.00
SOUNDS IN SPACE			
❏ RCA Victor SP-33-13 [S]		1958	50.00
—*Narrated by Ken Nordine with songs by various artists*			
SOUTH SIDE JAZZ			
❏ Chess CHV-415		1971	30.00
THE SPANISH SIDE OF JAZZ			
❏ Roulette SR-42001		1968	50.00
SPIRITUALS TO SWING: JOHN HAMMOND'S 30TH ANNIVERSARY CONCERT 1967			
❏ Columbia G30776		1971	35.00
❏ Columbia CG30776		197?	30.00
—*CG" prefix is a reissue of "G*			
STABLE MATES			
❏ Savoy MG-12115 [M]		1957	150.00
STARS OF JAZZ '61			
❏ Jazzland JLP-1001 [M]		1961	75.00

Number	Title	Yr	NM
STARS OF THE APOLLO			
❏ Columbia G30788		1971	35.00
❏ Columbia CG30788		197?	30.00
—*CG" prefix is a reissue of "G*			
THE STASH CHRISTMAS ALBUM			
❏ Stash 125		1980	35.00
ST. LOUIS JAZZ, 1925-27			
❏ Herwin 114		197?	30.00
STRAIGHT NO CHASER			
❏ Blue Note B1-28263		1994	75.00
—*Compilation of original recordings that were sampled by US3, plus others*			
STRETCHING OUT			
❏ United Artists UAL-4023 [M]		1959	400.00
❏ United Artists UAS-5023 [S]		1959	300.00
STRICTLY BEBOP			
❏ Capitol M-11059		1973	30.00
STRICTLY FROM DIXIE			
❏ MGM E-3262 [M]		1956	75.00
A STRING OF SWINGIN' PEARLS			
❏ RCA Victor LPM-1373 [M]		1956	75.00
SUMMIT MEETING			
❏ Vanguard VSD-79390		1977	30.00
❏ Vee Jay LP-3026 [M]		1961	50.00
❏ Vee Jay SR-3026 [S]		1961	75.00
SWEDES FROM JAZZVILLE			
❏ Epic LN3309 [M]		1957	250.00
SWEDISH PASTRY			
❏ Discovery DL-2008 [10]		1954	300.00
SWING 1946			
❏ Prestige PRLP-7604		1969	35.00
SWING AGAIN!			
❏ Capitol T1386 [M]		1960	100.00
❏ Capitol DT1386 [R]		196?	75.00
SWING CLASSICS 1935			
❏ Prestige PRLP-7646		1969	35.00
THE SWING ERA, VOL. 1			
❏ X LVA-3030 [10]		1955	175.00
SWING GOES DIXIE			
❏ American Recording Society G-420 [M]		1957	75.00
SWING GUITARS			
❏ Norgran MGN-1033 [M]		1955	175.00
❏ Verve MGV-8124 [M]		1957	175.00
❏ Verve V-8124 [M]		1961	50.00
SWING HI, SWING LO			
❏ Blue Note BLP-5027 [10]		1953	250.00
❏ Blue Note B-6507 [M]		1969	35.00
SWINGIN': BIG BAND SWING AND JAZZ FROM THE 1930S AND 1940S			
❏ Folkways FJ-2861		1986	30.00
SWINGING BROADWAY			
❏ Kimberly 2024 [M]		1963	50.00
❏ Kimberly 11024 [S]		1963	75.00
SWINGING FOR THE KING			
❏ Mercury MG-20133 [M]		1956	175.00
A SWINGIN' GIG			
❏ Tampa TP-2 [M]		1957	300.00
—*Colored vinyl*			
❏ Tampa TP-2 [M]		1958	250.00
—*Black vinyl*			
SWINGING SMALL BANDS			
❏ MCA 1324		198?	25.00
SWINGING SOUNDTRACK			
❏ Kimberly 2016 [M]		1963	50.00
❏ Kimberly 11016 [S]		1963	75.00
SWINGIN' LIKE SIXTY, VOL. 1			
❏ World Pacific WP-1289 [M]		1960	175.00
❏ World Pacific ST-1289 [S]		1960	175.00
SWINGIN' LIKE SIXTY, VOL. 2			
❏ World Pacific ST-1290 [S]		1960	175.00
SWINGIN' LIKE SIXTY, VOL. 3			
❏ World Pacific ST-1291 [S]		1960	175.00
SWINGIN' SOUNDS			
❏ Columbia Special Products XTV82030 [M]		1962	75.00
—*Issued for the W.A. Sheaffer Pen Co.*			
SWING LIGHTLY			
❏ Jazztone J-1265 [M]		1957	75.00
SWING... NOT SPRING!			
❏ Savoy MG-12062 [M]		1956	150.00
SWING POTPOURRI			
❏ Audiophile AP-23 [M]		1953	75.00
SWINGTIME JIVE			
❏ Stash ST-108		197?	25.00
THE SWINGVILLE ALL-STARS			
❏ Swingville SVLP-2010 [M]		1960	40.00
—*Purple label*			

Number Title	Yr	NM
❏ Swingville SVLP-2010 [M]	1965	50.00
—Blue label, trident logo at right		
A TASTE OF JAZZ		
❏ Concord Jazz CJ-93	1979	25.00
TEA PAD SONGS, VOL. 1		
❏ Stash ST-103	197?	25.00
TEA PAD SONGS, VOL. 2		
❏ Stash ST-104	197?	25.00
TENOR CONCLAVE		
❏ Prestige PRLP-7074 [M]	1957	200.00
—Reissued as Prestige 7249; see JOHN COLTRANE.		
TENOR JAZZ		
❏ Mercury MG-20016 [10]	1950	300.00
—Issued in a paper sleeve		
TENORS ANYONE?		
❏ Dawn DLP-1126 [M]	1958	250.00
TENOR SAX		
❏ Concord 3012 [M]	195?	40.00
TENOR SAXES		
❏ Norgran MGN-1034 [M]	1955	300.00
❏ Verve MGV-8127 [M]	1957	175.00
❏ Verve V-8127 [M]	1961	50.00
TENOR SAX SOLOS, VOL. 1		
❏ Savoy MG-9008 [10]	1952	300.00
TENOR SAX SOLOS, VOL. 2		
❏ Savoy MG-9013 [10]	1952	300.00
TENOR SAX SOLOS, VOL. 3		
❏ Savoy MG-9021 [10]	1953	300.00
TERRITORY BANDS 1926-31		
❏ Historical 26	1969	25.00
TERRITORY BANDS 1929-33		
❏ Historical 24	1968	25.00
THAT'S THE WAY I FEEL NOW		
❏ A&M SP-6600	1984	35.00
—Includes Joe Jackson		
THAT'S THE WAY I FEEL NOW (A TRIBUTE TO THELONIOUS MONK)		
❏ A&M SP-6006	198?	35.00
THEME SONGS		
❏ Columbia CL6016 [10]	1949	40.00
❏ RCA Victor LPT-1 [10]	1951	40.00
THESAURUS OF CLASSIC JAZZ		
❏ Columbia C4L18	1961	150.00
THEY ALL PLAYED RAGTIME		
❏ Jazzology JCE-52	197?	25.00
THEY ALL PLAYED THE MAPLE LEAF RAG		
❏ Herwin 401	197?	30.00
A THIRD SESSION AT SQUIRREL'S		
❏ Paramount LP-110 [M]	1954	120.00
THIS COULD LEAD TO LOVE		
❏ Riverside RLP 12-808 [M]	195?	50.00
THIS IS THE BIG BAND ERA		
❏ RCA Victor VPM-6043	197?	35.00
THIS IS THE BLUES		
❏ Kimberly 2020 [M]	1963	50.00
❏ Kimberly 11020 [S]	1963	75.00
THIS IS THE BLUES, VOL. 1		
❏ Pacific Jazz PJ-13 [M]	1961	75.00
THIS IS THE BLUES, VOL. 2		
❏ Pacific Jazz PJ-30 [M]	1962	75.00
❏ Pacific Jazz ST-30 [M]	1962	75.00
THIS IS THEIR TIME, OH YEAH		
❏ Revelation REV-11	1970	35.00
THREE DECADES OF MUSIC, 1939-49, VOL. 1		
❏ Blue Note BST-89902	1969	75.00
THREE DECADES OF MUSIC, 1949-59, VOL. 1		
❏ Blue Note BST-89903	1969	75.00
THREE DECADES OF MUSIC, 1959-69, VOL. 1		
❏ Blue Note BST-89904	1969	75.00
THREE ROADS TO JAZZ		
❏ American Recording Society LP-100 [M]	1956	75.00
TIME SPEAKS: DEDICATED TO THE MEMORY OF CLIFFORD BROWN		
❏ Timeless LPSJP-187	1990	30.00
—With Benny Golson, Freddie Hubbard, Woody Shaw, Kenny Barron, Cecil McBee, Ben Riley		
TOOTIN' THROUGH THE ROOF, VOL. 1		
❏ Onyx 209	197?	30.00
TOOTIN' THROUGH THE ROOF, VOL. 2		
❏ Onyx 213	197?	30.00
TOWN HALL CONCERT		
❏ Mainstream S-6004 [R]	1965	30.00
❏ Mainstream 56004 [M]	1965	75.00

Number Title	Yr	NM
TRADITIONAL JAZZ		
❏ London LL1242 [M]	1955	75.00
TRADITIONAL JAZZ AT THE ROYAL FESTIVAL HALL		
❏ London LL1184 [M]	1955	75.00
TRIBUTE TO CHARLIE PARKER FROM THE NEWPORT JAZZ FESTIVAL		
❏ RCA Victor LPM-3738 [M]	1967	75.00
❏ RCA Victor LSP-3738 [S]	1967	50.00
A TRIBUTE TO DUKE		
❏ Concord Jazz CJ-50	197?	30.00
TRIBUTE TO MONK AND BIRD		
❏ Tomato TOM-9002	1979	35.00
TROMBONE BAND STAND		
❏ Bethlehem BCP-6036 [M]	1960	300.00
TROMBONES		
❏ Savoy MG-12086 [M]	1956	120.00
TROMBONE SCENE		
❏ Vik LX-1087 [M]	1957	75.00
TRUE BLUE		
❏ Xanadu 136	197?	25.00
THE TRUMPET ALBUM		
❏ Savoy Jazz SJL-2237	198?	30.00
TRUMPET BLUES 1925-29		
❏ Historical 27	1969	25.00
TRUMPETER'S HOLIDAY		
❏ Epic LN3252 [M]	1956	150.00
TRUMPET INTERLUDE		
❏ EmArcy MG-36017 [M]	1955	250.00
❏ Savoy MG-12096 [M]	1957	120.00
TRUMPET STYLISTS		
❏ Capitol H326 [10]	1952	175.00
TRUMPET TRIBUTE TO FATS NAVARRO, CLIFFORD BROWN, BOOKER LITTLE		
❏ Trip 5036	197?	30.00
24 KARAT GOLD FOR GROOVIN'		
❏ Verve V6-6654	1968	50.00
25 YEARS OF PRESTIGE		
❏ Prestige 24046	197?	35.00
UNDER ONE ROOF		
❏ EmArcy MG-36088 [M]	1956	250.00
UNEXPURGATED JAZZ		
❏ Audiophile AP-43 [M]	1953	75.00
UNFORGETTABLE PERFORMANCES BY THE JAZZ IMMORTALS		
❏ Dot DLP-3444 [M]	196?	85.00
UPRIGHT AND LOWDOWN		
❏ Columbia CL685 [M]	1955	75.00
UP SWING		
❏ RCA Victor LPT-12 [10]	1951	40.00
THE VERVE COMPENDIUM OF JAZZ, NO. 1		
❏ Verve MGV-8194 [M]	1957	150.00
❏ Verve V-8194 [M]	1961	50.00
THE VERVE COMPENDIUM OF JAZZ, NO. 2		
❏ Verve MGV-8195 [M]	1957	150.00
❏ Verve V-8195 [M]	1961	50.00
VERY SAXY		
❏ Fantasy OJC-458	1990	15.00
❏ Prestige PRST-7790	1971	50.00
—Reissue of 7167		
❏ Prestige PRLP-7167 [M]	1959	250.00
VICEROY CIGARETTES CAMPUS JAZZ FESTIVAL		
❏ RCA Custom KO7P-1544 [M]	1959	75.00
—Available thoruigh Viceroy cigarettes		
THE VIOLIN SUMMIT		
❏ Prestige PRLP-7631	1969	35.00
VOODOO DRUMS IN HI-FI		
❏ Atlantic 1296 [M]	1958	300.00
—Black label		
❏ Atlantic 1296 [M]	1961	175.00
—Multicolor label, white "fan" logo at right		
❏ Atlantic 1296 [M]	1963	50.00
—Multicolor label, black "fan" logo at right		
WASHBOARD RHYTHM KINGS, VOL. 1		
❏ X LVA-3021 [10]	1954	300.00
WE CUT THIS ALBUM FOR BREAD		
❏ Bethlehem BCP-86 [M]	1958	250.00
WEED: A RARE BATCH		
❏ Stash ST-107	197?	30.00
WE LIKE BANDS		
❏ Coral CRL57229 [M]	195?	15.00
WEST COAST JAZZ, VOL. 2		
❏ Jazztone J-(# unk) [M]	1957	75.00

Number Title	Yr	NM
WEST COAST VS. EAST COAST		
❏ MGM E-3390 [M]	1956	300.00
WE'VE BUILT A JAZZ ALBUM FOR YOU		
❏ Bethlehem BCP-89 [M]	1958	250.00
WHEELIN' AND DEALIN'		
❏ Prestige PRLP-7131 [M]	1957	350.00
—Reissued as Status 8327; see JOHN COLTRANE.		
THE WIDE, WIDE WORLD OF JAZZ		
❏ RCA Victor LPM-1325 [M]	1956	75.00
WILDFLOWERS: NEW YORK LOFT JAZZ 1		
❏ Douglas 7045	1976	30.00
WILDFLOWERS: NEW YORK LOFT JAZZ 2		
❏ Douglas 7046	1976	30.00
WILDFLOWERS: NEW YORK LOFT JAZZ 3		
❏ Douglas 7047	1976	30.00
WILDFLOWERS: NEW YORK LOFT JAZZ 4		
❏ Douglas 7048	1976	30.00
WILDFLOWERS: NEW YORK LOFT JAZZ 5		
❏ Douglas 7049	1976	30.00
WINNERS ALL! THE DOWN BEAT JAZZ POLL '64		
❏ Verve V-8579 [M]	1964	50.00
❏ Verve V6-8579 [S]	1964	75.00
WINNER'S CIRCLE		
❏ Bethlehem BCP-6024 [M]	1958	250.00
WINNERS CIRCLE LIMITED EDITION		
❏ Columbia GB-4 [M]	1959	75.00
THE WOMEN IN JAZZ		
❏ Storyville STLP-916 [M]	1956	150.00
WOMEN IN JAZZ, VOL. 1: ALL-WOMAN GROUPS		
❏ Stash ST-111	198?	25.00
WOMEN IN JAZZ, VOL. 2: PIANISTS		
❏ Stash ST-112	198?	25.00
WOMEN IN JAZZ, VOL. 3: SWINGTIME TO MODERN		
❏ Stash ST-113	198?	25.00
THE WORLD OF SWING		
❏ Columbia KG32945	1974	35.00
THE WORLD'S GREATEST MUSIC SERIES 'POP' -- JAZZ		
❏ Artia-Parliament WGM2AB	196?	200.00
—Box set of material from the Roulette label; also issued as two five-record boxes		
❏ Artia-Parliament WGM2B	196?	150.00
—Second of two five-record sets		
❏ Artia-Parliament WGM-2A [M]	196?	150.00
❏ Artia-Parliament WGM(S)-2A [S]	196?	120.00
XANADU AT MONTREUX, VOL. 1		
❏ Xanadu 162	198?	25.00
XANADU AT MONTREUX, VOL. 2		
❏ Xanadu 163	198?	25.00
XANADU AT MONTREUX, VOL. 3		
❏ Xanadu 164	198?	25.00
XANADU AT MONTREUX, VOL. 4		
❏ Xanadu 165	198?	25.00
XANADU IN AFRICA		
❏ Xanadu 180	1981	30.00
YAZOO'S HISTORY OF JAZZ		
❏ Yazoo 1070	197?	25.00
YESTERDAY		
❏ Mainstream MRL-364	197?	30.00
THE YOUNG AT BOP		
❏ EmArcy MG-26001 [10]	1954	350.00
THE YOUNG ONES OF JAZZ		
❏ EmArcy MG-36085 [M]	1956	250.00
YOURS		
❏ Harmony HL7042 [M]	1957	50.00
YOU'VE GOT TO HEAR IT TO BELIEVE IT		
❏ Solid State SS-94	1966	50.00
YULE STRUTTIN' -- A BLUE NOTE CHRISTMAS		
❏ Blue Note 1P8119	1990	30.00
—Available on vinyl through Columbia House only		
ZENITH SALUTES THE SWINGIN' BANDS		
❏ Columbia Special Products CSS525 [M]	1967	35.00
—Available from Zenith dealers		

RECORD STORE DIRECTORY

ALABAMA:

Charlemagne Record Exchange
1924-1/2 11th Ave. S.
Birmingham, AL 35218
Phone: 205-322-5349

Excalibur Vintage and Vinyl
215 Second Ave., Unit 2
Decatur, AL 35601
Phone: 256-345-0988

Mobile Records
140 S. Sage Ave., No. B
Mobile, AL 36606
Phone: 251-479-0096

OZ Music
506 14th St.
Tuscaloosa, AL 35401
Phone: 205-758-1222

Renaissance Records
2020 11th Ave. S.
Birmingham, AL 35205
Phone: 205-933-8000

ALASKA:

Beat Garden
3300 College Road
Fairbanks, AK 99709-3707

Hoitts Music
1698 Airport Way
Fairbanks, AK 99701-4004

ARKANSAS:

Arkansas Record-CD Exchange
4212 MacArthur Drive
North Little Rock, AR 72118
Phone: 501-753-7877

Sound Warehouse
17 N. Block Ave.
Fayetteville, AR 72702
Phone: 479-442-4822

Vintage Stock-Rogers
4505 W. Walnut, Suite 5
Rogers, AR 72756
Phone: (479) 936-5881

ARIZONA:

Renfield Record Exchange
403 Clark St., Suite B11
Jerome, AZ 86331
Phone: 928-634-1615

Revolver Records
918 N. Second St.
Phoenix, AZ 85001
Phone: 602-795-4980

Rockzone Records
2155 E. University, No. 104

Tempe, AZ 85281
Phone: 480-964-6301

Stinkweeds
12 W. Camelback Road
Phoenix, AZ 85013-2518
Phone: 602-248-9461

Tracks in Wax Records
4741 N. Central Ave.
Phoenix, AZ 85001
Phone: 602-274-2660
E-mail: tracksinwax44@cox.net

CALIFORNIA:

Amoeba Music Hollywood
6400 Sunset Blvd.
Los Angeles, CA 90028
Phone: 323-245-6400
Web: www.amoeba.com

Amoeba Music
2455 Telegraph Ave.
Berkeley, CA 94704a
Phone: 510-549-1125

Aquarius Records
1055 Valencia St.
San Francisco, CA 94110
e-mail: store@aquariusrecords.org
Web: www.aquariusrecords.org
Phone: 415-647-2272

Cheap Thrills Records
563 Higuera St.
San Luis Obispo, CA 93401

Dr. Strange Records
7136 Amethyst Ave.
Alta Loma, CA 91701
Phone: 909-944-1778

Dyzzy Vinyl
3004 E. Seventh St.
Long Beach, CA 90804
Phone: 562-438-8928

Folk Arts Rare Records
3072 El Cajon Blvd
San Diego, CA 92104
Phone: 619-282-7833
Web: folkartsrarerecords.com

Kool Kat Jazz Records
97 Linden St.
Oakland, CA 94607
Phone: 510-291-1223

The Last Record Store
1899 A-Mendocino Ave.
Santa Rosa, CA 95401
Phone: 7070-525-1963
E-mail: lastrecordstore@sonic.net

Old Town Records
42012 Main St.
Temecula, CA 92589
Phone: 951-693-2004
E-mail: oldtownrecords@yahoo.com

Rasputin Music
2401 Telegraph Ave.
Berkeley, CA 94720
Phone: 800-350-8700

The Record Collector
7809 Melrose Ave.Hollywood, CA 90046
Phone: 323-655-6653
Web: www.therecordcollector.net

The Record Parlour
6408 Selma Avenue, Hollywood, CA
  90028
Phone: 323-655-6653
www.therecordparlour.com

Record Surplus
12436 Santa Monica Blvd.
Los Angeles, CA 90025
Phone: 310-979-4577
Web: www.recordsurplusla.com

Rockaway Records
2395 Glendale Blvd.
Los Angeles, CA 90039
Phone: 323-664-3232
E-mail: sales@rockaway.com
Web: http://www.rockaway.com

Streetlight Records
2350 Market St.
San Francisco, CA
Phone: 888-396-2350
www.streetlightrecords.com

Streetlight Records
980 S. Bascom Ave.
San Jose, CA
Phone: 888-330-7776

Streetlight Records
939 S. Pacific Ave.
Santa Cruz, CA
Phone: 888-648-9201

Vinyl Revolution
230 Lighthouse Ave.
Monterey, CA 93940
Phone: 831-646-9020

Vinyl Solution Records
151 West 25th Ave.
San Mateo, CA. 94403
650-571-0440
www.vinylsolutionrecords.com

Zoinks Records
226 S. Main St.
Pomona, CA
Phone: 909-865-4755

COLORADO:

Absolute Vinyl Records and Stereo
4474 N. Broadway St.
Boulder, CO 80304-0506
Phone: 303-955-1519
E-mail: fortherecords@cs.com

Albums on the Hill
1128 13th St.
Boulder, CO 80302
Phone: 303-447-0159
E-mail: albums2001@comcast.net

Finest Record Store
1129 W. Elizabeth St.
Fort Collins, CO 80527
Phone: 970-484-6446
E-mail: finest74@yahoo.com

The Leechpit
708 N. Weber St.
Colorado Springs, CO 80903
Phone: 719-634-3675
E-mail: adam@csindy.com

LPHound's Vinyl House
6235 E. 14th Ave.
Denver, CO 80220
Phone: 303-593-2540
E-mail: LPHounds@gmail.com

Wax Trax Records
638 E. 13th Ave
Denver, CO 80262
Phone: 303-831-7246
E-mail: waxtraxdenver@qwestoffice.net

CONNECTICUT:

Brass City Records (and Old Tools)
489 Meadow St, Waterbury, CT 06702
Phone: 203-574-7805
www.brasscityrecords.com

Disc & Dat
107 Greenwood Ave.
Bethel, CT 06801-2528
Phone: 203-797-0067

Exile on Main St.
267 E. Main St.
Branford, CT 06405

Gerosa Records
246 Federal Rd C16, Brookfield, CT
    06804
Phone: 203-775-7074
www.gerosarecords.com

Johnny's Records
45 Tokeneke Road
Darien, CT 06820
Phone: 203-655-0157

Merle's Record Rack
307 Racebrook Road
Orange, CT 06477

Mystic Disc
10 Steamboat Wharf
Mystic, CT
Phone: 860-536-1312
E-mail: dandisc@sbcglobal.net

Redscroll Records
24 N Colony Rd, Wallingford, CT 06492
Phone: 203-265-7013
redscrollrecords.com

Replay Records
2586 Whitney Ave.
Hamden, CT 06518
Phone: 203-980-1277
E-mail: davidelliott87@gmail.com

Telegraph
19 Golden St.
New London, CT 06320
Phone: 860-701-0506

Tumbleweeds
325 Main St.
Niantic, CT 06357
Phone: 860-739-9018
Web: http://www.tumbleweedst.com

Willimantic Records
744 Main Street
Willimantic, CT 06226 USA
Phone: 860-450-7000

DELAWARE:

Bert's Music
2501 Concord Pike
Wilmington, DE 19803
Phone: 302-478-3724

Rainbow Music & Books
54 E. Main St.
Newark, DE 19702
Phone: 302-368-7738
E-mail: chrisavino@gmail.com

**Vintage Vinyl at The Barn Shops at
Five Points**
18388 Coastal Highway, Unit 6
Lewes, DE 19958
Phone: 410-960-2919
Facebook: https://www.facebook.com/
    pages/Vintage-Vinyl-at-the-Barn-
    Shops-at-Five-Points

FLORIDA

Budget Records
212 San Marco Ave.
Saint Augustine, FL 32084
E-mail: jamesrfrederick@gmail.com

Hot Wax
1524 E 7th Ave.
Tampa, FL 33605
Phone: 813-248-6999
E-mail: hotwax1200@aol.com

Rock & Roll Heaven Inc.
1814 N. Orange Ave.
Orlando, FL 32804
Phone: 407-896-1952
E-mail: sales@rock-n-rollheaven.com
Web: http://www.rock-n-rollheaven.com

Remember Wynn Records
7007 Lanier Drive
Pensacola, FL 32504
Phone: 800-476-8630
E-mail: rememberwynn@bellsouth.net

Vinyl Lover (online only)
217 N. 12th St.
Tampa, FL 33602
Phone: 813-418-6880
Fax: 435-514-7447
E-mail: webmaster@vinyl-lover.com
Web: http://vinyl-lover.com

Yesterday and Today Records
9274 SW 40th St.
Miami, FL 33175
Phone: 305-554-1020
E-mail: yandtrec@aol.com

GEORGIA:

Fantasyland Records
360 Pharr Road, NE Suite B
Atlanta, GA 30305
Phone: 404-237-3193
E-mail: fantasyland41@hotmail.com

Low Yo Yo Stuff
261 W. Washington St.
Athens, GA 30601
Phone: 706-606-0842
E-mail: chris@chrisrazz.com

Mojo Vinyl
34 Webb St., No. 8
Roswell, GA 30075
Phone: 678-534-5042

Wax 'n' Facts
432 Moreland Ave. NE
Atlanta, GA 30307,
Phone: 404-525-2275
E-mail: waxnfacts@gmail.com

Wuxtry Records
197 E. Clayton St.
Athens, GA 30601
Phone: 706-369-9428

HAWAII:

Hungry Ear Records
418 Kuulei Road
Kailua, HI 96734
Phone: 808-262-2175
E-mail: info@hungryear.com
Web: www.hungryear.com

Jelly's Hawaii
670 Auahi Stree I-19
Honolulu, HI 96813
Phone: 808-587-7001
Fax: 808-587-7005
E-mail: pb.hawaii.1983@gmail.com

Requests
10 N. Market
Wailuku, HI 96793
Phone: 808-244-9315
E-mail: requestshi@gmail.com

Stylus Honolulu
2615 S. King St. No, A-301
Honolulu, HI 96826
Phone: 808-951-4500

IDAHO:

Big Hole Music
60 East Little Ave.
Driggs, ID
Phone: 208-354-3659
E-mail: bigholemusic@hotmail.com

Budget Tapes & Records
416 S. Fifth St.
Pocatello, ID 83201
Phone: 208-233-9650
E-mail: budgetrecords@gmail.com

The Long Ear
2405 N. Fourth St.
Coeur d Alene, ID 83814
Phone: 208-765-3472
E-mail: thelongear@frontier.com

The Record Exchange
1105 W. Idaho St.
Boise, ID 83702
Phone: 208-343-0107, Ext. 1

ILLINOIS:

Algonquin Records
532 E. Algonquin Road
Des Plaines, IL 60016

Blue Jay Way Record
14 W. Peru St.
Princeton, IL 61356
Phone: (815) 872-1935
E-mail: bluejaywayrecs@yahoo.com
www.facebook.com/pages/Blue-Jay-
   Way-Records

Deadwax
3819 N. Lincoln
Chicago, IL 60613
Phone: 773-529-1932
E-mail: deadwax@sbcglobal.net

Hip Cat Records
3540 Lake Ave.
Wilmette, IL 60091

Jazz Record Mart
27 E. Illinois
Chicago, IL 60610
Phone: 800-684-3480
E-mail: jazzmart@delmark.com
Web site: http://www.jazzmart.com

The Old School Records
7446 W. Madison St.
Forest Park, IL 60130

Rainbow Records
421 N. Northwest Highway, Suite 103
Barrington, IL 60010
Phone: 847-304-0721
E-mail: jmthominet@gmail.com

Reverberation Vinyl
1302 N. Main St.
Bloomington, IL 61701
Phone: 309-830-3750
Website: www.reverberationvinyl.com

Rich's Record Emporium
131 W. Main St. Collinsville IL
Phone: 618-200-9287
www.richsrecordemporium.com

Toad Hall Books & Records
10333 Campbell Road
Durand, IL 61024

INDIANA:

Alpha Records
492 Park 800 Drive
Greenwood, IN 46143-9525

Alpha Records and Music
P.O. Box 17575
Indianapolis, IN 46217
Phone: 317-882-9978
Web site: www.alpha.gemm.com

Dan's Downtown Records
219 W. Main St.
Muncie, IN 47305
Phone: 765-284-7611

Indy CD & Vinyl
806 Broad Ripple Ave.
Indianapolis, IN 46220
Phone: 317-259-1012
E-mail: rickz@indycdandvinyl.com

Karma Records
2606 Shelden St
Warsaw, IN 46582
Phone: 574-267-2080
Fax: 574-267-0091

Landlocked Music
202 N. Walnut St.
Bloomington, IN 47404
Phone: 812-339-2574

IOWA

Kanesville Used Records
530 Fourth St.
Council Bluffs, IA 51503
Phone: 712-328-8731
E-mail: kanesvillerecord@aol.com

Metro Records
807 E. 18th St.
Cedar Falls, IA 50613
Phone: 319-266-5539

Record Collector
116 S. Linn St.
Iowa City, IA 52240
Phone: 319-337-5029

Vinyl Cafe
303 Kellogg Ave.
Ames, IA 50010
Phone: 515-230-4574
E-mail: amesvinylcafe@gmail.com

Weird Harold's
411 Jefferson ST.
Burlington, IA 52601-5319
Phone: 319-753-5353
Web: http://weirdharolds.com

Zzz Records
2200 Ingersoll
Des Moines, IA 50312
Phone: 515-284-1401
Web: http://www.zzzrecords.com

KANSAS

The Flipside
11212 W. 75th St.
Shawnee, KS 66214
Phone: 913-602-8660
E-mail: theflipsidekc@yahoo.com

Keep N It Real Records
1700 State Ave.
Kansas City, KS 66102
Phone: 913-514-0901
E-mail: burnett-mike@sbcglobal.net

Rewound Sounds
815 W. Douglas
Wichita, KS 67213
Phone: 316-269-1413
E-mail: rewind316@gmail.com

Sisters of Sound Records/SOS Music
1214 Moro St. (Aggieville U Clothing Co.)
Manhattan, KS 66502
Phone: 785-770-9767

Vinyl Renaissance
10922 Shawnee Mission Parkway
Shawnee, KS 66203

KENTUCKY

Ear X-Tacy
2226 Bardstown Road
Louisville, KY 40205
Phone: 502.452.1799
E-mail: manager@earx-tacy.com

The Great Escape Bowling Green
2945 Scottsville Road
Bowling Green, KY 42104
Phone: 270-782-8092

The Great Escape Louisville
2433 Bardstown Road
Louisville, KY 40205
Phone: 502-456-2216

Ticket to Ride
Flealand 229
London, KY
Phone: 606-309-1389
E-mail: tickettoride@alltel.net

Underground Sounds
2003 Highland Ave.
Louisville, KY 40204
Phone: 502-485-0174
E-mail: usoundsrecords@yahoo.com

LOUISIANA

Euclid Records NOLA
3401 Chartres St.
New Orleans, LA 70117
Phone: 504-947-4348
www.euclidnola.com

Odyssey Records
1012 Canal St.
New Orleans, LA 70112
Phone: 504-523-3506
E-mail: mistaodyssey@aol.com

Peaches Records
408 N. Peters St.
New Orleans, LA 70130
Phone: 504-282-3322
E-mail: lillie.rea@gmail.com

Spazz Records
231 Trenton St.
West Monroe, LA, LA 71291,
Phone: (318) 805-6337
E-mail: popshop.monroe@gmail.com

Atomic Pop Shop
2963 Government St.
Baton Rouge, LA 70806
Phone: 225-771-8455
http://www.atomicpopshop.com

MAINE

Bill O'Neil's House of Rock 'n' Roll*
840 Portland Road
Saco, ME 04072
Phone: 207-283-1966

Everyday Music
205 Broadway
Farmington, ME 04938
Phone: 207-778-3483
E-mail: everydaymusic@verizon.net

The Record Connection
252 Main St.
Waterville, ME 04901
Phone: 207-873-1798
E-mail: recconn@roadrunner.com

MARYLAND:

Blinding Sun Records
332 N. Market St.
Frederick, MD 21701
Phone: 410-279-8869

Joe's Record Paradise
8216 Georgia Ave.
Silver Spring, MD 20910
Phone: 3015853269
E-mail: timsheamusic@live.com

KA-CHUNK!! Records
78 Maryland Ave
Annapolis, MD 21401
Phone: (410) 571-5047
E-mail: kachunkrecords@gmail.com

Memory Lane CDS & Records Inc.
2809 Walters Lane
District Heights, MD 20747
Phone: 301-568-5032
E-mail: memorylanerecords@verizon.net

MASSACHUSETTS:

Armageddon Shop
12 B Eliot St.
Cambridge, MA 02909
Phone: 617-492-1235
E-mail: armageddonshop@gmail.com

Planet Records, CDs, Tapes
54-B JFK Street
Cambridge, MA 02138
Phone: 617-492-0693
E-mail: planet@tiac.net

Rhythm and Muse
470 Centre St.
Jamaica Plain, MA 02130
Phone: 617-524-6622
Fax: 617-524-6039
E-mail: muse3@comcast.net

Turn It Up!
5 Pleasant St.
Northampton, MA 01060
Phone: 413-582-1885

MICHIGAN:

Dearborn Music
22501 Michigan Ave.
Dearborn, MI
313-561-1000

Flat Black & Circular
541 E. Grand River
East Lansing, MI 48823

Slick Disc
1625 West Road
Trenton, MI 48183
Phone: 734-692-1881
E-mail: SlickDisc@hotmail.com

Underground Sounds
255 E. Liberty St. Suite 249
Ann Arbor, MI 48104
Phone: 734-327-9239
E-mail: undergroundsoundsmi@gmail.
  com

MINNESOTA:

Dusty Pixels
2443 Hennepin Ave. S.
Minneapolis, MN 55405
Phone: 612-377-3371
E-mail: heydustypixels@gmail.com

Electric Fetus Records
• 2000 Fourth Ave. S.
Minneapolis, MN 55404
Phone: 612-870-9300
• 12 E. Superior St.
Duluth, MN 55802
Phone: 218-722-9970
• 28 S. Fifth Ave.
St. Cloud, MN 56301
Phone: 320-251-2569
Web: http://www.electricfetus.com

Hymie's Vintage Records
3820 E. Lake St.
Minneapolis, MN 55406
Phone: 612-729-8890

Mother's Music
431 Main Ave
Moorhead, MN 56560
Phone: (218)287-9601

Record Collectors' Co-op
3755 Bloomington Ave.
Minneapolis, MN 55407
Phone: 612-724-7070

MISSISSIPPI:

Disc-O-Tech
1030 Goodman Road E.
Southaven, MS 38671
Phone: 662-349-0303
E-mail: kcounce1106@yahoo.com

Rusty Robots
15222 Lemoyne Blvd.
Biloxi, MS 39532
Phone: 228-392-3255

MISSOURI:

Earwaxx Records & More
6408 N. Oak Trafficway
Gladstone, MO 64118
Phone: 816-436-9299
E-mail: earwaxxrecords@att.net

Euclid Records
601 East Lockwood Ave.
St. Louis, MO 63119
Phone: 314-961-8978
Web site: www.euclidrecords.com

Vintage Vinyl
6610 Delmar Blvd
St Louis, MO 63130-4503
Phone: (314) 721-4096

Webster Records
117 W. Lockwood Ave.
Webster Groves, MO 63119
Phone: 314-961-4656

MONTANA:

Cactus Records & Gifts
29 W. Main St.
Bozeman, MT 59715
Phone: 406-587-0245
E-mail: cactusrecords@yahoo.com

Ear Candy Music
624 S. Higgins Ave.
Missoula, MT 59807
Phone: 406-542-5029
E-mail: earcandymusic@live.com

Rockin' Rudy's
237 Blaine
Missoula, MT 59801
Phone: 406-542-0077

NEBRASKA:

Backtrack Records
1549 N. Cotner Blvd., Studio A
Lincoln, NE 68505-1627
Phone: 402-464-4567
E-mail: backtrack@windstream.net

Drastic Plastic
1209 Howard St.
Omaha, NE 68139
Phone: 402-346-8843
E-mail: lizz@drasticplasticrecords.com

Recycled Sounds
909 O Street
Lincoln, NE 68508
Phone: 402-476-8240
E-mail: recycledsounds@hotmail.com

Spindle Records
122 N. 14th St
Lincoln, NE 68508
Phone: 402-435-8350
E-mail: spindlerecords@yahoo.com

NEVADA:

Discology CDs, DVDs, LPs
11 N. Sierra St. No. 100
Reno, NV 89504
Phone: 775-323-2121
E-mail: discology@sbcglobal.net

Sundance Bookstore and Music
1155 W. Fourth Street No. 106
Reno, NV 89512
Phone: 775-786-1188

Wax Trax Records Inc.
2909 S. Decatur Blvd.
Las Vegas, NV 89102-7043
Phone: 702-362-4300
E-mail: waxtraxinc@aol.com

Zia Records – Eastern
4225 S. Eastern Ave.
Las Vegas, NV 89119
Phone: 702-735-4942

Zia Records – Sahara
4503 W. Sahara Ave.
Las Vegas, NV 89102
Phone: 702-233-4942

NEW HAMPSHIRE:

Metro City Records
691 Somerville St.
Manchester, NH 03103
Phone: 603-665-9889

Odyssey And Oracle
100 Albany St.
Portsmouth, NH 03802
Phone: 1-603-319-1656
E-mail: Eggmanrulzzz@aol.com

Pitchfork Records
2 S. Main St.
Concord, NH 03301

Phone: 603-224-6700
E-mail: pfork3@aol.com

Spun
266 Central Ave.
Dover, NH 03820
Phone: 603-742-6939
E-mail: spunmusicllc@yahoo.com

NEW JERSEY:

A&M Music Center
238 Stuyvesant Ave.
Lyndhurst, N.J. 07071

21st Century Music
121 Gertrude Ave.
Paramus, NJ 07652
Phone: 201-343-4886
Web: http://www.21centurymusic.com

Groovy Graveyard
658 Cookman Ave.
Asbury Park, N.J. 07712
Phone: 732-877-7024
Web: www.groovygraveyard.com
E-mail: info@groovygraveyard.com

Vintage Vinyl
51 LaFayette Road
Fords, NJ 08863
Phone: 732-225-7717

Yesterday's Treasures
1265B Stuyvesant Ave.
Union, NJ 07083
Phone: 908-416-5519
E-mail: jpoe141@aol.com

Zig Zag
2367 Highway 36
Atlantic Highlands, NJ 07752
Phone: 732 708 1666
E-mail: dibeninc@aol.com

NEW MEXICO:

Guy in the Groove
215 N. Guadalupe (inside Constellation)
Santa Fe, NM 87501
Phone: 505-699-3332
E-mail: GuyInTheGroove@aol.com

Mecca Records
1404 Central Ave. SW
Albuquerque, NM 87104
Phone: 505 243-5041
E-mail: meccaworld@gmail.com

NEW YORK:

A1 Records
439 E 6th St
New York, NY 10009
Phone: 212-473-2870

Academy LPs
415 E. 12th St.
New York, NY 10116
Phone: 212-780-9166

Academy Record Annex
85 Oak St
Brooklyn, NY 11222
Phone: 718-218-8200

Academy Records & CDs
12 W. 18th St.
New York, NY 10011
Phone: 212-242-3000

Black Gold Records
461 Court St,
Brooklyn, NY 11231
Phone: 347-227-8227

Bleecker Street Records
188 West 4th Street
New York, NY 10014
Phone: 212-255-7899

CD Exchange
40 Jay Scutti Blvd.
Rochester, NY 14623
E-mail: cdxstore@frontiernet.net

Colony Records
1619 Broadway, corner of Fourth and
   Broadway
New York, NY 10019
Phone: 212-365-2050
www.colonymusic.com

CO-OP 87 Records
87 Guernsey St
Brooklyn, NY 11222
Phone: 347-294-4629

Darkside Records & Gallery
782 Main St.
Poughkeepsie, NY 12603
Phone: 845-452-8010
www.darksiderecordsandgallery.com

Downtown Music Gallery
13 Monroe St.
New York, NY 10002
Phone: 212-473-0043

Earwax Records
218 Bedford Ave.
Brooklyn, NY 11211
Phone: 718-486-3771
E-mail: plasticllc@yahoo.com

Generation Records
210 Thompson St
New York, NY 10012
Phone: 212-254-1100

Gimme Gimme Records
325 E. Fifth St.
New York, NY 10003
Phone: 212-475-2955
E-mail: dc@raremusic.com

Good Records
218 East 5th Street
New York, NY 10003
212-529-2081
www.goodrecordsnyc.com

Halcyon The Shop
57 Pearl St

Brooklyn, NY 11201 (DUMBO)
Phone: 718-260-9299

Heaven Street
167 N 9th St
Brooklyn, NY 11211
Phone: 718-486-3771

Human Head Records
168 Johnson Ave
Brooklyn, NY 11206
Phone: 347-987-3362

In Living Stereo
2 Great Jones St
New York, NY 10012
Phone: 929-600-2008

Infinity Records
510 Park Blvd.
Massapequa Park, NY 11762
Phone: 516-221-0634
www.infinityrecords.net

Jazz Record Center
236 W 26th #804
New York, NY 10001
Phone:212-675-4480

Music Matters
413 7th Ave
Brooklyn, NY 11215
Phone: 718-369-7087

Other Music
15 East 4th Street
New York, NY 10003
212-477-8150
www.othermusic.com

Rainbow Music 2002 Ltd
130 1st Avenue
New York, NY 10009
Phone: 212-505-1774

Rebel Rebel Records
319 Bleecker St
New York, NY 10014
Phone: 212-989-0770

Record Grouch
986 Manhattan Ave
Brooklyn, NY 11222

Record Runner
5 Jones Street
New York, NY 10014
Phone: 212-255-4280

Rhino Records of New Paltz
3 Church St.
New Paltz, NY 12561
Phone: 845-255-0230

Rough Trade
64 North 9th Street
Brooklyn, NY 11249
718-388-4111
www.roughtradenyc.com

Spiral Scratch Records
2531 Delaware Ave.
Buffalo, NY 14216
Phone: 716-873-1484

Symphony Music
791 B. Crown St.
Brooklyn, NY 11213
Phone: 718-363-0174
www.symusicsstore.com

The Thing
1001 Manhattan Ave.
Brooklyn, NY 11222
Phone: 718-349-8234

Westsider Records
233 W 72nd St
New York, NY 10023
Phone: 212-874-1588

Woodstock Music Shop
6 Rock City Road
Woodstock, NY 12498
Phone: 845-679-3224

Ye Olde Hippie Shoppe of Woodstock
69 Tinker Street
Woodstock, NY 12498
Phone: 845-679-2650

NORTH CAROLINA:

The Birdsnest
102 B S. Main St.
Davidson, NC 28036
Phone: 704-990-6378 (nest)

Bull City Records
1916 Perry St.
Durham, NC 27705, United States of
    America
Phone: (919)286-9640

Gravity Records LLC
125 S. Kerr Ave. Suite No. 1
Wilmington, NC 28403
Phone: 910.392.2414

Green Eggs and Jam
740 W. King St.
Boone, NC 28608
Phone: 828-264-3233

Lunchbox Records
1419-A Central Ave.
Charlotte, NC 28205
Phone: 704-331-0788

NORTH DAKOTA:

Orange Records
641 First Ave. N.
Fargo, ND 58102
Phone: 701-478-6240
E-mail: matthewoland@gmail.com

Whole Wheat Records & Comics
2 N. Third St.
Grand Forks, ND 58203
Phone: 701-215-8557
E-mail: upauat@msn.com

OHIO:

A Separate Reality Records
2678 W. 14th St.
Cleveland, OH 44113
Phone: 216-644-7934

Checkered Records
1954 Whipple Ave. NW
Canton, OH 44708
Phone: 3304799576

Everybody's Records
6106 Montgomery Road
Cincinnati, OH 45213

Evil Empire Records at What The Rock!?
1194 N. High St.
Columbus, OH 43234
Phone: 614-294-WHAT

Moles Records and CD
111 Calhoun St.
Cincinnati, OH 45219
Phone: 513-861-6291
Email: molesrecords@fuse.net

OKLAHOMA:

Guestroom Records
125 E. Main St.
Norman, OK 73070
Phone: 405-701-5974
E-mail: guestroomrecords@gmail.com

Guestroom Records
3701 N. Western Ave.
Oklahoma City, OK 73113
Phone: 405-601-3859
E-mail: guestroomrecords@gmail.com

Randy's M&M'S
3200 S. Blvd.
Edmond, OK 73113
Phone: (405) 340-0404
E-mail: krisabt@swbell.net

Reggie's Records
110 S. 4th St.
Ponca City, OK 74601
Phone: 580-762-2544

OREGON:

Exiled Records
4628 SE Hawthorne Blvd.
Portland, OR 97215
Phone: 503.232.0751

Jackpot Records
203 SW Ninth Ave.
Portland, OR 97205
503-222-0990

Mississippi Records
5202 N. Albina Ave.
Portland, OR 97217
Phone: 503-282-2990

Off the Record
2227 B Newmark Ave.

North Bend, OR 97459
Phone: 1-541-751-0301
E-mail: bubba1947@hotmail.com

Yesterday & Today
317 E. Second St.
The Dalles, OR 97058
Phone: 541-296-1441
E-mail: thomas01@earthlink.net

PENNSYLVANIA:

A.K.A. Music
27 North Second St.
Philadelphia, PA 08101
Phone: 215-922-3855
Fax: 215-922-3852
E-mail: aka-music@hotmail.com

Angry Young & Poor
356 W. Orange St.
Lancaster, PA 17603
Phone: 717-397-6116

Main St. Jukebox
606 Main St.
Stroudsburg, Pa 18360
Phone: 570-424-2246

Musical Energi
59 N. Main St.
Wilkes-Barre, PA 18701
Phone: 570-829-2929
Web site: www.musicalenergi.com

RHODE ISLAND:

Armageddon Shop
436 Broadway
Providence, RI 02909
Phone: 401-521-6667

In Your Ear
462 Main St.
Warren, RI 02885
Phone: 401-245-9840
E-mail: inyourear@fullchannel.net

Music Box
160 Thames St.
Newport, RI 02840
Phone: 401-849-6666

The Time Capsule
537 Pontiac Ave.
Cranston, RI 02910
Phone: 401-781-5017
E-mail: ryeremian@aol.com

What Cheer!
7 S. Angell St.
Providence, RI 02906
Phone: 401-861-4244
E-mail: what_cheer_records@yahoo.com

SOUTH DAKOTA:

Ernie November
1319 W. Main St.
Rapid City, SD 57701
Phone: 605-341-0768

Ernie November
1918 w. 41st
Sioux Falls, SD 57105
Phone: 605-221-0621
E-mail: ernienovember@hotmail.com

Last Stop CD Shop
3508 W. 41 St.
Sioux Falls, SD 57106
Phone: 605-361-4416
E-mail: onlyfactor@hotmail.com

TENNESSEE:

Chad's Records
321 Vine St.
Chattanooga, TN 37403
Phone: 423-756-7563

Disc Exchange
2615 Chapman Highway
Knoxville, TN 37920
Phone: 865-573-9691, x12

For The Record
1 Northgate Mall
Chattanooga, TN 37421
Phone: 423-504-9589

Lost and Found Records
3714 Walker Blvd.
Knoxville, TN 37917
Phone: 865-687-5556
Email: albumhunter@comcast.net

Spinstreet
3484 Poplar Ave., Space D-2
Memphis, TN 38111
Phone: 678-229-4215
E-mail: brianp@vcei.com

TEXAS:

All That Music & Video
6800 Gateway East, Suite 1B
El Paso, TX 79915
www.allthatmusic.com

Cactus Records
2110 Portsmouth
Houston, TX 77098
Phone:713-526-9272

Encore Records
1745 W. Anderson Lane
Austin, TX 78757
Phone: (512) 451-8111
E-mail: encoremusic@austin.rr.com

Forever Young Records
2955 S. Highway 360
Grand Prairie, TX 75052

Good Records
1808 Greenville Ave.
Dallas, TX 75206-7437
Phone: 214-752-4663

Jukebox Records
Irving, TX 75060
Phone: 972-278-4333

Sig's Lagoon
3622 Main St., Ste. E,
Houston, TX 77002
Phone: 713-533-9525
Website: www.sigslagoon.com

Snake Eyes Vinyl
1101 Navasota Suite 3
Austin, TX 78765
Phone: 512-600-6950

UTAH:

Graywhale
208 S. 1300 E.
Salt Lake City, UT 84102

Graywhale
1775 W. 4700 S.
Taylorsville, UT 84118

Graywhale
4066 Riverdale Road
Ogden, UT 84107

Graywhale
575 E. University Parkway
Orem, UT

Graywhale
390 North 500 W.
Bountiful UT 84010
Graywhale 1670 W. 9000 SW
Jordan, UT 84088
Phone: 801-712-5457
E-mail: jon@fatfin.com

Jay's Records
785 E. Main St.
Price, UT 84501
Phone: (801) 259-0036
Email: coltonhaight@yahoo.com

Positively 4th Street Music
249 E. 400 S.
Salt Lake City, UT 84110
Phone: 801-531-8181
E-mail: fourthstmusic@yahoo.com

Sgt. Peppers Music & Video
59 S. Main St. No. 1
Moab, UT 84532
Phone: 435-259-4405

Slowtrain
221 E. Broadway
Salt Lake City, UT 84111
Phone: 801-364-2611

VERMONT:

BCA Records
East Arlington Antique Center
1223 E. Arlington Road
Arlington, VT
Phone: 802-375-6144

Burlington Records
170 Bank St.
Burlington, VT 05402
Phone: 802-881-0303

Exile On Main Street
94 North Main St.
Barre, VT 05670
Phone: (802) 479-3107
E-mail: exile@vtlink.net

Pure Pop Records
115 S. Winooski Ave.
Burlington, VT 05402
Phone: 802 658 2652

VIRGINIA:

Birdland Music
951 Providence Square Shopping Center
Virginia Beach, VA 23464

Blue Groove Soundz
5852 N. Washington Blvd.
Arlington, VA 22205
Phone: 703-270-9075

Chester Records
185 N. Loudoun St.
Winchester, VA 22601
Phone: (540) 667-3444
E-mail: n8rhodes@gmail.com

Sidetracks Music
310 Second St. SE, Unit A
Charlottesville, VA 22902
Phone: 434-295-3080
E-mail: calicotunes@mail.com

Skinnies Records
2119 Colonial Ave.
Norfolk, VA 23517
Phone: 757 622-2241
E-mail: Steveathey@prodigy.net

WASHINGTON:

Bop Street Records
2220 NW Market St.
Seattle, WA 98107
www.bopstreetrecords.com

The Business
402 Commercial Ave.
Anacortes, WA 98221
Phone: 360-293-9788
E-mail: lizatthebiz@hotmail.com

Easy Street Records & Cafe
4559 California Ave SW No. 200,
Seattle, WA
Phone: (206) 938-EASY(3279)

Easy Street Records
20 Mercer St.
Seattle, WA
Phone: (206) 691-EASY(3279)

Everyday Music
115 E. Magnolia
Bellingham, WA 98225
Phone: 360-676-1404
E-mail: shefte@everydaymusic.com

Exploding Planet Records
320 N. Callow Ave.
Bremerton, WA 98312
Phone: 8602946165

Four Thousand Holes
1610 N Monroe St
Spokane, WA 99205
Phone: (509) 325-1914

Groove Merchants
905 W Garland Ave
Spokane, WA 99205
Phone: (509) 998-0410

Off the Record
901 Summitview, Suite 180
Yakima, WA 98902
Phone: 509-453-8652
E-mail: rich@offtherecord.com

Recorded Memories
1902 N Hamilton St
Spokane, WA 99207
Phone: (509) 483-4753

Sounds Great
3007 Judson St.
Gig Harbor, WA 98335
Phone: 253 851 8986
E-mail: Soundsgreat@harbornet.com

WEST VIRGINIA:

Cheap Thrills Records
102 Galleria Plaza
Beckley, WV 25801
Phone: 304-252-DISC
E-mail: chpthrlls@earthlink.net

Cheap Thrills Records
1130 Stafford Drive
Princeton, WV 24740
Phone: 304-487-0404
E-mail: chpthrlls@earthlink.net

Now Hear This
1101 Fourth Ave.
Huntington, WV 25701
Phone: 3045220021
E-mail: vincehebert03@gmail.com

WISCONSIN:

B-Side Records
436 State St.
Madison, WI 53702, United States of
   America
Phone: 608-255-1977
E-mail: store@b-sidemadison.com

Bullseye Records
1627 E. Irving Place
Milwaukee, WI 53202
Phone: 414-223-3177
E-mail: bullseyerecordshop@gmail.com

Inner Sleeve Records
209 Scott St.
Wausau, WI 54403
715-842-8297

The Exclusive Company
770 West Northland Ave.
Appleton, WI 54914
Phone: 920-731-6010
www.exclusivecompany.com

The Exclusive Company
144 N. Main St.
West Bend, WI 53095
Phone: 262-334-7101

The Exclusive Company
318 N. Main St.
Oshkosh, WI 54901
Phone: 920-235-1450

The Exclusive Company
423 Dousman St.
Green Bay, WI 54303
Phone: 920-435-0880

The Exclusive Company
1259 Milton Ave.
Janesville, WI 53545
Phone: 608-743-0786

The Exclusive Company
5026 S. 74th St.
Greenfield, WI 53220
Phone: 414-281-6644

The Exclusive Company
1669 N. Farwell
Milwaukee, WI 53202
Phone: 414-271-8590

The Exclusive Company
508 State St.
Madison, WI 53703
Phone: 608-255-2433

MadCity Music Exchange
600 Williamson St.
Madison, WI 53703
Phone: 608-251-8558

Rush Mor Records
2635 S. Kinnickinnic Ave.
Milwaukee, WI 53207
Phone: 414-481-6040

Radio Kaos
968 Main St.
Stevens Point, WI 54481

Strictly Discs
1900 Monroe St.
Madison, WI 53711
Phone: 6082599179
E-mail: angie@strictlydiscs.com

WYOMING:

Sonic Rainbow CDs
140 S. Center
Casper, WY 82601
Phone: 307-577-5947
E-mail: s.sonicrainbow@bresnan.net